12/92

DATE DUE

DEMCO 38-296

DICTIONARY OF OCCUPATIONAL TITLES

Fourth Edition, Revised 1991

Volume I
Occupational Definitions

U.S. Department of Labor
Employment and Training Administration

≡≣BERNAN PRESS
Lanham, MD

Bernan Press
4611-F Assembly Drive
Lanham, MD 20706

Printed in the United States of America. TM

The binding on this edition is Library quality, Smyth sewn, and
designed to withstand heavy use for a number of years.

ISBN 0-89059-002-8 (Volume I)
ISBN 0-89059-000-1 (2 Volume Set)

Library of Congress Catalog Card Number: 91-76504

FOREWORD TO THE
DICTIONARY OF OCCUPATIONAL TITLES

As a result of our conversations in both the public and private sectors with librarians, state and local labor officials, and other professionals across the United States, Bernan Press decided to publish a value-added edition of the *Dictionary of Occupational Titles* (DOT), originally published in softcover by the U.S. Department of Labor. While still preserving the occupational definitions in their original form, we have tried to make the DOT more user-friendly. We have added a durable binding, designed to withstand frequent use. Also, we have grouped all of the Occupational Definitions into the first volume, and placed the Glossary, Appendixes, and Indexes in the second volume for easier cross-reference. Furthermore, we have added the occupational category to the top of each page in the occupational definitions chapters, thus making searching must faster. We are sure that readers will find these changes will add years to the life span of the volumes and will, at the same time, facilitate their use.

As Lynn Martin, U.S. Secretary of Labor, states in her Message from the Secretary, the DOT "has provided basic occupational information to many and varied users in both public and private sectors of the United States economy." Its production represents the work of numerous agencies and groups. In the Foreword to the Government Printing Office (GPO) edition of the DOT, Robert A. Schaerfl, Director of the U.S. Employment Service (USES), refers to the *Dictionary* as "a vital part of the USES commitment to collect and disseminate occupational data that is comprehensive, up-to-date, and economically useful. This revision of the Fourth Edition of the DOT culminates a decade of research and verification by more than 40 job analysts at five Occupational Analysis centers across the Nation and reflects the changing skills, knowledges and abilities of the American workforce."

And, finally, in his Prefatory Note to the GPO edition, Robert T. Jones, Assistant Secretary for Employment and Training indicates that

> "the American workplace has undergone revolutionary change. . . .Too many of America's young people are entering the world of work inadequately prepared. The resulting dislocation—the so-called "skills gap"—presents those of us who prepare, hire, or support American workers with a serious challenge.

> ". . . It provides an updated picture of the occupations for which America's workforce must be prepared. It details the tasks to be performed and the levels of education that must be achieved. The DOT offers a starting place from which to address issues of training and education, career guidance and employment counseling, job definition and wage restructuring."

As an organization, Bernan Associates has been supplying U.S. Government publications to libraries, businesses, and state agencies for nearly forty years. We at Bernan Press think that you will find this Library Bound edition of the DOT to be a valuable and enduring addition to your collection. In the coming months, we look forward to publishing other relevant and informative materials to suit your needs.

October, 1991   DONALD H. HAGEN
Lanham, Maryland   Director, Bernan Press

ACKNOWLEDGMENTS FROM
THE ORIGINAL SOFTCOVER VOLUMES

The revised fourth edition of the *Dictionary of Occupational Titles* was produced by the U.S. Employment Service under the direction of Robert A. Schaerfl, Director. The Occupational Analysis Program was directed by Clay Cottrell, Chief, Division of Planning and Operations. Coordination and technical supervision of the data collection effort was directed by John Hawk, Personnel Research Psychologist, with additional technical planning and support from Russ Kile of the OA unit.

The new data for this edition were developed through the efforts of the following Occupational Analysis Field Centers, operated through the State Employment Services: Boston, Massachusetts, Paul Cleary, Supervisor; Detroit, Michigan, Tom Kearney, Supervisor; St. Louis, Missouri, Doris Phelan, Supervisor; Raleigh, North Carolina; and Salt Lake City, Utah, Barbara Smith, Supervisor. Grateful acknowledgement is also made for the contribution of Jerome Stevens, former Supervisor of the Missouri Field Center.

The North Carolina Occupational Analysis Field Center served a pivotal role in the planning, collection, preparation, and technical review of data for this revised edition, as well as its computerization and publication. Special recognition is due the staff of that center, including Mike Swaim, Bruce Paige, Larry Patterson, and Sammie Batchelor, and to their Supervisor, Stanley Rose.

Space does not permit a listing of their names, but grateful acknowledgement is also given to those associations, business firms, labor organizations, other Federal Agencies, and individuals whose assistance and cooperation contributed significantly to the development of this publication.

CONTENTS

VOLUME I

VOLUME II

SPECIAL NOTICE

Occupational information contained in the revised fourth edition DOT reflects jobs as they have been found to occur, but they may not coincide in every respect with the content of jobs as performed in particular establishments or at certain localities. DOT users demanding specific job requirements should supplement this data with local information detailing jobs within their community.

In using the DOT, it should be noted that the U.S. Employment Service has no responsibility for establishing appropriate wage levels for workers in the United States, or settling jurisdictional matters in relation to different occupations. In preparing occupational definitions, no data were collected concerning these and related matters. Therefore, the occupational information in this edition cannot be regarded as determining standards for any aspect of the employer-employee relationship. Data contained in this publication should not be considered a judicial or legislative standard for wages, hours, or other contractual or bargaining elements.

Material contained in this publication is in the public domain and may be reproduced fully or partially, without the permission of the Federal Government. Source credit is requested but not required.

Comments or inquiries regarding definitions or data elements included in the revised fourth edition DOT are invited and should be addressed to:

Mr. Stanley Rose, Supervisor
North Carolina Occupational Analysis Field Center
North Carolina Employment Security Commission
Post Office Box 27625
Raleigh, North Carolina 27611

Telephone inquiries may be made by calling (919) 733-7917.

INTRODUCTION

The *Dictionary of Occupational Titles* (DOT) was developed in response to the demand of an expanding public employment service for standardized occupational information to support job placement activities. The U.S. Employment Service recognized this need in the mid-1930's, soon after the passage of the Wagner-Peyser Act established a Federal-State employment service system, and initiated an occupational research program, utilizing analysts located in numerous field offices throughout the country, to collect the information required. The use of this information has expanded from job matching applications to various uses for employment counseling, occupational and career guidance, and labor market information services.

In order to properly match jobs and workers, the public employment service system requires that a uniform occupational language be used in all of its local job service offices. Highly trained occupational analysts must go out and collect reliable data which is provided to job interviewers so they may systematically compare and match the specifications of employer job openings with the qualifications of applicants who are seeking jobs through its facilities. The Occupational Analysis (OA) Program is currently supporting job analysis activity in the states of Michigan, Missouri, Massachusetts, and Utah, with North Carolina serving as the lead Field Center providing leadership and oversight.

Based on the data collected by occupational analysts, the first edition of the DOT was published in 1939. The first edition contained approximately 17,500 concise definitions presented alphabetically, by title, with a coding arrangement for occupational classification. Blocks of jobs were assigned 5- or 6-digit codes which placed them in one of 550 occupational groups and indicated whether the jobs were skilled, semi-skilled, or unskilled.

The second edition DOT, issued in March 1949, combined material in the first edition with several supplements issued throughout the World War II period. The second edition and its supplements reflected the impact of the war on jobs in the U.S. economy including new occupations in the plastics, paper and pulp, and radio manufacturing industries.

The third edition DOT, issued in 1965, eliminated the previous designation of a portion of the occupations as "skilled, semi-skilled, or unskilled" and substituted a classification system based on the nature of the work performed and the demands of such work activities upon the workers. These new indicators of work requirements included eight separate classification components: training time, aptitudes, interests, temperaments, physical demands, working conditions, work performed, and industry.

The fourth edition of the DOT published in 1977, contained over 2,100 new occupational definitions and several thousand other definitions were substantially modified or combined with related definitions. In order to document these changes, approximately 75,000 on-site job analysis studies were conducted from 1965 to the mid-1970's. These studies, supplemented by information obtained through extensive contacts with professional and trade associations, reflected the restructuring of the economy at that time.

Two supplements to the DOT have been released since the publication of the 1977 fourth edition DOT, one in 1982 and one in 1986. The 1982 supplement contained titles, codes, and definitions derived from Occupational Code Requests (see Appendix E) submitted by DOT users to local Job Service offices. The 1986 supplement continued this effort to publish new definitions as well as modify existing definitions consistent with new data collected. The 1986 supplement contained 840 occupational definitions; of these, 761 were not defined in the fourth edition.

Changes in occupational content and job characteristics due to technological advancement continue to occur at a rapid pace. This rapid change to occupations coupled with user demand for the most current information possible has resulted in a revised approach to the publication of the DOT. The OA network has focused its efforts on the study of selected industries in order to document the jobs that have undergone the most significant occupational changes since the publication, in 1977, of the fourth edition DOT.

This effort of gathering data and writing/revising definitions in these selected industries, including "new" and revised definitions from the 1986 fourth edition supplement, has resulted in the publication of this revised fourth edition DOT. This information is presented in the hope that it will provide the best "snapshot" of how jobs continue to be performed in the majority of industries across the country. Comments, suggestions, or criticism by DOT users concerning the content and format of this revised DOT are welcomed.

PARTS OF THE OCCUPATIONAL DEFINITION

Work is organized in a variety of ways. As a result of technological, economic, and sociological influences, nearly every job in the economy is performed slightly differently from any other job. Every job is also similar to a number of other jobs.

In order to look at the millions of jobs in the U.S. economy in an organized way, the DOT groups jobs into "occupations" based on their similarities and defines the structure and content of all listed occupations. Occupational definitions are the result of comprehensive studies of how similar jobs are performed in establishments across the nation and are composites of data collected from diverse sources. The term "occupation," as used in the DOT, refers to this collective description of a number of individual jobs performed, with minor variations, in many establishments.

There are seven basic parts to an occupational definition. They present data about a job in a systematic fashion. The parts are listed below in the order in which they appear in every definition:

(1) The Occupational Code Number
(2) The Occupational Title
(3) The Industry Designation
(4) Alternate Titles (if any)
(5) The Body of the Definition
    (a) Lead Statement
    (b) Task Element Statements
    (c) "May" Items
(6) Undefined Related Titles (if any)
(7) Definition Trailer

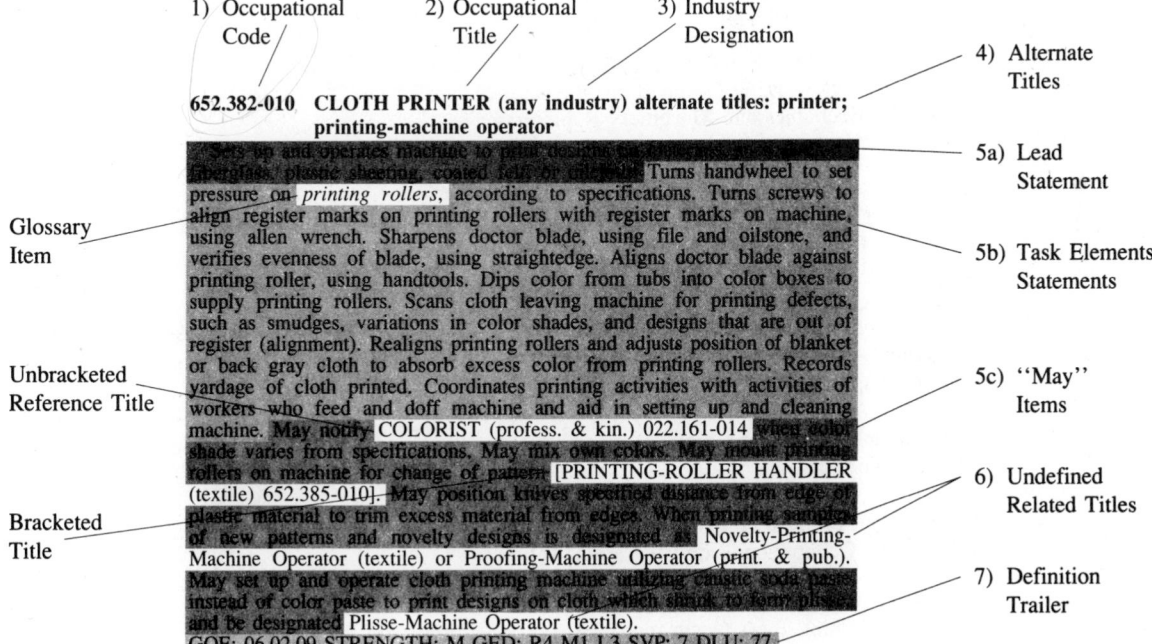

xi

(1) The Occupational Code Number

The first item in an occupational definition is the 9-digit occupational code (in the preceding example, 652.382-010). In the DOT occupational classification system, each set of three digits in the 9-digit code number has a specific purpose or meaning. Together, they provide a unique identification code for a particular occupation which differentiates it from all others.

The *first three digits* identify a particular occupational group. All occupations are clustered into one of nine broad "categories" (first digit), such as professional, technical and managerial, or clerical and sales occupations. These categories break down into 83 occupationally specific "divisions" (the first two digits), such as occupations in architecture and engineering within the professional category, or stenography, typing, and related occupations in the clerical and sales category. Divisions, in turn, are divided into small, homogeneous "groups" (the first three digits)—564 such groups are identified in the DOT. The nine primary occupational categories are listed below:

0/1	Professional, Technical, and Managerial Occupations
2	Clerical and Sales Occupations
3	Service Occupations
4	Agricultural, Fishery, Forestry, and Related Occupations
5	Processing Occupations
6	Machine Trades Occupations
7	Benchwork Occupations
8	Structural Work Occupations
9	Miscellaneous Occupations

In the example, the first digit (6) indicates that this particular occupation is found in the category, "Machine Trades Occupations." (For a listing of all occupational categories, divisions, and groups see page xxix.)

The second digit refers to a division within the category. The divisions within the "Machine Trades Occupations" category are as follows:

60	Metal Machining Occupations
61	Metalworking Occupations, n.e.c.
62/63	Mechanics and Machinery Repairers
64	Paperworking Occupations
65	Printing Occupations
66	Wood Machining Occupations
67	Occupations in Machining Stone, Clay, Glass, and Related Materials
68	Textile Occupations
69	Machine Trades Occupations, n.e.c.

Some divisions or groups end in the designation "n.e.c." (not elsewhere classified). This indicates that the occupations do not logically fit into precisely defined divisions or groups, or that they could fit into two or more of them equally well.

In the example, the second digit (5) locates the occupation in the "Printing Occupations" division.

The third digit defines the occupational group within the division. The groups within the "Printing Occupations" division are as follows:

650	Typesetters and Composers
651	Printing Press Occupations
652	Printing Machine Occupations
653	Bookbinding-Machine Operators and Related Occupations
654	Typecasters and Related Occupations
659	Printing Occupations, n.e.c.

In the example, the third digit (2) locates the occupation in the "Printing Machine Occupations" group.

The *middle three digits* of the DOT occupational code are the Worker Functions ratings of the tasks performed in the occupation. Every job requires a worker to function to some degree in relation to data, people, and things. A separate digit expresses the worker's relationship to each of these three groups:

DATA (4th Digit)	PEOPLE (5th Digit)	THINGS (6th Digit)
0 Synthesizing	0 Mentoring	0 Setting Up
1 Coordinating	1 Negotiating	1 Precision Working
2 Analyzing	2 Instructing	2 Operating-Controlling
3 Compiling	3 Supervising	3 Driving-Operating
4 Computing	4 Diverting	4 Manipulating
5 Copying	5 Persuading	5 Tending
6 Comparing	6 Speaking-Signalling	6 Feeding-Offbearing
	7 Serving	7 Handling
	8 Taking Instructions-Helping	

As a general rule, Worker Functions involving more complex responsibility and judgment are assigned lower numbers in these three lists while functions which are less complicated have higher numbers. For example, "synthesizing" and "coordinating" data are more complex tasks than "copying" data; "instructing" people involves a broader responsibility than "taking instructions-helping"; and "operating" things is a more complicated task than "handling" things.

The Worker Functions code in the example (382) relates to the middle three digits of the DOT occupational code and has a different meaning and no connection with group code 652 (first three digits).

The Worker Functions code (382) may be found in any occupational group. It signifies that the worker is "compiling" (3) in relation to data; "taking instructions-helping" (8) in relation to people; and "operating-controlling" (2) in relation to things. The Worker Functions code indicates the broadest level of responsibility or judgment required in relation to data, people, or things. It is assumed that, if the job requires it, the worker can generally perform any higher numbered function listed in each of the three categories. (See Appendix B for a more detailed discussion of Worker Functions codes.)

The *last three digits* of the occupational code number serve to differentiate a particular occupation from all others. A number of occupations may have the same first six digits, but no two can have the same nine digits. If a 6-digit code is applicable to only one occupational title, the final three digits assigned are always 010 (as in the example). If there is more than one occupation with the same first six digits, the final three digits are usually assigned in alphabetical order of titles in multiples of four (010, 014, 018, 022, etc.). If another printing machine occupation had the same six digits as CLOTH PRINTER (any industry) 652.382-010, and began with the letter "D," it would be assigned the occupational code 652.382-014. In order to minimize the number of changes made to the existing occupational classification structure, "new" occupations added to the DOT since the publication of the Fourth Edition have simply been added sequentially following the previous last entry for each of the 6-digit codes. The full nine digits thus provide each occupation with a unique code suitable for computerized operations.

(2) The Occupational Title

Immediately following the occupational code in every definition is the occupational base title. The base title is always in upper-case boldface letters. It is the most common type of title found in the DOT, and is the title by which the occupation is known in the majority of establishments in which it was found. In the example, CLOTH PRINTER (any industry) 652.382-010 is a base title.

(a) Master Titles

Some titles are classified as master titles. These titles are designed to eliminate unnecessary repetition of tasks common to a large number of occupations. Master titles define the common job tasks having a wide variety of job variables and wide variety of titles. An example is the title "SUPERVISOR (any industry)". Each individual supervisory occupation has its own separate definition in the DOT describing its unique duties, but at the end of the definition the reader is referred to the master definition; in this case by a sentence reading: "Performs other duties as described under SUPERVISOR (any industry) Master Title". By referring to this master definition, the user will learn about the typical supervisory duties which are commonly performed.

(b) Term Titles

Another type of DOT title is a term title. These include occupations with the same title but few common duties. An example of a term definition is:

CONSULTING ENGINEER (profess. & kin.): A term applied to workers who consult with and advise clients on specialized engineering matters in a particular field of endeavor, such as chemical engineering, civil engineering, or mechanical engineering.

Since neither master nor term definitions are occupations, they are not coded in the Occupational Group Arrangement but are found in separate sections of the DOT (see Contents).

There are other major types of titles used in the DOT, including *alternate titles* and *undefined related titles*. These are discussed later in this section.

(3) Industry Designation

The industry designation is in parentheses immediately following the occupational base title. It often differentiates between two or more occupations with identical titles but different duties. Because of this, it is an integral and inseparable part of any occupational title. An industry designation often tells one or more things about an occupation such as:

- location of the occupation (hotel & rest.; machine shop)

- types of duties associated with the occupation (education; forging)

- products manufactured (optical goods; textile)

- processes used (electroplating; petrol. refin.)

- raw materials used (nonfer. metal; stonework)

While a definition usually receives the designation of the industry or industries in which it occurs, certain occupations occur in a large number of industries. When this happens, the industry assigned is a cross-industry designation. For example, clerical occupations are found in almost every industry. To show the broad, cross-industry nature of clerical occupations, "clerical" is an industry designation in itself. Among other cross-industry designations are: "profess. & kin.", "machine shop", and "woodworking".

Occupations which characteristically occur in nearly all industries, or which occur in a number of industries, but not in most industries and which are not considered to have any particular industrial attachment, are assigned the designation of "any industry." The job title in the example is assigned this designation. It should always be identified as CLOTH PRINTER (any industry) 652.382-010.

In compiling information for the DOT, analysts were not able to study each occupation in all industries where it occurs. The industry designation, therefore, shows in what industries the occupation was studied but does not mean that it may not be found in others. Therefore, industry designations are to be regarded as indicative of industrial location, but not necessarily restrictive.

(4) Alternate Titles

An alternate title is a synonym for the base title. It is not as commonly used as the base title. Alternate titles are shown in lower-case letters immediately after the base title and its industrial designation. In the example, two alternate titles are given: "printer" and "printing-machine operator". Alternate titles may not be used by public employment service offices in assigning occupational classifications. Alternate titles are cross-referenced to their base titles in the Alphabetical Index of Occupational Titles (p. 1225). A particular occupation may have a large number of alternate titles or none at all. Alternate titles carry the code numbers and industry designations of the base title.

(5) The Body of the Definition

The body of the definition usually consists of two or three main parts: a lead statement, a number of task element statements, and a third part known as a "may" item.

(a) The Lead Statement

The first sentence following the industry designation and alternate titles (if any) is the lead statement. It is followed by a colon (:). The lead statement summarizes the entire occupation. It offers essential information such as:

—worker actions
—objective or purpose of the worker actions
—machines, tools, equipment, or work aids used by the worker
—materials used, products made, subject matter dealt with, or services rendered
—instructions followed or judgments made

In the example, the sentence "Sets up and operates machine to print designs on materials, such as cloth, fiberglass, plastics sheeting, coated felt, or oilcloth:" is the lead statement. From it, the user can obtain an overview of the occupation.

(b) Task Element Statements

Task element statements indicate the specific tasks the worker performs to accomplish the overall job purpose described in the lead statement. The sentences in the example beginning with "Turns handwheel . . .", "Turns screws . . .", "Sharpens doctor . . .", "Aligns doctor . . .", "Dips color . . .", etc. are all task element statements. They indicate how the worker actually carries out the job duties.

(c) "May" Items

Many definitions contain one or more sentences beginning with the word "May". They describe duties required of workers in this occupation in some establishments but not in others. The word "May" does not indicate that a worker will sometimes perform this task but rather that some workers in different establishments generally perform one of the varied tasks listed. In the example, the three sentences beginning "May notify. . .", "May mount. . .", "May position. . .", are "May" items. Do not confuse "May" items with the "May be designated. . ." sentence which introduces undefined related titles.

The definition also contains a number of additional information elements designed to assist the user. Among these elements are:

Italicized words: Any word in a definition shown in italics is defined in the "Glossary" (p. 993). Italicized words are technical or special uses of words not ordinarily found in a dictionary. In the example, the words "printing rollers" are italicized. Their precise meaning can be found in the "Glossary"

Bracketed titles: A bracketed title indicates that the worker in the base title occupation performs some duties of the bracketed occupation as a part of the worker's regular duties. In the example, the CLOTH PRINTER (any industry) 652.382-010 "May mount printing rollers. . ." Since this task is usually performed by a PRINTING-ROLLER HANDLER (textile) 652.385-010, this occupation is bracketed. To learn more about this particular aspect of the occupation, the user can read the definition of the bracketed occupational title.

Unbracketed titles: Unbracketed titles are used for occupations that have a frequent working relationship with the occupation defined. In the example, the CLOTH PRINTER (any industry) 652.382-010 has a close working relationship with a COLORIST (profess. & kin.) 022.161-014. This unbracketed title is therefore included in the definition.

Roman numerals: Several somewhat different occupations with the same job title may be found in the same industry. In this event, a Roman numeral follows each title. For example, there are two titles in the DOT listed as ASSEMBLER (ordnance). In order to distinguish between them, a Roman numeral is assigned to each one: ASSEMBLER (ordnance) I 736.381-010 and ASSEMBLER (ordnance) II 736.684-014. There is no connection in the sequence of these numbers with the level of complexity of these occupations or the frequency with which they occur in the U.S. economy.

Statement of significant variables: Another element found in some definitions is a statement of significant variables. It appears near the end of a definition and indicates possible variations that can occur in jobs. This eliminates the need to include a large number of almost identical definitions in the DOT. The statement begins with "Important variations include. . .". There is no statement of significant variables in the definition of CLOTH PRINTER (any industry) 652.382-010.

(6) Undefined Related Titles

Undefined related titles, when applicable, appear at the end of the occupational definition, with initial capital letters, preceded by a phrase, such as "May be designated according to. . .". In the example, three undefined related titles are given: Novelty-Printing-Machine-Operator (textile), Proofing-Machine Operator (print. & pub.), and Plisse-Machine Operator (textile). This type of title indicates a variation or specialization of the base occupation. It resembles the base enough to accompany it, but differs from it enough to require an explanatory phrase and its own unique title. An undefined related title has the same code as its base title. Undefined related titles found in occupational definitions are listed in the Alphabetical Index of Occupational Titles in initial capital letters. The entry includes the industry designation and the 9-digit code of the corresponding base title. In addition, undefined related titles appear in alphabetical order with their nine-digit code under their appropriate industry in the list of Occupational Titles Arranged by Industry Designation.

(7) Definition Trailer

Selected characteristics and auxiliary profile data are contained in a "trailer" appended to each definition. The trailer contains the following selected occupational analysis characteristics: GOE Code; Strength rating; R, M, and L of GED; and SVP. (Refer to Appendix C for a detailed explanation of these characteristics.)

The Date of Last Update (DLU), the last item in the trailer, is the date of the most recent material gathered in support of that occupation. The date "1977" indicates that the job has not been studied since the publication of the Fourth Edition DOT in 1977 (See page 1003, Appendix A.) This entry allows the reader to identify the currency of each definition. It will also provide easy identification of definitions "new" to the DOT or alert the reader to previously published and recently updated definitions.

HOW TO FIND AN OCCUPATIONAL TITLE AND CODE

Occupational titles and codes in the *Dictionary of Occupational Titles* (DOT) are based on the type of information presented in the lead statement and task element statements described in the previous section: worker actions; the purpose or objective of these actions; machines, tools, equipment, or work aids used; materials processed, products made, subject matter dealt with, or service rendered; the nature and complexity of instructions followed; and the job tasks actually performed by the worker. The more complete and comprehensive the information you are able to assemble about the tasks performed by a worker or required by an employer on a particular job, the easier it will be to determine the appropriate classification.

The Three Occupational Arrangements

There are three different arrangements of occupational titles in the DOT: the Occupational Group Arrangement, the Alphabetical Index, and the Industry Arrangement. All of these can assist you in identifying and classifying jobs.

(1) The Occupational Group Arrangement

In this revised edition, as in the fourth edition, the primary method of identifying or classifying jobs is by use of the Occupational Group Arrangement (pp. 13 - 991). For job placement and referral purposes, if you have obtained sufficient information from the worker seeking a job, or the employer placing an order, this is the preferred method to use. The other two arrangements of titles are supplementary and should be used in conjunction with the Occupational Group Arrangement. Using the Occupational Group Arrangement saves time by eliminating the extra step of referring to other sections of the DOT.

To use the Occupational Group Arrangement:

(a) Obtain all the relevant facts about the job.
(b) Find the 1-digit occupational category which seems most likely to contain the job.
(c) Find the most appropriate 2-digit occupational division of the category.
(d) Find the best 3-digit group within the division.
(e) Examine the occupational definition under the group you have selected and choose the most appropriate title. *Read the definition for the title selected carefully before deciding if this is the best possible classification. If it does not correspond closely with the information you have collected, repeat steps (b) to (d) to find the most appropriate classification.*

In the process of choosing the appropriate occupational category, division, and group (steps b - d) you will develop information about the job which will be helpful in classifying it. When you are trying to find the most appropriate definition in the occupational group selected (step e), remember that jobs requiring more responsibility and independent judgment have lower worker functions numerals and will be found near the beginning of the occupational group, while those requiring less responsibility and independent judgment have higher numbers and will be found nearer the end.

(2) The Alphabetical Index of Occupational Titles

The Alphabetical Index is the second basic arrangement of codes and titles in the DOT. In this section, titles are shown first, including their industry designation. Titles with two or more words, such as AC-COUNT-CLASSIFICATION CLERK (clerical), are treated as one word for purposes of alphabetizing. Following the industry designation, you will find the 9-digit code for the occupation. This will help to find quickly the title and its definition in the Occupational Group Arrangement (OGA). The Alphabetical Index is useful if you are sure of an occupational title, including its industry designation, and just need the 9-digit code, or if you are reasonably sure of a title and its industry designation, but there is more than one such title in the same industry (indicated by a Roman numeral), you could use this index to get the 9-digit codes of the various titles in order to locate and check out their definitions in the OGA. Although it is unwise to classify a job or application based on its title alone, the Alphabetical Index is useful in some situations to identify definitions that are possibly relevant.

To use the Alphabetical Index:

(a) Look through the index for the title of the job as you know it. If you find it, write down the 9-digit code printed to the right of the title. Using this code as a guide, find the definition for the title in the Occupational Group Arrangement. *Read the entire definition before deciding whether it is the most appropriate classification.*

(b) If you cannot find the job title, or if the definition appears inappropriate, look for another title. Some clues are:

Invert the title: maintenance carpenter
CARPENTER, MAINTENANCE

Contract the title: rubber-belt repairer
BELT REPAIRER

Find a synonym: car mechanic
AUTOMOBILE MECHANIC

Consider such factors as:

- *Job location*
  PARKING LOT ATTENDANT; STOREROOM CLERK
- *Machines used*
  PUNCH-PRESS OPERATOR; MACHINE FEEDER
- *Materials used*
  LOG LOADER; PLASTIC-TILE LAYER
- *Subject matter*
  ACCOUNTING CLERK; CREDIT ANALYST
- *Services involved*
  CLEANER AND PRESSER; BROKER
- *Activity performed*
  TEACHER; INSPECTOR
- *Job complexity*
  MACHINE SETTER; WELDING-MACHINE TENDER

If you have information on several of these factors, however, it may be more appropriate to use the Occupational Group Arrangement.

Some titles listed in the Alphabetical Index are not used in public employment service operations. "Master" and "Term" titles do not have occupational codes and consequently cannot be used. They are easily recognized since the words "Master Title" or "Term Title" appear in place of the code to the right of the title. Alternate titles, which are synonyms for, but less commonly used than base titles, are not standard titles for classification purposes in Job Service operations. They are also easily recognizable since they are in lower-case letters.

(3) Occupational Titles Arranged by Industry Designation

The Industry Arrangement of titles (pp.1027-1224) may be useful if you have limited information about a job. You may know the industry in which the job is located, but have little or no information about such things as products made, materials used, services rendered, and other essential data. The Industry Arrangement can also be of assistance if a person wants to work in a particular industry, or if you need to learn more about related jobs in the industry.

To use the Industry Arrangement:

(a) Look through the industry titles and read their definitions. Select the one most likely to contain the particular job.

(b) Survey the occupational titles listed under the selected industry. Choose the title which seems appropriate to the job, and write down the nine-digit code to the right of the title. Using this code as a guide, find the definition in the Occupational Group Arrangement. *Read the entire occupational definition before deciding if it is the most appropriate classification.*

Summary

The basic purpose and use of each of the three arrangements of occupational titles is shown below:

Use . . .	If you . . .
THE	have sufficient information about the job tasks
OCCUPATIONAL	want to know about other closely related occupations
GROUP ARRANGEMENT	want to be sure you have chosen the most appropriate classification using the other arrangements
OCCUPATIONAL TITLES	know only the industry in which the job is located
ARRANGED BY	want to know about other jobs in an industry
INDUSTRY DESIGNATION	your client wants to work in a specific industry
THE	know only the job title and cannot obtain better information
ALPHABETICAL INDEX OF	
OCCUPATIONAL TITLES	

OCCUPATIONAL CATEGORIES, DIVISIONS, AND GROUPS

ONE-DIGIT OCCUPATIONAL CATEGORIES

0/1	PROFESSIONAL, TECHNICAL, AND MANAGERIAL OCCUPATIONS	5	PROCESSING OCCUPATIONS
2	CLERICAL AND SALES OCCUPATIONS	6	MACHINE TRADES OCCUPATIONS
3	SERVICE OCCUPATIONS	7	BENCHWORK OCCUPATIONS
4	AGRICULTURAL, FISHERY, FORESTRY, AND RELATED OCCUPATIONS	8	STRUCTURAL WORK OCCUPATIONS
		9	MISCELLANEOUS OCCUPATIONS

TWO-DIGIT OCCUPATIONAL DIVISIONS

0/1 PROFESSIONAL, TECHNICAL, AND MANAGERIAL OCCUPATIONS
00/01 OCCUPATIONS IN ARCHITECTURE, ENGINEERING, AND SURVEYING
02 OCCUPATIONS IN MATHEMATICS AND PHYSICAL SCIENCES
03 COMPUTER-RELATED OCCUPATIONS
04 OCCUPATIONS IN LIFE SCIENCES
05 OCCUPATIONS IN SOCIAL SCIENCES
07 OCCUPATIONS IN MEDICINE AND HEALTH
09 OCCUPATIONS IN EDUCATION
10 OCCUPATIONS IN MUSEUM, LIBRARY, AND ARCHIVAL SCIENCES
11 OCCUPATIONS IN LAW AND JURISPRUDENCE
12 OCCUPATIONS IN RELIGION AND THEOLOGY
13 OCCUPATIONS IN WRITING
14 OCCUPATIONS IN ART
15 OCCUPATIONS IN ENTERTAINMENT AND RECREATION
16 OCCUPATIONS IN ADMINISTRATIVE SPECIALIZATIONS
18 MANAGERS AND OFFICIALS, N.E.C.
19 MISCELLANEOUS PROFESSIONAL, TECHNICAL, AND MANAGERIAL OCCUPATIONS

2 CLERICAL AND SALES OCCUPATIONS
20 STENOGRAPHY, TYPING, FILING, AND RELATED OCCUPATIONS
21 COMPUTING AND ACCOUNT-RECORDING OCCUPATIONS
22 PRODUCTION AND STOCK CLERKS AND RELATED OCCUPATIONS
23 INFORMATION AND MESSAGE DISTRIBUTION OCCUPATIONS
24 MISCELLANEOUS CLERICAL OCCUPATIONS
25 SALES OCCUPATIONS, SERVICES
26 SALES OCCUPATIONS, CONSUMABLE COMMODITIES
27 SALES OCCUPATIONS, COMMODITIES, N.E.C.
29 MISCELLANEOUS SALES OCCUPATIONS

3 SERVICE OCCUPATIONS
30 DOMESTIC SERVICE OCCUPATIONS
31 FOOD AND BEVERAGE PREPARATION AND SERVICE OCCUPATIONS
32 LODGING AND RELATED SERVICE OCCUPATIONS
33 BARBERING, COSMETOLOGY, AND RELATED SERVICE OCCUPATIONS
34 AMUSEMENT AND RECREATION SERVICE OCCUPATIONS
35 MISCELLANEOUS PERSONAL SERVICE OCCUPATIONS
36 APPAREL AND FURNISHINGS SERVICE OCCUPATIONS
37 PROTECTIVE SERVICE OCCUPATIONS
38 BUILDING AND RELATED SERVICE OCCUPATIONS

4 AGRICULTURAL, FISHERY, FORESTRY, AND RELATED OCCUPATIONS
40 PLANT FARMING OCCUPATIONS
41 ANIMAL FARMING OCCUPATIONS
42 MISCELLANEOUS AGRICULTURAL AND RELATED OCCUPATIONS
44 FISHERY AND RELATED OCCUPATIONS
45 FORESTRY OCCUPATIONS

46 HUNTING, TRAPPING, AND RELATED OCCUPATIONS

5 PROCESSING OCCUPATIONS
50 OCCUPATIONS IN PROCESSING OF METAL
51 ORE REFINING AND FOUNDRY OCCUPATIONS
52 OCCUPATIONS IN PROCESSING OF FOOD, TOBACCO, AND RELATED PRODUCTS
53 OCCUPATIONS IN PROCESSING OF PAPER AND RELATED MATERIALS
54 OCCUPATIONS IN PROCESSING OF PETROLEUM, COAL, NATURAL AND MANUFACTURED GAS, AND RELATED PRODUCTS
55 OCCUPATIONS IN PROCESSING OF CHEMICALS, PLASTICS, SYNTHETICS, RUBBER, PAINT, AND RELATED PRODUCTS
56 OCCUPATIONS IN PROCESSING OF WOOD AND WOOD PRODUCTS
57 OCCUPATIONS IN PROCESSING OF STONE, CLAY, GLASS, AND RELATED PRODUCTS
58 OCCUPATIONS IN PROCESSING OF LEATHER, TEXTILES, AND RELATED PRODUCTS
59 PROCESSING OCCUPATIONS, N.E.C.

6 MACHINE TRADES OCCUPATIONS
60 METAL MACHINING OCCUPATIONS
61 METALWORKING OCCUPATIONS, N.E.C.
62/63 MECHANICS AND MACHINERY REPAIRERS
64 PAPERWORKING OCCUPATIONS
65 PRINTING OCCUPATIONS
66 WOOD MACHINING OCCUPATIONS
67 OCCUPATIONS IN MACHINING STONE, CLAY, GLASS, AND RELATED MATERIALS
68 TEXTILE OCCUPATIONS
69 MACHINE TRADES OCCUPATIONS, N.E.C.

7 BENCHWORK OCCUPATIONS
70 OCCUPATIONS IN FABRICATION, ASSEMBLY, AND REPAIR OF METAL PRODUCTS, N.E.C.
71 OCCUPATIONS IN FABRICATION AND REPAIR OF SCIENTIFIC, MEDICAL, PHOTOGRAPHIC, OPTICAL, HOROLOGICAL, AND RELATED PRODUCTS
72 OCCUPATIONS IN ASSEMBLY AND REPAIR OF ELECTRICAL EQUIPMENT
73 OCCUPATIONS IN FABRICATION AND REPAIR OF PRODUCTS MADE FROM ASSORTED MATERIALS
74 PAINTING, DECORATING, AND RELATED OCCUPATIONS
75 OCCUPATIONS IN FABRICATION AND REPAIR OF PLASTICS, SYNTHETICS, RUBBER, AND RELATED PRODUCTS
76 OCCUPATIONS IN FABRICATION AND REPAIR OF WOOD PRODUCTS
77 OCCUPATIONS IN FABRICATION AND REPAIR OF SAND, STONE, CLAY, AND GLASS PRODUCTS
78 OCCUPATIONS IN FABRICATION AND REPAIR OF TEXTILE, LEATHER, AND RELATED PRODUCTS
79 BENCHWORK OCCUPATIONS, N.E.C.

8 STRUCTURAL WORK OCCUPATIONS
80 OCCUPATIONS IN METAL FABRICATING, N.E.C.
81 WELDERS, CUTTERS, AND RELATED OCCUPATIONS
82 ELECTRICAL ASSEMBLING, INSTALLING, AND REPAIRING OCCUPATIONS
84 PAINTING, PLASTERING, WATERPROOFING, CEMENTING, AND RELATED OCCUPATIONS
85 EXCAVATING, GRADING, PAVING, AND RELATED OCCUPATIONS
86 CONSTRUCTION OCCUPATIONS, N.E.C.
89 STRUCTURAL WORK OCCUPATIONS, N.E.C.

9 MISCELLANEOUS OCCUPATIONS
90 MOTOR FREIGHT OCCUPATIONS
91 TRANSPORTATION OCCUPATIONS, N.E.C.
92 PACKAGING AND MATERIALS HANDLING OCCUPATIONS
93 OCCUPATIONS IN EXTRACTION OF MINERALS
95 OCCUPATIONS IN PRODUCTION AND DISTRIBUTION OF UTILITIES
96 AMUSEMENT, RECREATION, MOTION PICTURE, RADIO AND TELEVISION OCCUPATIONS, N.E.C.
97 OCCUPATIONS IN GRAPHIC ART WORK

THREE-DIGIT OCCUPATIONAL GROUPS

PROFESSIONAL, TECHNICAL, AND MANAGERIAL OCCUPATIONS

00/01 OCCUPATIONS IN ARCHITECTURE, ENGINEERING, AND SURVEYING
001 ARCHITECTURAL OCCUPATIONS
002 AERONAUTICAL ENGINEERING OCCUPATIONS
003 ELECTRICAL/ELECTRONICS ENGINEERING OCCUPATIONS
005 CIVIL ENGINEERING OCCUPATIONS
006 CERAMIC ENGINEERING OCCUPATIONS
007 MECHANICAL ENGINEERING OCCUPATIONS
008 CHEMICAL ENGINEERING OCCUPATIONS
010 MINING AND PETROLEUM ENGINEERING OCCUPATIONS
011 METALLURGY AND METALLURGICAL ENGINEERING OCCUPATIONS
012 INDUSTRIAL ENGINEERING OCCUPATIONS
013 AGRICULTURAL ENGINEERING OCCUPATIONS
014 MARINE ENGINEERING OCCUPATIONS
015 NUCLEAR ENGINEERING OCCUPATIONS
017 DRAFTERS, N.E.C.
018 SURVEYING/CARTOGRAPHIC OCCUPATIONS
019 OCCUPATIONS IN ARCHITECTURE, ENGINEERING, AND SURVEYING, N.E.C.

02 OCCUPATIONS IN MATHEMATICS AND PHYSICAL SCIENCES
020 OCCUPATIONS IN MATHEMATICS
021 OCCUPATIONS IN ASTRONOMY
022 OCCUPATIONS IN CHEMISTRY
023 OCCUPATIONS IN PHYSICS
024 OCCUPATIONS IN GEOLOGY
025 OCCUPATIONS IN METEOROLOGY
029 OCCUPATIONS IN MATHEMATICS AND PHYSICAL SCIENCES, N.E.C.

03 COMPUTER-RELATED OCCUPATIONS
030 OCCUPATIONS IN SYSTEMS ANALYSIS AND PROGRAMMING
031 OCCUPATIONS IN DATA COMMUNICATIONS AND NETWORKS
032 OCCUPATIONS IN COMPUTER SYSTEM USER SUPPORT
033 OCCUPATIONS IN COMPUTER SYSTEMS TECHNICAL SUPPORT
039 COMPUTER-RELATED OCCUPATIONS, N.E.C.

04 OCCUPATIONS IN LIFE SCIENCES
040 OCCUPATIONS IN AGRICULTURAL SCIENCES
041 OCCUPATIONS IN BIOLOGICAL SCIENCES
045 OCCUPATIONS IN PSYCHOLOGY
049 OCCUPATIONS IN LIFE SCIENCES, N.E.C.

05 OCCUPATIONS IN SOCIAL SCIENCES
050 OCCUPATIONS IN ECONOMICS
051 OCCUPATIONS IN POLITICAL SCIENCE
052 OCCUPATIONS IN HISTORY
054 OCCUPATIONS IN SOCIOLOGY
055 OCCUPATIONS IN ANTHROPOLOGY
059 OCCUPATIONS IN SOCIAL SCIENCES, N.E.C.

07 OCCUPATIONS IN MEDICINE AND HEALTH
070 PHYSICIANS AND SURGEONS
071 OSTEOPATHS
072 DENTISTS
073 VETERINARIANS
074 PHARMACISTS
075 REGISTERED NURSES
076 THERAPISTS
077 DIETITIANS
078 OCCUPATIONS IN MEDICAL AND DENTAL TECHNOLOGY
079 OCCUPATIONS IN MEDICINE AND HEALTH, N.E.C.

09 OCCUPATIONS IN EDUCATION
090 OCCUPATIONS IN COLLEGE AND UNIVERSITY EDUCATION
091 OCCUPATIONS IN SECONDARY SCHOOL EDUCATION
092 OCCUPATIONS IN PRESCHOOL, PRIMARY SCHOOL, AND KINDERGARTEN EDUCATION
094 OCCUPATIONS IN EDUCATION OF PERSONS WITH DISABILITIES
096 HOME ECONOMISTS AND FARM ADVISERS
097 OCCUPATIONS IN VOCATIONAL EDUCATION
099 OCCUPATIONS IN EDUCATION, N.E.C.

10 OCCUPATIONS IN MUSEUM, LIBRARY, AND ARCHIVAL SCIENCES
100 LIBRARIANS
101 ARCHIVISTS
102 MUSEUM CURATORS AND RELATED OCCUPATIONS
109 OCCUPATIONS IN MUSEUM, LIBRARY, AND ARCHIVAL SCIENCES, N.E.C.

11 OCCUPATIONS IN LAW AND JURISPRUDENCE
110 LAWYERS
111 JUDGES
119 OCCUPATIONS IN LAW AND JURISPRUDENCE, N.E.C.

12 OCCUPATIONS IN RELIGION AND THEOLOGY
120 CLERGY
129 OCCUPATIONS IN RELIGION AND THEOLOGY, N.E.C.

13 OCCUPATIONS IN WRITING
131 WRITERS
132 EDITORS: PUBLICATION, BROADCAST, AND SCRIPT
137 INTERPRETERS AND TRANSLATORS
139 OCCUPATIONS IN WRITING, N.E.C.

14 OCCUPATIONS IN ART
141 COMMERCIAL ARTISTS: DESIGNERS AND ILLUSTRATORS, GRAPHIC ARTS
142 ENVIRONMENTAL, PRODUCT, AND RELATED DESIGNERS
143 OCCUPATIONS IN PHOTOGRAPHY
144 FINE ARTISTS: PAINTERS, SCULPTORS, AND RELATED OCCUPATIONS
149 OCCUPATIONS IN ART, N.E.C.

CLERICAL AND SALES OCCUPATIONS

277 SALES OCCUPATIONS, SPORTING, HOBBY, STATIONERY, AND RELATED GOODS
279 SALES OCCUPATIONS, MISCELLANEOUS COMMODITIES, N.E.C.
29 MISCELLANEOUS SALES OCCUPATIONS
290 SALES CLERKS
291 VENDING AND DOOR-TO-DOOR SELLING OCCUPATIONS
292 ROUTE SALES AND DELIVERY OCCUPATIONS
293 SOLICITORS
294 AUCTIONEERS
295 RENTAL CLERKS
296 SHOPPERS
297 SALES PROMOTION OCCUPATIONS
298 MERCHANDISE DISPLAYERS
299 MISCELLANEOUS SALES OCCUPATIONS, N.E.C.

SERVICE OCCUPATIONS

30 DOMESTIC SERVICE OCCUPATIONS
301 HOUSEHOLD AND RELATED WORK
302 LAUNDERERS, PRIVATE FAMILY
305 COOKS, DOMESTIC
309 DOMESTIC SERVICE OCCUPATIONS, N.E.C.
31 FOOD AND BEVERAGE PREPARATION AND SERVICE OCCUPATIONS
310 HOSTS/HOSTESSES AND STEWARDS/STEWARDESSES, FOOD AND BEVERAGE SERVICE, EXCEPT SHIP STEWARDS/STEWARDESSES
311 WAITERS/WAITRESSES, AND RELATED FOOD SERVICE OCCUPATIONS
312 BARTENDERS
313 CHEFS AND COOKS, HOTELS AND RESTAURANTS
315 MISCELLANEOUS COOKS, EXCEPT DOMESTIC
316 MEATCUTTERS, EXCEPT IN SLAUGHTERING AND PACKING HOUSES
317 MISCELLANEOUS FOOD AND BEVERAGE PREPARATION OCCUPATIONS
318 KITCHEN WORKERS, N.E.C.
319 FOOD AND BEVERAGE PREPARATION AND SERVICE OCCUPATIONS, N.E.C.
32 LODGING AND RELATED SERVICE OCCUPATIONS
320 BOARDING-HOUSE AND LODGING-HOUSE KEEPERS
321 HOUSEKEEPERS, HOTELS AND INSTITUTIONS
323 HOUSECLEANERS, HOTELS, RESTAURANTS, AND RELATED ESTABLISHMENTS
324 BELLHOPS AND RELATED OCCUPATIONS
329 LODGING AND RELATED SERVICE OCCUPATIONS, N.E.C.
33 BARBERING, COSMETOLOGY, AND RELATED SERVICE OCCUPATIONS
330 BARBERS
331 MANICURISTS
332 HAIRDRESSERS AND COSMETOLOGISTS
333 MAKE-UP OCCUPATIONS
334 MASSEURS AND RELATED OCCUPATIONS
335 BATH ATTENDANTS
338 EMBALMERS AND RELATED OCCUPATIONS
339 BARBERING, COSMETOLOGY, AND RELATED SERVICE OCCUPATIONS, N.E.C.
34 AMUSEMENT AND RECREATION SERVICE OCCUPATIONS
340 ATTENDANTS, BOWLING ALLEY AND BILLIARD PARLOR
341 ATTENDANTS, GOLF COURSE, TENNIS COURT, SKATING RINK, AND RELATED FACILITIES
342 AMUSEMENT DEVICE AND CONCESSION ATTENDANTS
343 GAMBLING HALL ATTENDANTS
344 USHERS
346 WARDROBE AND DRESSING-ROOM ATTENDANTS
349 AMUSEMENT AND RECREATION SERVICE OCCUPATIONS, N.E.C.
35 MISCELLANEOUS PERSONAL SERVICE OCCUPATIONS
350 SHIP STEWARDS/STEWARDESSES AND RELATED OCCUPATIONS
351 TRAIN ATTENDANTS
352 HOSTS/HOSTESSES AND STEWARDS/STEWARDESSES, N.E.C.
353 GUIDES
354 UNLICENSED BIRTH ATTENDANTS AND PRACTICAL NURSES
355 ATTENDANTS, HOSPITALS, MORGUES, AND RELATED HEALTH SERVICES
357 BAGGAGE HANDLERS
358 CHECKROOM, LOCKER ROOM, AND REST ROOM ATTENDANTS
359 MISCELLANEOUS PERSONAL SERVICE OCCUPATIONS, N.E.C.
36 APPAREL AND FURNISHINGS SERVICE OCCUPATIONS
361 LAUNDERING OCCUPATIONS
362 DRY CLEANING OCCUPATIONS
363 PRESSING OCCUPATIONS
364 DYEING AND RELATED OCCUPATIONS
365 SHOE AND LUGGAGE REPAIRER AND RELATED OCCUPATIONS
366 BOOTBLACKS AND RELATED OCCUPATIONS
369 APPAREL AND FURNISHINGS SERVICE OCCUPATIONS, N.E.C.
37 PROTECTIVE SERVICE OCCUPATIONS
371 CROSSING TENDERS AND BRIDGE OPERATORS
372 SECURITY GUARDS AND CORRECTION OFFICERS, EXCEPT CROSSING TENDERS
373 FIRE FIGHTERS, FIRE DEPARTMENT
375 POLICE OFFICERS AND DETECTIVES, PUBLIC SERVICE
376 POLICE OFFICERS AND DETECTIVES, EXCEPT IN PUBLIC SERVICE
377 SHERIFFS AND BAILIFFS
378 ARMED FORCES ENLISTED PERSONNEL
379 PROTECTIVE SERVICE OCCUPATIONS, N.E.C.
38 BUILDING AND RELATED SERVICE OCCUPATIONS
381 PORTERS AND CLEANERS
382 JANITORS
383 BUILDING PEST CONTROL SERVICE OCCUPATIONS
388 ELEVATOR OPERATORS
389 BUILDING AND RELATED SERVICE OCCUPATIONS, N.E.C.

AGRICULTURAL, FISHERY, FORESTRY, AND RELATED OCCUPATIONS

40 PLANT FARMING OCCUPATIONS
401 GRAIN FARMING OCCUPATIONS
402 VEGETABLE FARMING OCCUPATIONS
403 FRUIT AND NUT FARMING OCCUPATIONS
404 FIELD CROP FARMING OCCUPATIONS, N.E.C.
405 HORTICULTURAL SPECIALTY OCCUPATIONS
406 GARDENING AND GROUNDSKEEPING OCCUPATIONS
407 DIVERSIFIED CROP FARMING OCCUPATIONS
408 PLANT LIFE AND RELATED SERVICE OCCUPATIONS
409 PLANT FARMING AND RELATED OCCUPATIONS, N.E.C.

41 ANIMAL FARMING OCCUPATIONS
410 DOMESTIC ANIMAL FARMING OCCUPATIONS
411 DOMESTIC FOWL FARMING OCCUPATIONS
412 GAME FARMING OCCUPATIONS
413 LOWER ANIMAL FARMING OCCUPATIONS
418 ANIMAL SERVICE OCCUPATIONS
419 ANIMAL FARMING OCCUPATIONS, N.E.C.

42 MISCELLANEOUS AGRICULTURAL AND RELATED OCCUPATIONS
421 GENERAL FARMING OCCUPATIONS

429 MISCELLANEOUS AGRICULTURAL AND RELATED OCCUPATIONS, N.E.C.

44 FISHERY AND RELATED OCCUPATIONS
441 NET, SEINE, AND TRAP FISHERS
442 LINE FISHERS
443 FISHERS, MISCELLANEOUS EQUIPMENT
446 AQUATIC LIFE CULTIVATION AND RELATED OCCUPATIONS
447 SPONGE AND SEAWEED GATHERERS
449 FISHERY AND RELATED OCCUPATIONS, N.E.C.

45 FORESTRY OCCUPATIONS
451 TREE FARMING AND RELATED OCCUPATIONS
452 FOREST CONSERVATION OCCUPATIONS
453 OCCUPATIONS IN HARVESTING FOREST PRODUCTS, EXCEPT LOGGING
454 LOGGING AND RELATED OCCUPATIONS
455 LOG GRADING, SCALING, SORTING, RAFTING, AND RELATED OCCUPATIONS
459 FORESTRY OCCUPATIONS, N.E.C.

46 HUNTING, TRAPPING, AND RELATED OCCUPATIONS
461 HUNTING AND TRAPPING OCCUPATIONS

PROCESSING OCCUPATIONS

50 OCCUPATIONS IN PROCESSING OF METAL
500 ELECTROPLATING OCCUPATIONS
501 DIP PLATING OCCUPATIONS
502 MELTING, POURING, CASTING, AND RELATED OCCUPATIONS
503 PICKLING, CLEANING, DEGREASING, AND RELATED OCCUPATIONS
504 HEAT-TREATING OCCUPATIONS
505 METAL SPRAYING, COATING, AND RELATED OCCUPATIONS
509 OCCUPATIONS IN PROCESSING OF METAL, N.E.C.

51 ORE REFINING AND FOUNDRY OCCUPATIONS
510 MIXING AND RELATED OCCUPATIONS
511 SEPARATING, FILTERING, AND RELATED OCCUPATIONS
512 MELTING OCCUPATIONS
513 ROASTING OCCUPATIONS
514 POURING AND CASTING OCCUPATIONS
515 CRUSHING AND GRINDING OCCUPATIONS
518 MOLDERS, COREMAKERS, AND RELATED OCCUPATIONS
519 ORE REFINING AND FOUNDRY OCCUPATIONS, N.E.C.

52 OCCUPATIONS IN PROCESSING OF FOOD, TOBACCO, AND RELATED PRODUCTS
520 MIXING, COMPOUNDING, BLENDING, KNEADING, SHAPING, AND RELATED OCCUPATIONS
521 SEPARATING, CRUSHING, MILLING, CHOPPING, GRINDING, AND RELATED OCCUPATIONS
522 CULTURING, MELTING, FERMENTING, DISTILLING, SATURATING, PICKLING, AGING, AND RELATED OCCUPATIONS
523 HEATING, RENDERING, MELTING, DRYING, COOLING, FREEZING, AND RELATED OCCUPATIONS
524 COATING, ICING, DECORATING, AND RELATED OCCUPATIONS
525 SLAUGHTERING, BREAKING, CURING, AND RELATED OCCUPATIONS
526 COOKING AND BAKING OCCUPATIONS, N.E.C.
529 OCCUPATIONS IN PROCESSING OF FOOD, TOBACCO, AND RELATED PRODUCTS, N.E.C.

53 OCCUPATIONS IN PROCESSING OF PAPER AND RELATED MATERIALS
530 GRINDING, BEATING, AND MIXING OCCUPATIONS
532 COOKING AND DRYING OCCUPATIONS

533 COOLING, BLEACHING, SCREENING, WASHING, AND RELATED OCCUPATIONS
534 CALENDERING, SIZING, COATING, AND RELATED OCCUPATIONS
535 FORMING OCCUPATIONS, N.E.C.
539 OCCUPATIONS IN PROCESSING OF PAPER AND RELATED MATERIALS, N.E.C.

54 OCCUPATIONS IN PROCESSING OF PETROLEUM, COAL, NATURAL AND MANUFACTURED GAS, AND RELATED PRODUCTS
540 MIXING AND BLENDING OCCUPATIONS
541 FILTERING, STRAINING, AND SEPARATING OCCUPATIONS
542 DISTILLING, SUBLIMING, AND CARBONIZING OCCUPATIONS
543 DRYING, HEATING, AND MELTING OCCUPATIONS
544 GRINDING AND CRUSHING OCCUPATIONS
546 REACTING OCCUPATIONS, N.E.C.
549 OCCUPATIONS IN PROCESSING OF PETROLEUM, COAL, NATURAL AND MANUFACTURED GAS, AND RELATED PRODUCTS, N.E.C.

55 OCCUPATIONS IN PROCESSING OF CHEMICALS, PLASTICS, SYNTHETICS, RUBBER, PAINT, AND RELATED PRODUCTS
550 MIXING AND BLENDING OCCUPATIONS
551 FILTERING, STRAINING, AND SEPARATING OCCUPATIONS
552 DISTILLING OCCUPATIONS
553 HEATING, BAKING, DRYING, SEASONING, MELTING, AND HEAT-TREATING OCCUPATIONS
554 COATING, CALENDERING, LAMINATING, AND FINISHING OCCUPATIONS
555 GRINDING AND CRUSHING OCCUPATIONS
556 CASTING AND MOLDING OCCUPATIONS, N.E.C.
557 EXTRUDING OCCUPATIONS
558 REACTING OCCUPATIONS, N.E.C.
559 OCCUPATIONS IN PROCESSING OF CHEMICALS, PLASTICS, SYNTHETICS, RUBBER, PAINT, AND RELATED PRODUCTS, N.E.C.

56 OCCUPATIONS IN PROCESSING OF WOOD AND WOOD PRODUCTS
560 MIXING AND RELATED OCCUPATIONS
561 WOOD PRESERVING AND RELATED OCCUPATIONS
562 SATURATING, COATING, AND RELATED OCCUPATIONS, N.E.C.

MACHINE TRADES OCCUPATIONS

BENCHWORK OCCUPATIONS

776 OCCUPATIONS IN FABRICATION AND REPAIR OF ASBESTOS AND POLISHING PRODUCTS, ABRASIVES, AND RELATED MATERIALS

777 MODELMAKERS, PATTERNMAKERS, MOLDMAKERS, AND RELATED OCCUPATIONS

779 OCCUPATIONS IN FABRICATION AND REPAIR OF SAND, STONE, CLAY, AND GLASS PRODUCTS, N.E.C.

78 OCCUPATIONS IN FABRICATION AND REPAIR OF TEXTILE, LEATHER, AND RELATED PRODUCTS

780 OCCUPATIONS IN UPHOLSTERING AND IN FABRICATION AND REPAIR OF STUFFED FURNITURE, MATTRESSES, AND RELATED PRODUCTS

781 LAYING OUT, MARKING, CUTTING, AND PUNCHING OCCUPATIONS, N.E.C.

782 HAND SEWERS, MENDERS, EMBROIDERERS, KNITTERS, AND RELATED OCCUPATIONS, N.E.C.

783 FUR AND LEATHER WORKING OCCUPATIONS

784 OCCUPATIONS IN FABRICATION AND REPAIR OF HATS, CAPS, GLOVES, AND RELATED PRODUCTS

785 TAILORS AND DRESSMAKERS

786 SEWING MACHINE OPERATORS, GARMENT

787 SEWING MACHINE OPERATORS, NONGARMENT

788 OCCUPATIONS IN FABRICATION AND REPAIR OF FOOTWEAR

789 OCCUPATIONS IN FABRICATION AND REPAIR OF TEXTILE, LEATHER, AND RELATED PRODUCTS, N.E.C.

79 BENCH WORK OCCUPATIONS, N.E.C.

790 OCCUPATIONS IN PREPARATION OF FOOD, TOBACCO, AND RELATED PRODUCTS, N.E.C.

794 OCCUPATIONS IN FABRICATION OF PAPER PRODUCTS, N.E.C.

795 GLUING OCCUPATIONS, N.E.C.

STRUCTURAL WORK OCCUPATIONS

80 OCCUPATIONS IN METAL FABRICATING, N.E.C.

800 RIVETERS, N.E.C.

801 FITTING, BOLTING, SCREWING, AND RELATED OCCUPATIONS

804 TINSMITHS, COPPERSMITHS, AND SHEET METAL WORKERS

805 BOILERMAKERS

806 TRANSPORTATION EQUIPMENT ASSEMBLERS AND RELATED OCCUPATIONS

807 STRUCTURAL REPAIRERS, TRANSPORTATION EQUIPMENT

809 MISCELLANEOUS OCCUPATIONS IN METAL FABRICATING, N.E.C.

81 WELDERS, CUTTERS, AND RELATED OCCUPATIONS

810 ARC WELDERS AND CUTTERS

811 GAS WELDERS

812 RESISTANCE WELDERS

813 BRAZING, BRAZE-WELDING, AND SOLDERING OCCUPATIONS

814 SOLID STATE WELDERS

815 ELECTRON-BEAM; ELECTROSLAG; THERMIT; INDUCTION; AND LASER-BEAM WELDERS

816 THERMAL CUTTERS AND ARC CUTTERS

819 WELDERS, CUTTERS, AND RELATED OCCUPATIONS, N.E.C.

82 ELECTRICAL ASSEMBLING, INSTALLING, AND REPAIRING OCCUPATIONS

820 OCCUPATIONS IN ASSEMBLY, INSTALLATION, AND REPAIR OF GENERATORS, MOTORS, ACCESSORIES, AND RELATED POWERPLANT EQUIPMENT

821 OCCUPATIONS IN ASSEMBLY, INSTALLATION, AND REPAIR OF TRANSMISSION AND DISTRIBUTION LINES AND CIRCUITS

822 OCCUPATIONS IN ASSEMBLY, INSTALLATION, AND REPAIR OF WIRE COMMUNICATION, DETECTION AND SIGNALING EQUIPMENT

823 OCCUPATIONS IN ASSEMBLY, INSTALLATION, AND REPAIR OF ELECTRONIC COMMUNICATION, DETECTION, AND SIGNALING EQUIPMENT

824 OCCUPATIONS IN ASSEMBLY, INSTALLATION, AND REPAIR OF LIGHTING EQUIPMENT AND BUILDING WIRING, N.E.C.

825 OCCUPATIONS IN ASSEMBLY, INSTALLATION, AND REPAIR OF TRANSPORTATION AND MATERIAL-HANDLING EQUIPMENT, N.E.C.

826 OCCUPATIONS IN ASSEMBLY, INSTALLATION, AND REPAIR OF INDUSTRIAL APPARATUS, N.E.C.

827 OCCUPATIONS IN ASSEMBLY, INSTALLATION, AND REPAIR OF LARGE HOUSEHOLD APPLIANCES AND SIMILAR COMMERCIAL AND INDUSTRIAL EQUIPMENT

828 OCCUPATIONS IN FABRICATION, INSTALLATION, AND REPAIR OF ELECTRICAL AND ELECTRONICS PRODUCTS, N.E.C.

829 OCCUPATIONS IN INSTALLATION AND REPAIR OF ELECTRICAL PRODUCTS, N.E.C.

84 PAINTING, PLASTERING, WATERPROOFING, CEMENTING, AND RELATED OCCUPATIONS

840 CONSTRUCTION AND MAINTENANCE PAINTERS AND RELATED OCCUPATIONS

841 PAPERHANGERS

842 PLASTERERS AND RELATED OCCUPATIONS

843 WATERPROOFING AND RELATED OCCUPATIONS

844 CEMENT AND CONCRETE FINISHING AND RELATED OCCUPATIONS

845 TRANSPORTATION EQUIPMENT PAINTERS AND RELATED OCCUPATIONS

849 PAINTING, PLASTERING, WATERPROOFING, CEMENTING, AND RELATED OCCUPATIONS, N.E.C.

85 EXCAVATING, GRADING, PAVING, AND RELATED OCCUPATIONS

850 EXCAVATING, GRADING, AND RELATED OCCUPATIONS

851 DRAINAGE AND RELATED OCCUPATIONS

853 PAVING OCCUPATIONS, ASPHALT AND CONCRETE

859 EXCAVATING, GRADING, PAVING, AND RELATED OCCUPATIONS, N.E.C.

86 CONSTRUCTION OCCUPATIONS, N.E.C.

860 CARPENTERS AND RELATED OCCUPATIONS

861 BRICK AND STONE MASONS AND TILE SETTERS

862 PLUMBERS, GAS FITTERS, STEAM FITTERS, AND RELATED OCCUPATIONS

863 ASBESTOS AND INSULATION WORKERS

864 FLOOR LAYING AND FINISHING OCCUPATIONS

865 GLAZIERS AND RELATED OCCUPATIONS

866 ROOFERS AND RELATED OCCUPATIONS

869 MISCELLANEOUS CONSTRUCTION OCCUPATIONS, N.E.C.

89 STRUCTURAL WORK OCCUPATIONS, N.E.C.

891 OCCUPATIONS IN STRUCTURAL MAINTENANCE, N.E.C.

899 MISCELLANEOUS STRUCTURAL WORK OCCUPATIONS, N.E.C.

MISCELLANEOUS OCCUPATIONS

MASTER TITLES AND DEFINITIONS

Master definitions describe work duties that are common or potentially common to a number of jobs. Jobs in which the common duties are an essential part refer to the Master definition title as a device to save space and to avoid repetition of the common duties. Clues to classifications of jobs utilizing Master definitions are provided.

APPRENTICE (any industry)

A worker who learns, according to written or oral contractual agreement, a recognized skilled craft or trade requiring one or more years of on-the-job training through job experience supplemented by related instruction, prior to being considered a qualified skilled worker. High school or vocational school education is often a prerequisite for entry into an apprenticeship program. Provisions of apprenticeship agreement regularly include length of apprenticeship; a progressive scale of wages; work processes to be taught; and amount of instruction in subjects related to the craft or trade, such as characteristics of materials used, physics, mathematics, estimating, and blueprint reading. Apprenticeability of a particular craft or trade is best evidenced by its acceptability for registration as a trade by a State Apprenticeship agency or the Federal Bureau of Apprenticeship and Training. Generally, where employees are represented by a union, apprenticeship programs come under the guidance of joint apprenticeship committees composed of representatives of the employers or the employer association and representatives of the employees. These committees may determine need for apprentices in a locality and establish minimum apprenticeship standards of education, experience, and training. In instances where committees do not exist, apprenticeship agreement is made between apprentice and employer, or an employer group. The title APPRENTICE is often loosely used as a synonym for beginner, HELPER (any industry), or TRAINEE (any industry). This practice is technically incorrect and leads to confusion in determining what is meant. Typical classifications for apprentices are BLACKSMITH APPRENTICE (forging); MACHINIST APPRENTICE (machine shop); PLUMBER APPRENTICE (construction).

CLEANER I (any industry)

Maintains premises of commercial, institutional, or industrial establishments, office buildings, hotels and motels, apartment houses, retirement homes, nursing homes, hospitals, schools, or similar establishments in clean and orderly condition, performing the following duties: Cleans rooms, hallways, lobbies, lounges, rest rooms, corridors, elevators, stairways, and locker rooms and other work areas. Sweeps, scrubs, waxes, and polishes floors, using brooms and mops and powered scrubbing and waxing machines. Cleans rugs, carpets, upholstered furniture, and draperies, using vacuum cleaner. Dusts furniture and equipment. Polishes metalwork, such as fixtures and fittings. Washes walls, ceiling, and woodwork. Washes windows, door panels, and sills. Empties wastebaskets, and empties and cleans ashtrays. Transports trash and waste to disposal area. Replenishes bathroom supplies. Replaces light bulbs. Classifications are made according to type of establishment in which work is performed. Typical classifications are CLEANER, COMMERCIAL OR INSTITUTIONAL (any industry); CLEANER, HOSPITAL (medical ser.); CLEANER, HOUSEKEEPING (any industry); CLEANER, INDUSTRIAL (any industry); HOUSECLEANER (hotel & rest.).

DESIGN ENGINEER, FACILITIES (profess. & kin.)

Applies engineering principles to design, modify, or develop facilities, testing, machines, equipment, or processes used in processing or manufacturing products: Analyzes product or equipment specifications and performance requirements to determine designs which can be produced by existing manufacturing or processing facilities and methods. Analyzes engineering proposals, process requirements, and related technical data pertaining to industrial machinery and equipment design. Determines feasibility of designing new plant equipment or modifying existing facilities considering costs, available space, time limitations, company planning, and other technical and economic factors. Provides technical information concerning manufacturing or processing techniques, materials, properties, and process advantages and limitations which affect long range plant and product engineering planning. Compiles and analyzes operational, test, and research data to establish performance standards for newly designed or modified equipment. Studies engineering and technical publications to keep abreast of technological changes and developments in industry. Classifications are made according to type of process or specialization. May use computer-assisted engineering software and equipment.

DESIGN ENGINEER, PRODUCTS (profess. & kin.)

Conducts analytical studies on engineering proposals to develop design for products, such as engines, equipment, machines, associated and subsystems components, and aerospace structures, utilizing and applying engineering principles, research data, and proposed product specifications. Analyzes data to determine feasibility of product proposal. Confers with research personnel to clarify or resolve problems and develops design. Prepares or directs preparation of product or system layout and detailed drawings and schematics. Directs and coordinates manufacturing or building of prototype product or system. Plans and develops experimental test programs. Analyzes test data and reports to determine if design meets functional and performance specifications. Confers with research and other engineering personnel and prepares design modifications as required. Evaluates engineering test results for possible application to development of systems or other uses. Design engineering personnel are classified according to discipline. May use computer-assisted engineering software and equipment.

DRAFTER (profess. & kin.)

Prepares working plans and detail drawings from rough or detailed sketches and notes for engineering or manufacturing purposes according to dimensional specifications: Calculates and lays out dimensions, angles, curvature of parts, materials to be used, relationship of one part to another, and relationship of various parts to entire structure or project, utilizing knowledge of engineering practices, mathematics, building materials, manufacturing technology, and related physical sciences. Creates preliminary or final sketch of proposed drawing, using standard drafting techniques and devices, such as drawing board, T-square, protractor, and drafting machine, or using computer-assisted design/drafting equipment. Modifies drawings as directed by engineer or architect. Classifications are made according to type of drafting, such as electrical, electronic, aeronautical, civil, mechanical, or architectural.

HELPER (any industry)

A worker who assists another worker, usually of a higher level of competence or expertness, by performing a variety of duties, such as furnishing another worker with materials, tools, and supplies; cleaning work area, machines, and equipment; feeding or off bearing machines; holding materials or tools; and performing other routine duties. A HELPER (any industry) may learn a trade but does so without an agreement with employer that such is the purpose of their relationship. Consequently, the title HELPER (any industry) is sometimes used as synonym for APPRENTICE (any industry), a practice that is incorrect technically. A worker whose duties are limited or restricted to one type of activity, such as moving materials from one department to another, feeding machines, removing products from conveyors or machines, or cleaning machines or work areas is not technically a HELPER (any industry) and is classified according to duties performed as MATERIAL HANDLER (any industry); MACHINE CLEANER (any industry); CLEANER, INDUSTRIAL (any industry). A worker who performs a variety of duties to assist another worker is a HELPER (any industry) technically and is classified according to worker assisted as BRICKLAYER HELPER (construction); DRY-CLEANER HELPER (laundry & rel.).

RESEARCH ENGINEER (profess. & kin.) alternate titles: development engineer

Conducts research in a field or specialization of an engineering discipline to discover facts, or performs research directed toward investigation, evaluation, and application of known engineering theories and principles. Plans and conducts, or directs engineering personnel performing, complex engineering experiments to test, prove, or modify theoretical propositions on basis of research findings and experiences of others researching in related technological areas. Evaluates findings to develop new concepts, products, equipment, or processes; or to develop applications of findings to new uses. Prepares technical reports for use by engineering or management personnel for long- and short-range planning, or for use by sales engineering personnel in sales or technical services activities. Classifications are made according to discipline. May use computer-assisted engineering software and equipment.

SALES ENGINEER (profess. & kin.) alternate titles: marketing engineer

Sells chemical, mechanical, electromechanical, electrical, electronic equipment and supplies or services requiring knowledge of engineering and cost effectiveness: Calls on management representatives, such as engineers, architects, or other professional and technical personnel at commercial, industrial, and other establishments in attempt to convince prospective client of desirability and practicability of products or services offered. Reviews blueprints, plans, and other customer documents to develop and prepare cost estimates or projected increases in production from client's use of proposed equipment or services. Draws up or proposes changes in equipment, processes, or use of materials or services which would result in cost reduction or improvement in operations. Provides technical services to clients relating to use, operation, and maintenance of equipment. May draw up sales or service contract for products or services. May provide technical training to employees of client. Usually specializes in sale of one or more closely related group of products or types of services, such as electrical or electronic equipment or systems, industrial machinery, processing equipment or systems, air-conditioning and refrigeration equipment, electric power equipment, or chemical goods.

1

SALES REPRESENTATIVE (retail trade; wholesale tr.) alternate titles: sales agent; sales associate

Sells products to business and industrial establishments or individual for manufacturer or distributor at sales office, store, showroom, or customer's place of business, utilizing knowledge of product sold: Compiles lists of prospective customers for use as sales leads, based on information from newspapers, business directories, and other sources. Travels throughout assigned territory to call on regular and prospective customers to solicit orders or talks with customers on sales floor or by phone. Displays or demonstrates product, using samples or catalog, and emphasizes salable features. Quotes prices and credit terms and prepares sales contracts for orders obtained. Estimates date of delivery to customer, based on knowledge of own firm's production and delivery schedules. Prepares reports of business transactions and keeps expense accounts. Classifications are made according to products sold as SALES REPRESENTATIVE, FOOD PRODUCTS (wholesale tr.); SALES REPRESENTATIVE, INDUSTRIAL MACHINERY (wholesale tr.).

SALESPERSON (retail trade; wholesale tr.)

Sells merchandise to individuals in store or showroom, utilizing knowledge of products sold: Greets customer on sales floor and ascertains make, type, and quality of merchandise desired. Displays merchandise, suggests selections that meet customer's needs, and emphasizes selling points of article, such as quality and utility. Prepares sales slip or sales contract. Receives payment or obtains credit authorization. Places new merchandise on display. May wrap merchandise for customer. May take inventory of stock. May requisition merchandise from stockroom. May visit customer's home by appointment to sell merchandise on shop-at-home basis. Classifications are made according to products sold as SALESPERSON, AUTOMOBILE ACCESSORIES (retail trade; wholesale tr.); SALESPERSON, BOOKS (retail trade); SALESPERSON, SURGICAL APPLIANCES (retail trade).

SEWING-MACHINE OPERATOR, AUTOMATIC (any industry)

Tends one or more sewing machines that automatically join, reinforce, or decorate material or fabricated articles: Places spool of thread on spindle and draws thread through guides, tensions, and eye of needle. Inserts bobbin into shuttle and draws thread through slot in shuttle wall, or draws thread through guides and looper eyes. May pull boxes of flatfolded material into feeding position or place roll of material on brackets at entry end of machine. May thread material through feed rollers and guides. Depresses pedal or moves lever to raise presser foot; positions article parts or material under needle, using edges, seams, or markings on fabric as guides, and lowers presser foot. Presses pedal or button to start machine that stops as material runs out or thread breaks. May cut material, using scissors, when specified length of cloth has been sewn. Observes sewing operation to detect defective stitching, breaks in thread, or machine malfunction. Rethreads machine, replaces defective or broken needles, using pliers, or notifies SEWING-MACHINE REPAIRER (any industry) of machine malfunction. May remove rolls or trucks of material from discharge end of machine. May select supplies, such as fasteners or thread, according to specifications or color of fabric. May oil machine. May cut excess thread, using scissors or blade attachment on machine. May tend machine equipped with blade attachment that automatically trims selvages. May tend multiple-needle machine that joins two or more layers of cloth to reinforce them. Classifications are usually made according to function of machine as FASTENER-SEWING-MACHINE OPERATOR (any industry); HEMMER, AUTOMATIC (tex. prod., nec); SERGING-MACHINE OPERATOR, AUTOMATIC (any industry); TACKING-MACHINE OPERATOR (any industry).

SEWING-MACHINE OPERATOR, REGULAR EQUIPMENT (any industry)

Operates various sewing machines to join parts of fabricated articles or garments: Places spool of thread on spindle of machine and draws thread through machine guides, tensions, and eye of needle. Inserts bobbin into shuttle and draws thread through slot in shuttle wall, or draws thread through guide and looper eye. Presses knee lever, depresses pedal, or moves hand lever to raise presser foot or spread feed cups. Positions parts to be joined under presser foot and needle and lowers presser foot. Starts, stops, and controls speed of machine, using pedal or knee lever. Guides parts under needle, using fingers and hands, and following edges, seams, guides on machine bed, or markings on part. Observes stitching to detect defects and notifies supervisor or SEWING-MACHINE REPAIRER (any industry) when defects are caused by machine malfunction. May select sewing supplies, such as binding, braid, cord, piping, tape, thread, or welt, according to specifications or color of material. May cut excess material or thread, using blade attached to machine or scissors. May oil machine, change needles, or secure modifying attachments to machine. Classifications are usually made according to type of machine, garment part sewn, product fabricated, or modifying attachment on machine.

SUPERVISOR (any industry) alternate titles: boss; chief; leader; manager; overseer; principal; section chief; section leader

Supervises and coordinates activities of workers engaged in one or more occupations: Studies production schedules and estimates worker-hour requirements for completion of job assignment. Interprets company policies to workers and enforces safety regulations. Interprets specifications, blueprints, and job orders to workers, and assigns duties. Establishes or adjusts work procedures to meet production schedules, using knowledge of capacities of machines and equipment. Recommends measures to improve production methods, equipment performance, and quality of product, and suggests changes in working conditions and use of equipment to increase efficiency of shop, department, or work crew. Analyzes and resolves work problems, or assists workers in solving work problems. Initiates or suggests plans to motivate workers to achieve work goals. Recommends or initiates personnel actions, such as promotions, transfers, discharges, and disciplinary measures. May train new workers. Maintains time and production records. May estimate, requisition, and inspect materials. May confer with other SUPERVISORS (any industry) to coordinate activities of individual departments. May confer with workers' representatives to resolve grievances. May set up machines and equipment. When supervising workers engaged chiefly in one occupation or craft, is required to be adept in the activities of the workers supervised. When supervising workers engaged in several occupations, is required to possess general knowledge of the activities involved. Classifications are made according to process involved, craft of workers supervised, product manufactured, or according to industry in which work occurs. Classifications are made according to workers supervised.

SUPERVISOR (clerical) alternate titles: section chief; section head

Supervises and coordinates activities of clerical workers: Determines work procedures, prepares work schedules, and expedites workflow. Issues written and oral instructions. Assigns duties and examines work for exactness, neatness, and conformance to policies and procedures. Studies and standardizes procedures to improve efficiency of subordinates. Prepares composite reports from individual reports of subordinates. Adjusts errors and complaints. May perform or assist subordinates in performing duties. May keep time and personnel records, and oversee preparation of payrolls. May hire, train, and discharge workers. Classifications are made according to type of work or functions of unit supervised as SUPERVISOR, COMPUTER OPERATIONS (clerical) 213.132-010; SUPERVISOR, TELEPHONE CLERKS (tel. & tel.) 239.132-010; TYPING SECTION CHIEF (clerical) 203.137-014.

TEST ENGINEER (profess. & kin.)

Conducts environmental, operational, or performance tests on electrical, mechanical, electromechanical, general industrial, or experimental products, such as aircraft, automotive equipment, industrial machinery and equipment, controls, and systems: Designs, and directs engineering and technical personnel in fabrication of testing and test-control apparatus and equipment. Directs and coordinates engineering activities concerned with development, procurement, installation, and calibration of instruments, equipment, and control devices required to test, telemeter, record, and reduce test data. Determines conditions under which tests are to be conducted and sequences and phases of test operations. Directs and exercises control over operational, functional, and performance phases of tests. Confers with scientific, engineering, and technical personnel to resolve testing problems, such as product or system malfunctions, incomplete test data, and data interpretation, considering such factors as conditions under which test was conducted and instrumentation, procedures, and phase of test used to obtain and record data. Analyzes and interprets test data and prepares technical reports for use by engineering and management personnel. Testing engineers are classified by field of engineering. May use computer-assisted engineering software and equipment.

TERM TITLES AND DEFINITIONS

Terms are titles that are common to a number of jobs that may differ widely in job knowledge required, tasks performed, and job location. Definitions for Terms indicate broadly the jobs that are known by the title and provide information to aid in finding appropriate specific job titles and codes.

ACCOUNTANT, CERTIFIED PUBLIC (profess. & kin.) alternate titles: certified public accountant; c.p.a.
A term applied to an accountant who has met state legal requirements for public practice, and who has been certified by a state as possessing appropriate education and experience as evidenced by passing grade in nationally uniform examination. ACCOUNTANTS, CERTIFIED PUBLIC (profess. & kin.) may be employed by individual establishments, but usually provide a variety of accounting services to general public, either as individual on fee basis or as member or salaried employee of firm which provides such services.

AEROSPACE ENGINEER (profess. & kin.)
A term applied to engineering personnel engaged in research, planning, and development of flight systems and aerovehicles for use in terrestrial atmosphere and outer space. Includes engineering work on aerovehicles, missiles, rockets, space systems research and development, and test and evaluation functions. Classifications are made according to specialization as AERONAUTICAL ENGINEER (aircraft mfg.); ELECTRICAL ENGINEER (profess. & kin.); MECHANICAL ENGINEER (profess. & kin.).

AGRICULTURAL AIDE (agriculture)
A term applied to farm workers who plant, harvest, and cultivate crops and tend animals according to specific instructions of research workers. Classifications are made according to work performed as ANIMAL CARETAKER (any industry); FARMWORKER, POULTRY (agriculture); FARMWORKER, VEGETABLE (agriculture) I.

AGRICULTURIST (profess. & kin.)
A term applied to persons with broad scientific knowledge of theoretical and actual agricultural practices and of livestock, such as varieties, breeds, feeding problems, and propagation of livestock; harvesting and marketing methods; and specialized areas of production. Provides technical and professional advice concerning agriculture to interested persons. Classifications are made according to specialty as AGRONOMIST (profess. & kin.); COUNTY-AGRICULTURAL AGENT (government ser.).

AIR-PRESS OPERATOR (any industry) alternate titles: pneumatic-press operator
A term applied to workers who operate, tend, or feed *power presses* actuated by air pressure to cut, form, forge, straighten, attach, compress, or imprint materials. Classifications are made according to type of press as ASSEMBLY-PRESS OPERATOR (any industry); PLATEN-PRESS FEEDER (print. & pub.); PUNCH-PRESS OPERATOR (any industry) I; PUNCH-PRESS OPERATOR (any industry) II.

AIR-TOOL OPERATOR (construction) alternate titles: pneumatic-tool operator
A term applied to any worker when operating a tool driven by compressed air to perform such work as breaking old pavement, loosening or digging hard earth, trimming bottom and sides of trenches, breaking large rocks, driving sheeting, chipping concrete, trimming or cutting stone, or caulking steel plates. Classifications are made according to kind of work performed as ROCK-DRILL OPERATOR (construction) I; SHEET-PILE-HAMMER OPERATOR (construction); STEEL-PLATE CAULKER (any industry); STONE DRILLER (stonework).

APPLIANCE REPAIRER (any industry)
A term applied to workers engaged in installing, servicing, and repairing electrical or gas appliances. Classifications are made according to type of appliance serviced as ELECTRICAL-APPLIANCE REPAIRER (any industry); ELECTRICAL-APPLIANCE SERVICER (any industry); GAS-APPLIANCE SERVICER (any industry).

APPLICATIONS ENGINEER (profess. & kin.)
A term for engineers concerned with developing new applications for products and systems, and providing technical sales and marketing support to customers, distributors, and sales representatives. Classifications are made according to engineering specialization as ELECTRONICS ENGINEER (profess. & kin.); MECHANICAL ENGINEER (profess. & kin.).

AREA ENGINEER (profess. & kin.)
A term applied to an engineer who is assigned duties within a specific manufacturing area or department of industrial organization. Classifications are made according to field of engineering specialization.

ASSISTANT (any industry) alternate titles: assistant superintendent; assistant supervisor
A term applied to a worker who assists another by performing similar duties and by assuming authority and responsibilities of worker assisted during worker's absence. The same classification should be assigned an ASSISTANT (any industry) as is assigned worker assisted. When duties performed by ASSISTANT (any industry) are clearly subordinate to and different from those of worker assisted, job may be that of HELPER (any industry), or possibly APPRENTICE (any industry) if there is a contractual agreement according to which worker receives training to learn job. See TECHNICIAN (profess. & kin.) for workers assisting engineers and other scientists.

AUTHOR (profess. & kin.)
A term applied to individuals who produce original written works, such as articles, biographies, fiction, plays, poems, and essays. Classifications are made according to type of writing as HUMORIST (profess. & kin.); LIBRETTIST (profess. & kin.); PLAYWRIGHT (profess. & kin.); POET (profess. & kin.); WRITER, PROSE, FICTION AND NONFICTION (profess. & kin.).

BACKFILLER OPERATOR (any industry)
A term applied to a worker who operates power equipment to replace dirt removed from an excavation, such as a pipeline trench or foundation pit. Classifications are made according to type of equipment operated as BULLDOZER OPERATOR (any industry) I; DRAGLINE OPERATOR (any industry); POWER-SHOVEL OPERATOR (any industry).

BELTER (construction)
A term applied to a CEMENT-MASON HELPER (construction) when pushing and pulling a canvas belt or burlap strip back and forth across finished surface of concrete pavement to smooth surface and remove trowel and float marks left by CEMENT MASON, HIGHWAYS AND STREETS (construction).

BRIMMER (hat & cap)
A term for workers who perform any of various operations on brims of hats. Classifications are made according to type of work performed as BRIM-STRETCHING-MACHINE OPERATOR (hat & cap); HYDRAULIC BLOCKER (hat & cap).

BRUSHER (any industry)
A term applied to workers who clean or finish materials or articles. Operations may involve brushing, grinding, or scraping by hand or machine. Classifications are made according to article processed as BISQUE CLEANER (pottery & porc.); WARE DRESSER (pottery & porc.); or method employed as DUSTER (hat & cap); NAPPER TENDER (tex. prod., nec; textile).

BRUSHER (construction; furniture)
A term applied to a PAINTER (construction) or FURNITURE FINISHER (woodworking) when applying coloring, decorative, or protective coats of finish to structures or furniture by means of a brush rather than spray gun.

BUILDING SUPERVISOR (construction)
A term applied to a SUPERVISOR (any industry) who supervises work crew engaged in building construction activities, such as installing electrical, heating, plumbing, and other fixtures and equipment, painting and decorating the building, and other work related to building construction. Classifications are made according to activity of workers supervised. Classifications are SUPERVISOR, ADJUSTABLE-STEEL-JOIST-SETTING (construction); SUPERVISOR, CARPENTERS (construction); CARPENTER-LABOR SUPERVISOR (construction); CLEARING SUPERVISOR (construction); CONCRETING SUPERVISOR (construction); SUPERVISOR, GRADING (construction); SUPERVISOR, REINFORCED-STEEL-PLACING (construction); SUPERVISOR, WATERPROOFING (construction).

BULL-GANG WORKER (construction)
A term applied to any member of a crew engaged in manually lifting or moving heavy objects or materials. Usually these workers exercise considerable physical exertion to accomplish a specified task. Classifications are made according to the nature of the work activity as CONSTRUCTION WORKER (construction) II; LABORER, STORES (any industry); or MATERIAL HANDLER (any industry).

CABLESHIP WORKER (tel. & tel.)
A term applied to officers and crew of cable-laying or cable-repair ships trained in special duties of maneuvering ship and handling submarine cable. Classifications are based on position held as MATE, SHIP (water trans.); ORDINARY SEAMAN (water trans.).

CAISSON WORKER (construction)
A term applied to a CONSTRUCTION WORKER (construction) II or other worker when performing manual labor within compressed-air chamber or caisson in connection with submarine or other foundation work where compressed air is required to keep out water during construction.

3

CARDROOM WORKER (nonmet. min.; textile)

A term applied to workers in carding department of textile mill who prepare natural or synthetic fibers for spinning into yarn or thread. Classifications are made according to process performed or machine tended as CARD TENDER (nonmet. min.; textile); SLIVER-LAP-MACHINE TENDER (textile).

CARETAKER, FARM (agriculture)

A term applied to workers engaged to live on and care for farm in absence of owner. Classifications are made according to duties performed as ANIMAL CARETAKER (any industry); FARMWORKER, GENERAL (agriculture) II; YARD WORKER (domestic ser.).

CARTOGRAPHIC TECHNICIAN (profess. & kin.)

A term applied to workers who collect, evaluate, and select source materials to be used in constructing maps and charts; and compile, draft, and edit maps and charts of the earth and extraterrestrial bodies. Classifications are made according to area of specialization as DRAFTER, CARTOGRAPHIC (profess. & kin.); PHOTOGRAMMETRIST (profess. & kin.); STEREO-PLOTTER OPERATOR (profess. & kin.).

CATALYST OPERATOR (chemical)

A term applied to workers engaged in preparation of catalysts for use in the manufacture of chemicals, such as butadiene and styrene. Classifications are made according to processing step in production of catalytic material as DISSOLVER OPERATOR (chemical); GRINDER OPERATOR (chemical).

CAULKER (construction; ship-boat mfg.)

A term applied to any worker who makes watertight or airtight joints in pipes, tunnel linings, and steel plates by forcing sealing material into joints with hand or compressed-air-driven caulking tool. Classifications are made according to material being caulked as PIPE CAULKER (construction); STEEL-PLATE CAULKER (any industry); WOOD CAULKER (ship-boat mfg.).

CHEMICAL-DEPARTMENT WORKER (plastic-synth.) alternate titles: chemical-building worker; chemical operator

A term for workers engaged in treating raw materials to produce chemical constituents of synthetic fibers. Classifications are made according to equipment utilized as CHURN TENDER (plastic-synth.); RIPENING-ROOM ATTENDANT (plastic-synth.).

CHEMICAL OPERATOR I (chemical)

A term for workers engaged in tending or controlling equipment used in processing chemical products. Classifications are made according to equipment unit operated as BATCH-STILL OPERATOR (chemical) I; BLEACHER OPERATOR (chemical; soap & rel.); ELECTRIC-CELL TENDER (chemical); or process involved as ABSORPTION OPERATOR (chemical).

CHIMNEY ERECTOR (construction)

A term applied to workers engaged in the construction and repair of brick or concrete chimneys. Classifications are made according to work performed as CHIMNEY BUILDER, BRICK (construction); CHIMNEY BUILDER, REINFORCED CONCRETE (construction); CHIMNEY REPAIRER (construction).

CHLOROPRENE OPERATOR (chemical)

A term applied to workers engaged in production or refining of chlorobutadiene (chloroprene) for polymerization into synthetic rubber. Classifications are made according to equipment-unit operated or tended as CD-REACTOR OPERATOR (chemical); CD-REACTOR OPERATOR, HEAD (chemical).

CIGAR MAKER, LONG-FILLER MACHINE (tobacco)

A term applied to any of the four operators of a fresh-work or long-filler cigar machine. Classifications are made according to work performed as BINDER LAYER (tobacco); FILLER FEEDER (tobacco); FRESH-WORK INSPECTOR (tobacco); WRAPPER LAYER (tobacco).

CLOTH FOLDER (textile)

A term applied to workers engaged in folding cloth for shipment. Classifications are made according to task performed as CLOTH FOLDER, HAND (tex. prod., nec; textile); or according to machine tended as FOLDING-MACHINE OPERATOR (textile).

CLOTHING MAKER (garment) alternate titles: clothing operator; garment maker

A term applied to garment workers engaged in laying out, marking, and cutting material; operating or tending sewing machines or sewing by hand to join, hem, reinforce, or decorate garments and garment parts; and performing finishing operations, such as pressing and folding. For classifications see three-digit groups 781, 782, 785, and 786.

COLOR MIXER (textile)

A term applied to workers engaged in weighing and blending ingredients to make dyestuffs and color for dyeing, printing, or coating of cloth and yarn. Classifications are made according to task performed as COLOR-PASTE MIXER (textile); DYE WEIGHER (any industry); or according to machine tended as GUM MIXER (textile).

COMMERCIAL DECORATOR (any industry)

A term applied to workers who paint designs on commercial products, such as china, novelties, furniture, and tinware. Classifications are made according to work performed as LINER (pottery & porc.); PAINTER, HAND (any industry).

CONCRETE CHIPPER (construction)

A term applied to a CONCRETE RUBBER (concrete prod.); CONSTRUCTION WORKER (construction) I; or CONSTRUCTION WORKER (construction) II when chipping away concrete with chisel driven by hammer or air tool to remove bulges, rough spots, and defective concrete from walls, beams, and other parts of concrete structures.

CONCRETE CURER (construction) alternate titles: pavement curer

A term applied to a CONSTRUCTION WORKER (construction) I; or CONSTRUCTION WORKER (construction) II when covering fresh concrete with curing mats (light canvas mats quilted with cotton to retain water), earth, straw, or waterproof paper, and sprinkling water over concrete with hose to prevent too rapid drying.

CONCRETE PUDDLER (construction) alternate titles: concrete shoveler; concrete spader; concrete spreader; concrete tamper

A term applied to a CONSTRUCTION WORKER (construction) II; LABORER, CONCRETE-MIXING PLANT (construction); or LABORER, PRESTRESSED CONCRETE (concrete prod.) when spreading wet concrete evenly over subgrade in front of concrete-paving finishing machine or in concrete forms, using shovel, and tamping it around form and reinforcing material, using puddling pole, tamper, or concrete vibrator.

CONCRETE SCREEDER (construction)

A term applied to a CEMENT MASON (construction); CONSTRUCTION WORKER (construction) II; or LABORER, CONCRETE-MIXING PLANT (construction) when leveling surface of fresh concrete to desired shape and grade by pushing screed over surface of concrete.

CONSULTING ENGINEER (profess. & kin.)

A term applied to workers who consult with and advise clients on specialized engineering matters in particular field of endeavor, such as chemical engineering, civil engineering, or mechanical engineering.

COOK, BREAKFAST (hotel & rest.)

A term applied to any COOK (hotel & rest.; medical ser.) or COOK, FAST FOOD (hotel & rest.) when preparing, cooking, and portioning all foods on breakfast menu, such as hot cereals, bacon, and eggs.

COOK, SECOND (hotel & rest.)

A term applied to a SOUS CHEF (hotel & rest.) when acting as assistant to CHEF (hotel & rest.); EXECUTIVE CHEF (hotel & rest.); or SUPERVISING CHEF (hotel & rest.), performing their duties in their absence. Typically found in large establishments.

COUPLE (any industry)

A term used for designating two jobs or positions found in the same environment or industry where two persons are required to perform duties. The workers are usually furnished board and room or lodging in addition to remuneration for services performed. Classifications are made according to specific duties performed by each worker, such as BUTLER (domestic ser.) and COOK (domestic ser.) or where both workers participate in performing overall duties, such as maintenance, housekeeping, and managing as MANAGER, MOTEL (hotel & rest.); MANAGER, TOURIST CAMP (hotel & rest.); MANAGER, TRAILER PARK (hotel & rest.); or as MAINTENANCE REPAIRER, BUILDING (any industry).

CRANE OPERATOR (any industry) alternate titles: crane engineer

A term applied to workers who operate cranes to hoist, move, and place materials and objects, using attachments, such as sling, electromagnet, grapple hook, bucket, demolition ball, and clamshell. Classifications are made according to type of crane operated as OVERHEAD CRANE OPERATOR (any industry) 921.663-010; LOCOMOTIVE-CRANE OPERATOR (any industry) 921.663-038; MONORAIL CRANE OPERATOR (any industry) 921.663-042; TRUCK-CRANE OPERATOR (any industry) 921.663-062.

CUTTER (any industry)

A term applied to workers engaged in cutting materials, such as cloth, leather, or plastic, by hand or machine, according to pattern, layout lines, or specified dimensions. Classifications are made according to method of cutting as CUTTER, HAND (any industry) I; CUTTER, MACHINE (any industry) I; DIE CUTTER (any industry); or according to material cut as LEATHER CUTTER (leather prod.).

DIAMOND CUTTER (jewelry-silver.)

A term applied to workers who prepare diamonds for use in making jewelry. Classifications are made according to specific occupations as BRILLIANDEER-LOPPER (jewelry-silver.); DIAMOND CLEAVER (jewelry-silver.); GEM CUTTER (jewelry-silver.); GIRDLER (jewelry-silver.); LATHE OPERATOR (jewelry-silver.).

DIETITIAN (profess. & kin.)

A term applied to persons who possess educational qualifications, work experience, and license or certificate for employment in various fields of dietetics, such as research, consultation, administration, community, and clinical. Classifications are made according to specialized area of employment as DIETITIAN, CLINICAL (profess. & kin.); DIETITIAN, CONSULTANT (profess. & kin.); DIETITIAN, RESEARCH (profess. & kin.).

DITCH DIGGER (construction) alternate titles: backfiller, hand; laborer, excavation; trench backfiller; trench digger

A term applied to a CONSTRUCTION WORKER (construction) I; CONSTRUCTION WORKER (construction) II; or LABORER, CONCRETE-MIXING PLANT (construction) when digging trenches, footing holes, and similar excavations to specified depth and width, and refilling trenches with excavated material, using pick and shovel.

DIVISION OFFICER (r.r. trans.)

A term applied to railroad officials who administer activities of specified sector of railroad operations, such as segment of line between prescribed points, terminal, classification yard, or other facility. Classifications are made according to operations or facility administered as SUPERINTENDENT, DIVISION (motor trans.; r.r. trans.); YARD MANAGER (r.r. trans.).

DYEING-MACHINE OPERATOR (knitting)

A term applied to workers engaged in dyeing yarn, stockings, and knitted cloth, garments, and tubing. Workers are classified according to material dyed as DYE-REEL OPERATOR (textile); SKEIN-YARN DYER (textile); or according to type of machine utilized as DYE-TUB OPERATOR (knitting).

ECOLOGIST (profess. & kin.)

A term applied to persons who study plants or animals in relation to effect of environmental influences, such as rainfall, temperature, altitude, and kind and quantity of food. Classifications are made according to field of specialization as BOTANIST (profess. & kin.); ZOOLOGIST (profess. & kin.).

ELECTRICAL TESTER (utilities)

A term applied to a worker who carries out prescribed tests on electric power equipment used in production, transmission, distribution, and utilization of electricity, using various types of electrical testing equipment. Classifications are made according to type of equipment tested as RELAY TESTER (utilities); TRANSFORMER TESTER (utilities); or according to purpose of test as VOLTAGE TESTER (utilities).

ENGINEER (profess. & kin.) alternate titles: professional engineer

A term applied to persons who possess educational qualifications, work experience, and legal certification where required as established by engineering schools, employers, and licensing authorities for employment in various fields of engineering. Engineers typically function in one or more activities, such as research, development, design, production, consulting, administration and management, teaching, technical writing, or technical sales and service. Classifications are made according to one or more engineering fields in which individual is qualified for employment, such as aeronautical, electrical, mechanical, chemical, mining, marine, or nuclear engineering.

ENTERTAINER (amuse. & rec.; motion pictureradio-tv broad.) alternate titles: performer; theatrical performer

A term for persons who entertain and amuse audiences by means of an act or skit, dance, reading, feat of skill, songs, or comedy act. Classifications are made according to type of entertainment provided.

ENVIRONMENTAL ENGINEER (profess. & kin.) alternate titles: public-health engineer

A term applied to engineering personnel who utilize engineering knowledge and technology to identify, solve, or alleviate environmental problems. ENVIRONMENTAL ENGINEERS (profess. & kin.) typically apply knowledge of chemical, civil, mechanical, or other engineering discipline to preserve the quality of life by correcting and improving various areas of environmental concern, such as air, soil, or water pollution. However, any engineer whose technology is adaptable to solution of environmental problems, generates a need for environmental impact analysis, or affects the quality of life, is included in this term. This term may be used to denote engineering personnel in specific industries, such as mining and quarrying, petroleum production, or petroleum refining, who function at an administrative level to plan and coordinate pollution monitoring activities within a particular industrial framework. Classifications are made according to area or specialization as INDUSTRIAL-HEALTH ENGINEER (profess. & kin.); NUCLEAR ENGINEER (profess. & kin.); POLLUTION-CONTROL ENGINEER (profess. & kin.); PROJECT MANAGER, ENVIRONMENTAL RESEARCH (profess. & kin.); SANITARY ENGINEER (profess. & kin.).

ENVIRONMENTALIST (profess. & kin.) alternate titles: ecologist

A term applied to workers who study, analyze, and evaluate environmental problems; apply scientific knowledge to prevent pollution; develop solutions to existing environmental problems; and predict possibility of future environmental pollution, including that concerned with air, water, land and land use, noise, and radioactivity. May prepare environmental impact reports or studies detailing types and causes of pollution and probability of future environmental problems. May work with federal, state, and local governmental agencies and community groups in establishing and promoting environmental policies. General classifications are ENVIRONMENTAL ANALYST (profess. & kin.) and POLLUTION-CONTROL ENGINEER (profess. & kin.). Since environmental work activities are interdisciplinary in nature, classifications are also made according to spe-

cific fields of specialization, such as civil engineering, soils engineering, chemistry, biology, geophysics, geology, geography, architecture, or forestry. Workers may direct and coordinate activities of other environmental scientists and be classified PROJECT MANAGER, ENVIRONMENTAL RESEARCH (profess. & kin.). Workers may function at the technician level, providing scientific or engineering support to environmental projects, and be classified BIOLOGICAL AIDE (agriculture); LABORATORY TESTER (any industry); POLLUTION-CONTROL TECHNICIAN (profess. & kin.); SCIENTIFIC HELPER (profess. & kin.); or LABORATORY TESTER (any industry).

EQUIPMENT MECHANIC (tel. & tel.)

A term applied to workers who install, relocate, and remove telephone and telegraph equipment. Classifications are made according to type of equipment worked on as TELEGRAPH-PLANT MAINTAINER (tel. & tel.); EQUIPMENT INSTALLER (tel. & tel.).

EXECUTIVE TRAINEE (any industry)

A term for a worker who acts in junior supervisory capacities, such as assistant department manager or staff assistant supervisor in an organization, to learn company policies and procedures, and functions and activities of departments with view toward acquiring knowledge of all business phases. Attends personnel training classes to acquire knowledge of organizational setup, staff and line functions, and long and short range business objectives. Acquires, through on-the-job training in departments, such as credit, sales, engineering, production, and personnel, an overall knowledge of company business functions and activities. Workers are classified according to designation of supervisory personnel assisted or department staff activity.

EXPLOSIVE HANDLER (chemical)

A term applied to any worker who processes, stores, or otherwise handles explosives, observing specified safety regulations to prevent explosions. Classifications are made according to equipment used as BOILING-TUB OPERATOR (chemical); MIXER OPERATOR (chemical) I; POACHER OPERATOR (chemical); or according to material handled as DYNAMITE-CARTRIDGE CRIMPER (chemical); NITROGLYCERIN NEUTRALIZER (chemical); TETRYL-DISSOLVER OPERATOR (chemical).

FARMER (agriculture)

A term used to designate a person who manages a tract of land devoted to production or exploitation of plants and animals. Classifications are made according to duties performed as FARMER, FIELD CROP (agriculture); FARMER, GENERAL (agriculture); FARMER, FRUIT CROPS, BUSH AND VINE (agriculture); LIVESTOCK RANCHER (agriculture); POULTRY FARMER (agriculture).

FARMER, CONTRACT (agriculture)

A term applied to a farmer working on a contract basis for another farmer. Classifications are made according to kind of work contracted for as FARM-MACHINE OPERATOR (agriculture); FARMWORKER, GRAIN (agriculture) I.

FARMER, DRY LAND (agriculture)

A term applied to one who practices diversified or specialized farming and depends on limited rainfall for moisture as opposed to one who irrigates. Classifications are made according to type of crop grown as FARMER, CASH GRAIN (agriculture); FARMER, VEGETABLE (agriculture); FLOWER GROWER (agriculture); HAY FARMER (agriculture).

FARMER, TENANT (agriculture)

A term used to designate a worker who plants, cultivates, and harvests crops or raises animals on rented land for which payment is made in specified amount of money or fixed quantity of crops or animals. Machinery, tools, livestock, labor, seed, and fertilizer are provided by tenant. Classifications are made according to kind of farm rented or crop raised as FARMER, CASH GRAIN (agriculture); FARMER, FIELD CROP (agriculture); FARMER, VEGETABLE (agriculture).

FARMWORKER (agriculture)

A term applied to worker who performs variety of duties on farm including planting, cultivating, and harvesting crops, operating farm equipment, and attending to livestock. Classifications are made according to duties performed as FARM-MACHINE OPERATOR (agriculture); FARMWORKER, POULTRY (agriculture); FARMWORKER, VEGETABLE (agriculture) I; FARMWORKER, VEGETABLE (agriculture) II; HARVEST WORKER, FRUIT (agriculture).

FARMWORKER, SEASONAL (agriculture) alternate titles: wage worker

A term applied to workers who are engaged in farm work on seasonal basis. Workers may specialize in planting, weeding, irrigating, harvesting, or packing crops, but do not follow crop maturities over wide areas. Classifications are made according to duties performed, as FARM-MACHINE OPERATOR (agriculture); HARVEST WORKER, FRUIT (agriculture); HARVEST WORKER, VEGETABLE (agriculture); IRRIGATOR, GRAVITY FLOW (agriculture); PACKER, AGRICULTURAL PRODUCE (agriculture); SORTER, AGRICULTURAL PRODUCE (agriculture; can. & preserv.; wholesale tr.); WEEDER-THINNER (agriculture).

FEATURED PLAYER (amuse. & rec.)

A term applied to any stage, motion picture, or television performer who receives prominent billing for an entertainment production. Classifications are made according to type of role as ACTOR (amuse. & rec.); COMEDIAN (amuse. & rec.).

FISHER (fishing & hunt.)

A term applied to any worker who hunts, catches, and traps aquatic animals, such as finfish and shellfish, including mollusks and crustaceans, or gathers aquatic shells, mosses, seaweeds, and sponges. Classifications are made according to equipment used as FISHER, LINE (fishing & hunt.); FISHER, NET (fishing & hunt.); FISHER, POT (fishing & hunt.); SHELLFISH DREDGE OPERATOR (fishing & hunt.); or according to type of aquatic life taken as IRISH-MOSS GATHERER (fishing & hunt.); KELP CUTTER (fishing & hunt.); SPONGE HOOKER (fishing & hunt.).

FISHER, SPONGE (fishing & hunt.)

A term applied to any worker when gathering sponges from the sea. Classifications are made according to method used as FISHER, DIVING (fishing & hunt.); SPONGE HOOKER (fishing & hunt.).

FOREIGN-BROADCAST SPECIALIST (radio-tv broad.)

A term applied to individuals who are involved with planning, writing, producing, and announcing for or acting in radio and television programs produced for broadcast to or in another country. Classifications are made according to work performed, without regard to specific language requirements. Typical classifications include NEWSCASTER (radio-tv broad.); NEWSWRITER (print. & pub.; radio-tv broad.); REPORTER (print. & pub.; radio-tv broad.); SCREEN WRITER (motion picture; radio-tv broad.); TRANSLATOR (profess. & kin.).

FORM CLEANER (construction) alternate titles: form scraper

A term applied to a CARPENTER HELPER, HARDWOOD FLOORING (construction); FORM-SETTER HELPER (construction); LABORER, CONCRETE-MIXING PLANT (construction) or LABORER, CONCRETE PAVING (construction) when cleaning wooden or metal concrete molds, using scraper, pick, shovel, or other tools to remove hardened concrete.

FORM STRIPPER (construction) alternate titles: form puller; form remover; form wrecker; paving-form mover

A term applied to a CARPENTER HELPER, HARDWOOD FLOORING (construction); FORM-SETTER HELPER (construction); or LABORER, CONCRETE PAVING (construction) when removing wooden or steel forms from concrete paving or other concrete work after concrete has hardened.

FRUIT WORKER (agriculture)

A term applied to a worker who cultivates, picks, grades, or packs fruits. Classifications are made according to duties performed as FARMWORKER, FRUIT (agriculture) I; HARVEST WORKER, FRUIT (agriculture); PACKER, AGRICULTURAL PRODUCE (agriculture); SORTER, AGRICULTURAL PRODUCE (agriculture; can. & preserv.; wholesale tr.).

GAS-METER TESTER (utilities)

A term applied to workers performing tasks concerned with dismantling, testing, and repairing gasmeters. Classifications are made according to work performed as GAS-METER MECHANIC (utilities) I; GAS-METER MECHANIC (utilities) II; GAS-METER PROVER (utilities).

GENERATOR OPERATOR (utilities) alternate titles: dynamo operator

A term applied to a worker who controls operation of generator producing electricity for plant processes or for distribution by tending driving engine. Classifications are made according to type of driving engine as DIESEL-PLANT OPERATOR (utilities); TURBINE OPERATOR (utilities).

GOAT-TRUCK DRIVER (agriculture)

A term applied to workers who drive truck or farm equipment to transport empty containers to workers engaged in picking fruit and vegetables and to transport filled containers to shed or warehouse. Classifications are made according to equipment used as FARM-MACHINE OPERATOR (agriculture); TRUCK DRIVER, HEAVY (any industry).

GREIGE-ROOM WORKER (textile) alternate titles: greige-goods worker

A term applied to workers engaged in receiving and processing greige (unfinished) cloth or yarn in textile mill. Classifications are made according to process performed as GOODS LAYER (textile) 781.687-038; GREIGE-GOODS MARKER (textile) 229.587-010; or according to machine tended as GRAY-CLOTH TENDER, PRINTING (textile) 652.686-018.

GROUP LEADER (any industry) alternate titles: leader

A term applied to a worker who takes the lead and gives directions to workers while performing same duties as workers. Regularly performs all tasks of workers in group. Supervisory functions are secondary to the production duties performed and worker receives same classifications as workers led. Distinguished from STRAW BOSS (any industry).

HATTER (hat & cap)

A term for a worker who performs any of the operations connected with making felt hats or strawhats. Classifications are made according to the operation performed as BLOCKER, HAND (hat & cap) I; FUR-BLOWER OPERATOR (hat & cap); HAT-BLOCKING-MACHINE OPERATOR (hat & cap) I; HAT FINISHER (hat & cap).

HEALER (medical ser.)

A term applied to persons engaged in healing arts other than those requiring recognized legal, educational, or experience requirements. Usually restricted by law from performing such medical services as prescribing drugs or treating by surgery. Generally limited to such types of healing as physical culture and mental suggestion.

HIGHWAY SUPERVISOR (construction)

A term applied to a SUPERVISOR (any industry) who supervises work crews engaged in highway construction activities, such as clearing right-of-way, preparing subgrade, laying road surface, and installing curbing and guardrails. Classifications are made according to activity of workers supervised. Typical classifications are CLEARING SUPERVISOR (construction); CONCRETING SUPERVISOR (construction); SUPERVISOR, GRADING (construction).

INSTALLATION ENGINEER (profess. & kin.)

A term applied to an engineer who specializes in installing equipment. Classifications are made according to field of engineering specialization.

INSTRUCTOR, MACHINE (any industry)

A term applied to workers who instruct new employees in machine operations by giving on-the-job training. Workers are classified according to major work assignments as MACHINIST (machine shop); WEAVER (nonmet. min.; textile). Workers with supervisory duties are classified as SUPERVISOR (any industry).

INSTRUMENTATION ENGINEER (profess. & kin.)

A term applied to a worker who designs and supervises operation and maintenance of electrical, mechanical, and thermal instruments and control equipment necessary for safe and efficient operation of industrial plant. Classifications are made according to field of engineering specialization.

JOB-PRESS OPERATOR (print. & pub.)

A term applied to workers engaged in operation of printing presses used for printing small quantities, usually one sheet at a time, requiring frequent changes of press make-ready. Classifications are made according to type of press operated as CYLINDER-PRESS OPERATOR (print. & pub.) 651.362-010; PLATEN-PRESS OPERATOR (print. & pub.) 651.362-018.

JOURNEY WORKER (any industry)

A term applied to a worker who has completed a specified training program as an APPRENTICE (any industry) in learning a trade or craft, or who can give written proof of a specified number of years of qualifying experience for such trade or craft.

KETTLE TENDER (any industry)

A term applied to a worker who melts, cooks, or dyes material or substances in a container heated by electricity, flame, or steam. Workers are usually classified according to material or substance treated as COOK, KETTLE (beverage; can. & preserv.; grain-feed mills); DIPPER (any industry); RENDERING-EQUIPMENT TENDER (meat products).

LABORATORY CHIEF (profess. & kin.) alternate titles: director, laboratory

A term applied to persons who serve as administrative heads of chemical, physical, electrical, biological, or other scientific laboratories. Classifications are made according to particular science or branch of engineering as CHEMICAL LABORATORY CHIEF (profess. & kin.).

LABORATORY WORKER (any industry)

A term for any worker in a laboratory performing routine or special tests, or research. Classifications are made according to type of work as BIOCHEMIST (profess. & kin.); FOOD TESTER (any industry); LABORATORY TESTER (any industry); SCIENTIFIC HELPER (profess. & kin.).

LAUNDRY HAND (laundry & rel.)

A term applied to any laundry worker. Classifications are made according to work performed as FLATWORK FINISHER (laundry & rel.); SHIRT PRESSER (laundry & rel.); WASHER, MACHINE (laundry & rel.).

LINGUIST (profess. & kin.)

A term applied to any person who has become skilled in languages, particularly living languages. Classifications are made according to occupation in which this skill is utilized, as INTERPRETER (profess. & kin.); TRANSLATOR (profess. & kin.).

LOGGER (logging)

A term applied to any worker engaged in logging. Classifications are made according to type of activity as BUCKER (logging); CHOKE SETTER (logging); FALLER (logging) I; FALLER (logging) II; LIMBER (logging); LOGGER, ALL-ROUND (logging); RIGGING SLINGER (logging).

LOG-YARD CRANE OPERATOR (saw. & plan.)

A term applied to LOCOMOTIVE-CRANE OPERATOR (any industry); TRACTOR-CRANE OPERATOR (any industry); or TRUCK-CRANE OPERATOR (any industry) when operating a crane to lift and move logs in log storage yard.

MACHINE ADJUSTER (any industry) alternate titles: adjuster

A term applied to workers who set up and adjust a battery of machines designed to perform a particular function in a manufacturing process. Classifications are made according to type of material or article produced as MACHINE SET-UP OPERATOR, PAPER GOODS (paper goods); ROPE-MACHINE SETTER (tex. prod., nec.).

MACHINE RUNNER (mine & quarry) alternate titles: mining-machine operator

A term applied to workers who operate one or more mining machines to drill, undercut, load, and continuously mine in an underground mine. Classifications are made according to specific duties as CONTINUOUS-MINING-MACHINE OPERATOR (mine & quarry); CUTTER OPERATOR (mine & quarry); DRILLING-MACHINE OPERATOR (mine & quarry); LOADING-MACHINE OPERATOR (mine & quarry).

MAINTENANCE WORKER (any industry) alternate titles: service worker; trouble shooter

A term applied to workers engaged in repairing and maintaining buildings, machinery, and electrical and mechanical equipment in commercial, governmental, or industrial establishments. Classifications are made according to trade as CARPENTER, MAINTENANCE (any industry); ELECTRICIAN, MAINTENANCE (any industry); or according to structure repaired or maintained as BOILERHOUSE MECHANIC (any industry); MAINTENANCE REPAIRER, BUILDING (any industry); or according to machinery and equipment repaired or maintained as CELLOPHANE-CASTING-MACHINE REPAIRER (plastic prod.); ELEVATOR REPAIRER (any industry).

MANAGER, BAR (hotel & rest.)

A term applied to a BARTENDER (hotel & rest.) or WINE STEWARD/STEWARDESS (hotel & rest.) when supervising personnel engaged in mixing and serving drinks and performing related duties, such as purchasing supplies for the bar.

MANAGER, FACILITATING SERVICES (any industry)

A term applied to workers in industrial organizations who plan, organize, and direct overhead services, such as employment, public relations, and safety. Classifications are made according to work performed as MANAGER, EMPLOYMENT (profess. & kin.); MANAGER, PERSONNEL (profess. & kin.); PUBLIC-RELATIONS REPRESENTATIVE (profess. & kin.); SAFETY ENGINEER (profess. & kin.).

MANAGER, SERVICE ESTABLISHMENT (any industry) alternate titles: superintendent, service establishment

A term applied to workers who manage an organization that renders service to public, such as business-service, repair-service, or personal-service establishment. Typical classifications are MANAGER, BARBER OR BEAUTY SHOP (personal ser.); MANAGER, MARINE SERVICE (ship-boat mfg.); MANAGER, RETAIL STORE (retail trade); MANAGER, SERVICE DEPARTMENT (wholesale tr.); SUPERVISOR, CAB (motor trans.).

MASON (construction)

A term applied to any worker when working with artificial stone, brick, concrete, stone, and the like. Classifications are made according to material worked with as BRICKLAYER (construction); CEMENT MASON (construction); STONEMASON (construction).

MASON HELPER (construction)

A term applied to a BRICKLAYER HELPER (construction); CEMENT-MASON HELPER (construction); or STONEMASON HELPER (construction) when assisting one of the masons.

MASTER (water trans.) alternate titles: captain; skipper

A term applied to a worker who commands a self-propelled watercraft. May be licensed by U.S. Coast Guard depending on type and tonnage of craft and water navigated. Classifications are made according to type of watercraft commanded as CAPTAIN, FISHING VESSEL (fishing & hunt.); DREDGE CAPTAIN (water trans.); FERRYBOAT CAPTAIN (water trans.); MASTER, RIVERBOAT (water trans.); MASTER, SHIP (water trans.); TUGBOAT CAPTAIN (water trans.).

MIGRANT WORKER (agriculture)

A term applied to a worker who moves about the country, working as member of farm crew to grow and harvest vegetables, grains, and fruits: Usually contracts for work with MIGRANT LEADER (agriculture) and receives pay, subsistence, and transportation from same. Drives farm equipment to plow, plant, or cultivate crops. Plants, weeds, thins, picks, washes, ties, grades, or packs fruits and vegetables by hand or with handtools. Classifications are made according to duties performed as FARM-MACHINE OPERATOR (agriculture); HARVEST WORKER, FRUIT (agriculture); HARVEST WORKER, VEGETABLE (agriculture); IRRIGATOR, GRAVITY FLOW (agriculture); WEEDER-THINNER (agriculture).

MILLER (any industry)

A term applied to a worker who grinds material, such as coal, cocoa beans, coffee, grain, or ore, using a machine. Classifications are made according to material ground or method employed as MILLER, WET PROCESS (grain-feed mills); WASH-MILL OPERATOR (chemical).

MILL HAND (any industry)

A term applied to workers performing various duties in a mill. Classifications are made according to type of machine operated or work performed as MILL

OPERATOR (any industry); ROD-MILL TENDER (cement; smelt. & refin.); ROUGHER (steel & rel.); WASH-MILL OPERATOR (chemical).

MILL HAND (grain-feed mills)

A term applied to workers in a grain or feed mill whose duties require no previous experience and who work under the direction of other workers. Classifications are made according to tasks performed or worker assisted as BIN CLEANER (beverage; grain-feed mills); CUT-IN WORKER (grain-feed mills).

MILL WORKER (any industry)

A term applied to a worker who grinds and pulverizes materials, cleans and smooths articles and materials, treats hides and skins, or extracts metallic constituents from ore. Classifications are made according to machine or method used as FLOTATION TENDER (smelt. & refin.); TANNING DRUM OPERATOR (leather mfg.); TUMBLER OPERATOR (any industry).

MINER II (mine & quarry)

A term applied to any mine worker. Classifications are made according to work performed as CUTTER OPERATOR (mine & quarry); STRIPPING-SHOVEL OPERATOR (mine & quarry); TIMBER FRAMER (mine & quarry). In some areas the term MINER indicates only workers who have passed qualifying examinations for state miner's certificate.

MODEL MAKER II (any industry)

A term applied to workers who apply trade knowledge and skills to construct full scale experimental working models of electrical, electronic, or mechanical machines, controls, or tools, or to construct scale models for testing or display, or models to form molds for cast products. Workers are classified according to trade skill and knowledge applied as CONCRETE SCULPTOR (concrete prod.); PATTERNMAKER, WOOD (foundry); TOOL-AND-DIE MAKER (machine shop).

MUNICIPAL-SERVICES SUPERVISOR (government ser.)

A term for supervisory workers engaged in the maintenance of a public works program. Classifications are made according to municipal service rendered as SNOW-REMOVING SUPERVISOR (government ser.).

MUSEUM INTERN (museums)

A term applied to individuals who perform curatorial, administrative, educational, conservation, or research duties in museum or similar institution, to assist professional staff in utilization of institution's collections and other resources and to gain practical experience and knowledge to enhance personal qualifications for career. Classifications are made according to assignment which is usually based upon academic specialization as CRAFT DEMONSTRATOR (museums) 109.364-010; PAINTINGS RESTORER (profess. & kin.) 102.261-014; RESEARCH ASSISTANT (profess. & kin.) 109.267-010; RESEARCH ASSOCIATE (museums) 109.067-014.

NATURALIST (profess. & kin.)

A term applied to persons specializing in study of plants or animals. Classifications are made according to division studied as BOTANIST (profess. & kin.); ZOOLOGIST (profess. & kin.).

NEEDLE-TRADE WORKER (garment)

A term applied to workers engaged in sewing by hand in garment manufacturing establishment. Classifications are made according to type of sewing performed as BASTER, HAND (garment); FELLER, HAND (garment); SEWER, HAND (any industry).

NUMISMATIST (profess. & kin.)

A term for persons who specialize in science and collection of rare coins, medals, tokens, and paper money. Persons engaged in sale of coins are classified as SALESPERSON, STAMPS OR COINS (retail trade; wholesale tr.); those engaged in management of collections are classified CURATOR (museums).

NURSE, PROFESSIONAL (medical ser.) alternate titles: nurse, certified; nurse, licensed; nurse; nurse, registered

A term applied to persons meeting the educational, legal, and training requirements to practice as professional nurses, as required by a State Board of Nursing. Performs acts requiring substantial specialized judgment and skill in observation, care, and counsel of ill, injured, or infirm persons and in promotion of health and prevention of illness. Classifications are made according to type of nursing activity engaged in as DIRECTOR, NURSING SERVICE (medical ser.); NURSE, GENERAL DUTY (medical ser.); NURSE, PRIVATE DUTY (medical ser.).

PACE SETTER (agriculture)

A term applied to a lead worker engaged in picking fruit or truck crops, who picks at specified rate that determines production of workers. Classifications are made according to workers involved or crop picked as FARMWORKER, VEGETABLE (agriculture) II; HARVEST WORKER, FRUIT (agriculture).

PAINT GRINDER (paint & varnish) alternate titles: grinder operator; stock grinder

A term applied to workers engaged in reducing and dispersing dry particles in liquid vehicle for use in producing paint and related products. Classifications are made according to type of equipment used as ROLLER-MILL OPERATOR (paint & varnish); STONE-MILL OPERATOR (paint & varnish).

PHILATELIST (profess. & kin.)

A term applied to a worker who collects and studies stamps, stamped envelopes, and related material. Persons employed in sale or purchase of stamps are classified as MANAGER, RETAIL STORE (retail trade); SALESPERSON, STAMPS OR COINS (retail trade; wholesale tr.); those in charge of museum collections are classified CURATOR (museums).

PHYSICIAN, RESEARCH (medical ser.)

A term applied to persons with degree of doctor of medicine who conduct medical experiments and investigations to discover causes of various diseases; facts concerning diseases; and remedies for diseases. Classifications are made according to specialty.

PILE DRIVER (construction)

A term applied to a HOLDER, PILE DRIVING (construction); LABORER, PILE DRIVING, GROUND WORK (construction); LOFT WORKER, PILE DRIVING (construction); or RIGGER (construction) when driving piles.

PIPE CUTTER (construction)

A term applied to a PIPE FITTER (construction); PIPE-FITTER APPRENTICE (construction); PIPE-FITTER HELPER (construction); PLUMBER (construction) or PLUMBER APPRENTICE (construction) when cutting pipe for use in an air, water, steam, gas, or waste disposal system.

PIPELINE SUPERVISOR (construction)

A term applied to a SUPERVISOR (any industry) who supervises work crews engaged in pipeline-construction activities, such as clearing pipeline right-of-way, laying pipe, and backfilling ditches. Classifications are made according to activity of workers supervised. Typical classifications are CLEARING SUPERVISOR (construction); SUPERVISOR, LABOR GANG (construction).

PIPE THREADER, HAND (construction)

A term applied to a PIPE FITTER (construction); PIPE-FITTER APPRENTICE (construction); PIPE-FITTER HELPER (construction); PLUMBER (construction); PLUMBER APPRENTICE (construction); or PLUMBER HELPER (construction) when threading pipe.

PLANTER (agriculture)

A term applied to farmers, usually large-scale entrepreneurs, who specialize in growing cotton, rice, tobacco, or other crops. Classifications are made according to crop as COTTON GROWER (agriculture); PEANUT FARMER (agriculture); SOYBEAN GROWER (agriculture); TOBACCO GROWER (agriculture).

POLYMERIZATION OPERATOR (chemical; plastic-synth.)

A term applied to workers engaged in polymerization of chlorobutadiene into neoprene rubber, including preparation of constituent solutions. Classifications are made according to equipment operated as KETTLE OPERATOR (plastic-synth.).

POWER-PRESS OPERATOR (any industry)

A term applied to workers who operate, tend, or feed one or more power driven presses that cut, bend, punch, trim, compress, forge, rivet, emboss, upset, or force together materials to shape, fabricate, or assemble them by action of dies mounted on bed and ram of machine. Material may be manually or automatically fed into such press. Classifications are made according to function of machine as ASSEMBLY-PRESS OPERATOR (any industry); COMPRESSION-MOLDING-MACHINE TENDER (plastic prod.); EMBOSSING-PRESS OPERATOR (any industry); FORGING-PRESS OPERATOR (forging) I; FORGING-PRESS OPERATOR (forging) II; PUNCH-PRESS OPERATOR (any industry) I; PUNCH-PRESS OPERATOR (any industry) II; PUNCH-PRESS OPERATOR (any industry) III.

PRECIPITATOR OPERATOR (smelt. & refin.)

A term applied to workers engaged in precipitating aluminum hydroxide from rich liquor in the process of extracting alumina from bauxite. Classifications are made according to work performed as BOTTOM-PRECIPITATOR OPERATOR (smelt. & refin.); TOP-PRECIPITATOR OPERATOR (smelt. & refin.).

PRECISION-OPTICAL WORKER (optical goods)

A term applied to workers engaged in preparation of precision glass elements, working to close tolerances. Classifications are made according to work performed as OPTICAL-GLASS ETCHER (optical goods); OPTICAL-GLASS SILVERER (optical goods); PRECISION-LENS GRINDER (optical goods); PRECISION-LENS POLISHER (optical goods).

PRESS FEEDER (print. & pub.)

A term applied to workers who feed paper into printing presses. Classifications are made according to type of press fed.

PRESS OPERATOR (print. & pub.)

A term applied to workers who make ready and operate printing presses. Classifications are made according to type of press operated as CYLINDER-PRESS OPERATOR (print. & pub.) 651.362-010; OFFSET-PRESS OPERATOR (print. & pub.) I 651.382-042; PLATEN-PRESS OPERATOR (print. & pub.) 651.362-018.

PUBLIC-UTILITIES ENGINEER (profess. & kin.)

A term for persons who perform professional engineering work in field of regulation and control of public and private electric, natural gas, and water utilities. Classifications are made according to area of specialization, such as CIVIL ENGINEER (profess. & kin.); ELECTRICAL ENGINEER (profess. & kin.);

ELECTROLYSIS-AND-CORROSION-CONTROL ENGINEER (profess. & kin.); POWER-DISTRIBUTION ENGINEER (utilities); RATE ENGINEER (profess. & kin.); VALUATION ENGINEER (profess. & kin.).

PUBLISHER (print. & pub.)

A term applied to the individual who publishes printed materials, such as newspapers, books, and magazines, and directs marketing of these products. Classifications are made according to executive capacity in which engaged as EDITOR, BOOK (print. & pub.) 132.067-014; EDITOR, MANAGING, NEWSPAPER (print. & pub.) 132.017-010; MANAGER, CIRCULATION (print. & pub.) 163.167-014; PRESIDENT (any industry) 189.117-026.

RAILROAD SUPERVISOR (construction)

A term applied to a SUPERVISOR (any industry) who supervises work crews engaged in railroad construction activities, such as clearing railroad right-of-way, installing pipe culverts, and laying ties and rails. Classifications are made according to activity of workers supervised. Typical classifications are CLEARING SUPERVISOR (construction); TRACK-LAYING SUPERVISOR (construction).

REAMER (construction)

A term applied to a RIVETER HELPER (any industry); or RIVETER, PNEUMATIC (any industry) when shaping misaligned rivet holes in structural-steel members, using a hand or electrically powered reaming tool.

REHABILITATION THERAPIST (profess. & kin.)

A term applied to persons engaged in restoring physical, emotional, social, and economic effectiveness of medical patients and other disabled persons. Classifications are made according to type of therapy applied as CORRECTIVE THERAPIST (medical ser.); TEACHER, EMOTIONALLY IMPAIRED (education); MANUAL-ARTS THERAPIST (medical ser.); MUSIC THERAPIST (medical ser.); OCCUPATIONAL THERAPIST (medical ser.); ORIENTATION AND MOBILITY THERAPIST FOR THE BLIND (education; medical ser.; nonprofit org.); PHYSICAL THERAPIST (medical ser.); RECREATIONAL THERAPIST (medical ser.).

RELIEF WORKER (tobacco) alternate titles: packing-machine relief-operator-and-salvager; utility hand

A term applied to workers who relieve other employees engaged in packing or export department of cigarette manufacturing firm. Classifications are made according to work performed as CARTON-PACKAGING-MACHINE OPERATOR (tobacco); CIGARETTE-MAKING-MACHINE CATCHER (tobacco); CIGARETTE-PACKING-MACHINE OPERATOR (tobacco).

RESEARCH ASSOCIATE (profess. & kin.)

A term applied to persons who conduct independent research in scientific, legal, medical, political, academic, or other specialized fields. Individuals working at this level are required to have a graduate degree. Classifications are made according to field of specialization as AERODYNAMIST (aircraft mfg.) 002.061-010; METALLURGIST, PHYSICAL (profess. & kin.) 011.061-022; MICROBIOLOGIST (profess. & kin.) 041.061-058; PATHOLOGIST (medical ser.) 070.061-010; POLITICAL SCIENTIST (profess. & kin.) 051.067-010.

RIVER-AND-HARBOR SUPERVISOR (construction)

A term applied to a SUPERVISOR (any industry) who supervises work crews engaged in activities, such as deepening and widening harbors, canalizing streams, and impounding waters. Classifications are made according to activity of workers supervised. Typical classifications are BANK BOSS (construction); CONCRETING SUPERVISOR (construction); SUCTION-DREDGE-PIPE-LINE-PLACING SUPERVISOR (construction).

ROLL OPERATOR II (any industry)

A term applied to workers who operate machines to form, forge, bend, or straighten hot or cold metal by passing metal between or under revolving cylinders. Typical classifications are ANGLE-ROLL OPERATOR (any industry); FLANGING-ROLL OPERATOR (any industry); FORMING-ROLL OPERATOR (any industry) II; ROLL-FORMING-MACHINE OPERATOR (any industry) II; STRAIGHTENING-ROLL OPERATOR (any industry).

SAILOR (water trans.) alternate titles: sailor-merchant mariner

A term applied to workers aboard seagoing vessels. Classifications are made according to duties performed as MARINE OILER (water trans.); ORDINARY SEAMAN (water trans.).

SALESPERSON, CONTINGENT (retail trade) alternate titles: relief clerk; salesperson, part time; salesperson, relief

A term applied to a SALESPERSON (retail trade; wholesale tr.) who works only when called and works for period shorter than work period of regular SALESPERSONS (retail trade; wholesale tr.). May be employed for specified number of hours or days per week or month.

SAND HOG (construction)

A term applied to persons working under compressed air as in caisson or tunnel. Classifications are made according to work performed as LOCK TENDER (construction) I; MINER (construction); MUCKER (construction).

SAWYER (stonework)

A term applied to workers engaged in cutting stone with power-driven saws. The techniques required and types of machines vary considerably. Classifications are made according to type of saw as CIRCULAR SAWYER, STONE (stonework); GANG SAWYER, STONE (stonework); WIRE SAWYER (stonework).

SCIENTIST (profess. & kin.)
A term applied to a worker engaged in scientific studies and research. Classifications are made according to scientific specialties, such as ASTRONOMER (profess. & kin.); BIOLOGIST (profess. & kin.); MATHEMATICIAN (profess. & kin.); PHYSICIST (profess. & kin.); ZOOLOGIST (profess. & kin.).

SECOND HAND (textile)
A term applied to supervisors who supervise part of department in textile mill. Classifications are made according to name of department in which supervision is exercised as SUPERVISOR, PREPARATION DEPARTMENT (textile); SUPERVISOR, WINDING AND TWISTING DEPARTMENT (textile).

SECTION HAND (textile)
A term applied to supervisors, usually subordinate to SECOND HAND (textile), who supervise part of department in textile mill. Classifications are made according to name of department in which supervision is exercised as SUPERVISOR, PREPARATION DEPARTMENT (textile); SUPERVISOR, WINDING AND TWISTING DEPARTMENT (textile).

SERGING-MACHINE OPERATOR (any industry) alternate titles: edging-machine operator; overcasting-machine operator; overedge-machine operator; overlock-machine operator; overseaming-machine operator; serger
A term applied to sewing-machine operators when operating machine that trims raw edges from fabric and simultaneously binds trimmed edge with an overlock stitch. For classification of sewing-machine operators, see three-digit groups 786-787.

SEWER-AND-WATERWORKS SUPERVISOR (construction)
A term applied to a SUPERVISOR (any industry) who supervises work crews engaged in sewer-and-waterworks-construction activities, such as clearing right-of-way, loading materials, mixing concrete, and laying pipe. Classifications are made according to activity of workers supervised. Typical classifications are CLEARING SUPERVISOR (construction); CONCRETE-BATCHING AND MIXING-PLANT SUPERVISOR (construction); LABOR-CREW SUPERVISOR (construction; utilities); MATERIAL-CREW SUPERVISOR (construction; mfd. bldgs.).

SHARECROPPER (agriculture)
A term applied to a farmer who plants, cultivates, and harvests crops on land owned by another for specified share of receipts of sale of crop. Usually equipment, seed, and fertilizer are provided by land owner who may also specify crops to be grown and when planting and harvesting will take place. Classifications are made according to crop grown as FARMER, FIELD CROP (agriculture); FARMER, VEGETABLE (agriculture).

SHED WORKER (agriculture)
A term applied to farm workers when they are working in a building or lean-to which provides protection from weather or which is used for drying and storing crops. Classifications are made according to kind of crop, such as HARVEST WORKER, FIELD CROP (agriculture); HARVEST WORKER, VEGETABLE (agriculture); or according to duties performed as PACKER, AGRICULTURAL PRODUCE (agriculture); SORTER, AGRICULTURAL PRODUCE (agriculture; can. & preserv.; wholesale tr.); SUPERVISOR, SHED WORKERS (agriculture).

SHOP STEWARD (any industry)
A term applied to a worker who negotiates with company officials as a representative of fellow employees for the protection of their working interests or contractual rights. Acts as representative for other workers in the settlement of individual grievances. May keep overtime records. Workers whose union functions are incidental to their production work should be classified according to the production or administrative duties performed. Workers who spend full time in union activities should be classified as BUSINESS REPRESENTATIVE, LABOR UNION (profess. & kin.).

SMELTERY WORKER (smelt. & refin.)
A term applied to any worker in a smeltery where ores are melted to separate and recover the metals contained therein and the latter refined to a state of purity demanded for commercial use. Classifications are made according to type of activity or equipment used as FLOTATION TENDER (smelt. & refin.); KETTLE TENDER (smelt. & refin.) I; RAW SAMPLER (smelt. & refin.).

SOCIAL-WORK CONSULTANT (profess. & kin.)
A term applied to workers who render advisory service to agencies, groups, or individuals in fields of social work, employing their knowledge and skills gained through training, graduate-level education, and experience. Classifications are made according to areas of social work in which training, education, and experience have been acquired.

SOCIAL WORKER (profess. & kin.)
A term applied to a worker performing social service functions, based on university-level education in social-welfare human services, or equivalency, in a public or voluntary social welfare agency, organization, or department, or in other settings, as in housing projects or in schools. Classifications are made according to work performed as SOCIAL GROUP WORKER (social ser.); SO-CIAL WORKER, DELINQUENCY PREVENTION (social ser.); SOCIAL WORKER, PSYCHIATRIC (profess. & kin.).

SOLDERER, SILVER (welding)
A term applied to workers who braze together components of metal assemblies with a brazing alloy, usually containing silver (hard solder), by any brazing method. Workers are classified according to function or equipment used as BRAZER, ASSEMBLER (welding); BRAZER, CONTROLLED ATMOSPHERIC FURNACE (welding); BRAZER, INDUCTION (welding); BRAZER, REPAIR AND SALVAGE (welding); BRAZING-MACHINE OPERATOR (welding).

SPECIAL-DELIVERY DRIVER (any industry)
A term applied to TRUCK DRIVER, HEAVY (any industry); or TRUCK DRIVER, LIGHT (any industry) when delivering orders that cannot be handled by regular delivery system because order must reach customer immediately, customer's address is not on regular route, or for other reasons.

SPECIALTY CHEF (hotel & rest.) alternate titles: chef, department; chef, station
A term applied to the head cook of a station when specializing in a given type of cooking, such as frying foods or cooking sauces. Classifications are made according to specialty as SOUS CHEF (hotel & rest.).

SPINNING-ROOM WORKER (plastic-synth.)
A term for workers employed in the spinning department of a synthetic-fiber plant. Classifications are made according to work performed as BOX TENDER (plastic-synth.); PUMP TESTER (plastic-synth.); SPINNER (plastic-synth.); SPINNING-BATH PATROLLER (plastic-synth.); TEMPERATURE-CONTROL INSPECTOR (plastic-synth.).

SPONSOR (retail trade) alternate titles: instructor, training; coach
A term applied to MANAGER, DEPARTMENT (retail trade), his or her assistant, or to experienced salesperson who instructs and supervises new sales employees in store system, care and location of stock, merchandise information, and selling methods.

SPREADER II (any industry)
A term applied to a worker who lays out, coats, places, or spreads material to be cut, joined, stretched, or smoothed. Classifications are made according to material spread as CANDY SPREADER (sugar & conf.); FLATWORK FINISHER (laundry & rel.).

STAGE HAND (amuse. & rec.) alternate titles: stage technician
A term applied to all workers backstage of theater who handle props, curtains, or electrical equipment. Classifications are made according to type of activity in which engaged as PROPERTY COORDINATOR (amuse. & rec.; radio-tv broad.).

STILL OPERATOR (any industry)
A term applied to a worker who operates or tends equipment for distilling, purifying, reclaiming, or refining materials. Usually designated according to type of duties performed as BATCH-STILL OPERATOR (chemical) II; DISTILLER (chemical) I; DISTILLER (chemical) II; and REFINERY OPERATOR (petrol. refin.).

STITCHER, MACHINE (boot & shoe)
A term applied to workers who operate single, double, or multiple needle standard or special stitching machines to join, decorate, or reinforce shoe parts. Classification are made according to type of machine used as STITCHER, SPECIAL MACHINE (boot & shoe); STITCHER, STANDARD MACHINE (boot & shoe).

STONE MECHANIC (stonework) alternate titles: stone finisher
A term applied to a worker who is skilled in layout work and the use of handtools and machines for cutting, polishing, and sandblasting building and monument stone. Classifications should be made according to work performed as SANDBLASTER, STONE (stonework); STONECUTTER, HAND (stonework); STONECUTTER, MACHINE (stonework); STONE POLISHER, HAND (stonework).

STONE RENOVATOR (construction)
A term applied to a BRICKLAYER (construction); CEMENT MASON (construction); PLASTERER (construction); or STONEMASON (construction) when resurfacing stone to restore and renovate building.

STRAW BOSS (any industry) alternate titles: gang leader; group leader; head; pacer; pusher
A term applied to a worker who takes the lead in a construction or laboring crew and is selected to expedite the work of the crew, usually small in number. Regularly performs all duties of workers in crew. Explains tasks to new workers. The supervisory functions are incidental to the duties performed as a member of the crew. Classifications are made according to type of work performed by crew.

STRIPPER (any industry)
A term applied to a worker who dismantles or separates articles or material, removes coverings, trims and decorates products, or otherwise works with strips of material. Classifications are made according to article or material processed as CARD STRIPPER (textile); COVER STRIPPER (paper goods); FORM STRIPPER (concrete prod.; construction); FRAME STRIPPER (soap & rel.).

9

STUD-DRIVER OPERATOR (construction) alternate titles: cartridge-actuated-tool operator; explosive-actuated-tool operator; powder-actuated-tool operator

A term applied to a CARPENTER (construction) or ELECTRICIAN (construction) when driving steel studs into concrete, steel, or masonry base to anchor construction materials and equipment, using powder-actuated stud driver.

STYRENE OPERATOR (chemical)

A term applied to workers in a styrene manufacturing plant who operate or tend panel-controlled equipment, such as stills and catalytic converter units, to facilitate production of product meeting plant standards. Classifications are made according to equipment operated or tended as CATALYTIC-CONVERTER OPERATOR (chemical); CONTINUOUS-STILL OPERATOR (chemical).

SWITCHYARD WORKER (r.r. trans.)

A term applied to workers when switching or supervising workers engaged in switching cars within yard of railroad, industrial plant, quarry, construction project, or other similar location for purpose of loading, unloading, making up, and breaking up of trains. Classifications are made according to type of activity engaged in as CONDUCTOR, YARD (r.r. trans.); SWITCH TENDER (r.r. trans.); YARD COUPLER (r.r. trans.).

TAILINGS MACHINERY TENDER (smelt. & refin.)

A term applied to worker who tends equipment used to dispose of tailings (worthless material) after valuable minerals have been removed by ore-dressing processes. The equipment used varies with each individual mill, with pumps, bucket elevators, desliming cones, thickeners, launders, and settling tanks commonly being used. Usually designated according to type of equipment tended as CLASSIFIER TENDER (smelt. & refin.).

TEACHER, HOME (education)

A term applied to a TEACHER, ELEMENTARY SCHOOL (education) or a TEACHER, SECONDARY SCHOOL (education) who instructs students unable to attend classes because of confinement at home or hospital.

TECHNICIAN (profess. & kin.) alternate titles: engineering aide; technical aide; technical assistant

A term applied to a worker who works in direct support of ENGINEERS (profess. & kin.) or SCIENTISTS (profess. & kin.), utilizing theoretical knowledge of fundamental scientific, engineering, mathematical, or draft design principles. Solves practical problems encountered in fields of specialization, such as those concerned with development of electrical and electronic circuits, and establishment of testing methods for electrical, electronic, electromechanical, and hydromechanical devices and mechanisms; application of engineering principles in solving design, development, and modification problems of parts or assemblies for products or systems; and application of natural and physical science principles to basic or applied research problems in fields, such as metallurgy, chemistry, and physics. Classifications are made according to specialization as ELECTRONICS TECHNICIAN (profess. & kin.); MATHEMATICAL TECHNICIAN (profess. & kin.).

TEXTILE ENGINEER (profess. & kin.)

A term applied to workers possessing college degrees or equivalent experience in textile technology. These workers usually enter textile industry as trainees for any one of several supervisory or technical occupations. Classifications are made according to specialty as CLOTH DESIGNER (profess. & kin.); MANAGER, QUALITY CONTROL (profess. & kin.); DYER, SUPERVISOR (knitting; tex. prod., nec; textile); PRODUCTION SUPERINTENDENT (any industry); WEAVING SUPERVISOR (nonmet. min.; textile). Professional engineers who refer to themselves as textile engineers because of their experience in the textile industry should be classified according to their specialty as CHEMICAL ENGINEER (profess. & kin.); ELECTRICAL ENGINEER (profess. & kin.); MECHANICAL ENGINEER (profess. & kin.).

TIRE BUILDER (rubber tire)

A term applied to workers engaged in building parts of tires or assembling whole tires. Classifications are made according to part of tire being made as BAND BUILDER (rubber tire); or according to tire assembled as TIRE BUILDER, AUTOMOBILE (rubber tire); TIRE BUILDER, HEAVY SERVICE (rubber tire).

TOWER OPERATOR I (chemical)

A term applied to workers who operate or tend columns or towers in chemical absorption, distillation, stripping, rectification, or related processes. Classifications are made according to process operated as ABSORPTION OPERATOR (chemical) or according to equipment unit as TOWER HELPER (chemical).

TOXIC OPERATOR (chemical)

A term applied to any worker who processes or otherwise handles toxic explosives, such as tetryl and nitroglycerin, or toxic ingredients, such as acids and benzene. Classifications are made according to equipment used or according to material handled as TETRYL-SCREEN OPERATOR (chemical).

TRAINEE (any industry)

A term applied to workers who are engaged, under direct supervision, in learning a job or trade that may require up to several months of continuous on-the-job training, with or without related schooling in vocational subjects, before the worker may be considered fully qualified to perform the job. Such workers should be treated as entry applicants except that, if they have completed their training requirements, they should be classified according to the job learned. Workers who are learning a trade through apprenticeship training should be classified in accordance with the procedure set forth under APPRENTICE (any industry).

TRAINEE ENGINEER (profess. & kin.)

A term applied to an engineer who works under supervision of experienced engineers to gain qualifying experience in a particular field. Classifications are made according to field of specialization as CHEMICAL ENGINEER (profess. & kin.); ELECTRICAL ENGINEER (profess. & kin.); MECHANICAL ENGINEER (profess. & kin.).

TRUCK DRIVER (any industry) alternate titles: truck operator

A term applied to workers who drive trucks to transport materials, merchandise, equipment, or people. Workers are classified according to type of truck as DUMP-TRUCK DRIVER (any industry); TRACTOR-TRAILER-TRUCK DRIVER (any industry); TRUCK DRIVER, LIGHT (any industry).

TUNNEL WORKER (construction)

A term applied to a person working in tunnel. Classifications are made according to work performed as LOCK TENDER (construction) I; PIPE CAULKER (construction); SHIELD RUNNER (construction).

TYPESETTER (print. & pub.)

A term applied to a worker who, prior to actual printing operations, sets and assembles type and cuts in chases for printing articles, headings, and other printed matter; or who composes type by operating various typesetting machines. Typically is required to complete a lengthy apprenticeship and is thoroughly versed in type style, printed page makeup, and printing techniques involved in newspaper or commercial printing. Classifications are made according to type of printing activity engaged in as COMPOSITOR (print. & pub.) 973.381-010; LINOTYPE OPERATOR (print. & pub.) 650.582-010; MAKE-UP ARRANGER (print. & pub.) 973.381-026; MONOTYPE-KEYBOARD OPERATOR (machinery mfg.; print. & pub.) 650.582-014; TYPE-CASTING MACHINE OPERATOR (print. & pub.) 654.582-010; TYPESETTER-PERFORATOR OPERATOR (print. & pub.) 203.582-062.

VISUAL-INFORMATION SPECIALIST (profess. & kin.)

A term applied to civil service workers who plan and design visual material used in publications, exhibits, speeches, briefings, television, motion pictures, film strips, and similar visual media. Classifications are made according to duties and area of specialization as ART DIRECTOR (profess. & kin.); AUDIO-VISUAL PRODUCTION SPECIALIST (profess. & kin.); DISPLAY DESIGNER (profess. & kin.); GRAPHIC DESIGNER (profess. & kin.); ILLUSTRATOR (profess. & kin.); PUBLIC-RELATIONS REPRESENTATIVE (profess. & kin.); SET DESIGNER (motion picture; radio-tv broad.).

WARE FORMER (pottery & porc.)

A term applied to workers who form clay into vessels or other objects by hand or by using molds or presses. Classifications are made according to method used as CASTER (pottery & porc.); DIE PRESSER (pottery & porc.); JOLLIER (pottery & porc.); POTTERY-MACHINE OPERATOR (pottery & porc.); THROWER (pottery & porc.).

WASTE HAND (textile)

A term designating workers who handle waste materials in textile mill. Classifications are made according to task performed as LABORER, SALVAGE (any industry); or according to machine tended as WASTE-MACHINE TENDER (tex. prod., nec; textile).

WELDER, CERTIFIED (welding) alternate titles: certified welder

A term applied to a welder who possesses a written certification from an employer or certifying agent, such as governmental agency, and professional or technical association, verifying that worker's production of specified welds meets prescribed standards. Not all welders are certified. Certified and non-certified welders are classified according to welding process or workpiece, such as WELDER, ARC (welding); WELDER, BOILERMAKER (struct. metal); WELDER-FITTER (welding).

WELL-POINT SETTER (construction)

A term applied to a LABORER, PLUMBING (construction); MUCKER, COFFERDAM (construction); or PIPE-LAYER HELPER (construction) when assisting in the installation of well-point pumps and in setting well-point pipe into sand or loose earth to provide subsoil drainage systems for excavation work below ground water level.

WHEELER (construction) alternate titles: buggy pusher; chute worker; loader; wheelbarrow pusher

A term applied to a BRICKLAYER HELPER (construction); CARPENTER HELPER, HARDWOOD FLOORING (construction); LABORER, CONCRETE-MIXING PLANT (construction); LABORER, PLUMBING (construction); LABORER, ROAD (construction); PLASTERER HELPER (construction); or STONEMASON HELPER (construction) when pushing wheelbarrow or buggy (two-wheeled push cart with deep body) to transport concrete, mortar, sand, or other material.

YARD SUPERVISOR (any industry) alternate titles: yard boss

A term applied to a worker who supervises and directs activities of workers engaged in such duties as stacking materials, loading and unloading incoming

10

and outgoing shipments, or sorting scrap materials for salvage, in yard of an industrial plant. Classifications are made according to activity supervised as STOCK SUPERVISOR (clerical); SUPERVISOR, FRAMING MILL (wood prod., nec); SUPERVISOR, SCRAP PREPARATION (steel & rel.).

YEOMAN (water trans.)
A term applied to an ADMINISTRATIVE CLERK (clerical) who performs clerical duties on board ship.

OCCUPATIONAL GROUP ARRANGEMENT

0/1 PROFESSIONAL, TECHNICAL, AND MANAGERIAL OCCUPATIONS

This category includes occupations concerned with the theoretical or practical aspects of such fields of human endeavor as art, science, engineering, education, medicine, law, business relations, and administrative, managerial, and technical work. Most of these occupations require substantial educational preparation (usually at the university, junior college, or technical institute level).

00/01 OCCUPATIONS IN ARCHITECTURE, ENGINEERING, AND SURVEYING

This division includes occupations concerned with the practical application of physical laws and principles of engineering or architecture for the development and utilization of machines, materials, instruments, structures, processes, and services. Typical specializations are research, design, construction, testing, procurement, production, operations, and sales. Also includes preparation of drawings, specifications, and cost estimates, and participation in verification tests.

001 ARCHITECTURAL OCCUPATIONS

This group includes occupations concerned with the design and construction of buildings and related structures, or landscaping, and floating structures, according to aesthetic and functional factors.

001.061-010 ARCHITECT (profess. & kin.)
Researches, plans, designs, and administers building projects for clients, applying knowledge of design, construction procedures, zoning and building codes, and building materials: Consults with client to determine functional and spatial requirements of new structure or renovation, and prepares information regarding design, specifications, materials, color, equipment, estimated costs, and construction time. Plans layout of project and integrates engineering elements into unified design for client review and approval. Prepares scale drawings and contract documents for building contractors. Represents client in obtaining bids and awarding construction contracts. Administers construction contracts and conducts periodic on-site observation of work during construction to monitor compliance with plans. May prepare operating and maintenance manuals, studies, and reports. May use computer-assisted design software and equipment to prepare project designs and plans. May direct activities of workers engaged in preparing drawings and specification documents.
GOE: 05.01.07 STRENGTH: L GED: R6 M6 L6 SVP: 8 DLU: 81

001.061-014 ARCHITECT, MARINE (profess. & kin.) alternate titles: architect, naval; naval designer
Designs and oversees construction and repair of marine craft and floating structures, such as ships, barges, tugs, dredges, submarines, torpedoes, floats, and buoys: Studies design proposals and specifications to establish basic characteristics of craft, such as size, weight, speed, propulsion, armament, cargo, displacement, draft, crew and passenger complements, and fresh or salt water service. Oversees construction and testing of prototype in model basin and develops sectional and waterline curves of hull to establish center of gravity, ideal hull form, and buoyancy and stability data. Designs complete hull and superstructure according to specifications and test data, in conformity with standards of safety, efficiency, and economy. Designs layout of craft interior including cargo space, passenger compartments, ladder wells, and elevators. Confers with MARINE ENGINEERS (profess. & kin.) to establish arrangement of boiler room equipment and propulsion machinery, heating and ventilating systems, refrigeration equipment, piping, and other functional equipment. Evaluates performance of craft during dock and sea trials to determine design changes and conformance with national and international standards.
GOE: 05.01.07 STRENGTH: L GED: R6 M6 L6 SVP: 9 DLU: 77

001.061-018 LANDSCAPE ARCHITECT (profess. & kin.) alternate titles: community planner; environmental planner; land planner; site planner
Plans and designs development of land areas for projects, such as parks and other recreational facilities, airports, highways, and parkways, hospitals, schools, land subdivisions, and commercial, industrial, and residential sites: Confers with clients, engineering personnel, and ARCHITECTS (profess. & kin.) on overall program. Compiles and analyzes data on such site conditions as geographic location; soil, vegetation, and rock features; drainage; and location of structures for preparation of environmental impact report and development of landscaping plans. Prepares site plans, working drawings, specifications, and cost estimates for land development, showing ground contours, vegetation, locations of structures, and such facilities as roads, walks, parking areas, fences, walls, and utilities, coordinating arrangement of existing and proposed land features and structures. Inspects construction work in progress to ensure compliance with landscape specifications, to approve quality of materials and work, and to advise client and construction personnel on landscape features.

May be designated according to project as Highway-Landscape Architect (profess. & kin.); Park-Landscape Architect (profess. & kin.).
GOE: 05.01.07 STRENGTH: L GED: R5 M5 L5 SVP: 8 DLU: 77

001.167-010 SCHOOL-PLANT CONSULTANT (education)
Formulates and enforces standards for construction and alteration of public school facilities throughout state: Develops legislation relative to school building sites and school design and construction. Guides school districts in development of long range comprehensive master plans, including such factors as site selection and expected population growth and mobility, and school finance and specifications. Coordinates activities, jurisdictions, and responsibilities of adjacent school districts and evaluates entire systems of schools. Provides technical information and advice to local school authorities considering construction or renovation of school plant. Inspects proposed sites and schools under construction or undergoing alteration to enforce applicable standards. Prepares suggested classroom plans and layouts, taking into consideration such factors as climate, construction costs, availability of materials, and accepted principles of institutional construction. Reviews plans for construction and renovation of school buildings and approves or disapproves plans in accordance with standards and policies of department. Confers with representatives of school boards, educators, and architects to explain and reach agreement on design concepts and construction standards. Arbitrates difficult and unusual construction disputes. Conducts special research studies concerned with lighting, heating, ventilation, air-conditioning, and acoustics. Prepares reports for state education department and state legislature.
GOE: 05.01.08 STRENGTH: S GED: R5 M5 L5 SVP: 6 DLU: 77

001.261-010 DRAFTER, ARCHITECTURAL (profess. & kin.)
Prepares detailed drawings of architectural designs and plans for buildings, according to specifications, sketches, and rough drafts provided by ARCHITECT (profess. & kin.) 001.061-010: Draws rough and detailed sketches, drawings, and plans to scale [DRAFTER (profess. & kin.) Master Title].
GOE: 05.03.02 STRENGTH: S GED: R4 M4 L4 SVP: 7 DLU: 81

001.261-014 DRAFTER, LANDSCAPE (profess. & kin.)
Prepares detailed scale drawings and tracings from rough sketches or other data provided by LANDSCAPE ARCHITECT (profess. & kin.), performing duties described under DRAFTER (profess. & kin.) Master Title. May prepare separate detailed site plan, grading and drainage plan, lighting plan, paving plan, irrigation plan, planting plan, and drawings and detail of garden structures. May build models of proposed landscape construction and prepare colored drawings for presentation to client.
GOE: 05.03.02 STRENGTH: S GED: R4 M4 L3 SVP: 7 DLU: 77

002 AERONAUTICAL ENGINEERING OCCUPATIONS

This group includes occupations concerned with design and development of aircraft, space vehicles, surface effect vehicles, missiles, weapons, and related systems. Accessory techniques needed are those found in electronic and electrical engineering, mechanical and electromechanical engineering, metallurgy, propulsion systems design, ordnance engineering, and human factors and test engineering.

002.061-010 AERODYNAMICIST (aircraft mfg.) alternate titles: aerodynamics engineer; aerophysics engineer
Plans and conducts analysis of aerodynamic, thermodynamic, aerothermodynamic, and aerophysics concepts, systems, and designs to resolve problems and determine suitability and application to aircraft and aerospace products: Establishes computational methods and computer input data for analyzing problems. Analyzes designs and develops configurations to ensure satisfactory static and dynamic stability and control characteristics for completed vehicle. Initiates and assists in formulating and evaluating laboratory, flight, and wind tunnel test programs, and prepares reports and conclusions for other engineering and design personnel. Coordinates activities of model design group and model shop to assure required configuration of wind tunnel models. Prepares air load data on vehicle to conform to aerodynamic requirements. May prepare reports on results of analyses, such as flight performance validation, aircraft configuration, trade studies, and aircraft certification. May confer with customer on performance problems during operational life of vehicle. May specialize in analysis of thermodynamic effects and be designated Thermodynamics Engineer (aircraft mfg.).

GOE: 05.01.01 STRENGTH: L GED: R6 M6 L6 SVP: 8 DLU: 88

002.061-014 AERONAUTICAL ENGINEER (aircraft mfg.)
Designs, develops, and tests aircraft, space vehicles, surface effect vehicles, missiles, and related component systems, applying engineering principles and techniques: Designs and develops commercial, military, executive, general aviation, or special purpose aircraft, space vehicles, satellites, missiles, or related hardware or systems. Tests models, prototypes, subassemblies, or production vehicles to study and evaluate operational characteristics and effects of stress imposed during actual or simulated flight conditions. May specialize in design and development of structural components, such as wings, fuselage, rib assemblies, landing gear, or operational control systems. May specialize in analytical programs concerned with ground or flight testing, or development of acoustic, thermodynamic, or propulsion systems. May assist in planning technical phases of air transportation systems or other aspects of flight operations, maintenance, or logistics.
GOE: 05.01.07 STRENGTH: L GED: R6 M6 L6 SVP: 8 DLU: 86

002.061-018 AERONAUTICAL TEST ENGINEER (aircraft mfg.)
Conducts testing activities on aerospace and aircraft products, performing duties as described under TEST ENGINEER (profess. & kin.) Master Title.
GOE: 05.01.04 STRENGTH: L GED: R5 M5 L5 SVP: 8 DLU: 88

002.061-022 AERONAUTICAL-DESIGN ENGINEER (aircraft mfg.)
Develops basic design concepts used in design, development, and production of aeronautical and aerospace products and systems, performing duties as described under DESIGN ENGINEER, PRODUCTS (profess. & kin.) Master Title.
GOE: 05.01.07 STRENGTH: S GED: R5 M5 L5 SVP: 8 DLU: 88

002.061-026 AERONAUTICAL-RESEARCH ENGINEER (aircraft mfg.)
Conducts research in field of aeronautics, performing duties as described under RESEARCH ENGINEER (profess. & kin.) Master Title.
GOE: 05.01.01 STRENGTH: L GED: R6 M6 L6 SVP: 8 DLU: 88

002.061-030 STRESS ANALYST (aircraft mfg.)
Conducts stress analyses on designs of experimental, prototype, or production aircraft, space vehicles, surface effect vehicles, missiles, and related components to evaluate ability to withstand stresses imposed during flight or ground operations: Analyzes ability of structural components to withstand stresses imposed by static, dynamic, or thermal loads, due to operational or test conditions. Studies preliminary specifications and design requirements to determine strength and bending characteristics of parts, assemblies, and total airframe. Consults with design personnel regarding results of analyses and need for additional analysis, testing, or design modifications. Formulates *mathematical model* of stress problem or devises other methods of computer analysis or simulation to assist in stress analysis.
GOE: 05.01.04 STRENGTH: S GED: R5 M5 L5 SVP: 8 DLU: 88

002.151-010 SALES ENGINEER, AERONAUTICAL PRODUCTS (aircraft mfg.)
Sells aeronautical products and provides customers with technical engineering services as described under SALES ENGINEER (profess. & kin.) Master Title.
GOE: 05.01.05 STRENGTH: L GED: R5 M5 L5 SVP: 8 DLU: 89

002.167-010 VALUE ENGINEER (aircraft mfg.) alternate titles: cost development engineer; design specialist, producibility, cost and component technology
Plans and coordinates engineering activities to develop and apply standardized design criteria and production requirements for parts and equipment used in aircraft and aerospace vehicles: Establishes and maintains liaison between engineering and other departments to formulate and apply design criteria and production requirements for proposed products. Analyzes product design data to determine conformance to established design selection criteria, use of standardized parts and equipment, and design-to-cost ratio. Approves initial design or recommends modifications based on producibility, cost, and component technology factors. Coordinates testing of new parts and equipment, evaluates test results, and approves or rejects usage of parts and equipment based on test results. Evaluates and approves selection of vendors. Initiates and provides technical direction for research and development programs to enhance production methods, improve parts and equipment technology, and reduce costs. Develops methods and programs to predict, track, and report production costs during design development.
GOE: 05.01.06 STRENGTH: S GED: R6 M5 L6 SVP: 8 DLU: 89

002.167-014 FIELD-SERVICE ENGINEER (aircraft mfg.)
Plans and coordinates activities concerned with investigating and resolving customer reports of technical problems with aircraft or aerospace vehicles and eliminating future operational or service difficulties: Reviews performance reports and documentation from customers and field representatives, and inspects malfunctioning or damaged product to determine nature and scope of problem. Analyzes review and inspection findings to determine source of problem, and recommends repair, replacement, or other corrective action. Coordinates problem resolution with engineering, customer service, and other personnel to expedite repairs. Maintains records of performance reports. Analyzes reports of technical problems to determine trends affecting future design, production, service, and maintenance processes, and recommends modifications to eliminate future problems. May prepare service handbooks and bulletins based on field investigations, engineering changes, and overall knowledge of product. May provide on-site technical assistance to oversee repairs.

GOE: 05.01.04 STRENGTH: L GED: R5 M5 L5 SVP: 8 DLU: 89

002.167-018 AERONAUTICAL PROJECT ENGINEER (aircraft mfg.) alternate titles: aerospace project engineer
Directs and coordinates activities of personnel engaged in designing mechanisms, structures, systems, and equipment for aeronautical or aerospace products, applying knowledge of engineering theory and technology: Reviews and evaluates product request from customer, and formulates conceptual design to meet customer requirements. Analyzes project proposal to determine feasibility, producibility, cost, and production time, and discusses proposal with customer representatives, engineers, and other personnel. Assigns project personnel to specific aspects or phases of project, such as analysis, development, or design. Evaluates product design for conformance to engineering principles, customer requirements, quality standards, and specifications. Evaluates and approves design changes and drawing releases. Coordinates design, production, testing, and related activities. Consults with project personnel and others to provide technical assistance and information.
GOE: 05.01.08 STRENGTH: L GED: R6 M6 L6 SVP: 9 DLU: 88

002.261-010 DRAFTER, AERONAUTICAL (aircraft mfg.)
Drafts engineering drawings of developmental or production airplanes, missiles, and component and ancillary equipment, including launch mechanisms and scale models of prototype aircraft, as planned by AERONAUTICAL ENGINEER (aircraft mfg.) 002.061-014. Performs other duties as described under DRAFTER (profess. & kin.) Master Title.
GOE: 05.03.02 STRENGTH: S GED: R5 M5 L4 SVP: 7 DLU: 87

002.261-014 RESEARCH MECHANIC (aircraft mfg.) alternate titles: laboratory test mechanic
Lays out, fabricates, assembles, and tests mechanical, electromechanical, structural, hydraulic, and pneumatic aircraft parts, assemblies, and mechanisms to assist engineers in determining faulty design or fabrication procedures: Lays out, fabricates, and assembles parts, assemblies, and mechanisms to be tested, according to blueprints, specifications, sketches, templates, or verbal instructions. Installs test specimens, such as rib assemblies, struts, landing gears, valves, ducts, fuselage sections, and control surfaces, in test equipment, and connects wiring, tubing, couplings, and power sources, using handtools and power tools. Operates test equipment to gather data on performance of parts, assemblies, and mechanisms under simulated flight and operational conditions. Measures induced variations from normal, using precision instruments, such as micrometers, verniers, calipers, pressure gauges, flowmeters, strain gauges, and dynamometers. Records and interprets test data. Confers with engineering personnel regarding test procedures and test results. Fabricates and assembles test equipment, tooling, shop aids, or other devices for experimental test projects.
GOE: 05.01.04 STRENGTH: M GED: R4 M4 L4 SVP: 7 DLU: 87

002.262-010 FLIGHT-TEST DATA ACQUISITION TECHNICIAN (aircraft mfg.) alternate titles: data acquisition laboratory technician; technical aide, flight test data
Sets up, operates, monitors, modifies, calibrates, and maintains computer systems and devices for acquisition and analysis of flight test data, utilizing knowledge of electronic theory and operation of computer systems: Reviews engineering notification of flight test to determine data required for post-flight analysis. Plans method and sequence of operations to acquire data, and sets up required electronic data acquisition, test, and measurement equipment and accessories. Inputs flight test data and program information into computer console for specific test requested. Enters commands to modify program to accommodate additional or revised test requirements. Calculates calibration values used as model for comparison and measurement of test data. Monitors lights, displays, and other operating features of computer equipment, such as console, receivers, and printers, to detect malfunctions and ensure integrity of processed data. Diagnoses cause of equipment malfunctioning, and adjusts, repairs, or replaces faulty components. Enters information to update flight test data base and to maintain records, such as electronic parts inventory and manuals for equipment maintenance and calibrations. Discusses flight test requirements and results with engineers and other personnel.
GOE: 05.03.05 STRENGTH: L GED: R5 M4 L4 SVP: 7 DLU: 89

003 ELECTRICAL/ELECTRONICS ENGINEERING OCCUPATIONS

This group includes occupations concerned with the application of the laws of electrical energy and the principles of engineering for the generation, transmission, and use of electricity. Also includes the design and development of machinery and equipment for production and utilization of electric power. Accessory techniques needed are those used in mechanical and process engineering. Typical specializations are electrical power generation, transmission, and distribution, atomic power generation, electrical and electronic components, equipment, and systems manufacturing, radio and television broadcasting, telephone, telegraph, and electronic computer engineering, and bioengineering.

003.061-010 ELECTRICAL ENGINEER (profess. & kin.)
Researches, develops, designs, and tests electrical components, equipment, and systems, applying principles and techniques of electrical engineering: Designs electrical equipment, facilities, components, products, and systems for commercial, industrial, and domestic purposes [DESIGN ENGINEER, FACILITIES (profess. & kin.) Master Title; DESIGN ENGINEER, PRODUCTS (pro-

fess. & kin.) Master Title]. Designs and directs engineering personnel in fabrication of test control apparatus and equipment, and determines methods, procedures, and conditions for testing products [TEST ENGINEER (profess. & kin.) Master Title]. Develops applications of controls, instruments, and systems for new commercial, domestic, and industrial uses. Directs activities to ensure that manufacturing, construction, installation, and operational testing conform to functional specifications and customer requirements. May direct and coordinate operation, maintenance, and repair of equipment and systems in field installations. May specialize in specific area of discipline, such as electrical energy generation, transmission, and distribution systems; products, such as appliances, generators, transformers, control devices, and relays; or area of work, such as manufacturing, applications, or installation. May use computer-assisted engineering and design software and equipment to perform engineering tasks.
GOE: 05.01.08 STRENGTH: L GED: R5 M5 L5 SVP: 8 DLU: 88

003.061-014 ELECTRICAL TEST ENGINEER (profess. & kin.)
Conducts tests on electrical equipment and systems, performing duties as described under TEST ENGINEER (profess. & kin.) Master Title.
GOE: 05.01.04 STRENGTH: L GED: R5 M5 L5 SVP: 8 DLU: 77

003.061-018 ELECTRICAL-DESIGN ENGINEER (profess. & kin.)
Designs electrical equipment and products, performing duties as described under DESIGN ENGINEER, FACILITIES (profess. & kin.) Master Title; DESIGN ENGINEER, PRODUCTS (profess. & kin.) Master Title.
GOE: 05.01.07 STRENGTH: L GED: R5 M5 L5 SVP: 8 DLU: 77

003.061-022 ELECTRICAL-PROSPECTING ENGINEER (profess. & kin.) alternate titles: electrical engineer, geophysical prospecting
Designs and develops electrical and electronic instruments and equipment used in petroleum prospecting with the seismograph, magnetometer, or other instruments which detect and measure various physical properties of the earth's crust.
GOE: 05.01.07 STRENGTH: S GED: R6 M6 L6 SVP: 8 DLU: 77

003.061-026 ELECTRICAL-RESEARCH ENGINEER (profess. & kin.)
Conducts research in various fields of electrical phenomena performing duties as described under RESEARCH ENGINEER (profess. & kin.) Master Title.
GOE: 05.01.01 STRENGTH: L GED: R5 M5 L5 SVP: 8 DLU: 77

003.061-030 ELECTRONICS ENGINEER (profess. & kin.)
Researches, develops, designs, and tests electronic components, products, and systems for commercial, industrial, medical, military, and scientific applications, applying principles and techniques of electronic engineering: Designs electronic circuits, components and integrated systems, utilizing ferroelectric, nonlinear, dielectric, phosphorescent, photo-conductive, and thermoelectric properties of materials [DESIGN ENGINEER, PRODUCTS (profess. & kin.) Master Title]. Designs test control apparatus and equipment, determines procedures for testing products [TEST ENGINEER (profess. & kin.) Master Title], and directs engineering personnel in fabrication of test control apparatus and equipment. Develops new applications of conductive properties of metallic and nonmetallic materials used in components, and in application of components to products or systems. May direct field operations and maintenance of electronic installations. May evaluate operational systems and recommend design modifications to eliminate causes of malfunctions or changes in system requirements. May specialize in development of electronic principles and technology in fields, such as telecommunications, telemetry, aerospace guidance, missile propulsion control, counter-measures, acoustics, nucleonic instrumentation, industrial controls and measurements, high-frequency heating, computers, radiation detection, encephalography, electron optics, and biomedical research. May use computer-assisted engineering and design software and equipment to perform engineering tasks.
GOE: 05.01.08 STRENGTH: L GED: R5 M5 L5 SVP: 8 DLU: 88

003.061-034 ELECTRONICS-DESIGN ENGINEER (profess. & kin.)
Designs and develops electronic components, equipment, systems, and products, applying knowledge and principles of electronic theory, design, and engineering. Performs duties as described under DESIGN ENGINEER, PRODUCTS (profess. & kin.) Master Title. May use computer-assisted engineering and design software and equipment to formulate and test electronic designs.
GOE: 05.01.07 STRENGTH: L GED: R5 M5 L5 SVP: 8 DLU: 89

003.061-038 ELECTRONICS-RESEARCH ENGINEER (profess. & kin.)
Conducts research on electronic phenomena, performing duties as described under RESEARCH ENGINEER (profess. & kin.) Master Title.
GOE: 05.01.01 STRENGTH: L GED: R5 M5 L5 SVP: 8 DLU: 77

003.061-042 ELECTRONICS-TEST ENGINEER (profess. & kin.)
Plans, develops, and conducts tests on electronic components, products, and systems, applying knowledge and principles of electronic theory, testing methodology and procedures, and electronic engineering. Performs duties described under TEST ENGINEER (profess. & kin.) Master Title. May develop or use computer software and hardware to conduct tests on electronic products and systems.
GOE: 05.01.04 STRENGTH: L GED: R5 M5 L5 SVP: 8 DLU: 87

003.061-046 ILLUMINATING ENGINEER (profess. & kin.)
Designs and directs installation of illuminating equipment and systems for buildings, plants, streets, stadia, tunnels, and outdoor displays: Studies lighting requirements of client to determine lighting equipment and arrangement of lamps that will provide optimum illumination with economy of installation and operation. Designs lamps of required light intensity and output, light control reflectors and lenses, and lamp arrangement required to meet illuminating standards. Plans and prepares drawings for installation of lighting system in accordance with client's specifications and municipal codes. Directs installation of system to ensure conformance with engineering specifications and compliance with electrical codes. May be designated according to type or location of illumination system designed and installed as Building-Illuminating Engineer (profess. & kin.); Industrial-Illuminating Engineer (profess. & kin.); Outdoor-Illuminating Engineer (profess. & kin.).
GOE: 05.01.03 STRENGTH: S GED: R5 M5 L5 SVP: 8 DLU: 77

003.061-050 PLANNING ENGINEER, CENTRAL OFFICE FACILITIES (tel. & tel.)
Conducts studies to develop data required for planning central office switching facilities, and prepares plans and schedules for acquisition and installation of equipment to meet long term and current relief requirements: Conducts studies to accumulate information on current services, equipment capacities, current traffic data and estimated acquisition and installation costs. Analyzes data and forecasts on subscriber demands and projected traffic to determine type, size, and quantity of switching equipment required. Plans and schedules equipment acquisition, and installation, considering such factors as availability, current and future costs, and other economic projections. Reviews implementation schedules on continuing basis to ensure switching facilities have capacity within objective limits for subscriber demands. Prepares modifications on implementation schedules for acquisition and installation of switching equipment due to unforeseen increase or decrease of demands for services.
GOE: 05.01.03 STRENGTH: S GED: R6 M6 L6 SVP: 8 DLU: 77

003.131-010 SUPERVISOR, DRAFTING AND PRINTED CIRCUIT DESIGN (profess. & kin.)
Supervises and coordinates activities of workers engaged in drafting and designing layouts of printed circuit boards (PCBs) for use in manufacture of electronic equipment: Confers with PCB vendors to resolve problems encountered with board design. Reviews cost quotations for equipment and attends demonstrations to select equipment for purchase. Requisitions supplies, such as film positives. May design or change design of layout for PCBs [DRAFTER (profess. & kin.) Master Title]. Performs duties as described under SUPERVISOR (any industry) Master Title.
GOE: 05.03.02 STRENGTH: S GED: R4 M4 L4 SVP: 8 DLU: 86

003.151-010 SALES-ENGINEER, ELECTRICAL PRODUCTS (profess. & kin.)
Sells electrical products, power, and systems and provides technical services to clients, performing duties as described under SALES ENGINEER (profess. & kin.) Master Title.
GOE: 05.01.05 STRENGTH: L GED: R5 M5 L5 SVP: 8 DLU: 77

003.151-014 SALES-ENGINEER, ELECTRONICS PRODUCTS AND SYSTEMS (profess. & kin.)
Sells electronic products and systems and provides technical services to clients, performing duties as described under SALES ENGINEER (profess. & kin.) Master Title.
GOE: 05.01.05 STRENGTH: L GED: R5 M5 L5 SVP: 8 DLU: 77

003.161-010 ELECTRICAL TECHNICIAN (profess. & kin.) alternate titles: electrical-laboratory technician
Applies electrical theory and related knowledge to test and modify developmental or operational electrical machinery and electrical control equipment and circuitry in industrial or commercial plants and laboratories: Assembles and tests experimental motor-control devices, switch panels, transformers, generator windings, solenoids, and other electrical equipment and components according to engineering data and knowledge of electrical principles. Modifies electrical prototypes to correct functional deviations under direction of ELECTRICAL ENGINEER (profess. & kin.). Diagnoses cause of electrical or mechanical malfunction or failure of operational equipment and performs preventative and corrective maintenance. Develops wiring diagrams, layout drawings, and engineering specifications for system or equipment modifications or expansion, and directs personnel performing routine installation and maintenance duties. Plans, directs, and records periodic electrical testing, and recommends or initiates modification or replacement of equipment which fails to meet acceptable operating standards.
GOE: 05.01.01 STRENGTH: L GED: R4 M4 L4 SVP: 7 DLU: 77

003.161-014 ELECTRONICS TECHNICIAN (profess. & kin.)
Lays out, builds, tests, troubleshoots, repairs and modifies developmental and production electronic components, parts, equipment, and systems, such as computer equipment, missile control instrumentation, electron tubes, test equipment, and machine tool numerical controls, applying principles and theories of electronics, electrical circuitry, engineering mathematics, electronic and electrical testing, and physics: Discusses layout and assembly procedures and problems with ELECTRONICS ENGINEER (profess. & kin.) 003.061-030 and draws sketches to clarify design details and functional criteria of electronic units. Assembles experimental circuitry (breadboard) or complete prototype model according to engineering instructions, technical manuals, and knowledge of electronic systems and components. Recommends changes in circuitry or installation specifications to simplify assembly and maintenance. Sets up standard test

apparatus or devises test equipment and circuitry to conduct functional, operational, environmental, and life tests to evaluate performance and reliability of prototype or production model. Analyzes and interprets test data. Adjusts, calibrates, aligns, and modifies circuitry and components and records effects on unit performance. Writes technical reports and develops charts, graphs, and schematics to describe and illustrate system's operating characteristics, malfunctions, deviations from design specifications, and functional limitations for consideration by engineers in broader determinations affecting system design and laboratory procedures. May operate bench lathes, drills, or other machine tools to fabricate parts, such as coils, terminal boards, and chassis. May check functioning of newly installed equipment in aircraft, ships, and structures to evaluate system performance under actual operating conditions. May instruct and supervise other technical personnel. May be designated according to specialization in electronic applications as Computer-Laboratory Technician (profess. & kin.); Development-Instrumentation Technician (profess. & kin.); Electronic-Communications Technician (profess. & kin); Electronics Technician, Nuclear Reactor (profess. & kin.); Experimental Electronics Developer (aircraft mfg.); Systems-Testing-Laboratory Technician (profess. & kin.).
GOE: 05.01.01 STRENGTH: L GED: R5 M5 L4 SVP: 7 DLU: 88

003.161-018 TECHNICIAN, SEMICONDUCTOR DEVELOPMENT (profess. & kin.)

Tests developmental semiconductor devices or sample production units, and evaluates test equipment to develop data for engineering evaluation of new designs or special production yield study, applying knowledge of electronic theory and test equipment operating principles: Designs basic circuitry and prepares rough sketches for design documentation as directed by engineers, using drafting instruments and computer-assisted design/drafting equipment. Evaluates, calibrates, and tests new equipment circuits and fixtures, using testing equipment, such as oscilloscopes, logic and test probes, and calibrators. Builds and modifies electronic components, using handtools and power tools. Assists engineers in development of testing techniques and laboratory equipment. Assists with equipment maintenance. Liaises between test project sites to ensure orderly flow of information and materials. May supervise other technicians in unit.
GOE: 05.01.01 STRENGTH: L GED: R5 M5 L4 SVP: 8 DLU: 86

003.167-010 CABLE ENGINEER, OUTSIDE PLANT (tel. & tel.)

Plans, directs, and coordinates activities concerned with laying and repairing submarine telecommunication cables: Devises plans for laying cable lines, taking into consideration ocean currents and ocean depths. Determines where and how cables should be laid and decides such matters as where to place buoys, where to cut cable, what grapnel to use, what length of rope to use for a given depth, what type of cable to use, and what route to follow. Keeps charts and records to show depth and location of all cables laid. Analyzes test figures made when cable fault occurs to determine exact location of cable break. Oversees work of locating and repairing damaged cables.
GOE: 05.01.03 STRENGTH: L GED: R5 M5 L5 SVP: 8 DLU: 77

003.167-014 DISTRIBUTION-FIELD ENGINEER (utilities) alternate titles: line inspector

Plans and outlines changes in power distribution facilities to overcome unsatisfactory conditions, such as overloaded or underloaded circuits, and to provide for new or anticipated load increases: Reviews complaints and reports of load requirements for area under question to determine nature of adjustment to be made. Makes field surveys or studies maps showing relays, line intersections, overhead and underground connections, feeder lines, and other component elements of power system area under observation to ascertain where changes can be made. Makes calculations, following standardized procedures, to determine amount and type of replacing, switching, or other system revisions necessary to improve service. Recommends installation of additional facilities if changes within existing system cannot meet increased load. Makes notes and sketches of proposed changes and refers sketch to DRAFTER, CARTOGRAPHIC (profess. & kin.) for detailed work drawings. May investigate low voltage complaints by visiting area and determining if excessive load or power leakage causes defect.
GOE: 05.01.03 STRENGTH: L GED: R5 M5 L5 SVP: 8 DLU: 77

003.167-018 ELECTRICAL ENGINEER, POWER SYSTEM (utilities) alternate titles: power engineer

Designs power system facilities and equipment and coordinates construction, operation, and maintenance of electric power generating, receiving, and distribution stations, transmission lines, and distribution systems and equipment: Designs and plans layout of generating plants, transmission and distribution lines, and receiving and distribution stations. Directs preparation of, or prepares drawings and specific type of equipment and materials to be used, in construction and equipment installation. Estimates labor, material, construction, and equipment costs. Inspects completed installations for conformance with design and equipment specifications and safety standards. Observes operation of installation for conformance with operational standards. Coordinates operation and maintenance activities to ensure opitimum utilization of power system facilities and meet customer demands for electrical energy. May compile power rates and direct others in evaluating properties and developing utilities in new territories. May be designated according to type of engineering functions as Engineer, Design-And-Construction (utilities); Engineer, Operations-And-Maintenance (utilities).
GOE: 05.01.03 STRENGTH: L GED: R6 M6 L6 SVP: 8 DLU: 77

003.167-022 ELECTROLYSIS-AND-CORROSION-CONTROL ENGINEER (profess. & kin.) alternate titles: corrosion-control specialist; corrosion engineer; electrolysis engineer; electrolysis investigator

Investigates causes and devises means to combat or eliminate electrolysis of water, gas, and oil mains and pipelines resulting from stray electric currents flowing in earth: Determines existence and locates sources of stray electric currents creating electrolytic conditions, using voltmeters, ammeters, and other electrical testing apparatus. Recommends preventive and corrective measures for protection of pipe and underground structures, such as use of insulating and corrosion resisting materials. Confers with power company personnel and power consumers and suggests methods to eliminate sources of power leakage. Studies destructive properties of soil, corrosive actions, and other problems of deterioration, and suggests methods of preventing or mitigating trouble. Writes reports of studies and investigations conducted. May design and direct installation of cathodic protection stations to minimize and control electrolysis. May design and construct apparatus for use in testing materials or determining location of stray electric currents.
GOE: 05.01.03 STRENGTH: L GED: R5 M5 L5 SVP: 8 DLU: 77

003.167-026 ENGINEER OF SYSTEM DEVELOPMENT (utilities) alternate titles: development-and-planning engineer; planning engineer; system-planning engineer

Plans and coordinates activities to provide for orderly development and improve operating efficiency of electric power system: Coordinates scheduling, conducting, and analysis of special studies, such as commercial and residential developments in surrounding territory, population estimates, and advantages of and facilities for interconnections with other power systems. Coordinates collection and analysis of operational data, such as system-load demands and generating capacity. Evaluates analyses and recommends additional facilities to meet requirements of new, increased, or future loads, and to improve system.
GOE: 05.01.03 STRENGTH: S GED: R5 M5 L5 SVP: 8 DLU: 77

003.167-030 ENGINEER-IN-CHARGE, STUDIO OPERATIONS (radio-tv broad.) alternate titles: chief engineer; chief engineer, broadcasting operations; transmission engineer

Directs and coordinates radio or television station activities concerned with acquisition, installation, and maintenance, or with modification of studio broadcasting equipment: Evaluates studio needs for new broadcasting equipment to determine if acquisition would be justified considering such factors as cost, availability, and improvement gain in technical performance, and authorizes acquisition according to evaluation. Directs activities concerned with layout and design of electrical circuitry for acquired equipment to ensure conformance with codes and safety regulations. Establishes procedures for operation and maintenance of studio, remote control, and microwave transmission equipment. Inspects, and directs testing and maintenance of studio, remote, and airborne broadcasting equipment to ensure operational performance meets company standards and rules and regulations of Federal Communications Commission. Develops modification plans for existing broadcasting equipment to improve technical performance. Directs modification and testing of equipment to ensure operational performance meets specified standards. Prepares repair and maintenance schedules for studio, remote, and airborne broadcasting equipment to prevent interruption of broadcasts. Contacts telephone company personnel to ensure leased landlines or microwave facilities are operative and available for network broadcasting [COMMERCIAL ENGINEER (radio-tv broad.) 003.187-014]. Prepares annual budget for engineering department and controls expenditures within budget limitations. May direct and coordinate activities of transmitter personnel [ENGINEER-IN-CHARGE, TRANSMITTER (radio-tv broad.) 003.167-034]. May operate and maintain transmitter equipment to broadcast radio and television programs [TRANSMITTER OPERATOR (radio-tv broad.) 193.262-038]. May inspect and direct repair and maintenance of unmanned stations. Must hold First Class Radiotelephone License issued by FCC.
GOE: 05.01.03 STRENGTH: L GED: R5 M5 L5 SVP: 8 DLU: 89

003.167-034 ENGINEER-IN-CHARGE, TRANSMITTER (radio-tv broad.) alternate titles: director of engineering; engineer, chief; transmitter engineer

Directs and coordinates operation and maintenance activities of radio, television broadcasting, or satellite uplink transmitter station in accordance with rules and regulations of Federal Communications Commission: Establishes procedures and standards for operation and maintenance of transmitter equipment. Trains workers to interpret readings and indicator lights on control console and picture on video monitor, and to determine operating adjustments required to obtain uniform audio sound level and video picture of specified clarity and color. Tunes or directs worker to tune transmitter to ensure signal emissions and radiation do not infringe on frequencies or broadcast area of other stations, and to obtain optimum operational performance of transmitting equipment. Trains workers in diagnosing causes of transmitter malfunctions, using test equipment, and in repairing (or jury-rigging equipment (making temporary hookup) to return transmitter to operational status. Establishes procedures for testing of transmitter equipment, performance of preventative maintenance activities, and operation of equipment during test of Emergency Broadcast System. Develops, plans, and prepares schematic drawings designed to modify and improve existing transmitter equipment, and directs and coordinates equipment modification activities to prevent interruptions in transmitting operations. Prepares work schedules for TRANSMITTER OPERATORS (radio-tv broad.) 193.262-038.

May remove and repair, or assist workers to remove and repair equipment, using handtools, such as screwdrivers, wrenches, and pliers. Must hold first class radiotelephone license issued by Federal Communications Commission.
GOE: 05.01.03 STRENGTH: M GED: R5 M5 L5 SVP: 8 DLU: 89

003.167-038 INDUCTION-COORDINATION POWER ENGINEER (utilities)

Investigates and eliminates inductive interference by power transmission systems in telephones and radio receivers: Conducts technical investigations relating to inductive-coordination problems, including joint field investigations with engineers of communications and railroad companies. Checks proposed parallels between power and communications circuits and recommends installation of facilities to eliminate or reduce inductive interference. Consults with transmission and distribution line engineers on design of lines for prevention or reduction of radio interference. Conducts research in detection and elimination of the causes of radio noises in transmission systems. Assists municipalities on problems related to control equipment for alarm systems.
GOE: 05.01.03 STRENGTH: L GED: R5 M5 L5 SVP: 8 DLU: 77

003.167-042 OUTSIDE-PLANT ENGINEER (tel. & tel.)

Plans and prepares drawings for construction of new, and removal or rearrangement of existing, overhead or underground lines, cables, and conduits to obtain optimum and economical utilization of communications facilities: Analyzes traffic loads, available and existing lines, and estimates or forecasts of projected traffic to determine new construction or rearrangements and removals required. Selects routing of lines and equipment required for work projects. Prepares detailed construction and installation drawings, estimates equipment, labor, and material costs. Initiates work authorization request and submits request with substantiating drawings and documents to management for approval. Orders materials and equipment required and directs work activities to ensure conformance with engineering specifications and work authorization.
GOE: 05.01.03 STRENGTH: L GED: R5 M5 L5 SVP: 8 DLU: 77

003.167-046 POWER-DISTRIBUTION ENGINEER (utilities) alternate titles: electric-distribution engineer

Plans construction and coordinates operation of facilities for transmitting power from distribution points to consumers: Lays out substations and overhead and underground lines in urban and rural areas. Prepares specifications and estimates costs. Makes complex electrical computations to determine type and arrangement of circuits and size, type and number of pieces of equipment, such as transformers, circuit breakers, switches, and lightning arresters. Computes sag and stress for specifications on wire and cable. Plans layout of pole lines and underground cable and solves problems, such as determining height, location, spacing, guying, and insulating of poles. May be designated according to specialization as Overhead-Distribution Engineer (utilities); Rural-Service Engineer (utilities); Substation Engineer (utilities); Underground-Distribution Engineer (utilities).
GOE: 05.01.03 STRENGTH: S GED: R5 M5 L5 SVP: 8 DLU: 77

003.167-050 POWER-TRANSMISSION ENGINEER (utilities) alternate titles: electrical-transmission engineer; transmission-and-coordination engineer; transmission-line engineer

Lays out plans and estimates costs for constructing transmission lines (high-tension facilities for carrying power from source to distributing points): Visits proposed construction site and selects best and shortest route to avoid interference with telephone or other lines. Submits data on proposed route to right-of-way department for obtaining necessary easements. Arranges for aerial, topographical, and other surveys to be made to obtain pertinent data for planning lines. Devises steel and wood supporting structures for cables and draws sketch showing their location. Performs detailed engineering calculations to draw up construction specifications, such as cable sag, pole strength, and necessary grounding. Estimates labor, material, and construction costs, and draws up specifications for purchase of materials and equipment. Keeps informed on new developments in electric power transmission. Assists various departments of power company on problems involving transmission-line operation and maintenance. Inspects completed installation. Does not usually plan facilities for distributing power to consumers [POWER-DISTRIBUTION ENGINEER (utilities)].
GOE: 05.01.03 STRENGTH: L GED: R5 M5 L5 SVP: 8 DLU: 77

003.167-054 PROTECTION ENGINEER (utilities)

Plans layout and oversees maintenance of protection equipment of an electric power distribution system to minimize interruption to service and danger to lives and equipment from abnormalities, such as overload, no load, and short circuits: Studies drawings of power system and makes complex calculations to determine type, number, location, and correlation of protectors, such as relays, circuit breakers, fuses, and grounding devices. Plans adjustments and additions to protective system necessitated by increased demands in development of new residential areas and unusual requirements of heavy industry. Coordinates testing, repair, and installation of equipment. Studies new developments to determine suitability of their application to protection system. May program and direct computer analyses of system operating characteristics, such as power flow under normal and short-circuit conditions, system stability, and voltage and load limitations to obtain data used for such purposes as timing major system changes and additions, and analyzing interconnecting system problems. May be designated according to specialization as Grounding Engineer (utilities); Relay Engineer (utilities).

GOE: 05.01.03 STRENGTH: S GED: R5 M5 L5 SVP: 8 DLU: 77

003.167-058 SUPERVISOR, MICROWAVE (radio-tv broad.)

Plans relocation, installation, repair, and maintenance of microwave transmitters and receivers for cable-television broadcasting and gives technical advice and direction to laboratory and field staff regarding microwave transmission and reception: Plans installation or relocation of microwave transmitters and receivers for improved cable-television reception, new channels, or on-site live-broadcast transmission, using knowledge of microwave and electronic theory and electronic measuring and testing instruments. Directs laboratory and field supervisors and technicians in technical aspects of relocating, installing, repairing, and maintaining microwave transmitters and receivers. Monitors field and laboratory technicians to see that FCC regulations regarding microwave equipment are observed. Advises field and laboratory staff on technical problems of microwave equipment, commercial-FM radios used in company trucks, and portable radios used by field staff.
GOE: 05.01.03 STRENGTH: S GED: R5 M5 L5 SVP: 8 DLU: 77

003.167-066 TRANSMISSION-AND-PROTECTION ENGINEER (tel. & tel.) alternate titles: transmission engineer

Plans and lays out telephone transmitting facilities from engineering sketches: Advises and assists operation forces on application of transmission methods, devices, and standards affecting telephone equipment. Provides engineering services for protection of telephone service and facilities from noise, cross-talk, electrolysis, lightning, and other adverse electrical effects. Investigates causes of personal injury resulting from contact with high voltage communication equipment.
GOE: 05.01.03 STRENGTH: L GED: R5 M5 L5 SVP: 8 DLU: 77

003.167-070 ENGINEERING MANAGER, ELECTRONICS (profess. & kin.)

Directs and coordinates activities of engineering department to design, manufacture, and test electronic components, products, and systems: Directs department activities, through subordinates, to design new products, modify existing designs, improve production techniques, and develop test procedures. Analyzes technology trends, human resource needs, and market demand to plan projects. Confers with management, production, and marketing staff to determine engineering feasibility, cost effectiveness, and customer demand for new and existing products. Forecasts operating costs of department and directs preparation of budget requests. Directs personnel activities of department, such as recruitment, hiring, performance evaluations, and salary adjustments. May direct field testing of products and systems performed by field staff.
GOE: 05.01.08 STRENGTH: S GED: R6 M6 L5 SVP: 9 DLU: 88

003.187-010 CENTRAL-OFFICE EQUIPMENT ENGINEER (tel. & tel.)

Directs implementation of planning schedule for installation of central office toll or local switching facilities, or interoffice transmission facilities equipment, such as radio, TV, camera, and repeaters: Reviews planning schedule or equipment request and data on projected traffic to determine quantities of specific types of equipment required. Plans arrangement of equipment, prepares cost estimates for equipment and installation, and submits data to management for authorization approval. Prepares drawings and equipment specifications for installation. Monitors installation activities to solve any problems concerning arrangement or specifications. Assigns equipment and installation expenditures to specific program or project accounts. Closes out installation authorization when equipment has been tested and put in service.
GOE: 05.01.03 STRENGTH: S GED: R6 M6 L6 SVP: 8 DLU: 77

003.187-014 COMMERCIAL ENGINEER (radio-tv broad.) alternate titles: traffic engineer

Plans use of wire facilities connecting stations comprising a network to cover changing conditions and requirements: Evaluates technical capabilities of wire facilities, according to availability and range, to obtain most effective method of transmission. Reviews network program schedule to be linked to network stations, and projects use of wire facilities. Subdivides wire facilities linking network stations for simultaneous broadcasting of different programs to stations. Tests facilities prior to broadcast time to determine readiness of transmission line. May prepare engineering estimates of equipment installations or modification of existing equipment.
GOE: 05.01.03 STRENGTH: S GED: R5 M5 L5 SVP: 7 DLU: 77

003.187-018 CUSTOMER-EQUIPMENT ENGINEER (tel. & tel.) alternate titles: services engineer

Directs activities concerned with selection and installation of telephone facilities and special equipment on customer's premises to meet customer's communication requirements: Reviews sales order to ascertain extent of telephone facilities and equipment required. Inspects customer premises to ascertain space available for installation of equipment and to determine type and quantity of designated equipment that can be installed to provide specific communication facilities. Prepares floor plan of equipment arrangement for customer or architect approval. Prepares cost estimate for equipment and installation and submits data to management for authorization to proceed with job. Orders equipment, prepares installation specifications, and monitors progress of installation to ensure facilities are ready on specified date. Prepares all job-related paper work and closes out work authorization when equipment is in service.
GOE: 05.01.08 STRENGTH: L GED: R5 M5 L5 SVP: 8 DLU: 77

003.261-010 INSTRUMENTATION TECHNICIAN (profess. & kin.)

Devises, selects, sets up, and operates electronic instrumentation and related electromechanical or electrohydraulic apparatus used for operational and envi-

ronmental testing of mechanical, structural, or electrical equipment, and translates test data for engineering personnel to formulate engineering design and evaluation decisions: Selects, installs, calibrates, and checks sensing, telemetering, and recording instrumentation and circuitry, and develops specifications for nonstandard apparatus according to engineering data, characteristics of equipment under test, and capabilities of procurable test apparatus. Sketches and builds or modifies jigs, fixtures, and instruments and related apparatus, and verifies dimensional and functional acceptability of devices fabricated by craft or technical personnel. Performs preventive and corrective maintenance of test apparatus and peripheral equipment. Installs or directs technical personnel in installation of unit in test chamber or other test facility. Operates test apparatus during test cycle to produce, regulate, and record effects of actual or simulated conditions, such as vibration, stress, temperature, humidity, pressure, altitude, and acceleration. Analyzes and converts test data to usable form, using mathematical formulas, and prepares graphs and written reports to translate test results. May plan test program. May use computerized equipment and software to perform testing functions and produce graphs. May be designated according to equipment tested as Rocket-Control Technician (profess. & kin.); or according to nature of test as Environmental-Research Test Technician (profess. & kin.); Vibration Technician (profess. & kin.).
GOE: 05.01.01 STRENGTH: L GED: R5 M5 L4 SVP: 7 DLU: 90

003.261-014   CONTROLS DESIGNER (profess. & kin.) alternate titles: controls project engineer

Designs and drafts systems of electrical, hydraulic, and pneumatic controls for machines and equipment, such as arc welders, robots, conveyors, and *programmable controllers,* applying knowledge of electricity, electronics, hydraulics, and pneumatics: Discusses project with SUPERVISOR (any industry) Master Title and APPLICATIONS ENGINEER, MANUFACTURING (profess. & kin.) 007.061-038 to review functions of machines and equipment. Designs and drafts arrangement of linkage of conductors, relays, and other components of electrical, electronic, hydraulic, pneumatic, and lubrication devices, using drafting tools, and applying knowledge of electrical engineering and drafting [DRAFTER (profess. & kin.) Master Title]. Diagrams logic system for functions such as sequence and timing control. Designs and drafts diagrams of cable connection for robots, robot end-of-arm tool, *robot controller,* and other machines. Illustrates and describes installation and maintenance details, such as where bearings should be lubricated, types of lubrication, and which parts are lubricated automatically and manually. Confers with ASSEMBLER AND WIRER, INDUSTRIAL EQUIPMENT (elec. equip.; machinery mfg.) 826.361-010 to resolve problems regarding building of controls systems. Reviews schematics with customer's representatives to answer questions during installation of robot systems. Observes gauges during trial run of programmed machine and equipment operation to verify that electrical signals in system conform to specifications. May design controls for energy conversion or other industrial plant monitoring systems. May use computer and software programs to produce design drawings and be designated Controls Designer, Computer-Assisted (profess. & kin.).
GOE: 05.03.02 STRENGTH: S GED: R5 M4 L4 SVP: 8 DLU: 86

003.261-018   INTEGRATED CIRCUIT LAYOUT DESIGNER (profess. & kin.) alternate titles: mask designer

Designs layout for integrated circuits (IC), according to engineering specifications, using computer-assisted design (CAD) equipment and software, and utilizing knowledge of electronics, drafting, and IC design rules (standard IC manufacturing process requirements): Reviews and analyzes engineering design schematics and supporting documents, such as logic diagrams and design rules to plan layout of IC. Confers with engineering staff to resolve design details or problems. Enters engineering specifications into computer memory of CAD equipment and composes configurations on equipment display screen of IC logic elements (basic components of integrated circuit, such as resistors and transistors) for all IC layers, using keyboard, digitizing work aids (light pen or digitizing tablet), and engineering design schematics, and applying knowledge of design rules, programmed CAD functions, and electronics. Compares logic element configuration on equipment display screen with engineering schematics and redesigns or modifies logic elements, as needed, using digitizing work aids (light pen or digitizing tablet), keyboard, and programmed CAD functions. Lays out, redesigns, and modifies arrangement and interconnections of logic elements for each layer of integrated circuit, using digitizing work aids (light pen or digitizing tablet), keyboard and programmed CAD functions listed on display screen. Keys in specified commands, using CAD equipment keyboard, to test final IC layout for errors in design rules, using design rule software package. May generate copy of logic element design, using plotter to verify that logic element design copy meets design requirements and for use in laying out IC layer design for Very Large Scale (VLS) integrated circuits. May generate tape of final layout design for use in producing photo masks for each layer of IC, using CAD equipment. May program CAD equipment to change CAD functions listed on display screen, using keyboard. May be designated according to complexity of IC designed as IC Designer, Custom (profess. & kin.); IC Designer, Gate Arrays (profess. & kin.); IC Designer, Standard Cells (profess. & kin.).
GOE: 05.03.02 STRENGTH: S GED: R4 M4 L4 SVP: 8 DLU: 86

003.261-022   PRINTED CIRCUIT DESIGNER (profess. & kin.)

Designs and drafts layout for printed circuit boards (PCB's) according to engineering specifications, utilizing knowledge of electronics, drafting, and PCB design: Reviews and analyzes engineering design schematics and supporting documents to plan layout of PCB components and printed circuitry. Confers with engineering staff to resolve design details and problems. Drafts detailed drawings [DRAFTER (profess. & kin.) Master Title] and composes master layout of design components and circuitry. Examines and verifies master layout for electrical and mechanical accuracy. May verify accuracy of film reproductions of master layout. May prepare copies of drawings for use in PCB fabrication, using blueprint or diazo print machine. May generate computer tape for use in photo plotting design onto film, using digitizing equipment.
GOE: 05.03.02 STRENGTH: S GED: R4 M4 L4 SVP: 7 DLU: 88

003.281-010   DRAFTER, ELECTRICAL (profess. & kin.)

Drafts electrical equipment working drawings and wiring diagrams used by construction crews and repairers who erect, install, and repair electrical equipment and wiring in communications centers, power plants, industrial establishments, commercial or domestic buildings, or electrical distribution systems, performing duties as described under DRAFTER (profess. & kin.) Master Title. May use computer-assisted drafting (CAD) equipment and software and be designated Drafter (CAD), Electrical (profess. & kin.). May prepare detail cable layout and diagrams for cable installation and be designated Electric-Cable Diagrammer (elec. equip.).
GOE: 05.03.02 STRENGTH: S GED: R5 M5 L4 SVP: 7 DLU: 86

003.281-014   DRAFTER, ELECTRONIC (profess. & kin.) alternate titles: drafter, electromechanical

Drafts detailed drawings, such as wiring diagrams, layout drawings, mechanical detail drawings, and drawings of intermediate and final assemblies, used in manufacture, assembly, installation, and repair of electronic components, printed circuit boards, and equipment. Examines electronic schematics and supporting documents received from design engineering department to develop, compute, and verify specifications drafting data, such as configuration of parts, dimensions, and tolerances. Performs duties as described under DRAFTER (profess. & kin.) Master Title. May use computer-assisted drafting (CAD) equipment and software and be designated Drafter (CAD), Electronic (profess. & kin.).
GOE: 05.03.02 STRENGTH: S GED: R5 M5 L4 SVP: 7 DLU: 89

003.362-010   DESIGN TECHNICIAN, COMPUTER-AIDED (electron. comp.) alternate titles: digitizer

Operates computer-aided design (CAD) system and peripheral equipment to resize or modify integrated circuit designs (artwork) and to generate computer tape of artwork for use in producing mask plates used in manufacturing integrated circuits: Reviews work order and procedural manuals to determine critical dimensions of design. Calculates figures to convert design dimensions to resizing dimensions specified for subsequent production processes, using conversion chart and calculator. Locates file relating to specified design projection data base library and loads program into computer. Enters specified commands into computer, using keyboard, to retrieve design information from file and display design on CAD equipment display screen. Types commands on keyboard to enter resizing specifications into computer. Confers with engineering and design staff to determine design modifications and enters editing information into computer. Keys in specified information, using keyboard connected to on-line or off-line peripheral equipment (plotter), to produce graphic representation (hard copy) of design for review and approval by engineering and design staff. Enters specified information into computer, using keyboard, to generate computer tape of approved design.
GOE: 05.03.02 STRENGTH: L GED: R3 M3 L3 SVP: 5 DLU: 86

005   CIVIL ENGINEERING OCCUPATIONS

This group includes occupations concerned with the planning, design, and construction of structures and facilities, such as buildings, bridges, roads, harbors, airfields, dams, tunnels, and water supply and sewage systems. Also included are occupations concerned with the engineering aspects of environmental health systems and urban planning or renewal. Frequently requires a knowledge of industrial trends, population growth, zoning laws, and state and local building codes and ordinances. Accessory techniques needed are those used in agricultural, ceramic, chemical, electrical, geological, mechanical, metallurgical, and mining engineering. Typical specializations are structures, hydraulics, transportation systems, sanitation, water utility systems, airports, city planning, environmental protection, construction, engineering mechanics, irrigation and drainage, power, soil mechanics and foundations, pipeline engineering, and waterways and harbors.

005.061-010   AIRPORT ENGINEER (profess. & kin.)

Plans and lays out airports and landing fields and directs construction work involved in leveling fields, laying out and surfacing runways, and providing drainage: Designs runways based on weight and size of aircraft and prepares material and construction specifications. Directs or participates in surveying to lay out installations and establish reference points, grades, and elevations to guide construction. Estimates costs to provide basis for payments to contractor. Observes progress of construction to ensure workmanship is in conformity with specifications and advises SUPERINTENDENT, CONSTRUCTION (construction) regarding necessary corrections. May serve as agent or employee of contractor and study plans and specifications to recommend special equipment or procedures to reduce time and cost of construction. May schedule delivery of

materials, analyze costs, and provide technical advice in solution of construction problems.
GOE: 05.01.07 STRENGTH: L GED: R5 M5 L5 SVP: 8 DLU: 77

005.061-014 CIVIL ENGINEER (profess. & kin.)

Plans, designs, and directs civil engineering projects, such as roads, railroads, airports, bridges, harbors, channels, dams, irrigation systems, pipelines, and powerplants: Analyzes reports, maps, drawings, blueprints, tests, and aerial photographs on soil composition, terrain, hydrological characteristics, and other topographical and geologic data to plan and design project. Calculates cost and determines feasibility of project based on analysis of collected data, applying knowledge and techniques of engineering, and advanced mathematics. Prepares or directs preparation and modification of reports, specifications, plans, construction schedules, environmental impact studies, and designs for project. Inspects construction site to monitor progress and ensure conformance to engineering plans, specifications, and construction and safety standards. May direct construction and maintenance activities at project site. May use computer-assisted engineering and design software and equipment to prepare engineering and design documents. May be designated according to specialty or product.
GOE: 05.01.07 STRENGTH: L GED: R5 M5 L5 SVP: 8 DLU: 81

005.061-018 HYDRAULIC ENGINEER (profess. & kin.) alternate titles: hydrologic engineer

Designs and directs construction of power and other hydraulic engineering projects for control and use of water: Computes and estimates rates of waterflow. Specifies type and size of equipment, such as conduits, pumps, turbines, pressure valves, and surge tanks, used in transporting water and converting water power into electricity. Directs, through subordinate supervisors, activities of workers engaged in dredging, digging cutoffs, placing jetties, and constructing levees to stabilize streams or open water ways. Designs and coordinates construction of artificial canals, conduits, and mains to transport and distribute water; and plans reservoirs, pressure valves, and booster stations to obtain proper water pressure at all levels. Frequently builds laboratory models to study construction and flow problems.
GOE: 05.01.03 STRENGTH: L GED: R5 M5 L5 SVP: 7 DLU: 77

005.061-022 IRRIGATION ENGINEER (profess. & kin.)

Plans, designs, and oversees construction of irrigation projects for transporting and distributing water to agricultural lands: Plans and designs irrigation fixtures and installation of fixtures to requirements and specifications. Directs, through subordinate supervisors, construction of such irrigation systems as dams, canals, and ditches, according to type of soil, climatic characteristics, water supply, return flow, and other factors affecting irrigation requirements. Conducts research on problems of soil drainage and conservation, applying knowledge of civil engineering [RESEARCH ENGINEER (profess. & kin.)].
GOE: 05.01.03 STRENGTH: L GED: R5 M5 L4 SVP: 8 DLU: 77

005.061-026 RAILROAD ENGINEER (profess. & kin.)

Designs railroad and street railway tracks, terminals, yards, and other facilities and directs and coordinates construction and relocation of facilities: Plans roadbed, rail size, and curves to meet train speed and load requirements. Directs, through subordinate supervisors, construction of bridges, culverts, buildings, and other structures. Directs track and roadway maintenance. Surveys traffic problems related to street railway system and recommends grade revisions, additional trackage, use of heavier power, and other changes to relieve congestion and reduce hazards.
GOE: 05.01.07 STRENGTH: L GED: R5 M5 L5 SVP: 8 DLU: 77

005.061-030 SANITARY ENGINEER (profess. & kin.) alternate titles: public-health engineer

Designs and directs construction and operation of hygienic projects such as waterworks, sewage, garbage and trash disposal plants, drainage systems, and insect and rodent control projects: Plans development of watersheds and directs building of aqueducts, filtration plants, and storage and distribution systems for water supply. Directs swamp drainage, insect spraying, and design of insect-proof buildings. Plans and directs workers in building and operation of sewage-disposal plants. Designs and controls operation of incinerators, sanitary fills, and garbage-reduction plants to dispose of garbage and other refuse. Advises industrial plants in disposal of obnoxious gases, oils, greases, and other chemicals. Inspects and regulates sanitary condition of public places, such as markets, parks, and camps. May plan and direct operation of water treatment plant to soften and purify water for human consumption or industrial use and be known as Water-Treatment-Plant Engineer (profess. & kin.).
GOE: 05.01.03 STRENGTH: L GED: R5 M5 L5 SVP: 8 DLU: 77

005.061-034 STRUCTURAL ENGINEER (construction)

Directs or participates in planning, designing, or reviewing plans for erection of structures requiring stress analysis: Designs structure to meet estimated load requirements, computing size, shape, strength, and type of structural members, or performs structural analysis of plans and structures prepared by private engineers. May inspect existing projects and recommend repair and replacement of defective members or rebuilding of entire structure.
GOE: 05.01.08 STRENGTH: L GED: R5 M5 L5 SVP: 8 DLU: 77

005.061-038 TRANSPORTATION ENGINEER (profess. & kin.)

Develops plans for surface transportation projects according to established engineering standards and state or federal construction policy: Prepares plans, estimates, and specifications to design transportation facilities. Plans alterations

and modifications of existing streets, highways, and freeways to improve traffic flow. Prepares deeds, property descriptions, and right-of-way maps. Performs field engineering calculations to compensate for change orders and contract estimates. May prepare and present public reports of environmental analysis statements and other transportation information. May specialize in particular phase of work, such as making surveys, improving signs or lighting, preparing plans, or directing and coordinating construction or maintenance activities. May be designated Highway Engineer (government ser.). May specialize in studying vehicular and pedestrian traffic conditions and be designated Traffic Engineer (government ser.). May plan, organize, and direct work in transportation studies to plan surface systems and be designated Transportation Planning Engineer (government ser.).
GOE: 05.01.08 STRENGTH: L GED: R5 M5 L5 SVP: 8 DLU: 77

005.061-042 WASTE-MANAGEMENT ENGINEER, RADIOACTIVE MATERIALS (profess. & kin.)

Designs, implements, and tests systems and procedures to reduce volume and dispose of nuclear waste materials and contaminated objects: Identifies objects contaminated by exposure to radiation, such as trash, workers' clothing, and discarded tools and equipment. Analyzes samples of sludge and liquid effluents resulting from operation of nuclear reactors to determine level of radioactivity in substances and potential for retention of radioactivity, using radioactivity counters and chemical and electronic analyzers. Refers to state and federal regulations and technical manuals to determine disposal method recommended for prevention of leakage or absorption of radioactive waste. Compares costs of transporting waste to designated nuclear waste disposal sites and reducing volume and storing waste on plant site. Confers with equipment manufacturers' representatives and plant technical and management personnel to discuss alternatives and to choose most suitable plan on basis of safety, efficiency, and cost-effectiveness. Designs and draws plans for systems to reduce volume of waste by solidification, compaction, or incineration. Oversees construction, testing, and implementation of waste disposal systems, and resolves operational problems. Develops plans for modification of operating procedures to reduce volume and radioactive level of effluents, and writes manuals to instruct workers in changes in work procedures. Advises management on selection of lands suitable for use as nuclear waste disposal sites and on establishment of effective safety, operating, and closure procedures.
GOE: 05.01.03 STRENGTH: L GED: R5 M5 L5 SVP: 8 DLU: 86

005.167-010 CHIEF ENGINEER, WATERWORKS (waterworks)

Plans and directs activities concerned with water utility systems installation, operation, maintenance, and service: Directs activities of engineers engaged in preparing designs and plans to construct, enlarge, and modify such facilities as water treatment plants, watersheds, and dams, hydroelectric stations, pumping stations, and to install water mains, and other appurtenances. Provides engineering and technical direction for planning and design of water utility projects. Reviews plans and specifications prior to instituting project to determine whether they meet organizational requirements. Analyzes and compiles data received from engineers to prepare budget estimates. Directs and coordinates engineers in conducting studies, such as economics of systems operation, water distribution, and water treatment plants or relative equipment performance to determine most feasible approach to meeting organizational and technical problems. Confers with municipal authorities concerning budget requirements, changes in organizational policy, regulation of water rates, and plumbing requirements, or other problems affecting community.
GOE: 05.01.03 STRENGTH: L GED: R5 M5 L5 SVP: 9 DLU: 77

005.167-014 DRAINAGE-DESIGN COORDINATOR (waterworks)

Plans, designs, and coordinates construction of drainage systems in irrigation district, based on knowledge of soils, slope of land, and availability and economic use of existing drainage canals: Requests engineering surveys and soil tests to determine surface profile, types of soil, and characteristics such as salinity, water table, and areas of subnormal crop growth. Studies data and sketches scale drawing of tile and open ditch drains for area, using triangles, scales, dividers, and other drawing instruments. Indicates depth, spacing, and size of tiling for crop area leading to district drainage canals. Considers drainage cost to improve fertility, at least cost to farmer and district. Recommends deepening of drainage canals when field elevation prevents gravity flow, or provides for installation of sumps and electric pumps to drain low areas. Arranges for sale to farmers of district approved drainage materials, such as concrete wells and pipes. Determines need for securing easements and right-of-way deeds for district drainage structures. Inspects completed systems to determine that installation conforms to plan.
GOE: 05.01.03 STRENGTH: S GED: R5 M5 L4 SVP: 8 DLU: 77

005.167-018 FOREST ENGINEER (forestry; logging)

Lays out and directs construction, installation, and use of structures, equipment, and road or rail systems, and performs other engineering duties concerned with removal of logs from timber area: Surveys timber land and draws maps to show topographical features of area. Determines locations of loading points and storage areas and selects methods and equipment for handling logs. Lays out and directs construction of roads or rail network used to transport logs from cutting areas to loading sites and storage areas. Plans and directs construction of campsites, loading docks, bridges and culverts, equipment shelters, and water and sewage systems to maintain efficient and safe removal of logs from constantly shifting cutting areas.
GOE: 05.01.06 STRENGTH: L GED: R5 M5 L5 SVP: 7 DLU: 77

005.167-022 HIGHWAY-ADMINISTRATIVE ENGINEER (government ser.) alternate titles: director, traffic and planning

Administers statewide highway planning, design, construction, and maintenance programs: Coordinates activities of state highway engineering agencies. Reviews highway and bridge plans, location, contracts, and cost estimates for technical and legal accuracy, and approves acceptable proposals or makes corrective recommendations. Directs workers in research activities related to highway planning and engineering, and formulates highway engineering policies and procedures. Directs preparation of state agency budgets. Directs workers in preparation of reports to state and federal government officials and represents state highway commissioner at hearings with public officials, contractors, and engineering personnel. Speaks before civic groups and public gatherings to disseminate highway planning information and to solicit public support.
GOE: 11.05.03 STRENGTH: S GED: R6 M5 L6 SVP: 9 DLU: 77

005.167-026 PRODUCTION ENGINEER, TRACK (r.r. trans.)

Plans, directs, and coordinates, through supervisory personnel, activities of track maintenance crews of railway system: Analyzes engineering data and inspects repair site to determine priority of proposed track repair and maintenance projects. Coordinates scheduling of track maintenance and activities within designated region. Determines frequency of track use and project costs, utilizing computerized data and knowledge of railroad operations and maintenance expense to formulate recommendations for revising established project priorities. Reviews production reports and confers with engineering personnel to identify causes of low productivity of repair crews. Visits work sites to observe work crews and to inspect repairs. Directs engineering supervisors to correct substandard repairs.
GOE: 05.01.06 STRENGTH: L GED: R5 M3 L4 SVP: 9 DLU: 86

005.261-014 CIVIL ENGINEERING TECHNICIAN (profess. & kin.)

Assists CIVIL ENGINEER (profess. & kin.) 005.061-014 in application of principles, methods, and techniques of civil engineering technology: Reviews project specifications and confers with CIVIL ENGINEER (profess. & kin.) concerning assistance required, such as plan preparation, acceptance testing, evaluation of field conditions, design changes, and reports. Conducts materials testing and analysis, using tools and equipment and applying engineering knowledge necessary to conduct tests. Prepares reports detailing tests conducted and results. Surveys project sites to obtain and analyze topographical details of sites, using maps and surveying equipment. Drafts detailed dimensional drawings, such as those needed for highway plans, structural steel fabrication, and water control projects, performing duties as described under DRAFTER (profess. & kin.) Master Title. Calculates dimensions, profile specifications, and quantities of materials such as steel, concrete, and asphalt, using calculator. Inspects construction site to determine conformance of site to design specifications. May assist engineers to ensure that construction and repair of water and wastewater treatment systems meet pollution control requirements.
GOE: 05.03.02 STRENGTH: L GED: R4 M4 L4 SVP: 7 DLU: 86

005.281-010 DRAFTER, CIVIL (profess. & kin.) alternate titles: drafter, civil engineering; drafter, construction; drafter, engineering

Drafts detailed construction drawings, topographical profiles, and related maps and specifications used in planning and construction of civil engineering projects, such as highways, river and harbor improvements, flood control, and drainage: Reviews rough sketches, drawings, specifications, and other engineering data received from CIVIL ENGINEER (profess. & kin.) 005.061-014. Plots maps and charts showing profiles and cross-sections, indicating relation of topographical contours and elevations to buildings, retaining walls, tunnels, overhead power lines, and other structures. Drafts detailed drawings of structures and installations, such as roads, culverts, fresh water supply, sewage disposal systems, dikes, wharfs, and breakwaters. Computes volume of tonnage of excavations and fills and prepares graphs and hauling diagrams used in earthmoving operations. Performs other duties as described under DRAFTER (profess. & kin.) Master Title. May accompany survey crew in field to locate grading markers or to collect data required for revision of construction drawings. May specialize in drafting and modifying topographical maps from surveying notes and aerial photographs and be designated Drafter, Topographical (profess. & kin.). May use computer-assisted drafting (CAD) equipment and software and be designated Drafter, Civil (CAD) (profess. & kin.).
GOE: 05.03.02 STRENGTH: S GED: R4 M4 L4 SVP: 7 DLU: 81

005.281-014 DRAFTER, STRUCTURAL (profess. & kin.)

Performs duties of DRAFTER (profess. & kin.) Master Title by drawing plans and details for structures employing structural reinforcing steel, concrete, masonry, wood, and other structural materials. Produces plans and details of foundations, building frame, floor and roof framing, and other structural elements.
GOE: 05.03.02 STRENGTH: S GED: R5 M5 L4 SVP: 7 DLU: 77

006   CERAMIC ENGINEERING OCCUPATIONS

This group includes occupations concerned with the design, manufacture, and application of products made from nonmetallic minerals and rocks; and the design, construction, and control of necessary equipment and tools for the manufacture of such products. Accessory techniques include those used in chemical, mechanical, and electrical engineering, and physics and mineralogy. Typical specializations are structural materials, abrasives, cements, glass, whiteware,

and refractories. Occupations which are involved in only one phase of engineering, such as research, design, testing, sales, or project control, are found in Group 019.

006.061-010 CERAMIC DESIGN ENGINEER (profess. & kin.)

Designs ceramics manufacturing equipment and products, performing duties as described under DESIGN ENGINEER, FACILITIES (profess. & kin.) Master Title; DESIGN ENGINEER, PRODUCTS (profess. & kin.) Master Title.
GOE: 05.01.07 STRENGTH: L GED: R5 M5 L5 SVP: 8 DLU: 77

006.061-014 CERAMIC ENGINEER (profess. & kin.)

Conducts research, designs machinery, develops processing techniques, and directs technical work concerned with manufacture of ceramic products: Directs testing of physical, chemical, and heat-resisting properties of materials, such as clays and silicas. Analyzes results of test to determine combinations of materials which will improve quality of products. Conducts research into methods of processing, forming, and firing of clays to develop new ceramic products, such as ceramic machine tools, refractories for space vehicles, and for use in glass and steel furnaces. Designs equipment and apparatus for forming, firing, and handling products. Coordinates testing activities of finished products for characteristics, such as texture, color, durability, glazing, and refractory properties. May specialize in one branch of ceramic production, such as brick, glass, crockery, tile, pipe, or refractories. May specialize in developing heat-resistant and corrosion-resistant materials for use in aerospace, electronics, and nuclear energy fields. nuclear energy field.
GOE: 05.01.07 STRENGTH: L GED: R6 M6 L6 SVP: 8 DLU: 77

006.061-018 CERAMIC RESEARCH ENGINEER (profess. & kin.)

Conducts research to develop new ceramic products performing duties as described under RESEARCH ENGINEER (profess. & kin.) Master Title.
GOE: 05.01.01 STRENGTH: L GED: R5 M5 L5 SVP: 8 DLU: 77

006.061-022 CERAMICS TEST ENGINEER (profess. & kin.)

Conducts tests on ceramic products performing duties as described under TEST ENGINEER (profess. & kin.) Master Title.
GOE: 05.01.04 STRENGTH: L GED: R5 M5 L5 SVP: 8 DLU: 77

006.151-010 SALES ENGINEER, CERAMIC PRODUCTS (profess. & kin.)

Sells ceramic products and provides technical services for client performing duties as described under SALES ENGINEER (profess. & kin.) Master Title.
GOE: 05.01.05 STRENGTH: L GED: R5 M5 L5 SVP: 8 DLU: 77

006.261-010 SCIENTIFIC GLASS BLOWER (glass products) alternate titles: glass technician; glass technologist

Fabricates, modifies, and repairs experimental and laboratory glass products, using variety of machines and tools, and provides technical advice to scientific and engineering staff on function, properties, and proposed design of products, applying knowledge of glass technology: Confers with scientific or engineering personnel to exchange information and suggest design modifications regarding proposed glass apparatus, such as distillation and high-vacuum systems. Cuts glass tubing of specified type, using cutting tools, such as glass saw and hot-wire cutter. Heats glass tubing until pliable, using gas torch, and blows, bends, and shapes tubing to specified form, using blowhose, handtools, and manual pressure. Performs finishing operations to fabricate glass product or section, using machines and equipment, such as *lapping* and polishing wheels, spot-welding and sandblasting machines, internal-plating equipment, and drill press. Measures products to verify dimensions, using *optical scanner*, micrometers, and calipers, and examines glass coloration for degree of internal stress, using polariscope, to determine annealing requirements. Anneals products, using annealing oven. Joins and seals subassemblies to assemble finished product, using gas torch, handtools, and vacuum pump. May operate special equipment, such as radio-frequency-fusing machine, to bond glass to metal, quartz, and ceramic materials. May identify glass of unknown composition by heating with gas torch and evaluating curvature, bondability, and color characteristics. May direct and train GLASS BLOWERS, LABORATORY APPARATUS (glass products; inst. & app.). May design fixtures for use in production of prototype glass products and prepare sketches for machine-shop personnel. May prepare cost estimates for prototype glass products. May requisition or recommend purchase of materials, tools, and equipment. May specialize in specific types of glass scientific apparatus and have knowledge of effects of special environments on glass, such as radioactivity, vacuums, gases, chemicals, and electricity.
GOE: 05.05.11 STRENGTH: L GED: R4 M4 L4 SVP: 8 DLU: 77

007   MECHANICAL ENGINEERING OCCUPATIONS

This group includes occupations concerned with application of principles of physics and engineering for the generation, transmission, and utilization of heat and mechanical power; and the design, production, installation, and maintenance of fabricated products, tools, machines, machinery, and associated or auxiliary systems. Accessory techniques needed may be those used in electrical, metallurgical, nuclear, and civil engineering. Typical specializations are steam and mechanical power generation, transmission, and utilization; hydraulics; instrumentation; controls; automotive engineering; tooling; heating and ventilating; air-conditioning and refrigeration; bioengineering; pollution control; systems engineering; research; design; testing; sales; and project control.

007.061-010 AUTOMOTIVE ENGINEER (auto. mfg.)

Develops improved or new designs for automotive structural members, engines, transmissions, and associated automotive equipment or modifies existing

equipment on production vehicles, and directs building, modification, and testing of vehicle, using computerized work aids: Conducts experiments and tests on existing designs and equipment to obtain data on function of and performance of equipment. Analyzes data to develop new designs for motors, chassis, and other related mechanical, hydraulic, and electromechanical components and systems in automotive equipment. Designs components and systems to provide maximum customer value and vehicle function, including improved economy and safety of operation, control of emissions, and operational performance, at optimum costs. Directs and coordinates building, or modification of, automotive equipment or vehicle to ensure conformance with engineering design. Directs testing activities on components and equipment under designated conditions to ensure operational performance meets design specifications. Alters or modifies design to obtain specified functional and operational performance. May assist DRAFTER, AUTOMOTIVE DESIGN (auto. mfg.) 017.261-042 in developing structural design for auto body. May conduct research studies to develop new concepts in automotive engineering field.
GOE: 05.01.08 STRENGTH: L GED: R5 M5 L5 SVP: 8 DLU: 90

007.061-014 MECHANICAL ENGINEER (profess. & kin.)
Researches, plans, and designs mechanical and electromechanical products and systems, and directs and coordinates activities involved in fabrication, operation, application, installation, and repair of mechanical or electromechanical products and systems: Researches and analyzes data, such as customer design proposal, specifications, and manuals to determine feasibility of design or application. Designs products or systems, such as instruments, controls, robots, engines, machines, and mechanical, thermal, hydraulic, or heat transfer systems, applying knowledge of engineering principles [DESIGN ENGINEER, PRODUCTS (profess. & kin.) Master Title]. Plans and directs engineering personnel in fabrication of test control apparatus and equipment, and development of methods and procedures for testing products or systems [TEST ENGINEER (profess. & kin.) Master Title]. Directs and coordinates fabrication and installation activities to ensure products and systems conform to engineering design and customer specifications. Coordinates operation, maintenance, and repair activities to obtain optimum utilization of machines and equipment. May design products and systems to interface machines, hardware, and software. May evaluate field installations and recommend design modifications to eliminate machine or system malfunctions. May specialize in specific field of mechanical engineering, such as heat transfer, hydraulics, electromechanics, controls and instrumentation, robotics, nuclear systems, tooling, air-conditioning and refrigeration; or in type of product, such as propulsion systems or machinery and mechanical equipment; or in type of work, such as steam or gas generation and distribution, steam plant engineering, or system planning.
GOE: 05.01.08 STRENGTH: L GED: R5 M5 L5 SVP: 8 DLU: 88

007.061-018 MECHANICAL-DESIGN ENGINEER, FACILITIES (profess. & kin.)
Designs and directs installation of plant systems or product lines performing duties as described under DESIGN ENGINEER, FACILITIES (profess. & kin.) Master Title.
GOE: 05.01.07 STRENGTH: S GED: R5 M5 L5 SVP: 8 DLU: 77

007.061-022 MECHANICAL-DESIGN ENGINEER, PRODUCTS (profess. & kin.)
Designs mechanical or electromechanical products or systems performing duties as described under DESIGN ENGINEER, PRODUCTS (profess. & kin.) Master Title.
GOE: 05.01.07 STRENGTH: S GED: R5 M5 L5 SVP: 8 DLU: 77

007.061-026 TOOL DESIGNER (profess. & kin.)
Designs single- or multiple-edged machine cutting tools, such as broaches, milling-machine cutters, and drills, and related jigs, dies, and fixtures: Studies specifications, engineering blueprints, tool orders, and shop data and confers with engineering and shop personnel to resolve design problems related to material characteristics, dimensional tolerances, service requirements, manufacturing procedures, and cost. Applies algebraic and geometric formulas and standard tool engineering data to develop tool configuration. Selects standard items, such as bushings and tool bits, to incorporate into tool design. Draws preliminary sketches and prepares layout and detail drawings, using standard drafting tools and equipment or computer-assisted design/drafting equipment and software. Modifies tool designs according to trial or production service data to improve tool life or performance.
GOE: 05.01.07 STRENGTH: L GED: R5 M5 L5 SVP: 8 DLU: 88

007.061-030 TOOL-DESIGNER APPRENTICE (profess. & kin.)
Performs duties as described under APPRENTICE (any industry) Master Title.
GOE: 05.01.07 STRENGTH: L GED: R5 M5 L5 SVP: 8 DLU: 77

007.061-034 UTILIZATION ENGINEER (utilities)
Solves engineering problems concerned with industrial utilization of gas as source of power: Studies industrial processes to determine where and how application of gas fuel-consuming equipment can be made. Designs equipment to meet process requirements. Examines gas-powered equipment after installation to ensure proper functioning. Investigates equipment failures and difficulties and diagnoses faulty operation. Corrects or makes recommendations to maintenance crew to correct faults. Conducts safety, breakdown, and other engineering tests on gas fuel-consuming equipment to ascertain efficiency and safety of design and construction. May solve problems concerned with other gas-consuming equipment, such as air-conditioning and heating.

GOE: 05.01.06 STRENGTH: S GED: R5 M5 L5 SVP: 8 DLU: 77

007.061-038 APPLICATIONS ENGINEER, MANUFACTURING (profess. & kin.)
Plans, designs, and coordinates integration of machinery and equipment into manufacturing process of industrial establishment, applying knowledge of engineering and programming, and using computer, precision-measuring instruments, and drafting tools: Develops and writes equipment specifications, performance requirements, cost analysis, and proposal for integrating machinery and equipment, such as robots, *robot controllers,* and *programmable controllers* into manufacturing process, applying knowledge of mechanics, hydraulics, pneumatics, electrical wiring, electronics, programming, and manufacturing requirements, and using computer and calculator. Selects or designs robot end-of-arm tools to meet specifications, using robot manuals and either drafting tools or computer and software programs. Writes operating programs, using existing computer program, or writes own computer programs, applying knowledge of programming language and computer. Oversees installation to ensure machines and equipment are installed and functioning according to specifications. Tests ability of machines, such as robot, to perform tasks, using *teach pendant* and precision measuring instruments and following specifications. Confers with establishment personnel to implement operating procedures and resolve system malfunctions. Determines parts supply, maintenance tasks, safety procedures, and service schedule required to maintain machines and equipment in prescribed condition. Develops models of alternate processing methods to test feasibility of new applications of system components, and recommends implementation of improved procedures. Participates in meetings, seminars, and training sessions to stay apprised of new developments in field. Confers with workers in other departments, such as marketing, legal, and engineering, to provide technical information. May develop and conduct robot and related equipment training programs and demonstrate skills to trainees, using teach pendant, handtools, precision-measuring instruments, and following schematics, plant drawings, and manufacturer's specifications.
GOE: 05.01.08 STRENGTH: L GED: R5 M5 L5 SVP: 8 DLU: 86

007.061-042 STRESS ANALYST (profess. & kin.)
Conducts stress analyses on engineering designs for electronic components, systems, and products, using mathematical formulas and computer-aided engineering (CAE) systems: Analyzes engineering designs, schematics, and customer specifications to determine stress requirements on product. Formulates *mathematical model* or three-dimensional computer graphic model of product, using calculator or CAE system. Analyzes ability of product to withstand stress imposed by conditions such as temperature, loads, motion, and vibration, using mathematical formulas and computer simulation. Builds product model of wood or other material, performs physical stress tests on model, and evaluates test results. Consults with ELECTRONICS-DESIGN ENGINEER (profess. & kin.) 003.061-034 to recommend design modifications of product based on results of stress analysis. Prepares stress analysis reports.
GOE: 05.01.04 STRENGTH: S GED: R6 M6 L5 SVP: 8 DLU: 86

007.151-010 SALES ENGINEER, MECHANICAL EQUIPMENT (utilities)
Sells mechanical equipment and provides technical-services to clients as described under SALES ENGINEER (profess. & kin.) Master Title.
GOE: 05.01.05 STRENGTH: L GED: R5 M5 L5 SVP: 8 DLU: 77

007.161-010 DIE DESIGNER (machine shop) alternate titles: design leader; die design drafter; die developer
Develops plans for single stage or progressive stage dies for stamping, forming, forging, or extrusion presses, according to blueprints of product and knowledge of press characteristics and process limitations: Drafts drawings of dies necessary to form complete forging, stamping, or other part. Determines sequence and number of die stages in which single or progressive cutting, punching, and forming will be accomplished, and type of die sets required to produce complete part, based on knowledge of dies, forming processes, and machines. Drafts scale drawings of each die set, delineating contours and dimensions for manufacture of die. Compares part drawings with wood patterns of cast dies to determine correctness of pattern dimensions and form. May observe setup and tryout of newly developed die set in production machine to determine need for redesign or readiness for production use.
GOE: 05.03.02 STRENGTH: S GED: R4 M4 L4 SVP: 7 DLU: 77

007.161-014 DIE-DESIGNER APPRENTICE (machine shop)
Performs duties as described under APPRENTICE (any industry) Master Title.
GOE: 05.03.02 STRENGTH: S GED: R4 M4 L4 SVP: 7 DLU: 77

007.161-018 ENGINEERING ASSISTANT, MECHANICAL EQUIPMENT (profess. & kin.) alternate titles: mechanical design technician
Develops detailed design drawings and related specifications of mechanical equipment, according to engineering sketches and design proposal specifications: Analyzes engineering sketches, specifications, and related data and drawings to determine design factors, such as size, shape, and arrangement of parts. Sketches rough layout of machine and computes angles, weights, surface areas, dimensions, radii, clearances, tolerances, leverages, and location of holes. Computes magnitude, direction, and point of application of tension, compression, and bending forces, and develops geometric shape of machine parts to accommodate operating loads. Drafts detailed multiview drawings of machine and

21

subassemblies, including specifications for gear ratios, bearing loads, and direction of moving parts, using engineering data and standard references. Compiles and analyzes test data to determine effect of machine design on various factors, such as temperature, pressures, speed, horsepower, and fuel consumption. Modifies machine design to correct operating deficiencies or to reduce production problems. May measure machine and parts during production to ensure compliance with design specifications, using precision measuring instruments. May specialize in specific type of machine, such as air-cooled internal combustion engines, diesel engines, or machine tools. May use computer-assisted design/drafting equipment and software to develop designs.
GOE: 05.03.02 STRENGTH: S GED: R5 M5 L5 SVP: 7 DLU: 88

007.161-022 MECHANICAL RESEARCH ENGINEER (profess. & kin.)
Conducts research to develop mechanical equipment and machinery, performing duties as described under RESEARCH ENGINEER (profess. & kin.) Master Title.
GOE: 05.01.01 STRENGTH: L GED: R5 M5 L5 SVP: 8 DLU: 77

007.161-026 MECHANICAL-ENGINEERING TECHNICIAN (profess. & kin.) alternate titles: engineering technician; experimental technician; laboratory-development technician; mechanical technician
Develops and tests machinery and equipment, applying knowledge of mechanical engineering technology, under direction of engineering and scientific staff: Reviews project instructions and blueprints to ascertain test specifications, procedures, objectives, test equipment, nature of technical problem, and possible solutions, such as part redesign, substitution of material or parts, or rearrangement of parts or subassemblies. Drafts detail drawing or sketch for drafting room completion or to request parts fabrication by machine, sheet metal or wood shops. Devises, fabricates, and assembles new or modified mechanical components or assemblies for products, such as industrial equipment and machinery, power equipment, servosystems, machine tools, and measuring instruments. Sets up and conducts tests of complete units and components under operational conditions to investigate design proposals for improving equipment performance or other factors, or to obtain data for development, standardization, and quality control. Analyzes indicated and calculated test results in relation to design or rated specifications and test objectives, and modifies or adjusts equipment to meet specifications. Records test procedures and results, numercial and graphical data, and recommendations for changes in product or test method.
GOE: 05.01.01 STRENGTH: L GED: R5 M4 L4 SVP: 7 DLU: 77

007.161-030 OPTOMECHANICAL TECHNICIAN (optical goods; photo. appar.)
Applies engineering theory and practical knowledge, under direction of engineering staff, to build and test prototype optomechanical devices to be used in such equipment as aerial cameras, gun sights, and telescopes: Reviews project instructions, and preliminary specifications to identify and plan requirements for parts fabrication, purchase, assembly, and test. Prepares sketches and writes work orders and purchase requests for items to be furnished by others, and follows up delivery. Designs, builds, or modifies fixtures used to assemble parts. Lays out cutting lines for machining, using drafting tools. Assembles and adjusts parts and related electrical units of prototype to prepare for test. Sets up prototype and test apparatus, such as control console, collimator, recording equipment, and cables in accordance with specifications. Operates controls of test apparatus and prototype to observe and record test results. Computes test data on laboratory forms for engineers. Confers in technical meetings, recommending design and material changes to reduce cost and lead time. May be assigned as group leader to coordinate work of technicians, model makers, and others assigned to assist.
GOE: 05.01.01 STRENGTH: L GED: R5 M4 L4 SVP: 8 DLU: 77

007.161-034 TEST ENGINEER, MECHANICAL EQUIPMENT (profess. & kin.)
Conducts tests on mechanical equipment performing duties as described under TEST ENGINEER (profess. & kin.) Master Title.
GOE: 05.01.04 STRENGTH: S GED: R5 M5 L5 SVP: 8 DLU: 77

007.161-038 SOLAR-ENERGY-SYSTEMS DESIGNER (profess. & kin.)
Designs solar domestic hot water and space heating systems for new and existing structures, applying knowledge of energy requirements of structure, local climatological conditions, solar technology, and thermodynamics: Estimates energy requirements of new or existing structures, based on analysis of utility bills of structure, calculations of thermal efficiency of structure, and prevailing climatological conditions. Determines type of solar system, such as water, glycol, or silicone, which functions most efficiently under prevailing climatological conditions. Calculates on-site heat generating capacity of different solar panels to determine optimum size and type of panels which meet structure's energy requirements. Arranges location of solar system components, such as panel, pumps, and storage tanks, to minimize length and number of direction changes in pipes and reconstruction of existing structures. Studies engineering tables to determine size of pipes and pumps required to maintain specified flow rate through solar panels. Specifies types of electrical controls, such as differential thermostat, temperature sensors, and solenoid valves, compatible with other system components, using knowledge of control systems. Completes parts list, specifying components of system. Draws wiring, piping, and other diagrams, using drafting tools. May inspect structures to compile data used in solar system design, such as structure's angle of alignment with sun and temperature

of incoming cold water. May inspect construction of system to ensure adherence to design specifications.
GOE: 05.03.07 STRENGTH: L GED: R5 M4 L4 SVP: 5 DLU: 86

007.167-010 DIE-DRAWING CHECKER (profess. & kin.)
Examines die design drawings prepared by DIE DESIGNER (machine shop) for accuracy of design detail and to assure production feasibility of die sets: Computes dimensions of drawings to check accuracy of figures and proper placement of layout. Ascertains that production parts can be fabricated with dies as designed by applying thorough knowledge of machine capacities. Returns erroneous drawings to original designer for correction, indicating orally, or in writing, changes to be made.
GOE: 05.03.02 STRENGTH: S GED: R5 M5 L4 SVP: 7 DLU: 77

007.167-014 PLANT ENGINEER (profess. & kin.) alternate titles: factory engineer; superintendent, mechanical
Plans, directs, and coordinates activities concerned with design, construction, modification, and maintenance of equipment and machinery in industrial plant: Establishes standards and policies for pollution control, installation, modification, quality control, testing, operating procedure, inspection, and maintenance of equipment, according to engineering principles and safety regulations. Directs maintenance of plant buildings and coordinates requirements for new designs, surveys, and maintenance schedules for equipment and machinery. Prepares bid sheets and contracts for construction and facilities acquisition. Tests newly installed machines and equipment to ensure fulfillment of contract specifications.
GOE: 05.01.08 STRENGTH: L GED: R5 M5 L5 SVP: 8 DLU: 87

007.167-018 TOOL PROGRAMMER, NUMERICAL CONTROL (any industry) alternate titles: computer-programmer, numerical control; programmer, numerical control; tool programmer
Plans numerical control program to control contour-path machining of metal parts on automatic machine tools: Analyzes drawings, sketches, and design data of part to determine dimension and configuration of cuts, selection of cutting tools, and machine speeds and feed rates, according to knowledge of machine shop processes, part specifications, and machine capabilities. Determines reference points and direction of machine cutting paths. Computes angular and linear dimensions, radii, and curvatures, and outlines sequence of operations required to machine part. Prepares geometric layout on graph paper or using computer-assisted drafting software to show location of reference points and direction of cutting paths, using drafting instruments or computer. Writes instruction sheets and cutter lists to guide setup and operation of machine. Writes program of machine instructions in symbolic language to encode numerical control tape or direct numerical control data base to regulate movement of machine along cutting path. Compares encoded tape or computer printout with original program sheet to assure accuracy of machine instructions. Revises program to eliminate instruction errors or omissions. Observes operation of machine on trial run to prove taped or programmed instructions.
GOE: 05.01.06 STRENGTH: S GED: R5 M4 L4 SVP: 7 DLU: 87

007.181-010 HEAT-TRANSFER TECHNICIAN (profess. & kin.)
Plans requirements for fabricating, installing, testing, and servicing climate control and heat transfer assemblies and systems to assist engineering personnel, utilizing knowledge of heat transfer technology and engineering methods: Calculates required capacities for equipment units of proposed system to obtain specified performance and submits data to engineering personnel for approval. Studies supplier catalogs and technical data to recommend equipment unit selections for system. Prepares unit design layouts and detail drawings for fabricating parts and assembling system. Estimates cost factors, such as labor and material for purchased and fabricated parts, and costs for assembling, testing and installing in customer's premises. Fabricates nonstandard parts for system, using metalworking machinery and assembles system, using handtools and power tools. Installs test fixtures, apparatus, and controls and conducts operational tests under specified conditions. Analyzes test data and prepares report for evaluation by engineering personnel. Installs system in customer premises and tests operational performance for compliance with contract specifications and applicable codes. Diagnoses special service problems of systems under service contract and writes instructions for service or repair personnel. May be designated according to specialty as Air-Conditioning Technician (profess. & kin.); Heating Technician (profess. & kin.); Refrigerating Technician (profess. & kin.).
GOE: 05.03.07 STRENGTH: L GED: R5 M5 L5 SVP: 7 DLU: 77

007.261-010 CHIEF DRAFTER (profess. & kin.) alternate titles: layer-out drafter
Draws rough layout and sketches, and assigns work to and directs subordinate drafting workers: Sketches layout according to design proposal and standard specifications and practices. Assigns drafting of detail drawings to subordinate personnel and verifies accuracy and completeness of finished drawings. May perform duties described under DRAFTER (profess. & kin.) Master Title.
GOE: 05.03.02 STRENGTH: S GED: R5 M5 L5 SVP: 7 DLU: 77

007.261-014 DRAFTER, CASTINGS (profess. & kin.)
Drafts detailed drawings for castings which require special knowledge and attention to shrinkage allowances and such factors as minimum radii of fillets and rounds. Performs other duties as described under DRAFTER (profess. & kin.) Master Title.
GOE: 05.03.02 STRENGTH: S GED: R4 M4 L4 SVP: 7 DLU: 77

007.261-018 DRAFTER, PATENT (profess. & kin.)
Drafts clear and accurate drawings of varied sorts of mechanical devices for use of LAWYER, PATENT (profess. & kin.) in obtaining patent rights. Performs other duties as described under DRAFTER (profess. & kin.) Master Title.
GOE: 05.03.02 STRENGTH: S GED: R5 M5 L5 SVP: 7 DLU: 77

007.261-022 DRAFTER, TOOL DESIGN (profess. & kin.)
Drafts detailed drawing plans for manufacture of tools, usually following designs and specifications indicated by TOOL DESIGNER (profess. & kin.). Performs other duties as described under DRAFTER (profess. & kin.) Master Title.
GOE: 05.03.02 STRENGTH: S GED: R5 M5 L5 SVP: 7 DLU: 77

007.267-010 DRAWINGS CHECKER, ENGINEERING (profess. & kin.) alternate titles: standards analyst
Examines engineering drawings of military and commercial parts, assemblies, and installations to detect errors in design documents: Compares figures and lines on production drawing or diagram with production layout, examining angles, dimensions, bend allowances, and tolerances for accuracy. Determines practicality of design, material selection, available tooling, and fabrication process, applying knowledge of drafting and manufacturing methods. Confers with design personnel to resolve drawing and design discrepancies. May specialize in checking specific types of designs, such as mechanical assemblies, microelectronic circuitry, or fluid-flow systems. May operate copier equipment to make duplicates of designs.
GOE: 05.03.02 STRENGTH: S GED: R4 M4 L4 SVP: 6 DLU: 88

007.267-014 TOOL DESIGN CHECKER (aircraft mfg.) alternate titles: tool drawing checker
Examines tool drawings prepared by TOOL DESIGNER (profess. & kin.) 007.061-026 for inaccuracies of detail and evaluates overall tool design for fit, form, and function, utilizing knowledge of engineering principles, tool design methods, and manufacturing processes: Measures drawing dimensions, and compares figures with dimensions on original layout, specifications, or sample part to verify measurements conform to scale. Marks verified or out-of-scale dimensions on drawings. Inspects lines and figures on drawings for clarity. Evaluates overall tool design for functionality, conformance to drawing standards and design specifications, and manufacturing feasibility. Reviews material requirements for standardization and conformance to industry specification manuals. Discusses design, manufacturing, and related issues with engineering, production, or other personnel. Approves or rejects design. May operate computer to examine and evaluate computer-generated tool designs.
GOE: 05.01.07 STRENGTH: S GED: R5 M5 L5 SVP: 8 DLU: 88

007.281-010 DRAFTER, MECHANICAL (profess. & kin.) alternate titles: drafter, engineering
Drafts detailed drawings of machinery and mechanical devices, indicating dimensions and tolerances, fasteners and joining requirements, and other engineering data: Reviews rough sketches and engineering specifications received from engineer or architect. Drafts multiple-view assembly, subassembly, and layout drawings as required for manufacture and repair of machines and equipment. Performs other duties as described under DRAFTER (profess. & kin.) Master Title.
GOE: 05.03.02 STRENGTH: S GED: R5 M5 L5 SVP: 7 DLU: 87

007.362-010 NESTING OPERATOR, NUMERICAL CONTROL (aircraft mfg.) alternate titles: computer-numerical-control nesting operator; pattern data operator
Operates computer to lay out graphic display of parts to be machined in optimum arrangement (nest) and generate control media for numerical-control drilling, routing, and cutting machines: Reviews shop orders to determine job specifications and nesting requirements. Sorts shop orders into groups according to compatibility factors, such as quantity and shape of parts, and type, size, alloy, and gauge of material to be machined to produce nest that maximizes material utilization and minimizes machine setup and operation. Enters computer commands to retrieve stored parts data and graphic displays, such as simulated patterns or templates, and displays and manipulates part images on computer screen into optimum arrangement. Calculates and codes machine controlling criteria, such as table movement, type and size of cutting and drilling tools, spindle location, and machining start point, feed rate, and speed, utilizing knowledge of numerical-control machine operation. Enters commands to title and store nest layouts in computer memory and to build and maintain source files. Keys in commands to transfer nest data, listings, or layouts to other media, such as hardcopy, tape, or floppy disk, or to route nest data by direct link to direct-numerical-control machines. Loads and unloads disk packs, tapes, or floppy disks. May operate digitizing equipment to produce patterns. May discuss nesting or machining problems with machine operators or other personnel.
GOE: 05.03.02 STRENGTH: L GED: R4 M3 L3 SVP: 6 DLU: 89

008 CHEMICAL ENGINEERING OCCUPATIONS

This group includes occupations concerned with the application of chemistry and other sciences, such as physics and mathematics, and of engineering principles to manufacturing operations which involve chemical processes. Also includes the design, construction, and operation of industrial plants carrying out chemical processes. Typical specializations are heat transfer and energy conversion, food and pharmaceutical products, forest products, petrochemicals and fuels, and materials handling.

008.061-010 ABSORPTION-AND-ADSORPTION ENGINEER (profess. & kin.) alternate titles: adsorption-and-absorption engineer
Designs equipment and devises chemical processes to remove and separate components of gas mixture or liquid solutions by absorption and adsorption, using knowledge of chemistry and engineering: Devises processes and directs workers, using equipment, such as crushers, grinders, kilns, screens, pumps, compressors, pipelines, valves, tanks, and separators. Directs workers controlling flow of liquid or gas through an adsorbent, such as fuller's earth, clays, carbons, charcoal, and bone char in granular form (percolation method); or mixing adsorbent with liquid or gas and removing adsorbent by filtration, settling, or combination of both (contact filtration method). Directs workers, using absorption method to remove soluble constituent of gas or vapor by dissolving it in a liquid, using packed columns or towers into which liquid is sprayed.
GOE: 05.01.08 STRENGTH: S GED: R6 M6 L6 SVP: 8 DLU: 77

008.061-014 CHEMICAL DESIGN ENGINEER, PROCESSES (profess. & kin.)
Designs equipment and processes to produce chemical changes in elements and compounds, performing duties as described under DESIGN ENGINEER, FACILITIES (profess. & kin.) Master Title.
GOE: 05.01.07 STRENGTH: S GED: R5 M5 L5 SVP: 8 DLU: 77

008.061-018 CHEMICAL ENGINEER (profess. & kin.)
Designs equipment and develops processes for manufacturing chemicals and related products utilizing principles and technology of chemistry, physics, mathematics, engineering and related physical and natural sciences: Conducts research to develop new and improved chemical manufacturing processes. Designs, plans layout, and oversees workers engaged in constructing, controlling, and improving equipment to carry out chemical processes on commercial scale. Analyzes operating procedures and equipment and machinery functions to reduce processing time and cost. Designs equipment to control movement, storage, and packaging of solids, liquids, and gases. Designs and plans measurement and control systems for chemical plants based on data collected in laboratory experiments and pilot plant operations. Determines most effective arrangement of unit operations such as mixing, grinding, crushing, heat transfer, size reduction, hydrogenation, distillation, purification, oxidation, polymerization, evaporation, and fermentation, exercising judgement to compromise between process requirements, economic evaluation, operator effectiveness, and physical and health hazards. Directs activities of workers who operate and control such equipment as condensers, absorption and evaporation towers, kilns, pumps, stills, valves, tanks, boilers, compressors, grinders, pipelines, electromagnets, and centrifuges to effect required chemical or physical change. Performs tests and takes measurements throughout stages of production to determine degree of control over variables such as temperature, density, specific gravity, and pressure. May apply principles of chemical engineering to solve environmental problems. May apply principles of chemical engineering to solve bio-medical problems. May develop electro-chemical processes to generate electric currents, using controlled chemical reactions or to produce chemical changes, using electric currents. May specialize in heat transfer and energy conversion, petrochemicals and fuels, materials handling, pharmaceuticals, foods, forest products, or products such as plastics, detergents, rubber, or synthetic textiles. May be designated according to area of specialization.
GOE: 05.01.07 STRENGTH: L GED: R6 M6 L6 SVP: 8 DLU: 77

008.061-022 CHEMICAL RESEARCH ENGINEER (profess. & kin.)
Conducts research on chemical processes and equipment, performing duties as described under RESEARCH ENGINEER (profess. & kin.) Master Title.
GOE: 05.01.01 STRENGTH: L GED: R5 M5 L5 SVP: 8 DLU: 77

008.061-026 CHEMICAL-TEST ENGINEER (profess. & kin.)
Conducts tests on chemicals, fuels, and processes performing, duties as described under TEST ENGINEER (profess. & kin.) Master Title.
GOE: 05.01.04 STRENGTH: L GED: R5 M5 L5 SVP: 8 DLU: 77

008.151-010 CHEMICAL-EQUIPMENT SALES ENGINEER (profess. & kin.)
Sells chemical processing equipment and provides technical services to clients, performing duties as described under SALES ENGINEER (profess. & kin.) Master Title.
GOE: 05.01.05 STRENGTH: L GED: R5 M5 L5 SVP: 8 DLU: 77

008.167-010 TECHNICAL DIRECTOR, CHEMICAL PLANT (profess. & kin.) alternate titles: technical manager, chemical plant
Plans and coordinates technical activities in chemical plant, pilot-plant, or chemical-engineering department: Directs activities of engineering personnel engaged in preparing plans, designs, cost estimates, and specifications for experimental, maintenance, or modernization programs to determine most feasible approach to technical problems. Directs activities of engineers and technicians setting up prototype units designed to perform experimental operations. Coordinates activities of workers engaged in testing and metering unit operations, and collecting and interpreting processing records. Evaluates performance records of chemical processes and physical operations and submits report of findings to management. May prepare reports on cost of plant operation.
GOE: 05.01.08 STRENGTH: L GED: R6 M6 L5 SVP: 8 DLU: 77

008.261-010 CHEMICAL-ENGINEERING TECHNICIAN (profess. & kin.)
Applies chemical engineering principles and technical skills to assist CHEMICAL ENGINEER (profess. & kin.) in developing, improving, and testing

chemical-plant processes, products, and equipment: Prepares charts, sketches, diagrams, flow charts, and compiles and records engineering data to clarify design details or functional criteria of chemical processing and physical operation units. Participates in fabricating, installing, and modifying equipment to ensure that critical standards are met. Tests developmental equipment and formulates standard operating procedures. Tests processing equipment and instruments to observe and record operating characteristics and performance of specified design or process. Observes chemical or physical operation processes and recommends modification or change. Observes and confers with equipment operators to ensure specified techniques are used. Writes technical reports and submits finding to CHEMICAL ENGINEER (profess. & kin.). Performs preventive and corrective maintenance of chemical processing equipment. May prepare chemical solutions for use in processing materials, such as synthetic textiles, detergents, and fertilizers following formula. May set up test apparatus. May instruct or direct activities of technical personnel. May assist in developing and testing prototype processing systems and be designated Chemical-Engineering Technician, Prototype-Development (profess. & kin.). May assist in development of pilot-plant units and be designated Pilot-Plant Research-Technician (petrol. refin.).
GOE: 05.01.08 STRENGTH: L GED: R5 M5 L5 SVP: 8 DLU: 77

010   MINING AND PETROLEUM ENGINEERING OCCUPATIONS

This group includes occupations concerned with the extraction of minerals from the earth, including planning the development of the mine. Accessory techniques include those used in geology and in civil, mechanical, electrical, metallurgical, and chemical engineering. Typical specializations are according to activities involved, such as exploration, extraction, mine layout, oil well development, safety, research, and supervision and management; or according to type of substance involved, such as metals, nonmetallic minerals, coal, or petroleum and natural gas.

010.061-010 DESIGN ENGINEER, MINING-AND-OIL-FIELD EQUIPMENT (profess. & kin.)
Designs mining and oil field machinery, performing duties as described under DESIGN ENGINEER, PRODUCTS (profess. & kin.) Master Title.
GOE: 05.01.07 STRENGTH: L GED: R5 M5 L5 SVP: 8 DLU: 77

010.061-014 MINING ENGINEER (mine & quarry)
Conducts research to determine location and methods of extracting minerals, such as metallic ores and nonmetallic substances, such as coal, stone, and gravel: Conducts or collaborates in geological exploration, and reviews maps and drilling logs to determine location, size, accessibility, and estimated value of mineral deposit. Determines methods to extract minerals, considering factors such as safety, operational costs, deposit characteristics, overburden depth, and surrounding strata. Plans, recommends, and coordinates mining process, type and capacity of haulage equipment, such as power shovels and trucks, and labor utilization. Lays out and directs mine construction operations, such as location and development of shafts, tunnels, chambers, position of excavation benches (levels), and access roads. Designs, implements, and monitors facility projects, such as water and power supply, ventilation system, rock-dust and radon gas control, drainage, rail and conveyor systems, and material cleaning, grading, and reduction systems. May devise methods and locations to store and replace excavated soil to reclaim mine sites. May analyze labor requirements, equipment needs, and operational costs to compute and prepare annual budget reports. May apply knowledge of mining engineering to solve problems concerned with environment.
GOE: 05.01.06 STRENGTH: L GED: R5 M5 L5 SVP: 7 DLU: 80

010.061-018 PETROLEUM ENGINEER (petrol. & gas)
Analyzes technical and cost factors to plan methods to recover maximum oil and gas in oil-field operations, utilizing knowledge of petroleum engineering and related technologies: Examines map of subsurface oil and gas reservoir locations to recommend placement of wells to maximize economical production from reservoir. Evaluates probable well production rate during natural or stimulated-flow production phases. Recommends supplementary processes to enhance recovery involving stimulation of flow by use of processes, such as pressurizing or heating in subsurface regions. Analyzes recommendations of reservoir engineering specialist for placement of well in oil field. Develops well drilling plan for management approval, specifying factors including drilling time, number of special operations, such as directional drilling, and testing, and material requirements and costs including well casing and drilling muds. Provides technical consultation during drilling operations to resolve problems such as bore directional change, unsatisfactory drilling rate or invasion of subsurface water in well bore. Advises substitution of drilling mud compounds or tool bits to improve drilling conditions. Inspects well to determine that final casing and tubing installations are completed. Plans oil and gas field recovery containers, piping, and treatment vessels to receive, remove contaminants, and separate oil and gas products flowing from well. Monitors production rate of gas or oil from established wells and plans rework process to correct well production, such as repacking of well bore and additional perforation of subsurface sands adjacent to well bottom. May apply knowledge of petroleum engineering to solve problems concerned with environment [ENVIRONMENTAL ENGINEER (profess. & kin.)]. May be designated according to specialty as Development Engineer, Geothermal Operations (profess. & kin.); Drilling Engineer (petrol. & gas); Production Engineer (petrol. & gas); Reservoir Engineer (petrol. & gas).

GOE: 05.01.08 STRENGTH: L GED: R5 M5 L5 SVP: 8 DLU: 77

010.061-022 RESEARCH ENGINEER, MINING-AND-OIL-WELL EQUIPMENT (mine & quarry; petrol. & gas)
Conducts research to develop improved mining and oil well equipment, performing duties as described under RESEARCH ENGINEER (profess. & kin.) Master Title.
GOE: 05.01.01 STRENGTH: L GED: R5 M5 L5 SVP: 8 DLU: 77

010.061-026 SAFETY ENGINEER, MINES (mine & quarry) alternate titles: director, safety
Inspects underground or open-pit mining areas and trains mine personnel to ensure compliance with state and federal laws and accepted mining practices designed to prevent mine accidents: Inspects mine workings to detect unsafe timbers, cribbing, roof bolts, electric wiring, elevators, explosives storage, equipment, and working conditions. Examines walls and roof surfaces for evidence of strata faults indicating cave-in or rock slide hazards. Tests air to detect concentrations of toxic gases and explosive dusts, using safety lamp, methane detector, carbon monoxide register, and anemometer. Recommends alteration or installation of ventilation shafts, partitions, or equipment to remedy inadequate air circulation of air-conditioning. Applies principles of mining engineering and human engineering to design protective equipment and safety devices for mine machinery. Gives instructions to mine personnel in safe working practices and first aid, and strives to promote and maintain safety-mindedness of workers. Investigates explosions, fires, and accidents and reports causes and recommendations for remedial action to insurance companies, mine management, and state authorities. May lead rescue activities during emergencies and maintain mine rescue equipment.
GOE: 05.01.02 STRENGTH: L GED: R5 M5 L5 SVP: 8 DLU: 80

010.061-030 TEST ENGINEER, MINING-AND-OIL-FIELD EQUIPMENT (mine & quarry; petrol. & gas)
Conducts tests on mining and oil field machinery and equipment, performing duties as described under TEST ENGINEER (profess. & kin.) Master Title.
GOE: 05.01.04 STRENGTH: L GED: R5 M5 L5 SVP: 8 DLU: 77

010.131-010 WELL-LOGGING CAPTAIN, MUD ANALYSIS (petrol. & gas) alternate titles: mud-analysis-well-logging captain
Supervises and coordinates activities of workers engaged in analysis of oil well drilling mud and well cuttings during drilling operations to detect presence of oil or gas and identify productive strata: Coordinates work of WELL-LOGGING OPERATORS, MUD ANALYSIS (petrol. & gas) engaged in continuous sampling and analysis of mud circulating through wells being drilled and preparation of mud analysis logs. Reviews analysis made by workers of cores cut from wells to determine nature of earth formations penetrated. Summarizes log data and core analysis records for engineering personnel. Initiates or recommends personnel actions, such as pay increase, transfer or discipline.
GOE: 02.04.01 STRENGTH: L GED: R5 M5 L4 SVP: 7 DLU: 77

010.151-010 SALES ENGINEER, MINING-AND-OIL-WELL EQUIPMENT AND SERVICES (mine & quarry; petrol. & gas)
Sells mining and oilwell equipment and provides technical services to clients, performing duties as described under SALES ENGINEER (profess. & kin.) Master Title.
GOE: 05.01.05 STRENGTH: L GED: R5 M5 L5 SVP: 8 DLU: 77

010.161-010 CHIEF ENGINEER, RESEARCH (petrol. & gas)
Coordinates research activities to develop new and improved methods of drilling wells and producing oil or gas: Directs, through subordinate engineering personnel, planning and progress of experimental projects in drilling and production operations, such as projects investigating composition of drilling mud, recovery of natural gasoline from crude oil and gas solutions, or dehydration of crude petroleum. Assists CHIEF PETROLEUM ENGINEER (petrol. & gas) in solution of technical operating problems. May direct research activities in geochemical or other petroleum prospecting methods.
GOE: 05.01.01 STRENGTH: S GED: R6 M6 L6 SVP: 8 DLU: 77

010.161-014 CHIEF PETROLEUM ENGINEER (petrol. & gas)
Plans and directs engineering activities of a petroleum company to develop oil fields and produce oil and gas: Formulates programs for developing oil fields, planning schedules for drilling wells and for constructing pumping units, crude-oil treating units, and other production facilities. Coordinates projected activities with civil, electrical, and other engineering departments. Directs, through subordinate workers, selection, installation, use, and repair of oil field equipment. Directs PETROLEUM ENGINEERS (petrol. & gas) in engineering work concerned with drilling new wells and producing flow of oil or gas from wells, in maintaining well logs, and in other engineering activities. Directs laboratory and field research to develop new or to improve old methods and equipment for recovery of oil and gas. Keeps abreast of new developments in petroleum engineering. Selects, trains, and promotes engineering personnel. May direct mechanical, civil, electrical, and other engineering activities. May direct engineering and drilling activities in developing geothermal field and be designated Director, Geothermal Operations (petrol. & gas).
GOE: 05.01.08 STRENGTH: S GED: R6 M6 L6 SVP: 9 DLU: 77

010.161-018 OBSERVER, SEISMIC PROSPECTING (petrol. & gas) alternate titles: field seismologist; geophysical operator; section-plotter operator
Plans and directs activities of field party engaged in collecting seismic data used in prospecting for oil or gas: Designates location of shot holes and place-

ment of seismometers and connecting cables over blast area according to plot drawn by SURVEYOR, GEOPHYSICAL PROSPECTING (petrol. & gas). Plans and directs activities of workers engaged in laying out seismographic measuring apparatus over test area. Surveys area to verify that equipment is in position specified and tests electrical circuits for continuity. Directs SHOOTER, SEISMOGRAPH (petrol. & gas) to detonate charges placed in shot holes, using short wave radio. Observes reaction of recording instruments to detect irregularity. Develops picture of seismic wave pattern in photographic developing solution. Examines wave pattern on subterranean strata for evidence of distortion caused by electronic crossfeed, short circuit, or loose connection. Orders redrilling of shot holes and equipment layout to repeat shot. Directs repair or repairs instruments or equipment, using manufacturers' manuals and handtools.
GOE: 05.03.04 STRENGTH: L GED: R4 M4 L4 SVP: 7 DLU: 77

010.167-010 CHIEF ENGINEER (petrol. & gas; pipe lines)
Directs activities of workers in engineering department of petroleum production or pipeline company and advises management on engineering problems: Apportions work among engineering staff according to specialized training. Reviews engineering designs for neatness and accuracy. Directs engineering personnel in formulating plans, designs, cost estimates, and specifications for oil field or pipeline construction, maintenance, and modernization programs. Supervises engineering office workers computing operating budgets, compiling reports, and conducting special investigations and studies to evaluate efficiency of engineering programs. May apply knowledge of petroleum engineering to coordinate work of engineers engaged in solving problems concerned with environment [ENVIRONMENTAL ENGINEER (profess. & kin.)]. May be designated according to engineering department supervised as Chief Engineer, Drilling And Recovery (petrol. & gas); Chief Engineer, Pipeline (petrol. & gas); Chief Engineer, Production (petrol. & gas); Chief, Reservoir Engineering (petrol. & gas).
GOE: 05.01.08 STRENGTH: S GED: R6 M6 L6 SVP: 9 DLU: 77

010.167-014 DISTRICT SUPERVISOR, MUD-ANALYSIS WELL LOG-GING (petrol. & gas) alternate titles: mud-analysis-well-logging supervisor, district; mud engineer; mud-logging superintendent
Plans and directs mud-sample testing operations: Consults with SUPERINTENDENT, OIL-FIELD DRILLING (petrol. & gas) and interprets drilling logs to determine status of wells being drilled. Plans and coordinates itinerary for WELL-LOGGING CAPTAIN, MUD ANALYSIS (petrol. & gas); WELL-LOGGING OPERATOR, MUD ANALYSIS (petrol. & gas) and other members of mobile field-laboratory crews to obtain maximum utilization of personnel with minimum disruption of drilling operations. Interprets mud analysis logs obtained by crews, for PETROLEUM ENGINEER (petrol. & gas).
GOE: 05.02.03 STRENGTH: S GED: R5 M5 L5 SVP: 8 DLU: 77

010.167-018 SUPERINTENDENT, OIL-WELL SERVICES (petrol. & gas) alternate titles: manager, oil-well services
Directs activities concerned with providing technical services, such as electrical well logging, gun perforating, directional or caliper surveying, and cementing, acidizing, and formation fracturing, to assist in solving special oil well drilling and production problems: Advises SUPERINTENDENT, DRILLING AND PRODUCTION (petrol. & gas) on specific servicing problems and recommends use of specialized tools, techniques, and services. Directs organization and training of personnel, and directly or through subordinate personnel supervises servicing operations. Supervises repair and maintenance of equipment. Keeps records of operations and prepares reports.
GOE: 05.02.01 STRENGTH: S GED: R5 M5 L5 SVP: 8 DLU: 77

010.261-010 FIELD ENGINEER, SPECIALIST (petrol. & gas)
Collects fluid samples from oil-or gas-bearing formations and analyzes sample to determine potential productivity of formation: Moves controls on panel to fire charge into formation and to operate hydraulic mechanism which thrusts and seals probe into perforation. Analyzes fluid in sample to determine potential productivity of formation.
GOE: 05.03.04 STRENGTH: L GED: R4 M4 L4 SVP: 7 DLU: 77

010.261-014 OBSERVER, ELECTRICAL PROSPECTING (petrol. & gas) alternate titles: electrical-logging engineer; electrical-prospecting operator
Measures resistance of earth formations to electrical charges, using electrical apparatus to obtain data for locating rock strata favorable to further petroleum exploration activities: Transports electrical equipment and instruments to designated locations, and directs and assists in laying out and connecting cables, electrodes, instrument panels, and other electrical equipment. Adjusts electrical instruments to eliminate electrical interferences from earth currents or weather conditions. Opens and closes circuits to send electrical current through electrodes into earth. Reads dials and records data of millivoltmeter readings at various receptor points along cable to detect loss of potential due to resistance of earth formations. Diagnoses cause of malfunctioning of instruments and cables and makes repairs.
GOE: 05.03.04 STRENGTH: L GED: R4 M4 L4 SVP: 6 DLU: 77

010.261-018 OBSERVER, GRAVITY PROSPECTING (petrol. & gas) alternate titles: gravity-prospecting operator; recorder, gravity prospecting
Records readings of gravity meter, torsion balance, and other gravity-measuring instruments at various points in terrain to obtain data regarding gravity

characteristics indicating potential source of metallic ore or petroleum deposits: Sets up or directs set-up of instruments at specified location and records readings. Examines readings for accurate registration and adjusts instruments to specifications. Reads thermometers, barometers, and other instruments and records variations in temperature, barometric pressure, elevation, and other physical factors that affect instrument readings. May be designated according to instrument used as Gravity-Meter Observer (mine & quarry; petrol. & gas); Magnetometer Operator (mine & quarry; petrol. & gas).
GOE: 05.03.04 STRENGTH: L GED: R4 M4 L4 SVP: 6 DLU: 77

010.261-022 SURVEYOR, OIL-WELL DIRECTIONAL (petrol. & gas) alternate titles: oil-well-logging engineer
Measures sonar, electrical, or radioactive characteristics of earth formations in oil- or gas-well boreholes to evaluate productivity of oil- or gas-bearing reservoirs, using sonic, electronic, or nuclear measuring instruments: Signals HOISTING ENGINEER (any industry) to lower instruments into well, observing oscillograph and meters on control panel to verify operating condition of instruments. Turns dials on control panel to adjust instrument for specified recording and starts recording device when instruments reach bottom of borehole. Prints copies of recorded graphs in truck darkroom [DEVELOPER (photofinishing)]. Interprets graphs for customer to indicate identity, porosity, oil- or gas-bearing content, and productivity of geological formations. Measures borehole diameters, direction of borehole, and inclination of geological strata, using microcalipers, directional indicators (clinometers), and dipmeters. May be designated according to measuring instruments used as Acoustical Logging Engineer (petrol. & gas); Nuclear Logging Engineer (petrol. & gas).
GOE: 05.03.04 STRENGTH: L GED: R5 M5 L5 SVP: 7 DLU: 77

010.261-026 TEST-ENGINE EVALUATOR (petrol. refin.) alternate titles: research-test-engine evaluator
Collects and assists in evaluation of data obtained in testing petroleum fuels and lubricants under simulated operating conditions: Inspects engines after test runs have been made by TEST-ENGINE OPERATOR (petrol. refin.), for wear, deposits, and defective parts, using microscope and precision weighing and measuring devices to obtain accurate data. Records findings and assists in analyzing data. Assists in dismantling and reassembling engines during test runs. May obtain and analyze samples of engine-exhaust gas.
GOE: 05.01.04 STRENGTH: M GED: R4 M4 L4 SVP: 7 DLU: 77

010.267-010 SCOUT (petrol. & gas)
Investigates and collects information concerning oil well drilling operations, geological and geophysical prospecting, and land and lease contracts from other oil fields, the press, lease brokers, individuals, and organizations leading to possible discovery of new oil fields: Interviews individuals and observes field operations to obtain data, such as locations and depths of oil or gas wells or exploratory boreholes or of producing wells, subsurface and geophysical survey results, methods of well completion, and volume of oil or gas flow. Collects rock samples and cuttings and samples of oil or gas from wells. Inspects cores and notes recurrence of specific strata in various boreholes to confirm or disprove concepts of stratigraphy. Obtains information on purpose and locations of lease purchases, royalty contracts, and other agreements made by competitive companies. Observations may be confined to prospecting or to include drilling and producing activities. Must have knowledge of production engineering, oil field practices, and geology. May sketch subsurface contours of geological formations as indicated by data obtained. May negotiate with landowners for drilling leases, ore royalties, and land options [LEASE BUYER (mine & quarry; petrol. & gas)].
GOE: 05.03.04 STRENGTH: L GED: R5 M4 L4 SVP: 6 DLU: 77

010.281-010 DRAFTER, DIRECTIONAL SURVEY (petrol. & gas)
Plots oil- or gas-well boreholes from photographic subsurface survey recordings and other data. Computes and represents diameter, depth, degree, and direction of inclination, location of equipment, and other dimensions and characteristics of borehole. Performs other duties as described under DRAFTER (profess. & kin.) Master Title.
GOE: 05.03.02 STRENGTH: L GED: R5 M5 L5 SVP: 7 DLU: 77

010.281-014 DRAFTER, GEOLOGICAL (petrol. & gas)
Draws maps, diagrams, profiles, cross sections, directional surveys, and subsurface formations to represent geological or geophysical stratigraphy and locations of gas and oil deposits, performing duties as described under DRAFTER (profess. & kin.) Master Title: Correlates and interprets data obtained from topographical surveys, well logs, or geophysical prospecting reports, utilizing special symbols to denote geological and geophysical formations or oil field installations. May finish drawings in mediums and according to specifications required for reproduction by blueprinting, photographing, or other duplication methods.
GOE: 05.03.02 STRENGTH: S GED: R5 M5 L5 SVP: 6 DLU: 77

010.281-018 DRAFTER, GEOPHYSICAL (petrol. & gas)
Draws subsurface contours in rock formations from data obtained by geophysical prospecting party. Plots maps and diagrams from computations based on recordings of seismograph, gravity meter, magnetometer, and other petroleum prospecting instruments and from prospecting and surveying field notes. Performs other duties as described under DRAFTER (profess. & kin.) Master Title. May be designated according to method of prospecting as Drafter, Seismograph (petrol. & gas).
GOE: 05.03.02 STRENGTH: L GED: R5 M5 L5 SVP: 7 DLU: 77

010.281-022 WELL-LOGGING OPERATOR, MUD ANALYSIS (petrol. & gas) alternate titles: mud-analysis-well-logging operator

Analyzes mud and drill cuttings that are circulated through oil- or gas-well boreholes during drilling operations, using special testing equipment, to detect presence of oil or gas, and interprets findings to locate productive stratum: Attaches pump-stroke counter, mud-tank level indicator, and other measurement devices to drilling rig equipment, and connects electrical conductor cables to measurement devices and drilling rig monitoring instruments to prepare field laboratory for testing of mud and well cuttings. Detects presence of gas in mud by reading dial of gas-detection meter hooked up to detection devices in mud. Collects mud and drill cutting samples during drilling operations, and inspects samples to determine nature of earth formations encountered and presence of oil or gas in formation, using ultraviolet light, microscope, and other laboratory equipment. Keeps records of dial readings and tests made, and calculates depth of formations found to contain gas or oil. Performs minor repairs to electrical and mechanical equipment.
GOE: 02.04.01 STRENGTH: L GED: R4 M4 L4 SVP: 5 DLU: 77

011 METALLURGY AND METALLURGICAL ENGINEERING OCCUPATIONS

This group includes occupations concerned with the extraction of metals from ores, and their processing and conversion into final shape. Also includes the design and development of process methods. Accessory techniques needed include those used in chemistry, geology, ceramics, mineralogy, and in mining, chemical, and mechanical engineering.

011.061-010 FOUNDRY METALLURGIST (foundry) alternate titles: foundry technician

Conducts research to develop and improve methods of sand molding, melting, alloying, and pouring of metals: Makes experimental sand molds, and tests sand for permeability, strength, and chemical composition. Calculates quantity of alloying metals required. Melts alloys and pours metals under controlled conditions to make castings. Performs physical and radiographic tests and evaluates data to develop improved alloys and foundry techniques.
GOE: 05.01.01 STRENGTH: L GED: R5 M5 L5 SVP: 8 DLU: 77

011.061-014 METALLOGRAPHER (profess. & kin.)

Conducts microscopic, macroscopic, and other tests and investigations on samples of metals and alloys for purposes as metallurgical control over products or use in developing new or improved grades and types of metals, alloys, or production methods: Directs laboratory personnel in preparing of samples, such as polishing or etching, and designates area of sample where microscopic or macroscopic examination is to be made. Studies photomicrographs and performs microscopic examinations on samples to determine metal characteristics, such as crystal structure, porosity, and homogeneity. Interprets findings and prepares drawings, charts, and graphs for inclusion in reports for reference or instruction purposes, and writes reports regarding findings, conclusions, and recommendations. Coordinates and participates in performing special tests, such as end-quench hardenability, bend and tensile, and grain size tests.
GOE: 05.01.04 STRENGTH: S GED: R5 M5 L5 SVP: 8 DLU: 77

011.061-018 METALLURGIST, EXTRACTIVE (profess. & kin.) alternate titles: metallurgist, process

Originates, controls, and develops flotation, smelting, electrolytic, and other processes used in winning metals from their ores, for producing iron and steel, or for refining gold, silver, zinc, copper, and other metals: Studies ore reduction problems to determine most efficient methods of producing metals commercially. Controls temperature adjustments, charge mixtures, and other variables in blast-furnace operations and steel-melting furnaces to obtain pig iron and steel of specified metallurgical characteristics and qualities. Investigates methods of improving metallurgical processes, as in the reduction of alumina by electrolytic methods to produce aluminum, the distillation of molten ore to purify zinc, or selective oxidation methods to extract lead, nickel, mercury, and other nonferrous metals from their ores.
GOE: 05.01.06 STRENGTH: L GED: R6 M6 L6 SVP: 8 DLU: 77

011.061-022 METALLURGIST, PHYSICAL (profess. & kin.)

Investigates and conducts experiments concerned with physical characteristics, properties, and processing of metals to develop new alloys, applications, and methods of commercially fabricating products from metals: Conducts microscopic, x ray, x-ray diffraction, and spectroscopic studies of metals and alloys, such as steel, cast iron, and nonferrous alloys, to determine their physical characteristics, such as crystal structure, dispersion of alloy particles through basic metal, and presence of impurities, fractures, and other defects in metal samples. Develops melting, hot-working, cold-working, and heat-treating processes to obtain desired characteristics, such as ductility, malleability, elongation ability, durability, and hardness. Tests alloys in tension, compression, impact, bending, or fatigue devices to study physical characteristics for manufacturing purposes or determine compliance with manufacturing specifications and standards. Consults with engineers and officials to develop methods of manufacturing alloys at minimum costs. May specialize in particular area of physical metallurgy, such as development of improved techniques and materials, for use in production of pressed metallic-powder products.
GOE: 02.01.02 STRENGTH: L GED: R6 M6 L6 SVP: 8 DLU: 77

011.061-026 WELDING ENGINEER (profess. & kin.)

Develops welding techniques, procedures, and application of welding equipment to problems involving fabrication of metals, utilizing knowledge of pro-

duction specifications, properties and characteristics of metals and metal alloys, and engineering principles: Conducts research and development investigations to develop and test new fabrication processes and procedures, improve existing or develop new welding equipment, develop new or modify current welding methods, techniques, and procedures, discover new patterns of welding phenomena, or to correlate and substanitate hypotheses. Prepares technical reports as result of research and development and preventive maintenance investigations. Establishes welding procedures to guide production and welding personnel relating to specification restrictions, material processes, pre- and post-heating requirements which involve use of complex alloys, unusual fabrication methods, welding of critical joints, and complex postheating requirements. Evaluates new developments in welding field for possible application to current welding problems or production processes. Directs and coordinates technical personnel in performing inspections to ensure workers' compliance with established welding procedures, restrictions, and standards; in testing welds for conformance with national code requirements; or testing welding personnel for certification. Contacts personnel of other agencies, engineering personnel, or clients to exchange ideas, information, or offer technical advice concerning welding matters. May perform experimental welding to evaluate new equipment, techniques, and materials.
GOE: 05.01.08 STRENGTH: L GED: R5 M5 L5 SVP: 8 DLU: 77

011.161-010 SUPERVISOR, METALLURGICAL-AND-QUALITY-CONTROL-TESTING (profess. & kin.) alternate titles: physical-testing supervisor

Directs and coordinates, through subordinate supervisory personnel, activities of workers engaged in testing finished and semifinished metal sample specimens to determine if metallurgical and physical properties meet manufacturing specifications: Reviews production schedules to ascertain work load and prepares schedules and priorities for work. Assigns personnel to specific work assignments and reviews test reports to determine if physical characteristics of sample specimens meet metallurgical specifications and quality control standards. Investigates causes of defective material and advises supervisory personnel of production department responsible of processing defects. Determines disposition of substandard material, according to established precedent or practice or upon approval of superior, such as downgrading, reprocessing, or scrapping material. Advises metallurgical personnel on problems involving quality control and testing techniques and methods and on application of metallurgical specifications to metal products.
GOE: 02.04.01 STRENGTH: L GED: R5 M5 L5 SVP: 8 DLU: 77

011.261-010 METALLURGICAL TECHNICIAN (profess. & kin.) alternate titles: metallurgical-laboratory assistant; metallurgical tester; physical-laboratory assistant

Examines and tests metal samples to determine their physical properties, under direction of METALLOGRAPHER (profess. & kin.): Conducts routine microscopic examinations of metals and alloys to determine their crystal structure, porosity, homogeneity, and other characteristics. Polishes or etches metal specimens and photographs samples, using photomicroscope, or directs photography technical personnel to take, develop, and mount photomicrographs. Examines metal and alloy samples with x-ray, gamma-ray, and magnetic-flux equipment to detect internal fractures, impurities, and similar defects in metals. Tests samples in pressure devices, hot-acid baths, and other apparatus to determine strength, hardness, elasticity, toughness, or other properties of metal.
GOE: 02.04.01 STRENGTH: L GED: R4 M4 L4 SVP: 6 DLU: 77

011.261-014 WELDING TECHNICIAN (profess. & kin.)

Conducts experiments and tests and evaluates data to assist welding engineering personnel in development and application of new or improved welding equipment; welding techniques, procedures, and practices; and specifications for material heat treating: Assists engineering personnel in testing and evaluating welding equipment, metals, and alloys. Evaluates data and conducts experiments to develop application of new equipment or improved techniques, procedures, or practices. Recommends adoption of new developments and applications to engineering personnel and demonstrates practicability of recommendations. Inspects welded joints and conducts tests to ensure welds meet company standards, national code requirements, and customer job specifications. Records inspection and test results and prepares and submits reports to welding engineering personnel. Conducts certification tests for qualification of personnel with national code requirements.
GOE: 05.01.01 STRENGTH: L GED: R4 M3 L3 SVP: 8 DLU: 77

011.261-018 NONDESTRUCTIVE TESTER (profess. & kin.)

Conducts radiographic, penetrant, ultrasonic, and magnetic particle tests on metal parts to determine if parts meet nondestructive specifications: Reviews test orders to determine type of test requested, test procedures to follow, and part acceptability criteria. Applies agents, such as cleaners, penetrants, and developers, and couplant (light oil which acts as medium), to parts, or heats parts in oven, to prepare parts for testing. Determines test equipment settings according to type of metal, thickness, distance from test equipment, and related variables, using standard formulas. Calibrates test equipment, such as magnetic particle, x-ray, and ultrasonic contact machines, to standard settings, following manual instructions. Sets up equipment to perform tests, and conducts tests on parts, following procedures established for specified tests performed. Examines surface-treated materials during penetrant and magnetic particle tests to locate and identify cracks or other defects, using black light. Moves transducer probe across part when conducting ultrasonic tests and observes CRT (cathode ray

tube) screen to detect and locate discontinuities in metal structure [ULTRA-SONIC TESTER (any industry) 739.281-014]. Examines film when conducting radiographic tests to locate structural or welding flaws. Marks tested parts to indicate defective areas. Evaluates test results against designated standards, utilizing knowledge of metals and testing experience. Prepares reports outlining findings and conclusions. May perform similar tests on nonmetallic parts or structures.
GOE: 05.07.01 STRENGTH: M GED: R4 M3 L3 SVP: 6 DLU: 88

011.261-022 LABORATORY ASSISTANT, METALLURGICAL (steel & rel.) alternate titles: metallurgical analyst; metallurgical inspector
Analyzes data obtained from investigation of physical and chemical properties of metals, or processes used in recovering metals from their ores to select method, standards, and procedures of examination and testing and conducts tests: Analyzes operating records and test reports, or by personal observation and investigation, determines conformance to established procedures, methods, and standards. Conducts physical, chemical, and process examinations, using metallurgical equipment and instruments for routine, special, and experimental investigations. Writes report indicating deviations from specifications and recommends corrective measures for approval.
GOE: 02.04.01 STRENGTH: L GED: R4 M4 L4 SVP: 7 DLU: 77

011.281-014 SPECTROSCOPIST (profess. & kin.) alternate titles: spectrographer; spectrographic analyst
Conducts spectrographic examinations of metal and mineral samples under established procedures, using spectrograph, spectrometer, densitometer, and other measuring instruments: Analyzes densitometer or spectrometer readings to measure density ratio of specific elements in sample. Computes percentage composition of sample by comparing intensity ratio with standard charts. Investigates deviations from standard, performing further examinations by other spectrographic procedures and methods to establish degree of conformance to standard. Records quantitative determination, procedure, and standard applied for each sample examined.
GOE: 02.04.01 STRENGTH: L GED: R4 M4 L4 SVP: 7 DLU: 77

011.361-010 TESTER (profess. & kin.) alternate titles: physical tester; testing-machine operator
Measures tensile strength, hardness, ductility, or other physical properties of metal specimens, using following prescribed series of operations: Determines tensile strength on tension-testing machines. Measures dimensions of specimen with scales and micrometers and records measurements. Screws or clamps specimen in holders on machine. Clamps extensometer onto specimen and connects wire from extensometer to automatic stress-strain recorder. Turns handwheels or moves levers to apply tension to specimen at specified rate. Notes reading of indicator dial on control panel of machine or observes stress-strain curve (curve obtained by plotting applied tension against resultant elongation) being drawn by recorder to determine yield point and tensile strength of specimen. Removes pieces of broken specimen from machine, fits them together, and measures amount of elongation. Makes simple calculations of values, such as unit tensile strength and percentage elongation, using tables. Records readings and calculations on special forms. Measures hardness of specimens [HARDNESS INSPECTOR (heat treating) 504.387-010]. Measures ductility of sheet metal specimens in sheet metal testing machine. May test specimens for plasticity and compression. May specialize in testing iron or steel sheets for ductility and be designated Sheet Tester (steel & rel.).
GOE: 02.04.01 STRENGTH: L GED: R4 M4 L3 SVP: 5 DLU: 77

012 INDUSTRIAL ENGINEERING OCCUPATIONS

This group includes occupations concerned with the design and installation of integrated systems of personnel, materials, machinery, and equipment. Accessory techniques may include those used in mechanical and various other engineering specialities. Typical specializations are plant layout; production methods and standards; cost control; quality control; time, motion, and incentive studies; and methods, production, and safety engineering.

012.061-010 PRODUCT-SAFETY ENGINEER (profess. & kin.)
Develops and conducts tests to evaluate product safety levels and recommends measures to reduce or eliminate hazards: Establishes procedures for detection and elimination of physical and chemical hazards and avoidance of potential toxic effects and other product hazards. Investigates causes of accidents, injuries, and illnesses resulting from product usage and develops solutions. Evaluates potential health hazards or damage which could result from misuse of products and applies engineering principles and product standards to improve safety. May participate in preparation of product usage and precautionary label instructions.
GOE: 05.01.02 STRENGTH: S GED: R6 M6 L6 SVP: 8 DLU: 77

012.061-014 SAFETY ENGINEER (profess. & kin.)
Develops and implements safety program to prevent or correct unsafe environmental working conditions, utilizing knowledge of industrial processes, mechanics, chemistry, psychology, and industrial health and safety laws: Examines plans and specifications for new machinery or equipment to determine if all safety precautions have been included. Determines amount of weight that can be safely placed on plant floor. Tours plant to inspect fire and safety equipment, machinery, and facilities to identify and correct potential hazards and en-

sure compliance with safety regulations. Determines requirements for safety clothing and devices, and designs, builds, and installs, or directs installation of safety devices on machinery. Conducts or coordinates safety and first aid training to educate workers about safety policies, laws, and practices. Investigates industrial accidents to minimize recurrence and prepares accident reports. May conduct air quality tests for presence of harmful gases and vapors.
GOE: 05.01.02 STRENGTH: L GED: R6 M6 L6 SVP: 8 DLU: 88

012.061-018 STANDARDS ENGINEER (profess. & kin.)
Establishes engineering and technical limitations and applications for items, materials, processes, methods, designs, and engineering practices for use by designers of machines and equipment, such as aircraft, automobiles, and space vehicles: Communicates with management of industrial organization to maintain knowledge of current and proposed projects in order to develop appropriate standards for design and production of new items. Evaluates data in scientific journals, suppliers' catalogs, government standards documents, and other sources of information on materials, processes, and parts to update knowledge of available resources. Prepares specification sheets and standard drawings designating parts and materials acceptable for specific uses, using knowledge of primary engineering discipline and related disciplines. Examines all factors involved to confirm that standards will result in most economic use of material and labor consistent with safety and durability of final product. Reviews standards prepared with other departmental specialists to assure consistency with existing standards and those in other specialized disciplines. Communicates with user personnel to confirm knowledge of standards and cooperation of various project groups. Follows established procedures for retention of data developed to assure optimum storage and retrieval by manual or automated methods.
GOE: 05.01.06 STRENGTH: S GED: R5 M5 L5 SVP: 8 DLU: 77

012.067-010 METROLOGIST (profess. & kin.)
Develops and evaluates calibration systems that measure characteristics of objects, substances, or phenomena, such as length, mass, time, temperature, electric current, luminous intensity, and derived units of physical or chemical measure: Identifies magnitude of error sources contributing to uncertainty of results to determine reliability of measurement process in quantitative terms. Redesigns or adjusts measurement capability to minimize errors. Develops calibration methods and techniques based on principles of measurement science, technical analysis of measurement problems, and accuracy and precision requirements. Directs engineering, quality, and laboratory personnel in design, manufacture, evaluation, and calibration of measurement standards, instruments, and test systems to ensure selection of approved instrumentation. Advises others on methods of resolving measurement problems and exchanges information with other metrology personnel through participation in government and industrial standardization committees and professional societies.
GOE: 05.01.04 STRENGTH: S GED: R6 M6 L6 SVP: 8 DLU: 77

012.167-010 CONFIGURATION MANAGEMENT ANALYST (profess. & kin.)
Analyzes proposed changes of product design to determine effect on overall system, and coordinates recording of modifications for management control: Confers with manufacturer or customer representatives to establish change-reporting procedure, and prepares directives for change authorization and documentation by company and subcontractor personnel. Analyzes proposed part-design changes and exhibits to prepare report of effect on overall product for management action, using knowledge of engineering, manufacturing, and procurement activities. Confers with department managers to obtain additional information or to interpret policies and procedures for reporting changes in product design. Audits subcontractor's inspection or technical documents preparation procedure to verify compliance with contract requirements. Coordinates activities of personnel preparing manual or automated records of part-design change documents and *first-article configuration inspection.*
GOE: 05.01.06 STRENGTH: L GED: R5 M4 L5 SVP: 8 DLU: 77

012.167-014 MANAGER, QUALITY CONTROL (profess. & kin.)
Plans, coordinates, and directs quality control program designed to ensure continuous production of products consistent with established standards: Develops and analyzes statistical data and product specifications to determine present standards and establish proposed quality and reliability expectancy of finished product. Formulates and maintains quality control objectives and coordinates objectives with production procedures in cooperation with other plant managers to maximize product reliability and minimize costs. Directs, through intermediate personnel, workers engaged in inspection and testing activities to ensure continuous control over materials, facilities, and products. Plans, promotes, and organizes training activities related to product quality and reliability. May investigate and adjust customer complaints regarding quality.
GOE: 05.02.03 STRENGTH: L GED: R5 M5 L5 SVP: 8 DLU: 88

012.167-018 FACTORY LAY-OUT ENGINEER (profess. & kin.) alternate titles: planning engineer
Plans layout of complete departments of industrial plant or commercial establishment to provide maximum possible operating efficiency: Measures and studies available floor space and draws plan of floor space to scale, using drafting tools. Studies sequence of operations to be performed and flow of materials. Studies and measures machines, conveyors, benches, furnaces, and other equipment. Coordinates all available knowledge and information into finished scale drawing, showing most efficient location for each piece of equipment and necessary working area around each. May use computer-assisted design/drafting equipment.

GOE: 05.01.06 STRENGTH: L GED: R5 M5 L5 SVP: 8 DLU: 88

012.167-022 FIRE-PREVENTION RESEARCH ENGINEER (profess. & kin.) alternate titles: loss-prevention research engineer

Conducts research to determine cause and methods of preventing fires and prepares educational materials concerning fire prevention for insurance companies, performing duties as described under RESEARCH ENGINEER (profess. & kin.) Master Title.
GOE: 05.01.01 STRENGTH: S GED: R5 M5 L5 SVP: 7 DLU: 77

012.167-026 FIRE-PROTECTION ENGINEER (profess. & kin.) alternate titles: fire-loss-prevention engineer

Advises and assists private and public organizations and military services for purposes of safeguarding life and property against fire, explosion, and related hazards: Makes studies of industrial, mercantile, and public buildings, homes, and other property before and after construction, considering factors, such as fire resistance of construction, usage or contents of buildings, water supplies and water delivery, and egress facilities. Designs or recommends materials or equipment, such as structural components protection, fire-detection equipment, alarm systems, fire extinguishing devices and systems, and advises on location, handling, installation, and maintenance. Recommends materials, equipment, or methods for alleviation of conditions conducive to fire. Devises fire protection programs, and organizes and trains personnel to carry out such programs. May evaluate fire departments and adequacy of laws, ordinances, and regulations affecting fire prevention or firesafety. Conducts research and tests on fire retardants and firesafety of materials and devices and to determine fire causes and methods of fire prevention. May determine fire causes and methods of fire prevention. May teach courses on fire prevention and protection at accredited educational institutions. May advise and plan for prevention of destruction by fire, wind, water, or other causes of damage.
GOE: 05.01.02 STRENGTH: L GED: R5 M5 L5 SVP: 7 DLU: 77

012.167-030 INDUSTRIAL ENGINEER (profess. & kin.)

Plans utilization of facilities, equipment, materials, and personnel to improve efficiency of operations: Studies functional statements, organization charts, and project information to determine functions and responsibilities of workers and work units and to identify areas of duplication. Establishes work measurement programs and analyzes work samples to develop standards for labor utilization. Analyzes work force utilization, facility layout, and operational data, such as production costs, process flow charts, and production schedules, to determine efficient utilization of workers and equipment. Recommends methods for improving worker efficiency and reducing waste of materials and utilities, such as restructuring job duties, reorganizing work flow, relocating work stations and equipment, and purchase of equipment. Confers with management and engineering staff to implement plans and recommendations. May develop management systems for cost analysis, financial planning, wage and salary administration, and job evaluation.
GOE: 05.01.06 STRENGTH: S GED: R5 M5 L5 SVP: 7 DLU: 90

012.167-034 INDUSTRIAL-HEALTH ENGINEER (profess. & kin.) alternate titles: industrial hygiene engineer

Plans and coordinates private or government industrial health program requiring application of engineering principles and technology to analyze and control conditions contributing to occupational hazards and diseases: Conducts plant or area surveys to determine safe limits of exposure to materials or conditions, such as temperatures, noise, dusts, fumes, vapors, mists, gases, solvents, and radiation which are known or suspected of being real or potential detriments to health, and implements or recommends control measures. Directs workers engaged in field and laboratory verification of compliance with health regulations. Provides technical guidance to management, labor organizations, government agencies, and civic groups regarding health-related problems, such as stream and air pollution and correct use of protective clothing or accessories.
GOE: 05.01.02 STRENGTH: S GED: R5 M5 L5 SVP: 7 DLU: 77

012.167-038 LIAISON ENGINEER (aircraft mfg.)

Coordinates activities to evaluate and resolve engineering-related production problems encountered in assigned area of aircraft manufacturing facility: Reviews production schedules, engineering specifications, orders, and related information to maintain current knowledge of manufacturing methods, procedures, and activities in assigned area. Confers with quality control, material, manufacturing, and other department personnel to provide technical support. Interprets engineering drawings and facilitates correction of errors on drawings and documents identified during manufacturing operations. Investigates reports of defective, damaged, or malfunctioning parts, assemblies, equipment, or systems to determine nature and scope of problem. Examines, measures, inspects, or tests defective part for conformance to engineering design drawings or blueprint specifications, using precision measuring and testing instruments, devices, and equipment. Consults with project engineers to obtain specialized information. Evaluates findings to formulate corrective action plan and coordinates implementation of plan. Maintains records or oversees recording of information by others to ensure engineering drawings and documents are current and that engineering-related production problems and resolutions are documented. Serves as member of material review board to determine disposition of defective or damaged parts. May specialize in investigating and resolving tooling problems and be designated Tool Liaison (aircraft mfg.).
GOE: 05.01.06 STRENGTH: L GED: R5 M5 L4 SVP: 7 DLU: 88

012.167-042 MANUFACTURING ENGINEER (profess. & kin.)

Plans, directs, and coordinates manufacturing processes in industrial plant: Develops, evaluates, and improves manufacturing methods, utilizing knowledge of product design, materials and parts, fabrication processes, tooling and production equipment capabilities, assembly methods, and quality control standards. Analyzes and plans work force utilization, space requirements, and workflow, and designs layout of equipment and workspace for maximum efficiency [INDUSTRIAL ENGINEER (profess. & kin.) 012.167-030]. Confers with planning and design staff concerning product design and tooling to ensure efficient production methods. Confers with vendors to determine product specifications and arrange for purchase of equipment, materials, or parts, and evaluates products according to specifications and quality standards. Estimates production times, staffing requirements, and related costs to provide information for management decisions. Confers with management, engineering, and other staff regarding manufacturing capabilities, production schedules, and other considerations to facilitate production processes. Applies statistical methods to estimate future manufacturing requirements and potential.
GOE: 05.01.06 STRENGTH: L GED: R5 M5 L5 SVP: 8 DLU: 89

012.167-046 PRODUCTION ENGINEER (profess. & kin.)

Plans and coordinates production procedures in industrial plant: Directs production departments. Regulates and coordinates functions of office and shop. Introduces efficient production line methods. Initiates and directs procedures to increase company output.
GOE: 05.01.06 STRENGTH: L GED: R5 M5 L5 SVP: 8 DLU: 87

012.167-050 PRODUCTION PLANNER (profess. & kin.) alternate titles: planner, chief; planning supervisor; process planner; production-planning supervisor; production scheduler; scheduler; tool-and-production planner

Plans and prepares production schedules for manufacture of industrial or commercial products: Draws up master schedule to establish sequence and lead time of each operation to meet shipping dates according to sales forecasts or customer orders. Analyzes production specifications and plant capacity data and performs mathematical calculations to determine manufacturing processes, tools, and human resource requirements. Plans and schedules workflow for each department and operation according to previously established manufacturing sequences and lead times. Plans sequence of fabrication, assembly, installation, and other manufacturing operations for guidance of production workers. Confers with department supervisors to determine status of assigned projects. Expedites operations that delay schedules and alters schedules to meet unforeseen conditions. Prepares production reports. May prepare lists of required materials, tools, and equipment. May prepare purchase orders to obtain materials, tools, and equipment.
GOE: 05.01.06 STRENGTH: L GED: R5 M4 L4 SVP: 7 DLU: 86

012.167-054 QUALITY CONTROL ENGINEER (profess. & kin.)

Plans and directs activities concerned with development, application, and maintenance of quality standards for industrial processes, materials, and products: Develops and initiates standards and methods for inspection, testing, and evaluation, utilizing knowledge in engineering fields such as chemical, electrical, or mechanical. Devises sampling procedures and designs and develops forms and instructions for recording, evaluating, and reporting quality and reliability data. Establishes program to evaluate precision and accuracy of production equipment and testing, measurement, and analytical equipment and facilities. Develops and implements methods and procedures for disposition of discrepant material and devises methods to assess cost and responsibility. Directs workers engaged in measuring and testing product and tabulating data concerning materials, product, or process quality and reliability. Compiles and writes training material and conducts training sessions on quality control activities. May specialize in areas of quality control engineering, such as design, incoming material, process control, product evaluation, product reliability, inventory control, metrology, automated testing, software, research and development, and administrative application. May manage quality control program [MANAGER, QUALITY CONTROL (profess. & kin.) 012.167-014].
GOE: 05.01.04 STRENGTH: L GED: R6 M6 L6 SVP: 8 DLU: 89

012.167-058 SAFETY MANAGER (profess. & kin.)

Plans, implements, and coordinates program to reduce or eliminate occupational injuries, illnesses, deaths, and financial losses: Identifies and appraises conditions which could produce accidents and financial losses and evaluates potential extent of injuries resulting from accidents. Conducts or directs research studies to identify hazards and evaluate loss producing potential of given system, operation or process. Develops accident-prevention and loss-control systems and programs for incorporation into operational policies of organization. Coordinates safety activities of unit managers to ensure implementation of safety activities throughout organization. Compiles, analyzes, and interprets statistical data related to exposure factors concerning occupational illnesses and accidents and prepares reports for information of personnel concerned. Maintains liaison with outside organizations, such as fire departments, mutual aid societies, and rescue teams to assure information exchange and mutual assistance. Devises methods to evaluate safety program and conducts or directs evaluations. Evaluates technical and scientific publications concerned with safety management and participates in activities of related professional organizations to update knowledge of safety program developments. May store and retrieve statistical data, using computer.
GOE: 05.01.02 STRENGTH: S GED: R6 M6 L6 SVP: 8 DLU: 88

012.167-062 SUPERVISOR, VENDOR QUALITY (any industry) alternate titles: chief, vendor quality

Directs and coordinates quality inspection of parts, components, and materials produced by subcontractors and vendors, and surveillance of sub-

contractors' manufacturing processes: Directs sampling inspection, and testing of received parts, components, and materials to determine conformance to standards. Conducts periodic and special surveys of subcontractors' facilities and manufacturing processes to determine adequacy and capability of quality control and ability to comply with complete quality specifications. Reviews quality problems with engineering personnel and directs action required to correct defects. Prepares periodic and special reports concerning departmental activities, problems, subcontractor's quality system, schedules, and rejected items. Aids in organizational planning by participating in departmental conferences.
GOE: 05.03.06 STRENGTH: S GED: R5 M5 L5 SVP: 7 DLU: 77

012.167-070 TIME-STUDY ENGINEER (profess. & kin.) alternate titles: efficiency expert; manager, production; methods-and-procedures analyst; production engineer; production expert; time-study analyst; work-measurement engineer
Develops work measurement procedures and directs time-and-motion studies to promote efficient and economical utilization of personnel and facilities: Directs or conducts observation and analysis of personnel and work procedures to determine time-and-motion requirements of job duties. Analyzes work study data and equipment specifications to establish time and production standards. Applies mathematical analysis to determine validity and reliability of sampling and work study statistics. Applies principles of industrial engineering and applied psychology to evaluate work methods proposals and to develop recommendations to management affecting work methods, wage rates, and budget decisions. Trains INDUSTRIAL ENGINEERING TECHNICIAN (profess. & kin.) in time-and-motion study principles and techniques.
GOE: 05.01.06 STRENGTH: L GED: R5 M5 L5 SVP: 8 DLU: 77

012.167-074 TOOL PLANNER (any industry) alternate titles: processor
Analyzes blueprints or prototype parts to determine tools, fixtures, and equipment needed for manufacture and plans sequence of operations for fabrication and assembly of products, such as aircraft assemblies, automobile parts, cutting tools, or ball bearings: Studies engineering blueprints, drawings, models, and other specifications to obtain data on proposed part. Applies knowledge of functions and processes of various departments and capacities of machines and equipment to determine tool requirements and establish sequence of operations to fabricate and assemble parts. Lists operations to be performed on routing card or paper, indicates machines, cutting tools, fixtures, and other equipment to be used, and estimates times needed to perform each operation. May prepare reports for PRODUCTION PLANNER (profess. & kin.) in scheduling work for entire plant. May plan tool and operation sequences for only one department. May specify type of material to be used in construction of tools.
GOE: 05.01.06 STRENGTH: S GED: R5 M5 L5 SVP: 8 DLU: 77

012.167-078 DOCUMENTATION ENGINEER (profess. & kin.)
Plans, directs, and coordinates preparation of project documentation, such as engineering drawings, production specifications and schedules, and contract modifications, to ensure customer contract requirements are met: Reviews contract to determine documentation required for each phase of project, applying knowledge of engineering and manufacturing processes. Schedules due dates for drawings, specifications, software, technical manuals, and other documents. Monitors status of project to ensure documentation is submitted according to schedule. Reviews and verifies project documents for completeness, format, and compliance with contract requirements. Submits project documentation to management for approval, and transmits approved documents to customer. Confers with engineers, managers, customers, and others to discuss project, prepare documents, or modify contract schedules.
GOE: 05.01.06 STRENGTH: L GED: R5 M5 L5 SVP: 8 DLU: 86

012.167-082 MATERIAL SCHEDULER (aircraft mfg.) alternate titles: commodities requirements analyst; material planning and acquisition analyst; production control scheduler
Develops and analyzes lists of raw materials, purchased parts, equipment, and other items required to manufacture aircraft and aerospace products: Reviews and evaluates engineering drawings and blueprints to estimate quantity and type of materials, parts, or other items required. Converts requirements to orders of conventional sizes and quantities, considering factors such as existing inventories, unavoidable waste, and kind of material to be used. Reviews material lists for conformance to company standard practices in regard to parts and materials used. Schedules deliveries based on production forecasts, material substitutions, storage and handling facilities, and maintenance requirements. Prepares or authorizes preparation of purchase requisitions. Estimates need to reorder supplies due to rejections and engineering changes during manufacturing cycle. Confers with purchasing, engineering, planning, and other personnel to exchange information regarding inventories, schedules, and related issues.
GOE: 05.03.03 STRENGTH: S GED: R5 M5 L5 SVP: 7 DLU: 87

012.187-014 SHOE-LAY-OUT PLANNER (boot & shoe) alternate titles: shoe planner
Plans detailed instructions of operations in manufacture of newly designed shoes: Compiles manufacturing data from designer specifications, such as last to be used, size runs, ornamentation, saddle height, strap width, and color. Computes sizes of parts, such as inserts, linings, quarters, or vamps according to shoe size specifications or following *standard size system*. Lists specifications, such as materials, stitching, and findings for each shoe size. May cut paper patterns of shoe design. May cut traced design into pattern of shoe parts.
GOE: 05.03.02 STRENGTH: S GED: R5 M5 L4 SVP: 8 DLU: 77

012.261-010 AIR ANALYST (profess. & kin.) alternate titles: air tester
Analyzes samples of air in industrial establishments or other work areas to determine amount of suspended foreign particles and effectiveness of control methods, using dust collectors: Starts dust collector apparatus that draws air through machine and precipitates dust on tubes, plates, electrodes, or in flasks. Weighs or otherwise determines amount of collected particles, such as lead, rock, or coal dust. Compares weight or count of particles with volume of air passed through machine, and computes percentage of concentration per cubic foot of air tested, using mathematical and chemical formulas. Prepares summary of findings for submission to appropriate department. May recommend remedial measures.
GOE: 05.01.04 STRENGTH: L GED: R5 M5 L4 SVP: 5 DLU: 77

012.261-014 QUALITY CONTROL TECHNICIAN (profess. & kin.)
Tests and inspects products at various stages of production process and compiles and evaluates statistical data to determine and maintain quality and reliability of products: Interprets engineering drawings, schematic diagrams, or formulas and confers with management or engineering staff to determine quality and reliability standards. Selects products for tests at specified stages in production process, and tests products for variety of qualities, such as dimensions, performance, and mechanical, electrical, or chemical characteristics. Records test data, applying statistical quality control procedures. Evaluates data and writes reports to validate or indicate deviations from existing standards. Recommends modifications of existing quality or production standards to achieve optimum quality within limits of equipment capability. May set up and perform destructive and nondestructive tests on materials, parts, or products to measure performance, life, or material characteristics. May prepare graphs or charts of data or enter data into computer for analysis. May specialize in particular area of quality control engineering, such as design, incoming material, process control, product evaluation, inventory control, product reliability, research and development, and administrative application.
GOE: 02.04.01 STRENGTH: L GED: R5 M5 L4 SVP: 7 DLU: 89

012.267-010 INDUSTRIAL ENGINEERING TECHNICIAN (profess. & kin.)
Studies and records time, motion, methods, and speed involved in performance of maintenance, production, clerical, and other worker operations to establish standard production rate and to improve efficiency: Prepares charts, graphs, and diagrams to illustrate workflow, routing, floor layouts, material handling, and machine utilization. Observes workers operating equipment or performing tasks to determine time involved and fatigue rate, using stop watch, motion-picture camera, electrical recorder, and similar equipment. Recommends revision of methods of operation or material handling, alterations in equipment layout, or other changes to increase production or improve standards. Aids in planning work assignments in accordance with worker performance, machine capacity, production schedules, and anticipated delays. May be designated according to type of studies analyzed as Methods-Study Analyst (profess. & kin.); Motion-Study Analyst (profess. & kin.); Pace Analyst (profess. & kin.); Time-Study Analyst (profess. & kin.).
GOE: 05.03.06 STRENGTH: L GED: R5 M5 L4 SVP: 7 DLU: 81

012.281-010 SMOKE TESTER (smelt. & refin.)
Tests emissions from smokestack to determine if electrostatic precipitator and flue recovery systems are operating within prescribed standards: Measures force of gas flow by observing manometer attached to Pitot tube placed at various points in stack. Obtains solids contained in gas by drawing metered quantity of flue exhaust through filter bag. Computes total amount of gases and solids lost, using specified formula.
GOE: 02.04.01 STRENGTH: L GED: R4 M4 L3 SVP: 5 DLU: 77

013 AGRICULTURAL ENGINEERING OCCUPATIONS

This group includes occupations concerned with the application of engineering principles and techniques for the solution of agricultural problems. Also includes the design and development of agricultural machinery and structures. Accessory techniques needed may be those used in civil, mechanical, power, and electrical engineering; mineralogy; chemistry; and biology. Typical specializations are soil and water conservation; farm electrification; farm fire protection; pest control; and farm power and machinery, farm structures, and rural roads engineering.

013.061-010 AGRICULTURAL ENGINEER (profess. & kin.)
Applies engineering technology and knowledge of biological sciences to agricultural problems concerned with power and machinery, electrification, structures, soil and water conservation, and processing of agricultural products: Develops criteria for design, manufacture, or construction of equipment, structures, and facilities. Designs and uses sensing, measuring, and recording devices and instrumentation to study such problems as effects of temperature, humidity, and light, on plants or animals, or relative effectiveness of different methods of applying insecticides. Designs and directs manufacture of equipment for land tillage and fertilization, plant and animal disease and insect control, and for harvesting or moving commodities. Designs and supervises erection of structures for crop storage, animal shelter, and human dwelling, including light, heat, air-conditioning, water supply, and waste disposal. Plans and directs construction of rural electric-power distribution systems, and irrigation, drainage, and flood-

control systems for soil and water conservation. Designs and supervises installation of equipment and instruments used to evaluate and process farm products, and to automate agricultural operations. May conduct radio and television educational programs to provide assistance to farmers, local groups, and related farm cooperatives. Workers are usually designated according to area of specialty or product.
GOE: 05.01.08 STRENGTH: L GED: R5 M5 L5 SVP: 8 DLU: 77

013.061-014 AGRICULTURAL-RESEARCH ENGINEER (profess. & kin.)
Conducts research to develop agricultural machinery and equipment, performing duties as described under RESEARCH ENGINEER (profess. & kin.) Master Title.
GOE: 05.01.01 STRENGTH: L GED: R5 M5 L5 SVP: 8 DLU: 77

013.061-018 DESIGN-ENGINEER, AGRICULTURAL EQUIPMENT (profess. & kin.)
Designs agricultural machinery and equipment, performing duties as described under DESIGN ENGINEER, PRODUCTS (profess. & kin.) Master Title.
GOE: 05.01.07 STRENGTH: L GED: R5 M5 L5 SVP: 8 DLU: 77

013.061-022 TEST ENGINEER, AGRICULTURAL EQUIPMENT (profess. & kin.)
Conducts tests on agricultural machinery and equipment, performing duties as described under TEST ENGINEER (profess. & kin.) Master Title.
GOE: 05.01.04 STRENGTH: L GED: R5 M5 L5 SVP: 8 DLU: 77

013.151-010 SALES ENGINEER, AGRICULTURAL EQUIPMENT (profess. & kin.)
Sells agricultural machinery and equipment and provides technical services to client, performing duties as described under SALES ENGINEER (profess. & kin.) Master Title.
GOE: 05.01.05 STRENGTH: L GED: R5 M5 L5 SVP: 8 DLU: 77

013.161-010 AGRICULTURAL-ENGINEERING TECHNICIAN (profess. & kin.)
Prepares original layout and completes detailed drawings of agricultural machinery and equipment, such as farm machinery, irrigation, power, and electrification systems, soil and water conservation equipment and agricultural harvesting and processing equipment: Applies biological and engineering knowledge, design principles, and theories to ensure compliance with company policy, and an end product which will perform as required. Maintains working knowledge of functions, operations, and maintenance of various types of equipment and materials used in the industry to assure appropriate utilization.
GOE: 05.01.07 STRENGTH: S GED: R5 M5 L4 SVP: 7 DLU: 77

014   MARINE ENGINEERING OCCUPATIONS

This group includes occupations concerned with the design, development, and installation of ship machinery and related equipment, including propulsion machines and power supply systems. Accessory techniques needed are those used in mechanical and electrical engineering. Typical specializations are construction and repair, design and layout, consulting, research, and the administration of engineering enterprises and government regulatory activities.

014.061-010 DESIGN ENGINEER, MARINE EQUIPMENT (profess. & kin.)
Designs marine machinery and equipment performing duties as described under DESIGN ENGINEER, PRODUCTS (profess. & kin.) Master Title.
GOE: 05.01.07 STRENGTH: L GED: R5 M5 L5 SVP: 8 DLU: 77

014.061-014 MARINE ENGINEER (profess. & kin.)
Designs and oversees installation and repair of marine powerplants, propulsion systems, heating and ventilating systems, and other mechanical and electrical equipment in ships, docks, and marine facilities: Studies drawings and specifications and performs complex calculations to conceive equipment and systems designed to meet requirements of marine craft or facility. Oversees and evaluates operation of equipment during acceptance testing and shakedown cruises. May specialize in design of equipment, such as boilers, steam-driven reciprocating engines, heat exchangers, fire-control and communication systems, electric power systems, or piping and related fittings and valves.
GOE: 05.01.03 STRENGTH: L GED: R6 M5 L5 SVP: 8 DLU: 77

014.061-018 RESEARCH ENGINEER, MARINE EQUIPMENT (profess. & kin.)
Conducts research on marine machinery and equipment, performing duties as described under RESEARCH ENGINEER (profess. & kin.) Master Title.
GOE: 05.01.01 STRENGTH: L GED: R5 M5 L5 SVP: 8 DLU: 77

014.061-022 TEST ENGINEER, MARINE EQUIPMENT (profess. & kin.)
Conducts tests on marine machinery and equipment, performing duties as described under TEST ENGINEER (profess. & kin.) Master Title.
GOE: 05.01.04 STRENGTH: L GED: R5 M5 L5 SVP: 8 DLU: 77

014.151-010 SALES ENGINEER, MARINE EQUIPMENT (profess. & kin.)
Sells marine machinery and equipment and provides technical services to client, performing duties as described under SALES ENGINEER (profess. & kin.) Master Title.

GOE: 05.01.05 STRENGTH: L GED: R5 M5 L5 SVP: 8 DLU: 77

014.167-010 MARINE SURVEYOR (profess. & kin.) alternate titles: ship surveyor
Surveys marine vessels and watercraft, such as ships, boats, tankers, and dredges, to ascertain condition of hull, machinery, equipment, and equipage, and to determine repairs required for vessel to meet requirements for insuring: Examines underwater section of hull while ship is drydocked to ascertain conditions that indicate repairs are required. Takes readings on tailshaft and tailshaft bearings. Inspects condition of propellers, rudders, and sea valves. Inspects above waterline section of ship, such as hatchways, freeing ports, ventilators, bulkheads, fittings, and attachments, for compliance with operating standards, and compliance with standards for protection of crew. Observes operating tests on machinery and equipment and inspects opened up machinery for interior condition. Observes testing of cargo gear for compliance with testing standards and issues or endorses certificate for gear tested. Prepares reports on types of surveys conducted, recommended actions and repairs, or conditions remedied. Submits report to client.
GOE: 05.03.06 STRENGTH: L GED: R5 M4 L4 SVP: 8 DLU: 77

014.167-014 PORT ENGINEER (ship-boat mfg.; water trans.)
Coordinates repair and maintenance functions furnished operating fleet to minimize loss of revenue and cost of repairs: Reviews repair request and compares request with previous work accomplished on ship concerned and similar vessels to determine that expenditures are economically sound. Prepares recommendations for work, and initiates procurement of materials. Inspects machinery, equipment, or spaces outlined in work request, draws up job specifications, and obtains bids from contractors or shipyards to perform repairs. Maintains contact with contractors to ensure completion of work at minimum cost. Investigates machinery casualties to determine cause, and advises ship's officers in methods of operation to prevent recurrence of casualty or maloperation. Maintains records of engineering costs for each vessel, such as repairs, supplies, and personnel. Cooperates with regulatory bodies to ensure that requirements for alterations, repair, or modifications are kept at minimum cost consistent with safety. May represent ferry system interests in ferry and terminal construction and maintenance activities, and in union contract negotiations.
GOE: 05.01.06 STRENGTH: S GED: R5 M4 L3 SVP: 8 DLU: 77

014.281-010 DRAFTER, MARINE (profess. & kin.)
Draws structural and mechanical features of ships, docks, and other marine structures and equipment, performing duties of DRAFTER (profess. & kin.) Master Title. Works from general design drawings and notes made by ARCHITECT, MARINE (profess. & kin.) or MARINE ENGINEER (profess. & kin.).
GOE: 05.03.02 STRENGTH: S GED: R5 M5 L4 SVP: 7 DLU: 77

015   NUCLEAR ENGINEERING OCCUPATIONS

This group includes occupations concerned with the reasearch, development, and application of scientific knowledge of nuclear reactions and radiations, and principles of engineering applied to the production of heat and power, transmutation of elements, and production of neutrons, gamma radiation, and radioisotopes.

015.021-010 HEALTH PHYSICIST (profess. & kin.)
Devises and directs research, training, and monitoring programs to protect plant and laboratory personnel from radiation hazards: Conducts research to develop inspection standards, radiation exposure limits for personnel, safe work methods, and decontamination procedures, and tests surrounding areas to ensure that radiation is not in excess of permissible standards. Develops criteria for design and modification of health physics equipment, such as detectors and counters, to improve radiation protection. Assists in developing standards of permissible concentrations of radioisotopes in liquids and gases. Directs testing and monitoring of equipment and recording of personnel and plant area radiation exposure data. Requests bioassay samples from individuals believed to be exposed. Consults with scientific personnel regarding new experiments to determine that equipment or plant design conforms to health physics standards for protection of personnel. Conducts research pertaining to potential environmental impact of proposed atomic energy related industrial development to determine qualifications for licensing. Requisitions and maintains inventory of instruments. Instructs personnel in principles and regulations related to radiation hazards. Assigns film badges and dosimeters to personnel, and recommends changes in assignment for health reasons. Advises public authorities on methods of dealing with radiation hazards, and procedures to be followed in radiation incidents, and assists in civil defense planning. May specialize in research concerning decontamination of radioactive equipment and work areas in nuclear plants, laboratories, and other facilities and be designated Nuclear-Decontamination Research Specialist (profess. & kin.).
GOE: 05.01.02 STRENGTH: L GED: R6 M5 L5 SVP: 8 DLU: 81

015.061-010 DESIGN ENGINEER, NUCLEAR EQUIPMENT (profess. & kin.)
Designs nuclear machinery and equipment, performing duties as described under DESIGN ENGINEER, PRODUCTS (profess. & kin.) Master Title.
GOE: 05.01.07 STRENGTH: L GED: R5 M5 L5 SVP: 8 DLU: 77

015.061-014 NUCLEAR ENGINEER (profess. & kin.)
Conducts research into problems of nuclear energy systems; designs and develops nuclear equipment; and monitors testing, operation, and maintenance of

nuclear reactors: Plans and conducts nuclear research to discover facts or to test, prove, or modify known nuclear theories concerning release, control, and utilization of nuclear energy. Evaluates findings to develop new concepts of thermonuclear analysis and new uses of radioactive processes. Plans, designs, and develops nuclear equipment such as reactor cores, radiation shielding, and associated instrumentation and control mechanisms. Studies nuclear fuel cycle to define most economical uses of nuclear material and safest means of waste products disposal. Monitors nuclear tests and examines operations of facilities which process or utilize radioactive or fissionable material to ensure efficient functioning and conformance with safety specifications, regulations, and laws. Prepares technical reports, utilizing knowledge obtained during research and development activities and inspectional functions. May direct operating and maintenance activities of operational nuclear facility.
GOE: 05.01.03 STRENGTH: S GED: R6 M6 L5 SVP: 8 DLU: 77

015.061-018 RESEARCH ENGINEER, NUCLEAR EQUIPMENT (profess. & kin.)
Conducts research on nuclear equipment and machinery, performing duties as described under RESEARCH ENGINEER (profess. & kin.) Master Title.
GOE: 05.01.01 STRENGTH: L GED: R5 M5 L5 SVP: 8 DLU: 77

015.061-022 TEST ENGINEER, NUCLEAR EQUIPMENT (profess. & kin.)
Conducts tests on nuclear machinery and equipment, performing duties as described under TEST ENGINEER (profess. & kin.) Master Title.
GOE: 05.01.04 STRENGTH: L GED: R5 M5 L5 SVP: 8 DLU: 77

015.061-026 NUCLEAR-FUELS RECLAMATION ENGINEER (profess. & kin.)
Plans, designs, and oversees construction and operation of nuclear fuels reprocessing systems: Performs research and experiments to determine acceptable methods of reclaiming various types of nuclear fuels. Designs nuclear fuel reclamation systems and equipment for pilot plants. Communicates with vendors and contractors, and computes cost estimates of reclamation systems. Writes project proposals and submits them to company review board. Studies safety procedures, guidelines, and controls, and confers with safety officials to ensure that safety limits are not violated in design, construction, or operation of systems and equipment. Oversees nuclear fuels reprocessing system construction and operation, conferring with construction supervisory and operating personnel. Tests system equipment and approves equipment for operation. Monitors operations to detect potential or inherent problems. Initiates corrective actions and orders plant shutdown in emergency situations. Identifies operational and processing problems and recommends solutions. Maintains log of plant operations, and prepares reports for review by plant officials.
GOE: 05.01.03 STRENGTH: L GED: R6 M5 L5 SVP: 7 DLU: 86

015.061-030 NUCLEAR-FUELS RESEARCH ENGINEER (profess. & kin.)
Studies behavior of various fuels and fuel configurations in differentiated reactor environments to determine safest and most efficient usage of nuclear fuels, applying theoretical and experiential knowledge of reactor physics and thermal and metallurgical characteristics of nuclear fuels and fuel cell claddings: Analyzes available data and consults with other scientists to determine parameters of experimentation and suitability of analytical models. Designs fuels behavior tests and coordinates activities of experimental research team in performance and analysis of test operations. Monitors test reactor indicators of factors such as neutron power level, coolant level, and vital pressure, temperature and humidity readings, and changes or modifies procedures to meet test goals. Synthesizes analyses of test results and prepares technical reports to disseminate findings and recommendations. Formulates equations that describe phenomena occurring during fissioning of nuclear fuels and develops analytical models for nuclear fuels research.
GOE: 05.01.03 STRENGTH: L GED: R6 M6 L6 SVP: 8 DLU: 86

015.067-010 NUCLEAR-CRITICALITY SAFETY ENGINEER (profess. & kin.)
Conducts research and analyzes and evaluates proposed and existing methods of transportation, handling, and storage of nuclear fuel to preclude accidental nuclear reaction at nuclear facilities: Reviews and evaluates fuel transfer and storage plans received from nuclear plants. Studies reports of nuclear fuel characteristics to determine potential or inherent problems. Reads blueprints of proposed storage facilities and visits storage sites to determine adequacy of storage plans. Forecasts nuclear fuel criticality (point at which nuclear chain reaction becomes self-sustaining), given various factors which may exist in fuel handling and storage, using knowledge of nuclear physics, calculator, and computer terminal. Determines potential hazards and accident conditions which may exist in fuel handling and storage and recommends preventive measures. Summarizes findings and writes reports. Confers with project officials to resolve situations where hazard is beyond acceptable levels. Prepares proposal reports for handling and storage of fuels to be submitted to government review board. Studies existing procedures and recommends changes or additions to guidelines and controls to ensure prevention of self-sustaining nuclear chain reaction.
GOE: 05.01.02 STRENGTH: L GED: R6 M6 L5 SVP: 8 DLU: 86

015.137-010 RADIATION-PROTECTION ENGINEER (profess. & kin.)
Supervises and coordinates activities of workers engaged in monitoring radiation levels and condition of equipment used to generate nuclear energy to ensure safe operation of plant facilities: Evaluates water chemical analysis data

in primary and supportive plant systems to determine compliance with radiation content and corrosion control regulations. Investigates problems, such as radioactive leaks in reactors and auxiliary systems, or excessive radiation or corrosion of equipment, applying knowledge of radiation protection techniques and principles of chemistry and engineering to correct conditions. Confers with departmental supervisors, manufacturing representatives, and regulatory agency staff to discuss problems, to develop tests to detect radioactive leaks, and to design plans to monitor equipment and safety programs. Directs workers in testing and analyzing water samples and monitoring processing system. Prepares reports, such as environmental monitoring operation report, radioactive waste releases, and shipping reports, for review by administrative personnel and submission to regulatory agency. May prepare employee performance reviews and related reports.
GOE: 05.01.02 STRENGTH: L GED: R5 M4 L5 SVP: 8 DLU: 86

015.151-010 SALES ENGINEER, NUCLEAR EQUIPMENT (profess. & kin.)
Sells nuclear machinery and equipment and provides technical services to client, performing duties as described under SALES ENGINEER (profess. & kin.) Master Title.
GOE: 05.01.05 STRENGTH: L GED: R5 M5 L5 SVP: 8 DLU: 77

015.167-010 NUCLEAR-PLANT TECHNICAL ADVISOR (utilities)
Monitors plant safety status, advises operations staff, and prepares technical reports for operation of thermal-nuclear reactor at electric-power generating station: Observes control-room instrumentation systems and confers with operating personnel to ensure safe operation of plant. Walks throughout plant and observes machinery, equipment, and operating procedures to identify potential hazards. Examines locations of accidents and transients (sudden changes of voltage or load) and obtains data to formulate preventive measures. Implements changes in systems, procedures, structure, or equipment to improve safety. Compares critical parameters with plant transient predictions and accident analysis and determines whether response of plant safety systems is sufficient. Formulates corrective actions, calculates critical parameters from raw data, and computes rate of control rod withdrawal during reactor startup. Confers with operating personnel to provide technical assistance and to discuss maintenance activities, abnormal conditions, and safe operation of plant. Prepares reports to inform management officials of any proposed changes or irregularities in plant operation or systems.
GOE: 05.01.02 STRENGTH: L GED: R6 M5 L5 SVP: 8 DLU: 86

015.167-014 NUCLEAR-TEST-REACTOR PROGRAM COORDINATOR (profess. & kin.)
Evaluates, coordinates, and oversees testing of nuclear reactor equipment: Analyzes test proposal to ensure that test is valid and feasible. Identifies and resolves problems, such as incompatibilities between proposal and nuclear test-reactor system. Coordinates technical and financial agreements involving feasibility, scope, purpose, and cost of project in nuclear test facility. Assists engineering personnel in interpretation of test language, mathematical formulas, and computer codes used in test. Writes operational instructions. Inspects general condition of nuclear test-reactor vessel and related systems. Verifies setup of nuclear test-reactor for compliance with specifications. Observes control room instrumentation to ensure that performance factors such as neutron power level, chemical composition of coolant, and reactor temperatures and pressures are carried out as prescribed. Evaluates and resolves operational problems. Coordinates activities directed toward removal of test specimens from reactors and subsequent chemical, metallurgical, or mechanical analysis. Compiles report of test results.
GOE: 05.01.04 STRENGTH: L GED: R5 M5 L5 SVP: 8 DLU: 86

015.261-010 CHEMICAL-RADIATION TECHNICIAN (government ser.)
Tests materials and monitors operations of nuclear-powered electric generating plant, using specialized laboratory equipment and chemical and radiation detection instruments: Collects samples of water, gases, and solids at specified intervals during production process, using automatic sampling equipment. Analyzes materials, according to specified procedures, to determine if chemical components and radiation levels are within established limits. Records test results and prepares reports for review by supervisor. Assists workers to set up equipment and monitors equipment that automatically detects deviations from standard operations. Notifies personnel to adjust processing equipment, quantity of additives, and rate of discharge of waste materials, when test results and monitoring of equipment indicate that radiation levels, chemical balance, and discharge of radionuclide materials are in excess of standards. Carries out decontamination procedures to ensure safety of workers and continued operation of processing equipment in plant. Calibrates and maintains chemical instrumentation sensing elements and sampling system equipment, using handtools. Assists workers in diagnosis and correction of problems in instruments and processing equipment. Advises plant personnel of methods of protection from excessive exposure to radiation.
GOE: 11.10.03 STRENGTH: L GED: R4 M3 L3 SVP: 6 DLU: 86

015.362-010 ACCELERATOR OPERATOR (profess. & kin.)
Controls operation of particle accelerator used in research experiments involving properties of subatomic particles: Reviews experiment schedule to ascertain particle beam parameters specified by experimenter (scientist), such as energy, intensity, and repetition rate. Communicates with accelerator maintenance personnel to ensure readiness of support systems, such as vacuum, water

cooling, and radiofrequency power source. Sets control panel switches, according to standard procedures, to route electric power from source and direct particle beam through injector unit. Turns panel controls and watches meters and panel lights to adjust beam steering units and direct beam to accelerator. Pushes console buttons in prescribed sequence to control beam path in accelerator. Adjusts controls to increase beam pulse rate, energy, and intensity to specified levels. Notifies experimenter in target control room when beam parameters meet specifications. Pushes control levers to steer beam to experimenter's target, as directed. Monitors readings at console during experiment to ensure accelerator systems meet specifications and notifies experimenter of condition. Alters beam parameters during experiment as directed. Ensures that maintenance workers vacate hazardous locations before operations. Records data in log relative to beam specifications, equipment settings used, and beam conditions obtained for future reference. Participates in maintenance and modification of systems as member of team. May be designated according to type of accelerator operated.
GOE: 02.04.01 STRENGTH: L GED: R5 M4 L5 SVP: 7 DLU: 77

015.362-014 GAMMA-FACILITIES OPERATOR (profess. & kin.) alternate titles: pile operator; reactor-service operator
Controls gamma radiation equipment to irradiate materials for scientific research: Inserts capsules of materials to be irradiated into tubes leading to reactor core, using extension tool. Computes radiation time and dosage for experiments, and gamma intensities required at various distances from grid, using standard formulas, conversion tables, and slide rule, and submits data to supervisor for review. Tends cutoff saw, mounted on water-filled canal floor (radiation shield), that cuts fuel elements to size to fit into shielding boxes, using extension tools. Places fuel elements in geometric configurations around tube in gamma facility according to radiation intensity specifications. Lowers experimental materials, such as foods, plastics, or metal, into tube to subject material to irradiation for specified period of time. Lowers extension tool into floor of canal and transfers materials from completed experiments, and spent fuel elements discharged from reactor, to storage area on canal floor or into cask for subsequent shipment. Writes summary of irradiation activities performed. Monitors instruments and gauges that control heating, ventilating, steam, and water systems, and instruments that record gamma intensity, temperatures of experiments, and fuel elements in canal.
GOE: 02.04.01 STRENGTH: M GED: R4 M4 L4 SVP: 7 DLU: 77

015.362-018 HOT-CELL TECHNICIAN (profess. & kin.) alternate titles: irradiation technician
Operates remote-controlled equipment in hot cell to conduct metallurgical and chemical tests on radioactive materials: Controls slave manipulators from outside cell to remove metal or chemical materials from shielded containers inside hot cell and places on bench or equipment work station. Tests chemical or metallurgical properties of materials according to standardized procedures, and observes reaction through cell window. Sets up and operates machines to cut, lap, and polish test pieces, following blueprints, x-ray negatives, and sketches. Tests physical properties, using equipment, such as tensile tester, hardness tester, metallographic unit, micrometer, and gauges. Immerses test sample in chemical compound to prepare for testing. Places irradiated nuclear fuel materials in environmental chamber to test reaction to temperature changes. Records results of tests for further analysis by engineers, scientists, or customers. Places specimen in shielded container for removal from cell, using manipulators. Participates in cleaning and decontamination of cell during maintenance shutdown. May devise adapters and fixtures for use in hot cell operations.
GOE: 02.04.01 STRENGTH: L GED: R4 M3 L4 SVP: 7 DLU: 77

015.362-022 RADIOISOTOPE-PRODUCTION OPERATOR (profess. & kin.) alternate titles: isotope-production technician
Controls laboratory compounding equipment enclosed in protective hot cell to prepare radioisotopes and other radioactive materials for use as tracers for biological, biomedical, physiological, and industrial purposes according to written procedures: Places specified amounts of chemicals into container to be irradiated at nuclear reactor or with other irradiation equipment. Secures vacuum pump head to outlet valve on special container to replace air with inert gas, and routes container to irradiation facility. Receives irradiated chemicals delivered in shielded cell. Moves manipulator to open container and transfer irradiated contents into glass vessel. Opens pneumatic valves or uses manipulators to add specified types and quantities of chemical reagents into glass vessel to produce radioactive product. Controls manipulators to pour liquids required to perform standard chemical analyses involving titration and filtration. Withdraws radioactive sample for transport to chemical laboratory for analysis. Fills shipping container inside cell with prescribed quantity of radioisotope material for shipment pending sample approval.
GOE: 02.04.01 STRENGTH: L GED: R4 M3 L4 SVP: 6 DLU: 77

015.362-026 REACTOR OPERATOR, TEST-AND-RESEARCH (profess. & kin.)
Controls operation of nuclear reactor to create fissionable materials used for research purposes, study structure of atoms, and determine properties of materials: Positions fuel elements (uranium) and object to be irradiated in position in reactor core, using slave manipulators. Installs instrumentation leads in core to measure operating temperature and pressure in reactor working from mockups, blueprints, and wiring and instrumentation diagrams. Activates reactor and inserts object to be irradiated into rabbit (pneumatic) tube, beam hole, or irradiation tunnel according to size of object and nature of experiment. Mon-

itors instruments at console and reactor panels to control chain reaction, following directions of nuclear experimenters. Calculates applicable limits of operating factors, such as temperature and pressure, using standard formulas, and adjusts controls to maintain operating conditions, such as power level, airflow and waterflow, temperature, and radiation and neutron levels in reactor within operating limits. Records data, such as type of material irradiated, exposure time, pile atmospheric conditions, and position of control rods in core. Disassembles reactor parts, such as core plug (shield) and control rods, using crane and handtools. Lifts spent fuel elements and irradiated objects from core, using extension tool, and drops them through chute into canal for recovery of fissionable material. May work as member of team and alternate between operating reactor controls and monitoring instruments, gauges, and other recording devices in control room.
GOE: 02.04.01 STRENGTH: L GED: R4 M4 L4 SVP: 7 DLU: 77

015.384-010 SCANNER (profess. & kin.)
Compiles lists of events (collisions of atomic nuclei) from photographs of bubble chamber, cloud chamber, or other particle detector, and operates machine to record characteristics of events into computers: Observes projected photographs to locate particle tracks, locate and count events indicated by tracks, and identify nature of observed events. Receives instructions from scientist directing project as to specific events that are important in experiment, and identifies such events from other events. Turns cranks to move projector and locates point on track under crosshairs of eyepiece. Enters data into computer to record coordinates of particles. Repeats process to record successive stages of tracks resulting from each event to provide information for scientists to identify particles. May use microscope fitted with scales and protractors to scan photographic emulsions previously exposed to direct radiation and to compute direction, angle, length, curvature, density, and depth of tracks from standard formulas.
GOE: 02.04.01 STRENGTH: S GED: R4 M3 L4 SVP: 6 DLU: 77

017   DRAFTERS, N.E.C.

This group includes occupations, not elsewhere classified, concerned with preparing drawings used to communicate engineering ideas and information.

017.161-010 DRAFTER, CHIEF, DESIGN (utilities)
Oversees DRAFTERS, ARCHITECTURAL (profess. & kin.); DRAFTERS, ELECTRICAL (profess. & kin.); DRAFTERS, MECHANICAL (profess. & kin.); and DRAFTERS, STRUCTURAL (profess. & kin.) in drawing designs of indoor and outdoor facilities and structures of electrical or gas power plants and substations. Consults with engineering staff on development of plans and designs for buildings and installations and prepares layout diagrams to ensure accurate interpretation of designs by workers supervised.
GOE: 05.03.02 STRENGTH: L GED: R5 M5 L5 SVP: 8 DLU: 77

017.261-010 AUTO-DESIGN CHECKER (auto. mfg.) alternate titles: checker, product design
Examines detail, layout, and master drawings of either auto-body or chassis parts, assemblies, and systems, for practicality of design, accuracy of mathematical calculations, dimensional accuracy, projection, and conformity to specifications and standards, using computerized work aids. Applies knowledge of auto-body and chassis design, methods of manufacture and assembly, and drafting techniques and procedures. Discusses necessary changes with staff members and coordinates corrections.
GOE: 05.03.02 STRENGTH: L GED: R5 M4 L4 SVP: 8 DLU: 90

017.261-014 DESIGN DRAFTER, ELECTROMECHANISMS (profess. & kin.)
Drafts designs of electromechanical equipment such as aircraft engine subassemblies, electronic optical-character-recognition and related data processing systems, gyroscopes, rocket engine control systems, automatic materials handling and processing machinery, or bio-medical equipment: Confers with engineers and other drafters to interpret design concepts, determine nature and type of required detailed working drawings, and coordinate work with others. Drafts detail and assembly drawings performing duties described under DRAFTER (profess. & kin.) Master Title. Compiles data, computes quantities, determines materials needed, and prepares cost estimates.
GOE: 05.03.02 STRENGTH: S GED: R5 M5 L4 SVP: 7 DLU: 77

017.261-018 DETAILER (profess. & kin.)
Drafts detailed drawings of parts of machines or structures from rough or general design drawings: Shows dimensions, material to be used, and other information necessary to make detailed drawing clear and complete. Makes tracing of finished drawing on semitransparent paper from which blueprints can be made. Performs other duties as described under DRAFTER (profess. & kin.) Master Title. May specialize in preparing detail drawings for specific type of machine, structure, or product.
GOE: 05.03.02 STRENGTH: S GED: R4 M4 L4 SVP: 7 DLU: 77

017.261-022 DETAILER, FURNITURE (profess. & kin.)
Prepares detailed shop drawings in scale or full size, from blueprints of FURNITURE DESIGNER (furniture), showing methods of construction and upholstering, and indicating sizes and kinds of material to be used. Performs other duties as described under DRAFTER (profess. & kin.) Master Title.
GOE: 05.03.02 STRENGTH: L GED: R4 M4 L4 SVP: 7 DLU: 77

017.261-026 DRAFTER, COMMERCIAL (profess. & kin.)
Performs general duties of DRAFTER (profess. & kin.) Master Title in all-round drafting, such as laying out location of buildings, planning of arrangements in offices, large rooms, store buildings, and factories, and drawing of charts, forms, and records. Paints and washes colored drawings when required.
GOE: 05.03.02 STRENGTH: S GED: R5 M5 L4 SVP: 6 DLU: 77

017.261-030 DRAFTER, DETAIL (profess. & kin.)
Makes detailed drawings, in accordance with customers' orders, to provide shop departments with accurate information for manufacture of structural and ornamental construction parts: Confers with customers. Makes freehand sketches of designs and drawings of approved sketches. Advises supervisory personnel on difficult or obscure problems.
GOE: 05.03.02 STRENGTH: S GED: R4 M4 L4 SVP: 7 DLU: 77

017.261-034 DRAFTER, HEATING AND VENTILATING (profess. & kin.)
Draws plans for installation of heating, air-conditioning, and ventilating equipment, performing duties of DRAFTER (profess. & kin.) Master Title. May calculate heat loss and heat gain for buildings for use in determining equipment specifications, using calculator and following standardized procedures. May specialize in drawing plans for installation of refrigeration equipment only and be designated Drafter, Refrigeration (profess. & kin.).
GOE: 05.03.02 STRENGTH: S GED: R5 M5 L4 SVP: 7 DLU: 77

017.261-038 DRAFTER, PLUMBING (profess. & kin.)
Performs duties of DRAFTER (profess. & kin.) Master Title but specializes in drawing of plans for installation of plumbing equipment.
GOE: 05.03.02 STRENGTH: S GED: R5 M5 L4 SVP: 7 DLU: 77

017.261-042 DRAFTER, AUTOMOTIVE DESIGN (auto. mfg.)
Designs and drafts working layouts and master drawings of automotive vehicle components, assemblies, and systems from specifications, sketches, models, prototype or verbal instructions, applying knowledge of automotive vehicle design, engineering principles, manufacturing processes and limitations, and conventional and computer drafting techniques and procedures, using drafting instruments and computerized work aids: Analyzes specifications, sketches, engineering drawings, ideas and related design data to determine critical factors affecting design of components based on knowledge of previous designs and manufacturing processes and limitations. Draws rough sketches and performs mathematical computations to develop design and work out detailed specifications of components. Applies knowledge of mathematical formulas and physical laws and uses conventional and computerized work aids to make calculations. Performs preliminary and advanced work in development of working layouts and final master drawings adequate for detailing parts and units of design. Makes revisions to size, shape and arrangement of parts to create practical design. Confers with AUTOMOTIVE ENGINEER (auto. mfg.) 007.061-010 and others on staff to resolve design problems. Specializes in design of specific type of body or chassis components, assemblies or systems, such as door panels, chassis frame and supports, or braking system.
GOE: 05.03.02 STRENGTH: L GED: R5 M4 L4 SVP: 7 DLU: 90

017.281-010 AUTO-DESIGN DETAILER (auto. mfg.)
Drafts full-size or scale detail drawings of either auto-body or chassis parts and assemblies from specifications, master drawings, layouts, models, prototypes, sketches, or verbal instructions, for engineering and manufacturing purposes [DRAFTER (profess. & kin.) Master Title], applying knowledge of auto-body or chassis structure and methods of manufacture and assembly.
GOE: 05.03.02 STRENGTH: L GED: R4 M4 L3 SVP: 6 DLU: 90

017.281-014 DRAFTER APPRENTICE (profess. & kin.)
Performs duties as described under APPRENTICE (any industry) Master Title.
GOE: 05.03.02 STRENGTH: S GED: R5 M5 L4 SVP: 6 DLU: 77

017.281-018 DRAFTER, ASSISTANT (profess. & kin.)
Copies plans and drawings prepared by DRAFTER (profess. & kin.) Master Title by tracing them with ink and pencil on transparent paper or cloth spread over drawings, using triangle, T-square, compass, pens, and other drafting instruments. Makes simple sketches or drawings under close supervision.
GOE: 05.03.02 STRENGTH: S GED: R4 M4 L3 SVP: 7 DLU: 77

017.281-026 DRAFTER, AUTOMOTIVE DESIGN LAYOUT (auto. mfg.)
Prepares working layouts and master drawings of automotive vehicle components, assemblies, or systems from specifications, prior layouts, well-defined sketches, models or verbal instructions sufficient for detailing, applying knowledge of conventional and computerized drafting techniques and procedures, automotive vehicle design, manufacturing processes and limitations, using conventional drafting instruments and computerized work aids: Studies specifications, sketches, notes, and other design data and measures prior layouts, using scales and dividers, to determine details and dimensions of components being laid out from superimposed views and sections of parts on layouts. Lays out on vellum major or minor components, assemblies, or systems in full-scale working layouts. Performs mathematical calculations to work out detailed additions to specifications, applying knowledge of mathematical formulas, using slide rule or digital calculators. Develops design of details not completely defined. Projects sections and auxiliary views of components on layouts. Makes corrections, revisions, and changes to layouts as directed by AUTO-DESIGN CHECKER (auto. mfg.) 017.261-010 or DRAFTER, AUTOMOTIVE DESIGN

(auto. mfg.) 017.261-042. Drafts master drawing of approved design on mylar, aluminum, or other materials. Specializes in laying out specific type of body or chassis components, assemblies, or systems. Coordinates and works in conjunction with other workers designing, laying out, or detailing same or related structures. May direct activities of detailers.
GOE: 05.03.02 STRENGTH: L GED: R4 M4 L3 SVP: 7 DLU: 90

017.281-030 DRAFTER, OIL AND GAS (petrol. & gas; petrol. refin.)
Drafts plans and drawings for layout, construction, and operation of oil fields, refineries, and pipeline systems from field notes, rough or detailed sketches, and specifications: Develops detail drawings for construction of equipment and structures, such as drilling derricks, compressor stations, gasoline plants, frame, steel, and masonry buildings, piping manifolds and pipeline systems, and for manufacture, fabrication, and assembly of machines and machine parts [DRAFTER, ARCHITECTURAL (profess. & kin.); DRAFTER, CIVIL (profess. & kin.); DRAFTER, MECHANICAL (profess. & kin.)]. Prepares maps of pipeline systems and oil and gas locations, using field survey notes and aerial photographs [DRAFTER, CARTOGRAPHIC (profess. & kin.)]. May draft topographical maps or develop maps to represent geological stratigraphy and locations of oil and gas deposits, using geological and geophysical prospecting and surveying data [DRAFTER, GEOLOGICAL (petrol. & gas); DRAFTER, GEOPHYSICAL (petrol. & gas)].
GOE: 05.03.02 STRENGTH: L GED: R4 M4 L3 SVP: 7 DLU: 77

017.281-034 TECHNICAL ILLUSTRATOR (profess. & kin.) alternate titles: engineering illustrator; production illustrator
Lays out and draws illustrations for reproduction in reference works, brochures, and technical manuals dealing with assembly, installation, operation, maintenance, and repair of machines, tools, and equipment: Prepares drawings from blueprints, designs, mockups, and photoprints by methods and techniques suited to specified reproduction process or final use, such as blueprint, photo-offset, and projection transparencies, using drafting and optical equipment. Lays out and draws schematic, perspective, orthographic, or oblique-angle views to depict function, relationship, and assembly-sequence of parts and assemblies, such as gears, engines, and instruments. Shades or colors drawing to emphasize details or to eliminate undesired background, using ink, crayon, airbrush, and overlays. Pastes instructions and comments in position on drawing. May draw cartoons and caricatures to illustrate operation, maintenance, and safety manuals and posters.
GOE: 05.03.02 STRENGTH: S GED: R5 M5 L4 SVP: 7 DLU: 77

017.684-010 TAPER, PRINTED CIRCUIT LAYOUT (electron. comp.)
Places (tapes) adhesive symbols and precision tape on sheets of mylar in conformance with preliminary drawing of printed circuit board (PCB) to produce master layout: Places, aligns, and secures preliminary drawing of PCB and successive layers of transparent sheets of mylar on lighted drafting table, using register bar. Selects specified symbols and width of tape to indicate peak voltage potential. Cuts tape and places tape and adhesive symbols on specified sheets of mylar to outline board size, to indicate connector pads, placement of various components, and to trace circuitry of PCB as indicated on underlying preliminary drawing, using utility knife, precision grid, and straightedge. Places specified adhesive identification and reference numbers on master layout. Reproduces blueprint copy of master layout, using print machine. Inspects copy to verify accuracy.
GOE: 05.03.02 STRENGTH: S GED: R2 M2 L2 SVP: 2 DLU: 86

018   SURVEYING/CARTOGRAPHIC OCCUPATIONS

This group includes occupations concerned with determining, delineating, planning, and positioning tracts of land, natural and constructed features, coastlines, and land areas. Typical specialized surveys include property, cartography, construction, geodesy, hydrography, mining, photogrammetry, topography, land development, and mapping.

018.131-010 SUPERVISOR, CARTOGRAPHY (profess. & kin.)
Supervises and coordinates activities of DRAFTERS, CARTOGRAPHIC (profess. & kin.); PHOTOGRAMMETRISTS (profess. & kin.); and other personnel concerned with preparation of maps or map components: Develops design concept of map product. Defines production specifications, such as projection, scale, size, and colors. Provides guidelines for source material to be used, such as maps, automated mapping products, photographs, survey data, and place names. Supervises and coordinates compilation and editing of product components and monitors reproduction. Performs other duties as described under SUPERVISOR (any industry) Master Title.
GOE: 05.03.02 STRENGTH: S GED: R5 M5 L5 SVP: 8 DLU: 77

018.161-010 SURVEYOR, MINE (profess. & kin.)
Conducts surveys at surface and subsurface mine sites to obtain data used in planning mining operations: Takes instrument readings of sun or stars and calculates longitude and latitude to determine mine location. Directs survey technicians and helpers [SURVEYOR HELPER (any industry) 869.567-010] in use of electronic surveying equipment, light emitting systems, or other instruments to transfer surface survey positions and directions to underground areas and to survey assigned sections. Computes data necessary for driving and connecting underground passages to control direction and extent of mining operation. Computes volume of coal or ore in portions of mine, using survey data. Surveys and calculates volume of material deposits, spoil piles, or veins, and

amount of overburden to be removed. Drafts or directs others to draft maps of survey data. May assist MINE SUPERINTENDENT (mine & quarry) 181.117-014 and MINING ENGINEER (mine & quarry) 101.061-014 in planning mining operations. May conduct surveys of tunnels, subway sites, and underground storage facilities.
GOE: 05.03.01 STRENGTH: L GED: R5 M5 L4 SVP: 7 DLU: 80

018.167-010   CHIEF OF PARTY (profess. & kin.)
Leads work of survey party under direction of LAND SURVEYOR (profess. & kin.), performing surveying duties not requiring licensure.
GOE: 05.03.01 STRENGTH: L GED: R5 M5 L4 SVP: 7 DLU: 77

018.167-014   GEODETIC COMPUTATOR (profess. & kin.) alternate titles: topographic computator
Calculates latitude, longitude, angles, areas, and other information for map-making from field notes secured by engineering survey party, using reference tables and calculating machine or computer.
GOE: 05.03.01 STRENGTH: S GED: R5 M5 L4 SVP: 6 DLU: 77

018.167-018   LAND SURVEYOR (profess. & kin.)
Plans, organizes, and directs work of one or more survey parties engaged in surveying earth's surface to determine precise location and measurements of points, elevations, lines, areas, and contours for construction, mapmaking, land division, titles, mining or other purposes: Researches previous survey evidence, maps, deeds, physical evidence, and other records to obtain data needed for surveys. Develops new data from photogrammetric records. Determines methods and procedures for establishing or reestablishing survey control. Keeps accurate notes, records, and sketches to describe and certify work performed. Coordinates findings with work of engineering and architectural personnel, clients, and others concerned with project. Assumes legal responsibility for work and is licensed by state.
GOE: 05.01.06 STRENGTH: L GED: R5 M5 L4 SVP: 7 DLU: 77

018.167-022   MANAGER, LAND SURVEYING (profess. & kin.)
Plans, directs, and coordinates work of survey parties, and related staff, engaged in surveying earth's surface and preparing reports and legal descriptions of land: Develops organization policy or interprets it to staff. Prepares or approves budget for unit or organization within assigned area of responsibility. Coordinates work of LAND SURVEYOR (profess. & kin.) with that of legal, engineering, architectural, and other staff on project. Directs survey parties and projects, and reviews and certifies completed work to satisfy legal requirements. Writes or directs the writing of descriptions of land to satisfy legal requirements according to standard surveying practices. Appears as expert witness in court in cases involving land or boundary disputes. Monitors new technology, and evaluates and purchases or authorizes purchase of new equipment and supplies. Selects new staff for employment and takes disciplinary action when necessary. Assumes legal responsibility for work performed and is licensed by state.
GOE: 05.02.06 STRENGTH: L GED: R5 M5 L4 SVP: 8 DLU: 77

018.167-026   PHOTOGRAMMETRIC ENGINEER (profess. & kin.)
Plans, coordinates, and directs activities of workers concerned with conducting aerial surveys and preparing topographic materials from aerial photographs and other data: Analyzes survey objectives and specifications, utilizing knowledge of survey uses, such as municipal and ecological planning, property and utility mapping, and petroleum and mineral exploration. Selects most appropriate and economical survey methods, using knowledge of capabilities of aerial photography and applications of remote sensing (imagery through electronic scanning). Estimates cost of survey. Advises customers and department supervisors regarding flights for aerial photography and plans for ground surveys designed to establish base lines, elevations, and other geodetic measurements. Prepares charts and tables for aerial navigation, to specify flight path, altitude, and airspeed of camera-carrying aircraft. Computes geodetic measurements and interprets survey data from ground or aerial photographs or remote-sensing images to determine position, shape, and elevation of geomorphic and topographic features. Conducts research in surveying and mapping methods and procedures, using knowledge of techniques of photogrammetric map compilation, electronic data processing, and flight and control planning. May direct one or more phases of technical operations concerned with preparing survey proposals, negotiating with clients, scheduling activities, conducting surveys, processing data, reviewing work quality, and training and assigning personnel.
GOE: 05.03.01 STRENGTH: S GED: R6 M6 L5 SVP: 8 DLU: 77

018.167-030   SUPERVISOR, MAPPING (petrol. & gas; pipe lines)
Supervises and coordinates activities of workers engaged in mapping production areas of petroleum or natural gas company: Supervises drafting personnel in drafting maps used for exploration, leasing of lands, and construction and operation of production facilities, such as pumping stations, storage tanks, drilling derricks, and pipelines. Reviews completed maps for neatness and accuracy. May supervise production of blueprints, photostats, and photographs.
GOE: 05.03.02 STRENGTH: S GED: R4 M4 L4 SVP: 7 DLU: 77

018.167-034   SURVEYOR ASSISTANT, INSTRUMENTS (profess. & kin.)
Obtains data pertaining to angles, elevations, points, and contours used for construction, map making, mining, or other purposes, using alidade, level, transit, plane table, Theodolite, electronic distance measuring equipment, and other surveying instruments. Compiles notes, sketches, and records of data obtained and work performed. Directs work of subordinate members of survey team. Performs other duties relating to surveying work as directed by CHIEF OF PARTY (profess. & kin.).

GOE: 05.03.01 STRENGTH: L GED: R5 M5 L4 SVP: 7 DLU: 77

018.167-038   SURVEYOR, GEODETIC (profess. & kin.)
Plans, directs, or conducts surveys of land areas of such size that shape and size of earth exerts sufficient influence on survey measurements to require use of special high-accuracy techniques, including astronomical observations and complex computations to compile data used in preparation of geodetic maps and charts.
GOE: 05.03.01 STRENGTH: L GED: R5 M5 L4 SVP: 7 DLU: 77

018.167-042   SURVEYOR, GEOPHYSICAL PROSPECTING (petrol. & gas)
Locates and marks sites selected for conducting geophysical prospecting activities concerned with locating subsurface earth formations likely to contain petroleum deposits. Makes precise determinations of elevations and records other characteristics of terrain. May obtain permits for prospecting from property owner.
GOE: 05.03.01 STRENGTH: L GED: R5 M4 L4 SVP: 6 DLU: 77

018.167-046   SURVEYOR, MARINE (profess. & kin.) alternate titles: surveyor, hydrographic
Makes surveys of harbors, rivers, and other bodies of water to determine shore lines, topography of bottom, or other items for such purposes as determining navigable channels, and securing data for construction of breakwaters, piers, and other marine structures.
GOE: 05.03.01 STRENGTH: M GED: R5 M5 L4 SVP: 7 DLU: 77

018.261-010   DRAFTER, CARTOGRAPHIC (profess. & kin.) alternate titles: map maker; mapper
Draws maps of geographical areas to show natural and constructed features, political boundaries, and other features, performing duties described under DRAFTER (profess. & kin.) Master Title: Analyzes survey data, source maps and photographs, computer or automated mapping products, and other records to determine location and names of features. Studies legal records to establish boundries of properties, and local, national, and international areas of political, economic, social, or other significance. Geological maps are drawn by DRAFTER, GEOLOGICAL (petrol. & gas).
GOE: 05.03.02 STRENGTH: S GED: R4 M4 L3 SVP: 7 DLU: 77

018.261-018   EDITOR, MAP (profess. & kin.)
Verifies accuracy and completeness of topographical maps from aerial photographs and specifications: Views photographs and other reference materials, such as old maps and records and examines corresponding area of map to verify correct identification of specified topographical features and accuracy of contour lines. Verifies correct location and accuracy of scaled distances between control points and reference lines. Examines reference materials to detect omission of topographical features, poor register, or other defects in photography or draftsmanship. Marks errors and makes corrections, such as numbering grid lines or lettering names of rivers or towns.
GOE: 05.03.02 STRENGTH: L GED: R4 M4 L4 SVP: 7 DLU: 77

018.261-022   MOSAICIST (profess. & kin.)
Lays out and matches aerial photographs to form photographic mosaic of geographic area for subsequent use in photogrammetric activities, such as topographical mapping: Lays out photographic prints on table according to sequence in which photographs were taken during flightpath of aircraft. Examines prints to locate established landmarks and notes absence of normal overlap of adjacent prints indicating deflection of aircraft from prescribed flightpath. Locates and marks specified reference points, such as structures and highway or rail junctions. Computes and measures scaled distances between reference points to establish exact relative position of adjoining prints. Trims excess from edges of overlapping prints and glues prints to backing board, maintaining scaled distances between reference points and alignment of adjoining prints.
GOE: 05.03.02 STRENGTH: S GED: R4 M4 L4 SVP: 7 DLU: 77

018.261-026   PHOTOGRAMMETRIST (profess. & kin.) alternate titles: cartographic technician
Analyzes source data and prepares mosaic prints, contour maps, profile sheets, and related cartographic materials requiring technical mastery of photogrammetric techniques and principles: Prepares original maps, charts, and drawings, from aerial photographs, and survey data and applies standard mathematical formulas and photogrammetric techniques to identify, scale, and orient geodetic points, elevations, and other planimetric or topographic features and cartographic detail. Graphically delineates aerial photographic detail, such as control points, hydrography, topography, and cultural features, using precision stereoplotting apparatus or drafting instruments. Revises existing maps and charts and corrects maps in various stages of compilation. May prepare rubber, plastic, or plaster three-dimensional relief models.
GOE: 05.03.02 STRENGTH: S GED: R4 M4 L4 SVP: 7 DLU: 77

018.262-010   FIELD-MAP EDITOR (profess. & kin.)
Identifies and verifies information shown on aerial photographs used in map making: Travels over photographed area to observe and record all cultural and drainage features shown and not shown on photograph. Verifies numbers, names, and classes of roads and highways, location and number of railroads, location of state and county lines, and location and identification of streams, rivers, lakes, schools, and major buildings. Marks observations on map overlay, using specified symbols. Determines elevation of hills, trees, and buildings, using geometry. Obtains boundary and other official information from county records. May use stereoscope to combine information from two aerial maps.

GOE: 05.03.02 STRENGTH: L GED: R4 M3 L3 SVP: 6 DLU: 77

018.281-010 STEREO-PLOTTER OPERATOR (profess. & kin.) alternate titles: stereo operator; stereoptic projection topographer

Draws topographical maps from aerial photographs, using instruments that produce simultaneous projections of two photographs, taken from different positions, in manner that permits steroscopic viewing for delineation of planimetric detail and drawing of contours: Orients plotting instruments to form three dimensional stereo image. Orients plotting instruments to form three dimensional stereo image. Views stereoscopic image by using anaglyphic, binocular, or image alternator techniques. Determines contour interval and vertical scale of image, using mathematical table. Traces contours and topographical details to produce map.

GOE: 05.03.02 STRENGTH: L GED: R4 M4 L4 SVP: 7 DLU: 77

019 OCCUPATIONS IN ARCHITECTURE, ENGINEERING, AND SURVEYING, N.E.C.

This group includes occupations, not elsewhere classified, concerned with the application of the theoretical and practical aspects of engineering and architecture.

019.061-010 BIOMEDICAL ENGINEER (profess. & kin.)

Conducts research into biological aspects of humans or other animals to develop new theories and facts, or test, prove, or modify known theories of life systems, and to design life-support apparatus, utilizing principles of engineering and bio-behavioral sciences: Plans and conducts research concerning behavioral, biological, psychological, or other life systems. Studies engineering aspects of bio-behavioral systems of humans, utilizing knowledge of electrical, mechanical, chemical, or other engineering principles and knowledge of human anatomy and physiology. Develops *mathematical models* to simulate human bio-behavioral systems in order to obtain data for measuring or controlling life processes, utilizing knowledge of computer, graphics, and other related technologies. Designs and develops instruments and devices, such as artificial organs, cardiac pacemakers, or ultrasonic imaging devices, capable of assisting medical or other health-care personnel in observing, repairing, or treating physical ailments or deformities, using knowledge of materials compatible with body tissues, energy exchanges within the body, and instrumentation capable of measuring and controlling body functions. May specialize in design and development of biomedical equipment used by medical facilities and be known as Clinical Engineer (profess. & kin.).

GOE: 02.02.01 STRENGTH: S GED: R6 M6 L5 SVP: 8 DLU: 77

019.061-014 MATERIALS ENGINEER (profess. & kin.)

Evaluates technical and economic factors, recommending engineering and manufacturing actions for attainment of design objectives of process or product by applying knowledge of material science and related technologies: Reviews plans for new product and factors, such as strength, weight, and cost to submit material selection recommendations ensuring attainment of design objectives. Plans and implements laboratory operations to develop material and fabrication procedures for new materials to fulfill product cost and performance standards. Confers with producers of materials, such as metals, ceramics, or polymers, during investigation and evaluation of materials suitable for specific product applications. Reviews product failure data and interprets laboratory tests and analyses to establish or rule out material and process causes.

GOE: 05.01.06 STRENGTH: S GED: R5 M5 L5 SVP: 8 DLU: 77

019.061-018 OPTICAL ENGINEER (profess. & kin.) alternate titles: optical designer

Designs optical systems with specific characteristics to fit within specified physical limits of precision optical instruments, such as still- and motion-picture cameras, lens systems, telescopes, and viewing and display devices: Determines specifications for operations and makes adjustments to calibrate and obtain specified operational performance. Determines proper operation of optical system and makes adjustments to perfect system. Designs mounts for components to hold them in proper planes in relation to each other and instrument in which they will be used. Designs inspection instruments to test optical systems for defects, such as abberations and deviations. May work with electrical and mechanical engineering staff to develop overall design of optical system.

GOE: 05.01.07 STRENGTH: L GED: R6 M5 L5 SVP: 8 DLU: 77

019.061-022 ORDNANCE ENGINEER (chemical; ordnance)

Designs, tests, and coordinates development of explosive ordnance material to meet military procurement specifications and to prepare project proposals for negotiating production contracts: Participates in discussions with military authorities to determine characteristics desired in explosive material, nature of target objective, and type of delivery system to be used. Prepares or directs preparation of design drawings and specifications for approval by procurement authorities, according to knowledge of explosives and plastics chemistry, ballistics theory, fuse technology, metallurgy, electronics, fluidics, and techniques of efficient production. Tests sample shells, warheads, or similar material under simulated military conditions [PROOF TECHNICIAN (ordnance)]. Evaluates tests to determine acceptability of ordnance items or need for redesign. Presents findings orally and in writing to procurement authorities and demonstrates successful designs on proving ground. May negotiate procurement contracts. May coordinate pilot or serial production of ordnance items. May participate in development of delivery systems, fire-control components, and nonexplosive material. May be designated according to type of ordnance item developed.

GOE: 05.01.08 STRENGTH: L GED: R6 M6 L5 SVP: 8 DLU: 77

019.061-026 RELIABILITY ENGINEER (profess. & kin.)

Analyzes preliminary engineering-design concepts of major product, such as aircraft, naval vessel, or electronic communication or control system to recommend design or test methods for attaining customer-specified operational reliability, using knowledge of reliability engineering and other technologies: Analyzes preliminary plans and develops reliability engineering program to achieve customer reliability objectives. Analyzes projected product utilization and calculates cumulative effect on final system reliability of individual part reliabilities. Drafts *failure mode and effect analysis* sheets or formulates *mathematical models,* using computer-aided engineering equipment, to identify units posing excessive failure risks and support proposed changes in design. Enters data to simulate electrical inputs, transient conditions, temperature, stress, and other factors to develop computer models, and analyzes and adjusts design to predict and improve system reliability. Advises and confers with engineers in design review meetings to give reliability findings and recommendations. Determines units requiring environmental testing and specifies minimum number of samples to obtain statistically valid data. Reviews subcontractors' proposals for reliability program and submits evaluation for decision. Reviews engineering specifications and drawings, proposing design modifications to improve reliability within cost and other performance requirements. Observes conduct of tests at supplier, plant, or field locations to evaluate reliability factors, such as numbers and causes of unit failures. Monitors failure data generated by customer using product to ascertain potential requirement for product improvement.

GOE: 05.01.04 STRENGTH: S GED: R6 M6 L5 SVP: 8 DLU: 86

019.081-010 MAINTAINABILITY ENGINEER (profess. & kin.)

Analyzes engineering design of proposed product, such as aircraft, naval vessel, or electronic control or navigation system, and submits specifications for maintenance requirements, utilizing knowledge of maintainability engineering and related technologies: Analyzes customer's initial proposal for product utilization and recommends basic product specifications and techniques for satisfying customer requirements. Reviews engineering specifications and drawings during development and proposes design refinements to improve ratio of operational time to maintenance time. Participates in engineering discussions concerning design alternatives effecting product maintainability. Determines crew makeup, training requirements, and maintenance time by evaluating data from tests and maintainability programs of related products. Reviews subcontractor's technical practices for assuring maintainability of equipment and parts and submits evaluation for managment decision. Specifies standardized tests or drafts new test programs for demonstrating product maintainability in company or supplier test. Observes maintainability tests at supplier and plant locations to verify operations are conducted according to standards.

GOE: 05.01.08 STRENGTH: S GED: R5 M4 L5 SVP: 8 DLU: 77

019.081-014 PHOTOGRAPHIC ENGINEER (profess. & kin.) alternate titles: photo-optical instrumentation engineer

Designs and constructs special-purpose photographic equipment and materials for use in scientific or industrial applications, utilizing knowledge of various engineering disciplines, chemistry, and photographic equipment and techniques. Plans setup of equipment, specific procedures, and materials needed to meet data acquisition and measurement requirements. May advise others in such fields as high speed photography, radiography, graphic arts, and aerial and space photography.

GOE: 05.01.07 STRENGTH: L GED: R5 M4 L4 SVP: 8 DLU: 77

019.081-018 POLLUTION-CONTROL ENGINEER (profess. & kin.)

Plans and conducts engineering studies to analyze and evaluate pollution problems, methods of pollution control, and methods of testing pollution sources to determine physiochemical nature and concentration of contaminants: Reviews data collected by POLLUTION-CONTROL TECHNICIAN (profess. & kin.) from pollution emission sources. Performs engineering calculations to determine pollution emissions from various industrial sources and to evaluate effectiveness of pollution control equipment. Reviews compliance schedules and inspection reports to ensure compliance with pollution control regulations. Recommends issuance or denial of permits for industries to construct or operate facilities. Advises enforcement personnel of noncompliance or unsatisfactory compliance with regulations. Develops or modifies techniques for monitoring pollution. Calibrates and adjusts pollution control monitors to ensure accurate functioning of instruments. May be designated according to specialty as Air-Pollution Engineer (profess. & kin.); Noise-Abatement Engineer (profess. & kin.); Water Quality-Control Engineer (profess. & kin.).

GOE: 05.01.02 STRENGTH: L GED: R6 M6 L6 SVP: 8 DLU: 77

019.161-010 SUPERVISOR, ESTIMATOR AND DRAFTER (utilities)

Supervises ESTIMATORS AND DRAFTERS (utilities) in drawing up specifications, instructions, and cost estimates for installation of gas or electric-power distribution systems: Studies work orders or construction proposals and selects appropriate survey procedures and schedules work assignments. Reviews completed construction drawings and cost estimates for accuracy and conformity to standards and regulations. Confers with engineers and subordinates and assists in field surveys to resolve problems. Directs maintenance of files of blueprints, maps, construction sketches, cost estimates, and related records.

GOE: 05.03.02 STRENGTH: S GED: R5 M5 L5 SVP: 8 DLU: 77

019.161-014 TEST TECHNICIAN (profess. & kin.)

Prepares specifications for fabrication, assembly, and installation of apparatus and control instrumentation used to test experimental or prototype mechanical,

electrical, electromechanical, hydromechanical, or structural products, and conducts tests and records results, utilizing engineering principles and test technology: Confers with engineering personnel to resolve fabrication problems relating to specifications and to review test plans, such as types and cycles of tests, conditions under which tests are to be conducted, and duration of tests. Fabricates precision parts for test apparatus, using metalworking machines such as lathes, milling machines, and welding equipment, or interprets specifications for workers fabricating parts. Examines parts for conformance with dimensional specifications, using precision measuring instruments. Coordinates and participates in installing unit or system to be tested in test fixtures, connecting valves, pumps, hydraulic, mechanical or electrical controls, cabling, tubing, power source, and indicating instruments. Activates controls to apply electrical, hydraulic, pneumatic, or mechanical power and subject test item to successive steps in test cycle. Monitors controls and instruments and records test data for engineer's use. May recommend changes in test methods or equipment for engineering review. Workers are classified according to engineering specialty or type of product tested.
GOE: 05.01.04 STRENGTH: L GED: R5 M4 L4 SVP: 7 DLU: 77

019.167-010 LOGISTICS ENGINEER (profess. & kin.) alternate titles: logistics specialist
Directs and coordinates program activities designed to provide subcontractors, management, and customers with logistics technology that ensures effective and economical support concerned for manufacturing or servicing of products, systems, or equipment: Analyzes contractual commitments, customer specifications, design changes, and other data to plan and develop logistic program activities from conceptual stage through life-cycle of product. Develops and implements program activities, coordinates efforts of subcontractors, production departments, and field service personnel, and resolves problems in area of logistics to ensure meeting of contractual commitments. Develops and initiates preparation of handbooks, bulletins, and information systems to provide and supply logistics support. Compiles data on standardization and interchangeability of parts to expedite logistics activities. Determines logistic support sequences and time phasing, problems arising from location of operational area, and other factors, such as environmental and human factors affecting personnel. May perform special research or technical studies critical to logistic support functions. May utilize computer techniques for analysis, simulation or information systems and documentation.
GOE: 05.01.06 STRENGTH: S GED: R5 M5 L5 SVP: 8 DLU: 77

019.167-014 PROJECT ENGINEER (profess. & kin.) alternate titles: chief engineer
Directs, coordinates, and exercises functional authority for planning, organization, control, integration, and completion of engineering project within area of assigned responsibility: Plans and formulates engineering program and organizes project staff according to project requirements. Assigns project personnel to specific phases or aspects of project, such as technical studies, product design, preparation of specifications and technical plans, and product testing, in accordance with engineering disciplines of staff. Reviews product design for compliance with engineering principles, company standards, customer contract requirements, and related specifications. Coordinates activities concerned with technical developments, scheduling, and resolving engineering design and test problems. Directs integration of technical activities and products. Evaluates and approves design changes, specifications, and drawing releases. Controls expenditures within limitations of project budget. Prepares interim and completion project reports.
GOE: 05.01.08 STRENGTH: L GED: R5 M5 L5 SVP: 8 DLU: 87

019.167-018 RESOURCE-RECOVERY ENGINEER (government ser.)
Plans and participates in activities concerned with study, development, and inspection of solid-waste resource recovery systems and marketability of solid-waste recovery products: Conducts studies of chemical and mechanical solid-waste recovery processes and system designs to evaluate efficiency and cost-effectiveness of proposed operations. Inspects solid-waste resource recovery facilities to determine compliance with regulations governing construction and use. Collects data on resource recovery systems and analyzes alternate plans to determine most feasible systems for specific solid-waste recovery purposes. Prepares recommendations for development of resource recovery programs, based on analysis of alternate plans and knowledge of physical properties of various solid-waste materials. Confers with design engineers, management personnel, and others concerned with recovery of solid-waste resources to discuss problems and provide technical advice. Coordinates activities of workers engaged in study of potential markets for reclaimable materials. Lectures civic and professional organizations and provides information about practices to media representatives to promote interest and participation in solid-waste recovery practices.
GOE: 05.01.02 STRENGTH: S GED: R6 M6 L5 SVP: 8 DLU: 86

019.187-010 PACKAGING ENGINEER (profess. & kin.)
Plans and directs activities concerned with design and development of protective packaging containers: Analyzes engineering drawings and specifications of product to determine physical characteristics of item, special-handling and safety requirements, and type of materials required for container. Consults with establishment's purchasing and production departments to determine costs and feasibility of producing proposed packaging. Develops or directs development of sketches, specifications, samples, and written analyses of proposed packaging in order to present design for approval. May confer with customers or sales

representatives to draw up contracts. May advise employer or customers on efficient packing procedures, innovations in packaging materials, and utilization of sealing and fastening devices.
GOE: 05.03.09 STRENGTH: S GED: R5 M4 L5 SVP: 7 DLU: 77

019.261-010 BIOMEDICAL EQUIPMENT TECHNICIAN (profess. & kin.) alternate titles: biomedical electronics technician; biomedical engineering technician
Repairs, calibrates, and maintains medical equipment and instrumentation used in health-care delivery field: Inspects and installs medical and related technical equipment in medical and research facilities for use by physicians, nurses, scientists, or engineers involved in researching, monitoring, diagnosing, and treating physical ailments or dysfunctions. Services various equipment and apparatus, such as patient monitors, electrocardiographs, blood-gas analyzers, x-ray units, defibrillators, electrosurgical units, anesthesia apparatus, pacemakers, blood-pressure transducers, spirometers, sterilizers, diathermy equipment, in-house television systems, patient-care computers, and other related technical paraphernalia. Repairs, calibrates, and maintains equipment, using handtools, power tools, measuring devices, and knowledge of manufacturers' manuals, troubleshooting techniques, and preventive-maintenance schedules. Safety-tests medical equipment and health-care facility's structural environment to ensure patient and staff safety from electrical or mechanical hazards. Consults with medical or research staff to ascertain that equipment functions properly and safely, utilizing knowledge of electronics, medical terminology, human anatomy and physiology, chemistry, and physics. May demonstrate and explain correct operation of equipment to medical personnel. May modify or develop instruments or devices, under supervision of medical or engineering staff. May work as salesperson or service technician for equipment manufacturers or their sales representatives.
GOE: 02.04.02 STRENGTH: L GED: R4 M4 L4 SVP: 6 DLU: 77

019.261-014 ESTIMATOR AND DRAFTER (utilities) alternate titles: detail and lay-out drafter; distribution estimator; lay-out and detail drafter
Draws up specifications and instructions for installation of voltage transformers, overhead or underground cables, and related electrical equipment used to conduct electrical energy from transmission lines or high-voltage distribution lines to consumers: Studies work order request to determine type of service, such as lighting or power, demanded by installation. Visits site of proposed installation and draws rough sketch of location. Takes measurements, such as street dimensions, distances to be spanned by wire and cable, or space available in existing buildings and underground vaults which affect installation and arrangement of equipment. Estimates materials, equipment, and incidentals needed for installation. Draws master sketch showing relation of proposed installation to existing facilities. Makes other drawings, such as pertaining to wiring connections or cross sections of underground cables, as required for instructions to installation crew. Consults POWER-DISTRIBUTION ENGINEER (utilities) 003.167-046 on difficulties encountered. May draft sketches to scale [DRAFTER, ELECTRICAL (profess. & kin.) 003.281-010]. May estimate labor and material costs, using pricelists and records on previous projects. May inspect completed installation of electrical equipment and related building circuitry to verify conformance with specifications. May perform duties of LAND SURVEYOR (profess. & kin.) 018.167-018 and prepare specifications and diagrams for installation of gas distribution pipes owned by gas-electric utility.
GOE: 05.03.02 STRENGTH: L GED: R5 M5 L5 SVP: 7 DLU: 77

019.261-018 FACILITIES PLANNER (any industry) alternate titles: office-planning representative
Plans utilization of space and facilities for government agency or unit or business establishment consistent with requirements of organizational efficiency and available facilities and funds: Inspects buildings and office areas to evaluate suitability for occupancy, considering such factors as air circulation, lighting, location, and size. Measures or directs workers engaged in measurement of facilities to determine total square footage available for occupancy. Computes square footage available for each member of staff to determine whether minimum space restrictions can be met. Draws design layout, showing location of furniture, equipment, doorways, electrical and telephone outlets, and other facilities. May review real estate contracts for compliance with government specifications and suitability for occupancy of employing agency. May direct workers engaged in moving furniture and equipment and preparing facilities for occupancy.
GOE: 05.01.06 STRENGTH: L GED: R5 M5 L5 SVP: 7 DLU: 77

019.261-022 TEST TECHNICIAN (agric. equip.)
Tests experimental and production agricultural equipment, such as tractors and power mowers and components to evaluate their performance, using test equipment and recording instruments: Reads data sheet denoting operating specification for unit or component and type of evaluation required. Tests unit for conformance with operating requirements, such as resistance to vibration, specified horsepower, and tensile strength and hardness of parts, using test equipment, such as bend-fatigue machine, dynamometer, strength tester, hardness tester, analytical balance, and electronic recorder. Records data from dial readings and graphs and computes values, such as horse-power and tensile strength, using algebraic formulas. Operates unit to evaluate attachment performance, such as depth of tillage or harvesting capabilities for different types of crops. Draws sketches and describes test procedures and results in test data log.
GOE: 05.03.07 STRENGTH: L GED: R4 M4 L4 SVP: 6 DLU: 77

019.261-026 FIRE-PROTECTION ENGINEERING TECHNICIAN (profess. & kin.)

Designs and drafts plans and estimates costs for installation of fire protection systems for facilities and structures, applying knowledge of drafting, physical science, engineering principles, and fire protection codes: Analyzes blueprints and specifications prepared by ARCHITECT (profess. & kin.) 001.061-010 to determine dimensions of system to meet fire protection codes. Determines design and size of system components, using calculator or computer. Drafts detailed drawing of system to ensure conformance to specifications and applicable codes. May negotiate relocation of system components with SUPERINTENDENT, CONSTRUCTION (construction) 182.167-026 to resolve conflicts of colocation with other systems. May inspect fire-damaged structures to detect malfunctions. May specialize in one type of fire protection system, such as foam, water, dry chemical, or vaporous gas or specialize in one type of establishment, such as construction, insurance, or government.

GOE: 05.03.02 STRENGTH: L GED: R4 M4 L4 SVP: 7 DLU: 86

019.261-030 LABORATORY TECHNICIAN (auto. mfg.)

Tests chemical and physical properties of materials used in manufacturing or assembling motor vehicles: Performs standard chemical and physical tests on parts, solutions, and materials used in producing motor vehicles, using conventional and computerized machines and work aids. Conducts quantitative and qualitative analyses to determine chemical and physical properties of experimental and developmental materials [LABORATORY TESTER (any industry) 029.261-010].

GOE: 02.04.01 STRENGTH: L GED: R4 M4 L4 SVP: 5 DLU: 90

019.261-034 LASER TECHNICIAN (electron. comp.; inst. & app.)

Constructs and tests prototype gas or solid-state laser devices, applying theory and principles of laser engineering and electronic circuits: Reviews project instructions, such as assembly layout, blueprints, and sketches, and confers with engineering personnel to clarify laser device specifications. Interprets production details, such as dimensions and functional requirements, for workers engaged in grinding mirror blanks, coating mirror surfaces, and machining metal parts. Installs and aligns optical parts, such as mirrors and waveplates, in laser body, using precision instruments. Turns controls of vacuum pump and gas transfer equipment to purge, evacuate, and fill laser body with specified volume and pressure of gases, such as helium, neon, or carbon dioxide, to test laser beam. Assembles completed laser body in chassis, and installs and aligns electronic components, tubing, and wiring to connect controls, such as valves, regulators, dials, and switches. Sets up precision electronic and optical instruments to test laser device, using specified electrical or optical inputs. Tests laser for gas leaks, using leak detector. Analyzes test data and reports results to engineering personnel. May prepare and write technical reports to recommend solutions to technical problems.

GOE: 05.03.05 STRENGTH: M GED: R5 M4 L4 SVP: 7 DLU: 90

019.267-010 SPECIFICATION WRITER (profess. & kin.)

Interprets architectural or engineering plans and prepares material lists and specifications to be used as standards by plant employees or contracting personnel in material processing or in manufacturing or construction activities: Analyzes plans and diagrams, or observes and makes notes on material processing, to determine material and material processing specifications, or specifications for manufacturing or construction activities. Writes technical descriptions specifying material qualities and properties, utilizing knowledge of material standards, industrial processes, and manufacturing procedures. May draw rough sketches or arrange for finished drawings or photographs to illustrate specified materials or assembly sequence. Workers usually specialize and are designated according to engineering specialization, product, or process.

GOE: 05.03.02 STRENGTH: S GED: R5 M4 L4 SVP: 7 DLU: 77

019.281-010 CALIBRATION LABORATORY TECHNICIAN (aircraft mfg.; electron. comp.) alternate titles: engineering laboratory technician; quality assurance calibrator; standards laboratory technician; test equipment certification technician

Tests, calibrates, and repairs electrical, mechanical, electromechanical, and electronic measuring, recording, and indicating instruments and equipment for conformance to established standards, and assists in formulating calibration standards: Plans sequence of testing and calibration procedures for instruments and equipment, according to blueprints, schematics, technical manuals, and other specifications. Sets up standard and special purpose laboratory equipment to test, evaluate, and calibrate other instruments and test equipment. Disassembles instruments and equipment, using handtools, and inspects components for defects. Measures parts for conformity with specifications, using micrometers, calipers, and other precision instruments. Aligns, repairs, replaces, and balances component parts and circuitry. Reassembles and calibrates instruments and equipment. Devises formulas to solve problems in measurements and calibrations. Assists engineers in formulating test, calibration, repair, and evaluation plans and procedures to maintain precision accuracy of measuring, recording, and indicating instruments and equipment.

GOE: 02.04.01 STRENGTH: L GED: R5 M5 L4 SVP: 7 DLU: 88

02 OCCUPATIONS IN MATHEMATICS AND PHYSICAL SCIENCES

This division includes occupations concerned with research pertaining to the physical universe, and the application of established mathematical and scientific laws and principles to specific problems and situations.

020 OCCUPATIONS IN MATHEMATICS

This group includes occupations concerned with the development of methodology in mathematics, statistics, and actuarial science; and the application of original and standardized mathematical techniques to the solution of problems in the social and physical sciences, engineering, and business.

020.067-014 MATHEMATICIAN (profess. & kin.)

Conducts research in fundamental mathematics and in application of mathematical techniques to science, management, and other fields, and solves or directs solutions to problems in various fields by mathematical methods: Conducts research in such branches of mathematics as algebra, geometry, number theory, logic, and topology, and studies and tests hypotheses and alternative theories. Conceives and develops ideas for application of mathematics to wide variety of fields, including science, engineering, military planning, electronic data processing, and management. Applies mathematics or mathematical methods to solution of problems in research, development, production, logistics, and other functional areas, utilizing knowledge of subject or field to which applied, such as physics, engineering, astronomy, biology, economics, business and industrial management, or cryptography. Performs computations, applies methods of numerical analysis, and operates or directs operation of desk calculators and mechanical and electronic computation machines, analyzers, and plotters in solving problems in support of mathematical, scientific, or industrial research activity. Acts as advisor or consultant to research personnel concerning mathematical methods and applications. May be designated according to function as Mathematician, Applied (profess. & kin.); Mathematician, Research (profess. & kin.).

GOE: 02.01.01 STRENGTH: S GED: R6 M6 L6 SVP: 8 DLU: 81

020.067-018 OPERATIONS-RESEARCH ANALYST (profess. & kin.)

Conducts analyses of management and operational problems and formulates mathematical or simulation models of problem for solution by computers or other methods: Analyzes problem in terms of management information and conceptualizes and defines problem. Studies information and selects plan from competitive proposals that affords maximum probability of profit or effectiveness in relation to cost or risk. Prepares model of problem in form of one or several equations that relates constants and variables, restrictions, alternatives, conflicting objectives and their numerical parameters. Defines data requirements and gathers and validates information applying judgment and statistical tests. Specifies manipulative or computational methods to be applied to model. Performs validation and testing of model to ensure adequacy, or determines need for reformulation. Prepares reports to management defining problem, evaluation, and possible solution. Evaluates implementation and effectiveness of research. May design, conduct, and evaluate experimental operational models where insufficient data exists to formulate model. May specialize in research and preparation of contract proposals specifying competence of organization to perform research, development, or production work. May develop and apply time and cost networks, such as Program Evaluation and Review Techniques (PERT), to plan and control large projects. May work in association with engineers, scientists, and management personnel in business, government, health, transportation, energy, manufacturing, environmental sciences or other technologies.

GOE: 11.01.01 STRENGTH: S GED: R6 M6 L6 SVP: 7 DLU: 77

020.067-022 STATISTICIAN, MATHEMATICAL (profess. & kin.) alternate titles: statistician, theoretical

Conducts research into mathematical theories and proofs that form basis of science of statistics and develops statistical methodology: Examines theories, such as those of probability and inference, to discover mathematical bases for new or improved methods of obtaining and evaluating numerical data. Develops and tests experimental designs, sampling techniques, and analytical methods, and prepares recommendations concerning their utilization in statistical surveys, experiments, and tests. Investigates, evaluates, and prepares reports on applicability, efficiency, and accuracy of statistical methods used by physical and social scientists, including STATISTICIANS, APPLIED (profess. & kin.), in obtaining and evaluating data.

GOE: 11.01.01 STRENGTH: S GED: R6 M6 L6 SVP: 8 DLU: 77

020.162-010 MATHEMATICAL TECHNICIAN (profess. & kin.) alternate titles: data-reduction technician

Applies standardized mathematical formulas, principles, and methodology to technological problems in engineering and physical sciences in relation to specific industrial and research objectives, processes, equipment and products: Confers with professional, scientific, and engineering personnel to plan project. Analyzes raw data from computer or recorded on photographic film or other media. Selects most practical and accurate combination and sequence of computational methods, using algebra, trigonometry, geometry, vector analysis and calculus to reduce raw data to meaningful and manageable terms. Selects most

economical and reliable combination of manual, mechanical, or data processing methods and equipment consistent with data reduction requirements. Modifies standard formulas to conform to data processing method selected. Translates data into numerical values, equations, flow charts, graphs or other media. Analyzes processed data to detect errors. May operate calculator or computer.
GOE: 11.01.02 STRENGTH: S GED: R5 M5 L5 SVP: 7 DLU: 77

020.167-010 ACTUARY (profess. & kin.)
Applies knowledge of mathematics, probability, statistics, principles of finance and business to problems in life, health, social, and casualty insurance, annuities, and pensions: Determines mortality, accident, sickness, disability, and retirement rates; constructs probability tables regarding fire, natural disasters, and unemployment, based on analysis of statistical data and other pertinent information. Designs or reviews insurance and pension plans and calculates premiums. Ascertains premium rates required and cash reserves and liabilities necessary to ensure payment of future benefits. Determines equitable basis for distributing surplus earnings under participating insurance and annuity contracts in mutual companies. May specialize in one type of insurance and be designated Actuary, Casualty (profess. & kin.); Actuary, Life (profess. & kin.).
GOE: 11.01.02 STRENGTH: S GED: R5 M5 L5 SVP: 8 DLU: 77

020.167-026 STATISTICIAN, APPLIED (profess. & kin.)
Plans data collection, and analyzes and interprets numerical data from experiments, studies, surveys, and other sources and applies statistical methodology to provide information for scientific research and statistical analysis: Plans methods to collect information and develops questionnaire techniques according to survey design. Conducts surveys utilizing sampling techniques or complete enumeration bases. Evaluates reliability of source information, adjusts and weighs raw data, and organizes results into form compatible with analysis by computers or other methods. Presents numerical information by computer readouts, graphs, charts, tables, written reports or other methods. Describes sources of information, and limitations on reliability and usability. May analyze and interpret statistics to point up significant differences in relationships among sources of information, and prepare conclusions and forecasts based on data summaries. May specialize in specific aspect of statistics or industrial activity reporting and be designated by specialty as Demographer (profess. & kin.) I; Statistician, Analytical (profess. & kin.); Statistician, Engineering And Physical Science (profess. & kin.).
GOE: 11.01.02 STRENGTH: S GED: R5 M5 L4 SVP: 7 DLU: 77

020.167-030 WEIGHT ANALYST (profess. & kin.) alternate titles: weight engineer
Analyzes and calculates weight data of structural assemblies, components, and loads for purposes of weight, balance, loading, and operational functions of ships, aircraft, space vehicles, missiles, research instrumentation, and commercial and industrial products and systems: Studies weight factors involved in new designs or modifications, utilizing computer techniques for analysis and simulation. Analyzes data and prepares reports of weight distribution estimates for use in design studies. Confers with design engineering personnel in such departments as preliminary design, structures, aerodynamics, and sub-systems to ensure coordination of weight, balance, and load specifications with other phases of product development. Weighs parts, assemblies, or completed product, estimates weight of parts from engineering drawings, and calculates weight distribution to determine balance. Prepares reports or graphic data for designers when weight and balance requires engineering changes. Prepares technical reports on mass moments of inertia, static and dynamic balance, dead weight distributions, cargo and fuselage compartments, and fuel center of gravity travel. May prepare cargo and equipment loading sequences to maintain balance of aircraft or space vehicle within specified load limits. May analyze various systems, structures, and support equipment designs to obtain information on most efficient compromise between weight, operations, and cost. May conduct research and analysis to develop new techniques for weights estimating criteria.
GOE: 07.02.03 STRENGTH: M GED: R5 M5 L5 SVP: 7 DLU: 77

021 OCCUPATIONS IN ASTRONOMY

This group includes occupations concerned with the investigation of celestial phenomena to increase basic scientific knowledge, or for practical application in such fields as navigation and guidance. Also includes occupations concerned with the visual and instrumental observation of astronomical phenomena and the recording and evaluation of data.

021.067-010 ASTRONOMER (profess. & kin.)
Observes and interprets celestial phenomena and relates research to basic scientific knowledge or to practical problems, such as navigation: Studies celestial phenomena by means of optical, radio, or other telescopes, equipped with such devices as cameras, spectrometers, radiometers, photometers, and micrometers, which may either be on ground or carried above atmosphere with balloons, rockets, satellites, or space probes. Interprets information obtained in terms of basic physical laws. Determines sizes, shapes, brightness, spectra, and motions, and computes positions of sun, moon, planets, stars, nebulae, and galaxies. Calculates orbits of various celestial bodies. Determines exact time by celestial observations, and conducts research into relationships between time and space. Develops mathematical tables giving positions of sun, moon, planets, and stars at given times for use by air and sea navigators. Conducts research on statistical theory of motions of celestial bodies. Analyzes wave lengths of radiation from

celestial bodies, as observed in all ranges of spectrum. Studies history, structure, extent, and evolution of stars, stellar systems, and universe. May design new and improved optical, mechanical, and electronics instruments for astronomical research. May specialize in either observational or theoretical aspects of stellar astronomy, stellar astrophysics, interstellar medium, galactic structure, extragalactic astronomy, or cosmology.
GOE: 02.01.01 STRENGTH: L GED: R6 M6 L6 SVP: 8 DLU: 77

022 OCCUPATIONS IN CHEMISTRY

This group includes occupations concerned with research and development in the chemical and physical properties and compositional changes of substances. Specialization generally occurs in one or more branches of chemistry, such as organic chemistry, inorganic chemistry, physical chemistry and analytical chemistry. Chemistry specializations within the field of environmental control are also included here. Occupations concerned with biochemistry are found in Group 041.

022.061-010 CHEMIST (profess. & kin.)
Conducts research, analysis, synthesis, and experimentation on substances, for such purposes as product and process development and application, quantitative and qualitative analysis, and improvement of analytical methodologies: Devises new equipment, and develops formulas, processes, and methods for solution of technical problems. Analyzes organic and inorganic compounds to determine chemical and physical properties, utilizing such techniques as chromatography, spectroscopy, and spectrophotometry. Induces changes in composition of substances by introduction of heat, light, energy, and chemical catalysts. Conducts research on manufactured products to develop and improve products. Conducts research into composition, structure, properties, relationships, and reactions of matter. Confers with scientists and engineers regarding research, and prepares technical papers and reports. Prepares standards and specifications for processes, facilities, products, and tests. May be designated according to chemistry specialty as CHEMIST, ANALYTICAL (profess. & kin.); CHEMIST, INORGANIC (profess. & kin.); CHEMIST, ORGANIC (profess. & kin.); CHEMIST, PHYSICAL (profess. & kin.).
GOE: 02.01.01 STRENGTH: L GED: R6 M6 L5 SVP: 8 DLU: 81

022.061-014 CHEMIST, FOOD (profess. & kin.)
Conducts research and analysis concerning chemistry of foods to develop and improve foods and beverages: Experiments with natural and synthetic materials or byproducts to develop new foods, additives, preservatives, anti-adulteration agents, and related products. Studies effects of various methods of processing, preservation, and packaging on composition and properties of foods, such as color, texture, aroma, taste, shelf life, and nutritive content. Tests food and beverage samples, such as starch, sugar, cereals, beer, canned and dehydrated food products, meats, vegetables, dairy foods, and other products to ensure compliance with food laws, and standards of quality and purity. May perform, or supervise workers performing, quality control tests in food processing, canning, freezing, brewing or distilling. May specialize in particular food or process.
GOE: 02.02.04 STRENGTH: L GED: R6 M5 L5 SVP: 7 DLU: 77

022.081-010 TOXICOLOGIST (pharmaceut.)
Conducts research on toxic effects of cosmetic products and ingredients on laboratory animals for manufacturer of cosmetics: Applies cosmetic ingredient or cosmetic being developed to exposed shaved skin area of test animal and observes and examines skin periodically for possible development of abnormalities, inflammation, or irritation. Injects ingredient into test animal, using hypodermic needle and syringe, and periodically observes animal for signs of toxicity. Injects antidotes to determine which antidote best neutralizes toxic effects. Tests and analyzes blood samples for presence of toxic conditions, using microscope and laboratory test equipment. Dissects dead animals, using surgical instruments, and examines organs to determine effects of cosmetic ingredients being tested. Prepares formal reports of test results.
GOE: 02.04.02 STRENGTH: L GED: R5 M4 L5 SVP: 8 DLU: 86

022.137-010 LABORATORY SUPERVISOR (profess. & kin.)
Supervises and coordinates activities of personnel engaged in performing chemical and physical tests required for quality control of processes and products: Directs and advises personnel in special test procedures to analyze components and physical properties of materials. Compiles and analyzes test information to determine operating efficiency of process or equipment and to diagnose malfunctions. Confers with scientists or engineers to conduct analyses, interpret test results, or develop nonstandard tests. Performs other duties as described under SUPERVISOR (any industry) Master Title. May adjust formulas and processes based on test results. May test and analyze sample products. May prepare test solutions, compounds, and reagents for use by laboratory personnel in conducting tests. May conduct research to develop custom products and investigate complaints on existing products.
GOE: 02.04.01 STRENGTH: L GED: R5 M5 L4 SVP: 7 DLU: 86

022.161-010 CHEMICAL LABORATORY CHIEF (profess. & kin.) alternate titles: chief chemist; director, chemical laboratory
Plans and directs activities of chemical laboratory in industrial, research, governmental, or other organization: Plans, coordinates, and directs programs for research, product development, improvement of manufacturing processes; or for analysis and testing of substances to support criminal investigations, to detect toxins, or to verify composition of manufactured and agricultural products, and

natural resources, such as air, soil, and water. Coordinates research and analysis activities according to applicable government regulations, manufacturing processes, or other considerations, and approves modification of formulas, standards, specifications, and processes. Reviews research, testing, quality control, and other operational reports to ensure that quality standards, efficiency, and schedules are met. Interprets results of laboratory activities to laboratory personnel, management, and professional and technical societies, and prepares reports and technical papers. May prepare and administer budgets. May advise and assist in obtaining patents for products, processes, or equipment.
GOE: 02.01.02 STRENGTH: L GED: R6 M6 L6 SVP: 8 DLU: 78

022.161-014 COLORIST (profess. & kin.) alternate titles: color maker; color matcher

Develops color formulas for printing textile and plastic materials and compares customer's sample with standard color card, or blends pigments into vinyl solution and compares results with sample to determine formula required to duplicate colors. Selects dyes according to properties desired by customer. Records color formula and issues formula and mixing procedure to SUPERVISOR, COLOR-PASTE MIXING (textile) for assignment to appropriate workers. Prepares color sequence chart to guide CLOTH PRINTER (any industry) in setting up printing machine. Compares printed patch with customer's sample to verify color shade and position of design. Files folder containing color patch and formula for each design for use as printing standard. Coordinates color shop activities with printing department production schedule. May inspect printed material to ensure adherence to customer and plant specifications. May mix colors. May inventory and requisition supplies.
GOE: 02.04.01 STRENGTH: L GED: R5 M5 L4 SVP: 7 DLU: 77

022.161-018 PERFUMER (chemical)

Evaluates odors of aromatic chemicals to set production standards and ensure adherence by workers engaged in compounding and finishing operations: Directs workers engaged in preparation of work orders for compounding department and reviews batch sheets prepared for distillation department to ensure compliance with formulas devised in perfume laboratory. Visits compounding and distillation areas and determines, by smelling, odor qualities of prepared materials. Approves batches for finishing, from knowledge of odor characteristics and odor blends conforming with customer or laboratory standards. Resmells sample in air-filtered room, using blotter strips dipped in aromatic chemicals to evaluate fragrances for specific characteristics, such as odor, body, harmony, strength, and permanence. Compares odor and color of current sample with samples of previous batches. Rejects batches not meeting criteria, and notifies distillation personnel to redistill product. May devise production formulas and be designated Creative Perfumer (chemical).
GOE: 02.01.02 STRENGTH: L GED: R5 M5 L4 SVP: 7 DLU: 77

022.261-010 CHEMICAL LABORATORY TECHNICIAN (profess. & kin.)

Conducts chemical and physical laboratory tests of solid materials, liquids, and gases, and analyzes test data for variety of purposes, such as research, product development, quality control, criminal investigation, and establishing standards, involving experimental, theoretical, or practical application of chemistry and related sciences: Sets up laboratory equipment and instrumentation required for tests, research, or process control. Tests and analyzes products, such as food, drugs, fertilizers, plastics, paints, detergents, paper, petroleum, and cement, to determine strength, stability, purity, chemical content, and other characteristics. Tests and analyzes materials and substances, such as ores, minerals, gases, soil, water, and pollutants. Documents results of tests and analyses. May prepare chemical solutions for use in processing materials, following standardized formulas or experimental procedures. May test and analyze radioactive and biological materials, applying knowledge of radiochemical procedures, emission spectrometry, and related techniques.
GOE: 02.04.01 STRENGTH: L GED: R5 M4 L4 SVP: 7 DLU: 88

022.261-014 MALT-SPECIFICATIONS-CONTROL ASSISTANT (beverage)

Keeps perpetual inventory of malt and barley in storage elevators and determines formulas for blending malt: Compiles continuous records of malt and barley supplies by location, amount, physical characteristics, and chemical analysis. Writes orders to malt house to produce and blend standard malt types. Notifies purchasing department of barley supplies in storage. Analyzes physical and chemical test results to classify incoming barley shipments. Selects tanks and issues orders for storing barley and malt in elevators. Analyzes customer orders to determine if special malt blends are needed. Determines blend formulas, using established chemical and mathematical procedures. Mixes sample of blend by hand, orders chemical and physical testing by laboratory, and compares results with specifications. Sends formula and sample to malt elevators and customers.
GOE: 05.02.03 STRENGTH: S GED: R4 M4 L3 SVP: 7 DLU: 77

022.261-018 CHEMIST, INSTRUMENTATION (profess. & kin.)

Conducts chemical analyses of wastewater discharges of industrial users of municipal wastewater treatment plant to determine industrial waste surcharge assessments and to ensure that users meet pollution control requirements: Conducts chemical analyses of samples, using special instrumentation, such as gas chromatograph with electron capture, flame ionization, and thermal conductivity detectors, ultraviolet-visible recording spectrophotometer with photometry attachments, and infrared spectrophotometer. Compares findings with industry declared data and legal requirements and notes variations to be used in determining industrial waste surcharge assessments and to regulate industrial waste discharges. Develops new procedures in use of equipment and procedures for analyzing samples. Directs subordinate laboratory personnel in routine tests.
GOE: 02.01.01 STRENGTH: L GED: R5 M5 L4 SVP: 7 DLU: 87

022.261-022 CHEMIST, WASTEWATER-TREATMENT PLANT (profess. & kin.)

Analyzes samples of streams, raw and treated wastewater, sludge, and other byproducts of wastewater treatment process to determine efficiency of plant processes and to ensure that plant effluent meets water pollution control requirements, using standard laboratory equipment: Conducts tests for settleable solids, suspended solids, total solids, volatile solids, volatile acids, alkalinity, pH, dissolved oxygen demand, turbidity, and other substances. Initiates changes in laboratory procedures and equipment in order to increase efficiency of laboratory. Directs laboratory personnel in prescribed laboratory techniques and performance of routine tests.
GOE: 02.04.02 STRENGTH: L GED: R5 M5 L4 SVP: 7 DLU: 87

022.281-010 ASSAYER (profess. & kin.)

Tests ores and minerals and analyzes results to determine value and properties of components, using spectrographic analysis, chemical solutions, and chemical or laboratory equipment, such as furnaces, beakers, graduates, pipettes, and crucibles: Separates metals or other components from dross materials by solution, flotation, or other liquid processes, or by dry methods, such as application of heat to form slags of lead, borax, and other impurities. Weighs residues on balance scale to determine proportion of pure gold, silver, platinum, or other metals or components. May specialize in testing and analyzing precious metals and be designated Gold-And-Silver Assayer (profess. & kin.).
GOE: 02.04.01 STRENGTH: L GED: R5 M5 L4 SVP: 7 DLU: 77

022.281-014 CHEMIST, WATER PURIFICATION (waterworks)

Analyzes water in purification plant to control chemical processes which soften it or make it suitable for drinking: Analyzes samples of filtered water to ensure that quantities of solids left in suspension are below prescribed limits. Determines amounts of liquid chlorine to be used in chlorinators to destroy microbes and other harmful organisms, basing amounts on findings of MICROBIOLOGIST (profess. & kin.). Determines kinds and amounts of chemicals to be used in removing minerals, acids, salts, and other inorganic compounds from water to soften it. Tests samples extracted from various points in distribution system, such as mains, tanks, pumps, and outlets, to discover possible sources of water contamination.
GOE: 02.04.02 STRENGTH: L GED: R6 M6 L6 SVP: 7 DLU: 77

022.281-018 LABORATORY TESTER (plastic-synth.)

Examines, measures, photographs, and tests synthetic fiber samples to facilitate quality control of forming, treating, and texturing processes, performing any combination of following tasks: Dips several twisted threads in melted wax and directs stream of cold water over threads to congeal wax. Slices threads crosswise, using microtome. Dissolves wax, using solvent, and positions thread sample on microscope slide. Inserts slide in microscope and photographs sample, using standard microphotographic equipment and techniques. Develops, prints, and labels photographs. Analyzes photographs to determine whether structure and other characteristics of thread meet plant standards. Determines tensile strength of thread samples, using device that draws material between two jaws until breakage occurs. Measures cross-sectional area of thread samples, using planimeter. Immerses samples in water, corrosives, or cleaning agents to detect shrinkage or damage. Places thread samples in dye bath to evaluate permeability of dye and exposes samples to controlled light source to ascertain fade resistance. Prepares and submits reports of findings to production personnel to facilitate quality control of product.
GOE: 02.04.01 STRENGTH: L GED: R4 M3 L3 SVP: 6 DLU: 77

022.381-010 YEAST-CULTURE DEVELOPER (beverage)

Selects and cultivates yeast cells to develop pure yeast culture for brewing beer and malt liquors: Samples beer in fermenting stages to select specimens containing yeast cells having specific reproduction characteristics. Prepares cover glasses and slides with smears of yeast preparation taken from beer samples. Examines slides under microscope to isolate specific cells and record position of cells. Incubates slides to allow colonies of cells to form. Inoculates cells with hopped wort, using sterile needle to transfer cells from slides to flasks containing wort. Cultivates cells in flasks by incubation and propagates single cell cultures by transferring cells to additional flasks. Siphons developing yeast culture from flasks to tanks and pumps yeast culture from tanks to sterile barrels. Seals barrels with sterile bung and packs sealed barrels in dry ice to prevent yeast degeneration. Cleans and sterilizes equipment.
GOE: 02.04.02 STRENGTH: M GED: R4 M2 L4 SVP: 5 DLU: 77

023 OCCUPATIONS IN PHYSICS

This group includes occupations concerned with the investigation of the laws of matter and energy and their application to problems in such fields as science, engineering, medicine, environment, and production.

023.061-010 ELECTRO-OPTICAL ENGINEER (profess. & kin.)

Conducts research and plans development and design of gas and solid state lasers, masers, infrared, and other light emitting and light sensitive devices: De-

signs electronic circuitry and optical components with specific characteristics to fit within specified mechanical limits and to perform according to specifications. Designs suitable mounts for optics and power supply systems. Incorporates methods for maintenance and repair of components and designs, and develops test instrumentation and test procedures. Confers with engineering and technical personnel regarding fabrication and testing of prototype systems, and modifies design as required. May conduct application analysis to determine commercial, industrial, scientific, medical, military, or other use for electro-optical devices. May assist with development of manufacturing, assembly, and fabrication processes.
GOE: 05.01.07 STRENGTH: S GED: R6 M6 L6 SVP: 8 DLU: 77

023.061-014 PHYSICIST (profess. & kin.)
Conducts research into phases of physical phenomena, develops theories and laws on basis of observation and experiments, and devises methods to apply laws and theories of physics to industry, medicine, and other fields: Performs experiments with masers, lasers, cyclotrons, betatrons, telescopes, mass spectrometers, electron microscopes, and other equipment to observe structure and properties of matter, transformation and propagation of energy, relationships between matter and energy, and other physical phenomena. Describes and expresses observations and conclusions in mathematical terms. Devises procedures for physical testing of materials. Conducts instrumental analyses to determine physical properties of materials. May specialize in one or more branches of physics and be designated Physicist, Acoustics (profess. & kin.); Physicist, Astrophysics (profess. & kin.); Physicist, Atomic, Electronic And Molecular (profess. & kin.); Physicist, Cryogenics (profess. & kin.); Physicist, Electricity And Magnetism (profess. & kin.); Physicist, Fluids (profess. & kin.). May be designated: Physicist, Light And Optics (profess. & kin.); Physicist, Nuclear (profess. & kin.); Physicist, Plasma (profess. & kin.); Physicist, Solid Earth (profess. & kin.); Physicist, Solid State (profess. & kin.); Physicist, Thermodynamics (profess. & kin.).
GOE: 02.01.01 STRENGTH: L GED: R6 M6 L6 SVP: 8 DLU: 77

023.067-010 PHYSICIST, THEORETICAL (profess. & kin.)
Designs, conceives, and interprets experiments in physics and formulates theories consistent with data obtained: Analyzes results of experiments designed to detect and measure previously unobserved physical phenomena. Applies mathematical methods to solution of physical problems.
GOE: 02.01.01 STRENGTH: S GED: R6 M6 L6 SVP: 8 DLU: 77

024   OCCUPATIONS IN GEOLOGY

This group includes occupations concerned with the investigation of the composition, structure, and physical and biological history of the earth's crust and the application of this knowledge in such fields as archeology, mining, construction, and environmental impact. Typical specializations are ecomonic geology, historical geology, mineralogy, mining geology, paleontology, petroleum geology, petrology, physiography, structural geology, subsurface geology.

024.061-010 CRYSTALLOGRAPHER (clock & watch)
Conducts studies of nonmetallic minerals used in horological industry. Performs experimental research concerned with projects, such as development of diamond tools and dies, fabrication of jeweled bearings, and development of grinding *laps III* and wheels. Tests industrial diamonds and abrasives to determine grain size, pattern, crystalline orientation, goniometric features and other factors in order to appraise their suitability for use, using optical, x-ray, and other precision instruments. Repairs diamond and abrasive tools. Develops improved methods of fabricating silicon-carbide compounds into bearings and investigates substitution of other materials.
GOE: 02.01.02 STRENGTH: L GED: R6 M6 L6 SVP: 8 DLU: 77

024.061-014 GEODESIST (profess. & kin.)
Studies size, shape, and gravitational field of earth: Employs surveying and geodetic instruments, such as transits, theodolites, and other engineering instruments, in setting up and improving network of triangulation over earth's surface, in order to provide fixed points for use in making maps. Establishes bench marks (known points of elevation). Performs gravimetric surveying to determine variations in earth's gravitational field, and provides data used in determination of weight, size, and mass of earth.
GOE: 02.01.01 STRENGTH: L GED: R6 M6 L6 SVP: 8 DLU: 77

024.061-018 GEOLOGIST (profess. & kin.)
Studies composition, structure, and history of earth's crust: Examines rocks, minerals, and fossil remains to identify and determine sequence of processes affecting development of earth. Applies knowledge of chemistry, physics, biology, and mathematics to explain these phenomena and to help locate mineral, geothermal, and petroleum deposits and underground water resources. Studies ocean bottom. Applies geological knowledge to engineering problems encountered in construction projects, such as dams, tunnels, and large buildings. Studies fossil plants and animals to determine their evolutionary sequence and age. Prepares geologic reports and maps, interprets research data, and recommends further study or action. May specialize in area of study and be designated Geomorphologist (profess. & kin.); Oceanographer, Geological (profess. & kin.); Photogeologist (profess. & kin.). May conduct or participate in environmental studies and prepare environmental reports. Workers applying principles of rock and soil mechanics for engineering projects may be designated Geological Engineer (profess. & kin.). Workers applying all branches of geologic

knowledge to conditions that affect planning, design, construction, operation and safety to engineering projects may be designated Engineering Geologist (profess. & kin.).
GOE: 02.01.01 STRENGTH: L GED: R6 M6 L6 SVP: 8 DLU: 77

024.061-022 GEOLOGIST, PETROLEUM (petrol. & gas)
Explores and charts stratigraphic arrangement and structure of earth to locate gas and oil deposits: Studies well logs, analyzes cores and cuttings from well drillings, and interprets data obtained by electrical or radioactive well logging and other subsurface surveys to identify earth strata. Examines aerial photographs, evaluates results of geophysical prospecting, and prepares surface and subsurface maps and diagrams depicting stratigraphic arrangement and composition of earth and probable deposits of gas and oil. Recommends acquisition, retention, or release of property leases or contracts. Estimates oil reserves in proven or prospective fields, and consults with PETROLEUM ENGINEERS (petrol. & gas) concerning drilling and production methods. May direct drilling of shallow exploratory wells.
GOE: 02.01.02 STRENGTH: L GED: R6 M6 L5 SVP: 8 DLU: 77

024.061-026 GEOPHYSICAL PROSPECTOR (petrol. & gas)
Studies structure of subsurface rock formations to locate petroleum deposits: Conducts research, using geophysical instruments such as seismograph, gravimeter, torsion balance, and magnetometer, pendulum devices, and electrical-resistivity apparatus to measure characteristics of earth. Computes variations in physical forces existing at different locations and interprets data to reveal subsurface structures likely to contain petroleum deposits. Prepares charts, profiles or subsurface contour maps, and determines desirable locations for drilling operations. Directs field crews drilling boreholes and collecting samples of rock and soil for chemical analysis of hydrocarbon content. May specialize in particular instrumentation and be designated Electrical Prospector (petrol. & gas); Gravity Prospector (petrol. & gas); Magnetic Prospector (petrol. & gas); Seismic Prospector (petrol. & gas).
GOE: 02.01.02 STRENGTH: L GED: R6 M6 L6 SVP: 8 DLU: 77

024.061-030 GEOPHYSICIST (profess. & kin.)
Studies physical aspects of earth, including its atmosphere and hydrosphere: Investigates and measures seismic, gravitational, electrical, thermal, and magnetic forces affecting earth, utilizing principles of physics, mathematics, and chemistry. Analyzes data obtained to compute shape of earth, estimate composition and structure of earth's interior, determine flow pattern of ocean tides and currents, study physical properties of atmosphere, and help locate petroleum and mineral deposits. Investigates origin and activity of glaciers, volcanoes, and earthquakes. Compiles data to prepare navigational charts and maps, predict atmospheric conditions, prepare environmental reports, and establish water supply and flood-control programs. May study specific aspect of geophysics and be designated Geomagnetician (profess. & kin.); Glaciologist (profess. & kin.); Oceanographer, Physical (profess. & kin.); Tectonophysicist (profess. & kin.); Volcanologist (profess. & kin.).
GOE: 02.01.01 STRENGTH: L GED: R6 M5 L5 SVP: 8 DLU: 77

024.061-034 HYDROLOGIST (profess. & kin.)
Studies distribution, disposition, and development of waters of land areas, including form and intensity of precipitation, and modes of return to ocean and atmosphere: Maps and charts water flow and disposition of sediment. Measures changes in water volume due to evaporation and melting of snow. Studies storm occurrences and nature and movement of glaciers, and determines rate of ground absorption and ultimate disposition of water. Evaluates data obtained in reference to such problems as flood and drought forecasting, soil and water conservation programs, and planning water supply, water power, flood control, drainage, irrigation, crop production, and inland navigation projects.
GOE: 02.01.01 STRENGTH: L GED: R6 M6 L6 SVP: 8 DLU: 77

024.061-038 MINERALOGIST (profess. & kin.)
Examines, analyzes, and classifies minerals, gems, and precious stones: Isolates specimen from ore, rocks, or matrices. Makes microscopic examination to determine shape, surface markings, and other physical characteristics. Performs physical and chemical tests and makes x-ray examinations to determine composition of specimen and type of crystalline structure. Identifies and classifies samples. Develops data and theories on mode of origin, occurrence, and possible uses of minerals.
GOE: 02.01.01 STRENGTH: L GED: R6 M6 L6 SVP: 8 DLU: 77

024.061-042 PALEONTOLOGIST (profess. & kin.)
Studies fossilized remains of plants and animals found in geological formations to trace evolution and development of past life and identify geological formations according to nature and chronology: Recovers and assembles fossilized specimens, notes their positions, and classifies them according to their botanical or zoological family and probable age. Prepares treatises on findings for furtherance of scientific study, or as in aid to location of natural resources, such as petroleum-bearing formations. May organize scientific expeditions and supervise removal of fossils from deposits and matrix rock formations. May specialize in study of plant fossils and be designated Paleobotanist (profess. & kin.). May specialize in study of fossilized micro-organisms and be designated Micropaleontologist (profess. & kin.).
GOE: 02.01.01 STRENGTH: L GED: R6 M6 L6 SVP: 8 DLU: 77

024.061-046 PETROLOGIST (profess. & kin.)
Investigates composition, structure, and history of rock masses forming earth's crust. Applies findings to such fields of investigation as causes of for-

mations, breaking down and weathering, chemical composition and forms of deposition of sedimentary rocks, methods of eruption, and origin and causes of metamorphosis.
GOE: 02.01.01 STRENGTH: L GED: R6 M6 L5 SVP: 8 DLU: 77

024.061-050 SEISMOLOGIST (profess. & kin.)
Studies and interprets seismic data to locate earthquakes and earthquake faults: Reviews, analyzes, and interprets data from seismographs and geophysical instruments. Establishes existence and activity of faults, and direction, motion, and stress of earth movements before, during, and after earthquakes. Conducts research on seismic forces affecting deformative movements of earth. May issue maps or reports indicating areas of seismic risk to existing or proposed construction or development.
GOE: 02.01.01 STRENGTH: L GED: R6 M6 L6 SVP: 8 DLU: 77

024.061-054 STRATIGRAPHER (profess. & kin.)
Studies relative position and order of succession of deposits containing or separating archaeological fossil or plant material. Studies relation of life of past ages, evolutionary changes as recorded by fossil animals and plants, and successive changes in distribution of land and sea as interpreted from character of fossil content of sedimentary rocks.
GOE: 02.01.01 STRENGTH: L GED: R6 M6 L5 SVP: 8 DLU: 77

024.161-010 ENGINEER, SOILS (profess. & kin.)
Studies and analyzes surface and subsurface soils to determine characteristics for construction, development, or land planning: Inspects proposed construction site, and sets up test equipment and drilling machinery to obtain data and soil and rock samples. Analyzes data and soil samples through field and laboratory analysis, to determine type, classification, characteristics, and stability of soil. Computes bearing weights, prepares maps, charts, and reports of test results. May make recommendations regarding foundation design, slope angles, grading or building heights. May participate in environmental studies and prepare environmental impact reports.
GOE: 05.01.08 STRENGTH: L GED: R6 M5 L6 SVP: 7 DLU: 77

024.167-010 GEOPHYSICAL-LABORATORY CHIEF (profess. & kin.) alternate titles: director, geophysical laboratory; engineer, geophysical laboratory; research engineer, geophysical laboratory; superintendent, geophysical laboratory
Plans, directs, and coordinates research activities of geophysical laboratory to develop new or improved instruments and methods for measuring physical characteristics of earth's crust which provide data for petroleum or mineral exploration: Consults with management and field and laboratory technical personnel to determine specific phases of geophysical prospecting in which improved processes might be evolved by study and experimentation. Plans research programs and initiates and directs experiments to improve prospecting procedures, explore possibilities of new theories, and develop improved or new instruments. Directs and coordinates activities concerned with designing, building, and field testing experimental instruments and maintenance and repair of laboratory and prospecting instruments.
GOE: 02.04.01 STRENGTH: L GED: R6 M6 L6 SVP: 9 DLU: 77

024.267-010 GEOLOGICAL AIDE (petrol. & gas)
Examines and compiles geological information to provide technical data to GEOLOGIST, PETROLEUM (petrol. & gas) 024.061-022, using surface and subsurface maps, oil and gas well activity reports, and sand and core analysis studies: Studies geological reports to extract well data and posts data to maps and logs. Draws subsurface formation contours on charts to lay out and prepare geological cross section charts. Compiles information regarding well tests, completions, and formation tops to prepare oil or gas well records. Records net sand and sand percentage counts and calculates isopachous values to compile sand analysis data. Studies directional logs and surveys to calculate and plot formation tops. Reads well activity reports and records key well locations in drilling activity book. Assembles and distributes prepared charts, maps, and reports to geologist requesting material. Maintains file record systems and geological library. Attends SCOUT (petrol. & gas) 010.267-010 meeting to compile information on well activity. Contacts competitors to acquire oil and gas samples from wells. Operates computer terminal for input and retrieval of geological data.
GOE: 02.04.01 STRENGTH: L GED: R5 M5 L5 SVP: 8 DLU: 86

024.284-010 PROSPECTOR (any industry)
Explores likely regions to discover valuable mineral deposits, using topographical maps, surveys, reports, and knowledge of geology and mineralogy: Examines outcrops, placer, and stream channels for mineral content. Drills, dynamites, or digs trenches or pits along rock formations or creek beds to obtain rock samples. Breaks off samples and tests them for presence of minerals with heat, acid, magnifying glass, or by pulverizing and washing or panning. Assays samples for preliminary quantitative estimate. Collects data on rock formations, using geophysical instruments and devices, such as geiger counters and electronic sounding equipment, and determines feasibility of staking and developing claim. Stakes claim according to federal or state legal requirements. Develops mineral deposits by means of placer or hard rock mining. May sell interests in discovered areas.
GOE: 05.03.04 STRENGTH: H GED: R4 M4 L4 SVP: 7 DLU: 77

024.364-010 PALEONTOLOGICAL HELPER (profess. & kin.)
Prepares, classifies, and sorts rock and fossil specimens: Records receipt of

fossil and rock samples from outcroppings, quarries, oil or gas wells, boreholes, or other sources. Cleans, washes, and prepares samples, using probes, brushes, or cleaning solutions to remove extraneous matter. Separates rock and fossil specimens and classifies them into general categories of fossilization. Compiles background data of rock or fossil. Sacks and labels specimens. Mounts specimen for study or experimentation.
GOE: 02.04.01 STRENGTH: L GED: R3 M2 L2 SVP: 6 DLU: 77

024.381-010 LABORATORY ASSISTANT (petrol. & gas) alternate titles: analyst, geochemical prospecting; core analyst; laboratory tester
Tests sand, shale, and other earth materials to determine petroleum and mineral content and physical characteristics: Performs routine chemical or physical tests of earth samples in field or laboratory to determine content of hydrocarbon or other minerals indicating presence of petroleum and mineral deposits. Tests core samples brought up during well drilling to determine permeability and porosity of sample, fluid content of sand and shale, salinity of drilling mud, and other conditions affecting oil well drilling operations.
GOE: 02.04.01 STRENGTH: L GED: R4 M4 L3 SVP: 5 DLU: 77

025   OCCUPATIONS IN METEOROLOGY

This group includes occupations concerned with the investigation of atmospheric phenomena with specializations, such as synoptic meterology, climatology, dynamic meterology, physical meterology, radar and radio meterology, and hydrometerology.

025.062-010 METEOROLOGIST (profess. & kin.) alternate titles: weather forecaster
Analyzes and interprets meteorological data gathered by surface and upper-air stations, satellites, and radar to prepare reports and forecasts for public and other users: Studies and interprets synoptic reports, maps, photographs, and prognosic charts to predict long and short range weather conditions. Operates computer graphic equipment to produce weather reports and maps for analysis, distribution to users, or for use in televised weather broadcast. Issues hurricane and other severe weather warnings. May broadcast weather forecast over television or radio. May prepare special forecasts and briefings for particular audiences, such as those involved in air and sea transportation, agriculture, fire prevention, air-pollution control, and school groups. May direct forecasting services at weather station, or at radio or television broadcasting facility. May conduct basic or applied research in meteorology. May establish and staff weather observation stations.
GOE: 02.01.01 STRENGTH: L GED: R5 M5 L5 SVP: 7 DLU: 89

025.264-010 HYDROGRAPHER (waterworks)
Analyzes hydrographic data to determine trends in movement and utilization of water: Reads meters and gauges to measure waterflow and presure in streams, conduits, and pipelines, and records data. Measures water level in lakes, reservoirs, and tanks. Calculates seepage and evaporation rates for dams and reservoirs. Measures depth of water in wells and test holes to determine ground water level. Measures snow characteristics to evaluate water yield from snow runoff. Prepares graphs and charts to illustrate water patterns. Positions sluice gates to direct water onto spreading grounds. Installs, calibrates, and maintains metering instruments. Recommends locations for metering stations and instrument placement.
GOE: 02.04.01 STRENGTH: M GED: R4 M4 L4 SVP: 6 DLU: 77

025.267-010 OCEANOGRAPHER, ASSISTANT (military ser.)
Analyzes and records oceanographic and meteorological data to forecast changes in weather or sea condition: Collects weather and oceanographic data, using meteorological and oceanographic equipment and visual observation. Sketches surface weather charts, upper air charts, sea condition charts, and other charts and maps to indicate weather and sea conditions. Prepares and forecasts warnings of severe and hazardous weather and sea conditions and prepares briefings of current and predicted environmental conditions and their effect on military operations. Performs preventative maintenance on meteorological and oceanographic equipment.
GOE: 02.04.01 STRENGTH: M GED: R5 M5 L4 SVP: 7 DLU: 77

025.267-014 WEATHER OBSERVER (profess. & kin.) alternate titles: meteorological technician
Observes and records weather conditions for use in forecasting: Periodically observes general weather, sky and visibility conditions, and reads weather instruments including thermometers, barometers, and hygrometers to ascertain elements, such as temperature, barometric pressure, humidity, wind velocity, and precipitation. Transmits and receives weather data from other stations over teletype machine. May collect upper-air data on temperature, humidity, and winds, using weather balloon and radiosonde equipment. May conduct pilot briefings.
GOE: 02.04.01 STRENGTH: L GED: R4 M4 L4 SVP: 6 DLU: 77

029   OCCUPATIONS IN MATHEMATICS AND PHYSICAL SCIENCES, N.E.C.

This group includes occupations, not elsewhere classified, concerned with mathematics and the physical sciences.

029.067-010   GEOGRAPHER (profess. & kin.)
Studies nature and use of areas of earth's surface, relating and interpreting interactions of physical and cultural phenomena: Conducts research on physical and climatic aspects of area or region, making direct observation of landforms, climates, soils, plants, and animals within area under study and incorporating available knowledge from related scientific fields, such as physics, geology, oceanography, meteorology, and biology. Studies human activities within given area, such as ethnic distribution, economic activity, and political organization. Acts as adviser or consultant to governments and international organizations on subjects, such as economic exploitation of regions and determination of ethnic and natural boundaries between nations or administrative areas. May use surveying equipment or meteorological instruments. May construct and interpret maps, graphs, and diagrams. May specialize in particular branch of cultural geography, such as economic, political, urban, social, or historical geography.
GOE: 02.01.01 STRENGTH: L GED: R6 M6 L6 SVP: 7 DLU: 77

029.067-014   GEOGRAPHER, PHYSICAL (profess. & kin.)
Studies origins, nature, and distribution of features of earth's surface, including landforms, climates, soils, plants, and animals: Makes surveys of physical characteristics of specific regions, conducting studies of features, such as elevations, drainage, geological formations, climate, vegetation, and access to other regions. May conduct environmental studies and prepare environmental impact reports.
GOE: 02.01.01 STRENGTH: L GED: R6 M6 L6 SVP: 7 DLU: 77

029.081-010   ENVIRONMENTAL ANALYST (profess. & kin.) alternate titles: environmental scientist
Conducts research studies to develop theories or methods of abating or controlling sources of environmental pollutants, utilizing knowledge of principles and concepts of various scientific and engineering disciplines: Determines data collection methods to be employed in research projects and surveys. Plans and develops research models, using knowledge of mathematical, statistical, and physical science concepts and approaches. Identifies and analyzes sources of pollution to determine their effects. Collects and synthesizes data derived from pollution emission measurements, atmospheric monitoring, meteorological and minerological information, and soil or water samples. Prepares graphs, charts, and statistical models from synthesized data, using knowledge of mathematical, statistical, and engineering analysis techniques. Analyzes data to assess pollution problems, establish standards, and develop approaches for control of pollution. May be designated according to aspect of environment in which engaged as Air Pollution Analyst (profess. & kin.); Soils Analyst (profess. & kin.); Water Quality Analyst (profess. & kin.).
GOE: 02.01.02 STRENGTH: L GED: R6 M6 L6 SVP: 8 DLU: 77

029.081-014   MATERIALS SCIENTIST (profess. & kin.)
Conducts scientific studies for understanding, characterizing and developing materials leading to potential uses for the benefit of science and emerging technologies: Conducts programs for studying structures and properties of various materials, such as metals, alloys, ceramics, semiconductors and polymers to obtain research data. Plans experimental laboratory production of materials having special characteristics to confirm feasibility of processes and techniques for potential users. Prepares reports of materials studies for information of other scientists and requestors. May guide technical staff engaged in developing materials for specific use in projected product or device.
GOE: 02.01.02 STRENGTH: S GED: R6 M6 L5 SVP: 7 DLU: 77

029.167-010   AERIAL-PHOTOGRAPH INTERPRETER (government ser.)
Analyzes aerial photographs to detect significant military, industrial, resource, or topographical data: Studies photographs to locate enemy positions, camouflaged military installations and equipment, roads, industrial centers, rivers, wooded areas, and to determine nature of terrain. Interprets photographs to evaluate enemy strength and to predict military intentions. May draw maps for use of field commanders in planning deployment of troops. May interpret photographs for timber evaluation, water shed management, construction, or mining. May request enlargement of photograph for more detailed analysis. May use computers and data banks to store, retrieve, and compare information.
GOE: 02.01.02 STRENGTH: S GED: R5 M5 L5 SVP: 7 DLU: 77

029.167-014   PROJECT MANAGER, ENVIRONMENTAL RESEARCH (profess. & kin.)
Plans, directs, and coordinates activities of staff involved in developing procedures, equipment, and techniques to solve pollution problems, using scientific research methods: Schedules and assigns duties to staff research scientists and engineers based on evaluation of their knowledge of specific disciplines. Confers with project scientists and research engineers to formulate research plan, coordinate project activities, and establish reporting procedures. Prepares environmental research project feasibility and progress reports. Coordinates activities of research personnel conducting successive phases of problem analysis, solution proposals, and testing. Reviews technical aspects of project to assist staff and assess productivity of lines of research. Reviews project operations to ensure coordination of efforts and timely submission of reports. Analyzes reports to evaluate program effectiveness and budgetary needs. Approves expenditures necessary for completion of project. Coordinates planning, testing, and operating phases to complete project. Confers with local regulatory agencies to discover local environmental quality standards, industrial practices, and new developments in pollution abatement. May provide technical assistance to agencies conducting related environmental studies.

GOE: 02.01.02 STRENGTH: L GED: R5 M5 L5 SVP: 8 DLU: 77

029.261-010   LABORATORY TESTER (any industry)
Performs laboratory tests according to prescribed standards to determine chemical and physical characteristics or composition of solid, liquid, or gaseous materials for such purposes as quality control, process control, or product development: Sets up, adjusts and operates laboratory equipment and instruments, such as microscopes, centrifuge, agitators, viscosimeter, chemical balance scales, spectrophotometer, gas chromatograph, colorimeter, and other equipment. Tests materials used as ingredients in adhesives, cement, propellants, lubricants, refractories, synthetic rubber, plastics, paint, paper, cloth, and other products for such qualities as purity, stability, viscosity, density, absorption, burning rate, and melting or flash point. Tests solutions used in processes, such as anodizing, waterproofing, cleaning, bleaching, and pickling for chemical concentration, specific gravity, or other characteristics. Tests materials for presence and content of elements or substances, such as hydrocarbons, manganese, natural grease, tungsten, sulfur, cyanide, ash, dust, or impurities. Tests samples of manufactured products to verify conformity to specifications. Records test results on standardized forms and writes test reports describing procedures used. Cleans and sterilizes laboratory equipment. May prepare graphs and charts. May prepare chemical solutions according to standard formulas. May add chemicals or raw materials to process solutions or product batches to correct or establish formulation required to meet specifications. May calibrate laboratory instruments. May be designated according to product or material tested. For testing of food products see FOOD TESTER (any industry) 029.361-014.
GOE: 02.04.01 STRENGTH: L GED: R4 M4 L4 SVP: 6 DLU: 86

029.261-014   POLLUTION-CONTROL TECHNICIAN (profess. & kin.) alternate titles: environmental technician
Conducts tests and field investigations to obtain data for use by environmental, engineering, and scientific personnel in determining sources and methods of controlling pollutants in air, water, and soil, utilizing knowledge of agriculture, chemistry, meteorology, and engineering principles and applied technologies: Conducts chemical and physical laboratory and field tests according to prescribed standards to determine characteristics or composition of solid, liquid, or gaseous materials and substances, using pH meter, chemicals, autoclaves, centrifuge, spectrophotometer, microscope, analytical instrumentation, and chemical laboratory equipment. Collects samples of gases from smokestacks, and collects other air samples and meteorological data to assist in evaluation of atmospheric pollutants. Collects water samples from streams and lakes, or raw, semiprocessed or processed water, industrial waste water, or water from other sources to assess pollution problem. Collects soil, silt, or mud to determine chemical composition and nature of pollutants. Prepares sample for testing, records data, and prepares summaries and charts for review. Sets monitoring equipment to provide flow of information. Installs, operates, and performs routine maintenance on gas and fluid flow systems, chemical reaction systems, mechanical equipment, and other test instrumentation. May operate fixed or mobile monitoring or data collection station. May conduct bacteriological or other tests related to research in environmental or pollution control activity. May collect and analyze engine exhaust emissions to determine type and amount of pollutants and be designated Engine Emission Technician (profess. & kin.). May specialize in one phase or type of environmental pollution or protection and be identified according to specialty.
GOE: 05.03.08 STRENGTH: L GED: R4 M4 L4 SVP: 6 DLU: 77

029.261-018   TEST-ENGINE OPERATOR (petrol. refin.) alternate titles: research-test-engine operator
Subjects petroleum fuels and lubricants to simulated operating conditions in full-scale test engines to obtain evaluating data: Runs tests with gasoline, diesel, aviation, and supercharged research test engines, dynamometers, and other mechanical testing equipment, varying such factors as speed, temperature, load, fuel, and bearing, motor, or chassis lubricants as specified. Records horsepower ratings and other performance data. Tests fuels in standardized knock-rating test engines to obtain data for determination of octane or cetene values. Adjusts and makes minor repairs to engines during test runs.
GOE: 05.03.07 STRENGTH: L GED: R4 M4 L3 SVP: 6 DLU: 77

029.261-022   TESTER (petrol. refin.) alternate titles: crude tester; gas analyst; laboratory inspector; laboratory technician; laboratory tester; oil tester
Tests and analyzes samples of crude oil and petroleum products during processing stages, using laboratory apparatus, testing equipment, and following standard test procedures to determine physical and chemical properties and ensure products meet quality control standards: Tests samples of crude and blended oils, gases, asphalts, and pressure distillates to determine characteristics, such as boiling, vapor, freeze, condensation, flash and aniline points, viscosity, specific gravity, penetration, doctor solution, distillation, and corrosion, using test and laboratory equipment, such as hydrometers, fractionators, distillation apparatus, and analytical scales. Analyzes content of products to determine presence of gases, such as propane, iso-butane, butane, iso-pentane, and ethene. Determines hydrocarbon composition of gasolines, blending stocks and gases, using fractional distillation equipment, gas chromatography, and mass spectrometer. Operates fractionation column to separate crude oil into oils with different boiling points to determine their properties. Analyzes composition of products to determine quantitative presence of gum, sulfur, aromatics, olefins, water, and sediment. Compares color of liquid product with charts to determine processing factors measurable by color. May test air and water samples to detect industrial pollutants.

GOE: 02.04.01 STRENGTH: L GED: R4 M4 L3 SVP: 6 DLU: 77

029.261-026　CRIMINALIST (profess. & kin.) alternate titles: crime laboratory analyst; police chemist

Applies scientific principles to analysis, identification, and classification of mechanical devices, chemical and physical substances, materials, liquids, or other physical evidence related to criminology, law enforcement, or investigative work: Searches for, collects, photographs, and preserves evidence. Performs variety of analytical examinations, utilizing chemistry, physics, mechanics, and other sciences. Analyzes items, such as paint, glass, printed matter, paper, ink, fabric, dust, dirt, gases, or other substances, using spectroscope, microscope, infrared and ultraviolet light, microphotography, gas chromatograph, or other recording, measuring, or testing instruments. Identifies hair, skin, tissue, blood, bones, or human organs. Examines and classifies explosives, firearms, bullets, shells, and other weapons. Interprets laboratory findings relative to drugs, poisons, narcotics, alcohol, or other compounds ingested or injected into body. Reconstructs crime scene, preserving marks or impressions made by shoes, tires, or other objects by plaster or moulage casts. Prepares reports or presentations of findings, methods, and techniques used to support conclusions, and prepares results for court or other formal hearings. May testify as expert witness on evidence or crime laboratory techniques. Confers with experts in such specialties as ballistics, fingerprinting, handwriting, documents, electronics, metallurgy, biochemistry, medicine, or others.

GOE: 02.04.01 STRENGTH: L GED: R5 M5 L5 SVP: 7 DLU: 78

029.280-010　PHOTO-OPTICS TECHNICIAN (profess. & kin.)

Sets up and operates photo-optical instrumentation to record and photograph data for scientific and engineering projects: Operates and calibrates photo-optical equipment according to formalized procedures, maintenance manuals, and schematic diagrams. Operates test equipment and performs analysis of data for engineering and scientific personnel. May install and calibrate optical and photographic data collection equipment in missiles, aircraft, weaponry, weather or communication satelites, underwater devices, or other installations. May evaluate adequacy of data obtained to determine need for future changes in instrumentation. May modify existing equipment and participate in planning and testing modified equipment and instrumentation procedures.

GOE: 02.04.01 STRENGTH: L GED: R5 M4 L3 SVP: 6 DLU: 77

029.361-010　BOTTLE-HOUSE QUALITY-CONTROL TECHNICIAN (beverage) alternate titles: quality-control technician

Performs physical measuring and chemical analysis tests of packaged beer and materials in quality control laboratory of brewery bottle house: Selects test samples of crowns, cans, lids, bottles, labels, and cartons from packaging lines following established procedures as to time, place, and sequence. Measures dimensions of crowns, cans, bottles, lids, and labels with scales and micrometers. Conducts abrasion tests on cans, lids, bottles, crowns, and labels with abrasion machine. Measures hardness of crowns, lids, and cans, using hardness tester. Measures bursting strength of bottles, using hydraulic bursting machine. Tests wet and dry tearing strengths of labels and cartons. Weighs filled cans and bottles to measure volume of beer. Records test results and prepares graphs and charts.

GOE: 02.04.02 STRENGTH: L GED: R4 M4 L4 SVP: 6 DLU: 77

029.361-014　FOOD TESTER (any industry)

Performs standardized qualitative and quantitative tests to determine physical or chemical properties of food or beverage products, or to ensure compliance with company or government quality standards: Conducts standardized tests of food, beverages, additives, and preservatives for flavor, color, texture, nutritional value, or other factors, using incubator, autoclave, ovens, balance scales, refractometer, or other equipment. Tests flavoring and spices for moisture, oil content, coloring, and pungency, using spectrophotometer, stereomicroscope, and ovens. Tests production samples of food for compliance with standards, using spectrometer, pH meter, distillation equipment, balance scales, and other equipment. Refers to tables or computes such factors as moisture, salt content, sediment, or solubility. Smells samples of food for odors or tastes for prescribed flavor. Observes sample smear, sediment disk, or agar sample through microscope to identify bacterial or extraneous matter. Compares test results with standards and records results. Cleans laboratory equipment. May mix ingredients to make reagents. May operate calculating machine to compute percentages of ingredients in finished product. May be identified according to quality or product tested.

GOE: 02.04.02 STRENGTH: L GED: R4 M3 L3 SVP: 5 DLU: 79

029.361-018　LABORATORY ASSISTANT (utilities) alternate titles: laboratory technician

Performs standardized physical and chemical tests on materials and supplies used throughout power system to ensure compliance with specifications: Tests water used in boilers of steam generating plant for alkalinity and silica and phosphate content, using colorimeter and spectrophotometer. Notifies POWER-PLANT OPERATOR (utilities) or AUXILIARY-EQUIPMENT OPERATOR (utilities) of amount of chemical additives required to bring water to prescribed level of purity. Tests coal to determine Btu content by burning coal samples in colorimeter. Tests oil used in circuit breakers for dielectric strength by placing sample of oil in ceramic cup positioned between two electrodes, and measuring current conducted by oil, using ohmmeter. Ascertains heat resisting qualities of insulating paints and varnishes by coating pieces of sheet metal with paint and varnish and subjecting them to high temperatures. May determine vis-

cosity index of lubricating oils, using viscosimeter. May inspect rubber protective equipment, such as aprons, gloves, and blankets for flaws.

GOE: 02.04.01 STRENGTH: L GED: R5 M5 L5 SVP: 6 DLU: 77

029.381-010　CLOTH TESTER (garment; textile)

Performs standardized chemical and physical tests on samples of cloth to verify adherence to specifications: Compares test results with specimens of cloth or prepared standard cards, graphs, or tables. Examines cloth microscopically or through magnifying glass to determine number of threads per inch, whether woven, warped or knitted, and to identify type of fibers, such as wool, nylon, cotton, polyester, acrylic, or a blend. Tests cloth for weight, fastness of dye, color, type of material, tensile strength, shrinkage, absorbency, or fire retardancy, using special testing devices, chemicals, water, heat, drying oven, dehumidifier and scale. May test items, such as buttons, buckles, bindings, webbing, laces, and threads. May mix and apply chemicals to remove stains from garments or fabric soiled in manufacture or transit.

GOE: 02.04.01 STRENGTH: L GED: R4 M3 L4 SVP: 5 DLU: 77

029.381-014　LABORATORY ASSISTANT (textile) alternate titles: laboratory tester

Performs standardized laboratory tests to verify chemical characteristics or composition of textile fibers, yarns, and products, and materials used in processing textiles: Tests oil and soap products to determine fitness for use in cloth and yarn finishing processes. Tests dyed goods for stripping (removing dye). Tests greige goods to determine if goods are of specified quality for dyeing, printing, and finishing. Verifies dye formulas used to develop or match colors by dyeing samples of cloth, yarn or textile fibers, and determines fastness of dyes, using laboratory equipment. Tests raw stock for moisture content with meter-equipped probe. Verifies efficiency of scouring process by testing wool samples to determine percentage of natural greases removed, using scales, solvents, and ovens. Measures tear strength and wet and dry tensile strength, using tensile-testing equipment. Determines color value by subjecting material to lights. Visually inspects yarns and finished material. May classify finished product according to quality and estimate amount of mending required.

GOE: 02.04.01 STRENGTH: L GED: R3 M3 L3 SVP: 4 DLU: 80

029.383-010　PILOT, SUBMERSIBLE (any industry)

Pilots submersible craft to conduct research in fields of oceanography or marine biology, test capabilities and performance of craft and auxiliary equipment, or perform underwater activities, such as exploration, mapping, photography, or construction, salvage or rescue work: Plans and develops operational procedures or techniques in order to investigate and test theories, or carry out specific underwater activities. Conducts predive operational tests on craft, life support systems, and other equipment. Pilots and controls craft to carry out mission in accordance with operational plans. Conducts scientific tests on effect of underwater life, life support systems, and habitats on human or other animals. Performs maintenance and repair on underwater facilities, well-heads, or pipelines. Carries out specific salvage or rescue operations. May perform activities outside of craft, using scuba equipment [SCUBA DIVER (any industry)]. May prepare technical reports or provide data for use by scientific or engineering personnel.

GOE: 05.04.02 STRENGTH: L GED: R5 M3 L4 SVP: 5 DLU: 77

03　COMPUTER-RELATED OCCUPATIONS

This division includes occupations concerned with the application of computers and computer languages and the utilization of the computer in the design and solution of business, scientific, engineering and other technical problems. This division does not include workers, such as accountants, stock brokers, and secretaries, who use computers to aid them in performing their work. Occupations concerned with the mathematical statement of problems for solution by computers are included in Group 020. Occupations concerned with the application of electronics and the principles of engineering to design and develop computing equipment are included in Group 003. Occupations concerned with writing user instructions for computer application programs are included in Group 131. Occupations concerned with training workers to use new or modified information processing procedures are included in Group 166. Occupations concerned with operating and monitoring computers are included in Group 213.

030　OCCUPATIONS IN SYSTEMS ANALYSIS AND PROGRAMMING

This group includes occupations concerned with the analysis and evaluation of procedures and processes to design a sequence of steps for processing data by a computer. These activities may require the conversion of a sequence of steps into a computer language code which will be processed by the computer. Included are testing, locating and correcting program errors, enhancing, maintaining, and executing the coded instructions.

030.062-010　SOFTWARE ENGINEER (profess. & kin.)

Researches, designs, and develops computer software systems, in conjunction with hardware product development, for medical, industrial, military, communications, aerospace, and scientific applications, applying principles and techniques of computer science, engineering, and mathematical analysis: Analyzes software requirements to determine feasibility of design within time and cost constraints. Consults with hardware engineers and other engineering staff to evaluate interface between hardware and software, and operational and perform-

ance requirements of overall system. Formulates and designs software system, using scientific analysis and *mathematical models* to predict and measure outcome and consequences of design. Develops and directs software system testing procedures, programming, and documentation. Consults with customer concerning maintenance of software system. May coordinate installation of software system.
GOE: 11.01.01 STRENGTH: S GED: R5 M5 L5 SVP: 8 DLU: 90

030.162-010 · COMPUTER PROGRAMMER (profess. & kin.) alternate titles: applications programmer; programmer, business
Converts data from project specifications and statements of problems and procedures to create or modify computer programs: Prepares, or receives from SYSTEMS ANALYST (profess. & kin.) 030.167-014, detailed workflow chart and diagram to illustrate sequence of steps that program must follow and to describe input, output, and logical operations involved. Analyzes workflow chart and diagram, applying knowledge of computer capabilities, subject matter, and symbolic logic. Confers with supervisor and representatives of departments concerned with program to resolve questions of program intent, data input, output requirements, and inclusion of internal checks and controls. Converts detailed logical flow chart to language processable by computer. Enters program codes into computer system. Inputs test data into computer. Observes computer monitor screen to interpret program operating codes. Corrects program errors, using methods such as modifying program or altering sequence of program steps. Writes instructions to guide operating personnel during production runs. Analyzes, reviews, and rewrites programs to increase operating efficiency or to adapt program to new requirements. Compiles and writes documentation of program development and subsequent revisions. May train workers to use program. May assist COMPUTER OPERATOR (clerical) 213.362-010 to resolve problems in running computer program. May work with SYSTEMS ANALYST (profess. & kin.) to obtain and analyze project specifications and flow charts. May direct and coordinate work of others to write, test, and modify computer programs.
GOE: 11.01.01 STRENGTH: S GED: R5 M4 L5 SVP: 7 DLU: 90

030.162-014 PROGRAMMER-ANALYST (profess. & kin.) alternate titles: applications analyst-programmer
Plans, develops, tests, and documents computer programs, applying knowledge of programming techniques and computer systems: Evaluates user request for new or modified program, such as for financial or human resource management system, clinical research trial results, statistical study of traffic patterns, or analyzing and developing specifications for bridge design, to determine feasibility, cost and time required, compatibility with current system, and computer capabilities. Consults with user to identify current operating procedures and clarify program objectives. Reads manuals, periodicals, and technical reports to learn ways to develop programs that meet user requirements. Formulates plan outlining steps required to develop program, using structured analysis and design. Submits plans to user for approval. Prepares flowcharts and diagrams to illustrate sequence of steps program must follow and to describe logical operations involved. Designs computer terminal screen displays to accomplish goals of user request. Converts project specifications, using flowcharts and diagrams, into sequence of detailed instructions and logical steps for coding into language processable by computer, applying knowledge of computer programming techniques and computer languages. Enters program codes into computer system. Enters commands into computer to run and test program. Reads computer printouts or observes display screen to detect syntax or logic errors during program test, or uses diagnostic software to detect errors. Replaces, deletes, or modifies codes to correct errors. Analyzes, reviews, and alters program to increase operating efficiency or adapt to new requirements. Writes documentation to describe program development, logic, coding, and corrections. Writes manual for users to describe installation and operating procedures. Assists users to solve operating problems. Recreates steps taken by user to locate source of problem and rewrites program to correct errors. May use computer-aided software tools, such as flowchart design and code generation, in each stage of system development. May train users to use program. May oversee installation of hardware and software. May provide technical assistance to program users. May install and test program at user site. May monitor performance of program after implementation. May specialize in developing programs for business or technical applications.
GOE: 11.01.01 STRENGTH: S GED: R5 M5 L5 SVP: 7 DLU: 90

030.162-018 PROGRAMMER, ENGINEERING AND SCIENTIFIC (profess. & kin.)
Converts scientific, engineering, and other technical problem formulations to format processable by computer: Resolves symbolic formulations, prepares flow charts and block diagrams, and encodes resultant equations for processing by applying extensive knowledge of branch of science, engineering, or advanced mathematics, such as differential equations or numerical analysis, and understanding of capabilities and limitations of computer. Confers with other engineering and technical personnel to resolve problems of intent, inaccuracy, or feasibility of computer processing. Enters program into computer system. Reviews results of computer runs with interested personnel to determine necessity for modifications or reruns. Develops new subroutines or expands program to simplify statement, programming, or coding of future problems. May direct and coordinate activities of COMPUTER PROGRAMMERS (profess. & kin.) 030.162-010 working as part of project team.
GOE: 11.01.01 STRENGTH: S GED: R6 M6 L6 SVP: 8 DLU: 90

030.162-022 SYSTEMS PROGRAMMER (profess. & kin.)
Coordinates installation of computer operating system software and tests, maintains, and modifies software, using computer terminal: Reads loading and running instructions for system software, such as task scheduling, memory management, computer file system, or controlling computer input and output, and loads tape into tape drive or transfers software to magnetic disk. Initiates test of system program and observes readout on monitor of computer system to detect errors or work stoppage. Enters code changes into computer system to correct errors. Analyzes performance indicators, such as system's response time, number of transactions per second, and number of programs being processed at once, to ensure that system is operating efficiently. Changes system software so that system performance will meet objectives. Reviews computer system capabilities, workflow, and scheduling limitations to determine if requested changes to operating system are possible. Writes description of steps taken to modify system and procedures required to implement new software. Assists users having problems with use of system software. May train users, COMPUTER OPERATOR (clerical) 213.362-010, and COMPUTER PROGRAMMER (profess. & kin.) 030.162-010 to use system software. May prepare workflow charts and diagrams to modify system software. May visit vendors to observe demonstration of systems software. May administer and monitor computer program that controls user access to system. May review productivity reports and problem records to evaluate performance of computer system.
GOE: 11.01.01 STRENGTH: S GED: R5 M4 L5 SVP: 7 DLU: 90

030.167-010 CHIEF, COMPUTER PROGRAMMER (profess. & kin.) alternate titles: coordinator, computer programming
Plans, schedules, and directs preparation of programs to process data and solve problems by use of computers: Consults with managerial and systems analysis personnel to clarify program intent, identify problems, suggest changes, and determine extent of programming and coding required. Assigns, coordinates, and reviews work of programming personnel. Develops programs from workflow charts or diagrams, considering factors, such as computer storage capacity and speed, extent of peripheral equipment, and intended use of output data. Converts workflow charts to language processable by computer. Enters program codes into computer. Enters test data into computer. Analyzes test runs on computer to correct or direct correction of coded program and input data. Revises or directs revision of existing programs to increase operating efficiency or adapt to new requirements. Compiles documentation of program development and subsequent revisions. Trains subordinates in programming and program coding. Prescribes standards for terms and symbols used to simplify interpretation of programs. Collaborates with computer manufacturers and other users to develop new programming methods. Prepares records and reports.
GOE: 11.01.01 STRENGTH: S GED: R5 M4 L5 SVP: 8 DLU: 89

030.167-014 SYSTEMS ANALYST (profess. & kin.)
Analyzes user requirements, procedures, and problems to automate processing or to improve existing computer system: Confers with personnel of organizational units involved to analyze current operational procedures, identify problems, and learn specific input and output requirements, such as forms of data input, how data is to be summarized, and formats for reports. Writes detailed description of user needs, program functions, and steps required to develop or modify computer program. Reviews computer system capabilities, workflow, and scheduling limitations to determine if requested program or program change is possible within existing system. Studies existing information processing systems to evaluate effectiveness and develops new systems to improve production or workflow as required. Prepares workflow charts and diagrams to specify in detail operations to be performed by equipment and computer programs and operations to be performed by personnel in system. Conducts studies pertaining to development of new information systems to meet current and projected needs. Plans and prepares technical reports, memoranda, and instructional manuals as documentation of program development. Upgrades system and corrects errors to maintain system after implementation. May assist COMPUTER PROGRAMMER (profess. & kin.) 030.162-010 in resolution of work problems related to flow charts, project specifications, or programming. May prepare time and cost estimates for completing projects. May direct and coordinate work of others to develop, test, install, and modify programs.
GOE: 11.01.01 STRENGTH: S GED: R5 M4 L5 SVP: 7 DLU: 90

031   OCCUPATIONS IN DATA COMMUNICATIONS AND NETWORKS

This group includes occupations concerned with the evaluation of data communications and network hardware and software, coordinating data communications activities, and the transmission and reception of data or information sent electronically. Includes providing support to users of data communications. Occupations concerned with installing, maintaining, and repairing data communications equipment are included in Group 823.

031.132-010 SUPERVISOR, NETWORK CONTROL OPERATORS (any industry) alternate titles: data communications technician supervisor
Supervises and coordinates activities of workers engaged in monitoring or installing data communication lines and resolving user data communication problems: Distributes work assignments and monitors daily logs of NETWORK CONTROL OPERATORS (any industry) 031.262-014, using microcomputer. Explains data communications diagnostic and monitoring procedures to opera-

tors, using computer terminal and following vendor's equipment and software instructions. Explains and demonstrates installation of data communication lines and equipment to operators, using handtools and following vendor manuals. Enters diagnostic commands into computer and determines nature of problem to assist operators to resolve data communication problems. Enters record of actions taken to resolve problem in daily log, using microcomputer. Attends staff meetings to report on and resolve recurrent data communications problems. Attends vendor seminars to learn about changes in data communications technology. Performs other duties as described under SUPERVISOR (any industry) Master Title.
GOE: 07.01.02 STRENGTH: L GED: R4 M4 L4 SVP: 7 DLU: 88

031.262-010 DATA COMMUNICATIONS ANALYST (profess. & kin.)
Researches, tests, evaluates, and recommends data communications hardware and software: Identifies areas of operation which need upgraded equipment, such as modems, fiber optic cables, and telephone wires. Conducts survey to determine user needs. Reads technical manuals and brochures to determine equipment which meets establishment requirements. Visits vendors to learn about available products or services. Tests and evaluates hardware and software to determine efficiency, reliability, and compatibility with existing system, using equipment such as computer terminal and modem. Analyzes test data and recommends hardware or software for purchase. Develops and writes procedures for installation, use, and solving problems of communications hardware and software. Monitors system performance. Trains users in use of equipment. Assists users to identify and solve data communication problems. May write technical specifications to send to vendors for bid. May oversee or assist in installation of communications hardware. May perform minor equipment repairs.
GOE: 11.01.01 STRENGTH: L GED: R5 M3 L5 SVP: 7 DLU: 90

031.262-014 NETWORK CONTROL OPERATOR (any industry)
Monitors data communications network to ensure that network is available to all system users and resolves data communications problems: Receives telephone call from user with data communications problem, such as failure of data to be transmitted to another location. Reviews procedures user followed to determine if specified steps were taken. Explains user procedures necessary to transmit data. Monitors modems and display screen of terminal to mainframe computer to detect error messages that signal malfunction in communications software or hardware. Enters diagnostic commands into computer to determine nature of problem, and reads codes on screen to diagnose problem. Attaches diagnostic equipment to phone line to learn if line meets specification. Reads technical reference manuals for communications hardware and software to learn cause of problem. Instructs user to enter specified commands into computer to resolve problem. Calls service technician for service when problem cannot be resolved. Enters operating commands into computer to restart program. Records number of daily data communications transactions and number of problems and actions taken, using computer terminal. Updates documentation to record new equipment installed, new sites, and changes to computer configurations. May inspect communications wires and cables. May train staff and users to use equipment. May coordinate installation of or install communications lines.
GOE: 07.06.01 STRENGTH: L GED: R4 M3 L4 SVP: 6 DLU: 90

032 OCCUPATIONS IN COMPUTER SYSTEMS USER SUPPORT

This group includes occupations concerned with investigating, resolving, and explaining computer-related problems to users of computer systems. Occupations concerned with support for data communications users are included in Group 031.

032.132-010 USER SUPPORT ANALYST SUPERVISOR (profess. & kin.) alternate titles: help desk supervisor
Supervises and coordinates activities of workers who provide problem-solving support to computer users: Assists USER SUPPORT ANALYST (profess. & kin.) 032.262-010 in solving nonroutine software, hardware, and procedure problems, using computer and manuals. Talks with staff, computer users, supervisors, and managers to determine requirements for new or modified software and hardware. Writes recommendations for management review. Coordinates installation of hardware and software, and implementation of procedure changes. Performs duties described under SUPERVISOR (any industry) Master Title.
GOE: 11.01.01 STRENGTH: S GED: R4 M3 L4 SVP: 8 DLU: 88

032.262-010 USER SUPPORT ANALYST (profess. & kin.) alternate titles: customer service representative; end user consultant; help desk representative; information center specialist; office automation analyst
Investigates and resolves computer software and hardware problems of users: Receives telephone calls from users having problems using computer software and hardware or inquiring how to use specific software, such as statistical, graphics, data base, printing, word processing, programming languages, electronic mail, and operating systems. Talks to user to learn procedures followed and source of error. Answers questions, applying knowledge of computer software, hardware, and procedures. Asks user with problem to use telephone and participate in diagnostic procedures, using diagnostic software, or by listening to and following instructions. Determines whether problem is caused by hardware, such as modem, printer, cables, or telephone. Talks with coworkers to

research problem and find solution. Talks to programmers to explain software errors or to recommend changes to programs. Calls software and hardware vendors to request service regarding defective products. Reads trade magazines and attends computer trade shows to obtain current information about computers. May test software and hardware to evaluate ease of use and whether product will aid user in performing work. May write software and hardware evaluation and recommendation for management review. May write or revise user training manuals and procedures. May develop training materials, such as exercises and visual displays. May train users on software and hardware on-site or in classroom, or recommend outside contractors to provide training. May install microcomputers, software, and peripheral equipment, following procedures and using handtools [MICROCOMPUTER SUPPORT SPECIALIST (profess & kin.) 039.264-010]. May work as in-house consultant and research alternate approaches to existing software and hardware when standardized approaches cannot be applied. May conduct office automation feasibility studies, including work flow analysis, space design, and cost comparison analysis. May specialize by type of software, computer language, or computer operating system.
GOE: 11.01.01 STRENGTH: S GED: R4 M3 L4 SVP: 7 DLU: 90

033 OCCUPATIONS IN COMPUTER SYSTEMS TECHNICAL SUPPORT

This group includes occupations concerned with providing technical support for computer systems, rather than to users of computer systems. Includes the development, installation, and maintenance of computer operating systems software.

033.162-010 COMPUTER SECURITY COORDINATOR (profess. & kin.) alternate titles: data security coordinator; information security
Plans, coordinates, and implements security measures to safeguard information in computer files against accidental or unauthorized modification, destruction, or disclosure: Confers with computer user department personnel and COMPUTER PROGRAMMER (profess. & kin.) 030.162-010 to plan data security for new or modified software, discussing issues, such as employee data access needs and risk of data loss or disclosure. Reviews plan to ensure compatibility of planned security measures with establishment computer security system software. Modifies security data files to incorporate new software security into establishment security software, using computer terminal, or meets with SYSTEMS PROGRAMMER (profess. & kin.) 030.162-022 to request needed programming changes. Enters commands into computer in attempt to circumvent new security measures to test system. Reviews employee violations of computer security procedures recorded by computer and reports violations to user department managers or talks with employee to ensure that violation is not repeated. Coordinates implementation of vendor-issued security software update. Develops and writes computer security department policies and procedures. May assign computer access passwords to employees [COMPUTER SECURITY SPECIALIST (profess. & kin.) 033.362-010]. May develop, coordinate implementation of, and test plan to continue establishment data processing activities at off-site location in case of emergency, such as fire, at main site [DATA RECOVERY PLANNER (profess. & kin.) 033.162-014].
GOE: 11.10.05 STRENGTH: S GED: R5 M3 L4 SVP: 8 DLU: 90

033.162-014 DATA RECOVERY PLANNER (profess. & kin.) alternate titles: disaster recovery coordinator
Develops, coordinates implementation of, and tests plan to continue establishment data processing activities at off-site location in case of emergency, such as fire, at main site: Establishes priority of data processing activities according to importance to business. Determines hardware, software, data files, safe storage facilities, and other resources required. Develops plan to meet emergency data processing needs. Identifies personnel needed to implement plan. Presents plan to management and recommends means of obtaining required facilities, such as contracting with off-site vendor. Coordinates implementation of plan. Tests emergency data processing system, using computer and test data. Writes report to document test results and updates emergency recovery procedures.
GOE: 11.01.01 STRENGTH: L GED: R5 M3 L5 SVP: 8 DLU: 89

033.162-018 TECHNICAL SUPPORT SPECIALIST (profess. & kin.) alternate titles: project development coordinator; technical operations specialist
Performs any combination of following duties to provide technical support to workers in information processing departments: Develops work goals and department projects. Assigns and coordinates work projects, such as converting to new hardware or software. Designates staff assignments, establishes work priorities, and evaluates cost and time requirements. Reviews completed projects or computer programs to ensure that goals are met and that programs are compatible with other programs already in use. Evaluates work load and capacity of computer system to determine feasibility of expanding or enhancing computer operations. Makes recommendations for improvements in computer system. Reviews and tests programs written by PROGRAMMER-ANALYST (profess. & kin.) 030.162-014 or COMPUTER PROGRAMMER (profess. & kin.) 030.162-010 to ensure that programs meet objectives and specifications. Consults with QUALITY ASSURANCE ANALYST (profess. & kin.) 033.262-010 to ensure that program follows establishment standards. Modifies, tests, and corrects existing programs. Evaluates and tests vendor-supplied software packages for mainframe computer or microcomputers to determine compatibility

with existing system, ease of use, and if software meets user needs. Enters commands into computer to place programs in production status. Inactivates, individually or in combination, each component of computer system, such as central processing unit, tape drives, and mainframe coolers. Tests computer system to determine criticality of component loss. Prioritizes importance of components and writes recommendations for recovering losses and using backup equipment. Assists user to resolve computer-related problems, such as inoperative hardware or software. Trains workers in use of new software or hardware. Reads technical journals or manuals and attends vendor seminars to learn about new computer hardware and software. Writes project reports and documentation for new or modified software and hardware.
GOE: 11.01.01 STRENGTH: L GED: R5 M4 L5 SVP: 7 DLU: 88

033.167-010 COMPUTER SYSTEMS HARDWARE ANALYST (profess. & kin.) alternate titles: computer systems engineer; information processing engineer; methods analyst, data processing
Analyzes data processing requirements to plan data processing system that will provide system capabilities required for projected work loads, and plans layout and installation of new system or modification of existing system: Confers with data processing and project managers to obtain information on limitations and capabilities of existing system and capabilities required for data processing projects and projected work load. Evaluates factors such as number of departments serviced by data processing equipment, reporting formats required, volume of transactions, time requirements and cost constraints, and need for security and access restrictions to determine hardware configurations. Analyzes information to determine, recommend, and plan layout for type of computers and peripheral equipment, or modifications to existing equipment and system, that will provide capability for proposed project or work load, efficient operation, and effective use of allotted space. May enter data into computer terminal to store, retrieve, and manipulate data for analysis of system capabilities and requirements. May specify power supply requirements and configuration. May recommend purchase of equipment to control dust, temperature, and humidity in area of system installation. May specialize in one area of system application or in one type or make of equipment. May train users to use new or modified equipment. May monitor functioning of equipment to ensure system operates in conformance with specifications.
GOE: 05.01.03 STRENGTH: S GED: R5 M5 L5 SVP: 7 DLU: 88

033.262-010 QUALITY ASSURANCE ANALYST (profess. & kin.)
Evaluates and tests new or modified software programs and software development procedures used to verify that programs function according to user requirements and conform to establishment guidelines: Writes, revises, and verifies quality standards and test procedures for program design and product evaluation to attain quality of software economically and efficiently. Reviews new or modified program, including documentation, diagram, and flow chart, to determine if program will perform according to user request and conform to guidelines. Recommends program improvements or corrections to programmers. Reviews computer operating log to identify program processing errors. Enters instructions into computer to test program for validity of results, accuracy, reliability, and conformance to establishment standards. Observes computer monitor screen during program test to detect error codes or interruption of program and corrects errors. Identifies differences between establishment standards and user applications and suggests modifications to conform to standards. Sets up tests at request of user to locate and correct program operating error following installation of program. Conducts compatibility tests with vendor-provided programs. Monitors program performance after implementation to prevent reoccurrence of program operating problems and ensure efficiency of operation. Writes documentation to describe program evaluation, testing, and correction. May evaluate proposed software or software enhancement for feasibility. May develop utility program to test, track, and verify defects in software program. May write programs to create new procedures or modify existing procedures. May train software program users.
GOE: 11.01.01 STRENGTH: L GED: R4 M4 L4 SVP: 6 DLU: 89

033.362-010 COMPUTER SECURITY SPECIALIST (profess. & kin.)
Regulates access to computer data files, monitors data file use, and updates computer security files: Enters commands into computer to allow access to computer system for employee who forgot password. Reads computer security files to determine whether denial of data access reported by employee is justified. Modifies security files to correct error, or explains that employee authorization does not permit access. Answers employee questions about computer security. Modifies security files to add new employees, delete former employees, and change employee name, following notice received from computer user departments and personnel office. Sends printouts listing employee data authorization to computer user departments to verify or correct information in security files. Reviews data use records and compares user names listed in records with employee authorization to ensure that all employees who accessed data files were entitled to do so. Deletes data access of unauthorized users, and for users who have not used data for specified time.
GOE: 11.10.05 STRENGTH: S GED: R4 M2 L3 SVP: 6 DLU: 89

039   COMPUTER-RELATED OCCUPATIONS, N.E.C.

This group includes occupations, not elsewhere classified, concerned with computers.

039.162-010 DATA BASE ADMINISTRATOR (profess. & kin.)
Coordinates physical changes to computer data bases; and codes, tests, and implements physical data base, applying knowledge of data base management

system: Designs logical and physical data bases [DATA BASE DESIGN ANALYST (profess. & kin.) 039.162-014] or reviews description of changes to data base design to understand how changes to be made affect physical data base (how data is stored in terms of physical characteristics, such as location, amount of space, and access method). Establishes physical data base parameters. Codes data base descriptions and specifies identifiers of data base to data base management system or directs others in coding data base descriptions. Calculates optimum values for data base parameters, such as amount of computer memory to be used by data base, following manuals and using calculator. Specifies user access level for each segment of one or more data items, such as insert, replace, retrieve, or delete data.Specifies which users can access data bases and what data can be accessed by user. Tests and corrects errors, and refines changes to data base. Enters codes to create production data base. Selects and enters codes of utility program to monitor data base performance, such as distribution of records and amount of available memory. Directs programmers and analysts to make changes to data base management system. Reviews and corrects programs. Answers user questions. Confers with coworkers to determine impact of data base changes on other systems and staff cost for making changes to data base. Modifies data base programs to increase processing performance, referred to as performance tuning. Workers typically specialize in one or more types of data base management systems. May train users.
GOE: 11.01.01 STRENGTH: S GED: R5 M4 L5 SVP: 8 DLU: 90

039.162-014 DATA BASE DESIGN ANALYST (profess. & kin.)
Designs logical and physical data bases and coordinates data base development as part of project team, applying knowledge of data base design standards and data base management system: Reviews project request describing data base user needs. Estimates time and cost required to accomplish project. Determines if project requires creating series of new programs or modifying existing programs that access data stored in data bases. Attends specification meeting with project team workers to determine scope and limitations of project. Reviews workflow chart developed by PROGRAMMER-ANALYST (profess. & kin.) 030.162-014 to understand tasks computer will perform, such as updating records. Reviews procedures in data base management system manuals for making changes to data base, such as defining, creating, revising, and controlling data base. Revises company definition of data as defined in data dictionary (information about data, including name, description, source of data item, and key words for categorizing and searching for data item descriptions). Determines and enters changes to data dictionary descriptions, including type, structure, and intended use of data within system, using computer or assigns data entry work to programmer. Develops data model describing data elements and how they are used, following procedures and using pen and template or computer software. Creates description to enable PROGRAMMER-ANALYST (profess. & kin.) to understand how programs should access data. Writes description of how user accesses data, referred to as logical data base. Writes physical data base description, such as location, space requirements, and access method, to protect company data resources against unauthorized access and accidental destruction, according to computer industry standards and knowledge of data base management system. May specialize in adding, deleting, and modifying data items in data dictionary and be designated Data Dictionary Administrator (profess. and kin.). Workers typically specialize in one or more types of data base management systems.
GOE: 11.01.01 STRENGTH: S GED: R5 M4 L5 SVP: 8 DLU: 90

039.264-010 MICROCOMPUTER SUPPORT SPECIALIST (profess. & kin.)
Installs, modifies, and makes minor repairs to microcomputer hardware and software systems and provides technical assistance and training to system users: Inspects microcomputer equipment and reads order sheet listing user requirements to prepare microcomputer for delivery. Installs or assists service personnel in installation of hardware and peripheral components, such as monitors, keyboards, printers, and disk drives on user's premises, following design or installation specifications. Loads specified software packages, such as operating systems, word processing, or spreadsheet programs into computer. Enters commands and observes system functions to verify correct system operation. Instructs user in use of equipment, software, and manuals. Answers client's inquiries in person and via telephone concerning systems operation; diagnoses system hardware, software, and operator problems; and recommends or performs minor remedial actions to correct problems based on knowledge of system operation. Replaces defective or inadequate software packages. Refers major hardware problems to service personnel for correction. Attends technical conferences and seminars to keep abreast of new software and hardware product developments.
GOE: 05.05.05 STRENGTH: M GED: R4 M3 L4 SVP: 7 DLU: 90

04   OCCUPATIONS IN LIFE SCIENCES

This division includes occupations concerned with research to increase basic knowledge of living organisms, including humans and the practical application of biological and behavioral theories.

040   OCCUPATIONS IN AGRICULTURAL SCIENCES

This group includes occupations concerned with the application of scientific principles to problems related to agriculture, horticulture, forestry, and environmental impact. Also includes development of improved methods in cultivation, processing, handling, and storing of products; land conservation practices; pest control; landscape planning; and related activities.

040.061-010 AGRONOMIST (profess. & kin.) alternate titles: crop-research scientist; crop scientist

Conducts experiments or investigations in field-crop problems and develops new methods of growing crops to secure more efficient production, higher yield, and improved quality: Plans and carries out breeding studies at experiment stations or farms to develop and improve varieties of field crops, such as cotton, tobacco, or cereal with respect to characteristics, such as yield, quality, adaptation to specific soils or climates, and resistance to diseases and pests [PLANT BREEDER (profess. & kin.)]. Studies crop production to discover best methods of planting, cultivation, harvesting, and effects of various climatic conditions on crops. Develops methods for control of noxious weeds, crop diseases, and insect pests [PLANT PATHOLOGIST (profess. & kin.)]. May specialize in specific field crop, group of field crops, or specific agronomic problem.
GOE: 02.02.02 STRENGTH: L GED: R6 M6 L6 SVP: 8 DLU: 77

040.061-014 ANIMAL SCIENTIST (profess. & kin.)

Conducts research in selection, breeding, feeding, management, and marketing of beef and dual-purpose cattle, horses, mules, sheep, dogs, goats, and pet animals: Develops improved practices in feeding, housing, sanitation, and parasite and disease control. Controls breeding practices to improve strains of animals. May specialize in animal nutritional research and be designated Animal Nutritionist (profess. & kin.). May be designated according to animal specialty.
GOE: 02.02.01 STRENGTH: M GED: R6 M6 L6 SVP: 8 DLU: 77

040.061-018 DAIRY SCIENTIST (profess. & kin.)

Conducts research in selection, breeding, feeding, and management of dairy cattle: Studies feed requirements of dairy animals and nutritive value of feed materials. Carries out experiments to determine effects of different kinds of feed and environmental conditions on quantity, quality, and nutritive value of milk produced. Develops improved practices in care and management of dairy herds and use of improved buildings and equipment. Studies physiology of reproduction and lactation, and carries out breeding programs to improve dairy breeds [ANIMAL BREEDER (agriculture)]. May be designated according to specialty as Dairy-Management Specialist (profess. & kin.); Dairy-Nutrition Specialist (profess. & kin.).
GOE: 02.02.01 STRENGTH: L GED: R6 M6 L6 SVP: 8 DLU: 77

040.061-022 DAIRY TECHNOLOGIST (profess. & kin.) alternate titles: dairy-manufacturing technologist; dairy-products technologist

Applies principles of bacteriology, chemistry, physics, engineering, and economics to develop new and improved methods in production, preservation, and utilization of milk, cheese, ice cream, and other dairy products: Conducts experiments in such problems as preventing bacterial increase in milk during handling and processing, improving pasteurization methods, and designing better packaging materials, dairy equipment, or supplies. May specialize according to product, as ice cream or cheese, or according to functional activity, as sanitation research or storage problems.
GOE: 02.02.04 STRENGTH: L GED: R6 M6 L6 SVP: 8 DLU: 77

040.061-026 FIBER TECHNOLOGIST (profess. & kin.)

Studies nature, origin, use, improvement, and processing methods of plant, animal, and synthetic fibers: Analyzes wool, mohair, cashmere, camel's hair, alpaca, bristles, feathers, and similar animal and fowl fibers, plant fibers, such as cotton, linen, and jute, and synthetic fibers and products made from these fibers. Applies principles of science to improve growth and quality of fibers. Conducts experiments in blending fibers and develops improved manufacturing methods for converting fibers into articles, such as cloth, felts, rugs, mattresses, and brushes. Conducts tests on fibrous structures for quality control, such as tensile strength and stability to heat, light, and chemicals. May be identified according to fibers studied.
GOE: 05.01.08 STRENGTH: L GED: R6 M6 L6 SVP: 8 DLU: 77

040.061-030 FOREST ECOLOGIST (profess. & kin.)

Conducts research in environmental factors affecting forests: Carries out studies to determine what conditions account for prevalence of different varieties of trees. Studies classification, life history, light and soil requirements, and resistance to disease and insects of different species. Investigates adaptability of different species to new environmental conditions, such as changes in soil type, climate, and altitude.
GOE: 02.02.02 STRENGTH: L GED: R6 M6 L6 SVP: 8 DLU: 77

040.061-038 HORTICULTURIST (profess. & kin.)

Conducts experiments and investigations to determine methods of breeding, producing, storing, processing, and transporting of fruits, nuts, berries, vegetables, flowers, bushes, and trees: Experiments to develop new or improved varieties having higher yield, quality, nutritional value, resistance to disease, or adaptability to climates, soils, uses, or processes. Determines best methods of planting, spraying, cultivating, and harvesting. May specialize in research, breeding, production, or shipping and storage of fruits, nuts, berries, vegetables, ornamental plants, or other horticultural products and be identified according to specialty. May prepare articles and give lectures on horticultural specialty.
GOE: 02.02.02 STRENGTH: M GED: R6 M6 L6 SVP: 8 DLU: 79

040.061-042 POULTRY SCIENTIST (profess. & kin.)

Conducts research in breeding, feeding, and management of poultry: Examines selection and breeding practices to increase efficiency of production and improve quality of poultry products [ANIMAL BREEDER (agriculture)]. Studies nutritional requirements of various classes of poultry. Develops improved practices in incubation, brooding, feeding, rearing, housing, artificial insemination, and disease and parasite prevention and control. Studies effects of management practices and processing methods on quality of eggs and other poultry products. May specialize in artificial insemination.
GOE: 02.02.01 STRENGTH: L GED: R6 M6 L6 SVP: 8 DLU: 77

040.061-046 RANGE MANAGER (profess. & kin.) alternate titles: range-management specialist

Conducts research in range problems to provide sustained production of forage, livestock, and wildlife: Studies range lands to determine best grazing seasons and number and kind of livestock that can be most profitably grazed. Plans and directs construction and maintenance of range improvements, such as fencing, corrals, reservoirs for stock watering, and structures for soil-erosion control. Develops improved practices for range reseeding. Studies forage plants and their growth requirements to determine varieties best suited to particular range. Develops methods for controlling poisonous plants, and for protecting range from fire and rodent damage. May specialize in particular area and be designated Range Conservationist (profess. & kin.).
GOE: 02.02.02 STRENGTH: L GED: R6 M6 L6 SVP: 8 DLU: 77

040.061-050 SILVICULTURIST (profess. & kin.)

Establishes and cares for forest stands: Manages tree nurseries and thins forests to encourage natural growth of sprouts or seedlings of desired varieties. Conducts research in such problems of forest propagation and culture as tree growth rate, effects of thinning on forest yield, duration of seed viability, and effects of fire and animal grazing on growth, seed production, and germination of different species. Develops techniques for measuring and identifying trees.
GOE: 02.02.02 STRENGTH: L GED: R5 M5 L5 SVP: 7 DLU: 77

040.061-054 SOIL CONSERVATIONIST (profess. & kin.)

Plans and develops coordinated practices for soil erosion control, moisture conservation, and sound land use: Conducts surveys and investigations on rural or urban planning, agriculture, construction, forestry, or mining on measures needed to maintain or restore proper soil management. Plans soil management practices, such as crop rotation, reforestation, permanent vegetation, contour plowing, or terracing as related to soil and water conservation. Prepares soil conservation plans in cooperation with state, county, or local government, farmers, foresters, miners, or urban planners to provide for use and treatment of land according to needs and capability. Applies principles of two or more specialized fields of science, such as agronomy, soil science, forestry, or agriculture to achieve objectives of conservation. May develop or participate in environmental studies.
GOE: 02.02.02 STRENGTH: L GED: R6 M6 L6 SVP: 8 DLU: 77

040.061-058 SOIL SCIENTIST (profess. & kin.)

Studies soil characteristics and maps soil types, and investigates responses of soils to known management practices to determine use capabilities of soils and effects of alternative practices on soil productivity: Classifies soils according to standard types. Conducts experiments on farms or experimental stations to determine best soil types for different plants. Performs chemical analysis on micro-organism content of soil to determine microbial reactions and chemical and mineralogical relationship to plant growth. Investigates responses of specific soil types to tillage, fertilization, nutrient transformations, crop rotation, environmental consequences, water, gas or heat flow, industrial waste control and other soil management practices. Advises interested persons on rural or urban land use. May specialize in one or more types of activities relative to soil management and productivity and be designated Soil Fertility Expert (profess. & kin.).
GOE: 02.02.02 STRENGTH: L GED: R6 M6 L6 SVP: 8 DLU: 77

040.061-062 WOOD TECHNOLOGIST (profess. & kin.)

Conducts research to determine composition, properties, behavior, utilization, development, treatments, and processing methods of wood and wood products: Analyzes physical, chemical, and biological properties of wood. Studies methods of curing wood to determine best and most economical procedure. Develops and improves methods of seasoning, preservation, and treating wood with substances to increase resistance to wear, fire, fungi, insects, and marine borers. Conducts tests to determine ability of wood adhesives to withstand water, oil penetration, temperature extremes, and stability, strength, hardness and crystallinity of wood under variety of conditions. Evaluates and improves effectiveness of industrial equipment and production processes. Investigates processes for converting wood into commodities, such as alcohol, veneer, plywood, wood plastics, and other uses. Determines best type of wood for specific application, and investigates methods of turning waste wood materials into useful products. May specialize in research, quality control, marketing and sales, materials engineering, management or administration, manufacturing, production, or process development.
GOE: 02.02.02 STRENGTH: L GED: R6 M5 L5 SVP: 8 DLU: 77

040.167-010 FORESTER (profess. & kin.)

Manages and develops forest lands and resources for economic and recreational purposes: Plans and directs forestation and reforestation projects. Maps forest areas, estimates standing timber and future growth, and manages timber sales. Plans cutting programs to assure continuous production of timber or to assist timber companies achieve production goals. Determines methods of cutting and removing timber with minimum waste and environmental damage and

suggests methods of processing wood for various uses. Directs suppression of forest fires and conducts fire-prevention programs. Plans and directs construction and maintenance of recreation facilities, fire towers, trails, roads, and fire breaks. Assists in planning and implementing projects for control of floods, soil erosion, tree diseases, and insect pests in forests [ENTOMOLOGIST (profess. & kin.) 041.061-046; PLANT PATHOLOGIST (profess. & kin.) 041.061-086; SOIL CONSERVATIONIST (profess. & kin.) 040.061-054]. Advises landowners on forestry management techniques and conducts public educational programs on forest care and conservation. May participate in environmental studies and prepare environmental reports. May supervise activities of other forestry workers [SUPERVISOR (any industry) Master Title]. May patrol forests, enforce laws, and fight forest fires. May administer budgets. May conduct research to improve knowledge of forest management. May specialize in one aspect of forest management. May be designated Forestry Supervisor (profess. & kin.); Woods Manager (profess. & kin.).
GOE: 03.01.04 STRENGTH: L GED: R5 M5 L5 SVP: 8 DLU: 81

040.261-010 SOIL-CONSERVATION TECHNICIAN (profess. & kin.)
Provides technical assistance to land users in planning and applying soil and water conservation practices, utilizing basic engineering and surveying tools, instruments, and techniques and knowledge of agricultural and related sciences, such as agronomy, soil conservation, and hydrology: Analyzes conservation problems of land and discusses alternative solutions to problems with land users. Advises land users in developing plans for conservation practices, such as conservation cropping systems, woodlands management, pasture planning, and engineering systems, based on cost estimates of different practices, needs of land users, maintenance requirements, and life expectancy of practices. Computes design specification for particular practices to be installed, using survey and field information technical guides, engineering field manuals, and calculator. Submits copy of engineering design specifications to land users for implementation by land user or contractor. Surveys property to mark locations and measurements, using surveying instruments. Monitors projects during and after construction to ensure projects conform to design specifications. Periodically revisits land users to view implemented land use practices and plans.
GOE: 02.02.02 STRENGTH: L GED: R5 M4 L4 SVP: 7 DLU: 86

040.361-010 LABORATORY TECHNICIAN, ARTIFICIAL BREEDING (agriculture)
Measures purity and potency of animal semen to develop improved methods of processing and preserving for artificial insemination: Observes sample of freshly collected semen under microscope to determine mobility of sperm cells. Measures density, using densiometer. Adds measured amounts of extender, sodium citrate, and antibiotics to dilute and preserve sample. Transfers to refrigeration unit. Records data for use in compiling histroy of sire. Cleans and sterilizes laboratory equipment. Performs experimental tests, as directed, for purposes such as extension of cell survival rate and development of improved preservation processes. Cultivates, isolates, and identifies pathogenic bacteria and other micro-organisms in semen.
GOE: 02.04.02 STRENGTH: L GED: R4 M4 L4 SVP: 5 DLU: 77

040.361-014 SEED ANALYST (profess. & kin.) alternate titles: farm-seed specialist
Tests seed for germination, purity, and weed content: Plants definite number of seeds in box of pure soil and counts number of plants that grow to calculate percentage of germination. Inspects seed with magnifying glass or microscope for chaff, bits of wood, and weed content (any seed other than the one under consideration).
GOE: 02.04.02 STRENGTH: L GED: R4 M4 L4 SVP: 7 DLU: 77

041 OCCUPATIONS IN BIOLOGICAL SCIENCES

This group includes occupations concerned with research in the reproduction, growth and development, structure, life processes, behavior, and classification of living organisms and the application of findings to the prevention of disease in the maintenance and promotion of health in plant and animal life. Also includes investigations into economic utilization, environmental impact, or harmful aspects of specific animals and plants.

041.061-010 ANATOMIST (profess. & kin.)
Studies form and structure of animal bodies: Examines large organs and organ systems of body by systematic observation and dissection, and examines minute structure of organs, tissues, and cells, using microscope. Compares structure of one species with that of another. Determines ability of animal bodies to regenerate destroyed or damaged parts, and investigates possibility of transplanting organs and skin segments from one living body to another. Conducts research into basic laws of biological science to determine application to human medicine.
GOE: 02.02.01 STRENGTH: L GED: R6 M6 L6 SVP: 8 DLU: 77

041.061-014 ANIMAL BREEDER (profess. & kin.)
Develops systems of breeding desirable characteristics, such as improvement in strength, maturity rate, disease resistance, and meat quality, into economically important animals: Determines generic composition of animal populations, and heritability of traits, utilizing principles of genetics. Crossbreeds animals within existing strains, or crosses strains to obtain new combinations of desirable characteristics. Selects progeny having desired strains of both parents, and continues process until acceptable result is obtained.

GOE: 02.02.01 STRENGTH: L GED: R6 M6 L6 SVP: 8 DLU: 77

041.061-018 APICULTURIST (profess. & kin.)
Studies bee culture and breeding: Conducts experiments regarding causes and controls of bee diseases and factors affecting yields of nectar and pollen on various plants visited by bees. Conducts research into various phases of pollination. Improves bee strains, utilizing selective breeding by artificial insemination.
GOE: 02.02.01 STRENGTH: L GED: R6 M6 L6 SVP: 8 DLU: 77

041.061-022 AQUATIC BIOLOGIST (profess. & kin.) alternate titles: aquatic ecologist
Studies plants and animals living in water, and environmental conditions affecting them: Investigates salinity, temperature, acidity, light, oxygen content, and other physical conditions of water to determine their relationship to aquatic life. Examines various types of water life, such as plankton, worms, clams, mussels, and snails. May specialize in study of salt water aquatic life and be designated Marine Biologist (profess. & kin.); or fresh water aquatic life and be designated Limnologist (profess. & kin.). May specialize in culture, breeding, and raising of aquatic life, such as shrimp, lobsters, clams, oysters, or fish, and commercial fish farm operations and be designated Aquaculturist (profess. & kin.).
GOE: 02.02.03 STRENGTH: L GED: R6 M6 L6 SVP: 8 DLU: 77

041.061-026 BIOCHEMIST (profess. & kin.) alternate titles: chemist, biological
Studies chemical processes of living organisms: Conducts research to determine action of foods, drugs, serums, hormones, and other substances on tissues and vital processes of living organisms. Isolates, analyzes, and identifies hormones, vitamins, allergens, minerals, and enzymes and determines effects on body functions. Examines chemical aspects of formation of antibodies, and conducts research into chemistry of cells and blood corpuscles. Studies chemistry of living processes, such as mechanisims of development of normal and abnormal cells, breathing and digestion, and of living energy changes, such as growth, aging, and death. May specialize in particular area or field of work and be designated Chemist, Clinical (profess. & kin.); Chemist, Enzymes (profess. & kin.); Chemist, Proteins (profess. & kin.); Chemist, Steroids (profess. & kin.). May clean, purify, refine, and otherwise prepare pharmaceutical compounds for commercial distribution and develop new drugs and medications and be designated Chemist, Pharmaceutical (profess. & kin.).
GOE: 02.02.03 STRENGTH: L GED: R6 M6 L6 SVP: 8 DLU: 77

041.061-030 BIOLOGIST (profess. & kin.)
Studies basic principles of plant and animal life, such as origin, relationship, development, anatomy, and functions: May collect and analyze biological data to determine environmental effects of present and potential use of land and water areas, record data, and inform public, state, and federal representatives regarding test results. May prepare environmental impact reports. May specialize in research centering around particular plant, animal, or aspect of biology. May teach. May specialize in wildlife research and management and be designated Wildlife Biologist (profess. & kin.).
GOE: 02.02.03 STRENGTH: L GED: R6 M6 L6 SVP: 8 DLU: 81

041.061-034 BIOPHYSICIST (profess. & kin.)
Studies physical principles of living cells and organisms, their electrical and mechanical energy, and related phenomena: Conducts research to investigate dynamics in such areas as seeing and hearing; the transmission of electrical impulses along nerves and muscles, and damage to cells and tissues caused by x rays and nuclear particles; manner in which characteristics of plants and animals are carried forward through successive generations; and absorption of light by chlorophyll in photosynthesis or by pigments of eye involved in vision. Analyzes functions of electronic and human brains, such as transfer of information into brain from outside (learning), transfer and manipulation of information within brain (thinking), and storage of information (memory). Studies spatial configuration of submicroscopic molecules, such as proteins, using x ray and electron microscope. May specialize in one activity, such as use of radiation and nuclear particles for treating cancer or use of atomic isotopes to discover transformation of substances in cells.
GOE: 02.02.03 STRENGTH: L GED: R6 M6 L6 SVP: 8 DLU: 77

041.061-038 BOTANIST (profess. & kin.)
Studies development and life processes, physiology, heredity, environment, distribution, anatomy, morphology, and economic value of plants for application in such fields as agronomy, forestry, horticulture, and pharmacology: Studies behavior of chromosomes and reproduction, internal and external structures, and examines mechanics and biochemistry of plants and plant cells, using microscopes, staining techniques, and scientific equipment. Investigates environment and plant communities and effect of rainfall, temperature, climate, soil, and elevation on plant growth from seed to mature plants. Identifies and classifies plants. May conduct environmental studies and prepare reports. May be designated according to field of specialization as Plant Ecologist (profess. & kin.); Plant Taxonomist (profess. & kin.).
GOE: 02.02.02 STRENGTH: L GED: R6 M6 L6 SVP: 8 DLU: 77

041.061-042 CYTOLOGIST (profess. & kin.)
Studies plant and animal cells: Selects and sections minute particles of animal or plant tissue for microscopic study, using microtome and other equipment and employs stain techniques to make cell structures visible or to differentiate

parts: Studies parts of cells and details of cell division into new cells, using microscope. Analyzes cells concerned with reproduction, and means by which chromosomes divide or unite. Studies formation of sperm and eggs in animal sex glands and origin of blood and tissue cells. Conducts research in physiology of unicellular organisms, such as protozoa, to ascertain physical and chemical factors involved in growth. Studies influence of physical and chemical factors upon malignant and normal cells. Evaluates exfoliated, asperated, or abraded cells to assess hormonal status and presence of atypical or malignant changes. May be designated according to specialty as Animal Cytologist (profess. & kin.); Plant Cytologist (profess. & kin.).
GOE: 02.02.03 STRENGTH: L GED: R6 M6 L6 SVP: 8 DLU: 77

041.061-046 ENTOMOLOGIST (profess. & kin.)
   Studies insects and their relation to plant and animal life: Identifies and classifies species of insects and allied forms, such as mites and spiders. Aids in control and elimination of agricultural, structural, and forest pests by developing new and improved pesticides and cultural and biological methods, including use of natural enemies of pests. Studies insect distribution and habitat and recommends methods to prevent importation and spread of injurious species.
GOE: 02.02.01 STRENGTH: L GED: R6 M6 L6 SVP: 8 DLU: 77

041.061-050 GENETICIST (profess. & kin.)
   Studies inheritance and variation of characteristics in forms of life: Performs experiments to determine laws, mechanisms, and environmental factors in origin, transmission, and development of inherited traits. Analyzes determinants responsible for specific inherited traits, such as color differences, size, and disease resistance to improve or to understand relationship of heredity to maturity, fertility, or other factors. Devises methods for altering or producing new traits, making use of chemicals, heat, light, or other means. May specialize in particular branch of genetics, such as molecular genetics or population genetics. May perform human genetic counseling or medical genetics.
GOE: 02.02.01 STRENGTH: S GED: R6 M6 L6 SVP: 8 DLU: 77

041.061-054 HISTOPATHOLOGIST (medical ser.) alternate titles: histologist
   Studies human or animal tissue to provide data to delineate cause and progress of disease that impairs body function: Trains and oversees laboratory personnel in preparing tissue sections or prepares tissue sections from surgical and diagnostic cases and autopsies. Examines tissue under microscope to detect characteristics of cell structure indicative of disease and writes diagnostic reports. Devises and directs use of special stains and methods for isolating, identifying, and studying function, morphology, and pathology of obscure or difficult-to-identify cells, tissues, and connecting fibers. May conduct autopsies to select tissue specimens for study. May engage in research to develop techniques for diagnosing and identifying pathological conditions. May study anatomy of body tissues, formation of organs, and related problems to obtain data on body functions.
GOE: 02.02.01 STRENGTH: L GED: R6 M6 L6 SVP: 8 DLU: 89

041.061-058 MICROBIOLOGIST (profess. & kin.) alternate titles: bacteriologist
   Studies growth, structure, development, and general characteristics of bacteria and other micro-organisms: Isolates and makes cultures of significant bacteria or other micro-organisms in prescribed or standard inhibitory media, controlling factors, such as moisture, aeration, temperature, and nutrition. Identifies micro-organisms by microscopic examination of physiological, morphological, and cultural characteristics. Observes action of micro-organisms upon living tissues of plants, higher animals, and other micro-organisms and on dead organic matter. Makes chemical analyses of substances, such as acids, alcohols, and enzymes, produced by bacteria and other micro-organisms on organic matter. May specialize in study of viruses and rickettsiae and be designated Virologist (profess. & kin.). May specialize in particular material or product field and be designated Bacteriologist, Dairy (profess. & kin.); Bacteriologist, Fishery (profess. & kin.); Bacteriologist, Food (profess. & kin.); Bacteriologist, Industrial (profess. & kin.); Bacteriologist, Medical (profess. & kin.); Bacteriologist, Pharmaceutical (profess. & kin.); or Bacteriologist, Soil (profess. & kin.).
GOE: 02.02.03 STRENGTH: L GED: R6 M6 L6 SVP: 8 DLU: 77

041.061-062 MYCOLOGIST (profess. & kin.)
   Studies mechanism of life processes of edible, poisonous, and parasitic fungi to discover those that are useful to medicine, agriculture, and industry: Studies structure, affinities, classification, genetics, physiology, and growth of fungi. Applies findings to agriculture, medicine, and industry for development of drugs, medicines, molds, and yeasts. May specialize in research and development in such fields as antibiotics or fabric deterioration. May develop improved methods of propagating and growing edible fungi, as mushrooms and be designated Mushroom-Spawn Maker (profess. & kin.).
GOE: 02.02.02 STRENGTH: L GED: R6 M6 L6 SVP: 8 DLU: 77

041.061-066 NEMATOLOGIST (profess. & kin.)
   Studies nematodes (roundworms) that are plant parasitic, transmit diseases, attack insects, or attack soil, fresh water, or marine nematodes: Identifies and classifies nematodes and studies structure, behavior, biology, ecology, physiology, nutrition, culture, and distribution. Studies reactions of plants to parasitic nematodes and associations with other plant disease agents. Develops methods and apparatus for securing representative soil samples containing nematodes, and for isolating, mounting, counting, and identifying specimens. Investigates and develops pest management and control measures, such as chemical, hot

water and steam treatments, soil fumigation, biological crop rotations, and cultural practices. See PARASITOLOGIST (profess. & kin.) for scientists who specialize in study of nematodes that are parasitic in man or animals.
GOE: 02.02.01 STRENGTH: L GED: R6 M6 L6 SVP: 8 DLU: 77

041.061-070 PARASITOLOGIST (profess. & kin.)
   Studies characteristics, habits, and life cycles of animal parasites, such as protozoans, tapeworms, roundworms, flukes, and other parasitic organisms, to determine manner in which they attack human beings and animals and effects produced: Investigates modes of transmission from host to host. Develops methods and agents to combat parasites. May specialize in study of one variety of parasite, such as animal parasites that attack man, and be designated Medical Parasitologist (profess. & kin.); of parasitic worms and be designated Helminthologist (profess. & kin.); of one celled free living and parasitic organisms and be designated Protozoologist (profess. & kin.).
GOE: 02.02.01 STRENGTH: L GED: R6 M6 L6 SVP: 8 DLU: 77

041.061-074 PHARMACOLOGIST (profess. & kin.)
   Studies effects of drugs, gases, dusts, and other materials on tissue and physiological processes of animals and human beings: Experiments with animals, such as rats, guinea pigs, and mice, to determine reactions of drugs and other substances on functioning of organs and tissues, noting effects on circulation, respiration, digestion, or other vital processes. Standardizes drug dosages or methods of immunizing against industrial diseases by correlating results of animal experiments with results obtained from clinical experimentation on human beings. Investigates preventative methods and remedies for diseases, such as silicosis and lead, mercury, and ammonia poisoning. Analyzes food preservatives and colorings, vermin poisons, and other materials to determine toxic or nontoxic properties. Standardizes procedures for manufacture of drugs and medicinal compounds.
GOE: 02.02.01 STRENGTH: L GED: R6 M6 L6 SVP: 8 DLU: 77

041.061-078 PHYSIOLOGIST (profess. & kin.)
   Conducts research on cellular structure and organ-system functions of plants and animals: Studies growth, respiration, circulation, excretion, movement, reproduction, and other functions of plants and animals under normal and abnormal conditions. Performs experiments to determine effects of internal and external environmental factors on life processes and functions, using microscope, x-ray equipment, spectroscope, and other equipment. Studies glands and their relationship to bodily functions. May specialize in physiology of particular body area, function, or system. May specialize in physiology of animals and be designated Animal Physiologist (profess. & kin.); of plants and be designated Plant Physiologist (profess. & kin.); of human organisms and be designated Medical Physiologist (medical ser.).
GOE: 02.02.03 STRENGTH: L GED: R6 M6 L6 SVP: 8 DLU: 77

041.061-082 PLANT BREEDER (profess. & kin.)
   Plans and carries out breeding studies to develop and improve varieties of crops: Improves specific characteristics, such as yield, size, quality, maturity, and resistance to frost, drought, disease and insect pests in plants, utilizing principles of genetics and knowledge of plant growth. Develops variety and selects most desirable plants for crossing. Breeds plants, using methods such as inbreeding, crossbreeding, backcrossing, outcrossing, mutating, or interspecific hybridization and selection. Selects progeny having desired characteristics and continues breeding and selection process to reach desired objectives.
GOE: 02.02.02 STRENGTH: L GED: R6 M6 L6 SVP: 8 DLU: 77

041.061-086 PLANT PATHOLOGIST (profess. & kin.)
   Conducts research in nature, cause, and control of plant diseases and decay of plant products: Studies and compares healthy and diseased plants to determine symptoms of diseased condition. Inoculates healthy plants with culture of suspected agents taken from diseased plants and studies effects to determine agents responsible for disease. Isolates disease-causing agent, studies habits and life cycle, and devises methods of destroying or controlling agent [MICROBIOLOGIST (profess. & kin.)]. Tests possible control measures under laboratory and field conditions for comparative effectiveness, practicality, and economy. Investigates comparative susceptibility of different varieties of plants and develops varieties immune to disease [PLANT BREEDER (profess. & kin.)]. Studies rates of spread and intensity of disease under different conditions of soil, climate, and geography, and predicts outbreaks of plant diseases. Determines kinds of plants and insects that harbor or transmit disease. Studies losses from deterioration of perishable plant products in transit or storage and develops practices to prevent or reduce losses. Determines presence of disease producing agents in seed stocks to reduce losses from seed borne diseases. May specialize in type of plant affected, such as cereal crops, fruit, or forest trees, or by type of disease, such as bacterial, virus, fungus, mycoplasma, or nematode. May inspect flower and vegetable seeds and flowering bulbs for diseases, infections, and insect injuries.
GOE: 02.02.02 STRENGTH: L GED: R6 M6 L6 SVP: 8 DLU: 77

041.061-090 ZOOLOGIST (profess. & kin.)
   Studies origin, interrelationships, classification, life histories, habits, life processes, diseases, relation to environment, growth and development, genetics, and distribution of animals: Studies animals in natural habitat and collects specimens for laboratory study. Dissects and examines specimens under microscope and uses chemicals and various types of scientific equipment to carry out experimental studies. Prepares collections of preserved specimens or microscopic slides for such purposes as identification of species, study of species develop-

ment, and study of animal diseases. May raise specimens for experimental purposes. May specialize in one aspect of animal study, such as functioning of animal as an organism, or development of organism from egg to embryo stage. May specialize in study of reptiles, frogs, and salamanders and be designated Herpetologist (profess. & kin.); of fish and fishlike forms and be designated Ichthyologist (profess. & kin.); of sponges, jellyfish, and protozoa and be designated Invertebrate Zoologist (profess. & kin.); of birds and be designated Ornithologist (profess. & kin.); of mammals and be designated Mammalogist (profess. & kin.). May study animals for purposes of identification and classification and be designated Animal Taxonomist (profess. & kin.); or study effects of environment on animals and be designated Animal Ecologist (profess. & kin.).
GOE: 02.02.01 STRENGTH: L GED: R6 M6 L6 SVP: 8 DLU: 77

041.061-094   STAFF TOXICOLOGIST (government ser.)
Studies effects of toxic substances on physiological functions of human beings, animals, and plants to develop data for use in consumer protection and industrial safety programs: Designs and conducts studies to determine physiological effects of various substances on laboratory animals, plants, and human tissue, using biological and biochemical techniques. Interprets results of studies in terms of toxicological properties of substances and hazards associated with misuse of products containing substances. Provides information concerning toxicological properties of products and materials to regulatory agency personnel and industrial firms. Reviews toxicological data submitted by others for adequacy, and suggests amendment or expansion of data to clarify or correct information. Confers with governmental and industrial personnel to provide advice on precautionary labeling for hazardous materials and products and on nature and degree of hazard in cases of accidental exposure or ingestion. Prepares and maintains records of studies for use as toxicological resource material. Testifies as expert witness on toxicology in hearings and court proceedings.
GOE: 02.02.01 STRENGTH: L GED: R6 M6 L5 SVP: 8 DLU: 86

041.067-010   MEDICAL COORDINATOR, PESTICIDE USE (government ser.)
Studies human health-and-safety aspects of pesticides and other agricultural chemicals: Studies long-term health implications of low-dose pesticide exposure and determines safe worker reentry intervals. Reviews and provides recommendations on medical regulations governing use of pesticides. Reviews information and recommendations pertaining to safe levels of pesticide residues on agricultural products. Recommends specifications for safe working conditions for workers exposed to pesticides or their residues, and makes recommendations on public safety aspects of pesticide exposure. Confers with health department personnel to develop programs to improve ability of physicians and other medical personnel to diagnose, treat, and report pesticide-related illnesses. Confers with government agency representatives, physicians, university staff members, and other research workers to develop health and safety standards related to pesticide exposure. Advises industry representatives on organization of adequate medical supervision programs for employers. Prepares reports on research studies. Addresses interested groups as requested.
GOE: 02.02.01 STRENGTH: S GED: R6 M5 L6 SVP: 9 DLU: 86

041.081-010   FOOD TECHNOLOGIST (profess. & kin.) alternate titles: food scientist
Applies scientific and engineering principles in research, development, production technology, quality control, packaging, processing, and utilization of foods: Conducts basic research, and new product research and development of foods. Develops new and improved methods and systems for food processing, production, quality control, packaging, and distribution. Studies methods to improve quality of foods, such as flavor, color, texture, nutritional value, convenience, or physical, chemical, and microbiological composition of foods. Develops food standards, safety and sanitary regulations, and waste management and water supply specifications. Tests new products in test kitchen and develops specific processing methods in laboratory pilot plant, and confers with process engineers, flavor experts, and packaging and marketing specialists to resolve problems. May specialize in one phase of food technology, such as product development, quality control, or production inspection, technical writing, teaching, or consulting. May specialize in particular branch of food technology, such as cereal grains, meat and poultry, fats and oils, seafood, animal foods, beverages, dairy products, flavors, sugars and starches, stabilizers, preservatives, colors, and nutritional additives, and be identified according to branch of food technology.
GOE: 02.02.04 STRENGTH: L GED: R6 M5 L4 SVP: 7 DLU: 77

041.167-010   ENVIRONMENTAL EPIDEMIOLOGIST (government ser.)
Plans, directs, and conducts studies concerned with incidence of disease in industrial settings and effects of industrial chemicals on health: Confers with industry representatives to select occupational groups for study and to arrange for collection of data concerning work history of individuals and disease concentration and mortality rates among groups. Plans methods of conducting epidemiological studies and provides detailed specifications for collecting data to personnel participating in studies. Develops codes to facilitate computer input of demographic and epidemiological data for use by data processing personnel engaged in programming epidemiological statistics. Compares statistics on causes of death among members of selected working populations with those among general population, using life-table analyses. Analyzes data collected to determine probable effects of work settings and activities on disease and mortality rates, using valid statistical techniques and knowledge of epidemiology.

Presents data in designated statistical format to illustrate common patterns among workers in selected occupations. Initiates and maintains contacts with statistical and data processing managers in other agencies to maintain access to epidemiological source materials. Evaluates materials from all sources for addition to or amendment of epidemiological data bank. Plans and directs activities of clerical and statistical personnel engaged in tabulation and analysis of epidemiological information to ensure accomplishment of objectives.
GOE: 02.02.01 STRENGTH: L GED: R6 M6 L5 SVP: 8 DLU: 86

041.261-010   PUBLIC-HEALTH MICROBIOLOGIST (government ser.)
Conducts experiments to detect presence of harmful or pathogenic bacteria in water, food supply, or general environment of community and to control or eliminate sources of possible pollution or contagion: Makes periodic laboratory counts of bacteria in water supply. Analyzes samples of sewage for harmful micro-organisms and for rate of sludge purification by aerobic bacteria. Examines milk, shellfish, and other food items for micro-organisms constituting menace to public health. Cooperates with hospitals and clinical laboratories in identifying micro-organisms taken from diseased persons to determine presence of bacteria causing contagious or epidemic diseases. May inoculate members of community against contagious diseases.
GOE: 02.04.02 STRENGTH: L GED: R6 M6 L6 SVP: 7 DLU: 77

041.381-010   BIOLOGY SPECIMEN TECHNICIAN (profess. & kin.)
Prepares and embeds in plastic, biological specimens of plant and animal life for use as instructional aids: Selects plant or animal specimen in preserved or dried state. Dissects animal and cleans all matter from skeletal structures. Prepares slices or cross sections of small animals, embryos, or cross sections of animal organs, such as glands, kidneys, hearts, or eyes. Selects, trims, and stains a variety of stalks, flowers, and leaves to show plant structure and systems. Selects different stains to clearly indicate support structure, circulatory system, or other feature of plant or animal. Assembles and positions components of specimen in mold, using pins and holding devices. Mixes polylite plastic or other material and completes embedding by varied molding techniques. Works with plants, animals, mollusks, insects, and other classes of plants and animals. Identifies type and age of specimen, date of preparation, and type of embedding material used. May operate incubator to grow chicken eggs for embryo specimens. May prepare ecological kits which demonstrate polluting conditions in water, soil, or air.
GOE: 02.04.02 STRENGTH: S GED: R4 M3 L3 SVP: 7 DLU: 77

041.384-010   HERBARIUM WORKER (profess. & kin.)
Fumigates, presses, and mounts plant specimens, and maintains collection records of herbarium maintained by botanical garden, museum, or other institution: Records identification information concerning incoming plants. Places specimens in fumigation cabinet and turns valves to release toxic fumes that destroy insects, fungus, or parasites adhering to specimens. Arranges specimens between sheets of unsized paper so that upper and under portions of leaves, blossoms, and other components are visible, and pads paper with layers of felt and newsprint to protect specimens and form stacks. Places specified number of stacks in pressing frame and writes identification information on top layer of paper on each stack. Secures frame around stacks by tightening frame section with screws, fastening with leather straps, or tying with twine, to compress stacks and press and dry specimens in desired configuration. Mounts dried specimens on heavy paper, using glue, adhesive strips, or needle and thread, taking care to prevent distortion or breakage of specimens. Writes identification information on papers and inserts mounted specimens in labeled envelopes or folders. Files folders in drawers or cabinets according to standard botanical classification system. Maintains card files of specimens in herbarium collection and records of acquisitions, loans, exchanges, or sales of specimens.
GOE: 02.04.02 STRENGTH: L GED: R4 M3 L4 SVP: 5 DLU: 86

045   OCCUPATIONS IN PSYCHOLOGY

This group includes occupations concerned with the collection, interpretation, and application of scientific data relating to human behavior and mental processes. Activities are in either applied fields of psychology or in basic science fields and research.

045.061-010   PSYCHOLOGIST, DEVELOPMENTAL (profess. & kin.)
Investigates problems concerning growth and development of emotional, mental, physical, and social aspects of individuals, to increase understanding of origins of behavior and processes of human growth and decline: Formulates hypothesis or research problem and selects or develops method of investigation to test hypothesis. Studies behavior of children to analyze processes of learning, development of language in children, and parents' influence on children's behavior. Administers intelligence and performance tests to establish and measure patterns of intellectual and psychological growth, development, and decline in children and adults. Observes and records behavior of infants to establish patterns of social, motor, and sensory development. Analyzes growth of social values and attitudes, using information obtained from observation, questionnaires, and interviews. Formulates theories based on research findings for application in such fields as juvenile delinquency, education and guidance of children, parent education, and welfare of aged. Experiments with animals [PSYCHOLOGIST, EXPERIMENTAL (profess. & kin.)], to make comparative studies across species lines to contribute to understanding of human behavior. May specialize in study and treatment of children and be designated Child Psychologist (profess. & kin.).

GOE: 11.03.01 STRENGTH: L GED: R6 M6 L5 SVP: 7 DLU: 77

045.061-014 PSYCHOLOGIST, ENGINEERING (profess. & kin.) alternate titles: human factors specialist

Conducts research, development, application, and evaluation of psychological principles relating human behavior to characteristics, design, and use of environments and systems within which human beings work and live: Collaborates with equipment designers in design, development, and utilization of man-machine systems to obtain optimum efficiency in terms of human capabilities. Advises on human factors to be considered in design of man-machine systems, military equipment, and industrial products. Participates in solving such problems as determining numbers and kinds of workers required to operate machines, allocation of functions to machines and operators, and layout and arrangement of work sites. Analyzes jobs to establish requirements for use in classification, selection, placement, and training of personnel [JOB ANALYST (profess. & kin.)]. Develops training methods and materials, such as curriculums, lectures, and films, and prepares handbooks of human engineering data for use by equipment and system designers. May conduct research to develop psychological theories concerning such subjects as effects of physical factors (temperature, humidity, vibration, noise, and illumination) on worker's behavior; functional design of dials, scales, meters, and other instruments to minimize sensory requirements; specifications for optimal size, shape, direction and speed of motion, and location of equipment controls; and effects of environmental, organismic, and task or job variables on work behavior and life quality.
GOE: 11.03.01 STRENGTH: S GED: R6 M6 L6 SVP: 8 DLU: 77

045.061-018 PSYCHOLOGIST, EXPERIMENTAL (profess. & kin.)

Plans, designs, conducts, and analyzes results of experiments to study problems in psychology: Formulates hypotheses and experimental designs to investigate problems of perception, memory, learning, personality, and cognitive processes. Designs and constructs equipment and apparatus for laboratory study. Selects, controls, and modifies variables in laboratory experiments with humans or animals, and observes and records behavior in relation to variables. Analyzes test results, using statistical techniques, and evaluates significance of data in relation to original hypothesis. Collaborates with other scientists in such fields as physiology, biology, and sociology in conducting interdisciplinary studies of behavior and formulating theories of behavior. Writes papers describing experiments and interpreting test results for publication or for presentation at scientific meetings. May specialize in aesthetics, memory, learning, autonomic functions, electroencephalography, feeling and emotion, motivation, motor skills, perception, or higher order cognitive processes. May conduct experiments to study relationship of behavior to various bodily mechanisms and be designated Psychologist, Physiological (profess. & kin.). May specialize in study of animal behavior to develop theories of animal and human behavior and be designated Psychologist, Comparative (profess. & kin.).
GOE: 11.03.01 STRENGTH: L GED: R6 M6 L5 SVP: 8 DLU: 77

045.067-010 PSYCHOLOGIST, EDUCATIONAL (profess. & kin.)

Investigates processes of learning and teaching and develops psychological principles and techniques applicable to educational problems to foster intellectual, social, and emotional development of individuals: Conducts experiments to study importance of motivation in learning, implications of transfer of training in teaching, and nature and causes of individual differences in mental abilities to promote differentiated educational procedures to meet individual needs of students. Analyzes characteristics and adjustment needs of superior and inferior students and recommends educational program to promote maximum adjustment. Formulates achievement, diagnostic, and predictive tests to aid teachers in planning methods and content of instruction. Administers standardized tests to diagnose disabilities and difficulties among students and to develop special methods of remedial instruction. Investigates traits and attitudes of teachers to study conditions that contribute to or detract from optimal mental health of teachers. Studies effects of teachers' feelings and attitudes upon pupils, and characteristics of successful teachers to aid school administrators in selection and adjustment of teachers. Collaborates with education specialists in developing curriculum content and methods of organizing and conducting classroom work. May specialize in educational measurement, school adjustment, school learning, or special education.
GOE: 11.03.01 STRENGTH: L GED: R6 M6 L5 SVP: 8 DLU: 77

045.067-014 PSYCHOLOGIST, SOCIAL (profess. & kin.)

Investigates psychological aspects of human interrelationships to gain understanding of individual and group thought, feeling, and behavior, utilizing behavioral observation, experimentation, or survey techniques: Evaluates individual and group behavior, developing such techniques as rating scales and sampling methods to collect and measure data. Conducts surveys and polls to measure and analyze attitudes and opinions as basis for predicting economic, political, and other behavior, using interviews, questionnaires, and other techniques, and adhering to principles of statistical sampling in selecting people. Observes and analyzes relations of individuals to religious, racial, political, occupational, and other groups to evaluate behavior of individuals toward one another in groups, attitudes that exist in groups, and influence of group on individual. Investigates social behavior of individuals to study such problems as origin and nature of prejudice and stereotyping, transmission of values and attitudes in child rearing, and contribution of factors in social environment to individual mental health and illness. Conducts experimental studies on motivation, morale, and leadership, and prepares reports on findings.
GOE: 11.03.01 STRENGTH: S GED: R6 M6 L5 SVP: 8 DLU: 77

045.067-018 PSYCHOMETRIST (profess. & kin.)

Administers, scores, and interprets intelligence, aptitude, achievement, and other psychological tests to provide test information to teachers, counselors, students, or other specified entitled party: Gives paper and pencil tests or utilizes testing equipment, such as picture tests and dexterity boards, under standard conditions. Times tests and records results. Interprets test results in light of standard norms, and limitations of test in terms of validity and reliability.
GOE: 11.03.01 STRENGTH: S GED: R5 M5 L5 SVP: 7 DLU: 87

045.107-010 COUNSELOR (profess. & kin.)

Counsels individuals and provides group educational and vocational guidance services: Collects, organizes, and analyzes information about individuals through records, tests, interviews, and professional sources, to appraise their interests, aptitudes, abilities, and personality characteristics, for vocational and educational planning. Compiles and studies occupational, educational, and economic information to aid counselees in making and carrying out vocational and educational objectives. Refers students to placement service. Assists individuals to understand and overcome social and emotional problems. May engage in research and follow-up activities to evaluate counseling techniques. May teach classes. May be designated according to area of activity as Academic Counselor (education); Career Placement Services Counselor (education); Employment Counselor (government ser.); Guidance Counselor (education); Vocational Advisor (education).
GOE: 10.01.02 STRENGTH: S GED: R5 M5 L5 SVP: 7 DLU: 81

045.107-014 COUNSELOR, NURSES' ASSOCIATION (medical ser.)

Offers vocational, educational, and professional counseling to registered professional nurses, licensed practical nurses, and prospective professional and practical nurse students: Compiles credentials and prepares biographies of counselees. Provides information relative to qualifications required, opportunities for placement and advancement, wages, hours, and other data pertaining to selected field of work to assist nurses in determining educational and vocational objectives. Refers qualified nurses to employers for placement. Assists in establishing personnel policies relative to placement. Aids applicants in obtaining vocational, health, or other assistance from community agencies. May assist in recruitment.
GOE: 10.01.02 STRENGTH: S GED: R5 M4 L5 SVP: 8 DLU: 77

045.107-018 DIRECTOR OF COUNSELING (profess. & kin.) alternate titles: counseling-center manager; director, counseling bureau; director, vocational counseling; head counselor

Directs personnel engaged in providing educational and vocational guidance for students and graduates: Assigns and evaluates work of personnel. Conducts in-service training program for professional staff. Coordinates counseling bureau with school and community services. Analyzes counseling and guidance procedures and techniques to improve quality of service. Counsels individuals and groups relative to personal and social problems, and educational and vocational objectives. Addresses community groups and faculty members to interpret counseling service. Supervises maintenance of occupational library for use by counseling personnel. Directs activities of testing and occupational service center. May supervise auxiliary services, such as student learning center. May supervise in-service training programs in counseling, testing, or occupational information for graduate students. May teach graduate courses in psychology, guidance, and related subjects. May participate in appraising qualifications of candidates for faculty positions and eligibility of students for admission to medical, nursing, and engineering schools.
GOE: 10.01.02 STRENGTH: S GED: R5 M5 L5 SVP: 8 DLU: 77

045.107-022 CLINICAL PSYCHOLOGIST (profess. & kin.) alternate titles: psychologist, clinical

Diagnoses or evaluates mental and emotional disorders of individuals, and administers programs of treatment: Interviews patients in clinics, hospitals, prisons, and other institutions, and studies medical and social case histories. Observes patients in play or other situations, and selects, administers, and interprets intelligence, achievement, interest, personality, and other psychological tests to diagnose disorders and formulate plans of treatment. Treats psychological disorders to effect improved adjustments utilizing various psychological techniques, such as milieu therapy, psychodrama, play therapy and hypnosis. Selects approach to use in individual therapy, such as directive, nondirective, and supportive therapy, and plans frequency, intensity, and duration of therapy. May collaborate with PSYCHIATRIST (medical ser.) 070.107-014, and other specialists in developing treatment programs for patients. May instruct and direct students serving psychological internships in hospitals and clinics. May develop experimental designs and conduct research in fields of personality development and adjustment, diagnosis, treatment, and prevention of mental disorders. May serve as consultant to industrial, social, educational, welfare, and other agencies on individual cases or in evaluation, planning, and development of mental health programs. May specialize in behavior problems and therapy, crime and delinquency, group therapy, individual diagnosis and therapy, mental deficiency, objective tests, projective techniques, or speech pathology.
GOE: 10.01.02 STRENGTH: S GED: R6 M5 L6 SVP: 8 DLU: 81

045.107-026 PSYCHOLOGIST, COUNSELING (profess. & kin.)

Provides individual and group counseling services in universities and colleges, schools, clinics, rehabilitation centers, Veterans Administration hospitals, and industry, to assist individuals in achieving more effective personal, social, educational, and vocational development and adjustment: Collects data about in-

dividual through use of interview, case history, and observational techniques. Selects and interprets psychological tests designed to assess individual's intelligence, aptitudes, abilities, and interests, applying knowledge of statistical analysis. Evaluates data to identify causes of problem of individuals and to determine advisability of counseling or referral to other specialists or institutions. Conducts counseling or therapeutic interviews to assist individual to gain insight into personal problems, define goals, and plan action reflecting interests, abilities, and needs. Provides occupational, educational, and other information to enable individual to formulate realistic educational and vocational plans. Follows up results of counseling to determine reliability and validity of treatment used. May engage in research to develop and improve diagnostic and counseling techniques. May administer and score psychological tests.
GOE: 10.01.02 STRENGTH: S GED: R6 M5 L5 SVP: 8 DLU: 77

045.107-030   PSYCHOLOGIST,   INDUSTRIAL-ORGANIZATIONAL (profess. & kin.)

Develops and applies psychological techniques to personnel administration, management, and marketing problems: Observes details of work and interviews workers and supervisors to establish physical, mental, educational, and other job requirements. Develops interview techniques, rating scales, and psychological tests to assess skills, abilities, aptitudes, and interests as aids in selection, placement, and promotion. Organizes training programs, applying principles of learning and individual differences, and evaluates and measures effectiveness of training methods by statistical analysis of production rate, reduction of accidents, absenteeism, and turnover. Counsels workers to improve job and personal adjustments. Conducts research studies of organizational structure, communication systems, group interactions, and motivational systems, and recommends changes to improve efficiency and effectiveness of individuals, organizational units, and organization. Investigates problems related to physical environment of work, such as illumination, noise, temperature, and ventilation, and recommends changes to increase efficiency and decrease accident rate. Conducts surveys and research studies to ascertain nature of effective supervision and leadership and to analyze factors affecting morale and motivation. Studies consumer reaction to new products and package designs, using surveys and tests, and measures effectiveness of advertising media to aid in sale of goods and services. May advise management on personnel policies and labor-management relations. May adapt machinery, equipment, workspace, and environment to human use. May specialize in development and application of such techniques as job analysis and classification, personnel interviewing, ratings, and vocational tests for use in selection, placement, promotion, and training of workers and be designated Psychologist, Personnel (profess. & kin.). May apply psychological principles and techniques to selection, training, classification, and assignment of military personnel and be designated Psychologist, Military Personnel (profess. & kin.). May conduct surveys and tests to study consumer reaction to new products and package design and to measure effectiveness of advertising media to aid manufacturers in sale of goods and services and be designated Market-Research Analyst (profess. & kin.). II.
GOE: 11.03.01 STRENGTH: L GED: R6 M6 L5 SVP: 8 DLU: 77

045.107-034   PSYCHOLOGIST, SCHOOL (profess. & kin.)

Evaluates needs of average, gifted, handicapped, and disturbed children within educational system or school, and plans and carries out programs to enable children to attain maximum achievement and adjustment: Conducts diagnostic studies to identify child's needs, limitations, and potentials, observing child in classroom and at play, studying school records, consulting with parents and school personnel, and administering and interpreting diagnostic findings. Plans special placement or other treatment programs. Counsels pupils individually and in groups, using psychodrama, play therapy, personal interviews, and other psychological methods to assist pupils to achieve personal, social, and emotional adjustment. Carries out research to aid in introduction of programs in schools to meet current psychological, educational, and sociological needs of children. Advises teachers and other school personnel on methods to enhance school and classroom atmosphere to provide motivating educational environment. Refers individuals to community agencies to secure medical, vocational, or social services for child or family. Participates in planning of remedial classes and testing programs designed to meet needs of students. Serves as consultant to school board, superintendent, administrative committees, and parent-teacher groups in matters involving psychological services within educational system or school.
GOE: 10.01.02 STRENGTH: S GED: R6 M5 L5 SVP: 8 DLU: 77

045.107-038   RESIDENCE COUNSELOR (education) alternate titles: counselor, dormitory; dormitory supervisor; head resident, dormitory

Provides individual and group guidance services relative to problems of scholastic, educational, and personal-social nature to dormitory students: Suggests remedial or corrective actions and assists students in making better adjustments and in planning intelligent life goals. Plans and directs program to orient new students and assists in their integration into campus life. Initiates and conducts group conferences to plan and discuss programs and policies related to assignment of quarters, social and recreational activities, and dormitory living. Supervises dormitory activities. Investigates reports of misconduct and attempts to resolve or eliminate causes of conflict. May interview all dormitory students to determine need for counseling.
GOE: 10.01.02 STRENGTH: S GED: R5 M4 L5 SVP: 7 DLU: 77

045.107-042   VOCATIONAL REHABILITATION COUNSELOR (government ser.) alternate titles: counselor, vocational rehabilitation

Counsels handicapped individuals to provide vocational rehabilitation services: Interviews and evaluates handicapped applicants, and confers with medical and professional personnel to determine type and degree of handicap, eligibility for service, and feasibility of vocational rehabilitation. Accepts or recommends acceptance of suitable candidates. Determines suitable job or business consistent with applicant's desires, aptitudes, and physical, mental, and emotional limitations. Plans and arranges for applicant to study or train for job. Assists applicant with personal adjustment throughout rehabilitation program. Aids applicant in obtaining medical and social services during training. Promotes and develops job openings and places qualified applicant in employment. May specialize in type of disability, such as mental illness, alcohol abuse, hearing and visual impairment, or readjustment after prison release.
GOE: 10.01.02 STRENGTH: S GED: R5 M3 L5 SVP: 8 DLU: 81

045.107-046   PSYCHOLOGIST, CHIEF (profess. & kin.)

Plans psychological service programs and directs, coordinates, and participates in activities of personnel engaged in providing psychological services to clients in psychiatric center or hospital: Reviews reports, case management reviews, and psychiatric center's or hospital's procedural manual to assess need for psychological services. Plans psychological treatment programs that meet standards of accreditation. Plans utilization of available staff, assigns staff to treatment units, and recruits professional and nonprofessional psychological staff. Develops, directs, and participates in training programs. Directs testing and evaluation of new admissions and re-evaluation of present clients. Participates in staff conferences to evaluate and plan treatment programs. Interviews clients that present difficult and complex diagnostic problems and assesses their psychological status. Reviews management of cases, assignments, case problems, issues, and methods of treatment. Works with community agencies to develop effective corrective programs and to arrange to provide psychological services. Plans and supervises psychological research. Collaborates with psychiatrists and other professional staff to help develop comprehensive program of therapy, evaluation, and treatment.
GOE: 10.01.02 STRENGTH: S GED: R6 M5 L6 SVP: 8 DLU: 86

045.107-050   CLINICAL THERAPIST (profess. & kin.) alternate titles: clinical counselor

Counsels individuals or groups regarding psychological or emotional problems, such as stress, substance abuse, or family situations, using evaluative techniques, and develops and implements therapeutic treatment plan in medical setting: Interviews patient to obtain information concerning medical history or other pertinent information. Observes client to detect indications of abnormal physical or mental behavior. Selects and administers various tests, such as psychological tests, personality inventories, and intelligence quotient tests, to identify behavioral or personality traits and intelligence levels, and records results. Reviews results of tests to evaluate client needs. Plans and administers therapeutic treatment, such as behavior modification and stress management therapy, using biofeedback equipment, to assist patient in controlling disorders and other problems. Changes method and degree of therapy when indicated by client reactions. Discusses progress toward goals with client, such as controlling weight, stress, or substance abuse. Consults with medical doctor or other specialists concerning treatment plan and amends plan as directed. Conducts relaxation exercises, peer counseling groups, and family counseling during clinical therapy sessions. Refers client to supportive services to supplement treatment and counseling. May conduct research in treatment and test validation. May develop evaluative studies of therapy and treatment outcome.
GOE: 10.01.02 STRENGTH: S GED: R5 M5 L5 SVP: 7 DLU: 89

045.107-054   COUNSELOR, MARRIAGE AND FAMILY (profess. & kin.)

Provides individual, marital, and family counseling services to adults and children, to assist clients to identify personal and interactive problems, and to achieve effective personal, marital, and family development and adjustment: Collects information about clients (individuals, married couples, or families), using interview, case history, and observation techniques, *funnel approach*, and appraisal and assessment methods. Analyzes information collected to determine advisability of counseling or referral to other specialists or institutions. Reviews notes and information collected to identify problems and concerns. Consults reference material, such as textbooks, manuals, and journals, to identify symptoms, make diagnoses, and develop therapeutic or treatment plan. Counsels clients, using counseling methods and procedures, such as psychotherapy and hypnosis, to assist clients in gaining insight into personal and interactive problems, to define goals, and to plan action reflecting interests, abilities, and needs. Evaluates results of counseling methods to determine reliability and validity of treatment used. Interacts with other professionals to discuss therapy or treatment, new resources or techniques, and to share information.
GOE: 10.01.02 STRENGTH: S GED: R5 M3 L5 SVP: 8 DLU: 90

045.107-058   SUBSTANCE ABUSE COUNSELOR (profess. & kin.)

Counsels and aids individuals and families requiring assistance dealing with substance abuse problems, such as alcohol or drug abuse: Interviews clients, reviews records, and confers with other professionals to evaluate condition of client. Formulates program for treatment and rehabilitation of client, using knowledge of drug and alcohol abuse problems and counseling and treatment techniques. Counsels clients individually and in group sessions to assist client in overcoming alcohol and drug dependency. Counsels family members to assist

family in dealing with and providing support for client. Refers client to other support services as needed, such as medical evaluation and treatment, social services, and employment services. Monitors condition of client to evaluate success of therapy, and adapts treatment as needed. Prepares and maintains reports and case histories. May formulate and conduct programs to promote prevention of alcohol and drug abuse. May prepare documents for presentation in court and accompany client to court as needed.
GOE: 10.01.02 STRENGTH: S GED: R5 M3 L5 SVP: 8 DLU: 78

045.117-010 DIRECTOR OF GUIDANCE IN PUBLIC SCHOOLS (education) alternate titles: supervisor, counseling and guidance; supervisor of guidance and testing; supervisor of research
Organizes, administers, and coordinates guidance program in public school system: Formulates guidance policies and procedures. Plans and conducts in-service training program for guidance workers and selected teachers. Plans and supervises testing program in school system and devises and directs use of records, reports, and other material essential to program. Supervises school placement service. Establishes and supervises maintenance of occupational libraries in schools. Coordinates guidance activities with community agencies and other areas of school system. Conducts or supervises research studies to evaluate effectiveness of guidance program. May counsel students on referral basis relative to educational and vocational objectives and personal and social problems.
GOE: 11.07.03 STRENGTH: L GED: R5 M5 L5 SVP: 8 DLU: 77

049   OCCUPATIONS IN LIFE SCIENCES, N.E.C.

This group includes occupations, not elsewhere classified, concerned with the application of theoretical or practical aspects of life science.

049.127-010 PARK NATURALIST (government ser.)
Plans, develops, and conducts programs to inform public of historical, natural, and scientific features of national, state, or local park: Confers with park staff to determine subjects to be presented and program schedule. Surveys park to determine forest conditions and distribution and abundance of fauna and flora. Interviews specialists in desired fields to obtain and develop data for programs. Takes photographs and motion pictures to illustrate lectures and publications and to develop displays. Plans and develops audiovisual devices, prepares and presents illustrated lectures, constructs visitor-center displays, and conducts field trips to point out scientific, historic, and natural features of park. Performs emergency duties to protect human life, government property, and natural features of park. May plan, organize, and direct activities of seasonal staff members. May maintain official photographic and informational files for department.
GOE: 11.07.03 STRENGTH: M GED: R5 M4 L5 SVP: 7 DLU: 77

049.364-010 FEED-RESEARCH AIDE (agriculture)
Feeds rations of experimental feeds to animals, such as poultry, dogs, and cows, and compiles data on growth, productivity, and health of animals: Weighs feed rations and livestock and gathers eggs and milks cows. Observes livestock to note changes in health and preference for certain foods. Records data for evaluation by professional personnel. Waters stock and cleans pens.
GOE: 02.04.02 STRENGTH: M GED: R3 M2 L2 SVP: 4 DLU: 77

049.364-014 VECTOR CONTROL ASSISTANT (government ser.)
Assists public health staff in activities concerned with identification, prevention, and control of vectors (disease-carrying insects and rodents): Carries and sets up field equipment to be used in surveys of number and type of vectors in area. Sets traps and cuts through brush and weeds to obtain specimens of vector population for use in laboratory tests, using sweep. Prepares, mounts, and stores specimens, following instructions of supervisor. Prepares reports of field surveys and laboratory tests based upon information obtained from personnel involved in specific activities, for use in planning and carrying out projects for prevention and control of vectors.
GOE: 02.04.02 STRENGTH: L GED: R4 M2 L3 SVP: 5 DLU: 86

049.364-018 BIOLOGICAL AIDE (agriculture)
Assists research workers in experiments in biology, bacteriology, plant pathology, mycology, and related agricultural sciences: Sets up laboratory and field equipment, performs routine tests, and keeps records of plant growth, experimental plots, greenhouse activity, use of insecticides, bee hives, and other agricultural experimentation. Cleans and maintains field and laboratory equipment.
GOE: 02.04.02 STRENGTH: M GED: R3 M3 L3 SVP: 6 DLU: 77

05   OCCUPATIONS IN SOCIAL SCIENCES

This division includes occupations concerned with human society and its characteristic elements, such as origin, race, or state; and with economic and social relations and institutions involved in man's existence as a member of an organized community.

050   OCCUPATIONS IN ECONOMICS

This group includes occupations concerned with research and application of economic principles relating to sources of income, expenditures, development of natural resources, and production and consumption of goods. Includes devel-

oping theories based on research data and formulating plans to aid in the solution of economic problems in such fields as agriculture, credit and financing, taxation, industry, international trade, and labor supply.

050.067-010 ECONOMIST (profess. & kin.) alternate titles: economic analyst
Plans, designs, and conducts research to aid in interpretation of economic relationships and in solution of problems arising from production and distribution of goods and services: Studies economic and statistical data in area of specialization, such as finance, labor, or agriculture. Devises methods and procedures for collecting and processing data, utilizing knowledge of available sources of data and various econometric and sampling techniques. Compiles data relating to research area, such as employment, productivity, and wages and hours. Reviews and analyzes economic data in order to prepare reports detailing results of investigation, and to stay abreast of economic changes. Organizes data into report format and arranges for preparation of graphic illustrations of research findings. Formulates recommendations, policies, or plans to aid in market interpretation or solution of economic problems, such as recommending changes in methods of agricultural financing, domestic, and international monetary policies, or policies that regulate investment and transfer of capital. May testify at regulatory or legislative hearings to present recommendations. May specialize in specific economic area or commodity and be designated Agricultural Economist (profess. & kin.); Commodity-Industry Analyst (profess. & kin.); Financial Economist (profess. & kin.); Industrial Economist (profess. & kin); International-Trade Economist (profess. & kin.); Labor Economist (profess. & kin.); Price Economist (profess. & kin.); Tax Economist (profess. & kin.).
GOE: 11.03.05 STRENGTH: S GED: R5 M5 L5 SVP: 8 DLU: 81

050.067-014 MARKET-RESEARCH ANALYST I (profess. & kin.)
Researches market conditions in local, regional, or national area to determine potential sales of product or service: Establishes research methodology and designs format for data gathering, such as surveys, opinion polls, or questionaires. Examines and analyzes statistical data to forecast future marketing trends. Gathers data on competitors and analyzes prices, sales, and methods of marketing and distribution. Collects data on customer preferences and buying habits. Prepares reports and graphic illustrations of findings.
GOE: 11.06.03 STRENGTH: S GED: R5 M5 L5 SVP: 7 DLU: 77

050.117-010 DIRECTOR, EMPLOYMENT RESEARCH AND PLANNING (government ser.)
Directs activities of personnel engaged in compiling, analyzing, and presenting data on employment problems, unemployment compensation benefits, and labor market activities: Plans and directs research projects and surveys to develop data for administration of federal or state laws governing employment service activities. Directs analysis of statistical data for implementing employment service programs and for supplying information to legislative bodies in revising employment legislation. Confers with government officials, employers, labor leaders, and other parties to disseminate and secure information on employment problems and assist in formulating policies to meet demonstrated needs. Advises legislators on implications of employment and training planning and program activities.
GOE: 11.01.02 STRENGTH: S GED: R5 M5 L5 SVP: 8 DLU: 77

051   OCCUPATIONS IN POLITICAL SCIENCE

This group includes occupations concerned with research in the origin, development, and organization of formal and informal political entities. Includes developing theories based on research data; and making recommendations for the solution of problems in such fields as organization and administration of national and local governments, international organizations and relations, governmental policies in foreign and domestic matters, and the relations between governments and special interest groups.

051.067-010 POLITICAL SCIENTIST (profess. & kin.)
Studies phenomena of political behavior, such as origin, development, operation, and interrelationships of political institutions, to formulate and develop political theory: Conducts research into political philosophy and theories of political systems, utilizing information available on political phenomena, such as governmental institutions, public laws and administration, political party systems, and international law. Consults with government officials, civic bodies, research agencies, and political parties. Analyzes and interprets results of studies, and prepares reports detailing findings, recommendations or conclusions. May organize and conduct public opinion surveys and interpret results. May specialize in specific geographical, political, or philosophical aspect of political behavior.
GOE: 11.03.02 STRENGTH: S GED: R6 M5 L5 SVP: 8 DLU: 77

052   OCCUPATIONS IN HISTORY

This group includes occupations concerned with recording past or current events dealing with some phase of human activity, either in terms of individuals or social, ethnic, political, or geographic groups. Includes occupations in biography and genealogy.

052.067-010 BIOGRAPHER (profess. & kin.)
Specializes in reconstruction in narrative form of career or phase in life of individual: Assembles biographical material from sources, such as news ac-

counts, diaries, personal papers and correspondence, written accounts of events in which subject participated, and consultation with associates and relatives of subject. Portrays character and behavior of subject on basis of historical environment and application of psychological analysis, relating subject's activities to pertinent events during subject's lifetime [WRITER, PROSE, FICTION AND NONFICTION (profess. & kin.)].
GOE: 01.01.02 STRENGTH: S GED: R5 M2 L5 SVP: 7 DLU: 77

052.067-014 DIRECTOR, STATE-HISTORICAL SOCIETY (profess. & kin.)

Directs activities of state historical society: Directs and coordinates activities of research staff. Reviews publications and exhibits prepared by staff prior to public release in order to ensure historical accuracy of presentations. Speaks before various groups, organizations, and clubs to promote society aims and activities. Consults with or advises other individuals on historical authenticity of various materials. Conducts historical research on subjects or topics of import to society. Performs administrative duties, such as budget preparation, employee evaluation, and program planning. May edit society publications. May conduct campaigns to raise funds for society programs and projects.
GOE: 11.03.03 STRENGTH: S GED: R5 M3 L5 SVP: 8 DLU: 77

052.067-018 GENEALOGIST (profess. & kin.)

Conducts research into genealogical background of individual or family in order to establish descent from specific ancestor or to discover and identify forebears of individual or family: Consults American and foreign genealogical tables and publications and documents, such as church and court records, for evidence of births, baptisms, marriages, deaths, and legacies in order to trace lines of descent or succession. Constructs chart showing lines of descent and family relationships. Prepares history of family in narrative form or writes brief sketches emphasizing points of interest in family background.
GOE: 11.03.03 STRENGTH: S GED: R5 M2 L5 SVP: 7 DLU: 77

052.067-022 HISTORIAN (profess. & kin.)

Prepares in narrative, brief, or outline form chronological account or record of past or current events dealing with some phase of human activity, either in terms of individuals, or social, ethnic, political, or geographic groupings: Assembles historical data by consulting sources of information, such as historical indexes and catalogs, archives, court records, diaries, news files, and miscellaneous published and unpublished materials. Organizes and evaluates data on basis of authenticity and relative significance. Acts as adviser or consultant, and performs research for individuals, institutions, and commercial organizations on subjects, such as technological evolution within industry or manners and customs peculiar to certain historical period. May trace historical development within restricted field of research, such as economics, sociology, or philosophy.
GOE: 11.03.03 STRENGTH: S GED: R5 M2 L5 SVP: 7 DLU: 77

052.067-026 HISTORIAN, DRAMATIC ARTS (profess. & kin.)

Conducts research to authenticate details, such as customs, costumes, manners of speech, architectural styles, modes of transportation, and other items peculiar to given historical period or specific locality, to avoid anachronisms and inaccuracies in presentation of stage or radio dramas or motion pictures. Reads written historical texts and documents and pictorial material in libraries and museums, consults experts or witnesses of historical events, and visits and observes peculiarities of areas to be used as locale of drama to procure information.
GOE: 11.03.03 STRENGTH: S GED: R5 M2 L5 SVP: 7 DLU: 77

052.167-010 DIRECTOR, RESEARCH (motion picture; radio-tv broad.)

Directs activities of motion picture or television production research department, and conducts research on various subjects to ensure historical authenticity of productions: Researches specific period, locality or historical event to obtain authentic background for production, such as customs, speech characteristics, or dress, and architectural style of era. Advises members of production staff on matters relating to historical details of subject being photographed or recorded. Reviews and collects data, such as books, pamphlets, periodicals, and rare newspapers, to provide source material for research. Approves or recommends purchase of library reference materials for department, and coordinates activities of workers engaged in cataloging and filing materials. May translate or request translation of reference materials.
GOE: 11.03.03 STRENGTH: S GED: R5 M4 L5 SVP: 8 DLU: 77

054 OCCUPATIONS IN SOCIOLOGY

This group includes occupations concerned with research on the development, structure, and processes of society, its institutions and cultures, and the behavior of human beings as members of collectivities and of social systems; on development and consequences of expected and deviant behavior; and on economic, political, and other differences in customs and institutions among cultures. Occupations in social work are included in Group 195.

054.067-010 RESEARCH WORKER, SOCIAL WELFARE (profess. & kin.)

Plans, organizes, and conducts research for use in understanding social problems and for planning and carrying out social welfare programs: Develops research designs on basis of existing knowledge and evolving theory. Constructs and tests methods of data collection. Collects information and makes judgments through observation, interview, and review of documents. Analyzes and evaluates data. Writes reports containing descriptive, analytical, and evaluative content. Interprets methods employed and findings to individuals within agency and community. May direct work of statistical clerks, statisticians, and others. May collaborate with research workers in other disciplines. May be employed in voluntary or governmental social welfare agencies, community welfare councils, and schools of social work.
GOE: 11.03.02 STRENGTH: S GED: R6 M5 L5 SVP: 7 DLU: 77

054.067-014 SOCIOLOGIST (profess. & kin.)

Conducts research into development, structure, and behavior of groups of human beings and patterns of culture and social organization which have arisen out of group life in society. Collects and analyzes scientific data concerning social phenomena, such as community, associations, social institutions, ethnic minorities, social classes, and social change. May teach sociology, direct research, prepare technical publications, or act as consultant to lawmakers, administrators, and other officials dealing with problems of social policy. May specialize in research on relationship between criminal law and social order in causes of crime and behavior of criminals and be designated Criminologist (profess. & kin.). May specialize in research on punishment for crime and control and prevention of crime, management of penal institutions, and rehabilitation of criminal offenders and be designated Penologist (profess. & kin.). May specialize in research on group relationships and processes in an industrial organization and be designated Industrial Sociologist (profess. & kin.). May specialize in research on rural communities in contrast with urban communities and special problems occasioned by impact of scientific and industrial revolutions on rural way of life and be designated Rural Sociologist (profess. & kin.). May specialize in research on interrelations between physical environment and technology in spatial distribution of people and their activities and be designated Social Ecologist (profess. & kin.). May specialize in research on social problems arising from individual or group deviation from commonly accepted standards of conduct, such as crime and delinquency, or social problems and racial discrimination rooted in failure of society to achieve its collective purposes and be designated Social Problems Specialist (profess. & kin.). May specialize in research on origin, growth, structure, and demographic characteristics of cities and social patterns and distinctive problems that result from urban environment and be designated Urban Sociologist (profess. & kin.). May specialize in research on social factors affecting health care, including definition of illness, patient and practitioner behavior, social epidemiology, and delivery of health care, and be designated Medical Sociologist (profess. & kin.). May plan and conduct demographic research, surveys, and experiments to study human populations and affecting trends and be designated Demographer (profess. & kin.) II.
GOE: 11.03.02 STRENGTH: S GED: R6 M5 L5 SVP: 7 DLU: 77

054.107-010 CLINICAL SOCIOLOGIST (profess. & kin.)

Develops and implements corrective procedures to alleviate group dysfunctions: Confers with individuals and groups to determine nature of group dysfunction. Observes group interaction and interviews group members to identify problems related to factors such as group organization, authority relationships, and role conflicts. Develops approaches to solution of group's problems, based on findings and incorporating sociological research and study in related disciplines. Develops intervention procedures, utilizing techniques such as interviews, consultations, role playing, and participant observation of group interaction, to facilitate resolution of group problems. Monitors group interaction and role affiliations to evaluate progress and to determine need for additional change.
GOE: 11.03.02 STRENGTH: S GED: R5 M4 L5 SVP: 6 DLU: 86

055 OCCUPATIONS IN ANTHROPOLOGY

This group includes occupations concerned with research to determine the origin and development of the human race by comparing physical characteristics of fossilized human remains with those of existing racial groups; and research in the cultural and social development of civilization from data previously recorded or from the study of relics and ruins encountered in excavations.

055.067-010 ANTHROPOLOGIST (profess. & kin.)

Makes comparative studies in relations to distribution, origin, evolution, and races of humans, cultures they have created, and their distribution and physical characteristics: Gathers, analyzes, and reports data on human physique, social customs, and artifacts, such as weapons, tools, pottery, and clothing. May apply anthropological data and techniques to solution of problems in human relations in fields, such as industrial relations, race and ethnic relations, social work, political administration, education, public health, and programs involving transcultural or foreign relations. May specialize in application of anthropological concepts to current problems and be designated Applied Anthropologist (profess. & kin.). May specialize in study of relationships between language and culture and socialinguistic studies and be designated Anthropological Linguist (profess. & kin.); or in study of relationship between individual personality and culture and be designated Psychological Anthropologist (profess. & kin.); or in study of complex, industrialized societies and be designated Urban Anthropologist (profess. & kin.).
GOE: 11.03.03 STRENGTH: L GED: R6 M5 L5 SVP: 7 DLU: 77

055.067-014 ANTHROPOLOGIST, PHYSICAL (profess. & kin.)

Studies meanings and causes of human physical differences and interrelated effects of culture, heredity, and environment on human form: Studies human

fossils and their meaning in terms of long-range human evolution. Observes and measures bodily variations and physical attributes of existing human types. Studies physical and physiological adaptations to differing environments and hereditary characteristics of living populations. Studies growth patterns, sexual differences, and aging phenomena of human groups, current and past. May study museum collections of skeletal remains. May specialize in measurement of body or skeleton and be designated Anthropometrist (profess. & kin.). May specialize in epidemiology and nutritional studies, especially in developing or preliterate societies, and be designated Medical Anthropologist (profess. & kin.).
GOE: 02.02.01 STRENGTH: L GED: R6 M5 L5 SVP: 7 DLU: 77

055.067-018   ARCHEOLOGIST (profess. & kin.)
Reconstructs record of extinct cultures, especially preliterate cultures: Studies, classifies, and interprets artifacts, architectural features, and types of structures recovered by excavation in order to determine age and cultural identity. Establishes chronological sequence of development of each culture from simpler to more advanced levels. May specialize in study of literate periods of major civilizations in Near and Middle East and be designated Archeologist, Classical (profess. & kin.). May specialize in study of past Columbian history of the Americas and be designated Historical Archeologist (profess. & kin.).
GOE: 11.03.03 STRENGTH: L GED: R6 M5 L5 SVP: 7 DLU: 77

055.067-022   ETHNOLOGIST (profess. & kin.)
Makes comparative studies of cultures or of selected aspects of cultures of living peoples and of peoples no longer in existence in order to determine historical relations, arrive at typological classifications, and make generalizations concerning cultural process and human behavior: Studies cultures of societies, particularly preindustrial and non-Western societies, including social and political organization, religion, economics, mythology and traditions, and intellectual and artistic life. May formulate general laws of cultural development, general rules of social and cultural behavior, or general value orientations. May specialize in description of details of custom and belief and their interrelations in one culture at a time and be designated Ethnographer (profess. & kin.).
GOE: 11.03.03 STRENGTH: L GED: R6 M5 L5 SVP: 7 DLU: 77

055.381-010   CONSERVATOR, ARTIFACTS (profess. & kin.) alternate titles: preservationist
Cleans, restores, and preserves archeological specimens and historical artifacts according to accepted chemical and physical techniques and training in archeological science: Cleans and repairs or reinforces specimens, such as weapons, mummified remains, and pottery, using handtools and prescribed chemical agents. Restores artifacts by polishing, joining together broken fragments, or other procedures, using handtools, power tools, and acid, chemical, or electrolytic corrosion-removal baths. Treats specimens to prevent or minimize deterioriation, according to accepted procedures. Records treatment of each artifact. Prepares reports of activities. May plan and conduct research to improve methods of restoring and preserving specimen.
GOE: 01.06.02 STRENGTH: L GED: R4 M4 L4 SVP: 6 DLU: 77

059   OCCUPATIONS IN SOCIAL SCIENCES, N.E.C.

This group includes occupations, not elsewhere classified, concerned with the application of the theoretical or practical aspects of social sciences.

059.067-010   PHILOLOGIST (profess. & kin.)
Studies structure and development of specific language or language group: Traces origin and evolution of words and syntax through comparative analysis of ancient parent languages and modern language groups, studying word and structural characteristics, such as morphology, semantics, phonology, accent, grammar, and literature. Identifies and classifies obscure languages, both ancient and modern, according to family and origin. Reconstructs and deciphers ancient languages from examples found in archeological remains of past civilizations. May specialize in study of origin, history, and development of words and be designated Etymologist (profess. & kin.).
GOE: 11.03.02 STRENGTH: S GED: R5 M1 L5 SVP: 8 DLU: 77

059.067-014   SCIENTIFIC LINGUIST (profess. & kin.) alternate titles: linguist
Studies components, structure, and relationships within specified language to provide comprehension of its social functioning: Prepares description of sounds, forms, and vocabulary of language. Contributes to development of linguistic theory. Applies linguistic theory to any of following areas: development of improved methods in translation, including computerization; teaching of language to other than native speakers; preparation of language-teaching materials, dictionaries, and handbooks; reducing previously unwritten languages to standardized written form; preparation of literacy materials; preparation of tests for language-learning aptitudes and language proficiency; consultation with government agencies regarding language programs; or preparation of descriptions of comparative languages to facilitate improvement of teaching and translation.
GOE: 11.03.02 STRENGTH: S GED: R6 M5 L6 SVP: 8 DLU: 77

059.167-010   INTELLIGENCE RESEARCH SPECIALIST (profess. & kin.)
Plans and directs research into proposed problem solutions or courses of action to determine feasibility of military planning alternatives: Confers with military leaders and supporting personnel to determine dimensions of problem and

discuss proposals for solution. Develops plans for predicting such factors as cost and probable success of each alternative, according to accepted operations research techniques and mathematical or computer formulations. Evaluates results of research and prepares recommendations for implementing or rejecting proposed solutions or plans. May be designated according to nature of research conducted as Air Intelligence Specialist (profess. & kin.); Combat Operations Research Specialist (profess. & kin.).
GOE: 11.03.02 STRENGTH: S GED: R6 M5 L5 SVP: 8 DLU: 77

059.267-010   INTELLIGENCE SPECIALIST (government ser.)
Evaluates data concerning subversive activities, enemy propaganda, and military or political conditions in foreign countries to facilitate counteraction by United States, according to familiarity with geography, cultural traditions, and social, political, and economic structure of countries under consideration.
GOE: 11.03.02 STRENGTH: S GED: R5 M4 L4 SVP: 7 DLU: 77

059.267-014   INTELLIGENCE SPECIALIST (military ser.)
Collects, records, analyzes, and disseminates tactical, strategic, or technical intelligence information: Segregates and records incoming intelligence data according to type of data to facilitate comparison, study, and accessibility. Prepares and analyzes information concerning strength, equipment, location, disposition, organization, and movement of enemy forces. Assists intelligence officers in analysis and selection of aerial bombardment targets. Compiles intelligence information to be used in preparing situation maps, charts, visual aids, briefing papers, reports, and publications. Briefs and debriefs ground or aviation personnel prior to and after missions. Maintains intelligence libraries, including maps, charts, documents, and other items. Plans or assists superiors in planning and supervising intelligence activities of unit assigned. May examine source materials and compile terrain intelligence, such as condition of travel routes over land, port facilities, and sources of water, sand, gravel, rock, and timbers.
GOE: 04.01.02 STRENGTH: L GED: R4 M4 L4 SVP: 7 DLU: 77

07   OCCUPATIONS IN MEDICINE AND HEALTH

This division includes occupations concerned with the health care of humans or animals in the fields of medicine, surgery, and dentistry; and in related patient-care areas, such as nursing, therapy, dietetics, prosthetics, rehabilitation, diagnostic imaging, and pharmacy. Also includeed are occupations in sanitation, environmental and public health, and in laboratories and other health facilities. Many occupations in this category require licensing or registration to practice or use a specific title.

070   PHYSICIANS AND SURGEONS

This group includes occupations concerned with diagnosis, prevention, and treatment of diseases and injuries; and research in the causes, transmission, and control of diseases and other ailments.

070.061-010   PATHOLOGIST (medical ser.) alternate titles: medical pathologist
Studies nature, cause, and development of diseases, and structural and functional changes caused by them: Diagnoses, from body tissue, fluids, secretions, and other specimens, presence and stage of disease, utilizing laboratory procedures. Acts as consultant to other medical practitioners. Performs autopsies to determine nature and extent of disease, cause of death, and effects of treatment. May direct activities of pathology department in medical school, hospital, clinic, medical examiner's office, or research institute. May be designated according to specialty as Clinical Pathologist (medical ser.); Forensic Pathologist (medical ser.); Neuropathologist (medical ser.); Surgical Pathologist (medical ser.).
GOE: 02.03.01 STRENGTH: L GED: R6 M5 L6 SVP: 8 DLU: 87

070.101-010   ANESTHESIOLOGIST (medical ser.)
Administers anesthetics to render patients insensible to pain during surgical, obstetrical, and other medical procedures: Examines patient to determine degree of surgical risk, and type of anesthetic and sedation to administer, and discusses findings with medical practitioner concerned with case. Positions patient on operating table and administers local, intravenous, spinal, caudal, or other anesthetic according to prescribed medical standards. Institutes remedial measures to counteract adverse reactions or complications. Records type and amount of anesthetic and sedation administered and condition of patient before, during, and after anesthesia. May instruct medical students and other personnel in characteristics and methods of administering various types of anesthetics, signs and symptoms of reactions and complications, and emergency measures to employ.
GOE: 02.03.01 STRENGTH: L GED: R6 M5 L6 SVP: 8 DLU: 87

070.101-014   CARDIOLOGIST (medical ser.) alternate titles: heart specialist
Diagnoses and treats diseases of heart and its functions: Examines patient for symptoms indicative of heart disorders, using medical instruments and equipment. Studies diagnostic images and electrocardiograph recordings to aid in making diagnoses. Prescribes medications, and recommends dietary and activity program, as indicated. Refers patient to SURGEON (medical ser.) 070.101-094 specializing in cardiac cases when need for corrective surgery is indicated. May engage in research to study anatomy of and diseases peculiar to heart.
GOE: 02.03.01 STRENGTH: L GED: R6 M5 L6 SVP: 9 DLU: 87

070.101-018 DERMATOLOGIST (medical ser.) alternate titles: skin specialist

Diagnoses and treats diseases of human skin: Examines skin to determine nature of disease, taking blood samples and smears from affected areas, and performing other laboratory procedures. Examines specimens under microscope, and makes various chemical and biological analyses and performs other tests to identify disease-causing organisms or pathological conditions. Prescribes and administers medications, and applies superficial radiotherapy and other localized treatments. Treats abscesses, skin injuries, and other skin infections, and surgically excises cutaneous malignancies, cysts, birthmarks, and other growths. Treats scars, using dermabrasion.
GOE: 02.03.01 STRENGTH: L GED: R6 M5 L6 SVP: 8 DLU: 87

070.101-022 GENERAL PRACTITIONER (medical ser.) alternate titles: physician, general practice

Diagnoses and treats variety of diseases and injuries in general practice: Examines patients, using medical instruments and equipment. Orders or executes various tests, analyses, and diagnostic images to provide information on patient's condition. Analyzes reports and findings of tests and of examination, and diagnoses condition. Administers or prescribes treatments and drugs. Inoculates and vaccinates patients to immunize patients from communicable diseases. Advises patients concerning diet, hygiene, and methods for prevention of disease. Provides prenatal care to pregnant women, delivers babies, and provides postnatal care to mother and infant [OBSTETRICIAN (medical ser.) 070.101-054]. Reports births, deaths, and outbreak of contagious diseases to governmental authorities. Refers patients to medical specialist or other practitioner for specialized treatment. Performs minor surgery. May make house and emergency calls to attend to patients unable to visit office or clinic. May conduct physical examinations to provide information needed for admission to school, consideration for jobs, or eligibility for insurance coverage. May provide care for passengers and crew aboard ship and be designated Ship's Doctor (medical ser.).
GOE: 02.03.01 STRENGTH: L GED: R6 M5 L6 SVP: 8 DLU: 87

070.101-026 FAMILY PRACTITIONER (medical ser.) alternate titles: family physician

Provides comprehensive medical services for members of family, regardless of age or sex, on continuing basis: Examines patients, using medical instruments and equipment. Elicits and records information about patient's medical history. Orders or executes various tests, analyses, and diagnostic images to provide information on patient's condition. Analyzes reports and findings of tests and examination, and diagnoses condition of patient. Administers or prescribes treatments and medications. Promotes health by advising patients concerning diet, hygiene, and methods for prevention of disease. Innoculates and vaccinates patients to immunize patients from communicable diseases. Provides prenatal care to pregnant women, delivers babies, and provides postnatal care to mothers and infants [OBSTETRICIAN (medical ser.) 070.101-054]. Performs surgical procedures commensurate with surgical competency. Refers patients to medical specialist for consultant services when necessary for patient's well-being.
GOE: 02.03.01 STRENGTH: L GED: R6 M5 L6 SVP: 8 DLU: 90

070.101-034 GYNECOLOGIST (medical ser.)

Diagnoses and treats diseases and disorders of female genital, urinary, and rectal organs: Examines patient to determine medical problem, utilizing physical findings, diagnostic images, laboratory test results, and patient's statements as diagnostic aids. Discusses problem with patient, and prescribes medication and exercise or hygiene regimen, or performs surgery as needed to correct malfunctions or remove diseased organ. May care for patient throughout pregnancy and deliver babies [OBSTETRICIAN (medical ser.) 070.101-054].
GOE: 02.03.01 STRENGTH: L GED: R6 M5 L6 SVP: 8 DLU: 87

070.101-042 INTERNIST (medical ser.) alternate titles: internal medicine specialist

Diagnoses and treats diseases and injuries of human internal organ systems: Examines patient for symptoms of organic or congenital disorders and determines nature and extent of injury or disorder, referring to diagnostic images and tests, and using medical instruments and equipment. Prescribes medication and recommends dietary and activity program, as indicated by diagnosis. Refers patient to medical specialist when indicated.
GOE: 02.03.01 STRENGTH: L GED: R6 M5 L6 SVP: 8 DLU: 87

070.101-046 PUBLIC HEALTH PHYSICIAN (government ser.)

Plans and participates in medical care or research program in hospital, clinic, or other public medical facility: Provides medical care for eligible persons, and institutes program of preventive health care in county, city, or other government or civic division. Gives vaccinations, imposes quarantines, and establishes standards for hospitals, restaurants, and other areas of possible danger. May conduct research in particular areas of medicine to aid in cure and control of disease. May be designated Medical Officer (government ser.).
GOE: 02.03.01 STRENGTH: L GED: R6 M5 L6 SVP: 8 DLU: 90

070.101-050 NEUROLOGIST (medical ser.) alternate titles: nerve specialist

Diagnoses and treats organic diseases and disorders of nervous system: Orders and studies results of chemical, microscopic, biological, and bacteriological analyses of patient's blood and cerebro-spinal fluid to determine nature and extent of disease or disorder. Identifies presence of pathological blood conditions or parasites and prescribes and administers medications and drugs. Orders and studies results of electroencephalograms or x rays to detect abnormalities in brain wave patterns, or indications of abnormalities in brain structure. Advises patient to contact other medical specialist, as indicated.
GOE: 02.03.01 STRENGTH: L GED: R6 M5 L6 SVP: 8 DLU: 87

070.101-054 OBSTETRICIAN (medical ser.)

Treats women during prenatal, natal, and postnatal periods: Examines patient to ascertain condition, utilizing physical findings, laboratory results, and patient's statements as diagnostic aids. Determines need for modified diet and physical activities, and recommends plan. Periodically examines patient, prescribing medication or surgery, if indicated. Delivers infant, and cares for mother for prescribed period of time following childbirth. Performs cesarean section or other surgical procedure as needed to preserve patient's health and deliver infant safely. May treat patients for diseases of generative organs [GYNECOLOGIST (medical ser.) 070.101-034].
GOE: 02.03.01 STRENGTH: L GED: R6 M5 L6 SVP: 8 DLU: 87

070.101-058 OPHTHALMOLOGIST (medical ser.) alternate titles: eye specialist; oculist

Diagnoses and treats diseases and injuries of eyes: Examines patient for symptoms indicative of organic or congenital ocular disorders, and determines nature and extent of injury or disorder. Performs various tests to determine vision loss. Prescribes and administers medications, and performs surgery, if indicated. Directs remedial activities to aid in regaining vision, or to utilize sight remaining, by writing prescriptions for corrective glasses, and instructing patient in eye exercises.
GOE: 02.03.01 STRENGTH: L GED: R6 M5 L6 SVP: 8 DLU: 87

070.101-062 OTOLARYNGOLOGIST (medical ser.) alternate titles: otorhinolaryngologist

Diagnoses and treats diseases of ear, nose, and throat: Examines affected organs, using equipment such as audiometers, prisms, nasoscopes, microscopes, x-ray machines, and fluoroscopes. Determines nature and extent of disorder, and prescribes and administers medications, or performs surgery. Performs tests to determine extent of loss of hearing due to aural or other injury, and speech loss as result of diseases or injuries to larynx. May specialize in treating throat, ear, or nose and be designated Laryngologist (medical ser.); Otologist (medical ser.); Rhinologist (medical ser.).
GOE: 02.03.01 STRENGTH: L GED: R6 M5 L6 SVP: 9 DLU: 87

070.101-066 PEDIATRICIAN (medical ser.)

Plans and carries out medical care program for children from birth through adolescence to aid in mental and physical growth and development: Examines patients to determine presence of disease and to establish preventive health practices. Determines nature and extent of disease or injury, prescribes and administers medications and immunizations, and performs variety of medical duties.
GOE: 02.03.01 STRENGTH: L GED: R6 M5 L6 SVP: 8 DLU: 87

070.101-070 PHYSIATRIST (medical ser.) alternate titles: physical medicine specialist

Specializes in clinical and diagnostic use of physical agents and exercises to provide physiotherapy for physical, mental, and occupational rehabilitation of patients: Examines patient, utilizing electrodiagnosis and other diagnostic procedures to determine need for and extent of therapy. Prescribes and administers treatment, using therapeutic methods and procedures, such as light therapy, diathermy, hydrotherapy, iontophoresis, and cryotherapy. Instructs PHYSICAL THERAPIST (medical ser.) 076.121-014 and other personnel in nature and duration or dosage of treatment, and determines that treatments are administered as specified. Prescribes exercises designed to develop functions of specific anatomical parts or specific muscle groups. Recommends occupational therapy activities for patients with extended convalescent periods and for those whose disability requires change of occupation.
GOE: 02.03.01 STRENGTH: M GED: R6 M5 L6 SVP: 8 DLU: 90

070.101-078 PHYSICIAN, OCCUPATIONAL (medical ser.) alternate titles: company doctor; physician, industrial

Diagnoses and treats work-related illnesses and injuries of employees, and conducts fitness-for-duty physical examinations: Attends patients in plant or hospital, and reexamines disability cases periodically to verify progress. Oversees maintenance of case histories, health examination reports, and other medical records. Formulates and administers health programs. Inspects plant and makes recommendations regarding sanitation and elimination of health hazards.
GOE: 02.03.01 STRENGTH: L GED: R6 M5 L6 SVP: 8 DLU: 90

070.101-082 POLICE SURGEON (government ser.) alternate titles: surgeon, chief

Examines and treats members of municipal police force for duty-related injuries and illnesses and gives first-aid treatment to civilians under arrest: Examines and reports physical condition of applicants for police force. Maintains records of sick personnel. Examines officers who claim disability and, upon proof of such disability, issues required certificate. Reports charges against officers who feign illness or injury to evade duty or whose illness or injury results from improper conduct, intemperance, or habits. Prepares annual report on activities and evaluation of physical condition of police force.
GOE: 02.03.01 STRENGTH: L GED: R6 M5 L6 SVP: 8 DLU: 90

070.101-086 PROCTOLOGIST (medical ser.)

Diagnoses and treats diseases and disorders of anus, rectum, and colon: Diagnoses diseases and disorders utilizing techniques, such as discussion of symp-

toms and medical history with patient, instrumental inspection of rectum and colon, examination of diagnostic images of affected parts, and evaluation of laboratory test results. Treats diseases and disorders by surgical removal or repair of diseased or malfunctioning parts, or by prescription of medication and suggestions for adaptation of patient's living habits.
GOE: 02.03.01 STRENGTH: L GED: R6 M5 L6 SVP: 8 DLU: 87

070.101-090 RADIOLOGIST (medical ser.)
Diagnoses and treats diseases of human body, using x-ray and radioactive substances: Examines internal structures and functions of organ systems, making diagnoses after correlation of x-ray findings with other examinations and tests. Treats benign and malignant internal and external growths by exposure to radiation from x-rays, high energy sources, and natural and manmade radioisotopes directed at or implanted in affected areas of body. Administers radiopaque substances by injection, orally, or as enemas to render internal structures and organs visible on x-ray films or fluoroscopic screens. May specialize in diagnostic radiology or radiation oncology. May diagnose and treat diseases of human body, using radioactive substances, and be certified in Nuclear Radiology or Nuclear Medicine.
GOE: 02.03.01 STRENGTH: L GED: R6 M5 L6 SVP: 8 DLU: 87

070.101-094 SURGEON (medical ser.)
Performs surgery to correct deformities, repair injuries, prevent diseases, and improve function in patients: Examines patient to verify necessity of operation, estimate possible risk to patient, and determine best operational procedure. Reviews reports of patient's general physical condition, reactions to medications, and medical history. Examines instruments, equipment, and surgical setup to ensure that antiseptic and aseptic methods have been followed. Performs operations, using variety of surgical instruments and employing established surgical techniques appropriate for specific procedures. May specialize in particular type of operation, as on nervous system, and be designated Neurosurgeon (medical ser.) May specialize in repair, restoration, or improvement of lost, injured, defective, or misshapen body parts and be designated Plastic Surgeon (medical ser.). May specialize in correction or prevention of skeletal abnormalities, utilizing surgical, medical, and physical methodologies, and be designated Orthopedic Surgeon (medical ser.).
GOE: 02.03.01 STRENGTH: L GED: R6 M5 L6 SVP: 9 DLU: 88

070.101-098 UROLOGIST (medical ser.)
Diagnoses and treats diseases and disorders of genitourinary organs and tract: Examines patient, using x-ray machine, fluoroscope, and other equipment to aid in determining nature and extent of disorder or injury. Treats patient, using diathermy machine, catheter, cystoscope, radium emanation tube, and similar equipment. Performs surgery, as indicated. Prescribes and administers urinary antiseptics to combat infection.
GOE: 02.03.01 STRENGTH: L GED: R6 M5 L6 SVP: 9 DLU: 88

070.101-102 ALLERGIST-IMMUNOLOGIST (medical ser.) alternate titles: allergist; allergy specialist
Diagnoses and treats diseases and conditions with allergic or immunologic causes: Examines patient, utilizing medical instruments and equipment, patch tests, and blood tests as diagnostic aids. Elicits and records information about patient's history. Analyses reports and test results and prescribes treatment or medication for conditions, such as bronchial asthma, dermatological disorders, connective tissue syndromes, transplantation, and autoimmunity. Refers patients to ancillary and consultant services when indicated.
GOE: 02.03.01 STRENGTH: L GED: R6 M5 L6 SVP: 9 DLU: 88

070.107-014 PSYCHIATRIST (medical ser.)
Diagnoses and treats patients with mental, emotional, and behavioral disorders: Organizes data concerning patient's family, medical history, and onset of symptoms obtained from patient, relatives, and other sources, such as NURSE, GENERAL DUTY (medical ser.) 075.364-010 and SOCIAL WORKER, PSYCHIATRIC (profess. & kin.) 195.107-034. Examines patient to determine general physical condition, following standard medical procedures. Orders laboratory and other special diagnostic tests and evaluates data obtained. Determines nature and extent of mental disorder, and formulates treatment program. Treats or directs treatment of patient, utilizing variety of psychotherapeutic methods and medications.
GOE: 02.03.01 STRENGTH: L GED: R6 M5 L6 SVP: 8 DLU: 88

071 OSTEOPATHS

This group includes occupations concerned with the application of manipulative procedures in treating patients, in addition to the other accepted methods of medical care. Includes diagnosis, prevention, and treatment of diseases and injuries; research in the causes, transmission, and control of disease and other ailments.

071.101-010 OSTEOPATHIC PHYSICIAN (medical ser.) alternate titles: doctor, osteopathic; osteopath
Diagnoses and treats diseases and injuries of human body, relying upon accepted medical and surgical modalities: Examines patient to determine symptoms attributable to impairments in musculoskeletal system. Corrects disorders and afflictions of bones, muscles, nerves, and other body systems by medicinal and surgical procedures and, when deemed beneficial, manipulative therapy. Employs diagnostic images, drugs, and other aids to diagnose and treat bodily impairments. May practice medical or surgical speciality.

GOE: 02.03.01 STRENGTH: M GED: R6 M5 L6 SVP: 8 DLU: 89

072 DENTISTS

This group includes occupations concerned with examination, diagnosis, prevention, and treatment of ailments or abnormalities of gums ,jaws, soft tissue, and teeth. Includes oral surgery.

072.061-010 ORAL PATHOLOGIST (medical ser.)
Studies nature, cause, and development of diseases associated with mouth: Examines patient's mouth, jaw, face, and associated areas and obtains specimen, using medical instruments. Examines specimen from patient's mouth or associated area to determine pathological conditions, such as tumors and lesions, using microscope and other laboratory equipment and applying knowledge of medical pathology and dentistry. Discusses diagnosis with patient and referring practitioner.
GOE: 02.03.02 STRENGTH: L GED: R6 M5 L5 SVP: 8 DLU: 89

072.101-010 DENTIST (medical ser.)
Diagnoses and treats diseases, injuries, and malformations of teeth and gums, and related oral structures: Examines patient to determine nature of condition, utilizing x rays, dental instruments, and other diagnostic procedures. Cleans, fills, extracts, and replaces teeth, using rotary and hand instruments, dental appliances, medications, and surgical implements. Provides preventive dental services to patient, such as applications of fluoride and sealants to teeth, and education in oral and dental hygiene.
GOE: 02.03.02 STRENGTH: L GED: R6 M5 L5 SVP: 8 DLU: 89

072.101-014 ENDODONTIST (medical ser.)
Examines, diagnoses, and treats diseases of nerve, pulp, and other dental tissues affecting vitality of teeth: Examines teeth, gums, and related tissues to determine condition, using dental instruments, x ray, and other diagnostic equipment. Diagnoses condition and plans treatment. Treats exposure of pulp by pulp capping or removal of pulp from pulp chamber and root canal, using dental instruments. Performs partial or total removal of pulp, using surgical instruments. Treats infected root canal and related tissues, and fills pulp chamber and canal with endodontic materials. Removes pathologic tissue at apex of tooth, surgically. Reinserts teeth that have been knocked out of mouth by accident. Bleaches discolored teeth to restore natural color.
GOE: 02.03.02 STRENGTH: L GED: R6 M5 L5 SVP: 8 DLU: 89

072.101-018 ORAL AND MAXILLOFACIAL SURGEON (medical ser.) alternate titles: oral surgeon
Performs surgery on mouth, jaws, and related head and neck structure: Executes difficult and multiple extraction of teeth. Removes tumors and other abnormal growths. Performs preprosthetic surgery to prepare mouth for insertion of dental prosthesis. Corrects abnormal jaw relations by mandibular or maxillary revision. Treats fractures of jaws. Administers general and local anesthetics. May treat patients in hospital.
GOE: 02.03.02 STRENGTH: L GED: R6 M5 L5 SVP: 8 DLU: 89

072.101-022 ORTHODONTIST (medical ser.)
Examines, diagnoses, and treats abnormalities in development of jaws, position of teeth, and other dental-facial structures: Plans treatment, using cephalometric, height, and weight records, dental x rays, and front and lateral dental photographs. Designs and fabricates appliances, such as space maintainers, retainers, and labial and lingual arch wires, to alter position and relationship of teeth and jaws, and to realign teeth to produce and maintain normal function.
GOE: 02.03.02 STRENGTH: L GED: R6 M5 L5 SVP: 8 DLU: 89

072.101-026 PEDIATRIC DENTIST (medical ser.) alternate titles: pedodontist
Provides dental care for infants, children, and adolescents: Fabricates space maintainers designed for patients. Treats primary and secondary teeth and constructs and places bridges, dentures, and obturating appliances suitable for growing arches. Manages patients with behavioral problems or handicapping conditions. Counsels and advises patients and family on growth and development dental problems of patient. Provides preventive services through use of fluorides and sealants and instructs patient and family members on dental care.
GOE: 02.03.02 STRENGTH: L GED: R6 M5 L5 SVP: 8 DLU: 88

072.101-030 PERIODONTIST (medical ser.)
Diagnoses and treats inflammatory and destructive diseases of investing and supporting tissue of teeth: Cleans and polishes teeth, eliminates irritating margins of fillings, and corrects occlusions. Performs surgical procedures to remove diseased tissue, using dental instruments. Establishes recall treatment program to monitor oral health practices.
GOE: 02.03.02 STRENGTH: L GED: R6 M5 L5 SVP: 8 DLU: 89

072.101-034 PROSTHODONTIST (medical ser.) alternate titles: prosthetic dentist
Restores and maintains oral functions: Records physiologic position of jaws to determine shape and size of dental prostheses, using face bows, dental articulators, and other recording devices. Replaces missing teeth and associated oral structures with artificial teeth to improve chewing, speech, and appearance. Corrects natural and acquired deformation of mouth and jaws through use of prosthetic appliances.

GOE: 02.03.02 STRENGTH: L GED: R6 M5 L5 SVP: 8 DLU: 89

072.101-038   PUBLIC-HEALTH DENTIST (government ser.)

Plans, organizes, and maintains dental health program of public health agency: Analyzes dental needs of community to determine changes and trends in patterns of dental disease. Instructs community, school, and other groups on preventive oral health care services. Produces and evaluates dental health educational materials. Provides clinical and laboratory dental care and services. Instigates methods for evaluating changes in dental health status and needs of community.

GOE: 02.03.02 STRENGTH: L GED: R6 M5 L5 SVP: 8 DLU: 89

072.117-010   DIRECTOR, DENTAL SERVICES (medical ser.)

Administers dental program in hospital and directs departmental activities in accordance with accepted national standards and administrative policies: Confers with hospital administrators to formulate policies and recommend procedural changes. Establishes training program to advance knowledge and clinical skill levels of resident dentists studying for dental specializations. Implements procedures for hiring of professional staff and approves hiring and promotion of staff members. Establishes work schedules and assigns staff members to duty stations to maximize efficient use of staff. Observes and assists staff members at work to ensure safe and ethical practices and to solve problems and demonstrate techniques. Confers with hospital administrator to submit budget and statistical reports used to justify expenditures for equipment, supplies, and personnel.

GOE: 02.03.02 STRENGTH: S GED: R6 M5 L5 SVP: 8 DLU: 89

073   VETERINARIANS

This group includes occupations concerned with diagnosis, prevention, and treatment of animal disorders. Includes occupations in veterinary bacteriology, epidemiology, virology, pathology, and pharmacology.

073.061-010   VETERINARIAN, LABORATORY ANIMAL CARE (medical ser.)

Examines, diagnoses, and treats diseases of laboratory animals to ensure health of animals used in scientific research and to comply with regulations governing their humane and ethical treatment: Examines animals to detect indications of disease or injury, and treats animals when indications are found, to prevent spread of disease to other animals or workers. Discusses research projects with associates to plan procedures and selects animals for specific research based on knowledge of species and research principles and techniques. Participates in research projects. Oversees activities concerned with feeding, care, and maintenance of animal quarters to ensure compliance with laboratory regulations.

GOE: 02.02.01 STRENGTH: M GED: R6 M4 L5 SVP: 8 DLU: 89

073.061-014   VETERINARY ANATOMIST (profess. & kin.)

Studies form and structure of animals, both gross and microscopic. Required to hold degree of Doctor of Veterinary Medicine.

GOE: 02.02.01 STRENGTH: L GED: R5 M4 L5 SVP: 8 DLU: 77

073.061-018   VETERINARY MICROBIOLOGIST (profess. & kin.)

Studies biology, ecology, etiology, bacteriology, virology, and immunology of micro-organisms causing diseases in animals: Prepares laboratory cultures of micro-organisms taken from body fluids and tissues of diseased animals and identifies them by microscopic examination and bacteriological tests. Tests virulence of pathogenic organisms by observing effects of inoculations on laboratory and other animals. Investigates efficiency of vaccines, antigens, antibiotics, and other materials in prevention, diagnosis, and control of animal diseases. May specialize in bacteria causing animal diseases and be known as Veterinary Bacteriologist (profess & kin.). May specialize in study of viruses and rickettsiae and be known as Veterinary Virologist (profess. & kin.). May be required to hold degree of Doctor of Veterinary Medicine.

GOE: 02.02.01 STRENGTH: L GED: R6 M5 L6 SVP: 8 DLU: 88

073.061-022   VETERINARY EPIDEMIOLOGIST (profess. & kin.)

Studies factors influencing existence and spread of diseases among humans and animals, particularly those diseases transmissible from animals to humans. Required to hold degree of Doctor of Veterinary Medicine.

GOE: 02.02.01 STRENGTH: L GED: R5 M4 L5 SVP: 8 DLU: 77

073.061-026   VETERINARY PARASITOLOGIST (profess. & kin.)

Studies animal parasites that attack domestic animals and poultry: Conducts research to determine control and preventive measures, utilizing chemicals, heat, electricity, and other methods. Required to hold degree of Doctor of Veterinary Medicine.

GOE: 02.02.01 STRENGTH: L GED: R5 M4 L5 SVP: 8 DLU: 77

073.061-030   VETERINARY PATHOLOGIST (medical ser.) alternate titles: clinical veterinarian

Studies nature, cause, and development of animal diseases, and structural and functional changes resulting from them: Conducts tests, performs biopsies, and analyzes body tissue, fluids and other specimens to diagnose presence and stage of disease in animals, and probable source of contamination or infection. Conducts further research to expand scope of findings, or recommends treatment to consulting veterinary personnel. May direct activities of veterinary pathology department in educational institution or industrial establishment.

GOE: 02.02.01 STRENGTH: M GED: R6 M5 L5 SVP: 8 DLU: 88

073.061-034   VETERINARY PHARMACOLOGIST (profess. & kin.)

Studies drugs, including materia medica and therapeutics, as related to veterinary medicine. Required to hold degree of Doctor of Veterinary Medicine.

GOE: 02.02.01 STRENGTH: S GED: R5 M4 L4 SVP: 8 DLU: 77

073.061-038   VETERINARY PHYSIOLOGIST (profess. & kin.)

Studies function and mechanism of systems and organs in healthy and diseased animals. Required to hold degree of Doctor of Veterinary Medicine.

GOE: 02.02.01 STRENGTH: L GED: R5 M4 L5 SVP: 8 DLU: 77

073.101-010   VETERINARIAN (medical ser.)

Diagnoses, and treats diseases and injuries of pets, such as dogs and cats, and farm animals, such as cattle or sheep: Examines animal to determine nature of disease or injury and treats animal surgically or medically. Tests dairy herds, horses, sheep, and other animals for diseases and inoculates animals against rabies, brucellosis, and other disorders. Advises animal owners about sanitary measures, feeding, and general care to promote health of animals. May engage in research, teaching, or production of commercial products. May specialize in prevention and control of communicable animal diseases and be designated Veterinarian, Public Health (government ser.). May specialize in diagnosis and treatment of animal diseases, using roentgen rays and radioactive substances, and be designated Veterinary Radiologist (medical ser.).

GOE: 02.03.03 STRENGTH: M GED: R5 M4 L5 SVP: 8 DLU: 88

073.101-014   VETERINARIAN, POULTRY (agriculture)

Advises individual poultry raisers on poultry problems: Gathers from owner information on care, condition, performance, and action of birds. Inspects flocks, pens, and housing. Diagnoses disease and prescribes treatment. Culls undesirable birds from flock. Suggests feed changes to increase egg production or growth of fowls.

GOE: 02.03.03 STRENGTH: L GED: R5 M4 L5 SVP: 8 DLU: 77

073.101-018   ZOO VETERINARIAN (medical ser.)

Plans, directs, and participates in health care program of veterinary clinic in zoo: Establishes and conducts effective quarantine and testing procedures for all incoming animals to ensure health of collection, prevent spread of disease, and comply with government regulations. Conducts regularly scheduled immunization and preventive care programs to maintain health of animals and guard against communicable diseases. Provides immediate medical attention to diseased or traumatized animals. Participates with other personnel in planning and executing nutrition and reproduction programs for animals in zoo. Develops special programs to encourage reproduction among animals designated as endangered species, based on knowledge of native habitat and instincts. Participates in employee training in handling and care of animals. Conducts postmortem studies and analyses. Cooperates with zoo and aquarium personnel to exchange information concerning care of animals, to arrange transfer, sale, or trade of animals, and to maintain nationwide inventory of every species, including notation of live births. Acts as consultant to veterinarians in general practice seeking advice in treatment of exotic animals.

GOE: 02.03.03 STRENGTH: M GED: R6 M5 L6 SVP: 8 DLU: 89

073.161-010   VETERINARY LIVESTOCK INSPECTOR (government ser.)

Inspects animals for presence of disease: Performs standard clinical tests and submits specimens of tissues and other parts for laboratory analysis. Reports existence of disease conditions to state and federal authorities. Advises livestock owners of economic aspects of disease eradication and advises consumers of public health implications of diseases transmissible from animals to humans. May institute and enforce quarantine or other regulations governing import, export, and interstate movement of livestock. Required to hold degree of Doctor of Veterinary Medicine.

GOE: 02.03.03 STRENGTH: M GED: R5 M4 L4 SVP: 7 DLU: 77

073.261-010   VETERINARY VIRUS-SERUM INSPECTOR (government ser.)

Inspects establishments where serums, toxins, and similar products, used in treatment of animals, are manufactured to enforce state or federal standards of sanitation, purity, labeling, and storage. Examines animals used in production process to determine if diseases are present. Inspects production areas to determine that standards of sanitation are being maintained. Required to hold degree of Doctor of Veterinary Medicine.

GOE: 02.03.03 STRENGTH: L GED: R5 M4 L4 SVP: 7 DLU: 77

073.264-010   VETERINARY MEAT-INSPECTOR (government ser.) alternate titles: veterinary medical officer

Inspects establishments engaged in slaughtering livestock and processing meat intended for intrastate, interstate, and foreign shipment to enforce municipal, state, or federal standards: Examines animal and carcass before and after slaughtering to detect evidence of disease or other abnormal conditions. Determines that ingredients used in processing and marketing meat and meat products comply with standards of purity and grading, and that products are not adulterated or misbranded. Inspects processing areas to ensure sanitary conditions are maintained. Required to hold degree of Doctor of Veterinary Medicine. May specialize in inspecting establishments engaged in processing milk and milk products and be designated Veterinary Milk-Specialist (government ser.); or inspecting establishments engaged in processing poultry and edible poultry products and be designated Veterinary-Poultry Inspector (government ser.).

GOE: 02.03.03 STRENGTH: M GED: R5 M4 L5 SVP: 8 DLU: 78

074   PHARMACISTS

This group includes occupations concerned with compounding prescriptions of physicians, dentists, and other practitioners; and the bulk selection, compounding, dispensing, and preservation of drugs and medicines.

074.161-010 PHARMACIST (medical ser.) alternate titles: druggist
Compounds and dispenses prescribed medications, drugs, and other pharmaceuticals for patient care, according to professional standards and state and federal legal requirements: Reviews prescriptions issued by physician, or other authorized prescriber to assure accuracy and determine formulas and ingredients needed. Compounds medications, using standard formulas and processes, such as weighing, measuring, and mixing ingredients. Directs pharmacy workers engaged in mixing, packaging, and labeling pharmaceuticals. Answers questions and provides information to pharmacy customers on drug interactions, side effects, dosage and storage of pharmaceuticals. Maintains established procedures concerning quality assurance, security of controlled substances, and disposal of hazardous waste drugs. Enters data, such as patient name, prescribed medication and cost, to maintain pharmacy files, charge system, and inventory. May assay medications to determine identity, purity, and strength. May instruct interns and other medical personnel on matters pertaining to pharmacy, or teach in college of pharmacy. May work in hospital pharmacy and be designated Pharmacist, Hospital (medical ser.)
GOE: 02.04.01 STRENGTH: L GED: R5 M5 L5 SVP: 7 DLU: 87

074.161-014 RADIOPHARMACIST (medical ser.)
Prepares and dispenses radioactive pharmaceuticals used for patient diagnosis and therapy, applying principles and practices of pharmacy and radiochemistry: Receives radiopharmaceutical prescription from physician and reviews prescription to determine suitability of radiopharmaceutical for intended use. Verifies that specified radioactive substance and reagent will give desired results in examination or treatment procedures, utilizing knowledge of radiopharmaceutical preparation and principles of drug biodistribution. Calculates volume of radioactive pharmaceutical required to provide patient with desired level of radioactivity at prescribed time, according to established rates of radioisotope decay. Compounds radioactive substances and reagents to prepare radiopharmaceutical, following radiopharmacy laboratory procedures. Assays prepared radiopharmaceutical, using measuring and analysis instruments and equipment, such as ionization chamber, pulse-height analyzer, and radioisotope dose calibrator, to verify rate of drug disintegration and to ensure that patient receives required dose. Consults with physician following patient treatment or procedure to review and evaluate quality and effectiveness of radiopharmaceutical. Conducts research to develop or improve radiopharmaceuticals. Prepares reports for regulatory agencies to obtain approval for testing and use of new radiopharmaceuticals. Maintains control records for receipt, storage, preparation, and disposal of radioactive nuclei. Occasionally conducts training for students and medical professionals concerning radiopharmacy use, characteristics, and compounding procedures.
GOE: 02.04.01 STRENGTH: L GED: R6 M5 L5 SVP: 7 DLU: 87

074.167-010 DIRECTOR, PHARMACY SERVICES (medical ser.)
Directs and coordinates, through subordinate supervisory personnel, activities and functions of hospital pharmacy: Plans and implements procedures in hospital pharmacy according to hospital policies and legal requirements. Directs pharmacy personnel programs, such as hiring, training, and intern programs. Confers with computer personnel to develop computer programs for pharmacy information management systems, patient and department charge systems, and inventory control. Analyzes records to indicate prescribing trends and excessive usage. Prepares pharmacy budget and department reports required by hospital administrators. Attends staff meetings to advise and inform hospital medical staff of drug applications and characteristics. Observes pharmacy personnel at work and develops quality assurance techniques to ensure safe, legal, and ethical practices. Oversees preparation and dispensation of experimental drugs.
GOE: 02.04.01 STRENGTH: L GED: R6 M6 L6 SVP: 8 DLU: 87

074.381-010 PHARMACIST ASSISTANT (military ser.)
Mixes and dispenses prescribed medicines and pharmaceutical preparations in absence of or under supervision of PHARMACIST (medical ser.): Compounds preparations according to prescriptions issued by medical, dental, or veterinary officers. Pours, weighs, or measures dosages and grinds, heats, filters, or dissolves and mixes liquid or soluble drugs and chemicals. Procures, stores, and issues pharmaceutical materials and supplies. Maintains files and records and submits required pharmacy reports.
GOE: 02.04.01 STRENGTH: L GED: R4 M4 L3 SVP: 6 DLU: 77

074.382-010 PHARMACY TECHNICIAN (medical ser.) alternate titles: pharmacy clerk
Performs any combination of following duties to assist PHARMACIST (medical ser.) 074.161-010 in hospital pharmacy or retail establishment: Mixes pharmaceutical preparations, fills bottles with prescribed tablets and capsules, and types labels for bottles. Assists PHARMACIST (medical ser.) to prepare and dispense medication. Receives and stores incoming supplies. Counts stock and enters data in computer to maintain inventory records. Processes records of medication and equipment dispensed to hospital patient, computes charges, and enters data in computer. Prepares intravenous (IV) packs, using sterile technique, under supervision of hospital pharmacist. Cleans equipment and sterilizes glassware according to prescribed methods.
GOE: 05.09.01 STRENGTH: L GED: R3 M3 L3 SVP: 3 DLU: 87

075   REGISTERED NURSES

This group includes occupations concerned with administering nursing care to the ill or injured. Includes nursing administration and instruction; and public health, industrial, private duty, and surgical nursing. Licensing or registration is required.

075.117-010 CONSULTANT, EDUCATIONAL, STATE BOARD OF NURSING (government ser.) alternate titles: director, educational board of nurse examiners
Directs activities concerned with maintaining educational standards established by board of nursing or other legally authorized agency: Participates in development and implementation of philosophy, purpose, policies, and plans of board of agency, and consults with and advises administrators of nursing schools in regard to curricula and facilities for instruction. Plans and conducts surveys of nursing schools and advises institutions desiring to establish schools on policies and procedures. Maintains current and comprehensive records and reports and keeps informed on trends and developments within the profession. May assist with administrative functions.
GOE: 11.07.02 STRENGTH: S GED: R5 M4 L5 SVP: 8 DLU: 77

075.117-014 DIRECTOR, COMMUNITY-HEALTH NURSING (medical ser.) alternate titles: director, public-health nursing
Administers nursing service in community health agency: Coordinates and evaluates nursing activities in agency to ensure balanced and adequate program, and to formulate progressive program designed to meet changing needs of community. Directs collection, analysis, and interpretation of statistics significant to program planning and budget preparation. Prepares and submits budget estimates for nursing activities. Participates in establishing programs for guidance and professional development of nursing staff, and in establishing personnel policies, qualifications, and salaries. Recruits, selects, and assigns personnel for nursing services. Plans nursing consulting services. Participates in community planning concerning health and social welfare problems. Consults with advisory committee in establishment of medical policies of community health agency.
GOE: 11.07.02 STRENGTH: S GED: R5 M4 L5 SVP: 8 DLU: 77

075.117-018 DIRECTOR, EDUCATIONAL, COMMUNITY-HEALTH NURSING (medical ser.) alternate titles: director, educational, public-health nursing
Plans and directs educational program for community health agency: Develops educational plans for in-service education and orientation of health personnel. Confers with supervisors and staff to ensure efficiency of program. Cooperates with nursing specialists and supervisors to organize educational programs for staff and community. Obtains educational materials for use in teaching and demonstrating nursing and other health related activities. Confers with administrative personnel to determine procedures and techniques for patient care and to implement new programs. Assists in selecting nursing candidates and in orienting new employees. Cooperates with nursing schools and colleges in providing supervised field instruction for students to gain work experience and observe nursing techniques. Conducts surveys and analyses to determine adequacy of educational materials and effectiveness of program.
GOE: 10.02.01 STRENGTH: S GED: R5 M4 L5 SVP: 8 DLU: 77

075.117-022 DIRECTOR, NURSING SERVICE (medical ser.)
Administers nursing program in hospital, nursing home, or other medical facility to maintain standards of patient care, and advises medical staff, department heads, and administrators in matters related to nursing service: Recommends establishment or revision of policies and develops organizational structure and standards of performance. Interprets policies and objectives of nursing service to staff and community groups. Promotes working relationships with community agencies and with other establishment departments. Assists in preparation of departmental budget. Establishes personnel qualification requirements, drafts procedure manuals, initiates in-service programs, installs record and reporting system, and performs other personnel management tasks. Initiates studies to evaluate effectiveness of nursing services in relation to their objectives and costs. May assist nursing schools with curricular problems.
GOE: 11.07.02 STRENGTH: S GED: R5 M4 L5 SVP: 8 DLU: 89

075.117-026 DIRECTOR, OCCUPATIONAL HEALTH NURSING (medical ser.) alternate titles: director, industrial nursing
Plans with management, medical director, and legal counsel scope and objectives of nursing service in industrial establishment, and directs nursing activities: Determines qualifications, duties, and responsibilities of nursing staff, and assists in selection. Arranges for orientation of newly appointed nursing staff in company policy and nursing procedures. Prepares and maintains nursing policy and procedure manual. Evaluates nursing service and assists in evaluation of total health service. Establishes system of records and reports. Advises management in development and maintenance of plant sanitation and housekeeping practices. Develops nursing procedures for emergency and followup care of occupational and nonoccupational injuries and illnesses. Provides for health counseling and health education on individual or group basis. Interprets nursing functions in interdepartmental planning and coordination of health and welfare benefit programs. May visit branches and subsidiaries of company periodically to evaluate nursing service.

GOE: 11.07.02 STRENGTH: S GED: R5 M4 L5 SVP: 8 DLU: 77

075.117-030 DIRECTOR, SCHOOL OF NURSING (medical ser.) alternate titles: dean, school of nursing

Directs and administers educational program in school of nursing: Assists in preparation of budget, and administers program within budgetary limitations. Defines and interprets aims and policies of school. Interviews and appoints faculty and administrative staff. Participates in planning curriculums and schedule of instruction. Participates in establishing qualifications for faculty, staff, and students and in recruiting eligible candidates. Arranges with hospital and other institutions and agencies for students to use their facilities, under faculty supervision, for clinical experience. Maintains student records of educational experience and achievement. May arrange student living accommodations, and social and recreational opportunities. May advise institutions on educational problems.
GOE: 11.07.02 STRENGTH: S GED: R5 M4 L5 SVP: 8 DLU: 77

075.117-034 EXECUTIVE DIRECTOR, NURSES' ASSOCIATION (medical ser.) alternate titles: executive secretary, nurses' association

Administers program of professional nurses' association, as formulated by board of directors and association members: Participates in establishing objectives and policies of association, and interprets program to members and general public at general and professional meetings. Assists in organizing committees and aids in attaining objectives in such matters as legislation affecting nursing, employment conditions, health programs, and research designed to facilitate professional growth and efficiency. Publicizes program of association through various media.
GOE: 11.05.02 STRENGTH: S GED: R6 M4 L6 SVP: 8 DLU: 77

075.124-010 NURSE, SCHOOL (medical ser.)

Provides health care services to students: Plans school health program, in cooperation with medical authority and administrative school personnel. Participates in medical examinations and reviews findings to evaluate health status of pupils and progress of program. Instructs classes in subjects, such as child care, first aid, and home nursing, and establishes nursing policies to meet emergencies. Cooperates with school personnel in identifying and meeting social, emotional, and physical needs of school children. Administers immunizations, provides first-aid, and maintains health records of students. Counsels students in good health habits. Works with community agencies in planning facilities to meet needs of children outside school situation. May assist in program for care of handicapped children. May work in college and be designated Nurse, College (medical ser.).
GOE: 10.02.01 STRENGTH: L GED: R5 M4 L5 SVP: 7 DLU: 80

075.124-014 NURSE, STAFF, COMMUNITY HEALTH (medical ser.) alternate titles: public-health nurse

Instructs individuals and families in health education and disease prevention in community health agency: Visits homes to determine patient and family needs, develops plan to meet needs, and provides nursing services. Instructs family in care and rehabilitation of patient, and in maintenance of health and prevention of disease for family members. Gives treatments to patient following physician's instructions. Assists community members and health field personnel to assess, plan for, and provide needed health and related services. Refers patients with social and emotional problems to other community agencies for assistance. Teaches home nursing, maternal and child care, and other subjects related to individual and community welfare. Participates in programs to safeguard health of children, including child health conferences, school health, group instruction for parents, and immunization programs. Assists in preparation of special studies and in research programs. Directs treatment of patient by NURSE, LICENSED PRACTICAL (medical ser.) 079.374-014 and HOME ATTENDANT (personal ser.) 354.377-014. Cooperates with families, community agencies, and medical personnel to arrange for convalescent and rehabilitative care of sick or injured persons. May specialize in one phase of community health nursing, such as clinical pediatrics or tuberculosis.
GOE: 10.02.01 STRENGTH: M GED: R5 M4 L5 SVP: 7 DLU: 77

075.124-018 NURSE, INSTRUCTOR (medical ser.)

Demonstrates and teaches patient care in classroom and clinical units to nursing students and instructs students in principles and application of physical, biological, and psychological subjects related to nursing: Lectures to students, conducts and supervises laboratory work, issues assignments, and directs seminars and panels. Supervises student nurses and demonstrates patient care in clinical units of hospital. Prepares and administers examinations, evaluates student progress, and maintains records of student classroom and clinical experience. Participates in planning curriculum, teaching schedule, and course outline. Cooperates with medical and nursing personnel in evaluating and improving teaching and nursing practices. May specialize in specific subject, such as anatomy, chemistry, psychology, or nutrition, or in type of nursing activity, such as nursing of medical or surgical patients. May conduct classes for patients in health practices and procedures.
GOE: 10.02.01 STRENGTH: L GED: R5 M4 L5 SVP: 8 DLU: 86

075.127-010 INSTRUCTOR, PSYCHIATRIC AIDE (education)

Provides clinical and academic instruction in psychiatric nursing methods and procedures for PSYCHIATRIC AIDES (medical ser.): Plans curricular content and sequence. Prepares schedules and arranges for lectures given by members of hospital staff, or prepares orientation course for psychiatric aide trainees. Prepares study material and presents lectures and demonstrations. Observes student progress, conducts examinations, and compiles records. Confers with students and evaluates performances at end of training course. Assists with assignment of students to units.
GOE: 10.02.01 STRENGTH: L GED: R5 M4 L5 SVP: 7 DLU: 77

075.127-014 NURSE, CONSULTANT (medical ser.)

Advises hospitals, schools of nursing, industrial organizations, and public health groups on problems related to nursing activities and health services: Reviews and suggests changes in nursing organization and administrative procedures. Analyzes nursing techniques and recommends modifications. Aids schools in planning nursing curriculums, and hospitals and public health nursing services in developing and carrying out staff education programs. Provides assistance in developing guides and manuals for specific aspects of nursing services. Prepares educational materials and assists in planning and developing health and educational programs for industrial and community groups. Advises in services available through community resources. Consults with nursing groups concerning professional and educational problems. Prepares or furnishes data for articles and lectures. Participates in surveys and research studies.
GOE: 10.02.01 STRENGTH: S GED: R5 M4 L5 SVP: 7 DLU: 77

075.127-026 NURSE, SUPERVISOR, COMMUNITY-HEALTH NURSING (medical ser.) alternate titles: supervisor, public-health nursing

Supervises and coordinates activities of nursing personnel in community health agency: Serves as liaison between staff and administrative personnel. Develops standards and procedures for providing nursing care and for evaluating service. Provides orientation, teaching, and guidance to staff to improve quality and quantity of service. Evaluates performance of personnel and interprets nursing standards to staff, advisory boards, nursing committees, and community groups. Recommends duty assignment of nursing personnel and coordinates services with other health and social agencies to render program more effective. Reviews, evaluates, and interprets nursing records, vital statistics, and other data affecting health service in order to assess community needs and to plan and implement programs to meet these needs. Assists in planning educational programs for nurses, related professional workers, and community groups to meet needs of personnel and practitioners. Assists in preparation of agency budget. May plan for and participate in field research related to community health nursing.
GOE: 10.02.01 STRENGTH: L GED: R5 M4 L5 SVP: 7 DLU: 77

075.127-030 NURSE, SUPERVISOR, EVENING-OR-NIGHT (medical ser.)

Plans, organizes, and directs activities for evening or night shift of hospital nursing department: Establishes policies and procedures for nursing department, following directions of hospital administrators. Observes techniques of and services rendered by nursing staff to ensure adherence to hospital guidelines. Demonstrates techniques for nursing students and new personnel to provide training and direction. Identifies problem areas in nursing department, such as understaffing, absenteeism, and wastefulness, and takes corrective action. Monitors use of supplies and equipment to avoid abuses and requisitions supplies. Responds to various departments requesting emergency assistance and assigns staff accordingly during emergencies. Prepares work schedule and assigns duties to nursing staff in department for efficient use of personnel.
GOE: 10.02.01 STRENGTH: L GED: R5 M4 L5 SVP: 8 DLU: 86

075.127-034 NURSE, INFECTION CONTROL (medical ser.)

Directs and coordinates infection control program in hospital: Compares laboratory reports with communicable diseases list to identify conditions that require infection control procedures. Advises and consults with physicians, nurses, and hospital personnel concerning precautions to be taken to protect patients, staff, and other persons from possible contamination or infection. Investigates infection control problems and arranges for follow-up care for persons exposed to infection or disease. Instructs hospital personnel in universal and specific infection control procedures.
GOE: 10.02.01 STRENGTH: L GED: R5 M4 L5 SVP: 7 DLU: 90

075.137-010 NURSE, SUPERVISOR, OCCUPATIONAL HEALTH NURSING (medical ser.) alternate titles: nurse supervisor, industrial nursing

Directs employee health services of industrial organization: Interprets plant and departmental health policies and regulations to nursing staff and employees. Coordinates activities of personnel rendering assistance to physician and nursing care to employees. Trains nursing staff in techniques of industrial nursing. Participates in planning and executing health information programs designed to improve efficiency and reduce absentee and accident rates. Assists workers in securing medical or other aid. Establishes work schedules for nursing staff and requisitions supplies. May conduct classes in first aid and home nursing for employees. May recommend appointment of nursing personnel.
GOE: 10.02.01 STRENGTH: L GED: R5 M4 L5 SVP: 7 DLU: 77

075.137-014 NURSE, HEAD (medical ser.)

Supervises and coordinates nursing activities in hospital unit: Assigns duties and coordinates nursing service. Evaluates nursing activities to ensure patient care, staff relations, and efficiency of service. Observes nursing care and visits patients to ensure that nursing care is carried out as directed, and treatment administered in accordance with physician's instructions. Directs preparation and maintenance of patients' clinical records. Inspects rooms and wards for cleanliness and comfort. Accompanies physician on rounds, and keeps informed of

special orders concerning patients. Participates in orientation and training of personnel. Orders, or directs ordering of drugs, solutions, and equipment, and maintains records on narcotics. Investigates and resolves complaints, or refers unusual problems to superior.
GOE: 10.02.01 STRENGTH: M GED: R5 M4 L5 SVP: 7 DLU: 87

075.167-010 NURSE, SUPERVISOR (medical ser.)

Directs, through head nurses, activities of nursing staff: Plans and organizes activities in nursing services, such as obstetrics, pediatrics, or surgery, or for two or more patient-care units to ensure patient needs are met in accordance with instructions of physician and hospital administrative procedures. Coordinates activities with other patient care units. Consults with NURSE, HEAD (medical ser.) 075.137-014 on nursing problems and interpretation of hospital policies to ensure patient needs are met. Plans and organizes orientation and in-service training for unit staff members, and participates in guidance and educational programs. Assists in formulating budget. Engages in studies and investigations related to improving nursing care.
GOE: 10.02.01 STRENGTH: L GED: R5 M4 L5 SVP: 7 DLU: 87

075.167-014   QUALITY ASSURANCE COORDINATOR (medical ser.)

Interprets and implements quality assurance standards in hospital to ensure quality care to patients: Reviews quality assurance standards, studies existing hospital policies and procedures, and interviews hospital personnel and patients to evaluate effectiveness of quality assurance program. Writes quality assurance policies and procedures. Reviews and evaluates patients' medical records, applying quality assurance criteria. Selects specific topics for review, such as problem procedures, drugs, high volume cases, high risk cases, or other factors. Compiles statistical data and writes narrative reports summarizing quality assurance findings. May review patient records, applying utilization review criteria, to determine need for admission and continued stay in hospital. May oversee personnel engaged in quality assurance review of medical records.
GOE: 10.02.01 STRENGTH: L GED: R5 M4 L5 SVP: 7 DLU: 90

075.264-010   NURSE PRACTITIONER (medical ser.) alternate titles: primary care nurse practitioner

Provides general medical care and treatment to patients in medical facility, such as clinic, health center, or public health agency, under direction of physician: Performs physical examinations and preventive health measures within prescribed guidelines and instructions of physician. Orders, interprets, and evaluates diagnostic tests to identify and assess patient's clinical problems and health care needs. Records physical findings, and formulates plan and prognosis, based on patient's condition. Discusses case with physician and other health professionals to prepare comprehensive patient care plan. Submits health care plan and goals of individual patients for periodic review and evaluation by physician. Prescribes or recommends drugs or other forms of treatment such as physical therapy, inhalation therapy, or related therapeutic procedures. May refer patients to physician for consultation or to specialized health resources for treatment. May be designated according to field of specialization as Pediatric Nurse Practitioner (medical ser.). Where state law permits, may engage in independent practice.
GOE: 10.02.01 STRENGTH: L GED: R5 M5 L5 SVP: 8 DLU: 89

075.264-014   NURSE-MIDWIFE (medical ser.)

Provides medical care and treatment to obstetrical patients under supervision of OBSTETRICIAN (medical ser.), delivers babies, and instructs patients in prenatal and postnatal health practices: Participates in initial examination of obstetrical patient, and is assigned responsibility for care, treatment, and delivery of patient. Examines patient during pregnancy, utilizing physical findings, laboratory test results, and patient's statements to evaluate condition and ensure that patient's progress is normal. Discusses case with OBSTETRICIAN (medical ser.) to assure observation of specified practices. Instructs patient in diet and prenatal health practices. Stays with patient during labor to reassure patient and to administer medication. Delivers infant and performs postpartum examinations and treatments to ensure that patient and infant are responding normally. When deviations from standard are encountered during pregnancy or delivery, administers stipulated emergency measures, and arranges for immediate contact of OBSTETRICIAN (medical ser.). Visits patient during postpartum period in hospital and at home to instruct patient in care of self and infant and examine patient. Maintains records of cases for inclusion in establishment file. Conducts classes for groups of patients and families to provide information concerning pregnancy, childbirth, and family orientation. May direct activities of other workers. May instruct in midwifery in establishment providing such training.
GOE: 10.02.01 STRENGTH: M GED: R5 M5 L3 SVP: 7 DLU: 77

075.364-010   NURSE, GENERAL DUTY (medical ser.) alternate titles: nurse, staff

Provides general nursing care to patients in hospital, nursing home, infirmary, or similar health care facility: Administers prescribed medications and treatments in accordance with approved nursing techniques. Prepares equipment and aids physician during treatments and examinations of patients. Observes patient, records significant conditions and reactions, and notifies supervisor or physician of patient's condition and reaction to drugs, treatments, and significant incidents. Takes temperature, pulse, blood pressure, and other vital signs to detect deviations from normal and assess condition of patient. May rotate among various clinical services of institution, such as obstetrics, surgery, orthopedics, outpatient and admitting, pediatrics, and psychiatry. May prepare rooms, sterile instruments, equipment and supplies, and hand items to SURGEON (medical ser.)

070.101-094; OBSTETRICIAN (medical ser.) 070.101-054, or other medical practitioner. May make beds, bathe, and feed patients. May serve as leader for group of personnel rendering nursing care to number of patients.
GOE: 10.02.01 STRENGTH: M GED: R5 M4 L5 SVP: 7 DLU: 89

075.371-010   NURSE ANESTHETIST (medical ser.)

Administers local, inhalation, intravenous, and other anesthetics prescribed by ANESTHESIOLOGIST (medical ser.) 070.101-010 to induce total or partial loss of sensation or consciousness in patients during surgery, deliveries, or other medical and dental procedures: Fits mask to patient's face, turns dials and sets gauges of equipment to regulate flow of oxygen and gases to administer anesthetic by inhalation method, according to prescribed medical standards. Prepares prescribed solutions and administers local, intravenous, spinal, or other anesthetic, following specified methods and procedures. Notes patient's skin color and dilation of pupils and observes video screen and digital display of computerized equipment to monitor patient's vital signs during anesthesia. Initiates remedial measures to prevent surgical shock or other adverse conditions. Informs physician of patient's condition during anesthesia.
GOE: 10.02.01 STRENGTH: L GED: R5 M5 L5 SVP: 8 DLU: 90

075.374-014   NURSE, OFFICE (medical ser.)

Cares for and treats patients in medical office, as directed by physician: Prepares patient for and assists with examinations. Administers injections and medications, dresses wounds and incisions, interprets physician's instructions to patients, assists with emergency and minor surgery, and performs related tasks as directed. Maintains records of vital statistics and other pertinent data of patient. Cleans and sterilizes instruments and equipment, and maintains stock of supplies. May conduct specified laboratory tests. May record and develop electrocardiograms. May act as receptionist, perform secretarial duties, and prepare monthly statements.
GOE: 10.02.01 STRENGTH: L GED: R5 M3 L5 SVP: 7 DLU: 89

075.374-018   NURSE, PRIVATE DUTY (medical ser.) alternate titles: nurse, special

Contracts independently to render nursing care, usually to one patient, in hospital or private home: Administers medications, treatments, dressings, and other nursing services, according to physician's instructions and condition of patient. Observes, evaluates, and records symptoms. Applies independent emergency measures to counteract adverse developments and notifies physician of patient's condition. Directs patient in good health habits. Gives information to family in treatment of patient and maintenance of healthful environment. Maintains equipment and supplies. Cooperates with community agencies furnishing assistance to patient. May supervise diet when employed in private home. May specialize in one field of nursing, such as obstetrics, psychiatry, or tuberculosis.
GOE: 10.02.01 STRENGTH: M GED: R5 M4 L5 SVP: 7 DLU: 77

075.374-022   NURSE, STAFF, OCCUPATIONAL HEALTH NURSING (medical ser.) alternate titles: nurse, staff, industrial

Provides nursing service and first aid to employees or persons who become ill or injured on premises of department store, industrial plant, or other establishment: Takes patient's vital signs, treats wounds, evaluates physical condition of patient, and contacts physician and hospital to arrange for further medical treatment, when needed. Maintains record of persons treated, and prepares accident reports and insurance forms. Develops employee programs, such as health education, accident prevention, alcohol abuse counseling, curtailment of smoking, and weight control regimens. May assist physician in physical examination of new employees.
GOE: 10.02.01 STRENGTH: L GED: R5 M4 L5 SVP: 7 DLU: 87

076   THERAPISTS

This group includes occupations concerned with the treatment and rehabilitation of persons with physical or mental disabilities or disorders, to develop or restore functions, prevent loss of physical capacities, and maintain optimum performance. Includes occupations utilizing means, such as exercise, massage, heat, light, water, electricity, and specific therapeutic apparatus, usually as prescribed by a physician; or participation in medically oriented rehabilitative programs, including educational, occupational, and recreational activities.

076.101-010   AUDIOLOGIST (medical ser.)

Determines type and degree of hearing impairment and implements habilitation and rehabilitation services for patient: Administers and interprets variety of tests, such as air and bone conduction, and speech reception and discrimination tests, to determine type and degree of hearing impairment, site of damage, and effects on comprehension and speech. Evaluates test results in relation to behavioral, social, educational, and medical information obtained from patients, families, teachers, SPEECH PATHOLOGISTS (profess. & kin.) 076.107-010 and other professionals to determine communication problems related to hearing disability. Plans and implements prevention, habilitation, or rehabilitation services, including hearing aid selection and orientation, counseling, auditory training, lip reading, language habilitation, speech conservation, and other treatment programs developed in consultation with SPEECH PATHOLOGIST (profess. & kin.) and other professionals. May refer patient to physician or surgeon if medical treatment is determined necessary. May conduct research in physiology, pathology, biophysics, or psychophysics of auditory systems, or design and develop clinical and research procedures and apparatus. May act as consultant to educational, medical, legal, and other professional groups. May teach art and science of audiology and direct scientific projects.

GOE: 02.03.04 STRENGTH: L GED: R5 M4 L5 SVP: 7 DLU: 80

076.104-010   VOICE PATHOLOGIST (profess. & kin.)

Diagnoses and treats voice disorders, such as those associated with professional use of voice: Develops and implements perceptual evaluation procedures and psychophysical methods for voice assessment. Collects diagnostic data on individuals, such as output pressures, airflow, chestwall movements, and articular and laryngeal displacement, using scopes and other measuring instruments. Analyzes and interprets diagnostic data and consults with OTOLARYNGOLOGIST (medical ser.) 070.101-062 and other professionals to determine method of treatment, such as surgery, vocal modification, or voice therapy. Plans and conducts voice therapy sessions, applying auditory, visual, kinematic, and biofeedback techniques. Plans and conducts voice hygiene workshops. Calibrates equipment. May teach voice science to associates and direct research in area of voice. May establish procedures and direct operation of laboratory specializing in diagnosing and treating voice disorders and be designated Director, Bio-Communications Laboratory (medical ser.).

GOE: 02.03.04 STRENGTH: L GED: R5 M5 L5 SVP: 8 DLU: 86

076.107-010   SPEECH PATHOLOGIST (profess. & kin.) alternate titles: speech clinician; speech therapist

Specializes in diagnosis and treatment of speech and language problems, and engages in scientific study of human communication: Diagnoses and evaluates speech and language skills as related to educational, medical, social, and psychological factors. Plans, directs, or conducts habilitative and rehabilitative treatment programs to restore communicative efficiency of individuals with communication problems of organic and nonorganic etiology. Provides counseling and guidance and language development therapy to handicapped individuals. Reviews individual file to obtain background information prior to evaluation to determine appropriate tests and to ensure that adequate information is available. Administers, scores, and interprets specialized hearing and speech tests. Develops and implements individualized plans for assigned clients to meet individual needs, interests, and abilities. Evaluates and monitors individuals, using audio-visual equipment, such as tape recorders, overhead projectors, filmstrips, and demonstrative materials. Reviews treatment plan, and assesses individual performance to modify, change, or write new programs. Maintains records as required by law, establishment's policy, and administrative regulations. Attends meetings and conferences and participates in other activities to promote professional growth. Instructs individuals to monitor their own speech and provides ways to practice new skills. May act as consultant to educational, medical, and other professional groups. May conduct research to develop diagnostic and remedial techniques. May serve as consultant to classroom teachers to incorporate speech and language development activities into daily schedule. May teach manual sign language to student incapable of speaking. May instruct staff in use of special equipment designed to serve handicapped. See AUDIOLOGIST (medical ser.) 076.101-010 for one who specializes in diagnosis of, and provision of rehabilitative services for, auditory problems.

GOE: 02.03.04 STRENGTH: L GED: R5 M5 L5 SVP: 7 DLU: 89

076.117-010   COORDINATOR OF REHABILITATION SERVICES (medical ser.) alternate titles: director of rehabilitative services

Plans, administers, and directs operation of health rehabilitation programs, such as physical, occupational, recreational, and speech therapies: Consults with medical and professional staff of other departments and personnel from associated health care fields to plan and coordinate joint patient and management objectives. Conducts staff conferences and plans training programs to maintain proficiency of staff in therapy techniques and use of new methods and equipment to meet patients' needs. Allocates personnel on basis of work load, space, and equipment available. Analyzes operating costs and prepares department budget. Recommends staffing fees for therapy based on use of equipment and therapy staff. May coordinate research projects to develop new approaches to rehabilitative therapy. May serve as rehabilitative therapy consultant to employers, educational institutions, and community organizations.

GOE: 11.07.01 STRENGTH: L GED: R5 M5 L5 SVP: 8 DLU: 89

076.121-010   OCCUPATIONAL THERAPIST (medical ser.)

Plans, organizes, and conducts occupational therapy program in hospital, institution, or community setting to facilitate development and rehabilitation of mentally, physically, or emotionally handicapped: Plans program involving activities, such as manual arts and crafts; practice in functional, prevocational, vocational, and homemaking skills, and activities of daily living; and participation in sensorimotor, educational, recreational, and social activities designed to help patients or handicapped persons develop or regain physical or mental functioning or adjust to handicaps. Consults with other members of rehabilitation team to select activity program consistent with needs and capabilities of individual and to coordinate occupational therapy with other therapeutic activities. Selects constructive activities suited to individual's physical capacity, intelligence level, and interest to upgrade individual to maximum independence, prepare individual for return to employment, assist in restoration of functions, and aid in adjustment to disability. Teaches individuals skills and techniques required for participation in activities and evaluates individual's progress. Designs and constructs special equipment for individual and suggests adaptation of individual's work-living environment. Requisitions supplies and equipment. Lays out materials for individual's use and cleans and repairs tools at end of sessions. May conduct training programs or participate in training medical and nursing students and other workers in occupational therapy techniques and objectives. May plan, direct, and coordinate occupational therapy program and be designated Director, Occupational Therapy (medical ser.).

GOE: 10.02.02 STRENGTH: M GED: R5 M4 L5 SVP: 7 DLU: 89

076.121-014   PHYSICAL THERAPIST (education; medical ser.) alternate titles: physiotherapist

Plans and administers medically prescribed physical therapy treatment for patients suffering from injuries, or muscle, nerve, joint and bone diseases, to restore function, relieve pain, and prevent disability: Reviews physician's referral (prescription) and patient's condition and medical records to determine physical therapy treatment required. Tests and measures patient's strength, motor development, sensory perception, functional capacity, and respiratory and circulatory efficiency, and records findings to develop or revise treatment programs. Plans and prepares written treatment program based on evaluation of patient data. Administers manual exercises to improve and maintain function. Instructs, motivates, and assists patient to perform various physical activities, such as nonmanual exercises, ambulatory functional activities, daily-living activities, and in use of assistant and supportive devices, such as crutches, canes, and prostheses. Administers treatments involving application of physical agents, using equipment, such as hydrotherapy tanks and whirlpool baths, moist packs, ultraviolet and infrared lamps, and ultrasound machines. Evaluates effects of treatment at various stages and adjusts treatments to achieve maximum benefit. Administers massage, applying knowledge of massage techniques and body physiology. Administers traction to relieve pain, using traction equipment. Records treatment, response, and progress in patient's chart or enters information into computer. Instructs patient and family in treatment procedures to be continued at home. Evaluates, fits, and adjusts prosthetic and orthotic devices and recommends modification to ORTHOTIST (medical ser.) 078.261-018. Confers with physician and other practitioners to obtain additional patient information, suggest revisions in treatment program, and integrate physical therapy treatment with other aspects of patient's health care. Orients, instructs, and directs work activities of assistants, aides, and students. May plan and conduct lectures and training programs on physical therapy and related topics for medical staff, students, and community groups. May plan and develop physical therapy research programs and participate in conducting research. May write technical articles and reports for publications. May teach physical therapy techniques and procedures in educational institutions. May limit treatment to specific patient group or disability or specialize in conducting physical therapy research. In facilities where assistants are also employed, may primarily administer complex treatment, such as certain types of manual exercises and functional training, and monitor administration of other treatments. May plan, direct, and coordinate physical therapy program and be designated Director, Physical Therapy (medical ser.). Must comply with state requirement for licensure.

GOE: 10.02.02 STRENGTH: M GED: R5 M4 L5 SVP: 7 DLU: 89

076.121-018   EXERCISE PHYSIOLOGIST (medical ser.)

Develops, implements, and coordinates exercise programs and administers medical tests, under physician's supervision, to program participants to promote physical fitness: Explains program and test procedures to participant. Interviews participant to obtain vital statistics and medical history and records information. Records heart activity, using electrocardiograph (EKG) machine, while participant undergoes stress test on treadmill, under physician's supervision. Measures oxygen consumption and lung functioning, using spirometer. Measures amount of fat in body, using such equipment as hydrostatic scale, skinfold calipers, and tape measure, to assess body composition. Performs routine laboratory test of blood samples for cholesterol level and glucose tolerance, or interprets test results. Schedules other examinations and tests, such as physical examination, chest x ray, and urinalysis. Records test data in patient's chart or enters data into computer. Writes initial and follow-up exercise prescriptions for participants, following physician's recommendation, specifying equipment, such as treadmill, track, or bike. Demonstrates correct use of exercise equipment and exercise routines. Conducts individual and group aerobic, strength, and flexibility exercises. Observes participants during exercise for signs of stress. Teaches behavior modification classes, such as stress management, weight control, and related subjects. Orders material and supplies and calibrates equipment. May supervise work activities of other staff members.

GOE: 10.02.02 STRENGTH: M GED: R5 M4 L5 SVP: 7 DLU: 90

076.124-010   MANUAL-ARTS THERAPIST (medical ser.)

Instructs patients in prescribed manual arts activities to prevent anatomical and physiological deconditioning, and to assist in maintaining, improving, or developing work skills: Collaborates with other members of rehabilitation team in planning and organizing work activities consonant with patients' capabilities and disabilities. Teaches, by means of actual or simulated work situations, activities, such as woodworking, photography, metalworking, agriculture, electricity, and graphic arts. Prepares reports showing development of patient's work tolerance, and emotional and social adjustment to aid medical personnel in evaluating patient's progress and ability to meet physical and mental demands of employment.

GOE: 10.02.02 STRENGTH: L GED: R4 M4 L4 SVP: 7 DLU: 77

076.124-014   RECREATIONAL THERAPIST (medical ser.) alternate titles: therapeutic recreation worker

Plans, organizes, and directs medically approved recreation program for patients in hospitals and other institutions: Directs and organizes such activities as sports, dramatics, games, and arts and crafts to assist patients to develop interpersonal relationships, to socialize effectively, and to develop confidence needed to participate in group activities. Regulates content of program in accordance with patients' capabilities, needs and interests. Instructs patients in re-

laxation techniques, such as deep breathing, concentration, and other activities, to reduce stress and tension. Instructs patients in calisthenics, stretching and limbering exercises, and individual and group sports. Counsels and encourages patients to develop leisure activities. Organizes and coordinates special outings and accompanies patients on outings, such as ball games, sightseeing, or picnics to make patients aware of available recreational resources. Prepares progress charts and periodic reports for medical staff and other members of treatment team, reflecting patients' reactions and evidence of progress or regression. May supervise and conduct in-service training of other staff members, review their assessments and program goals, and consult with them on selected cases. May train groups of volunteers and students in techniques of recreation therapy. May serve as consultant to employers, educational institutions, and community health programs. May prepare and submit requisition for needed supplies.
GOE: 10.02.02 STRENGTH: L GED: R4 M2 L4 SVP: 6 DLU: 89

076.124-018 HORTICULTURAL THERAPIST (medical ser.)
Plans, coordinates, and conducts therapeutic gardening program to facilitate rehabilitation of physically and mentally handicapped patients: Confers with medical staff and patients to determine patients' needs. Evaluates patients' disabilities to determine gardening programs. Conducts gardening sessions to rehabilitate, train, and provide recreation for patients. Revises gardening program, based on observations and evaluation of patients' progress.
GOE: 10.02.02 STRENGTH: L GED: R5 M4 L5 SVP: 7 DLU: 86

076.127-010 ART THERAPIST (medical ser.)
Plans and conducts art therapy programs in public and private institutions to rehabilitate mentally and physically disabled clients: Confers with members of medically oriented team to determine physical and psychological needs of client. Devises art therapy program to fulfill physical and psychological needs. Instructs individuals and groups in use of various art materials, such as paint, clay, and yarn. Appraises client's art projections and recovery progress. Reports findings to other members of treatment team and counsels on client's response until art therapy is discontinued. Maintains and repairs art materials and equipment.
GOE: 10.02.02 STRENGTH: L GED: R5 M4 L5 SVP: 7 DLU: 89

076.127-014 MUSIC THERAPIST (medical ser.)
Plans, organizes, and directs medically prescribed music therapy activities as part of mental and physical health care and treatment of patients to influence behavioral and psychological changes leading to restoration, maintenance, and improvement of health and increased comprehension of self, environment, and physical ability: Collaborates with other members of rehabilitation team in planning music activities in accordance with patients' physical or psychological needs, capabilities, and interests. Develops treatment plan, using individualized needs assessment, depending on focus of therapy, such as hospice, psychiatric, or obstetrics. Directs and participates in instrumental and vocal music activities designed to meet patients' physical or psychological needs, such as solo or group singing, rhythmic and other creative music activities, music listening, or attending concerts. Instructs patients individually or in groups in prescribed instrumental or vocal music and music projective techniques, such as guided imagery, progressive relaxation, awareness of conscious feelings, or musically intergraded Lamaze Method. Studies and analyzes patients' reactions to various experiences and prepares reports describing symptoms indicative of progress or regression. Submits periodic reports to treatment team or physician to provide clinical data for evaluation. May oversee practicum and approved internships.
GOE: 10.02.02 STRENGTH: L GED: R5 M5 L5 SVP: 7 DLU: 89

076.127-018 DANCE THERAPIST (medical ser.)
Plans, organizes, and leads dance and body movement activities to improve patients' mental outlooks and physical well-beings: Observes and evaluates patient's mental and physical disabilities to determine dance and body movement treatment. Confers with patient and medical personnel to develop dance therapy program. Conducts individual and group dance sessions to improve patient's mental and physical well-being. Makes changes in patient's program based on observation and evaluation of progress. Attends and participates in professional conferences and workshops to enhance efficiency and knowledge.
GOE: 10.02.02 STRENGTH: L GED: R5 M3 L5 SVP: 8 DLU: 86

076.167-010 INDUSTRIAL THERAPIST (medical ser.)
Arranges salaried, productive employment in actual work environment for mentally ill patients, to enable patients to perform medically prescribed work activities, and to motivate and prepare patients to resume employment outside hospital environment: Determines work activities for greatest therapeutic value for particular patient within limits of patient's disability. Plans work activities in coordination with other members of rehabilitation team. Assigns patient to work activity and evaluates patient's progress. Processes payroll records and salary distribution.
GOE: 10.02.02 STRENGTH: L GED: R5 M5 L5 SVP: 7 DLU: 77

076.224-010 PHYSICAL THERAPIST ASSISTANT (medical ser.) alternate titles: physical therapy assistant; physical therapy technician
Administers physical therapy treatments to patients, working under direction of and as assistant to PHYSICAL THERAPIST (medical ser.) 076.121-014: Administers active and passive manual therapeutic exercises, therapeutic massage, and heat, light, sound, water, and electrical modality treatments, such as ultrasound, electrical stimulation, ultraviolet, infrared, and hot and cold packs. Administers traction to relieve neck and back pain, using intermittent and static

traction equipment. Instructs, motivates, and assists patients to learn and improve functional activities, such as preambulation, transfer, ambulation, and daily-living activities. Observes patients during treatments and compiles and evaluates data on patients' responses to treatments and progress and reports orally or in writing to PHYSICAL THERAPIST (medical ser.). Fits patients for, adjusts, and trains patients in use and care of orthopedic braces, prostheses, and supportive devices, such as crutches, canes, walkers, and wheelchairs. Confers with members of physical therapy staff and other health team members, individually and in conference, to exchange, discuss, and evaluate patient information for planning, modifying, and coordinating treatment programs. Gives orientation to new PHYSICAL THERAPIST ASSISTANTS (medical ser.) and directs and gives instructions to PHYSICAL THERAPY AIDES (medical ser.) 355.354-010. Performs clerical duties, such as taking inventory, ordering supplies, answering telephone, taking messages, and filling out forms. May measure patient's range-of-joint motion, length and girth of body parts, and vital signs to determine effects of specific treatments or to assist PHYSICAL THERAPIST (medical ser.) to compile data for patient evaluations. May monitor treatments administered by PHYSICAL THERAPY AIDES (medical ser.).
GOE: 10.02.02 STRENGTH: M GED: R4 M3 L4 SVP: 6 DLU: 87

076.224-014 ORIENTATION AND MOBILITY THERAPIST FOR THE BLIND (education; medical ser.; nonprofit org.) alternate titles: counselor, orientation and mobility; instructor of blind; orientor; orientation therapist for blind; therapist for blind
Assists blind and visually impaired clients to achieve personal adjustment and maximum independence through training in techniques of daily living: Interviews clients, analyzes client's lifestyle, and administers assessment tests to determine present and required or desired orientation and mobility skills. Trains clients in awareness of physical environment through sense of smell, hearing, and touch, and to travel alone, with or without cane, through use of variety of actual or simulated travel situations and exercises. Teaches clients personal and home management skills, and communication skills, such as eating, grooming, dressing, coin and money identification, cooking, and use of telephone and bathroom facilities. Teaches clients to protect body, using hands and arms to detect obstacles. Instructs clients in arts, crafts, and recreational skills, such as macrame, leatherworking, sewing, ceramics, and playing piano to improve sense of touch, coordination, and motor skills. Teaches clients to read and write Braille. Instructs client in use of reading machines and common electrical devices, and in development of effective listening techniques. Instructs clients in group activities, such as swimming, dancing, or playing modified sports activities to encourage and increase capacity for social participation and improve general health. Prepares progress report to allow members of rehabilitation team to evaluate clients' ability to perform varied activities essential to daily living. May develop and implement individualized orientation and mobility instructional program for blind and visually impaired and be designated Orientation And Mobility Instructor (education).
GOE: 10.02.02 STRENGTH: L GED: R5 M2 L5 SVP: 6 DLU: 80

076.264-010 PHYSICAL-INTEGRATION PRACTITIONER (medical ser.)
Conducts physical integration program to improve client's muscular function and flexibility: Determines client's medical history regarding accidents, operations, or chronic health complaints to plan objectives of program, using questionnaire. Photographs client to obtain different views of client's posture to facilitate treatment, using camera. Instructs client to demonstrate arm and leg movement and flexion of spine to evaluate client against established program norms. Determines program treatment procedures and discusses goals of program with client. Applies skin lubricant to section of body specified for treatment and massages muscles to release subclinical adhesions either manually or using hand held tool, utilizing knowledge of anatomy. Demonstrates and directs client's participation in specific exercises designed to fatigue desired muscle groups and release tension. Observes client's progress during program through such factors as increased joint movement, improved posture, or coordination. Records client's treatment, response, and progress.
GOE: 10.02.02 STRENGTH: L GED: R3 M1 L2 SVP: 6 DLU: 86

076.361-010 CORRECTIVE THERAPIST (medical ser.)
Provides medically prescribed program of physical exercises and activities designed to prevent muscular deterioration resulting from long convalescence or inactivity due to chronic illness: Collaborates with other members of rehabilitation team in organizing patients' course of treatment. Establishes rapport with patients to motivate them, choosing exercises and activities in accordance with prescription. Utilizes any or combination of resistive, assistive, or free movement exercises, utilizing bars, or hydrogymnastics. Instructs patients in use, function, and care of prostheses and devices, such as braces, crutches, or canes and in use of manually controlled vehicles. Directs blind persons in foot travel. Prepares progress reports of patient's emotional reactions to and progress in training by observing patient during exercises to provide clinical data for diagnosis and prognosis by rehabilitation team. Directs patients in techniques of personal hygiene to compensate for permanent disabilities.
GOE: 10.02.02 STRENGTH: M GED: R4 M2 L4 SVP: 7 DLU: 77

076.361-014 RESPIRATORY THERAPIST (medical ser.)
Administers respiratory therapy care and life support to patients with deficiencies and abnormalities of cardiopulmonary system, under supervision of physician and by prescription: Reads prescription, measures arterial blood gases, and reviews patient information to assess patient condition and determine

requirements for treatment, such as type and duration of therapy, and medication and dosages. Determines most suitable method of administering inhalants, precautions to be observed, and modifications which may be needed that will be compatible with physician's orders. Sets up and operates devices, such as mechanical ventilators, therapeutic gas administration apparatus, environmental control systems, and aerosol generators. Operates equipment to ensure specified parameters of treatment, such as volume, gas concentration, humidity, and temperature, and to administer medicinal gases and aerosol drugs to patients. Monitors patient's physiological responses to therapy, such as vital signs, arterial blood gases, and blood chemistry changes. Performs bronchopulmonary drainage and assists patient in performing breathing exercises. Performs pulmonary function tests to be used by physician in diagnosis of case. Observes equipment function and adjusts equipment to obtain optimum results to therapy. Consults with physician in event of adverse reactions. Maintains patient's chart that contains pertinent identification and therapy information. Inspects and tests respiratory therapy equipment to ensure equipment is functioning safely and efficiently. Orders repairs when needed. Demonstrates respiratory care procedures to trainees and other health care personnel.
GOE: 10.02.02 STRENGTH: M GED: R4 M3 L3 SVP: 6 DLU: 88

076.364-010 OCCUPATIONAL THERAPY ASSISTANT (medical ser.) alternate titles: educational/development assistant
Assists OCCUPATIONAL THERAPIST (medical ser.) 076.121-010 in administering occupational therapy program in hospital, related facility, or community setting for physically, developmentally, mentally retarded, or emotionally handicapped clients: Assists in evaluation of clients daily living skills and capacities to determine extent of abilities amd limitations. Assists in planning and implementing educational, vocational, and recreational programs and activities established by registered OCCUPATIONAL THERAPIST (medical ser.), designed to restore, reinforce, and enhance task performances, diminish or correct pathology, and to promote and maintain health and self-sufficiency. Designs and adapts equipment and working-living environment. Fabricates splints and other assistant devices. Reports information and observations to supervisor. Carries out general activity program for individuals or groups. Assists in instructing patient and family in home programs as well as care and use of adaptive equipment. Prepares work materials, assists in maintenance of equipment, and orders supplies. May be responsible for maintaining observed information in client records and preparing reports. May teach basic living skills to institutionalized, mentally retarded adults. May assist EDUCATIONAL SPECIALIST (education) 099.167-022 or CLINICAL PSYCHOLOGIST (profess. & kin.) 045.107-010 in administering situational or diagnostic tests to measure client's abilities or progress.
GOE: 10.02.02 STRENGTH: M GED: R4 M3 L4 SVP: 6 DLU: 86

077   DIETITIANS

This group includes occupations concerned with the application of the principles of nutrition to plan and supervise the preparation and serving of meals. Includes planning menus and diets for special nutritional requirements; participating in research; or instructing in the field of nutrition.

077.061-010 DIETITIAN, RESEARCH (profess. & kin.) alternate titles: research nutritionist
Conducts nutritional research to expand knowledge in one or more phases of dietetics: Plans, organizes, and conducts programs in nutrition, foods, and food service systems, evaluating and utilizing appropriate methodology and tools to carry out program. Studies and analyzes recent scientific discoveries in nutrition for application in current research, for development of tools for future research, and for interpretation to public. Communicates findings through reports and publications.
GOE: 02.02.04 STRENGTH: L GED: R6 M5 L5 SVP: 8 DLU: 77

077.117-010 DIETITIAN, CHIEF (profess. & kin.) alternate titles: dietitian, administrative; director, dietetics department
Directs activities of institution department providing quantity food service and nutritional care: Administers, plans, and directs activities of department providing quantity food service. Establishes policies and procedures, and provides administrative direction for menu formulation, food preparation and service, purchasing, sanitation standards, safety practices, and personnel utilization. Selects professional dietetic staff, and directs departmental educational programs. Coordinates interdepartmental professional activities, and serves as consultant to management on matters pertaining to dietetics.
GOE: 11.05.02 STRENGTH: S GED: R5 M4 L5 SVP: 8 DLU: 77

077.124-010 DIETETIC TECHNICIAN (profess. & kin.)
Provides services in assigned areas of food service management, teaches principles of food and nutrition, and provides dietary consultation, under direction of DIETITIAN, CLINICAL (profess. & kin.) 077.127-014: Plans menus based on established guidelines. Standardizes recipes and tests new products for use in facility. Supervises food production and service. Obtains and evaluates dietary histories of individuals to plan nutritional programs. Guides individuals and families in food selection, preparation, and menu planning, based upon nutritional needs. Assists in referrals for continuity of patient care. May select, schedule, and conduct orientation and in-service education programs. May develop job specifications, job descriptions, and work schedules. May assist in implementing established cost control procedures.

GOE: 05.05.17 STRENGTH: L GED: R5 M4 L5 SVP: 7 DLU: 89

077.127-010 COMMUNITY DIETITIAN (profess. & kin.)
Plans, organizes, coordinates, and evaluates nutritional component of health care services for organization: Develops and implements plan of care based on assessment of nutritional needs and available sources and correlates plan with other health care. Evaluates nutritional care and provides followup continuity of care. Instructs individuals and families in nutritional principles, diet, food selection, and economics and adapts teaching plans to individual life style. Provides consultation to and works with community groups. Conducts or participates in in-service education and consultation with professional staff and supporting personnel of own and related organizations. Plans or participates in development of program proposals for funding. Plans, conducts, and evaluates dietary studies and participates in nutritional and epidemiologic studies with nutritional component. Evaluates food service systems and makes recommendation for conformance level that will provide optional nutrition and quality food if associated with group care institutions. May be employed by public health agency and be designated Nutritionist, Public Health (government ser.).
GOE: 11.02.03 STRENGTH: L GED: R5 M4 L5 SVP: 8 DLU: 77

077.127-014 DIETITIAN, CLINICAL (profess. & kin.) alternate titles: dietitian, therapeutic
Plans therapeutic diets and implements preparation and service of meals for patients in hospital, clinic, or other health care facility: Consults with physician and other health care personnel to determine nutritional needs and diet restrictions, such as low fat or salt free, of patients. Formulates menus for therapeutic diets based on medical and physical condition of patients and integrates patient's menus with basic institutional menus. Inspects meals served for conformance to prescribed diets and for standards of palatability and appearance. Instructs patients and their families in nutritional principles, dietary plans, food selection, and preparation. May supervise activities of workers engaged in food preparation and service. May engage in research [DIETITIAN, RESEARCH (profess. & kin.) 077.061-010]. May teach nutrition and diet therapy to medical students and hospital personnel [DIETITIAN, TEACHING (profess. & kin.) 077.127-022].
GOE: 05.05.17 STRENGTH: L GED: R5 M4 L5 SVP: 7 DLU: 86

077.127-018 DIETITIAN, CONSULTANT (profess. & kin.) alternate titles: institutional-nutrition consultant
Advises and assists personnel in public and private establishments, such as hospitals, health-related facilities, child-care centers, and schools, in food service systems and nutritional care of clients: Evaluates and monitors all aspects of food service operation, making recommendations for conformance level that will provide nutritionally adequate, quality food. Plans, organizes, and conducts orientation and in-service educational programs for food service personnel. Develops menu patterns. Assesses, develops, implements, and evaluates nutritional-care plans and provides for followup, including written reports. Consults with health care team concerning nutritional care of client. Confers with designers, builders, and equipment personnel in planning for building or remodeling food service units.
GOE: 05.05.17 STRENGTH: L GED: R5 M4 L5 SVP: 8 DLU: 77

077.127-022 DIETITIAN, TEACHING (profess. & kin.)
Plans, organizes, and conducts educational programs in dietetics, nutrition, and institution management for DIETETIC INTERNS (profess. & kin.), nursing students, and other medical personnel: Develops curriculum and prepares manuals, visual aids, course outlines, and other material used in teaching. Lectures students on composition and values of foods, principles of nutrition, menu planning, diet therapy, food cost control, marketing, and administration of dietary department. May engage in research.
GOE: 11.02.02 STRENGTH: L GED: R5 M4 L5 SVP: 8 DLU: 77

078   OCCUPATIONS IN MEDICAL AND DENTAL TECHNOLOGY

This group includes occupations concerned with the application of technical knowledge in fields of medicine or dentistry for examination and treatment of patients or for research. Occupations occur in a doctor's or dentist's office, hospital, or laboratory.

078.121-010 MEDICAL TECHNOLOGIST, TEACHING SUPERVISOR (medical ser.)
Teaches one or more phases of medical technology to students of medicine, medical technology, or nursing arts, or to INTERNS (medical ser.): Organizes and directs medical technology training program. Formulates curriculums, outlines course materials, and establishes criteria in other matters affecting education and welfare of students. Develops educational policies concerning teaching methods. Supervises other instructors. May act as liaison officer between college or university and laboratory or hospital to coordinate academic and clinical training. May specialize in teaching one phase of medical technology.
GOE: 02.04.02 STRENGTH: S GED: R5 M4 L5 SVP: 7 DLU: 77

078.131-010 CHIEF TECHNOLOGIST, NUCLEAR MEDICINE (medical ser.) alternate titles: chief, nuclear medicine technologist
Supervises and coordinates activities of NUCLEAR MEDICINE TECHNOLOGISTS (medical ser.) 078.361-018 engaged in preparing, administering, and measuring radioactive isotopes in therapeutic, diagnostic, and tracer studies:

Assigns workers to prepare radiopharmaceuticals, perform nuclear medicine studies, and conduct laboratory tests, and monitors activities to ensure efficiency and accuracy of procedures. Writes computer protocols for diagnostic studies. Develops protocols for new and revised procedures and trains department workers in overall operation of department and use of equipment. Administers radiopharmaceuticals under direction of physician or other qualified medical personnel. Implements and supervises radiation safety policies and procedures to ensure safety of personnel and legal requirements are met for handling and disposing of radioactive materials. Assists in coordinating activities with other departments and in resolving operating problems. Performs duties of NUCLEAR MEDICINE TECHNOLOGIST (medical ser.) as needed.
GOE: 02.04.02 STRENGTH: L GED: R5 M4 L5 SVP: 8 DLU: 89

078.161-010 MEDICAL TECHNOLOGIST (medical ser.) alternate titles: medical laboratory manager
Directs and coordinates activities of workers engaged in performing chemical, microscopic, and bacteriologic tests to obtain data for use in diagnosis and treatment of diseases: Assigns workers to duties and oversees performance of tests in fields of microbiology, chemistry, histology, hematology, immunohematology, and serology. Purchases or directs purchase of laboratory equipment and supplies. Reviews test results to ensure quality control. Coordinates and conducts education and training programs for medical technology students and personnel.
GOE: 02.04.02 STRENGTH: L GED: R5 M4 L5 SVP: 8 DLU: 89

078.161-014 CARDIOPULMONARY TECHNOLOGIST, CHIEF (medical ser.)
Coordinates activities of CARDIOPULMONARY TECHNOLOGISTS (medical ser.) 078.362-030 engaged in performing diagnostic testing and treatment of patients with heart, lung, and blood vessel disorders: Establishes methods for conducting tests and treatments, applying knowledge of medical requirements and laboratory procedures. Schedules patients for tests and treatment by staff members. Reviews reports to ensure compliance with test and treatment procedures. Develops and modifies training program for assigned personnel. Evaluates worker performances and recommends promotions, transfers, and dismissals.
GOE: 02.04.02 STRENGTH: L GED: R5 M4 L5 SVP: 7 DLU: 86

078.162-010 RADIOLOGIC TECHNOLOGIST, CHIEF (medical ser.) alternate titles: chief, radiology
Directs and coordinates activities of radiology or diagnostic imaging department in hospital or other medical facility: Reviews work schedules and assigns duties to workers to maintain patient flow and achieve production goals. Oversees staff in operation of imaging equipment, such as x-ray machine, fluoroscope, CT (computerized tomography) scanner, or MRI (magnetic resonance imaging) equipment, evaluates accuracy and quality of images, and provides technical assistance. Demonstrates new techniques, equipment, and procedures to staff. Implements and monitors radiation safety measures to ensure safety of patients and staff and compliance with government regulatory requirements. Recommends personnel actions, such as performance evaluations, promotions, and disciplinary measures. Coordinates purchase of supplies and equipment and makes recommendations concerning department operating budget.
GOE: 10.02.02 STRENGTH: L GED: R5 M4 L5 SVP: 8 DLU: 89

078.221-010 IMMUNOHEMATOLOGIST (medical ser.)
Performs immunohematology tests, recommends blood problem solutions to doctors, and serves as consultant to blood bank and community: Visually inspects blood in specimen tubes for hemolysis. Centrifuges blood specimen to separate red cells from serum and tests separated serum to detect presence of antibodies. Interprets reactions observed to devise experiments and suggest techniques that will resolve patient's blood problems. Combines known and unknown cells with serum in test tubes and selects reagents, such as albumin, protolytic enzymes, and anti-human globutin, for individual tests to enhance and make visible reactions of agglutination and hemolysis. Processes various combinations in centrifuge and examines resulting samples under microscope to identify evidence of agglutination or hemolysis. Repeats and varies tests until normal suspension of reagents, serum, and red cells is attained. Interprets results obtained and identifies specific antibodies. Writes blood specifications to meet patient's need, on basis of test results, and applies knowledge of blood classification system to locate donor's blood. Performs immunohematology tests on donor's blood to confirm matching blood types. Requisitions and sends blood to supply patient's need, and prepares written report to inform physician of test results and of required volume of blood to administer. Evaluates completeness of immunohematology tests. May advise MEDICAL TECHNOLOGISTS (medical ser.) 078.261-038 in techniques of microscopic identification of precipitation, agglutination, or hemolysis in blood that leads to resolution of problems.
GOE: 02.04.02 STRENGTH: L GED: R5 M3 L5 SVP: 8 DLU: 89

078.261-010 BIOCHEMISTRY TECHNOLOGIST (medical ser.) alternate titles: medical technologist, chemistry; technologist, biochemistry
Performs qualitative and quantitative chemical analyses of body fluids and exudates, following instructions, to provide information used in diagnosis and treatment of diseases: Tests specimens, such as urine, blood, spinal fluid, and gastric juices, for presence and quantity of sugar, albumin, drugs, toxins, and blood gases such as oxygen. Prepares solutions used in chemical analysis. Calibrates and maintains manual and computer-controlled analyzers, spectrophotometers, colorimeters, flame photometers, and other equipment used in quantitative and qualitative analysis. May take blood samples.
GOE: 02.04.02 STRENGTH: L GED: R5 M4 L5 SVP: 7 DLU: 89

078.261-014 MICROBIOLOGY TECHNOLOGIST (medical ser.) alternate titles: medical technologist, microbiology
Cultivates, isolates, and assists in identifying bacteria and other microbial organisms, and performs various bacteriological, mycological, virological, mycobacteriological, and parasitological tests: Receives human or animal body materials from autopsy or diagnostic cases, or collects specimens directly from patients, under supervision of laboratory director. Examines materials for evidence of microbial organisms. Makes parasitological tests of specimens. May instruct medical laboratory students and other medical personnel in laboratory procedures. May supervise other technologists and be known as Supervisor, Microbiology Technologists (medical ser.).
GOE: 02.04.02 STRENGTH: L GED: R5 M4 L5 SVP: 7 DLU: 87

078.261-018 ORTHOTIST (medical ser.)
Provides care to patients with disabling conditions of limbs and spine by fitting and preparing orthopedic braces, under direction of and in consultation with physician: Assists in formulation of specifications for braces. Examines and evaluates patient's needs in relation to disease and functional loss. Formulates design of orthopedic brace. Selects materials, making cast measurements, model modifications, and layouts. Performs fitting, including static and dynamic alignments. Evaluates brace on patient and makes adjustments to assure fit, function, and quality of work. Instructs patient in use of orthopedic brace. Maintains patient records. May supervise ORTHOTICS ASSISTANTS (medical ser.) 078.361-022 and other support personnel. May supervise laboratory activities relating to development of orthopedic braces. May lecture and demonstrate to colleagues and other professionals concerned with orthotics. May participate in research. May perform functions of PROSTHETIST (medical ser.) 078.261-022 and be designated Orthotist-Prosthetist (medical ser.).
GOE: 05.05.11 STRENGTH: M GED: R5 M4 L4 SVP: 8 DLU: 77

078.261-022 PROSTHETIST (medical ser.)
Provides care to patients with partial or total absence of limb by planning fabrication of, writing specifications for, and fitting prosthesis under guidance of and in consultation with physician: Assists physician in formulation of prescription. Examines and evaluates patient's prosthetic needs in relation to disease entity and functional loss. Formulates design of prosthesis and selects materials and components. Makes casts, measurements, and model modifications. Performs fitting, including static and dynamic alignments. Evaluates prosthesis on patient and makes adjustments to assure fit, function, comfort, and workmanship. Instructs patient in prosthesis use. Maintains patient records. May supervise PROSTHETICS ASSISTANTS (medical ser.) 078.361-026 and other personnel. May supervise laboratory activities relating to development of prosthesis. May lecture and demonstrate to colleagues and other professionals concerned with practice of prosthetics. May participate in research. May also perform functions of ORTHOTIST (medical ser.) 078.261-018.
GOE: 05.05.11 STRENGTH: M GED: R5 M4 L4 SVP: 8 DLU: 77

078.261-026 CYTOGENETIC TECHNOLOGIST (medical ser.)
Prepares, examines, and analyzes chromosomes found in biological specimens, such as amniotic fluids, bone marrow, and blood, to aid in diagnosis and treatment of genetic diseases: Selects and prepares specimen and media for cell culture, using aseptic technique, knowledge of medium components, and cell nutritional requirements. Harvests cell culture at optimum time sequence based on knowledge of cell cycle differences and culture conditions. Prepares slide of cell culture, selects banding technique, and stains slide to make chromosomes visible under microscope, following standard laboratory procedures. Views slide through photomicroscope to count and identify chromosome number and presence of structural abnormality. Photographs slide and prints picture. Cuts images of chromosomes from photograph, identifies number and types of chromosomes, and arranges and attaches chromosomes in numbered pairs on karyotype chart, using standard genetics laboratory practices and nomenclature to identify normal or abnormal chromosomes. Communicates with physicians, family members, and researchers requesting technical information or test results. May supervise subordinate laboratory personnel and be known as Supervisor, Cytogenetic Laboratory (medical ser.).
GOE: 02.04.02 STRENGTH: S GED: R5 M4 L5 SVP: 7 DLU: 90

078.261-030 HISTOTECHNOLOGIST (medical ser.) alternate titles: histologic technologist; tissue technologist
Prepares histologic slides from tissue sections for microscopic examination and diagnosis by PATHOLOGIST (medical ser.) 070.061-010: Prepares sections of human or animal tissue for immediate examination, using rapid tissue processing and frozen section technique to freeze, cut, mount and stain tissue specimen received from surgery. Operates computerized laboratory equipment to fix, dehydrate, and infiltrate with wax, tissue specimens to be preserved for study by PATHOLOGIST (medical ser.). Prepares slides of specimens, using specified stain, to enhance visibility under microscope. Examines slides under microscope to ensure tissue preparation meets laboratory requirements. May study slides under microscope to detect deviations from norm and report abnormalities for further study. May supervise activities of laboratory personnel and be known as Supervisor, Histology (medical ser.).
GOE: 02.04.02 STRENGTH: L GED: R5 M4 L5 SVP: 6 DLU: 87

078.261-034 MEDICAL RADIATION DOSIMETRIST (medical ser.) alternate titles: dosimetrist

Measures and calculates radiation dose and develops optimum arrangement of radiation fields and exposures to treat patient: Studies prescription, x rays showing area to be treated, and requirements for dose calculation. Selects beam energy, optimum multiple beam arrangement, beam modifying devices, and other factors, using computer, manuals, and guides. Develops several possible treatment arrangements that meet physician's criteria and submits arrangements for selection by physician. Measures and calculates prescribed radiation dose based upon field sizes, depth of tumor, treatment unit, beam modifying devices, and other information, using manuals, guides, and computer. Calculates and records daily prescribed radiation dose. Explains treatment plan to RADIATION-THERAPY TECHNOLOGISTS (medical ser.) 078.361-034. May operate x-ray equipment to obtain diagnostic x ray of patient in treatment position. May simulate treatment procedure to assist in planning treatment.
GOE: 10.02.02 STRENGTH: L GED: R5 M4 L5 SVP: 8 DLU: 90

078.261-038 MEDICAL TECHNOLOGIST (medical ser.)

Performs medical laboratory tests, procedures, experiments, and analyses to provide data for diagnosis, treatment, and prevention of disease: Conducts chemical analyses of body fluids, such as blood, urine, and spinal fluid, to determine presence of normal and abnormal components. Studies blood cells, their numbers, and morphology, using microscopic technique. Performs blood group, type, and compatibility tests for transfusion purposes. Analyzes test results and enters findings in computer. Engages in medical research under direction of MEDICAL TECHNOLOGIST, CHIEF (medical ser.) 078.161-010. May train and supervise students. May specialize in area such as hematology, blood-bank, serology, immunohematology, bacteriology, histology, or chemistry.
GOE: 02.04.02 STRENGTH: L GED: R5 M4 L5 SVP: 7 DLU: 88

078.261-042 PHERESIS SPECIALIST (medical ser.) alternate titles: hemotherapist

Collects blood components and provides therapeutic treatments, such as replacement of plasma, or removal of white blood cells or platelets, to patients, using blood cell separator equipment: Compiles and evaluates donor information to ensure that donor meets screening criteria. Connects and installs tubing, transfer pack units, saline solution unit, other solution packs, and collection and separation containers to set up blood cell separator equipment. Explains procedures to donor or patient to reduce anxieties and obtain cooperation of donor or patient. Performs venipuncture on donor or patient to connect donor or patient to tubing of equipment to prepare for procedure. Sets controls and starts equipment that collects specific blood component or adds, reduces, or replaces blood component, and replaces remaining blood in vein of patient or donor. Monitors operation of equipment and observes trouble lights indicating equipment problems. Talks to and observes donor or patient for signs of distress or side effects such as pallor, nausea, fainting, or other problems during procedure. Forwards collection bag to laboratory for testing or further processing. Records information following collection or treatment procedures, such as flow rate, body site at which needle was inserted, anticoagulant rate, amount of fluids used, volume processed, red cells lost, and other information.
GOE: 10.02.02 STRENGTH: L GED: R5 M4 L5 SVP: 7 DLU: 89

078.262-010 PULMONARY-FUNCTION TECHNICIAN (medical ser.) alternate titles: pulmonary-function technologist

Performs pulmonary-function, lung-capacity, diffusion capacity, and blood-and-oxygen tests to gather data for use by physician in diagnosis and treatment of pulmonary disorders: Confers with patient in treatment room to explain test procedures. Explains specified methods of breathing to patient and conducts pulmonary-function tests, such as helium dilution and pulmonary mechanics (flow of air rate in lungs), arterial blood gas analyses, and lung-capacity tests, such as vital capacity and maximum breathing capacity tests, using spirometer or other equipment. Measures expired air, using various analyzers. Observes and records readings on metering devices of analysis equipment, and conveys findings of tests and analyses to physician for interpretation. May perform blood analysis tests to measure such factors as oxygen and carbon dioxide tensions, hemoglobin saturation and levels, and pH of blood, using blood gas analyzer. May measure sweat chloride to test for cystic fibrosis, using computerized analyzer. May assist physician in special procedures such as bronchoscopy.
GOE: 10.03.01 STRENGTH: L GED: R4 M4 L4 SVP: 6 DLU: 89

078.264-010 HOLTER SCANNING TECHNICIAN (medical ser.) alternate titles: holter technician

Analyzes data from cardiac-function monitoring device (Holter monitor) worn by patient for use in diagnosis of cardiovascular disorders: Places magnetic tape or cassette from Holter monitor worn by patient in scanner and starts scanner that produces audio and visual representation of heart activity. Adjusts scanner controls that regulate taped sounds associated with heart activity and focus video representation of sounds on scanner screen. Observes scanner screen to identify irregularities in patient cardiac patterns, utilizing knowledge of regular and irregular cardiac-function patterns, or verifies data provided by computer program that automatically scans, analyzes, identifies, and prints irregular heart patterns. Prints sections of abnormal heart patterns or full disclosure tape for physician. Analyzes information in patient diary to identify incidents that correspond to heart pattern irregularities detected on heart monitor. Records findings on report form and forwards tapes, form, patient diary, and printouts of heart patterns to interpreting physician. May attach electrodes to patient's chest and connect electrodes to heart monitor, following standard pro-

cedure. May measure distances between peaks and valleys of heart activity patterns, using calipers, to obtain data for further analysis. May perform other diagnostic procedures, such as electrocardiography and stress testing, to aid in medical evaluation of patient.
GOE: 10.03.01 STRENGTH: S GED: R3 M3 L3 SVP: 6 DLU: 88

078.281-010 CYTOTECHNOLOGIST (medical ser.)

Stains, mounts, and studies cells of human body to detect evidence of cancer, hormonal abnormalities, and other pathological conditions, following established standards and practices: Prepares microscopic slides from specimens of blood, scrappings, or other bodily exudates, and fixes and stains slide to preserve specimen and enhance visibility of cells under microscope. Examines slide under microscope to identify abnormalities in cell structure. Reports abnormalities to PATHOLOGIST (medical ser.) 070.061-010. May supervise and coordinate activities of staff of cytology laboratory and be known as Supervisor, Cytology (medical ser.).
GOE: 02.04.02 STRENGTH: S GED: R5 M4 L5 SVP: 6 DLU: 88

078.361-010 DENTAL HYGIENIST (medical ser.)

Performs dental prophylaxis: Cleans calcareous deposits, accretions, and stains from teeth and beneath margins of gums, using dental instruments. Feels lymph nodes under patient's chin to detect swelling or tenderness that could indicate presence of oral cancer. Feels and visually examines gums for sores and signs of disease. Examines gums, using probes, to locate periodontal recessed gums and signs of gum disease. Applies fluorides and other cavity preventing agents to arrest dental decay. Charts conditions of decay and disease for diagnosis and treatment by dentist. Exposes and develops x-ray film. Makes impressions for study casts. May remove sutures and dressings. May administer local anesthetic agents. May place and remove rubber dams, matrices, and temporary restorations. May place, carve, and finish amalgam restorations. May remove excess cement from coronal surfaces of teeth. May provide clinical services and health education to improve and maintain oral health of school children. May conduct dental health clinics for community groups to augment services of dentist.
GOE: 10.02.02 STRENGTH: L GED: R4 M3 L4 SVP: 6 DLU: 89

078.361-018 NUCLEAR MEDICINE TECHNOLOGIST (medical ser.)

Prepares, measures, and administers radiopharmaceuticals in diagnostic and therapeutic studies, utilizing variety of equipment and following prescribed procedures: Prepares stock solutions of radiopharmaceutical materials, calculates doses, and administers doses, under direction of physician. Calibrates equipment. Performs diagnostic studies on patients as prescribed by physician, using scanners or scintillation cameras to detect radiation emitted and to produce image of organ on photographic film. Measures radioactivity, using Geiger counters, scalers, and scintillation detecters. Administers therapeutic doses of radiopharmaceuticals under direction of physician. Follows radiation safety techniques in use and disposal of radioactive materials.
GOE: 10.02.02 STRENGTH: M GED: R5 M4 L5 SVP: 7 DLU: 89

078.361-022 ORTHOTICS ASSISTANT (medical ser.)

Assists ORTHOTIST (medical ser.) 078.261-018 in providing care and fabricating and fitting orthopedic braces to patients with disabling conditions of limbs and spine: Under guidance of and in consultation with ORTHOTIST (medical ser.), makes assigned casts, measurements, model modifications, and layouts. Performs fitting, including static and dynamic alignments. Evaluates orthopedic braces on patient to ensure fit, function, and workmanship. Repairs and maintains orthopedic braces. May be responsible for performance of other personnel. May also perform functions of PROSTHETICS ASSISTANT (medical ser.) 078.361-026 and be designated Orthotics-Prosthetics Assistant (medical ser.).
GOE: 05.05.11 STRENGTH: M GED: R4 M4 L4 SVP: 7 DLU: 77

078.361-026 PROSTHETICS ASSISTANT (medical ser.)

Assists PROSTHETIST (medical ser.) 078.261-022 in providing care to and fabricating and fitting prostheses for patients with partial or total absence of limb: Under direction of PROSTHETIST (medical ser.), makes assigned casts, measurements, and model modifications. Performs fitting, including static and dynamic alignments. Evaluates prosthesis on patient to ensure fit, function, and quality of work. Repairs and maintains prostheses. May be responsible for performance of other personnel. May also perform functions of ORTHOTICS ASSISTANT (medical ser.) 078.361-022.
GOE: 05.05.11 STRENGTH: M GED: R4 M4 L4 SVP: 7 DLU: 77

078.361-034 RADIATION-THERAPY TECHNOLOGIST (medical ser.)

Provides radiation therapy to patients as prescribed by RADIOLOGIST (medical ser.) 070.101-090, according to established practices and standards: Reviews prescription, diagnosis, patient chart, and identification. Acts as liaison with physicist and supportive care personnel. Prepares equipment, such as immobilization, treatment, and protection devices, and positions patient according to prescription. Enters data into computer and sets controls to operate and adjust equipment and regulate dosage. Observes and reassures patient during treatment and reports unusual reactions to physician. Photographs treated area of patient and processes film. Maintains records, reports, and files as required. Follows principles of radiation protection for patient, self, and others. May assist in dosimetry procedures and tumor localization. May train therapy students.
GOE: 10.02.02 STRENGTH: L GED: R5 M4 L5 SVP: 7 DLU: 89

078.361-038 OPHTHALMIC TECHNICIAN (medical ser.)

Tests and measures eye function to assist OPHTHALMOLOGIST (medical ser.) 070.101-058 to diagnose and treat eye disorders and disease: Tests pa-

tient's far acuity, near acuity, peripheral vision, depth perception, and color perception to assist OPHTHALMOLOGIST (medical ser.) to diagnose and treat eye disorders and disease. Examines eye, using slit lamp, for abnormalities of cornea, and anterior and posterior chambers. Applies drops to anesthetize, dilate, or medicate eyes. Measures intraocular pressure of eyes (glaucoma test). Tests patient's field of vision, including central and peripheral vision, for defects, and charts test results on graph paper. Measures axial length of eye, using ultrasound equipment. Performs other tests and measurements as requested by physician. Gives instructions to patients concerning eye care. May supervise other technicians and be known as Chief Ophthalmic Technician (medical ser.).
GOE: 10.03.01 STRENGTH: L GED: R4 M4 L4 SVP: 6 DLU: 89

078.362-010 AUDIOMETRIST (profess. & kin.) alternate titles: audiometric technician; hearing-test technician

Administers audiometric screening and threshold tests, generally pure-tone air conduction, to individuals or groups, under supervision of AUDIOLOGIST (medical ser.) or OTOLARYNGOLOGIST (medical ser.). Fits earphones on subject and provides instruction on procedures to be followed. Adjusts audiometer to control sound emitted and records subjects' responses. Refers individuals to AUDIOLOGIST (medical ser.) for interpretation of test results and need for more definitive hearing examination or to physician for medical examination.
GOE: 10.03.01 STRENGTH: L GED: R4 M3 L4 SVP: 6 DLU: 77

078.362-014 DIALYSIS TECHNICIAN (medical ser.) alternate titles: hemodialysis technician

Sets up and operates hemodialysis machine to provide dialysis treatment for patients with kidney failure: Attaches dialyzer and tubing to machine to assemble for use. Mixes dialysate, according to formula. Primes dialyzer with saline or heparinized solution to prepare machine for use. Transports patient to dialysis room and positions patient on lounge chair at hemodialysis machine. Takes and records patient's predialysis weight, temperature, blood pressure, pulse rate, and respiration rate. Explains dialysis procedure and operation of hemodialysis machine to patient before treatment to allay anxieties. Cleans area of access (fistula, graft, or catheter), using antiseptic solution. Connects hemodialysis machine to access in patient's forearm or catheter site to start blood circulating through dialyzer. Inspects equipment settings, including pressures, conductivity (proportion of chemicals to water), and temperature to ensure conformance to safety standards. Starts blood flow pump at prescribed rate. Inspects venous and arterial pressures as registered on equipment to ensure pressures are within established limits. Calculates fluid removal or replacement to be achieved during dialysis procedure. Monitors patient for adverse reaction and hemodialysis machine for malfunction. Takes and records patient's postdialysis weight, temperature, blood pressure, pulse rate, and respiration rate. May fabricate parts, such as cannulas, tubing, catheters, connectors, and fittings, using handtools.
GOE: 10.02.02 STRENGTH: L GED: R4 M3 L3 SVP: 6 DLU: 89

078.362-018 ELECTROCARDIOGRAPH TECHNICIAN (medical ser.) alternate titles: ecg technician; ekg technician

Produces recordings of electromotive variations in patient's heart muscle, using electrocardiograph (ECG), to provide data for diagnosis of heart ailments: Attaches electrodes to chest, arms, and legs of patient. Connects electrode leads to electrocardiograph and starts machine. Moves electrodes along specified area of chest to produce electrocardiogram that records electromotive variations occurring in different areas of heart muscle. Monitors electrocardiogram for abnormal patterns. Keys information into machine or marks tracing to indicate positions of chest electrodes. Replenishes supply of paper and ink in machine and reports malfunctions. Edits and forwards final test results to attending phsyician for analysis and interpretation. May attach electrodes of Holter monitor (electrocardiograph) to patient to record data over extended period of time.
GOE: 10.03.01 STRENGTH: L GED: R3 M3 L3 SVP: 4 DLU: 87

078.362-022 ELECTROENCEPHALOGRAPHIC   TECHNOLOGIST (medical ser.) alternate titles: eeg technologist

Measures electrical activity of brain waves, using electroencephalograph (EEG) instrument, and conducts evoked potential response tests for use in diagnosis of brain and nervous system disorders: Measures patient's head and other body parts, using tape measure, and marks points where electrodes are to be placed. Attaches electrodes to predetermined locations, and verifies functioning of electrodes and recording instrument. Operates recording instruments (EEG and evoked potentials) and supplemental equipment and chooses settings for optimal viewing of nervous system. Records montage (electrode combination) and instrument settings, and observes and notes patient's behavior during test. Conducts visual, auditory, and somatosensory evoked potential response tests to measure latency of response to stimuli. Writes technical reports summarizing test results to assist physician in diagnosis of brain disorders. May perform other physiological tests, such as electrocardiogram, electrooculogram, and ambulatory electroencephalogram. May perform video monitoring of patient's actions during test. May monitor patient during surgery, using EEG or evoked potential instrument. May supervise other technologists and be known as Chief Electroencephalographic Technologist (medical ser.).
GOE: 10.03.01 STRENGTH: M GED: R4 M4 L4 SVP: 6 DLU: 89

078.362-026 RADIOLOGIC TECHNOLOGIST (medical ser.) alternate titles: radiographer; x-ray technologist

Operates radiologic equipment to produce radiographs (x rays) of body for diagnostic purposes, as directed by RADIOLOGIST (medical ser.) 070.101-090: Positions patient on examining table and adjusts immobilization devices to obtain optimum views of specified area of body requested by physician. Explains procedures to patient to reduce anxieties and obtain patient cooperation. Moves x-ray equipment into specified position and adjusts equipment controls to set exposure factors, such as time and distance, based on knowledge of radiographic exposure techniques and protocols. Practices radiation protection techniques, using beam restrictive devices, patient shielding skills, and knowledge of applicable exposure factors, to minimize radiation to patient and staff. May operate mobile x-ray equipment in operating room, emergency room, or at patient's bedside. May specialize in production of screening and diagnostic x rays for detection of breast tumors and be known as Radiologic Technologist, Mammogram (medical ser.).
GOE: 10.02.02 STRENGTH: L GED: R5 M4 L5 SVP: 7 DLU: 89

078.362-030 CARDIOPULMONARY TECHNOLOGIST (medical ser.) alternate titles: cardiovascular technologist

Performs diagnostic tests of cardiovascular and pulmonary systems of patients to aid physician in diagnosis and treatment of heart, lung, and blood vessel disorders: Prepares patient for test and explains procedures to obtain cooperation and reassure patient. Conducts electrocardiogram, phonocardiogram, echocardiogram, stress testing, and other tests to aid in diagnosis of cardiovascular system, using variety of specialized electronic test equipment, recording devices, and laboratory instruments. Conducts tests of pulmonary system to aid physician in diagnosis of pulmonary disorders, using spirometer and other respiratory testing equipment. Operates multichannel physiologic monitor, as part of cardiac catheterization team, to measure and record functions of cardiovascular and pulmonary systems of patient during cardiac catheterization. Alerts physician to instrument readings outside normal ranges during cardiac catheterization procedures. Provides test results to physician.
GOE: 10.03.01 STRENGTH: L GED: R4 M4 L4 SVP: 5 DLU: 89

078.362-034 PERFUSIONIST (medical ser.)

Sets up and operates heart-lung machine in hospital to take over functions of patient's heart and lungs during surgery or respiratory failure: Reviews patient medical history and chart, and consults with surgeon or physician to obtain patient information needed to set up heart-lung machine and associated equipment. Selects, assembles, sets up, and tests heart-lung machine to ensure that machine and associated equipment function according to specifications. Operates heart-lung machine to regulate blood circulation and composition, to administer drugs and anesthetic agents, and to control body temperature during surgery or respiratory failure of patient. Monitors and observes operation of heart-lung machine and patient's physiologic variables such as blood temperature, blood composition, and flow rate, and adjusts equipment to maintain normal body functions. Cleans and adjusts parts of heart-lung machine.
GOE: 10.03.02 STRENGTH: M GED: R4 M3 L4 SVP: 7 DLU: 88

078.362-038 ELECTROMYOGRAPHIC TECHNICIAN (medical ser.) alternate titles: emg technician

Measures electrical activity in peripheral nerves, using electromyograph (EMG) instrument, for use by physician in diagnosing neuromuscular disorders: Explains procedures to patient to obtain cooperation and relieve anxieties during test. Rubs electrode paste on patient's skin to ensure contact of electrodes. Attaches surface recording electrodes to extremity in which activity is being measured to detect electrical impulse. Attaches electrodes to electrode cables or leads connected to EMG instrument and selects nerve conduction mode on EMG. Operates EMG instrument to record electrical activity in peripheral nerves. Presses button on manually held surface stimulator electrode to deliver pulse and send electrical charge along peripheral nerve. Monitors response on oscilloscope and presses button to record nerve conduction velocity. Measures and records time and distance between stimulus and response, manually or using computer, and calculates velocity of electrical impulse in peripheral nerve. Removes electrodes from patient upon conclusion of test and cleans electrode paste from skin, using alcohol and cotton.
GOE: 10.03.01 STRENGTH: L GED: R4 M4 L4 SVP: 5 DLU: 90

078.362-042 POLYSOMNOGRAPHIC TECHNICIAN (medical ser.) alternate titles: polysomnographic technologist

Measures electrical activity of patient's brain waves and other physiological variables, using *polysomnograph*, to aid physician in diagnosis and treatment of sleep disorders: Applies surface electrodes to patient's head, using adhesive paste or tape, to obtain electroencephalogram (EEG) measurement and applies other combinations of sensors and electrodes to patient to obtain measurements such as electromyogram (EMG), electrooculogram (EOG), electrocardiogram (EKG), air flow respiratory effort, and oxygen saturation, as requested by physician and following established procedures. Operates closed circuit television camera to observe patient during test and to record patient's sleep activities. Operates polysomnograph equipment to record electrical activity of brain waves and other physiological variables and records notes on graph to eliminate from consideration physiological measurements caused by such activities as patient opening eyes, turning head, or turning body. Studies polysomnogram to recognize arrhythmias and abnormal respiratory patterns and calls physician or other emergency personnel if needed. Measures durations of brain waves recorded on polysomnograms, using millimeter ruler. Studies characteristics of completed polysomnogram tracings and summarizes data showing stages of sleep, abnormal breathing events, periodic leg movements, arrhythmias, and other information, applying knowledge of polysomnograph testing principles. Enters data into computer and writes report incorporating patient's medical history, completed patient questionnaires, previous and current polysomnogram in-

formation, presence and type of abnormality, and other information for analysis by physician or other health professional. May apply electrodes to patient's head, using pins. May supervise and coordinate activities of other technicians and be known as Chief Polysomnographic Technician (medical ser.).
GOE: 10.03.01 STRENGTH: M GED: R4 M4 L4 SVP: 4 DLU: 89

078.362-046 SPECIAL   PROCEDURES   TECHNOLOGIST, ANGIOGRAM (medical ser.) alternate titles: angiographer; radiographer, angiogram

Operates diagnostic imaging equipment to produce contrast enhanced radiographs of blood vessels to aid physician in diagnosis and treatment of disease: Positions patient in examining position, using immobilization devices, such as head or shoulder braces. Operates fluoroscope to aid physician to view and guide wire or catheter through blood vessel to area of interest. Fills automatic injector with contrast media, sets flow rate, and activates injection of contrast media into blood vessels of patient, as directed by physician. Monitors video display of area of interest and adjusts density and contrast to obtain optimum exposure. Starts filming sequence. Delivers film to dark room to be developed and reviews developed x rays for accuracy of positioning and quality of exposure techniques.
GOE: 10.02.02 STRENGTH: M GED: R5 M4 L5 SVP: 7 DLU: 89

078.362-050 SPECIAL PROCEDURES TECHNOLOGIST, CARDIAC CATHETERIZATION (medical ser.) alternate titles: radiographer, cardiac catheterization; special vascular imaging technologist

Operates diagnostic imaging equipment to produce contrast enhanced radiographs of heart and cardiovascular system (angiocardiograms), during cardiac catheterization, to aid physician in diagnostic evaluation and treatment: Positions and immobilizes patient on examining table, using head and shoulder braces and following specified protocols. Enters technical factors determined by protocol such as amount and quality of radiation beam, and specified filming sequence, into computer. Raises and lowers examining table and manipulates and positions x-ray tube in response to instructions from physician. Starts automatic injection of contrast medium into blood vessels of patient. Activates fluoroscope and 35 mm motion picture camera (cinefluorography) to produce images that assist physician in guiding catheter through cardiovascular system of patient. Observes gauges, recorder, and video screens of multichannel data analysis system that indicates blood pressure, cardiac output, and respiration, during imaging of cardiovascular system. Alerts physician to changes in patient responses. May assist physician in interventional procedures, such as instilling enzymes or inserting balloon in blood vessels to remove plaque or other blockage.
GOE: 10.02.02 STRENGTH: M GED: R5 M4 L5 SVP: 7 DLU: 89

078.362-054 SPECIAL PROCEDURES TECHNOLOGIST, CT SCAN (medical ser.) alternate titles: ct technologist

Operates computed tomography (CT) scanner to produce cross-sectional radiographs of patient's body for diagnostic purposes: Positions and immobilizes patient on examining table, using supportive devices to obtain precise patient position and following protocols specified by RADIOLOGIST (medical ser.) 070.101-090. Administers contrast media orally or assists physician in intravenous administration. Enters data, such as type of scan requested, slice thickness, scan time, and other technical data into computer, using knowledge of radiologic technology and computed tomography. Starts CT scanner to scan designated anatomical area of patient. Talks to patient over intercom system and observes patient through window of control room to monitor patient safety and comfort. Views images of organs or tissue on video display screen to ensure quality of pictures. Starts camera to produce radiographs. Evaluates radiographs, video tape, and computer generated information for technical quality.
GOE: 10.02.02 STRENGTH: M GED: R5 M4 L5 SVP: 7 DLU: 89

078.362-058 SPECIAL PROCEDURES TECHNOLOGIST, MAGNETIC RESONANCE IMAGING (MRI) (medical ser.) alternate titles: magnetic resonance imaging technologist

Operates magnetic resonance imaging equipment to produce cross-sectional images (photographs) of patient's body for diagnostic purposes: Interviews patient to explain magnetic resonance imaging procedures and to request removal of metal objects which are hazardous to patient and equipment when magnet is activated. Positions patient on examining table and places specified coil (receiver) such as head coil or knee coil, close to area of interest, following protocols requested by RADIOLOGIST (medical ser.) 070.101-090. Demonstrates use of microphone that allows patient and technologist to communicate during examination. Enters data, such as patient history, anatomical area to be scanned, orientation specified, and position of entry into aperture of magnetic resonance imaging equipment (head or feet first), into computer. Keys commands to specify scan sequences, and adjust transmitters and receivers, into computer. Observes patient through window of control room and on closed circuit TV screen to monitor patient safety and comfort. Views images of area being scanned on video display screen to ensure quality of pictures. Keys in data on keyboard of camera to photograph images. Alerts staff entering magnet room to danger of wearing or carrying metal around magnet.
GOE: 10.02.02 STRENGTH: M GED: R5 M4 L5 SVP: 7 DLU: 90

078.362-062 STRESS TEST TECHNICIAN (medical ser.) alternate titles: stress technician

Produces recordings of electromotive variations in action of heart muscle,

using electrocardiograph, while patient walks on treadmill, under direction of physician, to provide data for diagnosis of heart ailments: Attaches electrodes to patient's arms, legs, and chest area, according to specified pattern, and connects electrode leads to electrocardiograph, to obtain electrocardiogram. Explains testing procedures to patient and obtains consent form. Starts treadmill at speed directed by physician. Starts electrocardiograph and records data, such as angle and speed of treadmill, patient's indications of pain, and measurements of blood pressure. Informs physician of wave abnormalities on electrocardiogram. Stands alongside patient during test to lend support if necessary. Removes recorder strip printout from machine upon conclusion of test to obtain permanent record of test. Edits and mounts representative samples of tracings for patient's record, indicating time of test measurement and bodily factors that could have affected recording. May conduct electrocardiograph test of resting patient.
GOE: 10.03.01 STRENGTH: L GED: R4 M3 L3 SVP: 6 DLU: 88

078.364-010 ULTRASOUND TECHNOLOGIST (medical ser.) alternate titles: diagnostic medical sonographer

Produces two-dimensional ultrasonic recordings of internal organs, using ultrasound equipment, for use by physician in diagnosis of disease and study of malfunction of organs: Selects equipment for use in ultrasound setup according to specifications of examination. Explains process to patient, and instructs and assists patient in assuming physical position for examination. Selects transducer and adjusts equipment controls according to organ to be examined, depth of field, and other specifications of test. Keys test data and patient information into computer of ultrasound equipment to maintain record of test results. Moves transducer, by hand, over specified area of body and observes sound wave display screen to monitor quality of ultrasonic pattern produced. Starts equipment which produces images of internal organs and records diagnostic data on magnetic tape, computer disk, strip printout, or film. Photographs images of organs shown on display module, or removes strip printout from equipment, to obtain permanent record of internal examination. Discusses test results with supervisor or attending physician.
GOE: 02.04.01 STRENGTH: L GED: R5 M4 L4 SVP: 7 DLU: 89

078.364-014 ECHOCARDIOGRAPH TECHNICIAN (medical ser.) alternate titles: diagnostic cardiac sonographer

Produces two-dimensional ultrasonic recordings and Doppler flow analyses of heart and related structures, using ultrasound equipment, for use by physician in diagnosis of heart disease and study of heart: Explains procedures to patient to obtain cooperation and reduce anxieties of patient. Attaches electrodes to patient's chest to monitor heart rhythm and connects electrodes to electrode leads of ultrasound equipment. Adjusts equipment controls according to physician's orders and areas of heart to be examined. Keys patient information into computer keyboard on equipment to record information on video cassette and strip printout of test. Starts ultrasound equipment that produces images of real time tomographic cardiac anatomy, and adjusts equipment to obtain quality images. Moves transducer, by hand, over patient's heart areas, observes ultrasound display screen, and listens to Doppler signals to acquire data for measurement of blood flow velocities. Prints pictures of graphic analysis recordings and removes video cassette for permanent record of internal examination. Measures heart wall thicknesses and chamber sizes recorded on strip printout, using calipers and ruler, or keys commands into computer to measure thicknesses and chamber sizes of heart on video tape, and compares measurement to standard norms to identify abnormalities in heart. Measures blood flow velocities and calculates data, such as cardiac physiology and valve areas for evaluation of cardiac function by physician. Reviews test results with interpreting physician.
GOE: 10.03.01 STRENGTH: L GED: R4 M3 L4 SVP: 7 DLU: 88

078.367-010 CARDIAC MONITOR TECHNICIAN (medical ser.) alternate titles: telemetry technician

Monitors heart rhythm pattern of patients in special care unit of hospital to detect abnormal pattern variances, using telemetry equipment: Reviews patient information to determine normal heart rhythm pattern, current pattern, and prior variances. Observes screen of cardiac monitor and listens for alarm to identify abnormal variation in heart rhythm. Informs supervisor or NURSE, GENERAL DUTY (medical ser.) 075.364-010 of variances to initiate examination of patient. Measures length and height of patient's heart rhythm pattern on graphic tape readout, using calipers, and posts information on patient records. Answers calls for assistance from patients and inquiries concerning patients from medical staff, using intercom and call director. May perform duties as described under ELECTROCARDIOGRAPH TECHNICIAN (medical ser.) 078.362-018.
GOE: 10.03.01 STRENGTH: S GED: R3 M2 L2 SVP: 5 DLU: 86

078.381-014 MEDICAL-LABORATORY TECHNICIAN (medical ser.) alternate titles: laboratory assistant; medical technician

Performs routine tests in medical laboratory to provide data for use in diagnosis and treatment of disease: Conducts quantitative and qualitative chemical analyses of body fluids, such as blood, urine, and spinal fluid, under supervision of MEDICAL TECHNOLOGIST (medical ser.) 078.261-038. Performs blood counts, using microscope. Conducts blood tests for transfusion purposes. May draw blood from patient's finger, ear lobe, or vein, observing principles of asepsis to obtain blood samples. May specialize in hematology, blood bank, cytology, histology, or chemistry.
GOE: 02.04.02 STRENGTH: L GED: R4 M4 L4 SVP: 5 DLU: 89

078.384-010 CEPHALOMETRIC ANALYST (medical ser.) alternate titles: cephalometric technician; cephalometric tracer; tracer

Traces head x rays and illustrates cosmetic result of proposed orthodontic treatment: Traces frontal and lateral head x rays onto transparent paper, using template, compass, protractor, and knowledge of cranial-facial skeletal structure. Traces lower teeth from occlusal x ray or photograph to locate key points defining true curve of lower dental arch. Records cephalometric measurements to prepare data for computer analysis, using electronic data recording equipment. Compiles data from tracings and computer plot sheets to illustrate results of proposed surgery or other orthodontic treatment.
GOE: 02.04.02 STRENGTH: S GED: R4 M4 L4 SVP: 6 DLU: 77

078.664-010 ORTHOPEDIC ASSISTANT (medical ser.) alternate titles: orthopedic cast specialist

Applies, adjusts, and removes casts, assembles traction apparatus, and fits strappings and splints for orthopedic patients according to medical staff instructions, using handtools: Covers injured areas with specified protective materials, such as stockinette bandages, gauze, or rubber pads, preparatory to cast application. Wets, wraps, and molds plaster bandages around area of fracture. Trims plaster, using electric cutter. Removes whole and broken casts and alters position of cast to change setting of patient's limb or body part as directed. Assembles wooden, metal, plastic, or plaster material to make orthopedic splints, using handtools. Rigs pulleys, ropes, and frames to assemble fracture beds, using handtools. Attaches traction supports to patient's limb and adjusts support to specified tension. Assembles exercise frames, using handtools. Adjusts crutches and canes to fit patient. Instructs patients in care of and assists patients in walking with casts, braces, and crutches.
GOE: 10.03.02 STRENGTH: M GED: R3 M2 L3 SVP: 4 DLU: 77

078.687-010 LABORATORY ASSISTANT, BLOOD AND PLASMA (medical ser.; pharmaceut.)

Performs routine laboratory tasks related to processing whole blood and blood components: Centrifuges whole blood to produce various components including packed red cells, platelet concentrate, washed red cells, and plasma. Examines blood stock at designated intervals to confirm that all units are in satisfactory condition. Observes thermostats on storage units to confirm that temperature remains constant at designated temperature. Inspects blood units returned from hospitals to determine whether plasma can be salvaged and if so refers to plasma salvage unit. Confirms that sedimentation has occurred, that color is normal, and that containers are in satisfactory condition. Cleans and maintains laboratory equipment, supplies, and laboratory. Performs related clerical duties including updating statistical records, labeling tubes, and scheduling processing runs.
GOE: 02.04.02 STRENGTH: L GED: R3 M3 L3 SVP: 6 DLU: 77

079 OCCUPATIONS IN MEDICINE AND HEALTH, N.E.C.

This group includes occupations, not elsewhere classified, concerned with the health care of humans or animals.

079.021-014 MEDICAL PHYSICIST (profess. & kin.)

Applies knowledge and methodology of science of physics to all aspects of medicine, to address problems related to diagnosis and treatment of human disease: Advises and consults with physicians in such applications as use of ionizing radiation in diagnosis, therapy, treatment planning with externally delivered radiation as well as use of internally implanted radioactive sources; complete subject of x-ray equipment, calibration, and dosimetry; medical uses of ultrasound and infrared; bioelectrical investigation of brain and heart; mathematical analysis and applications of computers in medicine; formulation of radiation protection guides and procedures specific to hospital environment; development of instrumentation for improved patient care and clinical service. Plans, directs, conducts, and participates in supporting programs to ensure effective and safe use of radiation and radionuclides in human beings by physician specialist. Teaches principles of medical physics to physicians, residents, graduate students, medical students, and technologists by means of lectures, problem solving, and laboratory sessions. Directs and participates in investigations of biophysical techniques associated with any branch of medicine. Conducts research in development of diagnostic and remedial procedures and develops instrumentation for specific medical applications. Acts as consultant to education, medical research, and other professional groups and organizations.
GOE: 02.02.01 STRENGTH: L GED: R6 M6 L6 SVP: 8 DLU: 77

079.101-010 CHIROPRACTOR (medical ser.) alternate titles: chiropractic; doctor, chiropractic

Diagnoses and treats musculoskeletal conditions of spinal column and extremities to prevent disease and correct abnormalities of body believed to be caused by interference with nervous system: Examines patient to determine nature and extent of disorder. Performs diagnostic procedures including physical, neurologic, and orthopedic examinations, laboratory tests, and other procedures, using x-ray machine, proctoscope, electrocardiograph, otoscope, and other instruments and equipment. Manipulates spinal column and other extremities to adjust, align, or correct abnormalities caused by neurologic and kinetic articular dysfunction. Utilizes supplementary measures, such as exercise, rest, water, light, heat, and nutritional therapy.
GOE: 02.03.04 STRENGTH: M GED: R5 M4 L5 SVP: 8 DLU: 89

079.101-014 DOCTOR, NATUROPATHIC (medical ser.)

Diagnoses, treats, and cares for patients, using system of practice that bases treatment of physiological functions and abnormal conditions on natural laws governing human body: Utilizes physiological, psychological, and mechanical methods, such as air, water, light, heat, earth, phytotherapy, food and herb therapy, psychotherapy, electrotherapy, physiotherapy, minor and orificial surgery, mechanotherapy, naturopathic corrections and manipulation, and natural methods or modalities, together with natural medicines, natural processed foods, and herbs and nature's remedies. Excludes major surgery, therapeutic use of x ray and radium, and use of drugs, except those assimilable substances containing elements or compounds which are components of body tissues and are physiologically compatible to body processes for maintenance of life.
GOE: 02.03.04 STRENGTH: L GED: R5 M4 L5 SVP: 7 DLU: 77

079.101-018 OPTOMETRIST (medical ser.)

Examines eyes to determine nature and degree of vision problem or eye disease and prescribes corrective lenses or procedures: Examines eyes and performs various tests to determine visual acuity and perception and to diagnose diseases and other abnormalities, such as glaucoma and color blindness. Prescribes eyeglasses, contact lenses, and other vision aids or therapeutic procedures to correct or conserve vision. Consults with and refers patients to OPHTHALMOLOGIST (medical ser.) 070.101-058 or other health care practitioner if additional medical treatment is determined necessary. May prescribe medications to treat eye diseases if state laws permit. May specialize in type of services provided, such as contact lenses, low vision aids or vision therapy, or in treatment of specific groups, such as children or elderly patients. May conduct research, instruct in college or university, act as consultant, or work in public health field.
GOE: 02.03.04 STRENGTH: L GED: R5 M4 L5 SVP: 7 DLU: 80

079.101-022 PODIATRIST (medical ser.)

Diagnoses and treats diseases and deformities of human foot: Diagnoses foot ailments, such as tumors, ulcers, fractures, skin or nail diseases, and congenital or acquired deformities, utilizing diagnostic aids, such as urinalysis, blood tests, and x-ray analysis. Treats deformities, such as flat or weak feet and foot imbalance, by mechanical and electrical methods, such as whirlpool or paraffin baths and short wave and low voltage currents. Treats conditions, such as corns, calluses, ingrowing nails, tumors, shortened tendons, bunions, cysts, and abscesses by surgical methods, including suturing, medications, and administration of local anesthetics. Prescribes drugs. Does not perform foot amputations. Corrects deformities by means of plaster casts and strappings. Makes and fits prosthetic appliances. Prescribes corrective footwear. Advises patients concerning continued treatment of disorders and proper foot care to prevent recurrence. Refers patients to physician when symptoms observed in feet and legs indicate systemic disorders, such as arthritis, heart disease, diabetes, or kidney trouble. May treat bone, muscle, and joint disorders and be designated Podiatrist, Orthopedic (medical ser.); childrens' foot diseases and be designated Popopediatrician (medical ser.), or perform surgery and be designated Podiatric Surgeon (medical ser.).
GOE: 02.03.01 STRENGTH: L GED: R5 M4 L5 SVP: 7 DLU: 77

079.117-010 EMERGENCY MEDICAL SERVICES COORDINATOR (medical ser.)

Directs medical emergency service program: Coordinates activities of persons involved in rescue, transportation, and care of accident or catastrophe victims, and others requiring emergency medical assistance. Arranges for establishment of emergency medical facilities, staffing of facilities by emergency-trained medical and auxiliary personnel, installation of telecommunication network components, and acquisition of emergency vehicles. Maintains records of facilities and personnel, and periodically inspects facilities to ensure capability of meeting area's emergency needs. Maintains telecommunication contact with mobile and stationary units comprising emergency service network to coordinate activities of personnel, enlist services of other protective agencies, or provide alternate directions to onscene emergency personnel when planned procedures are not feasible. Develops, plans, and participates in training programs for ambulance and rescue personnel. Cooperates with schools and community organizations to encourage public interest in and knowledge of basic and advanced first aid training, and assists groups in development and presentation of classes. Maintains records of emergency medical service activities, for coordination with records prepared by cooperating institutions, to provide data for evaluation of program. Prepares reports stating progress, problems, and plans for future implementation of emergency service for community or area, for review by officials of sponsoring agency. Confers with coordinators of emergency programs in other areas to discuss problems, coordinate activities, and cooperate in area or statewide plans.
GOE: 11.07.02 STRENGTH: L GED: R4 M4 L4 SVP: 8 DLU: 77

079.117-014 PUBLIC HEALTH EDUCATOR (profess. & kin.)

Plans, organizes, and directs health education programs for group and community needs: Conducts community surveys and collaborates with other health specialists and civic groups to ascertain health needs, develop desirable health goals, and determine availability of professional health services. Develops and maintains cooperation between public, civic, professional, and voluntary agencies. Prepares and disseminates educational and informational materials. Promotes health discussions in schools, industry, and community agencies. May plan for and provide educational opportunities for health personnel.
GOE: 11.07.02 STRENGTH: L GED: R5 M4 L5 SVP: 8 DLU: 77

079.117-018   SANITARIAN (profess. & kin.)
Plans, develops, and executes environmental health program: Organizes and conducts training program in environmental health practices for schools and other groups. Determines and sets health and sanitation standards and enforces regulations concerned with food processing and serving, collection and disposal of solid wastes, sewage treatment and disposal, plumbing, vector control, recreational areas, hospitals and other institutions, noise, ventilation, air pollution, radiation, and other areas. Confers with government, community, industrial, civil defense, and private organizations to interpret and promote environmental health programs. Collaborates with other health personnel in epidemiological investigations and control. Advises civic and other officials in development of environmental health laws and regulations.
GOE: 11.10.03 STRENGTH: M GED: R6 M5 L6 SVP: 8 DLU: 77

**079.127-010   INSERVICE COORDINATOR, AUXILIARY PERSONNEL
            (medical ser.)**
Plans and conducts orientation and training program for nonprofessional nursing personnel: Organizes and writes nursing procedure manuals and guides for use by auxiliary nursing personnel. Schedules classes, and teaches routine nursing procedures to auxiliary personnel. Explains policies, rules, employee benefits, and organizational structure of institution. Discusses functions of various hospital departments and arranges for tour of physical plant. Assists nursing service supervisory personnel in solving problems of in-service training, promotions, transfers, and discipline of auxiliary personnel.
GOE: 10.02.01 STRENGTH: L GED: R5 M4 L5 SVP: 7 DLU: 77

079.131-010   DIRECTOR, SPEECH-AND-HEARING (medical ser.)
Directs and coordinates activities of personnel in hospital speech and hearing department engaged in research and in testing and treating patients according to established policies: Organizes and establishes personnel procedures, including hiring and training, counsels employees, and evaluates work performance. Confers with ADMINISTRATOR, HEALTH CARE FACILITY (medical ser.) 187.117-010 and committee members to request expenditures for equipment, supplies, and personnel. Meets with ADMINISTRATOR, HEALTH CARE FACILITY (medical ser.), department officials, and staff members to explain new techniques and procedures or to demonstrate new and innovative equipment. Plans and directs research and treatment programs to provide direction and assistance to staff members. Conducts workshops and seminars to develop staff expertise and knowledge. Analyzes data and maintains records of research and treatment programs.
GOE: 11.07.02 STRENGTH: S GED: R6 M5 L5 SVP: 8 DLU: 86

079.151-010   TRANSPLANT COORDINATOR (medical ser.) alternate titles: organ transplant coordinator
Plans and coordinates in-hospital transplant services, solicits organ donors, and assists medical staff in organ retrieval for patients undergoing organ or tissue transplantation: Communicates with donors, patients, and health team members to ensure comprehensive documentation, including informed consent of potential organ donor and transplant recipient, equitable access to transplantation system, and access to treatment alternatives. Analyzes medical data of potential organ donors and transplant recipients from medical and social records, physical examination, and consultation with health team members to perform preliminary physical assessment and screen potential recipients and donors. Schedules recipient and donor laboratory tests to determine histocompatibility of blood or tissue of recipient and donor. Compares collected data to normal values and correlates and summarizes laboratory reports, x rays, and other tests to assist physician to determine medical suitability of procedure, to identify potential complicating factors, and to evaluate recipient and donor compatibility. Solicits medical and community groups for organ donors and assists medical team in retrieval of organs for transplantation, using medical instruments. Coordinates in-hospital services and counsels recipient and donor to alleviate anxieties and assist recipient and donor throughout procedure. Advises post-operative patients on therapies for managing health after transplant and serves as team member to monitor and assess progress of patient and offer advice and assistance to patient following transplant. May coordinate in-hospital services and be known as Clinical Transplant Coordinator (medical ser.). May coordinate organ and tissue procurement services and be known as Procurement Transplant Coordinator (medical ser.).
GOE: 10.02.01 STRENGTH: L GED: R5 M5 L5 SVP: 7 DLU: 89

079.157-010   HYPNOTHERAPIST (profess. & kin.)
Induces hypnotic state in client to increase motivation or alter behavior patterns: Consults with client to determine nature of problem. Prepares client to enter hypnotic state by explaining how hypnosis works and what client will experience. Tests subject to determine degree of physical and emotional suggestibility. Induces hypnotic state in client, using individualized methods and techniques of hypnosis based on interpretation of test results and analysis of client's problem. May train client in self-hypnosis conditioning.
GOE: 10.02.02 STRENGTH: S GED: R4 M3 L4 SVP: 7 DLU: 77

079.161-010   INDUSTRIAL HYGIENIST (profess. & kin.)
Conducts health program in industrial plant or governmental organization to recognize, eliminate, and control occupational health hazards and diseases: Collects samples of dust, gases, vapors, and other potentially toxic materials for analysis. Investigates adequacy of ventilation, exhaust equipment, lighting, and other conditions which may affect employee health, comfort, or efficiency. Conducts evaluations of exposure to ionizing and nonionizing radiation and to

noise, and recommends measures to ensure maximum employee protection. Collaborates with INDUSTRIAL-HEALTH ENGINEER (profess. & kin.) and PHYSICIAN, OCCUPATIONAL (medical ser.) to institute control and remedial measures for hazardous and potentially hazardous conditions and equipment. Prepares reports including observations, analysis of contaminants, and recommendations for control and correction of hazards. Participates in educational meetings to instruct employees in matters pertaining to occupational health and prevention of accidents. May specialize in particular area, such as collection and analysis of samples.
GOE: 11.10.03 STRENGTH: M GED: R5 M4 L5 SVP: 8 DLU: 77

**079.167-010   COMMUNITY-SERVICES-AND-HEALTH-EDUCATION
            OFFICER (government ser.)**
Plans and directs statewide program of public health education and promotes establishment of local health services: Directs workers engaged in preparation and distribution of health information materials, such as brochures, films, weight charts, and first-aid kits. Promotes establishment or expansion of local health services and provides technical assistance to individuals and groups conducting [health conferences, workshops, and training courses. Answers health information requests received by department or reviews correspondence prepared by others. Coordinates special health education campaigns during epidemics, rabies outbreaks, instances of food poisoning, and similar emergencies. May direct health education activities in public schools.
GOE: 11.07.02 STRENGTH: S GED: R6 M5 L6 SVP: 8 DLU: 77

079.167-014   MEDICAL-RECORD ADMINISTRATOR (medical ser.)
Plans, develops, and administers health information system for health care facility consistent with standards of accrediting and regulatory agencies and requirements of health care system: Develops and implements policies and procedures for documenting, storing, and retrieving information, and for processing medical-legal documents, insurance data, and correspondence requests, in conformance with federal, state, and local statutes. Supervises staff, directly or through subordinates, in preparing and analyzing medical documents. Participates in development and design of computer software for computerized health information system. Coordinates medical care evaluation with medical staff and develops criteria and methods for such evaluation. Develops in-service educational materials and conducts instructional programs for health care personnel. Analyzes patient data for reimbursement, facility planning, quality of patient care, risk management, utilization management, and research. May manage medical records department and be known as Director, Medical Records (medical ser.).
GOE: 11.07.02 STRENGTH: L GED: R6 M5 L6 SVP: 8 DLU: 88

079.267-010   UTILIZATION-REVIEW COORDINATOR (medical ser.)
Analyzes patient records to determine legitimacy of admission, treatment, and length of stay in health-care facility to comply with government and insurance company reimbursement policies: Analyzes insurance, governmental, and accrediting agency standards to determine criteria concerning admissions, treatment, and length of stay of patients. Reviews application for patient admission and approves admission or refers case to facility utilization review committee for review and course of action when case fails to meet admission standards. Compares inpatient medical records to established criteria and confers with medical and nursing personnel and other professional staff to determine legitimacy of treatment and length of stay. Abstracts data from records and maintains statistics. Determines patient review dates according to established diagnostic criteria. May assist review committee in planning and holding federally mandated quality assurance reviews. May supervise and coordinate activities of utilization review staff.
GOE: 11.07.02 STRENGTH: L GED: R5 M4 L5 SVP: 7 DLU: 89

079.271-010   ACUPUNCTURIST (medical ser.)
Administers specific theraputic treatment of symptoms and disorders amenable to acupuncture procedures, as specifically indicated by supervising physician: Reviews patient's medical history, physical findings, and diagnosis made by physician to ascertain symptoms or disorder to be treated. Selects needles of various lengths, according to location of insertion. Inserts needles at locations of body known to be efficacious to certain disorders, utilizing knowledge of acupuncture points and their functions. Leaves needles in patient for specific length of time, according to symptom or disorder treated, and removes needles. Burns bark of mugwort tree in small strainer to administer moxibustion treatment. Covers insertion area with cloth and rubs strainer over cloth to impart heat and assist in relieving patient's symptoms.
GOE: 02.03.04 STRENGTH: L GED: R5 M4 L5 SVP: 6 DLU: 77

079.271-014   ACUPRESSURIST (medical ser.)
Examines clients with pain, stress, or tension, determines acupressure techniques required to relieve problems, and demonstrates techniques to client, according to knowledge of acupressure methods and techniques. Directs client to lie on couch and positions client's arms and legs in relaxed position to facilitate examination and demonstration techniques. Questions clients, examines client's muscular system visually, and feels tissue around muscles, nerves, and blood vessels to locate knots and other blockages which indicate excessive accumulations of blood, fluids, and other substances in tissue. Determines cause of accumulations and acupressure techniques needed to increase circulation, according to knowledge of Asian acupuncture and pressure points and Western medical trigger points, bodywork techniques, such as Jin Shin, Do-In, Shiatsu, Swedish, and Esalen, and experience. Feels tissue around muscles, nerves, and blood ves-

sels to locate points and applies specified pressure at specified pressure points or muscles, using thumbs, fingers, palms, or elbows, to redirect accumulated body fluids into normal channels, according to acupressure knowledge, techniques, and experience. Discusses findings with client and explains diet and methods to prevent recurrence of problem. May be known according to specific method or combination of methods used, such as Gia Ahp, Jin Shin, Do-In, or Shiatsu.
GOE: 10.02.02 STRENGTH: M GED: R5 M3 L4 SVP: 5 DLU: 86

079.361-014 VETERINARY TECHNICIAN (medical ser.) alternate titles: animal health technician; animal technician; veterinary assistant

Performs variety of animal health care duties to assist VETERINARIAN (medical ser.) 073.101-010 in settings such as veterinarians' clinics, zoos, research laboratories, kennels, and commercial facilities: Prepares treatment room for examination of animals, and holds or restrains animals during examination, treatment, or innoculation. Administers injections, performs venipunctures, applies wound dressings, cleans teeth, and takes vital signs of animal, under supervision of veterinarian. Prepares patient, medications, and equipment for surgery, and hands instruments and materials to veterinarian during surgical procedures. Peforms routine laboratory tests, cares for and feeds laboratory animals, and assists professional personnel with research projects in commercial, public health, or research laboratories. Inspects products or carcasses when employed in food processing plants to ensure compliance with health standards. May assist veterinarian to artificially inseminate animals. May bathe and groom small animals.
GOE: 02.03.03 STRENGTH: M GED: R4 M3 L4 SVP: 6 DLU: 90

079.361-018 DENTAL ASSISTANT (medical ser.)

Assists dentist during examination and treatment of patients: Prepares patient, sterilizes and disinfects instruments, sets up instrument trays, prepares materials, and assists dentist during dental procedures. Takes and records medical and dental histories and vital signs of patient. Exposes dental diagnostic x rays. Makes preliminary impressions for study casts and occlusal registrations for mounting study casts. Pours, trims, and polishes study casts, fabricates custom impression trays from preliminary impressions, cleans and polishes removable appliances, and fabricates temporary restorations. Assists dentist in management of medical and dental emergencies. Instructs patients in oral hygiene and plaque control programs. Provides postoperative instructions prescribed by dentist. Records treatment information in patient records. Schedules appointments, prepares bills and receives payment for dental services, completes insurance forms, and maintains clerical records, manually or using computer. May clean teeth, using dental instruments. May apply protective coating of fluoride to teeth.
GOE: 10.03.02 STRENGTH: L GED: R4 M3 L4 SVP: 6 DLU: 89

079.362-010 MEDICAL ASSISTANT (medical ser.)

Performs any combination of following duties under direction of physician to assist in examination and treatment of patients: Interviews patients, measures vital signs, such as pulse rate, temperature, blood pressure, weight, and height, and records information on patients' charts. Prepares treatment rooms for examination of patients. Drapes patients with covering and positions instruments and equipment. Hands instruments and materials to doctor as directed. Cleans and sterilizes instruments. Inventories and orders medical supplies and materials. Operates x ray, electrocardiograph (EKG), and other equipment to administer routine diagnostic test or calls medical facility or department to schedule patients for tests. Gives injections or treatments, and performs routine laboratory tests. Schedules appointments, receives money for bills, keeps x ray and other medical records, performs secretarial tasks, and completes insurance forms. May key data into computer to maintain office and patient records. May keep billing records, enter financial transactions into bookeeping ledgers, and compute and mail monthly statements to patients.
GOE: 10.03.02 STRENGTH: L GED: R4 M3 L4 SVP: 6 DLU: 88

079.362-014 MEDICAL RECORD TECHNICIAN (medical ser.)

Compiles and maintains medical records of patients of health care delivery system to document patient condition and treatment: Reviews medical records for completeness and to abstract and code clinical data, such as diseases, operations, procedures and therapies, using standard classification systems. Compiles medical care and census data for statistical reports on types of diseases treated, surgery performed, and use of hospital beds, in response to inquiries from law firms, insurance companies, and government agencies. Maintains and utilizes variety of health record indexes and storage and retrieval systems. Operates computer to process, store, and retrieve health information. Assists MEDICAL-RECORD ADMINISTRATOR (medical ser.) 079.167-014 in special studies or research, as needed.
GOE: 07.05.03 STRENGTH: L GED: R4 M3 L4 SVP: 6 DLU: 88

079.362-018 TUMOR REGISTRAR (medical ser.)

Compiles and maintains records of hospital patients treated for cancer to provide data for physicians and research studies, utilizing tumor registry data system: Reviews hospital records to identify and compile patient data for use in cancer managment program and to comply with government regulations. Reviews patient's medical record, abstracts and codes information, such as demographic characteristics, history and extent of disease, diagnostic procedures and treatment, and enters data into computer. Contacts discharged patients, their families, and physicians to maintain registry with follow-up information, such as quality of life and length of survival of cancer patients. Prepares statistical

reports, narrative reports and graphic presentations of tumor registry data for use by hospital staff, researchers, and other users of registry data. May supervise subordinate tumor registry staff and be known as Manager, Tumor Registry (medical ser.).
GOE: 07.05.03 STRENGTH: S GED: R5 M4 L5 SVP: 7 DLU: 89

079.364-010 CHIROPRACTOR ASSISTANT (medical ser.)

Aids CHIROPRACTOR (medical ser.) during physical examination of patients, gives specified office treatments, and keeps patients' records: Writes history of patient's accident or illness, and shows patient to examining room. Aids CHIROPRACTOR (medical ser.) in lifting and turning patient under treatment. Gives physiotherapy treatments, such as diathermy, galvanics, or hydrotherapy, following directions of CHIROPRACTOR (medical ser.). Takes and records patient's temperature and blood pressure, assists in x-ray procedures, and gives first aid. Answers telephone, schedules appointments, records treatment information on patient's chart, and fills out insurance forms. Prepares and mails patient's bills.
GOE: 10.03.02 STRENGTH: M GED: R4 M3 L4 SVP: 6 DLU: 77

079.364-014 OPTOMETRIC ASSISTANT (medical ser.)

Performs any combination of following tasks to assist OPTOMETRIST (medical ser) 079.101-018: Obtains and records patient's preliminary case history. Maintains records, schedules appointments, performs bookkeeping, correspondence, and filing. Prepares patient for vision examination; assists in testing for near and far acuity, depth perception, macula integrity, color perception, and visual field, utilizing ocular testing apparatus. Instructs patient in care and use of glasses or contact lenses. Works with patient in vision therapy. Assists patient in frame selection. Adjusts and repairs glasses. Modifies contact lenses. Maintains inventory of materials and cleans instruments. Assists in fabrication of eye glasses or contact lenses.
GOE: 10.03.02 STRENGTH: S GED: R4 M4 L4 SVP: 6 DLU: 77

079.364-018 PHYSICIAN ASSISTANT (medical ser.)

Provides health care services to patients under direction and responsibility of physician: Examines patient, performs comprehensive physical examination, and compiles patient medical data, including health history and results of physical examination. Administers or orders diagnostic tests, such as x ray, electrocardiogram, and laboratory tests, and interprets test results for deviations from normal. Performs therapeutic procedures, such as injections, immunizations, suturing and wound care, and managing infection. Develops and implements patient management plans, records progress notes, and assists in provision of continuity of care. Instructs and counsels patients regarding compliance with prescribed therapeutic regimens, normal growth and development, family planning, emotional problems of daily living, and health maintenance. May have training in particular medical specialty and be designated Anesthesiologist Assistant (medical ser.) or Surgeon Assistant (medical ser.).
GOE: 10.02.01 STRENGTH: L GED: R5 M4 L5 SVP: 7 DLU: 89

079.364-022 PHLEBOTOMIST (medical ser.)

Draws blood from patients or donors in hospital, blood bank, or similar facility for analysis or other medical purposes: Assembles equipment, such as tourniquet, needles, disposable containers for needles, blood collection devices, gauze, cotton, and alcohol on work tray, according to requirements for specified tests or procedures. Verifies or records identity of patient or donor and converses with patient or donor to allay fear of procedure. Applies tourniquet to arm, locates accessible vein, swabs puncture area with antiseptic, and inserts needle into vein to draw blood into collection tube or bag. Withdraws needle, applies treatment to puncture site, and labels and stores blood container for subsequent processing. May prick finger to draw blood. May conduct interviews, take vital signs, and draw and test blood samples to screen donors at blood bank.
GOE: 02.04.02 STRENGTH: L GED: R3 M2 L3 SVP: 3 DLU: 88

079.364-026 PARAMEDIC (medical ser.) alternate titles: emt-paramedic

Administers life support care to sick and injured persons in prehospital setting as authorized and directed by physician: Assesses nature and extent of illness or injury to establish and prioritize medical procedures to be followed or need for additional assistance. Restores and stabilizes heart rhythm on pulseless, nonbreathing patient, using defibrillator, or as directed by physician. Monitors cardiac patient, using electrocardiograph. Initiates intravenous fluids to administer medication or drugs, or to replace fluids lacking in body. Performs endotracheal intubation to open airways and ventilate patient. Administers injections of medications and drugs, following established protocols. Inflates pneumatic anti-shock garment on patient to improve blood circulation. Administers initial treatment at emergency scene and takes and records patient's vital signs. Assists in extricating trapped victims and transports sick and injured persons to treatment center. Observes, records, and reports to physician patient's condition and reaction to drugs, treatments, and significant incidents. May drive mobile intensive care unit to emergency scene. May serve as team leader for EMERGENCY MEDICAL TECHNICIANS (medical ser.) 079.374-010. May communicate with physician and other medical personnel via radio-telephone.
GOE: 10.03.02 STRENGTH: V GED: R4 M3 L4 SVP: 6 DLU: 89

079.367-018 MEDICAL-SERVICE TECHNICIAN (military ser.)

Administers medical aid to personnel aboard submarines, small ships, and isolated areas in absence of or under supervision of medical superior: Examines patients and diagnoses condition. Prescribes medication to treat condition of patient. Inoculates and vaccinates patients to immunize patients from commu-

71

nicable diseases. Treats cuts and burns, performs minor surgery and administers emergency medical care to patients during emergency situations in absence of superior. Inspects food and facilities to determine conformance to sanitary regulations. Recommends necessary measures to ensure sanitary conditions are maintained. Records, transcribes, and files medical case histories. Prepares requisitions for supplies, services, and equipment.
GOE: 07.05.03 STRENGTH: L GED: R4 M3 L3 SVP: 7 DLU: 77

079.371-014   ORTHOPTIST (medical ser.)
Aids persons with correctable focusing defects to develop and use binocular vision (focusing of both eyes): Measures visual acuity, focusing ability, and eye-motor movement of eyes, separately and jointly. Aids patient to move, focus, and coordinate both eyes to aid in visual development. Develops visual skills, near-visual discrimination, and depth perception, using developmental glasses and prisms. Instructs adult patients or parents of young patients in utilization of corrective methods at home.
GOE: 10.02.02 STRENGTH: L GED: R4 M4 L4 SVP: 6 DLU: 77

079.374-010   EMERGENCY MEDICAL TECHNICIAN (medical ser.)
Administers first-aid treatment to and transports sick or injured persons to medical facility, working as member of emergency medical team: Responds to instructions from emergency medical dispatcher and drives specially equipped emergency vehicle to specified location. Monitors communication equipment to maintain contact with dispatcher. Removes or assists in removal of victims from scene of accident or catastrophe. Determines nature and extent of illness or injury, or magnitude of catastrophe, to establish first aid procedures to be followed or need for additional assistance, basing decisions on statements of persons involved, examination of victim or victims, and knowledge of emergency medical practice. Administers prescribed first-aid treatment at site of emergency, or in specially equipped vehicle, performing such activities as application of splints, administration of oxygen or intravenous injections, treatment of minor wounds or abrasions, or administration of artificial resuscitation. Communicates with professional medical personnel at emergency treatment facility to obtain instructions regarding further treatment and to arrange for reception of victims at treatment facility. Assists in removal of victims from vehicle and transfer of victims to treatment center. Assists treatment center admitting personnel to obtain and record information related to victims' vital statistics and circumstances of emergency. Maintains vehicles and medical and communication equipment and replenishes first-aid equipment and supplies. May assist in controlling crowds, protecting valuables, or performing other duties at scene of catastrophe. May assist professional medical personnel in emergency treatment administered at medical facility.
GOE: 10.03.02 STRENGTH: M GED: R4 M3 L4 SVP: 5 DLU: 77

079.374-014   NURSE, LICENSED PRACTICAL (medical ser.)
Provides prescribed medical treatment and personal care services to ill, injured, convalescent, and handicapped persons in such settings as hospitals, clinics, private homes, schools, sanitariums, and similar institutions: Takes and records patients' vital signs. Dresses wounds, gives enemas, douches, alcohol rubs, and massages. Applies compresses, ice bags, and hot water bottles. Observes patients and reports adverse reactions to medication or treatment to medical personnel in charge. Administers specified medication, orally or by subcutaneous or intermuscular injection, and notes time and amount on patients' charts. Assembles and uses such equipment as catheters, tracheotomy tubes, and oxygen suppliers. Collects samples, such as urine, blood, and sputum, from patients for testing and performs routine laboratory tests on samples. Sterilizes equipment and supplies, using germicides, sterilizer, or autoclave. Prepares or examines food trays for prescribed diet and feeds patients. Records food and fluid intake and output. Bathes, dresses, and assists patients in walking and turning. Cleans rooms, makes beds, and answers patients' calls. Washes and dresses bodies of deceased persons. Must pass state board examination and be licensed. May assist in delivery, care, and feeding of infants. May inventory and requisition supplies. May provide medical treatment and personal care to patients in private home settings and be designated Home Health Nurse, Licensed Practical (medical ser.).
GOE: 10.02.01 STRENGTH: M GED: R4 M3 L4 SVP: 6 DLU: 87

079.374-018   PODIATRIC ASSISTANT (medical ser.)
Assists PODIATRIST (medical ser.) in patient care. Prepares patients for treatment, sterilizes instruments, performs general office duties, and assists PODIATRIST (medical ser.) in preparing dressings, administering treatments, and developing x rays.
GOE: 10.03.02 STRENGTH: L GED: R4 M2 L4 SVP: 6 DLU: 77

079.374-022   SURGICAL TECHNICIAN (medical ser.) alternate titles: operating-room technician
Performs any combination of following tasks before, during, and after surgery to assist surgical team: Places equipment and supplies in operating room and arranges instruments, according to instructions. Assists team members to place and position patient on table. Scrubs arms and hands and dons gown and gloves. Aids team to don gowns and gloves. Maintains supply of fluids, such as plasma, saline, blood, and glucose for use during operation. Hands instruments and supplies to surgeon, holds retractors, cuts sutures, and performs other tasks as directed by surgeon during operation. Puts dressings on patient following surgery. Counts sponges, needles, and instruments before and after operation. Washes and sterilizes equipment, using germicides and sterilizers. Cleans operating room.

GOE: 10.03.02 STRENGTH: L GED: R4 M4 L3 SVP: 6 DLU: 88

079.374-026   PSYCHIATRIC TECHNICIAN (medical ser.)
Provides nursing care to mentally ill, emotionally disturbed, or mentally retarded patients in psychiatric hospital or mental health clinic and participates in rehabilitation and treatment programs: Helps patients with their personal hygiene, such as bathing and keeping beds, clothing, and living areas clean. Administers oral medications and hypodermic injections, following physician's prescriptions and hospital procedures. Takes and records measures of patient's general physical condition, such as pulse, temperature, and respiration, to provide daily information. Observes patients to detect behavior patterns and reports observations to medical staff. Intervenes to restrain violent or potentially violent or suicidal patients by verbal or physical means as required. Leads prescribed individual or group therapy sessions as part of specific therapeutic procedures. May complete initial admittance forms for new patients. May contact patient's relatives by telephone to arrange family conferences. May issue medications from dispensary and maintain records in accordance with specified procedures. May be required to hold state license.
GOE: 10.02.02 STRENGTH: M GED: R4 M3 L4 SVP: 6 DLU: 86

09   OCCUPATIONS IN EDUCATION

This division includes occupations in education concerned with research, administration, and teaching. Includes occupations in the administration of federal, state, and private programs for which a background in education is required. Includes aides who assist classroom teachers by instructing sections of classes, coaching invidivual pupils, and grading papers, but excludes aides where educational preparation is not specific and tasks of jobs include various clerical or service tasks. Classroom aide occupations in primary and secondary school are included in Group 249. Occupations concerned with teaching art other than in primary and secondary schools are included in Group 149. Occupations concerned with teaching dramatics, dancing, music, athletics, games of mental skill, e.g., bridge and chess, and sports, other than in primary and secondary schools, are included in appropriate groups under Division 15. Occupations concerned with student and teacher personnel work and vocational guidance are included in Groups 045 and 166. Administrative occupations which do not require a background of education are included in groups under Division 16.

090   OCCUPATIONS IN COLLEGE AND UNIVERSITY EDUCATION

This group includes occupations concerned with research, administration, and teaching in schools beyond the secondary school level (including junior colleges, technical institutes, and specialized post-secondary vocational schools, such as secretarial, laboratory technology, and aviation-training schools, as well as the graduate and undergraduate facilities and professional schools of colleges and universities). Teachers at this level usually specialize in one academic subject, professional discipline, or technical skill.

090.107-010   FOREIGN-STUDENT ADVISER (education) alternate titles: visiting-student counselor
Assists foreign students in making academic, personal-social, and environmental adjustment to campus and community life: Evaluates students' qualifications in light of admission requirements and makes recommendations relative to admission. Develops and maintains case histories, noting language, educational, social, religious, or physical problems affecting students' adjustments. Provides informal counseling and orientation regarding recreational and religious outlets, study habits, and personal adjustments. Interprets university regulations and requirements. Assists students in complying with government regulations concerning status, immigration, visas, passports, permission to work, and related matters. Represents students in cases involving conflict with regulations. Cooperates with other personnel service bureaus to assist in adjustment of students. Approves students' proposed budgets and requests release of funds from students' home governments to meet financial obligations. Recommends students for scholarships, grants-in-aid, and waivers of tuition fees on basis of scholarship, character, and financial need. Encourages and coordinates activities of groups which promote understanding of foreign cultures. May assist in curriculum planning.
GOE: 10.01.02 STRENGTH: S GED: R5 M2 L5 SVP: 7 DLU: 77

090.117-010   ACADEMIC DEAN (education) alternate titles: academic vice president; dean of instruction; faculty dean; provost; university dean; vice president for instruction
Develops academic policies and programs for college or university: Directs and coordinates activities of deans and chairpersons of individual colleges. Advises on personnel matters. Determines scheduling of courses and recommends implementation of additional courses. Coordinates activities of student advisors. Participates in activities of faculty committees, and in development of academic budget. Advises PRESIDENT, EDUCATIONAL INSTITUTION (education) on academic matters. Serves as liaison officer with accrediting agencies which evaluate academic programs. May serve as chief administrative officer in absence of PRESIDENT, EDUCATIONAL INSTITUTION (education). May provide general direction to LIBRARIAN (library); DIRECTOR OF ADMISSIONS (education); and REGISTRAR, COLLEGE OR UNIVERSITY (education).

GOE: 11.07.03 STRENGTH: S GED: R5 M3 L5 SVP: 9 DLU: 77

090.117-014 ALUMNI SECRETARY (education) alternate titles: director, alumni relations

Directs and coordinates activities of college or university alumni organization: Communicates with alumni and former students. Organizes and directs alumni organizational functions, regional alumni meetings, and production of alumni publications. Coordinates activities of clerical and publications staff. Promotes alumni endorsement of institutional activities and enlists alumni aid in recruiting students and fund raising. Secures publicity for alumni functions. May promote athletic events. May assist in followup studies of graduates. May supervise alumni field officers.
GOE: 11.09.02 STRENGTH: S GED: R5 M3 L5 SVP: 8 DLU: 77

090.117-018 DEAN OF STUDENTS (education) alternate titles: dean of student affairs; director of student services; vice president of student affairs

Directs and coordinates student programs of college or university: Formulates and develops student personnel policies. Advises staff members on problems relating to policy, program, and administration. Directs and assists in planning social, recreational, and curricular programs. Counsels or advises individuals and groups on matters pertaining to personal problems, educational and vocational objectives, social and recreational activities, and financial assistance. Reviews reports of student misconduct cases that require disciplinary action to ensure recommendations conform to university policies. Sponsors and advises student organizations. Reviews budget and directs appropriations of student services unit. Represents university in community on matters pertaining to student personnel program and activities. May teach. May direct admissions, foreign student services, health services, student union, and testing services. May be designated Dean Of Men (education); Dean Of Women (education).
GOE: 10.01.02 STRENGTH: S GED: R5 M3 L5 SVP: 8 DLU: 77

090.117-022 DIRECTOR, ATHLETIC (education)

Plans, administers, and directs intercollegiate athletic activities in college or university: Interprets and participates in formulating extramural athletic policies. Employs and discharges coaching staff and other department employees on own initiative or at direction of board in charge of athletics. Directs preparation and dissemination of publicity to promote athletic events. Plans and coordinates activities of coaching staff. Prepares budget and authorizes department expenditures. Plans and schedules sports events, and oversees ticket sales activities. Certifies reports of income produced from ticket sales. May direct programs for students of physical education.
GOE: 11.07.03 STRENGTH: S GED: R5 M3 L5 SVP: 9 DLU: 77

090.117-026 DIRECTOR, EXTENSION WORK (education)

Directs college or university extension service to provide educational programs for adults in extended day, evening, and off-campus classes and in special interest seminar and convention courses: Consults staff members to determine community educational needs and to ascertain feasibility of proposed programs. Develops academic objectives for specific programs and for long range extension services. Consults with staff and outside experts and formulates program scope and content. Meets with academic and administrative personnel to disseminate information regarding program objectives and to ensure that program goals are met. Establishes operational policies and procedures. Reviews program progress reports to ensure that objectives are met. Reviews and approves budget. Oversees activities of operational and program departments. Directs activities of administrative staff.
GOE: 11.07.03 STRENGTH: S GED: R6 M3 L5 SVP: 9 DLU: 77

090.117-030 FINANCIAL-AIDS OFFICER (education) alternate titles: director of financial aid and placements; director of student aid

Directs scholarship, grant-in-aid, and loan programs to provide financial assistance to students in college or university: Selects candidates and determines types and amounts of aid. Organizes and oversees student financial counseling activities. Coordinates activities with other departmental staff engaged in issuing or collecting student payments. May teach. May select financial aid candidates as members of committee and be designated Chairperson, Scholarship And Loan Committee (education).
GOE: 11.07.03 STRENGTH: S GED: R5 M3 L5 SVP: 8 DLU: 77

090.117-034 PRESIDENT, EDUCATIONAL INSTITUTION (education) alternate titles: chancellor

Formulates plans and programs for and directs administration of college, school, or university, within authority delegated by governing board: Confers with board of control to plan and initiate programs concerning organizational, operational, and academic functions of campus, and oversees their execution. Administers fiscal and physical planning activities, such as development of budget and building expansion programs, and recommends their adoption. Negotiates with administrative officials and representatives of business, community, and civic groups to promote educational, research, and public service objectives and policies of institution as formulated by board of control. Establishes operational procedures, rules, and standards relating to faculty and staff classification standards, financial disbursements, and accounting requirements. Represents campus on board of control and at formal functions. May be designated according to type of institution presided over as President, Business School (education); President, College Or University (education).
GOE: 11.07.03 STRENGTH: S GED: R5 M3 L5 SVP: 9 DLU: 77

090.164-010 LABORATORY MANAGER (education)

Coordinates activities of university science laboratory to assist faculty in teaching and research programs: Consults with faculty laboratory coordinator to determine equipment purchase priorities based on budget allowances, condition of existing equipment, and scheduled laboratory activities. Prepares and puts in place equipment scheduled for use during laboratory teaching sessions. Demonstrates care and use of equipment to teaching assistants. Builds prototype equipment, applying electromechanical knowledge and using handtools and power tools. Trains teaching staff and students in application and use of new equipment. Diagnoses equipment malfunctions and dismantles and repairs equipment, applying knowledge of shop mechanics and using gauges, meters, handtools, and power tools. Develops methods of laboratory experimentation, applying knowledge of scientific theory and computer capability. Confers with teaching staff periodically to evaluate new equipment and methods. Teaches laboratory sessions in absence of teaching assistant.
GOE: 11.07.03 STRENGTH: L GED: R5 M5 L4 SVP: 7 DLU: 86

090.167-010 DEPARTMENT HEAD, COLLEGE OR UNIVERSITY (education) alternate titles: department chairperson, college or university

Administers affairs of college department, such as English, biological sciences, or mathematics department: Arranges schedules of classes and assigns teaching staff to conduct classes. Prepares lists of budgetary and other needs. Interviews applicants for teaching positions. Performs other administrative duties in addition to teaching assignment. May administer department's budget and recruit academic personnel. May head department in two-year college and be designated Department Head, Junior College (education).
GOE: 11.07.03 STRENGTH: S GED: R6 M5 L5 SVP: 8 DLU: 77

090.167-014 DIRECTOR OF ADMISSIONS (education) alternate titles: dean of admissions

Directs and coordinates admissions program of public or private college or university, according to policies developed by governing board: Directs program of admissions counseling and reviews exceptional admissions cases. Confers with staff of other schools to explain admission requirements and student transfer credit policies. Evaluates courses offered by other schools to determine their equivalency to courses offered on campus. Directs preparation of printed materials explaining admission requirements and transfer credit policies for dissemination to other schools. May counsel students having problems relating to admissions or may supervise professionally trained admissions counseling staff. May serve on policy making admissions committee. May participate in or conduct student recruitment programs with other members of faculty and staff. May administer financial aid programs.
GOE: 11.07.03 STRENGTH: S GED: R5 M3 L5 SVP: 8 DLU: 77

090.167-018 DIRECTOR OF INSTITUTIONAL RESEARCH (education) alternate titles: administrative analyst; director of institutional studies; vice president for institutional research

Directs and coordinates activities concerned with research and evaluation of operations and programs of college or university: Identifies problem areas, such as admission patterns, fiscal and management analysis, and sources of financial support in order to develop research procedures. Coordinates research efforts and assists in evaluating research findings. Coordinates activities of research staff. May teach.
GOE: 11.07.03 STRENGTH: S GED: R6 M5 L5 SVP: 8 DLU: 77

090.167-022 DIRECTOR OF STUDENT AFFAIRS (education) alternate titles: director, student union; manager, student union; student-activities adviser; student-union consultant

Plans and arranges social, cultural, and recreational activities of various student groups, according to university policies and regulations: Meets with student and faculty groups to plan activities. Evaluates programs and suggests modifications. Schedules events to prevent overlapping and coordinates activities with sports and other university programs. Contacts caterers, entertainers, decorators, and others to arrange for scheduled events. Conducts orientation program for new students with other members of faculty and staff. Advises student groups on financial status of and methods for improving their organizations. Promotes student participation in social, cultural, and recreational activities. May coordinate preparation and publishing of student affairs calendar. May provide individual or group counseling on selection of social activities and use of leisure time. May be designated according to activity performed as Fraternity Adviser (education); Women's-Activities Adviser (education).
GOE: 11.07.03 STRENGTH: S GED: R5 M3 L5 SVP: 8 DLU: 77

090.167-026 DIRECTOR, SUMMER SESSIONS (education)

Coordinates and directs summer session program of college or university: Analyzes past records and confers with faculty and staff on enrollment trends to anticipate size of enrollment. Estimates budget requirements on basis of expected income and expenditures and requests allotment of funds. Discusses apportionment of funds with heads of departments and approves or alters detailed budgets according to past financial success of proposed course offerings. Issues invitations to and appoints teaching staff upon recommendations of department heads. Directs preparation and distribution of summer session bulletin and publicity releases. Oversees registration of summer session students. May establish tuition fees as member of committee on basis of expected enrollment to provide income equal to expenses.
GOE: 11.07.03 STRENGTH: S GED: R5 M3 L5 SVP: 9 DLU: 77

090.167-030   REGISTRAR, COLLEGE OR UNIVERSITY (education) alternate titles: director of admissions

Directs and coordinates college or university registration activities: Consults with other officials to devise registration schedules and procedures. Analyzes statistical data on registration for administrative use in formulating policies. Exchanges student information with other colleges or universities. Directs preparation of student transcripts. Prepares commencement list. Directs preparation of statistical reports on educational activities for government and educational agencies and interprets registration policies to faculty and students. Directs activities of workers engaged in transcribing and evaluating academic records of students applying for permission to enter college or university. Directs compilation of information, such as class schedules and graduation requirements, for publication in school bulletins and catalogs. Coordinates dissemination of information on courses offered and procedures students are required to follow in order to obtain grade transcripts. Issues official transcripts. Coordinates class schedules with room assignments for optimum use of buildings and equipment. May assign rooms for student activities.
GOE: 11.07.03 STRENGTH: S GED: R5 M5 L5 SVP: 8 DLU: 77

090.167-034   DIRECTOR, FIELD SERVICES (education) alternate titles: director of recruitment

Directs and plans recruitment activities of community college: Plans comprehensive program of marketing services in recruitment of students and outreach activities with business, industry, community organizations, and public agencies to establish educational programs and to identify educational needs of community. Develops and distributes recruiting literature in locations, such as high schools and shopping centers. Plans publicity campaign and contacts target groups directly through visits with school counselors, career day activities, and meetings with industry groups to explain college educational programs and services. Studies federal and state regulations and local demographic and employment trends to determine impact on enrollment. Coordinates recruitment activities with other colleges. Advises administrative staff on need for new programs and courses. Prepares budget and annual reports.
GOE: 11.07.03 STRENGTH: M GED: R5 M4 L5 SVP: 8 DLU: 86

090.222-010   INSTRUCTOR, BUSINESS EDUCATION (education)

Instructs students in commercial subjects, such as typing, filing, secretarial procedures, business mathematics, office equipment use, and personality development, in business schools, community colleges, or training programs: Instructs students in subject matter, utilizing various methods, such as lecture and demonstration, and uses audiovisual aids and other materials to supplement presentations. Prepares or follows teaching outline for course of study, assigns lessons, and corrects homework and classroom papers. Administers tests to evaluate students' progress, records results, and issues reports to inform students of their progress. Maintains discipline in classroom.
GOE: 11.02.01 STRENGTH: L GED: R5 M4 L5 SVP: 8 DLU: 86

090.227-010   FACULTY MEMBER, COLLEGE OR UNIVERSITY (education)

Conducts college or university courses for undergraduate or graduate students: Teaches one or more subjects, such as economics, chemistry, law, or medicine, within prescribed curriculum. Prepares and delivers lectures to students. Compiles bibliographies of specialized materials for outside reading assignments. Stimulates class discussions. Compiles, administers, and grades examinations, or assigns this work to others. Directs research of other teachers or graduate students working for advanced academic degrees. Conducts research in particular field of knowledge and publishes findings in professional journals. Performs related duties, such as advising students on academic and vocational curricula, and acting as adviser to student organizations. Serves on faculty committee providing professional consulting services to government and industry. May be designated according to faculty rank in traditional hierarchy as determined by institution's estimate of scholarly maturity as Associate Professor (education); Professor (education); or according to rank distinguished by duties assigned or amount of time devoted to academic work as Research Assistant (education); Visiting Professor (education). May teach in two-year college and be designated Teacher, Junior College (education); or in technical institute and be designated Faculty Member, Technical Institute (education). May be designated: Acting Professor (education); Assistant Professor (education); Clinical Instructor (education); Instructor (education); Lecturer (education); Teaching Assistant (education).
GOE: 11.02.01 STRENGTH: L GED: R6 M5 L5 SVP: 8 DLU: 81

090.227-014   GRADUATE ASSISTANT (education)

Assists department chairperson, faculty members or other professional staff members in college or university, by performing any combination of following duties: Assists in library, develops teaching materials, such as syllabi and visual aids, assists in laboratory or field research, prepares and gives examinations, assists in student conferences, grades examinations and papers, and teaches lower-level courses. May be designated by duties performed, or equipment operated.
GOE: 11.02.01 STRENGTH: L GED: R6 M4 L6 SVP: 8 DLU: 77

090.227-018   INSTRUCTOR, EXTENSION WORK (education)

Conducts evening classes for extension service of college or university: Prepares course of study designed to meet community, organization, and student needs. Conducts and corrects examinations, and assigns course grades.

GOE: 11.02.01 STRENGTH: S GED: R5 M3 L5 SVP: 8 DLU: 77

091   OCCUPATIONS IN SECONDARY SCHOOL EDUCATION

This group includes occupations concerned with research, administration, and teaching at the secondary school level (intermediate grades between primary school and college). Teaching at this level is generally specialized according to one group of related subjects, such as physics, math, history, literature, home economics, industrial arts, or music. Occupations concerned with relieving teachers of duties which do not require academic training, such as clerical tasks or attending to personal needs of students, are included in Group 249.

091.107-010   ASSISTANT PRINCIPAL (education)

Administers school student personnel program in primary or secondary school, and counsels and disciplines students, performing any combination of following tasks: Formulates student personnel policies, such as code of ethics. Plans and supervises school student activity programs. Gives individual and group guidance for personal problems, educational and vocational objectives, and social and recreational activities. Talks with and disciplines students in cases of attendance and behavior problems. Supervises students in attendance at assemblies and athletic events. Walks about school building and property to monitor safety and security or directs and coordinates teacher supervision of areas such as halls and cafeteria. Observes and evaluates teacher performance. Maintains records of student attendance. Arranges for and oversees substitute teachers. Works with administrators to coordinate and supervise student teachers program. Teaches courses. Assists PRINCIPAL (education) 099.117-018 to interview and hire teachers. Organizes and administers in-service teacher training. Acts as PRINCIPAL (education) in absence of PRINCIPAL (education). May be required to have certification from state.
GOE: 10.01.02 STRENGTH: L GED: R5 M3 L5 SVP: 8 DLU: 80

091.221-010   TEACHER, INDUSTRIAL ARTS (education) alternate titles: shop teacher

Teaches students basic techniques and assists in development of manipulative skills in industrial arts courses in secondary schools: Prepares lesson plans for courses and establishes goals. Lectures, illustrates, and demonstrates when teaching use of handtools; machines, such as lathe, planer, power saws, and drill press; safety practices; precision measuring instruments, such as micrometer; and industrial arts techniques. Evaluates student progress. Talks with parents and counselor to resolve behavioral and academic problems. May teach shop math. May specialize in one or more areas, such as woodworking, metalworking, electricity, graphic arts, automobile repair, or drafting. May teach students with disabilities. May be required to have certification from state.
GOE: 11.02.02 STRENGTH: L GED: R5 M4 L5 SVP: 7 DLU: 80

091.227-010   TEACHER, SECONDARY SCHOOL (education) alternate titles: high school teacher

Teaches one or more subjects to students in public or private secondary schools: Instructs students, using various teaching methods, such as lecture and demonstration, and uses audiovisual aids and other materials to supplement presentations. Prepares course objectives and outline for course of study following curriculum guidelines or requirements of state and school. Assigns lessons and corrects homework. Administers tests to evaluate pupil progress, records results, and issues reports to inform parents of progress. Keeps attendance records. Maintains discipline in classroom. Meets with parents to discuss student progress and problems. Participates in faculty and professional meetings, educational conferences, and teacher training workshops. Performs related duties, such as sponsoring one or more activities or student organizations, assisting pupils in selecting course of study, and counseling student in adjustment and academic problems. May be identified according to subject matter taught. May be required to hold certification from state.
GOE: 11.02.01 STRENGTH: L GED: R5 M4 L5 SVP: 7 DLU: 80

092   OCCUPATIONS IN PRESCHOOL, PRIMARY SCHOOL, AND KINDERGARTEN EDUCATION

This group includes occupations concerned with research, administration, and teaching below the secondary school level. Teaching at this level is generally not specialized according to subject matter. Some specialization does occur in music, art, science, or physical training. Occupations concerned with relieving teachers of duties which do not require academic training, such as clerical tasks or attending to personal needs of children, are included in Group 249.

092.167-010   DIRECTOR, DAY CARE CENTER (education)

Directs activities of preschool, day care center, or other child development facility to provide instruction and care for children: Prepares and submits facility budget to board of trustees, administrative agency, or owner for approval. Authorizes purchase of instructional materials and teaching aids, such as books, toys, and games designed to stimulate learning. Interviews and recommends hiring of teaching and service staff. Confers with parents regarding facility activities, policies, and enrollment procedures. Confers with teaching staff regarding child's behavioral or learning problems, and recommends methods of modifying inappropriate behavior and encouraging learning experiences. Reviews and evaluates facility activities to ensure conformance to state and local regulations. Re-

views and approves menu plans and food purchases. May arrange medical attention for ill or injured child in accordance with parental instructions. May perform classroom teaching duties during absence of regular teacher. May be designated Director, Child Development Center (education); Director, Nursery School (education).
GOE: 11.07.03 STRENGTH: S GED: R4 M3 L4 SVP: 7 DLU: 77

092.227-010 TEACHER, ELEMENTARY SCHOOL (education)
Teaches elementary school students academic, social, and motor skills in public or private schools: Prepares course objectives and outline for course of study following curriculum guidelines or requirements of state and school. Lectures, demonstrates, and uses audiovisual teaching aids to present subject matter to class. Prepares, administers, and corrects tests, and records results. Assigns lessons, corrects papers, and hears oral presentations. Teaches rules of conduct. Maintains order in classroom and on playground. Counsels pupils when adjustment and academic problems arise. Discusses pupils' academic and behavioral attitudes and achievements with parents. Keeps attendance and grade records as required by school. May coordinate class field trips. May teach combined grade classes. May specialize in subject taught, such as math, science, or social studies. May be required to hold state certification.
GOE: 11.02.01 STRENGTH: L GED: R5 M4 L5 SVP: 7 DLU: 81

092.227-014 TEACHER, KINDERGARTEN (education) alternate titles: instructor, kindergarten
Teaches elemental natural and social science, personal hygiene, music, art, and literature to children from 4 to 6 years old, to promote their physical, mental, and social development: Supervises activities, such as field visits, group discussions, and dramatic play acting, to stimulate students' interest in and broaden understanding of their physical and social environment. Fosters cooperative social behavior through games and group projects to assist children in forming satisfying relationships with other children and adults. Encourages students in singing, dancing, rhythmic activities, and in use of art materials, to promote self-expression and appreciation of esthetic experience. Instructs children in practices of personal cleanliness and self care. Alternates periods of strenuous activity with periods of rest or light activity to avoid overstimulation and fatigue. Observes children to detect signs of ill health or emotional disturbance, and to evaluate progress. Discusses students' problems and progress with parents.
GOE: 10.02.03 STRENGTH: L GED: R5 M2 L4 SVP: 7 DLU: 77

092.227-018 TEACHER, PRESCHOOL (education)
Instructs children in activities designed to promote social, physical, and intellectual growth needed for primary school in preschool, day care center, or other child development facility. Plans individual and group activities to stimulate growth in language, social, and motor skills, such as learning to listen to instructions, playing with others, and using play equipment. May be required to have certification from state. May be designated Teacher, Child Development Center (education); Teacher, Day Care Center (education); Teacher, Early Childhood Development (education); Teacher, Nursery School (education).
GOE: 10.02.03 STRENGTH: L GED: R4 M2 L3 SVP: 7 DLU: 81

094 OCCUPATIONS IN EDUCATION OF PERSONS WITH DISABILITIES

This group includes occupations concerned with research in the education and training of persons with disabilities; the administration of schools or programs for persons with disabilities; and teaching in such schools and programs which require specialized techniques and procedures. Includes teaching persons with visual impairments to read books imprinted in braille and to develop their sense of touch; instructing persons who are hearing impaired in sign language and lip reading; and instructing persons with mental, neurological, and emotional disabilities.

094.107-010 WORK-STUDY COORDINATOR, SPECIAL EDUCATION (education)
Plans and conducts special education work and study program for in-school youth: Establishes contacts with employers and employment agencies and surveys newspapers and other sources to locate work opportunities for students. Confers with potential employers to communicate objectives of work study program and to solicit cooperation in adapting work situations to special needs of students. Evaluates and selects program participants according to specified criteria and counsels and instructs selected students in matters such as vocational choices, job readiness, and job retention skills and behaviors. Assists students in applying for jobs and accompanies students to employment interviews. Confers with employer and visits work site to monitor progress of student and to determine support needed to meet employer requirements and fulfill program goals. Counsels students to foster development of satisfactory job performance. Confers with school and community personnel to impart information about program and to coordinate program functions with related activities.
GOE: 10.02.03 STRENGTH: L GED: R5 M3 L5 SVP: 7 DLU: 86

094.117-010 DIRECTOR, COMMISSION FOR THE BLIND (government ser.)
Directs activities of State Commission for the Blind to facilitate vocational and social adjustment of visually handicapped individuals: Directs, through subordinates, activities of workers engaged in training visually handicapped in vocational and other skills. Plans and organizes training programs and self-employment opportunities for blind persons. Confers with representatives of civic groups and charitable organizations to coordinate programs and services. Recommends changes in legislation affecting visually handicapped individuals. Represents Commission at conventions and addresses public gatherings to promote understanding of problems of blind and partially sighted and activities of Commission. Authorizes purchase of materials and equipment within allocated budget.
GOE: 11.07.01 STRENGTH: S GED: R5 M4 L5 SVP: 8 DLU: 77

094.117-018 VOCATIONAL REHABILITATION CONSULTANT (government ser.)
Develops and coordinates implementation of vocational rehabilitation programs: Consults with members of local communities and personnel of rehabilitation facilities, such as sheltered workshops and skills training centers, to identify need for new programs or modification of existing programs. Collects and analyzes data to define problems and develops proposals for programs to provide needed services, utilizing knowledge of vocational rehabilitation theory and practice, program funding sources, and government regulations. Provides staff training, negotiates contracts for equipment and supplies, and performs related functions to implement program changes. Monitors program operations and recommends additional measures to ensure programs meet defined needs.
GOE: 11.07.03 STRENGTH: S GED: R5 M4 L5 SVP: 8 DLU: 86

094.167-010 SUPERVISOR, SPECIAL EDUCATION (education)
Directs and coordinates activities of teachers and other staff providing home or school instruction, evaluation services, job placement, or other special education services to physically, mentally, emotionally, or neurologically handicapped children: Reviews referrals and diagnoses and participates in conferences with administrators, staff, parents, children, and other concerned parties to formulate recommendations for student placement and provision of services. Monitors staff activities and gives technical assistance in areas, such as assessment, curriculum development, use of materials and equipment, and management of student behavior. Plans and conducts in-service training. Interviews applicants, recommends hirings, and evaluates staff performance. May write grant proposals. May assist program administrators in preparation of budget and development of program policy and goals. May address public to elicit support and explain program objectives.
GOE: 10.02.03 STRENGTH: L GED: R5 M4 L5 SVP: 8 DLU: 86

094.167-014 DIRECTOR, SPECIAL EDUCATION (education) alternate titles: administrative assistant, special education; assistant superintendent, special education
Directs and coordinates special education programs in public school systems, public agencies, and state institutions to teach students with mental or physical disabilities: Formulates policies and procedures for new or revised programs or activities, such as screening, placement, education, and training of students. Evaluates special education programs to ensure that objectives for student education are met. Interprets laws, rules, and regulations to students, parents, and staff. Recruits, selects, and evaluates staff. Prepares budget and solicits funds to provide financial support for programs. Prepares reports for federal, state, and local regulatory agencies. May contract with agencies for needed services, such as residential care. May administer achievement tests to measure student level of performance.
GOE: 11.07.03 STRENGTH: S GED: R6 M5 L5 SVP: 8 DLU: 81

094.224-010 TEACHER, HEARING IMPAIRED (education)
Teaches elementary and secondary school subjects to hearing impaired students, using various methods of communication to receive and convey language: Plans curriculum and prepares lessons and other instructional materials according to grade level of students, utilizing visual media, such as computer, films, television, and charts. Confers with committee of parents, administrators, testing specialists, social worker, and others to develop individual educational program. Instructs students in academic subjects. Instructs students in various forms of communication, such as gestures, sign language, finger spelling, and speech cues. Encourages students to participate in verbal communication classroom learning experiences to ensure their comprehension of subject matter, development of social skills, and ability to communicate in situations encountered in daily living. Tests students' hearing aids to ensure hearing aids are functioning. May attend and interpret lectures and instructions for students enrolled in regular classes. May teach parents how to participate in and enhance students' learning experiences. May teach students to use computer. May specialize in teaching lip reading and be designated Teacher, Lip Reading (education). May be required to have certification from state.
GOE: 10.02.03 STRENGTH: L GED: R5 M4 L5 SVP: 7 DLU: 86

094.224-014 TEACHER, PHYSICALLY IMPAIRED (education)
Teaches elementary and secondary school subjects to physically impaired students, adapting teaching techniques and methods of instruction to meet individual needs of students in schools, hospitals, and students' homes: Plans curriculum and prepares lessons and other materials, considering factors, such as individual needs, abilities, learning levels, and physical limitations of students. Confers with parents, administrators, testing specialists, social worker, and others to develop educational program for student. Instructs students with observable orthopedic impairments, as well as those with internal impairment, such as heart condition. Arranges and adjusts tools, work aids, and equipment utilized by students in classroom, such as specially equipped worktables, computers, typewriters, and mechanized page turners. Devises special teaching tools,

75

techniques, and equipment. Instructs students in academic subjects and other activities designed to provide learning experience. Confers with other members of staff to develop programs to maximize students' potentials. May assist members of medical staff in rehabilitation programs for students. May be required to have certification from state.
GOE: 10.02.03 STRENGTH: L GED: R5 M4 L5 SVP: 7 DLU: 86

094.224-018   TEACHER, VISUALLY IMPAIRED (education)
 Teaches elementary and secondary school subjects and daily living skills to visually impaired students: Instructs students in reading and writing, using magnification equipment and large print material or braille system. Confers with parents, administrator, testing specialists, social worker, and others to develop individual educational program for students. Plans curriculum and prepares lessons and other instructional materials, according to grade level of students. Transcribes lessons and other materials into braille for blind students or large print for low vision students. Reviews and corrects completed assignments, using such aids as braille writer, slate and stylus, or computer. Arranges for and conducts field trips designed to promote experiential learning. Instructs students in academic subject areas and daily living skills, such as hygiene, safety, and food preparation. Encourages students to participate in verbal and sensory classroom learning experiences to ensure their comprehension of subject matter, development of social skills, and ability to identify objects encountered in daily living. Meets with parents to discuss how parents can encourage student's independence and well-being and to provide guidance in using community resources. May counsel students. May teach braille to individuals with sight and be designated Instructor, Braille (education).
GOE: 10.02.03 STRENGTH: L GED: R5 M4 L5 SVP: 7 DLU: 81

094.227-010   TEACHER, EMOTIONALLY IMPAIRED (education)
 Teaches elementary and secondary school subjects to students with emotional impairments in schools, institutions, or other specialized facilities: Plans curriculum and prepares lessons and other instructional materials to meet individual needs of students, considering such factors as physical, emotional, and educational levels of development. Confers with parents, administrators, testing specialists, social workers, and others to develop individual educational plan for student. Instructs students in academic subjects and social interaction skills. Observes students for signs of disruptive behavior, such as violence, verbal outbursts, and episodes of destructiveness. Teaches socially acceptable behavior employing techniques such as behavior modification and positive reinforcement. Confers with other staff members to plan programs designed to promote educational, physical, and social development of students. May be required to have certification from local, state, and federal government.
GOE: 10.02.03 STRENGTH: L GED: R5 M4 L5 SVP: 7 DLU: 86

094.227-022   TEACHER, MENTALLY IMPAIRED (education)
 Teaches basic academic and living skills to mentally impaired students in schools and other institutions: Plans curriculum and prepares lessons and other instructional materials according to achievement levels of students. Confers with parents, administrators, testing specialists, social workers, and others to develop individual educational program for students who are at different learning ability levels, including educable, trainable, and severely impaired. Instructs students in academic subjects, utilizing various teaching techniques, such as phonetics, multisensory learning, and repetition to reinforce learning. Instructs students in daily living skills required for independent maintenance and economic self-sufficiency, such as hygiene, safety, and food preparation. Observes, evaluates, and prepares reports on progress of students. Meets with parents to provide support and guidance in using community resources. May administer and interpret results of ability and achievement tests. May be required to hold state certification.
GOE: 10.02.03 STRENGTH: L GED: R5 M4 L5 SVP: 7 DLU: 86

094.227-026   TEACHER, VOCATIONAL TRAINING (education)
 Teaches vocational skills to handicapped students: Confers with students, parents, school personnel, and other individuals to plan vocational training that meets needs, interests, and abilities of students. Instructs students in areas such as personal-social skills and work-related attitudes and behaviors. Develops work opportunities that allow students to experience success in performing tasks of increasing difficulty and that teach work values, such as self-improvement, independence, dependability, productivity, and pride of workmanship. Conducts field trips to enable students to learn about job activities and to explore work environments. May teach academic skills to students. May instruct students in one or more vocational skills, such as woodworking, building maintenance, cosmetology, food preparation, gardening, sewing, or nurse aiding.
GOE: 10.02.03 STRENGTH: L GED: R5 M3 L5 SVP: 7 DLU: 86

094.227-030   TEACHER, LEARNING DISABLED (education)
 Teaches elementary and secondary school subjects in schools, institutions, or other specialized facilities to students with neurological problems in learning: Plans curriculum and prepares lessons and other instructional materials to meet individual need of students, considering state and school requirements, physical, emotional, and educational levels of development. Confers with parents, administrators, testing specialists, social worker, and others to develop individual educational program for student. Instructs students in all academic subjects. Creates learning materials geared to each student's ability and interest. Instructs students, using special educational strategies and techniques, to improve sensory-motor and perceptual-motor development, perception, memory, language, cognition, and social and emotional development. Works with students to increase

motivation, provide consistent reinforcement to learning, continuous assessment of level of functioning, and continuous feedback to student for all learning activities. Works with parents to accept and develop skills in dealing with student's learning impairment. May work as consultant, teach in self-contained classroom, or teach in resource room. May be required to hold certification from state.
GOE: 10.02.03 STRENGTH: L GED: R5 M4 L5 SVP: 7 DLU: 81

094.267-010   EVALUATOR (education)
 Assesses type and degree of disability of handicapped children to aid in determining special programs and services required to meet educational needs: Reviews referrals of children having or suspected of having learning disabilities, mental retardation, behaviorial disorders, or physical handicaps to determine evaluation procedure. Confers with school or other personnel and scrutinizes records to obtain additional information on nature and severity of disability. Observes student behavior and rates strength and weakness of factors such as rapport, motivation, cooperativeness, aggression, attention span, and task completion. Selects, administers, and scores variety of preliminary tests to measure individual's aptitudes, educational achievements, perceptual motor skills, vision, and hearing. Reports findings for staff consideration in placement of children in educational programs. May test preschool children to detect learning handicaps' and recommend followup activities, consultation, or services. May administer work related tests and review records and other data to assess student vocational interests and abilities. May specialize in evaluating student readiness to transfer from special classes to regular classroom, and in providing supportive services to regular classroom teacher and be designated Mainstreaming Facilitator (education).
GOE: 10.02.03 STRENGTH: L GED: R5 M4 L5 SVP: 7 DLU: 86

096   HOME ECONOMISTS AND FARM ADVISERS

 This group includes occupations concerned with informing and advising homemakers, farmers, and farm youth in the arts and techniques of homemaking or farming, usually in the home or on the farm, in consultation, or in locally organized groups and meetings.

096.121-010   COUNTY HOME-DEMONSTRATION AGENT (government ser.) alternate titles: home agent; home-demonstration agent; home-extension agent
 Develops, organizes, and conducts programs for individuals in rural communities to improve farm and family life: Lectures and demonstrates techniques in such subjects as nutrition, clothing, home management, home furnishing, and child care. Visits homes to advise families on problems, such as family budgeting and home remodeling. Organizes and advises clubs, and assists in selecting and training leaders to guide group discussions and demonstrations in subjects, such as sewing, food preparation, and home decoration. Writes leaflets and articles and talks over radio and television to disseminate information. Participates in community activities, such as judging at rural fairs and speaking before parent-teachers associations. May direct 4-H Club activities [FOUR-H CLUB AGENT (education)].
GOE: 11.02.03 STRENGTH: L GED: R5 M3 L5 SVP: 7 DLU: 77

096.121-014   HOME ECONOMIST (profess. & kin.) alternate titles: consumer services consultant
 Organizes and conducts consumer education service or research program for equipment, food, textile, or utility company, utilizing principles of home economics: Advises homemakers in selection and utilization of household equipment, food, and clothing, and interprets homemakers' needs to manufacturers of household products. Writes advertising copy and articles of interest to homemakers, tests recipes, equipment, and new household products, conducts radio and television homemakers' programs, and performs other public relations and promotion work for business firms, newspapers, magazines, and radio and television stations. Advises individuals and families on home management practices, such as budget planning, meal preparation, and energy conservation. Teaches improved homemaking practices to homemakers and youths through educational programs, demonstrations, discussions, and home visits. May engage in research in government, private industry, and colleges and universities to explore family relations or child development, develop new products for home, discover facts on food nutrition, and test serviceability of new materials. May specialize in specific area of home economics and be designated Equipment Specialist (profess. & kin.); Fashion Consultant (profess. & kin.); Home Economist, Consumer Service (profess. & kin.); Nutritionist (profess. & kin.); Product Representative (profess. & kin.); Research-Home Economist (profess. & kin.); Test-Kitchen-Home Economist (profess. & kin.).
GOE: 11.02.03 STRENGTH: L GED: R5 M3 L5 SVP: 7 DLU: 77

096.127-010   COUNTY-AGRICULTURAL AGENT (government ser.) alternate titles: agricultural agent; county adviser; county agent; extension agent; extension-service agent; extension worker; farm adviser; farm agent
 Organizes and conducts cooperative extension program to advise and instruct farmers and individuals engaged in agri-business in applications of agricultural research findings: Collects, analyzes, and evaluates agricultural data; plans and develops techniques; and advises farmers to assist in solving problems, such as crop rotation and soil erosion. Delivers lectures and prepares articles concerning subjects, such as farm management and soil conservation. Demonstrates prac-

tical procedures used in solving agricultural problems. Discusses extension program with representatives of commercial organizations, county government, and other groups to inform them of program services and to obtain their cooperation in encouraging use of services. Prepares activity, planning, and other reports and maintains program records. Prepares budget requests, or assists in their preparation. May supervise and coordinate activities of other county extension workers. May direct 4-H Club activities. May be designated by specific program assignment as Agri-Business Agent (government ser.); Farm-Management Agent (government ser.); Horticultural Agent (government ser.); Livestock Agent (government ser.); Resource Agent (government ser.).
GOE: 11.02.03 STRENGTH: L GED: R5 M3 L5 SVP: 7 DLU: 77

096.127-014 EXTENSION SERVICE SPECIALIST (government ser.) alternate titles: cooperative extension advisor specialist
Instructs extension workers and develops specialized service activities in area of agriculture or home economics: Plans, develops, organizes, and evaluates training programs in subjects, such as home management, horticulture, and consumer information. Prepares leaflets, pamphlets, and other material for use as training aids. Conducts classes to train extension workers in specialized fields and in teaching techniques. Delivers lectures to commercial and community organizations and over radio and television to promote development of agricultural or domestic skills. Analyzes research data and plans activities to coordinate services with those offered by other departments, agencies, and organizations. May be designated according to field of specialization as Agricultural-Extension Specialist (government ser.); Home Economics Specialist (government ser.).
GOE: 11.02.03 STRENGTH: L GED: R5 M3 L5 SVP: 8 DLU: 77

096.127-018 FEED AND FARM MANAGEMENT ADVISER (agriculture; retail trade)
Instructs farmers and retail grain and feed-store customers in modern and scientific feed and farm management techniques: Discusses feeding problems for fowl, swine, cattle, and other livestock with farmers. Examines poultry or livestock and recommends medication and remedial measures to prevent spread of disease and to maintain healthy poultry or livestock. Advises and assists farmers in securing services of VETERINARIAN (medical ser.) for treating larger animals. Assists farmers in setting up cost and production records to determine most economical method of farm operation. May give lectures and demonstrations to farm groups. May take feed orders.
GOE: 11.02.03 STRENGTH: L GED: R4 M3 L4 SVP: 7 DLU: 77

096.127-022 FOUR-H CLUB AGENT (education)
Organizes and directs educational projects and activities of 4-H Club: Recruits and trains volunteer leaders to plan and guide 4-H Club program to meet needs and interests of individuals and community. Directs selection of educational projects, such as sewing, woodworking, photography, and livestock raising. Procures, develops, distributes, and presents teaching materials, such as visual aids and literature for educational projects. Arranges for 4-H Clubs to exhibit or participate in events, such as county and state fairs and state 4-H Club events. Develops and maintains recognition and incentive program for members and leaders of 4-H Clubs. May specialize in directing 4-H Club activities for girls and be designated Youth Agent (education).
GOE: 11.02.03 STRENGTH: L GED: R5 M3 L5 SVP: 7 DLU: 77

096.161-010 HOME-SERVICE DIRECTOR (profess. & kin.) alternate titles: director of home economics
Plans, coordinates, and directs consumer education service or research program for equipment, food, or utility company to promote goodwill and sale of products or services: Studies and interprets data concerning consumer habits and preferences obtained from surveys, letters, and other customer contacts to aid company in product development. Plans and organizes program to educate consumers in use of equipment, product, or service. Develops and plans methods of instruction and techniques of demonstrating principles of home economics, such as food preparation and equipment use, to community and school groups. Directs and coordinates testing of recipes and development of new uses for equipment or product. Instructs dealers, sales personnel, and other employees in home management practices and in operation and care of equipment. Contacts organizations, such as school, professional, and women's groups, to promote company product and services. Writes articles and plans preparation of instruction manuals, booklets on product uses, and other consumer publications. Advises on content and accuracy of sales promotional material, such as newspaper, radio, and television advertising copy.
GOE: 11.02.03 STRENGTH: L GED: R5 M3 L5 SVP: 8 DLU: 77

096.167-010 DISTRICT EXTENSION SERVICE AGENT (government ser.) alternate titles: extension supervisor; regional extension-service specialist
Directs and coordinates activities of workers engaged in agricultural or home economics services of agricultural extension program within group of counties: Determines methods and procedures or services and assigns tasks to workers according to extension program policies. Examines county methods and procedures to evaluate content and effectiveness of services within district. Delivers lectures to groups, such as commercial and community organizations, and directs county extension workers to deliver lectures to publicize and promote extension services activities. Reviews personnel data and recommends personnel action, such as hiring and discharging workers and adjusting salaries. Prepares, or assists in preparing, activity and planning reports and directs county exten-

sion workers to prepare reports. May formulate or assist in formulating budget requests to obtain operating funds. May be designated according to field of specialization as District Agricultural Agent (government ser.); District Home Economics Agent (government ser.).
GOE: 11.07.03 STRENGTH: S GED: R5 M3 L5 SVP: 8 DLU: 77

096.167-014 SPECIALIST-IN-CHARGE, EXTENSION SERVICE (government ser.)
Directs and coordinates activities of extension service specialists and develops educational programs in agriculture and home economics: Plans procedures and analyzes data for use by extension service specialists. Meets with specialists, volunteers, and other staff to discuss program problems and to disseminate information pertaining to practical applications of research findings in specific program areas. Coordinates activities of specialists to ensure program goals are met. Recruits and hires workers for specialized extension program services, and plans, organizes, and conducts training programs for new employees. Prepares activity, planning, and other reports, and maintains service records. Prepares or assists in preparation of budget requests.
GOE: 11.02.03 STRENGTH: S GED: R5 M3 L5 SVP: 8 DLU: 77

097 OCCUPATIONS IN VOCATIONAL EDUCATION

This group includes occupations concerned with research, administration, and teaching in vocational education.

097.167-010 DIRECTOR, VOCATIONAL TRAINING (education)
Directs and coordinates vocational training programs for public school system, according to board of education policies and state education code: Confers with members of industrial and business communities to determine human resource training needs for apprenticeable and nonapprenticeable occupations. Reviews and interprets federal and state vocational education codes to ensure that program conforms to legislation. Prepares budget and funding allocations for vocational programs. Reviews and approves new programs. Evaluates apprenticeable and nonapprenticeable programs, considering factors, such as selection, training, and placement of enrollees. Plans and develops joint programs in conjunction with other members of education staff. Organizes committees to provide technical and advisory assistance to programs. Coordinates on-the-job training programs with employers, and evaluates progress of enrollees in conjunction with program contract goals.
GOE: 11.07.03 STRENGTH: S GED: R5 M3 L5 SVP: 8 DLU: 77

097.221-010 INSTRUCTOR, VOCATIONAL TRAINING (education) alternate titles: teacher, vocational training
Teaches vocational training subjects to students in public or private schools or in industrial plants: Organizes program of practical and technical instruction, including demonstrations of skills required in trade, and lectures on theory, techniques, and terminology. Instructs students in subject areas, such as mathematics, science, drawing, use and maintenance of tools and equipment, codes or regulations related to trade, and safety precautions. Plans and supervises work of students, individually or in small groups, in shop or laboratory. Tests and evaluates achievement of student in technical knowledge and trade skills. May be identified according to trade or theory taught or type of establishment in which training is conducted, such as plumbing, electronics, or dental assistance. May place students in job training. May teach students with disabilities. May be required to have certification from state.
GOE: 11.02.02 STRENGTH: L GED: R4 M4 L4 SVP: 7 DLU: 81

097.227-010 INSTRUCTOR, FLYING II (education)
Instructs student pilots in flight procedures and techniques and in ground school courses: Develops and prepares course outlines, study materials, and instructional procedures for students enrolled in basic, advanced, or instrument ground school. Lectures on various subjects, such as aircraft construction, federal aviation regulations, and radio navigation. Demonstrates operation of various aircraft components and instruments, and techniques for controlling aircraft during maneuvers, such as taxiing, takeoff, and landing, using synthetic instrument trainers. Observes student's actions during training flights to ensure assimilation of classroom instruction and to comply with federal aviation regulations. Tests and evaluates students' progress, using written and performance tests and oral interviews. May teach advanced, basic, or instrument courses and be designated Ground Instructor, Advanced (education); Ground Instructor, Basic (education); Ground Instructor, Instrument (education). Must be certified by Federal Aviation Administration.
GOE: 05.04.01 STRENGTH: L GED: R4 M4 L3 SVP: 6 DLU: 77

099 OCCUPATIONS IN EDUCATION, N.E.C.

This group includes occupations in education, not elsewhere classified, concerned with research, administration, and teaching.

099.117-010 DIRECTOR, EDUCATIONAL PROGRAM (education)
Plans, develops, and administers programs to provide educational opportunities for students: Cooperates with business, civic, and other organizations to develop curriculums to meet needs and interests of students and community. Interviews and selects staff members and provides in-service training for teachers. Prepares budget and determines allocation of funds for staff, supplies and equipment, and facilities. Analyzes data from questionaires, interviews, and group discussions to evaluate curriculums, teaching methods, and community

participation in educational and other programs. May direct preparation of publicity to promote activities, such as personnel recruitment, educational programs or other services. May specialize in elementary, secondary, adult, or junior college education.

GOE: 11.07.03 STRENGTH: S GED: R5 M3 L5 SVP: 8 DLU: 77

099.117-014   EDUCATION SUPERVISOR, CORRECTIONAL INSTITUTION (education)

Plans and administers program of correlated academic, vocational, and social education in federal, state, or local correctional institution: Prepares courses of study and training materials designed to aid in rehabilitation process. Observes and advises instructors on improvements of methods and techniques. Institutes and directs vocational training programs for development of work habits, skills, and abilities. Conducts followup studies to evaluate effectiveness of academic and vocational training programs. Correlates educational programs with recreation program and other activities of institution and with parole program. Prepares budget requests for education programs, orders school supplies, and prepares records and reports. May supervise preparation of institutional publications. May be designated according to type of correctional facility as Education Supervisor, Penal Institution (education); Education Supervisor, Youth Authority (education).

GOE: 11.07.03 STRENGTH: S GED: R5 M3 L5 SVP: 8 DLU: 77

099.117-018   PRINCIPAL (education)

Directs and coordinates educational, administrative, and counseling activities of primary or secondary school: Develops and evaluates educational program to ensure conformance to state and school board standards. Develops and coordinates educational programs through meetings with staff, review of teachers' activities, and issuance of directives. Confers with teachers, students, and parents concerning educational and behavioral problems in school. Establishes and maintains relationships with colleges, community organizations, and other schools to coordinate educational services. Requisitions and allocates supplies, equipment, and instructional material as needed. Directs preparation of class schedules, cumulative records, and attendance reports. Observes and evaluates teacher performance. Interviews and hires teachers. Walks about school building and property to monitor safety and security. Plans and monitors school budget. May plan and direct building maintenance. May develop and administer educational programs for students with mental or physical handicaps. May be required to have certification from state.

GOE: 11.07.03 STRENGTH: L GED: R5 M3 L5 SVP: 8 DLU: 81

099.117-022   SUPERINTENDENT, SCHOOLS (education)

Directs and coordinates activities concerned with administration of city, county, or other school system in accordance with board of education standards: Formulates plans and policies for educational program and submits them to school board for approval. Administers program for selection of school sites, construction of buildings, and provision of equipment and supplies. Directs preparation and presentation of school budget and determines amount of school bond issues required to finance educational program. Addresses community and civic groups to enlist their support. Interprets program and policies of school system to school personnel, to individuals and community groups, and to governmental agencies. Coordinates work of school system with related activities of other school districts and agencies. May ensure that laws applying to attendance of children at school are enforced. May supervise examining, appointing, training, and promotion of teaching personnel. May specialize in areas, such as personnel services, curriculum development, or business administration.

GOE: 11.07.03 STRENGTH: S GED: R5 M3 L5 SVP: 9 DLU: 77

099.117-026   SUPERVISOR, EDUCATION (education)

Develops program curriculum and directs teaching personnel of school system: Confers with teaching and administrative staff to plan and develop curriculum designed to meet needs of students. Visits classrooms to observe effectiveness of instructional methods and material. Evaluates teaching techniques and recommends changes for improving them. Provides teachers with supplies, equipment, and visual and other instructional aids. Conducts workshops and conferences for teachers to study new classroom procedures, new instructional materials, and other aids to teaching. Assists in recruitment and in-service training of teachers. May be designated according to subject matter field or department administered as Supervisor, Adult Education (education); Supervisor, Agricultural Education (education); Supervisor, Elementary Education (education); Supervisor, Home Economics (education); Supervisor, Industrial Arts Education (education); Supervisor, Modern Languages (education); Supervisor, Trade And Industrial Education (education).

GOE: 11.07.03 STRENGTH: L GED: R5 M3 L5 SVP: 8 DLU: 77

099.117-030   DIRECTOR, EDUCATION (museums)

Plans, develops, and administers educational program of museum, zoo, or similar institution: Confers with administrative personnel to decide scope of program to be offered. Prepares schedules of classes and rough drafts of course content to determine number and background of instructors needed. Interviews, hires, trains, and evaluates work performance of education department staff. Contacts and arranges for services of guest lecturers from academic institutions, industry, and other establishments to augment education staff members in presentation of classes. Assists instructors in preparation of course descriptions and informational materials for publicity or distribution to class members. Prepares budget for education programs and directs maintenance of records of expenditures, receipts, and public and school participation in programs. Works with

other staff members to plan and present lecture series, film programs, field trips, and other special activities. May teach classes. May speak before school and community groups and appear on radio or television to promote institution programs. May coordinate institution educational activities with those of other area organizations to maximize utilization of resources. May train establishment volunteers to assist in presentation of classes or tours. May develop and submit program and activity grant proposals and applications and implement programs funded as result of successful applications.

GOE: 11.07.03 STRENGTH: S GED: R5 M4 L5 SVP: 7 DLU: 86

099.167-010   CERTIFICATION AND SELECTION SPECIALIST (education)

Interviews, examines, and evaluates qualifications of applicants for teaching positions in public school system, using guidelines established by school district and state education licensing codes: Reviews and evaluates construction of written examinations to ensure that questions meet district's testing standards. Confers with other members of staff in order to coordinate district's teacher recruiting efforts. Reviews transcripts and interviews candidates to ascertain qualifications for positions within district. Corrects and scores essay portions of examinations, utilizing knowledge of teaching methods. Authorizes preparation of paper work assigning teaching candidates to positions. Analyzes reports and statistical data on criteria used to select, examine, and recruit teaching staff to ensure that methods conform to predetermined policies, standards, and codes, and recommends procedure revisions as needed. Informs candidates of employment possibilities within district. May evaluate qualifications of candidates applying for other certificated positions within district.

GOE: 11.03.04 STRENGTH: S GED: R6 M5 L5 SVP: 8 DLU: 77

099.167-014   CONSULTANT, EDUCATION (education)

Plans and coordinates educational policies for specific subject area or grade level: Develops programs for in-service education of teaching personnel. Confers with federal, state, and local school officials to develop curricula and establish guidelines for educational programs. Confers with lay and professional groups to disseminate and receive input on teaching methods. Reviews and evaluates curricula for use in schools and assists in adaptation to local needs. Interprets and enforces provisions of state education codes and rules and regulations of State Board of Education. Conducts or participates in workshops, committees, and conferences designed to promote intellectual, social, and physical welfare of students. Studies and prepares recommendations on instructional materials, teaching aids, and related equipment. Prepares or approves manuals, guidelines, and reports on state educational policies and practices for distribution to school districts. Advises school officials on implementation of state and federal programs and procedures. Conducts research into areas, such as teaching methods and techniques. May perform tasks at local school district level or as independent consultant in area of expertise. May be designated as consultant in specific area, such as reading, elementary education, or audio-visual education.

GOE: 11.07.03 STRENGTH: S GED: R6 M6 L5 SVP: 8 DLU: 77

099.167-018   DIRECTOR, INSTRUCTIONAL MATERIAL (education)

Directs and coordinates preparation, development, and use of educational material in public school system: Confers with members of various educational committees and advisory groups to obtain knowledge of subject teaching areas, and to relate curriculum materials to specific subjects, individual student needs, and occupational areas. Coordinates activities of workers engaged in cataloging, distributing, and maintaining educational materials and equipment in curriculum library and laboratory. Reviews educational materials, such as video tapes, slides, and programmed texts, for educational content, and recommends acquisition of materials that meet district's standards. Advises staff members in techniques and methods of developing and evaluating specialized materials and instructional units. Organizes and implements use of new instructional systems. May train teachers and other staff in use of materials and equipment.

GOE: 11.07.03 STRENGTH: L GED: R5 M4 L5 SVP: 8 DLU: 77

099.167-022   EDUCATIONAL SPECIALIST (education) alternate titles: director, evaluation and research

Directs research activities concerned with educational programs and services in school system: Formulates and designs procedures to determine if program objectives are being met. Develops tests to measure effectiveness of curriculum or services and to interpret pupil intellectual and social development and group and school progress. Develops questionnaires and interviews school staff and administrators to obtain information about curriculum. Evaluates data obtained from study and prepares narrative and statistical reports for dissemination to school administrators. Formulates recommendations and procedures for current and proposed units of instruction. Develops in-service training program for staff. May devise questionnaire to evaluate training program. May specialize in research activities concerned with elementary, secondary, college, or other specialized educational programs. May evaluate staff performance. May plan budget.

GOE: 11.07.03 STRENGTH: S GED: R6 M5 L5 SVP: 8 DLU: 81

099.167-026   MUSIC SUPERVISOR (education)

Directs and coordinates activities of teaching personnel engaged in instructing students in vocal and instrumental music in school system: Consults with teaching and administrative staff to plan and develop music education curriculum. Observes, evaluates, and recommends changes in work of teaching staff to strengthen teaching skills in classroom. Analyzes music education program

to evaluate instructional methods and materials. Orders instructional materials, supplies, equipment, and visual aids designed to meet training needs of students. Authorizes purchase of musical instruments for school system. Inspects and authorizes repair of instruments. Establishes interschool orchestra, band, and choral group to represent schools at civic and community events.
GOE: 11.07.03 STRENGTH: S GED: R5 M2 L5 SVP: 8 DLU: 77

099.167-030 EDUCATIONAL RESOURCE COORDINATOR (museums)
Directs operation of educational resource center of museum, zoo, or similar establishment: Maintains collections of slides, video tapes, programmed texts, and other educational materials related to institution specialty, storing or filing materials according to subject matter, geographic or ethnic association, or historical period. Composes or directs others in composition of descriptions of materials, and prepares catalog listing materials for use of museum staff members, area school teachers, and others. Compiles list of books, periodicals, and other materials designed to augment items available in resource center. Explains storage and cataloging systems to teachers and others who visit center and suggests materials for various projects, such as preparing school classes for tour of institution or presentation of lecture for community group. Issues loan materials to teachers or lecturer, or schedules and coordinates delivery of materials to designated locations. Maintains records of loans and prepares circulation reports for review by administrative personnel. Conducts workshops to acquaint educators with use of institution's facilities and materials. Attends teacher meetings and conventions to promote use of institution services.
GOE: 11.07.03 STRENGTH: L GED: R5 M2 L5 SVP: 7 DLU: 86

099.167-034 DIRECTOR OF PUPIL PERSONNEL PROGRAM (education)
Directs pupil information data system program in support of educational services, in accordance with governmental laws and regulations for school district: Develops and maintains compliance program to meet legal requirements concerning students rights to privacy and due process of law in accordance to applicable laws and regulations. Directs and coordinates activities of clerical staff engaged in compiling, maintaining, and releasing pupil records and information. Confers with staff and reviews records management system to recommend changes to improve system, utilizing knowledge of filing methods and coding system, equipment, legal problems, and Board of Education requirements. Provides in-service training on topics, such as legal requirements concerning pupil records and information and to improve quality of report writing. Prepares departmental budget, records, and reports.
GOE: 11.07.03 STRENGTH: S GED: R5 M4 L5 SVP: 8 DLU: 86

099.223-010 INSTRUCTOR, DRIVING (education)
Instructs individuals and groups in theory and application of automobile driving skills: Demonstrates and explains handling of automobile in emergencies, driving techniques, and mechanical operation of automobile, using blackboard diagrams, audiovisual aids, and driving simulators. Observes individual's driving habits and reactions under various driving conditions to ensure conformance with vehicle operational standards and state vehicle code. May test hearing and vision of individuals, using lettered charts and colored lights. May teach motor vehicle regulations and insurance laws. May teach operation of vehicles other than automobile and be identified according to type of vehicle.
GOE: 09.03.03 STRENGTH: L GED: R4 M2 L3 SVP: 4 DLU: 77

099.224-010 INSTRUCTOR, PHYSICAL EDUCATION (education) alternate titles: teacher, physical education
Instructs students in physical education activities in educational institution: Plans physical education program to promote development of student's physical attributes and social skills. Teaches individual and team sports to students, utilizing knowledge of sports techniques and of physical capabilities of students. Organizes, leads, instructs, and referees indoor and outdoor games, such as volleyball, baseball, and basketball. Instructs individuals or groups in beginning or advanced calisthenics, gymnastics, or corrective exercises, determining type and level of difficulty of exercises, corrections needed, and prescribed movements, applying knowledge of sports, physiology, and corrective techniques. Teaches and demonstrates use of gymnastic and training apparatus, such as trampolines and weights. Confers with students, parents, and school counselor to resolve student problem. May select, store, order, issue, and inventory equipment, materials, and supplies used in physical education program. May specialize in instructing specific sport, such as tennis, swimming, or basketball. May teach students with disabilities. May be required to have certification from state.
GOE: 11.02.01 STRENGTH: L GED: R5 M3 L5 SVP: 7 DLU: 81

099.224-014 TEACHER, ADVENTURE EDUCATION (education)
Instructs and leads students in variety of stressful and challenging activities, such as rock climbing, canoeing, spelunking, and skiing to build student confidence and promote physical, mental, and social development: Appraises students' tolerance to stress and selects and structures learning environment that provides for success in activities appropriate to maturity, interests, and abilities of students. Demonstrates basic skills, safety precautions, and other techniques to prepare students for activities. Arranges for provisions, such as transportation, food, and equipment. Teaches camping and related outdoor skills to students, staff, and volunteers.
GOE: 10.02.03 STRENGTH: M GED: R5 M4 L5 SVP: 7 DLU: 86

099.227-010 CHILDREN'S TUTOR (domestic ser.)
Cares for children in private home, overseeing their recreation, diet, health, and deportment: Teaches children foreign languages, and good health and per-

sonal habits. Arranges parties, outings, and picnics for children. Takes disciplinary measures to control children's behavior. Ascertains cause of behavior problems of children and devises means for solving them. When duties are confined to care of young children may be designated Children's Tutor, Nursery (domestic ser.).
GOE: 10.03.03 STRENGTH: L GED: R4 M2 L4 SVP: 5 DLU: 77

099.227-014 INSTRUCTOR, CORRESPONDENCE SCHOOL (education)
Plans course of study for students enrolled in correspondence courses to obtain high school, college, or other specialized subject area instruction: Reviews enrollment applications and oversees mailing of course materials to students. Corrects, grades, and comments on lesson assignments submitted by students. Corresponds with students to answer questions pertaining to course.
GOE: 11.02.01 STRENGTH: S GED: R5 M3 L5 SVP: 7 DLU: 77

099.227-018 INSTRUCTOR, GROUND SERVICES (air trans.)
Conducts classroom instruction, on-the-job training, and orientation sessions for new and experienced ground personnel on various subjects, such as aircraft and station familiarization, company policies and procedures, and specific job duties: Develops and prepares course outlines, instructional procedures, and study materials for nontechnical occupations in such areas as airfreight, customer services load planning, ramp services, reservations, and ticketing. Presents course material through use of audiovisual aids, classroom lectures, on-the-job training, and printed handouts. Tests student's progress, using oral interviews, written examinations, and performance tests to ascertain comprehension of subject matter. Prepares reports of attendance, grades, and training activities. Keeps records of training accomplishments and confers with supervisory personnel regarding training needs. Conducts recurrent on-the-job training or classroom instruction to acquaint experienced workers with changing procedures or with use of new equipment. Coordinates training activities with local station manager. May conduct special training programs in company and industry procedures, regulations, rules, and techniques relating to passenger travel for workers employed by travel agencies.
GOE: 11.02.02 STRENGTH: L GED: R5 M3 L5 SVP: 7 DLU: 77

099.227-022 INSTRUCTOR, MILITARY SCIENCE (education)
Teaches military subjects, such as employment and deployment of weapons systems, military aspects of geopolitics, and defense concepts in public and private secondary schools and colleges and universities offering Reserve Officers' Training program. Specializes in teaching subjects concerned with particular branch of military tactics, such as aerospace science, naval science, or military science.
GOE: 11.02.01 STRENGTH: S GED: R5 M3 L5 SVP: 9 DLU: 77

099.227-026 INSTRUCTOR, MODELING (education)
Instructs individuals and groups in techniques and methods of self-improvement, utilizing principles of modeling, such as visual poise, wardrobe coordination, and cosmetic application: Analyzes appearance of individual to determine self-improvement considering factors, such as figure, complexion, and body posture. Explains and demonstrates methods and techniques of self-improvement. Observes student, such as ascending and descending stairs, walking, and in cosmetic application sessions to ensure comformance to classroom instruction. Instructs students in selecting and coordinating wardrobe.
GOE: 01.08.01 STRENGTH: L GED: R4 M2 L4 SVP: 4 DLU: 77

099.227-030 TEACHER, ADULT EDUCATION (education)
Instructs out-of-school youths and adults in academic and nonacademic courses in public or private schools or other organizations: Prepares outline of instructional program and studies and assembles material to be presented. Presents lectures and discussions to group to increase students' knowledge or vocational competence. Tests and grades students on achievement in class. Teaches courses, such as citizenship, fine arts, and homemaking, to enrich students' cultural and academic backgrounds. Conducts workshops and demonstrations to teach such skills as driving, sports, and dancing, or to provide training for parenthood. May teach basic courses in American history, principles, ideas, and customs and in English to foreign-born and be designated Teacher, Citizenship (education).
GOE: 11.02.01 STRENGTH: L GED: R4 M2 L4 SVP: 7 DLU: 77

099.227-034 TUTOR (education)
Teaches academic subjects, such as English, mathematics, and foreign languages to pupils requiring private instruction, adapting curriculum to meet individual's needs. May teach in pupil's home.
GOE: 11.02.01 STRENGTH: L GED: R5 M3 L5 SVP: 7 DLU: 77

099.227-038 TEACHER (museums)
Teaches classes, presents lectures, conducts workshops, and participates in other activities to further educational program of museum, zoo, or similar institution: Plans course content and method of presentation, and prepares outline of material to be covered and submits it for approval. Selects and assembles materials to be used in teaching assignment, such as pieces of pottery or samples of plant life, and arranges use of audiovisual equipment or other teaching aids. Conducts classes for children in various scientific, history, or art subjects, utilizing museum displays to augment standard teaching methods and adapting course content and complexity to ages and interests of students. Teaches adult classes in such subjects as art, history, astronomy, or horticulture, using audiovisual aids, demonstration, or laboratory techniques appropriate to subject matter. Presents series of lectures on subjects related to institution collections, often

incorporating films or slides into presentation. Conducts seminars or workshops for school system teachers or lay persons to demonstrate methods of using institution facilities and collections to enhance school programs or to enrich other activities. Conducts workshops or field trips for students or community groups and plans and directs activities associated with projects. Plans and presents vacation or weekend programs for elementary or preschool children, combining recreational activities with teaching methods geared to age groups. Conducts classes for academic credit in cooperation with area schools or universities. Teaches courses in museum work to participants in work-study programs. Works with adult leaders of youth groups to assist youths to earn merit badges or fulfill other group requirements. Maintains records of attendance. Evaluates success of courses, basing evaluation on number and enthusiasm of persons participating and recommends retaining or dropping course in future plans. When course is offered for academic credit, evaluates class member performances, administers tests, and issues grades in accordance with methods used by cooperating educational institution.
GOE: 11.02.01 STRENGTH: L GED: R5 M4 L5 SVP: 7 DLU: 86

099.227-042 TEACHER, RESOURCE (education)
  Teaches basic academic subjects to students requiring remedial work, using special help programs to improve scholastic level: Teaches basic subjects, such as reading and math, applying lesson techniques designed for short attention spans. Administers achievement tests and evaluates test results to discover level of language and math skills. Selects and teaches reading material and math problems related to everyday life of individual student. Confers with school counselors and teaching staff to obtain additional testing information and to gain insight on student behavioral disorders affecting learning process. Designs special help programs for low achievers and encourages parent-teacher cooperation. Attends professional meetings, writes reports, and maintains records.
GOE: 11.02.01 STRENGTH: L GED: R5 M5 L5 SVP: 7 DLU: 86

099.327-010 TEACHER AIDE I (education) alternate titles: teacher assistant
  Performs any combination of following instructional tasks in classroom to assist teaching staff of public or private elementary or secondary school: Discusses assigned teaching area with classroom teacher to coordinate instructional efforts. Prepares lesson outline and plan in assigned area and submits outline to teacher for review. Plans, prepares, and develops various teaching aids, such as bibliographies, charts, and graphs. Presents subject matter to students, utilizing variety of methods and techniques, such as lecture, discussion, and supervised role playing. Prepares, administers, and grades examinations. Assists students, individually or in groups, with lesson assignments to present or reinforce learning concepts. Confers with parents on progress of students. May specialize in single subject area. May be required to have completed specified number of college education credits.
GOE: 11.02.01 STRENGTH: L GED: R4 M3 L4 SVP: 6 DLU: 86

10 OCCUPATIONS IN MUSEUM, LIBRARY, AND ARCHIVAL SCIENCES

  This division includes occupations concerned with library and archival sciences, including public and private libraries and archives, and with maintaining museums, galleries, and related exhibits.

100 LIBRARIANS

  This group includes occupations concerned with administering libraries and performing related library services. Includes selecting, acquiring, cataloging, classifying, circulating, and maintaining library materials; furnishing reference, bibliographical, and reader's advisory services.

100.117-010 LIBRARY DIRECTOR (library) alternate titles: librarian, head
  Plans and administers program of library services: Submits recommendations on library policies and services to governing body, such as board of directors or board of trustees, and implements policy decisions. Analyzes, selects, and executes recommendations of personnel, such as department chiefs or branch supervisors. Coordinates activities of branch or departmental libraries. Analyzes and coordinates departmental budget estimates and controls expenditures to administer approved budget. Reviews and evaluates orders for books and audiovisual materials. Examines trade publications and materials, interviews publishers' representatives, and consults with others to select materials. Administers personnel regulations, interviews and appoints job applicants, rates staff performance, and promotes and discharges employees. Plans and conducts staff meetings and participates in community and professional meetings to discuss and act on library problems. Delivers book reviews and lectures to publicize library activities and services. Provides library public relations services. May examine and select materials to be discarded, repaired, or replaced. May be designated according to governmental subdivision served as City-Library Director (library); County-Library Director (library).
GOE: 11.07.04 STRENGTH: S GED: R6 M4 L5 SVP: 8 DLU: 81

100.117-014 LIBRARY CONSULTANT (library)
  Advises administrators of public libraries: Analyzes administrative policies, observes work procedures, and reviews data relative to book collections to determine effectiveness of library service to public. Compares allocations for

building funds, salaries, and book collections with statewide and national standards, to determine effectiveness of fiscal operations. Gathers statistical data, such as population and community growth rates, and analyzes building plans to determine adequacy of programs for expansion. Prepares evaluation of library systems based on observations and surveys, and recommends measures to improve organization and administration of systems.
GOE: 11.07.04 STRENGTH: S GED: R6 M4 L6 SVP: 8 DLU: 86

100.127-010 CHIEF LIBRARIAN, BRANCH OR DEPARTMENT (library) alternate titles: principal librarian; senior librarian; supervising librarian
  Coordinates activities of library branch or department, and assists patrons in selection and location of books, audiovisual materials, and other materials: Trains and directs workers in performance of such tasks as receiving, shelving, and locating materials. Examines book reviews, publishers' catalogs, and other information sources to recommend material acquisition. Searches catalog files, biographical dictionaries, and indexes, and examines content of reference materials to assist patrons in locating and selecting materials. May assemble and arrange materials for display. May prepare replies to mail requests for information. May be designated according to type of library as Chief Librarian, Branch (library); or according to department as Chief Librarian, Circulation Department (library); Chief Librarian, Extension Department (library); Chief Librarian, General Reference Department (library); Chief Librarian, Music Department (library); Chief Librarian, Periodical Reading Room (library); Chief Librarian, Readers' Advisory Service (library); Chief Librarian, Work With Blind (library).
GOE: 11.07.04 STRENGTH: L GED: R5 M3 L5 SVP: 7 DLU: 77

100.127-014 LIBRARIAN (library)
  Maintains library collections of books, serial publications, documents, audiovisual, and other materials, and assists groups and individuals in locating and obtaining materials: Furnishes information on library activities, facilities, rules, and services. Explains and assists in use of reference sources, such as card or book catalog or book and periodical indexes to locate information. Describes or demonstrates procedures for searching catalog files. Searches catalog files and shelves to locate information. Issues and receives materials for circulation or for use in library. Assembles and arranges displays of books and other library materials. Maintains reference and circulation materials. Answers correspondence on special reference subjects. May compile list of library materials according to subject or interests, using computer. May select, order, catalog, and classify materials . May prepare or assist in preparation of budget. May plan and direct or carry out special projects involving library promotion and outreach activity and be designated Outreach Librarian (library). May be designated according to specialized function as Circulation Librarian (library); Readers'-Advisory-Service Librarian (library); or Reference Librarian (library).
GOE: 11.02.04 STRENGTH: L GED: R5 M3 L4 SVP: 7 DLU: 81

100.167-010 AUDIOVISUAL LIBRARIAN (library) alternate titles: film librarian; recordings librarian
  Plans audiovisual programs and administers library of film and other audiovisual materials: Assists patrons in selection of materials, utilizing knowledge of collections. Advises other library personnel on audiovisual materials and appropriate selection for particular needs and uses. Establishes and maintains contact with major film distributors and resources for procurement of tapes and cassettes. Evaluates materials, considering their technical, informational, and aesthetic qualities, and selects materials for library collections. Prepares summaries of acquisitions for catalog. Prepares and arranges audiovisual programs for presentation to groups and may lead discussions after film showings. Advises those planning audiovisual programs on technical problems, such as acoustics, lighting, and program content. Evaluates audiovisual equipment and gives advice in selection of equipment, considering factors, such as. intended use, quality, and price. May advise in planning and layout of physical facilities for audiovisual services. May operate film projectors, splicers, rewinders, film inspection equipment, and tape and record playing equipment. May train personnel in operation and maintenance of audiovisual equipment. May select, procure, and maintain framed art prints collection.
GOE: 11.02.04 STRENGTH: L GED: R5 M3 L3 SVP: 7 DLU: 77

100.167-014 BOOKMOBILE LIBRARIAN (library)
  Provides library services from mobile library within given geographical area: Surveys needs and selects books and materials for library. Publicizes visits to area to stimulate reading interest. May prepare special collections for schools and other groups. May arrange bookmobile schedule. May drive bookmobile.
GOE: 11.02.04 STRENGTH: L GED: R4 M3 L4 SVP: 7 DLU: 77

100.167-018 CHILDREN'S LIBRARIAN (library)
  Manages library program for children: Selects books and audiovisual materials of interest to children to be acquired by library. Assists children in selecting and locating library materials. Plans and conducts programs for children to encourage reading, viewing, and listening and use of library materials and facilities. Confers with teachers, parents, and community groups to assist in developing programs to encourage and improve children's communication skills. Compiles lists of materials of interest to children. Activities may include story telling, book talks, puppet shows, and film and multimedia programs.
GOE: 11.02.04 STRENGTH: L GED: R5 M3 L5 SVP: 7 DLU: 77

100.167-022 INSTITUTION LIBRARIAN (library) alternate titles: hospital librarian; patient's librarian; prison librarian
  Plans and directs library program for residents and staff of extended care facilities, such as mental institutions, correctional institutions, or institutions for

physically handicapped or mentally retarded: Develops library policies and programs and prepares operational budgets. Selects, acquires, and organizes library materials for convenient access. Provides readers' advisory services on basis of knowledge of current reviews and bibliographies. Reviews requests, and selects books and other library materials according to mental state, educational background, and special needs of residents. Assembles book reviews for institution's bulletins or newspapers, and circulates reviews among residents. Provides handicapped or bedridden residents with reading aids, such as prism glasses, page turners, bookstands, or talking books, and with phonograph records.
GOE: 11.02.04 STRENGTH: L GED: R5 M4 L5 SVP: 7 DLU: 80

100.167-026 LIBRARIAN, SPECIAL LIBRARY (library)

Manages library or section containing specialized materials for industrial, commercial, or governmental organizations, or for such institutions as schools and hospitals: Selects, orders, catalogs, and classifies special collections of technical books, manufacturers' catalogs and specifications, periodicals, magazines, newspapers, audio-visual material, microforms, journal reprints, and other materials. Searches literature, compiles accession lists, and annotates or abstracts materials. Assists patrons in research problems. May key information into computer to store or search for selected material. May translate or order translation of materials from foreign languages into English. May train other workers engaged in cataloguing, locating, filing, or copying selected material. May be designated according to subject matter, specialty or library, or department as Art Librarian (library); Business Librarian (library); Engineering Librarian (library); Law Librarian (library); Map Librarian (library); Medical Librarian (library).
GOE: 11.02.04 STRENGTH: L GED: R5 M4 L5 SVP: 8 DLU: 81

100.167-030 MEDIA SPECIALIST, SCHOOL LIBRARY (library) alternate titles: librarian, school; media center director, school

Assesses and meets needs of students and faculty for information, and develops programs to stimulate students' interests in reading and use of types of resources: Selects and organizes books, films, tapes, records, and other materials and equipment. Suggests appropriate books to students for classroom assignments and personal readings. Plans and carries out program of instruction in use by school library media center. Prepares and administers budget for media center. Confers with faculty to provide materials for classroom instruction. Confers with parents, faculty, public librarians, and community organizations to develop programs to enrich students' communications skills. Reviews records to compile lists of overdue materials and notifies borrowers to arrange for their return.
GOE: 11.02.04 STRENGTH: L GED: R5 M3 L5 SVP: 8 DLU: 80

100.167-034 YOUNG-ADULT LIBRARIAN (library)

Plans and conducts library program to provide special services for young adults: Selects books and audiovisual materials of interest to young adults to be acquired by library. Assists young adults in selecting materials. Plans and organizes young adult activities, such as film programs, chess clubs, creative writing clubs, and photography contests. Delivers talks on books to stimulate reading. Compiles lists of library materials of interest to young adults. Confers with parents, teachers, and community organizations to assist in developing programs to stimulate reading and develop communication skills.
GOE: 11.02.04 STRENGTH: L GED: R5 M2 L5 SVP: 7 DLU: 77

100.167-038 NEWS LIBRARIAN (library) alternate titles: news information resource manager; news library director; newspaper library manager

Manages information resources library stored in files, on tape or microfilm, or in computers for use by news and editorial staff in publishing establishments, such as newspaper and magazine publishers, and in broadcasting establishments, such as radio and television stations: Directs activities of workers engaged in clipping, classifying, cataloging, indexing, storing, editing, and retrieving library information, or performs these activities as needed. Researches, retrieves, and disseminates information in resource library or commercial data bases in response to requests from news or editorial staff, using knowledge of classification system or computer data base. Maintains records and statistics on use of data bases and information services provided. May manage in-house data base of news information, assign classification terms to news articles, input news articles into data base, and research news information in in-house data base. May develop data bases for data storage and retrieval, according to needs of news staff. May hire, train, schedule, and evaluate library staff. May prepare library budgets. May promote and market library products and services to public. May coordinate activities of library with activities of other departments. May select and purchase reference books for library collection. May manage graphics library, assign classification terms to graphics, and research graphics and be designated Photo-Graphics Librarian (library).
GOE: 11.02.04 STRENGTH: L GED: R5 M4 L5 SVP: 7 DLU: 90

100.267-010 ACQUISITIONS LIBRARIAN (library)

Selects and orders books, periodicals, films, and other materials for library: Reviews publishers' announcements and catalogs, and compiles list of publications to be purchased. Compares selections with card catalog and orders-in-process to avoid duplication. Circulates selection lists to branches and departments for comments. Selects vendors on basis of such factors as discount allowance and delivery dates. Compiles statistics on purchases, such as total purchases, average price, and fund allocations. May recommend acquisition of materials from individuals or organizations or by exchange with other libraries.
GOE: 11.02.04 STRENGTH: L GED: R4 M3 L4 SVP: 6 DLU: 77

100.267-014 LIBRARIAN, SPECIAL COLLECTIONS (library)

Collects and organizes books, pamphlets, manuscripts, and other materials on select subjects to be used for research: Organizes collections according to field of interest. Examines reference works and consults specialists preparatory to selecting materials for collections. Compiles bibliographies. Appraises books, using references, such as bibliographies, book auction records, and special catalogs on incunabula (printing prior to 1500). Publishes papers and bibliographies on special collections to notify scholars of available materials. Lectures on booklore, such as history of printing, bindings, and illuminations. May plan and arrange displays for library exhibits. May index and reproduce materials for sale to other libraries.
GOE: 11.02.04 STRENGTH: L GED: R5 M2 L5 SVP: 8 DLU: 77

100.367-010 BIBLIOGRAPHER (profess. & kin.)

Compiles lists of books, periodical articles, and audiovisual materials, on specialized subjects. Annotates bibliographies with physical description and analysis of subject content of materials. Recommends acquisition of materials in specialized subject.
GOE: 11.02.04 STRENGTH: S GED: R4 M2 L4 SVP: 7 DLU: 77

100.367-014 CLASSIFIER (library)

Classifies library materials, such as books, audiovisual materials, and periodicals, according to subject matter: Reviews materials to be classified and searches information sources, such as book reviews, encyclopedias, and technical publications to determine subject matter of materials. Selects classification numbers and descriptive headings according to Dewey Decimal, Library of Congress, or other classification systems. Makes sample cards containing author, title, and classification number to guide CATALOG LIBRARIAN (library) in preparing catalog cards for books and periodicals. Assigns classification numbers, descriptive headings, and explanatory summaries to book and catalog cards to facilitate locating and obtaining materials. Composes annotations (explanatory summaries) of material content.
GOE: 11.02.04 STRENGTH: L GED: R4 M3 L4 SVP: 6 DLU: 77

100.367-018 LIBRARY TECHNICAL ASSISTANT (library) alternate titles: library assistant; library technician

Provides information service, such as answering questions regarding card catalogs, and assists public in use of bibliographic tools, such as Library of Congress catalog: Performs routine descriptive cataloging, such as fiction and children's literature. Files cards in catalog drawers according to system used. Answers routine inquiries, and refers persons requiring professional assistance to LIBRARIAN (library). Verifies bibliographic information on order requests. Directs activities of workers in maintenance of stacks or in section of department or division, such as ordering or receiving section of acquisitions department, card preparation activities in catalog department, or limited loan or reserve desk operation of circulation department.
GOE: 11.02.04 STRENGTH: L GED: R4 M3 L3 SVP: 5 DLU: 77

100.367-022 MUSIC LIBRARIAN (radio-tv broad.) alternate titles: librarian; music director

Classifies and files musical recordings, sheet music, original arrangements, and scores for individual instruments. Selects music for subject matter of program or for specific visual or spoken action. Suggests musical selections to DIRECTOR, MUSIC (motion picture; radio-tv broad.) 152.047-018 or DIRECTOR, PROGRAM (radio-tv broad.) 184.167-030 or DISK JOCKEY (radio-tv broad.) 159.147-014. May issue music required music to CONDUCTOR, ORCHESTRA (profess. & kin.) 152.047-014, or other studio personnel. May track musical selections broadcasted, using computer. May listen to music, using playback equipment, to verify quality of recordings meet broadcast standards.
GOE: 11.02.04 STRENGTH: L GED: R4 M2 L4 SVP: 6 DLU: 89

100.367-026 MUSIC LIBRARIAN, INTERNATIONAL BROADCAST (radio-tv broad.)

Maintains script archive and music library used for preparing programs for foreign broadcast, utilizing knowledge of foreign languages and of listening tastes of people of foreign countries. Compiles statistical and financial library reports.
GOE: 11.02.04 STRENGTH: S GED: R4 M3 L4 SVP: 6 DLU: 77

100.387-010 CATALOG LIBRARIAN (library) alternate titles: cataloger; descriptive catalog librarian

Compiles information on library materials, such as books and periodicals, and prepares catalog cards to identify materials and to integrate information into library catalog: Verifies author, title, and classification number on sample catalog card received from CLASSIFIER (library) against corresponding data on title page. Fills in additional information, such as publisher, date of publication, and edition. Examines material and notes additional information, such as bibliographies, illustrations, maps, and appendices. Copies classification number from sample card into library material for identification. Files cards into assigned sections of catalog. Tabulates number of sample cards according to quantity of material and catalog subject headings to determine amount of new cards to be ordered or reproduced. Prepares inventory card to record purchase information and location of library material. Requisitions additional cards. Records new information, such as death date of author and revised edition date, to amend cataloged cards. May supervise activities of other workers in unit.

GOE: 11.02.04 STRENGTH: L GED: R4 M2 L4 SVP: 5 DLU: 77

101 ARCHIVISTS

This group includes occupations concerned with collecting, evaluating, systemizing, preserving, and making available for reference public records and documents of historical significance.

101.167-010 ARCHIVIST (profess. & kin.)
Appraises and edits permanent records and historically valuable documents, participates in research activities based on archival materials, and directs safekeeping of archival documents and materials: Analyzes documents, such as government records, minutes of corporate board meetings, letters from famous persons, and charters of nonprofit foundations, by ascertaining date of writing, author, or original recipient of letter, to appraise value to posterity or to employing organization. Directs activities of workers engaged in cataloging and safekeeping of valuable materials and directs disposition of worthless materials. Prepares or directs preparation of document descriptions and reference aids for use of archives, such as accession lists, indexes, guides, bibliographies, abstracts, and microfilmed copies of documents. Directs filing and cross indexing of selected documents in alphabetical and chronological order. Advises government agencies, scholars, journalists, and others conducting research by supplying available materials and information according to familiarity with archives and with political, economic, military, and social history of period. Requests or recommends pertinent materials available in libraries, private colllections, or other archives. Selects and edits documents for publication and display, according to knowledge of subject, literary or journalistic expression, and techniques for presentation and display. May be designated according to subject matter specialty as Archivist, Economic History (profess. & kin.); Archivist, Military History (profess. & kin.); Archivist, Political History (profess. & kin.); or according to nature of employing institution as Archivist, Nonprofit Foundation (nonprofit organ.). In smaller organizations, may direct activities of libraries.
GOE: 11.03.03 STRENGTH: S GED: R5 M3 L5 SVP: 8 DLU: 77

102 MUSEUM CURATORS AND RELATED OCCUPATIONS

This group includes occupations concerned with administering museums, art galleries, arboreta, historical sites, and botanical and zoological gardens, and performing related services. Includes activities in collecting, authenticating, preserving, maintaining, exhibiting, researching, and furnishing information on collections of historical, artistic, scientific, or technological significance or of general public interest.

102.017-010 CURATOR (museums)
Directs and coordinates activities of workers engaged in operating exhibiting institution, such as museum, botanical garden, arboretum, art gallery, herbarium, or zoo: Directs activities concerned with instructional, acquisition, exhibitory, safekeeping, research, and public service objectives of institution. Assists in formulating and interpreting administrative policies of institution. Formulates plans for special research projects. Oversees curatorial, personnel, fiscal, technical, research, and clerical staff. Administers affairs of institution by corresponding and negotiating with administrators of other institutions to obtain exchange of loan collections or to exchange information or data, maintaining inventories, preparing budget, representing institution at scientific or association conferences, soliciting support for institution, and interviewing and hiring personnel. Obtains, develops, and organizes new collections to expand and improve educational and research facilities. Writes articles for publication in scientific journals. Consults with board of directors and professional personnel to plan and implement acquisitional, research, display and public service activities of institution. May participate in research activities. May be designated according to field of specialization as Curator, Art Gallery (museums); Curator, Herbarium (museums); Curator, Horticultural Museum (museums); Curator, Medical Museum (museums); Curator, Natural History Museum (museums); Curator, Zoological Museum (museums); Director, Industrial Museum (museums).
GOE: 11.07.04 STRENGTH: L GED: R6 M5 L6 SVP: 9 DLU: 77

102.117-010 SUPERVISOR, HISTORIC SITES (government ser.)
Directs and coordinates activities of personnel engaged in investigating, acquiring, marking, improving, and preserving historic sites and natural phenomena in conformity with state policy. Authorizes acquisition and improvement of sites, such as historic homes and battlefields, within allocated budget. Recommends appropriation of additional funds where necessary to purchase or restore landmarks. Negotiates with representatives of local governments, philanthropic organizations, and other interested groups to acquire properties. Provides information and encouragement to private individuals or civic groups attempting to acquire and maintain landmarks not considered feasible for state acquisition. Directs or participates in archeological research efforts in state parks. Directs design, preparation, and installation of museum exhibits and historical markers. Directs workers engaged in preparation of brochures, exhibits, maps, photographs, and similar materials to stimulate public interest in visiting sites. Serves as custodian of historic documents acquired during research efforts.
GOE: 11.05.03 STRENGTH: L GED: R5 M4 L5 SVP: 7 DLU: 77

102.117-014 DIRECTOR, MUSEUM-OR-ZOO (museums)
Administers affairs of museum, zoo, or similar establishment: Confers with institution's board of directors to formulate policies and plan overall operations.

Directs acquisition, education, research, public service, and development activities of institution, consulting with curatorial, administrative, and maintenance staff members to implement policies and initiate programs. Works with members of curatorial and administrative staffs to acquire additions to collections. Confers with administrative staff members to determine budget requirements, plan fund raising drives, prepare applications for grants from government agencies or private foundations, and solicit financial support for institution. Establishes and maintains contact with administrators of other institutions to exchange information concerning operations and plan, coordinate, or consolidate community service and education programs. Represents institution at professional and civic social events, conventions, and other gatherings to strengthen relationships with cultural and civic leaders, present lectures or participate in seminars, or explain institution's functions and seek financial support for projects. Reviews materials prepared by staff members, such as articles for journals, requests for grants, and reports on institution programs, and approves materials or suggests changes. Instructs classes in institution's education program or as guest lecturer at university. Writes articles for technical journals or other publications.
GOE: 11.02.01 STRENGTH: S GED: R6 M4 L6 SVP: 8 DLU: 86

102.167-010 ART CONSERVATOR (museums)
Coordinates activities of subordinates engaged in examination, repair, and conservation of art objects: Examines art objects to determine condition, need for repair, method of preservation, and authenticity, using x rays, radiographs, and special lights. Directs curatorial and technical staffs on handling, mounting, care, and storage of art objects. Estimates cost of restoration work.
GOE: 01.06.02 STRENGTH: L GED: R5 M4 L4 SVP: 8 DLU: 77

102.167-014 HISTORIC-SITE ADMINISTRATOR (museums)
Manages operation of historic structure or site: Discusses house or site operation with governing body representatives to form or change policies. Oversees activities of building and grounds maintenance staff and other employees. Maintains roster of volunteer guides, and contacts volunteers to conduct tours of premises according to schedule. Conducts tours, explaining points of interest and answers visitors' questions. Studies documents, books, and other materials to obtain information concerning history of site or structure. Conducts classes in tour presentation methods for volunteer guides. Accepts group reservations for house tours and special social events. Arranges for refreshments, entertainment, and decorations for special events. Collects admission and special event fees, and maintains records of receipts, expenses, and numbers of persons served. Assists in planning publicity, and arranges for printing of brochures or placement of information in media. Inspects premises for evidence of deterioration and need for repair, and notifies governing body of such need.
GOE: 11.02.01 STRENGTH: L GED: R5 M4 L5 SVP: 5 DLU: 86

102.167-018 REGISTRAR, MUSEUM (museums)
Maintains records of accession, condition, and location of objects in museum collection, and oversees movement, packing, and shipping of objects to conform to insurance regulations: Observes unpacking of objects acquired by museum through gift, purchase, or loan to determine that damage or deterioration to objects has not occurred. Registers and assigns accession and catalog numbers to all objects in collection, according to established registration system. Composes concise description of objects, and records descriptions on file cards and in collection catalogs. Oversees handling, packing, movement, and inspection of all objects entering or leaving establishment, including traveling exhibits, and confers with other personnel to develop and initiate most practical methods of packing and shipping fragile or valuable objects. Maintains records of storage, exhibit, and loan locations of all objects in collection for use of establishment personnel, insurance representatives, and other persons utilizing facilities. Prepares acquisition reports for review of curatorial and administrative staff. Periodically reviews and evaluates registration and catalog system to maintain applicability, consistency, and operation. Recommends changes in recordkeeping procedures to achieve maximum accessibility to and efficient retrieval of collection objects. Arranges for insurance of objects on loan or special exhibition, or recommends insurance coverage on parts of or entire collection.
GOE: 07.01.02 STRENGTH: S GED: R5 M4 L5 SVP: 6 DLU: 86

102.261-010 CONSERVATION TECHNICIAN (museums)
Repairs and cleans art objects, such as pottery, statuary, etchings, or tapestries, to restore art objects' natural appearance: Studies descriptive information on object or conducts standard chemical and physical tests to determine such factors as age, composition, and original appearance, and plans methods or procedures for restoring object. Cleans object or broken pieces, using such methods as scraping and applying solvents to metal objects; washing statuary, using soap solutions; or cleaning and polishing furniture and silver objects. Repairs objects, using glue or solder, to assemble broken pieces, buffing assembled object where repaired, or repainting faded or incomplete designs with paint of same chemical composition and color in order to restore original appearance. Notifies superior when problem of restoration requires outside experts. Fabricates or repairs picture frames for paintings, using handtools and power tools and machines. Mounts pictures in frames.
GOE: 01.06.02 STRENGTH: M GED: R4 M4 L4 SVP: 6 DLU: 77

102.261-014 PAINTINGS RESTORER (profess. & kin.) alternate titles: paintings conservator
Restores damaged and faded paintings and preserves paintings, using techniques based on knowledge of art and art materials: Examines surfaces of paint

82

ing, using magnifying device, and performs tests to determine factors, such as age, structure, pigment stability, and probable reaction to various cleaning agents and solvents. Removes painting from frame. Applies select solvents and cleaning agents and uses predetermined method to clean surface of painting and remove accretions, discolorations, and deteriorated varnish. Stretches new linen backing, applies paste material to back of painting, and laminates parts together, using laminating press. Dries laminated painting under controlled conditions to prevent shrinkage. Applies beeswax or other substance to damaged or faded areas where restoration is needed. Studies style, techniques, colors, textures, and materials used by artist to maintain consistency in reconstruction or retouching procedures. Reconstructs or retouches damaged areas and blends area into adjacent areas to restore painting to original condition. Applies varnish or other preservative to surface of painting and dries under controlled conditions. May remove paint layer from backing and remount on canvas, wood, or metal support using pressure and special adhesives. May apply neutral color powder to damaged areas to restore areas.
GOE: 01.02.02 STRENGTH: L GED: R5 M4 L4 SVP: 8 DLU: 77

102.361-010 RESTORER, LACE AND TEXTILES (museums)
Restores and prepares ancient textile and lace materials for display in textile museum: Cleans fabric, using cleaning compounds and techniques based on historical knowledge of fabric manufacture and effect of cleaning upon fabric. Develops new cleaning compounds and methods when available means are inadequate or tend to harm fabric. Repairs and reweaves worn, torn, and decayed fabrics, using techniques based on knowledge of weaving and lace methods. Mounts fabric in frame or other suitable background.
GOE: 01.06.02 STRENGTH: M GED: R5 M4 L4 SVP: 7 DLU: 77

102.361-014 RESTORER, CERAMIC (museums)
Cleans, preserves, restores, and repairs objects made of glass, porcelain, china, fired clay, and other ceramic materials: Coats excavated objects with surface-active agents to loosen adhering mud or clay and washes objects with clear water. Places cleaned objects in dilute hydrochloric acid or other solution to remove remaining deposits of lime or chalk, basing choice of solution on knowledge of physical and chemical structure of objects and destructive qualities of solvents. Cleans glass, porcelain, or similar objects by such methods as soaking objects in lukewarm water with ammonia added, wiping gilded or enameled objects with solvent-saturated swab, or rubbing objects with paste cleanser. Rubs objects with jewelers' rouge or other mild cleanser, soaks objects in distilled water with bleach or solvent added, or applies paste or liquid solvent, such as magnesium silicate or acetone, basing choice of method and material on age, condition, and chemical structure of objects, to remove stains from objects. Recommends preservation measures, such as control of temperature, humidity, and exposure to light, to curatorial and building maintenance staff to prevent damage to or deterioration of object. Impregnates surfaces with diluted synthetic lacquers to reduce porosity of material to increase durability of ancient earthenware. Restores or simulates original appearance of objects by such methods as polishing surfaces to restore translucency, removing crackled glaze and applying soluble synthetic coating, grinding or cutting out chipped edges and repolishing surfaces, or applying matt paints, gold leaf, or other coating to object, basing methods and materials used on knowledge of original craft and condition of objects. Repairs broken objects, employing such techniques as bonding edges together with adhesive, inserting dowel pins in sections and cementing together, or affixing adhesive coated strips to inner portions of broken objects. Replaces missing sections of objects by constructing wire frames of missing sections, shaping plasticene or other materials over frames, affixing modeled sections to objects with dowels or adhesive, and painting attached sections to reproduce original appearance. Constructs replicas of archaeological artifacts or historically significant ceramic ware, basing construction design on size, curvature, and thickness of excavated shards or pieces of objects available and knowledge of techniques and designs characteristic of period.
GOE: 01.06.02 STRENGTH: L GED: R5 M5 L5 SVP: 7 DLU: 86

102.367-010 FINE ARTS PACKER (museums) alternate titles: art preparator
Specifies types of packing materials, crating, containerization, and special handling procedures for shipping or storing art objects, scientific specimens, and historical artifacts to minimize damage and deterioration: Confers with curatorial personnel regarding status of museum projects and proposed shipping or transfer dates of exhibitions. Develops methods and procedures for packing or containerization of art objects, according to weight and characteristics of shipment. Selects protective or preservative materials, such as excelsior, chemical agents, or moistureproof wrapping, to protect shipment against vibration, moisture, impact, or other hazards. Designs special crates, modules, brackets, and traveling frames to meet insurance and museum shipping specifications. Shapes and contours internal support modules, based on size and type of paintings, sculptures, bronzes, glass, and other art objects. Directs workers engaged in moving art objects from receiving or storage areas to galleries of museum, in packing shipments, or in rigging sculptures for installation of exhibition. Inspects incoming shipment to detect damages for insurance purposes. Keeps records and documents of incoming and outgoing shipments, or location of traveling exhibitions and loan materials. Prepares and attaches written or pictorial instructions for unpacking, storage, or for exhibition of contents of shipment. May specify type of carrier, such as barge, train, or messenger according to cost considerations and nature of shipment.
GOE: 05.03.09 STRENGTH: M GED: R4 M3 L3 SVP: 7 DLU: 77

102.381-010 MUSEUM TECHNICIAN (museums) alternate titles: museum preparator
Prepares specimens for museum collections and exhibits: Cleans rock matrix from fossil specimens, using electric drills, awls, dental tools, chisels, and mallets. Brushes preservatives, such as plaster, resin, hardeners, and shellac on specimens. Molds and restores skeletal parts of fossil animals, using modeling clays and special molding and casting techniques. Constructs skeletal mounts of fossil animals, using tools, such as drill presses, pipe threaders, welding and soldering apparatus, and carpenter's tools. Constructs duplicate specimens, using plaster, glue, latex, and plastiflex-molding techniques. Reassembles fragmented artifacts, and fabricates substitute pieces. Maintains museum files. Cleans, catalogs, labels, and stores specimens. May install, arrange, and exhibit materials.
GOE: 01.06.02 STRENGTH: M GED: R4 M3 L4 SVP: 7 DLU: 77

109 OCCUPATIONS IN MUSEUM, LIBRARY, AND ARCHIVAL SCIENCES, N.E.C.

This group includes occupations, not elsewhere classified, concerned with museum, library, and archival science.

109.067-010 INFORMATION SCIENTIST (profess. & kin.) alternate titles: chief information officer; information broker; information manager; information resources director; information resources manager
Designs information system to provide management or clients with specific data from computer storage, utilizing knowledge of electronic data processing principles, mathematics, and computer capabilities: Develops and designs methods and procedures for collecting, organizing, interpreting, and classifying information for input into computer and retrieval of specific information from computer, utilizing knowledge of symbolic language and optical or pattern recognition principles. Develops alternate designs to resolve problems in input, storage, and retrieval of information. May specialize in specific field of information science, such as scientific or engineering research, or in specific discipline, such as business, medicine, education, aerospace, or library science.
GOE: 11.01.01 STRENGTH: S GED: R5 M5 L5 SVP: 7 DLU: 77

109.067-014 RESEARCH ASSOCIATE (museums)
Plans, organizes, and conducts research in scientific, cultural, historical, or artistic field for use in own work or in project of sponsoring institution: Develops plans for project or studies guidelines for project prepared by professional staff member to outline research procedures to be followed. Plans schedule according to variety of methods to be used, availability and quantity of resources, and number of subordinate personnel assigned to participate in project. Conducts research, utilizing institution library, archives, and collections, and other sources of information, to collect, record, analyze, and evaluate facts. Discusses findings with other personnel to evaluate validity of findings. Prepares reports of completed projects for publication in technical journals, for presentation to agency requesting project, or for use in further applied or theoretical research activities.
GOE: 11.03.03 STRENGTH: S GED: R6 M6 L6 SVP: 7 DLU: 86

109.137-010 SHELVING SUPERVISOR (library)
Supervises and coordinates activities of library workers engaged in replacing books and other materials on shelves according to library classification system: Assigns duties to workers. Trains and directs workers in performance of shelving tasks. Examines materials on shelves to verify accuracy of placement. Counts number of materials placed on shelves to record shelving activity. Marks designated classification number on material, using pen and ink, to facilitate placement on shelves. May sort material, according to author, classification number, subject matter, or title, to arrange material for shelving.
GOE: 11.02.04 STRENGTH: L GED: R4 M2 L4 SVP: 6 DLU: 77

109.267-010 RESEARCH ASSISTANT I (profess. & kin.)
Conducts research on historic monuments, buildings, and scenes to reconstruct exhibits to scale in dioramas for use of fine-arts students or other purposes. Collects information from libraries, museums, and art institutes. Monitors construction of dioramas to ensure authenticity of proportions, color, and costumes in diorama.
GOE: 11.03.03 STRENGTH: L GED: R5 M4 L4 SVP: 7 DLU: 77

109.267-014 RESEARCH WORKER, ENCYCLOPEDIA (profess. & kin.)
Analyzes information on specified subjects to answer inquiries from encyclopedia owners, referring to library reference sources or consulting with experts in field of knowledge involved. Prepares written summary of research findings for mailing to inquirers.
GOE: 11.08.02 STRENGTH: S GED: R5 M3 L5 SVP: 6 DLU: 77

109.281-010 ARMORER TECHNICIAN (museums)
Specializes in restoring and preparing exhibits of medieval arms and armor: Assembles parts of armor, helmets, guns, swords, and similar items. Designs and fabricates missing or broken parts. Conducts research to determine authenticity and classifies and catalogs articles. Prepares articles for exhibition.
GOE: 01.06.02 STRENGTH: L GED: R5 M4 L5 SVP: 7 DLU: 77

109.361-010 RESTORER, PAPER-AND-PRINTS (library; museums)
Cleans, preserves, restores, and repairs books, documents, maps, prints, photographs, and other paper objects of historic or artistic significance: Examines

or tests objects to determine physical condition and chemical structure of paper, ink, paint, or other coating, in order to identify problem and plan safest and most effective method of treating material. Cleans objects by such methods as sprinkling crumbled art gum or draft powder over surface and rotating soft cloth over cleaning agent to absorb soil (dry cleaning), immersing objects in circulating bath of water or mild chemical solution (wet cleaning), or applying solvent to remove rust, fly specks, mildew, or other stains, basing choice of method on knowledge of physical and chemical structure of objects and effects of various kinds of treatment. Preserves or directs preservation of objects by such methods as immersing paper in deacidification baths to remove acidity from papers and ink to prevent deterioration, sealing documents or other papers in cellulose cases and passing sealed objects through heated rollers to laminate them, spraying objects, storage containers, or areas with fungicides, insecticides, or pesticides, and controlling temperature, humidity, and exposure to natural or artificial light in areas where objects are displayed or stored. Restores objects to original appearance by such methods as immersing papers in mild bleach solution to brighten faded backgrounds, removing old varnish from such art works as engravings and mezzotints, or strengthening papers by resizing in bath of gelatin solution. Repairs objects by such methods as mending tears with adhesive and tissue, patching and filling worm holes, torn corners, or large tears by chamfering, inserting, affixing, and staining paper of similar weight and weave to simulate original appearance, or retouching stained, faded, or blurred watercolors, prints, or documents, using colors and strokes to reproduce those of original artist or writer.
GOE: 01.06.03 STRENGTH: S GED: R5 M5 L5 SVP: 7 DLU: 86

109.364-010 CRAFT DEMONSTRATOR (museums)
Demonstrates and explains techniques and purposes of handicraft or other activity, such as candle dipping, horseshoeing, or soap making, as part of display in history or folk museum, or restored or refurbished farm, village, or neighborhood: Studies historical and technical literature to acquire information about time period and lifestyle depicted in display and craft techniques associated with time and area, to devise plan for authentic presentation of craft. Drafts outline of talk, assisted by research personnel, to acquaint visitors with customs and crafts associated with folk life depicted. Practices techniques involved in handicraft to ensure accurate and skillful demonstrations. Molds candles, shoes horses, operates looms, or engages in other crafts or activities, working in appropriate period setting, to demonstrate craft to visitors. Explains techniques of craft, and points out relationship of craft to lifestyle depicted to assist visitors to comprehend traditional techniques of work and play peculiar to time and area. Answers visitor questions or refers visitor to other sources for information.
GOE: 09.01.02 STRENGTH: L GED: R4 M2 L4 SVP: 4 DLU: 86

109.367-010 MUSEUM ATTENDANT (museums)
Conducts operation of museum and provides information about regulations, facilities, and exhibits to visitors: Opens museum at designated hours, greets visitors, and invites visitors to sign museum register. Monitors visitors viewing exhibits, cautions persons not complying with museum regulations, distributes promotional materials, and answers questions concerning exhibits, regulations, and facilities. Arranges tours of facility for schools or other groups, and schedules volunteers or other staff members to conduct tours. Examines exhibit facilities and collection objects periodically and notifies museum professional personnel or governing body when need for repair or replacement is observed.
GOE: 07.04.04 STRENGTH: L GED: R4 M3 L4 SVP: 3 DLU: 86

11   OCCUPATIONS IN LAW AND JURISPRUDENCE

This division includes occupations concerned with the application of principles relating to statute law and its administration.

110   LAWYERS

This group includes occupations concerned with the practice of one or more phases of law. Includes representing individuals, organizations, or government; and the preparation of legal documents.

110.107-010 LAWYER (profess. & kin.) alternate titles: advocate; attorney; counselor; counselor-at-law
Conducts criminal and civil lawsuits, draws up legal documents, advises clients as to legal rights, and practices other phases of law: Gathers evidence in divorce, civil, criminal, and other cases to formulate defense or to initiate legal action. Conducts research, interviews clients, and witnesses and handles other details in preparation for trial. Prepares legal briefs, develops strategy, arguments and testimony in preparation for presentation of case. Files brief with court clerk. Represents client in court, and before quasi-judicial or administrative agencies of government. Interprets laws, rulings, and regulations for individuals and businesses. May confer with colleagues with specialty in area of lawsuit to establish and verify basis for legal proceedings. May act as trustee, guardian, or executor. May draft wills, trusts, transfer of assets, gifts and other documents. May advise corporate clients concerning transactions of business involving internal affairs, stockholders, directors, officers and corporate relations with general public. May supervise and coordinate activities of subordinate legal personnel. May prepare business contracts, pay taxes, settle labor disputes, and administer other legal matters. May teach college courses in law. May specialize in specific phase of law.

GOE: 11.04.02 STRENGTH: S GED: R6 M4 L6 SVP: 8 DLU: 87

110.107-014 LAWYER, CRIMINAL (profess. & kin.)
Specializes in law cases dealing with offenses against society or state, such as theft, murder, and arson: Interviews clients and witnesses to ascertain facts of case. Correlates findings and prepares case. Prosecutes, or defends defendant against charges. Conducts case, examining and cross examining witnesses. Summarizes case to jury.
GOE: 11.04.02 STRENGTH: S GED: R6 M4 L6 SVP: 8 DLU: 77

110.117-010 DISTRICT ATTORNEY (government ser.) alternate titles: prosecuting attorney; prosecutor; solicitor, city or state; state's attorney; united states attorney
Conducts prosecution in court proceedings in behalf of city, county, state, or federal government: Gathers and analyzes evidence in case and reviews pertinent decisions, policies, regulations, and other legal matters pertaining to case. Presents evidence against accused to grand jury for indictment or release of accused. Appears against accused in court of law and presents evidence before JUDGE (government ser.) or other judiciary and jury.
GOE: 11.04.02 STRENGTH: S GED: R6 M4 L6 SVP: 8 DLU: 77

110.117-014 INSURANCE ATTORNEY (insurance) alternate titles: claim attorney; insurance counsel
Advises management of insurance company on legality of insurance transactions: Studies court decisions, and recommends changes in wording of insurance policies to conform with law or to protect company from unwarranted claims. Advises claims department personnel of legality of claims filed on company to ensure against undue payments. Advises personnel engaged in drawing up of legal documents, such as insurance contracts and release papers. May specialize in one phase of legal work, such as claims or contracts.
GOE: 11.04.02 STRENGTH: S GED: R6 M4 L6 SVP: 8 DLU: 77

110.117-018 LAWYER, ADMIRALTY (profess. & kin.)
Specializes in law applicable to matters occurring on inland navigable waters or on high seas: Conducts lawsuits in matters involving ship personnel, collisions, matters of cargo, and damage to objects by vessels. Draws legal documents, including charter parties, applications for registry of vessels under flags of a particular country, and bills of sale for vessels. Determines law applicable by study of the Constitution, statutes, previous decisions, and regulations. Advises clients as to advisability of prosecuting and defending law suits, or as to legal rights and obligations in other matters.
GOE: 11.04.02 STRENGTH: S GED: R6 M4 L6 SVP: 8 DLU: 77

110.117-022 LAWYER, CORPORATION (profess. & kin.) alternate titles: business and financial counsel; corporate counsel
Advises corporation concerning legal rights, obligations, and privileges: Studies Constitution, statutes, decisions, and ordinances of quasi-judicial bodies. Examines legal data to determine advisability of defending or prosecuting lawsuit. May act as agent of corporation in various transactions.
GOE: 11.04.02 STRENGTH: S GED: R6 M4 L6 SVP: 8 DLU: 77

110.117-026 LAWYER, PATENT (profess. & kin.) alternate titles: patent attorney; solicitor, patent
Specializes in patent law: Advises clients, such as inventors, investors, and manufacturers, concerning patentability of inventions, infringement of patents, validity of patents, and similar items. Prepares applications for patents and presents applications to U.S. Patent Office. Prosecutes or defends clients in patent infringement litigations. May specialize in protecting American trademarks and copyrights in foreign countries.
GOE: 11.04.02 STRENGTH: S GED: R6 M4 L6 SVP: 8 DLU: 77

110.117-030 LAWYER, PROBATE (profess. & kin.)
Specializes in settlement and planning of estates: Drafts wills, deeds of trusts, and similar documents to carry out estate planning of clients. Probates wills and represents and advises executors and administrators of estates.
GOE: 11.04.02 STRENGTH: S GED: R6 M4 L6 SVP: 8 DLU: 77

110.117-034 LAWYER, REAL ESTATE (profess. & kin.)
Specializes in sale and transfer of real property: Institutes title search to establish ownership. Draws up documents, such as deeds, mortgages, and leases. May act as trustee of property and hold funds for investment or issuance. May act as agent in real estate transactions.
GOE: 11.04.02 STRENGTH: S GED: R6 M4 L6 SVP: 8 DLU: 77

110.117-038 TAX ATTORNEY (profess. & kin.) alternate titles: tax agent; tax representative
Advises individuals, business concerns, and other organizations concerning income, estate, gift, excise, property, and other federal, state, local, and foreign taxes. Prepares opinions on tax liability resulting from prospective and past transactions. Represents clients in tax litigation.
GOE: 11.04.02 STRENGTH: S GED: R6 M4 L6 SVP: 8 DLU: 77

110.117-042 TITLE ATTORNEY (profess. & kin.) alternate titles: title examiner
Examines abstracts of titles, leases, contracts, and other legal documents to determine ownership of land, and gas, oil, and mineral rights: Draws up legal documents covering purchase and sale of land, and oil, gas, and mineral rights, drafts deeds and affidavits, and presents other evidence to meet legal requirements of documents. Examines instruments and opinions prepared by other attorneys and advises officials of organization as to legal requirements in connec-

tion with titles. Searches for and examines public records and writes opinions on titles. Prepares cases for trial and tries or assists in trial of lawsuits involving titles to land, and gas, oil, and mineral rights.
GOE: 11.04.02 STRENGTH: L GED: R6 M4 L6 SVP: 8 DLU: 90

110.167-010 BAR EXAMINER (profess. & kin.) alternate titles: law examiner

Determines qualifications of candidates seeking admission to practice of law: Prepares written examinations dealing with law subjects, such as contracts, property, and criminal law based on legal code of examining jurisdiction. Corrects and marks papers. Announces names of candidates earning passing grades. Submits each candidate to oral examination concerning qualifications. Recommends candidates meeting prescribed standards be admitted to practice.
GOE: 11.04.02 STRENGTH: S GED: R6 M4 L6 SVP: 8 DLU: 77

111 JUDGES

This group includes occupations concerned with presiding as arbitrator, advisor, and administrator of the judicial system in a court of law.

111.107-010 JUDGE (government ser.) alternate titles: justice

Arbitrates disputes, advises counsel, jury, litigants, or court personnel, and administers judicial system: Establishes rules of procedure on questions for which standard procedures have not been established by law or by superior court. Reads or listens to allegations made by plaintiff in civil suits to determine their sufficiency. Examines evidence in criminal cases to determine if evidence will support charges. Listens to presentation of case, rules on admissibility of evidence and methods of conducting testimony, and settles disputes between opposing attorneys. Instructs jury on applicable law and directs jury to deduce facts from evidence presented. Sentences defendant in criminal cases, on conviction by jury, according to statutes of state or federal government, or awards judicial relief to litigants in civil cases in relation to findings by jury or by court. May be designated according to level of court in judicial hierarchy as Appellate-Court Judge (government ser.); District-Court Judge (government ser.); Municipal-Court Judge (government ser.); Superior-Court Judge (government ser.); Supreme-Court Justice (government ser.). May preside over particular court department and be designated Conciliation-Court Judge (government ser.); Criminal-Court Judge (government ser.); Juvenile-Court Judge (government ser.); Probate Judge (government ser.).
GOE: 11.04.01 STRENGTH: S GED: R6 M4 L6 SVP: 9 DLU: 77

111.107-014 MAGISTRATE (government ser.) alternate titles: justice-court judge; justice of the peace; police judge; police justice; police magistrate

Adjudicates civil cases in which damages do not exceed prescribed maximum established by state law, and minor misdemeanor cases not involving penitentiary sentences or fines in excess of maximum amount allowed to be levied under state law. Conducts preliminary hearings in felony cases to determine whether there is reasonable and probable cause to hold defendant for further proceedings or trial by superior court. May perform wedding ceremonies. May perform duties at night and be designated Night-Court Magistrate (government ser.). May adjudicate cases involving motor vehicle laws and be designated Traffic-Court Magistrate (government ser.).
GOE: 11.04.01 STRENGTH: S GED: R6 M4 L6 SVP: 9 DLU: 77

119 OCCUPATIONS IN LAW AND JURISPRUDENCE, N.E.C.

This group includes occupations, not elsewhere classified, concerned with law and jurisprudence.

119.107-010 HEARING OFFICER (government ser.) alternate titles: appeals board referee; referee

Reviews previously adjudicated social welfare tax or eligibility issues, as member of appeals board, utilizing knowledge of regulations, policy, and precedent decisions: Researches laws, regulations, policies, and precedent decisions to prepare for appeal hearings. Schedules hearing, issues subpoenas, counsels parties, and administers oaths to prepare for formal hearing. Conducts hearing to obtain information and evidence relative to disposition of appeal. Questions witnesses and rules on exceptions, motions, and admissibility of evidence. Analyzes evidence and applicable law, regulations, policy, and precedent decisions to determine appropriate and permissible conclusions. Prepares written decision. May hear disability insurance appeals and be designated Disability-Insurance-Hearing Officer (government ser.). May hear unemployment insurance appeals and be designated Unemployment-Insurance-Hearing Officer (government ser.).
GOE: 11.04.01 STRENGTH: S GED: R6 M3 L6 SVP: 9 DLU: 77

119.117-010 APPEALS REVIEWER, VETERAN (government ser.)

Adjudicates military service veterans' claims for allowances: Conducts hearings and determines validity of claim in accordance with federal and state laws and precedents. Renders decision and writes opinion on questions appealed. Prepares interpretations and advisory opinions on points of law requested by state or federal agencies engaged in admininstration of veterans' programs. Conducts studies of appeals procedures in field agencies to ensure adherence to legal requirements and facilitate determination of cases.
GOE: 11.04.01 STRENGTH: S GED: R6 M5 L5 SVP: 9 DLU: 77

119.167-010 ADJUDICATOR (government ser.)

Adjudicates claims filed by government against individuals or organizations: Determines existence and amount of liability, according to law, administrative and judicial precedents and other evidence. Recommends acceptance or rejection of compromise settlement offers.
GOE: 11.04.03 STRENGTH: S GED: R5 M4 L5 SVP: 7 DLU: 77

119.167-014 PATENT AGENT (profess. & kin.)

Prepares and presents patent application to U.S. Patent Office and in patent courts, according to familiarity with patent law and filing procedures. Must be registered by U.S. Patent Office. Cannot practice law or appear in other courts.
GOE: 11.04.04 STRENGTH: S GED: R6 M5 L6 SVP: 7 DLU: 77

119.167-018 TITLE SUPERVISOR (profess. & kin.)

Directs and coordinates activities of subordinates engaged in searching public records and examining titles to determine legal condition of property title.
GOE: 07.01.05 STRENGTH: S GED: R5 M3 L5 SVP: 8 DLU: 77

119.267-010 ABSTRACTOR (profess. & kin.) alternate titles: abstract clerk; abstract maker; abstract searcher; abstract writer; court abstractor; title abstractor

Analyzes pertinent legal or insurance details or section of statute or case law to summarize for purposes of examination, proof, or ready reference. May search out titles to determine if title deed is correct [TITLE EXAMINER (profess. & kin.)].
GOE: 11.04.04 STRENGTH: S GED: R5 M3 L5 SVP: 6 DLU: 77

119.267-014 APPEALS REFEREE (government ser.)

Adjudicates social welfare tax or benefit eligibility issues filed by disabled or unemployed claimants or employers: Arranges and conducts hearings to discover pertinent facts bearing on claim in accord with federal and state laws and procedures. Renders decisions affirming or denying previous ruling, based on testimony, claim records, applicable provisions of law, and established precedents. Writes decision explaining ruling and informs interested parties of results. Confers with personnel of employer or agency involved to obtain additional information bearing on appeal, and to clarify future implications of decisions. May participate in court proceedings against claimants attempting to obtain benefits through fraud. May render informal opinions on points of law in questionable cases to facilitate initial determination of benefit eligibility or imposition of penalties. May be required to hold law degree or license to practice law.
GOE: 11.04.01 STRENGTH: S GED: R6 M3 L6 SVP: 8 DLU: 77

119.267-018 CONTRACT CLERK (profess. & kin.) alternate titles: contract consultant; contract technician

Reviews agreements or proposed agreements for conformity to company rates, rules, and regulations: Analyzes contracts and confers with various department heads to detect ambiguities, inaccurate statements, omissions of essential terms, and conflicts with possible legal prohibitions. Recommends modifications. Converts agreements into contract form or prepares amended agreement for approval by legal department. May initiate changes in standard form contracts.
GOE: 07.01.05 STRENGTH: S GED: R5 M2 L5 SVP: 7 DLU: 77

119.267-022 LEGAL INVESTIGATOR (profess. & kin.) alternate titles: legal assistant

Researches and prepares cases relating to administrative appeals of civil service members: Examines state government, personnel, college, or university rules and regulations. Answers members' questions regarding rights and benefits and advises on how rules apply to individual situations. Presents arguments and evidence to support appeal at appeal hearing. Calls upon witnesses to testify at hearing.
GOE: 11.04.02 STRENGTH: S GED: R5 M2 L5 SVP: 7 DLU: 77

119.267-026 PARALEGAL (profess. & kin.) alternate titles: law clerk; legal aid; legal assistant

Researches law, investigates facts, and prepares documents to assist LAWYER (profess. & kin.) 110.107-010: Researches and analyzes law sources such as statutes, recorded judicial decisions, legal articles, treaties, constitutions, and legal codes to prepare legal documents, such as briefs, pleadings, appeals, wills, contracts, initial and amended articles of incorporation, stock certificates and other securities, buy-sell agreements, closing papers and binders, deeds, and trust instruments for review, approval, and use by attorney. Appraises and inventories real and personal property for estate planning. Investigates facts and law of case to determine causes of action and to prepare case accordingly. Files pleadings with court clerk. Prepares affidavits of documents and maintains document file. Delivers or directs delivery of subpoenas to witnesses and parties to action. May direct and coordinate activities of law office employees. May prepare office accounts and tax returns. May specialize in litigation, probate, real estate, or corporation law. May prepare real estate closing statement and assist in closing process. May act as arbitrator and liaison between disputing parties. May act as law librarian, keeping and monitoring legal volumes and ensuring legal volumes are up-to-date. May search patent files to ascertain originality of patent application and be designated Patent Clerk (government ser.).
GOE: 11.04.02 STRENGTH: L GED: R5 M2 L5 SVP: 7 DLU: 87

119.287-010 TITLE EXAMINER (profess. & kin.)

Searches public records and examines titles to determine legal condition of property title: Examines copies of records, such as mortgages, liens, judgments,

easements, vital statistics, and plat and map books to determine ownership and legal restrictions and to verify legal description of property. Copies or summarizes (abstracts) recorded documents, such as mortgages, trust deeds, and contracts affecting condition of title to property. Analyzes restrictions and prepares report outlining restrictions and actions required to clear title. When working in title-insurance company, prepares and issues policy that guarantees legality of title.
GOE: 07.01.05 STRENGTH: S GED: R5 M3 L5 SVP: 7 DLU: 77

119.367-010　ESCROW OFFICER (profess. & kin.)
Holds in escrow, funds, legal papers, and other collateral posted by contracting parties to ensure fulfillment of contracts or trust agreements: Prepares escrow agreement. Executes terms of contract or trust agreement, such as holding money or legal papers, paying off mortgages, or paying sums to designated parties. Files and delivers deeds and other legal papers. May assist buyer to secure financing.
GOE: 07.01.04 STRENGTH: S GED: R4 M3 L3 SVP: 8 DLU: 77

12　　OCCUPATIONS IN RELIGION AND THEOLOGY

This division includes occupations concerned with religious worship and observance, and with theological research and history of religion.

120　CLERGY

This group includes occupations concerned with serving spiritual needs of congregation members, usually as minister, priest, or rabbi. Includes delivering sermons, conducting services, administering religious rites, instructing prospective congregation members, and counseling members in need of spiritual advice.

120.107-010　CLERGY MEMBER (profess. & kin.) alternate titles: minister; preacher; priest; rabbi
Conducts religious worship and performs other spiritual functions associated with beliefs and practices of religious faith or denomination as authorized, and provides spiritual and moral guidance and assistance to members: Leads congregation in worship services. Prepares and delivers sermons and other talks. Interprets doctrine of religion. Instructs people who seek conversion to faith. Conducts wedding and funeral services. Administers religious rites or ordinances. Visits sick and shut-ins, and helps poor. Counsels those in spiritual need and comforts bereaved. Oversees religious education programs. May write articles for publication and engage in interfaith, community, civic, educational, and recreational activities sponsored by or related to interest of denomination. May teach in seminaries and universities. May serve in armed forces, institutions, or industry and be designated Chaplain (profess. & kin.). When in charge of Christian church, congregation, or parish, may be designated Pastor (profess. & kin.) or Rector (profess. & kin.). May carry religious message and medical or educational aid to nonchristian lands and people to obtain converts and establish native church and be designated Missionary (profess. & kin.).
GOE: 10.01.01 STRENGTH: L GED: R6 M4 L6 SVP: 8 DLU: 77

129　　OCCUPATIONS IN RELIGION AND THEOLOGY, N.E.C.

This group includes occupations, not elsewhere classified, concerned with religion and theology.

129.027-010　CANTOR (profess. & kin.)
Chants and reads portions of ritual during religious services, and directs congregants in musical activities: Arranges musical portion of religious services in consultation with leader of congregation. Chants or recites religious texts during worship services or other observances and trains and leads congregants in musical responses. May create variations of traditional music or compose music for services. May train and direct choir or teach vocal music to youth or other groups of congregants.
GOE: 11.07.03 STRENGTH: L GED: R5 M1 L4 SVP: 8 DLU: 86

129.107-010　CHRISTIAN SCIENCE NURSE (profess. & kin.)
Provides support and nonmedical physical care, through practical knowledge of Christian Science, to patients receiving treatment from CHRISTIAN SCIENCE PRACTITIONERS (profess. & kin.). May work on staff of Christian Science sanatorium or Christian Science visiting nurse service. May contract independently, usually with one patient, to provide individual care in Christian Science sanatorium or private home.
GOE: 10.03.02 STRENGTH: L GED: R4 M3 L4 SVP: 7 DLU: 77

129.107-014　CHRISTIAN SCIENCE PRACTITIONER (profess. & kin.)
Practices spiritual healing through prayer alone in accordance with religious teaching of Christian Science.
GOE: 10.01.01 STRENGTH: S GED: R5 M2 L3 SVP: 6 DLU: 77

129.107-018　DIRECTOR OF RELIGIOUS ACTIVITIES (education) alternate titles: dean of chapel; director of religious life
Directs and coordinates activities of various denominational groups to meet religious needs of students: Meets with religious advisers and councils to coordinate overall religious program. Assists and advises groups in promoting interfaith understanding. Interprets policies of university to community religious

workers and confers with administrative officials concerning suggestions and requests for religious activities. Provides counseling and guidance relative to marital, health, financial, and religious problems. Plans and conducts conferences and courses to assist in interpretation of religion to various academic groups and to promote understanding of individual faiths and convictions of other groups.
GOE: 10.01.01 STRENGTH: S GED: R5 M3 L5 SVP: 8 DLU: 77

129.107-022　DIRECTOR, RELIGIOUS EDUCATION (nonprofit org.)
Plans, organizes, and directs religious education program designed to promote religious education among congregation membership and counsels members concerning personal problems: Analyzes revenue and program cost data to determine budget priorities. Analyzes member participation, and changes in congregation emphasis to determine needs for religious education. Develops study courses and supervises instructional staff. Counsels students. Plans congregational activities and projects to attract attention to, and encourage active participation in programs. Promotes student participation in extracurricular congregational activities. Visits homes of congregation members and confers with CLERGY MEMBER (profess. & kin.) 120.107-010, congregation officials, and congregation organizations to solicit support and participation, and to stimulate interest in religious and educational programs. Participates in such denominational activities as giving help to new congregations and small congregations. Interprets work of school to public through speaking or discussion-leading in related fields, and contributes articles to local and national publications. Orders and distributes school supplies.
GOE: 11.07.03 STRENGTH: S GED: R5 M3 L5 SVP: 8 DLU: 77

129.107-026　PASTORAL ASSISTANT (nonprofit org.)
Assists ordained clergy in conducting worship services; provides spiritual guidance to church members; and plans and arranges educational, social, and recreational programs for congregation: Assists CLERGY MEMBER (profess. & kin.) 120.107-010 in conducting worship, wedding, funeral, and other services and in coordinating activities of lay participants, such as organist, choir, and ushers. Visits church members in hospitals and convalescent facilities or at home to offer spiritual guidance and assistance, such as emergency financial aid or referral to community support services. Assists CLERGY MEMBER (profess. & kin.) and lay teachers in selecting books and reference materials for religious education classes and in adapting content to meet needs of different age groups. May write and deliver sermons. May teach history and doctrine of church to church members. May assist CLERGY MEMBER (profess. & kin.) in coordinating committees that oversee social and recreational programs.
GOE: 10.01.01 STRENGTH: L GED: R5 M3 L5 SVP: 6 DLU: 86

129.271-010　MOHEL (profess. & kin.) alternate titles: ritual circumciser
Circumcises Jewish male infants in accordance with tenets of faith: Reviews infant's family medical history to determine possibility of hemorrhage. Examines infant for infection and other conditions to determine best operational time and procedure. Disinfects surgical instruments, hands, and operative area. Affixes lyre-shaped shield to penis and excises foreskin and membrane along line of shield, using scalpel. Removes blood from wound, using suction, and applies sterile dressing. Recites prescribed benedictions and announces Hebrew name of child.
GOE: 10.01.01 STRENGTH: L GED: R4 M2 L4 SVP: 6 DLU: 77

13　　OCCUPATIONS IN WRITING

This division includes occupations concerned with reporting, editing, promoting, and interpreting ideas and facts in written form. Occupations concerned with translating and interpreting written and spoken words from one language to another are also included in this division.

131　WRITERS

This group includes occupations primarily concerned with researching and writing material for performance, publication, or broadcast. Includes reporting, analyzing, and interpreting facts, events, and personalities; developing fiction or nonfiction ideas, using various literary techniques to produce plays, novels, poems, or other related works; critically evaluating art, music, drama, and other artistic presentations; and persuading the general public to favor personalities, goods, and services. Writers often rewrite material developed by others and perform editorial duties but are distinguished from editors because they are primarily responsible for originating written material. Technical writers are also included in this group. Occupations which include writing but are primarily involved with other disciplines, such as economics, psychology, and history, are grouped according to primary involvement.

131.067-010　COLUMNIST/COMMENTATOR (print. & pub.; radio-tv broad.)
Analyzes news and writes column or commentary, based on personal knowledge and experience with subject matter, for publication or broadcast: Gathers information and develops subject perspective through research, interview, experience, and attendance at functions, such as political conventions, news meetings, sports events, and social activities. Analyzes and interprets information to formulate and outline story idea. Selects material most pertinent to presentation, organizes material into acceptable media form and format, and writes column

or commentary. Records commentary or presents commentary live when working in broadcast medium. May be required to develop material to fit media time or space requirements. May analyze current news items and be designated News Analyst (radio-tv broad.). May be designated according to medium worked in as Columnist (print. & pub.); Commentator (radio-tv broad.). May specialize in particular field, such as sports, fashion, society, or politics. May analyze topics chosen by publication or broadcast facility editorial board. May enter information into computer to prepare commentaries.
GOE: 11.08.03 STRENGTH: S GED: R6 M3 L6 SVP: 7 DLU: 88

131.067-014 COPY WRITER (profess. & kin.)
Writes advertising copy for use by publication or broadcast media to promote sale of goods and services: Consults with sales media, and marketing representatives to obtain information on product or service and discuss style and length of advertising copy. Obtains additional background and current development information through research and interview. Reviews advertising trends, consumer surveys, and other data regarding marketing of specific and related goods and services to formulate presentation approach. Writes preliminary draft of copy and sends to supervisor for approval. Corrects and revises copy as necessary. May write articles, bulletins, sales letters, speeches, and other related informative and promotional material. May enter information into computer to prepare advertising copy.
GOE: 01.01.02 STRENGTH: S GED: R5 M2 L5 SVP: 7 DLU: 89

131.067-018 CRITIC (print. & pub.; radio-tv broad.)
Writes critical reviews of literary, musical, or artistic works and performances for broadcast and publication: Attends art exhibitions, musical or dramatic performances, reads books, or previews motion picture or television presentations. Analyzes factors such as theme, expression, and technique, and makes comparisons to other works and standards. Forms critical opinions based on personal knowledge, judgement, and experience. Organizes material to emphasize prominent features, and writes review. Presents oral review in live or recorded form when working in broadcasting medium. May enter information into computer to prepare reviews. May be designated according to field of specialization as Art Critic (print. & pub.; radio-tv broad.); Book Critic (print. & pub.; radio-tv broad.); Drama Critic (print. & pub.; radio-tv broad.); Movie Critic (print. & pub.; radio-tv broad.); Music Critic (print. & pub.; radio-tv broad.).
GOE: 01.01.03 STRENGTH: S GED: R6 M2 L6 SVP: 8 DLU: 88

131.067-022 EDITORIAL WRITER (print. & pub.)
Writes comments on topics of reader interest to stimulate or mold public opinion, in accordance with viewpoints and policies of publication: Prepares assigned or unassigned articles from knowledge of topic and editorial position of publication, supplemented by additional study and research. Submits and discusses copy with editor for approval. May specialize in one or more fields, such as international affairs, fiscal matters, or national or local politics. May participate in conferences of editorial policy committee to recommend topics and position to be taken by publication on specific public issues.
GOE: 01.01.02 STRENGTH: S GED: R5 M3 L5 SVP: 8 DLU: 77

131.067-026 HUMORIST (profess. & kin.)
Writes humorous material for publication or performance: Selects topic according to personal preference or assignment. Writes and makes changes and revisions to material until it meets personal standards. Submits material for approval and confers with client regarding additional changes or revisions. May conduct research to obtain factual information regarding subject matter. May specialize in writing comedy routines, gags, or special material for entertainers and be designated Gag Writer (profess. & kin.). May write comedy shows for presentation on radio or television and be designated Comedy Writer (profess. & kin.). May work as a member of writing team and be assigned to develop segment of comedy show.
GOE: 01.01.02 STRENGTH: S GED: R6 M2 L6 SVP: 8 DLU: 77

131.067-030 LIBRETTIST (profess. & kin.)
Composes text for opera, musical play, or extended choral work, fitting words to music composed by another. Adapts text to accommodate musical requirements of COMPOSER (profess. & kin.) and SINGER (amuse. & rec.; motion picture; radio-tv broad.).
GOE: 01.01.02 STRENGTH: S GED: R6 M2 L6 SVP: 7 DLU: 77

131.067-034 LYRICIST (profess. & kin.) alternate titles: lyric writer; song writer
Writes words to be sung or spoken to accompaniment of music. Expresses sentiment, ideas, or narration, usually in verse, to fit music.
GOE: 01.01.02 STRENGTH: S GED: R6 M2 L6 SVP: 7 DLU: 77

131.067-038 PLAYWRIGHT (profess. & kin.) alternate titles: dramatist
Writes original plays, such as tragedies, comedies, or dramas, or adapts themes from fictional, historical, or narrative sources, for dramatic presentation: Writes plays, usually involving action, conflict, purpose, and resolution, to depict series of events from imaginary or real life. Writes dialogue and describes action to be followed during enactment of play. Revises script during rehearsals and preparation for initial showing.
GOE: 01.01.02 STRENGTH: S GED: R6 M2 L6 SVP: 8 DLU: 77

131.067-042 POET (profess. & kin.)
Writes narrative, dramatic, or lyric poetry for magazines, books, and other publications: Chooses subject matter and suitable form to express personal feel-

ing and individual experience, or to narrate story or event. May write doggerel or other type verse.
GOE: 01.01.02 STRENGTH: S GED: R6 M2 L6 SVP: 7 DLU: 77

131.067-046 WRITER, PROSE, FICTION AND NONFICTION (profess. & kin.) alternate titles: writer
Writes original prose material for publication: Selects subject matter based on personal interest or receives specific assignment from publisher. Conducts research and makes notes to retain ideas, develop factual information, and obtain authentic detail. Organizes material and plans arrangement or outline. Develops factors, such as theme, plot, order, characterization, and story line. Writes draft of manuscript. Reviews, revises, and corrects it and submits material for publication. Confers with publisher's representative regarding manuscript changes. May specialize in one or more styles or types of writing, such as descriptive or critical interpretations or analyses, essays, magazine articles, short stories, novels, and biographies.
GOE: 01.01.02 STRENGTH: S GED: R6 M3 L6 SVP: 8 DLU: 77

131.067-050 SCREEN WRITER (motion picture; radio-tv broad.) alternate titles: scenario writer; script writer
Writes scripts for motion pictures or television: Selects subject and theme for script based on personal interests or assignment. Conducts research to obtain accurate factual background information and authentic detail. Writes plot outline, narrative synopsis, or treatment and submits for approval. Confers with PRODUCER (motion picture) 187.167-174 or PRODUCER (radio-tv broad.) 159.117-010 and DIRECTOR, MOTION PICTURE (motion picture) 159.067-010 or DIRECTOR, TELEVISION (radio-tv broad.) 159.067-014 regarding script development, revisions, and other changes. Writes one or more drafts of script. May work in collaboration with other writers. May adapt books or plays into scripts for use in television or motion picture production. May write continuity or comedy routines. May specialize in particular type of script or writing.
GOE: 01.01.02 STRENGTH: S GED: R6 M2 L6 SVP: 7 DLU: 77

131.087-010 CONTINUITY WRITER (radio-tv broad.)
Originates and prepares material that is read by ANNOUNCER (radio-tv broad.) 159.147-010 to introduce and connect various parts of musical, news, and sports programs.
GOE: 01.01.02 STRENGTH: S GED: R5 M2 L5 SVP: 7 DLU: 77

131.087-014 READER (motion picture; radio-tv broad.) alternate titles: script reader; story analyst
Reads novels, stories, and plays and prepares synopses for review by editorial department or PRODUCER (motion picture) or PRODUCER (radio-tv broad.). Suggests possible treatment of selected materials. May read foreign story material in original language.
GOE: 01.01.01 STRENGTH: S GED: R5 M2 L5 SVP: 6 DLU: 77

131.262-010 NEWSCASTER (radio-tv broad.) alternate titles: newsperson
Analyzes and broadcasts news received from various sources: Examines news items of local, national, and international significance to determine selection or is assigned news items for broadcast by editorial staff. Prepares or assists in preparation of script [NEWSWRITER (print. & pub.; radio-tv broad.) 131.262-014]. Presents news over radio or television. May specialize in particular field of news broadcasting, such as political, economic, or military. May gather information about newsworthy events [REPORTER (print. & pub.; radio-tv broad.) 131.262-018]. May introduce broadcasters who specialize in particular fields, such as sports or weather, and be designated Anchorperson (radio-tv broad.) or News Anchor (radio-tv broad.).
GOE: 11.08.03 STRENGTH: L GED: R5 M2 L5 SVP: 7 DLU: 89

131.262-014 NEWSWRITER (print. & pub.; radio-tv broad.) alternate titles: rewriter
Writes news stories for publication or broadcast from written or recorded notes supplied by reporting staff, using computer or typewriter: Reviews and evaluates written or recorded notes obtained from reporting staff to isolate pertinent facts and details. Verifies accuracy of questionable facts and obtains supplemental material and additional details from files, reference libraries, and interviews with knowledgeable sources. Organizes material and writes story conforming to specified length, style, and format requirements. May discuss story length and format with EDITOR, CITY (print. & pub.) 132.037-014 or with PRODUCER (radio-tv broad.) 159.117-010 and FILM OR VIDEOTAPE EDITOR (motion picture; radio-tv broad.) 962.262-010. May write news stories in foreign language.
GOE: 11.08.02 STRENGTH: L GED: R5 M2 L5 SVP: 7 DLU: 89

131.262-018 REPORTER (print. & pub.; radio-tv broad.) alternate titles: newsperson
Collects and analyzes information about newsworthy events to write news stories for publication or broadcast: Receives assignment or evaluates news leads and news tips to develop story idea. Gathers and verifies factual information regarding story through interview, observation, and research. Organizes material, determines slant or emphasis, and writes story according to prescribed editorial style and format standards. May monitor police and fire department radio communications to obtain story leads. May take photographs or shoot video to illustrate stories. May edit, or assist in editing, videos for broadcast. May appear on television program when conducting taped or filmed interviews or narration. May give live reports from site of event or mobile broadcast unit.

May transmit information to NEWSWRITER (print. & pub.; radio-tv broad.) 131.262-014 for story writing. May specialize in one type of reporting, such as sports, fires, accidents, political affairs, court trials, or police activities. May be assigned to outlying areas or foreign countries and be designated Correspondent (print. & pub.; radio-tv broad.) or Foreign Correspondent (print. & pub.; radio-tv broad.).
GOE: 11.08.02 STRENGTH: L GED: R5 M3 L5 SVP: 7 DLU: 89

131.267-022 SCRIPT READER (radio-tv broad.) alternate titles: copy reader; editor
Reads book or script of radio and television programs and commercials or views and listens to video and sound tapes to detect and recommend deletion of vulgar, immoral, libelous, or misleading statements, applying knowledge of FCC and station standards and regulations: Types recommended editorial revisions in script. Confers with sales or advertising agency personnel to report on revised or disallowed commercials. When reading continuity, may be designated Continuity Reader (radio-tv broad.).
GOE: 07.05.02 STRENGTH: S GED: R4 M2 L4 SVP: 6 DLU: 77

131.267-026 WRITER, TECHNICAL PUBLICATIONS (profess. & kin.)
Develops, writes, and edits material for reports, manuals, briefs, proposals, instruction books, catalogs, and related technical and administrative publications concerned with work methods and procedures, and installation, operation, and maintenance of machinery and other equipment: Receives assignment from supervisor. Observes production, developmental, and experimental activities to determine operating procedure and detail. Interviews production and engineering personnel and reads journals, reports, and other material to become familiar with product technologies and production methods. Reviews manufacturer's and trade catalogs, drawings and other data relative to operation, maintenance, and service of equipment. Studies blueprints, sketches, drawings, parts lists, specifications, mock ups, and product samples to integrate and delineate technology, operating procedure, and production sequence and detail. Organizes material and completes writing assignment according to set standards regarding order, clarity, conciseness, style, and terminology. Reviews published materials and recommends revisions or changes in scope, format, content, and methods of reproduction and binding. May maintain records and files of work and revisions. May select photographs, drawings, sketches, diagrams, and charts to illustrate material. May assist in laying out material for publication. May arrange for typing, duplication, and distribution of material. May write speeches, articles, and public or employee relations releases. May edit, standardize, or make changes to material prepared by other writers or plant personnel and be designated Standard-Practice Analyst (profess. & kin.). May specialize in writing material regarding work methods and procedures and be designated Process-Description Writer (profess. & kin.).
GOE: 11.08.02 STRENGTH: S GED: R5 M3 L5 SVP: 8 DLU: 81

132   EDITORS: PUBLICATION, BROADCAST, AND SCRIPT

This group includes occupations concerned with assigning, selecting, and preparing written materials for publication, broadcast, or motion picture production. This includes planning arrangement of material, rewriting, verifying, compiling, and abstracting according to standards of consistency, organization, development or specified viewpoint. Editors coordinate the work of authors, designers, production personnel, and printers. Editors of specialized types of written material are also included.

132.017-010 EDITOR, MANAGING, NEWSPAPER (print. & pub.) alternate titles: managing editor
Negotiates with newspaper owner's representative to establish publication policies, and directs editorial activities of newspaper departments: Confers with executive staff to discuss editorial policy, makeup plans, changes in staff organization, news coverage of special events, and similar decisions. Relays information to department heads. Coordinates work of editorial departments in accordance with newspaper policy. Directs general page makeup of publication. Inspects final makeup of editions and rearranges makeup to meet emergency news situations. Originates plans for special features or projects and assigns department heads to implement them. May write leading or policy editorials. In smaller establishments may perform duties of EDITOR, NEWS (print. & pub.) 132.067-026; and EDITOR, CITY (print. & pub.) 132.037-014.
GOE: 11.05.01 STRENGTH: S GED: R6 M3 L6 SVP: 8 DLU: 77

132.017-014 EDITOR, NEWSPAPER (print. & pub.) alternate titles: editor-in-chief, newspaper
Formulates editorial policy and directs operation of newspaper: Confers with editorial policy committee and heads of production, advertising, and circulation departments to develop editorial and operating procedures and negotiate decisions affecting publication. Appoints editorial heads and supervises work of their departments in accordance with newspaper policy. Writes leading or policy editorials or notifies editorial department head of position to be taken on specific public issues. Reviews financial reports and takes appropriate action with respect to costs and revenues. Represents publication at professional and community functions. In smaller establishments may perform duties of one or more subordinate editors and direct activities of advertising, circulation, or production personnel.
GOE: 11.08.01 STRENGTH: S GED: R6 M3 L6 SVP: 9 DLU: 77

132.017-018 EDITOR, TECHNICAL AND SCIENTIFIC PUBLICATIONS (profess. & kin.) alternate titles: manager, technical and scientific publications; supervisor, publications
Directs and coordinates activities of writers engaged in preparing technical, scientific, medical, or other material for publication in conjunction with or independent from manufacturing, research, and related activities: Analyzes developments in specific field to determine need for revisions, corrections, and changes in previously published materials, and development of new material. Confers with customer representatives, vendors, plant executives, or publisher to establish technical specifications, determine specific or general subject material to be developed for publication, and resolve problems concerned with developing and publishing subject material. Assigns staff writer or contracts with specialist in subject area to produce draft of manuscript. Supervises staff writers and delineates standard procedures for gathering data and writing. Reviews draft of manuscript and makes recommendations for changes. May edit and correct final draft to prepare for typesetting. May perform similar duties to those supervised. May select or recommend graphics, such as drawings, diagrams, pictures, and charts to illustrate manuscript. May specialize in particular type of publication, such as manuals, handbooks, articles, or proposals.
GOE: 11.08.01 STRENGTH: S GED: R6 M3 L6 SVP: 9 DLU: 77

132.037-010 CONTINUITY DIRECTOR (radio-tv broad.) alternate titles: editor, continuity and script
Coordinates activities of continuity department of radio or television station: Assigns duties to staff and freelance writers. Supervises staff writers preparing program continuity and scripts for broadcasting, and edits material to ensure conformance with company policy, laws, and regulations. May be responsible for nonmusical copyright material. May read book or script of television programs and commercials or view and listen to videotapes to detect and recommend deletion of vulgar, immoral, libelous, or misleading statements, applying knowledge of Federal Communications Commission and station standards and regulations. May supervise administrative research workers and employees receiving and examining program ideas and scripts suggested by public for station or network presentation.
GOE: 01.01.01 STRENGTH: S GED: R5 M2 L5 SVP: 8 DLU: 88

132.037-014 EDITOR, CITY (print. & pub.) alternate titles: city editor; metropolitan editor
Directs and supervises personnel engaged in selecting, gathering, and editing local news and news photographs for edition of newspaper: Receives information regarding developing news events or originates story ideas and assigns coverage to members of reporting and photography staff. Reviews news copy and confers with executive staff members regarding allocation of news space. Sends copy to copy desk for editing. Reviews edited copy and sends to EDITOR, NEWS (print. & pub.) or composing room. May write or direct writing of headlines. May hire and discharge members of reporting staff. May perform other editorial duties as required. Designated State Editor (print. & pub.) when working with State news and National Editor (print. & pub.) when working with National news.
GOE: 11.08.01 STRENGTH: S GED: R6 M3 L6 SVP: 8 DLU: 77

132.037-018 EDITOR, DEPARTMENT (print. & pub.)
Supervises personnel engaged in selecting, gathering, and editing news and news photographs for one or more specialized news departments of newspaper: May select submitted material such as letters or articles for publication. May assign cartoons or editorials to staff members. May perform duties of REPORTER (print. & pub.; radio-tv broad.). May edit copy and perform related duties as required. Usually identified according to individual specialty or specialties.
GOE: 11.08.01 STRENGTH: S GED: R5 M3 L5 SVP: 8 DLU: 77

132.037-022 EDITOR, PUBLICATIONS (print. & pub.)
Formulates policy; plans, coordinates, and directs editorial activities; and supervises workers who assist in selecting and preparing material for publication in magazines, trade journals, house organs, and related publications: Confers with executives, department heads, and editorial staff to formulate policy, coordinate department activities, establish production schedules, solve publication problems, and discuss makeup plans and organizational changes. Determines theme of issue and gathers related material. Writes or assigns staff members or freelance writers to write articles, reports, editorials, reviews, and other material. Reads and evaluates material submitted for publication consideration. Secures graphic material from picture sources and assigns artists and photographers to produce pictures and illustrations. Assigns staff member, or personally interviews individuals and attends gatherings, to obtain items for publication, verify facts, and clarify information. Assigns research and other editorial duties to assistants. Organizes material, plans overall and individual page layouts, and selects type. Marks dummy pages to indicate position and size of printed and graphic material. Reviews final proofs and approves or makes changes. Reviews and evaluates work of staff members and makes recommendations and changes. May perform related editorial duties listed under EDITORIAL ASSISTANT (print. & pub.). May direct activities of production, circulation, or promotion personnel. May prepare news or public relations releases, special brochures, and similar materials. May be designated according to type of publication worked on as Communications Manager (print. & pub.); Editor, Farm Journal (print. & pub.); Editor, House Organ (print. & pub.); Editor, Magazine (print. & pub.); Editor, Trade Journal (print. & pub.); Industrial Editor (print. & pub.).

GOE: 01.01.01 STRENGTH: S GED: R6 M3 L6 SVP: 8 DLU: 77

132.037-026 STORY EDITOR (motion picture; radio-tv broad.)

Selects and secures written material and supervises staff writers who prepare scripts to be used for television or motion picture productions: Reviews and evaluates writers' work developed during previous associations, samples presented by agents, and material received from other sources to select writers and subject material compatible with established styles, concepts, and formats. Recommends purchase of material judged to be suitable in developing scripts. Confers with production head regarding selection of writers and material. Hires, assigns, and supervises writers who prepare scripts for production. Reviews writers' work and gives instruction and direction regarding changes, additions, and corrections. Rewrites, combines, and polishes draft scripts, as necessary, to prepare scripts for production. Reads stories and other material obtained from various sources and evaluates potential for development into scripts. May assign staff members to write synopses, treatments, adaptations, scripts, and continuity when working on motion pictures.

GOE: 01.01.01 STRENGTH: S GED: R6 M2 L6 SVP: 8 DLU: 77

132.067-010 BUREAU CHIEF (print. & pub.)

Directs and coordinates activities of personnel engaged in selecting, gathering, and editing news and news pictures in remote location or foreign country and transmitting to home office of newspaper or press syndicate: May translate dispatches into English or cable language. May perform duties of REPORTER (print. & pub.; radio-tv broad.).

GOE: 11.08.01 STRENGTH: S GED: R5 M3 L5 SVP: 8 DLU: 77

132.067-014 EDITOR, BOOK (print. & pub.)

Secures, selects, and coordinates publication of manuscripts in book form: Reviews submitted manuscript, determines demand based on consumer trends and personal knowledge, and makes recommendations regarding procurement and revision. Confers with author and publisher to arrange purchase and details, such as publication date, royalties, and number of copies to be printed. Coordinates design and production activities. May assign and supervise editorial staff. May contract design and production or personally design and produce book.

GOE: 01.01.01 STRENGTH: S GED: R6 M3 L6 SVP: 8 DLU: 77

132.067-018 EDITOR, DICTIONARY (profess. & kin.) alternate titles: lexicographer

Researches information about words that make up language and writes and reviews definitions for publication in dictionary: Conducts or directs research to discover origin, spelling, syllabication, pronunciation, meaning, and usage of words. Organizes research material and writes dictionary definition. May study or conduct surveys to determine factors, such as frequency of use for a specific word, or word use by particular segment of population in order to select words for inclusion in dictionary. May perform related editorial duties. May select drawings or other graphic material to illustrate word meaning. May specialize in particular type of dictionary, such as medical, electronic, or industrial.

GOE: 11.08.01 STRENGTH: S GED: R6 M3 L6 SVP: 8 DLU: 77

132.067-022 EDITOR, GREETING CARD (print. & pub.)

Selects and edits original sentiments for use on greeting cards: Reads material submitted by freelance and staff writers and determines suitability based on knowledge of market trends, company standards, and personal tastes. Edits material to meet greeting card requirements. Maintains file of sentiments for future use. May write greeting card verses. May supervise writing staff. May design cards. May coordinate activities of art, photographic, and printing staff.

GOE: 01.01.01 STRENGTH: S GED: R5 M2 L5 SVP: 6 DLU: 77

132.067-026 EDITOR, NEWS (print. & pub.) alternate titles: makeup editor

Plans layout of newspaper edition: Receives news copy, photographs, and dummy page layouts marked to indicate columns occupied by advertising. Confers with management and editorial staff members regarding placement of developing news stories. Determines placement of stories based on relative significance, available space, and knowledge of layout principles. Marks layout sheets to indicate position of each story and accompanying photographs. Approves proofs submitted by composing room. May write or revise headlines. May edit copy. May perform related editorial duties as required.

GOE: 11.08.01 STRENGTH: S GED: R5 M3 L5 SVP: 8 DLU: 77

132.067-030 PROGRAM PROPOSALS COORDINATOR (radio-tv broad.) alternate titles: coordinator, program planning

Develops, writes, and edits proposals for new radio or television programs: Reviews program proposals submitted by staff, station and independent producers, and other sources to determine proposal feasibility, based on knowledge of station's programming needs, policy and budgetary considerations, and potential underwriting (funding) sources. Edits proposals, or writes proposals for original program concepts, and submits proposals for review of programming, financial, and other departmental personnel. Participates in selection of researchers, consultants, producers, and on-air personalities to facilitate development of program ideas. Authorizes preparation of budget for final proposals. Maintains liaison between program production department and proposal originators to inform originators of status of accepted projects.

GOE: 11.05.02 STRENGTH: S GED: R5 M3 L5 SVP: 7 DLU: 86

132.132-010 ASSIGNMENT EDITOR (radio-tv broad.) alternate titles: managing editor

Supervises and coordinates activities of radio or television news gathering staff: Maintains contact with outside news agencies, police and fire depart-

ments, and other news sources to obtain information regarding developing news items. Determines priority and assigns coverage to news units. Originates or approves ideas for news features. Confers with DIRECTOR, NEWS (radio-tv broad.) 184.167-014 and department heads to coordinate production activities. Reads and edits news copy to ensure that slanderous, libelous, and profane statements are avoided or deleted. Prepares rundown of news stories and assignment sheets, using computer. Communicates with reporters on assignments, using two-way radio. May direct or participate in writing and editing activities.

GOE: 11.08.01 STRENGTH: S GED: R5 M2 L5 SVP: 8 DLU: 89

132.267-010 EDITOR, TELEGRAPH (print. & pub.; radio-tv broad.) alternate titles: editor, wire

Selects and edits state, national, and international news items received by wire from press associations: Corrects errors of spelling and punctuation in telegraph copy. Deletes less important paragraphs, according to importance and amount of space available for story. Issues selected items to EDITOR, NEWS (print. & pub.), with notations of desired length of story in accordance with predetermined space allotment. Monitors teleprinter machines for new leads on important news items received before press time of edition, and reserves space for copy on such items. May select news of local events of national or international interest, and prepare copy to be forwarded to central news associations by wire. May rewrite stories to include information of special interest to subscribers of publication.

GOE: 11.08.01 STRENGTH: S GED: R4 M3 L4 SVP: 7 DLU: 77

132.267-014 EDITORIAL ASSISTANT (print. & pub.) alternate titles: assistant editor; associate editor

Prepares written material for publication, performing any combination of following duties: Reads copy to detect errors in spelling, punctuation, and syntax. Verifies facts, dates, and statistics, using standard reference sources. Rewrites or modifies copy to conform to publication's style and editorial policy and marks copy for typesetter, using standard symbols to indicate how type should be set. Reads galley and page proofs to detect errors and indicates corrections, using standard proofreading symbols. May confer with authors regarding changes made to manuscript. May select and crop photographs and illustrative materials to conform to space and subject matter requirements. May prepare page layouts to position and space articles and illustrations. May write or rewrite headlines, captions, columns, articles, and stories according to publication requirements. May initiate or reply to correspondence regarding material published or being considered for publication. May read and evaluate submitted manuscripts and be designated Manuscript Reader (print. & pub.). May be designated according to type of publication worked on as Copy Reader (print. & pub.) when working on newspaper; Copy Reader, Book (print. & pub.) when working on books.

GOE: 11.08.01 STRENGTH: S GED: R5 M3 L5 SVP: 7 DLU: 77

132.367-010 EDITOR, INDEX (print. & pub.) alternate titles: indexer

Prepares indices for books and other publications: Reads material to determine which items should be in index. Arranges topical or alphabetical list of index items, according to page or chapter, indicating location of item in text. Classifies items of topical interest, and inserts cross references in index to refer reader to related subjects appearing elsewhere in text. Directs activities of clerical staff engaged in typing index, filing subject-cards, and performing related duties. May prepare related items, such as glossaries, bibliographies, and explanatory footnotes, following literary style of manuscript author.

GOE: 11.08.01 STRENGTH: S GED: R5 M3 L5 SVP: 7 DLU: 77

137 INTERPRETERS AND TRANSLATORS

This group includes occupations concerned with translating spoken or written words from one language into another, and translating spoken language into sign language.

137.137-010 DIRECTOR, TRANSLATION (profess. & kin.)

Directs and coordinates activities of INTERPRETERS (profess. & kin.) and TRANSLATORS (profess. & kin.) engaged in translating spoken passages, documents, and other material from one language to another for business establishments, government agencies, and academic institutions: Studies material, using knowledge of language and linguistics, to determine best qualified personnel for specific projects. Assigns projects to personnel and reviews work for quality. Attends meetings of groups and organizations engaged in international relations to promote translation service. Prepares budget for department and determines allocation of funds. Interviews and selects personnel for staff positions.

GOE: 11.08.04 STRENGTH: S GED: R5 M3 L5 SVP: 8 DLU: 77

137.267-010 INTERPRETER (profess. & kin.)

Translates spoken passages from one language into another: Provides consecutive or simultaneous translation between languages. In consecutive interpreting listens to complete statements in one language, translates to second, and translates responses from second into first language. Expresses either approximate or exact translation, depending on nature of occasion. In simultaneous interpreting renders oral translation of material at time it is being spoken, usually hearing material over electronic audio system and broadcasting translation to listeners. Usually receives briefing on subject discussed prior to interpreting session. May be designated according to language or languages interpreted. May specialize in specific subject area.

GOE: 11.08.04 STRENGTH: S GED: R5 M2 L5 SVP: 6 DLU: 77

137.267-014 INTERPRETER, DEAF (profess. & kin.) alternate titles: translator, deaf

Provides translation between spoken and manual (sign language) communication: Translates spoken material into sign language for understanding of deaf. Interprets sign language of deaf into oral or written language for hearing individuals or others not conversant in sign language. May translate television news and other broadcasts for deaf viewers.
GOE: 01.03.02 STRENGTH: L GED: R4 M3 L4 SVP: 5 DLU: 77

137.267-018 TRANSLATOR (profess. & kin.)

Translates documents and other material from one language to another: Reads material and rewrites material in specified language or languages, following established rules pertaining to factors, such as word meanings, sentence structure, grammar, punctuation, and mechanics. May specialize in particular type of material, such as news, legal documents, or scientific reports and be designated accordingly. May be identified according to language translated. May represent or spell characters of another alphabet and be designated Transliterator (profess. & kin.).
GOE: 11.08.04 STRENGTH: S GED: R6 M3 L6 SVP: 7 DLU: 77

139   OCCUPATIONS IN WRITING, N.E.C.

This group includes occupations, not elsewhere classified, concerned with writing.

139.087-010 CROSSWORD-PUZZLE MAKER (print. & pub.)

Devises and creates crossword puzzles: Draws form setting up numbered blank squares for insertion of words and black squares to complete design. Fits words, whose spelling coincides vertically and horizontally, into blank areas and composes short definitions numbered correspondingly with matching series of blank squares. Sets up filled puzzle as key to solution. May originate puzzles for specific purposes, such as advertisements or holiday specialities.
GOE: 01.01.02 STRENGTH: S GED: R5 M2 L5 SVP: 6 DLU: 77

139.167-010 PROGRAM COORDINATOR (amuse. & rec.)

Coordinates activities of amusement park educational department to present educational scripts during animal performances: Reviews educational materials to gather information for scripts. Confers with animal trainer to verify format of performance, and writes script to coincide with performance, or reviews scripts prepared by department researchers for suggested changes in format. Prepares brochures containing information, such as time of performances, theme of performances, and map of park facilities. Reads reservation log to determine information, such as name of visiting groups, size of groups, and time of arrival. Greets visitors, passes out brochures, answers questions, and escorts visitors to site of performance. May introduce trainer to audience and present memorized script during performance over speaker system and be designated Narrator (amuse. & rec.).
GOE: 01.03.03 STRENGTH: L GED: R4 M2 L4 SVP: 8 DLU: 86

14   OCCUPATIONS IN ART

This division includes occupations concerned with integrating personal expression, knowledge of subject matter, and art concepts, techniques, and processes to develop ideas and create environments, products, and art works which elicit an emotional or esthetic response. Occupations concerned with teaching are included in Groups 091, 092, and 097. Occupations in performing arts are included in Groups 150, 151, and 152. Occupations in art museums are included in Group 102.

141   COMMERCIAL ARTISTS: DESIGNERS AND ILLUSTRATORS, GRAPHIC ARTS

This group includes occupations concerned with designing and executing artwork to promote public consumption of materials, products, or services; influence others in their opinions of individuals or organizations; or illustrate and adorn subject matter. Includes preparing animated cartoons.

141.031-010 ART DIRECTOR (profess. & kin.)

Formulates concepts and supervises workers engaged in executing layout designs for art work and copy to be presented by visual communications media, such as magazines, books, newspapers, television, posters, and packaging: Reviews illustrative material and confers with client or individual responsible for presentation regarding budget, background information, objectives, presentation approaches, styles, techniques, and related production factors. Formulates basic layout design concept and conducts research to select and secure suitable illustrative material, or conceives and assigns production of material and detail to artists and photographers. Assigns and directs staff members to develop design concepts into art layouts and prepare layouts for printing. Reviews, approves, and presents final layouts to client or department head for approval. May perform duties of GRAPHIC DESIGNER (profess. & kin.) to design art layouts. May mark up, paste up, and finish layouts to prepare layouts for printing. May draw illustrations. May prepare detailed story board showing sequence and timing of story development when producing material for television. May specialize in particular field, media, or type of layout.
GOE: 01.02.03 STRENGTH: S GED: R5 M3 L5 SVP: 8 DLU: 77

141.051-010 COLOR EXPERT (profess. & kin.) alternate titles: color consultant; colorist; color specialist

Advises clients relative to fashionable shades and color combinations in paper, paint, draperies, floor coverings, and other permanent installations for furnishing interiors of homes, offices, and other commercial establishments.
GOE: 01.02.03 STRENGTH: L GED: R5 M2 L4 SVP: 7 DLU: 77

141.061-010 CARTOONIST (print. & pub.)

Draws cartoons for publications to amuse readers and interpret or illustrate news highlights, advertising, stories, or articles: Develops personal ideas or reads written material to develop ideas from context. Discusses ideas with editor or publisher's representative or sketches cartoon drawing and submits drawing for approval. Makes changes and corrections as necessary and finishes drawing. May develop and draw comic strips. May be designated according to type of cartoons drawn as Editorial Cartoonist (print. & pub.); Sports Cartoonist (print. & pub.).
GOE: 01.02.03 STRENGTH: S GED: R5 M2 L4 SVP: 7 DLU: 77

141.061-014 FASHION ARTIST (retail trade)

Draws or paints apparel and accessory illustrations for newspaper or related advertisements: Positions garment, accessory, or model to accentuate desired sales features. Renders drawing of garment or accessory, complementary articles, and background, using various art media and materials. May use models, props, and settings to accentuate subject materials. May draw lettering.
GOE: 01.02.03 STRENGTH: S GED: R5 M2 L4 SVP: 7 DLU: 77

141.061-018 GRAPHIC DESIGNER (profess. & kin.) alternate titles: layout artist

Designs art and copy layouts for material to be presented by visual communications media such as books, magazines, newspapers, television, and packaging: Studies illustrations and photographs to plan presentation of material, product, or service. Determines size and arrangement of illustrative material and copy, selects style and size of type, and arranges layout based upon available space, knowledge of layout principles, and esthetic design concepts. Draws sample of finished layout and presents sample to ART DIRECTOR (profess. & kin.) 141.031-010 for approval. Prepares notes and instructions for workers who assemble and prepare final layouts for printing. Reviews final layout and suggests improvements as needed. May prepare illustrations or rough sketches of material according to instructions of client or supervisor. May prepare series of drawings to illustrate sequence and timing of story development for television production. May mark up, paste, and assemble final layouts to prepare layouts for printer. May specialize in particular field, medium, or type of layout. May produce still and animated graphic formats for on-air and taped portions of television news broadcasts, using electronic video equipment. May photograph layouts, using camera, to make layout prints for supervisor or client. May develop negatives and prints, using negative and print developing equipment, tools and work aids to produce layout photographs for client or supervisor. May key information into computer equipment to create layouts for client or supervisor.
GOE: 01.02.03 STRENGTH: S GED: R5 M3 L4 SVP: 7 DLU: 89

141.061-022 ILLUSTRATOR (profess. & kin.) alternate titles: artist; commercial artist; graphic artist

Draws or paints illustrations for use by various media to explain or adorn printed or spoken word: Studies layouts, sketches of proposed illustrations, and related materials to become familiar with assignment. Determines style, technique, and medium best suited to produce desired effects and conform with reproduction requirements, or receives specific instructions regarding these variables. Formulates concept and renders illustration and detail from models, sketches, memory, and imagination. Discusses illustration at various stages of completion and makes changes as necessary. May select type, draw lettering, lay out material, or perform related duties. May be identified according to specific style, technique, medium, subject material or combination of variables. May draw or paint graphic material and lettering to be used for title, background, screen advertising, commercial logo, and other visual layouts for motion picture production and television programming and be designated Title Artist (motion picture; radio-tv broad.).
GOE: 01.02.03 STRENGTH: S GED: R5 M2 L4 SVP: 7 DLU: 77

141.061-026 ILLUSTRATOR, MEDICAL AND SCIENTIFIC (profess. & kin.) alternate titles: artist, scientific

Creates illustrations, graphics, and three dimensional models to demonstrate medical or biological subjects, using variety of artistic techniques: Develops drawings, paintings, diagrams, and models of medical or biological subjects in fields such as anatomy, physiology, histology, pathology, or in surgical procedures, for use in publications, exhibits, consultations, research, and teaching activities. Completes illustrations in pen and ink, oil, monochromatic wash, watercolor, carbon dust, and mixed media. Constructs or advises in construction of models in plaster, wax, plastics, and other materials. Devises visual aids, such as films, video tapes, charts, and computer graphics, to assist in teaching and research programs.
GOE: 01.02.03 STRENGTH: S GED: R5 M4 L5 SVP: 7 DLU: 89

141.061-030 ILLUSTRATOR, SET (motion picture; radio-tv broad.) alternate titles: sketch maker

Plans, develops, and prepares illustrations of scenes and backgrounds against which action is filmed for use in motion picture or television production: Reads script, reviews working drawings, conducts research and consults with ART DI-

RECTOR (motion picture; radio-tv broad.) to develop illustration ideas. Performs duties of ILLUSTRATOR (profess. & kin.) to render illustrations.
GOE: 01.02.03 STRENGTH: S GED: R5 M3 L4 SVP: 8 DLU: 77

141.061-034 POLICE ARTIST (government ser.) alternate titles: forensic artist
Sketches likenesses of criminal suspects, according to descriptions of victims and witnesses, and prepares schematic drawings depicting scenes of crimes: Interviews crime victims and witnesses to obtain descriptive information concerning physical build, sex, nationality, facial features, and related characteristics of unidentified suspect. Prepares series of simple line drawings conforming to description of suspect and presents drawings to informant for selection of sketch that most resembles suspect. Questions informant to obtain additional descriptive information and draws and verifies details of features to improve resemblance of conception to recollection of informant. Measures distances and sketches layout of crime scene, or develops sketches from photographs and measurements taken at scene of crime by other police personnel to prepare schematic drawing of scene of crime.
GOE: 01.02.03 STRENGTH: L GED: R5 M3 L4 SVP: 7 DLU: 86

141.061-038 COMMERCIAL DESIGNER (profess. & kin.)
Creates and designs graphic material for use as ornamentation, illustration, advertising, or cosmetic on manufactured materials and packaging: Receives assignment from customer or supervisor. Studies traditional, period, and contemporary design styles and motifs to obtain perspective. Reviews marketing trends and preferences of target and related markets. Integrates findings with personal interests, knowledge of design, and limitations presented by methods and materials. Creates, draws, modifies, and changes design to achieve desired effect. Confers with customer or supervisor regarding approval or desired changes to design. May be required to have specialized knowledge of material designed. May prepare original artwork and design model. May perform related duties, such as fabricating silk screens, drawing full size patterns, or cutting stencils. May work with specific items, such as signs, packaging, wallpaper, ceramics, tile, glassware, monograms, crests, emblems, or embroidery. See INDUSTRIAL DESIGNER (profess. & kin.) 142.061-026 for workers who design both product form and associated graphic materials.
GOE: 01.02.03 STRENGTH: S GED: R5 M3 L4 SVP: 7 DLU: 81

141.067-010 CREATIVE DIRECTOR (profess. & kin.)
Develops basic presentation approaches and directs layout design and copy writing for promotional material, such as books, magazines, newspapers, television, posters, and packaging: Reviews materials and information presented by client and discusses various production factors to determine most desirable presentation concept. Confers with heads of art, copy writing, and production departments to discuss client requirements and scheduling, outline basic presentation concepts, and coordinate creative activities. Reviews and approves art and copy materials developed by staff and presents final layouts to client for approval.
GOE: 01.02.03 STRENGTH: S GED: R5 M3 L5 SVP: 8 DLU: 77

141.081-010 CARTOONIST, MOTION PICTURES (motion picture; radio-tv broad.) alternate titles: animated-cartoon artist; animator
Draws animated cartoons for use in motion pictures or television: Renders series of sequential drawings of characters or other subject material which when photographed and projected at specific speed becomes animated. May label each section with designated colors when colors are used. May create and prepare sketches and model drawings of characters. May prepare successive drawings to portray wind, rain, fire, and similar effects and be designated Cartoonist, Special Effects (motion picture; radio-tv broad.). May develop color patterns and moods and paint background layouts to dramatize action for animated cartoon scenes and be designated Cartoon-Background Artist (motion picture; radio-tv broad.).
GOE: 01.02.03 STRENGTH: S GED: R5 M2 L4 SVP: 7 DLU: 77

141.137-010 PRODUCTION MANAGER, ADVERTISING (profess. & kin.)
Coordinates activities of design, illustration, photography, paste-up, and typography personnel to prepare advertisements for publication, and supervises workers engaged in pasting-up advertising layouts in art department or studio: Determines arrangement of art work and photographs and selects style and size of type, considering factors such as size of advertisement, design, layout, sketches, and method or printing specified. Submits copy and typography instructions to printing firm or department for typesetting. Reviews proofs of printed copy for conformance to specifications. Assigns personnel to mount printed copy and illustration on final layouts, coordinating assignments with completion of art work to ensure that schedules are maintained. Writes instructions for final margin widths and type sizes, and submits layout for printing. Examines layout proofs for quality of printing and conformance to layout.
GOE: 01.02.03 STRENGTH: S GED: R4 M3 L4 SVP: 7 DLU: 86

142 ENVIRONMENTAL, PRODUCT, AND RELATED DESIGNERS

This group includes occupations concerned with designing or arranging objects and materials to achieve aesthetically pleasing and functional effect for apparel, interiors, and other commercial items.

142.031-014 MANAGER, DISPLAY (retail trade)
Develops advertising displays for window or interior use and supervises and coordinates activities of workers engaged in laying out and assembling displays: Consults with advertising and sales officials to ascertain type of merchandise to be featured and time and place for each display. Develops layout and selects theme, colors, and props to be used. Oversees requisitioning and construction of decorative props from such materials as wood, plastics, paper, and glass. Plans lighting arrangement and selects coloring medium. May design store fixtures. May prepare sketches or floor plans of proposed displays. May develop merchandise displays at special exhibits, such as trade shows.
GOE: 01.02.03 STRENGTH: L GED: R5 M3 L4 SVP: 7 DLU: 77

142.051-010 DISPLAY DESIGNER (profess. & kin.) alternate titles: display and banner designer; flag decorator and designer
Designs displays, using paper, cloth, plastic, and other material to decorate streets, fairgrounds, buildings, and other places for celebrations, fairs, and special occasions: Confers with client regarding budget, theme, materials, colors, emblem styles, and related factors. Plans display and sketches rough design for client's approval. Selects stock decorations or directs construction according to design concepts. May construct decorations. May direct and supervise workers who put up decorations. May design, draw, paint, or sketch backgrounds and fixtures made of wood, cardboard, paper, plaster, canvas, or other material for use in windows or interior displays and be designated Display Artist (profess. & kin.). May specialize in designing outdoor displays and be designated Display Designer, Outside (profess. & kin.).
GOE: 01.02.03 STRENGTH: S GED: R5 M3 L4 SVP: 7 DLU: 77

142.051-014 INTERIOR DESIGNER (profess. & kin.)
Plans, designs, and furnishes interior environments of residential, commercial, and industrial buildings: Confers with client to determine architectural preferences, purpose and function of environment, budget, types of construction, equipment to be installed, and other factors which affect planning interior environments. Integrates findings with knowledge of interior design and formulates environmental plan to be practical, esthetic, and conducive to intended purposes, such as raising productivity, selling merchandise, or improving life style of occupants. Advises client on interior design factors, such as space planning, layout and utilization of furnishings and equipment, color schemes, and color coordination. Renders design ideas in form of paste ups, drawings, or illustrations, estimates material requirements and costs, and presents design to client for approval. Selects or designs and purchases furnishings, art works, and accessories. Subcontracts fabrication, installation, and arrangement of carpeting, fixtures, accessories, draperies, paint and wall coverings, art work, furniture, and related items. May plan and design interior environments for boats, planes, buses, trains, and other enclosed spaces. May specialize in particular field, style, or phase of interior design. May specialize in decorative aspects of interior design and be designated Interior Decorator (profess. & kin.).
GOE: 01.02.03 STRENGTH: L GED: R5 M3 L4 SVP: 7 DLU: 85

142.061-010 BANK-NOTE DESIGNER (government ser.)
Designs engraving plate for printing government securities, such as currency, stamps, and bonds, according to preliminary drawings and knowledge of engraving and printing techniques: Examines preliminary sketch of design from government agency desiring to issue new or modified design. Modifies design to conform with technical characteristics and limitations of reproduction, engraving, and printing equipment and to introduce design elements to discourage counterfeiting, using drawing instruments. Selects or suggests colored inks pleasing to eye, consistent with dignity of security and need to discourage counterfeiting. Confers with representatives of issuing agency to obtain design approval. May originate designs and design suggestions for securities.
GOE: 01.06.01 STRENGTH: S GED: R4 M3 L4 SVP: 8 DLU: 77

142.061-014 CLOTH DESIGNER (profess. & kin.) alternate titles: cloth pattern maker; pattern designer; textile stylist
Originates designs for fabrication of cloth, specifying weave pattern, color, and gauge of thread, to create new fabrics according to functional requirements and fashion preferences of consumers: Develops new ideas for fabrics, utilizing knowledge of textiles and fashion trends. Consults with technical and merchandising staff to obtain design ideas, and to estimate consumer acceptance of new types of fabrics. Sketches designs for patterns on graph paper, using water colors, brushes, pens, and rulers, or prepares written instructions to specify details, such as finish, color, and construction of fabric. Examines fabricated sample on loom and modifies design as required. May be designated according to product designed as Rug Designer (carpet & rug); Woven-Label Designer (narrow fabrics).
GOE: 01.02.03 STRENGTH: S GED: R4 M3 L4 SVP: 7 DLU: 77

142.061-018 FASHION DESIGNER (profess. & kin.) alternate titles: clothes designer
Designs men's, women's, and children's clothing and accessories: Analyzes fashion trends and predictions, confers with sales and management executives, compares leather, fabrics, and other apparel materials, and integrates findings with personal interests, tastes, and knowledge of design to create new designs for clothing, shoes, handbags, and other accessories. Sketches rough and detailed drawings of apparel and writes specifications describing factors, such as color scheme, construction, and type of material to be used. Confers with and coordinates activities of workers who draw and cut patterns and construct garments to fabricate sample garment. Examines sample garment on and off model

91

and modifies design as necessary to achieve desired effect. May draw pattern for article designed, using measuring and drawing instruments. May cut patterns. May construct sample, using sewing equipment. May arrange for showing of sample garments at sales meetings or fashion shows. May attend fashion and fabric shows to observe new fashions and materials. May be identified according to specific group designed for, such as men, women, or children or areas of specialization, such as sportswear, coats, dresses, suits, lingerie, or swimwear. May design custom garments for clients and be designated Custom Garment Designer (retail trade). May conduct research and design authentic period, country, or social class costumes to be worn by film, television, concert, stage, and other performers and be designated Costume Designer (profess. & kin.). May design, fabricate, repair, and sell leather articles and be designated Leather Crafter (leather prod.). May design, copy, or modify clothing accessories and be designated according to article designed as Handbag Designer (leather prod.); Hat Designer (hat & cap); or Shoe Designer (boot & shoe).
GOE: 01.02.03 STRENGTH: L GED: R5 M3 L4 SVP: 7 DLU: 78

142.061-022   FURNITURE DESIGNER (furniture)

Designs furniture for manufacture, according to knowledge of design trends, offerings of competition, production costs, capability of production facilities, and characteristics of company's market: Confers with production, design, and sales personnel to obtain design suggestions and customer orders. Evaluates orders and proposals to determine feasibility of producing item. Sketches freehand design of article. Obtains approval from customer, design committee, or authorized company officials, and originates scale or full size drawing, using drawing instruments. Prepares itemized production requirements to produce item. Traces drawing on material for use in production of blueprints, using drawing instruments. Prepares or directs preparation of blueprints containing manufacturing specifications, such as dimensions, kind of wood, and upholstery fabrics to be used in manufacturing article. Attends staff conference with plant personnel to explain and resolve production requirements. May design and prepare detailed drawings of jigs, fixtures, forms, or tools required to be used in production. May plan modifications for completed furniture to conform to changes in design trends and increase customer acceptance. May design custom pieces or styles according to specific period or country. May build or oversee construction of models or prototypes. May design fixtures and equipment, such as counters and display cases, and be designated Fixture Designer (furniture).
GOE: 01.02.03 STRENGTH: S GED: R5 M4 L4 SVP: 7 DLU: 77

142.061-026   INDUSTRIAL DESIGNER (profess. & kin.)

Originates and develops ideas to design the form of manufactured products: Reads publications, attends showings, and consults with engineering, marketing, production, and sales representatives to establish design concepts. Evaluates design ideas based on factors such as appealing appearance, design-function relationships, serviceability, materials and methods engineering, application, budget, price, production costs, methods of production, market characteristics, and client specifications. Integrates findings and concepts and sketches design ideas. Presents design to client or design committee and discusses need for modification and change. May design product packaging and graphics for advertising. May build simulated model, using hand and power tools and various materials. May prepare illustrations. May prepare or coordinate preparation of working drawings from sketches and design specifications. May design products for custom applications. May be required to have specialized product knowledge. Usually specializes in specific product or type of product including, but not limited to hardware, motor vehicle exteriors and interiors, scientific instruments, industrial equipment, luggage, jewelry, housewares, toys, or novelties and is designated accordingly.
GOE: 01.02.03 STRENGTH: S GED: R5 M4 L4 SVP: 7 DLU: 77

142.061-030   MEMORIAL DESIGNER (stonework)

Designs and builds plaster models of monuments, statues, and memorials: Interviews customer to obtain information regarding size, style, and motif of memorial. Draws sketches and detailed plans of memorial according to customer's suggestions. Casts plaster block and carves design in block, using chisels, mallets, knives, and files to form model of memorial. Routes finished model and work order specifications to STONE CARVER (stonework). May draw detailed sketches or plans of family burial plots. May build models of cemeteries used as displays.
GOE: 01.02.03 STRENGTH: L GED: R4 M4 L3 SVP: 7 DLU: 77

142.061-034   ORNAMENTAL-METALWORK DESIGNER (struct. metal) alternate titles: art-metal designer

Designs ornamental metal items, such as grills, lattice work, statuary, railings, displays, plaques, and light fixtures, and tooling for fabrication, utilizing knowledge of properties of metal, fabrication techniques, principles of design, and artistic talent: Analyzes sketches or observes and measures physical surroundings prior to installation. Selects designs from pattern book, alters or originates designs according to customer specifications. Draws detail sketches and prescribes fabricating techniques. Forges tools, such as peening hammers, bending jigs, and scroll forms, using forge, machine tools, welding equipment, and hand forming tools. May sculpture plastic patterns to form molding castings. Builds products from original design or working models [ORNAMENTAL-METAL WORKER (metal prod., nec)]. May prescribe colors for painted parts.
GOE: 01.02.02 STRENGTH: L GED: R5 M4 L4 SVP: 8 DLU: 77

142.061-038   SAFETY-CLOTHING-AND-EQUIPMENT   DEVELOPER (profess. & kin.) alternate titles: protective-clothing-and-equipment specialist

Designs safety clothing and equipment to protect personnel against hazards, such as fire and toxic fumes: Consults with employers and technical personnel to determine safety problem involved. Designs clothing and equipment, such as suits, helmets, and gloves, incorporating such devices as mechanical breathing apparatus and communication systems to meet specific hazards. Drafts pattern of garment parts on pattern paper in full scale, using ruler, drawing instruments, pattern blocks, and cuts material to make first pattern. Gives instructions to workers engaged in cutting material and assembling sample garment. May estimate cost of production.
GOE: 05.01.07 STRENGTH: L GED: R5 M3 L5 SVP: 8 DLU: 77

142.061-042   SET DECORATOR (motion picture; radio-tv broad.)

Selects decorations and coordinates activities of workers who decorate sets for motion picture or television production: Reads script to determine decoration requirements. Selects furniture, draperies, pictures, lamps, and rugs for decorative quality and appearance on film. Gives directions to GRIP (motion picture; radio-tv broad.) in placing items on set. Examines dressed sets to ensure props and scenery do not interfere with moovements of cast or view of camera.
GOE: 01.02.03 STRENGTH: S GED: R5 M2 L4 SVP: 8 DLU: 77

142.061-046   SET DESIGNER (motion picture; radio-tv broad.)

Designs motion picture or television production sets, signs, props, or scenic effects, and prepares scale drawings for use in construction, modification, or alteration: Confers with ART DIRECTOR (motion picture; radio-tv broad.) 142.061-062 and reviews illustrations to determine set requirements and discuss preliminary design ideas. Integrates requirements and concepts to conceive set design. Prepares rough draft and scale working drawings of set [DRAFTER (profess. & kin.) Master Title]. Presents drawings for approval and makes changes and corrections as directed. May design miniature motion picture or television production sets used in filming backgrounds, titles, and special effects and be designated Miniature Set Designer (motion picture; radio-tv broad.). May purchase construction materials and ready made props to ensure availability for use by freelance workers. May schedule times television production sets and props are to be used, and coordinate setup and storage of television production sets and props.
GOE: 01.02.03 STRENGTH: L GED: R5 M3 L4 SVP: 8 DLU: 88

142.061-050   SET DESIGNER (amuse. & rec.) alternate titles: scenic designer; theatrical-scenic designer

Designs sets for theatrical productions: Confers with play's director regarding interpretation and set requirements. Conducts research to determine appropriate architectural and furnishing styles. Integrates requirements, interpretation, research, design concepts, and practical considerations regarding factors, such as mobility, interchangeability, and budget to plan sets. Renders drawing or illustration of design concept, estimates costs, and presents drawing for approval. Prepares working drawings of floor plan, front elevation, scenery, and properties to be constructed. Prepares charts to indicate where items, such as curtains and borders are to be hung. Oversees building of sets, furniture, and properties. May build scale models from cardboard, plaster, or sponge. May design stage lighting to achieve dramatic or decorative effects.
GOE: 01.02.03 STRENGTH: L GED: R5 M3 L4 SVP: 8 DLU: 77

142.061-054   STAINED GLASS ARTIST (profess. & kin.)

Creates original stained glass designs and artwork, draws cartoons (full size working drawings), and prepares glass for fabrication into windows, art objects, and other decorative articles: Consults client regarding theme and subject to be portrayed. Studies style of building architecture and shape of windows to plan conforming design. Integrates knowledge of glass cutting, stresses, portraiture, symbolism, heraldry, ornamental styles, and related factors with functional requirements to conceptualize design idea. Renders illustration of design and detail, estimates costs, and presents to client for approval. Prepares full size, detailed color cartoon indicating size, shape, shading, and detail of individual glass pieces. Transfers cartoon into pattern, selects colored glass, and cuts glass according to pattern. Assembles cut pieces into design pattern and waxes pieces in place to secure glass for painting. Paints artwork and detail on glass, using artist's brushes and ground glass mixed with enamel, and copper or iron oxide. Stains back of glass pieces prior to or after firing. Fires glass to fuse and stabilize colors. May assemble, lead, and solder finished glass to fabricate designed article. May install finished window in window frame or door. May restore damaged or broken stained glass objects. May only design, paint, or draw cartoons.
GOE: 01.02.02 STRENGTH: S GED: R5 M3 L4 SVP: 8 DLU: 77

142.061-058   EXHIBIT DESIGNER (museums)

Plans, designs, and oversees construction and installation of permanent and temporary exhibits and displays: Confers with administrative, curatorial, and exhibit staff members to determine theme, content, interpretative or informational purpose, and planned location of exhibit, to discuss budget, promotion, and time limitations, and to plan production schedule for fabrication and installation of exhibit components. Prepares preliminary drawings of proposed exhibit, including detailed construction, layout, and special effect diagrams and material specifications, for final drawing rendition by other personnel, basing design and specifications on knowledge of artistic and technical concepts, principles, and techniques. Submits plan for approval, and adapts plan as needed to serve in-

tended purpose or to conform to budget or fabrication restrictions. Oversees preparation of artwork and construction of exhibit components to ensure intended interpretation of concepts and conformance to structural and material specifications. Arranges for acquisition of specimens or graphics or building of exhibit structures by outside contractors as needed to complete exhibit. Inspects installed exhibit for conformance to specifications and satisfactory operation of special effects components. Oversees placement of collection objects or informational materials in exhibit framework.
GOE: 01.02.03 STRENGTH: S GED: R5 M4 L5 SVP: 7 DLU: 86

142.061-062 ART DIRECTOR (motion picture; radio-tv broad.)
Formulates design concepts, selects locations and settings, and directs and coordinates set design, construction, and erection activities to produce sets for motion picture and television productions: Reads script and confers with heads of production and direction to establish budget, schedules, and determine setting requirement. Conducts research and consults experts to establish architectural styles which accurately depict given periods and locations. Conducts search for suitable locations and constructed sets. Assigns assistants and staff members to complete design ideas and prepare sketches, illustrations, and detailed drawings of sets. Directs design and production of graphics or animation to produce graphics or animation for on-air programs. Estimates construction costs and presents plans and estimates for approval. Directs and coordinates set construction, erection, and decoration activities to ensure that they conform to design, budget, and schedule requirements. Reviews budget and expenditures reports to monitor costs. May make rough drawings of design concepts. May formulate design concepts for costumes, makeup, photographic effects, titles, and related production items.
GOE: 01.02.03 STRENGTH: S GED: R5 M3 L5 SVP: 8 DLU: 89

142.081-010 FLORAL DESIGNER (retail trade) alternate titles: florist
Designs and fashions live, cut, dried, and artificial floral and foliar arrangements for events, such as holidays, anniversaries, weddings, balls, and funerals: Confers with client regarding price and type of arrangement desired. Plans arrangement according to client's requirements and costs, utilizing knowledge of design and properties of materials, or selects appropriate standard design pattern. Selects flora and foliage necessary for arrangement. Trims material and arranges bouquets, sprays, wreaths, dish gardens, terrariums, and other items, using wire, pins, floral tape, foam, trimmers, cutters, shapers, and other materials and tools. May decorate buildings, halls, churches, or other facilities where events are planned. May pack and wrap completed arrangements. May estimate costs and price arrangements. May conduct classes or demonstrations. May instruct and direct other workers. May arrange according to standard designs or under instruction of designer and be designated Floral Arranger (retail trade).
GOE: 01.02.03 STRENGTH: L GED: R4 M3 L3 SVP: 6 DLU: 77

142.081-014 FUR DESIGNER (fur goods)
Designs or redesigns custom and commercial fur garments: Analyzes fashion trends and predictions and confers with client or sales and management executives regarding design ideas. Sketches design on paper to make or restyle garment, utilizing knowledge of various kinds of fur, techniques for handling fur, and fashion trends. Obtains customer measurements, using tape measure. Draws pattern on paper according to customer measurements and cuts out pattern. Lays pattern on canvas and cuts out material, using scissors. Sews together sections of canvas to form mockup of garment. Fits mockup on customer and makes necessary alterations. Directs workers engaged in cutting and sewing garment. Examines completed garments for defects. May estimate cost of restyling or of making new garment.
GOE: 01.02.03 STRENGTH: L GED: R4 M2 L4 SVP: 7 DLU: 77

142.081-018 PACKAGE DESIGNER (profess. & kin.)
Designs containers for products, such as foods, beverages, toiletries, cigarettes, and medicines: Confers with representatives of engineering, marketing, management, and other departments to determine packaging requirements and type of product market. Sketches design of container for specific product, considering factors, such as convenience in handling and storing, distinctiveness for identification by consumer, and simplicity to minimize production costs. Renders design, including exterior markings and labels, using paints and brushes. Typically fabricates model in paper, wood, glass, plastic, or metal, depending on material to be used in package. Makes changes or modifications required by approving authority.
GOE: 01.02.03 STRENGTH: S GED: R5 M3 L4 SVP: 7 DLU: 77

142.281-010 COPYIST (garment)
Gathers information on current trends in garment styling and sketches representations of competitors' garments, such as dresses, coats, and trousers: Attends garment fashion shows, concerts, and other public activities and reviews garment magazines and manuals to obtain information concerning style trends, consumer preferences, and price ranges. Sketches garments in pencil, crayon, or other medium to illustrate such details as garment style and type of fabric. May design original garments, incorporating features of observed garments.
GOE: 01.02.03 STRENGTH: L GED: R4 M2 L4 SVP: 6 DLU: 77

143 OCCUPATIONS IN PHOTOGRAPHY

This group includes occupations concerned with photographing people, events, fictionalized scenes, materials, and products with still or motion-picture cameras. Includes conceiving artistic photographic effects and arranging and preparing subject matter.

143.062-010 DIRECTOR OF PHOTOGRAPHY (motion picture; radio-tv broad.) alternate titles: camera operator, first; camera operator, head; cinematographer
Plans, directs, and coordinates motion picture filming: Confers with DIRECTOR, MOTION PICTURE (motion picture) regarding interpretation of scene and desired effects. Observes set or location and reviews drawings and other information relating to natural or artificial conditions to determine filming and lighting requirements. Reads charts and computes ratios to determine required lighting, film, shutter angles, filter factors, camera distance, depth of field and focus, angles of view, and other variables to produce desired effects. Confers with ELECTRICIAN, CHIEF (motion picture) to establish lighting requirements. Selects cameras, accessories, equipment, and film stock, utilizing knowledge of filming techniques, filming requirements, and computations. Instructs camera operators regarding camera setup, angles, distances, movement, and other variables and signals cues for starting and stopping filming. Surveys set or location for potential problems, observes effects of lighting, measures lighting levels, and coordinates necessary changes prior to filming. Views film after processing and makes adjustments, as necessary, to achieve desired effects. May direct television productions which utilize electronic cameras. May specialize in special effects and be designated Director Of Photography, Special Effects (motion picture; radio-tv broad.).
GOE: 01.02.03 STRENGTH: L GED: R5 M4 L4 SVP: 8 DLU: 77

143.062-014 PHOTOGRAPHER, AERIAL (profess. & kin.)
Photographs segments of earth and other subject material from aircraft to produce pictures used in surveying, mapping, volumetric surveying, or related purposes, such as recording effects of pollution or natural disasters, determining condition of crops and timberland, and planning cities or other large scale projects: Sets up and mounts camera in aircraft. Confers with pilot regarding plotted course, speed, altitude, and area to be photographed. Communicates with pilot during flight to ensure adherence to flight plan or make adjustments to equipment to compensate for changes. Calculates number of exposures and time lapse between them, using standard formulas to determine requirements for adequate area coverage. Adjusts camera shutter speed, lens aperture opening, and focus. Adjusts automatic exposure interval on camera equipped with time lapse control or times intervals with stopwatch and manually trips shutter. Maintains camera in level position and oriented to flight path when making photographs for mapping or surveying. May match individual photographs to form terrain map of photographed area.
GOE: 01.06.01 STRENGTH: L GED: R4 M3 L3 SVP: 7 DLU: 77

143.062-018 PHOTOGRAPHER, APPRENTICE (profess. & kin.) alternate titles: commercial photographer apprentice; portrait photographer apprentice
Performs duties as described under APPRENTICE (any industry) Master Title.
GOE: 01.02.03 STRENGTH: L GED: R4 M3 L4 SVP: 7 DLU: 77

143.062-022 CAMERA OPERATOR (motion picture; radio-tv broad.)
Photographs various subjects and subject material, using motion picture, television broadcasting, or video recording cameras and equipment, utilizing knowledge of motion picture, television broadcasting, or video recording techniques, limitations, and advantages to photograph scenes: Resolves problems presented by exposure control, subject and camera movement, changes in subject distance during filming, and related variables. May receive directives from PRODUCER (radio-tv broad.) 159.117-010 or DIRECTOR, TELEVISION (radio-tv broad.) 159.067-014 over headset. May set up and operate dollies, cranes, camera mounting heads, power zooms, and related motion picture, television broadcasting, or video recording equipment and accessories. May maintain or repair equipment and accessories. May specialize in particular subject material or field, such as medical, scientific, news, or commercial. May photograph action on motion picture or television sets and locations, using shoulder held camera, and be designated Camera Operator, Second (motion picture; radio-tv broad.) or photograph special effects and be designated Camera Operator, Special Effects (motion picture; radio-tv broad.). May specialize in operation of television cameras and be designated Camera Operator, Television (radio-tv broad.). May specialize in operation of motion picture cameras and be designated Photographer, Motion Picture (motion picture).
GOE: 01.02.03 STRENGTH: M GED: R4 M3 L4 SVP: 7 DLU: 88

143.062-026 PHOTOGRAPHER, SCIENTIFIC (profess. & kin.)
Photographs variety of subject material to illustrate or record scientific data or phenomena, utilizing knowledge of scientific procedures and photographic technology and techniques: Plans methods and procedures for photographing subject material and setup of equipment required, such as microscopes, telescopes, infrared or ultraviolet lighting, and x ray. Sets up and positions camera for photographing material or subject. Trips shutter to expose film. May prepare microscope slides. May make photographic copies of fragile documents and other material. May engage in research to develop new photographic procedures, methods, and materials. May process film and photographic paper to produce transparencies, prints, slides, and motion picture film. Usually specializes in specific field, such as chemistry, biology, medicine, metallurgy, physiology, astronomy, aerodynamics, ballistics, or engineering and is designated accordingly.
GOE: 02.04.01 STRENGTH: L GED: R4 M3 L4 SVP: 7 DLU: 77

143.062-030 PHOTOGRAPHER, STILL (profess. & kin.) alternate titles: commercial photographer
Photographs subjects, using still cameras, color or black-and-white film, and variety of photographic accessories: Selects and assembles equipment according

to subject material, anticipated conditions, and knowledge of function and limitations of various types of cameras, lenses, films, and accessories. Views subject and setting and plans composition, camera position, and camera angle to produce desired effect. Arranges subject material, poses subject, or maneuvers into position to take candid photo. Estimates or measures light level, using light meter or creates artificial lighting with flash units, lights, and lighting equipment. Adjusts lens aperture and shutter speed based on combination of factors, such as lighting, depth of field, subject motion, and film speed. Determines subject-to-lens distance, using tape measure, range finder, ground glass, or reflex viewing system to adjust focus. Positions camera and trips shutter to expose film. May calculate variables, such as exposure time, exposure interval, filter effect, and color temperature using tables, standard formulas, and mechanical or electronic measuring instruments. May make adjustments to camera, lens, or equipment to compensate for factors, such as distorted perspective and parallax. May design, build, arrange, or secure properties and settings to be used as background for subject material. May direct activities of other workers. May mix chemicals, process film and photographic paper, and make contact and enlarged prints. May spot and retouch prints and negatives. May conceive and plan photographic sequence for effective presentation. May specialize in particular type of photography, such as illustrative, fashion, architectural, or portrait. May be required to have detailed knowledge of use and characteristics of various types of film, including specialty films, such as infrared.
GOE: 01.02.03 STRENGTH: L GED: R4 M3 L4 SVP: 7 DLU: 88

143.062-034 PHOTOJOURNALIST (print. & pub.; radio-tv broad.) alternate titles: photographer, news
  Photographs newsworthy events, locations, people, or other illustrative or educational material for use in publications or telecasts, using still cameras: Travels to assigned location and takes pictures. Develops negatives and prints film. Submits negatives and pictures to editorial personnel. Usually specializes in one phase of photography, as news, sports, special features, or as freelance photographer.
GOE: 01.02.03 STRENGTH: L GED: R4 M2 L4 SVP: 7 DLU: 77

143.260-010 OPTICAL-EFFECTS-CAMERA OPERATOR (motion picture)
  Sets up and operates optical printers and related equipment to produce fades, dissolves, superimpositions, and other optical effects required in motion pictures, applying knowledge of optical effects printing and photography: Reads work order and count sheet to ascertain optical effects specifications and location of subject material on original photography film. Analyzes specifications to determine work procedures, sequence of operations, and machine setup, using knowledge of optical effects techniques and procedures. Loads camera of optical effects printer with magazine of unexposed film stock. Mounts original photography film in transport and masking mechanism of optical-printer projector and moves film into designated position for optical effect, using counter and film markings to determine placement. Adjusts camera position, lens position, mask opening, lens aperture, focus, shutter angle, film transport speed, and related controls, using precision measuring instruments and knowledge of optical effects techniques to determine settings. Selects designated color and neutral density filters and mounts in filter holder to control light and intensity. Sets controls in automatic or manual mode, moves control to start camera, and observes printer operation and footage counter during filming. Adjusts controls during filming operation when operating in manual mode, and stops camera when designated counter reading is observed. Moves controls to rewind camera film and original photography film and repeats select portions or entire operation number of times necessary to produce designated effect. Sets up and operates animation and matte cameras and related equipment to photograph artwork, such as titles and painted mattes. Sets up and operates single pass optical printers when enlarging or reducing film or performing related operations. Sets up and operates subtitle camera and related equipment to photograph film subtitles. Examines frames of film exposed with different combinations of color filters (wedges) to select optimum color balance based on experience and judgment.
GOE: 01.02.03 STRENGTH: L GED: R4 M3 L3 SVP: 7 DLU: 86

143.362-010 BIOLOGICAL PHOTOGRAPHER (profess. & kin.)
  Photographs medical, biological, and allied phenomena to provide illustrations for scientific publications, records, and research and teaching activities: Makes still and motion picture reproductions of patients, anatomical structures, gross and microscopic specimens, plant and animal tissues, and physiological and pathological processes. Makes copies of x rays and similar materials, utilizing photographic techniques, such as time-lapse and ultraspeed pictures, and ultraviolet or infrared light to produce visible record of normally invisible phenomena. Processes photosensitive materials to make transparencies, lantern slides, photomontages, and color prints. Engages in research activities related to biological photography and presentation of scientific data. May design special equipment and processing formulas. May specialize in a particular technique, such as cinematography, color photography, or photomicrography. May specialize in a particular field, such as medicine, and be designated Medical Photographer (medical ser.).
GOE: 02.04.02 STRENGTH: L GED: R4 M3 L3 SVP: 6 DLU: 77

143.362-014 OPHTHALMIC PHOTOGRAPHER (medical ser.)
  Photographs medical phenomena of eye to document diseases, surgeries, treatments, and congenital problems, to aid OPHTHALMOLOGIST (medical ser.) 070.101-058 in diagnosis and treatment of eye disorders: Focuses specialized microscope and cameras to take two- and three-dimensional photographs

of external, anterior, and posterior segments of eye. Monitors patient's gaze through lens of microscope and camera to ensure that patient complies with instructions to obtain desired results. Selects filters to modify light. Injects contrast medium into vein of patient and photographs fluorescent dye as it flows through retina or iris vessels to obtain angiogram of eye. Develops exposed film, and mounts and labels slides for inclusion on patient's medical chart. May photograph eye to document research studies.
GOE: 02.04.02 STRENGTH: L GED: R4 M4 L4 SVP: 6 DLU: 89

143.382-010 CAMERA OPERATOR, ANIMATION (motion picture)
  Operates special camera to make animated cartoon motion picture films: Places background drawing on horizontal easel over which camera is suspended. Positions transparent celluloid slide on which animation has been drawn over background and covers it with glass plate. Exposes frame of motion picture film and repeats process, using next drawing in animation sequence. Regulates exposure and aperture to obtain special effects, such as fade out or fade-ins.
GOE: 05.10.05 STRENGTH: L GED: R4 M3 L3 SVP: 6 DLU: 77

143.382-014 PHOTOGRAPHER, FINISH (amuse. & rec.) alternate titles: photo-finish photographer
  Operates photographic equipment to photograph finish of horse race: Loads film into camera and advances to picture taking position. Sights camera on finish line and adjusts exposure controls and focus. Observes race and starts camera as horses approach finish line. Stops camera after last horse has crossed finish line. Removes exposed film from camera and places it into film-developing machine that automatically develops film. Prints and enlarges photographs used to determine winner of race when finish is close.
GOE: 05.10.05 STRENGTH: L GED: R4 M2 L3 SVP: 6 DLU: 77

143.457-010 PHOTOGRAPHER (amuse. & rec.)
  Persuades nightclub and restaurant patrons to pose for pictures and operates camera to photograph them: Carries camera and flashbulb equipment to tables and solicits customers' patronage. Adjusts camera and photographs customers. Takes exposed film to darkroom on premises for immediate processing by DEVELOPER (photofinishing). Returns to customers with finished photographs or proofs and writes orders for additional prints selected. Receives payment for photographs. May use camera which produces instant picture.
GOE: 08.03.01 STRENGTH: L GED: R3 M1 L3 SVP: 3 DLU: 77

144 FINE ARTISTS: PAINTERS, SCULPTORS, AND RELATED OCCUPATIONS

  This group includes occupations concerned with creating fine arts works whose primary purpose is to be viewed for esthetic content. The major factor distinguishing occupations in this group from those in commercial art is the retention of responsibility for selection of theme, subject matter, medium, and manner of execution.

144.061-010 PAINTER (profess. & kin.) alternate titles: artist
  Paints variety of original subject material, such as landscapes, portraits, still lifes, and abstracts, using watercolors, oils, acrylics, tempera, or other paint medium: Conceives and develops ideas for painting, based on assignment, personality, interests, and knowledge of painting methods and techniques. Applies color medium to canvas or other surface, using brushes, pallet knives, and various other artist's tools and equipment. Integrates and develops visual elements, such as line, space, mass, color, and perspective to produce desired effect. May make preliminary sketch of painting. May coat finished painting with varnish or other preservative. May paint in particular style, such as realism, impressionism, naturalism, or regionalism. May specialize in particular media, or subject material. May teach painting [TEACHER, ART (education)]. May work in other art mediums, such as etching, drawing, or sculpture. May be identified according to specialization, style, media, technique, or subject matter. May paint scenic backgrounds, murals, portraiture, and other items for use on motion picture and television production sets and be designated Scenic Artist (motion picture; radio-tv broad.).
GOE: 01.02.02 STRENGTH: L GED: R5 M2 L4 SVP: 8 DLU: 77

144.061-014 PRINTMAKER (profess. & kin.)
  Conceives and develops drawings and other art work and prepares printmaking medium used to print fine arts graphics: Determines printmaking method, such as recessed (intaglio), raised (relief), or flat (lithograph), which will be most effective to reproduce conceived art work. Renders art work on stone, metal, wood, linoleum, or other material, using various tools, procedures, and processes to etch, engrave, carve, paint, draw, or perform some similar operation, utilizing knowledge of art and printing to prepare image capable of being transferred. Inks surface of medium and transfers image to paper, using hand or machine press. Examines proofs and makes corrections to art work, if necessary. Approves and signs final proof. May prepare preliminary sketches. May use photographic or silk screen process to produce image. May use any suitable textured surface for printmaking medium. May use more than one process on single graphic. May print entire edition or instruct other workers to print it. May teach printmaking.
GOE: 01.02.03 STRENGTH: S GED: R5 M2 L4 SVP: 8 DLU: 77

144.061-018 SCULPTOR (profess. & kin.) alternate titles: statue maker
  Designs and constructs three-dimensional art works, utilizing any combination of mediums, methods, and techniques: Carves objects from stone, con-

crete, plaster, wood, or other material, using abrasives, chisels, gouges, mallets, and other handtools and power tools. Models plastic substance, such as clay or wax, using fingers and small handtools to form objects which may be cast in bronze or concrete, or fired to harden objects. Constructs artistic forms from metal or stone, using metalworking, welding, or masonry tools and equipment. Cuts, bends, laminates, arranges, and fastens individual or mixed raw and manufactured materials and products to form art works. Usually works under contract or commission. May teach sculpturing [TEACHER, ART (education)]. May specialize in one technique or medium and be identified accordingly.
GOE: 01.02.02 STRENGTH: L GED: R5 M3 L4 SVP: 8 DLU: 77

149   OCCUPATIONS IN ART, N.E.C.

This group includes occupations, not elsewhere classified, concerned with art.

149.021-010   TEACHER, ART (education) alternate titles: art instructor
Instructs pupils in art, such as painting, sketching, designing, and sculpturing: Prepares lesson plans and establishes course goals. Selects books and art supplies for courses. Demonstrates method and procedure to pupils. Observes and evaluates pupils' work to determine student progress or to make suggestions for improvement. Confers with student, parent, and counselor to resolve student problem. Accompanies students on field trips to museums or art galleries. May specialize in teaching one or more areas of art, such as illustration, art history, or commercial art. May direct planning and supervision of student contests and arranging of art exhibits. May teach students with disabilities. May be required to have certification from state. May be designated according to subject taught as Instructor, Illustration (education); Instructor, Industrial Design (education).
GOE: 01.02.01 STRENGTH: L GED: R5 M4 L5 SVP: 7 DLU: 80

149.031-010   SUPERVISOR, SCENIC ARTS (motion picture; radio-tv broad.)
Creates layouts of scenery and backdrops for motion picture and television sets according to instructions, and supervises and coordinates activities of artists who paint them: Confers with ART DIRECTOR (motion picture; radio-tv broad.) 142.061-062 regarding details of background against which action is to be photographed. Directs preparation of sketches and designs or assigns work based on illustrations received from ART DIRECTOR (motion picture; radio-tv broad.). Computes amount of surface to be covered by specific color scheme in proportion to its application in scene. Requisitions paint and materials. Estimates costs of paints and other materials, using price lists and records of previous productions, to prepare budget. Estimates number of workers and time required to complete project. May prepare sketches or work drawings, including coloring details of scenery.
GOE: 01.02.03 STRENGTH: L GED: R5 M4 L4 SVP: 8 DLU: 77

149.041-010   QUICK SKETCH ARTIST (amuse. & rec.)
Sketches likeness of customers: Poses subject to accentuate most pleasing features and draws likeness, using pencil, charcoal, pastels, or other medium. May draw sketch from photograph. May only draw exaggerated likenesses and be designated Caricaturist (amuse. & rec.). May be identified according to medium worked in.
GOE: 01.02.02 STRENGTH: S GED: R5 M1 L3 SVP: 6 DLU: 77

149.051-010   SILHOUETTE ARTIST (amuse. & rec.)
Cuts silhouettes of customers: Poses subject to present pleasing profile and cuts freehand outline of profile from paper (silhouette). Glues silhouette on paper of constrasting color or mounts silhouette in frame or folder. May draw profile prior to cutting it. May cut profile from photograph. May use strong lights adjusted to cast subject's shadow on backdrop as aid in viewing subject's profile.
GOE: 01.02.02 STRENGTH: S GED: R5 M1 L3 SVP: 6 DLU: 77

149.061-010   AUDIOVISUAL PRODUCTION SPECIALIST (profess. & kin.) alternate titles: instructional technology specialist
Plans and produces audio, visual, and audiovisual material for communication and learning: Develops production ideas based on assignment or generates own ideas based on objectives and personal interest. Conducts research or utilizes knowledge and training to determine format, approach, content, level, and medium which will be most effective, meet objectives, and remain within budget. Plans and develops, or directs assistants to develop, preproduction ideas into outlines, scripts, continuity, story boards, and graphics. Executes, or directs assistants to execute, rough and finished graphics and graphic designs. Locates and secures settings, properties, effects, and other production necessities. Directs and coordinates activities of assistants and other personnel during production. May review, evaluate, and direct modifications to material produced independently by other personnel. May set up, adjust, and operate equipment, such as cameras, sound mixers, and recorders during production. May perform narration or present announcements. May construct and place in position properties, sets, lighting equipment, and other equipment. May develop manuals, texts, workbooks, or related materials for use in conjunction with production materials. May conduct training sessions on selection, use, and design of audiovisual materials, and operation of presentation equipment. May perform duties listed under DIRECTOR, INSTRUCTIONAL MATERIAL (education) 099.167-018.
GOE: 01.02.03 STRENGTH: L GED: R5 M4 L5 SVP: 7 DLU: 80

149.261-010   EXHIBIT ARTIST (museums)
Produces artwork for use in permanent or temporary exhibit settings of museum, zoo, or similar establishment, performing any combination of following duties to prepare exhibit setting and accessories for installation: Confers with professional museum personnel to discuss objectives of exhibits and type of artwork needed. Makes scale drawing of exhibit design, indicating size, position, and general outlines of artwork needed for use of installation and other fabrication personnel. Paints scenic, panoramic, or abstract composition on canvas, board, burlap, or other material to be used as background or component of exhibit, following layout prepared by designer. Paints or stencils exhibit titles and legends on boards, or cuts letters from plastic or plywood to form title and legend copy, and mounts letters on panel or board, using adhesives or handtools. Photographs persons, artifacts, scenes, plants, or other objects, and develops negatives to obtain prints to be used in exhibits. Enlarges, intensifies, or otherwise modifies prints, according to exhibit design specifications. Fashions exhibit accessories, such as human figures, tree parts, or relief maps, from clay, plastic, wood, fiberglass, papier mache, or other materials, using hands, handtools, or molding equipment to cut, carve, scrape, mold, or otherwise shape material to specified dimensions. Brushes or sprays protective or decorative finish on completed background panels, informational legends, and exhibit accessories. Maintains files of photographs, paintings, and accessories for use in exhibits.
GOE: 01.02.03 STRENGTH: L GED: R5 M3 L4 SVP: 6 DLU: 86

149.281-010   FURNITURE REPRODUCER (furniture)
Prepares working drawings and templates of antique or custom furniture to facilitate reproduction: Draws sketches of piece, freehand or with drawing instruments. Measures piece with rule and calipers and notes dimensions on drawing. Makes detailed drawing of joints, carvings, and milled sections for shop use [DRAFTER (profess. & kin.)]. Traces or draws outlines of parts on plywood or cardboard and cuts out part along outline to make template. Marks templates to indicate name of part, type of construction, variety of wood, and finish. May make drawings from pictures when models are not available.
GOE: 05.03.02 STRENGTH: S GED: R5 M3 L4 SVP: 7 DLU: 77

15   OCCUPATIONS IN ENTERTAINMENT AND RECREATION

This division includes occupations concerned with amusing, diverting, or informing others by such means as sound or physical movement. Includes teaching these skills (except occupations in primary, secondary, and vocational schools which are included in Groups 091, 092, and 097).

150   OCCUPATIONS IN DRAMATICS

This group includes occupations concerned with interpreting roles to audiences in dramatic productions or readings.

150.027-010   DRAMATIC COACH (profess. & kin.)
Coaches performers in acting techniques: Conducts reading to evaluate performer's acting ability. Adapts training methods to improve and develop performer's competence. Coaches performers in camera or stage techniques, script analysis, voice projection, and character interpretation, to prepare them for stage, motion picture, or television production. Advises clients regarding wardrobe, grooming, and audition methods, to prepare them for professional contacts. May be designated according to area of specialization as Screen Coach (profess. & kin.); Theater Coach (profess. & kin.).
GOE: 01.03.01 STRENGTH: L GED: R5 M2 L5 SVP: 7 DLU: 77

150.027-014   TEACHER, DRAMA (education) alternate titles: instructor, dramatic arts; teacher, dramatics; teacher, theater arts
Teaches acting principles and techniques to individuals or groups: Conducts readings to evaluate student's talent. Adapts course of study and training methods to meet student's need and ability. Teaches enunciation, diction, voice development, and dialects, using voice exercises, speech drills, explanation, lectures, and improvisation. Discusses and demonstrates vocal and body expression to teach acting styles, character development, and personality projection. Produces and directs plays for school and public performances. Auditions students to select cast and assign parts. Rehearses and drills students to ensure they master parts. Assigns nonperforming students to backstage production tasks, such as constructing, painting, moving scenery, operating stage light, and sound equipment. May direct activities of students involved in constructing, painting, and lighting scenery. May teach elements of stagecraft, stage makeup, costume craft, play writing, or play direction.
GOE: 01.03.01 STRENGTH: L GED: R5 M2 L5 SVP: 7 DLU: 77

150.047-010   ACTOR (amuse. & rec.)
Portrays role in dramatic production to interpret character or present characterization to audience: Rehearses part to learn lines and cues as directed. Interprets serious or comic role by speech, gesture, and body movement to entertain or inform audience for stage, motion picture, television, radio, or other media production. May write or adapt own material. May dance and sing. May direct self and others in production [DIRECTOR, MOTION PICTURE (motion picture); DIRECTOR, STAGE (amuse. & rec.)]. May read from script or book, utilizing minimum number of stage properties and relying mainly on changes of voice and inflection to hold audience's attention and be designated Dramatic Reader (amuse. & rec.). May be designated according to gender of worker or type of role portrayed as Actress (amuse. & rec.); Character Actor (amuse. &

rec.); Character Actress (amuse. & rec.); Ingenue (amuse. & rec.); Juvenile (amuse. & rec.).
GOE: 01.03.02 STRENGTH: L GED: R5 M2 L5 SVP: 7 DLU: 77

150.067-010 DIRECTOR, STAGE (amuse. & rec.)
Interprets script, directs technicians, and conducts rehearsals to create stage presentation: Confers with PLAYWRIGHT (profess. & kin.) and PRODUCER (amuse. & rec.) to discuss script changes. Confers with MANAGER, STAGE (amuse. & rec.) to coordinate production plans. Rehearses cast in individual roles to elicit best possible performance. Suggests changes, such as voice and movement, to develop performance based on script interpretation and using knowledge of acting techniques. Approves scenic and costume designs, sound, special effects, and choreography. May select cast. May select SET DESIGNER (amuse. & rec.).
GOE: 01.03.01 STRENGTH: L GED: R5 M3 L5 SVP: 8 DLU: 77

150.147-010 NARRATOR (motion picture) alternate titles: motion-picture commentator
Makes explanatory comments to accompany action parts of motion picture: Reads from script and speaks into microphone as film is being projected, timing comments to fit action portrayed. May write script.
GOE: 01.03.03 STRENGTH: L GED: R5 M2 L5 SVP: 5 DLU: 77

151 OCCUPATIONS IN DANCING

This group includes occupations concerned with the interpretation of ideas through rhythmic expression.

151.027-010 CHOREOGRAPHER (amuse. & rec.) alternate titles: director, dance
Creates and teaches original dances for ballet, musical, or revue to be performed for stage, television, motion picture, or nightclub production: Composes dance designed to suggest story, interpret emotion, or enliven show, coordinating dance with music. Instructs performers at rehearsals to achieve desired effect. May audition performers for specific parts. May direct and stage presentation.
GOE: 01.05.01 STRENGTH: L GED: R5 M3 L5 SVP: 8 DLU: 77

151.027-014 INSTRUCTOR, DANCING (education) alternate titles: professor, dance; teacher, dancing
Instructs pupils in ballet, ballroom, tap, and other forms of dancing: Observes students to determine physical and artistic qualifications and limitations and plans programs to meet students' needs and aspirations. Explains and demonstrates techniques and methods of regulating movements of body to musical or rhythmic accompaniment. Drills pupils in execution of dance steps. May teach history of dance. May teach theory and practice of dance notation. May choreograph and direct dance performance. May be designated according to style of dancing taught as Instructor, Ballroom Dancing (education); Instructor, Tap Dancing (education); Teacher, Ballet (education). May be employed by ballet company to train corps de ballet and be designated Ballet Master/Mistress (education).
GOE: 01.05.01 STRENGTH: H GED: R5 M2 L5 SVP: 6 DLU: 80

151.047-010 DANCER (amuse. & rec.)
Dances alone, with partner, or in group to entertain audience: Performs classical, modern, or acrobatic dances, coordinating body movements to musical accompaniment. Rehearses dance movements developed by CHOREOGRAPHER (amuse. & rec.). May choreograph own dance. May sing and provide other forms of entertainment. May specialize in particular style of dancing and be designated according to specialty as Acrobatic Dancer (amuse. & rec.); Ballet Dancer (amuse. & rec.); Ballroom Dancer (amuse. & rec.); Belly Dancer (amuse. & rec.); Chorus Dancer (amuse. & rec.); Interpretative Dancer (amuse. & rec.); Strip-Tease Dancer (amuse. & rec.); Tap Dancer (amuse. & rec.).
GOE: 01.05.02 STRENGTH: H GED: R4 M2 L4 SVP: 7 DLU: 77

152 OCCUPATIONS IN MUSIC

This group includes occupations concerned with the composition, arrangement, rendition, or direction of instrumental or vocal music.

152.021-010 TEACHER, MUSIC (education) alternate titles: music instructor
Teaches individuals or groups instrumental or vocal music in public or private school: Plans daily classroom work based on teaching outline prepared for course of study to meet curriculum requirements. Evaluates students' interests, aptitudes, temperament, and individual characteristics to determine suitable instrument for beginner. Sings or plays instrument to demonstrate musical scales, tones, and rhythm. Instructs students in music theory, harmony, score and sight reading, composition, music appreciation, and provides individual or group vocal and instrumental lessons using technical knowledge, aesthetic appreciation, and prescribed teaching techniques. Conducts group rehearsals and instructs and coaches members in their individual parts, in fundamentals of musicianship, and ensemble performance. Critiques performance to identify errors and reinforce correct techniques. Leads orchestra and choral groups in regular and special performances for school program, community activities, concerts, and festivals. Meets with parents of student to resolve student problem. May accompany students on field trips to musical performances. May order, store,

and inventory musical instruments, music, and supplies. May teach students with disabilities. May be required to have certification from state. May be designated Teacher, Instrumental (education); Teacher, Vocal (education).
GOE: 01.04.01 STRENGTH: L GED: R5 M3 L5 SVP: 7 DLU: 81

152.041-010 MUSICIAN, INSTRUMENTAL (amuse. & rec.)
Plays musical instrument as soloist or as member of musical group, such as orchestra or band, to entertain audience: Studies and rehearses music to learn and interpret score. Plays from memory or by following score. May transpose music to play in alternate key. May improvise. May compose. May play instrument to signal activity, such as flag raising, post time, or arrival of dignitaries at sporting or other events. May be designated according to instrument played as Calliope Player (amuse. & rec.); Drummer (amuse. & rec.); Harpist (amuse. & rec.); Organist (amuse. & rec.); Pianist (amuse. & rec.); Violinist (amuse. & rec.). May accompany soloist or another MUSICIAN, INSTRUMENTAL (amuse. & rec.) and be designated Accompanist (amuse. & rec.).
GOE: 01.04.04 STRENGTH: L GED: R5 M3 L3 SVP: 8 DLU: 77

152.047-010 CHORAL DIRECTOR (profess. & kin.) alternate titles: choir leader;
Conducts vocal music groups, such as choirs and glee clubs: Auditions and selects members of group. Selects music to suit performance requirements and accommodate talent and ability of group. Directs group at rehearsals and performance to achieve desired effects, such as tonal and harmonic balance, dynamics, rhythm, tempo, and shading, utilizing knowledge of conducting techniques and music theory. May schedule tours and performances and arrange for transportation and lodging. May transcribe musical compositions and melodic lines to adapt them to or create particular style for group [ARRANGER (profess. & kin.)]. May conduct group with instrumental accompaniment [CONDUCTOR, ORCHESTRA (profess. & kin.)].
GOE: 01.04.01 STRENGTH: L GED: R5 M3 L5 SVP: 8 DLU: 77

152.047-014 CONDUCTOR, ORCHESTRA (profess. & kin.) alternate titles: band leader; director, music; orchestra leader
Conducts instrumental music groups, such as orchestras and dance bands: Auditions and selects members of group. Selects music to accommodate talents and abilities of group and to suit type of performance to be given. Positions members within group to obtain balance among instrumental sections. Directs group at rehearsals and performances to achieve desired effects, such as tonal and harmonic balance, dynamics, rhythms, tempos, and shadings, utilizing knowledge of conducting techniques, music theory and harmony, range and characteristics of instruments, and talents of individual performers. May transcribe musical compositions and melodic lines to adapt them to or create particular style for group [ARRANGER (profess. & kin.)]. May schedule tours and performances and arrange for transportation and lodging. May be designated according to specialization as Conductor, Dance Band (profess. & kin.); Conductor, Symphonic-Orchestra (profess. & kin.).
GOE: 01.04.01 STRENGTH: L GED: R5 M3 L3 SVP: 9 DLU: 77

152.047-018 DIRECTOR, MUSIC (motion picture; radio-tv broad.) alternate titles: musical director; music department head
Plans and directs activities of personnel in studio music department and conducts studio orchestra: Selects vocal, instrumental, and recorded music suitable to type of program or motion picture and to entertainers who are to render selections. Engages services of COMPOSER (profess. & kin.) 152.067-014, as required, to write score for motion picture or television program. Issues assignments and reviews work of staff in such areas as scoring, arranging, and copying music, lyric writing, and vocal coaching. Auditions and selects vocal and instrumental talent for musical shows. Auditions and hires studio music personnel. Conducts orchestra in recording or broadcast of music [CONDUCTOR, ORCHESTRA (profess. & kin.) 152.047-014].
GOE: 01.04.01 STRENGTH: L GED: R5 M4 L5 SVP: 9 DLU: 77

152.047-022 SINGER (amuse. & rec.; motion picture; radio-tv broad.)
Sings as soloist or member of vocal ensemble: Interprets music, using knowledge of harmony, melody, rhythm, and voice production, to present characterization or to achieve individual style of vocal delivery. Sings, following printed text and musical notation, or memorizes score. May sing a cappella or with musical accompaniment. May watch CHORAL DIRECTOR (profess. & kin.) or CONDUCTOR, ORCHESTRA (profess. & kin.) for directions and cues. May be known according to voice range as soprano, contralto, tenor, baritone, or bass. May specialize in one type of music, such as opera, lieder, choral, gospel, folk, or country and western and be identified according to specialty.
GOE: 01.04.03 STRENGTH: L GED: R4 M3 L4 SVP: 8 DLU: 77

152.067-010 ARRANGER (profess. & kin.) alternate titles: adapter; transcriber; transcripter
Transcribes musical composition for orchestra, band, choral group, or individual to adapt composition to particular style for which it was not originally written: Determines voice, instrument, harmonic structure, rhythm, tempo, and tone balance to achieve desired effect. Writes score, utilizing knowledge of music theory and instrumental and vocal capabilities [ORCHESTRATOR (profess. & kin.)]. May copy parts from score for individual performers within group [COPYIST (any industry)].
GOE: 01.04.02 STRENGTH: S GED: R6 M4 L5 SVP: 8 DLU: 77

152.067-014 COMPOSER (profess. & kin.)
Writes musical compositions: Creates musical ideas, using knowledge of harmonic, rhythmic, melodic, and tonal structure and other elements of music the-

ory, such as instrumental and vocal capabilities. Creates original musical form or writes within circumscribed musical form, such as sonata, symphony, or opera. Transcribes ideas into musical notation.
GOE: 01.04.02 STRENGTH: S GED: R6 M4 L6 SVP: 9 DLU: 77

152.067-018 CUE SELECTOR (radio-tv broad.)
Integrates prerecorded theme, background, and bridge music with story line and film sequence to arrange musical score for episode of television series, using knowledge of film scoring: Reads script of episode to become familiar with story line. Confers with DIRECTOR, TELEVISION (radio-tv broad.) to coordinate interpretation of script, including mood to be conveyed or quality of character stressed. Listens to tape recording of theme, background, and bridge music to become familiar with them. Notes key of music, length of passage, and identification number. Selects passages which match story line of script to form tentative score. Views episode to align selections with action on screen. Gives directions to technical personnel during electronic recording of score from tapes, making changes as needed.
GOE: 01.04.02 STRENGTH: L GED: R6 M4 L5 SVP: 9 DLU: 77

152.067-022 ORCHESTRATOR (profess. & kin.)
Writes score for orchestra, band, choral group, or individual instrumentalist or vocalist: Transposes music from one voice or instrument to another to accommodate particular musician or musical group. Scores composition consistent with instrumental and vocal capabilities, such as range and key, using knowledge of music theory. May transcribe composition to adapt it to particular style [ARRANGER (profess. & kin.)]. May copy parts from score for individual performers [COPYIST (any industry)].
GOE: 01.04.02 STRENGTH: S GED: R6 M4 L5 SVP: 8 DLU: 77

152.267-010 COPYIST (any industry)
Transcribes musical parts onto staff paper from score written by ARRANGER (profess. & kin.) or ORCHESTRATOR (profess. & kin.) for each instrument or voice, utilizing knowledge of music notation and experience and background in music. May transpose score to different key.
GOE: 01.04.02 STRENGTH: S GED: R5 M3 L5 SVP: 7 DLU: 77

152.367-010 PROMPTER (amuse. & rec.)
Prompts performers in operatic productions: Marks copy of vocal score to note cues. Observes CONDUCTOR, ORCHESTRA (profess. & kin.) and follows vocal score to time cues accurately. Speaks or sings in language required by opera to prompt performers.
GOE: 01.04.02 STRENGTH: L GED: R4 M3 L4 SVP: 7 DLU: 77

153   OCCUPATIONS IN ATHLETICS AND SPORTS

This group includes occupations concerned with application of the theoretical or practical aspects of athletics and sports. Includes teaching physical education at speciality schools or health clubs; scouting for professional athletes; coaching nonschool athletes; and giving instructions in golf, skiing, and similar activities.

153.117-010 HEAD COACH (amuse. & rec.) alternate titles: manager, athletic team
Plans and directs training and recommends acquisition or trade of players for professional athletic team: Directs conditioning of players to achieve maximum athletic performance. Assesses player's skills and assigns team positions. Evaluates own and opposition team capabilities to determine game strategy. Coaches or directs COACH, PROFESSIONAL ATHLETES (amuse. & rec.) to instruct players in techniques of game. Participates in discussions with other clubs to sell or trade players. May participate on team managed and be designated Coach-Player (amuse. & rec.); Player-Manager (amuse. & rec.).
GOE: 12.01.01 STRENGTH: L GED: R5 M4 L4 SVP: 9 DLU: 77

153.117-014 MANAGER, ATHLETE (amuse. & rec.)
Manages affairs of PROFESSIONAL ATHLETE (amuse. & rec.) by negotiating with promoters or others to settle contracts and business matters and directs training: Negotiates with team management and promoters to obtain favorable contracts for client [BUSINESS MANAGER (amuse. & rec.)]. May prescribe exercises, rest periods, and diet to be followed by PROFESSIONAL ATHLETE (amuse. & rec.). May direct ATHLETIC TRAINER (amuse. & rec.; education) in conditioning PROFESSIONAL ATHLETE (amuse. & rec.). May give directions to protege in athletic techniques. May determine strategy to be followed by PROFESSIONAL ATHLETE (amuse. & rec.) in competition with others. May be designated according to type of PROFESSIONAL ATHLETE (amuse. & rec.) managed as Manager, Boxer (amuse. & rec.); Manager, Wrestler (amuse. & rec.).
GOE: 11.12.03 STRENGTH: L GED: R5 M5 L5 SVP: 7 DLU: 77

153.117-018 SCOUT, PROFESSIONAL SPORTS (amuse. & rec.)
Evaluates athletic skills of PROFESSIONAL ATHLETES (amuse. & rec.) to determine fitness and potentiality for professional sports and negotiates with them to obtain services: Reviews prospects' exhibitions and past performance records. Negotiates with PROFESSIONAL ATHLETES (amuse. & rec.) to arrange contracts. Reports to team management results of scouting assignments, such as selection or rejection of PROFESSIONAL ATHLETES (amuse. & rec.) scouted and persons and areas sighted for future recruitment. May be designated according to type of sport in which engaged as Baseball Scout (amuse. & rec.); Basketball Scout (amuse. & rec.); Football Scout (amuse. & rec.).
GOE: 12.01.01 STRENGTH: S GED: R4 M3 L4 SVP: 8 DLU: 77

153.117-022 STEWARD, RACETRACK (amuse. & rec.)
Coordinates and directs racing activities at racetrack: Confers with track management and studies prior racing and attendance records to plan types of races to schedule. Confers with officials of other tracks to plan racing dates to coincide with number of days allotted by state racing commission. Assigns workers to duties, such as inspecting entrants, starting, and judging races to comply with racing commission regulations. Observes workers performing duties to ensure compliance with commission rules and track policy. Approves or disapproves requests of handlers to change equipment on horses. Confers with veterinary personnel regarding horses unfit to race. Serves as member of judiciary board that exercises control over racing participants and makes decisions in accordance with state racing commission rules on such matters as validity of complaints and order of finishes. Writes reports to comply with state racing commission rules, such as recording and reporting all complaints, actions taken, penalties imposed, and voting record of board members.
GOE: 12.01.02 STRENGTH: L GED: R5 M4 L5 SVP: 8 DLU: 77

153.137-010 MANAGER, POOL (amuse. & rec.)
Supervises and coordinates activities of swimming pool staff to prevent accidents and provide assistance to swimmers, and conducts swimming classes: Assigns duties to lifeguards, locker room attendants, and clerical staff. Schedules swimming classes for basic and specialty techniques, according to enrollment, age, and number of instructors. Meets with employees to discuss and resolve work related problems. Completes staff evaluation forms reflecting information such as work habits, effectiveness in interpersonal relations, and acceptance of responsibility. Instructs individuals or groups in swimming classes, principles of water confidence, and lifesaving. Administers first aid, according to prescribed procedures, or calls emergency medical facility, when necessary. Determines chlorine content, pH value, and color of pool water at periodic intervals during day, using testing kit. Completes forms indicating time, date, and pool water test results. Routes forms to supervisor for evaluation and filing. Maintains required forms, such as time and attendance, inventory list, and program of facility activities.
GOE: 11.11.02 STRENGTH: H GED: R3 M3 L3 SVP: 4 DLU: 86

153.167-010 PADDOCK JUDGE (amuse. & rec.)
Inspects equipment of horses and riders in paddock at racetrack before each race to determine that equipment meets track and state racing commission specifications: Reads racing programs to schedule arrival of horses and riders in paddock area. Examines horse's equipment and rider's attire to assure compliance with racing specifications. Orders equipment changes to conform to racing rules. Refers requests for equipment changes to racing officials. Tells riders to mount and dismount. Signals winning horse and rider to winner's circle. Reports delays in paddock area and equipment changes to racing officials. Examines credentials to prevent unauthorized persons from entering paddock area.
GOE: 12.01.02 STRENGTH: L GED: R4 M2 L3 SVP: 7 DLU: 77

153.167-014 PIT STEWARD (amuse. & rec.) alternate titles: pit boss; referee
Directs activities at automobile or motorcycle racetrack: Determines qualifying order of vehicles for each race based on trial event results or by drawing numbers. Assigns STARTERS (amuse. & rec.) to position on track. Controls traffic to ensure only authorized number of vehicles are in pit. Directs vehicles to assigned places in pit. Ascertains legality of pit stops according to rules set by sanctioning body authorizing race. Consults with SCORERS (amuse. & rec.) to resolve scoring disputes. Determines penalties to be assessed for rules violation. May inspect vehicles and drivers for safety equipment, such as seat belts, harnesses, and helmets.
GOE: 12.01.02 STRENGTH: L GED: R4 M3 L4 SVP: 6 DLU: 77

153.167-018 RACING SECRETARY AND HANDICAPPER (amuse. & rec.)
Plans and arranges racing schedules and assigns handicapped weights to horses at racetrack: Analyzes official workout and past performance records to arrange races between horses of equal experience and ability. Handicaps horse in each race by assigning weight it will carry, using knowledge of handicapping and based on data, such as age, sex, total winnings of horse, and distances of races won. Confers with track management personnel to plan types of races to schedule and to determine purse for each race. Reviews application requesting permission to enter and train horse for competition. Accepts application and entrance fee from owner. Registers names of persons having financial interest in horse. Reviews racing information to be published in newspaper, racing form, and daily racing program. Directs activities of workers engaged in duties, such as compiling racing information and assigning stable space. Records information regarding official racing result to keep file on each horse's ability. Records changes of ownership and submits report to track officials. May observe race to study ability and form of horse, verify selection of entries, and assignment of handicap weights.
GOE: 12.01.02 STRENGTH: S GED: R4 M4 L4 SVP: 8 DLU: 77

153.224-010 ATHLETIC TRAINER (amuse. & rec.; education)
Evaluates physical condition and advises and treats professional and amateur athletes to maintain maximum physical fitness for participation in athletic competition: Prescribes routine and corrective exercises to strengthen muscles. Recommends special diets to build up health and reduce overweight athletes. Massages parts of players' bodies to relieve soreness, strains, and bruises. Renders first aid to injured players, such as giving artificial respiration, cleaning and

bandaging wounds, and applying heat and cold to promote healing. Calls physician for injured persons as required. Wraps ankles, fingers, or wrists of athletes in synthetic skin, protecting gauze, and adhesive tape to support muscles and ligaments. Treats chronic minor injuries and related disabilities to maintain athletes' performance. May give heat and diathermy treatments as prescribed by health service. Workers are identified according to type of sport.
GOE: 10.02.02 STRENGTH: M GED: R5 M4 L4 SVP: 8 DLU: 77

153.227-010   COACH, PROFESSIONAL ATHLETES (amuse. & rec.) alternate titles: coach

Analyzes performance and instructs PROFESSIONAL ATHLETES (amuse. & rec.) in game strategies and techniques to prepare them for athletic competition: Observes players while they perform to determine need for individual or team improvement. Coaches players individually or in groups, demonstrating techniques of sport coached. Oversees daily practice of players to instruct them in areas of deficiency. Determines strategy during game, independently or in conference with other COACH, PROFESSIONAL ATHLETES (amuse. & rec.) or HEAD COACH (amuse. & rec.) based on factors as weakness in opposing team. May be designated according to phase of game coached as Defensive-Line Coach (amuse. & rec.); Pitching Coach (amuse. & rec.). May be designated according to game coached as Basketball Coach (amuse. & rec.); Football Coach (amuse. & rec.); Swimming Coach (amuse. & rec.); Tennis Coach (amuse. & rec.).
GOE: 12.01.01 STRENGTH: H GED: R5 M3 L4 SVP: 8 DLU: 77

153.227-014   INSTRUCTOR, PHYSICAL (amuse. & rec.; education)

Teaches individuals or groups beginning or advanced calisthenics, gymnastics, and reducing or corrective exercises, in private health club or gymnasium, evaluating abilities of individual to determine suitable training program: Teaches and demonstrates use of gymnastic apparatus, such as trampolines, corrective weights, and mechanical exercisers. Demonstrates and teaches body movements and skills used in sports. Advises clients in use of heat or ultraviolet treatments and hot baths. Lubricates mechanical equipment and reports malfunctioning equipment to maintenance personnel.
GOE: 10.02.02 STRENGTH: L GED: R3 M3 L3 SVP: 6 DLU: 77

153.227-018   INSTRUCTOR, SPORTS (amuse. & rec.; education) alternate titles: athletic coach

Teaches sport activity to individual or groups at private or public recreational facility or school: Explains and demonstrates use of apparatus and equipment. Explains and demonstrates principles, techniques, and methods of regulating movement of body, hands, or feet to achieve proficiency in activity. Observes students during practice to detect and correct mistakes. Explains and enforces safety rules and regulations. Explains method of keeping score. May organize and conduct competition and tournaments. May participate in competition to demonstrate skill. May purchase, display, sell, maintain, or repair equipment. May keep record of receipts and expenditures. May lecture on history and purpose of sport. Workers are identified according to sport instructed, such as golf, fencing, or tennis.
GOE: 12.01.01 STRENGTH: M GED: R4 M3 L4 SVP: 7 DLU: 81

153.243-010   AUTOMOBILE RACER (amuse. & rec.)

Drives automobile racing car in competition road races: Drives car over track where race is to be run to familiarize self with course. Participates in speed and elimination trial races to qualify car for race. Drives car in race and analyzes speed and position of other cars to determine when and where to drive car so as to be in favorable position to win. Observes fuel, oil, and compression gauges on dashboard of car to ensure that car is operating efficiently. Watches for warning signs, such as flags or flares, that indicate an accident is present and drives car accordingly. May perform maintenance work on car.
GOE: 12.01.03 STRENGTH: M GED: R4 M3 L3 SVP: 6 DLU: 77

153.243-014   MOTORCYCLE RACER (amuse. & rec.)

Rides motorcycle over track, course, or natural terrain in competitive races: Operates motorcycle, using hands and feet to manipulate controls. Evaluates power, speed, maneuverability, and position of own and other motorcycles in race to determine strategy. Listens to engine and reads tachometer to determine gear change and maximum speed which obstacles, such as turns and jumps can be taken. Maneuvers motorcycles to avoid track accident, unexpected barrier, or other emergency situation. Watches for warning flags, and other signals to follow instructions given by track officials. May perform maintenance work on motorcycle. May specialize in one type of competition, such as road, dirt track, motocross, off road, or speedway racing.
GOE: 12.01.03 STRENGTH: H GED: R3 M2 L3 SVP: 5 DLU: 77

153.244-010   JOCKEY (amuse. & rec.)

Rides racehorse at racetrack: Confers with training personnel to plan strategy for race, based on ability and peculiarities of own and other horses in competition. Mounts horse in paddock after weighing-in, and rides horse to specified numbered stall of starting gate. Races from starting gate to finish line. Talks to training personnel after race to analyze horse's performance.
GOE: 12.01.03 STRENGTH: M GED: R4 M2 L3 SVP: 6 DLU: 77

153.244-014   SULKY DRIVER (amuse. & rec.) alternate titles: harness racer

Drives horse-drawn, two-wheel sulky in harness race: Studies performance record of competing horses to plan race strategy. Controls speed of horse in specific sections of racetrack, applying knowledge of harness racing to deter-

mine when to challenge for lead of race. May train own harness racing horses. May direct activities of workers involved in grooming, training, feeding, stabling, handling and transporting harness race horses.
GOE: 12.01.03 STRENGTH: M GED: R4 M2 L3 SVP: 6 DLU: 77

153.267-010   HORSE-RACE STARTER (amuse. & rec.) alternate titles: starter

Determines entry sequence into starting gate and gives directions to riders and other track personnel to get horses into position for horse race: Evaluates performance and training record and observes horse's behavior to determine entry sequence. Directs entry of horse and rider into starting gate according to planned sequence and stall number. Gives directions to track personnel to assist rider when horse refuses to enter starting gate. Reports undue starting delay to racing officials. Presses button to open gate automatically when horses are correctly aligned. May recommend removal of horse unfit to start race. May schedule morning workouts for horses requiring familiarization with starting gate procedures.
GOE: 12.01.02 STRENGTH: L GED: R3 M3 L3 SVP: 4 DLU: 77

153.267-014   PATROL JUDGE (amuse. & rec.)

Observes horse race at racetrack to detect infractions of racing rules and resolve claims of fouls committed: Watches race from elevated stand at one of several locations around track, using binoculars to detect infractions of rules, such as action of JOCKEY (amuse. & rec.) causing another horse to change stride. Reports name and number of horse and rider guilty of foul to racing officials for disciplinary action. Confers with racing officials and watches motion picture of race to verify infractions and to determine validity of complaints lodged by participants. Submits report to racing officials concerning infractions of rules and disciplinary action taken. When flashing numbers of first three horses as race progresses or observing horses in stretch in order to post first four horses crossing finish line, is designated Placing Judge (amuse. & rec.).
GOE: 12.01.01 STRENGTH: L GED: R4 M3 L4 SVP: 8 DLU: 77

153.267-018   UMPIRE (amuse. & rec.) alternate titles: field captain; judge; referee

Officiates at sporting events: Observes actions of participants to detect infractions of rules. Decides disputable matters according to established regulations. When concerned only with determining validity of goals, finish line order, or out-of-bound plays, may be designated Finish Judge (amuse. & rec.); Goal Umpire (amuse. & rec.); Line Umpire (amuse. & rec.).
GOE: 12.01.02 STRENGTH: L GED: R4 M3 L4 SVP: 8 DLU: 77

153.287-010   HOOF AND SHOE INSPECTOR (amuse. & rec.) alternate titles: plating inspector

Inspects hoofs and shoes (plates) of horses at racetrack to determine that hoofs have been trimmed to prevent stumbling during race and to detect loose or broken shoes: Records names of horse, owner, and RACEHORSE TRAINER (amuse. & rec.) and condition of horse's hoofs and shoes. Presents information to STEWARD, RACETRACK (amuse. & rec.) for further action. May remove and replace broken or cracked plates. May instruct handlers to secure plates or trim horses hoofs as required.
GOE: 03.03.02 STRENGTH: L GED: R4 M1 L3 SVP: 6 DLU: 77

153.341-010   PROFESSIONAL ATHLETE (amuse. & rec.)

Participates in professional competitive athletic events, such as football, boxing, and hockey, to entertain audience: Exercises and practices under direction of ATHLETIC TRAINER (amuse. & rec.; education) 153.224-010 or COACH, PROFESSIONAL ATHLETES (amuse. & rec.) 153.227-010 to train for sport. Plays game and engages in sport conforming to established rules and regulations. Athletes are identified according to professional sport in which engaged. May speak, as representative of team or professional sports club, to groups involved in activities, such as sports clinics and fund raisers.
GOE: 12.01.03 STRENGTH: M GED: R4 M2 L3 SVP: 6 DLU: 81

153.367-010   CLOCKER (amuse. & rec.)

Clocks (times) racehorses at racetrack during morning workouts to obtain speed information: Identifies each horse on track by its particular identifying marks and color, and records name. Observes horse during workout and assigns speed rating according to effort extended by horse and rider, distance run, and time required as measured by stopwatch. Records information and submits it to track management.
GOE: 12.01.02 STRENGTH: L GED: R3 M2 L2 SVP: 2 DLU: 77

153.367-014   HORSE-RACE TIMER (amuse. & rec.)

Clocks and records time required for horse leading in race to run specified distance: Observes signal for official start and activates stopwatch to time race. Observes leading horse crossing markers denoting fractional parts and finish line of race to note and record time elapsed. Compares recorded results with those obtained by automatic electronic timer and reports difference to racing officials. Writes daily report of name, number of leading horse, fractional and total time required for each race to submit to track officials.
GOE: 12.01.02 STRENGTH: L GED: R3 M3 L3 SVP: 3 DLU: 77

153.384-010   MARSHAL (amuse. & rec.)

Rides saddle horse to lead parade of horserace entrants onto track to mobile-starting-gate assembly area. Mounts quarter horse and chases and restrains runaways to prevent injury to horses and thrown riders and disruption of race.
GOE: 12.01.02 STRENGTH: H GED: R3 M1 L1 SVP: 4 DLU: 77

153.387-010   IDENTIFIER, HORSE (amuse. & rec.)

Verifies identification of horses at receiving barn of racetrack: Checks identifying features, such as tattooed registration number on lip and physical appear-

ance with official records and photographs to ensure only horses scheduled to race are permitted in paddock. Releases identified horses to handlers for transfer to paddock for saddling. Notifies track officials when doubt exists as to horses' identity. Records physical changes in horses, such as weight increase or scar received since last inspection, to keep identification records current.
GOE: 12.01.02 STRENGTH: L GED: R3 M3 L3 SVP: 3 DLU: 77

153.387-014 SCORER (amuse. & rec.) alternate titles: lap checker
Records laps completed by drivers in automobile or motorcycle race: Observes vehicles passing start-finish line to obtain count of laps completed by each competitor. Enters lap count onto scoresheet. Totals laps at end of race to determine winner, order of finish, and lap count for each racer. May clock and record time during race and be designated Timer (amuse. & rec.). May give directions to other SCORERS (amuse. & rec.) and be designated Head Scorer (amuse. & rec.).
GOE: 12.01.02 STRENGTH: S GED: R3 M3 L3 SVP: 4 DLU: 77

153.467-010 CLERK-OF-SCALES (amuse. & rec.)
Weighs rider and riding equipment before and after each race to ensure that assigned handicapped weights have been carried during race: Weighs rider and saddle on scale to assure that weight is as specified on racing program. Directs rider to insert or remove lead pads from saddle pocket to meet specified weight. Notifies racing officials of rider unable to meet weight limit. Weighs rider and equipment after race to assure that lead pads were not lost during race.
GOE: 12.01.02 STRENGTH: L GED: R3 M3 L3 SVP: 3 DLU: 77

153.667-010 STARTER (amuse. & rec.)
Waves signal flags of different color and design to start and stop automobile or motorcycle race and to inform drivers of track condition: Signals slower driver to move aside to allow passage of faster vehicles. Signals drivers to slow down or stops race for clearing of track following accidents. Signals specific driver to return to pit for consultation upon request of AUTOMOBILE MECHANIC (automotive ser.); MOTORCYCLE REPAIRER (automotive ser.); PIT STEWARD (amuse. & rec.), or other track official.
GOE: 12.01.02 STRENGTH: L GED: R3 M2 L2 SVP: 4 DLU: 77

153.674-010 EXERCISER, HORSE (amuse. & rec.)
Rides racehorses to exercise and condition them for racing: Rides racehorse during workout and training races, following specific instructions of training personnel. Informs training personnel of horses' temperament, peculiarities, and physical condition as demonstrated during exercise so that training plans can be modified to prepare horse for racing.
GOE: 03.03.01 STRENGTH: M GED: R2 M1 L1 SVP: 3 DLU: 77

153.674-014 LEAD PONY RIDER (amuse. & rec.)
Rides lead pony to lead JOCKEY (amuse. & rec.) and mount from paddock to starting gate at racetrack: Leads horse scheduled to race from receiving barn to paddock to be saddled. Leads procession of riders in post position order to starting gate. Rides after runaway horse to aid rider regain control. Diverts riders from competitor involved in accident on racetrack. Leads race horse to paddock or receiving barn after race. Assists horse ambulance workers to remove injured horse from track, using block and tackle. Grooms and feeds lead pony.
GOE: 12.01.02 STRENGTH: M GED: R2 M1 L1 SVP: 2 DLU: 77

159 OCCUPATIONS IN ENTERTAINMENT AND RECREATION, N.E.C.

This group includes occupations, not elsewhere classified, concerned with entertainment.

159.041-010 MAGICIAN (amuse. & rec.)
Performs original and stock tricks of illusion and sleight of hand to entertain and mystify audience, using props, such as illusion boxes, scarf, cards, rabbit, and jewelry. May include participant from audience in act to remove personal valuables, such as wallets or jewelry, without participant's knowledge.
GOE: 01.03.02 STRENGTH: L GED: R4 M3 L4 SVP: 6 DLU: 77

159.041-014 PUPPETEER (amuse. & rec.)
Originates puppet shows, designs and constructs puppets and moves controls of puppets to animate them for entertainment of audience: Studies media for ideas that relate to fads, stories, plays, and seasonal themes and confers with other staff to develop ideas for new show. Writes or adapts script for use in puppet theater. Sketches designs for puppets based on script. Constructs hand, string, rod, and shadow puppets from materials, such as wood, papier mache, styrofoam, wires, metal, and rubber, using handtools and machine tools. Sews clothing for puppets by hand or machine. Animates puppets, using string, wire, rod, fingers or hand from position above, below, or at level with stage. Talks or sings during performance to give illusion of voice to puppets. May operate audio equipment, such as tape deck, during performance and simultaneously move puppet's mouth in synchronization with music to create illusion of singing.
GOE: 01.03.02 STRENGTH: L GED: R4 M3 L4 SVP: 8 DLU: 79

159.042-010 LASERIST (amuse. & rec.)
Creates optical designs-and-effects show for entertainment of audiences, using control console and related laser projection and recording equipment: Sets up and operates console to control laser projection, recording equipment, and

house lights. Presses switches and turns dials to dim house lights, cue opening music, and begin programmed laser sequence. Moves controls to orchestrate colors, patterns, and movements in concert with musical accompaniment. Tests, repairs, and adjusts laser and sound systems, using circuit schematics and test equipment. Examines, cleans, and maintains system cooling, optical, and sound equipment according to preventive maintenance schedule. Discusses show concepts and laser equipment operation with press representatives to promote public relations.
GOE: 05.03.05 STRENGTH: L GED: R5 M3 L4 SVP: 6 DLU: 86

159.044-010 VENTRILOQUIST (amuse. & rec.)
Entertains audience by projecting voice so that it appears to come from dummy or puppet: Changes position of dummy or puppet during performance to give illusion of life. May construct puppet or dummy. May write script for show.
GOE: 01.03.02 STRENGTH: L GED: R4 M2 L4 SVP: 7 DLU: 77

159.047-010 CLOWN (amuse. & rec.)
Dresses in comical costume and makeup and performs original or stock comedy routines to entertain audience.
GOE: 01.03.02 STRENGTH: L GED: R4 M2 L3 SVP: 6 DLU: 77

159.047-014 COMEDIAN (amuse. & rec.) alternate titles: comic
Attempts to make audience laugh by telling jokes, delivering comic lines, singing humorous songs, performing comedy dances or walks, or facial contortions, wearing funny costumes, or resorting to any similar device to amuse audience. May do impersonations [IMPERSONATOR (amuse. & rec.)].
GOE: 01.03.02 STRENGTH: L GED: R5 M2 L4 SVP: 5 DLU: 77

159.047-018 IMPERSONATOR (amuse. & rec.) alternate titles: imitator; mimic
Entertains by impersonating another person, or type of person, or animal, or some inanimate object, usually by copying mannerisms, form, expression, dress, voice, or sound of character or thing impersonated. May be designated according to character impersonated as Animal Impersonator (amuse. & rec.); Female Impersonator (amuse. & rec.); Male Impersonator (amuse. & rec.).
GOE: 01.03.02 STRENGTH: L GED: R4 M2 L4 SVP: 6 DLU: 77

159.047-022 MIME (amuse. & rec.) alternate titles: pantomimist
Presents serious, humorous, or burlesqued interpretations of emotions, dramatic actions, and various situations through body movements, facial expressions, and gestures.
GOE: 01.03.02 STRENGTH: L GED: R5 M2 L3 SVP: 7 DLU: 77

159.067-010 DIRECTOR, MOTION PICTURE (motion picture)
Reads and interprets script, conducts rehearsals, and directs activities of cast and technical crew for motion picture film: Confers with ART DIRECTOR (motion picture; radio-tv broad.) to ensure that music, sets, scenic effects, and costumes conform to script interpretation. Confers with DIRECTOR OF PHOTOGRAPHY (motion picture) to explain details of scene to be photographed and to consider utilization of miniatures, stock film, inserts, transparencies, backgrounds, or trick shots. Schedules sequences of scenes to be filmed for each day of shooting, grouping scenes together according to set and cast of characters. Rehearses cast and suggests changes, using knowledge of acting, voice, and movement to elicit best possible performance. Informs technicians of scenery, lights, props, and other equipment desired. Approves scenery, costumes, choreography, and music. Directs cast, DIRECTOR OF PHOTOGRAPHY (motion picture; radio-tv broad.), and other technicians during rehearsals and final filming. May audition and select cast. May cut and edit film. May direct film for television.
GOE: 01.03.01 STRENGTH: S GED: R5 M4 L5 SVP: 8 DLU: 77

159.067-014 DIRECTOR, TELEVISION (radio-tv broad.)
Plans and directs audio and video aspects of television programs, based on program specifications and knowledge of television programming techniques: Interprets script, rehearses cast, and establishes pace of program to stay within time requirements. Informs technicians of scenery, lights, props, and other equipment desired. Approves scenery, costumes, choreography, and music. Issues instructions to technicians from control room during telecast to keep them informed of effects desired, such as dissolves, long shots, medium shots, superimpositions, fade-ins, and fade-outs. May move controls to integrate material from multisite origins into live program. May direct news and special events programs. May direct program for live broadcast or for electronic video recording. May direct nonbroadcast television presentation, such as program for sales, medical, educational, or industrial purposes. May direct commercials. May operate viewing/editing equipment to review and edit program tapes, using personal knowledge of television programming and editing techniques. May key information into computer, using keyboard, to compile letters, memos, and other program material, such as scripts and notes. May be designated Producer-Director (radio-tv broad.) in small station.
GOE: 01.03.01 STRENGTH: L GED: R5 M4 L5 SVP: 8 DLU: 89

159.117-010 PRODUCER (radio-tv broad.) alternate titles: associate producer
Plans and coordinates various aspects of radio, television, or cable television programs: Interviews and selects SCREEN WRITERS (motion picture; radio-tv broad.) 131.067-050 and cast principals from staff members or outside talent. Outlines program to be produced to SCREEN WRITERS (motion picture; radio-tv broad.) and evaluates finished script. Composes or edits program script

to meet management or other requirements, using typewriter or computer terminal. Coordinates various aspects of production, such as audio work, scenes, music, timing, camera work, and script writing. Gives instructions to staff to schedule broadcast and to develop and coordinate details to obtain desired production. Reviews production to ensure objectives are attained. Views taped program to select scenes to be used for promotional purposes, using video equipment. Listens to audio tape recording to verify program, script, or sound effects conform to broadcast standards, using audio equipment. May obtain costumes, props, music, or other equipment or personnel to complete production. May represent television network, acting as liaison to independent producer of television series produced for network broadcast. May review budget and expenditures for programs or commercial productions for conformance to budgetary restrictions. May coordinate production details to produce live television programs from locations distant from station. May be designated according to level of responsibility and by type of show produced as Executive Producer (radio-tv broad.); or by type of media as Radio Producer (radio-tv broad.); Television Producer (radio-tv broad.).
GOE: 01.03.01 STRENGTH: L GED: R6 M4 L6 SVP: 8 DLU: 89

159.124-010 COUNSELOR, CAMP (amuse. & rec.)
Directs activities of children at vacation camp: Plans activities, such as hikes, cookouts, and campfires, to provide wide variety of camping experiences. Demonstrates use of camping equipment and explains principles and techniques of activities, such as backpacking, nature study, and outdoor cooking, to increase campers' knowledge and competence. Plans and arranges competition in activities, such as team sports or housekeeping, to stimulate campers interest and participation. Demonstrates use of materials and tools to instruct children in arts and crafts. Instructs campers in skills, such as canoeing, sailing, swimming, archery, horseback riding, and animal care, explaining and demonstrating procedures and safety techniques. Organizes, leads, instructs, and referees games. Enforces camp rules and regulations to guide conduct, maintain discipline, and safeguard health of campers. May be identified according to type of camp activity.
GOE: 09.01.01 STRENGTH: M GED: R4 M2 L4 SVP: 5 DLU: 80

159.147-010 ANNOUNCER (radio-tv broad.) alternate titles: radio board operator-announcer
Announces radio and television programs to audience: Memorizes script, reads, or ad-libs to identify station, introduce and close shows, and announce station breaks, commercials, or public service information. Cues worker to transmit program from network central station or other pick-up points according to schedule. Reads news flashes to keep audience informed of important events. May rewrite news bulletin from wire service teletype to fit specific time slot. May describe public event such as parade or convention. May interview guest, such as sport or other public personality, and moderate panel or discussion show to entertain audience. May keep daily program log. May operate control console (radio board). May perform additional duties in small stations, such as operating radio transmitter [TRANSMITTER OPERATOR (radio-tv broad.) 193.262-038], selling time, or writing advertising copy. May be designated according to media as Radio Announcer (radio-tv broad.); Television Announcer (radio-tv broad.). May announce program of local interest and be designated Local Announcer (radio-tv broad.). May announce program for transmission over network and affiliated stations and be designated Network Announcer (radio-tv broad.). May announce in foreign language for international broadcast and be designated Announcer, International Broadcast (radio-tv broad.). May describe sporting event during game from direct observation or announce sports news received at station for radio or television broadcasting and be designated Sports Announcer (radio-tv broad.).
GOE: 01.03.03 STRENGTH: L GED: R5 M3 L4 SVP: 6 DLU: 89

159.147-014 DISC JOCKEY (radio-tv broad.)
Announces radio program of musical selections: Selects phonograph or tape recording to be played based on program specialty, knowledge of audience taste, or listening audience requests. Comments on music and other matters of interest to audience, such as weather, time, or traffic conditions. May interview musical personalities. May interview members of listening audience who telephone musical requests. May specialize in one type of music, such as classical, pop, rock, or country and western. May write entries onto log to provide information on all elements aired during broadcast, such as musical selections and station promotions. May be designated Combination Operator (radio-tv broad.) when operating transmitter or control console.
GOE: 01.03.03 STRENGTH: L GED: R5 M3 L5 SVP: 5 DLU: 89

159.147-018 SHOW HOST/HOSTESS (radio-tv broad.) alternate titles: game show host/hostess; talent; talk show host/hostess
Performs any combination of following duties to broadcast program over television or radio: Discusses and prepares program content with PRODUCER (radio-tv broad.) 159.117-010 and assistants. Interviews show guests about their lives, their work, or topics of current interest. Discusses various topics over telephone with viewers or listeners. Asks questions of contestants, or manages play of game, to enable contestants to win prizes. Describes or demonstrates products that viewers may purchase by telephoning show or by mail, or may purchase in stores. Acts as Host/Hostess at civic, charitable, or promotional events that are broadcast over television or radio.
GOE: 01.03.03 STRENGTH: L GED: R5 M3 L5 SVP: 6 DLU: 89

159.167-010 ARTIST AND REPERTOIRE MANAGER (amuse. & rec.)
Selects recording artists and musical selections for production of phonograph records: Auditions recording artist or record to select most appropriate talent

for each recording, using knowledge of vocal and instrumental technique and familiarity with popular taste in music. May direct recording sessions. May promote record sales by personal appearances and contacts with broadcasting personalities.
GOE: 01.04.01 STRENGTH: L GED: R4 M3 L4 SVP: 7 DLU: 77

159.167-014 DIRECTOR, RADIO (radio-tv broad.) alternate titles: director, broadcast
Directs rehearsals and broadcast of one or more radio programs for live broadcast or electronic recording: Selects assisting staff and performers for radio program or commercial announcement. Integrates various parts of program or commercial announcement to produce entertainment balance. Rehearses staff and performers to elicit effects desired and best possible performance. Establishes pace of program or commercial announcement to stay within time requirements. Cues ANNOUNCERS (radio-tv broad.) 159.147-010 and technicians during program to insert spot announcements or commercials.
GOE: 01.03.01 STRENGTH: L GED: R4 M3 L4 SVP: 6 DLU: 89

159.167-018 MANAGER, STAGE (amuse. & rec.; radio-tv broad.)
Coordinates production plans and directs activities of stage crew and performers during rehearsals and performance: Confers with DIRECTOR, STAGE (amuse. & rec.) 150.067-010 concerning production plans. Arranges conference times for cast, crew, and DIRECTOR, STAGE (amuse. & rec.), and disseminates general information about production. Reads script during each performance and gives cues for curtain, lights, sound effects, and prompting performers. Interprets stage-set diagrams to determine stage layout. Supervises stage crew engaged in placing scenery and properties. Devises emergency substitutes for stage equipment or properties. Keeps records to advise PRODUCER (amuse. & rec.) 187.167-178 on matters of time, attendance, and employee benefits. Compiles cue words and phrases to form prompt book. Directs activities of one or more assistants. May instruct understudy, replacement, or extra. May call performers at specified interval before curtain time. May operate production equipment to transmit or record performance.
GOE: 01.03.01 STRENGTH: L GED: R4 M3 L4 SVP: 7 DLU: 87

159.167-022 EXECUTIVE PRODUCER, PROMOS (radio-tv broad.)
Directs and coordinates production of promos (promotional spot announcements) for local or national broadcasting service: Directs activities of workers involved in production of promos, utilizing knowledge of continuity writing, on-air promotion guidelines, filming and videotaping techniques, and usage of equipment. Edits scripts for continuity, applying knowledge of continuity writing. Contacts vendors to secure needed props, audio visual materials, and sound effects. Confers with operations and support services personnel to coordinate unit activities with those of other departments. Reviews and edits audio and video tapes, completed promos, and filler continuity, and schedules approved productions for broadcast. Arranges for timely delivery of promo materials to local or network promotion departments. Serves as liaison between station and advertising service of program sponsors or underwriters to coordinate unit activities with client promotional campaigns in other media.
GOE: 11.09.01 STRENGTH: S GED: R5 M3 L5 SVP: 7 DLU: 89

159.207-010 ASTROLOGER (amuse. & rec.)
Prepares and analyzes horoscope to advise clients regarding future trends and events: Prepares horoscope by computing position of planets, their relationship to each other and to zodiacal signs, based on factors, such as time and place subject was born. Analyzes horoscope chart to advise client, such as person or company, regarding conditions which lie ahead, course of action to follow, and probability of success or failure of that action.
GOE: 10.01.02 STRENGTH: S GED: R4 M4 L4 SVP: 4 DLU: 77

159.224-010 ANIMAL TRAINER (amuse. & rec.)
Trains animals to obey commands, compete in shows, or perform tricks to entertain audience: Evaluates animal to determine temperament, ability, and aptitude for training. Conducts training program to develop desired behavior. May organize format of show. May conduct show. May cue or signal animal during performance. May rehearse animal according to script for motion picture or television film or stage or circus program. May train guard dog to protect property. May teach guide dog and master to function as team. May feed, exercise, and give general care to animal. May observe animal's physical condition to detect illness or unhealthy condition requiring medical care. May be designated according to specific animal trained. May be designated Head Animal Trainer (amuse. & rec.) or Senior Animal Trainer (amuse. & rec.) when directing activities of other workers.
GOE: 03.03.01 STRENGTH: L GED: R4 M3 L3 SVP: 6 DLU: 82

159.227-010 INSTRUCTOR, BRIDGE (education) alternate titles: bridge expert
Teaches individuals or groups contract bridge, evaluating individual abilities to determine method and technique of instruction: Explains card suits and values and methods of scoring. Lectures, illustrates, and demonstrates to teach conventions and playing of bridge hands. Supervises individual and group practice, using prearranged decks of cards. Prepares instructional materials for outside study assignments. Usually specializes in one system of bidding. May participate in bridge tournaments. May direct bridge tournaments. May write instructional bridge columns and articles on bridge tournaments for local newspaper.
GOE: 09.01.01 STRENGTH: S GED: R4 M4 L4 SVP: 8 DLU: 77

159.247-010 ACROBAT (amuse. & rec.) alternate titles: tumbler
Entertains audience by performing difficult and spectacular feats, such as leaping, tumbling, and balancing, alone or as member of team. Originates act

or adapts stock presentations. May use equipment, such as chairs and teeter board. May juggle various articles [JUGGLER (amuse. & rec.)]. May perform feats requiring bodily contortions and be designated Contortionist (amuse. & rec.).
GOE: 12.02.01 STRENGTH: V GED: R3 M2 L2 SVP: 5 DLU: 77

159.247-014 AERIALIST (amuse. & rec.) alternate titles: trapeze artist; trapeze performer
Performs gymnastic feats of skill and balance while swinging on trapeze, turning somersaults, or executing flying stunts alone or as member of team.
GOE: 12.02.01 STRENGTH: V GED: R3 M3 L2 SVP: 6 DLU: 77

159.267-010 DIRECTOR, CASTING (motion picture; radio-tv broad.) alternate titles: talent director
Auditions and interviews performers for specific parts, considering such factors as physical size and appearance, quality of voice, expressiveness, and experience: Submits list of suitable performers to PRODUCER (radio-tv broad.) or DIRECTOR, MOTION PICTURE (motion picture); DIRECTOR, RADIO (radio-tv broad.); DIRECTOR, TELEVISION (radio-tv broad.) for final selection. Keeps talent file, including information, such as personality types, specialties, past performances, and availability of performers. May arrange for screen tests of new performers. May obtain contractual agreement from performers on such items as salary or fees, program credits, residual payments, performance dates, and production schedules.
GOE: 01.03.01 STRENGTH: L GED: R5 M3 L4 SVP: 7 DLU: 77

159.341-010 JUGGLER (amuse. & rec.)
Juggles and balances objects, such as balls, knives, plates, tenpins, and hats, to entertain audience.
GOE: 12.02.01 STRENGTH: L GED: R3 M2 L2 SVP: 6 DLU: 77

159.341-014 STUNT PERFORMER (amuse. & rec.; motion picture; radio-tv broad.)
Performs stunts, such as overturning speeding automobile or falling from runaway horse, and participates in fight-action scenes for motion picture, television, or stage production: Reads script and confers with DIRECTOR, MOTION PICTURE (motion picture) and DIRECTOR OF PHOTOGRAPHY (motion picture; radio-tv broad.) to ascertain positions of cameras and other performers. Examines terrain and inspects equipment, such as harness, rigging bars, or nets to avoid injury. Coordinates body movement and facial expression to simulate giving and receiving violent blows. Rehearses stunt routines alone or with other STUNT PERFORMER (amuse. & rec.; motion picture; radio-tv broad.). May design, build, or repair own safety equipment.
GOE: 12.02.01 STRENGTH: M GED: R3 M3 L3 SVP: 6 DLU: 77

159.344-010 EQUESTRIAN (amuse. & rec.)
Rides horses at circus, carnival, exhibition, or horse show, performing acrobatic stunts on saddled or saddleless horse or feats of equestrian skill and daring to entertain audience. When performing stunts on horse without saddle, may be designated Bareback Rider (amuse. & rec.).
GOE: 12.02.01 STRENGTH: M GED: R3 M3 L1 SVP: 6 DLU: 77

159.344-014 RODEO PERFORMER (amuse. & rec.)
Demonstrates daring and skill by bronc riding, calf roping, bull riding, steer wrestling, or similar feats in rodeo competition to entertain spectators and compete for prize money.
GOE: 12.02.01 STRENGTH: H GED: R3 M2 L3 SVP: 5 DLU: 77

159.344-018 SHOW-HORSE DRIVER (amuse. & rec.)
Rides or drives horse before judges in horse show, exercising care to display best points of animal to judges and spectators.
GOE: 12.02.01 STRENGTH: L GED: R3 M2 L2 SVP: 5 DLU: 77

159.347-010 ANNOUNCER (amuse. & rec.) alternate titles: public-address announcer
Announces information of interest to patrons of sporting and other entertainment events, using public address system: Announces program and substitutions or other changes to patrons. Informs patrons of coming events or emergency calls. May observe sporting event to make running commentary, such as play-by-play description or explanation of official decisions. May speak extemporaneously to audience on items of interest, such as background and past record of players. May read prepared script to describe acts or tricks during performance. May furnish information concerning play to SCOREBOARD OPERATOR (amuse. & rec.).
GOE: 01.07.02 STRENGTH: S GED: R4 M2 L4 SVP: 6 DLU: 77

159.347-014 AQUATIC PERFORMER (amuse. & rec.)
Performs water-ballet routines to entertain audience, utilizing synchronized techniques of swimming: May swim underwater, using air lines. May serve as LIFEGUARD (amuse. & rec.), sell tickets, or perform other duties when not participating in show.
GOE: 12.02.01 STRENGTH: M GED: R3 M3 L3 SVP: 5 DLU: 77

159.347-018 THRILL PERFORMER (amuse. & rec.)
Entertains audience at fairs, carnivals, and circuses by performing daredevil feats, such as diving from high diving board into tank of water, parachuting from airplane, or being shot from cannon onto net. May be designated according to specialty as Comedy Diver (amuse. & rec.); Human Projectile (amuse. & rec.); Parachutist (amuse. & rec.).
GOE: 12.02.01 STRENGTH: M GED: R3 M2 L2 SVP: 5 DLU: 77

159.347-022 WIRE WALKER (amuse. & rec.) alternate titles: high-wire artist; tight-rope walker
Walks across high wire or rope fastened between two stands or other uprights, performing acrobatic feats of balance, such as headstands, lie-downs, and somersaults to entertain audience. May walk ascending or descending wire or cable. May ride unicycle, bicycle, or motorcycle across wire. May perform as member of team.
GOE: 12.02.01 STRENGTH: M GED: R3 M2 L1 SVP: 6 DLU: 77

159.367-010 RING CONDUCTOR (amuse. & rec.)
Introduces circus acts, using presence and manner, to set style desired by circus management: Signals start and finish of individual acts, using knowledge of circus performance running order. Signals performers to coordinate smooth transition of acts and addresses audience to alleviate their concern in emergencies, such as accidents or equipment failure.
GOE: 01.07.02 STRENGTH: L GED: R4 M2 L4 SVP: 6 DLU: 77

159.647-010 AMUSEMENT PARK ENTERTAINER (amuse. & rec.)
Entertains audience in amusement park by exhibiting special skills. Designated according to specialty act performed as Fire Eater (amuse. & rec.); Hypnotist (amuse. & rec.); Organ Grinder (amuse. & rec.); Phrenologist (amuse. & rec.); Physiognomist (amuse. & rec.); Snake Charmer (amuse. & rec.); Sword Swallower (amuse. & rec.). May be designated Side-Show Entertainer (amuse. & rec.). May entertain in nightclubs and similar establishments. May entertain for live variety show or for television production.
GOE: 01.07.03 STRENGTH: L GED: R2 M2 L2 SVP: 2 DLU: 77

159.647-014 EXTRA (amuse. & rec.; motion picture; radio-tv broad.)
Performs as nonspeaking member of scene in stage, motion picture, or television productions: Stands, walks, or sits in scenes as background for stars actions, or performs actions requiring special skills, such as dancing, swimming, skating, riding, or handling livestock. Rehearses and performs pantomime, portraying points essential in staging of scene. Workers may be designated according to registration in union as General Extra (amuse. & rec.; motion picture; radio-tv broad.); Special Ability Extra (amuse. & rec.; motion picture; radio-tv broad.); Silent Bit Extra (amuse. & rec.; motion picture; radio-tv broad.).
GOE: 01.08.01 STRENGTH: L GED: R2 M2 L2 SVP: 2 DLU: 77

159.647-018 PSYCHIC READER (amuse. & rec.)
Entertains client or audience by professing to tell past, present, or future events through extraordinary spiritual insight or by perceiving another's thoughts. Designated according to specialty or medium used as Card Reader (amuse. & rec.); Crystal Gazer (amuse. & rec.); Fortune Teller (amuse. & rec.); Mind Reader (amuse. & rec.); Palmist (amuse. & rec.); Tea-Leaf Reader (amuse. & rec.).
GOE: 01.07.01 STRENGTH: S GED: R3 M2 L3 SVP: 3 DLU: 77

159.647-022 SHOW GIRL (amuse. & rec.)
Parades across stage to display costumes and provide background for chorus line to entertain audience.
GOE: 01.08.01 STRENGTH: L GED: R2 M1 L1 SVP: 2 DLU: 77

16 OCCUPATIONS IN ADMINISTRATIVE SPECIALIZATIONS

This division includes occupations concerned with specialized administrative and managerial functions which are common to many types of organizations. (Managerial occupations which are peculiar to one or a few related types of organizations are included in Division 18). In general, occupations included in the group listed below demand a knowledge of a particular function rather than a knowledge of the operations of an organization included in Division 18. Includes occupations which involve the more routine nonclerical duties or a combination of clerical and administrative work. Occupations involving clerical work exclusively in these fields are not included.

160 ACCOUNTANTS, AUDITORS, AND RELATED OCCUPATIONS

This group includes occupations concerned with examining, analyzing, and interpreting accounting records for the purpose of giving advice or preparing statements. It also includes occupations involved in devising or installing accounting systems and advising on cost-recording systems or other financial and budgetary data.

160.162-010 ACCOUNTANT, TAX (profess. & kin.)
Prepares federal, state, or local tax returns of individual, business establishment, or other organization: Examines accounts and records and computes taxes owed according to prescribed rates, laws, and regulations, using computer. Advises management regarding effects of business activities on taxes, and on strategies for minimizing tax liability. Ensures that establishment complies with periodic tax payment, information reporting, and other taxing authority requirements. Represents principal before taxing bodies. May devise and install tax record systems. May specialize in various aspects of tax accounting, such as tax laws applied to particular industry, or in individual, fiduciary, or partnership income tax preparation.
GOE: 11.06.01 STRENGTH: S GED: R5 M5 L5 SVP: 8 DLU: 87

160.162-018 ACCOUNTANT (profess. & kin.)
Applies principles of accounting to analyze financial information and prepare financial reports: Compiles and analyzes financial information to prepare entries to accounts, such as general ledger accounts, documenting business transactions. Analyzes financial information detailing assets, liabilities, and capital, and prepares balance sheet, profit and loss statement, and other reports to summarize current and projected company financial position, using calculator or computer. Audits contracts, orders, and vouchers, and prepares reports to substantiate individual transactions prior to settlement. May establish, modify, document, and coordinate implementation of accounting and accounting control procedures. May devise and implement manual or computer-based system for general accounting. May direct and coordinate activities of other accountants and clerical workers performing accounting and bookkeeping tasks.
GOE: 11.06.01 STRENGTH: S GED: R5 M5 L5 SVP: 8 DLU: 88

160.162-022 ACCOUNTANT, BUDGET (profess. & kin.)
Applies principles of accounting to analyze past and present financial operations and estimates future revenues and expenditures to prepare budget: Analyzes records of present and past operations, trends and costs, estimated and realized revenues, administrative commitments, and obligations incurred to project future revenues and expenses, using computer. Documents revenues and expenditures expected and submits to management. Maintains budgeting systems which provide control of expenditures made to carry out activities, such as advertising and marketing, production, maintenance, or to project activities, such as construction of buildings. Advises management on matters, such as effective use of resources and assumptions underlying budget forecasts. Interprets budgets to management. May develop and install manual or computer-based budgeting system. May assist in financial analysis of legislative projects to develop capital improvement budget and be designated Program Analyst (government ser.). May assist communities to develop budget and efficient use of funds and be designated Public Finance Specialist (government ser.).
GOE: 11.06.01 STRENGTH: S GED: R5 M5 L5 SVP: 8 DLU: 89

160.162-026 ACCOUNTANT, COST (profess. & kin.)
Applies principles of cost accounting to conduct studies which provide detailed cost information not supplied by general accounting systems: Plans study and collects data to determine costs of business activity, such as raw material purchases, inventory, and labor. Analyzes data obtained and records results, using computer. Analyzes changes in product design, raw materials, manufacturing methods, or services provided, to determine effects on costs. Analyzes actual manufacturing costs and prepares periodic report comparing standard costs to actual production costs. Provides management with reports specifying and comparing factors affecting prices and profitability of products or services. May develop and install manual or computer-based cost accounting system. May specialize in analyzing costs relating to public utility rate schedule and be designated Rate Engineer (profess. & kin.). May specialize in appraisal and evaluation of real property or equipment for sale, acquisition, or tax purposes for public utility and be designated Valuation Engineer (profess. & kin.).
GOE: 11.06.01 STRENGTH: S GED: R5 M5 L5 SVP: 8 DLU: 88

160.162-030 AUDITOR, DATA PROCESSING (profess. & kin.) alternate titles: auditor, information systems
Plans and conducts audits of data processing systems and applications to safeguard assets, ensure accuracy of data, and promote operational efficiency: Establishes audit objectives and devises audit plan, following general audit plan and previous audit reports. Interviews workers and examines records to gather data, following audit plan, and using computer. Analyzes data gathered to evaluate effectiveness of controls and determine accuracy of reports and efficiency and security of operations. Writes audit report to document findings and recommendations, using computer. Devises, writes, and tests computer program required to obtain information needed from computer for audit, using computer. Devises controls for new or modified computer application to prevent inaccurate calculations and data loss, and to ensure discovery of errors.
GOE: 11.06.01 STRENGTH: S GED: R5 M4 L5 SVP: 7 DLU: 89

160.167-022 ACCOUNTANT, PROPERTY (profess. & kin.)
Identifies and keeps record of company owned or leased equipment, buildings, and other property: Records description, value, location, and other pertinent information of each item. Conducts periodic inventories to keep records current and ensure that equipment is properly maintained. Distributes cost of maintenance to proper accounts. Examines records to determine that acquisition, sale, retirement, and other entries have been made. Prepares statements reflecting monthly appreciated and depreciated values. Summarizes statements on annual basis for income tax purposes. Prepares schedules for amortization of buildings and equipment. Develops and recommends property accounting methods to provide effective controls.
GOE: 11.06.01 STRENGTH: S GED: R5 M5 L5 SVP: 8 DLU: 77

160.167-026 ACCOUNTANT, SYSTEMS (profess. & kin.) alternate titles: accounting-system expert
Devises and installs special accounting systems and related procedures in establishment which cannot use standardized system: Conducts survey of operations to ascertain needs of establishment. Sets up classification of accounts and organizes accounting procedures and machine methods support. Devises forms and prepares manuals required to guide activities of bookkeeping and clerical personnel who post data and keep records. May adapt conventional accounting and recordkeeping functions to machine accounting processes and be designated Accountant, Machine Processing (profess. & kin.).

GOE: 11.06.01 STRENGTH: S GED: R5 M5 L5 SVP: 8 DLU: 77

160.167-030 AUDITOR, COUNTY OR CITY (government ser.)
Directs activities of personnel engaged in recording deeds and similar legal instruments, keeping records of county or municipal accounts, compiling and transmitting fiscal records to appropriate state officials, preparing financial statements of county or municipal finances for publication in local newspaper, and auditing books of city or county offices and departments. May be designated according to jurisdiction as City Auditor (government ser.); County Auditor (government ser.). In smaller communities or counties, may personally discharge all duties of office.
GOE: 11.06.01 STRENGTH: S GED: R5 M5 L5 SVP: 6 DLU: 77

160.167-034 AUDITOR, INTERNAL (profess. & kin.)
Conducts audits for management to assess effectiveness of controls, accuracy of financial records, and efficiency of operations: Examines records of departments and interviews workers to ensure recording of transactions and compliance with applicable laws and regulations. Inspects accounting systems to determine their efficiency and protective value. Reviews records pertaining to material assets, such as equipment and buildings, and staff to determine degree to which they are utilized. Analyzes data obtained for evidence of deficiencies in controls, duplication of effort, extravagance, fraud, or lack of compliance with laws, government regulations, and management policies or procedures. Prepares reports of findings and recommendations for management. May conduct special studies for management, such as those required to discover mechanics of detected fraud and to develop controls for fraud prevention. May audit employer business records for governmental agency to determine unemployment insurance premiums, liabilities, and employer compliance with state tax laws.
GOE: 11.06.01 STRENGTH: L GED: R5 M5 L5 SVP: 7 DLU: 89

160.167-038 AUDITOR, TAX (profess. & kin.)
Audits financial records to determine tax liability: Reviews information gathered from taxpayer, such as material assets, income, surpluses, liabilities, and expenditures to verify net worth or reported financial status and identify potential tax issues. Analyzes issues to determine nature, scope, and direction of investigation required. Develops and evaluates evidence of taxpayer finances to determine tax liability, using knowledge of interest and discount, annuities, valuation of stocks and bonds, sinking funds, and amortization valuation of depletable assets. Prepares written explanation of findings to notify taxpayer of tax liability. Advises taxpayer of appeal rights. May conduct on-site audits at taxpayer's place of business and be designated Field Auditor (government ser.). May audit individuals and small businesses through correspondence or by summoning taxpayer to branch office for interview and be designated Office Auditor (government ser.). May perform legal and accounting work in examination of records, tax returns, and related documents pertaining to tax settlement of decedent's estates and be designated Tax Analyst (government ser.). May review most complicated taxpayer accounts and be designated Tax Examiner (government ser.).
GOE: 11.06.01 STRENGTH: L GED: R5 M5 L5 SVP: 8 DLU: 77

160.167-042 BURSAR (education)
Directs and coordinates activities of workers engaged in keeping complete books of tuition fees and other receipts for educational institution. Periodically reports receipts to board of trustees or other body ultimately responsible for financial condition of institution.
GOE: 11.06.01 STRENGTH: S GED: R5 M5 L5 SVP: 7 DLU: 77

160.167-046 CHIEF BANK EXAMINER (government ser.)
Directs investigation of financial institutions for state or federal regulatory agency to enforce laws and regulations governing establishment, operation, and solvency of financial institutions: Schedules audits according to departmental policy, availability of personnel, and financial condition of institution. Evaluates examination reports to determine action required to protect solvency of institution and interests of shareholders and depositors. Confers with financial advisors and other regulatory officials to recommend or initiate action against banks failing to comply with laws and regulations. Confers with officials of financial institutions industry to exchange views and discuss issues. Reviews application for merger, acquisition, establishment of new institution, acceptance in Federal Reserve System, or other action, and evaluates results of investigations undertaken to determine whether such action is in public interest. Recommends acceptance or rejection of application on basis of findings.
GOE: 11.10.01 STRENGTH: S GED: R5 M5 L5 SVP: 8 DLU: 77

160.167-050 REVENUE AGENT (government ser.)
Conducts independent field audits and investigations of federal income tax returns to verify or amend tax liabilities: Examines selected tax returns to determine nature and extent of audits to be performed. Analyzes accounting books and records to determine appropriateness of accounting methods employed and compliance with statutory provisions. Investigates documents, financial transactions, operation methods, industry practices and such legal instruments as vouchers, leases, contracts, and wills, to develop information regarding inclusiveness of accounting records and tax returns. Confers with taxpayer or representative to explain issues involved and applicability of pertinent tax laws and regulations. [Workers who investigate and collect federal tax delinquencies are defined under REVENUE OFFICER (government ser.).] Secures taxpayer's agreement to discharge tax assment or submits contested determination to other administrative or judicial conferees for appeals hearings. May participate in informal appeals hearings on contested cases from other agents. May serve as

102

member of regional appeals board to reexamine unresolved issues in terms of relevant laws and regulations and be designated Appellate Conferee (government ser.).
GOE: 11.06.01 STRENGTH: L GED: R5 M4 L4 SVP: 7 DLU: 77

160.167-054   AUDITOR (profess. & kin.)
Examines and analyzes accounting records to determine financial status of establishment and prepares financial reports concerning operating procedures: Reviews data regarding material assets, net worth, liabilities, capital stock, surplus, income, and expenditures. Inspects items in books of original entry to determine if accepted accounting procedure was followed in recording transactions. Counts cash on hand, inspects notes receivable and payable, negotiable securities, and cancelled checks. Verifies journal and ledger entries of cash and check payments, purchases, expenses, and trial balances by examining and authenticating inventory items. Prepares reports for management concerning scope of audit, financial conditions found, and source and application of funds. May make recommendations regarding improving operations and financial position of company. May supervise and coordinate activities of auditors specializing in specific operations of establishments undergoing audit. May audit banks and financial institutions and be designated Bank Examiner (government ser.). May examine company payroll and personnel records to determine worker's compensation coverage and be designated Payroll Auditor (insurance).
GOE: 11.06.01 STRENGTH: S GED: R5 M5 L5 SVP: 8 DLU: 81

160.167-058   CONTROLLER (profess. & kin.) alternate titles: comptroller
Directs financial activities of organization or subdivision of organization: Prepares, using computer or calculator, or directs preparation of, reports which summarize and forecast company business activity and financial position in areas of income, expenses, and earnings, based on past, present, and expected operations. Directs determination of depreciation rates to apply to capital assets. Establishes, or recommends to management, major economic objectives and policies for company or subdivision. May manage accounting department. May direct preparation of budgets. May prepare reports required by regulatory agencies. May advise management on desirable operational adjustments due to tax code revisions. May arrange for audits of company accounts. May advise management about property and liability insurance coverage needed. May direct financial planning, procurement, and investment of funds for organization [TREASURER (profess. & kin.) 161.117-018].
GOE: 11.06.02 STRENGTH: S GED: R5 M5 L4 SVP: 8 DLU: 88

160.207-010   CREDIT COUNSELOR (profess. & kin.)
Provides financial counseling to individuals in debt: Confers with client to ascertain available monthly income after living expenses to meet credit obligations. Calculates amount of debt and funds available to plan method of payoff and estimate time for debt liquidation. Contacts creditors to explain client's financial situation and to arrange for payment adjustments so that payments are feasible for client and agreeable to creditors. Establishes payment priorities to reduce client's overall costs by liquidating high-interest, short-term loans or contracts first. Opens account for client and disburses funds from account to creditors as agent for client. Keeps records of account activity. May counsel client on personal and family financial problems, such as excessive spending and borrowing of funds, and be designated Budget Consultant (profess. & kin.). May be required to be licensed by state agency.
GOE: 07.01.01 STRENGTH: S GED: R5 M5 L5 SVP: 7 DLU: 77

160.267-014   DIRECTOR, UTILITY ACCOUNTS (government ser.)
Evaluates financial condition of electric, telephone, gas, water, and public transit utility companies to facilitate work of regulatory commissions in setting rates: Analyzes annual reports, financial statements, and other records submitted by utility companies, applying accepted accounting and statistical analysis procedures to determine current financial condition of company. Evaluates reports from commission staff members and field investigators regarding condition of company property and other factors influencing solvency and profitability of company. Prepares and presents exhibits and testifies during commission hearings on regulatory or rate adjustments. Confers with company officials to discuss financial problems and regulatory matters. Directs workers engaged in filing company financial records. May conduct specialized studies, such as cost of service, revenue requirement, and cost allocation studies for commission, or design new rates in accordance with findings of commission and be designated Rate Analyst (government ser.).
GOE: 11.06.03 STRENGTH: S GED: R5 M5 L5 SVP: 8 DLU: 77

160.267-022   CREDIT ANALYST (financial)
Analyzes credit information to determine risk involved in lending money to commercial customers, and prepares report of findings: Selects information, including company financial statements and balance sheet and records data on spreadsheet, using computer. Enters codes for computer program to generate ratios for use in evaluating commercial customer's financial status. Compares items, such as liquidity, profitability, credit history, and cash, with other companies of same industry, size, and geographic location. Analyzes such factors as income growth, quality of management, market share, potential risks of industry, and collateral appraisal. Writes offering sheet (loan application), including results of credit analysis and summary of loan request. Describes credit risk and amount of loan profit. Submits offering sheet to loan committee for decision. May visit company to collect information as part of analysis.
GOE: 11.06.03 STRENGTH: S GED: R5 M4 L5 SVP: 8 DLU: 89

160.267-026   INVESTMENT ANALYST (financial; insurance) alternate titles: securities analyst; securities-research analyst
Analyzes financial information to forecast business, industry, and economic conditions, for use in making investment decisions: Gathers and analyzes company financial statements, industry, regulatory and economic information, and financial periodicals and newspapers. Interprets data concerning price, yield, stability, and future trends of investments. Summarizes data describing current and long term trends in investment risks and economic influences pertinent to investments. Draws charts and graphs to illustrate reports, using computer. Recommends investment timing and buy-and-sell orders to company or to staff of investment establishment for advising clients. May call brokers and purchase investments for company, according to company policy. May recommend modifications to management's investment policy. May specialize in specific investment area, such as bond, commodity, equity, currency, or portfolio management.
GOE: 11.06.03 STRENGTH: S GED: R5 M5 L5 SVP: 8 DLU: 89

161   BUDGET AND MANAGEMENT SYSTEMS ANALYSIS OCCUPATIONS

This group includes occupations concerned with reviewing, examining, and evaluating the organizational structures, administrative policies, and management systems of organizations, such as governmental units, industrial concerns, business firms, and nonprofit groups. Includes the preparation of reports summarizing findings and recommending to line management changes in organization, programs, methods, policies, procedures, or practices concerning such management systems as budget forecasting and records and information management. Includes consolidating the budget estimates of several organizational units and preparing a unitary budget itemizing production costs, for consideration and action by upper echelons of management.

161.117-010   BUDGET OFFICER (profess. & kin.)
Directs and coordinates activities of personnel responsible for formulation, monitoring and presentation of budgets for controlling funds to implement program objectives of public and private organizations: Directs compilation of data based on statistical studies and analyses of past and current years to prepare budgets and to justify funds requested. Correlates appropriations for specific programs with appropriations for divisional programs and includes items for emergency funds. Reviews operating budgets periodically to analyze trends affecting budget needs. Consults with unit heads to ensure adjustments are made in accordance with program changes in order to facilitate long-term planning. Directs preparation of regular and special budget reports to interpret budget directives and to establish policies for carrying out directives. Prepares comparative analyses of operating programs by analyzing costs in relation to services performed during previous fiscal years and submits reports to director of organization with recommendations for budget revisions. Testifies regarding proposed budgets before examining and fund-granting authorities to clarify reports and gain support for estimated budget needs. Administers personnel functions of budget department, such as training, work scheduling, promotions, transfers, and performance ratings.
GOE: 11.06.05 STRENGTH: S GED: R5 M5 L5 SVP: 8 DLU: 87

161.117-014   DIRECTOR, RECORDS MANAGEMENT (profess. & kin.)
Plans, develops, and administers records management policies designed to facilitate effective and efficient handling of business records and other information: Plans development and implementation of records management policies intended to standardize filing, protecting, and retrieving records, reports, and other information contained on paper, microfilm, computer program, or other media. Coordinates and directs, through subordinate managers, activities of departments involved with records management analysis, reports analysis, and supporting technical, clerical micrographics, and printing services. Evaluates staff reports, utilizing knowledge of principles of records and information management, administrative processes and systems, cost control, governmental recordkeeping requirements, and organizational objectives. Confers with other administrators to assure compliance with policies, procedures, and practices of records management program.
GOE: 11.01.01 STRENGTH: S GED: R5 M4 L5 SVP: 8 DLU: 77

161.117-018   TREASURER (profess. & kin.) alternate titles: treasury representative
Directs financial planning, procurement, and investment of funds for an organization: Delegates authority for receipt, disbursement, banking, protection and custody of funds, securities, and financial instruments. Analyzes financial records to forecast future financial position and budget requirements. Evaluates need for procurement of funds and investment of surplus. Advises management on investments and loans for short- and long-range financial plans. Prepares financial reports for management. Develops policies and procedures for account collections and extension of credit to customers. Signs notes of indebtedness as approved by management. May act as CONTROLLER (profess. & kin.) 160.167-058.
GOE: 11.06.03 STRENGTH: S GED: R5 M5 L5 SVP: 8 DLU: 77

161.167-010   MANAGEMENT ANALYST (profess. & kin.) alternate titles: systems analyst
Analyzes business or operating procedures to devise most efficient methods of accomplishing work: Plans study of work problems and procedures, such as

organizational change, communications, information flow, integrated production methods, inventory control, or cost analysis. Gathers and organizes information on problem or procedures including present operating procedures. Analyzes data gathered, develops information and considers available solutions or alternate methods of proceeding. Organizes and documents findings of studies and prepares recommendations for implementation of new systems, procedures or organizational changes. Confers with personnel concerned to assure smooth functioning of newly implemented systems or procedure. May install new systems and train personnel in application. May conduct operational effectiveness reviews to ensure functional or project systems are applied and functioning as designed. May develop or update functional or operational manuals outlining established methods of performing work in accordance with organizational policy.
GOE: 05.01.06 STRENGTH: S GED: R5 M5 L5 SVP: 7 DLU: 89

161.167-014 MANAGER, FORMS ANALYSIS (profess. & kin.)
Directs and coordinates activities of workers involved with analyzing business forms: Plans and directs compilation and updating of cost and control records, utilizing knowledge of forms inventories, usage, and operating practices. Coordinates activities of personnel engaged in forms analysis, such as format design, increasing content effectiveness, and reducing production and processing costs. Plans and directs activities of workers involved in identifying form deficiencies and recommending solution, utilizing knowledge of principles and techniques of records management, government recordkeeping requirements, printing and microfilm processes, and cost specifications. Analyzes and evaluates staff recommendations and approves implementation of change, utilizing knowledge of forms analysis and standardization, managerial processes and systems, budgetary limitations, and organizational policies and procedures.
GOE: 11.06.02 STRENGTH: S GED: R5 M4 L4 SVP: 8 DLU: 77

161.167-018 MANAGER, RECORDS ANALYSIS (profess. & kin.)
Directs and coordinates activities of workers involved with analyzing systems of records management: Plans and directs compilation and updating of cost and control records, utilizing knowledge of records inventories, usage, costs, and operating practices. Coordinates activities of personnel engaged in studying such matters as simplification of filing and retrieval systems, protection of vital records and economical utilization of paper, microfilm, computer program, or other information-bearing media according to organizational and governmental recordkeeping schedules and requirements. Analyzes and evaluates staff reports and approves implementation of recommendations, utilizing knowledge of principles and techniques of records and information management, managerial processes and systems, budgetary limitations and organizational policies and procedures.
GOE: 11.06.02 STRENGTH: S GED: R5 M4 L4 SVP: 8 DLU: 77

161.167-022 MANAGER, REPORTS ANALYSIS (profess. & kin.)
Directs and coordinates activities of workers involved with analysis of business reports: Plans and directs compilation and updating of cost and control records, utilizing knowledge of reports inventories, usage, cost, distribution, frequency, and operating practices. Coordinates activities of personnel engaged in reports analysis, such as determining necessity of report, simplification of reports format, increasing content effectiveness, and reduction of processing costs. Plans and directs activities intended to develop new or revised reports format, utilizing knowledge of principles and techniques of information and documents management, vital records protection, and cost-control practices. Analyzes and evaluates staff recommendations and approves implementation of changes, utilizing knowledge of reports analysis and standardization, managerial processes and systems, budgetary limitations, and organizational policies and procedures.
GOE: 11.06.02 STRENGTH: S GED: R5 M4 L4 SVP: 8 DLU: 77

161.267-010 CLERICAL-METHODS ANALYST (profess. & kin.)
Examines and evaluates clerical work methods to develop new or improved standardized methods and procedures: Interviews clerical workers and supervisory personnel and conducts on-site observation to ascertain unit functions, work performed, methods and equipment used, and personnel involved. Sketches office layout to show location of equipment required for originating, processing, and filing business records and information. Confers with managerial personnel to obtain suggestions for improvements, such as modifying existing procedures, using alternate work method, or introducing new business forms, reports standards, or coding system. Evaluates findings, using knowledge of principles and techniques of work simplification, governmental record keeping requirements, and company policies to recommend methods or equipment intended to improve clerical operations. May prepare training manuals and train clerical workers in new procedure or operation and maintenance of machines and equipment. May assist in preparation of job descriptions or specifications. May specialize in one phase of clerical methods analysis, such as filing, workflow, or coding systems. May be designated according to location where work is performed as in-house staff or customer field-representative.
GOE: 05.01.06 STRENGTH: S GED: R5 M5 L4 SVP: 7 DLU: 77

161.267-018 FORMS ANALYST (profess. & kin.)
Examines and evaluates format and function of business forms to develop new, or improve existing forms format, usage, and control: Reviews forms to evaluate need for revision, consolidation, or discontinuation, using knowledge of form use, workflow, document flow, and compatibility with manual or machine processing. Confers with form users to gather recommendations for improvements, considering such characteristics as form necessity, completeness,

design, text, and specifications as to size and color of paper, style of typeface, and number of copies. May design, draft or prepare finished master copy for new or modified form, or confer with printer's representative to specify changes in format and approve proof copies. Prepares and issues written instructions for use of forms in accordance with organizational policies, procedures, and practices. Keeps records to update information concerning form origin, function, necessity, usage, cost, and stock level.
GOE: 11.01.01 STRENGTH: S GED: R4 M3 L4 SVP: 7 DLU: 77

161.267-022 RECORDS-MANAGEMENT ANALYST (profess. & kin.)
Examines and evaluates records-management systems to develop new or improve existing methods for efficient handling, protecting, and disposing of business records and information: Reviews records and reports to ascertain media (paper, microfilm, or computer tape) used, reproduction process, or electronic data processing involved. Drafts office and storage area layout to plot location of equipment and to compute space available. Confers with clerical and supervisory personnel to gather suggestions for improvements and to detect records-management problems. Reviews records retention schedules and governmental recordkeeping requirements to determine timetables for transferring active records to inactive or archival storage, for reducing paper records to micrographic form, or for destroying obsolete or unnecessary records. Evaluates findings and recommends changes or modifications in procedures, utilizing knowledge of functions of operating units, coding systems and filing methods. Recommends purchase of storage, retrieval, or disposal equipment according to knowledge of equipment capability and cost.
GOE: 11.06.02 STRENGTH: S GED: R4 M3 L4 SVP: 7 DLU: 77

161.267-026 REPORTS ANALYST (profess. & kin.)
Examines and evaluates purpose and content of business reports to develop new, or improve existing format, use, and control: Reviews reports to determine basic characteristics, such as origin and report flow, format, frequency, distribution and purpose or function of report. Confers with persons originating, handling, processing, or receiving reports to identify problems and to gather suggestions for improvements. Evaluates findings, using knowledge of workflow, operating practices, records retention schedules, and office equipment layout. Recommends establishment of new or modified reporting methods and procedures to improve report content and completeness of information. May prepare and issue instructions concerning generation, completion, and distribution of reports according to new or revised practices, procedures, or policies of reports management.
GOE: 11.06.02 STRENGTH: S GED: R4 M3 L4 SVP: 7 DLU: 77

161.267-030 BUDGET ANALYST (government ser.)
Analyzes current and past budgets, prepares and justifies budget requests, and allocates funds according to spending priorities in governmental service agency: Analyzes accounting records to determine financial resources required to implement program and submits recommendations for budget allocations. Recommends approval or disapproval of requests for funds. Advises staff on cost analysis and fiscal allocations.
GOE: 11.06.05 STRENGTH: S GED: R5 M3 L4 SVP: 7 DLU: 86

162 PURCHASING MANAGEMENT OCCUPATIONS

This group includes occupations concerned with negotiating and contracting for the purchase of equipment, products, and supplies for industrial plants, utilities, governmental units, or other establishments, and the purchasing of merchandise for resale; determining quantity and quality to be purchased, costs, delivery dates, contract conditions, sources of supply, and taking inventories.

162.117-010 CHRISTMAS-TREE CONTRACTOR (any industry) alternate titles: field technician
Contacts landowners to negotiate purchase of Christmas trees and arranges with contractors to cut trees: Contacts owners of forest lands prior to cutting season to negotiate contracts for purchase of trees. Surveys stumpage (standing timber) to determine approximate tree yield and informs property owner of types and sizes of trees desired. Confers with cutting contractors to arrange for cutting trees on leased lands and establishes piecework rate based on grade and size of trees cut. May supervise operations in district during cutting season.
GOE: 08.01.03 STRENGTH: L GED: R5 M3 L5 SVP: 7 DLU: 77

162.117-014 CONTRACT ADMINISTRATOR (any industry)
Directs activities concerned with contracts for purchase or sale of equipment, materials, products, or services: Examines performance requirements, delivery schedules, and estimates of costs of material, equipment, and production to ensure completeness and accuracy. Prepares bids, process specifications, test and progress reports, and other exhibits that may be required. Reviews bids from other firms for conformity to contract requirements and determines acceptable bids. Negotiates contract with customer or bidder. Requests or approves amendments to or extensions of contracts. Advises planning and production departments of contractual rights and obligations. May compile data for preparing estimates. May coordinate work of sales department with production and shipping department to implement fulfillment of contracts. May act as liaison between company and subcontractors. May direct sales program [MANAGER, SALES (any industry) 163.167-018].
GOE: 11.12.04 STRENGTH: S GED: R5 M3 L5 SVP: 8 DLU: 86

162.117-018 CONTRACT SPECIALIST (profess. & kin.) alternate titles: contract coordinator
Negotiates with suppliers to draw up procurement contracts: Negotiates, administers, extends, terminates, and renegotiates contracts. Formulates and co

ordinates procurement proposals. Directs and coordinates activities of workers engaged in formulating bid proposals. Evaluates or monitors contract performance to determine necessity for amendments or extensions of contracts, and compliance to contractual obligations. Approves or rejects requests for deviations from contract specifications and delivery schedules. Arbitrates claims or complaints occurring in performance of contracts. Analyzes price proposals, financial reports, and other data to determine reasonableness of prices. May negotiate collective bargaining agreements. May serve as liaison officer to ensure fulfillment of obligations by contractors.
GOE: 11.12.04 STRENGTH: L GED: R5 M3 L5 SVP: 8 DLU: 87

162.117-022   FIELD CONTRACTOR (any industry)
Negotiates contracts with growers to raise or purchase crops, such as fruits and vegetables, performing any combination of the following duties: Contacts grower to negotiate contracts and to explain terms and conditions of contract and contractual responsibilities. Determines production possibilities of land by studying data, such as history of crop rotation, type and fertility of soil, location, topography, and irrigation facilities. Negotiates amount of acreage to be planted or purchased and selects fields to be planted. Advises grower on preparing land, planting, cultivating, thinning, harvesting, and related problems. Supplies seed and fertilizer. May estimate crop yield. Arranges for financing and advances funds to purchase supplies and equipment or services of contractor. May arrange for loans of company-owned machinery. Arranges for transportation of crops to processing plants. Inspects growing crops for evidence of disease and insect damage and recommends corrective measures. May assist in recruiting extra labor during peak seasons. May conduct lectures for farm groups on specific phases of agricultural activities. May write articles for publication and for scientific groups. May specialize in one crop and be designated according to crop bought.
GOE: 03.01.01 STRENGTH: L GED: R5 M3 L5 SVP: 7 DLU: 77

162.117-026   FIELD-CONTACT TECHNICIAN (dairy products)
Contacts dairy farmers to negotiate contracts for purchase of dairy products and to discuss methods for improving milk production: Negotiates with farmers for long-term contracts to purchase milk or cream of specified butterfat content. Discusses milk production problems and tests milk for butterfat content, sediment, and bacteria. Suggests methods of feeding, housing, and milking to improve production and to comply with sanitary regulations. May set up truck routes to haul milk to dairy. May solicit memberships in cooperative association. May sell items, such as dairy farm equipment, chemicals, and feed.
GOE: 08.01.03 STRENGTH: L GED: R5 M3 L5 SVP: 7 DLU: 77

162.117-030   RESEARCH-CONTRACTS SUPERVISOR (government ser.)
Directs activities of workers engaged in negotiating and servicing research contracts with universities and other institutions conducting research projects for federal agencies. Evaluates contract proposals and directs awarding of contracts according to knowledge of contract law and other fields, such as engineering development and metallurgical laboratory techniques, depending on nature of project.
GOE: 11.12.04 STRENGTH: S GED: R6 M5 L5 SVP: 8 DLU: 77

162.157-010   BROKER-AND-MARKET OPERATOR, GRAIN (financial; wholesale tr.) alternate titles: grain trader
Buys and sells grain on commission, for customers, through commodity exchange: Advises customers on probable price changes and factors which may affect prices, such as crop carryover, normal grain production and consumption, foreign and domestic crop conditions, and price differentials among various grades of grains. Notifies customer when additional margin is required because of price fluctuations and governmental regulations. May buy and sell grain futures for customer or brokerage firm and be designated Buyer Grain (wolesale tr.).
GOE: 11.06.04 STRENGTH: S GED: R5 M4 L4 SVP: 7 DLU: 77

162.157-018   BUYER (profess. & kin.) alternate titles: broker
Purchases merchandise or commodities for resale: Inspects and grades or appraises agricultural commodities, durable goods, apparel, furniture, livestock, or other merchandise offered for sale to determine value and yield. Selects and orders merchandise from showings by manufacturing representatives, growers, or other sellers, or purchases merchandise on open market for cash, basing selection on nature of clientele or demand for specific commodity, merchandise, or other property, utilizing knowledge of various articles of commerce and experience as buyer. Transports purchases or contacts carriers to arrange transportation of purchases. Authorizes payment of invoices or return of merchandise. May negotiate contracts for severance of agricultural or forestry products from land. May conduct staff meeetings with sales personnel to introduce new merchandise. May price items for resale. May be required to be licensed by state. May be identified according to type of commodities, merchandise, or goods purchased.
GOE: 08.01.03 STRENGTH: L GED: R4 M3 L4 SVP: 6 DLU: 86

162.157-022   BUYER, ASSISTANT (retail trade)
Performs following duties in connection with purchase and sale of merchandise to aid BUYER (profess. & kin.): Verifies quantity and quality of stock received from manufacturer. Authorizes payment of invoices or return of shipment. Approves advertising copy for newspaper. Gives MARKERS (retail trade; wholesale tr.) information, such as price mark-ups or mark-downs, manufacturer number, season code, and style number to print on price tickets. Inspects exchanged or refunded merchandise. May sell merchandise to become familiar with customers' attitudes, preferences, and purchasing problems.

GOE: 08.01.03 STRENGTH: L GED: R4 M3 L3 SVP: 6 DLU: 77

162.157-026   COMMISSION AGENT, LIVESTOCK (wholesale tr.)
Sells livestock at stockyards as agent for owner: Receives, appraises, and sorts livestock according to factors, such as weight, sex, age, and appearance, to determine value and facilitate sale. Contacts purchasing agents and informs them of livestock available for sale. Shows livestock to buyers and receives bids. Informs interested buyers of other bids received. Sells livestock to highest bidder. May purchase livestock as agent for farmer. May specialize in purchase of one species of livestock.
GOE: 08.01.03 STRENGTH: L GED: R4 M3 L4 SVP: 6 DLU: 77

162.157-030   OUTSIDE PROPERTY AGENT (motion picture) alternate titles: buyer-renter
Locates and arranges for purchase or rental of props specified for use in motion pictures when such props are not in studio stock and are not to be constructed by studio personnel. May purchase stock, such as lumber, to be used in fabrication of props.
GOE: 08.01.03 STRENGTH: S GED: R4 M4 L4 SVP: 7 DLU: 77

162.157-034   PROCUREMENT ENGINEER (aircraft mfg.)
Develops specifications and performance test requirements to facilitate procurement of parts and equipment for aeronautical and aerospace products: Analyzes technical data, designs, preliminary specifications, manufacturing limitations, supplier facilities, and availability of parts and equipment. Consults with engineering personnel to establish performance criteria and specifications for manufacturing and testing. Investigates potential suppliers and recommends those most desirable. Advises company personnel, suppliers, and customers of nature and function of parts and equipment. Interviews supplier representatives regarding specifications, costs, inspection, and similar problems relating to parts and equipment. Arranges and participates in conferences between suppliers and engineers, purchasers, inspectors, and other company personnel to facilitate material inspection, substitution, standardization, rework, salvage, utilization, and economical procurement of parts and equipment installed in aircraft, spacecraft, or related products.
GOE: 05.03.03 STRENGTH: S GED: R5 M5 L5 SVP: 7 DLU: 89

162.157-038   PURCHASING AGENT (profess. & kin.) alternate titles: buyer
Coordinates activities involved with procuring goods and services, such as raw materials, equipment, tools, parts, supplies, and advertising, for establishment: Reviews requisitions. Confers with vendors to obtain product or service information, such as price, availability, and delivery schedule. Selects products for purchase by testing, observing, or examining items. Estimates values according to knowledge of market price. Determines method of procurement, such as direct purchase or bid. Prepares purchase orders or bid requests. Reviews bid proposals and negotiates contracts within budgetary limitations and scope of authority. Maintains manual or computerized procurement records, such as items or services purchased, costs, delivery, product quality or performance, and inventories. Discusses defective or unacceptable goods or services with inspection or quality control personnel, users, vendors, and others to determine source of trouble and take corrective action. May approve invoices for payment. May expedite delivery of goods to users.
GOE: 11.05.04 STRENGTH: L GED: R4 M3 L4 SVP: 7 DLU: 87

162.167-010   BUYER, GRAIN (grain-feed mills; wholesale tr.) alternate titles: grain-elevator agent; manager, grain elevator
Manages grain elevator: Examines samples to extent of dirt, burrs, hulls, seeds, and other dockage. Extracts samples and forwards them to local grain exchange for analysis and certification of moisture and protein content. Reviews analysis to ascertain amount of moisture and protein present in sample. Calculates market value and bargains with sellers to obtain grain at favorable price. Buys grain or issues storage certificates. Computes shipping cost to determine most economical way of transporting grain. Reviews and approves grain settlements to ensure that payments are made according to weight, moisture, and protein content. Keeps daily records on kinds and grades of grain received, prices paid, amount purchased, and amount in storage. Directs workers engaged in unloading, loading, storing, and mixing of grain for shipment and milling.
GOE: 08.01.03 STRENGTH: L GED: R5 M3 L4 SVP: 8 DLU: 77

162.167-014   BUYER, TOBACCO, HEAD (wholesale tr.) alternate titles: buyer, head; circuit rider; circuit walker
Coordinates activities of workers engaged in buying tobacco on auction warehouse floor: Tells BUYER (profess. & kin.) which grades and quantities of tobacco to buy and prices to be paid, and observes purchases for conformance to company regulations. May buy tobacco on auction market. May inspect and regrade tobacco in processing plant.
GOE: 08.01.03 STRENGTH: L GED: R4 M3 L4 SVP: 7 DLU: 77

162.167-018   CLEAN-RICE BROKER (grain-feed mills) alternate titles: milled-rice broker
Coordinates rice buying and milling operations with demand and sells clean (milled) rice on domestic and foreign markets: Contacts prospective purchasers, sends or displays samples of grades and varieties of rice offered for sale, states selling price, and arranges sales. Ascertains from orders, quantity and varieties of rice required, and notifies buyers purchasing rice from growers. Prepares instructions for operating personnel of lots of rice to be milled and sequence and method of milling. Directs workers keeping records and preparing contracts and shipping data.

GOE: 11.05.04 STRENGTH: S GED: R5 M5 L5 SVP: 7 DLU: 77

162.167-022 MANAGER, PROCUREMENT SERVICES (profess. & kin.) alternate titles: director, procurement services; manager, material control

Directs and coordinates activities of personnel engaged in purchasing and distributing raw materials, equipment, machinery, and supplies in industrial plant, public utility, or other organization: Prepares instructions regarding purchasing systems and procedures. Prepares and issues purchase orders and change notices to PURCHASING AGENTS (profess. & kin.). Analyzes market and delivery conditions to determine present and future material availability and prepares market analysis reports. Reviews purchase order claims and contracts for conformance to company policy. Develops and installs clerical and office procedures and practices, and studies work flow, sequence of operations, and office arrangement to determine expediency of installing new or improved office machines. Arranges for disposal of surplus materials.
GOE: 11.05.02 STRENGTH: S GED: R4 M4 L4 SVP: 7 DLU: 77

162.167-026 PRIZE COORDINATOR (radio-tv broad.)

Coordinates use of assorted merchandise for prizes on television game shows: Verifies receipt and accuracy of manufacturer's contract guaranteeing availability of promised merchandise. Sends contract to network for approval. Prepares and sends details of contract (fact sheet), with mounted pictures of manufacturer's products (flip cards), to production company for approval. Inspects flip cards and display merchandise before show is taped to verify their match with prepared script. Views taping of shows to verify promotional use of merchandise and records each episode's winners. Writes status reports for all merchandise used on shows, including amount of contestants' gratuitous awards and type and retail value of merchandise advertised and won during each episode. Obtains contestants' signatures on contestant prize forms after each show and gives written rules and instructions to winners for receiving and using prizes. Notifies manufacturers, or their representatives, of date taped show will be telecast, including names of winners and prizes awarded. Contacts manufacturers to assist winners in resolving complaints about prizes. May solicit use of manufacturer's product. May assist production company in selecting prizes for each taped episode.
GOE: 07.01.02 STRENGTH: L GED: R4 M3 L4 SVP: 5 DLU: 77

162.167-030 PURCHASE-PRICE ANALYST (profess. & kin.)

Compiles and analyzes statistical data to determine feasibility of buying products and to establish price objectives for contract transactions: Compiles information from periodicals, catalogs, and other sources to keep informed on price trends and manufacturing processes. Obtains data for cost analysis studies by determining manufacturing costs within divisions of company. Confers with vendors and analyzes vendor's operations to determine factors that affect prices. Prepares reports, charts, and graphs of findings. Evaluates findings and makes recommendations to purchasing personnel regarding feasibility of manufacturing or buying needed products. May recommend use of alternative parts, materials, or manufacturing methods to reduce costs.
GOE: 11.06.03 STRENGTH: S GED: R5 M5 L4 SVP: 7 DLU: 77

162.167-034 FLOOR BROKER (financial) alternate titles: broker; floor representative; floor trader; trader

Buys and sells securities on floor of securities exchange: Analyzes market conditions and trends to determine best time to execute securities transaction orders. Buys and sells securities based on market quotation and competition in market. Informs REGISTERED REPRESENTATIVE (financial) 250.257-018 of market fluctuations and securities transactions affecting accounts. Must meet exchange requirements, which may include state license, to be member of exchange. May specialize in trading specific securities to stabilize market and be designated Independent Trader (financial) or Specialist (financial).
GOE: 11.06.04 STRENGTH: L GED: R5 M3 L4 SVP: 6 DLU: 90

162.167-038 SECURITIES TRADER (financial) alternate titles: broker; trader

Purchases and sells securities for brokerage firm: Receives sales order ticket from REGISTERED REPRESENTATIVE (financial) 250.257-018, and inspects form to ensure accuracy of information. Contacts market maker (securities exchange or brokerage firm that is trading requested securities) to execute client orders for purchase or sale of securities, or completes transaction independently if brokerage firm is market maker in requested securities. Writes and signs sales order confirmation forms to record and approve securities transactions. Reviews all securities transactions to ensure that trades conform to regulations of Securities and Exchange Commission, National Association of Securities Dealers, and other government agencies. Must pass state examination to receive license and become registered to trade securities. May prepare financial reports to monitor corporate finances. May have management or supervisory responsibility for department employees. May provide clients with information on investments, and sell securities and other financial services [REGISTERED REPRESENTATIVE (financial)].
GOE: 11.06.03 STRENGTH: S GED: R5 M4 L5 SVP: 7 DLU: 89

162.267-010 TITLE CLERK (petrol. & gas; petrol. refin.; pipe lines)

Procures testimonial documents required to remove restrictions affecting title of landowners to property, and requisitions purchase orders and bank checks to satisfy requirements of contracts and agreements covering lease or purchase of land and gas, oil, and mineral rights: Examines leases, contracts, and purchase agreements to assure conformity to specified requirements. Examines ab-

stract to assure complete title-coverage of land described, completeness of land description, and to detect lapses of time in abstract coverage of landowner's title. Prepares correspondence and other records to transmit leases and abstracts. Reviews title opinion to determine nature of testimonial documents needed to meet legal objections and to assure accuracy in terms of trade. Confers with personnel of abstract company, landowners, and LEASE BUYERS (mine & quarry; petrol. & gas) to explain reasons for and to obtain testimonial documents needed to clear title. Prepares or requests deeds, affidavits, and other documents and transmits them to appropriate persons for execution to meet title requirements. Investigates whether delinquent taxes are due on land involved in agreements and confers or corresponds with landowner to assure payment. Verifies computations of fees, rentals, bonuses, brokerage commissions and other expenses and prepares records to initiate requests for payment. Prepares purchase data sheet for records unit covering each trade or exchange. Answers queries regarding leases and contracts by mail, telephone, or personal discussion.
GOE: 07.01.05 STRENGTH: S GED: R5 M4 L5 SVP: 6 DLU: 77

163 SALES AND DISTRIBUTION MANAGEMENT OCCUPATIONS

This group includes occupations concerned with managing sales and marketing for a manufacturer, retail or wholesale house, jobber, or other establishment. Includes market research and analysis; establishing and managing a sales organization; and evaluating sales statistics and reports.

163.117-010 MANAGER, CONTRACTS (petrol. & gas; petrol. refin.; pipe lines) alternate titles: supply representative, petroleum products

Negotiates contracts with representatives of oil producers, refiners, and pipeline carriers for purchase, sale, or delivery of crude oil, petroleum distillates, and natural gas and gasoline: Analyzes records of petroleum supply sources, movements of materials from plants to refineries, and current and prospective refinery demands. Coordinates work of sales, production, and shipping departments to implement procurance of products in accordance with refinery needs. Performs liaison work with engineering and production departments concerning contractual rights and obligations. May manage contracts for entire company, department, or for specified product, such as crude oil or natural gas. May be designated according to product contracted as Supply Representative, Dry Gas (petrol. & gas; petrol. refin.; pipe lines); Manager, Natural-Gas Utilization (petrol. & gas).
GOE: 11.05.02 STRENGTH: S GED: R5 M5 L5 SVP: 7 DLU: 77

163.117-014 MANAGER, EXPORT (any industry)

Directs foreign sales and service outlets of an organization: Negotiates contracts with foreign sales and distribution centers to establish outlets. Directs clerical staff in expediting export correspondence, bid requests, and credit collections. Directs conversion of products from American to foreign standards and specifications to ensure efficient operation under foreign conditions. Arranges shipping details, such as export licenses, customs declarations, and packing, shipping, and routing of product. Directs clerical and technical staff in preparation of foreign language sales manuals. Expedites import-export arrangements and maintains current information on import-export tariffs, licenses, and restrictions.
GOE: 11.05.04 STRENGTH: S GED: R5 M5 L5 SVP: 8 DLU: 77

163.117-018 MANAGER, PROMOTION (hotel & rest.) alternate titles: director, sales; manager, business promotion; manager, sales

Plans and administers sales policies and programs to foster and promote hotel patronage: Consults newspapers, trade journals, and other publications to learn about contemplated conventions and social functions. Organizes prospect files by listing information, such as names of officials and plans for conventions, to be used for promotional purposes. Directs workers engaged in preparing promotional correspondence with travel bureaus, business and social groups. Confers with department heads to discuss and formulate plans for soliciting business. Contacts executives of organizations to explain services and facilities offered by hotel and to solicit their business. Supervises and trains service representatives. Plans and prepares advertising and promotional material and arranges for newspaper and other publicity.
GOE: 11.09.01 STRENGTH: L GED: R5 M3 L4 SVP: 8 DLU: 77

163.117-022 DIRECTOR, MEDIA MARKETING (radio-tv broad.)

Plans and administers marketing and distribution of broadcasting television programs and negotiates agreements for ancillary properties, such as copyrights and distribution rights for films and audiovisual materials: Reviews inventory of television programs and films produced and distribution rights of broadcasting station to determine potential markets. Develops marketing strategy, based on knowledge of establishment policy, nature of market, copyright and royalty requirements, and cost and markup factors. Compiles catalog of audiovisual offerings and sets prices and rental fees. Negotiates with media agents to secure agreements for translation of materials into other media. Arranges for reproduction of materials for distribution and examines reproductions for conformity to standards. Edits materials according to specific market or customer requirements. Confers with legal staff to resolve problems, such as copyrights and royalty sharing with outside producers and distributors.
GOE: 11.05.04 STRENGTH: S GED: R5 M4 L5 SVP: 8 DLU: 86

163.117-026 DIRECTOR, UNDERWRITER SOLICITATION (radio-tv broad.) alternate titles: director, underwriter sales

Plans and directs activities to secure and maintain underwriting (funding) of public television or radio programming: Reviews reports, periodicals, and other materials to identify prospective funding sources for proposed broadcast programs. Directs and counsels subordinates in developing strategies to secure program funding and negotiates final agreements with funding establishment representatives. Serves as liaison between station's legal, programming, public information, and other departmental staff and funding establishment personnel to provide information on status of projects and to resolve problems. May specialize in solicitation of funding from government, foundation, or corporation sources.
GOE: 11.05.04 STRENGTH: S GED: R5 M3 L4 SVP: 8 DLU: 86

163.167-010 MANAGER, ADVERTISING (print. & pub.)

Directs sale of display and classified advertising services for a publication: Plans sales campaigns. Consults with department heads and other officials to plan special campaigns and to promote sale of advertising services to various industry or trade groups. Corresponds with customers relative to advertising rates and policies, or to solicit new business. May select and train new sales personnel. May be designated according to type of advertising sold as Manager, Classified Advertising (print. & pub.); Manager, Display Advertising (print. & pub.); or area or region served as Manager, Local Advertising (print. & pub.); Manager, National Advertising (print. & pub.).
GOE: 11.09.01 STRENGTH: S GED: R5 M3 L5 SVP: 8 DLU: 77

163.167-014 MANAGER, CIRCULATION (print. & pub.)

Directs sale and distribution of newspapers, books, and periodicals: Directs staffing, training, and performance evaluations to develop and control sales and distribution program. Establishes geographical areas of responsibility for subordinates to coordinate sales and distribution activities. May be designated according to type of circulation activity managed as Manager, Newspaper Circulation (print. & pub.); or area served as Manager, City Circulation (print. & pub.).
GOE: 11.05.04 STRENGTH: S GED: R5 M3 L4 SVP: 8 DLU: 77

163.167-018 MANAGER, SALES (any industry)

Manages activities of establishment: Directs staffing, training, and performance evaluations to develop and control sales program. Coordinates sales distribution by establishing sales territories, quotas, and goals and advises dealers, distributors, and clients concerning sales and advertising techniques. Assigns sales territory to sales personnel. Analyzes sales statistics to formulate policy and to assist dealers in promoting sales. Reviews market analyses to determine customer needs, volume potential, price schedules, and discount rates, and develops sales campaigns to accommodate goals of company. Directs product simplification and standardization to eliminate unprofitable items from sales line. Represents company at trade association meetings to promote product. Coordinates liaison between sales department and other sales-related units. Analyzes and controls expenditures of division to conform to budgetary requirements. Assists other departments within establishment to prepare manuals and technical publications. Prepares periodic sales report showing sales volume and potential sales. May direct sales for manufacturer, retail store, wholesale house, jobber, or other establishment. May direct product research and development. May recommend or approve budget, expenditures, and appropriations for research and development work.
GOE: 11.05.04 STRENGTH: S GED: R5 M3 L5 SVP: 8 DLU: 89

163.167-022 MANAGER, UTILITY SALES AND SERVICE (utilities) alternate titles: general superintendent, power sales and service

Directs program to promote sales and provide service to consumers of electric power and gas: Coordinates activities of home-service department in demonstrating use of appliances and home lighting methods with promotional work of sales department. Confers with manufacturers to secure current information on gas and electric appliances and equipment. Estimates area consumer demands for use in planning budget. May be designated according to specialized activity as Manager, Commercial Sales (utilities); Manager, Industrial Sales (utilities); Manager, Residential Sales (utilities).
GOE: 11.05.04 STRENGTH: S GED: R5 M4 L4 SVP: 8 DLU: 77

163.167-026 PROPERTY-DISPOSAL OFFICER (any industry) alternate titles: redistribution-and-marketing officer; surplus-property disposal agent; surplus sales officer

Disposes of surplus property, other than real property, using knowledge of merchandising practices: Inspects property to ascertain condition and estimate market value. Investigates market conditions and facilities to determine time, place, type of sale, and whether items shall be sold individually or in lots. Prepares advertising material and selects media for its release. Assigns and directs activities of sales personnel. Determines method of property display and sets prices of items to be sold in conformity with value and market. Advises interested parties of salvage possibilities. Recommends destruction or abandonment of property not deemed possible or practical to sell or salvage.
GOE: 11.05.04 STRENGTH: L GED: R5 M5 L5 SVP: 7 DLU: 77

163.267-010 FIELD REPRESENTATIVE (business ser.; wholesale tr.) alternate titles: distribution manager

Monitors dealers and distributors to ensure efficiency of franchise operation: Surveys proposed locations to determine feasibility of establishing dealerships or distributorships. Advises dealers and distributors of policies and operating procedures to ensure functional effectiveness of business, and also develops information concerning planning and developing of business modifications and expansions. Reviews operations records to evaluate effectiveness.
GOE: 11.05.04 STRENGTH: L GED: R5 M4 L3 SVP: 6 DLU: 77

164 ADVERTISING MANAGEMENT OCCUPATIONS

This group includes occupations concerned with influencing consumer preference for goods and services, either as an employee of the organization served or as a member of an agency under contract; managing advertising programs and campaigns; and, in advertising agencies, managing customers' accounts. Occupations concerned with planning and executing artwork are included in Group 141. Occupations concerned with writing copy are included in Group 131.

164.117-010 MANAGER, ADVERTISING (any industry) alternate titles: director, advertising; sales promotion director

Plans and executes advertising policies of organization: Confers with department heads to discuss possible new accounts and to outline new policies or sales promotion campaigns. Confers with officials of newspapers, radio, and television stations, billboard advertisers, and advertising agencies to negotiate advertising contracts. Allocates advertising space to departments or products of establishment. Reviews and approves television and radio advertisements before release. Reviews rates and classifications applicable to various types of advertising and provides authorization. Directs workers in advertising department engaged in developing and producing advertisements. Directs research activities concerned with gathering information or with compilation of statistics pertinent to planning and execution of advertising sales promotion campaign. May authorize information for publication, such as interviews with reporters or articles describing phases of establishment activity. May serve as establishment representative for geographical district or department. May transact business as agent for advertising accounts. May direct preparation of special promotional features. May monitor and analyze sales promotion results to determine cost effectiveness of promotion campaign.
GOE: 11.09.01 STRENGTH: S GED: R6 M5 L5 SVP: 8 DLU: 89

164.117-014 MANAGER, ADVERTISING AGENCY (business ser.)

Directs activities of advertising agency: Formulates plans to extend business with established accounts, to solicit new accounts, and to establish new advertising policies and procedures. Coordinates activities of departments, such as sales, graphic arts, media, finance, and research. Inspects layouts and advertising copy, and edits radio and television scripts for adherence to specifications. Conducts meetings with agency personnel to outline and initiate new advertising policies or procedures. May confer with clients to provide marketing or technical advice.
GOE: 11.09.01 STRENGTH: L GED: R5 M3 L4 SVP: 8 DLU: 78

164.117-018 MEDIA DIRECTOR (profess. & kin.)

Plans and administers media programs in advertising department: Confers with representatives of advertising agencies, product managers, and corporate advertising staff to establish media goals, objectives, and strategies within corporate advertising budget. Confers with advertising agents or media representatives to select specific programs and negotiate advertising to ensure optimum use of budgeted funds and long-term contracts. Adjusts broadcasting schedules due to program cancellations. Studies demographic data and consumer profiles to identify target audiences of media advertising. Reads trade journals and professional literature to stay informed of trends, innovations, and changes that affect media planning.
GOE: 11.09.01 STRENGTH: S GED: R5 M4 L5 SVP: 8 DLU: 89

164.167-010 ACCOUNT EXECUTIVE (business ser.)

Plans, coordinates, and directs advertising campaign for clients of advertising agency: Confers with client to determine advertising requirements and budgetary limitations, utilizing knowledge of product or service to be advertised, media capabilities, and audience characteristics. Confers with agency artists, copywriters, photographers, and other media-production specialists to select media to be used and to estimate costs. Submits proposed program and estimated budget to client for approval. Coordinates activities of workers engaged in marketing research, writing copy, laying out artwork, purchasing media time and space, developing special displays and promotional items, and performing other media-production activities, in order to carry out approved campaign.
GOE: 11.09.01 STRENGTH: S GED: R5 M3 L4 SVP: 8 DLU: 77

165 PUBLIC RELATIONS MANAGEMENT OCCUPATIONS

This group includes occupations concerned with selection or development of favorable persuasive material and its distribution through personal contact or various communications media, in order to promote goodwill, develop credibility, or create favorable public image for individual, establishment, group, or organization. Includes both generalists and specialists working either as outside consultant or in-house staff member.

165.017-010 LOBBYIST (profess. & kin.) alternate titles: legislative advocate

Contacts and confers with members of legislature and other holders of public office to persuade them to support legislation favorable to client's interest:

Studies proposed legislation to determine possible effect on interest of client, who may be person, specific group, or general public. Confers with legislators and officials to emphasize supposed weaknesses or merits of specific bills to influence passage, defeat, or amendment of measure, or introduction of legislation more favorable to client's interests. Contacts individuals and groups having similar interests in order to encourage them also to contact legislators and present views. Prepares news releases and informational pamphlets and conducts news conferences in order to state client's views and to inform public of features of proposed legislation considered desirable or undesirable. Plans and coordinates meetings between members and elected officials to discuss legislative issues and proposals and allow officials to respond to membership concerns. May contact regulatory agencies and testify at public hearings to enlist support for client's interests. May be legally required to register with governmental authorities as lobbyist and to submit reports of regulated expenditures incurred during lobbying activities. May attend and represent local organization at state and national association meetings. May instruct individuals or organization members in lobbying techniques.
GOE: 11.09.03 STRENGTH: S GED: R5 M3 L5 SVP: 7 DLU: 88

165.117-010 DIRECTOR, FUNDRAISING (nonprofit org.)
 Directs and coordinates solicitation and disbursement of funds for community social-welfare organization: Establishes fund-raising goals according to financial need of agency. Formulates policies for collecting and safeguarding contributions. Initiates public relations program to promote community understanding and support for organization's objectives. Develops schedule for disbursing solicited funds. Issues instructions to volunteer and paid workers regarding solicitations, public relations, and clerical duties.
GOE: 11.09.02 STRENGTH: S GED: R5 M4 L4 SVP: 8 DLU: 80

165.117-014 DIRECTOR, FUNDS DEVELOPMENT (profess. & kin.) alternate titles: director of major or capital gifts
 Plans, organizes, directs, and coordinates ongoing and special project funding programs for museum, zoo, public broadcasting station, or similar institution: Prepares statement of planned activities and enlists support from members of institution staff and volunteer organizations. Develops public relations materials to enhance institution image and promote fund raising program. Identifies potential contributors to special project funds and supporters of institution ongoing operations through examination of past records, individual and corporate contracts, and knowledge of community. Plans and coordinates fund drives for special projects. Assigns responsibilities for personal solicitation to members of staff, volunteer organizations, and governing body according to special interests or capabilities. Organizes direct mail campaign to reach other potential contributors. Plans and coordinates benefit events, such as banquets, balls, or auctions. Organizes solicitation drives for pledges of ongoing support from individuals, corporations, and foundations. Informs potential contributors of special needs of institution, and encourages individuals, corporations, and foundations to establish or contribute to special funds through endowments, trusts, donations of gifts-in-kind, or bequests, conferring with attorneys to establish methods of transferring funds to benefit both donors and institution. Researches public and private grant agencies and foundations to identify other sources of funding for research, community service, or other projects. Supervises and coordinates activities of workers engaged in maintaining records of contributors and grants and preparing letters of appreciation to be sent to contributors. May purchase mailing list of potential donors. May negotiate agreements with representatives of other organizations for exchange of mailing lists, information, and cooperative programs.
GOE: 11.09.02 STRENGTH: S GED: R5 M4 L5 SVP: 7 DLU: 87

165.157-010 SONG PLUGGER (recording)
 Persuades producers and announcers of radio and television musical shows to broadcast recordings produced by employer: Contacts broadcasting station officials by telephone, letter, or in person. Represents phonograph recording manufacturer in dealing with broadcasters.
GOE: 08.02.08 STRENGTH: S GED: R4 M2 L4 SVP: 5 DLU: 77

165.167-010 SALES-SERVICE PROMOTER (any industry)
 Promotes sales and creates goodwill for firm's products or services by preparing displays, touring country, making speeches at retail dealers conventions, and calling on individual merchants to advise on ways and means for increasing sales. May demonstrate products representing technological advances in industry.
GOE: 11.09.01 STRENGTH: L GED: R5 M3 L5 SVP: 7 DLU: 77

165.167-014 PUBLIC-RELATIONS REPRESENTATIVE (profess. & kin.) alternate titles: public-relations practitioner
 Plans and conducts public relations program designed to create and maintain favorable public image for employer or client: Plans and directs development and communication of information designed to keep public informed of employer's programs, accomplishments, or point of view. Arranges for public relations efforts in order to meet needs, objectives, and policies of individual, special interest group, business concern, nonprofit organization, or governmental agency, serving as in-house staff member or as outside consultant. Prepares and distributes fact sheets, news releases, photographs, scripts, motion pictures, or tape recordings to media representatives and other persons who may be interested in learning about or publicizing employer's activities or message. Purchases advertising space and time as required. Arranges for and conducts public-contact programs designed to meet employer's objectives, utilizing knowl-

edge of changing attitudes and opinions of consumers, clients, employees, or other interest groups. Promotes goodwill through such publicity efforts as speeches, exhibits, films, tours, and question/answer sessions. Represents employer during community projects and at public, social, and business gatherings. May research data, create ideas, write copy, lay out artwork, contact media representatives, or represent employer directly before general public. May develop special projects such as campaign fund raisers or public awareness about political issues. May direct activities of subordinates. May confer with production and support personnel to coordinate production of television advertisements and on-air promotions. May prepare press releases and fact sheets, and compose letters, using computer. May disseminate facts and information about organization's activities or governmental agency's programs to general public and be known as Public Information Officer (profess. & kin.).
GOE: 11.09.03 STRENGTH: S GED: R5 M4 L5 SVP: 7 DLU: 89

166 PERSONNEL ADMINISTRATION OCCUPATIONS

 This group includes occupations concerned with formulating policies relating to the personnel administration of an organization and conducting programs concerning employee recruitment, selection, training, development, retention, promotion, compensation, benefits, labor relations, and occupational safety. Occupations in personnel research and in administration of testing and counseling programs, for which a background in psychology is required, are included in Group 045.

166.067-010 OCCUPATIONAL ANALYST (profess. & kin.)
 Researches occupations and analyzes and integrates data to develop and devise concepts of worker relationships, modify and maintain occupational classification system, and provide business, industry, and government with technical occupational information necessary for utilization of work force: Confers with business, industry, government, and union officials to arrange for and develop plans for studies and surveys. Devises methods and establishes criteria for conducting studies and surveys. Researches jobs, industry and organizational concepts and techniques, and worker characteristics to determine job relationships, job functions and content, worker traits, and occupational trends. Prepares results of research for publication in form of books, brochures, charts, film, and manuals. Identifies need for and develops job analysis tools, such as manuals, reporting forms, training films, and slides. Prepares management tools, such as personnel distribution reports, organization and flow charts, job descriptions, tables of job relationships, and worker trait analysis. Conducts training and provides technical assistance to promote use of job analysis materials, tools, and concepts in areas of curriculum development, career planning, job restructuring, and government and employment training programs. May specialize in providing technical assistance to private, public, or governmental organizations and be designated Industrial Occupational Analyst (profess. & kin.).
GOE: 11.03.04 STRENGTH: L GED: R5 M4 L5 SVP: 7 DLU: 77

166.117-010 DIRECTOR, INDUSTRIAL RELATIONS (profess. & kin.) alternate titles: employee relations administrator; vice president, industrial relations
 Formulates policy and directs and coordinates industrial relations activities of organization: Formulates policy for subordinate managers of departments, such as employment, compensation, labor relations, and employee services, according to knowledge of company objectives, government regulations, and labor contract terms. Writes directives advising department managers of company policy regarding equal employment opportunities, compensation, and employee benefits. Analyzes wage and salary reports and data to determine competitive compensation plan. Studies legislation, arbitration decisions, and collective bargaining contracts to assess industry trends. Consults legal staff to ensure that policies comply with federal and state law. Prepares personnel forecast to project employment needs. Writes and delivers presentation to corporate officers or government officials regarding industrial relations policies and practices.
GOE: 11.05.02 STRENGTH: L GED: R6 M4 L5 SVP: 8 DLU: 81

166.117-014 MANAGER, EMPLOYEE WELFARE (profess. & kin.) alternate titles: employee-service officer; manager, welfare
 Directs welfare activities for employees of stores, factories, and other industrial and commercial establishments: Arranges for physical examinations, first aid, and other medical attention. Arranges for installation and operation of libraries, lunchrooms, recreational facilities, and educational courses. Organizes dances, entertainment, and outings. Ensures that lighting is sufficient, sanitary facilities are adequate and in good order, and machinery safeguarded. May visit workers' homes to observe their housing and general living conditions and recommend improvements if necessary. May assist employees in the solution of personal problems, such as recommending day nurseries for their children and counseling them on personality frictions or emotional maladjustments.
GOE: 11.05.02 STRENGTH: S GED: R5 M4 L5 SVP: 7 DLU: 77

166.117-018 MANAGER, PERSONNEL (profess. & kin.) alternate titles: manager, human resources
 Plans and carries out policies relating to all phases of personnel activity: Recruits, interviews, and selects employees to fill vacant positions. Plans and conducts new employee orientation to foster positive attitude toward company goals. Keeps record of insurance coverage, pension plan, and personnel transactions, such as hires, promotions, transfers, and terminations. Investigates acci-

dents and prepares reports for insurance carrier. Conducts wage survey within labor market to determine competitive wage rate. Prepares budget of personnel operations. Meets with shop stewards and supervisors to resolve grievances. Writes separation notices for employees separating with cause and conducts exit interviews to determine reasons behind separations. Prepares reports and recommends procedures to reduce absenteeism and turnover. Represents company at personnel-related hearings and investigations. Contracts with outside suppliers to provide employee services, such as canteen, transportation, or relocation service. May prepare budget of personnel operations, using computer terminal. May administer manual and dexterity tests to applicants. May supervise clerical workers. May keep records of hired employee characteristics for governmental reporting purposes. May negotiate collective bargaining agreement with BUSINESS REPRESENTATIVE, LABOR UNION (profess & kin.) 187.167-018.
GOE: 11.05.02 STRENGTH: S GED: R5 M5 L5 SVP: 8 DLU: 88

166.167-010 CONTESTANT COORDINATOR (radio-tv broad.)
Interviews applicants for television game shows and coordinates studio activities of contestants: Provides information to applicants concerning show objectives, show format, and screens applicants for compliance with needs of show and established rules. Keeps file of applicants and arranges call-back for mock game before PRODUCER (radio-tv broad.). Notifies chosen applicants of selection and provides required information for applicant's participation in show. Performs other personal services, such as attending to needs and comforts of applicants, briefing applicants on studio procedures, and reviewing rules of show. May confer with television game show PRODUCER (radio-tv broad.) to aid in establishing selection standards for contestants. May devise testing procedure and materials used during applicant screening. May operate camera to photograph applicants. May be responsible for final selection of contestants. May interview applicants from studio audience and at such locations as shopping centers, colleges, or theaters to select contestants and be designated Interviewer (radio-tv broad.).
GOE: 07.01.01 STRENGTH: L GED: R4 M3 L4 SVP: 5 DLU: 77

166.167-014 DIRECTOR OF PLACEMENT (education) alternate titles: coordinator of placement; director of career planning and placement; director of career resources; manager of student placement service
Coordinates activities of job placement service for students and graduates: Develops placement office procedures. Establishes work loads, assigns tasks, and reviews results. Conducts in-service training program for placement personnel. Interviews applicants to determine qualifications and eligibility for employment. Assists individuals to develop employment plans based on appraisals of aptitudes, interests, and personality characteristics, and to plan curriculums accordingly. Contacts prospective employers to determine needs and to explain placement service. Arranges on-campus interviews between employers and graduating students to facilitate placement of graduates. Collects, organizes, and analyzes occupational, educational, and economic information for use in job placement activities. Directs maintenance of occupational library. Assists in conducting community surveys to gather labor market information, such as prevailing wages, hours, training, and employment possibilities. Coordinates program for analyzing campus jobs.
GOE: 10.01.02 STRENGTH: S GED: R6 M5 L5 SVP: 8 DLU: 77

166.167-018 MANAGER, BENEFITS (profess. & kin.) alternate titles: manager, employee benefits; manager, employee services; manager, personnel services
Manages employee benefits program for organization: Plans and directs implementation and administration of benefits programs designed to insure employees against loss of income due to illness, injury, layoff, or retirement. Directs preparation and distribution of written and verbal information to inform employees of benefits programs, such as insurance and pension plans, paid time off, bonus pay, and special employer sponsored activities. Analyzes existing benefits policies of organization, and prevailing practices among similar organizations, to establish competitive benefits programs. Evaluates services, coverage, and options available through insurance and investment companies, to determine programs best meeting needs of organization. Plans modification of existing benefits programs, utilizing knowledge of laws concerning employee insurance coverage, and agreements with labor unions, to ensure compliance with legal requirements. Recommends benefits plan changes to management. Notifies employees and labor union representatives of changes in benefits programs. Directs performance of clerical functions, such as updating records and processing insurance claims. May interview, select, hire, and train employees.
GOE: 11.05.02 STRENGTH: S GED: R4 M4 L4 SVP: 7 DLU: 87

166.167-022 MANAGER, COMPENSATION (profess. & kin.) alternate titles: wage and salary administrator
Manages compensation program in establishment: Directs development and application of techniques of job analysis, job descriptions, evaluations, grading, and pricing in order to determine and record job factors and to determine and convert relative job worth into monetary values to be administered according to pay-scale guidelines and policy formulated by DIRECTOR, INDUSTRIAL RELATIONS (profess. & kin.). Analyzes company compensation policies, government regulations concerning payment of minimum wages and overtime pay, prevailing rates in similar organizations and industries, and agreements with labor unions, in order to comply with legal requirements and to establish competitive rates designed to attract, retain, and motivate employees. Recommends compensation adjustments according to findings, utilizing knowledge of prevail-

ing rates of straight-time pay, types of wage incentive systems, and special compensation programs for professional, technical, sales, supervisory, managerial, and executive personnel. Approves merit increases permitted within budgetary limits and according to pay policies. Duties may also include administration of employee benefits program [MANAGER, BENEFITS (profess. & kin.)].
GOE: 11.05.02 STRENGTH: S GED: R5 M5 L5 SVP: 8 DLU: 77

166.167-026 MANAGER, EDUCATION AND TRAINING (education) alternate titles: training administrator
Plans, coordinates, and directs personnel training and staff development programs for industrial, commercial, service, or governmental establishment: Confers with management and supervisory personnel in order to determine training needs. Compiles data and analyzes past and current year training requirements to prepare budgets and justify funds requested, using calculator or computer. Formulates training policies and schedules, utilizing knowledge of identified training needs, company production processes, business systems, or changes in products, procedures, or services. Designates training procedures, utilizing knowledge of effectiveness of such methods as individual training, group instruction, lectures, on-the-job training, demonstrations, conferences, meetings, and workshops. Organizes and develops training manuals, reference library, testing and evaluation procedures, multimedia visual aids, and other educational materials. Trains assigned instructors and supervisors in effective techniques for training in such areas as those concerned with new employee orientation, specific on-the-job training, apprenticeship programs, sales techniques, health and safety practices, public relations, refresher training, promotional development, upgrading, retraining, and leadership development. Updates records and compiles statistical reports on interviews, transfers, performance rating, and promotions to evaluate performance of instructors and monitor progress of trainees. May coordinate established courses with technical and professional courses offered by community schools. May screen, test, counsel, and recommend employees for educational programs or for promotion or transfer. May write applications and proposals to submit to fund-granting authorities, such as government and foundations.
GOE: 11.07.03 STRENGTH: L GED: R5 M4 L5 SVP: 7 DLU: 88

166.167-030 MANAGER, EMPLOYMENT (profess. & kin.) alternate titles: employment supervisor
Manages employment activities of establishment: Plans and directs activities of staff workers concerned with such functions as developing sources of qualified applicants, conducting screening interviews, administering tests, checking references and background, evaluating applicants' qualifications, and arranging for preliminary indoctrination and training for newly hired employees according to policy formulated by DIRECTOR, INDUSTRIAL RELATIONS (profess. & kin.) 166.117-010. Keeps records and compiles statistical reports concerning recruitments, interviews, hires, transfers, promotions, terminations, and performance appraisals, utilizing knowledge of job requirements, valid selection processes, and legislation concerning equal employment practices. Coordinates employment activities, such as those concerned with preparing job requisitions; interviewing, selecting, and hiring candidates; on-the-job indoctrination and additional training; supervisory follow-up, development, and rating of employees; and conducting exit interviews. Analyzes statistical data and other reports concerning all aspects of employment function in order to identify and determine causes of personnel problems and to develop and present recommendations for improvement of establishment's employment policies, processes, and practices.
GOE: 11.05.02 STRENGTH: S GED: R5 M4 L5 SVP: 8 DLU: 87

166.167-034 MANAGER, LABOR RELATIONS (profess. & kin.) alternate titles: labor relations representative
Manages labor relations program of organization: Analyzes collective bargaining agreement to develop interpretation of intent, spirit, and terms of contract. Advises management and union officials in development, application, and interpretation of labor relations policies and practices, according to policy formulated by DIRECTOR, INDUSTRIAL RELATIONS (profess. & kin.) 166.117-010. Arranges and schedules meetings between grieving workers, supervisory and managerial personnel, and BUSINESS REPRESENTATIVE, LABOR UNION (profess. & kin.) 187.167-018, to investigate and resolve grievances. Prepares statistical reports, using records of actions taken concerning grievances, arbitration and mediation cases, and related labor relations activities, to identify problem areas. Monitors implementation of policies concerning wages, hours, and working conditions, to ensure compliance with terms of labor contract. Furnishes information, such as reference documents and statistical data concerning labor legislation, labor market conditions, prevailing union and management practices, wage and salary surveys, and employee benefits programs, for use in review of current contract provisions and proposed changes. May represent management in labor contract negotiations. May supervise employees and be known as Labor Relations Supervisor (profess. & kin.). May be employed by firm offering labor relations advisory services to either management or labor and be known as Labor Relation Consultant (profess. & kin.). May be employed by governmental agency to study, interpret, and report on relations between management and labor and be known as Industrial Relations Representative (government ser.).
GOE: 11.05.02 STRENGTH: L GED: R5 M4 L5 SVP: 8 DLU: 81

166.167-038 PORT PURSER (water trans.)
Coordinates activities and trains workers concerned with shipboard business functions and social activities for passengers: Screens applicants applying for positions. Assigns trainees to vessels, considering their duties and responsibil-

109

ities. Plans training and rotation of trainees between ship and shore positions. Hires entertainment and medical staff and plans replacement programs to ensure that qualified personnel are available in case of sickness or resignation. Adjusts complaints of passengers which cannot be resolved during voyage.
GOE: 11.11.03 STRENGTH: S GED: R5 M4 L4 SVP: 8 DLU: 77

166.167-042   SENIOR ENLISTED ADVISOR (military ser.)

Advises commander on such matters as troop welfare, health, and morale: Assists commander on official visits and at military ceremonies. Assists in inspection of facilities and personnel to determine if established standards are met. Counsels enlisted personnel concerning attitude, personal problems, and similar matters, and to elicit their cooperation and self improvement. Reviews activities of subordinate noncommissioned officers, and initiates appropriate corrective action for discrepancies noted. May assists commander in reception of visitors. May supervise clerical or administrative personnel.
GOE: 11.10.03 STRENGTH: L GED: R3 M3 L3 SVP: 5 DLU: 77

166.167-046   SPECIAL AGENT (insurance) alternate titles: sales representative

Recruits independent SALES AGENTS, INSURANCE (insurance) in field and maintains contact between agent and home office: Selects SALES AGENT, INSURANCE (insurance), based on experience with other insurance companies. Drafts contract between agent and company. Advises agent on matters pertaining to conduct of business, such as cancellations, overdue accounts, and new business prospects. May gather information for UNDERWRITER (insurance). When working in life insurance, is designated Brokerage Manager (insurance).
GOE: 11.05.02 STRENGTH: S GED: R5 M3 L5 SVP: 8 DLU: 77

166.167-050   PROGRAM SPECIALIST, EMPLOYEE-HEALTH MAINTENANCE (profess. & kin.)

Coordinates activities of area employers in setting up local government funded program within establishments to help employees who are not functioning at satisfactory levels of job performance due to alcoholism or other behavioral medical problems: Writes and prepares newspaper advertisements, newsletters, and questionnaires and speaks before community groups to promote employee assistance program within business community. Analyzes character and type of business establishments in area, and compiles list of prospective employers appropriate for implementing assistance program. Contacts prospective employers, explains program and fees, points out advantages of program, and reaches agreement with interested employers on extent of proposed program. Develops program within establishment. Establishes committee composed of company officials and workers to develop statement of employee assistance program and policy and procedures. Plans and conducts training sessions for company officials to develop skills in identifying and handling employees troubled by alcoholism or other personal problems. Assists employer in setting up in-plant educational program to prevent alcoholism, using posters, pamphlets, and films, and establishes referral network providing for in-plant and out-of-plant group or individual counseling for troubled employees. Confers with team member of assistance program who provides counseling regarding planning and progress of counseling components. Confers with staff of employee assistance program regarding progress and evaluation of current programs and proposals for developing new programs.
GOE: 11.05.02 STRENGTH: S GED: R5 M3 L5 SVP: 6 DLU: 86

166.167-054   TECHNICAL TRAINING COORDINATOR (education)

Coordinates activities of instructors engaged in training employees or customers of industrial or commercial establishment: Confers with managers, instructors, or customer's representative to determine training needs. Assigns instructors to conduct training. Schedules classes, based on availability of classrooms, equipment, and instructors. Evaluates training packages, including outline, text, and handouts written by instructors. Assigns instructors to in-service or out-service training classes to learn new skills as needed. Monitors budget to ensure that training costs do not exceed allocated funds. Writes budget report listing training costs, such as instructors' wages and equipment costs, to justify expenditures. Attends meetings and seminars to obtain information useful to training staff and to inform management of training programs and goals. Monitors instructors during lectures and laboratory demonstrations to evaluate performance. May perform other duties as described under SUPERVISOR (any industry) Master Title. May develop and conduct training programs for employees or customers of industrial or commercial establishment [INSTRUCTOR, TECHNICAL TRAINING (education) 166.221-010].
GOE: 11.07.03 STRENGTH: L GED: R5 M3 L5 SVP: 8 DLU: 87

166.221-010   INSTRUCTOR, TECHNICAL TRAINING (education) alternate titles: training specialist

Develops and conducts programs to train employees or customers of industrial or commercial establishment in installation, programming, safety, maintenance, and repair of machinery and equipment, such as robots, *programmable controllers,* and *robot controllers,* following manuals, specifications, blueprints, and schematics, and using handtools, measuring instruments, and testing equipment: Confers with management and staff or TECHNICAL TRAINING COORDINATOR (education) 166.167-054 to determine training objectives. Writes training program, including outline, text, handouts, and tests, and designs laboratory exercises, applying knowledge of electronics, mechanics, hydraulics, pneumatics, and programming, and following machine, equipment, and tooling manuals. Schedules classes based on classroom and equipment availability. Lectures class on safety, installation, programming, maintenance, and repair of machinery and equipment, following outline, handouts, and texts, and using visual aids, such as graphs, charts, videotape, and slides. Demonstrates procedures being taught, such as programming and repair, applying knowledge of electrical wire color coding, programming, electronics, mechanics, hydraulics, and pneumatics, using handtools, measuring instruments, and testing equipment, and following course outline. Observes trainees in laboratory and answers trainees' questions. Administers written and practical exams and writes performance reports to evaluate trainees' performance. Participates in meetings, seminars, and training sessions to obtain information useful to training facility and integrates information into training program. May repair electrical and electronic components of robots in industrial establishments. May install, program, maintain, and repair robots in customer's establishment [FIELD SERVICE TECHNICIAN (machinery mfg.) 638.261-026]. May be designated according to subject taught as Instructor, Programmable Controllers (education); Instructor, Robotics (education).
GOE: 11.02.02 STRENGTH: L GED: R5 M4 L5 SVP: 8 DLU: 86

166.227-010   TRAINING REPRESENTATIVE (education) alternate titles: training instructor

Develops and conducts training programs for employees of industrial, commercial, service, or government establishment: Confers with management to gain knowledge of work situation requiring training for employees to better understand changes in policies, procedures, regulations, and technologies. Formulates teaching outline and determines instructional methods, utilizing knowledge of specified training needs and effectiveness of such methods as individual training, group instruction, lectures, demonstrations, conferences, meetings, and workshops. Selects or develops teaching aids, such as training handbooks, demonstration models, multimedia visual aids, computer tutorials, and reference works. Conducts training sessions covering specified areas such as those concerned with new employee orientation, on-the-job training, use of computers and software, apprenticeship programs, sales techniques, health and safety practices, public relations, refresher training, promotional development, upgrading, retraining displaced workers, and leadership development. Tests trainees to measure progress and to evaluate effectiveness of training. May specialize in developing instructional software.
GOE: 11.02.02 STRENGTH: L GED: R5 M4 L5 SVP: 7 DLU: 88

166.257-010   EMPLOYER RELATIONS REPRESENTATIVE (profess. & kin.)

Establishes and maintains working relationships with local employers to promote use of public employment programs and services: Contacts employers new to area or company requiring revisit and arranges appointment to visit company representative or employer responsible for hiring workers. Establishes rapport between Employment Service and company to promote use of agency programs and services. Confers with employer to resolve problems, such as local employment office effectiveness, employer complaints, and alternative employer actions for recruiting qualified applicants. Answers employer questions concerning Employment Service programs or services available. Solicits employers to list job openings with Employment Service. Receives job orders from employers by phone or in person and records information to facilitate selection and referral process.
GOE: 11.09.03 STRENGTH: L GED: R5 M2 L4 SVP: 6 DLU: 86

166.267-010   EMPLOYMENT INTERVIEWER (profess. & kin.) alternate titles: personnel interviewer; placement interviewer

Interviews job applicants to select people meeting employer qualifications: Reviews employment applications and evaluates work history, education and training, job skills, compensation needs, and other qualifications of applicants. Records additional knowledge, skills, abilities, interests, test results, and other data pertinent to selection and referral of applicants. Reviews job orders and matches applicants with job requirements, utilizing manual or computerized file search. Informs applicants of job duties and responsibilities, compensation and benefits, work schedules and working conditions, company and union policies, promotional opportunities, and other related information. Refers selected applicants to person placing job order, according to policy of organization. Keeps records of applicants not selected for employment. May perform reference and background checks on applicants. May refer applicants to vocational counseling services. May conduct or arrange for skills, intelligence, or psychological testing of applicants. May evaluate selection and placement techniques by conducting research or follow-up activities and conferring with management and supervisory personnel. May specialize in interviewing and referring certain types of personnel, such as professional, technical, managerial, clerical, and other types of skilled or unskilled workers. May search for and recruit applicants for open positions [PERSONNEL RECRUITER (profess. & kin.) 166.267-038]. May contact employers in writing, in person, or by telephone to solicit orders for job vacancies for clientele or for specified applicants and record information about job openings on job order forms to describe duties, hiring requirements, and related data.
GOE: 11.03.04 STRENGTH: S GED: R5 M3 L5 SVP: 6 DLU: 87

166.267-014   HOSPITAL-INSURANCE REPRESENTATIVE (insurance)

Interprets hospital and medical insurance services and benefits to contracting hospital personnel: Discusses contract provisions and hospital claims forms with medical and hospital personnel. Instructs hospital clerical staff in resolving problems concerning billing and admitting procedures. Writes reports outlining hospital and contract benefits for incorporation into brochures and pamphlets. May travel from city to city.

GOE: 07.01.05 STRENGTH: S GED: R4 M3 L4 SVP: 6 DLU: 77

166.267-018 JOB ANALYST (profess. & kin.) alternate titles: personnel analyst
Collects, analyzes, and prepares occupational information to facilitate personnel, administration, and management functions of organization: Consults with management to determine type, scope, and purpose of study. Studies current organizational occupational data and compiles distribution reports, organization and flow charts, and other background information required for study. Observes jobs and interviews workers and supervisory personnel to determine job and worker requirements. Analyzes occupational data, such as physical, mental, and training requirements of jobs and workers and develops written summaries, such as job descriptions, job specifications, and lines of career movement. Utilizes developed occupational data to evaluate or improve methods and techniques for recruiting, selecting, promoting, evaluating, and training workers, and administration of related personnel programs. May specialize in classifying positions according to regulated guidelines to meet job classification requirements of civil service system and be known as Position Classifier (government ser.).
GOE: 11.03.04 STRENGTH: L GED: R5 M4 L5 SVP: 6 DLU: 77

166.267-022 PRISONER-CLASSIFICATION INTERVIEWER (profess. & kin.)
Interviews new prison inmates to obtain social and criminal histories to aid in classification and assignment of prisoners to appropriate work and other activities: Gathers data, such as work history, school, criminal, and military records, family background, habits, religious beliefs, and prisoner's version of crime committed. Analyzes prisoner's social attitudes, mental capacity, character, and physical capabilities and prepares admission summary based on data obtained. Explains prison rules and regulations.
GOE: 11.03.04 STRENGTH: S GED: R5 M3 L4 SVP: 7 DLU: 77

166.267-026 RECRUITER (military ser.) alternate titles: career counselor
Interviews military and civilian personnel to recruit and inform individuals on matters concerning career opportunities, incentives, military rights and benefits, and advantages of military career: Assists and advises military commands in organizing, preparing, and implementing enlisted recruiting and retention program. Interviews individuals to determine their suitability for placement into specific military occupation. Occasionally lectures to civic and social groups, military dependents, school officials, and religious leaders concerning military career opportunities.
GOE: 11.03.04 STRENGTH: L GED: R4 M2 L3 SVP: 5 DLU: 86

166.267-030 RETIREMENT OFFICER (government ser.)
Provides information and advice concerning provisions and regulations of state-administered retirement program for public employees: Explains retirement annuity system to personnel officers of local or state governmental entities covered by system, utilizing knowledge of rules and policies of retirement plan. Explains retirement policies and regulations of retirement board to covered employee groups, utilizing knowledge of annuity payments, procedure manuals, and official interpretations. Audits retirement accounts and examines records of employing entities to ensure compliance with prescribed standards and regulations. Attends and addresses conferences and other meetings of employees concerned, as representative of retirement board.
GOE: 07.01.01 STRENGTH: L GED: R5 M5 L4 SVP: 7 DLU: 77

166.267-034 JOB DEVELOPMENT SPECIALIST (profess. & kin.)
Promotes and develops employment and on-the-job training opportunities for disadvantaged applicants: Assists employers in revising standards which exclude applicants from jobs. Demonstrates to employers effectiveness and profitability of employing chronically unemployed by identifying jobs that workers could perform. Establishes relationships with employers regarding problems, complaints, and progress of recently placed disadvantaged applicants and recommends corrective action. Assists employers in establishing wage scales commensurate with prevailing rates. Promotes, develops, and terminates on-the-job training program opportunities with employers and assists in writing contracts. Identifies need for and assists in development of auxiliary services to facilitate bringing disadvantaged applicants into job-ready status. Informs business, labor, and public about training programs through various media. May instruct applicants in resume writing, job search, and interviewing techniques.
GOE: 11.03.04 STRENGTH: S GED: R4 M3 L4 SVP: 5 DLU: 86

166.267-038 PERSONNEL RECRUITER (profess. & kin.)
Seeks out, interviews, screens, and recruits job applicants to fill existing company job openings: Discusses personnel needs with department supervisors to prepare and implement recruitment program. Contacts colleges to arrange on-campus interviews. Provides information on company facilities and job opportunities to potential applicants. Interviews college applicants to obtain work history, education, training, job skills, and salary requirements. Screens and refers qualified applicants to company hiring personnel for follow-up interview. Arranges travel and lodging for selected applicants at company expense. Performs reference and background checks on applicants. Corresponds with job applicants to notify them of employment consideration. Files and maintains employment records for future references. Projects yearly recruitment expenditures for budgetary control.
GOE: 11.03.04 STRENGTH: S GED: R5 M3 L5 SVP: 7 DLU: 86

166.267-042 EMPLOYEE RELATIONS SPECIALIST (profess. & kin.)
Interviews workers to gather information on worker attitudes toward work environment and supervision received to facilitate resolution of employee rela-

tions problems: Explains to workers company and governmental rules, regulations, and procedures, and need for compliance. Gathers information on workers' feelings about factors that affect worker morale, motivation, and efficiency. Meets with management to discuss possible actions to be taken. Inspects work stations to ensure required changes or actions are implemented. Interviews workers to determine reactions to specific actions taken. Prepares reports on workers' comments and actions taken. Enrolls eligible workers in company programs, such as pension and savings plans. Maintains medical, insurance, and other personnel records and forms. May operate computer to compile, store, or retrieve worker related information, such as medical, insurance, pension, and savings plans.
GOE: 11.03.04 STRENGTH: S GED: R4 M2 L2 SVP: 7 DLU: 87

166.267-046 HUMAN RESOURCE ADVISOR (profess. & kin.)
Provides establishment personnel assistance in identifying, evaluating, and resolving human relations and work performance problems within establishment to facilitate communication and improve employee human relations skills and work performance: Talks informally with establishment personnel and attends meetings of managers, supervisors, and work units to facilitate effective interpersonal communication among participants and to ascertain human relations and work related problems that adversely affect employee morale and establishment productivity. Evaluates human relations and work related problems and meets with supervisors and managers to determine effective remediation techniques, such as job skill training or personal intervention, to resolve human relations issues among personnel. Develops and conducts training to instruct establishment managers, supervisors, and workers in human relation skills, such as supervisory skills, conflict resolution skills, interpersonal communication skills, and effective group interaction skills. Schedules individuals for technical job-related skills training to improve individual work performance. May participate in resolving labor relations issues. May assist in screening applicants for establishment training programs. May write employee newsletter. May operate audio-visual equipment to review or to present audio-visual tapes for training program.
GOE: 11.02.02 STRENGTH: L GED: R5 M3 L5 SVP: 7 DLU: 87

168   INSPECTORS AND INVESTIGATORS, MANAGERIAL AND PUBLIC SERVICE

This group includes occupations concerned with examining the condition of persons, plants, and animals; the quality of consumer products and services; and the operations of establishments, serving in the capacity of a governmental or private inspector or investigator in order to verify compliance with and enforcement of regulatory laws, health, and safety laws, or the establishment's quality standards. Occupations for public service and private detectives concerned with enforcement of criminal laws are found in Groups 375 and 376. Occupations concerned with performing laboratory or other scientific tests in order to ascertain the nature or quality of items are generally to be found in the group of the basic physical or life science with which they are concerned. Occupations which involve working in a specific professional discipline, such as engineering, medicine, or the physical and life sciences and which involve working for a governmental agency in the capacity of an inspector or investigator still belong to the basic group of their specific discipline.

168.161-010 CORONER (government ser.) alternate titles: medical examiner
Directs investigation of deaths occurring within jurisdiction as required by law: Directs activities of staff physicians, technicians, and investigators involved with conducting inquests, performing autopsies, conducting pathological and toxicological analyses, and investigating circumstances of deaths in order to determine cause and fix responsibility for accidental, violent, or unexplained deaths, or contracts for such services with outside physicians, medical laboratories, and law enforcement agencies. Testifies at inquests, hearings, and court trials. Confers with officials of public health and law enforcement agencies to coordinate interdepartmental activities. Coordinates activities for disposition of unclaimed corpse and personal effects of deceased. Directs activities of workers involved in preparing documents for permanent records. May assist relatives of deceased in negotiations concerning payment of insurance policies or burial benefits by providing information concerning circumstances of death. May be required by law or ordinance to have specified medical or legal training.
GOE: 02.02.01 STRENGTH: L GED: R5 M5 L4 SVP: 7 DLU: 77

168.161-014 INDUSTRIAL-SAFETY-AND-HEALTH TECHNICIAN (any industry)
Plans and directs safety and health activities in industrial plant to evaluate and control environmental hazards: Tests noise levels and measures air quality, using precision instruments. Maintains and calibrates instruments. Administers hearing tests to employees. Trains forklift operators to qualify for licensing. Enforces use of safety equipment. Lectures employees to obtain compliance with regulations. Develops and monitors emergency action plans. Investigates accidents and prepares accident reports. Assists management to prepare safety and health budget. Recommends changes in policies and procedures to prevent accidents and illness.
GOE: 11.10.03 STRENGTH: L GED: R5 M4 L4 SVP: 6 DLU: 86

168.167-010 CUSTOMS PATROL OFFICER (government ser.)
Conducts surveillance, inspection, and patrol by foot, vehicle, boat, or aircraft at assigned points of entry into the United States to prohibit smuggled mer-

chandise and contraband and to detect violations of Customs and related laws: Inspects vessels, aircraft, and vehicles at docking, landing, crossing, and entry points. Establishes working rapport with local residents, law enforcement agencies, and businesses. Observes activity and regularity of vessels, planes, cargo, and storage arrangements in assigned area. Gathers and evaluates information from informers and other sources. Locates and apprehends customs violators. Assists in developing and testing new enforcement techniques and equipment. Develops intelligence information and forwards data for use by U.S. Customs Service. Testifies in courts of law against customs violators.
GOE: 04.01.02 STRENGTH: L GED: R5 M3 L4 SVP: 8 DLU: 77

168.167-014 EQUAL-OPPORTUNITY REPRESENTATIVE (government ser.)
Organizes and implements federally funded programs related to equal employment opportunity by providing consultation, encouraging good will between employers and minority communities, and evaluating employment practices: Consults with community representatives to develop technical assistance agreements in accordance with statutory regulations. Informs minority community on civil rights laws. Assists employers to interpret state and federal laws. Develops guidelines for nondiscriminatory employment practices for use by employers. Acts as liaison representative between minority placement agencies and large employers. Investigates existing employment practices to detect and correct discriminatory factors. Conducts surveys and evaluates findings to determine existence of systematic discrimination.
GOE: 11.10.02 STRENGTH: S GED: R5 M3 L5 SVP: 8 DLU: 77

168.167-018 HEALTH OFFICER, FIELD (government ser.) alternate titles: investigator, communicable disease
Investigates reported cases of communicable diseases and advises exposed persons to obtain medical treatment and to prevent further spread of disease: Locates and interviews exposed person, using information obtained from records of state or local public health departments and from individual already under treatment for communicable disease. Advises person to obtain treatment from private physician or public health clinic. May take blood sample to assist in identifying presence of disease in suspected victim. Questions exposed person to obtain information concerning other persons who may have received exposure. Conducts follow-up interviews with patients and suspected carriers. Writes report of activities and findings. Visits physicians, laboratories, and community health facilities to stimulate reporting of cases and to provide information about government-sponsored health programs concerning immunization efforts, VD control, mosquito abatement, and rodent control.
GOE: 11.10.03 STRENGTH: L GED: R5 M3 L5 SVP: 6 DLU: 77

168.167-022 IMMIGRATION INSPECTOR (government ser.)
Regulates entry of persons into United States at designated port of entry in accordance with immigration laws: Examines applications, visas, and passports and interviews persons to determine eligibility for admission, residence, and travel privileges in United States. Interprets laws and explains decisions to persons seeking entry. Arrests, detains, paroles, or arranges for deportation of persons according to laws, regulations, and departmental orders. Writes reports of activities and decisions. May patrol border on foot or horseback, or by airplane, automobile, or boat to detect and apprehend persons entering United States illegally and be designated Immigration Patrol Inspector (government ser.).
GOE: 11.10.04 STRENGTH: L GED: R4 M3 L4 SVP: 5 DLU: 77

168.167-026 INSPECTOR, BOILER (profess. & kin.) alternate titles: safety-engineer, pressure vessels
Inspects boilers, pressure vessels, and accessories for conformance to safety laws and standards regulating their design, fabrication, installation, repair, and operation: Inspects steam boilers, air tanks, liquefied gas tanks, and other pressure vessels under construction or already installed in ships or in residential, commercial, or industrial buildings to verify conformance to safety codes and standards issued by governmental agency, recognized professional technical organization, or insurance underwriting company. Inspects drawings, designs, and specifications for boilers and other vessels. Inspects materials used, safety devices, regulators, construction quality, brace and rivet tension, riveting, welding, pitting, corrosion, cracking, safety valve operation, and other factors affecting condition and operation of equipment. Performs standard tests such as hammer, accumulation, and hydrostatic tests to verify condition of boilers and other vessels. Calculates allowable limits of pressure, strength, and stresses. Witnesses acceptance and installation tests. Recommends changes to correct unsafe conditions. Orders correction of faulty work or materials or other conditions which violate legal requirements. Checks permits and methods of operation for boiler and other pressure vessel installations. Confers with engineers, manufacturers, contractors, owners, and operators concerning problems in construction, operation, and repair of pressure vessels and accessories. Investigates accidents involving pressure vessels to determine causes and to develop methods of preventing recurrences. Keeps records and prepares reports of inspections and investigations for administrative or legal authorities. May be required to possess Federal, State, or local license.
GOE: 05.03.06 STRENGTH: L GED: R5 M4 L5 SVP: 8 DLU: 77

168.167-030 INSPECTOR, BUILDING (government ser.)
Inspects new and existing buildings and structures to enforce conformance to building, grading, and zoning laws and approved plans, specifications, and standards: Inspects residential, commercial, industrial, and other buildings during and after construction to ensure that components, such as footings, floor

framing, completed framing, chimneys, and stairways meet provisions of building, grading, zoning, and safety laws and approved plans, specifications, and standards. Observes conditions and issues notices for corrections to persons responsible for conformance. Obtains evidence and prepares report concerning violations which have not been corrected. Interprets legal requirements and recommends compliance procedures to contractors, craftworkers, and owners. Keeps inspection records and prepares reports for use by administrative or judicial authorities. May conduct surveys of existing buildings to determine lack of prescribed maintenance, housing violations, or hazardous conditions. May review request for and issue building permits. May specialize in inspecting multifamily residences, temporary structures, buildings to be moved, or building appendages, such as chimneys, signs, swimming pools, retaining walls, and excavations and fills. May specialize in inspecting single-family residences for enforcement of full range of building, zoning, grading, and mechanical codes, including electrical, plumbing, heating and refrigeration, ventilating, and air-conditioning regulations and be designated Residential Building Inspector (government ser.).
GOE: 05.03.06 STRENGTH: L GED: R4 M4 L4 SVP: 7 DLU: 81

168.167-034 INSPECTOR, ELECTRICAL (government ser.)
Inspects electrical installations to verify conformance with safety laws and ordinances: Inspects electrical installations during construction or remodeling to enforce laws and ordinances establishing and maintaining minimum standards for residential, commercial, and industrial electrical installation and appliances. Reviews electrical plans and materials list to interpret specifications and methods of installation. Verifies loads, demand factors, and number of circuits to ensure that circuits are capable of operating without overloads. Inspects electric wiring, fixtures, and equipment, and issues notices to repair, remove, or refrain from using items found to be unsafe. Interprets legal requirements and recommends compliance procedures to contractors, craftworkers, and owners. Keeps records of inspections and prepares reports for use by administrative or judicial authorities.
GOE: 05.03.06 STRENGTH: L GED: R5 M4 L4 SVP: 7 DLU: 77

168.167-038 INSPECTOR, ELEVATORS (government ser.) alternate titles: safety engineer, elevators
Inspects lifting and conveying devices, such as elevators, escalators, moving sidewalks, and other similar mechanisms to verify conformance to laws and ordinances regulating design, installation, and safe operation: Inspects mechanical and electrical features of elevator installations, including elevator cars, beams, safety devices, control circuits, cables, guide rails, governors, switch boxes, counterweights, and buffers for conformance to governmental safety orders and regulations concerning standards of design, installation, maintenance, and operation. Conducts time tests of elevator's speed. Computes allowable loads for elevators and other devices. Observes running and drop test of elevators to determine if brakes and safety devices work properly. Inspects escalators, dumbwaiters, personnel lifts and hoists, platform hoists, inclined railways, aerial tramways, ski lifts, and various amusement rides to determine if safety precautions are observed. Recommends corrections for unsafe conditions. Seals operating device of unsafe elevators and other equipment. Investigates accidents involving elevators and similar lifting devices to determine causes and to develop means of preventing recurrence. Inspects equipment damaged by fire and recommends repair. Consults with engineers, installers, and owners regarding solution to problems connected with installation, maintenance, and repair of elevating equipment. Keeps records and prepares reports of inspections and investigations for use by administrative and legal authorities.
GOE: 05.03.06 STRENGTH: L GED: R5 M4 L5 SVP: 8 DLU: 77

168.167-042 INSPECTOR, HEALTH CARE FACILITIES (government ser.)
Inspects health care facilities, such as hospitals, nursing homes, sheltered care homes, maternity homes, and day care centers, to enforce public health laws and to investigate complaints: Inspects physical facilities, equipment, accommodations, and operating procedures to ensure compliance with laws governing standards of sanitation, acceptability of facilities, record keeping, staff competence qualifications, and ethical practices. Reviews reports concerning staffing, personal references, floor plans, fire inspections, and sanitation. Recommends changes in facilities, standards, and administrative methods in order to improve services and efficiency, utilizing knowledge of good practices and legal requirements. Advises applicants for approval of health care facilities on license application and rules governing operation of such facilities. May testify at hearings or in court. May compile data on conditions of health care facilities, for use in determining construction needs in community or region.
GOE: 11.10.03 STRENGTH: S GED: R4 M3 L4 SVP: 6 DLU: 77

168.167-046 INSPECTOR, HEATING AND REFRIGERATION (government ser.)
Inspects heating, ventilating, air-conditioning, and refrigeration installations for conformance to safety laws and regulations and approved plans and specifications: Inspects heating, ventilating, air-conditioning, and refrigeration equipment and installations in residential, commercial, and industrial buildings and facilities for conformance to safety laws and ordinances designed to prevent use of faulty equipment. Issues notices for correction of defective installations and issues citations to violators of safety code. Inspects gas heating appliances in retail stores and notifies dealers to remove unapproved appliances. Confers with property owners or agents to discuss and approve alteration plans to heating, ventilating, air-conditioning, and refrigeration equipment that comply with safe-

ty regulations. Investigates complaints regarding installation of heating and re-frigeration equipment by unlicensed contractors. Keeps records and prepares reports of inspections and investigations for use by administrative or judicial authorities. May investigate installations where fire or death has occurred. May determine percentage and acceptability of contract work completed for purposes of progress payments.
GOE: 05.07.02 STRENGTH: L GED: R5 M4 L4 SVP: 7 DLU: 77

168.167-050 INSPECTOR, PLUMBING (government ser.)
Inspects plumbing installations for conformance to governmental codes, sanitation standards, and construction specifications: Inspects commercial and industrial plumbing systems for conformance to plumbing laws and codes and approved plans and specifications. Inspects water-supply systems, drainage and sewer systems, water heater installations, fire sprinkler systems, and air and gas piping systems for approved materials, specified pipe sizes and connections, required grade and fitting, approved back-flow prevention devices, required bracing, ventilation, and air- and- water-tightness. Inspects building sites for soil type to determine fill conditions, water table level, site layout, seepage rate, and other conditions. Advises owners and contractors on acceptable locations for septic tanks, cesspools, and seepage pits. Interviews PLUMBER (construction) working in jurisdiction to determine possession of valid occupational licenses. Reviews plumbing permit applications and verifies payment of fees. Reviews complaints concerning alleged violations of plumbing code, gathers evidence, and appears in court as witness. Keeps records of inspections performed, actions taken, and corrections recommended and secured.
GOE: 05.03.06 STRENGTH: L GED: R5 M4 L4 SVP: 7 DLU: 77

168.167-058 MANAGER, CUSTOMER SERVICE (tel. & tel.)
Plans, directs, and coordinates activities of workers engaged in receiving, investigating, evaluating, settling complaints and claims of telegraph customers: Directs workers to investigate complaints, such as those concerning rates or service in connection with domestic, international, or special-gift telegrams. Analyzes reports of findings and recommends response to complaint, considering nature and complexity of complaint, requirements of governmental utility-regulation agencies, and policies of company. Reviews actions of subordinates to ensure settlements are made correctly. Authorizes retention of data and preparation of documents for use during governmental or customer inquiries.
GOE: 11.12.01 STRENGTH: S GED: R5 M5 L5 SVP: 8 DLU: 77

168.167-062 OCCUPATIONAL-SAFETY-AND-HEALTH INSPECTOR (government ser.) alternate titles: occupational-safety-and-health-compliance officer
Inspects places of employment to detect unsafe or unhealthy working conditions: Inspects work environment, machinery, and equipment in establishments and other work sites for conformance with governmental standards according to procedure or in response to complaint or accident. Interviews supervisors and employees to obtain facts about work practice or accident. Rates unsafe condition according to factors, such as severity of potential injury, likelihood of recurrence, employers' accident record, and evidence of voluntary compliance. Observes employees at work to determine compliance with safety precautions and safety equipment used. Orders suspension of activity posing threat to workers. Writes new safety order proposal designed to protect workers from work methods, processes, or other hazard not previously covered, using knowledge of safety-engineering practices, available protective devices, safety testing, and occupational safety and health standards. Discusses reason for inspection and penalty rating system with employer. Reviews log of reportable accidents and preventive actions taken to determine employers' attitude toward compliance with regulations. Documents findings and code sections violated. Interprets applicable laws and regulations to advise employer on legal requirements. May specialize in inspection of specific machine, apparatus, or device. May specialize in inspection of specific industry, such as construction, manufacturing, mining, petroleum, or transportation. May testify in legal proceedings. May photograph work environment suspected of endangering workers to provide evidence in legal proceedings.
GOE: 11.10.03 STRENGTH: L GED: R5 M5 L5 SVP: 6 DLU: 77

168.167-066 QUALITY-CONTROL COORDINATOR (pharmaceut.)
Coordinates activities of workers engaged in testing and evaluating ethical and proprietary pharmaceuticals in order to control quality of manufacture and to ensure compliance with legal standards: Participates with management personnel in establishing procedures for testing drugs and related products, applying knowledge of controlled production, sampling techniques, testing procedures, and statistical analysis. Assigns subordinates to specific testing functions. Reviews laboratory reports of test batches. Recommends full-scale production of batches meeting company or consumer specifications and complying with federal purity standards. Orders destruction of substandard batches, as authorized by supervisor. Directs and coordinates investigation of complaints concerning defective products. Recommends response to complaints, considering test reports, production records, legal standards, and complaint validity. Reviews legislative developments to determine changes in legal requirements and probable effects on company's manufacturing activities. Directs retention of data and preparation of documents for use by self or other company personnel during inquiries concerning suspect products.
GOE: 05.02.03 STRENGTH: S GED: R4 M4 L4 SVP: 6 DLU: 77

168.167-070 REGULATORY ADMINISTRATOR (tel. & tel.)
Directs and coordinates activities of workers engaged in investigating and responding to complaints from telephone subscribers or regulatory agencies con-

cerning rates and services: Directs investigations of telephone company rates and services to ensure that subscribers' complaints are answered and requirements of governmental utility-regulation agencies are met. Analyzes reports of resulting data and recommends response to complaint, considering nature of complaint and company interests and policies. Directs preparation of documents for use by company witnesses summoned to testify at governmental hearings. Reviews governmental rulings to determine changes in legal stipulations and probable effects on company activities. May provide advice and source data to management personnel concerned with preparing applications to regulatory bodies for changes in rates or service.
GOE: 11.10.05 STRENGTH: S GED: R5 M5 L5 SVP: 8 DLU: 77

168.167-074 REVIEWING OFFICER, DRIVER'S LICENSE (government ser.)
Evaluates traffic record and other aspects of driver's attitude and behavior to recommend suspension, revocation, or reinstatement of state operator's license: Reviews written record of driver, considering applicable laws and factors, such as number and nature of accidents, interval between accidents or convictions, driver's occupation, and number and gravity of traffic convictions, to evaluate driver's attitude and determine probability of repeated offenses. Recommends probation, suspension, or revocation of license, following rules, regulations, and policies of agency. Conducts hearings at request of persons whose licenses have been suspended or revoked to receive testimony and facts bearing on action. Receives petitions for reinstatement of licenses and approves or disapproves petitions according to evaluation of all pertinent facts. Confers with police and court officials to compile information, facilitate location or punishment of violators, and promote traffic safety. May allocate points for accidents or convictions and mail warnings to violators facing automatic penalties.
GOE: 11.10.03 STRENGTH: S GED: R4 M3 L4 SVP: 7 DLU: 77

168.167-078 SAFETY INSPECTOR (insurance) alternate titles: loss-control technician; safety engineer
Inspects insured properties to evaluate physical conditions and promote safety programs: Inspects properties such as buildings, industrial operations, vehicles, and recreational facilities to evaluate physical conditions, safety practices, and hazardous situations according to knowledge of safety and casualty underwriting standards and governmental regulations. Measures insured area, calculates frontage, and records description and amount of stock, and photographs or drafts scale drawings of properties, to identify factors affecting insurance premiums. Analyzes history of accidents and claims against insured and inspects scenes of accidents to determine causes and to develop accident-prevention programs. Prepares written report of findings and recommendations for correction of unsafe or unsanitary conditions. Confers with employees of insured to induce compliance with safety standards, codes, and regulations. Conducts informational meetings among various educational, civic, and industrial groups to promote general safety concepts, utilizing audiovisual aids and insurance statistics. May specialize in specific type of accident-prevention or safety program, such as fire safety or traffic safety.
GOE: 11.10.03 STRENGTH: L GED: R5 M4 L5 SVP: 8 DLU: 77

168.167-082 TRANSPORTATION INSPECTOR (motor trans.; r.r. trans.) alternate titles: service inspector; undercover agent
Compiles information concerning service activities and conduct of employees on railroads, streetcars, and buses and submits written reports of findings: Observes employees performing assigned duties, assuming role of passenger to note their deportment, treatment of passengers, and adherence to company regulations and schedules. Observes and records time required to load and unload passengers or freight, volume of traffic at different stops or stations, and on streetcars and buses, at different times of day. Inspects company vehicles and other property for damage and evidence of abuse. Submits written reports to management with recommendations for improving service.
GOE: 11.10.05 STRENGTH: L GED: R4 M3 L4 SVP: 7 DLU: 77

168.167-086 SAFETY MANAGER (medical ser.)
Plans, implements, coordinates, and assesses hospital accident, fire prevention, and occupational safety and health programs under general direction of hospital officials, utilizing knowledge of industrial safety-related engineering discipline and operating regulations: Develops and recommends new procedures and approaches to safety and loss prevention based on reports of incidents, accidents, and other data gathered from hospital personnel. Disseminates information to department heads and others regarding toxic substances, hazards, carcinogens, and other safety information. Assists department heads and administrators in enforcing safety regulations and codes. Measures and evaluates effectiveness of safety program, using established goals. Conducts building and grounds surveys on periodic and regular basis to detect code violations, hazards, and incorrect work practices and procedures. Develops and reviews safety training for hospital staff. Maintains administrative control of records related to safety and health programs. Prepares and disseminates memos and reports. Maintains required records. Assists personnel department in administering worker compensation program.
GOE: 11.10.03 STRENGTH: L GED: R5 M5 L5 SVP: 7 DLU: 86

168.167-090 MANAGER, REGULATED PROGRAM (government ser.)
Directs and coordinates activities of departmental personnel engaged in investigating regulated activities to ensure compliance with federal, state, or municipal laws, utilizing knowledge of agency's purposes, rules, regulations, procedures, and practices: Reviews agency's current work load status, schedules,

and individual personnel assignments and expertise to establish priorities and to determine ability to accept and complete future commitments. Assigns specific duties to inspectors or INVESTIGATOR (government ser.) 168.267-062 either directly or through subordinate supervisors. Reviews work reports, papers, rulings, and other records prepared by subordinate personnel for clarity, completeness, accuracy, and conformance with agency policies. Routes approved reports and records to designated individuals, such as DIRECTOR, REGULATORY AGENCY (government ser.) 188.117-134 for action or for information. May participate in or make initial or advanced level investigations, tests, or rulings. May testify in court or before control or review board. May be required to be certified in designated speciality area. May be designated according to function or agency as Business Regulation Investigator (government ser.); Child Day Care Program Supervisor (government ser.); Feed Inspection Supervisor (government ser.); Insurance Licensing Supervisor (government ser.); Meat And Poultry Specialist Supervisor (government ser.); Petroleum Products District Supervisor (government ser.); Poultry Specialist Supervisor (government ser.); Public Utilities Complaint Analyst Supervisor (government ser.); Supervisor, Weights And Measures, Gas And Oil Inspection (government ser.). Workers involved in these activities may be identified by different titles according to classification used by various agencies.
GOE: 11.05.03 STRENGTH: L GED: R5 M5 L5 SVP: 8 DLU: 86

168.261-010   RADIATION-PROTECTION   SPECIALIST   (government ser.)

Tests x-ray equipment, inspects areas where equipment is used, and evaluates operating procedures to detect and control radiation hazards: Visits hospitals, medical offices, and other establishments to test x-ray machines and fluoroscopes and to inspect premises. Tests equipment to determine that kilovolt potential, alignment of components, and other elements of equipment meet standards for safe operation, using specialized instruments and procedures. Operates equipment to determine need for calibration, repair, or replacement of tubes or other parts. Measures density of lead shielding in walls, using radiometric equipment. Computes cumulative radiation levels and refers to regulations to determine if amount of shielding is sufficient to absorb radiation emissions. Examines license of equipment operator for authenticity and observes operating practices to determine competence of operator to use equipment. Confers with physicians, dentists, and x-ray personnel to explain procedures and legal requirements pertaining to use of equipment. Demonstrates exposure techniques to improve procedures and minimize amount of radiation delivered to patient and operator. Reviews plans and specifications for proposed x-ray installations for conformance to legal requirements and radiation safety practices. Contacts organizations submitting inadequate specifications to explain changes in shielding or layout needed to conform to regulations.
GOE: 11.10.03 STRENGTH: L GED: R5 M4 L5 SVP: 8 DLU: 86

168.264-010   INSPECTOR, AIR-CARRIER (government ser.) alternate titles: aviation-safety officer; operations inspector

Inspects aircraft and maintenance base facilities to assure conformance with federal safety and qualifications standards: Examines aircraft maintenance record and flight log to determine if service checks, maintenance checks, and overhauls were performed at intervals prescribed. Inspects landing gear, tires, and exterior of fuselage, wings, and engine for evidence of damage or corrosion and recommends repair. Examines access plates and doors for security. Inspects new, repaired, or modified aircraft, according to checklist, to determine structural and mechanical airworthiness, using handtools and test instruments. Starts aircraft and observes gauges, meters, and other instruments to detect evidence of malfunction. Examines electrical systems and accompanies flight crew on proving flight to test instruments. Inventories spare parts to determine whether stock meets requirements. Analyzes training programs to assure competency of persons operating, installing, and repairing equipment. Informs airline officials of deficiencies. Prepares report of inspection to document findings. Approves or disapproves issuance of certificate of airworthiness. Conducts examinations to test theoretical and practical knowledge of construction, maintenance, repair, and trouble diagnosis for aircraft mechanics license candidates. Investigates air accidents to determine whether cause was due to structural or mechanical malfunction. Required to have federal aviation rating for type of aircraft inspected and pass federal aviation medical certification. May be designated according to specialty as Air-Carrier Electronics Inspector (government ser.); Air-Carrier Maintenance Inspector (government ser.).
GOE: 05.03.06 STRENGTH: L GED: R5 M5 L4 SVP: 7 DLU: 77

168.264-014   SAFETY INSPECTOR (any industry) alternate titles: safety technician

Inspects machinery, equipment, and working conditions in industrial or other setting to ensure compliance with occupational safety and health regulations: Inspects machines and equipment for accident prevention devices. Observes workers to determine use of prescribed safety equipment, such as glasses, helmets, goggles, respirators, and clothing. Inspects specified areas for fire-prevention equipment and other safety and first-aid supplies. Tests working areas for noise, toxic, and other hazards, using decibel meter, gas detector, and light meter. Prepares report of findings with recommendations for corrective action. Investigates accidents to ascertain causes for use in recommending preventive safety measures and developing safety program. May demonstrate use of safety equipment.
GOE: 11.10.03 STRENGTH: L GED: R4 M3 L4 SVP: 6 DLU: 77

168.264-018   GAS INSPECTOR (utilities)

Inspects equipment and facilities used to store, transport, distribute, and measure liquefied petroleum or compressed or natural gas: Examines establishment inspection records to determine that establishment inspection schedule and remedial actions conform to procedures and regulations. Examines containers, piping, tubing, and fittings for leaks and for adherence to government specifications for pressure level, design, construction, and installation. Examines and tests components and support systems, such as relief valves, steam vaporizers, safety devices, electrical equipment, exhaust systems, and vehicles, for conformance with standards and regulations. Connects test equipment, using handtools, and tests calibration of meters and gauges. Inspects above and below ground gas mains to determine that rate of flow, pressure, location, construction, or installation conform to establishment or regulated standards. Maintains records and prepares reports of results of inspections. Discusses and explains procedures and regulations or need for corrective action with establishment or regulatory agency personnel. May be designated according to function, agency, or establishment where employed as Division Field Inspector (utilities); Gas Inspector, Liquefied (government ser.).
GOE: 11.10.03 STRENGTH: L GED: R5 M4 L5 SVP: 7 DLU: 87

168.267-010   BUILDING INSPECTOR (insurance)

Inspects buildings to determine fire insurance rates: Examines building for type of construction, condition of roof, and fireproofing. Determines risk represented by adjoining buildings, by nature of business, and building contents. Determines availability of fireplugs and firefighting equipment. Completes inspection report. May compute insurance rate.
GOE: 05.03.06 STRENGTH: L GED: R4 M3 L4 SVP: 7 DLU: 77

168.267-014   CLAIM EXAMINER (insurance)

Reviews settled insurance claims to determine that payments and settlements have been made in accordance with company practices and procedures: Analyzes data used in settling claim to determine its validity in payment of claims. Reports overpayments, underpayments, and other irregularities. Confers with legal counsel on claims requiring litigation.
GOE: 07.02.03 STRENGTH: S GED: R5 M3 L4 SVP: 7 DLU: 77

168.267-018   CUSTOMS IMPORT SPECIALIST (government ser.) alternate titles: customs examiner

Examines, classifies, and appraises imported merchandise according to federal revenue laws, in order to enforce regulations of U.S. Customs Service: Examines and appraises merchandise and accompanying documentation according to import requirements, considering legal restrictions, country of origin, import quotas, and current market values. Requests laboratory testing and analyses of merchandise as needed. Determines duty and taxes to be paid on imported merchandise, considering its classification and value. Interviews importers and examines their records to verify integrity of invoices. Determines and reports evidence of intent to defraud and violations of trademark, copyright, and marking laws. Notifies other governmental agencies responsible for particular import inspection, or when apparent import violations concern other agency regulations. Issues or denies permits to release imported merchandise for delivery, depending on importer's meeting legal requirements. Appraises seized and unclaimed merchandise to be sold at public auction. Assists federal attorneys in preparation and trial of cases in customs court by supplying technical information and advice, securing qualified witnesses and evidence, and appearing as a government witness. May plan, coordinate, and evaluate work of import inspection team. May defend appraisal of merchandise during court appeals by importers.
GOE: 11.10.04 STRENGTH: L GED: R5 M3 L5 SVP: 8 DLU: 77

168.267-022   CUSTOMS INSPECTOR (government ser.)

Inspects cargo, baggage, articles worn or carried by persons, and vessels, vehicles, or aircraft entering or leaving United States to enforce customs and related laws: Boards carriers arriving from foreign ports, and inspects and searches carriers to determine nature of cargoes. Superintends loading and unloading of cargo to ensure compliance with customs, neutrality, and commerce laws. Weighs, measures, and gauges imported goods, using calipers, measuring rods, scale, and hydrometer. Examines baggage of passengers arriving from foreign territory to discover contraband or undeclared merchandise. Conducts body search of passengers or crewmembers. Questions suspicious persons to clarify irregularities and explains laws and regulations to tourists or others unfamiliar with customs statutes and procedures. Seals hold and compartments containing sea stores (supplies for ship's personnel) to prevent illegal sale or smuggling of dutiable merchandise. Examines crew and passenger lists, manifests, pratiques, store lists, declarations of merchandise, and ships' documents and issues required permits. Classifies articles and assesses and collects duty on merchandise. Writes reports of findings, transactions, violations, and discrepancies. Seizes contraband and undeclared merchandise and detains or arrests persons involved in violations. May perform preliminary immigration screening of persons entering United States. May take samples of merchandise for appraising. May be designated according to type of inspection performed as Baggage Inspector (government ser.); Border Inspector (government ser.); Cargo Inspector (government ser.).
GOE: 11.10.04 STRENGTH: L GED: R4 M4 L4 SVP: 6 DLU: 77

168.267-026   DEALER-COMPLIANCE REPRESENTATIVE (retail trade; wholesale tr.) alternate titles: field representative

Inspects franchise dealerships and distributorships to ascertain compliance with company operating policies and procedures and to require adherence in detected instances: Inspects inventory and operating records to ascertain that only approved products are sold and approved operating procedures followed by

dealer. Inspects premises and observes working conditions to ensure compliance with company and governmental standards of safety and sanitation. May ascertain that dealers are paying bills due company and may collect monies due. May advise dealers on financial aspects of operating franchise.
GOE: 11.10.05 STRENGTH: L GED: R4 M3 L3 SVP: 6 DLU: 77

168.267-030 DINING-SERVICE INSPECTOR (r.r. trans.) alternate titles: service inspector

Inspects railroad dining car facilities and service and investigates complaints to ensure that cleanliness and service standards are maintained: Inspects cooking area and utensils to ensure that they are clean and sanitary. Inspects food and observes preparation to ensure that food is served in sanitary and appetizing manner. Observes WAITERS/WAITRESSES, DINING CAR (r.r. trans.) as they serve food to patrons to ensure that service is efficient and courteous. Investigates complaints by patrons of poor service or discourtesy. Recommends service improvements and operating efficiencies. Prepares reports of complaints and action taken.
GOE: 11.10.05 STRENGTH: L GED: R4 M2 L3 SVP: 7 DLU: 77

168.267-034 DRIVER'S LICENSE EXAMINER (government ser.)

Gives written and visual acuity tests and conducts road performance tests to determine applicant's eligibility for driver's license: Scores written and visual acuity tests and issues and collects fees for instruction permits. Conducts road tests and observes applicant's driving ability throughout specified maneuvers and compliance with traffic safety rules. Rates ability for each maneuver. Collects fees and issues licenses. Lectures to school and community groups concerning driver improvement program. May inspect brakes, stop and signal lights, and horn to determine if applicant's vehicle is safe to operate.
GOE: 07.01.07 STRENGTH: L GED: R3 M2 L3 SVP: 4 DLU: 77

168.267-038 ELIGIBILITY-AND-OCCUPANCY INTERVIEWER (government ser.)

Interviews and investigates prospective tenants to determine eligibility for public low-rent housing: Receives and processes initial or reactivated applications for public housing. Interviews applicant to obtain additional information such as family composition, health and social problems, veteran status, rent paying ability, net assets, and need for housing assistance. Advises applicant on eligibility requirements, methods of selecting tenants, and housing opportunities. Contacts employers, and public and private health and welfare agencies to verify applicant information. Provides information to tenant or applicant on availability of community resources for financial or social welfare assistance. Determines applicant eligibility according to agency rules and policies. Selects and refers eligible applicant to MANAGER, HOUSING PROJECT (profess. & kin.). Notifies eligible applicant of vacancy and assignment procedures. Computes rent in proportion to applicant's income. Receives and records security deposit and advance rent from selected applicant. Conducts annual, interim, and special housing reviews with tenants. May assist in resolving tenant complaints on maintenance problems. May visit home to determine housekeeping habits, verify housing condition, and establish housing need.
GOE: 07.01.01 STRENGTH: L GED: R4 M4 L4 SVP: 5 DLU: 77

168.267-042 FOOD AND DRUG INSPECTOR (government ser.)

Inspects establishment where foods, drugs, cosmetics, and similar consumer items are manufactured, handled, stored, or sold to enforce legal standards of sanitation, purity, and grading: Visits specified establishments to investigate sanitary conditions and health and hygiene habits of persons handling consumer products. Collects samples of products for bacteriological and chemical laboratory analysis. Informs individuals concerned of specific regulations affecting establishments. Destroys subgrades, or prohibits sale of impure, toxic, damaged, or misbranded items. Questions employees, vendors, consumers, and other principals to obtain evidence for prosecuting violators. Ascertains that required licenses and permits have been obtained and are displayed. Prepares reports on each establishment visited, including findings and recommendations for action. May negotiate with marketers and processors to effect changes in facilities and practices, where undesirable conditions are discovered that are not specifically prohibited by law. May grade products according to specified standards. May test products, using variety of specialized test equipment, such as ultraviolet lights and filter guns. May investigate compliance with or violation of public sanitation laws and regulations and be designated Sanitary Inspector (government ser.).
GOE: 11.10.03 STRENGTH: L GED: R5 M4 L5 SVP: 6 DLU: 77

168.267-046 INSPECTOR, FURNITURE AND BEDDING (government ser.)

Inspects bedding materials and furniture padding to enforce public health laws and to investigate consumer complaints: Inspects premises and operations at furniture and bedding factories, warehouses, renovating plants, and sales outlets to ascertain compliance with state furniture and bedding sanitation laws. Examines labels on furniture and bedding items to ascertain compliance with fiber content and labeling regulations. Examines stock of used goods, condition of fumigation chambers, and use of prescribed chemicals. Conducts laboratory analyses on sample fibers, feathers, and materials to determine usability and cleanliness, utilizing standardized microscopic examination and chemical tests. May cite or arrest suspected violators and testify in court.
GOE: 11.10.03 STRENGTH: M GED: R4 M3 L4 SVP: 6 DLU: 77

168.267-050 INSPECTOR, GOVERNMENT PROPERTY (government ser.)

Inspects government-owned equipment and materials in hands of private contractors to prevent waste, damage, theft, and other irregularities. Reviews inventory reports and similar records to detect discrepancies in utilization of materials. Recommends legal or administrative action to protect government property.
GOE: 11.10.01 STRENGTH: L GED: R4 M3 L4 SVP: 6 DLU: 77

168.267-054 INSPECTOR, INDUSTRIAL WASTE (government ser.)

Inspects industrial and commercial waste disposal facilities and investigates source of pollutants in municipal sewage and storm-drainage system to ensure conformance with ordinance and permit requirements: Visits establishments to determine possession of industrial waste permits and to inspect waste treatment facilities, such as floor drains, sand traps, settling and neutralizing tanks, and grease removal equipment for conformance with regulations. Extracts samples of waste from sewers, storm drains, and water courses for laboratory tests. Conducts field tests for acidity, alkalinity, and other characteristics to determine if discharged wastes will cause water pollution or deterioration of sewerage facilities. Inspects sewers and storm drains to determine presence of explosive gases, using gas-analysis equipment. Reviews plans of proposed waste-treatment facilities and inspects construction to ensure conformance with ordinances. Issues citations to apparent violators of sanitation code or water-quality regulations. Compiles written reports of investigations and findings, and actions taken or recommended. May enforce ordinances concerned with commercial hauling and disposal of contents from cesspools and septic tanks into sewers. May inspect water wells for contamination and conformance with legal construction standards, and order closing of unsanitary or unsafe wells. May inspect solid waste disposal facilities, such as sanitary landfills and chemical disposal sites.
GOE: 05.03.06 STRENGTH: M GED: R5 M4 L5 SVP: 6 DLU: 79

168.267-058 INSPECTOR, MOTOR VEHICLES (government ser.) alternate titles: automobile inspector; motor-transport inspector; weigh-station inspector

Inspects motor vehicles and cargoes for compliance with statutory regulations: Reviews employer records to determine that accidents, traffic violations, and medical information are recorded according to federal and state regulations. Advises shipper of methods to improve cargo security and record keeping to account for shortage or theft. Interprets applicable regulations and suggests method of self-inspection to accomplish voluntary compliance with code. Inspects vehicle systems, such as lights, brakes, tires, directional signals, exhaust systems, and warning devices, to detect excessive wear or malfunction. Measures interior and exterior noise levels, using decibel meter. Measures efficiency of emission-control devices, using electronic test apparatus. Reviews shipping papers to identify hazardous cargo, such as explosives, poisons, or combustibles. Inspects manner in which hazardous cargo is secured to prevent accidental spillage. Computes and records weight of commercial trucks at highway weigh station or uses portable scale to determine gross weight and distribution of load over axles. Reviews commercial vehicle log to verify driver has not exceeded allowable driving hours and required permits and licenses are displayed. Declares vehicle or driver out-of-service for violation of intra- or interstate commerce regulations. Inspects buses to determine compliance with public transport regulations. May accompany bus drivers to observe conduct and observance with safety precautions. May inspect establishments that rebuild containers used to hold hazardous materials. May testify in legal proceedings.
GOE: 11.10.03 STRENGTH: L GED: R4 M3 L4 SVP: 5 DLU: 78

168.267-062 INVESTIGATOR (government ser.)

Investigates regulated activities to assure compliance with federal, state, or municipal laws: Locates and interviews plaintiffs, witnesses, or representatives of business or government to gather facts relating to alleged violation. Observes conditions to verify facts indicating violation of law relating to such activities as revenue collection, employment practices, or fraudulent benefit claims. Examines business, personal, or public records and documents to establish facts and authenticity of data. Investigates character of applicant for special license or permit. Investigates suspected misuses of license or permit. Prepares correspondence and reports of investigations for use by administrative or legal authorities. Testifies in court or at administrative proceedings concerning findings of investigation. May serve legal papers. May be required to meet licensing or certification standards established by regulatory agency concerned. May be designated according to function or agency where employed as Inspector, Weights And Measures (government ser.); Investigator, Internal Revenue (government ser.); Investigator, Welfare (government ser.); Postal Inspector (government ser.); Investigator, Claims (government ser.).
GOE: 11.10.01 STRENGTH: L GED: R5 M4 L4 SVP: 6 DLU: 77

168.267-066 LICENSE INSPECTOR (government ser.)

Visits establishments licensed by local governments to ascertain that valid licenses and permits are displayed and that licensing standards are being upheld. Prepares report on violators and recommends action. Warns violators of minor or unintentional infractions. May arrest violators. May be designated according to class of establishment visited as Rooming-House Inspector (government ser.); Tavern Inspector (government ser.).
GOE: 11.10.03 STRENGTH: L GED: R4 M3 L3 SVP: 7 DLU: 77

168.267-070 LOGGING-OPERATIONS INSPECTOR (forestry; logging)

Inspects contract logging operations to ensure adherence to contract provisions and safety laws and to prevent loss of timber through breakage and damage to residual stand: Examines logging area for utilization practices, slash disposal, sanitation, observance of boundaries, and safety precautions. Issues remedial instructions for violations of contract agreement and fire and safety regula-

tions, and prepares report of logging method, efficiency, and progress. May initiate bid requests and negotiate terms of contracts with logging contractors.
GOE: 03.01.04 STRENGTH: L GED: R5 M3 L4 SVP: 7 DLU: 77

168.267-074 MINE INSPECTOR (mine & quarry) alternate titles: check viewer; safety inspector
Inspects underground or open-pit mines to ascertain compliance with contractual agreements and with health and safety laws: Inspects for rotted or incorrectly placed timbers, dangerously placed or defective electrical and mechanical equipment, improperly stored explosives, and other hazardous conditions. Tests air quality to detect toxic or explosive gas or dust, using portable gas-analysis equipment, in order to control health hazards and to reduce injuries and fatalities. Observes mine activities to detect violations of federal and state health and safety standards. Inspects mine workings to verify compliance with contractual agreements concerning production rates or mining within specified limits. May instruct mine workers in safety and first aid procedures. May be designated according to type of mine inspected as Coal-Mine Inspector (mine & quarry); Metal-Mine Inspector (mine & quarry). May specialize in inspection of specific conditions and be designated Gas Inspector (mine & quarry). When employed by governmental agency (instead of mine operator), conducts periodic mine inspections specifically to enforce federal or state mining laws and is known as Mine Inspector, Federal (government ser.); Mine Inspector, State (government ser.).
GOE: 11.10.03 STRENGTH: L GED: R4 M3 L4 SVP: 6 DLU: 80

168.267-078 MORTICIAN INVESTIGATOR (government ser.)
Inspects mortuaries for sanitary conditions, equipment and procedures, and competence of personnel. Examines registration credentials of trainees and licenses of funeral directors to ensure compliance with state licensing requirements. Investigates complaints and recommends license revocation or other action. May be required to hold mortician's license.
GOE: 11.10.03 STRENGTH: L GED: R4 M3 L4 SVP: 6 DLU: 77

168.267-082 AGRICULTURAL-CHEMICALS INSPECTOR (government ser.)
Inspects establishments where agricultural service products, such as livestock feed and remedies, fertilizers, and pesticides, are manufactured, sold, or used to ensure conformance to laws regulating product quality and labeling: Visits processing plants, distribution warehouses, sales outlets, agricultural pest control service organizations, and farmers to collect product samples for analysis and to examine fresh and dried produce for spray residue. Inspects product label information concerning ingredients and advertising claims for conformance to chemical analysis of ingredients and documented effects of use. Investigates suspected violations of product quality and labeling laws. Interviews farmers, merchants, and others to determine nature of suspected violations and to obtain documented evidence to be used in legal action against violators. Calls on dealers to determine that licensing requirements have been met, and calls on manufacturers and distributors to collect delinquent tonnage reports. Prepares reports of all inspections and investigations for review by supervisory personnel and for use as evidence in legal action initiated by others.
GOE: 11.10.03 STRENGTH: L GED: R4 M2 L3 SVP: 7 DLU: 86

168.267-086 HAZARDOUS-WASTE MANAGEMENT SPECIALIST (government ser.)
Conducts studies on hazardous waste management projects and provides information on treatment and containment of hazardous waste: Participates in developing hazardous waste rules and regulations to protect people and environment. Surveys industries to determine type and magnitude of disposal problem. Assesses available hazardous waste treatment and disposal alternatives, and costs involved, to compare economic impact of alternative methods. Assists in developing comprehensive spill prevention programs and reviews facility plans for spill prevention. Participates in developing spill-reporting regulations and environmental damage assessment programs. Prepares reports of findings concerning spills and prepares material for use in legal actions. Answers inquiries and prepares informational literature to provide technical assistance to representatives of industry, government agencies, and to general public. Provides technical assistance in event of hazardous chemical spill and identifies pollutant, determines hazardous impact, and recommends corrective action.
GOE: 11.10.03 STRENGTH: S GED: R5 M3 L5 SVP: 7 DLU: 86

168.267-090 INSPECTOR, WATER-POLLUTION CONTROL (government ser.)
Inspects sites where discharges enter state waters and investigates complaints concerning water pollution problems: Inspects wastewater treatment facilities at sites, such as mobile home parks, sewage treatment plants, and other sources of pollution. Inspects lagoons and area where effluent enters state waters for such features as obvious discoloration of water, sludge, algae, rodents, and other conditions. Informs owner when unacceptable or questionable conditions are present and recommends corrective action. Notifies mobile laboratory technicians when sampling is required. Advises property owners, facility managers, and equipment operators concerning pollution control regulations. Investigates complaints concerning water pollution problems. Compiles information for pollution control discharge permits. Prepares technical reports of investigations.
GOE: 11.10.03 STRENGTH: L GED: R5 M4 L5 SVP: 7 DLU: 86

168.267-094 MARINE-CARGO SURVEYOR (business ser.)
Inspects cargoes of seagoing vessels to certify compliance with national and international health and safety regulations in cargo handling and stowage:

Reads vessel documents that set forth cargo loading and securing procedures, capacities, and stability factors to ascertain cargo capabilities according to design and cargo regulations. Advises crew in techniques of stowing dangerous and heavy cargo, such as use of extra support beams (deck bedding), shoring, and additional stronger lashings, according to knowledge of hazards present when shipping grain, explosives, logs, and heavy machinery. Inspects loaded, secured cargo in holds and lashed to decks to ascertain that pertinent cargo handling regulations have been observed. Issues certificate of compliance when violations are not detected. Recommends remedial procedures to correct deficiencies. Measures ship holds and depth of fuel and water in tanks, using sounding line and tape measure, and reads draft markings to ascertain depth of vessel in water. Times roll of ship, using stopwatch. Calculates hold capacities, volume of stored fuel and water, weight of cargo, and ship stability factors, using standard mathematical formulas and calculator. Analyzes data obtained from survey, formulates recommendations pertaining to vessel capacities, and writes report of findings. Inspects cargo handling devices, such as boom, hoists, and derricks, to identify need for maintenance.
GOE: 11.10.03 STRENGTH: L GED: R4 M4 L4 SVP: 9 DLU: 86

168.267-098 PESTICIDE-CONTROL INSPECTOR (government ser.)
Inspects operations of distributors and commercial applicators of pesticides to determine compliance with government regulations on handling, sale, and use of pesticides: Inspects premises of wholesale and retail distributors to ensure that registered pesticides are handled in accordance with state and federal regulations. Determines that handlers possess permits and sell restricted pesticides only to authorized users. Evaluates pesticides for correct labeling, misbranding, misrepresentation, or adulteration, and confiscates or quarantines unacceptable pesticides. Inspects operations of commercial applicators of pesticides and observes application methods to ensure correct use of equipment, application procedures, and that applicators possess valid permits. Determines that accurate records are kept to show pesticides used, dosage, times, places, and methods of applications. Inspects premises to ensure that storage and disposal of pesticides conform to regulations. Investigates complaints concerning pesticides and uses. Identifies insect or disease, recommends treatment, and authorizes emergency use of suitable restricted pesticides to respond to emergency situations, such as insect infestations or outbreaks of plant disease.
GOE: 11.10.03 STRENGTH: L GED: R4 M2 L3 SVP: 7 DLU: 86

168.267-102 PLAN CHECKER (government ser.)
Examines commercial and private building plans and inspects construction sites to ensure compliance with building code regulations: Reviews building plans for completeness and accuracy. Examines individual plan components to ensure that all code mandated items are included. Calculates footage between building components, such as doors, windows, and parking areas and amount of area occupied by components to ensure compliance with code. Notes instances of noncompliance on plans and correction sheet and suggests modifications to bring plans into compliance. Approves and signs plans meeting code requirements. Inspects building sites and buildings to ensure construction follows plans. Submits reports detailing items of noncompliance to builder for correction. Provides code information to individuals planning buildings. Issues occupancy certificates to building owners when completed buildings are in compliance with codes. Tours jurisdictional area to detect unapproved or noncompliance construction. Proposes studies to improve or update building codes. Testifies at appeal hearings regarding buildings alleged to be not in compliance with codes.
GOE: 05.03.06 STRENGTH: L GED: R4 M4 L4 SVP: 7 DLU: 86

168.267-106 REGISTRATION SPECIALIST, AGRICULTURAL CHEMICALS (government ser.)
Reviews and evaluates information on applications for registration of products containing dangerous chemicals for compliance with statutory regulations: Reads registration applications from manufacturers and distributors of pesticides, fertilizers, and other products containing dangerous chemicals. Evaluates label information to determine that directions for use and claims for effectiveness of product are stated clearly and accurately. Reviews statements concerning product ingredients, effects of misuse, and administration of antidotes for adequacy of information and conformance to regulatory requirements for substances. Forwards approved applications to other personnel for registration. Contacts manufacturers and distributors of products not meeting standards to clarify regulations and to suggest changes in label information to permit registration. Prepares, organizes, and maintains records to document activities and provide reference materials. Conducts studies and investigations of faulty labeling or use of products as directed by agricultural agency personnel.
GOE: 11.10.03 STRENGTH: S GED: R5 M3 L4 SVP: 7 DLU: 86

168.267-110 SANITATION INSPECTOR (government ser.)
Inspects community land areas and investigates complaints concerning neglect of property and illegal dumping of refuse to ensure compliance with municipal code: Inspects designated areas periodically for evidence of neglect, excessive litter, and presence of unsightly or hazardous refuse. Interviews residents and inspects area to investigate reports of illegal dumping and neglected land. Locates property owners to explain nature of inspection and investigation findings and to encourage voluntary action to resolve problems. Studies laws and statutes in municipal code to determine specific nature of code violation and type of action to be taken. Issues notices of violation to land owners not complying with request for voluntary correction of problems. Issues notices of abatement to known violators of dumping regulations and informs other munici-

pal agencies of need to post signs forbidding illegal dumping at designated sites. Prepares case materials when legal action is required to solve problems. Conducts informational meetings for residents, organizes neighborhood cleanup projects, and participates in campaigns to beautify city to promote community interest in eliminating dangerous and unsightly land use practices.
GOE: 11.10.03 STRENGTH: L GED: R3 M2 L3 SVP: 5 DLU: 86

168.117-114 EQUAL OPPORTUNITY OFFICER (any industry)
Monitors company contracts to determine affirmative action requirements and facilitate compliance: Reviews contracts to determine company actions required to meet equal opportunity provisions of local, state, or federal laws. Studies equal opportunity complaints to clarify issues, and meets with personnel involved to arbitrate and settle disputes. Confers with supervisory personnel to verify or document alleged violations of law, such as failure to post notices, process grievances, or correct ethnic or other imbalances. Prepares report of findings and makes recommendations for corrective action. Participates with MANAGER, PERSONNEL (profess. & kin.) 166.117-018 in addressing and resolving issues involving company hiring and related personnel policies.
GOE: 11.10.02 STRENGTH: S GED: R5 M3 L5 SVP: 7 DLU: 87

168.287-010 INSPECTOR, AGRICULTURAL COMMODITIES (government ser.)
Inspects agricultural commodities, processing equipment, and facilities to enforce compliance with governmental regulations: Inspects horticultural products, such as fruits, vegetables, and ornamental plants to detect disease or infestations harmful to consumers or agricultural economy. Inspects live animals and processing establishments to detect disease or unsanitary conditions. Compares brand with registry to identify owner. Examines, weighs, and measures commodities such as poultry, eggs, mutton, beef, and seafood to certify wholesomeness, grade, and weight. Examines viscera to detect spots or abnormal growths. Collects sample of pests or suspected diseased material and routes to laboratory for identification and analysis. Writes report of findings and advises grower or processor of corrective action. May testify in legal proceedings. May be required to hold U.S. Department of Agriculture license for each product inspected. May be designated according to type of commodity or animal inspected.
GOE: 11.10.03 STRENGTH: L GED: R4 M3 L4 SVP: 7 DLU: 77

168.287-014 INSPECTOR, QUALITY ASSURANCE (government ser.) alternate titles: procurement inspector
Inspects products manufactured or processed by private companies for government use to ensure compliance with contract specifications: Examines company's records to secure such information as size and weight of product and results of quality tests. Inspects product to determine compliance with order specifications, company's quality control system for compliance with legal requirements, and shipping and packing facilities for conformity to specified standards. Submits samples of product to government laboratory for testing as indicated by department procedures. Stamps mark of approval or rejection on product and writes report of examinations. May specialize in lumber, machinery, petroleum products, paper products, electronic equipment, furniture, or other specific product or group of related products.
GOE: 05.03.06 STRENGTH: L GED: R5 M5 L5 SVP: 7 DLU: 77

168.287-018 INSPECTOR, RAILROAD (government ser.)
Examines railroad equipment and systems to verify compliance with Federal safety regulations: Inspects railroad locomotives, engines, and cars to ensure adherence to safety standards governing condition of mechanical, structural, electrical, pneumatic, and hydraulic elements or systems, using blueprints, schematic diagrams, gauges, handtools, and test equipment. Tests railroad signals to determine warning light responses to commands from dispatcher or tripswitches, using simulator. Inspects roadbeds to detect damaged, worn, or defective equipment, such as rails, ties, bolts, fishplates, or switches. Inspects condition and movement of railroad cars containing flammable or explosive materials to ensure safe loading, switching, and transport. Reviews records, operating practices, and accident history to verify compliance with safety regulations. Issues citations to railroad employees of condition or equipment found in violation of standards. Investigates accidents and inspects wreckage to determine causes. Prepares inspection reports for use by administrative or judicial authorities.
GOE: 05.03.06 STRENGTH: M GED: R4 M3 L4 SVP: 7 DLU: 77

168.367-010 ATTENDANCE OFFICER (education) alternate titles: truant officer
Investigates continued absences of pupils from public schools to determine if such absences are lawful and known to parents.
GOE: 07.01.06 STRENGTH: L GED: R4 M2 L4 SVP: 7 DLU: 77

168.367-014 RATER, TRAVEL ACCOMMODATIONS (profess. & kin.)
Inspects and evaluates travel and tourist accommodations in order to rate facilities to be listed in guidebook produced by employing organization, such as automobile club, tourism promoters, or travel guide publishers: Travels to and inspects travel accommodations and tourist facilities, such as hotels, motels, restaurants, campgrounds, vacation resorts, and other similar year-round or seasonal recreational establishments in order to observe conditions and gather data to be used in determining ratings. Rates or re-rates establishment according to predetermined standards concerning quantity and quality of such factors as convenience of location, variety of facilities available, degree of cleanliness maintained, efficiency of services offered, range of rates charged, and other matters

of concern to travelers. Reports findings to employer by filling out forms containing ratings and reasons for conclusions and judgments. May sell to establishments concerned advertising space in publication (such as dining guide, tourist magazine, or recreational-area catalogs) in which ratings are to appear.
GOE: 11.10.05 STRENGTH: L GED: R3 M3 L3 SVP: 6 DLU: 77

168.367-018 CODE INSPECTOR (government ser.)
Inspects existing residential buildings and dwelling units, visually, to determine compliance with city ordinance standards and explains ordinance requirements to concerned personnel: Obtains permission from owners and tenants to enter dwellings. Visually examines all areas to determine compliance with ordinance standards for heating, lighting, ventilating, and plumbing installations. Measures dwelling units and rooms to determine compliance with ordinance space requirements, using tape measure. Inspects premises for overall cleanliness, adequate disposal of garbage and rubbish, and for signs of vermin infestation. Prepares forms and letters advising property owners and tenants of possible violations and time allowed for correcting deficiencies. Consults file of violation reports and revisits dwellings at periodic intervals to verify correction of violations by property owners and tenants. Explains requirements of housing standards ordinance to property owners, building contractors, and other interested parties.
GOE: 05.03.06 STRENGTH: L GED: R3 M2 L3 SVP: 5 DLU: 86

168.367-022 PERSONNEL QUALITY ASSURANCE AUDITOR (electron. comp.)
Audits work activities of processing production workers to verify conformance of activities to quality assurance standards, applying knowledge of job performance requirements, equipment operation standards, and product processing specifications: Obtains quality assurance personnel check list. Observes and asks worker questions pertaining to job functions. Reads processing information, such as worker logs, product processing sheets, and specification sheets, to verify that records adhere to quality assurance specifications. Observes worker using equipment to verify that equipment is being operated and maintained according to quality assurance standards, applying knowledge of equipment operation. Writes audit information on quality assurance form and keys information into computer, using keyboard. Submits audit report to supervisory personnel.
GOE: 11.10.05 STRENGTH: L GED: R3 M2 L3 SVP: 6 DLU: 86

168.387-010 OPENER-VERIFIER-PACKER, CUSTOMS (government ser.)
Unpacks, verifies, and repacks mail shipments of imported merchandise to assure compliance with federal revenue laws and U.S. Customs Service Regulations: Determines containers to open, according to nature of merchandise, country of origin, and shipper. Unpacks containers and visually verifies identity and quantity of commodities against declaration or invoice. Weighs and measures commodities. May write descriptive verification as compared with declaration or invoice. Lists damaged goods. Records evidence of tampering, pilfering, shortages, excesses, or other unusual condition of merchandise. Inspects goods for violations of marking, trademark, or copyright regulations. Inspects containers for contraband and smuggled goods. May disassemble and drill into merchandise and containers suspected of containing contraband or undeclared items, using handtools and electric power drill. Records date, name, and address of importer or sender on mail entry form. Unpacks and lays out representative samples of merchandise for examination by CUSTOMS IMPORT SPECIALIST (government ser.). Repacks merchandise after examination, for release to postal service and subsequent delivery. Attaches envelope containing completed mail entry form to container. Hand stamps container to indicate examination completed and need to collect duty. May testify during court appeals by importers.
GOE: 05.09.03 STRENGTH: H GED: R3 M3 L3 SVP: 5 DLU: 77

169 OCCUPATIONS IN ADMINISTRATIVE SPECIALIZATIONS, N.E.C.

This group includes occupations, not elsewhere classified, concerned with administrative specializations.

169.107-010 ARBITRATOR (profess. & kin.)
Arbitrates disputes between labor and management to bind both to specific terms and conditions of labor contract: Conducts hearing to evaluate contentions of parties regarding disputed contract provisions. Analyzes information obtained, using knowledge of facts in issue and industry practices. Renders binding decision to settle dispute, protect public interests, prevent employee wage loss, and minimize business interruptions. Issues report concerning results of arbitration. May serve exclusively for particular case for which selected by parties and be known as Ad Hoc Arbitrator (profess. & kin.). May serve for all disputes concerning specific agreements and be known as Umpire (profess. & kin.); Referee (profess. & kin.).
GOE: 11.04.03 STRENGTH: S GED: R5 M4 L5 SVP: 8 DLU: 77

169.117-010 EXECUTIVE SECRETARY, STATE BOARD OF NURSING (government ser.)
Directs activities of State Board of Nursing: Develops procedures relative to licensure by examination or endorsement, renewal of licenses, certification to other states, and discipline of licensees. Assumes responsibility for keeping board informed of relevant matter to aid in policy-making and decisions. Determines specific needs of program and provides for written plans and statement

of policies. Ascertains number, scope, and responsibility of positions on board, selects staff, and delegates duties. Directs and supervises activities of staff and evaluates performance. Establishes system of record keeping and maintains up-to-date, comprehensive records of board activities and office procedures. Estimates and submits request for budget. Collects, analyzes, and prepares for publication data relating to nursing education and licensure. Initiates and cooperates in research projects. Participates in interpreting nursing laws, board rules and policies, and trends in nursing and nursing education. Issues licenses and recommends revocations and suspensions. Surveys schools of nursing to ensure compliance with legal requirements.
GOE: 11.05.03 STRENGTH: S GED: R5 M5 L5 SVP: 8 DLU: 77

169.117-014　GRANT COORDINATOR (profess. & kin.)
　Develops and coordinates grant-funded programs for agencies, institutions, local government, or units of local government, such as school systems or metropolitan police departments: Reviews literature dealing with funds available through grants from governmental agencies and private foundations to determine feasibility of developing programs to supplement local annual budget allocations. Discusses program requirements and sources of funds available with administrative personnel. Confers with personnel affected by proposed program to develop program goals and objectives, outline how funds are to be used, and explain procedures necessary to obtain funding. Works with fiscal officer in preparing narrative justification for purchase of new equipment and other budgetary expenditures. Submits proposal to officials for approval. Writes grant application, according to format required, and submits application to funding agency or foundation. Meets with representatives of funding sources to work out final details of proposal. Directs and coordinates evaluation and monitoring of grant-funded programs, or writes specifications for evaluation or monitoring of program by outside agency. Assists department personnel in writing periodic reports to comply with grant requirements. Maintains master files on grants. Monitors paperwork connected with grant-funded programs.
GOE: 11.05.02 STRENGTH: S GED: R5 M4 L5 SVP: 8 DLU: 86

169.127-010　CIVIL PREPAREDNESS TRAINING OFFICER (government ser.)
　Instructs paid and volunteer workers in techniques for meeting disaster situations: Conducts classes in emergency techniques, such as first aid, flood protection, firefighting, shelter management, disaster communications and organization, use of radiological monitoring equipment, and post-attack operations. Confers with local government and federal authorities and with representatives of police, fire, sanitation, and public works departments to coordinate training. May direct or participate in preparation of geographic surveys of local areas to aid in formulating emergency survival plans. May specialize in preparing and distributing emergency preparedness information and be designated Civil Preparedness Public Information Officer (government ser.).
GOE: 11.07.02 STRENGTH: L GED: R4 M3 L4 SVP: 6 DLU: 77

169.167-010　ADMINISTRATIVE ASSISTANT (any industry) alternate titles: administrative analyst; administrative officer
　Aids executive in staff capacity by coordinating office services, such as personnel, budget preparation and control, housekeeping, records control, and special management studies: Studies management methods in order to improve workflow, simplify reporting procedures, or implement cost reductions. Analyzes unit operating practices, such as recordkeeping systems, forms control, office layout, suggestion systems, personnel and budgetary requirements, and performance standards to create new systems or revise established procedures. Analyzes jobs to delimit position responsibilities for use in wage and salary adjustments, promotions, and evaluation of workflow. Studies methods of improving work measurements or performance standards. Coordinates collection and preparation of operating reports, such as time-and-attendance records, terminations, new hires, transfers, budget expenditures, and statistical records of performance data. Prepares reports including conclusions and recommendations for solution of administrative problems. Issues and interprets operating policies. Reviews and answers correspondence. May assist in preparation of budget needs and annual reports of organization. May interview job applicants, conduct orientation of new employees, and plan training programs. May direct services, such as maintenance, repair, supplies, mail, and files. May compile, store, and retrieve management data, using computer.
GOE: 11.05.02 STRENGTH: S GED: R5 M3 L5 SVP: 7 DLU: 88

169.167-014　ADMINISTRATIVE SECRETARY (any industry) alternate titles: executive secretary
　Keeps official corporation records and executes administrative policies determined by or in conjunction with other officials: Prepares memorandums outlining and explaining administrative procedures and policies to supervisory workers. Plans conferences. Directs preparation of records, such as notices, minutes, and resolutions for stockholders' and directors' meetings. Directs recording of company stock issues and transfers. Acts as custodian of corporate documents and records. Directs preparation and filing of corporate legal documents with government agencies to conform with statutes. In small organizations, such as trade, civic, or welfare associations, often performs publicity work. Depending on organization, works in line or staff capacity.
GOE: 07.01.02 STRENGTH: S GED: R5 M4 L5 SVP: 8 DLU: 77

169.167-018　CONTACT REPRESENTATIVE (government ser.)
　Provides information and assistance to public on government agency programs and procedures: Explains regulations, agency policies, form completion

procedures, and determinations of agency to advise individuals regarding obtainment of required documents and eligibility requirements for receiving benefits. Analyzes applications and information for benefits, privileges, or relief from obligations, using knowledge of rules, regulations, and precedent decisions to determine qualifications for benefits and privileges or liability for obligations. Investigates errors or delays in processing of applications for benefits and initiates corrective action. May be designated according to title of agency represented.
GOE: 07.01.01 STRENGTH: S GED: R5 M3 L5 SVP: 6 DLU: 79

169.167-022　FIRE ASSISTANT (government ser.) alternate titles: fire-control assistant; fire deputy
　Advises local governments, public, and timber interests on prevention and control of forest fires: Inspects forest areas and standby fire fighting crews in fire prevention and control program. Prepares public-information materials and campaigns on fire prevention techniques. Gives instructions to fire fighting crews in methods of controlling forest fires, considering such factors as terrain, wind conditions, history of rainfall in fire area, and location of population centers. Gives public lectures to campers, youth groups, and hunters to promote responsible use of fire and inflammable materials in forest areas. May direct activities of fire suppression crews. May participate in fighting fires.
GOE: 04.01.01 STRENGTH: L GED: R4 M3 L4 SVP: 6 DLU: 77

169.167-026　LABORATORY ASSISTANT, LIAISON INSPECTION (steel & rel.) alternate titles: laboratory coordinator
　Acts as liaison between manufacturer and private consumer or government agency to expedite testing and inspection of products according to contract specifications: Notifies consumer representative or government inspector of availability of products for testing. Designates tests required according to individual specifications. Reviews laboratory reports for completeness and accuracy and for test characteristics, such as strength, hardness, and quality of products. Promotes good will among plant divisions to facilitate expediting of orders.
GOE: 02.04.01 STRENGTH: L GED: R5 M5 L5 SVP: 7 DLU: 77

169.167-030　MANAGER, DATA PROCESSING (profess. & kin.) alternate titles: director, data processing; director, management information systems
　Directs and coordinates development and production activities of data processing department: Consults with management to determine information requirements of management, scientists, or engineers, determine boundaries and priorities of new projects, and discuss system capacity and equipment acquisitions. Confers with department heads involved with proposed projects to ensure cooperation and further define nature of project. Consults with COMPUTER SYSTEMS HARDWARE ANALYST (profess. & kin.) 033.167-010 to define equipment needs. Reviews project feasibility studies. Establishes work standards. Assigns and schedules work, or delegates work to subordinate managers and supervisors, and reviews work. Interprets policies, purposes, and goals of organization to subordinates. Prepares progress reports to inform management of project status and deviation from goals. Contracts with management specialists, technical personnel, or vendors to solve problems. Directs COMPUTER PROCESSING SCHEDULER (clerical) 221.362-030 to change computer operating schedule to meet department priorities. Reviews reports of computer and peripheral equipment production, malfunctions, and maintenance to ascertain costs and plan department operating changes. Analyzes department workflow and workers' job duties to recommend reorganization or departmental realignment within company. Participates in decisions concerning staffing and promotions within data processing department. Directs training of subordinates. May prepare proposals and solicit sale of systems analysis, programming, and computer services to outside firms. May assist staff to diagnose and solve computer equipment problems. May participate in technical projects, such as writing equipment specifications or developing computer programs for specified applications.
GOE: 11.01.01 STRENGTH: S GED: R5 M4 L5 SVP: 8 DLU: 88

169.167-034　MANAGER, OFFICE (any industry) alternate titles: chief clerk; manager, administrative services
　Coordinates activities of clerical personnel in establishment or organization: Analyses and organizes office operations and procedures, such as typing, bookkeeping, preparation of payrolls, flow of correspondence, filing, requisition of supplies, and other clerical services. Evaluates office production, revises procedures, or devises new forms to improve efficiency of workflow. Establishes uniform correspondence procedures and style practices. Formulates procedures for systematic retention, protection, retrieval, transfer, and disposal of records. Plans office layouts and initiates cost reduction programs. Reviews clerical and personnel records to ensure completeness, accuracy, and timeliness. Prepares activities reports for guidance of management, using computer. Prepares employee ratings and conducts employee benefit and insurance programs, using computer. Coordinates activities of various clerical departments or workers within department. May prepare organizational budget and monthly financial reports. May hire, train, and supervise clerical staff. May compile, store, and retrieve managerial data, using computer.
GOE: 07.01.02 STRENGTH: S GED: R4 M3 L4 SVP: 7 DLU: 88

169.167-038　ORDER DEPARTMENT SUPERVISOR (any industry)
　Coordinates activities of personnel of order-writing department: Plans and initiates order-writing procedures, using knowledge of company products, pricing methods, and discount classifications. Directs establishment and mainte-

nance of customer order records, such as discount classifications, cost basis, special routing, and transportation information. Supervises workers writing master orders used by production, shipping, invoicing, advertising, cost, and estimating departments.
GOE: 07.05.03 STRENGTH: S GED: R4 M3 L4 SVP: 7 DLU: 86

169.167-042 PARK RANGER (government ser.) alternate titles: ranger

Enforces laws, regulations, and policies in state or national park: Registers vehicles and visitors, collects fees, and issues parking and use permits. Provides information pertaining to park use, safety requirements, and points of interest. Directs traffic, investigates accidents, and patrols area to prevent fires, vandalism, and theft. Cautions, evicts, or apprehends violators of laws and regulations. Directs or participates in first aid and rescue activities. May supervise workers engaged in construction and maintenance of park facilities and enforces standards of cleanliness and sanitation. May compile specified park-use statistics, keep records, and prepare reports of area activities. May train and supervise park workers and concession attendants. May specialize in snow safety and avalanche control and be designated Snow Ranger (government ser.).
GOE: 04.02.03 STRENGTH: L GED: R4 M3 L4 SVP: 7 DLU: 82

169.167-046 PUBLIC HEALTH REGISTRAR (government ser.)

Records and maintains birth and death certificates and communicable disease reports, and prepares statistical data and medical reports for city or county public health department: Registers birth, death, and communicable disease statistics from information supplied by physicians, hospital personnel, funeral directors, and representatives from other agencies. Analyzes cause of death statements and communicable disease reports for compliance with laws and local regulations, consistency, and completeness. Contacts information sources concerning vital statistics and disease reports to resolve discrepancies and obtain additional information. Makes certified copies of documents and issues permits to remove and bury bodies. Prepares reports, such as epidemiological case history and morbidity report and keeps file of communicable disease cases. Refers tuberculosis cases and contacts to appropriate health agencies for consultation, treatment referral, and assistance in disease control. Obtains medical, statistical, and sociological data for use by workers in various public health departments. Assists in maintaining statistical data file and medical information reference library.
GOE: 07.04.03 STRENGTH: L GED: R4 M3 L4 SVP: 7 DLU: 77

169.167-050 SPECIAL AGENT, GROUP INSURANCE (insurance)

Explains group insurance programs to promote sale of insurance to prospective clients and establishes bookkeeping system for insurance plan: Explains types of insurance coverage, such as health, accident, life, or liability, and accounting documentation required by company, as requested by SALES AGENT, INSURANCE (insurance). Plans and oversees incorporation of insurance program into a company's bookkeeping system. Establishes client's method of payment. May install accounting systems and resolve system problems.
GOE: 08.01.02 STRENGTH: S GED: R5 M3 L5 SVP: 7 DLU: 77

169.167-054 TOOLING COORDINATOR, PRODUCTION ENGINEERING (aircraft mfg.) alternate titles: tool procurement coordinator

Coordinates activities of engineering, tool design, purchasing, and other departments, to facilitate production or procurement of tooling: Evaluates tooling orders received from production engineering department to determine whether tooling should be manufactured in-house or procured from outside vendor. Examines blueprints to determine tool requirements and special materials or items to be ordered. Calculates and records tool requirement data on tooling order, and routes order to tool design or purchasing department. Prepares requisitions for items to be purchased. Contacts tool room, purchasing, receiving, or other personnel to follow up on procurement or production activities and to expedite movement of tools between departments or vendors. Maintains manual or computerized records of tooling procurement, status, and disposition information. Examines tools and tool records to determine disposition of tools. Processes requests for tool repair. May transport tooling between departments or vendors to expedite handling.
GOE: 05.02.03 STRENGTH: L GED: R4 M4 L4 SVP: 7 DLU: 88

169.167-062 COORDINATOR, SKILL-TRAINING PROGRAM (government ser.)

Plans and arranges for cooperation with and participation in skill training program by private industry, agencies, and concerned individuals: Organizes and coordinates recruiting, training, and placement of participants. Contacts various service agencies on behalf of trainees with social problems and refers trainees to appropriate agencies to ensure trainees receive maximum available assistance. Prepares periodic reports to monitor and evaluate progress of program.
GOE: 07.01.02 STRENGTH: S GED: R5 M4 L4 SVP: 6 DLU: 86

169.167-066 LEGISLATIVE ASSISTANT (government ser.)

Assists legislator in preparation of proposed legislation: Conducts research into subject of proposed legislation and develops preliminary draft of bill. Analyzes pending legislation and suggests to legislator action to be taken. Briefs legislator on policy issues. Attends committee meetings and prepares reports of proceedings. Speaks with lobbyists, constituents, and members of press to gather and provide information on behalf of legislator. Analyzes voting records of other legislators and political activity in legislator home district to derive data for legislator consideration. Maintains liaison with government agencies af-

fected by proposed or pending legislation. Assists in campaign activities and drafts speeches for legislator.
GOE: 11.05.03 STRENGTH: S GED: R5 M3 L5 SVP: 7 DLU: 86

169.167-070 DIRECTOR, EDUCATIONAL PROGRAMMING (radio-tv broad.)

Plans, develops, and administers programs to promote educational uses of television programs and auxiliary services of public broadcasting station: Reviews past and current educational and instructional programs produced by station and others to determine improvements needed in production and presentation of programs and auxiliary services, such as teaching guides and workshops. Analyzes data to determine prospective users, audiences, and potential funding sources. Confers with education officials and administrators to develop programs and services consistent with mandated curriculum requirements. Plans, initiates, and administers, through subordinates, preparation of written proposals and implementation of special educational projects, such as instructional programs for in-school and home-viewing courses. Confers with representatives of international educational and broadcasting agencies to ascertain availability of programs from foreign sources and to promote use of station's programs and services by foreign stations and schools. Directs printing, publishing, and dissemination of educational and promotional materials, such as newsletters, lesson plans, and study guides. May prepare budget for contracting programs and services to educational institutions.
GOE: 11.05.02 STRENGTH: S GED: R5 M4 L5 SVP: 7 DLU: 86

169.167-074 PREVENTIVE MAINTENANCE COORDINATOR (any industry)

Plans and coordinates schedule of preventive maintenance for equipment, machinery, tools, or buildings: Reviews manufacturers' service manuals, own establishment's usage schedules, and records of maintenance problems to determine optimum frequency of preventive maintenance. Studies production and operation schedules and confers with other staff and with maintenance supervisors to determine when planned maintenance will least interfere with operation of establishment. Estimates costs of personnel, parts, and supplies to be used during scheduled maintenance. Maintains records of planned and completed maintenance. May develop and coordinate plans for reconstruction or installation of new equipment, machinery, or buildings. May direct and coordinate activities of subordinate staff, such as MAINTENANCE DATA ANALYST (military ser.) 221.367-038. May direct and coordinate activities of maintenance workers.
GOE: 05.01.06 STRENGTH: L GED: R4 M3 L3 SVP: 7 DLU: 86

169.167-078 UTILIZATION COORDINATOR (radio-tv broad.)

Coordinates subscriber utilization of instructional television programming: Communicates with administrators, teaching staff, audiovisual specialists, and other personnel to assist subscribers in incorporating programs and related materials into planned curricula. Conducts surveys to determine problems in use of programs and materials and develops workshops and other services to address identified needs. Confers with prospective users of programs to elicit interest in subscribing to services. Participates with other station personnel in developing advertising and promotional material. Oversees activities of workers engaged in processing subscriber accounts.
GOE: 11.05.02 STRENGTH: S GED: R5 M3 L5 SVP: 7 DLU: 86

169.167-082 MANAGER, COMPUTER OPERATIONS (profess. & kin.)

Directs and coordinates activities of workers engaged in computer operations: Plans and develops policies and procedures for carrying out computer operations. Meets with subordinate supervisors to discuss progress of work, resolve problems, and ensure that standards for quality and quantity of work are met. Adjusts hours of work, priorities, and staff assignments to ensure efficient operation, based on work load. Reviews daily logs and reports to detect recurring slowdowns or errors, using computer terminal. Consults with software and hardware vendors and other establishment workers to solve problems impeding computer processing. Meets with users to determine quality of service and identify needs. Meets with data processing managers to determine impact of proposed changes in hardware or software on computer operations and service to users. Evaluates new software and hardware to determine usefulness and compatibility with existing software and hardware. Evaluates proposed data processing projects to assess adequacy of existing hardware, and recommends purchase of equipment. Develops budget and monitors expenditures. May direct and coordinate activities of tape library and supervise TAPE LIBRARIAN (clerical) 206.367-018.
GOE: 11.01.01 STRENGTH: S GED: R5 M4 L4 SVP: 8 DLU: 90

169.167-086 MANAGER, CREDIT AND COLLECTION (any industry)

Directs and coordinates activities of workers engaged in conducting credit investigations and collecting delinquent accounts of customers: Assigns workers, directly or through subordinate supervisors, responsibility for investigating and verifying financial status and reputation of prospective customers applying for credit, preparing documents to substantiate findings, and recommending rejection or approval of applications. Establishes credit limitations on customer account. Assigns responsibility for investigation of fraud cases and possible legal action and collection for worthless checks and delinquent bills. Reviews collection reports to ascertain status of collections-and-balances outstanding and to evaluate effectiveness of current collection policies and procedures. Audits delinquent accounts considered to be uncollectible to ensure maximum efforts have been taken before assigning bad-debt status to account. Coordinates with others, including personnel in company branches and credit card companies, to

exchange information and update controls. May submit delinquent accounts to attorney or outside agency for collection. May compile and analyze statistical data on fraudulent use of credit cards to develop procedures designed to deter or prevent use of cards. May specialize in credit and collection activities for credit cards and be designated Manager, Credit Card Operations (any industry).
GOE: 11.06.03 STRENGTH: S GED: R4 M4 L4 SVP: 8 DLU: 88

169.171-010 GAMEKEEPER (agriculture)
Breeds, raises, and protects game animals and birds on state game farm or private game preserves: Cares for breeding stocks in pens. Selects pairs for mating on basis of size, color, vigor, or desired characteristics. Gathers eggs for artificial incubation, and transfers young to rearing pens. Mixes feed according to formulas and fills feeding stations. Cleans and fills water containers. Sets and maintains traps for predatory and noxious animals and birds that may prey upon or carry disease to charges. Drives birds into portable coops to prepare them for transportation to release area. May liberate birds and animals in designated areas.
GOE: 03.01.02 STRENGTH: H GED: R4 M3 L3 SVP: 6 DLU: 77

169.207-010 CONCILIATOR (profess. & kin.) alternate titles: mediator
Mediates and conciliates disputes over negotiations of labor agreements or other labor relations disputes: Promotes use of fact-finding and advisory services to prevent labor disputes and to maintain sound labor relationships. Promotes use of mediation and conciliation services to resolve labor disputes. Advises and counsels parties to solve labor problems. Investigates and mediates labor disputes upon request of any bona fide party, using knowledge of labor law, industry practices, and social policies involved in labor relations. Urges expeditious settlement of negotiations to prevent employee wage loss, to minimize business interruptions, and to achieve labor-management peace. Interrogates parties and clarifies problems to focus discussion on crucial points of disagreement. Assists parties to compromise and settle deadlocked negotiations. Prepares reports of decisions reached or outcome of negotiations. May assist in arranging arbitration. May conduct representation elections according to written consent agreement of concerned parties. May oversee balloting procedures to assist in ratification of labor agreements.
GOE: 11.04.03 STRENGTH: S GED: R5 M4 L5 SVP: 8 DLU: 77

169.262-010 CASEWORKER (government ser.)
Performs research into laws of United States and procedures of federal agencies and prepares correspondence in office of Member of Congress to resolve problems or complaints of constituents: Confers with individuals who have requested assistance to determine nature and extent of problems. Analyzes U.S. Code to become familiar with laws relating to specific complaints of constituents. Researches procedures and systems of governmental agencies and contacts representatives of federal agencies to obtain information on policies. Contacts Congressional Research Service to collect information relating to agency policies and laws. Contacts colleges and universities to obtain information relating to constituent problems. Determines action to facilitate resolution of constituent problems. Composes and types letters to Federal agencies and Congressional Committees concerning resolution of problems of constituents. Prepares memoranda to inform Member of Congress of problems which require legislative attention. Confers with personnel assisting Member of Congress to discuss introduction of legislation to solve constituent problems. Calculates social security benefits, veterans' benefits, tax assessments, and other data concerning constituent complaints, using desk calculator.
GOE: 07.01.06 STRENGTH: S GED: R5 M3 L4 SVP: 5 DLU: 86

169.267-010 CLAIMS ADJUDICATOR (government ser.)
Adjudicates claims for benefits offered under governmental social insurance program, such as those dealing with unemployed, retired, or disabled workers, veterans, dependents, or survivors: Reviews and evaluates data on documents and forms, such as claim applications, birth or death certificates, physician's statements, employer's records, vocational evaluation reports, and other similar records. Interviews or corresponds with claimants or agents to elicit information, correct errors or omissions on claim forms, and to investigate questionable data. Authorizes payment of valid claims, or notifies claimant of denied claim and appeal rights. Reevaluates evidence and procures additional information in connection with claims under appeal or in cases requiring investigation of claimant's continuing eligibility for benefits. Prepares written reports of findings. May specialize in one phase of claim program, such as assisting claimant to prepare forms, rating degree of disability, investigating appeals, or answering questions concerning filing requirements and benefits provided. May be designated according to type of benefit-claim adjudicated. May act as consultant to board rating disability.
GOE: 11.12.01 STRENGTH: S GED: R5 M4 L4 SVP: 7 DLU: 77

169.267-014 EXAMINER (government ser.)
Examines and evaluates data to determine persons' or organizations' eligibility for, conformity with, or liability under, government regulated activity or program: Examines data contained in application forms, agency reports, business records, public documents or other records to gather facts, verify correctness, or establish authenticity. Interviews persons, visits establishments, or confers with technical or professional specialists, to obtain information or clarify facts. Analyzes data obtained, utilizing knowledge of administrative policies, regulatory codes, legislative directives, precedent, or other guidelines. Determines eligibility for participation in activity, conformity to program requirements, or liability for damages or financial losses incurred, based on findings.

Prepares correspondence to inform concerned parties of decision and rights to appeal. Prepares reports of examinations, evaluations, and decisions. May be classified according to job function, program involved, or agency concerned.
GOE: 07.01.05 STRENGTH: S GED: R4 M4 L4 SVP: 6 DLU: 77

169.267-018 FINANCIAL-AID COUNSELOR (education)
Interviews students applying for financial aid, such as loans, grants-in-aid, or scholarships, to determine eligibility for assistance in college or university: Confers with individuals and groups to disseminate information and answer questions relating to financial assistance available to students enrolled in college or university. Interviews students to obtain information needed to determine eligibility for aid. Compares data on students' applications, such as proposed budget, family income, or transcript of grades, with eligibility requirements of assistance program. Determines amount of aid, considering such factors as funds available, extent of demand, and needs of students. Authorizes release of funds to students and prepares required records and reports. May assist in selection of candidates for financial awards or aid granted by specific department. May specialize in specific aid program and be designated Loan Counselor (education); Scholarship Counselor (education).
GOE: 07.01.01 STRENGTH: S GED: R4 M4 L4 SVP: 5 DLU: 77

169.267-022 SECRETARY, BOARD-OF-EDUCATION (education)
Evaluates academic records and maintains personnel file on school employees, compiles budget estimates, and prepares reports: Reviews applications of teaching, administrative, and clerical personnel entering school system to determine that educational and experience qualifications meet city, county, and state requirements, and that such information as state certificates and military records are included. Sets up and maintains records for personnel of entire system according to established procedures. Prepares correspondence and answers inquiries regarding employees and other school matters. Compiles reports for various boards of education and other officials. Compiles statistical and other data from questionnaires and surveys requested by local, state, and national organizations. Estimates budget requirements and prepares master payroll for system's schools. Records minutes of board meetings. Studies new regulations and applies them in preparing reports and maintaining records.
GOE: 07.01.02 STRENGTH: S GED: R5 M5 L5 SVP: 7 DLU: 77

169.267-026 SUPERVISOR, SPECIAL SERVICES (education) alternate titles: veterans' coordinator
Provides special informational services to veterans, potential military enlistees, and physically handicapped students of college or university: Advises students regarding eligibility for veterans benefits, ways of fulfilling military obligation, or availability of public assistance. Interprets selective service and veterans' assistance laws to students. Refers handicapped students for counseling regarding vocational choice. Directs workers engaged in processing students' application and certification forms.
GOE: 07.01.01 STRENGTH: S GED: R5 M4 L5 SVP: 6 DLU: 77

169.267-030 PASSPORT-APPLICATION EXAMINER (government ser.)
Approves applications for United States passports and related privileges and services: Reviews information on applications, such as applicant's birthplace and birthplaces of applicant's parents, to determine eligibility according to nationality laws and governmental policies. Examines supporting documents, such as affidavits, records, newspaper files, and Bibles, to evaluate relevance and authenticity of documents. Queries applicants to obtain additional or clarifying data. Forwards approved applications to designated official, and prepares summaries for cases not approved, indicating points of law. Answers questions of individuals concerning passport applications and related services.
GOE: 07.01.05 STRENGTH: L GED: R4 M3 L4 SVP: 5 DLU: 86

169.267-034 RESEARCH ANALYST (insurance)
Evaluates insurance industry developments to update company products and procedures: Reviews industry publications and monitors pending legislation and regulations to determine impact of new developments on company insurance products. Consults with designated company personnel to disseminate information necessitating changes in language or provisions of insurance contracts and assists in preparation of documents or directives needed to implement changes. Corresponds or consults with agents, brokers, and other interested persons to determine feasibility and marketability of new products to meet competition and increase sales. Develops procedures and materials for introduction and administration of new products, and submits package for review by company personnel and regulatory bodies. May recommend lobbying activities to management. May direct or coordinate activities of other workers. May specialize in analyzing developments in group insurance operations and be designated Group-Contract Analyst (insurance).
GOE: 11.05.02 STRENGTH: L GED: R5 M4 L5 SVP: 8 DLU: 86

169.267-038 ESTIMATOR (profess. & kin.) alternate titles: cost estimator; production estimator
Analyzes blueprints, specifications, proposals, and other documentation to prepare time, cost, and labor estimates for products, projects, or services, applying knowledge of specialized methodologies, techniques, principles, or processes: Reviews data to determine material and labor requirements and prepares itemized lists. Computes cost factors and prepares estimates used for management purposes, such as planning, organizing, and scheduling work, preparing bids, selecting vendors or subcontractors, and determining cost effectiveness. Conducts special studies to develop and establish standard hour and related cost data or effect cost reductions. Consults with clients, vendors, or other individ-

uals to discuss and formulate estimates and resolve issues. May specialize according to particular service performed, type of product manufactured, or phase of work involved, such as tool and fixture costs, production costs, construction costs, or material costs.

GOE: 05.03.02 STRENGTH: S GED: R4 M4 L4 SVP: 7 DLU: 88

169.267-042 LETTER-OF-CREDIT DOCUMENT EXAMINER (financial)

Authorizes payment on letters of credit used in international banking: Examines documents, such as bills of lading, certificates of origin, and shipping manifests, for accuracy and completeness and to ensure that conditions of letters of credit are in accordance with establishment policy and international uniform custom and practice. Verifies document computations, using calculator. Talks with customers and recommends acceptable wording for letters of credit. Explains regulatory and legal implications of terms and conditions, including U.S. trade restrictions. Instructs workers in preparing amendments to letters of credit. Contacts foreign banks, suppliers, or other sources to obtain required documents. Authorizes method of payment against letter of credit in accordance with client instructions.

GOE: 11.06.03 STRENGTH: S GED: R5 M4 L4 SVP: 7 DLU: 89

169.267-046 UNDERWRITER (insurance)

Reviews insurance applications to evaluate, classify, and rate individuals and groups for insurance and accepts or rejects applications, following establishment underwriting standards: Examines such documents as application form, inspection report, insurance maps, and medical reports to determine degree of risk from such factors as applicant financial standing, age, occupation, accident experience, and value and condition of property. Reviews company records to determine amount of insurance in force on single risk or group of closely related risks, and evaluates possibility of losses due to catastrophe or excessive insurance. Writes to field representatives, medical personnel, and other insurance or inspection companies to obtain further information, quote rates, or explain company underwriting policies. Declines excessive risks. Authorizes reinsurance of policy when risk is high. Decreases value of policy when risk is substandard to limit company obligation, and specifies applicable endorsements, or applies rating to insure safe and profitable distribution of risks, using rate books, tables, code books, computer records, and other reference materials. Workers typically specialize by type of insurance coverage, such as life, health, property and liability, or multiline insurance; and by individual or group underwriting. Within different types of coverage, workers may further specialize in areas, such as pension, workers' compensation, property, marine, automoblile, homeowner, or fire.

GOE: 11.06.03 STRENGTH: S GED: R5 M4 L5 SVP: 7 DLU: 78

169.284-010 ADMEASURER (government ser.)

Compiles data and prepares certificates of admeasurement to document ships, and determine type of license and safety equipment required, net tonnage, and applicable tolls and wharfage fees: Examines blueprints of ship and takes physical measurements to determine capacity, using rule and tape measure. Computes gross and net tonnage and deductible space of vessel required by laws. Prepares sketches of vessels, using drafting instruments. Writes certificates of admeasurement, listing such details as design, length, depth, and breadth of vessel, and method of propulsion.

GOE: 05.03.02 STRENGTH: L GED: R5 M4 L5 SVP: 7 DLU: 77

169.367-010 EMPLOYMENT-AND-CLAIMS AIDE (government ser.)

Assists applicants completing application forms for job referrals or unemployment compensation claims: Answers questions concerning registration for jobs or application for unemployment insurance benefits. Reviews data on job application to claim forms to ensure completeness. Refers applicants to job opening or interview with EMPLOYMENT INTERVIEWER (profess. & kin.), in accordance with administrative guidelines or office procedures. Schedules unemployment insurance claimants for interview by CLAIMS ADJUDICATOR (government ser.) when question of eligibility arises. Interviews claimants returning at specified intervals to certify claimants for continuing benefits. May assist applicants in filling out forms using knowledge of information required or native language of applicant.

GOE: 07.04.01 STRENGTH: S GED: R3 M3 L3 SVP: 5 DLU: 77

18   MANAGERS AND OFFICIALS, N.E.C.

This division includes managerial occupations which require a knowledge of the management and operations of an organization, rather than a scientific, technical, or administrative specialty. Generally speaking, these are line management occupations in contrast to the staff and specialist occupations included in Division 16. Also includes such occupations as officers and executives of government, corporations, and nonprofit organizations; general managers; general supervisors; and department heads and their assistants in industrial establishments. Many general administrators and managers are former scientific, professional, and administrative specialists. Care must be taken to classify occupations according to duties and requirements rather than an incumbent's education or experience. Occupations in the administration of a scientific, technical, or professional activity must be carefully scrutinized to determine whether they are concerned primarily with technical supervision or with general management or specialized administrative work.

180   AGRICULTURE, FORESTRY, AND FISHING INDUSTRY MANAGERS AND OFFICIALS

This group includes managerial occupations concerned with operation for owners or other entities of all types of farms, ranches, hatcheries, and game preserves, including crop production and care of livestock for commercial use; care of timber tracts and reforestation activities; and commercial fishing, and related managerial services incidental to the industries. Occupations concerned with logging and related services are included under Group 183.

180.117-010 MANAGER, CHRISTMAS-TREE FARM (forestry)

Plans, directs, and coordinates district operations of Christmas tree farm: Plans activities of district according to executive directives, budget, projected sales volume, and other guidelines. Negotiates contracts for lease of private lands for farming, and purchase of wild (uncultivated) trees for harvesting. Issues instructions to supervisors pertaining to variety and density of tree planting, cultural practices to apply, harvesting dates and locations, and shipping schedules. Contracts for trucks to haul trees from cutting areas to sorting yard. Hires workers and coordinates planting and cultivating of seedlings, and pruning, harvesting, grading, and shipping of trees. Directs office activities, such as compilation of production reports, preparation of payroll, and maintenance of office records.

GOE: 03.01.01 STRENGTH: L GED: R5 M3 L4 SVP: 7 DLU: 77

180.161-010 MANAGER, PRODUCTION, SEED CORN (agriculture) alternate titles: manager, regional

Plans and directs development and production of hybrid seed corn for commercial seed companies: Plans and executes experimental field studies to develop and improve varieties of hybrid corn with desired characteristics, such as greater yield, resistance to disease and insects, and adaptability to specific soils and climate. Selects and inbreeds plants until specific inbred line is produced, using various breeding techniques, such as crossbreeding, backcrossing, and outcrossing. Confers with farmers to arrange contracts for raising hybrid corn. Distributes seeds, specifies areas of farm to be planted, directs workers engaged in corn planting to make most effective use of land, and oversees fertilizing, cultivating, detasseling, and harvesting [FIELD SUPERVISOR, SEED PRODUCTION (agriculture)]. Directs, through subordinate supervisors, workers engaged in shelling and grading corn. Examines equipment used to clean and grade shelled corn for proper functioning and plans changes in drying, grading, storage, and shipment of seed corn for greater efficiency and accuracy. Interprets company policies and hires, discharges, transfers, and promotes workers. Records production, farm management practices, parent stock, or other data.

GOE: 03.01.01 STRENGTH: L GED: R5 M4 L4 SVP: 7 DLU: 77

180.161-014 SUPERINTENDENT, HORTICULTURE (museums)

Plans, coordinates, and directs activities concerned with breeding, growing, and displaying ornamental flowers, shrubs, and other plants in botanical garden, arboretum, park, or similar facility: Confers with administrative, technical, and maintenance staff members to plan activities for maintenance of growing stock and production of plants for display on grounds, installation in special exhibits, sale to public, or use in research projects. Discusses plans for renovation or additions to facility with administrative personnel and devises designs for floral exhibits to complement theme of new or renovated sections. Prepares scale drawings of outdoor or greenhouse exhibits for use of gardening staff members. Issues instructions to supervisory personnel in charge of plant growing, greenhouse, and display activities. Inspects greenhouse, hothouses, potting sheds, experimental growing areas, and other areas to determine need for repair and to observe activities of workers. Maintains inventory of propagation and growing equipment and supplies, and orders additional materials as needed. Arranges purchase, sale, or exchange of plants with representatives of similar institutions. Confers with research personnel to discuss development of new strains of plants and to devise methods to exhibit, publicize, or market new products. Represents establishment at civic or professional meetings. Participates in radio or television shows or prepares articles for newspapers to provide horticultural information to public.

GOE: 02.02.02 STRENGTH: L GED: R5 M4 L5 SVP: 8 DLU: 86

180.167-010 ARTIFICIAL-BREEDING DISTRIBUTOR (agriculture)

Manages distributorship concerned with collecting and packaging bull semen and inseminating cows: Hires, trains, and supervises ARTIFICIAL-BREEDING TECHNICIAN (agriculture). Prepares and issues advertising, speaks at farm organization meetings, and judges cattle shows to develop contacts with potential farmer-customers and to promote artificial breeding of cattle. Trains technicians in product knowledge, artificial insemination methods, and sales techniques. Organizes and coordinates sales and service functions and publishes material to motivate technicians and inform them of current breeding developments. Keeps customers' accounts and breeding and herd records for distributorship. Collects accounts due. Orders supplies, equipment, and promotional materials for technicians. May perform breeding services.

GOE: 03.01.02 STRENGTH: L GED: R4 M3 L4 SVP: 7 DLU: 77

180.167-014 FIELD SUPERVISOR, SEED PRODUCTION (agriculture)

Coordinates activities of FARMERS (agriculture) engaged in producing seed stocks for commercial seed companies: Inspects and analyzes soil and water

supplies of farm and studies wind currents, land contours, and windbreaks to plan production areas for effective utilization of land, prevention of cross-pollination, and avoid recurrence of previously planted crops. Distributes seed stock to FARMERS (agriculture) and specifies areas and number of acres to be planted. Gives instructions to workers engaged in cultivation procedures, such as fertilization, tilling, and detasseling. Determines harvesting dates and methods of harvesting. Plans and directs storage and shipment of harvested seed crop to ensure protection of seed life.
GOE: 03.02.01 STRENGTH: L GED: R5 M4 L4 SVP: 6 DLU: 77

180.167-018   GENERAL MANAGER, FARM (agriculture; wholesale tr.) alternate titles: ranch manager
Manages farm concerned with raising, harvesting, packing, and marketing farm products for corporations, cooperatives, and other owners: Analyzes market conditions to determine acreage allocations. Negotiates with bank officials to obtain credit from bank. Purchases farm machinery and equipment and supplies, such as tractors, seed, fertilizer, and chemicals. Hires and discharges personnel. Prepares financial and other management reports. Supervises office personnel engaged in preparing payrolls and keeping records. Visits orchards and fields to inspect and estimate maturity dates of crops and potential crop damage due to harsh weather conditions. Confers with purchasers, and determines when and under what conditions to sell crops, marine life, or forest products. May be designated according to type of crop.
GOE: 03.01.01 STRENGTH: L GED: R5 M4 L4 SVP: 8 DLU: 79

180.167-022   GROUP LEADER (agriculture) alternate titles: crew boss; crew leader; row boss
Coordinates activities of group of FARMWORKERS, GENERAL (agriculture) I engaged in planting, cultivating, and harvesting diversified crops: Recruits members for group. Locates jobs for group and accompanies group on job. May be required to hold state registration certificate. Performs other duties as described under SUPERVISOR (any industry) Master Title.
GOE: 03.01.01 STRENGTH: L GED: R3 M2 L2 SVP: 7 DLU: 77

180.167-026   MANAGER, DAIRY FARM (agriculture)
Manages dairy farm: Plans, develops, and implements policies, procedures, and practices for operation of dairy farm to ensure compliance with company's or owner's standards for farm production, propagation of herd, and regulations of regulatory agencies. Directs and coordinates, through subordinate supervisory personnel, farm activities, such as breeding and rearing livestock, feeding and milking of cows, storage of milk, and sterilizing and maintaining facilities and equipment. Reviews breeding and milk production records to determine bulls and cows that are unproductive and should be sold. Inspects facilities and equipment to ensure compliance with sanitation standards, and to determine maintenance and repair requirements. Authorizes, requisitions, or purchases supplies and equipment, such as feed, disinfective and sanitation chemicals, and replacements for defective equipment. Secures services of VETERINARIAN (medical ser.) for treatment of herd or when cows are calving. Prepares farm activity reports for evaluation by management or owner. May direct and coordinate activities concerned with planting, growing, harvesting, and storage of feed forage crops. May directly supervise dairy workers on small farms.
GOE: 03.01.01 STRENGTH: L GED: R4 M3 L3 SVP: 8 DLU: 77

180.167-030   MANAGER, FISH HATCHERY (fishing & hunt.) alternate titles: fish culturist; superintendent, fish hatchery
Manages public or private fish hatchery, applying knowledge of management and fish culturing techniques: Determines, administers, and executes policies relating to administration, standards of hatchery operations, and maintenance of facilities. Confers with BIOLOGISTS (profess. & kin.) and other fishery personnel to obtain data concerning fish habits; food and environmental requirements; and techniques for collecting, fertilizing, incubating spawn, and treatment of spawn and fry. Oversees trapping and spawning of fish; incubating of eggs; rearing of fry; and movement of fish to lakes, ponds, and streams or commercial tanks. Prepares reports required by state and federal laws. Prepares budget reports, and receives, accounts for, and dispenses funds. May approve employment and discharge of employees, sign payrolls, and perform similar personnel duties. May manage hatchery concerned with culturing shellfish and other marine life and be designated Manager, Marine Life Hatchery (fishing & hunt.); Manager, Shellfish Hatchery (fishing & hunt.).
GOE: 03.01.02 STRENGTH: L GED: R5 M3 L4 SVP: 7 DLU: 77

180.167-034   MANAGER, GAME BREEDING FARM (agriculture)
Directs and coordinates activities concerned with operation of private or state game breeding farm: Consults with professional personnel and reviews technical publications and other literature to obtain data on breeding, rearing, habits, diets, and diseases and treatment, of various species of game birds and animals. Evaluates data in order to plan game breeding and rearing activities. Plans, formulates, and implements policies, methods, and procedures required to attain game farm objectives. Directs and coordinates farm activities, such as incubation and hatching of game bird eggs and rearing of birds; selection, pairing, and rearing of game animals; treatment of diseased or ill game birds and animals; and repair and maintenance of farm facilities. Inspects facilities and equipment for needed repairs or maintenance. Examines game for sign of illness or disease and notifies designated personnel of actions to be taken. May contract with state agencies or private game preserves to provide establishments with birds or animals. May contract with food establishments to furnish game birds and game animal meat. Must be licensed as breeder by state department

of fish and game. May be designated according to type of game bred as Manager, Game-Animal Farm (agriculture); Manager, Game-Bird Farm (agriculture).
GOE: 03.01.02 STRENGTH: L GED: R5 M3 L4 SVP: 7 DLU: 77

180.167-038   MANAGER, GAME PRESERVE (agriculture)
Directs and coordinates activities concerned with operation of state or private game preserve: Determines nature of habitat required for propagation and subsistence of species of game animals or birds on preserve, utilizing knowledge of habits and natural propagation of animals and birds. Directs and coordinates activities of workers engaged in constructing and maintaining habitats required, conducting game surveys, protection of game from predatory animals, and maintaining buildings and facilities of preserve. Determines from surveys number of birds or animals that may be hunted or killed in order to eliminate imbalances resulting from natural propagation of game and limitations imposed by area habitat. Posts signs restricting areas where game may be hunted and enforces fish and game laws. Prepares reports required by county, state, or federal government regulatory agencies. May breed, rear, and liberate game on preserve. May contract with breeding personnel for stocking purposes and liberate game on preserve. May arrange contracts for movie studios to film on preserve or for sale of game to zoos. May present lectures on objectives, policies, and practices of state fish and game department to inform and aquaint civic or other interested groups on wildlife and preserve programs.
GOE: 03.01.01 STRENGTH: L GED: R5 M4 L4 SVP: 8 DLU: 77

180.167-042   MANAGER, NURSERY (agriculture; retail trade; wholesale tr.)
Manages nursery to grow horticultural plants, such as trees, shrubs, flowers, ornamental plants, or vegetables for sale to trade or retail customers: Determines type and quantity of horticultural plants to be grown, considering such factors as whether plants will be grown under controlled conditions in hothouse or greenhouse or under natural weather conditions in field, and market demand or conditions, utilizing knowledge of plant germination, growing habits of plants, soil conditions, plant nutrients, and disease control requirements. Selects and purchases seed, plant nutrients, and disease control chemicals according to type of horticultural plants and conditions under which plants will be grown. Tours work areas to observe quality and quantity of work being done, to inspect crops and to evaluate horticultural conditions, such as plant disease and soil conditions. Directs and coordinates, through subordinate supervisory personnel, activities of workers engaged in planting of seed, raising, feeding, and controlling growth and disease of plants, and transplanting, potting, or cutting plants for marketing. Coordinates clerical, record keeping, accounting, and marketing activities. May purchase nursery stock for resale and sell gardening accessories, such as sprays, garden implements, and plant nutrients and be known as Manager, Retail Nursery (agriculture; retail trade). May grow horticultural plants under controlled conditions hydroponically and be known as Manager, Hydroponics Nursery (agriculture).
GOE: 03.01.03 STRENGTH: L GED: R5 M4 L5 SVP: 8 DLU: 81

180.167-046   MANAGER, POULTRY HATCHERY (agriculture)
Manages poultry hatchery: Plans, develops, and implements policies and practices for operation of hatchery to ensure attainment of goals and profitable operation. Arranges with farmers to supply eggs or obtains eggs from company owned flocks. Directs and coordinates, through subordinate supervisory personnel, hatchery activities, such as hatching of eggs, sorting, vaccinating and shipping of chicks, and maintenance of facilities and equipment. Prepares hatching schedules for variety of chicks considering such factors as customer orders, market forecasts, and hatchery facilities and equipment. Arranges for sale of chicks to farmers or commercial growers. Interprets hatchery records and genetic data on chicks and advises customers regarding breeding, brooding, feeding, and sanitation practices to follow for various species of poultry. Arranges for purchases of equipment and supplies, such as brooders, incubators, feeds, and medicines. Prepares reports on hatchery activities, such as chick production and sales and reports required by regulatory bodies. May be designated by species of poultry hatched as Manager, Chicken Hatchery (agriculture); Manager, Duck Hatchery (agriculture); Manager, Turkey Hatchery (agriculture).
GOE: 03.01.01 STRENGTH: L GED: R4 M3 L3 SVP: 7 DLU: 77

180.167-050   MIGRANT LEADER (agriculture) alternate titles: crew leader; farm-crew leader
Contracts seasonal farm employment of MIGRANT WORKERS (agriculture): Consults employment agencies to locate work and confers with FARMERS (agriculture) to obtain suitable contracts for crew. Recruits and organizes crew and furnishes transportation to work site. Schedules en-route rest stops that afford shelters, benches or beds, cooking facilities, fuel and water, and adequate toilet and sanitary provisions. Confers with employer and community officials at site of employment to ensure availability of living quarters for families and single individuals, educational and recreational facilities, medical care, and day care for children. Supplies farm implements and machinery to crew and directs them in methods of cultivation, harvesting, and packaging of crop. Prepares payroll and production records. May provide initial financing of trips and advance funds to workers during idle periods. May be required to hold state registration certificate. Performs other duties as described under SUPERVISOR (any industry) Master Title.
GOE: 03.01.01 STRENGTH: L GED: R3 M2 L2 SVP: 7 DLU: 77

180.167-054   SUPERINTENDENT (agriculture; can. & preserv.)
Coordinates packinghouse activities with harvesting of crops: Inspects farms to ascertain quantity of crops to be processed by packinghouse. Advises grow-

ers of best time for harvesting crops, considering such factors as maturity of and demand for products. Informs packinghouse supervisor and sales agents of crops to be processed to plan packinghouse activities and sales campaigns. Oversees packinghouse activities and assigns duties to subordinate supervisors. Reports needed packinghouse repairs and replacements to superiors. May hire and discharge packinghouse employees.
GOE: 03.01.01 STRENGTH: L GED: R5 M4 L4 SVP: 7 DLU: 77

180.167-058 SUPERINTENDENT, PRODUCTION (agriculture) alternate titles: grove superintendent; manager, production
Directs and coordinates activities of workers engaged in laying out of new citrus groves and maintenance of mature groves, owned by packinghouses or other absentee companies. Analyzes soil to determine type and quantity of plant food required for maximum production. Directs amount and kind of insecticides and fungicides to be used and method of application. Keeps company officials informed of condition of groves, quantity of crops estimated for harvesting, and other factors affecting production of citrus fruits. May contract to maintain groves for independent owners. May purchase supplies for grove care.
GOE: 03.01.01 STRENGTH: L GED: R4 M3 L3 SVP: 7 DLU: 77

180.167-062 MANAGER, AERIAL PLANTING AND CULTIVATION (agriculture)
Manages operations of aerial seed sowing and crop dusting establishment: Negotiates contracts with farm personnel to sow seeds of specified varieties or to spray or dust fields or crops with specified agricultural chemicals. Confers with AIRPLANE PILOT (agriculture) 196.263-010 to determine materials and conditions required to meet terms of contract and schedules flights according to factors, such as client requests, weather conditions, aircraft availability, and legal and safety considerations. Monitors AIRPLANE-PILOT HELPER (agriculture) 409.667-010 mixing chemicals, loading chemicals and seeds into hopper of aircraft, and indicating flight passes to pilot from ground to ensure efficient and safe operations. Purchases seeds and chemicals from suppliers. Oversees repair and maintenance of aircraft and contracts for repair and maintenance of hangars, runway, and related company facilities. Maintains records for billing and payroll purposes. Initiates personnel actions, such as hiring, firing, and disciplining workers.
GOE: 11.11.03 STRENGTH: S GED: R4 M4 L4 SVP: 7 DLU: 86

180.167-066 MANAGER, ORCHARD (agriculture)
Manages orchards: Directs and coordinates, through subordinate supervisory personnel, orchard activities, such as orchard development, irrigation, chemical application, and harvesting to ensure that company production goals are met. Evaluates oral and written reports and observes operations to monitor progress of work and to detect and resolve problems. Determines and authorizes alternative procedures to accommodate variables, such as weather conditions, water supply, stage of crop or tree development, and new legislation. Coordinates orchard department activities with those of engineering, equipment maintenance, packing house, and other related departments. Analyzes financial statements and makes budget proposals. May initiate personnel actions, interpret company policy, and enforce safety regulations.
GOE: 03.01.01 STRENGTH: L GED: R5 M4 L5 SVP: 8 DLU: 86

181 MINING INDUSTRY MANAGERS AND OFFICIALS

This group includes managerial occupations concerned with exploration and development of mineral properties; extracting minerals, such as coal and ores, liquid petroleum, and gases; quarrying, well operation, and mining.

181.117-010 MANAGER, BULK PLANT (petrol. refin.; retail trade) alternate titles: field operating superintendent; terminal superintendent
Manages plant in which gasoline, lubricants, and petroleum fuels are stored and distributed in bulk lots, formulating policies in regard to storage, distribution, and other operating policies: Determines type and quantities of products according to consumer demand. Contacts refineries and petroleum canning plants to schedule shipment of products. Establishes operating procedures for incoming shipments, indicating storage tanks and warehouse facilities to be used. Formulates policies for distribution and sale of products to wholesale and retail outlets and consumers.
GOE: 05.02.07 STRENGTH: L GED: R5 M4 L4 SVP: 8 DLU: 77

181.117-014 MINE SUPERINTENDENT (mine & quarry) alternate titles: superintendent, colliery; superintendent, quarry
Plans and coordinates activities of personnel engaged in extracting minerals, such as coal, ore, or rock, from underground or surface mines, pits, or quarries: Reviews data, such as maps, survey reports, and geological records, and confers with engineering, maintenance, and supervisory personnel to plan and direct mine development. Calculates mining or quarrying operational costs, estimates potential income, and instructs PIT SUPERVISOR (mine & quarry) 939.137-014 to abandon or open mine sections, pits, or other working areas. Studies maps and blueprints to determine location for haulageways, access roads, ventilation shafts, rail tracks, and conveyor systems. Studies land contours and rock formations, and specifies locations to install pillars, timbers, and roof bolts, and use of equipment for cutting, drilling, blasting and loading minerals. Reads mining laws and safety regulations, and issues directives to workers to ensure adherence to applicable rules and regulations. Reviews and consolidates

records, such as ore grade, air quality, safety reports, and production records. Tours and inspects mine to detect and resolve production, equipment maintenance, safety, atmospheric, and personnel problems. Negotiates with workers, union personnel, and other parties to settle grievances.
GOE: 05.02.05 STRENGTH: L GED: R5 M4 L4 SVP: 8 DLU: 80

181.167-010 MANAGER, FIELD PARTY, GEOPHYSICAL PROSPECTING (petrol. & gas) alternate titles: field-party manager
Directs activities in petroleum company or geophysical exploration service concerned with providing transportation, supplies, housing, and other requirements for field party prospecting for petroleum reserves: Purchases and maintains flow of supplies to party. Arranges for housing and other living facilities. Discharges financial obligations. Arranges for and directs repair of automotive and drilling equipment.
GOE: 11.11.04 STRENGTH: L GED: R4 M4 L4 SVP: 6 DLU: 77

181.167-014 SUPERINTENDENT, DRILLING AND PRODUCTION (petrol. & gas) alternate titles: district superintendent; division superintendent
Directs activities concerned with exploratory drilling, and drilling oil wells and producing oil and gas from wells within one or more oil fields: Plans erection of drilling rigs, and installation and maintenance of equipment, such as pumping units and compressor stations. Directs technical processes, such as treatment of oil and gas to reduce moisture and sediment content, mud analysis, well logging, and formation testing. Determines procedures to resolve drilling problems, such as nonvertical bore holes and broken drilling tools. Formulates methods to control production of wells in accordance with proration regulations. Schedules dismantling and storing derricks and drilling equipment, cleaning wells, and servicing well equipment. Analyzes production reports, initiates personnel actions, and revises drilling and production procedures to control operating costs and production efficiency of oil field. Directs petroleum exploration parties engaged in drilling for samples (cores) of subsurface stratigraphy and in seismic prospecting. May be designated according to specialty as Superintendent, Oil-Field Drilling (petrol. & gas); Superintendent, Production (petrol. & gas).
GOE: 05.02.01 STRENGTH: L GED: R5 M5 L4 SVP: 8 DLU: 77

181.167-018 SUPERVISOR, MINE (mine & quarry) alternate titles: supervisor, general
Supervises and coordinates activities of personnel, such as PIT SUPERVISOR (mine & quarry); SECTION SUPERVISOR (mine & quarry) in one or more underground or surface mines, pits, or quarries: Directs opening of new surface cuts or pits or underground rooms and passageways, or construction and installation of equipment as designated by MINE SUPERINTENDENT (mine & quarry). Coordinates activities with those of SAFETY ENGINEER, MINES (mine & quarry) and reports safety violations. Inspects mines and instructs supervisors to take necessary measures to improve production and working conditions.
GOE: 05.02.05 STRENGTH: L GED: R4 M3 L3 SVP: 8 DLU: 77

182 CONSTRUCTION INDUSTRY MANAGERS AND OFFICIALS

This group includes managerial and contractual occupations concerned with construction of dwellings, office buildings, stores, farm buildings, bridges, roads, and similar structures; plumbing, painting, electrical, carpentry, site preparation, and landscaping work.

182.167-010 CONTRACTOR (construction)
Contracts to perform specified construction work in accordance with architect's plans, blueprints, codes, and other specifications: Estimates costs of materials, labor, and use of equipment required to fulfill provisions of contract and prepares bids. Confers with clients to negotiate terms of contract. Subcontracts specialized craft work, such as electrical, structural steel, concrete, and plumbing. Purchases material for construction. Supervises workers directly or through subordinate supervisors. May be designated according to specialty license or scope of principal activities as Contractor, General Engineering (construction); Contractor, General Building (construction).
GOE: 11.12.04 STRENGTH: L GED: R4 M4 L4 SVP: 7 DLU: 77

182.167-014 LANDSCAPE CONTRACTOR (construction)
Contracts to landscape grounds of houses, industrial plants, other buildings, or areas around highways: Confers with prospective client, studies landscape designs or drawings, and bills of materials to ascertain scope of landscaping work required, such as installation of lighting or sprinkler systems, erection of fences, concrete work, and types of trees, shrubs, or ornamental plants specified. Inspects grounds or area to determine equipment requirements for grading, tilling, or replacing top soil, and labor requirements to install sprinkler or lighting system, build fences, or perform concreting and planting work. Calculates labor, equipment, material, and overhead costs to determine minimum estimate or bid which will provide for margin of profit. Prepares and submits estimate for client or bid to industrial concern or governmental agency. Prepares contract for client to sign or signs contract if successful bidder. Plans landscaping functions and sequences of work at various sites to obtain optimum utilization of work force and equipment. Directs and coordinates, through subordinate supervisory personnel, activities of workers engaged in performing landscaping func-

tions in contractual agreement. Purchases and ensures that materials are on-site as needed. Inspects work at sites for compliance with terms and specifications of contract. May personally supervise workers. May participate in performing landscaping functions. May be required to possess state license as landscape contractor. May subcontract electrical installation or concrete work if not equipped to provide those services.
GOE: 03.01.03 STRENGTH: L GED: R4 M4 L4 SVP: 8 DLU: 77

182.167-018 RAILROAD-CONSTRUCTION DIRECTOR (r.r. trans.)
Plans and coordinates activities of workers engaged in constructing, installing, inspecting, and maintaining railroad track and rights-of-way within assigned district of railroad: Plans work assignments and schedules. Requisitions supplies and materials to complete construction projects. Dispatches workers and equipment to scenes of accidents and impassable roadbeds or tunnels to repair damage and restore service. Investigates accidents, defective tracks, and obstructions to rights-of-way and issues restorative work orders. Prepares reports stating causes of accidents or concerning condition of tracks and issues recommendations to prevent future accidents, damage, or track deterioration. Recommends construction of new tracks.
GOE: 05.02.02 STRENGTH: L GED: R4 M3 L3 SVP: 8 DLU: 77

182.167-022 SUPERINTENDENT, CONCRETE-MIXING PLANT (construction)
Manages ready-mix concrete plant: Determines work procedure and assigns duties to personnel concerned with mixing and dispatching of concrete and maintenance of plant and equipment. Inspects personnel performance for quality and quantity. Prepares reports on cost of plant operation and maintains personnel records. Hires, trains, and discharges workers. Coordinates activities of sales personnel.
GOE: 05.02.03 STRENGTH: S GED: R4 M4 L4 SVP: 6 DLU: 77

182.167-026 SUPERINTENDENT, CONSTRUCTION (construction) alternate titles: superintendent, job
Directs activities of workers concerned with construction of buildings, dams, highways, pipelines, or other construction projects: Studies specifications to plan procedures for construction on basis of starting and completion times and staffing requirements for each phase of construction, based on knowledge of available tools and equipment and various building methods. Assembles members of organization (supervisory, clerical, engineering, and other workers) at start of project. Orders procurement of tools and materials to be delivered at specified times to conform to work schedules. Confers with and directs supervisory personnel and subcontractors engaged in planning and executing work procedures, interpreting specifications, and coordinating various phases of construction to prevent delays. Confers with supervisory personnel and labor representatives to resolve complaints and grievances within work force. Confers with supervisory and engineering personnel and inspectors and suppliers of tools and materials to resolve construction problems and improve construction methods. Inspects work in progress to ensure that work conforms to specifications and that construction schedules are adhered to. Prepares, or receives from subordinates, reports on progress, materials used and costs, and adjusts work schedules as indicated by reports. May direct workers concerned with major maintenance or reconditioning projects for existing installations. Workers are usually designated according to type of project, work, or construction activity directed.
GOE: 05.02.02 STRENGTH: L GED: R5 M5 L4 SVP: 7 DLU: 80

182.167-030 SUPERINTENDENT, MAINTENANCE OF WAY (r.r. trans.)
Plans and coordinates construction and maintenance of railroad right-of-way: Approves repair and construction projects and assigns work to specified departments. Reviews progress and production charts to ascertain that work is proceeding on schedule. Reviews and authorizes construction and maintenance projects or plans for budget, staff, and equipment requests. Coordinates activities of workers engaged in maintaining right-of-way. Visits sites damaged by wreck, derailment, or natural disaster, and prepares report identifying such factors as amount of damage, repairs to be done, and reasons for derailment or wreck. May consult with public-service agencies to resolve issues of unsafe crossings, bridges, trestles, and installation of additional warning devices. May direct construction and maintenance of buildings and other structures, such as bridges, trestles, and tunnels.
GOE: 05.02.02 STRENGTH: L GED: R5 M4 L4 SVP: 8 DLU: 81

182.167-034 SUPERVISOR, BRIDGES AND BUILDINGS (r.r. trans.)
Directs and coordinates activities of workers engaged in construction and repair of railroad structures, such as bridges, culverts, tunnels, and buildings: Plans work schedules for construction and maintenance projects. Interprets and explains plans for construction of new projects. Ensures that workers are supplied with tools, materials, and equipment for completion of construction or maintenance projects. Ensures that railroad construction specifications are followed. Dispatches workers and equipment to scenes of accidents to repair damaged bridges, tunnels, or right-of-way. Investigates reports of damage or accidents to determine and correct cause, if attributable to faulty construction or maintenance. Inspects right-of-way and structures to detect need for repairs. Prepares reports of hours, equipment, and materials used to complete each construction or maintenance project. May cooperate with engineering department to develop plans for new projects.
GOE: 05.02.02 STRENGTH: L GED: R5 M5 L4 SVP: 7 DLU: 77

182.267-010 CONSTRUCTION INSPECTOR (construction)
Inspects and oversees construction of bridges, buildings, dams, highways, and other types of construction work to ensure that procedures and materials comply with plans and specifications: Measures distances to verify accuracy of dimensions of structural installations and layouts. Verifies levels, alignment, and elevation of installations, using surveyor's level and transit. Observes work in progress to ensure that procedures followed and materials used conform to specifications. Prepares samples of unapproved materials for laboratory testing. Examines workmanship of finished installations for conformity to standard and approves installation. Interprets blueprints and specifications for CONTRACTOR (construction) and discusses deviations from specified construction procedures to ensure compliance with regulations governing construction. Records quantities of materials received or used during specified periods. Maintains daily log of construction and inspection activities and compares progress reports. Computes monthly estimates of work completed and approves payment for contractors. Prepares sketches of construction installations that deviate from blueprints and reports such changes for incorporation on master blueprints. May be designated according to structure or material inspected as Building-Construction Inspector (construction); Ditch Inspector (construction); Highway Inspector (construction); Masonry Inspector (construction); Reinforced-Concrete Inspector (construction); Rod Inspector (construction). May be designated: Pipeline Inspector (construction); Structural-Steel Inspector (construction); Tunnel-Heading Inspector (construction).
GOE: 05.03.06 STRENGTH: L GED: R4 M4 L3 SVP: 6 DLU: 77

183   MANUFACTURING INDUSTRY MANAGERS AND OFFICIALS

This group includes managerial occupations concerned with plants, factories, or mills which use power-driven machines and materials-handling equipment to bring about mechanical or chemical transformation of organic or inorganic substances into products. Includes establishments engaged in assembling component parts of manufactured products where the product is not a structure.

183.117-010 MANAGER, BRANCH (any industry) alternate titles: agent; manager, area; manager, division; manager, plant
Directs production, distribution, and marketing operations for branch plant, or assigned territory of industrial organization: Coordinates production, distribution, warehousing, and sales in accordance with policies, principles, and procedures established by MANAGER, INDUSTRIAL ORGANIZATION (any industry) 189.117-022. Confers with customers and representatives of associated industries to evaluate and promote improved and expanded services in area. Develops plans for efficient use of materials, machines, and employees. Reviews production costs and product quality, and modifies production and inventory control programs to maintain and enhance profitable operation of division. Reviews operations of competing organizations, and plans and directs sales program to develop new markets, using sales aids, advertising, promotional programs, and field services. Directs personnel program. Directs preparation of accounting records. Recommends budgets to management. May be designated according to title of area of jurisdiction as Manager, District (any industry); Manager, Local (any industry); Manager Regional (any industry).
GOE: 11.05.02 STRENGTH: S GED: R5 M4 L4 SVP: 8 DLU: 78

183.117-014 PRODUCTION SUPERINTENDENT (any industry) alternate titles: manager, factory; manager, general; manager, plant; manager, production; plant supervisor; superintendent, factory; superintendent, general; superintendent, mill; superintendent, plant
Directs and coordinates, through subordinate supervisory personnel, activities concerned with production of company product(s), utilizing knowledge of product technology, production methods and procedures, and capabilities of machines and equipment: Confers with management personnel to establish production and quality control standards, develop budget and cost controls, and to obtain data regarding types, quantities, specifications, and delivery dates of products ordered. Plans and directs production activities and establishes production priorities for products in keeping with effective operations and cost factors. Coordinates production activities with procurement, maintenance, and quality control activities to obtain optimum production and utilization of human resources, machines, and equipment. Reviews and analyzes production, quality control, maintenance, and operational reports to determine causes of nonconformity with product specifications, and operating or production problems. Develops and implements operating methods and procedures designed to eliminate operating problems and improve product quality. Revises production schedules and priorities as result of equipment failure or operating problems. Consults with engineering personnel relative to modification of machines and equipment in order to improve production and quality of products. Conducts hearings to resolve or effect settlement of grievances and refers unresolved grievances for management-union negotiations. Supervises subordinates directly in plants having no GENERAL SUPERVISOR (any industry) 183.167-018. PRODUCTION SUPERINTENDENTS (any industry) 183.117-014 are usually designated according to product produced or by type of plant, industry, or activity. May compile, store, and retrieve production data, using computer.
GOE: 05.02.03 STRENGTH: L GED: R5 M4 L4 SVP: 8 DLU: 89

183.161-014 WINE MAKER (beverage) alternate titles: enologist
Directs and coordinates all activities of winery concerned with production of wine: Contracts with growers to provide fruit for processing or cooperates with

HORTICULTURIST (profess. & kin.) of company vineyard in grape production. Examines grape samples to ascertain presence and extent of such factors as sugar and acid content, and ripeness. Orders grapes picked when analysis indicates they are at degree of ripeness desired. Coordinates processes and directs workers concerned with testing and crushing grapes, fermenting juice, fortifying, clarifying, aging, and finishing of wine, including cooling, filtering, and bottling. Blends wines according to formulas or knowledge and experience in wine making. May develop new processes to improve product. When processing champagne, may be designated Champagne Maker (beverage). When processing wine into vinegar, is designated Vinegar Maker (beverage).
GOE: 05.02.03 STRENGTH: L GED: R5 M3 L4 SVP: 8 DLU: 77

183.167-010 BREWING DIRECTOR (beverage) alternate titles: brewing superintendent

Develops new or modifies existing brewing formulas and processing techniques and coordinates, through subordinate supervisors, brewing, fermenting, lagering, and malting departments of a brewery: Devises brewing formulas and processes or works in conjunction with research personnel to develop or modify formulas and processes. Directs and coordinates activities of departments to control processing, according to formula specifications. Confers with technical and administrative personnel to resolve formula and process problems. Reviews and analyzes production orders to determine brewing schedules and human resource requirements. Tests and inspects beer, grain, malt, wort, and yeast, using saccharimeter, hydrometer, and other test equipment and correlates results with quality control analyses. Advises and recommends to management methods and procedures for selecting, installing, and maintaining equipment. Reviews and resolves personnel actions. Prepares and submits production reports. May confer with worker's representatives to resolve grievances.
GOE: 05.02.03 STRENGTH: L GED: R5 M4 L4 SVP: 8 DLU: 77

183.167-014 GENERAL SUPERINTENDENT, MILLING (grain-feed mills) alternate titles: milling superintendent

Directs operations of number of grain and feed mills under one establishment: Estimates operating time of each mill to produce various kinds of grain or feed products, basing estimates on experience, sales records, and anticipated need of stock. Prepares comparative data for each mill and type of product, and issues orders to each MILLER SUPERVISOR (grain-feed mills) concerning his particular mill. Plans new mills, selects milling machinery, and ensures that machinery is installed according to specifications. May supervise workers engaged in changing existing mills to improve production.
GOE: 05.02.03 STRENGTH: L GED: R5 M4 L4 SVP: 8 DLU: 77

183.167-018 GENERAL SUPERVISOR (any industry) alternate titles: department supervisor; division supervisor; process supervisor; production supervisor

Directs and coordinates, through subordinate supervisory personnel, activities of production department(s) in processing materials or manufacturing products in industrial establishment, applying knowledge of production methods, processes, machines and equipment, plant layout, and production capacities of each department: Reviews production orders or schedules to ascertain product data, such as types, quantities, and specifications of products and scheduled delivery dates in order to plan department operations. Plans production operations, establishing priorities and sequences for manufacturing products, utilizing knowledge of production processes and methods, machine and equipment capabilities, and human resource requirements. Prepares operational schedules and coordinates manufacturing activities to ensure production and quality of products meets specifications. Reviews production and operating reports and resolves operational, manufacturing, and maintenance problems to ensure minimum costs and prevent operational delays. Inspects machines and equipment to ensure specific operational performance and optimum utilization. Develops or revises standard operational and working practices and observes workers to ensure compliance with standards. Initiates personnel actions, such as promotions, transfers, discharges, or disciplinary measures. Resolves worker grievances or submits unsettled grievances to PRODUCTION SUPERINTENDENT (any industry) 183.117-014 for action. Workers are usually designated according to department processes, operations, activity, or industry. May compile, store, and retrieve production data, using computer.
GOE: 05.02.03 STRENGTH: L GED: R5 M4 L4 SVP: 8 DLU: 88

183.167-022 GENERAL SUPERVISOR (beverage)

Supervises and coordinates activities of supervisory personnel engaged in brewing operations: Recommends improvements in processing, sanitation, and safety procedures. Reviews and approves requests for minor repairs and maintenance. Assists BREWING DIRECTOR (beverage) in departmental operations.
GOE: 05.02.03 STRENGTH: L GED: R4 M3 L4 SVP: 8 DLU: 77

183.167-026 MANAGER, FOOD PROCESSING PLANT (can. & preserv.)

Directs and coordinates activities of food processing plant: Contacts buyers or growers to arrange for purchasing or harvesting and delivery of agricultural products, seafoods, meat, or other raw materials to plant for processing. Directs, through subordinate supervisory personnel, workers engaged in processing, canning, freezing, storing, and shipping food products. Directs and coordinates activities concerned with dismantling, moving, installing, or repairing of machines and equipment. Approves plant payroll and payments for purchased materials or products. Estimates quantities of foods for processing required and orders foods, materials, supplies, and equipment needed. Hires, transfers, and dis-

charges employees. May provide suppliers with transportation to expedite delivery of purchased products or supplies to plant. May arrange for freezing of packaged products by other food processing plants. May negotiate with suppliers or growers prices to be paid for purchases.
GOE: 05.02.03 STRENGTH: L GED: R5 M4 L4 SVP: 8 DLU: 77

183.167-030 SERVICE SUPERVISOR, LEASED MACHINERY AND EQUIPMENT (any industry)

Directs and coordinates activities of service department of establishment concerned with providing lessees of machinery and equipment with maintenance and repair services as stipulated in leasing contract: Organizes field service offices and facilities in locations that will provide greatest number of customers with services. Stocks offices with spare parts and supplies to enable offices to provide required services. May arrange for transportation of machinery to and from customer's establishment when repairs cannot be performed on-site. May contact potential customers concerning leasing of machinery and equipment. May negotiate leasing and service contracts for machinery and equipment.
GOE: 11.11.05 STRENGTH: L GED: R4 M4 L4 SVP: 7 DLU: 77

183.167-034 SUPERINTENDENT, CAR CONSTRUCTION (railroad equip.)

Coordinates, through subordinates, activities of workers engaged in constructing and repairing railroad freight cars: Reviews plans for construction of new cars and reports of cars requiring repairs and confers with subordinate department supervisors to estimate time, supplies, human resources, and equipment required to complete work. Schedules work to departments, such as metal, paint, or structural shops. Reviews progress reports and reschedules work for departments completing work in order to meet schedule deadlines. Recommends salvaging or scrapping of cars. Interprets and enforces company safety rules, building codes, and regulations.
GOE: 05.02.03 STRENGTH: S GED: R5 M5 L4 SVP: 8 DLU: 77

183.167-038 SUPERINTENDENT, LOGGING (logging) alternate titles: cutting supervisor; yarding supervisor

Directs and coordinates, through subordinate supervisory personnel, activities of workers engaged in logging operations: Reviews logging orders and inspects designated timber tract and terrain to determine methods for logging operations, size of crew, and equipment requirements. Confers with mill, company, and government forestry officials regarding methods for logging tract in order to determine safest and most efficient method. Engages personnel and directs setting up of equipment at logging site. Plans, schedules, and coordinates logging operations in accordance with production requirements and in compliance with safety laws and government regulations. Observes logging operations to detect unsafe working conditions and noncompliance of workers with safety regulations. Changes logging procedures or methods to eliminate unsafe conditions and warns or disciplines workers disregarding safety regulations. Prepares production and personnel time records for management. May negotiate contract with mill, logging company, governmental agency, or individuals to perform logging operations and be designated Logging Contractor (logging).
GOE: 05.02.05 STRENGTH: L GED: R5 M4 L4 SVP: 8 DLU: 77

184 TRANSPORTATION, COMMUNICATION, AND UTILITIES INDUSTRY MANAGERS AND OFFICIALS

This group includes managerial occupations concerned with passenger and freight transportation by railway, highway, water, or air; furnishing services relating to transportation; petroleum pipeline transportation; warehousing; telephone and telegraph communication services; radio broadcasting and television; and the supplying of electricity, gas, steam, water, or sanitary services.

184.117-010 DIRECTOR, PUBLIC SERVICE (radio-tv broad.) alternate titles: manager, public service

Plans, schedules, and coordinates broadcasting of public service radio or television programs in various fields, such as education, religion, and civic and government affairs: Directs activities of public relations staff that maintains contacts between station or network and governmental and educational organizations. Evaluates proposed programs for suitability within station or network policy. Makes recommendations to formulate policy. Attends and addresses conventions and conferences of various groups to interest them in educational uses of radio and television. Interviews community officials and leaders to identify community problems and concerns. Examines station or network programming to ascertain available time and schedules public service programs. Contacts member network stations to promote public service programs on national scale. May research and write information on proposed program topics. May contact potential guests to solicit participation in program. May plan and schedule meetings with community organizations. May write or type notes on meeting agendas, minutes of meetings, letters, memos, and reports. May be designated according to specialization as Director, Educational Radio (radio-tv broad.).
GOE: 11.09.03 STRENGTH: L GED: R5 M4 L5 SVP: 8 DLU: 89

184.117-014 DIRECTOR, TRANSPORTATION (motor trans.)

Formulates policies, programs, and procedures for transportation system, including schedules, rates, routes, assignment of drivers and vehicles and other terminal operations: Submits recommendations for development of, and compli-

ance with transportation policies, procedures, and programs. Plans, directs, and implements vehicle scheduling, allocation, dispatching, licensing, and communication functions in accordance with established policies and objectives to effect economical utilization of vehicle facilities. Directs compilation and issuance of timetables. Conducts continuous analyses of vehicle and driver assignments and analyzes scheduling for possible consolidation. Reviews and revises driver schedules to ensure increased efficiency and to lower costs. Conducts field surveys to evaluate operations and recommends changes. Directs compilation and preparation of statistical surveys to determine traffic trends. Reviews and analyzes reports, such as revenue and performance records, and seat occupancy patterns to secure information for recommended changes. Analyzes proposed schedules and rates, initiates preparation and distribution of proposed trip schedule changes, and submits analyses of data and rescheduling recommendations to administration. Directs operation and maintenance of communication systems, reviews procedures, provides guidance to resolve technical problems, analyzes costs and recommends cost control measures. Reviews cost statements to locate excessive expenses, and develops plans, policies, and budgets. Selects and recommends personnel for staff positions and trains and assigns personnel for supervisory positions.
GOE: 11.05.01 STRENGTH: S GED: R5 M5 L5 SVP: 8 DLU: 77

184.117-018   DISTRICT SUPERVISOR (motor trans.) alternate titles: city service supervisor
Selects passenger bus depot sites along routes and sets up agreement between company and agent. Inspects depots to ensure maintenance of company standards for food and passenger comfort facilities. Collects and audits ticket sales and computes agent's commission. Advises agent of bus schedule changes. Investigates accidents and arranges settlements.
GOE: 11.12.02 STRENGTH: L GED: R5 M5 L5 SVP: 6 DLU: 77

184.117-022   IMPORT-EXPORT AGENT (any industry) alternate titles: foreign agent
Coordinates activities of international traffic division of import-export agency and negotiates settlements between foreign and domestic shippers: Plans and directs flow of air and surface traffic moving to overseas destinations. Supervises workers engaged in receiving and shipping freight, documentation, waybilling, assessing charges, and collecting fees for shipments. Negotiates with domestic customers, as intermediary for foreign customers, to resolve problems and arrive at mutual agreements. Negotiates with foreign shipping interests to contract for reciprocal freight-handling agreements. May examine invoices and shipping manifests for conformity to tariff and customs regulations. May contact customs officials to effect release of incoming freight and resolve customs delays. May prepare reports of transactions to facilitate billing of shippers and foreign carriers.
GOE: 11.05.02 STRENGTH: S GED: R5 M4 L5 SVP: 7 DLU: 77

184.117-026   MANAGER, AIRPORT (air trans.) alternate titles: director, airport; superintendent, airport
Plans, directs, and coordinates, through subordinate personnel, activities concerned with construction and maintenance of airport facilities and operation of airport in accordance with governmental agency or commission policies and regulations: Consults with commission members, governmental officials, or representatives of airlines to discuss and plan such matters as design and development of airport facilities, formulation of operating rules, regulations, and procedures, and aircraft landing, taxiing, and take-off patterns for various types of aircraft. Negotiates with representatives of airlines, utility companies, or individuals for acquisition of property for development of airport, lease of airport buildings and facilities, or use of rights-of-way over private property. Formulates procedures for use in event of aircraft accidents, fires, or other emergencies. Inspects airport facilities, such as runways, buildings, beacons and lighting, and automotive or construction equipment, or reviews inspection reports, to determine repairs, replacement, or improvements required. Coordinates activities of personnel involved in repair and maintenance of airport facilities, buildings, and equipment to minimize interruption of airport operations and improve efficiency. Directs personnel in investigating violations of aerial or ground traffic regulations, reviews investigation reports, and initiates actions to be taken against violators. Directs studies on noise abatement resulting from complaints of excessive noise from low flying aircraft or other operations. Reviews reports of expenditures for previous fiscal year, proposed improvements to facilities, and estimated increase in volume of traffic, in order to prepare budget estimates for upcoming fiscal year. Represents airport before civic or other organizational groups, courts, boards, and commissions. When management functions are divided at large or international airports, workers may be designated according to activities directed as Director, Airport Operations (air trans.); Manager, Airport-Property-And-Development (air trans.); Superintendent, Airport-Buildings-Maintenance (air trans.); Superintendent, Airport-Facilities-Repair-And-Maintenance (air trans.).
GOE: 11.05.01 STRENGTH: L GED: R5 M5 L5 SVP: 8 DLU: 77

184.117-030   MANAGER, AREA DEVELOPMENT (utilities) alternate titles: area-development consultant
Negotiates with representatives of industrial, commercial, agricultural, or other interests utilizing electric power or fuel gas to encourage location of facilities in area served by utility: Directs and coordinates activities of workers engaged in preparation of surveys and studies of prospective development area to compile information of interest to companies desirous of relocation. Analyzes compiled data and formulates methods and procedures for developing industrial

areas to determine industries that would enhance developmental plan. Plans promotional sales program and advertising to promote maximum utilization of land and consumption of electric power. Contacts companies to persuade them to locate in service area.
GOE: 11.09.03 STRENGTH: S GED: R5 M3 L4 SVP: 8 DLU: 77

184.117-034   MANAGER, AUTOMOTIVE SERVICES (any industry)
Directs and coordinates activities concerned with acquisition of automotive equipment and operation and maintenance of automotive fleet repair and storage facilities for public utility, transportation, commercial, or industrial company: Coordinates activities of staff personnel conducting research and testing program on automotive equipment considered for acquisition for such factors as operational performance, operational and maintenance costs, safety of operation, and compliance with environmental laws and regulations. Reviews and submits staff proposals for modifications to vendor or manufacturer. Directs procurement of all types of company-owned-and-operated automotive equipment, and materials, supplies, and parts required to maintain automotive equipment, garages, and storage facilities. Coordinates automotive repair and maintenance services to obtain maximum utilization of automotive equipment and prevent operational delays in other departments.
GOE: 11.11.03 STRENGTH: S GED: R5 M4 L4 SVP: 8 DLU: 77

184.117-038   MANAGER, FLIGHT OPERATIONS (air trans.)
Directs and coordinates through subordinate management personnel, flight operation and control activities of air transport company terminal station: Reviews flight schedules, flight crew bid sheet for routes, and crew schedules to ensure assignments for schedules and routes are in accordance with personnel qualifications for type of aircraft, federal safety and operational regulations, union contract provisions, and company policy. Confers with flight crew personnel to resolve any differences regarding schedule and route assignments. Coordinates activities of sections in flight operations department, such as dispatching, flight control, flight training and meterology, to ensure maximum operating efficiency. Confers with administrative personnel, government regulatory agencies, and representatives of other airlines to propose revision and adoption of rules and procedures governing flight operation activities. Directs preparation of supplemental training materials or revision of operational manuals resulting from changes in rules and procedures. Conducts investigations in cooperation with federal agencies to determine causes of aircraft accidents and to establish accident prevention and emergency methods and procedures. May check out flight crew personnel on aircraft.
GOE: 11.05.02 STRENGTH: S GED: R5 M5 L5 SVP: 8 DLU: 77

184.117-042   MANAGER, HARBOR DEPARTMENT (water trans.)
Manages operations of municipal harbor department or port authority: Enforces orders, rules, and regulations, concerning use and control of navigable waters, tidelands, and submerged lands within harbor. Authorizes acquisition and maintenance of water craft and erection of facilities for department. Directs assignment of berths and wharves to steamship companies. Negotiates leases for office space and warehouses. Coordinates activities of purchasing, traffic, wharfage, and accounting divisions. Analyzes reports of harbor operations to plan and develop future operations, taking into consideration such factors as economic conditions, tariff changes, and commodity movements. Prepares and submits reports and recommendations to board or authority. Prepares budget and authorizes expenditures within departments.
GOE: 11.05.03 STRENGTH: S GED: R6 M4 L4 SVP: 9 DLU: 77

184.117-046   MANAGER, IRRIGATION DISTRICT (waterworks) alternate titles: manager, water department
Plans and directs construction, maintenance, and operation of irrigation system within area delegated by board of directors: Establishes company policies relating to matters such as regulation of distribution and use of water, setting up of operation and maintenance standards, and standards concerned with construction of drainage systems. Recommends changes in policy, basing recommendations on study of capacity of present facilities, agricultural requirements, crop trends, and probable future water needs. Prepares directives to carry out policies approved by board. Confers with farmers, officials of city water systems, and representatives of county, state, and federal government to discuss matters such as water delivery schedules, construction problems at road and highway intersections, and diversion of river water for district use. Visits division offices, inspects field operations, and reviews periodic reports from subordinates to determine progress of construction and maintenance projects, distribution of water within divisions, collection of charges to users, and status of other phases of operation. Reviews budget estimates and compiles and approves estimates for district. Approves employment and discharge of employees, signs payrolls, and performs similar personnel duties.
GOE: 11.05.03 STRENGTH: L GED: R5 M4 L4 SVP: 9 DLU: 77

184.117-050   MANAGER, OPERATIONS (air trans.; motor trans.; r.r. trans.; water trans.) alternates titles: operations manager
Directs and coordinates activities of operations department of air, motor, railroad, or water transportation organization: Confers and cooperates with management personnel in formulating administrative and operational policies and procedures. Directs and coordinates, through subordinate managerial personnel, activities of operations department to obtain optimum use of equipment, facilities, and personnel. Reviews and analyzes expenditure, financial, and operations reports to determine requirements for increasing profits, such as need for increase in fares or tariffs, expansion of existing schedules, or extension of routes or

new routes. Prepares recommendations on findings for management evaluation. Recommends capital expenditures for acquisition of new equipment which would increase efficiency and services of operations department. Approves requisitions for equipment, materials, and supplies within limits of operations department budget. Enforces compliance of operations personnel with administrative policies, procedures, safety rules, and governmental regulations. Directs investigations into causes of customer or shipper complaints relating to operations department. May negotiate contracts with equipment and materials suppliers. May act as representative of transportation organization before government commissions or regulatory bodies during hearings for increased fares or tariffs and on extensions of or new routes.
GOE: 11.05.02 STRENGTH: S GED: R5 M4 L5 SVP: 8 DLU: 81

184.117-054 MANAGER, REGIONAL (motor trans.)
Directs and coordinates regional activities of motor transportation company: Examines and analyzes rates, tariffs, operating costs, and revenues to determine such needs or requirements as increase in rates and tariffs, reduction of operations and maintenance costs, and expansion of or changes in schedules or routes. Prepares, for management evaluation, recommendations designed to increase efficiency and revenues and lower costs. Directs, through subordinate management personnel, compliance of workers with established company policies, procedures, and standards, such as safekeeping of funds and tickets, personnel employment and grievance practices, and enforcement of union contracts and government regulations. Reviews operational records and reports and refers to manuals, company instructions, and government regulations to detect deviations from operational practices and prepares directives to eliminate such infractions. Investigates safeguards and inspects regional premises to ensure that adequate protection exists for company assets, property, and equipment. Participates in union contract negotiations and settling of grievances. Coordinates advertising and sales promotion programs for region. Reviews replies to passenger complaints and settlement of claims for conformance with company public relations policies and procedures. Inspects terminals for conformance with standards for cleanliness, appearance, and need of repair or maintenance, and directs corrective measures required to meet standards.
GOE: 11.05.02 STRENGTH: S GED: R5 M5 L5 SVP: 8 DLU: 77

184.117-058 MANAGER, SCHEDULE PLANNING (air trans.)
Negotiates with governmental regulatory body to change company's route application (fixed schedule for flights) over authorized routes as representative of certificated air carrier: Analyzes documentation on company operations and recommended changes in route application, prepared by subordinates, to determine if company position warrants requesting route application hearing, considering such factors as current and projected traffic load, route application of competitive carriers over same route, and profitability of route operations. Submits current and proposed schedules to Schedule Committee for consideration and approval to request hearing before regulatory body. Prepares company's position and arguments for presentation at route application hearing and negotiates with body for additional route applications or deletion of route applications on unprofitable routes in order to improve efficient utilization of flight personnel and equipment and to reduce losses or increase revenues. Directs and coordinates activities of workers compiling documentation on route application, analyzing data, and preparing recommendations for schedule changes.
GOE: 11.05.02 STRENGTH: S GED: R5 M4 L5 SVP: 8 DLU: 77

184.117-062 MANAGER, STATION (radio-tv broad.)
Directs and coordinates activities of radio or television station, or of cable television franchise: Supervises directly, or through subordinates, personnel engaged in departments, such as sales, program, engineering, and personnel. Observes activities to ensure compliance with government regulations. Discusses plans with marketing personnel to promote sales of programs and time periods to advertisers and their agencies. Confers with owners or company senior management to discuss station policy and administrative procedures. May prepare operational budget and monitor expenses for station or franchise. May negotiate with motion picture companies for purchase of independent film programs. May negotiate cable franchise contract with local issuing authority. May develop strategy to promote sales of new cable television service, or upgraded service, to customers within franchise area. May contact prospective buyers of station time to promote sale of station services. May manage station engaged in transmitting broadcasts to foreign countries and be known as Director, International Broadcasting (radio-tv broad.). May perform different duties and responsibilities, according to station size and network affiliation, and be designated General Manager, Broadcasting (radio-tv broad.).
GOE: 11.05.02 STRENGTH: L GED: R5 M4 L5 SVP: 8 DLU: 89

184.117-066 MANAGER, TRAFFIC (air trans.; motor trans.; water trans.) alternate titles: manager, rates and schedules
Conducts studies on company freight and passenger classifications, rates, and tariffs and formulates changes required to provide for increased revenues and profitability of operations: Analyzes financial reports on operations and evaluates existing classifications, rates, and tariffs to determine changes required and need for expansion or curtailment of schedules and routes. Documents data to support proposals for increased revenues, expansion of schedules or routes, and files application for new rates, schedules, or routes with regulatory agencies. Testifies before regulatory agencies to present company's position and need for increased revenues in order to operate profitably. Negotiates with personnel of other transportation companies on division of interline revenues and signs contract on terms of agreement. Consults with officials of other companies on traf-

fic movement problems, such as freight handling, transfer, and in-transit storage. Directs and coordinates activities of workers in classification of shipments and in applying and enforcing rates and tariffs.
GOE: 11.11.03 STRENGTH: S GED: R5 M5 L5 SVP: 8 DLU: 77

184.117-070 OPERATIONS MANAGER (tel. & tel.)
Directs activities of main and branch offices of telegraph communications systems division: Interprets and implements company policies, and develops operating procedures to facilitate branch office operations. Conducts management studies, collecting and interpreting economic and statistical data to prepare budget estimates, determine work load, personnel, and equipment requirements, and to forecast future community needs. Approves branch office personnel assignments and requisition and installation of new equipment. Locates and appraises properties for proposed office locations and negotiates lease agreements with property owners. Prepares telegraph office layouts and drawings for administrative review. Inspects branch office installations and facilities to ensure that company service and operating standards are followed. Audits branch office accounts and verifies cash balances to determine accuracy and completeness of financial accounts and records. Directs security measures for protection of funds and personnel against injury or loss from sources, such as fire or theft.
GOE: 11.05.02 STRENGTH: S GED: R5 M5 L5 SVP: 8 DLU: 77

184.117-074 REVENUE-SETTLEMENTS ADMINISTRATOR (tel. & tel.)
Directs activities concerned with intercompany negotiations on revenue settlements: Negotiates revenue settlements with intercompany representatives on proposed facility arrangements, such as cables and switching equipment, and changes in operations and procedures. Supervises workers engaged in analyzing settlement agreements. Analyzes results of studies to determine effects on revenue, expense, and investment. Prepares settlement contracts, following guidelines developed during negotiations. Prepares or supervises preparation of revenue budget estimates for accounting purposes. May represent company at Public Utilities Commission hearings.
GOE: 11.12.01 STRENGTH: S GED: R5 M5 L5 SVP: 8 DLU: 77

184.117-078 SUPERINTENDENT, COMMISSARY (water trans.)
Manages commissary department of company operating sea-going vessels: Processes requisitions for supplies and equipment from vessels and approves or denies request. Negotiates contracts with supply houses, manufacturers, or wholesalers for equipment, supplies, and furnishings. Formulates and issues instructions for management commissary department aboard vessels. Represents company in formulating policies when negotiating contracts with union. Resolves labor-management problems of commissary department personnel. Inventories food supplies aboard vessels and examines menus to ensure that vessels are serving balanced diets. Inspects vessels to ensure that housekeeping functions conform to sanitary regulations and that repairs and improvements are made. Analyzes food costs and prepares reports for management.
GOE: 11.05.02 STRENGTH: S GED: R5 M4 L4 SVP: 8 DLU: 77

184.117-082 SUPERINTENDENT, COMMUNICATIONS (tel. & tel.) alternate titles: plant chief
Directs construction, operation, and maintenance of telephone or telegraph communication systems: Studies and accepts or rejects recommendations for improvement or additions to communication facilities. Investigates availability and approves cost estimates of new equipment requested. Approves or rejects equipment rental and electric-power contracts. Supervises personnel and performs other administrative duties to ensure efficient operation. May direct installation and operation of radio communications systems.
GOE: 05.02.01 STRENGTH: S GED: R5 M4 L4 SVP: 8 DLU: 77

184.117-086 MANAGER, CAR INSPECTION AND REPAIR (r.r. trans.)
Plans, directs, and coordinates, through subordinate supervisors, activities concerned with inspection, repair, and maintenance of railroad equipment: Confers with department heads to establish administrative and operational policies and procedures for following federal, Railroad Association, and union regulations and agreements. Interprets policies and procedures for subordinate supervisors, and monitors activities to ensure that policies and procedures are followed. Analyzes records of daily operations, such as freight car inspections, repairs completed or scheduled, or worker absenteeism, to maintain knowledge of department activities. Instructs subordinates to institute specific measures, such as studies and maintaining bar graphs, to monitor productivity. Discusses freight car repairs with shippers or consignees and inspection and repair violations with federal and public representatives to resolve concerns, such as time of repair, repair cost, and methods of preventing future violations. Monitors inventory of parts and materials and prepares requisition forms for items in short supply. Conducts investigations of personnel matters, such as continued tardiness, excessive absenteeism, or safety violations; negotiates with union representative matters, such as contract violations, job abolishment, and reallocation of human resources; and prepares required reports, according to prescribed procedures.
GOE: 11.11.03 STRENGTH: S GED: R5 M4 L5 SVP: 8 DLU: 86

184.117-090 REGIONAL SUPERINTENDENT, RAILROAD CAR INSPECTION AND REPAIR (r.r. trans.)
Plans and coordinates inspection, maintenance, and repair of railroad equipment within assigned railroad region: Analyzes productivity and budget reports to determine allocation of work force, and equipment and productivity of inspection and repair facilities within assigned region. Confers with shop and yard supervisory personnel and shippers to stay apprised of daily work sched-

ules and to ensure priority scheduling of repairs for railcars needed back in service. Oversees administrative matters, such as training policies, budget allocations, and equipment replacement. Monitors administration of safety program, according to company rules, union agreements, and federal regulations.
GOE: 11.11.03 STRENGTH: S GED: R5 M4 L4 SVP: 9 DLU: 86

184.161-010 CABLE SUPERVISOR (tel. & tel.)
Directs and coordinates, through subordinate supervisory personnel, activities of workers engaged in installation, maintenance, and repair of underground, buried, aerial, or submarine telephone carrier cables in plant district: Reviews proposed construction plans and schematic drawings to ensure that proposals are compatible with existing equipment and that plans adhere to specifications. Inspects construction sites and installations to ensure service deadlines are being met. Directs and coordinates testing and inspecting of plant equipment for operational performance. Prepares budget, determines work force requirements, and establishes production schedules to meet service loads.
GOE: 05.05.05 STRENGTH: L GED: R4 M2 L4 SVP: 8 DLU: 77

184.161-014 SUPERINTENDENT, WATER-AND-SEWER SYSTEMS (waterworks)
Directs and coordinates activities of workers engaged in installation, maintenance, repair, expansion, and relocation of water distribution and sewage facilities: Analyzes trends, such as population and industrial growth of area being served to determine adequacy of current facilities and to project community demands for future facilities. Develops plans to meet and serve expanding community needs, such as increasing capacity of water storage and filtration facilities, or arranging new sources of water supply. Plans methods and sequence of operations to facilitate additions, deletions and modifications to the system. Directs activities of subordinate personnel who oversee installation, maintenance, and repair of water distribution and sewage facilities. Inspects field projects to confirm conformance to specifications. Confers with administrative and technical personnel and personnel of other utilities to coordinate departmental activities. Evaluates new developments in materials, tools, and equipment to recommend or deny purchase. Prepares budget estimates based on anticipated needs of department. For classification of workers concerned only with water supply see SUPERVISOR, WATERWORKS (waterworks); for those concerned only with sewage disposal see SUPERVISOR, SEWER SYSTEM (waterworks).
GOE: 05.02.01 STRENGTH: S GED: R6 M6 L6 SVP: 9 DLU: 77

184.162-010 MANAGER, PRODUCTION (radio-tv broad.)
Coordinates work of various departments to produce radio or television programs and commercial announcements: Trains, assigns duties, and supervises employees engaged in production and taping such programs as game shows, talk broadcasts, and special programs. Ensures that slanderous, libelous, and profane statements are avoided or deleted and that program is in conformance with station or network policy and regulations. Schedules usage of studio and editing facilities needed by PRODUCERS (radio-tv broad.) 159.117-010, and engineering and maintenance staff to maximize use of facilities, according to scheduled events. Operates television broadcasting equipment, such as switcher, video and color monitors, tape decks, lights and microphones to train workers or to substitute for absent employees. Operates portable, shoulder-mounted camera to record or broadcast live programs from location of event. May direct subordinates in auditioning talent and proposed programs. May coordinate audio work, scenes, music, timing, camera work, and script writing, to develop desired production, and review production to ensure objectives are obtained.
GOE: 11.05.02 STRENGTH: H GED: R5 M4 L4 SVP: 7 DLU: 89

184.163-010 TRAFFIC INSPECTOR (motor trans.; r.r. trans.) alternate titles: dispatcher; transportation inspector
Coordinates scheduled service within assigned territory of streetcar, bus, or railway transportation system: Periodically observes vehicles along route to ensure that service is provided according to schedule. Investigates schedule delays, accidents, equipment failures, and complaints, and files written report. Reports disruptions to service, using radiotelephone. Determines need for changes in service, such as additional coaches, route changes, and revised schedules to increase operating efficiency and improve service. Drives automobile along route to detect conditions hazardous to equipment and passengers, and negotiates with local government personnel to eliminate hazards. Assists in dispatching equipment when necessary. Recommends promotions and disciplinary actions involving transportation personnel. Inspects mechanical malfunctions of vehicles along route and directs repair.
GOE: 11.10.05 STRENGTH: L GED: R4 M2 L3 SVP: 7 DLU: 77

184.167-010 BOAT DISPATCHER (water trans.)
Coordinates movement of freight by barge or lighter to provide most efficient service to shippers consistent with available equipment and facilities: Determines number and kind of barges and lighters needed to transport cargo. Coordinates movement of vessels to ensure most efficient service. Assigns barges and lighters to individual haulage jobs and issues orders to TUGBOAT CAPTAINS (water trans.). Compiles or directs activities of workers engaged in compilation of periodic reports on freight tonnage transported and cost of operations.
GOE: 07.05.01 STRENGTH: S GED: R4 M3 L3 SVP: 7 DLU: 77

184.167-014 DIRECTOR, NEWS (radio-tv broad.)
Directs and coordinates activities of news department of radio or television network or station: Confers with executives and production staff members re-

garding budget, station policy, news coverage of special events, and production problems. Originates or approves feature ideas and sends ideas to personnel of assignment department for implementation. Monitors news development and reviews edited copy and news film. Approves program content or issues directions for changes or modification. Coordinates news staff activities with radio or television programming, traffic, and film editing departments. Hires, discharges, and evaluates performance of news staff. May operate video equipment to review and approve news film or tape, using knowledge of usage of equipment. May write or type news copy, letters, and memos. May perform production duties or directly supervise those performing them in smaller station. May be designated according to media as Director, Radio News (radio-tv broad.); Director, Television News (radio-tv broad.).
GOE: 11.08.01 STRENGTH: L GED: R5 M3 L5 SVP: 8 DLU: 89

184.167-018 DIRECTOR, OPERATIONS (radio-tv broad.)
Directs and coordinates operations departments of radio, television or cable television station: Carries out general policies established by company officers. Prepares and administers budget for program department. Makes decisions pertaining to general policies beyond scope of authority of department heads under jurisdiction. Approves hiring and discharging of department personnel. May compose memos on budgetary and policy matters, using computer.
GOE: 11.05.02 STRENGTH: S GED: R5 M4 L5 SVP: 8 DLU: 89

184.167-022 DIRECTOR, OPERATIONS, BROADCAST (radio-tv broad.)
Coordinates activities of personnel engaged in preparation of station and network program schedules: Reviews program schedules in advance and issues daily corrections. Arranges for split network programs furnishing stations not carrying sponsored programs with noncommercial programs. Notifies traffic department to install or cancel programs originating at points remote from broadcasting station. Advises affiliated stations regarding their schedules. Examines expenditures for programs to determine compliance with budgetary restrictions. Prepares schedules for talent and assigns talent to broadcast periods. Arranges for office space and equipment.
GOE: 11.05.02 STRENGTH: L GED: R5 M3 L5 SVP: 8 DLU: 88

184.167-034 DIRECTOR, SPORTS (radio-tv broad.)
Directs and coordinates activities of personnel engaged in broadcasting sports news or sports events over radio or television network or for individual station: Plans broadcast coverage of sports events, such as baseball, basketball, and football games or boxing matches. Directs or arranges for setup of remote broadcast facilities. Hires and assigns staff personnel to operate and direct broadcasting activities and to announce event. Directs preparation and broadcast of sports news and commentaries. Plans for and arranges employment of well-known individuals (personalities) to serve as guest commentators for special events or programs. May participate in broadcasts and interview sport personalities during broadcast, depending on size of station.
GOE: 11.05.02 STRENGTH: S GED: R5 M4 L5 SVP: 8 DLU: 89

184.167-038 DISPATCHER, CHIEF I (petrol. & gas; petrol. refin.; pipe lines) alternate titles: superintendent, scheduling
Plans transmission schedules and operating procedures to direct movement of crude oil, petroleum products, natural gas, or coal slurry through pipelines from transmission terminal to distribution points or destinations: Contacts customers or shippers to ascertain volume or quantities of products to be transported, reviews consumption records and forecasts on consumer demands, and estimates peak delivery periods in order to plan and determine quantities, pressures, or volume of products required in transmission lines. Schedules movement of petroleum products to minimize contamination of various grades or types of products. Prepares operating schedules for compressor or pump stations, tank farms and refineries, as to type and quantities of product movement, time of movement, pressures or volumes specified in pipeline, and destination for specified products. Issues instructions relative to gauging, switching, sampling, and testing of products. Reviews operating reports on receipts, movements, withdrawals, deliveries, and on-hand storage stocks to ensure safe and efficient operation of pipelines. Prepares emergency operating procedures to meet schedules, provide for specified volumes and pressures in pipeline, and recover losses resulting from breakdown of equipment. May communicate with field personnel, using teletype or telephone. May be designated according to type of product scheduled as Dispatcher, Chief, Coal Slurry (pipe lines); Dispatcher, Chief, Natural Gas (petrol. & gas; pipe lines); Dispatcher, Chief, Oil (pipe lines); Dispatcher, Chief, Petroleum Products (petrol. refin.; pipe lines).
GOE: 05.02.01 STRENGTH: S GED: R5 M4 L4 SVP: 8 DLU: 77

184.167-042 GENERAL AGENT, OPERATIONS (air trans.; motor trans.; r.r. trans.) alternate titles: service center manager
Directs and coordinates activities of personnel involved in transportation of freight by air, motor, and railway transportation systems: Coordinates transportation and handling of express shipments within geographic subdivision by directing activities of airport field offices, branch agencies, and railway terminals. Recruits, hires, and administers training of employees. Establishes procedures and standards to implement policies of company. Inspects operations to evaluate efficiency of methods and submits reports to regional manager.
GOE: 11.05.02 STRENGTH: S GED: R4 M3 L4 SVP: 8 DLU: 77

184.167-046 INCINERATOR-PLANT-GENERAL SUPERVISOR (sanitary ser.)
Supervises and coordinates activities of workers engaged in operating one or more incinerator plants: Schedules work and assigns crews to shifts or plants.

Plans routine for receiving and incinerating rubbish and refuse. Instructs employees in work methods and interprets and enforces operating orders and procedures. Issues orders and directives regarding operation, repair, and maintenance of facilities and equipment. Inspects plant operations and directs compilation of operating records. Analyzes cause of operating failure and recommends repair methods and procedures. Interviews and recommends prospective employees. Directs preparation of timesheets and personnel records, and initiates requests for supplies and contract repair work.
GOE: 05.06.04 STRENGTH: S GED: R4 M3 L4 SVP: 6 DLU: 77

184.167-050 MAINTENANCE SUPERVISOR (utilities)
Directs and coordinates activities of workers engaged in mechanical and electrical repair and maintenance of electric-power generating equipment, and transmission, distribution, and control equipment of electric power utility: Confers with management and other department heads to plan preventive maintenance programs and to schedule inspections and major overhauls in coordination with other operating activities. Reviews technical papers, catalogs, and other reference materials, and confers with equipment sales representatives to select and recommend new supplies and maintenance methods to improve plant operations. Confers with contractors to resolve problems in installation of new equipment and to assist in start of new plants or additions. Reviews inspection and repair reports and observes progress of work on major overhauls to evaluate efficiency and work quality. May prepare annual departmental budget. May specialize in supervision of maintenance work and be designated Maintenance Supervisor, Electrical (utilities); Maintenance Supervisor, Mechanical (utilities).
GOE: 05.02.02 STRENGTH: L GED: R4 M4 L4 SVP: 7 DLU: 81

184.167-054 MANAGER, BUS TRANSPORTATION (motor trans.)
Directs and coordinates activities of motor bus company to provide passengers with fast, efficient, and safe transportation, either performing following duties personally or through subordinate supervisory personnel: Applies for or recommends fare revisions, extension of routes, or changes in schedules in order to improve passenger services and increase revenues. Coordinates terminal and dispatching activities, communication operations, and assignment of driving personnel to obtain optimum use of facilities, equipment, and human resources. Inspects physical facilities of terminal and buses for such factors as cleanliness, safety, and appearance, and takes required actions in order to meet prescribed standards. Processes passenger complaints and initiates corrective actions designed to improve customer relations and services. Initiates investigations into causes of accidents, interviews operators concerned to determine responsibility, and takes actions on findings or submits reports to management. Directs preparation and issuance of new schedules to terminal and operating personnel. Dispatches replacement buses for vehicles involved in accidents and buses and operators for special charter or tours. Directs and participates in training of personnel and issues manuals, bulletins, and technical guides to improve services and operational activities. Reviews operator bids for routes to determine assignments for driving personnel. Checks trip and dispatch logs for conformance with schedules. Verifies cash fares with operator reports and reviews errors with personnel concerned. Directs preparation of and keeping of dispatch and vehicle operations records and reports.
GOE: 11.11.03 STRENGTH: S GED: R4 M4 L4 SVP: 8 DLU: 77

184.167-058 MANAGER, CARGO-AND-RAMP-SERVICES (air trans.)
Directs and coordinates, through subordinate supervisory personnel, air transport terminal cargo and ramp activities to provide fast and efficient services for clients and passengers: Reviews data on incoming flights, such as scheduled or estimated times of arrival or departure, destinations and downline station stops, and air cargo and passenger manifests in order to plan work activities. Directs preparation of loading plans for each departing flight, and confers with supervisory personnel to ensure workers and equipment are available for air cargo and baggage loading, unloading, and handling activities and for ramp service activities. Analyzes reports and records of operations and inspects facilities to determine effectiveness of existing methods and procedures and physical condition of facilities and equipment. Prepares and submits recommendations designed to improve efficiency of cargo and ramp services. Investigates causes of accidents and recommends safety measures for preventing further occurrences. Reviews performance evaluations of personnel for conformance to standards, recommends personnel actions, and directs and coordinates training activities to increase workers' efficiency and proficiency. Interprets and enforces, through supervisory personnel, company policies, procedures, and safety regulations.
GOE: 11.11.03 STRENGTH: S GED: R5 M4 L4 SVP: 8 DLU: 77

184.167-062 MANAGER, COMMUNICATIONS STATION (tel. & tel.)
Directs and coordinates, through shift supervisory personnel, operation and maintenance activities of submarine-cable head, microwave-satellite, or coastal radio-telephone station of communications company: Reviews station logs and confers with supervisory personnel to ascertain apparatus or equipment malfunctions and remedial procedures taken. Plans station activities, prepares work schedules, and assigns technical personnel to operating or maintenance duties. Authorizes requisitions for replacement parts, materials, and supplies. Prepares reports and records on station activities. May personally supervise workers in stations where shift supervisory personnel are not utilized. May be designated according to type of communications station managed.
GOE: 05.02.04 STRENGTH: S GED: R5 M4 L4 SVP: 8 DLU: 77

184.167-066 MANAGER, FLIGHT CONTROL (air trans.)
Directs and coordinates activities of commercial airline flight control center concerned with dispatching aircraft on scheduled flights and controlling flight movements on routes in accordance with federal and company regulations and policies: Assigns aircraft dispatching and flight controlling duties for specific scheduled flights on designated routes to center personnel, basing assignments on knowledge and abilities of personnel and human resource requirements for operation of flight control center. Reviews dispatching and flight control actions taken by control center personnel for conformance with federal and company regulations and procedures. Explains to center personnel prescribed methods and procedures for planning flight operations and sequences to be followed in dispatching (releasing) flight and controlling aircraft on route. Interviews prescreened applicants for center staff to ascertain abilities and qualifications and recommends qualified applicants to personnel department. Instructs new employees on federal and company regulations and procedures for dispatch of aircraft and control of flight movements. Evaluates center personnel on job proficiency and recommends such personnel actions as salary increases, promotions, disciplinary actions, and dismissals. Must possess valid Aircraft Dispatchers Certificate of Competency issued by Federal Aviation Agency.
GOE: 05.02.04 STRENGTH: S GED: R5 M4 L4 SVP: 8 DLU: 77

184.167-070 MANAGER, FLIGHT-RESERVATIONS (air trans.)
Directs and coordinates, through subordinate supervisory personnel, flight reservation activities for certificated commercial or transport company: Reviews flight reservation reports, statistical data on passenger miles flown, and conducts comparison studies on other airline reservations to develop methods and procedures designed to improve operating efficiency and increase reservations for company flights. Interprets and implements, through supervisory personnel, company policies and procedures regarding customer relations and contact with public. Analyzes economic statistics as applied to air transportation and other factors, such as weather conditions, special flight rates, and package deals, to estimate future volume of flight reservations. Prepares estimates of work force required to process work load and equipment requirements in order to formulate budget estimate. Reviews performance evaluations on reservations personnel and initiates personnel actions as required. Schedules notation of worker assignments to improve capabilities of personnel and develop worker overall knowledge of department activities. Directs investigation of customer complaints regarding reservation services and prepares correspondence designed to improve customer relations. Endeavors to resolve personnel grievances and submits unresolved grievances to higher authority.
GOE: 11.11.03 STRENGTH: S GED: R5 M4 L4 SVP: 8 DLU: 77

184.167-078 MANAGER, SOLID-WASTE-DISPOSAL (government ser.)
alternate titles: superintendent, landfill operations
Directs and coordinates, through subordinate supervisory personnel, landfill site activities concerned with solid-waste disposal for governmental sanitation agency or private refuse-disposal company: Inspects site and confers with supervisory personnel to determine procedures and methods for utilizing site area for disposal activities and to remain in compliance with specifications of environmental impact study. Plans sequences of waste disposal operations to obtain optimum utilization of site basing plans on such factors as past and predicted solid-waste disposal and land reclamation requirements, quantity of waste handled daily, and space in site required for waste handled. Ensures that waste disposal activities are in compliance with public health insect and rodent control laws and regulations. Prepares records and reports on disposal activities, such as quantities of waste handled, receipts from operations, and actions taken to comply with public health and environmental regulations. May prepare operational budget for landfill waste disposal activities and submit budget to agency management. May examine loads of waste for recyclable material and direct sorting, handling, and recycling operations. May supervise workers engaged in waste disposal operations. May operate heavy equipment to compact and bury waste in private landfill disposal dump.
GOE: 05.02.06 STRENGTH: L GED: R4 M3 L3 SVP: 7 DLU: 77

184.167-082 MANAGER, STATION (air trans.)
Directs and coordinates airline station activities at transport station or terminal point located at airport to provide services for scheduled flight operations: Reviews station activity reports to ascertain data required for planning station operations. Directs preparation of work schedules to obtain optimum utilization of human resources and facilities. Coordinates activities of passenger reservations and ticketing, passenger services, ramp and cargo services, commissary services, and dispatching of aircraft to ensure operations meet company and government policies and regulations. Directs preparation of passenger lists, cargo manifests, and plans for stowage of cargo and baggage aboard aircraft. Evaluates training and performance records of employees to determine and formulate training designed to increase employee efficiency. May direct activities of TRANSPORTATION AGENTS (air trans.) in expediting movement of freight, mail, baggage, and passengers through station or from other company's terminal to station. May be designated in large airlines according to specific station activity directed as Manager, Commissary Service (air trans.); Manager, Flight Dispatching (air trans.); Manager, Flight Service (air trans.); Manager, Passenger Service (air trans.); Manager, Reservations-And-Ticketing (air trans.).
GOE: 11.11.03 STRENGTH: S GED: R5 M4 L4 SVP: 8 DLU: 77

184.167-086 MANAGER, TELEGRAPH OFFICE (tel. & tel.)
Manages activities of branch or local telegraph office: Directs handling of circuits and telegrams. Supervises personnel, and coordinates work of various departments. Answers customer inquiries, suggests services, and adjusts complaints to promote goodwill. Reviews financial accounts and records, verifies accuracy of daily cash balances, remittances, and bank deposits. Compiles and analyzes statistical and operating reports and data. Writes correspondence.

GOE: 07.01.02 STRENGTH: S GED: R4 M3 L4 SVP: 8 DLU: 77

184.167-090 MANAGER, TRAFFIC (radio-tv broad.)
Arranges for leasing of wire facilities to transmit radio and television programs to individual stations of network: Contacts communication companies and arranges for facilities to transmit programs from point of origin to network stations. Informs stations of noncommercial programs available for broadcast. Informs affiliated stations of charges to be made for commercial broadcasts and programs requiring special facility hookups. Directs activities of workers engaged in transmitting messages by teletype or simplex systems.
GOE: 11.12.02 STRENGTH: S GED: R5 M3 L5 SVP: 7 DLU: 77

184.167-094 MANAGER, TRAFFIC (any industry)
Directs and coordinates traffic activities of organization: Develops methods and procedures for transportation of raw materials to processing and production areas and commodities from departments to customers, warehouses, or other storage facilities. Determines most efficient and economical routing and mode of transportation, using rate and tariff manuals and motor freight and railroad guidebooks. Directs scheduling of shipments and notifies concerned departments or customers of arrival dates. Initiates investigations into causes of damages or shortages in consignments or overcharges for freight or insurance. Conducts studies in areas of packaging, warehousing, and loading of commodities and evaluates existing procedures and standards. Initiates changes designed to improve control and efficiency of traffic department. May negotiate contracts for leasing of transportation equipment or property. May assist in preparing department budget.
GOE: 11.05.02 STRENGTH: S GED: R5 M4 L4 SVP: 8 DLU: 77

184.167-098 MANAGER, TRAFFIC I (tel. & tel.)
Directs traffic operations in central telegraph office: Directs transmitting and receiving of telegrams and facsimile recordings and clearing of communications circuits. Evaluates data, such as traffic loads, speed and accuracy of message handling, and cost factors to improve services. Coordinates work activities of various operational departments. Hires, promotes, discharges, or transfers employees. Regulates production and performs other administrative or supervisory functions.
GOE: 07.01.02 STRENGTH: S GED: R4 M3 L4 SVP: 8 DLU: 77

184.167-102 MANAGER, TRAFFIC I (motor trans.)
Directs and coordinates activities concerned with documentation and routing of outgoing freight, and verification and reshipment of incoming freight, at motor-transportation company warehouse: Directs activities of workers engaged in assigning tariff classifications according to type and weight of freight or merchandise, routing and scheduling shipment by air, rail, or truck, and preparing billings from tariff and classification manuals. Reviews documents to ensure that assigned classifications and tariffs are in accordance with mode of transportation and destination of shipment. Investigates shipper or consignee complaints regarding lost or damaged merchandise or shortages in shipment to determine responsibility. Directs preparation of claims against carrier responsible and corresponds with shipper or consignee to effect settlement. Schedules shipments to ensure compliance with interstate traffic laws and regulations and company policies.
GOE: 07.01.02 STRENGTH: S GED: R5 M4 L5 SVP: 8 DLU: 77

184.167-106 MANAGER, TRAFFIC II (tel. & tel.) alternate titles: traffic chief; traffic superintendent
Directs and coordinates telephone traffic activities within specific geographical area: Directs activities, such as customer service, traffic measurements and operations, and traffic studies. Directs preparation of budgets and control and assignment of personnel to meet traffic-volume requirements. Participates in public relations activities with customer representatives and attends service and professional organizational meetings as part of company's public relations program. Consults with representatives of connecting telephone companies to resolve service problems.
GOE: 11.11.03 STRENGTH: S GED: R5 M4 L5 SVP: 8 DLU: 77

184.167-110 MANAGER, TRUCK TERMINAL (motor trans.) alternate titles: terminal manager
Directs and coordinates activities of terminal used by trucking concerns as intermediate freight distribution or shipping point: Reviews schedules to ascertain trucking concerns having freight consignments for terminal and shipments originating from terminal in order to plan activities. Assigns workers to specific duties, such as loading or unloading trucks, checking incoming and outgoing shipments against bills of ladings, and moving freight into and out of storage. May hire terminal personnel or order workers from union dispatch office. May provide garage services for trucks.
GOE: 11.11.03 STRENGTH: S GED: R4 M3 L3 SVP: 8 DLU: 77

184.167-114 MANAGER, WAREHOUSE (any industry) alternate titles: storekeeper; superintendent, storage area; superintendent, warehouse; warehouse supervisor
Directs warehousing activities for commercial or industrial establishment: Establishes operational procedures for activities, such as verification of incoming and outgoing shipments, handling and disposition of materials, and keeping warehouse inventory current. Inspects physical condition of warehouse and equipment and prepares work order for repairs and requisitions for replacement of equipment. Confers with department heads to ensure coordination of warehouse activities with such activities as production, sales, records control, and

purchasing. Screens and hires warehouse personnel and issues work assignments. Directs salvage of damaged or used material. May participate in planning personnel-safety and plant-protection activities.
GOE: 11.11.03 STRENGTH: L GED: R4 M3 L4 SVP: 8 DLU: 88

184.167-118 OPERATIONS MANAGER (motor trans.)
Directs and coordinates activities of workers engaged in crating, moving, and storing household goods and furniture: Inspects warehouse facilities and equipment and recommends changes in allocation of space, and crating procedures to WAREHOUSE SUPERVISOR (motor trans.). Purchases moving equipment such as dollies, pads, trucks, and trailers. Plans pickup and delivery schedules for TRUCK DRIVERS, HEAVY (any industry). Answers such inquiries as type of service offered, rates, schedules, and areas serviced. Examines items to be moved, to ascertain approximate weights and type of crating required. Investigates customers' complaints involving such matters as damaged items, overcharges, and delay in shipment, and makes necessary adjustment. Interviews, selects, trains, and assigns new personnel. May call on customers to solicit new business. May prepare cost estimates for clients.
GOE: 11.11.03 STRENGTH: L GED: R4 M3 L3 SVP: 6 DLU: 77

184.167-122 PORT-TRAFFIC MANAGER (water trans.)
Manages operations of traffic division for port authorities: Enforces rules and regulations, such as berthing of ships, handling and storing of cargo, and use of port facilities. Directs policing and cleaning activities of harbor department land, streets, buildings, and water areas. Ensures that activities concerning revenue are documented and submitted to accounting division. Advises port authorities on rates and revisions of port tariff. Solicits steamship companies to use port facilities. Directs activities concerned with compiling daily and annual ship and cargo statistics.
GOE: 11.05.03 STRENGTH: S GED: R5 M5 L5 SVP: 8 DLU: 77

184.167-126 SERVICE SUPERVISOR III (utilities)
Directs and coordinates, through subordinates, activities of workers who inspect, maintain, and test distribution lines, and install meters and customer service drops, but does not supervise major repair activities involving use of line crews.
GOE: 05.02.02 STRENGTH: L GED: R4 M4 L4 SVP: 8 DLU: 77

184.167-130 STATION MANAGER (r.r. trans.)
Directs and coordinates activities of railroad station employees and authorizes departure of trains: Notifies employees of changes in arrival and departure times of trains, boarding track numbers, and other information affecting passengers for announcement over loudspeaker and for posting on callboard. Ensures that shift workers and train crews report as scheduled, or that replacements are obtained. Authorizes departure of passenger trains after transfer of mail and baggage is completed, delaying departure for arrival of connecting train if necessary. Authorizes repairs to station facilities and directs activities of custodial and maintenance workers. Investigates passenger service complaints to ensure efficient and courteous service. May negotiate with concessionaires to lease station space or facilities for restaurants, newsstands, advertising displays, and parking.
GOE: 11.11.03 STRENGTH: L GED: R4 M3 L3 SVP: 7 DLU: 77

184.167-134 STATIONS-RELATIONS-CONTACT REPRESENTATIVE (radio-tv broad.)
Coordinates program presentations between network and independently owned radio and television stations comprising network: Aids in formulating network policies. Advises station personnel on operating procedures to disseminate programs to all parts of network. Acts as liaison officer between various stations and networks.
GOE: 11.05.02 STRENGTH: S GED: R5 M4 L5 SVP: 8 DLU: 77

184.167-138 SUPERINTENDENT OF GENERATION (utilities) alternate titles: superintendent, operations
Directs and coordinates generation of electrical energy by interconnected generating stations throughout electric utility system: Analyzes fuel consumption and power output reports to determine need for plant maintenance and repair work. Coordinates plant shutdowns for emergency and periodic inspection and repair. Directs and coordinates testing activities and analyzes test data as heat input, heat output, and boiler and turbine efficiency, to evaluate capability and efficiency of generating stations. Directs activities of maintenance crews servicing scattered generating stations. May direct operation of substations and transmission lines [SUPERINTENDENT, TRANSMISSION (utilities)].
GOE: 05.02.01 STRENGTH: S GED: R5 M5 L4 SVP: 8 DLU: 77

184.167-142 SUPERINTENDENT, COLD STORAGE (any industry)
Coordinates activities of workers in cold storage plant to ensure perishable commodities are stored with minimum spoilage: Specifies refrigeration temperatures for commodities, such as vegetables, milk products, and meat to be stored and supervises REFRIGERATING ENGINEERS (any industry) in maintaining temperatures within specified limits.
GOE: 05.06.02 STRENGTH: L GED: R4 M3 L3 SVP: 8 DLU: 77

184.167-146 SUPERINTENDENT, COMPRESSOR STATIONS (pipe lines)
Directs and coordinates operational and maintenance activities of system of compressor stations, located at transmission terminals and at intermittent points along pipeline, to boost pressure in pipeline and expedite transmission of natural gas to distribution points: Directs preparation of operation, safety, and main-

tenance manuals for compressor stations. Directs and coordinates, through COMPRESSOR-STATION ENGINEER, CHIEF (pipe lines), activities of personnel to ensure adjustments of gas pressures for transmission are performed safely and in accordance with prescribed procedures. Selects, and directs training of, supervisory personnel for compressor stations. Develops plans for additional stations, as required, and recommends design of station structures and types of machinery, such as compressors, driving engines, generators, and auxiliary equipment to engineering personnel. Directs and coordinates activities, such as testing of new or repaired machinery, and maintenance and repair of machinery and station structures, to ensure uninterrupted transmission of gas.
GOE: 05.02.01 STRENGTH: S GED: R5 M4 L4 SVP: 8 DLU: 77

184.167-150 SUPERINTENDENT, DISTRIBUTION I (utilities) alternate titles: chief power dispatcher; district manager; manager, electric distribution department

Supervises and coordinates activities of workers engaged in maintenance and extension of power-distribution facilities, adjustment of customer complaints, and other activities concerned with distribution of electrical energy from substations to customers of electric power company. May be designated Superintendent, Overhead Distribution (utilities); Superintendent, Underground Distribution (utilities).
GOE: 05.02.01 STRENGTH: S GED: R5 M5 L4 SVP: 9 DLU: 77

184.167-154 SUPERINTENDENT, DISTRIBUTION II (utilities) alternate titles: superintendent, city plant; superintendent, gas distribution; superintendent, operations division

Directs and coordinates activities of workers in city gas-distribution plant to ensure adequate facilities and gas supply to meet consumer demands with minimum interruptions to service: Schedules activities, such as gas dispatching, pressure regulation, pumping of drips, odorization of gas, and patrolling and inspection of facilities. Authorizes and supervises, through subordinate supervisory personnel, repair and construction or installation of structures, mains, services (pipes leading from mains to residences), meters, regulators, gas appliances, and other distribution equipment. Formulates policies for promoting customer relationships and directs activities of workers engaged in investigating and adjusting distribution or appliance complaints.
GOE: 05.02.01 STRENGTH: L GED: R5 M4 L4 SVP: 8 DLU: 77

184.167-158 SUPERINTENDENT, DIVISION (motor trans.; r.r. trans.) alternate titles: division superintendent

Plans and administers operations of railroad or bus transportation system within geographic division, consistent with safe and efficient utilization of human resources and equipment, and convenience of shippers and passengers: Establishes and enforces admininstrative policies and procedures. Evaluates reports of train or bus movements, emergency changes in schedules, accidents, weather conditions, and other factors influencing operations to make decisions affecting service. Coordinates repair and maintenance of equipment within division, and recommends capital investments and erection of structures or other facilities. Investigates causes of accidents and delays in traffic and takes steps to ensure that they will not recur. Reviews complaints from shippers and passengers regarding improper or discourteous service. Interprets company agreements for subordinate officials to resolve or prevent labor-relations problems. Confers with state government regulatory commissions and other transportation systems to establish new fares, schedules, routes, and traffic agreements. May personally inspect company facilities and equipment throughout division.
GOE: 11.05.02 STRENGTH: L GED: R5 M3 L5 SVP: 8 DLU: 77

184.167-162 SUPERINTENDENT, ELECTRIC POWER (utilities) alternate titles: manager, public utility, rural

Plans and directs activities of major division, district, plant, or department of utility company, or directs particular phase of operation, concerned with production and distribution of electrical power: Interprets company policies and methods and develops specific operating procedures. Delegates functional activities to workers and establishes supervisory schedules to define authority for independent decisions imperative to continuous service to public and safety of workers. Recruits, trains, and supervises workers directly or through subordinate supervisors. Investigates, evaluates, and determines best application of new developments in electric power industry, and devises other means of securing maximum efficiency of personnel and equipment within his jurisdiction. Anticipates and forecasts power consumption and economic trends, prepares budget recommendations, and makes related decisions in order to keep facilities and system operation concurrent with economic changes. Cooperates with other SUPERINTENDENTS, ELECTRIC POWER (utilities) in solving interrelated administrative, organizational, and technical problems. Directs maintenance of property records and upkeep of equipment and structures. Is usually required to possess an electrical or mechanical engineering background, extensive familiarity with electric power systems, and experience directly related to particular phase of electrical activity superintended.
GOE: 05.02.01 STRENGTH: S GED: R5 M5 L5 SVP: 8 DLU: 77

184.167-166 SUPERINTENDENT, GENERATING PLANT (utilities) alternate titles: chief operating engineer

Directs and coordinates operation of major generating plant of electric power system: Directs and coordinates periodic plant inspections to evaluate condition of equipment. Prepares work orders for major maintenance or repairs. Reviews daily operating reports and other records to ensure specified operating characteristics in control of steam and electric power generating equipment. Confers

with personnel, such as SWITCHBOARD OPERATOR (utilities) 952.362-034 to diagnose equipment malfunctions during emergencies and directs activities to restore normal operation or to shutdown malfunctioning unit. Notifies LOAD DISPATCHER (utilities) 952.167-014 of shutdown or major changes in power output of unit preparatory to transfer of load to other units. Cooperates with SUPERINTENDENT, TESTS (utilities) 184.167-218 and SAFETY INSPECTOR (utilities) 821.367-014 in routine and special tests and plant inspections to improve operations and maintain safe working conditions. May prepare operating budget. May perform personnel activities of department, such as recruitment, hiring, and training.
GOE: 05.02.01 STRENGTH: S GED: R5 M5 L5 SVP: 8 DLU: 81

184.167-170 SUPERINTENDENT, MAINTENANCE (motor trans.) alternate titles: shop superintendent

Directs and coordinates activities of workers engaged in repairing and maintaining motor freight transportation equipment to ensure safe and efficient operation. Purchases parts and records expenditures. Determines specifications for new equipment and directs construction of truck bodies. Contracts for repair services not performed in shop.
GOE: 05.02.02 STRENGTH: S GED: R4 M4 L3 SVP: 7 DLU: 77

184.167-174 SUPERINTENDENT, MAINTENANCE (air trans.)

Directs and coordinates work of employees engaged in maintaining and repairing aircraft: Plans, schedules, and directs, through subordinates, activities of maintenance department concerned with maintaining and repairing engines, airframes, and electrical and hydraulic systems of aircraft. Reviews production records and time-cost statistics, and confers with supervisory personnel to ensure adherence to company standards and to locate areas of inefficient operation. Confers with management to recommend modifications of factors, such as employee and equipment utilization, supervisory and production methods, and procedures to increase efficiency of department. Provides technical advice to subordinates on operating problems. May participate in collective bargaining and settlement of grievances.
GOE: 05.02.02 STRENGTH: S GED: R5 M4 L4 SVP: 8 DLU: 77

184.167-178 SUPERINTENDENT, MAINTENANCE OF EQUIPMENT (motor trans.; r.r. trans.)

Directs and coordinates activities of workers engaged in servicing and repairing buses, trolley cars, or other operating vehicles of busline or railway transit system: Establishes policies for inspection, maintenance, and repair of vehicles. Supervises subordinate supervisors who assign and direct activities in servicing and repairing equipment. Authorizes and arranges for purchasing supplies, tools, and machinery. Consults with officials of operating and servicing divisions on vehicle replacement needs. May investigate and evaluate cause and extent of damage to vehicles involved in accidents.
GOE: 11.11.03 STRENGTH: S GED: R4 M3 L4 SVP: 8 DLU: 77

184.167-182 SUPERINTENDENT, MARINE (water trans.)

Manages on-shore activities for company vessels: Reads radio message from MASTER, SHIP (water trans.) to determine services requested. Requisitions ship's stores or equipment to be delivered on dock at vessel's arrival. Places orders for fuel oil and arranges for time of delivery. Orders personnel replacements from unions. Arranges for other services, such as inspections, tests, overhauls, as required by federal regulations or by company. Notifies MASTER, SHIP (water trans.) by radio of arrangements made. When licensed to command ship, may be designated Port Captain (water trans.).
GOE: 11.11.03 STRENGTH: S GED: R5 M5 L4 SVP: 8 DLU: 77

184.167-186 SUPERINTENDENT, MARINE OIL TERMINAL (water trans.)

Directs and coordinates marine petroleum terminal activities concerned with delivery of crude and fuel oil, gasoline, and other petroleum products to, and receipt from, tankers, barges, or ships; storing of products in terminal tanks; and transfer of products by pipelines: Reviews data, such as vessel arrival date and manifest of cargo showing types and quantities of products to be offloaded or delivered, in order to plan work activities. Determines if storage tanks have capacity to hold quantities of products being discharged or quantities of products to be loaded, using gauging reports showing contents and levels in each tank. Notifies pipeline or refinery personnel of transfer requirements. Directs and coordinates, through subordinate supervisory personnel, connecting of oil transfer hoses, lining up of cross-connections and valves to pump products into or from vessels' tanks or storage tanks. Coordinates activities, such as gauging of tanks, recording tank contents temperature, and obtaining samples of products for analysis, to ensure specified quantities and types of products are received or delivered. Directs preparation of reports on receipt or delivery to and from vessels, pipeline, or storage tanks. Prepares report on status of storage tanks' contents and quantities of products in each tank. Requisitions and schedules repair and maintenance work on terminal facilities and equipment for periods when oil movements are not scheduled.
GOE: 05.02.07 STRENGTH: S GED: R4 M3 L4 SVP: 8 DLU: 77

184.167-190 SUPERINTENDENT, MEASUREMENT (petrol. & gas; pipe lines) alternate titles: measurement superintendent

Directs and coordinates activities concerned with operation and maintenance of control stations used to regulate, measure, and direct flow of crude oil, petroleum products, or natural gas in pipeline system. Plans and directs studies on flow control and measurement of petroleum products and gas and directs activities of workers evaluating newly developed devices. Refers selected devices to

engineering personnel for feasibility and test studies prior to purchase and installation in system. Ascertains need for new control stations, extensions of existing pipelines, and determines locations and sizes of lines from data on forecasts of estimated sales volume and potential customers available at distribution points. Recommends design features of control stations to engineering personnel and directs activities concerned with installation, testing, and maintenance of control and measurement equipment, such as pressure gauges, thermostats, and specialized metering devices in system. Develops plans for coordinating station activities of pipeline system to regulate and measure flow of products from point of origin into and from distribution points in system.
GOE: 05.02.01 STRENGTH: S GED: R5 M5 L4 SVP: 8 DLU: 77

184.167-194 SUPERINTENDENT, METERS (utilities) alternate titles: meter shop superintendent

Coordinates activities of workers engaged in installation, testing, maintenance, and repair of meters used in electric, gas, steam, and water utilities: Develops testing procedures and standards for meters and installations. Provides technical advice and assistance to customers, contractors, and utility personnel concerning metering problems. Directs training of personnel in testing and maintenance of meters and metering installations.
GOE: 05.10.02 STRENGTH: L GED: R5 M4 L4 SVP: 8 DLU: 77

184.167-198 SUPERINTENDENT, PIPELINES (pipe lines)

Coordinates engineering, construction, operation, and maintenance activities of cross-country pipeline used to transport crude oil, petroleum products, natural gas, or coal slurry from transmission to distribution terminal: Reviews forecasts of customer demands to determine additional pipeline construction or alteration requirements on pipeline system and facilities. Develops plans to meet expanded demands and requests engineering section to design and prepare specifications for expanded facilities and capacity, award construction contracts, and assign project engineering personnel for on-site direction. Directs and coordinates, through other management personnel, scheduling, measuring, transmission, and maintenance activities to ensure efficient operation of pipelines and minimize losses. Authorizes procurement of equipment, materials, and supplies required for operations and maintenance. May be designated according to area of pipeline for which responsible as Pipeline Superintendent, District (pipe lines); Pipeline Superintendent, Division (pipe lines).
GOE: 05.02.01 STRENGTH: S GED: R5 M5 L5 SVP: 8 DLU: 77

184.167-202 SUPERINTENDENT, POWER (r.r. trans.) alternate titles: superintendent, electrical department

Directs procurement of electric power for street-railway or electrical railway system, and directs and coordinates activities of workers engaged in planning, installing, and maintaining power generation and distribution facilities: Confers with officials of power companies to arrange for power. Directs activities of company-owned generating plant through subordinate officials. Directs subordinates who supervise construction, maintenance, and repair of distribution system including trolley wire, power lines, poles, underground conduits, and trolley contact signals, when working for street-railway system. Approves plans and designs for electrical distribution equipment.
GOE: 05.02.01 STRENGTH: S GED: R5 M4 L4 SVP: 8 DLU: 77

184.167-206 SUPERINTENDENT, STATIONS (motor trans.; r.r. trans.)

Manages stations and terminals of busline, subway, elevated or interurban railway transit system and confers with other transportation companies on matters, such as fares, routes, and schedules: Examines books and records of stations and terminals. Analyzes financial reports from stations and terminals and prepares reports for management showing profits and expenditures. Analyzes statistics to determine which areas require additional terminals and stations to provide adequate service to public. Reviews agreements with other transportation companies to ensure against or settle disputes concerning fares, routes, and schedules. Confers with governmental commissions and management to establish policy concerning adequate service to public.
GOE: 11.05.02 STRENGTH: S GED: R5 M5 L4 SVP: 6 DLU: 77

184.167-210 SUPERINTENDENT, SYSTEM OPERATION (utilities) alternate titles: planning-division superintendent

Directs activities of system-planning department of electric power company to ensure safe, economical, efficient scheduling of loads and use of facilities to meet normal and emergency power demands. Supervises such personnel as PROTECTION ENGINEERS (utilities) and ENGINEER OF SYSTEM DEVELOPMENT (utilities) concerned with planning and development responsibilities to promote maximum operating efficiency and safety of system.
GOE: 05.02.01 STRENGTH: L GED: R5 M5 L4 SVP: 8 DLU: 77

184.167-214 SUPERINTENDENT, TERMINAL (water trans.)

Manages operations of freight terminal to load and discharge ships' cargoes: Studies ship's manifests to determine whether cargo should be stored in transit sheds or on wharves and to determine what equipment is needed to handle cargo. Notifies SUPERINTENDENT, STEVEDORING (water trans.) to assign workers to jobs and arrange dock space for freight. Computes cost of operations for tonnage handled. Directs purchase of cargo-handling gear and maintenance of terminal and company equipment. May order railroad cars or hire trucks and tractors for transporting freight from docks. When working with company whose terminal has piers located at different places, may be designated Superintendent, Pier (water trans.). May direct operations at container terminal and be designated Superintendent, Container Terminal (water trans.).
GOE: 11.11.03 STRENGTH: S GED: R5 M4 L4 SVP: 8 DLU: 77

184.167-218 SUPERINTENDENT, TESTS (utilities)

Directs and coordinates activities of workers conducting chemical, physical, mechanical, and electrical tests on materials, apparatus, and equipment used in electric power utility: Develops and prepares standard testing procedures manuals for conducting tests and fault analysis research in system. Plans testing activities and prepares schedules for conducting tests, considering such factors as priorities, budget limitations, available human resources, testing facilities, and equipment, in order to obtain optimum utilization of human resources and equipment. Analyzes test results and reports on newly developed apparatus and equipment, malfunctioning and repaired apparatus and equipment, system disturbances, and materials. Consults with other engineering personnel, manufacturers' representatives, and personnel of other utilities to keep abreast of newly developed apparatus and equipment, testing policies and procedures, and modifications of existing equipment. Directs design and testing of new equipment or modification of existing testing equipment. Recommends awarding of contracts for purchase of new equipment, apparatus and materials, basing recommendations on results of tests. May be designated according to testing operations directed as Electrical-Tests Supervisor (utilities); Superintendent, Materials-And-Apparatus Tests (utilities); Superintendent, Meter Tests (utilities); Superintendent, Research-And-Fault-Analysis Tests (utilities); Superintendent, Station-And-Protection-System Tests (utilities).
GOE: 05.01.03 STRENGTH: S GED: R5 M5 L4 SVP: 9 DLU: 77

184.167-222 SUPERINTENDENT, TRANSMISSION (utilities)

Directs operation and maintenance of substations and transmissions lines located at various points throughout electric power system, and the transmission of electrical energy from source to substations: Confers with management and executives of other divisions on such matters as design, construction, operation, and maintenance of system equipment. Formulates and interprets company policies and operating procedures to subordinate supervisory personnel. Prepares budget estimates. Reviews and approves material requisitions and work authorization. Investigates, evaluates, and prepares reports on application of new developments. Reviews and approves drawings for facilities. Prepares, or directs preparation of specifications for materials and work methods. Analyzes bids for materials, equipment, and services, and recommends purchases and awarding of contracts. Directs selection and training of new workers through subordinates. Schedules operation and maintenance work programs and periodically inspects work activities to ensure compliance with company and government regulations. Prepares monthly operating reports.
GOE: 05.02.01 STRENGTH: L GED: R5 M5 L4 SVP: 8 DLU: 77

184.167-226 SUPERINTENDENT, TRANSPORTATION (any industry) alternate titles: manager, transportation; motor vehicles supervisor; superintendent, automotive; transportation department head

Directs and coordinates operational activities of automotive equipment department of an establishment: Procures state-required certificates of title and arranges for registrations and state inspections. Inspects automotive equipment, scheduling needed repair or service work. Coordinates operation and maintenance of equipment, storage facilities, and repair facilities. Directs recording of expenses and analyzes purchase and repair costs to control expenditures. May arrange for insurance coverage on vehicles. May plan and direct safety campaigns. May negotiate with vendors to purchase automotive equipment, materials, and supplies. May assign trucks and passenger cars for use [DISPATCHER, MOTOR VEHICLE (clerical)].
GOE: 11.05.02 STRENGTH: L GED: R5 M4 L5 SVP: 8 DLU: 77

184.167-230 SUPERVISOR OF COMMUNICATIONS (any industry)

Directs and coordinates activities concerned with acquisition, installation, and maintenance of equipment in private communications system of commercial, financial, industrial, transportation firm, or public utility: Directs studies to be conducted on existing communications system and equipment, such as present and projected volume of communications, effectiveness and adequacy of system, and estimated equipment replacement and maintenance costs. Coordinates engineering studies to obtain data on new equipment and systems developments in communications field and adaptability of equipment to existing system. Analyzes reports, records, and recommendations to determine whether equipment should be repaired or replaced, additional equipment installed, or newly developed equipment acquired considering such factors as predicted volume of communications traffic, acquisition and installation costs, estimated improvement in efficiency and effectiveness of operations, and changes in operational procedures resulting from new system installation. Prepares recommendations for acquisition of newly developed, additional, or replacement equipment based on analyses for action by management. Directs preparation of, or prepares, equipment specifications and floor plans for installation in offices or departments. Contacts vendors to arrange for bids for lease or purchase of equipment. Approves acquisition and installation of equipment within limitations approved by management. Coordinates equipment installation and maintenance activities with operations to avoid disruptions in communications and ensure efficiency of operations.
GOE: 05.02.04 STRENGTH: S GED: R4 M4 L4 SVP: 8 DLU: 77

184.167-234 SUPERVISOR OF WAY (r.r. trans.) alternate titles: maintenance-of-way supervisor

Directs personnel in maintenance-of-way department and coordinates maintenance and repair activities with other functions of street-railway system: Issues instructions to personnel engaged in removal of snow or other obstruction from

tracks, and construction, maintenance, and repair of roadway, bridges, and other structures. Dispatches crews of workers and equipment during emergencies, such as breakdowns, derailments, floods, and landslides, to make necessary repairs for restoration of service. Inspects equipment along way, periodically, to ascertain that it is maintained according to standards. Directs personnel engaged in maintaining time and work records.
GOE: 05.02.02 STRENGTH: S GED: R5 M5 L4 SVP: 7 DLU: 77

184.167-238 SUPERVISOR, SEWER SYSTEM (waterworks)
Directs and coordinates work of subordinate personnel engaged in installing, maintaining, repairing, servicing, enlarging, and relocating sewage facilities: Studies proposed projects to evaluate most feasible approach for excavations and repairs, using land plats, topographical maps, and other source data. Determines need for material and equipment required to complete project, such as type and size of pipe, fittings and unions, cranes, bulldozers, welders, or trenching machines, according to size and nature of project. Inspects project to evaluate progress and assure conformance to specifications. Confers with representatives of other utilities to coordinate work schedules for most effective and economic repair activities. Writes reports concerning human resource utilization, work progress, and disposition of materials. Prepares budget estimates based on anticipated material and personnel needs. May effect liaison between field operations and top management or assume regional or zonal responsibility.
GOE: 05.02.01 STRENGTH: L GED: R5 M5 L5 SVP: 8 DLU: 77

184.167-242 SUPERVISOR, TERMINAL OPERATIONS (motor trans.)
Manages terminal operations of passenger or freight motor transportation company: Observes personnel performing duties and studies terminal operations reports on revenues derived, costs of operation, accidents, and frequency of personal or merchandise claims for losses or damages, to determine changes in work practices and procedures necessary to improve operations and reduce claims. Inspects terminal facilities for conformance to prescribed standards of safety and cleanliness, and for maintenance or repair required, and initiates requisitions for corrective actions. Enforces worker compliance with established safety rules and regulations and measures to protect safety of employees and customers and security of merchandise, property, and equipment. Reviews accident reports and takes actions prescribed by company policy. Evaluates worker performance and recommends or initiates personnel actions. May process or attempt to resolve employee grievances according to union contract procedures.
GOE: 11.05.02 STRENGTH: L GED: R4 M3 L3 SVP: 7 DLU: 78

184.167-246 SUPERVISOR, WATERWORKS (waterworks)
Plans and coordinates activities of workers in operation and maintenance of waterworks system to ensure adequate water supply for human consumption, industrial or agricultural use: Schedules and coordinates activities concerned with processing and distributing water. Assigns personnel to shifts to operate filtering and chemical treatment, coagulating and settling basins, and other plant facilities. Determines action to be taken in event of emergencies such as machine, equipment or power failure, or need to release dammed water to effect flood control. Prepares plans and specifications for new equipment or modification of existing equipment to effect increased operational capacity or efficiency. Reviews and evaluates water reports, records, logs, and graphs to confirm adequacy of present and projected water needs. Prepares budget estimates based on anticipated material and personnel needs. May prepare reports concerned with chemical and bacteriological analyses of water for administrative purposes and governmental agencies. May direct construction and maintenance of roads and communication lines used in operating water supply system.
GOE: 05.02.01 STRENGTH: L GED: R5 M5 L5 SVP: 7 DLU: 77

184.167-250 TARIFF PUBLISHING AGENT (business ser.)
Files applications with state and federal regulatory agencies, on behalf of certificated carrier or public utility and under power of attorney, to establish schedule of rates and charges: Receives rates compiled by clerical personnel. Analyzes and arranges tariff to cover one or more carrier or utility and validate power of attorney for any new coverage. Files with federal and state commissions new or revised tariff with new power of attorney. May participate in federal tariff proceedings. May assist attorneys preparing transportation or utility documents.
GOE: 11.04.04 STRENGTH: S GED: R4 M3 L3 SVP: 8 DLU: 77

184.167-254 TERMINAL SUPERINTENDENT (r.r. trans.) alternate titles: assistant superintendent, transportation
Directs and coordinates activities of personnel involved in transportation and handling of freight within geographic subdivision of railroad. Investigates train derailments or other accidents and directs clean-up operations. Directs activities of workers within railroad stations and terminals.
GOE: 11.11.03 STRENGTH: S GED: R4 M3 L4 SVP: 8 DLU: 77

184.167-258 TESTING-AND-REGULATING CHIEF (tel. & tel.)
Directs and coordinates, through shift supervisory personnel, activities concerned with testing, regulating, and maintaining telegraphic channels and circuits and associated terminal apparatus to ensure continuity of wire services: Reviews logs and reports and confers with shift supervisory personnel to ascertain data required for planning, testing, and regulating activities. Prepares work schedules assigning workers to shift supervisory personnel, considering workers' expertise in diagnosing and isolating circuit and apparatus malfunctions and knowledge and experience in adjusting and maintaining telegraphic circuits, channels, and apparatus, such as teleprinters, repeaters, and carriers. Authorizes requisitions for replacement parts, materials, and supplies. Prepares reports and

records on testing and regulating activities, circuit and apparatus malfunctions, and resulting adjustment and maintenance functions.
GOE: 05.02.01 STRENGTH: S GED: R5 M4 L4 SVP: 8 DLU: 77

184.167-262 TRAIN DISPATCHER (r.r. trans.) alternate titles: ctc operator; dispatcher; traffic-control operator
Coordinates railroad traffic on specified section of line from CTC (centralized-traffic-control) unit that electrically activates track switches and signals: Reads train orders and schedules to familiarize self with scheduled runs, destination of trains, times of arrivals and departures, and priority of trains. Monitors CTC panelboard that indicates location of trains by lights that illuminate as train passes specified positions on run. Operates controls to activate track switches and traffic signals. Reroutes trains or signals LOCOMOTIVE ENGINEER (r.r. trans.) to stop train or change speed according to traffic conditions. Talks by telephone with crewmembers to relay changes in train orders and schedules, and to receive notification of emergency stops, delays, or accidents. Records time each train reaches specified point, time messages are given or received, and name of person giving or receiving message. May chart train movements on graph to estimate arrival times at specified points. May operate teletypewriter to transmit messages to freight offices or other points along line.
GOE: 07.04.05 STRENGTH: S GED: R4 M3 L4 SVP: 7 DLU: 77

184.167-266 TRANSPORTATION-MAINTENANCE SUPERVISOR (any industry)
Directs and coordinates, through supervisory personnel, activities of workers engaged in maintenance of transportation equipment in industrial establishment: Confers with department heads to arrange for equipment, such as motor vehicles, railroad rolling stock and equipment, and within-plant trackage systems, to be released from service for inspection, service, or repair. Schedules repairs and follows up on repairs made.
GOE: 05.02.02 STRENGTH: S GED: R5 M4 L4 SVP: 8 DLU: 77

184.167-270 WATER CONTROL SUPERVISOR (waterworks)
Directs and coordinates, through subordinate supervisory personnel, activities of workers engaged in allocation, regulation, and delivery of government controlled water in irrigation district, and in repair and maintenance of irrigation facilities: Reviews water-rights agreements, irrigation contracts, and departmental policies and regulations to determine equitable distribution of water. Schedules time and amount of water to be delivered to users in accordance with instructions. Inspects channels, siphons, tunnels, weirs, roads, bridges, buildings, and equipment for need of repair and maintenance. Assigns supervisory personnel to sanitation, maintenance and repair activities and inspects work for compliance with prescribed operational procedures and methods. Confers with water users to investigate and resolve complaints and public relations problems. Notifies water users of changes in policies and procedures.
GOE: 05.02.01 STRENGTH: L GED: R5 M4 L4 SVP: 8 DLU: 77

184.167-274 WHARFINGER, CHIEF (water trans.)
Plans and directs activities of persons in wharfage department to ensure that fees assessed shipping companies, using municipal facilities, are in accordance with port tariff: Assigns responsibility to personnel for berthing, compiling dockage, wharfage, demurrage, and storage reports, and enforcing safety regulations. Reviews department reports to verify accuracy of assessments. Assigns berth, dock, and shed space for incoming ships. Prepares recommendations for assignment of facilities to companies on a continuous basis. Analyzes reports to determine efficiency of dock operations and recommends improvements. Contacts representatives of shipping companies to resolve problems pertaining to facilities and to maintain business relationship.
GOE: 11.11.03 STRENGTH: S GED: R4 M4 L4 SVP: 8 DLU: 77

184.167-278 YARD MANAGER (r.r. trans.)
Directs and coordinates activities of workers engaged in makeup and breakup of trains and switching inbound and outbound traffic of railroad yard: Reviews train schedules and switching orders, and observes traffic movement in yard to determine which tracks can be made available to accommodate inbound and outbound traffic. Directs routing of inbound and outbound traffic to specific tracks. Reviews waybills or other shipping records indicating material to be loaded or unloaded, tonnage of cargo, type of carrier, and planned routes. Provides instruction concerning switching of cars, makeup and breakup of trains, and routing of inbound and outbound traffic to ensure safe and efficient conduct of yard activities.
GOE: 11.11.03 STRENGTH: S GED: R4 M3 L3 SVP: 7 DLU: 77

184.167-282 DIVISION ROAD SUPERVISOR (r.r. trans.)
Directs and coordinates through supervisory personnel activities of railroad engine crews to ensure efficient operation of railroad in specified jurisdictions: Interviews engine crew personnel to evaluate workers' knowledge of operating and train-handling rules and of railroad route characteristics, such as locations and meanings of signals and types of grades on routes. Rides trains and observes personnel to determine conformance to regulations governing matters, such as train signals, train timetables, and emergency procedures. Determines speed of trains, using radar gun and electrical speed-recording device, and documents detected violations. Conducts investigations of train wrecks to determine causes, to assess equipment damage, to identify personnel responsible, and issues reports of findings.
GOE: 05.02.02 STRENGTH: L GED: R4 M3 L4 SVP: 8 DLU: 86

184.167-286 GENERAL CAR SUPERVISOR, YARD (r.r. trans.)
Directs and coordinates, through subordinate supervisors, activities of workers engaged in inspection, repair, and maintenance of railroad freight cars, uti-

lizing knowledge of railroad maintenance regulations: Analyzes production reports, work schedules, and freight car repair list to determine efficient utilization of human resourcs, and recommends to superiors increasing, reducing, or shifting human resources as necessary to complete work requirements. Fills out daily worksheets identifying defective freight cars, necessary repairs, and priority of repairs for use of subordinate supervisors. Notifies YARD MANAGER (r.r. trans.) 184.167-278 to close tracks on which freight trains are being inspected to other rail traffic. Coordinates dispatching of wreck crews and heavy equipment to wreck site within yard or assigned geographic area. Contacts private contractors to rent equipment needed at wreck site. Informs consignees of damaged freight cars and obtains permission to transfer loads when necessary. Observes work in yard and repair shop to determine that areas are clean and free of hazards. Serves on committees to investigate causes of wrecks. Conducts investigations to determine cause of accidental worker injuries. Submits written reports of findings to superiors.
GOE: 05.02.02 STRENGTH: L GED: R4 M3 L3 SVP: 7 DLU: 86

184.167-290 SUPERVISOR, COMMUNICATIONS-AND-SIGNALS (r.r. trans.)

Directs and coordinates, through subordinate supervisory personnel, activities of workers engaged in installing, maintaining, and testing communications and signalling equipment within specified jurisdiction of railroad: Reviews reports that describe handling of communications and signal irregularities to discern whether deployment of personnel and maintenance procedures followed administrative and labor regulations. Discusses causes of irregularities with supervisor who directed repairs to suggest changes in inspection or maintenance techniques that would prevent recurrence of irregularities, utilizing knowledge of communication and signal functioning. Writes summary of reports indicating worker overtime involved and nature of equipment malfunctions and routes reports to superior. Confers with company engineers regarding major repairs or installation projects in communication and signal system to stay apprised of changes within system. Confers with supervisors throughout projects to provide technical assistance and to ensure availability of equipment needed to complete project.
GOE: 11.11.03 STRENGTH: L GED: R4 M4 L4 SVP: 8 DLU: 86

184.167-294 SUPERVISOR, TRAIN OPERATIONS (r.r. trans.)

Directs and coordinates activities of personnel engaged in scheduling and routing trains and engines in specified railroad territory: Observes record entries and monitors railroad radio communications and lights on train location panelboard to oversee train and engine movements along specified territory of railroad. Confers with railroad dispatchers to determine scheduling of trains and engines. Directs delays of train departures upon notification of substandard track conditions. Coordinates train movements to utilize train crews efficiently to schedule engines to arrive at service locations when due for maintenance and to maximize use of local trains versus special work trains. Scrutinizes train schedules and advises specified personnel of availability of tracks for scheduled repair and maintenance. Issues directives to subordinates to coordinate movement of expedited, late, or special railroad trains, using information received through railroad information network.
GOE: 05.02.02 STRENGTH: L GED: R4 M3 L4 SVP: 8 DLU: 86

184.267-010 FREIGHT-TRAFFIC CONSULTANT (business ser.) alternate titles: transportation consultant

Advises industries, business firms, and individuals concerning methods of preparation of freight for shipment, rates to be applied, and mode of transportation to be used: Consults with client regarding packing procedures and inspects packed or crated goods for conformance to shipping specifications to prevent damage, delay, or penalties. Selects mode of transportation, such as air, water, railroad, or truck without regard to higher rates when speed is necessary. Confers with shipping brokers concerning export and import papers, docking facilities, or packing and marking procedures. Files claims with insurance company for losses, damages, and overcharges of freight shipments.
GOE: 11.05.02 STRENGTH: S GED: R5 M4 L4 SVP: 8 DLU: 77

184.387-010 WHARFINGER (water trans.)

Compiles reports, such as dockage, demurrage, wharfage, and storage, to ensure that shipping companies are assessed specified harbor fees: Compares information on statements, records, and reports with ship's manifest to determine that weight, measurement, and classification of commodities are in accordance with tariff. Calculates tariff assessment from ship's manifest to ensure that charges are correct. Prepares and submits reports. Inspects sheds and wharves to determine need for repair. Arranges for temporary connection of water and electrical services from wharves. Reads service meters to determine charges to be made.
GOE: 07.02.04 STRENGTH: L GED: R3 M3 L2 SVP: 5 DLU: 77

185 WHOLESALE AND RETAIL TRADE MANAGERS AND OFFICIALS

This group includes managerial occupations concerned with selling merchandise to retailers; to industrial, commercial, institutional or professional users; or to other wholesalers; or acting as agents in buying merchandise for or selling merchandise to such persons or companies.

185.117-010 MANAGER, DEPARTMENT STORE (retail trade)

Directs and coordinates, through subordinate managerial personnel, activities of department store selling lines of merchandise in specialized departments:

Formulates pricing policies for sale of merchandise, or implements policies set forth by merchandising board. Coordinates activities of nonmerchandising departments, as purchasing, credit, accounting, and advertising with merchandising departments to obtain optimum efficiency of operations with minimum costs in order to maximize profits. Develops and implements, through subordinate managerial personnel, policies and procedures for store and departmental operations and customer personnel and community relations. Negotiates or approves contracts negotiated with suppliers of merchandise, or with other establishments providing security, maintenance, or cleaning services. Reviews operating and financial statements and departmental sales records to determine merchandising activities that require additional sales promotion, clearance sales, or other sales procedures in order to turn over merchandise and achieve profitability of store operations and merchandising objectives.
GOE: 11.05.02 STRENGTH: S GED: R5 M4 L5 SVP: 8 DLU: 77

185.117-014 AREA SUPERVISOR, RETAIL CHAIN STORE (retail trade) alternate titles: operations manager

Directs and coordinates activities of subordinate managerial personnel involved in operating retail chain stores in assigned area: Interviews and selects individuals to fill managerial vacancies. Maintains employment records for each manager. Terminates employment of store managers whose performance does not meet company standards. Directs, through subordinate managerial personnel, compliance of workers with established company policies, procedures, and standards, such as safekeeping of company funds and property, personnel and grievance practices, and adherence to policies governing acceptance and processing of customer credit card charges. Inspects premises of assigned area stores to ensure that adequate security exists and that physical facilities comply with safety and environmental codes and ordinances. Reviews operational records and reports of store managers to project sales and to determine store profitability. Coordinates sales and promotional activities of store managers. Analyzes marketing potential of new and existing store locations and recommends additional sites or deletion of existing area stores. Negotiates with vendors to enter into contracts for merchandise and determines allocations to each store manager.
GOE: 11.11.05 STRENGTH: L GED: R4 M3 L4 SVP: 7 DLU: 86

185.137-010 MANAGER, FAST FOOD SERVICES (retail trade; wholesale tr.)

Manages franchised or independent fast food or wholesale prepared food establishment: Directs, coordinates, and participates in preparation of, and cooking, wrapping or packing types of food served or prepared by establishment, collecting of monies from in-house or take-out customers, or assembling food orders for wholesale customers. Coordinates activities of workers engaged in keeping business records, collecting and paying accounts, ordering or purchasing supplies, and delivery of foodstuffs to wholesale or retail customers. Interviews, hires, and trains personnel. May contact prospective wholesale customers, such as mobile food vendors, vending machine operators, bar and tavern owners, and institutional personnel, to promote sale of prepared foods, such as doughnuts, sandwiches, and specialty food items. May establish delivery routes and schedules for supplying wholesale customers. Workers may be known according to type or name of franchised establishment or type of prepared foodstuff retailed or wholesaled.
GOE: 11.11.04 STRENGTH: L GED: R4 M4 L4 SVP: 5 DLU: 81

185.157-010 FASHION COORDINATOR (retail trade) alternate titles: fashion stylist

Promotes new fashions and coordinates promotional activities, such as fashion shows, to induce consumer acceptance: Studies fashion and trade journals, travels to garment centers, attends fashion shows, and visits manufacturers and merchandise markets to obtain information on fashion trends. Consults with buying personnel to gain advice regarding type of fashions store will purchase and feature for season. Advises publicity and display departments of merchandise to be publicized. Selects garments and accessories to be shown at fashion shows. Provides information on current fashions, style trends, and use of accessories. May contract with models, musicians, caterers, and other personnel to manage staging of shows. May conduct teenage fashion shows and direct activities of store-sponsored club for teenage girls.
GOE: 11.09.01 STRENGTH: L GED: R5 M4 L5 SVP: 7 DLU: 77

185.157-014 SUPERVISOR OF SALES (business ser.)

Coordinates and publicizes tobacco marketing activities within specified area: Visits tobacco growers, buyers, and auction warehouses to cultivate interest and goodwill. Develops publicity for tobacco industry. Investigates and confirms eligibility of buyers. Collects membership dues for tobacco Board of Trade. Schedules tobacco auction dates. Records quantity and purchase price of tobacco sold daily, and prepares reports specified by board. May prepare report of marketing activities for state and federal agencies. May review and verify reports for individual warehouses. May examine quality and growth of tobacco in fields of individual growers and inform buyers of results.
GOE: 11.09.01 STRENGTH: L GED: R4 M4 L4 SVP: 7 DLU: 77

185.157-018 WHOLESALER II (wholesale tr.)

Exports domestic merchandise to foreign merchants and consumers and imports foreign merchandise for sale to domestic merchants or consumers: Arranges for purchase and transportation of imports through company representatives abroad and sells imports to local customers. Sells domestic goods, materials, or products to representatives of foreign companies. May be required

to be fluent in language of country in which import or export business is conducted. May specialize in only one phase of foreign trade and be designated Exporter (wholesale tr.); Importer (retail trade; wholesale tr.).
GOE: 11.05.04 STRENGTH: S GED: R5 M4 L5 SVP: 7 DLU: 77

185.164-010 SERVICE MANAGER (retail trade)
Coordinates activities of service department in lawnmower sales and service establishment: Directs activities of workers through supervisory staff. Discusses with supervisory staff methods of assembling and repairing lawnmowers to ensure compliance with prescribed procedures. Interviews and hires workers. Maintains time and production records. Answers questions and discusses complaints with customers regarding services as specified in equipment warranty agreement. Assembles and tests operation of new lawnmowers to prepare mowers for sales floor, following assembly and test procedures and using handtools.
GOE: 05.10.02 STRENGTH: H GED: R4 M3 L3 SVP: 7 DLU: 86

185.167-010 COMMISSARY MANAGER (any industry)
Directs and coordinates activities of commissary store to sell to or provide company employees or other eligible customers with foodstuffs, clothing, or other merchandise: Determines quantities of foodstuffs or other merchandise required to stock commissary, from inventory records, and prepares requisitions or buys merchandise to replenish stock. Sells merchandise to company employees or other eligible customers or issues merchandise upon requisition by authorized personnel. Keeps records pertaining to purchases, sales, and requisitions. May issue foodstuffs and supplies to COOKS, CAMP (any industry) for preparation of meals.
GOE: 11.11.05 STRENGTH: L GED: R4 M4 L3 SVP: 6 DLU: 77

185.167-014 MANAGER, AUTOMOBILE SERVICE STATION (retail trade)
Manages automobile service station: Plans, develops, and implements policies for operating station, such as hours of operation, workers required and duties, scope of operations, and prices for products and services. Hires and trains workers, prepares work schedules, and assigns workers to specific duties, such as customer service, automobile maintenance, or repair work. Directs, coordinates, and participates in performing customer service activities, such as pumping gasoline, checking engine oil, tires, battery, and washing windows and windshield. Notifies customer when oil is dirty or low, tires are worn, hoses or fanbelts are defective, or evidece indicates battery defects, to promote sale of products and services, such as oil change and lubrication, tires, battery, or other automotive accessories. Reconciles cash with gasoline pump meter readings, sales slips, and credit card charges. Orders, receives, and inventories gasoline, oil, automotive accessories and parts. May perform automotive maintenance and repair work, such as adjusting or relining brakes, motor tune-ups, valve grinding, and changing and repairing tires. May sell only gasoline and oil on self-service basis and be designated Manager, Self-Service Gasoline Station (retail trade).
GOE: 11.11.05 STRENGTH: H GED: R4 M4 L4 SVP: 7 DLU: 81

185.167-018 MANAGER, DISTRIBUTION WAREHOUSE (wholesale tr.)
Directs and coordinates activities of wholesaler's distribution warehouse: Reviews bills of lading for incoming merchandise and customer orders in order to plan work activities. Assigns workers to specific duties, such as verifying amounts of and storing incoming merchandise and assembling customer orders for delivery. Establishes operational procedures for verification of incoming and outgoing shipments, handling and disposition of merchandise, and keeping of warehouse inventory. Coordinates activities of distribution warehouse with activities of sales, record control, and purchasing departments to ensure availability of merchandise. Directs reclamation of damaged merchandise.
GOE: 11.11.03 STRENGTH: S GED: R5 M3 L4 SVP: 6 DLU: 77

185.167-022 MANAGER, FOOD CONCESSION (hotel & rest.)
Manages refreshment stand or other food concession at public gatherings, sports events, amusement park, or similar facility: Purchases refreshments, according to anticipated demand and familiarity with public taste in food and beverages. Directs storage, preparation, and serving of refreshments by other workers at refreshment stand or circulating throughout audience. Assigns VENDORS (amuse. & rec.) to locations. Tabulates receipts and balances accounts. Inventories supplies on hand at end of each day or other designated period.
GOE: 09.04.01 STRENGTH: L GED: R3 M3 L3 SVP: 6 DLU: 77

185.167-026 MANAGER, MACHINERY-OR-EQUIPMENT, RENTAL AND LEASING (any industry)
Directs and coordinates activities of establishment engaged in renting or leasing machinery, tools and equipment to companies involved in business operations such as manufacturing, petroleum production, construction or materials handling, or to individuals for personal use: Confers with customer to ascertain article required, duration of rental time, and responsibility for maintenance and repair, in order to determine rental or leasing charges based on such factors as type and cost of article, type of usage, duration of rental or lease, and overhead costs. Prepares rental or lease agreement, specifying charges and payment procedures, for use of machinery, tools, or equipment. Directs activities of workers engaged in bookkeeping, record and inventory keeping, and in checking, handling, servicing or maintaining in-house, leased, or rented machines, tools and equipment. Managers of leasing or renting establishments may be designated according to type or use of machinery, tools or equipment.
GOE: 11.11.05 STRENGTH: L GED: R4 M4 L4 SVP: 6 DLU: 77

185.167-030 MANAGER, MEAT SALES AND STORAGE (retail trade; wholesale tr.)
Coordinates activities of workers engaged in buying, processing, and selling meats and poultry and renting frozen food lockers: Prepares daily schedule and directs activities of employees. Examines products bought for resale or received for storage. Cuts, trims, bones, and cleans meats and poultry. Displays and sells different cuts of meats and poultry to customers and advises customers on quality of food, method of handling, and other factors affecting preparing, freezing, and storing food. Conducts in-service training for employees.
GOE: 11.11.05 STRENGTH: M GED: R4 M3 L3 SVP: 6 DLU: 77

185.167-034 MANAGER, MERCHANDISE (retail trade; wholesale tr.) alternate titles: director, merchandise
Formulates merchandising policies and coordinates merchandising activities in wholesale or retail establishment: Determines mark-up and mark-down percentages necessary to ensure profit, based on estimated budget, profit goals, and average rate of stock turnover. Determines amount of merchandise to be stocked and directs buyers in purchase of supplies for resale. Consults with other personnel to plan sales promotion programs.
GOE: 11.05.04 STRENGTH: S GED: R4 M3 L4 SVP: 7 DLU: 77

185.167-038 MANAGER, PARTS (retail trade; wholesale tr.) alternate titles: manager, stockroom
Manages retail or wholesale automotive parts establishment or department of repair shop or service station: Requisitions new stock. Verifies cash receipts and keeps sales records. Hires, trains, and discharges workers. Confirms credit references of customers by mail or telephone. May sell parts.
GOE: 11.11.05 STRENGTH: L GED: R4 M3 L3 SVP: 7 DLU: 77

185.167-042 MANAGER, PROFESSIONAL EQUIPMENT SALES-AND-SERVICE (business ser.)
Directs and coordinates activities of establishment engaged in sale of professional equipment and supplies, and providing customer services, to organizations in such fields as medicine and medical services, engineering, and education: Plans and directs sales and service programs to promote new markets, improve competitive position in area, and provide fast and efficient customer service. Confers with potential customer to ascertain equipment, supplies, and service needs. Advises customer on types of equipment to purchase, considering such factors as costs, space availability, and intended use. Directs and coordinates activities of personnel engaged in sales and service accounting and record keeping, and receiving and shipping operations. Reviews articles in trade publications to keep abreast of technological developments in types of professional equipment merchandised. Resolves customer complaints regarding equipment, supplies, and services. Workers are usually classified according to type of firm managed or type of equipment and supplies sold such as dental, hospital, school, medical, or laboratory supply house.
GOE: 11.05.04 STRENGTH: S GED: R5 M4 L4 SVP: 7 DLU: 77

185.167-046 MANAGER, RETAIL STORE (retail trade) alternate titles: store manager
Manages retail store engaged in selling specific line of merchandise, such as groceries, meat, liquor, apparel, jewelry, or furniture; related lines of merchandise, such as radios, televisions, or household appliances; or general line of merchandise, performing following duties personally or supervising employees performing duties: Plans and prepares work schedules and assigns employees to specific duties. Formulates pricing policies on merchandise according to requirements for profitability of store operations. Coordinates sales promotion activities and prepares, or directs workers preparing, merchandise displays and advertising copy. Supervises employees engaged in sales work, taking of inventories, reconciling cash with sales receipts, keeping operating records, or preparing daily record of transactions for ACCOUNTANT (profess & kin.) 160.162-018, or performs work of subordinates, as needed. Orders merchandise or prepares requisitions to replenish merchandise on hand. Ensures compliance of employees with established security, sales, and record keeping procedures and practices. May answer customer's complaints or inquiries. May lock and secure store. May interview, hire, and train employees. May be designated according to specific line of merchandise sold, such as women's apparel or furniture; related lines of merchandise, such as camera and photographic supplies, or gifts, novelties, and souvenirs; type of business, such as mail order establishment or auto supply house; or general line of merchandise, such as sporting goods, drugs and sundries, or variety store.
GOE: 11.11.05 STRENGTH: L GED: R4 M4 L4 SVP: 7 DLU: 81

185.167-050 MANAGER, TEXTILE CONVERSION (business ser.; wholesale tr.)
Directs and coordinates activities of firm engaged in purchasing, finishing, and wholesaling textile fabrics, or in finishing fabrics for trade on commission basis: Purchases textile fabrics from mills or receives fabrics from apparel or other finished fabric product manufacturers. Directs and coordinates finishing operations, such as bleaching, dyeing, and printing (roller, screen, flock, or plisse techniques), preshrinking, calendering, or napping, according to customer specifications. May direct other chemical finishing treatments of fabric to develop qualities, such as water repellency, fire resistance, or mildew proofing.
GOE: 11.11.05 STRENGTH: L GED: R4 M4 L4 SVP: 6 DLU: 77

185.167-054 MANAGER, TOBACCO WAREHOUSE (wholesale tr.)
Manages tobacco warehouse: Oversees auction sale of consigned tobacco to wholesale buyers. Ascertains eligibility of each purchaser before completing

sale. Supervises workers engaged in collecting payment from buyers and paying growers for tobacco sold. Directs advertisement of firm through printed matter and subordinates who contact prospective customers.
GOE: 11.11.05 STRENGTH: L GED: R4 M3 L3 SVP: 8 DLU: 77

185.167-058 SERVICE MANAGER (automotive ser.)
Coordinates activities of workers in one or more service departments of automobile accessories sales-service establishment: Directs activities of workers, such as TIRE REPAIRER (automotive ser.) and BRAKE REPAIRER (automotive ser.). Assists sales personnel in adjusting customers' service complaints. Hires, transfers, and discharges workers. Directs activities of workers engaged in testing new equipment and recommends purchase or rejection of equipment. Determines work standards and evaluates workers' performance. May handle claims regarding defective factory work quality. May determine need and cost of automobile repair [AUTOMOBILE-REPAIR-SERVICE ESTIMATOR (automotive ser.)].
GOE: 05.10.02 STRENGTH: L GED: R4 M3 L4 SVP: 6 DLU: 77

185.167-062 SUPERVISOR, LIQUOR STORES AND AGENCIES (government ser.)
Directs activities of alcoholic beverage control authority in counties or other governmental units of states operating retail liquor stores: Coordinates, through subordinates, purchasing, sale, inventory control, display, tabulating of receipts, and warehousing of beverages in stores according to public demand and established policy of control authority. Visits stores to inspect facilities and procedures and evaluate condition of stock. Authorizes transfer of beverages among stores to maintain fresh, balanced stock. Recommends expansion, remodeling, or relocation of stores according to accepted merchandising principles and policy of authority. Reviews sales and inventory reports to develop more efficient procedures and to supply data on beverage consumption to legislative officials or other interested parties. May plan window displays or other merchandising techniques to stimulate sales. May direct activities of state self-service stores and be designated Supervisor, Self-Service Store (government ser.).
GOE: 11.05.03 STRENGTH: S GED: R5 M4 L4 SVP: 8 DLU: 77

185.167-066 VENDING-STAND SUPERVISOR (government ser.) alternate titles: operations supervisor; vending-enterprises supervisor
Coordinates activities of persons engaged in vending-stand operations of state program for rehabilitation of the blind: Observes stand operation and advises blind vendor on merchandise purchase and display, improved methods of operation, personal appearance, and sanitation. Inspects condition of stock and fixtures to ascertain adherence to regulations and to determine need for maintenance and repairs. Examines invoices and receipts to determine equity of charges and to prepare monthly profit and loss statement. Investigates and resolves problems varying from nuisance complaints to breach-of-contract. May address civic groups to promote public relations. May collect cash, invoices, receipts, and specified assessments as determined by state program requirements. May plan, locate, and arrange for installation of stands, train vendors, and negotiate contracts with building managers for stand operation [BUSINESS-ENTERPRISE OFFICER (government ser.)].
GOE: 09.04.01 STRENGTH: L GED: R5 M4 L4 SVP: 7 DLU: 77

185.167-070 WHOLESALER I (wholesale tr.)
Manages establishment engaged in purchasing, wholesaling, and distributing merchandise, such as furniture and home furnishings, construction materials and supplies, metals and minerals, electrical goods, drugs and drug proprietaries, groceries and foodstuffs, and professional equipment and supplies to retailers, industrial and commercial consumers, or professional personnel: Estimates stock requirements based on sales orders, inventory, projected volume of sales, and current condition of economy. Authorizes purchase of merchandise based on estimates. Directs assembly of and storing of merchandise by workers, filling of orders, and distribution to customers according to sales orders. Directs and coordinates activities of workers engaged in wholesaling merchandise and extending credit to purchasers. Advises customers concerning current and future market conditions and availability of merchandise. Workers are classified according to type of merchandise, product, or material wholesaled and distributed.
GOE: 11.05.04 STRENGTH: S GED: R5 M5 L4 SVP: 8 DLU: 77

185.167-074 MANAGER, AUTO SPECIALTY SERVICES (automotive ser.)
Manages establishment engaged in automotive specialty services, such as engine tune-up, front-end alignment, or muffler installation: Directs and coordinates, through subordinate personnel, activities of workers engaged in diagnosing and repairing automobile malfunctions. Monitors operations to ensure that services rendered conform to company policy and standards. Resolves customer complaints. Reviews operational expenses and collection reports for accuracy. Authorizes acquisition of tools, equipment, and parts. Hires, discharges, and assists in training workers. May contact advertising media to publicize services.
GOE: 11.11.04 STRENGTH: L GED: R5 M4 L4 SVP: 7 DLU: 86

186   FINANCE, INSURANCE, AND REAL ESTATE MANAGERS AND OFFICIALS

This group includes managerial and management related occupations concerned with banks and trust companies, credit agencies other than banks, investment companies, brokers, and dealers in securities and commodity contracts,

and security and commodity exchanges; all types of insurance, and insurance agents and brokers; owners, lessors, lessees, buyers, sellers, agents, and developers of real estate.

186.117-010 BUSINESS MANAGER, COLLEGE OR UNIVERSITY (education)
Administers business affairs of college or university: Prepares operating budget draft for submission through PRESIDENT, COLLEGE OR UNIVERSITY (education) to board of trustees. Directs control of budget upon its approval by board, including collection, custody, investment, disbursement, accounting, and auditing of all college funds. Recruits, supervises, and oversees training of clerical staff. Formulates, with DIRECTOR OF STUDENT AFFAIRS (education), policies and procedures governing financial relations with students, dormitories, cafeterias, bookstores, and recreational and parking facilities. Audits financial status of student organization accounts, campus food service, housing, and bookstores. Administers financial aspects of student loans, scholarships, and student credit. Negotiates with groups, such as foundations, for university loans. Keeps financial records and prepares annual financial report. Formulates and administers policies and procedures for development and management of physical plant, including custodial care, sanitation, and fire and police protection. Negotiates with industry representatives on costs and materials for building construction. Develops policies and procedures for procurement of goods and nonpersonal services for university. Coordinates service operations, such as printing, duplicating, mail and messenger service, bindery, and machine computing and tabulating.
GOE: 11.05.02 STRENGTH: S GED: R5 M5 L5 SVP: 8 DLU: 77

186.117-018 CUSTOMS BROKER (financial) alternate titles: customs-house broker
Prepares and compiles documents required by federal government for discharge of foreign cargo at domestic port to serve as intermediary between importers, merchant shipping companies, airlines, railroads, trucking companies, pipeline operators, and the United States Customs Service: Prepares entry papers from shipper's invoice in accordance with U.S. Customs Service regulations, and regulations of other federal agencies bearing on importation of goods, such as Environmental Protection Agency and Food And Drug Administration. Files papers with Customs Service and arranges for payment of duties. Quotes duty rates on goods to be imported, based on knowledge of federal tariffs and excise taxes. Prepares papers for shippers desiring to appeal duty charges imposed by Customs Service. Provides for storage of imported goods and for transportation of imported goods from port to final destination. May register foreign ships with U.S. Coast Guard. Must be licensed by U.S. Treasury Department or operate under corporate license granted to employer by Treasury Department.
GOE: 11.04.04 STRENGTH: S GED: R5 M4 L5 SVP: 7 DLU: 89

186.117-022 DEPUTY INSURANCE COMMISSIONER (government ser.)
Directs investigative, examining, and surety bonding activities of State Insurance Commission to ensure that companies and agents comply with provisions of insurance regulations and laws: Reviews insurance policies for conformance with prescribed underwriting standards or directs this work by others. Coordinates staff investigative activities concerning complaints of fraud, misrepresentation, excessive rates, financial irresponsibility, and other improprieties. Reviews financial statements of companies and agents to determine adherence to licensing requirements and state laws. Conducts examination of agents or other insurance personnel to determine qualifications for licensing. Receives and validates surety bonds from company representatives. Recommends or initiates punitive action, such as prosecution or license revocation, in cases of company or agent impropriety.
GOE: 11.10.01 STRENGTH: S GED: R5 M5 L5 SVP: 8 DLU: 77

186.117-030 GENERAL CLAIMS AGENT (air trans.; motor trans.; r.r. trans.; water trans.)
Directs and coordinates activities involving claims against transportation company for shortages in or damaged freight, accidental death or injury to persons or employees, and private property damages: Directs activities of workers investigating claims to ascertain validity of claims and extent of company liability. Processes freight and property claims for which company is liable and submits claims to head office for settlement, or negotiates settlement with claimant and authorizes payment. Reviews employee accident reports to determine compensation program under which accidents are covered, and doctor reports for type of injury and length of time disabled. Authorizes payment of disability compensation according to state or federal acts. Contacts medical personnel to ascertain need for extension of payments beyond specified recovery date. Negotiates with persons having valid claims against company or death or injury to effect out-of-court settlement and refers cases that cannot be settled to legal department. Represents company at industrial accident or compensation board hearings to present company position on accident liability. May testify at court hearings to present evidence on company liability from investigation documents.
GOE: 11.12.01 STRENGTH: S GED: R4 M4 L4 SVP: 8 DLU: 77

186.117-034 MANAGER, BROKERAGE OFFICE (financial) alternate titles: branch manager; office manager
Directs and coordinates activities concerned with buying or selling investment products and financial services, such as securities, insurance, and real estate, for clients of brokerage firm: Screens, selects, and hires REGISTERED

REPRESENTATIVES (financial) 250.257-018 and other employees. Directs in-service training to improve client services and increase sales volume. Develops and implements plans to ensure compliance of workers with established programs, procedures, and practices. Establishes internal control procedures to control margin accounts, short sales, and options and to reduce office errors and client complaints. Reviews recapitulation of daily transactions to ensure accordance with rules and regulations of government agencies, regulatory bodies, and securities exchanges. Analyzes operations to determine areas where cost reductions could be implemented or program improvements initiated. Evaluates profitability of gross sales and transactions. Conducts staff meetings of personnel to discuss changes in policy, redirection of sales emphasis to other programs, or to propose methods and procedures to increase firm's share of local market and trade volume. Explains firm's research and customer service facilities and how use of facilities can promote customer relations and sales. Prepares activity reports for evaluation by management. May be required to have securities agent license. May be required to have experience in certain type of brokerage office managed, such as full-service brokerage office, discount brokerage office, or full-service/discount brokerage office.
GOE: 11.05.04 STRENGTH: S GED: R5 M4 L5 SVP: 8 DLU: 89

186.117-042 MANAGER, LAND DEVELOPMENT (real estate)
Coordinates activities of land development company and negotiates with representatives of real estate, private enterprise and industrial organizations, and community leaders to acquire and develop land: Supervises staff engaged in such activities as preparing appraisal reports on available land, preparing feasibility studies, showing availability and quality of water resources, mineral deposits, electric power, and labor supply. Prepares or directs preparation of statistical abstracts to reveal trends in tax rates in given communities, and proportion of total work force having specified skills. Plans, oversees, and directs activities of field staff engaged in sampling mineral deposits, surveying land boundaries, and testing water supply to determine optimum usage of land. Negotiates with community, business, and public utility representatives to eliminate obstacles to land purchase, development, sale, or lease. Negotiates mortgage loans. Directs collection and auditing of funds from sale or lease of property. May perform duties of REAL-ESTATE AGENT (profess. & kin.) 186.117-058. May cooperate with representatives of public utilities, universities, and other groups to coordinate research activities. May work for railroad and specialize in industrial development and be designated Manager, Industrial Development (r.r. trans.). May work for government and be designated Property Manager (government ser.).
GOE: 11.05.01 STRENGTH: L GED: R5 M5 L5 SVP: 8 DLU: 89

186.117-046 MANAGER, LEASING (petrol. & gas) alternate titles: general manager, land department; land-and-leases supervisor; land department head; lease agent; leases-and-land supervisor; manager, land department; superintendent, land department
Directs land and leasing department of petroleum company to secure leases, options, rights-of-way, and special agreements covering land and mineral rights for drilling wells and producing gas and oil: Studies leases bought, prices paid, and other negotiations of competing companies in specified areas and determines expenditure necessary to obtain leases and other contracts in those areas. Determines and specifies date of termination of lease rentals. Negotiates with brokers or other individuals to sell interests in leases owned. Executes general policies established by company officials. May make final decisions on and sign agreements and contracts for purchase, sale and acquisition of land leases, mineral and royalty rights. May be designated according to area of operations as Manager, Divisional Leasing (petrol. & gas).
GOE: 11.12.02 STRENGTH: S GED: R5 M5 L5 SVP: 8 DLU: 77

186.117-054 PRESIDENT, FINANCIAL INSTITUTION (financial)
Plans, develops, and directs financial policies and practices of bank, savings bank, commercial bank, trust company, mortgage company, credit union, or company dealing in consumer credit, such as finance company, to ensure that financial objectives, goals, and institutional growth are met and in accordance with policies of Board of Directors or corporate charter and government regulations: Plans and develops investment, loan, interest, and reserve policies to ensure optimum monetary returns in accordance with availability of investment funds, government restrictions, and sound financial practices. Coordinates communication and reporting activities between divisions, departments, and branch offices to ensure availability of data required for efficient daily operations. Delegates to subordinate corporate officers authority for administering activities and operations under their control. Reviews reports and financial statements to determine policy changes due to changes in economic conditions. May serve as bank representative in professional, business, and community organizations to promote bank services. May plan budget and monitor financial activities, using computer. May serve on Board of Directors. May be designated according to type of financial institution as President, Commercial Bank (financial); President, Credit Union (financial); President, Finance Company (financial); President, Mortgage Company (financial); President, Savings Bank (financial); President, Trust Company (financial).
GOE: 11.05.01 STRENGTH: S GED: R6 M5 L5 SVP: 9 DLU: 89

186.117-058 REAL-ESTATE AGENT (profess. & kin.) alternate titles: land agent
Coordinates activities of real-estate department of company and negotiates acquisition and disposition of properties in most beneficial manner: Supervises staff engaged in preparing lease agreements, recording rental receipts, and performing other activities necessary to efficient management of company properties, or in performing routine research on zoning ordinances and condemnation considerations. Directs appraiser to inspect properties and land under consideration for acquisition, and recommends acquisition, lease, disposition, improvement, or other action consistent with best interest of company. Authorizes or requests authorization for maintenance of company properties not under control of operating departments, such as dwellings, hotels, or commissaries. Evaluates and promotes industrial-development potential of company properties. Negotiates contracts with sellers of land and renters of properties.
GOE: 11.12.02 STRENGTH: L GED: R5 M5 L5 SVP: 8 DLU: 77

186.117-062 RENTAL MANAGER, PUBLIC EVENTS FACILITIES (business ser.)
Negotiates contracts for leasing arenas, auditoriums, stadiums, or other public events facilities: Solicits new business and renews established contracts to promote rental of facilities. Maintains schedule of rentals to determine availability of facilities for bookings. Oversees operation and maintenance of facilities. Notifies fire and police departments of scheduled use of buildings to provide protection. Studies reports to ascertain time lessee used facilities and if damage was incurred to facilities or contents. Submits bills and receives and accounts for monies paid for rentals.
GOE: 11.12.02 STRENGTH: L GED: R5 M4 L4 SVP: 8 DLU: 77

186.117-066 RISK AND INSURANCE MANAGER (any industry) alternate titles: insurance and risk manager
Plans, directs, and coordinates risk and insurance programs of establishment to control risks and losses: Analyzes and classifies risks as to frequency and potential severity, and measures financial impact of risk on company. Selects appropriate technique to minimize loss, such as avoidance (reducing chance of loss to zero), loss prevention and reduction (reducing frequency and severity of loss), retention (including self-insurance and planned noninsurance), grouping of exposure units (to increase predictability of loss), and transfer (placement of property, activity, or risk with other establishment or insurers). Directs insurance negotiations, selects insurance brokers and carriers, and places insurance. Appoints claims and self-insurance administrators, and allocates program costs. Prepares operational and risk reports for management analysis. Manages insurance programs, such as fidelity, surety, liability, property, group life, medical, pension plans, and workers' compensation. Prepares operational and risk reports for management analysis. May direct loss prevention and safety programs. May select and direct activities of safety, engineering, and loss prevention experts. May negotiate with unions for employee benefits.
GOE: 11.06.03 STRENGTH: S GED: R5 M4 L4 SVP: 8 DLU: 77

186.117-070 TREASURER, FINANCIAL INSTITUTION (financial) alternate titles: cashier
Directs and coordinates programs, transactions, and security measures of financial institution: Examines institution operations to evaluate efficiency. Plans and implements new operating procedures to improve efficiency and reduce costs. Directs receipt and disbursement of funds and acquisition and sale of other assets. Approves agreements affecting capital transactions. Directs safekeeping, control, and accounting of assets and securities. Ensures that institution reserves meet legal requirements. Analyzes financial and operating statements of institution, and reports and makes recommendations to management or board of directors in regard to financial policies and programs. May participate as member of committee deciding on extending lines of credit to commercial enterprises and other organizations. May be designated according to type of financial institution, such as Treasurer, Savings Bank (financial).
GOE: 11.06.05 STRENGTH: S GED: R5 M5 L5 SVP: 9 DLU: 77

186.117-074 TRUST OFFICER (financial) alternate titles: trust administrator
Directs and coordinates activities relative to creating and administering personal, corporate, probate, and court-ordered guardianship trusts in accordance with terms creating trust, will, or court order: Directs drafting of, drafts, or consults with client's attorney who drafts, legal documents specifying details, conditions, and duration of trust. Locates and places funds, securities, and other assets in trust account. Interviews trust beneficiaries of court-ordered guardianship trusts in order to locate probable sources of assets. Negotiates with public agencies, such as Social Security Administration and Worker's Compensation Commission, in effort to accumulate all assets into trust. Directs collection of earnings, dividends, or sale of assets and placement of proceeds in trust account. Directs realization of assets, liquidation of liabilities, and payment of debts for trusts. Directs disbursement of funds according to conditions of trust or needs of court ward or beneficiary. Ensures that excess or surplus funds are invested according to terms of trust and wishes of trust client. May specialize in promoting trust services and establishing new trust accounts. May prepare federal and state tax returns for trusts. May be designated according to type of trust as Corporate Trust Officer (financial); Personal Trust Officer (financial).
GOE: 11.06.05 STRENGTH: L GED: R5 M4 L5 SVP: 7 DLU: 89

186.117-078 VICE PRESIDENT, FINANCIAL INSTITUTION (financial)
Directs and coordinates, through subordinate managerial personnel, activities of department, region, administrative division, or specific function of financial institution, such as lending, trusts, mortgages, investments, acting under authority and responsibility delegated by corporate executive officer: Coordinates ac-

tivities of assigned program, such as sales, operations, or electronic financial services, determines methods and procedures for carrying out program, and assists in interpreting policies and practices. Directs or conducts management studies, prepares work load and budget estimates for specified or assigned operations, analyzes operational reports, and submits activity reports. Develops and recommends plans for expansion of programs, operations, and financial activities. May solicit new business or participate in community or service organizations. May authorize loans of specified types and amounts when permitted by institution regulations. May be designated according to type of financial institution as Vice President, Commercial Bank (financial); or according to activity as Vice President, Lending (financial).
GOE: 11.05.02 STRENGTH: S GED: R5 M5 L5 SVP: 8 DLU: 89

186.117-082 FOREIGN-EXCHANGE DEALER (financial) alternate titles: foreign-exchange trader
Maintains bank's balances on deposit in foreign banks to ensure foreign exchange position, and negotiates prices at which such exchanges shall be purchased and sold, based on demand, supply, and stability of currency: Refers to international bank market rate to determine foreign exchange rates. Establishes local rates based upon international bank rates, size of transaction involved, stability of market, and bank's balances available to fund customer requirements. Negotiates purchase and sale of foreign exchange drafts on foreign exchange market and calculates U.S. dollar equivalents, using calculator or computer. Adjusts deposit balances with foreign banks. May direct foreign exchange personnel in transactions relating to international monetary business.
GOE: 11.06.03 STRENGTH: S GED: R5 M4 L4 SVP: 8 DLU: 89

186.117-086 MANAGER, EXCHANGE FLOOR (financial) alternate titles: manager, floor operations; manager, floor services
Directs floor operations of brokerage firm engaged in buying and selling securities at exchange: Monitors order flow and transactions that brokerage firm executes on floor of exchange. Reviews reports of securities transactions and price lists, using computer, to analyze market conditions. Informs staff of changes affecting firm or exchange. Calculates profit made by firm and estimates business volume lost to competition. Develops plan to increase firm's market share of business. Negotiates business contracts with exchange officials, and represents firm by membership in various exchange committees. Interviews, selects, and hires employees, such as FLOOR BROKER (financial) 162.167-034 and clerical workers. Develops and implements plans to ensure compliance of workers with established programs and procedures. Conducts staff meetings to discuss changes in policy or to propose methods and procedures which could increase profit and trade volume. Monitors employee attendance and takes disciplinary action when regulations are violated. Evaluates employee job performance and promotes or terminates personnel. May place orders with independent trader when additional help is needed to fill orders for brokerage firm. May buy and sell securities on floor of exchange [FLOOR BROKER (financial)]. May specialize according to type of securities traded at exchange and be designated Manager, Commodity Exchange Floor (financial); Manager, Options Exchange Floor (financial); Manager, Stock Exchange Floor (financial).
GOE: 11.05.04 STRENGTH: L GED: R5 M4 L5 SVP: 8 DLU: 90

186.137-014 OPERATIONS OFFICER (financial)
Supervises and coordinates activities of personnel involved in performing internal operations in department or branch office of financial institution: Prepares work schedules and assigns duties to operations personnel to ensure efficient operation of department or branch. Audits accounts, records of proof, and certifications to ensure compliance of workers with established standard procedures and practices. Compiles required and special reports on operating functions of department or branch. Interviews, selects, and hires new employees. Directs employee training to improve efficiency and ensure conformance with standard procedures and practices. Verifies workers' count of incoming cash shipments. Controls supply of money on hand to meet branch's daily needs and legal requirements. Conducts staff meetings of operations personnel, or confers with subordinate personnel to discuss operational problems or explain procedural changes or practices. May be designated according to type of financial operations supervised as Operations Officer, Branch Office (financial); Operations Officer, Trust Department (financial).
GOE: 11.06.01 STRENGTH: S GED: R5 M4 L4 SVP: 7 DLU: 89

186.167-010 ESTATE PLANNER (insurance)
Reviews assets and liabilities of estate to determine that insurance is adequate for financial protection of estate: Studies legal instruments, such as wills, trusts, business agreements, life insurance policies, and government benefits to estimate value and expenses of estate. Computes expenses, taxes, and debts to determine value of adjusted gross estate, using knowledge of accounting and tax laws. Prepares and discusses insurance program with client that will provide maximum financial security for family and protect investments. Suggests purchase of additional or new life insurance when analysis of estate indicates need for meeting cash demands at death. Discusses legal instruments with family attorney if study indicates need for change. May be required to hold state license.
GOE: 08.01.02 STRENGTH: S GED: R5 M4 L5 SVP: 7 DLU: 77

186.167-018 MANAGER, APARTMENT HOUSE (real estate)
Manages apartment house complex or development for owners or property management firm: Shows prospective tenants apartments and explains occupancy terms. Informs prospective tenants of availability of nearby schools, shopping malls, recreational facilities, and public transportation. Rents or leases

apartments, collects security deposit as required, and completes lease form outlining conditions and terms of occupancy when required. Collects rents due and issues receipts. Investigates tenant complaints concerning malfunctions of utilities or furnished household appliances or goods, and inspects vacated apartments to determine need for repairs or maintenance. Directs and coordinates activities of maintenance staff engaged in repairing plumbing or electrical malfunctions, painting apartments or buildings, and performing landscaping or gardening work, or arranges for outside personnel to perform repairs. Resolves tenant complaints concerning other tenants or visitors. May arrange for other services, such as trash collection, extermination, or carpet cleaning. May clean public areas of building and make minor repairs to equipment or appliances.
GOE: 11.11.01 STRENGTH: L GED: R4 M3 L4 SVP: 5 DLU: 81

186.167-030 MANAGER, HOUSING PROJECT (profess. & kin.)
Directs operations of housing project to provide low-income or military families, welfare recipients, or other eligible individuals with furnished or unfurnished housing in single or multiunit dwellings or house trailers: Develops and implements plans for administration of housing project and procedures for making housing assignments. Reviews occupancy reports to ensure that applications, selection of tenants and assignment of dwelling units are in accordance with rules and regulations. Conducts surveys of local rental rates and participates in setting of rental rates according to occupants' income and accommodation requirements. Prepares operational budget requests and receives accounts for and disburses funds. Conducts analyses of management and maintenance costs to determine areas where cost reductions can be effected. Plans long range schedule of major repairs on units, such as reroofing or painting exterior of dwellings. Studies housing demands occupancy and turnover rates and accommodation requirements of applicants to recommend policy and physical requirement changes. Promotes harmonious relations among tenants, housing project personnel, and persons of the community. Directs work activities of office and clerical staff in processing applications, collecting of rents and accounting for monies collected, and assigns building and grounds maintenance personnel to specific duties. Requisitions furnishings and furniture for housing units. May direct activities of other management personnel in housing project having commercial shops, concessions, theater, library, and recreational facilities. May refer applicants to private housing if all available units are occupied or if accommodation requirements are inadequate.
GOE: 11.05.03 STRENGTH: S GED: R5 M4 L4 SVP: 7 DLU: 77

186.167-034 MANAGER, INSURANCE OFFICE (insurance) alternate titles: district agent
Directs and coordinates activities of branch or district office of insurance company, agency or insurance brokerage firm: Hires and trains workers in performing activities, such as selling insurance, processing insurance claims, or underwriting. Reviews activity reports to ensure that personnel have achieved sales quotas, processed claims promptly, or credited collections to policyholders' accounts. Confers with company officials to plan and develop methods and procedures to increase sales, lower costs, and obtain greater efficiency. Interprets, implements, and enforces company policies. Prepares and submits activity reports. May reconcile earned commissions with commission advances on sales personnel. May be designated according to type of office managed as District Branch Manager (insurance); District Claims Manager (insurance); District Sales Manager (insurance); Manager, Farm Underwriters (insurance); Manager, Field Underwriters (insurance); Manager, Insurance Agency (insurance).
GOE: 11.11.04 STRENGTH: S GED: R5 M4 L5 SVP: 8 DLU: 78

186.167-038 MANAGER, LAND LEASES-AND-RENTALS (petrol. & gas)
Directs and coordinates recordkeeping activities concerning land leases, agreements, and contracts relative to petroleum company rights for drilling wells on public or private lands and producing gas and oil: Directs activities of workers engaged in keeping current files and records on terms, conditions, and expiration dates of land documents. Prepares reports on expiration dates, disposition of, and for renegotiation of existing contracts, leases, and agreements for use by management or other land department personnel. Coordinates activities of lease and rental section with activities of other sections of land department to ensure that files and records are current and that company is in compliance with terms and conditions set forth in documents. Requests title searches, procurement of deeds and affidavits, or other substantiating data to ensure legality of documents. May authorize payment of royalties, bonuses, or other compensation as provided for in terms and conditions of documents. May be designated according to activity directed as Manager, Contracts-And-Titles (petrol. & gas); Manager, Titles-And-Land-Records (petrol. & gas).
GOE: 11.05.02 STRENGTH: L GED: R4 M4 L4 SVP: 7 DLU: 77

186.167-042 MANAGER, MARKET (retail trade; wholesale tr.)
Directs and coordinates activities of municipal, regional, or state fruit, vegetable, or meat market or exchange: Negotiates contracts between wholesalers and market authority or rents space to food buyers and sellers. Directs through subordinate supervisory personnel collection of fees or monies due market, maintenance and cleaning of buildings and grounds, and enforcement of market sanitation and security rules and regulations. Keeps records of current sales prices of food items and total sales volume. May endeavor to resolve differences arising between buyers and sellers. May prepare market activity reports for management or board.
GOE: 11.11.05 STRENGTH: S GED: R4 M3 L3 SVP: 7 DLU: 77

186.167-046 MANAGER, PROPERTY (real estate)

Manages commercial, industrial, or residential real estate properties for clients: Discusses with client terms and conditions for providing management services, and drafts agreement stipulating extent and scope of management responsibilities, services to be performed, and costs for services. Prepares lease or rental agreements for lessees and collects specified rents and impounds. Directs bookkeeping functions, or credits client account for receipts and debits account for disbursements, such as mortgage, taxes, and insurance premium payments, management sevices costs, and upkeep and maintenance costs. Arranges for alterations to, or maintenance, upkeep, or reconditioning of property as specified in management services or lessee's agreement. Employs, or contracts for services of, security, maintenance, and groundskeeping personnel and on-site management personnel if required. Purchases supplies and equipment for use on leased properties. Directs preparation of financial statements and reports on status of properties, such as occupancy rates and dates of expiration of leases. Directs issuance of check for monies due client. May advise client relative to financing, purchasing, or selling property. Usually required to have real estate broker's license and be certified in property management. May prepare periodic inventory of building contents and forward listing to owner for review. May contact utility companies to arrange for transfer of service for tenants. May assist with eviction of tenants in compliance with court order and directions from LAWYER (profess. & kin.) 110.107-010 and owner.
GOE: 11.11.04 STRENGTH: L GED: R4 M3 L4 SVP: 8 DLU: 89

186.167-054 RESERVE OFFICER (financial; insurance) alternate titles: collateral placement officer; money position officer; portfolio administrator

Directs purchase, sale, and redemption of bonds and securities, and placement of collateral funds in safekeeping accounts of correspondent or reserve banks to maintain institution reserve position mandated by regulatory bodies: Arranges deposit agreements with correspondent banks or designated reserve bank, and directs placement of funds to fulfill agreements. Reviews financial statements to determine reserve needed, and adjusts reserve to obtain specified ratio of reserves to liabilities. Directs purchase and sale of government bonds and other securities, redemption of bonds, and disbursement of funds to branch offices, correspondent banks, and reserve banks to ensure that funds are kept at level specified by reserve regulations and deposit agreements. Prepares reports on reserve position for management.
GOE: 11.06.03 STRENGTH: S GED: R5 M5 L4 SVP: 9 DLU: 77

186.167-062 CONDOMINIUM MANAGER (real estate)

Manages condominium complex in accordance with homeowners' property management contract: Confers with representatives of homeowners' association or board of directors to review financial status of association and to determine management priorities. Attends monthly board meetings, records minutes, and prepares copies for distribution to board members. Arranges for and oversees activities of contract service representatives, such as exterminators, trash collector, major repair contractors, utility service repairers, and swimming pool management personnel. Investigates tenant disturbances, violations, or complaints, and resolves problems in accordance with regulations established by board of directors. Directs collection of monthly assessments from residents and payment of incurred operating expenses. Directs maintenance staff in routine repair and maintenance of buildings and grounds of complex. Prepares and maintains record of work assignments, and prepares performance evaluations. Prepares annual budget and activity reports and submits reports to association members. May recruit, hire, train, and supervise maintenance, janitorial, guard, and groundskeeping staff who perform routine repairs, maintain buildings and grounds, and patrol area to maintain secure environment of complex. May maintain contact with insurance carrier, fire protection and police departments, and other agencies having jurisdiction over property to ensure that association is complying with codes and regulations of each agency. May issue and maintain records of special permits, such as vehicle and pet registration, required by condominium association.
GOE: 11.11.01 STRENGTH: L GED: R4 M3 L4 SVP: 7 DLU: 89

186.167-066 MANAGER, REAL-ESTATE FIRM (real estate)

Directs and coordinates activities of sales staff for real estate firm: Screens and hires sales agents. Conducts training sessions to present and discuss sales techniques, ethics, and methods of maintaining sales quotas. Accompanies sales agents and clients to observe sales methods utilized, and counsels agents regarding matters, such as professionalism, financing, and sales closings. Confers with agents and clients to resolve problems, such as adjusting sales price, repairing property, or accepting closing costs. Sells or rents property for clients [SALES AGENT, REAL ESTATE (real estate) 250.357-018]. Manages residential and commercial properties for clients [MANAGER, PROPERTY (real estate) 186.167-046]. May own real estate firm or be employed by nationwide franchise. May confer with legal authority to determine if transactions are handled in accordance with state laws and with regulations governing real estate industry. May assist in negotiating development contracts with land developers, contractors, and architects. May review closing statements and attend closing transactions to represent real estate establishment.
GOE: 11.11.04 STRENGTH: L GED: R4 M3 L4 SVP: 8 DLU: 89

186.167-070 ASSISTANT BRANCH MANAGER, FINANCIAL INSTITUTION (financial)

Directs and coordinates activities of workers engaged in providing financial services to customers, and assists in cash management activities: Trains new employees, prepares work schedules, and monitors work performance. Examines documents prepared by subordinates, such as savings bond applications and safe deposit vault entry and exit records, to ensure compliance with establishment policies and procedures. Monitors branch office operations to ensure that security procedures are being followed. Evaluates establishment procedures and recommends changes to MANAGER, FINANCIAL INSTITUTION (financial) 186.167-086. Talks to customers to resolve account-related problems and to ensure positive public relations. Explains services to potential personal and business account customers to generate additional business for establishment. Assists workers to balance daily transactions, using calculator and computer terminal. Manages office in absence of MANAGER, FINANCIAL INSTITUTION (financial). May remove, count, and record cash from automated teller machine. May examine, evaluate, and process loan applications. May prepare, type, and maintain records of financial transactions.
GOE: 11.11.04 STRENGTH: L GED: R5 M4 L5 SVP: 7 DLU: 89

186.167-074 CLOSER (real estate)

Coordinates closing transactions in real estate company: Receives and deposits escrow monies in established accounts and disburses funds from each account. Reviews closing documents to determine accuracy of information and need for additional documents. Contacts courthouse personnel, buyer and seller, and other real estate personnel to obtain additional information. Confers with legal counsel regarding legal aspects of closing transactions. Calculates prorated balances on mortgages, taxes, and fire insurance premiums, as of closing date, and records balances on closing statement form to provide both parties with accurate and complete financial and legal information regarding property ownership transfer transaction. Reviews contract between buyer and seller to ensure seller can convey acceptable property title to prospective buyer. Prepares closing statement for purchase of property, using figures gathered in previous transactions and listing financial settlement between buyer and seller. Compiles figures to determine closing cost of final transaction, including loan, title, appraisal, and other fees included in sale of property. Schedules appointment to complete closing process and to answer any questions regarding procedures. Presides over closing meeting, reviews and explains contract documents and terms of transaction to buyer and seller, and obtains and notarizes signatures that ensure acceptance of agreement. Collects down payment from buyer for deposit in trust fund account. Disburses funds, based on final statement, to pay seller's debts against property, such as liens, taxes, and assessments. Reviews documents to determine that they have been executed according to regulations and are ready to be recorded. Disburses completed documents to concerned parties to effect transfer of property ownership. May prepare and type legal documents, contracts, warranty deeds, and deeds of trust. May notify contract inspection or pest control businesses to perform needed service. May prepare work assignments and complete closing work schedules to maintain efficient work flow. May compile statistical reports and keep daily log on closing activities.
GOE: 07.01.04 STRENGTH: S GED: R4 M3 L4 SVP: 7 DLU: 89

186.167-078 COMMERCIAL LOAN COLLECTION OFFICER (financial) alternate titles: special loan officer

Coordinates activities to collect delinquent commercial loans: Reviews files of commercial loans in default to determine collateral held by bank. Writes letter to customer to demand payment of loan balance. Calls or visits customer to determine if repayment plan can be established. Computes repayment schedule, using calculator. Determines if status of customer's financial position prevents repayment of loan and justifies re-classifying loan as non-revenue producing. Initiates collateral liquidation when customer does not repay loan. Petitions court to transfer title and deeds of collateral to bank. Coordinates maintenance and repairs to property. Coordinates activities to maintain income flow related to seized assets, such as notifying renters to mail payments to financial institution. Calls real estate broker to initiate sale of real estate. Calls auctioneer or liquidation specialist to sell specified property, such as machines, equipment, and inventory at public auction. Specifies changes to bank records on value of loan. May testify at legal proceedings.
GOE: 11.05.02 STRENGTH: S GED: R5 M4 L5 SVP: 8 DLU: 89

186.167-082 FACTOR (financial)

Factors (purchases at discount) accounts receivable from businesses needing operating capital: Directs collection of facts about prospective client's business, such as credit rating of customers, evaluation of past losses, terms of sales, due dates, average amount of invoices, and expected volume and turnover of accounts receivable. Evaluates data collected to determine type of factoring plan to propose and percentage of net face value of accounts to advance which will yield favorable profit margin and alleviate client's cash shortage. Determines charge from fee schedule. Explains factoring agreement to client. Prepares and signs contract specifying terms of agreement and rights and obligations of both parties. May provide clients with other business services, such as credit and collection services, accounts receivable bookkeeping, and management consulting, on contract or fee basis. May specialize in factoring agreements in one or more industries.
GOE: 11.06.03 STRENGTH: S GED: R5 M4 L4 SVP: 8 DLU: 89

186.167-086 MANAGER, FINANCIAL INSTITUTION (financial)

Manages branch or office of financial institutions, such as commercial bank, credit union, finance company, mortgage company, savings bank, or trust company: Directs and coordinates activities to implement institution policies, procedures, and practices concerning granting or extending lines of credit, commer-

employment through productive work: Reviews evaluation made on individual to ascertain type of work recommended and limitations due to specific handicap. Assigns individual to specific tasks, such as cleaning, sorting, assembling, or repairing products or components, and demonstrates methods and procedures for performing work. Observes worker to ensure that work is performed according to prescribed methods and meets established standards. Explains and redemonstrates tasks to resolve work related problems or difficulties. Assigns individual to simpler tasks when worker cannot perform assigned duties. Evaluates individual's work performance and makes reassignments to different tasks within shop to improve vocational skills. Endeavors to place individual in gainful employment after acquisition of marketable skills. May train handicapped individuals under contract with state agency. May pay workers under contract and license of state agency or by piecework according to contract. May solicit industrial establishment for subcontract work on products or components and be designated Executive Director, Contract Shop (nonprofit org.).
GOE: 11.07.01 STRENGTH: L GED: R5 M4 L4 SVP: 8 DLU: 80

187.117-030 EXECUTIVE VICE PRESIDENT, CHAMBER OF COMMERCE (nonprofit org.) alternate titles: manager, chamber of commerce
Directs activities of chamber of commerce to promote business, industrial and job development, and civic improvements in community: Administers programs of departments and committees which perform such functions as providing members economic and marketing information, promoting economic growth and stability in community, and counseling business organizations and industry on problems affecting local economy. Coordinates work with that of other community agencies to provide public services. Writes and gives speeches to government, and business organizations to create greater understanding between community, government, and business organizations. Prepares and submits annual budget to elected official for approval. Studies governmental legislation, taxation, and other fiscal matters to determine effect on community interests, and makes recommendations based on organizational policy.
GOE: 11.05.02 STRENGTH: S GED: R5 M5 L5 SVP: 8 DLU: 78

187.117-034 GENERAL MANAGER, ROAD PRODUCTION (amuse. & rec.)
Directs and coordinates activities concerned with setting up facility for performances of circus, ice skating show, rodeo, or similar touring road show: Plans layout of performance and backstage areas to conform with specification considering such factors, as type and space of facility. Negotiates with local renting agent to arrange personal space for entertainers and animals at each facility used on tour. Coordinates activities of various departments to ensure arrangements are made for providing water and feed for animals and disposal of rubbish and garbage, and to ensure that work crew has equipment and other facilities prepared for each performance. May count daily receipts and verify amount against number of tickets sold. May be designated according to type of show as Superintendent, Circus (amuse. & rec.).
GOE: 11.11.04 STRENGTH: L GED: R4 M3 L4 SVP: 8 DLU: 77

187.117-038 MANAGER, HOTEL OR MOTEL (hotel & rest.) alternate titles: manager, general; manager, motor hotel; manager, motor inn; manager, resident
Manages hotel or motel to ensure efficient and profitable operation: Establishes standards for personnel administration and performance, service to patrons, room rates, advertising, publicity, credit, food selection and service, and type of patronage to be solicited. Plans dining room, bar, and banquet operations. Allocates funds, authorizes expenditures, and assists in planning budgets for departments. Interviews, hires, and evaluates personnel. Answers patrons' complaints and resolves problems. Delegates authority and assigns responsibilities to department heads. Inspects guests' rooms, public access areas, and outside grounds for cleanliness and appearance. Processes reservations and adjusts guests' complaints when working in small motels or hotels.
GOE: 11.11.01 STRENGTH: S GED: R5 M4 L4 SVP: 7 DLU: 81

187.117-042 MANAGER, RECREATION ESTABLISHMENT (amuse. & rec.)
Manages recreation establishment, such as dancehall, sports arena, or auditorium, to provide entertainment to public: Negotiates with promoters to contract and schedule entertainment. Compiles record of future engagements. Supervises clerical, service, and other employees. Hires and discharges workers. Complies with state and local fire and liquor regulations governing operation of establishment. May order supplies. May oversee workers engaged in keeping premises of establishment clean and in good repair. May be designated according to type of recreational facility directed as Manager, Dance Floor (amuse. & rec.).
GOE: 11.11.02 STRENGTH: L GED: R5 M4 L4 SVP: 7 DLU: 77

187.117-046 PROGRAM DIRECTOR, GROUP WORK (profess. & kin.)
Plans, organizes, and directs activity program of group work agency or department, or scouting organization: Coordinates activities of program committees and other groups to plan procedures. Studies and analyzes member and community needs for basis of program development. Directs selection and training of staff and volunteer workers. Assigns work and evaluates performance of staff members and recommends indicated actions. Assists staff through individual and group conferences in analysis of specific programs, understanding of program development, and increasing use of individual skills. Interprets agency program and services to individuals or groups in community. May be designated according to agency or program directed as Activities Director, Scout-

ing (nonprofit org.); Director, Teen Post (profess. & kin.); Program Director, Scouting (nonprofit org.).
GOE: 11.07.01 STRENGTH: L GED: R5 M5 L5 SVP: 8 DLU: 77

187.117-050 PUBLIC HEALTH SERVICE OFFICER (government ser.)
Administers public-health program of county or city: Inspects public facilities for health hazards or directs inspection by others. Negotiates with school, state, federal, or other authorities and with community groups to formulate health standards and legislation affecting jurisdiction. Participates in establishing free clinics, cancer detection centers, and other programs to improve public health. Develops and coordinates public relations campaigns to promote programs and services and participates in radio and television discussions, public meetings, and other activities. Conducts examinations of hospitals, indigent care centers, and other institutions under control of municipality to ensure conformance to accepted standards. Prohibits sale of unsafe milk and other food and dairy products. May impose quarantines on area, animals, or persons with contagious disease. May order closing of establishments not conforming to prescribed health standards.
GOE: 11.10.03 STRENGTH: S GED: R5 M5 L5 SVP: 8 DLU: 77

187.117-054 SUPERINTENDENT, RECREATION (government ser.) alternate titles: director, recreation
Plans, promotes, organizes, and administers public recreation service for entire community, under policies established by public managing authority: Selects, develops, and supervises paid staff and volunteers. Superintends acquisition, planning, design, construction, and maintenance of recreation facilities. Evaluates effectiveness of recreation areas, facilities, and services. Studies local conditions and develops immediate and long range plans to meet recreational needs of all age groups. Prepares budget and directs expenditure of department funds and keeping of department records. Interprets recreation program to public and maintains cooperative planning and working relationships with allied public and voluntary agencies. Serves as technical adviser to managing authority and as recreation consultant to community.
GOE: 11.07.04 STRENGTH: L GED: R5 M3 L5 SVP: 8 DLU: 77

187.117-058 DIRECTOR, OUTPATIENT SERVICES (medical ser.)
Supervises and directs activities of outpatient clinic and coordinates activities of clinic with those of other hospital departments: Establishes clinic policies and procedures in cooperation with other hospital officials. Interprets and administers personnel policies and provides for training program. Reviews clinic activities and recommends changes in, or better utilization of, facilities, services, and staff. Establishes and maintains work schedules and assignments of resident professional staff members. Authorizes purchase of supplies and equipment. Prepares and submits budget, records, reports, and statistical data to ADMINISTRATOR, HEALTH CARE FACILITY (medical ser.) 187.117-010. Meets with personnel of other local institutions and organizations to promote public health and educational services. Oversees operation of clinic and recommends procedures, treatments, or other course of action to assist medical staff.
GOE: 11.07.02 STRENGTH: S GED: R6 M5 L6 SVP: 8 DLU: 86

187.117-062 RADIOLOGY ADMINISTRATOR (medical ser.)
Plans, directs, and coordinates administrative activities of radiology department of hospital medical center: Conducts studies and implements changes to improve internal operations of department. Advises staff and supervisors on administrative changes. Assists hospital officials in preparation of department budget. Conducts specified classes and provides training material to assist in student training program. Directs and coordinates personnel activities of department. Recommends cost saving methods and hospital supply changes to effect economy of department operations. Interprets, prepares, and distributes statistical data regarding department operations.
GOE: 11.07.02 STRENGTH: S GED: R5 M5 L5 SVP: 7 DLU: 86

187.117-066 EXECUTIVE DIRECTOR, RED CROSS (nonprofit org.)
Directs and coordinates operations of nonprofit agency to provide blood, medical care, financial aid, and other special services: Oversees agency volunteer operations in areas such as blood donor program, nursing, and financial assistance to assure program adherence to agency charter. Participates in community activities to develop opportunities to ascertain needs, serve clients, and promote agency goals. Establishes and maintains close working relationships with cooperating agencies to avoid duplication of services. Prepares budget in consultation with departmental directors to allocate funds, control costs, and maintain operations at level consistent with agency guidelines. Recommends new policy and procedures to agency governing board. Advises volunteer leaders of potential problems and recommends alternative methods of providing service. Negotiates with community organizations to plan joint fund-raising campaigns. Hires paid staff in consultation with agency head. Confers with staff and disseminates written materials to inform staff of current developments.
GOE: 11.07.01 STRENGTH: L GED: R5 M4 L5 SVP: 8 DLU: 86

187.134-010 SUPERVISOR, CONTRACT-SHELTERED WORKSHOP (nonprofit org.)
Supervises and coordinates activities of handicapped individuals in sheltered workshop to train and improve vocational skills for gainful employment through productive work: Assigns individual to specific tasks, such as cleaning, sorting, assembling, repairing, or hand packing products or components. Demonstrates job duties to handicapped individual and observes worker performing tasks to ensure understanding of job duties. Monitors work performance at each

individual's work station to ensure compliance with procedures and safety regulations and to note behavior deviations. Examines workpiece visually to verify adherence to specifications. Confers with individuals to explain or to demonstrate task again to resolve work related difficulties. Reassigns individual to simpler tasks when worker cannot perform assigned tasks, or to tasks containing higher degrees of complexity as level of competence is reached. Performs other duties described under SUPERVISOR (any industry) Master Title.
GOE: 11.07.03 STRENGTH: L GED: R4 M3 L3 SVP: 7 DLU: 86

187.137-014 SUPERVISOR, VOLUNTEER SERVICES (profess. & kin.) alternate titles: volunteer services assistant

Supervises volunteer workers and coordinates activities in specified project or work area within organization to help strengthen and extend selected public or private programs and projects: Recruits, interviews, and classifies applicants for volunteer work and trains and supervises volunteers in specific assignments. Informs volunteers of policies, procedures, and standards of volunteer service. Reviews written reports and observes work activities of volunteers to evaluate work performance. Confers with volunteers to resolve grievances and promote cooperation and interest. Participates in programs of public recognition for volunteer workers. Supervises workers engaged in preparing and maintaining records of volunteer service programs, needs, and donations. May perform volunteer work in such areas as teaching, corrections, medical specialty, or social work and be known accordingly. May develop, organize, and direct special activities or programs of volunteer agency or department of organization and be designated Program Director (profess. & kin.).
GOE: 11.07.01 STRENGTH: L GED: R4 M3 L4 SVP: 7 DLU: 78

187.137-018 MANAGER, FRONT OFFICE (hotel & rest.)

Coordinates front-office activities of hotel or motel and resolves problems arising from guests' complaints, reservation and room assignment activities, and unusual requests and inquiries: Assigns duties and shifts to workers and observes performances to ensure adherence to hotel policies and established operating procedures. Confers and cooperates with other department heads to ensure coordination of hotel activities. Answers inquiries pertaining to hotel policies and services. Greets important guests. Arranges for private telephone line and other special services. May patrol public rooms, investigate disturbances, and warn troublemakers. May interview and hire applicants. May receive and process advance registration payments. May send out letters of confirmation or return checks when registration cannot be accepted.
GOE: 11.11.01 STRENGTH: L GED: R4 M4 L4 SVP: 6 DLU: 80

187.161-010 EXECUTIVE CHEF (hotel & rest.) alternate titles: chef de cuisine; chef, head; manager, food production

Coordinates activities of and directs indoctrination and training of CHEFS (hotel & rest.); COOKS (hotel & rest.); and other kitchen workers engaged in preparing and cooking foods in hotels or restaurants to ensure an efficient and profitable food service: Plans or participates in planning menus and utilization of food surpluses and leftovers, taking into account probable number of guests, marketing conditions, popularity of various dishes, and recency of menu. Estimates food consumption, and purchases or requisitions foodstuffs and kitchen supplies. Reviews menus, analyzes recipes, determines food, labor, and overhead costs, and assigns prices to menu items. Directs food apportionment policy to control costs. Supervises cooking and other kitchen personnel and coordinates their assignments to ensure economical and timely food production. Observes methods of food preparation and cooking, sizes of portions, and garnishing of foods to ensure food is prepared in prescribed manner. Tests cooked foods by tasting and smelling them. Devises special dishes and develops recipes. Hires and discharges employees. Familarizes newly hired CHEFS (hotel & rest.) and COOKS (hotel & rest.) with practices of restaurant kitchen and oversees training of COOK APPRENTICES (hotel & rest.). Maintains time and payroll records. Establishes and enforces nutrition and sanitation standards for restaurant. May supervise or cooperate with STEWARD/STEWARDESS (hotel & rest.) in matters pertaining to kitchen, pantry, and storeroom.
GOE: 11.05.02 STRENGTH: L GED: R5 M4 L3 SVP: 8 DLU: 77

187.161-014 MANAGER, HANDICRAFT-OR-HOBBY SHOP (amuse. & rec.)

Manages hobby shops and coordinates activities of workers engaged in conducting classes in one or more crafts, such as woodworking, photography, and leather tooling for hobby or craft shop: Plans and initiates promotional projects to publicize recreational facilities. Prepares budget request for additional craft facilities. Conducts surveys to determine which crafts are in demand to ensure that facilities are acquired. Inventories and requisitions supplies. Plans and coordinates activities of subordinates conducting classes. Prepares accounting reports on disbursement of funds. Demonstrates use of machines and equipment to enforce safety rules and regulations.
GOE: 11.11.02 STRENGTH: L GED: R4 M4 L4 SVP: 7 DLU: 77

187.167-010 APPLIANCE-SERVICE SUPERVISOR (utilities) alternate titles: electrical-appliance service supervisor; merchandise supervisor; utilization supervisor

Coordinates activities of merchandise-servicing department of gas or electric appliance distributors: Supervises, trains, and assigns duties to workers engaged in servicing appliances, pricing, and disposition of returned merchandise and excess repair parts. Develops company policies and procedures regarding servicing of appliances and disposition of defective parts. Consults manufacturers to obtain advice on unusual service problems and to obtain service instructions

and parts catalogs. May write instructions on care and use of appliances for distribution to public.
GOE: 05.02.06 STRENGTH: L GED: R4 M4 L4 SVP: 7 DLU: 77

187.167-014 BOOKMAKER (amuse. & rec.) alternate titles: bookie

Manages establishment to receive and pay off bets placed by horse racing patrons: Prepares and issues lists of approximate handicap odds on each horse prior to race, from knowledge of previous performance of horse under existing conditions of weather and track. Determines risks on each horse to refuse additional bets after maximum desired limit of liability has been reached. Records bets placed over counter or by telephone or teletype. Issues betting receipts. Pays off bets on track parimutuel basis. May supervise and coordinate activities of CASHIERS, GAMBLING (amuse. & rec.). May balance betting accounts and keep records as required by state or municipal authorities. May place customers' bets with cooperating BOOKMAKERS (amuse. & rec.) to limit liability and apportion risk. May be designated Sports Bookmaker (amuse. & rec.) when taking bets on sports, such as football, boxing, baseball, and hockey.
GOE: 11.06.03 STRENGTH: L GED: R4 M3 L3 SVP: 6 DLU: 77

187.167-018 BUSINESS REPRESENTATIVE, LABOR UNION (profess. & kin.)

Manages business affairs of labor union: Coordinates and directs such union functions as promoting local membership, placing union members on jobs, arranging local meetings, and maintaining relations between union and employers and press representatives. Visits work sites to ensure management and labor employees adhere to union contract specifications. May assist in developing plant production and safety and health measures. May negotiate with management on hours, wages, individual grievances, and other work-related matters affecting employees.
GOE: 11.05.02 STRENGTH: S GED: R5 M3 L4 SVP: 8 DLU: 77

187.167-022 COORDINATOR, VOLUNTEER SERVICES (social ser.) alternate titles: volunteer coordinator

Coordinates student and community volunteer services program in organizations engaged in public, social, and welfare activities: Consults administrators and staff to determine organization needs for various volunteer services and plans for volunteer recruitment. Interviews, screens, and refers applicants to appropriate units. Orients and trains volunteers prior to assignment in specific units. Arranges for on-the-job and other required training and supervision and evaluation of volunteers. Resolves personnel problems. Serves as liaison between administration, staff, and volunteers. Prepares and maintains procedural and training manuals. Speaks to community groups, explaining organization activities and role of volunteer program. Publishes agency newsletter, and prepares news items for other news media. Maintains personnel records. Prepares statistical reports on extent, nature, and value of volunteer service.
GOE: 11.07.01 STRENGTH: S GED: R5 M3 L5 SVP: 7 DLU: 77

187.167-026 DIRECTOR, FOOD SERVICES (hotel & rest.) alternate titles: manager, school lunch program

Coordinates activities of workers engaged in preparing noon meals in school or school system cafeterias: Plans menus of nutritional value. Purchases foods and supplies. Consults with administrative staff and PRINCIPAL (education) 099.117-018 to develop policies and procedures for operating school kitchens and cafeterias. Conducts research program to improve existing practices and services. Keeps records required by other governmental agencies regarding milk subsidies and surplus foods. Directs hiring and training of employees. Prepares budgetary reports.
GOE: 11.11.04 STRENGTH: L GED: R5 M4 L4 SVP: 7 DLU: 80

187.167-030 DIRECTOR, FUNERAL (personal ser.) alternate titles: manager, funeral home; mortician; undertaker

Arranges and directs funeral services: Coordinates activities of workers to remove body to mortuary for embalming. Interviews family or other authorized person to arrange details, such as preparation of obituary notice, selection of urn or casket, determination of location and time of cremation or burial, selection of PALLBEARERS (personal ser.), procurement of official for religious rites, and transportation of mourners. Plans placement of casket in parlor or chapel and adjusts lights, fixtures, and floral displays. Directs PALLBEARERS (personal ser.) in placement and removal of casket from hearse. Closes casket and leads funeral cortege to church or burial site. Directs preparations and shipment of body for out-of-state burial. May prepare body for interment [EMBALMER (personal ser.)].
GOE: 11.11.04 STRENGTH: L GED: R4 M4 L4 SVP: 7 DLU: 77

187.167-034 DIRECTOR, NURSES' REGISTRY (medical ser.) alternate titles: registrar, nurses' registry

Directs registry services for NURSES, PRIVATE DUTY (medical ser.) according to regulations established by state or district professional nurses' association: Maintains roster of nurses available for duty. Refers nurses in response to requests. Keeps record of number and type of calls received. Analyzes problems of registry to render more efficient service and operations. Informs registrants of new and revised requirements and regulations. May assist in recruiting nurses for emergencies. May be responsible for financial administration of registry.
GOE: 07.01.02 STRENGTH: S GED: R5 M4 L5 SVP: 6 DLU: 77

187.167-038 DIRECTOR, VOLUNTEER SERVICES (social ser.)

Directs activities of volunteer agencies and workers offering their services to hospitals, social service, and community agencies: Confers with administrative

staff to plan volunteer program consistent with needs of institution or agency. Recommends establishment of policies and procedures for inservice training, work hours, and types of service to be performed by volunteers. Secures services of volunteer workers. Organizes classes of instruction for volunteers to teach procedures and techniques. Suggests and directs projects to be carried out by volunteer workers. Assigns workers to various services with hospital or agency. Conducts surveys to evaluate effectiveness of volunteer service program. Arranges for recognition of volunteers for their services.
GOE: 11.07.02 STRENGTH: S GED: R5 M4 L4 SVP: 7 DLU: 77

187.167-042 DIVISION MANAGER, CHAMBER OF COMMERCE (nonprofit org.) alternate titles: department manager, chamber of commerce

Directs and administers activities of department of chamber of commerce, such as domestic trade, construction industries, or aviation and space departments: Analyzes market trends and economic conditions to forecast potential sales of products or services in area. Assists business and industrial organizations on such problems as expansions, cost reductions, and community development. Advises business organizations and industrial groups on tax problems and legislation. Studies agricultural economy for exploitation of rural resources, production and marketing of farm products, improving farm income, and effecting favorable agricultural legislation. Suggests civic improvements, such as community zoning, planning, public housing programs, and airport expansions, based on surveys of community needs. Plans and directs educational campaigns to promote public support of such community programs as housing, transportation, and hospital facilities. Stimulates civic and economic growth of community by writing and giving speeches to promote tourist travel, to solicit convention business, and to induce labor and industry to immigrate into area. May represent chamber at public, social and business receptions, or before governmental agencies. May be designated according to field of specialization or department managed as Manager, Aviation And Space (nonprofit org.); Manager, Construction Industries (nonprofit org.); Manager, Domestic Trade (nonprofit org.).
GOE: 11.05.02 STRENGTH: S GED: R5 M4 L5 SVP: 7 DLU: 79

187.167-046 EXECUTIVE HOUSEKEEPER (any industry) alternate titles: custodial services manager; director, housekeeping; housekeeper, administrative; housekeeper, head

Directs institutional housekeeping program to ensure clean, orderly, and attractive conditions of establishment: Establishes standards and procedures for work of housekeeping staff, and plans work schedules to ensure adequate service. Inspects and evaluates physical condition of establishment, and submits to management recommendations for painting, repairs, furnishings, relocation of equipment, and reallocation of space. Periodically inventories supplies and equipment. Reads trade journals to keep informed of new and improved cleaning methods, products, supplies, and equipment. Organizes and directs departmental training programs, resolves personnel problems, hires new employees, and evaluates employees performance and working relationship. Maintains records and prepares periodic activity and personnel reports for review by management. Coordinates activities with those of other departments. May select and purchase new furnishings. May evaluate records to forecast department personnel requirements, and to prepare budget. May perform cleaning duties in cases of emergency or staff shortage.
GOE: 11.11.01 STRENGTH: L GED: R5 M4 L4 SVP: 8 DLU: 87

187.167-050 MANAGER, AGRICULTURAL-LABOR CAMP (profess. & kin.) alternate titles: superintendent, camp

Coordinates activities of residential camp for seasonal agricultural workers: Directs activities, such as maintenance of buildings and facilities, preparation of meals and type of food served, compliance with state health and fire regulations, and assignment of living quarters. Arranges medical care for sick or injured workers. Assists underage employees in obtaining health and birth certificates and work permits. Administers recreation programs. Prepares periodic reports of camp operation. May recruit and employ workers prior to camp opening.
GOE: 11.11.04 STRENGTH: L GED: R5 M4 L4 SVP: 7 DLU: 77

187.167-054 MANAGER, AQUATIC FACILITY (amuse. & rec.)

Manages sea circus facility: Establishes operational procedures relating to purchasing, accounting, and budgeting. Hires and coordinates activities of subordinates and performers. Reviews operational expense and other financial reports for accuracy and budget preparation. Inspects facility for compliance with occupational, health, and safety regulations.
GOE: 11.11.02 STRENGTH: S GED: R4 M4 L4 SVP: 7 DLU: 77

187.167-058 MANAGER, BARBER OR BEAUTY SHOP (personal ser.)

Manages business operations and directs personal service functions of barber or beauty shop: Confers with employees to ensure quality services for patrons, such as haircuts, facials, hair styling, shaves, massages, shampoos, and manicures. Makes appointments and assigns patrons to BARBERS (personal ser.) or COSMETOLOGIST (personal ser.) to maintain uniform employee schedules. Adjusts customer complaints and promotes new business by expressing personal interest in efficient service for patrons. Directs sanitary maintenance of shop in compliance with health regulations and requires cleanliness, neatness, and courtesy of employees. Negotiates leases and orders equipment and supplies. Keeps accounts of receipts and expenditures and makes up payroll. Performs services of BARBER (personal ser.) or COSMETOLOGIST (personal ser.) in addition to management functions. May supervise on-the-job training and

school attendance of apprentice. May train apprentice and master barbers. May supervise MANICURIST (personal ser.); SHOE SHINER (personal ser.) and other workers.
GOE: 11.11.04 STRENGTH: L GED: R4 M4 L4 SVP: 7 DLU: 77

187.167-062 MANAGER, BRANCH OPERATION EVALUATION (hotel & rest.)

Examines, analyzes, and evaluates operations of individual branches of chain of restaurants, motels, or other facilities to ensure adherence to company standards and policies: Travels from branch to branch and visually checks physical structures and surroundings, noting degree of maintenance provided or required and unusual wear and tear. Notes condition of furniture, linens, and supplies and recommends replacements where necessary. Evaluates adequacy of return of investment on individual branches and alters or initiates procedures to improve service and reduce expenses. Examines books of account of individual establishment. Prepares report, summarizing findings and including recommendations for maintenance, repair, changes in operational procedures, and purchase requirements, and submits report to home office.
GOE: 11.05.02 STRENGTH: L GED: R4 M3 L4 SVP: 6 DLU: 77

187.167-066 MANAGER, CAMP (construction; logging)

Directs and coordinates activities of workers concerned with preparing and maintaining buildings and facilities in residential construction or logging camp: Coordinates through subordinate personnel or personally directs workers engaged in preparing and maintaining such camp facilities as dining halls and barracks used by resident laborers. Directs activities of food service workers. Schedules purchase and delivery of food supplies. Enforces safety and sanitation regulations.
GOE: 05.10.04 STRENGTH: L GED: R4 M3 L3 SVP: 6 DLU: 77

187.167-070 MANAGER, CASINO (amuse. & rec.)

Manages casino operation: Establishes policy on types of gambling to be offered, extension of credit, and serving food and beverages. Hires and delegates authority to subordinates. Reviews operational expense and collection reports for accuracy. Resolves complaints requiring explanation and interpretation of house rules.
GOE: 11.11.02 STRENGTH: L GED: R4 M4 L4 SVP: 7 DLU: 77

187.167-074 MANAGER, CEMETERY (real estate) alternate titles: superintendent, cemetery

Directs cemetery program and coordinates, through subordinate personnel, activities of workers engaged in providing burial services and maintaining cemetery grounds: Formulates and administers cemetery policy and services under authority of governing board. Analyzes and coordinates budget estimates and regulates expenditures to administer budget. Periodically observes monuments to determine needs for repair or replacement. Oversees hiring and firing of applicants and workers. Directs activities of clerical staff and other workers engaged in burial services, landscaping, or maintenance of cemetery grounds. Directs subordinates to arrange details, such as site of burial, digging of grave or opening of crypt, and placement of equipment and protective covering, with DIRECTOR, FUNERAL (personal ser.) 187.167-030 or other official for burial services. Directs subordinates to carry out burial arrangements. May participate in layout, planning and preparing paperwork on construction projects. May confer with suppliers, architects, contractors, paving company officials, and plumbers to plan and oversee major projects. May supervise sales staff or sell burial lots to patrons.
GOE: 11.11.04 STRENGTH: L GED: R4 M4 L4 SVP: 7 DLU: 86

187.167-078 MANAGER, CONVENTION (hotel & rest.)

Coordinates activities of staff and convention personnel to make arrangements for group meetings and conventions to be held in hotel: Consults with representatives of group or organization to plan details, such as number of persons expected, display space desired, and food-service schedule. Obtains permits from fire and health departments to erect displays and exhibits and serve food in rooms other than dining rooms. Notifies various department heads of arrangements made. Directs workers in preparing banquet and convention rooms and erecting displays and exhibits. Inspects rooms and displays for conformance to needs and desires of group. Arranges publicity, special functions, adjusts complaints, and performs other duties to promote goodwill.
GOE: 11.11.01 STRENGTH: L GED: R5 M4 L4 SVP: 7 DLU: 77

187.167-082 MANAGER, CUSTOMER SERVICES (business ser.; retail trade)

Directs and coordinates customer service activities of establishment to install, service, maintain, and repair durable goods, such as machines, equipment, major appliances, or other items sold, leased, or rented with service contract or warranty: Reviews customer requests for service to ascertain cause for service request, type of malfunction, and customer address. Determines staff hours, number of personnel, and parts and equipment required for service call, utilizing knowledge of product, typical malfunctions, and service procedures and practices. Prepares schedules for service personnel, assigns personnel to routes or to specific repair and maintenance work according to workers' knowledge, experience, and repair capabilities on specific types of products. Arranges for transportation of machines and equipment to customer's location for installation or from customer's location to shop for repairs that cannot be performed on premises. Keeps records of work hours and parts utilized, and work performed for each service call. Requisitions replacement parts and supplies. May contact service personnel over radio-telephone to obtain or give information and directions regarding service or installation activities.

GOE: 05.10.02 STRENGTH: L GED: R4 M4 L4 SVP: 8 DLU: 77

187.167-086   MANAGER, DANCE STUDIO (education)
Sells dancing lessons and coordinates activities of branch dance studio, in accord with policies established by head office of chain: Directs sales activities, dance instruction of patrons, and maintenance of required records. Selects, trains, promotes, and discharges instructional, sales, and clerical personnel. Coordinates advertising activities of studio in print media, on radio and television, or through other channels, using prepared materials supplied by head office. Interviews prospective patrons and attempts to persuade them to sign instructional contracts. Gives dancing demonstrations for prospective patrons to stimulate sales. May give instruction [INSTRUCTOR, DANCING (education)].
GOE: 01.05.01 STRENGTH: L GED: R4 M3 L4 SVP: 6 DLU: 77

187.167-090   MANAGER, DENTAL LABORATORY (protective dev.)
Coordinates activities of workers in dental laboratory engaged in making and repairing full or partial dentures, crowns, inlays, and bridgework: Coordinates production schedules to ensure that work is completed by delivery date. Studies processing methods to determine reasons for production difficulties. Analyzes cost and production records to ensure that operation is efficient and profitable. Institutes measures or approves suggestions to improve efficiency of operation and working conditions. Examines finished products for conformance to specifications. May contact DENTISTS (medical ser.) 072.101-010 to solicit business. May make and repair dental appliances [DENTAL-LABORATORY TECHNICIAN (protective dev.) 712.381-018].
GOE: 05.05.11 STRENGTH: L GED: R5 M4 L4 SVP: 7 DLU: 77

187.167-094   MANAGER, DUDE RANCH (amuse. & rec.)
Directs operation of dude ranch: Formulates policy on advertising, publicity, guest rates, and credit. Plans recreational and entertainment activities, such as camping, fishing, hunting, horseback riding, and dancing. Directs activities of DUDE WRANGLERS (amuse. & rec.). Directs preparation and maintenance of financial records. Directs other activities, such as breeding, raising, and showing horses, mules, and livestock.
GOE: 11.11.02 STRENGTH: L GED: R4 M4 L4 SVP: 7 DLU: 77

187.167-098   MANAGER, EMPLOYMENT AGENCY (profess. & kin.)
Manages employment services and business operations of private employment agency: Directs hiring, training, and evaluation of employees. Analyzes placement reports to determine effectiveness of EMPLOYMENT INTERVIEWERS (profess. & kin.). Participates in development and utilization of job development methods to promote business for agency. Enforces, through subordinate staff, agency policies, procedures, safety rules, and regulations. Approves or disapproves requests for purchase of new equipment and supplies. Ensures maintenance and repair of facilities and equipment. Prepares budget requests. Investigates and resolves customer complaints. May negotiate leases and order equipment and supplies for agency.
GOE: 11.11.04 STRENGTH: S GED: R4 M3 L4 SVP: 7 DLU: 77

187.167-102   MANAGER, FISH-AND-GAME CLUB (amuse. & rec.)
Manages fish and game club for owner or membership: Hires and coordinates activities of club personnel. Allots camps, fishing areas, and hunting grounds to parties, and arranges for guide services, provisions, and transportation. Purchases and inventories equipment and supplies, and directs workers engaged in maintaining camp property, equipment, and supplies. Ensures that personnel and patrons adhere to fish and game laws.
GOE: 11.11.02 STRENGTH: L GED: R4 M4 L4 SVP: 6 DLU: 77

187.167-106   MANAGER, FOOD SERVICE (hotel & rest.; personal ser.)
Coordinates food service activities of hotel, restaurant, or other similar establishment or at social functions: Estimates food and beverage costs and requisitions or purchases supplies. Confers with food preparation and other personnel to plan menus and related activities, such as dining room, bar, and banquet operations. Directs hiring and assignment of personnel. Investigates and resolves food quality and service complaints. May review financial transactions and monitor budget to ensure efficient operation, and to ensure expenditures stay within budget limitations. May be designated according to type of establishment or specialty as Caterer (personal ser.); Manager, Banquet (hotel & rest.); Manager, Cafeteria Or Lunchroom (hotel & rest.); Manager, Catering (hotel & rest.); Manager, Food And Beverage (hotel & rest.); Manager, Restaurant Or Coffee Shop (hotel & rest.).
GOE: 11.11.04 STRENGTH: L GED: R4 M4 L4 SVP: 7 DLU: 80

187.167-114   MANAGER, GOLF CLUB (amuse. & rec.)
Manages golf club to provide entertainment for patrons: Directs activities of dining room and kitchen workers and crews that maintain club buildings, equipment, and golf course in good condition. Hires and discharges workers. Estimates quantities and costs of foodstuffs, beverages, and groundskeeping equipment to prepare operating budget. Explains necessity of items on budget to board of directors and requests approval. Inspects club buildings, equipment, and golf course. Requisitions materials, such as foodstuffs, beverages, seeds, fertilizers, and groundskeeping equipment. Keeps accounts of receipts and expenditures. May assist in planning tournaments.
GOE: 11.11.02 STRENGTH: S GED: R4 M4 L4 SVP: 6 DLU: 77

187.167-118   MANAGER, GUN CLUB (amuse. & rec.) alternate titles: manager, range; range master
Manages activities of gun club: Confers with governing body, and other gun clubs, organizations and associations to arrange competitive shooting meets.

Publicizes events and club facilities to acquaint public with sport and to solicit members. Informs club members of coming events through bulletin notices or club paper. Purchases ammunition, firearms, and supplies. Sells supplies and firearms to club members. Coordinates events to determine eligible participants, type of competition, and time meet is held. Advises participants of changes in rules and regulations governing meet. Keeps records of expenditures, dues, and membership. Enforces safety rules and regulations. Directs maintenance crew activities, such as placing shooting targets in designated area, repairing targets, keeping yards and grounds clean, and performing landscaping. May instruct new members on use of firearms. May act as judge in competition trap or skeet shooting meets. May repair skeet and trap-bird throwing machines.
GOE: 11.11.02 STRENGTH: L GED: R4 M3 L4 SVP: 6 DLU: 77

187.167-122   MANAGER, HOTEL RECREATIONAL FACILITIES (amuse. & rec.)
Manages hotel or motel recreational facilities: Advises guests of available activities, such as swimming, skating, boating, and other sports. Processes applications for rental of cabanas, docking of yachts, and membership. Hires and directs activities of subordinates. Compiles record of receipts collected for use of facilities. Requisitions supplies and equipment.
GOE: 11.11.02 STRENGTH: L GED: R4 M4 L4 SVP: 7 DLU: 77

187.167-126   MANAGER, LIQUOR ESTABLISHMENT (hotel & rest.) alternate titles: manager, club
Coordinates activities of workers engaged in selling alcoholic beverages for consumption on premises: Estimates and orders foodstuffs, liquors, wines, or other beverages, and supplies. Interviews, hires, trains, and discharges workers. Adjusts customer's complaints concerning service, food, and beverages. Inspects establishment and observes workers and patrons to ensure compliance with occupational, health, and safety standards and local liquor regulations. May plan and arrange promotional programs and advertisement. May hire entertainers. May be designated according to kind of establishment managed as Manager, Beer Parlor (hotel & rest.); Manager, Cocktail Lounge (hotel & rest.); Manager, Night Club (hotel & rest.); Manager, Tavern (hotel & rest.).
GOE: 11.11.04 STRENGTH: L GED: R4 M4 L4 SVP: 6 DLU: 77

187.167-130   MANAGER, MARINE SERVICE (ship-boat mfg.)
Directs activities of boat-repair service, according to knowledge of maintenance needs of small craft and marine safety requirements: Confers with owner or crew of vessel to obtain maintenance history and details concerning condition of craft. Observes and listens to vessel in operation to detect unsafe or malfunctioning equipment and leaks or other flaws in hull and superstructure. Performs tests on vessel and equipment, using gauges and other standard testing devices. Estimates cost of repairs according to familiarity with labor and materials requirements or fee schedule. Directs and coordinates activities of workers engaged in repairing, painting, and otherwise restoring vessels to seaworthy condition. May repair vessels, assisted by other workers.
GOE: 05.05.09 STRENGTH: L GED: R4 M3 L3 SVP: 8 DLU: 77

187.167-134   MANAGER, MUTUEL DEPARTMENT (amuse. & rec.)
Coordinates activities of workers engaged in selling parimutuel tickets and calculating amount of money to be paid to patrons holding winning tickets at racetrack: Directs workers compiling summary sheets for each race to show total amount of money wagered, total number of tickets sold on each horse, and calculating amount of money to be paid to patrons holding winning tickets. Keeps attendance records. Hires workers, schedules working hours, and assigns work stations. Examines calculations of workers periodically to detect errors. Adjusts customer complaints.
GOE: 07.03.01 STRENGTH: S GED: R4 M4 L4 SVP: 5 DLU: 77

187.167-138   MANAGER, SALES (laundry & rel.)
Manages sales functions of drycleaning establishment: Coordinates activities of SERVICE-ESTABLISHMENT ATTENDANT (laundry & rel.; personal ser.) and DRIVERS, SALES ROUTE (retail trade; wholesale tr.). Visits customers to make estimates on proposed work, such as cleaning draperies, rugs, and upholstered furniture. Adjusts customers' complaints. Directs advertising and promotion campaigns.
GOE: 11.11.04 STRENGTH: L GED: R4 M4 L4 SVP: 7 DLU: 77

187.167-142   MANAGER, SERVICE DEPARTMENT (wholesale tr.) alternate titles: manager, service; service supervisor
Manages farm machinery service department and warehouse: Directs workers engaged in servicing equipment, such as mowers, cotton pickers, hay balers, and combines. Analyzes requests for service and records repairs, replacements, or service required. Informs field service personnel of location and work to be done. Authorizes issuance of replacement parts. Provides training for service personnel. May replenish warehouse stock.
GOE: 11.11.04 STRENGTH: L GED: R4 M4 L4 SVP: 7 DLU: 77

187.167-146   MANAGER, SKATING RINK (amuse. & rec.)
Manages ice or roller skating rink and coordinates activities of workers engaged in selling admission tickets, issuing skates to patrons, and enforcing skating rules and regulations on floor: Establishes hours that rink is open for business. Plans and initiates promotional projects to advertise establishment. Arranges private parties. Purchases skates and skating supplies. Sells skates and skating supplies to patrons. Keeps record of budget. Arranges for individual or group skating instruction. Inspects building to detect need for maintenance. Inspects floor to determine need for resanding or for scraping of ice. May repair

broken skates. May be designated according to type of rink managed as Manager, Ice-Skating Rink (amuse. & rec.); Manager, Roller-Skating Rink (amuse. & rec.).
GOE: 11.11.02 STRENGTH: L GED: R4 M4 L4 SVP: 6 DLU: 77

187.167-150 MANAGER, STORAGE GARAGE (automotive ser.)
Supervises attendants and coordinates operation of automobile storage garage or parking lot: Plans work schedule, assigns duties to PARKING-LOT ATTENDANTS (automotive ser.), and supervises worker's activities to ensure compliance with established rules and regulations. Coordinates issuance of parking tickets, stickers, and validations. Keeps daily record of operations, including money received, services performed, and accidents reported. Advises customers on garage or parking lot services and insurance rules. May balance amount of cash received against daily receipts and records. May order gas if garage has operating pumps. May perform duties of PARKING-LOT ATTENDANT (automotive ser.).
GOE: 11.11.03 STRENGTH: L GED: R3 M3 L3 SVP: 6 DLU: 77

187.167-154 MANAGER, THEATER (amuse. & rec.) alternate titles: manager, house
Manages theater for stage productions or motion pictures: Coordinates activities of personnel to ensure efficient operation and to promote patronage of theater. Directs workers in making alterations to and repair of building. Manages financial business of theater. Determines price of admission and promotes theater events. Orders and sells theater tickets. Requisitions or purchases supplies. May book pictures or stage attractions designed to meet tastes of patrons. May negotiate contracts for scripts or performers. May solicit advertisements from business and community groups. May prepare and monitor theater schedules and budget.
GOE: 11.11.02 STRENGTH: L GED: R5 M3 L4 SVP: 7 DLU: 80

187.167-158 MANAGER, TRAVEL AGENCY (business ser.; retail trade)
Manages travel agency: Directs, coordinates, and participates in merchandising travel agency services, such as sale of transportation company carrier tickets, packaged or specialized tours, or vacation packages. Plans work schedules for employees. Trains employees in advising customers on current traveling conditions, planning customer travel and itineraries, ticketing and booking functions, and in calculating costs for transportation and accommodations from current transportation schedules and tariff books and accommodation rate books. Sells travel tickets, packaged and specialized tours, and advises customers on travel plans. Reviews employee ticketing and sales activities to ensure cost calculations, booking, and transportation scheduling are in accordance with current transportation carrier schedules, tariff rates, and regulations and that charges are made for accommodations. Reconciles sales slips and cash daily. Coordinates sales promotion activities, approves advertising copy, and travel display work. Keeps employee records and hires and discharges employees.
GOE: 11.11.04 STRENGTH: L GED: R4 M4 L4 SVP: 7 DLU: 77

187.167-162 MANAGER, VEHICLE LEASING AND RENTAL (automotive ser.)
Manages automobile and truck leasing business: Directs and evaluates leasing, sales, advertising, and administrative procedures, including collections, inventory financing, and used car sales. Directs and monitors audit of financial accounts to assure compliance with prescribed standards. May visit franchised dealers to stimulate interest in establishment or expansion of leasing programs.
GOE: 11.11.05 STRENGTH: L GED: R5 M4 L4 SVP: 8 DLU: 77

187.167-166 MANAGER, WINTER SPORTS (amuse. & rec.)
Directs sports program at winter resort and coordinates activities of resort employees: Advises resort management or owner of optimum dates for opening and closing resort, taking into consideration weather predictions, reservations backlog from guests, and experience of previous season. Orders supplies, such as skiing and skating rental gear and provisions. Coordinates activities of custodial staff, food-service workers, and other resort employees to ensure availability of facilities on opening date. Trains winter-sports instructors and service personnel. Ensures that skating rink and ski slopes are suitable for use by public, notifying resort personnel to take appropriate action according to weather conditions. Inventories supplies and keeps records of weather conditions. Issues weather reports to resort management. Arranges for snow removal from roads by public authorities. May give instruction to guests in winter sports participation.
GOE: 11.11.02 STRENGTH: L GED: R4 M4 L4 SVP: 6 DLU: 77

187.167-170 MANAGER, WORLD TRADE AND MARITIME DIVISION (nonprofit org.)
Directs activities of world trade department in chamber of commerce to assist business concerns in developing and utilizing foreign markets: Conducts economic and commercial surveys in foreign countries to locate markets for products and services. Analyzes data and publishes bulletins concerning business developments in other countries, regulations affecting world trade, and opportunities for selling and buying products. Advises business and other groups on local, national, and international legislation affecting world trade. Advises exporters and importers on documentation procedures and certifies commercial documents that are required by foreign countries. Entertains foreign governmental officials and business representatives to promote trade relations. Promotes travel to other countries.
GOE: 11.05.02 STRENGTH: S GED: R5 M4 L5 SVP: 7 DLU: 77

187.167-174 PRODUCER (motion picture)
Coordinates activities of personnel engaged in writing, directing, editing, and producing motion pictures: Reviews synopses and scripts and directs adaptation for screen. Determines treatment and scope of proposed productions and establishes departmental operating budgets. Selects principal members of cast and key production staff members. Reviews filmed scenes of each day's shooting, orders retakes, and approves final editing of filmed productions. Conducts meetings with DIRECTOR, MOTION PICTURE (motion picture), SCREEN WRITER (motion picture; radio-tv broad.), and other staff members to discuss production progress and results.
GOE: 01.01.01 STRENGTH: S GED: R6 M5 L6 SVP: 8 DLU: 77

187.167-178 PRODUCER (amuse. & rec.)
Selects play for stage performance, arranges finances, and coordinates play production activities: Reads manuscripts and selects play on basis of plot, timeliness, and quality of writing. Sells shares to investors to finance production. Hires DIRECTOR, STAGE (amuse. & rec.); MANAGER, STAGE (amuse. & rec.), cast, and crew. Formulates business management policies and coordinates production schedules. Suggests or approves changes in script and staging. Arbitrates personnel disputes. May direct production of play [DIRECTOR, STAGE (amuse. & rec.)]. May produce shows for special occasions, such as fund-raising events or testimonial banquets.
GOE: 01.03.01 STRENGTH: L GED: R5 M4 L5 SVP: 7 DLU: 77

187.167-182 PRODUCER, ASSISTANT (motion picture)
Directs activities of one or more departments of motion picture studio. May direct preparation of daily production schedules and operating cost reports.
GOE: 11.05.02 STRENGTH: S GED: R5 M5 L5 SVP: 7 DLU: 77

187.167-186 RESIDENCE SUPERVISOR (any industry) alternate titles: adviser; chaperon; cottage parent; house manager
Coordinates variety of activities for residents of boarding school, college fraternity or sorority house, care and treatment institution, children's home, or similar establishment: Orders supplies and determines need for maintenance, repairs, and furnishings. Assigns rooms, assists in planning recreational activities, and supervises work and study programs. Counsels residents in identifying and resolving social or other problems. Compiles records of daily activities of residents. Chaperones group-sponsored trips and social functions. Ascertains need for and secures services of physician. Answers telephone and sorts and distributes mail. May escort individuals on trips outside establishment for shopping or to obtain medical or dental services. May hire and supervise activities of housekeeping personnel. May plan menus.
GOE: 11.07.01 STRENGTH: S GED: R4 M3 L4 SVP: 6 DLU: 77

187.167-190 SUPERINTENDENT, BUILDING (any industry) alternate titles: building-service supervisor; manager, building
Directs activities of workers engaged in operating and maintaining facilities and equipment in buildings such as apartment houses or office buildings: Inspects facilities and equipment to determine need and extent of service, equipment required, and type and number of operation and maintenance personnel needed. Hires, trains, and supervises building service personnel. Assigns workers to duties such as maintenance, repair, or renovation and obtains bids for additional work from outside contractors. Directs contracted projects to ensure adherence to specifications. Purchases building and maintenance supplies, machinery, equipment, and furniture. Plans and administers building department budget. Compiles records of labor and material cost for operating building and issues cost reports to owner or managing agents. May prepare construction specifications or plans, obtaining advice from engineering consultants, assemble and analyze contract bids, and submit bids and recommendations to superiors for action.
GOE: 05.02.02 STRENGTH: L GED: R4 M4 L4 SVP: 7 DLU: 87

187.167-194 SUPERINTENDENT, LAUNDRY (laundry & rel.)
Manages laundry plant in linen supply establishment or commercial or industrial laundry: Schedules flow of work through sorting, washing, and ironing departments, taking into consideration amount of clothes to be laundered and capacity of equipment. Hires, discharges, and transfers employees according to work performance and production needs. Purchases supplies, such as soap, starch, and bleach. Prepares and analyzes reports on labor cost and production operations to determine whether operating cost standards are being met. Tests strength of bleach, using chemical test kit. Performs other administrative and supervisory duties to ensure efficient and profitable operation. Supervises workers directly or through subordinates.
GOE: 11.11.04 STRENGTH: L GED: R4 M3 L3 SVP: 7 DLU: 78

187.167-198 VETERANS CONTACT REPRESENTATIVE (nonprofit org.) alternate titles: liaison officer; national insurance officer; rehabilitation officer; service officer; veterans' claims representative; veterans' counselor; veterans' service officer
Advises and aids veterans or dependents in presenting disability, insurance, or pension claims for benefits under federal, state, or local laws: Reviews legislation, regulations, and precedents and studies veteran's medical report and service history to evaluate and determine validity of claim. Obtains claimant's power of attorney. Prepares claim forms and briefs and assembles pertinent evidence. Requests hearing before government board and presents brief. Reviews board decision for grounds for appeal. Advises veteran on insurance, vocational, and other matters, working in cooperation with Veterans Administration and other agencies. Prepares bulletins and correspondence to acquaint field rep-

resentatives with current activities and legislation. Participates in or initiates civic functions, such as panel discussions and mass communication programs, to inform public of services rendered and rights and benefits of veterans and dependents. May offer technical advice at congressional or other governmental hearings.
GOE: 10.01.02 STRENGTH: S GED: R5 M4 L5 SVP: 7 DLU: 77

187.167-202 DIRECTOR, CRAFT CENTER (profess. & kin.)
Plans, organizes, and directs activities of craft center operated by folk or history museum, historic or ethnic area or community, or historic or regional theme park: Consults with administrative personnel to plan activities, such as craft classes, exhibits, and other projects conducted in cooperation with sponsoring institution. Orders supplies needed for basketry, leatherwork, candlemaking, macrame, tole painting, beadwork, or other crafts compatible with institution theme. Plans and writes publicity material for craft classes, and coordinates presentation of craft shows and exhibits, arranging for participants, and overseeing installation of exhibit booths, distribution of publicity materials, and scheduling of craft demonstrations. Maintains inventory, personnel, and accounting records. Arranges for consignment of craft items for sale, directs sales personnel, and maintains records of operation. Reports operational activities to institution administrative staff or governing body, and confers with staff to plan and implement changes in operation of facilities.
GOE: 11.07.04 STRENGTH: L GED: R5 M4 L5 SVP: 7 DLU: 86

187.167-206 DIETARY MANAGER (hotel & rest.)
Directs and coordinates food service activities of hospital, nursing home, or related facility: Confers with DIETITIAN, CHIEF (profess. & kin.) 077.117-010 to ensure that menus and department policies conform to nutritional standards and government and establishment regulations and procedures. Reviews patient diet information and discusses requests, changes, and inconsistencies with patient, professional staff, or resident food committee. Plans and coordinates through subordinate supervisors, such as KITCHEN SUPERVISOR (hotel & rest.) 319.137-030, standards and procedures of food storage, preparation, and service; equipment and department sanitation; employee safety; and personnel policies and procedures. Inspects food and food preparation and storage areas, using thermometers and knowledge of health and sanitation regulations. Tastes, smells, and observes food to ensure conformance with recipes and appearance standards. Attends meetings with employees, union, establishment, administrative, and regulatory personnel to discuss regulations, procedures, grievances, and recommendations for improving food service. Computes operating costs for own information and for information of administrative personnel. May be required to have competency certificate.
GOE: 11.11.04 STRENGTH: S GED: R5 M5 L5 SVP: 8 DLU: 86

187.167-210 DIRECTOR, FOOD AND BEVERAGE (amuse. & rec.)
Directs and coordinates activities of food service facilities at amusement park, through subordinate managers: Reviews food and beverage lists submitted by each facility manager to determine that sufficient items are ordered weekly. Eliminates or adds items to list, utilizing experience and knowledge of facility operations. Inspects food service facilities to ensure that equipment and buildings meet company, state, and local health laws. Analyzes information concerning facility operation, such as daily food sales, patron attendance, and labor costs to prepare budget and to maintain cost control of facility operations, using calculator and following standard business procedures. Inspects and tastes prepared foods to maintain quality standards and sanitation regulations.
GOE: 11.11.04 STRENGTH: L GED: R4 M4 L4 SVP: 8 DLU: 86

187.167-214 DIRECTOR, SERVICE (nonprofit org.)
Directs and coordinates regional program activities of nonprofit agency to provide specialized human services, such as water safety programs, disaster relief, and emergency transportation: Consults with cooperating agencies, such as police, firefighters, and emergency ambulance services, to coordinate efforts and define areas of jurisdiction. Participates in program activities to serve clients of agency. Prepares budgets to control costs and to allocate funds in accordance with provisions and agency charter. May instruct agency staff and volunteers in skills required to provide services. May requisition and arrange for maintenance of equipment, such as two-way radios and agency vehicles. May coordinate services to disaster victims and be designated Disaster Director (nonprofit org.). May coordinate safety programs, such as water safety and emergency first aid, and be designated Safety Director (nonprofit org.). May coordinate transportation of agency clients, blood, and medical supplies and equipment and be designated Transportation Director (nonprofit org.).
GOE: 11.07.01 STRENGTH: M GED: R5 M3 L5 SVP: 8 DLU: 86

187.167-218 MANAGER, ANIMAL SHELTER (nonprofit org.)
Manages animal shelter: Sets standards for and monitors conduct of shelter employees to ensure that humane philosophy is projected to public and implemented in care of animals: Develops work plans and assigns priorities for organizational units. Reviews shelter practices and procedures to ensure efficient and economical use of resources. Recommends to board of directors policy and personnel changes and budget expenditures. Directs actions to provide followup on animal neglect and cruelty complaints appearing to justify prosecution. Answers mail and maintains file of documents such as animal adoption and burial contracts and reports of shelter activities. Verifies cash receipts and deposits cash to shelter accounts. Delivers lectures, prepares materials for media broadcasts, and prepares and publishes newsletters to report agency activities and interpret organizational philosophy to public.

GOE: 11.07.01 STRENGTH: L GED: R5 M3 L5 SVP: 6 DLU: 86

187.167-222 MANAGER, BOWLING ALLEY (amuse. & rec.)
Manages bowling alley: Directs activities of workers engaged in providing services to patrons and in maintaining facilities and equipment. Assigns alleys for use, issues score sheets, and pushes controls to actuate automatic game-scoring equipment. Records number of games played and collects payment. Inspects alleys to ensure equipment is operative and observes patrons to detect disruptive behavior and misuse of alleys and equipment. Rents bowling shoes to patrons. Organizes bowling leagues and informs members of league requirements. Prepares and distributes announcements of league activities, collects member fees, and distributes tournament prizes. May sell bowling equipment. May hire and train workers.
GOE: 11.11.02 STRENGTH: L GED: R4 M2 L3 SVP: 5 DLU: 86

187.167-226 MANAGER, MARINA DRY DOCK (amuse. & rec.; water trans.)
Directs and coordinates dry docking activities at marina: Administers affairs of department, such as planning and coordinating work schedules, assigning storage crib for each boat, and maintaining department budget. Directs workers in maintenance of boats and trailers, such as painting or washing boats, lubricating and repairing motors, and retrofitting trailers and cars with lights and turn signals. Monitors fuel dock operation to ensure services to patrons. Operates, or supervises workers operating, equipment to lift boats from water and transport and dry dock boats, using crane or forklift. Hires, orients, and trains personnel in job duties, safety practices, employer policy, and performance requirements.
GOE: 05.02.07 STRENGTH: H GED: R4 M3 L3 SVP: 6 DLU: 86

187.167-230 MANAGER, RECREATION FACILITY (amuse. & rec.)
Manages recreation facilities, such as tennis courts, golf courses, or arcade, and coordinates activities of workers engaged in providing services of facility: Determines work activities necessary to operate facility, hires workers, and assigns specific tasks and work hours, accordingly. Initiates projects, such as promotional mailing or telephone campaigns, to acquaint public with activities of facility. Discusses fees of facility with interested persons. Registers patrons and explains rules and regulations. Confers with patrons to resolve grievances. Hires workers, such as carpenters, plumbers, and electricians, to make needed facility repairs. Maintains financial records. Collects coins from arcade machines. Purchases items such as golf balls, tennis balls, and paper supplies.
GOE: 11.11.02 STRENGTH: L GED: R4 M3 L4 SVP: 6 DLU: 86

187.167-234 DIRECTOR, COMMUNITY ORGANIZATION (nonprofit org.) alternate titles: community planning director, community chest; director, council of social agencies; director, federated fund; director, united fund; executive, community planning
Directs activities of organization to coordinate functions of various community health and welfare programs: Organizes and develops planning program to ascertain community requirements and problems in specific fields of welfare work, and to determine agency responsibility for administering program. Surveys functions of member agencies to avoid duplication of efforts and recommends curtailment, extension, modification, or initiation of services. Advises health and welfare agencies in planning and providing services based on community surveys and analyses. Reviews estimated budgets of member agencies. Prepares and releases reports, studies, and publications to promote public understanding of and support for community programs. May recruit and train volunteer workers. May organize and direct campaign for solicitation of funds. May visit agency sites to evaluate effectiveness of services provided.
GOE: 11.07.01 STRENGTH: S GED: R5 M3 L4 SVP: 8 DLU: 80

187.167-238 RECREATION SUPERVISOR (profess. & kin.) alternate titles: area supervisor; district director; recreation specialist
Coordinates activities of paid and volunteer recreation service personnel in public department, voluntary agency, or similar type facility, such as community centers or swimming pools: Develops and promotes recreation program, including music, dance, arts and crafts, cultural arts, nature study, swimming, social recreation and games, or camping. Adapts recreation programs to meet needs of individual agency or institution, such as hospital, armed services, institution for children or aged, settlement house, or penal institution. Introduces new program activities, equipment, and materials to staff. Trains personnel and evaluates performance. Interprets recreation service to public and participates in community meetings and organizational planning. May work in team with administrative or other professional personnel, such as those engaged in medicine, social work, nursing, psychology, and therapy, to ensure that recreation is well balanced, coordinated, and integrated with special services.
GOE: 11.07.04 STRENGTH: L GED: R5 M3 L5 SVP: 7 DLU: 80

188 PUBLIC ADMINISTRATION MANAGERS AND OFFICIALS

This group includes managerial occupations concerned with federal, state, local, and international government activities, such as the legislative, judicial, and administrative functions, as well as government owned and operated business enterprises.

188.117-010 APPRENTICESHIP CONSULTANT (government ser.) alternate titles: area representative

Directs and coordinates apprenticeship training programs in accord with state and federal policies and standards: Interprets and clarifies state and federal policies governing apprenticeship training programs, and provides information and assistance to trainees and labor and management representatives. Visits establishments to ensure that existing programs conform with training standards, investigates discrepancies, and submits progress reports. Suggests operational methods to improve existing programs, to adapt programs to production needs, to develop new training programs, and to recruit and select trainees. Negotiates with labor and management representatives to resolve training problems and to promote establishment of effective new programs. Reviews and evaluates requests for training programs and investigates establishments to ascertain if facilities, supervision, and training methods meet government standards. Evaluates training programs to determine eligibility for application of veterans benefits. May assist in resolving labor relations issues relating to training programs, such as wages, hours, supervision, and bargaining agreements.
GOE: 11.07.03 STRENGTH: L GED: R5 M4 L5 SVP: 8 DLU: 77

188.117-014 BUSINESS-ENTERPRISE OFFICER (government ser.) alternate titles: area specialist

Plans and directs self-employment rehabilitation programs for handicapped persons throughout state or region: Interviews handicapped applicants to determine suitable job or business consistent with applicant's experience, training, aptitude, and physical limitations. Accepts or recommends acceptance of suitable candidates. Develops training methods and trains handicapped persons in operation of business, according to knowledge of retail merchandising principles and techniques. Plans desirable locations for enterprises, considering available facilities, traffic volume, fixtures and equipment costs, and character of business. Negotiates lease or donation of space with property owners and other interested parties. Establishes statistical and accounting procedures to evaluate productivity of business and success of proprietor. Coordinates activities with religious, charitable, and other agencies carrying out related programs to benefit handicapped persons. Prepares public information materials explaining program for radio, television, and printed media and presents lectures to interested groups to increase public awareness of handicapped citizens' problems. Confers with state purchasing officials to obtain fixtures and initial stock for retail operations at most favorable prices available. Supervises activities of VENDING-STAND SUPERVISORS (government ser.) within territory assigned. May confer with contractors and inspect construction of retail stands for conformity with contract provisions.
GOE: 11.07.01 STRENGTH: L GED: R5 M4 L5 SVP: 6 DLU: 77

188.117-018 CHIEF, FISHERY DIVISION (government ser.)

Directs state fish conservation program for benefit of sport and commercial fishing interests, consistent with state policy and accepted principles of game management: Directs activities of personnel engaged in conducting fish count, managing hatcheries, stocking streams, destroying superfluous or undesirable fish, and enforcing restrictions governing sport and commercial fishing. Modifies regulations on size, species, length of fishing season, acceptable fishing practices, and other considerations according to fluctuations in fish population. Organizes programs to correct unfavorable conditions, such as water pollution, silting of streams, excessive mortality of given species of fish, and diversion of waterways. Delivers speeches, writes articles, and prepares other informational material to explain conservation principles and acquaint public with fishing regulations. Recommends changes in legislation and administrative procedures as necessary to maintain conservation activities consistent with current needs. Prepares or directs preparation of budget requests covering staff and equipment requirements.
GOE: 03.01.02 STRENGTH: L GED: R5 M4 L5 SVP: 8 DLU: 77

188.117-022 CIVIL PREPAREDNESS OFFICER (government ser.)

Coordinates activities of workers engaged in preparing for or combating disaster situations and negotiates with civic and professional leaders to develop and implement survival plans in accord with local needs and state and federal policies: Directs marking and stocking of radiation shelters to meet specified standards. Obtains cooperation of property owners, civic leaders, and professional groups in providing facilities and services for emergency preparedness. Confers with business and governmental representatives to assist in local emergency planning. Reviews emergency plans to coordinate with changes in state or federal policies and military technology. Addresses interested civic, social, and religious groups to stimulate awareness of emergency preparedness activities. Directs inspection and inventory of emergency supplies and equipment and requisitions needed materials or arranges for equipment maintenance. May assist in providing warnings and survival information to communities before, during, and after community emergencies. May direct activities of headquarters technical, clerical, and administrative staffs and assign paid or volunteer workers to duty during simulated or actual emergencies. May review and recommend alterations in local emergency planning to coordinate with changes in economic character of community or region. May be designated according to specific function as Civil Preparedness Operations Officer (government ser.); Civil Preparedness Radiological Officer (government ser.); Civil Preparedness Supply Specialist (government ser.); Director, Civil Preparedness Warden (government ser.); Shelter Management Officer (government ser.). May assume responsibility for local, regional, or state civil preparedness or emergency activities and be designated Director, Civil Preparedness (government ser.). May plan

and coordinate procedures for meeting civil preparedness emergencies in industrial establishments and be designated Civil Preparedness Coordinator (profess. & kin.). Workers involved in these and other civil preparedness activities may be identified by different titles according to classifications used by local or national authorities.
GOE: 11.05.03 STRENGTH: L GED: R5 M3 L5 SVP: 6 DLU: 77

188.117-026 COMMISSIONER, CONSERVATION OF RESOURCES (government ser.)

Directs conservation of natural resources within state and negotiates with interested parties to promote maximum utilization of resources consistent with public interest: Initiates conservation programs according to accepted principles and familiarity with characteristics of natural resources and economy of state. Establishes standards for resource depletion, such as annual oil production quotas or limitations on extraction of iron ore deposits. Negotiates with mining interests, petroleum production companies, and other parties to promote conservation principles, encourage technological advancement, and stimulate efficient exploitation of resources. Delivers speeches and participates in discussions with representatives of government, labor, and industry to resolve problems related to conservation and economic development. Participates in establishment and implementation of rehabilitation programs for workers affected by changing technology or loss of markets. Supervises and coordinates, through subordinates, activities of workers engaged in preparing reports, statistics, and other data on departmental activities. May be designated according to resource involved as Commissioner, Iron Range Resources And Rehabilitation (government ser.).
GOE: 11.05.03 STRENGTH: S GED: R5 M4 L4 SVP: 8 DLU: 77

188.117-030 COMMISSIONER, PUBLIC WORKS (government ser.) alternate titles: public-works commissioner

Directs and coordinates activities of city departments of public works and utilities: Confers with officials responsible for street and building construction and maintenance, and for supplying water, power, sanitation, or other services to coordinate use of human resources and equipment and to consolidate purchasing requests. Reviews preliminary budgets and adjusts items for conformance to anticipated needs. Attends city council meetings to present budgets, activity reports, and plans for future activities. Confers with suppliers and sellers and places orders for equipment, materials, and supplies. May hire, promote, and discipline employees of departments supervised.
GOE: 11.05.03 STRENGTH: S GED: R5 M5 L5 SVP: 8 DLU: 77

188.117-034 DIRECTOR, AERONAUTICS COMMISSION (government ser.)

Directs activities of state commission or department of aeronautics: Authorizes airport construction and expansion, and inspection of state aircraft and facilities, and regulation of aviation activities under state control. Formulates policies and work programs. Recommends and drafts rules, regulations, and statutes governing aeronautics in state. Coordinates activities of commission or department with private organizations and other government units to ensure effective aviation programs.
GOE: 11.05.03 STRENGTH: S GED: R5 M4 L5 SVP: 8 DLU: 77

188.117-038 DIRECTOR, AGRICULTURAL SERVICES (government ser.)

Administers state agricultural program: Develops and coordinates programs for producing and marketing commodities, such as livestock, grain, dairy products, and produce. Interprets and enforces laws, rules, and regulations governing agricultural commodities. Directs programs, such as weights and measures, inspection of grain and livestock facilities, and processing, packaging, and distribution of agricultural products to ensure compliance with federal and state regulations. Conducts hearings to determine violations and penalties. Represents agency at meetings, conventions, and other forums to promote program objectives. Prepares and releases reports, studies, and other publications relating to marketing trends and program accomplishments. Develops and directs training program for staff personnel.
GOE: 11.05.03 STRENGTH: L GED: R5 M5 L5 SVP: 8 DLU: 77

188.117-042 DIRECTOR, ARTS-AND-HUMANITIES COUNCIL (government ser.)

Administers program to promote visual and performing arts and humanities: Plans, organizes, and executes creative arts program under authority of governing board. Negotiates contracts and agreements with federal and state agencies and other cultural organizations for funding and implementation of programs. Establishes statewide councils and provides guidance in obtaining grants, initiating local projects, and disseminating cultural information. Exchanges ideas through seminars, conferences, and other forums and media to accomplish program objectives.
GOE: 11.05.03 STRENGTH: L GED: R5 M5 L5 SVP: 8 DLU: 77

188.117-046 DIRECTOR, COMPLIANCE (government ser.)

Directs human relations program: Plans, organizes, and executes compliance programs in areas of employment, housing, and education under authority of federal, state, or local discriminatory legislation. Establishes and coordinates activities of local community relations committees. Conducts investigations to resolve complaints and report violations for adjudication. Plans informational programs to stimulate and maintain community interest and support. Cooperates with local, state, and federal governmental units and other organizations in identifying needs and providing assistance in enforcement of statutes.

GOE: 11.10.02 STRENGTH: L GED: R5 M4 L5 SVP: 7 DLU: 77

188.117-050   DIRECTOR, CONSUMER AFFAIRS (government ser.)
Administers consumer affairs program: Plans and implements policies and procedures governing program. Develops and conducts program to inform public of departmental objectives. Conducts investigations and cooperates with federal, state, and local agencies, business community, and private organizations to resolve violations of consumer protection laws. Advocates consumer interests before legislative body, regulatory agencies, and other judicial forums. Recommends changes in legislation affecting consumer protection. Directs hiring, training, and evaluation of staff personnel.
GOE: 11.10.02 STRENGTH: L GED: R5 M5 L5 SVP: 8 DLU: 77

188.117-054   DIRECTOR, CORRECTIONAL AGENCY (government ser.)
Administers state correction program, such as parole, probation, work release, or custodial care: Organizes, develops, and executes departmental policies in accordance with state and federal regulations and under direction of governing board. Establishes cooperative agreements with other state agencies and criminal justice department to plan and promote rehabilitative programs and projects. Investigates complaints or incidents to resolve inmate grievances. Coordinates staff activities, such as fiscal, management, training, and other supportive services. Establishes system of records and reports. Testifies at legislative or other hearings to recommend changes in existing statutes.
GOE: 11.05.03 STRENGTH: L GED: R6 M5 L5 SVP: 8 DLU: 77

188.117-058   DIRECTOR, COUNCIL ON AGING (government ser.) alternate titles: regional coordinator for aging
Directs local or statewide services to promote understanding and resolution of senior citizens' problems: Plans and directs surveys and research studies of such problems as health needs and employment difficulties of older persons. Evaluates findings to formulate policies and techniques for improving adjustment of older citizens. Promotes establishment of or directs local programs and services, such as clinics and hobby groups. Coordinates programs of government, charitable, and religious organizations to avoid duplication. Prepares and distributes public information materials dealing with group problems. Delivers speeches and participates in discussions with community leaders and other interested parties to promote objectives of program. Recommends changes in legislation and public policy to promote interests of aged.
GOE: 11.07.01 STRENGTH: S GED: R5 M4 L5 SVP: 8 DLU: 80

188.117-062   DIRECTOR, FIELD REPRESENTATIVES (government ser.)
Administers educational and job training programs for veterans of armed services, as established by government regulations, and directs activities of field representatives: Develops and presents reports concerning activities, expenses, budget, new or revised government statutes and rulings, and other items affecting program. Evaluates curriculums, and reviews and approves or rejects applications of schools, establishments, or individuals offering educational or training facilities. Determines eligibility of veterans to receive education or training. Confers with government agencies on problems and other matters relating to program. Interprets regulatory or administrative decisions to execute legal requirements, establishes guides for making decisions in field, and assigns work load to subordinates.
GOE: 11.07.03 STRENGTH: S GED: R5 M5 L5 SVP: 8 DLU: 77

188.117-066   DIRECTOR, LABOR STANDARDS (government ser.)
Directs labor standards program: Establishes operational procedures and guidelines for enforcing statutes and regulations governing minimum wage, working hours and conditions, employment of minors, and licensing of private employment agencies. Effects liaison with federal agencies to coordinate activities and avoid duplication of effort. Mediates disputes and violations of laws. Conducts research projects to establish standards and proposes legislative changes to implement findings. Develops and directs training program for staff in licensing, inspection, and investigative functions.
GOE: 11.10.02 STRENGTH: L GED: R5 M5 L5 SVP: 8 DLU: 77

188.117-070   DIRECTOR, LAW ENFORCEMENT (government ser.)
Administers state law enforcement program: Plans and organizes program for units of local and State agencies concerned with law enforcement, criminal justice, corrections, juvenile delinquency, and rehabilitation. Develops and coordinates training program for staff and law enforcement personnel. Promotes community acceptance of crime and delinquency programs through news and other media. Coordinates reporting activities of local and state cooperating agencies.
GOE: 11.05.03 STRENGTH: L GED: R5 M5 L5 SVP: 7 DLU: 77

188.117-074   DIRECTOR, LICENSING AND REGISTRATION (government ser.)
Administers state program for licensing motorists and motor vehicles: Formulates procedures and guidelines for examining and licensing drivers and registering vehicles in accordance with statutes, rules, and regulations. Coordinates departmental activities, such as clerical, inspection, licensing, registration, and insurance and financial liability. Recommends legislative changes in vehicle and driver license laws. Directs compilation of statistics, such as accidents, fatalities and injuries, and driver characteristics. Directs investigations to resolve problems, such as financial responsibility, license revocations, and related matters. Confers with other state or federal agencies to coordinate safety and other traffic programs.
GOE: 11.05.03 STRENGTH: L GED: R5 M5 L5 SVP: 8 DLU: 77

188.117-078   DIRECTOR, EMPLOYMENT SERVICES (government ser.)
Administers employment service program: Plans and executes policies and procedures to provide statewide employment services under authority of federal and state regulations. Coordinates local office operations with staff services, such as counseling, testing, job analysis, farm placement, recruitment and staff training, and human resource development to achieve program objectives. Negotiates agreements with other state agencies to provide assistance in cooperative projects. Reviews operating reports to determine effectiveness of program. Attends conferences with government officials, employers, labor leaders, and other parties to secure assistance in formulating policies for new or ongoing programs.
GOE: 11.05.03 STRENGTH: L GED: R5 M5 L5 SVP: 8 DLU: 77

188.117-082   DIRECTOR, MEDICAL FACILITIES SECTION (government ser.)
Administers activities of state department of hospital licensing and construction: Directs inspection of public and private hospitals, nursing homes, diagnostic centers and similar facilities in operation or under construction. Recommends or disapproves licensing in accord with findings, state laws, and established policy. Prepares and coordinates state plan for construction of medical facilities, in accordance with demonstrated need, available funds, and availability of medical service personnel. Prepares and enforces standards for operation of medical facilities. Confers with medical service personnel, representative of local medical societies, and other interested parties to implement policies and programs in accordance with public interest. May administer activities of state-operated clinics and hospitals.
GOE: 11.10.03 STRENGTH: S GED: R5 M5 L5 SVP: 8 DLU: 77

188.117-086   DIRECTOR, MERIT SYSTEM (government ser.)
Directs administration of statewide merit system qualifying examinations: Formulates policies and procedures on recruitment, testing, placement, classification, and salary administration. Confers with school officials and superintendents of public buildings to arrange for space to conduct examinations. Verifies applicability and authenticity of examination and inventories examination materials to prevent errors and unauthorized use. Effects liaison with public officials, employee groups, and general public to promote program objectives. May proctor examinations and participate in oral interviews with applicants.
GOE: 11.05.03 STRENGTH: L GED: R4 M4 L4 SVP: 5 DLU: 77

188.117-090   DIRECTOR, REVENUE (government ser.)
Administers state revenue program for collection of taxes, such as income, inheritance, gasoline, and sales: Devises and implements policies and procedures for collecting taxes and auditing accounts in compliance with state statutory regulations. Schedules and holds hearings to resolve delinquency and other tax violations. Reviews reports and prepares revenue estimates for legislative budgetary action. Disseminates tax information to public, using radio, television, and other media.
GOE: 11.05.03 STRENGTH: L GED: R6 M5 L5 SVP: 8 DLU: 77

188.117-094   DIRECTOR, UNEMPLOYMENT INSURANCE (government ser.)
Administers unemployment insurance program: Interprets policies, rules, and regulations under authority of governing commission and federal and state legislation. Plans and coordinates staff activities, such as maintenance of records of employer contributions, employee wages, benefit payment, administrative expenditures, and related matters. Directs investigations of employer liability, payroll records, and employee coverage. Prepares and releases operating reports. Attends conferences with government officials, employers, labor leaders, and other parties to promote support for program objectives. Recommends changes in legislation affecting program.
GOE: 11.05.03 STRENGTH: L GED: R5 M5 L5 SVP: 8 DLU: 77

188.117-098   DISTRICT CUSTOMS DIRECTOR (government ser.)
Directs and coordinates administrative activities of customs collection district and negotiates with interested parties to enforce federal customs laws and collections: Prepares, reviews, and submits reports of district's activities to customs office and other government agencies. Represents Bureau of Customs in meetings with individuals, representatives of private industry, government agencies, and in court. Recommends and approves personnel appointments, promotions, transfers, and reassignments within district. Directs submission of customs receipts and preparation of accounts as required by law and procedures of Bureau.
GOE: 11.10.04 STRENGTH: S GED: R5 M5 L5 SVP: 8 DLU: 77

188.117-102   ECONOMIC DEVELOPMENT COORDINATOR (government ser.)
Directs economic development planning activities for city, state, or region: Negotiates with industry representatives to encourage location in area. Directs activities, such as research, analysis, and evaluation of technical information to determine feasibility and economic impact of proposed expansions and developments. Confers with governmental officials to effect changes in local policies or ordinances discouraging effective development.
GOE: 11.05.03 STRENGTH: L GED: R5 M4 L5 SVP: 8 DLU: 77

188.117-106   FOREIGN-SERVICE OFFICER (government ser.)
Represents interests of United States Government and Nationals by conducting relations with foreign nations and international organizations; protecting and advancing political, economic, and commercial interests overseas; and rendering

personal services to Americans abroad and to foreign nationals traveling to the United States: Manages and administers diplomatic or consular post abroad. Conveys views of U.S. Government to host government. Reports political and other developments in host country to superior or Secretary of State. Analyzes basic economic data, trends, and developments in host country or region. Advances trade by alerting U.S. business personnel to potential foreign trade and investment opportunities. Provides medical, legal, familial, and traveling advice and assistance to U.S. citizens. Issues passports to Americans and visas to foreigners wishing to enter the United States. Offers notarial services and assistance on benefit programs to Americans and eligible foreigners. Determines eligibility of persons to be documented as U.S. citizens. Takes testimony abroad for use in U.S. Courts. May negotiate agreements between host and United States Government. May recommend how American policy can help improve foreign economic conditions. May coordinate American economic assistance programs. May serve in Washington, D.C. as counterpart to outstationed colleagues, relating foreign service administrative needs to Department of State or United States Information Agency. May disseminate information overseas about the United States and its policies by engaging in cultural and educational interaction through United States Information Agency. May be designated according to basic field of specialization as Administrative Officer (government ser.); Commercial Officer (government ser.); Consular Officer (government ser.); Cultural Affairs Officer (government ser.); Diplomatic Officer (government ser.); Economic Officer (government ser.). May be designated: Information Officer (government ser.); Political Officer (government ser.); Public Affairs Officer (government ser.).
GOE: 11.09.03 STRENGTH: S GED: R5 M4 L5 SVP: 8 DLU: 77

188.117-110 HOUSING-MANAGEMENT OFFICER (government ser.)
Directs and coordinates activities concerned with providing advice and technical assistance to housing authorities and evaluating housing management programs: Develops policy and standards for guidance of local housing organizations in establishing and maintaining uniformity in operation of housing projects. Studies operation of housing projects, notes trends and needs, and evaluates efficiency of housing programs. Prepares regulations, procedures, and instructions for operation of housing projects based on analysis of operations. Approves or disapproves requests for waivers to policies, standards, and procedures. Consults with and advises housing personnel of public and private groups concerning needed improvements in housing operations. Advises and assists MANAGERS, HOUSING PROJECT (profess. & kin.) and staffs of local housing authorities concerning problems, such as eliminating excess costs, improving livability features and maintenance care of dwelling units, making more effective use of project facilities and community services, and promoting satisfactory relationships among tenants, housing project personnel, public officials, and private agencies. Leads public meetings and serves on committees to stimulate efforts of national, local, and private housing agencies and to emphasize housing needs of military personnel and low-income families.
GOE: 11.05.03 STRENGTH: L GED: R5 M3 L4 SVP: 8 DLU: 77

188.117-114 MANAGER, CITY (government ser.) alternate titles: manager, county; manager, town
Directs and coordinates administration of city or county government in accordance with policies determined by city council or other authorized elected officials: Appoints department heads and staffs as provided by state laws or local ordinances. Supervises activities of departments performing functions such as collection and disbursement of taxes, law enforcement, maintenance of public health, construction of public works, and purchase of supplies and equipment. Prepares annual budget and submits estimates to authorized elected officials for approval. Plans for future development of urban and nonurban areas to provide for population growth and expansion of public services. May recommend zoning regulation controlling location and development of residential and commercial areas [URBAN PLANNER (profess. & kin.)]. May perform duties of one or more city or county officials as designated by local laws.
GOE: 11.05.03 STRENGTH: S GED: R5 M4 L5 SVP: 8 DLU: 77

188.117-118 POLICE COMMISSIONER I (government ser.)
Administers municipal police department: Participates in decisions of Board to purchase supplies and equipment; to administer funds and care for property of department; to set number and salary of officers and employees of department; to modify classification standards of service; to hear and act on charges of incompetence, disobedience, and dishonesty filed against members of force; to appoint, assign to duty, or transfer members of force; to establish rules and regulations for department; and to perform other necessary functions. Receives and acts upon recommendations of officers in service and of committees appointed by Board to whom implementation of Board responsibilities may be delegated.
GOE: 04.01.01 STRENGTH: S GED: R5 M4 L5 SVP: 8 DLU: 77

188.117-122 PROPERTY-UTILIZATION OFFICER (government ser.) alternate titles: business-service officer; manager, surplus property
Coordinates property procurement and maintenance activities, and negotiates with representatives to effect property transfers and sales, rental, and leasing contracts for government agency: Reviews property-related data, such as inventories, budgets, planning reports, vendor brochures, and excess property and property request reports, to obtain information on property status, needs, and availability. Writes, fills out, and reviews bids, contract specifications, purchase orders and estimates, and transfer forms to effect property transactions. Con-

tacts vendors and potential users, and inspects and inventories acquired and transferred property through visits to government installations and vendor sites. Negotiates and confers with administrators, vendors, or users to effect agreement on property transfer details, such as price, model, packaging, transportation, land boundaries, or building layout. Authorizes expenditures within specified limits for purchases of supplies and equipment, equipment repair and maintenance, and alterations to premises. Fills government agency or other qualifying organization requests from surplus inventories, considering factors such as donation criteria, actual needs, and justification. Prepares plans, standards, and specifications for building and equipment maintenance, repair, and inspection. May be designated according to property involved as Real-Estate-Utilization Officer (government ser.); State-Surplus-Commodity-And-Property Representative (government ser.).
GOE: 11.12.02 STRENGTH: L GED: R5 M4 L4 SVP: 8 DLU: 77

188.117-126 WELFARE DIRECTOR (government ser.) alternate titles: director of social services
Directs administration of public welfare program in county or city, in conformity with policies of welfare board and availability of funds: Consults with members of welfare board to plan activities and expenditures. Coordinates, directly or through subordinates, activities of staff engaged in investigating and counseling welfare claimants and in processing welfare claims. Participates in discussions with community leaders and other interested parties to improve conditions of welfare recipients and to coordinate public assistance programs with efforts of religious and charitable organizations. Coordinates distribution of government surplus commodities in conformity with federal standards. Prepares welfare budget and adjusts welfare services in accordance with available funds. In smaller communities may interview welfare recipients, assist them in resolving personal or financial problems, and perform related activities [CASEWORKER (social ser.)]. May be designated according to jurisdiction as County Director, Welfare (government ser.).
GOE: 11.07.01 STRENGTH: S GED: R5 M5 L5 SVP: 8 DLU: 77

188.117-130 COURT ADMINISTRATOR (government ser.)
Administers nonjudicial functions of court: Coordinates activities such as jury selection, notification, and utilization, case scheduling and tracking, personnel assignment, and space and equipment allocation to accomplish orderly processing of court cases. Investigates problems that affect case flow and recommends or implements corrective measures. Compiles and analyzes data on court activity to monitor management performance and prepare activity reports. Conducts research to analyze current and alternative personnel, facilities, and data management systems and consults with judicial staff of court to evaluate findings and recommendations. May oversee accounting of revenues and expenditures and prepare and justify budget. May resolve questions and complaints raised by court personnel, attorneys, and members of other organizations and public.
GOE: 11.05.03 STRENGTH: L GED: R5 M4 L5 SVP: 8 DLU: 86

188.117-134 DIRECTOR, REGULATORY AGENCY (government ser.)
Directs agency, division, or major function of agency or division charged with investigating regulated activities to assure compliance with federal, state, or municipal laws: Interprets and clarifies federal, state, or municipal laws. Represents agency at meetings, conventions, and other forums to promote and explain agency objectives. Consults with other governmental agencies, business community, and private organizations to resolve problems. Plans and directs surveys and research studies to ensure effective program operation and to establish or modify standards. Recommends changes in legislation and administrative procedures to reflect technological and ecological changes and public sentiment. Confers with legislative liaison individuals or committees to develop legislative bills involving inspection procedures and to obtain wording for proposed inspection codes. Prepares or directs preparation and release of reports, studies, and other publications relating to program trends and accomplishments. Reviews and evaluates work of MANAGER, REGULATED PROGRAM (government ser.) 168.167-090 through conversations, meetings, and reports. Prepares or directs preparation of budget requests. May be required to testify in court or before control or review board. May be designated according to function or agency administered as Administrator, Pesticide (government ser.); Administrator, Structural Pest Control (government ser.); Agricultural Commodity Grading Supervisor (government ser.); Director, Reactor Projects (government ser.); Director, Transportation Utilities Regulation (government ser.); Director, Weights And Measures (government ser.); Manager For Health, Safety, And Environment (government ser.); Petroleum Products Inspection Supervisor (government ser.).
GOE: 11.05.03 STRENGTH: S GED: R5 M4 L5 SVP: 8 DLU: 86

188.137-010 SUPERVISOR (government ser.)
Supervises and coordinates activities of personnel engaged in carrying out departmental objectives in unit of governmental agency, utilizing knowledge of agency purposes, rules, regulations, procedures, and practices: Reviews unit's work load, schedules, personnel assignments, status of on-going work, projects, and available personnel for work assignment in order to plan unit activities. Assigns specific duties to personnel, such as enforcing of agency rules and regulations or government laws and codes; conducting investigations or research; writing technical, informative, or operational reports and papers; or working on special projects, considering individual's knowledge and experience. Reviews reports, papers, and other records prepared by personnel for clarity, completeness, accuracy, and conformance with agency policies. Routes approved reports and records to superior for action. Coordinates work activities of unit with other

units, sections, or agencies to prevent delays in actions required or to improve services to public. Plans and conducts, or arranges for, indoctrination and training of personnel. Approves leave requests, evaluates personnel performance, and initiates disciplinary actions. Interviews job applicants on eligibility lists and prepares individual recommendations for consideration by superior. May be designated according to agency unit supervised or purpose of unit.
GOE: 11.05.03 STRENGTH: L GED: R5 M3 L4 SVP: 7 DLU: 80

188.167-010 APPRAISER (government ser.) alternate titles: deputy assessor

Appraises real and personal property to determine fair value and assesses taxes in accordance with prescribed schedules: Inspects property and considers factors such as current market value, location of property, and building or replacement costs to make property appraisal. Computes amount of tax to be levied, using applicable tax tables, and writes reports of determinations for public record. May interpret laws, formulate policies, and direct activities of assessment office. May be designated according to type of property assessed as Appraiser, Aircraft (government ser.); Appraiser, Auditor (government ser.); Appraiser, Boats And Marine (government ser.); Appraiser, Buildings (government ser.); Appraiser, Land (government ser.); Appraiser, Oil And Water (government ser.); Appraiser, Personal Property (government ser.); Appraiser, Real Estate (government ser.); Appraiser, Timber (government ser.).
GOE: 11.06.03 STRENGTH: L GED: R5 M5 L5 SVP: 7 DLU: 77

188.167-014 ASSESSOR-COLLECTOR, IRRIGATION TAX (government ser.) alternate titles: appraiser, irrigation tax

Directs activities of workers engaged in assessing and collecting property tax levies for operation and maintenance of irrigation system: Supervises and participates with workers in determining value of municipal and rural properties within irrigation district. Directs activities of clerical workers engaged in preparing tax bills, collecting taxes, and keeping tax rolls, maps, and records of taxes levied and paid. Authorizes addition of penalties on delinquent tax accounts. Draws up and issues certificate of sale in favor of water district to satisfy unpaid taxes. Interviews property owners to resolve complaints, and answer questions concerning taxes and appraisal values.
GOE: 11.05.03 STRENGTH: L GED: R5 M5 L5 SVP: 8 DLU: 77

188.167-018 CHIEF WARDEN (government ser.)

Coordinates activities of FISH AND GAME WARDENS (government ser.) and other personnel within state or conservation district: Determines effectiveness of training administered by others, according to review of personnel records and supervisory evaluations. Coordinates special enforcement campaigns, such as rabies control activities and investigations into cause of excessive fish mortality. Assigns personnel to enforcement territories or to aid other divisions in seasonal conservation activities. Prepares public information materials, delivers speeches, and confers with representatives of sports groups to promote conservation activities. Answers correspondence concerning enforcement or other activities. Keeps records of hunting accidents, drownings, hunting law violations, and related data. Prepares budget for submission to state legislature.
GOE: 11.05.03 STRENGTH: L GED: R5 M4 L4 SVP: 6 DLU: 77

188.167-022 DIRECTOR OF VITAL STATISTICS (government ser.) alternate titles: chief of vital statistics

Directs collection, recording, and tabulation of vital statistics and implementation of special statistical studies required by state government: Directs activities of workers engaged in compiling statistical data, such as births, deaths, marriages, incidence of various diseases, and supplementary material. Formulates procedures for converting raw data into statistical form, according to knowledge of accepted statistical analysis procedures. Conducts special studies on request from legislative officials, private organizations, and other interested groups, by defining dimensions of study, size of statistical sampling, data collection procedures, and methods of presenting findings. Develops and implements, through subordinates, procedures for registration and certification of births, marriages, and similar occurrences in communities throughout state.
GOE: 11.01.02 STRENGTH: S GED: R5 M5 L5 SVP: 8 DLU: 77

188.167-026 DIRECTOR, CLASSIFICATION AND TREATMENT (government ser.) alternate titles: assignment officer; correctional officer

Directs prison rehabilitation programs and assignment of inmates under direction of DIRECTOR, INSTITUTION (any industry): Plans and coordinates programs for providing educational, recreational, and spiritual services; supplying medical, dental, and psychiatric treatment; and meeting other needs of inmates in conformity with established policies of correctional institution. Administers and scores intelligence, aptitude, and other standard tests to evaluate inmates' suitability for rehabilitation. Reviews case reports of prisoners to recommend parole, vocational training, transfer, psychiatric treatment, custody status, or other disposition according to findings. Directs workers engaged in maintenance of inmate records. Confers with other members of prison staff to coordinate all program activities in conformity with prison routine and security requirements. Prepares and delivers speeches to promote understanding of prison services and characteristics of offenders.
GOE: 11.07.01 STRENGTH: S GED: R5 M4 L5 SVP: 7 DLU: 77

188.167-030 DIRECTOR, FINANCIAL RESPONSIBILITY DIVISION (government ser.)

Directs administration of state financial responsibility law requiring deposit of surety bonds by uninsured motorists involved in highway accidents: Coordi-

nates activities of personnel engaged in compiling and analyzing personal injury and property damage reports and related data to determine applicability of law and amount of surety deposit required for compliance. Formulates or interprets regulations and policies for implementation by staff and to supply information to attorneys and litigants in accident cases. Coordinates activities of workers engaged in preparing receipts for surety deposits, making disbursements and refunds, and forwarding deposits to appropriate state office. Notifies motor vehicle licensing officials of motorists' failure to meet requirements of law to facilitate license revocation or other official action. Recommends changes in law to remove inequities and maintain surety requirements consistent with trends in accident statistics and jury damage awards.
GOE: 11.05.03 STRENGTH: S GED: R4 M4 L4 SVP: 6 DLU: 77

188.167-034 DIRECTOR, SAFETY COUNCIL (government ser.)

Directs activities of State Highway Safety Council to promote driver education and safety of roads and vehicles: Directs workers engaged in compilation of traffic safety statistics, such as fatalities and injuries, causes of accidents, and characteristics of drivers involved in accidents. Evaluates statistics according to accepted statistical analysis procedures and formulates plans for improving driver education and highway engineering. Prepares or directs workers engaged in preparation of pamphlets, advertisements, radio commercials, and other educational materials concerned with highway safety. Delivers speeches and participates in public forums and broadcasts to educate motorists in safety habits. Confers with officials of other departments, such as state police and highway engineering and with national safety leaders to coordinate program activities. Recommends changes in legislation and highway user regulations to improve safety conditions.
GOE: 11.05.03 STRENGTH: S GED: R5 M5 L5 SVP: 8 DLU: 77

188.167-038 DIRECTOR, SECURITIES AND REAL ESTATE (government ser.)

Directs activities of state department governing securities and real estate transactions: Interprets laws regarding transactions and recommends action by law enforcement agencies or appropriate state board. Investigates applications for registration of securities sales. Investigates complaints of fraudulent or irregular transactions and recommends legal action if necessary. Prepares agenda and participates in meetings with Securities Commission and Board of Real Estate Examiners to discuss pending cases and present or future problems. Directs workers engaged in publishing manuals, bulletins, and reports for information of dealers, brokers, and public. Conducts educational classes and approves written examinations required of applicants for registration and licenses.
GOE: 11.10.01 STRENGTH: S GED: R5 M4 L5 SVP: 7 DLU: 77

188.167-042 DIRECTOR, STATE-ASSESSED PROPERTIES (government ser.)

Directs local or statewide program of real estate and property assessment equalization to facilitate adjustments in tax base and rates resulting from changes in property values: Devises procedures for compiling, computing, and analyzing valuation data according to knowledge of statistical principles and accepted valuation theories [VALUATION ENGINEER (profess. & kin.)]. Assigns APPRAISERS (government ser.) to interview industrial, commercial, and residential property owners and inspect properties in prescribed areas to obtain current valuation data. Directs personnel engaged in assembling and analyzing data into statistical groupings to facilitate comparisons with previous assessments. Prepares or directs preparation of reports and graphs to illustrate findings. Derives assessment equalization factors from computed data according to accepted valuation principles and knowledge of real estate market relationships. Allocates expected revenue among state tax districts according to computations and departmental regulations. Recommends changes in valuation procedures, tax rates, and tax policy to appropriate officials. Represents tax commission at meetings of boards of equalization, at tax appeal hearings, and in court.
GOE: 11.05.03 STRENGTH: S GED: R5 M5 L5 SVP: 7 DLU: 77

188.167-046 DISTRICT CUSTOMS DIRECTOR, DEPUTY (government ser.)

Directs and coordinates activities of customs collection district personnel and cooperates with officials of other government agencies to enforce federal customs laws and collections, under supervision of DISTRICT CUSTOMS DIRECTOR (government ser.): Dictates correspondence and prepares or verifies district reports. Answers inquiries of confidential or technical nature. Confers with officials of other government agencies to effect mutual cooperation in enforcement activities. Reviews civil case reports on customs violations to determine disposition. Schedules training and work assignments. Serves as consultant to DISTRICT CUSTOMS DIRECTOR (government ser.).
GOE: 11.10.04 STRENGTH: S GED: R5 M5 L5 SVP: 7 DLU: 77

188.167-050 ELECTION ASSISTANT (government ser.) alternate titles: election supervisor

Directs compliance with official election procedures throughout state and recommends procedural changes to improve efficiency and equity of voting: Participates in training election workers and advising local election officials prior to elections. Directs workers engaged in printing ballots and conducting of censuses, elections, and referendums. Studies election laws in other states and jurisdictions to recommend changes in procedures governing registration, filing, voting, reporting, and other requirements. Alters official legislative procedures as manual recommendations are accepted by legislature.
GOE: 11.05.03 STRENGTH: S GED: R5 M3 L4 SVP: 7 DLU: 77

188.167-054 FEDERAL AID COORDINATOR (government ser.)

Coordinates project activities to ensure administrative efficiency and compliance with federal laws, regulations, and standards and directs disbursement of federal funds and administration of federal projects to implement fish and wildlife conservation programs in state: Analyzes conservation problems and needs in state to recommend or authorize establishment of conservation programs. Confers with conservation officials to provide coordination of project and liaison between federal and state authorities. Reviews accounting records and authorizes reimbursement of project funds to state. Prepares budget estimates for activities and projects.
GOE: 11.05.03 STRENGTH: S GED: R5 M4 L5 SVP: 7 DLU: 77

188.167-058 MANAGER, OFFICE (government ser.)

Manages local, district, or regional office of governmental agency or department to provide public or other individuals with designated services, or implement laws, codes, programs, or policies prescribed by legislative bodies: Reviews official directives and correspondence to ascertain such data as changes prescribed in agency programs, policies, and procedures, and new assignments or responsibilities delegated to office. Confers with subordinate supervisory personnel and reads staff reports and records to obtain data, such as status of ongoing work or projects, cases and investigations pending, indications of probable conclusions, and projected completion dates. Plans office activities and work projects and assigns unit supervisory personnel responsibility for carrying out and completing specific projects and duties. Coordinates activities of various office units in order to provide designated functions or services with minimum delay and optimum efficiency and accuracy. Informs supervisory personnel of changes or interpretations of laws, codes, programs, policies, or procedures. Conducts staff meetings for dissemination of pertinent information. Trains and evaluates performance of supervisory personnel and reviews performance reports prepared on staff. Prepares reports on office activities required by agency. May be designated according to type of office and agency or department managed or by type of work performed by office staff.
GOE: 11.05.03 STRENGTH: S GED: R4 M4 L4 SVP: 8 DLU: 79

188.167-062 PARK SUPERINTENDENT (government ser.) alternate titles: supervisory park ranger

Coordinates activities of PARK RANGERS (government ser.) and other workers engaged in development, protection, and utilization of national, state, or regional park: Tours areas to assess development possibilities and determine maintenance needs. Prepares estimates of costs to plan and provide or improve fish and wildlife protection, recreation, and visitor safety. Selects, trains, and supervises PARK RANGERS (government ser.). Directs workers engaged in rescue activities and fire suppression in park area. Investigates accidents, vandalism, theft, poaching, and other violations and presents evidence before court or designated legal authority. Answers letters of inquiry and addresses visitors and civic organizations to inform public of park regulations and available recreational facilities, and to point out historical, and scenic features of park. Prepares reports of area activities. May maintain records of attendance, permits issued, and monies received.
GOE: 04.01.01 STRENGTH: L GED: R5 M3 L4 SVP: 7 DLU: 77

188.167-066 POSTMASTER (government ser.)

Coordinates activities of workers engaged in postal and related work in assigned post office: Organizes and supervises directly, or through subordinates, such activities as processing incoming and outgoing mail; issuing and cashing money orders; selling stamps, bonds and certificates; and collecting box rents to ensure efficient service to patrons. Resolves customer complaints and informs public of postal laws and regulations. Confers with suppliers to obtain bids for proposed purchases, requisitions supplies, and disburses funds as specified by law. Prepares and submits detailed and summary reports of post office activities to designated superior. Selects, trains, and evaluates performance of employees and prepares work schedules. May perform or participate in post office activities depending on size of post office. May plan and implement labor relations program. May confer with employees to negotiate labor disputes.
GOE: 11.05.03 STRENGTH: S GED: R4 M4 L4 SVP: 7 DLU: 77

188.167-070 RELOCATION COMMISSIONER (government ser.) alternate titles: commissioner of relocation services

Directs relocation program to assist individuals and businesses affected by condemnation proceedings necessary to public improvement programs, such as highway or flood-control projects: Confers with individuals and businesses to ascertain necessary action. Analyzes housing data to determine availability, values, trends, and existing rental and zoning patterns. Coordinates plans to effect relocation of homes, businesses, or other property affected by improvement. Prepares program budget. May arrange moving of houses, fences, and other improvements. May arrange drilling of wells and construction of foundations for affected residents.
GOE: 11.12.02 STRENGTH: L GED: R5 M4 L5 SVP: 8 DLU: 79

188.167-074 REVENUE OFFICER (government ser.)

Investigates and collects delinquent federal taxes and secures delinquent tax returns from individuals or business firms according to prescribed laws and regulations: Investigates delinquent tax cases referred by agency investigators, as well as leads found in newspapers, trade journals, and public stockbroker records. Confers with individuals or business representatives by telephone, correspondence, or in person to determine amount of delinquent taxes and enforce collection. Examines and analyzes tax assets and liabilities to determine solu-

tion for resolving tax problem. Selects appropriate remedy for delinquent taxes when necessary, such as part-payment agreements, offers of compromise, or seizure and sale of property. Directs service of legal documents, such as subpoenas, warrants, notices of assessment, and garnishments. Recommends criminal prosecutions and civil penalties when necessary. Writes reports of determinations and actions taken for departmental files. (Workers who examine and audit tax records to determine tax liabilities are defined under title REVENUE AGENT (government ser.).
GOE: 11.10.01 STRENGTH: L GED: R5 M4 L4 SVP: 7 DLU: 77

188.167-078 ROADS SUPERVISOR (government ser.)

Directs construction and maintenance of roads or streets within jurisdiction: Assures that work is in conformity with federal and state standards, accepted principles of design and engineering, and available funds. Addresses meetings of realtors, citizens, members of financial community, and other interested parties to explain plans and activities of department.
GOE: 05.02.02 STRENGTH: S GED: R5 M5 L5 SVP: 8 DLU: 77

188.167-082 SECRETARY OF STATE (government ser.)

Directs and coordinates activities of Secretary of State office to assist Executive and Legislative Branches of State Government under authority of state statutory and constitutional provisions: Directs activities of workers engaged in preserving records of official acts performed by Governor and Legislative bodies. Directs distribution of laws, resolutions, and other official state documents. Examines corporate articles or corporate statements of qualification to approve or disallow petitions for incorporation, amendments to corporate articles, dissolutions, and agreements of merger or consolidation. Administers Uniform Commercial Code to protect secured interest of retail merchants and lending institutions. Approves licensing of notaries public. Receives for processing, recording, and filing documents, such as deeds to state lands, claims to fraternal names and insignia, manuscripts, oaths of office, organization and boundaries of public districts, administrative rules and regulations adopted by state agencies, and statements of trust receipt financing. Directs activities involved in preserving historical documents and public records in state archives. May interpret and enforce election laws. May tabulate and certify accuracy of election returns.
GOE: 11.05.03 STRENGTH: S GED: R5 M4 L4 SVP: 8 DLU: 77

188.167-086 SECTIONAL CENTER MANAGER, POSTAL SERVICE (government ser.)

Directs and coordinates operational, management, and supportive services of associate post offices within district area known as sectional center: Plans and implements facility programs in accordance with regional and national policy and to meet established objectives for providing efficient and effective postal services. Approves operating budgets of associate post offices. Directs such supportive services as personnel administration, finance, safety, and plant and vehicle maintenance. Participates in selecting, training, and removing POSTMASTERS (government ser.) and top level management of associate postal units. Provides postal information to news media, business representatives, and local governmental agencies. May direct and coordinate operations of various sectional centers within a district and be designated District Manager, Postal Service (government ser.).
GOE: 11.05.03 STRENGTH: S GED: R5 M3 L4 SVP: 8 DLU: 77

188.167-090 SPECIAL AGENT, CUSTOMS (government ser.) alternate titles: criminal investigator, customs

Investigates persons, common carriers, and merchandise, arriving in or departing from the United States, to protect government and business interests and prevent irregular or prohibited importing and exporting: Develops sources of information to complete investigations of customs violations. Examines private and public records, interrogates and investigates persons, and uses technical and scientific devices to establish facts, verify data, and secure legal evidence. Determines investigative and arrest or seizure techniques to be used and directs activities of assisting agents. Analyzes and assembles facts and evidence. Seizes contraband, vehicles, and air or sea craft suspected of carrying smuggled merchandise. Arrests violators of customs and related laws. Institutes civil and criminal prosecutions. Investigates applications for duty refunds. Petitions for remission or mitigation of penalties. Testifies in administrative and judicial proceedings. Coordinates activities with other federal or state agencies to enforce customs and related laws. May be required to carry weapon.
GOE: 04.01.02 STRENGTH: L GED: R5 M3 L5 SVP: 8 DLU: 77

188.167-094 SUPERINTENDENT, INDUSTRIES, CORRECTIONAL FACILITY (government ser.)

Directs and coordinates vocational work programs in governmental correctional institution: Confers with administrative and supervisory staff of prison to schedule work programs consistent with security regulations, maintenance needs, and established vocational policy. Interviews and assigns inmates to vocational rehabilitation programs or work details in conformity with their education, previous skills, and available facilities of institution. Plans production assignments to meet output requirements and vocational instruction schedule. Establishes production standards and plans layout according to capacity of equipment, qualifications of staff, and procurement specifications of customers for prison-made products. Inspects equipment and facilities to recommend maintenance and replacement of obsolete machinery. Inventories and requisitions supplies to maintain efficient production. May prepare design drawings for production, according to customer specifications. May negotiate with purchasers to conclude contracts for manufactured products. May evaluate ade-

quacy of vocational instruction and recommend changes in established curriculum, policies, and standards.
GOE: 11.07.01 STRENGTH: S GED: R4 M4 L4 SVP: 8 DLU: 77

188.167-098 SUPERINTENDENT, SANITATION (government ser.) alternate titles: director, sanitation bureau
Plans and directs establishment of collection routes and assignment of personnel and equipment: Coordinates activities of workers concerned with sewage treatment, recycling or incineration plants, and landfill activities of disposal sites. Conducts field inspections to evaluate efficiency of sanitation program and to determine that residents are adhering to regulations. Notifies individuals of violations and initiates actions to obtain compliance with regulations. Supervises workers engaged in investigation of complaints and collection of delinquent accounts, where user assessments are imposed. Supervises persons engaged in preparation of cost and operational reports and compiles budget estimates for review and approval of authorities. Confers with engineering and other technical personnel to advise and assist in development, design, and installation of sanitation facilities. Prepares material such as handbills or press releases to keep public informed of changes in regulations. May direct one phase of sanitation services, as recycling, incineration, or sewage treatment, and be designated Superintendent, Refuse Disposal (government ser.); Superintendent, Sewage-Treatment (government ser.).
GOE: 05.02.01 STRENGTH: L GED: R5 M4 L5 SVP: 7 DLU: 77

188.167-102 TRAFFIC-SAFETY ADMINISTRATOR (government ser.)
Directs traffic-safety program of municipality in accord with accident and traffic data compiled by subordinates. Plans and directs safety campaigns and coordinates activities of auxiliaries such as volunteer school-crossing personnel and motorist groups pledged to safety. Administers tests to determine driving proficiency and attitude of municipal employees. Keeps files of accident reports and maps accident locations to facilitate corrective measures.
GOE: 11.07.02 STRENGTH: S GED: R5 M4 L4 SVP: 8 DLU: 77

188.167-106 UNCLAIMED PROPERTY OFFICER (government ser.)
Directs activities of state unclaimed property disposal office: Directs, through subordinates, search for owners of unclaimed property, such as abandoned automobiles, cash, or property of deceased individuals leaving no known heirs. Receives and directs processing of recovery claims, according to results of investigation or other evidence of ownership. Authorizes deposit of unclaimed property in trust fund or arranges for public auctions, depending upon nature of property.
GOE: 11.12.01 STRENGTH: L GED: R4 M4 L4 SVP: 7 DLU: 77

188.167-110 PLANNER, PROGRAM SERVICES (government ser.)
Conducts studies, prepares reports, and advises public and private sector administrators on feasibility, cost-effectiveness, and regulatory conformance of proposals for special projects or ongoing programs in such fields as transportation, conservation, or health care: Consults with administrators or planning councils to discuss overall intent of programs or projects, and determines broad guidelines for studies, utilizing knowledge of subject area, research techniques, and regulatory limitations. Reviews and evaluates materials provided with proposals, such as environmental impact statements, construction specifications, or budget or staffing estimates, to determine additional data requirements. Conducts field investigations, economic or public opinion surveys, demographic studies, or other research to gather required information. Organizes data from all sources, using statistical methods to ensure validity of materials. Evaluates information to determine feasibility of proposals or to identify factors requiring amendment. Develops alternate plans for program or project, incorporating recommendations, for review of officials. Maintains collection of socioeconomic, environmental, and regulatory data related to agency functions, for use by planning and administrative personnel in government and private sectors. Reviews plans and proposals submitted by other governmental planning commissions or private organizations to assist in formulation of overall plans for region.
GOE: 11.03.02 STRENGTH: L GED: R5 M5 L5 SVP: 7 DLU: 86

188.217-010 COMMISSIONER OF CONCILIATION (government ser.)
Conducts conference of employer and employee representatives to analyze and resolve labor disputes, as directed by federal government: Contacts parties in labor controversy and arranges meeting. Compiles all information on disagreement and determines points at issue, according to knowledge of labor, business, and government responsibilities under law and precedent. Attempts reconciliation of opposing claims and demands by ascertaining and exposing facts, by suggesting concessions, or by proposing adoption of new procedures. Prepares reports of cases, findings, and recommendations for resolving issues.
GOE: 11.04.03 STRENGTH: S GED: R5 M5 L5 SVP: 8 DLU: 77

189 MISCELLANEOUS MANAGERS AND OFFICIALS, N.E.C.

This group includes miscellaneous managers and officials, not elsewhere classified.

189.117-010 ASSOCIATION EXECUTIVE (profess. & kin.)
Directs and coordinates activities of professional or trade association in accordance with established policies to further achievement of goals, objectives, and standards of profession or association: Directs research surveys, compilation, and analysis of factors, such as average income, benefits, standards, and common problems of profession, for presentation to association committees for action. Confers with officers to ensure that membership roster is current and complete and that members receive equal treatment regarding services and information provided by Board. Directs or participates in preparation of educational and informative materials for presentation to membership or public in newsletters, magazines, news releases, or on radio or television. Provides information and technical assistance to members, clients of members, or public, relating to business operations. Represents association in negotiations with representatives of government, business, labor, and other organizations, and holds news conferences, delivers speeches, and appears before legislative bodies to present association's viewpoints and encourage acceptance of goals and objectives. Oversees finances of Board of Directors, including preparation of long range forecast and monthly and annual budget reports. Plans, develops, and implements new programs and ideas, and confers with committee leaders to evaluate services and recommend methods to promote and increase membership involvement. Directs and coordinates association functions, such as conventions, exhibits, or local or regional workshops, to present membership with committee proposals on goals or objectives, familiarize membership or public with new technology or products, and increase public acceptance of membership objectives. Prepares and updates procedural manual. May conduct investigations on members' professional ethics, competence, or conduct, or financial responsibility of members to enforce quasi-legal standards of membership. May visit members' businesses to maintain goodwill, to encourage greater participation in organization activities, and to offer assistance to businesses experiencing reverses. May be designated according to area of responsibility or activity directed as Director Of Publications (profess. & kin.); Executive Secretary (profess. & kin.); Membership Secretary (profess. & kin.); Representative, Government Relations (profess. & kin.); Research Director (profess. & kin.).
GOE: 11.05.01 STRENGTH: L GED: R5 M4 L5 SVP: 8 DLU: 88

189.117-014 DIRECTOR, RESEARCH AND DEVELOPMENT (any industry) alternate titles: manager, product development; manager, research and development; manufacturing engineer, chief
Directs and coordinates research and development activities for organizational products, services, or ideologies: Plans and formulates aspects of research and development proposals, such as objective or purpose of project, applications that can be utilized from findings, costs of project, and equipment and human resource requirements. Reviews and analyzes proposals submitted to determine if benefits derived and possible applications justify expenditures. Approves and submits proposals considered feasible to management for consideration and allocation of funds or allocates funds from department budget. Develops and implements methods and procedures for monitoring projects, such as preparation of records of expenditures and research findings, progress reports, and staff conferences, in order to inform management of current status of each project. May recruit, hire, and train department staff, evaluate staff performance, and develop goals and objectives for staff. May negotiate contracts with consulting firms to perform research studies. May specialize in one type of research and be designated Director, Marketing Research and Analysis (profess. & kin); Director, Product Research and Development (profess. & kin.).
GOE: 05.01.01 STRENGTH: S GED: R5 M5 L5 SVP: 8 DLU: 88

189.117-018 MANAGER, CUSTOMER TECHNICAL SERVICES (profess. & kin.)
Directs and coordinates activities of department in manufacturing establishment concerned with providing customers technical services in conjunction with marketing activities: Coordinates technical liaison services between management, production department, sales department, and customers with newly developed techniques or practices in processing company products, and to inform customers of new types, specifications, and end-uses of products. Confers with production department managers to assist in specific classification of products from quality assurance position, report on new product or process technology of competitors, and to discuss new specifications required by customers. Directs investigation of customer complaints regarding quality, tolerances, specifications, and delivered condition of products. Records, analyzes, and informs concerned personnel of production quality assurance, and sales departments of status and disposition of customer complaints and claims. Negotiates settlement of claims, for which company is responsible, within limits prescribed by management. May survey potential markets for increasing sales.
GOE: 05.02.03 STRENGTH: S GED: R5 M4 L4 SVP: 8 DLU: 77

189.117-022 MANAGER, INDUSTRIAL ORGANIZATION (any industry) alternate titles: general manager, industrial organization; manager, general; plant superintendent, industrial organization
Directs and coordinates activities of industrial organization to obtain optimum efficiency and economy of operations and maximize profits: Plans and develops organization policies and goals, and implements goals through subordinate administrative personnel. Coordinates activities of divisions or departments, such as operating, manufacturing, engineering, planning, sales, maintenance, or research and development, to effect operational efficiency and economy. Directs and coordinates promotion of products manufactured or services performed to develop new markets, increase share of market, and obtain competitive position in industry. Analyzes division or department budget requests to identify areas in which reductions can be made, and allocates operating budget. Confers with administrative personnel, and reviews activity, operating,

and sales reports to determine changes in programs or operations required. Directs preparation of directives to division or department administrator outlining policy, program, or operations changes to be implemented. Promotes organization in industry, manufacturing or trade associations. Workers are usually identified according to industry in which employed, such as petroleum production or refining, iron and steel, electrical equipment; type of organization, such as air, rail, motor or water transportation; or type of product, such as paper, chemical, or plastics products.
GOE: 11.05.01 STRENGTH: L GED: R5 M4 L5 SVP: 8 DLU: 86

189.117-026 PRESIDENT (any industry)
Plans, develops, and establishes policies and objectives of business organization in accordance with board directives and corporation charter: Confers with company officials to plan business objectives, to develop organizational policies to coordinate functions and operations between divisions and departments, and to establish responsibilities and procedures for attaining objectives. Reviews activity reports and financial statements to determine progress and status in attaining objectives and revises objectives and plans in accordance with current conditions. Directs and coordinates formulation of financial programs to provide funding for new or continuing operations to maximize returns on investments, and to increase productivity. Plans and develops industrial, labor, and public relations policies designed to improve company's image and relations with customers, employees, stockholders, and public. Evaluates performance of executives for compliance with established policies and objectives of firm and contributions in attaining objectives. May preside over board of directors. May serve as chairman of committees, such as management, executive, engineering, and sales.
GOE: 11.05.01 STRENGTH: S GED: R5 M5 L5 SVP: 8 DLU: 89

189.117-030 PROJECT DIRECTOR (profess. & kin.) alternate titles: project manager
Plans, directs, and coordinates activities of designated project to ensure that goals or objectives of project are accomplished within prescribed time frame and funding parameters: Reviews project proposal or plan to determine time frame, funding limitations, procedures for accomplishing project, staffing requirements, and allotment of available resources to various phases of project. Establishes work plan and staffing for each phase of project, and arranges for recruitment or assignment of project personnel. Confers with project staff to outline workplan and to assign duties, responsibilities, and scope of authority. Directs and coordinates activities of project personnel to ensure project progresses on schedule and within prescribed budget. Reviews status reports prepared by project personnel and modifies schedules or plans as required. Prepares project reports for management, client, or others. Confers with project personnel to provide technical advice and to resolve problems. May coordinate project activities with activities of government regulatory or other governmental agencies. See PROJECT ENGINEER (profess. & kin.) 019.167-014 for engineering projects.
GOE: 11.05.02 STRENGTH: S GED: R5 M5 L5 SVP: 8 DLU: 81

189.117-034 VICE PRESIDENT (any industry)
Directs and coordinates activities of one or more departments, such as engineering, operations, or sales, or major division of business organization, and aids chief administrative officer in formulating and administering organization policies: Participates in formulating and administering company policies and developing long range goals and objectives. Directs and coordinates activities of department or division for which responsibility is delegated to further attainment of goals and objectives. Reviews analyses of activities, costs, operations, and forecast data to determine department or division progress toward stated goals and objectives. Confers with chief administrative officer and other administrative personnel to review achievements and discuss required changes in goals or objectives resulting from current status and conditions. May perform duties of PRESIDENT (any industry) 189.117-026 during absence. May serve as member of management committees on special studies.
GOE: 11.05.02 STRENGTH: S GED: R5 M4 L5 SVP: 8 DLU: 88

189.117-038 USER REPRESENTATIVE, INTERNATIONAL ACCOUNTING (profess. & kin.)
Directs activities of information systems group engaged in designing, developing, implementing, and maintaining worldwide integrated finance and accounting system utilized by multinational organization: Studies and analyzes general plan proposal, confers with corporate officials to obtain details of general plan, and obtains systems requirements from corporate and international accounting and management personnel to compile raw data for plan development. Develops methods and procedures for project accomplishment, applying knowledge of foreign monetary and tax systems and international accounting conventions. Prepares specifications documenting systems and project requirements, including time frame, staffing, activity schedule, and methods and procedures. Interprets international finance and accounting policies and procedures to provide coding assistance to others engaged in systems design and coding. Oversees entering of source data and programs into computer, analyzes output to identify existence and nature of problems, and orders indicated corrections to design or program. Writes procedures manuals for users, reflecting and adapting individual accounting conventions and monetary and tax systems into overall integrated system. Prepares training plan and trains user staff prior to implementation of system. Edits and audits financial and accounting reports to identify problems in installed system and initiates corrective measures.
GOE: 11.05.02 STRENGTH: S GED: R5 M5 L5 SVP: 8 DLU: 86

189.117-042 DIRECTOR, QUALITY ASSURANCE (profess. & kin.) alternate titles: director, product assurance
Participates, as member of management team, in formulating and establishing organizational policies and operating procedures for company and develops, implements, and coordinates, through support staff and lower echelon managers, product assurance program to prevent or eliminate defects in new or existing products: Analyzes, evaluates, and presents information concerning factors, such as business situations, production capabilities, manufacturing problems, economic trends, and design and development of new products for consideration by other members of management team. Suggests and debates alternative methods and procedures in solving problems and meeting changing market opportunities. Cooperates with other top management personnel in formulating and establishing company policies, operating procedures, and goals. Develops initial and subsequent modifications of product assurance program to delineate areas of responsibility, personnel requirements, and operational procedures within program, according to and consistent with company goals and policies. Evaluates contents of reports from product assurance program department heads and confers with top management personnel preparatory to formulating fiscal budget for product assurance program. Conducts management meetings with product assurance program department heads to establish, delineate, and review program organizational policies, to coordinate functions and operations between departments, and to establish responsibilities and procedures for attaining objectives. Reviews technical problems and procedures of departments and recommends solutions to problems or changes in procedures. Visits and confers with representatives of material and component vendors to obtain information related to supply quality, capacity of vendor to meet orders, and vendor quality standards. Confers with engineers about quality assurance of new products designed and manufactured products on market to rectify problems. Reviews technical publications, articles, and abstracts to stay abreast of technical developments in industry.
GOE: 11.05.02 STRENGTH: L GED: R5 M5 L5 SVP: 8 DLU: 86

189.117-046 MANAGER, BAKERY (bakery products)
Directs and coordinates activities involved with production, sale, and distribution of bakery products: Determines variety and quantity of bakery products to be produced, according to orders and sales projections. Develops budget for bakery operation, utilizing experience and knowledge of current market conditions. Directs sales activities, following standard business practices. Plans product distribution to customers, and negotiates with suppliers to arrange purchase and delivery of bakery supplies. Implements, through subordinate managerial personnel, policies to utilize human resources, machines, and materials productively. Hires and discharges employees. May train subordinates in all phases of bakery activities. May manage bakery that produces only specialty products, such as bagels or pastries. May manage bakery that sells products to general public. May prepare bakery products.
GOE: 11.05.01 STRENGTH: S GED: R5 M4 L4 SVP: 8 DLU: 86

189.157-010 BUSINESS-OPPORTUNITY-AND-PROPERTY-INVESTMENT BROKER (business ser.; real estate) alternate titles: business investor; property investor
Buys and sells business enterprises or investment property on speculative or commission basis: Reviews trade journals, business opportunity advertisements, or other publications to ascertain business enterprises or investment property up for sale. Investigates financial rating of business, customer appeal for type of merchandise, and desirability of location for type of business, or condition and location of investment property. Estimates cost of improving business or property and potential market value to determine resale value. Purchases business or property on speculative basis or on commission basis for client. Repairs, remodels, or redecorates building; purchases competitive merchandise; and installs sound management practices to improve value of property or business acquisition. Contacts prospective clients through newspaper advertisements or mailing lists. Describes to client selling points of property or business, emphasizing such factors as improvements made and profit potential. Sells business or property to buyer and makes arrangements for escrow and title change. Must be licensed by state.
GOE: 08.01.03 STRENGTH: L GED: R5 M4 L4 SVP: 7 DLU: 77

189.167-010 CONSULTANT (profess. & kin.)
Consults with client to define need or problem, conducts studies and surveys to obtain data, and analyzes data to advise on or recommend solution, utilizing knowledge of theory, principles, or technology of specific discipline or field of specialization: Consults with client to ascertain and define need or problem area, and determine scope of investigation required to obtain solution. Conducts study or survey on need or problem to obtain data required for solution. Analyzes data to determine solution, such as installation of alternate methods and procedures, changes in processing methods and practices, modification of machines or equipment, or redesign of products or services. Advises client on alternate methods of solving need or problem, or recommends specific solution. May negotiate contract for consulting service. May specialize in providing consulting service to government in field of specialization. May be designated according to field of specialization such as engineering or science discipline, economics, education, labor, or in specialized field of work as health services, social services, or investment services.
GOE: 11.01.02 STRENGTH: S GED: R5 M5 L5 SVP: 8 DLU: 77

189.167-014   DIRECTOR, SERVICE (retail trade) alternate titles: manager, operating and occupancy; superintendent, nonselling; superintendent, operating

Directs operating and nonselling services, such as building maintenance, warehousing, and payroll, in department store: Controls expenditures for items, such as remodeling and repairing of building, upkeep of elevators and air-conditioning system, and repairing electrical system. Arranges for storage and display space for new merchandise. Acts as liaison for trucking company that delivers merchandise to customers. May hire and train new employees.
GOE: 11.05.02 STRENGTH: S GED: R5 M4 L4 SVP: 7 DLU: 77

189.167-018   MANAGEMENT TRAINEE (any industry)

Performs assigned duties, under direction of experienced personnel, to gain knowledge and experience required for promotion to management positions: Receives training and performs duties in several departments, such as credit, customer relations, accounting, or sales, to become familiar with line and staff functions, operations, management viewpoints, and company policies and practices that affect each phase of business. Observes experienced workers to acquire knowledge of methods, procedures, and standards required for performance of departmental duties. Workers are usually trained in functions and operations of related departments to facilitate subsequent transferability between departments and to provide greater promotional opportunities. May be required to attend company-sponsored training classes.
GOE: 11.05.02 STRENGTH: L GED: R5 M3 L4 SVP: 6 DLU: 87

189.167-022   MANAGER, DEPARTMENT (any industry) alternate titles: department head; superintendent

Directs and coordinates, through subordinate supervisors, department activities in commercial, industrial, or service establishment: Reviews and analyzes reports, records, and directives, and confers with supervisors to obtain data required for planning department activities, such as new commitments, status of work in progress, and problems encountered. Assigns, or delegates responsibility for, specified work or functional activities and disseminates policy to supervisors. Gives work directions, resolves problems, prepares schedules, and sets deadlines to ensure timely completion of work. Coordinates activities of department with related activities of other departments to ensure efficiency and economy. Monitors and analyzes costs and prepares budget, using computer. Prepares reports and records on department activities for management, using computer. Evaluates current procedures and practices for accomplishing department objectives to develop and implement improved procedures and practices. May initiate or authorize employee hire, promotion, discharge, or transfer. Workers are designated according to functions, activities, or type of department managed.
GOE: 11.05.02 STRENGTH: S GED: R5 M4 L4 SVP: 7 DLU: 89

189.167-026   MEMBERSHIP DIRECTOR (profess. & kin.)

Organizes chapters of fraternal society, lodge, or similar organization and surveys conditions in branches already established: Contacts interested parties to present aims and ideals of organization. Coordinates group efforts in petitioning parent organization for charter and recognition. Advises societies or lodges having financial, organizational, and membership problems.
GOE: 11.09.02 STRENGTH: L GED: R5 M4 L4 SVP: 7 DLU: 77

189.167-030   PROGRAM MANAGER (profess. & kin.)

Manages program to ensure that implementation and prescribed activities are carried out in accordance with specified objectives: Plans and develops methods and procedures for implementing program, directs and coordinates program activities, and exercises control over personnel responsible for specific functions or phases of program. Selects personnel according to knowledge and experience in area with which program is concerned, such as social or public welfare, education, economics, or public relations. Confers with staff to explain program and individual responsibilities for functions and phases of program. Directs and coordinates personally, or through subordinate managerial personnel, activities concerned with implementation and carrying out objectives of program. Reviews reports and records of activities to ensure progress is being accomplished toward specified program objective and modifies or changes methodology as required to redirect activities and attain objectives. Prepares program reports for superiors. Controls expenditures in accordance with budget allocations. May specialize in managing governmental programs set up by legislative body or directive and be designated Manager, Governmental Program (government ser.).
GOE: 11.05.02 STRENGTH: S GED: R5 M5 L5 SVP: 8 DLU: 77

189.167-034   SECURITY OFFICER (any industry)

Plans and establishes security procedures for company engaged in manufacturing products or processing data or material for federal government: Studies federal security regulations and restrictions relative to company operations. Directs activities of personnel in developing company security measures which comply with federal regulations. Consults with local, district, or other federal representatives for interpretation or application of particular regulations applying to company operations. Prepares security manual outlining and establishing measures and procedures for handling, storing, safekeeping, and destroying classified records and documents, and for granting company personnel or visitors access to classified material or entry into restricted areas. Directs and coordinates activities of personnel in revising or updating security measures due to new or revised regulations. May request deviations from restrictive regulations that interfere with normal operations. May interview and hire applicants to fill security guard vacancies.

GOE: 11.05.02 STRENGTH: S GED: R4 M3 L4 SVP: 7 DLU: 82

189.167-038   SUPERINTENDENT, AMMUNITION STORAGE (ordnance)

Directs and coordinates, through subordinate supervisory personnel, activities concerned with handling and storing ammunition, rockets, mines, and other explosive components at ammunition supply depot or arsenal: Reviews invoices and requisitions to plan work activities. Prepares schedules for storing incoming and issuing ammunition specifying magazine or bunker number for storing each type of ammunition, quantity to store in bunker or magazine, and numerical order of bunkers or magazines from which to issue requisitioned ammunition. Enforces, through subordinate personnel, worker compliance with established safety regulations, and method and procedures for handling and storing each type of ammunition. Inspects bunkers and magazines to ensure that automatic safeguards and control instrumentation are operative and security measures are in force. Prepares reports and correspondence and directs clerical personnel in typing reports and record keeping activities.
GOE: 05.02.07 STRENGTH: L GED: R4 M4 L4 SVP: 8 DLU: 77

189.167-042   SUPERINTENDENT, LABOR UTILIZATION (any industry)

Directs and coordinates activities concerned with utilization and work of labor pool in industrial establishment: Inspects plant buildings, structures, and grounds and reviews human resource requests from other departments for workers to perform such work as cleaning tanks, digging ditches, or assisting craft workers, in order to plan labor pool utilization and establish priorities, projects, and schedules. Confers with subordinate supervisory personnel on status of on-going projects and number of workers required in order to determine allocation and assignment of human resources in labor pool. Assigns supervisory personnel and workers to perform work requested, complete on-going projects, or to assist craft workers, considering such factors as priority of project or work, type of work, and available human resources in labor pool. Inspects projects to ensure work performed meets standards and that workers are observing established safety rules and regulations for type of work being performed. Reassigns workers to meet unforeseen emergencies or work requests. Prepares activity reports on utilization of labor pool human resources, status of projects, and workers assigned work with other departments.
GOE: 11.05.02 STRENGTH: L GED: R4 M3 L4 SVP: 8 DLU: 77

189.167-046   SUPERINTENDENT, MAINTENANCE (any industry)

Directs and coordinates, through subordinate supervisory personnel, activities of workers engaged in repair, maintenance, and installation of machines, tools, and equipment, and in maintenance of buildings, grounds, and utility systems of mill, industrial plant, or other establishment: Reviews job orders to determine work priorities. Schedules repair, maintenance, and installation of machines, tools, and equipment to ensure continuous production operations. Coordinates activities of workers fabricating or modifying machines, tools, or equipment to manufacture new products or improve existing products. Directs maintenance activities on utility systems to provide continuous supply of heat, steam, electric power, gas, or air required for operations. Develops preventive maintenance program in conjunction with engineering and maintenance staff. Reviews production, quality control, and maintenance reports and statistics to plan and modify maintenance activities. Inspects operating machines and equipment for conformance with operational standards. Plans, develops, and implements new methods and procedures designed to improve operations, minimize operating costs, and effect greater utilization of labor and materials. Reviews new product plans and discusses equipment needs and modifications with design engineers. Requisitions tools, equipment, and supplies required for operations. Directs training and indoctrination of workers to improve work performance and acquaint workers with company policies and procedures. Confers with management, engineering, and quality control personnel to resolve maintenance problems and recommend measures to improve operations and conditions of machines and equipment. May confer with workers' representatives to resolve grievances. May perform supervisory functions in establishments where subordinate supervisory personnel are not utilized. May prepare department budget and monitor expenditure of funds in budget.
GOE: 05.05.02 STRENGTH: L GED: R5 M5 L5 SVP: 8 DLU: 86

189.167-050   SUPERINTENDENT, PLANT PROTECTION (any industry) alternate titles: protection chief, industrial plant; security manager

Directs personnel involved in establishing, promoting, and maintaining firm's security and property-protection programs: Establishes and supervises through subordinates, operational procedures for activities, such as fire prevention and firefighting, traffic control, guarding and patrolling physical property, orienting and monitoring of personnel involved with classified information, and investigation of accidents and criminal acts. Confers with representatives of management to formulate policies, determine need for programs, and coordinate programs with plant activities. Confers with representatives of local government to ensure cooperation and coordination of plant activities with law enforcement and firefighting agencies. May direct activities of workers involved in industrial safety programs. May direct activities of workers engaged in performing building maintenance and janitorial services.
GOE: 11.05.02 STRENGTH: S GED: R5 M4 L4 SVP: 8 DLU: 77

189.167-054   SECURITY CONSULTANT (business ser.; personal ser.)

Plans, directs, and oversees implementation of comprehensive security systems for protection of individuals and homes, and business, commercial, and

industrial organizations, and investigates various crimes against client: Inspects premises to determine security needs. Studies physical conditions, observes activities, and confers with client's staff to obtain data regarding internal operations. Analyzes compiled data and plans and directs installation of electronic security systems, such as closed circuit surveillance, entry controls, burglar alarms, ultrasonic motion detectors, electric eyes, and outdoor perimeter and microwave alarms. Directs installation and checks operation of electronic security equipment. Plans and directs personal security and safety of individual, family, or group for contracted period. Provides bulletproof limousine and bodyguards to ensure client protection during trips and outings. Suggests wearing bulletproof vest when appropriate. Plans and reviews client travel itinerary, mode of transportation, and accommodations. Travels with client and directs security operations. Investigates crimes committed against client, such as fraud, robbery, arson, and patent infringement. Reviews personnel records of client staff and conducts background investigation of selected members to obtain personal histories, character references, and financial status. Conducts or directs surveillance of suspects and premises to apprehend culprits. Notifies client of security weaknesses and implements procedures for handling, storing, safekeeping, and destroying classified materials. Reports criminal information to authorities and testifies in court.
GOE: 04.02.02 STRENGTH: L GED: R5 M3 L5 SVP: 7 DLU: 86

189.267-010 FIELD REPRESENTATIVE (profess. & kin.)
Reviews and evaluates program operations of national or state affiliated or nonaffiliated social service agency or organization, or community group to provide assistance and services in achieving goals: Interprets standards and program goals of national or state agency to assist local boards, committees, groups, or agencies in establishing program goals and standards. Confers with community councils to advise members on matters relating to program. Evaluates capabilities of local or community agencies or groups to achieve goals, considering such factors as administration and program finances, facilities and personnel staffing, and changing community needs. Prepares reports to inform national or state agency on conditions in local agencies or organizations and developing trends in local communities. May organize or conduct training or staff development programs. May organize regional meetings. May plan or conduct studies or surveys of local agency operation. May assist communities in establishing new local affiliates or programs. May confer with field representatives of other national agencies.
GOE: 11.07.01 STRENGTH: S GED: R5 M4 L5 SVP: 8 DLU: 77

19 MISCELLANEOUS PROFESSIONAL, TECHNICAL, AND MANAGERIAL OCCUPATIONS

This division includes miscellaneous occupations concerned with professional, technical, and managerial work.

191 AGENTS AND APPRAISERS, N.E.C.

This group includes occupations, not elsewhere classified, concerned with representing clients in business operations; and determining value, quantity, or quality of a product, property, or object. Included are those classified in one group as both agents and appraisers.

191.117-010 ARTIST'S MANAGER (amuse. & rec.) alternate titles: artist's representative; artist consultant; personal agent; personal manager; talent agent
Manages affairs of entertainers by participating in negotiations with agents and others concerning contracts and business matters affecting clients' interests, and advises clients on career development and advancement: Represents client in negotiations with officials of unions, motion picture or television studios, theatrical productions, or entertainment house, for favorable contracts and financial fees to be received for engagements. Advises client concerning contracts, wardrobe, and effective presentation of act, according to knowledge of show business. Procures services of professional personnel in particular phase of show business to create or design format of original act, or prepare special material for new act to advance client's career. Manages business details of tours and engagements, such as obtaining reservations for transportation and hotel accommodations, and making disbursements for road expenses. Represents client in public contacts, such as handling fan mail, telephone inquiries, and requests for personal appearances. May audition new talent for representation purposes. May procure bookings for clients.
GOE: 11.12.03 STRENGTH: S GED: R5 M4 L5 SVP: 7 DLU: 77

191.117-014 BOOKING MANAGER (amuse. & rec.) alternate titles: booker; booking agent
Books performers, theatrical or ballet productions, variety or nightclub acts, concert or lecture series, trade shows, or other popular or classical attractions for entertainment in various establishments, such as theaters, showplaces, clubs, or halls: Schedules attractions for season, considering such factors as entertainment policy, budget, and tastes of patrons of particular establishment represented. Negotiates with booking representatives or producers of attractions to arrange terms of contract, play dates, and fees to be paid for engagements. Auditions new talent. Arranges for billing in accordance with contract agreement. Books motion pictures for exhibit into theater chains or independent houses. Se-

lects and rents pictures to be exhibited on basis of potential box-office sales, cast of players, advertising allotment allowed by distributor, and similar factors. May specialize in in-house bookings and be designated according to establishment as Concert Or Lecture Hall Manager (amuse. & rec.); Showplace Manager (amuse. & rec.). May specialize in independent bookings and be designated according to type of talent or of entertainment package represented and placed as Artists' Booking Representative (amuse. & rec.); Theatrical Variety Agent (amuse. & rec.). May specialize in rental and distribution of motion pictures and be designated Film Booker (amuse. & rec.). May represent popular or rock musical groups only and be designated Band Booker (amuse. & rec.). When sponsoring, managing, and producing an entertainment, may be designated Impresario (amuse. & rec.).
GOE: 11.12.03 STRENGTH: S GED: R4 M4 L4 SVP: 6 DLU: 77

191.117-018 BUSINESS MANAGER (amuse. & rec.) alternate titles: business agent
Manages financial affairs of entertainers and negotiates with agents and representatives for contracts and appearances: Negotiates with officials of unions, motion picture or television studios, stage productions, or entertainment houses for contracts and financial return to be received for engagements. Promotes client's interests by advising on income, investments, taxes, legal, and other financial matters. Provides liaison between client and representatives concerning contractual rights and obligations to settle contracts. Summarizes statements on periodic basis concerning client's investments, property, and financial status.
GOE: 11.12.03 STRENGTH: S GED: R5 M4 L5 SVP: 7 DLU: 77

191.117-022 CIRCUS AGENT (amuse. & rec.)
Plans and arranges route of circus for following season, coordinating date and location schedules: Obtains information about facilities of new locations to determine feasibility of presenting show. Consults with circus officials to arrange route and obtain approval of tour. Schedules dates of performance for each location, taking into consideration length of travel time to transport circus from one location to another, climatic conditions, budget, and previous year's attendance records. Rearranges tour in event of unexpected occurrences.
GOE: 11.12.03 STRENGTH: S GED: R4 M3 L4 SVP: 7 DLU: 77

191.117-026 JOCKEY AGENT (amuse. & rec.)
Represents riders of race horses in negotiations with owners to arrange for riding engagements at racetrack: Contacts riders to ascertain races and dates they are available for hire. Confers with owners of horses scheduled to race to inform them of riders available. Negotiates with owners for riding fees. Records name of owner, horse, date, and number of race in engagement book. Notifies riders of contracted engagements, and terms agreed on. Notifies riders to report to owner for briefing on horse's temperament and behavior, and other riding instructions. Collects hiring fees from riders.
GOE: 11.12.03 STRENGTH: L GED: R4 M3 L4 SVP: 5 DLU: 77

191.117-030 LEASE BUYER (mine & quarry; petrol. & gas) alternate titles: leaser
Contacts landowners and representatives of other oil or coal producing firms to negotiate agreements, such as leases, options, and royalty contracts covering oil or coal exploration, drilling, and producing activities in specified oil or coal fields: Discusses and draws up unitization agreements (pooling oil and gas production from wells located in same field with other oil producers). Discusses land leases and options and royalty payments with landowners and obtains signatures to documents. Applies knowledge of company policies and local, state, and federal laws relating to petroleum or coal leases to prepare agreements. May examine abstracts to verify clearance of title to oil or coal properties and write purchase orders and bank checks to satisfy requirements of leases, agreements, and contracts [TITLE CLERK (petrol. & gas; petrol. refin.; pipe lines)].
GOE: 11.12.02 STRENGTH: L GED: R5 M4 L5 SVP: 7 DLU: 77

191.117-034 LITERARY AGENT (business ser.) alternate titles: author's agent; writer's representative
Markets clients' manuscripts to editors, publishers, and other buyers: Reads and appraises manuscripts and suggests revisions. Contacts prospective purchaser of material, basing selection upon knowledge of market and specific content of manuscript. Negotiates contract between publisher and client. Usually works on commission basis.
GOE: 11.12.03 STRENGTH: S GED: R5 M4 L5 SVP: 7 DLU: 77

191.117-038 MANAGER, TOURING PRODUCTION (amuse. & rec.) alternate titles: manager, theatrical production; manager, touring
Travels with and manages business affairs of theatrical company on tour: Completes various arrangements, such as contracting union agreements, hiring stage hands, and procuring legal permits for performance. Approves budgetary items for advertising and promotional purposes. Audits box-office receipts and files accounting statements according to legal requirements. May compile payroll records and distribute paychecks. When coordinating business affairs of first touring company on road, may be designated Company Manager (amuse. & rec.). When managing second and third road show companies, may be designated Road Manager (amuse. & rec.).
GOE: 11.11.04 STRENGTH: S GED: R4 M3 L4 SVP: 7 DLU: 77

191.117-042 PERMIT AGENT, GEOPHYSICAL PROSPECTING (petrol. & gas)
Negotiates permits with property owners to allow prospecting, surveying, and testing for petroleum and gas deposits: Searches public records to determine

legal ownerships of proposed exploration sites. Precedes prospecting party to area and interviews local authorities and landowners to determine legal and highway regulations and to draw up trespass agreements. Draws sketches of prospecting locations and terrain to be traversed. Drives stakes in ground to indicate locations of shot holes and recording instruments for use in surveying land and conducting seismic, magnetic, and gravity tests.
GOE: 11.12.02 STRENGTH: L GED: R5 M4 L5 SVP: 6 DLU: 77

191.117-046   RIGHT-OF-WAY AGENT (any industry) alternate titles: claims agent, right-of-way; permit agent
Negotiates with property owners and public officials to secure purchase or lease of land and right-of-way for utility lines, pipelines, and other construction projects: Determines roads, bridges, and utility systems that must be maintained during construction. Negotiates with landholders for access routes and restoration of roads and surfaces. May examine public records to determine ownership and property rights. May be required to know property law.
GOE: 11.12.02 STRENGTH: L GED: R5 M4 L5 SVP: 7 DLU: 77

191.117-050   RIGHT-OF-WAY SUPERVISOR (any industry) alternate titles: supervisor, permits, easements, and right-of-way
Coordinates activities of field agents and contacts property owners and public officials to obtain permits and easements or to purchase right-of-way for utility lines, pipelines, and other construction projects: Directs activities involved in search of city and county records to ascertain ownership of properties, and disposition of rights along streets, alleys, and highways. Interprets company policy for RIGHT-OF-WAY AGENTS (any industry) regarding purchase of property, or payments and terms of agreements for permits and easements to install facilities on property belonging to other parties. Purchases or directs acquisition of right-of-way or obtaining permits, licenses, and agreements. Settles claims for property or crop damage resulting from construction activities. Releases information to public regarding right-of-way agreements and arranges for modification or release of existing agreements. May direct activities of surveying crews in surveying right-of-way and lines for new construction.
GOE: 11.12.02 STRENGTH: L GED: R5 M4 L5 SVP: 8 DLU: 77

191.157-010   PAWNBROKER (retail trade)
Estimates pawn or pledge value of articles, such as jewelry, cameras, and musical instruments, and lends money to customer: Examines article to determine condition and worth. Weighs gold or silver articles on coin scales or employs acid tests to determine carat content and purity to verify value of articles. Inspects diamonds and other gems for flaws and color, using loupe (magnifying glass). Assigns pledge value to article based on knowledge of values or listing of wholesale prices. Rejects articles in unsatisfactory condition or having no pledge value. Issues pledge tickets and keeps record of loans. Computes interest when pledges are redeemed or extended. Sells unredeemed pledged items. May examine customer's identification and record thumbprints for police reports. May testify in court proceedings involving stolen merchandise.
GOE: 08.01.03 STRENGTH: L GED: R4 M4 L4 SVP: 6 DLU: 77

191.167-010   ADVANCE AGENT (amuse. & rec.)
Coordinates business and promotional activities concerned with production of entertainment in advance of touring theatrical company, circus, road show, motion picture, or other attraction: Inspects performance location and reports condition, and if stage presentation, inspects equipment and accommodations of theatre, such as size of stage, seating capacity, and number of dressing rooms. Completes business details, such as advance sale of tickets and lodging for members of touring group. Purchases advertising space or spot announcements in newspapers, radio and television, and other media. Distributes posters, signs, and other displays to stimulate interest in coming attraction and promote box-office sales [PUBLIC-RELATIONS REPRESENTATIVE (profess. & kin.)].
GOE: 11.12.03 STRENGTH: L GED: R4 M4 L4 SVP: 7 DLU: 77

191.167-014   CLAIM AGENT (petrol. & gas; pipe lines)
Interviews property holders and adjusts damage claims resulting from activities connected with prospecting, drilling, and production of oil and gas, and laying of pipelines on private property: Examines titles to property to determine their validity and acts as company agent in transactions with property owners. Investigates and assesses damage to crops, fences, and other properties, and negotiates claim settlements with property owners. Collects and prepares evidence to support contested damage claims in courts.
GOE: 11.12.01 STRENGTH: S GED: R6 M3 L6 SVP: 7 DLU: 77

191.167-018   LOCATION MANAGER (motion picture; radio-tv broad.)
Arranges for leasing of suitable property for use as location for television or motion picture production: Confers with production or unit manager and DIRECTOR, TELEVISION (radio-tv broad.) or DIRECTOR, MOTION PICTURE (motion picture) regarding scenic backgrounds, terrain, and other topographical details of locations required for photographing exterior scenes. Searches files for pictures or descriptions of suitable locations or seeks new locations. Contacts property owners and local officials to arrange leasing and use of public and private property, rental of housing facilities, hiring of extras, and to obtain sanction for production activities. Arranges for transportation of troupe to location.
GOE: 11.12.02 STRENGTH: L GED: R4 M3 L4 SVP: 6 DLU: 77

191.167-022   SERVICE REPRESENTATIVE (auto. mfg.)
Investigates dealer's claims for reimbursement of defective automotive parts: Reviews claims for labor or material adjustments with automobile dealer, exam-

ines parts claimed to be defective, and approves or disapproves dealer's claim. Assists dealers in handling unsettled claims by consulting with service personnel or customers. Prepares reports showing volume, types, and disposition of claims handled, or settlement allowed. May train dealers or service personnel in service operations or construction of products. May study dealers' organizational needs and advise them on matters, such as parts, tools, equipment, and personnel needed to handle service volume. May contact customers to survey customer satisfaction with purchase of new motor vehicle.
GOE: 11.12.01 STRENGTH: S GED: R5 M4 L4 SVP: 7 DLU: 90

191.267-010   APPRAISER, REAL ESTATE (real estate)
Appraises improved or unimproved real property to determine value for purchase, sale, investment, mortgage, or loan purposes: Interviews persons familiar with property and immediate surroundings, such as contractors, home owners, and other realtors to obtain pertinent information. Inspects property for construction, condition, and functional design and takes property measurements. Considers factors, such as depreciation, reproduction costs, value comparison of similar property, and income potential, when computing final estimation of property value. Considers location and trends or impending changes that could influence future value of property. Searches public records for transactions, such as sales, leases, and assessments. Photographs interiors and exteriors of property, to assist in estimating property value, to substantiate findings, and to complete appraisal report. Prepares written report, utilizing data collected and submits report to corroborate value established. May direct activities of appraisers. May evaluate staff job performance and recommend measures to improve performance according to establishment policies and procedures.
GOE: 11.06.03 STRENGTH: L GED: R5 M4 L4 SVP: 7 DLU: 89

191.287-010   APPRAISER (any industry)
Appraises merchandise, fixtures, machinery, and equipment of business firms to ascertain values for such purposes as approval of loans, issuance of insurance policies, disposition of estates, and liquidation of assets of bankrupt firms: Examines items and estimates their wholesale or auction-sale values, basing estimate on knowledge of equipment or goods, current market values, and industrial and economic trends. Prepares and submits reports of estimates to clients, such as insurance firms, lending agencies, government offices, creditors, courts, or attorneys.
GOE: 11.06.03 STRENGTH: L GED: R5 M5 L5 SVP: 7 DLU: 77

191.287-014   APPRAISER, ART (profess. & kin.)
Examines works of art, such as paintings, sculpture, and antiques, to determine their authenticity and value: Examines work for color values, style of brushstroke, esthetic correctness, and other characteristics, to establish art period or identify artist. Judges authenticity and value, based on knowledge of art history, materials employed, techniques of individual artists, and current market. May illuminate work with quartz light to determine whether discoloration is present. May x ray painting and perform chemical tests on paint sample to detect forgery or to authenticate work. May specialize in particular categories of art or in specific types of artistic articles appraised.
GOE: 01.02.01 STRENGTH: L GED: R5 M4 L4 SVP: 8 DLU: 77

191.367-010   PERSONAL PROPERTY ASSESSOR (government ser.) alternate titles: deputy assessor
Prepares lists of personal property owned by householders and merchants in assigned area to facilitate tax assessment, showing number and estimated value of taxable items designated in regulations.
GOE: 11.06.03 STRENGTH: L GED: R3 M3 L3 SVP: 4 DLU: 77

193   RADIO OPERATORS

This group includes occupations concerned with receiving and transmitting communications, using radiotelegraph or radiotelephone equipment, in accordance with government regulations. Must be federally licensed.

193.162-010   AIR-TRAFFIC COORDINATOR (government ser.)
Coordinates movement of air traffic between altitude sectors and control centers to provide maximum separation and safety for aircraft: Maintains radio and telephone contact with AIR-TRAFFIC COORDINATORS (government ser.) in adjoining control centers. Relays information regarding air traffic by radio to AIR-TRAFFIC-CONTROL SPECIALIST, TOWER (government ser.) and AIR-TRAFFIC-CONTROL SPECIALIST, STATION (government ser.), monitoring each sector, for transmittal to AIRPLANE PILOT, COMMERCIAL (air trans.). Relays information, such as altitude, expected time of arrival, and course. Determines procedure and time for altitude changes to prevent collisions and excessive traffic buildup in flight sector. Completes daily activity report.
GOE: 05.03.03 STRENGTH: L GED: R4 M3 L4 SVP: 8 DLU: 77

193.162-014   AIR-TRAFFIC-CONTROL SPECIALIST, STATION (government ser.)
Receives and transmits flight plans, meteorological, navigational, and other information in air traffic control station to perform preflight and emergency service for airplane pilots: Accepts flight plans from pilots in person or by telephone and reviews them for completeness. Routes plans for operating under instrument flight rules to control center and for operating under visual flight rules to station in vicinity of destination airport, using radio, teletype, radiotelephone, radiotelegraph, telephone, or interphone. Provides meteorological, navigational, and other information to pilots during flight, using radio. Relays traffic control

and other instructions concerned with aircraft safety to pilots. Radios such information as identifying landmarks, beacons, and available landing fields to pilots in flight. Maintains file of plans for operating under visual flight rules until completion of flight, and contacts facilities along route of flight to secure information on overdue aircraft. Reports lost aircraft to control center for rescue or local emergency services. Monitors such radio aids to navigation as range stations, fan markers, and voice communication facilities, and notifies air personnel of availability of these facilities. Maintains written records of messages transmitted and received.
GOE: 05.03.03 STRENGTH: L GED: R4 M3 L4 SVP: 8 DLU: 81

193.162-018 AIR-TRAFFIC-CONTROL SPECIALIST, TOWER (government ser.) alternate titles: airport-control operator; control-tower-radio operator; flight-control-tower operator
Controls air traffic on and within vicinity of airport according to established procedures and policies to prevent collisions and to minimize delays arising from traffic congestion: Answers radio calls from arriving and departing aircraft and issues landing and take-off instructions and information, such as runway to use, wind velocity and direction, visibility, taxiing instructions, and pertinent data on other aircraft operating in vicinity. Transfers control of departing flights to and accepts control of arriving flights from air traffic control center, using telephone or interphone. Alerts airport emergency crew and other designated personnel by radio or telephone when airplanes are having flight difficulties. Pushes buttons or pulls switches to control airport floodlights and boundary, runway, and hazard lights. Scans control panel to ascertain that lights are functioning. Operates radio and monitors radarscope to control aircraft operating in vicinity of airport. Receives cross-country flight plans and transmits them to air traffic control center. Signals aircraft flying under visual flight rules, using electric signal light or flags. May control cross-runway traffic by radio directions to guards or maintenance vehicles. May keep written record of messages received from aircraft. May control traffic within designated sector of airspace between centers and beyond airport control tower area and be designated Air-Traffic-Control Specialist, Center (government ser.).
GOE: 05.03.03 STRENGTH: L GED: R4 M3 L4 SVP: 8 DLU: 81

193.162-022 AIRLINE-RADIO OPERATOR, CHIEF (air trans.; business ser.) alternate titles: senior radio operator; watch supervisor
Coordinates activities of AIRLINE-RADIO OPERATORS (air trans.; business ser.) in maintaining radio communications with aircraft and other ground stations: Establishes and maintains standards of operation by periodic inspections of equipment and tests of AIRLINE-RADIO OPERATORS (air trans.; business ser.) Periodically reviews company and Federal Aviation Authority regulations regarding radio communications. Assigns personnel to individual jobs. Coordinates radio searches for overdue or lost airplanes. Inspects radio reports. Makes emergency repairs to equipment or gives instructions for such repairs. Examines and operates new equipment prior to installation in airport radio stations.
GOE: 07.04.05 STRENGTH: S GED: R4 M4 L4 SVP: 8 DLU: 77

193.167-010 CHIEF CONTROLLER (government ser.) alternate titles: air-traffic-control supervisor
Coordinates activities of and supervises personnel engaged in operation of air traffic control tower, station, or center: Interprets Federal Aviation Agency directives and places them into effect. Adapts procedures to deal with problems or situations not covered by established procedures or policies. Organizes and conducts on-the-job training of AIR-TRAFFIC-CONTROL SPECIALIST, STATION (government ser.); AIR-TRAFFIC-CONTROL SPECIALIST, TOWER (government ser.). Directs radio searches for overdue or lost aircraft. Inspects radio equipment for frequency adjustments and reviews records and reports for clarity and completeness. May be designated according to control activity supervised as Chief Controller, Center (government ser.); Chief Controller, Station (government ser.); Chief Controller, Tower (government ser.).
GOE: 05.03.03 STRENGTH: S GED: R5 M4 L4 SVP: 7 DLU: 77

193.167-014 FIELD SUPERVISOR, BROADCAST (radio-tv broad.)
Coordinates activities of FIELD ENGINEERS (radio-tv broad.) in installing, testing, and operating portable field equipment used to broadcast programs or events from points distant from studio: Assigns FIELD ENGINEERS (radio-tv broad.) with audio and relay equipment to various field pick-up points, to test equipment prior to broadcast. Directs workers in maintaining field transmission equipment in operating order.
GOE: 05.03.05 STRENGTH: L GED: R5 M4 L5 SVP: 7 DLU: 77

193.167-018 SUPERINTENDENT, RADIO COMMUNICATIONS (government ser.) alternate titles: commanding officer, radio division communications officer
Directs and coordinates various activities of personnel engaged in installing and maintaining municipal emergency and business radio communications equipment, and in operating police, fire, or other municipal radio transmitters: Ensures that government regulations concerning installation and operation of municipal radio stations are complied with. Participates in operation, testing, and development of all types of police, fire, or other municipal communication systems. Submits requirements reports to designated authorities concerning communications equipment status, such as nature of business transacted over radio station, character of radio repairs made or needed, and general condition of municipal communications system. Confers with municipal authorities for approval of major capital investments needed in establishing and maintaining system. Co-

operates with fire, weather station, and civil defense authorities to originate or relay emergency messages. In communities where equipment is used primarily for police broadcasts, may be a police officer and be designated according to rank as Radio-Division Captain (government ser.); Radio-Division Lieutenant (government ser.).
GOE: 05.02.04 STRENGTH: S GED: R5 M4 L5 SVP: 8 DLU: 77

193.262-010 AIRLINE-RADIO OPERATOR (air trans.; business ser.)
Transmits and receives messages between station and aircraft or other ground stations by radiotelephone: Sends meteorological data to aircraft by radiotelephone. Relays by telegraphic typewriter to DISPATCHER (air trans.) transmissions from aircraft, such as number of passengers aboard, estimated time of arrival, mechanical condition of plane, and requests for repairs. Relays instructions of air traffic control centers to airplane when communication fails. Makes connections between telephone and radio equipment to permit direct communication between DISPATCHER (air trans.) and airplane. Must be licensed by Federal Communications Commission.
GOE: 07.04.05 STRENGTH: S GED: R4 M4 L4 SVP: 7 DLU: 77

193.262-014 DISPATCHER (government ser.)
Operates radio and telephone equipment to receive reports and requests from firefighting crews, fire-lookout stations, and mobile units, and relays information or orders to officials concerned. Maintains communications log and maps location of fires, men, and equipment from field reports. May organize and direct activities of firefighting crew.
GOE: 07.04.05 STRENGTH: S GED: R4 M3 L4 SVP: 6 DLU: 77

193.262-018 FIELD ENGINEER (radio-tv broad.) alternate titles: field technician
Installs and operates portable field transmission equipment to broadcast programs or events originating at points distant from studio: Determines availability of telephone wire facilities for use in making connections between microphones, amplifier, telephone line, and auxiliary power supply to relay broadcast to master control. Sets up, tests, and operates microwave transmitter to broadcast program in absence of telephone wire system. Conducts broadcast from field. Must be licensed by Federal Communications Commission. May perform duties of RECORDING ENGINEER (recording; radio-tv broad.) 194.362-010; ANNOUNCER (radio-tv broad.) 159.147-010. May be designated Microwave Engineer (radio-tv broad.) when restricted to operating microwave transmitter.
GOE: 05.03.05 STRENGTH: L GED: R5 M4 L5 SVP: 7 DLU: 88

193.262-022 RADIO OFFICER (water trans.) alternate titles: radio operator
Operates and maintains radiotelegraph and radiotelephone equipment and accessories aboard ship: Turns on power to activate generator, and throws switches to cut in transmitters and antennas. Turns dials to obtain sending frequency and volume. Receives and transmits messages following procedure prescribed by federal regulations. Maintains log of messages transmitted and received. Monitors emergency frequency for ship and distress calls. Performs minor repairs and adjustments on ships' radio equipment and lifeboat radios. Charges batteries. May perform minor repairs to radar, loran, auto-alarm, and gyrocompass systems. May copy broadcast schedules, such as Merfox (U.S. Navy broadcast), Mercast (weather information and navigational hazards), and news (wire-press). Must be licensed by Federal Communications Commission as Radiotelegraph Operator and Radiotelephone Operator, and by U.S. Coast Guard as Radio Officer.
GOE: 07.04.05 STRENGTH: S GED: R4 M3 L3 SVP: 7 DLU: 77

193.262-026 RADIO STATION OPERATOR (aircraft mfg.) alternate titles: radio operator, ground
Operates radio and associated test equipment at aircraft factory radio station to transmit and receive information during flight testing and delivery of aircraft: Communicates with TEST PILOT (aircraft mfg.) 196.263-042, engineering personnel, and others during flight testing to relay information. Observes aircraft prior to landing or takeoff and advises plane crew of observations. Maintains station log and other flight test records. May dispatch firetrucks, emergency equipment, and personnel during test flights. May operate radar and specialized test equipment during flight testing or preflight checkout to assist engineers in evaluating aircraft or equipment.
GOE: 07.04.05 STRENGTH: L GED: R5 M4 L4 SVP: 6 DLU: 87

193.262-030 RADIOTELEGRAPH OPERATOR (tel. & tel.) alternate titles: cw operator; radiotelegraphist
Operates and keeps in repair equipment used in radiotelegraph communications: Watches frequency lights on receiver to ascertain if station is being called. Snaps toggle switch that sets receiver to frequency when call is indicated. Opens circuit and manipulates key to acknowledge call. Listens to telegraph signal, types message on form, and relays it to addressee by telephone or teletype. Manipulates key to call ships or stations by code, and to send messages after acknowledgement. Monitors emergency frequency for distress calls, and Conelrad (civil defense circuit) as required by regulations. Performs routine repairs and maintenance, such as changing tubes, resistors, and transmitters. Is required to have Radiotelegraph License issued by Federal Communications Commission.
GOE: 07.04.05 STRENGTH: S GED: R4 M2 L3 SVP: 7 DLU: 77

193.262-034 RADIOTELEPHONE OPERATOR (any industry) alternate titles: phone-circuit operator; radiophone operator; radio-telephone-technical operator
Operates and keeps in repair radiotelephone transmitter and receiving equipment for commercial communication: Throws switches to cut in power to

stages of transmitter. Cuts in antennas and connects transmitting and receiving equipment into telephone system. Turns controls to adjust voice volume and modulation, and to set transmitter on specified frequency. Conducts routine tests and repairs transmitting equipment, using electronic testing equipment, handtools, and power tools, to maintain communication system in operative condition. Must hold Radiotelephone Operator's License issued by Federal Communications Commission.
GOE: 05.03.05 STRENGTH: L GED: R4 M3 L4 SVP: 7 DLU: 77

193.262-038   TRANSMITTER OPERATOR (radio-tv broad.) alternate titles: transmitter engineer

Operates and maintains radio transmitter to broadcast radio and television programs: Moves switches to cut in power to units and stages of transmitter. Monitors lights on console panel to ascertain that components are operative and that transmitter is ready to emit signal. Turns controls to set transmitter on FM, AM, or TV frequency assigned by Federal Communications Commission. Monitors signal emission and spurious radiations outside of licensed transmission frequency to ensure signal is not infringing on frequencies assigned other stations. Notifies broadcast studio when ready to transmit. Observes indicators and adjusts controls to maintain constant sound modulation and ensure that transmitted signal is sharp and clear. Maintains log of programs transmitted as required by Federal Communications Commission. Tests components of malfunctioning transmitter to diagnose trouble, using test equipment, such as oscilloscope, voltmeters, and ammeters. Disassembles and repairs equipment, using handtools [RADIO MECHANIC (any industry) 823.261-018]. May converse with studio personnel to determine cause of equipment failure and to solve problem. May operate microwave transmitter and receiver to receive or send programs to or from other broadcast stations. Must possess license issued by Federal Communications Commission.
GOE: 05.03.05 STRENGTH: M GED: R4 M4 L4 SVP: 7 DLU: 89

193.362-010   PHOTORADIO OPERATOR (print. & pub.; tel. & tel.) alternate titles: facsimile operator; radio-photo technician; telephoto engineer

Operates electronic equipment to transmit and receive radio photographs and repairs equipment: Mounts photographs or printed matter on cylinder and secures with gripper bar. Turns dials to set frequency controls. Starts equipment that scans material and converts light and dark areas into electrical impulses for transmission. Communicates with receiving operator to give and receive instructions for transmission. Positions negative on cylinder, sets controls, and listens for signals to receive transmission. Develops negatives, prints photographs, and keeps log of transmissions. Maintains and repairs electronic equipment, such as wire circuits, dials, and gauges, using schematic diagram, handtools, and test instruments. Reruns transmission when photograph is substandard. May send or receive Morse code messages when voice communication is not possible. May transmit and receive news photographs, using automated telephoto equipment. May be required to hold Federal Communications Commission operator's license.
GOE: 07.04.05 STRENGTH: S GED: R4 M4 L4 SVP: 6 DLU: 77

193.362-014   RADIO-INTELLIGENCE OPERATOR (government ser.)

Controls equipment to intercept, locate, identify, and record radio transmissions of enemy or potential enemy: Tunes receiver over assigned frequency band. Obtains bearings on source of transmission, using electronic direction-finding equipment. Informs location plotters of bearings obtained to locate and identify station. Monitors stations, records intercepted transmissions, and forwards transcripts for decoding. May operate sound-recording equipment to preserve broadcast for analysis by other intelligence personnel.
GOE: 05.03.05 STRENGTH: S GED: R4 M3 L4 SVP: 6 DLU: 77

193.382-010   ELECTRONIC INTELLIGENCE OPERATIONS SPECIALIST (military ser.)

Operates electronic monitoring and related equipment to detect electronic emissions: Conducts continuous search and monitoring of assigned portions of radio frequency spectrum, using special search or monitoring equipment. Observes video presentations or listens to signal to determine primary characteristics of monitored signals. Operates cameras to photograph signals. Operates recorders to record signals. Determines azimuth from which signal originated, using direction finder procedures. Determines accurately and rapidly parameters, directional bearing, and point of origin of electronic data recorded on photographic film and magnetic tape through operation of technical laboratory analysis equipment, such as electronic parameter display consoles, oscilloscope, electronic counters and sorters, X-Y plotters, sonographs, visographs, brush recorders, video and audio playback units, complex viewers, visual projectors, and associated analog and digital equipment.
GOE: 05.03.05 STRENGTH: S GED: R4 M3 L4 SVP: 7 DLU: 77

194   SOUND, FILM, AND VIDEOTAPE RECORDING, AND REPRODUCTION OCCUPATIONS

This group includes occupations concerned with recording, transcribing, reproducing and regulating quality of voice, music, and other sounds by use of electronic equipment. Includes occupations concerned with motion picture film, video tape, and phonograph record production. Occupations concerned with radio and television broadcasting must be federally licensed. Occupations concerned with creating and editing sound and visual effects are found in Group 962. Cutting and splicing of film and videotape are included in Group 976.

194.062-010   TELEVISION TECHNICIAN (radio-tv broad.) alternate titles: production assistant; production technician

Performs any combination of following duties to record and transmit broadcasts: Operates studio and mini-television (portable, shoulder-mounted) cameras [CAMERA OPERATOR (motion picture; radio-tv broad.) 143.062-022]. Controls console to regulate transmission of television scenes [VIDEO OPERATOR (radio-tv broad.) 194.282-010]. Produces educational and training films and video tapes [COMMUNICATIONS TECHNICIAN (education) 962.362-010]. Sets up and controls television production equipment, such as cameras [CAMERA OPERATOR (radio-tv broad.)], lights [LIGHT TECHNICIAN (motion picture; radio-tv broad.) 962.362-014], microphones and microphone booms [MICROPHONE-BOOM OPERATOR (motion picture; radio-tv broad.) 962.384-010], and recording equipment [RECORDIST (motion picture) 962.382-010], in studio and at locations outside of studio, to record or transmit broadcasts. Performs preventive and minor equipment maintenance, using work tools. Maintains log to record equipment usage and location of equipment. May perform duties of other related occupations depending upon specific production needs of individual airwave or closed-circuit station where workers must be able to set up and operate equipment.
GOE: 01.02.03 STRENGTH: H GED: R5 M4 L5 SVP: 7 DLU: 89

194.122-010   ACCESS COORDINATOR, CABLE TELEVISION (radio-tv broad.)

Instructs trainees in use of equipment; and operates equipment, such as camera, sound mixer, and videotape deck, to film events, to copy/edit graphics, voice, and music onto videotape, for broadcast on cable television: Determines time and day of class and plans outline of material to be covered. Distributes manuals, and instructs and demonstrates to trainees, care, setup and operation of equipment, such as tripods, microphones and portable camera. Prepares and administers written and practical tests to test trainees' knowledge. Determines equipment required to film event, and sets up and operates equipment, such as lights and portable camera to film event. Prepares script of filmed event. Loads videotape deck with videotape and instructs assistant to read script. Sets recording level, and records verbal description of event onto videotape, using videotaping equipment. Reviews videotape of filmed event, using videotaping equipment, to determine quality of video and color. Observes scales in video and color monitors and operates controls to adjust video and color levels. Enters written information about filmed event into graphic equipment. Plays musical selection, using stereo equipment, and adjusts controls to improve clarity and balance music. Sets *inpoints* and *outpoints* for graphics, voice, and music. Records graphics, voice, and music onto videotape, using audio/video equipment. Observes monitors to verify that video, voice, and music are synchronized during editing/copying process. Reviews assembled videotape, using videotaping equipment, to discern quality of video and audio signals, and operates controls to clarify and adjust video and audio signals. Edits manuals and schedules programs. May prepare report outlining past programs and future programs to be aired, and contents of programs.
GOE: 05.03.05 STRENGTH: H GED: R4 M3 L4 SVP: 7 DLU: 88

194.162-010   PROGRAM DIRECTOR, CABLE TELEVISION (radio-tv broad.) alternate titles: production supervisor

Directs and coordinates activities of workers engaged in selection and production of cable television programs, and operates equipment to film events, and to copy/edit graphics, voice, and music onto videotape: Interviews and hires workers. Instructs workers in operation and maintenance of equipment, such as cameras and microphones, or directs instruction of workers through subordinate personnel. Gives work directives, resolves problems, interprets policies and procedures and prepares work schedules. Initiates disciplinary action for rules infractions and terminates workers. Contacts talent (entertainers) and companies to determine interest in program(s) and interest in supplying prizes to audience participants. Writes script and rehearses script with talent. Coordinates audio work, music, camera work and script to produce show. Operates equipment, such as camera, sound mixer, and videotape deck, to film events, and to edit/copy graphics, voice and music onto videotape. Performs public relations duties, such as contacting school personnel to discuss company's internship program for students, and prepares press releases for newspapers, indicating company trends and direction. Prepares and monitors budget to verify expenditures stay within budgetary restrictions. Prepares forms for government agencies and contract renewal. Prepares invoices and bills customers for services rendered. May operate broadcast equipment to transmit program to viewing audience.
GOE: 05.02.04 STRENGTH: H GED: R5 M3 L5 SVP: 8 DLU: 88

194.262-010   AUDIO OPERATOR (radio-tv broad.) alternate titles: audio engineer; audio technician; sound engineer, audio control

Controls audio equipment to regulate volume level and quality of sound during television broadcasts, according to script and instructions of DIRECTOR, TECHNICAL (radio-tv broad.) 962.162-010: Places microphones or directs worker in placing microphones in locations that ensure quality of sound reproduction. Cuts microphones in, and blends output of individual microphones by adjusting volume, fader, and mixer controls. Monitors audio signals by earphone, loudspeaker, and by observing dials on control panel to verify quality of sound reproduction. Sets keys, switches, and dials to synchronize sound with picture presentation. Obtains tapes, records, and themes from library according to program schedule. Operates turntables and tape recording machines to reproduce music and audio sounds for specific programs. May direct adjustment of acoustical curtains and blinds within studio.

GOE: 05.10.05 STRENGTH: L GED: R4 M4 L3 SVP: 7 DLU: 89

194.262-014 SOUND CONTROLLER (amuse. & rec.)

Operates sound-mixing board to control output of voices, music, and previously taped sound effects during stage performances: Analyzes script of dialog, music, and sound effects as applied to particular scene to determine sound requirements. Confers with producing personnel concerning microphone placement, special sound effects, cues, and acoustical characteristics of theater. Locates sound-mixing board backstage or in theater control room. Arranges microphones in theater to achieve best sound pickup. Moves control to turn microphones on or off and adjusts volume, fader, and mixer controls to blend output of individual microphones. Listens to overall effect on monitor loudspeaker and observes dials on control panel to verify suitability of sounds. May modify design of sound equipment used. May operate record and electrical transcription turntables to supply musical selections and other sound material.
GOE: 05.10.03 STRENGTH: L GED: R4 M4 L3 SVP: 7 DLU: 77

194.262-018 SOUND MIXER (motion picture; radio-tv broad.; recording) alternate titles: board operator; mixer operator; music mixer; studio engineer; studio technician

Operates console to regulate volume level and quality of sound during filming of motion picture, phonograph recording session, or television and radio productions: Determines acoustics of recording studio and adjusts controls to specified levels. Directs installation of microphones and amplifiers for use in sound pickup. Turns knobs and dials on console while recording to cut microphones in and out, and to blend output of individual microphones to obtain balance between music, dialog, and sound effects. Instructs performers to project voices for pickup by microphones. Copies and edits recordings, using recording and editing equipment. May test machines and equipment, using electronic testing equipment, such as ohm and voltage meters, to detect defects. May repair and replace audio amplifier parts.
GOE: 05.10.05 STRENGTH: S GED: R4 M4 L3 SVP: 7 DLU: 89

194.262-022 MASTER CONTROL OPERATOR (radio-tv broad.) alternate titles: master control engineer

Sets up, controls and monitors television broadcasting equipment to transmit television programs and station breaks to viewing audience: Reads television programming log to ascertain name of program or station break, and at what time program or station break is scheduled to air. Verifies voice-over recording, using tape equipment, and informs supervisor of inconsistencies. Loads videotape equipment with videotapes containing program or station break or presses button on switching equipment to access videotape equipment. Subtracts *preroll* time from on-air time to determine at what time to begin preroll. Turns video and color monitors on and presses button to start videotape equipment. Observes scales in video and color monitors and turns knobs to set video and color levels to specifications. Turns knob to set audio level to specification. Observes clock, and presses buttons on switching equipment to begin preroll and to transmit program or station break to viewing audience. Observes on-air monitor to ascertain problems with transmission, such as loss of audio or video signals, and presses buttons to access and transmit technical difficulties sign or station identification to viewing audience. Presses buttons to access voice-over recording indicating nature of problem, name of station or name of next scheduled program. Troubleshoots equipment and observes lights on transmitter control panel to determine cause and area of problem and informs engineering personnel of transmission problems. Records onto television programming log actual time program or station break was aired. Prepares report describing problems encountered during transmission of program or station break and reason for problems. May control transmitting equipment to route television program to affiliated station. May take and record transmitter readings onto transmitter log. May be required to hold license issued by Federal Communications Commission.
GOE: 05.03.05 STRENGTH: S GED: R4 M3 L4 SVP: 8 DLU: 89

194.282-010 VIDEO OPERATOR (radio-tv broad.) alternate titles: camera control operator; color-television console monitor; video engineer

Controls video console to regulate transmission of television scenes, including test patterns and filmed and live black-and-white or color telecast: Views action on television monitor and sets switches and observes dials on console to control framing, contrast, brilliance, color balance, and fidelity of image being transmitted. Monitors on-air programs to ensure technical quality of broadcast. Previews upcoming program to determine that signal is functioning and that program will be ready for transmission at required time. May maintain log on studio-to-transmitter microwave link.
GOE: 05.03.05 STRENGTH: S GED: R4 M4 L3 SVP: 7 DLU: 88

194.362-010 RECORDING ENGINEER (radio-tv broad.; recording) alternate titles: sound recording technician

Operates disk or tape recording machine to record music, dialog, or sound effects of phonograph recording sessions, radio broadcasts, television shows, training courses, or conferences, or to transfer transcribed material to sound-recording medium: Threads tape through recording device or places blank disk on turntable. Moves lever to regulate speed of turntable. Places cutting stylus on record. Examines grooves during cutting by stylus to determine if grooves are level, using microscope. Turns knobs on cutting arm to shift or adjust weight of stylus and cause grooves to be cut evenly. Starts recording machine and moves switches to open microphone and tune in live or recorded programs.

Listens through earphone to detect imperfections of recording machines or extraneous noises emanating from recording studio or production stage. Observes dials, mounted on machine, to ensure that volume level and intensity remain within specified limits. Removes filled reel or completed recordings from machine and attaches identifying labels. Keeps record of recordings in logbook. May service and repair recording machines and allied equipment. May be designated according to type of machine used as Disk-Recording-Machine Operator (radio-tv broad.; recording); Tape-Recording-Machine Operator (radio-tv broad.; recording). When transcribing to disk used in production of phonograph records, may be designated Dubbing-Machine Operator (recording). When recording live television programs in monochrome or color on magnetic tape is designated Videotape-Recording Engineer (radio-tv broad.).
GOE: 05.10.05 STRENGTH: L GED: R3 M3 L3 SVP: 7 DLU: 77

194.362-014 RERECORDING MIXER (motion picture; radio-tv broad.)

Operates console to synchronize and equalize prerecorded dialog, music, and sound effects with action of motion picture or television production: Reads script and dupe sheets of film and tape or video tape to learn sequence of speaking parts, music, and sound effects to be synchronized and integrated in film or tape or video tape. Informs DUBBING-MACHINE OPERATOR (motion picture; radio-tv broad.) 962.665-010 to load sound tracks onto dubbing machine and MOTION-PICTURE PROJECTIONIST (amuse. & rec.; motion picture) 960.362-010 to place film in projector. Operates console to control starting and stopping of projector and dubbing machine. Observes film or video tape projected onto screen, listens to sound over loud speakers, and turns knobs on panel of console to balance intensity and volume. Informs MOTION-PICTURE PROJECTIONIST (amuse. & rec.; motion picture) to project film onto screen. Observes projection and listens to determine that sound is synchronized and equalized with action on film.
GOE: 05.10.05 STRENGTH: S GED: R4 M4 L4 SVP: 7 DLU: 87

194.362-018 TELECINE OPERATOR (radio-tv broad.)

Controls equipment, such as tape recording and playback units, film projectors, and slide projectors in television broadcasting studio, synchronizing equipment with program content and activities of other technical personnel to maintain prescribed professional programming standards. Threads film or tape through equipment and inserts slides in slide projector. Installs, adjusts, and repairs equipment to facilitate uninterrupted service during broadcast.
GOE: 05.10.05 STRENGTH: S GED: R4 M4 L3 SVP: 7 DLU: 77

194.362-022 TECHNICIAN, NEWS GATHERING (radio-tv broad.) alternate titles: technician-photographer/editor

Locates news events, and sets up and controls field transmission equipment to record or transmit news events to television station: Drives vehicle to locate news events, such as fire or public rally, or receives information over two-way radio and scanner about location of news events. Turns power supply and monitors on, and activates air compressor to raise mast. Selects channel for transmission of audio and video signals. Converses with station operator, using two-way radio, while controlling lever to align antennae with receiving dish to obtain clearest signal for transmission of news event to station. Lays electrical cord and audio and video cables between vehicle, microphone, camera, and REPORTER (print. & pub.; radio-tv broad.) 131.262-018, or person being interviewed, to allow for receiving of off-air signal and transmission of audio and video signals to station. Observes scale in video monitor and sets video level to specifications. Observes audio level to specifications. Observes monitor and transmission light, and converses with station operator, using two-way radio, to verify transmission of news event to station, and makes adjustments to equipment. Records news event onto videotape, using recording equipment, during transmission of news event to studio, or receives videotape from CAMERA OPERATOR (motion picture; radio-tv broad.) 143.062-022 and makes dub, using recording equipment. Records information, such as location and news events recorded or transmitted to station, onto log. Is required to hold license issued by Federal Communications Commission.
GOE: 05.03.05 STRENGTH: M GED: R4 M3 L3 SVP: 8 DLU: 89

194.381-010 TECHNICAL TESTING ENGINEER (motion picture) alternate titles: sound installation worker

Tests and adjusts optical, electrical, and audio-frequency equipment used to transmit, record, and reproduce sounds on motion picture set: Inspects sound circuit patch cords to ensure flow of current from sound stage to recording equipment. Tests sound circuits and equipment, such as light valves, galvanometers, microphones, and magnetic recording heads to verify standard operating condition; using portable testing instruments. Replaces defective components and wiring and adjusts equipment to correct defects, using handtools.
GOE: 05.10.03 STRENGTH: L GED: R4 M4 L3 SVP: 6 DLU: 77

194.382-010 SECTION-PLOTTER OPERATOR (petrol. & gas) alternate titles: playback operator

Operates electronically controlled sound reproducing and photographic equipment (section plotter) to record seismic waves from magnetic tape recordings of explosions reflected or refracted from subsurface strata: Starts equipment and moves controls to align adjacent recordings uniformly on positive photographic film, following tracings of wave form shown on indicator. Verifies identification data on magnetic tape container to ensure specified order of sound reproduction. Clamps magnetic tape around drum of sound reproducer, starts machine, and observes wave form on oscillograph to detect malfunctions. May develop and print photographic recordings in darkroom. May test circuits, resis-

159

tors, transistors, and related equipment parts, using schematic drawings, wiring diagrams, and electronic test equipment. May replace defective parts and repair faulty connections, using soldering iron.
GOE: 05.10.05 STRENGTH: L GED: R3 M3 L3 SVP: 5 DLU: 77

194.382-014 TAPE TRANSFERRER (radio-tv broad.; recording) alternate titles: tape duplicator

Operates machines to reproduce tape recordings from master tapes (original tape recording): Consults charts to determine amount of tape needed, considering running time of master tape. Positions master tape in master-reproducing machine and mounts blank tape on spindle of tape-recording machine. Threads tapes through machines. Interconnects and starts machines to record selection on blank tape. Stops machines and reverses tape in recording machine to record second selection on reverse side of tape. Operates recording machine to play back reproduced recording to test quality of reproduced sound.
GOE: 05.10.05 STRENGTH: L GED: R3 M3 L3 SVP: 5 DLU: 77

194.382-018 VIDEOTAPE OPERATOR (radio-tv broad.) alternate titles: studio technician-video operator; videotape engineer

Sets up and operates videotaping equipment to record and play back television programs, applying knowledge of videotaping equipment operation: Reads television programming log to ascertain program to be recorded or program to be aired. Selects source, such as satellite or studio, from which program will be recorded, and selects videotaping equipment on which program will be recorded. Observes monitor to verify that station is on-air, and informs supervisor if station not on-air. Cleans videotape path to remove contaminants that would affect quality of recording or playback, and mounts videotape onto videotaping equipment. Sets audio level, and records test pattern and program onto videotape, using videotaping equipment. Verifies quality of recording, using videotape equipment, and informs designated personnel of quality of recording. Inspects tape for defective ends, removes defective end, using cutting tool, and mounts videotape onto videotaping equipment to play back program. Starts videotaping equipment and turns video and color monitors on to verify setting of video and color levels. Observes scales in video and color monitors and operates controls to adjust video and color levels. Cues program, using videotaping equipment, and places videotaping equipment in remote control mode for use by other operator. May operate videotaping equipment to dub and edit tapes. May wire audio and video patch bays (socketed equipment that allows for transfer of audio and video signals between different pieces of equipment, via cables). May set up videotaping equipment to play station breaks. May set up film equipment to play program. May make minor repairs to equipment.
GOE: 05.03.05 STRENGTH: L GED: R4 M2 L3 SVP: 8 DLU: 89

194.387-010 QUALITY-CONTROL INSPECTOR (recording) alternate titles: matrix inspector; mother tester

Inspects metal phonograph record *mothers* for surface defects, using optical and sound-reproducing equipment: Places matrix on turntable and measures grooved surface and width of grooves in matrix, using ruler and calibrated microscope. Places tone arm on matrix and starts sound-reproducing machine. Listens for defects in matrix, such as pops and ticks, and observes meter that indicates surface noise and sound level. Stops machine and locates defects in matrix, using microscope and magnifying glass. Marks location of defects with bar soap and returns matrix for repair. Notes reasons for rejection on worksheet. Listens to repaired matrices to ensure that defects have been eliminated.
GOE: 06.03.01 STRENGTH: S GED: R3 M2 L2 SVP: 4 DLU: 77

194.387-014 RECORD TESTER (recording)

Inspects and tests sample phonograph records, using optical instruments and audio equipment: Inspects record for defects, such as bumps, stains, or scratches. Compares number imprinted on record with serial number on label to ensure correct labeling. Places record on turntable and guides calibrated microscope over revolving record, observing movement of off-center line of record, to determine if groove centering is within specified tolerances. Plays record on sound-producing equipment, listening for defects, such as pops, ticks, or distortion, and to verify that selections on record conform to printed label. Notes defects and returns record to pressing department.
GOE: 06.03.01 STRENGTH: S GED: R3 M2 L3 SVP: 4 DLU: 77

195 OCCUPATIONS IN SOCIAL AND WELFARE WORK

This group includes occupations concerned with rendering assistance to individuals and groups with problems, such as poverty, illness, family maladjustment, antisocial behavior, financial mismanagement, limited recreation opportunities, and inadequate housing.

195.107-010 CASEWORKER (social ser.) alternate titles: community placement worker; intake worker; social service worker

Counsels and aids individuals and families requiring assistance of social service agency: Interviews clients with problems, such as personal and family adjustments, finances, employment, food, clothing, housing, and physical and mental impairments to determine nature and degree of problem. Secures information, such as medical, psychological, and social factors contributing to client's situation, and evaluates these and client's capacities. Counsels client individually, in family, or in other small groups regarding plans for meeting needs, and aids client to mobilize inner capacities and environmental resources to im-

prove social functioning. Helps client to modify attitudes and patterns of behavior by increasing understanding of self, personal problems, and client's part in creating them. Refers clients to community resources and other organizations. Compiles records and prepares reports. Reviews service plan and performs follow-up to determine quantity and quality of service provided client and status of client's case. Accesses and records client and community resource information, manually or using computer equipped with keyboard, to input and retrieve information. May secure supplementary information, such as employment, medical records, or school reports. May specialize in providing, monitoring, and evaluating services provided to older adults. May determine client's eligibility for financial assistance. May work in collaboration with other professional disciplines. May be required to visit clients in their homes or in institutions. Usually required to have knowledge and skill in case work method acquired through degree program at school of social work. May be required to possess state license or certificate. When rendering advisory services to agencies, groups, or individuals, may be designated Social-Work Consultant, Casework (social ser.). May aid parents with child rearing problems and children and youth with difficulties in social adjustments [CASEWORKER, CHILD WELFARE (social ser.) 195.107-014].
GOE: 10.01.02 STRENGTH: S GED: R5 M3 L5 SVP: 7 DLU: 81

195.107-014 CASEWORKER, CHILD WELFARE (social ser.)

Aids parents with child rearing problems and children and youth with difficulties in social adjustments: Investigates home conditions to protect children from harmful environment. Evaluates children's physical and psychological makeup to determine needs. Refers child and parent or guardian to community resources according to needs of child. Evaluates foster home environmental factors and personal characteristics of adoption applicants to determine suitability of foster home and adoption applicants. Places and is responsible for children and their well-being in foster or adoptive homes, institutions, and medical treatment centers. Counsels children and parents, guardians, foster parents, or institution staff, concerning adjustment to foster home situation, plans for child's care, interactional behavior modifications needed, or rehabilitation. Places children in adoptive homes and counsels adoptive parents pending legal adoption. Provides service to unmarried parents, including care during pregnancy and planning for child. Arranges for day care or homemaker service. Employed in establishments such as child placement (foster care or adoption), protective service, or institution. Maintains case history records and reports. Usually required to have knowledge and skill in casework methods acquired through degree program at school of social work. May specialize in specific area of child-directed casework and be designated according to work performed as Caseworker, Child Placement (social ser.); Caseworker, Protective Services (social ser.). May interview clients for purpose of screening to determine eligibility for agency services and be designated Caseworker, Intake (social ser.).
GOE: 10.01.02 STRENGTH: L GED: R5 M3 L5 SVP: 7 DLU: 81

195.107-018 CASEWORKER, FAMILY (social ser.) alternate titles: family counselor

Aids individuals and families having problems concerning family relationships or other aspects of their social functioning affecting unity of family and welfare of community: Counsels clients on problems, such as unsatisfactory relationships between marriage partners or between parents and children; unwed parenthood; home management; work adjustment; vocational training; need for financial assistance; care of the ill, handicapped, or aged, care of other family members at time of physical or mental illness; desertion of parent; or difficulties encountered in travel or stabilization in new community. Helps clients to use agency's services, such as homemaker, or day care, and other community resources. In a public assistance or voluntary agency ascertains client's eligibility for financial assistance and determines amount of grant and assumes responsibility for services rendered. May assist travelers, runaways of any age, migrants, transients, refugees, repatriated Americans, and problem families drifting from community to community, encountering difficulty in traveling or needing help toward stabilization. Employed in organizations, such as public assistance, family service, Travelers Aid, and American Red Cross Home Service. Usually required to have knowledge and skill in casework methods acquired through degree program at school of social work.
GOE: 10.01.02 STRENGTH: S GED: R5 M4 L5 SVP: 7 DLU: 77

195.107-022 SOCIAL GROUP WORKER (social ser.)

Develops program content, organizes, and leads activities planned to enhance social development of individual members and accomplishment of group goals: Interviews individual members to assess social and emotional capabilities and plans group composition in relation to personal and social compatibility of members. Selects program appropriate to particular group goals, level of development, needs, capacities, and interests of group members. Involves members in planning and assuming responsibility for activities. Helps members through group experience to develop attitudes and social skills for improved family relations and community responsibility. May secure supplementary information, such as medical records and school reports. May work in collaboration with other professional disciplines. Refers members, when indicated, to community resources and other organizations. Employed in agencies, such as community center, settlement house, youth serving organization, institution for children or aged, hospital, or penal institution. Usually required to have skills acquired through degree program at school of social work.
GOE: 10.01.02 STRENGTH: S GED: R5 M3 L5 SVP: 8 DLU: 77

195.107-026 SOCIAL WORKER, DELINQUENCY PREVENTION (social ser.)

Works through community action programs to ameliorate social conditions tending to cause juvenile delinquency and provides counseling and guidance to juveniles: Aids civil authorities to plan urban, suburban, and rural development to ensure provisions for meeting social needs of youth. Works with individuals and groups in danger of becoming delinquent, through individual and group guidance and through use of community resources. Refers juveniles to community agencies, such as settlement houses, child guidance clinics, and health clinics, for mental, physical, and social rehabilitation. Works closely with law enforcement agencies, schools, employers, health, welfare, and recreation agencies. Usually attached to public agency.
GOE: 10.01.02 STRENGTH: L GED: R5 M3 L5 SVP: 8 DLU: 80

195.107-030 SOCIAL WORKER, MEDICAL (profess. & kin.) alternate titles: social worker, clinical; social worker, health services

Assists patients and their families with personal and environmental difficulties which predispose illness or interfere with obtaining maximum benefits from medical care: Works in close collaboration with physicians and other health care personnel in patient evaluation and treatment to further their understanding of significant social and emotional factors underlying patient's health problem. Helps patient and family through individual or group conferences to understand, accept, and follow medical recommendations. Provides service planned to restore patient to optimum social and health adjustment within patient's capacity. Utilizes community resources to assist patient to resume life in community or to learn to live within limits of disability. Prepares patient histories, service plans, and reports. Participates in planning for improving health services by interpreting social factors pertinent to development of program. Provides general direction and supervision to workers engaged in clinic home service program activities. Works in general hospitals, clinics, rehabilitation centers, drug and alcohol abuse centers, or related health programs. May be employed as consultant in other agencies. Usually required to have knowledge and skill in casework methods acquired through degree program at school of social work.
GOE: 10.01.02 STRENGTH: S GED: R5 M3 L5 SVP: 7 DLU: 89

195.107-034 SOCIAL WORKER, PSYCHIATRIC (profess. & kin.) alternate titles: social worker, clinical; social worker, mental

Provides psychiatric social work assistance to mentally or emotionally disturbed patients of hospitals, clinics, and other medical centers, and to their families, collaborating with psychiatric and allied team in diagnosis and treatment plan: Investigates case situations and presents information to PSYCHIATRIST (medical ser.) 070.107-014 and PSYCHOLOGIST, CLINICAL (profess. & kin.) 045.107-022 and other members of health team, on patient's family and social background pertinent to diagnosis and treatment. Helps patients to respond constructively to treatment and assist in adjustment leading to and following discharge. Interprets psychiatric treatment to patient's family and helps to reduce fear and other attitudes obstructing acceptance of psychiatric care and continuation of treatment. Serves as link between patient, psychiatric agency, and community. May work directly in treatment relationship with patients, individually or in groups, in consultation with PSYCHIATRIST (medical ser.). May refer patient or patient's family to other community resources. Usually required to have knowledge and skill in casework methods acquired through degree program at school of social work.
GOE: 10.01.02 STRENGTH: S GED: R5 M3 L5 SVP: 8 DLU: 78

195.107-038 SOCIAL WORKER, SCHOOL (profess. & kin.) alternate titles: home and school visitor; school adjustment counselor; visiting teacher

Aids students with behavioral, mental, emotional or physical problems: Counsels students whose behavior, school progress, or mental or physical handicap or condition indicates need for assistance. Consults with parents, teachers, and other school personnel to determine causes of problems and effect solutions. Arranges for medical, psychiatric, and other tests and examinations that may disclose causes of difficulties and indicate remedial measures. Attempts to alter attitudes and behavior of parents and teachers that cause or aggravate problems. Recommends change of class or school, special tutoring, or other treatment to effect remedy. Serves as liaison between student, home, school, and community resources, such as family service agencies, child guidance clinics, courts, protective services, doctors, and clergy members. Serves as consultant to school personnel regarding students or situations which are not referred for direct service. May lead group counseling sessions to enhance social development of individual members and provide peer support in areas such as grief, stress, or chemical dependency. Usually required to have knowledge and skill in casework methods acquired through degree program at school of social work and certification by state department of education.
GOE: 10.01.02 STRENGTH: L GED: R5 M3 L5 SVP: 7 DLU: 81

195.107-042 CORRECTIONAL-TREATMENT SPECIALIST (social ser.)

Provides casework services for inmates of penal or correctional institution: Interviews inmate and confers with attorneys, judges, and probation officers to compile social history reflecting such factors as nature and extent of inmate's criminality and current and prospective social problems. Analyzes collected data and develops and initiates treatment plan. Interviews inmate and consults with employees of institution, such as supervisory personnel, CLINICAL PSYCHOLOGIST (profess. & kin.) 045.107-022, and CLERGY MEMBER (profess. & kin.) 120.107-010, to evaluate inmate's social progress, and counsels inmate concerning perceived problems. Reports inmate's progress and makes rec-

ommendations to parole officials. Assists inmate with matters concerning detainers, sentences in other jurisdictions, and writs. Confers with inmate's family to identify family needs prior to inmate's release. Occasionally conducts collective counseling for small groups of inmates. Lectures groups of newly admitted inmates to inform them of institution rules and regulations.
GOE: 10.01.02 STRENGTH: S GED: R5 M3 L5 SVP: 7 DLU: 86

195.107-046 PROBATION-AND-PAROLE OFFICER (profess. & kin.)

Counsels juvenile or adult offenders in activities related to legal conditions of probation or parole: Confers with offender, legal representatives, family, and other concerned persons, and reviews documents pertaining to legal and social history of offender to conduct prehearing or presentencing investigations and to formulate rehabilitation plan. Compiles reports, testifies in court, and makes recommendations concerning conditional release or institutionalization of offender. Informs offender or guardian of legal requirements of conditional release, such as visits to office, restitution payments, or educational and employment stipulations. Counsels offender and family or guardian, helps offender to secure education and employment, arranges custodial care, and refers offender to social resources of community to aid in rehabilitation. Evaluates offender's progress on follow-up basis including visits to home, school, and place of employment. Secures remedial action by court if necessary. May be employed by correctional institution, parole board, courts system, or separate agency serving court. May specialize in working with either juvenile or adult offenders. May specialize in working with offenders on probation and be designated Probation Officer (profess. & kin.). May specialize in working with offenders on parole and be designated Parole Officer (profess. & kin.).
GOE: 10.01.02 STRENGTH: L GED: R5 M3 L5 SVP: 7 DLU: 86

195.117-010 ADMINISTRATOR, SOCIAL WELFARE (profess. & kin.) alternate titles: director, social welfare; executive secretary, social welfare; general secretary, social welfare

Directs agency or major function of public or voluntary organization providing services in social welfare field to individuals, groups, or community: Works with board of directors and committees to establish policies and programs and administers such programs. Determines policies and defines scope of services to be rendered within legislative regulations for public welfare agency functioning without board of directors. Assumes responsibility for development and administration of standards and procedures related to personnel, including staff development, budget, and physical facilities. Interprets agency purpose and program to community. Establishes and maintains relationships with other agencies and organizations in community toward meeting community needs and services. Prepares, distributes, and maintains variety of reports. Inspects agency operations and facilities to ensure agency meets standards and procedures criteria. May direct or coordinate fund raising, public relations, and fact finding or research activities. Employed in settings such as child welfare, community welfare councils, family casework, youth serving agencies, health organizations, informal education, and recreation, including scouting and Y's, public welfare, and fund raising. May work in specific area of social welfare and be designated Director, Child Support Enforcement Program (profess. & kin.); Director, Community Center (profess. & kin.); Director, Social Service (profess. & kin.); Director, Rehabilitation Program (profess. & kin.); Director, Mental Health Agency (profess. & kin.).
GOE: 11.07.01 STRENGTH: S GED: R5 M3 L5 SVP: 8 DLU: 80

195.137-010 CASEWORK SUPERVISOR (social ser.) alternate titles: case supervisor; social work unit supervisor

Supervises and coordinates activities of social-service-agency staff and volunteers, and students of school of social work: Assigns caseloads and related duties, and coordinates activities of staff in providing counseling services to assist clients with problems of emergency or crisis nature. Assists agency staff members through individual and group conferences in analyzing case problems and in improving their diagnostic and helping skills. Reviews case records and evaluates performance of staff members and recommends indicated action. Participates in developing and implementing agency administrative policy. Counsels clients individually or in groups on planned or experimental basis and in emergencies. Trains new employees in areas such as agency policy, department procedures, and agency or government regulations. Provides in-service training for experienced workers in areas such as new policies, procedures, and regulations. Represents agency in community or in interagency activities. May conduct or direct staff development programs. May train workers in use of computer. Employed in areas such as child welfare, community welfare councils, family casework, youth services, senior citizen services, health services, public welfare, probation and parole, housing relocation, education, and rehabilitation. Usually required to have master's degree from school of social work.
GOE: 10.01.02 STRENGTH: S GED: R5 M3 L5 SVP: 7 DLU: 80

195.164-010 GROUP WORKER (social ser.)

Organizes and leads groups, such as senior citizens, children, and street gangs, in activities that meet interests of individual members: Develops recreational, physical education, and cultural programs for various age groups. Demonstrates and instructs participants in activities, such as active sports, group dances and games, arts, crafts, and dramatics. Organizes current-events discussion groups, conducts consumer problem surveys, and performs similar activities to stimulate interest in civic responsibility. Promotes group work concept of enabling members to develop their own program activities through encouragement and leadership of membership discussions. Consults with other community resources regarding specific individuals, and makes referral when indi-

cated. Keeps records. May recruit, train, and supervise paid staff and volunteers. Employed in settings, such as community center, neighborhood or settlement house, hospital, institution for children or aged, youth centers, and housing projects.
GOE: 09.01.01 STRENGTH: L GED: R5 M4 L5 SVP: 7 DLU: 77

195.167-010 COMMUNITY ORGANIZATION WORKER (social ser.) alternate titles: community service consultant; information and referral director; program consultant
Plans, organizes, and coordinates programs with agencies and groups concerned with social problems of community: Promotes and coordinates activities of agencies, groups, and individuals to meet identified needs. Studies and assesses strength and weakness of existing resources. Interprets needs, programs, and services to agencies, groups, and individuals involved and provides leadership and assistance. Prepares reports and disseminates information. Maintains contact with representatives of other organizations to exchange and update information on resources and services available. May write proposals to obtain government or private funding for projects designed to meet needs of community. May assist in budget preparation and presentation. May assist in raising funds. Works in specialized fields such as housing, urban renewal and redevelopment, and health or in public or voluntary coordinating agency, such as community welfare or health council, or combined fund raising and welfare planning council. Works with special groups such as elderly, financially disadvantaged, juvenile delinquents, or physically or mentally handicapped. Usually required to have degree from school of social work. May direct and coordinate activities of volunteers or practicum students.
GOE: 11.07.01 STRENGTH: S GED: R5 M3 L5 SVP: 8 DLU: 81

195.167-014 COMMUNITY-RELATIONS-AND-SERVICES ADVISOR, PUBLIC HOUSING (social ser.) alternate titles: tenant relations coordinator
Promotes tenant welfare in low income public housing developments: Initiates and maintains liaison between local housing authority and voluntary and public agencies for development and managements of public housing developments. Facilitates establishment of constructive relationships between tenants and housing management, and among tenants. Secures social services, such as health, welfare, and education programs for improving family and community standards. Provides leadership to tenants in development of group activities, such as adult education and recreation. Refers families with personal problems to community resources. Cooperates with other organizations in development of understanding and interest among voluntary and public agencies participating in long range plans for urban improvement.
GOE: 11.07.01 STRENGTH: S GED: R5 M3 L5 SVP: 7 DLU: 77

195.167-018 DIRECTOR, CAMP (social ser.)
Directs activities of recreation or youth work camp: Plans programs of recreational and educational activities. Hires and supervises camp staff. Arranges for required licenses, certificates, and insurance coverage to meet health, safety, and welfare standards for campers and for camp operation. Keeps records regarding finances, personnel actions, enrollments, and program activities related to camp business operations and budget allotments.
GOE: 11.11.02 STRENGTH: S GED: R5 M4 L5 SVP: 7 DLU: 77

195.167-022 DIRECTOR, FIELD (social ser.) alternate titles: field director
Coordinates activities of civilian aids engaged in providing recreational and welfare services to armed forces personnel: Directs staff in planning and arranging recreational activities. Oversees activities of welfare workers in assisting service personnel to solve personal and family problems. May plan and direct organization of specialized services in foreign cities to meet needs of service personnel and dependents stationed abroad.
GOE: 11.07.01 STRENGTH: S GED: R5 M4 L5 SVP: 7 DLU: 77

195.167-026 DIRECTOR, RECREATION CENTER (social ser.)
Plans, organizes, and directs comprehensive public and voluntary recreation programs at recreation building, indoor center, playground, playfield, or day camp: Studies and analyzes recreational needs and resources. Oversees and assigns duties to staff. Interprets recreation programs and their philosophy to individuals and groups through personal participation and staff assignments. Schedules maintenance and use of facilities. Coordinates recreation program of host agency, such as settlement house, institution for children or aged, hospital, armed services, or penal institution, with related activity programs of other services or allied agencies. Cooperates with recreation and nonrecreation personnel. Works under direction of RECREATION SUPERVISOR (profess. & kin.).
GOE: 11.11.02 STRENGTH: L GED: R5 M3 L5 SVP: 7 DLU: 77

195.167-038 REHABILITATION CENTER MANAGER (government ser.)
Coordinates activities and provides for physical and emotional needs of public-welfare recipients housed in indigent camp: Cooperates with welfare department investigators, psychologists, and physicians in assigning activities to indigents and in providing specialized attention to them in accordance with recommendations. Appoints leaders of activities, such as food preparation and maintenance of grounds, from camp inmates in accord with democratic leadership principles and welfare department policy. Coordinates sanitation, food management, health, education, spiritual counseling, and vocational activity programs in conformity with available facilities, needs of camp inmates, and policy

of department. Interviews inmates and arranges with business and community leaders to place them in jobs. Maintains discipline and arbitrates disputes. Arranges for entertainment, such as movies, lectures, and musical programs. Maintains camp records, inventories supplies, and submits requisitions for camp needs.
GOE: 11.07.01 STRENGTH: L GED: R5 M4 L5 SVP: 7 DLU: 77

195.167-042 ALCOHOL-AND-DRUG-ABUSE-ASSISTANCE PROGRAM ADMINISTRATOR (government ser.)
Coordinates government programs dealing with prevention and treatment of alcohol and drug abuse problems affecting work performance of employees in private and public sectors of work force: Studies composition of industrial and business communities and state agencies to determine methods of promoting information concerning alcohol and drug abuse prevention and treatment programs to executives and administrators in industry and government. Confers with management personnel to explain purpose and benefits of Employee Assistance Program, and attempts to establish programs in establishments, organizations, and agencies. Consults with representatives of Area Service Providers (professionals in health care, counseling, and other special services) to develop participation in prevention and treatment programs. Instructs personnel in methods of recognizing and identifying employee problems, referring employee to community Area Service Providers, and maintaining records of program-related activities. Consults with management and administrators of participating organizations and Area Service Providers to evaluate progress of program and identify administrative problems. Implements corrective action plan to solve problems. Develops training materials to be used by participating organizations and Area Service Providers. Prepares articles for newspaper and other media to explain purpose of program. Lectures and participates in workshops, radio and television interviews, community meetings, and other organizational functions to promote acceptance and support of program. Prepares grant proposals and reports for submission to department supervisor.
GOE: 11.07.01 STRENGTH: L GED: R5 M3 L5 SVP: 7 DLU: 86

195.227-010 PROGRAM AIDE, GROUP WORK (social ser.) alternate titles: group leader
Leads group work activities, as directed by agency program staff: Receives instructions from PROGRAM DIRECTOR, GROUP WORK (profess. & kin.) 187.117-046 or GROUP WORKER (social ser.) 195.164-010 prior to initiating therapeutic group activities. Plans program details to meet needs and interests of individual members. Interests participants in various activities, such as arts and crafts and dramatics. Demonstrates techniques for active sports, group dances, and games. Helps develop new skills and interests. May work with part-time or volunteer staff. Works for social service agencies, such as community center, neighborhood house, settlement house, hospital, geriatric residential center, and health care facility.
GOE: 10.02.02 STRENGTH: L GED: R5 M3 L4 SVP: 6 DLU: 89

195.227-014 RECREATION LEADER (social ser.)
Conducts recreation activities with assigned groups in public department of voluntary agency: Organizes, promotes, and develops interest in activities, such as arts and crafts, sports, games, music, dramatics, social recreation, camping, and hobbies. Cooperates with other staff members in conducting community wide events and works with neighborhood groups to determine recreation interests and needs of persons of all ages. Works under close supervision of RECREATION SUPERVISOR (profess. & kin.) 187.167-238. Cooperates with recreation and nonrecreation personnel when in agency setting, such as settlement house, institution for children or aged, hospital, armed services, or penal institution.
GOE: 09.01.01 STRENGTH: L GED: R4 M3 L4 SVP: 6 DLU: 81

195.227-018 TEACHER, HOME THERAPY (social ser.) alternate titles: child development specialist; development disability specialist; infant educator; parent trainer
Instructs parent of mentally- and physically-handicapped children in therapy techniques and behavior modification: Observes and plays with child and confers with child's parents and other professionals periodically to obtain information relating to child's mental and physical development. Evaluates child's responses to determine levels of child's physical and mental development. Determines parent's ability to comprehend and apply therapeutic and behavior modification techniques and parent's social and emotional needs to formulate teaching plan. Develops individual teaching plan covering self-help, motor, social, cognitive, and language skills development for parents to implement in home. Instructs parents individually or in groups in behavior modification, physical development, language development, and conceptual learning exercises and activities. Revises teaching plan to correspond with child's rate of development. Counsels parents and organizes groups of parents in similar situations to provide social and emotional support for parents. Refers parents and child to social service agencies and facilities for additional services and financial assistance. Consults and coordinates plans with other professionals. Teaches preschool subjects, such as limited vocabulary sign language and color recognition, to children capable of learning such subjects.
GOE: 10.02.03 STRENGTH: L GED: R5 M3 L5 SVP: 7 DLU: 86

195.267-010 ELIGIBILITY WORKER (government ser.)
Interviews applicants or recipients to determine eligibility for public assistance: Interprets and explains rules and regulations governing eligibility and grants, methods of payment, and legal rights to applicant or recipient. Records

and evaluates personal and financial data obtained from applicant or recipient to determine initial or continuing eligibility, according to departmental directives. Initiates procedures to grant, modify, deny, or terminate eligibility and grants for various aid programs, such as public welfare, employment, and medical assistance. Authorizes amount of grants, based on determination of eligibility for amount of money payments, food stamps, medical care, or other general assistance. Identifies need for social services, and makes referrals to various agencies and community resources available. Prepares regular and special reports as required, and submits individual recommendations for consideration by supervisor. Prepares and keeps records of assigned cases.
GOE: 07.01.01 STRENGTH: S GED: R4 M3 L4 SVP: 6 DLU: 77

195.267-018 PATIENT-RESOURCES-AND-REIMBURSEMENT AGENT (government ser.)

Investigates financial assets, properties, and resources of hospitalized retarded and brain-damaged clients to protect financial interests and provide reimbursement of hospital costs: Visits and interviews or contacts by mail or telephone relatives, friends, former employers, pension funds, fraternal and veterans organizations and government agencies. Records documentation of financial resources in patient files. Analyzes data accumulated, such as disability allowances, medicare, medicaid, social security pension, dividends, interest, and insurance, and determines ability to pay for hospitalization. Determines additional sources from which reimbursements can be obtained. Prepares reports and enumerates amounts and sources of reimbursements, including public assistance from social agencies in behalf of patients and families. Reviews patients' records to ensure that reimbursements are maintained. Applies for appointment of conservators to financially protect patients with assets over statutory limits and submits names of appointees to courts. Occasionally attends court hearings to protect patient interests.
GOE: 10.01.02 STRENGTH: L GED: R5 M3 L5 SVP: 7 DLU: 86

195.267-022 CHILD SUPPORT OFFICER (government ser.)

Investigates and analyzes child welfare cases and initiates administrative action to facilitate enforcement of child support laws: Reviews application for child support received from client and examines case file to determine that divorce decree and court ordered judgement for payment are in order. Interviews client to obtain information, such as relocation of absent parent, amount of child support previously awarded, and names of persons who can act as witnesses to support client's claim for support. Locates absent parent and interviews parent to gather data, such as support award, and discusses case with parent to resolve issues in lieu of filing court proceedings. Contacts friends and relatives of child's parents to verify gathered information about case. Computes amount of child support payments. Prepares file indicating data, such as wage records of accused, witnesses, and blood test results. Confers with prosecuting attorney to prepare court case. Determines type of court jurisdiction, according to facts and circumstances surrounding case, and files court action. Confers with court clerk to obtain arrest warrant and to schedule court date for hearing or trial. Monitors child support payments awarded by court to ensure compliance and enforcement of child support laws. Prepares report of legal action taken when delinquency in payments occurs.
GOE: 10.01.02 STRENGTH: S GED: R5 M3 L5 SVP: 7 DLU: 89

195.367-010 CASE AIDE (social ser.) alternate titles: community program aide

Performs community contact work on simpler aspects of programs or cases and assists in providing services to clients and family members, under close and regular supervision and tutorage of CASEWORKER (social ser.) 195.107-010 or CASEWORK SUPERVISOR (social ser.) 195.137-010. Assists in locating housing for displaced individuals and families. Monitors free, supplementary meal program administered by agencies for children and youth from low-income families to ensure cleanliness of facility and that eligibility guidelines are met for persons receiving meals. Assists elderly clients in preparation of forms, such as tax and rent refund forms. Accompanies elderly clients on visits to social, charitable, and government agencies to assist clients with their problems. Submits to and reviews reports and problems with superior. May be designated according to clients serviced as Senior Service Aide (social ser.); Youth Nutritional Monitor (social ser.).
GOE: 10.01.02 STRENGTH: L GED: R4 M3 L3 SVP: 3 DLU: 80

195.367-014 MANAGEMENT AIDE (social ser.)

Aids residents of public and private housing projects and apartments in relocation and provides information concerning regulations, facilities, and services: Explains rules established by owner or management, such as sanitation and maintenance requirements, and parking regulations. Demonstrates use and care of equipment for tenant use. Informs tenants of facilities, such as laundries and playgrounds. Advises homemakers needing assistance in child care, food, money management, and housekeeping problems. Provides information on location and nature of available community services, such as clinics and recreation centers. Keeps records and prepares reports for owner or manangement.
GOE: 07.01.01 STRENGTH: L GED: R4 M3 L4 SVP: 5 DLU: 77

195.367-018 COMMUNITY WORKER (government ser.)

Investigates problems of assigned community and of individuals disadvantaged because of income, age, or other economic or personal handicaps to determine needs: Seeks out, interviews, and assists persons in need of agency services, under direction of professional staff, or refers persons to specific agencies for service. Visits individuals and families in their homes to explain sup-

portive services and resources available to persons needing special assistance. Speaks before neighborhood groups to establish communication and rapport between persons in community and agency, to publicize supportive services available, and to assist in resolving problems facing community concerning housing, urban renewal, education, welfare, unemployment insurance, and crime prevention. Follows up all contacts and prepares and submits reports of activities. May maintain files and records of work activities to provide access to and retrieval of data. May work for police department for purpose of establishing communication between citizens and police officials to promote understanding of functions, purpose, and goals of police in community and assists in resolution of community problems.
GOE: 10.01.02 STRENGTH: L GED: R4 M3 L4 SVP: 6 DLU: 86

195.367-022 FOOD-MANAGEMENT AIDE (government ser.) alternate titles: nutrition aide

Advises low-income family members how to plan, budget, shop, prepare balanced meals, and handle and store food, following prescribed standards: Advises clients of advantages of food stamps, how to obtain stamps, and use of stamps during shopping trips. Transports clients to shopping area, using automobile. Observes clients' food selections. Recommends alternate economical and nutritional food choices. Observes and discusses meal preparation. Suggests alternate methods of food preparation. Assists in planning of food budget, utilizing charts and sample budgets. Advises clients on preferred methods of sanitation. Consults with supervisor concerning programs for individual families. Maintains records concerning results of family visits.
GOE: 10.01.02 STRENGTH: L GED: R3 M2 L3 SVP: 3 DLU: 86

195.367-026 PREPAROLE-COUNSELING AIDE (government ser.)

Provides individual and group guidance to inmates of correctional facility, who are eligible for parole, and assists in developing vocational and educational plans in preparing inmates for reentry into community life: Conducts inmate orientation sessions to explain programs and resources available to inmates and to induce inmates to join programs. Interviews inmates to record data on individual problems, needs, interests, and attitude. Holds individual and group counseling sessions to discuss programs available that affect inmate's reentry into community life, such as housing and financial aid, veteran's benefits, work release programs, vocational rehabilitation, and job search assistance. Prepares and maintains case folder for each inmate and discusses findings with supervisor to obtain assistance in establishing goals and plan of action for inmates. Conducts followup interview to ascertain inmate progress. Prepares correspondence and applications for medicare, medicaid, veteran benefits, food stamps, and housing. Telephones and corresponds with persons and agencies outside facility to ensure that family and business matters are attended to. Meets with family members at facility to discuss and resolve problems prior to release of inmate. Develops and prepares informational packets for inmate, listing outside agencies and programs that could assist ex-offender upon release.
GOE: 10.01.02 STRENGTH: S GED: R4 M2 L4 SVP: 6 DLU: 86

195.367-030 RECREATION AIDE (social ser.)

Assists RECREATION LEADER (social ser.) 195.227-014 in conducting recreation activities in community center or other voluntary recreation facility: Arranges chairs, tables, and sporting or exercise equipment in designated rooms or other areas for scheduled group activities, such as banquets, wedding receptions, parties, group meetings, or sports events. Welcomes visitors and answers incoming telephone calls. Notifies patrons of activity schedules and registration requirements. Monitors spectators and participants at sports events to ensure orderly conduct. Receives, stores, and issues sports equipment and supplies. May keep attendance records or scores at sporting events, operate audiovisual equipment, monitor activities of children during recreational trips or tours, or perform other duties as directed by RECREATION LEADER (social ser.) 195.227-014.
GOE: 09.01.01 STRENGTH: L GED: R3 M2 L3 SVP: 2 DLU: 86

195.367-034 SOCIAL-SERVICES AIDE (social ser.)

Assists professional staff of public social service agency, performing any combination of following tasks: Interviews individuals and family members to compile information on social, educational, criminal, institutional, or drug history. Visits individuals in homes or attends group meetings to provide information on agency services, requirements, and procedures. Provides rudimentary counseling to agency clients. Oversees day-to-day group activities of residents in institution. Meets with youth groups to acquaint them with consequences of delinquent acts. Refers individuals to various public or private agencies for assistance. May care for children in client's home during client's appointments. May accompany handicapped individuals to appointments.
GOE: 10.01.02 STRENGTH: L GED: R4 M3 L4 SVP: 6 DLU: 86

196   AIRPLANE PILOTS AND NAVIGATORS

This group includes occupations concerned with piloting airplanes for the transportation of passengers, freight, and mail, and other purposes, such as crop dusting and the testing of new models; and charting the courses of planes by the use of instruments, charts, celestial observation, and dead reckoning. Must be federally licensed. Includes occupations concerned with the supervision of flight operations and maintenance when a pilot's or navigator's license is required. Includes flight instructors. Ground school instructors are included in Group 099.

196.163-010 FLIGHT-OPERATIONS INSPECTOR (government ser.) alternate titles: air-carrier operations inspector

Conducts examinations and flight tests to determine individual's ability to qualify for aircraft pilot's license. Administers both oral and written examinations to determine applicant's knowledge of flight rules and regulations, communications, and airport landing procedures. Accompanies pilot on check flight to assess flying skill, stability under emergency conditions, and ability to maintain control of aircraft under flying emergencies. Issues pilot's license to individuals meeting standards. Investigates aircraft accidents and complaints to determine cause and responsibility. Prepares accident and flight activity reports. Recommends changes in federal flight rules and regulations based on knowledge of operating conditions, aircraft improvements, and other factors. Observes flight activities of crop dusters, flying schools charter services, private pilots, and other licensed aircraft owners within assigned geographical area to ensure conformance to flight and safety regulations.

GOE: 05.04.01 STRENGTH: L GED: R5 M4 L5 SVP: 8 DLU: 77

196.163-014 SUPERVISING AIRPLANE PILOT (government ser.)

Plans, supervises, and participates in activities of personnel engaged in Federal Aviation Administration inflight testing of air navigational aids, air traffic controls, communications equipment, and sites of proposed equipment installations: Schedules and coordinates inflight testing program with ground support crews, air traffic, and military personnel to assure ground tracking, equipment monitoring, and related services. Conducts regularly scheduled and special flights to test equipment under all types of flight conditions including adverse weather, using both manual and automatic controls. Prepares evaluation reports of flight activities and reviews reports prepared by FACILITIES-FLIGHT-CHECK PILOTS (government ser.). Recommends promotion, transfer, and discharge of personnel and authorizes leave. Recommends purchase, repair, or modification of equipment.

GOE: 05.04.01 STRENGTH: L GED: R5 M5 L5 SVP: 8 DLU: 77

196.167-010 CHIEF PILOT (air trans.) alternate titles: airplane pilot, chief

Directs operation of flight department of airline: Conducts indoctrination training for new pilots and refresher training for experienced pilots. Reviews reports on pilot performance and forwards reports to Federal Aviation Administration. Discusses operational and personal problems with subordinates to improve morale and efficiency. Studies technical manuals of airplane and equipment manufacturers and government regulations affecting flight operations to ensure that company training manuals adhere to legal requirements and are adapted to type of aircraft in use. Represents company in advisory capacity during contract negotiations with pilots' union. Accompanies flights to observe performance of pilots [CHECK PILOT (air trans.)]. Conducts training classes for flight personnel covering emergency procedures and use of survival equipment. Directs preparation of flight-crew schedules and assignment of personnel. May interview and hire flight personnel. May pilot airplane on scheduled flights.

GOE: 05.04.01 STRENGTH: L GED: R5 M4 L5 SVP: 9 DLU: 77

196.167-014 NAVIGATOR (air trans.) alternate titles: aerial navigator; airplane navigator

Locates position and directs course of airplane on international flights, using navigational aids, such as charts, maps, sextant, and slide rule: Establishes position of airplane by use of navigation instruments and charts, celestial observation, or dead reckoning. Directs deviations from course required by weather conditions, such as wind drifts and forecasted atmospheric changes. Utilizes navigation aids, such as radio beams and beacons, when available. Keeps log of flight. Must be licensed by Federal Aviation Administration.

GOE: 05.03.01 STRENGTH: S GED: R5 M5 L4 SVP: 6 DLU: 77

196.223-010 INSTRUCTOR, FLYING I (education)

Instructs student pilots in flight procedures and techniques: Accompanies students on training flights and demonstrates techniques for controlling aircraft during taxiing, takeoff, spins, stalls, turns, and landings. Explains operation of aircraft components, such as rudder, flaps, ailerons, compass, altimeter, and tachometer. May give student proficiency tests at termination of training. Is required to hold Commercial Pilot's Certificate, with Instructor's Rating, issued by Federal Aviation Administration.

GOE: 05.04.01 STRENGTH: L GED: R5 M4 L5 SVP: 7 DLU: 77

196.223-014 INSTRUCTOR, PILOT (air trans.)

Trains new and experienced company AIRLINE PILOTS (air trans.) in policy and in use of equipment: Instructs new pilots in company regulations and procedures and trains pilots in operation of types of aircraft used by company. Conducts courses for experienced company pilots to familiarize them with new equipment. May conduct review courses in navigation and meteorology. May make flights to observe performance of pilots [CHECK PILOT (air trans.)]. Must hold Commercial Pilot's Certificate, with Instructor's Rating, issued by Federal Aviation Administration.

GOE: 05.04.01 STRENGTH: L GED: R5 M4 L5 SVP: 8 DLU: 77

196.263-010 AIRPLANE PILOT (agriculture) alternate titles: aerial-applicator pilot; agricultural-aircraft pilot; aircraft pilot; airplane pilot, crop dusting

Pilots airplane or helicopter, at low altitudes, over agricultural fields to dust or spray fields with seeds, fertilizers, or pesticides: Pilots aircraft over field, or drives to field, or studies maps to become acquainted with obstacles or haz-

ards, such as air turbulence, hedgerows, and hills, peculiar to particular field. Arranges for warning signals to be posted. Notifies livestock owners to move livestock from property over which harmful material may drift. Signals AIRPLANE-PILOT HELPER (agriculture) 409.667-010 to load aircraft. Pilots aircraft to dust or spray fields with seeds, fertilizers, or pesticides, and observes field markers and flag waved by AIRPLANE-PILOT HELPER (agriculture) on ground to prevent overlaps of application and to ensure coverage of field. May be accompanied by property owner when piloting aircraft to survey field. May specialize in application of pesticides and be designated Pest-Control Pilot (agriculture).

GOE: 05.04.01 STRENGTH: L GED: R4 M4 L4 SVP: 6 DLU: 81

196.263-014 AIRPLANE PILOT, COMMERCIAL (air trans.) alternate titles: commercial pilot; pilot

Pilots airplane to transport passengers, mail, or freight, or for other commercial purposes: Reviews ship's papers to ascertain factors, such as load weight, fuel supply, weather conditions, and flight route and schedule. Orders changes in fuel supply, load, route, or schedule to ensure safety of flight. Reads gauges to verify that oil, hydraulic fluid, fuel quantities, and cabin pressure are at prescribed levels prior to starting engines. Starts engines and taxies airplane to runway. Sets brakes, and accelerates engines to verify operational readiness of components, such as superchargers, carburetor-heaters, and controls. Contacts control tower by radio to obtain takeoff clearance and instructions. Releases brakes and moves throttles and hand and foot controls to take off and control airplane in flight. Pilots airplane to destination adhering to flight plan and regulations and procedures of federal government, company, and airport. Logs information, such as time in flight, altitude flown, and fuel consumed. Must hold commercial pilot's certificate issued by Federal Aviation Administration. May instruct students or pilots in operation of aircraft. May be designated according to federal license held as Transport Pilot (air trans.), or type of commercial activity engaged in as Airplane Pilot (air trans.) or Corporate Pilot (air trans.). May be designated Airplane-Patrol Pilot (business ser.) when piloting airplane over pipelines, train tracks, and communications systems to detect and radio location and nature of damage. May be designated Airplane Captain (air trans.) when in command of aircraft and crew or Airplane First-Officer (air trans.) or Copilot (air trans.) when second in command.

GOE: 05.04.01 STRENGTH: L GED: R5 M4 L4 SVP: 8 DLU: 81

196.263-018 AIRPLANE PILOT, PHOTOGRAMMETRY (business ser.)

Pilots airplane or helicopter at specified altitudes and airspeeds, following designated flight lines, to photograph areas of earth's surface for mapping and other photogrammetric purposes: Sights along pointers (window blocking) on aircraft to topographical landmarks. Adjusts controls to hold aircraft on course, to ensure required overlap with photographs taken on previous flight line, and to select landmark points as guide for next flight line. Observes dials and moves controls to hold aircraft in level flight to eliminate contour errors in photographs caused by forward and lateral tilt of aircraft.

GOE: 05.04.01 STRENGTH: L GED: R5 M4 L4 SVP: 7 DLU: 77

196.263-022 CHECK PILOT (air trans.)

Accompanies AIRPLANE CAPTAINS (air trans.) and AIRPLANE FIRST-OFFICERS (air trans.) periodically, to test and review their proficiency: Observes and evaluates pilot knowledge and skills, utilizing such means as technical manuals, check lists, and proficiency tests. Notes compliance with and infringement of company or Federal Aviation Administration flight regulations. Compiles and issues reports on findings to appropriate company and Federal Aviation Administration officials.

GOE: 05.04.01 STRENGTH: S GED: R5 M4 L5 SVP: 8 DLU: 77

196.263-026 CONTROLLER, REMOTELY-PILOTED VEHICLE (aircraft mfg.)

Directs flight path of remotely-piloted (drone) photo reconnaissance or target aircraft along predetermined flight course from command center in guide aircraft or ground station: Operates aircraft controls from command center by remote radio and closed circuit video transmission to direct aircraft to take off, follow flight path, and land, utilizing knowledge of aircraft navigation and aircraft flight characteristics. Analyzes performance data and prepares reports covering airframe, guidance, power plant, and mechanical controls of aircraft after ground or flight testing. Confers with engineering, inspecting, and manufacturing personnel concerning success of flight tested aircraft or need for corrective action. May assist with preflight inspection of aircraft. May direct flight path of guided missiles, utilizing remote computerized controls, and be designated Missile-Control Pilot (aircraft mfg.).

GOE: 05.04.01 STRENGTH: L GED: R5 M5 L4 SVP: 8 DLU: 87

196.263-030 EXECUTIVE PILOT (any industry) alternate titles: company pilot; corporation pilot; private pilot

Pilots company-owned aircraft to transport company officials or customers, and makes preflight and inflight tests to ensure safety of flight: Files flight plan with airport officials. Obtains weather data and interprets data based on flight plan. Operates radio equipment aboard airplane. May maintain and repair aircraft according to limitations set by A&E license. May represent company on executive level when dealing with business associates, officials, and customers.

GOE: 05.04.01 STRENGTH: L GED: R5 M4 L5 SVP: 7 DLU: 77

196.263-034 FACILITIES-FLIGHT-CHECK PILOT (government ser.)

Operates airplane equipped with special radio, radar, and other electronic equipment to conduct in-flight testing of air navigational aids, air traffic con-

trols, and communications equipment, and to evaluate sites of proposed equipment installation: Plans flight activities in accordance with test schedule. Plots flight pattern and files flight plan. Informs crewmembers of flight and test procedures. Coordinates flight activities with ground-support crews and air-traffic control. Operates aircraft over designated area at specified altitudes in all types of weather to determine receptivity and other characteristics of airport-control signal and navigation and communications equipment and systems, such as racon, tacan, scater, and atis. Prepares evaluation reports of each flight. Conducts periodic preflight checks of aircraft to ensure proper maintenance and safe operation.
GOE: 05.04.01 STRENGTH: L GED: R5 M5 L4 SVP: 8 DLU: 77

196.263-038 HELICOPTER PILOT (any industry)
Pilots helicopter for purposes such as transporting passengers and cargo: Plans flight, following government and company regulations, and using aeronautical charts and navigation instruments. Inspects helicopter prior to departure to detect leaking hydraulic fluid, inoperative control, low fuel level, or other unsafe condition, following checklist. Pilots helicopter to transport passengers and cargo, conduct search and rescue missions, fight fires, report on traffic conditions, or other purpose. Writes specified information in flight record. May instruct students in operation of helicopter and equipment. Must hold type of pilot's license and certification specified by Federal Aviation Administration for work performed.
GOE: 05.04.01 STRENGTH: L GED: R4 M4 L4 SVP: 7 DLU: 81

196.263-042 TEST PILOT (aircraft mfg.) alternate titles: engineering test pilot
Pilots new, prototype, experimental, modified, and production aircraft to evaluate factors such as aircraft's airworthiness, performance, systems operation, and design: Inspects or oversees inspection of aircraft prior to flight to ensure aircraft's readiness for flight. Starts and warms engine, listens to engine sounds at various speeds, and monitors instruments to detect malfunctions. Taxies aircraft to test controls, brakes, and shock absorbers. Radios control tower for takeoff instructions, releases brakes, and moves throttles and hand and foot controls to take off and control aircraft in flight. Operates aircraft controls to perform maneuvers, such as stalls, dives, loops, rolls, turns, and speed runs, to test and evaluate stability, control characteristics, and aerodynamic design. Observes recording, measuring, and operating instruments and equipment during test flight to evaluate aircraft's performance. Prepares report of test results and collaborates with engineering personnel to analyze test data. Assists engineers in preparing master flight plans for testing purposes. May provide instructions for adjustments or replacement of parts. May deliver aircraft to designated receiving point. May train customer in operation of aircraft.
GOE: 05.04.01 STRENGTH: M GED: R5 M4 L4 SVP: 8 DLU: 88

197 SHIP CAPTAINS, MATES, PILOTS, AND ENGINEERS

This group includes occupations concerned with managing and operating vessels. Includes occupations concerned with technical supervision of marine operations for a group of vessels; administrative and technical responsibility for the operation, maintenance, and safety of a passenger or cargo vessel; the planning and supervision of operations and maintenance in the deck and engine departments of a vessel; administration of business affairs, such as purchasing, disbursing, and ensuring compliance with customs and immigration regulations, aboard a vessel; and piloting vessels through rivers, straits, and harbors.

197.130-010 ENGINEER (water trans.) alternate titles: marine engineer; mechanic, marine engine
Supervises and coordinates activities of crew engaged in operating and maintaining propulsion engines and other engines, boilers, deck machinery, and electrical, refrigeration, and sanitary equipment aboard ship: Inspects engines and other equipment and orders crew to repair or replace defective parts. Starts engines to propel ship and regulates engines and power transmission to control speed of ship. Stands engine-room watch during specified periods, observing that required water levels are maintained in boilers, condensers, and evaporators, load on generators is within acceptable limits, and oil and grease cups are kept full. Repairs machinery, using handtools and power tools. Maintains engineering log and bell book (orders for changes in speed and direction of ship). May be required to hold appropriate U.S. Coast Guard license, depending upon tonnage of ship, type of engines, and means of transmitting power to propeller shaft. When more than one ENGINEER (water trans.) is required, may be designated Engineer, Chief (water trans.); Engineer, First Assistant (water trans.); Engineer, Second Assistant (water trans.); Engineer, Third Assistant (water trans.). May be designated according to ship assigned as Barge Engineer (water trans.); Cannery-Tender Engineer (water trans.); Engineer, Fishing Vessel (water trans.); Tugboat Engineer (water trans.). May be designated Cadet Engineer (water trans.) when in training.
GOE: 05.06.02 STRENGTH: M GED: R4 M3 L3 SVP: 8 DLU: 77

197.133-010 CAPTAIN, FISHING VESSEL (fishing & hunt.) alternate titles: skipper
Commands fishing vessel crew engaged in catching fish and other marine life: Interviews, hires, and gives instructions to crew, and assigns crew to watches and quarters. Plots courses on navigation charts and computes positions, using standard navigation aids, such as compass, sextant, clock, radio fix,

and navigation tables. Steers vessel and operates electronic equipment, such as radio, sonic depth finder, and radar. Directs fishing operations, using knowledge of fishing grounds and work load capacities of vessel and crew. Records daily activities in ship's log. May purchase supplies and equipment for boat, such as food, fuel, webbing, rope, and cable. May tow and maneuver fish barges at cannery wharf. May contact buyers and make arrangements for sale of catch. May buy fish for resale and be designated Buy-Boat Operator (fishing & hunt.), or haul fish from other fishing vessels to cannery and be designated Captain, Cannery Tender (fishing & hunt.).
GOE: 05.04.02 STRENGTH: L GED: R4 M4 L4 SVP: 7 DLU: 77

197.133-014 MASTER, YACHT (water trans.)
Commands yacht cruising on oceans, bays, lakes, and coastal waters: Sets course of yacht, using navigational aids, such as charts, area plotting sheets, compass, and sextant, and steers yacht to avoid reefs, outlying shoals, and other hazards to shipping. Determines geographical position of yacht, using loran or azimuths of celestial bodies. Signals passing ships, using whistle, flashing lights, flags, and radio. Calculates landfall (sighting of land), using electronic sounding devices and following contour lines on chart. Approaches land, utilizing aids to navigation, such as lights, lighthouses, and buoys. Relinquishes command of yacht to PILOT, SHIP (water trans.) to guide yacht through hazardous waters. Maintains yacht's log. May be licensed by U.S. Coast Guard for steam or motor yacht according to waters navigated and tonnage of yacht. May be designated according to waters licensed to navigate as Master, Coastwise Yacht (water trans.); Master, Ocean Yacht (water trans.); or according to yacht commanded as Master, Steam Yacht (water trans.).
GOE: 05.04.02 STRENGTH: L GED: R4 M4 L4 SVP: 8 DLU: 77

197.133-018 MATE, FISHING VESSEL (fishing & hunt.) alternate titles: fishing captain
Supervises and coordinates activities of crew aboard fishing vessel: Examines fishing gear and life-saving equipment and orders crew to repair or replace defective gear and equipment. Stands watch during specified periods and determines geographical position of vessel upon request of CAPTAIN, FISHING VESSEL (fishing & hunt.), using loran and azimuths of celestial bodies. Directs activities of workers engaged in capture, preservation, stowing, and refrigeration of fish aboard fishing vessel. Assumes command of fishing vessel in event CAPTAIN, FISHING VESSEL (fishing & hunt.) becomes incapacitated. May locate schools of finfish and other marine life by observation from masthead and relay navigating directions to CAPTAIN, FISHING VESSEL (fishing & hunt.). May be required to hold license issued by U.S. Coast Guard.
GOE: 03.04.03 STRENGTH: M GED: R4 M4 L4 SVP: 7 DLU: 77

197.133-022 MATE, SHIP (water trans.) alternate titles: ship officer
Supervises and coordinates activities of crew aboard ship: Inspects holds of ship during loading to ensure that cargo is stowed according to specifications. Examines cargo-handling gear and lifesaving equipment and orders crew to repair or replace defective gear and equipment. Supervises crew engaged in cleaning and maintaining decks, superstructure, and bridge of ship. Stands watch during specified periods and determines geographical position of ship, upon request of MASTER, SHIP (water trans.), using loran and azimuths of celestial bodies. Assumes command of ship in event MASTER, SHIP (water trans.) becomes incapacitated. May be required to hold license issued by U.S. Coast Guard, depending on waters navigated and tonnage of ship. When more than one MATE, SHIP (water trans.) is required, may be designated Mate, Chief (water trans.) (usually on vessels inspected by U.S. Coast Guard); Mate, First (water trans.) (usually on uninspected vessels); Mate, Fourth (water trans.); Mate, Second (water trans.); Mate, Third (water trans.). May remain in port to relieve another MATE, SHIP (water trans.) who desires to go ashore while ship is in port and be designated Mate, Relief (water trans.).
GOE: 05.04.02 STRENGTH: L GED: R4 M4 L4 SVP: 7 DLU: 77

197.133-026 PILOT, SHIP (water trans.)
Commands ships to steer them into and out of harbors, estuaries, straits, and sounds, and on rivers, lakes, and bays: Directs course and speed of ship on basis of specialized knowledge of local winds, weather, tides, and current. Orders worker at helm to steer ship, and navigates ship to avoid reefs, outlying shoals, and other hazards to shipping, utilizing aids to navigation, such as lighthouses and buoys. Signals TUGBOAT CAPTAIN (water trans.) to berth and unberth ship. Must be licensed by U.S. Coast Guard with limitations indicating class and tonnage of vessels for which license is valid and route and waters that may be piloted. May be designated according to vessel commanded as Pilot, Steam Yacht (water trans.); Pilot, Tank Vessel (water trans.).
GOE: 05.04.02 STRENGTH: L GED: R4 M4 L3 SVP: 8 DLU: 77

197.133-030 TUGBOAT CAPTAIN (water trans.)
Commands tugboat to tow barges and ships into and out of harbors, estuaries, straits, and sounds, and on rivers, lakes, and bays: Signals workers on deck to rig towlines to barges or ship to be towed. Determines course and towing speed on basis of specialized knowledge of local winds, weather, tides, and current. Steers tugboat to push or pull barges to destination and to berth and unberth ships, avoiding reefs, outlying shoals, and other hazards to shipping, utilizing navigation devices, such as radar, sonic depth finder, compass and sextant and aids to navigation, such as lighthouses and buoys. Directs placement of suction hose or siphon to pump water from hold of barge, and signals workers to repair leak. Is required to hold license issued by U.S. Coast Guard.
GOE: 05.04.02 STRENGTH: M GED: R4 M3 L3 SVP: 8 DLU: 77

197.133-034 TUGBOAT MATE (water trans.)

Supervises and coordinates activities of crew aboard tugboat: Inspects towing gear and lifesaving equipment, and orders crew to repair or replace defective equipment. Directs activities of crew engaged in rigging towlines to barges or ship to be towed. Supervises crew engaged in cleaning and painting of boat. Stands watch during specified periods, and determines geographical position of boat upon request of TUGBOAT CAPTAIN (water trans.), using loran and azimuths of celestial bodies. Steers tugboat, upon request of TUGBOAT CAPTAIN (water trans.), to push or pull barges to destination and to berth and unberth ships, avoiding reefs, outlying shoals, and other hazards to navigation, utilizing navigation devices, such as compass and sextant, and aids to navigation, such as lighthouses and buoys. Assumes command of tugboat in event TUGBOAT CAPTAIN (water trans.) becomes incapacitated. Is required to hold license issued by U.S. Coast Guard.
GOE: 05.04.02 STRENGTH: M GED: R4 M3 L3 SVP: 7 DLU: 77

197.137-010 DREDGE MATE (water trans.)

Supervises and coordinates activities of crew aboard dredge (vessel equipped with machinery to excavate under water) used in building of structures in harbors, estuaries, straits, sounds, rivers, lakes, bays, and oceans: Examines dredging gear and lifesaving equipment, and orders crew to repair or replace defective gear and equipment. Stands watch during specified periods, and determines geographical position of ship, upon request of DREDGE CAPTAIN (water trans.), using loran and azimuths of celestial bodies. Directs activities of crew engaged in dredging operations. Assumes command of ship in event DREDGE CAPTAIN (water trans.) becomes incapacitated. Worker required to hold license issued by U.S. Coast Guard.
GOE: 05.12.01 STRENGTH: L GED: R4 M4 L3 SVP: 7 DLU: 77

197.161-010 DREDGE CAPTAIN (water trans.) alternate titles: dredge operator; dredge runner

Commands vessel equipped with machinery for excavating under water to facilitate building structures in harbors, estuaries, straits, sounds, rivers, lakes, bays, and oceans: Sets course of vessel, using navigational aids, such as charts, area plotting sheets, compass, and sextant, and orders worker at helm to steer ship toward excavation site. Determines geographical position of ship, using loran or azimuths of celestial bodies. Directs crew engaged in operating deck winches and lowering dredging equipment. Supervises crew engaged in dredging operations. Verifies depth of excavations to ensure that excavations are made according to requirements. Maintains ship's log. Must be licensed by U.S. Coast Guard for steam, motor, or sail ship according to waters navigated and tonnage of ship.
GOE: 05.04.02 STRENGTH: L GED: R4 M4 L3 SVP: 8 DLU: 77

197.163-010 FERRYBOAT CAPTAIN (water trans.)

Commands ferryboat to transport passengers, motor vehicles, or freight across lakes, bays, sounds, or rivers: Signals crew to close ferry gates and raise loading ramp, and signals engine room to start engines. Determines course and speed of ferryboat on basis of specialized knowledge of local winds, weather, tides, and current. Steers ferryboat, or orders worker at helm to steer ferryboat toward slip (landing pier) on opposite side of water. Inspects ferryboat to ensure that passengers and crew observe regulations pertaining to safe and efficient operation of ferryboat. Signals engine room to reverse engines, and maneuvers ferryboat into slip. Maintains ferryboat's log. Must hold license issued by U.S. Coast Guard, depending on tonnage of ferryboat and waters crossed.
GOE: 05.04.02 STRENGTH: L GED: R4 M4 L4 SVP: 7 DLU: 77

197.163-014 MASTER, PASSENGER BARGE (water trans.) alternate titles: barge captain

Commands barge to transport passengers on inland waterways, such as estuaries, lakes, bays, sounds, and rivers: Sets course of barge, using navigational aids, such as charts, area plotting sheets, compass, and sextant. Steers or orders crew worker at helm to steer barge and navigates barge to avoid reefs, outlying shoals, and other hazards to shipping, utilizing aids, such as lights, lighthouses, and buoys. Determines geographical position of barge, using loran and azimuths of celestial bodies. Inspects barge to ensure that passengers and crew observe regulations pertaining to safe and efficient operation of barge. Relinquishes command of barge to PILOT, SHIP (water trans.) to guide barge through hazardous waters. Maintains barge's log. Must be licensed by U.S. Coast Guard for steam or motor barge according to waters navigated and tonnage of barge.
GOE: 05.04.02 STRENGTH: L GED: R4 M4 L4 SVP: 7 DLU: 77

197.163-018 MASTER, RIVERBOAT (water trans.) alternate titles: riverboat captain

Commands riverboat to transport passengers, freight, or other cargo along rivers: Determines course and speed of riverboat on basis of knowledge of winds, weather, tides, and current. Steers riverboat or orders crew worker at helm to steer riverboat and navigates boat to avoid reefs, outlying shoals, and other hazards to shipping, utilizing aids to navigation, such as lighthouses and buoys. Inspects riverboat to ensure that passengers and crew observe regulations pertaining to safe and efficient operation of riverboat. Relinquishes command of riverboat to PILOT, SHIP (water trans.) to guide riverboat through hazardous waters. Maintains riverboat's log. Must be licensed by U.S. Coast Guard for steam or motor riverboat according to waters navigated and tonnage of riverboat.
GOE: 05.04.02 STRENGTH: L GED: R4 M4 L4 SVP: 7 DLU: 77

197.167-010 MASTER, SHIP (water trans.) alternate titles: ship's captain

Commands ship to transport passengers, freight, and other cargo across oceans, bays, lakes, and in coastal waters: Sets course of ship, using naviga-tional aids, such as charts, area plotting sheets, compass, and sextant, and orders crew worker at helm to steer ship. Determines geographical position of ship, using loran or azimuths of celestial bodies. Inspects ship to ensure that crew and passengers observe regulations pertaining to safety and efficient operation of ship. Coordinates activities of crewmembers responsible for signaling devices, such as ship's whistle, flashing lights, flags, and radio, to signal ships in vicinity. Calculates landfall (sighting of land), using electronic sounding devices and following contour lines on chart. Avoids reefs, outlying shoals, and other hazards to shipping, utilizing aids to navigation, such as lights, light-houses, and buoys. Relinquishes command of ship to PILOT, SHIP (water trans.) to guide ship through hazardous waters. Signals TUGBOAT CAPTAIN (water trans.) to berth ship. Maintains ship's log. Must be licensed by U.S. Coast Guard for steam, motor, or sail ship according to waters navigated and tonnage of ship. May be designated according to waters licensed to navigate as Master, Bays, Sounds, And Lakes (water trans.); Master, Coastal Waters (water trans.); Master, Great Lakes (water trans.); Master, Ocean (water trans.).
GOE: 05.04.02 STRENGTH: L GED: R6 M6 L5 SVP: 8 DLU: 77

197.167-014 PURSER (water trans.) alternate titles: ship purser

Coordinates activities of workers aboard ship concerned with shipboard business functions and social activities for passengers: Prepares shipping articles and signs on crew. Maintains payroll records and pays off crews at completion of voyage. Submits passenger and crew sailing lists to governmental agencies as required by regulations. Assists passengers in preparing declarations for customs, arranging for inspections of horticultural items being brought into country, and inspection of documents by immigration authorities. Prepares ship's entrance and clearance papers for foreign ports, and ship's cargo manifests when discharging cargo. Supervises stowage, care, and removal of hold baggage. Arranges for travel and scenic tours at ports of call. Provides banking services and safekeeping of valuables for passengers. Supervises preparing, editing, printing, and distribution of ship's daily newspaper. Plans and conducts games, tournaments, and parties for passengers' enjoyment. May conduct religious services. May provide first aid for passengers and crew.
GOE: 11.11.03 STRENGTH: S GED: R4 M3 L3 SVP: 7 DLU: 77

198 RAILROAD CONDUCTORS

This group includes occupations concerned with directing the activities of crews on trains carrying passengers, freight, or mail.

198.167-010 CONDUCTOR, PASSENGER CAR (r.r. trans.)

Coordinates activities of train crew engaged in transporting passengers on passenger train: Reads train orders, timetable schedules, and other written instructions received from TRAIN DISPATCHER (r.r. trans.) and discusses contents with LOCOMOTIVE ENGINEER (r.r. trans.) and train crew. Compares watch with that of LOCOMOTIVE ENGINEER (r.r. trans.) to ensure that departure time from station or terminal is in accordance with timetable schedules. Assists passengers to board train. Signals LOCOMOTIVE ENGINEER (r.r. trans.) to begin train run, using radiotelephone, giving hand signals, or by waving lantern. Collects tickets, fares, or passes from passengers. Answers passengers' questions concerning train rules and regulations and timetable schedules. Announces names of train stations and terminals to passengers. Supervises workers who inspect air brakes, airhoses, couplings, and journal boxes and who regulate air-conditioning, lighting, and heating to ensure safety and comfort to passengers. Assists passengers to get off train at stations or terminals. Prepares reports at end of run to explain accidents, unscheduled stops, or delays.
GOE: 11.11.03 STRENGTH: L GED: R4 M3 L4 SVP: 8 DLU: 77

198.167-014 CONDUCTOR, PULLMAN (r.r. trans.) alternate titles: conductor, sleeping car

Coordinates activities of workers engaged in providing services to passengers of railroad sleeping and lounge cars during trip: Collects tickets and fares from passengers. Supervises workers engaged in providing porter, maid, and meal services. Observes and talks with passengers to ascertain passengers are comfortable, and to answer passenger inquiries. Compiles record of tickets and money received, and destination of each and accommodations furnished passengers.
GOE: 09.01.04 STRENGTH: L GED: R4 M3 L4 SVP: 6 DLU: 77

198.167-018 CONDUCTOR, ROAD FREIGHT (r.r. trans.)

Coordinates activities of train crew engaged in transporting freight on freight train: Reads train orders, schedules, and other written instructions received from TRAIN DISPATCHER (r.r. trans.) and discusses their contents with LOCOMOTIVE ENGINEER (r.r. trans.) and train crew. Inspects couplings and airhoses to ensure that they are securely fastened. Inspects journal boxes to ensure that they are lubricated. Inspects handbrakes on cars to ensure that they are released before train begins to run. Inspects freight cars to ensure that they are securely sealed. Records number of car and corresponding seal number and compares listing with waybill to ensure accuracy of routes and destinations. Compares watch with watch of LOCOMOTIVE ENGINEER (r.r. trans.) to ensure that departure time from station or terminal is in accordance with timetable schedules. Signals LOCOMOTIVE ENGINEER (r.r. trans.) via radiotelephone or by waving lantern to begin train run. Talks to LOCOMOTIVE ENGINEER (r.r. trans.) and traffic control center personnel via telephone during run to give or receive instructions or information concerning stops, delays, or oncoming trains. Instructs workers to set warning signals in front of and at rear of train during emergency stops to warn oncoming trains. Supervises workers engaged

in inspection and maintenance of cars and mechanical equipment during run to ensure that train is operating efficiently and safely. Records time of departures and arrivals at all destinations. Prepares reports at end of run to explain accidents, unscheduled stops, or delays.
GOE: 11.11.03 STRENGTH: L GED: R4 M3 L3 SVP: 8 DLU: 77

199   MISCELLANEOUS PROFESSIONAL, TECHNICAL, AND MANAGERIAL OCCUPATIONS, N.E.C.

This group includes occupations concerned with professional, technical, and managerial work, not elsewhere classified.

199.167-010 RADIATION MONITOR (profess. & kin.) alternate titles: health-physics technician; personnel monitor

Monitors personnel, plant facilities, and work environment to detect radioactive contamination, using radiation detectors and other instruments: Measures intensity and identifies type of radiation in working areas, using devices, such as beta-gamma survey meter, gamma-background monitor, and alphabeta-gamma counter. Collects air samples to determine airborne concentration of radioactivity, and collects and analyzes monitoring equipment worn by personnel, such as film badges and pocket detection chambers, to measure individual exposure to radiation. Takes smear test of suspected contaminated area by wiping floor with filter paper and placing paper in scaler to obtain contamination count. Informs supervisors when individual exposures and area radiation levels approach maximum permissible limits. Recommends work stoppage in unsafe areas, posts warning signs, and ropes off contaminated areas. Calculates amount of time personnel may be exposed safely to radiation in area, taking into account contamination count and HEALTH PHYSICIST'S (profess. & kin.) determinations concerning exposure limits of personnel. Instructs personnel in radiation safety procedures and demonstrates use of protective clothing and equipment. Monitors time and intensity of exposure of personnel working in radiation-waste disposal areas. Inspects shipments for contamination, using counter, and tags shipments in which radiation count exceeds specifications. May make periodic urinalyses of personnel and notify supervisors when overexposure to radiation is indicated. Logs data, such as status of areas being decontaminated, rate of radiation exposure to personnel, and location and intensity of radioactivity in contaminated areas. Tests detection instruments against standards to ensure their accuracy. May recommend decontamination procedures.
GOE: 05.03.08 STRENGTH: L GED: R4 M4 L4 SVP: 6 DLU: 77

199.167-014 URBAN PLANNER (profess. & kin.) alternate titles: city planner; city-planning engineer; land planner; town planner

Develops comprehensive plans and programs for utilization of land and physical facilities of cities, counties, and metropolitan areas: Compiles and analyzes data on economic, social, and physical factors affecting land use, and prepares or requisitions graphic and narrative reports on data. Confers with local authorities, civic leaders, social scientists, and land planning and development specialists to devise and recommend arrangements of land and physical facilities for residential, commercial, industrial, and community uses. Recommends governmental measures affecting land use, public utilities, community facilities, and housing and transportation to control and guide community development and renewal. May review and evaluate environmental impact reports applying to specified private and public planning projects and programs. When directing activities of planning department, is known as Chief Planner (profess. & kin.); Director, Planning (profess. & kin.). Usually employed by local government jurisdictions, but may work for any level of government, or private consulting firms.
GOE: 11.03.02 STRENGTH: S GED: R5 M4 L5 SVP: 8 DLU: 77

199.167-018 ENERGY-CONTROL OFFICER (education)

Monitors energy use and develops, promotes, implements, and coordinates energy conservation program in county school district facilities: Compiles monthly energy report on consumption of electricity, fuel, oil, coal, LP gas, and water in school facilities, listing units consumed and costs. Sets up energy monitoring devices in school facilities that graphically plot energy usage and temperature changes during extended periods of time. Visits school facilities on regular basis to inspect monitoring devices and utilities usage. Determines areas in which energy conservation measures are needed, and compiles needs-assessment report of all school facilities. Monitors energy usage of extracurricular activities in school facilities. Coordinates energy conservation activities in areas with those of local, state, and federal conservation groups. Recommends energy conservation policies to board of education. Presents lectures on resource conservation at teachers' meetings and to civic groups.
GOE: 05.03.08 STRENGTH: L GED: R4 M4 L4 SVP: 7 DLU: 86

199.167-022 ENVIRONMENTAL ANALYST (government ser.)

Directs, develops, and administers state governmental program for assessment of environmental impact of proposed recreational projects: Directs assessment of environmental impact and preparation of impact statements required for final evaluation of proposed actions. Directs identification and analysis of alternative proposals for handling projects in environmentally sensitive manner. Plans for enhancement of environmental setting for each proposed recreational project. Designs and directs special studies to obtain technical environmental information regarding planned projects, contacting and utilizing various sources, such as regional engineering offices, park region laboratories, and other govern-

mental agencies. Prepares and controls budget for functions of impact-statement preparation program. Attends meetings and represents department on subjects related to program.
GOE: 11.05.03 STRENGTH: S GED: R5 M3 L4 SVP: 8 DLU: 86

199.171-010 PROOF TECHNICIAN (ordnance)

Test-fires small arms, artillery weapons, ammunition, and bombs to evaluate mechanical performance and ballistic qualities, such as range, accuracy, bursting effect, and armor-piercing ability: Erects heavy weapons and connects electrical fire-control apparatus according to diagrams and written instructions. Positions small arms in holding fixtures and rigs trigger-pulling device. Loads, aims, and fires weapons. Measures gun barrel pressures and computes velocities of projectile. Examines and measures targets to verify accuracy of weapons and ammunition. Refrigerates, heats, or immerses ammunition in water before firing to verify performance under severe temperature and moisture conditions. Keeps records of observations. Prepares aerial bombs for test-dropping and loads bombs into aircraft. May prepare experimental ammunition and bombs and devise firing methods. May direct helpers. May specialize in testing of specific ordnance and be designated according to type of item involved.
GOE: 02.04.01 STRENGTH: L GED: R4 M4 L4 SVP: 6 DLU: 77

199.207-010 DIANETIC COUNSELOR (profess. & kin.) alternate titles: dianeticist; scientologist; scientology auditor

Conducts auditing (counseling) sessions designed to guide clients to emotional well-being by relieving clients from effects of past experiences: Questions client according to prescribed procedures while client is in contact with E-meter (electrometer). Listens to client's responses to questioning and observes indicator needle on meter. Interprets movement of needle to determine effectiveness of auditing, utilizing knowledge of dianetic auditing practice. Compiles notes on client responses during session. May be known by titles which reflect various levels of proficiency and responsibility in Scientology organization.
GOE: 10.01.02 STRENGTH: S GED: R5 M3 L4 SVP: 6 DLU: 77

199.251-010 TESTER, FOOD PRODUCTS (any industry) alternate titles: consultant; director of consumer services; nutrition consultant

Develops, tests, and promotes various types of food products: Selects recipes from conventional cookbooks, or develops new recipes for company food products. Prepares and cooks food according to recipe to test quality and standardize procedures and ingredients. Evaluates prepared item as to texture, appearance, flavor, and nutritional value. Records amount and kinds of ingredients and various test results. Suggests new products, product improvements, and promotions for company use or for resale to dealers, manufacturers, or other users. Presents food items at demonstration functions to promote desired qualities, nutritional values, and related characteristics. Samples shipments to verify weights, measures, coding data, and other evaluations for product control. Answers consumer mail.
GOE: 05.05.17 STRENGTH: L GED: R4 M3 L4 SVP: 6 DLU: 77

199.261-010 TAXIDERMIST (profess. & kin.)

Prepares, stuffs, and mounts skins of birds or animals in lifelike form: Removes skin from dead body with special knives, scissors, and pliers, taking care to preserve hair and feathers in natural state. Rubs preservative solutions into skin. Forms body foundation by building up on wire foundation with papier mache and adhesive tape, to give natural attitude and show form and muscles of specimen. Covers foundation with skin, using specified adhesive or modeling clay. Affixes eyes, teeth, and claws; dresses feathers, and brushes fur to enhance lifelike appearance of specimen. May mount specimen in case with representations of natural surroundings. May make plaster cast of specimen to enhance physical details preparatory to making papier mache mold. May dress-out, preserve, or otherwise prepare animal carcasses preparatory to scientific or exhibition purposes.
GOE: 01.06.02 STRENGTH: M GED: R5 M3 L4 SVP: 7 DLU: 77

199.261-014 PARKING ANALYST (government ser.) alternate titles: engineering technician, parking

Develops plans for construction and utilization of revenue-producing vehicle parking facilitites: Plans and conducts comprehensive field surveys to locate sites for new parking facilities. Analyzes factors such as capacity, turnover, rates, and required property changes relative to proposed sites, and prepares maps, graphs, tracings, and diagrams to illustrate findings. Designs parking lot facilities, including spaces, aisles, driveways, lighting, gates, landscaping, cashier booths, storm drains, grades, and paving details, and prepares cost estimates. Evaluates work performed by contractors to verify conformity to specifications. Keeps log of construction projects and prepares final reports. Reports maintenance problems occurring at facilities to supervisor. Prepares replies to public suggestions and complaints.
GOE: 05.03.06 STRENGTH: L GED: R5 M4 L5 SVP: 7 DLU: 86

199.267-010 BALLISTICS EXPERT, FORENSIC (government ser.) alternate titles: firearms expert

Examines and tests firearms, spent bullets, and related evidence in criminal cases to develop facts useful in apprehension and prosecution of suspects: Examines bullets, bullet fragments, cartridge clips, firearms, and related evidence found at scene of crime or in possession of suspect to identify make and caliber of weapon. Test-fires weapons allegedly used to facilitate microscopic comparison of bullets from test weapon with those discovered at scene of crime. Determines, from knowledge of ballistics theory and standard test procedures, prob-

able angle and distance from which crime weapon was fired, revealing origin of shot. Prepares reports of findings and testifies at inquests, trials, and other hearings to facilitate prosecution or exoneration of suspects on basis of determinations. May perform standardized tests on other articles of evidence, using chemical agents, physical-testing equipment, measuring instruments, and prescribed procedure, to determine relationship of evidence to suspect and to crime. May order and maintain departmental weapons and related equipment. May be designated by rank as Lieutenant, Ballistics (government ser.).
GOE: 02.04.01 STRENGTH: L GED: R5 M5 L5 SVP: 7 DLU: 77

199.267-014 CRYPTANALYST (government ser.) alternate titles: cipher expert; cryptographer; secret-code expert
Analyzes secret coding systems and decodes messages for military, political, or law enforcement agencies or organizations: Examines secret messages for characteristics that reveal coding system employed in message. Analyzes message, using formulas, code books, chemicals, mechanical devices, computers, and knowledge of commonly used coding keys. Decodes entire message and consults books, magazines, government publications, and police files to obtain corroborative evidence. May develop codes or new coding methods.
GOE: 11.08.04 STRENGTH: S GED: R5 M5 L5 SVP: 8 DLU: 77

199.267-018 EXAMINATION PROCTOR (government ser.)
Administers civil service qualifying examinations: Verifies admissions credentials of examinees, maintains order, distributes and collects examination materials, keeps time, and answers questions relative to examination procedures. May participate in oral interviews of candidates. May score examinations, using scoring template or answer sheet.
GOE: 07.01.07 STRENGTH: L GED: R4 M3 L4 SVP: 5 DLU: 77

199.267-022 EXAMINER, QUESTIONED DOCUMENTS (government ser.) alternate titles: handwriting expert
Examines handwritten material or other questioned documents to identify author, detect forgery, or determine method used to alter documents: Confers with laboratory specialists, such as chemists and photographers, to determine which scientific processes are necessary to effect analysis. Examines hand or typewritten sample to detect characteristics, such as open loop, quaver, or t-cross peculiar to an individual, using microscope. Measures angle or slant to estimate degree to which letters and lines vary from perpendicular, using protractor. Compares paper specimen with manufacturer's samples to ascertain type and source. Compares photographic blowup of written or typed specimen obtained from separate sources to ascertain similarity or differences. Works in consultative capacity to various agencies or organizations, including police force, and testifies in legal proceedings.
GOE: 02.04.01 STRENGTH: L GED: R5 M2 L4 SVP: 6 DLU: 77

199.267-026 POLYGRAPH EXAMINER (profess. & kin.) alternate titles: lie-detection examiner
Interrogates and screens individuals to detect deception or to verify truthfulness, using polygraph equipment and standard polygraph techniques: Attaches apparatus to individual to measure and record changes in respiration, blood pressure, and electrical resistance of skin as result of perspiration changes. Evaluates reactions to questions of a non-emotional nature. Interprets and diagnoses individual's emotional responses to key questions recorded on graph. Visits morgues, examines scene of crime, or contacts other sources, when assigned to criminal case, to gather information for use in interrogating suspects, witnesses, and other persons. Appears in court as witness on matters relating to polygraph examinations, according to formalized procedures. Prepares reports and keeps records on polygraph examinations. May instruct classes in polygraph interrogation techniques, methods, and uses. When analyzing voice stress charted on moving tape by needle of recording device for deception or truthfulness verification, may be designated Psychological Stress Evaluator (profess. & kin.).
GOE: 02.04.02 STRENGTH: L GED: R5 M3 L5 SVP: 5 DLU: 77

199.267-030 TRAFFIC TECHNICIAN (government ser.)
Conducts field studies to determine traffic volume, speed, effectiveness of signals, adequacy of lighting, and other factors influencing traffic conditions: Analyzes traffic volume and interviews motorists at assigned intersections or other areas where congestion exists or where disproportionate number of accidents have occurred [TRAFFIC CHECKER (government ser.)]. Determines average speed of vehicles, using electrical timing devices or radar equipment. Times stoplight or other delays, using stopwatch. Observes lighting, visibility of signs and pavement markings, location of traffic signals, width of street or roadway, and other considerations affecting traffic conditions. Draws graphs, charts, diagrams, and similar aids to illustrate observations and conclusions. Computes mathematical factors for adjusting timing of traffic signals, speed restrictions, and related data, using standard formulas. Prepares drawings of proposed signal installations or other control devices, using drafting instruments. May prepare statistical studies of traffic conditions. May recommend changes in traffic control devices and regulations on basis of findings.
GOE: 05.03.06 STRENGTH: L GED: R5 M4 L5 SVP: 7 DLU: 77

199.267-034 RESEARCH ASSISTANT II (profess. & kin.) alternate titles: researcher
Analyzes verbal or statistical data to prepare reports and studies for use by professional workers in variety of areas, such as science, social science, law, medicine, or politics: Searches sources, such as reference works, literature, documents, newspapers, and statistical records, to obtain data on assigned subject.

Analyzes and evaluates applicability of collected data. Prepares statistical tabulations, using calculator or computer. Writes reports or presents data in formats such as abstracts, bibliographies, graphs, or maps. May interview individuals to obtain data or draft correspondence to answer inquiries. May be designated Legislative Aide (government ser.) when conducting studies to assist lawmakers.
GOE: 11.08.02 STRENGTH: S GED: R5 M3 L5 SVP: 6 DLU: 87

199.267-038 GRAPHOLOGIST (profess. & kin.)
Analyzes handwriting to appraise personal characteristics: Obtains handwriting specimen to observe overall appearance of writing and detailed formation of letters. Measures height of letters and slant of writing, using calibrated templates. Observes individual writing strokes to determine unique or distinguishing characteristics, using ruler and low-power magnifying glass or microscope. Evaluates handwriting sample and interprets findings, according to theories of handwriting analysis. May use diagram to plot writing characteristics.
GOE: 02.04.01 STRENGTH: S GED: R4 M3 L3 SVP: 6 DLU: 89

199.281-010 GEMOLOGIST (jewelry-silver.) alternate titles: gem expert
Examines gemstones, such as jade, sapphires, and rubies, to evaluate their genuineness, quality, and value, utilizing knowledge of gems and market valuations: Examines gem surfaces and internal structure, using polariscope, refractometer, microscope, and other optical instruments, to differentiate between stones, identify rare specimens, or to detect flaws, defects, or peculiarities affecting gem values. Immerses stones in prescribed chemical solutions to determine specific gravities and key properties of gemstones or substitutes, which indicate physical characteristics of stone for gem identification, quality determination, and for appraisal. Grades stones for color, perfection, and quality of cut. Estimates wholesale and retail value of gems, following pricing guides, market fluctuations, and various economic changes that affect distribution of precious stones. May advise customers and others in use of gems to create attractive jewelry items.
GOE: 05.05.14 STRENGTH: L GED: R4 M3 L4 SVP: 7 DLU: 77

199.361-010 RADIOGRAPHER (any industry) alternate titles: industrial x-ray operator
Radiographs metal, plastics, concrete, or other materials, such as castings, sample parts, pipes, and structural members for flaws, cracks, or presence of foreign materials, utilizing knowledge of radiography equipment, techniques, and procedures: Aligns object on stand between source of x rays and film or plate; or aligns source of gamma rays, such as cobalt or iridium isotope and film or plate on opposite sides of object, manually or using hand or electric truck, chain hoist, or crane. Masks peripheral areas with lead shields. Selects type of radiation source and type of film, and applies standard mathematical formulas to determine exposure distance and time, considering size, mobility, and strength of radiation sources in relation to density and mobility of object. Verifies radiation intensities, using radiation meters. Adjusts controls of x-ray equipment on console or exposes source of radioactivity to take radiograph. Removes and develops film or plate. Monitors working area, using survey meters, to protect personnel area. May replace radioactive isotope source in containers by manipulating tongs from behind protective lead shield. Marks defects appearing on film and assists in analyzing findings. May specialize in x-ray work and be designated X-Ray Technician (any industry).
GOE: 05.03.05 STRENGTH: L GED: R4 M4 L4 SVP: 5 DLU: 77

199.364-010 CITY PLANNING AIDE (profess. & kin.) alternate titles: planning assistant
Compiles data for use by URBAN PLANNER (profess. & kin.) in making planning studies: Summarizes information from maps, reports, field and file investigations, and books. Traces maps and prepares statistical tabulations, computations, charts, and graphs to illustrate planning studies in areas, such as population, transportation, traffic, land use, proposed subdivisions, and public utilities. Prepares and updates files and records. May answer public inquiries, conduct field interviews and make surveys of traffic flow, parking, housing, educational facilities, recreation, zoning, and other conditions which affect planning studies.
GOE: 11.03.02 STRENGTH: L GED: R4 M4 L4 SVP: 6 DLU: 77

199.364-014 SCIENTIFIC HELPER (profess. & kin.) alternate titles: laboratory assistant; research assistant
Performs duties according to type of research in which supervising scientist is engaged, such as collecting rock samples for study by GEOLOGIST (profess. & kin.) or plant specimens for study by BOTANIST (profess. & kin.). Prepares samples for analysis or examination and performs routine laboratory tests. May participate in field explorations, such as mineralogical or geophysical expeditions. May be designated according to field of scientific research.
GOE: 02.04.01 STRENGTH: M GED: R4 M4 L4 SVP: 6 DLU: 77

199.382-010 TELEVISION-SCHEDULE COORDINATOR (radio-tv broad.) alternate titles: log operations coordinator; media coordinator; program schedule clerk
Enters data, such as program and commercial formats, into computer to prepare daily operations schedules and advance program log for newspapers, magazines, traffic or broadcast department: Provides for clearance and rotation of spot-commercial films and slides for television programs, and performs related clerical duties for DIRECTOR PROGRAM (radio-tv broad.) 184.167-030. May compose courtesy, apology, and stay-tuned announcements, using computer. May review overnight television ratings to determine number of viewers watching television programs containing station promotions.

GOE: 07.05.01 STRENGTH: L GED: R4 M3 L4 SVP: 4 DLU: 89

199.384-010 DECONTAMINATOR (any industry)

Decontaminates radioactive materials and equipment, using chemical solutions, and sandblasting machine: Reads contamination level, using radiation meter, and sorts contaminated items by size and radiation level, following specifications. Weighs out and mixes chemical solutions in tank according to prescribed formula, and heats solution, using steam hose. Immerses objects, such as pipes, motors, valves, hose, and containers, in solution for specified time, using hoist. Places smaller objects in sandblasting machine, using manipulators or protective gloves, and starts machine to remove greater proportion of contamination and reduce immersion time. Places hot (radioactive) waste, such as sweepings and broken sample bottles, into disposal containers to be processed for land or sea burial. Cleans objects having radiation count under specified amount, using cloth, soap, solvents, wire brush, and buffing wheel. Records type of material and equipment decontaminated and method used. May accompany coffins of waste to disposal area. May monitor radiation-exposed equipment, plant and hospital areas, and materials, using radiation-detector measuring instruments, such as portable gamma survey meter, Geiger counter, and alpha-beta-gamma survey meter. May determine method of decontamination according to size and nature of equipment, and degree of contamination.
GOE: 02.04.01 STRENGTH: M GED: R3 M3 L3 SVP: 6 DLU: 77

199.682-010 AEROSPACE PHYSIOLOGICAL TECHNICIAN (military ser.)

Operates physiological training devices, such as pressure suits, pressure chamber, parasail equipment, and ejection seats, that simulate flying conditions, to indoctrinate flying personnel to physical and physiological stresses encountered in flight: Interviews trainees to obtain physiological and medical histories to detect evidence of disqualifying conditions, prior to simulated flight. Moves levers, turns knobs, and presses buttons on control panel to regulate gas and airflow, temperature, and barometric pressure in pressure chamber to simulate flying conditions at varying altitudes and speeds. Operates altitude pressure suit control console which adjusts pressure inside flying suits and helmets. Operates parasail training equipment, such as tow reel, tow truck, radio equipment, and meteorological devices. Adjusts seat, harness, and headrest of ejection tower for safety of personnel. Places ammunition in catapult chamber to load catapult for firing. Fires catapult that ejects seat to simulate ejection from aircraft.
GOE: 02.04.02 STRENGTH: S GED: R4 M3 L3 SVP: 6 DLU: 77

2 CLERICAL AND SALES OCCUPATIONS

This category encompasses two occupational fields: Clerical (Divisions 20 - 24) which includes occupations concerned with compiling, recording, communicating, computing, and otherwise systematizing data; Sales (Divisions 25 - 29) which includes occupations concerned with influencing customers in favor of a commodity or service. Includes occupations closely identified with sales transactions even though they do not involve actual participation. Excluded from this category are clerical occupations primarily associated with a manufacturing process.

20 STENOGRAPHY, TYPING, FILING, AND RELATED OCCUPATIONS

This division includes occupations concerned with making, classifying, and filing primarily verbal records. Includes activities, such as transmitting and receiving data by machines equipped with a typewriter-like keyboard, cold type typesetting, word processing, and operating machines to duplicate records, correspondence, and reports; to emboss data on metal or plastic plates for addressing and similar identification purposes; to sort, fold, insert, seal, address, and stamp mail; and to open envelopes. Occupations concerned primarily with statistical, financial, or other numerical data are found in Division 21.

201 SECRETARIES

This group includes occupations concerned with carrying out minor administrative and general office duties in addition to taking and transcribing dictation. Occupations concerned primarily with taking and transcribing dictation are included in Group 202.

201.162-010 SOCIAL SECRETARY (clerical)

Coordinates social, business, and personal affairs of employer. Confers with employer on contemplated social functions, sends invitations, and arranges for decorations and entertainment. Advises employer on etiquette, dress, and current events. Reads and answers routine correspondence, using typewriter or in own handwriting as situation demands. May manage financial affairs of entire house.
GOE: 07.01.03 STRENGTH: S GED: R4 M2 L4 SVP: 6 DLU: 77

201.362-010 LEGAL SECRETARY (clerical)

Prepares legal papers and correspondence of legal nature, such as summonses, complaints, motions, and subpoenas, using typewriter, word processor, or personal computer. May review law journals and other legal publications to identify court decisions pertinent to pending cases and submit articles to company officials.
GOE: 07.01.03 STRENGTH: S GED: R4 M2 L4 SVP: 6 DLU: 82

201.362-014 MEDICAL SECRETARY (medical ser.)

Performs secretarial duties, utilizing knowledge of medical terminology and hospital, clinic, or laboratory procedures: Takes dictation in shorthand or using dictaphone. Compiles and records medical charts, reports, and correspondence, using typewriter or word processor. Answers telephone, schedules appointments, and greets and directs visitors. Maintains files.
GOE: 07.01.03 STRENGTH: S GED: R4 M3 L4 SVP: 6 DLU: 86

201.362-018 MEMBERSHIP SECRETARY (nonprofit org.)

Compiles and maintains membership lists, records receipts of dues and contributions, and gives information to members of nonprofit organization: Compiles and maintains membership lists and contribution records. Welcomes new members and issues membership cards. Explains privileges and obligations of membership, discusses organization problems, adjusts complaints, and provides other information to members. Types and sends notices of dues. Collects and records receipts of dues and contributions. Sends newsletters, promotional materials, and other publications to persons on mailing list. May prepare and distribute monthly financial reports to department heads. May assign numbers and codes to new corporate and individual members and input billing schedule into computer. May revise existing membership records, compile list of delinquent dues, and forward information to president.
GOE: 07.01.02 STRENGTH: S GED: R4 M3 L4 SVP: 5 DLU: 88

201.362-022 SCHOOL SECRETARY (education)

Performs secretarial duties in public or private school: Composes, or transcribes from rough draft, correspondence, bulletins, memorandums, and other material, using typewriter or computer. Compiles and files student grade and attendance reports and other school records. Greets visitors to school, determines nature of business, and directs visitors to destination. Talks with student encountering problem and resolves problem or directs student to other worker. Answers telephone to provide information, take message, or transfer calls. May order and dispense school supplies. May accept and deposit funds for lunches, school supplies, and student activities. May disburse funds, record financial transactions, and audit and balance student-organization and other school-fund accounts. May take dictation in shorthand and transcribe notes, using typewriter or computer. May maintain calendar of school events. May oversee student playground activities and monitor classroom during temporary absence of teacher.

GOE: 07.01.03 STRENGTH: S GED: R4 M3 L3 SVP: 5 DLU: 81

201.362-026 SCRIPT SUPERVISOR (motion picture; radio-tv broad.)

Compiles and records details of scenes, such as action sequences, physical layout, and costumes used during photographing of motion pictures and television film productions to relieve DIRECTOR, MOTION PICTURE (motion picture) of minor administrative and clerical detail: Reads script and prepares notes of action, properties, and costumes to be used for each scene. Observes filming of production, records scene details, such as position, facial expression, and coiffure of cast members, camera position in relation to cast, position of properties, and condition of costumes, and refers to previously prepared notes to ensure continuity of sequence during subsequent scenes. Listens to dialog and informs cast of deviations from script. Times length of scenes, using stopwatch. Types and distributes script changes to cast and production personnel. Keeps records, such as type of camera and lighting equipment used for each scene, and prepares daily activity and progress reports. May take dictation. May write synopsis of production for advertising or publicity purposes.
GOE: 01.03.01 STRENGTH: L GED: R4 M2 L4 SVP: 6 DLU: 77

201.362-030 SECRETARY (clerical) alternate titles: secretarial stenographer

Schedules appointments, gives information to callers, takes dictation, and otherwise relieves officials of clerical work and minor administrative and business detail: Reads and routes incoming mail. Locates and attaches appropriate file to correspondence to be answered by employer. Takes dictation in shorthand or by machine [STENOTYPE OPERATOR (clerical) 202.362-022] and transcribes notes on typewriter, or transcribes from voice recordings [TRANSCRIBING-MACHINE OPERATOR (clerical) 203.582-058]. Composes and types routine correspondence. Files correspondence and other records. Answers telephone and gives information to callers or routes call to appropriate official and places outgoing calls. Schedules appointments for employer. Greets visitors, ascertains nature of business, and conducts visitors to employer or appropriate person. May not take dictation. May arrange travel schedule and reservations. May compile and type statistical reports. May oversee clerical workers. May keep personnel records [PERSONNEL CLERK (clerical) 209.362-026]. May record minutes of staff meetings. May make copies of correspondence or other printed matter, using copying or duplicating machine. May prepare outgoing mail, using postage-metering machine. May prepare notes, correspondence, and reports, using word processor or computer terminal.
GOE: 07.01.03 STRENGTH: S GED: R4 M3 L4 SVP: 6 DLU: 89

202 STENOGRAPHERS

This group includes occupations concerned with taking shorthand or speedwriting notes by hand or machine and transcribing them. Occupations concerned with carrying out minor administrative and general office duties in addition to taking and transcribing dictation are found in Group 201.

202.132-010 SUPERVISOR, STENO POOL (clerical)

Supervises and coordinates activities of workers engaged in taking and transcribing dictation of correspondence and reports: Assigns stenographers to executives and department heads to take dictation and transcribe correspondence and memos. Assigns manuscript or recorded messages to workers for transcription. Verifies typed copy for neatness, spelling, and punctuation. Performs other duties as described under SUPERVISOR (clerical) Master Title.
GOE: 07.05.03 STRENGTH: S GED: R4 M2 L4 SVP: 6 DLU: 77

202.362-010 SHORTHAND REPORTER (clerical) alternate titles: court reporter; law reporter

Records examination, testimony, judicial opinions, judge's charge to jury, judgment or sentence of court, or other proceedings in court of law by machine shorthand [STENOTYPE OPERATOR (clerical)], takes shorthand notes, or reports proceedings into *steno-mask*. Reads portions of transcript during trial on judge's request, and asks speakers to clarify inaudible statements. Operates typewriter to transcribe recorded material, or dictates material into recording machine. May record proceedings of quasi-judicial hearings and formal and informal meetings and be designated Hearings Reporter (clerical). May be self-employed, performing duties in court of law or at hearings and meetings, and be designated Freelance Reporter (clerical).
GOE: 07.05.03 STRENGTH: S GED: R3 M2 L3 SVP: 6 DLU: 77

202.362-014 STENOGRAPHER (clerical) alternate titles: clerk-stenographer

Takes dictation in shorthand of correspondence, reports, and other matter, and operates typewriter to transcribe dictated material. Performs variety of cleri-

cal duties [ADMINISTRATIVE CLERK (clerical) 219.362-010], except when working in stenographic pool. May transcribe material from sound recordings [TRANSCRIBING-MACHINE OPERATOR (clerical) 203.582-058]. May perform stenographic duties in professional office and be designated Legal Stenographer (clerical); Medical Stenographer (clerical); Technical Stenographer (clerical). May take dictation in foreign language and be known as Foreign-Language Stenographer (clerical). May be designated according to department in which employed as Police Stenographer (government ser.). May work for public stenographic service and be designated Public Stenographer (clerical).
GOE: 07.05.03 STRENGTH: S GED: R3 M2 L3 SVP: 5 DLU: 87

202.362-018 STENOGRAPHER, PRINT SHOP (print. & pub.)
Takes dictation and operates typewriter to transcribe dictated material and to prepare metal printing plates for use in addressing machines: Takes and transcribes dictation. Operates typewriter to type manuscript in English or foreign language. Operates electromagnetic typewriter to imprint metal printing plates for use in addressing machines. May operate justifying typewriter to produce typed matter with uniform margins. May cut stencils for use in mimeographing machine.
GOE: 07.05.03 STRENGTH: S GED: R3 M2 L3 SVP: 5 DLU: 77

202.362-022 STENOTYPE OPERATOR (clerical) alternate titles: steno-type-machine operator; steno-typist
Takes dictation of correspondence, reports, and other matter on machine that writes contractions or symbols for full words on paper roll. Operates typewriter to transcribe notes. May dictate notes into recording machine for TRANSCRIBING-MACHINE OPERATOR (clerical) to transcribe.
GOE: 07.05.03 STRENGTH: S GED: R4 M2 L4 SVP: 5 DLU: 77

202.382-010 STENOCAPTIONER (radio-tv broad.)
Operates computerized stenographic captioning equipment to provide *captions* of live television broadcast for hearing-impaired viewers: Discusses program or news story content with broadcast's PRODUCER (radio-tv broad.) 159.117-010 to learn new words and terms which are not included in computer's stenographic glossary. Devises stenographic equivalents of new words or terms and adds them to stenographic glossary. Reviews glossary items before broadcast for words and terms that are likely to be used on-air. Listens to live program dialogue and types stenographic equivalents for words and phrases to provide on-screen captions. May type captions for movie or taped television program [CAPTION WRITER (motion picture; radio-tv broad.) 203.362-026].
GOE: 07.05.03 STRENGTH: S GED: R4 M2 L4 SVP: 8 DLU: 87

203 TYPISTS AND TYPEWRITING-MACHINE OPERATORS

This group includes occupations concerned primarily with recording, transcribing, transmitting, duplicating, and receiving data by means of a typewriter or a machine equipped with a typewriter-like keyboard. Also included are occupations whose duties include substantial typing tasks and occupations concerned with cold-type setting of type. Occupations involving typesetting by metal type or other traditional methods are included in Group 650.

203.132-010 SUPERVISOR, TELEGRAPHIC-TYPEWRITER OPERATORS (clerical) alternate titles: telegraphic-typewriter operator, chief
Supervises and coordinates activities of TELEGRAPHIC-TYPEWRITER OPERATORS (clerical): Assigns duties and monitors sending and receiving of messages. Directs workers keeping files, such as messages, correspondence, instructions, and reports. Inspects equipment and orders repairs of machinery. May operate telegraphic typewriter [TELEGRAPHIC-TYPEWRITER OPERATOR (clerical)]. May transfer operators or regulate work load between stations to ensure even distribution of traffic. Performs other duties as described under SUPERVISOR (clerical) Master Title.
GOE: 07.06.02 STRENGTH: L GED: R4 M2 L4 SVP: 7 DLU: 77

203.132-014 SUPERVISOR, TRANSCRIBING OPERATORS (clerical) alternate titles: transcribing operator, head
Supervises and coordinates activities of TRANSCRIBING-MACHINE OPERATORS (clerical) in a bank or other business organization, performing duties as described under SUPERVISOR (clerical) Master Title.
GOE: 07.06.02 STRENGTH: L GED: R4 M2 L4 SVP: 6 DLU: 77

203.137-010 SUPERVISOR, WORD PROCESSING (clerical)
Supervises and coordinates activities of workers engaged in operating word processing equipment to prepare correspondence, records, reports, insurance policies, and similar items: Advises other departmental personnel in techniques and style of dictation and letter writing. Recommends changes in procedures to effect savings in time, labor and other costs, and to improve operating efficiency. Assigns new workers to experienced workers for training. Assists subordinates in resolving problems in nonstandard situations. Evaluates job performance of subordinates and recommends appropriate personnel action. Performs duties as described under SUPERVISOR (clerical) Master Title.
GOE: 07.06.02 STRENGTH: S GED: R4 M3 L4 SVP: 6 DLU: 77

203.137-014 TYPING SECTION CHIEF (clerical)
Supervises and coordinates activities of TYPISTS (clerical) engaged in transcribing correspondence from longhand copy, typing reports, and making duplicate copies of correspondence. Performs duties as described under SUPERVISOR (clerical) Master Title.

GOE: 07.06.02 STRENGTH: L GED: R4 M2 L3 SVP: 6 DLU: 77

203.362-010 CLERK-TYPIST (clerical)
Compiles data and operates typewriter or computer in performance of routine clerical duties to maintain business records and reports: Types reports, business correspondence, application forms, shipping tickets, and other material. Files records and reports, posts information to records, sorts and distributes mail, answers telephone, and performs similar duties. May compute amounts, using adding or calculating machine. May type on or from specialized forms and be designated Guest-History Clerk (hotel & rest.); Storage-Receipt Poster (clerical). May compile reports and type prescription data on labels in hospital pharmacy and be designated Dispensary Clerk (medical ser.). May be designated: Collection-Card Clerk (clerical); Motor-Pool Clerk (clerical); Order Clerk (utilities); Policy-Issue Clerk (insurance). May operate telex machine to produce records and reports.
GOE: 07.06.02 STRENGTH: S GED: R3 M3 L3 SVP: 4 DLU: 88

203.362-014 CREDIT REPORTING CLERK (business ser.) alternate titles: crt operator
Compiles, posts, and retrieves credit information, using computer, and reports credit information to subscribers of credit reporting agency: Answers requests received by computer modem, mail, or telephone from subscribers for information about credit applicants. Identifies caller by code. Enters inquiry into computer to retrieve requested information. Transmits information to subscriber, using computer and modem, reads information to subscriber over telephone, or generates printout for mailing to subscriber. Compiles and enters credit information into computer.
GOE: 07.06.01 STRENGTH: S GED: R3 M2 L3 SVP: 4 DLU: 77

203.362-026 CAPTION WRITER (motion picture; radio-tv broad.) alternate titles: subtitle writer
Operates computerized captioning system to provide *captions* for movies or taped television productions for hearing-impaired viewers, and to provide captions (subtitles) in English or foreign language: Listens to dialogue of production and writes caption phrases for dialogue. Watches production and reviews captions simultaneously to determine which caption phrases to leave in, which to revise, and where captions should be placed on screen. Enters commands to edit and place captions, and to synchronize captions with dialogue. May write captions to describe music and background noises. May discuss captions with DIRECTOR, MOTION PICTURE (motion picture) 159.067-010, DIRECTOR, TELEVISION (radio-tv broad.) 159.067-014, PRODUCER (motion picture) 187.167-174, or PRODUCER (radio-tv broad.) 159.117-010. May translate foreign language dialogue into English language captions, or translate English dialogue into foreign language captions. May oversee encoding of captions to master tape of television production.
GOE: 07.05.03 STRENGTH: L GED: R4 M2 L4 SVP: 6 DLU: 87

203.382-014 CANCELLATION CLERK (insurance) alternate titles: memorandum-statement clerk; policy-cancellation clerk; premium-cancellation clerk; premium-card-cancellation clerk; termination clerk
Cancels insurance policies as requested by agents: Receives computer printout of cancellation data or retrieves expiration card from file. Checks number on card with number of policy. Computes refunds, using calculator, adding machine, and rate tables. Types cancellation correspondence and mails with canceled policy to policyholder. Types cancellation notice and routes to bookkeeping department for recording. Mails cancellation notice to agent.
GOE: 07.02.02 STRENGTH: S GED: R3 M3 L3 SVP: 5 DLU: 77

203.382-018 MAGNETIC-TAPE-COMPOSER OPERATOR (print. & pub.) alternate titles: composing-machine operator
Operates magnetic-tape recording and typographic composing machine to prepare copy used for offset printing of forms, documents, advertisements, and other matter, following copy and layout instructions and using knowledge of typesetting and typing techniques: Clips copy and instructions to copy holder. Inserts blank tape cartridges on tape-station hubs and starts recorder to thread tape. Selects and attaches specified type-font element to typewriter carrier. Adjusts margins and other spacing mechanisms to set line justification. Types from marked copy, using electric typewriter that simultaneously produces proof copy and master tape. Types in composer control codes according to program sequence to allow change of type font and format. Proofreads copy. Makes corrections by strikeover on proof copy, automatically correcting identical material on master tape, or retypes corrected portions only, generating correction tape. Reference codes correction tape to error location in original copy and tape. Removes tape cartridges from recorder and installs cartridges, with correction tape, if any, into composer-output printer. Installs specified type font and sets escapement and vertical spacing controls. Keys in layout and composing codes on control panel, following program sequence. Inserts coated paper and starts composer. Operates composer controls in response to function-light indicators and changes type font and format as work progresses. Removes copy from composer, examines copy for errors, and makes necessary corrections. May specialize in operation of recorder or composer units. May operate varitype machine to set headline copy [VARITYPE OPERATOR (clerical)]. May prepare final camera-ready copy and layout, using waxing machine and drafting tools and equipment.
GOE: 07.06.02 STRENGTH: S GED: R4 M3 L3 SVP: 5 DLU: 77

203.382-026 VARITYPE OPERATOR (clerical)
Operates one or variety of electrically powered typewriting machines equipped with changeable type fonts to typeset master copies, such as stencils,

direct plates, photo-offsets, and tracings, for reproduction of copies having printed appearance: Plans layout of page elements (illustrations, headlines, and text) from rough draft or specifications, using knowledge of design. Pastes up preprinted type and reproduction proofs on master layout, using paste and brush. Determines size and style of type, horizontal and vertical spacing, and margins, using knowledge of typesetting. Calculates anticipated dimensions of photo-offset copy to be enlarged or reduced, using arithmetic percentages. Attaches fonts to type holder. Attaches gear to platen to control spacing between lines. Moves lever to control spacing between characters. Sets stops to control right margin. Changes style and size of type by pressing type-change key and turning font from reserve to typing position. May draw decorative or illustrative designs on copy. May lay out and rule forms and charts, using drafting tools.
GOE: 07.06.02 STRENGTH: S GED: R3 M2 L3 SVP: 5 DLU: 77

203.382-030 WORD PROCESSING MACHINE OPERATOR (clerical)
   Operates word processing equipment to compile, type, revise, combine, edit, print, and store documents: Compiles material to be typed, following written or oral instructions. Reads instructions accompanying material, or follows verbal instructions from supervisor or person requesting document, to determine format and content required. Enters commands, flips switches, and presses buttons to establish spacing, margins, type size, style, and color, and other parameters, using computer and word processing software or other word processing equipment. Types, revises, and combines material such as correspondence, reports, records, forms, minutes of meetings, scientific or technical material, numerical data, and tabular information, from rough draft, corrected copy, recorded voice dictation, or previous version displayed on screen. Checks completed document on screen for spelling errors, using software. Proofreads and edits document for grammar, spelling, punctuation, and format. Corrects errors. Stores completed document in machine memory or on data storage medium, such as disk. Enters commands to print document. May load paper in printer and change printer ribbon, print wheel, or fluid cartridges. May keep record of work performed. May input data for revision or editing, using data entry device other than keyboard, such as optical scanner. Variations in means by which tasks are accomplished result from brand of computer, printer, other word processing equipment, and software used.
GOE: 07.06.02 STRENGTH: S GED: R3 M2 L3 SVP: 5 DLU: 86

203.562-010 WIRE-TRANSFER CLERK (financial) alternate titles: funds transfer clerk
   Transfers funds or securities and maintains records of transactions, using computer: Types, transmits, and receives funds transfer messages on computer terminal to or from other banks and Federal Reserve Bank. Records funds or securities transferred and disposition, using computer. May maintain file of customers requiring daily transfer of funds or securities. May verify or assign code number to telecommunication messages.
GOE: 07.06.02 STRENGTH: S GED: R3 M3 L3 SVP: 4 DLU: 89

203.582-010 BRAILLE OPERATOR (print. & pub.)
   Operates machine, similar to typewriter, to impress dots in metal sheets for making braille books, transcribing from prepared copy or original script: Inserts metal sheet into machine carriage. Depresses one or combination of keys to form braille letter. Depresses pedal that forces punches to impress on metal sheet combinations of dots that distinguish braille letters. If worker is blind, transcribes from recorded rather than manuscript copy.
GOE: 07.06.02 STRENGTH: L GED: R3 M1 L3 SVP: 4 DLU: 77

203.582-014 BRAILLE TYPIST (education; nonprofit organ.; print. & pub.) alternate titles: braille coder; braille transcriber
   Operates braille typewriter to transcribe reading matter for use by the blind: Reads copy and operates braille typewriter to emboss specially treated paper with various combinations of dots that characterize braille alphabet, using braille code form.
GOE: 07.06.02 STRENGTH: S GED: R4 M1 L3 SVP: 5 DLU: 77

203.582-018 CRYPTOGRAPHIC-MACHINE OPERATOR (clerical) alternate titles: code clerk; cryptographic technician
   Operates cryptographic equipment to code, transmit, and decode secret messages for units of armed forces, law enforcement agencies, or business organizations: Selects required code according to instructions, using code book. Inserts specified code card into machine station to program encoding machine. Types plain text data on keyboard of automatic machine which encrypts and transmits message, or on semiautomatic machine which converts plain text into taped code for transmission via teletype machine. Feeds incoming tape into decoder device on semiautomatic machine and distributes decoded messages. Resolves garbled or undecipherable messages, using cryptographic procedures and equipment or requests retransmission of message. May operate teletype or teleprinter equipment to transmit messages. May operate radio to send and receive data.
GOE: 07.06.02 STRENGTH: S GED: R4 M2 L3 SVP: 5 DLU: 77

203.582-038 PERFORATOR TYPIST (clerical)
   Operates special typewriter that perforates tape or paper for subsequent automatic reproduction of data, such as letters, reports, and other material from master copy: Pastes gummed paper over holes to correct errors. May file perforated rolls. May operate automatic typewriter that reproduces material from perforated tape or paper and be designated Typewriter Operator, Automatic (clerical). Important variations are kinds (trade names) of machines used.
GOE: 07.06.02 STRENGTH: S GED: R3 M1 L3 SVP: 4 DLU: 77

203.582-042 PHOTOCOMPOSING-PERFORATOR-MACHINE OPERATOR (print. & pub.)
   Operates automatic photocomposing-perforator machine equipped with keyboard to copy data from manuscript onto tape used in photocomposing machine: Inserts *paper tape* in perforator. Clips copy in copy holder and starts perforator mechanism. Sets indexed dials to select line length, type size, film feed, and type face specified on manuscript. Depresses keys of keyboard to perforate coded signals in paper tape for subsequent activation of photocomposing machine. Removes perforated tape from perforator. Important variables are trade names of system operated. May operate similar machine equipped with video display terminal to edit and correct perforated tape as indicated by PROOFREADER (print. & pub.) on reproduction proof.
GOE: 07.06.02 STRENGTH: S GED: R4 M3 L3 SVP: 6 DLU: 77

203.582-046 PHOTOCOMPOSITION-KEYBOARD OPERATOR (print. & pub.)
   Operates keyboard of computer terminal equipped with video display screen to record data from manuscript for storage and retrieval into and from computer system for subsequent reproduction as printed matter: Reads instructions on worksheet to obtain codes which direct specific computer activity and depresses command keys on terminal keyboard to store or retrieve data. Reads manuscript and types on keyboard to record and store data into computer memory. Reads corrected proof sheet and depresses keys to retrieve specified portions of text for display on video screen. Observes screen to locate text to be corrected and types corrections. Maintains log of activities. If worker operates similar equipment to perforate *paper tape* used to activate photocomposing machine, see PHOTOCOMPOSING-PERFORATOR-MACHINE OPERATOR (print. & pub.).
GOE: 07.06.02 STRENGTH: S GED: R3 M2 L3 SVP: 4 DLU: 77

203.582-050 TELEGRAPHIC-TYPEWRITER OPERATOR (clerical) alternate titles: telegraph operator, automatic
   Operates telegraphic typewriter to send and receive messages: Turns on machine and types identifying code for station called or acknowledges calls from other stations. Types outgoing messages when stations are connected. Reads incoming messages to detect errors and presses lever to stop transmission when messages are garbled or overlined. Types requests for clarification. Enters date, time, and serial number on messages sent and received. Pastes messages received on tape on paper forms. May type messages on tape attachment and transmit them by inserting tape into machine when stations are connected. May be designated according to system used as Multiplex-Machine Operator (tel. & tel.). Important variations are kinds (trade names) of telegraphic typewriters operated.
GOE: 07.06.02 STRENGTH: S GED: R3 M2 L3 SVP: 4 DLU: 77

203.582-054 DATA ENTRY CLERK (clerical) alternate titles: data entry operator
   Operates keyboard or other data entry device to enter data into computer or onto magnetic tape or disk for subsequent processing: Enters alphabetic, numeric, or symbolic data from source documents into computer, using data entry device, such as keyboard or optical scanner, and following format displayed on screen. Compares data entered with source documents, or re-enters data in verification format on screen to detect errors. Deletes incorrectly entered data, and re-enters correct data. May compile, sort, and verify accuracy of data to be entered. May keep record of work completed.
GOE: 07.06.01 STRENGTH: S GED: R3 M2 L3 SVP: 4 DLU: 89

203.582-058 TRANSCRIBING-MACHINE OPERATOR (clerical) alternate titles: dictating-machine transcriber; dictating-machine typist
   Operates typewriter or word processor/computer to transcribe letters, reports, or other recorded data heard through earphones of transcribing machine: Inserts cassette tape into cassette player or positions tape on machine spindle and threads tape through machine. Positions earphones on ears and presses buttons on transcribing machine to listen to recorded data. Turns dials to control volume, tone, and speed of voice reproduction. Depresses pedal to pause tape. Types message heard through earphones. Reads chart prepared by dictator to determine length of message and corrections to be made. May type unrecorded information, such as name, address, and date. May keep file of records. May receive and route callers [RECEPTIONIST (clerical) 237.367-038]. May be designated by subject matter transcribed as Legal Transcriber (clerical); Medical Transcriber (clerical).
GOE: 07.06.02 STRENGTH: S GED: R3 M1 L3 SVP: 5 DLU: 86

203.582-062 TYPESETTER-PERFORATOR OPERATOR (print. & pub.) alternate titles: perforator operator
   Operates keyboard of tape perforator machine to type visible proof copy and copy data from manuscript onto tape used for producing automatic type composition: Secures roll of tape and blank stationery in machine magazine. Turns adjustment screws to set indicator scale that controls counting mechanism according to type size and width of line to be composed. Positions copy in copyholder and depresses keys on keyboard to punch tape. Observes justification (even margin) points on indicator scale to determine when to end line. Removes completed roll of tape for delivery to typesetting machines. May be designated by type of machine operated as Justowriter Operator (print. & pub.).
GOE: 07.06.02 STRENGTH: S GED: R3 M1 L3 SVP: 4 DLU: 77

203.582-066 TYPIST (clerical)
   Operates typewriter or computer to type and revise documents: Compiles material to be typed. Reads instructions accompanying material, or follows verbal

instructions from supervisor or person requesting document, to determine format desired, number of copies needed, priority, and other requirements. Types and revises material such as correspondence, reports, statistical tables, addresses, and forms, from rough draft, corrected copy, recorded voice dictation, or previous version displayed on screen, using typewriter or computer and word processing software. May verify totals on report forms, requisitions, or bills. May operate duplicating machine to reproduce copy. May be designated according to material typed, as Address-Change Clerk (insurance); Endorsement Clerk (insurance); Policy Writer (insurance); Record Clerk (hotel & rest.); Statistical Typist (clerical). May be designated: Application-Register Clerk (insurance); Filing Writer (insurance); Master-Sheet Clerk (insurance); Mortgage-Papers-Assignment-and-Assembly Clerk (insurance); Stencil Cutter (clerical); Tabular Typist (clerical); Title Clerk, Automobile (clerical).
GOE: 07.06.02 STRENGTH: S GED: R3 M2 L3 SVP: 3 DLU: 88

203.582-078 NOTEREADER (clerical)
Operates typewriter to transcribe stenotyped notes of court proceedings, following standard formats for type of material transcribed: Reads work order to obtain information, such as type of case, case number, number of copies required, and spelling of participants' names. Reviews form books to ascertain format required for specified document, and adjusts typewriter settings for indentation, line spacing, and other style requirements. Operates typewriter to transcribe contractions and symbols of stenotyped text into standard language form. Proofreads typed copy to identify and correct errors and to verify format specifications. Copies typed documents, using copying machines. May use automatic or manual stenotype noteholder.
GOE: 07.06.02 STRENGTH: S GED: R3 M1 L3 SVP: 5 DLU: 86

205 INTERVIEWING CLERKS

This group includes occupations concerned with interviewing and eliciting information. Work frequently involves assisting persons in completing application forms, verifying information obtained, and performing various clerical tasks in relation to records prepared. Clerical occupations concerned with eliciting and recording information and making determinations for such purposes as extending credit, resolving customer complaints, and adjusting claims, are found in Group 241.

205.137-014 SUPERVISOR, SURVEY WORKERS (clerical) alternate titles: area coordinator; field supervisor
Supervises and coordinates activities of workers engaged in interviewing people to compile statistical information about topics, such as public issues or consumer buying habits: Recruits and hires interviewers. Trains interviewers in method of approaching public, asking questions, and recording answers. Supplies interviewers with names or addresses of persons to contact or instructs them in sampling methods used in compiling contact lists. Reviews questionnaires for completeness and accuracy. Verifies work of interviewers by telephoning persons interviewed to review answers and evaluate personal manner of interviewers. Tallies number of calls made and questionnaires completed by interviewers. Reviews, classifies, and sorts questionnaires, following specified procedures and criteria.
GOE: 07.04.01 STRENGTH: L GED: R4 M3 L3 SVP: 6 DLU: 77

205.162-010 ADMITTING OFFICER (medical ser.)
Coordinates activities related to admission of patients in hospital or other medical facility: Confers with physicians, and nursing, housekeeping, transport, and other staff members to coordinate and schedule admission of patient. Assigns accommodations based on physician's admittance orders, patient's preference, nature of illness, availability of space, and other information, and enters bed assignment information into computer. Prepares records of admission, transfer, and other required data. Notifies departments of patient's admission. Reviews clerical work of interviewers and other personnel. Keeps records of admissions and discharges, and compiles occupancy-census data. May interview patient or patient's representative to obtain necessary personal and financial data to determine eligibility for admission. May perform duties described under SUPERVISOR (clerical) Master Title.
GOE: 07.04.01 STRENGTH: S GED: R4 M2 L3 SVP: 7 DLU: 89

205.362-010 CIVIL-SERVICE CLERK (government ser.) alternate titles: appointment clerk; recruitment clerk
Keeps records of selection and assignment of personnel in office that recruits workers from civil service register: Mails announcements of examinations and blank application forms in response to requests. Performs reception duties and answers questions about examinations, eligibility, salaries, benefits, and other pertinent information. Issues application forms to applicants at counter. Reviews applications for completeness, accuracy, and eligibility requirements. Files application forms, test papers, and records. Reviews examination ratings and places names of eligibles on register. Refers names from register to agency head and notifies eligible applicants of appointment. Posts results of interviews on file cards. Requests references from present or past employers concerning applicants. Types reports and forms. May keep records, such as group life insurance and retirement payments. May administer civil service examinations to applicants.
GOE: 07.04.04 STRENGTH: S GED: R3 M2 L3 SVP: 3 DLU: 77

205.362-014 EMPLOYMENT CLERK (clerical) alternate titles: interviewer; reception interviewer
Interviews applicants for employment and processes application forms: Interviews applicants to obtain information, such as age, marital status, work experience, education, training, and occupational interest. Informs applicants of company employment policies. Refers qualified applicants to employing official. Types letters to references indicated on application, or telephones agencies, such as credit bureaus and finance companies. Files applications forms. Compiles and types reports for supervisors on applicants and employees from personnel records. May review credentials to establish eligibility of applicant in regard to identification and naturalization. May telephone or write applicant to inform applicant of acceptance or rejection for employment. May administer aptitude, personality, and interest tests. May compile personnel records [PERSONNEL CLERK (clerical)].
GOE: 07.04.01 STRENGTH: S GED: R4 M2 L4 SVP: 5 DLU: 77

205.362-018 HOSPITAL-ADMITTING CLERK (medical ser.) alternate titles: admissions clerk; clinic clerk; hospital-receiving clerk; medical clerk
Interviews incoming patient or representative and enters information required for admission into computer: Interviews patient or representative to obtain and record name, address, age, religion, persons to notify in case of emergency, attending physician, and individual or insurance company responsible for payment of bill. Explains hospital regulations, such as visiting hours, payment of accounts, and schedule of charges. Escorts patient or arranges for escort to assigned room or ward. Enters patient admitting information into computer and routes printed copy to designated department. Obtains signed statement from patient to protect hospital's interests. May assign patient to room or ward. May compile data for occupancy and census records. May store patient's valuables. May receive payments on account.
GOE: 07.04.01 STRENGTH: S GED: R3 M2 L3 SVP: 4 DLU: 88

205.362-022 IDENTIFICATION CLERK (clerical) alternate titles: security clerk
Compiles and records personal data about civilian workers, vendors, contractors, military personnel, and dependents of military personnel at defense installation and prepares badges, passes, and identification cards: Interviews applicants to obtain and verify information, such as name, date of birth, physical description, and type of security clearance held. Corresponds with law enforcement officials, previous employers, and other references to obtain applicant's social, moral, and political background for use by department in determining employment acceptability. Photographs new workers, using automatic identification camera. May fingerprint workers and keep other supplemental identification systems. May keep records of badges issued, lost, and reissued. May issue temporary identification badges to visitors.
GOE: 07.04.01 STRENGTH: S GED: R3 M1 L3 SVP: 3 DLU: 77

205.362-026 CUSTOMER SERVICE REPRESENTATIVE (financial)
Opens accounts, explains and processes investments and other financial services, and corrects records: Interviews customers to obtain information and explain available financial services, such as savings and checking accounts, Individual Retirement Account, Certificates of Deposit, savings bonds, and securities. Rents safe deposit boxes. Types account information obtained from customer on record card or form, and enters into computer. Answers customer questions and investigates and corrects errors, following customer and establishment records, and using calculator or computer. Presents funds received from customer to TELLER (financial) 211.362-018 for deposit, and obtains receipt for customer. May help customer complete loan application. May obtain credit records from credit reporting agency. May admit customers to safe deposit vault. May execute wire transfers of funds.
GOE: 07.04.01 STRENGTH: L GED: R4 M3 L4 SVP: 6 DLU: 90

205.362-030 OUTPATIENT-ADMITTING CLERK (medical ser.)
Interviews new outpatients at hospital or clinic and records data on medical charts: Obtains specified information from patient, such as age, insurance coverage, and symptoms, and types information onto prescribed forms. Places records and blank history sheets in order and files them in folder. Schedules appointments for examinations in hospital clinics, according to nature of illness. Gives general information about outpatient care and answers telephone. May tally number of outpatients entering each day or week. May give first aid.
GOE: 07.04.01 STRENGTH: S GED: R3 M2 L3 SVP: 4 DLU: 77

205.367-010 ADMISSIONS EVALUATOR (education) alternate titles: administrative assistant; degree clerk
Examines academic records of students to determine eligibility for graduation or for admission to college, university, or graduate school: Compares transcripts of courses with school entrance or degree requirements and prepares evaluation form listing courses for graduation. Studies course prerequisites, degree equivalents, and accreditation of schools, and computes grade-point averages to establish students' qualifications for admission, transfer, or graduation. Explains evaluations to students. Refers students with academic discrepancies to proper department heads for further action. Types list of accepted applicants or of degree candidates and submits it for approval. Issues registration permits and records acceptances and fees paid. Performs related duties, such as preparing commencement programs and computing student averages for honors. May advise students concerning their eligibility for teacher certificates. May specialize in evaluation of transfer students' records and be designated Evaluator, Transfer Students (education).
GOE: 07.01.05 STRENGTH: S GED: R4 M2 L4 SVP: 6 DLU: 77

205.367-014 CHARGE-ACCOUNT CLERK (clerical) alternate titles: credit-card interviewer; new-account interviewer
Interviews customers applying for charge accounts: Confers with customer to explain type of charge plans available. Assists customer in filling out applica-

tion or completes application for customer. Reviews applications received by mail. Files credit applications after credit department approves or disapproves credit. May check references by phone or form letter and notify customer of acceptance or rejection of credit [CREDIT CLERK (clerical)]. May verify entries and correct errors on charge accounts [CUSTOMER-COMPLAINT CLERK (clerical)], using adding machine. May answer credit rating requests from banks and credit bureaus. May issue temporary shopping slip when credit references appear satisfactory.
GOE: 07.04.01 STRENGTH: S GED: R3 M2 L3 SVP: 2 DLU: 77

205.367-018 CLAIMS CLERK II (insurance) alternate titles: loss-claim clerk

Prepares reports and insurance-claim forms for damage or loss against insurance companies: Obtains information from insured to prepare claim form. Forwards report of claim or claim form to insurance company. Acts as intermediary between company and insured. May assist in settling claims.
GOE: 07.04.02 STRENGTH: S GED: R3 M3 L3 SVP: 4 DLU: 77

205.367-022 CREDIT CLERK (clerical) alternate titles: loan clerk

Processes applications of individuals applying for loans and credit: Interviews applicant to obtain personal and financial data and fills out application. Calls or writes to credit bureaus, employers, and personal references to check credit and personal references. Establishes credit limit, considering such factors as applicant's assets, credit experience, and personal references, based on predetermined standards. Notifies customer by mail, telephone, or in person of acceptance or rejection of application. May keep record or file of credit transactions, deposits, and payments, and sends letters or confers with customers having delinquent accounts to make payment [COLLECTION CLERK (clerical) 241.357-010]. May send form letters and brochures to solicit business from prospective customers. May adjust incorrect credit charges and grant extensions of credit on overdue accounts. May accept payment on accounts. May keep record of applications for loans and credit, using computer. May compute interest and payments, using calculator. May provide customer credit information or rating on request to retail stores, credit agencies, or banks. May check value of customer's collateral, such as securities, held as security for loan. May advise customer by phone or in writing about loan or credit information. May assist customer in filling out loan or credit application.
GOE: 07.04.01 STRENGTH: S GED: R4 M3 L4 SVP: 4 DLU: 88

205.367-026 CREEL CLERK (government ser.)

Interviews anglers and inspects catch to compile statistical data concerning recreational fishing: Greets anglers returning from recreational fishing and solicits permission to examine catch. Counts and examines fish to ascertain total caught and to identify species and sex. Collects deformed or diseased fish for analysis by others. Measures and weighs fish, using ruler and scale. Interviews anglers to determine state of residence, method and location of fishing, and type of bait used. Records data obtained and tabulates results.
GOE: 07.04.01 STRENGTH: L GED: R3 M3 L3 SVP: 2 DLU: 77

205.367-030 ELECTION CLERK (government ser.) alternate titles: poll clerk; returning officer

Performs any combination of the following duties during elections: Compiles and verifies voter lists from official registration records. Requests identification of voters at polling place. Obtains signatures and records names of voters to prevent voting of unauthorized persons. Distributes ballots to voters and answers questions concerning voting procedure. Counts valid ballots and prepares official reports of election results.
GOE: 07.04.03 STRENGTH: S GED: R3 M2 L2 SVP: 2 DLU: 77

205.367-034 LICENSE CLERK (government ser.)

Issues licenses or permits to qualified applicants: Questions applicant to obtain information, such as name, address, and age, and records data on prescribed forms. Evaluates information obtained to determine applicant qualification for licensure. Collects prescribed fee. Issues driver, automobile, marriage, or other license. May conduct oral, visual, written, or performance test to determine applicant qualifications.
GOE: 07.04.03 STRENGTH: L GED: R3 M2 L3 SVP: 3 DLU: 78

205.367-038 REGISTRAR (government ser.) alternate titles: entrance guard

Registers visitors to public facilities, such as national or state parks, military bases, and monuments: Stops vehicles and pedestrians at gate and records name, nationality, home address, license plate number of vehicle, and time of entrance and departure. Cautions visitors about fires, wild animals, travel hazards, and domestic pets and informs them of laws and regulations pertaining to area. May issue information leaflets. May collect fees and issue entry and fire permits. May give talks describing historical, natural, or scenic points of area.
GOE: 07.04.03 STRENGTH: L GED: R3 M2 L3 SVP: 5 DLU: 77

205.367-042 REGISTRATION CLERK (government ser.)

Interviews persons to compile information for legal or other records: Records answers to personal history queries, such as date of birth, length of residence in United States, and change of address to enroll persons for voting, citizenship applications, or other purposes. May record number of applicants registered. May fingerprint registrants [FINGERPRINT CLERK (government ser.) I]. May take affidavits concerning registrants' statement.
GOE: 07.04.01 STRENGTH: S GED: R3 M2 L3 SVP: 3 DLU: 77

205.367-046 REHABILITATION CLERK (nonprofit org.)

Compiles, verifies, and records client data in vocational rehabilitation facility: Interviews clients to obtain information, such as medical history and work limitations. Prepares and assists clients to complete routine intake and personnel forms. Gives and receives client information in person, by telephone, or mail to authorized persons. Prepares and types client attendance, training, and counseling reports from client records. Reviews training approval forms and payment vouchers for completeness and accuracy.
GOE: 07.04.01 STRENGTH: S GED: R3 M2 L2 SVP: 4 DLU: 77

205.367-050 SUPERVISOR, CONTINGENTS (retail trade)

Interviews and hires applicants for contingent (temporary and part-time) work and keeps employment records: Reviews applications and hires applicants. Notifies applicants by mail or telephone to report for work. Prepares and approves payroll vouchers. Keeps employment records. Compiles list of workers qualified for contingent employment. May schedule work assignments.
GOE: 07.04.01 STRENGTH: S GED: R4 M2 L4 SVP: 6 DLU: 77

205.367-054 SURVEY WORKER (clerical) alternate titles: interviewer; merchandising representative; public interviewer

Interviews people and compiles statistical information on topics, such as public issues or consumer buying habits: Contacts people at home or place of business, or approaches persons at random on street, or contacts them by telephone, following specified sampling procedures. Asks questions following specified outline on questionnaire and records answers. Reviews, classifies, and sorts questionnaires following specified procedures and criteria. May participate in federal, state, or local population survey and be known as Census Enumerator (government ser.).
GOE: 07.04.01 STRENGTH: L GED: R3 M1 L2 SVP: 2 DLU: 81

205.367-058 TRAFFIC CHECKER (government ser.)

Interviews motor vehicle drivers at specified road intersection or highway to secure information for use in highway planning: Places equipment, such as barricades, signs, and automatic vehicle counting devices. Signals driver to stop, presents identification credentials, and explains reason for halting vehicle. Questions driver to obtain data, such as itinerary and purpose of trip. Records results of interview, and permits driver to continue journey. May secure information on load (either passenger or cargo) carried and type and weight of vehicle.
GOE: 07.04.01 STRENGTH: L GED: R2 M2 L2 SVP: 2 DLU: 77

205.367-062 REFERRAL CLERK, TEMPORARY HELP AGENCY (clerical) alternate titles: referral clerk; staffing clerk

Compiles and records information about temporary job openings and refers qualified applicants from register of temporary help agency: Answers call from hospital, business, or other type of organization requesting temporary workers and obtains and records job requirements. Reviews records to locate registered workers who match job requirements and are available for scheduled shift. Notifies selected workers of job availability and records referral information on agency records. Sorts mail, files records, and performs other clerical duties. May give employment applications to applicants, schedule interviews with agency registration interviewers, or administer skill tests. May refer workers in specific occupations, such as nursing.
GOE: 07.05.03 STRENGTH: S GED: R3 M3 L3 SVP: 3 DLU: 86

205.567-010 BENEFITS CLERK II (clerical) alternate titles: insurance and benefits clerk

Answers employees' questions and records employee enrollment in benefits and group insurance programs: Explains and interprets company insurance program to employees and dependents. Answers questions regarding benefits, such as pension and retirement plan, and group insurance, such as life, hospitalization, and workers' compensation. Fills out application forms or verifies information on forms submitted by employees. Mails applications to insurance company. Files records of claims and fills out cancellation forms when employees leave company service. May correspond with or telephone physicians, hospitals, and employees regarding claims.
GOE: 07.05.03 STRENGTH: S GED: R3 M3 L3 SVP: 4 DLU: 80

206   FILE CLERKS

This group includes occupations concerned with classifying, sorting, and filing correspondence, records, and other data.

206.137-010 SUPERVISOR, FILES (clerical) alternate titles: records-section supervisor

Supervises and coordinates activities of workers engaged in maintaining central records files: Directs and assists workers in storing, retrieving, checking, correcting, and copying paper documents, microfilm, or other company records. Directs workers in searching files to retrieve lost or missing records, utilizing knowledge of frequent filing errors. Routes erroneously removed files to workers for refiling. Directs and assists workers in periodic disposal of obsolete files, following company policy and legal requirements. Conducts and coordinates studies of files and filing system as directed by management. May recommend changes in work procedures to improve filing-system efficiency. May supervise workers engaged in microfilming records. Performs duties as described under SUPERVISOR (clerical) Master Title.
GOE: 07.05.03 STRENGTH: L GED: R4 M2 L4 SVP: 7 DLU: 88

206.367-010   ENGINEERING-DOCUMENT-CONTROL CLERK (aircraft mfg.; electron. comp.) alternate titles: blueprint control clerk; drawing-release clerk; engineering-release clerk; release and technical records clerk

Compiles and maintains control records and related files to release blueprints, drawings, and engineering documents to manufacturing and other operating departments: Examines documents, such as blueprints, drawings, change orders, and specifications to verify completeness and accuracy of data. Confers with document originators or engineering liaison personnel to resolve discrepancies and compiles required changes to documents. Posts changes to computerized or manual control records, releases documents, and notifies affected departments. Maintains related files. May prepare requests for reproduction of documents. May operate reproduction equipment. May prepare reports and memorandums.
GOE: 07.05.03 STRENGTH: L GED: R4 M3 L4 SVP: 6 DLU: 89

206.367-014   FILE CLERK II (clerical)

Files correspondence, cards, invoices, receipts, and other records in alphabetical or numerical order, or according to subject matter, or other system [FILE CLERK (clerical) I 206.387-034], searches for and investigates information contained in files, inserts additional data on file records, completes reports, keeps files current, and supplies information from file data. Classifies material when classification is not readily discernible [CLASSIFICATION CLERK (clerical) 206.387-010]. Disposes of obsolete files in accordance with established retirement schedule or legal requirements. May copy records on photocopying or microfilming machines. May type labels or reports. May make calculations or use calculating machine to keep files current. May be designated according to material filed.
GOE: 07.05.03 STRENGTH: L GED: R3 M2 L3 SVP: 3 DLU: 87

206.367-018   TAPE LIBRARIAN (clerical)

Classifies, catalogs, and maintains library of computer tapes: Classifies reels and cartridges of magnetic computer tape according to content, purpose, principal user, date generated, or other criteria. Assigns identification number, following standard system. Prepares catalog of tapes classified, using logbook and computer. Stores tapes according to classification and identification number. Issues tapes and maintains charge-out record. Inspects returned tapes and notifies supervisor when tapes are worn or damaged. Removes obsolete tapes from library, following data retention requirements. May send tapes to vendor for cleaning and to off-site location for secure storage. May maintain files of program developmental records and operating instructions. May work in computer room operations, performing tasks such as loading and removing paper and printouts and reels of tape.
GOE: 07.05.03 STRENGTH: L GED: R4 M2 L3 SVP: 4 DLU: 89

206.387-010   CLASSIFICATION CLERK (clerical) alternate titles: coding file clerk

Classifies materials according to subject matter and assigns numbers or symbols from predetermined coding system to facilitate accurate filing and reference: Scans correspondence, reports, drawings, and other materials to be filed to determine subject matter. Ascertains specified number or symbol, using code book or chart, and marks or stamps code on material. Assigns cross-indexing numbers if subject matter should be classified and filed under more than one heading. May revise coding system to improve code usage.
GOE: 07.05.03 STRENGTH: S GED: R3 M2 L3 SVP: 5 DLU: 80

206.387-014   FINGERPRINT CLERK II (government ser.)

Examines fingerprint patterns and classifies prints according to standard system: Examines fingerprints, using magnifying glass, to determine pattern formations. Classifies fingerprints according to standard system and records classification on file cards. Files records, following prescribed sequence. Searches fingerprint identification files to provide information to authorized persons.
GOE: 07.05.03 STRENGTH: S GED: R4 M2 L3 SVP: 4 DLU: 77

206.387-022   RECORD CLERK (textile)

Keeps files of sample pads, slubbings (slightly twisted fibers), and yarns for color comparison and stock reference: Attaches identification tags indicating data, such as color blend, batch number, and date of shipment, to sample pads, slubbings, and yarns, and files them. Files order forms, formula cards, and color percentage cards. May make sample pads from slubbings [PAD MAKER (textile)].
GOE: 07.07.01 STRENGTH: L GED: R3 M2 L2 SVP: 3 DLU: 77

206.387-034   FILE CLERK I (clerical)

Files records in alphabetical or numerical order, or according to subject matter or other system: Reads incoming material and sorts according to file system. Places cards, forms, microfiche, or other material in storage receptacle, such as file cabinet, drawer, or box. Locates and removes files upon request. Keeps records of material removed, stamps material received, traces missing files, and types indexing information on folders. May verify accuracy of material to be filed. May enter information on records. May examine microfilm and microfiche for legibility, using microfilm and microfiche viewers. May color-code material to be filed to reduce filing errors. May be designated according to subject matter filed, such as Change-of-Address Clerk (clerical); or according to material filed, such as File Clerk, Correspondence (clerical).
GOE: 07.07.01 STRENGTH: L GED: R3 M1 L2 SVP: 3 DLU: 87

206.587-010   BRAND RECORDER (government ser.)

Records brand marks used to identify cattle, produce, or other commodities, to facilitate identification: Receives applications for new brands and verifies against official brand records to prevent duplication. Records assignment or reassignment of brands beside name of appropriate individual or organization. Receives and records brand recording fees and submits brand certificates for approval. Keeps files of reports compiled by field inspectors to prevent frauds and unauthorized use of brands.
GOE: 07.05.03 STRENGTH: S GED: R3 M1 L2 SVP: 4 DLU: 77

207   DUPLICATING-MACHINE OPERATORS AND TENDERS

This group includes occupations concerned with making copies by means of office machines. Three major duplicating processes used are: photocopy (including photographic), spirit (or fluid), and stencil (ink). An image created by one of these processes is either transferred directly, as with the photocopying machine, or indirectly, as with the offset duplicating machine. Also included is the duplicating of braille-printed pages on chemically treated plastic paper. This group does not include offset printing machine and press occupations which are found in Groups 651 and 652.

207.137-010   CHIEF CLERK, PRINT SHOP (clerical)

Supervises and coordinates activities of workers in duplicating department: Analyzes requisitions for duplicating to determine method of reproduction, based on requested completion date, and availability and specialization of machines and machine operators. Keeps file indicating priority, date due, and status of job. Examines material in process and suggests improved methods of reproduction. Oversees machine preventive-maintenance program. May confer with persons requesting printing or duplicating to determine preference of methods and materials. May keep stock of duplicating material and requisition material. May keep supply of standard forms and issue forms on requisition. Performs other duties as described under SUPERVISOR (clerical) Master Title. May supervise workers engaged in making microfilm or microfiche copies of records and be designated Micrographics-Services Supervisor (clerical).
GOE: 05.10.05 STRENGTH: L GED: R4 M2 L3 SVP: 6 DLU: 77

207.682-010   DUPLICATING-MACHINE OPERATOR I (clerical)

Operates machine to reproduce data or ruled forms on paper from type in flat impression bed or plates on revolving cylinder: Selects type or embossed plate and positions type or plate on cylinder or flat bed of machine. Loads paper in feed tray and makes adjustments to parts, such as inking rolls or ribbon and feeding mechanism. Starts machine which automatically pushes sheets under revolving cylinder or against flat impression bed of type where paper is printed. May keep record of number of copies made. Important variations may be indicated by trade name of machines used.
GOE: 05.10.05 STRENGTH: L GED: R3 M2 L1 SVP: 4 DLU: 77

207.682-014   DUPLICATING-MACHINE OPERATOR II (clerical)

Operates duplicating machine to print typewritten or handwritten matter directly from master copy: Places master copy on drum of machine and blank paper in feed tray. Adjusts machine for speed, size of paper, and flow of process liquid to moistening pad. Starts machine that pulls blank sheets across moistening pad and transfers image from master copy onto copy sheet. May type or draw diagram to prepare original copy. Important variations may be indicated by trade name of machine operated.
GOE: 05.12.19 STRENGTH: L GED: R2 M1 L1 SVP: 4 DLU: 77

207.682-018   OFFSET-DUPLICATING-MACHINE OPERATOR (clerical)

Operates offset-duplicating machine to reproduce single or multicolor copies of charts, schedules, bulletins, and related matter, according to oral instructions or layout and stock specifications on job order: Installs sensitized metal printing plate or master copy of plastic-coated paper around press cylinder of machine and locks plate or master copy into position, using handtools. Turns handwheel and ink fountain screws to regulate ink flow. Selects paper stock to be printed according to color, size, thickness, and quantity specified, stacks paper on feed table, and positions spring guide on side of paper stack. Turns elevator crank to raise feed table to paper height. Sets dial controls to adjust speed and feed of machine according to weight of paper. Starts machine that automatically reproduces copy by offset process. Cleans and files master copy or plate. Cleans and oils machine. May prepare printing plates. May operate stencil-process or spirit-duplicating machines and photocopy equipment. Important variations may be indicated by trade names of machines used.
GOE: 05.10.05 STRENGTH: M GED: R3 M2 L1 SVP: 5 DLU: 77

207.685-010   BRAILLE-DUPLICATING-MACHINE OPERATOR (print. & pub.) alternate titles: braille-thermoform operator

Tends equipment to reproduce braille-embossed pages, using one of following methods: (1) Places master page on screen bed. Places roll of treated paper on stand. Threads paper through equipment and locks paper in clamping frame. Pulls heat unit over clamping frame. Depresses pedal or handle to lower clamping frame onto screen bed and to create vacuum that forms braille impressions. Pushes heat unit from bed. Releases pedal or handle to raise clamping frame, and releases catch on frame to draw reproduced copy through equipment. Repeats process to make required number of copies. Cuts copies apart, using scissors. Writes identifying information, such as page number or title, on each copy. (2) Positions master page on screen bed. Places sheet of heat-sensitive plastic paper over page and lowers clamping frame to lock page into position on bed. Pulls heat unit over clamping frame to activate vacuum pump trip-lever. Holds heat unit over frame to form braille impressions. Pushes heat

unit from bed to release vacuum. Raises frame to release individual copy. Repeats process to make required number of copies. Most workers in this occupation are blind.
GOE: 05.12.19 STRENGTH: M GED: R2 M1 L2 SVP: 2 DLU: 77

207.685-014 PHOTOCOPYING-MACHINE OPERATOR (clerical)
Tends duplicating machine to reproduce handwritten or typewritten matter: Places original copy on glass plate in machine. Places blank paper on loading tray. Sets control switch for number of copies. Presses button to start machine which transfers image of original copy onto blank paper by photographic and static electricity process. May clean and repair machine. May receive payment for duplicate copies. Important variables may be indicated by trade name of machine tended.
GOE: 05.12.19 STRENGTH: L GED: R2 M1 L1 SVP: 2 DLU: 77

207.685-018 PHOTOGRAPHIC-MACHINE OPERATOR (clerical)
Tends machine that photographs original documents, such as bills, statements, receipts, and checks: Loads machine with film. Feeds records to be photographed into feed rolls that carry material to be photographed past camera lens, or positions records on table beneath camera lens. May adjust camera distance from document, focus, and exposure settings to accommodate size of record and ensure clarity and resolution of image. May tend equipment which encases roll film in cartridges or mounts microfiche (sheet of microfilm) on aperture card.
GOE: 05.12.19 STRENGTH: L GED: R3 M2 L2 SVP: 2 DLU: 87

208 MAILING AND MISCELLANEOUS OFFICE MACHINE OPERATORS

This group includes mailing and miscellaneous office machine occupations, not elsewhere classified, concerned with using machines to record data; to emboss data on metal or plastic plates for addressing and identification purposes; to sort and fold printed or typewritten matter; to insert, seal, address, and stamp mail; and to open envelopes. Occupations involving substantial typing duties and use of machines equipped with typewriter-like keyboards to record data or to typeset printed matter, using methods other than preparation of metal plates or 'slugs' are found in Group 203. Occupations concerned with operating automatic data processing equipment are found in Group 213.

208.382-010 TERMINAL-MAKEUP OPERATOR (print. & pub.) alternate titles: ad-terminal-makeup operator
Operates computer terminal and related equipment to transfer and typeset display advertising data from perforated tape onto computer tapes for subsequent reproduction as printed matter: Secures perforated tape roll on machine reel and presses button to feed perforated tape into terminal console. Presses button to activate video display screen. Reads work order to determine combination of type style, point size, line width, and spacing to be set. Pushes terminal controls and depresses keys to observe and arrange elements on screen according to specifications. Measures copy margins to verify margin specifications, using ruler. Presses buttons to transfer typeset copy onto computer tape and into computer for storage.
GOE: 07.06.01 STRENGTH: S GED: R3 M2 L3 SVP: 5 DLU: 77

208.462-010 MAILING-MACHINE OPERATOR (print. & pub.)
Operates machine that automatically addresses, weighs, and ties into bundles printed publications, such as magazines, catalogs, and pamphlets, for mailing according to zip code: Reads production order to determine type and size of publication scheduled for mailing. Adjusts guides, rollers, loose card inserter, weighing machine, and tying arm, using rule and handtools. Fills paste reservoir. Mounts roll of subscriber address labels onto machine spindle and threads twine through tying arm. Starts machine and observes operation to detect evidence of malfunctions throughout production run. Stops machine to make adjustments or clear jams. Records production according to customer name and zip code, and machine down time due to malfunctions or lack of work.
GOE: 06.04.38 STRENGTH: M GED: R4 M2 L3 SVP: 5 DLU: 77

208.582-010 ADDRESSING-MACHINE OPERATOR (clerical)
Operates machine to print addresses, code numbers, and similar information on items, such as envelopes, accounting forms, packages, and advertising literature: Positions plates, stencils, or tapes in machine magazine and places articles to be addressed into loading rack. Starts machine that automatically feeds plates, stencils, or tapes through mechanism. Adjusts flow of ink and guides to fit size of paper and sets stops and selectors so that only certain plates will be printed, using wrench and pliers. Maintains plate file and operates embossing machine or typewriter to make corrections, additions, and changes on plates. May type statistical lists of plate files and correspondence concerning addressing jobs.
GOE: 05.12.19 STRENGTH: L GED: R3 M2 L2 SVP: 4 DLU: 77

208.582-014 EMBOSSING-MACHINE OPERATOR I (clerical) alternate titles: name-plate-stamping-machine operator; plate embosser
Operates machine to emboss names and addresses on metallic and nonmetallic plates for use in duplicating or addressing machines or for use as nameplates and tags: Adjusts plate carriage for each size plate, and clamps blank plates in holder. Reads copy to be embossed and turns handwheel to set

character or letter die in embossing position. Pulls lever to lower die and emboss character on plate. Trips levers or presets automatic controls to space letters, words, and lines. May insert plates in envelopes. May insert plates in frames and file alphabetically. May operate pantograph type engraving machine to engrave plates [ENGRAVER PANTOGRAPH (engraving) I]. Important variations may be indicated by trade name of machine operated.
GOE: 06.02.02 STRENGTH: S GED: R3 M1 L2 SVP: 4 DLU: 77

208.682-010 EMBOSSING-MACHINE OPERATOR II (clerical) alternate titles: embosser operator; plate embosser
Operates electrically powered machine to emboss metal plates for use in duplicating and addressing machines: Places blank plate in holder. Depresses keys on keyboard to imprint characters on plate, copying name and address from form or work ticket. Removes embossed plate and inserts plate in indexed file according to work ticket specifications. May operate manually powered embossing machine [EMBOSSING-MACHINE OPERATOR (clerical) I]. May operate addressing and duplicating machines.
GOE: 06.02.02 STRENGTH: S GED: R3 M1 L2 SVP: 4 DLU: 77

208.685-010 COLLATOR OPERATOR (clerical)
Tends machine that assembles pages of printed material in numerical sequence: Adjusts control that regulates stroke of paper pusher, according to size of paper. Places pages to be assembled in holding trays. Starts machine. Removes assembled pages from machine.
GOE: 05.12.19 STRENGTH: L GED: R2 M1 L1 SVP: 2 DLU: 77

208.685-014 FOLDING-MACHINE OPERATOR (clerical) alternate titles: folder operator
Tends machine that folds advertising literature, forms, letters, or other paper sheets: Turns indicator knobs to adjust folding rollers, side guides, and stops, according to specified size and number of folds. Starts machine and feeds paper sheets between folding rollers. Removes folded sheets. May place folded sheets into envelopes preparatory to mailing.
GOE: 05.12.19 STRENGTH: L GED: R2 M1 L1 SVP: 2 DLU: 77

208.685-018 INSERTING-MACHINE OPERATOR (clerical)
Tends machine that inserts printed matter, such as letters or booklets into folders or envelopes: Stacks quantities of inserts and covers into machine feedboxes and turns setscrews to adjust feeder mechanisms, according to thickness of material. Starts machine and replenishes feedboxes with inserts and covers.
GOE: 05.12.19 STRENGTH: L GED: R2 M1 L2 SVP: 2 DLU: 77

208.685-022 MICROFILM MOUNTER (clerical)
Tends machine that automatically mounts developed microfilm onto cards for filing purposes: Inserts roll of microfilm into machine. Fills hopper with presorted cards. Pours specified amount of adhesive solution into hopper to coat cards. Starts machine and observes coating of cards with adhesive solution and mounting of film onto cards.
GOE: 05.12.19 STRENGTH: L GED: R2 M1 L1 SVP: 2 DLU: 77

208.685-026 SEALING-AND-CANCELING-MACHINE OPERATOR (clerical) alternate titles: envelope-stamping-machine operator; letter-stamping-machine operator; postage-machine operator
Tends machine that automatically seals envelopes and prints postage and postmark onto envelopes or tape to be affixed onto packages: Turns indicator dials to specified letters and numbers to be printed. Starts machine and positions envelopes onto feed tray or secures roll of tape on machine spindles. Removes postmarked envelopes or tape. May weigh articles to determine required postage, using scale and postal code book. May be designated according to particular function as Canceling-Machine Operator (clerical); Envelope-Sealing-Machine Operator (clerical); Stamping-Machine Operator (clerical).
GOE: 05.12.19 STRENGTH: L GED: R2 M2 L2 SVP: 2 DLU: 77

208.685-034 WING-MAILER-MACHINE OPERATOR (print. & pub.)
Tends machine that affixes address labels to advertising matter preparatory to mailing: Adjusts wing (feed guides) to accommodate size of article to be labeled and places stack of unlabeled articles between guides. Mounts roll of preaddressed labels onto machine spindle. Fills reservoir with water or paste. Moves handle and turns rubber wheel to feed label over roller or brush that applies water or paste and under blade that automatically cuts labels from roll and applies label to mailing piece. Removes labeled article from machine and stacks on table, exposing unlabeled article for labeling.
GOE: 05.12.19 STRENGTH: L GED: R2 M1 L1 SVP: 2 DLU: 77

209 STENOGRAPHY, TYPING, FILING, AND RELATED OCCUPATIONS, N.E.C.

This group includes occupations, not elsewhere classified, concerned with making, classifying, and filing records.

209.132-010 SUPERVISOR, PERSONNEL CLERKS (clerical)
Supervises and coordinates activities of workers engaged in compilation and maintenance of personnel records: Coordinates recording and filing of information about company personnel, such as promotions, wage scales, absences, training status, and discharges. Compiles reports of absences, accession rates, salaries, and other matters of interest to company management, using typewriter

and calculator. Performs other duties as described under SUPERVISOR (clerical) Master Title. May hire and discharge subordinates. May discuss merit ratings with company employees to inform employees of progress or to assist in correcting deficiencies.
GOE: 07.05.03 STRENGTH: S GED: R4 M2 L4 SVP: 6 DLU: 77

209.132-014 TECHNICAL COORDINATOR (government ser.)
Supervises and coordinates activities of workers engaged in processing applications and claims in water rights office: Prepares correspondence and takes dictation. Examines applications for errors. Prepares notices for owners to close, clean, deepen, repair, or replace wells. Prepares closing notices for publication. Plats descriptions on documents, using drafting tools. Answers telephone and personal inquiries. Performs other duties as described under SUPERVISOR (clerical) Master Title.
GOE: 07.05.03 STRENGTH: S GED: R4 M4 L4 SVP: 7 DLU: 77

209.137-010 MAILROOM SUPERVISOR (clerical)
Supervises and coordinates activities of clerks who open, sort, and route mail, and prepare outgoing material for mailing: Reads letters and determines department or official for whom mail is intended and informs MAIL CLERK (clerical) of routing. Computes amount of postage required for outgoing mail according to weight and classification. Computes cost of mail permits from postage meter readings. Performs other duties as described under SUPERVISOR (clerical) Master Title. May interview and recommend hiring of mailroom employees. May train new employees. May maintain personnel records [PERSONNEL CLERK (clerical)].
GOE: 07.05.04 STRENGTH: L GED: R4 M3 L4 SVP: 6 DLU: 77

209.137-014 METER READER, CHIEF (utilities; waterworks)
Supervises and coordinates activities of METER READERS (utilities; waterworks): Verifies rates and addresses of new service accounts. Reviews reports and notifies authorities of attempted diversions, defective meters, and other irregularities. Investigates customer complaints concerning METER READERS (utilities; waterworks). Performs duties as described under SUPERVISOR (clerical) Master Title.
GOE: 07.05.02 STRENGTH: S GED: R4 M2 L3 SVP: 6 DLU: 77

209.137-018 SUPERVISOR, AGENCY APPOINTMENTS (insurance)
Supervises and coordinates activities of workers engaged in maintaining records of insurance company agents' appointments, licenses, certification, and sales contracts: Confers with superior, subordinates, and personnel in other departments to plan and coordinate work schedules. Evaluates work of AGENT-LICENSING CLERKS (insurance) and returns faulty work with instructions for correction or rework. Conducts periodic job-performance reviews and recommends appropriate personnel action. Gives orientation to and trains new workers, or assigns employee to experienced worker for training. Performs work of and assists subordinates to maintain production schedules. Performs duties as described under SUPERVISOR (clerical) Master Title.
GOE: 07.05.03 STRENGTH: S GED: R4 M3 L4 SVP: 7 DLU: 77

209.137-026 SUPERVISOR, MARKING ROOM (retail trade)
Supervises and coordinates activities of workers engaged in marking and attaching price tickets or tags to merchandise in marking room of retail establishment: Reviews invoices and purchase orders and makes rounds of work stations to determine type and amount of marking tickets required for each shipment of goods. Periodically examines test run of tickets printed by TICKETERS (any industry), to detect machine skips or other printing errors. Obtains completed batches of marking tickets, distributes tickets with purchase orders, and initiates correction form when discrepancies between merchandise and purchase order entries are noted by MARKERS (retail trade; wholesale tr.). Regularly participates in marking and tagging merchandise to assist workers and maintain production. Performs other duties as described under SUPERVISOR (clerical) Master Title.
GOE: 05.09.03 STRENGTH: L GED: R3 M2 L3 SVP: 6 DLU: 77

209.362-010 CIRCULATION CLERK (print. & pub.) alternate titles: subscription clerk
Compiles records concerned with delivery or mail order distribution of newspapers or magazines to subscribers, carriers, or dealers and adjusts complaints: Examines delivery tickets and records number of newspapers or magazines delivered to each city carrier or dealer. Types changes and corrections in names and addresses of subscribers, carriers, and dealers on distribution lists. Writes or types receipts for mail order subscriptions and forwards them to customers. Examines subscription date file and sends form letters to solicit renewal of expiring subscriptions. Receives telephoned and written complaints from subscribers and notifies distributor. Sells back copies of publication as requested. When concerned with distribution of publications within city may be designated City-Distribution Clerk (print. & pub.).
GOE: 07.05.03 STRENGTH: S GED: R3 M2 L3 SVP: 3 DLU: 77

209.362-014 CONTROL CLERK, AUDITING (insurance)
Maintains audit-control files, assigns insurance cases to field auditors, and compiles reports of audits accomplished: Assigns insurance cases to field auditors for investigation or settlement according to designated territory and type of audit, following established procedures. Maintains card control files to indicate location and status of audits. Reviews audit reports and compares reports with data in files to compile production reports, using calculator and typewriter.
GOE: 07.05.03 STRENGTH: S GED: R3 M3 L3 SVP: 3 DLU: 77

209.362-018 CREDIT REFERENCE CLERK (financial; retail trade)
Telephones or writes to references listed on application form to investigate credit standing of applicant. Records information on previous employment, received from employers, using typewriter or computer. Reciprocates credit information with credit bureaus.
GOE: 07.05.02 STRENGTH: S GED: R3 M2 L3 SVP: 3 DLU: 86

209.362-022 IDENTIFICATION CLERK (government ser.)
Performs any combination of following duties to compile and transmit records, relay information, microfilm documents, and take and classify fingerprints in police agency: Retrieves and prints copies of police records and reports requested by public and police personnel, using computer and printer. Retrieves information on vehicles and persons requested by patrolling police officers, and provides information to officers over police radio communications system. Operates equipment to microfilm crime and accident reports. Files microfilm. Retrieves microfilmed information upon request of police officials or public, and operates equipment to copy requested information. Tends facsimile machine to transmit and receive photographs, fingerprints, and accompanying information. Fingerprints applicants for licenses and assists in preparation of applications. Classifies fingerprints and matches fingerprints with prints previously filed as evidence in unsolved crimes [FINGERPRINT CLASSIFIER (government ser.) 375.387-010]. Compiles and submits periodic reports pertaining to police department activities.
GOE: 07.05.03 STRENGTH: L GED: R3 M2 L3 SVP: 4 DLU: 78

209.362-026 PERSONNEL CLERK (clerical) alternate titles: human resources clerk; personnel records clerk
Compiles and maintains personnel records: Records employee information, such as personal data; compensation, benefits, and tax data; attendance; performance reviews or evaluations; and termination date and reason. Processes employment applications and assists in other employment activities. Updates employee files to document personnel actions and to provide information for payroll and other uses. Examines employee files to answer inquiries and provides information to authorized persons. Compiles data from personnel records and prepares reports using typewriter or computer. May administer and score aptitude, personality, and interest tests. May explain bonding procedure required by company, and assist in completion of bonding application. May compute wages and record data for use in payroll processing [PAYROLL CLERK (clerical) 215.382-014]. May compile and maintain records for use in employee benefits administration and be designated Benefits Clerk (clerical) I. May prepare and file reports of accidents and injuries at establishment and be designated Accident-Report Clerk (clerical).
GOE: 07.05.03 STRENGTH: S GED: R4 M2 L4 SVP: 4 DLU: 88

209.362-030 CONGRESSIONAL-DISTRICT AIDE (government ser.)
Provides information and assistance to public and performs variety of clerical tasks in office of congressional legislator: Answers requests for information and assistance from constituents and other members of public, by phone or in person, using knowledge of governmental agencies and programs and source materials, such as agency listings and directories. Transcribes reports and types letters, using electric typewriter. Operates telecopier to receive and send messages, reports, and other documents. Opens and sorts mail according to addressee or type of assistance or information requested. Maintains record of telephone calls. Files correspondence, reports, and documents. Occasionally composes correspondence in response to written requests. Occasionally contacts other governmental or private agencies to act as liaison on behalf of constituents.
GOE: 07.04.04 STRENGTH: S GED: R4 M3 L4 SVP: 5 DLU: 86

209.362-034 CORRESPONDENCE CLERK (clerical)
Composes letters in reply to correspondence concerning such items as requests for merchandise, damage claims, credit information, delinquent accounts, incorrect billing, unsatisfactory service, or to request information: Reads incoming correspondence and gathers data to formulate reply. Operates typewriter to prepare correspondence or to complete form letters, or dictates reply. May route correspondence to other departments for reply. May keep files of correspondence sent, received, or requiring further action. May process purchase orders, prepare order forms, and check progress of orders [ORDER CLERK (clerical) 249.362-026]. May be designated according to type of correspondence handled as Claim Clerk (clerical); Credit-Correspondence Clerk (clerical); Fan-Mail Clerk (amuse. & rec.); Sales-Correspondence Clerk (clerical).
GOE: 07.04.02 STRENGTH: S GED: R3 M2 L2 SVP: 6 DLU: 78

209.367-010 AGENT-LICENSING CLERK (insurance) alternate titles: agents'-records clerk
Processes new and prospective agents' licensing, certification, or bonding applications and forms to ensure conformance with regulations of State Insurance Commissions and bonding companies: Prepares or reviews licensing applications and other forms for completeness and accuracy, in accordance with insurance commission or bonding company requirements. Mails applications, documents, and fees to authorities and arranges appointments for examinations. Notifies company officials of applicants' acceptance or rejection. Maintains files of correspondence, records, and reports. May compile, type, and mail to field offices changes to approved lists of medical examiners.
GOE: 07.05.03 STRENGTH: S GED: R4 M1 L4 SVP: 5 DLU: 77

209.367-014 BRAILLE PROOFREADER (nonprofit org.; print. & pub.)
Verifies proof copy of braille transcription against original script, such as pamphlet, book, or newspaper, to detect grammatical, typographical, or

compositional errors and marks proof for correction: Reads original script to compare it with proof copy (if sighted); or listens to reading or recording of original and slides fingers over braille characters to feel discrepancies in proof (if blind). Consults reference books or secures aid of reader to check references to rules of grammar and composition. Marks proof with braille stylus or pencil to correct errors, using standard printers' marks. May direct workers in use of braille slates (printing devices). May select material for transcription.
GOE: 07.05.02 STRENGTH: S GED: R4 M1 L4 SVP: 5 DLU: 77

209.367-018 CORRESPONDENCE-REVIEW CLERK (clerical)
Reads and routes incoming correspondence to individual or department concerned: Reviews correspondence, determines appropriate routing, and requisitions records needed to process correspondence. Types acknowledgement letter to person sending correspondence. Reviews requested records for completeness and accuracy and attaches records to correspondence for reply by other workers. May maintain files and control records to show status of action in processing correspondence. May compile data from records to prepare periodic reports. May investigate discrepancies in reports and records and confer with personnel in affected departments to ensure accuracy and compliance with procedures.
GOE: 07.05.04 STRENGTH: S GED: R3 M1 L3 SVP: 5 DLU: 77

209.367-026 FINGERPRINT CLERK I (government ser.)
Transfers fingerprints of persons onto cards for purposes of identification: Directs individual to extend fingers and presses fingers on ink pad or glass plate and rolls them in specified spaces on card. Writes or types identifying information, such as name, address, and occupation on card. May administer oath of allegiance and perform other clerical duties.
GOE: 07.04.03 STRENGTH: L GED: R3 M2 L2 SVP: 2 DLU: 77

209.367-034 LOST-CHARGE-CARD CLERK (clerical)
Records data concerning lost or stolen charge cards: Receives by telephone, letter, or in person, and records information concerning loss, theft, or destruction of charge cards. Records information in customer-account record to avoid further billing of customer. Compiles reports to notify other personnel of possible need for further investigation and action, such as issuance of lost or stolen-card bulletin to subscribing merchants, to prevent fraudulent use of lost or stolen charge cards by others, or to issue new charge card to customer. May issue reward checks to merchants or other people who turn in lost or stolen charge cards. May send form letter to customers in reply to inquiries about lost, stolen, or replacement charge cards.
GOE: 07.05.03 STRENGTH: S GED: R3 M2 L3 SVP: 3 DLU: 77

209.367-038 NEWS ASSISTANT (radio-tv broad.) alternate titles: desk assistant
Compiles, dispenses, and files newsstories and related copy to assist editorial personnel in broadcasting newsroom: Telephones government agencies and sports facilities and monitors other stations to obtain weather, traffic, and sports information. Telephones people involved in news events to obtain further information or to arrange for on-air or background interviews by news broadcasting personnel. Files and retrieves news scripts, printouts, and recording tapes. May make written copies of newsstories called in from remote locations. May record, edit, and play back tapes of newsstories to assist COLUMNIST/COMMENTATOR (print. & pub.; radio-tv broad.), using recording and splicing machines and equipment.
GOE: 07.05.03 STRENGTH: L GED: R4 M2 L4 SVP: 3 DLU: 77

209.367-042 RECONSIGNMENT CLERK (clerical) alternate titles: disposition clerk; diversion clerk
Reroutes freight shipments to new destinations following request from shipper: Receives request from shipper for reconsignment or change in destination of freight shipment. Searches for original bill of lading, waybill, and freight bills to ascertain original route or destination. Telephones station at next scheduled stop on original route and issues instructions to reroute freight shipment. Sends telegram to confirm instructions issued over telephone. Prepares new bill of lading to record shipper's request for new destination, reconsignment, and route selected. May prepare waybills.
GOE: 07.05.04 STRENGTH: S GED: R3 M3 L3 SVP: 4 DLU: 77

209.367-046 TITLE SEARCHER (real estate) alternate titles: abstractor
Searches public and private records and indices to compile list of legal instruments pertaining to property titles, such as mortgages, deeds, and assessments, for insurance, real estate, or tax purposes: Reads search request to ascertain type of title evidence required, and to obtain legal description of property and names of involved parties. Compares legal description of property with legal description contained in records and indices, to verify such factors as deed of ownership, tax code and parcel number, and description of property's boundaries. Requisitions maps or drawings delineating property from company title plant, county surveyor, or assessor's office. Confers with realtors, lending institution personnel, buyers, sellers, contractors, surveyors, and courthouse personnel to obtain additional information. Compiles list of transactions pertaining to property, using legal description or name of owner to search lot books, geographic and general indices, or assessor's rolls. Examines title to determine if there are any restrictions which would limit use of property, prepares report listing restrictions, and indicates action needed to remove restrictions to clear title. Compiles information and documents required for title binder. Prepares title commitment and final policy of title insurance based on information compiled from title search. May specialize in searching tax records and be des-

ignated Tax Searcher (real estate). May use computerized system to retrieve additional documentation needed to complete real estate transaction. May retrieve and examine closing files to determine accuracy of information and to ensure that information included is recorded and executed according to regulations governing real estate industry. May prepare closing statement, utilizing knowledge of and expertise in real estate procedures.
GOE: 07.05.02 STRENGTH: L GED: R3 M1 L3 SVP: 5 DLU: 89

209.367-050 TRIP FOLLOWER (air trans.) alternate titles: flight follower
Posts positions of various aircraft flying within boundaries of dispatch area, on flight-following board: Reads messages received over telegraphic typewriter and posts data pertaining to position of airplanes on flight-following board. Notifies DISPATCHER (air trans.) or FLIGHT-INFORMATION EXPEDITER (air trans.) of messages received regarding departure times, delays, mechanical difficulties, or unusual weather conditions.
GOE: 07.04.05 STRENGTH: L GED: R3 M3 L3 SVP: 3 DLU: 77

209.367-054 YARD CLERK (r.r. trans.) alternate titles: check clerk
Prepares switching orders for railroad yard switching crew: Types or writes switching orders to inform switching crew of railroad yard, location, disposition, and number of railroad cars to be switched for loading, unloading, makeup, and breakup of trains, based on information received from YARD MANAGER (r.r. trans.) and other personnel or records. Keeps record of and reports movement and disposition of railroad cars for YARD MANAGER (r.r. trans.). May count and record number of cars remaining in yard each day. May telephone various personnel to verify location of railroad cars.
GOE: 07.05.03 STRENGTH: S GED: R3 M2 L2 SVP: 3 DLU: 77

209.382-010 CONTINUITY CLERK (motion picture)
Types descriptive record of motion picture scenes, including dialog, and such details as wardrobe, hairdress, and on-scene entrances and exits of ACTORS (amuse. & rec.); ACTRESS (amuse. & rec.) to aid editorial personnel in editing and assembling complete film: Mounts film on spindle of film viewer and starts equipment. Observes film on screen to determine action being depicted and pertinent details. Types brief narrative description and identifying information for each scene. Keeps records of completed work.
GOE: 07.05.03 STRENGTH: S GED: R3 M1 L3 SVP: 5 DLU: 77

209.382-014 SPECIAL-CERTIFICATE DICTATOR (insurance) alternate titles: settlement technician
Drafts endorsement to basic life insurance agreement, consistent with company and legal requirements, to denote method of payment to beneficiary: Reviews insured's request and examines basic policy to determine modifications required in basic agreement. Types or dictates text of modifying agreement to be appended to basic policy.
GOE: 07.05.03 STRENGTH: S GED: R3 M2 L3 SVP: 6 DLU: 77

209.382-022 TRAFFIC CLERK (radio-tv broad.) alternate titles: traffic manager
Compiles log (broadcast schedule) of radio, television, or cable television commercial and public-service spot announcements, using computer: Reviews on-air time sales orders and public-service announcements to verify completeness of data required for log, such as sponsor identity, date, time, and duration of announcement, and whether live or recorded announcements. Enters information, such as sponsor identity, date, maximum time and frequency of commercials, and established network or local news announcement times, into computer to generate log. Contacts station staff for missing information. Reviews sponsors' requests for specific dates and times of announcements, and recommends alternate dates and times, or keys information into computer to revise log to avoid conflicts. Enters information into computer to compose daily log, and prints and distributes log to operations personnel and on-air talent. Reviews daily log after use for authorized changes made during broadcast date. May review content of commercial or public-service announcements for objectionable material. May operate viewing and or audio equipment to ascertain content and length of commercial or public-service announcements. May perform additional clerical duties, such as billing, typing correspondence, reception, and filing sales orders, commercial and public-service announcement tapes, and daily logs.
GOE: 07.05.03 STRENGTH: L GED: R3 M2 L3 SVP: 4 DLU: 89

209.387-014 COMPILER (clerical)
Compiles directories, survey findings, opinion polls, and census reports from data obtained from surveys or census: Compiles names, addresses, vital statistics, and other facts or opinions from business subscribers or persons in communities or cities. Verifies information for completeness and accuracy. Records and arranges information in specified order or groupings, such as by name, location, sex, occupation, or affiliation. May use typewriter or other recording device to duplicate information for filing or distribution. May prepare graphs or charts to show survey results. May be designated according to type of information compiled as Directory Compiler (clerical); Survey Compiler (clerical). May compile lists of prospective customers and be designated Mailing-List Compiler (clerical).
GOE: 07.05.03 STRENGTH: S GED: R3 M2 L3 SVP: 4 DLU: 77

209.387-018 CONTACT CLERK (utilities)
Sorts and lists gas- and electric-power service-connection orders for distribution to various service centers and compiles data from completed orders for reports: Sorts orders into groups for delivery to service centers, locating ad-

dress of customer on zoned map to determine appropriate center. Compiles list of each type of order (dispatch list) for use as control record. Reviews completed orders for compliance with reporting procedures and compiles data for various reports. Reviews incompleted orders and forwards them for processing.
GOE: 07.05.04 STRENGTH: S GED: R3 M2 L3 SVP: 4 DLU: 77

209.387-022 DATA-EXAMINATION CLERK (clerical)
Reviews computer input and output documents to ensure accuracy, completeness, and adherence to establishment standards: Reviews documents, such as surveys, to ensure completeness and appropriateness prior to data entry. Reads notes and instructions written on source documents and compares information with printouts to detect errors and ensure completeness and conformity with establishment policies and procedures. Notifies supervisor when errors and shortage of output are detected, and corrects errors or refers work to other workers for correction. Compares corrected input and output data with source documents, worksheets, and data displayed on screen of computer terminal to verify corrections. May review only computer input or output. May operate machines to separate and remove carbon paper from computer generated forms. May retype mutilated forms, using typewriter. May sort printouts for distribution.
GOE: 07.05.02 STRENGTH: S GED: R3 M2 L3 SVP: 3 DLU: 87

209.387-026 LIBRARY CLERK, TALKING BOOKS (library)
Selects talking books for mailing to blind library patrons: Compares borrower's written request with list or chart of available titles. Selects books or materials, such as large type or braille volumes, tape cassettes, and open reel tape talking books, following borrower's request, or selects substitute titles, following such criteria as age, education, interest, and sex of borrower. Obtains books or materials from shelves. Types address label to prepare books or materials for mailing. May type records, such as material or issue cards. May receive and inspect talking books returned to library [BRAILLE-AND-TALKING BOOKS CLERK (library)].
GOE: 05.09.01 STRENGTH: L GED: R3 M1 L3 SVP: 3 DLU: 77

209.387-030 PROOFREADER (print. & pub.)
Reads typescript (original copy) or proof of type setup to detect and mark for correction any grammatical, typographical, or compositional errors, by either of following methods: (1) Places proof and copy side by side on reading board. Reads proof against copy, marking by standardized code, errors that appear in proof. Returns marked proof for correction and later checks corrected proof against copy. (2) Reads and corrects proof while COPY HOLDER (print. & pub.) reads aloud from original copy or reads proof aloud to COPY HOLDER (print. & pub.) who calls out discrepancies between proof and copy. May measure dimensions, spacing, and positioning of page elements (copy and illustrations) to verify conformance to specifications, using printer's ruler.
GOE: 07.05.02 STRENGTH: L GED: R4 M1 L4 SVP: 5 DLU: 77

209.387-034 SUGGESTION CLERK (clerical)
Compiles and records suggestions submitted to suggestion committee: Reads suggestions submitted and records suggestions on control cards. Writes memorandum to acknowledge receipt of suggestion. Requisitions amount of cash award recommended for accepted suggestions. Schedules distribution of awards to winners, or forwards checks and award certificates to appropriate department heads for presentation to winners. Writes or types letters to originators of rejected suggestions, explaining reasons for nonacceptance. Maintains record of suggestions received. May review suggestions for clarity and legibility before presenting copies to review committee.
GOE: 07.05.03 STRENGTH: S GED: R3 M1 L3 SVP: 4 DLU: 77

209.562-010 CLERK, GENERAL (clerical) alternate titles: office clerk, routine
Performs any combination of following and similar clerical duties requiring limited knowledge of systems or procedures: Writes, types, or enters information into computer, using keyboard, to prepare correspondence, bills, statements, receipts, checks, or other documents, copying information from one record to another. Proofreads records or forms. Counts, weighs, or measures material. Sorts and files records. Receives money from customers and deposits money in bank. Addresses envelopes or packages by hand or with typewriter or addressograph machine. Stuffs envelopes by hand or with envelope stuffing machine. Answers telephone, conveys messages, and runs errands. Stamps, sorts, and distributes mail. Stamps or numbers forms by hand or machine. Photocopies documents, using photocopier.
GOE: 07.07.03 STRENGTH: L GED: R3 M2 L3 SVP: 3 DLU: 89

209.567-010 METER READER (utilities; waterworks)
Reads electric, gas, water, or steam consumption meters and records volume used by residential and commercial consumers: Walks or drives truck over established route and takes readings of meter dials. Inspects meters and connections for defects, damage, and unauthorized connections. Indicates irregularities on forms for necessary action by servicing department. Verifies readings to locate abnormal consumption and records reasons for fluctuations. Turns service off for nonpayment of charges in vacant premises, or on for new occupants. Collects bills in arrears. Returns route book to business office for billing purposes. May be designated according to type of meter read as Electric-Meter Reader (utilities); Gas-Meter Reader (utilities); Steam-Meter Reader (utilities); Water-Meter Reader (waterworks).
GOE: 05.09.03 STRENGTH: L GED: R3 M2 L2 SVP: 3 DLU: 81

209.567-014 ORDER CLERK, FOOD AND BEVERAGE (hotel & rest.)
Takes food and beverage orders over telephone or intercom system and records order on ticket: Records order and time received on ticket to ensure

prompt service, using time-stamping device. Suggests menu items, and substitutions for items not available, and answers questions regarding food or service. Distributes order tickets or calls out order to kitchen employees. May collect charge vouchers and cash for service and keep record of transactions. May be designated according to type of order handled as Telephone-Order Clerk, Drive-In (hotel & rest.); Telephone-Order Clerk, Room Service (hotel & rest.).
GOE: 07.04.02 STRENGTH: S GED: R3 M1 L2 SVP: 2 DLU: 77

209.582-010 MUSIC COPYIST (print. & pub.) alternate titles: music typographer
Copies musical scores onto stencils or manuscript paper for reproduction: Writes or types, using typewriter equipped with musical-symbol keyboard, musical notations indicating instrumental parts and choral arrangement. Draws or types lines to block out spacing of words and music. Types stencils and other materials concerned with reproduction of musical scores.
GOE: 07.06.02 STRENGTH: S GED: R3 M2 L2 SVP: 5 DLU: 77

209.584-010 BRAILLE TRANSCRIBER, HAND (education; nonprofit organ.; print. & pub.) alternate titles: braille coder
Transcribes reading matter into braille for use by the blind, using hand stylus: Reads copy and manipulates hand stylus to emboss special paper with various combinations of dots that characterize braille alphabet, using braille code form.
GOE: 07.05.03 STRENGTH: S GED: R3 M1 L3 SVP: 4 DLU: 77

209.587-010 ADDRESSER (clerical) alternate titles: addressing clerk; envelope addresser
Addresses by hand or typewriter, envelopes, cards, advertising literature, packages, and similar items for mailing. May sort mail.
GOE: 07.07.02 STRENGTH: S GED: R2 M1 L2 SVP: 2 DLU: 77

209.587-014 CREDIT-CARD CLERK (retail trade)
Issues credit cards to customers for use as identification when purchasing articles to be charged to their account. Assigns and records card identification number on customer's account. Keeps records of cards reported lost and issues replacement cards.
GOE: 07.05.03 STRENGTH: S GED: R3 M1 L3 SVP: 3 DLU: 77

209.587-018 DIRECT-MAIL CLERK (clerical)
Mails letters, merchandise samples, and promotional literature to prospective customers. Receives requests for samples and prepares required shipping slips. Maintains files and records of customer transactions.
GOE: 07.07.02 STRENGTH: L GED: R3 M1 L2 SVP: 4 DLU: 77

209.587-022 HISTORY-CARD CLERK (utilities) alternate titles: meter-changes records clerk; meter-record clerk
Copies information such as name and address of customer, meter size and type, servicing and inspection dates, and results of installation or disconnection to maintain records of electric, gas, or steam meters. Supplies meter repair and maintenance workers with information from files as requested. May record date of receipt and completion of meter service orders to keep control register of work orders. May match permits with work orders and verify completeness of orders to show required measurements and sketch of meter location. May assist with periodic physical inventory of meters in meter shop. May make periodic reports of meters set, removed, or changed.
GOE: 07.05.03 STRENGTH: S GED: R3 M2 L3 SVP: 4 DLU: 77

209.587-030 MAP CLERK (insurance)
Records insurance information, such as policy number, amount and type of coverage, and expiration date, on street maps showing locations of buildings on which insurance company has written insurance. Compares insurance coverage with adjoining buildings to check justification of coverage.
GOE: 07.05.03 STRENGTH: S GED: R3 M2 L2 SVP: 3 DLU: 77

209.587-034 MARKER (retail trade; wholesale tr.) alternate titles: marking clerk; merchandise marker; price marker; ticket maker
Marks and attaches price tickets to articles of merchandise to record price and identifying information: Marks selling price by hand on boxes containing merchandise, or on price tickets. Ties, glues, sews, or staples price ticket to each article. Presses lever or plunger of mechanism that pins, pastes, ties, or staples ticket to article. May record number and types of articles marked and pack them in boxes. May compare printed price tickets with entries on purchase order to verify accuracy and notify supervisor of discrepancies. May print information on tickets, using ticket-printing machine [TICKETER (any industry)]; [TICKET PRINTER AND TAGGER (garment)].
GOE: 05.09.03 STRENGTH: L GED: R2 M1 L1 SVP: 2 DLU: 77

209.587-042 RETURN-TO-FACTORY CLERK (clerical) alternate titles: returns clerk
Records information pertaining to merchandise to be returned to manufacturer because of defects, wrong amount, or type: Examines and compares merchandise with original requisition to record information, such as quantity, type of defects, and date on invoice or other forms. Prepares invoices and other forms for all returned goods. May type letters or information on records to explain reason for returned goods. May compile and file list of merchandise handled.
GOE: 07.05.03 STRENGTH: L GED: R3 M2 L2 SVP: 3 DLU: 77

209.587-046 SAMPLE CLERK, PAPER (paper & pulp; paper goods) alternate titles: laboratory assistant
Prepares samples of paper and paper products for filing and mailing, performing any combination of following tasks: Collects samples of paper from

paper machines, coating machines, supercalenders and cutting machines. Cuts samples to specified dimensions, using paper cutter. Marks samples with identifying information, such as customer order number, batch number, and grade and color of paper, or pastes labels on samples. Files samples for use in tracing technical defects or to facilitate processing of repeat orders, mails samples to customers, or distributes them to plant officials for examination. May compare samples with standard or customer's sample to ascertain that paper meets specifications of grade and color. May send samples to laboratory for testing and compare test reports with specifications. May address packages of samples to be mailed to customers, by hand or using typewriter.
GOE: 06.04.26 STRENGTH: M GED: R3 M2 L2 SVP: 3 DLU: 77

209.587-050 WRONG-ADDRESS CLERK (retail trade)
Verifies addresses and corrects illegible or misaddressed shipping tags or labels, using credit files or directory information: Searches company credit files and directories, such as telephone, city, and postal directories, to find correct name and address. Marks revision on tags and labels, using marking pencil. Records adjusted information on delivery records.
GOE: 07.07.02 STRENGTH: L GED: R2 M1 L2 SVP: 3 DLU: 77

209.667-010 COPY HOLDER (print. & pub.)
Reads copy to PROOFREADER (print. & pub.) I to correct proofsheets of printed matter: Reads original copy aloud, calling out punctuation marks and spelling unusual words and proper names. Follows original copy word for word as PROOFREADER (print. & pub.) reads proofsheet aloud. Calls attention to discrepancies between copy and proof.
GOE: 07.05.02 STRENGTH: S GED: R4 M1 L4 SVP: 4 DLU: 77

209.667-014 ORDER CALLER (clerical) alternate titles: caller; call-out clerk; order-desk caller
Reads items listed on order sheets to LABORER, STORES (any industry) who gathers and assembles items or to BILLING TYPIST (clerical) who prepares bills for items. Indicates on order sheets items located and items that are not available. May read items to CHECKER (clerical) I who examines articles prior to shipping. May be designated by kind of data called out to other worker as Weight Caller (clerical); Yardage Caller (textile).
GOE: 05.09.03 STRENGTH: L GED: R2 M1 L2 SVP: 2 DLU: 77

209.667-018 CODE AND TEST CLERK (financial)
Verifies and assigns code numbers on telecommunications messages used in banking transactions: Reads code (test) number on incoming messages and compares code number to previously agreed-upon number to verify authenticity of message. Assigns specified code number to outgoing messages, using computer or code sheets. May translate decoded foreign language messages into English.
GOE: 11.08.04 STRENGTH: S GED: R4 M3 L4 SVP: 5 DLU: 89

209.687-010 CHECKER II (clerical) alternate titles: check clerk; data clerk; proofreader; report checker
Performs routine checking duties to ensure accuracy of recorded data: Compares information or figures on one record against same data on other records. Corrects or records omissions, errors, or inconsistencies found. Is not characteristically engaged in making computations [AUDIT CLERK (clerical); CALCULATING-MACHINE OPERATOR (clerical)] but does use arithmetic. Does not check incoming or outgoing shipments, or record or keep tallies [RECEIVING CHECKER (clerical); SHIPPING CHECKER (clerical)]. May be designated according to type of clerical work checked as Billing Checker (clerical); Entry Examiner (clerical); Installment-Account Checker (clerical). May be designated: Asset-Card Clerk (clerical); Coupon-Manifest Clerk (clerical); Outlaw-Loan-Record Clerk (clerical); Price Checker (clerical); Printed-Forms Proofreader (clerical); Typing Checker (clerical).
GOE: 07.05.02 STRENGTH: S GED: R3 M2 L2 SVP: 4 DLU: 77

209.687-014 MAIL HANDLER (government ser.) alternate titles: distribution clerk
Sorts and processes mail in post office: Sorts incoming or outgoing mail into mail rack pigeonholes or into mail sacks according to destination. May feed letters into electric canceling machine or hand-stamp mail with rubber stamp to cancel postage. May serve at public window or counter. May transport mail within post office [MATERIAL HANDLER (any industry)]. May sort mail in mobile post office and be designated Distribution Clerk, Railway Or Highway Post Office (government ser.). May sort mail which other workers have been unable to sort and be designated Speical-Distribution Clerk (government ser.).
GOE: 07.05.04 STRENGTH: L GED: R3 M2 L2 SVP: 4 DLU: 77

209.687-018 REVIEWER (insurance) alternate titles: final-application reviewer; new-business clerk; sales-review clerk
Reviews insurance applications to ensure that all questions have been answered. Corresponds with sales personnel to inform them of status of application being processed, and to encourage prompt delivery of policies to policyholders. May collect initial premiums and issue receipts. May compile periodic reports on new business for management.
GOE: 07.05.02 STRENGTH: S GED: R3 M1 L3 SVP: 4 DLU: 77

209.687-022 SORTER (clerical)
Sorts data, such as forms, correspondence, checks, receipts, bills, and sales tickets, into specified sequence or grouping, such as by address, code, quantity, and class, for such purposes as filing, mailing, copying, or preparing records. May be designated according to work performed as Bill Sorter (clerical); Sales-Slip Sorter (clerical).

GOE: 07.07.02 STRENGTH: S GED: R2 M1 L2 SVP: 3 DLU: 77

209.687-026 MAIL CLERK (clerical) alternate titles: mailroom clerk; mail sorter; postal clerk
Sorts incoming mail for distribution and dispatches outgoing mail: Opens envelopes by hand or machine. Stamps date and time of receipt on incoming mail. Sorts mail according to destination and type, such as returned letters, adjustments, bills, orders, and payments. Readdresses undeliverable mail bearing incomplete or incorrect address. Examines outgoing mail for appearance and seals envelopes by hand or machine. Stamps outgoing mail by hand or with postage meter. May fold letters or circulars and insert in envelopes [FOLDING-MACHINE OPERATOR (clerical) 208.685-014]. May distribute and collect mail. May weigh mail to determine that postage is correct. May keep record of registered mail. May address mail, using addressing machine [ADDRESSING-MACHINE OPERATOR (clerical) 208.582-010]. May be designated according to type of mail handled as Mail Clerk, Bills (clerical).
GOE: 07.05.04 STRENGTH: L GED: R3 M1 L2 SVP: 2 DLU: 87

21 COMPUTING AND ACCOUNT-RECORDING OCCUPATIONS

This division includes occupations concerned with sytematizing information about transactions and activities into accounts and quantitative records, and paying and receiving money. It includes such activities as keeping and verifying records of business and financial transactions; receiving and disbursing money in banks and other establishments; operating data processing and peripheral equipment; computing and verifying amounts due for goods and services; preparing payrolls, timekeeping records, and duty rosters; combining data and performing computations to create statistical records; and computing costs of production in relation to other factors to determine profit and loss. Activities concerned with computing amounts of materials, equipment, and labor to determine production costs; and activities concerned with coordinating, scheduling, or monitoring production processes are found in Division 22.

210 BOOKKEEPERS AND RELATED OCCUPATIONS

This group includes occupations which require knowledge of bookkeeping principles and which are concerned with classifying, recording, and summarizing numerical data and with making computations to compile and keep financial records. Included in this group are occupations involving use of computers to maintain aggregated financial records, such as ledgers and general ledgers, and to compile financial reports. Occupations concerned primarily with making computations to prepare or verify documents, such as bills and statements, are found in Group 214. Occupations requiring limited or no knowledge of bookkeeping principles and concerned with performing computations to systematize information on transactions and activities into accounts and other numerical records are found in Group 216.

210.132-010 SUPERVISOR, AUDIT CLERKS (clerical)
Supervises and coordinates activities of workers engaged in examining bookkeeping and accounting entries of other workers or computer-rejected items, computing to reconcile errors, and recording corrections. Performs duties as described under SUPERVISOR (clerical) Master Title.
GOE: 07.02.01 STRENGTH: L GED: R4 M4 L3 SVP: 6 DLU: 77

210.362-010 DISTRIBUTION-ACCOUNTING CLERK (utilities)
Audits time and material charges on work orders for construction, maintenance, and operation of electric-power distribution lines: Reviews construction sketches and bills of materials at time work order is issued to ensure accurate listings of material quantities and assignment of accounting classifications. Audits chargeouts and return of materials from storeroom and time and material reports from construction crew to ensure accurate accounting of materials issued, used, or returned to storeroom. Summarizes charges and returns upon completion of job, using adding machine and calculator, and compares with construction sketch and bill of materials to detect differences between actual and estimated charges. May maintain field construction files.
GOE: 07.02.02 STRENGTH: S GED: R3 M3 L2 SVP: 5 DLU: 77

210.367-010 ACCOUNT-INFORMATION CLERK (utilities)
Keeps accounting records and compiles information requested by customer and others pertaining to customer accounts: Keeps records and prepares report of meters registering use of gas- or electric-power, showing results of investigations and amounts recovered or lost. Prepares lists and enters charges and payments to customers' accounts for losses, additional deposits, special and irregular charges. Keeps records of overpayments on customer accounts. Applies overpayments to charges on customers' account or prepares voucher for refund. Investigates incorrect billings due to charges or credits on customers' accounts and prepares written instructions for correction. Reviews accounts not billed and prepares bill from available information. Enters information in meter books which was received too late for billing, such as meter test reports and missed meter readings. Prepares lists of special billing instructions, incorporating charges shown on customers' account. Processes final bills that exceed amount of deposit to enter amount of net bill. Prepares and mails duplicate bills as requested. Interviews customers and others in person or by telephone to answer

inquiries and complaints pertaining to bills, customer deposits, and accounts. May specialize in handling inquiries received by mail, compiling information from customer accounting records for replies dictated by others.
GOE: 07.02.03 STRENGTH: S GED: R4 M3 L3 SVP: 6 DLU: 77

210.367-014 FOREIGN-EXCHANGE-POSITION CLERK (financial)
Maintains current record of bank's funds on deposit (position) in foreign banks: Records bank's balances on deposit in foreign banks, outstanding (future) purchase and sales contracts, and undelivered items, to maintain record, using computer. Lists totals in holdover register and posts net balances to daily position reports to determine new position. Reviews records to determine when balances need replenishing. Computes net balances and informs trading personnel. May compare current and previous balance sheets to eliminate double-posting to transactions and verification of limits. May assist trading personnel in preparing monthly revaluation of foreign currency accounts. May answer inquiries regarding foreign exchange trading regulations. May quote established conversion rates for bank branch staff and customers.
GOE: 07.02.01 STRENGTH: S GED: R4 M4 L3 SVP: 5 DLU: 89

210.382-010 AUDIT CLERK (clerical)
Verifies accuracy of figures, calculations, and postings pertaining to business transactions recorded by other workers: Examines expense accounts, commissions paid to employees, loans made on insurance policies, interest and account payments, cash receipts, sales tickets, bank records, inventory and stock-record sheets, and similar items to verify accuracy of recorded data. Corrects errors or lists discrepancies for adjustment. Computes percentages and totals, using adding or calculating machines, and compares results with recorded entries. May be designated according to type of records audited as Cash-Sales-Audit Clerk (clerical); Charge-Accounts-Audit Clerk (clerical); C.O.D. Audit Clerk (clerical); Commission Auditor (insurance); Expense Clerk (clerical); Federal-Housing-Administration-Loan Auditor (insurance). May be designated: Inventory-Audit Clerk (clerical); Journal-Entry-Audit Clerk (clerical); Medical-Records Auditor (medical ser.); Remittance-On-Farm-Rental-And-Soil-Conservation Auditor (insurance).
GOE: 07.02.01 STRENGTH: S GED: R4 M4 L3 SVP: 7 DLU: 80

210.382-014 BOOKKEEPER (clerical)
Keeps records of financial transactions for establishment, using calculator and computer: Verifies, allocates, and posts details of business transactions to subsidiary accounts in journals or computer files from documents, such as sales slips, invoices, receipts, check stubs, and computer printouts. Summarizes details in separate ledgers or computer files and transfers data to general ledger, using calculator or computer. Reconciles and balances accounts. May compile reports to show statistics, such as cash receipts and expenditures, accounts payable and receivable, profit and loss, and other items pertinent to operation of business. May calculate employee wages from plant records or time cards and prepare checks for payment of wages. May prepare withholding, Social Security, and other tax reports. May compute, type, and mail monthly statements to customers. May be designated according to kind of records of financial transactions kept, such as Accounts-Receivable Bookkeeper (clerical), and Accounts-Payable Bookkeeper (clerical). May complete records to or through trial balance.
GOE: 07.02.01 STRENGTH: S GED: R4 M4 L3 SVP: 6 DLU: 87

210.382-030 CLASSIFICATION-CONTROL CLERK (clerical)
Classifies, for bookkeeping purposes, each item on reports, work orders, material requisitions, and invoices, noting after each item ledger account to which it is to be charged, or classifies items for statistical purposes according to predetermined system. May specialize in item classified and be designated Account-Classification Clerk (clerical); Invoice-Classification Clerk (clerical).
GOE: 07.02.01 STRENGTH: S GED: R4 M3 L3 SVP: 5 DLU: 77

210.382-038 CREDIT-CARD CLERK (hotel & rest.)
Compiles and verifies credit-card data from vouchers and other records and computes charges and payments due to establishment to keep records of hotel credit-card transactions: Compares charges on vouchers with audit tape to detect errors and corrects faulty vouchers. Sorts and combines vouchers and other credit transaction records by individual card-issuing firm. Computes totals, discounts, net charges, and amounts due, using calculator and adding machine, and posts to account journals. Prepares invoices for payment by card-issuing firms.
GOE: 07.02.02 STRENGTH: S GED: R3 M3 L2 SVP: 3 DLU: 77

210.382-042 FIXED-CAPITAL CLERK (utilities)
Keeps records of fixed-capital accounts: Posts completed gas or electric work orders to respective accounts in plant ledgers. Appraises retirement values of equipment, such as gas mains, regulators, meters, and transformers and posts retirements to fixed-capital record books. Balances fixed-capital record books with respective control accounts in general ledger. Prepares journal vouchers, makes trial balances, and compiles reports of money charged to fixed-capital accounts.
GOE: 07.02.02 STRENGTH: S GED: R4 M3 L3 SVP: 5 DLU: 77

210.382-046 GENERAL-LEDGER BOOKKEEPER (clerical)
Compiles and posts in general ledgers information or summaries concerning various business transactions that have been recorded in separate ledgers by other clerks, using calculating or adding machine.
GOE: 07.02.01 STRENGTH: S GED: R4 M4 L3 SVP: 5 DLU: 77

210.382-050 MORTGAGE-LOAN-COMPUTATION CLERK (insurance)
Compiles ledger accounts on mortgage loans, using calculating machine. Examines ledger card for balance owed by debtor. Computes interest, principal,

and added charges, such as taxes or insurance. Enters results of calculations in ledger accounts.
GOE: 07.02.02 STRENGTH: S GED: R3 M3 L2 SVP: 3 DLU: 77

210.382-054 NIGHT AUDITOR (hotel & rest.) alternate titles: night-clerk auditor
Verifies and balances entries and records of financial transactions reported by various hotel departments during day, using adding, bookkeeping, and calculating machines. May perform duties of HOTEL CLERK (hotel & rest.) 238.367-038 in smaller establishment.
GOE: 07.02.02 STRENGTH: S GED: R4 M4 L3 SVP: 5 DLU: 80

210.382-062 SECURITIES CLERK (clerical)
Compiles and maintains records of firm's securities transactions: Reviews statements of transactions such as purchases and sales of securities, compares items with records to verify accuracy, and enters details in journals. Computes amounts, such as cash balances, dividends, gain or loss, and other investment data to verify accuracy of records, using adding machine, and reconciles discrepancies. Distributes investment income to various accounts, according to budgeted percentages, to compile investment journals. Computes amounts to determine cash position of various accounts and prepares vouchers to transfer funds needed to meet payments due.
GOE: 07.02.03 STRENGTH: S GED: R4 M4 L3 SVP: 6 DLU: 77

211 CASHIERS AND TELLERS

This group includes occupations concerned with receiving and disbursing money and recording transactions. Most occupations involve use of calculators, cash registers, change makers, or computer terminals. Some machines, such as cash registers, may be connected to computers and use a scanner to record customer purchases. It includes occupations concerned with receiving and disbursing money in banks and other financial institutions.

211.132-010 TELLER, HEAD (financial)
Supervises and coordinates activities of workers engaged in receiving and paying out money and keeping records of transactions in banks and similar financial institutions: Assigns duties and work schedules to workers to ensure efficient functioning of department. Trains employees in customer service and banking procedures. Approves checks for payment. Examines TELLERS' (financial) 211.362-018 reports of daily transactions for accuracy. Consolidates and balances daily transactions, using adding machine and computer. Ensures supply of money for financial institution's needs based on legal requirements and business demand. May allow customers access to safe deposit boxes, following specified procedures. May monitor and review financial institution's security procedures and control access to vault. May count and record currency and coin in vault. Performs other duties as described under SUPERVISOR (clerical) Master Title.
GOE: 07.03.01 STRENGTH: L GED: R4 M3 L4 SVP: 8 DLU: 88

211.137-010 SUPERVISOR, CASHIERS (hotel & rest.; retail trade)
Supervises and coordinates activities of workers engaged in receiving cash or credit-card payment for merchandise or services and keeping records of funds received in retail establishments or places of public accommodation: Performs cashiering and other clerical duties to relieve subordinates during peak work periods. Searches records to assist subordinates in locating and reconciling posting errors on customers' invoices, such as hotel bills or sales tickets, or compares cash register totals with receipts in register to verify accuracy of transactions. Withdraws monies from bank and keeps custody of operating funds, or retains next day's operating funds from daily receipts. Allocates operating funds to cashiering stations. Totals and summarizes funds received, endorses checks, and prepares bank deposit slip. Performs duties as described under SUPERVISOR (clerical) Master Title.
GOE: 07.03.01 STRENGTH: L GED: R4 M3 L3 SVP: 7 DLU: 77

211.137-014 SUPERVISOR, FOOD CHECKERS AND CASHIERS (hotel & rest.)
Plans, supervises, and coordinates activities of FOOD-AND-BEVERAGE CHECKERS (hotel & rest.) and CASHIERS (clerical) II at multiple stations in large food-service establishment: Establishes food-checking and cashiering stations to support activities, such as dining rooms, bars, clubs, banquets, and social functions. Hires and trains workers. Observes food-checking, billing, and cashiering activities; counts cash; and reconciles charge sales and cash receipts with total sales to verify accuracy of transactions. Compiles reports, such as cash receipts, guest-bill charges, and sales for accounting and management purposes, or supervises clerical workers preparing reports.
GOE: 07.03.01 STRENGTH: L GED: R4 M4 L3 SVP: 7 DLU: 77

211.137-018 SUPERVISOR, MONEY-ROOM (amuse. & rec.)
Supervises and coordinates activities of money-room workers engaged in keeping account of money wagered on each race at racetrack: Keeps continuous balance sheet of cash transactions and verifies with cash on hand. Requisitions additional cash as needed. Determines workers needed each day and assigns their duties. Performs duties as described under SUPERVISOR (clerical) Master Title.
GOE: 07.02.02 STRENGTH: L GED: R4 M4 L3 SVP: 6 DLU: 77

211.137-022 SUPERVISOR, TELLERS (utilities)
Supervises and coordinates activities of TELLERS (utilities) in accepting payments for gas and electric-power bills from customers and keeps records of

money received: Interprets company policies and work procedures. Calculates monthly commissions for authorized collection agencies, such as neighborhood stores, from daily summaries of cash receipts by agents. Dictates correspondence or contacts agents by telephone to reconcile errors in their reports. Traces payments made to agents when customer does not receive credit for payment. Interviews customers to assist workers in resolving questions not covered by specified procedures. Prepares regular reports on operations of section. Maintains records of daily overage or shortage in cash receipts. Performs other duties as described under SUPERVISOR (clerical) Master Title.
GOE: 07.03.01 STRENGTH: S GED: R4 M4 L4 SVP: 8 DLU: 77

211.362-010 CASHIER I (clerical) alternate titles: cash-accounting clerk
Receives funds from customers and employees, disburses funds, and records monetary transactions in business establishment or place of public accommodation: Receives cash or checks or completes credit-card charge transactions. Counts money to verify amounts and issues receipts for funds received. Issues change and cashes checks. Compares totals on cash register with amount of currency in register to verify balances. Endorses checks and lists and totals cash and checks for bank deposit. Prepares bank deposit slips. Withdraws cash from bank accounts and keeps custody of cash fund. Disburses cash and writes vouchers and checks in payment of company expenditures. Posts data and balances accounts. Compiles collection, disbursement, and bank-reconciliation reports. Operates office machines, such as typewriter, computer terminal, and adding, calculating, bookkeeping, and check-writing machines. May authorize various plant expenditures and purchases. May prepare payroll and paychecks. May issue itemized statement to customer. May be designated according to specialization as Agency Cashier (insurance); Cashier, Front Office (hotel & rest.). When disbursing money in payment of wages, materials, taxes, plant maintenance, and other company expenses, is designated Disbursement Clerk (clerical).
GOE: 07.03.01 STRENGTH: S GED: R4 M3 L3 SVP: 5 DLU: 88

211.362-014 FOREIGN BANKNOTE TELLER-TRADER (financial)
Buys and sells foreign currencies and drafts and sells travelers' checks, according to daily international exchange rates, working at counter in foreign exchange office: Questions patrons to determine type of currency or draft desired or offered for sale. Quotes unit exchange rate, following daily international rate sheet or computer display. Computes exchange value including fee for transaction, using calculator, and counts out currency. Sells foreign and domestic travelers' checks. Prepares sales slips and records transactions in daily log. Gives information to patrons about foreign currency regulations. Prepares daily inventory of currency, drafts, and travelers' checks. Computes amounts on logsheets and reconciles totals with inventory report.
GOE: 08.01.03 STRENGTH: S GED: R4 M4 L4 SVP: 5 DLU: 78

211.362-018 TELLER (financial) alternate titles: general teller
Receives and pays out money, and keeps records of money and negotiable instruments involved in financial transactions: Receives checks and cash for deposit, verifies amount, and examines checks for endorsements. Cashes checks and pays out money after verification of signatures and customer balances. Enters customers' transactions into computer to record transactions, and issues computer-generated receipts. Places holds on accounts for uncollected funds. Orders daily supply of cash, and counts incoming cash. Balances currency, coin, and checks in cash drawer at end of shift, using calculator, and compares totaled amounts with data displayed on computer screen. Explains, promotes, or sells products or services, such as travelers checks, savings bonds, money orders, and cashier's checks. May open new accounts. May remove deposits from, and count and balance cash in, automated teller machines and night depository. May accept utility bill and loan payments. May use typewriter, photocopier, and check protector to prepare checks and financial documents.
GOE: 07.03.01 STRENGTH: L GED: R4 M3 L3 SVP: 5 DLU: 88

211.367-010 PAYMASTER OF PURSES (amuse. & rec.)
Pays purses (winnings) to owners of winning horses and receives deposits from owners for expenses at racetrack: Receives deposits from owners desiring to claim horses in claiming race and for racing expenses, such as entry and rider fees and stable expenses. Pays owners of winning horses amounts specified on official programs. Pays claiming price to sellers, pays racing expenses for owners, and debits accounts. Periodically balances owners' accounts. Notifies owners when accounts are overdrawn or writes checks to close accounts. Compiles and records information concerning ownership of horses for submission to racing officials.
GOE: 07.03.01 STRENGTH: S GED: R4 M4 L3 SVP: 6 DLU: 77

211.382-010 TELLER, VAULT (financial)
Fills orders for currency and coins, and counts and records cash deposits in vault of commercial bank: Counts currency, coins, and checks received for deposit in vault from business or branch bank, by hand and using currency-counting machine. Totals currency and checks, using computer or calculator, to verify amount on deposit slip or other form. Records deposit in customer account record. Removes specified amount of currency and coins from vault and places cash in bag for shipment to business or branch bank. Records amount of cash shipped. Counts and records large denomination bills, mutilated currency, and food stamps, by hand and using currency-counting machine, for shipment to Federal Reserve Bank. Balances transactions for day, using computer or calculator, and records results.
GOE: 07.03.01 STRENGTH: M GED: R4 M3 L3 SVP: 4 DLU: 88

211.462-010 CASHIER II (clerical) alternate titles: cash clerk; cashier, general; cashier, office; ticket clerk
Receives cash from customers or employees in payment for goods or services and records amounts received: Recomputes or computes bill, itemized lists, and tickets showing amount due, using adding machine or cash register. Makes change, cashes checks, and issues receipts or tickets to customers. Records amounts received and prepares reports of transactions. Reads and records totals shown on cash register tape and verifies against cash on hand. May be required to know value and features of items for which money is received. May give cash refunds or issue credit memorandums to customers for returned merchandise. May operate ticket-dispensing machine. May operate cash register with peripheral electronic data processing equipment by passing individual price coded items across electronic scanner to record price, compile printed list, and display cost of customer purchase, tax, and rebates on monitor screen. May sell candy, cigarettes, gum, and gift certificates, and issue trading stamps. May be designated according to nature of establishment as Cafeteria Cashier (hotel & rest.); Cashier, Parking Lot (automotive ser.); Dining-Room Cashier (hotel & rest.); Service-Bar Cashier (hotel & rest.); Store Cashier (clerical); or according to type of account as Cashier, Credit (clerical); Cashier, Payments Received (clerical). May press numeric keys of computer corresponding to gasoline pump to reset meter on pump and to record amount of sale and be designated Cashier, Self-Service Gasoline (automotive ser.). May receive money, make change, and cash checks for sales personnel on same floor and be designated Floor Cashier (clerical). May make change for patrons at places of amusement other than gambling establishments and be designated Change-Booth Cashier (amuse. & rec.).
GOE: 07.03.01 STRENGTH: L GED: R3 M2 L2 SVP: 2 DLU: 81

211.462-014 CASHIER-CHECKER (retail trade)
Operates cash register to itemize and total customer's purchases in grocery, department, or other retail store: Reviews price sheets to note price changes and sale items. Records prices and departments, subtotals taxable items, and totals purchases on cash register. Collects cash, check, or charge payment from customer and makes change for cash transactions. Stocks shelves and marks prices on items. Counts money in cash drawer at beginning and end of work shift. May record daily transaction amounts from cash register to balance cash drawer. May weigh items, bag merchandise, issue trading stamps, and redeem food stamps and promotional coupons. May cash checks. May use electronic scanner to record price. May be designated according to items checked as Grocery Checker (retail trade).
GOE: 07.03.01 STRENGTH: L GED: R3 M2 L2 SVP: 3 DLU: 81

211.462-018 CASHIER-WRAPPER (retail trade)
Operates cash register to compute and record total sale and wraps merchandise for customers in department, variety, and specialty stores: Receives sales slip, money, and merchandise from salesperson or customer. Records amount of sale on cash register and makes change. Obtains credit authorization on charge purchases in excess of floor limit from designated official, using telephone or pneumatic tube carrier. Inspects merchandise prior to wrapping to see that it is in satisfactory condition and verifies sales slip with price tickets on merchandise. Places merchandise in bags or boxes and gives change and packages to selling personnel. Wraps packages for shipment and routes to delivery department. Balances cash received with cash sales daily. May gift wrap merchandise.
GOE: 09.04.02 STRENGTH: L GED: R3 M2 L2 SVP: 3 DLU: 77

211.462-022 CASHIER, GAMBLING (amuse. & rec.)
Accepts and pays off bets placed by patrons of cardrooms, bookmaking, or other gambling establishments: Sells color-coded gambling chips or tickets to patrons or to other workers for resale to patrons. Records transaction, using cash register. Accepts cash or checks for chips or approves patrons' credit and charges individual accounts for amount issued. Reconciles daily summaries of transactions to balance books. May accept patrons' credit applications and verify credit references to obtain check-cashing authorization. May accept bets only and be designated Bet Taker (amuse. & rec.).
GOE: 07.03.01 STRENGTH: S GED: R3 M3 L2 SVP: 4 DLU: 77

211.462-026 CHECK CASHIER (business ser.) alternate titles: cashier, check-cashing agency
Cashes checks, prepares money orders, receives payment for utilities bills, and collects and records fees charged for check-cashing service. May receive payment and issue receipts for such items as license plates.
GOE: 07.03.01 STRENGTH: S GED: R3 M3 L2 SVP: 3 DLU: 77

211.462-030 DRIVERS'-CASH CLERK (motor trans.)
Receives monies and drivers' route sheets, and issues receipts to truck drivers for cash collected on shipment. Records bills for which cash has been received on collection sheets. Verifies totals of cash on hand against bills, using calculating machine. May endorse checks and wrap currency and coins.
GOE: 07.02.02 STRENGTH: L GED: R3 M2 L1 SVP: 3 DLU: 77

211.462-034 TELLER (utilities) alternate titles: remittance clerk
Computes and collects payments from customers for utility services or appliances: Receives cash or check from customer or through mail. Totals items on bill, using adding machine. Records transaction on cash register and issues receipt and any change due customer. Balances totals received with totals on billing stubs. Explains charges on bill to customer and initiates action to adjust complaints. May collect customer's deposit for service connection. May specialize in handling delinquent bills or those presented for partial payment.

GOE: 07.03.01 STRENGTH: L GED: R3 M2 L2 SVP: 3 DLU: 77

211.462-038 TOLL COLLECTOR (government ser.)
Collects toll charged for use of bridges, highways, or tunnels by motor vehicles, or fare for vehicle and passengers on ferryboats: Collects money and gives customer change. Accepts toll and fare tickets previously purchased. At end of shift balances cash and records money and tickets received. May sell round-trip booklets. May be designated according to place of employment as Toll-Bridge Attendant (government ser.); or type of fare as Vehicle-Fare Collector (motor trans.; water trans.). May admit passengers through turnstile and be designated Turnstile Collector (water trans.).
GOE: 07.03.01 STRENGTH: L GED: R3 M2 L2 SVP: 2 DLU: 77

211.467-010 CASHIER, COURTESY BOOTH (retail trade)
Cashes checks for customers and monitors checkout stations in self-service store: Cashes personal and payroll checks. Provides information to customers. Receives customer's complaints and resolves complaints when possible. Monitors checkout stations to reduce customer delay. Calls additional workers to stations when situation warrants. Issues cash to stations and removes excess cash. Audits cash register tapes. May compile reports, verify employee time records, and prepare payroll.
GOE: 09.04.02 STRENGTH: L GED: R3 M3 L3 SVP: 4 DLU: 77

211.467-014 MONEY COUNTER (amuse. & rec.) alternate titles: money-room teller
Counts, sorts, and issues money to PARIMUTUEL-TICKET SELLERS (amuse. & rec.), and PARIMUTUEL-TICKET CASHIERS (amuse. & rec.) to conduct daily transactions at racetrack. Observes totaling board for official race results and issues money to cashiering stations to pay holders of winning tickets. Compares workers' reports of cash collected and paid out to verify accuracy of transactions.
GOE: 07.07.02 STRENGTH: L GED: R3 M3 L2 SVP: 3 DLU: 77

211.467-018 PARIMUTUEL-TICKET CASHIER (amuse. & rec.) alternate titles: mutuel cashier; parimutuel cashier
Cashes winning parimutuel tickets for patrons at race track: Posts official race results and value of winning tickets on worksheet to compute payouts. Compares ticket submitted by patron with sample to determine validity. Pays winnings to patron. Summons security personnel to apprehend persons attempting to cash fraudulent tickets, or directs patron to INFORMATION CLERK-CASHIER (amuse. & rec.) or to supervisory personnel to resolve questions of ticket validity. Records number of tickets cashed and amount paid out after each race. Requisitions additional cash from MONEY COUNTER (amuse. & rec.) as required. Keeps daily balance sheet of amount and number of transactions.
GOE: 07.03.01 STRENGTH: L GED: R3 M2 L2 SVP: 2 DLU: 77

211.467-022 PARIMUTUEL-TICKET SELLER (amuse. & rec.) alternate titles: mutuel clerk; parimutuel clerk
Sells parimutuel tickets to patrons at racetrack: Reads entry sheets to ascertain entry number of specific horses in designated race and depresses corresponding numbered key of ticket-dispensing machine that automatically ejects ticket requested by patron. Accepts money and makes change. After start of race records totals of tickets sold and cash received and forwards to money room for counting and verification.
GOE: 07.03.01 STRENGTH: L GED: R3 M2 L2 SVP: 2 DLU: 77

211.467-026 SHEET WRITER (amuse. & rec.)
Cashes winning tickets in bookmaking establishment: Records on sheets final odds on winning horses as odds are received at bookmaking establishment. Computes winnings due and pays bettors. Balances cash disbursed against total of winning tickets. Computes total monies received for tickets sold on each race.
GOE: 07.03.01 STRENGTH: L GED: R3 M2 L2 SVP: 2 DLU: 77

211.467-030 TICKET SELLER (clerical) alternate titles: cashier, ticket selling
Sells tickets for travel on ferryboats, street railroads, buses, and for admission to places of entertainment, such as skating rinks, baseball parks, stadiums, and amusement parks: Depresses key on ticket-dispensing machine that automatically ejects number of tickets requested by patron or tears tickets from roll and hands ticket to patron. Accepts payment and makes change. Answers questions concerning fares, routes, schedules, and reservations, and gives information concerning coming attractions. Keeps daily balance sheet of cash received and tickets sold. May fill reservations for seats by telephone or mail. May sell tickets from box office and be designated Cashier, Box Office (amuse. & rec.). May collect fares from repeat riders at amusement park and be designated Second-Ride-Fare Collector (amuse. & rec.). May collect fares from railroad passengers at station and sell commuter tickets and be designated Station Agent (r.r. trans.) II.
GOE: 07.03.01 STRENGTH: L GED: R3 M2 L2 SVP: 2 DLU: 80

211.467-034 CHANGE PERSON (amuse. & rec.)
Exchanges coins for customer's paper money in slot machine area of gambling establishment: Walks and carries money belt in assigned section to exchange size and value of coins desired by customers. Listens for jackpot alarm bell, issues payoffs, and obtains customer's signature on receipt when winnings exceed amount contained in machine.
GOE: 07.03.01 STRENGTH: M GED: R2 M2 L1 SVP: 2 DLU: 86

211.482-010 CASHIER, TUBE ROOM (retail trade)
Computes and records cash receipts, issues operating funds, receives money and makes change, via pneumatic tube, to assist cashiering personnel in department store: Issues bank (operating funds) to cashiering stations. Receives, via pneumatic tube, carriers containing money and sales slips from sales departments, and makes change, using cash drawer and change dispenser. Records individual payments received, using adding machine. Inserts change into carrier and routes, via tube, for return to specified department. Receives bank and cash receipts from departments and c.o.d. collections from delivery-truck drivers, tallies cash receipts, and verifies cash against accompanying reports. Sorts and counts currency, checks, refunds, and gift certificates. Stacks currency manually and sorts, counts, and wraps coins, using machine. Computes totals, using adding machine, and records on daily report. Corrects faulty entries on individual cash reports received. May perform tasks without use of pneumatic tube.
GOE: 07.02.02 STRENGTH: S GED: R3 M2 L2 SVP: 3 DLU: 77

211.482-014 FOOD CHECKER (hotel & rest.)
Scans loaded trays carried by patrons in hotel or restaurant cafeteria to compute bill: Operates machine similar to cash register to compute bill and presents check to patron for payment to CASHIER (clerical) II. May operate adding machine and present tape rather than check to customer for payment. May act as CASHIER (clerical) II.
GOE: 07.06.02 STRENGTH: S GED: R3 M2 L1 SVP: 3 DLU: 77

211.482-018 FOOD-AND-BEVERAGE CHECKER (hotel & rest.)
Computes food or beverage service bills and verifies completeness of customer orders in hotel kitchen, dining room, restaurant, or service bar: Examines food on tray enroute from kitchen or beverages enroute from service bar and compares items with listing on customer order to verify completeness and accuracy of order. Operates machine similar to cash register to compute charges. May take telephone orders for room service [ORDER CLERK, FOOD AND BEVERAGE (hotel & rest.)].
GOE: 05.09.03 STRENGTH: L GED: R3 M2 L2 SVP: 3 DLU: 77

213 COMPUTER AND PERIPHERAL EQUIPMENT OPERATORS

This group includes occupations concerned with managing, controlling, and monitoring operations of computers and peripheral equipment that record, store, retrieve, and print processed information. Activities involving the primary input of data into computer systems using machines equipped with typewriter-like keyboards are found in Group 203. Occupations concerned with computer scheduling are found in Group 221.

213.132-010 SUPERVISOR, COMPUTER OPERATIONS (clerical) alternate titles: chief console operator; supervisor, data processing
Supervises and coordinates activities of workers operating computers and peripheral equipment: Assigns staff and schedules work to facilitate production. Directs training or trains workers to operate computer and peripheral equipment. Confers with programmers and operates computer to test new and modified programs. Directs operation of computer to execute program, and observes operation to detect error or failure in progress of program. Reads monitor and enters commands to help computer operators identify and correct errors. Revises input data and program to continue operation of program, using computer terminal. Notifies programming and maintenance personnel if unable to locate and correct cause of processing error or failure. Revises operation schedule to adjust for delays, or notifies scheduling workers of need to adjust schedule. Prepares or reviews production, operating, and down time records and reports. Recommends changes in programs, routines, and quality control standards to improve computer operating efficiency. Consults with supervisor about problems, such as equipment performance, output quality, and maintenance schedule. Coordinates flow of work between shifts to ensure continuity. Performs other duties as described under SUPERVISOR (clerical) Master Title.
GOE: 07.06.01 STRENGTH: L GED: R5 M4 L4 SVP: 7 DLU: 90

213.362-010 COMPUTER OPERATOR (clerical)
Operates computer and peripheral equipment to process business, scientific, engineering, or other data, according to operating instructions: Enters commands, using keyboard of computer terminal, and presses buttons and flips switches on computer and peripheral equipment, such as tape drive, printer, data communications equipment, and plotter, to integrate and operate equipment, following operating instructions and schedule. Loads peripheral equipment with selected materials, such as tapes and printer paper for operating runs, or oversees loading of peripheral equipment by peripheral equipment operators. Enters commands to clear computer system and start operation, using keyboard of computer terminal. Observes peripheral equipment and error messages displayed on monitor of terminal to detect faulty output or machine stoppage. Enters commands to correct error or stoppage and resume operations. Notifies supervisor of errors or equipment stoppage. Clears equipment at end of operating run and reviews schedule to determine next assignment. Records problems which occurred, such as down time, and actions taken. May answer telephone calls to assist computer users encountering problem. May assist workers in classifying, cataloging, and maintaining tapes [TAPE LIBRARIAN (clerical) 206.367-018].
GOE: 07.06.01 STRENGTH: L GED: R4 M2 L3 SVP: 6 DLU: 90

213.382-010 COMPUTER PERIPHERAL EQUIPMENT OPERATOR (clerical)

Operates computer peripheral equipment, such as printer, plotter, computer output microfiche machine, and document reader-sorter to transfer data to and from computer and to convert data from one format to another: Reads instructions and schedule, such as schedule of documents to be printed, or receives instructions from supervisor orally, to determine work for shift. Mounts reels and cartridges of magnetic tape in tape drives, loads paper in printer, loads checks or other documents in magnetic ink reader-sorter or optical character reader, sets guides, keys, and switches, enters commands into computer, using computer terminal, and performs other tasks, to start and operate peripheral machines. Observes machine operation and error lights on machines to detect malfunction. Observes materials printed for defects, such as creases and tears. Removes faulty materials and notifies supervisor of error or machine stoppage. Unloads and labels magnetic tape for delivery to other worker or tape library. May separate, sort, and distribute output. May clean and supply equipment operated with paper, ink, film, developing solution, and other materials.
GOE: 07.06.01 STRENGTH: L GED: R3 M2 L3 SVP: 4 DLU: 88

213.582-010 DIGITIZER OPERATOR (business ser.; petrol. & gas)

Operates encoding machine to trace coordinates on documents, such as maps or drawings, and to encode document points into computer: Reads work order to determine document points to be digitized (encoded). Positions document on digitizer (encoding machine) table. Guides digitizer cursor over document to trace coordinates, stops at specified points, and punches cursor key to digitize points into computer memory unit. Observes monitor screen periodically to verify completeness of encoding. Types command on keyboard to transfer encoded data from memory unit to magnetic tape. Keeps record of work orders, time, and tape production.
GOE: 07.06.01 STRENGTH: S GED: R3 M3 L2 SVP: 5 DLU: 86

214 BILLING AND RATE CLERKS

This group includes occupations concerned with making computations with or without machines for purposes of preparing or verifying bills, invoices, rates, tariffs, duties, and statements of amounts due for items purchased or services rendered. It includes counting or tallying to obtain data on which payments are based. Occupations concerned with preparing bills and invoices involving substantial use of typewriter are found in Group 203. Occupations concerned with using knowledge of bookkeeping principles and procedures to compute, classify, and record numerical data to keep sets of financial records are found in Group 210. Occupations concerned with preparing numerical records of time worked or units produced for payroll or timekeeping purposes are found in Group 215. Occupations concerned with making computations involving various aspects of production are found in Group 221.

214.137-010 DOCUMENTATION SUPERVISOR (water trans.)

Supervises and coordinates activities of workers engaged in preparing shipping documents and related reports and in classifying and rating cargo according to established tariff rates: Reviews ships' schedules and booking records to plan and schedule work activities. Assigns rating activities to workers and reviews ratings to ensure that cargo has been classified in accordance with established tariff rates. Verifies cargo assigned shippers against bills of lading and assigns codes to new accounts. Assigns documentation activities to workers, such as preparing dock receipts, bills of lading, and manifests, and compiling tonnage, demurrage, and storage reports. Examines reports and documents for completeness and accuracy and gives instructions to workers regarding corrections. Issues bills of lading to shippers upon verification of documents. Confers with other supervisory personnel and shippers' representatives to clarify problems and resolve complaints. May supervise and coordinate activities of workers engaged in passenger baggage handling. Performs other duties as described under SUPERVISOR (clerical) Master Title.
GOE: 07.02.04 STRENGTH: L GED: R4 M3 L3 SVP: 7 DLU: 77

214.137-014 SUPERVISOR, STATEMENT CLERKS (financial)

Supervises and coordinates activities of workers engaged in preparing customer bank statements for distribution, maintaining cancelled checks and customer signature files, and adjusting customer accounts: Coordinates assignments of workers preparing bank statements for delivery, reconciling account differences, and filing checks. Writes letters and makes telephone calls to recover checks returned in error and to adjust customer accounts and complaints. Assists customers in establishing depository arrangements for large accounts. Accepts stop-payment orders and directs workers in flagging customer accounts to prevent withdrawal of uncollected portions of deposits, or to prevent payment of protested checks. Performs other duties as described under SUPERVISOR (clerical) Master Title.
GOE: 07.01.04 STRENGTH: L GED: R4 M3 L4 SVP: 7 DLU: 87

214.137-018 RATE SUPERVISOR (clerical)

Supervises and coordinates activities of TRAFFIC-RATE CLERKS (clerical) engaged in determining and quoting rates and classifications applicable to shipments of merchandise, products, and equipment: Analyzes existing rates and routes to effect reduction in transportation costs, and prepares reports of estimated savings. Confers with carriers for reduction in rates. Performs other duties as described under SUPERVISOR (clerical) Master Title.
GOE: 07.02.02 STRENGTH: S GED: R4 M3 L3 SVP: 6 DLU: 77

214.137-022 SUPERVISOR, ACCOUNTS RECEIVABLE (utilities; water-works) alternate titles: billing supervisor

Supervises and coordinates activities of workers engaged in tracing sources of error and correcting billing records for gas, electric-power, and water supply customers, and in processing records for advance or final billings: Interprets work procedures for subordinates. Confers with subordinates to resolve procedural problems in tracing sources of error. Reviews and corrects customer accounts to determine amounts over or under paid as result of irregular connection (meter tampering) investigations. Prepares corrected bills to reconcile errors in meter readings, using calculator. Traces source and corrects customer accounts for errors in billing rates, misapplied credits, or identifying information, such as name and address received from customer. Confers with employees of other departments to trace payments on bills under investigation by collection department and to give information pertaining to accuracy of charges on customer's bills. Performs other duties described under SUPERVISOR (clerical) Master Title.
GOE: 07.02.02 STRENGTH: S GED: R4 M4 L3 SVP: 8 DLU: 77

214.267-010 RATE ANALYST, FREIGHT (air trans.; motor trans.; r.r. trans.; water trans.)

Analyzes existing freight rates, tariff regulations, and proposed or government-approved changes in rates to revise or recommend changes in rate structures, rules, and regulations for freight carrier: Analyzes proposals and applications for changes in rates, rules, or regulations received from rate bureaus, shippers, sales offices, and other carriers, and reviews regulations and regulatory agencies' decisions on applications filed by other carriers governing established rates and newly approved rate changes to determine required changes in company's rate charts. Compiles rate-manual sections in accordance with governmental regulations, based on factors such as handling costs, classes of merchandise transported, fuel costs, refrigeration required, business volume, and potential return trip loads. Confers with shippers, sales and rate bureau personnel, and others to discuss revised rates, rules, and regulations. Prepares revised rate schedules or submits data for publication. May propose rates for activities or services not previously rated.
GOE: 11.06.03 STRENGTH: S GED: R4 M4 L4 SVP: 6 DLU: 77

214.362-010 DEMURRAGE CLERK (r.r. trans.) alternate titles: car-record clerk

Compiles demurrage charges, using basic rates from rate tables: Communicates with consignee by telephone or letter to notify consignee of date and time of arrival of freight shipment, location, and allowable time for moving or unloading freight before demurrage charges are levied. Reviews bills of lading and other shipping documents to ascertain number of carloads of shipment and computes demurrage charges, using basic rates from rate table and adding or calculating machine. Prepares demurrage bill and forwards it to consignee or shipper. May reconsign or reroute cars on order from shippers. May prepare new waybills and bills of lading on receipt of notice of sale of carload of freight from shipper.
GOE: 07.02.04 STRENGTH: S GED: R3 M3 L3 SVP: 5 DLU: 77

214.362-014 DOCUMENTATION-BILLING CLERK (air trans.; motor trans.; r.r. trans.; water trans.)

Compiles and types transportation billing documents listing details of freight shipped by carrier: Types information on manifest, such as name of shipper, weight, destination, and charges from bills of lading and shipper's declaration. Computes totals of document items, using adding machine. Compares figures and totals on documents with statement of accounts submitted by accounting department to verify accuracy of documents. Notifies CARGO CHECKER (water trans.) to examine shipment when discrepancies are found. Resolves discrepancies on accounting records or manifest. May prepare manifest, using billing machine. May notify shipper's agent of consular visa and official stamps required and attach stamps to documents when presented by agent. May be designated by type of document prepared as Manifest Clerk (air trans.; motor trans.; r.r. trans.; water trans.); Waybill Clerk (air trans.; motor trans.; r.r. trans.; water trans.).
GOE: 07.02.04 STRENGTH: S GED: R3 M3 L3 SVP: 4 DLU: 77

214.362-022 INSURANCE CLERK (medical ser.) alternate titles: hospital-insurance clerk; patient-insurance clerk

Verifies hospitalization insurance coverage, computes patients' benefits, and compiles itemized hospital bills: Types insurance assignment form with data, such as names of insurance company and policy holder, policy number, and physician's diagnosis. Telephones, writes, or wires insurance company to verify patient's coverage and to obtain information concerning extent of benefits. Computes total hospital bill showing amounts to be paid by insurance company and by patient, using adding and calculating machines. Answers patient's questions regarding statements and insurance coverage. Telephones or writes companies with unpaid insurance claims to obtain settlement of claim. Prepares forms outlining hospital expenses for governmental, welfare, and other agencies paying bill of specified patient.
GOE: 07.02.04 STRENGTH: S GED: R4 M3 L4 SVP: 5 DLU: 77

214.362-026 INVOICE-CONTROL CLERK (clerical) alternate titles: purchase-order checker

Compiles data from vendor invoices and supporting documents to verify accuracy of billing data and to ensure receipt of items ordered, using calculator and computer: Compares invoices against purchase orders and shipping and re-

ceiving documents to verify receipt of items ordered. Reads computer files or computes figures to determine prices and discounts, following invoices and credit memorandums, and using calculator. Records data in control records. Contacts vendors or buyers regarding errors in partial or duplicate shipments, prices, and substitutions. Maintains file of returnable items received from or returned to vendors. Writes check or prepares voucher authorizing payment to vendors.
GOE: 07.02.04 STRENGTH: S GED: R4 M3 L3 SVP: 4 DLU: 88

214.362-030 RATE CLERK, PASSENGER (motor trans.) alternate titles: charter representative

Provides fare information to passengers traveling on nonscheduled or chartered motor trips, using rate tables: Interviews customer or reviews written requests to obtain data on proposed trips. Studies maps to select or lay out and measure travel route. Refers to rate tables to gather rate data considering such items as type of vehicle, distance, destination, estimated travel and waiting time, cost of tolls, and passenger or freight service. Computes rates, using calculator. Prepares written report on rates or informs customer orally. May arrange travel accommodations for tourists [TRAVEL CLERK (hotel & rest.)].
GOE: 07.04.04 STRENGTH: S GED: R4 M3 L3 SVP: 4 DLU: 77

214.362-034 TARIFF INSPECTOR (r.r. trans.)

Verifies use of current tariff rates at railroad freight, passenger agent, and ticket offices. Visits offices and examines records, such as freight bills, to ascertain whether current rates are in use, in accordance with tariff schedules. Computes and verifies tariff rates applied, using calculating machine and rate books. Issues instructions to agent regarding correction of errors in rates. Compiles reports for management, identifying names of agents and locations using incorrect tariffs.
GOE: 11.10.01 STRENGTH: L GED: R4 M4 L4 SVP: 5 DLU: 77

214.362-038 TRAFFIC-RATE CLERK (clerical) alternate titles: freight-rate clerk; rate clerk

Compiles and computes freight rates, passenger fares, and other charges for transportation services, according to rate tables and tariff regulations: Examines shipping bills to obtain description of freight, and classifies freight according to rate-book description. Consults rate schedule to obtain specific rate for each item classified depending on distance shipped. Computes total freight charge, using calculator and records charges on shipping order. Calculates and records storage, redelivery, and reconsignment charges when applicable. Answers mail or telephone inquiries from shippers regarding rates, routing, packing procedures and interline transportation procedures. May examine bills of lading and file claims with transportation companies for overcharges. May keep records of freight movements.
GOE: 07.02.04 STRENGTH: S GED: R4 M3 L3 SVP: 5 DLU: 77

214.362-042 BILLING CLERK (clerical)

Operates calculator and typewriter to compile and prepare customer charges, such as labor and material costs: Reads computer printout to ascertain monthly costs, schedule of work completed, and type of work performed for customer, such as plumbing, sheet metal, and insulation. Computes costs and percentage of work completed, using calculator. Compiles data for billing personnel. Types invoices indicating total items for project and cost amounts.
GOE: 07.02.04 STRENGTH: S GED: R4 M3 L3 SVP: 4 DLU: 86

214.362-046 STATEMENT CLERK (financial)

Compares previously prepared bank statements with cancelled checks, prepares statements for distribution to customers, and reconciles discrepancies in records and accounts: Matches statement with batch of cancelled checks by account number. Inserts statements and cancelled checks in envelopes and affixes postage, or inserts statements and checks in feeder of machine which automatically stuffs envelopes and meters postage. Routes statements for mailing or over-the-counter delivery to customers. Keeps cancelled checks and customer signature files. May recover checks returned to customer in error, adjust customer account, and answer inquiries. May post stop-payment notices to prevent payment of protested checks. May encode and cancel checks, using machine. May take orders for imprinted checks.
GOE: 07.02.02 STRENGTH: S GED: R3 M2 L3 SVP: 4 DLU: 87

214.382-014 BILLING TYPIST (clerical) alternate titles: billing clerk; invoice clerk; order clerk

Compiles data and types invoices and bills: Reads computer files or gathers records, such as purchase orders, sales tickets, and charge slips, to compile needed data. Enters information into computer or computes amounts due, using calculator. Types invoices, listing items sold, amounts due, credit terms, and dates of shipment, using typewriter or computer. Types bills of lading and lists weight and serial number of items sold, using specification book. May type shipping labels. May type credit memorandums to indicate returned or incorrectly billed merchandise. May type credit forms for customers or finance companies. May post transactions to accounting records, such as work sheet, ledger, or computer files. May be designated according to type of billing done, such as Bill-Of-Lading Clerk (clerical); C.O.D. Biller (clerical) and Mail-Order Biller (retail trade; wholesale tr.). If worker is involved with compiling and typing transportation billing documents and verifying related accounting records, see DOCUMENTATION-BILLING CLERK (air trans.; motor trans.; r.r. trans.; water trans.) 214.362-014.
GOE: 07.02.04 STRENGTH: S GED: R3 M3 L3 SVP: 4 DLU: 80

214.382-018 C.O.D. CLERK (clerical) alternate titles: cash-on-delivery clerk; collect-on-delivery clerk

Sorts c.o.d. bills according to type of delivery or consignor and computes charges on bills and amounts collected: Sorts c.o.d. bills according to type of delivery or consignor, such as will-call parcel post, or store delivery. Computes total of bills and verifies total against accounting records. Calculates and records amount of money collected on delivery route for c.o.d. bills, using adding and calculating machines. May search customer records to correct addresses on misdirected packages [WRONG-ADDRESS CLERK (retail trade)].
GOE: 07.02.04 STRENGTH: S GED: R3 M2 L2 SVP: 3 DLU: 77

214.382-022 INTERLINE CLERK (motor trans.; r.r. trans.)

Compiles and computes freight and passenger charges payable to participating carriers on interline business: Examines waybills and ticket sales records to compute number of miles each carrier transported freight or passengers. Computes freight or passenger charges payable to each carrier, using basic rates from rate table and calculating machine. Records results of calculations on special forms. Reviews statements submitted by other companies to determine if portion of charges received is correct. May distribute, to appropriate airlines, revenue from passengers traveling on more than one carrier on through passage and be designated Passenger-Interline Clerk (air trans.). May compile records of daily freight car rental fees due to other carriers and be designated Per Diem Clerk (r.r. trans.).
GOE: 07.02.04 STRENGTH: S GED: R4 M3 L3 SVP: 5 DLU: 77

214.382-026 REVISING CLERK (motor trans.; r.r. trans.)

Verifies and revises freight and tariff charges on bills for freight shipments, using freight and tariff rate tables and schedules, according to classification of items shipped. Computes additional charges for reconsignment of freight, using adding machine. Records on special form additional, excess, or short charges made for each freight bill.
GOE: 07.02.04 STRENGTH: S GED: R3 M3 L3 SVP: 4 DLU: 77

214.382-030 SETTLEMENT CLERK (smelt. & refin.)

Compiles and computes payment due shipper for ores, concentrates, scrap metal, and other metal products forwarded to plant for processing, using adding machine and calculator. Bases computations on weight figures from freight bills and laboratory report of moisture content and ore analysis. May obtain registered check for required amount and remit to shipper.
GOE: 07.02.04 STRENGTH: S GED: R3 M3 L3 SVP: 4 DLU: 77

214.387-010 BILLING-CONTROL CLERK (utilities)

Reviews and posts data from meter books, computes charges for utility services, and marks special accounts for billing purposes: Marks accounts with fixed demands, combined bills for more than one meter connection, and those requiring use of constant multipliers to extend meter reading to actual consumption. Posts late and special meter readings and estimated readings. Examines meter-reading entries for evidence of irregular conditions, such as defective meters or use of service without contract, and prepares forms for corrective actions by others. Marks accounts for no bill when irregular conditions cannot be resolved before billing date.
GOE: 07.02.04 STRENGTH: S GED: R3 M3 L3 SVP: 5 DLU: 77

214.387-014 RATE REVIEWER (utilities)

Reviews rates for conformity to regulations, and compiles data pertaining to operating costs, revenues, and volume of gas or electric power: Reviews reports of changes in gas or consumption and complaints about high bills. Reviews rate investigation reports, analyses of billings, and rate assignments for completeness and conformity to regulation. Reviews special rate accounts to determine changes which will benefit customer. Compiles data for reports pertaining to costs, revenues, and volumes of gas or electricity consumed. Draws graphs and charts to illustrate changing trends, using drafting instruments.
GOE: 11.06.03 STRENGTH: S GED: R4 M3 L4 SVP: 6 DLU: 77

214.387-018 SERVICES CLERK (water trans.)

Compiles reports and calculates tariff assessments for services rendered vessels using harbor facilities: Reads register of merchant vessels to verify tonnage, registry, and ship's owner. Calculates charges and types tariff form for service furnished, such as gallons of water and kilowatts of electricity used during vessel's stay in harbor. Keeps records of ships entering port and tonnage of cargo unloaded or loaded. Submits reports to accounting and traffic departments for billing purposes.
GOE: 07.02.04 STRENGTH: S GED: R4 M3 L3 SVP: 5 DLU: 77

214.462-010 ACCOUNTS-ADJUSTABLE CLERK (r.r. trans.)

Computes corrected freight charges from waybill data, using comptometer, and posts corrections on freight bills. Corresponds with other railroads to determine accuracy of billing and to arrange for settlement of adjusted accounts.
GOE: 07.02.04 STRENGTH: S GED: R3 M3 L3 SVP: 3 DLU: 77

214.467-010 FOREIGN CLERK (clerical)

Computes duties, tariffs, and weight, volume, and price conversions of merchandise exported to or imported from foreign countries: Examines documents, such as invoices, bills of lading, and shipping statements, to verify conversion of merchandise weights or volumes into system used by other country. Converts foreign currency figures into United States monetary equivalents, or domestic currency into foreign equivalents, using rate charts. Calculates duties or tariffs to be paid on merchandise, using calculating machine. May correspond with foreign companies. May be designated according to type of transaction as Customs-Entry Clerk (clerical); Export Clerk (clerical); Import Clerk (clerical).

GOE: 07.02.04 STRENGTH: S GED: R4 M4 L3 SVP: 5 DLU: 77

214.467-014 PRICER, MESSAGE AND DELIVERY SERVICE (business ser.)

Computes charges for pickup and delivery of items, such as documents, messages, and packages, using rate manuals and zone maps: Sorts dispatch tickets and reads postal zone maps and street directories to determine zone categories for pickup and delivery of items. Computes charges for services in various zones, using rate manuals, and quotes rates to customers upon request. Records charges on report form.
GOE: 07.02.04 STRENGTH: S GED: R3 M2 L2 SVP: 3 DLU: 86

214.482-010 BILLING-MACHINE OPERATOR (clerical) alternate titles: bill clerk; biller; billing clerk; invoicing-machine operator

Operates billing machines with or without computing devices to prepare bills, statements, and invoices to be sent to customers, itemizing amounts customers owe: Inserts blank billing sheets in machine and sets carriage. Transcribes data from office records, such as customer's name, address, and items purchased or services rendered. Calculates totals, net amounts, and discounts by addition, subtraction, and multiplication, and records computations. May make computations on separate adding and calculating machines. May be designated according to type of bill prepared as Delinquent-Notice-Machine Operator (clerical).
GOE: 07.06.02 STRENGTH: S GED: R3 M3 L3 SVP: 4 DLU: 87

214.482-014 DEPOSIT-REFUND CLERK (utilities)

Prepares final bills for mailing to gas and electric-power customers: Computes and prepares final bills, using adding machine and calculator. Keeps file of deposit certificates surrendered by customer and attaches certificates to final bills for refund of deposit. Reviews accounting records to ensure that all charges and credits are included in final bills. May compute interest due customers for amounts on deposit.
GOE: 07.02.04 STRENGTH: S GED: R3 M3 L3 SVP: 4 DLU: 77

214.482-018 MEDICAL-VOUCHER CLERK (insurance) alternate titles: examiner-rating clerk; medical-fee clerk

Examines vouchers forwarded to insurance carrier by doctors who have made medical examinations of insurance applicants, and approves vouchers for payment, based on standard rates. Computes fees for multiple examinations, using adding machine. Notes fee on form and forwards forms and vouchers to appropriate personnel for further approval and payment.
GOE: 07.02.04 STRENGTH: S GED: R3 M2 L3 SVP: 3 DLU: 77

214.482-022 RATER (insurance) alternate titles: policy rater; rate inserter; rating clerk

Calculates amount of premium to be charged for various types of insurance, using rate book, calculator, and adding machine: Selects premium rate based on information in case record folder relating to type and amount of policy based on standard risk factors, such as use and age of automobile, location and value of property, or age of applicant. Adds premium rates of basic policy and endorsements to compute total annual premium. Records rates on abstract sheet (worksheet), from which policies will be typed. May calculate commissions.
GOE: 07.02.04 STRENGTH: S GED: R3 M3 L3 SVP: 4 DLU: 77

214.487-010 CHART CALCULATOR (utilities)

Computes power factor and net amount of electric power consumed by commercial customers and determines peak load demand to verify application of appropriate rates. Enters information on record forms for monthly billing purposes. If worker compiles data for statistical reports or reviews rates to determine possible adjustments for commercial consumers of gas and electric power, see RATE REVIEWER (utilities).
GOE: 07.02.04 STRENGTH: S GED: R4 M4 L3 SVP: 5 DLU: 77

214.587-010 TELEGRAPH-SERVICE RATER (tel. & tel.) alternate titles: clerk, rating; rate marker

Counts number of words in telegrams dispatched from telegraph office, consults rates in rate book, and marks charges on duplicates of messages for use in billing customers.
GOE: 07.07.03 STRENGTH: S GED: R2 M2 L2 SVP: 2 DLU: 77

214.587-014 TRAFFIC CLERK (clerical)

Records incoming and outgoing freight data, such as destination, weight, route-initiating department, and charges: Ensures accuracy of rate charges by comparing classification of materials with rate chart. May keep file of claims for overcharges and for damages to goods in transit.
GOE: 07.02.04 STRENGTH: S GED: R3 M3 L2 SVP: 4 DLU: 77

215   PAYROLL, TIMEKEEPING, AND DUTY-ROSTER CLERKS

This group includes occupations concerned with making computations for and transcribing data to payroll and timekeeping records; computing earnings based on units produced or services rendered; preparing and distributing pay envelopes; and preparing duty rosters and work schedules.

215.137-010 CREW SCHEDULER, CHIEF (air trans.)

Supervises CREW SCHEDULERS (air trans.) and participates in preparation of duty rosters for crewmembers of scheduled airline flights: Assigns crews according to seniority, choice, and qualifications. May prepare or assist in preparation of section's budget. May audit expense vouchers and related invoices.

215.137-014 SUPERVISOR, PAYROLL (clerical) alternate titles: payroll clerk, chief; timekeeper supervisor

Supervises and coordinates activities of workers engaged in recording hours of work, processing time records, compiling payroll statistics, maintaining payroll control records, and calculating payrolls: Reviews, or directs review of, personnel records to determine names, rates of pay, and occupations of newly hired workers, and changes in wage rates and occupations of employees on payroll. Records, or directs recording of, new or changed pay rates in payroll register or computer files. Directs computation of pay according to company policy. Directs compilation and preparation of other payroll data, such as pension, insurance, and credit union payments. Reviews and approves payroll deductions. Interprets company policies and government regulations affecting payroll procedures. Directs preparation of government reports. Reviews payroll to ensure accuracy. May direct activities of workers engaged in computing costs of production, such as labor and equipment. Performs duties described under SUPERVISOR (clerical) Master Title.
GOE: 07.02.05 STRENGTH: S GED: R4 M3 L4 SVP: 7 DLU: 80

215.137-018 SUPERVISOR, FORCE ADJUSTMENT (tel. & tel.) alternate titles: force dispatcher

Coordinates work assignments and supervises clerical personnel preparing work schedules: Plans and prepares work force schedules from statistical data, such as budget estimates and telephone or telegraphic service and traffic records. Compiles previous traffic-flow counts from transmitting and receiving records, or supervises clerks engaged in compiling flow data to aid in predicting operating needs. Analyzes past flow counts, and personnel data, such as turnover, absenteeism, or overtime. Prepares or revises personnel schedules for long- or short-range periods, considering vacations and budget allotments. May direct preparation of comparative reports and charts to identify operating deficiencies. When working in telegraph offices, assigns personnel to branch offices within geographical area upon receipt of personnel shortage reports. Performs other duties as described under SUPERVISOR (clerical) Master Title.
GOE: 07.05.01 STRENGTH: S GED: R4 M3 L4 SVP: 7 DLU: 77

215.167-010 CAR CLERK, PULLMAN (r.r. trans.) alternate titles: pullman clerk

Assigns and dispatches sleeping cars to railroad company requesting cars: Keeps record of car movement and where assigned, using train schedules and movement charts. Assigns CONDUCTORS, PULLMAN (r.r. trans.) to trains for trips and notifies them of assignments.
GOE: 07.05.01 STRENGTH: S GED: R4 M3 L3 SVP: 6 DLU: 77

215.362-010 CREW SCHEDULER (air trans.)

Compiles duty rosters of flight crews and maintains records of crewmembers' flying time for scheduled airline flights: Prepares flight register which crewmembers sign to indicate their preference and availability for flights and time they wish to be called prior to each flight. Types names of crewmembers onto flight schedule in order of seniority to indicate flights to which crewmembers are assigned. Posts names of extra crewmembers in order of seniority on reserve list. Selects replacements from reserve list and notifies replacement when needed. Computes and logs cumulative flight time for crewmembers and removes crewmember's name from flight schedule when flying time limit as prescribed by Federal Aviation Administration has been reached. Schedules vacations as requested by crewmembers. May notify crewmembers of assignments, using telephone.
GOE: 07.05.01 STRENGTH: S GED: R3 M3 L3 SVP: 5 DLU: 77

215.362-014 DISPATCHER CLERK (r.r. trans.)

Schedules work for train crew or individual workers and keeps time records: Enters names of workers on assignment sheet for each trip on basis of seniority. Notifies workers of assignment, establishes availability, and assigns replacement crew when needed. Keeps record of departure and return of crew or worker for each trip, recording total time worked, and number of miles covered, using calculator.
GOE: 07.02.05 STRENGTH: S GED: R3 M2 L2 SVP: 4 DLU: 77

215.362-018 FLIGHT-CREW-TIME CLERK (air trans.)

Compiles flight time record of flight officers for payroll and crew-scheduling departments to ensure accuracy of payroll and legality of flights: Posts data, such as time in flight, type of aircraft, mileage flown, and weight of aircraft, onto flight time records, using posting machine. Reviews union agreements to ascertain payroll factors, such as meal expense allowance, billeting allotment, and rates of pay. Computes pay [PAYROLL CLERK (clerical)]. Compares figures with flight officers's log to detect and reconcile discrepancies. Notifies CREW SCHEDULERS (air trans.) of total accumulated flight time of each officer and submits pay records to payroll section.
GOE: 07.02.05 STRENGTH: S GED: R4 M3 L4 SVP: 5 DLU: 77

215.362-022 TIMEKEEPER (clerical)

Compiles employees' time and production records, using calculator or computer: Reviews timesheets, workcharts, and timecards for completeness. Computes total time worked by employees, using calculator or computer, posts time worked to master timesheet, and routes timesheet to payroll department. May pay employees. May calculate time worked and units produced by piece-work or bonus work employees, using calculator or computer, and be designated Time Checker (clerical) or Work Checker (clerical). May locate workers on

jobs at various times to verify attendance of workers listed on daily spot sheet and be designated Spotter (any industry). May interview employees to discuss hours worked and pay adjustments to be made and be designated Pay Agent (clerical).
GOE: 07.02.05 STRENGTH: S GED: R3 M2 L2 SVP: 3 DLU: 80

215.367-010   ASSIGNMENT CLERK (motor trans.) alternate titles: assignment agent; bulletin clerk
Assigns operating personnel of busline to partial, temporary, or rush hour runs to meet daily human resource and transportation needs of company: Records driver staffing requirements for unstaffed scheduled runs from data received from personnel department. Prepares list of extra drivers available in ready room for assignment for regular, special, or charter trips. Selects drivers according to such considerations as seniority, experience, and time, location, and duration of assignment. Records and submits data on assignments to personnel department. May prepare and issue bulletins regarding policy, procedure, and schedule changes.
GOE: 07.05.01 STRENGTH: S GED: R3 M2 L2 SVP: 3 DLU: 77

215.367-014   PERSONNEL SCHEDULER (clerical) alternate titles: scheduler and planner
Compiles weekly personnel assignment schedules for production department in manufacturing plant: Studies production schedules and staffing tables to ascertain personnel requirements. Determines and records work assignments according to worker availability, seniority, job classification, and preferences. Compiles and oversees in-plant distribution of work schedule. Adjusts schedules to meet emergencies caused by extended leave or increased production demands. Compiles annual seniority lists on which employees indicate vacation preferences and approves leave requests to prevent production losses.
GOE: 07.05.01 STRENGTH: S GED: R4 M3 L3 SVP: 4 DLU: 77

215.367-018   TAXICAB COORDINATOR (motor trans.)
Assigns taxicabs to TAXI DRIVERS (motor trans.) and maintains record of assignments and trip data. Reviews report of meter readings taken from incoming cabs for accuracy or takes and records taximeter readings. Compiles and maintains records of mileage traveled and fuel used.
GOE: 07.05.03 STRENGTH: S GED: R3 M2 L2 SVP: 5 DLU: 77

215.382-014   PAYROLL CLERK (clerical)
Compiles payroll data, and enters data or computes and posts wages, and reconciles errors, to maintain payroll records, using computer or calculator: Compiles payroll data, such as hours worked, sales or piecework, taxes, insurance, and union dues to be withheld, and employee identification number, from time sheets and other records. Prepares computer input forms, enters data into computer files, or computes wages and deductions, using calculator, and posts to payroll records. Reviews wages computed and corrects errors to ensure accuracy of payroll. Records changes affecting net wages, such as exemptions, insurance coverage, and loan payments for each employee to update master payroll records. Records data concerning transfer of employees between departments. May prorate expenses to be debited or credited to each department for cost accounting records. May prepare periodic reports of earnings, taxes, and deductions. May keep records of leave pay and nontaxable wages. May prepare and issue paychecks.
GOE: 07.02.05 STRENGTH: S GED: R4 M3 L3 SVP: 4 DLU: 88

215.563-010   CALLER (r.r. trans.)
Notifies members of train, engine, or yard crews to report for duty or meetings: Obtains addresses and telephone numbers from personnel records. Talks to workers by telephone to inform them of time to report. Positions worker's name tag on assignment board. Records reason given by worker unable to report and gives information to TRAIN DISPATCHER (r.r. trans.) or DISPATCHER CLERK (r.r. trans.).
GOE: 07.07.03 STRENGTH: L GED: R2 M2 L2 SVP: 2 DLU: 77

216   ACCOUNTING AND STATISTICAL CLERKS

This group includes occupations concerned with computing, calculating, and posting of financial, statistical, and numerical data to maintain accounting records, to use in statistical studies, and to record details of business transactions. Occupations which require knowledge of bookkeeping principles and which are concerned with classifying, recording, and summarizing numerical data, and with making computations to compile and keep financial records are found in Group 210. Occupations concerned with managing, controlling, and monitoring operations of computers and peripheral equipment are found in Group 213. Occupations concerned with making computations for purposes of preparing or verifying bills and statements of amounts due for items purchased or services rendered are found in Group 214. Occupations concerned with making computations and transcribing data to payroll and timekeeping records are found in Group 215.

216.132-010   SUPERVISOR, ACCOUNTING CLERKS (clerical)
Supervises and coordinates activities of workers engaged in calculating, posting, verifying, and typing duties to obtain and record financial data for use in maintaining accounting and statistical records: Compiles reports required by management or government agencies. May perform duties of ACCOUNTING CLERK (clerical) 216.482-010 and BOOKKEEPER (clerical) 210.382-014. Performs duties as described under SUPERVISOR (clerical) Master Title.

GOE: 07.02.02 STRENGTH: S GED: R4 M4 L4 SVP: 7 DLU: 87

216.132-014   SUPERVISOR, SECURITIES VAULT (financial)
Supervises and coordinates activities of workers engaged in recording securities transactions and receiving and delivering securities to and from trust vault and oversees vault safekeeping procedures and controls: Plans and directs activities of workers engaged in recording securities interest and dividends and maintaining securities transaction records. Plans and implements procedures for safekeeping of securities. Explains safekeeping policies and procedures to workers and oversees compliance with procedures. Assigns vault combination numbers and changes combination periodically. Sets vault clock daily for following morning opening time. Reviews visitor register to verify that only authorized persons were admitted to vault. Examines trust securities stored in vault, verifies descriptions, signatures, and certificate or serial numbers, and computes total value of all securities, using calculator or computer, to assist bank AUDITOR (profess. & kin.) 160.167-054 in performing audits. Reviews securities documents to ensure that documents correspond with descriptions on delivery-request ticket prepared by TRUST-VAULT CLERK (financial) 216.367-014 for delivery to authorized persons. Performs duties as described under SUPERVISOR (clerical) Master Title.
GOE: 07.02.02 STRENGTH: L GED: R4 M3 L4 SVP: 7 DLU: 78

216.137-010   COST-AND-SALES-RECORD SUPERVISOR (utilities) alternate titles: rate-and-cost analyst; statistician
Supervises and coordinates activities of STATISTICAL CLERKS (clerical) engaged in compiling power-generation and transmission data, preparing charts and graphs, and in making statistical computation for utility district: Directs maintenance and storage of records, such as maps, right-of-way deeds, and joint-use agreements. Compiles running totals of power produced by various generating units and totals of power exchanged with connecting systems, using calculator and adding machine. Analyzes and interprets trends to assist in planning budgets and construction expenditures, conferring with management, department heads, and large industrial customers. Directs preparation of power-generation and transmission charts and graphs to show trends in sales, operating costs, and revenue of company. May assist in making rate analyses, applying statistical method to investigate comparative rates with other utilities and to calculate rate formulas. May compile data for various power consumption reports required by government and utility associations. May compute percentages of monthly increase or decrease in gas consumption. May calculate sellers' weekly commissions. Performs other duties as described under SUPERVISOR (clerical) Master Title.
GOE: 07.02.03 STRENGTH: S GED: R5 M5 L4 SVP: 7 DLU: 77

216.137-014   TRANSFER CLERK, HEAD (financial)
Supervises and coordinates activities of TRANSFER CLERKS (financial) 216.362-046 in transactions relating to stock certificates, applying knowledge of company policies and procedures, and commercial law: Explains company policies to stockholders with regard to stock transfers and payment of dividends. Examines certificates presented for transfer to verify legality of transactions. Answers inquiries concerning stock transfer requirements, dividend payments, and tax on certificates. Performs duties as described under SUPERVISOR (clerical) Master Title. May arrange meetings for bank-shareholders.
GOE: 07.01.02 STRENGTH: S GED: R4 M4 L4 SVP: 6 DLU: 77

216.362-014   COLLECTION CLERK (financial)
Receives and processes collection items (negotiable instruments), such as checks, drafts, and coupons presented to bank by customers or corresponding banks: Reads letter of instructions accompanying negotiable instruments to determine disposition of items. Debits bank account and credits customer's account to liquidate outstanding collections. Computes interest on bills of exchange (drafts), using adding machine or computer terminal, and lists debits and credits on liability sheet, or enters information into computer system, to record customer's outstanding balance. Examines, calculates interest on, endorses, records, and issues receipts, and mails outgoing collections for payment. Traces unpaid items to determine reasons for nonpayment and notifies customer of disposition. May prove and balance daily transactions. May act as agent for collections payable in United States and possessions and be designated Out-of-Town-Collection Clerk (financial). May process collection items drawn on local bond and securities exchanges or transfers within a locality and be designated Local Collection Clerk (financial). May collect foreign bills of exchange and be designated Foreign-Collection Clerk (financial). May process matured bonds and coupons and be designated Coupon-and-Bond-Collection Clerk (financial); Coupon-Collection Clerk (financial).
GOE: 07.02.02 STRENGTH: S GED: R4 M4 L4 SVP: 5 DLU: 77

216.362-022   FOOD-AND-BEVERAGE CONTROLLER (hotel & rest.) alternate titles: control clerk, food-and-beverage
Compiles and computes amounts and costs of food bought and sold from records of CASHIER (clerical) II and other summaries. Operates calculating machine to compute profit or loss on each item of food or beverages sold in restaurant and individual departments and records data to keep perpetual inventory.
GOE: 07.02.02 STRENGTH: S GED: R4 M3 L2 SVP: 5 DLU: 77

216.362-026   MORTGAGE-ACCOUNTING CLERK (clerical) alternate titles: amortization-schedule clerk
Keeps records of mortgage loans in mortgage loan establishment, performing any of following clerical duties: Records data, such as loan number, selling

price, and taxes of mortgaged property. Computes interest and principal payments on loans, using calculating machines. Prepares applications for insurance on property and for extensions on delinquent loans. Types or posts by hand, such data as legal description of property, name of mortgager, amount and type of hazard insurance on property, and results of computations that break down monthly payments into principal, interest, taxes, and optional items. Prepares copies of documents for filing and mailing. May file documents and records.
GOE: 07.02.02 STRENGTH: S GED: R4 M3 L3 SVP: 3 DLU: 77

216.362-034 RESERVES CLERK (financial)
Compiles records of fund reserves of bank and branches to ensure conformity with Federal Reserve requirements: Reviews cash orders from branches to determine that order follows established procedure and amount meets with bank limitations and requirements. Posts order to department record sheet, or computer files, using computer. Telephones order to Federal Reserve Bank, and prepares letter to Federal Reserve confirming order, using computer or typewriter. Charges or credits accounts, following bank regulations. Keeps records of bank balance with Federal Reserve Bank.
GOE: 07.02.01 STRENGTH: S GED: R4 M3 L3 SVP: 5 DLU: 77

216.362-038 ELECTRONIC FUNDS TRANSFER COORDINATOR (financial)
Compiles and reconciles data involving electronic transfer of funds to maintain accounting records: Examines electronic funds transaction entries on documents, such as bank statements and printouts, for completeness and accuracy. Adds debits and credits, using adding machine or calculator, to ensure that figures balance. Identifies and corrects errors or calls customers, other bank personnel, or personnel from other financial institutions, such as correspondent banks, Automated Clearing House, or Federal Reserve Bank, to obtain information needed to reconcile differences. Posts transaction data to specified accounts, using ledger sheets or computer. May prepare checks to deposit funds in specified accounts. May transmit funds between specified accounts by wire [WIRES-TRANSFER CLERK (financial) 203.562-010].
GOE: 07.02.01 STRENGTH: L GED: R4 M4 L4 SVP: 7 DLU: 89

216.362-042 MARGIN CLERK I (financial)
Compiles data, using computer, to determine customer margin (equity) in stock purchased: Totals customer accounts and computes difference between purchase price of stock and present market value, using calculator, to show amount due for brokerage fees. Notifies REGISTERED REPRESENTATIVE (financial) 250.257-018 or other workers when customer margin is less than government regulations or brokerage firm requirements. May solve customer margin account problems, using customer account information and transaction records.
GOE: 07.02.02 STRENGTH: S GED: R3 M3 L3 SVP: 6 DLU: 89

216.362-046 TRANSFER CLERK (financial) alternate titles: operations clerk; stock-transfer clerk; stock-transfer technician
Records transfer of securities and corrects problems related to transfer: Enters information, such as type and amount of securities that client wishes to purchase or sell, into computer terminal. Reviews client instructions for transfer of securities. Examines securities certificates to verify that information is correct, and mails certificates to department or company specializing in transfer of securities certificates. Receives new certificates from department or company, and sends certificates to client to complete transfer. Talks with coworkers, including REGISTERED REPRESENTATIVES (financial) 250.257-018 to correct problems related to transfer of securities.
GOE: 07.02.02 STRENGTH: L GED: R3 M2 L3 SVP: 6 DLU: 89

216.367-014 TRUST-VAULT CLERK (financial) alternate titles: securities auditor; vault custodian
Compiles security transaction records and receives and delivers securities to and from trust vault: Opens combinations on cabinets in vault. Examines securities deposited for safekeeping, verifies descriptions and signatures, and files securities according to customer names and account number. Records securities transactions including purchases, exchanges, and stock splits to maintain control of customer accounts. Releases securities from vault upon authorized request. Acts as agent for bank by observing bank auditors auditing securities in vault. May examine collateral to ensure conformity with loan specifications.
GOE: 07.02.02 STRENGTH: S GED: R4 M3 L3 SVP: 6 DLU: 77

216.382-022 BUDGET CLERK (clerical) alternate titles: budget-record clerk; budget-report clerk; fiscal clerk
Prepares budgets based on previous budget figures or estimated revenue and expense: Reviews records of sales and actual operating expenses, such as payrolls and material costs. Compiles tables of revenues and expenses to show current budget status. Writes justifications for overrun or underrun of budget estimates. Computes ratios and percentages to make interdepartmental comparisons, indicate trends, and show other selected factors. Prepares charts and graphs. Tabulates statistical data for presentation in miscellaneous budget reports, using calculator and typewriter or computer. May prepare financial statement showing profit and loss. May examine budget and requisition funds and be designated Expenditure-Requisition Clerk (utilities).
GOE: 07.01.04 STRENGTH: S GED: R4 M4 L3 SVP: 5 DLU: 87

216.382-026 CLEARING-HOUSE CLERK (financial) alternate titles: clearing-distribution clerk
Compiles settlement data and submits checks, drafts, and other items to clearinghouse association for exchange and settlement with other banks: Sorts items

into bundles, lists items, and totals amounts, using adding machine or calculator. Posts totals to clearinghouse settlement sheet. Mails or delivers items to clearinghouse. Accepts items from clearinghouse that have been drawn on own bank and posts totals on settlement sheet. Totals debit and credit columns and computes net balance. Submits sheet to clearinghouse for verification. May maintain telephone contact with bank personnel and others to locate missing checks, correct errors, and reconcile differences in records.
GOE: 07.02.01 STRENGTH: L GED: R4 M3 L3 SVP: 5 DLU: 77

216.382-034 COST CLERK (clerical) alternate titles: cost-accounting clerk; expense clerk
Compiles production or sales cost reports on unit or total basis for department or working unit: Calculates individual items, such as labor, material, and time costs, relationship of sales or revenues to cost, and overhead expenditures, using calculating machine. Examines records, such as time and production sheets, payrolls, operations charts and schedules, to obtain data for calculations. Prepares reports showing total cost, selling prices, or rates profits. May be designated according to work performed as Cost-Estimating Clerk (utilities); Operating-Cost Clerk (clerical).
GOE: 07.02.02 STRENGTH: S GED: R3 M3 L3 SVP: 4 DLU: 88

216.382-046 MARGIN CLERK II (financial)
Compiles daily stock quotations and compares data with customer margin accounts to determine market prices in relation to collateral held by bank. Computes and records fluctuations and reports need of additional collateral to secure loans. May discuss price fluctuations with customers, REGISTERED REPRESENTATIVES (financial) 250.257-018, and others to monitor stock trends in relation to bank's margin loan accounts.
GOE: 07.02.02 STRENGTH: S GED: R4 M3 L3 SVP: 5 DLU: 77

216.382-050 POLICY-VALUE CALCULATOR (insurance)
Compiles and computes loan or surrender value of life insurance policy, using calculator, and rate books and tables: Computes amount payable to policyholder who drops insurance, allows insurance to lapse, or requests loan on policy, considering factors, such as unclaimed dividends, premiums paid in advance, length of time held, and principal sum (loan value), using calculator. Records values on sheet for preparation of correspondence to policyholder and entry onto master file. When working on dropped policies and policyholder requests full cash value, is known as Cash-Surrender Calculator (insurance). When working on dropped policies and policyholder does not request full cash value, prorates cash value to determine time policy may be kept in force and is known as Extended-Insurance Clerk (insurance). When working on policy loans, calculates repayments, using interest tables, and is known as Policy-Load Calculator (insurance). May specialize in data related to pension plans and life insurance, such as premiums, dividends, retirements, and death benefits, and be designated Calculation Clerk (insurance). May verify and recompute calculations made by other workers and be designated Calculation Reviewer (insurance).
GOE: 07.02.03 STRENGTH: S GED: R3 M2 L2 SVP: 5 DLU: 77

216.382-054 RECEIPT-AND-REPORT CLERK (water trans.) alternate titles: cost-report clerk
Prepares reports of labor and equipment costs incurred in loading and unloading ship cargoes: Compiles reports of tonnage and type of cargo handled, labor charges involved in loading and unloading cargo, and charges for equipment used, such as cranes, barges, and conveyors. Computes cost per ton for each type of cargo handled and prepares report of total costs for each ship.
GOE: 07.02.03 STRENGTH: S GED: R4 M3 L3 SVP: 5 DLU: 77

216.382-058 RETURNED-ITEM CLERK (financial) alternate titles: rejected-items clerk
Returns unpaid checks from correspondent banks, branches, or individual customers to adjust and balance accounts: Sorts returned checks into debit and credit groups. Types debit and credit forms listing amount, date, name of maker, name of bank, and reason for return, in order to adjust accounts and inform customers of nonpayment, using typewriter or computer. Totals and balances checks received, using adding machine or calculator, and submits checks and recapitulation sheet to department head. Visually examines checks to determine which checks to process, setting aside checks with no account, no signature on file, or forgeries for review by law enforcement official. Exchanges checks received by mistake with representatives of other banks. Photographs items returned to customers and other banks [PHOTOGRAPHIC-MACHINE OPERATOR (clerical) 207.685-018]. Files copies of forms.
GOE: 07.02.02 STRENGTH: S GED: R3 M3 L3 SVP: 4 DLU: 87

216.382-062 STATISTICAL CLERK (clerical) alternate titles: record clerk; report clerk; tabulating clerk
Compiles data and computes statistics for use in statistical studies, using calculator and adding machine: Compiles statistics from source materials, such as production and sales records, quality control and test records, personnel records, timesheets, survey sheets, and questionnaires. Assembles and classifies statistics, following prescribed procedures. Computes statistical data according to formulas, using calculator. May compile and compute statistics, using computer. May verify authenticity of source material. May be designated according to type of statistics compiled as Census Clerk (government ser.); Mileage Clerk (r.r. trans.); Production-Statistical Clerk (clerical); Sales-Record Clerk (clerical); Steam-Plant Records Clerk (utilities); Time-Analysis Clerk (clerical); Traffic Enumerator (clerical). May compile actuarial statistics, charts, and graphs and

be designated Actuarial Clerk (insurance). May compile data and statistics from media guides and team data for use during televised sporting event and be designated Statistician (radio-tv broad.).
GOE: 07.02.03 STRENGTH: S GED: R3 M3 L3 SVP: 4 DLU: 88

216.382-066 STATISTICAL CLERK, ADVERTISING (retail trade) alternate titles: advertising clerk
Compiles and tabulates statistical records showing cost of advertising, volume of advertising as compared with competitors, amount of merchandise sold following advertisements as compared to amount sold without advertising, and other pertinent statistics. Operates calculating and adding machines to compute data. Files copies of advertisements.
GOE: 07.02.03 STRENGTH: S GED: R3 M3 L2 SVP: 4 DLU: 77

216.462-010 BOOKING PRIZER (tobacco)
Verifies weight and identifying data stenciled on hogsheads of tobacco and records data in prize books (ledgers): Removes ticket from hogshead and verifies computations of net weight to determine whether figures recorded by WEIGHER, PRODUCTION (any industry) are correct. Listens as BULL-GANG WORKER (tobacco) calls out hogshead number and grade stenciled on hogshead and compares data with that recorded on hogshead ticket. Instructs STENCILER (any industry) to correct markings. Records hogshead number, tobacco grade, and weight in appropriate prize book. Computes total weight for each page of prize book, using adding machine, and records totals.
GOE: 05.09.03 STRENGTH: L GED: R3 M3 L3 SVP: 3 DLU: 77

216.482-010 ACCOUNTING CLERK (clerical)
Performs any combination of following calculating, posting, and verifying duties to obtain financial data for use in maintaining accounting records: Compiles and sorts documents, such as invoices and checks, substantiating business transactions. Verifies and posts details of business transactions, such as funds received and disbursed, and totals accounts, using calculator or computer. Computes and records charges, refunds, cost of lost or damaged goods, freight charges, rentals, and similar items. May type vouchers, invoices, checks, account statements, reports, and other records, using typewriter or computer. May reconcile bank statements. May be designated according to type of accounting performed, such as Accounts-Payable Clerk (clerical); Accounts-Receivable Clerk (clerical); Bill-Recapitulation Clerk (utilities); Rent and Miscellaneous Remittance Clerk (insurance); Tax-Record Clerk (utilities).
GOE: 07.02.02 STRENGTH: S GED: R4 M3 L3 SVP: 5 DLU: 88

216.482-018 AUDIT-MACHINE OPERATOR (clerical)
Adds sales slips or register tapes, using electrically powered auditing machine. Computes subtotals for individual sales departments and types of sales, such as cash, charge, installment, and will-call. Verifies daily or periodic balances against predetermined figures.
GOE: 07.06.02 STRENGTH: S GED: R3 M2 L2 SVP: 4 DLU: 77

216.482-022 CALCULATING-MACHINE OPERATOR (clerical) alternate titles: calculator operator
Computes and records statistical, accounting and other numerical data, utilizing knowledge of mathematics and using machine that automatically performs mathematical processes, such as addition, subtraction, multiplication, division, and extraction of roots: Calculates statistical, accounting, and other numerical data, using calculating machine, and posts totals to records, such as inventories and summary sheets. May verify computations made by other workers. May be designated according to subject matter as Formula Figurer (paint & varnish); Premium-Note Interest-Calculator Clerk (insurance). May compute and record inventory data from audio transcription, using transcribing machine and calculator, and be designated Inventory Transcriber (business ser.). May be designated according to type of computations made as Weight Calculator (shipboat mfg.).
GOE: 07.02.02 STRENGTH: S GED: R3 M3 L2 SVP: 3 DLU: 81

216.482-026 DIVIDEND-DEPOSIT-VOUCHER CLERK (insurance) alternate titles: dividend-deposit-entry clerk
Keeps record of accruing dividends on insurance policies and calculates and records interest due on them, using adding machine, calculator, statistical manuals, and rate tables.
GOE: 07.02.02 STRENGTH: S GED: R3 M2 L2 SVP: 3 DLU: 77

216.482-030 LAUNDRY PRICING CLERK (laundry & rel.) alternate titles: pricer
Computes cost of customers' laundry by pricing each item on customers' lists, using adding machine, calculating machine, or comptometer. May keep inventory of customers' laundered articles. May prepare statements to be sent to customers.
GOE: 07.02.04 STRENGTH: S GED: R3 M3 L2 SVP: 3 DLU: 77

216.482-034 DIVIDEND CLERK (financial) alternate titles: operations clerk
Computes, records, and pays dividends to customers of brokerage firm: Reviews stock records and reports to determine customer stock ownership on record date. Totals stock owned by customers and computes dividends due, using calculator. Records dividends due, and enters information into customer accounts, using computer. Reviews customer accounts to obtain dividend payment instructions, and pays dividends and interest due to customers. Solves dividend related problems with customer accounts, applying knowledge of policies and procedures concerning payment of dividends and interest. May perform other clerical tasks such as filing, typing, and operating office machines.

GOE: 07.02.02 STRENGTH: L GED: R3 M3 L3 SVP: 5 DLU: 90

216.567-010 TICKET MARKER (wholesale tr.)
Records price, name of buyer, and grade of tobacco on tickets attached to piles or baskets of tobacco as tobacco is auctioned to highest bidder. Signals purchaser to raise bids that are below government support price. May perform other clerical tasks during periods between auction sales.
GOE: 05.09.03 STRENGTH: L GED: R3 M2 L3 SVP: 3 DLU: 77

216.587-010 BOOKING CLERK (wholesale tr.)
Copies name of buyer, grade, and price per pound from tickets attached to baskets of tobacco onto sales sheets with prelisted number of pounds in each basket. Submits sales sheets to auction warehouse office for computation of total amount due each grower.
GOE: 05.09.02 STRENGTH: L GED: R2 M1 L1 SVP: 3 DLU: 77

216.685-010 GAS USAGE METER CLERK (petrol. refin.; pipe lines; utilities) alternate titles: chart clerk
Tends machine, equipped with pen attachments and meter charts, that computes volume of gas flowing through meter: Positions chart on chart plate. Starts machine to revolve chart and actuate computing mechanism. Pulls levers to guide pens along static pressure and volume curve lines. Removes chart and records computation on back of chart.
GOE: 05.09.03 STRENGTH: L GED: R3 M2 L3 SVP: 3 DLU: 77

217 ACCOUNT-RECORDING-MACHINE OPERATORS, N.E.C.

This group includes occupations, not elsewhere classified, concerned with operating machines to keep quantitative records and accounts. Occupations which require knowledge of bookkeeping principles and which are concerned with classifying, recording, and summarizing numerical data, and with making computations to compile and keep financial records are found in Group 210. Occupations concerned with operating machines to receive and disburse money are found in Group 211. Occupations concerned with managing, controlling, and monitoring operations of computers and peripheral equipment are found in Group 213. Occupations concerned with operating machines to prepare bills, invoices, and statements are found in Group 214. Occupations concerned with operating machines to prepare payroll records are found in Group 215. Occupations concerned with operating machines to perform computing, calculating, and posting of financial, statistical, and numerical data are found in Group 216.

217.132-010 PROOF-MACHINE-OPERATOR SUPERVISOR (financial)
Supervises and coordinates activities of workers engaged in operating machines to encode, add, cancel, photocopy, and sort checks, drafts, and money orders for collection, and to prove records of transactions: Locates check copies and proof records to answer inquiries from staff or customers. Prepares journal voucher to correct account when error is found. Requests equipment maintenance and repair from vendors. Participates in work of subordinates. May compile check processing cost information for management use in determining service fees. May supervise retention and retrieval of microfilmed checks [SUPERVISOR, FILES (clerical) 206.137-010]. Performs duties as described under SUPERVISOR (clerical) Master Title.
GOE: 07.06.02 STRENGTH: S GED: R4 M3 L4 SVP: 6 DLU: 87

217.382-010 PROOF-MACHINE OPERATOR (financial) alternate titles: proof clerk; transit clerk
Operates machines to encode, add, cancel, photocopy, and sort checks, drafts, and money orders for collection and to prove records of transactions: Places checks into machine that encodes amounts in magnetic ink, adds amounts, and cancels check. Enters amount of each check, using keyboard. Places encoded checks in sorter and activates machine to automatically microfilm, sort, and total checks according to bank drawn on. Observes panel light to note check machine cannot read. Reads check and enters data, such as amount, bank, or account number, using keyboard. Compares machine totals to listing received with batch of checks and rechecks each item if totals differ. Encodes correct amount or prepares transaction correction record, if error is found. Bundles sorted check with tape listing each item to prepare checks, drawn on other banks, for collection. May enter commands to transfer data from machine to computer. May operate separate photocopying machine. May clean machine and replace printer ribbons, film, and tape. May manually sort and list items for proof or collection. May record, sort, and prove other transaction documents, such as deposit and withdrawal slips, using proof machine.
GOE: 07.06.02 STRENGTH: S GED: R3 M3 L3 SVP: 4 DLU: 87

217.485-010 CURRENCY COUNTER (financial) alternate titles: currency-machine operator
Sorts and counts paper money, using automatic currency-counting machine: Examines money to detect and remove counterfeit, mutilated, and worn bills. Requisitions replacements. Sorts bills according to denomination or federal reserve district number, and inserts bills into slot or hopper of machine to be automatically counted. Verifies totals registered on machine against amount of deposit reported by member bank or depositor, using calculator, and posts shortage or overage to account. Bundles and wraps counted money to be placed in vault. May sort, count, and wrap coins [COIN-COUNTER-AND-WRAPPER (financial) 217.585-010].
GOE: 05.12.19 STRENGTH: L GED: R3 M2 L2 SVP: 3 DLU: 89

217.585-010 COIN-COUNTER-AND-WRAPPER (clerical) alternate titles: coin-machine operator; coin teller

Sorts, counts, and wraps coins, using various machines: Sorts coins according to denomination, using coin-separating machine. Removes counterfeit and mutilated coins. Feeds coins into hopper of counting machine that counts and bags them. Removes, seals, and weighs bags of counted coins. Wraps coins, using coin-wrapping machine, and places rolls of coins into bags or boxes for distribution. Records machine totals, shortages or overages, and kind and value of coins removed from circulation. Verifies totals against deposit slips or other documents and prepares coins for shipment. May sort, count, and wrap paper money by hand or machine [CURRENCY SORTER (financial) 217.485-010].
GOE: 05.12.19 STRENGTH: M GED: R3 M2 L2 SVP: 3 DLU: 89

219 COMPUTING AND ACCOUNT-RECORDING OCCUPATIONS, N.E.C.

This group includes occupations, not elsewhere classified, concerned with systemizing information about transactions and activities into accounts and quantitative records, and paying and receiving money.

219.132-010 SUPERVISOR, POLICY-CHANGE CLERKS (insurance) alternate titles: supervisor, records change

Supervises and coordinates activities of workers engaged in compiling data on changes to insurance policies in force, changing provisions of policies to conform to insured's specifications, and computing premium rates based on changes to policies: Reviews correspondence from insured or agents requesting policy changes to determine work assignments based on types of changes requested. Assigns duties to POLICY-CHANGE CLERKS (insurance) 219.362-042; POLICY-VALUE CALCULATORS (insurance) 216.382-050; POLICY-HOLDER-INFORMATION CLERKS (insurance) 249.262-010, and related clerical workers. Interprets policy provisions to workers, as needed, to assist workers in effecting changes according to company regulations. Assists workers in locating and changing policy information, using computer. Verifies accuracy of premium computations, using calculator. Performs other duties as described under SUPERVISOR (clerical) Master Title.
GOE: 07.02.02 STRENGTH: S GED: R4 M3 L4 SVP: 7 DLU: 78

219.132-014 SUPERVISOR, TRUST ACCOUNTS (financial)

Supervises and coordinates activities of workers engaged in processing settlement of cash or securities transactions for trust-account customers in trust division of commercial bank: Reviews debit and credit entries to customer trust accounts pertaining to cash or securities transactions to determine whether funds were received or disbursed according to predetermined schedules, trust or investment-department instructions, or instructions on customer account records, using computer terminal and computer printouts. Assists workers with more difficult aspects of preparing records and transmittal documents for transactions involving purchase or sale of customer assets, recording interest and balance on contracts and notes, recording stock dividends, and placing insurance for customer property held in trust. Trains new workers. Performs other duties as described under SUPERVISOR (clerical) Master Title. May be designated according to specialized area of work as Securities Supervisor (financial).
GOE: 07.02.02 STRENGTH: S GED: R4 M3 L4 SVP: 7 DLU: 89

219.132-022 SUPERVISOR, UNDERWRITING CLERKS (insurance) alternate titles: policy-issue supervisor

Supervises and coordinates activities of workers engaged in computing premiums, recording, and issuing insurance policies following acceptance of insurance applications by underwriting department. Performs duties as described under SUPERVISOR (clerical) Master Title.
GOE: 07.02.02 STRENGTH: L GED: R4 M3 L4 SVP: 7 DLU: 77

219.137-010 FIELD CASHIER (construction)

Supervises and coordinates activities of clerical workers in field office of construction project, engaged in performing such office work as compiling and distributing payrolls, keeping inventories, compiling cost data, and keeping account books. Performs duties as described under SUPERVISOR (clerical) Master Title.
GOE: 07.02.02 STRENGTH: S GED: R4 M4 L4 SVP: 7 DLU: 77

219.267-010 HANDICAPPER, HARNESS RACING (amuse. & rec.)

Determines winning odds on each race of harness-racing program by analyzing data, such as horses' and drivers' past performances, post position, and race distance, for use in racing publications: Reviews data on each horse entered in same race, such as past performance, assigned-racing classification, and race distance and reviews past performance of assigned drivers, and analyzes compiled data to estimate probable order of finish for each horse in each race. Assigns winning odds to horses by using estimated order of finish and standard-odds ratios, occasionally making adjustments of winning odds as dictated by judgment. Determines winning odds on horses in maiden races, based on breeding and qualifying-times data. Mails or telephones opening or revised winning odds to printers of racing programs and other harness-race publications.
GOE: 11.06.03 STRENGTH: S GED: R4 M3 L3 SVP: 4 DLU: 77

219.362-010 ADMINISTRATIVE CLERK (clerical) alternate titles: clerk, general office

Compiles and maintains records of business transactions and office activities of establishment, performing variety of following or similar clerical duties and utilizing knowledge of systems or procedures: Copies data and compiles records and reports. Tabulates and posts data in record books. Computes wages, taxes, premiums, commissions, and payments. Records orders for merchandise or service. Gives information to and interviews customers, claimants, employees, and sales personnel. Receives, counts, and pays out cash. Prepares, issues, and sends out receipts, bills, policies, invoices, statements, and checks. Prepares stock inventory. Adjusts complaints. Operates office machines, such as typewriter, adding, calculating, and duplicating machines. Opens and routes incoming mail, answers correspondence, and prepares outgoing mail. May take dictation. May greet and assist visitors. May prepare payroll. May keep books. May purchase supplies. May operate computer terminal to input and retrieve data. May be designated according to field of activity or according to location of employment as Adjustment Clerk (retail trade; tel. & tel.); Airport Clerk (air trans.); Colliery Clerk (mine & quarry); Death-Claim Clerk (insurance); Field Clerk (clerical). May be designated: Agency Clerk (insurance); Auction Clerk (clerical); Construction-Records Clerk (construction; utilities); Shop Clerk (clerical).
GOE: 07.01.02 STRENGTH: L GED: R4 M3 L3 SVP: 4 DLU: 88

219.362-014 ATTENDANCE CLERK (education)

Compiles attendance records for school district, issues attendance permits, and answers inquiries: Obtains district attendance figures from each school daily, using telephone. Records figures by grade level and for special classes, such as mentally retarded or gifted, in workbook. Totals figures, using calculator. Collates data and prepares standard state reports, using typewriter. Computes average daily attendance figures and forwards to state for compensation and to school cafeteria for meal planning. Interviews applicants for interdistrict attendance permits to attend elementary and secondary schools in district and issues permits, if requirements are met. Sends copy of permit to applicable school and retains file copy. Maintains file of interdistrict attendance agreements, bills outside districts for attendance within district, and notifies supervisor of agreement expirations. Answers inquiries from parents and school officials, using state education code as guide. Prepares special reports, such as ethnic or racial-distribution surveys, requested by state or district education officials.
GOE: 07.05.03 STRENGTH: S GED: R4 M3 L4 SVP: 6 DLU: 77

219.362-018 BROKERAGE CLERK II (financial)

Compiles security purchases and sales made for client and records information in journal. Totals daily transactions, using calculator, and summarizes effects on customers' accounts and earnings of REGISTERED REPRESENTATIVE (financial) 250.257-018. Calls customers to inform them of market fluctuations and purchase and sale of securities affecting their accounts.
GOE: 07.02.02 STRENGTH: L GED: R3 M3 L3 SVP: 4 DLU: 77

219.362-022 CLERK, TELEGRAPH SERVICE (tel. & tel.) alternate titles: clerk, personal service bureau; clerk, private wire-billing and control

Compiles and maintains statistical records relating to telegraph services, performing any combination of following duties: Answers telephone requests from private wire or tie-line patrons regarding handling of messages and repair service. Writes and issues work orders for equipment installation or repair. Compiles statistical data concerning pricing and telegraph services for use in preparing studies and proposals. Verifies accuracy of billing charges. Posts charges to service accounts. Posts revenue received from charge accounts and other sales data to card index files. Writes or types statements. Sorts and distributes mail. Takes and transcribes dictation. Types letters, reports, and proposals. Files records and correspondence.
GOE: 07.02.02 STRENGTH: S GED: R4 M3 L3 SVP: 5 DLU: 77

219.362-026 CONTRACT CLERK, AUTOMOBILE (retail trade)

Verifies accuracy of automobile sales contracts: Calculates tax, transfer and license fees, insurance premiums, and interest rates, using tables, schedules, and calculating machine. Verifies amount and number of payments, trade-in allowance, and total price of automobile. Interviews customer to obtain additional information and explain terms of contract. Corresponds with motor vehicle agencies to clear automobile titles. Obtains license, signs registration documents on cars traded in, and transfers titles on cars sold. Keeps file of sales contracts.
GOE: 07.02.02 STRENGTH: S GED: R4 M3 L3 SVP: 5 DLU: 77

219.362-030 EXTENSION CLERK (utilities)

Processes requisitions for gas main or electric-power line extensions and keeps control records to report and coordinate construction activities between utility and contractors: Compiles information required for preparation of line- or main-extension contracts from construction sketches. Computes or verifies charges for customer. Reviews completed contracts and construction work orders for completeness and accuracy. Annotates subdivision plat books (maps) to indicate location and nature of construction shown on work order. Compiles reports from extension requisitions and work orders. Receives orders from customers by telephone and in person for services requiring extensions in main or distribution lines.
GOE: 07.05.03 STRENGTH: S GED: R4 M3 L3 SVP: 5 DLU: 77

219.362-038 MORTGAGE-CLOSING CLERK (clerical) alternate titles: loan closer

Completes mortgage transactions between loan establishment, sellers, and borrowers after loans have been approved: Verifies completeness of data on loan papers. Answers questions of buyers and sellers relating to details of trans-

action and obtains signatures of principal parties on necessary documents. Closes out seller's interest in property by presenting seller with check to cover seller's equity. Operates office machines to compute rebates or adjustments. Prepares and mails rebates and other papers to clients.
GOE: 07.05.02 STRENGTH: S GED: R4 M3 L4 SVP: 5 DLU: 77

219.362-042 POLICY-CHANGE CLERK (insurance)
Compiles data and records changes in insurance policies: Examines letter from insured or agent, original application, and other company documents to determine how to effect proposed changes, such as change in beneficiary or method of payment, increase in principal sum or type of insurance. Corresponds with insured or agent to obtain supplemental information or to explain how change would not conform to company regulations or state laws, or routes file to POLICYHOLDER-INFORMATION CLERK (insurance) 249.262-010. Calculates premium, commission adjustments, and new reserve requirements, using rate books, statistical tables, and calculator or computer, and knowledge of specific types of policies. Transcribes data to abstract (work sheet) or enters data into computer for use in preparing documents and adjusting accounts. May write abstract or enter data into computer to prepare new policy or rider to existing policy. May underwrite changes when increase in amount of risk occurs.
GOE: 07.02.02 STRENGTH: S GED: R4 M3 L4 SVP: 5 DLU: 78

219.362-046 REAL-ESTATE CLERK (real estate)
Maintains records concerned with rental, sale, and management of real estate, performing any combination of following duties: Types copies of listings of real estate rentals and sales for distribution to trade publications, and for use as reference data by other departments. Computes interest owed, penalty payment, amount of principal, and taxes due on mortgage loans, using calculating machine. Holds in escrow collateral posted to ensure fulfillment of contracts in transferring real estate and property titles. Checks due notices on taxes and renewal dates of insurance and mortgage loans to take follow-up action. Sends out rent notices to tenants. Writes checks in payment of bills due, keeps record of disbursements, and examines cancelled returned checks for endorsement. Secures estimates from contractors for building repairs. May compile list of prospects from leads in newspapers and trade periodicals to locate prospective purchasers of real estate. May open, sort, and distribute mail. May submit photographs and descriptions of property to newspaper for publication. May maintain and balance bank accounts for sales transactions and operating expenses. May maintain log of sales and commissions received by SALES AGENT, REAL ESTATE (real estate) 250.357-018. May scan records and files to identify dates requiring administrative action, such as insurance premium due dates, tax due notices, and lease expiration dates. May compose and prepare routine correspondence, rental notices, letters, and material for advertisement.
GOE: 07.01.04 STRENGTH: S GED: R4 M3 L3 SVP: 5 DLU: 88

219.362-050 REVIVAL CLERK (insurance) alternate titles: reinstatement clerk
Compiles data on lapsed insurance policies to determine automatic reinstatement according to company policies: Determines if overdue premium is received within specified time limit. Compares answers given by insured on reinstatement application with those approved by company and examines company records to determine if there are circumstances which may make reinstatement impossible. Approves reinstatement when criteria for automatic reinstatement are met. Calculates irregular premium and reinstatement penalty due when reinstatement is approved. Types notices of reinstatement approval or denial, and of payment due, and sends notices to insured.
GOE: 07.05.02 STRENGTH: S GED: R3 M2 L3 SVP: 4 DLU: 77

219.362-054 SECURITIES CLERK (financial)
Records security transactions, such as purchases and sales, stock dividends and splits, conversions, and redemptions: Issues receipts for securities received from customers. Prepares transmittal papers or endorsements for securities sold to ensure payment, transfer, and delivery. Issues vault withdrawal orders at customer request. Computes dividends to be disbursed to customers. Writes letters to customers to answer inquiries on security transactions. May prepare reports on individual customer accounts.
GOE: 07.01.04 STRENGTH: S GED: R4 M4 L3 SVP: 5 DLU: 89

219.362-066 VOUCHER CLERK (r.r. trans.) alternate titles: claims clerk
Compiles data to prorate cost of lost or damaged goods among interline railroad carriers: Receives claim for lost or damaged goods filed by shipper of consignee. Verifies records to substantiate claim of shipment and requests CUSTOMER-COMPLAINT CLERK (clerical) to investigate claim and to submit estimate of value of lost or damaged goods. Receives estimate and verifies records to ascertain names of carriers involved in transporting goods. Computes number of miles each carrier transported goods. Prorates and computes cost to be charged to interline carriers according to comparative mileage in transit over each railroad, using calculating machine. Records name of each interline carrier involved and amount prorated to each.
GOE: 07.02.04 STRENGTH: S GED: R4 M4 L3 SVP: 4 DLU: 77

219.362-070 TAX PREPARER (business ser.) alternate titles: income-tax-return preparer; tax form preparer
Prepares income tax return forms for individuals and small businesses: Reviews financial records, such as prior tax return forms, income statements, and documentation of expenditures to determine forms needed to prepare return. Interviews client to obtain additional information on taxable income and deductible expenses and allowances. Computes taxes owed, using adding machine,

and completes entries on forms, following tax form instructions and tax tables. Consults tax law handbooks or bulletins to determine procedure for preparation of atypical returns. Occasionally verifies totals on forms prepared by others to detect errors of arithmetic or procedure. Calculates form preparation fee according to complexity of return and amount of time required to prepare forms.
GOE: 07.02.02 STRENGTH: S GED: R4 M4 L3 SVP: 4 DLU: 86

219.362-074 TRUST OPERATIONS ASSISTANT (financial)
Opens and closes trust accounts; arranges transfer of trust assets; updates trust account records; pays bills, dividends, and interest; and performs clerical duties in personal or corporate trust department: Compiles, records, and enters names and addresses, description of assets, and other information, or deletes information previously entered, to open or close trust account, using computer. Calls or writes holders of assets, trust customer, stock transfer company, and other parties, and transmits specified documents to arrange for transfer of securities and other trust assets to or from trust account. Documents funds received or disbursed and updates records. Prepares and mails checks, or enters commands to generate checks, to pay bills for personal trust customers, disburse loan proceeds, and remit dividends, interest, and other funds to recipients. Composes and types business letters, using computer or typewriter. Opens mail and answers telephone. May call investment department to obtain information on investments and market conditions requested by trust customer. May place customer order for purchase or sale of investment with establishment investment department.
GOE: 07.01.03 STRENGTH: L GED: R4 M3 L4 SVP: 6 DLU: 89

219.367-010 CHECKER, DUMP GROUNDS (business ser.)
Estimates size of load on truck entering dump grounds. Collects fees based on size of load and type of material dumped. Keeps record of truckloads and money received. Directs truck drivers to designated dumping areas. May weigh truck, using scale, to determine amount of load.
GOE: 05.09.03 STRENGTH: L GED: R3 M3 L2 SVP: 3 DLU: 77

219.367-014 INSURANCE CLERK (financial; insurance)
Orders insurance policies to ensure coverage for property owned by establishment and for property held as security for loan: Reviews premium notices from insurance companies for property owned by establishment. Types check or voucher requesting payment of premium. Reviews notification from insurance companies of lapse in premium paid by customer for loan collateral, such as real estate, automobile, aircraft, or boat. Orders payment of premium and notifies customer of delinquency in premium. Arranges for renewal, transfer or cancellation of insurance coverage. Records dates of insurance expiration and cancellation, using computer.
GOE: 07.05.03 STRENGTH: S GED: R3 M3 L3 SVP: 4 DLU: 78

219.367-018 MERCHANDISE DISTRIBUTOR (retail trade)
Compiles reports of stock on hand and kind and amount sold: Dispatches inventory data to units of retail chain. Routes merchandise from one branch store to another on the basis of sales. Usually specializes in one type of merchandise, such as dresses, sportswear, or lingerie. May give directions to one or more workers.
GOE: 07.05.04 STRENGTH: L GED: R3 M2 L2 SVP: 3 DLU: 77

219.367-022 PAPER-CONTROL CLERK (water trans.)
Prepares control form of space available for cargo in company's ships scheduled for loading: Records onto control sheet previous day's bookings by ship and type of cargo. Calculates remaining space available, according to type of space, such as refrigeration, container, and general cargo.
GOE: 07.02.03 STRENGTH: S GED: R3 M3 L3 SVP: 5 DLU: 77

219.367-030 SHIPPING-ORDER CLERK (clerical)
Requisitions transportation from freight carriers to ship plant products: Reads shipping orders to determine quantity and type of transportation needed. Contacts carrier representative to make arrangements and to issue instructions for loading products. Annotates shipping orders to inform shipping department of loading location and time of arrival of transportation. May perform other clerical tasks, such as typing and mailing bills, typing correspondence, and keeping files.
GOE: 07.05.04 STRENGTH: L GED: R3 M2 L3 SVP: 4 DLU: 77

219.367-038 UNDERWRITING CLERK (insurance) alternate titles: underwriting analyst
Compiles data and performs routine clerical tasks to relieve UNDERWRITER (insurance) of minor administrative detail, using knowledge of underwriting and policy issuing procedures: Reviews correspondence, records, and reports to select routine matters for processing. Routes risk-involved matters to UNDERWRITER (insurance) for evaluation. Prepares requisitions for and reviews credit and motor vehicle reports and results of investigations to compile and summarize pertinent data onto underwriting worksheets. Consults manuals to determine rate classifications and assigns rates to pending applications, using adding machine. Corresponds with or telephones field personnel to inform them of underwriting actions taken. Maintains related files.
GOE: 07.01.04 STRENGTH: L GED: R3 M3 L3 SVP: 4 DLU: 77

219.367-042 CANCELING AND CUTTING CONTROL CLERK (financial)
Verifies amount and denominations of worn or mutilated currency for canceling and cutting in unit of Federal Reserve Bank: Counts amounts and denominations of worn or mutilated currency, using automatic counting machine.

Verifies entries on delivery and debit tickets. Records amounts, denominations, and types (notes, certificates, old series) of currency processed and shipped for destruction. Totals figures daily in ledger to prove transactions, using adding machine or calculator. Oversees canceling and cutting operations to ensure custody of currency during operations. Notifies U.S. Treasury Department of daily disposition of specified categories of currency. Compiles and prepares statistical reports.
GOE: 07.03.01 STRENGTH: S GED: R4 M3 L3 SVP: 7 DLU: 86

219.367-046 DISBURSEMENT CLERK (financial)
Verifies accuracy of consumer loan applications and records loan: Compares original application against credit report. Types checks for approved loans. Prepares loan work sheet, insurance record, credit report, and application copy for each loan. Records loan and types daily report of loan transactions, using computer. Prepares payment book and mails payment book to customer. Answers customer's question, such as current rates and date loan checks were issued.
GOE: 07.05.02 STRENGTH: S GED: R3 M3 L3 SVP: 4 DLU: 86

219.367-050 LETTER-OF-CREDIT CLERK (financial)
Issues import and export letters of credit and accepts payments: Notifies exporters and importers of issuance of letters of credit covering shipment of merchandise. Reviews letter of credit documents to determine compliance with international standards. Verifies terms of credit, such as amount, insurance coverage, and shipping conditions to determine compliance with established standards. Coordinates customer credit information and collateral papers with LOAN OFFICER (financial) 186.267-018 to comply with bank credit standards. Types letters of credit and related documents, using typewriter or computer. Records payments and liabilities and other customer account information, using computer. May translate correspondence into English or foreign language.
GOE: 07.05.02 STRENGTH: S GED: R4 M3 L3 SVP: 5 DLU: 89

219.382-010 CHECK WRITER (retail trade)
Imprints payment data on checks, records payment details on check register, using checkwriting machine, and compiles summaries of daily disbursements: Receives checks and vouchers authorized for payment, selects specified check register form, and inserts form into checkwriting-machine slot. Depresses buttons to transcribe payment data from voucher into machine. Inserts blank check into additional slot and presses bar to imprint details on check register and check. Removes check and repeats procedure to process batch of checks. Turns key to release signature plate and removes plate when processing checks totalling more than designated amount and sets such checks aside for handwritten signature by authorized personnel. Pulls lever to clear machine and print total on individual register. Compares register total with total on adding-machine tape to verify accuracy of register totals. Corrects errors or returns vouchers to other personnel for correction. Compiles daily summary of payment amounts by bank, merchandise, and expense categories and totals amounts, using adding machine.
GOE: 07.06.02 STRENGTH: S GED: R4 M4 L2 SVP: 3 DLU: 77

219.387-010 ASSIGNMENT CLERK (tel. & tel.) alternate titles: clerk, cable transfer
Compiles records and authorizations to facilitate installation or rewiring of telephone or telegraph lines resulting from subscribers' address changes or other changes in service: Selects, assigns, and posts cable-assignment data and telephone numbers on service orders. Routes orders to service department, information operators, and directory-compilation personnel for action. Reviews completed disconnection orders to update cable-assignment records. Prepares statistical reports and assembles data for subscriber-analysis studies, as directed. May request field investigation by FACILITY EXAMINER (tel. & tel.) where records do not indicate available facilities for subscriber service.
GOE: 07.05.03 STRENGTH: S GED: R3 M3 L3 SVP: 4 DLU: 77

219.387-014 INSURANCE CLERK (clerical)
Compiles records of insurance policies covering risks to property and equipment of industrial organization: Files records of insurance transactions and keeps calendar of premiums due and expiration dates of policies. Prepares vouchers for payment of premiums and verifies that payments have been made. Fills in data on renewal policy applications and forwards applications to insurance company. Compiles statistical data for reports to insurance company and departments in organization. May notify insurance company of changes in property or equipment affecting insurance coverage. May type amortization schedules.
GOE: 07.05.03 STRENGTH: S GED: R4 M3 L3 SVP: 4 DLU: 77

219.387-022 PLANIMETER OPERATOR (government ser.)
Traces boundary lines of land plots on aerial photographs to determine acreage, using planimeter: Centers *tracer point* of planimeter arm on plot to be measured and places pivot arm at right angle to tracer point. Moves tracer point to starting point on photograph according to shape of area to be measured and traces boundary until point of beginning is reached. Records figures shown on dial and measuring wheels of planimeter at beginning and ending of tracing and subtracts figures from each other to determine acreage.
GOE: 07.07.03 STRENGTH: S GED: R3 M2 L1 SVP: 3 DLU: 77

219.387-026 SPACE-AND-STORAGE CLERK (ordnance)
Keeps records of weights and amounts of ammunition and components stored in magazines (storage areas) of arsenal: Posts ledger showing gross weights and amounts of each type of ammunition on hand according to information con-

tained in receiving, shipping, and transfer reports. Keeps charts of floor plan of magazines, indicating utilization of space and type of ammunition stored, according to reports on movement of stores. Compiles periodic reports on amounts of each type of ammunition on hand and floor space available for each type (dangerous explosives are segregated).
GOE: 07.05.03 STRENGTH: L GED: R3 M2 L2 SVP: 3 DLU: 77

219.387-030 STOCK CONTROL CLERK (clerical) alternate titles: inventory clerk; inventory control clerk; stock order lister
Performs any combination of following tasks to compile records concerned with ordering, receiving, storing, issuing, and shipping materials, supplies, and equipment: Compiles data from sources, such as contracts, purchase orders, invoices, requisitions, and accounting reports and writes, types, or enters information into computer to maintain inventory, purchasing, shipping, or other records. Keeps back order file in established sequence and releases back orders for issue or shipment as stock becomes available. Compiles stock control records and information, such as consumption rate, characteristics of items in storage, and current market conditions, to determine stock supply and need for replenishment. Prepares requisitions, orders, or other documents for purchasing or requisitioning new or additional stock items. Compares nomenclature, stock numbers, authorized substitutes, and other listed information with catalogs, manuals, parts lists, and similar references to verify accuracy of requisitions and shipping orders. Reviews files to determine unused items and recommends disposal of excess stock.
GOE: 07.05.03 STRENGTH: L GED: R4 M3 L3 SVP: 5 DLU: 87

219.462-010 COUPON CLERK (financial)
Receives matured bond coupons from bank departments, local banks, and customers to effect collection on cash basis, or for payment when future collection is made: Examines coupons presented for payment to verify issue, payment date, and amount due. Enters credit in customer's passbook or into computer system, for coupons accepted for payment. Liquidates collection payment by debiting and crediting accounts. Issues checks to bond owners in settlement of transactions. Totals and proves daily transactions, using adding machine or calculator. Composes, types, and mails correspondence relating to discrepancies, errors, and outstanding unpaid items. Totals outstanding unpaid cash coupons, using adding machine or calculator, and records amounts in ledgers or into computer system.
GOE: 07.02.02 STRENGTH: S GED: R4 M3 L4 SVP: 5 DLU: 77

219.462-014 TRAIN CLERK (r.r. trans.) alternate titles: schedule clerk
Records time each train arrives and departs from station or terminal: Records number of train, engine, and exact time train departs or arrives. Compares time of arrival or departure with train schedules to ascertain number of minutes train was off schedule. Ascertains from train crew or YARD MANAGER (r.r. trans.) reasons or causes for delays. Transmits train-movement data to electronic data processing system, using on-line console or telegraphic typewriter. May type operating information, such as switching lists and personnel assignments, according to instructions from YARD MANAGER (r.r. trans.).
GOE: 07.05.03 STRENGTH: S GED: R3 M2 L2 SVP: 3 DLU: 77

219.467-010 GRADING CLERK (education) alternate titles: grade recorder; test clerk
Scores objective-type examination papers and computes and records test grades and averages of students in school or college: Grades papers, using electric marking machine. Totals errors found and computes and records percentage grade on student's grade card. Averages test grades to compute student's grade for course. May use weight factors in computing test grades and arriving at final averages.
GOE: 07.02.03 STRENGTH: S GED: R4 M3 L3 SVP: 3 DLU: 77

219.482-010 BROKERAGE CLERK I (financial)
Records purchase and sale of securities, such as stocks and bonds, for investment firm: Computes federal and state transfer taxes and commissions, using calculator and rate tables. Verifies information, such as owners' names, transaction dates, and distribution instructions, on securities certificates to ensure accuracy and conformance with government regulations. Posts transaction data to accounting ledgers and certificate records. Types data on confirmation form to effect transfer of securities purchased and sold. Receives securities and cash and schedules delivery of customer securities.
GOE: 07.02.02 STRENGTH: S GED: R4 M3 L3 SVP: 5 DLU: 77

219.482-014 INSURANCE CHECKER (insurance)
Verifies accuracy of insurance company records, performing any combination of following duties: Compares computations on premiums paid, interest, and dividends due with same data on other records. Verifies data on applications and policies, such as age, name, and address, principal sums, and value of property. Proofreads printed material concerning insurance programs. Verifies computations on interest accrued, premiums due, and settlement surrender or loan values, using calculator, manuals, and rate books. May train new employees. May be designated according to data checked as Abstract Checker (insurance); Policy Checker (insurance).
GOE: 07.05.02 STRENGTH: S GED: R3 M3 L3 SVP: 5 DLU: 78

219.482-018 REINSURANCE CLERK (insurance)
Types reinsurance applications and contracts and calculates reinsurance liability, working for either prime insurer or reinsurer and by either of following methods: (1) Calculates reinsurance required on each risk, considering limit of

liability. Selects reinsurers who may accept part of ceded liability. Types applications. Computes amount of each premium due, using calculating machine. Accepts reinsurers and their liability for cash values and dividends. Prepares abstract for typing of contracts. (2) Receives reinsurance application from prime insurer. Determines amount of insurance already held on risk from company records and calculates reinsurance that company can accept, based on limit of liability. Determines if reinsurance is automatic from treaty provisions and sends application to underwriting department when it is not automatic. Types notice of acceptance or rejection, based on limit of liability, and action of UNDERWRITER (insurance). Operates calculator to verify computations made by prime insurer.
GOE: 07.02.04 STRENGTH: S GED: R4 M3 L3 SVP: 5 DLU: 77

219.487-010 TAX CLERK (clerical) alternate titles: revenue-stamp clerk
Computes state or federal taxes on sales transactions, production processes, or articles produced, and keeps record of amount due and paid. May affix revenue stamps to tax reports to cover amount of tax due.
GOE: 07.02.04 STRENGTH: S GED: R3 M2 L2 SVP: 3 DLU: 77

219.587-010 PARIMUTUEL-TICKET CHECKER (amuse. & rec.) alternate titles: ticket counter
Counts and records number of parimutuel tickets cashed at race track to verify records of cashiers. Compares totals with entries on daily balance sheet. Compares each ticket with sample or examines tickets under fluorescent light to verify validity of tickets. Reports discrepancies.
GOE: 07.05.02 STRENGTH: S GED: R3 M3 L3 SVP: 2 DLU: 77

22 PRODUCTION AND STOCK CLERKS AND RELATED OCCUPATIONS

This division includes occupations concerned with compiling and maintaining production records, expediting flow of work and materials, and receiving, storing, shipping, issuing, requisitioning, and accounting for materials and goods.

221 PRODUCTION CLERKS

This group includes occupations concerned with compiling records and reports on various aspects of production, such as materials and parts used, products produced, and frequency of defects; estimating or measuring amount of material needed and computing material and production costs; counting, measuring, or weighing goods produced or material on hand to tally data for production control or payroll purposes; charting production progress; preparing or distributing work tickets, formula cards, or other production guides; scheduling and expediting flow of work and materials for production or repair; coordinating, scheduling or monitoring production, using electronic equipment; and observing production operations to log products produced, materials used, processes completed, and machine and instrument readings. Occupations concerned with preparing payroll and timekeeping records from production data are found in Group 215.

221.132-010 CHIEF CLERK, MEASUREMENT DEPARTMENT (petrol. & gas; pipe lines)
Supervises and coordinates activities of workers engaged in compiling reports concerning quality and quantity of oil or natural gas produced, purchased, transported, and sold: Directs clerks in compiling of production and sales reports, purchase orders, and transportation records. Oversees consolidation of data used to determine heating quality of natural gas. Directs clerks in compiling production records and other reports. Calculates factors used to compute petroleum or gas volumes transported by pipelines, using adding machine or calculator. Performs duties as described under SUPERVISOR (clerical) Master Title. May direct CHART CLERKS (clerical) in compiling data relating to volume of petroleum or gas products passing specified points on pipeline system and be designated Chart Clerk, Chief (clerical).
GOE: 07.02.03 STRENGTH: S GED: R4 M4 L4 SVP: 7 DLU: 77

221.137-010 CONTROL CLERK, HEAD (clock & watch)
Supervises and coordinates activities of CONTROL CLERKS (clock & watch) engaged in distributing material to workers and keeping records of parts worked on and completed: Keeps perpetual inventory of watches in department. Totals hours worked by subordinates for payroll purposes. Issues work tickets. Performs duties as described under SUPERVISOR (clerical) Master Title.
GOE: 05.09.02 STRENGTH: L GED: R4 M3 L4 SVP: 6 DLU: 77

221.137-014 SUPERVISOR, PRODUCTION CLERKS (clerical)
Supervises and coordinates activities of PRODUCTION CLERKS (clerical) engaged in keeping records and preparing statistical statements and reports on production of manufactured goods, consumption of raw materials, and other production data, performing duties as described under SUPERVISOR (clerical) Master Title.
GOE: 07.02.03 STRENGTH: S GED: R4 M4 L4 SVP: 7 DLU: 77

221.137-018 SUPERVISOR, PRODUCTION CONTROL (clerical)
Supervises and coordinates activities of MATERIAL COORDINATORS (clerical) engaged in expediting flow of material, parts, and assemblies within or between departments of industrial plant, and of PRODUCTION COORDINATORS (clerical) engaged in scheduling production operations: Evaluates written data, such as job orders, product specifications and operations sheets,

parts and materials inventory lists, and machine and worker production rates, to establish efficient allocation and scheduling of parts, materials, machines, and sequences of operations and workflow. Confers with production personnel to resolve problems affecting production schedules. Performs duties as described under SUPERVISOR (clerical) Master Title.
GOE: 05.09.02 STRENGTH: L GED: R4 M3 L4 SVP: 8 DLU: 77

221.162-010 PRODUCTION SCHEDULER, PAPERBOARD PRODUCTS (paper goods) alternate titles: production clerk; production planner; scheduler
Prepares production schedules and miscellaneous reports for manufacturing such paperboard products as corrugated and folded cartons, boxes, and containers: Examines blueprint or drawings to determine type and quantity of material and equipment required to manufacture number of containers specified. Confers with production personnel to clarify processing methods or establish sequence of operations. Prepares production schedules, issues work orders, and keeps progress records [PRODUCTION CLERK (clerical)]. Calculates unit and job-lot manufacturing costs of containers, based on size and type, and involving such factors as labor, material, handling, and shipping costs.
GOE: 05.03.03 STRENGTH: S GED: R4 M4 L4 SVP: 6 DLU: 77

221.167-010 COPY CUTTER (print. & pub.)
Coordinates activities of workers engaged in setting of copy into type: Examines, apportions, and distributes editorial and classified advertising copy to COMPOSITORS (print. & pub.); LINOTYPE OPERATORS (print. & pub.); or MONOTYPE-KEYBOARD OPERATORS (machinery mfg.; print. & pub.). Examines copy to determine time and date for publication, type style, and size specified for headings and body. Determines size of sections to be cut and distributed, according to time available for setting type. Cuts copy into sections, marks sections with type size if cuts are to be used, and distributes to composing room. May mark sections to aid in assembling type and cuts in galley.
GOE: 05.10.05 STRENGTH: S GED: R4 M3 L3 SVP: 8 DLU: 77

221.167-014 MATERIAL COORDINATOR (clerical) alternate titles: material control expediter; production control scheduler
Coordinates and expedites flow of materials, parts, and assemblies between sections or departments, according to production and shipping schedules or department priorities, and compiles and maintains manual or computerized records: Reviews production schedules and related information and confers with department supervisors to determine material requirements to identify overdue materials and to track material. Requisitions material and establishes sequential delivery dates to departments, according to job order priorities and material availability. Examines material delivered to production departments to verify conformance to specifications. Arranges in-plant transfer of materials to meet production schedules. Computes amount of material required to complete job orders, applying knowledge of product and manufacturing processes. Compiles and maintains manual or computerized records, such as material inventory, in-process production reports, and status and location of materials. May move or transport materials from one department to another, manually or using material handling equipment. May arrange for repair and assembly of material or part. May monitor and control movement of material and parts on automated conveyor system.
GOE: 05.09.02 STRENGTH: L GED: R4 M3 L4 SVP: 6 DLU: 90

221.167-018 PRODUCTION COORDINATOR (clerical) alternate titles: production controller; production expediter; production scheduler; progress clerk; schedule clerk; scheduler
Schedules and coordinates flow of work within or between departments of manufacturing plant to expedite production: Reviews master production schedule and work orders, establishes priorities for specific customer orders, and revises schedule according to work order specifications, established priorities, and availability or capability of workers, parts, material, machines, and equipment. Reschedules identical processes to eliminate duplicate machine setups. Distributes work orders to departments, denoting number, type, and proposed completion date of units to be produced. Confers with department supervisors to determine progress of work and to provide information on changes in processing methods received from methods or engineering departments. Compiles reports concerning progress of work and downtime due to failures of machines and equipment to apprise production planning personnel of production delays. Maintains inventory of materials and parts needed to complete production. May expedite material [MATERIAL COORDINATOR (clerical) 221.167-014]. May expedite production of spare parts and establish delivery dates for spare parts orders and be designated Spares Scheduler (clerical). May coordinate and expedite work in automobile repair and service establishment from control tower, using public address system, and be designated Work Coordinator, Tower Control (automotive ser.). May use computer system to track and locate production units.
GOE: 05.09.02 STRENGTH: S GED: R4 M3 L4 SVP: 6 DLU: 87

221.167-022 RETORT-LOAD EXPEDITER (wood prod., nec) alternate titles: load tallier
Coordinates tram-car loading activities in wood-preserving plant to expedite movement of wood products into treatment retorts, tallies products loaded to verify against customer orders, and records product-load data for use by processing personnel: Confers with supervisors to determine processing schedule. Determines combinations of orders which can be processed together and number and sizes of tram cars required for each retort charge, according to retort

capacities, wood types, and estimate of product volume. Directs RIGGER (any industry) 921.260-010 and OVERHEAD CRANE OPERATOR (any industry) 921.663-010 in tram-car loading operations. Examines loaded tram cars to verify linkage between cars and determine need for securing load. Counts products in each car by size and wood type and compares total against customer specifications to ensure that orders are complete. Times loading activities for each order and posts time in tally book. Computes displacement (volume in cubic feet) of each retort charge, using calculator, records displacement figure onto record form, and delivers form to TREATING-PLANT SUPERVISOR (wood prod., nec) 561.131-010 to clear load for processing and provide processing data.
GOE: 05.09.02 STRENGTH: L GED: R3 M3 L3 SVP: 5 DLU: 77

221.167-026 CUSTOMER SERVICES COORDINATOR (print. & pub.)
    Coordinates production of printed materials, prepress or printing services with customers' requirements: Confers with customers throughout production to keep them informed of status of job, to solicit and resolve inquiries and complaints, to obtain approval of materials, such as artwork, color separations (film for each primary color), ink samples, and proofs, and to procure information and materials needed by establishment personnel to process order. Determines supplies, materials, and equipment needed for job order, plans and draws layout of job, and routes supplies and materials, such as paste-ups, artwork, copy, film, or prints, to work areas to put job order into production. Monitors progress of job order throughout production, confers with establishment personnel, orders supplies, contracts services with outside vendors, and alters production schedule and job order to expedite timely processing of job in accordance with customers' requirements and company standards.
GOE: 05.09.02 STRENGTH: L GED: R5 M4 L4 SVP: 6 DLU: 89

221.362-010 AIRCRAFT-LOG CLERK (air trans.) alternate titles: aircraft-inspection-record clerk; aircraft-time clerk; equipment scheduler; maintenance-planning clerk
    Keeps records of usage and time intervals between inspection and maintenance of designated airplane parts: Compiles data from flight schedules and computes and posts amount of time airplanes and individual parts are in use daily, using calculating machine. Maintains card file for individual parts with notations of time used and facts taken from inspection records. Notifies inspection department when parts and airplanes approach date for inspection, including accummulated time and routing schedule. Records work notations onto inspection report forms, using typewriter. Prepares reports on schedule delays caused by mechanical difficulties to be filed with Federal Aviation Administration. May keep reports on amounts of gasoline used daily. May keep employees' time records [TIMEKEEPER (clerical)].
GOE: 07.05.03 STRENGTH: S GED: R3 M3 L3 SVP: 4 DLU: 77

221.362-014 DISPATCHER, RELAY (pipe lines)
    Compiles and transmits dispatching information and instructions between central office, pipeline terminals, tank farms, and pumping and compressor stations: Relays messages to stations to direct flow of oil and gas, using PBX switchboard. Transmits, receives, and posts information pertaining to pumping schedules, oil and gas pressures, gauging reports, oil stocks and storage capacities, and physical characteristics of gas and oil in storage and lines, such as temperatures, specific gravities, Btu, and sediment content. Receives, records, and prepares reports of quantities of oil and gas pumped or compressed and received by stations and tank farms. Performs other clerical duties, such as typing reports and records and keeping files. May communicate with field personnel, using radio-telephone equipment.
GOE: 07.04.05 STRENGTH: S GED: R3 M3 L3 SVP: 5 DLU: 77

221.362-018 ESTIMATOR, PAPERBOARD BOXES (paper goods)
    Estimates cost of manufacturing paperboard boxes, according to specifications, blueprints, and diagrams, using tables, charts, and arithmetic calculations: Confers with plant production personnel to select machines for possible use in manufacturing boxes. Reads tables to estimate cost of each production operation. Determines positions of pattern on blank (paperboard sheet) to minimize waste and facilitate operations on machines. Calculates total material to be used and total material cost, using calculator and considering quantity, quality, and style of box, packaging, and delivery rates. Submits total estimate to sales department. May estimate cost of manufacturing boxes made from other types of materials.
GOE: 05.09.02 STRENGTH: L GED: R4 M4 L4 SVP: 6 DLU: 77

221.362-022 PROGRESS CLERK (construction)
    Records and reports progress of construction work: Reviews information, such as daily record of activities (log), records of materials received and used, and reports from various workers. Prepares and types report. May inspect and measure work completed. May photograph construction work at various stages of completion to report progress pictorially.
GOE: 07.05.03 STRENGTH: L GED: R4 M3 L3 SVP: 5 DLU: 77

221.362-026 RAILROAD-MAINTENANCE CLERK (r.r. trans.)
    Compiles and records information pertaining to track and right-of-way repair and maintenance by railroad section crews, such as materials used, types and locations of repairs made, and hours expended. Types or writes requisitions for materials needed. May keep daily time records [TIMEKEEPER (clerical)] and compile maintenance reports for specific section crew and be designated Road Clerk (r.r. trans.). May compile daily, weekly, and monthly composite reports and be designated Section-Crews-Activities Clerk (r.r. trans.).

GOE: 07.05.03 STRENGTH: S GED: R3 M3 L3 SVP: 4 DLU: 77

221.362-030 COMPUTER PROCESSING SCHEDULER (clerical)
    Schedules work for computer processing and monitors execution of schedule, using software and computer terminal: Reviews computer processing job requests received from programmers and computer users, and talks with programmers and users to determine processing requirements, such as computer time and memory required, and priority. Develops processing schedule, using computer terminal and job scheduling software. Reviews completed schedule to detect conflicts and ensure availability of memory and other computer resources, using computer terminal. Talks with programmers and users to resolve conflicts in schedule. Enters commands to ensure that new processing jobs do not hinder computer operation, following programmers' specifications. Monitors computer terminal display to detect problem, and to ensure that data entered are correct and that jobs will run as scheduled. Corrects problem, such as failure of program to run, or program running incorrect sequence. May establish guidelines for scheduling work. May train other workers in use of scheduling software.
GOE: 07.05.01 STRENGTH: S GED: R4 M2 L4 SVP: 6 DLU: 90

221.367-010 ALTERATIONS WORKROOM CLERK (retail trade)
    Schedules distribution of garments received for alterations within alteration workroom of retail store: Receives garment from sales floor, checks accuracy of entries on sales slip against garment tag, and removes section of tag for record purposes. Segregates garments on racks and distributes work according to nature of alteration and completion date specified on tag. Receives tags from alteration workers upon completion of alterations and matches with tags in file. Transcribes figures from tag to production record of each worker and computes daily and weekly figures, using adding machine. Answers telephone calls from customers regarding status of garments being altered and complaints about unsatisfactory alterations on completed garments.
GOE: 05.09.02 STRENGTH: L GED: R3 M2 L2 SVP: 3 DLU: 77

221.367-014 ESTIMATOR, PRINTING (print. & pub.)
    Estimates labor and material costs of printing and binding books, pamphlets, periodicals, and other printed matter, based on specifications outlined on sales order or submitted by prospective customer: Examines specifications, sketches, and sample layouts, and calculates unit and production costs, using labor and material pricing schedules, and considering factors such as size and number of sheets or pages, paper stock requirements, binding operations, halftones, number and units of colors, and quality of finished product, to determine cost effective and competitive price. Confers with department heads or production personnel to develop or confirm information regarding various cost elements. May estimate cost of mailing finished printed matter if specified on order. May estimate labor and material cost of specific phase of printing, such as plate making or binding, and be designated according to specialty as Estimator, Printing-Plate-Making (print. & pub.) or Estimator, Binding (print. & pub.).
GOE: 05.09.02 STRENGTH: L GED: R4 M3 L3 SVP: 6 DLU: 89

221.367-018 FOLLOW-UP CLERK (elec. equip.)
    Locates, gathers, and groups, according to specifications, parts required to complete switchgear units at place of installation: Prepares list of parts and materials, such as circuit breakers, transformers, bus-bars, wiring materials, insulation, hardware, paints, and ventilating pipes. Locates parts in plant by consulting production records, supervisors, and production personnel. Gathers parts dismantled from switchgear units. Fills orders for accessory parts from stockroom and withdraws repaired items from repair department. Groups parts according to pattern in which switchgear units are split up for shipment. Tags items with identifying information and routes to inspection and shipping department. Posts information on status of accessory, split, and repair orders in production book.
GOE: 05.09.02 STRENGTH: M GED: R4 M3 L3 SVP: 6 DLU: 77

221.367-022 INDUSTRIAL-ORDER CLERK (clerical)
    Verifies completion of industrial orders and conformance of product to specifications: Compares blueprints with contract or order to ascertain that product meets engineering specifications. Communicates with customer and delivery personnel to verify delivery of product. Fills out completion slip after order is filled. May route products not meeting specifications to production units for correction.
GOE: 05.09.03 STRENGTH: S GED: R4 M3 L4 SVP: 4 DLU: 77

221.367-026 LINE-UP WORKER (auto. mfg.) alternate titles: scheduler; scheduler, conveyor; transfer and line-up worker
    Relays scheduling information to workers on automotive assembly line: Reads production schedule and computer printouts and relays information orally or by written instructions. Verifies conformity of assemblies and parts on conveyor lines with scheduling information. Notifies workers to switch parts and assemblies not in sequence. Enters production data in computer, using keyboard or laser reader.
GOE: 05.09.02 STRENGTH: L GED: R3 M2 L2 SVP: 3 DLU: 78

221.367-030 LOCOMOTIVE LUBRICATING-SYSTEMS CLERK (r.r. trans.)
    Keeps and reviews records and reports pertaining to locomotive lubricating systems and advises railroad repair shops when locomotives require oil change or repair to lubricating systems: Scans incoming reports to identify locomotives with oil contamination. Dials computer dial phone to obtain location of oil-contaminated locomotives. Telephones and directs clerks at reported locations to

notify maintenance personnel to determine contamination causes and make necessary repairs. Requests that locomotives be pushed to nearest repair shops when bad-oil reports indicate need for major repairs. Reviews reports to identify locomotives requiring repeated repairs and advises need for major repairs to prevent possible crankshaft damage. Verifies and records informational data on all repairs. Plots weekly and 10-week-average graphs and prepares reports on locomotives' lubrication oil and lubrication systems. May test locomotive water for chromate contents, using spectrophotometer, and notify repair shops of need for rust or clogging-preventative additives.
GOE: 07.05.01 STRENGTH: S GED: R3 M2 L3 SVP: 5 DLU: 77

221.367-034 MACHINE-STOPPAGE-FREQUENCY CHECKER (textile) alternate titles: frequency checker; survey hand
Records number and cause of machine stoppage on textile machines, such as looms and spinning frames, for payroll, work assignment, and quality control purposes: Observes machine and questions worker to determine reason for machine stoppage. Records information on forms for analysis by management. May perform quality control tests on samples, such as measuring variations in thickness and testing tensile strength, using testing equipment. May record and total items, such as material and labor costs to determine plant processing costs. May be known as Loom-Stop Checker (textile) when working in weave room. May be known as Ends-Down Checker (textile) when observing spinning or roving frames.
GOE: 05.09.03 STRENGTH: L GED: R3 M3 L3 SVP: 3 DLU: 78

221.367-038 MAINTENANCE DATA ANALYST (military ser.)
Prepares schedules for preventive maintenance of equipment to ensure uninterrupted operation of equipment: Reviews maintenance schedule to determine preventive maintenance to be performed on equipment. Compares maintenance and staff-hour data against monthly maintenance plans, work load estimates, and standards. Calculates amount of human resources required to perform maintenance work. Notifies superiors of maintenance to be performed. Identifies and assists superiors in analysis of material deficiencies, high staff-hour action areas, and trends and deviations from schedules and standards. Prepares inspection tests, repair, modification, alignment service, and load schedules for aircraft, missiles, and machinery. Maintains maintenance index file for individual equipment maintenance.
GOE: 05.09.02 STRENGTH: L GED: R3 M3 L3 SVP: 5 DLU: 77

221.367-042 MATERIAL EXPEDITER (clerical) alternate titles: expediter; stock chaser
Compiles and maintains material and parts inventory and status information to expedite movement of material and parts between production areas, according to predetermined production schedules and order priorities: Reads production schedules, inventory reports, and work orders to determine type and quantity of materials required, availability of stock, and order priority. Confers with department supervisors to determine overdue material and parts and to inform supervisors of material status. Locates and distributes materials to specified production areas, manually or using handcart, handtruck, or forklift. Records and maintains perpetual inventory of quantity and type of materials and parts received, stocked, and distributed, manually or using computer. Compiles and maintains records, such as material inventory records, production records, and timecards, manually or using computer. May direct INDUSTRIAL-TRUCK OPERATOR (any industry) 921.683-050 or MATERIAL HANDLER (any industry) 929.687-030 to expedite transfer of materials from stock area to production areas. May examine material received, verify part numbers, and check discrepancies, such as damaged or unmarked parts. May compare work ticket specifications to material used at work stations to verify appropriate assignment. May drive truck to outlying work areas to check status of orders or to deliver materials.
GOE: 05.09.02 STRENGTH: M GED: R3 M3 L3 SVP: 4 DLU: 87

221.367-046 MILL RECORDER, COMPUTERIZED MILL (steel & rel.)
Compiles and feeds input data into computer that controls reduction processing of steel slabs on roughing section of hot-strip rolling mill and records mill production and operating data: Reviews rolling schedule to ascertain operational data, such as slab sizes, metallurgical analysis, and rolling sequences. Contacts heating personnel by intercom system to ascertain stock of scheduled slabs and notifies crew of deviations from rolling schedule. Notifies supervisor when data is in computer. Monitors computer readout and adjusts input data according to read failures, data errors, or when notified by heating personnel of out-of-sequence changes, no changes, or runback of slabs due to insufficient rolling temperature. Prepares production and delay reports from data in logs and information received from mill crew.
GOE: 05.03.03 STRENGTH: L GED: R3 M2 L3 SVP: 5 DLU: 77

221.367-050 RECORDER (steel & rel.)
Records data concerning steel production to ensure that processing procedures are carried out according to specifications: Reads production, heating, or rolling schedule to determine processing specifications. Distributes copies of orders to operating personnel. Observes processing of material; reads gauges, clocks, and automatic recorder; and records and compares information with schedules to ensure compliance with processing specifications. Marks billets (bars) with tags or chalk. Informs supervisor of deviations from processing instructions. Writes reports describing processing delays and deviations. Records steel production information for different types of processes, such as oxygen-furnace pit, open-hearth pit, structural mill, blooming mill, and slabbing mill.

GOE: 05.09.02 STRENGTH: L GED: R3 M2 L3 SVP: 5 DLU: 79

221.367-054 RELAY-RECORD CLERK (utilities)
Compiles, classifies, and keeps reports and records of tests performed by relay field-test crews and transmits supervisor's instructions to relay test crews of electric power company: Prepares reports and verifies accuracy of data submitted by field-test crews in company plant and substation installations. Prepares reports on maintenance and new-installation tests performed at customer's substation. Classifies, files, and issues blueprints and related documents used on construction work by field-test crews. Verifies accuracy of calculations on test reports, such as power or current transformer ratio, circuit breaker time-performance, and transformer winding resistance, using calculator. Summarizes daily field-test reports and posts data in logbooks. Relays supervisor's instructions to test crews, using communication system.
GOE: 07.05.03 STRENGTH: S GED: R3 M3 L3 SVP: 5 DLU: 77

221.367-058 REPRODUCTION ORDER PROCESSOR (clerical)
Reviews request orders for duplication of printed, typed, and handwritten materials and determines appropriate reproduction method, based on knowledge of cost factors and duplicating machines and processes: Reads duplication requests to ascertain number of copies to be made and completion date requested. Confers with order requestor when additional information is necessary to facilitate completion of order. Designates method of duplication, such as photocopying or offset, and routes request orders for processing. Examines completed reproduced material for adherence to order specifications. Keeps files on status of request orders. Keeps supply of standard forms and issues forms as requested.
GOE: 07.05.03 STRENGTH: S GED: R3 M2 L3 SVP: 5 DLU: 77

221.367-062 SALES CORRESPONDENT (clerical)
Compiles data pertinent to manufacture of special products for customers: Reads correspondence from customers to determine needs of customer not met by standard products. Confers with engineering department to ascertain feasibility of designing special equipment. Confers with production personnel to determine feasibility of fabrication and to obtain estimate of cost and production time. Corresponds with customer to inform of production progress and costs. May specialize in correspondence dealing with customer service agreements and be designated Service Correspondent (clerical).
GOE: 05.09.02 STRENGTH: L GED: R4 M2 L4 SVP: 6 DLU: 77

221.367-066 SCHEDULER, MAINTENANCE (clerical) alternate titles: dispatcher, maintenance
Schedules repairs and lubrication of motor vehicles for vehicle-maintenance concern or company automotive-service shop: Schedules vehicles for lubrication or repairs based on date of last lubrication and mileage traveled or urgency of repairs. Contacts garage to verify availability of facilities. Notifies parking garage workers to deliver specified vehicles. Maintains file of requests for services.
GOE: 07.05.01 STRENGTH: S GED: R3 M2 L3 SVP: 4 DLU: 77

221.367-070 SERVICE CLERK (clerical) alternate titles: repair-service clerk; service-order dispatcher
Receives, records, and distributes work orders to service crews upon customers' requests for service on articles or utilities purchased from wholesale or retail establishment or utility company: Records information, such as name, address, article to be repaired, or service to be rendered. Prepares work order and distributes to service crew. Schedules service call and dispatches service crew. Calls or writes customer to ensure satisfactory performance of service. Keeps record of service calls and work orders. May dispatch orders and relay messages and special instructions to mobile crews and other departments, using radio-telephone equipment.
GOE: 07.04.05 STRENGTH: S GED: R3 M2 L2 SVP: 4 DLU: 77

221.367-078 TRAFFIC CLERK (business ser.)
Compiles schedules and control records on work in process in advertising agency to ensure completion of artwork, copy, and layouts prior to deadline and notifies staff and clients of schedule changes: Keeps schedules and records on work to ensure arrival of printing and artwork, as needed, and to ensure completion of copy. Contacts vendors and notifies agency personnel and clients of changes in schedules.
GOE: 07.05.01 STRENGTH: S GED: R4 M2 L3 SVP: 4 DLU: 77

221.367-082 WORK-ORDER-SORTING CLERK (utilities)
Sorts and routes work orders for construction of gas or electric mains, service connections, or meter installations: Relays work orders, messages and special instructions by telephone or personal notification to service crews. Keeps control register showing number of work orders received and date completed.
GOE: 07.05.04 STRENGTH: S GED: R3 M2 L3 SVP: 5 DLU: 77

221.367-086 CLERK, TELEVISION PRODUCTION (radio-tv broad.)
Schedules use of facility and equipment and compiles and maintains employee work schedules and equipment and facility usage records for public broadcasting station: Schedules personnel based on written or oral requisition for studio usage, equipment needed for television production, and availability of workers. Compiles leave and vacation schedules. Prepares daily and weekly charts that indicate worker assignment and usage of facilities and equipment. Duplicates charts for distribution to staff, using photocopy machine. Revises schedule charts to accommodate changing priorities and worker absences. Compiles and submits timesheet information to payroll office.
GOE: 07.05.01 STRENGTH: S GED: R4 M3 L3 SVP: 6 DLU: 86

221.367-090 FORMULA CLERK (textile)
Adapts basic dye formulas for use in dyeing goods in accordance with customer specifications: Reads production orders scheduled for processing to determine number of pounds of yarn or fabric to be dyed. Reviews basic dye formula developed for dyeing specified customer lot to ascertain weights of dyes and chemicals used in basic formula. Computes amounts of dyes and chemicals required to dye specified number of pounds of goods in conformity with customer specifications, utilizing knowledge of machine capacity, applying mathematical formulas and using calculator. Records lot size and dye machine number onto adjusted formula and places formula in designated location for use by dye department personnel. Compiles department production records [PRODUCTION CLERK (clerical) 221.382-018].
GOE: 05.09.02 STRENGTH: S GED: R3 M3 L3 SVP: 3 DLU: 86

221.382-010 CHART CLERK (clerical) alternate titles: yield clerk
Performs any combination of following duties to extract statistical data from charts taken from flowmeters and other measuring and recording devices used on pipelines: Calculates volume of natural gas, manufactured gas, and petroleum handled by specific pipelines, using adding machine, calculator, or planimeter, and meter records of gas pressure, temperature, and specific gravity. Compiles reports from measurement charts to indicate quantity of gas produced, transported, and sold. Posts and files charts.
GOE: 07.02.03 STRENGTH: S GED: R3 M3 L3 SVP: 4 DLU: 77

221.382-018 PRODUCTION CLERK (clerical) alternate titles: plant clerk; production checker; production-control clerk; production-posting clerk
Compiles and records production data for industrial establishment to prepare records and reports on volume of production, consumption of raw material, quality control, and other aspects of production, performing any combination of following duties: Compiles and records production data from such documents as customer orders, work tickets, product specifications, and individual-worker production sheets, following prescribed recordkeeping procedures, using typewriter, computer terminal, and writing instruments. Calculates factors, such as types and quantities of items produced, materials used, amount of scrap, frequency of defects, and worker and department production rates, using adding machine or calculator. Writes production reports based on data compiled, tabulated, and computed, following prescribed formats. Maintains files of documents used and prepared. Compiles from customer orders and other specifications detailed production sheet or work tickets for use by production workers as guides in assembly or manufacture of product [ORDER DETAILER (clerical) 221.387-046]. Prepares written work schedules based on established guidelines and priorities. Compiles material inventory records and prepares requisitions for procurement of materials and supplies [MATERIAL CLERK (clerical) 222.387-034]. Charts production, using wall chart, graph, or pegboard, based on statistics compiled, for reference by production and management personnel. Sorts and distributes work tickets or material to workers. May compute wages from employee timecards and post wage data on records used for preparation of payroll [PAYROLL CLERK (clerical) 215.382-014]. May be designated according to type of data recorded as Machine-Load Clerk (woodworking); department or division of establishment to which data pertains as Production Clerk, Lace Tearing (tex. prod., nec); Mill Recorder (nonfer. metal); or work aids used as Production Control Pegboard Clerk (garment).
GOE: 05.03.03 STRENGTH: S GED: R3 M3 L3 SVP: 4 DLU: 86

221.382-022 REPAIR-ORDER CLERK (clerical) alternate titles: work-order clerk
Receives interdepartmental work orders for construction or repairs, routes work orders to maintenance shop, and compiles cost reports: Files copy of each work order received, and routes original copy to maintenance shop. Receives and files cost reports of work accomplished, and prepares bills to be charged against department requesting construction or repairs. Types cost reports of work completed or in progress.
GOE: 07.05.03 STRENGTH: S GED: R3 M3 L3 SVP: 3 DLU: 77

221.382-026 SAMPLE CLERK (furniture)
Operates pantograph, camera, and adding machine in pattern department of furniture plant to estimate upholstery costs: Places cardboard pattern on workbed and plastic sheet on mounting plate of reduction machine. Moves stylus on tracing arm of pantograph around edge of pattern to control movement of heated cutting needle that cuts reduced plastic pattern of upholstery part. Arranges pattern pieces on scaled table to facilitate maximum fabric usage from standard spread of cloth. Operates camera mounted on adjustable stand to photograph pattern layout. Files pattern parts and developed camera print for reference by other workers. Compiles cutting, sewing, and fabric cost data, using adding machine, standardized computation sheets and formulas, and pattern layout information.
GOE: 05.09.02 STRENGTH: L GED: R3 M3 L3 SVP: 5 DLU: 86

221.387-010 BACK-SHOE WORKER (boot & shoe)
Compiles production records and replaces damaged or missing shoes or shoe parts to complete departmental order: Records each completed step in shoe assembly by entering identifying number of workers who performed operation. Posts record of shoe shortages caused by damage or lack of material. Completes orders by gathering parts or completed shoes from bins and racks to replace items damaged or lost in processing.
GOE: 05.09.02 STRENGTH: L GED: R3 M2 L3 SVP: 4 DLU: 77

221.387-014 COMPLAINT CLERK (boot & shoe) alternate titles: repair clerk; returns clerk
Examines shoes returned by customers and distributes shoes for repair: Examines shoes to determine repairs required and responsibility for repair charges. Writes work order, specifying repairs to be made. Carries shoes with work orders to worker or department responsible for repair. May contact customers by mail or telephone to give or obtain information regarding complaints and repairs.
GOE: 05.09.02 STRENGTH: L GED: R3 M1 L3 SVP: 4 DLU: 77

221.387-018 CONTROL CLERK (clock & watch) alternate titles: production-control clerk
Keeps record of clock and watch parts being worked on and completed, and distributes material and parts to workers: Requisitions parts, based on production orders, and distributes parts to designated work stations. Moves completed work to next operation to keep workers supplied with material. Keeps records of quantity and type of material received, completed, and being worked on. Determines number of hours worked by employees in department, and collects work tickets from which pay is calculated. May be designated according to section of plant as Control Clerk, Repairs (clock & watch); Control Clerk, Subassembly (clock & watch); Control Clerk, Training And Mechanism (clock & watch).
GOE: 05.09.02 STRENGTH: L GED: R3 M3 L3 SVP: 6 DLU: 77

221.387-022 ESTIMATOR, JEWELRY (jewelry-silver.)
Estimates amount of material and labor required to produce particular types of jewelry, utilizing knowledge gained from experience of designs and orders. Keeps record of estimations.
GOE: 05.09.02 STRENGTH: S GED: R4 M3 L3 SVP: 6 DLU: 77

221.387-026 EXPEDITER CLERK (optical goods)
Keeps production records to ensure that optical goods are delivered as promised: Reads prescription to determine date and time work is needed to meet mail or delivery schedule. Keeps chronological list of due dates for prescriptions. Removes work not meeting production schedule from production line and places at head of line. Records on prescription work order date and time material was delivered or shipped.
GOE: 05.09.02 STRENGTH: L GED: R3 M2 L3 SVP: 3 DLU: 77

221.387-030 JACKET PREPARER (print. & pub.)
Prepares jacket (worksheet) for guide in revising customer's printing job order: Compares new order with old one on file and records changes in format, such as size or color of sheet and content of material. Rewrites order listing changes and routes order to production department.
GOE: 07.05.03 STRENGTH: S GED: R3 M2 L3 SVP: 3 DLU: 77

221.387-034 JOB TRACER (clerical) alternate titles: job checker; job spotter; progress clerk
Locates and determines progress of job orders in various stages of production, such as fabrication, assembly, and inspection, and compiles reports used by scheduling and production personnel.
GOE: 05.09.02 STRENGTH: L GED: R3 M2 L3 SVP: 4 DLU: 77

221.387-038 LAUNDRY CLERK (clerical) alternate titles: floor clerk
Compiles and maintains work-production records of each employee for use in payroll and efficiency records. Frequently performs other clerical duties, such as recording weights of laundry bundles. May convert count of each type of garment to production points achieved, following prepared charts or verbal instructions.
GOE: 05.09.02 STRENGTH: L GED: R3 M2 L3 SVP: 3 DLU: 77

221.387-042 MELTER CLERK (foundry) alternate titles: weight-and-test-bar clerk
Records heat (crucible) numbers, composition of alloys, and identification of castings poured from each heat. Calculates amount of each metal for alloys according to standard formula. May stamp heat number on metal tags, using hand-operated press. May insert end of tag wire into metal to identify each casting.
GOE: 05.09.02 STRENGTH: L GED: R3 M3 L3 SVP: 4 DLU: 77

221.387-046 ORDER DETAILER (clerical) alternate titles: job-order clerk; ticketer; work-order detailer
Compiles purchase orders and product specifications to prepare worksheets used in assembly or manufacture of products: Compares customer purchase order with specifications to determine method of assembly or manufacture and materials needed. Records data, such as quantity, quality, type, and size of material, and expected completion date, on worksheet. Obtains documents, such as assembly instructions and blueprints, from files and attaches to worksheet. Routes worksheet and other assembly documents to specified department. May keep inventory of stock on hand and requisition needed material and supplies. May compile purchase order data, maintain stock and production records, and prepare production worksheets, using computer. May prepare worksheets pertaining to cloth printing and mixing of printing colors and be designated Formula Checker (tex. prod., nec; textile). May prepare worksheets and order steel stock for rolling mill and be designated Provider (steel & rel.). May prepare work order and allocate silicon crystal ingots that meet customer specifications for use in manufacturing semiconductor wafers and be designated Allocations Clerk (electronics). May compile process specification sheets and prepare and issue materials for use in semiconductor crystal growing and be designated Production Material Coordinator (electron. comp.).

GOE: 05.09.02 STRENGTH: L GED: R3 M3 L3 SVP: 4 DLU: 89

221.387-050 PRODUCTION ASSISTANT (chemical)
  Estimates and orders quantities of raw materials, such as benzene, acetone, and alcohol, used in manufacture of explosives, and schedules their delivery to processing units. Prepares monthly inventory [INVENTORY CLERK (clerical)].
GOE: 05.09.02 STRENGTH: L GED: R3 M3 L3 SVP: 4 DLU: 77

221.387-054 BATCH-RECORDS CLERK (plastic prod.)
  Compiles and maintains plastic-mixing and ingredient records, and prepares daily mixing instructions for use by MATERIAL MIXERS (plastic prod.) 550.685-130: Compiles and maintains daily mixing and perpetual inventory records from work orders, mixing logs, and formula cards that indicate production information, such as type and quantity of plastic ingredients mixed, ingredient formulas, number of products molded, and identification numbers of molds and molding machines utilized. Copies formula for each plastic mixture from specified formula card onto display card for use by MATERIAL MIXER (plastic prod.). Determines and records amount of plastic mixture required for each molding machine in daily mixing log, based on amount of mixture stored at each machine and knowledge of machine's consumption rate.
GOE: 05.09.02 STRENGTH: S GED: R3 M2 L2 SVP: 3 DLU: 86

221.467-010 GIN CLERK (agriculture) alternate titles: scale clerk
  Weighs incoming cotton, computes ginning charges, and records production in cotton ginning establishment: Weighs truck or trailer loaded with cotton and records gross, tare, and net weights. Computes and records quantity of cotton ginned and baled, and records weight of cottonseed removed from cotton. Questions cotton owners to obtain baling and ginning instructions and records instructions on bale tags. Computes and records ginning charges, using rate chart and adding machine. May prepare payrolls and records of payments to growers and quantity of seed cotton received. May prepare cotton-classing samples and mail samples and ginning figures of individual growers to U.S. Department of Agriculture.
GOE: 05.09.02 STRENGTH: L GED: R3 M2 L2 SVP: 3 DLU: 77

221.482-010 FABRIC-AND-ACCESSORIES ESTIMATOR (garment)
  Computes yardage and determines number of accessories, such as belts, linings, and labels, required in manufacture of women's garments: Reads cutting ticket to determine number of belts, buttons, labels, and amount of lining required for each style garment. Computes number of yards of material used for each style garment to ascertain number of yards per dozen. Types copies of cutting tickets and orders for various dressmaker's supplies. Keeps records of patterns.
GOE: 05.09.02 STRENGTH: S GED: R3 M3 L3 SVP: 3 DLU: 77

221.482-014 LUMBER ESTIMATOR (wood. container) alternate titles: estimator, lumber
  Calculates number of board feet of lumber necessary to manufacture boxes and crates of specified size and number: Reviews customer order to determine quantity, size, weight, and shape of product to be packed. Computes number of board feet of lumber needed, using standardized measurement tables, calculator, and adding machine. Submits estimate to be used as basis for determining selling price of boxes or crates.
GOE: 05.09.02 STRENGTH: S GED: R3 M3 L3 SVP: 5 DLU: 77

221.482-018 TICKET WORKER (tobacco)
  Collects weight tickets for leaf tobacco fed onto blending conveyor line during designated intervals. Computes and records total weight blended and percentage of each tobacco grade in blend, using adding machine and grade formulas, to provide production data for use by blending department supervisor. Occasionally performs miscellaneous nonclerical duties, such as feeding tobacco leaves onto conveyors, hand-straightening tobacco leaves, and sweeping floors.
GOE: 05.09.02 STRENGTH: L GED: R3 M2 L2 SVP: 2 DLU: 77

221.484-010 YARDAGE ESTIMATOR (garment)
  Computes amount of fabric required to produce specified styles of garments in various sizes: Measures parts of sample garments or paper patterns to determine amount of fabric required to produce particular style of garment. Calculates amount of fabric required to produce specified style of garment in various sizes, using size charts. Positions parts of sample or paper patterns on length of fabric to estimate amount of fabric to be used from bolts for minimization of waste during marking operations. May calculate cost of fabric for specified size and style of garment, based on yardage required and estimated wastage. May cut paper patterns, using shears.
GOE: 05.09.02 STRENGTH: L GED: R3 M3 L3 SVP: 6 DLU: 77

221.487-010 LUMBER SCALER (woodworking) alternate titles: lumber tallier
  Measures width of each board of lumber supplied to plant in stacks (lots) of standard lengths and thicknesses to determine board footage, using *lumber scale*. Tallies footage of each board and computes total footage of stack, using calculator. Records thickness, species, grade, length, and board footage of lumber in each stack.
GOE: 05.09.01 STRENGTH: M GED: R3 M3 L2 SVP: 3 DLU: 77

221.584-010 CHART CHANGER (clerical) alternate titles: chart collector
  Changes charts and records data from industrial recording instruments, such as pyrometers and flowmeters: Removes and replaces charts, adjusts recording pen and refills pen with ink, and winds clock springs on mechanical models. Records chart readings and time and date of chart removal. Repairs and adjusts instruments, using handtools. May compare recordings, compute and record average readings, and report discrepancies for use in interpretation of chart data.
GOE: 05.09.03 STRENGTH: L GED: R3 M2 L3 SVP: 4 DLU: 77

221.587-010 CHECKER (textile)
  Reads tickets attached to bundles of cut or wrapped towels to determine worker identity and weight and style of towels. Counts bundles of wrapped towels or estimates quantity of cut towels in bundle, using conversion chart based on weight and style, and records on production sheet quantity of bundles wrapped or towels cut by each worker for use in payroll computation. May load bundles on handtruck and move to next production area.
GOE: 05.09.02 STRENGTH: L GED: R2 M1 L2 SVP: 2 DLU: 77

221.587-014 CHECKER-IN (boot & shoe)
  Copies identifying data from work ticket into department record book to record receipt of shoes or parts. May attach colored production route tags onto shoes to indicate specified production operation. May peel protective coating from uppers. May hang uppers in muller (humidifier) to soften uppers and record time of storage on work ticket, or hang uppers on storage beams outside humidifier. May tack insoles onto outer soles of shoes, using automatic tacking gun.
GOE: 05.09.03 STRENGTH: M GED: R2 M1 L2 SVP: 2 DLU: 77

221.587-018 ODD-PIECE CHECKER (knitting) alternate titles: shortage worker
  Obtains missing garment parts from stockroom to complete specified lots of knitted garments. Distributes parts to production workers. Records quantity, size, and style of parts distributed.
GOE: 05.09.01 STRENGTH: L GED: R2 M1 L2 SVP: 2 DLU: 77

221.587-022 OUTSOLE SCHEDULER (boot & shoe)
  Copies code number from production control book onto work ticket to indicate storage bin location of outsoles for use in casing operations. May prepare outsole requisitions according to inventory records.
GOE: 05.09.03 STRENGTH: L GED: R2 M1 L2 SVP: 2 DLU: 77

221.587-026 RECORDER (knitting)
  Records on identification tickets yardage, weight, and identity of cloth processed on finishing *range:* Sets yardage meter to zero position prior to each cloth-lot processing run. Records yardage reading from meter and copies weight and style and lot numbers from job order onto roll (identification) ticket. Clips roll ticket onto roll of finished cloth. Stops range in event of obvious visible cloth defects and notifies supervisor. Adjusts and repairs yardage meter, using handtools.
GOE: 05.09.03 STRENGTH: L GED: R3 M1 L2 SVP: 2 DLU: 77

221.587-030 TALLIER (clerical) alternate titles: checker; counter; counter-weigher; scale clerk; weigher; weight clerk
  Performs any combination of following duties to tally products or raw materials, such as field crops, fish, livestock, typewriter and watch parts, and steel ingots, received from suppliers or by and from workers, for payroll, payment, and production control purposes, using weight scales, counting devices, and tally sheets: Computes and records totals of tallied figures, using adding machine. Examines and sorts items tallied. Records number and types of defects for quality control purposes. Counts sample quantity of parts onto ratio balance scale and computes total number of parts. Issues receipts. Moves tallied items to storage, shipping, or production areas, manually or by handtruck. May be required to have weigh master's license. May be designated according to product tallied as Apple Checker (agriculture); Boxcar Weigher (railroad equip.); Cotton Weigher (agriculture); Fish Checker (can. & preserv.); Ingot Weigher (steel & rel.); Livestock Counter (agriculture); Lumber Checker (woodworking); Parts Counter-Weigher (clock & watch; electron. comp.; office machines).
GOE: 05.09.01 STRENGTH: L GED: R3 M2 L2 SVP: 3 DLU: 86

221.587-034 TARE WEIGHER (meat products; sugar & conf.; tobacco)
  Weighs sample quantities of product received by establishment for processing, removes tare (waste), and reweighs and records weight of usable product for payment or quality control purposes: Selects specified sample of unprocessed product, such as sugar beets, tobacco leaves, and slaughtered poultry, weighs sample on scale, and records weight. Washes off, strips, trims, or otherwise removes unusable portions of product, such as stems, caked dirt, and spoiled sections. Reweighs sample and records weight. May compute tare in pounds or as percentage of original weight. May prepare and attach weight and identification tickets to product. May send sample to laboratory for analysis.
GOE: 05.09.02 STRENGTH: M GED: R2 M2 L2 SVP: 3 DLU: 78

221.587-038 TICKET SCHEDULER (boot & shoe)
  Copies specifications from master schedule (listing of shoe sizes with heel designations) onto work ticket. Batches tickets for delivery to other workers. May compute department production and record production data from work tickets. May sort heel covers.
GOE: 05.09.03 STRENGTH: L GED: R2 M2 L2 SVP: 3 DLU: 77

221.587-042 WEAVE-DEFECT-CHARTING CLERK (textile)
  Plots weaving defects on graph charts to depict frequency and types of defects charged to each textile weaver: Shades chart boxes of bar graph to plot weaving defects for each· weaver by type and workshift, using inspection re-

ports and colored pencils. Posts charts in weaving room for weavers' reference. Copies data, such as frequency and types of defects, loom numbers, and cloth style from inspection reports onto defect-report form for quality control use.
GOE: 07.07.03 STRENGTH: S GED: R2 M1 L2 SVP: 2 DLU: 77

221.587-046 WHEEL-PRESS CLERK (railroad equip.)
Reads machine pressure readings and wheel and axle serial numbers after each wheel-press operation by WHEEL-PRESS OPERATORS (railroad equip.) and records data on production record form and on masking-tape labels. Applies labels onto axles of completed wheel assemblies to facilitate inspection.
GOE: 05.09.02 STRENGTH: L GED: R2 M1 L2 SVP: 2 DLU: 77

221.587-050 YARDAGE-CONTROL CLERK (carpet & rug)
Measures number of skeins of carpet yarn wound onto cardboard cones, using calibrated board. Records amount of yarn and identification of worker who wound cone for quality and production control purposes.
GOE: 05.09.02 STRENGTH: L GED: R2 M1 L2 SVP: 2 DLU: 77

221.667-010 WORK-TICKET DISTRIBUTOR (knitting) alternate titles: knitting-order distributor
Distributes workcards that contain instructions, such as type of yarn, type of stitch or stitches, and length and width of tubing, to workers engaged in knitting knit tubing. May file workcards according to knitting machine number and style of cloth.
GOE: 05.09.02 STRENGTH: L GED: R2 M1 L2 SVP: 2 DLU: 77

221.687-014 TICKET PULLER (tobacco)
Removes warehouse tickets from baskets or sheets of tobacco on processing floor and compares grades recorded with processor's grade to detect discrepancies in grading and prevent processing of mixed grades. Removes tobacco of questionable grade from processing line or directs MATERIAL HANDLER (any industry) to set basket aside until grade can be ascertained. Writes grade on back of ticket, using felt pen, and carries tickets from each truckload to office for comparison with bill-of-lading. May remove processor's grade ticket and file it with warehouse ticket for production records. May call out grade on sheet of tobacco as it moves along conveyor to facilitate removal by MATERIAL HANDLER (any industry). May attach tickets to full pallet to facilitate bulk feeding process.
GOE: 05.09.03 STRENGTH: L GED: R2 M1 L1 SVP: 2 DLU: 77

222 SHIPPING, RECEIVING, STOCK, AND RELATED CLERICAL OCCUPATIONS

This group includes occupations concerned with receiving, storing, shipping, distributing, and issuing supplies, equipment, and merchandise within a stockroom, toolcrib, receiving room, shipping room, freight yard, or warehouse environment, but excludes occupations not requiring direct contact with materials or products involved. This group also includes checking incoming or outgoing shipments by such methods as counting, measuring, and weighing; distributing, issuing and requisitioning items; taking and maintaining inventories; and keeping related clerical records; gathering, sorting, and packing items for shipment; manually addressing and affixing postage to packages; and unpacking and storing incoming products. Occupations concerned with adding or removing materials or products to or from containers to achieve specified weight are included in Categories 5 through 9. Occupations concerned with computing and recording data related to shipping, receiving, storing and related activities, but having no direct contact with materials or products involved, are found in Division 20 or 21.

222.137-010 FILM-VAULT SUPERVISOR (motion picture)
Supervises and coordinates activities of workers engaged in receiving, identifying, storing, and issuing motion picture films stored in vaults: Prepares custody cards to record receipt of films. Supervises workers assembling and coding films to be stored in vault. Inspects films being issued to ensure that they are packaged and identified as required. Performs other duties as described under SUPERVISOR (clerical) Master Title.
GOE: 05.09.01 STRENGTH: L GED: R4 M3 L3 SVP: 7 DLU: 77

222.137-014 LINEN-ROOM SUPERVISOR (laundry & rel.) alternate titles: supervisor, industrial garment
Supervises and coordinates activites of workers engaged in storing linens and wearing apparel, assembling loads for DRIVER, SALES ROUTE (retail trade; wholesale tr.), and maintaining stock in linen supply establishments: Assigns duties to workers. Inventories articles in stock, such as table linens, bed sheets, towels, and uniforms, and confers with SUPERINTENDENT, LAUNDRY (laundry & rel.) to request replacement of articles in short supply. Counts articles in loads for DRIVER, SALES ROUTE (retail trade; wholesale tr.) to ensure agreement with quantity specified on load sheet. Confers with DRIVER, SALES ROUTE (retail trade; wholesale tr.) and with customers to resolve complaints, and to modify orders according to size, color, and type of articles specified. Interviews employees to resolve complaints and grievances. May supervise workers engaged in attaching labels and emblems, repairing, and altering linens and wearing apparel. May purchase linen supplies. Performs other duties as described under SUPERVISOR (clerical) Master Title.
GOE: 05.09.01 STRENGTH: L GED: R4 M3 L3 SVP: 6 DLU: 77

222.137-018 MAGAZINE SUPERVISOR (chemical; ordnance) alternate titles: ammunition storekeeper; ammunition supervisor
Supervises and coordinates activities of workers engaged in storing, issuing, and accounting for ammunition or explosives, performing duties as described under SUPERVISOR (clerical) Master Title.
GOE: 06.02.01 STRENGTH: L GED: R4 M2 L3 SVP: 6 DLU: 77

222.137-022 MAILROOM SUPERVISOR (print. & pub.)
Supervises and coordinates activities of workers engaged in wrapping and addressing printed material, such as periodicals, books, and newspapers, for mailing and dispatching: Revises local, state, and out-of-state mailing lists. Inspects work stations to ensure that material is wrapped and addressed in time to meet scheduled departure of buses, trains, and airlines. Records distribution of material to subscribers and dealers in city, suburban, home, and country divisions, working from shipping and mailing reports. Maintains file of bus, train, and airline schedules and transfer points, and baggage, express, air, or postal mailing rates. Performs other duties as described under SUPERVISOR (clerical) Master Title.
GOE: 07.07.02 STRENGTH: L GED: R4 M2 L3 SVP: 7 DLU: 77

222.137-026 PETROLEUM-INSPECTOR SUPERVISOR (business ser.)
Supervises and coordinates activities of PETROLEUM INSPECTORS (business ser.) engaged in inspecting petroleum products consigned to clients: Writes consignment order, listing quantity, grade, and kind of petroleum product in consignment. Dispatches workers to inspect products and verify quantities received. Reviews inspection report and laboratory analyses of consignment for conformance to client's specifications. Contacts client and arranges for additional inspections and analyses when variances from contract specifications occur. Performs other duties as described under SUPERVISOR (clerical) Master Title.
GOE: 05.07.05 STRENGTH: S GED: R4 M3 L3 SVP: 7 DLU: 77

222.137-030 SHIPPING-AND-RECEIVING SUPERVISOR (clerical)
Supervises and coordinates activities of workers engaged in verifying and keeping records on incoming and outgoing shipments, and preparing items for shipment: Studies shipping notices, bills of lading, invoices, orders, and other records to determine shipping priorities, work assignments, and shipping methods required to meet shipping and receiving schedules, utilizing knowledge of shipping procedures, routes, and rates. Oversees incoming and outgoing shipping activities to ensure accuracy, completeness, and condition of shipments. Determines space requirements and position of shipment in boxcars and trucks and lays out position of shipment. Determines routing and legal load limits of trucks, according to established schedules and weight limits of states. Inspects loading operations to ensure compliance with shipping specifications, and seals loaded boxcars and truck doors. Inspects material handling equipment for defects and notifies maintenance personnel or contacts outside service facility for repair. Maintains vehicle maintenance report. Directs movement of shipments from shipping and receiving platform to storage and work areas. Compiles records of unfilled orders. Posts weight and shipping charges. Prepares bills of lading. Performs other duties as described under SUPERVISOR (clerical) Master Title. May assist workers in shipping and receiving activities. May be designated according to function supervised as Receiving Supervisor (clerical); Shipping Supervisor (clerical).
GOE: 05.09.01 STRENGTH: L GED: R4 M3 L4 SVP: 6 DLU: 86

222.137-034 STOCK SUPERVISOR (clerical) alternate titles: manager, stockroom; stockroom supervisor; storeroom supervisor; warehouse supervisor
Supervises and coordinates activities of workers concerned with ordering, receiving, storing, inventorying, issuing, and shipping materials, supplies, tools, equipment, and parts, in stockroom, warehouse, or yard: Plans layout of stockroom, warehouse, and other storage areas, considering turnover, size, weight, and related factors of items stored. Advises employee on care and preservation of items received, stored, and shipped, methods and use of equipment in handling, storing, maintaining, and shipping stock, and related problems. Studies records and recommends remedial actions for reported nonusable, slow-moving, and excess stock. Reviews records for accuracy of information and compliance with established procedures, and to determine adequacy of stock levels. Schedules work for special and periodic inventories. Traces history of items to determine reasons for discrepancies between inventory and stock-control records and recommends remedial actions to resolve discrepancies. Performs other duties as described under SUPERVISOR (clerical) Master Title. May supervise and coordinate activities of workers engaged in handling of merchandise in stockroom or warehouse of retail store and be known as Head of Stock (retail trade).
GOE: 05.09.01 STRENGTH: L GED: R4 M3 L3 SVP: 6 DLU: 86

222.137-038 STOCK-CONTROL SUPERVISOR (clerical)
Supervises and coordinates activities of STOCK-CONTROL CLERKS (clerical) engaged in keeping records of sales, keeping perpetual inventory or taking periodical physical inventory, and issuing production orders for stock. Performs duties as described under SUPERVISOR (clerical) Master Title. May supervise and coordinate activities of workers engaged in keeping inventory records of equipment and rolling stock and be known as Equipment-Records Supervisor (construction).
GOE: 07.05.03 STRENGTH: L GED: R4 M3 L3 SVP: 6 DLU: 77

222.137-042 SUPERVISOR, ASSEMBLY STOCK (clerical)
Supervises and coordinates activities of stock control personnel engaged in supplying progressive assembly line, and keeps stock control records: Deter-

mines if parts removed from production departments are to be stored or spotted on assembly line. Assigns duties to stock control personnel, such as INDUSTRIAL-TRUCK OPERATOR (any industry) and STOCK CLERK (clerical), to coordinate movement of parts from production departments or storage areas to assembly line. Keeps records, such as personnel, nonproduction time of lines due to stock difficulties, goods returned to production department or salvage department because of defects, and amount and location of goods in storage. Discusses stock supply or removal requirements with line or department supervisor. Performs other duties as described under SUPERVISOR (clerical) Master Title.
GOE: 05.09.02 STRENGTH: L GED: R4 M2 L3 SVP: 6 DLU: 77

222.137-046 TOOL-CRIB SUPERVISOR (clerical)

Supervises and coordinates activities of TOOL-CRIB ATTENDANTS (clerical) engaged in receiving, storing, and issuing tools and equipment to other workers in industrial establishment and keeping records of same, applying knowledge of types of tools and procedures of tool storage and recordkeeping. Performs other duties as described under SUPERVISOR (clerical) Master Title. May be specified by employer according to experience in particular type of plant or with specific type of tools or equipment.
GOE: 05.09.01 STRENGTH: L GED: R4 M3 L3 SVP: 6 DLU: 77

222.137-050 VAULT CASHIER (business ser.) alternate titles: vault supervisor

Supervises and coordinates activities of workers engaged in receiving, processing, routing, and shipping money and other valuables in armored car firm: Prepares route and work schedules. Oversees loading, unloading, and moving of money and other valuables to and from vault. Issues work and route sheets to workers and collects delivery and pickup receipts from guards. Supervises workers preparing payroll envelopes for customers. Observes workers to ensure that security regulations are followed. Performs other duties as described under SUPERVISOR (clerical) Master Title.
GOE: 07.01.04 STRENGTH: L GED: R4 M3 L3 SVP: 5 DLU: 77

222.167-010 METAL-CONTROL COORDINATOR (nonfer. metal) alternate titles: materials-handling coordinator

Expedites movement of metal stock and supplies used in producing nonferrous metal sheets, bars, tubing, and alloys: Inspects incoming material to ascertain condition, and attaches identification tag to containers or uncrated items. Directs workers weighing or counting metal or supplies, and records amounts received. Directs workers in unloading and storing metal stock and supplies in designated storage areas. Keeps records of materials stored in specific areas. May obtain samples of incoming material and deliver to laboratory for analysis.
GOE: 05.09.01 STRENGTH: L GED: R4 M3 L3 SVP: 6 DLU: 77

222.367-010 CARGO CHECKER (water trans.) alternate titles: freight checker; marine clerk

Compiles records of amount, kind, and condition of cargo loaded on or unloaded from ship: Verifies amount of cargo against lists compiled from bills of lading or shipping manifests. Measures and records dimensions of cargo and computes cubic feet required for stowage aboard ship. Records condition of damaged cargo unloaded from ship. May prepare stowage plan showing location of cargo stowed aboard ship or rail car.
GOE: 05.09.03 STRENGTH: L GED: R3 M2 L3 SVP: 4 DLU: 78

222.367-014 CUT-FILE CLERK (print. & pub.)

Stores, files, and issues advertising and layout cuts, mats, and electrotypes used in newspaper printing: Tags or marks cuts, mats, or plates with identifying information and places them in filing cabinets or cases. Prepares card index for each item filed. Removes requested items from file and records date of removal on file card. Washes plates to remove dirt, ink, and oxides. Applies gum solution to plate surface to protect plate during storage. May discard obsolete materials and records according to established schedule or instructions.
GOE: 05.09.01 STRENGTH: L GED: R3 M1 L2 SVP: 4 DLU: 77

222.367-018 EXPEDITER (clerical)

Contacts vendors and shippers to ensure that merchandise, supplies, and equipment are forwarded on specified shipping date: Contacts vendor by mail, phone, or visit to verify shipment of goods on specified date. Communicates with transportation company to preclude delays in transit. May arrange for distribution of materials upon arrival. May contact vendors to requisition materials. May inspect products for quality and quantity to ensure adherence to specifications.
GOE: 07.05.01 STRENGTH: S GED: R3 M3 L3 SVP: 6 DLU: 81

222.367-022 EXPRESS CLERK (motor trans.; r.r. trans.)

Receives express consignments (parcels) from customers, computes charges, routes consignment according to destination, and releases consignments to consignee: Weighs parcels received from customer and refers to rate chart to compute charges. Writes receipts and bill of charges, accepts payment, or routes parcel c.o.d. Sorts parcels and places them in bins or sacks according to destination. Releases parcels to consignee upon presentation of written notice or other identification. Answers inquiries regarding shipping policies. May be designated according to type of transportation used as Motor-Express Clerk (motor trans.); Rail-Express Clerk (r.r. trans.).
GOE: 07.03.01 STRENGTH: M GED: R3 M3 L3 SVP: 4 DLU: 77

222.367-026 FILM-OR-TAPE LIBRARIAN (clerical)

Classifies, catalogs, and maintains library of motion picture films, photographic slides, and video and audio tapes: Classifies and catalogs items accord-

ing to contents and purpose and prepares index cards for file reference. Maintains records of items received, stored, issued, and returned. Stores items and records according to classification and catalog number. Delivers and retrieves items to and from departments by hand or push cart. May prepare, store, and retrieve classification and catalog information, lecture notes, or other documents related to documents stored, using computer. May be designated according to items stored as Audio-Tape Librarian (clerical); Film Librarian (motion picture).
GOE: 11.02.04 STRENGTH: L GED: R3 M2 L3 SVP: 5 DLU: 89

222.367-030 FLOOR-SPACE ALLOCATOR (tobacco; wholesale tr.)

Allocates space on auction warehouse floor and gives directions to workers placing tobacco in warehouse: Ascertains quality of tobacco offered for sale and assigns floor space according to number of baskets. Shows customers space reserved for their tobacco. Directs workers placing tobacco in assigned spaces, and in keeping tobacco in rows. May assist workers in placing tobacco on warehouse floor.
GOE: 05.09.01 STRENGTH: L GED: R3 M2 L2 SVP: 3 DLU: 77

222.367-034 LOST-AND-FOUND CLERK (clerical)

Receives and returns to owner articles lost in stores, public conveyances, or buildings, and keeps records of articles lost, found, and claimed: Inspects articles and telephones or sends letters to owners when identification is known. Tags and places articles in drawers, shelves, racks, or safe, according to type of article and where it was found. Discusses lost articles by telephone or in person, and returns articles to owners upon positive identification.
GOE: 07.07.03 STRENGTH: L GED: R3 M2 L2 SVP: 3 DLU: 77

222.367-038 MAGAZINE KEEPER (clerical) alternate titles: powder monkey; powder nipper; priller

Stores and issues explosive materials, such as blasting powder, ammonium nitrate, dynamite, fireworks, and munitions, in magazine of explosives or munitions factory, mine, arsenal, or construction project: Records nature and quantity of materials received, shipped, or issued to workers. Enforces observance of safety regulations by persons entering magazine. May direct workers engaged in moving and loading explosives into trucks or boxcars. May thaw frozen explosives. May fill bags, using loading machine. May mix fuel oil with powder to increase combustibility. May assemble fuses and detonators. May insert detonators into sticks of explosives and attach fuse or electric wire to prepare primer charges. May pack and unpack explosives, fireworks, and munitions.
GOE: 05.09.02 STRENGTH: M GED: R3 M2 L2 SVP: 5 DLU: 77

222.367-042 PARTS CLERK (clerical) alternate titles: shop clerk; spare-parts clerk

Receives, stores, and issues spare and replacement parts, equipment, and expendable items used in repair or maintenance shop. Takes inventory of parts and equipment and maintains inventory records. May drive truck to pick up incoming stock or to pick up and deliver parts to units in other buildings or locations. May sell auto parts to customers. May be designated according to type of parts issued as Parts Clerk, Automobile Repair (clerical); Parts Clerk, Plant Maintenance (clerical).
GOE: 05.09.01 STRENGTH: H GED: R3 M3 L3 SVP: 3 DLU: 80

222.367-046 PETROLEUM INSPECTOR (business ser.)

Inspects consignments of crude or refined petroleum to certify that consignments conform to contract specifications: Lowers container into tank and withdraws samples from top, middle, and bottom of tank. Pours samples into bottles and routes samples to laboratory for analysis. Examines petroleum during transfer into receiving tank for discoloration or water. Sounds shore tank with steel tape and consults calibration tables to determine quantity of consignment. Writes report of findings. May conduct laboratory analyses. May calibrate tanks, meters, and tank cars [TANK CALIBRATOR (business ser.)].
GOE: 05.07.05 STRENGTH: L GED: R3 M2 L2 SVP: 5 DLU: 77

222.367-050 PRESCRIPTION CLERK, LENS-AND-FRAMES (optical goods)

Selects lens blanks and frames for production of eyeglasses, according to prescription specifications, and keeps stock inventory at specified level: Reads prescription to determine specifications, such as lens power and base curve and frame style and color. Selects lens blanks and frames from stock and routes them with prescription to production section. Requisitions lens blanks and eyeglass frames and communicates by letter and telephone with suppliers to keep stock at specified level. May work with only lenses or frames and be designated Prescription Clerk, Frames (optical goods); Prescription Clerk, Lenses (optical goods).
GOE: 05.09.02 STRENGTH: L GED: R3 M2 L2 SVP: 5 DLU: 77

222.367-054 PROPERTY CLERK (government ser.) alternate titles: property custodian

Receives, stores, records, and issues money, valuables, and other articles seized as evidence, removed from prisoner, or recovered, lost, or stolen property: Prepares record of articles and valuables received, including description of article, name of owner (if known), name of police officer from whom received, and reason for retention. Issues property being retained as evidence to officer at time of trial upon receipt of authorization. Telephones owners or mails letters to notify owners to claim property, and releases lost or stolen property to owners upon proof of ownership. Returns property to released prisoners. Prepares list of articles required by law to be destroyed and destroys narcotics and drugs (upon authorization) in presence of official witnesses. Sends

alcoholic beverages to state liquor commission. Lists and sends unclaimed or confiscated money to auditor's office. Sends unclaimed and illegal weapons for official destruction. Prepares inventory of unclaimed articles for possible sale at auction or donation to charitable organization.
GOE: 07.05.03 STRENGTH: L GED: R3 M2 L3 SVP: 5 DLU: 77

222.367-062 TOOL-CRIB ATTENDANT (clerical) alternate titles: tool clerk

Receives, stores, and issues handtools, machine tools, dies, materials, and equipment in industrial establishment: Issues tools and equipment to workers and maintains records of tools and equipment issued and returned, manually or using computer. Locates lost or misplaced tools and equipment. Prepares periodic inventory or maintains perpetual inventory of tools and equipment, manually or using computer. Receives, unpacks, and stores incoming tools and equipment, and requisitions stock to replenish inventory. Inspects and measures tools and equipment for defects and wear, visually or using micrometer, and reports damage or wear to supervisors. Repairs, services, and lubricates tools and equipment, using handtools, spray gun, or pressurized spray can. May deliver tools or equipment to workers, manually or using handtruck. May mark and identify tools and equipment, using identification tag, stamp, or electric marking tool.
GOE: 05.09.01 STRENGTH: M GED: R3 M2 L2 SVP: 5 DLU: 88

222.367-066 TRUCKLOAD CHECKER (construction)

Examines and records materials transported by truck to or from site of excavation: Examines load delivered to verify quantity and type of material. Writes ticket showing quantity and type of material, truck number, job location, and time. Reports on amount of materials transported. May signal driver in aligning and spacing loads according to specifications. May hammer stakes in ground to indicate place for unloading of materials.
GOE: 05.09.03 STRENGTH: L GED: R3 M2 L3 SVP: 3 DLU: 77

222.367-070 EXPEDITER, SERVICE ORDER (furniture)

Reviews and verifies information on bills of lading to expedite orders and to ensure that customer furniture orders are shipped in accordance with production and shipping schedules: Reads bills of lading to determine items being shipped, destination, priority of order, and shipping date. Confers with department personnel to ascertain items available for shipment and production shortages. Notifies shipping personnel and department supervisors of items listed on shipping orders as available, but not located, in attempt to expedite processing of items required for immediate shipment. Maintains bills of lading files.
GOE: 07.05.01 STRENGTH: L GED: R3 M3 L3 SVP: 3 DLU: 86

222.384-010 INSPECTOR, RECEIVING (aircraft mfg.; elec. equip.; electron. comp.)

Inspects purchased parts, assemblies, accessories, and materials for conformance to specifications, using precision measuring instruments and devices: Examines items for defects in materials, workmanship, and damage occurring in transit. Compares quantity and part number of items received with procurement data and other specifications to ensure completeness and accuracy of order. Inspects and measures items for dimensional accuracy, fit, alignment, and functional operation, according to blueprints, parts manuals, company or military standards, and other specifications, using precision measuring instruments and devices. Approves or rejects items, and records inspection and disposition information. May test hardness of metals, using testing equipment. May examine x rays of welded parts to determine that welds conform to established standards. May inspect outgoing and production line parts and materials. May prepare inspection procedure outlines for reference use in subsequent inspections, using data obtained from blueprints, customer specifications, and catalogs.
GOE: 06.03.01 STRENGTH: M GED: R3 M2 L3 SVP: 5 DLU: 88

222.387-010 AIRCRAFT-SHIPPING CHECKER (aircraft mfg.) alternate titles: aircraft-delivery checker

Examines completed aircraft to ensure that spare parts, accessories, or subassemblies, itemized on packing and loading sheet, are aboard craft before delivery to customer: Examines blueprints showing location of parts in aircraft, verifies that part is aboard, and records part serial numbers on packing sheet. Reports shortages of parts and subassemblies, as indicated by packing and loading sheet, to designated department. Reads various work orders and operational records and enters such data as contract number, test flight time, maintenance and repair orders, and engine run-up time (engine test time) of aircraft in logbooks that accompany completed aircraft. May obtain spare parts from storeroom and forward them for packing and crating. May load crated or loose parts into aircraft.
GOE: 05.09.03 STRENGTH: L GED: R3 M3 L3 SVP: 5 DLU: 87

222.387-014 CAR CHECKER (r.r. trans.)

Verifies identity of freight cars entering classification yard to ensure that trains are complete upon arrival: Records information, such as car number, type of car, car owner, and date and time of arrival. Compares information with manifest and prepares report showing discrepancies. Examines door seals on cars to determine that seals have not been tampered with or broken. Marks code number or symbol on cars to indicate disposition of cars by switching crew. May record date, mileage, and number of cars switched by switching crew and be known as Switching Clerk (r.r. trans.).
GOE: 05.09.03 STRENGTH: L GED: R3 M2 L3 SVP: 2 DLU: 77

222.387-018 FUEL-OIL CLERK (clerical)

Maintains records and prepares reports regarding quantity and value of fuel oil purchased, received, stored, and used in steam-electric generating plants: Witnesses receipt of fuel oil by company tank-farm operating personnel to verify oil-gaging reports. Examines supplier documents and generating plant records to obtain fuel oil use and loss data. Verifies computation of gross and net barrels of oil received, using standard conversion tables and simple arithmetic. Computes quantity of fuel oil burned, Btu's per barrel, and quantity in storage from operating records and laboratory reports. Posts computations and other related data to fuel-oil ledgers and records and compares data with contract specifications and delivery documents to detect errors and verify accuracy of entries. Telephones representatives of fuel-oil suppliers, railroads, and company traffic department to verify delivery dates and quantities, to determine cause of variations in loading and unloading temperatures and to correct discrepancies in delivery documents or errors in invoices. Notifies supervisory personnel when discrepancies and errors cannot be resolved. Prepares receipts for oil received. Prepares reports of quantity and value of oil purchased, received, lost in delivery, burned, and in storage tanks.
GOE: 07.02.03 STRENGTH: S GED: R3 M3 L2 SVP: 7 DLU: 77

222.387-022 GUN-REPAIR CLERK (ordnance) alternate titles: package opener

Receives and examines small arms and keeps records of arms returned by customers for repair: Receives, unpacks, and examines weapons for live ammunition or mutilated serial numbers. Prepares repair order from customer's request and routes with gun to repair department or sends weapon to GUN EXAMINER (ordnance) and types work order based on report. Verifies repairs made to gun and delivers with invoices to shipping department. Files copies of invoices, cost estimates, and other correspondence concerning receipt, repair, and return of weapon to customer in order to keep record of transaction. May keep inventory of spare parts.
GOE: 05.09.01 STRENGTH: L GED: R3 M2 L2 SVP: 3 DLU: 77

222.387-026 INVENTORY CLERK (clerical)

Compiles and maintains records of quantity, type, and value of material, equipment, merchandise, or supplies stocked in establishment: Counts material, equipment, merchandise, or supplies in stock and posts totals to inventory records, manually or using computer. Compares inventories to office records or computes figures from records, such as sales orders, production records, or purchase invoices to obtain current inventory. Verifies clerical computations against physical count of stock and adjusts errors in computation or count, or investigates and reports reasons for discrepancies. Compiles information on receipt or disbursement of material, equipment, merchandise, or supplies, and computes inventory balance, price, and cost. Prepares reports, such as inventory balance, price lists, and shortages. Prepares list of depleted items and recommends survey of defective or unusable items. May operate office machines, such as typewriter or calculator. May stock and issue materials or merchandise. May be designated according to item inventoried as Property-And-Equipment Clerk (petrol. & gas); or type of inventory as Inventory Clerk, Physical (clerical).
GOE: 05.09.01 STRENGTH: M GED: R3 M3 L3 SVP: 4 DLU: 88

222.387-030 LINEN-ROOM ATTENDANT (hotel & rest.; medical ser.) alternate titles: linen checker; linen clerk; linen-exchange attendant; linen-room houseperson; uniform attendant

Stores, inventories, and issues or distributes bed and table linen and uniforms in establishments, such as hotels, hospitals, and clinics: Collects or receives, and segregates, counts, and records number of items of soiled linen and uniforms for repair or laundry, and places items in containers. Examines laundered items to ensure cleanliness and serviceability. Stamps items with identifying marks. Stores laundered items on shelves, after verifying numbers and types of items. Counts and assembles laundered items on cart or linen truck, records amounts of linens and uniforms to fill requisitions, and transports carts to floors. Conducts monthly and yearly inventories to identify items for replacement. Keeps linen room in clean and orderly condition. May mend torn articles with needle and thread or sewing machine or send articles to SEWER, LINEN ROOM (hotel & rest.) 787.682-030.
GOE: 05.09.01 STRENGTH: M GED: R3 M2 L2 SVP: 2 DLU: 86

222.387-034 MATERIAL CLERK (clerical) alternate titles: stock-record clerk

Compiles and maintains records of quantity, cost, and type of material received, stocked, and issued, and prepares material requisitions: Compares information on requisitions, invoices, and shipping notices to material received or issued to verify accuracy of order. Compiles and maintains inventory of material received, stocked, and issued [INVENTORY CLERK (clerical) 222.387-026]. Prepares requests for procurement of material. May inspect, accept or reject material received. May mark identifying information on material. May be designated according to location of goods as Warehouse-Record Clerk (clerical).
GOE: 05.09.03 STRENGTH: L GED: R3 M3 L3 SVP: 5 DLU: 80

222.387-038 PARCEL POST CLERK (clerical) alternate titles: parcel post packer; parcel post weigher

Wraps, inspects, weighs, and affixes postage to parcel post packages, and records c.o.d. and insurance information: Wraps packages or inspects wrapping for conformance to company standards and postal regulations. Weighs packages and determines postage, using scale and parcel post zone book, and affixes postage stamps to packages. Records information, such as value, charges, and destination of insured and c.o.d. packages. Copies and attaches c.o.d. card to

packages to indicate amount to be collected. Addresses packages or compares addresses with records to verify accuracy. May compute cost of merchandise, shipping fees, and other charges, and bill customer. May sort parcels for shipment, according to destination or other classification, and place parcels in mail bags or bins and be designated Mail-Order Sorter (retail trade). May process incoming and outgoing mail [MAIL CLERK (clerical) 209.687-026]. May fill orders from stock and be designated Parcel-Post Order-Clerk (clerical).
GOE: 07.05.04 STRENGTH: H GED: R3 M2 L3 SVP: 3 DLU: 81

222.387-042 PROPERTY CUSTODIAN (motion picture)
Receives, stores, and issues properties in motion picture studio prop room: Examines incoming property for breaks and flaws and notifies supervisor of damage. Attaches identification tags or labels to property according to type of object. Keeps records of incoming and outgoing props, props in inventory, and rented props. May work in makeup department of motion picture or television film studio and be known as Stock Clerk, Makeup (motion picture).
GOE: 05.09.01 STRENGTH: L GED: R3 M3 L2 SVP: 5 DLU: 77

222.387-046 RETURNED-TELEPHONE-EQUIPMENT   APPRAISER (comm. equip.)
Appraises and classifies telephone equipment returned by telephone companies to determine disposition and price: Examines returned supplies and apparatus to identify and classify returns according to price lists and catalogs. Determines adaptability for current use. Records classification, price, and disposition.
GOE: 06.03.01 STRENGTH: L GED: R3 M3 L2 SVP: 5 DLU: 77

222.387-050 SHIPPING AND RECEIVING CLERK (clerical)
Verifies and keeps records on incoming and outgoing shipments and prepares items for shipment: Compares identifying information and counts, weighs, or measures items of incoming and outgoing shipments to verify information against bills of lading, invoices, orders, or other records. Determines method of shipment, utilizing knowledge of shipping procedures, routes, and rates. Affixes shipping labels on packed cartons or stencils identifying shipping information on cartons, using stenciling equipment. Assembles wooden or cardboard containers or selects preassembled containers. Inserts items into containers, using spacers, fillers, and protective padding. Nails covers on wooden crates and binds containers with metal tape, using strapping machine. Stamps, stencils, or glues identifying information and shipping instructions onto crates or containers. Posts weights and shipping charges, and affixes postage. Unpacks and examines incoming shipments, rejects damaged items, records shortages, and corresponds with shipper to rectify damages and shortages. Routes items to departments. Examines outgoing shipments to ensure shipments meet specifications. Maintains inventory of shipping materials and supplies. May operate tier-lift truck or use handtruck to move, convey, or hoist shipments from shipping-and-receiving platform to storage or work area. May direct others in preparing outgoing and receiving incoming shipments. May perform only shipping or receiving activities and be known as Shipping Clerk (clerical) or Receiving Clerk (clerical). May be designated according to specialty as Freight Clerk (clerical); Reshipping Clerk (clerical). May receive damaged or defective goods returned to establishment and be designated Returned-Goods Receiving Clerk (clerical). May receive unsold products returned by DRIVER, SALES ROUTE (retail trade; wholesale tr.) 292.353-010 and be designated Route Returner (clerical).
GOE: 05.09.01 STRENGTH: M GED: R3 M3 L2 SVP: 5 DLU: 88

222.387-054 SORTER-PRICER (nonprofit org.) alternate titles: pricer-sorter
Sorts used merchandise received from donors and appraises, prices, wraps, packs, and allocates merchandise for resale in retail outlets of nonprofit organization and maintains related records. Discards unsalable items or sets them aside for salvage or repair. May make minor repairs on damaged merchandise. May be designated according to merchandise sorted as Book Sorter (nonprofit org.); Clothing Sorter (nonprofit org.); Jewelry Sorter (nonprofit org.); Wares Sorter (nonprofit org.).
GOE: 05.09.03 STRENGTH: L GED: R3 M2 L2 SVP: 5 DLU: 77

222.387-058 STOCK CLERK (clerical) alternate titles: stock checker; stockroom clerk; storekeeper; storeroom clerk; storeroom keeper; stores clerk; supply clerk; supply-room clerk
Receives, stores, and issues equipment, material, supplies, merchandise, foodstuffs, or tools, and compiles stock records in stockroom, warehouse, or storage yard: Counts, sorts, or weighs incoming articles to verify receipt of items on requisition or invoices. Examines stock to verify conformance to specifications. Stores articles in bins, on floor, or on shelves, according to identifying information, such as style, size, or type of material. Fills orders or issues supplies from stock. Prepares periodic, special, or perpetual inventory of stock. Requisitions articles to fill incoming orders. Compiles reports on use of stock handling equipment, adjustments of inventory counts and stock records, spoilage of or damage to stock, location changes, and refusal of shipments. May mark identifying codes, figures, or letters on articles, using labeling equipment. May distribute stock among production workers, keeping records of material issued. May make adjustments or repairs to articles carried in stock. May determine methods of storage, identification, and stock location, considering temperature, humidity, height and weight limits, turnover, floor loading capacities, and required space. May cut stock to size to fill order. May move or transport material or supplies to other departments, using hand or industrial truck. May maintain inventory and other stock records, using computer terminal. May be designated according to material, equipment, or product stored as Camera-Store-

room Clerk (motion p'cture); Oil-House Attendant (clerical); Wire Stockkeeper (steel & rel.); or work location as Wine-Cellar Stock Clerk (hotel & rest.); or stage in manufacture of material or goods as Finished-Goods Stock Clerk (clerical); or container in which goods are stored as Drum-Stock Clerk (clerical). May receive and store incoming shipments of yarn, thread, or jute stock and verify color standards of shipment and be known as Color Standards Clerk (clerical). May be designated: Custodian, Blood Bank (medical ser.); Food Storeroom Clerk (hotel & rest.); Hogshead-Stock Clerk (tobacco); Material Stockkeeper, Yard (petrol. & gas); Mold Picker (rubber goods); Paint Stocker (aircraft mfg.); Pattern-Room Attendant (foundry); Printing-Plate (clerical); Refrigerator-Room Clerk (clerical). May receive, store, and sort unserviceable equipment and supplies for sale, disposal, or reclamation and be known as Salvage Clerk (clerical).
GOE: 05.09.01 STRENGTH: H GED: R3 M3 L2 SVP: 4 DLU: 88

222.387-062 STOREKEEPER (water trans.) alternate titles: cargo-gear mechanic
Receives, stores, and issues supplies and equipment and compiles records of supply transactions aboard ship: Verifies that supplies received are listed on requisitions and invoices. Stores supplies and equipment in storerooms. Issues supplies. Inventories supplies and equipment at end of each voyage. Compiles report of expenditures. May be designated according to department worked in as Storekeeper, Deck (water trans.); Storekeeper, Engineering (water trans.); Storekeeper, Steward (water trans.).
GOE: 05.09.01 STRENGTH: L GED: R3 M2 L2 SVP: 5 DLU: 77

222.387-066 SAMPLE CLERK (plastic prod.)
Receives and fills requisitions for samples of fabricated plastic products and inspects samples for conformance to company standards: Collects sample products from production lines and inspects samples for conformance to company standards, using specification sheets, gauges, and color standard chart. Stores selected samples in sample room, pending requests for samples from sales representatives and customers. Wraps and packs samples, upon request, for shipment. Maintains records of requests received and filled. Maintains perpetual inventory of samples and replenishes sample stock to maintain required levels.
GOE: 05.09.01 STRENGTH: L GED: R3 M3 L3 SVP: 5 DLU: 86

222.387-074 SHIPPING-AND-RECEIVING WEIGHER (clerical) alternate titles: weight recorder
Weighs and records weight of filled containers, cargo of loaded vehicles, or rolls of materials, such as cotton, sugarcane, paper, cloth, plastic, and tobacco, to keep receiving and shipping records: Reads scale dial to ascertain weight and records weight on ticket, product, or material; or subtracts tare from gross weight to obtain net weight of product or material; or inserts ticket into automatic scale recorder that prints weight on ticket. May convey objects to scale, using handtruck, and lift objects onto scale. May record information on weight ticket, such as grade and yardage. May be designated according to item weighed as Cloth Weigher (knitting); Garment Weigher (knitting); Roll Weigher (paper & pulp; paper goods; plastics-synth.); Tobacco Weigher (clerical). May signal YARD ENGINEER (r.r. trans.) 910.363-018 to move cars on and off scale and be designated Scaler (r.r. trans.). May weigh only incoming or outgoing materials or products and be designated Receiving Weigher (clerical); Shipping Weigher (cerical).
GOE: 05.09.01 STRENGTH: L GED: R3 M2 L2 SVP: 2 DLU: 80

222.485-010 MILK-RECEIVER, TANK TRUCK (dairy products) alternate titles: bulk intake worker
Tends pump that pumps incoming milk from tank trucks to storage tank, and computes and records volume of milk received: Weighs loaded truck on platform scale and records weight on record sheet. Dips and pours sample of milk from vent hole of truck into bottle for laboratory analysis. Tastes and takes temperature of milk, and records taste data and temperature reading. Connects plastic hose between sanitary valves of truck and storage tank, starts pump, and turns valves to transfer milk to tank. Stops pump when transfer is completed, reads milk-flow meter, and records volume pumped on record sheet. Disconnects plastic hose from truck tank and connects nozzle of tank-cleaning system to vent hole of tank. Starts equipment that automatically rinses, washes, and sanitizes interior of tank. Removes nozzle and seals vent hole. Washes exterior of truck and pumping equipment, using brushes, detergent solution, and water hose. Weighs empty truck and records weight. Computes difference between loaded and unloaded weights of truck to verify accuracy of meter.
GOE: 05.09.01 STRENGTH: M GED: R3 M2 L2 SVP: 3 DLU: 77

222.487-010 CHECKER, BAKERY PRODUCTS (bakery products) alternate titles: order filler, bakery products
Loads racks with bakery products to prepare orders for shipping, according to products available and following order slips: Adjusts amount of products going to routes according to supply and route-return records of DRIVER, SALES ROUTE (retail trade; wholesale tr.) 292.353-010. Loads products onto tiered racks and pushes racks to loading area. Records adjustments on route slips.
GOE: 05.09.01 STRENGTH: H GED: R2 M2 L2 SVP: 2 DLU: 78

222.487-014 ORDER FILLER (retail trade; wholesale tr.)
Fills customers' mail and telephone orders and marks price of merchandise on order form: Reads order to ascertain catalog number, size, color, and quantity of merchandise. Obtains merchandise from bins or shelves. Computes price of each group of items. Places merchandise on conveyor leading to wrapping area.

GOE: 05.09.01 STRENGTH: L GED: R3 M2 L2 SVP: 3 DLU: 77

222.567-010 GRAIN ELEVATOR CLERK (beverage; grain-feed mills) alternate titles: grain weigher

Records data pertaining to receiving, storing, and shipping of grain at grain elevators: Examines bin slips or track list to determine type, destination, and estimated weight of railroad car. Signals workers to dump or load cars, using bell, light, or telephone. Pulls lever to open slide gate on storage hopper to dump grain into scale hopper. Weighs grain and inserts ticket into automatic recorder on scale that stamps weight on ticket. Notifies government inspector to examine beam scale balance and stamped ticket. Records weight, description, and destination of grain shipped and received. Keeps charts indicating location and contents of storage tanks. Assigns workers to jobs according to work schedules, and reviews timecards. Grades and weighs grain samples, using hand graders and scales, and records results. Reads thermometers on control panel to ascertain grain temperatures at various levels in storage tank. May start conveyors, select flow pipes, set trippers, and select storage tanks to convey grain into storage or to loading department.
GOE: 05.09.01 STRENGTH: L GED: R3 M2 L2 SVP: 4 DLU: 77

222.567-014 SHIP RUNNER (water trans.) alternate titles: floor runner; runner

Determines location for merchandise on dock preparatory to being stowed on ship or transported to receivers: Inspects freight to determine amount of dock space freight will occupy. Directs movement and disposition of freight on dock. Marks destination of outgoing freight in large letters on dock, using chalk. Records deliveries in record book.
GOE: 05.09.01 STRENGTH: L GED: R3 M2 L2 SVP: 4 DLU: 77

222.567-018 SLOT-TAG INSERTER (clerical)

Inserts address tags into slots (holders) of mailsacks used for bulk mailing of subscription magazines and catalogs: Receives and deposits, in mailsacks, stacked or tied bundles of magazines addressed to same city or state. Selects printed destination tag from labeled compartment of wall rack, and inserts tag into metal holder attached to mail bag. Marks tag indicating to postal employees whether magazines in mailsack are all addressed to one city or to various cities within same state. Notifies co-worker to tie, lock, and remove filled sacks. Handwrites mail slot-tags when printed tags are not supplied for specified destination area, referring to list of postal terminals.
GOE: 07.07.02 STRENGTH: L GED: R2 M2 L2 SVP: 2 DLU: 77

222.585-010 MILK RECEIVER (dairy products) alternate titles: can intake worker

Dumps, weighs, and records weight of incoming milk received in milk cans by dairy, and tends washing machine that sterilizes empty cans: Presses switch to activate conveyor of can washing machine and turns valves to admit steam and water to machine. Presses switch to activate conveyor that moves individual producer's milk cans from unloading dock to dumping station. Removes cover from each can, smells milk to detect sourness, and tilts can to dump milk into weigh tank. Places emptied cans and covers on conveyor of washing machine. Reads scale and records total weight of milk in producer's shipment and identification number of producer on record sheet. Dips and pours sample of producer's milk from weigh tank into bottle for laboratory analysis. Pulls lever to open valve and empty weigh tank. Cleans and lubricates washing machine and conveyors.
GOE: 05.09.01 STRENGTH: H GED: R3 M2 L2 SVP: 3 DLU: 77

222.587-014 BRAILLE-AND-TALKING BOOKS CLERK (library)

Prepares braille and talking books for mailing to blind library patrons and receives books returned by patrons: Stamps issue date on book card to maintain record of location of borrowed books. Stamps due date on issue card and inserts card and return mailing label in book pocket. Places books in mailing container and affixes address label to container, securing container with straps for mailing. Receives and examines returned books for damage, such as torn paper and scratched record surfaces. Stamps return date on book card. Shelves returned books alphabetically by author's name or by title.
GOE: 07.05.04 STRENGTH: L GED: R3 M2 L3 SVP: 3 DLU: 77

222.587-018 DISTRIBUTING CLERK (clerical) alternate titles: packing-and-shipping clerk; publications-distribution clerk

Assembles and routes various types of printed material: Assembles specified number of forms, manuals, or circulars for each addressee as indicated by distribution tables or instructions. Wraps, ties, or places material in envelopes, boxes, or other containers. Stamps, types, or writes addresses on packaged materials. Forwards packages by mail, messenger, or through message center. Keeps records of materials sent. May requisition and store materials to maintain stock [STOCK CLERK (clerical)].
GOE: 07.07.02 STRENGTH: L GED: R3 M2 L3 SVP: 3 DLU: 77

222.587-022 KITCHEN CLERK (hotel & rest.) alternate titles: storeroom food-checker

Verifies quantity and quality of foodstuffs issued to kitchen from storeroom. Weighs and measures foodstuffs to verify quantity received. Oversees distribution of all foodstuffs. Prepares inventory of foodstuffs on hand in kitchen.
GOE: 05.09.03 STRENGTH: M GED: R3 M2 L2 SVP: 4 DLU: 77

222.587-026 LABORATORY CLERK (clerical)

Keeps records of chemicals, apparatus, and samples, such as coal, ash, and oil, received for testing in control laboratory. Weighs and prepares for shipment chemical supplies furnished by laboratory. Cleans glassware and other laboratory apparatus, and salvages sample bottles or containers for reuse. Returns unused chemicals to designated cabinets and cleans work area, using mop.
GOE: 05.09.01 STRENGTH: L GED: R3 M2 L2 SVP: 3 DLU: 77

222.587-030 MAILER (print. & pub.)

Mails or dispatches newspapers, periodicals, envelopes, cartons, or other bulk printed matter by performing any combination of following duties: Wraps or bundles printed matter by hand or using tying machine. Addresses bundle or wrapped printed matter by hand or stamps, tags, or labels them according to mailing lists and dispatching orders, using stencils and stamping machine. Sorts bundles according to zip code and places bundles to be mailed in specified mail bags. Stacks bundles for shipment and loads and unloads bundles onto and from trucks and conveyors. Files and corrects stencils. Counts and records number of bundles and copies handled. May keep card record distribution file of units mailed or dispatched to subscribers and dealers.
GOE: 05.09.01 STRENGTH: L GED: R2 M2 L2 SVP: 3 DLU: 77

222.587-032 MAILER APPRENTICE (print. & pub.)

Performs duties as described under APPRENTICE (any industry) Master Title.
GOE: 05.09.01 STRENGTH: L GED: R2 M2 L2 SVP: 3 DLU: 77

222.587-034 ROUTE-DELIVERY CLERK (clerical)

Prepares itemized delivery sheet for items of merchandise to be delivered by truck drivers, grouping and routing deliveries according to designated districts: Copies information, such as name, address of consignee, type of merchandise, number of pieces, and mailing designation, from records onto delivery sheet. Locates and selects merchandise and verifies against delivery sheet specifications. May arrange for unloading of merchandise from freight cars, transport trucks, or ships, into consignees' trucks. May keep records of and arrange for storage of undelivered merchandise.
GOE: 07.05.04 STRENGTH: L GED: R2 M2 L2 SVP: 3 DLU: 77

222.587-038 ROUTER (clerical) alternate titles: dispatcher; marker, delivery; routing clerk

Stamps, stencils, letters, or tags packages, boxes, or lots of merchandise to indicate delivery routes. Reads addresses on articles and determines route, using standard charts.
GOE: 07.07.02 STRENGTH: L GED: R2 M1 L2 SVP: 2 DLU: 77

222.587-042 SAMPLER, WOOL (wholesale tr.)

Records wool lot numbers and forwards samples to wool-buying house: Observes manner in which sample is drilled from sacks to ensure representative sample. Records lot number from which sample is taken. Packs and forwards samples to wool-buying house.
GOE: 05.09.03 STRENGTH: L GED: R2 M2 L2 SVP: 3 DLU: 77

222.587-046 STACKER (leather prod.) alternate titles: bundler

Counts novelty case parts to verify amount specified on work ticket and stacks and bundles parts prior to spraying. May burn off feather edges from bundled leather parts, using gas torch.
GOE: 05.09.03 STRENGTH: M GED: R2 M2 L1 SVP: 2 DLU: 77

222.587-050 SWATCH CLERK (garment)

Collects cloth samples (swatches) from cutting rooms and marks each lot to identify webs (bolts) of cloth from which samples were cut. Files and keeps inventory of swatch cards that are used to show prospective customers available fabrics. Mails swatches to customers on request. Checks swatch cards prepared by outside firm to ensure conformance to original order.
GOE: 05.09.03 STRENGTH: L GED: R2 M2 L2 SVP: 2 DLU: 77

222.587-054 TRANSFORMER-STOCK CLERK (utilities)

Receives, stores, and issues transformers used in electric power system: Moves new transformers to storage space, using hoist. Drains oil from used transformers. Starts motor-driven pump which forces used oil through filtering machine and into storage tank. Selects type and size of transformer to fill requisition. Fills oil container of transformers to be issued with new or reclaimed oil. Hoists transformers onto truck for delivery. Keeps stock records.
GOE: 05.09.01 STRENGTH: M GED: R3 M2 L2 SVP: 3 DLU: 77

222.587-058 VAULT WORKER (business ser.)

Keeps records of, sorts, and routes sealed money bags received at and dispatched from vault of armored car firm: Receives bags and signs routing slip to acknowledge receipt. Sorts bags according to delivery routes. Records data, such as origin, routing, and destination of bags. Delivers bags to ARMORED-CAR GUARD (business ser.) for loading onto truck and verifies that guard has signed routing slip. Submits logs and routing slips to VAULT CASHIER (business ser.) for review.
GOE: 07.05.04 STRENGTH: M GED: R3 M2 L2 SVP: 3 DLU: 77

222.684-010 MEAT CLERK (retail trade)

Receives, stores, and grinds meats in retail establishment: Unloads fresh, cured, and boxed meats and poultry from delivery truck and transports them to storage room on conveyor and with handtruck. Counts and weighs incoming articles and compares results against invoice. Examines meats in storage and rotates meats to avoid aging. Cuts meat into small pieces suitable for grinding, and grinds for use as hamburgers, meat loaf, and sausage, using powered grinding machine. Cleans grinder, meat containers, and storage room with water hose and broom. May take meat orders from customers.

GOE: 05.09.01 STRENGTH: M GED: R2 M1 L1 SVP: 2 DLU: 77

222.687-010   CHECKER I (clerical)
Verifies quantities, quality, condition, value, and type of articles purchased, sold, or produced against records or reports. May sort data or items into predetermined sequence or groups. May record items verified. May be designated according to type of establishment as Warehouse Checker (clerical).
GOE: 07.07.02 STRENGTH: L GED: R2 M2 L2 SVP: 2 DLU: 80

222.687-014   GARMENT SORTER (garment)
Sorts finished garments, such as shirts, dresses, and pajamas, according to lot and size numbers recorded on tags and labels attached to garments. May fold and package garments in boxes and bags. May iron garments prior to folding [PRESSER, HAND (any industry)]. May be designated according to garment sorted as Shirt Sorter (garment).
GOE: 06.03.02 STRENGTH: L GED: R2 M2 L1 SVP: 2 DLU: 77

222.687-018   RECEIVING CHECKER (clerical) alternate titles: checking clerk; order checker; receiving inspector; unloading checker
Counts, measures, or weighs articles to verify contents of shipments against bills of lading, invoices, or storage receipts. May examine articles for defects and sort articles according to extent of defect. May attach identification data onto article. May record factors causing goods to be returned. May unload and unpack incoming shipments.
GOE: 05.09.03 STRENGTH: M GED: R3 M2 L2 SVP: 3 DLU: 80

222.687-022   ROUTING CLERK (clerical) alternate titles: route clerk; router
Sorts bundles, boxes, or lots of articles for delivery: Reads delivery or route numbers marked on articles or delivery slips, or determines locations of addresses indicated on delivery slips, using charts. Places or stacks articles in bins designated according to route, driver, or type. May be designated according to work station as Conveyor Belt Package Sorter (retail trade). May sort sacks of mail and be known as Mail Sorter (r.r. trans.).
GOE: 07.07.02 STRENGTH: L GED: R2 M2 L2 SVP: 2 DLU: 77

222.687-026   SAMPLE DISPLAY PREPARER (knitting)
Fills orders for sample hose for sales personnel and customers: Selects hose, pantyhose, surgical hose, and socks according to specifications and examines hose for defects. Pairs hose according to size, color, and length. Attaches label designating size, color, and style to top of hose. Folds and packs hose in boxes. Records name of customer or seller, size, style, color, and quantity of hose, and shipping date. May stamp identifying information on hose, using transfer paper and stamping iron.
GOE: 05.09.01 STRENGTH: L GED: R3 M2 L2 SVP: 4 DLU: 81

222.687-030   SHIPPING CHECKER (clerical) alternate titles: loading checker; order checker; packing checker
Verifies quantity, quality, labeling, and addressing of products and items of merchandise ready for shipment at manufacturing or commercial establishment: Counts, weighs, measures, or examines packaging and contents of items for conformance to company specifications. Affixes postage on packages, using postal meter. Compares items packed with customer's order and other identifying data. May keep records on number of baskets of tobacco sold and removed from auction warehouse and be designated Tobacco-Checkout Clerk (wholesale tr.). May oversee crew of workers engaged in loading and bracing material in railroad cars or trucks.
GOE: 05.09.01 STRENGTH: L GED: R3 M3 L2 SVP: 4 DLU: 77

222.687-034   STUBBER (retail trade)
Removes sales-slip stubs from packages at loading dock and sorts stubs, according to size of package or type of merchandise, to keep record of store deliveries. Returns illegibly addressed or mutilated packages for rewrapping or readdressing. Totals number of stubs at end of day and prepares report.
GOE: 05.09.03 STRENGTH: M GED: R2 M2 L2 SVP: 2 DLU: 77

222.687-038   TOOTH CLERK (protective dev.)
Selects false teeth used to make dental plates: Selects teeth of color specified and according to shape of jaw. Matches teeth with teeth of mold made by DENTIST (medical ser.) 072.101-010 preparatory to assembly of dentures by DENTAL-LABORATORY TECHNICIAN (protective dev.) 712.381-018.
GOE: 05.12.19 STRENGTH: S GED: R3 M2 L2 SVP: 4 DLU: 77

222.687-042   INSPECTOR, HANDBAG FRAMES (leather prod.) alternate titles: frame opener
Inspects metal or plastic frames used in manufacture of women's handbags: Removes frames from packing case and verifies order with invoice and shipping order. Examines frames for defects, such as scratches, discolorations, or missing hinge pins. Opens and closes frames to test frame construction and ease of fastening. Discards defective frames for repair or return to manufacturer. Compiles inventory of acceptable and unacceptable frames received.
GOE: 06.03.02 STRENGTH: L GED: R2 M2 L2 SVP: 2 DLU: 86

222.687-046   PROTECTIVE-CLOTHING ISSUER (chemical)
Sorts and issues protective clothing and related supplies to workers: Receives delivery of items such as coveralls, underwear, gloves, and towels from laundry, checks items against list to verify completeness of delivery, and sorts items by type and size. Opens workers' lockers, using master key, and places clean items in locker. Removes, sorts, and counts soiled items stored in hamper. Disposes of worn items. Maintains inventory of clean laundry received and issued.

GOE: 07.07.02 STRENGTH: L GED: R2 M2 L2 SVP: 2 DLU: 86

229   PRODUCTION AND STOCK CLERKS AND RELATED OCCUPATIONS, N.E.C.

This group includes occupations, not elsewhere classified, concerned with maintaining production records, expediting flow of work and materials, and receiving, storing, shipping, issuing, requisitioning, and accounting for materials and goods. Similar occupations, not elsewhere classified, concerned primarily with loading and moving materials and products are found in Group 929.

229.137-010   SACK-DEPARTMENT SUPERVISOR (grain-feed mills)
Supervises and coordinates activities of workers engaged in receiving, storing, and distributing such grain and feed mill supplies as bags, cartons, sacks, and twine, and in cleaning, sorting, and repairing sacks. Schedules distribution of sacks, bags, and other supplies to packing machines according to packing orders. Performs duties as described under SUPERVISOR (any industry) Master Title.
GOE: 05.09.01 STRENGTH: L GED: R4 M3 L2 SVP: 6 DLU: 77

229.137-014   YARD SUPERVISOR (construction)
Supervises and coordinates activities of workers engaged in receiving, storing, issuing, and maintaining machines, equipment, materials, and supplies in construction storage building or yard: Dispatches materials and equipment to construction sites. May requisition materials and supplies. May operate crane to move items in yard. May repair machines and equipment. May supervise workers engaged in fabricating metal structural members and concrete forms and products used on construction projects. Performs other duties as described under SUPERVISOR (any industry) Master Title.
GOE: 05.09.02 STRENGTH: L GED: R4 M3 L4 SVP: 7 DLU: 77

229.267-010   PARTS CATALOGER (any industry) alternate titles: engineering clerk; parts data writer; technical release analyst
Reviews blueprints, change orders, and other engineering data to prepare and maintain master parts listings, catalogs, and other documentation used for material requisitioning and disbursement, inventory control, production planning, scheduling, and related manufacturing activities: Examines engineering drawings, blueprints, orders, and other documentation for conformance to established criteria regarding materials, parts, and equipment specified, and initiates requests for changes to ensure compliance with standards. Reviews engineering data and compiles list of materials, parts, and equipment required for manufacturing product. Prepares and maintains manual or computerized record systems providing detailed parts information, such as complete description, quantities, operational characteristics, functions, and specifications [PARTS LISTER (electron. comp.) 229.367-014]. Prepares and updates parts catalogs, manuals, and related documentation. Releases parts data and documentation to authorized departments and organizations. May determine material requirements for fabricating parts, considering size, cutting, and forming involved. May assist in determining adequate spare parts inventory requirements for customers.
GOE: 05.03.02 STRENGTH: S GED: R4 M3 L4 SVP: 6 DLU: 88

229.367-010   FIELD RECORDER (utilities) alternate titles: field clerk
Maintains records of equipment, materials, and supplies used in construction, installation, and maintenance of electric-power distribution lines and facilities: Observes operations of field crew, and records data, such as equipment installed or replaced, materials and supplies used, and labor costs. Prepares sketches or enters on drawing type of equipment installed and location of equipment in order that circuit maps and blueprints can be corrected. Prepares and attaches identification tags to equipment, such as transformers and switches removed from service for repair or storage. Prepares and nails metal tags on pole indicating circuit and station in transmission or distribution line. Maintains inventory of equipment in field truck and prepares requisitions for replacement parts, materials, and supplies.
GOE: 05.09.02 STRENGTH: L GED: R3 M3 L3 SVP: 4 DLU: 77

229.367-014   PARTS LISTER (electron. comp.)
Compiles master lists of replaceable parts in electronic equipment to ensure inventories and to provide government and other customers with information on source of parts: Reads master bill of materials to obtain complete list of parts used in product. Identifies each item by part number, manufacturer, and brief description. Contacts purchasing department, engineering department, and vendor representatives regarding procurement and availability of specially designed components. May operate computer to access and compile master lists.
GOE: 05.09.01 STRENGTH: L GED: R3 M3 L3 SVP: 4 DLU: 88

229.387-010   MATERIAL LISTER (construction)
Reviews blueprint and material specifications to determine amount, size, kind, grade, and type of delivery of materials for building construction projects. May list suppliers and bid prices for each type of material used. May prepare material schedules showing promised delivery data for each type of material. May keep records of materials received and used on project.
GOE: 05.03.02 STRENGTH: S GED: R4 M3 L4 SVP: 5 DLU: 77

229.387-014   TANK CALIBRATOR (business ser.)
Measures tanks of varying sizes and shapes to determine incremental and total liquid capacities, using one or both of following methods: (1) Extends tape to encircle tanks at specified level to measure circumference. Lowers tape to measure outside and inside heights at specified places. Measures width, height,

and thickness of projections, such as flanges, boltheads, shell plate, butt-welded joint, rivets, overflows, and floating roofs, using tapes, calipers, and straight-edge. Records measurements and calculates total and incremental tank capacities to prepare gauging tables, following formulas. (2) Measures tank, using liquid calibration methods. Turns valves to admit measured quantities of liquid from calibrated container into tank being calibrated. Lowers tape into tank at specified places and records measurements. Repeats process to obtain measurements at various levels. Takes temperature, samples, and records type of calibration liquid, using thermometer and sample container. Prepares gauging tables, following formulas. May prepare sketches and drawings of tanks and tank projections.
GOE: 05.09.03 STRENGTH: M GED: R4 M4 L3 SVP: 5 DLU: 77

229.587-010 GREIGE-GOODS MARKER (textile) alternate titles: marker, hand
Assigns identifying numbers to cuts of greige cloth received for finishing. Records numbers on cloth and on lot sheet to ensure return of cloth to customer after finishing. May record numbers on tag or ticket and attach to cloth. May cut open bundles of cloth, using knife, and verify that cloth meets specifications on customer order.
GOE: 05.09.03 STRENGTH: L GED: R2 M1 L2 SVP: 2 DLU: 77

229.587-014 QUALITY-CONTROL CLERK (pharmaceut.)
Stores samples of materials tested and records test result data for product stability study program: Files bottles of raw materials used in pharmaceutical compounding, samples of purchased and plant-processed intermediate products, lot control samples, and samples of finished pharmaceutical batches. Stores samples of finished products in cartons labeled with type of product (cream, liquid, tablet) and records identifying data in alphabetical index listing. Keeps tickler file for withdrawal of samples for testing. Withdraws samples on dates indicated and takes them to laboratory. Keeps file of product stability study control charts. Records on charts test result data, such as appearance, color, and melting point.
GOE: 07.05.03 STRENGTH: L GED: R3 M2 L3 SVP: 3 DLU: 77

229.587-018 TICKETER (textile) alternate titles: labeler; tagger; ticket stamper
Records or stamps information, such as price, size, style, color, and inspection results on tags, tickets, and labels, using rubber stamp or writing instrument. Pastes, staples, sews, or otherwise fastens tickets, tags, labels, or shipping documents to cloth or carpeting. May compute number of rolls of cloth to be produced from each lot to determine required number of tickets, tags, or labels. May trim excess threads from selvage (finished edge) of cloth, using scissors or shears. May keep records of production, returned goods, and personnel transactions.
GOE: 05.09.03 STRENGTH: L GED: R2 M1 L2 SVP: 2 DLU: 77

229.687-010 SAMPLE CHECKER (carpet & rug; textile)
Examines cloth samples mounted in books or tagged to verify that samples are neatly mounted and are identical in color, weave, and hand with swatch previously approved by customer. Compares style number marked on sample with that on customer's order and on standard swatch. May assemble cards or books for shipment to sales department.
GOE: 05.09.03 STRENGTH: L GED: R3 M1 L2 SVP: 3 DLU: 77

23 INFORMATION AND MESSAGE DISTRIBUTION OCCUPATIONS

This division includes occupations concerned with the distribution of information and messages by direct personal or telephone contact, involving such activities as delivering mail, relaying messages by telephone or telegraph equipment, arranging travel accommodations, and directing visitors at reception points.

230 HAND DELIVERY AND DISTRIBUTION OCCUPATIONS

This group includes occupations concerned with the hand delivery or distribution of mail, messages, packages, telephone directories, product samples, and handbills to the public or to industrial or commercial establishments, generally involving outside travel on foot or by bicycle or motor vehicle. Occupations concerned with the delivery of goods by truck involving collection of payment for goods delivered or delivery of goods to a distribution site are included in Groups 905 and 906, or in Group 292 if concerned with the delivery and sale of products over an established route. Occupations concerned with the delivery of messages and documents or the distribution of office supplies within an establishment are included in Group 239.

230.137-010 SUPERVISOR, ADVERTISING-MATERIAL DISTRIBUTORS (business ser.)
Supervises and coordinates activities of crew of workers engaged in distributing sample merchandise, handbills, or coupons: Issues advertising material to ADVERTISING-MATERIAL DISTRIBUTORS (any industry) and instructs them in methods of distribution. Assigns workers to specified routes and tours area to ensure coverage of assigned territory. Records information, such as area covered, material distributed, and working hours. May hire crewmembers. Performs other duties as described under SUPERVISOR (clerical) Master Title.

GOE: 07.07.02 STRENGTH: L GED: R4 M2 L4 SVP: 6 DLU: 77

230.137-014 SUPERVISOR, DELIVERY DEPARTMENT (tel. & tel.)
Supervises and coordinates activities of workers engaged in telegram and package pickup and delivery service of telegraph office: Trains and supervises TELEGRAM MESSENGERS (tel. & tel.). Assigns pickup and delivery routes on basis of knowledge of area served. May keep time and activity records of department employees. May train and supervise TELEGRAPH-SERVICE RATERS (tel. & tel.). Performs other duties as described under SUPERVISOR (clerical) Master Title.
GOE: 07.07.02 STRENGTH: L GED: R4 M2 L3 SVP: 6 DLU: 77

230.137-018 SUPERVISOR, MAIL CARRIERS (government ser.)
Supervises and coordinates activities of workers engaged in collecting, sorting, and delivering mail: Receives, investigates, and initiates action on patron's complaints. May analyze carrier routes and recommend changes of route boundaries to regulate amount of mail being delivered. Performs other duties as described under SUPERVISOR (clerical) Master Title.
GOE: 07.05.04 STRENGTH: L GED: R4 M3 L4 SVP: 6 DLU: 77

230.363-010 RURAL MAIL CARRIER (government ser.)
Delivers mail along established route outside town or city corporate limits: Sorts mail for delivery according to location along route. Delivers mail over route by motor vehicle. Picks up outgoing mail, sells stamps, and issues money orders.
GOE: 07.05.04 STRENGTH: M GED: R3 M3 L2 SVP: 2 DLU: 86

230.367-010 MAIL CARRIER (government ser.) alternate titles: city carrier; letter carrier
Sorts mail for delivery and delivers mail on established route: Inserts mail into slots of mail rack to sort for delivery. Delivers mail to residences and business establishments along route. Completes delivery forms, collects charges, and obtains signature on receipts for delivery of specified types of mail. Enters changes of address in route book and re-addresses mail to be forwarded. May drive vehicle over established route. May deliver specialized types of mail and be designated Parcel-Post Carrier (government ser.); Special-Delivery Carrier (government ser.).
GOE: 07.05.04 STRENGTH: M GED: R3 M2 L3 SVP: 4 DLU: 86

230.647-010 SINGING MESSENGER (business ser.)
Performs song and dance routines to deliver messages and entertain specified individuals for customers of message delivery service: Practices song and dance routines with experienced worker to become familiar with routines offered by service. Receives customer instructions from dispatcher, selects standard message supplied by service, or records customer's personalized message on form, using typewriter or pen. Applies theatrical makeup and dresses in costume, when necessary, and travels to destination, using vehicle, maps, and customer instructions. Locates recipient of message and performs routine, basing time frame of routine on recipient's reaction. May play musical instruments, such as kazoo or finger cymbals, during routine. May present gift items at conclusion of performance.
GOE: 07.07.02 STRENGTH: L GED: R3 M2 L3 SVP: 2 DLU: 86

230.663-010 DELIVERER, OUTSIDE (clerical) alternate titles: courier; messenger
Delivers messages, telegrams, documents, packages, and other items to business establishments and private homes, traveling on foot or by bicycle, motorcycle, automobile, or public conveyance. May keep log of items received and delivered. May obtain receipts or payment for articles delivered. May service vehicle driven, such as checking fluid levels and replenishing fuel. May be designated according to item delivered, as Telegram Messenger (tel. & tel.).
GOE: 07.07.02 STRENGTH: L GED: R2 M1 L2 SVP: 2 DLU: 88

230.667-014 TELEPHONE-DIRECTORY DELIVERER (business ser.) alternate titles: phone-book deliverer
Delivers telephone directories to residences and business establishments, on foot: Receives supply of directories from TELEPHONE-DIRECTORY-DISTRIBUTOR DRIVER (business ser.) or from other individual at central distribution point or from vehicle parked in distribution area, places books on handtruck or in sacks or other containers, and delivers books, following verbal instructions or address list. May pick up outdated directories for return for salvage purposes.
GOE: 07.07.02 STRENGTH: H GED: R1 M1 L1 SVP: 1 DLU: 77

230.687-010 ADVERTISING-MATERIAL DISTRIBUTOR (any industry) alternate titles: distributor, advertising material
Distributes advertising material, such as merchandise samples, handbills, and coupons, from house to house, to business establishments, or to persons on street, following oral instructions, street maps, or address lists. May be designated according to type of advertising material distributed as Handbill Distributor (any industry); Pamphlet Distributor (any industry); Sample Distributor (any industry).
GOE: 07.07.02 STRENGTH: L GED: R1 M1 L1 SVP: 2 DLU: 77

235 TELEPHONE OPERATORS

This group includes occupations concerned with operating telephone switchboards to relay incoming and interoffice calls, make connections with outside

205

lines for outgoing calls, establish connections between subscribers, supply information, and calculate long-distance charges.

235.132-010 CENTRAL-OFFICE-OPERATOR SUPERVISOR (tel. & tel.)

Supervises and coordinates activities of CENTRAL-OFFICE OPERATORS (tel. & tel.) engaged in operating telephone switchboards: Conducts on-the-job training for inexperienced operators. Assists operators in placing unusual types of calls. May discuss service problems directly with customers. Performs other duties as described under SUPERVISOR (clerical) Master Title.
GOE: 07.04.06 STRENGTH: L GED: R4 M2 L3 SVP: 6 DLU: 77

235.132-014 COMMUNICATION-CENTER COORDINATOR (air trans.)

Supervises and coordinates activities of airport terminal personnel engaged in receiving and issuing communications on telephone, internal radio, and public-address system, and monitoring electronic equipment. Receives telephone or radio requests for repair of electronic equipment, such as elevator-monitoring devices, and relays requests to maintenance department. Telephones key personnel in emergencies, such as bomb threats. Records activities in logs. Performs other duties as described under SUPERVISOR (clerical) Master Title.
GOE: 07.04.05 STRENGTH: S GED: R4 M3 L4 SVP: 5 DLU: 77

235.137-010 TELEPHONE OPERATOR, CHIEF (clerical)

Supervises and coordinates activities of TELEPHONE OPERATORS (clerical) 235.662-022 in telephone or telegraph office or in industrial establishment: Notifies telephone company maintenance department of switchboard operational difficulties reported by operators. Prepares work schedules and assigns switchboard positions. Trains new employees and keeps attendance records. Maintains record of incoming and outgoing long-distance and tie line calls, noting duration and time of calls. Keeps record of employees' personal calls and forwards record to department head for collection. Compiles plant phone directory, arranges for distribution to designated personnel, and keeps record of directories distributed. Performs other duties as described under SUPERVISOR (clerical) Master Title. May relieve operators. May supervise operators of telephone answering and message service and be designated Supervisor, Telephone-Answering-Service (business ser.).
GOE: 07.04.06 STRENGTH: S GED: R4 M3 L4 SVP: 6 DLU: 78

235.222-010 PRIVATE-BRANCH-EXCHANGE SERVICE ADVISER (tel. & tel.)

Conducts training classes in operation of switchboard and teletype equipment: Explains mechanical construction and operation of switchboards and demonstrates procedures for receiving and completing incoming and interoffice calls. Observes operators handling calls and recommends methods to improve service. Analyzes traffic loads and conducts studies to determine equipment needs. Keeps records of equipment in subscribers' establishments.
GOE: 07.04.05 STRENGTH: L GED: R4 M2 L4 SVP: 6 DLU: 77

235.387-010 RADIO-MESSAGE ROUTER (tel. & tel.)

Classifies messages at central-office exchange and routes messages for transmission: Places routing information on message, such as method of transmission, route, and operator's code. Places message in pneumatic tube or basket for delivery to operator.
GOE: 07.05.04 STRENGTH: S GED: R3 M1 L3 SVP: 5 DLU: 77

235.462-010 CENTRAL-OFFICE OPERATOR (tel. & tel.) alternate titles: switchboard operator; telephone operator

Operates telephone switchboard to establish or assist customers in establishing local or long-distance telephone connections: Observes signal light on switchboard, plugs cords into trunk-jack, and dials or presses button to make connections. Inserts tickets in calculagraph (time-stamping device) to record time of toll calls. Consults charts to determine charges for pay-telephone calls, and requests coin deposits for calls. May give information regarding subscribers' telephone numbers [DIRECTORY-ASSISTANCE OPERATOR (tel. & tel.)]. Calculates and quotes charges on long-distance calls. May make long-distance connections and be designated Long-Distance Operator (tel. & tel.).
GOE: 07.04.06 STRENGTH: L GED: R3 M1 L3 SVP: 3 DLU: 77

235.562-010 CLERK, ROUTE (tel. & tel.)

Sorts and routes telegrams received by pickup and delivery section of telegraph office: Folds and places messages in envelopes for delivery. Receives requests for message pickup within area served by telegraph office. Routes messages to customers within city via private telegraph wire or telephone, and to customers in distant cities via telegraphic-typewriter or Morse telegraphy. Reads maps to sort messages and pick-up requests into routes. Dispatches TELEGRAM MESSENGER (tel. & tel.). Receives and records remittances returned for messages picked up. Reads messages for errors.
GOE: 07.05.04 STRENGTH: S GED: R3 M2 L3 SVP: 4 DLU: 77

235.562-014 SWITCHBOARD OPERATOR, POLICE DISTRICT (government ser.)

Operates switchboard to receive and transmit police communications: Talks to police officers reporting from callboxes and records messages on special forms. Enters time of call and callbox number. Telephones for ambulances or fire-fighting equipment when requested. Routes messages for radio broadcast to DISPATCHER, RADIO (government ser.).
GOE: 07.04.05 STRENGTH: L GED: R3 M1 L2 SVP: 4 DLU: 77

235.662-010 COMMAND AND CONTROL SPECIALIST (military ser.)

Operates and monitors communication console to receive and relay command and control information or instructions: Observes signal light on communication console and presses switch to open or close communication channel. Receives communiques concerning such items as unknown aircraft, deployment of equipment and troops, or emergency situation. Records message and notifies designated personnel concerning communique, following manual procedures, or presses switch to facilitate direct communication between originator and appropriate action addressee. Relays information to originating source or specified individuals to initiate action to be taken.
GOE: 07.04.05 STRENGTH: S GED: R3 M3 L3 SVP: 5 DLU: 77

235.662-014 COMMUNICATION-CENTER OPERATOR (air trans.)

Operates airport authority communication systems and monitors electronic equipment alarms: Operates public address system to page passengers or visitors. Operates telephone switchboard to receive or place calls to and from terminal. Operates two-way internal radio system to communicate with departments. Operates terminal courtesy telephone system to communicate with passengers or visitors. Observes electronic monitoring panel to detect serious malfunction of elevators, escalators, shuttle train, fire alarms, emergency doors, heating, air-conditioning, or ventilating systems.
GOE: 07.04.05 STRENGTH: S GED: R3 M2 L3 SVP: 5 DLU: 77

235.662-018 DIRECTORY-ASSISTANCE OPERATOR (tel. & tel.)

Provides telephone information from cord or cordless central office switchboard: Plugs in headphones when signal light flashes on cord switchboard, or pushes switch keys on cordless switchboard to make connections. Refers to alphabetical or geographical reels or directories to answer questions and suggests alternate locations and spelling under which number could be listed. May type location and spelling of name on computer terminal keyboard, and scan directory or microfilm viewer to locate number. May keep record of calls received. May keep reels and directories up to date.
GOE: 07.04.06 STRENGTH: S GED: R3 M2 L3 SVP: 3 DLU: 77

235.662-022 TELEPHONE OPERATOR (clerical) alternate titles: control-board operator; pbx operator; private-branch-exchange operator; switchboard operator; telephone-switchboard operator

Operates cord or cordless switchboard to relay incoming, outgoing, and interoffice calls: Pushes switch keys on cordless switchboard to make connections and relay calls. Plugs cord of cord type equipment into switchboard jacks to make connections and relay calls. May supply information to callers and record messages. May keep record of calls placed and toll charges. May perform clerical duties, such as typing, proofreading, and sorting mail. May operate system of bells or buzzers to call individuals in establishment to phone. May receive visitors, obtain name and nature of business, and schedule appointments [RECEPTIONIST (clerical) 237.367-038].
GOE: 07.04.06 STRENGTH: S GED: R3 M2 L3 SVP: 3 DLU: 87

235.662-026 TELEPHONE-ANSWERING-SERVICE OPERATOR (business ser.) alternate titles: interceptor operator; telephone-interceptor operator

Operates cord or cordless switchboard to provide answering service for clients. Greets caller and announces name or phone number of client. Records and delivers messages, furnishes information, accepts orders, and relays calls. Places telephone calls at request of client and to locate client in emergencies. Date stamps and files messages.
GOE: 07.04.06 STRENGTH: S GED: R3 M2 L3 SVP: 3 DLU: 77

236 TELEGRAPH OPERATORS

This group includes occupations concerned with operating telegraph equipment to transmit and receive signals or messages, including transmitting train-delay reports, train orders, etc. Occupations concerning use of telegraphic typewriters are included in Group 203.

236.252-010 REPRESENTATIVE, PERSONAL SERVICE (tel. & tel.)

Visits agents, tie line customers, and private wire patrons to demonstrate to employees use and operation of telegraph equipment and facilities: Demonstrates use of telegraph equipment and operating procedures. Explains rates and company services. Consults with customers concerning communication needs and suggests methods of eliminating operational difficulties. Suggests modifications of customer's private wire switching equipment. Prepares written reports of services rendered to customers, including descriptions of difficulties encountered. Aids in development and preparation of operating procedures.
GOE: 05.02.06 STRENGTH: L GED: R5 M3 L5 SVP: 6 DLU: 77

236.562-010 TELEGRAPHER (r.r. trans.) alternate titles: telephoner; teletype-telegrapher

Operates telegraph key, Teletype machine, or talks over telephone to transmit and receive train orders and messages: Records time and date messages were received or transmitted. Operates Teletype machine to transmit messages and train orders. Reads messages received and marks for distribution. Informs TRAIN DISPATCHER (r.r. trans.) by telephone of departure of outbound trains from yard or terminal. Replaces rolls of Teletype paper in machine as required.
GOE: 07.04.05 STRENGTH: S GED: R4 M3 L3 SVP: 4 DLU: 77

236.562-014 TELEGRAPHER AGENT (r.r. trans.) alternate titles: station telegrapher

Transmits and receives messages, train orders, and car reports in Morse code, using manual or semiautomatic key: In small railroad station performs duties,

such as selling tickets and forwarding and receiving baggage and freight [BAG-GAGE-AND-MAIL AGENT (r.r. trans.); STATION AGENT (r.r. trans.) I]. May move controls to change block signals and semaphores.
GOE: 07.04.05 STRENGTH: S GED: R3 M2 L3 SVP: 5 DLU: 77

237 INFORMATION AND RECEPTION CLERKS

This group includes occupations primarily concerned with giving information to employers, customers, visitors, or the general public, inquiring in person, or by telephone, regarding such matters as activities of establishment, location of offices within firm, stock quotations, and credit status. It also includes scheduling appointments and keeping records of callers and nature of inquiries. Occupations primarily concerned with interviewing persons to elicit and record information on registrations or other records are found in Group 205.

237.137-010 SUPERVISOR, TELEPHONE INFORMATION (motor trans.)

Supervises and coordinates activities of workers engaged in giving bus service information, by telephone, to callers for motor transportation company: Confers with management and examines past activity records to project staffing, budget, and equipment requirements, performing duties as described under SUPERVISOR (clerical) Master Title. Issues oral and written instructions on schedule changes and rates to keep workers informed and maintain accuracy of information given to public. Monitors telephone conversations between workers and callers to evaluate technical accuracy. Reads telephone operator's meter to determine volume of calls handled and hourly total of lost calls to compile record for planning purposes. Conducts classroom and on-the-job training to maintain and improve service standards. Submits reports, as required, to provide information for accounting department.
GOE: 07.04.04 STRENGTH: S GED: R4 M3 L4 SVP: 7 DLU: 77

237.137-014 SUPERVISOR, TRAVEL-INFORMATION CENTER (government ser.)

Supervises and coordinates activities of workers engaged in greeting and welcoming motorists at State Highway Information Center: Provides information, such as directions, road conditions, and vehicular travel regulations. Provides maps, brochures, and pamphlets to assist motorist in locating points of interest or in reaching destination. Performs duties as described under SUPERVISOR (clerical) Master Title. May direct tourists to rest areas, camps, resorts, historical points, or other tourist attractions.
GOE: 07.04.04 STRENGTH: L GED: R4 M3 L4 SVP: 6 DLU: 77

237.267-010 INFORMATION CLERK, AUTOMOBILE CLUB (nonprofit org.)

Provides telephone inquirers with information concerning activities and programs of automobile club: Provides information on matters, such as traffic engineering and motor-vehicle safety, applicable motor vehicle laws, licensing regulations, automobile insurance and financing, and legal actions. Receives and records complaints on road conditions. Participates in traffic surveys. May specialize in assisting members file insurance claims for motor vehicle property damage and be designated Claims And Insurance Information Clerk, Automobile Club (nonprofit org.).
GOE: 07.04.04 STRENGTH: S GED: R4 M3 L4 SVP: 5 DLU: 77

237.367-010 APPOINTMENT CLERK (clerical) alternate titles: reception clerk

Schedules appointments with employer or other employees for clients or customers by mail, phone, or in person, and records time and date of appointment in appointment book. Indicates in appointment book when appointments have been filled or cancelled. May telephone or write clients to remind them of appointments. May receive payments for services, and record them in ledger. May receive callers [RECEPTIONIST (clerical)]. May operate switchboard [TELEPHONE OPERATOR (clerical)].
GOE: 07.04.04 STRENGTH: S GED: R3 M2 L3 SVP: 3 DLU: 77

237.367-014 CALL-OUT OPERATOR (business ser.; retail trade)

Compiles credit information, such as status of credit accounts, personal references, and bank accounts to fulfill subscribers' requests, using telephone. Copies information onto form to update information for credit record on file, or for computer input. Telephones subscriber to relay requested information or submits data obtained for typewritten report to subscriber.
GOE: 07.05.03 STRENGTH: S GED: R3 M2 L3 SVP: 2 DLU: 77

237.367-018 INFORMATION CLERK (motor trans.; r.r. trans.; water trans.) alternate titles: travel clerk

Provides travel information for bus or train patrons: Answers inquiries regarding departures, arrivals, stops, and destinations of scheduled buses or trains. Describes routes, services, and accommodations available. Furnishes patrons with timetables and travel literature. Computes and quotes rates for interline trips, group tours, and special discounts for children and military personnel, using rate tables.
GOE: 07.04.04 STRENGTH: L GED: R4 M2 L3 SVP: 2 DLU: 77

237.367-022 INFORMATION CLERK (clerical)

Answers inquiries from persons entering establishment: Provides information regarding activities conducted at establishment, and location of departments, offices, and employees within organization. Informs customer of location of store merchandise in retail establishment. Provides information concerning services,

such as laundry and valet services, in hotel. Receives and answers requests for information from company officials and employees. May call employees or officials to information desk to answer inquiries. May keep record of questions asked.
GOE: 07.04.04 STRENGTH: S GED: R4 M2 L3 SVP: 4 DLU: 86

237.367-026 LAND-LEASING EXAMINER (government ser.) alternate titles: land-lease-information clerk

Furnishes information to public concerning status of state-owned lands for lease, and assists applicants to file documents required to lease land: Answers public inquiries concerning types of land leases available. Furnishes current information concerning land classification, withdrawals from market, or mineral reservations. Assists applicant in completing required documents. Examines applications, transfers, and supporting documents for conformance with agency specifications. Processes documents, collects fees, and maintains history ledgers of state-owned land.
GOE: 07.04.04 STRENGTH: S GED: R4 M3 L4 SVP: 7 DLU: 77

237.367-030 MANAGER, TRAFFIC II (motor trans.)

Quotes freight rates and gives information on truck arrivals to trucking-transportation firm's customers. May investigate and settle claims against firm for damaged, short, or overcharged freight shipments [CUSTOMER-COMPLAINT CLERK (clerical)].
GOE: 07.04.04 STRENGTH: S GED: R3 M2 L2 SVP: 6 DLU: 77

237.367-034 PAY-STATION ATTENDANT (tel. & tel.)

Obtains telephone numbers at pay stations for persons with visual impairment, persons unfamiliar with local telephone exchanges, or others unable to secure satisfactory telephone service. Usually stationed at hotels, military bases, or similar places frequented by strangers. Contacts international operator or direct-dials to place international telephone calls, and collects toll from caller. Periodically verifies operating condition of telephones within facility and advises supervisor of location of malfunctioning equipment.
GOE: 09.04.02 STRENGTH: L GED: R3 M2 L3 SVP: 5 DLU: 77

237.367-038 RECEPTIONIST (clerical) alternate titles: reception clerk

Receives callers at establishment, determines nature of business, and directs callers to destination: Obtains caller's name and arranges for appointment with person called upon. Directs caller to destination and records name, time of call, nature of business, and person called upon. May operate PBX telephone console to receive incoming messages. May type memos, correspondence, reports, and other documents. May work in office of medical practitioner or in other health care facility and be designated Outpatient Receptionist (medical ser.) or Receptionist, Doctor's Office (medical ser.). May issue visitor's pass when required. May make future appointments and answer inquiries [INFORMATION CLERK (clerical) 237.367-022]. May perform variety of clerical duties [ADMINISTRATIVE CLERK (clerical) 219.362-010] and other duties pertinent to type of establishment. May collect and distribute mail and messages.
GOE: 07.04.04 STRENGTH: S GED: R3 M2 L3 SVP: 4 DLU: 88

237.367-042 REFERRAL-AND-INFORMATION AIDE (government ser.)

Receives callers and responds to complaints in person or by telephone for government agency: Questions callers to ascertain nature of complaints against government agency; records complaint on standard form; and routes form to appropriate department or office for action. Contacts department or office to which complaint was referred to determine disposition. Contacts complainant to verify data and follow-up on results of referral. Compiles complaint records, by category, department office, and disposition. Notifies supervisor of patterns of poor provision of service. Maintains up-to-date reference materials and files.
GOE: 07.04.02 STRENGTH: S GED: R3 M2 L3 SVP: 3 DLU: 77

237.367-046 TELEPHONE QUOTATION CLERK (financial) alternate titles: information clerk, brokerage; quote clerk; telephone-information clerk

Answers telephone calls from customers requesting current stock quotations and provides information posted on electronic quote board. Relays calls to REGISTERED REPRESENTATIVE (financial) 250.257-018 as requested by customer. May call customers to inform them of stock quotations.
GOE: 07.04.04 STRENGTH: S GED: R3 M2 L3 SVP: 2 DLU: 77

237.367-050 TOURIST-INFORMATION ASSISTANT (government ser.)

Provides travel information and other services to tourists at State Information Center: Greets tourists, in person or by telephone, and answers questions and gives information on resorts, historical sites, scenic areas, and other tourist attractions. Assists tourists in planning itineraries and advises them of traffic regulations. Sells hunting and fishing licenses and provides information on fishing, hunting, and camping regulations. Composes letters in response to inquiries. Maintains personnel, license-sales, and other records. Contacts motel, hotel, and resort operators by mail or telephone to obtain advertising literature.
GOE: 07.04.04 STRENGTH: S GED: R4 M3 L4 SVP: 6 DLU: 77

238 ACCOMMODATION CLERKS AND GATE AND TICKET AGENTS

This group includes occupations concerned with planning, scheduling, reserving, or otherwise arranging accommodations, such as transportation, lodging, and recreation, for customers, guests, employees, and government and military personnel, when direct personal or telephone contact is involved. Includes ticket agents engaged in assigning and reserving space, selling tickets, and providing travel information to patrons of transportation agency. Also included in this group are gate agents who check tickets and assist passengers at airports. Travel agents engaged in selling and arranging travel and lodging services on a commission basis are found in Group 252.

238.137-010 MANAGER, RESERVATIONS (hotel & rest.)

Supervises and coordinates activities of workers engaged in taking, recording, and canceling reservations in front office of hotel: Sorts reservations received by mail into current (up to 3 days) and future (over 3 days). Sends futures to reservation center in other hotel of chain. Gives current reservations to clerks for computerization. Receives contracts detailing room allotments for conventions from sales representative and feeds information into terminal. Corresponds with groups and travel agents to answer special requests for rooms and rates. Verifies that daily printouts listing guests' arrivals and individual guest folios are received by ROOM CLERKS (hotel & rest.). Maintains weekly attendance sheet and sends to payroll department. Delegates assistants to train clerks in taking telephone reservations and in operating computer terminals and printers to store and receive reservation data. Reschedules workers to accommodate arrivals of conventions and other groups. Recommmends promotion and discharge of workers to MANAGER, FRONT OFFICE (hotel & rest.). Performs other duties as described under SUPERVISOR (clerical) Master Title.
GOE: 07.05.01 STRENGTH: L GED: R4 M2 L3 SVP: 5 DLU: 77

238.137-014 SENIOR RESERVATIONS AGENT (air trans.)

Supervises and coordinates activities of workers engaged in reserving seat space for passengers on scheduled airline flights: Assigns workers to tasks in accordance with abilities and personnel requirements. Observes work procedures, monitors telephone calls, and reviews completed work to ensure adherence to quality and efficiency standards and to rules and regulations. Directs, explains, and demonstrates improved work practices and procedures to attain efficient utilization of personnel. Writes revisions to procedure guides and memoranda describing changes in reservations methods, flight schedules, and rates. Records teletypewriter messages and telephones passenger service personnel to obtain information regarding flight cancellations and schedule changes and to determine disposition of passengers holding reservations on cancelled or rescheduled flights. Posts flight schedule changes and passenger disposition information on bulletin board, and directs staff to telephone passengers to notify of schedule and reservation changes. Performs other duties as described under SUPERVISOR (clerical) Master Title.
GOE: 07.05.01 STRENGTH: L GED: R4 M3 L3 SVP: 6 DLU: 77

238.137-018 SUPERVISOR, GATE SERVICES (air trans.) alternate titles: senior gate agent

Supervises and coordinates activities of workers engaged in admitting departing passengers to airplanes and assisting passengers disembark at terminal exit of commercial airline: Reviews flight schedules, passenger manifests, and information obtained from staff to ascertain staffing requirements that will ensure efficient passenger embarking and disembarking; and assigns staff accordingly. Observes workers to ensure that services to passengers are performed courteously and correctly. Directs, explains, and demonstrates improved work practices and procedures to attain efficient utilization of human resources. Evaluates work performance of personnel and prepares recommendations for retention, dismissal, transfer, or promotion. Prepares daily personnel and activity reports. May perform tasks of GATE AGENT (air trans.).
GOE: 09.05.04 STRENGTH: L GED: R4 M2 L4 SVP: 7 DLU: 77

238.137-022 SUPERVISOR, TICKET SALES (air trans.) alternate titles: lead ticket-sales agent; senior passenger agent; senior ticket-sales agent

Supervises and coordinates activities of personnel engaged in selling tickets for scheduled airline flights in airline ticket office or terminal: Instructs and trains agents. Adjusts disputes between customers and agents. Prepares reports, such as volume of ticket sales and cash received. Maintains records on data, such as weight and location of passengers, cargo, and mail to ensure compliance with load specifications. Suggests travel itineraries for customers. May reserve space for passengers [RESERVATIONS AGENT (air trans.)] and sell tickets for scheduled flights [TICKET AGENT (any industry)]. Performs other duties as described under SUPERVISOR (clerical) Master Title.
GOE: 07.03.01 STRENGTH: L GED: R4 M3 L4 SVP: 6 DLU: 77

238.167-010 TRAVEL CLERK (government ser.)

Plans itinerary and schedules travel accommodations for military and civilian personnel and dependents according to travel orders, using knowledge of routes, types of carriers, and travel regulations: Verifies travel orders to ensure authorization. Studies routes and regulations and considers cost, availability, and convenience of different types of carriers to select most advantageous route and carrier. Notifies personnel of travel dates, baggage limits, and medical and visa requirements, and determines that all clearances have been obtained. Assists personnel in completing travel forms and other business transactions pertaining to travel. May deliver personnel files and travel orders to persons prior to departure. May meet and inform arriving personnel of available facilities and housing, and furnish other information. May arrange for motor transportation for arriving or departing personnel.
GOE: 07.05.01 STRENGTH: S GED: R4 M3 L4 SVP: 7 DLU: 77

238.167-014 TRAVEL COUNSELOR, AUTOMOBILE CLUB (nonprofit org.) alternate titles: touring counselor; traveling clerk

Plans trips for members of automobile club: Confers with member in person or by telephone to answer questions and explain services. Marks suitable roads

and possible detours on road map, showing route from point of origin to destination and return. Indicates points of interest, restaurants, hotels or other housing accommodations, and emergency repair services available along route. Reserves hotel, motel, or resort accommodations by telephone, telegraph, or letter. Calculates mileage of marked route and estimates travel expenses. Informs patron of bus, ship, train, and plane connections. Consults hotel directories, road maps, circulars, timetables, and other sources to obtain current information. Provides members with guides, directories, brochures and maps. May plan trips for members in response to mail requests. May plan foreign trips and perform duties, such as arranging for automobile rental, purchase, and shipment, and be designated World-Travel Counselor (nonprofit org.). May review itineraries prepared by other travel counselors for factors such as accuracy, pricing, and date and timetable sequencing and be designated Travel-Ticketing Reviewer (nonprofit org.).
GOE: 07.05.01 STRENGTH: S GED: R4 M4 L3 SVP: 5 DLU: 77

238.362-014 RESERVATION CLERK (clerical) alternate titles: clerk, travel reservations; travel clerk

Obtains travel and hotel accommodations for guests and employees of industrial concern, issues tickets, types itineraries, and compiles reports of transactions: Obtains confirmation of travel and lodging space and rate information. Issues and validates airline tickets from stock or *teleticketer* and obtains rail and bus tickets from carriers. Prepares passenger travel booklet containing tickets, copy of itinerary, written lodging confirmations, pertinent credit cards, and travel suggestions. Keeps current directory of hotels, motels, and timetables, and answers inquiries concerning routes, fares, and accommodations. Reviews routine invoices of transportation charges, and types and submits reports to company and to transportation agencies. Prepares and types claim forms for refunds and adjustments and reports of transactions processed.
GOE: 07.05.01 STRENGTH: S GED: R3 M3 L3 SVP: 5 DLU: 77

238.367-010 GATE AGENT (air trans.)

Assists passengers and checks flight tickets at entrance gate or station when boarding or disembarking airplane of commercial airline: Examines passenger tickets to ensure that passengers have correct flight or seat, or directs passengers to correct boarding area, using passenger manifest, seating chart, and flight schedules. Verifies names on passenger manifest or separates portions of passenger's ticket and stamps or marks ticket or issues boarding pass to authorize passenger to board airplane. Directs passengers to air-terminal facilities. Opens gate or allows passengers to board airplane. Assists elderly, disabled, or young passengers to board or depart from airplane, such as moving passengers in wheelchairs. May announce flight information, using public-address system. May post flight information on flight board.
GOE: 09.05.04 STRENGTH: L GED: R3 M2 L3 SVP: 4 DLU: 77

238.367-014 RESERVATION CLERK (r.r. trans.)

Receives requests for and assigns space on trains to passengers on railroad passenger trains. Accepts requests for space assignments and examines diagram charts of each car on train to verify available space on specified train. Informs STATION AGENTS (r.r. trans.) I or INFORMATION CLERKS (clerical) of available space. Marks blocks on diagram to indicate that space is reserved. Prepares Teletype requests to other interline carriers to complete passage. Informs STATION AGENTS (r.r. trans.) I and INFORMATION CLERKS (clerical) upon completion of booking arrangements. Informs RESERVATION CLERKS (r.r. trans.) at other cities and towns of space reserved or space remaining available.
GOE: 07.05.01 STRENGTH: S GED: R3 M2 L3 SVP: 3 DLU: 77

238.367-018 RESERVATIONS AGENT (air trans.) alternate titles: telephone-sales agent

Makes and confirms reservations for passengers on scheduled airline flights: Arranges reservations and routing for passengers at request of TICKET AGENT (any industry) 238.367-026 or customer, using timetables, airline manuals, reference guides, and tariff book. Types requested flight number on keyboard of on-line computer reservation system and scans screen to determine space availability. Telephones customer or TICKET AGENT (any industry) to advise of changes in flight plan or to cancel or confirm reservation. May maintain advance or current inventory of available passenger space on flights. May advise load control personnel and other stations of changes in passenger itinerary to control space and ensure utilization of seating capacity on flights.
GOE: 07.04.03 STRENGTH: S GED: R4 M3 L3 SVP: 4 DLU: 82

238.367-022 SPACE SCHEDULER (clerical) alternate titles: conference service coordinator

Compiles lists of individuals or groups requesting space for activities in business establishment or institution and schedules needed facilities: Receives requests from company officials, staff, students, and community groups requiring space for activities. Consults charts and records to determine space availability for dates and times requested. Determines suitability of space for requested activities, such as sales meetings, lectures, film screenings, musical programs, and laboratory work, and assigns conference rooms, lecture halls, and other facilities. Notifies program participants of location assigned. Maintains schedules and records of available space, space used, and cancellations. May requisition needed equipment, such as audiovisual aids, music stands, and additional seats. May arrange for cleaning of rooms after use.
GOE: 07.05.01 STRENGTH: S GED: R4 M2 L3 SVP: 4 DLU: 77

238.367-026 TICKET AGENT (any industry) alternate titles: passenger agent; passenger-booking clerk; reservation clerk; ticket clerk; ticket seller

Sells tickets for transportation agencies, such as airlines, bus companies (other than city buses), railroads (other than street railways), and steamship lines: Plans route and computes ticket cost, using schedules, rate books, and computer terminals. Ensures that cabins, seats, or space is available. Answers inquiries regarding airplane, train, bus, or boat schedules and accommodations. May check baggage and direct passenger to designated concourse, pier, or track for loading. May make public address announcements of arrivals and departures. May sell travel insurance.
GOE: 07.03.01 STRENGTH: L GED: R4 M3 L3 SVP: 5 DLU: 80

238.367-030 TRAVEL CLERK (hotel & rest.) alternate titles: transportation clerk

Provides travel information and arranges accommodations for tourists: Answers inquiries, offers suggestions, and provides descriptive literature pertaining to trips, excursions, sports events, concerts, and plays. Discusses routes, time schedules, rates, and types of accommodations with patrons to determine preferences and makes reservations. Verifies arrival and departure times, traces routes on maps, and arranges for baggage handling and other services requested by guests. May deliver tickets. May arrange for visas and other documents required by foreign travelers. May contact individuals and groups to inform them of package tours.
GOE: 07.04.04 STRENGTH: S GED: R3 M3 L3 SVP: 4 DLU: 77

238.367-034 SCHEDULER (museums) alternate titles: education department registrar; museum service scheduler

Makes reservations and accepts payment for group tours, classes, field trips, and other educational activities offered by museum, zoo, or similar establishment: Provides information regarding tours for school, civic, or other groups, suggests tours on institution calendar, and contacts group leaders prior to scheduled dates to confirm reservations. Provides information regarding classes, workshops, field trips, and other educational programs designed for such special groups as school or college students, teachers, or handicapped persons. Registers groups and individuals for participation in programs, enters registration information in department records, and contacts participants prior to program dates to confirm registration and provide preparatory information. Prepares lists of groups scheduled for tours and persons registered for other activities for use of DIRECTOR, EDUCATION (museums) 099.117-030 or other personnel. Collects and records receipts of fees for tours, classes, and other activities. Maintains records of participating groups, fees received, and other data related to educational programs for use in preparation of department reports. May take reservations and sell advance tickets to exhibits, concerts, and other events sponsored by institution, prepare periodic summaries of department activities for review by administrative personnel, or arrange for various support services to facilitate presentation of special activities.
GOE: 07.05.01 STRENGTH: S GED: R3 M3 L3 SVP: 3 DLU: 86

238.367-038 HOTEL CLERK (hotel & rest.) alternate titles: motel clerk; motor-lodge clerk

Performs any combination of following duties for guests of hotel or motel: Greets, registers, and assigns rooms to guests. Issues room key and escort instructions to BELLHOP (hotel & rest.) 324.677-010. Date-stamps, sorts, and racks incoming mail and messages. Transmits and receives messages, using telephone or telephone switchboard. Answers inquiries pertaining to hotel services; registration of guests; and shopping, dining, entertainment, and travel directions. Keeps records of room availability and guests' accounts, manually or using computer. Computes bill, collects payment, and makes change for guests [CASHIER (clerical) I 211.362-010]. Makes and confirms reservations. May post charges, such as room, food, liquor, or telephone, to ledger, manually or using computer [BOOKKEEPER (clerical) 210.382-014]. May make restaurant, transportation, or entertainment reservation, and arrange for tours. May deposit guests' valuables in hotel safe or safe-deposit box. May order complimentary flowers or champagne for guests. May rent dock space at marina-hotel. May work on one floor and be designated Floor Clerk (hotel & rest.). May be known as Key Clerk (hotel & rest.); Reservation Clerk (hotel & rest.); Room Clerk (hotel & rest.) or according to specific area in which employed as Front Desk Clerk (hotel & rest.).
GOE: 07.04.03 STRENGTH: L GED: R3 M3 L3 SVP: 4 DLU: 81

239 INFORMATION AND MESSAGE DISTRIBUTION OCCUPATIONS, N.E.C.

This group includes occupations, not elsewhere classified, concerned with distribution of information and messages by direct personal or telephone contact.

239.132-010 SUPERVISOR, TELEPHONE CLERKS (tel. & tel.) alternate titles: telephone supervisor

Supervises and coordinates activities of TELEPHONE CLERKS, TELEGRAPH OFFICE (tel. & tel.) engaged in relaying telegraph and radio messages by telephone, performing duties as described under SUPERVISOR (clerical) Master Title.
GOE: 07.04.06 STRENGTH: L GED: R4 M2 L4 SVP: 5 DLU: 77

239.137-010 COMMERCIAL-INSTRUCTOR SUPERVISOR (tel. & tel.; utilities; waterworks)

Supervises and coordinates activities of CUSTOMER-SERVICE-REPRESENTATIVE INSTRUCTORS (tel. & tel.; utilities; waterworks): Confers with department managers to determine training needs. Determines training requirements and assists instructors in securing required training aids and scheduling classroom space. Assigns instructors to teach subjects, such as principles of supervision, customer interviewing techniques, account collection, and processing of service and repair orders. Monitors (audits) classes to determine effectiveness of instruction and suggests methods designed to improve training program. Performs duties as described under SUPERVISOR (clerical) Master Title. Maintains records and compiles reports of training activities as required.
GOE: 11.07.03 STRENGTH: S GED: R4 M3 L4 SVP: 8 DLU: 77

239.137-014 CUSTOMER SERVICE REPRESENTATIVE SUPERVISOR (radio-tv broad.; tel. & tel.; utilities; waterworks)

Supervises and coordinates activities of CUSTOMER SERVICE REPRESENTATIVES (radio-tv broad.; tel. & tel.; utilities; waterworks) 239.362-014 engaged in handling service orders and telephone complaints of customers: Monitors service calls [SERVICE OBSERVER (tel. & tel.) 239.367-026] to observe employee's demeanor, technical accuracy, and conformity to company policies. Recommends corrective services to adjust customer complaints. Answers questions about service. Keys information into computer to compile work volume statistics for accounting purposes and to keep records of customer service requests and complaints. Checks accounting ledger and order postings for errors. Performs other duties as described under SUPERVISOR (clerical) Master Title.
GOE: 07.04.01 STRENGTH: S GED: R4 M2 L3 SVP: 6 DLU: 88

239.137-018 ROUTE SUPERVISOR (tel. & tel.)

Supervises and coordinates activities of workers engaged in routing telegraph messages, such as CLERKS, ROUTE (tel. & tel.) and ROUTE AIDES (tel. & tel.), performing duties as described under SUPERVISOR (clerical) Master Title.
GOE: 07.05.04 STRENGTH: L GED: R4 M2 L3 SVP: 6 DLU: 77

239.137-022 SERVICE OBSERVER, CHIEF (tel. & tel.) alternate titles: monitor chief

Supervises and coordinates activities of group of SERVICE OBSERVERS (tel. & tel.) in telegraph office. Performs duties as described under SUPERVISOR (clerical) Master Title.
GOE: 07.04.05 STRENGTH: L GED: R4 M2 L4 SVP: 7 DLU: 77

239.137-026 SUPERVISOR, PUBLIC MESSAGE SERVICE (tel. & tel.) alternate titles: traffic controller, cable

Supervises and coordinates activities of workers involved in local distribution and transmission of international message traffic: Directs and controls movement of traffic. Examines messages before transmission for proper routing and censorship marks and determines that no international regulations have been violated. Performs other duties as described under SUPERVISOR (clerical) Master Title.
GOE: 07.05.04 STRENGTH: S GED: R4 M3 L4 SVP: 7 DLU: 77

239.167-010 COMMUNICATIONS COORDINATOR (medical ser.)

Coordinates telephone communications services in hospital: Confers with administrative personnel to determine hospital requirements for communications equipment, such as switchboards, public-address paging systems, and extension telephones. Determines equipment to be installed, based on anticipated volume of calls, and knowledge of available equipment. Writes instruction and procedure manuals for switchboard operation and training, applying knowledge of hospital procedures, departmental functions, and equipment. Determines methods of improving telephone service from discussions with supervisory personnel, observation of switchboard operations, and analysis of service complaints. Arranges with telephone company personnel for special training of workers, as necessary. May estimate telephone services costs for use in preparing hospital budget. May prepare records and reports for management, concerning telephone services.
05.03.05 STRENGTH: S GED: R4 M3 L3 SVP: 7 DLU: 77

239.167-014 DISPATCHER (tel. & tel.) alternate titles: cable dispatcher

Establishes and reroutes telegraph and submarine cable circuits to ensure flow of messages: Orders irregular routing of telegrams to prevent congestion or wire shortage. Receives reports of delays in transmission of messages, and issues orders to facilitate transmission. Directs flow of messages during emergencies, such as storms, floods, and fires.
GOE: 07.04.05 STRENGTH: S GED: R4 M3 L4 SVP: 7 DLU: 77

239.227-010 CUSTOMER-SERVICE-REPRESENTATIVE INSTRUCTOR (tel. & tel.; utilities; waterworks)

Conducts classroom and on-the-job training for CUSTOMER-SERVICE REPRESENTATIVES (tel. & tel.; utilities; waterworks): Instructs employees on company policies, systems, and routines for handling customer service requests, following prescribed training program. Explains service forms and company procedures, using training aids, such as tape recorder, motion picture films, and slides. Listens to or takes recordings of trainees handling customer service calls to detect errors. Discusses errors and problems to improve techniques in handling calls.
GOE: 07.04.02 STRENGTH: S GED: R4 M2 L3 SVP: 6 DLU: 77

239.267-010 PLACER (insurance)

Advises clients of broker (independent agent) in selecting casualty, life, or property insurance: Discusses advantages and disadvantages of various policies to help client make choice. Selects company that offers type of coverage requested by client to underwrite policy. Contacts underwriter and submits forms to obtain binder coverage. Contacts company to determine if policy was issued or rejected.

GOE: 08.01.02 STRENGTH: S GED: R4 M3 L4 SVP: 5 DLU: 77

239.362-010 TELEPHONE CLERK, TELEGRAPH OFFICE (tel. & tel.) alternate titles: clerk-operator

Relays telegraph and radio messages by telephone: Calls addressee, using telephone directories and card indexes to locate telephone number. Reads message and spells misunderstood words, using phonetic alphabet. Solicits reply to promote sale of services. Records message to be sent, using pen, pencil, or typewriter. Suggests rewording, if necessary, for clarity and conciseness. Quotes rates, explains classifications, and reads sample messages to aid customer in preparing message. Counts message units, reads rates in rate book, and records rate on customer bill. May operate telephone switchboard equipment.

GOE: 07.04.05 STRENGTH: S GED: R3 M2 L3 SVP: 3 DLU: 77

239.362-014 CUSTOMER SERVICE REPRESENTATIVE (radio-tv broad.; tel. & tel.; utilities; waterworks) alternates titles: adjustment clerk; application clerk; order clerk; outside contact clerk; service representative

Interviews applicants and records interview information into computer for water, gas, electric, telephone, or cable television system service: Talks with customers by phone or in person and receives orders for installation, turn-on, discontinuance, or change in service. Fills out contract forms, determines charges for service requested, collects deposits, prepares change of address records, and issues discontinuance orders, using computer. May solicit sale of new or additional services. May adjust complaints concerning billing or service rendered, referring complaints of service failures, such as low voltage or low pressure, to designated departments for investigation. May visit customers at their place of residence to investigate conditions preventing completion of service-connection orders and to obtain contract and deposit when service is being used without contract. May discuss cable television equipment operation with customer over telephone to explain equipment usage and to troubleshoot equipment problems.

GOE: 07.04.01 STRENGTH: S GED: R3 M2 L3 SVP: 5 DLU: 88

239.367-014 DISPATCHER, MAINTENANCE SERVICE (clerical) alternate titles: dispatcher; maintenance clerk

Receives telephone and written orders from plant departments for maintenance service, such as repair work, machine adjustments, and renewals or installation of other plant property, and relays requests to appropriate maintenance division. Keeps record of requests and services rendered. Requisitions supplies for maintenance and clerical workers.

GOE: 07.04.05 STRENGTH: S GED: R3 M2 L3 SVP: 3 DLU: 77

239.367-018 MAIL-DISTRIBUTION-SCHEME EXAMINER (government ser.) alternate titles: scheme examiner

Devises and conducts tests that indicate knowledge of postal clerks concerning city, state, and regional addresses and tests skill in placing mail into designated boxes. Conducts and scores tests and forwards results to personnel department. Instructs postal clerks on distribution scheme requirements. Reviews and revises distribution schemes.

GOE: 07.01.07 STRENGTH: S GED: R4 M2 L4 SVP: 5 DLU: 77

239.367-022 RECEIVER-DISPATCHER (nonprofit org.) alternate titles: service aide

Receives and records requests for emergency road service from automobile club members, and dispatches tow truck or service truck to stranded vehicle: Answers telephone and obtains and records on road service card such information as name of club member, location of disabled vehicle, and nature of vehicle malfunction. Routes card to dispatch station, or relays information to service station or tow truck in motorist's vicinity, using telephone or two-way radio. May locate site of stranded vehicle, using maps. May maintain file of road service cards.

GOE: 07.04.05 STRENGTH: L GED: R3 M2 L3 SVP: 4 DLU: 77

239.367-026 SERVICE OBSERVER (tel. & tel.) alternate titles: monitor; observer

Monitors telephone conversations or telegraph messages between operators, business office employees, and subscribers to observe employees' demeanor, technical accuracy, and conformity to company policies. Plugs headphones into switchboard, listens to conversations, and records errors. Submits lists of errors to supervisors for remedial action.

GOE: 07.04.05 STRENGTH: L GED: R4 M2 L4 SVP: 4 DLU: 77

239.367-030 DISPATCHER, STREET DEPARTMENT (government ser.)

Receives and records public requests for street maintenance services, and relays work orders to maintenance crews, using telephone and two-way radio: Receives telephone requests from public for services, such as street repair, repair of traffic signals, erection of traffic barricades, and snow removal. Relays work orders, messages, and information to or from work crews, supervisors, and field inspectors. Answers routine questions from public and directs requests for other information to designated personnel. Maintains daily log of work orders, messages, or reports received and relayed.

GOE: 07.04.05 STRENGTH: S GED: R3 M1 L2 SVP: 3 DLU: 86

239.367-034 UTILITY CLERK (utilities)

Responds to telephone requests for information concerning location of underground utility distribution lines: Informs construction contractors and others excavating near company installations of buried line locations to prevent safety hazards and damage to company equipment, utilizing plat and distribution line maps. Updates maps to indicate extensions and revisions of utility distribution lines within specified jurisdiction. May relay telephone reports of gas emergencies to specified personnel [GAS-DISTRIBUTION-AND-EMERGENCY CLERK (utilities) 249.367-042] or radio customer service requests to mobile service crews, using two-way radio. May issue tools and parts used by company work crews [STOCK CLERK (clerical) 222.387-058].

GOE: 07.04.05 STRENGTH: L GED: R4 M3 L3 SVP: 5 DLU: 86

239.382-010 WIRE-PHOTO OPERATOR, NEWS (print. & pub.) alternate titles: telephoto operator

Operates news wirephoto machine to transmit syndicated news photographs over telecommunication wires to newspapers and magazines: Inserts developed photographic print in camera chamber equipped with electric eye which scans and transmits photographs over transcontinental telephone or telegraph wires. Adjusts controls to coordinate machine processes involving detecting, screening, and converting photographic highlights and shadows into sound signals for wire transmission. May operate machine to receive news photographs. May develop film and print positives.

GOE: 05.10.05 STRENGTH: S GED: R4 M2 L3 SVP: 5 DLU: 77

239.567-010 OFFICE HELPER (clerical)

Performs any combination of following duties in business office of commercial or industrial establishment: Furnishes workers with clerical supplies. Opens, sorts, and distributes incoming mail, and collects, seals, and stamps outgoing mail. Delivers oral or written messages. Collects and distributes paperwork, such as records or timecards, from one department to another. Marks, tabulates, and files articles and records. May use office equipment, such as envelope-sealing machine, letter opener, record shaver, stamping machine, and transcribing machine. May deliver items to other business establishments [DELIVERER, OUTSIDE (clerical) 230.663-010]. May specialize in delivering mail, messages, documents, and packages between departments of establishment and be designated Messenger, Office (clerical). May deliver stock certificates and bonds within and between stock brokerage offices and be designated Runner (financial).

GOE: 07.07.03 STRENGTH: L GED: R2 M2 L2 SVP: 2 DLU: 81

239.677-010 MESSENGER, COPY (print. & pub.) alternate titles: proof runner

Delivers and illustration material to and from advertisers and other outside agencies and within office. May read competitors' publications, clip items or stories not printed in own publication, and submit clippings to editor.

GOE: 07.07.02 STRENGTH: L GED: R2 M1 L2 SVP: 2 DLU: 77

239.687-010 ROUTE AIDE (tel. & tel.)

Delivers messages to and from conveyor belts, terminals, tube locations, and other transmitting points within telegraph office. May microfilm copies of telegrams, using automatic microfilming equipment. May search for and retrieve messages stuck in equipment between transmitting points.

GOE: 07.07.02 STRENGTH: L GED: R2 M1 L2 SVP: 2 DLU: 77

239.687-014 TUBE OPERATOR (clerical) alternate titles: pneumatic-tube operator; tube clerk; tube dispatcher; tube-station attendant

Receives and routes messages through pneumatic-tube system: Opens incoming pneumatic-tube carriers containing items, such as mail correspondence, bills, and receipts. Reads and sorts items according to department. Inserts items into carriers, and carriers into tube system, and routes to specified locations.

GOE: 07.07.02 STRENGTH: S GED: R2 M1 L2 SVP: 2 DLU: 77

24 MISCELLANEOUS CLERICAL OCCUPATIONS

This division includes miscellaneous occupations concerned with clerical work.

241 INVESTIGATORS, ADJUSTERS, AND RELATED OCCUPATIONS

This group includes occupations concerned with investigating and making determinations pertaining to such matters as the eligibility or qualifications of applicants for insurance, credit, or employment; adjustment of insurance claims; and resolution of customer complaints. This group also includes occupations concerned with activities, such as locating persons and arranging for payment of debts and repossessing merchandise. Occupations concerned with interviewing persons and taking applications, registrations, or public opinion surveys without making determinations regarding information elicited are found in Group 205.

241.137-010 SUPERVISOR, CREDIT AND LOAN COLLECTIONS (clerical)

Supervises and coordinates activities of workers engaged in collecting overdue payments for charge accounts, credit card accounts, or loans from cus-

tomers of banks, loan companies, department stores, oil companies, or other credit-card-issuing companies: Reviews delinquent account records to determine which customers must be contacted for collection of overdue accounts. Organizes collection work load according to degree and amount of delinquency and assigns accounts to workers for collection. Writes letters or approves form letters for use in collection attempts. Recommends telephone techniques used by COLLECTOR (clerical) 241.367-010. Verifies accuracy of accounts, using calculator and computer. Authorizes or refers accounts to manager for repossession and legal actions against debtors. May assist subordinates with collection activities in difficult cases. May supervise and coordinate activities of clerical workers in related activities. Performs duties as described under SUPERVISOR (clerical) Master Title.
GOE: 07.04.02 STRENGTH: S GED: R4 M3 L4 SVP: 7 DLU: 89

241.137-014 SUPERVISOR, CUSTOMER-COMPLAINT SERVICE (clerical)

Supervises and coordinates activities of workers engaged in resolving customer problems and complaints concerning matters, such as merchandise, service, and billing: Reviews customer-complaint correspondence, notes any suggestions, and assigns complaint to CUSTOMER-COMPLAINT CLERK (clerical) 241.367-014 for action. Advises subordinates on handling difficult customer complaints, or may handle complaint personally. Confers with other supervisory or managerial personnel to recommend changes in order to avoid recurring customer complaints. May explain to customer by telephone or letter action taken on complaint. May follow up with customer to see that complaint was satisfactorily resolved. May be designated according to type of problem as Supervisor, Lost and Found (air trans.; motor trans.). Performs other duties as described under SUPERVISOR (clerical) Master Title.
GOE: 07.04.02 STRENGTH: S GED: R4 M3 L4 SVP: 6 DLU: 88

241.137-018 SUPERVISOR, CLAIMS (insurance) alternate titles: claims administrator

Supervises and coordinates activities of workers engaged in examining insurance claims for payment in claims division of insurance company: Analyzes and approves insurance and matured endowment claims. Conducts personal interviews with policy owners and beneficiaries to explain procedure for filing claims. Submits statement of claim liabilities to actuarial department for review. Informs departmental supervisors on claims status. Evaluates job performance of subordinates. Performs duties described under SUPERVISOR (clerical) Master Title.
GOE: 11.12.01 STRENGTH: S GED: R4 M3 L4 SVP: 7 DLU: 86

241.217-010 CLAIM ADJUSTER (business ser.; insurance) alternate titles: insurance adjustor; insurance-claim representative; insurance investigator

Investigates claims against insurance or other companies for personal, casualty, or property loss or damages and attempts to effect out-of-court settlement with claimant: Examines claim form and other records to determine insurance coverage. Interviews, telephones, or corresponds with claimant and witnesses; consults police and hospital records; and inspects property damage to determine extent of company's liability, varying method of investigation according to type of insurance. Prepares report of findings and negotiates settlement with claimant. Recommends litigation by legal department when settlement cannot be negotiated. May attend litigation hearings. May be designated according to type of claim adjusted as Automobile-Insurance-Claim Adjuster (business ser.; insurance); Casualty-Insurance-Claim Adjuster (clerical); Fidelity-And-Surety-Bonds-Claim Adjuster (business ser.; insurance); Fire-Insurance-Claim Adjuster (business ser.; insurance); Marine-Insurance-Claim Adjuster (business ser.; insurance); Property-Loss-Insurance-Claim Adjuster (clerical).
GOE: 11.12.01 STRENGTH: L GED: R5 M3 L5 SVP: 6 DLU: 77

241.267-010 AGENT-CONTRACT CLERK (insurance) alternate titles: contract administrator

Evaluates character and ability of prospective agents, and approves their contracts to sell insurance for company: Reviews prospect's application for employment, inspection report, and recommendations to evaluate applicant's character and qualifications. Approves contract if applicant meets company requirements. Corresponds with agency to explain rejection of prospect. Sends application and fee for license to licensing agency. Notifies licensing agency of agent's contract termination. May prepare bulletins to inform insurance agency personnel of revisions in company practices and procedures.
GOE: 07.01.05 STRENGTH: S GED: R5 M1 L4 SVP: 5 DLU: 77

241.267-014 APPRAISER, AUTOMOBILE DAMAGE (business ser.; insurance) alternate titles: automobile-damage appraiser; estimator, automobile damage

Appraises automobile or other vehicle damage to determine cost of repair for insurance claim settlement and attempts to secure agreement with automobile repair shop on cost of repair: Examines damaged vehicle to determine extent of structural, body, mechanical, electrical, or interior damage. Estimates cost of labor and parts to repair or replace each item of damage, using standard automotive labor and parts cost manuals and knowledge of automotive repair. Determines salvage value on total-loss vehicle. Evaluates practicality of repair as opposed to payment of market value of vehicle before accident. Prepares insurance forms to indicate repair-cost estimates and recommendations. Reviews repair-cost estimates with automobile-repair shop to secure agreement on cost of repairs. Occasionally arranges to have damage appraised by another appraiser to resolve disagreement with repair shop on repair cost.

GOE: 11.12.01 STRENGTH: L GED: R4 M2 L4 SVP: 7 DLU: 77

241.267-018 CLAIM EXAMINER (business ser.; insurance) alternate titles: insurance-claim approver; insurance-claim auditor

Analyzes insurance claims to determine extent of insurance carrier's liability and settles claims with claimants in accordance with policy provisions: Compares data on claim application, death certificate, or physician's statement with policy file and other company records to ascertain completeness and validity of claim. Corresponds with agents and claimants or interviews them in person to correct errors or omissions on claim forms, and to investigate questionable entries. Pays claimant amount due. Refers most questionable claims to INVESTIGATOR (clerical) or to CLAIM ADJUSTER (business ser.; insurance) for investigation and settlement. May investigate claims in field. May be designated according to type of claim handled as Accident-And-Health-Insurance-Claim Examiner (insurance); Automobile-Insurance-Claim Examiner (business ser.; insurance); Death-Claim Examiner (insurance); Disability-Insurance-Claim Examiner (insurance); Fire-Insurance-Claim Examiner (business ser.; insurance); Marine-Insurance-Claim Examiner (business ser.; insurance).
GOE: 11.12.01 STRENGTH: S GED: R4 M3 L4 SVP: 7 DLU: 77

241.267-022 CREDIT ANALYST (clerical)

Analyzes paying habits of customers who are delinquent in payment of bills and recommends action: Reviews files to select delinquent accounts for collection efforts. Evaluates customer records and recommends that account be closed, credit limit reduced or extended, or collection attempted, based on earnings and savings data, payment history, and purchase activity of customer. Confers with representatives of credit associations and other businesses to exchange information concerning credit ratings and forwarding addresses. Interviews customers in person or by telephone to investigate complaints, verify accuracy of charges, or to correct errors in accounts [BILL ADJUSTER (clerical)].
GOE: 07.01.04 STRENGTH: S GED: R4 M3 L4 SVP: 7 DLU: 77

241.267-026 DEPOSIT CLERK (utilities)

Interviews commercial or industrial applicants for gas or electric-power service to determine amount of cash deposit required as guaranty against loss and to approve refund or waiver of deposits: Studies service rates to estimate applicants' service bill, considering such factors as type of business, previous bills at same address, and estimates of load from reports by contractors or information obtained regarding motor sizes, capacities and hours of operation. Investigates credit standing [CREDIT CLERK (clerical)] and approves or disapproves requests. Investigates credit standing of persons given as guarantors. Approves refunds on checks made out in excess of payment and requests for allowance of discounts on bills. Receives cash deposits and issue receipts.
GOE: 07.01.04 STRENGTH: S GED: R4 M3 L4 SVP: 6 DLU: 77

241.267-030 INVESTIGATOR (clerical)

Investigates persons or business establishments applying for credit, employment, insurance, loans, or settlement of claims: Contacts former employers, neighbors, trade associations, and others by telephone or in person, to verify employment record and to obtain health history and history of moral and social behavior. Examines city directories and public records to verify residence history, convictions and arrests, property ownership, bankruptcies, liens, and unpaid taxes of applicant. Obtains credit rating from banks and credit services. Analyzes information gathered by investigation and prepares reports of findings and recommendations, using typewriter or computer. May interview applicant on telephone or in person to obtain other financial and personal data to complete report. May be designated according to type of investigation as Credit Reporter (business ser.); Insurance Application Investigator (insurance).
GOE: 11.06.03 STRENGTH: S GED: R4 M3 L4 SVP: 5 DLU: 81

241.267-034 INVESTIGATOR, UTILITY-BILL COMPLAINTS (utilities) alternate titles: customer-service representative

Investigates customers' bill complaints for gas and electric-power service: Examines weather reports for weather conditions during billing period that might have contributed to increased use of service. Examines meter reading schedules to determine if early readings increased billing period. Reviews meter books, microfilm, computer printouts, and machine accounting records for errors causing high bill. Orders tests to detect meter malfunctions. Confers with customer in person, by telephone, or dictates correspondence to explain reasons for high bill. Prepares forms required for correction of meter reading or billing errors.
GOE: 07.05.02 STRENGTH: L GED: R4 M4 L4 SVP: 6 DLU: 77

241.357-010 COLLECTION CLERK (clerical) alternate titles: delinquent-account clerk; past-due-accounts clerk

Notifies or locates customers with delinquent accounts and attempts to secure payment, using postal services, telephone, or personal visit: Mails form letters to customers to encourage payment of delinquent accounts. Confers with customer by telephone in attempt to determine reason for overdue payment, reviewing terms of sales, service, or credit contract with customer. Notifies credit department if customer fails to respond. Contacts delinquent account customers in person [COLLECTOR (clerical) 241.367-010]. Records information about financial status of customer and status of collection efforts. May order repossession or service disconnection, or turn over account to attorney. May sort and file correspondence. May receive payments and post amount paid to customer account. May grant extensions of credit. May use automated telephone dialing system to contact customers and computer to record customer account information. May void sales tickets for unclaimed c.o.d. and lay-away merchandise.

May trace customer to new address by inquiring at post office or by questioning neighbors [SKIP TRACER (clerical) 241.367-026]. May attempt to repossess merchandise, such as automobile, furniture, and appliances when customer fails to make payment [REPOSSESSOR (clerical) 241.367-022]. May be designated according to type of establishment as Bank-Credit-Card-Collection Clerk (financial); Department-Store-Collection Clerk (retail trade); Hospital Collection Clerk (medical ser.); Utility-Bill-Collection Clerk (clerical).
GOE: 07.04.02 STRENGTH: S GED: R4 M3 L4 SVP: 5 DLU: 88

241.362-010 CLAIMS CLERK I (insurance)
Reviews insurance-claim forms for completeness; secures and adds missing data; and transmits claims for payment or further investigation: Reviews insurance-claim forms and related documents for completeness; calls or writes insured or other involved persons for missing information; and posts or attaches information to claim file. Reviews insurance policy to determine coverage. Calculates amount of claim, using desk calculator. Transmits routine claims for payment or advises claims supervisor if further investigation is indicated.
GOE: 07.05.02 STRENGTH: S GED: R4 M3 L3 SVP: 4 DLU: 77

241.367-010 COLLECTOR (clerical) alternate titles: bill collector; collection agent; outside collector
Locates customers to collect installments or overdue accounts, damage claims, or nonpayable checks: Visits or phones customer and attempts to persuade customer to pay amount due or arranges for payment at later date. Questions neighbors and postal workers at post office to determine new address of customers. May have service discontinued or merchandise repossessed. Keeps record of collections and status of accounts. May deliver bills. May sell insurance or other service. May be designated according to type of collection as Claims Collector (clerical); Insurance Collector (insurance); Utility-Bill-Collector (clerical).
GOE: 07.03.01 STRENGTH: L GED: R3 M3 L3 SVP: 4 DLU: 81

241.367-014 CUSTOMER-COMPLAINT CLERK (clerical) alternate titles: adjustment clerk; consumer-relations-complaint clerk
Investigates customer complaints about merchandise, service, billing, or credit rating: Examines records, such as bills, computer printouts, microfilm, meter readings, bills of lading, and related documents and correspondence, and converses or corresponds with customer and other company personnel, such as billing, credit, sales, service, or shipping, to obtain facts regarding customer complaint. Examines pertinent information to determine accuracy of customer complaint and to determine responsibility for errors. Notifies customer and designated personnel of findings, adjustments, and recommendations, such as exchange of merchandise, refund of money, credit of customer's account, or adjustment of customer's bill. May recommend to management improvements in product, packaging, shipping methods, service, or billing methods and procedures to prevent future complaints of similar nature. May examine merchandise to determine accuracy of complaint. May follow up on recommended adjustments to ensure customer satisfaction. May key information into computer to obtain computerized records. May trace missing merchandise and be designated Tracer Clerk (clerical). May investigate overdue and damaged shipments or shortages in shipments for common carrier and be designated Over-Short-And-Damage Clerk (clerical). May be designated according to type of complaint adjusted as Bill Adjuster (clerical); Merchandise-Adjustment Clerk (retail trade); Service Investigator (utilities; tel. & tel.).
GOE: 07.05.02 STRENGTH: S GED: R4 M3 L4 SVP: 5 DLU: 89

241.367-018 LOAN INTERVIEWER, MORTGAGE (financial) alternate titles: loan officer
Interviews applicants applying for mortgage loans: Interviews loan applicants to document income, debt, and credit history. Requests documents, such as income tax return, bank account number, purchase agreement, and property description, for verification. Determines if applicant meets establishment standards for further consideration, following manual and using calculator. Informs applicant of closing costs, such as appraisal, credit report, and notary fees. Answers applicant's questions and asks for signature on information authorization forms. Submits application forms to MORTGAGE LOAN PROCESSOR (financial) 249.362-022 for verification of application information. Calls applicant or other persons to resolve discrepancies, such as credit report showing late payment history. Informs applicant of loan denial or acceptance. May visit establishments, such as branch banks, credit unions, real estate brokers, and builders, to promote mortgage service. May work on commission basis.
GOE: 07.04.01 STRENGTH: S GED: R4 M3 L3 SVP: 6 DLU: 89

241.367-022 REPOSSESSOR (clerical)
Locates debtors and solicits payment for delinquent accounts and removes merchandise for nonpayment of account. May initiate repossession proceedings. May drive truck to return merchandise to creditor. May locate, enter, and start vehicle being repossessed, using special tools, if key cannot be obtained from debtor, and return vehicle to creditor. May be designated according to merchandise repossessed as Automobile Repossessor (clerical).
GOE: 04.02.03 STRENGTH: M GED: R3 M2 L2 SVP: 3 DLU: 77

241.367-026 SKIP TRACER (clerical) alternate titles: debtor; tracer
Traces skips (debtors who change residence without notifying creditors to evade payment of bills) for creditors or other concerned parties: Searches city and telephone directories, and street listings, and inquires at post office. Interviews, telephones, or writes former neighbors, stores, friends, relatives, and former employers to elicit information pertaining to whereabouts of skips. Fol-

lows up each lead and prepares report of investigation to creditor. May trace individuals for purposes of serving legal papers. May contact debtors by mail or phone to attempt collection of money owed [COLLECTION CLERK (clerical)].
GOE: 07.04.01 STRENGTH: S GED: R4 M2 L4 SVP: 4 DLU: 77

241.367-030 THROW-OUT CLERK (retail trade) alternate titles: charge-account identification clerk
Processes records of department-store transactions which cannot be applied to customer's account by routine procedures in order that charges, cash payments, and refunds may be recorded, collected, or credited: Reviews and talks to sales-audit, charge-account-authorization, and collection personnel to identify missing information or compare signatures on sales or credit slips. Telephones or writes to customers for additional information. Corrects or adds information to customer accounts as necessary. Mails dunning correspondence to customers in arrears on their charge accounts [COLLECTION CLERK (clerical)].
GOE: 07.05.02 STRENGTH: S GED: R3 M3 L3 SVP: 4 DLU: 77

241.367-034 TIRE ADJUSTER (retail trade)
Examines defective tires and tubes returned by customers to determine allowance due on replacement: Visually and tactually examines tire to determine if defect resulted from faulty construction or curing. Measures tread depth, using tread depth gauge, to determine remaining tire life. Prorates allowances based on tread wear, warranty provisions, and knowledge of tire characteristics. Explains basis for allowance to customer, sales representative, or distributor. May train new workers.
GOE: 05.09.01 STRENGTH: M GED: R3 M3 L2 SVP: 3 DLU: 77

241.367-038 INVESTIGATOR, DEALER ACCOUNTS (financial) alternate titles: floor plan adjuster
Visits dealers to verify purchases financed by bank against physical inventory of merchandise: Reviews computer printouts listing customer names, addresses, and descriptions of merchandise financed through bank credit and chattel mortgage accounts to plan itinerary of unannounced visits to dealer premises. Explains purpose of visit and locates merchandise in areas, such as showroom, storage room, or car lot. Observes features of merchandise, such as size, color, model, and serial number, to verify item against computer printout. Examines records and questions dealer to determine disposition of items missing from inventory and to elicit information on dealer arrangement for payment to bank for merchandise sold. Records findings on printout and notifies supervisor of unusual findings.
GOE: 07.05.02 STRENGTH: L GED: R4 M3 L4 SVP: 2 DLU: 89

241.367-042 PROPERTY-ASSESSMENT MONITOR (government ser.)
Gathers property assessment data at owner premises, verifies data against previously recorded data, and records discrepancies: Visits property, observes premises, and confers with owner to collect and verify property assessment data, using data cards (property assessment records) as guides. Measures and records size of land boundaries and house, using tape measure. Records type of exterior coverings and physical condition of exterior and interior of house. Counts and records number of bathrooms, stoves, and fireplaces. Verifies findings against recorded data and notes discrepancies. Occasionally attends town meetings to answer taxpayer questions regarding use of information contained on data cards.
GOE: 07.05.02 STRENGTH: L GED: R4 M4 L4 SVP: 3 DLU: 86

241.387-010 CLAIMS CLERK (auto. mfg.)
Examines and processes automotive warranty claims from dealers requesting reimbursement for defective parts, using computerized records system. Reviews claims for completeness, and determines if expenses comply with established policies. Completes reports for further action or returns incomplete claims to dealers for additional data.
GOE: 07.05.02 STRENGTH: S GED: R4 M3 L3 SVP: 4 DLU: 90

243 GOVERNMENT SERVICE CLERKS, N.E.C.

This group includes occupations, not elsewhere classified, concerned with performing clerical duties for federal, state, county, city, or town governments.

243.137-010 SUPERVISOR, MAILS (government ser.) alternate titles: post-office supervisor
Supervises and coordinates activities of workers processing mail in post office. Keeps records of processed mail, mail in process, and changes in worker assignments. May analyze and recommend changes in distribution schemes. Performs other duties as described under SUPERVISOR (clerical) Master Title.
GOE: 07.05.04 STRENGTH: L GED: R4 M2 L3 SVP: 6 DLU: 77

243.362-010 COURT CLERK (government ser.)
Performs clerical duties in court of law: Prepares docket or calendar of cases to be called, using typewriter. Examines legal documents submitted to court for adherence to law or court procedures, prepares case folders, and posts, files, or routes documents. Explains procedures or forms to parties in case. Secures information for judges, and contacts witnesses, attorneys, and litigants to obtain information for court, and instructs parties when to appear in court. Notifies district attorney's office of cases prosecuted by district attorney. Administers oath to witnesses. Records minutes of court proceedings, using stenotype machine or shorthand, and trsnscribes testimony, using typewriter. Records case disposition, court orders, and arrangement for payment of court fees. Collects court fees or fines and records amounts collected.

GOE: 07.01.02 STRENGTH: S GED: R4 M2 L4 SVP: 6 DLU: 77

243.362-014 POLICE AIDE (government ser.)

Performs any combination of following tasks in police department to relieve police officers of clerical duties: Types and files police forms, such as accident reports, arrest records, evidence cards, and attendance records and schedules. Posts information to police records, manually or using typewriter or computer. Gives information to public, over phone or in person, concerning arrests, missing persons, or other police related business. Operates telephone system to take or relay information. Receives and records physical evidence recovered from crime scenes by police officers.
GOE: 07.04.05 STRENGTH: S GED: R3 M2 L3 SVP: 3 DLU: 79

243.367-010 MAIL CENSOR (government ser.)

Opens and inspects incoming and outgoing correspondence and packages to ensure compliance with prison security rules: Reads incoming and outgoing correspondence (with permission of appropriate jurisdiction) of prisoners with adjustment problems or suspected of forbidden activities, such as planning escapes or attempting to contact confederates outside prison. Removes money mailed to prisoners, prepares receipt, and forwards to security office for safekeeping. Impounds contraband articles, such as weapons and drugs, and notifies proper authorities of rules violations. Returns to sender, articles prisoners are forbidden to possess. May evaluate content of incoming correspondence, conferring with psychiatric staff to protect inmate against information considered injurious to prisoner's emotional welfare or adjustment.
GOE: 07.05.02 STRENGTH: S GED: R4 M2 L3 SVP: 5 DLU: 77

243.367-014 POST-OFFICE CLERK (government ser.) alternate titles: postal clerk

Performs any combination of following tasks in post office: Sells postage stamps, postal cards, and stamped envelopes. Issues money orders. Registers and insures mail and computes mailing costs of letters and parcels. Places mail into pigeonholes of mail rack, or into bags, according to state, address, name of person, organization, or other scheme. Examines mail for correct postage and cancels mail, using rubber stamp or canceling machine. Weighs parcels and letters on scale and computes mailing cost based on weight and destination. Records daily transactions. Receives complaints concerning mail delivery, mail theft, and lost mail, completes and routes appropriate forms for investigation. Answers questions pertaining to mail regulations or procedures. Posts circulars on bulletin board for public information; distributes public announcements; and assists public in complying with other federal agency requirements, such as registration of aliens. May drive motorcycle or light truck to deliver special delivery letters. May be employed in remote retail store contracted by post office to provide postal services and be designated Contract-Post-Office Clerk (retail trade).
GOE: 07.03.01 STRENGTH: L GED: R3 M3 L3 SVP: 4 DLU: 77

243.367-018 TOWN CLERK (government ser.)

Performs variety of clerical and administrative duties required by municipal government: Prepares agendas and bylaws for town council; records minutes of council meetings; answers official correspondence; keeps fiscal records and accounts; and prepares reports on civic needs.
GOE: 07.01.02 STRENGTH: S GED: R4 M4 L3 SVP: 5 DLU: 77

245 MEDICAL SERVICE CLERKS, N.E.C.

This group includes occupations, not elsewhere classified, concerned with performing clerical duties in hospitals, clinics, medical laboratories, blood banks, or related medical service establishments.

245.362-010 MEDICAL-RECORD CLERK (medical ser.)

Compiles, verifies, types, and files medical records of hospital or other health care facility: Prepares folders and maintains records of newly admitted patients. Reviews medical records for completeness, assembles records into standard order, and files records in designated areas according to applicable alphabetic and numeric filing system. Locates, signs out, and delivers medical records requested by hospital departments. Compiles statistical data, such as admissions, discharges, deaths, births, and types of treatment given. Operates computer to enter and retrieve data and type correspondence and reports. May assist other workers with coding of records. May post results of laboratory tests to records and be designated Charting Clerk (medical ser.).
GOE: 07.05.03 STRENGTH: L GED: R4 M3 L3 SVP: 4 DLU: 88

245.362-014 UNIT CLERK (medical ser.) alternate titles: health unit clerk; ward clerk

Prepares and compiles records in nursing unit of hospital or medical facility: Records name of patient, address, and name of attending physician to prepare medical records on new patients. Copies information, such as patient's temperature, pulse rate, and blood pressure from nurses' records onto patient's medical records. Records information, such as physicians' orders and instructions, dietary requirements, and medication information, on patient charts and medical records. Keeps file of medical records on patients in unit. Prepares notice of patient's discharge to inform business office. Requisitions supplies designated by nursing staff. Answers telephone and intercom calls and provides information or relays messages to patients and medical staff. Directs visitors to patients' rooms. Distributes mail, newspapers, and flowers to patients. Compiles census of patients. May keep record of absences and hours worked by unit personnel. May transport patients in wheelchair or conveyance to locations within facility. May key patient information into computer.
GOE: 07.05.03 STRENGTH: L GED: R3 M3 L3 SVP: 3 DLU: 87

245.367-010 ANIMAL-HOSPITAL CLERK (medical ser.)

Registers and admits animals brought to animal hospital; advises owners about condition of pets being treated; prepares case records of treated animals; and computes and records payment of fees: Questions animal owners to determine symptoms and to complete admission form. Answers questions by phone, letter, or in person about condition of animals treated, visiting hours, first aid, and discharge date. Prepares case record on each animal treated, including identifying information, diagnosis, and treatment. Computes treatment cost and records fees collected.
GOE: 07.04.03 STRENGTH: S GED: R3 M2 L3 SVP: 4 DLU: 77

245.367-014 BLOOD-DONOR-UNIT ASSISTANT (medical ser.)

Performs any combination of following supportive duties at blood-collection unit of blood bank: Schedules appointments over telephone for blood donors. Interviews blood donors and records identifying and blood-credit information on registration form. Notifies nurse if donor appears to be underweight or too old to give blood. Takes blood donor's temperature and pulse to assist during medical interview. Unpacks, labels, and stamps date on empty blood packs. Posts donor names, blood-control numbers, and donor-group numbers to unit logsheet. Seals filled blood packs and sample tubes, using handtools and heat-sealing machine. Serves refreshments, such as coffee, juice, cookies, and jelly beans, to donors to prevent or relieve adverse reactions and to begin replenishment of blood fluids.
GOE: 07.04.01 STRENGTH: L GED: R2 M1 L2 SVP: 2 DLU: 77

245.367-018 CALENDAR-CONTROL CLERK, BLOOD BANK (medical ser.) alternate titles: blood-bank-booking clerk

Schedules dates for mobile blood collection units to visit blood-donor groups for nonprofit blood bank: Determines available date to schedule mobile blood collection units to visit blood-donor group, such as business or fraternal organizations, labor unions, or schools, or for blood-donor groups to visit temporary blood collection stations, based on uncommitted dates, availability of mobile units, location of donor groups, anticipated number of blood donors, and total daily blood collection capacity of blood bank. Prepares tentative weekly schedule and distributes schedule to mobile units and BLOOD-DONOR RECRUITERS (medical ser.). Notifies staff when change occurs in schedules. Confers with mobile-unit supervisor and BLOOD DONOR RECRUITERS (medical ser.) to learn changes in information and to advise of any late changes in scheduling. Prepares reports on anticipated and actual blood donations for management.
GOE: 07.05.01 STRENGTH: S GED: R3 M2 L2 SVP: 3 DLU: 77

245.367-022 CREDIT CLERK, BLOOD BANK (medical ser.)

Reviews and verifies applications for blood credit for members of blood donor groups; informs hospital of result of verification; and answers inquiries regarding blood credit from patients, donor groups, hospitals, and health insurance organizations: Checks blood credit release form received from blood donor groups for completeness and legibility and reviews blood bank records to determine eligibility for donor blood credit. Records amounts of blood or components used by patient and issues credit slip to blood bank accounting department. Sends copies of credit slips to hospitals and health insurance organizations. Processes reciprocity forms being sent to or received from Red Cross clearance agency authorizing blood credit from one blood bank region to another. Answers inquiries by phone or letter from patients and family, blood donor groups, hospital staff, and health insurance staff regarding blood credit information.
GOE: 07.05.02 STRENGTH: S GED: R3 M2 L3 SVP: 3 DLU: 77

245.367-026 ORDER-CONTROL CLERK, BLOOD BANK (medical ser.; nonprofit organ.)

Receives and processes requests for blood from hospitals: Records amount and type of whole blood or blood component requested and checks inventory control board, or phones blood storage units, laboratories, doctors, or other hospitals to determine availability of whole blood and blood components. Questions hospital ordering blood as to urgency and use of blood. Advises supervisor or staff doctor when blood request is excessive, unusual, or for rare blood type or component, or when blood inventory is low. Relays orders to blood storage units to prepare and ship blood or components to designated hospitals. Adjusts figures on blood inventory control board and records transfer of blood from one hospital to another.
GOE: 07.05.04 STRENGTH: S GED: R3 M2 L3 SVP: 3 DLU: 77

245.587-010 DIET CLERK (medical ser.)

Prepares dietary information for use by kitchen personnel in preparation of foods for hospital patients: Examines diet orders and menus received from hospital units and tallies portions and foods of general and soft diets. Tallies quantities of specific foods, such as vegetables and meats, to be prepared in kitchen. Marks tally on master menu to inform kitchen personnel of food requirements. Processes new diets and changes as required. May calculate diabetic diets, using calculator, and following standards established by DIETITIAN, CLINICAL (profess. & kin.) 077.127-014. May answer telephone and intercom calls and relay information to kitchen concerning meal changes, complaints, or patient discharge. May prepare and deliver formula and special nourishments to unit pantries.

GOE: 07.05.03 STRENGTH: S GED: R3 M3 L3 SVP: 3 DLU: 86

247 ADVERTISING-SERVICE CLERKS, N.E.C.

This group includes occupations, not elsewhere classified, concerned with performing clerical duties related to advertising products and services.

247.137-010 SUPERVISOR, ADVERTISING-DISPATCH CLERKS (print. & pub.)

Supervises and coordinates activities of ADVERTISING-DISPATCH CLERKS (print. & pub.) engaged in compiling and dispatching advertising schedules and materials to composing room of daily or weekly publication and maintaining advertising files: Confers with advertising and composing-room personnel to organize and file customer advertising copy. Confers with customers by telephone to discuss copy revisions. Reviews customer advertising files to ensure that information is correct and that files are maintained according to company standards. Performs other duties as described under SUPERVISOR (clerical) Master Title.

GOE: 07.05.01 STRENGTH: L GED: R4 M2 L4 SVP: 5 DLU: 77

247.137-014 SUPERVISOR, CLASSIFIED ADVERTISING (print. & pub.)

Supervises and coordinates activities of workers engaged in preparing classified advertisements: Reviews advertisement and suggests changes to improve its effectiveness. Reviews customer accounts and approves credit or refers matter to credit department. Edits copy of accepted advertisements and forwards copy to composing room. Trains new personnel in work procedures. May make personal or telephone contacts to solicit new accounts or to increase use of advertising by current customers. Performs other duties as described under SUPERVISOR (clerical) Master Title.

GOE: 07.05.02 STRENGTH: L GED: R4 M3 L4 SVP: 6 DLU: 77

247.367-010 CLASSIFIED-AD CLERK I (print. & pub.) alternate titles: ad clerk

Receives orders for classified advertising for newspaper or magazine by telephone or in person: Talks to customer to determine wording and dates of publication of classified advertisement. Determines word, line, or day rates, using rate schedule, and calculates total charge for customer. Assigns box number for anonymous advertisements. Collects payments for advertisements. Writes order form to customer's specification and transmits to production personnel for publication. Writes receipts and keeps records of transactions. May mark advertising that has expired and indicate number of days other advertisements are to continue. May record customer's request for cancellations or corrections of classified advertisement. May solicit orders for classified advertisements over telephone [TELEPHONE SOLICITOR (any industry)]. When taking order over telephone, may be designated Telephone Ad Taker (print. & pub.).

GOE: 07.04.02 STRENGTH: S GED: R3 M2 L3 SVP: 5 DLU: 77

247.382-010 MEDIA CLERK (business ser.)

Keeps record of clients' advertising schedules for advertising agency: Computes cost of space allotment and advertising program from standard rates and data. Records media used, such as newspapers and magazines, and expenses. Types contract after receiving client's approval. Determines cost of advertising space in various media in other areas considering factors, such as size and population of city, space rates, and kind and frequency of publication for comparison.

GOE: 07.02.04 STRENGTH: S GED: R4 M3 L3 SVP: 5 DLU: 77

247.387-010 ADVERTISING CLERK (business ser.)

Compiles advertising orders for submission to publishers and verifies conformance of published advertisements to specifications, for billing purposes: Reviews order received from advertising agency or client to determine specifications. Computes cost of advertisement, based on size, date, position, number of insertions, and other requirements, using rate charts. Posts cost data on order and worksheet. Types and mails order and specifications to designated publishers. Files order data pending receipt of publication. Scans publication to locate published advertisement. Measures advertisement, using ruler or transparent calibrated overlay, to verify conformance to size specifications [ADVERTISING-SPACE CLERK (print. & pub.)]. Compares advertisement with order to verify conformance to other specifications. Computes difference in cost when published advertisement varies from specifications and posts corrected costs on order controls. Separates tear sheet (page upon which advertisement appears) from publication, types and attaches identifying information to tear sheet; and routes with order and worksheet to billing department.

GOE: 07.02.04 STRENGTH: S GED: R3 M2 L2 SVP: 4 DLU: 77

247.387-014 ADVERTISING-DISPATCH CLERK (print. & pub.) alternate titles: schedule clerk

Compiles and dispatches advertising schedule and material to composing room of daily or weekly publication: Reviews advertising order and prepares advertising schedule, listing size of ad, date(s) to appear, and page and position of ad. Searches advertising files and selects mat that corresponds to advertising layout. Dispatches mat, advertising layout and copy, and advertising schedule to composing department. Obtains advertising proofs from composing department and dispatches them to advertising department for proofreading. Maintains files of all advertising material. May proofread and correct advertising proofs. May read advertisement in first edition of publication for errors.

GOE: 07.05.01 STRENGTH: S GED: R3 M2 L3 SVP: 4 DLU: 77

247.387-018 ADVERTISING-SPACE CLERK (print. & pub.) alternate titles: space clerk

Measures and draws outlines of advertising space on dummy newspaper copy and compiles and records identifying data on dummy copy and other worksheets used as guides for production workers: Computes total inches of advertising and news copy for next day's edition, using adding machine, and reads chart to determine required number of newspaper pages. Measures and draws outlines of advertisements in sizes specified onto dummy copy sheets, using pencil and ruler and arranging advertisements on each sheet so that competitive ones do not appear on same page and balance is attained. Records name of advertiser and dimensions of advertisement within ruled outlines and date and page number on each sheet. Extracts data from dummy copy and other sources and records onto lineage breakdown sheets (production worksheets). Delivers dummy copy and lineage breakdown sheets to designated production and administrative personnel for review and use.

GOE: 01.06.01 STRENGTH: S GED: R3 M3 L3 SVP: 5 DLU: 77

247.387-022 CLASSIFIED-AD CLERK II (print. & pub.) alternate titles: classified-copy-control clerk

Examines and marks classified advertisements of newspaper according to copy sheet specifications to guide composing room in assembling type: Marks advertisements that have expired and indicates number of days others are to continue, using classified file copy and copy sheet for current day. Computes and records total number of lines expired and number of lines for new advertisements.

GOE: 07.05.02 STRENGTH: S GED: R3 M3 L2 SVP: 5 DLU: 77

247.667-010 PRODUCTION PROOFREADER (print. & pub.; retail trade)

Compares proofs of store advertisements with original copy to detect errors in printed material. Reads proofs and corrects errors in type, arrangement, grammar, punctuation, or spelling, using proofreader's marks. Routes proofs with corrections to be reprinted and reads corrected proofs.

GOE: 07.05.02 STRENGTH: S GED: R3 M2 L3 SVP: 4 DLU: 77

248 TRANSPORTATION-SERVICE CLERKS, N.E.C

This group includes occupations, not elsewhere classified, concerned with performing clerical duties in the air-, motor-, rail-, or water-transportation industries.

248.137-010 BOOKING SUPERVISOR (water trans.)

Supervises and coordinates activities of workers engaged in booking shipments of cargo on ships and keeping booking control records to ensure maximum utilization of cargo spaces: Reviews records of bookings and studies plans of cargo spaces to determine type of tonnage that can be booked on each ship in order to obtain maximum revenue and utilize available cargo space. Assigns booking duties to workers and gives work directions regarding tonnage or cubic feet of storage space that can be booked for refrigerated cargo, or container cargo. Coordinates booking and space control activities to ensure that each ship is booked to capacity. Trains workers in booking procedures and demonstrates methods of converting cubic feet of storage space into tonnage. Submits booking sheets to documentation department for preparation of shipping documents. Performs other duties as described under SUPERVISOR (clerical) Master Title.

GOE: 07.05.01 STRENGTH: L GED: R4 M3 L3 SVP: 6 DLU: 77

248.137-014 PURCHASING-AND-CLAIMS SUPERVISOR (water trans.)

Supervises and coordinates activities of workers in purchasing-and-claims department of ferryboat service: Reviews and approves requisitions for supplies and designates approved supplier. Reviews and forwards for approval requisitions for ferry or terminal maintenance or repair. Recommends contractors or vendors for notification to bid for repair or supply contracts. Supervises and coordinates activities of workers engaged in typing correspondence, preparing requisitions, obtaining price quotations, and verifying accuracy of billing. Performs other duties as described under SUPERVISOR (clerical) Master Title. Reviews claims by passengers of ferry service for property damage or personal injury and authorizes payment or submits claims to insurance carrier.

GOE: 07.01.02 STRENGTH: S GED: R4 M3 L4 SVP: 6 DLU: 77

248.137-018 SUPERVISOR, CUSTOMER SERVICES (motor trans.)

Supervises and coordinates activities of workers engaged in servicing and promoting shipper accounts for parcel-delivery firm: Reviews records indicating shipper parcel volume, claims for damaged and lost parcels, and deficiencies in parcel preparation for pickup and delivery. Discusses service to shippers with assigned representatives to develop plans of service. Meets with, or directs representatives to meet with, shippers to resolve problems in wrapping and handling of parcels and relationships between firm's employees and shippers. Assigns representatives to solicit prospective accounts. Evaluates performance and productivity of workers and reports to management. Performs other duties as described under SUPERVISOR (clerical) Master Title.

GOE: 07.01.02 STRENGTH: L GED: R4 M3 L4 SVP: 6 DLU: 77

248.167-010 SUPERCARGO (water trans.) alternate titles: freight clerk

Plans and coordinates loading and unloading of ships' cargo and prepares reports on type, amount, and condition of cargo to protect company from claims for damage or shortage: Examines cargo lists to determine types of cargo that

can be loaded together. Prepares loading and stowage plan to ensure that weight of cargo is equally distributed in hatches. Informs shippers and supervisor of CARGO CHECKERS (water trans.) of loading time and point, and supervisors of STEVEDORES (water trans.) II of cargo to load and location of load. Prepares reports, such as tonnage carried, breakage, overages, and shortages. Acts as agent of shipowners in foreign ports.
GOE: 05.09.02 STRENGTH: L GED: R4 M3 L3 SVP: 7 DLU: 77

248.362-010 INCOMING-FREIGHT CLERK (water trans.) alternate titles: storage-wharfage clerk
Compiles documents on incoming cargo shipments to expedite removal of cargo from dock and prepares bill for shipping charges: Examines ship's manifest and bills of lading to determine work procedures for releasing cargo. Contacts terminal employees by telephone to determine when cargo will be available for removal from dock. Notifies consignee or agent by telephone or letter of arrival dates of shipment, customs clearance requirements, and tonnage of shipment. Stamps bill of lading so that cargo can be removed from dock. Computes from bills of lading, shipping, storage, and demurrage charges, using calculator. Prepares bill for charges and submits it to accounting department for collection.
GOE: 07.02.04 STRENGTH: L GED: R3 M3 L3 SVP: 5 DLU: 77

248.362-014 WEATHER CLERK (air trans.)
Assembles and distributes weather charts and bulletins to provide data for DISPATCHER (air trans.) in making flight plans: Reads messages and charts received by telegraphic typewriter and teleautograph. Assembles and fastens together individual messages, using tape. Prints copies of weather reports, charts, and maps, using duplicating machine [DUPLICATING-MACHINE OPERATOR (clerical) II]. Posts charts on flight crew bulletin board or distributes to AIRPLANE PILOTS, COMMERCIAL (air trans.).
GOE: 07.07.03 STRENGTH: L GED: R3 M2 L3 SVP: 3 DLU: 77

248.367-010 AIRPLANE-DISPATCH CLERK (air trans.) alternate titles: flight-operations-dispatch clerk
Compiles flight information to expedite movement of aircraft between and through airports: Compiles aircraft dispatch data, such as scheduled arrival and departure times at checkpoints and scheduled stops, amount of fuel needed for flight, and maximum allowable gross takeoff and landing weight. Submits data to DISPATCHER (air trans.) for approval and flight authorization. Receives messages on progress of flights. Posts flight schedules and weather information on bulletin board. Compiles such information as flight plans, ramp delays, and weather reports, using Teletype, computer-printout terminal, and two-way radio, to anticipate off-schedule arrivals or departures and notifies flight operations of schedule changes. Prepares messages concerning flights for transmittal by radio, telegraph, or telegraphic typewriter to other stations on routes. May operate telegraphic typewriter or two-way radio to send messages. May issue maps to pilot. May duplicate weather maps and telegraph or radio messages [DUPLICATING-MACHINE OPERATOR (clerical) II]. May record flight and weather information on tape recorder for playback to passengers in waiting areas. May verify presence or locate scheduled flight crews, and post changes in flight crew schedule on bulletin board.
GOE: 07.05.03 STRENGTH: L GED: R4 M3 L4 SVP: 5 DLU: 77

248.367-014 BOOKING CLERK (water trans.)
Books outbound freight shipments to ensure maximum use of available cargo space on company ships: Obtains cargo data from shipper, such as type, tonnage, destination, and shipping date, in order to determine allocation of cargo and fully utilize capacity of each ship. Consults booking sheet to ascertain availability of cargo space. Informs shipper of ship's name on which cargo is booked, sailing date, and cargo delivery date. Records cargo data on booking control sheet, listing tonnage, type of cargo, shipper's name, and cargo destination. May be designated according to type of cargo booked as Container-Cargo Clerk (water trans.); General-Cargo Clerk (water trans.); Refrigerated-Cargo Clerk (water trans.).
GOE: 07.05.01 STRENGTH: S GED: R3 M2 L2 SVP: 5 DLU: 77

248.367-018 CARGO AGENT (air trans.) alternate titles: air-freight agent; customer service agent
Routes inbound and outbound air freight shipments to their destinations: Takes telephone orders from customers and arranges for pickup of freight and delivery to loading platform. Assembles cargo according to destination. Weighs items and determines cost, using rate book. Itemizes charges, prepares freight bills, accepts payments and issues refunds. Prepares manifest to accompany shipments. Notifies shippers of delays in departure of shipment. Unloads inbound freight and notifies consignees on arrival of shipments and arranges for delivery to consignees. May force conditioned air into interior of plane for passenger comfort prior to departure, using mobile aircraft-air-conditioning-unit.
GOE: 05.09.01 STRENGTH: M GED: R3 M3 L3 SVP: 5 DLU: 77

248.367-022 CONTAINER COORDINATOR (water trans.)
Expedites movement of cargo containers between ports to ensure adequate supply of empty containers for shipper: Records movement of loaded and unloaded cargo containers between ports and number of containers available for shipping cargo. Expedites delivery of loaded containers to consignee, using telephone or Teletype. Computes storage and demurrage charges on containers for use by accounting department, using calculating machine.
GOE: 07.05.01 STRENGTH: S GED: R4 M3 L3 SVP: 6 DLU: 77

248.367-026 DISPATCHER, SHIP PILOT (water trans.)
Dispatches PILOT, SHIP (water trans.) to ships entering or leaving port: Writes order showing name of ship, berth, tugboat company, and time of arrival

or departure, and notifies PILOT, SHIP (water trans.) and pilot boat operator of assignment. Obtains receipt of pilotage from pilot upon return from ship. Records charges on receipt, using tariff book as guide. Compiles reports of activities, such as number of ships piloted and charges made. Keeps records of ships entering port, showing owner, name of ship, displacement tonnage, agent, and country of registration. May be required to possess radiotelephone operator's license issued by Federal Communications Commission, and operate radar to fix position and speed of ships entering and leaving port.
GOE: 07.04.05 STRENGTH: S GED: R3 M3 L3 SVP: 4 DLU: 77

248.367-030 WATERWAY TRAFFIC CHECKER (water trans.)
Observes vessels passing inland-waterway checkpoint, using binoculars, to verify identity and ascertain speed and direction. Telephones observations to designated control point, such as drawbridge or lock station. Reports movements of overdue vessels to estimate arrival time at specified points along waterway. Notifies waterway officials or other authorities of accidents, distress signals from passing vessels, obstructions, and other unusual conditions observed from checkpoint. Records observations in log.
GOE: 07.04.05 STRENGTH: S GED: R3 M3 L3 SVP: 3 DLU: 77

248.382-010 TICKETING CLERK (air trans.) alternate titles: teleticketing agent; ticket agent
Compiles and records information to assemble airline tickets for transmittal or mailing to passengers: Reads coded data on booking card to ascertain destination, carrier, flight number, type of accommodation, and stopovers enroute. Selects ticket blank, invoice, and customer account card if applicable, and compiles, computes, and records identification and fare data, using tariff manuals, rate tables, flight schedules, and pen or ticket imprinter. Separates and files copies of completed tickets. Clips completed tickets and invoices to booking cards and routes to other workers for Teletype transmittal or mails tickets to customers. Computes total daily fares, using adding machine, to compile daily revenue report.
GOE: 07.02.04 STRENGTH: S GED: R3 M3 L3 SVP: 4 DLU: 77

248.387-010 FLIGHT OPERATIONS SPECIALIST (military ser.)
Maintains aviation operations files and records, and prepares and types reports, orders, and schedules pertaining to aviation operations and aviation safety: Displays flight planning information to include airfield diagram, status of navigational aids, map of local flying area, special use airspace, and crash grid chart. Maintains and issues flying regulations and pilot's and flight crew's information file. Keeps files of extended flight and navigational information, such as weight and balance data, cross-country kits, navigational publications, radio and landing facility charts, flight information manuals, maps, and other pertinent guides and notices. Compiles, prepares, and distributes correspondence, such as aviation operations reports, aviation safety reports, and flight schedules. Assists flight-line personnel in assigning crew and passengers to aircraft and assists aviators in preparing flight plans, processes flight plans and arrival reports for transmission to flight and air traffic control centers.
GOE: 07.05.03 STRENGTH: L GED: R3 M3 L2 SVP: 6 DLU: 77

248.387-014 TONNAGE-COMPILATION CLERK (water trans.)
Calculates tonnage of specified components of ship's cargo to compile report for use in assessing tariffs: Calculates tonnage of each commodity from ship's manifest. Converts cubic feet of cargo volume into tonnage assessable. Converts metric volume of cargo into pounds and cubic feet, using formulas and calculating machine. Compiles tonnage list for each commodity in ship's cargo and submits lists to accounting department.
GOE: 07.02.04 STRENGTH: S GED: R4 M3 L3 SVP: 5 DLU: 77

249 MISCELLANEOUS CLERICAL OCCUPATIONS, N.E.C.

This group includes clerical occupations, not elsewhere classified.

249.137-010 OFFICE SUPERVISOR, ANIMAL HOSPITAL (nonprofit org.)
Supervises and coordinates activities of clerical staff in nonprofit animal hospital. Performs duties as described under SUPERVISOR (clerical) Master Title. May interview pet owners to compile information on financial status and make determinations regarding eligibility for free services, reduced fees, or deferred payments. May supervise clerical staff in animal shelter section and be designated Chief Clerk, Shelter (nonprofit org.).
GOE: 07.05.03 STRENGTH: S GED: R4 M3 L4 SVP: 6 DLU: 77

249.137-014 SUPERVISOR, CONTACT AND SERVICE CLERKS (utilities)
Supervises and coordinates activities of CONTACT CLERKS (utilities) engaged in preparing gas and electric-power service orders and SERVICE CLERKS (clerical) engaged in receiving service requests on telephone: Routes service orders to service departments and outlying service centers. Reviews completed orders for accuracy, completeness, and conformity to specified procedures. Reviews incomplete or rejected orders to determine actions to facilitate completion. Answers telephone questions from customers, contractors, building inspectors, and other company departments pertaining to progress in completion of orders. Performs other duties as described under SUPERVISOR (clerical) Master Title.
GOE: 07.04.02 STRENGTH: S GED: R4 M2 L4 SVP: 7 DLU: 77

249.137-018 SUPERVISOR, CORRESPONDENCE SECTION (insurance)

Supervises and coordinates activities of workers engaged in preparing correspondence, policies, and related clerical activities in headquarters or branch office of insurance company: Reads policyholder and company field personnel correspondence, studies policy records, and examines replies prepared by CORRESPONDENCE CLERKS (clerical) 209.362-034 and POLICYHOLDER-INFORMATION CLERKS (insurance) 249.262-010 to determine completeness of replies and appropriateness of actions taken. Proofreads copy for style, appearance, accuracy of spelling, punctuation, grammar, and conformity with company standards. Returns faulty work with instructions for revision. Performs other duties as described under SUPERVISOR (clerical) Master Title. May verify accuracy of computations, using calculator. May dictate replies to nonroutine correspondence. May review and correct records, using computer.
GOE: 07.05.03 STRENGTH: S GED: R4 M2 L4 SVP: 6 DLU: 78

249.137-022 SUPERVISOR, CUSTOMER RECORDS DIVISION (utilities)

Supervises and coordinates activities of workers engaged in receiving requests from customers pertaining to connection, transfer, or disconnection of gas and electric-power services, issuing service connection orders, and maintaining records concerning service connection: Interprets company policies and work procedures for employees pertaining to customer contacts, service complaints, preparation and disposition of work orders, and maintenance of service records. Sorts and distributes completed meter orders. Reviews completed meter orders to assure entry of rates, constants, and demand. Reviews incomplete orders to determine procedure for disposition. Prepares annual operating budget, and special and regular reports. May receive money collected by workers for special connections. Performs other duties described under SUPERVISOR (clerical) Master Title.
GOE: 07.04.02 STRENGTH: S GED: R4 M3 L4 SVP: 7 DLU: 77

249.137-026 SUPERVISOR, ORDER TAKERS (clerical) alternate titles: sales-service supervisor

Supervises and coordinates activities of workers taking customer orders for products and merchandise by telephone, mail, or in person: Monitors ORDER CLERKS (clerical) to evaluate order-taking performance and to assist in responding to customer inquiries and complaints. Consults with sales, technical, shipping, or administrative staff and telephones or writes letters to answer or advise customer. Reviews completed orders for errors or omissions. Trains ORDER CLERKS (clerical) in order-taking procedures and customer-relations techniques, and advises workers of new or revised information on products or merchandise, such as product capability, pricing, credit, warranties, and shipping. Performs other duties as described under SUPERVISOR (clerical) Master Title.
GOE: 07.04.02 STRENGTH: S GED: R4 M3 L4 SVP: 5 DLU: 77

249.137-030 SUPERVISOR, REAL-ESTATE OFFICE (real estate)

Supervises and coordinates activities of clerical personnel in real estate office: Interviews clerical applicants, gives performance tests, and evaluates applicant data to determine new hires. Verifies completeness, accuracy, and timeliness of clerical personnel production. Prepares or assists in preparaing papers for closings of real estate transactions, such as sales contracts and purchase agreements. Analyzes financial activities of establishment and prepares reports for review of SALES AGENT, REAL ESTATE (real estate) 250.357-018 or other personnel. Schedules government inspections of properties to ensure that offerings meet code regulations. Contacts mortgage companies to determine insurance status of properties. Notifies utility companies of transfer of property to new owners. Performs other duties as described under SUPERVISOR (clerical) Master Title.
GOE: 07.01.04 STRENGTH: S GED: R4 M3 L4 SVP: 7 DLU: 86

249.137-034 SUPERVISOR, LENDING ACTIVITIES (financial)

Supervises and coordinates activities of workers engaged in processing and recording commercial, residential, and consumer loans: Answers workers' and customers' questions regarding procedures. Reviews and authorizes corrections to loan records. Supervises MORTGAGE LOAN PROCESSOR (financial) 249.362-022; MORTGAGE LOAN CLOSER (financial) 249.362-018; CLERK-TYPIST (clerical) 203.362-010; and others. Performs other duties as described under SUPERVISOR (clerical) Master Title. Workers who supervise loan collection are classified under SUPERVISOR, CREDIT AND LOAN COLLECTIONS (clerical) 241.137-010.
GOE: 07.01.02 STRENGTH: S GED: R4 M3 L4 SVP: 8 DLU: 88

249.167-010 AUTOMOBILE-CLUB-SAFETY-PROGRAM COORDINATOR (nonprofit org.)

Coordinates activities and gives information and advice regarding traffic-engineering and safety programs of automobile club: Develops and revises automobile-club procedures regarding traffic-engineering and safety programs. Arranges for speakers to address gatherings to promote and explain traffic-engineering and safety programs. Schedules, monitors, and keeps records on program activities. Advises club members about traffic summonses and violations and contacts courts to expedite processing or clarify disposition of summonses. Answers questions and gives information to callers or visitors about traffic-engineering and safety programs of automobile club. Prepares reports about road or traffic-control conditions based on information received from club members or other staff members.
GOE: 07.01.02 STRENGTH: S GED: R4 M3 L4 SVP: 6 DLU: 77

249.167-014 DISPATCHER, MOTOR VEHICLE (clerical)

Assigns motor vehicles and drivers for conveyance of freight or passengers: Compiles list of available vehicles. Assigns vehicles according to factors, such as length and purpose of trip, freight or passenger requirements, and preference of user. Issues keys, record sheets, and credentials to drivers. Records time of departure, destination, cargo, and expected time of return. Investigates overdue vehicles. Directs activities of drivers, using two-way radio. May confer with customers to expedite or locate missing, misrouted, delayed, or damaged merchandise. May maintain record of mileage, fuel used, repairs made, and other expenses. May establish service or delivery routes. May issue equipment to drivers, such as handtrucks, dollies, and blankets. May assign helpers to drivers. May be designated according to type of motor vehicle dispatched as Dispatcher, Automobile Rental (automotive ser.); Dispatcher, Tow Truck (automotive ser.).
GOE: 07.05.01 STRENGTH: S GED: R3 M2 L3 SVP: 5 DLU: 78

249.167-018 LABOR EXPEDITER (construction)

Expedites movement of labor to construction locations: Contacts representatives of transportation, feeding, and housing facilities to arrange for servicing workers at transient points. Issues permits, identification cards, and tickets to workers for travel to specified areas. May contact labor union with jurisdiction, where project is located, to inform labor official of recruited workers and to determine union regulations in area. May direct workers to report to local union after arrival in area. May meet recruited workers at designated depot, airport, or dock.
GOE: 07.01.02 STRENGTH: L GED: R4 M3 L4 SVP: 5 DLU: 77

249.262-010 POLICYHOLDER-INFORMATION CLERK (insurance) alternate titles: correspondent; customer-service clerk

Analyzes and answers requests by mail, telephone, or in person from policyholders, beneficiaries, or others for information concerning insurance policies: Searches company records to obtain information requested by customer. Estimates loan or cash value of policy for policyholders, using rate books and calculating machine. Interprets policy provisions to determine methods of effecting desired changes, such as change of beneficiary or type of insurance, or change in method of payment. Mails or gives out specified forms and routes completed forms to various units for processing. Analyzes policy transactions and corrects company records to adjust errors. May compose formal synopses of company and competitor policies for use by sales force. May provide information for pensioners and be designated Pensionholder-Information Clerk (insurance).
GOE: 07.04.04 STRENGTH: S GED: R4 M2 L4 SVP: 6 DLU: 77

249.267-010 COPYRIGHT EXPERT (radio-tv broad.) alternate titles: copyright clerk

Examines script of radio and television musical programs prior to broadcasting to ascertain that permission has been secured for use of copyrighted materials: Investigates musical compositions as to author, owner, and publisher to verify that license has been granted company to use programmed material and to arrange for payment to copyright owner. Examines musical arrangements to determine whether they constitute an infringement on other copyrighted arrangements.
GOE: 07.05.02 STRENGTH: S GED: R4 M2 L4 SVP: 7 DLU: 77

249.362-010 COUNTER CLERK (tel. & tel.)

Receives, types, routes, and collects payment for telegraph messages and cashes money order warrants at counter in telegraph office: Quotes rates for telegrams and collects amount due for message. Types message from customer's copy and places message in pneumatic tube for routing. Pays customer amount due on money order warrant. Keeps records of receipts and disbursements and balances cash on hand at end of day. May be assigned to process money orders only and be designated Money-Order Clerk (tel. & tel.).
GOE: 07.03.01 STRENGTH: L GED: R4 M2 L4 SVP: 5 DLU: 77

249.362-014 MORTGAGE CLERK (financial)

Performs any combination of following duties to process payments and maintain records of mortgage loans: Types letters, forms, checks, and other documents used for collecting, disbursing, and recording mortgage principal, interest, and escrow account payments, using computer. Answers customer questions regarding mortgage account and corrects records, using computer. Examines documents such as deeds, assignments, and mortgages, to ensure compliance with escrow instructions, institution policy, and legal requirements. Records disbursement of funds to pay insurance and tax. Types notices to government, specifying changes to loan documents, such as discharge of mortgage. Orders property insurance policies to ensure protection against loss on mortgaged property. Enters data in computer to generate tax and insurance premium payment notices to customers. Reviews printouts of allocations for interest, principal, insurance, or tax payments to locate errors. Corrects errors, using computer. May call or write loan applicants to obtain information from bank official. May be designated according to type of work assigned as Escrow Clerk (financial); Foreclosure Clerk (financial); Insurance Clerk (financial); Tax Clerk (financial).
GOE: 07.01.04 STRENGTH: S GED: R3 M3 L3 SVP: 5 DLU: 88

249.362-018 MORTGAGE LOAN CLOSER (financial)

Schedules loan closing and compiles and types closing documents: Reviews approved mortgage loan to determine conditions that must be met prior to closing, such as purchase of private mortgage insurance. Calls borrower, real estate broker, and title company to request specified documents, such as receipt for payment of outstanding tax bill. Verifies accuracy and consistency of specifications on documents, such as title abstract and insurance forms. Calls borrower,

broker, and other specified individuals to arrange time and date for closing. Answers questions regarding closing requirements. Enters numbers and calculates loan interest and principal payment, and closing costs, using computer or factor table and calculator. Types closing documents. Assembles documents for delivery to title company, real estate broker, or lending officer for closing. Records loan information in log and on government reporting forms, using computer. May compile closed loan forms for delivery to marketing department for sale to investors.
GOE: 07.01.04 STRENGTH: S GED: R4 M3 L4 SVP: 5 DLU: 88

249.362-022 MORTGAGE LOAN PROCESSOR (financial)
Verifies, compiles, and types application information for mortgage loans: Reviews residential loan application file to verify that application data is complete and meets establishment standards, including type and amount of mortgage, borrower assets, liabilities, and length of employment. Recommends that loan not meeting standards be denied. Calls or writes credit bureau and employer to verify accuracy of information. Types loan application forms, using computer. Calls specified companies to obtain property abstract, survey, and appraisal. Informs supervisor of discrepancies in title or survey. Submits mortgage loan application file for underwriting approval. Types and mails approval and denial letters to applicants. Submits approved mortgage loan file to MORTGAGE LOAN CLOSER (financial) 249.362-018 for settlement. Records data on status of loans, including number of new applications and loans approved, canceled, or denied, using computer.
GOE: 07.05.02 STRENGTH: S GED: R3 M3 L3 SVP: 5 DLU: 88

249.362-026 ORDER CLERK (clerical) alternate titles: customer-order clerk; order filler; order taker
Processes orders for material or merchandise received by mail, telephone, or personally from customer or company employee, manually or using computer or calculating machine: Edits orders received for price and nomenclature. Informs customer of unit prices, shipping date, anticipated delays, and any additional information needed by customer, using mail or telephone. Writes or types order form, or enters data into computer, to determine total cost for customer. Records or files copy of orders received according to expected delivery date. May ascertain credit rating of customer [CREDIT CLERK (clerical) 205.367-022]. May check inventory control and notify stock control departments of orders that would deplete stock. May initiate purchase requisitions. May route orders to departments for filling and follow up on orders to ensure delivery by specified dates and be designated Telephone-Order Dispatcher (clerical). May compute price, discount, sales representative's commission, and shipping charges. May prepare invoices and shipping documents, such as bill of lading [BILLING TYPIST (clerical) 214.382-014]. May recommend type of packing or labeling needed on order. May receive and check customer complaints [CUSTOMER-COMPLAINT CLERK (clerical) 241.367-014]. May confer with production, sales, shipping, warehouse, or common carrier personnel to expedite or trace missing or delayed shipments. May attempt to sell additional merchandise to customer [TELEPHONE SOLICITOR (any industry) 299.357-014]. May compile statistics and prepare various reports for management. May be designated according to method of receiving orders as Mail-Order Clerk (clerical); Telephone-Order Clerk (clerical).
GOE: 07.05.03 STRENGTH: S GED: R3 M3 L3 SVP: 4 DLU: 88

249.363-010 BOOKMOBILE DRIVER (library)
Drives bookmobile or light truck that pulls book trailer, and assists in providing library services in mobile library: Drives vehicle to specified locations on predetermined schedule. Places books and periodicals on shelves according to such groupings as subject matter, reader's age grouping, or reading level. Stamps dates on library cards, files cards, and collects fines. Compiles reports of mileage, number of books issued, and amount of fines collected. Drives vehicle to garage for repairs, such as motor or transmission overhauls, and for preventive maintenance, such as chassis lubrication and oil change. May operate microfilm camera to photograph library cards [PHOTOGRAPHIC-MACHINE OPERATOR (clerical) 207.685-018].
GOE: 05.09.01 STRENGTH: L GED: R3 M2 L2 SVP: 3 DLU: 77

249.365-010 REGISTRATION CLERK (library)
Registers library patrons to permit them to borrow books, periodicals, and other library materials: Copies identifying data, such as name and address, from application onto registration list and borrowers' cards to register borrowers, and issues cards to borrowers. Records change of address or name onto registration list and borrowers' cards to amend records. Tends microfilm machine to record identification of borrower and materials issued [PHOTOGRAPHIC-MACHINE OPERATOR (clerical)]. Reviews records, such as microfilm and issue cards, to determine title of overdue materials and to identify borrower. Types notices to notify borrower of overdue material and amount of fine due.
GOE: 07.04.03 STRENGTH: L GED: R3 M1 L3 SVP: 5 DLU: 77

249.366-010 COUNTER CLERK (photofinishing)
Receives film for processing, loads film into equipment that automatically processes film for subsequent photo printing, and collects payment from customers of photofinishing establishment: Answers customer's questions regarding prices and services. Receives film to be processed from customer and enters identification data and printing instructions on service log and customer order envelope. Loads film into equipment that automatically processes film, and routes processed film for subsequent photo printing. Files processed film and photographic prints according to customer's name. Locates processed film and

prints for customer. Totals charges, using cash register, collects payment, and returns prints and processed film to customer. Sells photo supplies, such as film, batteries, and flashcubes.
GOE: 07.03.01 STRENGTH: L GED: R2 M2 L2 SVP: 2 DLU: 86

249.367-010 ANIMAL-SHELTER CLERK (nonprofit org.)
Assists public to adopt animals in animal shelter and compiles records of impounded animals: Assists prospective owners in selection of animals for adoption and in preparation of adoption forms. Advises new owners of pet-examination and neuterization services. Maintains list of prospective dog owners and contacts them when desired type of dog is available. Prepares dog-license forms and collects fees. Reviews shelter records of licensed-dog owners to identify owners of lost dogs; reviews other shelter records to help owners find lost pets. Compiles daily records required by animal shelter describing stray animals found by shelter workers and animals turned in by public.
GOE: 07.04.03 STRENGTH: S GED: R3 M2 L3 SVP: 3 DLU: 77

249.367-014 CAREER-GUIDANCE TECHNICIAN (education) alternate titles: career-information specialist; career resource technician
Collects and organizes occupational data to provide source materials for school career information center, and assists students and teachers to locate and obtain materials: Orders, catalogues, and maintains files on materials relating to job opportunities, careers, technical schools, colleges, scholarships, armed forces, and other programs. Assists students and teachers to locate career information related to students' interests and aptitudes, or demonstrates use of files, shelf collections, and other information retrieval systems. Assists students to take and score self-administered vocational interest and aptitude tests. Keeps records of students enrolled in work experience program and other vocational programs to assist counseling and guidance staff. Schedules appointments with school guidance and counseling staff for students requiring professional assistance. May make presentations to parent and other groups to publicize activities of career center. May operate audio-visual equipment, such as tape recorders, record players, and film or slide projectors.
GOE: 11.02.04 STRENGTH: L GED: R4 M3 L4 SVP: 6 DLU: 77

249.367-018 CHARTER (amuse. & rec.)
Observes horserace, calls out description of race to other worker, and records statistical and related data on race for use in racing publication: Focuses binoculars on distance markers along track during race and calls out horses' numbers, positions, estimate of distances of horses from inside rail and between horses, and related observable data for other worker to record. Revises record of order and distance between horses at finish line if different from intercom announcement of official results. Copies identifying information, such as horses' names and drivers, from racing form onto record. Transcribes race results, such as winning and intermediate times, purse, and prices paid to bettors from tote board onto record. Contacts judges, using intercom, for decisions on foul claims and notes record accordingly. Computes race completion times for all but winning horses, using formula. Mails completed record to printer for use in printing race results in racing publications.
GOE: 12.01.02 STRENGTH: S GED: R3 M2 L3 SVP: 3 DLU: 77

249.367-022 CREDIT AUTHORIZER (clerical) alternate titles: authorizer; charge-account authorizer
Authorizes credit charges against customer's account: Receives charge slip or credit application by mail, or receives information from salespeople or merchants over telephone. Verifies credit standing of customer from information in files, and approves or disapproves credit, based on predetermined standards. May file sales slips in customer's ledger for billing purposes. May prepare credit cards or charge account plates. May keep record of customer's charges and payments and mail charge statement to customer.
GOE: 07.05.02 STRENGTH: S GED: R3 M2 L2 SVP: 3 DLU: 77

249.367-026 CREDIT CARD CONTROL CLERK (financial) alternate titles: card processing clerk
Compiles, verifies, and files records and forms to control issuing, blocking (withholding), or renewal of credit cards, performing any combination of following duties: Receives shipments of plastic credit card blanks and verifies totals received against invoices. Assigns consecutive batch numbers to blank cards and stores cards in vault. Issues blank cards for imprinting, on requisition, and keeps records of batch numbers issued. Receives new or reissued printed cards, verifies number sequence, and compares identifying data on cards with data on application files to detect errors. Compiles lists of cards containing errors and initiates correction forms. Places completed credit cards and establishment literature into envelopes for mailing. Receives returned cards and reviews correspondence or searches records to determine customer reasons for return. Receives blocking notices from officials and places designated cards in hold file until release is authorized. Destroys inaccurate, mutilated, undelivered, withheld, or expired cards, in presence of witnesses, using scissors. Compiles list of destroyed cards and records reasons for destruction, using computer. Occasionally verifies customers' account balances to expedite issuance or renewal of cards. Maintains related files and control records. Issues cards for automated teller machines.
GOE: 07.05.03 STRENGTH: S GED: R3 M2 L2 SVP: 3 DLU: 87

249.367-030 DOG LICENSER (nonprofit org.)
Canvasses assigned area to locate and advise dog owners of licensing law; to assist with license applications; and to collect license fees: Visits homes and

questions dog owners to determine compliance with licensing law. Explains requirements to dog owners, fills out applications, and collects license fees or gives application to owners for mailing. Counts collected fees and applications. Submits fees and reports to department for record.
GOE: 07.04.03 STRENGTH: L GED: R3 M2 L3 SVP: 4 DLU: 77

249.367-034 EVALUATOR (nonprofit org.)
Estimates market value of items donated to vocational rehabilitation organization and prepares and mails tax receipts to donors: Sorts collection receipts by type of items donated. Estimates market value of items, using standard formula, and totals amount donated. Prepares tax receipt and mails to donor.
GOE: 05.09.02 STRENGTH: L GED: R4 M2 L2 SVP: 4 DLU: 77

249.367-042 GAS-DISTRIBUTION-AND-EMERGENCY CLERK (utilities)
Receives and relays telephone reports of gas emergencies and control-panel readings for gas-distribution-control-center of public utility company: Answers telephone reports of gas emergencies, such as leaks and fires, from general public, police, and fire departments, and notifies company personnel responsible for dispatch of service crews and issuance of reports to governmental agencies. Files charts and records of gas pressure, volume, and flow, and posts by category in daily logbook. Calculates statistical data from recorded readings and prepares gas supply-and-demand charts for use by GAS DISPATCHER (pipe lines; utilities).
GOE: 07.04.05 STRENGTH: S GED: R4 M3 L3 SVP: 6 DLU: 77

249.367-046 LIBRARY ASSISTANT (library) alternate titles: book-loan clerk; circulation clerk; desk attendant; library attendant; library clerk; library helper
Compiles records, sorts and shelves books, and issues and receives library materials, such as books, films, slides, and phonograph records: Records identifying data and due date on cards by hand or using photographic equipment to issue books to patrons. Inspects returned books for damage, verifies due-date, and computes and receives overdue fines. Reviews records to compile list of overdue books and issues overdue notices to borrowers. Sorts books, publications, and other items according to classification code and returns them to shelves, files, or other designated storage area. Locates books and publications for patrons. Issues borrower's identification card according to established procedures. Files cards in catalog drawers according to system. Repairs books, using mending tape and paste and brush, and places plastic covers on new books. Answers inquiries of nonprofessional nature on telephone and in person and refers persons requiring professional assistance to LIBRARIAN (library) 100.127-014. May type material cards or issue cards and duty schedules. May be designated according to type of library as Bookmobile Clerk (library); Branch-Library Clerk (library); or according to assigned department as Library Clerk, Art Department (library).
GOE: 11.02.04 STRENGTH: L GED: R3 M2 L3 SVP: 5 DLU: 82

249.367-058 PARTS-ORDER-AND-STOCK CLERK (clerical) alternate titles: purchaser, automotive parts
Purchases, stores, and issues spare parts for motor vehicles or industrial equipment: Obtains purchase order number from purchasing department and assigns identifying number. Reads shop manuals to ascertain type and specification of part. Visits, telephones, telegraphs, or contacts vendors by mail to order parts. Compares invoices against requisitions to verify quality and quantity of merchandise received. Stores purchased parts in storeroom bins and issues parts to workers upon request. Keeps records of parts received and issued, and inventories parts in storeroom periodically. May record repair time expended by mechanics. May requisition parts from central parts department for national organization.
GOE: 05.09.01 STRENGTH: L GED: R3 M2 L2 SVP: 5 DLU: 77

249.367-062 PROCESS SERVER (business ser.)
Serves court orders and processes, such as summonses and subpoenas: Receives papers to be served from magistrate, court clerk, or attorney. Locates person to be served, using telephone directories, state, county, and city records, or public utility records, and delivers document. Records time and place of delivery. May deliver general messages and documents between courts and attorneys.
GOE: 07.07.02 STRENGTH: L GED: R3 M2 L3 SVP: 3 DLU: 77

249.367-066 PROCUREMENT CLERK (clerical) alternate titles: award clerk; bid clerk; buyer, assistant; purchase-request editor; purchasing-and-fiscal clerk; purchasing clerk; purchasing-contracting clerk
Compiles information and records to prepare purchase orders for procurement of material for industrial firm, governmental agency, or other establishment: Verifies nomenclature and specifications of purchase requests. Searches inventory records or warehouse to determine if material on hand is in sufficient quantity. Consults catalogs and interviews suppliers to obtain prices and specifications. Types or writes invitation-of-bid forms and mails forms to supplier firms or for public posting. Writes or types purchase order and sends copy to supplier and department originating request. Compiles records of items purchased or transferred between departments, prices, deliveries, and inventories. Computes total cost of items purchased, using calculator. Confers with suppliers concerning late deliveries. May compare prices, specifications, and delivery dates and award contract to bidders or place orders with suppliers or mail order firms. May verify bills from suppliers with bids and purchase orders and approve bills for payment. May classify priority regulations.

GOE: 07.01.02 STRENGTH: S GED: R4 M3 L3 SVP: 4 DLU: 86

249.367-070 ROUTING CLERK (nonprofit org.)
Determines truck routes involved and issues route slips to drivers to pick up donated clothing, furniture, and general merchandise for vocational rehabilitation organization: Reviews presorted route slips and reviews street maps to determine appropriate route, based on type and quantity of merchandise pledged and location of donor. Issues route slips to drivers. Answers telephone and mail inquiries and complaints from donors concerning pickups; and advises drivers of problems or reschedules pickup. Occasionally takes pickup orders. Prepares daily truck-collection report based on information from drivers, and keeps attendance, safety, and maintenance records.
GOE: 07.05.04 STRENGTH: S GED: R3 M2 L3 SVP: 3 DLU: 77

249.367-074 TEACHER AIDE II (education) alternate titles: teacher aide, clerical
Performs any combination of following duties in classroom to assist teaching staff of public or private elementary or secondary school: Takes attendance. Grades homework and tests, using answer sheets, and records results. Distributes teaching materials to students, such as textbooks, workbooks, or paper and pencils. Maintains order within school and on school grounds. Operates learning aids, such as film and slide projectors and tape recorders. Prepares requisitions for library materials and stockroom supplies. Types material and operates duplicating equipment to reproduce instructional materials.
GOE: 07.01.02 STRENGTH: L GED: R3 M3 L3 SVP: 3 DLU: 86

249.367-078 TEST TECHNICIAN (clerical) alternate titles: evaluation aide; test examiner
Administers and scores psychological, vocational, or educational tests: Distributes test blanks or apparatus to individuals being tested. Reads directions orally from testing manual, or gives other standardized directions. Demonstrates use of test apparatus or discusses practice exercises to familiarize individuals with testing material. Monitors test group to ensure compliance with directions. Times test with stop watch or electric timer. Scores test with test-scoring key or machine. May schedule time and place for test to be administered. May administer test designed to measure work skills of mentally or physically handicapped individuals. Records results on test paper, work application, or test profile form.
GOE: 07.01.07 STRENGTH: L GED: R3 M2 L3 SVP: 4 DLU: 80

249.367-082 PARK AIDE (government ser.) alternate titles: park technician; ranger aide
Assists PARK RANGER (government ser.) 169.167-042 or PARK SUPERINTENDENT (government ser.) 188.167-062 in operation of state or national park, monument, historic site, or recreational area through performance of any combination of clerical and other duties: Greets visitors at facility entrance and explains regulations. Assigns campground or recreational vehicle sites, and collects fees at park offering camping facilities. Monitors campgrounds, cautions visitors against infractions of rules, and notifies PARK RANGER (government ser.) of problems. Replenishes firewood, and assists in maintaining camping and recreational areas in clean and orderly condition. Conducts tours of premises and answers visitors' questions when stationed at historic park, site, or monument. Operates projection and sound equipment and assists PARK RANGER (government ser.) in presentation of interpretive programs. Provides simple first-aid treatment to visitors injured on premises and assists persons with more serious injuries to obtain appropriate medical care. Participates in carrying out fire-fighting or conservation activities. Assists other workers in activities concerned with restoration of buildings and other facilities or excavation and preservation of artifacts when stationed at historic or archeological site.
GOE: 07.04.03 STRENGTH: L GED: R4 M3 L4 SVP: 3 DLU: 86

249.367-086 SATELLITE-INSTRUCTION FACILITATOR (education) alternate titles: satellite-project site monitor
Monitors training programs transmitted by communication satellite from institution of higher learning to remote educational institution or facility: Registers students for satellite communication courses and sells and distributes textbooks and other classroom materials. Activates audiovisual receiver and monitors classroom viewing of live or recorded courses transmitted by communication satellite. Stimulates classroom discussion immediately after broadcast, following standardized format. Monitors live seminar transmittals from institute of higher learning, elicits responses from classroom students, and consolidates and transmits students' questions by teletype or telephone to seminar participants for direct response via satellite. Distributes homework assignments and test blanks to students. Collects completed assignments and tests and mails them to institute of higher learning. Maintains class attendance records.
GOE: 07.01.02 STRENGTH: S GED: R3 M2 L3 SVP: 3 DLU: 86

249.367-090 ASSIGNMENT CLERK (clerical)
Compiles data to notify establishment personnel of position vacancies, and identifies and assigns qualified applicants, following specified guidelines and procedures: Scans reports to detect listings of vacancies or receives telephone notices of vacancies from establishment personnel. Types or writes information, such as position titles, shifts, days off, and application deadlines, on vacancy advertisement forms. Reviews bid slips or similar application forms submitted by employees in response to advertisement and verifies relevant data on application against data in personnel records. Selects applicants meeting specified criterion, such as seniority, and notifies concerned personnel of selection. Compiles and disperses position assignment notices to notify other establishment

personnel of applicants selected to fill vacancies. Records data on specified forms to update personnel and employment records.
GOE: 07.05.03 STRENGTH: S GED: R3 M2 L2 SVP: 5 DLU: 86

249.387-010 BROADCAST CHECKER (radio-tv broad.) alternate titles: log clerk; program checker

Monitors radio and television programs to detect contract violations with advertisers and program producers and violations of Federal Communications Commission (FCC) regulations and to detect audio and video irregularities: Times program elements, such as commercials, public service announcements, and news bulletins, using stopwatch. Observes and listens to programs to determine if FCC regulations and contract provisions with advertisers and program producers have been violated and whether quality of broadcast conforms to station and FCC standards. Logs length, type, and time of irregularities.
GOE: 11.10.02 STRENGTH: S GED: R3 M2 L3 SVP: 4 DLU: 77

249.387-014 INTELLIGENCE CLERK (military ser.)

Collects and organizes intelligence information from various established sources for production of intelligence documents: Reviews data to ascertain accuracy of data and reliability of sources. Compiles intelligence information and disseminates data through media, such as situation maps, charts, briefings, reports, and publications. Maintains intelligence libraries.
GOE: 07.05.03 STRENGTH: M GED: R3 M3 L3 SVP: 6 DLU: 77

249.387-018 PEDIGREE TRACER (clerical) alternate titles: pedigree researcher

Traces animal genealogy to certify or establish individual pedigree. Consults charts, books, and breeding records to ascertain lineage, names, ownerships, and show or racing performance records of ancestors. Records data and issues certificates.
GOE: 07.05.02 STRENGTH: S GED: R3 M2 L3 SVP: 3 DLU: 77

249.387-022 READER (business ser.) alternate titles: clipping marker; press reader; press-service reader

Reads newspapers, magazines, and other periodicals for articles of prescribed subject matter, and marks items to be clipped, using colored pencils and customer code system.
GOE: 07.05.02 STRENGTH: S GED: R3 M1 L3 SVP: 4 DLU: 77

249.467-010 INFORMATION CLERK-CASHIER (amuse. & rec.)

Cashes checks for patrons and provides information concerning racetrack activities: Receives specified amounts of monies from money room for check-cashing funds. Examines patrons' credentials and cashes checks. Directs patrons to such facilities as betting and paying windows and food and beverage concessions. Resolves patrons' claims of winning tickets not honored by PARI-MUTUEL-TICKET CASHIER (amuse. & rec.). Examines tickets under fluorescent light to verify watermark and establish validity. Confers with payment personnel to effect payment or refers disputed claims to supervisory personnel for resolution. Keeps records of customer complaints and suggestions regarding facilities and submits records to supervisory personnel.
GOE: 07.03.01 STRENGTH: L GED: R3 M2 L3 SVP: 5 DLU: 77

249.587-010 BOARD ATTENDANT (amuse. & rec.) alternate titles: gambling broker; racing-board marker; wall attendant

Writes racing information, such as betting odds, entries, and winning time, on paper sheets affixed to walls or on blackboards of bookmaking establishment. Works from stepladder.
GOE: 09.05.05 STRENGTH: L GED: R3 M2 L2 SVP: 2 DLU: 77

249.587-014 CUTTER-AND-PASTER, PRESS CLIPPINGS (business ser.) alternate titles: tearer, press clipping; trimmer, press clippings

Tears or cuts out marked articles or advertisements from newspapers and magazines, using knife or scissors. Records name of publication, page and location, date, and name of customer on label, and affixes label to clipping.
GOE: 07.07.03 STRENGTH: S GED: R2 M1 L1 SVP: 2 DLU: 77

249.587-018 DOCUMENT PREPARER, MICROFILMING (business ser.)

Prepares documents, such as brochures, pamphlets, and catalogs, for microfilming, using paper cutter, photocopying machine, rubber stamps, and other work devices: Cuts documents into individual pages of standard microfilming size and format when allowed by margin space, using paper cutter or razor knife. Reproduces document pages as necessary to improve clarity or to reduce one or more pages into single page of standard microfilming size, using photocopying machine. Stamps standard symbols on pages or inserts instruction cards between pages of material to notify MICROFILM-CAMERA OPERATOR (business ser.) 976.682-022 of special handling, such as manual repositioning, during microfilming. Prepares cover sheet and document folder for material and index card for company files indicating information, such as firm name and address, product category, and index code, to identify material. Inserts material to be filmed in document folder and files folder for processing according to index code and filming priority schedule.
GOE: 07.05.03 STRENGTH: S GED: R3 M1 L2 SVP: 2 DLU: 86

249.687-010 OFFICE COPY SELECTOR (print. & pub.)

Inspects publications, such as magazines, catalogs, and pamphlets for conformance to quality standards, and selects copies of highest quality for distribution to management, publishers, and clients according to distribution list: Reviews distribution list for specific publication in order to ascertain number of copies required for distribution. Examines overall appearance of copies received from production department for conformance to quality standards. Examines each page of copies for uniformity of margins, quality of multicolored and monocolored illustrations, missing pages, and other defects. Sorts copies with highest overall quality and routes stack to management. Selects copies which have highest quality reproductions of advertisements and feature articles, tags individual copies or bundles according to distribution sheet, and routes stacks to mailing room. Keeps records of copies distributed.
GOE: 07.05.04 STRENGTH: L GED: R3 M1 L2 SVP: 3 DLU: 77

249.687-014 PAGE (library) alternate titles: runner; shelver; shelving clerk; stack clerk

Locates library materials, such as books, periodicals, and pictures for loan, and replaces material in shelving area (stacks) or files, according to identification number and title. Trucks or carries material between shelving area and issue desk. May clip premarked articles from periodicals.
GOE: 07.07.02 STRENGTH: L GED: R2 M1 L2 SVP: 2 DLU: 77

25 SALES OCCUPATIONS, SERVICES

This division includes occupations concerned with selling real estate, insurance, securities, and other business, financial, and consumer services.

250 SALES OCCUPATIONS, REAL ESTATE, INSURANCE, SECURITIES, AND FINANCIAL SERVICES

This group includes occupations concerned with renting, buying, and selling real property for clients; selling insurance to clients; buying and selling securities; and selling financial services, such as accounting, auditing, tax, credit checking, financial planning, lending and other services of financial institutions.

250.157-010 SUPERINTENDENT, SALES (construction) alternate titles: sales representative

Plans and promotes sale of new and custom-built homes for building contractor: Plans and organizes sales promotion programs and techniques in cooperation with suppliers of household appliances, furnishings, and equipment. Locates and appraises undeveloped areas for building sites, based on evaluation of area market conditions. Interviews prospective clients and shows homes under construction to display construction features and quality of work. Reviews plans and specifications for custom-built homes with client and ARCHITECT (profess. & kin.) to clarify costs and construction details in preliminary negotiations for contract. Recommends construction features and available decorating options, such as cabinet installations, to aid client in formulating plans. Answers questions regarding work under construction. May assess clients' financial status to determine eligibility for financing home through contractor. May arrange for sale of client's present home [SALES AGENT, REAL ESTATE (real estate)].
GOE: 08.02.04 STRENGTH: L GED: R5 M4 L5 SVP: 7 DLU: 77

250.257-010 SALES AGENT, INSURANCE (insurance) alternate titles: insurance agent

Sells insurance to new and current clients: Compiles lists of prospective clients to provide leads for additional business. Contacts prospective clients and explains features and merits of policies offered, recommending amount and type of coverage based on analysis of prospect's circumstances, and utilizing persuasive sales techniques. Calculates and quotes premium rates for recommended policies, using calculator and rate books. Calls on policyholders to deliver and explain policy, to suggest additions or changes in insurance program, or to make changes in beneficiaries. May collect premiums from policyholders and keep record of payments. Must hold license issued by state. May be designated according to type of insurance sold as Sales Agent, Casualty Insurance (insurance); Sales Agent, Fire Insurance (insurance); Sales Agent, Life Insurance (insurance); Sales Agent, Marine Insurance (insurance). May work independently selling variety of insurance, such as life, fire, casualty, and marine, for many companies and be designated Insurance Broker (insurance). May work independently selling for one company and be designated General Agent (insurance).
GOE: 08.01.02 STRENGTH: L GED: R4 M3 L4 SVP: 6 DLU: 81

250.257-014 FINANCIAL PLANNER (profess. & kin.)

Develops and implements financial plans for individuals, businesses, and organizations, utilizing knowledge of tax and investment strategies, securities, insurance, pension plans, and real estate: Interviews client to determine client's assets, liabilities, cash flow, insurance coverage, tax status, and financial objectives. Analyzes client's financial status, develops financial plan based on analysis of data, and discusses financial options with client. Prepares and submits documents to implement plan selected by client. Maintains contact with client to revise plan based on modified needs of client or changes in investment market. May refer client to other establishments to obtain services outlined in financial plan. May sell insurance to client, recommending amount and type of coverage [SALES AGENT, INSURANCE (insurance) 250.257-010]. May buy and sell stocks and bonds for client [SALES AGENT, SECURITIES (financial) 251.157-010]. May rent, buy, and sell property for client [SALES AGENT, REAL ESTATE (real estate) 250.357-018]. May be registered with professional

self-regulatory association and be designated Certified Financial Planner (profess. & kin.).
GOE: 08.01.02 STRENGTH: S GED: R5 M3 L4 SVP: 8 DLU: 86

250.257-018 REGISTERED REPRESENTATIVE (financial) alternate titles: account executive; broker; investment executive; securities broker; stock-broker

Sells financial products and services to clients for investment purposes, applying knowledge of securities, investment plans, market conditions, regulations, and financial situation of clients: Identifies potential clients, using advertising campaigns, mailing lists, and personal contacts. Solicits business from potential clients. Interviews clients to determine financial position, resources, assets available to invest, and financial goals. Provides clients with information and advice on purchase or sale of securities, financial services, and investment plans, based on review of professional publications and other financial literature, and knowledge of securities market and financial services industry. Completes sales order tickets and submits completed tickets to support personnel for processing of client requested transaction. Must pass state examination to receive license and become registered to sell securities. May read status reports and perform calculations to monitor client accounts and verify transactions. May work for firm that offers discounted brokerage fees and does not offer advice to clients. May develop and implement financial plans, and sell insurance, real estate, or securities [FINANCIAL PLANNER (profess. & kin.) 250.257-014].
GOE: 11.06.04 STRENGTH: S GED: R4 M3 L4 SVP: 7 DLU: 89

250.257-022 SALES REPRESENTATIVE, FINANCIAL SERVICES (financial)

Sells financial services to customers of financial institution: Develops prospects from current commercial customers, referral leads, and other sources. Contacts prospective customers to present information on available services, such as deposit accounts, lines-of-credit, sales or inventory financing, cash management, or investment services. Determines customers' financial services needs and prepares proposals to sell services. Reviews business trends and advises customers regarding expected fluctuations. Attends sales and trade meetings to develop new business prospects. May make presentations on financial services to groups to attract new clients. May prepare forms or agreement to complete sale. May evaluate costs and revenue of agreements to determine if they are profitable to continue. May sell services, such as check processing and collecting, record keeping and reporting, trust, investment, or safekeeping services, or products such as travelers checks, to other financial institutions. May solicit businesses to participate in consumer credit card program.
GOE: 08.01.02 STRENGTH: L GED: R5 M4 L5 SVP: 7 DLU: 89

250.357-010 BUILDING CONSULTANT (wholesale tr.)

Sells new home construction to property owners: Displays and explains features of company house plans, using such visual aids as brochures, architectural drawings, samples of construction materials, and photographic slides. Secures construction financing with own firm or mortgage company. Contacts utility companies for service hookup to client's property. May appraise client's unimproved property to determine loan value. May investigate client's credit status. May search public records to ascertain that client has clear title to property. May contact utility companies for service hookup in customer's property.
GOE: 08.02.04 STRENGTH: L GED: R4 M3 L4 SVP: 5 DLU: 77

250.357-014 LEASING AGENT, RESIDENCE (real estate) alternate titles: rental agent

Shows and leases apartments, condominiums, homes, or mobile home lots to prospective tenants: Interviews prospective tenants and records information to ascertain needs and qualifications. Accompanies prospects to model homes and apartments and discusses size and layout of rooms, available facilities, such as swimming pool and saunas, location of shopping centers, services available, and terms of lease. Completes lease form or agreement and collects rental deposit. May inspect condition of premises periodically and arrange for necessary maintenance. May compile listings of available rental property. May compose newspaper advertisements. May be required to have real estate agent's license. May contact credit bureau to obtain credit report on prospective tenant.
GOE: 08.02.04 STRENGTH: L GED: R4 M2 L4 SVP: 5 DLU: 89

250.357-018 SALES AGENT, REAL ESTATE (real estate) alternate titles: real-estate agent

Rents, buys, and sells property for clients on commission basis: Studies property listings to become familiar with properties for sale. Reviews trade journals and attends staff and association meetings to keep informed of marketing conditions, property values, and legislation which would affect real estate industry. Interviews prospective clients to solicit listings. Accompanies prospects to property sites, quotes purchase price, describes features, and discusses conditions of sale or terms of lease. Draws up real estate contracts, such as deeds, leases, and mortgages, and negotiates loans on property. Must have license issued by state. May hold broker's license and be designated Real-Estate Broker (real estate). May assist buyer and seller in obtaining pertinent information or services, such as finance, maintenance, repair, or obtaining an appraisal. May obtain pictures and measurements of rooms, doors, windows, or any other specified areas for inclusion in newspaper advertisement and real estate booklets listing description of property. May inspect property to determine if repairs are needed and notify owner. May conduct seminars and training sessions for sales agents to improve sales techniques. May prepare closing statements, oversee signing of real estate documents, disburse funds, and coordinate closing activities.

GOE: 08.02.04 STRENGTH: L GED: R4 M3 L4 SVP: 5 DLU: 89

250.357-022 SALES REPRESENTATIVE (motor trans.)

Sells warehouse space and services to manufacturers and jobbers, performing duties as described under SALESPERSON (retail trade; wholesale tr.) Master Title.
GOE: 08.02.06 STRENGTH: L GED: R3 M3 L3 SVP: 5 DLU: 77

250.357-026 SALES AGENT, FINANCIAL-REPORT SERVICE (business ser.) alternate titles: sales agent, credit services

Sells services, such as credit, financial, insurance, employee investigation reports, and credit-rating books to business establishments: Calls on establishments, such as financial institutions and commercial and industrial firms, to explain services offered by agency. Explains advantages of using impartial and factual reports and data as basis for assigning credit ratings, insurance, or security risks. May also sell equipment, such as portable teletype terminal units, for use in immediate retrieval of computerized data.
GOE: 08.01.02 STRENGTH: L GED: R4 M3 L4 SVP: 5 DLU: 77

251 SALES OCCUPATIONS, BUSINESS SERVICES, EXCEPT REAL ESTATE, INSURANCE, SECURITIES, AND FINANCIAL SERVICES

This group includes occupations concerned with selling business services, such as management consulting, data processing, clerical, janitorial, and exterminating services.

251.157-014 SALES REPRESENTATIVE, DATA PROCESSING SERVICES (business ser.)

Contacts representatives of government, business, and industrial organizations to solicit business for data processing establishment: Calls on prospective clients to explain types of services provided by establishment, such as inventory control, payroll processing, data conversion, sales analysis, and financial reporting. Analyzes data processing requirements of prospective client and draws up prospectus of data processing plan designed specifically to serve client's needs. Consults SYSTEMS ANALYST (profess. & kin.) 030.167-014 and COMPUTER SYSTEMS HARDWARE ANALYST (profess. & kin.) 033.167-010 employed by data processing establishment to secure information concerning methodology for solving unusual problems. Quotes prices for services outlined in prospectus. Revises or expands prospectus to meet client's needs. Writes order and schedules initiation of services. Periodically confers with clients and establishment personnel to verify satisfaction with service or to resolve complaints.
GOE: 08.01.02 STRENGTH: L GED: R5 M5 L5 SVP: 7 DLU: 86

251.257-014 SALES AGENT, PSYCHOLOGICAL TESTS AND INDUSTRIAL RELATIONS (business ser.; print. & pub.)

Sells programs of industrial relations, public relations, psychological counseling, and psychological, intelligence, and aptitude testing to schools and business organizations, working for industrial psychological firm or for book publisher: Interviews management officials of business to explain advantages of utilizing services offered. Analyzes program needs of organization and recommends appropriate psychological or testing program. Answers questions about services. Takes orders for services. Aids in integrating program into firm's method of operation. May give instructions to organization personnel in administration, scoring, and interpretation of tests.
GOE: 08.01.02 STRENGTH: L GED: R5 M4 L5 SVP: 7 DLU: 77

251.357-010 SALES AGENT, BUSINESS SERVICES (business ser.)

Sells business service, such as food-vending, trading stamps, detective, armored truck, telephone-answering, linen supply, and cleaning service: Develops list of prospective customers by studying business and telephone directories, consulting business associates, and observing business establishment while driving through sales territory. Reviews orders for ideas to expand services available to present customers. Calls on prospects to explain features of services, cost, and advantages. Writes orders and schedules initiation of services. Confers with customers and company officials to resolve complaints. May collect payments on accounts. May be designated according to service sold as Sales Agent, Food-Vending Service (wholesale tr.); Sales Agent, Protective Service (business ser.); Sales Agent, Trading Stamps (business ser.).
GOE: 08.02.06 STRENGTH: L GED: R4 M3 L4 SVP: 5 DLU: 77

251.357-018 SALES AGENT, PEST CONTROL SERVICE (business ser.) alternate titles: sales agent, exterminating service

Sells pest-control service to home owners and commercial concerns: Selects prospects in assigned territory from account file, list of firms with possible need, and from potential customers who have requested service. Calls on prospect to explain service. Inspects premises to ascertain presence of vermin. Prepares contract for customers including such information as name of pest, area of infestation, and remedy required, based on knowledge of pest, structural damage, kinds of insecticides, and conditions conducive to pest development. Quotes price, obtains consent of customer, and schedules EXTERMINATOR (any industry) to initiate treatment. May treat infested areas [EXTERMINATOR, TERMITE (business ser.)].
GOE: 08.02.06 STRENGTH: L GED: R4 M3 L4 SVP: 6 DLU: 77

251.357-022 SALES REPRESENTATIVE, FRANCHISE (business ser.)

Solicits purchase of franchise operation by contacting persons who meet organization's standards: Visits prospects to explain advantages of franchised

business, services to be rendered, costs, location, and financial arrangements. Performs other duties as described under SALES REPRESENTATIVE (retail trade; wholesale tr.) Master Title. May assist franchise purchaser in early stages of operating business, May confer with purchaser and company officials to resolve complaints.
GOE: 08.02.06 STRENGTH: L GED: R4 M3 L4 SVP: 5 DLU: 77

251.357-026 SALES REPRESENTATIVE, HERBICIDE SERVICE (business ser.)
    Sells weed-eradication service to firms desiring right-of-way maintenance, performing duties as described under SALES REPRESENTATIVE (retail trade; wholesale tr.) Master Title. Confers with prospective customer to determine amount of ground surface to be treated, unusual vegetation problems, terrain, and other factors influencing price of service. Consults with technical staff, when needed, to arrive at proposal and price quotation.
GOE: 08.02.06 STRENGTH: L GED: R4 M3 L4 SVP: 5 DLU: 77

252   SALES OCCUPATIONS, TRANSPORTATION SERVICES

    This group includes occupations concerned with selling passenger and freight transportation services. Includes arranging passenger travel and lodging accommodations by travel agents.

252.152-010 TRAVEL AGENT (business ser.; motor trans.; retail trade) alternate titles: travel counselor
    Plans itineraries, and arranges accommodations and other travel services for customers of travel agency: Converses with customer to determine destination, mode of transportation, travel dates, financial considerations, and accommodations required. Provides customer with brochures and publications containing travel information, such as local customs, points of interest, and special events occurring in various locations, or foreign country regulations, such as consular requirements and currency limitations. Computes cost of travel and accommodations, using calculator, computer, carrier tariff books, and hotel rate books, or quotes package tours' costs. Books transportation and hotel reservations, using computer terminal or telephone. Prints or requests transportation carrier tickets, using computer printer system or system link to travel carrier. Collects payment for transportation and accommodations from customer. Plans, describes, arranges, and sells itinerary tour packages and promotional travel incentives offered by various travel carriers, utilizing knowledge of available travel services and promotional techniques. May specialize in foreign or domestic travel, individual or group travel, specific geographic area, airplane charters, or package tours. May be located in transportation terminal and specialize in group and individual escorted tours and be designated Tour Agent (motor trans.).
GOE: 08.02.06 STRENGTH: S GED: R4 M3 L4 SVP: 5 DLU: 81

252.257-010 TRAFFIC AGENT (air trans.; motor trans.; r.r. trans.; water trans.) alternates titles: sales representative
    Solicits freight business from industrial and commercial firms and passenger-travel business from travel agencies, schools, clubs, and other organizations: Calls on prospective shippers to explain advantages of using company facilities. Quotes tariffs, rates, and train schedules. Explains available routes, load limits, and special equipment available, and offers suggestions in method of loading, crating, and handling freight. Calls on travel agents, schools, clubs, and other organizations to explain available accommodations offered by company. Quotes fares, schedules, and available itineraries offered to groups by company. Speaks to members of groups and organizations and exhibits travel movies showing points of interest along routes to stimulate interest in travel. Distributes descriptive pamphlets. Acts as liaison between shipper and carrier to obtain information for settling complaints. May specialize in soliciting freight or passenger contracts or may travel from community to community to solicit freight and passenger patronage and be designated Freight-Traffic Agent (air trans.; motor trans.; r.r. trans.; water trans.); Passenger Traffic Agent (air trans.; motor trans.; r.r. trans.; water trans.); Traveling-Freight-And-Passenger Agent (air trans.; motor trans.; r.r. trans.; water trans.).
GOE: 08.01.02 STRENGTH: L GED: R5 M3 L4 SVP: 7 DLU: 77

252.357-010 CRATING-AND-MOVING ESTIMATOR (motor trans.; r.r. trans.)
    Solicits freight or storage business from homeowners and business establishments and estimates packing, crating, moving, and storage costs: Develops lists of prospective customers from review of publications and contacts with business and real estate firms, providing such information as personnel transfers and home-sales listings. Calls on prospect at home or business establishment and describes services provided by company. Examines goods to be moved or stored, estimates cubic feet of storage or shipping space required, using comparison chart, and computes cost of packing, crating, moving, shipping, and delivering household goods, machinery, or other material. Records details on itemized sales contract, such as value and description of goods, packing instructions, and charge for each service.
GOE: 08.02.06 STRENGTH: L GED: R4 M3 L4 SVP: 5 DLU: 77

252.357-014 SALES REPRESENTATIVE, SHIPPING SERVICES (motor trans.)
    Solicits shipper's account for parcel-delivery firm: Visits management of new businesses and those with change of ownership to promote new business and obtain contracts for service. Explains shipping rates and regulations regarding wrapping, size, handling, and weight of parcels. Completes service contract form. Reviews shipper's accounts to identify problems, such as overdue accounts, proposed changes in pickup and delivery schedules, failure of shipper to follow parcel wrapping and handling requirements, and frequency and type of shipper's claims. Calls on shipper's representatives to discuss and resolve problems.
GOE: 08.01.02 STRENGTH: L GED: R3 M3 L3 SVP: 5 DLU: 77

253   SALES OCCUPATIONS, UTILITIES

    This group includes occupations concerned with selling utility services, such as gas, electric power, and telephone and telegraph services.

253.157-010 COMMUNICATIONS CONSULTANT (tel. & tel.) alternate titles: special-service representative
    Contacts residential, commercial, and industrial telephone company subscribers to ascertain communication problems and needs and promote use of telephone services, utilizing knowledge of marketing conditions, contracts, sales methods, and communications services and equipment: Discusses communication services, such as telephone, teletypewriter, or ticker tape, with subscriber representative to inform representative of services available, and obtains information, such as size of physical plant, range of desired communication, and type of equipment or service desired. Consults with other workers regarding communication needs of subscriber to obtain information, such as availability and cost of services or equipment requested. Analyzes information obtained to determine practicability of subscriber request and advises subscriber representative on selection and utilization of services. Prepares sales contracts. Reviews subscriber accounts to determine and evaluate utilization of communication services. May specialize in sales of commercial, industrial, or residential telephone services and be designated Communications Consultant, Commercial Services (tel. & tel.); Communications Consultant, Industrial Services (tel. & tel.); Communications Consultant, Residential Services (tel. & tel.).
GOE: 08.01.01 STRENGTH: L GED: R5 M3 L4 SVP: 6 DLU: 87

253.257-010 SALES REPRESENTATIVE, TELEPHONE SERVICES (tel. & tel.) alternate titles: commercial representative
    Sells telephone services to business accounts: Contacts and visits commercial customers to review telephone service. Analyzes communication needs of business establishments, using knowledge of type of business, available telephone equipment, and traffic studies. Recommends services, such as additional telephone instruments and lines, switchboard systems, dial- and key-telephone systems, private-branch exchanges, and speaker telephones. Quotes rates for equipment and writes up orders. Explains equipment usage, using brochures and demonstration equipment. May specialize in selling services to a particular industry.
GOE: 08.01.02 STRENGTH: L GED: R5 M3 L4 SVP: 6 DLU: 77

253.357-010 SALES REPRESENTATIVE, PUBLIC UTILITIES (tel. & tel.; utilities) alternate titles: commercial service representative
    Solicits prospective and existing commercial and residential clients to promote increased or economical use of public utilities, such as gas, electric power, telephone, and telegraph service: Inspects installations in existing establishments or reviews plans for new construction to determine potential need or necessity for extension of utility service. Advises customers in most economical use of utility to promote energy conservation and reduce cost. Quotes approximate rates, installation charges, and operating costs and explains company services. Writes construction requisitions and service applications, conforming to needs and requests of consumer. May investigate customers' complaints concerning bills. May be designated by type of utility sold as Sales Representative, Electric Service (utilities); Sales Representative, Gas Service (utilities); Sales Representative, Telephone and Telegraph Services (tel. & tel.) or by area in which utility is sold as Sales Representative, Rural Power (utilities).
GOE: 08.01.02 STRENGTH: L GED: R4 M3 L4 SVP: 6 DLU: 78

254   SALES OCCUPATIONS, PRINTING AND ADVERTISING

    This group includes occupations concerned with selling printing services, display and classified advertising for publications, outdoor advertising, and art works used for advertising purposes.

254.251-010 SALES REPRESENTATIVE, GRAPHIC ART (business ser.)
    Sells graphic art, such as layout, illustration, and photography, to advertising agencies and industrial organizations for use in advertising and illustration: Plans and sketches layouts to meet customer needs. Advises customer in methods of composing layouts, utilizing knowledge of photographic and illustrative art and printing terminology. Informs customer of types of artwork available by providing samples. Computes job costs. Delivers advertising or illustration proofs to customer for approval. May write copy as part of layout.
GOE: 08.01.01 STRENGTH: L GED: R5 M3 L4 SVP: 7 DLU: 77

254.257-010 SALES REPRESENTATIVE, SIGNS AND DISPLAYS (fabrication, nec)
    Solicits and draws up contracts for signs and displays: Calls on advertisers and sales promotion people to obtain information concerning prospects for cur-

rent advertising and sales promotion. Discusses advantages of and suggests ideas for signs and displays. Submits rendering or drawing of proposed sign or display to prospect. Draws up contract covering arrangements for designing, fabricating, erecting, and maintaining sign or display, depending on type of job and customer's wishes. May confer with architect in determining type of sign. May select and arrange for lease of site [SALES AGENT, REAL ESTATE (real estate)].
GOE: 08.01.01 STRENGTH: L GED: R4 M3 L4 SVP: 6 DLU: 77

254.357-010   LEASING AGENT, OUTDOOR ADVERTISING (business ser.)
Obtains leases to sites for outdoor advertising: Persuades property owners to lease sites for erection of billboard signs used in outdoor advertising. Arranges price and draws up lease. May locate potential billboard sites, using automobile to travel through assigned district. May search legal records for land ownership.
GOE: 11.12.02 STRENGTH: L GED: R3 M2 L3 SVP: 4 DLU: 77

254.357-014   SALES REPRESENTATIVE, ADVERTISING (print. & pub.) alternate titles: advertising-sales representative; advertising solicitor
Sells classified and display advertising space for publication: Prepares list of prospects from leads in other papers and from old accounts. Obtains pertinent information concerning prospect's past and current advertising for use in sales presentation. Visits advertisers to point out advantages of own publication and exhibits prepared layouts with mats and copy with headings. May collect payments due. Usually designated by type of advertising sold as Sales Representative, Classified Advertising (print. & pub.); Sales Representative, Display Advertising (print. & pub.).
GOE: 08.01.02 STRENGTH: L GED: R4 M3 L4 SVP: 6 DLU: 77

254.357-018   SALES REPRESENTATIVE, PRINTING (wholesale tr.)
Visits business establishments to solicit business for printing firm: Interviews purchasing personnel and quotes prices on printed material from schedule or secures price from ESTIMATOR, PRINTING (print. & pub.). Explains technical phases, such as type size and style, paper stock, binding materials, and various methods of reproduction. Contacts prospects, following leads submitted by management, established customers, or developed through other sources. May prepare sales promotional letters to be sent to prospective customers. May submit formal bids on large orders of printed matter.
GOE: 08.01.02 STRENGTH: L GED: R4 M3 L4 SVP: 5 DLU: 77

254.357-022   SALES REPRESENTATIVE, SIGNS (fabrication, nec)
Sells electric, cutout, neon, engraved, or painted signs, to be made according to customers' specifications, from materials, such as wood, metal, or plastic, utilizing knowledge of lettering, color harmony, and processes involved in making various signs. Performs other duties as described under SALESPERSON (retail trade; wholesale tr.) Master Title.
GOE: 08.01.01 STRENGTH: L GED: R4 M3 L4 SVP: 6 DLU: 77

259   SALES OCCUPATIONS, SERVICES, N.E.C.

This group includes occupations, not elsewhere classified, concerned with selling services.

259.157-010   SALES REPRESENTATIVE, AUDIOVISUAL PROGRAM PRODUCTIONS (motion picture)
Contacts prospective customers to sell service of producing motion pictures or recordings designed to inform specific audiences about goods, services, or procedures, performing duties as described under SALES REPRESENTATIVE (retail trade; wholesale tr.) Master Title: Records customer's instructions and plans preliminary programs commensurate with customer's objectives and budget limitations. Obtains information necessary for production specialists to produce programs that accomplish customer's aims. Consults with production specialists to obtain cost estimate of program and submits estimate to customer for approval.
GOE: 08.02.06 STRENGTH: L GED: R4 M3 L4 SVP: 5 DLU: 77

259.157-014   SALES REPRESENTATIVE, HOTEL SERVICES (hotel & rest.)
Contacts representatives of government, business, associations, and social groups to solicit business for hotel, motel, or resort: Reviews information on sales meetings, conventions, training classes, overnight travel, and other functions held by organization members to select prospective customers for hotel services. Calls on prospects to solicit business, analyzes requirements of function, outlines available hotel facilities and services offered, and quotes prices. Verifies reservations by letter, or draws up contract and obtains signatures. Confers with customer and hotel department heads to plan function details, such as space requirements, publicity, time schedule, food service, and decorations. May serve as convention advisor or coordinator during function to minimize confusion and resolve problems, such as space adjustment and need for additional equipment. May select and release hotel publicity. May prepare and mail advance brochures to prospective customers.
GOE: 08.01.02 STRENGTH: S GED: R4 M3 L4 SVP: 7 DLU: 81

259.257-010   SALES REPRESENTATIVE, EDUCATION COURSES (education)
Solicits applications for enrollment in technical, commercial, and industrial schools: Contacts prospects, explains courses offered by school, and quotes fees. Advises prospective students on selection of courses based on their education and vocational objectives. Compiles registration information. May accept registration fees or tuition payments. May be designated according to type of school as Sales Representative, Business Courses (education); Sales Representative, Correspondence Courses (education).
GOE: 08.01.02 STRENGTH: L GED: R4 M3 L4 SVP: 5 DLU: 77

259.257-014   SALES REPRESENTATIVE, ELECTROPLATING (wholesale tr.)
Sells electroplating services to manufacturers of formed metal and plastic products: Visits industrial establishments that manufacture formed metal and plastic products, such as metal automotive parts and plastic radio and television control panels. Evaluates structural characteristics and properties of products and determines specifications of finishing process, such as plating, anodizing, and coloring, utilizing knowledge of electroplating processes on metal and plastic. Confers with production staff of electroplating establishment to analyze special problems related to customer's product. Performs other duties as described under SALES REPRESENTATIVE (retail trade; wholesale tr.) Master Title.
GOE: 08.01.01 STRENGTH: L GED: R5 M4 L4 SVP: 7 DLU: 77

259.257-018   SERVICE REPRESENTATIVE, ELEVATORS, ESCALATORS, AND DUMBWAITERS (wholesale tr.)
Sells maintenance service and engineering improvements for elevators, escalators, and dumbwaiters, applying knowledge of mechanical engineering: Compiles list of prospective customers and schedules contacts according to sales potential and geographical location. Explains type of service available and quotes cost of servicing equipment, explains tasks performed to achieve maximum performance, such as lubrication, electronic testing, and inspection of cables. Writes service contracts for new customers and renewal contracts for current customers. Explains benefits of modernizing equipment, such as improved speed, safety, and appearance. Inspects equipment and tallies traffic in building. Writes report of equipment to be modernized and changes to be made, and submits to engineering department for cost quotations. Presents proposal to customer for approval. Prepares monthly report of contracts sold, details of business transactions, and customers contacted. May sell elevator, escalator, and dumbwaiter parts to owners who maintain own equipment.
GOE: 08.01.01 STRENGTH: L GED: R5 M4 L4 SVP: 5 DLU: 77

259.257-022   SALES REPRESENTATIVE, SECURITY SYSTEMS (business ser.)
Sells burglar, fire, and medical emergency alarm systems and security monitoring services to individuals and businesses: Contacts prospective customers to explain security monitoring services and to demonstrate alarm systems. Examines customer's home or business and analyzes customer's requirements to recommend security system to meet customer's needs. Explains operation of security system after installation. Performs other duties as described under SALES REPRESENTATIVE (retail trade; wholesale tr.) Master Title.
GOE: 08.01.02 STRENGTH: M GED: R4 M3 L4 SVP: 5 DLU: 86

259.357-010   GROUP-SALES REPRESENTATIVE (amuse. & rec.) alternate titles: promotor, group-ticket sales
Promotes sale of group or season tickets for sports or other entertainment events: Telephones, visits, or writes to organizations, such as chambers of commerce, corporate-employee-recreation clubs, social clubs, and professional groups, to persuade them to purchase group tickets or season tickets to sports or other entertainment events, such as baseball, horseracing, or stage plays. Quotes group-ticket rates, arranges for sale of tickets and seating for group on specific date(s), and obtains payment. May arrange for club to sponsor sports event, such as one of races at horseracing track.
GOE: 08.02.08 STRENGTH: L GED: R3 M2 L3 SVP: 3 DLU: 77

259.357-014   SALES REPRESENTATIVE, DANCING INSTRUCTIONS (education)
Sells dancing instructions to patrons at dance studio: Interviews patron to ascertain dancing background. Dances with patron to determine dancing ability and discusses ability with patron. Devises plan of instruction and persuades patron to purchase lessons. May prepare sales contracts and receive payments. May instruct patron in dancing [INSTRUCTOR, DANCING (education)].
GOE: 08.02.05 STRENGTH: L GED: R3 M2 L3 SVP: 4 DLU: 77

259.357-018   SALES REPRESENTATIVE, RADIO AND TELEVISION TIME (radio-tv broad.) alternate titles: account executive
Contacts prospective customers to sell radio and television time or captioning services for broadcasting station, network, or cable television franchise: Calls on prospects and presents outlines of various programs or commercial announcements. Discusses current popularity of various types of programs, such as news, drama, and variety. Drives auto vehicle to prospective customer's location. May arrange for and accompany prospect to commercial taping sessions. May prepare promotional plans, sales literature, and sales contracts, using computer.
GOE: 08.01.02 STRENGTH: L GED: R4 M3 L4 SVP: 6 DLU: 89

259.357-022   SALES REPRESENTATIVE, TELEVISION CABLE SERVICE (radio-tv broad.)
Contacts homeowners, apartment managers, and other prospects to sell cable television service: Compiles list of prospective customers from lists of homes that do not have cable television and lists of residential addresses with names of owners and occupants. Travels throughout assigned territory to call on pro-

spective customers in their homes to solicit orders. Performs duties as described under SALES REPRESENTATIVE (retail trade; wholesale tr.) Master Title.
GOE: 08.02.06 STRENGTH: L GED: R4 M3 L4 SVP: 3 DLU: 88

259.357-026 SALES REPRESENTATIVE, UPHOLSTERY AND FUR-NITURE REPAIR (retail trade)

Calls on prospective customers to sell and estimate cost of furniture repair and upholstery service, utilizing knowledge of upholstery and repair procedures and material and labor costs: Examines worn or damaged furniture to determine extent of repairs required. Estimates amount of material required based on style and dimensions of furniture. Advises customer on color and type of fabric. Completes estimate form and gives form to customer. Prepares sales contract for upholstery work.
GOE: 08.02.06 STRENGTH: L GED: R4 M3 L3 SVP: 5 DLU: 77

259.357-030 SALES REPRESENTATIVE, WEATHER-FORECASTING SERVICE (business ser.)

Sells weather forecasting services to business establishments: Calls on or writes to establishments, such as construction contractors and airlines, explains services, and quotes prices to gain new customers or renew current accounts. Writes customer orders and maintains order files. May write advertising and sales promotion aids.
GOE: 08.01.02 STRENGTH: L GED: R4 M3 L4 SVP: 4 DLU: 77

259.357-034 TICKET BROKER (amuse. & rec.)

Purchases entertainment tickets in blocks at box-office prices, usually before attraction opens: Prices tickets for profitable resale, based on such factors as availability and demand for tickets and location of seats. Sells tickets to public in accordance with legal regulations concerning amount of profit or place of sale. May trade as well as buy and sell tickets. May pick up and deliver, by automobile, tickets bought, sold, or traded.
GOE: 11.06.04 STRENGTH: L GED: R4 M3 L4 SVP: 6 DLU: 77

259.357-038 TOBACCO-WAREHOUSE AGENT (business ser.)

Solicits business for tobacco auction warehouse and rents space for display of tobacco on warehouse floor: Meets tobacco growers at warehouse entrance, on streets, or visits growers prior to sale to solicit their business. Informs customers or prospective customers of warehouse space available for tobacco display. Issues tickets to growers reserving warehouse space and ascertains that space has been reserved.
GOE: 08.01.02 STRENGTH: L GED: R3 M2 L3 SVP: 3 DLU: 77

26 SALES OCCUPATIONS, CONSUMABLE COMMODITIES

This division includes occupations concerned with selling consumable commodities, such as farm produce and livestock, foodstuffs, textiles, apparel, fuels and petroleum products, chemicals, and drug preparations, when knowledge of the commodities sold is required.

260 SALES OCCUPATIONS, AGRICULTURAL AND FOOD PRODUCTS

This group includes occupations concerned with selling farm products, such as grains, vegetables, fruits, nuts, poultry, livestock, and raw wool; cut flowers; animal hides, skins, and fur pelts; milled products, such as flour, meal, and cereals (except farm-animal feed); food staples and specialties, such as meat, seafood, dairy and bakery products, canned goods, coffee, candy, and tobacco; pet foods; and beverages, such as soft drinks, wine, and liquor. Occupations concerned with selling farm-animal feed and horticultural and nursery products, such as seeds, bulbs, shrubs, and trees, are found in Group 272.

260.257-010 SALES REPRESENTATIVE, LIVESTOCK (wholesale tr.)

Sells cattle, horses, hogs, and other livestock on commission to packing houses, farmers, or other purchasers: Contacts prospective buyers to persuade them to purchase livestock. Reviews current market information and inspects livestock to determine their value. Informs buyers of market conditions, care, and breeding of livestock. Attends livestock meetings to keep informed of livestock trends and developments.
GOE: 08.01.03 STRENGTH: L GED: R4 M3 L4 SVP: 5 DLU: 77

260.357-010 COMMISSION AGENT, AGRICULTURAL PRODUCE (wholesale tr.) alternate titles: broker, agricultural produce

Sells bulk shipments of agricultural produce on commission basis to WHOLESALERS (wholesale tr.) I or other buyers for growers or shippers. Deducts expenses and commission from payment received from sale of produce, and remits balance to shipper. May call on wholesalers' customers, such as restaurants and institutional food services, to promote sales and provide nutritional and other information about products. May be required to be licensed and bonded by state.
GOE: 08.01.03 STRENGTH: S GED: R4 M3 L4 SVP: 6 DLU: 77

260.357-014 SALES REPRESENTATIVE, FOOD PRODUCTS (wholesale tr.)

Sells food products, such as bakery products, confectionery, canned goods, coffee, tea, spices, poultry, meats, and seafood, to retail food stores, wholesale grocers, restaurants, hotels, or institutions. Performs other duties as described

under SALES REPRESENTATIVE (retail trade; wholesale tr.) Master Title. May be designated according to kind of food sold as Sales Representative, Flour And Cereals (wholesale tr.); Sales Representative, Groceries (wholesale tr.); Sales Representative, Meats (wholesale tr.).
GOE: 08.02.01 STRENGTH: L GED: R4 M3 L4 SVP: 5 DLU: 77

260.357-018 SALES REPRESENTATIVE, MALT LIQUORS (wholesale tr.)

Sells beer and other malt liquors to taverns, hotels, restaurants, cocktail lounges, bowling alleys, steamship companies, railroads, military establishments, delicatessens, and supermarkets for wholesale distributor. Performs other duties as described under SALES REPRESENTATIVE (retail trade; wholesale tr.) Master Title. Confers with SALES SUPERVISOR, MALT LIQUORS (wholesale tr.) to resolve customer problems.
GOE: 08.02.01 STRENGTH: L GED: R4 M3 L3 SVP: 4 DLU: 77

260.357-022 SALES REPRESENTATIVE, TOBACCO PRODUCTS AND SMOKING SUPPLIES (retail trade; wholesale tr.)

Sells tobacco products, such as cigars, cigarettes, and pipe tobacco, and smoking supplies, such as pipes and tobacco pouches, performing duties as described under SALES REPRESENTATIVE (retail trade; wholesale tr.) Master Title. May also sell confectionery and chewing gum products.
GOE: 08.02.03 STRENGTH: L GED: R4 M3 L3 SVP: 5 DLU: 77

260.357-026 SALESPERSON, FLOWERS (retail trade)

Sells natural and artificial flowers, potted plants, floral pieces, and accessories: Advises customer regarding type of flowers, floral arrangements, and decorations desirable for specific occasions, utilizing knowledge of social and religious customs. Arranges display of flowers and decorative accessories, such as vases and ceramics. Performs other duties as described under SALESPERSON (retail trade; wholesale tr.) Master Title. May contact florists in other communities by telegraph or telephone to place orders for out-of-town delivery. May design and make up corsages, wreaths, sprays, and other floral decorations.
GOE: 08.02.02 STRENGTH: L GED: R4 M3 L3 SVP: 4 DLU: 77

261 SALES OCCUPATIONS, TEXTILE PRODUCTS, APPAREL, AND NOTIONS

This group includes occupations concerned with selling textile products, such as canvas, jute, and felt products, parachutes, and fish nets; yard goods, such as woolen, cotton, and synthetic fabrics; apparel and accessories, including footwear (except orthopedic), hats, wigs, belts, neckties, fur garments, and corsets; trimmings, such as embroidery, waistbands, and cording; safety apparel, such as goggles, safety belts, and fireproof suits; and notions, such as buttons, buckles, pins, needles, hooks and eyes, and slide and snap fasteners. Occupations concerned with selling textile fibers, jewelry, and leather goods other than belts and apparel, such as billfolds, luggage, and saddlery, are included in Group 269. Occupations concerned with selling orthopedic shoes are included in Group 276.

261.351-010 SALESPERSON, WIGS (personal ser.; retail trade)

Sells wigs, wiglets, falls, and other hairpieces in salon, department store, specialty shop, or customer's home, performing duties as described under SALESPERSON (retail trade; wholesale tr.) Master Title: Observes customer's facial features and complexion and selects wig for customer's consideration. Fits and styles wig on customer, combing and brushing wig to achieve desired effect. Advises customer on care and homestyling of wig. Styles wigs and hairpieces for display purposes, using combs, brushes, hair sprays, and cleaning compounds. May clean, cut, and style hairpieces for customer and be designated Wig Stylist (personal ser.).
GOE: 08.02.02 STRENGTH: L GED: R3 M3 L3 SVP: 4 DLU: 77

261.354-010 SALESPERSON, CORSETS (retail trade) alternate titles: corsetier

Sells corsets, girdles, brassieres, and other foundation garments: Measures customer, using tape measure, and selects garment to fit customer. Assists customer in trying on garments. Advises customer on type of garment for reducing, surgical, maternity, or corrective purposes that will support and mold figure, based on knowledge of foundation garments. May fit garment on customer and indicate necessary alterations, using pins. Performs other duties as described under SALESPERSON (retail trade; wholesale tr.) Master Title.
GOE: 08.02.02 STRENGTH: L GED: R4 M3 L4 SVP: 5 DLU: 77

261.357-010 SALES REPRESENTATIVE, APPAREL TRIMMINGS (wholesale tr.)

Contacts apparel manufacturers to sell trimmings for apparel, such as dresses, blouses, shirts, and sweaters, and service of applying trim to apparel: Suggests design and trimming, such as embroidery, applique, tucking, or cording, to use on apparel. Performs other duties as described under SALES REPRESENTATIVE (retail trade; wholesale tr.) Master Title.
GOE: 08.02.01 STRENGTH: L GED: R4 M3 L4 SVP: 5 DLU: 77

261.357-014 SALES REPRESENTATIVE, CANVAS PRODUCTS (wholesale tr.)

Sells canvas goods, such as awnings, tents, tarpaulins, covers, and bags, to retail outlets and industrial and commercial establishments, performing duties as described under SALES REPRESENTATIVE (retail trade; wholesale tr.)

Master Title. May rent tents for events, such as circuses, conventions, or revival meetings. May measure area to be covered by canvas product. May deliver and install awnings [AWNING HANGER (construction; retail trade; tex. prod., nec)].
GOE: 08.02.01 STRENGTH: L GED: R4 M3 L4 SVP: 6 DLU: 77

261.357-018 SALES REPRESENTATIVE, FOOTWEAR (wholesale tr.)
Sells footwear, such as shoes, boots, overshoes, and slippers, performing duties as described under SALES REPRESENTATIVE (retail trade; wholesale tr.) Master Title.
GOE: 08.02.01 STRENGTH: L GED: R4 M3 L4 SVP: 6 DLU: 77

261.357-022 SALES REPRESENTATIVE, MEN'S AND BOYS' APPAREL (wholesale tr.)
Sells men's and boys' clothing, such as suits, coats, sport jackets, and slacks, utilizing knowledge of garment construction, fabrics, and styles. Performs other duties as described under SALES REPRESENTATIVE (retail trade; wholesale tr.) Master Title.
GOE: 08.02.01 STRENGTH: L GED: R4 M3 L4 SVP: 6 DLU: 77

261.357-026 SALES REPRESENTATIVE, SAFETY APPAREL AND EQUIPMENT (wholesale tr.)
Sells safety apparel and equipment, such as goggles, masks, shoes, belts, helmets, fireproof suits, and hearing-protection devices, performing duties as described under SALES REPRESENTATIVE (retail trade; wholesale tr.) Master Title. Tours industrial plant and suggests protective clothing and devices to prevent accidents.
GOE: 08.02.01 STRENGTH: L GED: R4 M3 L4 SVP: 4 DLU: 77

261.357-030 SALES REPRESENTATIVE, TEXTILES (wholesale tr.)
Sells textile fabrics, such as cottons, wools, synthetics, and combination blends, to garment manufacturers, retail stores, textile converters, and buying offices, utilizing knowledge of textile construction, fabrics, fashion, and textile products. Performs duties as described under SALES REPRESENTATIVE (retail trade; wholesale tr.) Master Title. May sell raw fibers to spinning mills and be designated Sales Representative, Raw Fibers (wholesale tr.).
GOE: 08.02.01 STRENGTH: L GED: R4 M3 L4 SVP: 6 DLU: 77

261.357-034 SALES REPRESENTATIVE, UNIFORMS (retail trade; wholesale tr.)
Sells men's and women's uniforms for use in industrial and commercial establishments, medical-service organizations, and for such groups as bands and private organizations, performing duties as described under SALES REPRESENTATIVE (retail trade; wholesale tr.) Master Title. May take individual measurements for uniforms.
GOE: 08.02.03 STRENGTH: L GED: R4 M3 L4 SVP: 6 DLU: 77

261.357-038 SALES REPRESENTATIVE, WOMEN'S AND GIRLS' APPAREL (wholesale tr.)
Sells women's and girls' apparel, such as coats, dresses, lingerie, and accessories, utilizing knowledge of fabrics, style, and prices. Performs other duties as described under SALES REPRESENTATIVE (retail trade; wholesale tr.) Master Title. May specialize according to price range of garment sold. May sell only girls' or women's apparel and be designated Sales Representative, Girls' Apparel (wholesale tr.); Sales Representative, Women's Apparel (wholesale tr.).
GOE: 08.02.01 STRENGTH: L GED: R4 M3 L4 SVP: 5 DLU: 77

261.357-042 SALESPERSON, FURS (retail trade)
Sells ready-to-wear or custom-made fur garments and pieces, such as capes, coats, neckpieces, and stoles: Displays garments from stock and assists customer in trying on garment. Explains qualities of various kinds of fur, how fur garments are made, number of skins used, and when particular types of furs should be worn. Displays samples of fur skins and linings at request of customer desiring custom-made garment. Estimates cost of altering, remodeling, or repairing garment. Receives fur garment for storage, writes description on ticket, and estimates value of garment and storage cost. Performs other duties as described under SALESPERSON (retail trade; wholesale tr.) Master Title.
GOE: 08.02.02 STRENGTH: L GED: R4 M3 L4 SVP: 5 DLU: 77

261.357-046 SALESPERSON, INFANTS' AND CHILDREN'S WEAR (retail trade)
Sells infants' and children's wearing apparel, nursery furniture, and bedding: Advises customer on durability of merchandise and quantity to purchase for infants. Suggests gift items or sizes of infants' clothes. May sell infants' and children's shoes. Performs other duties as described under SALESPERSON (retail trade; wholesale tr.) Master Title.
GOE: 08.02.02 STRENGTH: L GED: R4 M3 L4 SVP: 3 DLU: 77

261.357-050 SALESPERSON, MEN'S AND BOYS' CLOTHING (retail trade)
Sells men's and boys' outer garments, such as suits, pants, and coats: Advises customer about prevailing styles and appropriateness of garments for particular occasions. Answers questions about fabric, design, and quality of garment. Selects standard-size garments nearest customer's measurements. May measure customer to determine garment size required, using measuring tape. May mark garment for alterations. Performs other duties as described under SALESPERSON (retail trade; wholesale tr.) Master Title.
GOE: 08.02.02 STRENGTH: L GED: R3 M3 L3 SVP: 4 DLU: 81

261.357-054 SALESPERSON, MEN'S FURNISHINGS (retail trade) alternate titles: haberdasher
Sells men's furnishings, such as neckties, shirts, belts, hats, and accessories: Advises customer on coordination of accessories based on knowledge of current fashions. Answers questions relating to fabrics and quality of merchandise. Performs other duties as described under SALESPERSON (retail trade; wholesale tr.) Master Title. May be designated according to type of furnishing sold as Salesperson, Men's Hats (retail trade); Salesperson, Neckties (retail trade).
GOE: 08.02.02 STRENGTH: L GED: R4 M3 L4 SVP: 4 DLU: 77

261.357-058 SALESPERSON, MILLINERY (retail trade) alternate titles: salesperson, women's hats
Displays, fits, and sells women's hats and related accessories: Observes customer's age, coloring, figure, and shape of face and selects hats for customer's consideration. Fits hats on customer. May manually adjust headband to alter hat size for customer. May also sell wigs and other hairpieces [SALESPERSON, WIGS (personal ser.; retail trade)]. Performs other duties as described under SALESPERSON (retail trade; wholesale tr.) Master Title.
GOE: 08.02.02 STRENGTH: L GED: R4 M3 L4 SVP: 3 DLU: 77

261.357-062 SALESPERSON, SHOES (retail trade)
Fits and sells shoes, boots, and other footwear: Ascertains style and color of shoe customer wishes. Asks customer shoe size or measures customer's foot, using measuring device. Obtains footwear of specified style, color, and size from stock. Helps customer try on shoes, observes and questions customer about fit, and feels customer's feet through shoes to ensure fit. May stretch shoes, using hand stretcher, or insert insoles or instep pads to improve fit. May sell related products, such as handbags, hosiery, shoetrees, and shoe polish. Performs other duties as described under SALESPERSON (retail trade; wholesale tr.) Master Title. May be designated according to type of shoes sold as Salesperson, Children's Shoes (retail trade); Salesperson, Men's Shoes (retail trade); Salesperson, Women's Shoes (retail trade).
GOE: 08.02.02 STRENGTH: L GED: R3 M2 L3 SVP: 4 DLU: 81

261.357-066 SALESPERSON, WOMEN'S APPAREL AND ACCESSORIES (retail trade) alternate titles: salesperson, ladies' wear
Sells women's clothing and accessories, such as coats, sportswear, suits, dresses, formal gowns, lingerie, hosiery, belts, gloves, costume jewelry, handbags, and scarfs: Advises customer on current fashion and coordinating accessories. Answers questions regarding washability, durability, and color fastness of fabrics. May mark garments for alterations. Performs other duties as described under SALESPERSON (retail trade; wholesale trade) Master Title. May be designated according to specific category or type of item sold as Salesperson, Fashion Accessories (retail trade); Salesperson, Handbags (retail trade); Salesperson, Hosiery (retail trade); Salesperson, Lingerie (retail trade); Salesperson, Women's Dresses (retail trade); Salesperson, Women's Sportswear (retail trade).
GOE: 08.02.02 STRENGTH: L GED: R3 M2 L3 SVP: 3 DLU: 81

261.357-070 SALESPERSON, YARD GOODS (retail trade)
Sells yard goods made from cotton, linen, wool, silk, synthetic fibers, and other materials: Unrolls bolts of cloth to display assortment of fabrics to customer. Advises customer as to kind and quantity of material required to make garments, bed clothes, curtains, and other articles. Discusses features and qualities of fabric, such as weave, texture, color, and washability. Suggests harmonizing or matching colors of fabrics. Measures and cuts length of fabric from bolt, using scissors and measuring machine or yardstick. Performs other duties as described under SALESPERSON (retail trade; wholesale tr.) Master Title. May sell sewing accessories and notions, such as dress patterns, needlecraft books, needles, thread, buttons, and zippers.
GOE: 08.02.02 STRENGTH: L GED: R4 M3 L4 SVP: 3 DLU: 77

261.357-074 SALESPERSON, LEATHER-AND-SUEDE APPAREL-AND-ACCESSORIES (retail trade)
Sells suede and leather apparel and accessories: Advises customer on selection of apparel and on coordination of accessories, such as handbags, belts, and boots. Answers questions regarding cleaning requirements, color fastness, and durability of article. Packs or wraps customer purchase. Checks merchandise deliveries against packing slips. Tickets merchandise, using ticket gun. Inventories stock. Posts daily sales from sales slips onto inventory sheet. Performs other duties as described under SALESPERSON (retail trade; wholesale tr.) Master Title.
GOE: 08.02.02 STRENGTH: L GED: R3 M3 L3 SVP: 5 DLU: 86

262 SALES OCCUPATIONS, CHEMICALS, DRUGS, AND SUNDRIES

This group includes occupations concerned with selling organic and inorganic chemicals, drugs, medicines, cosmetics, toiletries, and allied products.

262.157-010 PHARMACEUTICAL DETAILER (wholesale tr.) alternate titles: detailer, pharmaceuticals
Promotes use of and sells ethical drugs and other pharmaceutical products to physicians, DENTISTS (medical ser.) 072.101-010, hospitals, and retail and wholesale drug establishments, utilizing knowledge of medical practices, drugs, and medicines: Calls on customers, informs customer of new drugs, and explains characteristics and clinical studies conducted with drug. Discusses dosage, use, and effect of new drugs and medicinal preparations. Gives samples of new drugs to customer. Promotes and sells other drugs and medicines manufactured by company. May sell and take orders for pharmaceutical supply items from persons contacted.

GOE: 08.01.01 STRENGTH: L GED: R5 M3 L5 SVP: 7 DLU: 77

262.357-010 SALES REPRESENTATIVE, CHEMICALS AND DRUGS (wholesale tr.)

Sells chemical or pharmaceutical products, such as explosives, acids, industrial or agricultural chemicals, medicines, and drugs, performing duties as described under SALES REPRESENTATIVE (retail trade; wholesale tr.) Master Title.

GOE: 08.01.01 STRENGTH: L GED: R4 M3 L4 SVP: 5 DLU: 77

262.357-014 SALES REPRESENTATIVE, TOILET PREPARATIONS (wholesale tr.)

Sells toilet preparations, such as cosmetics, perfumes, soaps, bath oils, and facial and hair preparations, utilizing knowledge of promotion and display techniques. Performs other duties as described under SALES REPRESENTATIVE (retail trade; wholesale tr.) Master Title.

GOE: 08.02.01 STRENGTH: L GED: R4 M3 L4 SVP: 5 DLU: 77

262.357-018 SALESPERSON, COSMETICS AND TOILETRIES (retail trade)

Sells cosmetics and toiletries, such as skin creams, hair preparations, face powder, lipstick, and perfume, to customers in department store or specialty shop: Demonstrates methods of application of various preparations to customer. Explains beneficial properties of preparations and suggests shades or varieties of makeup to suit customer's complexion. May weigh and mix facial powders, according to established formula, to obtain desired shade, using spatula and scale. Performs other duties as described under SALESPERSON (retail trade; wholesale tr.) Master Title.

GOE: 08.02.02 STRENGTH: L GED: R3 M3 L3 SVP: 4 DLU: 77

262.357-022 SALES REPRESENTATIVE, WATER-TREATMENT CHEMICALS (wholesale tr.)

Contacts prospective customers to sell chemicals that treat water in boilers, cooling towers, and air wash systems: Schedules appointment to explain products and services available, inspects customer water system equipment, and prepares service estimates. Obtains sample of water to be analyzed, and ships sample to home office for analysis. Receives and reviews analysis, and contacts customers to recommend treatment to control levels of substances in water. Explains merits of program to persuade customer to purchase treatment package. Attempts to resolve problems encountered with customer's water-treatment process. Sells water-treatment chemicals to customer. Performs follow-up test on water in customer water system, utilizing test kit, knowledge of chemical treatment, and reference manual. Explains test results to customers. Observes changes in water color and recommends to customer amount and type of chemical additives for necessary water treatment.

GOE: 08.02.01 STRENGTH: S GED: R3 M3 L3 SVP: 7 DLU: 86

269 SALES OCCUPATIONS, MISCELLANEOUS CONSUMABLE COMMODITIES, N.E.C.

This group includes occupations, not elsewhere classified, concerned with selling consumable commodities.

269.357-010 SALES REPRESENTATIVE, FUELS (retail trade; wholesale tr.)

Sells fuels, other than petroleum, such as coal, coke, and wood, performing duties as described under SALES REPRESENTATIVE (retail trade; wholesale tr.) Master Title.

GOE: 08.02.03 STRENGTH: L GED: R4 M3 L4 SVP: 4 DLU: 77

269.357-014 SALES REPRESENTATIVE, PETROLEUM PRODUCTS (wholesale tr.)

Sells petroleum products, such as gasoline, oil, greases, and lubricants, performing duties as described under SALES REPRESENTATIVE (retail trade; wholesale tr.) Master Title. May be designated according to specific petroleum product sold as Sales Representative, Industrial Lubricants (wholesale tr.).

GOE: 08.02.01 STRENGTH: L GED: R4 M3 L4 SVP: 6 DLU: 77

269.357-018 SALES-PROMOTION REPRESENTATIVE (wholesale tr.)

Persuades customers to use sales promotion display items of wholesale commodity distributor: Visits retail establishments, such as department stores, taverns, supermarkets, and clubs to persuade customers to use display items to promote sale of company products. Delivers promotion items, such as posters, glasses, napkins, and samples of product, and arranges display of items in customer's establishment. May take sales order from customer.

GOE: 08.02.01 STRENGTH: L GED: R4 M2 L3 SVP: 3 DLU: 77

27 SALES OCCUPATIONS, COMMODITIES, N.E.C.

This division includes occupations concerned with selling commodities, not included in Division 26, when knowledge of the commodities sold is required.

270 SALES OCCUPATIONS, HOME FURNITURE, FURNISHINGS, AND APPLIANCES

This group includes occupations concerned with selling household furniture; housefurnishings, such as china, glassware, silverware, floor coverings, bedding, curtains, draperies, upholstery, linens, brooms, and other household accessories; and home appliances, such as refrigerators, dishwashers, clothes washers and driers, sewing machines, vacuum cleaners, radios, television sets, phonograph and high fidelity equipment, household lamps, toasters, and room air-conditioners. Occupations concerned with selling industrial and commercial air-conditioning units and refrigerators are included in Group 274.

270.352-010 SALESPERSON, SEWING MACHINES (retail trade)

Demonstrates and sells sewing machines: Explains and demonstrates to prospective customers how to thread and adjust tensions on machine, use various attachments, and set machine to sew various stitches. Estimates and quotes trade-in allowance for customer's old machine. Determines extent of repair service required in response to customer's call and advises customer on minor repair procedures or arranges for service. May prepare machine rental contracts. May clean and maintain store demonstrator machines. May sell vacuum cleaners and sewing accessories. Performs other duties as described under SALESPERSON (retail trade; wholesale tr.) Master Title.

GOE: 08.02.02 STRENGTH: M GED: R4 M3 L4 SVP: 6 DLU: 77

270.357-010 SALES REPRESENTATIVE, HOME FURNISHINGS (wholesale tr.)

Sells home furnishings, such as china, glassware, floor coverings, furniture, linens, brooms, and kitchen articles, performing duties as described under SALES REPRESENTATIVE (retail trade; wholesale tr.) Master Title.

GOE: 08.02.01 STRENGTH: L GED: R4 M3 L4 SVP: 5 DLU: 77

270.357-014 SALES REPRESENTATIVE, HOUSEHOLD APPLIANCES (wholesale tr.)

Sells household appliances, such as refrigerators, ranges, laundry equipment, dishwashers, vacuum cleaners, and room air-conditioning units. Performs duties as described under SALES REPRESENTATIVE (retail trade; wholesale tr.) Master Title. May train dealers in operation and use of appliances.

GOE: 08.02.01 STRENGTH: L GED: R4 M3 L4 SVP: 5 DLU: 77

270.357-018 SALESPERSON, CHINA AND SILVERWARE (retail trade; wholesale tr.)

Displays and sells china, glassware, and silver flatware and hollow ware: Advises customer on use of various silverware, china, and glassware items for specific purposes or decorative schemes. May be required to have knowledge of manufacturing methods, materials, and methods of decoration of china. Performs other duties as described under SALESPERSON (retail trade; wholesale tr.) Master Title. May be designated according to category of items sold as Salesperson, China And Glassware (retail trade; wholesale tr.); Salesperson, Silverware (retail trade).

GOE: 08.02.03 STRENGTH: L GED: R4 M3 L4 SVP: 4 DLU: 77

270.357-022 SALESPERSON, CURTAINS AND DRAPERIES (retail trade)

Sells curtains, draperies, slipcovers, bedspreads, and yard goods from which these may be made: Displays samples of fabric and advises customer regarding color and pattern of material or style that will complement furnishings in customer's home. Selects size or number of curtains or drapes required, based on customer's specifications or window measurements. May estimate cost of fabricating draperies, curtains, or slipcovers. May measure and cut fabric from bolt. May also sell curtain and drapery rods and window shades. Performs other duties as described under SALESPERSON (retail trade; wholesale tr.) Master Title. May sell custom-made draperies to customers in their homes and be designated Salesperson, Custom Draperies (retail trade).

GOE: 08.02.02 STRENGTH: L GED: R4 M3 L4 SVP: 4 DLU: 77

270.357-026 SALESPERSON, FLOOR COVERINGS (retail trade; wholesale tr.)

Displays and sells floor coverings, such as carpets, rugs, and linoleum, in department store, specialty store, or showroom: Shows rugs or samples of carpets to customer. Explains qualities of various rugs and carpets, such as composition, method of fabrication, and wearing qualities. Estimates cost and amount of covering required, referring to customer's floor plans. Performs other duties as described under SALESPERSON (retail trade; wholesale tr.) Master Title. May measure floor and sell floor coverings in customer's home or place of business and be designated Floor-Coverings Estimator (retail trade; wholesale tr.); Salesperson, Terrazzo Tiles (retail trade; wholesale tr.).

GOE: 08.02.03 STRENGTH: L GED: R4 M3 L4 SVP: 4 DLU: 77

270.357-030 SALESPERSON, FURNITURE (retail trade)

Sells furniture and bedding in furniture or department store: Suggests furniture size, period style, color, fabric, and wood that will complement customer's home and other furnishings. Discusses quality of fabric and finish, and type and quality of construction with customer. May resolve customer complaints regarding delivery of damaged or incorrect merchandise. Performs other duties as described under SALESPERSON (retail trade; wholesale tr.) Master Title.

GOE: 08.02.02 STRENGTH: L GED: R3 M3 L3 SVP: 4 DLU: 81

270.357-034 SALESPERSON, HOUSEHOLD APPLIANCES (retail trade)

Sells radios, television sets, and other household appliances to customers: Explains features of appliances, such as stoves, refrigerators, vacuum cleaners, and washing machines. Demonstrates television, radio, and phonograph sets. Performs other duties as described under SALESPERSON (retail trade; wholesale tr.) Master Title. May sell service contracts for appliances sold. May dem-

onstrate appliances on display floor of utility company and refer interested customers to appliance dealers for purchase.
GOE: 08.02.02 STRENGTH: L GED: R4 M3 L4 SVP: 4 DLU: 77

270.357-038 SALESPERSON, STEREO EQUIPMENT (retail trade)
Sells home-entertainment electronic sound equipment and parts, such as stereophonic phonographs, recording equipment, radios, speakers, tuners, amplifiers, microphones, and record changers. Explains features of various brands, meaning of technical manufacturers' specifications, and method of installation, applying knowledge of electronics. Performs other duties as described under SALESPERSON (retail trade; wholesale tr.) Master Title.
GOE: 08.02.02 STRENGTH: M GED: R4 M3 L4 SVP: 4 DLU: 77

271   SALES OCCUPATIONS, ELECTRICAL GOODS, EXCEPT HOME APPLIANCES

This group includes occupations concerned with selling electrical industrial apparatus, electric transmission and distribution equipment, electric lighting and wiring equipment, communications equipment, and electrical and electronic components and accessories.

271.257-010 SALES REPRESENTATIVE, COMMUNICATION EQUIPMENT (wholesale tr.)
Sells communication equipment, such as telephone and telegraph apparatus, intercommunication equipment, and radio broadcasting equipment, utilizing knowledge of electronics. Analyzes customer's communication needs and recommends equipment needed. Performs other duties as described under SALES REPRESENTATIVE (retail trade; wholesale tr.) Master Title. May train personnel of business establishments in use of equipment.
GOE: 08.01.01 STRENGTH: L GED: R4 M4 L4 SVP: 6 DLU: 77

271.352-010 SALES REPRESENTATIVE, RADIOGRAPHIC-INSPECTION EQUIPMENT AND SERVICES (wholesale tr.)
Sells radiographic equipment, supplies, and inspection services to foundries, railroads, and other establishments requiring radiographic devices and materials for such purposes as inspecting welds, detecting variances in product quality, and conducting research into structure of metals. Performs duties as described under SALES REPRESENTATIVE (retail trade; wholesale tr.) Master Title.
GOE: 08.01.01 STRENGTH: L GED: R4 M3 L4 SVP: 6 DLU: 77

271.352-014 SALES REPRESENTATIVE, ULTRASONIC EQUIPMENT (wholesale tr.)
Sells electronic devices that clean, test, or process materials by means of ultrahigh frequency sound waves, such as disintegrators for cleaning surgical instruments, electronic guns for bonding plastics, and sonic devices for detecting flaws in metals, cutting steel and diamonds, and separating fossils from rocks. Performs duties as described under SALES REPRESENTATIVE (retail trade; wholesale tr.) Master Title.
GOE: 08.01.01 STRENGTH: L GED: R4 M3 L4 SVP: 5 DLU: 77

271.354-010 SALESPERSON, ELECTRIC MOTORS (retail trade; wholesale tr.) alternate titles: electric-motor-repair clerk
Sells new and used fractional horsepower electric motors and estimates costs of repairs in manufacturing, retail, or repair establishment: Determines malfunction of motors received for repair, using test equipment. Estimates repair cost, using pricelist for parts and labor. Receives motors in exchange for new or used motors. Keeps records of exchange or sales of new and used motors. Performs other duties as described under SALESPERSON (retail trade; wholesale tr.) Master Title. May repair motors [ELECTRIC-MOTOR REPAIRER (any industry)].
GOE: 08.02.03 STRENGTH: L GED: R4 M3 L4 SVP: 6 DLU: 77

271.357-010 SALES REPRESENTATIVE, ELECTRONICS PARTS (wholesale tr.)
Sells radio, television, and other electronics parts to establishments, such as appliance stores, dealers, and repair shops or electronics and aircraft manufacturing firms, performing duties as described under SALES REPRESENTATIVE (retail trade; wholesale tr.) Master Title.
GOE: 08.01.01 STRENGTH: L GED: R4 M3 L4 SVP: 6 DLU: 77

271.357-014 SALES REPRESENTATIVE, VIDEOTAPE (wholesale tr.)
Sells television tape, used to record programs for delayed play-back, performing duties as described under SALES REPRESENTATIVE (retail trade; wholesale tr.) Master Title.
GOE: 08.02.01 STRENGTH: L GED: R4 M3 L4 SVP: 3 DLU: 77

272   SALES OCCUPATIONS, FARM AND GARDENING EQUIPMENT AND SUPPLIES

This group includes occupations concerned with selling such items as tractors, farm implements and machinery, feed and feed supplements, fertilizer, and lawn and gardening tools, equipment, and accessories; and horticultural and nursery products, such as shrubs, trees, seeds, and bulbs.

272.357-010 SALES REPRESENTATIVE, ANIMAL-FEED PRODUCTS (wholesale tr.)
Sells livestock- and poultry-feed products to farmers and retail establishments: Suggests feed changes to improve breeding of fowl and stock. Performs

other duties as described under SALES REPRESENTATIVE (retail trade; wholesale tr.) Master Title. May specialize in selling feed supplements and be designated Sales Representative, Cattle-And-Poultry Feed Supplements (wholesale tr.).
GOE: 08.02.01 STRENGTH: L GED: R4 M3 L4 SVP: 6 DLU: 77

272.357-014 SALES REPRESENTATIVE, FARM AND GARDEN EQUIPMENT AND SUPPLIES (wholesale tr.)
Sells farm and garden machinery, equipment, and supplies, such as tractors, feed, fertilizer, seed, insecticide, and farm and garden implements, performing duties as described under SALES REPRESENTATIVE (retail trade; wholesale tr.) Master Title. May sell spare parts and service contracts for machinery and equipment.
GOE: 08.02.01 STRENGTH: L GED: R4 M3 L4 SVP: 5 DLU: 77

272.357-018 SALES REPRESENTATIVE, POULTRY EQUIPMENT AND SUPPLIES (retail trade; wholesale tr.)
Sells poultry equipment and supplies, such as brooders, coolers, feeders, graders, and washers: Advises customers on care and feeding of poultry, setting up of poultry equipment, and egg production problems, and suggests remedial measures for diseased poultry. Performs other duties as described under SALES REPRESENTATIVE (retail trade; wholesale tr.) Master Title. May sell chicks. May tend battery of brooders to hatch chicks.
GOE: 08.02.03 STRENGTH: M GED: R4 M3 L4 SVP: 6 DLU: 77

272.357-022 SALESPERSON, HORTICULTURAL AND NURSERY PRODUCTS (retail trade; wholesale tr.)
Sells container-grown plants and garden supplies in nursery, greenhouse, or department store: Advises customer on selection of plants and methods of planting and cultivation. Suggests trees and shrubbery suitable for specified growing conditions. Performs other duties as described under SALESPERSON (retail trade; wholesale tr.) Master Title. May water and trim growing plants on sales floor.
GOE: 08.02.03 STRENGTH: L GED: R4 M3 L4 SVP: 4 DLU: 77

273   SALES OCCUPATIONS, TRANSPORTATION EQUIPMENT, PARTS, AND SUPPLIES

This group includes occupations concerned with selling transportation equipment, such as motor vehicles (automobiles, trucks, motorcycles, and motor homes and campers) and equipment, aircraft and parts, boats, ships, marine supplies, railroad equipment, and camping, house, and utility trailers; and accessories, such as tires, tubes, and batteries. Occupations concerned with selling bicycles and small recreational vehicles, such as powered golf carts and snowmobiles, are included in Group 277. Occupations concerned with selling tractors, farm vehicles, and parts are included in Group 272.

273.253-010 SALES REPRESENTATIVE, AIRCRAFT (retail trade; wholesale tr.)
Sells aircraft to individuals and to business and industrial establishments: Discusses suitability of different types of aircraft to meet customer's requirements. Demonstrates aircraft in flight, stressing maneuverability, safety factors, and ease of handling. Verifies customer's credit rating. Prepares contracts for plane storage and maintenance service. Performs other duties as described under SALES REPRESENTATIVE (retail trade; wholesale tr.) Master Title. May appraise aircraft traded-in on new plane. May rent aircraft to customers [AIRPLANE-CHARTER CLERK (air trans.)]. May pilot aircraft during demonstrations and be required to have private pilot's license issued by Federal Aviation Administration.
GOE: 08.01.01 STRENGTH: L GED: R5 M3 L4 SVP: 6 DLU: 77

273.353-010 SALESPERSON, AUTOMOBILES (retail trade)
Sells new or used automobiles, trucks, and vans on premises of vehicle sales establishment: Explains features and demonstrates operation of car in showroom or on road. Suggests optional equipment for customer to purchase. Computes and quotes sales price, including tax, trade-in allowance, license fee, and discount, and requirements for financing payment of vehicle on credit. Performs other duties as described under SALESPERSON (retail trade; wholesale tr.) Master Title. May be designated Salesperson, New Cars (retail trade); Salesperson, Used Cars (retail trade).
GOE: 08.02.02 STRENGTH: L GED: R4 M3 L4 SVP: 6 DLU: 81

273.357-010 SALES REPRESENTATIVE, AIRCRAFT EQUIPMENT AND PARTS (wholesale tr.)
Sells aircraft equipment and parts, such as engines, body-and-wing assemblies, power transmission assemblies, fuel tanks, bolts, fittings, tires, and electric motors or servomotors, performing duties as described under SALES REPRESENTATIVE (retail trade; wholesale tr.) Master Title.
GOE: 08.01.01 STRENGTH: L GED: R4 M3 L4 SVP: 6 DLU: 77

273.357-014 SALES REPRESENTATIVE, AUTOMOTIVE-LEASING (business ser.)
Sells automotive-leasing services to businesses and individuals: Visits prospective customers to stimulate interest in establishing or expanding automotive-leasing programs. Explains advantages of leasing automotive equipment, such as tax savings and reduced capital expenditures. Recommends types and number of vehicles needed to satisfactorily perform job with minimal expense. Computes leasing charges, based on such factors as length of contract, antici-

pated mileage, and applicable taxes. Prepares and sends leasing contract to leasing agency. Performs other tasks to increase sales, such as evaluating advertising campaigns or revising administrative procedures. Performs other duties as described under SALES REPRESENTATIVE (retail trade; wholesale tr.) Master Title.
GOE: 08.02.06 STRENGTH: L GED: R4 M3 L4 SVP: 5 DLU: 77

273.357-018 SALES REPRESENTATIVE, BOATS AND MARINE SUPPLIES (retail trade; wholesale tr.)

Sells boats and marine equipment and supplies, such as fixtures, pumps, instruments, cordage, paints, and motor parts: Shows boat on sales floor or shows catalog pictures and blueprints. Explains construction and performance of boat and differences between various types of marine equipment. Advises boat owners on selection of new equipment and problems pertaining to repairs. Performs other duties as described under SALES REPRESENTATIVE (retail trade; wholesale tr.) Master Title. May demonstrate boat in water. May arrange for delivery, registration, and inspection of boat. May sell water-sports equipment, such as water skis and scuba gear. May sell marine equipment and supplies, except boats, and be designated Sales Representative, Marine Supplies (retail trade; wholesale tr.).
GOE: 08.02.03 STRENGTH: L GED: R4 M3 L4 SVP: 5 DLU: 77

273.357-022 SALES REPRESENTATIVE, MOTOR VEHICLES AND SUPPLIES (wholesale tr.) alternate titles: distributor, motor vehicles and supplies

Sells motor vehicles, such as automobiles, motorcycles, tractors, and trucks, and parts and supplies, such as batteries, tires, motors, chassis parts, tools, equipment, and lubricants, to dealers and service stations: Confers with dealer and reviews sales records to determine number of vehicles to order. Advises customer in methods of increasing sales volume, utilizing knowledge of sales promotion techniques. Performs other duties as described under SALES REPRESENTATIVE (retail trade; wholesale tr.) Master Title. May be designated according to items sold as Sales Representative, Automobile Parts And Supplies (wholesale tr.).
GOE: 08.02.01 STRENGTH: L GED: R4 M3 L4 SVP: 5 DLU: 77

273.357-026 SALES REPRESENTATIVE, RAILROAD EQUIPMENT AND SUPPLIES (wholesale tr.)

Sells railroad equipment and supplies, such as rolling stock, signaling or braking devices, or switches: Performs duties as described under SALES REPRESENTATIVE (retail trade; wholesale tr.) Master Title. May arrange for installation of equipment.
GOE: 08.02.01 STRENGTH: L GED: R4 M3 L4 SVP: 6 DLU: 77

273.357-030 SALESPERSON, AUTOMOBILE ACCESSORIES (retail trade; wholesale tr.)

Sells automobile supplies and accessories, such as tires, batteries, seat covers, mufflers, and headlights: Ascertains make and year of automobile and reads catalog for stock number of item. Performs other duties as described under SALESPERSON (retail trade; wholesale tr.) Master Title.
GOE: 08.02.03 STRENGTH: L GED: R4 M3 L4 SVP: 4 DLU: 77

273.357-034 SALESPERSON, TRAILERS AND MOTOR HOMES (retail trade) alternate titles: salesperson, recreational vehicles

Sells travel and camping trailers, motor homes, and truck campers to individuals: Determines customer's needs and exhibits vehicle of particular type or model. Demonstrates use of equipment and furnishings. Performs other duties as described under SALESPERSON (retail trade; wholesale tr.) Master Title. May prepare sales contract. May arrange financing and insurance. May sell mobile homes, motorcycles, and snowmobiles.
GOE: 08.02.02 STRENGTH: L GED: R4 M3 L4 SVP: 5 DLU: 77

274 SALES OCCUPATIONS, INDUSTRIAL AND RELATED EQUIPMENT AND SUPPLIES

This group includes occupations concerned with selling construction machinery, such as power shovels, bulldozers, and concrete mixers; mining and well-drilling equipment; building equipment, materials, and supplies, such as commercial heating, air-conditioning, and refrigerating equipment, plumbing fixtures, roofing, glass, insulation, bricks, and lumber; and industrial machinery, equipment, and supplies, such as textile machines, lubricating and material-handling equipment, abrasives, gears, pipefittings, wire rope, cartons, drums, and barrels.

274.157-010 SALES REPRESENTATIVE, ELEVATORS, ESCALATORS, AND DUMBWAITERS (wholesale tr.)

Sells passenger and freight elevators, escalators, and dumbwaiters to building owners and contractors: Contacts property owners and agents of prospective customers to obtain blueprints of proposed new construction and submits to engineering department for bid. Confers with owners of existing structures to determine type of installation required. Inspects premises to verify feasibility of request and recommends changes for more efficient operation. Submits specifications, such as number, size, type, load capacity, and speed of elevator to engineering department. Presents bid to customer, explains cost factors, emphasizing characteristics, such as construction, performance, durability, and appearance of equipment. Follows up order to ensure lists of materials ordered are correct and work will be completed by project deadline. Contacts owner peri-

odically to advise of progress of work, and attends sales and trade meetings and reads journals to keep informed of market conditions, business trends, and new developments in industry. Performs other duties as described under SALES REPRESENTATIVE (retail trade; wholesale tr.) Master Title. If worker sells service and modernization contracts see SERVICE REPRESENTATIVE, ELEVATORS, ESCALATORS, AND DUMBWAITERS (wholesale tr.).
GOE: 08.01.01 STRENGTH: L GED: R5 M4 L4 SVP: 7 DLU: 77

274.257-010 SALES REPRESENTATIVE, FOUNDRY AND MACHINE SHOP PRODUCTS (wholesale tr.)

Solicits from industrial establishments job contracts for manufacture of foundry or machine shop products, such as castings, machine parts, pipefittings, jigs, fixtures, and gears: Prepares price quotations or bids based on knowledge of material and labor costs and manufacturing schedules and processes. Submits bid to customer for examination and approval. Performs other duties as described under SALES REPRESENTATIVE (retail trade; wholesale tr.) Master Title.
GOE: 08.01.01 STRENGTH: L GED: R5 M4 L4 SVP: 7 DLU: 77

274.357-010 SALES REPRESENTATIVE, ABRASIVES (wholesale tr.)

Sells abrasive materials in granulated or pellet form, and abrasive products, such as wheels, disks, and belts: Advises engineering, production, and purchasing staffs on processes and methods in use of abrasive materials. Determines abrasive requirements for specific grinding, buffing, and polishing operations on metal, plastic, ceramics, or wood materials. Performs other duties as described under SALES REPRESENTATIVE (retail trade; wholesale tr.) Master Title.
GOE: 08.01.01 STRENGTH: L GED: R4 M3 L4 SVP: 6 DLU: 77

274.357-014 SALES REPRESENTATIVE, BOTTLES AND BOTTLING EQUIPMENT (wholesale tr.)

Sells bottles and bottling equipment, such as glass and plastic bottles and jars, bottle washers, and milk pasteurizers: Recommends specific types of bottles and equipment according to customer's specifications and type of bottling operation. Performs other duties as described under SALES REPRESENTATIVE (retail trade; wholesale tr.) Master Title. May specialize in selling either bottles or equipment and be designated Sales Representative, Bottles And Jars (wholesale tr.); Sales Representative, Bottling Equipment (wholesale tr.).
GOE: 08.02.01 STRENGTH: L GED: R4 M3 L4 SVP: 5 DLU: 77

274.357-018 SALES REPRESENTATIVE, BUILDING EQUIPMENT AND SUPPLIES (wholesale tr.)

Sells building materials, equipment, and supplies, such as heating or air-conditioning equipment, insulation, glass, floor tiles, bricks, lumber, plumbing fixtures, and roofing, following blueprints and applying knowledge of building construction. Performs other duties as described under SALES REPRESENTATIVE (retail trade; wholesale tr.) Master Title.
GOE: 08.01.01 STRENGTH: L GED: R4 M3 L4 SVP: 6 DLU: 80

274.357-022 SALES REPRESENTATIVE, CONSTRUCTION MACHINERY (wholesale tr.) alternate titles: sales representative, heavy equipment

Sells construction machinery, such as truck cranes, bulldozers, graders, concrete mixers, and trenchers: Recommends specific standard or modified machine best suited for customer's use. Performs other duties as described under SALES REPRESENTATIVE (retail trade; wholesale tr.) Master Title. May test-operate machinery at customer work site. May sell machine maintenance and repair services.
GOE: 08.01.01 STRENGTH: L GED: R4 M3 L4 SVP: 6 DLU: 77

274.357-026 SALES REPRESENTATIVE, CONTAINERS (wholesale tr.)

Sells fiberboard, metal, plastic, or wood containers, such as corrugated cartons, tin cans, steel pails and drums, and barrels, utilizing knowledge of sizes and uses of containers. Performs other duties as described under SALES REPRESENTATIVE (retail trade; wholesale tr.) Master Title.
GOE: 08.02.01 STRENGTH: L GED: R4 M3 L4 SVP: 5 DLU: 77

274.357-030 SALES REPRESENTATIVE, DAIRY SUPPLIES (wholesale tr.)

Sells dairy supplies, such as cheese wrappings, rennet, filters, cheese coloring, thickening and stabilizing agents, and test indicators, performing duties as described under SALES REPRESENTATIVE (retail trade; wholesale tr.) Master Title. May sell food and dairy machines and equipment. May sketch floor plans to indicate placement of machines and equipment for maximum utilization of space.
GOE: 08.02.01 STRENGTH: L GED: R4 M3 L4 SVP: 6 DLU: 77

274.357-034 SALES REPRESENTATIVE, HARDWARE SUPPLIES (wholesale tr.)

Sells hardware supplies, such as plumbing and electrical supplies, power tools and handtools, paints and varnishes, plate glass, and builder's hardware, performing duties as described under SALES REPRESENTATIVE (retail trade; wholesale tr.) Master Title.
GOE: 08.02.01 STRENGTH: L GED: R4 M3 L4 SVP: 5 DLU: 77

274.357-038 SALES REPRESENTATIVE, INDUSTRIAL MACHINERY (wholesale tr.)

Sells industrial machinery, such as metalworking, woodworking, food processing, and plastic fabricating machines, utilizing knowledge of manufacture,

operation, and uses of machinery: Computes cost of installing machinery and anticipated savings in production costs. Reviews existing plant machinery layout and draws diagrams of proposed machinery layout to effect more efficient space utilization, using standard measuring devices and templates. Arranges for installation of machinery. Performs other duties as described under SALES REPRESENTATIVE (retail trade; wholesale tr.) Master Title. Worker is not required to become as involved in technical knowledge and plant efficiency as SALES ENGINEER (profess. & kin.) Master Title.
GOE: 08.01.01 STRENGTH: L GED: R4 M3 L4 SVP: 5 DLU: 77

274.357-042 SALES REPRESENTATIVE, INDUSTRIAL RUBBER GOODS (wholesale tr.)

Sells rubber products, such as gaskets, hose, belts, and washers, made to customer's specifications, performing duties as described under SALES REPRESENTATIVE (retail trade; wholesale tr.) Master Title.
GOE: 08.02.01 STRENGTH: L GED: R4 M3 L4 SVP: 6 DLU: 77

274.357-046 SALES REPRESENTATIVE, LUBRICATING EQUIPMENT (wholesale tr.)

Sells lubricating equipment and parts to industrial establishments: Reviews existing plant layout and draws diagrams indicating proposed location of lubricating equipment. Recommends lubricants for particular equipment and machinery. Arranges for installation of lubricating equipment. Demonstrates operation of installed equipment. Performs other duties as described under SALES REPRESENTATIVE (retail trade; wholesale tr.) Master Title.
GOE: 08.02.01 STRENGTH: L GED: R4 M3 L4 SVP: 5 DLU: 77

274.357-050 SALES REPRESENTATIVE, MATERIAL-HANDLING EQUIPMENT (wholesale tr.)

Sells material-handling equipment, such as conveyor systems, forklift trucks, chain hoists, and powered drum dumpers, to commercial and industrial establishments, performing duties as described under SALES REPRESENTATIVE (retail trade; wholesale tr.) Master Title. May contract for maintenance and repair service. May survey plant and recommend installation of specific type equipment.
GOE: 08.02.01 STRENGTH: L GED: R4 M3 L4 SVP: 5 DLU: 77

274.357-054 SALES REPRESENTATIVE, METALS (wholesale tr.)

Sells nonfabricated metals, such as brass, copper, iron, and steel, to industrial establishments, utilizing knowledge of metallurgy and applications of various metals. Performs other duties as described under SALES REPRESENTATIVE (retail trade; wholesale tr.) Master Title.
GOE: 08.01.01 STRENGTH: L GED: R4 M3 L4 SVP: 6 DLU: 77

274.357-058 SALES REPRESENTATIVE, OIL FIELD SUPPLIES AND EQUIPMENT (wholesale tr.)

Sells and rents oil field supplies, machinery, equipment, and oil well services, such as directional drilling, electrical well logging, well fishing (recovering equipment from well bottoms), perforating, and temperature and pressure surveying, performing duties as described under SALES REPRESENTATIVE (retail trade; wholesale tr.) Master Title: May interpret graphs and survey data for customer. May be designated according to type of sales as Sales Representative, Oil Field Supplies (wholesale tr.); Sales Representative, Oil-Well Equipment Rentals (wholesale tr.); Sales Representative, Oil-Well Services (wholesale tr.).
GOE: 08.01.01 STRENGTH: L GED: R4 M3 L4 SVP: 6 DLU: 77

274.357-062 SALES REPRESENTATIVE, PRINTING SUPPLIES (wholesale tr.)

Sells printing supplies, such as ink, plates, rollers, and type, performing duties as described under SALES REPRESENTATIVE (retail trade; wholesale tr.) Master Title.
GOE: 08.02.01 STRENGTH: L GED: R4 M3 L4 SVP: 5 DLU: 77

274.357-066 SALES REPRESENTATIVE, TEXTILE DESIGNS (wholesale tr.)

Sells textile-pattern designs, and screens and rollers for printing patterns on greige, to textile converters: Displays design drawings to customer, examines sample of customer's greige on which pattern is to be printed, and aids customer in selection of colors and designs, utilizing knowledge of textile, inks, and types of weaves. Submits greige sample to own firm for printing of selected design and shows printed sample to customer for approval. Writes sales orders for designs and required printing screens and rollers. Performs other duties as described under SALES REPRESENTATIVE (retail trade; wholesale tr.) Master Title.
GOE: 08.02.01 STRENGTH: L GED: R4 M3 L4 SVP: 5 DLU: 77

274.357-070 SALES REPRESENTATIVE, TEXTILE MACHINERY (wholesale tr.)

Sells textile machinery, such as knitting machines, carding machines, looms, and spinning frames, utilizing knowledge of uses and operation of machinery and performing duties as described under SALES REPRESENTATIVE (retail trade; wholesale tr.) Master Title.
GOE: 08.02.01 STRENGTH: L GED: R4 M3 L4 SVP: 6 DLU: 77

274.357-074 SALES REPRESENTATIVE, WELDING EQUIPMENT (wholesale tr.)

Sells welding equipment, materials, and supplies to machine shops and other industrial establishments, utilizing knowledge of tool-and-die making, welding

techniques, and metalworking processes. Performs duties as described under SALES REPRESENTATIVE (retail trade; wholesale tr.) Master Title.
GOE: 08.01.01 STRENGTH: L GED: R4 M3 L4 SVP: 6 DLU: 77

274.357-078 SALES REPRESENTATIVE, WIRE ROPE (wholesale tr.)

Sells wire rope and cable for use in towing, hoisting, and related activities to logging companies, construction contractors, marine supply houses, and similar establishments, utilizing knowledge of construction industry and uses and application of wire rope. Performs other duties as described under SALES REPRESENTATIVE (retail trade; wholesale tr.) Master Title.
GOE: 08.02.01 STRENGTH: L GED: R4 M3 L4 SVP: 6 DLU: 77

275 SALES OCCUPATIONS, BUSINESS AND COMMERCIAL EQUIPMENT AND SUPPLIES

This group includes occupations concerned with selling office machines, such as typewriters and data processing, computing, accounting, and duplicating machines; service industry machines, such as commercial vacuum cleaners and refrigerators; hotel and restaurant equipment and supplies; barber and florist supplies; shoe leather and findings; vending machines and cash registers; commercial laundry machinery and equipment; office and institutional furniture; and photocopy and microfilm equipment.

275.257-010 SALES REPRESENTATIVE, COMPUTERS AND EDP SYSTEMS (wholesale tr.)

Sells computers and electronic data processing systems to business or industrial establishments, performing duties as described under SALES REPRESENTATIVE (retail trade; wholesale tr.) Master Title. Analyzes customer's needs and recommends computer system that best meets customer's requirements. Emphasizes salable features, such as flexibility, cost, capacity, and economy of operation. Consults with staff engineers on highly technical problems.
GOE: 08.01.01 STRENGTH: L GED: R5 M4 L4 SVP: 6 DLU: 77

275.357-010 SALES REPRESENTATIVE, BARBER AND BEAUTY EQUIPMENT AND SUPPLIES (wholesale tr.)

Sells barber and beauty equipment and supplies, such as hydraulic chairs, counters, mirrors, hair driers, clippers, brushes, cosmetics, hairdressings, and shampoos, to barber and beauty shops: Advises customers on layout of shop fixtures and equipment. Performs other duties as described under SALES REPRESENTATIVE (retail trade; wholesale tr.) Master Title.
GOE: 08.02.01 STRENGTH: L GED: R4 M3 L4 SVP: 5 DLU: 77

275.357-014 SALES REPRESENTATIVE, CHURCH FURNITURE AND RELIGIOUS SUPPLIES (wholesale tr.)

Sells church furniture and supplies, such as pews, pulpits, lecterns, altarware, candles, statuary, and prayer books: Measures area to be furnished. Prepares drawings, estimates, and bids. Performs other duties as described under SALES REPRESENTATIVE (retail trade; wholesale tr.) Master Title. May be designated Sales Representative, Church Furniture (wholesale tr.); Sales Representative, Religious Supplies (wholesale tr.).
GOE: 08.02.01 STRENGTH: L GED: R4 M3 L4 SVP: 5 DLU: 77

275.357-018 SALES REPRESENTATIVE, COMMERCIAL EQUIPMENT AND SUPPLIES (wholesale tr.)

Sells commercial furniture, equipment, and supplies other than office machines to business establishments: Performs duties as described under SALES REPRESENTATIVE (retail trade; wholesale tr.) Master Title. May oversee installation of equipment. May train employees in use of equipment.
GOE: 08.02.01 STRENGTH: L GED: R4 M3 L4 SVP: 4 DLU: 77

275.357-022 SALES REPRESENTATIVE, CORDAGE (wholesale tr.)

Sells cordage and twine, such as manila, sisal, nylon, orlon, and cotton, to business and commercial establishments, performing duties as described under SALES REPRESENTATIVE (retail trade; wholesale tr.) Master Title.
GOE: 08.02.01 STRENGTH: L GED: R4 M3 L4 SVP: 5 DLU: 77

275.357-026 SALES REPRESENTATIVE, HOTEL AND RESTAURANT EQUIPMENT AND SUPPLIES (wholesale tr.)

Sells hotel and restaurant equipment and supplies, such as dishwashers, ranges, refrigerators, counters and booths, china, glassware, silverware, drapery and carpeting, and furniture, utilizing knowledge of design and layout of furniture or equipment. Performs other duties as described under SALES REPRESENTATIVE (retail trade; wholesale tr.) Master Title.
GOE: 08.02.01 STRENGTH: L GED: R4 M3 L4 SVP: 6 DLU: 77

275.357-030 SALES REPRESENTATIVE, MORTICIAN SUPPLIES (wholesale tr.) alternate titles: sales representative, funeral equipment; sales representative, undertaker supplies

Sells funeral equipment and supplies, such as caskets, embalming fluids, and cosmetics, performing duties as described under SALES REPRESENTATIVE (retail trade; wholesale tr.) Master Title.
GOE: 08.02.01 STRENGTH: L GED: R4 M3 L4 SVP: 6 DLU: 77

275.357-034 SALES REPRESENTATIVE, OFFICE MACHINES (retail trade; wholesale tr.)

Sells office machines, such as typewriters and adding, calculating, and duplicating machines, to business establishments: Performs duties as described under SALES REPRESENTATIVE (retail trade; wholesale tr.) Master Title. May instruct employees or purchasers in use of machine. May make machine adjust-

ments. May sell office supplies, such as paper, ribbons, ink, and tapes. May rent or lease office machines. May be designated according to type of machine sold as Sales Representative, Adding Machines (wholesale tr.); Sales Representative, Calculating Machines (wholesale tr.); Sales Representative, Cash Registers (wholesale tr.); Sales Representative, Dictating Machines (wholesale tr.); Sales Representative, Duplicating Machines (wholesale tr.); Sales Representative, Typewriters (wholesale tr.). May be designated: Sales Representative, Addressing Machines (wholesale tr.); Sales Representative, Bookkeeping-And-Accounting Machines (wholesale tr.); Sales Representative, Check-Endorsing-And-Signing Machines (wholesale tr.); Sales Representative, Stenographic Machines (wholesale tr.).
GOE: 08.02.03 STRENGTH: M GED: R4 M3 L4 SVP: 5 DLU: 77

275.357-038 SALES REPRESENTATIVE, PRESSURE-SENSITIVE TAPE (wholesale tr.)

Sells pressure-sensitive tape used to seal shipping containers and packages and for masking purposes, performing duties as described under SALES REPRESENTATIVE (retail trade; wholesale tr.) Master Title.
GOE: 08.02.01 STRENGTH: L GED: R4 M3 L4 SVP: 4 DLU: 77

275.357-042 SALES REPRESENTATIVE, SCHOOL EQUIPMENT AND SUPPLIES (wholesale tr.)

Sells school equipment and supplies, such as blackboards, art supplies, science and homemaking equipment, and school furniture, performing duties as described under SALES REPRESENTATIVE (retail trade; wholesale tr.) Master Title.
GOE: 08.02.01 STRENGTH: L GED: R4 M3 L4 SVP: 5 DLU: 77

275.357-046 SALES REPRESENTATIVE, SHOE LEATHER AND FINDINGS (wholesale tr.)

Sells shoe leather and shoe repairing supplies, such as eyelets, welts, polish, and handtools, performing duties as described under SALES REPRESENTATIVE (retail trade; wholesale tr.) Master Title.
GOE: 08.02.01 STRENGTH: L GED: R4 M3 L4 SVP: 5 DLU: 77

275.357-050 SALES REPRESENTATIVE, VENDING AND COIN MACHINES (wholesale tr.)

Sells coin-operated amusement and food vending machines, performing duties as described under SALES REPRESENTATIVE (retail trade; wholesale tr.) Master Title.
GOE: 08.02.01 STRENGTH: L GED: R4 M3 L4 SVP: 5 DLU: 77

275.357-054 SALESPERSON, FLORIST SUPPLIES (wholesale tr.)

Sells florist supplies, such as artificial flowers, vases, ribbon, and wire, performing duties as described under SALESPERSON (retail trade; wholesale tr.) Master Title.
GOE: 08.02.01 STRENGTH: L GED: R4 M3 L4 SVP: 4 DLU: 77

276 SALES OCCUPATIONS, MEDICAL AND SCIENTIFIC EQUIPMENT AND SUPPLIES

This group includes occupations concerned with selling dental, medical, veterinary, and ophthalmic equipment and supplies, such as surgical instruments, dental tools, eyeglasses, hearing aids, orthopedic appliances, artificial limbs, and related hospital supplies; and engineering, laboratory, and scientific instruments and supplies, such as slide rules, drafting implements, measuring and controlling instruments, lenses and optical instruments, and navigation and surveying instruments.

276.257-010 SALES REPRESENTATIVE, DENTAL AND MEDICAL EQUIPMENT AND SUPPLIES (wholesale tr.)

Sells medical and dental equipment and supplies, except drugs and medicines, to doctors, dentists, hospitals, medical schools, and retail establishments: Studies data describing new products to develop sales approach. Compiles data on equipment and supplies preferred by customers. Advises customers of equipment for given need based on technical knowledge of products. Provides customers with advice in such areas as office layout, legal and insurance regulations, cost analysis, and collection methods to develop goodwill and promote sales. Performs other duties as described under SALES REPRESENTATIVE (retail trade; wholesale tr.) Master Title. May be designated according to type of equipment and supplies sold as Sales Representative, Dental Equipment And Supplies (wholesale tr.). May sell orthopedic appliances, trusses, and artificial limbs and be designated Sales Representative, Prosthetic And Orthotic Appliances (wholesale tr.). May sell services of dental laboratory and be designated Sales Representative, Dental Prosthetics (wholesale tr.).
GOE: 08.01.01 STRENGTH: L GED: R4 M3 L4 SVP: 6 DLU: 77

276.257-014 SALES REPRESENTATIVE, WEIGHING AND FORCE-MEASUREMENT INSTRUMENTS (wholesale tr.)

Sells spring scales and dynamometers, performing duties as described under SALES REPRESENTATIVE (retail trade; wholesale tr.) Master Title. Evaluates customer's needs and emphasizes salable features, utilizing technical knowledge of capabilities and limitations of spring scales and dynamometers, engineering specifications, and catalogs. Worker is not required to be as technically knowledgeable as SALES ENGINEER (profess. & kin.) Master Title.
GOE: 08.01.01 STRENGTH: S GED: R5 M4 L5 SVP: 6 DLU: 77

276.257-018 SALESPERSON, ORTHOPEDIC SHOES (retail trade) alternate titles: orthopedic-shoe fitter

Evaluates customers' foot conditions and fits and sells corrective shoes, using knowledge of orthopedics or following prescription: Examines malformed or injured joints and bone structure of customer's feet, or reads physician's prescription to determine type of corrective shoe required. Selects shoes from stock or draws outline and takes measurements of customer's feet to order custom-made shoes. Examines shoes on customer's feet to verify correctness of fit. Performs other duties as described under SALESPERSON (retail trade; wholesale tr.) Master Title.
GOE: 08.02.02 STRENGTH: L GED: R4 M3 L4 SVP: 6 DLU: 77

276.257-022 SALESPERSON, SURGICAL APPLIANCES (retail trade) alternate titles: fitter; surgical-appliance fitter

Fits and sells surgical appliances, such as trusses, abdominal supports, braces, cervical collars, and artificial limbs, using knowledge of anatomy, orthopedics, orthotics, and prosthetics: Measures customer with tape measure or follows prescription from physician to determine type and size of appliance required. Selects appliance from stock and fits appliance on customer. Writes specifications for and orders custom-made appliances. Performs other duties as described under SALESPERSON (retail trade; wholesale tr.) Master Title. May design and fabricate, or direct fabrication of custom-made appliances.
GOE: 08.02.02 STRENGTH: L GED: R5 M3 L4 SVP: 6 DLU: 77

276.354-010 HEARING AID SPECIALIST (retail trade) alternate titles: hearing instrument specialist; salesperson, hearing aids

Fits and sells hearing amplification systems to individuals in retail establishment: Tests auditory system of hearing-impaired individuals, using test equipment and applying standardized evaluation procedures; or receives individuals referred by physician for fitting and purchasing of hearing amplification systems. Interprets and evaluates auditory test results and confers with hearing-impaired individuals to demonstrate, select, fit, adapt, and modify hearing amplification systems for individuals. Performs other duties as described under SALESPERSON (retail trade; wholesale tr.) Master Title. May replace defective parts or make repairs to hearing amplification systems returned by customers. May make impression of client's ear to facilitate shaping of hearing aid. May visit homes of confined individuals to administer auditory system tests. May assist individuals in aural rehabilitation methods.
GOE: 08.02.02 STRENGTH: L GED: R4 M3 L4 SVP: 6 DLU: 78

276.357-010 SALES REPRESENTATIVE, ARCHITECTURAL AND ENGINEERING SUPPLIES (wholesale tr.)

Sells architectural and engineering supplies, such as protractors, slide rules, triangles, and T-squares, to business and industrial establishments: Performs other duties as described under SALES REPRESENTATIVE (retail trade; wholesale tr.) Master Title. May deliver supplies ordered and collect payment for orders.
GOE: 08.02.01 STRENGTH: L GED: R4 M3 L4 SVP: 6 DLU: 77

276.357-014 SALES REPRESENTATIVE, PRECISION INSTRUMENTS (wholesale tr.)

Sells precision instruments, such as laboratory, navigation, and surveying instruments, performing duties as described under SALES REPRESENTATIVE (retail trade; wholesale tr.) Master Title.
GOE: 08.01.01 STRENGTH: L GED: R4 M3 L4 SVP: 6 DLU: 77

276.357-018 SALES REPRESENTATIVE, VETERINARIAN SUPPLIES (wholesale tr.)

Sells veterinarian and animal hospital instruments, drugs, equipment, supplies, and packaged food, performing duties as described under SALES REPRESENTATIVE (retail trade; wholesale tr.) Master Title.
GOE: 08.02.01 STRENGTH: L GED: R4 M3 L4 SVP: 6 DLU: 77

277 SALES OCCUPATIONS, SPORTING, HOBBY, STATIONERY, AND RELATED GOODS

This group includes occupations concerned with selling amusement devices, such as games and toys; sporting and athletic goods, such as firearms and ammunition, fishing tackle, golf and tennis goods, bicycles, billiard tables, skates, and gymnasium and playground equipment; photographic equipment and supplies, such as cameras, projectors, film, and enlargers; musical instruments and accessories, sheet music, phonograph records, and prerecorded tapes; pets and pet supplies; hobby goods, including stamps and coins for collectors; souvenirs, trinkets, and novelties; books and periodicals; and stationery goods and greeting cards. Occupations concerned with selling industrial photographic equipment, such as blueprinting and diazotype (white printing) equipment, are included in Group 274. Occupations concerned with selling commercial photographic equipment, such as photocopy and microfilm equipment, are included in Group 275.

277.354-010 SALESPERSON, PIANOS AND ORGANS (retail trade)

Sells pianos or organs: Plays instrument to demonstrate tonal qualities of piano or combinations of tones on organ. Discusses construction and operating techniques of organs, or construction of piano with effect on tone, quality, and limitations. Advises customer on style of organ or piano to harmonize with other furniture. May appraise used organs or pianos for trade-in allowance. May rent pianos or organs and prepare rental contracts. Performs duties as described under SALESPERSON (retail trade; wholesale tr.) Master Title.
GOE: 08.02.02 STRENGTH: L GED: R4 M3 L4 SVP: 6 DLU: 77

277.357-010 SALES REPRESENTATIVE, HOBBIES AND CRAFTS (retail trade; wholesale tr.)

Sells hobby and craft materials, such as leather, leatherworking tools, ceramic clay, paints, and model kits: Explains and demonstrates use of tools and mate-

rials to retail dealers. Performs other duties as described under SALES REP-RESENTATIVE (retail trade; wholesale tr.) Master Title.
GOE: 08.02.03 STRENGTH: L GED: R4 M3 L4 SVP: 5 DLU: 77

277.357-014 SALES REPRESENTATIVE, MUSICAL INSTRUMENTS AND ACCESSORIES (wholesale tr.)
Sells brass, percussion, stringed, and woodwind musical instruments, accessories, and supplies, performing duties as described under SALES REPRESENTATIVE (retail trade; wholesale tr.) Master Title.
GOE: 08.02.01 STRENGTH: L GED: R4 M3 L4 SVP: 6 DLU: 77

277.357-018 SALES REPRESENTATIVE, NOVELTIES (wholesale tr.)
Sells novelties, such as souvenirs, toys, statuettes, glassware, and trinkets, to variety stores, toy stores, and carnivals, performing duties as described under SALES REPRESENTATIVE (retail trade; wholesale tr.) Master Title.
GOE: 08.02.01 STRENGTH: L GED: R4 M3 L4 SVP: 4 DLU: 77

277.357-022 SALES REPRESENTATIVE, PUBLICATIONS (wholesale tr.) alternate titles: distributor, publications
Sells publications, such as books and periodicals: Suggests sales promotion techniques to retail dealers to increase sales. Performs other duties as described under SALES REPRESENTATIVE (retail trade; wholesale tr.) Master Title.
GOE: 08.02.01 STRENGTH: L GED: R4 M3 L4 SVP: 5 DLU: 77

277.357-026 SALES REPRESENTATIVE, RECREATION AND SPORTING GOODS (wholesale tr.)
Sells amusement and sporting goods, such as hunting and fishing equipment, camping equipment, athletic equipment, playground equipment, toys, and games: Performs duties as described under SALES REPRESENTATIVE (retail trade; wholesale tr.) Master Title. May be designated according to product sold as Sales Representative, Playground Equipment (wholesale tr.); Sales Representative, Sporting Goods (wholesale tr.); Sales Representative, Toys And Games (retail trade; wholesale tr.).
GOE: 08.02.01 STRENGTH: L GED: R4 M3 L4 SVP: 5 DLU: 77

277.357-030 SALES REPRESENTATIVE, WRITING AND MARKING PENS (wholesale tr.)
Sells ballpoint, fountain, and felt-tipped pens to retail dealers, performing duties as described under SALES REPRESENTATIVE (retail trade; wholesale tr.) Master Title.
GOE: 08.02.01 STRENGTH: L GED: R4 M3 L4 SVP: 3 DLU: 77

277.357-034 SALESPERSON, BOOKS (retail trade)
Sells books in book or department store: Suggests selection of books, based on knowledge of current literature and familiarity with publishers' catalogs and book reviews. Arranges books on shelves and racks according to type, author, or subject matter. Performs other duties as described under SALESPERSON (retail trade; wholesale tr.) Master Title. May specialize in selling technical publications.
GOE: 08.02.02 STRENGTH: L GED: R4 M3 L4 SVP: 4 DLU: 77

277.357-038 SALESPERSON, MUSICAL INSTRUMENTS AND ACCESSORIES (retail trade)
Sells brass, percussion, stringed, and woodwind musical instruments, musical accessories, equipment, and supplies: Explains function, mechanisms, and care of musical instruments to customer. Demonstrates and discusses quality of tone and variations in instruments of different prices. Performs other duties as described under SALESPERSON (retail trade; wholesale tr.) Master Title. May make repairs. May solicit business of orchestras or other musical groups. May rent instruments to customers and prepare rental contracts.
GOE: 08.02.02 STRENGTH: L GED: R4 M3 L4 SVP: 6 DLU: 77

277.357-042 SALESPERSON, PETS AND PET SUPPLIES (retail trade)
Sells pets and pet accessories, equipment, food, and remedies: Advises customer on care, training, feeding, living habits, and characteristics of pets, such as dogs, cats, birds, fish, and hamsters. Explains use of equipment, such as aquarium pumps and filters. Feeds and provides water for pets. Performs other duties as described under SALESPERSON (retail trade; wholesale tr.) Master Title. May clean cages and tanks. May suggest remedies for certain animal diseases or recommend services of VETERINARIAN (medical ser.).
GOE: 08.02.02 STRENGTH: L GED: R4 M3 L4 SVP: 4 DLU: 77

277.357-046 SALESPERSON, PHONOGRAPH RECORDS AND TAPE RECORDINGS (retail trade)
Sells phonograph records and tape recordings in music store, record shop, or department store, performing duties as described under SALESPERSON (retail trade; wholesale tr.) Master Title. Assists customers in selection of instrumental and vocal recordings in musical categories, such as popular, classical, folk, and religious, using knowledge of available releases, catalogs, and lists. May also sell recording maintenance equipment and supplies.
GOE: 08.02.02 STRENGTH: L GED: R3 M3 L3 SVP: 3 DLU: 77

277.357-050 SALESPERSON, PHOTOGRAPHIC SUPPLIES AND EQUIPMENT (retail trade; wholesale tr.)
Sells photographic and optical equipment and supplies, such as cameras, projectors, film, and binoculars: Demonstrates equipment to customer and explains functioning of various cameras, filters, lenses, and other photographic accessories. Receives film for processing. Performs other duties as described under SALESPERSON (retail trade; wholesale tr.) Master Title. May repair photographic or optical equipment.

GOE: 08.02.03 STRENGTH: L GED: R4 M3 L4 SVP: 5 DLU: 77

277.357-054 SALESPERSON, SHEET MUSIC (retail trade)
Sells books and sheet music for instrumental and vocal groups or soloists, utilizing knowledge of composers, compositions, and types of music, such as classical, popular, and sacred. Performs duties as described under SALESPERSON (retail trade; wholesale tr.) Master Title.
GOE: 08.02.02 STRENGTH: L GED: R4 M3 L4 SVP: 5 DLU: 77

277.357-058 SALESPERSON, SPORTING GOODS (retail trade)
Sells sporting goods and athletic equipment: Advises customer on type of equipment for specific purposes, such as length of golf club, size of grip on tennis racket, weight of bowling ball, length of skis and poles, and caliber and make of gun or rifle. Explains care of equipment, regulations of games, and fish and game laws. Informs customer of areas for hunting, fishing, or skiing, and cost of such outings. Performs other duties as described under SALESPERSON (retail trade; wholesale tr.) Master Title. May repair sporting goods.
GOE: 08.02.02 STRENGTH: L GED: R4 M3 L4 SVP: 5 DLU: 77

277.357-062 SALESPERSON, STAMPS OR COINS (retail trade; wholesale tr.)
Sells stamps or coins, or both, to collectors: Locates stamp or coin desired by customer. Discusses value of items with customer. Performs other duties as described under SALESPERSON (retail trade; wholesale tr.) Master Title. May appraise and classify stamps or coins, using magnifier and catalogs. May buy coins or stamps from collectors and wholesalers for resale.
GOE: 08.02.03 STRENGTH: L GED: R4 M3 L4 SVP: 5 DLU: 77

277.357-066 SALESPERSON, TOY TRAINS AND ACCESSORIES (retail trade)
Sells toy trains, model train kits, and accessories, such as tracks, batteries, tunnels, and signal lights, performing duties as described under SALESPERSON (retail trade; wholesale tr.) Master Title.
GOE: 08.02.02 STRENGTH: L GED: R4 M3 L4 SVP: 3 DLU: 77

277.457-010 SALESPERSON, ART OBJECTS (retail trade)
Sells paintings, art materials, curios, and mirror and picture frames, performing duties as described under SALESPERSON (retail trade; wholesale tr.) Master Title.
GOE: 08.02.02 STRENGTH: L GED: R3 M2 L3 SVP: 4 DLU: 77

279 SALES OCCUPATIONS, MISCELLANEOUS COMMODITIES, N.E.C.

This group includes occupations, not elsewhere classified, concerned with selling commodities.

279.157-010 MANUFACTURERS' REPRESENTATIVE (wholesale tr.) alternate titles: manufacturers' agent
Sells single, allied, diversified, or multiline products to WHOLESALERS (wholesale tr.) I 185.167-070 or other customers for one or more manufacturers on commission basis: Contacts manufacturers and arranges to sell their products. Calls on regular or prospective customers to solicit orders. Demonstrates products and points out salable features. Answers questions concerning products, such as price, credit terms, and durability. Completes sales contracts or forms to record required sales information. May forward orders to manufacturer. May promote products at trade shows and conferences.
GOE: 08.02.01 STRENGTH: L GED: R4 M3 L4 SVP: 6 DLU: 81

279.357-010 SALES EXHIBITOR (nonprofit org.)
Sells variety of products made by the blind, such as wallets, mops, neckties, rugs, aprons, and babywear: Contacts businesses and civic establishments and arranges to exhibit and sell merchandise made by the blind on their premises. Sets up and displays merchandise to attract attention of prospective customers. Performs other duties as described under SALESPERSON (retail trade; wholesale tr.) Master Title.
GOE: 08.02.02 STRENGTH: L GED: R3 M2 L3 SVP: 3 DLU: 77

279.357-014 SALES REPRESENTATIVE, GENERAL MERCHANDISE (wholesale tr.)
Sells variety of merchandise, such as dry goods, notions, and housewares, to retail stores or other outlets, performing duties as described under SALES REPRESENTATIVE (retail trade; wholesale tr.) Master Title. May assemble and stock product displays in retail stores. May obtain credit information on prospective customers and forward findings to home office.
GOE: 08.02.01 STRENGTH: L GED: R4 M3 L4 SVP: 5 DLU: 89

279.357-018 SALES REPRESENTATIVE, JEWELRY (wholesale tr.)
Sells jewelry, jewels, and watches, performing duties as described under SALES REPRESENTATIVE (retail trade; wholesale tr.) Master Title.
GOE: 08.02.01 STRENGTH: L GED: R4 M3 L4 SVP: 6 DLU: 77

279.357-022 SALES REPRESENTATIVE, LEATHER GOODS (wholesale tr.)
Sells leather goods, such as billfolds, luggage, handbags, and utility kits, utilizing knowledge of kinds and grades of leather and product manufacturing process. Performs duties as described under SALES REPRESENTATIVE (retail trade; wholesale tr.) Master Title.
GOE: 08.02.01 STRENGTH: L GED: R4 M3 L4 SVP: 6 DLU: 80

279.357-026 SALES REPRESENTATIVE, PAPER AND PAPER PROD-UCTS (wholesale tr.)

Sells paper and paper products, such as bags, containers, newsprint, wrapping paper, stationery, towels, and plates. Performs duties as described under SALES REPRESENTATIVE (retail trade; wholesale tr.) Master Title. May be designated according to type of paper as Sales Representative, Printing Paper (wholesale tr.); or paper product sold as Sales Representative, Envelope (wholesale tr.).
GOE: 08.02.01 STRENGTH: L GED: R4 M3 L4 SVP: 5 DLU: 77

279.357-030 SALES REPRESENTATIVE, PLASTIC PRODUCTS (wholesale tr.)

Sells fabricated plastic products, such as boxes, shipping containers, and refrigerator linings. Prepares sketches and specifications for items to meet specific needs of customer. Performs duties as described under SALES REPRESENTATIVE (retail trade; wholesale tr.) Master Title.
GOE: 08.02.01 STRENGTH: L GED: R4 M3 L4 SVP: 4 DLU: 77

279.357-034 SALES REPRESENTATIVE, WATER-SOFTENING EQUIPMENT (retail trade; wholesale tr.)

Sells water softener tanks and service contracts to home owners, laundries, apartment houses, and motel owners: Calls on prospective customers from list furnished by company, or develops own sales leads by door-to-door canvassing. Tests water at location for hardness, acidity, and iron and sulfur content, using water analysis kit. Persuades customer to purchase water softener tank, if test results indicate need. Prepares sales contract and service agreement for customer, collects deposit, and issues receipt. Determines interest on time payment plans, using interest table. May examine water pipes in building and suggest location for tank.
GOE: 08.02.03 STRENGTH: L GED: R4 M3 L4 SVP: 5 DLU: 77

279.357-038 SALESPERSON-DEMONSTRATOR, PARTY PLAN (retail trade)

Displays and sells merchandise, such as clothes, household items, jewelry, toiletries, or toys, to guests attending house party: Confers with party sponsor to arrange date, time, and number of guests. Sets up display of sample merchandise. Meets guests and converses with them to establish rapport. Discusses items on display or demonstrates uses of product, and explains program to guests. Hands out catalogs or brochures that picture merchandise available. Writes orders for merchandise and arranges for payment. Delivers orders to sponsor or individual and collects monies due. May give small sample items to guests. May discuss program with guests to persuade them to sponsor house party by describing benefits derived from sponsorship. May assist sponsor to serve refreshments.
GOE: 08.02.05 STRENGTH: L GED: R4 M3 L4 SVP: 4 DLU: 77

279.357-042 SALESPERSON, BURIAL NEEDS (retail trade) alternate titles: salesperson, cemetery

Sells burial needs, such as cemetery plots and crypts, grave coverings, markers, and mausoleums: Contacts prospects at their homes in response to telephone inquiries, referrals from funeral homes, and leads from obituary notices. May sell monuments and similar memorials, either in employ of cemetery or monument firm. May specialize in one type of burial need and be designated Salesperson, Burial Plots (retail trade); Salesperson, Grave Coverings And Markers (retail trade).
GOE: 08.02.02 STRENGTH: L GED: R4 M3 L4 SVP: 5 DLU: 77

279.357-046 SALESPERSON, FLYING SQUAD (retail trade) alternate titles: salesperson, utility staff

Sells merchandise in any assigned department of sales establishment in substitute or supplementary capacity, performing duties as described under SALESPERSON (retail trade; wholesale tr.) Master Title. Worker is experienced in selling merchandise in many departments and is assigned to particular department depending on store need.
GOE: 08.02.02 STRENGTH: L GED: R4 M3 L4 SVP: 6 DLU: 77

279.357-050 SALESPERSON, GENERAL HARDWARE (retail trade; wholesale tr.)

Sells hardware, such as nails, bolts, screws, hand-and-power tools, electrical equipment, plumbing supplies, garden tools, and paint: Advises customer on tools, hardware, and materials needed, and procedure to follow to complete task customer wishes to perform. Informs customer about quality of tools, hardware, and equipment, and demonstrates use. Performs related duties, such as estimating amount of paint required to cover given area, mixing paint, and cutting screen, glass, wire, or window shades to specified size. Performs other duties as described under SALESPERSON (retail trade; wholesale tr.) Master Title. May specialize in selling paint or wall coverings and be designated Salesperson, Paint (retail trade; wholesale tr.); Salesperson, Wall Coverings (retail trade; wholesale tr.).
GOE: 08.02.03 STRENGTH: L GED: R3 M2 L2 SVP: 4 DLU: 81

279.357-054 SALESPERSON, GENERAL MERCHANDISE (retail trade; wholesale tr.)

Sells variety of commodities in sales establishment, performing duties as described under SALESPERSON (retail trade; wholesale tr.) Master Title. May demonstrate use of merchandise. May examine defective article returned by customer to determine if refund or replacement should be made. May estimate quantity of merchandise required to fill customer's need.

GOE: 08.02.03 STRENGTH: L GED: R3 M2 L2 SVP: 3 DLU: 81

279.357-058 SALESPERSON, JEWELRY (retail trade)

Displays and sells jewelry and watches: Advises customer on quality, cuts, or value of jewelry and gems and in selecting mountings or settings for gems. Informs customer of various grades of watch movements and type of servicing offered by manufacturer. Performs other duties as described under SALESPERSON (retail trade; wholesale tr.) Master Title. May estimate cost of jewelry and watch repair. May suggest designs for custom jewelry. May sell flatware, hollowware, and tableware, and advise customer on quality, grades, and patterns.
GOE: 08.02.02 STRENGTH: L GED: R4 M3 L4 SVP: 5 DLU: 77

279.357-062 SALESPERSON, PARTS (retail trade; wholesale tr.) alternate titles: counter clerk; parts clerk

Sells automotive, appliance, electrical, and other parts and equipment in repair facility or parts store: Ascertains make, year, and type of part needed, inspects worn, damaged, or defective part to determine replacement required, or advises customer of part needed according to description of malfunction. Discusses use and features of various parts, based on knowledge of machine or equipment. Reads catalog, microfiche viewer, or computer for replacement part stock number and price. Advises customer on substitution or modification of part when replacement is not available. Examines returned part to determine if defective, and exchanges part or refunds money. Fills customer orders from stock. Marks and stores parts in stockroom according to prearranged system. Receives and fills telephone orders for parts. Performs other duties as described under SALESPERSON (retail trade; wholesale tr.) Master Title. May measure engine parts, using precision measuring instruments, to determine whether similar parts may be machined down or built up to required size. Usually specializes in selling parts for one type of machinery or equipment and is designated according to part sold, as Counter Clerk, Appliance Parts (retail trade; wholesale tr.); Counter Clerk, Automotive Parts (retail trade; wholesale tr.); Counter Clerk, Farm Equipment Parts (retail trade; wholesale tr.); Counter Clerk, Industrial Machinery and Equipment Parts (retail trade; wholesale tr.); Counter Clerk, Radio, Television, and Electronics Parts (retail trade; wholesale tr.); Counter Clerk, Tractor Parts (retail trade; wholesale tr.); Counter Clerk, Truck Parts (retail trade; wholesale tr.).
GOE: 08.02.03 STRENGTH: L GED: R4 M3 L3 SVP: 5 DLU: 81

29 MISCELLANEOUS SALES OCCUPATIONS

This division includes occupations concerned with sales transactions, except those of sales representatives and salespersons which are included in Divisions 25, 26, and 27, and occupations closely related to sales transactions, even though they do not involve actual participation in such transactions.

290 SALES CLERKS

This group includes occupations concerned with selling, usually in a retail store, any of a large variety of inexpensive merchandise, usually without specializing in any single commodity and not requiring much more knowledge of merchandise than price.

290.477-010 COUPON-REDEMPTION CLERK (retail trade)

Redeems books of trading stamps or coupons in exchange for merchandise and vacation trips: Shows customer selection of merchandise in display catalog and aids customer to make selection of merchandise. Counts books and verifies number of coupons required for requested articles, and cancels books exchanged for merchandise, using canceling machine. Collects sales tax on merchandise. Orders or obtains merchandise from stockroom. Fills out order form to request merchandise from warehouse when items requested by customer are not in stock. Talks to customers to resolve complaints or problems about merchandise and stamps. May keep record of books redeemed, taxes collected, and merchandise distributed. May take inventory of stock. May arrange merchandise for display on counters, racks, shelves, or stands. May wrap merchandise.
GOE: 07.03.01 STRENGTH: L GED: R3 M2 L2 SVP: 2 DLU: 77

290.477-014 SALES CLERK (retail trade)

Obtains or receives merchandise, totals bill, accepts payment, and makes change for customers in retail store such as tobacco shop, drug store, candy store, or liquor store: Stocks shelves, counters, or tables with merchandise. Sets up advertising displays or arranges merchandise on counters or tables to promote sales. Stamps, marks, or tags price on merchandise. Obtains merchandise requested by customer or receives merchandise selected by customer. Answers customer's questions concerning location, price, and use of merchandise. Totals price and tax on merchandise purchased by customer, using paper and pencil, cash register, or calculator, to determine bill. Accepts payment and makes change. Wraps or bags merchandise for customers. Cleans shelves, counters, or tables. Removes and records amount of cash in register at end of shift. May calculate sales discount to determine price. May keep record of sales, prepare inventory of stock, or order merchandise. May be designated according to product sold or type of store.
GOE: 09.04.02 STRENGTH: L GED: R3 M2 L2 SVP: 3 DLU: 82

290.477-018 SALES CLERK, FOOD (retail trade)

Obtains or prepares food items requested by customers in retail food store, totals customer bill, receives payment, and makes change: Fills customer order,

performing duties such as obtaining items from shelves, freezers, coolers, bins, tables, or containers; cleaning poultry; scaling and trimming fish; slicing meat or cheese, using slicing machine; preparing take-out sandwiches and salads; dispensing beverages; and warming food items in oven. Weighs items, such as produce, meat, and poultry to determine price. Lists and totals prices, using paper and pencil, calculator, or cash register. Informs customer of total price of purchases. Receives payment from customer for purchases and makes change. Bags or wraps purchases for customer. Cleans shelves, bins, tables, and coolers. Stamps, marks, or tags price on merchandise. Sets up displays and stocks shelves, coolers, counter, bins, tables, freezers, containers, or trays with new merchandise. May make deliveries to customer home or place of business [DELIVERER, MERCHANDISE (retail trade) 299.477-010]. May write orders, decorate cakes, or describe available specialty products, such as birthday cakes. May order merchandise from warehouse or supplier. May be designated according to type of food sold as Grocery Clerk (retail trade); Meat Counter Clerk (retail trade); Produce Clerk (retail trade) I; Sales Clerk, Fish (retail trade).
GOE: 09.04.02 STRENGTH: L GED: R3 M3 L2 SVP: 3 DLU: 82

291 VENDING AND DOOR-TO-DOOR SELLING OCCUPATIONS

This group includes occupations concerned with hawking and selling merchandise or services on street, door to door, or at amusement and recreational facilities, such as sports arenas and nightclubs, using basket, pushcart, horse and wagon, stand, carrying case, or truck to carry merchandise.

291.157-010 SUBSCRIPTION CREW LEADER (retail trade)
Supervises and coordinates activities of workers engaged in selling magazine subscriptions door to door. Gives training to crew in company methods and procedures in selling and writing sales contract. Assigns crews to specified area. Reviews orders received by crewmembers. Compiles magazine sales records. May hire crewmembers.
GOE: 08.02.08 STRENGTH: L GED: R3 M2 L3 SVP: 5 DLU: 77

291.357-010 SALES REPRESENTATIVE, DOOR-TO-DOOR (retail trade) alternate titles: canvasser; peddler; solicitor
Sells merchandise or service, such as books, magazines, notions, brushes, and cosmetics, going from door to door without making appointments or following leads from management, other workers, or from listings in city and telephone directories: Displays sample products, explains desirable qualities of products, and leaves samples, or distributes advertising literature explaining service or products. Writes and submits orders to company. Delivers merchandise, collects money, and makes change. May contact individuals previously solicited in person, by telephone, or by mail to close sale. May travel from one area to another, or be assigned to specified territory.
GOE: 08.02.08 STRENGTH: L GED: R3 M2 L3 SVP: 2 DLU: 81

291.454-010 LEI SELLER (retail trade) alternate titles: lei maker
Makes and sells leis (wreaths or garlands of flowers) to persons arriving or departing on ships, or attending social functions, such as dances. Does not operate stand or permanent place of business. Sells individual flowers, bouquets, and accessories.
GOE: 08.03.01 STRENGTH: L GED: R2 M2 L2 SVP: 2 DLU: 77

291.457-010 CIGARETTE VENDOR (hotel & rest.)
Sells cigars, cigarettes, corsages, and novelties to patrons in hotels, restaurants, and nightclubs: Walks among guests carrying tray of articles and persuades patrons to make purchases. May order supplies. May wire flowers and attach ribbons to form corsages.
GOE: 08.03.01 STRENGTH: L GED: R2 M2 L2 SVP: 2 DLU: 77

291.457-014 LOUNGE-CAR ATTENDANT (r.r. trans.) alternate titles: sandwich seller; vendor
Sells beverages, cakes, candies, cigarettes, and sandwiches to passengers in railroad passenger coaches: Walks down aisle of car, with basket or cart containing items for sale, and calls out offerings. Serves items to passengers. Accepts money for items purchased and returns change. May sell newspapers, magazines, postcards, playing cards, and similar nonfood items only and be designated News Agent (r.r. trans.).
GOE: 08.03.01 STRENGTH: M GED: R2 M2 L2 SVP: 2 DLU: 77

291.457-018 PEDDLER (retail trade) alternate titles: hawker; huckster; vendor
Sells merchandise, such as fruit, vegetables, flowers, or ice cream, on streets or from door to door, usually using basket, pushcart, or truck to carry products. May attract attention by playing chimes or chanting song. May be designated according to product sold as Ice-Cream Vendor (retail trade); Vegetable Vendor (retail trade).
GOE: 08.03.01 STRENGTH: M GED: R2 M2 L1 SVP: 3 DLU: 77

291.457-022 VENDOR (amuse. & rec.) alternate titles: peddler
Sells refreshments, programs, novelties, or cushions at sports events, parades, or other entertainments: Circulates among patrons or spectators, calling out items for sale. Hands, passes, or throws item to purchaser, receives payment, and makes change as required. Checks out items to replenish stock and turns in monies from sales.

GOE: 08.03.01 STRENGTH: M GED: R2 M2 L2 SVP: 2 DLU: 77

292 ROUTE SALES AND DELIVERY OCCUPATIONS

This group includes occupations concerned with selling and delivering such items as baked goods, milk, ice, newspapers, and laundry and dry cleaning to customers by driving truck or other vehicle or walking along established route. Includes collecting coins from vending or amusement machines, juke boxes, parking meters, and pay telephones along established route. Occupations concerned with selling merchandise on street, from vehicle, or door to door are found in Group 291. Occupations concerned only with transporting goods by truck are found in Division 90.

292.137-010 COIN-MACHINE-COLLECTOR SUPERVISOR (clerical)
Supervises and coordinates activities of workers engaged in collecting money from meters, pay phones, amusement machines, jukeboxes, or vending machines: Assigns workers to routes and keeps records of areas to be serviced. Counts coins and computes amount due to agents and subscribers. May pay refunds. May schedule and coordinate delivery of merchandise to vending machines. Performs other duties as described under SUPERVISOR (clerical) Master Title.
GOE: 07.07.03 STRENGTH: L GED: R3 M3 L3 SVP: 5 DLU: 77

292.137-014 SUPERVISOR, ROUTE SALES-DELIVERY DRIVERS (retail trade; wholesale tr.) alternate titles: dispatcher, route sales-delivery drivers; route supervisor
Supervises and coordinates activities of DRIVERS, SALES ROUTE (retail trade; wholesale tr.) engaged in selling and distributing products or services: Plans routes and schedules drivers, vehicles, and deliveries and pickups based on driver, company, and customer information. Records drivers' attendance and time for payroll records. Informs DRIVERS, SALES ROUTE (retail trade; wholesale tr.) of location of accounts and of collection procedures. Demonstrates sales methods. Oversees loading and dispatching of trucks. May collect overdue payments. May collect daily cash receipts from drivers and record amounts in records. May solicit new accounts. May investigate customer complaints and pay claims for damaged articles. May drive vehicle to designated areas. May load vehicles. May compute payroll and distribute pay to subordinates. Performs other duties as described under SUPERVISOR (any industry) Master Title. May be designated according to product sold as Supervisor, Newspaper Deliveries (wholesale tr.).
GOE: 08.02.07 STRENGTH: L GED: R4 M3 L4 SVP: 5 DLU: 77

292.353-010 DRIVER, SALES ROUTE (retail trade; wholesale tr.) alternate titles: delivery-route truck driver; route driver; truck driver, sales route
Drives truck or automobile over established route to deliver and sell products or render services, collects money from customers, and makes change: Drives truck to deliver such items as beer, soft drinks, bakery products, dry cleaning, laundry, specialty foods, and medical supplies to customer's home or place of business. Collects money from customers, makes change, and records transactions on customer receipt. Writes customer order and instructions. Records sales or deliveries information on daily sales or delivery record. Calls on prospective customers to solicit new business. Prepares order forms and sales contracts. Informs regular customers of new products or services. Listens to and resolves service complaints. May place stock on shelves or racks. May set up merchandise and sales promotion displays or issue sales promotion materials to customers. May collect or pick up empty containers or rejected or unsold merchandise. May load truck. May issue or obtain customer signature on receipt for pickup or delivery. May clean inside of truck. May perform routine maintenance on truck. May direct DRIVER HELPER, SALES ROUTE (retail trade; wholesale tr.) 292.667-010 to load and unload truck and carry merchandise. May be designated according to product delivered or service rendered.
GOE: 08.02.07 STRENGTH: M GED: R3 M2 L3 SVP: 3 DLU: 81

292.363-010 NEWSPAPER-DELIVERY DRIVER (wholesale tr.)
Drives truck or automobile over prescribed route to deliver newspapers to wholesale or retail newspaper dealers, or to bus, airline, or express stations for shipment: Loads newspapers onto vehicle. Reviews list of dealers, customers, or station drops for change in deliveries. Drives truck or automobile over prescribed route on city streets or rural roads. Delivers newspapers to dealers or individual subscribers at their homes or place of business, or to bus, airline, or express station for shipment. Keeps records of deliveries made. Collects receipts for deliveries to newsdealers. May pick up unsold newspapers and credit newsdealer's account. May collect payment for newspaper deliveries from customers. May keep records pertaining to driving expenses, such as mileage, oil, and gasoline. May stock newspapers in street sales rack, and collect coins from rack coin boxes. May distribute sales promotion material to customers with newspaper deliveries. May be designated according to publication delivered as Magazine-Delivery Driver (wholesale tr.).
GOE: 05.08.03 STRENGTH: M GED: R3 M2 L2 SVP: 4 DLU: 77

292.457-010 NEWSPAPER CARRIER (retail trade) alternate titles: carrier; newspaper deliverer
Delivers and sells newspapers to subscribers along prescribed route and collects money periodically: Purchases newspapers at wholesale price for resale to subscriber at retail rate. Walks or rides bicycle to deliver newspapers to subscribers. Keeps records of accounts. Contacts prospective subscribers along

route to solicit subscriptions. May attend training sessions to learn selling techniques. If worker delivers newspapers, using automobile or truck, see NEWS-PAPER-DELIVERY DRIVER (wholesale tr.).
GOE: 09.04.02 STRENGTH: L GED: R2 M2 L2 SVP: 2 DLU: 77

292.463-010 LUNCH-TRUCK DRIVER (hotel & rest.) alternate titles: catering-truck operator; lunch-truck operator
Drives lunch truck over regular scheduled route, and sells miscellaneous food specialties, such as sandwiches, box lunches, and beverages, to industrial and office workers, students, and to patrons of sports and public events. Loads and unloads truck. Maintains truck and food-dispensing equipment in sanitary condition and good working order. May prepare and wrap sandwiches for delivery. May push lunch-cart through departments of industrial establishment or office building to sell merchandise and be known as Lunch-Wagon Operator (hotel & rest.).
GOE: 09.04.01 STRENGTH: M GED: R2 M2 L2 SVP: 2 DLU: 77

292.483-010 COIN COLLECTOR (business ser.) alternate titles: route driver, coin machines; servicer, coin machines
Drives truck over established route to collect money from and refill coin-operated amusement-game machines, jukeboxes, and vending machines that dispense merchandise, such as cigarettes, coffee, food, beverages, and candy: Loads truck with supplies according to written or verbal instructions. Drives truck to establishment, collects coins, refills machine, cleans inside of machines that dispense food or beverages, and records amount of money collected. Turns in money to cashiering department at completion of route and unloads truck. Reports malfunctioning machines to maintenance department for repair. May perform minor repairs or adjustments on machines, using handtools, to correct malfunctions. May promote installation of new or additional coin-operated machines at locations of customers or potential customers. May be designated according to type of machine serviced as Amusement-Game Machine Coin Collector (business ser.); Jukebox Coin Collector (business ser.); Vending-Machine Coin Collector (business ser.).
GOE: 05.08.03 STRENGTH: M GED: R3 M2 L3 SVP: 3 DLU: 77

292.667-010 DRIVER HELPER, SALES ROUTE (retail trade; wholesale tr.) alternate titles: route driver helper
Aids DRIVER, SALES ROUTE (retail trade; wholesale tr.) in providing sales, services, or deliveries of goods to customers over an established route, performing any combination of the following duties: Loads and unloads truck at beginning and end of trip. Carries merchandise from truck to customer's home or store. Collects c.o.d. payments or obtains receipts. May drive to relieve driver. May solicit new business.
GOE: 08.02.07 STRENGTH: M GED: R2 M2 L2 SVP: 2 DLU: 77

292.687-010 COIN-MACHINE COLLECTOR (business ser.; tel. & tel.) alternate titles: coin-box collector; pay-station collector
Collects coins or coin boxes from parking meters or telephone pay stations: Unlocks telephone faceplate and removes box containing money. Inserts empty box and locks faceplate. Tags boxes to identify pay stations. Reports malfunctioning telephones or parking meters to repair department. Delivers boxes to central depot for machine counting, tabulating, and customer payment. May count coins and compute amount due subscriber, according to difference between minimum guaranteed rate and total cash in box. May pay subscriber percentage refund. May adjust or repair parking meters, using handtools. May keep records of collections, balances due, and refunds. May be designated according to type of equipment involved as Parking-Meter-Coin Collector (business ser.); Telephone Coin-Box Collector (tel. & tel.).
GOE: 07.07.03 STRENGTH: L GED: R2 M1 L2 SVP: 2 DLU: 87

293 SOLICITORS

This group includes occupations concerned with encouraging individuals to join, contribute to, or otherwise participate in activities or causes, such as joining clubs or organizations, contributing money or time to charitable causes, or donating blood.

293.137-010 SUPERVISOR, BLOOD-DONOR RECRUITERS (medical ser.)
Supervises and coordinates activities of BLOOD-DONOR RECRUITERS (medical ser.) engaged in soliciting blood donations from employees or members of companies, unions, and fraternal organizations: Selects, trains, and assigns BLOOD-DONOR RECRUITERS (medical ser.). Reviews records and reports to evaluate BLOOD-DONOR RECRUITER (medical ser.) performance and recommends personnel action when necessary. Analyzes and resolves work problems, or assists BLOOD-DONOR RECRUITER (medical ser.) in solving problems. Interprets blood-bank policies and procedures to staff. Attends management meetings to exchange ideas and information and discuss problems. Assists in preparation of annual budget by providing data and making recommendations. Serves as liaison between donor-enrollment unit and other units of blood bank. Occasionally answers requests for information from prospective or participating blood-donor groups. Occasionally speaks to interested donor groups about blood-bank program.
GOE: 11.09.02 STRENGTH: S GED: R4 M3 L4 SVP: 6 DLU: 77

293.157-010 FUND RAISER I (nonprofit org.)
Plans fund raising program for charities or other causes, and writes to, telephones, or visits individuals or establishments to solicit funds or gifts-in-kind:

Compiles and analyzes information about potential contributors to develop mailing or contact list and to plan selling approach. Writes, telephones, or visits potential contributors and persuades them to contribute funds or gifts-in-kind by explaining purpose and benefits of fund raising program. Takes pledges or funds from contributors. Records expenses incurred and contributions received. May organize volunteers and plan social functions to raise funds. May prepare fund raising brochures for mail-solicitation programs. May train volunteers to perform certain duties to assist fund raising.
GOE: 11.09.02 STRENGTH: L GED: R5 M3 L4 SVP: 6 DLU: 87

293.357-010 BLOOD-DONOR RECRUITER (medical ser.)
Contacts fraternal, business, and labor organizations by telephone, in person, or by mail to solicit blood donations from employees or members for nonprofit blood bank: Develops list of prospective donor groups by using organizational, professional, and industrial listings and directories. Contacts prospective donor groups to explain requirements and benefits of participation in blood donor program. Visits prospective or participating blood donor group to discuss blood program. Distributes promotional material and uses audio-visual aids to motivate groups to participate in blood-donor program. Keeps records of organizations participating in program. Arranges specific date of blood collection for blood-donor group and confirms appointment in writing. Records information for mobile blood-collection unit, such as space available, staffing required, and number of donors anticipated. Consults blood bank records to answer questions, monitor activity, or resolve problems of blood donor groups. Prepares reports of blood-donor program and recruitment activities. May identify donors with rare-type blood from blood-bank records, and telephone donors to solicit and arrange blood donation.
GOE: 11.09.02 STRENGTH: L GED: R4 M2 L4 SVP: 3 DLU: 77

293.357-014 FUND RAISER II (nonprofit org.) alternate titles: contribution solicitor
Contacts individuals and firms to solicit donations for charity or other causes: Confers with supervisor, or reads potential donor list, to determine which individuals or firms to approach. Contacts individuals and firms by telephone, in person, or by mail to solicit funds or gifts-in-kind. Takes pledges for amounts or gifts-in-kind to be contributed, or accepts immediate cash payments. May sell emblems or other tokens of organization represented. May write letter to express appreciation for donation. May arrange for pick-up of gifts-in-kind.
GOE: 08.02.08 STRENGTH: L GED: R3 M2 L3 SVP: 2 DLU: 87

293.357-018 GOODWILL AMBASSADOR (business ser.) alternate titles: welcome-wagon host/hostess
Promotes goodwill and solicits trade for local business firms who are members of parent organization: Develops list of prospective clients from such sources as newspaper items, utility companies' records, and local merchants. Visits homes of new residents, prospective parents, recently married couples, engaged persons, and other prospects to explain and sell services available from local merchants. Usually presents token gifts or gift certificates to induce clients to use local services or purchase local merchandise. Prepares reports of services rendered and visits made for parent organization and member firms. May solicit new organization membership. May explain community services available. May organize clubs and plan parties for new residents.
GOE: 11.09.01 STRENGTH: L GED: R3 M2 L3 SVP: 2 DLU: 77

293.357-022 MEMBERSHIP SOLICITOR (any industry)
Solicits membership for club or trade association: Visits or contacts prospective members to explain benefits and costs of membership and to describe organization and objectives of club or association. May collect dues and payments for publications from members. May solicit funds for club or association [FUND RAISER (nonprofit org.) II]. May speak to members at meetings about services available.
GOE: 08.02.08 STRENGTH: L GED: R4 M3 L4 SVP: 4 DLU: 77

294 AUCTIONEERS

This group includes occupations concerned with selling commodities to highest bidder at auctions.

294.257-010 AUCTIONEER (retail trade; wholesale tr.)
Sells articles at auction to highest bidder: Appraises merchandise before sale and assembles merchandise in lots according to estimated value of individual pieces or type of article. Selects article to be auctioned at suggestion of bidders or by own choice. Appraises article and determines or asks for starting bid. Describes merchandise and gives information about article, such as history and ownership, in order to encourage bidding. Continues to ask for bids, attempting to stimulate buying desire of bidders. Closes sale to highest bidder. May write auction catalog and advertising copy for local or trade newspapers and periodicals. May be designated according to property auctioned as Auctioneer, Art (retail trade; wholesale tr.); Auctioneer, Automobile (wholesale tr.); Auctioneer, Furniture (retail trade; wholesale tr.); Auctioneer, Livestock (retail trade; wholesale tr.); Auctioneer, Real Estate (retail trade; wholesale tr.); Auctioneer, Tobacco (wholesale tr.).
GOE: 08.02.03 STRENGTH: L GED: R3 M2 L3 SVP: 6 DLU: 77

294.567-010 AUCTION CLERK (retail trade; wholesale tr.)
Records amounts of final bids for merchandise at auction sales, and receives money from final bidders at auction: Locates lot and item number of article

up for bidding on record sheet. Listens to amount of bids called for by AUC-TIONEER (retail trade; wholesale tr.) and records final amount bid for article. Receives deposit money or full payment from final bidders.
GOE: 07.03.01 STRENGTH: S GED: R2 M2 L2 SVP: 3 DLU: 77

294.667-010 AUCTION ASSISTANT (retail trade; wholesale tr.) alternate titles: lot caller
   Assists AUCTIONEER (retail trade; wholesale tr.) at auction by tagging and arranging articles for sale, calling out lot and item numbers, and holding or displaying articles being auctioned: Receives and stores incoming merchandise to be auctioned. Writes assigned record numbers on tags and wires tags to articles. Arranges articles into group lots, according to similarity of type of merchandise, such as household goods, art objects, jewelry, and furniture. Assigns lot and item numbers to grouped articles and records numbers on tags and in record book. Calls out lot and item numbers of article being auctioned and holds or otherwise displays article during bidding. Assists final bidders in locating purchased items.
GOE: 07.07.02 STRENGTH: L GED: R2 M1 L2 SVP: 2 DLU: 77

295   RENTAL CLERKS

   This group includes occupations concerned with renting commodities, such as automobiles, bicycles, boats, films, televisions, tools and equipment, and trailers.

295.137-010 SUPERVISOR, SAFETY DEPOSIT (financial) alternate titles: safe deposit manager
   Supervises and coordinates activities of workers engaged in renting and maintaining safe-deposit boxes: Turns controls to set vault clock for reopening. Authorizes forcing, servicing, and repair of safe-deposit box locks. Approves or disapproves rentals and requests for admittance to safe-deposit boxes in accordance with bank regulations. Develops, implements, and evaluates improved procedures for safe deposit operations. Monitors prices charged by competitors, recommends rental fees for safe-deposit boxes, and develops marketing plan to advertise safe-deposit services. Prepares cost, expense, and budget reports. Keeps departmental records. Trains and assigns duties to new employees. May open and close vault. May admit customer to vault. Performs duties as described under SUPERVISOR (clerical) Master Title.
GOE: 07.01.02 STRENGTH: L GED: R4 M3 L3 SVP: 6 DLU: 89

295.357-010 APPAREL-RENTAL CLERK (retail trade)
   Rents formal clothes or costumes to customers: Talks to customer to determine clothing needs, date needed, quantity, style, color, and size. Shows customers available or appropriate garments. Explains rental fee to customer. Orders or reserves garment selected. Packages garments selected with complimentary accessories, such as cuff links, cummerbunds, neckties, and studs, and places in protective bag or box. Obtains suitable identification and deposit as security from customer. Computes rental charge and tax and prepares bill for customer. Collects money from customer or charges bill on customer's credit card. Examines garments for damages, and designates garments for cleaning or repair. May mark garments on customer for alteration. May sew buttons, hooks, hems, snaps, tears, or make minor alterations, by hand or using sewing machine. May mail or deliver rented garments to customer. May mail advertising material to customers. May return cleaned or repaired garments to stock. May be designated according to type of garments rented as Costume-Rental Clerk (retail trade); Formal-Wear-Rental Clerk (retail trade).
GOE: 09.04.02 STRENGTH: L GED: R3 M3 L3 SVP: 3 DLU: 77

295.357-014 TOOL-AND-EQUIPMENT-RENTAL CLERK (business ser.; retail trade) alternate titles: rental clerk, tool-and-equipment
   Rents tools and equipment to customers: Suggests tools or equipment, based on work to be done. Prepares rental form and quotes rental rates to customer. Starts power equipment to ensure performance prior to issuance to customer. Computes rental fee based on hourly or daily rate. Cleans, lubricates, and adjusts power tools and equipment. May drive truck or use handtruck to deliver tools or equipment to customer.
GOE: 09.04.02 STRENGTH: M GED: R3 M3 L3 SVP: 4 DLU: 77

295.357-018 FURNITURE-RENTAL CONSULTANT (retail trade) alternate titles: decorator consultant; rental clerk, furniture
   Rents furniture and accessories to customers: Talks to customer to determine furniture preferences and requirements. Guides or accompanies customer through showroom, answers questions, and advises customer on compatibility of various styles and colors of furniture items. Compiles list of customer-selected items. Computes rental fee, explains rental terms, and presents list to customer for approval. Prepares order form and lease agreement, explains terms of lease to customer, and obtains customer signature. Obtains credit information from customer. Forwards forms to credit office for verification of customer credit status and approval of order. Collects initial payment from customer. Contacts customers to encourage followup transactions. May visit commercial customer site to solicit rental contracts, or review floor plans of new construction and suggest suitable furnishings. May sell furniture or accessories [SALESPERSON, FURNITURE (retail trade) 270.357-030].
GOE: 09.04.02 STRENGTH: L GED: R3 M2 L2 SVP: 2 DLU: 86

295.367-010 AIRPLANE-CHARTER CLERK (air trans.) alternate titles: aircraft charter dispatcher; airplane-rental clerk
   Charters or rents airplanes to licensed pilots, licensed flight instructors, or charters aircraft to passenger-customers with company pilot: Determines pur-

pose, destination, dates and time of flight, and number of passengers to select appropriate airplane for charter. Examines pilot's license to assure customer is qualified to pilot aircraft or is qualified to train students, or notifies company pilot of requested flight. Prepares rental or charter forms and secures customer's signature. Reserves airplane and records flight information in logbook. Informs other workers to fuel, clean, and move airplane to flight line. Computes customer's charges based on hours flown and company rate schedule. Receives payment or records credit charges. Prepares monthly bills. Requisitions and keeps records of office and airplane supplies. May inspect airplanes periodically to check if they are properly cleaned and serviced. May file flight plans with airport traffic controller. May provide pilots with weather forecasts and airplane specifications.
GOE: 07.04.03 STRENGTH: L GED: R4 M3 L4 SVP: 3 DLU: 77

295.367-014 BABY-STROLLER AND WHEELCHAIR RENTAL CLERK (retail trade) alternate titles: stroller rental clerk; wheelchair and baby-stroller rental clerk
   Rents baby strollers and wheelchairs in shopping or recreation and amusement areas: Explains rental terms to customers. Unfolds or pushes stroller or wheelchair from storage area. Explains to customers how to use stroller or wheelchair. Accepts cash, driver's license, or credit cards as deposit for stroller or wheelchair. Accepts rental fee and makes change. Occasionally cleans strollers and wheelchairs and inspects for damage. May adjust parts of strollers or wheelchairs to correct defect, using handtools.
GOE: 09.04.02 STRENGTH: L GED: R3 M2 L3 SVP: 2 DLU: 77

295.367-018 FILM-RENTAL CLERK (business ser.; retail trade) alternate titles: audio-visual-equipment-rental clerk; film booker
   Rents films and audio-visual equipment to individuals and organizations, such as schools, churches, clubs, and business firms: Views incoming films to familiarize self with content. Recommends films on specific subjects to show to designated group, utilizing knowledge of film content, availability of film, and rental charge. Determines and quotes rental charges for film, depending on purpose for showing film, number of times to be shown, and size of audience. Writes orders, listing shipping date, show date, and method of shipping film. Posts film rental dates on office records to complete reservation. May write or type correspondence, invoices, and shipping labels. May visit prospective or current customers to sell film-rental and audio-visual-equipment-renting service.
GOE: 11.02.04 STRENGTH: L GED: R4 M3 L4 SVP: 5 DLU: 77

295.367-022 SAFE-DEPOSIT-BOX RENTAL CLERK (financial)
   Rents safe-deposit boxes to bank customers: Interviews customer to obtain information necessary to open account. Types rental contract and obtains customer signature. Collects initial rental fee from customer and writes receipt. Issues safe-deposit box key to customer. Files safe-deposit records, such as signature cards, rental contract, and access slips to vault. Admits customer to safe-deposit vault. Orders replacements for lost keys. Schedules repairs for safe-deposit box locks. Contacts vendor to forcibly open safe-deposit box when necessary, such as when customer loses key. Receives and records customer payment of yearly safe-deposit fee. May record box rental information, payment, and account changes, using computer terminal. May perform clerical duties.
GOE: 07.03.01 STRENGTH: L GED: R3 M3 L3 SVP: 4 DLU: 89

295.367-026 STORAGE-FACILITY RENTAL CLERK (business ser.; retail trade)
   Leases storage space to customers of rental storage facility: Informs customers of space availability, rental regulations, and rates. Assists customers in selection of storage unit size according to articles or material to be stored. Records terms of rental on rental agreement form and assists customer in completing form. Photographs completed form and customer to establish identification record, using security camera. Computes rental fee and collects payment. Maintains rental status record and waiting list for storage units. Notifies customers when rental term is about to expire or rent is overdue. Inspects storage area periodically to ensure storage units are locked. Observes individuals entering storage area to prevent access to or tampering with storage units by unauthorized persons. Loads film into security and surveillance cameras, records dates of film changes, and monitors camera operations to ensure performance as required. Cleans facility and maintains premises in orderly condition.
GOE: 09.04.02 STRENGTH: L GED: R3 M3 L3 SVP: 2 DLU: 86

295.467-010 BICYCLE-RENTAL CLERK (retail trade)
   Rents bicycles to patrons at beach, resort, or retail bicycle-rental store: Explains bicycle-rental rates and conditions to customer. Issues bicycle to customer and records time of transaction. Receives returned bicycles and examines them for abuse or breakage. Computes rental charge according to elapsed time and accepts payment, imposing specified fee for damage to bicycle. Records time bicycle was returned. Prepares cash report at end of shift. Tags bicycles needing repair or service. May adjust bicycle seat to suit customer. May receive money deposit or identification, such as driver's license, as security toward return of bicycle. May explain operation of bicycle and features of certain bicycles, such as gear shifting and hand brakes to customers.
GOE: 09.04.02 STRENGTH: L GED: R2 M2 L2 SVP: 2 DLU: 77

295.467-014 BOAT-RENTAL CLERK (amuse. & rec.)
   Rents canoes, motorboats, rowboats, sailboats, and fishing equipment: Explains rental rates and operation of boats and equipment to customer. Assists customers in and out of boats. Launches and moors boats. Tows disabled boats to shore, using motorboat. Calculates rental payment and collects payment from

customer. May make minor adjustments and repairs on motors of motorboats, such as replacing battery, using handtools. May pump water out of boats, using mechanical pump.
GOE: 09.04.02 STRENGTH: L GED: R3 M3 L3 SVP: 2 DLU: 77

295.467-018 HOSPITAL-TELEVISION-RENTAL CLERK (business ser.)
Rents television sets to hospital patients: Determines, from hospital staff and records, names of patients requesting television rental service. Visits patient's room and unlocks and adjusts television set. Explains operation of remote controls and informs patient of rental fee. Periodically collects rental fees. Keeps records of television rentals and fees due. May deliver and connect portable television sets.
GOE: 09.04.02 STRENGTH: L GED: R2 M2 L2 SVP: 2 DLU: 77

295.467-022 TRAILER-RENTAL CLERK (automotive ser.)
Rents trailers, trucks, and power-driven mobile machinery and equipment: Talks with customer to determine type of equipment needed, such as vacation, boat, or open trailer, or moving truck or moving-van trailer, or cement mixer. Quotes rental rates and collects security deposit. Prepares rental-agreement form. Directs yard personnel to hitch trailer to customer's vehicle or bring truck or power-driven mobile equipment to customer. Computes rental charges, collects money, makes change, and returns deposit. May pull trailer into position and fasten appropriate hitch to customer's vehicle. May splice wires from trailer's taillights onto wires of customer's vehicle's taillights to provide brake and turn signals to trailer. May advise customer on type of equipment to rent, depending on work to be done. May rent power tools and equipment [TOOL-AND-EQUIPMENT-RENTAL CLERK (business ser.; retail trade)]. May be designated according to type of equipment rented as Construction-Machinery-And-Equipment-Rental Clerk (business ser.); Farm-Machinery-And-Equipment-Rental Clerk (business ser.); Truck Rental Clerk (automotive ser.).
GOE: 09.04.02 STRENGTH: L GED: R3 M3 L3 SVP: 4 DLU: 77

295.467-026 AUTOMOBILE RENTAL CLERK (automotive ser.) alternate titles: automobile rental agent; automobile rental representative; car rental clerk
Rents automobiles to customers: Talks with customer to determine type of automobile and accessories desired, such as power steering and air-conditioning, location for pick up and return of automobile, and number of days needed for rental. Quotes cost of rental, based on type of automobile, daily rates, estimated mileage, insurance coverages requested, and amount of deposit required. Examines customer's driver's license and credit card, to determine validity of identification and eligibility for rental. Completes rental contract, explains rental policies and procedures, verifies credit, and obtains customer signature and deposit. Calls storage or service area to determine automobile availability and request delivery, and to check automobile upon return for damage and to record mileage and fuel level reading. Accepts automobiles returned by customer and computes rental charges based on type of automobile, length of time, distance traveled, taxes, and other expenses, such as late charges or damage fees incurred during rental. May reconcile cash or credit card slips with rental agreements and send to management. May inspect automobile fluid levels and add fluids, such as fuel, oil, and engine coolant to maintain automobile. May deliver automobile to customer. May keep log to track location of rented automobiles. May be designated according to type of automobile rented as Limousine Rental Clerk (automotive ser.).
GOE: 09.04.02 STRENGTH: L GED: R3 M3 L3 SVP: 4 DLU: 81

296 SHOPPERS

This group includes occupations concerned with visiting competing stores to gather information, such as style, quality, and prices of competitive merchandise, to aid employing establishment in setting its prices and determining its buying policy; suggesting suitable purchases to customers; and purchasing items from other stores for individual customers.

296.357-010 PERSONAL SHOPPER (retail trade) alternate titles: professional shopper; shopper's aid; special shopper
Selects and purchases merchandise for department store customers, according to mail or telephone requests. Visits wholesale establishments or other department stores to purchase merchandise which is out-of-stock or which store does not carry. Records and processes mail orders and merchandise returned for exchange. May escort customer through store.
GOE: 09.04.02 STRENGTH: L GED: R4 M3 L3 SVP: 5 DLU: 77

296.367-010 AUTOMOBILE LOCATOR (retail trade)
Phones other new or used automobile dealers to locate type of automobile desired by customer. Prepares papers for transfer of automobile. Keeps records of automobiles traded.
GOE: 07.05.03 STRENGTH: S GED: R3 M2 L3 SVP: 3 DLU: 77

296.367-014 COMPARISON SHOPPER (retail trade; wholesale tr.)
Compares prices, packaging, physical characteristics, and styles of merchandise in competing stores: Visits stores to observe details of merchandise and gather information that will be valuable to employer in setting prices and determining buying policies. Verifies complaints of customers on price of merchandise by shopping at designated store to ascertain same quality and style for specified price. Prepares reports of findings. May check with BUYER (profess. & kin.) to verify that advertised merchandise will be available for cus-

tomer purchase, and that merchandise, price, and sales dates are accurately described in advertising copy and illustration. May purchase merchandise in various locations for quality comparison tests.
GOE: 08.01.03 STRENGTH: L GED: R4 M2 L3 SVP: 3 DLU: 77

297 SALES PROMOTION OCCUPATIONS

This group includes occupations concerned with promoting interest on the part of customers to buy or rent merchandise or real estate by indirect selling techniques, such as modeling or demonstrating merchandise, instructing customers in arts and crafts involved in producing or using product, or giving guided tours to prospective buyers.

297.354-010 DEMONSTRATOR (retail trade; wholesale tr.)
Demonstrates merchandise and products to customers to promote sales: Displays product and explains features to customers. Answers customer's questions about product. Demonstrates use or production of product and simultaneously explains merits to persuade customers to buy product. May perform duties described under SALESPERSON (retail trade; wholesale tr.) Master Title. May suggest product improvements to employer. May use graphic aids, such as charts, slides, or films, to facilitate demonstration. May give product samples to customers. May conduct guided tours of plant where product is made. May train other demonstrators. May visit retail store or customer's home to demonstrate products. May be designated according to type merchandise demonstrated as Bakery Demonstrator (retail trade); Ceramic-Maker Demonstrator (retail trade); Cosmetics Demonstrator (retail trade); Food Demonstrator (retail trade; wholesale tr.); Glassware-Maker Demonstrator (retail trade); Housewares Demonstrator (retail trade; wholesale tr.).
GOE: 08.02.05 STRENGTH: L GED: R3 M3 L3 SVP: 3 DLU: 81

297.354-014 DEMONSTRATOR, KNITTING (retail trade)
Shows customers how to knit garments or accessories by hand: Demonstrates methods of holding needles and making various stitches. Interprets knitting terminology and how to read and follow knitting instructions for customer. Suggests yarn for use in particular style of garment and estimates amount to purchase. Takes customer's measurements for proposed garment and estimates number of stitches required for each part of garment. Sells customer yarn required for knitting specified garment or clothing accessory.
GOE: 08.02.05 STRENGTH: S GED: R4 M4 L4 SVP: 5 DLU: 77

297.357-010 DEMONSTRATOR, ELECTRIC-GAS APPLIANCES (utilities)
Demonstrates and explains operation and care of electric or gas appliances to utility company customers to promote appliance sales, and advises customers on energy conservation methods: Visits community organizations and schools to demonstrate operating features and care of appliances, such as air-conditioners, driers, ranges, and washers. Explains how electricity or gas is produced and transmitted, reasons for electricity and gas rate increases, and methods of efficiently using appliances to conserve energy and reduce utility bills. Lectures to dealers, sales personnel, and employees of utility company on efficient use and care of appliances, as part of training program. Answers telephone and written requests from customers for information about appliance use. May advise customers on related homemaking problems, such as kitchen planning, home lighting, heating-fuel conservation, food preparation, and laundering with new fabrics. May write articles and pamphlets on appliance use. May represent utility company as guest on radio or television programs to discuss conservation of electrical or gas energy.
GOE: 08.02.05 STRENGTH: L GED: R5 M3 L5 SVP: 6 DLU: 77

297.367-010 EXHIBIT-DISPLAY REPRESENTATIVE (any industry)
Attends trade, traveling, promotional, educational, or amusement exhibit to answer visitors' questions, explain or describe exhibit, and to protect it against theft or damage. May set up or arrange display. May demonstrate use of displayed items. May lecture and show slides. May collect fees or accept donations. May solicit patronage. May distribute brochures. May obtain names and addresses of prospective customers. May drive truck and trailer to transport exhibit. May be designated Trade-Show Representative (any industry).
GOE: 09.01.02 STRENGTH: L GED: R4 M2 L4 SVP: 5 DLU: 77

297.451-010 INSTRUCTOR, PAINTING (retail trade)
Selects and recommends materials for customers' use in ornamental painting, such as on plaques, lampshades, and fabrics. Demonstrates painting techniques and advises customers in various aspects of painting and materials to purchase. Does ornamental painting for other departments.
GOE: 01.06.03 STRENGTH: S GED: R3 M3 L3 SVP: 4 DLU: 77

297.454-010 DEMONSTRATOR, SEWING TECHNIQUES (retail trade)
Demonstrates sewing machines and their operation to retail store customers: Shows customers recommended procedures for cutting material from patterns, assembly and basting, and machine sewing. Explains and demonstrates use of various attachments, such as hemmer, edge stitcher, and ruffler. May instruct customers in alteration of garments.
GOE: 08.02.05 STRENGTH: L GED: R3 M3 L3 SVP: 3 DLU: 77

297.667-014 MODEL (garment; retail trade; wholesale tr.) alternate titles: fashion model; house model
Models garments, such as dresses, coats, underclothing, swimwear, and suits, for garment designers, BUYERS (profess. & kin.), sales personnel, and cus-

tomers: Dresses in sample or completed garments. Stands, turns, and walks to demonstrate features, such as garment quality, style, and design, to observers at fashion shows, private showings, and retail establishments. May inform prospective purchasers as to model, number, and price of garments and department where garment can be purchased. May select own accessories. May be designated according to size of garment modeled. May model for PHOTOGRAPHER, STILL (profess. & kin.) [MODEL, PHOTOGRAPHERS' (any industry)] or for ILLUSTRATOR (profess. & kin.) [MODEL, ARTISTS' (any industry)].
GOE: 01.08.01 STRENGTH: L GED: R3 M1 L2 SVP: 3 DLU: 77

298   MERCHANDISE DISPLAYERS

This group includes occupations concerned with planning and executing commercial displays, such as those in windows and interiors of retail stores and those used in trade exhibitions.

298.081-010 DISPLAYER, MERCHANDISE (retail trade) alternate titles: decorator, store; display trimmer
Displays merchandise, such as clothes, accessories, and furniture, in windows, showcases, and on sales floor of retail store to attract attention of prospective customers: Originates display ideas or follows suggestions or schedule of MANAGER, DISPLAY (retail trade) and constructs or assembles prefabricated display properties from wood, fabric, glass, paper, and plastic, using handtools. Arranges properties, mannequins, furniture, merchandise, and backdrop according to prearranged plan or own ideas. Places price and descriptive signs on backdrop, fixtures, merchandise, or floor. May dress mannequins for use in displays and be designated Model Dresser (retail trade). May be designated according to area trimmed or decorated as Showcase Trimmer (retail trade); Window Dresser (retail trade).
GOE: 01.02.03 STRENGTH: M GED: R4 M3 L3 SVP: 6 DLU: 77

298.381-010 DECORATOR (any industry) alternate titles: commercial decorator
Prepares and installs decorations and displays from blueprints or drawings for trade and industrial shows, expositions, festivals, and other special events: Cuts out designs on cardboard, hard board, and plywood, according to motif of event. Constructs portable installations according to specifications, using woodworking power tools. Installs booths, exhibits, displays, carpets, and drapes, as guided by floor plan of building. Arranges installations, furniture, and other accessories in position shown in prepared sketch. Installs decorations, such as flags, banners, festive lights, and bunting, on or in building, street, exhibit halls, and booths, to achieve special effects [DECORATOR, STREET AND BUILDING (any industry)]. Assembles and installs prefabricated parts to reconstruct traveling exhibits from sketch submitted by client, using handtools.
GOE: 01.06.02 STRENGTH: L GED: R4 M4 L3 SVP: 7 DLU: 77

299   MISCELLANEOUS SALES OCCUPATIONS, N.E.C.

This group includes occupations, not elsewhere classified, concerned with sales transactions.

299.137-010 MANAGER, DEPARTMENT (retail trade) alternate titles: department supervisor; manager, floor
Supervises and coordinates activities of workers in department of retail store: Interviews job applicants and evaluates worker performance to recommend personnel actions such as hiring, retention, promotion, transfer or dismissal of workers. Assigns duties to workers and schedules break periods, work hours, and vacations. Trains workers in store policies, department procedures, and job duties. Orders merchandise, supplies, and equipment. Records delivery of merchandise, compares record with merchandise ordered, and reports discrepancies to control costs and maintain correct inventory levels. Inspects merchandise to ensure it is correctly priced and displayed. Recommends additions to or deletions of merchandise to be sold in department. Prepares sales and inventory reports. Listens to customer complaints, examines returned merchandise, and resolves problems to restore and promote good public relations. May assist sales workers in completing difficult sales. May sell merchandise. May approve checks written for payment of merchandise purchased in department. May install and remove department cash-register-receipt tape and audit cash receipts. May perform customer service activities and be designated Customer Service Manager (retail trade). May plan department layout or merchandise or advertising display [DISPLAYER, MERCHANDISE (retail trade) 298.081-010]. May be designated according to department managed or type of merchandise sold as Candy-Department Manager (retail trade); Toy-Department Manager (retail trade); Produce-Department Manager (retail trade).
GOE: 11.11.05 STRENGTH: M GED: R4 M3 L3 SVP: 7 DLU: 78

299.137-014 SALES SUPERVISOR, MALT LIQUORS (wholesale tr.)
Supervises and coordinates activities of workers engaged in promoting and selling beer and other malt liquors for wholesale distributor: Accompanies workers on visits to customers to evaluate work performance, ascertain customer problems, and detect market trends. Reviews sales orders and records of new and delinquent accounts to ascertain market conditions and status of customers' accounts. Compiles sales figures and reports problems to management. Confers with management and sales personnel to formulate plans for meeting competition and improving sales. Adjusts customers' complaints.

GOE: 08.02.01 STRENGTH: L GED: R4 M3 L4 SVP: 5 DLU: 77

299.137-018 SAMPLE-ROOM SUPERVISOR (textile) alternate titles: sample supervisor
Supervises and coordinates activities of workers engaged in preparing such advertising media as sample books and swatches for sales force and customers of textile manufacturing or finishing concerns. Distributes sample books and other media to customers and advertising agencies. Performs other duties as described under SUPERVISOR (any industry) Master Title. May compare samples with cloth lots for style and color specifications.
GOE: 06.02.01 STRENGTH: L GED: R4 M3 L4 SVP: 7 DLU: 77

299.137-022 SUPERVISOR, ICE STORAGE, SALE, AND DELIVERY (food prep., nec) alternate titles: ice platform supervisor
Supervises and coordinates activities of workers engaged in storing, delivering, and selling ice. Performs duties as described under SUPERVISOR (any industry) Master Title.
GOE: 09.04.02 STRENGTH: L GED: R4 M3 L3 SVP: 6 DLU: 77

299.137-026 SUPERVISOR, MARINA SALES AND SERVICE (retail trade)
Supervises and coordinates activities of workers engaged in launching, retrieving, and servicing boats, and selling sport fishing equipment and supplies: Assists workers in launching and retrieving trailer-mounted boats, using dock crane and electric winch. Services boats with fuel and assists in casting off and tying up boats. Loads or unloads fishing and propulsion equipment from boats. Demonstrates sport fishing merchandise, such as fishing rods and reels, electronic communication and navigational equipment, and protective clothing to customers. Orders fuel for boats, and fishing equipment and supplies, such as rods and reels, bait, and ice. Inventories stock. Trains new workers in job duties.
GOE: 09.04.02 STRENGTH: L GED: R4 M3 L4 SVP: 5 DLU: 77

299.167-010 CIRCULATION-SALES REPRESENTATIVE (print. & pub.)
Promotes and coordinates sale and distribution of newspapers in areas served by franchised wholesale distributors: Surveys urban and suburban areas to determine newspaper sales potential, using statistical tables, and recommends new outlets and locations for newsstands, street-sale racks, and carrier routes. Schedules delivery and distribution of newspapers and regulates size of orders to maintain maximum sales with minimum return of unsold papers. Evaluates dealer sales and assists dealers through sales promotion and training programs. Inspects routes to ensure prompt and regular delivery of newspapers to distributors, dealers, carriers, and vending machines. Distributes and explains circulation instructions and changes to distributors and dealers, and investigates and adjusts dealer complaints. Examines and investigates applications for sale or transfer of franchises. Investigates delinquent accounts and makes collections. Instructs drivers, dealers, and carriers in sales techniques to improve sales. Lays out home delivery routes and organizes carrier crews. Analyzes sales statistics to assist management in circulation planning. Reports on sales and activities of competitors. Writes promotional bulletins to notify dealers and carriers of special sales promotions and offers. Arranges for sale of newspapers at special events and sale of special issues and editions in case of important news breaks.
GOE: 11.09.01 STRENGTH: L GED: R4 M3 L4 SVP: 6 DLU: 77

299.251-010 SALES-SERVICE REPRESENTATIVE, MILKING MACHINES (retail trade)
Sells, installs, and repairs milking equipment: Calls on farmers to solicit repair business and to sell new milking equipment, such as vacuum pumps, buckets, pipelines, and replacement parts. Demonstrates milking machines. Cuts and threads pipe and attaches fittings, using plumber's tools, to install pipelines. Cleans and flushes pipelines, and repairs pulsators and vacuum pumps.
GOE: 08.02.02 STRENGTH: M GED: R4 M3 L4 SVP: 6 DLU: 77

299.357-010 LINEN CONTROLLER (laundry & rel.)
Contacts customers of linen rental service to discuss inventory control and usage of rented articles and to solicit new business: Examines rented articles and discusses with customers selection and use of articles to prevent abuse. Reviews customer inventory records to determine charges for replacement of damaged articles. Recommends account cancellation when customers continue to ruin articles. Solicits new business and estimates required inventory. May inspect plant equipment for defects that stain or tear articles during laundry process.
GOE: 08.02.06 STRENGTH: L GED: R4 M2 L3 SVP: 6 DLU: 77

299.357-014 TELEPHONE SOLICITOR (any industry) alternate titles: telemarketer; telephone sales representative
Solicits orders for merchandise or services over telephone: Calls prospective customers to explain type of service or merchandise offered. Quotes prices and tries to persuade customer to buy, using prepared sales talk. Records names, addresses, purchases, and reactions of prospects solicited. Refers orders to other workers for filling. Keys data from order card into computer, using keyboard. May develop lists of prospects from city and telephone directories. May type report on sales activities. May contact DRIVER, SALES ROUTE (retail trade; wholesale tr.) 292.353-010 to arrange delivery of merchandise.
GOE: 08.02.08 STRENGTH: S GED: R3 M3 L3 SVP: 3 DLU: 88

299.357-018 WEDDING CONSULTANT (retail trade)
Advises prospective brides in all phases of wedding planning, such as etiquette, attire of wedding party, and selection of trousseau: Compiles list of pro-

spective brides from newspaper announcements of engagements. Mails promotional material to offer own and store's services as consultant. Recommends trousseau for bride, and costumes and accessories for attendants. Advises bride on selection of silverware style and pattern, china, glassware, stationery, invitations, flowers, and catering service. May display and sell wedding trousseau to bride, and attire for attendants, and silverware, china, and glassware to brides and wedding gift purchasers, performing duties as described under SALESPERSON (retail trade; wholesale tr.) Master Title. May compile and maintain gift register. May arrange for photographers to take pictures of wedding party. May attend rehearsals and wedding ceremony to give advice on etiquette. May accompany bride when shopping in store or shop for her.
GOE: 08.02.06 STRENGTH: L GED: R4 M3 L4 SVP: 6 DLU: 77

299.361-010 OPTICIAN, DISPENSING (optical goods; retail trade)
Fills ophthalmic eyeglass prescriptions and fits and adapts lenses and frames, utilizing written optical prescription: Evaluates prescription in conjunction with client's vocational and avocational visual requirements. Determines client's current lens prescription, when necessary, using lensometer or lens analyzer and client's eyeglasses. Recommends specific lenses, lens coatings, and frames to suit client needs. Assists client in selecting frames according to style and color, coordinating frames with facial and eye measurements and optical prescription. Measures client's bridge and eye size, temple length, vertex distance, pupillary distance, and optical centers of eyes, using millimeter rule and light reflex pupillometer. Prepares work order and instructions for grinding lenses and fabricating eyeglasses. Verifies finished lenses are ground to specification. Heats, shapes, or bends plastic or metal frames to adjust eyeglasses to fit client, using pliers and hands. Instructs clients in adapting to, wearing, and caring for eyeglasses. Sells optical goods, such as binoculars, plano sunglasses, magnifying glasses, and low vision aids. Repairs damaged frames. May be required to hold license issued by governing state. May fabricate lenses to prescription specifications. May select and order frames for display. May grind lens edges or apply coating to lenses. May manage one or more optical shops. May compute amount of sale and collect payment for services. May fit contact lenses only and be designated Optician, Contact-Lens Dispensing (optical goods; retail trade).
GOE: 05.10.01 STRENGTH: L GED: R4 M3 L4 SVP: 7 DLU: 81

299.361-014 OPTICIAN APPRENTICE, DISPENSING (optical goods; retail trade)
Performs duties as described under APPRENTICE (any industry) Master Title.
GOE: 05.10.01 STRENGTH: L GED: R4 M3 L4 SVP: 7 DLU: 77

299.364-010 DRAPERY AND UPHOLSTERY MEASURER (retail trade) alternate titles: upholstery and drapery measurer
Calls at customers' homes to take measurements for and estimate cost of fabricating draperies and window shades, slipcovers, and upholstery: Measures area of furniture to be covered. Draws sketches to scale of work to be done. Discusses selection of fabric and other materials with customer, using material samples, and informs customer of material, fabrication, and installations costs. May be designated according to specialty as Slip-Cover Estimator (retail trade); Window-Shade Estimator (retail trade).
GOE: 05.09.02 STRENGTH: L GED: R3 M3 L2 SVP: 6 DLU: 77

299.364-014 GIFT WRAPPER (retail trade) alternate titles: wrapper
Wraps and decorates customer's purchases with gift-wrapping paper, ribbons, bows, and tape in retail store. May collect money and make change for gift-wrapping service. May assist customer to select appropriate wrapping materials.
GOE: 01.06.03 STRENGTH: L GED: R3 M2 L1 SVP: 3 DLU: 77

299.367-010 CUSTOMER-SERVICE CLERK (retail trade) alternate titles: customer-service specialist, post exchange
Performs any combination of following tasks in post exchange: Arranges for gift wrapping, monogramming, printing, and fabrication of such items as desk nameplates and rubber stamps, and repair or replacement of defective items covered by warranty. Takes orders for such items as decorated cakes, cut flowers, personalized greeting cards and stationery, and merchandise rentals and repairs. Prepares special order worksheet. Keeps record of services in progress. Notifies customer when service is completed and accepts payment. Acts as WEDDING CONSULTANT (retail trade). Assists customers to select and purchase specified merchandise [PERSONAL SHOPPER (retail trade)]. Keeps records of items in layaway, receives and posts customer payments, and prepares and forwards delinquent notices [LAYAWAY CLERK (retail trade)]. Issues temporary identification cards from information on military records. Approves customer's checks and provides check cashing service according to exchange policy. Answers customer's telephone, mail, and in-person inquiries and directs customers to appropriate sales area [INFORMATION CLERK (clerical)]. Resolves customer complaints and requests for refunds, exchanges, and adjustments. Provides customers with catalogs and information concerning prices, shipping time, and costs.
GOE: 09.04.02 STRENGTH: L GED: R3 M3 L3 SVP: 4 DLU: 77

299.367-014 STOCK CLERK (retail trade) alternate titles: stock clerk, self-service store
Inventories, stores, prices, and restocks merchandise displays in retail store: Takes inventory or examines merchandise to identify items to be reordered or replenished. Requisitions merchandise from supplier based on available space, merchandise on hand, customer demand, or advertised specials. Receives,

opens, and unpacks cartons or crates of merchandise, checking invoice against items received. Stamps, attaches, or changes price tags on merchandise, referring to price list. Stocks storage areas and displays with new or transferred merchandise. Sets up advertising signs and displays merchandise on shelves, counters, or tables to attract customers and promote sales. Cleans display cases, shelves, and aisles. May itemize and total customer merchandise selection at check out counter, using cash register, and accept cash or charge card for purchases. May pack customer purchases in bags or cartons. May transport packages to specified vehicle for customer. May be designated according to type of merchandise handled as Baked-Goods Stock Clerk (retail trade); Delicatessen-Goods Stock Clerk (retail trade); Discount-Variety-Store Clerk (retail trade); Liquor-Store Stock Clerk (retail trade); Meat Stock Clerk (retail trade); Pharmacy Stock Clerk (retail trade); Produce Stock Clerk (retail trade); or type of store worked in as Supermarket Stock Clerk (retail trade).
GOE: 05.09.01 STRENGTH: H GED: R3 M2 L2 SVP: 4 DLU: 81

299.367-018 WATCH-AND-CLOCK-REPAIR CLERK (retail trade)
Receives clocks and watches for repairs: Examines defective timepieces to identify malfunction, using loupe and handtools, and estimates cost of repairs, using knowledge of repairs and cost charts. Forwards timepiece to workshop with notation of repairs needed. May keep list of repairs and costs. May make minor repairs, such as replacing crystals or bands. May estimate cost to repair jewelry.
GOE: 05.09.02 STRENGTH: L GED: R3 M3 L3 SVP: 5 DLU: 77

299.377-010 PLATFORM ATTENDANT (food prep., nec) alternate titles: ice seller
Sells ice to customers from platform of ice plant: Pulls ice from storage room chute or conveyor with pair of ice tongs in quantities desired by customer or as specified on written wholesale order and slides ice across platform and into delivery trucks. Obtains signature of driver or wholesale charge-account customers on order. Cuts portions of ice from block for retail customers, using ice pick, and loads ice into car, using tongs. Accepts payment for ice sold. Keeps daily inventory record of ice on hand, record of sales, cash received, and orders filled.
GOE: 09.04.02 STRENGTH: H GED: R3 M2 L2 SVP: 3 DLU: 77

299.387-010 DRAPERY AND UPHOLSTERY ESTIMATOR (retail trade)
Estimates price of making and installing household accessories, such as draperies, slipcovers, window shades, and furniture upholstery: Computes cost of fabric and hardware, according to measurements, work specifications, and type of fabric to be used, using calculator. Itemizes cost of labor in making and installing goods. Records total price on sales check or contract. May contact customer to obtain additional information about order. May confer with ARCHITECTS (profess. & kin.) and interior decorators to obtain additional information when computing estimates for commercial orders. May take measurements for draperies, upholstery, slip covers, or shades in customer's home [DRAPERY AND UPHOLSTERY MEASURER (retail trade)]. May specialize in estimating price of specific type of household accessory and be designated Drapery Estimator (retail trade); Upholstery Estimator (retail trade).
GOE: 05.09.02 STRENGTH: S GED: R3 M3 L2 SVP: 5 DLU: 77

299.387-014 STAMP ANALYST (retail trade) alternate titles: philatelic consultant
Selects stamps to mail to customers on approval, based on customers' current orders or record of amount and type of past purchases.
GOE: 07.07.02 STRENGTH: S GED: R4 M2 L3 SVP: 6 DLU: 77

299.387-018 STAMP CLASSIFIER (retail trade)
Classifies stamps according to value and condition preparatory to selling to collectors: Sorts stamps into various classes. Examines stamp and determines value, using stamp catalog as guide.
GOE: 05.09.01 STRENGTH: S GED: R4 M2 L3 SVP: 6 DLU: 77

299.467-010 LAYAWAY CLERK (retail trade) alternate titles: will-call clerk
Stores and releases merchandise and receives payments for merchandise held in layaway department: Places ordered merchandise on shelves in storeroom. Receives payments on account and final payments for merchandise and issues receipts, using cash register. Keeps records of packages held, amount of each payment, and balance due. Contacts customer when specified period of time has passed without payment to determine if customer still wants merchandise. Releases merchandise to customer upon receipt of final payment, or when customer opens charge account, or routes merchandise for delivery to shipping or delivery department. Packs merchandise when picked up by or being delivered to customer.
GOE: 07.03.01 STRENGTH: L GED: R3 M3 L3 SVP: 3 DLU: 77

299.477-010 DELIVERER, MERCHANDISE (retail trade)
Delivers merchandise from retail store to customers on foot, bicycle, or public conveyance: Unpacks incoming merchandise, marks prices on articles, and stacks them on counters and shelves [STOCK CLERK (retail trade) 299.367-014]. Walks, rides bicycle, or uses public conveyances to deliver merchandise to customer's home or place of business. Collects money from customers or signature from charge-account customers. Sweeps floors, runs errands, and waits on customers [SALES CLERK (retail trade) 290.477-014]. May drive light truck to deliver orders. May be designated according to merchandise delivered as Deliverer, Food (retail trade); Deliverer, Pharmacy (retail trade).

GOE: 09.04.02 STRENGTH: M GED: R2 M2 L2 SVP: 2 DLU: 77

299.587-010 PRODUCE WEIGHER (retail trade)
Weighs produce selected by customer in self-service store. Marks price on bag. May unpack produce, stock counters, arrange produce in attractive displays, and clean counters, display tables, and work area.
GOE: 09.04.02 STRENGTH: L GED: R1 M1 L1 SVP: 1 DLU: 77

299.647-010 IMPERSONATOR, CHARACTER (any industry)
Impersonates traditional holiday or storybook characters, such as Santa Claus, Snow White, and the Three Little Pigs, to promote sales activity in retail stores, at conventions or exhibits, and to amuse children at hospitals, amusement parks and private parties. Wears character costumes and impersonates characters portrayed to amuse children and adults. May hand out samples or presents, demonstrate toys, pose for pictures, and converse with children and adults. May appear in costume parade. May solicit donations on street for charitable purposes. May be designated according to character portrayed as Easter Bunny (any industry); Santa Claus (any industry); Santa's Helper (any industry).
GOE: 01.07.02 STRENGTH: L GED: R3 M1 L3 SVP: 2 DLU: 77

299.667-010 BILLPOSTER (any industry) alternate titles: sign poster
Places posters and banners in prominent places to advertise entertainment, political event, or product: Secures permission from owner to place posters and banners on private property. Displays posters in windows of stores, restaurants, and other public places. Fastens banners and posters to fences, poles, and sides of buildings, using paste, twine, tacks and hammer, hand staplers, and ladders.
GOE: 05.12.12 STRENGTH: M GED: R2 M1 L2 SVP: 2 DLU: 77

299.667-014 STOCK CHECKER, APPAREL (retail trade)
Gathers and counts garments tried on by customers in fitting rooms of retail store: Hangs garments according to size on display racks, and refastens belts, buttons, and zippers on garments tried by customers. Counts number of garments carried in and out of dressing rooms to assure no garments are missing. May sew on missing and loose buttons, hooks, and loops.
GOE: 05.09.03 STRENGTH: L GED: R2 M1 L1 SVP: 2 DLU: 77

299.677-010 SALES ATTENDANT (retail trade) alternate titles: attendant, self-service store
Performs any combination of following duties to provide customer service in self-service store: Aids customers in locating merchandise. Answers questions from and provides information to customer about merchandise for sale. Obtains merchandise from stockroom when merchandise is not on floor. Arranges stock on shelves or racks in sales area. Directs or escorts customer to fitting or dressing rooms or to cashier. Keeps merchandise in order. Marks or tickets merchandise. Inventories stock.
GOE: 09.04.02 STRENGTH: L GED: R3 M1 L2 SVP: 2 DLU: 81

299.677-014 SALES ATTENDANT, BUILDING MATERIALS (retail trade) alternate titles: yard salesperson
Assists customers and stocks merchandise in building materials and supplies department of self-service store: Answers questions and advises customer in selection of building materials and supplies. Cuts lumber, screening, glass, and related materials to size requested by customer, using power saws, holding fixtures, and various hand-cutting tools. Assists customer to load purchased materials into customer's vehicle. Moves materials and supplies from receiving area to display area, using forklift or hand truck. Marks prices on merchandise or price stickers, according to pricing guides, using marking devices. Straightens materials on display to maintain safe and orderly conditions in sales areas. Covers exposed materials, when required, to prevent weather damage. Counts materials and records totals on inventory sheets.
GOE: 09.04.02 STRENGTH: H GED: R2 M2 L2 SVP: 3 DLU: 86

299.687-010 PORTER, SAMPLE CASE (wholesale tr.)
Carries or rolls sample cases while accompanying sales representative on calls to wholesale or retail stores. Opens sample cases upon arrival at store, and assists sales representative in displaying merchandise to prospective buyers. Replaces merchandise when sales representative has completed visit. May transport samples cases, using automobile.
GOE: 09.05.06 STRENGTH: M GED: R2 M1 L1 SVP: 2 DLU: 77

299.687-014 SANDWICH-BOARD CARRIER (any industry)
Wears sign boards and walks in public to advertise merchandise, services, or belief. May distribute handbills to passers-by [ADVERTISING-MATERIAL DISTRIBUTOR (any industry)]. May wear costume to attract attention [IMPERSONATOR, CHARACTER (any industry)]. May work for labor organization and be designated Picket, Labor Union (nonprofit org.).
GOE: 08.03.02 STRENGTH: L GED: R1 M1 L1 SVP: 1 DLU: 77

3 SERVICE OCCUPATIONS

This category includes occupations concerned with performing tasks in and around private households; serving individuals in institutions and in commercial and other establishments; and protecting the public against crime, fire, accidents, and acts of war.

30 DOMESTIC SERVICE OCCUPATIONS

This division includes occupations concerned with tasks in and around a private household.

301 HOUSEHOLD AND RELATED WORK

This group includes occupations concerned with performing such duties in a private household as cleaning, making beds, caring for children, planning meals, marketing, and cooking. Includes workers managing private household and directing work activities of other workers performing these duties. Occupations concerned primarily with washing and ironing are included in Group 302, and preparation and cooking food in Group 305.

301.137-010 HOUSEKEEPER, HOME (domestic ser.) alternate titles: manager, household

Supervises and coordinates activities of household employees in a private residence: Informs new employees of employer's desires and gives instructions in work methods and routines. Assigns duties, such as cooking and serving meals, cleaning, washing, and ironing, adjusting work activities to accommodate family members. Orders foodstuffs and cleaning supplies. Keeps record of expenditures. May hire and discharge employees. Works in residence employing large staff.
GOE: 05.12.01 STRENGTH: L GED: R4 M2 L3 SVP: 6 DLU: 77

301.474-010 HOUSE WORKER, GENERAL (domestic ser.) alternate titles: housekeeper, home

Performs any combination of following duties to maintain private home clean and orderly, to cook and serve meals, and to render personal services to family members: Plans meals and purchases foodstuffs and household supplies. Prepares and cooks vegetables, meats, and other foods according to employer's instructions or following own methods. Serves meals and refreshments. Washes dishes and cleans silverware. Oversees activities of children, assisting them in dressing and bathing. Cleans furnishings, floors, and windows, using vacuum cleaner, mops, broom, cloths, and cleaning solutions. Changes linens and makes beds. Washes linens and other garments by hand or machine, and mends and irons clothing, linens, and other household articles, using hand iron or electric ironer. Answers telephone and doorbell. Feeds pets.
GOE: 05.12.18 STRENGTH: M GED: R3 M2 L2 SVP: 3 DLU: 86

301.677-010 CHILD MONITOR (domestic ser.) alternate titles: nurse, children's

Performs any combination of following duties to attend children in private home: Observes and monitors play activities or amuses children by reading to or playing games with them. Prepares and serves meals or formulas. Sterilizes bottles and other equipment used for feeding infants. Dresses or assists children to dress and bathe. Accompanies children on walks or other outings. Washes and irons clothing. Keeps children's quarters clean and tidy. Cleans other parts of home. May be designated Nurse, Infants' (domestic ser.) when in charge of infants. May be designated Baby Sitter (domestic ser.) when employed on daily or hourly basis.
GOE: 10.03.03 STRENGTH: M GED: R3 M1 L2 SVP: 3 DLU: 81

301.687-010 CARETAKER (domestic ser.) alternate titles: odd-job worker

Performs any combination of following duties in keeping private home clean and in good condition: Cleans and dusts furnishings, hallways, and lavatories. Beats and vacuums rugs and scrubs them with cleaning solutions. Washes windows and waxes and polishes floors. Removes and hangs draperies. Cleans and oils furnace. Shovels coal into furnace and removes ashes. Replaces light switches and repairs broken screens, latches, or doors. Paints exterior structures, such as fences, garages, and sheds. May drive family car. May mow and rake lawn. May groom and exercise pets. When duties are confined to upkeep of house, may be designated House Worker (domestic ser.).
GOE: 05.12.18 STRENGTH: M GED: R2 M1 L2 SVP: 2 DLU: 77

301.687-014 DAY WORKER (domestic ser.)

Performs any combination of following domestic duties: Cleans and dusts furnishings, hallways, and lavatories. Changes and makes beds. Washes and irons clothings by hand or machine. Vacuums carpets, using vacuum cleaner. May watch children to keep them out of mischief. May wash windows and wax and polish floors.
GOE: 05.12.18 STRENGTH: M GED: R2 M1 L1 SVP: 2 DLU: 81

301.687-018 YARD WORKER (domestic ser.)

Performs any combination of following duties, in accordance with instructions of employer, to keep grounds of private residence in neat and orderly condition: Plants, transplants, fertilizes, sprays with pesticides, prunes, cultivates, and waters flowers, shrubbery, and trees. Seeds and mows lawns, rakes leaves, and keeps ground free of other debris. Whitewashes or paints fences. Washes and polishes automobiles. Cleans patio furniture and garage. Shovels snow from walks. May cultivate flowers, shrubbery, and other plants in greenhouse. May wax floors, tend furnace, or groom and exercise pets. May divide time between several homes, working on hourly or daily basis. When duties are confined to upkeep of grounds, may be designated Gardener (domestic ser.).
GOE: 03.04.04 STRENGTH: H GED: R2 M2 L2 SVP: 2 DLU: 77

302 LAUNDERERS, PRIVATE FAMILY

This group includes occupations concerned with washing and ironing clothes and household linens for one or several private families.

302.685-010 LAUNDRY WORKER, DOMESTIC (domestic ser.)

Tends automatic washing and drying machines to clean and dry household articles and presses household articles, using hand iron: Sorts articles by color and fabric, and loads into automatic washing machine. Adjusts machine settings for temperature, water level, and time duration of wash. Adds measured amounts of detergent, bluing, starches, and fabric softener as required. Removes articles from washer and loads into dryer. Sorts, irons, and folds dried articles. May iron only [IRONER (domestic ser.)]. May perform other housework [HOUSE WORKER, GENERAL (domestic ser.)]. May use electric ironing machine.
GOE: 05.12.18 STRENGTH: L GED: R2 M1 L1 SVP: 2 DLU: 77

302.687-010 IRONER (domestic ser.)

Dampens and irons wearing apparel, household linens, and other household articles with hand iron. May use electric ironing machine (mangle). May be employed on hourly basis.
GOE: 05.12.18 STRENGTH: L GED: R1 M1 L1 SVP: 2 DLU: 77

305 COOKS, DOMESTIC

This group includes occupations concerned with preparing and cooking food, including special diets, for private household.

305.281-010 COOK (domestic ser.)

Plans menus and cooks meals, in private home, according to recipes or tastes of employer: Peels, washes, trims, and prepares vegetables and meats for cooking. Cooks vegetables and bakes breads and pastries. Boils, broils, fries, and roasts meats. Plans menus and orders foodstuffs. Cleans kitchen and cooking utensils. May serve meals. May perform seasonal cooking duties, such as preserving and canning fruits and vegetables, and making jellies. May prepare fancy dishes and pastries. May prepare food for special diets. May work closely with persons performing household or nursing duties. May specialize in preparing and serving dinner for employed, retired, or other persons and be designated Family-Dinner Service Specialist (domestic ser.).
GOE: 05.10.08 STRENGTH: L GED: R3 M2 L2 SVP: 6 DLU: 81

309 DOMESTIC SERVICE OCCUPATIONS, N.E.C.

This group includes occupations, not elsewhere classified, concerned with tasks in and around a private household.

309.137-010 BUTLER (domestic ser.)

Supervises and coordinates activities of household employees engaged in cooking, cleaning, and related domestic duties: Oversees serving of luncheon and dinner, sets table, directs workers in serving meals, or personally serves them. Performs other services as requested, such as mixing and serving cocktails and tea. Answers telephone and delivers messages. Receives and announces guests. May prepare salads. May keep silver service clean and intact. May employ and discharge other household employees.
GOE: 09.01.03 STRENGTH: L GED: R4 M2 L3 SVP: 6 DLU: 77

309.354-010 HOMEMAKER (social ser.)

Advises family in private home in dealing with problems, such as nutrition, cleanliness, and household utilities: Advises and assists family members in planning nutritious meals, purchasing and preparing foods, and utilizing commodities from surplus food programs. Assists head of household in training and disciplining children, assigns and schedules housekeeping duties to children according to their capabilities, and encourages parents to take interest in children's schoolwork and assist them in establishing good study habits. Explains fundamental hygiene principles and renders bedside care to individuals who are ill, and trains other family members to provide required care. Participates in evaluating needs of individuals served, and confers with CASEWORKER (social ser.) to plan for continuing additional services.

GOE: 11.02.03 STRENGTH: L GED: R4 M2 L4 SVP: 5 DLU: 77

309.367-010   HOUSE SITTER (domestic ser.)

Occupies and oversees house to maintain order and security of property and conduct necessary business transactions during temporary absence of owner, renter, or other occupant: Monitors entrances to property and secures locks and other devices to prevent access of unauthorized persons. Answers telephone and doorbell, takes messages, and forwards information to employer as requested. Forwards or files mail. Pays current bills from designated funds and makes deposits to accounts as required. Cleans, vacuums, and dusts house, using vacuum cleaner and other housecleaning aids. Feeds and waters pets and takes ill pets to veterinarian for treatment. Inspects utilities, such as plumbing and air-conditioning, to detect problems requiring services of repairer and contacts repair establishment to arrange for necessary repairs. May care for swimming pool or grounds or perform other related duties.

GOE: 09.05.06 STRENGTH: L GED: R3 M2 L2 SVP: 2 DLU: 86

309.674-010   BUTLER, SECOND (domestic ser.)

Performs variety of manual duties in large household, working under supervision of BUTLER (domestic ser.): Serves food and drink during meals, cleans and polishes silver, waxes floors, washes windows and performs other duties in dining room, living room, and other downstairs rooms. May answer telephone or doorbell and announce guests. Performs duties of BUTLER (domestic ser.) in his or her absence. Frequently lays out employer's clothes for wear, polishes shoes, and performs other valet duties.

GOE: 05.12.18 STRENGTH: L GED: R3 M1 L2 SVP: 3 DLU: 77

309.674-014   PERSONAL ATTENDANT (domestic ser.)

Performs personal services to employer in private household: Brushes, cleans, presses, mends employer's clothing. Lays out employer's clothing, and assists employer to dress. Packs clothing for travel. Cleans employer's quarters. Prepares bath. Purchases clothing and accessories. Answers telephone. Drives car to perform errands. Mixes and serves drinks. May prepare and serve refreshments. May shampoo and groom employer's hair, shave face, manicure nails, give body or facial massages, or apply cosmetics for employer. May change linens, and make employer's bed.

GOE: 09.05.06 STRENGTH: L GED: R2 M2 L2 SVP: 3 DLU: 77

309.677-010   COMPANION (domestic ser.)

Cares for elderly, handicapped, or convalescent persons: Attends to employer's personal needs [PERSONAL ATTENDANT (domestic ser.)]. Transacts social or business affairs [SOCIAL SECRETARY (clerical)]. Reads aloud, plays cards, or other games to entertain employer. Accompanies employer on trips and outings. May prepare and serve meals to employer.

GOE: 10.03.03 STRENGTH: L GED: R3 M2 L3 SVP: 3 DLU: 77

309.677-014   FOSTER PARENT (domestic ser.)

Rears homeless or parentless children in own home as members of family: Organizes and schedules activities, such as recreation, rest periods, and sleeping time. Ensures child has nutritious diet. Instructs children in good personal and health habits. Bathes, dresses, and undresses young children. Washes and irons clothing. Accompanies children on outings and walks. Disciplines children when required. May return children to parents' home during weekends and holidays. May work under supervision of welfare agency. May prepare periodic reports concerning progress and behavior of children for welfare agency.

GOE: 10.03.03 STRENGTH: M GED: R3 M2 L3 SVP: 3 DLU: 77

31   FOOD AND BEVERAGE PREPARATION AND SERVICE OCCUPATIONS

This division includes occupations concerned with preparing food and beverages and serving them to patrons of such establishments as hotels, clubs, restaurants, and cocktail lounges.

310   HOSTS/HOSTESSES AND STEWARDS/ STEWARDESSES, FOOD AND BEVERAGE SERVICE, EXCEPT SHIP STEWARDS/ STEWARDESSES

This group includes occupations concerned with greeting and seating customers of establishment; and supervising activities of waiters/waitresses, dining room attendants, storeroom workers, and kitchen and pantry workers, except those actually engaged in food preparation.

310.137-010   HOST/HOSTESS, RESTAURANT (hotel & rest.) alternate titles: dining-room manager; waiter/waitress, head

Supervises and coordinates activities of dining room personnel to provide fast and courteous service to patrons: Schedules dining reservations and arranges parties or special services for diners. Greets guests, escorts them to tables, and provides menus. Adjusts complaints of patrons. Assigns work tasks and coordinates activities of dining room personnel to ensure prompt and courteous service to patrons. Inspects dining room serving stations for neatness and cleanliness, and requisitions table linens and other dining room supplies for tables and serving stations. May interview, hire, and discharge dining room personnel. May train dining room employees. May schedule work hours and keep time records of dining room workers. May assist in planning menus. May prepare

beverages and expedite food orders. May total receipts, at end of shift, to verify sales and clear cash register. May collect payment from customers [CASHIER (clerical) II 211.462-010].

GOE: 09.01.03 STRENGTH: L GED: R4 M3 L4 SVP: 6 DLU: 80

310.137-018   STEWARD/STEWARDESS (hotel & rest.) alternate titles: chief steward/stewardess; executive steward/stewardess; house steward/stewardess

Supervises and coordinates activities of pantry, storeroom, and noncooking kitchen workers, and purchases or requisitions foodstuffs, kitchen supplies, and equipment: Inspects kitchens and storerooms to ensure that premises and equipment are clean and in order, and that sufficient foodstuffs and supplies are on hand to ensure efficient service. Examines incoming purchases for quality and to ensure that purchases are as specified in order. Approves invoices or bills for payment. Coordinates work of noncooking kitchen and storeroom workers engaged in activities, such as dishwashing, silver cleaning, and storage and distribution of foodstuffs and supplies. Establishes controls to guard against theft and wastage. Confers with EXECUTIVE CHEF (hotel & rest.) or MANAGER, CATERING (hotel & rest.) concerning banquet arrangements for food service, equipment, and extra employees. May plan and price menus, keep cost records, and establish budget controls to ensure profitable food service operation. May perform duties for recreational or business clubs. This job occurs in hotels as opposed to KITCHEN SUPERVISOR (hotel & rest.) which occurs in restaurants and cafeterias.

GOE: 05.12.01 STRENGTH: L GED: R4 M3 L4 SVP: 7 DLU: 77

310.137-022   STEWARD/STEWARDESS, BANQUET (hotel & rest.)

Supervises and coordinates activities of kitchen and dining-room workers during banquets to ensure that food is served promptly: Consults with MANAGER, CATERING (hotel & rest.) or EXECUTIVE CHEF (hotel & rest.) on such items as serving arrangements and additional employees and equipment needed. Hires and supervises temporary banquet employees. Requisitions table linen, china, glassware, and silverware. Orders preparation of salads and coffee. Observes food being served to ensure that food is correctly garnished and arranged on plates.

GOE: 09.05.02 STRENGTH: L GED: R4 M3 L4 SVP: 7 DLU: 77

310.137-026   STEWARD/STEWARDESS, RAILROAD DINING CAR (r.r. trans.)

Supervises and coordinates activities of workers engaged in preparing, cooking, and serving food to passengers on railroad dining car: Requisitions food supplies necessary to fill menu and prepares requisitions for linen, crockery, and silverware from commissary. Examines supplies for quality and completeness of orders. Supervises workers engaged in storing food in car. Receives bills and money from WAITER/WAITRESS, DINING CAR (r.r. trans.) and makes change. Maintains record of all cash received during each day. Informs COOK, RAILROAD (r.r. trans.) of approximate number of persons expected to board train. Assigns work stations to WAITERS/WAITRESSES DINING CAR (r.r. trans.). May coordinate sale and serving of beverages in lounge car and be designated Steward/Stewardess, Club Car (r.r. trans.).

GOE: 11.11.04 STRENGTH: L GED: R4 M3 L3 SVP: 7 DLU: 77

310.267-010   ANALYST, FOOD AND BEVERAGE (hotel & rest.) alternate titles: research worker, kitchen

Examines food samples and food service records and other data to determine sales appeal and cost of preparing and serving meals and beverages in establishments, such as restaurants and cafeterias or for chain of food establishments: Tastes food samples to determine palatability and customer appeal. Estimates number of servings obtainable from standard and original recipes and unit cost of preparation. Converts recipes for use in quantity preparation. Studies reservation lists and previous records and forecasts customer traffic and number of servings required for specified period of time. May investigate complaints relative to faulty cooking or quality of ingredients. May plan menus. May specialize in industrial-employee food service or cafeteria food service. May supervise FOOD-AND-BEVERAGE CONTROLLER (hotel & rest.) and kitchen employees.

GOE: 05.05.17 STRENGTH: L GED: R5 M4 L4 SVP: 8 DLU: 77

310.357-010   WINE STEWARD/STEWARDESS (hotel & rest.) alternate titles: sommelier

Selects, requisitions, stores, sells, and serves wines in restaurant: Keeps inventory and orders wine to replenish stock. Stores wines on racks or shelves. Discusses wines with patrons and assists patrons to make wine selection, applying knowledge of wines. Tastes wines prior to serving and serves wines to patrons.

GOE: 09.05.02 STRENGTH: L GED: R3 M3 L3 SVP: 6 DLU: 77

311   WAITERS/WAITRESSES, AND RELATED FOOD SERVICE OCCUPATIONS

This group includes occupations concerned with setting places at dining tables or counters, taking orders for and serving food and drink, answering inquiries relative to items on the menu, and otherwise attending to the wishes of customers.

311.137-010   COUNTER SUPERVISOR (hotel & rest.)

Supervises and coordinates activities of workers engaged in serving food from cafeteria counter: Directs workers engaged in stocking and arranging of

food, dishes, silverware, and other supplies at steamtables, ice counters, and serving stations. Inspects serving operations to ensure that supplies are adequate and that food portioning meets prescribed standards. Assigns duties to counter workers. Directs workers engaged in removing food after meals and cleaning counters and work areas. May assist workers in serving customers or in performing other duties.
GOE: 09.05.02 STRENGTH: L GED: R3 M2 L3 SVP: 6 DLU: 77

311.137-014 WAITER/WAITRESS, BANQUET, HEAD (hotel & rest.)
Plans details for banquets, receptions, and other social functions. Hires extra help, directs setting up of tables and decorations, and supervises WAITER/WAITRESS, FORMAL (hotel & rest.).
GOE: 09.01.03 STRENGTH: L GED: R4 M3 L3 SVP: 6 DLU: 77

311.137-018 WAITER/WAITRESS, CAPTAIN (hotel & rest.) alternate titles: captain
Supervises activities of workers in section of dining room: Receives guests and conducts them to tables. Describes or suggests food courses and appropriate wines. When serving banquets, may be designated Banquet Captain (hotel & rest.).
GOE: 09.01.03 STRENGTH: L GED: R4 M2 L3 SVP: 6 DLU: 77

311.137-022 WAITER/WAITRESS, HEAD (hotel & rest.)
Supervises and coordinates activities of dining-room employees engaged in providing courteous and rapid service to diners: Greets guests and escorts them to tables. Schedules dining reservations. Arranges parties for patrons. Adjusts complaints regarding food or service. Hires and trains dining-room employees. Notifies payroll department regarding work schedules and time records. May assist in preparing menus. May plan and execute details for banquets [STEWARD/STEWARDESS, BANQUET (hotel & rest.); MANAGER, CATERING (hotel & rest.)]. May supervise WAITERS/WAITRESSES, ROOM SERVICE (hotel & rest.) and be designated Captain, Room Service (hotel & rest.).
GOE: 09.01.03 STRENGTH: L GED: R4 M3 L4 SVP: 6 DLU: 77

311.472-010 FAST-FOODS WORKER (hotel & rest.) alternate titles: cashier, fast foods restaurant
Serves customer of fast food restaurant: Requests customer order and depresses keys of multicounting machine to simultaneously record order and compute bill. Selects requested food items from serving or storage areas and assembles items on serving tray or in takeout bag. Notifies kitchen personnel of shortages or special orders. Serves cold drinks, using drink-dispensing machine, or frozen milk drinks or desserts, using milkshake or frozen custard machine. Makes and serves hot beverages, using automatic water heater or coffeemaker. Presses lids onto beverages and places beverages on serving tray or in takeout container. Receives payment. May cook or apportion french fries or perform other minor duties to prepare food, serve customers, or maintain orderly eating or serving areas.
GOE: 09.04.01 STRENGTH: L GED: R2 M2 L2 SVP: 2 DLU: 86

311.477-010 CAR HOP (hotel & rest.) alternate titles: drive-in waiter/waitress
Serves food and refreshments to patrons in cars: Takes order and relays order to kitchen or serving counter to be filled. Places filled order on tray and fastens tray to car door. Totals and presents check to customer and accepts payment for service. Removes tray and stacks dishes for return to kitchen. Sweeps service area with broom. May prepare fountain drinks, such as sodas, milkshakes, and malted milks. May restock service counter with items, such as ice, napkins, and straws.
GOE: 09.04.01 STRENGTH: L GED: R2 M2 L2 SVP: 2 DLU: 80

311.477-014 COUNTER ATTENDANT, LUNCHROOM OR COFFEE SHOP (hotel & rest.) alternate titles: waiter/waitress, counter
Serves food or beverages to customers seated at counter: Calls order to kitchen and picks up and serves order when it is ready. Itemizes and totals check for service or totals takeout transaction on cash register and accepts payment. May prepare sandwiches, salads, and other short order items [COOK, SHORT ORDER (hotel & rest.) 313.374-014]. May perform other duties, such as cleaning counters, washing dishes, and selling cigars and cigarettes.
GOE: 09.04.01 STRENGTH: L GED: R2 M2 L2 SVP: 2 DLU: 81

311.477-018 WAITER/WAITRESS, BAR (hotel & rest.) alternate titles: waiter/waitress, cocktail lounge
Serves beverages to patrons seated at tables in bar or cocktail lounge. Computes bill and accepts payment. May take orders for and serve light meals and hors d'oeuvres. May request identification from customers when legal age is questioned. When working in establishment serving only beer and wine, is designated Waiter/Waitress, Tavern (hotel & rest.).
GOE: 09.04.01 STRENGTH: L GED: R3 M2 L2 SVP: 3 DLU: 79

311.477-022 WAITER/WAITRESS, DINING CAR (r.r. trans.)
Serves passengers in railroad dining car: Presents menu to patrons, makes suggestions, and answers questions regarding food and service. Takes order from patron and presents it to COOK, RAILROAD (r.r. trans.). Serves food to passenger. Computes cost of meal. Accepts money from patron and returns change. Removes dishes from table and carries them to kitchen. Places clean linen, silverware, and glassware on table according to rules of etiquette. Washes glassware and silverware. May prepare salads, appetizers, and cold dishes. May receive and store linen supplies. May prepare and serve mixed drinks. May be designated according to specialty as Bar Attendant (r.r. trans.); Pantry Attendant (r.r. trans.).

GOE: 09.04.01 STRENGTH: L GED: R3 M2 L2 SVP: 3 DLU: 77

311.477-026 WAITER/WAITRESS, FORMAL (hotel & rest.) alternate titles: server
Serves meals to patrons according to established rules of etiquette, working in formal setting: Presents menu to diner, suggesting dinner courses, appropriate wines, and answering questions regarding food preparation. Writes order on check or memorizes it. Relays order to kitchen and serves courses from kitchen and service bars. Garnishes and decorates dishes preparatory to serving. Serves patrons from chafing dish at table. Observes diners to respond to any additional requests and to determine when meal has been completed. Totals bill and accepts payment or refers patron to CASHIER (clerical) II 211.462-010. May carve meats, bone fish and fowl, and prepare flaming dishes and desserts at patron's table. May be designated Waiter/Waitress, Banquet (hotel & rest.) when serving at banquets.
GOE: 09.04.01 STRENGTH: L GED: R3 M2 L2 SVP: 4 DLU: 80

311.477-030 WAITER/WAITRESS, INFORMAL (hotel & rest.) alternate titles: server
Serves food to patrons at counters and tables of coffeeshops, lunchrooms, and other dining establishments where food service is informal: Presents menu, answers questions, and makes suggestions regarding food and service. Writes order on check or memorizes it. Relays order to kitchen and serves courses from kitchen and service bars. Observes guests to respond to additional requests and to determine when meal has been completed. Totals bill and accepts payment or refers patron to CASHIER (clerical) II 211.462-010. May ladle soup, toss salads, portion pies and desserts, brew coffee, and perform other services as determined by establishment's size and practices. May clear and reset counters or tables at conclusion of each course [DINING ROOM ATTENDANT (hotel & rest.) 311.677-018].
GOE: 09.04.01 STRENGTH: L GED: R3 M2 L2 SVP: 3 DLU: 80

311.477-034 WAITER/WAITRESS, ROOM SERVICE (hotel & rest.)
Serves meals to guests in their rooms. Carries silverware, linen, and food on tray or uses cart. Sets up table and serves food from cart. Removes equipment from rooms.
GOE: 09.05.02 STRENGTH: L GED: R3 M2 L2 SVP: 3 DLU: 77

311.477-038 WAITER/WAITRESS, TAKE OUT (hotel & rest.)
Serves customers at take out counter of restaurant or lunchroom: Writes items ordered on order tickets, totals orders, passes orders to cook, and gives ticket stubs to customers to identify filled orders. Wraps menu items, such as sandwiches, hot entrees, and desserts. Fills containers with requested beverages, such as coffee, tea, or carbonated drink. Receives payment for orders and makes change. May prepare fountain drinks, such as sodas and milkshakes. May record orders and compute bill simultaneously, using cash register.
GOE: 09.04.01 STRENGTH: L GED: R2 M2 L2 SVP: 3 DLU: 80

311.674-010 CANTEEN OPERATOR (any industry)
Serves sandwiches, salads, beverages, desserts, candies, and tobacco to employees in industrial establishment. May collect money for purchases. May order items to replace stocks. May serve hot dishes, such as soups. May serve employees from mobile canteen.
GOE: 09.04.01 STRENGTH: L GED: R2 M1 L2 SVP: 3 DLU: 77

311.674-014 RAW SHELLFISH PREPARER (hotel & rest.)
Cleans and prepares shellfish for serving to customers: Washes shellfish in water. Inserts blunt-edge knife between halves to open bivalves and cuts out inedible parts. Returns oysters and clams to half shell and arranges them on ice filled dishes or places them in cold storage. Removes shells from shrimp and meat from crab and lobster shells, and arranges meat in special glasses for serving as cocktails. Mixes meat with other ingredients and arranges mixture on plates for salads. Serves customers at bar. May place silverware, napkins, potato chips, and condiments on bar. May mix ketchup, horseradish, lemon juice, and other ingredients to make cocktail sauces. May prepare only oysters for use as food and be designated Oyster Preparer (hotel & rest.).
GOE: 09.05.02 STRENGTH: L GED: R2 M1 L2 SVP: 2 DLU: 77

311.674-018 WAITER/WAITRESS, BUFFET (hotel & rest.)
Serves or assists diners to serve themselves at buffet or smorgasbord table. Replenishes supplies of food and tableware. May carry trays of food to individual tables for diners.
GOE: 09.05.02 STRENGTH: L GED: R2 M2 L1 SVP: 3 DLU: 77

311.677-010 CAFETERIA ATTENDANT (hotel & rest.) alternate titles: dining-room attendant, cafeteria; service attendant, cafeteria; table attendant, cafeteria; waiter/waitress, cafeteria
Carries trays from food counters to tables for cafeteria patrons. Carries dirty dishes to kitchen. Wipes tables and seats with dampened cloth. Sets tables with clean linens, sugar bowls, and condiments. May wrap clean silver in napkins. May circulate among diners and serve coffee and be designated Coffee Server, Cafeteria Or Restaurant (hotel & rest.).
GOE: 09.05.02 STRENGTH: L GED: R2 M1 L1 SVP: 2 DLU: 81

311.677-014 COUNTER ATTENDANT, CAFETERIA (hotel & rest.) alternate titles: server; steamtable attendant
Serves food from counters and steamtables to cafeteria patrons: Serves salads, vegetables, meat, breads, and cocktails, ladles soups and sauces, portions desserts, and fills beverage cups and glasses as indicated by customer. Adds

relishes and garnishes according to instructions from COUNTER SUPERVISOR (hotel & rest.) 311.137-010. Scrubs and polishes counters, steamtables, and other equipment. May replenish foods at serving stations. May brew coffee and tea. May carve meat. May accept payment for food, using cash register or adding machine to total check. May prepare and serve salads and be known as Salad Counter Attendant (hotel & rest.). May serve food to passenger from steamtable on railroad dining car and be known as Steamtable Attendant, Railroad (r.r. trans.).
GOE: 09.05.02 STRENGTH: L GED: R2 M1 L2 SVP: 3 DLU: 86

311.677-018 DINING ROOM ATTENDANT (hotel & rest.) alternate titles: bus person
Performs any combination of following duties to facilitate food service: Carries dirty dishes from dining room to kitchen. Wipes table tops and chairs, using damp cloth. Replaces soiled table linens and sets tables with silverware and glassware. Replenishes supply of clean linens, silverware, glassware, and dishes in dining room. Supplies service bar with food, such as soups, salads, and desserts. Serves ice water and butter to patrons. Cleans and polishes glass shelves and doors of service bars and equipment, such as coffee urns and cream and milk dispensers. Makes coffee and fills fruit juice dispensers. May sweep and mop floors. May transfer food and dishes between floors of establishment, using dumbwaiter, and be designated Dumbwaiter Operator (hotel & rest.). May run errands and deliver food orders to offices and be designated Runner (hotel & rest.). May be designated according to type of activity or area of work as Clean-Up Helper, Banquet (hotel & rest.); Counter Dish Carrier (hotel & rest.); Dish Carrier (hotel & rest.); Glass Washer And Carrier (hotel & rest.); Room Service Assistant (hotel & rest.); Steamtable Worker (hotel & rest.); Table Setter (hotel & rest.); Water Server (hotel & rest.).
GOE: 09.05.02 STRENGTH: M GED: R2 M1 L1 SVP: 2 DLU: 80

312 BARTENDERS

This group includes occupations concerned with mixing and dispensing alcoholic drinks.

312.474-010 BARTENDER (hotel & rest.) alternate titles: bar attendant; barkeeper
Mixes and serves alcoholic and nonalcoholic drinks to patrons of bar, following standard recipes: Mixes ingredients, such as liquor, soda, water, sugar, and bitters, to prepare cocktails and other drinks. Serves wine and draught or bottled beer. Collects money for drinks served. Orders or requisitions liquors and supplies. Arranges bottles and glasses to make attractive display. May slice and pit fruit for garnishing drinks. May prepare appetizers, such as pickles, cheese, and cold meats. May tend service bar and be designated Service Bartender (hotel & rest.).
GOE: 09.04.01 STRENGTH: L GED: R3 M2 L3 SVP: 3 DLU: 80

312.477-010 BAR ATTENDANT (hotel & rest.)
Serves alcoholic drinks to patrons in taverns or combination bar and package-goods store: Takes orders from customers. Serves shots (jiggers) for consumption within establishment. Serves bottled beer or draws draught beer from kegs. Sells unopened bottles of alcoholic and nonalcoholic beverages to be taken from premises when licensed for sale of packaged goods. Receives payment for amount of sale and makes change. Usually does not serve mixed drinks.
GOE: 09.04.01 STRENGTH: L GED: R2 M2 L2 SVP: 2 DLU: 77

312.677-010 TAPROOM ATTENDANT (amuse. & rec.)
Fills glasses with beer drawn from tap and hands filled glasses to patron or to worker who serves patrons. Inserts hose couplings into fittings on barrel to connect beer tap and CO2 automatic pressure regulator to beer barrel. Twists valve control lever to pressurize beer barrel. Pulls tap control handle to pour beer. Wipes bar and equipment with cloth to clean. May wash and sterilize glasses. May order and inventory supplies. May wax bar.
GOE: 09.05.02 STRENGTH: L GED: R2 M1 L1 SVP: 2 DLU: 77

312.687-010 BARTENDER HELPER (hotel & rest.) alternate titles: bar porter; bar runner
Cleans bar and equipment, and replenishes bar supplies, such as liquor, fruit, ice, and dishes: Stocks refrigerating units with wines and bottled beer. Replaces empty beer kegs with full ones. Slices and pits fruit used to garnish drinks. Washes glasses, bar, and equipment, and polishes bar fixtures. Mops floors. Removes empty bottles and trash. May mix and prepare flavors for mixed drinks.
GOE: 05.12.18 STRENGTH: M GED: R2 M1 L1 SVP: 2 DLU: 77

313 CHEFS AND COOKS, HOTELS AND RESTAURANTS

This group includes occupations concerned with planning menus, estimating consumption, and cooking food in hotels or restaurants. Workers usually specialize in a particular area.

313.131-010 BAKER, HEAD (hotel & rest.) alternate titles: baker, bread, chief; baker chef
Supervises and coordinates activities of personnel in bread-baking department: Plans production according to daily requirements. Requisitions supplies and equipment. Maintains production records.

GOE: 05.10.08 STRENGTH: L GED: R4 M3 L3 SVP: 7 DLU: 77

313.131-014 CHEF (hotel & rest.) alternate titles: cook, chief; kitchen chef
Supervises, coordinates, and participates in activities of cooks and other kitchen personnel engaged in preparing and cooking foods in hotel, restaurant, cafeteria, or other establishment: Estimates food consumption, and requisitions or purchases foodstuffs. Receives and examines foodstuffs and supplies to ensure quality and quantity meet established standards and specifications. Selects and develops recipes based on type of food to be prepared and applying personal knowledge and experience in food preparation. Supervises personnel engaged in preparing, cooking, and serving meats, sauces, vegetables, soups, and other foods. Cooks or otherwise prepares food according to recipe [COOK (hotel & rest.) 313.361-014]. Cuts, trims, and bones meats and poultry for cooking. Portions cooked foods, or gives instructions to workers as to size of portions and methods of garnishing. Carves meats. May employ, train, and discharge workers. May maintain time and payroll records. May plan menus. May supervise kitchen staff, plan menus, purchase foodstuffs, and not prepare and cook foods [EXECUTIVE CHEF (hotel & rest.)] 187.167-010]. May be designated according to cuisine specialty as Chef, French (hotel & rest.); Chef, German (hotel & rest.); Chef, Italian (hotel & rest.); or according to food specialty as Chef, Broiler Or Fry (hotel & rest.); Chef, Saucier (hotel & rest.). May supervise worker preparing food for banquet and be designated Banquet Chef (hotel & rest.).
GOE: 05.05.17 STRENGTH: L GED: R4 M3 L3 SVP: 7 DLU: 81

313.131-018 COOK, HEAD, SCHOOL CAFETERIA (hotel & rest.) alternate titles: food service coordinator; head cook, school; preparation center coordinator
Supervises and coordinates activities of workers engaged in preparing, cooking, and serving food in school cafeteria, cafeterias, or central school district kitchen: Plans varied menus to ensure that food is appetizing and nutritionally suitable for children. Estimates daily or weekly needs and orders food supplies and equipment. Supervises and coordinates activities of workers who prepare, cook, serve food, clean premises, and wash dishware. Keeps daily record of meals served and takes inventory of supplies and equipment. Trains new employees. Participates in preparing and cooking meals. May direct activities of students engaged in washing dishes and utensils.
GOE: 05.10.08 STRENGTH: M GED: R4 M3 L3 SVP: 6 DLU: 80

313.131-022 PASTRY CHEF (hotel & rest.)
Supervises and coordinates activities of COOKS (hotel & rest.) engaged in preparation of desserts, pastries, confections, and ice cream: Plans production for pastry department, according to menu or special requirements. Supplies recipes for, and suggests methods and procedures to pastry workers. Fashions table and pastry decorations, such as statuaries and ornaments, from sugar paste and icings, using cream bag, spatula, and various decorating tools. Requisitions supplies and equipment. Maintains production records. May participate in preparing desserts.
GOE: 05.10.08 STRENGTH: L GED: R4 M3 L3 SVP: 8 DLU: 77

313.131-026 SOUS CHEF (hotel & rest.) alternate titles: chef assistant; chef, under; executive-chef assistant; supervising-chef assistant
Supervises and coordinates activities of COOKS (hotel & rest.) and other workers engaged in preparing and cooking foodstuffs: Observes workers engaged in preparing, portioning, and garnishing foods to ensure that methods of cooking and garnishing and sizes of portions are as prescribed. Gives instructions to cooking personnel in fine points of cooking. Cooks and carves meats, and prepares dishes, such as sauces, during rush periods and for banquets and other social functions. Assumes responsibility for kitchen in absence of EXECUTIVE CHEF (hotel & rest.). In establishments not employing EXECUTIVE CHEF (hotel & rest.), may be designated Supervising Chef (hotel & rest.).
GOE: 05.05.17 STRENGTH: M GED: R4 M3 L3 SVP: 8 DLU: 77

313.281-010 CHEF DE FROID (hotel & rest.)
Designs and prepares decorated foods and artistic food arrangements for buffets in formal restaurants: Confers with EXECUTIVE CHEF (hotel & rest.) and SOUS CHEF (hotel & rest.) and reviews advance menus to determine amount and type of food to be served and decor to be carried out. Prepares foods, such as hors d'oeuvres, cold whole salmon, roast suckling pig, casseroles, and fancy aspics, according to recipe, and decorates them following customer's specifications, designated color scheme, or theme, using colorful fruit, vegetables, and relishes. Molds butter into artistic forms, such as dancing girls or animals. Sculptures blocks of ice, using chisels and ice picks. Carves meats in patron's presence, employing showmanship. May prepare cold meats, casseroles, and other foods during slack periods [GARDE MANGER (hotel & rest.)].
GOE: 05.05.17 STRENGTH: M GED: R4 M3 L3 SVP: 7 DLU: 77

313.361-010 BAKER, SECOND (hotel & rest.)
Prepares bread, rolls, muffins, and biscuits in establishments where baking of various breads, cakes, and pastries is divided among several workers, and supervises other BAKERS (hotel & rest.) in absence of BAKER, HEAD (hotel & rest.).
GOE: 05.10.08 STRENGTH: H GED: R4 M3 L3 SVP: 7 DLU: 77

313.361-014 COOK (hotel & rest.) alternate titles: cook, restaurant
Prepares, seasons, and cooks soups, meats, vegetables, desserts, and other foodstuffs for consumption in eating establishments: Reads menu to estimate

food requirements and orders food from supplier or procures food from storage. Adjusts thermostat controls to regulate temperature of ovens, broilers, grills, roasters, and steam kettles. Measures and mixes ingredients according to recipe, using variety of kitchen utensils and equipment, such as blenders, mixers, grinders, slicers, and tenderizers, to prepare soups, salads, gravies, desserts, sauces, and casseroles. Bakes, roasts, broils, and steams meats, fish, vegetables, and other foods. Adds seasoning to foods during mixing or cooking, according to personal judgment and experience. Observes and tests foods being cooked by tasting, smelling, and piercing with fork to determine that it is cooked. Carves meats, portions food on serving plates, adds gravies and sauces, and garnishes servings to fill orders. May supervise other cooks and kitchen employees. May wash, peel, cut, and shred vegetables and fruits to prepare them for use. May butcher chickens, fish, and shellfish. May cut, trim, and bone meat prior to cooking. May bake bread, rolls, cakes, and pastry [BAKER (hotel & rest.) 313.381-010]. May price items on menu. May be designated according to meal cooked or shift worked as Cook, Dinner (hotel & rest.); Cook, Morning (hotel & rest.); or according to food item prepared as Cook, Roast (hotel & rest.); or according to method of cooking as Cook, Broiler (hotel & rest.). May substitute for and relieve or assist other cooks during emergencies or rush periods and be designated Cook, Relief (hotel & rest.). May prepare and cook meals for institutionalized patients requiring special diets and be designated Food-Service Worker (hotel & rest.). May be designated: Cook, Dessert (hotel & rest.); Cook, Fry (hotel & rest.); Cook, Night (hotel & rest.); Cook, Sauce (hotel & rest.); Cook, Soup (hotel & rest.); Cook, Special Diet (hotel & rest.); Cook, Vegetable (hotel & rest.). May oversee work of patients assigned to kitchen for work therapy purposes when working in psychiatric hospital.
GOE: 05.05.17 STRENGTH: M GED: R3 M3 L3 SVP: 7 DLU: 81

313.361-018 COOK APPRENTICE (hotel & rest.)
Performs duties as described under APPRENTICE (any industry) Master Title.
GOE: 05.05.17 STRENGTH: M GED: R3 M3 L3 SVP: 7 DLU: 77

313.361-026 COOK, SPECIALTY (hotel & rest.)
Prepares specialty foods, such as fish and chips, tacos, and pasties (Cornish meat pies) according to recipe and specific methods applicable to type of cookery. May serve orders to customers at window or counter. May prepare and serve beverages, such as coffee, clam nectar, and fountain drinks. May be required to exercise showmanship in preparation of food, such as flipping pancakes in air to turn or tossing pizza dough in air to lighten texture. May be designated according to food item prepared as Cook, Fish And Chips (hotel & rest.).
GOE: 05.10.08 STRENGTH: M GED: R3 M2 L2 SVP: 5 DLU: 77

313.361-030 COOK, SPECIALTY, FOREIGN FOOD (hotel & rest.)
Plans menus and cooks foreign-style dishes, dinners, desserts, and other foods, according to recipes: Prepares meats, soups, sauces, vegetables, and other foods prior to cooking. Seasons and cooks food according to prescribed method. Portions and garnishes food. Serves food to waiters on order. Estimates food consumption and requisitions or purchases supplies. Usually employed in restaurant specializing in foreign cuisine, such as French, Scandinavian, German, Swiss, Italian, Spanish, Hungarian, and Cantonese. May be designated according to type of food specialty prepared as Cook, Chinese-Style Food (hotel & rest.); Cook, Italian-Style Food (hotel & rest.); Cook, Kosher-Style Food (hotel & rest.); Cook, Spanish-Style Food (hotel & rest.).
GOE: 05.10.08 STRENGTH: M GED: R3 M3 L2 SVP: 7 DLU: 77

313.361-034 GARDE MANGER (hotel & rest.) alternate titles: cold-meat chef; cook, cold meat
Prepares cold dishes such as meat loaves and salads, utilizing leftover meats, seafoods, and poultry: Consults with supervisory staff to determine dishes that will use greatest amount of leftovers. Prepares appetizers, relishes, and hors d'oeuvres. Chops, dices, and grinds meats and vegetables. Slices cold meats and cheese. Arranges and garnishes cold meat dishes. Prepares cold meat sandwiches. Mixes and prepares cold sauces, meat glazes, jellies, salad dressings, and stuffings. May supervise pantry workers. May follow recipes to prepare foods.
GOE: 05.10.08 STRENGTH: L GED: R3 M2 L2 SVP: 7 DLU: 77

313.361-038 PIE MAKER (hotel & rest.) alternate titles: baker, pie; cook, pastry; cook, pie; pie chef
Mixes ingredients and bakes pies, tarts, and cobblers, according to recipes: Weighs and measures ingredients, using measuring cup and spoons. Mixes ingredients by hand or with electric mixer to form piecrust dough. Rolls and shapes dough, using rolling pin. Places portions of rolled dough in piepans and trims overlapping edges with knife. Cuts, peels, and prepares fruit for pie fillings. Mixes and cooks ingredients for fillings, such as creams and custards. Pours fillings into pie shells. Covers filling with top crust or spreads topping, such as cream or meringue, over filling. Places pie in oven to bake. Adjusts drafts or thermostat controls to regulate oven temperatures. Usually found in restaurant or cafeteria where no COOK, PASTRY (hotel & rest.) is employed and need not be able to bake other desserts or pastries as opposed to COOK, PASTRY (hotel & rest.).
GOE: 05.10.08 STRENGTH: L GED: R3 M2 L2 SVP: 6 DLU: 77

313.374-010 COOK, FAST FOOD (hotel & rest.)
Prepares and cooks to order foods requiring short preparation time: Reads food order slip or receives verbal instructions as to food required by patron,

and prepares and cooks food according to instructions. Prepares sandwiches [SANDWICH MAKER (hotel & rest.) 317.664-010]. Prepares salads and slices meats and cheese, using slicing machine, [PANTRY GOODS MAKER (hotel & rest.) 317.684-014]. Cleans work area and food preparation equipment. May prepare beverages [COFFEE MAKER (hotel & rest.) 317.684-010]. May serve meals to patrons over counter.
GOE: 05.10.08 STRENGTH: M GED: R3 M2 L2 SVP: 5 DLU: 81

313.374-014 COOK, SHORT ORDER (hotel & rest.)
Prepares food and serves restaurant patrons at counters or tables: Takes order from customer and cooks foods requiring short preparation time, according to customer requirements. Completes order from steamtable and serves customer at table or counter. Accepts payment and makes change, or writes charge slip. Carves meats, makes sandwiches, and brews coffee. May clean food preparation equipment and work area. May clean counter or tables.
GOE: 05.10.08 STRENGTH: L GED: R3 M2 L2 SVP: 3 DLU: 81

313.381-010 BAKER (hotel & rest.) alternate titles: baker, bread; bread maker; oven tender
Prepares bread, rolls, muffins, and biscuits according to recipe: Checks production schedule to determine variety and quantity of goods to bake. Measures ingredients, using measuring cups and spoons. Mixes ingredients to form dough or batter by hand or using electric mixer. Cuts dough into uniform portions with knife or divider. Molds dough into loaves or desired shapes. Places shaped dough in greased or floured pans. Spreads or sprinkles topping, such as jelly, cinnamon, and poppy seeds on specialties. Places pans of dough in proof box to rise. Inserts pans of raised dough in oven to bake, using peel. Adjusts drafts or thermostatic controls to regulate oven temperature. Removes baked goods from oven and places goods on cooling rack. May bake pies, cakes, cookies, and other pastries [COOK, PASTRY (hotel & rest.)]. May be designated according to specialty baked as Baker, Biscuit (hotel & rest.); Hot-Bread Baker (hotel & rest.); Rolls Baker (hotel & rest.); or according to shift worked as Night Baker (hotel & rest.).
GOE: 05.10.08 STRENGTH: M GED: R3 M2 L2 SVP: 6 DLU: 77

313.381-014 BAKER, PIZZA (hotel & rest.)
Prepares and bakes pizza pies: Measures ingredients, such as flour, water, and yeast, using measuring cup, spoon, and scale. Dumps specified ingredients into pan or bowl of mixing machine preparatory to mixing. Starts machine and observes operation until ingredients are mixed to desired consistency. Stops machine and dumps dough into proof box to allow dough to rise. Kneads fermented dough. Cuts out and weighs amount of dough required to produce pizza pies of desired thickness. Shapes dough sections into balls or mounds and sprinkles each section with flour to prevent crust forming until used. Greases pan. Stretches or spreads dough mixture to size of pan. Places dough in pan and adds olive oil and tomato puree, tomato sauce, mozarella cheese, meat, or other garnish on surface of dough, according to kind of pizza ordered. Sets thermostatic controls and inserts pizza into heated oven to bake for specified time. Removes product from oven and observes color to determine when pizza is done.
GOE: 05.10.08 STRENGTH: M GED: R3 M2 L1 SVP: 5 DLU: 77

313.381-018 COOK APPRENTICE, PASTRY (hotel & rest.) alternate titles: baker apprentice, pastry
Performs duties as described under APPRENTICE (any industry) Master Title.
GOE: 05.10.08 STRENGTH: M GED: R4 M3 L3 SVP: 7 DLU: 77

313.381-022 COOK, BARBECUE (hotel & rest.)
Prepares, seasons, and barbecues pork, beef, chicken, and other types of meat: Builds fire in pit below spit, using hickory wood or other fuel to obtain bed of live coals, or regulates gas or electric heat. Secures meat on spit which is slowly turned by hand or electric motor to cook meat uniformly. Seasons meat and bastes it frequently during roasting. May kill and dress animals or fowls or purchase meat from vendors. When cooking whole pigs, may be designated Cook, Roast Pig (hotel & rest.).
GOE: 05.10.08 STRENGTH: M GED: R3 M2 L2 SVP: 5 DLU: 77

313.381-026 COOK, PASTRY (hotel & rest.) alternate titles: baker, cake; baker, pastry; cake maker
Prepares and bakes cakes, cookies, pies, puddings, or desserts, according to recipe: Measures ingredients, using measuring cups and spoons. Mixes ingredients to form dough or batter, using electric mixer or beats and stirs ingredients by hand. Shapes dough for cookies, pies, and fancy pastries, using pie dough roller and cookie cutters or by hand. Places shaped dough portions in greased or floured pans and inserts them in oven, using long-handled paddle (peel). Adjusts drafts or thermostatic controls to regulate oven temperatures. Prepares and cooks ingredients for pie fillings, puddings, custards, or other desserts. Pours filling into pie shells and tops filling with meringue or cream. Mixes ingredients to make icings. Decorates cakes and pastries [CAKE DECORATOR (bakery product) 524.381-010]. Blends colors for icings and for shaped sugar ornaments and statuaries. May specialize in preparing one or more types of pastry or dessert when employed in large establishment. May oversee work of patients assigned to kitchen for work therapy purposes when working in psychiatric hospital.
GOE: 05.10.08 STRENGTH: M GED: R4 M3 L3 SVP: 7 DLU: 77

313.381-030 COOK, SCHOOL CAFETERIA (hotel & rest.)
Prepares soups, meats, vegetables, salads, dressings, and desserts for consumption in school cafeteria, utilizing cafeteria equipment and cooking experi-

ence. Specializes in providing lightly seasoned, nutritionally adequate, and varied diet. Inspects equipment for cleanliness and functional operation. Work is usually performed with other workers. May plan menus, order food supplies, and receive supplies delivered.
GOE: 05.10.08 STRENGTH: M GED: R3 M2 L2 SVP: 6 DLU: 81

313.381-034 ICE-CREAM CHEF (hotel & rest.) alternate titles: cook, frozen dessert; cook, ice cream
Mixes, cooks, and freezes ingredients to make frozen desserts, such as sherbets, ice cream, and custards: Measures and cooks ingredients for frozen desserts, according to recipes. Pours mixed ingredients into freezing machine reservoir, and starts machine to churn and freeze ingredients. Removes frozen dessert mixture from machine. Stores frozen desserts in refrigerated room or refrigerator. Molds ice cream or sherbet into various shapes, such as flowers or emblems, using paddle and mold forms. Tints and decorates molded figures with icing, using cream bag and tubes. Mixes and cooks sauces and syrups for use with frozen desserts. May portion frozen desserts for waiters. May carve decorations out of ice.
GOE: 05.10.08 STRENGTH: M GED: R3 M2 L2 SVP: 5 DLU: 77

313.684-010 BAKER HELPER (hotel & rest.)
Assists BAKER (hotel & rest.) by performing any combination of following duties in bread-baking department: Carries and distributes supplies, such as flour, shortening, and baking pans. Mixes, kneads, or shapes dough for bread, rolls, muffins, or biscuits. Cuts dough into uniform portions. Greases pans used to mold or bake breads and lines pans with waxed paper. Places pans of dough into oven to bake. Removes baked products from oven. Cleans bakery utensils, equipment, and work area. Performs other duties as described under HELPER (any industry) Master Title.
GOE: 05.12.17 STRENGTH: M GED: R2 M1 L1 SVP: 3 DLU: 77

313.687-010 COOK HELPER, PASTRY (hotel & rest.) alternate titles: bakeshop cleaner; pastry helper
Assists pastry shop workers, performing any combination of following duties: Carries and distributes supplies and equipment. Mixes, kneads, and shapes dough or batter to make pies, cakes, cookies, and other pastries. Washes and cuts up fruits for desserts and pies. Greases baking tins or lines them with waxed paper. Inserts cakes, pies, and cookies into oven, and removes baked products. Portions pastries, desserts, and ice cream. Washes and scours pots, pans, and other equipment. Performs other duties as described under HELPER (any industry) Master Title.
GOE: 05.12.17 STRENGTH: M GED: R2 M1 L1 SVP: 3 DLU: 77

315 MISCELLANEOUS COOKS, EXCEPT DOMESTIC

This group includes service occupations concerned with preparing and cooking food in places other than private houses, hotels, or restaurants.

315.131-010 COOK, CHIEF (water trans.)
Supervises and coordinates activities of kitchen personnel and participates in preparation of meals aboard cargo ship: Collaborates with STEWARD/STEWARDESS, CHIEF, CARGO VESSEL (water trans.) to plan menus. Determines time and sequence of cooking operations to meet meal-serving hours. Directs COOK, THIRD (water trans.); SECOND COOK AND BAKER (water trans.); and SCULLION (water trans.) in preparation of foods. Inspects galley and galley equipment, such as pots, ovens, and cutlery, for cleanliness. Butchers and prepares meat, fowl, and fish, and participates in cooking of meats and sauces. May requisition supplies.
GOE: 05.10.08 STRENGTH: M GED: R4 M2 L3 SVP: 7 DLU: 77

315.131-014 PASTRY CHEF (water trans.)
Supervises and coordinates activities of workers in pastry shop aboard passenger ship to produce puddings, icings, and fancy pastries, and creates new recipes: Receives orders from CHEF, PASSENGER VESSEL (water trans.) to prepare confections. Assigns specific baking tasks and directs workers in task performance. Measures and mixes ingredients, such as flour, flavoring, and fruit, to form concoctions. Kneads dough into desired shape and places dough in oven. Turns oven controls to regulate temperatures and to set time cycle for baking products. Decorates products with icing designs, using spatula and cream bag. Creates new designs and recipes. Inspects pastry shop, baking equipment, and workers for cleanliness. Requisitions supplies and equipment.
GOE: 05.10.08 STRENGTH: M GED: R4 M2 L3 SVP: 8 DLU: 77

315.137-010 CHEF, PASSENGER VESSEL (water trans.)
Supervises and coordinates activities of kitchen workers to prepare and cook food aboard passenger ship: Collaborates with STEWARD/STEWARDESS, CHIEF, PASSENGER SHIP (water trans.) to plan menus. Determines time and sequence of cooking operations to meet meal-serving hours. Delegates to SOUS CHEF (water trans.) responsibility for preparation of food. Directs cooks, bakers, butchers, and other kitchen personnel engaged in preparing, cooking, and serving food. Inspects galleys, bakery, and butcher shop for cleanliness. Requisitions food and galley supplies. Estimates cost of food consumed and compiles cost control records. Authorizes personnel to work overtime.
GOE: 05.05.17 STRENGTH: L GED: R4 M3 L3 SVP: 7 DLU: 77

315.137-014 SOUS CHEF (water trans.)
Supervises and coordinates activities of kitchen workers to prepare and cook food aboard passenger ship: Receives menus planned by CHEF, PASSENGER

VESSEL (water trans.) and STEWARD/STEWARDESS, CHIEF, PASSENGER SHIP (water trans.). Determines kinds and amounts of foodstuffs necessary to prepare items listed on menus. Plans sequence and time of cooking operations to meet meal-serving hours. Assigns specific tasks to cooks of several galleys. Directs cooks performing tasks. Determines size of food portions and observes workers serving food. Evaluates and solves problems encountered, such as substituting items on menus, reusing cooked food, and reducing excess waste and spoilage. Inspects galleys, pantries, serving stations, and butchering and baking shops for cleanliness. May assist in cooking tasks and in preparing hot and cold canapes and hors d'oeuvres for banquets, cocktail parties, and other social functions.
GOE: 05.05.17 STRENGTH: L GED: R4 M3 L4 SVP: 7 DLU: 77

315.361-010 COOK (any industry) alternate titles: cook, mess
Prepares and cooks family-style meals for crews or residents and employees of institutions: Cooks foodstuffs in quantities according to menu and number of persons to be served. Washes dishes. Bakes breads and pastry [BAKER (hotel & rest.)]. Cuts meat [BUTCHER, MEAT (hotel & rest.)]. Plans menu taking advantage of foods in season and local availability. May serve meals. May order supplies and keep records and accounts. May direct activities of one or more workers who assist in preparing and serving meals. May be designated according to work location as Cook, Camp (any industry); Cook, Institution (any industry); Cook, Ranch (agriculture); Cook, Ship (water trans.).
GOE: 05.10.08 STRENGTH: M GED: R3 M2 L2 SVP: 6 DLU: 77

315.361-022 COOK, STATION (water trans.)
Prepares, seasons, and cooks food on menu from station aboard passenger vessel: Prepares sauces, dressings, puddings, or relishes to be served with dish. Gives directions for setting up station so that food, garnishes, and service equipment are arranged in serving order. Portions and places food on plate, and arranges garnishes on plate. Must be certified as Food Handler and as Cook by U.S. Coast Guard. May be required to hold Life Boatman certificate. May be designated according to station as Cook, Station, Grill (water trans.); according to meal prepared as Cook, Station, Breakfast (water trans.); or according to food prepared as Cook, Station, Roast (water trans.); Cook, Station, Soup And Fish (water trans.).
GOE: 05.10.08 STRENGTH: M GED: R3 M2 L2 SVP: 6 DLU: 77

315.371-010 COOK, MESS (water trans.) alternate titles: cook, boat; cook, ship
Cooks and serves meals to crew on passenger ship: Cleans, cuts, and cooks meat, fish, and poultry. Serves food to crewmembers. Washes dishes and cleans galley and galley equipment. Requisitions supplies. Compiles cost records of food used.
GOE: 05.10.08 STRENGTH: M GED: R3 M2 L2 SVP: 6 DLU: 77

315.381-010 COOK (fishing & hunt.) alternate titles: cook, fishing vessel
Prepares meals for crew and officers on board fishing vessel or in shore fishery establishment. May assist in actual fishing. May purchase food supplies.
GOE: 05.10.08 STRENGTH: M GED: R3 M2 L2 SVP: 5 DLU: 77

315.381-014 COOK, LARDER (water trans.) alternate titles: garde manger
Prepares cold plate entrees, appetizers, and cocktails for lunch and dinner service, and makes canapes, hors d'oeuvres, and sandwiches for buffets: Slices roast, such as beef, veal, pork, and lamb, for cold plates or sandwiches. Cuts luncheon meats, such as head cheese, pork loaf, veal loaf, and ham. Mixes gelatins, grinds up leftover meats, and prepares hot and cold canapes, hors d'oeuvres, and goose liver pate to be served as appetizers. Prepares sandwiches for pantry service outside of meal hours. May prepare food showpieces. Mixes sauces and various seafoods, such as crab, lobster, and shrimp, to prepare cocktails.
GOE: 05.10.08 STRENGTH: L GED: R4 M2 L2 SVP: 7 DLU: 77

315.381-018 COOK, RAILROAD (r.r. trans.) alternate titles: chef
Prepares, seasons, and cooks food in railroad dining car, following recipes for preplanned menus: Broils steaks, chops, fish, and poultry. Toasts bread and prepares waffles and pancakes, using prepared mixes. Mixes ingredients for cooked and uncooked desserts, such as pudding, custard, gelatin, and fruit desserts. Washes, peels, cuts, seeds, and cooks vegetables. May inventory supplies of food and prepare requisitions. May carve meats. May supervise other kitchen workers. May be designated according to specialties prepared as Cook, Fry (r.r. trans.). When preparing and serving food to passengers in Pullman Lounge (combination sleeping and dining car) may be designated Pullman Attendant (r.r. trans.).
GOE: 05.10.08 STRENGTH: L GED: R3 M2 L2 SVP: 6 DLU: 77

315.381-022 COOK, THIRD (water trans.)
Prepares and cooks food aboard cargo vessel: Cleans, cuts, and cooks meat, fish, and poultry as directed by COOK, CHIEF (water trans.). Apportions food for servings. Cleans pots, pans, ranges, and other cooking equipment.
GOE: 05.10.08 STRENGTH: M GED: R3 M1 L2 SVP: 6 DLU: 77

315.381-026 SECOND COOK AND BAKER (water trans.)
Prepares food aboard cargo vessel, as directed by COOK, CHIEF (water trans.): Bakes bread, rolls, and pastries. Cooks vegetables and prepares desserts. Cleans baking area. May apportion cooked foods on plates.

GOE: 05.10.08 STRENGTH: H GED: R3 M2 L2 SVP: 6 DLU: 77

316 MEATCUTTERS, EXCEPT IN SLAUGHTERING AND PACKING HOUSES

This group includes occupations concerned with cutting and otherwise preparing meat for cooking in hotels and restaurants, or for sale in wholesale or retail trade. Meatcutter occupations in slaughtering and packing houses or centralized meat processing plants are included in Group 525.

316.661-010 CARVER (hotel & rest.) alternate titles: display carver; exhibition carver; meat carver

Carves individual portions from roasts and poultry to obtain maximum number of meat portions, using carving knives and meat-slicing machines: Disjoints roasts and poultry. Slices uniform portions of meat and places sliced meat in steamtable container, or arranges individual portions on plate. Ladles gravy over food and garnishes plate. Removes shells from seafood and bones fish, using forks. May weigh sliced meat to ensure that portions are uniform. May serve food from steamtable. May serve customers [WAITER/WAITRESS, FORMAL (hotel & rest.)].
GOE: 05.10.08 STRENGTH: L GED: R3 M2 L2 SVP: 4 DLU: 77

316.681-010 BUTCHER, MEAT (hotel & rest.) alternate titles: butcher; meat cutter

Cuts, trims, bones, ties, and grinds meats, using butcher's cutlery and powered equipment, such as electric grinder and bandsaw, to portion and prepare meat in cooking form: Cuts, trims, and bones carcass sections or prime cuts, using knives, meat saw, cleaver, and bandsaw, to reduce to cooking cuts, such as roasts, steaks, chops, stew cubes, and grinding meat. Cuts and weighs steaks and chops for individual servings. Tends electric grinder to grind meat. Shapes and ties roasts. May estimate requirements and requisition or order meat supply. May receive, inspect, and store meat upon delivery. May record quantity of meat received and issued to cooks. May clean fowl and fish [BUTCHER, CHICKEN AND FISH (hotel & rest.)]. May oversee other butchers and be designated Butcher, Head (hotel & rest.).
GOE: 05.10.08 STRENGTH: H GED: R3 M2 L2 SVP: 6 DLU: 77

316.684-010 BUTCHER, CHICKEN AND FISH (hotel & rest.) alternate titles: chicken-and-fish cleaner; poultry-and-fish butcher

Butchers and cleans fowl, fish, and shellfish preparatory to cooking: Cleans and prepares fowl, fish, and shellfish, using knife and fork. Discards inedible parts. Cuts up fowl, using knife and cleaver or bandsaw. Bones game fowl and fish, using boning knife. Reshapes boned fowl into natural form for cooking and serving. Cuts fillets and steaks from fish. May butcher poultry in retail establishment and be designated Sales Clerk, Fresh Poultry (retail trade).
GOE: 05.10.08 STRENGTH: L GED: R2 M2 L1 SVP: 3 DLU: 77

316.684-014 DELI CUTTER-SLICER (retail trade)

Cuts delicatessen meats and cheeses, using slicing machine, knives, or other cutters: Places meat or cheese on cutting board and cuts slices to designated thickness, using knives or other hand cutters. Positions and clamps meat or cheese on carriage of slicing machine. Adjusts knob to set machine for desired thickness. Presses button to start motor that moves carriage past rotary blade that slices meats and cheeses. Stacks cut pieces on tray or platter, separating portions with paper. May weigh and wrap sliced foods and affix sticker showing price and weight.
GOE: 05.12.17 STRENGTH: L GED: R2 M2 L1 SVP: 2 DLU: 77

316.684-018 MEAT CUTTER (retail trade; wholesale tr.) alternate titles: butcher; salesperson, meats

Cuts and trims meat to size for display or as ordered by customer, using handtools and power equipment, such as grinder, cubing machine, and power saw. Cleans and cuts fish and poultry. May shape, lace, and tie meat cuts by hand, using boning knife, skewer, and twine to form roasts. May place meat in containers to be wrapped by other workers. May place meat on trays in display counter. May clean work area. May unload meat from delivery truck and store meat into refrigerator. May wrap and weigh meat for customers and collect money for sales. May inspect and grade meats and be designated Meat Inspector (retail trade; wholesale tr.).
GOE: 05.10.08 STRENGTH: H GED: R3 M2 L3 SVP: 6 DLU: 81

316.684-022 MEAT-CUTTER APPRENTICE (retail trade; wholesale tr.) alternate titles: butcher apprentice; salesperson apprentice, meats

Performs duties as described under APPRENTICE (any industry) Master Title.
GOE: 05.10.08 STRENGTH: H GED: R3 M2 L3 SVP: 6 DLU: 77

317 MISCELLANEOUS FOOD AND BEVERAGE PREPARATION OCCUPATIONS

This group includes occupations concerned with preparing food and beverages.

317.384-010 SALAD MAKER (water trans.)

Prepares salads, fruits, melons, and gelatin desserts: Cleans vegetables, fruits, and berries for salads, relishes, and gelatin desserts. Mixes ingredients for green

salads, fruit salads, and potato salad. Prepares relish plates of green onions, celery, radishes, and olives. Prepares dressings, such as Thousand Island, French, and Roquefort, to be served on green salads. Peels, cleans, and cuts fruits, to be served for breakfast or compotes. Prepares cold sandwiches and cheeses. Requisitions supplies daily.
GOE: 05.10.08 STRENGTH: L GED: R3 M2 L3 SVP: 5 DLU: 77

317.664-010 SANDWICH MAKER (hotel & rest.) alternate titles: sandwich-counter attendant

Prepares sandwiches to individual order of customers: Receives sandwich orders from customers. Slices cold meats and cheese by hand or machine. Selects and cuts bread, such as white, whole wheat, or rye, and toasts or grills bread, according to order. Places meat or filling and garnish, such as chopped or sliced onion and lettuce, between bread slices. Prepares garnishes for sandwiches, such as sliced tomatoes and pickles. May cook, mix, and season ingredients to make dressings, fillings, and spreads. May fry hamburgers, bacon, steaks, and eggs for hot sandwiches. May butter bread slices, using knife.
GOE: 05.12.17 STRENGTH: M GED: R2 M1 L1 SVP: 2 DLU: 80

317.684-010 COFFEE MAKER (hotel & rest.) alternate titles: coffee-urn attendant

Brews coffee, tea, and chocolate, using coffee urns, drip or vacuum coffee makers, teapots, drink mixers, and other kitchen equipment. Performs various duties to assist in filling customers' orders, such as cooking hot cakes and waffles, boiling eggs, and making toast [PANTRY GOODS MAKER (hotel & rest.)]. Cleans and polishes utensils and equipment used in food and beverage preparation. May serve coffee. May prepare and issue iced beverages, such as coffee, tea, and fountain or bottled drinks, to be served by COUNTER ATTENDANT, LUNCHROOM OR COFFEE SHOP (hotel & rest.).
GOE: 05.12.17 STRENGTH: M GED: R2 M1 L1 SVP: 2 DLU: 77

317.684-014 PANTRY GOODS MAKER (hotel & rest.)

Prepares salads, appetizers, sandwich fillings, and other cold dishes: Washes, peels, slices, and mixes vegetables, fruits, or other ingredients for salads, cold plates, and garnishes. Carves and slices meats and cheese. Portions and arranges food on serving dishes. Prepares fruit or seafood cocktails and hors d'oeuvres. Measures and mixes ingredients to make salad dressings, cocktail sauces, gelatin salads, cold desserts, and waffles, following recipes. Makes sandwiches to order [SANDWICH MAKER (hotel & rest.) 317.664-010]. Brews tea and coffee [COFFEE MAKER (hotel & rest.) 317.684-010]. Prepares breakfast and dessert fruits, such as melons, grapefruit, and bananas. Portions fruit sauces and juices. Distributes food to waiters/waitresses to serve to customers. May serve food to customers. May be designated Salad Maker (hotel & rest.) when specializing in making salads.
GOE: 05.10.08 STRENGTH: L GED: R3 M2 L2 SVP: 4 DLU: 81

317.687-010 COOK HELPER (hotel & rest.)

Assists workers engaged in preparing foods for hotels, restaurants, or ready-to-serve packages by performing any combination of following duties: Washes, peels, cuts, and seeds vegetables and fruits. Cleans, cuts, and grinds meats, poultry, and seafood. Dips food items in crumbs, flour, and batter to bread them. Stirs and strains soups and sauces. Weighs and measures designated ingredients. Carries pans, kettles, and trays of food to and from work stations, stove, and refrigerator. Stores foods in designated areas, utilizing knowledge of temperature requirements and food spoilage. Cleans work areas, equipment and utensils, segregates and removes garbage, and steam-cleans or hoses garbage containers [KITCHEN HELPER (hotel & rest.) 318.687-010]. Distributes supplies, utensils, and portable equipment, using handtruck. May be designated according to worker assisted as Cook Helper, Broiler or Fry (hotel & rest.); Cook Helper, Dessert (hotel & rest.); Cook Helper, Vegetable (hotel & rest.); Pantry Goods Maker Helper (hotel & rest.). Performs other duties as described under HELPER (any industry) Master Title.
GOE: 05.12.17 STRENGTH: M GED: R2 M1 L1 SVP: 2 DLU: 81

318 KITCHEN WORKERS, N.E.C.

This group includes occupations, not elsewhere classified, concerned with performing such duties as washing and drying dishes; polishing silverware; and disposing of garbage and trash.

318.137-010 KITCHEN STEWARD/STEWARDESS (hotel & rest.)

Supervises kitchen employees not actively engaged in cooking to ensure clean, efficient, and economical food service: Assigns KITCHEN HELPER (hotel & rest.) and other noncooking employees to such activities as dishwashing and silver cleaning. Inspects kitchens, workrooms, and equipment for cleanliness and order. Hires and discharges employees, and posts time and production records. Observes and evaluates employees' performance to devise methods for improving efficiency and guard against theft and wastage. Takes inventories of china, silverware, and glassware. Reports shortages and requisitions replacement of equipment from STEWARD/STEWARDESS (hotel & rest.) or PURCHASING AGENT (profess. & kin.). May be working supervisor in establishments employing an EXECUTIVE CHEF (hotel & rest.), who devotes full time to supervising kitchen employees. May be designated according to area of work as Pantry Steward/Stewardess (hotel & rest.).
GOE: 05.12.01 STRENGTH: M GED: R4 M3 L4 SVP: 6 DLU: 77

318.687-010 KITCHEN HELPER (hotel & rest.) alternate titles: cookee; cook helper; kitchen hand; kitchen porter; kitchen runner

Performs any combination of following duties to maintain kitchen work areas and restaurant equipment and utensils in clean and orderly condition: Sweeps

and mops floors. Washes worktables, walls, refrigerators, and meat blocks. Segregates and removes trash and garbage and places it in designated containers. Steam-cleans or hoses-out garbage cans. Sorts bottles, and breaks disposable ones in bottle-crushing machine. Washes pots, pans, and trays by hand. Scrapes food from dirty dishes and washes them by hand or places them in racks or on conveyor to dishwashing machine. Polishes silver, using burnishing-machine tumbler, chemical dip, buffing wheel, and hand cloth. Holds inverted glasses over revolving brushes to clean inside surfaces. Transfers supplies and equipment between storage and work areas by hand or by use of handtruck. Sets up banquet tables. Washes and peels vegetables, using knife or peeling machine. Loads or unloads trucks picking up or delivering supplies and food.
GOE: 05.12.18 STRENGTH: M GED: R2 M1 L1 SVP: 2 DLU: 86

318.687-014 SCULLION (water trans.)
Performs any combination of tasks involved in cleaning ship's galleys, bakery, and butcher shop: Cleans pots and pans, dishes, chopping blocks, and service stations, by hand or using dishwashing machine. Polishes silver chafing dishes and coffee pots. Places washed glasses in rack to prevent breakage. Defrosts and cleans reefers and iceboxes. Cleans and culls vegetables and fruits. Dumps garbage and cleans can. Swabs deck of assigned area. Carries supplies from reefers and storerooms to galleys, pantries, bakery, and butcher shop. Stocks serving stations with dishes and stores. May be designated according to type of work performed as Baker Scullion (water trans.); Butcher Scullion (water trans.); Glass Scullion (water trans.); Silverware Washer (water trans.); Vegetable Scullion (water trans.); or according to area to which assigned as Main-Galley Scullion (water trans.). May give directions to workers and be designated Scullion Chief (water trans.). When work is performed on cargo ship, is usually known as Utility Hand (water trans.).
GOE: 05.12.18 STRENGTH: M GED: R2 M1 L1 SVP: 2 DLU: 77

318.687-018 SILVER WRAPPER (hotel & rest.)
Spreads silverware on absorbent cloth to remove moisture. Wraps individual place settings in napkins or inserts them with prescribed accessory condiments in plastic bag and closes bag with electric sealer. May immerse silverware in cleaning solution to remove soap stains before wrapping. May place tarnished and bent eating utensils aside.
GOE: 05.12.18 STRENGTH: L GED: R2 M1 L1 SVP: 1 DLU: 77

319 FOOD AND BEVERAGE PREPARATION AND SERVICE OCCUPATIONS, N.E.C.

This group includes occupations, not elsewhere classified, concerned with food and beverage preparation and service.

319.137-010 FOOD-SERVICE SUPERVISOR (hotel & rest.)
Supervises employees engaged in serving food in hospital, nursing home, school, or similiar institutions, and in maintaining cleanliness of food service areas and equipment: Trains workers in performance of duties. Assigns and coordinates work of employees to promote efficiency of operations. Supervises serving of meals. Inspects kitchen and dining areas and kitchen utensils and equipment to ensure sanitary standards are met. Keeps records, such as amount and cost of meals served and hours worked by employees. Requisitions and inspects foodstuffs, supplies, and equipment to maintain stock levels and ensure standards of quality are met. Prepares work schedules and evaluates work performance of employees. May direct preparation of foods and beverages. May assist DIETITIAN, CLINICAL (profess. & kin.) 077.127-014 in planning menus. May interview, select, or hire new employees. When supervising workers engaged in tray assembly may be designated Tray-Line Supervisor (medical ser.).
GOE: 09.05.02 STRENGTH: L GED: R4 M3 L3 SVP: 6 DLU: 86

319.137-014 MANAGER, FLIGHT KITCHEN (hotel & rest.)
Supervises and coordinates activities of kitchen employees engaged in purchasing and preparing food and supplies for food service department of airline: Reviews reservations and flight information to ascertain and compute types and quantities of food needed. Orders and schedules delivery of food and supplies from local vendors. Prepares work schedules for kitchen personnel to ensure presence of requisite labor force on each shift. Oversees and coordinates work of cooks and other kitchen employees engaged in preparing meals to ensure adherence to recipes and quality standards. Controls alcoholic beverage supply by perpetual inventory and prepares government forms as prescribed by law to account for consumption of taxable and nontaxable beverages. Inspects kitchen for conformance to government and company safety and sanitation requirements. Participates in collective bargaining and settling of union grievances involving department employees.
GOE: 11.11.04 STRENGTH: L GED: R4 M3 L3 SVP: 7 DLU: 77

319.137-018 MANAGER, INDUSTRIAL CAFETERIA (hotel & rest.) alternate titles: dining-service supervisor
Supervises and coordinates activities of workers engaged in preparing and serving balanced meals to employees of industrial plant: Plans daily menus to accommodate employees of all shifts, keeping expenses within budget. Purchases and keeps adequate supply of food and oversees storage and issuance of supplies. Supervises subordinates and coordinates activities of workers engaged in preparing food, serving meals, and cleaning kitchen and dining room. Keeps records and makes reports of expenditures. Cooperates with medical personnel in providing special diets for employees requiring individual attention.

May distribute pamphlets on food and health habits to employees. May balance receipts and prepare bank deposit slip. May interview and hire new workers.
GOE: 11.11.04 STRENGTH: L GED: R4 M3 L3 SVP: 6 DLU: 77

319.137-022 SUPERVISOR, COMMISSARY PRODUCTION (hotel & rest.) alternate titles: cooked foods supervisor
Supervises and coordinates activities of commissary workers engaged in preparing, assembling, packaging, and shipping ready-to-eat food items: Checks inventories and orders foodstuffs and supplies. Prescribes quantities, production sequence, and time for items to be prepared, cooked, assembled, and packaged to meet production schedule. Specifies arrangement of equipment, work stations, and staffing to prepare for production. Explains and demonstrates work methods to train employees and establish size of food portions. Performs other duties as described under SUPERVISOR (any industry) Master Title.
GOE: 11.11.04 STRENGTH: L GED: R4 M3 L3 SVP: 7 DLU: 77

319.137-026 SUPERVISOR, KOSHER DIETARY SERVICE (hotel & rest.) alternate titles: moshgiach; overseer, kosher kitchen; supervisor, kashruth
Supervises workers engaged in storing, preparing, and cooking meats, poultry, and other foods in restaurants, catering halls, hospitals, or other establishments to ensure observance of Hebrew dietary laws and customs: Examines incoming purchases of meat and fowl to ensure that slaughtering and selection of meat cuts have been performed according to dietary law. Inspects equipment, utensils, and food supplies to ascertain that separation of dairy and meat products is maintained and that kosher foods and supplies are kept separate from nonkosher foods. Ensures that silverware, dishes, and utensils are sent to prescribed meat kitchen or dairy kitchen for washing. Washes and salts meat and fowl in accordance with Hebrew ritual. Directs kitchen staff in methods of complying with dietary laws.
GOE: 05.10.08 STRENGTH: L GED: R4 M2 L3 SVP: 7 DLU: 77

319.137-030 KITCHEN SUPERVISOR (hotel & rest.) alternate titles: dietary assistant; manager, kitchen
Supervises and coordinates activities of food preparation, kitchen, pantry, and storeroom personnel and purchases or requisitions foodstuffs and kitchen supplies: Plans or participates in planning menus, preparing and apportioning foods, and utilizing food surpluses and leftovers. Specifies number of servings to be made from any vegetable, meat, beverage, and dessert to control portion costs. Supervises noncooking personnel, such as KITCHEN HELPER (hotel & rest.) 318.687-010, to ensure cleanliness of kitchen and equipment. Supervises COOK (hotel & rest.) 313.361-014 and tastes, smells, and observes food to ensure conformance with recipes and appearance standards. Supervises workers engaged in inventory, storage, and distribution of foodstuffs and supplies. Purchases foodstuffs, kitchen supplies, and equipment, or requisitions them from PURCHASING AGENT (profess. & kin.) 162.157-038. Hires and discharges employees. Trains new workers. Performs other duties as described under SUPERVISOR (any industry) Master Title. May set prices to be charged for food items. May meet with professional staff, customers, or client group to resolve menu inconsistencies or to plan menus for special occasions. May assist dietitian to plan, change, test, and standardize recipes to increase number of servings prepared. This job occurs typically in restaurants, cafeterias, and institutions as opposed to STEWARD/STEWARDESS (hotel & rest.) 310.137-018 which occurs typically in hotels.
GOE: 05.10.08 STRENGTH: M GED: R4 M3 L4 SVP: 7 DLU: 86

319.464-010 AUTOMAT-CAR ATTENDANT (r.r. trans.)
Stocks automatic food dispensing machines on railroad passenger car, makes change, and answers passengers' queries regarding food selections: Places portions of specified foods, beverages, and desserts on shelves in machine. Inserts labels below windows of machines to indicate type of food or drink on shelf and available for dispensing. Makes change for passengers and answers questions concerning selections. Observes gauges registering temperature in machine to ensure that food and drink is kept cool or warm. Corrects jamming and common malfunctions of machines. Prepares requisition for food and drink supplies. Cleans interior and exterior of machines, using damp cloth. Removes refuse from tables and wipes them clean.
GOE: 09.04.01 STRENGTH: L GED: R2 M2 L2 SVP: 2 DLU: 77

319.464-014 VENDING-MACHINE ATTENDANT (hotel & rest.)
Stocks machines and assists customers in facility where food is dispensed from coin-operated machines: Places food or drink items on shelves of vending machines and changes shelf labels as required to indicate selections. Makes change for customers and answers questions regarding selections. Adjusts temperature gauges to maintain food items at specified temperatures. Performs minor repairs or adjustments on machines to correct jams or similar malfunctions, using handtools. Prepares requisitions for food and drink supplies. Cleans interior and exterior of machines, using damp cloth. Maintains eating area in orderly condition. May sell precooked foods from hot table. May remove money from vending machines and keep records of receipts.
GOE: 09.04.01 STRENGTH: L GED: R2 M2 L2 SVP: 2 DLU: 86

319.467-010 FOOD ORDER EXPEDITER (hotel & rest.)
Calls out and verifies food orders in drive-in restaurant or restaurant specializing in fast service: Removes order placed on device, such as wheel or nail board, at kitchen service counter. Calls out food orders to cooks and pantry and fountain workers. Examines portioning and garnishing of completed food order. Reviews order for accuracy and tabulates check. Notifies serving personnel

when order is ready. May record count of items, such as entrees drawn from supply or entrees served, to accumulate food control data. May prepare and cook foods that can be completed in short time [COOK, FAST FOOD (hotel & rest.) 313.374-010].
GOE: 05.09.03 STRENGTH: L GED: R3 M2 L2 SVP: 3 DLU: 77

319.474-010 FOUNTAIN SERVER (hotel & rest.) alternate titles: fountain dispenser; ice cream dispenser; soda clerk; soda dispenser; soda jerker
Prepares and serves soft drinks and ice cream dishes, such as ice cream sundaes, malted milks, sodas, and fruitades, using memorized formulas and methods or following directions. Cleans glasses, dishes, and fountain equipment and polishes metalwork on fountain. May prepare and serve sandwiches [SANDWICH MAKER (hotel & rest.) 317.664-010] or other foods [COUNTER ATTENDANT, LUNCHROOM OR COFFEE SHOP (hotel & rest.) 311.477-014]. May verify and total customer's bill, accept cash, and make change.
GOE: 09.04.01 STRENGTH: L GED: R2 M2 L2 SVP: 2 DLU: 80

319.484-010 FOOD ASSEMBLER, KITCHEN (hotel & rest.) alternate titles: dining-service worker; food assembler, commissary kitchen; food-tray assembler; supply service worker; tray setter
Prepares meal trays in commissary kitchen for inflight service of airlines, multiunit restaurant chains, industrial caterers, or educational, and similar institutions, performing any combination of following duties: Reads charts to determine amount and kind of foods and supplies to be packaged. Fills individual serving cartons with portions of various foods and condiments, such as cream, jams, and sauces, by hand or using automatic filling machine. Portions and garnishes hot cooked foods, such as meat and vegetables, into individual serving dishes. Stores dishes of hot food on shelves of portable electric warming cabinet or food cart for stowing aboard airplane or transfer to restaurant or cafeteria dining unit. Removes pans of portioned salads, desserts, rolls, cream, and other cold food items from refrigerator or pantry, and places at appropriate stations of tray assembly counter to facilitate loading meal trays. Places food items, silverware, and dishes in depression of compartmented food tray passing on conveyor belt. Examines filled tray for completeness and appearance, and stores completed trays in refrigerated storage cabinets to be transported to airplane, dining room, or cafeteria. May be designated according to type of food assembled as Appetizer Packer (hotel & rest.); Casserole Preparer (hotel & rest.); Cold-Food Packer (hotel & rest.); Hot-Food Packer (hotel & rest.).
GOE: 05.12.17 STRENGTH: L GED: R2 M2 L1 SVP: 3 DLU: 77

319.677-010 CATERER HELPER (personal ser.)
Prepares and serves food and refreshments at social affairs, under supervision of CATERER (personal ser.): Arranges tables and decorations. Prepares hors d'oeuvres, fancy and plain sandwiches, and salads. Serves foods and beverages to guests. Washes and packs dishes and utensils for removal to catering establishment.
GOE: 09.05.02 STRENGTH: L GED: R3 M2 L2 SVP: 3 DLU: 77

319.677-014 FOOD-SERVICE WORKER, HOSPITAL (medical ser.) alternate titles: dietary aide; tray worker
Prepares and delivers food trays to hospital patients, performing any combination of following duties on tray line: Reads production orders on color-coded menu cards on trays to determine items to place on tray. Places items, such as eating utensils, napkins, and condiments on trays. Prepares food items, such as sandwiches, salads, soups, and beverages. Places servings in blender to make foods for soft or liquid diets. Apportions and places food servings on plates and trays according to diet list on menu card. Examines filled tray for completeness and places on cart, dumbwaiter, or conveyor belt. Pushes carts to halls or ward kitchen. Serves trays to patients. Collects and stacks dirty dishes on cart and returns cart to kitchen. Washes dishes and cleans work area, tables, cabinets, and ovens. Collects and places garbage and trash in designated containers. May record amount and types of special food items served to patients. May assemble and serve food items to hospital staff in cafeteria.
GOE: 09.05.02 STRENGTH: M GED: R3 M2 L2 SVP: 2 DLU: 89

319.687-010 COUNTER-SUPPLY WORKER (hotel & rest.)
Replenishes food and equipment at steamtables and serving counters of cafeteria to facilitate service to patrons: Carries food, dishes, trays, and silverware from kitchen and supply departments to serving counters. Garnishes foods and positions them on table to ensure their visibility to patrons and convenience in serving. Keeps assigned area and equipment free of spilled foods. Keeps shelves of vending machines stocked with food when working in automat.
GOE: 09.05.02 STRENGTH: M GED: R2 M1 L1 SVP: 2 DLU: 77

32 LODGING AND RELATED SERVICE OCCUPATIONS

This division includes occupations concerned with providing accommodations to guests in boarding houses or lodging houses.

320 BOARDING-HOUSE AND LODGING-HOUSE KEEPERS

This group includes occupations concerned with managing boarding or rooming houses to provide accommodations for transients and permanent guests.

320.137-010 MANAGER, BOARDING HOUSE (hotel & rest.) alternate titles: manager, guest house
Supervises and coordinates activities of workers in boarding house engaged in providing meals and lodging accommodations for transients and permanent guests: Advertises vacancies and shows and rents rooms. Supervises household employees engaged in such tasks as cleaning rooms, issuing linens, and cooking and serving meals. Plans menus and purchases supplies. Collects rents, pays bills, and posts information in records. Resolves complaints regarding food, accommodations, or service. May participate in cleaning and cooking activities. May make minor repairs to building and furnishings. When meal service is not provided, is designated Manager, Rooming House (hotel & rest.).
GOE: 11.11.01 STRENGTH: L GED: R3 M3 L3 SVP: 6 DLU: 77

320.137-014 MANAGER, LODGING FACILITIES (hotel & rest.)
Manages and maintains temporary or permanent lodging facilities, such as small apartment houses, motels, small hotels, trailer parks, and boat marinas: Shows and rents or assigns accommodations. Registers guests. Collects rents and records data pertaining to rent funds and expenditures. Resolves occupants' complaints. Purchases supplies and arranges for outside services, such as fuel delivery, laundry, maintenance and repair, and trash collection. Provides telephone answering service for tenants, delivers mail and packages, and answers inquiries concerning travel routes, recreational facilities, scenic attractions, and eating establishments. Cleans public areas, such as entrances, halls, and laundry rooms, and fires boilers. Makes minor electrical, plumbing, and structural repairs. Mows and waters lawns, and cultivates flower beds and shrubbery. Cleans accommodations after guests' departure. Provides daily maid service in overnight accommodations. May rent equipment, such as rowboats, water skis, and fishing tackle. May coordinate intramural activities of patrons of park. May arrange for medical aid for park patron. May sell light lunches, candy, tobacco, and other sundry items. May be designated according to type of establishment managed as Manager, Apartment House (hotel & rest.); Manager, Hotel (hotel & rest.); Manager, Marina (hotel & rest.); Manager, Motel (hotel & rest.); Manager, Tourist Camp (hotel & rest.); Manager, Trailer Park (hotel & rest.).
GOE: 11.11.01 STRENGTH: M GED: R4 M3 L4 SVP: 7 DLU: 86

321 HOUSEKEEPERS, HOTELS AND INSTITUTIONS

This group includes occupations concerned with supervising workers in maintaining cleanliness and orderliness in hotels or institutions. Some housekeepers purchase housekeeping supplies and equipment and take periodic inventories.

321.137-010 HOUSEKEEPER (hotel & rest.; medical ser.; real estate) alternate titles: floor housekeeper
Supervises work activities of cleaning personnel to ensure clean, orderly attractive rooms in hotels, hospitals, and similar establishments: Obtains list of vacant rooms which need to be cleaned immediately and list of prospective check-outs or discharges in order to prepare work assignments. Assigns workers their duties, and inspects work for conformance to prescribed standards of cleanliness. Advises manager, desk clerk, or admitting personnel of rooms ready for occupancy. Inventories stock to ensure adequate supplies. Issues supplies and equipment to workers. Investigates complaints regarding housekeeping service and equipment, and takes corrective action. Examines rooms, halls, and lobbies to determine need for repairs or replacement of furniture or equipment, and makes recommendations to management. Screens job applicants, hires new employees, and recommends promotions, transfers, or dismissals. Conducts orientation training of new employees and in-service training of other employees to explain company policies, housekeeping work procedures, and to demonstrate use and maintenance of equipment. Attends training seminars to perfect housekeeping techniques and procedures, and enhance supervisory skills. Records data concerning work assignments, personnel actions, and time cards, and prepares periodic reports. Attends periodic staff meetings with other department heads to discuss company policies and patrons' complaints, and to make recommendations to improve service and ensure more efficient operation. May prepare reports concerning room occupancy, payroll expenses, and department expenses.
GOE: 05.12.01 STRENGTH: L GED: R3 M2 L3 SVP: 6 DLU: 89

321.137-014 INSPECTOR (hotel & rest.)
Supervises cleaning personnel and inspects hotel guestrooms, bathrooms, corridors, and lobbies: Assigns work to cleaning personnel and trains personnel in housekeeping duties. Posts room occupancy records. Adjusts guests' complaints regarding housekeeping service or equipment. Writes requisitions for room supplies and furniture renovation or replacements. Reports need for room redecoration to HOUSEKEEPER (hotel & rest.; medical ser.; real estate). Examines carpets, drapes and furniture for stains, damage, or wear. Checks and counts linens and supplies. Records inspection results and notifies cleaning personnel of inadequacies. May perform cleaning duties. May be designated according to area supervised as Floor Supervisor (hotel & rest.).
GOE: 05.12.01 STRENGTH: L GED: R3 M2 L3 SVP: 6 DLU: 77

323 HOUSECLEANERS, HOTELS, RESTAURANTS, AND RELATED ESTABLISHMENTS

This group includes occupations concerned with general cleaning and upkeep in hotels, restaurants, hospitals, and other institutions. Includes heavy duties, such as laying carpets and rugs and arranging furniture, and light duties, such as making beds, dusting furniture and fixtures, and replenishing linens. Includes performing minor personal services for guests.

323.137-010 SUPERVISOR, HOUSECLEANER (hotel & rest.)

Supervises and coordinates activities of personnel engaged in preparing establishment's facilities for banquets and conventions: Assigns duties and instructs workers in collection, assembly, and arrangement of articles for convention or banquet hall and conference rooms, such as furnishings, decorations, displays, microphones, and tableware. Inspects facilities for completeness of arrangements and instructs personnel to correct errors. Prepares daily work assignments roster and maintains work performance records. May perform cleaning duties for banquets and conventions and may interview and hire [HOUSECLEANER (hotel & rest.)].
GOE: 05.12.01 STRENGTH: M GED: R3 M2 L3 SVP: 6 DLU: 77

323.687-010 CLEANER, HOSPITAL (medical ser.) alternate titles: housekeeper, hospital

Cleans hospital patient rooms, baths, laboratories, offices, halls, and other areas: Washes beds and mattresses, and remakes beds after dismissal of patients. Keeps utility and storage rooms in clean and orderly condition. Distributes laundered articles and linens. Replaces soiled drapes and cubicle curtains. Performs other duties as described under CLEANER (any industry) I Master Title. May disinfect and sterilize equipment and supplies, using germicides and sterilizing equipment.
GOE: 05.12.18 STRENGTH: M GED: R2 M1 L2 SVP: 2 DLU: 87

323.687-014 CLEANER, HOUSEKEEPING (any industry) alternate titles: maid

Cleans rooms and halls in commercial establishments, such as hotels, restaurants, clubs, beauty parlors, and dormitories, performing any combination of following duties: Sorts, counts, folds, marks, or carries linens. Makes beds. Replenishes supplies, such as drinking glasses and writing supplies. Checks wraps and renders personal assistance to patrons. Moves furniture, hangs drapes, and rolls carpets. Performs other duties as described under CLEANER (any industry) I Master Title. May be designated according to type of establishment cleaned as Beauty Parlor Cleaner (personal ser.); Motel Cleaner (hotel & rest.); or according to area cleaned as Sleeping Room Cleaner (hotel & rest.).
GOE: 05.12.18 STRENGTH: L GED: R1 M1 L1 SVP: 2 DLU: 86

323.687-018 HOUSECLEANER (hotel & rest.) alternate titles: hall cleaner; mover; night cleaner

Performs any combination of following duties to maintain hotel premises in clean and orderly manner: Moves and arranges furniture. Turns mattresses. Hangs draperies. Dusts venetian blinds. Polishes metalwork. Prepares sample rooms for sales meetings. Arranges decorations, apparatus, or furniture for banquets and social functions. Collects soiled linens for laundering, and receives and stores linen supplies in linen closet. Performs other duties as described under CLEANER (any industry) I Master Title. May deliver television sets, ironing boards, baby cribs, and rollaway beds to guests rooms. May clean swimming pool with vacuum. May clean and remove debris from driveway and garage areas. May be designated according to specialization as Curtain Cleaner (hotel & rest.); Housecleaner, Floor (hotel & rest.); Linen-Room Worker (hotel & rest.); Porter, Lobby (hotel & rest.); Vacuum Worker (hotel & rest.).
GOE: 05.12.18 STRENGTH: H GED: R2 M1 L1 SVP: 2 DLU: 81

324 BELLHOPS AND RELATED OCCUPATIONS

This group includes occupations concerned with catering to wants of guests at a hotel or related establishment, and performing general services, such as escorting guests to rooms, carrying luggage, running errands, delivering ice, beverages, and packages, and paging guests.

324.137-010 BAGGAGE PORTER, HEAD (hotel & rest.)

Supervises and directs activities of PORTERS, BAGGAGE (hotel & rest.) engaged in handling baggage and related work for hotel patrons: Adjusts work schedules according to work load and makes individual task assignments. Advises PORTERS, BAGGAGE (hotel & rest.) of action to be taken in response to unusual requests. Resolves guests' complaints pertaining to conduct of PORTERS, BAGGAGE (hotel & rest.) and lost or mishandled baggage. May perform personnel duties, such as screening, hiring, giving directions to new workers, and maintaining time records. May give travel information. May act as agent for transportation company. May participate in baggage handling activities and setting up sample rooms.
GOE: 09.05.03 STRENGTH: L GED: R3 M3 L3 SVP: 6 DLU: 77

324.137-014 BELL CAPTAIN (hotel & rest.)

Supervises BELLHOPS (hotel & rest.) engaged in duties, such as paging, running errands, and giving information. Calls BELLHOPS (hotel & rest.) to escort guests to rooms or perform related services. Determines work schedules and keeps time records. Inspects workers for neatness and uniform dress. Instructs workers in procedures regarding requests from guests, utilizing knowledge of hotel facilities and local merchants and attractions. Furnishes information, makes reservations, and obtains tickets for guests to social and recreational events or for travel. May report suspicious behavior of patrons to hotel security personnel. May pick up and bundle guests' laundry for outside cleaning service. May perform duties of subordinates.

GOE: 09.05.03 STRENGTH: M GED: R3 M2 L2 SVP: 6 DLU: 77

324.477-010 PORTER, BAGGAGE (hotel & rest.) alternate titles: porter, luggage

Delivers luggage to and from hotel rooms, sets up sample rooms for sales personnel and performs related services as requested by guest or BAGGAGE PORTER, HEAD (hotel & rest.). Transfers trunks, packages, and other baggage to room or loading area, using handtruck. Arranges for outgoing freight, express or mail shipments, computes charges, tags article, and records information, such as addressee, addressor, carrier, and charges, on specified forms. Sets up display tables, racks, or shelves and assists sales personnel in unpacking and arranging merchandise display. May supply guests with travel information, such as transportation rates, routes, and schedules. May escort incoming guest to room [BELLHOP (hotel & rest.)]. May arrange for cleaning, laundering, and repair of guests' clothing and other items. May compute charge slips for services rendered guests and forwards slips to bookkeeping department.
GOE: 09.05.03 STRENGTH: M GED: R2 M2 L2 SVP: 2 DLU: 77

324.577-010 ROOM-SERVICE CLERK (hotel & rest.) alternate titles: delivery-room clerk; package clerk; receiving-room clerk; runner

Performs any combination of following tasks related to serving guests in apartment hotels: Delivers and removes packages, laundry, clothes, groceries, and other articles to and from guests rooms or servidors (cabinets built into doors of hotel rooms). Collects supply orders from various departments and delivers to PURCHASING AGENT (profess. & kin.). Delivers mail to various departments and guests. Records information pertaining to services rendered. May arrange for pressing clothes and shining shoes, sending and receiving packages, and in maintaining valet service. May press clothes and shine shoes [SHOE SHINER (personal ser.)]. May supervise activities of workers engaged in delivering packages to hotel guests.
GOE: 09.05.03 STRENGTH: L GED: R2 M2 L2 SVP: 2 DLU: 77

324.677-010 BELLHOP (hotel & rest.)

Performs any combination of following duties to serve hotel guests: Escorts incoming hotel guests to rooms, assists with hand luggage, and offers information pertaining to available services and facilities of hotel, points of interest, and entertainment attractions. Inspects guest's room to ensure furnishings are in order and supplies are adequate. Explains features of room, such as operation of radio, television, and night-lock, and how to place telephone calls. Pages guests in lobby, dining room, or other parts of hotel. Delivers messages and runs errands. Delivers room service orders. Picks up articles for laundry and valet service. Calls taxi for guests. Transports guests about premises or local areas in car or motorized cart. Keeps record of calls for service. Delivers packages, suitcases, and trunks, and sets up sample rooms [PORTER, BAGGAGE (hotel & rest.) 324.477-010]. Tidies lobby [HOUSECLEANER (hotel & rest.) 323.687-018]. Operates elevator [ELEVATOR OPERATOR (any industry) 388.663-010]. May be known as Page (hotel & rest.) when paging guests.
GOE: 09.05.03 STRENGTH: H GED: R2 M2 L2 SVP: 2 DLU: 81

324.677-014 DOORKEEPER (any industry)

Serves residents, guests, or patrons of hotel, store, apartment building, hospital, or similar establishment by opening doors, hailing taxicabs, answering inquiries, assisting elderly or infirm persons into automobiles, and performing related services. Prevents entrance of unauthorized or undesirable persons. May forcibly eject inebriated or rowdy persons from premises. May notify guests by telephone of delivery of automobiles, packages, or arrival of visitors. May carry baggage.
GOE: 09.05.04 STRENGTH: M GED: R2 M1 L2 SVP: 2 DLU: 77

329 LODGING AND RELATED SERVICE OCCUPATIONS, N.E.C.

This group includes occupations, not elsewhere classified, concerned with providing accommodations to guests in boarding houses, marinas, or lodging houses.

329.137-010 SUPERINTENDENT, SERVICE (hotel & rest.) alternate titles: manager, service; service supervisor; superintendent, house

Supervises and coordinates activities of workers engaged in handling baggage, operating elevators, and cleaning public areas of hotel: Hires workers and makes assignments. Adjusts guests' complaints regarding service personnel. Conducts investigations for lost baggage. May arrange for services, such as stenographic, notary public or baby sitting. May perform tasks of subordinates.
GOE: 09.01.04 STRENGTH: L GED: R3 M3 L3 SVP: 7 DLU: 77

329.161-010 MANAGER, CAMP (amuse. & rec.)

Directs operation of recreation camp and coordinates activities of staff: Inspects camp facilities prior to campers' arrival for condition of pool, buildings, and recreation equipment. Assigns staff to camp maintenance duties in area, such as painting, plumbing, and carpentry; and inspects completed work, utilizing experience and knowledge. Inspects facilities prior to campers' departure to determine damage assessments. Registers and informs campers about camp accommodations and regulations. Prepares and collects fees, and issues receipts.
GOE: 11.11.02 STRENGTH: H GED: R4 M3 L3 SVP: 7 DLU: 86

329.467-010 ATTENDANT, LODGING FACILITIES (hotel & rest.) alternate titles: auto-camp attendant; caretaker, resort; tourist-camp attendant

Performs various clerical, housekeeping, and maintenance duties at tourist camp, motel, trailer park, vacation resort, or lodge: Informs guests concerning services and facilities available. Registers guests, assigns cabins, rooms, or trailer spaces, and collects rents. Issues soap, towels, and other supplies to guests. Sweeps and mops floors, mows lawn, maintains outside recreational areas, and performs other general cleaning and maintenance duties. May service tourists' cars with gasoline, oil, and water. May collect resort admission fees and direct parking of cars.
GOE: 05.10.04 STRENGTH: M GED: R2 M2 L2 SVP: 3 DLU: 77

329.677-010 PORTER, MARINA (water trans.)

Performs any of following services for patrons at dockside: Secures boat to dock with mooring lines. Connects utility lines (telephone, power, and water) to boat. Operates motor vehicle to transport patrons and baggage to and from dockside. Reports disturbances in dock area to superior. May pump water from boats. May deliver ice and written messages to patrons. May police dock area.
GOE: 09.05.03 STRENGTH: M GED: R2 M2 L2 SVP: 3 DLU: 77

329.683-010 ATTENDANT, CAMPGROUND (amuse. & rec.) alternate titles: campground hand;

Performs general maintenance on facilities and grounds at recreational camp or park: Operates riding lawn mower to mow grass. Checks buildings and furnishings, repairs minor damage, using handtools, and reports major repair needs to DIRECTOR, CAMP (social ser.). Replaces light bulbs. Carries and places supplies in storage areas. Cleans swimming pool, using vacuum cleaner and scrub brushes. Measures and pours chemicals into pool water to maintain chemical balance. Performs minor repairs to dock, and keeps lakefront swimming area clean and free from hazards. Drives truck to pick up trash and garbage for delivery to central area.
GOE: 05.12.18 STRENGTH: M GED: R2 M1 L1 SVP: 2 DLU: 77

33 BARBERING, COSMETOLOGY, AND RELATED SERVICE OCCUPATIONS

This division includes occupations concerned with rendering beauty and related treatments to individuals.

330 BARBERS

This group includes occupations concerned with cutting and shaping hair and mustaches, shaving whiskers and trimming beards, and giving facial massages, shampoos, and scalp treatments. Includes fitting hair pieces.

330.371-010 BARBER (personal ser.) alternate titles: haircutter; tonsorial artist

Provides customers with barbering services: Cuts, shapes, trims, and tapers hair, using clippers, comb, blow-out gun, and scissors. Applies lather and shaves beard or shapes hair contour (outline) on temple and neck, using razor. Performs other tonsorial services, such as applying hairdressings or lotions, dyeing, shampooing, singeing, or styling hair, and massaging face, neck, or scalp. Records service charge on ticket or receives payment. Cleans work area and work tools. Orders supplies. May sell lotions, tonics, or other cosmetic supplies.
GOE: 09.02.02 STRENGTH: L GED: R3 M2 L3 SVP: 6 DLU: 81

330.371-014 BARBER APPRENTICE (personal ser.)

Performs duties as described under APPRENTICE (any industry) Master Title.
GOE: 09.02.02 STRENGTH: L GED: R3 M2 L3 SVP: 6 DLU: 77

331 MANICURISTS

This group includes occupations concerned with cleaning, shaping, and polishing fingernails, rubbing lotions on hands and massaging them.

331.674-010 MANICURIST (personal ser.)

Cleans, shapes, and polishes customers' fingernails and toenails: Removes previously applied nail polish, using liquid remover and swabs. Shapes and smooths ends of nails, using scissors, files, and emery boards. Cleans customers' nails in soapy water, using swabs, files, and orange sticks. Softens nail cuticles with water and oil, pushes back cuticles, using cuticle knife, and trims cuticles, using scissors or nippers. Whitens underside of nails with white paste or pencil. Polishes nails, using powdered polish and buffer, or applies clear or colored liquid polish onto nails with brush. May perform other beauty services such as giving facials, and shampooing, tinting, and curling hair [COSMETOLOGIST (personal ser.)].
GOE: 09.05.01 STRENGTH: S GED: R2 M1 L2 SVP: 3 DLU: 77

331.674-014 FINGERNAIL FORMER (personal ser.)

Forms artificial fingernails on customer's fingers: Roughens surfaces of fingernails, using abrasive wheel. Attaches paper forms to tips of customer's fingers to support and shape artificial nails. Brushes coats of powder and solvent onto nails and paper forms with handbrush to extend nails to desired length. Removes paper forms and shapes and smooths edges of nails, using rotary abrasive wheel. Brushes additional powder and solvent onto new growth between cuticles and nails to maintain nail appearance. May soften, trim, or cut cuticles, using oil, water, knife, or scissors, to prepare customer's nails for application of artificial nails.
GOE: 09.05.01 STRENGTH: S GED: R2 M1 L2 SVP: 3 DLU: 86

332 HAIRDRESSERS AND COSMETOLOGISTS

This group includes occupations concerned with waving, cutting, styling, and coloring hair; giving scalp and facial treatments; and performing related tasks to improve the appearance of beauty shop patrons. Includes fitting and servicing wigs.

332.271-010 COSMETOLOGIST (personal ser.) alternate titles: beautician; beauty culturist; beauty operator; cosmetician

Provides beauty services for customers: Analyzes hair to ascertain condition of hair. Applies bleach, dye, or tint, using applicator or brush, to color customer's hair, first applying solution to portion of customer's skin to determine if customer is allergic to solution. Shampoos hair and scalp with water, liquid soap, dry powder, or egg, and rinses hair with vinegar, water, lemon, or prepared rinses. Massages scalp and gives other hair and scalp-conditioning treatments for hygienic or remedial purposes [SCALP-TREATMENT OPERATOR (personal ser.) 339.371-014]. Styles hair by blowing, cutting, trimming, and tapering, using clippers, scissors, razors, and blow-wave gun. Suggests coiffure according to physical features of patron and current styles, or determines coiffure from instructions of patron. Applies water or waving solutions to hair and winds hair around rollers, or pin curls and finger-waves hair. Sets hair by blow-dry or natural-set, or presses hair with straightening comb. Suggests cosmetics for conditions, such as dry or oily skin. Applies lotions and creams to customer's face and neck to soften skin and lubricate tissues. Performs other beauty services, such as massaging face or neck, shaping and coloring eyebrows or eyelashes, removing unwanted hair, applying solutions that straighten hair or retain curls or waves in hair, and waving or curling hair. Cleans, shapes, and polishes fingernails and toenails [MANICURIST (personal ser.) 331.674-010]. May be designated according to beauty service provided as Facial Operator (personal ser.); Finger Waver (personal ser.); Hair Colorist (personal ser.); Hair Tinter (personal ser.); Marceller (personal ser.); Permanent Waver (personal ser.); Shampooer (personal ser.).
GOE: 09.02.01 STRENGTH: L GED: R4 M3 L3 SVP: 6 DLU: 81

332.271-014 COSMETOLOGIST APPRENTICE (personal ser.) alternate titles: beautician apprentice; beauty-culturist apprentice; beauty-operator apprentice; cosmetician apprentice

Performs duties as described under APPRENTICE (any industry) Master Title.
GOE: 09.02.01 STRENGTH: L GED: R4 M3 L3 SVP: 6 DLU: 77

332.271-018 HAIR STYLIST (personal ser.) alternate titles: hairdresser

Specializes in dressing hair according to latest style, period, or character portrayal, following instructions of patron, MAKE-UP ARTIST (amuse. & rec.; motion picture; radio-tv broad.), or script: Questions patron or reads instructions of MAKE-UP ARTIST (amuse. & rec.; motion picture; radio-tv broad.) or script to determine hairdressing requirements. Studies facial features of patron or performing artist and arranges, shapes, and trims hair to achieve desired effect, using fingers, combs, barber scissors, hair-waving solutions, hairpins, and other accessories. Dyes, tints, bleaches, or curls or waves hair as required. May create new style especially for patron. May clean and style wigs. May style hairpieces and be designated Hairpiece Stylist (fabrication, nec).
GOE: 09.02.01 STRENGTH: L GED: R4 M3 L3 SVP: 6 DLU: 77

332.361-010 WIG DRESSER (fabrication, nec; personal ser.) alternate titles: hairdresser

Dresses wigs and hair pieces according to instructions, samples, sketches, or photographs: Attaches wig or hair piece onto model head, using hammer and tacks or pins. Combs and sets hair, using barber and beautician equipment. Arranges hair according to instructions, pictures, or photographs, using brush and comb. Sprays hair with lacquer to keep hair in place. May cut wigs and hair pieces to specified length and style, using scissors or razor. May wash and dry hair pieces.
GOE: 01.06.02 STRENGTH: L GED: R3 M2 L2 SVP: 6 DLU: 77

333 MAKE-UP OCCUPATIONS

This group includes occupations concerned with applying cosmetics to face or exposed body areas of actors and actresses to improve their appearance or to alter their expressions to those of the characters they are portraying.

333.271-010 BODY-MAKE-UP ARTIST (amuse. & rec.; motion picture)

Applies makeup to bodies of performers in color tone and texture to match facial cosmetics: Consults production schedule to plan work. Mixes oils, greases, and coloring to prepared grease paint for special color effects. Selects liquid makeup of desired shade from stock or adds water to cake of powder to form solutions. Applies grease paint, liquid makeup, and powder to exposed areas of bodies, using sponge, fingers, and powder puffs.

GOE: 01.06.02 STRENGTH: L GED: R3 M2 L2 SVP: 4 DLU: 77

334   MASSEURS AND RELATED OCCUPATIONS

This group includes occupations concerned with giving massages to patrons of public baths, beauty parlors, reducing salons, or health clubs, using hands or vibrating equipment.

334.374-010   MASSEUR/MASSEUSE (personal ser.) alternate titles: bath attendant; bath-house attendant; rubber

Massages customers and administers other body conditioning treatments for hygienic or remedial purposes: Applies alcohol, lubricants, or other rubbing compounds. Massages body, using such techniques as kneading, rubbing, and stroking flesh, to stimulate blood circulation, relax contracted muscles, facilitate elimination of waste matter, or to relieve other conditions, using hands or vibrating equipment. Administers steam or dry heat, ultraviolet or infrared, or water treatments on request of customer or instructions of physician. May give directions to clients in activities, such as reducing or remedial exercises. May examine client and recommend body conditioning activities or treatments. May record treatments furnished to customers.
GOE: 09.05.01 STRENGTH: M GED: R3 M2 L3 SVP: 4 DLU: 77

334.677-010   RUBBER (personal ser.) alternate titles: bath attendant

Massages and bathes customers in thermal bathhouse: Kneads, slaps, strokes, and rubs flesh with stiff-bristled brush or brush made of leaves and twigs to increase circulation, relax muscles, and relieve fatigue. Assists customer into tub or onto bench, slab, or table in dry heat or steam room. Adjusts thermostat that regulates flow of heat and turns steam valve or sprinkles water on heated rocks to control temperature and humidity. Splashes soapy water on customer's body, scrubs body with brush, mitt, or sponge to clean skin and remove dead cuticle, and splashes clear water on body to rinse soap from skin. May dry customer after bath, using towel. May supply customer with drinking water or wrap client's head in cold towel during bath [HOT-ROOM ATTENDANT (personal ser.)]. May massage customer after bath, using alcohol and oil, to soothe skin [COOLING-ROOM ATTENDANT (personal ser.)]. May bind leaves and twigs to form brush used in rubdown. May be designated according to type of massage given as Finnish Rubber (personal ser.); Russian Rubber (personal ser.); Turkish Rubber (personal ser.).
GOE: 09.05.01 STRENGTH: M GED: R2 M1 L2 SVP: 2 DLU: 77

335   BATH ATTENDANTS

This group includes occupations concerned with assisting clients of public bath houses to take Russian, Sauna, Turkish, electric cabinet, sweatbox, or steam baths; providing and stocking towels; and checking money and valuables.

335.677-010   COOLING-ROOM ATTENDANT (personal ser.) alternate titles: alcohol rubber; slumber-room attendant

Attends to comfort and needs of thermal bath customers cooling off and resting after bath and massage: Assigns cot to customer. Rubs customer's body with alcohol and oil to soothe skin. Covers customer with sheet. Times length of rest period. Procures beverage, food, or other items on request. May arrange for valet services. May change bedding on cots. May shine shoes [SHOE SHINER (personal ser.)]. May sweep and mop floors and dust furniture [CLEANER, COMMERCIAL OR INSTITUTIONAL (any industry)].
GOE: 09.05.01 STRENGTH: L GED: R2 M1 L2 SVP: 2 DLU: 77

335.677-014   HOT-ROOM ATTENDANT (personal ser.) alternate titles: electric-bath attendant; porter, bath; public-bath attendant; sweat-box attendant; tub attendant

Serves patrons in dry-heat cabinet or room or steamroom of athletic, bathing, or other establishment: Spreads sheet or towel over seating facility in cabinet or rooms and seats patrons. Supplies drinking water and renders other services requested, such as wrapping cool towels about patron's head, spraying body with water, or timing length of bath. Gives shower baths and furnishes towel or dries patron. Collects soiled linen and cleans bathing area and facilities, such as tubs and showers. May turn valves and switches to adjust heating equipment, regulating amount of steam or temperature. May pour water over heated rocks to prepare steamroom. May be designated according to bath facility served as Dry-Heat-Cabinet Attendant (personal ser.); Dry-Heat-Room Attendant (personal ser.); Shower Attendant (personal ser.); Steam-Room Attendant (personal ser.).
GOE: 09.05.01 STRENGTH: L GED: R2 M1 L2 SVP: 2 DLU: 77

338   EMBALMERS AND RELATED OCCUPATIONS

This group includes occupations concerned with preparing corpses for interment.

338.371-010   EMBALMER APPRENTICE (personal ser.)

Performs duties as described under APPRENTICE (any industry) Master Title.
GOE: 02.04.02 STRENGTH: H GED: R4 M4 L4 SVP: 7 DLU: 77

338.371-014   EMBALMER (personal ser.)

Prepares bodies for interment in conformity with legal requirements: Washes and dries body, using germicidal soap and towels or hot air drier. Inserts con-vex celluloid or cotton between eyeball and eyelid to prevent slipping and sinking of eyelid. Presses diaphragm to evacuate air from lungs. May join lips, using needle and thread or wire. Packs body orifices with cotton saturated with embalming fluid to prevent escape of gases or waste matter. Makes incision in arm or thigh, using scalpel, inserts pump tubes into artery, and starts pump that drains blood from circulatory system and replaces blood with embalming fluid. Incises stomach and abdominal walls and probes internal organs, such as bladder and liver, using trocar to withdraw blood and waste matter from organs. Attaches trocar to pump-tube, starts pump, and repeats probing to force embalming fluid into organs. Closes incisions, using needle and suture. Reshapes or reconstructs disfigured or maimed bodies, using materials, such as clay, cotton, plaster of paris, and wax. Applies cosmetics to impart lifelike appearance. Dresses body and places body in casket. May arrange funeral details, such as type of casket or burial dress and place of interment [DIRECTOR, FUNERAL (personal ser.)]. May maintain records, such as itemized list of clothing or valuables delivered with body and names of persons embalmed.
GOE: 02.04.02 STRENGTH: H GED: R4 M4 L4 SVP: 7 DLU: 77

339   BARBERING, COSMETOLOGY, AND RELATED SERVICE OCCUPATIONS, N.E.C.

This group includes occupations, not elsewhere classified, concerned with rendering beauty and related treatments to individuals.

339.137-010   MANAGER, HEALTH CLUB (personal ser.)

Supervises and coordinates activities of workers engaged in planning, selling, and instructing fitness plans for clients of health club: Assigns and adjusts work schedules to meet customer demand. Interviews, hires, and trains new employees. Observes workers in performance of duties and gives remedial training to correct worker deficiencies and ensure courteous service to patrons. Plans and sells figure-controlling programs to prospective patrons. Assists subordinates in interviewing, measuring, and evaluating patrons' physical condition to determine appropriate fitness program. Prepares contract forms, obtains signatures, collects deposits, and issues membership cards to patrons accepting plans. Demonstrates operation and explains purpose of equipment, such as treadmill exerciser and stationary bicycle, and instructs patrons in their use. Monitors patron's exercise program to ensure adherence to specified techniques.
GOE: 11.11.02 STRENGTH: L GED: R4 M3 L4 SVP: 7 DLU: 77

339.361-010   MORTUARY BEAUTICIAN (personal ser.) alternate titles: embalmer assistant; funeral-home attendant

Prepares embalmed bodies for interment: Manicures nails, using files and nail polish, and performs other grooming tasks, such as arching and plucking eyebrows and removing facial hair, using depilatory cream and tweezers. Shampoos, waves, presses, curls, brushes, and combs hair, and applies cosmetics on face to restore natural appearance, following photograph of deceased, or verbal or written description obtained from family. Dresses and arranges body in casket. May select casket or burial dress, arrange floral displays, and prepare obituary notices. May record personal effects delivered with body and information about deceased. May wash and dry bodies, using germicidal soap and towels or hot air drier. May reshape or reconstruct damaged or disfigured areas of body, using such materials as cotton or foam rubber.
GOE: 01.06.02 STRENGTH: M GED: R3 M2 L2 SVP: 6 DLU: 77

339.371-010   ELECTROLOGIST (personal ser.) alternate titles: electric-needle specialist; electrolysis operator; hypertrichologist

Removes hair from skin of patron by electrolysis: Positions sterile bulbous or round-tipped needles into holders (electrodes) of galvanic or short wave electrical equipment. Places secondary electrode in hand or immerses fingers or hand of patron in water-filled electrode cup to complete circuit and stabilize amount of electricity when equipment is operating. Swabs skin area with antiseptic solution to sterilize it. Inserts needle or needles into hair follicle and into organ beneath hair root (papilla). Presses switch and adjusts timing and rheostat controls of equipment that regulate amount of electricity flowing through needle or needles to decompose cells of papilla. Removes needle or needles, and pulls hair from follicle, using tweezers.
GOE: 09.05.01 STRENGTH: L GED: R3 M2 L3 SVP: 5 DLU: 77

339.371-014   SCALP-TREATMENT OPERATOR (personal ser.) alternate titles: hair-and-scalp specialist; scalp specialist; trichologist

Gives hair and scalp conditioning treatments for hygienic or remedial purposes: Massages, shampoos, and steams hair and scalp of patron to clean and remove excess oil, using liquid soap, rinses, and hot towels. Applies medication to and massages scalp to increase blood circulation, stimulate glandular activity, and promote growth of hair, using hands and fingers or vibrating equipment. Administers other remedial treatments to relieve such conditions as dandruff or itching scalp, using such therapeutic equipment as infrared or ultraviolet lamps. Advises patrons with chronic or potentially contagious scalp conditions to seek medical treatment. May maintain treatment records.
GOE: 09.02.01 STRENGTH: L GED: R3 M2 L3 SVP: 5 DLU: 77

339.571-010   TATTOO ARTIST (personal ser.) alternate titles: jagger; tattooer; tattooist

Pricks skin of patron, using needled electric tool, that inserts indelible nontoxic pigment into skin to form decorative or ornamental design: Shaves area to receive tattoo and washes it, using germicidal soap. Presses charcoal-coated stencil, draws design, or traces pattern of design onto skin of patron,

to mark outline of design. Dips needles of tool into colored pigment solution and presses needles into skin to insert indelible pigment into skin following outline of design. Applies sterile dressing to area. Sterilizes needles in steam-heated cabinet (sterilizer). Mixes nontoxic colored pigments according to formula. Adjusts and repairs needled electric tool, using handtools, such as screwdrivers and pliers. May draw original designs on paper, trace designs onto acetate sheet, and cut out design to form pattern or stencil, using stylus and knife.
GOE: 01.06.02 STRENGTH: S GED: R3 M2 L2 SVP: 5 DLU: 77

339.687-010 SUPPLY CLERK (personal ser.) alternate titles: dispensary attendant; storekeeper
Dispenses supplies in beauty parlor or barber shop: Counts, sorts, issues, and collects articles, such as towels, drapes, combs, brushes, curlers, and nets. Washes combs and brushes in antiseptic soap solution and places them in sterilizing cabinet. Dilutes concentrated shampoo, rinses, and waving solutions with water according to instructions. Dissolves cake soap in water to make shampoo. Assembles materials, solutions, and equipment specified for individual treatment, such as facial, permanent wave, and manicure. Maintains perpetual supply inventory and lists items needed to replace stock. Sweeps floor and tidies rooms.
GOE: 05.09.01 STRENGTH: L GED: R2 M2 L1 SVP: 3 DLU: 77

34 AMUSEMENT AND RECREATION SERVICE OCCUPATIONS

This division includes occupations concerned with amusement and recreation services.

340 ATTENDANTS, BOWLING ALLEY AND BILLIARD PARLOR

This group includes occupations concerned with assigning alleys and billiard tables to patrons, collecting fees for games played, setting pins, and preparing billiard tables for playing.

340.367-010 DESK CLERK, BOWLING FLOOR (amuse. & rec.)
Assigns bowling alleys to patrons and collects fees: Reserves alleys for bowling league or individuals. Issues scoresheets and alley numbers to patrons. Inspects alleys to ensure that bowling equipment is available. Observes players to determine misuse of alleys or other equipment. Records number of games played and receipts collected. Rents bowling shoes to patrons.
GOE: 09.04.02 STRENGTH: L GED: R3 M3 L3 SVP: 3 DLU: 77

340.477-010 RACKER (amuse. & rec.) alternate titles: ball racker; pool-room attendant; table attendant
Positions pool balls on table, using triangular rack. Performs such services as supplying chalk to players, cleaning table with brush, and placing cues in cue rack after game. Collects fees from players or writes fees on slips for collection by manager or cashier. May inspect cue tips and replace them, using glue and knife.
GOE: 09.05.05 STRENGTH: L GED: R2 M2 L1 SVP: 2 DLU: 77

341 ATTENDANTS, GOLF COURSE, TENNIS COURT, SKATING RINK, AND RELATED FACILITIES

This group includes occupations concerned with starting players on golf courses, assigning tennis courts, keeping records of players and receiving fees, giving skating instruction, and caddying for golfers. Includes caddies and workers who issue athletic equipment or skates, etc.

341.137-010 CADDIE SUPERVISOR (amuse. & rec.)
Supervises CADDIES (amuse. & rec.) and assigns them to players. May hire, train, and discharge CADDIES (amuse. & rec.). May admit players to course and start their play in order.
GOE: 09.05.06 STRENGTH: L GED: R3 M2 L2 SVP: 6 DLU: 77

341.367-010 RECREATION-FACILITY ATTENDANT (amuse. & rec.)
Schedules use of recreation facilities, such as golf courses, tennis courts, and softball and sandlot diamonds, in accordance with private club or public park rules: Makes reservations for use of facilities by players. Settles disputes between groups or individual players regarding use of facilities. Coordinates use of facilities to prevent players from interfering with one another. May collect fees from players. May inform players of rules concerning dress, conduct, or equipment and enforce rules or eject unruly player or unauthorized persons as necessary. May sell or rent golf and tennis balls, racquets, golf clubs, and other equipment. May render emergency first aid to injured or stricken players. May patrol facilities to detect damage to facilities and report damages to appropriate authority. May be designated according to facility tended as Golf-Course Starter (amuse. & rec.); Tennis-Court Attendant (amuse. & rec.).
GOE: 07.04.03 STRENGTH: L GED: R4 M2 L3 SVP: 3 DLU: 81

341.464-010 SKATE-SHOP ATTENDANT (amuse. & rec.)
Repairs, rents, or sells ice skates and equipment at ice-skating rink: Removes skate blade from shoe, places it in guide frame, and sharpens blade on grinding

wheel. Drills holes in shoe, using electric drill, and bolts blade to shoe, using wrench. Cleans skates with cloth or buffing tool and places them on shelf according to size. Issues skates to patrons and collects ticket or money for rental. Sells merchandise, such as skates, skate guards, and skating apparel.
GOE: 09.04.02 STRENGTH: L GED: R3 M2 L2 SVP: 3 DLU: 77

341.665-010 SKI-TOW OPERATOR (amuse. & rec.) alternate titles: ski-lift operator
Tends gasoline, diesel, or electric lift to transport skiers up slope or mountainside, and collects fares: Pulls levers to start, stop, and adjust speed of lifts, such as rope tow, chair lift, T-bar, or J-bar. Collects or punches ticket for passengers and assists them onto and from lift. May repair and maintain motor and lift equipment.
GOE: 09.05.08 STRENGTH: L GED: R3 M2 L3 SVP: 3 DLU: 77

341.677-010 CADDIE (amuse. & rec.) alternate titles: golf caddie
Carries golf bags or pushes or pulls cart that holds golf bags around golf course for players, handing clubs to players as requested: Advises players, as requested, on selection of proper club for stroke or concerning peculiarities of course. Locates driven balls and holds marker out of cup while players putt.
GOE: 09.05.06 STRENGTH: M GED: R2 M2 L2 SVP: 2 DLU: 77

341.683-010 GOLF-RANGE ATTENDANT (amuse. & rec.)
Performs combination of following duties at golf driving range: Picks up golf balls by hand or drives vehicle equipped with trailer that automatically picks up balls as vehicle moves over fairway. Starts revolving tumbler filled with soapy water and immerses golf balls to remove dirt, grass stain, and club marks. Removes and rinses washed balls. Applies liquid cleaner to head and shank of golf clubs and buffs with steel wool. Replaces golf balls and clubs in racks for use by driving range patrons. May perform minor maintenance on benches, using handtools.
GOE: 05.12.18 STRENGTH: M GED: R2 M1 L2 SVP: 2 DLU: 77

342 AMUSEMENT DEVICE AND CONCESSION ATTENDANTS

This group includes occupations concerned with operating games of chance or skill or other types of amusement equipment, such as the ferris wheel, roller coaster, and merry-go-round; and running fairs, carnivals, circuses, or amusement parks. Includes spielers or barkers who solicit patronage.

342.137-010 SUPERVISOR, RIDES (amuse. & rec.)
Supervises and coordinates activities of workers engaged in operating or tending rides in amusement parks, carnivals or similar recreational establishments. Inspects ride equipment for operating condition and safety. Trains workers and performs other duties as described under SUPERVISOR (any industry) Master Title.
GOE: 05.10.02 STRENGTH: L GED: R4 M3 L3 SVP: 7 DLU: 77

342.357-010 WEIGHT GUESSER (amuse. & rec.)
Guesses weight of patrons at amusement park, carnival, or similar place of entertainment: Attracts attention of passing public, vociferously proclaiming game and skill. Scrutinizes patron's physique and makes oral estimate of weight. Invites patron to stand on scale or to sit in seat attached to industrial scale, usually forfeiting prize if weight guessed is not correct within 2 or 3 pounds. May demonstrate personal skill in guessing patron's age, occupation, home state, or other related pertinent data.
GOE: 01.07.03 STRENGTH: L GED: R3 M2 L3 SVP: 2 DLU: 77

342.657-010 BARKER (amuse. & rec.) alternate titles: carney; spieler
Attempts to attract patrons to entertainment by exhorting passing public, describing attractions of show and emphasizing variety, novelty, beauty, or some other feature believed to incite listeners to attend entertainment. May conduct brief free show, introducing performers and describing acts to be given at feature performance.
GOE: 01.07.02 STRENGTH: L GED: R3 M2 L3 SVP: 2 DLU: 77

342.657-014 GAME ATTENDANT (amuse. & rec.) alternate titles: game operator
Induces customers to participate in games at concession booths in parks, carnivals, stadiums, or similar amusement places: Describes types of games available to passing public to attract customers. Supplies customers with game equipment, such as toss rings or balls, distributes prizes to customers who win games, and collects fees for services. Cleans and repairs booth and keeps equipment in serviceable condition. May be designated according to type of game operated as Shooting Gallery Operator (amuse. & rec.).
GOE: 09.04.02 STRENGTH: L GED: R3 M3 L3 SVP: 3 DLU: 78

342.663-010 RIDE OPERATOR (amuse. & rec.) alternate titles: amusement-equipment operator
Operates or informs patrons how to operate mechanical riding devices furnished by amusement parks, carnivals, or similar places of entertainment: Informs patron to fasten belt, bar, or other safety device. Moves controls to start and stop equipment, such as roller coaster, merry-go-round, and ferris wheel. Gives directions to patrons, usually over microphone, regarding safety and operation of such rides as midget autos and speedboats. Turns on current to permit operation of ride by patron and turns off current after allotted time. Drives vehicles, such as trains, on which persons ride, guiding and controlling their

speed. Adds to or removes equipment, according to amount of patronage. Oils, refuels, adjusts, and repairs device. Tests equipment daily before opening ride to patrons. May notify patron of expiration of period for which fee was paid to use device. May observe patrons boarding vehicle to ensure they are safely seated without being overcrowded and safety belts or bars are secure. May collect tickets or cash fares from patrons. May space rides operated in cars or sections to avoid danger of collisions. May be designated according to equipment operated as Auto-Speedway Operator (amuse. & rec.); Ferris-Wheel Operator (amuse. & rec.); Flume-Ride Operator (amuse. & rec.); Merry-Go-Round Operator (amuse. & rec.); Monorail Operator (amuse. & rec.); Railroad Operator (amuse. & rec.); Roller-Coaster Operator (amuse. & rec.); Speedboat Operator (amuse. & rec.); Swing-Ride Operator (amuse. & rec.); Train Operator (amuse. & rec.); Whip Operator (amuse. & rec.).
GOE: 05.10.02 STRENGTH: L GED: R2 M2 L2 SVP: 3 DLU: 79

342.665-010 FUN-HOUSE OPERATOR (amuse. & rec.) alternate titles: walk-through operator
Tends one or several pieces of automatic equipment designed to amuse, excite, or mystify patrons of fun house in amusement park: Switches on device that automatically blows blasts of air under women's skirts. Starts revolving turntables, conveyor belt, drum or similar device. Ejects rowdy persons from establishment. Observes equipment for efficient operation and repairs minor breakdowns in equipment.
GOE: 05.12.15 STRENGTH: L GED: R3 M1 L2 SVP: 3 DLU: 77

342.667-010 WHARF ATTENDANT (amuse. & rec.) alternate titles: boat-ride operator; dock attendant
Launches and moors boats on lake or similar amusement place and shows patrons how to guide crafts, such as rowboats, canoes, and electric or gasoline motorboats: Assists patrons stepping in or out of boats. Takes tickets from patrons. Demonstrates how to row, paddle, or guide boats. Tows disabled boats to dock for repair. Changes batteries of electric motorboats and refuels gasoline motors. Cleans, paints, varnishes, and makes minor repairs on motors, using handtools, to maintain boats in good condition. When working in boat-tank facility of amusement park, is designated Boat-Tank Attendant (amuse. & rec.). See BOAT-RENTAL CLERK (amuse. & rec.) for rental of canoes, motorboats, rowboats, sailboats, and fishing equipment.
GOE: 09.04.02 STRENGTH: M GED: R3 M2 L3 SVP: 3 DLU: 77

342.667-014 ATTENDANT, ARCADE (amuse. & rec.)
Assists patrons of amusement facility, and performs minor repairs on game machines: Explains operation of game machines to patrons and exchanges coins for paper currency. Listens to patron complaints regarding malfunction of machines. Removes coin accepter mechanism of machines, using key, and observes mechanism to detect causes of malfunctions, such as bent coins, slugs, or foreign material. Removes obstructions, repositions mechanism, inserts coins, and observes machine operation to determine whether malfunctions are still present. Places out-of-order signs on defective machines and returns money lost in defective machines to patrons. Notifies maintenance department of defective machines, and records times of machine malfunctions and repairs to maintain required records. Observes conduct of patrons in facility to ensure orderliness, and asks disruptive patrons to leave.
GOE: 09.04.02 STRENGTH: L GED: R2 M2 L2 SVP: 2 DLU: 86

342.677-010 RIDE ATTENDANT (amuse. & rec.)
Directs patrons of amusement park in getting on and off riding device: Erects barrier in front of ride, admitting only as many persons to loading platform as can be seated on ride. Keeps order among patrons waiting to ride device. Fastens patrons' safety belts or bars to prevent injuries during ride. Assists children and elderly patrons from ride. Directs patrons from unloading platform to park grounds. May space rides operated in cars or sections to avoid danger of collisions. May collect tickets or cash fares. May clean and polish equipment and perform other minor maintenance work, such as replacing light bulbs.
GOE: 09.05.08 STRENGTH: L GED: R2 M1 L2 SVP: 2 DLU: 77

343 GAMBLING HALL ATTENDANTS

This group includes occupations concerned with running games of chance in gambling establishments. Includes dealing cards or providing other gambling equipment.

343.137-010 MANAGER, CARDROOM (amuse. & rec.)
Supervises and coordinates activities of GAMBLING DEALERS (amuse. & rec.); CARD PLAYERS (amuse. & rec.); BOARD ATTENDANTS (amuse. & rec.); and other workers engaged in providing gambling activities in a gambling establishment: Prepares work schedule for gambling establishment workers and assigns work stations. Supervises overall operation to ensure that employees render prompt and courteous service to patrons. Resolves customer-service complaints and settles matters requiring explanation and interpretation of house rules. Reviews operational expenses and budget estimates. Trains new workers and evaluates their performance.
GOE: 11.11.02 STRENGTH: L GED: R4 M4 L4 SVP: 7 DLU: 77

343.137-014 SUPERVISOR, CARDROOM (amuse. & rec.)
Supervises and coordinates activities of CARDROOM ATTENDANTS (amuse. & rec.) I engaged in selling gambling chips, collecting house fees, and serving food and beverages to patrons of cardroom: Assigns workers to serve patrons at designated group of card tables. Examines collection reports, submitted for approval by workers, for accuracy and timeliness. Explains and interprets operating rules of house to patrons. Circulates among tables and observes operations to ensure player harmony and adjust service complaints. Notifies BOARD ATTENDANT (amuse. & rec.) of vacancies at tables so that waiting patrons may play.
GOE: 09.04.02 STRENGTH: L GED: R4 M4 L4 SVP: 6 DLU: 77

343.367-010 CARD PLAYER (amuse. & rec.) alternate titles: proposition player; public-relations player; shill; stakes player
Participates in card game, usually poker, for gambling establishment to provide minimum complement of players at table. Relinquishes seat on arrival of patron desiring to play cards.
GOE: 09.04.02 STRENGTH: S GED: R3 M2 L2 SVP: 4 DLU: 77

343.367-014 GAMBLING MONITOR (amuse. & rec.)
Observes patrons and employees participating in gambling activities to detect infractions of house rules: Watches participants in games such as dice or cards to detect cheating, identify rule violators, and observe persons designated by superior. Speaks or signals to supervising personnel using hand, telephone, or voice to identify and supply information about suspected violators. May examine dice periodically to check for damage or substitution. May calculate winnings to verify payment made by dealer.
GOE: 04.02.03 STRENGTH: L GED: R4 M3 L3 SVP: 7 DLU: 77

343.464-010 GAMBLING DEALER (amuse. & rec.)
Conducts gambling table, such as dice, roulette, or cards, in gambling establishment: Exchanges paper currency for playing chips or coin money. Ensures that wagers are placed before cards are dealt, roulette wheel is spun, or dice are tossed. Announces winning number or color to players. Computes payable odds to pay winning bets. Pays winning bets and collects losing bets. May be designated according to specialty as Baccarat Dealer (amuse. & rec.); Dice Dealer (amuse. & rec.); Roulette Dealer (amuse. & rec.); Twenty-One Dealer (amuse. & rec.).
GOE: 09.04.02 STRENGTH: L GED: R3 M3 L2 SVP: 5 DLU: 86

343.467-010 CARDROOM ATTENDANT I (amuse. & rec.) alternate titles: chip
Collects house fees from players and sells gambling chips, food, beverages, and tobacco in cardroom: Collects specified house fees periodically from card players. Prepares collection report for submission to supervisor. Sells gambling chips, food, beverages and tobacco to accommodate players upon request. May distribute new card decks to players as required. May explain and interpret operating rules of house to patrons requesting information.
GOE: 09.04.02 STRENGTH: L GED: R3 M2 L2 SVP: 4 DLU: 77

343.467-014 FLOOR ATTENDANT (amuse. & rec.)
Verifies winning bingo cards to award prize or pay prize money to players holding winning cards: Collects money (fee) for participation in game and issues game cards to players. Listens for shouts or looks for waving arms from players who have winning cards. Compares numbers on card with numbers called and displayed on board to verify winning cards. Gives prize or pays money to players holding winning cards.
GOE: 09.04.02 STRENGTH: L GED: R2 M1 L1 SVP: 2 DLU: 77

343.467-022 KENO WRITER (amuse. & rec.)
Conducts keno game in gambling establishment: Receives, verifies, and records cash wagers of customers. Starts gaming equipment that randomly selects numbered balls. Announces number of each ball selected until number of balls specified for each game is selected. Scans winning tickets presented by customers, calculates amount of winnings, and pays customers, utilizing knowledge of rules and payoffs of game.
GOE: 09.04.02 STRENGTH: L GED: R3 M3 L3 SVP: 4 DLU: 86

343.577-010 CARDROOM ATTENDANT II (amuse. & rec.)
Seats cardroom patrons: Takes name of patron requesting seat at table and adds name, with chalk, to waiting list on board. Pages customer over loudspeaker when notified by SUPERVISOR, CARDROOM (amuse. & rec.) that seat is available.
GOE: 09.05.05 STRENGTH: L GED: R2 M1 L2 SVP: 2 DLU: 77

343.687-010 PLASTIC-CARD GRADER, CARDROOM (amuse. & rec.) alternate titles: card grader
Examines plastic playing cards for reuse by patrons of public cardroom: Inspects cards for defects, such as scratches, cuts, and discoloration. Replaces defective cards with those matching others of deck in color, size, and pattern. Feels each card of deck for uniform thickness. Counts, sorts, and repackages cards in box. Grades decks according to condition and approximate usage.
GOE: 06.03.02 STRENGTH: S GED: R2 M1 L2 SVP: 4 DLU: 77

344 USHERS

This group includes occupations concerned with taking tickets, distributing programs, and escorting patrons to seats in public places.

344.137-010 USHER, HEAD (amuse. & rec.)
Supervises and coordinates activities of USHERS (amuse. & rec.) at entertainment events and directs patrons to area of seat location: Directs USHERS (amuse. & rec.) in job duties and assigns to work stations. Directs patrons to

area of seat location according to information on ticket stubs. Resolves complaints of patrons. Coordinates activities in emergencies such as fights or fires. May hire and discharge USHERS (amuse. & rec.). May keep records of workers' time.
GOE: 09.05.08 STRENGTH: L GED: R3 M2 L3 SVP: 4 DLU: 77

344.667-010 TICKET TAKER (amuse. & rec.)
Collects admission tickets and passes from patrons at entertainment events: Examines ticket or pass to verify authenticity, using criteria such as color and date issued. Refuses admitance to patrons without ticket or pass, or who are undesirable for reasons, such as intoxication or improper attire. May direct patrons to their seats. May distribute door checks to patrons temporarily leaving establishment. May count and record number of tickets collected. May issue and collect completed release forms for hazardous events, and photograph patron with release form for permanent records file. May be designated Gate Attendant (amuse. & rec.) or Turnstile Attendant (amuse. & rec.) when collecting tickets at open-air event.
GOE: 09.05.08 STRENGTH: L GED: R2 M1 L2 SVP: 2 DLU: 80

344.677-010 PRESS-BOX CUSTODIAN (amuse. & rec.)
Verifies credentials of patrons desiring entrance into press-box and permits only authorized persons to enter. Runs errands for patrons of press-box, performing such duties as obtaining refreshments, carrying news releases, and placing wagers.
GOE: 09.05.04 STRENGTH: L GED: R2 M1 L2 SVP: 2 DLU: 77

344.677-014 USHER (amuse. & rec.)
Assists patrons at entertainment events to find seats, search for lost articles, and locate facilities, such as restrooms and telephones. Distributes programs to patrons. Assists other workers to change advertising display.
GOE: 09.05.08 STRENGTH: L GED: R2 M1 L1 SVP: 2 DLU: 81

346 WARDROBE AND DRESSING-ROOM ATTENDANTS

This group includes occupations concerned with caring for costumes of entertainers, distributing them, keeping records of those issued and returned, and assisting entertainers in dressing.

346.261-010 COSTUMER (motion picture; radio-tv broad.)
Selects and fits costumes for cast members according to style of historical period and characters to be portrayed: Analyzes script or reviews analysis of SUPERVISOR, COSTUMING (motion picture; radio-tv broad.) to determine locale of story and number of costumes required for each character. Studies books, pictures, and examples of costumes to determine styles worn during specified period in history. Inventories stock to determine types and condition of costuming available and selects costumes based on script analysis and studies. Examines costume on cast member and sketches or writes notes designating alterations. Makes minor alterations and repairs to costume by hand, or using sewing machine. Sends costume to tailor for major alterations or repairs. May design and construct unusual costumes, applying creative ingenuity. May press and spot-clean costumes, using electric iron and cleaning fluid. May purchase or rent costumes and other wardrobe accessories.
GOE: 01.06.02 STRENGTH: L GED: R4 M3 L4 SVP: 7 DLU: 77

346.361-010 WARDROBE SUPERVISOR (amuse. & rec.)
Attends to costumes of members of cast of theatrical production: Examines costumes and cleans and mends them. Presses costumes, using electric iron. Refits costumes as necessary. Assists cast to don completed costumes, or assigns DRESSERS (amuse. & rec.) to assist specific cast members. Arranges costumes, or assigns DRESSERS (amuse. & rec.) to arrange costumes of cast on dress racks in sequence to appearance on stage to facilitate quick changes. Packs costumes for cast when accompanying them on tour.
GOE: 09.05.07 STRENGTH: L GED: R3 M2 L3 SVP: 7 DLU: 77

346.374-010 COSTUMER ASSISTANT (motion picture; radio-tv broad.) alternate titles: custodian, wardrobe; wardrobe draper
Assists COSTUMER (motion picture; radio-tv broad.) 346.261-010 in selecting costumes for and fitting them to performers: Distributes costumes and wardrobe accessories to principals, extras, and bit players. Alters, repairs, presses, and spot-cleans costumes by hand or using sewing machine, electric iron, and cleaning fluid. Keeps records of costumes issued and returned.
GOE: 09.05.07 STRENGTH: L GED: R3 M2 L3 SVP: 4 DLU: 77

346.667-010 JOCKEY-ROOM CUSTODIAN (amuse. & rec.)
Ensures that JOCKEYS (amuse. & rec.) scheduled to ride are present in jockey room at racetrack and that their dress and riding equipment meet track specifications: Notifies JOCKEYS (amuse. & rec.) when to dress. Inspects JOCKEYS (amuse. & rec.) for specified colors (silks), saddle numbers, and riding equipment. Informs STEWARD, RACETRACK (amuse. & rec.) of JOCKEYS (amuse. & rec.) not reporting to prepare for race. Maintains order in jockey room. Examines lead pads to determine that they meet track specifications. Gives directions to workers to clean jockey room.
GOE: 12.01.02 STRENGTH: L GED: R2 M1 L2 SVP: 3 DLU: 77

346.674-010 DRESSER (amuse. & rec.)
Aids entertainer to dress and attends to clothing and costumes: Arranges costumes in order of use. Unpacks clothes and costumes and places them for con-

venient use. Cleans spots from apparel. Presses costumes. Mends ripped seams or makes other minor repairs. May arrange for cleaning, pressing or laundering of costumes.
GOE: 09.05.06 STRENGTH: L GED: R2 M2 L2 SVP: 3 DLU: 77

346.677-010 JOCKEY VALET (amuse. & rec.)
Attends to JOCKEY (amuse. & rec.) at racetrack performing variety of services: Saddles horse and inserts lead pads in saddle pockets to meet weight specifications for race. Places number on saddle to correspond with horse's entry number in race. Reads color assignment chart and obtains specific colors of silks from color room corresponding to stable colors. Assists JOCKEY (amuse. & rec.) to dress for race. Unsaddles horse after race and returns riding equipment to storage area. Cleans saddles, washes silks, and shines boots for JOCKEY (amuse. & rec.).
GOE: 09.05.06 STRENGTH: L GED: R2 M2 L2 SVP: 3 DLU: 77

346.677-014 RIDING-SILKS CUSTODIAN (amuse. & rec.) alternate titles: colors custodian
Issues designated riding silks (colors) and identifying arm and saddle numbers to JOCKEYS (amuse. & rec.) before each race, according to colors and numbers printed on program. Collects and stores silks and numbers after each race. Issues jackets to LEAD PONY RIDERS (amuse. & rec.). Sends out soiled silks and jackets for cleaning.
GOE: 09.05.07 STRENGTH: L GED: R2 M1 L1 SVP: 2 DLU: 77

346.677-018 SECOND (amuse. & rec.)
Serves prizefighter between rounds by giving drinking water, sponging with water, and fanning with towel. Applies medications to minor injuries, such as cuts and bruises.
GOE: 09.05.01 STRENGTH: L GED: R2 M1 L1 SVP: 2 DLU: 77

349 AMUSEMENT AND RECREATION SERVICE OCCUPATIONS, N.E.C.

This group includes occupations, not elsewhere classified, concerned with amusement and recreation services.

349.224-010 ANIMAL-RIDE MANAGER (amuse. & rec.)
Manages stable of animals, trains animals for riding, and supervises workers engaged in handling and attending animals, selling rides, and assisting patrons to ride animals: Purchases animals, feed and supplies. Examines animals for injury or symptoms of illness and arranges for veterinarian services when required. Trains animals for riding, performing tasks, such as teaching animals to walk, trot or gallop. Inspects facilities for cleanliness. Supervises and coordinates workers engaged in feeding, watering, grooming, harnessing and training animals, selling rides and assisting patrons to mount and ride animals.
GOE: 03.03.01 STRENGTH: M GED: R4 M3 L3 SVP: 6 DLU: 77

349.247-010 DIVER (amuse. & rec.)
Feeds, describes, and identifies fish enclosed in aquarium or community fish tank for public amusement: Dons diving suit and helmet and drops to floor of tank to feed fish on scheduled show periods. Circulates among fish and delivers running commentary over sound system to amuse audience. Identifies for audience species of fish being fed, such as bat rays, sawfish, and sharks, and describes briefly life history of individual specimens, based on prepared text. Cleans bottom of tank, using suction hose, and clears algae from windows inside tank, using scrubbing brushes. Observes and reports diseased, injured, or dead fish. Gives routine medical treatment to fish as directed.
GOE: 01.07.02 STRENGTH: M GED: R3 M2 L3 SVP: 4 DLU: 77

349.367-010 KENNEL MANAGER, DOG TRACK (amuse. & rec.)
Verifies credentials and starting position of dogs in races and guards dogs against injury and illegal acts: Verifies credentials of each dog entered in race, comparing color, name, and sex of dog and name of owner with information on racing form. Ensures that dogs are admitted to assigned stalls, notifying other workers to round up designated dogs in advance of each race. Guards dogs to prevent persons from injuring them or attempting illegally to influence dog's performance. Notifies owner or veterinary personnel in cases of injury or suspected illness. Notifies track officials of irregularities as required by racing regulations. May clean racinng stalls after each race, using disinfectant solution.
GOE: 12.01.02 STRENGTH: L GED: R3 M1 L2 SVP: 6 DLU: 77

349.367-014 RECEIVING-BARN CUSTODIAN (amuse. & rec.)
Verifies credentials of persons at receiving barn of racetrack and notifies STABLE ATTENDANTS (any industry) to bring horses scheduled to race, to barn for examination and inspection: Compares credentials of persons requesting admittance with list of names authorized. Informs STABLE ATTENDANTS (any industry) to bring racehorses to receiving barn for examination and inspection by VETERINARIAN (medical ser.), HOOF AND SHOE INSPECTOR (amuse. & rec.), and IDENTIFIER, HORSE (amuse. & rec.). Notifies LEAD PONY RIDERS (amuse. & rec.) to lead racehorses to paddock for saddling. Informs racing officials of horses not meeting racing specifications or not present for examination and inspection. Issues instructions to workers to clean stable and barn area.
GOE: 09.05.04 STRENGTH: L GED: R3 M2 L3 SVP: 3 DLU: 77

349.477-010 JINRIKISHA DRIVER (amuse. & rec.) alternate titles: rickshaw driver
Conveys passengers to destinations, using three-wheeled vehicle: Pumps pedals and turns handlebars to propel and steer vehicle along roadway to attract

and convey passengers for novelty rides. Assists passengers into carriage of vehicle and asks their destination. Records time or odometer reading at start of trip. Conveys passengers to specified destination. Computes fare according to miles traveled or time expended and collects payment.
GOE: 01.07.03 STRENGTH: M GED: R2 M2 L2 SVP: 1 DLU: 86

349.664-010 AMUSEMENT PARK WORKER (amuse. & rec.)
Performs any combination of following duties in amusement park: Escorts patrons on tours of park's points of interest. Takes pictures of patrons to impart pictures onto T-shirts, using camera, automatic printing equipment, and heating press. Maintains and distributes uniforms worn by park employees. Cleans park grounds, office facilities, and rest room areas, using broom, dust pan, or vacuum cleaner. Distributes literature, such as maps, show schedules, and pass information, to acquaint visitors with park facilities. Monitors activities of children using park playground area to ensure safe use of equipment. Directs patrons to seats for park attractions and opens doors to assist patrons' entry and exit from attractions. Receives cash for tickets or items sold to patrons and records sales, using cash register.
GOE: 09.01.01 STRENGTH: M GED: R2 M2 L2 SVP: 2 DLU: 86

349.665-010 SCOREBOARD OPERATOR (amuse. & rec.)
Watches players and officials at athletic event and posts or moves indicators and buttons to record progress of game on scoreboard to inform spectators. Confers, by telephone, with ANNOUNCER (amuse. & rec.) or sideline officials to verify observation of plays.
GOE: 07.04.05 STRENGTH: S GED: R3 M2 L3 SVP: 2 DLU: 77

349.667-010 HOST/HOSTESS, DANCE HALL (amuse. & rec.)
Participates, as social partner, in dancing, dining, drinking, conversation with patrons to increase business of public dancehall. Collects tickets or fees from patrons for time spent in their company. Counts number of tickets collected from patrons and submits tickets to management for pay computation at end of shift.
GOE: 09.01.01 STRENGTH: L GED: R2 M2 L2 SVP: 2 DLU: 77

349.667-014 HOST/HOSTESS, HEAD (amuse. & rec.)
Introduces unaccompanied persons at dancehall to HOSTS/HOSTESSES, DANCE HALL (amuse. & rec.), explaining procedure of engaging social partner. Inspects dress of HOSTS/HOSTESSES, DANCE HALL (amuse. & rec.) to ensure that they present clean and pleasing personal appearance. Attempts to distribute patrons equally among HOSTS/HOSTESSES, DANCE HALL (amuse. & rec.).
GOE: 09.01.01 STRENGTH: L GED: R3 M2 L3 SVP: 2 DLU: 77

349.673-010 DRIVE-IN THEATER ATTENDANT (amuse. & rec.) alternate titles: field attendant
Performs any combination of following duties in rendering services to patrons of drive-in theaters: Greets patrons desiring to attend theater. Collects admission fee and purchases ticket for patron from TICKET SELLER (clerical). Parks car or directs patron to parking space, indicating available space with flashlight. Patrols theater on foot or bicycle to prevent disorderly conduct, rowdiness, or to detect other infractions of rules. Watches over children in playground during intermission. Serves patrons at refreshment stand during intermission. May attach loudspeaker to automobile door and turn controls to adjust volume.
GOE: 09.05.04 STRENGTH: L GED: R2 M1 L2 SVP: 2 DLU: 77

349.674-010 ANIMAL-RIDE ATTENDANT (amuse. & rec.)
Assists patrons to mount and ride animals, collects payment for ride, and attends animals in amusement facility: Selects animal to be ridden on basis of size and age of patron. Accepts payment for ride. Assists patron to mount and ride animal, performing tasks, such as lifting child into saddle, explaining safe riding techniques, leading animal, and observing patron to detect uneasiness or handling difficulty. Attends animals, performing tasks, such as harnessing, saddling, feeding, watering, grooming, observing symptoms of illness, and cleaning stable. May be designated according to type of animal ridden as Pony-Ride Attendant (amuse. & rec.).
GOE: 03.03.02 STRENGTH: H GED: R3 M1 L2 SVP: 2 DLU: 77

349.677-010 CABANA ATTENDANT (amuse. & rec.)
Performs combination of following tasks to serve patrons of private beach, club, or swimming pool having individual cabanas (bathhouses): Issues or rents swimsuits, bathing caps, soap, towels, umbrellas, beach chairs, and similar items. Obtains and serves refreshments to guests as requested. Collects soiled towels and rented swimming attire for laundering. Folds and stores chairs, blankets, and umbrellas at sundown. Picks up rubbish along beach or near pool. Participates in draining, cleaning, and refilling pool and changing pool filters.
GOE: 09.04.02 STRENGTH: L GED: R2 M2 L2 SVP: 3 DLU: 77

349.677-014 COACH DRIVER (business ser.)
Drives horse-drawn vehicle to provide background or special effects for activities such as advertising promotions, political campaigns, or wedding parties; or to transport passengers for purposes such as sightseeing or hay rides. Dons costume for occasion. May feed, water, harness and attend horses. May clean or polish vehicle such as carriage, wagon or cart.
GOE: 01.07.03 STRENGTH: L GED: R3 M1 L1 SVP: 3 DLU: 77

349.677-018 CHILDREN'S ATTENDANT (amuse. & rec.)
Monitors behavior of unaccompanied children in children's section of theater to maintain order: Escorts children who are unaccompanied by adult between theater entrance and children's section when children enter or leave theater. Maintains order among children and searches for lost articles. Notes when each child enters section and reminds child to go home after witnessing complete performance.
GOE: 09.05.08 STRENGTH: L GED: R2 M1 L1 SVP: 2 DLU: 86

349.680-010 TICKET-DISPENSER CHANGER (amuse. & rec.)
Changes code slugs (printing dies) and installs rolls of ticket tape in ticket dispensing machine before each race at racetrack: Unlocks machine with key and turns knob to reset number register to zero. Changes code slug so that different symbols are printed on tickets. Replaces depleted roll of ticket tape, threading end of tape through feed roller to type roller. Presses key of machine to obtain sample ticket. Examines ticket to ascertain that machine is printing correctly and adjusts machine to correct defects. Relocks machine.
GOE: 05.12.15 STRENGTH: L GED: R3 M2 L2 SVP: 3 DLU: 77

35   MISCELLANEOUS PERSONAL SERVICE OCCUPATIONS

This division includes occupations concerned with those duties performed by stewards and hostesses, not elsewhere classified, and attendants, guides, and the like.

350   SHIP STEWARDS/STEWARDESSES AND RELATED OCCUPATIONS

This group includes occupations concerned with serving passengers and crewmembers on cargo, passenger, or other vessels. Includes serving food and beverages in dining salon or on deck, and caring for staterooms, bathrooms, and public rooms.

350.137-010 HEADWAITER/HEADWAITRESS (water trans.)
Supervises and coordinates activities of dining room personnel to serve food aboard ship: Assigns duties, work stations, and responsibilities to personnel and directs their performances. Inspects dining tables and work areas for cleanliness. Greets patrons and shows them to dining tables. Requisitions supplies, such as glassware, china, and silverware. Authorizes personnel to work overtime. May suggest entrees, dinner courses, and wines to guests. May serve wine [STEWARD/STEWARDESS, WINE (water trans.)].
GOE: 09.01.03 STRENGTH: L GED: R3 M2 L3 SVP: 7 DLU: 77

350.137-014 STEWARD/STEWARDESS, CHIEF, CARGO VESSEL (water trans.)
Supervises and coordinates activities of personnel in steward's department aboard cargo vessel: Collaborates with COOK, CHIEF (water trans.) to plan menus. Requisitions and purchases expendable equipment and subsistence and sundry stores. Receives, checks, and issues stores. Inventories supplies. Authorizes personnel to work overtime. Estimates food costs per serving. Compiles supply, overtime, and cost control records.
GOE: 07.01.02 STRENGTH: L GED: R4 M3 L3 SVP: 7 DLU: 77

350.137-018 STEWARD/STEWARDESS, CHIEF, PASSENGER SHIP (water trans.)
Supervises and coordinates activities of personnel in steward's department aboard passenger vessel: Supervises workers engaged in housekeeping and meal serving. Arranges space for shipboard recreation activities. Inspects passenger areas for cleanliness. Observes services rendered by steward personnel for conformance to company standards. Collaborates with CHEF, PASSENGER VESSEL (water trans.) to plan menus. Requisitions stores, such as food, sundries, and furniture. Obtains replacements for personnel leaving ship.
GOE: 05.12.01 STRENGTH: L GED: R4 M3 L3 SVP: 7 DLU: 77

350.137-022 STEWARD/STEWARDESS, SECOND (water trans.)
Supervises and coordinates activities of workers engaged in providing accommodation services to first class passengers: Assigns personnel to work stations in passenger areas, such as staterooms, lounges, deck, and smokeroom and informs them of duties and responsibilities to passengers. Inspects work areas with STEWARD/STEWARDESS, CHIEF, PASSENGER SHIP (water trans.) to ascertain that service given passengers is in accordance with company standards. Coordinates work assignments so that additional help is available for recreational activities. May be designated according to shift worked as Second Steward/Stewardess, Night (water trans.); or according to class of passengers served as Steward/Stewardess, Economy Class (water trans.); Steward/Stewardess, Second Class (water trans.); Steward/Stewardess, Third Class (water trans.); Steward/Stewardess, Tourist Class (water trans.).
GOE: 09.01.04 STRENGTH: L GED: R4 M2 L3 SVP: 7 DLU: 77

350.137-026 STEWARD/STEWARDESS, THIRD (water trans.)
Supervises and coordinates activities of workers engaged in providing housekeeping services to officers and crew: Assigns personnel to work stations, such as officers' and crew's quarters, and messrooms. Inspects work stations for cleanliness. Requisitions stores, such as soap, scrubbing brushes, and mops.
GOE: 05.12.01 STRENGTH: L GED: R4 M2 L3 SVP: 7 DLU: 77

350.677-010 MESS ATTENDANT (water trans.)
Serves food to officers and crew aboard ship: Prepares hot and cold drinks, and fruits, for serving, and sets tables for meals. Serves food. Washes glassware

and silverware after meals, cleans messroom, and disposes of trash and garbage. Makes beds and cleans bedrooms and bathrooms assigned to ship's officers. May be designated according to area in which work is performed or personnel served as Mess Attendant, Crew (water trans.); Mess Attendant, Officers' Room (water trans.); Mess Attendant, Officers' Salon (water trans.).
GOE: 09.05.02 STRENGTH: M GED: R2 M1 L2 SVP: 3 DLU: 77

350.677-014 PASSENGER ATTENDANT (water trans.)
Serves passengers aboard ship by performing any combination of following duties: Answers bells from staterooms requesting service. Obtains food or beverage from galley, pantry, or bar, and carries it to staterooms. Demonstrates donning of life jackets during passenger boat drill. Serves hors d'oeuvres during entertainment. Cleans work area. Relieves ELEVATOR OPERATOR (any industry) during breaks.
GOE: 09.05.02 STRENGTH: L GED: R2 M1 L2 SVP: 2 DLU: 77

350.677-018 STEWARD/STEWARDESS, BATH (water trans.)
Services bathrooms aboard ship, and schedules passengers for baths and showers: Prepares baths and showers at times requested and informs passengers. Cleans bathrooms, showers, sinks, and other lavatory equipment. Replenishes supplies, such as towels, bathmat, and soap. May clean public toilets in assigned area.
GOE: 05.12.18 STRENGTH: L GED: R2 M1 L1 SVP: 3 DLU: 77

350.677-022 STEWARD/STEWARDESS (water trans.)
Attends to comfort of passengers aboard ship: Issues sun pads and sports equipment to passengers on deck. Arranges card tables and chairs and provides playing cards, pencils, and score pads for passengers in lounge. Carries passengers' baggage to assigned rooms, and cleans rooms, changes linens and towels, and makes up beds and berths. Issues and arranges game equipment for passengers in smoking room. Serves cold drinks and snacks to passengers. May be required to hold certficates issued by U.S. Coast Guard to handle food and man lifeboat. When attending to passengers at night, may be designated Steward/Stewardess, Night (water trans.). May be designated according to location of passengers attended as Steward/Stewardess, Deck (water trans.); Steward/Stewardess, Lounge (water trans.); Steward/Stewardess, Room (water trans.); Steward/Stewardess, Smoke Room (water trans.).
GOE: 09.01.04 STRENGTH: L GED: R3 M1 L2 SVP: 3 DLU: 77

350.677-026 STEWARD/STEWARDESS, WINE (water trans.)
Serves alcoholic beverages to guests in dining room and in other locations aboard passenger ship: Arranges linens, glassware, and stores on station prior to opening dining room. Chills wines to be served. Serves drinks to dining room guests. Serves wines, cocktails, and other spiritous liquors to passengers in ballroom or smoking room after dining hours and at shipboard sailing parties. Cleans assigned section of dining room. Must be certified by U.S. Coast Guard. May be required to hold Lifeboatman certificate.
GOE: 09.05.02 STRENGTH: M GED: R3 M2 L2 SVP: 4 DLU: 77

350.677-030 WAITER/WAITRESS (water trans.) alternate titles: steward/ stewardess, dining room
Serves passengers in ships' dining rooms: Obtains linen, silver, glassware, and china to set tables. Arranges settings on tables. Provides dining room service to passengers [WAITER/WAITRESS, FORMAL (hotel & rest.)]. Maintains assigned station, including table pieces, side stands, and chairs. May be designated according to class of passengers served as Waiter/Waitress, Cabin Class (water trans.); Waiter/Waitress, Economy Class (water trans.); Waiter/Waitress, First Class (water trans.); Waiter/Waitress, Second Class (water trans.); Waiter/ Waitress, Third Class (water trans.); Waiter/Waitress, Tourist Class (water trans.).
GOE: 09.05.02 STRENGTH: L GED: R3 M1 L2 SVP: 3 DLU: 77

351 TRAIN ATTENDANTS

This group includes occupations concerned with providing services to train passengers. Includes preparation of sleeping berths and private compartments; providing newspapers, food, drink, and personal articles on request; and dispensing general information.

351.677-010 SERVICE ATTENDANT, SLEEPING CAR (r.r. trans.) alternate titles: porter, pullman
Performs variety of personal services for railroad patrons: Carries hand baggage to station platform from seat. Makes berths. Supplies towels to washroom. Furnishes patrons with light lunches, drinks, card tables, or other articles they may request. When only one sleeping car is in train, may perform duties of CONDUCTOR, PULLMAN (r.r. trans.)..
GOE: 09.01.04 STRENGTH: M GED: R2 M2 L2 SVP: 2 DLU: 77

352 HOSTS/HOSTESSES AND STEWARDS/ STEWARDESSES, N.E.C.

This group includes occupations, not elsewhere classified, concerned with rendering a variety of personal services, such as seeing that travelers on board bus, airplane, or railroad are made comfortable; and arranging recreational activities for guests in hotels or at places of amusement, or introducing guests to each other.

352.137-010 SUPERVISOR, AIRPLANE-FLIGHT ATTENDANT (air trans.)
Supervises and coordinates activities of flight attendants: Assigns duties and areas of work to AIRPLANE-FLIGHT ATTENDANT (air trans.) to provide services for airline passengers. Observes activities of employees to evaluate work performance and maintains personnel records. Explains and demonstrates methods and procedures for performing tasks. Prepares evaluation reports on performance of employees. Analyzes, records, and prepares reports of personnel activities. Interprets company policies and practices for workers. May update local procedures manuals and guides according to directives and oral instructions.
GOE: 09.01.04 STRENGTH: L GED: R4 M3 L4 SVP: 7 DLU: 77

352.167-010 DIRECTOR, SOCIAL (hotel & rest.; water trans.) alternate titles: director, recreation
Plans and organizes recreational activities and creates friendly atmosphere for guests in hotels and resorts or for passengers on board ship: Greets new arrivals, introduces them to other guests, acquaints them with recreation facilities, and encourages them to participate in group activities. Ascertains interests of group and evaluates available equipment and facilities to plan activities, such as card parties, games, tournaments, dances, musicals, and field trips. Arranges for activity requirements, such as setting up equipment, transportation, decorations, refreshments, and entertainment. Associates with lonely guests and visits those who are ill. May greet and seat guests in dining room. May assist management in resolving guests' complaints.
GOE: 09.01.01 STRENGTH: L GED: R4 M3 L4 SVP: 6 DLU: 77

352.367-010 AIRPLANE-FLIGHT ATTENDANT (air trans.) alternate titles: airplane-cabin attendant
Performs variety of personal services conducive to safety and comfort of airline passengers during flight: Greets passengers, verifies tickets, records destinations, and directs passengers to assigned seats. Assists passengers to store carry-on luggage in overhead, garment, or under seat storage. Explains use of safety equipment, such as seat belts, oxygen masks, and life jackets. Walks aisle of plane to verify that passengers have complied with federal regulations prior to take off. Serves previously prepared meals and beverages. Observes passengers to detect signs of discomfort, and issues palliatives to relieve passenger ailments, such as airsickness and insomnia. Administers first aid according to passenger distress when needed. Answers questions regarding performance of aircraft, stopovers, and flight schedules. Performs other personal services, such as distributing reading material and pointing out places of interest. Prepares reports showing place of departure and destination, passenger ticket numbers, meal and beverage inventories, palliatives issued, and lost and found articles. May collect money for meals and beverages.
GOE: 09.01.04 STRENGTH: M GED: R4 M3 L3 SVP: 3 DLU: 81

352.367-014 FLIGHT ATTENDANT, RAMP (air trans.)
Checks AIRPLANE-FLIGHT ATTENDANT'S (air trans.) conformance to personal appearance standard and performance of preflight duties during boarding stage of scheduled airline flights, and compiles report of findings. Inspects appearance and grooming of personnel for conformance to company standards. Observes performance of on-board airplane preflight duties and inspections by personnel for conformance, adequacy, and completeness. Records errors, inadequacies, and reasons for deviation on daily checksheet and forwards checksheet to supervisor. Extracts information from checksheets and writes performance reports for inclusion in personnel folders. Consolidates trip report and daily checklist information regarding work performed, emergency equipment, safety procedures, and appearance standards for use by supervisor. Prepares flight register and schedules to indicate assignments. Notifies personnel of changes in schedules.
GOE: 09.01.04 STRENGTH: L GED: R4 M3 L3 SVP: 6 DLU: 77

352.377-010 HOST/HOSTESS, GROUND (air trans.)
Renders personal services to passengers in airline terminal to facilitate movement of passengers through terminal and create goodwill: Greets and welcomes passengers to terminal. Answers questions and advises passengers concerning flight schedules and accommodations, such as arrival or departure time, location of concourses and gates, and selection of seat on aircraft. Performs such tasks as assembling and forwarding luggage to departing flight, or guiding and escorting passengers to designated gate for boarding of aircraft, to expedite transfer of passengers between airline flights. Informs passengers, upon request, concerning fares, airline schedules, and travel itineraries, and distributes brochures to promote interest and sale of air travel. Informs passengers of terminal facilities, such as rest rooms and snackbar, to promote comfort and well being of passengers.
GOE: 09.01.04 STRENGTH: L GED: R3 M2 L3 SVP: 3 DLU: 77

352.577-010 BUS ATTENDANT (motor trans.)
Renders variety of personal services to bus passengers to make their trip pleasant: Welcomes passengers boarding bus. Adjusts seating arrangement to accommodate passengers when requested. Answers questions about bus schedules, travel routes, and bus services. Points out places of interest. Distributes magazines, newspapers, pillows and blankets. Mails passengers' letters and arranges for dispatch of telegrams. Tends tape recorder to provide music. Serves refreshments. Lists names of passengers on manifest. Maintains inventory to account for food served during trip and food on hand. May warm bottles for babies.

GOE: 09.01.04 STRENGTH: L GED: R3 M2 L3 SVP: 2 DLU: 77

352.667-010 HOST/HOSTESS (any industry) alternate titles: receptionist

Greets guests arriving at country club, catered social function, or other gathering place. Introduces guests and suggests planned activities, such as dancing or games. Gives directions to personnel engaged in serving of refreshments. May plan menus and supervise activities of food-service workers. May plan and participate in social activities, games, and sports, depending on nature of establishment or function. May deposit or pick up guests at railway station, home, or other location as directed.
GOE: 09.01.01 STRENGTH: L GED: R3 M2 L3 SVP: 3 DLU: 77

352.667-014 PARLOR CHAPERONE (hotel & rest.) alternate titles: counselor

Chaperones young people attending social functions held in hotels or restaurants: Greets guests and answers questions regarding program. Arranges for entertainment, such as games, concerts, and motion pictures. Asks guests to observe rules of establishment or reports offenders to HOUSE OFFICER (hotel & rest.). May collect tickets for admission to events.
GOE: 09.01.01 STRENGTH: L GED: R3 M1 L2 SVP: 2 DLU: 77

352.677-010 PASSENGER SERVICE REPRESENTATIVE I (r.r. trans.) alternate titles: host/hostess, railway

Renders personal services to railroad passengers to make their trip pleasant and comfortable: Straightens seat cushions and window shades to prepare cars for passengers. Greets passengers boarding trains and introduces passengers to each other. Answers questions about train schedules, travel routes, and railway services. Assists in feeding and caring for children during transit. Assists ill passengers.
GOE: 09.01.04 STRENGTH: L GED: R3 M2 L3 SVP: 3 DLU: 77

352.677-014 RECEPTIONIST, AIRLINE LOUNGE (air trans.)

Admits members and guests to airline lounge, serves beverages and snacks, and provides other personal services as requested: Opens door to lounge in response to sound of buzzer, verifies membership cards, and admits and seats members and guests. Serves refreshments such as cocktails, coffee and snacks. Answers questions regarding scheduled flights and terminal facilities. Verifies passengers' reservations. Directs or accompanies passengers to departure gates, rest rooms and other terminal facilities. Relays requests for paging service, using telephone. Opens cans, bottles, and packages; brews coffee; and arranges pastry, nuts, and appetizers on serving trays. Removes used ash trays, glasses, and dishes from tables and picks up trash.
GOE: 09.01.03 STRENGTH: L GED: R3 M2 L3 SVP: 3 DLU: 77

352.677-018 WAITER/WAITRESS, CLUB (hotel & rest.) alternate titles: page

Attends members in private club by performing duties, such as the following: Takes orders for food and beverages and serves members in dining room or clubrooms. Brings cards, chips, amusement devices, candies, tobacco, and other articles as requested. Places orders for clubroom reservation. Delivers telephone, telegraph, and personal messages. Removes card tables, sweeps and dusts furniture and woodwork, vacuums rugs, and otherwise keeps rooms and halls clean.
GOE: 09.05.02 STRENGTH: L GED: R2 M1 L2 SVP: 2 DLU: 77

353   GUIDES

This group includes occupations concerned with escorting individuals or groups on hunting and fishing trips, cruises, sightseeing tours, and through such places of interest as industrial establishments, public buildings, museums, and art galleries.

353.137-010 GUIDE, CHIEF AIRPORT (air trans.)

Supervises and coordinates activities of workers engaged in conducting guided tours at airport: Arranges tours according to interests of groups, such as school children, foreign visitors, and civic or private organizations. Schedules tours to avoid interruption of airport operations and minimize congestion. Assigns workers to guide tours. Provides information to workers about interests of specific groups. Coaches workers on organization, history, and function of airport, and use of airport facilities. Observes workers' dress and performance on guided tours to assure conformance to department standards. Confers with public relations personnel to plan special event programs. Prepares reports showing number of people taking tours, type of tours, and public reaction.
GOE: 09.01.02 STRENGTH: L GED: R4 M2 L3 SVP: 5 DLU: 77

353.161-010 GUIDE, HUNTING AND FISHING (amuse. & rec.)

Plans, organizes and conducts hunting and fishing trips for individuals and groups: Plans itinerary for hunting and fishing trips applying knowledge of countryside to determine best route and sites. Arranges for transporting sportsman, equipment and supplies to hunting or fishing area using horses, land vehicles, motorboat, or airplane. Explains hunting and fishing laws to ensure compliance. Instructs members of party in use of hunting or fishing gear. Prepares meals for members of party. Administers first aid to injured sportsmen. May care for animals. May sell or rent equipment, clothing and supplies. May pilot airplane or drive land and water vehicles.
GOE: 09.01.01 STRENGTH: H GED: R4 M3 L3 SVP: 7 DLU: 77

353.164-010 GUIDE, ALPINE (personal ser.)

Organizes and conducts mountain-climbing expeditions for adventurers or tourists: Arranges for camping and climbing equipment, transportation to site of ascent, and services of medical or other personnel as needed. Selects ascent consistent with experience and endurance of members of climbing party. Leads party to site of ascent and during climb. Gives advice and instruction to climbing novices in accepted techniques and use of equipment. May obtain permits to climb in restricted areas and verify quantity and quality of client-furnished equipment to ensure fulfillment of prerequisites prior to departure. May give classroom instructions in mountaineering and wilderness survival.
GOE: 09.01.01 STRENGTH: V GED: R4 M3 L4 SVP: 7 DLU: 77

353.167-010 GUIDE, TRAVEL (personal ser.) alternate titles: guide, excursion; guide, itinerary; guide, tour

Arranges transportation and other accommodations for groups of tourists, following planned itinerary, and escorts groups during entire trip, within single area or at specified stopping points of tour: Makes reservations on ships, trains, and other modes of transportation, and arranges for other accommodations, such as baggage handling, dining and lodging facilities, and recreational activities, using communication media, such as cable, telegraph, or telephone. Accompanies tour group and describes points of interest. May assist tourists to plan itinerary, obtain travel certificates, such as visas, passports, and health certificates, and convert currency into travelers' checks or foreign moneys. May be designated according to method of transportation used as Guide, Cruise (personal ser.); or locality of tour as Guide, Domestic Tour (personal ser.); Guide, Foreign Tour (personal ser.).
GOE: 07.05.01 STRENGTH: L GED: R4 M3 L4 SVP: 6 DLU: 77

353.363-010 GUIDE, SIGHTSEEING (amuse. & rec.; personal ser.) alternate titles: barker; cicerone; spieler

Drives motor vehicle to transport sightseers and lectures group concerning points of interest during sightseeing tour: Drives limousine or sightseeing bus, stopping vehicle at establishments or locations, such as art gallery, museum, battlefield, and cave, to permit group to be escorted through buildings by GUIDE, ESTABLISHMENT (any industry) 353.367-014. Describes points of interest along route of tour, using public address system or megaphone. May collect fees or tickets, and plan refreshment and rest stops. May escort group through establishment and describe points of interest. May operate tram to transport patrons through amusement park and be designated Tram Operator (amuse. & rec.).
GOE: 09.01.02 STRENGTH: L GED: R3 M2 L3 SVP: 4 DLU: 81

353.364-010 DUDE WRANGLER (amuse. & rec.)

Performs combination of the following services for patrons of dude ranch to enhance guests' enjoyment: Saddles and unsaddles horses, adjusting equipment to accommodate each guest. Assists guests in mounting and dismounting. Plans itinerary of trips, taking into consideration wishes and preferences of guests, knowledge of terrain, and location of suitable campsites. Packs horses with supplies and provisions for extended or overnight trips. Drives or leads pack horses. Pitches camp, prepares fire, and participates in cooking for camping parties. Advises guests concerning suitable hunting and fishing sites and applicable conservation and wildlife laws. Entertains guests by singing, telling stories, or playing guitar or other instrument. Escorts female guests to dances and other social functions. May participate in rodeos provided by ranch management for entertainment of guests. May repair saddles.
GOE: 12.01.02 STRENGTH: M GED: R3 M2 L3 SVP: 3 DLU: 77

353.367-010 GUIDE (personal ser.) alternate titles: guide, visitor

Escorts visitors around city or town: Advises visitors, such as convention delegates, foreign government personnel, or salesmen, as to location of buildings, points of interest, and other sites, or escorts visitors to designated locations, using private or public transportation. May carry equipment, luggage, or sample cases for visitors. May be required to speak foreign language when communicating with foreign visitors. May be designated according to type of visitor directed or escorted as Guide, Delegate (personal ser.).
GOE: 09.01.02 STRENGTH: L GED: R3 M1 L2 SVP: 3 DLU: 77

353.367-014 GUIDE, ESTABLISHMENT (any industry) alternate titles: guide, tour

Escorts group of people through establishment, such as museum, aquarium, or public or historical building, or through historic or scenic outdoor site, such as battlefield, park, or cave, usually following specified route: Lectures concerning size, value, and history of establishment, points out features of interest, and gives other information peculiar to establishment. Answers questions of group. Assumes responsibility for safety of group. May collect fees from members of group. May solicit patronage. May distribute brochures on establishment or historical site to visitors. May be designated Airport Guide (air trans.).
GOE: 09.01.02 STRENGTH: L GED: R3 M1 L3 SVP: 3 DLU: 80

353.367-018 GUIDE, PLANT (any industry) alternate titles: plant tour guide

Escorts group of people through industrial establishment, and describes features of interest: Leads way along specified route and explains various processes and operation of machines. Answers questions and supplies information on work of department or departments visited.
GOE: 09.01.02 STRENGTH: L GED: R3 M2 L3 SVP: 3 DLU: 77

353.367-022 PAGE (radio-tv broad.)

Conducts visitors on tours of radio and television station facilities and explains duties of staff, operation of equipment, and methods of broadcasting. Utilizing general knowledge of various phases of radio and television station operations. Runs errands within studio. May relieve telephone switchboard operator. May perform general clerical duties such as taking messages, filing, and typing. *GOE: 09.01.02 STRENGTH: L GED: R3 M2 L3 SVP: 2 DLU: 77*

353.667-010 ESCORT (any industry)
Guides visitors to destinations in industrial establishment: Escorts visitors to office, department, or section of plant. May collect and deliver mail and messages. May issue identification badges and safety devices to visitors. *GOE: 09.05.08 STRENGTH: L GED: R2 M1 L2 SVP: 2 DLU: 77*

354 UNLICENSED BIRTH ATTENDANTS AND PRACTICAL NURSES

This group includes occupations concerned with bathing patients, taking and recording pulse and temperature readings, giving injections, assisting women in childbirth, caring for and feeding infants, giving first aid, and performing similar routine nursing tasks. Knowledge is acquired primarily through practical experience. Licensed practical nursing occupations are included in Group 079.

354.374-010 NURSE, PRACTICAL (medical ser.)
Cares for patients and children in private homes, hospitals, sanitoriums, industrial plants, and similar institutions: Bathes and dresses bed patients, combs hair, and otherwise attends to their comfort and personal appearance. Cleans room, and changes bed linen. Takes and records temperature, pulse, and respiration rate. Gives medication as directed by physician or NURSE, GENERAL DUTY (medical ser.) 075.364-010, and makes notation of amount and time given. Gives enemas, douches, massages, and alcohol rubs. Applies hot and cold compresses and hot water bottles. Sterilizes equipment and supplies, using germicides, sterilizer, or autoclave. Prepares food trays, feeds patients, and records food and liquid intake and output. Cooks, washes, cleans, and does other housekeeping duties in private home. May give injections. May care for infants and small children in private home. For practical nurses meeting state licensing requirements see NURSE, LICENSED PRACTICAL (medical ser.) 079.374-014. *GOE: 10.03.02 STRENGTH: M GED: R3 M2 L3 SVP: 4 DLU: 77*

354.377-010 BIRTH ATTENDANT (medical ser.)
Provides assistance to women during childbirth, in absence of medical practitioner. May function under supervision of local or state health department. *GOE: 10.03.02 STRENGTH: M GED: R3 M1 L2 SVP: 4 DLU: 77*

354.377-014 HOME ATTENDANT (personal ser.) alternate titles: home health aide
Cares for elderly, convalescent, or handicapped persons in patient's home, performing any combination of following tasks: Changes bed linens, washes and irons patient's laundry, and cleans patient's quarters. Purchases, prepares, and serves food for patient and other members of family, following special prescribed diets. Assists patients into and out of bed, automobile, or wheelchair, to lavatory, and up and down stairs. Assists patient to dress, bathe, and groom self. Massages patient and applies preparations and treatments, such as liniment or alcohol rubs and heat-lamp stimulation. Administers prescribed oral medications under written direction of physician or as directed by home care nurse. Accompanies ambulatory patients outside home, serving as guide, companion, and aide. Entertains patient, reads aloud, and plays cards or other games with patient. Performs variety of miscellaneous duties as requested, such as obtaining household supplies and running errands. May maintain records of services performed and of apparent condition of patient. May visit several households to provide daily health care to patients. *GOE: 10.03.03 STRENGTH: M GED: R3 M2 L2 SVP: 3 DLU: 77*

354.677-010 FIRST-AID ATTENDANT (any industry) alternate titles: nurse, first aid
Renders first aid and subsequent treatment to injured or ill employees at industrial plant, commercial establishment, mine, or construction site: Sterilizes, disinfects, anoints, and bandages minor cuts and burns. Applies artificial respiration or administers oxygen, in cases of suffocation and asphyxiation. Administers medications, such as aspirin or antiseptic solution, to relieve pain or prevent infection until patient can receive professional care, and gives prescribed medicines and treatments for illness. Changes beds, cleans equipment, and maintains infirmary for ward patients. Aids physician during emergency situations. Keeps personal and medical records of employees. *GOE: 10.03.02 STRENGTH: L GED: R3 M2 L3 SVP: 3 DLU: 77*

355 ATTENDANTS, HOSPITALS, MORGUES, AND RELATED HEALTH SERVICES

This group includes occupations concerned with attending to the physical comfort, safety, and appearance of patients; performing routine menial tasks; and assisting in conducting occupational and recreational therapy.

355.354-010 PHYSICAL THERAPY AIDE (medical ser.)
Prepares patients for physical therapy treatments, assists PHYSICAL THERAPIST (medical ser.) 076.121-014 or PHYSICAL THERAPIST ASSISTANT (medical ser.) 076.224-010 during administration of treatments, and provides routine treatments: Assists patients to dress, undress, and put on and remove supportive devices, such as braces, splints, and slings, before and after treat-

ments. Secures patients into or onto therapy equipment. Safeguards, motivates, and assists patients practicing exercises and functional activities under direction of professional staff. Provides routine treatments, such as hydrotherapy, hot and cold packs, and paraffin bath. Transports patients to and from treatment area. Cleans work area and equipment after treatment. May record treatment given and equipment used. May inventory and requisition supplies and equipment. May adjust fit of supportive devices for patients, as instructed. May be assigned to specific type of treatment or patient service and be designated Physical Therapy Aide, Hydrotherapy (medical ser.); Physical Therapy Aide, Transport (medical ser.). *GOE: 10.03.02 STRENGTH: M GED: R3 M2 L3 SVP: 4 DLU: 87*

355.374-010 AMBULANCE ATTENDANT (medical ser.)
Accompanies and assists AMBULANCE DRIVER (medical ser.) on calls: Assists in lifting patient onto wheeled cart or stretcher and into and out of ambulance. Renders first aid, such as bandaging, splinting, and administering oxygen. May be required to have Red Cross first-aid training certificate. *GOE: 10.03.02 STRENGTH: M GED: R3 M2 L3 SVP: 3 DLU: 77*

355.374-014 CERTIFIED MEDICATION TECHNICIAN (medical ser.)
Administers prescribed medications to patients and maintains related medical records under supervision of NURSE, GENERAL DUTY (medical ser.) 075.364-010: Verifies identity of patient receiving medication and records name of drug, dosage, and time of administration on specified forms or records. Presents medication to patient and observes ingestion or other application, or administers medication, using specified procedures. Takes vital signs or observes patient to detect response to specified types of medications and prepares report or notifies designated personnel of unexpected reactions. Documents reasons prescribed drugs are not administered. Gives direct patient care, such as bathing, dressing, and feeding patients, and assisting in examinations and treatments [NURSE AIDE (medical ser.) 355.674-014]. May receive supply of ordered medications and apportion, mix, or assemble drugs for administration to patient. May record and restock medication inventories. *GOE: 10.03.02 STRENGTH: M GED: R3 M3 L3 SVP: 4 DLU: 89*

355.377-010 OCCUPATIONAL THERAPY AIDE (medical ser.)
Assists OCCUPATIONAL THERAPIST (medical ser.) 076.121-010 or OCCUPATIONAL THERAPY ASSISTANT (medical ser.) 076.364-010 in occupational therapy program in hospital or similar institution: Performs program support services, such as transporting patient, assembling equipment, and preparing and maintaining work areas, as directed by professional staff. Assists in maintaining supplies and equipment. May help professional staff demonstrate therapy techniques, such as manual and creative arts, games, and daily living activities to patients. May assist in selected aspects of patient services as assigned. *GOE: 10.03.02 STRENGTH: M GED: R3 M2 L2 SVP: 4 DLU: 81*

355.377-014 PSYCHIATRIC AIDE (medical ser.) alternate titles: assistant therapy aide; asylum attendant; charge attendant; chemical dependency attendant; psychiatric attendant; ward attendant
Assists patients, working under direction of nursing and medical staff in psychiatric, chemical dependency, or similar setting: Accompanies patients to shower rooms, and assists them in bathing, dressing, and grooming. Accompanies patients to and from wards for examination and treatment, administers prescribed medications, measures vital signs, performs routine nursing procedures, such as collecting laboratory specimens, giving enemas and douches, and drawing blood samples, and records information in patients' charts. Assists patients in becoming accustomed to hospital routine and encourages them to participate in social and recreational activities to promote rehabilitation. Observes patients to ensure that none wanders from ward areas or grounds. Feeds patients or attempts to persuade them to eat, and notes and records reasons for rejection of food. Observes patients to detect unusual behavior, and aids or restrains them to prevent injury to themselves or others. May escort patients off grounds to medical or dental appointments, library, church services, motion pictures, or athletic events. May clean rooms, ward furnishings, walls, and floors, using water, detergents, and disinfectants. May change bed linens. May interview patients upon admission and record data obtained. May be designated Ward Supervisor (medical ser.) when responsible for patient care and other services of single ward. *GOE: 10.03.02 STRENGTH: M GED: R3 M2 L3 SVP: 4 DLU: 89*

355.377-018 MENTAL-RETARDATION AIDE (medical ser.) alternate titles: resident care aide
Assists in providing self-care training and therapeutic treatments to residents of mental retardation center: Demonstrates activities such as bathing and dressing to train residents in daily self-care practices. Converses with residents to reinforce positive behaviors and to promote social interaction. Serves meals and eats with residents to act as role model. Accompanies residents on shopping trips and instructs and counsels residents in purchase of personal items. Aids staff in administering therapeutic activities, such as physical exercises, occupational arts and crafts, and recreational games, to residents. Restrains disruptive residents to prevent injury to themselves and others. Observes and documents residents' behaviors, such as speech production, feeding patterns, and toilet training, to facilitate assessment and development of treatment goals. Attends to routine health-care needs of residents under supervision of medical personnel. May give medications as prescribed by physician. May train parents or guardians in care of deinstitutionalized residents. *GOE: 10.03.02 STRENGTH: M GED: R4 M3 L3 SVP: 6 DLU: 87*

355.667-010 MORGUE ATTENDANT (medical ser.)
Prepares bodies, specimens of human organs, and morgue room to assist PATHOLOGIST (medical ser.) in postmortem examinations: Places body in compartment tray of refrigerator or on autopsy table, using portable hoist and stretcher. Lays out surgical instruments and laboratory supplies for postmortem examinations. Washes table, storage trays, and instruments, sharpens knives, and replaces soiled linens. Records identifying information for morgue file. Releases body to authorized person. May close post mortem incisions, using surgical needle and cord. May fill cranium with plaster. May feed, water, and clean quarters for animals used in medical research. May prepare preserving solutions according to formulas. May preserve specimens and stain slides. May photograph specimens.
GOE: 02.04.02 STRENGTH: M GED: R3 M2 L2 SVP: 4 DLU: 77

355.674-010 CHILD-CARE ATTENDANT, SCHOOL (personal ser.)
Attends to personal needs of handicapped children while in school to receive specialized academic and physical training: Wheels handicapped children to classes, lunchrooms, treatment rooms, and other areas of building. Secures children in equipment, such as chairs, slings, or stretchers, and places or hoists children into baths or pools. Monitors children using life support equipment to detect indications of malfunctioning of equipment and calls for medical assistance when needed. Helps children to walk, board buses, put on prosthetic appliances, eat, dress, bathe, and perform other physical activities as their needs require.
GOE: 10.03.03 STRENGTH: M GED: R3 M1 L2 SVP: 2 DLU: 81

355.674-014 NURSE ASSISTANT (medical ser.) alternate titles: nurse aide
Performs any combination of following duties in care of patients in hospital, nursing home, or other medical facility, under direction of nursing and medical staff: Answers signal lights, bells, or intercom system to determine patients' needs. Bathes, dresses, and undresses patients. Serves and collects food trays and feeds patients requiring help. Transports patients, using wheelchair or wheeled cart, or assists patients to walk. Drapes patients for examinations and treatments, and remains with patients, performing such duties as holding instruments and adjusting lights. Turns and repositions bedfast patients, alone or with assistance, to prevent bedsores. Changes bed linens, runs errands, directs visitors, and answers telephone. Takes and records temperature, blood pressure, pulse and respiration rates, and food and fluid intake and output, as directed. Cleans, sterilizes, stores, prepares, and issues dressing packs, treatment trays, and other supplies. Dusts and cleans patients' rooms. May be assigned to specific area of hospital, nursing home, or medical facility. May assist nursing staff in care of geriatric patients and be designated Geriatric Nurse Assistant (medical ser.). May assist in providing medical treatment and personal care to patients in private home settings and be designated Home Health Aide (medical ser.).
GOE: 10.03.02 STRENGTH: M GED: R3 M2 L2 SVP: 4 DLU: 89

355.674-018 ORDERLY (medical ser.)
Performs any combination of following tasks, as directed by nursing and medical staff, to care for patients in hospital, nursing home, or other medical facility: Bathes patients and gives alcohol rubs. Measures and records intake and output of liquids, and takes and records temperature, and pulse and respiration rate. Gives enemas. Carries meal trays to patients and feeds patients unable to feed themselves. Lifts patients onto and from bed, and transports patients to other areas, such as operating and x-ray rooms, by rolling bed, or using wheelchair or wheeled stretcher. Sets up equipment, such as oxygen tents, portable x-ray machines, and overhead irrigation bottles. Makes beds and collects soiled linen. Cleans rooms and corridors. Bathes deceased patients, accompanies body to morgue, and places personal belongings in mortuary box. Administers catheterizations and bladder irrigations. Accompanies discharged patients home or to other institutions.
GOE: 10.03.02 STRENGTH: H GED: R3 M2 L2 SVP: 4 DLU: 86

355.674-022 RESPIRATORY-THERAPY AIDE (medical ser.)
Performs any combination of following tasks to assist personnel in Respiratory Therapy Department: Cleans, disinfects, and sterilizes equipment used in administration of respiratory therapy. Examines equipment to detect worn tubes, loose connections, or other indications of disrepair, and notifies supervisor of need for maintenance. Starts equipment and observes gauges measuring pressure, rate of flow, and continuity to test equipment, and notifies supervisor of malfunctions. Assists in preparation of inventory records. Delivers oxygen tanks and other equipment and supplies to specified hospital locations. Assists in administration of gas or aerosol therapy as directed by RESPIRATORY THERAPIST (medical ser.) 076.361-014 and prescribed by physician.
GOE: 10.03.02 STRENGTH: M GED: R3 M3 L3 SVP: 4 DLU: 88

355.677-014 TRANSPORTER, PATIENTS (medical ser.) alternate titles: escort, patients
Escorts or transports patients within hospital or other medical facility: Determines patient name, destination, mode of travel, time, and other data, following written or oral instructions. Directs or escorts incoming patients from admitting office or reception desk to designated area. Carries patient's luggage. Assists patient in walking to prevent accidents by falling, or transports nonambulatory patient, using wheelchair. Transports patient, alone or with assistance, in bed, wheeled cart, or wheelchair to designated areas within facility during patient stay. Delivers messages, mail, medical records, and other items.

GOE: 10.03.03 STRENGTH: M GED: R2 M1 L2 SVP: 2 DLU: 88

355.687-014 GRAVES REGISTRATION SPECIALIST (military ser.)
Collects and identifies remains of deceased military personnel, both buried and unburied, and evacuates bodies to rear area for burial activities: Searches battlefields and other areas for unburied dead and for isolated and unmarked graves. Exhumes bodies of buried dead. Examines immediate area for identification items, such as dog tags, watches, and similar personal effects, and transports remains and personal effects to rear area. Takes fingerprints, skeletal x rays, and prepares teeth chart to aid in identifying remains. Examines remains, removes personal effects, and records property inventory on designated forms. Records identity of remains including name, military unit, location, and cause and date of death. Indicates location of temporary graves on map, sketch, or overlay for purposes of future recovery.
GOE: 02.04.02 STRENGTH: V GED: R2 M2 L2 SVP: 3 DLU: 77

357 BAGGAGE HANDLERS

This group includes occupations concerned with carrying bags for passengers in train, bus, marina and airplane terminals; checking baggage and calling taxicabs; pushing wheelchairs for invalids; and connecting marine utilities to boats for customers. Occupations concerned with handling of baggage for guests of hotels and related establishments are included in Group 324.

357.477-010 BAGGAGE CHECKER (air trans.; motor trans.) alternate titles: luggage checker
Receives and returns baggage to passengers at motorbus or airline terminals: Prepares and attaches baggage claim checks. Stacks baggage on specified carts or conveyors. Returns baggage to patrons on receipt of claim check. May receive, weigh, and bill parcels for express shipment by bus. May weigh baggage and collect excess weight charge. May complete baggage insurance forms, determine rate from schedule and collect charge from customer.
GOE: 09.05.03 STRENGTH: M GED: R3 M2 L3 SVP: 3 DLU: 77

357.677-010 PORTER (air trans.; motor trans.; r.r. trans.) alternate titles: porter, baggage; redcap
Carries baggage for passengers of airline, railroad, or motorbus by hand or handtruck, to waiting or baggage room, onto train or bus, or to taxicab or private automobile. Performs related services, such as calling taxicabs, directing persons to ticket windows and rest rooms, and assisting handicapped passengers upon their arrival or departure. May clean terminal floors; wash walls, windows and counters; and dust furniture. When employed in airline terminal, is designated Skycap (air trans.).
GOE: 09.05.03 STRENGTH: M GED: R2 M1 L2 SVP: 2 DLU: 77

358 CHECKROOM, LOCKER ROOM, AND REST ROOM ATTENDANTS

This group includes occupations concerned with serving clients of checkrooms, locker rooms, or rest rooms. Includes storing apparel or valuables, issuing claim checks and returning items on demand; providing towels or soap; and over-seeing children in shower or rest rooms of schools and institutions.

358.137-010 CHECKROOM CHIEF (any industry)
Supervises and coordinates activities of workers engaged in storing guests' wearing apparel, parcels and other articles in checkrooms of establishment. Reviews printed schedule of activities to determine services needed. Assigns work schedules and keeps time records of personnel. Receives customers' complaints concerning quality of service and rectifies or instructs workers to rectify complaints. Submits reports of unclaimed or lost articles to hotel security department. Performs duties as described under CHECKROOM ATTENDANT (any industry).
GOE: 09.05.03 STRENGTH: L GED: R3 M2 L3 SVP: 5 DLU: 77

358.677-010 CHECKROOM ATTENDANT (any industry)
Stores wearing apparel, luggage, bundles, and other articles for patrons of an establishment or employees of business establishment, issuing claim check for articles checked and returning articles on receipt of check. May be designated according to article stored as Baggage Checker (any industry); Coat Checker (any industry); Hat Checker (any industry); Stand-By (motion picture); Wrap Checker (any industry).
GOE: 09.05.03 STRENGTH: L GED: R2 M2 L2 SVP: 2 DLU: 77

358.677-014 LOCKER-ROOM ATTENDANT (personal ser.) alternate titles: cage clerk; dressing-room attendant; locker attendant; locker-room clerk; personal attendant; suit attendant
Assigns dressing room facilities, locker space or clothing containers, and supplies to patrons of athletic or bathing establishment: Issues dressing room or locker key. Receives patron's clothing-filled container, furnishes claim check, places container on storage shelf or rack, and returns container upon receipt of claim check. Issues athletic equipment, bathing suit, or supplies, such as soap and towels. May arrange for valet services, such as clothes pressing and shoeshining. May collect soiled linen and perform cleaning tasks, such as mop dressing room floors, wash shower room walls and clean bathroom facilities. May collect fees for use of facilities, equipment, or supplies. May pack athletic uniforms and equipment for individual or team out-of-town sporting events. May attend to needs of athletic team in team clubhouse and be designated

Clubhouse Attendant (amuse. & rec.). May provide baseball players with baseball bats, retrieve bats and foul balls from field, and supply balls to game officials and be designated Bat Boy/Girl (amuse. & rec.).
GOE: 09.05.07 STRENGTH: L GED: R2 M2 L2 SVP: 2 DLU: 81

358.677-018 REST ROOM ATTENDANT (any industry) alternate titles: lavatory attendant; toilet attendant; washroom attendant
Serves patrons of lavatories in store, public building, hotel, or similar establishment by providing soap and towels, brushing patrons' clothing, shining shoes, sewing on loose buttons, and performing related services. Replenishes rest room supplies. May scrub lavatory, floors, walls, mirrors, and fixtures, using brushes, detergent, and water. May administer first aid to ill or injured patrons.
GOE: 09.05.07 STRENGTH: L GED: R2 M1 L1 SVP: 2 DLU: 77

358.687-010 CHANGE-HOUSE ATTENDANT (any industry) alternate titles: dry boss; dry janitor; shower room attendant
Maintains building, such as locker room of golf club, change house of mining camp, or shower facilities of industrial plant, in which patrons or workers shower and change clothes: Sweeps floor and scrubs shower stalls, using broom, brushes, and soap and water. Opens windows to control ventilation or adjusts controls of automatic heating, cooling, or dehumidifying unit to maintain healthful and comfortable conditions. May fire boiler to heat water for bathing or heating facility. May place contaminated work clothes in vacuum chamber for removal of toxic chemical dust. May requisition and issue supplies, such as soap, towels, and protective clothing.
GOE: 05.12.18 STRENGTH: M GED: R2 M1 L2 SVP: 2 DLU: 77

359 MISCELLANEOUS PERSONAL SERVICE OCCUPATIONS, N.E.C.

This group includes occupations, not elsewhere classified, concerned with personal services.

359.137-010 SUPERVISOR, HOSPITALITY HOUSE (amuse. & rec.)
Supervises and coordinates activities of workers engaged in greeting, guiding, and serving patrons in amusement and recreation facilities: Formulates roster and personnel work assignments to assure work coverage. Explains work procedures for subordinates. Prepares written reports of operational activities to aid in planning future activities. Verifies cleanliness of facilities and operability of equipment and forwards work order forms on equipment requiring maintenance or repair to management. Inventories and orders supplies, checks and turns in receipts, and reviews correspondence. Attends meeting to plan future operational activities and implementation of plans with other department heads.
GOE: 09.01.01 STRENGTH: L GED: R4 M3 L4 SVP: 6 DLU: 77

359.363-010 HEALTH-EQUIPMENT SERVICER (medical ser.)
Delivers, installs, demonstrates, and maintains rental medical equipment, such as respirator, oxygen equipment, hospital beds, and wheelchairs, for use in private residences: Loads medical equipment on truck and delivers equipment to renter's or patient's residence. Unloads, installs, and sets up equipment, using handtools. Inspects and maintains rental oxygen equipment, performing such tasks as inspecting hoses and water traps to detect leaks and condensation; observing gauges of oxygen analyzer, pressure gauges, and other monitoring equipment to determine pressure and oxygen content of air output of compressors and concentrators; and changing filters. Maintains record on oxygen equipment by hours of usage to determine need for maintenance.
GOE: 05.08.03 STRENGTH: V GED: R3 M2 L3 SVP: 5 DLU: 86

359.367-010 ESCORT (personal ser.) alternate titles: guide escort
Acts as social partner for person of opposite sex to enable individual to attend functions, participate in activities requiring a partner, or provide companionship or protection while visiting public establishments, such as restaurants, night clubs, theaters, and gambling houses. May suggest places of entertainment and arrange for transportation and tickets. May speak one or more foreign languages. May accompany individual on sightseeing tour [GUIDE, SIGHTSEEING (amuse. & rec.; personal ser.) 353.363-010].
GOE: 09.01.01 STRENGTH: L GED: R3 M2 L3 SVP: 2 DLU: 77

359.367-014 WEIGHT-REDUCTION SPECIALIST (personal ser.) alternate titles: nutrition educator
Assists clients in devising and carrying out weight-loss plan, using established dietary programs and positive reinforcement procedures: Interviews client to obtain information on weight development history, eating habits, medical restrictions, and nutritional objectives. Weighs and measures client, using measuring instruments, and enters data on client record. Discusses eating habits with client to identify dispensable food items and to encourage increased consumption of high nutrition, low calorie food items, or selects established diet program which matches client goals and restrictions. Explains program and procedures which should be followed to lose desired amount of weight, and answers client questions. Reviews client food diary at regular intervals to identify eating habits which do not coincide with established or agreed upon dietary program, and reviews weight loss statistics to determine progress. Counsels client to promote established goals and to reinforce positive results. May photograph client during therapy to provide visual record of progress. May conduct aversion therapy, utilizing electric shock, rancid odors, and other physical or visual stimuli to promote negative association with food designated for elimination from diet.

May conduct positive conditioning therapy sessions, utilizing physical and visual stimuli to promote positive association with foods designated for increase in diet. May give client weight-loss aids, such as calorie counters, or sell nutritional products to be used in conjunction with diet program.
GOE: 09.05.01 STRENGTH: L GED: R3 M2 L3 SVP: 3 DLU: 86

359.567-010 REDUCING-SALON ATTENDANT (personal ser.)
Measures, weighs and records patron's body statistics, refers information to supervisor for evaluation and planning of exercise program, and demonstrates exercises and use of equipment. Monitors member's exercise activities to assure progress toward desired goals. Records patron's measurements periodically for re-evaluation.
GOE: 09.05.01 STRENGTH: M GED: R2 M2 L2 SVP: 2 DLU: 77

359.573-010 BLIND AIDE (personal ser.) alternate titles: clerk guide; escort, blind
Performs any combination of following duties to assist blind persons: Drives motor vehicle to transport blind persons to specified locations according to their personal and business activities. Carries brief or sample cases. Assists client with dressing, moving from one location to another, obtaining information or other personal service. Prepares and maintains records of assistance rendered. May type correspondence and reports [CLERK-TYPIST (clerical)]. May assist teacher of blind in routine classroom activities such as toiletry or group school activities.
GOE: 10.03.03 STRENGTH: L GED: R3 M2 L2 SVP: 3 DLU: 77

359.667-010 CHAPERON (personal ser.)
Accompanies minors on trips to educational institutions, public functions, or recreational activities such as dances, concerts, or sports events, to provide adult supervision in absence of parents. Follows parents' instructions regarding minors' activities and imposes limitations and restrictions to ensure their safety, well-being, and conformance to specified behavior standards. May plan free-time activities. May arrange for transportation, tickets, and meals.
GOE: 04.02.03 STRENGTH: L GED: R3 M2 L2 SVP: 2 DLU: 77

359.673-010 CHAUFFEUR (domestic ser.) alternate titles: driver
Drives private car as ordered by owner or other passenger and performs other miscellaneous duties: Assists passengers to enter and leave car and holds umbrellas in wet weather. Keeps car clean, polished, and in operating condition. May make minor repairs, such as fixing punctures, cleaning spark plugs, or adjusting carburetor. May assist CARETAKER (domestic ser.) with heavy work. May groom and exercise pets.
GOE: 09.03.02 STRENGTH: L GED: R2 M1 L2 SVP: 3 DLU: 77

359.673-014 CHAUFFEUR, FUNERAL CAR (personal ser.) alternate titles: funeral driver
Drives mortuary vehicles, such as hearses and limousines: Drives hearse to transport bodies to mortuary for embalming and from mortuary to place of funeral service or interment. Helps PALLBEARERS (personal ser.) to move casket from mortuary into hearse and from hearse to destination. Arranges flowers in hearse. Drives limousine in funeral procession, following prearranged schedule, to transport mourners. Assists passengers entering or leaving limousine. May clean vehicles prior to funeral. May dust furniture and sweep floors in mortuary. May be designated according to type of vehicle driven as Funeral-Limousine Driver (personal ser.); Hearse Driver (personal ser.).
GOE: 05.08.03 STRENGTH: V GED: R2 M1 L2 SVP: 4 DLU: 77

359.677-010 ATTENDANT, CHILDREN'S INSTITUTION (any industry) alternate titles: child-care attendant; house parent
Cares for group of children housed in city, county, private, or other similar institution, under supervision of superintendent of home: Awakens children each morning and ensures children are dressed, fed, and ready for school or other activity. Gives instructions to children regarding desirable health and personal habits. Plans and leads recreational activities and participates or instructs children in games. Disciplines children and recommends or initiates other measures to control behavior. May make minor repairs to clothing. May supervise housekeeping activities of other workers in assigned section of institution. May counsel or provide similar diagnostic or therapeutic services to mentally disturbed, delinquent, or handicapped children. May escort child to designated activities. May perform housekeeping duties in children's living area.
GOE: 10.03.03 STRENGTH: M GED: R3 M2 L3 SVP: 3 DLU: 81

359.677-014 FUNERAL ATTENDANT (personal ser.) alternate titles: undertaker assistant; usher
Performs variety of tasks during funeral: Places casket in parlor or chapel prior to wake or funeral service and arranges floral offerings and lights around casket, following instructions of DIRECTOR, FUNERAL (personal ser.) or EMBALMER (personal ser.). Directs or escorts mourners to parlor or chapel in which wake or funeral is held. Assists DIRECTOR, FUNERAL (personal ser.) to close coffin. Carries flowers to hearse or limousine for transportation to place of interment. Assists mourners into and out of limousines. Issues and stores funeral equipment, such as casket lowering devices and grass mats used at place of interment. May carry casket [PALLBEARER (personal ser.)].
GOE: 09.01.04 STRENGTH: M GED: R2 M1 L2 SVP: 3 DLU: 77

359.677-018 NURSERY SCHOOL ATTENDANT (any industry) alternate titles: child-care leader; child-day-care center worker; day care worker
Organizes and leads activities of prekindergarten children in nursery schools or in playrooms operated for patrons of theaters, department stores, hotels, and

similar organizations: Helps children remove outer garments. Organizes and participates in games, reads to children, and teaches them simple painting, drawing, handwork, songs, and similar activities. Directs children in eating, resting, and toileting. Helps children develop habits of caring for own clothing and picking up and putting away toys and books. Maintains discipline. May serve meals and refreshments to children and regulate rest periods. May assist in preparing food and cleaning quarters.
GOE: 10.03.03 STRENGTH: L GED: R3 M2 L3 SVP: 4 DLU: 81

359.677-022 PASSENGER SERVICE REPRESENTATIVE (air trans.)
Renders variety of personal services to airline passengers requiring other than normal service, such as company officials, distinguished persons, foreign speaking passengers, invalids, and unaccompanied children: Greets and escorts distinguished persons to lounge or waiting area. Transports special passengers between lobby and boarding area, using electric cart. Gives aid to ill or injured passengers and obtains medical assistance. Informs relatives of passengers whereabouts and condition. Assists elderly persons and unaccompanied children in claiming personal belongings and baggage. Prepares baby food for mothers with infants. Accompanies foreign speaking passengers, or aliens traveling without visas, aboard airplane and introduces them to AIRPLANE-FLIGHT ATTENDANT (air trans.). Arranges for air commuter and ground transportation. Teletypes or telephones down-line stations regarding special services for arriving passengers.
GOE: 09.01.04 STRENGTH: L GED: R3 M2 L3 SVP: 3 DLU: 77

359.677-026 PLAYROOM ATTENDANT (any industry) alternate titles: kindergartner
Entertains children in nursery of department store, country club, or similar establishment as service to patrons. Reads aloud, organizes and participates in games, and gives elementary lessons in arts or crafts.
GOE: 10.03.03 STRENGTH: L GED: R3 M2 L3 SVP: 3 DLU: 77

359.677-030 RESEARCH SUBJECT (any industry) alternate titles: subject, scientific research
Submits to scientifically conducted research relating to such fields as medicine, psychology, or consumer-product testing: Participates in activities such as performing physical tasks, taking psychological tests, or using experimental products, following instructions of researcher. Replies verbally or records responses to questionnaire to provide researcher with data for evaluation.
GOE: 09.05.06 STRENGTH: L GED: R3 M2 L3 SVP: 1 DLU: 86

359.685-010 CREMATOR (personal ser.)
Tends retort furnace that cremates human bodies: Slides casket containing body into furnace. Starts furnace. Adjusts valves to attain extreme heat and to maintain temperature for specified time. Allows furnace to cool. Removes unburned metal casket parts from furnace. Scrapes ashes of casket and body from furnace, using handtools. Sifts ashes through fine screen and removes extraneous material. Places remains in canister and attaches metal identification tag to canister. Cleans furnace and sweeps and washes floors. May place rings and jewelry in temporary box for return to relatives. May clean building and fixtures. May care for lawns and shrubs.
GOE: 06.04.19 STRENGTH: H GED: R3 M2 L2 SVP: 3 DLU: 77

359.687-010 PALLBEARER (personal ser.)
Acts as one of group to carry casket from mortuary to place of funeral service and interment.
GOE: 09.05.03 STRENGTH: M GED: R1 M1 L1 SVP: 1 DLU: 77

36   APPAREL AND FURNISHINGS SERVICE OCCUPATIONS

This division includes occupations concerned with improving the appearance of and repairing clothing, furnishings, and accessories.

361   LAUNDERING OCCUPATIONS

This group includes occupations concerned with washing, drying, and mending garments and household furnishings, such as blankets, curtains, and washable rugs, in commercial laundries. Includes sorting soiled articles; examining laundered articles for spots, tears, stains, wrinkles, and other defects; and folding laundered articles.

361.137-010 SUPERVISOR, LAUNDRY (laundry & rel.)
Supervises and coordinates activities of workers engaged in receiving, marking, washing, and ironing clothes or linen in laundry: Determines sequence in which flatwork, one-day service, and white and colored work are to be scheduled through laundry to provide quick and efficient service to customers and to regulate work loads. Inspects articles to determine methods of specific cleaning requirements. Inspects finished laundered articles to ensure conformance to standards. Observes operation of machines and equipment to detect possible malfunctions. Investigates and resolves customer complaints of unsatisfactory work or bundle shortage. Studies literature of launderers' and dry cleaners' associations, and confers with salespersons to obtain information on new or improved work methods and equipment. Performs other duties as described under SUPERVISOR (any industry) Master Title. May be designated according to activity supervised as Flatwork Supervisor (laundry & rel.); Laundry-Marker Supervisor (laundry & rel.); Receiving, Marking, And Washing Supervisor (laun-

dry & rel.); Shirt-Ironer Supervisor (laundry & rel.); Sorting-And-Folding Supervisor (laundry & rel.); Washroom Supervisor (laundry & rel.).
GOE: 05.09.02 STRENGTH: L GED: R3 M3 L3 SVP: 6 DLU: 78

361.587-010 FLATWORK TIER (laundry & rel.)
Folds, stacks, counts, and wraps ironed flatwork: Verifies customer's identification accompanying each group of flatwork. Records customer's name on company invoice. Completes folding of flatwork, such as sheets, pillowcases, and towels. Counts flatwork for each customer and records amount on production record and invoice. Verifies customer's count. Wraps flatwork, writes customer's name on bundle, and places bundle in storage bin.
GOE: 06.04.35 STRENGTH: L GED: R2 M2 L2 SVP: 2 DLU: 77

361.665-010 WASHER, MACHINE (laundry & rel.) alternate titles: steam cleaner, machine; wet cleaner, machine; wet washer, machine
Tends one or more machines that wash commercial, industrial, or household articles, such as garments, blankets, curtains, draperies, fine linens, and rags: Loads, or directs workers engaged in loading, machine with articles requiring identical treatment. Starts machine and turns valves to admit specified amounts of soap, detergent, water, bluing, and bleach. Adds starch to loads of such articles as curtains or linens, when bell signal indicates that washing cycle is completed. Removes, or directs workers in removing, articles from washer and into handtrucks or extractors. May wash delicate fabrics by hand. May mix solutions, such as bleach, bluing, or starch, and apply them to articles before or after washing to remove color or improve appearance. May spot-clean articles, before washing, to remove heavy stains. May sterilize items. May hang curtains, draperies, or blankets on stretch-frames to dry. May brush blankets, or feed blankets into carding machine, to raise and fluff nap. May pull trousers over heated metal forms to dry and stretch legs. May load and remove articles from extractor or drier by hand or hoist, using metal basket or cord mesh bag. May tend semiautomatic or computer-controlled washing machines that automatically select water levels, temperature, cleaning additives, and wash cycle according to type of articles to be laundered. May tend machines that dry articles. When washing contaminated laundry from hospital isolation wards, may be designated Isolation-Washer (laundry & rel.). May be designated according to type of articles washed as Flatwork Washer (laundry & rel.); Overall Washer (laundry & rel.); Rag Washer (laundry & rel.); Washer, Blanket (laundry & rel.).
GOE: 06.04.35 STRENGTH: M GED: R3 M2 L2 SVP: 4 DLU: 81

361.682-010 RUG CLEANER, MACHINE (laundry & rel.)
Operates machine that washes, rinses, and partially dries rugs and carpets: Starts machine, and turns valves to admit cleaning solutions and water. Feels rug to determine end to be fed into machine to retain natural lay of pile. Fastens edge of rug to pins on conveyor bar and guides rug into machine. Sprinkles chemical solutions on stained area to dissolve stains. Moves levers or turns handwheels to regulate roller clearance, sprayer, water force, and speed of machine to avoid damage to rugs. May soap and scrub rugs requiring special attention, using portable scrubber prior to cleaning in machine. May sort rugs according to pile before cleaning. May turn valve handle to regulate heat when machine is drier equipped. May sew rugs end-to-end, using rail-mounted sewing machine and portable sewing machine to obtain continuous rug lengths for processing through machine. May load and push handtruck to transport rugs within plant.
GOE: 06.02.18 STRENGTH: M GED: R3 M1 L1 SVP: 4 DLU: 77

361.684-010 LAUNDERER, HAND (laundry & rel.)
Washes, dries, and irons articles in hand-laundries and laundromats, using equipment, such as hand iron, and small washing and drying machines: Sorts articles on worktable or in baskets on floor to separate special washes, such as fugitives and starch work. Loads and unloads washing and drying machines, and adds detergent powder and bleach as required. Folds fluff-dry articles preparatory to wrapping. Presses wearing apparel, using hand iron [PRESSER, HAND (any industry)]. Assembles, wraps, or bags laundered articles for delivery to customer. Some hand laundries are machine-equipped and only touching-up is done by hand iron; in others, some articles, such as flatwork and shirts, are sent to larger machine-equipped plants.
GOE: 06.04.35 STRENGTH: M GED: R2 M1 L2 SVP: 2 DLU: 77

361.684-014 LAUNDRY WORKER I (any industry) alternate titles: camp-laundry operator; company laundry worker
Washes and irons wearing apparel, sheets, blankets, and other linens and clothes used by employees of logging, construction, mining, or other camp, or washes uniforms, aprons, and towels in establishments supplying employees with these linens. Uses equipment usually found in household or in small laundry.
GOE: 05.12.18 STRENGTH: M GED: R2 M1 L1 SVP: 2 DLU: 77

361.684-018 SPOTTER I (laundry & rel.)
Identifies stains in washable cotton and synthetic garments or household linens prior to laundering and applies chemicals until stain dissolves, using brush, sponge, or bone spatula: Sorts stained articles to segregate items stained with oil, grease or blood. Applies and rubs chemicals into garment, using bone spatula, sponge or brush, until stain dissolves. Places spotted articles in net bags for return to washroom. Bleaches and washes some articles in small washing machine.
GOE: 06.02.27 STRENGTH: L GED: R3 M1 L1 SVP: 3 DLU: 77

361.685-010 CONDITIONER-TUMBLER OPERATOR (laundry & rel.) alternate titles: tumbler operator

Tends conditioner machine that semidries and untangles flatwork preparatory to ironing: Inserts small pieces directly into drum and places large pieces, such as sheets, on conveyor which feeds into conditioner where items are heated, untangled, and discharged onto conveyor leading to flatwork ironing machine.
GOE: 06.04.35 STRENGTH: M GED: R2 M1 L2 SVP: 2 DLU: 77

361.685-014 CONTINUOUS-TOWEL ROLLER (laundry & rel.) alternate titles: towel-rolling-machine operator

Tends machine that winds washed, damp, or ironed roller towels into rolls preparatory to ironing or packaging: Wraps end of towel around metal rod and inserts ends of rod into slots in machine. Swings down hinged tension gate until it latches to put tension on towel. Pushes and pulls hand-operated clutch bar to start and stop machine. Inspects towel for stains and holes as it is being wound onto roll. Secures end of wound towel with tape. Lifts rolled towel from machine. May tend machine that unrolls and folds towels.
GOE: 06.04.35 STRENGTH: L GED: R2 M1 L1 SVP: 2 DLU: 77

361.685-018 LAUNDRY WORKER II (any industry)

Tends laundering machines to clean articles, such as rags, wiping cloths, filter cloths, bags, sacks, and work clothes: Loads articles into washer and adds specified amount of detergent, soap, or other cleaning agent. Turns valve to fill washer with water. Starts machine that automatically washes and rinses articles. Lifts clean, wet articles from washer and places them successively into wringers and driers for measured time cycles. Sorts dried articles according to identification numbers or type. Folds and places item in appropriate storage bin. Lubricates machines, using grease gun and oil can. May dissolve soap granules in hot water and steam to make liquid soap. May mend torn articles, using needle and thread. May sort and count articles to verify quantities on laundry lists. May soak contaminated articles in neutralizer solution in vat to precondition articles for washing. May mix dyes and bleaches according to formula, and dye and bleach specified articles. May be designated according to article cleaned as Bag Washer (any industry); Cloth Washer (any industry); Color-Straining-Bag Washer (textile); Oil-Rag Washer (any industry); Wiping-Rag Washer (tex. prod., nec).
GOE: 06.04.35 STRENGTH: M GED: R2 M1 L1 SVP: 2 DLU: 77

361.685-022 PATCHING-MACHINE OPERATOR (laundry & rel.)

Tends machine that patches articles, such as tablecloths, sheets, and uniforms: Positions damaged article between platens (heated irons) of machine. Selects adhesive patching material to match article to be repaired. Cuts out patch with scissors, and places patch over tear. Reads gauge on machine to ensure that ram is heated to specified temperature. Presses control button to close press and secure patch on article. May seal identification tapes on articles.
GOE: 06.04.35 STRENGTH: L GED: R1 M1 L1 SVP: 2 DLU: 77

361.686-010 WASHING-MACHINE LOADER-AND-PULLER (laundry & rel.)

Loads and unloads washing machines in laundry: Pushes handtruck containing soiled laundry from marking and classifying department to washing machine and loads articles into machine. Removes washed laundry from machine and places in extractor baskets. May lift loaded extractor baskets, using power hoist. May place baskets in extractor and start extractor. May be known according to task performed as Puller (laundry & rel.); Washer Helper, Machine (laundry & rel.); Washing-Machine Loader (laundry & rel.) I.
GOE: 06.04.35 STRENGTH: H GED: R2 M1 L1 SVP: 2 DLU: 77

361.687-010 ASSEMBLER, WET WASH (laundry & rel.) alternate titles: net checker-hanger

Reassembles washed laundry according to lot number or individual customer's bundles preparatory to subsequent processing, such as tumbling, starching, or ironing: Compares pin number on nets of laundry to numbers on laundry ticket and hangs nets in bins, or slides key-tag onto key-tag holder to assemble lots. Counts key-tags on holder or compares count of nets in bin to count of pin numbers written on laundry ticket to verify completed assembly. Loads assembled lots in basket trucks for delivery to other work stations.
GOE: 05.09.03 STRENGTH: M GED: R2 M1 L1 SVP: 2 DLU: 77

361.687-014 CLASSIFIER (laundry & rel.) alternate titles: assorter, laundry; separator; soiled linen distributor; sorter, laundry articles

Sorts laundry into lots, such as flatwork, starchwork, and colored articles prior to washing or ironing: Places sorted articles in bins, nets, or baskets, or onto conveyor belt. May weigh flatwork and record weight on laundry ticket. May affix customer's identification mark on articles or fasten identifying pin to nets.
GOE: 06.03.02 STRENGTH: L GED: R2 M1 L2 SVP: 2 DLU: 78

361.687-018 LAUNDRY LABORER (laundry & rel.) alternate titles: bundle clerk

Prepares laundry for processing and distributes laundry, performing any combination of following duties: Opens bundles of soiled laundry. Places bundles onto conveyor belt or drops down chute for distribution to marking and classification sections. Weighs laundry on scales and records weight on tickets. Removes bundles from conveyor and distributes to workers, using handtruck. Fastens identification pins or clips onto laundry to facilitate subsequent assembly of customers' orders. Sorts net bags containing clean wash according to customers' identification tags. Sorts empty net bags according to color and size. Collects identification tags from lots of laundered articles for reuse. Moistens clean wash preparatory to ironing. Operates power hoist to load and unload washing machines and extractors. Stacks linen supplies on storage room shelves. Unloads soiled linen from trucks. May be designated according to duties performed as Bundle Weigher (laundry & rel.); Chute Worker (laundry & rel.); Clipper (laundry & rel.); Linen-Supply-Room Worker (laundry & rel.); Net Sorter (laundry & rel.). May be designated: Pin Sorter And Bagger (laundry & rel.); Pin Worker (laundry & rel.); Washing-Machine Loader (laundry & rel.) II.
GOE: 06.04.35 STRENGTH: M GED: R1 M1 L1 SVP: 2 DLU: 77

361.687-022 LINEN GRADER (laundry & rel.)

Grades laundered towels and similar linens according to quality, condition, and kind of item. Ties them into bundles of specified size or number of articles and records contents of each bundle. Stores bundles in bins for delivery to customers of linen-rental service.
GOE: 06.03.02 STRENGTH: L GED: R2 M1 L1 SVP: 2 DLU: 77

361.687-026 SHAKER, WEARING APPAREL (laundry & rel.)

Shakes out semidry wearing apparel to prepare it for ironing, sorting, or folding. Inspects articles for tears or missing buttons, and routes damaged articles to repair department. Sorts, folds, and stacks articles on handtrucks or hangs them on moving conveyor. May starch shirt collars and cuffs.
GOE: 06.04.35 STRENGTH: L GED: R1 M1 L1 SVP: 2 DLU: 77

361.687-030 WASHER, HAND (laundry & rel.)

Washes articles, such as curtains, table linens, and lingerie by hand: Soaps and rubs articles, and rinses them in chemical solutions and clear water. Extracts excess moisture with hand wringer or tends small extractor [EXTRACTOR OPERATOR (any industry)]. Hangs articles on racks to dry. May immerse articles in tint or dye solutions to restore color. May operate small machines to wash articles. May wash and card blankets.
GOE: 06.04.35 STRENGTH: L GED: R2 M1 L1 SVP: 2 DLU: 77

362 DRY CLEANING OCCUPATIONS

This group includes occupations concerned with washing garments, furs, hats, rugs, and other household furnishings with cleaning solvents, in drycleaning plants. Includes washing unusually soiled articles with water, which may or may not be preparatory to washing them with solvents.

362.381-010 SPOTTER II (laundry & rel.)

Identifies stains in wool, synthetic, and silk garments and household fabrics and applies chemical solutions to remove stains, determining spotting procedures on basis of type of fabric and nature of stain: Spreads article on worktable and positions stain over vacuum head or on marble slab. Sprinkles chemical solvents over stain and pats area with brush or sponge until stain is removed. Applies chemicals to neutralize effect of solvents. Sprays steam, water, or air over spot to flush out chemicals and dry garment. Applies bleaching powder to spot and sprays with steam to remove stains from certain fabrics which do not respond to other cleaning solvents. May mix bleaching agent with hot water in vats and soak material until bleached. May operate drycleaning machine. May be designated according to type of material spotted as Silk Spotter (laundry & rel.); Wool Spotter (laundry & rel.).
GOE: 06.02.27 STRENGTH: L GED: R3 M2 L2 SVP: 4 DLU: 77

362.382-010 DRY-CLEANER APPRENTICE (laundry & rel.) alternate titles: dry-cleaning-machine-operator apprentice

Performs duties as described under APPRENTICE (any industry) Master Title.
GOE: 06.02.16 STRENGTH: M GED: R3 M2 L2 SVP: 5 DLU: 77

362.382-014 DRY CLEANER (laundry & rel.) alternate titles: dry-cleaning-machine operator

Operates dry cleaning machine to clean garments, drapes, and other materials, utilizing knowledge of cleaning processes, fabrics, and colors: Sorts articles, places lot of sorted articles in drum of dry cleaning machine. Fastens cover and starts drum rotating. Turns or pushes valves, levers, and switches to admit cleaning solvent into drum. Adds liquid soap or chemicals to facilitate cleaning process. Tends extractor that removes excess cleaning solvent from articles [EXTRACTOR OPERATOR (any industry) 581.685-038]. Tends tumbler that dries articles and removes odor of solvent from articles [TUMBLER OPERATOR (laundry & rel.) 369.685-034]. Opens valves of dry cleaning machine to drain dirty solvent into filter tank. Adds chemicals to solvent to facilitate filtration, and starts electric pumps, forcing solvent through filters to screen lint, dirt, and other impurities. Pulls sludge box from bottom of tank to remove sludge. Starts electric pumps and turns valves to operate distilling system that reclaims dirty solvent. May operate dry cleaning machine that automatically extracts excess cleaning solvent from articles. May clean by hand articles that cannot be cleaned by machine because of amount of soil on article or delicacy of fabric [DRY CLEANER, HAND (laundry & rel.) 362.684-010]. May add chemicals to dry cleaning machine to render garments water repellant. May spot articles [SPOTTER (laundry & rel.) II 362.381-010].
GOE: 06.02.16 STRENGTH: M GED: R3 M2 L2 SVP: 5 DLU: 81

362.684-010 DRY CLEANER, HAND (laundry & rel.)

Cleans, by hand, articles, such as garments, drapes, lampshades, and leather goods that require individual treatment or are too delicate for machine cleaning:

Determines whether article will be cleaned with water or drycleaning solvents. Determines work aids to use, such as cloths, brushes, or sponges. Immerses articles in water or cleaning solvent, or dips brush or sponge into liquid and rubs article until clean. Observes work methods to ensure that articles are not damaged. Rinses and dries cleaned article. May bleach articles, such as draperies and bedspreads, to strip articles of color or discoloration.
GOE: 06.04.35 STRENGTH: M GED: R2 M1 L1 SVP: 3 DLU: 77

362.684-014 FUR CLEANER (laundry & rel.) alternate titles: fur dry-cleaner; furrier; sawdust-machine operator

Cleans fur pieces and garments by hand or machine, using brushes, pads, sawdust, corncob dust, and cleaning fluids, determining procedure and type of cleaning agent from knowledge of difference in dyed, processed, or natural furs: Examines fur for damage and to identify type of fur. Cleans furs, using either of following methods: (1) rubbing lining of garment and brushing collar, cuffs, and soiled areas, using pad and brush dipped in cleaning solvent or (2) placing furs in drum of cleaning machine containing treated sawdust or corncob dust. Removes sawdust or corncob dust from cleaned garments, using compressed air line nozzle or rotating drum. Dries fluid-cleaned garments, using extractor and either drying cabinet or tumbler drier. Beats or rubs fur with rattan or bamboo stick to fluff fur. May spray glazing compound on fur and brush by hand. May wash fur garment linings. May iron fur.
GOE: 06.02.27 STRENGTH: L GED: R3 M2 L2 SVP: 5 DLU: 77

362.684-018 FUR CLEANER, HAND (laundry & rel.) alternate titles: fur dry-cleaner, hand

Cleans fur pieces and fur garments, by hand, that are too delicate to be cleaned by machine: Brushes fur pieces with handbrush dipped in cleaning fluid. Places garment or piece in box of sawdust or corncob dust and rubs dust through fur with hands to remove moisture and further clean fur. Removes cleaning dust from furs with electric blower. May brush or spray glazing compound on furs [FUR GLAZER (fur goods; laundry & rel.)].
GOE: 06.04.35 STRENGTH: L GED: R3 M1 L2 SVP: 5 DLU: 77

362.684-022 FURNITURE CLEANER (laundry & rel.) alternate titles: dry cleaner, furniture, hand; furniture shampooer

Cleans upholstered furniture in plant or on customer's premises, using vacuum cleaner, brush, sponge, drycleaning fluids, or detergent solutions: Cleans loose dust and dirt from furniture, using vacuum cleaner. Applies cleaning solutions selected according to stains and pats or rubs stained areas with brush or sponge to remove stains. Scrubs upholstery with brush and drycleaning solvents or detergent solutions and water to clean upholstery. Rubs leather or plastic surfaces with oiled cloth and buffs with cloth or hand buffer to restore softness and luster. May spray upholstery, using spray gun and solutions such as stain repellent or plastic fluid which reduces soil collection. May polish wooden parts of furniture.
GOE: 06.04.35 STRENGTH: M GED: R2 M1 L2 SVP: 3 DLU: 77

362.684-026 LEATHER CLEANER (laundry & rel.)

Cleans suede and leather garments, such as gloves, jackets, and coats: Sorts and classifies articles into lots according to color, degree of dirtiness, and work to be performed. Brushes or sponges stains with fatty liquors (leather oils extracted from hides) to spot garment preparatory to cleaning. Observes surface and modifies pressure on brush according to type of leather to avoid damage to garment. Loads sorted articles into drum of cleaning machine. Turns valve to admit cleaning fluid into drum. Loads cleaned garments into extractor and tumbler to dry and fluff garments. May hand clean articles that are too delicate or badly soiled for machine cleaning.
GOE: 06.04.35 STRENGTH: L GED: R3 M2 L2 SVP: 3 DLU: 77

362.685-010 FEATHER RENOVATOR (laundry & rel.) alternate titles: pillow cleaner

Tends renovator machine that cleans feathers for reuse in pillows: Cuts pillow along seam and empties feathers into hopper of machine that automatically cleans and sterilizes feathers with ultra violet light or steam and hot air. Clamps new or cleaned pillow tick over discharge spout to refill pillow. Opens air valve to blow feathers into pillow tick. May sew opening in tick, using power sewing machine.
GOE: 06.04.35 STRENGTH: L GED: R1 M1 L1 SVP: 2 DLU: 77

362.686-010 DRY-CLEANER HELPER (laundry & rel.) alternate titles: cleaner assistant; cleaner helper; dry-cleaning-machine-operator helper

Assists DRY CLEANER (laundry & rel.) to dryclean or wet-clean garments, drapes, and other articles: Starts drycleaning machines and adds filter powder and activated carbon to prepare machines for work. Loads and unloads drycleaning and washing machines, extractor, and tumbler. Moves articles to and from machines, using handtruck. Scrubs articles, such as shirts and raincoats which require more vigorous action than obtained from wet-cleaning machines, using brushes and soap solution. Cleans filter on drycleaning machines. Sorts and distributes cleaned garments to pressers. Performs other duties as described under HELPER (any industry) Master Title.
GOE: 06.04.35 STRENGTH: M GED: R2 M1 L1 SVP: 2 DLU: 77

362.686-014 RUG-CLEANER HELPER (laundry & rel.)

Performs variety of tasks to assist in cleaning rugs in plant or at customers' premises: Moves furniture to remove rug to plant or to clear room for cleaning rug on premises. Pushes vacuum cleaner over rug or feeds rug into machine

equipped with rotating straps or brushes that remove dirt and dust preparatory to scrubbing. Fastens rug to pins attached to conveyor chain of automatic cleaning machine, as directed by RUG CLEANER, MACHINE (laundry & rel.). Examines or rubs cleaned rugs with towel to determine cleanliness and notifies RUG CLEANER, MACHINE (laundry & rel.) if additional cleaning is required. Rolls and wraps rug with paper or ties it with cord for delivery to customer or storage. May brush or spray sizing on back of rug. May spray rugs, carpets, and upholstered furniture with insecticides to mothproof them.
GOE: 06.04.35 STRENGTH: M GED: R2 M1 L2 SVP: 2 DLU: 77

362.687-010 GLOVE CLEANER, HAND (laundry & rel.)

Cleans leather gloves with cleaning solvents, using handbrush: Soaks gloves in vessel containing cleaning solution. Lays soaked gloves on worktable and brushes gloves with handbrush until clean, observing texture of leather and controlling pressure on brush to avoid damage (scuffing) to leather. Clips gloves to hanger or fits gloves on heated form to dry. May immerse white gloves in solution to prevent yellowing. May dye gloves or jackets, following customer's specifications.
GOE: 06.04.35 STRENGTH: L GED: R2 M1 L2 SVP: 2 DLU: 77

362.687-014 LINING SCRUBBER (laundry & rel.) alternate titles: brusher-down; lining brusher; lining cleaner

Cleans linings of fur garments by scrubbing the linings with brush dipped in cleaning solvent.
GOE: 06.04.35 STRENGTH: L GED: R1 M1 L1 SVP: 2 DLU: 77

362.687-018 SHAVER (laundry & rel.)

Brushes surface of cleaned suede leather garments with stiff handbrush to raise nap. May position garment on form and actuate steam and air pressure to expand garment for ease in brushing.
GOE: 06.04.35 STRENGTH: L GED: R1 M1 L1 SVP: 2 DLU: 77

363 PRESSING OCCUPATIONS

This group includes occupations concerned with removing wrinkles from and restoring shape or giving finish to articles by the application of tension or pressure in commercial laundries, dry cleaning plants, and valet shops. The pressure method is usually accompanied by heat or steam.

363.681-010 SILK FINISHER (laundry & rel.)

Presses drycleaned and wet-cleaned silk and synthetic fiber garments, using hot-head press or steamtable, puff irons, and hand iron: Operates machine presses to finish those parts that can be pressed flat and completes other parts of garments by pressing with hand iron. Finishes parts difficult to reach, such as flounces, by fitting parts over puff irons. Finishes velvet garments by steaming on buck of hot-head press or steamtable, and brushing pile (nap) with handbrush. Finishes fancy garments, such as evening gowns and costumes, with hand iron, applying knowledge of fabrics and heats to produce high quality finishes which cannot be obtained on machine presses. Presses ties on small pressing machine or by inserting heated metal form into tie and touching up rough places with hand iron. Finishes pleated garments, determining size of pleat from evidence of old pleat or from work order (for new garments) and presses with machine press or hand iron. May press wool fabrics requiring precision finishing. In establishments where many SILK FINISHERS (laundry & rel.) are employed may be designated according to specialty as Finisher, Hand (laundry & rel.); Form-Finishing-Machine Operator (laundry & rel.); Hot-Head-Machine Operator (laundry & rel.); Pleat Presser (laundry & rel.); Puff-Iron Operator (laundry & rel.) I; Tie Presser (laundry & rel.); Velvet Steamer (laundry & rel.).
GOE: 06.04.35 STRENGTH: L GED: R3 M1 L2 SVP: 4 DLU: 77

363.682-010 LEATHER FINISHER (laundry & rel.) alternate titles: presser, leather garments

Operates hot-head pressing machine to press and shape drycleaned leather or suede garments: Positions garment on buck of machine and pushes buttons to lower pressing head of machine onto garment. Rearranges garment on buck, repeating process until pressing is completed. Brushes suede to raise nap.
GOE: 06.04.35 STRENGTH: L GED: R3 M1 L2 SVP: 4 DLU: 77

363.682-014 PRESSER, ALL-AROUND (laundry & rel.) alternate titles: combination presser

Operates steam pressing machine [PRESSER, MACHINE (any industry) 363.682-018] or uses hand iron [PRESSER, HAND (any industry) 363.684-018] to press garments, such as trousers, sweaters, and dresses, usually in small cleaning establishment. Presses silk garments [SILK FINISHER (laundry & rel.) 363.681-010] and wool garments [WOOL PRESSER (laundry & rel.) 363.682-018].
GOE: 06.04.35 STRENGTH: M GED: R2 M2 L1 SVP: 3 DLU: 80

363.682-018 PRESSER, MACHINE (any industry) alternate titles: buck presser; finisher, machine; flattening-machine operator; ironer, machine; pressing machine operator; steam flattener; steam presser; steam-press operator

Operates pressing machine to smooth surfaces, flatten seams, or shape articles, such as garments, drapes, slipcovers, and hose, in manufacturing or dry cleaning establishments, using either of following methods: (1) Spreads articles to be pressed on buck (padded table) of machine. Pulls pressing head onto article and depresses pedals or presses buttons to admit steam from buck through garments to press them and to exhaust steam from presser. Rearranges articles

on buck and repeats process until pressing is complete. (2) Positions garment on buck and depresses pedal to lower *jump iron* onto garment and to apply pressure. Pushes lever to release steam from iron. Pushes iron attached to movable arm back and forth over garment and shifts garment under iron until garment is pressed. Hangs pressed articles on wire hangers. May operate two presses simultaneously, positioning articles on one press while another article is steamed on other press. May finish pressed articles, using hand or puff irons. May tend machine that presses and shapes articles, such as shirts, blouses, and sweaters [PRESSER, FORM (any industry) 363.685-018]. May be designated according to article pressed as Coat Presser (any industry); Pants Presser (any industry); or according to fabric pressed as Silk Presser (garment) II; or according to part of garment pressed as Armhole-And-Shoulder Off-Presser (garment); Lining Presser (laundry & rel.); or according to type of machine used as Jump-Iron-Machine Presser (garment). May be designated according to article, part, type of fabric, or machine used as Band Presser (garment); Collar Fuser (garment); Form-Press Operator (laundry & rel.); Legger-Press Operator (laundry & rel.); Mushroom-Press Operator (laundry & rel.); Puff-Iron Operator (laundry & rel.) II; Shirt Finisher (garment); Topper-Press Operator (laundry & rel.); Topper-Press Operator, Automatic (laundry & rel.); Vest-Front Presser (garment); Wash-Clothes Presser (laundry & rel.); Wool Presser (laundry & rel.).
GOE: 06.04.05 STRENGTH: M GED: R2 M1 L1 SVP: 2 DLU: 80

363.684-010 BLOCKER (laundry & rel.) alternate titles: boucle finisher; knitted-garment finisher; knitted-goods shaper; presser-and-blocker, knitted goods; presser-and-shaper, knitted goods
Blocks (shapes) knitted garments after cleaning: Shrinks or stretches garment by hand until it conforms to original measurements and pins garment to cover of steamtable or back of pressing machine. Applies steam to garment, as it is held in shape, by means of hand valves or foot levers. Measures and records dimensions of garments, using yardstick, cloth tape, or by making perforated outline on paper. Compares cleaned garments with recorded measurements or perforated paper and returns garments that have shrunk or stretched for reprocessing. May hang garments on forms corresponding to desired shape and saturate with steam from nozzle to block garments. May measure customer and record measurements for use in blocking customer's garments. May fold and wrap garments.
GOE: 06.02.27 STRENGTH: L GED: R3 M2 L1 SVP: 3 DLU: 77

363.684-014 HAT BLOCKER (laundry & rel.) alternate titles: hat finisher
Blocks cleaned hats to specified size and shape: Selects wooden hat block according to size and shape of hat. Mounts hat on block and holds block over steamer to soften material. Pulls hat down over block to shape crown. Places hat on form of hat-ironing machine. Depresses pedal to engage automatic hat-ironing machine. Brushes crown with melted wax to ensure retention of shape during further processing. Removes hat from block and applies sizing to brim with sponge. Inserts hat in hollow, wooden brim form. Steams or wets brim and places under heated sandbag to press and shape brim. Rubs or brushes hat to smooth nap. Applies cleaning solvent with brush or sponge to remove spots. May insert finished hats in paper bags. May wait on patrons and collect payment. May be designated according to part of hat blocked as Brim Blocker (laundry & rel.); Crown Blocker (laundry & rel.); or according to machine operated as Crown-Ironer Operator (laundry & rel.).
GOE: 06.02.27 STRENGTH: L GED: R3 M1 L1 SVP: 4 DLU: 77

363.684-018 PRESSER, HAND (any industry) alternate titles: finisher, hand; ironer, hand
Presses articles, such as drapes, knit goods, millinery parts, parachutes, garments, and slip covers, or delicate textiles, such as lace, synthetics, and silks to remove wrinkles, flatten seams, and give shape to article, using hand iron: Places article in position on ironing board or worktable. Smooths and shapes fabric prior to pressing. Sprays water over fabric to soften fibers when not using steam iron. Adjusts temperature of iron, according to type of fabric, and uses covering cloths to prevent scorching or to avoid sheen on delicate fabrics. Pushes and pulls iron over surface of article, according to type of fabric. Fits odd-shaped pieces which cannot be pressed flat over puff iron. May pin, fold, and hang article after pressing. May be designated according to article or part pressed as Coat Ironer, Hand (any industry); Lining Presser (garment; laundry & rel.); Seam Presser (garment); Vest Presser (garment); or according to type of cloth pressed as Cotton Presser (garment); Silk Presser (garment) I or part pressed as: Flatwork Finisher, Hand (laundry & rel.); Piece Presser (garment); Pocket Presser (garment); Underpresser, Hand (garment); Waist Presser (garment); Wearing-Apparel Finisher, Hand (laundry & rel.).
GOE: 06.04.35 STRENGTH: L GED: R2 M1 L1 SVP: 2 DLU: 80

363.685-010 PRESS OPERATOR (laundry & rel.) alternate titles: wearing-apparel presser
Tends pressing-machine (hot-head type) to press washed wearing apparel, such as uniforms, jackets, aprons, and shirts: Smooths section of garment on buck (table) of machine, and moistens dry portions of garment with wet cloth or water spray. Pushes buttons to lower pressing head of machine to press and dry garment. Rearranges garment on buck, repeating process until pressing is completed. May work as part of team and press only portion of garment. May tend two or three presses simultaneously, positioning garment on one press while other presses are closed.
GOE: 06.04.35 STRENGTH: L GED: R2 M1 L1 SVP: 2 DLU: 77

363.685-014 PRESSER, AUTOMATIC (laundry & rel.) alternate titles: press operator, automatic
Tends automatic pressing machine equipped with single or double upright body forms to press front, yoke, and back of shirts, coats, and other garments: Fits garment on buck (table) and pulls lever to clamp neckband of garment to buck. Lowers pressing head to iron yoke. Depresses pedal to clamp tailband in position on buck, and release pressing head to raised position. Presses control buttons that rotate dressed buck into pressing cabinet for automatic ironing of front and back of garment. May pull sleeves over forms and shift levers to move forms into pressing cabinet for ironing. May finish one type of garment, such as duck or linen coats. May be designated according to type of garment pressed as Shirt Presser, Automatic (laundry & rel.); Pants Presser, Automatic (laundry & rel.).
GOE: 06.04.35 STRENGTH: L GED: R2 M1 L1 SVP: 3 DLU: 77

363.685-018 PRESSER, FORM (any industry) alternate titles: blocker; pressing-machine operator
Tends machine that presses and blocks (shapes) garments, such as blouses, coats, dresses, shirts, and sweaters in manufacturing or drycleaning establishment: Selects pressing form (dummy) according to shape of garment. Positions form on holder over steaming device, expands or contracts form according to size of garment, and inserts pin in slot to lock form. Pulls garment over form. Turns dial to regulate steam pressure according to type of material pressed. Depresses pedals that activate steam and air to press, block, and dry garment. Removes garment from form and lays garment on table.
GOE: 06.04.35 STRENGTH: L GED: R2 M2 L1 SVP: 2 DLU: 77

363.685-022 PRESSER, HANDKERCHIEF (laundry & rel.) alternate titles: handkerchief ironer
Tends machine that fluffs and irons flatwork articles, such as handkerchiefs and napkins: Dumps handkerchiefs from net into door-hopper of fluffer unit to condition for ironing. Places fluffed handkerchief on pad of machine and presses pedal to clamp edge. Pulls opposite edge to straighten and square handkerchief on pad. Pulls lever to revolve pad under steam chest to iron handkerchief and rotate second press in position. Removes handkerchief. May operate machine with sock attachment to press socks. May fold handkerchief and place in bag with identification tag. May tie bundles of handkerchiefs with paper ribbon.
GOE: 06.04.35 STRENGTH: L GED: R1 M1 L1 SVP: 2 DLU: 77

363.685-026 SHIRT PRESSER (laundry & rel.)
Performs any combination of following tasks in conjunction with other workers to finish and fold shirts: Places collar, cuffs, and yoke on curved, padded forms of pressing machine. Pushes button or moves lever to lower pressing head and press shirt parts. Pulls sleeves of shirt over heated form to finish, or pulls sleeve over padded forms and presses button to insert forms into cabinet to iron sleeves. Lays back of shirt on buck (table) of pressing machine. Depresses pedal or pushes button to lower pressing head onto shirt. Drapes shirt over form and pushes buttons to rotate form into steam cabinet to press shirt bosom. Folds finished shirts around piece of cardboard on folding board or on folding machine. Finishes detached collars by feeding collars into equipment for dampening, shaping, and pressing. May be designated according to part of garment ironed as Body Presser (laundry & rel.); Bosom Presser (laundry & rel.); Shirt-Collar-And-Cuff Presser (laundry & rel.); Shirt Folder (laundry & rel.) II; Yoke Presser (laundry & rel.).
GOE: 06.04.35 STRENGTH: L GED: R2 M1 L1 SVP: 2 DLU: 78

363.686-010 FLATWORK FINISHER (laundry & rel.)
Feeds laundered flatwork articles, such as sheets, pillowcases, tablecloths, and napkins into machine that automatically spreads and presses finished articles: Shakes wrinkles and folds from semidry flatwork. Lays edge of flatwork articles on feeder roller that conveys articles into machine, shaking, smoothing, and guiding by hand during ironing process to prevent folds and wrinkles. Folds flatwork pieces discharged from machine, and places articles on table for assembly. Rejects faulty articles for reprocessing. May be designated according to operation performed as Flatwork Catcher (laundry & rel.); Flatwork Feeder (laundry & rel.); Flatwork Folder (laundry & rel.); Shaker, Flatwork (laundry & rel.).
GOE: 06.04.35 STRENGTH: L GED: R2 M1 L1 SVP: 2 DLU: 77

363.687-010 GLOVE FORMER (glove & mit.; laundry & rel.) alternate titles: glove finisher; glove presser; glove turner and former; ironer; layer-off
Pulls gloves over heated, hand-shaped form and smooths with hands, cloth, or brush to shape and press gloves. Presses thick portion of heavy gloves by beating finger tips and seams with wooden block. May smooth glove between fingers (crotch) by pulling rake (pronged bar) over gloved form. May examine glove while pressing to detect defects. May turn seams inside [GLOVE TURNER (glove & mit.)]. May sew ripped seams and small tears by hand. May apply chemical solution and rub gloves with cloth to remove stains. May apply chemical or ready-mixed tint with cloth to restore original color to gloves.
GOE: 06.04.27 STRENGTH: L GED: R1 M1 L1 SVP: 3 DLU: 77

363.687-014 IRONER, SOCK (laundry & rel.) alternate titles: sock-and-stocking ironer; sock drier; sock folder
Pulls socks and stockings over heated metal forms to dry and finish them. Folds and stacks the ironed socks and stockings. May cover small hole with adhesive cloth patch and apply heat to secure patch to fabric of sock.

GOE: 06.04.35 STRENGTH: L GED: R1 M1 L1 SVP: 1 DLU: 77

363.687-018 PUFF IRONER (laundry & rel.) alternate titles: baller; puffer

Slides material back and forth over heated, metal, ball-shaped form to smooth and press portions of garments that cannot be satisfactorily pressed with flat presser or hand iron. May use hand iron to complete pressing of garment.
GOE: 06.04.27 STRENGTH: L GED: R1 M1 L1 SVP: 1 DLU: 77

363.687-022 STRETCHER-DRIER OPERATOR (laundry & rel.) alternate titles: carder, blankets; curtain drier; curtain framer; curtain stretcher; stretcher operator

Stretches and dries household articles, such as blankets, curtains, and linen tablecloths that require special treatment to protect delicate fabrics and retain desired measurements, using any of following methods: (1) Attaches article to projecting wires of adjustable stretcher and pushes, or rotates frame on locking pivot, to position article in drying cabinet. (2) Attaches curtains or blankets to horizontal frame mounted over steampipes and turns valve to allow steam to heat pipes and dry articles. (3) Adjusts levers to clamp and stretch drapes and comforts in horizontal frame of drapery former. May card (brush) blankets with wire-bristled handbrush to raise nap or feed blankets into carding machine. May touch-up (press) bindings and ruffles with hand iron. May guide ruffles of curtains through grooved, heated rollers to fluting machine that press fluting (grooves) in fabric. May fold and stack articles.
GOE: 06.04.35 STRENGTH: L GED: R2 M1 L1 SVP: 2 DLU: 77

364 DYEING AND RELATED OCCUPATIONS

This group includes occupations concerned with changing the color of articles by means of dyes. Involves knowledge of composition of textiles being dyed and of reagents, such as acids, alkalies, soap and dyes, and their effect on textiles.

364.361-010 DYER (laundry & rel.) alternate titles: sample dyer

Dyes articles, such as garments, drapes, and slipcovers in kettles or dyeing machines, and mixes dyes and chemicals according to standard formulas or by matching customers' samples against color cards that provide formulas: Examines garment to identify fabric and original dye by sight, touch, or by testing sample with fire or chemical reagent. Computes and weighs out powdered dye, oil, and acids, following formulas. Dissolves dye in boiling water and tests dye on swatch of fabric. Adds dyes to water until desired color is produced. Immerses garment in solution and stirs with stick, or dyes garment in rotary-drum or paddle-dyeing machine. Removes or directs DYER HELPER (laundry & rel.) to remove garments from kettle or machine, and rinses them in water and acetic acid solution to remove excess dye and to fix colors. Directs DYER HELPER (laundry & rel.) in operation of extractor and drier. May mix chemicals to make bleaching bath, and immerse garments in bath before dyeing to remove original colors. May use spray gun to spray dye onto garments.
GOE: 05.05.16 STRENGTH: M GED: R4 M3 L2 SVP: 7 DLU: 77

364.361-014 RUG DYER I (laundry & rel.)

Dyes rugs to match sample color, basing work procedure on knowledge of properties of bleaching agents and dyes, and on type, construction, condition, and colors of rug: Measures amounts of bleaches and dyes and mixes components with boiling water in vats. Immerses rug in bleaching bath to strip colors and in color bath to dye rug. May loop rug around reel that revolves rug in dye bath.
GOE: 05.05.16 STRENGTH: M GED: R4 M3 L3 SVP: 8 DLU: 77

364.381-010 PAINTER, RUG TOUCH-UP (laundry & rel.)

Touches up worn and faded spots on cleaned rugs, using oil paint to restore color and contour of original pattern: Examines rug to determine color to apply. Selects matching paint and works paint into pile of rug pattern with stylus. May use inks instead of paints. May mix colors to attain matching color and shade.
GOE: 01.06.03 STRENGTH: L GED: R3 M1 L2 SVP: 6 DLU: 77

364.684-010 RUG DYER II (laundry & rel.)

Dyes rugs on customers' premises, using spray gun and brushes: Mixes powdered dye with water according to prescribed formula. Sprays or brushes rugs with prepared solution to remove stains. Applies dye to rugs with spray gun, electrically rotated brush, and handbrushes.
GOE: 05.10.07 STRENGTH: L GED: R3 M2 L2 SVP: 5 DLU: 77

364.684-014 SHOE DYER (personal ser.) alternate titles: shoe tinter

Dyes or tints shoes for customers of shoe repair or shoe shining shops: Inserts shoetree or stuffs paper into shoe to stiffen shoe upper, forming smooth working surface on shoe. Cleans shoes with acetone, alcohol, water, or other solutions to remove dirt, dye, and grease, using brushes, cloths, and sponges. Selects prepared dye or mixes dyes to match shade specified by instructions or color chart. Applies coat of dye or tint onto shoe upper, using spray gun or swab. Ignites gas on shoe to drive dye into leather.
GOE: 05.12.14 STRENGTH: L GED: R2 M2 L1 SVP: 3 DLU: 77

364.684-018 SPRAYER, LEATHER (laundry & rel.) alternate titles: spray dyer

Sprays dyes on leather articles, such as gloves and jackets, to restore original color, using spray gun: Selects suede or leather dyes to match color of garment and fills spray gun container with dye. Places article on dress form and sprays

dye evenly over surface. Hangs finished garments on line to dry. Brushes (buffs) suede garments with handbrush to raise nap. Sprays some garments with water-repelling compounds. May prepare dye solutions by blending basic colors to obtain specified hue.
GOE: 05.12.14 STRENGTH: L GED: R2 M1 L2 SVP: 4 DLU: 77

364.687-010 DYER HELPER (laundry & rel.) alternate titles: dyer assistant; dye-room helper

Performs any combination of following tasks in dyeing textile products, such as garments, rugs, and drapes: Loads and unloads dyeing machines, extractor, and tumbler. Scrubs rugs with handbrush, soap, and water prior to dyeing. Bleaches articles, under direction of DYER (laundry & rel.), to strip them of original colors preparatory to dyeing by immersing articles in vat. May spread rug over steamtable and turn valves to admit steam through table and into rug, when dyeing rugs.
GOE: 06.04.35 STRENGTH: H GED: R2 M1 L1 SVP: 3 DLU: 77

364.687-014 RUG-DYER HELPER (laundry & rel.)

Performs any combination of following duties to dye and dry carpets and rugs: Sews scrap material onto odd shaped rugs to facilitate handling during dyeing process. Hangs rug over roller of dyeing machine and stitches ends together with needle and twine so that rug can be immersed in solution when roller is turned. Observes rug during dyeing process and keeps rug straight on roller. Lifts rug with power hoist to drain off excess solution. Moves rug to washing platform, using handtruck. Washes rug, using water hose to remove excess dye. Places rug in extractor or hangs rug on pole in drying room. Rolls dry rug and carries or transports rug to loading area, using handtruck. May remove dust from rug before dyeing process, using rug dusting machine or hand vacuum cleaner.
GOE: 05.12.14 STRENGTH: M GED: R2 M1 L1 SVP: 3 DLU: 77

365 SHOE AND LUGGAGE REPAIRER AND RELATED OCCUPATIONS

This group includes occupations concerned with resoling, reheeling, and otherwise repairing shoes. Includes repair and renovation of hand luggage, such as handbags, briefcases, golf club bags, and hatboxes, and also trunks and other heavy luggage made of leather, plastic, fiber, and other materials.

365.131-010 SHOE-REPAIR SUPERVISOR (personal ser.) alternate titles: rehabilitation technician

Supervises and coordinates activities of workers in repairing and refinishing shoes: Inspects donated new and used shoes to determine feasability of repair or saleability. Trains subordinates and handicapped individuals in job duties of SHOE REPAIRER (personal ser.). Performs periodic performance evaluations. Performs duties as described under SHOE REPAIRER (personal ser.).
GOE: 05.05.15 STRENGTH: L GED: R3 M1 L1 SVP: 7 DLU: 77

365.361-010 LUGGAGE REPAIRER (any industry) alternate titles: hand luggage repairer

Repairs and renovates worn or damaged luggage made of leather, fiber, and other materials: Sews rips by hand or machine, inserts and repairs linings, and replaces locks, catches, straps, buckles, corner protectors, and other parts to repair all types of hand luggage. Repairs and reconditions trunks and other heavy luggage, constructing and gluing together frame, cutting and bending fiberboard pieces together, and inserting on locks, catches, corner protectors, and other parts. May construct leather articles, such as purses, wallets, and briefcases, ordered specially by customers. May specialize in repairing trunks and other heavy luggage and be designated Trunk Repairer (any industry).
GOE: 05.10.01 STRENGTH: M GED: R3 M2 L2 SVP: 6 DLU: 77

365.361-014 SHOE REPAIRER (personal ser.) alternate titles: cobbler; shoemaker

Repairs or refinishes shoes, following customer specifications, or according to nature of damage, or type of shoe: Positions shoe on last and pulls and cuts off sole or heel with pincers and knife. Starts machine, and holds welt against rotating sanding wheel or rubs with sandpaper to bevel and roughen welt for attachment of new sole. Selects blank or cuts sole or heel piece to approximate size from material, using knife. Brushes cement on new sole or heel piece and on shoe welt and shoe heel. Positions sole over shoe welt or heel piece on shoe heel and pounds piece, using machine or hammer, so piece adheres to shoe; drives nails around sole or heel edge into shoe; or guides shoe and sole under needle of sewing machine to fasten sole to shoe. Trims sole or heel edge to shape of shoe with knife. Holds and turns shoe sole or heel against revolving abrasive wheel to smooth edge and remove excess material. Brushes edge with stain or polish and holds against revolving buffing wheels to polish edge. Nails heel and toe cleats to shoe. Restitches ripped portions or sews patches over holes in shoe uppers by hand or machine. Dampens portion of shoe and inserts and twists adjustable stretcher in shoes or pull portion of moistened shoe back and forth over warm iron to stretch shoe. May build up portions of shoes by nailing, stapling, or stitching additional material to shoe sole to add height or make other specified alterations to orthopedic shoes. May repair belts, luggage, purses, and other products made of materials, such as canvas, leather, and plastic. May quote charges, receive articles, and collect payment for repairs [SERVICE-ESTABLISHMENT ATTENDANT (laundry & rel.; personal ser.) 369.477-014].
GOE: 05.05.15 STRENGTH: L GED: R3 M2 L1 SVP: 6 DLU: 82

365.674-010 SHOE-REPAIRER HELPER (personal ser.)

Assists SHOE REPAIRER (personal ser.) to repair shoes by any combination of following tasks: Rips worn soles and heels from shoes, using handtools. Tacks new soles and heels in place and trims excess leather, using knife or revolving trimmer. Sands and finishes sole edges by holding against sanding rollers and revolving metal disk. Shines, stains, and dyes shoes. May sell merchandise, such as shoestrings, polishes, and other accessories. Performs other duties as described under HELPER (any industry) Master Title.
GOE: 05.05.15 STRENGTH: L GED: R2 M2 L1 SVP: 4 DLU: 77

366 BOOTBLACKS AND RELATED OCCUPATIONS

This group includes occupations concerned with cleaning and polishing shoes.

366.677-010 SHOE SHINER (personal ser.) alternate titles: bootblack; boot polisher; shoe polisher

Cleans and polishes footwear for customers: Removes surface dirt, using brush. Removes grime and old polish or wax from leather footwear, using brush or sponge dipped in cleaning fluid or soapy water. Applies coating of polish by hand or using dauber, and polishes leather, using brushes and cloths. Buffs buck or suede footwear with sandpaper or wire brush to clean areas or raise nap. Applies liquid dressing or dry wax by hand or dauber, and brushes surface to remove excess. Applies liquid dressing to fabric areas of footwear to restore appearance of cloth. Coats edges of sole and heel with sole dressing, using dauber or sponge. May dye or tint footwear [SHOE DYER (personal ser.)]. May brush lint from patron's clothing, using whiskbroom. May assist customers with wraps. May sweep and mop floors, dust and polish furnishings, and wash windows.
GOE: 09.05.07 STRENGTH: L GED: R1 M1 L1 SVP: 2 DLU: 77

369 APPAREL AND FURNISHINGS SERVICE OCCUPATIONS, N.E.C.

This group includes occupations, not elsewhere classified, concerned with improving appearance of, and repairing clothing, furnishings, and accessories.

369.137-010 SUPERVISOR, DRY CLEANING (laundry & rel.)

Supervises and coordinates activities of workers engaged in drycleaning and pressing wearing apparel and household articles, such as drapes, blankets, and linens: Determines standards and rates of production in accordance with company policy, type of equipment, and work load. Assigns duties to workers. Observes progress of work and transfers or hires new employees to maintain production. Confers with workers to resolve problems, complaints, and grievances. Confers with company officials and sellers of materials and equipment to plan improved methods. Reviews production and accounting records to determine cost levels of operation. Trains or assigns new employees to experienced workers for training. May supervise workers engaged in cleaning and pressing garments in hotel establishment and be known as Valet Manager (hotel & rest.).
GOE: 06.04.01 STRENGTH: M GED: R4 M3 L3 SVP: 7 DLU: 77

369.137-014 SUPERVISOR, RUG CLEANING (laundry & rel.)

Supervises and coordinates activities of workers engaged in repair, storage, and cleaning of rugs and carpets. Examines rug to determine cleaning method. May repair rugs [RUG REPAIRER (laundry & rel.)]. May measure and cut rugs to customer's specifications. Performs duties as described under SUPERVISOR (any industry) Master Title.
GOE: 05.12.01 STRENGTH: L GED: R4 M2 L3 SVP: 7 DLU: 77

369.167-010 MANAGER, LAUNDROMAT (laundry & rel.)

Manages coin-operated drycleaning and laundering business: Plans and implements hours of operations, types of services to be provided, and charges for services. Orders machines, equipment, and supplies for operation. Hires, trains, and supervises personnel to provide laundry and drycleaning services. Records and analyzes business data to determine performance record. May clean and perform repair services on machines.
GOE: 11.11.04 STRENGTH: S GED: R4 M3 L3 SVP: 6 DLU: 77

369.367-010 FUR-STORAGE CLERK (retail trade) alternate titles: fur-vault attendant

Tags and appraises fur garments received for storage: Examines garments to determine condition and estimate value. Records description of garment, estimated value, and name and address of owner. Computes and records charges. Attaches tag to garment. May take telephone orders. May prepare application for insurance, when customer gives approval, and forward application to insurance company.
GOE: 05.09.01 STRENGTH: L GED: R4 M3 L3 SVP: 6 DLU: 77

369.367-014 RUG MEASURER (laundry & rel.; retail trade) alternate titles: rug-receiving clerk

Determines type of rug received for cleaning, measures it, calculates area, and records information for use in case rug is lost and to facilitate proper billing to customer. Affixes identifying tag to rug which indicates type of work to be performed. May examine rugs for stains and holes, and determine from its condition if rug will withstand cleaning. May determine repairs which should be made and contact customer concerning repairs.
GOE: 05.09.02 STRENGTH: L GED: R3 M2 L2 SVP: 4 DLU: 77

369.384-010 HATTER (laundry & rel.)

Cleans, blocks, trims, and makes minor repairs to hats: Cuts threads to remove linings, sweatbands, hatbands and ornaments prior to cleaning. Immerses hat in solvent and rubs hat with sponge and brush to remove soil particles and stain. Tends extractor to remove moisture from hats. Shapes hat, using hat block, size ring, hat stretcher, turn-lathe, hat ironing machine and brim pressing machine. Rubs hat with pad to obtain finished appearance. Replaces linings, sweatbands, hatbands and ornaments, using needle and thread.
GOE: 06.02.27 STRENGTH: L GED: R3 M1 L2 SVP: 6 DLU: 77

369.384-014 RUG CLEANER, HAND (laundry & rel.) alternate titles: carpet cleaner; rug renovator; rug scrubber; rug shampooer; rug washer

Cleans rugs with chemical solutions in plant or on customer's premises, using handbrushes or portable scrubbing machine, determining washing method according to condition of rug: Vacuums rugs to remove loose dirt. Guides scrubbing machine over rug surface or sprays rug with cleaning solution under pressure to agitate nap and loosen embedded dirt. Removes excess suds and water from rug during scrubbing operation, using vacuum nozzle or squeegee. Identifies persistent stains and selects spotting agent to remove stain according to type of fiber, dye, and stain. Rubs chemical solution into rug with handbrush until stain disappears. Rinses rug, using water hose, and hangs rug on rack to dry. Pushes pilating (pile lifting) machine over surface of dried rug to raise and fluff nap or brushes pile, using broom. Removes excess water by feeding rugs between rollers of mechanical wringer, putting rugs in extractor, or going over surface with squeegee or vacuum nozzle. Brushes, sprays, or sprinkles sizing solutions on the backs of rugs, using handbrush, spray gun, or sprinkling can. May scrub fragile or oriental rugs, using handbrush, soap, and water. May spray acetic acid or salt solution over washed rugs to prevent colors from running. May measure rugs to determine cleaning fee. May clean upholstered furniture, using sponge, brush, and cleaning solutions. May trim frayed edges of carpet and rebind carpet edges, using scissors, knife, needle, and thread. May perform rug cleaning duties as employee of establishment, such as hotel.
GOE: 06.02.27 STRENGTH: M GED: R3 M1 L2 SVP: 5 DLU: 77

369.387-010 LAUNDRY WORKER III (any industry)

Prepares soiled clothing and linen for delivery to laundry and verifies contents of returned bundles: Prepares typed forms listing soiled articles received. Ties articles in bundle for transporting to laundry. Receives returned bundles and checks contents against lists, noting and reporting shortages. Stores clean linen on shelves and issues item on presentation of soiled articles for exchange.
GOE: 05.09.03 STRENGTH: L GED: R2 M1 L2 SVP: 3 DLU: 77

369.467-010 MANAGER, BRANCH STORE (laundry & rel.)

Manages store where customers deliver and call for articles to be cleaned, laundered, and pressed and keeps records of same: Receives article from customer. Writes identifying slip or tag giving name of customer, work to be done, and date of completion. Pins or staples tag on article. Delivers finished article to customer and collects amount due. Records cash receipts and articles received and delivered. May examine article in presence of customer to advise of possible damage that might result during processing, such as shrinkage, loss of shape, and fading. May measure garments liable to shrink. May remove ornaments and sew or replace them on finished garment upon return from plant.
GOE: 09.04.02 STRENGTH: L GED: R3 M2 L2 SVP: 3 DLU: 77

369.477-010 CURB ATTENDANT (laundry & rel.)

Gives curb service to customers: Receives and delivers articles to customers remaining in cars outside store or plant. Writes tickets to identify and to indicate work to be done. Receives amount due for servicing articles. Opens doors for customers entering or leaving store. May perform other duties, such as sweeping and dusting store, placing garments in paper bags, and running errands.
GOE: 09.04.02 STRENGTH: M GED: R2 M2 L2 SVP: 2 DLU: 77

369.477-014 SERVICE-ESTABLISHMENT ATTENDANT (laundry & rel.; personal ser.) alternate titles: counter attendant

Receives articles, such as shoes and clothing, to be repaired or cleaned, in personal-service establishment: Examines articles to determine nature of repair and advises customer of repairs needed. Quotes prices and prepares work ticket. Sends articles to work department. Returns finished articles to customer and collects amount due. May keep records of cash receipts and articles received and delivered. May sell articles, such as cleaner, polish, shoelaces, and accessories.
GOE: 09.04.02 STRENGTH: L GED: R3 M2 L2 SVP: 3 DLU: 77

369.587-010 VAULT CUSTODIAN (laundry & rel.)

Receives, identifies, fumigates, and places garments in cold-storage vaults: Marks incoming garments with identification tags, tape, or by some other method, and classifies and routes garments to cleaning and repair departments. Fills pans with fumigant and seals storage vaults to fumigate incoming and stored garments. Turns on ventilating system to remove fumigating gas from vaults. Hangs garments in specified place in storage vault. Removes stored garments at customer's request. Inspects or routes garments to INSPECTOR (laundry & rel.) and sends them to delivery department. May monitor vault room humidistat and adjust refrigeration thermostat to change temperature and relative humidity in vault. May record garment identifying information on control record.
GOE: 05.09.03 STRENGTH: M GED: R2 M1 L2 SVP: 3 DLU: 77

369.677-010 SELF-SERVICE-LAUNDRY-AND-DRY-CLEANING AT-TENDANT (laundry & rel.) alternate titles: attendant, coin-operated laundry; attendant, laundry-and-dry-cleaning service; washateria attendant

Assists customer to launder or dryclean clothes, or launders or drycleans clothes for customer paying for complete service, using self-service equipment: Gives instructions to customer in clothes preparation, such as weighing, sorting, fog-spraying spots, and removing perishable buttons. Assigns machine and directs customer or points out posted instructions regarding equipment operation. Weighs soiled items and calculates amount charged customer requiring complete services. Dampens garments with cleaning solvent and rubs with sponge or brush to remove spots or stains. Places clothes, cleaning material, bleach, and coins in laundering or drycleaning equipment, and sets automatic controls to clean or dry clothes. Removes clothes from equipment. Hangs, bags, folds, and bundles clothes for delivery to customer. Receives payment for service. May sell cleansing agents.
GOE: 09.04.02 STRENGTH: M GED: R3 M1 L3 SVP: 2 DLU: 77

369.684-010 FUR GLAZER (fur goods) alternate titles: fur glosser

Coats hair of fur garments with moisture or glazing compound to protect against shedding and restore glossy appearance: Fits garment over form and sprays glazing compound on garment with spray gun. Brushes, combs, or shakes garment to fluff fur. Allows garment to hang for specified period, or directs nozzle of compressed air line to dry fur. May iron fur and lining. May rub fur with stick to make hair fluffy. May tend sawdust-filled rotating drum to remove loose hairs. May trim garment section, using furrier's knife. May pull offcolored hair from fur, using tweezers.
GOE: 06.04.35 STRENGTH: L GED: R2 M1 L2 SVP: 2 DLU: 77

369.684-014 LAUNDRY OPERATOR (laundry & rel.)

Receives, marks, washes, finishes, checks, and wraps articles in laundry, performing any combination of following tasks: Classifies and marks incoming laundry with identifying code number, by hand or using machine [MARKER (laundry & rel.)]. Tends washing machine, extractor, and tumbler to clean and dry laundry. Finishes laundered articles, using hand iron, pressing machine, or feeds and folds flatwork on flatwork ironing machine. Sorts laundry and verifies count on laundry ticket [ASSEMBLER (laundry & rel.)]; CHECKER (laundry & rel.)]. May perform related tasks, such as mending torn articles, using sewing machine or by affixing adhesive patches. May wrap articles. May specialize in receiving and washing, or in finishing and checking, and be designated according to unit in which work is performed as Laundry Operator, Finishing (laundry & rel.); Laundry Operator, Wash Room (laundry & rel.).
GOE: 06.04.35 STRENGTH: M GED: R2 M1 L2 SVP: 3 DLU: 77

369.684-018 UMBRELLA REPAIRER (any industry)

Repairs defective umbrellas, using handtools: Replaces parts of umbrella frames, such as springs, ribs, shanks, and handles, using handtools. Sews umbrella cover to frame [UMBRELLA TIPPER, HAND (fabrication, nec)]. May repair wheels and casters on beds, carts, and similar rolling equipment [WHEEL-AND-CASTER REPAIRER (any industry)].
GOE: 05.10.01 STRENGTH: L GED: R2 M1 L2 SVP: 4 DLU: 77

369.685-010 FUR BLOWER (retail trade) alternate titles: blower

Tends equipment that fumigates and removes foreign matter from furs: Hangs furs in fumigating cabinet, pours fumigant into storage tank, and closes door. Turns switch to start blower that vaporizes and blows fumigant onto furs. Adjusts timing switch to stop fumigation process. Presses button to start ventilating system to exhaust vapors from cabinet, opens door, and removes furs. Adjusts valve on compressed air gun to regulate air pressure, according to condition or type of fur. Squeezes trigger of gun and directs stream of air on fur to remove dirt, insects, and loose fur.
GOE: 06.04.39 STRENGTH: L GED: R2 M1 L1 SVP: 2 DLU: 77

369.685-014 FUR CLEANER, MACHINE (fur goods; laundry & rel.; retail trade; wholesale tr.) alternates titles: fur beater; fur drummer; fur dry-cleaner; saw-dust machine operator

Tends drum that tumbles fur garments in dry or liquid cleaning agents to clean fur: Selects and pours liquid or drycleaning agent into drum. Places garments in drum and moves lever to start and stop drum rotation. Removes garments from drum. Dumps drycleaning agents from drum and repeats tumbling process or uses compressed air gun to remove cleaning agents from garment; or places garment in extractor to remove liquid cleaning agent. Hangs garments in heated cabinets or places in drying tumbler to dry garments. May glaze fur. May wash garment linings.
GOE: 06.04.35 STRENGTH: L GED: R2 M1 L2 SVP: 3 DLU: 77

369.685-018 FUR IRONER (laundry & rel.)

Tends fur ironing machine to remove lining wrinkles and highlight hair luster of fur garments, using either of following methods: (1) Irons lining and hair of garments, using heated hand iron to remove wrinkles from lining and produce luster on fur. (2) Positions garment on feed roll of machine. Sets temperature control of metal ironing roll according to type of fur. Depresses pedal to bring garment into contact with heated roll and guides garment under roll. Releases pedal, changes position of garment, and repeats operation to complete ironing of garment. May iron garment by hand.
GOE: 06.04.35 STRENGTH: L GED: R3 M1 L1 SVP: 3 DLU: 77

369.685-022 FUR-GLAZING-AND-POLISHING-MACHINE OPERATOR (laundry & rel.) alternate titles: fur ironer

Tends machine that combs and polishes furs, and manually applies glazing solution to restore luster: Sets thermostat to heat roller to specified temperature.

Presses button to start machine and arranges garment on feed roller. Applies water or glazing solution, using hand spray gun. Depresses pedal to raise feed roller to grooved heated roller that polishes and straightens fur. Releases feed roller and rearranges garment to remove wrinkles and restore luster to fur, using hand iron. May polish furs only and be designated Fur-Polishing-Machine Operator (laundry & rel.).
GOE: 06.04.35 STRENGTH: L GED: R2 M1 L1 SVP: 3 DLU: 77

369.685-026 RUG-DRY-ROOM ATTENDANT (laundry & rel.)

Tends rug conveyor or electric powered hoist that lifts and carries rugs to drying room, using either of following methods: (1) Pulls rug ejected from washing and wringing machines into drying room. Feeds end of rug to be sized through sizing rolls to distribute sizing compound evenly over back of rug. Fastens end of rug to pins attached to poles and pushes button to hoist and suspend rugs in drying room. (2) Feeds end of rug to be sized through sizing rolls and fastens ends to pin on rug poles. Pushes button to operate conveyor which hoists and transports rug through drying room. May adjust thermostat of heaters circulating hot air through drying room. May spray sizing compound on back of rugs with spray gun. May remove dried rugs from poles and wrap or tie for delivery to customer. May tend wrapping machine which wraps rug.
GOE: 06.04.35 STRENGTH: M GED: R2 M1 L1 SVP: 2 DLU: 77

369.685-030 SHIRT-FOLDING-MACHINE OPERATOR (garment; laundry & rel.)

Tends machine that automatically folds shirts: Positions shirt on bed of machine, places button strip and collar of shirt in clamps on machine bed, and closes clamps by hand. Pushes button to lower folding blade onto shirt and actuates folding bar and plates of machine to fold body and arms of shirt around folding blade. Depresses pedal to retract folding blade and plates and open heated collar-shaping clamp. Inserts cardboard band under collar to maintain shape. May place cardboard on shirt prior to folding to strengthen folded package. May place paper bands around folded shirts and pack shirts in bags. May separate and stack shirts according to customers' markings. May insert paper cuff links in dress shirts.
GOE: 06.04.05 STRENGTH: L GED: R2 M1 L2 SVP: 2 DLU: 77

369.685-034 TUMBLER OPERATOR (laundry & rel.) alternate titles: drier operator; drying-machine operator; drying-tumbler operator; tumbler-drier operator

Tends machines that fluff-dry laundered articles or dry and deodorize drycleaned items: Transfers partially dried articles from extractor by hand or by use of handtruck or overhead hoist, and places articles in drum of tumbler. Turns pointer on dial of machine timer for drying cycle, according to type of fabric and weight of items being dried. Starts drum and blower. May hang delicate fabrics in heated cabinet to dry. May tend extractor [EXTRACTOR OPERATOR (any industry) 581.685-038]. May fold, stack, and bundle finished articles.
GOE: 06.04.35 STRENGTH: M GED: R2 M1 L1 SVP: 2 DLU: 78

369.686-010 FOLDING-MACHINE OPERATOR (laundry & rel.)

Feeds laundered towels, pillowcases, and napkins onto feeder conveyor of machine that folds, stacks, and counts flatwork: Sorts items on feedstacks according to size. Lays aside stained articles for separate feeding and ticketing. Adjusts position of gear lever to regulate speed of machine. Removes jammed articles from machine. May unload rack and transfer stacks of folded napkins to be bundled to tying machine.
GOE: 06.04.35 STRENGTH: L GED: R2 M1 L1 SVP: 2 DLU: 78

369.687-010 ASSEMBLER (laundry & rel.) alternate titles: distributor; matcher; subsorter

Sorts laundered or drycleaned articles, such as linens, garments, blankets, and drapes, according to customer's identification mark or tag: Reads identification symbols on mark or tag attached to clean articles. Sorts articles with similar symbols into groups. Collects items belonging to each customer from group, using customer's list of articles received to verify completeness of order. Inspects items for quality of service. May be designated according to type of article assembled as Flatwork Assembler (laundry & rel.); Wearing-Apparel Assembler (laundry & rel.).
GOE: 06.03.02 STRENGTH: L GED: R2 M1 L2 SVP: 3 DLU: 78

369.687-014 CHECKER (laundry & rel.)

Verifies number and type of laundered or dry cleaned articles by checking against customers' lists: Inspects articles for cleanliness and neatness of finish. Returns incomplete laundry bundles to bin. Folds curtains lengthwise and drapes curtains over hangers. Hangs dry cleaned garments on hangers, covering articles with paper or bags. May fill customers' orders for clean linens, such as sheets, towels, aprons, and uniforms. May wrap and load bundles onto trucks for delivery to customers. May count linen supplies returned by DRIVER, SALES ROUTE (retail trade; wholesale tr.) 292.353-010 to verify quantities shown on return list and be designated Return Checker (laundry & rel.).
GOE: 05.09.03 STRENGTH: M GED: R2 M1 L1 SVP: 2 DLU: 78

369.687-018 FOLDER (laundry & rel.)

Folds fluff-dried or pressed laundry, such as shirts, towels, uniforms, and jackets: Shakes out, smooths, folds, sorts, and stacks wash according to identification tags. Inspects pressed laundry for holes or tears, and separates defective articles for transfer to repair department. Folds laundry, preparatory to wrap-

ping, for delivery to customer. Folds pressed shirts around cardboard forms and inserts assembly in plastic bags. May attach missing buttons to articles, using button-sewing-machine or button-attaching machine. May unload tumbler. May turn socks, match pairs, and tie socks into bundles. May be designated according to type of laundry folded as Shirt Folder (laundry & rel.) I; Wearing-Apparel Folder (laundry & rel.).
GOE: 06.04.35 STRENGTH: L GED: R2 M1 L1 SVP: 2 DLU: 78

369.687-022 INSPECTOR (laundry & rel.) alternate titles: garment examiner

Inspects garments or articles after cleaning and finishing, to verify items meet company standards: Returns articles having wrinkles, double creases, shine, spots, tears, broken seams, missing buttons, or missing belts to pressing, spotting, or repair units for correction. When examining garments to verify quality of alteration and repairs, may be designated Sewing Inspector (laundry & rel.).
GOE: 06.03.02 STRENGTH: L GED: R2 M1 L2 SVP: 3 DLU: 77

369.687-026 MARKER (laundry & rel.) alternate titles: clothes marker; entry clerk; garment marker; receiving checker; tagger

Performs any combination of following duties in marking, sorting, and recording soiled garments, linens, and other articles received for cleaning and laundering. Opens bundle or bag and spreads articles on worktable. Examines articles and records defects, such as holes, stains, tears, and ripped seams. Compares articles with customer's listing or records by hand or by using listing-pricing machine. Affixes or marks customer-identifying symbols on soiled articles by one of following methods: (1) Adjusts numbered disks of marking machine by hand to set code number; places article or cloth tag under disks; depresses pedal or pulls lever that forces disks against article or tag to print code; pins or staples tag to article. (2) Writes code number on garment or tag with pen and waterproof ink; pins, staples, or sews tag to garment. (3) Positions garment under stapling machine and pulls lever that staples short length of tape to garment; writes identifying code on tape. (4) Presses lever of clipping machine that fastens metal clip to garment. (5) Depresses keys of marking machine that prints identifying symbol on garment. (6) Seals identification tape on article, using patching machine and adhesive tape. Routes defective articles to MENDER (any industry) 787.682-030 for repairs. Sorts articles according to color, degree of soil, and type of materials or treatment. Measures articles with yardstick or measuring tape and records measurements to ensure articles are finished to original size. Removes buttons, ornaments, and other trimmings from soiled garments and replaces buttons on cleaned garments. Places sorted articles in different colored nets or ties articles in bundles and attaches tags that indicate work to be performed, such as method of cleaning, articles to be starched or tinted, and pretreatment of stained articles. Counts finished articles for completeness of order and verifies count with plant records.
GOE: 05.09.01 STRENGTH: M GED: R2 M1 L1 SVP: 2 DLU: 78

369.687-030 RUG INSPECTOR (laundry & rel.)

Examines cleaned rugs to detect deficiencies, such as inadequate cleaning, failure to remove spots or stains, and faulty brushing of pile. Returns imperfect rugs to workers responsible for defects. Rolls completed rugs by hand or guides rug into rug-rolling machine. May measure and calculate areas of rugs for billing purposes.
GOE: 06.03.02 STRENGTH: L GED: R3 M1 L2 SVP: 4 DLU: 77

37   PROTECTIVE SERVICE OCCUPATIONS

This division includes occupations concerned with protecting the public against crime, fire, accidents, and acts of war.

371   CROSSING TENDERS AND BRIDGE OPERATORS

This group includes occupations concerned with guarding crossings to warn motorists and pedestrians of approaching vehicles; and opening bridges so vessels may pass.

371.362-010 DRAWBRIDGE OPERATOR (r.r. trans.) alternate titles: bridge tender

Controls railroad or highway drawbridge over waterways to permit passage of vessels: Observes approaching vessels and listens for whistle signal from vessel indicating desire to pass. Moves levers that activate traffic signals and alarms, lower gates to halt street traffic, or activate interlocking railroad signals to warn oncoming railroad trains. Starts motors of drawbridge and moves levers to raise or turn drawbridge, giving vessels passage. Signals vessels to pass through opening. Inspects drawbridge and auxiliary equipment. Cleans, oils, and greases machinery. Writes and submits maintenance work requisitions. Prepares reports of accidents occurring on or to bridge. Records name of vessels passing and number of trains or vehicles crossing bridge. May relay messages to vessels in waterway. May make repairs and adjustment to drawbridge. May be required to hold Railway Signalman Certificate or similar license.
GOE: 05.11.04 STRENGTH: L GED: R3 M1 L2 SVP: 4 DLU: 77

371.567-010 GUARD, SCHOOL-CROSSING (government ser.)

Guards street crossings during hours when children are going to or coming from school: Directs actions of children and traffic at street intersections to en-

sure safe crossing. Records license numbers of vehicles disregarding traffic signals and reports infractions to police. May escort children across street. May place caution signs at designated points before going on duty and remove signs at end of shift. May stop speeding vehicles and warn drivers.
GOE: 10.03.03 STRENGTH: L GED: R2 M1 L2 SVP: 2 DLU: 77

371.667-010 CROSSING TENDER (any industry)

Guards railroad crossing to warn motorists and pedestrians of approaching trains: Consults train schedules and listens for approaching trains from watchtower. Presses button to flash warning signal lights. Presses control button to lower crossing gates until train passes, and raises gate when crossing is clear. May wave flags, signs, or lanterns in emergencies.
GOE: 05.12.20 STRENGTH: L GED: R2 M2 L2 SVP: 3 DLU: 77

372   SECURITY GUARDS AND CORRECTION OFFICERS, EXCEPT CROSSING TENDERS

This group includes occupations concerned with guarding property from illegal entry, fire, and theft, and enforcing safety regulations, including the custody and discipline of prisoners.

372.137-010 CORRECTION OFFICER, HEAD (government ser.)

Supervises and coordinates activities of CORRECTION OFFICERS (government ser.): Conducts roll call of officers and issues duty assignments. Directs release or transfer of prisoners based on court order instructions. Investigates and reports causes of inmate disturbances, such as assaults, fights, and thefts. Assists subordinates with unruly inmates and other assignments. Maintains prison records and prepares reports. Reviews work records of subordinates to evaluate efficiency and suitability for assignments.
GOE: 04.01.01 STRENGTH: L GED: R4 M2 L3 SVP: 6 DLU: 77

372.167-010 DISPATCHER, SECURITY GUARD (business ser.)

Dispatches security personnel to client's site for private, protective-service firm: Reads posted orders to ascertain personnel requirements and notifies guards of work assignments and changes in instructions by telephone. Posts assignment information on dispatch board. Compiles and records data for dispatch, payroll, billings, and personnel records. May issue regular and special equipment to guards. May interview applicants and recommend hiring or hire guards.
GOE: 04.02.02 STRENGTH: L GED: R4 M3 L3 SVP: 6 DLU: 77

372.167-014 GUARD, CHIEF (any industry)

Supervises and coordinates activities of guard force of establishment, such as industrial plant, department store, or museum: Assigns personnel to posts or patrol, according to size and nature of establishment and protection requirements. Interprets security rules and directs subordinates in enforcing compliance, such as issuance of security badges, photographing of employees, and safekeeping of forbidden articles carried by visitors. Responds to calls from subordinates to direct activities during fires, storms, riots, or other emergencies. Inspects or directs inspection of premises to test alarm systems, detect safety hazards, and to ensure that safety rules are posted and enforced. Examines fire extinguishers and other safety equipment for serviceability. Reports irregularities and hazards to appropriate personnel. Cooperates with police, fire, and civil defense authorities in problems affecting establishment. May select and train subordinates in protective procedures, first aid, fire safety, and other duties. May be designated according to rank as Guard, Captain (any industry); Guard, Lieutenant (any industry); Guard, Sergeant (any industry); or according to establishment served as Plant-Protection Supervisor (any industry); Security Chief, Museum (museums).
GOE: 04.01.01 STRENGTH: L GED: R3 M2 L3 SVP: 6 DLU: 77

372.167-018 JAILER, CHIEF (government ser.)

Supervises and coordinates activities of jail staff: Establishes rules, regulations, and procedures to be executed by JAILERS (government ser.). Prepares work schedules and assigns duties. Reviews commitment orders of new inmates to ensure that legal requirements are met. Classifies and segregates inmates according to status, such as pretrial, under-sentence, or witness. Communicates with court officials to ensure availability of inmates for trials or hearings. Escorts inmates to courts, hospitals, and other correctional institutions. Schedules visits of medical personnel to treat inmates. Directs search of inmates and all areas for contraband. Inspects facilities for cleanliness. Selects trustees for special work assignments. Accepts and records bail and fine payments, issues receipts, and arranges for release of inmates. Prepares reports concerning inmate population and jail functions, as required by law. Writes daily activity reports for superiors. Maintains financial records for use in budget preparation. Prepares requisitions for commissary, clothing, and housekeeping supplies. Evaluates work of subordinates and takes disciplinary measures for inefficiency or violation of regulations. Maintains personnel records of subordinates.
GOE: 04.01.01 STRENGTH: S GED: R4 M3 L4 SVP: 7 DLU: 77

372.167-022 MANAGER, ARMORED TRANSPORT SERVICE (business ser.)

Plans, directs, and coordinates activities of personnel engaged in providing armored car services: Analyzes capability based on customer requirements and develops work procedures to satisfy customer needs. Assigns tasks and interprets company policies and procedures for workers. Directs workers engaged in driving armored cars, guarding money and articles in transit, sorting, and

routing money bags, and clerical activities. Confers with customer and industry representatives to evaluate company services and promote expansion. Hires and discharges workers.
GOE: 11.11.04 STRENGTH: L GED: R4 M3 L4 SVP: 6 DLU: 77

372.267-010 SPECIAL AGENT (r.r. trans.)
   Guards shipments of valuables and investigates reports of theft or damage of shipments transported by railroad: Patrols railway express cars, baggage cars, and freight cars during run to guard shipments of valuables, such as money, bullion, strategic metals, or prototype machinery. Apprehends unauthorized persons and removes them from train at next stop or from railroad properties. Investigates report of theft [DETECTIVE (any industry) I]. Interviews train crew and other persons to gather information concerning theft. Cooperates with local law enforcement agencies to secure additional clues. Interviews neighbors, associates, and former employers of employment applicants to get personal and work history data. Prepares reports on findings of criminal and applicant investigations.
GOE: 04.02.02 STRENGTH: L GED: R4 M3 L4 SVP: 5 DLU: 77

372.363-010 PROTECTIVE OFFICER (government ser.) alternate titles: security inspector; security technician
   Guards government installations, materials, and documents against illegal acts, such as sabotage, riot, and espionage: Patrols area on foot, horseback, automobile, or aircraft to detect and prevent unauthorized activities, using weapons or physical force as necessary. Searches installation for explosive devices and notifies bomb disposal unit. Stands guard during secret and hazardous experiments. Performs routine police duties within installation. May travel throughout United States and foreign countries.
GOE: 04.02.02 STRENGTH: M GED: R3 M2 L3 SVP: 4 DLU: 77

372.367-010 COMMUNITY SERVICE OFFICER, PATROL (government ser.)
   Patrols city housing projects and community parks to prevent crimes, quell disturbances, and maintain civic harmony: Travels assigned area on foot or motor scooter to observe civil activity and maintain security. Confers with individuals involved in disturbances to determine cause and course of action to take. Attempts to resolve disputes and calls POLICE OFFICER (government ser.) I in situations requiring arrest authority. Refers individuals and families to social agencies for assistance in resolving social or health problems.
GOE: 04.02.03 STRENGTH: L GED: R3 M2 L3 SVP: 3 DLU: 77

372.367-014 JAILER (government ser.) alternate titles: jail keeper; turnkey
   Guards prisoners in precinct station house or municipal jail, assuming responsibility for all needs of prisoners during detention: Locks prisoner in cell after searching for weapons, valuables, or drugs. Serves meals to prisoner and provides or obtains medical aid if needed. May prepare arrest records identifying prisoner and charge assigned. May question prisoner to elicit information helpful in solving crime. May prepare meals for self and prisoner. May distribute commissary items purchased by inmates, such as candy, snacks, cigarettes, and toilet articles, and record payment on voucher. In small communities, may perform duties of SHERIFF, DEPUTY (government ser.) 377.263-010 or POLICE OFFICER (government ser.) I 375.263-014 when not engaged in guard duties.
GOE: 04.02.01 STRENGTH: L GED: R3 M2 L2 SVP: 4 DLU: 78

372.563-010 ARMORED-CAR GUARD AND DRIVER (business ser.) alternate titles: armored-car messenger
   Drives armored van to transport money and valuables, and guards money and valuables during transit: Loads and carries bags of cash, coin, and other valuables into and from armored van at protective service building, bank, or customer establishment. Drives armored van along established routes to transport valuables to destination. Guards bags of money and valuables during receipt and transfer to ensure safe delivery. Issues and receives receipts from customers to verify transfer of valuables. May drive truck along established route and collect coins from parking meters.
GOE: 04.02.02 STRENGTH: M GED: R3 M2 L2 SVP: 3 DLU: 77

372.567-010 ARMORED-CAR GUARD (business ser.) alternate titles: armored-car messenger
   Guards armored car enroute to business establishments to pick up or deliver money and valuables: Collects moneybags, receipts, daily guide sheet, and schedule from VAULT WORKER (business ser.). Guards money and valuables in transit to prevent theft. Records information, such as number of items received, destination, contents of packages, and delivery time at scheduled stops, on daily guide sheet. Deposits moneybags, receipts, daily guide sheet, change box, and money with cashiering department.
GOE: 04.02.02 STRENGTH: M GED: R3 M2 L2 SVP: 3 DLU: 77

372.567-014 GUARD, IMMIGRATION (government ser.)
   Guards aliens held by immigration service pending further investigation before being released or deported: Takes into custody and delivers aliens to designated jail, juvenile detention facility, hospital, court, claim's office, immigration facility, or other areas to transact business. Escorts aliens departing or arriving by airplane, train, car, ship, or bus. Prepares and maintains records relating to detention, release, transportation of alien, and completes application for travel documents. May prepare related correspondence. May be required to travel throughout nation and foreign countries.
GOE: 04.02.01 STRENGTH: M GED: R3 M2 L3 SVP: 4 DLU: 77

372.667-010 AIRLINE SECURITY REPRESENTATIVE (air trans.) alternate titles: customer security clerk; flight security specialist; screening representative
   Screens passengers and visitors for weapons, explosives, or other forbidden articles to prevent articles from being carried into restricted area of air terminal, performing any combination of following tasks: Greets individuals desiring to enter restricted area and informs them that they must be screened prior to entry. Asks individual to empty contents of pockets into tray. Examines contents of tray for forbidden articles and directs individual to pass through metal-detecting device. Asks individual to remove metal articles from person if metal detector signals presence of metal, or uses hand held metal detector to locate metal item on person. Places carry-on baggage or other containers onto x-ray device, actuates device controls, and monitors screen to detect forbidden articles. Requests owner to open baggage or containers when x ray shows questionable contents. Returns baggage and tray contents to individual if no forbidden articles are detected. Notifies GUARD, SECURITY (any industry) if forbidden articles are discovered or detector equipment indicates further search is needed. May turn on power and make adjustments to equipment. May perform duties of GUARD, SECURITY (any industry). May screen boarding passengers against Federal Aviation Administration approved profile of aircraft hijackers. May make reports.
GOE: 04.02.02 STRENGTH: L GED: R2 M1 L2 SVP: 2 DLU: 77

372.667-014 BODYGUARD (personal ser.)
   Escorts individuals to protect them from bodily injury, kidnapping, or invasion of privacy. May perform other duties, such as receiving and transcribing dictation or driving motor vehicle to transport individuals to disguise purpose of employment.
GOE: 04.02.02 STRENGTH: L GED: R2 M1 L2 SVP: 3 DLU: 77

372.667-018 CORRECTION OFFICER (government ser.) alternate titles: guard
   Guards inmates in penal institution in accordance with established policies, regulations, and procedures: Observes conduct and behavior of inmates to prevent disturbances and escapes. Inspects locks, window bars, grills, doors, and gates for tampering. Searches inmates and cells for contraband articles. Guards and directs inmates during work assignments. Patrols assigned areas for evidence of forbidden activities, infraction of rules, and unsatisfactory attitude or adjustment of prisoners. Reports observations to superior. Employs weapons or force to maintain discipline and order among prisoners, if necessary. May escort inmates to and from visiting room, medical office, and religious services. May guard entrance of jail to screen visitors. May prepare written report concerning incidences of inmate disturbances or injuries. May be designated according to institution as Correction Officer, City Or County Jail (government ser.); Correction Officer, Penitentiary (government ser.); Correction Officer, Reformatory (government ser.). May guard prisoners in transit between jail, courtroom, prison, or other point, traveling by automobile or public transportation and be designated Guard, Deputy (government ser.).
GOE: 04.02.01 STRENGTH: M GED: R3 M2 L2 SVP: 4 DLU: 86

372.667-022 FLAGGER (construction) alternate titles: traffic control signaler
   Controls movement of vehicular traffic through construction projects: Discusses traffic routing plans, and type and location of control points with superior. Distributes traffic control signs and markers along site in designated pattern. Directs movement of traffic through site, using sign, hand, and flag signals. Warns construction workers when approaching vehicle fails to heed signals to prevent accident and injury to workers. Informs drivers of detour routes through construction sites. Records license number of traffic control violators for police. May give hand marker to last driver in line up of one-way traffic for FLAGGER (construction) at opposite end of site, signaling clearance for reverse flow of traffic.
GOE: 05.12.20 STRENGTH: L GED: R2 M1 L2 SVP: 2 DLU: 77

372.667-026 FLAGGER (amuse. & rec.)
   Signals with checkered flag when first race horse crosses starting line after release from starting gate to notify racing timer when to start timing race.
GOE: 12.01.02 STRENGTH: L GED: R2 M1 L1 SVP: 2 DLU: 77

372.667-030 GATE GUARD (any industry) alternate titles: gatekeeper; guard; watch guard, gate
   Guards entrance gate of industrial plant and grounds, warehouse, or other property to control traffic to and from buildings and grounds: Opens gate to allow entrance or exit of employees, truckers, and authorized visitors. Checks credentials or approved roster before admitting anyone. Issues passes at own discretion or on instructions from superiors. Directs visitors and truckers to various parts of grounds or buildings. Inspects outgoing traffic to prevent unauthorized removal of company property or products. May record number of trucks or other carriers entering and leaving. May perform maintenance duties, such as mowing lawns and sweeping gate areas. May require permits from employees for tools or materials taken from premises. May supervise use of time clocks for recording arrival and departure of employees [TIMEKEEPER (clerical) 215.362-022]. May answer telephone and transfer calls when switchboard is closed. When stationed at entrance to restricted area, such as explosives shed or research laboratory, may be designated Controlled-Area Checker (any industry).
GOE: 04.02.02 STRENGTH: L GED: R3 M2 L2 SVP: 3 DLU: 80

372.667-034 GUARD, SECURITY (any industry) alternate titles: patrol guard; special police officer; watchguard

Guards industrial or commercial property against fire, theft, vandalism, and illegal entry, performing any combination of following duties: Patrols, periodically, buildings and grounds of industrial plant or commercial establishment, docks, logging camp area, or work site. Examines doors, windows, and gates to determine that they are secure. Warns violators of rule infractions, such as loitering, smoking, or carrying forbidden articles, and apprehends or expels miscreants. Inspects equipment and machinery to ascertain if tampering has occurred. Watches for and reports irregularities, such as fire hazards, leaking water pipes, and security doors left unlocked. Observes departing personnel to guard against theft of company property. Sounds alarm or calls police or fire department by telephone in case of fire or presence of unauthorized persons. Permits authorized persons to enter property. May register at watch stations to record time of inspection trips. May record data, such as property damage, unusual occurrences, and malfunctioning of machinery or equipment, for use of supervisory staff. May perform janitorial duties and set thermostatic controls to maintain specified temperature in buildings or cold storage rooms. May tend furnace or boiler. May be deputized to arrest trespassers. May regulate vehicle and pedestrian traffic at plant entrance to maintain orderly flow. May patrol site with guard dog on leash. May watch for fires and be designated Fire Patroller (logging). May be designated according to shift worked as Day Guard (any industry); area guarded as Dock Guard (any industry); Warehouse Guard (any industry); or property guarded as Powder Guard (construction). May be designated according to establishment guarded as Grounds Guard, Arboretum (any industry); Guard, Museum (museums); Watchguard, Racetrack (amuse. & rec.); or duty station as Coin-Vault Guard (any industry). May be designated Guard, Convoy (any industry) when accompanying or leading truck convoy carrying valuable shipments. May be designated: Armed Guard (r.r. trans.); Camp Guard (any industry); Deck Guard (fishing & hunt.; water trans.); Night Guard (any industry); Park Guard (amuse. & rec.).
GOE: 04.02.02 STRENGTH: L GED: R3 M1 L2 SVP: 3 DLU: 88

372.667-038 MERCHANT PATROLLER (business ser.) alternate titles: doorshaker; guard; security guard

Patrols assigned territory to protect persons or property: Tours buildings and property of clients, examining doors, windows, and gates to assure they are secured. Inspects premises for such irregularities as signs of intrusion and interruption of utility service. Inspects burglar alarm and fire extinguisher sprinkler systems to ascertain they are set to operate. Stands guard during counting of daily cash receipts. Answers alarms and investigates disturbances [ALARM INVESTIGATOR (business ser.)]. Apprehends unauthorized persons. Writes reports of irregularities. May call headquarters at regular intervals, using telephone or portable radio transmitter. May be armed with pistol and be uniformed. May check workers' packages and vehicles entering and leaving premises.
GOE: 04.02.02 STRENGTH: L GED: R2 M1 L2 SVP: 3 DLU: 77

372.667-042 SCHOOL BUS MONITOR (government ser.)

Monitors conduct of students on school bus to maintain discipline and safety: Directs loading of students on bus to prevent congestion and unsafe conditions. Rides school bus to prevent altercations between students and damage to bus. Participates in school bus safety drills. May disembark from school bus at railroad crossings and clear bus across tracks.
GOE: 04.02.03 STRENGTH: L GED: R2 M1 L2 SVP: 2 DLU: 77

372.677-010 PATROL CONDUCTOR (government ser.) alternate titles: correction officer

Guards prisoners being transported in correctional van between jail, courthouse, prison, mental institution, or other destination: Searches or assures that prisoners have been searched by POLICE OFFICER (government ser.) I and receives commitment papers before placing prisoner in van. Watches prisoner to prevent escape or violence. Delivers prisoner to appropriate authority and obtains signed receipt for prisoner. Searches inside of correctional van after each trip to determine if weapons or valuables have been hidden by prisoner. May administer first aid to injured or ill prisoners. May handcuff violent or dangerous prisoners.
GOE: 04.02.01 STRENGTH: L GED: R3 M2 L2 SVP: 3 DLU: 77

373 FIRE FIGHTERS, FIRE DEPARTMENT

This group includes occupations concerned with fighting fires; and inspecting fire-fighting equipment, factories, places of amusement and other establishments, to detect unsafe conditions and to recommend improvements or repairs which will reduce fire hazards. Includes investigative activities concerning causes of fire and other hazards.

373.117-010 FIRE CHIEF (government ser.) alternate titles: chief engineer

Directs activities of municipal fire department: Directs training of personnel and administers laws and regulations affecting department. Evaluates fire prevention and fire control policies by keeping abreast of new methods and conducting studies of departmental operations. Assumes personal command at multiple-alarm fires. Supervises firefighters engaged in operation and maintenance of fire stations and equipment. Coordinates mutual fire protection plans with surrounding municipalities. Surveys buildings, grounds, and equipment to esti-mate needs of department and prepare departmental budget. Confers with officials and community groups and conducts public relations campaigns to present need for changes in laws and policies and to encourage fire prevention. May investigate causes of fires and inspect buildings for fire hazards. May control issue of occupancy permits and similar licenses. May perform duties of BATTALION CHIEF (government ser.) 373.167-010 in smaller communities. May be designated Chief Of Field Operations (government ser.); District Fire Chief (government ser.); or Fire Chief, Deputy (government ser.) in larger organizations.
GOE: 04.01.01 STRENGTH: L GED: R5 M4 L5 SVP: 8 DLU: 78

373.134-010 FIRE CAPTAIN (government ser.)

Supervises and coordinates activities of company of FIRE FIGHTERS (any industry) assigned to specific firehouse: Inspects station house, buildings, grounds, and facilities, and examines firetrucks and equipment, such as ladders and hoses, to ensure compliance with departmental maintenance standards. Responds to fire alarms and determines from observation nature and extent of fire, condition of building, danger to adjacent buildings, and source of water supply, and directs firefighting crews accordingly. Trains subordinates in use of equipment and methods of extinguishing all types of fires. Evaluates efficiency of personnel. Inspects commercial establishments in assigned district and reports fire hazards or safety violations to FIRE INSPECTOR (government ser.). Compiles report of each fire call, listing location, type, probable cause, estimated damage, and disposition. May respond to emergency calls to render first aid. May recommend corrective measures for fire hazards or safety violations to building owners. May conduct fire drills for occupants of buildings. May supervise and coordinate activities of fire companies fighting multiple alarm fire until relieved by superiors. May write and submit proposal for new equipment or modification of existing equipment to superiors. May be designated Fire Lieutenant (government ser.) in larger organizations. May be designated according to specialty as Fire Captain, Marine (government ser.); Fire Lieutenant, Marine (government ser.).
GOE: 04.01.01 STRENGTH: M GED: R4 M3 L4 SVP: 7 DLU: 77

373.167-010 BATTALION CHIEF (government ser.)

Directs and coordinates firefighting activities of battalion of fire companies in municipality: Determines plan of action of fire companies for answering calls in fire, salvage, and rescue operations. Directs inspections of commerical buildings to ensure compliance with fire and safety regulations. Enters fire site during fires to coordinate and supervise fire fighting activities of companies onsite, and reports events to superior, using portable two-way radio. Plans for purchase of new equipment and use of new techniques in rescue, first aid, and firefighting operations. Directs personnel in use of firefighting equipment. Inspects fire stations, equipment, personnel, and records of assigned companies to ensure efficiency and enforcement of departmental regulations. Recommends awards for personnel for superior service. Prepares reports of accidents involving equipment and personnel. Keeps equipment and personnel records. May direct investigation of causes of incendiary and arson cases. May determine cause of fire and appraise amount of fire loss to building and other property. May promote fire prevention activities by organizing and training fire brigades in industrial plants.
GOE: 04.01.01 STRENGTH: L GED: R5 M4 L4 SVP: 8 DLU: 77

373.167-014 CAPTAIN, FIRE-PREVENTION BUREAU (government ser.)

Directs and coordinates activities of personnel of municipal fire prevention bureau: Directs building inspection, arson investigation, and distribution of fire prevention publicity material. Confers with officials or civic representatives to improve fire safety and fire education. Directs public information program for adults and juveniles, such as talks and demonstrations on resuscitation, fire safety, and home-safety inspections. Oversees review of new building plans to ensure compliance with laws, ordinances, and administrative rules for public fire safety. Studies and interprets fire safety codes to establish procedures for issuing permits regulating storage or use of hazardous and flammable substances. Assigns FIRE INSPECTORS (government ser.) to investigate hazards, cases of suspected arson, and false alarms. May participate in inspections and investigations made by subordinates. May train and evaluate employees and oversee performance of department's clerical activities.
GOE: 04.01.01 STRENGTH: L GED: R5 M4 L4 SVP: 8 DLU: 77

373.167-018 FIRE MARSHAL (any industry)

Supervises and coordinates activities of firefighting personnel of industrial establishment and inspects equipment and premises to ensure adherence to fire regulations: Inspects and orders replacement or servicing of firefighting equipment, such as sprinklers and extinguishers. Issues permits for storage and use of hazardous or flammable materials. Inspects premises to detect combustion hazards [FIRE INSPECTOR (any industry) 373.367-010]. Orders and directs fire drills. Directs firefighting and rescue activities according to knowledge of accepted procedures. May be designated according to employing establishment as Fire Chief (saw. & plan.); Fire Marshal, Refinery (petrol. refin.).
GOE: 04.01.01 STRENGTH: M GED: R4 M3 L3 SVP: 7 DLU: 77

373.267-010 FIRE INSPECTOR (government ser.) alternate titles: field inspector

Inspects buildings and equipment to detect fire hazards and enforce local ordinances and state laws: Observes tests of equipment, such as gasoline storage tanks and air compressors, and inspects storage conditions to ensure conform-

ance to fire and safety codes. Issues permits to attest to safe operating conditions. Examines interiors and exteriors of buildings to detect hazardous conditions or violations of fire ordinances and laws. Prepares report of violations or unsafe conditions. Discusses condition with owner or manager and recommends safe methods of storing flammables or other hazardous materials. Informs owner or manager of conditions requiring correction, such as faulty wiring. Issues summons for fire hazards not corrected on subsequent inspection and enforces code when owner refuses to cooperate. Keeps file of inspection records and prepares report of activities. May perform duties of FIRE FIGHTER (any industry) or FIRE CAPTAIN (government ser.). May collect fees for permits and licenses.
GOE: 11.10.03 STRENGTH: L GED: R4 M3 L4 SVP: 7 DLU: 77

373.267-014 FIRE MARSHAL (government ser.)
Investigates and gathers facts to determine cause of fires and explosions and enforces fire laws: Investigates case when either arson or criminal negligence is suspected; multialarm fire results in serious injury or death; or fire takes place in commercial establishment of public building. Examines fire site to determine *burn pattern* and detect presence of flammable materials and gases and incendiary devices, using various detectors. Performs match test to determine flash point of suspicious material at fire site. Subpoenas and interviews witnesses, building owners, and occupants to obtain sworn testimony of observed facts. Prepares reports on each investigation and submits data indicating arson to DISTRICT ATTORNEY (government ser.) 110.117-010. Arrests, logs, fingerprints, and detains arson suspect. Testifies in court, citing evidence obtained from investigation. Conducts inquiries into departmental employees delinquency in performance of duties and violation of laws or regulations.
GOE: 04.01.02 STRENGTH: L GED: R4 M3 L4 SVP: 7 DLU: 77

373.267-018 FIRE-INVESTIGATION LIEUTENANT (government ser.)
Investigates and analyzes evidence of fires to determine causes and testifies as expert witness in court: Examines sites of fires and collects evidence to ascertain causes of fires, utilizing knowledge and experience in fire fighting and fire investigation techniques and equipment. Photographs fire damage and evidence of fire causes and stores evidence in vault. Questions persons reporting fires, FIRE FIGHTER (any industry), police, and others to obtain information. Compiles investigation results, determines probable causes of fire, and reports results to superiors. Cooperates with police and insurance companies to investigate reports of fires and stolen flammable materials. Swears out warrants for arrest of suspected arsonists. Gives testimony in court cases involving fires, suspected arson, and false fire alarms. Investigates false fire alarm in cooperation with police. Maintains records of convicted arsonists and arson suspects. Responds to calls from schools and parents to instruct children in dangers of fires.
GOE: 11.10.03 STRENGTH: M GED: R5 M4 L5 SVP: 7 DLU: 77

373.363-010 FIRE CHIEF'S AIDE (government ser.)
Maintains administrative records, chauffeurs FIRE CHIEF (government ser.), and performs related duties in fire department: Compiles administrative records and types reports. Maintains sets of keys to high-rise buildings in area of responsibility. Drives car to transport and accompany FIRE CHIEF (government ser.) on rounds and to scenes of fire. Inspects scene of fire to assess extent of fire and needs of firefighting crew. Radios assessment to superior, using walkie-talkie. Participates in fire drills, and performs FIRE FIGHTER (any industry) duties on chief's instructions.
GOE: 04.02.04 STRENGTH: H GED: R4 M3 L3 SVP: 6 DLU: 77

373.364-010 FIRE FIGHTER (any industry)
Controls and extinguishes fires, protects life and property, and maintains equipment as volunteer or employee of city, township, or industrial plant: Responds to fire alarms and other emergency calls. Selects hose nozzle, depending on type of fire, and directs stream of water or chemicals onto fire. Positions and climbs ladders to gain access to upper levels of buildings or to assist individuals from burning structures. Creates openings in buildings for ventilation or entrance, using ax, chisel, crowbar, electric saw, *core cutter,* and other power equipment. Protects property from water and smoke by use of waterproof salvage covers, smoke ejectors, and deodorants. Administers first aid and artificial respiration to injured persons and those overcome by fire and smoke. Communicates with superior during fire, using portable two-way radio. Inspects buildings for fire hazards and compliance with fire prevention ordinances. Performs assigned duties in maintaining apparatus, quarters, buildings, equipment, grounds, and hydrants. Participates in drills, demonstrations, and courses in hydraulics, pump operation and maintenance, and firefighting techniques. May fill fire extinguishers in institutions or industrial plants. May issue forms to building owners, listing fire regulation violations to be corrected. May drive and operate firefighting vehicles and equipment. May be assigned duty in marine division of fire department and be designated Firefighter, Marine (any industry).
GOE: 04.02.04 STRENGTH: V GED: R4 M2 L3 SVP: 6 DLU: 81

373.367-010 FIRE INSPECTOR (any industry) alternate titles: fire watcher
Inspects premises of industrial plant to detect and eliminate fire hazards: Inspects fire-extinguishing and fire-protection equipment to ensure equipment is operable and prepares reports listing repairs and replacements needed. Patrols plant areas and notes and investigates unsafe conditions and practices which might cause or increase fire hazards. Reports findings to FIRE MARSHAL (any industry) with recommendations for eliminating or counteracting hazards. Ren-

ders first aid in emergencies. Patrols plant areas in which raw and combustible materials are stored, takes temperature and pressure readings from instruments, and reports undesirable conditions or takes steps to correct such conditions. May instruct employees in fire safety practices. May perform tests on fire-prevention equipment in plants where explosive or flammable materials are processed. May participate in fighting fires [FIRE FIGHTER (any industry)].
GOE: 04.02.02 STRENGTH: M GED: R3 M3 L3 SVP: 5 DLU: 77

373.663-010 FIRE FIGHTER, CRASH, FIRE, AND RESCUE (air trans.) alternate titles: fire fighter, airport
Responds to actual or potential air-crash emergencies to prevent or extinguish fires and rescue plane crew and passengers: Drives to scene of crash or to end of runway where distressed craft is expected to land. Sprays chemical foam onto runway surface to minimize danger of fire and explosion on impact, and water fog or chemical agents onto craft after landing. Participates in removal of trapped or injured crewmembers and passengers, using flame-cutting equipment if necessary to gain entry to damaged craft. Renders first aid to injured. Establishes firelines to prevent unauthorized persons from entering crash area. May participate in removal or neutralization of explosive ordnance material when military aircraft is involved. May deactivate aircraft electrical power to prevent fires or explosions.
GOE: 04.02.04 STRENGTH: V GED: R4 M2 L3 SVP: 5 DLU: 77

375 POLICE OFFICERS AND DETECTIVES, PUBLIC SERVICE

This group includes occupations concerned with protecting the public; maintaining law and order; detecting and preventing crime; directing and controlling motor traffic; and investigating and apprehending suspects in criminal cases.

375.117-010 POLICE CHIEF (government ser.) alternate titles: police inspector, chief; superintendent, police
Directs and coordinates activities of governmental police department in accordance with authority delegated by Board of Police: Promulgates rules and regulations for department as delegated by regulating code. Coordinates and administers daily police activities through subordinates. Coordinates internal investigation of members of department for alleged wrong doing. Suspends or demotes members of force for infractions of rules or inefficiency. Directs activities of personnel engaged in preparing budget proposals, maintaining police records, and recruiting staff. Approves police budget and negotiates with municipal officials for appropriation of funds. May command force during emergencies, such as fires and riots. May make inspection visits to precincts. May address various groups to inform public of goals and operations of department. May prepare requests for government agencies to obtain funds for special operations or for purchasing equipment for department. In smaller communities, may assist one or more subordinates in investigation or apprehension of offenders. In communities having no Board of Police, may be designated Police Commissioner (government ser.) II.
GOE: 04.01.01 STRENGTH: S GED: R5 M3 L4 SVP: 9 DLU: 81

375.133-010 POLICE SERGEANT, PRECINCT I (government ser.) alternate titles: detail sergeant; division sergeant; patrol sergeant; sergeant; squad sergeant
Supervises and coordinates activities of squad of POLICE OFFICERS (government ser.) I 375.263-014 assigned to patrol, in car or on foot, designated area of municipality: Assumes command of squad at precinct or headquarters, inspects uniforms and equipment, and reads orders to squad. Cruises in car to observe POLICE OFFICER (government ser.) I on post or in cars for efficiency and appearance and to direct them in duties. Reports infractions of rules to superiors. Notifies superior of major crimes or disturbances within area and takes necessary action until arrival of superior. Reports dangers in streets or sidewalks, such as holes, obstructions, or leaking gas mains. May be designated according to assigned duty of force members supervised as Police Sergeant, Radio Patrol (government ser.); or according to type facility assigned as Airport Safety And Security Duty Officer (government ser.).
GOE: 04.01.01 STRENGTH: L GED: R4 M2 L3 SVP: 6 DLU: 78

375.137-010 COMMANDER, IDENTIFICATION AND RECORDS (government ser.)
Supervises and coordinates activities of personnel engaged in gathering, cataloging, and identifying evidence, and maintaining police department records: Conceives, develops, and installs police record keeping and cross-filing system to ensure ready retrieval. Directs exchange of criminal records by mail or facsimile transmission between department and local, state, and federal law enforcement agencies. Maintains evidence file of active criminal cases. Assigns POLICE OFFICER, IDENTIFICATION AND RECORDS (government ser.) 375.384-010 to duties according to departmental work load. Reviews informational requests to determine whether release of information on cases to public is in accord with law and department policy. Directs subordinates in preparation of statistical and activity records and reviews reports for accuracy prior to release. Analyzes and resolves work problems or supervises subordinates in resolving problems. Prepares budget for unit and submits to POLICE CHIEF (government ser.) 375.117-010 for review. May perform duties of subordinate officers.
GOE: 07.01.06 STRENGTH: L GED: R4 M3 L3 SVP: 8 DLU: 78

375.137-014 DESK OFFICER (government ser.) alternate titles: operations officer

Supervises and coordinates activities of personnel assigned to police precinct station: Assumes responsibility for safekeeping of money and valuables taken from prisoners, lost or stolen articles, and property held as evidence. Supervises work of POLICE OFFICER (government ser.) II 375.367-010 or POLICE OFFICER (government ser.) I 375.263-014 who search suspects. Supervises TELEPHONE OPERATOR (clerical) 235.662-022 engaged in sending and receiving police communication by telephone and radio systems. Receives notification and informs commanding officer of calls and orders received over police communication systems. Records information, such as name of arresting officer and prisoner's name, address, and charge, to complete precinct activity reports for commanding officer. Commands subordinate officers and subordinate personnel on assigned duty and assumes responsibility for efficiency and discipline of workers under command. Assumes command of station house in absence of commanding officer. May make inspection tour of police beats in precinct area [TRAFFIC LIEUTENANT (government ser.) 375.167-046]. May supervise and coordinate activities of police clerical staff [SECRETARY OF POLICE (government ser.) 375.137-022]. May be designated according to rank as Desk Captain (government ser.); Desk Lieutenant (government ser.); Desk Sergeant (government ser.).
GOE: 04.01.01 STRENGTH: S GED: R4 M2 L3 SVP: 7 DLU: 78

375.137-018 POLICE LIEUTENANT, COMMUNITY RELATIONS (government ser.)

Supervises and coordinates activities of law enforcement personnel in endeavoring to resolve community social problems, and to create better understanding of police functions within community: Assigns subordinates to establish rapport with groups and individuals to identify and resolve grievances, problems, and needs. Consults social service agencies and public groups to determine community needs and to develop and coordinate remedial programs. Sponsors events, such as concerts, dances, and ball games for neighborhood youth groups. Lectures on specific aspects, functions, and goals of police departments to civic, school, and other community groups. Plans and initiates training of new employees. Compiles activity reports and prepares budget of unit for review by POLICE CHIEF (government ser.) 375.117-010.
GOE: 11.09.03 STRENGTH: L GED: R4 M3 L3 SVP: 8 DLU: 78

375.137-022 SECRETARY OF POLICE (government ser.) alternate titles: chief clerk; police-department secretary; secretary to board of commissioners

Supervises and coordinates activities of clerical workers of police department or personally maintains payroll, personnel, and similar records. Swears in and issues appointment papers to police recruits. May assume custody of valuables deposited with police [DESK OFFICER (government ser.)].
GOE: 07.01.02 STRENGTH: S GED: R4 M3 L4 SVP: 7 DLU: 77

375.137-026 TRAFFIC SERGEANT (government ser.)

Supervises and coordinates activities of officers performing traffic control duties: Visits officers at assigned traffic control stations to relay orders of TRAFFIC LIEUTENANT (government ser.) and observe activities of officers. Notifies superior of traffic conditions requiring additional personnel. Reports irregular conduct or inefficiency of personnel to superior. May supervise and coordinate activities of GUARD, SCHOOL-CROSSING (government ser.). May inspect and test police vehicles to verify operator maintenance reports and contact maintenance shop to perform repairs. May train new GUARDS, SCHOOL-CROSSING (government ser.).
GOE: 04.01.01 STRENGTH: L GED: R4 M2 L3 SVP: 7 DLU: 77

375.137-030 COMMANDER, POLICE RESERVES (government ser.)

Supervises and coordinates activities of police reserve officers to support police personnel at special functions: Writes news releases for press, radio, and television and speaks before community and business groups to recruit police reserve volunteers. Confers with potential reservists to explain policies, duties, responsibilities, and working conditions, and to provide other pertinent information. Reviews applications, results of physical and psychological examinations, oral interviews, and background information to determine suitability of candidates. Plans and coordinates instruction to train reservists in basic police techniques. Issues uniforms, arms, and equipment to reservists. Reviews schedules to determine areas of need and coordinates assignments of reservists to support police personnel at special functions, such as parades and sporting events. Observes reservists at work to evaluate work performance.
GOE: 04.01.01 STRENGTH: L GED: R4 M3 L3 SVP: 8 DLU: 86

375.137-034 COMMANDING OFFICER, POLICE (government ser.)

Supervises and coordinates activities of personnel engaged in locating and apprehending fugitives and others sought for various reasons and in locating missing persons: Supervises work of POLICE OFFICER (government ser.) III 375.267-038. Inspects vehicles to detect damage and determine maintenance needs. Prepares reports to document personnel activities and budget requirements. Performs other duties as described under SUPERVISOR (any industry) Master Title.
GOE: 04.01.01 STRENGTH: L GED: R4 M3 L4 SVP: 8 DLU: 86

375.137-038 COMPLAINT EVALUATION SUPERVISOR (government ser.)

Supervises and coordinates activities of workers engaged in receiving telephone requests for police services: Supervises work of COMPLAINT EVAL-

UATION OFFICER (government ser.) 375.367-014. Confers with workers to resolve problems when decision involving procedure or action to be taken is questionable. Performs other duties as described under SUPERVISOR (any industry) Master Title.
GOE: 07.04.05 STRENGTH: L GED: R4 M2 L3 SVP: 8 DLU: 86

375.163-010 COMMANDING OFFICER, MOTORIZED SQUAD (government ser.) alternate titles: commanding officer, highway district

Directs and coordinates activities of members of motorized (motorcycle and squad car) highway patrol who enforce state and municipal traffic laws and ordinances: Prepares reports on traffic conditions in patrol areas and recommends changes in traffic-control techniques and regulations to improve conditions. Directs members in safe use and care of motorcycles or cars, and assigns personnel to patrol areas. Evaluates work performance and disciplines immediate subordinates, and reviews evaluation of members of highway patrol unit for infraction of policy or procedures. May review changes in policy or law related to division activities to determine required revisions in operating procedures, and implements revisions. May prepare, or assign subordinate to prepare, revision of patrol training manual. May be designated according to rank as Motorized-Squad Captain (government ser.); Motorized-Squad Lieutenant (government ser.); Motorized-Squad Sergeant (government ser.). In some municipalities, may coordinate activities of all personnel engaged in enforcing traffic laws, directing traffic, and investigating accidents and be designated Commanding Officer, Traffic Division (government ser.).
GOE: 04.01.01 STRENGTH: L GED: R4 M3 L4 SVP: 8 DLU: 78

375.163-014 PILOT, HIGHWAY PATROL (government ser.)

Pilots airplane or drives automobile to engage in law enforcement activities: Patrols highway by aircraft to enforce traffic laws and coordinates air operations with ground personnel to apprehend traffic and other law violators. Flies emergency missions to deliver medical supplies. Prepares activities reports. Engages in routine police ground activities.
GOE: 04.01.02 STRENGTH: L GED: R5 M3 L4 SVP: 6 DLU: 77

375.167-010 COMMANDING OFFICER, HOMICIDE SQUAD (government ser.)

Coordinates activities of detectives investigating homicide cases for clues and evidence leading to arrest and conviction of guilty parties: Proceeds to scene of crime and takes charge of investigation. Orders detention of persons in vicinity of crime for questioning. Directs photographing position of body and other evidence. Directs DETECTIVES, HOMICIDE SQUAD (government ser.) in search for clues at crime scene. Questions witnesses and suspects. Prepares and submits report on crime to superior. May assign subordinates to specific cases. May evaluate and prepare work performance reports on subordinates. May be designated according to rank as Homicide-Squad Captain (government ser.); Homicide-Squad Lieutenant (government ser.); Homicide-Squad Sergeant (government ser.).
GOE: 04.01.01 STRENGTH: L GED: R4 M3 L4 SVP: 7 DLU: 77

375.167-014 COMMANDING OFFICER, INVESTIGATION DIVISION (government ser.) alternate titles: commanding officer, vice squad

Directs and coordinates activities of squad of law enforcement personnel engaged in investigating establishments and persons suspected of violating laws concerning gambling, liquor, narcotics, and prostitution: Conducts raids upon suspect establishments and directs arrest of persons involved. Directs persons engaged in collection of evidence to be used in prosecuting arrested suspects. Evaluates work performance of immediate subordinates. May train subordinates newly assigned to investigation division in performance of duties. May prepare and maintain various activity and personnel reports and records. May maintain budget of money to be utilized in purchasing of narcotics from sellers to effect arrest. May be designated according to rank of officer in charge as District Lieutenant (government ser.); Investigation Division Captain (government ser.); Investigation Division Lieutenant (government ser.); Investigation Division Sergeant (government ser.).
GOE: 04.01.01 STRENGTH: L GED: R4 M2 L3 SVP: 7 DLU: 77

375.167-018 COMMANDING OFFICER, MOTOR EQUIPMENT (government ser.) alternate titles: commanding officer, garage; commanding officer, motor transport division; commanding officer, vehicle maintenance unit

Directs and coordinates activities of personnel engaged in repairing, maintaining, and modifying motor vehicles used by municipal or metropolitan police force: Plans and schedules departmental activities to maintain police vehicles in operating condition. Reviews complaints about police vehicle malfunctions from field units and assigns technical research teams to develop corrective modifications or orders repairs. Evaluates work performance of immediate subordinates and reviews evaluations of other division personnel. Disciplines members for infractions of rules and regulations. Reviews productivity records of work force and operating procedures to identify work areas requiring improvements, and revises procedures. Discusses grievances of worker with supervisor to identify and resolve problem. Prepares division budget estimates, identifying operating cost, procurement of motor vehicles, replacement parts and materials, and cost of outside contractual services. Directs preparation of technical specifications for police vehicles to be purchased and submits to purchasing department. May be designated according to rank as Motor-Equipment Captain (gov-

ernment ser.); Motor-Equipment Lieutenant (government ser.); Motor-Equipment Sergeant (government ser.).
GOE: 11.05.03 STRENGTH: S GED: R4 M3 L4 SVP: 8 DLU: 77

375.167-022 DETECTIVE CHIEF (government ser.) alternate titles: commanding officer, detectives; detective-bureau chief

Directs and coordinates activities of detective squad engaged in investigation of criminal cases, such as auto theft, armed robbery, missing persons, homicide, vice, narcotics, fraud, and crimes involving youths: Assigns DETECTIVES (government ser.) 375.267-010 to designated posts or criminal cases. Reviews and submits reports of cases investigated to superiors. Ensures that apprehended criminals are fingerprinted. Directs photographing of crime scene, evidence, and suspects. Submits record of suspicions along with statement of witnesses and informants to office of DISTRICT ATTORNEY (government ser.) 110.117-010 for submission to MAGISTRATE (government ser.) 111.107-014 to obtain search warrant necessary to raid premises suspected of housing illegal activities. Conducts raids upon establishments suspected of violating such statutes as gambling or prostitution laws and oversees arrest of persons involved. Details officers to public gatherings to protect public from pickpockets and other criminals. May personally investigate criminal cases. May be designated according to nature of crime investigated as Commanding Officer, Automobile Section (government ser.); or according to rank as Detective Captain (government ser.); Detective Lieutenant (government ser.); Detective Sergeant (government ser.) I.
GOE: 04.01.01 STRENGTH: L GED: R4 M2 L3 SVP: 7 DLU: 78

375.167-026 HARBOR MASTER (government ser.) alternate titles: port warden

Directs and coordinates activities of harbor police force to ensure enforcement of laws, regulations, and policies governing navigable waters and property under jurisdiction of municipality or port district: Confers with officials, such as port authorities, Coast Guard officers, and members of city council to establish policies, define responsibilities, and determine operating requirements. Issues general instructions and outline of departmental policies regarding water-traffic control, public safety, theft prevention, and apprehension of law violators to subordinate officers and confers with them to determine operating procedures. Authorizes or approves departmental expenditures, personnel actions, and department's participation or assistance in activities not regularly assigned. Prepares periodic activity reports and annual budget. May evaluate work performance of captain and crew of ship. May direct rescue operations from patrol launch after major disaster, such as ship collision or downed aircraft.
GOE: 04.01.01 STRENGTH: S GED: R5 M3 L4 SVP: 8 DLU: 77

375.167-030 LAUNCH COMMANDER, HARBOR POLICE (government ser.)

Coordinates activities of crew patrolling municipal harbor to detect and apprehend criminals and render assistance to persons in distress: Directs navigation of power launch. Assigns stations and duties to crew as required by occurrences during patrol. Rescues drowning victims, recovers bodies, and attempts to prevent sinking of ships in distress. Cooperates with federal or other law enforcement officers in detection and apprehension of criminals, such as smugglers and illegal entrants. Investigates suspicious vessels and establishments in harbor area. Reports navigation hazards, faulty navigation aids, and fires or marine accidents to authorities concerned. Receives orders from and reports activities to POLICE CHIEF (government ser.) or HARBOR MASTER (government ser.), using radio or telephone. Inspects appearance and condition of vessel and crew for conformity with departmental standards. Maintains log of activities and fuel or other supplies consumed. Requisitions provisions and fuel. May participate in firefighting activities in dock area. May train crewmembers to rescue drowning victims, recover bodies, and prevent sinking of ships in distress. May be designated according to rank as Harbor-Police Captain (government ser.); Harbor-Police Lieutenant (government ser.).
GOE: 04.01.01 STRENGTH: L GED: R4 M2 L3 SVP: 6 DLU: 77

375.167-034 POLICE CAPTAIN, PRECINCT (government ser.) alternate titles: captain; commanding officer, precinct; district captain; patrol commander; precinct captain; uniform-force captain

Directs and coordinates activities of members of police force assigned to precinct or patrol division: Conducts roll call of officers at beginning and end of tour of duty. Explains general orders, special messages, and decisions of POLICE CHIEF (government ser.) 375.117-010 to subordinates. Assigns force members to designated posts. Informs members of command of changes in regulations and policies, implications of new or amended laws, and new techniques of police work. Submits report on condition of precinct or police station house and equipment and on daily precinct or patrol activities to superiors. Investigates charges of inefficiency or neglect of duty against force members and files charges based on evidence. Recommends merit awards for subordinates. Investigates charges filed against private citizens by complainants before issuing arrest orders. Reads and forwards reports of subordinates to POLICE CHIEF (government ser.). May review activity reports prepared by police personnel for quantity and quality of work performance. May read and answer police correspondence. May write and submit police press releases to media. May issue city permits signed by POLICE CHIEF (government ser.) for parades, street vendors and petitioners. May assign and work with ADMINISTRATIVE ASSISTANT (any industry) 169.167-010 to prepare budget of department. May be designated according to assignment as Chief, Airport Safety And Security (government ser.); Police Lieutenant, Precinct (government ser.); Police Sergeant, Precinct (government ser.) II.

375.167-038 POLICE LIEUTENANT, PATROL (government ser.)

Directs and coordinates activities of municipal police patrol force: Conducts roll call of subordinates. Relays orders and messages from superior. Inspects police logbooks to ascertain that information is recorded in conformance with regulations. Assists subordinates in performance of duties. Records information identifying arrested suspect in logbook and advises prisoner of charges. Sets bail for prisoners held on nonfelony charges, following court prepared instructions. May perform inspection tours of police beats.
GOE: 04.01.01 STRENGTH: L GED: R4 M3 L4 SVP: 8 DLU: 77

375.167-042 SPECIAL AGENT (government ser.) alternate titles: criminal investigator

Investigates alleged or suspected criminal violations of federal, state, or local laws to determine if evidence is sufficient to recommend prosecution: Analyzes charge, complaint, or allegation of law violation to identify issues involved and types of evidence needed. Assists in determining scope, timing, and direction of investigation. Develops and uses informants to get leads to information. Obtains evidence or establishes facts by interviewing, observing, and interrogating suspects and witnesses and analyzing records. Examines records to detect links in chain of evidence or information. Uses cameras and photostatic machines to record evidence and documents. Verifies information obtained to establish accuracy and authenticity of facts and evidence. Maintains surveillances and performs undercover assignments. Presents findings in clear, logical, impartial, and properly documented reports. Reports critical information to and coordinates activities with other offices or agencies when applicable. Testifies before grand juries. Serves subpoenas or other official papers. May lead or coordinate work of other SPECIAL AGENTS. May obtain and use search and arrest warrants. May serve on full-time, detail, or rotational protection assignments. May carry firearms and make arrests. May be designated according to agency worked for as Special Agent, FBI (government ser.); Special Agent, IRS (government ser.); Special Agent, Secret Service (government ser.).
GOE: 04.01.02 STRENGTH: M GED: R5 M5 L5 SVP: 7 DLU: 77

375.167-046 TRAFFIC LIEUTENANT (government ser.)

Directs and coordinates activities of police personnel in performance of traffic-control duties and removal of illegally parked vehicles: Recommends changes in traffic-control devices and regulations, considering suggestions of subordinates as well as own observations of traffic conditions at intersections or other points where police personnel are stationed. Evaluates work performance of subordinates. May cooperate with demonstration and parade officials to identify line of march and number of people involved in event. May analyze proposed parade plans to determine traffic rerouting requirements and number and disposition of police personnel; and prepares operations procedure to be utilized. May assume command of police personnel at site of unauthorized demonstrations to minimize traffic disruption and to maintain law and order.
GOE: 04.01.01 STRENGTH: L GED: R4 M2 L3 SVP: 7 DLU: 77

375.167-050 COMMANDER, INTERNAL AFFAIRS (government ser.)

Directs activities of workers engaged in investigating accusations against police personnel, administering disciplinary actions and inspecting police personnel and equipment: Directs investigative work of internal affairs personnel to gather information for presentation at hearings in response to accusations against police personnel or deficiencies in performance. Schedules hearings to permit complainant or accused officer to appeal recommended disciplinary action. Supervises work of POLICE INSPECTOR (government ser.) I 375.267-026.
GOE: 04.01.01 STRENGTH: L GED: R4 M3 L4 SVP: 8 DLU: 86

375.167-054 POLICE ACADEMY PROGRAM COORDINATOR (government ser.)

Plans and coordinates training programs for recruits, in-service police officers, licensed security guards, and other law enforcement personnel: Reviews police technology and law enforcement literature, surveys agency personnel, and confers with Police Academy and Police Department administrators to determine training needs, assess current programs, and propose new courses. Determines feasibility of proposed courses based on factors such as number of registrants, availability of instructors, and funds allocation. Arranges for course instructors, allocates space, and ensures availability of training materials and equipment. Assists instructors during training sessions and evaluates course effectiveness. Maintains enrollee records. May specialize in coordinating training in specific area, such as security, police vehicle driving, or firearms.
GOE: 04.01.01 STRENGTH: L GED: R4 M3 L4 SVP: 7 DLU: 86

375.227-010 POLICE-ACADEMY INSTRUCTOR (government ser.)

Instructs probationary and experienced POLICE OFFICERS (government ser.) I in such phases of police work as police science, police ethics, investigative methods and techniques, government, law, community relations, marksmanship, self defense, and care of firearms. Evaluates test results and classroom performance of students and prepares performance evaluation reports. May drill personnel at regular intervals or before parades and similar events.
GOE: 04.01.01 STRENGTH: L GED: R4 M2 L3 SVP: 7 DLU: 77

375.263-010 ACCIDENT-PREVENTION-SQUAD POLICE OFFICER (government ser.) alternate titles: crash-squad accident investigator

Investigates traffic accidents as member of squad to obtain details surrounding accident, determine if crime was committed, and to provide interested par-

Service Occupations

ties with reliable data surrounding accident for use in legal action or formulation or revision of traffic safety program: Photographs and diagrams accident scene and tests brakes and tires of involved vehicles, using testing equipment. Questions and records statements of principals and eye witnesses of accident. Reviews all facts to determine if crime, such as vehicular homicide, murder, manslaughter, or assault, or traffic violation was involved. Arrests perpetrator of criminal act or submits traffic citation to violator of motor vehicle ordinance. Files all facts, records, and information involved in case for possible use in criminal or civil legal action or safety program.
GOE: 04.01.02 STRENGTH: M GED: R4 M2 L3 SVP: 6 DLU: 77

375.263-014 POLICE OFFICER I (government ser.) alternate titles: patrol officer; traffic officer

Patrols assigned beat on foot, on motorcycle, in patrol car, or on horseback to control traffic, prevent crime or disturbance of peace, and arrest violators: Familiarizes self with beat and with persons living in area. Notes suspicious persons and establishments and reports to superior officer. Reports hazards. Disperses unruly crowds at public gatherings. Renders first aid at accidents, and investigates causes and results of accident. Directs and reroutes traffic around fire or other disruption. Inspects public establishments requiring licenses to ensure compliance with rules and regulations. Warns or arrests persons violating animal ordinances. Issues tickets to traffic violators. Registers at police call boxes at specified interval or time. Writes and files daily activity report with superior officer. May drive patrol wagon or police ambulance. May notify public works department of location of abandoned vehicles to tow away. May accompany parking meter personnel to protect money collected. May be designated according to assigned duty as Airport Safety And Security Officer (government ser.); Dance-Hall Inspector (government ser.); Traffic Police Officer (government ser.); or according to equipment used as Ambulance Driver (government ser.); Motorcycle Police Officer (government ser.); Mounted Police Officer (government ser.). May be designated: Emergency-Detail Driver (government ser.); Patrol Driver (government ser.); Pool-Hall Inspector (government ser.); Radio Police Officer (government ser.); Show Inspector (government ser.).
GOE: 04.01.02 STRENGTH: M GED: R4 M2 L3 SVP: 6 DLU: 81

375.263-018 STATE-HIGHWAY POLICE OFFICER (government ser.) alternate titles: state trooper

Patrols state highways within assigned area, in vehicle equipped with two-way radio, to enforce motor vehicle and criminal laws: Arrests or warns persons guilty of violating motor vehicle regulations and safe driving practices. Monitors passing traffic to detect stolen vehicles and arrests drivers where ownership is not apparent. Provides road information and assistance to motorists. Directs activities in accident or disaster area, rendering first aid and restoring traffic to normal. Investigates conditions and causes of accident. Directs traffic in congested areas and serves as escort for funeral processions, military convoys, and parades. Performs general police work by keeping order and apprehending criminals. Appears in court as witness in traffic violation and criminal cases. Keeps records and makes reports regarding activities. May assist law enforcement officers not under state jurisdiction. May serve as DISPATCHER, RADIO (government ser.) 379.362-010 at patrol substation. May supervise activities of station equipped to inspect automobiles for safe operating conditions.
GOE: 04.01.02 STRENGTH: M GED: R4 M2 L3 SVP: 6 DLU: 81

375.264-010 POLICE OFFICER, CRIME PREVENTION (government ser.)

Inspects dwellings and public buildings to evaluate security needs and to recommend measures to make premises less vulnerable to crime, and installs burglar alarm systems: Inspects locks, window barriers, alarms, lighting, and other features to evaluate needs and to recommend actions to strengthen security. Lends etching tools to individuals to inscribe identfying information on personal and household articles. Installs portable self-contained protective signal systems and positions sensing devices at strategic locations to detect burglary or other irregularities and to notify police. Inspects equipment to detect malfunctions. Addresses community groups to inform citizens of crime prevention and security methods. May compile and analyze data from patrol unit reports to identify patterns of crime and to recommend changes in police patrols to prevent further crimes.
GOE: 04.01.02 STRENGTH: M GED: R4 M3 L4 SVP: 7 DLU: 86

375.267-010 DETECTIVE (government ser.) alternate titles: detective, criminal investigation; plain-clothes officer

Carries out investigations to prevent crimes or solve criminal cases: Investigates known or suspected criminals or facts of particular case to detect planned criminal activity or clues. Frequents known haunts of criminals and becomes familiar with criminals to determine criminals' habits, associates, characteristics, aliases, and other personal information. Records and reports such information to commanding officer. Investigates crimes and questions witnesses. Examines scene of crime to obtain clues and gather evidence. Investigates suspected persons and reports progress of investigation. Arrests or assists in arrest of criminals or suspects. Prepares assigned cases for court, according to formalized procedures. Testifies before court and grand jury. May be designated according to nature of crime investigated as Detective, Automobile Section (government ser.); Detective, Homicide Squad (government ser.); according to rank as Detective Sergeant (government ser.) II; or according to administrative division to which assigned as Detective, Precinct (government ser.); Detective, Youth Bureau (government ser.).

GOE: 04.01.02 STRENGTH: L GED: R4 M2 L3 SVP: 7 DLU: 80

375.267-014 DETECTIVE, NARCOTICS AND VICE (government ser.)

Investigates and apprehends persons suspected of illegal sale or use of narcotics, or violating anti-vice laws: Examines prescriptions in pharmacies and physicians' records to ascertain legality of sale and distribution of narcotics, and determines amount of such drugs in stock. Investigates persons suspected of illegal sale or purchase of narcotics and arrests offenders. Investigates establishments and persons suspected of violating anti-vice laws, working as member of squad, and conducts or participates in raids of such establishments. Arrests suspects and obtains evidence to be used by DISTRICT ATTORNEY (government ser.) in prosecuting case in court. Obtains statements for prosecution of offenders and appears in court as witness. Records progress of investigation and reports to superior.
GOE: 04.01.02 STRENGTH: L GED: R4 M3 L4 SVP: 7 DLU: 77

375.267-018 INVESTIGATOR, NARCOTICS (government ser.) alternate titles: narcotics investigator

Investigates and apprehends persons suspected of illegal sale or use of narcotics: Compiles identifying information on suspects charged with selling narcotics. Maintains surveillance of suspect to detect modus operandi. Selects undercover officer best suited to contact suspect and purchase narcotics. Obtains police funds required to make purchase. Submits written report containing charges, available facts, and evidence to MAGISTRATE (government ser.) to authorize search warrant or wire tap. Observes and photographs narcotic purchase transaction to compile evidence and protect undercover investigator. Arrests narcotics offenders. Obtains statements for prosecution of offenders and appears in court as witness.
GOE: 04.01.02 STRENGTH: L GED: R4 M2 L3 SVP: 7 DLU: 77

375.267-022 INVESTIGATOR, VICE (government ser.) alternate titles: morals-squad police officer; vice-squad police officer

Investigates establishments and persons suspected of violating antivice laws, working as member of squad, and conducts raids upon such establishments: Arrests suspects and obtains evidence to be used by state or municipality in prosecuting suspects arrested. Records and maintains informational files on suspects and establishments. Reviews governmental agency files to obtain identifying data pertaining to suspects or establishments suspected of violating antivice laws. Maintains surveillance of establishments to attain identifying information on suspects. May operate as undercover agent to penetrate organized crime ring to obtain evidence necessary to arrest and prosecute.
GOE: 04.01.02 STRENGTH: M GED: R4 M2 L3 SVP: 7 DLU: 77

375.267-026 POLICE INSPECTOR I (government ser.) alternate titles: division commander; field control inspector; police captain, senior

Inspects police stations and examines personnel and case records to ensure that police personnel conform to prescribed standards of appearance, conduct, and efficiency: Inspects premises and police records and observes activities in assigned division for evidence of inefficiency and misconduct. Prepares reports concerning discipline, efficiency, and condition of force within division. Submits reports to superiors and recommends disciplinary action or changes in rules governing activities of force. Transmits orders from POLICE CHIEF (government ser.) 375.117-010 to commanding officers within division. Takes command of members of force during emergencies, such as fires and riots. May formulate procedures and human resource requirements, and direct personnel assigned to crowd control at such events as parades, demonstrations, and labor disputes. May serve as police liaison on public and civic boards engaged in planning and developing programs, and prepare procedures to identify police function in assisting board to improve community living. May be designated Police Chief, Deputy (government ser.) and report directly to POLICE CHIEF (government ser.).
GOE: 04.01.01 STRENGTH: L GED: R4 M3 L4 SVP: 7 DLU: 78

375.267-030 POLICE INSPECTOR II (government ser.)

Visits railroad stations, stores, theaters, places of amusement, or public gatherings to detect, prevent, and solve crimes: Notes actions of known criminals or suspicious persons to prevent crimes. Ascertains that establishments and publicly licensed gatherings conform to law. Arrests or warns unruly persons, law violators, and suspected criminals. Compares lists of stolen merchandise with items displayed in retail stores, pawn shops, used-car lots, and other outlets for such goods. Directs closing of illegal establishments and indecent amusement performances. Alerts other police officers or public authorities to take prescribed action after he has left the premises. Files reports of establishments visited, findings, and recommendations for action. May be designated according to assigned beat or establishment visited as Inspector, Pawnshop Detail (government ser.). May be permanently assigned to specific establishment, such as ballpark or recreation center.
GOE: 04.01.02 STRENGTH: L GED: R4 M3 L4 SVP: 5 DLU: 77

375.267-034 INVESTIGATOR, INTERNAL AFFAIRS (government ser.)

Investigates complaints filed against police officers by citizens: Interviews complainant to identify officers being accused and to obtain facts concerning complaints. Interviews accused officers to obtain responses to accusations. Records interviews, using recording device, and prepares charges and responses to charges, using recorded information as reference. Conducts investigations to establish facts supporting complainant or accused, using supportive information from witnesses or tangible evidence. Schedules polygraph test for consenting

273

parties, and records results of test interpretations for presentation with findings. Writes report of findings from results of investigation and submits reports to commanding officer for review. Testifies at hearings as requested.
GOE: 07.01.06 STRENGTH: L GED: R4 M3 L4 SVP: 7 DLU: 86

375.267-038 POLICE OFFICER III (government ser.)

Conducts investigations to locate, arrest, and return fugitives and persons wanted for nonpayment of support payments and unemployment insurance compensation fraud, and to locate missing persons: Reviews files and criminal records to develop possible leads, such as previous addresses and aliases. Contacts employers, neighbors, relatives, law enforcement agencies, and other persons to locate person sought. Obtains necessary legal documents, such as warrants or extradition papers, to bring about return of fugitive. Serves warrants and makes arrests to return persons sought. Examines medical and dental x rays, fingerprints, and other information to identify bodies held in morgue. Completes reports to document information acquired and actions taken. Testifies in court to present evidence regarding cases.
GOE: 04.01.02 STRENGTH: M GED: R4 M2 L3 SVP: 7 DLU: 86

375.267-042 POLICE OFFICER, SAFETY INSTRUCTION (government ser.)

Conducts training programs to enhance public and personal safety and law enforcement: Collects and organizes materials, prepares and delivers lectures, and plans and implements activities to educate and advise school students, teachers, parents, and civic and business groups on such topics as personal and public safety, drugs, safe driving, and law enforcement. Coordinates activities between schools, clubs and other organizations, and police department to administer crime prevention programs. Talks with students, teachers, parents, and other individuals to establish rapport, identify problems, offer assistance, and to aid students in danger of becoming delinquent. Carries out investigations to prevent crimes and solve criminal cases [DETECTIVE (government ser.) 375.267-010]. May survey premises of homes, businesses, and other establishments to evaluate needs and to recommend safety and security measures.
GOE: 04.01.02 STRENGTH: L GED: R3 M2 L3 SVP: 6 DLU: 86

375.362-010 POLICE CLERK (government ser.)

Compiles daily duty roster and types and maintains various records and reports in municipal police department to document information, such as daily work assignments, equipment issued, vacation scheduled, training records, and personnel data: Prepares duty roster to indicate such personnel information as days on, days off, equipment assigned, and watch. Arranges schedule to most efficiently use personnel and equipment and ensure availability of personnel for court dates. Submits roster to superior for approval. Compiles and records data to maintian personnel folders. Reviews duty roster, personnel folders, and training schedules to schedule training for police personnel. Performs other duties as described under POLICE AIDE (government ser.) 243.362-014.
GOE: 07.05.01 STRENGTH: S GED: R4 M3 L3 SVP: 6 DLU: 86

375.363-010 BORDER GUARD (government ser.) alternate titles: border patrol agent

Patrols on foot, by motor vehicle, power boat, or aircraft along border or seacoast of United States to detect persons attempting to enter country illegally. Apprehends and detains illegal entrants for subsequent action by immigration authorities. May question agricultural workers near border to identify and apprehend illegal aliens. May report evidence of smuggling observed on patrol to customs authorities.
GOE: 04.02.03 STRENGTH: M GED: R3 M2 L3 SVP: 5 DLU: 77

375.367-010 POLICE OFFICER II (government ser.) alternate titles: correction officer; supervisor, education and custody

Guards female and juvenile persons detained at police station house or detention room pending hearing, return to parents, or transfer to penal institution, and is responsible for inmates' care while incarcerated: Searches all female prisoners for weapons, contraband, drugs, and other harmful articles. Investigates background of first offenders and causes for arrest, and makes recommendations to MAGISTRATE (government ser.) concerning the disposition of case. Cares for and administers to female and juvenile prisoners who are sick or intoxicated. Cares for lost and runaway children until parents or guardians are contacted. Accompanies all female and juvenile prisoners to court and remains with prisoners until case has been disposed of. May observe inmates in cells to assure prisoners' well-being and adherence to regulations and rules. May maintain identification record of incarcerated females. May be responsible for cleanliness and sanitation of dormitory and cells of detention rooms.
GOE: 04.02.01 STRENGTH: L GED: R3 M1 L2 SVP: 5 DLU: 77

375.367-014 COMPLAINT EVALUATION OFFICER (government ser.)

Evaluates telephone requests for police services and monitors alarm systems to determine urgency of requests and need to dispatch patrol car: Converses with telephone caller to obtain information and respond to requests for police services. Evaluates information received to determine if patrol car should be dispatched immediately, dispatched on delayed basis, or if situation can be resolved without patrol car being dispatched. Observes light and sound signals on wall panel to monitor alarm systems of fire department, private protective agencies, citizen band radio, city hall, or other buildings. Relays information to DISPATCHER, RADIO (government ser.) 379.362-010 when patrol car is to be dispatched.
GOE: 07.04.05 STRENGTH: S GED: R4 M2 L3 SVP: 6 DLU: 86

375.367-018 POLICE OFFICER, BOOKING (government ser.)

Completes and maintains various records to book and process prisoners: Prepares reports to document arrest information, such as name, address, charge,

and arresting officer. Fingerprints and searches prisoners. Records personal property of prisoners and seals property in envelope. Logs and forwards arrest registers to teleprocessing unit to enter information into computer-based information system. Monitors arrest registers, using computer-based information system to ensure timely processing of prisoners in accordance with procedural requirements. Reviews booking reports of prisoners arrested in other districts to verify completeness and accuracy of reports. Schedules pretrial interviews, prepares court dockets, and releases prisoners in response to bail being posted to process prisoners. Answers inquiries to explain procedures, give status of individuals, verify information, and expedite processing of prisoners.
GOE: 04.02.01 STRENGTH: L GED: R3 M3 L3 SVP: 4 DLU: 86

375.384-010 POLICE OFFICER, IDENTIFICATION AND RECORDS (government ser.)

Collects evidence at scene of crime or fatal accident, classifies and identifies fingerprints, and photographs evidence for use in criminal and civil cases: Dusts selected areas of crime scene to locate and reveal latent fingerprints. Lifts prints from crime site, using special tape. Photographs crime or accident scene to obtain record of evidence. Photographs, records physical description, and fingerprints homicide victims and suspects for identification purposes. Classifies and files fingerprints FINGERPRINT CLASSIFIER (government ser.) 375.387-010. Develops film and prints, using photographic developing equipment. Submits evidence to COMMANDER, IDENTIFICATION AND RECORDS (government ser.) 375.137-010 for cataloging.
GOE: 07.01.06 STRENGTH: L GED: R4 M3 L3 SVP: 7 DLU: 78

375.387-010 FINGERPRINT CLASSIFIER (government ser.) alternate titles: fingerprint expert

Classifies fingerprints and compares fingerprints of unknown persons or suspects with fingerprint records to determine if prints were involved in previous crimes: Classifies record cards containing fingerprints of crime suspects according to specified grouping, and compares fingerprints with others in file to determine if prisoner has criminal record or is wanted for other crimes. Examines fingerprint evidence left at scene of crime, classifies prints, and endeavors to identify person. May fingerprint prisoner, using ink pad. May transfer residual fingerprints from objects, such as weapons or drinking glasses, to record cards, using standard technique. May keep files of criminals and suspects, containing such information as photographs, habits, and modus operandi of crimes with which individual has been connected.
GOE: 02.04.01 STRENGTH: L GED: R4 M2 L3 SVP: 6 DLU: 77

375.587-010 PARKING ENFORCEMENT OFFICER (government ser.) alternate titles: parking enforcement agent

Patrols assigned area, such as public parking lot or section of city, to issue tickets to overtime parking violators. Winds parking meter clocks. Surrenders ticket book at end of shift to supervisor to facilitate preparation of violation records. May report missing traffic signals or signs to superior at end of shift. May chalk tires of vehicles parked in unmetered spaces, record time, and return at specified intervals to ticket vehicles remaining in spaces illegally. May collect coins deposited in meters. When patrolling metered spaces, may be known as Meter Attendant (government ser.).
GOE: 04.02.02 STRENGTH: L GED: R2 M1 L2 SVP: 2 DLU: 77

376 POLICE OFFICERS AND DETECTIVES, EXCEPT IN PUBLIC SERVICE

This group includes occupations concerned with policing private property to prevent thievery, malicious damage, and dishonesty among employees or patrons; and to maintain order. Includes investigating irregularities concerning fire, sabotage, or unlawful intrusion, and conducting private investigations on a fee basis.

376.137-010 MANAGER, INTERNAL SECURITY (business ser.)

Supervises and coordinates activities of STORE DETECTIVES (retail trade), conducts private investigations, and sells internal protective service to wholesale and retail businesses: Assigns STORE DETECTIVES (retail trade) to shifts at various locations according to job requirements and worker's abilities, skills, and experience. Observes workers in performance of duties to evaluate efficiency and to detect and correct inefficient work practices. Interviews and hires workers to fill vacant positions. Demonstrates and explains methods of detecting and apprehending shoplifters. Explains state laws concerning arrest and detention to employees. Conducts private investigation to obtain information concerning such matters as divorce evidence, juvenile runaways, and background data on persons applying for employment, insurance, or bonding. Acts as undercover agent in retail stores to detect employee incompetency and dishonesty. Prepares detailed reports concerning matters investigated. Contacts business establishments to promote sales of security services. Analyzes security needs, estimates costs, and presents proposal to prospective customer.
GOE: 04.01.01 STRENGTH: L GED: R4 M3 L4 SVP: 7 DLU: 77

376.167-010 SPECIAL AGENT-IN-CHARGE (r.r. trans.)

Directs and coordinates activities of security staff to protect railroad passengers, employees, and property: Plans and implements programs to protect railroad passengers, employees, and property. Directs investigation of crimes on railroad property, freight theft claims, or suspicious damage and loss of passenger's valuables. Directs security activities at derailments and fires, floods and strikes involving railroad property or responsibility. Conducts investigations

and implements programs related to fire prevention and inspections, grade crossing accident prevention, and other special safety and prevention measures. Directs security training of new employees.
GOE: 04.01.01 STRENGTH: S GED: R4 M3 L4 SVP: 7 DLU: 77

376.267-010 INVESTIGATOR, CASH SHORTAGE (retail trade)
Investigates cash shortages occurring in sales section of department store: Receives notification regarding shortage of cash from audit or sales department. Discusses shortage with sales department and security department supervisors. Reviews sales checks and cash register tapes, and counts cash to verify shortages. Observes personnel on closed circuit television to detect thefts. Questions store personnel to obtain evidence and develop cases. Apprehends and turns suspect over to security department. Prepares case summaries and testifies at hearings of suspects.
GOE: 11.10.01 STRENGTH: S GED: R4 M3 L3 SVP: 6 DLU: 77

376.267-014 INVESTIGATOR, FRAUD (retail trade)
Investigates cases of fraud involving use of charge cards reported lost or stolen, cash refunds, and nonexistent accounts in retail stores: Receives information from credit, sales, and collection departments regarding suspected fraud cases. Interviews store personnel, and observes and questions suspected customers to obtain evidence. Compiles detailed reports on fraud cases, and submits and discusses cases with police. Consults with postal officials when charge cards are reported stolen in mail. Testifies at court trials of offenders. Prepares reports of fraud cases and submits reports to security department and other store officials.
GOE: 11.10.01 STRENGTH: S GED: R4 M4 L3 SVP: 7 DLU: 77

376.267-018 INVESTIGATOR, PRIVATE (business ser.) alternate titles: detective, private eye; undercover agent; undercover operator
Conducts private investigations to locate missing persons, obtain confidential information, and solve crimes: Questions individuals to locate missing persons. Conducts surveillance of suspects using binoculars and cameras. Conducts background investigation of individual to obtain data on character, financial status, and personal history. Examines scene of crime for clues and submits fingerprints and findings to laboratory for identification and analysis. Writes reports of investigations for clients. Reports criminal information to police and testifies in court. May investigate activities of individuals in divorce and child custody cases. May arrange lie detector tests for employees of clients or witnesses. May escort valuables to protect client's property. May be employed in commercial or industrial establishments for undercover work [DETECTIVE (any industry) I] or be assigned to guard persons [BODYGUARD (personal ser.)].
GOE: 04.01.02 STRENGTH: L GED: R4 M3 L4 SVP: 5 DLU: 77

376.267-022 SHOPPING INVESTIGATOR (business ser.) alternate titles: investigator; service auditor; shopping inspector; spotter
Shops in commercial, retail, and service establishments to test integrity of sales and service personnel, and evaluates sales techniques and services rendered customers: Reviews establishment's policies and standards to ascertain employee-performance requirements. Buys merchandise, orders food, or utilizes services to evaluate sales technique and courtesy of employee. Carries merchandise to check stand or sales counter and observes employee during sales transaction to detect irregularities in listing or calling prices, itemizing merchandise, or handling cash. Delivers purchases to agency conducting shopping investigation service. Writes report of investigations for each establishment visited. Usually works as member of shopping investigation crew.
GOE: 11.10.05 STRENGTH: L GED: R3 M3 L3 SVP: 3 DLU: 77

376.367-010 ALARM INVESTIGATOR (business ser.) alternate titles: armed guard; investigator operator; security agent
Investigates source of alarm and trouble signals on subscribers' premises, as recorded in central station of electrical protective signaling system: Drives radio-equipped car to subscriber's establishment, and locates source of alarm. Investigates disturbances, such as unlawful intrusion, fires, and property damage. Apprehends unauthorized persons found on property, using armed force if necessary, and releases them to custody of authorities. Contacts supervisor by radio or telephone to report irregularities and obtain further instructions. Adjusts and repairs subscriber's signaling equipment to restore service, using handtools. Coordinates activities with police and fire departments during alarms. Writes investigation and automobile usage reports.
GOE: 04.02.04 STRENGTH: L GED: R3 M1 L3 SVP: 3 DLU: 77

376.367-014 DETECTIVE I (any industry) alternate titles: investigator
Protects property of business establishment by detecting vandalism, thievery, shoplifting, or dishonesty among employees or patrons, performing any combination of following duties: Conducts investigations on own initiative or on request of management. Stakes out company grounds to apprehend suspects in illegal acts. Questions suspects and apprehends culprits. Files complaints against suspects and testifies in court as witness. Writes case reports. Alerts other retail establishments when person of known criminal character is observed in store. May be designated according to type of establishment as Store Detective (retail trade).
GOE: 04.02.02 STRENGTH: L GED: R3 M2 L3 SVP: 4 DLU: 77

376.367-018 HOUSE OFFICER (hotel & rest.) alternate titles: house detective; security officer; special officer
Patrols hotel or motel premises to maintain order, enforce regulations, and ensure observance of applicable laws: Patrols lobbies, corridors, and public

rooms, confers with management, interviews guests and employees, and interrogates persons to detect infringements and investigate disturbances, complaints, thefts, vandalism, and accidents. Patrols public areas to detect fires, unsafe conditions, and missing or inoperative safety equipment. Warns or ejects troublemakers, and cautions careless persons. Obtains assistance for accident victims and writes accident reports. Notifies staff of presence of persons with questionable reputations. Assists management and enforcement officers in emergency situations. Usually is not armed. May enter and check rooms of guests suspected of leaving without paying bill to confirm suspicions and to seize any remaining personal property.
GOE: 04.02.03 STRENGTH: L GED: R3 M1 L2 SVP: 4 DLU: 77

376.367-022 INVESTIGATOR (utilities)
Investigates persons suspected of securing services through fraud or error: Makes personal calls on individuals in question and tactfully attempts to secure evidence or personal admission that individual being investigated owes for previous service, or obtains pertinent data to show that suspicion was unwarranted.
GOE: 04.01.02 STRENGTH: L GED: R3 M2 L3 SVP: 6 DLU: 77

376.367-026 UNDERCOVER OPERATOR (retail trade) alternate titles: undercover agent
Detects thievery or problems of morality, or verifies employee conformance to company policies and procedures, working in any occupation of establishment: Talks to employees to gain their friendship and confidence. Observes daily routines of employees and unusual occurrences. Performs duties of regular employees, such as sales, stock control, or truck driving, depending on assignment and experience. Maintains record of activities and makes periodic reports to home office.
GOE: 04.02.03 STRENGTH: L GED: R3 M2 L3 SVP: 4 DLU: 77

376.667-010 BOUNCER (amuse. & rec.) alternate titles: house detective
Patrols place of entertainment to preserve order among patrons and protect property: Circulates among patrons to prevent improper dancing, skating, or similar activities, and to detect persons annoying other patrons or damaging furnishings of establishment. Warns patrons guilty of infractions and evicts them tactfully from premises if they become unruly or ejects them by force if necessary. Calls police if unable to quell disturbance. May be designated according to type of establishment patrolled as Fun-House Attendant (amuse. & rec.); Guard, Dance Hall (amuse. & rec.); Ice Guard, Skating Rink (amuse. & rec.).
GOE: 04.02.03 STRENGTH: L GED: R2 M1 L2 SVP: 3 DLU: 77

376.667-014 DETECTIVE II (any industry)
Patrols premises of business establishment to preserve order and enforce standards of decorum established by management: Requests patrons to conform with rules pertaining to dress, behavior, or sobriety. Requests undesirable persons, such as inebriates, rowdies, known criminals, or perverts to leave premises and forcibly ejects undesirables or notifies police. May be designated according to employing establishment as Detective, Bowling Alley (amuse. & rec.); Special Officer, Automat (hotel & rest.).
GOE: 04.02.03 STRENGTH: L GED: R3 M2 L3 SVP: 4 DLU: 77

376.667-018 PATROLLER (r.r. trans.)
Guards, patrols, and polices railroad yards, stations, and other facilities to protect company property: Examines credentials of persons desiring entrance to unauthorized areas. Patrols yards to apprehend unauthorized persons and remove them from yard. Walks about stations or terminal to maintain order. Polices right-of-way to prevent dumping of rubbish on company grounds. Arrests persons dumping rubbish on grounds. Cooperates with local law enforcement agencies in apprehending trespassers or thieves. May record seal numbers of boxcars containing high pilferage items, such as cigarettes and liquor, and verify record with electronic data processing list of original seal and car numbers to detect pilfered cars. May seal empty boxcars by twisting nails in door hasps, using nail twister. May be designated according to assigned post as Gate Guard (r.r. trans.); Right-Of-Way Inspector (r.r. trans.); Station Patroller (r.r. trans.); Yard Patroller (r.r. trans.).
GOE: 04.02.02 STRENGTH: L GED: R2 M1 L2 SVP: 3 DLU: 77

377 SHERIFFS AND BAILIFFS

This group includes occupations concerned with enforcing law and order in rural or unincorporated districts; maintaining order in court; and serving summonses.

377.134-010 SUPERVISOR, IDENTIFICATION AND COMMUNICATIONS (government ser.)
Supervises and coordinates activities of officers engaged in gathering and identifying evidence and operating radio relay transmitters to furnish information to fire and law enforcement departments: Designs and installs criminal identification filing systems, such as fingerprint, photograph, modus operandi and name, criminal-wanted and crimes reported files, to facilitate information retrieval. Directs exchange of criminal records between department and local, state, and federal law enforcement agencies. Prepares operator's work schedules to ensure round-the-clock coverage of radio transceivers. Assigns officers to duties according to work load. Verifies fingerprint classifications performed by IDENTIFICATION OFFICER (government ser.) to ensure accuracy. Collects and processes evidence in homicide cases [IDENTIFICATION OFFICER (government ser.)]. Testifies in court as qualified fingerprint expert. Determines

equipment needs and prepares and submits request for Federal grants upon approval of DEPUTY SHERIFF, CHIEF (government ser.). Checks permit prior to hook-up of commercial establishment's burglar alarm to department's communication system. Analyzes and resolves or assists subordinates in resolving work problems. Estimates annual expenditures, prepares budget, and submits to superior for review. Directs staff in preparation of activity and statistical reports.
GOE: 07.01.06 STRENGTH: L GED: R4 M3 L4 SVP: 8 DLU: 77

377.137-010 DEPUTY SHERIFF, COMMANDER, CIVIL DIVISION (government ser.)
Supervises and coordinates activities of personnel engaged in executing mandates of civil court: Reviews contents of orders, such as summonses, garnishments, property seizures, and arrest orders, for adherence to state laws and county ordinances. Assigns cases to DEPUTY SHERIFF, CIVIL DIVISION (government ser.) for execution of court orders. Discusses cases with subordinates and recommends course of action. Prepares legal notices of *sheriff's sales* by arranging for posting in public places and mailing copy to newspapers. Oversees or conducts sale of real and personal property legally confiscated by county. Reviews reports to determine progress and disposition of cases. Oversees collection, recording, and depositing of legal fees gathered by subordinates. Examines civil division accounts and financial records for completeness and accuracy. Submits data for audits by state and county officials. Writes reports on civil division activities and submits to superiors. Disciplines staff for violation of regulations and resolves personnel problems. Performs duties such as serving civil court orders, seizing property, and making arrests.
GOE: 04.01.01 STRENGTH: S GED: R4 M3 L4 SVP: 7 DLU: 77

377.137-014 DEPUTY SHERIFF, COMMANDER, CRIMINAL AND PATROL DIVISION (government ser.) alternate titles: squad leader; watch commander
Supervises and coordinates activities of one or more squad units in law enforcement activities of patrol and criminal division of county sheriff's department: Reviews duty log of previous shift. Assigns units to posts based on activities of log or on order of DEPUTY SHERIFF, CHIEF (government ser.). Tours patrol areas to ensure execution of orders and adherence to divisional work procedures. Inspects uniform appearance of officers and checks patrol vehicles for conformity to standards. Directs squad activities in cases of civil unrest or emergency to coordinate deployment of human resources and weapons, first aid units, sniper-suppression teams, search-rescue units, and mounted forces. Consults with state and local law enforcement agencies to provide or obtain information. Prepares reports about patrol activities, squad efficiency, discipline, and personnel evaluation and submits reports to superior. Prepares shift schedules and human resource projections. Conducts hearings in cases of misconduct of subordinates. Evaluates reports on undercover operations, determines priority, and assigns personnel to cases. Supervises officers in obtaining court orders and oversees procedures involved with arrests, fingerprinting, and filing of charges. Trains officers in police techniques. Assists subordinates in operations, such as surveillance, raids, and arrests. May speak before civic groups on law enforcement topics. May act as receiving officer for division when accepting delivery of equipment and supplies. May act as extradition officer for division. May perform duties of absent DEPUTY SHERIFF, CHIEF (government ser.).
GOE: 04.01.01 STRENGTH: S GED: R4 M3 L4 SVP: 8 DLU: 77

377.137-018 DEPUTY, COURT (government ser.)
Supervises and coordinates activities of court peace officers engaged in providing security and maintaining order within individual courtrooms and throughout courthouse: Tours and inspects duty stations of BAILIFF (government ser.) to ensure compliance with regulation job duties and correct appearance. Patrols courthouse to quell disturbances and to keep order. Trains newly appointed officers in performance of job duties. Communicates with COURT CLERKS (government ser.) to identify day's court calendar. Prepares and schedules work assignments of court officers, and issues daily duty assignments. Prepares jury's meal vouchers for court official assigned to escort jurors to restaurant. Secures lodging facilities and transportation for jurors deliberating lengthy trials. Prepares and submits activity and time reports to DEPUTY SHERIFF, CHIEF (government ser.). May witness name selection list of prospective jurors to ensure impartiality. May perform duties of BAILIFF (government ser.).
GOE: 04.01.01 STRENGTH: L GED: R3 M2 L3 SVP: 6 DLU: 77

377.167-010 DEPUTY SHERIFF, CHIEF (government ser.)
Directs and coordinates activities of county sheriff's department: Schedules work assignments and deployment of human resources in patrol division and transmits orders to subordinate officers for execution. Supervises investigations of narcotics traffic and auto theft, evaluates progress with investigators, and plans actions, such as raids, surveillance, or arrests. Issues funds to undercover operatives to buy information or contraband. Advises subordinates of procedures required to secure search and bench warrants. Reviews available evidence for suitability and consults with district attorney in preparation of grand jury cases. Develops departmental procedures to serve as guidelines for proper conduct of patrol division activities, based on legal information and previous law enforcement experience. Monitors effectiveness of procedures through follow-up with patrol officers. Reviews daily patrol activity log prepared by subordinates. Conducts meetings of patrol officers to evaluate operations and efficiency of squad members. Investigates civilian complaints against division members

and determines action to be taken based on evidence secured. Disciplines division members for violation of intradepartmental rules and regulations. Resolves personnel problems of division members or refers problems to supervisor if no solution is found. Inspects firearms in division armory to ensure operational readiness. Collects and analyzes data on division activities. Prepares regular and supplemental budgets for division and submits to superior. Requisitions equipment and services for division and assumes responsibility for receipt of items. Writes reports concerning division activities and submits to sheriff. Addresses civic and educational groups on law enforcement subjects. Conducts training sessions in police training school and within division and assumes field command of division during emergency operations.
GOE: 04.01.01 STRENGTH: S GED: R4 M3 L4 SVP: 8 DLU: 77

377.263-010 SHERIFF, DEPUTY (government ser.)
Maintains law and order and serves legal processes of courts: Patrols assigned area to enforce laws, investigate crimes, and arrest violators. Drives vehicle through assigned area, observing traffic violations and issuing citations. Assumes control at traffic accidents to maintain traffic flow, assist accident victims, and investigate causes of accidents. Investigates illegal or suspicious activities of persons, quells disturbances, and arrests law violators. Locates and takes persons into custody on arrest warrants. Transports or escorts prisoners between courtrooms, prison, and medical facilities. Serves subpoenas and summonses [PROCESS SERVER (business ser.)] and keeps record of dispositions. Keeps order in courtroom [BAILIFF (government ser.)]. May operate radio to deliver instructions to patrol units. May assist in dragging river to locate bodies.
GOE: 04.01.02 STRENGTH: M GED: R3 M2 L3 SVP: 5 DLU: 77

377.264-010 IDENTIFICATION OFFICER (government ser.)
Collects, analyzes, classifies and photographs physical evidence and fingerprints to identify criminals: Searches, for evidence and dusts surfaces to reveal latent fingerprints. Photographs crime site and fingerprints to obtain record of evidence. Lifts print on tape and transfers to permanent record cards. Vacuums site to collect physical evidence and submits to SUPERVISOR, IDENTIFICATION AND COMMUNICATIONS (government ser.) for verifications. Photographs, fingerprints, and measures height and weight of arrested suspects, noting physical characteristics, and posts data on record for filing. Prepares and photographs plastic moulage of footprints and tire tracks. Compares fingerprints obtained with suspect or unknown files to identify perpetrator [FINGERPRINT CLASSIFIER (government ser.)]. Manipulates *mask mirror* on specialized equipment to prepare montage of suspect according to description from witnesses. May fingerprint applicant for employment or federal clearance and forward prints to other law enforcement agencies. May testify in court as qualified fingerprint expert.
GOE: 07.01.06 STRENGTH: L GED: R4 M3 L4 SVP: 8 DLU: 77

377.267-010 DEPUTY UNITED STATES MARSHAL (government ser.)
Enforces law and order under jurisdiction of federal courts: Receives prisoners into federal custody. Escorts prisoners to and from jails and courts, and guards prisoners during hospitalization. Provides protection to court personnel, jurors, and witnesses or their families. Serves civil and criminal writs. Reviews records, gathers information, and traces and arrests individuals named in criminal warrants. Assists federal agencies in matters such as investigations, raids, and arrests as directed. Seizes property pursuant to court orders.
GOE: 04.01.02 STRENGTH: M GED: R3 M2 L3 SVP: 5 DLU: 86

377.363-010 DEPUTY SHERIFF, GRAND JURY (government ser.) alternate titles: deputy, grand jury
Guards grand jury room and district attorney's offices to provide security: Searches premises to ensure security of rooms. Questions individuals entering area to determine purpose of business and directs or reroutes individuals to destinations. Arrests persons violating law, and summons patrol unit to take custody. Notifies sheriff's patrol units of need for assistance or medical aid. Requests prisoner's arrest records be sent by criminal identification unit to DISTRICT ATTORNEY (government ser.). Prepares and validates receipts to reimburse witnesses for travel expenses. Occasionally transports prisoners between jail, district attorney's office, and penitentiary for questioning, trial, or incarceration.
GOE: 04.02.03 STRENGTH: L GED: R3 M1 L2 SVP: 6 DLU: 77

377.667-010 BAILIFF (government ser.) alternate titles: court officer
Maintains order in courtroom during trial and guards jury from outside contact: Checks courtroom for security and cleanliness. Assures availability of sundry supplies for use of JUDGE (government ser.). Enforces courtroom rules of behavior and warns persons not to smoke or disturb court procedure. Collects and retains unauthorized firearms from persons entering courtroom. Stops people from entering courtroom while JUDGE (government ser.) charges jury. Provides jury escort to restaurant and other areas outside of courtroom to prevent jury contact with public. Guards lodging of sequestered jury. Reports need for police or medical assistance to sheriff's office. May advise attorneys of dress required of witnesses. May announce entrance of JUDGE (government ser.).
GOE: 04.02.03 STRENGTH: L GED: R2 M1 L2 SVP: 3 DLU: 77

377.667-014 DEPUTY SHERIFF, BUILDING GUARD (government ser.) alternate titles: deputy, building guard
Patrols courthouse, guards court, and escorts defendants: Patrols courthouse to provide security. Escorts defendants to and from courtroom and stands guard during court proceedings. Records daily activities in log. May operate vehicle to transport prisoners to penal institutions. May direct traffic in courthouse parking areas.

GOE: 04.02.03 STRENGTH: L GED: R2 M1 L2 SVP: 3 DLU: 77

377.667-018 DEPUTY SHERIFF, CIVIL DIVISION (government ser.)

Serves orders of civil court: Delivers court orders, such as subpoenas, garnishments, property executions, commitments and show-cause orders to individuals. Collects money from garnishee and issues receipt. Confiscates real or personal property by court order for disposal at *sheriff's sale* and posts notice of sale in public places. Serves warrants and evicts persons from property designated by court order. Submits written report on disposition of assigned cases to superior. May conduct or assist at sheriff's sale.

GOE: 04.01.02 STRENGTH: L GED: R3 M3 L3 SVP: 3 DLU: 77

378 ARMED FORCES ENLISTED PERSONNEL

This group includes occupations, not elsewhere classified, concerned with protecting the nation from enemies and maintaining peace and order during times of martial law or civil disobedience.

378.132-010 FIELD ARTILLERY SENIOR SERGEANT (military ser.)

Supervises and coordinates activities of personnel engaged in direction of artillery fire, target acquisition, operation of field artillery, operation of radar equipment, and operation of survey and fire direction equipment incident to control of artillery fire and naval gunfire: Prepares field orders, training, and status reports, and intelligence reports. Advises superior on assignments, promotions, and other matters related to troop welfare. Prepares schedule for unit training. Conducts classes on unit drill, military courtesy, and similar subjects. Assists supervisor on inspection tour of artillery units, and prepares notes on discrepancies found. Initiates corrective action to correct discrepancies.

GOE: 05.03.05 STRENGTH: L GED: R3 M3 L3 SVP: 8 DLU: 77

378.137-010 INFANTRY UNIT LEADER (military ser.)

Supervises or assists in supervision of personnel during training and tactical employment of infantry unit: Directs personnel in preparing weapons and equipment for movement and combat operations. Directs personnel in establishment of unit command post and assists in operation of command post. Assists supervisor in formulating plans of employment of unit and in directing and leading infantry unit. Assists supervisor in coordinating employment of unit's fire and support weapons. Inspects unit weapons and equipment to determine functioning condition of weapons and equipment and initiates action to correct deficiencies. Directs personnel in preparation of unit correspondence, reports, schedules, and rosters. Directs personnel in distribution of ammunition, food, and other supplies.

GOE: 04.02.02 STRENGTH: V GED: R3 M2 L2 SVP: 7 DLU: 77

378.161-010 COMBAT SURVEILLANCE AND TARGET ACQUISITION NONCOMMISSIONED OFFICER (military ser.)

Supervises and coordinates activities of personnel engaged in providing combat surveillance and target acquisition information, such as sound, flash, or survey, in support of field artillery units: Confers with firing battery personnel to coordinate target acquisition and combat surveillance activities and to provide liaison between target acquisition or combat surveillance units and artillery units. Advises commanding officer on matters related to troop welfare, including personnel assignments, discipline, and training needs. Directs personnel in preparing charts, maps, and overlays.

GOE: 05.03.05 STRENGTH: M GED: R3 M3 L3 SVP: 7 DLU: 77

378.227-010 MARKSMANSHIP INSTRUCTOR (military ser.)

Instructs personnel in rifle, pistol, and shotgun marksmanship: Explains and demonstrates weapon safety, firing positions, sight picture, and alignment, breath and trigger control, and other specified fundamentals and techniques of marksmanship: Instructs personnel in nomenclature, weapon disassembly, weapon operation, weapon stoppages, and immediate corrective action for small arms weapons. Explains range safety regulations. Inspects small arms weapons to ensure that weapons are clean, properly lubricated, and in designated operating condition. Observes personnel during firing to ensure that safety procedures are followed. Offers corrective advice to personnel to improve marksmanship and to aid in correcting weapon malfunctions. Scores field firing results to include target detection, range estimation, firing positions, and other marksmanship principles.

GOE: 11.02.01 STRENGTH: M GED: R3 M2 L3 SVP: 4 DLU: 77

378.227-014 RECRUIT INSTRUCTOR (military ser.) alternate titles: drill sergeant

Instructs newly recruited military personnel, in accordance with training schedules and orders: Orients recruits in fundamentals of service life, discipline, physical fitness, pride and love of service and country. Trains recruits in close order drill. Instructs recruits in nomenclature, disassembly, assembly, and functioning of small arms weapons; and assists in weapons marksmanship instruction. Instructs recruits in general orders (standing requirements) for sentinels, interior guard duty, personal hygiene, first aid, military posture, and care of clothing and equipment. Lectures on military history and tradition, customs of the armed services, military courtesy, and regulations. Evaluates recruit performance in all facets of training. Assists superior in conduct of parades and reviews; maintains records and prepares reports. May instruct personnel in conduct of hand-to-hand combat and bayonet drill.

GOE: 11.02.01 STRENGTH: M GED: R3 M2 L2 SVP: 4 DLU: 77

378.227-018 SURVIVAL SPECIALIST (military ser.)

Instructs personnel in survival and rescue techniques and procedures and on how to evade, escape, and resist enemy interrogation, exploitation, and political indoctrination as prisoner of war: Demonstrates methods of constructing emergency shelter, building animal or fish traps and snares, improvising clothing and equipment and recognizing, procuring, preparing, and preserving water and various plant and animal life. Demonstrates use of life support and recovery equipment, basic survival kit items, and application of survival medicine. Instructs personnel in use of support and recovery equipment and procedures for signaling and guiding search vehicles. Discusses and demonstrates principles and techniques of escape and evasion, penetration of barriers, camouflage, and organization of prisoner of war groups.

GOE: 11.02.01 STRENGTH: V GED: R3 M2 L3 SVP: 5 DLU: 77

378.267-010 COUNTERINTELLIGENCE AGENT (military ser.)

Collects, evaluates, and disseminates counterintelligence information: Investigates activities of enemy agents, collaborationists or other specified personnel known or suspected to have knowledge or record of counterintelligence information. Interrogates suspects, informants, and witnesses while conducting investigations to obtain information pertaining to activities, such as actual, attempted, or suspected treason, sedition, subversion, disaffection, espionage, and sabotage. Conducts security surveys and inspections of installation, activities, and personnel. Evaluates information obtained and recommends remedial action. Prepares administrative forms and correspondence incident to granting security clearances. Conducts security lectures. Directs personnel engaged in general security indoctrination for military personnel or civilian employees. May plan, organize, and coordinate activities of counterintelligence agents and teams.

GOE: 04.01.02 STRENGTH: L GED: R5 M4 L5 SVP: 7 DLU: 77

378.267-014 DISASTER OR DAMAGE CONTROL SPECIALIST (military ser.)

Assists disaster preparedness officer in preparation and monitoring of disaster preparedness plans and procedures: Inspects protective equipment to determine operational readiness. Directs personnel in repair of equipment. Directs location, marking, and stocking of radiation shelters. Confers with superiors and civil defense personnel to provide information on radiological monitoring and survey; biological and chemical weapons and effects; protective measures and decontamination methods; and biological, chemical, and nuclear accident control to assist superior in development of local emergency plans. Tests suspected area to detect presence of toxic agents, using chemical detection equipment and identifies type of chemical agent. Tests areas for radioactive contamination, using portable measuring instruments. Collects biological samples and tests and identifies biological agents. Plots area of contamination on map. Informs superior of contaminated area and type of contamination. Recommends to superior method to be followed to decontaminate personnel, equipment, and area. Informs superior when decontamination has been completed. Conducts training in methods and techniques of defense during chemical, biological, and nuclear warfare.

GOE: 04.02.02 STRENGTH: M GED: R4 M3 L3 SVP: 6 DLU: 77

378.281-010 TARGET AIRCRAFT TECHNICIAN (military ser.)

Services, repairs, and overhauls drone target aircraft and aircraft engines: Repairs, replaces, and assembles parts, such as wings, cowlings, stabilizers, and propeller assembly, using power tools and handtools to rebuild or replace airframe or airframe components. Replaces worn or damaged parts, such as spark plugs, parachute, and battery, using handtools. Tests aircraft engine operation. Places aircraft on launching device, including catapult launcher. Installs JATO (Jet Assist Take-Off) or other launching propellant. Starts aircraft, using portable starting equipment. Adjusts carburetor to regulate fuel mixture to attain optimum engine performance. Performs preflight inspection of target aircraft. Inspects launching device prior to each launch. Diagnoses electronic malfunctions. Repairs and replaces defective parts and wiring.

GOE: 05.10.02 STRENGTH: M GED: R3 M3 L2 SVP: 6 DLU: 77

378.362-010 SOUND RANGING CREWMEMBER (military ser.)

Operates sound ranging equipment to detect location of enemy artillery fire during combat or training, serving as member of sound ranging crew: Patrols area and selects operating site. Deploys and positions sound detection equipment and monitors equipment to detect sounds of enemy artillery fire. Records sound data and computes location of enemy artillery. Notifies friendly artillery unit, using radio, of direction and location of enemy artillery.

GOE: 05.03.05 STRENGTH: V GED: R3 M3 L3 SVP: 5 DLU: 77

378.363-010 ARMOR RECONNAISSANCE SPECIALIST (military ser.)

Drives military wheeled or tracked vehicle and observes area to gather information concerning terrain features, enemy strength, and location, serving as member of ground armored reconnaissance unit: Reports information to commander, using secure voice communication procedure. Writes field messages to report combat reconnaissance information. Drives armored, tracked, and wheeled vehicles in support of tactical operations to harass, delay, and destroy enemy troops. Directs gunfire from vehicle to provide covering or flanking fire against enemy attack. Prepares and employs night firing aids to assist in delivering accurate fire. Tests surrounding air to determine presence and identity of chemical agents, using chemical agent detecting equipment, radiac, or radiological monitoring device. Drives vehicle to bridge locations to mark routes and control traffic. Requests and adjusts mortar and artillery fire on targets and reports effectiveness of fire.

GOE: 04.02.02 STRENGTH: M GED: R3 M3 L3 SVP: 5 DLU: 77

378.367-010 ARTILLERY OR NAVAL GUNFIRE OBSERVER (military ser.)

Observes and reports by specified means of communications, enemy and simulated enemy locations to coordinate and adjust artillery or naval gunfire during

combat or training: Selects sites for observation posts. Sets up observation and communication instruments and equipment. Informs infantry, artillery, or naval gunfire ships of enemy activity, location of friendly troops and other pertinent intelligence data, using radio. Confers with artillery and gunship personnel to request and adjust artillery and naval gunfire. Confers with fire direction center personnel to report gunfire results based on knowledge of characteristics, capabilities, and limitations of artillery, mortar, rocket, and naval gunfire, using radio.
GOE: 05.03.05 STRENGTH: V GED: R3 M3 L2 SVP: 4 DLU: 77

378.367-014 FIELD ARTILLERY OPERATIONS SPECIALIST (military ser.)
Collects, records, and evaluates information pertinent to location of enemy weapons for use by friendly artillery, using chronograph, gun direction computer, and other fire direction equipment: Observes enemy fire, using transit and records angle to firing position. Measures velocity of projectiles fired from enemy weapon, using chronograph. Determines direction of enemy weapons, using gun direction computer. Collects data and constructs firing chart to plot target location. Computes azimuth (direction), elevation, and other firing data (information to engage target). Communicates firing data to artillery unit personnel, using radio and transmits artillery fire adjustment data to artillery unit.
GOE: 05.03.05 STRENGTH: L GED: R4 M4 L3 SVP: 5 DLU: 77

378.367-018 FLASH RANGING CREWMEMBER (military ser.)
Measures range and horizontal and vertical angles to enemy artillery flashes and projectile bursts, using flash ranging equipment in observation post: Selects location site for observation post. Performs traverse survey to establish coordinate location of observation post. Orients and calibrates flash ranging instruments. Observes enemy weapon flashes during firing and projectile bursts, using flash ranging instrument, and records horizontal and vertical angles to flash or burst. Computes data to determine distance and direction of enemy emplacement. Confers with artillery personnel to report location of enemy forces and effectiveness of friendly fire weapons.
GOE: 05.03.05 STRENGTH: V GED: R4 M4 L3 SVP: 5 DLU: 77

378.367-022 INFANTRY OPERATIONS SPECIALIST (military ser.)
Collects, evaluates, and prepares operation and intelligence information at battalion or higher headquarters for combined arms combat operations: Assists superior in organizing and operating unit operations section when deployed in field. Prepares operation maps, maintains situation maps, indicating location, strength, tactical deployment and emplacements of friendly and enemy units. Receives and records on situation maps pertinent information obtained from intelligence and reconnaissance reports, using conventional signs and symbols. Prepares and maintains operations journal which contains briefs of important written and oral messages received and sent, notations of periodic reports, orders, and specified matters that pertain to section or unit. Assists superior in preparing war diaries and special reports upon completion of operation. Prepares orders, training orders, memorandums, schedules, status, and periodic reports.
GOE: 04.02.02 STRENGTH: M GED: R4 M4 L4 SVP: 6 DLU: 77

378.367-026 OPERATIONS AND INTELLIGENCE ASSISTANT (military ser.)
Collects, consolidates, and evaluates air defense intelligence information received from ground observers; radar sections; other supportive units; and prepares and revises operations and situation maps: Communicates with intelligence personnel from radar, ground observation, and other supportive units to collect air defense information, using field telephone and radiotelephone equipment, and plots early warning information on situation board. Prepares and revises operations and situation maps to indicate location, strength, and tactical employment of friendly and hostile units. Alerts personnel of firing batteries as to grid locations of incoming targets, using radio.
GOE: 04.02.02 STRENGTH: L GED: R3 M3 L3 SVP: 5 DLU: 77

378.367-030 RECONNAISSANCE CREWMEMBER (military ser.)
Observes, locates, and reports enemy force movements and terrain characteristics from vantage point: Conducts surveillance from vantage post to observe such places as bridges, airfields, roads, and rivers to detect enemy movements. Observes beach areas to determine possible amphibious landing site. Requests artillery, air, and naval gunfire to destroy enemy forces, using radio. Fires weapons, such as pistol, rifle, and grenade launcher. Studies maps and aerial photographs to locate enemy force.
GOE: 04.02.02 STRENGTH: V GED: R3 M3 L3 SVP: 4 DLU: 77

378.382-010 AIRBORNE SENSOR SPECIALIST (military ser.)
Operates airborne sensing equipment to locate and identify friendly and enemy aircraft: Places and secures sensing and monitoring equipment, such as IFF (Identification Friend or Foe), infrared, and radar, in aircraft. Pushes buttons, presses switches and turns knobs to start, control, and stop equipment. Observes equipment scopes and indicators to obtain data to determine location and identity of aircraft. Contacts Command Post personnel, using radio, to report presence of enemy aircraft. Examines equipment to detect malfunctions. Replaces malfunctioning components, including tubes and circuit boards, to repair equipment, using handtools.
GOE: 05.03.05 STRENGTH: V GED: R3 M3 L3 SVP: 6 DLU: 77

378.382-014 DEFENSIVE FIRE CONTROL SYSTEMS OPERATOR (military ser.)
Operates inflight fire control system to detect intrusion of enemy aerial vehicles and to evade or destroy airborne threat during combat or training: Observes radar scope to detect blips indicative of aerial vehicles. Identifies vehicles following manual procedures. Notifies superior of presence of enemy aircraft, missile, or other aerial vehicle. Presses buttons as directed by superior to activate automatic tracking system and to automatically fire weapons and infrared missile launcher to destroy enemy or simulated threat. Diagnoses equipment malfunction. Replaces defective parts and wiring and adjusts mechanical parts.
GOE: 05.03.05 STRENGTH: S GED: R3 M2 L3 SVP: 7 DLU: 77

378.382-018 UNATTENDED-GROUND-SENSOR SPECIALIST (military ser.)
Emplaces, records location, and operates remote surveillance devices and other monitoring equipment to gather intelligence information relating to enemy location, direction, and speed of movement: Examines air photographs and contour maps to determine best location for surveillance devices and monitoring equipment. Assists superiors in sensing equipment emplacement. Selects radio-relay sensor sites, and emplaces and activates relay stations. Installs and operates communications equipment. Uses authentication codes, signal operating instructions, and standing signal instructions when operating communication equipment. Camouflages sensor positions and tactical field positions. Observes monitoring, recording, and display devices and interprets and reports information gathered. Computes density, direction, rate of movement, and nature of targets detected. Performs preventive maintenance on unattended ground sensors, relay equipment, monitoring devices, and ancillary equipment. May recommend appropriate action and reaction to be taken and request supporting fire on targets.
GOE: 05.03.05 STRENGTH: V GED: R3 M3 L3 SVP: 6 DLU: 77

378.464-010 ANTITANK ASSAULT GUNNER (military ser.)
Positions, fires, and maintains antitank and assault weapons, such as recoilless rifle, portable flame thrower, and multishot portable flame weapon: Prepares weapons and equipment for movement. Designates location for and positions weapons. Computes firing data, loads and aims weapons preparatory to firing. Fires antitank and assault weapons at fixed and moving targets. Assists supervisor in leading antitank or assault units to assault positions during combat or training operations, furnishing supporting fire for other infantry units. Assists supervisor in coordinating unit's fire and movement with that of unit supported, adjacent units, and other support units. Constructs and camouflages positions and ground obstacles for antitank and assault squads. Employs, arms, disarms, and removes mines used for local security and antitank defense. Protects weapons and equipment against chemical warfare agents and decontaminates weapons and equipment when exposed to chemical attack. Performs minor repairs to weapons and equipment. May direct fire of other infantry crew-served weapons.
GOE: 04.02.02 STRENGTH: H GED: R2 M2 L2 SVP: 3 DLU: 77

378.663-010 VULCAN CREWMEMBER (military ser.)
Fires vehicle mounted Vulcan artillery system (multibarrel rapid firing weapon) during combat and training operations: Drives vehicle to transport Vulcan system into firing position. Lifts and carries ammunition from vehicle storage to Vulcan firing platform. Inserts ammunition into firing tube to load Vulcan for firing. Presses button to engage firing mechanism that automatically fires system. Operates support equipment, such as power generators, fire control devices, and radios. Repairs and maintains support equipment, using handtools, power tools, and measuring instruments, to ensure optimum operational efficiency.
GOE: 05.03.05 STRENGTH: V GED: R2 M1 L1 SVP: 3 DLU: 77

378.682-010 REDEYE GUNNER (military ser.)
Operates and fires Redeye Guided Missile Weapon System (short range ground to air missile) to destroy low flying enemy aircraft: Observes low flying enemy aircraft or receives radar information concerning low flying aircraft. Visually identifies aircraft detected. Evaluates enemy threat, and establishes priority of engagement. Notifies superior of target. Presses switches, upon order, to activate automatic tracking system and fires missile at target. Confers with supervisor, using radio, to transmit results of firing. Selects appropriate primary and alternate positions for Redeye employment, considering capabilities and limitations of weapon, friendly troop location and situation in area to be defended, and probable aircraft tactics and directions of attack.
GOE: 05.03.05 STRENGTH: V GED: R3 M3 L3 SVP: 3 DLU: 77

378.682-014 SMOKE AND FLAME SPECIALIST (military ser.)
Operates and controls smoke or flame and support equipment, such as self-propelled flamethrowers, smoke generators, and radio equipment, to provide smokescreen or flame support for military forces during combat or training: Observes terrain and weather conditions to determine location for smoke generators and smoke munitions. Starts smoke generator to form smokescreen. Observes smokescreen to ensure proper screening without interference to mission of adjacent friendly units. Adjusts smoke generators as needed to obtain optimum quality and quantity of screening smoke. Assists in loading flamethrower and on-vehicle weapons. Moves firing controls and fire control instruments to operate and fire vehicular mounted weapons and self-propelled flamethrowers. Moves driver controls to start, stop, and steer self-propelled flamethrower vehicles. Receives and stores on-vehicle materials, such as rations, fuel, and ammunition. Confers with squad or unit personnel to report observance of targets or other combat information, using visual signal, radio or telephone, in conformance with terminology and security procedures. Performs preventive maintenance and repairs on equipment and weapons, such as flamethrowers, radio equipment, and smoke generators.

GOE: 05.03.05 STRENGTH: H GED: R3 M2 L2 SVP: 4 DLU: 77

378.683-010 AMPHIBIAN CREWMEMBER (military ser.)
Drives or steers military amphibious equipment, such as tractors and armored vehicles on land and sea to transport personnel, supplies, and equipment in support of combat or training operations: Loads supplies and equipment aboard vehicle. Confers with superior to determine course to be followed. Drives or steers vehicle to transport personnel, supplies, and equipment between ship and shore. Confers with personnel aboard ship and on land, using radio to transmit and receive information concerning enemy location, troop movement, and enemy gunfire encountered. Loads ammunition into breech of weapon. Aims and fires weapon at enemy emplacement.
GOE: 04.02.02 STRENGTH: M GED: R2 M1 L1 SVP: 3 DLU: 77

378.683-014 POWERED BRIDGE SPECIALIST (military ser.)
Operates mobile military assault bridge vehicle and other power bridging equipment on land and water to position and connect bridge and raft sections across streams, rivers, and other water obstacles: Selects most suitable site for entering of streams and other water obstacles based on physical characteristics of water obstacles, such as depth, distance across, and swiftness of water, using depth charges, range indicators, and tide and current tables. Manipulates driver's controls and helm to start, stop, and steer vehicle and connects with other vehicles to form rafts and bridges. Pumps water out of vehicle, using bilge pump. Confers with other vehicle operators and unit personnel, using radio and interphone to provide information concerning progress of work, enemy troop movement, and similar tactical information.
GOE: 05.11.04 STRENGTH: V GED: R3 M3 L3 SVP: 5 DLU: 77

378.683-018 TANK CREWMEMBER (military ser.)
Drives military tank and fires tank weapons working as member of tank crew: Prepares tank and equipment for movement and combat. Drives tank over various types of terrain to locate target. Loads ammunition into breech of weapon. Aims weapon, using tank fire control equipment and fires weapon at target. Camouflages position and protects tank and equipment against chemical warfare agents. Decontaminates tank and equipment when exposed to contaminants.
GOE: 04.02.02 STRENGTH: M GED: R2 M2 L2 SVP: 4 DLU: 77

378.684-010 CAMOUFLAGE SPECIALIST (military ser.)
Camouflages military field equipment and installations, using items such as nets, paint, brush, and grass: Observes field areas to determine types of camouflage required. Applies specified garnishes to nets to prepare nets for use in camouflaging activities. Drapes and covers field equipment and activities with nets, employing rigging techniques. Camouflages equipment and structures, using paint and natural materials, such as grass and brush. Fabricates camouflage materials and decoys in shop, using handtools. Erects decoys, runs misleading tracks to decoys, and simulates activity to confuse enemy forces.
GOE: 04.02.02 STRENGTH: H GED: R2 M2 L2 SVP: 4 DLU: 77

378.684-014 COMBAT RIFLE CREWMEMBER (military ser.)
Opposes members of enemy ground force in effort to destroy or capture enemy forces, using rifle, during combat or training operations, and serving as member of infantry unit: Constructs field fortifications, including wire entanglements and road blocks, using handtools, barbed wire, and lumber. Camouflages combat equipment and weapons, using items such as paint, nets, leaves, and brush. Places and activates antitank or antipersonnel mines in mine field. Decontaminates weapons and equipment when exposed to chemical or nuclear contamination, using specified procedures. Observes compass, aerial photographs, and maps to determine field position for troop movements. Examines equipment and weapons to detect malfunctions. Repairs weapons and equipment, using items such as handtools, oil, and rags. Fires machine guns, grenade launchers, and rifles to inflict casualties on enemy force.
GOE: 04.02.02 STRENGTH: V GED: R2 M1 L1 SVP: 3 DLU: 77

378.684-018 FIELD ARTILLERY CREWMEMBER (military ser.)
Loads and fires field artillery gun or howitzer during combat or training situations: Selects firing site and positions cannon according to orders. Camouflages position if terrain and situation require camouflage. Loads ammunition into breech of cannon. Fires cannon upon order. Realigns cannon position to engage target and repeats cannon firing procedures to fulfill mission requirements on target. Inspects weapon and replaces worn or unserviceable parts, such as gears, springs, and ejectors. Cleans and lubricates hubs, wheels, and similar assemblies, using handtools, brushes, solvents, and rags.
GOE: 04.02.02 STRENGTH: H GED: R2 M1 L1 SVP: 3 DLU: 77

378.684-022 INFANTRY INDIRECT FIRE CREWMEMBER (military ser.)
Positions and fires mortar during combat or training operations: Selects site and positions mortar utilizing concealment and camouflage procedures to prevent detection by enemy. Studies maps and aerial photographs to locate friendly and enemy positions. Confers with friendly unit personnel and furnishes information concerning enemy location, troop movement and similar tactical information. Drops ammunition into mortar to discharge and fire ammunition at target. Observes projectile burst and readjusts mortar to obtain effective hit on target.
GOE: 04.02.02 STRENGTH: V GED: R2 M1 L1 SVP: 5 DLU: 77

378.684-026 INFANTRY WEAPONS CREWMEMBER (military ser.)
Deploys, positions, fires, and maintains crew-served weapons, such as recoilless rifle, tank destroying missile system, or light machine guns, during training

or combat mission: Disassembles, cleans, and loads weapons and equipment for movement and use in combat. Designates location of gun, sector of fire, and targets. Computes firing data, aims, and fires weapons at fixed and moving targets, employing direct fire techniques. Assists superior in leading and directing personnel in combat missions, and during maneuvers or tactical problems. Fires weapons at enemy forces to support and assist other infantry units. Assists superior in coordinating fire and movement with that of other friendly units. Constructs and camouflages weapon positions and ground obstacles. Emplaces and arms, or disarms and removes mines used for local security. Protects weapons and equipment against attack from chemical warfare agents. Decontaminates weapons and equipment when exposed to chemical attack. Performs preventive maintenance, routine tests, and authorized minor repairs to weapons and equipment.
GOE: 04.02.02 STRENGTH: V GED: R2 M1 L1 SVP: 3 DLU: 77

378.684-030 LIGHT AIR DEFENSE ARTILLERY CREWMEMBER (military ser.)
Fires variety of light air defense artillery automatic weapons or machine guns during combat or in training, serving as member of light air defense artillery unit: Removes ammunition from truck and stacks ammunition in storage pit. Positions light air defense artillery automatic weapons and machine guns in specified location. Camouflages ammunition, weapons, and equipment, using nets, paint, and similar items. Installs wire to specified locations to establish field communications. Loads ammunition in breech of weapon or machine gun and fires weapon or machine gun on order at aerial and surface targets during combat or training.
GOE: 04.02.02 STRENGTH: V GED: R2 M1 L1 SVP: 3 DLU: 77

378.687-010 COMBAT SURVEILLANCE AND TARGET ACQUISITION CREWMEMBER (military ser.)
Assists crewmembers of sound, flash, and other target acquisition units in detecting sound or flash of enemy artillery: Assists crewmembers to emplace sound, flash, or other target acquisition equipment. Plots sound or flash data on maps. Assists personnel in operating searchlights. Lays wire to establish field communications. Cleans and lubricates vehicles and equipment.
GOE: 05.03.05 STRENGTH: V GED: R2 M2 L2 SVP: 2 DLU: 77

379 PROTECTIVE SERVICE OCCUPATIONS, N.E.C.

This group includes occupations, not elsewhere classified, concerned with protective service.

379.132-010 SUPERVISOR, TELECOMMUNICATOR (government ser.)
Supervises and coordinates activities of workers engaged in receiving emergency or nonemergency calls, dispatching personnel and equipment, and providing prearrival instructions to callers: Prepares work schedules to ensure that sufficient shift personnel are available for work load demands, using knowledge of supervisory techniques, department regulations, and procedures. Teaches emergency medical dispatch course to new employees, using dispatch simulator. Reviews dispatch office operations to identify technical and operational training needs. Teaches courses dealing with hazardous materials, highrise fires, and medical triage to update training for TELECOMMUNICATOR (government ser.) 379.362-018. Meets with committees composed of representatives from fire and police departments, public, and other interested groups to develop, review, and update policies and procedures for dispatch office. Pushes buttons, flips power switches, and reads gauges to determine serviceability of backup emergency equipment. Performs other duties as described under SUPERVISOR (any industry) Master Title.
GOE: 07.04.05 STRENGTH: S GED: R4 M2 L4 SVP: 7 DLU: 86

379.137-010 SUPERVISOR, ANIMAL CRUELTY INVESTIGATION (nonprofit org.) alternate titles: animal humane agent supervisor; inspector
Supervises and coordinates activities of workers engaged in investigating complaints of cruelty to animals, inspecting establishments housing animals and monitoring public exhibitions featuring animals to enforce humane laws: Assigns ANIMAL TREATMENT INVESTIGATORS (nonprofit org.) to geographical work areas to investigate complaints. Inspects workers for proper attire. Telephones or writes to complainants to resolve complaints or to obtain additional information. Directs worker to investigate emergency complaints received, using telephone or two-way radio. Advises public and workers of provisions and applications of humane laws. Interviews and recommends hiring and firing of employees. Maintains records of workers' daily activities and submits records to superior. Supervises on-the-job training for new workers.
GOE: 11.10.03 STRENGTH: S GED: R4 M2 L4 SVP: 7 DLU: 77

379.137-014 SUPERVISOR, DOG LICENSE OFFICER (nonprofit org.) alternate titles: chief, dog license inspector
Supervises and coordinates activities of workers engaged in enforcing dog license laws and inspecting license books of pet shops: Assigns DOG LICENSERS (nonprofit org.) to crews to assure adequate staff to cover all geographical canvass areas. Reviews work of crews and recommends areas requiring coverage. Checks pet shop license books to assure that license applications and fees have been forwarded. Compares recorded number of dogs sold for period with number of applications completed to assure that pet shop is complying with dog license laws. Records results of visit on control cards. Performs personnel functions, such as interviewing new workers, recommending hiring, and resolving employee grievances.

GOE: 07.04.03 STRENGTH: L GED: R4 M2 L4 SVP: 7 DLU: 77

379.137-018 WILDLIFE AGENT, REGIONAL (government ser.)

Supervises and coordinates activities of FISH AND GAME WARDENS (government ser.) engaged in enforcing fish and game laws, reporting crops and property damage by wildlife, and compiling biological data: Studies and surveys assigned region to learn topography and available cover and feed for wildlife. Subdivides region into geographical districts and submits request for FISH AND GAME WARDENS (government ser.) to patrol districts. Plans location of access roads, trails, sanitary facilities, boat launching sites, and parking areas, based on number of people using area. Trains and assists subordinates to solve work problems and to interpret directives and regulations. Observes issuance of citations, apprehension of game law violators, and seizure of equipment to verify compliance with laws and regulations. Evaluates and submits efficiency reports on subordinates, and initiates personnel actions such as reprimand, disciplinary action, transfer, or discharge. Addresses school, civic, and sports groups on wildlife and recreational activities. Arranges for witnesses and evidence to be used at court trials of game law violators. Compiles consolidated report of region activities and approves requests for new equipment.

GOE: 04.01.02 STRENGTH: L GED: R5 M4 L4 SVP: 7 DLU: 77

379.137-022 SUPERVISOR, PROTECTIVE-SIGNAL OPERATIONS (business ser.)

Supervises and coordinates activities of workers engaged in monitoring protective-signaling system controls and investigating alarm signals transmitted from subscriber premises: Confers with workers to help resolve difficulties encountered during monitoring of system controls and investigation of alarms. Monitors system equipment displays, scans system operations reports, and talks to subscribers to ensure that systems operate according to company and subscriber specifications. Schedules repair of defective installations and equipment. Performs other duties as described under SUPERVISOR (any industry) Master Title.

GOE: 07.04.05 STRENGTH: L GED: R4 M3 L3 SVP: 7 DLU: 86

379.162-010 ALARM OPERATOR (government ser.) alternate titles: fire-alarm dispatcher

Operates municipal fire alarm system, radio transmitter and receiver, and telephone switchboard: Receives incoming fire calls by telephone or through alarm system. Questions caller, observes alarm register that codes location of fire, and scans map of city to determine whether fire is located within area served by city fire department. Determines type and number of units to respond to emergency. Notifies fire station, using radio, and starts alarm system that automatically contacts all fire stations and indicates location of fire. Relays messages from scene of fire, such as requests for additional help and medical assistance. Records date, time, type of call and destination of messages received or transmitted. Maintains activity, code, and locator files. Tests various communications systems and reports malfunctions to maintenance units. May operate telegraph to relay code as back-up if transmitter fails.

GOE: 07.04.05 STRENGTH: S GED: R4 M3 L4 SVP: 6 DLU: 77

379.167-010 FISH AND GAME WARDEN (government ser.) alternate titles: conservation officer; game and fish protector; game warden; guard, range

Patrols assigned area to prevent game law violations, investigate reports of damage to crops and property by wildlife, and compile biological data: Travels through area by car, boat, airplane, horse, and on foot to observe persons engaged in taking fish and game, to ensure method and equipment used are lawful, and to apprehend violators. Investigates reports of fish and game law violations and issues warnings or citations. Serves warrants, makes arrests, and prepares and presents evidence in court actions. Seizes equipment used in fish and game law violations and arranges for disposition of fish and game illegally taken or possessed. Collects and reports information on condition of fish and wildlife in their habitat, availability of game food and cover, and suspected pollution of waterways. Investigates hunting accidents and files reports of findings. Addresses schools and civic groups to disseminate information and promote public relations. May enlist aid of sporting groups in such programs as lake and stream rehabilitation, and game habitat improvement. May assist in promoting hunter safety training by arranging for materials and instructors. May be designated according to specialty as Fish Protector (government ser.); Game Protector (government ser.); or according to assigned patrol as Fish-And-Game Warden, Marine Patrol (government ser.).

GOE: 04.01.02 STRENGTH: M GED: R4 M3 L4 SVP: 6 DLU: 77

379.227-010 INSTRUCTOR-TRAINER, CANINE SERVICE (government ser.)

Instructs police officers in handling of dogs for police work in canine training facility: Instructs police officers in dog training techniques, such as obedience training, tracking, and crowd control. Demonstrates dog handling techniques with dog on and off leash, using trained dog. Instructs officers on subjects related to use of dogs in police work, such as theory of scent and narcotics and bomb detection. Informs officers (handlers) of health care of dogs and responsibilities of handlers. Observes officer and dog teams during practice sessions, and offers suggestions to improve handling techniques when necessary. Contacts representatives of other police departments and law enforcement agencies throughout country to keep training updated and to schedule training sessions. Conducts tours of facility and explains importance of dogs in police work. Purchases dog food and supplies and directs maintenance of facility.

GOE: 03.03.01 STRENGTH: L GED: R3 M2 L3 SVP: 7 DLU: 86

379.263-010 ANIMAL TREATMENT INVESTIGATOR (nonprofit org.) alternate titles: animal control officer

Investigates animal cruelty and neglect charges and performs related duties to promote compliance with laws regulating animal treatment: Observes areas of alleged violations and interviews available witnesses to determine if laws are being violated. Informs persons perpetrating inhumane acts of laws and penalties for violations. Reports violators to police or requests police to arrest violators. Aids animals in distress by feeding starving animals and freeing trapped animals. Removes animals from inhumane conditions and drives vehicle to transport animals to shelter for treatment and care. Inspects establishments housing or exhibiting animals to ascertain compliance with humane laws. Writes reports of activities.

GOE: 11.10.03 STRENGTH: L GED: R3 M1 L3 SVP: 5 DLU: 77

379.263-014 PUBLIC-SAFETY OFFICER (government ser.)

Patrols assigned beat and responds to emergency calls to protect persons or property from crimes, fires, or other hazards: Patrols assigned area on foot or horseback or using vehicle to regulate traffic, control crowds, prevent crime, or arrest violators. Responds to crimes in progress, initiating actions such as aid to victims and interrogation of suspects. Attends public gatherings to maintain order. Responds to fire alarms or other emergency calls. Forces openings in buildings for ventilation of fire or for entry, using ax or crowbar. Controls and extinguishes fires, using water and chemicals. Administers first aid and artificial respiration to injured persons. Participates in drills and emergency precautionary demonstrations. May inspect establishments for compliance with local regulations. May drive and operate firefighting and other emergency equipment.

GOE: 04.01.02 STRENGTH: V GED: R4 M3 L3 SVP: 7 DLU: 86

379.267-010 WILDLIFE CONTROL AGENT (government ser.)

Controls animal population in geographical district and investigates crop and property damage claims caused by wildlife: Conducts on-site surveys to estimate number of birds and animals, such as deer, pheasant, and mountain fox in designated areas and availability of game food and cover. Recommends changes in hunting and trapping seasons and relocation of animals in overpopulated areas to obtain balance of wildlife and habitat. Implements approved control measures, performing duties such as trapping beavers, dynamiting beaver dams, and tranquilizing and relocating deer, bear, cougar, and other animals. Resurveys area and totals bag counts of hunters to determine effectiveness of control measures. Recommends revised hunting and trapping regulations and other control measures and release of birds for restocking. Searches area of reported property damage for animal tracks, leavings and other evidence to identify specie of animal responsible. Photographs extent of damage, documents other evidence, estimates financial loss, and recommends compensation. Advises owner of methods to remedy future damages, and implements other measures, such as erecting fences, tranquilizing and relocating animal herds and spraying flower beds and bushes with repellants. Performs duties of wildlife agent during hunting season. Gives talks to civic groups, school assemblies and sports organizations to disseminate information about wildlife and department policies.

GOE: 03.01.02 STRENGTH: M GED: R4 M3 L3 SVP: 7 DLU: 77

379.362-010 DISPATCHER, RADIO (government ser.) alternate titles: dispatcher; police radio dispatcher; station operator

Receives complaints from public concerning crimes and police emergencies, broadcasts orders to police radio patrol units in vicinity to investigate complaint, and relays instructions or questions from remote units. Records calls broadcast and complaints received. In some municipalities coordinates all police, fire, ambulance, and other emergency requests, relaying instructions to radio unit concerned. May make operating adjustments to transmitting equipment where station is not automatic and be required to hold federal license. May transmit and receive messages between divisions of own agency and other law enforcement agencies. May monitor silent alarm system to detect illegal entry into business establishments. May contact POLICE OFFICERS (government ser.) I 375.263-014 and GUARDS, SCHOOL-CROSSING (government ser.) 371.567-010 to verify assignment locations.

GOE: 07.04.05 STRENGTH: S GED: R3 M2 L3 SVP: 4 DLU: 81

379.362-014 PROTECTIVE-SIGNAL OPERATOR (any industry) alternate titles: alarm-signal operator; drop-board operator; dx board operator; operator, circuit; operator, direct wire; signal timer

Reads and records coded signals received in central station of electrical protective signaling system: Interprets coded audible or visible signals received on alarm signal board by direct wire or register tape from subscribers' premises that indicate opening and closing of protected premises, progress of security guard, unlawful intrusions, or fire. Reports irregular signals for corrective action. Reports alarms to police or fire department. Posts changes of subscriber opening and closing schedules. Prepares daily alarm activity and subscriber service reports. May adjust central station equipment to ensure uninterrupted service. May dispatch security personnel to premises after receiving alarm.

GOE: 07.04.05 STRENGTH: S GED: R3 M2 L3 SVP: 5 DLU: 77

379.362-018 TELECOMMUNICATOR (government ser.) alternate titles: dispatcher

Operates communication equipment to receive incoming calls for assistance and dispatches personnel and equipment to scene of emergency: Operates tele-

phone console to receive incoming calls for assistance. Questions caller to determine nature of problem and type and number of personnel and equipment needed, following established guidelines. Scans status charts and computer screen to determine units available. Monitors alarm system signals that indicate location of fire or other emergency. Operates two-way radio to dispatch police, fire, medical, and other personnel and equipment and to relay instructions or information to remove units. Types commands on computer keyboard to update files and maintain logs. Tests communications and alarm equipment and backup systems to ensure serviceability. May provide prearrival instructions to caller, utilizing knowledge of emergency medical techniques. May activate alarm system to notify fire stations.
GOE: 07.04.05 STRENGTH: S GED: R4 M2 L4 SVP: 5 DLU: 86

379.364-010 AUTOMOBILE TESTER (government ser.) alternate titles: motor-vehicle inspector; vehicle-safety inspector
Inspects automobiles and trucks at state-operated inspection station to ensure compliance with state safety requirements: Examines or tests specified components of vehicle, such as brake system, tires, lighting system, directional signals, steering, horn, and exhaust line for evidence of wear, damage, or improper adjustment. Applies inspection sticker to vehicles that pass and rejection sticker to those that do not. May prepare records on condition of each vehicle for follow-up action by owner or police. May perform duties of STATE-HIGHWAY POLICE OFFICER (government ser.) when not assigned to inspection detail. May arrest or direct the arrest of vehicle owners having illegal equipment installed on vehicle. May utilize mechanical, electronic, or electrical devices and instruments to determine condition of vehicle components.
GOE: 05.07.02 STRENGTH: L GED: R3 M2 L2 SVP: 4 DLU: 77

379.364-014 BEACH LIFEGUARD (amuse. & rec.)
Patrols public beach area to monitor activities of swimmers and prevent illegal conduct: Observes activities in assigned area on foot, in vehicle, or from tower or headquarters building with binoculars to detect hazardous situations, such as swimmers in distress, disturbances, or safety infractions. Cautions people against use of unsafe beach areas or illegal conduct, such as drinking or fighting, using megaphone. Rescues distressed persons from ocean or adjacent cliffs, using rescue techniques and equipment. Examines injured individuals, administers first aid, and monitors vital signs, utilizing training, antiseptics, bandages, and instruments, such as stethoscope and sphygmomanometer. Administers artificial respiration, utilizing cardiopulmonary or mouth-to-mouth methods, or provides oxygen to revive persons. Compiles emergency and medical treatment report forms and maintains daily information on weather and beach conditions. Occasionally operates switchboard or two-way radio system to maintain contact and coordinate activities between emergency rescue units.
GOE: 04.02.03 STRENGTH: V GED: R3 M2 L2 SVP: 4 DLU: 86

379.367-010 SURVEILLANCE-SYSTEM MONITOR (government ser.)
Monitors premises of public transportation terminals to detect crimes or disturbances, using closed circuit television monitors, and notifies authorities by telephone of need for corrective action: Observes television screens that transmit in sequence views of transportation facility sites. Pushes hold button to maintain surveillance of location where incident is developing, and telephones police or other designated agency to notify authorities of location of disruptive activity. Adjusts monitor controls when required to improve reception, and notifies repair service of equipment malfunctions.
GOE: 04.02.03 STRENGTH: S GED: R3 M1 L3 SVP: 2 DLU: 86

379.384-010 SCUBA DIVER (any industry) alternate titles: salvage diver
Performs various underwater jobs, wearing diving gear, such as self-contained underwater breathing apparatus, mask, flippers, and insulated suit: Swims from boat, dock, or shore to job site. Dives to locate or recover submerged automobiles, boats, logs, and articles, such as purses, keys, and other valuables. Swims to bottom and fastens lines or chains around heavy objects and attaches to lowered hook. Picks up lightweight objects and carries to surface. May search for bodies. May fish for abalone, crab, or sponge. May use safety line, and communicate with tender by jerking on line. May repair underwater installations. May engage in fire fighting activities.
GOE: 05.10.01 STRENGTH: H GED: R3 M2 L2 SVP: 4 DLU: 77

379.664-010 SKI PATROLLER (amuse. & rec.)
Patrols ski trails and slope areas to provide assistance and protection to skiers and report condition of trails, ski lifts, and snow cover on slopes: Patrols assigned areas, using skis or snowshoes. Rescues injured skiers and renders first aid or transfers them to waiting ambulance, using toboggan. Notifies medical personnel in case of serious injury where moving skier might prove dangerous. Ensures that no skiers remain on slopes or trails at end of day or during inclement weather. Inspects ski lifts, such as rope tows, T-bar, J-bar, and chair lifts, to report safety hazards and evidence of damage or wear. May pack snow on slopes. May give ski instruction. May participate in skiing demonstrations for entertainment of resort guests. May assist demolition crew to blast for avalanche control.
GOE: 04.02.03 STRENGTH: H GED: R3 M2 L3 SVP: 6 DLU: 77

379.667-010 GOLF-COURSE RANGER (amuse. & rec.) alternate titles: golf-course patroller
Patrols golf course to prevent unauthorized persons from using facilities, keep play running smoothly, and assist injured or ill players: Inspects player and CADDIE (amuse. & rec.) registration and green fee tickets for validity. Prevents players from entering course beyond starting tee. Advises players to

speed up or slow down in order to alleviate bottlenecks. Explains rules of game to players to settle disputes. Locates damaged or hazardous areas and marks areas for repair, using lime marker or stake. Cautions players against tearing up turf or otherwise abusing course. Renders first aid to injured or ill players and carries their equipment to clubhouse. Returns lost equipment to owners or to clubhouse. Keeps log of daily activities. May deliver urgent messages to players on course.
GOE: 12.01.02 STRENGTH: L GED: R3 M2 L3 SVP: 4 DLU: 77

379.667-014 LIFEGUARD (amuse. & rec.)
Monitors activities in swimming areas to prevent accidents and provide assistance to swimmers: Cautions swimmers regarding unsafe areas. Rescues swimmers in danger of drowning and administers first aid. Maintains order in swimming areas. Inspects facilities for cleanliness. May clean and refill swimming pool. May determine chlorine content and pH value of water, using water testing kit. May conduct or officiate at swimming meets. May give swimming instructions.
GOE: 04.02.03 STRENGTH: M GED: R3 M1 L2 SVP: 4 DLU: 77

379.673-010 DOG CATCHER (government ser.) alternate titles: dog warden
Captures and impounds unlicensed, stray, and uncontrolled animals: Snares animal with net, rope, or device. Cages or secures animal in truck. Drives truck to shelter. Removes animal from truck to shelter cage or other enclosure. Supplies food, water, and personal care to detained animals. Investigates complaints of animal bite cases. Destroys rabid animals as directed. Examines dog licenses for validity and issues warnings or summonses to delinquent owners. May destroy unclaimed animals, using gun, or by gas or electrocution. May examine captured animals for injuries and deliver injured animals to VETERINARIAN (medical ser.) for medical treatment. May maintain file of number of animals impounded and disposition of each. May enforce regulations concerning treatment of domestic animals and be designated Humane Officer (government ser.).
GOE: 03.04.05 STRENGTH: M GED: R3 M1 L2 SVP: 3 DLU: 77

379.687-010 FIRE-EXTINGUISHER-SPRINKLER INSPECTOR (any industry) alternate titles: fire-apparatus sprinkler inspector
Inspects and tests sprinkler valves. Inspects pipes, hoses, and hose boxes of fire apparatus in plants, offices, apartment buildings, and similar structures. Fills out inspection report on condition of valves, pipes, tanks, pumps, and alarms for superiors and customers.
GOE: 05.07.01 STRENGTH: L GED: R3 M2 L2 SVP: 4 DLU: 77

379.687-014 MOSQUITO SPRAYER (government ser.) alternate titles: hand-spray operator; sanitarian; sprayer, insecticide
Sprays marshland, drainage ditches, or catch-basins with insecticide, using portable compressed-air spray tank, to control breeding of mosquitoes. Removes blockage from area being sprayed, using pick and shovel, to facilitate drainage. May drive truck equipped with gasoline-powered fogger to spray insecticide over designated areas. May place poison bait in storm sewers and ditches to exterminate rodents.
GOE: 03.04.05 STRENGTH: M GED: R1 M1 L1 SVP: 3 DLU: 77

38 BUILDING AND RELATED SERVICE OCCUPATIONS

This division includes occupations concerned with the cleaning and upkeep of building interiors and the conveying of passengers and freight by elevator.

381 PORTERS AND CLEANERS

This group includes occupations concerned with cleaning buildings, furniture, and equipment. Includes sweeping, dusting, mopping, polishing floors and walls, and disposing of trash.

381.137-010 SUPERVISOR, JANITORIAL SERVICES (any industry) alternate titles: janitor, head; lead janitor; porter, head; supervisor, building maintenance
Supervises and coordinates activities of workers engaged in cleaning and maintaining premises of commercial, industrial, or other establishments, such as schools, stores, or auditorium: Assigns tasks to workers, and inspects completed work for conformance to standards. Issues supplies and equipment. Resolves workers' problems or refers matters to supervisor. Trains new workers, records hours worked, recommends discharge of incompetent workers, and performs other personnel duties as required. May submit requests for repair of cleaning equipment to SUPERINTENDENT, BUILDING (any industry) 187.167-190. May hire new employees. May requisition or purchase cleaning supplies and equipment. May perform duties of workers supervised. May supervise employees of public school system and be designated Supervisor, Maintenance And Custodians (education).
GOE: 05.12.18 STRENGTH: M GED: R4 M2 L3 SVP: 6 DLU: 87

381.137-014 SUPERVISOR, CENTRAL SUPPLY (medical ser.)
Supervises and coordinates activities of personnel in medical central supply room engaged in furnishing sterile and nonsterile supplies and equipment for use in care and treatment of patients: Directs activities of workers engaged in cleaning, assembling, and packing of linens, gowns, dressings, gloves, treatment trays, instruments, and related items; preparation of solutions; arrangement of

stock; and requisitioning, issuing, controlling, and charging of supplies and equipment. Instructs personnel in use of sterilizing equipment and water distillation apparatus, setting up standardized treatment trays, and maintaining equipment of central supply room. Establishes standards of work performance and methods of operation for department. Inspects work activities to ensure workers are following prescribed procedures to meet hospital standards. Ensures that aseptic techniques are employed by personnel in preparing and handling sterile items. Inspects daily inventory, maintains records of supply usage, and compiles periodic reports.
GOE: 05.12.01 STRENGTH: L GED: R4 M3 L4 SVP: 7 DLU: 86

381.687-010 CENTRAL-SUPPLY WORKER (medical ser.) alternate titles: central-service technician
Performs any combination of following duties: Scrubs and washes surgical instruments, containers, and equipment, such as aspirators and suction units. Sterilizes instruments, equipment, surgical linens, and supplies, such as surgical packs and treatment trays, using autoclave, sterilizer, or antiseptic solutions. Prepares packs of supplies, instruments, and dressing and treatment trays, according to designated lists or codes, and wraps, labels, and seals packs. Stores prepared articles and supplies in designated areas. Fills requisitions, writes charges, and inventories supplies. May be assigned to hospital areas, such as surgery and delivery rooms.
GOE: 05.12.18 STRENGTH: L GED: R3 M2 L2 SVP: 4 DLU: 88

381.687-014 CLEANER, COMMERCIAL OR INSTITUTIONAL (any industry) alternate titles: clean-up worker; housekeeper; janitor; laborer, building maintenance; mopper; porter; scrubber; sweeper
Keeps premises of office building, apartment house, or other commercial or institutional building in clean and orderly condition: Cleans and polishes lighting fixtures, marble surfaces, and trim, and performs duties described in CLEANER (any industry) I Master Title. May cut and trim grass, and shovel snow, using power equipment or handtools. May deliver messages. May transport small equipment or tools between departments. May setup tables and chairs in auditorium or hall. May be designated according to duties performed as Hall Cleaner (hotel & rest.); Light-Fixture Cleaner (any industry); Marble Cleaner (any industry); Metal Polisher (any industry); Paint Cleaner (any industry); or according to equipment used as Scrubbing-Machine Operator (any industry).
GOE: 05.12.18 STRENGTH: H GED: R1 M1 L1 SVP: 2 DLU: 88

381.687-018 CLEANER, INDUSTRIAL (any industry) alternate titles: clean-up worker; janitor; sanitor; scrubber; sweeper; trash collector; vacuum cleaner; waste collector
Keeps working areas in production departments of industrial establishment in clean and orderly condition, performing any combination of following duties: Transports raw materials and semifinished products or supplies between departments or buildings to supply machine tenders or operators with materials for processing, using handtruck. Arranges boxes, material, and handtrucks or other industrial equipment in neat and orderly manner. Cleans lint, dust, oil, and grease from machines, overhead pipes, and conveyors, using brushes, airhoses, or steam cleaner. Cleans screens and filters. Scrubs processing tanks and vats. Cleans floors, using water hose, and applies floor drier. Picks up reusable scrap for salvage and stores in containers. Performs other duties as described under CLEANER (any industry) I Master Title. May burn waste and clean incinerator. May pick up refuse from plant grounds and maintain area by cutting grass or shoveling snow. May operate industrial truck to transport materials within plant. May start pumps to force cleaning solution through production machinery, piping, or vats. May start pumps to lubricate machines. May be designated according to area cleaned as Alley Cleaner (textile); Can-Filling-Room Sweeper (beverage); Casting-And-Locker-Room Servicer (plastic-synth.); Ceiling Cleaner (any industry); Engine-Room Cleaner (any industry); Floor Cleaner (any industry); Overhead Cleaner (any industry).
GOE: 05.12.18 STRENGTH: M GED: R2 M1 L2 SVP: 2 DLU: 88

381.687-022 CLEANER, LABORATORY EQUIPMENT (any industry) alternate titles: equipment washer; laboratory aide; laboratory assistant; laboratory helper; laborer, laboratory; tester helper
Cleans laboratory equipment, such as glassware, metal instruments, sinks, tables, and test panels, using solvents, brushes, and rags: Mixes water and detergents or acids in container to prepare cleaning solution according to specifications. Washes, rinses, and dries glassware and instruments, using water, acetone bath, and cloth or hot-air drier. Scrubs walls, floors, shelves, tables, and sinks, using cleaning solution and brush. May sterilize glassware and instruments, using autoclave. May fill tubes and bottles with specified solutions and apply identification labels. May label and file microscope slides. May arrange specimens and samples on trays to be placed in incubators and refrigerators. May deliver supplies and laboratory specimens to designated work areas, using handtruck. May tend still that supplies laboratory with distilled water. May be designated Glass Washer, Laboratory (any industry) when cleaning glassware. May maintain inventory reports and logs.
GOE: 05.12.18 STRENGTH: M GED: R2 M2 L1 SVP: 2 DLU: 88

381.687-026 CLEANER, WALL (any industry) alternate titles: wallpaper cleaner; wall washer
Cleans interior walls and ceilings of offices, apartments, and other buildings, by hand or by use of wall-washing machine: Cleans walls and ceilings by hand,

using sponge and soapy water or chemical solution, or presses lever in nozzle of machine to control flow of solution and moves nozzle fitted with porous pad over surfaces, exerting sufficient pressure to remove dirt and grease. May estimate cost of cleaning walls and submit bids.
GOE: 05.12.18 STRENGTH: M GED: R1 M1 L1 SVP: 2 DLU: 77

381.687-030 PATCH WORKER (agriculture)
Sweeps floors of cotton-bale compressing plant. Gathers loose cotton from floor. Carries or transfers light equipment to various workers, using handtruck.
GOE: 06.04.40 STRENGTH: L GED: R1 M1 L1 SVP: 2 DLU: 77

381.687-034 WAXER, FLOOR (any industry)
Cleans, waxes, and polishes floors by hand or machine: Removes dirt and blemishes from floor, using various cleaning solvents and compounds, according to composition of floor. Applies paste or liquid wax to floor with rags or machine. Polishes floor with electric polishing machine or weighted brush.
GOE: 05.12.18 STRENGTH: M GED: R1 M1 L1 SVP: 2 DLU: 77

382   JANITORS

This group includes occupations concerned with cleaning buildings and keeping them in good repair; performing minor painting, plumbing, and carpentry tasks; and firing and tending furnaces and boilers.

382.137-010 SUPERVISOR, MAINTENANCE (chemical) alternate titles: labor supervisor
Supervises and coordinates activities of workers engaged in maintenance of chemical plant. Performs duties as described under SUPERVISOR (any industry) Master Title.
GOE: 05.12.01 STRENGTH: M GED: R4 M3 L3 SVP: 6 DLU: 77

382.664-010 JANITOR (any industry) alternate titles: maintenance engineer; superintendent, building
Keeps hotel, office building, apartment house, or similar building in clean and orderly condition and tends furnace, air-conditioner, and boiler to provide heat, cool air, and hot water for tenants, performing any combination of following duties: Sweeps, mops, scrubs, and vacuums hallways, stairs and office space. Regulates flow of fuel into automatic furnace or shovels coal into handfired furnace. Empties tenants' trash and garbage containers. Maintains building, performing minor and routine painting, plumbing, electrical wiring, and other related maintenance activities, using handtools. Replaces air-conditioner filters. Cautions tenants regarding complaints about excessive noise, disorderly conduct, or misuse of property. Notifies management concerning need for major repairs or additions to lighting, heating, and ventilating equipment. Cleans snow and debris from sidewalk. Mows lawn, trims shrubbery, and cultivates flowers, using handtools and power tools. Posts signs to advertise vacancies and shows empty apartments to prospective tenants. May reside on property and be designated Manager, Resident (any industry).
GOE: 05.12.18 STRENGTH: M GED: R3 M2 L3 SVP: 3 DLU: 88

383   BUILDING PEST CONTROL SERVICE OCCUPATIONS

This group includes occupations concerned with pest control in buildings and surrounding areas.

383.361-010 FUMIGATOR (business ser.)
Releases poisonous gas and sets traps in buildings to kill dry-wood termites, beetles, vermin, and other pests, using cylinders of compressed gas and mechanical traps: Inspects infested building to identify pests causing damage and to determine treatment necessary. Examines porosity of walls and roof, based on knowledge of construction techniques, to determine method of sealing house. Measures inside dimensions of rooms with rule, and calculates volume of fumigant required and cost to owner. Tapes vents. Climbs ladder, pulls tarpaulins over building, and fastens edges of tarpaulins with clamps to make building airtight. Posts warning signs and padlocks doors. Turns valve on cylinder to discharge gas into building through hose. Holds halide lamp near seams of tarpaulins and building vents to detect leaking fumigant. Sprays or dusts chemicals in rooms or work areas and sets mechanical traps to destroy pests. May fumigate clothing and house furnishing in vaults at business establishment.
GOE: 05.10.09 STRENGTH: H GED: R4 M3 L3 SVP: 5 DLU: 77

383.364-010 EXTERMINATOR, TERMITE (business ser.) alternate titles: termite treater
Treats termite-infested and fungus-damaged wood in buildings: Studies report and diagram of infested area prepared by SALES AGENT, PEST CONTROL SERVICE (business ser.) to determine sequence of operations. Examines building to determine means of reaching infested areas. Cuts openings in building to gain access to infested areas, using handtools and power tools, such as electric drills, pneumatic hammers, saws, and chisels. Inserts nozzle into holes and opens compressed air valve of treating unit to force termicide into holes. Sprays pesticide under and around building, using pressure spray gun. Bores holes in concrete around buildings and injects termicide to impregnate ground. Keeps record of work performed. May direct EXTERMINATOR HELPER, TERMITE (business ser.). May replace damaged wood in sills, flooring, or walls, using carpenter's tools. May pour concrete or lay concrete blocks to raise height of foundation or isolate wood from contact with earth to prevent reinfestation.

GOE: 05.10.09 STRENGTH: H GED: R3 M2 L2 SVP: 6 DLU: 77

383.684-010 EXTERMINATOR HELPER (any industry) alternate titles: pest control worker helper

Assists EXTERMINATOR (any industry) 389.684-010 in destroying and controlling field rodents, noxious weeds, or other pests in or around buildings, performing any combination of following tasks: Sets traps and places poisonous bait in rodent infested areas. Fumigates burrows, using toxic gas, or kills rodents, using firearms. Secures tarpaulins over building to be fumigated, using ladder. Applies insecticides to buildings and grounds, using spray pumps and other equipment. Digs up, sprays with herbicides, or burns noxious weeds. Identifies and reports evidence of pest infestation. May drive service vehicles or equipment. Performs other duties as described under HELPER (any industry) Master Title.

GOE: 05.10.09 STRENGTH: M GED: R3 M2 L2 SVP: 4 DLU: 86

383.687-010 EXTERMINATOR, TERMITE (business ser.) alternate titles: termite-treater helper

Assists EXTERMINATOR, TERMITE (business ser.) in treating termite-infested buildings: Digs around foundations to be chemically treated and digs ditches for forms, using pick and shovel. Carries lumber, building materials, and tools to work site. Crawls underneath buildings to remove debris prior to spraying. Cleans work site after completion of job. Performs other duties as described under HELPER (any industry) Master Title.

GOE: 05.12.03 STRENGTH: H GED: R1 M1 L1 SVP: 2 DLU: 77

388 ELEVATOR OPERATORS

This group includes occupations concerned with conveying persons and freight between floors; giving information and directions to passengers; and frequently assisting passengers on and off cars.

388.367-010 ELEVATOR STARTER (any industry) alternate titles: elevator dispatcher; elevator supervisor; starter

Schedules, supervises, and coordinates activities of ELEVATOR OPERATORS (any industry) to provide efficient service to building patrons and employees: Provides elevator service according to demand by signaling operators or by establishing time schedules for each car. Enforces crowding and weight restrictions in cars. Answers questions regarding location of offices, individuals, or merchandise, and ushers passengers into waiting elevators. Gives instructions to new employees in elevator operation. Ensures that sufficient personnel are available to meet service demands, regulating shift assignments accordingly. Inspects equipment for safety and efficient operation. Reports need for maintenance to supervisor or elevator service company. May record employees' time on cards.

GOE: 09.05.09 STRENGTH: L GED: R3 M2 L2 SVP: 6 DLU: 77

388.663-010 ELEVATOR OPERATOR (any industry) alternate titles: service-car operator

Operates elevator to transport passengers between floors of office building, apartment house, department store, hotel, or similar establishment: Pushes buttons or moves lever to control movement of elevator on signal or instructions from passengers or others. Opens and closes safety gate and door of elevator at each floor where stop is made. Supplies information to passengers, such as location of offices, merchandise, and individuals. May perform other duties, such as distributing mail to various floors, answering telephone, preventing unauthorized persons from entering building, and assisting other employees to load and unload freight. May sweep or vacuum elevator. May be designated according to location of elevator operated as Front-Elevator Operator (hotel & rest.).

GOE: 09.05.09 STRENGTH: L GED: R2 M1 L2 SVP: 2 DLU: 77

389 BUILDING AND RELATED SERVICE OCCUPATIONS, N.E.C.

This group includes occupations, not elsewhere classified, concerned with building and related service occupations.

389.134-010 SUPERVISOR, EXTERMINATION (business ser.)

Supervises and coordinates activities of EXTERMINATORS (any industry) engaged in destroying vermin with insecticides, rodenticides or fumigants: Inspects infested structure and recommends treatment, basing diagnosis on knowledge of pests' habits, fumigants, rodenticides and insecticides, and structural conditions. Directs EXTERMINATORS (any industry) in type of chemicals to use and locations to be treated. Advises building owners on preventive measures against reinfestation. May spray or apply insecticides, rodenticides or fumigants and perform duties as described under EXTERMINATOR (any industry).

GOE: 05.10.09 STRENGTH: L GED: R4 M3 L3 SVP: 6 DLU: 77

389.137-010 SUPERVISOR, HOME RESTORATION SERVICE (any industry)

Supervises and coordinates activities of workers engaged in cleaning and restoring interiors of homes damaged by fire, smoke, or water: Schedules work crews according to type and extent of interior damage to home. Inventories, requisitions, and issues supplies and equipment. Trains and supervises workers in methods of cleaning and restoring interiors of homes, including floors, walls, ceilings, carpet, upholstery, and draperies. Inspects completed work and work

in progress for conformance to standards. Resolves workers' problems or refers matters to management. Explains methods of restoration and attempts to persuade prospective customers to contract for services.

GOE: 05.12.01 STRENGTH: M GED: R3 M3 L3 SVP: 7 DLU: 86

389.664-010 CLEANER, HOME RESTORATION SERVICE (any industry) alternate titles: cleaner, carpet and upholstery

Cleans and restores interiors of homes damaged by fire, smoke, or water, using commercial cleaning equipment: Receives work orders and schedules from supervisor. Drives van equipped with floor-mounted or portable commercial carpet, upholstery, and interior cleaning machines, tools, and supplies to work site. Cleans carpet, upholstery, floors, walls, ceilings, draperies, windows, and room accessories to remove effects of smoke and water damage such as dirt, soot, stains, mildew, and excess water and moisture, using commercial cleaning machines mounted in van with extension hoses or portable cleaning machines and variety of work aids, such as vacuum cleaners, chemical cleaning solutions, ladders, drop cloths, sponges, buckets, mops, and brushes. Places fans and dehumidifiers in strategic room locations to remove moisture from carpet, upholstery, and air. Verifies moisture presence and removal with moisture sensor. Sprays or fogs carpet, upholstery, and accessories with fabric conditioners and protectors, deodorizers, and disinfectants, using hand and power sprayers and electric foggers, applying knowledge of types of fabrics, dyes, and chemical sprays. Inspects completed restoration to ensure conformance to standards. Collects payments and discusses results of work with customers.

GOE: 05.12.18 STRENGTH: H GED: R2 M1 L2 SVP: 3 DLU: 86

389.667-010 SEXTON (nonprofit org.) alternate titles: janitor, church; verger

Takes care of church buildings and furnishings: Performs cleaning and routine maintenance duties in church and auxiliary buildings and in churchyard, or gives directions to other workers so engaged. Takes care of vestments and sacred vessels and prepares altar for religious services according to prescribed rite. Opens and locks church before and after services. Rings bells to announce services and other church events. Tends furnace and boiler to provide heat. May order cleaning supplies. May act as usher during services, maintain attendance count, and conduct visitors between services. May take part in conduct of services performing activities, such as lighting candles. May maintain church cemetery. May patrol church premises to provide security against vandalism and theft.

GOE: 05.12.18 STRENGTH: M GED: R2 M1 L2 SVP: 2 DLU: 77

389.683-010 SWEEPER-CLEANER, INDUSTRIAL (any industry) alternate titles: cleaner operator; power-cleaner operator; vacuum-cleaner operator

Drives industrial vacuum cleaner through designated areas, such as factory aisles and warehouses, to collect scrap, dirt, and other refuse. Empties trash collecting box or bag at end of each shift. May sift refuse to recover usable materials, such as screws, metal scrap, or machine parts. May clean machine, using rags and vacuum cleaner. May refuel machine and lubricate parts. May hand sweep areas inaccessible to machine and pick up scrap.

GOE: 05.12.18 STRENGTH: M GED: R1 M1 L1 SVP: 2 DLU: 77

389.684-010 EXTERMINATOR (business ser.) alternate titles: pest control worker; vermin exterminator

Sprays chemical solutions or toxic gases and sets mechanical traps to kill pests that infest buildings and surrounding areas: Fumigates rooms and buildings, using toxic gases. Sprays chemical solutions or dusts powders in rooms and work areas. Places poisonous paste or bait and mechanical traps where pests are present. May clean areas that harbor pests, using rakes, brooms, shovels, and mops, preparatory to fumigating. May be required to hold state license. May be designated according to type of pest eliminated as Rodent Exterminator (business ser.).

GOE: 05.10.09 STRENGTH: L GED: R3 M2 L2 SVP: 5 DLU: 81

389.687-010 AIR PURIFIER SERVICER (business ser.) alternate titles: air deodorizer servicer

Delivers, installs, and services air deodorizing and sanitizing devices in commercial, institutional, and public establishments: Drives delivery truck to convey deodorizing devices and chemical refills to building of customers. Attaches deodorizing devices (dispensers) to walls, using handtools, or places device unattached at various locations of customer's building. Places nontoxic chemical into deodorizing containers. May clean deodorizing device, using wire brush, or remove unit, if defective. May clean and disinfect equipment, such as urinals, toilet bowls, and washbasins, using brushes, sponges, and cleaning agents.

GOE: 05.12.12 STRENGTH: L GED: R1 M1 L1 SVP: 2 DLU: 77

389.687-014 CLEANER, WINDOW (any industry) alternate titles: window washer

Cleans windows, glass partitions, mirrors, and other glass surfaces of building interior or exterior, using pail of soapy water or other cleaner, sponge, and squeegee. Crawls through window from inside and hooks safety belt to brackets for support, sets and climbs ladder to reach second or third story, or uses bosun's chair, swing stage, or other scaffolding lowered from roof to reach outside windows, or stands to reach first floor or inside windows.

GOE: 05.12.18 STRENGTH: M GED: R1 M1 L1 SVP: 2 DLU: 77

389.687-018 LIGHT-FIXTURE SERVICER (any industry) alternate titles: fixture relamper; fluorescent lamp replacer; light-bulb replacer; light cleaner

Replaces electric light fixture parts, such as bulbs, fluorescent tubes, and starters. Repairs fixture parts, such as switches and sockets, using handtools.

Cleans fixtures and lamps, using soap, water and rags. Requisitions and keeps supply of bulbs, tubes, and replacement parts.

GOE: 05.12.18 STRENGTH: M GED: R1 M1 L1 SVP: 2 DLU: 77

4 AGRICULTURAL, FISHERY, FORESTRY, AND RELATED OCCUPATIONS

This category includes occupations concerned with propagating, growing, caring for, and gathering plant and animal life and products. Also included are occupations concerned with providing related support services; logging timber tracts; catching, hunting, and trapping animal life; and caring for parks, gardens, and grounds. Excluded are occupations requiring a primary knowledge or involvement with technologies, such as processing, packaging, and stock checking, regardless of their industry designation. Managerial occupations in agriculture, fishery, and forestry are included in Group 180.

40   PLANT FARMING OCCUPATIONS

This division includes occupations concerned with tilling soil; propagating, cultivating, and harvesting plant life; gathering products of plant life; and caring for parks, gardens, and grounds. Service occupations performed in support of these activities are also included.

401   GRAIN FARMING OCCUPATIONS

This group includes occupations concerned with growing and harvesting grain crops, such as corn, sorghum, wheat, barley, and rice; and field peas, field beans, and soybeans.

401.137-010 SUPERVISOR, AREA (agriculture)

Supervises and coordinates activities of workers engaged in detasseling corn on hybrid seed-corn farm: Examines ears of corn in field to determine time of emergence of silk and its retention of accompanying pollen from tassels, and schedules work load. Assigns block and field code numbers and identifies and marks male and female rows of stalks. Examines fields to find areas of rapidly growing tassels and orders crew to remove tassels before emergence of silk from ears of corn. Assigns fields to SUPERVISOR, DETASSELING CREW (agriculture). Determines frequency of detasseling according to factors, such as temperature, moisture, time of season, and variety of corn grown. Inspects fields for undetasseled corn plants, estimates number of plants in field, and computes percent of tassels pulled by making sample counts of plants. Registers corn detasseling crew and issues identification badges. Performs other duties as described under SUPERVISOR (any industry) Master Title.
GOE: 03.02.01 STRENGTH: L GED: R4 M3 L3 SVP: 7 DLU: 77

401.137-014 SUPERVISOR, DETASSELING CREW (agriculture)

Supervises and coordinates activites of workers engaged in breaking and pulling tassels from corn plants: Directs crewmembers in methods of pulling tassels and stems from corn plants. Designates rows of corn to be detasseled so that ears of corn will be pollenized by tassels of adjacent rows of corn. Records detasseling time and acreage covered. May direct workers in method of pulling corn suckers. May recruit crewmembers and transport them to fields. Performs other duties as described under SUPERVISOR (any industry) Master Title.
GOE: 03.04.01 STRENGTH: L GED: R3 M2 L3 SVP: 6 DLU: 77

401.161-010 FARMER, CASH GRAIN (agriculture) alternate titles: cash grain grower; grain farmer

Plants, cultivates, and harvests one or more grain crops, such as barley, corn, rice, soybeans, and wheat, for cash sale: Selects and buys type and amount of seed to be grown, taking into consideration local growing conditions and market demands. Operates equipment to plow, disk, harrow, and fertilize ground and to plant grain. Plans harvesting, considering ripeness and maturity of grain and weather conditions and operates grain-harvesting equipment. Sells grain or stores grain for future sale. Directs activities of workers. Hires and discharges workers. May be designated according to specific grain grown as Corn Grower (agriculture); Rice Farmer (agriculture); Soybean Grower (agriculture); Wheat Grower (agriculture).
GOE: 03.01.01 STRENGTH: H GED: R4 M3 L3 SVP: 7 DLU: 81

401.683-010 FARMWORKER, GRAIN I (agriculture)

Drives and operates farm machinery to plant, cultivate, harvest, and store grain crops, such as wheat, oats, rye, and corn: Attaches farm implements, such as plow, disc, and drill, to tractor and drives tractor in fields to till soil and plant and cultivate grain, according to instructions. Tows harvesting equipment or drives and operates self-propelled combine to harvest crop. Performs variety of other duties, such as husking and shelling corn, lubricating and repairing farm machinery, and unloading grain onto conveyors to storage bins or elevators. May plan and schedule plowing, cultivating, and harvesting operations.
GOE: 03.04.01 STRENGTH: M GED: R3 M1 L2 SVP: 4 DLU: 80

401.683-014 FARMWORKER, RICE (agriculture)

Drives and operates rice-farm machinery to prepare land, till soil, build ditches and levees, and harvest rice crop: Hitches farm implements to tractor, and drives tractor along existing swaths and contours of rice field to plow and level fields and build or shore up ditches and levees of flood-irrigation system. Plants rice seed, or soaks rice seed in water and loads germinated seed onto airplane for aerial seeding of field. Loads fertilizer and weed killer into airplane, and stands at edge of field or positions markers indicating field pass by

airplane to prevent overlap and gaps during aerial spraying. Drives tractor with harrow attachment over aerially seeded fields to cover seeds with dirt. Sets mowing controls and drives combine through fields to cut and thresh rice, stopping to adjust controls when amount of grain observed in chaff and amount of chaff observed in grain hoppers exceed allowable amounts. Transfers grain from combine hopper to grain truck, using transfer auger. Patrols irrigation ditches to detect obstructions and earthen deterioration, and removes debris and shores-up levees and ditches with shovel to ensure complete flooding of fields. Starts irrigation pumps, removes levee gates, and breaks apart levees to flood or drain field sections as directed. Performs miscellaneous duties, such as cleaning and lubricating farm equipment, loading and unloading trucks, and repairing buildings and fences.
GOE: 03.04.01 STRENGTH: M GED: R3 M2 L2 SVP: 5 DLU: 77

401.687-010 FARMWORKER, GRAIN II (agriculture)

Performs variety of manual tasks appropriate for grain crop being cultivated and harvested: Cultivates and thins crops, using hoe. Removes undesirable and excess growth, such as tassels, suckers, and weeds, by hand. Carries supplies, such as bags and baling wires, to workers in fields. Clears irrigation ditches, using shovel. Loads and unloads trucks. Repairs fences and buildings, using carpenter's handtools. Cleans and lubricates farm machines. May be identified with task being performed, such as hoeing, detasseling, and picking; or with crop being worked, such as hybrid seed-corn, field beans and peas, and wheat.
GOE: 03.04.01 STRENGTH: M GED: R1 M1 L1 SVP: 2 DLU: 77

402   VEGETABLE FARMING OCCUPATIONS

This group includes occupations concerned with growing and harvesting vegetable crops. Occupations concerned with growing and harvesting potatoes, sugar beets, and sugarcane are classified in Group 404. Occupations concerned with growing vegetables in a controlled environment, such as in greenhouses and sheds, are classified in Group 405.

402.131-010 SUPERVISOR, VEGETABLE FARMING (agriculture) alternate titles: field supervisor

Supervises and coordinates activities of workers engaged in planting, cultivating, and harvesting vegetable crops: Discusses seasonal crop-growing activities with management to determine sequence of operations and supplies, machinery, and work force needs. Assigns duties, such as tilling soil, planting, weeding, fertilizing, irrigating, harvesting, and maintaining machines, to subordinates, and specifies machines, tools, and supplies to be used. Observes workers to detect inefficient and unsafe work procedures, and demonstrates approved procedures. Performs other duties as described under SUPERVISOR (any industry) Master Title. May supervise workers engaged in mechanical repairs. May requisition machinery parts and record purchase data.
GOE: 03.02.01 STRENGTH: M GED: R4 M2 L3 SVP: 7 DLU: 77

402.161-010 FARMER, VEGETABLE (agriculture) alternate titles: garden farmer; vegetable grower

Raises vegetables: Determines kind and amount of crop to be grown, according to market conditions, weather, and size and location of farm. Selects and purchases seed, fertilizer, and farm machinery and arranges with buyers for sale of crop. Hires and directs farm workers engaged in planting, cultivating, and harvesting crop, such as beans, onions, and peas. Performs various duties of farm workers, depending on size and nature of farm, including setting up and operating farm machinery. May grow vegetables in greenhouse to produce out-of-season crops. May grow variety of vegetables and be designated Truck Farmer (agriculture). May specialize in growing single vegetable and be designated by name of vegetable as Onion Farmer (agriculture).
GOE: 03.01.01 STRENGTH: M GED: R4 M4 L4 SVP: 7 DLU: 81

402.663-010 FARMWORKER, VEGETABLE I (agriculture)

Drives and operates farm machinery to plant, cultivate, and harvest vegetables, such as peas, lettuce, tomatoes, and lima beans: Attaches farm implements, such as plow, planter, fertilizer applicator, and harvester, to tractor and drives tractor in fields to prepare soil and plant, fertilize, and harvest crops. Thins, hoes, and weeds row crops, using hand implements. Irrigates land to provide sufficient moisture for crop growth, using irrigation method appropriate to crop or locality. May mix spray solutions and spray crops. May supervise seasonal workers and keep time records of workers. May use horse-drawn equipment to plant, cultivate, and harvest crops. May adjust and maintain farm machinery. May be identified with crop raised.
GOE: 03.04.01 STRENGTH: M GED: R3 M2 L3 SVP: 4 DLU: 77

402.687-010 FARMWORKER, VEGETABLE II (agriculture) alternate titles: garden worker; laborer, vegetable farm; vegetable worker

Plants, cultivates, and harvests vegetables, working as crewmember: Dumps seed into hopper of planter towed by tractor. Rides on planter and brushes debris from seed spouts that discharge seeds into plowed furrow. Plants roots and bulbs, using hoe or trowel. Covers plants with sheet or caps of treated cloth or paper to protect plants from weather. Weeds and thins blocks of plants, using hoe or spoon-shaped tool. Transplants seedlings, using hand transplanter or by placing seedlings in rotating planting wheel while riding on power-drawn transplanter. Sets bean poles and strings them with wire or twine. Closes and ties leaves over heads of cauliflower and other cabbage and cabbagelike plants. Picks, cuts, pulls, or lifts crops to harvest them. Ties vegetables in bunches and removes tops from root crops. Pitches vine crops into viner (pea or bean shelling machine), using pitchfork or electric fork and boom, and cleans up spilled vines. May participate in irrigation activities. May be identified with work assigned, such as blocking, cutting, and stringing, or with crop raised, such as asparagus, beans, and celery.
GOE: 03.04.01 STRENGTH: M GED: R1 M1 L1 SVP: 2 DLU: 81

402.687-014 HARVEST WORKER, VEGETABLE (agriculture)

Harvests vegetables, such as cucumbers, onions, lettuce, and sweet corn, by hand or using knife, according to method appropriate for type of vegetable: Ascertains picking assignment from supervisor and places work aids, such as buckets and tie wires, in assigned area. Picks vegetable from plant, pulls vegetable from plant or soil, or cuts vegetable from stem or root. Puts vegetables in container or lays bunches of vegetables along row for collection. Carries containers or armloads of bunched vegetables to collection point. Loads vegetables on trucks or field conveyors. May tie vegetables into specified-size bunches, using wires or rubber bands. May cut top foliage from root vegetables, using knife. May wash vegetables. May be identified with tasks performed, such as picking, cutting, bunching, and washing; or with crop harvested as cucumbers, lettuce, onions, radishes, and sweet corn.
GOE: 03.04.01 STRENGTH: M GED: R1 M1 L1 SVP: 1 DLU: 81

403 FRUIT AND NUT FARMING OCCUPATIONS

This group includes occupations concerned with growing and harvesting fruit and nut crops. Occupations concerned with propagating and growing plants and tree stock for fruit and nut farms are classified in Group 405.

403.131-010 SUPERVISOR, TREE-FRUIT-AND-NUT FARMING (agriculture) alternate titles: supervisor, grove; supervisor, orchard

Supervises and coordinates activities of workers engaged in cultivating, pruning, spraying, thinning, propping, and harvesting tree crops, such as apples, lemons, oranges, peaches, and pecans: Assigns trees, rows, or blocks of trees to workers. Directs workers in spacing, thinning, irrigating, fertilizing, spraying, and pruning trees and in harvesting fruit. Issues ladders, pruning tools, and picking bags or buckets to workers. Inspects harvested fruit for bruises, maturity, and improper harvesting defects. Performs other duties as described under SUPERVISOR (any industry) Master Title. May dig up soil samples from various locations in grove to send to laboratory for analysis, using auger or shovel. May examine trees for blight and insect infestation and record degree of damage and location of affected trees. May requisition and purchase farm supplies, such as insecticides and machinery lubricants. May hire and discharge workers. May prepare daily tally sheets of worker hours and production.
GOE: 03.02.01 STRENGTH: M GED: R4 M3 L4 SVP: 7 DLU: 78

403.131-014 SUPERVISOR, VINE-FRUIT FARMING (agriculture)

Supervises and coordinates activities of workers engaged in planting, cultivating, and harvesting berry crops, such as cranberries and grapes: Confers with manager to evaluate weather and soil conditions and to develop plans and procedures. Hires workers and explains and demonstrates field work-techniques and safety-regulations to inexperienced workers. Assigns duties, such as tilling soil, planting, cultivating, and spraying vines, and gathering berries, to farmworkers and oversees work activities. Attaches farm implement, such as disc, planter, and fertilizer, and herbicide spreader, to tractor, and drives tractor in fields to plant and cultivate vines. Performs other duties as described under SUPERVISOR (any industry) Master Title. May adjust and repair farm machinery. May irrigate fields. May cut plant runners and uprights to thin vines and stimulate growth, using pruning tools. May be identified according to location as Cranberry-Farm Supervisor (agriculture); Vineyard Supervisor (agriculture).
GOE: 03.02.01 STRENGTH: M GED: R4 M3 L3 SVP: 6 DLU: 77

403.161-010 FARMER, TREE-FRUIT-AND-NUT CROPS (agriculture) alternate titles: orchardist

Plants and cultivates trees, such as apple, orange, and walnut, and harvests fruit and nut crops, applying knowledge of horticulture and market conditions: Determines varieties and quantities of trees to be grown, acreage to be tilled, and employees to be hired. Selects and purchases tree stock and farm machines, implements, and supplies. Decides when and how to plant, bud, graft, cultivate, irrigate, and prune trees and harvest crop, based on knowledge of tree-crop culture. Attaches farm implements, such as plow, disc, and harrow, to tractor and drives tractor in fields to till soil. Plants root stock, applies fertilizers, insecticides, and fungicides, and irrigates fields. Prunes growing trees to develop desired size and shape. Assigns duties to farmhands and explains orchard work techniques and safety regulations to inexperienced workers. Maintains employee and financial records. Arranges with buyers for sale of crops. Lubricates, adjusts, and makes minor repairs on farm machinery, implements, and equipment, using oilcan, grease gun, and handtools. May bud and graft stock. May plant ground crops to shade ground, conserve moisture, and improve soil. May be designated according to crop grown as Apple Grower (agriculture); Cherry Grower (agriculture); Filbert Grower (agriculture); Lemon Grower (agriculture); Nut Orchardist (agriculture); Orange Grower (agriculture). May be designated: Peach Grower (agriculture); Pecan Grower (agriculture); Tung-Nut Grower (agriculture); Walnut Grower (agriculture).
GOE: 03.01.01 STRENGTH: H GED: R4 M4 L4 SVP: 7 DLU: 77

403.161-014 FARMER, FRUIT CROPS, BUSH AND VINE (agriculture) alternate titles: berry grower

Plants and cultivates fruit bushes and vines and harvests crops, such as grapes, cranberries, and strawberries, applying knowledge of growth characteristics of specific varieties and soil, climate, and market conditions: Determines varieties and quantities of plants to be grown, acreage to be tilled, and employees to be hired. Selects and purchases plant stock and farm machines, implements, and supplies. Decides when and how to plant, bud, graft, prune, sucker, cultivate and irrigate plants, and harvest crop, based on knowledge of vine-crop culture. Attaches farm implements, such as harrow and ditcher, to tractor and drives tractor in fields to till soil. Drives and operates farm machinery to spray fertilizers, herbicides, and pesticides and haul fruit boxes. Hires, assigns duties to, and oversees activities of seasonal workers engaged in tilling and irrigating soil, pruning plants, and harvesting and marketing crop. Demonstrates and explains farm work techniques and safety regulations. Maintains employee and financial records. Makes arrangements with buyers for sale and shipment of crop. May make arrangements with AIRPLANE PILOT (agriculture) 196.263-010 to spray and dust fertilizers and pesticides on planted acreage. May install irrigation system(s) and irrigate fields. May set poles, string wires on poles to form trellises, and tie vines and canes to trellis wires. May prune vines and canes to size and shape growth. May lubricate, adjust, and make minor repairs on farm machinery, implements, and equipment, using oilcan, grease gun, and handtools, such as hammer and wrench. May be designated according to crop grown as Blueberry Grower (agriculture); Cranberry Grower (agriculture); Grape Grower (agriculture); Raspberry Grower (agriculture); Strawberry Grower (agriculture).
GOE: 03.01.01 STRENGTH: H GED: R4 M4 L4 SVP: 7 DLU: 81

403.683-010 FARMWORKER, FRUIT I (agriculture)

Drives and operates farm machinery to plant, cultivate, spray, and harvest fruit and nut crops, such as apples, oranges, strawberries, and pecans: Attaches farm implements, such as plow, planter, fertilizer applicator, and harvester to tractor and drives tractor in fields to prepare soil, and plant, fertilize, and harvest crops. Mixes chemical ingredients and sprays trees, vines, and grounds with solutions to control insects, fungus and weed growth, and diseases. Removes excess growth from trees and vines to improve fruit quality, using pruning saws and clippers. Irrigates soil, using portable-pipe or ditch system. Picks fruit during harvest. Drives truck or tractor to transport materials, supplies, workers, and products. Makes adjustments and minor repairs to farm machinery. May thin blossoms, runners, and immature fruit to obtain better-quality fruit. May select, cut, and graft stock-wood (scion) onto tree stem or trunk to propagate fruit and nut trees. May spray trees in spring to loosen and remove surplus fruit, and in fall to prevent early dropping and discoloration of fruit. May prop limbs to prevent them from breaking under weight of fruit. May start fans that circulate air or light smudge pots or torches to prevent frost damage. May be identified with work being performed, such as picking, plowing, and spraying; or according to crop worked such as cherries, cranberries, lemons, or walnuts.
GOE: 03.04.01 STRENGTH: M GED: R3 M2 L3 SVP: 5 DLU: 81

403.687-010 FARMWORKER, FRUIT II (agriculture)

Performs any combination of following tasks involved in planting, cultivating, and harvesting fruits and nuts, such as cranberries, apples, and pecans, according to instructions from supervisor or farmer: Tills soil, plants stock, prunes trees and bushes, and removes suckers and runners from vines and plants, using tools such as shovels, hoes, tampers, pruning hooks, and shears. Sprays plants with prescribed herbicides, fungicides, and pesticides to control diseases and insects. Removes blossoms and thins fruit to improve fruit quality. Harvests fruit [HARVEST WORKER, FRUIT (agriculture) 403.687-018]. May light smudge pots and torches or start wind machines that heat and circulate air about crop during cold weather to minimize frost damage. May lay out irrigation pipes, install sprinklers, and open and adjust water valves and gates to irrigate assigned fields. May repair wire fences and farm buildings, using handtools such as hammers and saws. May load and unload trucks. May guide harvester discharge spout over wooden bins to load fruit on trailer. May bag or box harvested fruit. May lay harvested fruit on trays in sun to sun-dry fruit. May clean, lubricate, and adjust farm machinery, such as weeders and harvesters, using tools such as wrenches and grease guns. May clear and burn roots and brush and gather ladders and containers to clean fields. May be identified with tasks being performed, such as thinning, smudging, and picking. May be designated according to crop grown as Farmworker, Berry (agriculture); Farmworker, Cranberry (agriculture); or according to work location as Laborer, Orchard (agriculture); Laborer, Vineyard (agriculture).

GOE: 03.04.01 STRENGTH: M GED: R2 M1 L2 SVP: 2 DLU: 81

403.687-014 FIG CAPRIFIER (agriculture)

Facilitates pollination of fig trees: Selects and picks mature figs which contain wasps or other small insects and places figs in hamper. Transfers figs from hampers to containers attached to infertile trees where wasps and other insects grow to maturity and expedite pollination.
GOE: 03.04.01 STRENGTH: M GED: R2 M1 L2 SVP: 2 DLU: 77

403.687-018 HARVEST WORKER, FRUIT (agriculture) alternate titles: fruit picker

Harvests fruits and nuts, such as cherries, strawberries, grapes, oranges, and pecans, according to method appropriate for type of fruit, by hand or using tools, such as shears, rubber mallet, pronged scoop, or hooked pole: Carries and positions work aids, such as ladders, canvas drop cloths, and buckets. Selects fruit to be harvested, according to size, shape, and color. Grasps, twists, and pulls fruit, snips stems, and shakes trees and vines to separate crop from plant and places fruit into bags, buckets, or trays, exercising care to avoid plant and fruit damage. Empties filled containers into collection boxes and bins. May stand on ladders or elevated platforms, stoop over plants, or crawl along rows to reach fruit. May measure fruit, using gauges. May pour fruit through screens when removing foreign matter, such as twigs and grasses. May position hand held vibrating device against branches of bushes to shake ripe fruit from branches. May dump fruit from containers onto conveyors or load containers onto trucks or wagons. May remove ladders, debris, boxes, and discarded fruit from fields and bogs to clean growing areas. May collect fallen nuts into piles, using rake. May carry and position irrigation pipes. May be identified with tasks being performed, such as rhubarb trimming, cranberry screening, and walnut knocking.
GOE: 03.04.01 STRENGTH: M GED: R1 M1 L1 SVP: 2 DLU: 81

403.687-022 VINE PRUNER (agriculture)

Prunes berry vines according to specific instructions: Walks along berry-plant row and observes plant foliage to ascertain vines requiring pruning. Cuts away excessive vine-growth, using pruning knife and shears.
GOE: 03.04.01 STRENGTH: L GED: R1 M1 L1 SVP: 1 DLU: 77

404 FIELD CROP FARMING OCCUPATIONS, N.E.C.

This group includes occupations concerned with growing and harvesting field crops, such as cotton, peanuts, potatoes, sugar beets, sugarcane, and tobacco; and miscellaneous crops, such as castor and mung beans, dill, ginseng, hops, and sesame. These crops usually require processing before being sold to the consumer and miscellaneous crops are those that cannot be classified as grain, vegetable, fruit, nut, horticultural, or field crops.

404.131-010 SUPERVISOR, FIELD-CROP FARMING (agriculture)

Supervises and coordinates activities of workers engaged in preparing fields and planting, cultivating, and harvesting crop specialties, such as cotton, mint, tobacco, and hops: Confers with manager to evaluate soil and weather conditions and to develop plans and procedures. Inspects fields and observes growing plants and harvested crop to determine work requirements, such as cultivating, spraying, thinning, weeding, irrigating, harvesting, and drying, according to time of year and condition of soil, plants, and crops. Determines number and kind of workers needed to perform required work and schedules activities. Inspects work performed, observes instrument and gauge readings, ascertains condition of crop, and performs related duties to verify worker adherence to instructions. Performs other duties as described under SUPERVISOR (any industry) Master Title. May hire workers. May train workers in work procedures, safety policies, and use of machinery and tools. May oversee packaging and transporting of harvested crop. May drive and operate farm machinery, such as tractor, baler, and self-propelled harvester. May examine machinery to ascertain maintenance, repair, and replacement requirements, and supervise workers engaged in machinery-maintenance activities. May issue tools to workers. May be designated Driver (agriculture) when supervising cotton workers. May be identified with crop grown.
GOE: 03.02.01 STRENGTH: M GED: R4 M3 L3 SVP: 7 DLU: 77

404.131-014 SUPERVISOR, SHED WORKERS (agriculture) alternate titles: shed boss

Supervises and coordinates activities of workers engaged in curing tobacco leaves on farm: Reads work schedule and ascertains number of available workers on day-haul bus. Assigns workers to tasks, such as stringing, handling, and hanging tobacco leaves for drying. Enforces company rules to promote safety and prevent waste. Investigates grievances and settles disputes to maintain harmony among workers. Keeps production records. Performs other duties as described under SUPERVISOR (any industry) Master Title.
GOE: 03.04.01 STRENGTH: L GED: R4 M3 L3 SVP: 7 DLU: 77

404.161-010 FARMER, FIELD CROP (agriculture)

Plants, cultivates, and harvests specialty crops, such as alfalfa, cotton, hops, peanuts, mint, sugarcane, and tobacco, applying knowledge of growth characteristics of individual crop, and soil, climate, and market conditions: Determines number and kind of employees to be hired, acreage to be tilled, and varieties and quantities of plants to be grown. Selects and purchases plant stock and farm machinery, implements, and supplies. Decides when and how to plant, cultivate, and irrigate plants and harvest crops, applying knowledge of plant

culture. Attaches farm implements, such as plow, disc, and seed drill to tractor and drives tractor in fields to till soil and plant and cultivate crops. Drives and operates farm machinery to spray fertilizers, herbicides, and pesticides and haul harvested crops. Hires, assigns duties to, and oversees activities of farm workers. Demonstrates and explains farm work techniques and safety regulations to new workers. Maintains employee and financial records. Arranges with buyers for sale and shipment of crop. May install irrigation system(s) and irrigate fields. May set poles and string wires and twine on poles to form trellises. May lubricate, adjust, and make minor repairs on farm machinery, implements, and equipment, using mechanic's handtools and work aids. May plant seeds in cold-frame bed and cover bed with cloth or glass to protect seedlings from weather. May transplant seedlings in rows, by hand or using transplanter machine. May grade and package crop for marketing. May be designated according to crop grown as Cotton Grower (agriculture); Ginseng Farmer (agriculture); Hay Farmer (agriculture); Hop Grower (agriculture); Peanut Farmer (agriculture); Sugarcane Planter (agriculture); Tobacco Grower (agriculture).
GOE: 03.01.01 STRENGTH: M GED: R4 M4 L4 SVP: 7 DLU: 77

404.663-010 FARMWORKER, FIELD CROP I (agriculture)

Performs following duties to prepare fields and plant, cultivate, and harvest field crops, such as cotton and weed cutter, to tractor, using bolts and mechanic's handtools. Drives tractor to field and tows attached implement back and forth across field or between crop rows, manipulating levers that activate and position implement parts to till soil. Loads and drives truck to transport farm supplies and tools, such as fertilizer and pesticide chemicals, trellis poles and wires, hoes and shovels, harvested crops, and farm workers to specified locations. Drives and operates self-propelled harvest machine to harvest crop. Adds oil, gasoline, and water to appropriate tanks on machinery. Makes minor mechanical adjustments and repairs on farm machinery, paints farm structures, and replaces fence and trellis wires when weather and season preclude driving activities. May irrigate fields. May oversee work crew engaged in planting, weeding, or harvesting activities. May weigh crop-filled containers and record weights. May spray fertilizer and pesticide solutions in assigned areas.
GOE: 03.04.01 STRENGTH: M GED: R3 M2 L3 SVP: 5 DLU: 77

404.685-010 SEED-POTATO ARRANGER (agriculture)

Tends machine that cuts potatoes into sections of uniform size for use as seed: Pushes button to start machinery that carries potatoes to, through, and from cutter blades. Arranges potatoes, according to size, on feed conveyor in line with knives. Discards diseased and rotting potatoes. Monitors potato flow and observes machinery operation to detect jams and malfunctions. Clears jams, and reports malfunctions to supervisor. Rakes up potatoes and potato sections that have fallen from conveyors.
GOE: 03.04.01 STRENGTH: L GED: R1 M1 L1 SVP: 2 DLU: 77

404.686-010 SEED CUTTER (agriculture) alternate titles: cutter; potato-seed cutter

Cuts seed potatoes into sections of uniform size for mechanical planting, using any of following methods: (1) Cuts potato into sections containing one or more eyes, using paring knife or draws potato along knife attached to table. (2) Dumps potatoes into hopper of machine that cuts potatoes in half. (3) Places potatoes on revolving arms of machine that cuts potatoes into quarters.
GOE: 03.04.01 STRENGTH: M GED: R1 M1 L1 SVP: 1 DLU: 77

404.687-010 FARMWORKER, FIELD CROP II (agriculture)

Plants, cultivates, and harvests field crops, such as cotton, hops, and tobacco, working as crewmember: Plants seeds or digs up and transplants seedlings and sets, using handtools such as hoes and scoops. Chops out weeds, thins plants to leave sturdier plants spaced at regular intervals, and hills up soil around plant roots to retain moisture and protect roots from temperature extremes, using hoe. Cuts vines from trellis, using knife, or pulls leaves from stalks to harvest crop. Stacks or packs crop in containers and loads containers on trucks or wagons. May propagate plants in covered cold-frame beds and pull up seedlings to be transplanted. May set up poles, string wires and twine among poles to form trellises, and secure plants and cloth netting to trellis structure to support growing plants and provide shade. May cut or pull away tops, leaves, and suckers from plants during growing season. May spray fungicides and pesticides on plants to destroy diseases and insects, using hand or engine-powered pump sprayer. May stack empty harvest containers in field area. May sharpen hoes, using portable grinding wheel and hand file. May be identified with task performed, such as pole setting, raking, suckering, and picking, or according to crop as Cotton Farmworker (agriculture); Hops Farmworker (agriculture); Tobacco Farmworker (agriculture).
GOE: 03.04.01 STRENGTH: H GED: R1 M1 L1 SVP: 2 DLU: 81

404.687-014 HARVEST WORKER, FIELD CROP (agriculture)

Harvests field crops, such as broomcorn, cotton, hops, peanuts, sugarcane, and tobacco, working as crewmember: Walks, stoops, crawls, or sits between plant rows to reach harvestable crop. Pulls, twists, or cuts fibers, leaves, stalks, straw, or vines, selected according to color, size, and shape, from bolls, roots, stalks, or trellises; by hand or using knife, machete, or sickle. Collects crop into containers, such as bags, boxes, and bundles, or piles and stacks crop in windrows. Picks up and carries bundles, bales, containers, or stacks of harvested crop to collection point, and loads crop onto truck or wagon, by hand or using hoist or hooks. May tie leaves, stalks, straws, or vines into bundles, using twine, clamps, or rubber bands. May shake dirt from vines and stack vines or

straw around stakes or stalks, by hand or using pitchfork, to protect crop from weathering on damp soil. May gather up and load scattered leaves, vines, or pods on truck. May burn debris, leaves, and stalks. May be identified with duties performed, such as cutting, picking, carrying, and loading; or with crop worked, such as alfalfa, mint, and sugar beets.
GOE: 03.04.01 STRENGTH: H GED: R1 M1 L1 SVP: 1 DLU: 80

405   HORTICULTURAL SPECIALTY OCCUPATIONS

This group includes occupations concerned with propagating and raising products, such as nursery stock, flowers, flowering plants, flower seeds, bulbs, and turf grasses. Also included are occupations concerned with growing food crops, such as mushrooms and rhubarb, which require controlled environmental conditions. Occupations concerned with propagating, raising, and transplanting forest trees are classified in Group 451.

405.131-010 SUPERVISOR, HORTICULTURAL-SPECIALTY FARMING (agriculture) alternate titles: green house manager; harvesting manager

Supervises and coordinates activities of workers engaged in propagating, cultivating, and harvesting horticultural specialties, such as trees, shrubs, flowering plants, flowers, and mushrooms, applying knowledge of environmental-control structures, systems, and techniques, and plant culture: Discusses plant growing activities with management personnel to plan planting and picking schedules and employee assignments; obtain authorization for changes in fertilizer, herbicide, and pesticide application techniques and formulas; resolve problems; and develop procedures for new species in product line and new cultivation techniques. Observes plants and flowers in greenhouses, pots, cold frames, and fields to ascertain condition, such as leaf texture and bloom size; and oversees changes in humidity and temperature levels and cultivation procedures to ensure conformance with quality control standards. Prepares and assigns work schedules. Trains new employees in gardening techniques, such as transplanting and weeding, and grading and packaging activities. Inspects facilities for signs of disrepair, such as missing glass panes and clogged sprinklers, and delegates repair duties to ensure refurbishing or replacement of parts in environmental-control structures and systems. May drive and operate heavy machinery, such as dump truck, four-wheeled tractor, and growth-media tiller, to handle materials and supplies. May perform variety of duties involving propagation, care, and marketing of plants and crops. Performs other duties as described under SUPERVISOR (any industry) Master Title. May be identified according to kind of establishment as Greenhouse Superintendent (agriculture); or crop as Mushroom-Growing Supervisor (agriculture); Orchid Superintendent (agriculture).
GOE: 03.02.03 STRENGTH: M GED: R4 M3 L4 SVP: 7 DLU: 80

405.137-010 SUPERVISOR, ROSE-GRADING (agriculture) alternate titles: head rose grader

Supervises and coordinates activities of workers engaged in grading flowers according to size and appearance characteristics, and packaging customer orders in greenhouse: Reads inventory records, customer orders, and shipping schedules to ascertain day's activity requirements. Assigns duties to subordinates and informs workers of departures from established routines. Collects, reviews, and compares daily work-tallies, and looks at and feels flower bunches and rejected flowers, to ascertain quantity and quality of subordinates' work. Prepares and submits written and oral reports of personnel actions, such as performance evaluations, hires, promotions, and discipline. Explains and demonstrates grading techniques and packing procedures to train new workers. Grades and packs flowers, according to specifications, to maintain workflow during emergencies and periods of increased work load. Performs other duties as described under SUPERVISOR (any industry) Master Title.
GOE: 03.04.04 STRENGTH: M GED: R4 M3 L4 SVP: 7 DLU: 77

405.161-010 BONSAI CULTURIST (agriculture) alternate titles: dwarf tree grower

Grows dwarf (Bonsai) trees: Selects seedlings or other small trees suitable for Bonsai. Stunts plant growth, using root and branch pruning techniques and soil and fertilizer mixtures. Trains limbs and branches to achieve artistic shape, using cutters and wires. Arranges plantings in containers, selected according to style, size, and shape complimentary to arrangement, and adds decorative materials, such as rocks, moss, and mirrors.
GOE: 03.01.03 STRENGTH: L GED: R4 M3 L3 SVP: 7 DLU: 77

405.161-014 HORTICULTURAL-SPECIALTY GROWER, FIELD (agriculture)

Propagates and grows horticultural-specialty products and crops, such as seeds, bulbs, rootstocks, sod, ornamental plants, and cut flowers: Plans acreage utilization and work schedules, according to knowledge of crop culture, climate and market conditions, seed, bulb, or rootstock availability, and employable work force and machinery. Attaches farm implements, such as disc and fertilizer spreader, to tractor and drives tractor in fields to till soil and plant and cultivate crop. Inspects fields periodically to ascertain nutrient deficiencies, detect insect, disease, and pest infestations, and identify foreign-plant growth, and selects, purchases, and schedules materials, such as fertilizers and herbicides, to ensure quality control. Hires field workers; assigns their duties according to scheduled activities, such as planting, irrigating, weeding, and harvesting; and oversees their activities. Maintains personnel and production records. Arranges with customers for sale of crop. May oversee activities, such as product cleaning, grading, and packaging. May provide customer services, such as planning and building planters, walls, and patios, and planting and caring for landscape and display arrangements. May bud or graft scion stock on plantings to alter growth characteristics. May develop new variations of species specialty to produce crops with specialized market-appeal, such as disease resistance or color brilliance. May cultivate out-of-season seedlings and crops, using greenhouse. May cultivate cover crop, such as hay or rye, in rotation with horticultural specialty to rejuvenate soil. May drive and operate self-propelled harvesting machine. May lubricate, adjust, and make minor repairs on farm machinery and equipment. May build, remove, and repair farm structures, such as fences and sheds. May be designated according to crop as Bulb Grower (agriculture); Flower Grower (agriculture); Grass Farmer (agriculture); Rose Grower (agriculture); Seed Grower (agriculture); Shrub Grower (agriculture).
GOE: 03.01.03 STRENGTH: M GED: R4 M3 L3 SVP: 7 DLU: 77

405.161-018 HORTICULTURAL-SPECIALTY GROWER, INSIDE (agriculture)

Grows horticultural-specialty products and crops, such as flowers, ornamental plants, and vegetables, under environmentally controlled conditions, applying knowledge of plant culture, environmental-control systems and structures, and market conditions: Determines types and quantities of plantings to grow; allocates space in structure, such as greenhouse or shed; and schedules growing activities. Plants seeds and transplants seedlings in material, such as bark, gravel, heated water, sandy soil, and stable straw to propagate seeds and nursery stock. Removes substandard plants to maintain quality control, prunes plants to enhance development, and positions plants to artistically display products. Monitors timing and metering devices that control frequency, amount, and type of nutrient applications; regulate humidity, ventilation, and carbon dioxide conditions; and dispense herbicides, fungicides, and pesticides. Explains and demonstrates care-taking techniques to subordinates. May assign their duties. May hire workers. May maintain personnel and production records. May deal with vendors to purchase supplies and materials, and arrange with customers to sell products and crops. May be identified with crop as Bean-Sprout Grower (agriculture); Mushroom Grower (agriculture); Orchid Grower (agriculture); or technique as Hydroponics Grower (agriculture).
GOE: 03.01.03 STRENGTH: M GED: R4 M3 L4 SVP: 7 DLU: 77

405.361-010 PLANT PROPAGATOR (agriculture)

Propagates plants, such as orchids and rhododendrons, applying knowledge of environmental controls and plant culture: Confers with management personnel to ascertain type and number of species to propagate and to develop and revise nutrient formulas and environmental-control specifications. Selects materials according to kind of plant; mixes growth media; and prepares containers, such as jars, pots, and trays. Initiates new plant growth, using methods such as following: (1) Cuts leaves, stems, or rhizomes from parent plant and places cuttings in growth media. (2) Bends, covers, or buries branches of parent plant in soil, securing branches with pegs or rocks. (3) Wounds stems of parent plant, using sharp knife, inserts pebble into wound, and binds wound with moss, burlap, or raffia. (4) Plants meristem and seeds in growth media. (5) Breaks off or cuts apart and plants roots, crowns, and tubers from parent plant. Inspects growing area to ascertain temperature and humidity conditions, and regulates systems of heaters, fans, and sprayers to ensure conformance with specifications. Gives transplanting and cultivation instructions to coworkers, and monitors activiies to assure adherence to established plant-culture procedures. May graft or divide developing plants to promote altered growth characteristics. May log activities, maintain propagation records, and compile periodic reports.
GOE: 03.04.04 STRENGTH: M GED: R4 M4 L4 SVP: 6 DLU: 77

405.683-010 FARMWORKER, BULBS (agriculture)

Performs any combination of following tasks involved with driving, operating, and maintaining farm machinery and equipment, planting, cultivating, and harvesting flower bulbs and flowers, and maintaining structures on nursery acreage or in greenhouse: Hitches farm implements, such as plow and disc, to tractor, and drives tractor while operating implements to till soil and plant, fertilize, cultivate, dust, and spray crops, such as tulip, hyacinth, and begonia. Adjusts conveyor speeds and height of digging mechanism, using wrench, and drives and operates harvesting machine to dig up bulbs, applying knowledge of terrain contours and type of bulb being harvested. Participates in indoor activities, such as setting flowers in chilled-water troughs, packing flowers in cartons, stacking cartons on pallets, handtrucking containers of flowers and bulbs to designated areas in warehouse or greenhouse, and repairing boxes. Loads truck with containers of bulbs or flowers, and drives truck to deliver products. Repairs and paints farm structures, using ladder, brushes, and carpentry handtools. Washes, paints, lubricates, and participates in repair of farm machinery, using mechanic's handtools.
GOE: 03.04.04 STRENGTH: M GED: R3 M2 L2 SVP: 5 DLU: 77

405.683-014 GROWTH-MEDIA MIXER, MUSHROOM (agriculture)

Drives and operates machinery, such as crane loader, dump truck, and manure-turning machine, to move and treat straw and manure and dirt for use in mushroom beds: Operates crane loader to scoop wet manure from wet pit and dry manure from dry stack and dumps dry and wet manure into dump truck bed. Drives dump truck to haul manure to shed-covered area and dumps manure into rows. Drives dump truck loaded with dirt to rows of manure and moves levers to dump dirt over manure. Operates manure-turning machine to turn and mix manure with dirt and specified additives. Drives scoop loader to push manure from place to place on mushroom farm and to load manure onto trucks.

GOE: 03.04.04 STRENGTH: M GED: R3 M2 L2 SVP: 3 DLU: 77

405.684-010 BUDDER (agriculture)
Buds field-grown rose plants with hybrid buds during rose-growing season: Crouches over rows of rose plants to reach plant rootstock. Cuts T-shaped incision on rootstock and opens incision, using budding knife. Slices hybrid bud from scion wood and inserts bud into incision. Observes tying of buds to ensure quality of tie. Repeats procedure, rapidly, throughout work period to maintain production.
GOE: 03.04.04 STRENGTH: M GED: R2 M1 L2 SVP: 2 DLU: 77

405.684-014 HORTICULTURAL WORKER I (agriculture)
Plants, cultivates, and harvests horticultural specialties, such as flowers and shrubs, and performs related duties in environmentally controlled structure, applying knowledge of environmental systems: Ascertains growing schedules and deviations from established procedures from grower or manager. Sows seed and plants cuttings. Looks at and feels leaf texture, bloom development, and soil condition to determine nutrient and moisture requirements and to detect and identify germ and pest infestations. Sets fertilizer timing and metering devices that control frequency and amount of nutrients to be introduced into irrigation system. Applies herbicides, fungicides, and pesticides to destroy undesirable growth and pests, using spray wand connected to solution tank. Reads and interprets sensing indicators and regulates humidity, ventilation, and carbon dioxide systems to control environmental conditions. Grafts scions to seedling stock. Pollinates, prunes, transplants, and pinches plants, and culls flowers, branches, fruit, and plants to ensure development of marketable products. Harvests, packs, and stores crop, using techniques appropriate for individual horticultural specialty. May maintain and repair hydroponic and environmental control systems. May mix planting soil, following prescribed procedures. May record information, such as chemicals used, grafting performed, and environmental conditions, to maintain required records. May maintain and repair structures, using materials, such as corrugated fiberglass panels, lath, glass panes, and putty, and tools, such as hammer, saw, and putty knife. May be designated according to work location as Greenhouse Worker (agriculture); according to techniques employed as Hydrophonics Worker (agriculture); or according to horticultural specialty as Orchid Worker (agriculture).
GOE: 03.04.04 STRENGTH: H GED: R3 M2 L3 SVP: 3 DLU: 81

405.687-010 FLOWER PICKER (agriculture)
Harvests flowers, such as daffodils and tulips, working as member of crew: Pinches or cuts flower stem to remove flower from plant. Bundles specified number of stems, using rubberband, and carries bundles to collection box.
GOE: 03.04.04 STRENGTH: L GED: R1 M1 L1 SVP: 1 DLU: 77

405.687-014 HORTICULTURAL WORKER II (agriculture)
Performs any combination of following duties concerned with preparing soil and growth media, cultivating, and otherwise participating in horticultural activities under close supervision on acreage, in nursery, or in environmentally controlled structure, such as greenhouse and shed: Hauls and spreads topsoil, fertilizer, peat moss, and other materials to condition land. Digs, rakes, and screens soil, and fills cold frames and hot beds to prepare them for planting. Fills growing tanks with water. Plants, sprays, weeds, and waters plants, shrubs, and trees. Sows grass seed and plants plugs of sod and cuts, rolls, and stacks sod. Prepares scion and ties buds to assist worker budding roses. Traps and poisons pests, such as moles, gophers, and mice. Plants shrubs and plants in containers. Ties, bunches, wraps, and packs flowers, plants, shrubs, and trees to fill orders. Moves containerized shrubs and trees, using wheelbarrow. Digs up shrubs and trees, and wraps their roots with burlap. May dip rose cuttings into vat to disinfect cuttings prior to storage. May fold and staple corrugated forms to make boxes used for packing horticultural products. May be designated according to employing establishment as Grass-Farm Laborer (agriculture); Greenhouse Laborer (agriculture); Nursery Laborer (agriculture); Rose-Farm Laborer (agriculture); or according to horticultural specialty as Bean-Sprout Laborer (agriculture); Mushroom Laborer (agriculture).
GOE: 03.04.04 STRENGTH: H GED: R2 M1 L1 SVP: 2 DLU: 81

405.687-018 TRANSPLANTER, ORCHID (agriculture)
Transplants orchids in greenhouse, according to specific instructions: Slides meristem from jars of nutrient solution, or lifts plants from trays or pots. Trims and cleans plant roots, using knife, tweezers, water, and fungicide. Spreads pebbles and inert growth-media in planting containers, positions plant on media, adds and presses media around roots, and sprinkles surface with water and fertilizer solution. Records species code and planting date on plastic marker, and inserts marker in container. Places planted orchids on designated greenhouse shelves. Washes jars and lids in sanitizing solution, and carries them to laboratory.
GOE: 03.04.04 STRENGTH: M GED: R2 M1 L2 SVP: 2 DLU: 77

406 GARDENING AND GROUNDSKEEPING OCCUPATIONS

This group includes occupations concerned with caring for areas, such as gardens, grounds, parks, and cemeteries. Landscaping occupations are classified in Group 408.

406.134-010 SUPERVISOR, CEMETERY WORKERS (real estate)
Supervises and coordinates activities of workers engaged in preparing graves, maintaining cemetery grounds, and performing related work in cemetery: Confers with manager to develop plans and schedules for routine maintenance of grounds and graves and to ascertain number, nature, and time schedule for priority activities, such as grave digging and lining, grave-marker placement, and disinterments. Determines crew and equipment requirements for each maintenance and priority activity and assigns specific tasks to subordinates. Periodically observes ongoing work to ascertain if work is being performed according to instructions and will be completed on schedule. Reassigns tasks of subordinates and confers with manager to adjust activity schedules. Demonstrates and explains tasks, such as pruning shrubs and finishing cement, and use of equipment, such as backhoe, power lawnmower, and casket lowering device, to train new workers and improve performance of other workers. Performs other duties as described under SUPERVISOR (any industry) Master Title. May supervise workers engaged in opening and closing mausoleum vaults. May supervise and oversee graveside services to ensure services are performed according to instructions. May perform minor repairs on equipment, using handtools and power tools and applying mechanical knowledge. May supervise and coordinate activities of workers engaged in installation of water and sewer lines, building and sealing of roads within cemetery, excavation of ground for preset vaults, and movement of equipment by trailer.
GOE: 03.02.03 STRENGTH: L GED: R4 M3 L3 SVP: 6 DLU: 86

406.134-014 SUPERVISOR, LANDSCAPE (museums; waterworks)
Supervises and coordinates activities of workers engaged in maintenance of areas, such as parks, botanical gardens, and playgrounds: Plans landscaping tasks, and instructs workers in taking care of nursery, planting of flowers, and transplanting and pruning of trees and shrubbery. Directs workers in maintenance and repair of driveways, walks, hedges, swings, benches, and other park equipment. Performs other duties as described under SUPERVISOR (any industry) Master Title. May patrol parks to guard against vandalism and destruction. May supervise workers engaged in maintenance of areas along highways, around rest areas, and federal or state facilities and be designated Supervisor, Grounds (government ser.); Supervisor, Rest Area (government ser.); or Supervisor, Park Workers (government ser.).
GOE: 03.02.03 STRENGTH: L GED: R4 M3 L4 SVP: 6 DLU: 81

406.137-010 GREENSKEEPER I (any industry) alternate titles: greenskeeper, head
Supervises and coordinates activities of workers engaged in preserving grounds and turf of golf course in playing condition: Confers with SUPERINTENDENT, GREENS (amuse. & rec.) 406.137-014 to plan and review work projects. Determines work priority and assigns workers to specific tasks, such as fertilizing, irrigating, seeding, mowing, raking, and spraying. Mixes and prepares recommended spray and dust solutions. Performs other duties as desribed under SUPERVISOR (any industry) Master Title. May direct and assist workers engaged in maintenance and repair of mechanical equipment. May assist workers to perform more critical duties.
GOE: 03.04.04 STRENGTH: M GED: R4 M3 L3 SVP: 6 DLU: 77

406.137-014 SUPERINTENDENT, GREENS (amuse. & rec.)
Supervises and coordinates activities of workers engaged in constructing new areas and preserving golf course grounds: Plans work programs, utilizing experience and established agronomic practices, to improve and maintain turf and playing condition of course. Plans new areas or changes in course and directs workers engaged in cultivation, grading, seeding, and sodding of area. Reviews test results of soil and turf samples and directs application of fertilizer, lime, insecticide, and fungicide. Tours grounds to ascertain work progress and condition of course. Inspects turf to designate height and frequency of mowing, and determine need for supplemental irrigation to sustain or force growth. Reviews and keeps employee time records. Interviews, hires, and discharges workers. Performs other duties as described under SUPERVISOR (any industry) Master Title. May assign workers to short-course training sessions related to course maintenance.
GOE: 03.01.03 STRENGTH: L GED: R4 M4 L4 SVP: 7 DLU: 77

406.381-010 GARDENER, SPECIAL EFFECTS AND INSTRUCTION MODELS (motion picture; museums)
Plants trees, shrubs, grass, flowers, and similar plant life in special display areas, such as motion picture sets and horticultural workshop beds, and as instruction models, such as terrariums and dish gardens, according to written, oral, and illustrated instructions and using gardening tools: Reads and studies instructions and discusses project with supervisor to ascertain material and tool requirements. Collects horticultural items and gathers materials, such as containers, charcoal, moss, and rock. Plants items, following plan and applying knowledge of appropriate gardening techniques. May weed, water, and fertilize displays, sets, and instruction models. May collect horticultural items, such as twigs, leaves and flowers for use as instruction materials. May be designated Greens Planter (motion picture) when working on motion picture sets.
GOE: 03.01.03 STRENGTH: M GED: R4 M3 L3 SVP: 5 DLU: 77

406.683-010 GREENSKEEPER II (any industry) alternate titles: laborer, golf course
Performs any combination of following duties, as directed by GREENSKEEPER (any industry) I, to maintain grounds and turf of golf course in playing condition: Operates tractor, using specific attachments, to till, cultivate, and grade new turf areas, to apply prescribed amounts of lime, fertilizer, insecticide, and fungicide, and to mow rough and fairway areas at designated cut, exercising care not to injure turf or shrubs. Cuts turf on green and tee

areas, using hand mower and power mower. Connects hose and sprinkler systems at designated points on course to irrigate turf. Digs and rakes ground to prepare new greens, grades and cleans traps, and repairs roadbeds, using shovels, rakes, spades, and other tools. May plant, trim, and spray trees and shrubs.
GOE: 03.04.04 STRENGTH: M GED: R2 M1 L2 SVP: 3 DLU: 77

406.684-010 CEMETERY WORKER (real estate) alternate titles: grave-digger

Prepares graves and maintains cemetery grounds: Locates grave site according to section, lot, and plot numbers, and marks area to be excavated. Removes sod from gravesite, using shovel. Digs grave to specified depth, using pick and shovel or backhoe. Places concrete slabs on bottom and around grave to line it. Mixes and pours concrete to construct foundation for grave marker, using premixed concrete, wheelbarrow, and handtools. Positions casket-lowering device on grave, covers dirt pile and sod with artificial grass carpet, erects canopy, and arranges folding chairs to prepare site for burial service. Builds wooden forms for concrete slabs, using hammer, saw, and nails. Sets grave marker in concrete on gravesite, using shovel and trowel. Mows grass, using hand or power mower. Prunes shrubs, trims trees, and plants flowers and shrubs on grave, using handtools. Removes leaves and other debris from graves, using leaf blowers and weed eaters. May drive vehicles, such as backhoe, trucks, and tractors. May repair and maintain tools and equipment, using handtools and power tools and applying mechanical knowledge. May open and close mausoleum vaults, using handtools.
GOE: 03.04.04 STRENGTH: H GED: R3 M1 L2 SVP: 5 DLU: 86

406.684-014 GROUNDSKEEPER, INDUSTRIAL-COMMERCIAL (any industry) alternate titles: caretaker, grounds; gardener

Maintains grounds of industrial, commercial, or public property, performing any combination of following tasks: Cuts lawns, using hand mower or power mower. Trims and edges around walks, flower beds, and walls, using clippers, weed cutters, and edging tools. Prunes shrubs and trees to shape and improve growth or remove damaged leaves, branches, or twigs, using shears, pruners, or chain saw. Sprays lawn, shrubs, and trees with fertilizer, herbicides, and insecticides, using hand or automatic sprayer. Rakes and bags or burns leaves, using rake. Cleans grounds and removes litter, using spiked stick or broom. Shovels snow from walks and driveways. Spreads salt on public passage ways to prevent ice buildup. Plants grass, flowers, trees, and shrubs, using gardening tools. Waters lawn and shrubs, using hose or by activating fixed or portable sprinkler system. May repair fences, gates, walls, and walks, using carpentry and masonry tools. May paint fences and outbuildings. May clean out drainage ditches and culverts, using shovel and rake. May perform ground maintenance duties, using tractor equipped with attachments, such as mowers, lime or fertilizer spreaders, lawn roller, and snow removal equipment. May sharpen tools, such as weed cutters, edging tools, and shears, using file or knife sharpener. May make minor repairs on equipment, such as lawn mower, spreader, and snow removal equipment, using handtools and power tools. May perform variety of laboring duties, common to type of employing establishment.
GOE: 03.04.04 STRENGTH: M GED: R2 M1 L2 SVP: 3 DLU: 86

406.684-018 GARDEN WORKER (agriculture; museums) alternate titles: gardener-florist

Cultivates and cares for ornamental plants and installs floral displays in indoor or outdoor settings through performance of any combination of following duties as directed by supervisory personnel: Conditions and prepares soils and plants seeds, seedlings, or bulbs in greenhouse or outdoor growing area, using spades, trowels, sprayers, sprinklers, cultivators, and other gardening handtools and equipment. Fertilizes, waters, weeds, transplants, or thins plants in growing areas. Mixes and applies pesticides to maintain health of plants and prepare plants for installation in greenhouse or outdoor display areas. Lays sod or artificial grass and builds framework for indoor floral displays, or prepares outdoor display beds according to work plan. Transplants plants from growing area to display beds, or places potted plants in beds according to work plans. Attends display beds to maintain health of plants and beauty of display. Maintains and repairs gardening handtools and equipment and structures, such as greenhouses and hot beds, using maintenance and carpentry tools. May mow lawns, prune trees, and perform other duties to maintain grounds.
GOE: 03.04.04 STRENGTH: M GED: R3 M2 L3 SVP: 4 DLU: 86

406.687-010 LANDSCAPE SPECIALIST (government ser.) alternate titles: park worker

Maintains grounds and areas along highway right-of-way of city, state, and national parks: Sows grass seed, using spreader, or plants trees, shrubs, or flowers, according to instructions and planned design of landscaped area, using handtools. Applies herbicide or mulch to designated areas, using sprayers. Grubs and weeds around bushes, trees, and flower beds. Trims hedges and prunes trees, using handtools. Mows lawns, using hand mower or power-driven lawnmower. Picks up and burns or carts away paper and rubbish. Repairs and paints benches, tables and guardrails, and assists in repair of roads, walks, buildings, and mechanical equipment, using handtools. May live on-site and be designated Campground Caretaker (government ser.). May be referred to as Groundskeeper, Parks and Grounds (government ser.).
GOE: 03.04.04 STRENGTH: M GED: R2 M1 L2 SVP: 2 DLU: 81

407 DIVERSIFIED CROP FARMING OCCUPATIONS

This group includes occupations concerned with growing and harvesting two or more kinds of crops, usually on the same farm.

407.131-010 SUPERVISOR, DIVERSIFIED CROPS (agriculture)

Supervises and coordinates activities of workers engaged in planting, cultivating, and harvesting more than one kind of crop, such as vegetable, cash grain, crop specialty, and fruit: Confers with management to evaluate weather and soil conditions and to develop and revise plans and procedures. Directs workers in preparing soil and in planting, cultivating, spraying, and harvesting crops, such as wheat, onions, sweet corn, and mint. Performs other duties as described under SUPERVISOR (any industry) Master Title. May supervise workers engaged in maintenance and repair of farm machines and facilities, such as mowers, root diggers, fences, and sheds. May adjust, lubricate, refuel and repair farm machines and facilities. May drive and operate farm machinery, such as trucks, tractors, and self-propelled harvesters. May compile and submit reports on farm conditions, such as machinery breakdowns, crop diseases, and labor problems. May hire and discharge workers.
GOE: 03.02.01 STRENGTH: M GED: R4 M3 L4 SVP: 7 DLU: 78

407.161-010 FARMER, DIVERSIFIED CROPS (agriculture)

Grows and harvests more than one kind of crop, such as fruit, grain, vegetable, and specialty crop, applying market condition and agricultural knowledge applicable to kinds of crops raised: Determines kinds and quantities of crops to grow according to market conditions, weather, and farm size and location. Selects and purchases supplies, such as seeds, fertilizers, and farm machinery, and arranges with buyers for sale of crops. Hires and directs activities of farm workers engaged in tilling soil and planting, cultivating, and harvesting crops. Performs various duties of farm workers, depending on farm size or season, including setting up and operating farm machinery, such as truck, tractor, disc harrow, and self-propelled harvester.
GOE: 03.01.01 STRENGTH: M GED: R4 M4 L4 SVP: 7 DLU: 77

407.663-010 FARMWORKER, DIVERSIFIED CROPS I (agriculture)

Drives and operates farm machines to grow and harvest combination of kinds of crops, such as grain, fruit, and vegetable: Attaches farm implements, such as plow, seed drill, and manure spreader to tractor, and drives tractor and operates implements in fields to till soil and plant, cultivate, and fertilize crops, such as sugar beets, asparagus, wheat, onions, and mint. Thins and weeds plants, such as field corn, lima beans, fresh peas, and dry beans, using handtools, such as hoes and shovels or power-drawn implement. Irrigates fields to provide moisture for crop growth, according to irrigation method appropriate for crops or locality. May mix chemical solutions, such as pesticides, herbicides, and fertilizers, and spray crops. May oversee activities of seasonal workers, and keep workers' time records. May adjust and maintain farm machines.
GOE: 03.04.01 STRENGTH: M GED: R3 M2 L3 SVP: 4 DLU: 77

407.687-010 FARMWORKER, DIVERSIFIED CROPS II (agriculture)

Performs any combination of following manual duties involved in planting, cultivating, and harvesting crops on diversified-crop farm, such as wheat, onion and sugar-beet farm and tomato and sweet-potato farm: Rides on planter and brushes debris from furrow-plowing spouts. Plants roots and bulbs, using hoe or trowel. Transplants seedlings, using hand transplanter. Covers plants to protect them from weather, using sheets or caps of treated cloth or paper. Weeds and thins plants, using hoe or spoon-shaped tool. Sets out poles and strings wires or twine to build trellises or fences. Positions and ties leaves or tendrils of plants, such as watermelons and cabbages, to promote market-quality development. Prunes limbs, runners, or buds from trees or vines to shape plants and promote productivity, using shears and saws. Harvests crops using appropriate method, such as picking, pulling, and cutting. Cuts off tops of root plants and sacks or bunches and ties harvested crops to facilitate handling. Picks out debris, such as vines and culls, to clean harvested crops, and cleans up area around harvesting machines. May be identified with work performed, such as planting, weeding, and picking.
GOE: 03.04.01 STRENGTH: M GED: R1 M1 L1 SVP: 2 DLU: 77

408 PLANT LIFE AND RELATED SERVICE OCCUPATIONS

This group includes occupations typically found in establishments providing blight, weed, and pest control; and landscaping, tree, and related services on a fee or contract basis. Farm equipment operators are classified in Group 409. Crop-preparation-service-for-market occupations, such as sorting, grading, and packing fruit and vegetables; and nut hulling and shelling are classified in Division 92.

408.131-010 SUPERVISOR, SPRAY, LAWN AND TREE SERVICE (agriculture) alternate titles: crew manager

Supervises and coordinates activities of workers engaged in pruning trees and shrubs, cultivating lawns, and applying pesticides and other chemicals according to service contract specifications: Reviews contracts to ascertain service, machine, and work force requirements and schedules work for crews according to weather conditions, availability of equipment, and seasonal limitations. Investigates customer complaints and spot checks completed work to ascertain quality of subordinates' work and effectiveness of chemicals applied. Suggests formula and procedure changes and orders corrective work to improve quality of service and ensure contract compliance. Answers inquiries from potential customers regarding methods, materials, and price ranges in person or by telephone. Prepares service estimates according to labor hour, material, and machine requirement costs determined from job site appraisal data, experience, and

records. Compiles reports of personnel matters, such as absenteeism and labor costs, for management. Performs other duties as described under SUPERVISOR (any industry) Master Title. May be designated according to kind of crew supervised as Spray Supervisor (agriculture); Tree-Service Supervisor (agriculture).
GOE: 03.02.03 STRENGTH: L GED: R4 M4 L4 SVP: 7 DLU: 77

408.137-010 SUPERVISOR, INSECT AND DISEASE INSPECTION (agriculture) alternate titles: disease-and-insect-control boss
Supervises and coordinates activities of workers engaged in detecting presence of noxious insects and plant diseases in field crops and counting insect population, applying knowledge of standard sampling techniques: Ascertains kinds of crops planted in each field and number of acreages involved to determine need for modifying sampling techniques and to determine number of workers needed. Assigns fields to workers, distributes sampling worksheets, and briefs new workers on identifying characteristics of prevalent insects and diseases. Compiles sampling-results data from worksheets to prepare composite insect and disease report for each field. Transports workers to and from fields using truck. Performs other duties as described under SUPERVISOR (any industry) Master Title.
GOE: 03.02.04 STRENGTH: L GED: R4 M4 L4 SVP: 6 DLU: 77

408.137-014 SUPERVISOR, TREE-TRIMMING (utilities)
Supervises and coordinates the activities of workers engaged in removing trees that interfere with electric power lines: Examines work order to determine location of trees to be pruned or felled by trimming crews. Reads street and road maps and drives truck to transport crew to work site. Inspects electric power lines near trees to be trimmed and secures clearance to work on lines if necessary. Directs placement of rigging for hoisting tools to workers in trees and for lowering severed tree limbs to ground. Supervises workers in cutting away branches of trees so that remaining tree limbs are at safe distance from electric power lines. Orders removal of trees when necessary. Explains tree trimming activities to consumers when working on consumers' property. Keeps daily work records. Occasionally trims trees. Performs other duties as described under SUPERVISOR (any industry) Master Title.
GOE: 03.04.05 STRENGTH: M GED: R4 M3 L4 SVP: 6 DLU: 77

408.161-010 LANDSCAPE GARDENER (agriculture) alternate titles: landscaper
Plans and executes small scale landscaping operations and maintains grounds and landscape of private and business residences: Participates with LABORER, LANDSCAPE (agriculture) in preparing and grading terrain, applying fertilizers, seeding and sodding lawns, and transplanting shrubs and plants, using manual and power-operated equipment. Plans lawns, and plants and cultivates them, using gardening implements and power-operated equipment. Plants new and repairs established lawns, using seed mixtures and fertilizers recommended for particular soil type and lawn location. Locates and plants shrubs, trees, and flowers selected by property owner or those recommended for particular landscape effect. Mows and trims lawns, using hand mower or power mower. Trims shrubs and cultivates gardens. Cleans grounds, using rakes, brooms, and hose. Sprays trees and shrubs, and applies supplemental liquid and dry nutrients to lawn and trees. May dig trenches and install drain tiles. May make repairs to concrete and asphalt walks and driveways.
GOE: 03.01.03 STRENGTH: H GED: R4 M4 L4 SVP: 7 DLU: 77

408.181-010 TREE SURGEON (agriculture)
Prunes and treats ornamental and shade trees and shrubs in yards and parks to improve their appearance, health, and value: Cuts out dead and undesirable limbs and trims trees to enhance beauty and growth. Scrapes decayed matter from cavities in trees, and fills holes with cement to promote healing and prevent further deterioration. Sprays and dusts pesticides on shrubs and trees to control pests and disease or sprays foliar fertilizers to increase plant growth, using hand or machine dusters and sprayers. Tops trees to control growth characteristics and to prevent interference with utility wires. May apply herbicides to kill brush and weeds. May fell and remove trees and bushes. May plant trees and shrubs.
GOE: 03.01.03 STRENGTH: M GED: R4 M2 L2 SVP: 6 DLU: 77

408.364-010 PLANT-CARE WORKER (agriculture) alternate titles: interior horticulturist; plant tender
Cares for ornamental plants on various customer premises, applying knowledge of horticultural requirements, and using items such as insecticides, fertilizers, and gardening tools: Reads work orders and supply requisitions to determine job requirements, and confers with supervisor to clarify work procedures. Loads plants and supplies onto truck in order of scheduled stops, using handtruck. Drives truck to premises and carries needed supplies to work area. Examines plants and soil to determine moisture level, using water sensor gauge, and waters plants according to requirements of species, using hose and watering can. Sponges plant leaves to apply moisture and remove dust. Observes plants under magnifying glass to detect insects and disease, and consults plant care books or confers with supervisor to identify problems and determine treatments. Selects and applies specified chemical solutions to feed plants, kill insects, and treat diseases, using hose or mist-sprayer. Transplants root-bound plants into larger containers. Pinches and prunes stems and leaves to remove dead and diseased leaves, to shape plants, and to induce growth, using shears. Removes diseased and dying plants from premises and replaces them with healthy plants. Informs customer of plant care needs. Enters record of actions taken at each stop in route book and prepares requisitions for materials needed on subsequent visit. Returns diseased, dying, and unused plants and supplies to employer premises.
GOE: 03.04.05 STRENGTH: M GED: R3 M2 L3 SVP: 3 DLU: 86

408.381-010 SCOUT (agriculture) alternate titles: pest-control worker
Locates and exterminates plant and tree pests and diseases: Searches fields, brush, trees, and warehouses to locate plant pests, such as witchweed, boll weevil, Japanese beetle, soybean cyst nematode, fire ant, gypsy moth, white-fringed beetles, and army worms. Mixes exterminating agents, such as herbicides, insecticides, and fungicides, according to type of infection or infestation to be treated. Applies exterminating agents, using spray equipment. Destroys clusters of gypsy-moth eggs by painting or spraying clusters with creosote. Collects samples of infected soil or plants for laboratory analysis. Marks infested area to determine effectiveness of treatment. May specialize in treatment of one type of infestation, such as gypsy moth or witchweed.
GOE: 03.04.05 STRENGTH: M GED: R3 M2 L3 SVP: 4 DLU: 77

408.381-014 WEED INSPECTOR (agriculture)
Locates and destroys noxious weeds in rural municipality: Inspects roadsides and ditches for noxious weeds and notifies landowners in areas where suspected weeds are located. Identifies weeds and prepares poisonous solution required to destroy them. Sprays infected area with solution.
GOE: 03.04.05 STRENGTH: L GED: R3 M2 L3 SVP: 5 DLU: 77

408.662-010 HYDRO-SPRAYER OPERATOR (agriculture)
Operates truck-mounted *hydro-sprayer* to cover areas, such as highway median strip, hillsides and fields with mixture of grass seed, fertilizer and mulch according to specifications: Pumps water and dumps seed, fertilizer, and wood fiber into hydro-sprayer tank according to formula. Connects hoses and nozzles, selected according to terrain and distribution pattern requirements, using pressure couplings and threaded fittings. Starts motors and engages machinery, such as hydro-sprayer agitator and pump. Lifts, pushes, and swings nozzle, hose, and tube to direct spray over designated area. Covers area to specified depth, applying knowledge of weather conditions, such as humidity and wind velocity; machinery capacities, such as droplet size and elevation-to-distance ratio; and obstructions, such as trees and buildings. Gives driving instructions to truck driver, using hand and horn signals, to ensure complete coverage of designated area. Cleans and services machinery to ensure operating efficiency, using water, gasoline, lubricants, and handtools. Occasionally plants grass with seed spreader and operates straw blower to cover seeded area with asphalt and straw mixture.
GOE: 03.04.04 STRENGTH: H GED: R3 M2 L2 SVP: 4 DLU: 77

408.664-010 TREE TRIMMER (tel. & tel.; utilities) alternate titles: tree trimmer, line clearance; tree-trimming-line technician
Trims trees to clear right-of-way for communications lines and electric power lines to minimize storm and short-circuit hazards: Climbs trees to reach branches interfering with wires and transmission towers, using climbing equipment. Prunes treetops, using saws or pruning shears. Repairs trees damaged by storm or lightning by trimming jagged stumps and painting them to prevent bleeding of sap. Removes broken limbs from wires, using hooked extension pole. Fells trees interfering with power service, using chain saw (portable power saw). May work from bucket of extended truck boom to reach limbs.
GOE: 03.04.05 STRENGTH: H GED: R3 M2 L2 SVP: 4 DLU: 77

408.667-010 TREE-TRIMMER HELPER (utilities) alternate titles: tree trimmer helper, line clearance
Assists TREE TRIMMER (tel. & tel.; utilities) in clearing trees and branches that interfere with communication lines and electric power lines: Hoists tools and equipment to TREE TRIMMER (tel. & tel.; utilities) and lowers branches with rope or block and tackle. Positions and steadies ladders. Saws and chops up branches, and loads debris, tree trunk and limbs on truck, using winch. Performs other duties as described under HELPER (any industry) Master Title.
GOE: 03.04.05 STRENGTH: M GED: R1 M1 L1 SVP: 2 DLU: 77

408.684-010 LAWN-SERVICE WORKER (agriculture)
Cultivates lawns, using power aerator and *thatcher* and chemicals according to specifications: Lifts dead leaves and grass from between growing grass and soil, using thatcher. Pierces soil to make holes for fertilizer and water, using aerator. Presses aerator fork into soil and pulls rake through grass to cultivate areas not accessible to machines. Distributes granulated fertilizers, pesticides, and fungicides on lawn, using spreader. Records services rendered, materials used, and charges assessed on specified form. Transports thatcher, aerator, tools, and materials to and from job site, using truck with hydraulic lift-gate. May care for athletic field turf and be designated Athletic Turf Worker (amuse. & rec.).
GOE: 03.04.04 STRENGTH: H GED: R3 M2 L2 SVP: 4 DLU: 77

408.684-014 SPRAYER, HAND (agriculture)
Sprays herbicides, pesticides, and fungicides on trees, shrubs, and lawns, using hoses and truck-mounted tank: Fills sprayer tank with water and chemicals according to formula, using hose or pump. Pulls spray hose from truck-mounted reel, turns knob, presses lever, and points nozzle selected according to job site characteristics, such as type of infestation, wind direction and velocity, plantings and terrain, to spray weeds, trees, shrubs, and lawns. Occasionally manipulates levers that control hydraulically powered, truck-mounted boom to position spray wands and release chemical solutions under pressure to spray ground areas. May use portable spray equipment. May grub out and burn infested bushes. May destroy diseased trees. May spray livestock with pesticides.

GOE: 03.04.04 STRENGTH: H GED: R3 M2 L2 SVP: 4 DLU: 77

408.684-018 TREE PRUNER (agriculture)

Cuts away dead and excess branches from fruit, nut, and shade trees, using handsaws, pruning hooks and shears, and long-handled clippers. Applies tar or other protective substances to cut surfaces to seal surfaces against insects. May use truck-mounted hydraulic lifts and pruners and power pruners. May climb trees, using climbing hooks and belts, or climb ladders to gain access to work area. May specialize in pruning fruit trees and be designated Orchard Pruner (agriculture). May prune, cut down, fertilize, and spray trees as directed by TREE SURGEON (agriculture) and be designated Tree-Surgeon Helper (agriculture) I.

GOE: 03.04.05 STRENGTH: M GED: R3 M2 L3 SVP: 4 DLU: 77

408.687-010 FIELD INSPECTOR, DISEASE AND INSECT CONTROL (agriculture)

Inspects fields to detect presence of noxious insects and plant diseases, applying knowledge of identifying characteristics of insects and diseases: Walks through fields, following standard sampling patterns, and examines plants at periodic intervals to detect presence of insects or diseases. Counts numbers of insects on examined plants or number of diseased plants within sample area. Records results of counts onto field worksheet. Collects samples of unidentifiable insects or diseased plants for identification by supervisor.

GOE: 03.02.04 STRENGTH: L GED: R2 M2 L2 SVP: 2 DLU: 77

408.687-014 LABORER, LANDSCAPE (agriculture)

Moves soil, equipment, and materials, digs holes, and performs related duties to assist LANDSCAPE GARDENER (agriculture) 408.161-010 in landscaping grounds: Digs holes for plants and trees, using pick and shovel. Mixes fertilizer or lime with dirt in bottom of holes to enrich soil, places plants or trees in holes, and adds dirt to fill holes. Attaches wires from planted trees to stakes to support trees. Hauls or spreads topsoil, using wheelbarrow and rake. Waters lawns, trees, and plants, using portable sprinkler system, hose, or watering can. Spreads straw over seeded soil to prevent movement of seed and soil. Builds forms for concrete borders, using lumber, hammer, and nails. Mixes and pours cement for garden borders. Places decorative stones and plants flowers in garden areas. Mows lawns, using power mower.

GOE: 03.04.04 STRENGTH: H GED: R2 M2 L2 SVP: 2 DLU: 81

408.687-018 TREE-SURGEON HELPER II (agriculture)

Hands or hoists tools and equipment to TREE PRUNER (agriculture) or TREE SURGEON (agriculture). Lowers pruned limbs and trunk sections, using ropes; sections limbs, using saw; and reduces sections to chips, using chipper. Rakes up debris and loads it on truck. Performs other duties as described under HELPER (any industry) Master Title.

GOE: 03.04.04 STRENGTH: H GED: R2 M1 L2 SVP: 2 DLU: 77

409 PLANT FARMING AND RELATED OCCUPATIONS, N.E.C.

This group includes occupations, not elsewhere classified, concerned with plant farming and related activities.

409.117-010 HARVEST CONTRACTOR (agriculture) alternate titles: farm-labor contractor

Provides harvest crews for farmers and directs, coordinates, and oversees crew activities, such as field hauling and threshing: Contacts crop growers to ascertain time and method of harvesting. Inspects crops and fields to estimate acreage yield and determine loading requirements, land contours, road accessibility, and distances to storage or processing area. Prepares and submits bids to farmer to obtain harvest contract. Recruits, hires and orients crewmembers. Assigns workers to tasks involved in harvesting, loading, moving, and storing crops. Prepares and submits bids to farmers to provide work crews for farming activities, such as planting, pruning, and thinning fruit trees, setting posts, and weeding field crops. May supply, tend, adjust, and repair trucks and farm machines. May transport or arrange for transportation of workers. May be required to be licensed by state and federal authorities. May prepare production records and crew payroll. May be identified with crew activity as Contractor, Broomcorn Threshing (agriculture); Contractor, Field Hauling (agriculture).

GOE: 03.01.01 STRENGTH: L GED: R4 M4 L4 SVP: 7 DLU: 77

409.131-010 SUPERVISOR, PICKING CREW (agriculture) alternate titles: harvest supervisor

Supervises and coordinates activities of workers engaged in picking fruits, vegetables, and row crops, by hand or machine, and loading and stacking filled containers on trucks: Examines crop to determine degree of maturity. Directs workers in methods of picking crops and specifies size of fruit or vegetable to pick. Ensures that equipment, such as ladders and containers, are available to workers. Directs distribution of field boxes along rows for convenience of workers. Checks harvested products for size, quality, and variety, and informs workers of discrepancies. Oversees loading and stacking filled containers on trucks. Performs other duties as described under SUPERVISOR (any industry) Master Title. May pay employees. May be designated according to type of crops harvested as Apple-Picking Supervisor (agriculture); Cauliflower-Harvesting-And-Packing Supervisor (agriculture); Orange-Picking Supervisor (agriculture); Onion-Harvesting Supervisor (agriculture); Peach-Harvesting Supervisor (agriculture); Watermelon-Harvesting Supervisor (agriculture).

GOE: 03.04.01 STRENGTH: M GED: R4 M3 L4 SVP: 7 DLU: 80

409.137-010 IRRIGATOR, HEAD (agriculture) alternate titles: supervisor, irrigation

Supervises and coordinates activities of workers engaged in irrigating crops: Inspects area irrigated to ensure adequate soaking and prevent waste of water. Opens head gate to permit entry of water into main ditches or pipes. Signals worker to start water flow. Directs workers in cleaning and repairing ditches or pipes. Keeps workers' time records. Performs other duties as described under SUPERVISOR (any industry) Master Title. May verify addition of liquid fertilizer to irrigation ditches by commercial firm.

GOE: 03.04.05 STRENGTH: M GED: R3 M2 L3 SVP: 5 DLU: 78

409.137-014 ROW BOSS, HOEING (agriculture)

Supervises and coordinates activities of workers engaged in hoeing, weeding, and thinning crops, such as sugar beets, lettuce, and watermelons: Assigns rows and distributes hoes to workers. Observes thinning, weeding, or cultivating process, notes evidence of unsatisfactory work, and initiates corrective measures. Keeps time and production records. Collects tools at end of workday. Performs other duties as described under SUPERVISOR (any industry) Master Title. May recruit workers.

GOE: 03.04.01 STRENGTH: L GED: R4 M3 L4 SVP: 7 DLU: 77

409.667-010 AIRPLANE-PILOT HELPER (agriculture)

Performs any combination of following duties to provide ground support for AIRPLANE PILOT (agriculture) 196.263-010 engaged in aerial seeding and fertilizing of fields and dusting of crops: Mixes fertilizers and pesticides according to prescribed formulas, and loads seeds, fertilizers, or pesticides onto airplane. Pours or pumps materials and seeds into feed hopper of airplane. Signals pilot when propeller is clear of people and obstructions to take off and to dust or spray fields. Waves flag or stands on edge of field to mark flight passes for pilot to prevent skips and overlaps.

GOE: 03.04.05 STRENGTH: M GED: R2 M2 L2 SVP: 3 DLU: 78

409.683-010 FARM-MACHINE OPERATOR (agriculture)

Drives and operates one or more farm machines, such as tractors, trucks, and harvesters to perform specified farm activity as cutting hay, picking cranberries, and harvesting wheat: Hitches soil conditioning implement, such as plow or harrow to tractor, and operates tractor and towed implement to furrow and grade soil. Drives tractor and operates designated towed machine, such as seed drill or manure spreader, to plant, fertilize, dust, and spray crops. Prepares harvesting machine by adjusting speeds of cutters, blowers, and conveyors and height of cutting head or depth of digging blades according to type, height, weight, and condition of crop being harvested, and contour of terrain. Attaches towed- or mounted-type harvesting machine to tractor, using handtools, or drives self-propelled harvesting machine to cut, pull up, dig, thresh, clean, chop, bag, or bundle crops, such as sod, vine fruits, or livestock feed. Moves switches, pulls levers, and turns knobs and wheels to activate and regulate mechanisms. Refuels engine, lubricates machine parts, and monitors machine operations to ensure optimum performance. Drives truck to haul materials, supplies, or harvested crops to designated locations. May load and unload containers of materials and products on trucks, trailers, or railcars by hand or driving forklift truck. May mix specified materials and dump solutions, powders, or seeds into planter or sprayer machinery. May oversee activities of field crews. May drive horses or mules to tow farm machinery. May be identified with crop, such as hay, onions, and cranberries, or machine, such as baler, chopper, and digger.

GOE: 03.04.01 STRENGTH: H GED: R3 M2 L2 SVP: 3 DLU: 82

409.683-014 FIELD HAULER (agriculture)

Drives truck or tractor with trailer attached to gather and transport harvested crop in field: Hauls trailer alongside crew loading crop or adjacent to harvesting machine and regulates speed to keep abreast of crew. Hauls loaded trailers from field to highway or packing shed, uncouples trailer, couples empty trailer to tractor and returns to field. May haul crop over public roads to storage shed or processing plant.

GOE: 03.04.01 STRENGTH: M GED: R2 M2 L2 SVP: 3 DLU: 77

409.684-010 IRRIGATOR, VALVE PIPE (agriculture)

Floods or row-irrigates field sections, using portable pipe sections equipped with valves connected to underground waterline: Secures gate attachment (water flow regulator) to vertical pipe. Connects length of valve pipe to gate and attaches additional pipe through field section or across ends of rows until area is spanned. Starts motor that pumps water through pipeline system, and opens valves to direct water over uneven terrain and fill rows or areas enclosed by checks (earth embankments). Observes rate of flow and adjusts valves accordingly. Shovels dirt into holes and low spots in levees and removes obstructions. Digs opening in embankment at end of row to direct overflow of water into spillway. Builds levees to prevent water from overflowing other crops or highways. Lubricates pumping equipment and makes minor repairs.

GOE: 03.04.05 STRENGTH: M GED: R2 M1 L1 SVP: 3 DLU: 77

409.685-010 FARM-MACHINE TENDER (agriculture)

Tends machines, such as corn shelling machine, winnowing machine, and grass-removing machine that separate crops from waste materials, such as grass, twigs, and cobs: Turns switches to activate machinery, such as conveyors, blowers, and shakers. Adjusts machinery to obtain optimum separations. Loads conveyors, hoppers, and wheels to feed machines. Positions boxes or attaches bags at discharge end of conveyor to catch products. Moves baffle lever that

channels product flow to container or stops flow during container exchanges. Observes machine operation to detect malfunctions and adjusts machine, lubricates parts, and replaces pieces to improve performance. Stops machinery and pulls debris or overloads from conveyors to avoid clogging. May level and smooth materials on conveyor to regulate flow through machine. May weigh containers to ensure conformance with specifications. May close filled sacks, using needle and thread or tie-string, and stencil identifying information on sack. May mix and pour chemical solutions, such as preservatives and insecticides, in treating tanks. May transport materials and products to and from machine, using dump truck. May be identified with machine tended.
GOE: 03.04.01 STRENGTH: H GED: R2 M1 L2 SVP: 2 DLU: 77

409.685-014 IRRIGATOR, SPRINKLING SYSTEM (agriculture) alternate titles: irrigator, overhead
Tends sprinkler system that irrigates land: Lays out strings (pipe) along designated pipeline settings in field. Connects pipe, using snap lock or wrench to tighten collar clamp. Attaches revolving sprinkler heads to vertical pipes at designated points along pipeline. Starts gasoline engine and adjusts controls that move self-propelled wheel line sprinkler system across field or pushes on switch that activates circle sprinkler system, and starts pump that forces water through system to irrigate crops. Observes revolving sprinklers to ensure uniform distribution of water to all areas. Lubricates, adjusts, and repairs or replaces parts, such as sprinkler heads and drive chains to maintain system, using handtools. Disassembles system and moves it to next location after specified time intervals.
GOE: 03.04.05 STRENGTH: M GED: R2 M1 L2 SVP: 2 DLU: 81

409.686-010 FARMWORKER, MACHINE (agriculture)
Performs any combination of following duties to feed or off bear farm machines used to plant, harvest, and clean crops: Loads containers of rooted cuttings, plants, seedlings, or bulbs on planting machine and pulls levers to start planting and watering mechanisms. Walks beside or rides on machine while inserting plants in planter-mechanism clamp, pocket, or tube at specified intervals. Dumps, pitches, scoops, or shovels materials and products, such as bulbs, onions, and nuts into feed hopper. Guides plants onto feed conveyor. Picks up spilled products and places them on feed mechanism. Notifies designated coworker when machine malfunctions are observed. Stacks empty boxes in conveyor discharge rack or hangs bags on hooks under discharge chute, and flips baffle lever that channels discharge flow to catch products. Closes ends of filled sacks, using tie wires. Loads sacks or boxes onto truck or trailer, or guides discharge spout over truck, trailer, or silo. Cleans machinery, such as planting or digging mechanism and chain conveyor. Lubricates, adjusts, and replaces machinery parts, using handtools.
GOE: 03.04.01 STRENGTH: H GED: R1 M1 L1 SVP: 1 DLU: 77

409.687-010 INSPECTOR-GRADER, AGRICULTURAL ESTABLISHMENT (agriculture)
Inspects and grades agricultural products, such as carrots, rose bushes, strawberry plants, and tobacco, in field or shed, according to marketing specifications: Estimates weight of product visually and by feel. Verifies count. Looks at, feels, and smells product, as required by its nature, to determine grade and identify substandard products. Places rejected products and individual grades of products in designated piles, containers, or areas. May pay harvest hands. May oversee field hauling. May be designated according to kind of product as Carrot Grader-Inspector (agriculture); Rose Grader (agriculture); Tobacco Grader (agriculture); Watermelon Inspector (agriculture).
GOE: 03.04.01 STRENGTH: M GED: R2 M2 L2 SVP: 2 DLU: 80

409.687-014 IRRIGATOR, GRAVITY FLOW (agriculture)
Irrigates field and row crops, using any of following gravity-flow methods: (1) Lifts gate in side of flooded irrigation ditch, permitting water to flow into bordered section of field. Shovels and packs dirt in low spots of embankment or cuts trenches in high areas to direct water flow. Closes gate in ditch when bordered section is flooded. (2) Removes plugs from portholes in pipes or wooden tunnels set in embankment at end of rows and observes water flowing through portholes. Removes obstructions from rows and builds up edges of rows with dirt. Plugs porthole as each row is filled. (3) Opens gate or connects standpipe (vertical pipe) to underground pipe system that releases waterflow into reservoir or ditch. Siphons water from flooded reservoir or gate or connects standpipe (vertical pipe) to underground pipe system that releases waterflow into reservoir or ditch. Shovels or hoes soil to clear ditches and furrows and build embankments that channel water in assigned area but avoid overflow into areas that could be damaged by water. May mix and apply cement solution to fill holes and cracks in concrete-lined pipes, ditches, and spillways, and make minor repairs to metal, concrete, and wooden frameworks in pipe and ditch valves and gates. May carry, lay out, and join portable irrigation-pipe sections to link up main ditch or pipe with field.
GOE: 03.04.05 STRENGTH: M GED: R2 M1 L1 SVP: 2 DLU: 77

409.687-018 WEEDER-THINNER (agriculture)
Weeds or thins crops, such as tobacco, strawberries, sugar beets, and carrots, by hand or using hoe: Breaks up soil around each plant. Pulls or cuts out weeds and surplus seedlings. Grooves dirt along row to facilitate irrigation, and mounds dirt around plants to protect roots. May be designated Hoer (agriculture) when job emphasis is on use of hoe.

GOE: 03.04.01 STRENGTH: M GED: R1 M1 L1 SVP: 1 DLU: 77

41   ANIMAL FARMING OCCUPATIONS

This division includes occupations concerned with breeding, raising, maintaining, gathering, and caring for land animals, collecting their products, and providing services in support of these activities. Occupations concerned with breeding and caring for aquatic animals are included in Division 44.

410   DOMESTIC ANIMAL FARMING OCCUPATIONS

This group includes occupations concerned with breeding, raising, gathering, and caring for domestic animals and domesticated wild animals, such as cattle, sheep, dogs, buffalo, and reindeer, and collecting their products, such as milk, wool, and fur. Occupations concerned with raising domestic fowl are included in Group 411, game animals in Group 412, and lower animals in Group 413.

410.131-010 BARN BOSS (any industry) alternate titles: corral boss; hostler; lot boss; stable manager
Supervises and coordinates activities of workers engaged in maintenance of stables and care of horses: Establishes amount and type of rations to feed animals according to past food consumption, health, activity, and size of animals. Inspects animals for evidence of disease or injury and treats animal according to experience or following instructions of VETERINARIAN (medical ser.). Inspects stables and animals for cleanliness. Supervises STABLE ATTENDANT (any industry) in upkeep of stalls, feed and water troughs, and equipment, and in care and feeding of animals. Performs other duties as described under SUPERVISOR (any industry) Master Title.
GOE: 03.02.04 STRENGTH: L GED: R4 M3 L3 SVP: 7 DLU: 77

410.131-014 SUPERVISOR, ARTIFICIAL BREEDING RANCH (agriculture)
Supervises and coordinates activities of workers engaged in caring for stud animals and collecting semen: Studies weight and activity records, nutritional requirements, and considers available feed, to determine feed rations. Considers animals' age, temperaments, fertility, and buyer demand to develop semen collection schedules. Observes animals for deviation in behavior and appearance, to detect illness and injury. Treats, or assigns workers to treat, ill or injured animals, or obtains services of VETERINARIAN (medical ser.) for serious illnesses or injuries. Assigns workers tasks, such as feeding animals, cleaning quarters, and maintaining facilities and equipment. Supervises workers engaged in collecting and processing semen and collects semen, using artificial vagina. Analyzes semen samples, using spectroscope and microscope, to determine number of services possible, or supervises workers analyzing semen samples. Demonstrates artificial insemination techniques to farmers to promote use of product. Trains workers in care of studs and collecting and processing semen. Orders supplies, such as feed and bedding. Performs other duties as described under SUPERVISOR (any industry) Master Title.
GOE: 03.02.01 STRENGTH: M GED: R4 M3 L3 SVP: 7 DLU: 77

410.131-018 SUPERVISOR, DAIRY FARM (agriculture)
Supervises and coordinates activities of workers engaged in milking, breeding, and caring for cows, and performs lay-veterinary duties on dairy farm: Assigns workers to tasks, such as feeding and milking cows, cleaning cattle, barns, and equipment, and assisting with breeding and health care. Inspects barns and milking parlor for cleanliness and maintenance and informs workers of actions required to ensure compliance with established standards. Studies feed and milk production records to determine feed formula required to produce maximum milk yield and notifies workers of diet changes. Studies genetic and health records to develop schedules for activities, such as breeding, dehorning, and sale of calves. Schedules breeding, vaccinating, and dehorning of cows and calves. Observes cows during estrus and artificially inseminates cows to produce desired offspring. Examines cows for evidence of illness, injuries, and calving, treats illnesses and injuries, delivers calves, and engages VETERINARIAN (medical ser.) to care for serious injuries and illnesses. Performs other duties as described under SUPERVISOR (any industry) Master Title.
GOE: 03.02.01 STRENGTH: M GED: R4 M3 L3 SVP: 7 DLU: 77

410.131-022 SUPERVISOR, STOCK RANCH (agriculture)
Supervises and coordinates activities of workers engaged in breeding, feeding, herding, marking, and segregating livestock and in construction and repair of fences, pens, and buildings: Inspects stock, buildings, fences, fields, pasturage and feed supply, notes tasks to be done, and assigns them to crews or individual workers. Performs other duties as described under SUPERVISOR (any industry) Master Title. May be designated according to type of stock raised.
GOE: 03.02.01 STRENGTH: M GED: R4 M3 L3 SVP: 7 DLU: 77

410.134-010 SUPERVISOR, LIVESTOCK-YARD (any industry)
Supervises and coordinates activities of workers engaged in care and movement of livestock in livestock yard: Assigns workers to feed, weigh, medically treat, and transfer livestock. Observes livestock handling and issues movement and health treatment instructions to direct livestock processing and transfer. Examines livestock to determine effectiveness of disease and injury control and instructs workers to take corrective action to rectify deficiencies. Observes condition of stockyard structures and equipment and arranges for needed maintenance and repairs. Performs other duties as described under SUPERVISOR (any industry) Master Title.

GOE: 03.02.04 STRENGTH: L GED: R3 M3 L3 SVP: 6 DLU: 77

410.134-014 SUPERVISOR, WOOL-SHEARING (agriculture)

Supervises and coordinates activities of workers engaged in shearing sheep on contract basis: Contacts SHEEP RANCHER (agriculture) to arrange terms of contract. Recruits, hires, trains, and supervises crew who shear sheep and perform related duties. Provides, sets up, and tests shearing equipment. Arranges for transportation, living quarters or campsite, food, and other accommodations for crew. Maintains time, production, and other records. Pays crewmembers. Performs duties as described under SUPERVISOR (any industry) Master Title. May participate in shearing sheep.

GOE: 03.04.01 STRENGTH: H GED: R4 M3 L3 SVP: 7 DLU: 77

410.134-018 SUPERVISOR, KENNEL (nonprofit org.) alternate titles: animal shelter supervisor

Supervises and coordinates activities of animal shelter workers, and performs maintenance on buildings and equipment: Establishes and coordinates work schedule to expedite accomplishment of essential and emergency tasks, issues instructions to workers, examines work results, and provides training to improve performance. Examines ailing animals to determine need of services from VETERINARIAN (medical ser.) 073.101-010. Replaces faulty electrical and plumbing fixtures, builds shelves, and paints structures and equipment to maintain shelter facilities. Greases water pump and observes water pumping system and pressure gauge to verify water pressure and to detect signs of leakage. Tunes-up, replaces parts, and maintains ambulance, pickup truck, lawnmower, and edger, using handtools, spare parts, and maintenance manuals. Cleans and disinfects shelter area, using high pressure water hose and bleach, to prepare shelter to receive visitors. Operates shelter euthanasia equipment to destroy designated animals. Drives ambulance and pickup truck in response to emergency calls and to investigate complaints of animal neglect or cruelty. Assists workers in interring coffins of heavy animals. Performs other duties as described under SUPERVISOR (any industry) Master Title.

GOE: 03.02.04 STRENGTH: H GED: R4 M2 L3 SVP: 4 DLU: 86

410.134-022 SUPERVISOR, RESEARCH DAIRY FARM (agriculture)

Supervises and coordinates activities of workers engaged in caring for bulls, cows, and young animal stock on research dairy farm: Demonstrates work methods of animal care, such as feeding, barn cleaning, milking, and tagging animals for identification to workers. Transports hay and grain from storage area to barn, using tractor or electric cart. Observes animals for signs of illness, injury, nervousness, or unnatural behavior. Notifies veterinarian when serious injury or illness occurs. Maintains records on medical care, breeding, and milk production. Observes living conditions of animal environment and informs workers of remedial actions to be taken. Informs maintenance crew of needed repairs on tractors and carts. May perform duties of caring for animals in absence of workers. Performs other duties as described under SUPERVISOR (any industry) Master Title.

GOE: 03.02.01 STRENGTH: H GED: R3 M2 L3 SVP: 6 DLU: 86

410.137-010 CAMP TENDER (agriculture)

Supervises and coordinates activities of workers engaged in tending bands of sheep on range or pasture and keeps them supplied with food and other necessities: Designates area to be used by each SHEEP HERDER (agriculture). Transports food, drinking water, fuel, mail, animal feed, and other supplies to SHEEP HERDER (agriculture). Observes condition of range, water, and animals, and gives directions to SHEEP HERDER (agriculture) when to move to another range, reporting findings to owner of band or to LIVESTOCK RANCHER (agriculture). Assists in moving camp to another location by hauling supply wagon, using horse or truck. Performs duties as described under SUPERVISOR (any industry) Master Title. May substitute for SHEEP HERDER (agriculture) during emergencies, vacations, or for other reasons. May lamb ewes and drench sheep.

GOE: 03.01.01 STRENGTH: L GED: R3 M2 L3 SVP: 6 DLU: 77

410.137-014 TOP SCREW (agriculture) alternate titles: lead rider; ramrod; top waddy

Supervises and coordinates activities of a group of COWPUNCHERS (agriculture) (colloquially called screws or waddies) riding after cattle on open range. Performs duties as described under SUPERVISOR (any industry) Master Title.

GOE: 03.04.01 STRENGTH: H GED: R4 M3 L3 SVP: 7 DLU: 77

410.137-018 SUPERVISOR, ANIMAL MAINTENANCE (pharmaceut.)

Supervises and coordinates activities of workers engaged in raising and caring for animals used in development of pharmaceutical products in pharmaceutical research and manufacturing facility: Visits animal maintenance areas and observes and discusses animal care, such as feeding, treatment, and breeding, with workers to identify problems or recommend changes. Prepares reports that indicate activity of unit, such as purchases, absenteeism of workers, and animal treatment. Contacts approved vendors to order and schedule arrival of animals, animal food, and equipment. Trains and observes workers in job duties and safety precautions. Contacts designated personnel to recruit new personnel or for repair of equipment. Performs other duties as described under SUPERVISOR (any industry) Master Title.

GOE: 03.03.02 STRENGTH: L GED: R4 M3 L3 SVP: 6 DLU: 86

410.161-010 ANIMAL BREEDER (agriculture)

Breeds and raises animals, such as cats, dogs, guinea pigs, mice, monkeys, rabbits, and rats: Selects and breeds animals, according to knowledge of animals, genealogy, traits, and offspring desired. Feeds and waters animals, and cleans pens, cages, yards, and hutches. Examines animals to detect symptoms of illness or injury. Treats minor injuries and ailments and engages VETERINARIAN (medical ser.) to treat animals with serious illnesses or injuries. Records weight, diet and other breeding data. Builds and maintains hutches, pens, and fenced yards. Adjusts controls to maintain specific temperature in building. Arranges for sale of animals to hospitals, research centers, pet shops, and food processing plants. May exhibit animals at shows. May be designated according to kind of animal bred and raised as Cat Breeder (agriculture); Dog Breeder (agriculture); Guinea-Pig Breeder (agriculture); Monkey Breeder (agriculture); Mouse Breeder (agriculture); Rabbit Breeder (agriculture); Rat Breeder (agriculture).

GOE: 03.01.02 STRENGTH: M GED: R4 M3 L3 SVP: 6 DLU: 77

410.161-014 FUR FARMER (agriculture)

Breeds and raises fur-bearing animals, such as mink, fox, or chinchilla: Buys or captures breeding stock. Breeds and raises animals in surroundings simulating their habitat. Feeds and waters animals and cleans their pens and yards. Kills animals in their prime and removes their pelts. Arranges with buyers for sale of pelts and breeding stock. Packs pelts in crates and ships to processing plants. Places live animals in crates and ships to buyers. May treat and preserve pelts at farm. May be designated according to type of animal raised as Chinchilla Farmer (agriculture); Fox Farmer (agriculture); Mink Farmer (agriculture).

GOE: 03.01.02 STRENGTH: L GED: R4 M3 L3 SVP: 6 DLU: 77

410.161-018 LIVESTOCK RANCHER (agriculture) alternate titles: livestock breeder; livestock farmer

Breeds and raises livestock, such as beef cattle, dairy cattle, goats, horses, reindeer, sheep, and swine, for such purposes as sale of meat, riding or working stock, breeding, or for show; and for products, such as milk, wool, and hair: Selects and breeds animals according to knowledge of animals, genealogy, characteristics, and offspring desired. Selects pasture, range, and crop lands to graze animals and produce feed crops. Mixes feed and feed supplements according to dietary requirements of animals and availability of grazing land. Feeds, waters, grazes, and distributes salt licks for animals. Observes animals to detect signs of illness and injury, treats minor injuries and ailments, disinfects and vaccinates animals, and engages VETERINARIAN (medical ser.) 073.101-010 to treat serious illnesses and injuries. Attends animals during and after birth of offspring. Castrates, docks, and dehorns animals. Brands, tatoos, notches ears, and attaches tags to identify animals. Milks cows and goats, shears sheep, and clips goats' hair. Operates farm machinery to plant, cultivate, and harvest feed crops. Cleans and fumigates barns, stalls, and pens, and sterilizes milking machines and equipment. Cools milk to prevent spoilage and packages wool and other products for shipment. Maintains and repairs farm machinery, equipment, buildings, pens, and fences. Arranges for sale of animals and products. Maintains cost and operation records. May butcher animals and cure meat. May hire and supervise workers. May exercise and train horses. May groom and exhibit animals at livestock shows. May be designated according to animal raised as Cattle Rancher (agriculture); Dairy Farmer (agriculture); Goat Farmer (agriculture); Horse Rancher (agriculture); Reindeer Rancher (agriculture); Sheep Rancher (agriculture); Swine Rancher (agriculture). May manage farm that raises and breeds thoroughbred horses and be designated Thoroughbred Horse Farm Manager (agriculture).

GOE: 03.01.01 STRENGTH: H GED: R4 M3 L3 SVP: 7 DLU: 81

410.161-022 HOG-CONFINEMENT-SYSTEM MANAGER (agriculture)

Breeds and raises swine in confinement buildings for purpose of selling pork to meatpacking establishments: Selects and breeds swine according to knowledge of animals, genealogy, characteristics, and offspring desired. Regulates breeding of sow herd to produce maximum number of litters. Attends sows during farrowing and helps baby pigs to survive birth and infancy. Castrates and docks pigs. Notches ears to identify animals. Determines weaning dates for pigs based on factors such as condition of sows, cost of feed, and available space in nursery. Vaccinates swine for disease and administers antibiotics and iron supplements, using syringes and hypodermic needles. Formulates rations for swine according to nutritional needs of animals and cost and availability of feeds. Grinds and mixes feed and adds supplements to satisfy dietary requirements. Stores and periodically examines feeds to ensure maintenance of appropriate temperatures and moisture levels. Operates water foggers, air-conditioners, fans, and heaters to maintain optimal temperature in swine confinement buildings. Flushes hog wastes into holding pit. Repairs and maintains machinery, plumbing, physical structures, and electrical wiring and fixtures in swine farrowing, nursery, and finishing buildings. May hire and supervise worker to assist in swine production activities.

GOE: 03.01.01 STRENGTH: M GED: R5 M4 L4 SVP: 7 DLU: 86

410.357-010 MILK SAMPLER (agriculture) alternate titles: sampler

Collects milk samples from farms, dairy plants, and tank cars and trucks for laboratory analysis: Removes sample from bulk tanks, tankers or milking machine, using dipper or pipette, and pours sample into sterile bottles. Weighs samples, using scale. Labels bottle with origin of sample, and packs samples in dry ice. Transports samples to laboratory for bacteriological and butterfat content analysis. Contacts potential customers to explain benefits of testing program to sell milk testing service. May assist customer in interpreting sample test results to maximize benefits to customer. May maintain individual milk production records for each cow in customer's herd.

GOE: 03.04.05 STRENGTH: M GED: R3 M2 L3 SVP: 4 DLU: 77

410.364-010 LAMBER (agriculture)

Attends to ewes during lambing: Observes ewes to determine delivery time and assists ewes during delivery. Places ewes and lambs in pens or erects canvas tents and places lambs and ewes inside to protect from elements. Assists weak lambs in suckling. Administers artificial respiration or stimulants as needed. Skins dead lambs and ties skins over live lambs to induce ewes to adopt rejected or orphaned lambs. Feeds orphaned lambs from bottle. Feeds and waters ewes while in enclosures. Docks lambs. May castrate lambs.

GOE: 03.04.01 STRENGTH: L GED: R3 M1 L2 SVP: 3 DLU: 77

410.664-010 FARMWORKER, LIVESTOCK (agriculture) alternate titles: laborer, livestock; ranch hand, livestock

Performs any combination of following tasks to attend livestock, such as cattle, sheep, swine, and goats on farm or ranch: Mixes feed and additives, fills feed troughs with feed, and waters livestock. Herds livestock to pasture for grazing. Examines animals to detect diseases and injuries. Vaccinates animals by placing vaccine in drinking water or feed or using syringes and hypodermic needles. Applies medications to cuts and bruises, sprays livestock with insecticide, and herds them into insecticide bath. Confines livestock in stalls, washes and clips them to prepare them for calving, and assists VETERINARIAN (medical ser.) 073.101-010 in delivery of offspring. Binds or clamps testes or surgically removes testes to castrate livestock. Clips identifying notches or symbols on animal or brands animal, using branding iron, to indicate ownership. Clamps metal rings into nostrils of livestock to permit easier handling and prevent rooting. Docks lambs, using hand snips. Cleans livestock stalls and sheds, using disinfectant solutions, brushes, and shovels. Grooms, clips, and trims animals for exhibition. May maintain ranch buildings and equipment. May plant, cultivate, and harvest feed grain for stock. May maintain breeding, feeding, and cost records. May shear sheep.

GOE: 03.04.01 STRENGTH: H GED: R3 M3 L3 SVP: 4 DLU: 81

410.674-010 ANIMAL CARETAKER (any industry) alternate titles: animal attendant; farmworker, animal

Performs any combination of following duties to attend animals, such as mice, canaries, guinea pigs, mink, dogs, and monkeys, on farms and in facilities, such as kennels, pounds, hospitals, and laboratories: Feeds and waters animals according to schedules. Cleans and disinfects cages, pens, and yards and sterilizes laboratory equipment and surgical instruments. Examines animals for signs of illness and treats them according to instructions. Transfers animals between quarters. Adjusts controls to regulate temperature and humidity of animals' quarters. Records information according to instructions, such as genealogy, diet, weight, medications, food intake, and license number. Anesthetizes, innoculates, shaves, bathes, clips, and grooms animals. Repairs cages, pens, or fenced yards. May kill and skin animals, such as fox and rabbit, and pack pelts in crates. May be designated according to place worked such as Dog-Pound Attendant (government ser.); Farmworker, Fur (agriculture); Helper, Animal Laboratory (pharmaceut.); Kennel Attendant (agriculture); Pet Shop Attendant (retail trade); Veterinary-Hospital Attendant (medical ser.).

GOE: 03.03.02 STRENGTH: M GED: R2 M1 L1 SVP: 4 DLU: 80

410.674-014 COWPUNCHER (agriculture) alternate titles: puncher; ranch rider; rider

Performs any combination of the following duties on a beef cattle ranch to attend to beef cattle: Herds, castrates, and brands cattle. Inspects and repairs fences, windmills, watering troughs, and feed containers. Feeds cattle supplemental food during shortages of natural forage. Trains saddle horses. Rides beside horse being trained to prevent bucking horse or rider from being injured.

GOE: 03.04.01 STRENGTH: M GED: R2 M2 L2 SVP: 4 DLU: 77

410.674-018 LIVESTOCK-YARD ATTENDANT (any industry)

Performs any combination of the following tasks to bed, feed, water, load, weigh, mark, and segregate livestock: Feeds grains, hay, and prepared feed and waters livestock according to schedule. Opens gates and drives livestock to scales, pens, trucks, railcars, and holding and slaughtering areas according to instructions, using electric prod and whip. Weighs animals and records weight. Segregates animals according to weight, age, color, and physical condition. Marks livestock to identify ownership and grade, using brands, tags, paint, or tattoos. Cleans ramps, scales, trucks, railcars, and pens, using hose, fork, shovel, and rake. Scatters new bedding material, such as sawdust and straw, in pens, railcars, and trucks. May vaccinate, apply liniment, drench, isolate, and mark animals to effect disease control program. May make routine repairs and perform general maintenance duties in stockyard.

GOE: 03.04.01 STRENGTH: H GED: R3 M2 L2 SVP: 2 DLU: 77

410.674-022 STABLE ATTENDANT (any industry) alternate titles: barnworker, groom

Cares for horses and mules to protect their health and improve their appearance: Waters animals and measures, mixes and apportions feed and feed supplements according to feeding instructions. Washes, brushes, trims and curries animals' coats to clean and improve their appearance. Inspects animals for disease, illness, and injury and treats animals according to instructions. Cleans animals' quarters and replenishes bedding. Exercises animals. Unloads and stores feed and supplies. May whitewash stables, using brush. May clean saddles and bridles. May saddle animals. May shoe animals. May be designated according to animal cared for as Horse Tender (any industry); Mule Tender (any industry); Stallion Keeper (agriculture).

GOE: 03.03.02 STRENGTH: H GED: R2 M1 L1 SVP: 2 DLU: 77

410.684-010 FARMWORKER, DAIRY (agriculture) alternate titles: laborer, dairy farm

Performs any combination of following tasks on dairy farm: Washes and sprays cows with water, insecticides, and repellants. Flushes, brushes, and scrapes refuse from walls and floors to minimize infestation. Examines cows and reports estrus, injuries, and disease to supervisor. Administers prescribed treatments and reports problems requiring veterinary attention to supervisor. Weighs, loads, mixes, and distributes feed. Replaces bedding in stalls. Herds cows from milking parlor to pasture. Loads animals to be sold onto trucks. Cleans and sterilizes milk containers and equipment, and tends pumps that automatically clean milk pipelines. Milks cows by hand and using milking machine. Cultivates, harvests, and stores feed crops, using farm equipment, such as trucks and tractors. May build and maintain fences and farm facilities. May repair and lubricate equipment and machinery. May maintain data, such as breeding and cost records.

GOE: 03.04.01 STRENGTH: H GED: R2 M1 L1 SVP: 4 DLU: 81

410.684-014 SHEEP SHEARER (agriculture) alternate titles: sheep clipper; stock clipper; wool shearer

Shears wool from live sheep, using power-driven clippers or hand shears: Places animal in shearing station. Clips wool close to hide so that fleece is removed in one piece and exercises care to nick or cut skin as little as possible. Herds shorn animal into runway leading to pen. Oils and sharpens clippers and shears. May tie fleece.

GOE: 03.04.01 STRENGTH: M GED: R2 M1 L1 SVP: 3 DLU: 77

410.685-010 MILKER, MACHINE (agriculture) alternate titles: milking-machine operator

Tends machine that milks dairy cows: Guides cow into stanchion and washes teats and udder of cow with disinfectant. Squeezes cow's teat to collect sample of milk in strainer cup and examines sample for curd and blood. Starts milking machine and attaches cups of machine to teats of cow. Removes cups when required amount of milk is obtained from cow. Dips cups of machine into disinfectant solution after each cow is milked. Pumps milk from receptacles into storage tank and cleans and sterilizes milking equipment. May notify farm manager of possible diseases or problems in milking cows.

GOE: 03.04.01 STRENGTH: M GED: R2 M1 L1 SVP: 2 DLU: 82

410.687-010 FLEECE TIER (agriculture)

Folds and ties wool fleece into bundle for sacking or grading: Removes heavy tags, dung locks, and badly stained wool from fleece. Spreads fleece on floor with hide side up. Folds loose ends inside and rolls fleece into compact bundle, tying bundle with twisted wool or paper twine. Tosses bundle aside for sacking or grading. May shear sheep [SHEEP SHEARER (agriculture)].

GOE: 03.04.01 STRENGTH: M GED: R2 M1 L1 SVP: 2 DLU: 77

410.687-014 GOAT HERDER (agriculture)

Attends herd of goats: Herds goats from corral to fresh pastures. Assists does during kidding season.

GOE: 03.04.01 STRENGTH: L GED: R2 M1 L1 SVP: 3 DLU: 77

410.687-018 PELTER (agriculture) alternate titles: skinner, pelts

Skins small fur-bearing animals, such as foxes, weasels, mink, and muskrats, for their pelts, using skinning knife.

GOE: 03.04.03 STRENGTH: M GED: R2 M2 L2 SVP: 2 DLU: 77

410.687-022 SHEEP HERDER (agriculture) alternate titles: herder; mutton puncher; shepherd

Attends sheep flock grazing on range: Herds sheep and rounds up strays using trained dogs. Beds down sheep near evening campsite. Guards flock from predatory animals and from eating poisonous plants. Drenches sheep. May assist in lambing, docking, and shearing. May feed sheep supplementary feed.

GOE: 03.04.01 STRENGTH: M GED: R2 M1 L1 SVP: 3 DLU: 77

410.687-026 WOOL-FLEECE SORTER (agriculture)

Inspects fleece for dungy locks and badly discolored areas. Segregates fleece in separate piles according to cleanliness of wool, preparatory to bundling or bagging.

GOE: 03.04.01 STRENGTH: M GED: R2 M1 L1 SVP: 3 DLU: 77

411 DOMESTIC FOWL FARMING OCCUPATIONS

This group includes occupations concerned with breeding, raising, gathering, and caring for domestic fowl and domesticated wild fowl, such as chickens, turkeys, ducks, parrots, and pea fowl, and collecting their products, such as eggs and feathers.

411.131-010 SUPERVISOR, POULTRY FARM (agriculture)

Supervises and coordinates activities of workers engaged in raising poultry, collecting eggs, crating fryers, and maintaining equipment and facilities on poultry farm: Confers with farm manager to ascertain production requirements and to discuss condition of equipment and status of supplies. Assigns workers to duties, such as collecting and candling eggs, feeding and vaccinating poultry, crating and shipping fryers, and cleaning and fumigating chicken houses. Directs maintenance and repair of facilities and equipment, such as chicken houses, automatic feeders, and layer nests. Trains new workers. Participates in work activities to expedite work load. Prepares worker attendance, egg produc-

tion, feed consumption and poultry mortality reports. Performs other duties as described under SUPERVISOR (any industry) Master Title. May be designated according to type of farm as Supervisor, Brooder Farm (agriculture); Supervisor, Egg-Producing Farm (agriculture); Supervisor, Fryer Farm (agriculture); Supervisor, Pullet Farm (agriculture); Supervisor, Turkey Farm (agriculture).
GOE: 03.02.01 STRENGTH: M GED: R4 M2 L3 SVP: 7 DLU: 77

411.137-010 SUPERVISOR, POULTRY HATCHERY (agriculture)
Supervises and coordinates activities of workers engaged in receiving and preparing eggs for incubation; incubating eggs; grading, preparing, and shipping chicks in poultry hatchery: Confers with hatchery manager to discuss equipment and supply needs, production and research requirements, and work schedules. Assigns workers to duties, such as egg candling, sorting and traying, incubating eggs, and grading and *debeaking* chicks. Monitors thermometers, gauges, and chart recorders to detect equipment malfunctions and to verify compliance with incubator temperature and ventilation standards. Adjusts controls to maintain specified incubating conditions. Periodically inspects eggs in incubator trays to ascertain hatching progress, and orders removal of chicks. Observes packing of chicks to verify adherence to customer's orders and shipping instructions. Prepares production reports, and requisitions equipment, materials, and supplies. Performs other duties as described under SUPERVISOR (any industry) Master Title. May be designated according to type of hatchery as Supervisor, Chicken Hatchery (agriculture); Supervisor, Turkey Hatchery (agriculture).
GOE: 03.02.01 STRENGTH: L GED: R4 M2 L3 SVP: 6 DLU: 77

411.161-010 CANARY BREEDER (agriculture)
Breeds and raises canaries: Places males with females to induce mating. Examines birds for disease and administers prescribed treatments. Maintains genetic and health records. Segregates them according to sex, color, health and vitality, and selects birds for mating to improve strain.
GOE: 03.01.02 STRENGTH: L GED: R4 M2 L3 SVP: 5 DLU: 77

411.161-014 POULTRY BREEDER (agriculture) alternate titles: chicken fancier
Breeds and raises poultry and fowl to improve strain and develop show stock: Selects and pairs birds for breeding or breeds birds by artificial insemination. Incubates eggs to induce hatching. Feeds and waters poultry. Cleans and disinfects poultry houses, cages, and nests. Places vaccines in drinking water, injects vaccines into poultry, or dusts air with vaccine powder to vaccinate poultry against diseases. Maintains growth, feed, and production records. Arranges with buyers for sale of pedigreed eggs, chicks, and birds. May hire and supervise workers.
GOE: 03.01.01 STRENGTH: L GED: R4 M3 L3 SVP: 7 DLU: 77

411.161-018 POULTRY FARMER (agriculture)
Raises poultry to produce eggs and meat: Selects and purchases poultry stock. Feeds and waters poultry. Cleans and disinfects poultry houses, cages, and nests. Places vaccines in drinking water, injects vaccines into poultry, or dusts air with vaccine powder to vaccinate poultry against diseases. Inspects and disposes of or segregates infected poultry. Collects, inspects, and packs eggs and selects and crates pullets and fryers for shipment. Maintains growth, feed, and production records. Arranges with wholesalers for sale of poultry and eggs. May hire and supervise workers. May incubate fertile eggs. May be designated according to kind of poultry raised as Duck Farmer (agriculture); Poultry Farmer, Egg (agriculture); Poultry Farmer, Meat (agriculture); Turkey Farmer (agriculture).
GOE: 03.01.01 STRENGTH: M GED: R4 M3 L3 SVP: 7 DLU: 77

411.267-010 FIELD SERVICE TECHNICIAN, POULTRY (agriculture)
Inspects farms for compliance with contract and cooperative agreement standards and advises farmers regarding development programs to aid in producing quality poultry products: Tours farms to inspect facilities and equipment for adequacy, sanitation and efficiency of operations. Examines chickens for evidence of disease and growth rate (according to weight and age) to determine effectiveness of medication and feeding programs. Recommends changes in facilities, equipment, and medication to improve production, based on knowledge of poultry farming, hatchery operations and processing. Informs farmers of new procedures and techniques, government regulations and company and association production standards to enable them to upgrade farms and meet requirements. Recommends laboratory testing of diseased chickens, feeds, and supplements or gathers samples and takes them to plant laboratory for analysis. Reports findings of farm conditions, laboratory tests, recommendations and farmers' reactions to keep superior apprised of farmers' efforts to furnish quality products.
GOE: 03.01.01 STRENGTH: L GED: R4 M3 L3 SVP: 7 DLU: 77

411.364-010 BLOOD TESTER, FOWL (agriculture)
Tests blood of poultry to ascertain presence of pullorum disease: Picks vein in bird's wing, using needle. Collects blood on wire loop and drops blood into pullorum reactor. Examines blood for specks that indicate presence of pullorum disease. Removes diseased birds from flock.
GOE: 03.04.05 STRENGTH: M GED: R3 M2 L2 SVP: 2 DLU: 77

411.364-014 POULTRY TENDER (agriculture)
Attends to poultry used in experimental tests that determine effects of various feeds and quantities of feed on growth and production of poultry: Segregates poultry into groups according to weight, age, and sex. Selects, weighs, and mixes feeds, according to specific instructions, and fills feeders for each group

of poultry with specified feeds. Regulates controls to maintain required temperatures in poultry houses. Maintains records of poultry weights, weights and kinds of feed consumed, eggs produced, deaths, and occurrence of poultry diseases, providing information about effects of various feeds. Places vaccines in drinking water, injects vaccines into poultry, or dusts air with vaccine powder to vaccinate poultry for diseases, such as fowl pox and bronchitis. Ascertains sex of chicks. May attach identification bands to legs or wings of poultry. May clip wings of fowl to prevent flying, wash and clean poultry houses and equipment, and debeak poultry.
GOE: 03.04.01 STRENGTH: H GED: R3 M2 L2 SVP: 5 DLU: 77

411.384-010 POULTRY INSEMINATOR (agriculture) alternate titles: artificial-insemination technician
Collects semen from roosters and fertilizes hens and eggs: Pinions bird, and collects semen in vial. Examines semen, using microscope, and records density and motility of gametes. Measures specified amount of semen into calibrated syringe and inserts syringe into inseminating gun. Injects semen into oviduct of hen or through hole in egg shell. Records dates of insemination of hens.
GOE: 03.04.05 STRENGTH: M GED: R3 M2 L2 SVP: 3 DLU: 77

411.584-010 FARMWORKER, POULTRY (agriculture) alternate titles: helper, chicken farm; poultry helper
Performs any combinations of following duties concerned with raising poultry for eggs and meat: Removes chicks from shipping cartons and places them in brooder houses. Cleans and fills feeders and water containers. Sprays poultry houses with disinfectants and vaccines. Inspects poultry for diseases and removes weak, ill, and dead poultry from flock. Collects eggs from trap nests, releases hens from nests, and records number of eggs laid by each hen. Packs eggs in cases or cartons; selects, weighs, and crates fryers and pullets; and records totals packed or crated on shipping or storage document. Maintains feeding and breeding reports. Monitors feed, water, illumination, and ventilation systems; and cleans, adjusts, lubricates, and replaces systems parts, using handtools. May cut off tips of beaks. May be designated according to type of farm or product as Farmworker, Brooder Farm (agriculture); Farmworker, Chicken Farm (agriculture); Farmworker, Egg-Producing Farm (agriculture); Farmworker, Fryer Farm (agriculture); Farmworker, Pullet Farm (agriculture); Farmworker, Turkey Farm (agriculture).
GOE: 03.04.01 STRENGTH: M GED: R2 M2 L2 SVP: 3 DLU: 77

411.684-010 CAPONIZER (agriculture)
Castrates cockerels to prevent development of sexual characteristics: Ascertains that cockerels have not been fed or watered for specified period of time. Binds legs and wings or pinions birds with weights and makes incision between cockerel's last two ribs or beneath and behind wings, using surgical knife or heated knife that cauterizes cut. Removes testicles, using forceps and heated knife or heated forceps.
GOE: 03.04.01 STRENGTH: L GED: R2 M1 L1 SVP: 2 DLU: 77

411.684-014 POULTRY VACCINATOR (agriculture)
Vaccinates poultry for diseases, such as pox and bronchitis, by placing vaccine in drinking water, dusting air with vaccine powder, injecting vaccine in eye, leg, vent, wing web, or nostril of bird, using medicine dropper or hypodermic needle. May be designated according to poultry vaccinated as Chicken Vaccinator (agriculture).
GOE: 03.04.01 STRENGTH: M GED: R2 M1 L1 SVP: 2 DLU: 77

411.687-010 CHICK GRADER (agriculture) alternate titles: poultry culler
Grades baby chicks according to appearance and separates healthy from deformed or diseased chicks: Examines baby chicks for curled toes, blindness, misshapened beaks, discolored downs, and abdominal rigidity. Examines chicks for symptoms of diseases, such as bronchitis and navel infection. Segregates healthy from diseased or deformed chicks. Places diseased chicks in incinerator. May press beak of chicks against hot wire to remove tip of beak. May pack chicks in cartons.
GOE: 03.04.01 STRENGTH: M GED: R2 M2 L2 SVP: 2 DLU: 77

411.687-014 CHICK SEXER (agriculture)
Examines chick genitalia to determine their sex: Turns back skin fold of external cloacal opening or inserts illuminating viewer into cloaca to observe genitals. Places chicks into boxes according to sex. May mark content data on boxes of segregated chicks.
GOE: 03.04.01 STRENGTH: L GED: R2 M1 L2 SVP: 4 DLU: 77

411.687-018 LABORER, POULTRY FARM (agriculture)
Performs any combination of following duties on poultry farm: Catches chickens and places them in crates and poultry houses. Sprays disinfectants or vaccines on chickens or in poultry houses. Spreads wood shavings over floor, using shovel. Cleans droppings and waste from floor, using broom and shovel, backhoe, or manure-cleaning machine. Dumps sacks of feed on conveyors and in feeders in brood houses. Fills water containers. Repairs farm buildings, fences, and shipping crates, using handtools. Lengthens and shortens ropes to adjust level of feed cans and water troughs. Moves equipment, using wheelbarrow, truck, and cart; or carries equipment from one area to another. Shovels manure onto truck. May stack and move crated eggs and poultry. May drive truck to move and deliver materials. May be designated according to type of farm or product as Laborer, Brooder Farm (agriculture); Laborer, Chicken Farm (agriculture); Laborer, Egg-Producing Farm (agriculture); Laborer, Fryer Farm

(agriculture); Laborer, Pullet Farm (agriculture); Laborer, Turkey Farm (agriculture).
GOE: 03.04.01 STRENGTH: M GED: R2 M1 L2 SVP: 2 DLU: 77

411.687-022 LABORER, POULTRY HATCHERY (agriculture) alternate titles: hatchery helper; incubator helper

Performs any combination of following duties in poultry hatchery: Places eggs in incubator trays, wads paper between eggs to secure them, and clips trays to incubator racks. Transfers trays from incubator to hatchery and removes paper wads from between eggs to make room for hatching chicks. Transfers hatched chicks from trays to chick boxes and counts out prescribed number of chicks to each box section. Supplies baby chicks to other workers for sexing, grading, and *debeaking*. May deliver cartons of chicks to designated farms or commercial growing establishments, using truck.
GOE: 03.04.01 STRENGTH: M GED: R2 M2 L2 SVP: 2 DLU: 77

411.687-026 POULTRY DEBEAKER (agriculture) alternate titles: debeaker

Trims and sears beaks, toes, and wings of baby chicks to prevent injury and flight: Inserts chick's beak in guide hole of heated trimmer and depresses pedal to cut off and sear tip of beak or trims and sears chick's beak, using heated hand shears. Trims and sears chick's toes and wings by pressing them against hot wire.
GOE: 03.04.01 STRENGTH: L GED: R2 M1 L1 SVP: 3 DLU: 77

412   GAME FARMING OCCUPATIONS

This group includes occupations concerned with breeding, raising, and caring for wild animals and birds, raised for game, exhibition, or preservation of species. Occupations concerned with raising and maintaining domesticated wild animals are included in groups 410 and 411.

412.131-010 SUPERVISOR, GAME FARM (agriculture)

Supervises and coordinates activities of workers engaged in breeding, raising, and protecting game on private or state game farm: Plans daily schedule and assigns workers to tasks, such as feeding and watering animals, cleaning pens and yards, gathering, incubating, and hatching eggs, planting cover crops, and maintaining buildings and equipment. Oversees preparation and transfer of game to zoos, filming locations, and release areas. Directs feeding and watering of game, cleaning of pens and yards, and maintenance of buildings and equipment. Observes game to detect signs of illnesses and injuries, treats minor ailments, and notifies MANAGER, GAME PRESERVE (agriculture) of serious illnesses and injuries. Trains workers in methods of raising, training, and transferring game. Records number and specie of game animals raised and location of release sites. Performs duties as described under SUPERVISOR (any industry) Master Title.
GOE: 03.02.01 STRENGTH: M GED: R4 M3 L4 SVP: 5 DLU: 77

412.137-010 ANIMAL KEEPER, HEAD (amuse. & rec.) alternate titles: keeper, head; superintendent, menagerie

Supervises and coordinates activities of workers engaged in care and exhibition of birds and animals at establishments, such as zoos or circuses. Observes animals to detect signs of illness and consults with VETERINARIAN (medical ser.) to determine type of medication or treatment required. Inspects cages, grottos, and pens for cleanliness and structural defects. Assigns workers to various tasks, and oversees treatment, preparation of food, feeding of animals, and maintenance and repair of animal quarters. Specifies type of animal to exhibit in zoo and location of exhibit, according to weather, animal behavior characteristics, and physical condition. Performs other duties as described under SUPERVISOR (any industry) Master Title. May hire, train, and discharge workers. May keep time records and prepare supply requisitions and reports. May coordinate training of animals for circus performance. May give lectures to public to stimulate interest in animals.
GOE: 03.03.02 STRENGTH: M GED: R4 M3 L3 SVP: 7 DLU: 77

412.161-010 GAME-BIRD FARMER (agriculture)

Breeds and raises wild birds, such as pheasant, quail, or partridge: Feeds and waters birds and cleans bird pens and yards. Examines birds to detect signs of illness and innoculates ill birds with antibiotics. Removes eggs from nests and hatches eggs in incubator. Clips birds' wings to prevent flight. Trims bills of birds to prevent injury. Exhibits prize birds at shows. Crossbreeds birds to improve strain and develop new types. Builds and repairs pens and yards. Arranges with hunting and gun clubs, game preserves, or poultry houses for sale of birds. May be designated according to type of game bird raised as Partridge Farmer (agriculture); Pheasant Farmer (agriculture); Quail Farmer (agriculture).
GOE: 03.01.02 STRENGTH: L GED: R4 M3 L3 SVP: 6 DLU: 77

412.674-010 ANIMAL KEEPER (amuse. & rec.) alternate titles: animal caretaker; menagerie caretaker; zoo caretaker

Feeds, waters, and cleans quarters of animals and birds in zoo, circus, or menagerie: Prepares food for charges by chopping or grinding meat, fish, fruit, or vegetables; mixing prepared, dry, or liquid commercial feeds; or unbaling forage grasses. Adds vitamins or medication to food as prescribed by VETERINARIAN (medical ser.) 073.101-010. Fills water containers and places food in cages as specified. Cleans animals' quarters, using rake, water hose, and disinfectant. Observes animals to detect illnesses and injuries and notifies ANIMAL KEEPER, HEAD (amuse. & rec.) 412.137-010 or VETERINARIAN

(medical ser.) of findings. Transfers animals from one enclosure to another for purposes such as breeding, giving birth, rearrangement of exhibits, or shipping. Sets temperature and humidity controls to specified. Answers visitors' questions concerning animals' habits or zoo operations. Bathes and grooms animals as required. May assist VETERINARIAN (medical ser.) in treatment of animals for illnesses and injuries. May assist ANIMAL TRAINER (amuse. & rec.) 159.224-010 or instructor in presentation of programs, shows, or lectures. May assist maintenance staff in cleaning zoo facilities. May be designated according to animal cared for as Bear Keeper (amuse. & rec.); Elephant Keeper (amuse. & rec.); Monkey Keeper (amuse. & rec.); or according to species as Bird Keeper (amuse. & rec.); Mammal Keeper (amuse. & rec.). May direct activities of other workers.
GOE: 03.03.02 STRENGTH: M GED: R3 M2 L2 SVP: 4 DLU: 81

412.674-014 ANIMAL-NURSERY WORKER (amuse. & rec.; museums) alternate titles: children's zoo caretaker

Cares for newborn and young animals in zoo nursery and exhibit area: Prepares liquid formula, cereal, and other foods for young animals according to direction of ZOO VETERINARIAN (medical ser.) 073.101-018 and prepares standard diet foods for mothers of newborn animals according to requirements of species. Fills sterilized nursing bottles with formula and feeds animals that have been orphaned or deserted, or that require food in addition to that provided by mother. Observes newborn animals to detect indications of abnormality or disease, and notifies ZOO VETERINARIAN (medical ser.) when such indications are evident. Periodically conducts physical examination of young animals, performing such tasks as taking temperatures, blood pressure, and pulse rate, and weighing and measuring animals. Maintains records of animal weights, sizes, and physical conditions to be used in zoo account of animals born in captivity. Adjusts humidity and temperature controls to maintain specified environmental conditions in nursery or exhibit area. Installs equipment such as infrared light stands, cribs, or feeding devices in young animal exhibit area. Explains to visitors procedures for care and feeding of young animals, and answers questions concerning factors such as native habitats and breeding habits. Observes children petting or feeding animals in designated area and cautions children against activities that might be harmful to animals.
GOE: 03.03.02 STRENGTH: M GED: R3 M2 L3 SVP: 4 DLU: 86

412.684-010 GAME-FARM HELPER (agriculture) alternate titles: laborer, game farm

Performs any combination of duties to attend game, such as ducks, pheasants, bears, cougars, and lions on private or state game farm: Feeds and waters game. Gathers bird eggs from field nests and places eggs in incubators. Brails (ties) wings of birds to prevent flying. Cleans water containers, pens, cages, and yards. Maintains and repairs fences, coops, pens, buildings, and equipment. Observes game to detect signs of illness and adds prescribed medications to food and water. Crates or cages game to prepare for movement. Transports game to release areas, filming locations, and zoos, using truck. Sets and maintains traps to protect birds from predatory animals. May operate farm equipment to cultivate and plant field crops.
GOE: 03.04.01 STRENGTH: M GED: R2 M2 L2 SVP: 3 DLU: 77

412.687-010 COMMISSARY ASSISTANT (amuse. & rec.; museums) alternate titles: commissary helper; food preparer

Stores, prepares, and delivers foods for zoo or aquarium animals: Unloads meats, produce, fodder, and other food items from delivery vehicle, using handtruck. Sorts and stores items on shelves, in bins, or in refrigerated storage room of commissary. Assembles food items needed for diet of various animals as directed by supervisory personnel. Measures, weighs, or counts items to obtain amount of food specified for diet plans. Bundles fodder, washes produce, and cuts away defects. Sorts assembled items according to destinations, loads items into truck, and drives truck to animal quarters. Assists ANIMAL KEEPER (amuse. & rec.) 412.674-010 in carrying food to preparation areas or in selecting and loading food into truck or cart.
GOE: 03.03.02 STRENGTH: H GED: R2 M2 L1 SVP: 2 DLU: 86

413   LOWER ANIMAL FARMING OCCUPATIONS

This group includes occupations concerned with breeding, raising, gathering, and caring for lower animals, such as bees, worms, and snakes, and collecting their products, such as honey and venom.

413.161-010 BEEKEEPER (agriculture) alternate titles: apiarist; bee farmer; bee raiser; bee rancher; honey producer

Raises bees to produce honey and pollinate crops: Assembles beehives, using handtools. Arranges with sellers for purchases of honeybee colonies. Inserts honeycomb of bees into beehive or inducts wild swarming bees into hive of prepared honeycomb frames. Places screen plug in hive entrance to confine bees and sets hive in orchard, clover field, or near other source of nectar and pollen. Forces bees from hive, using smoke pot or by placing carbolic acid soaked pad over hive to inspect hive and to harvest honeycombs. Scrapes out parasites, such as wax moth larvae, and removes vermin, such as birds and mice. Collects royal jelly from queen bee cells for sale as base for cosmetics and as health food. Destroys superfluous queen bee cells to prevent division of colony by swarming. Destroys diseased bee colonies, using cyanide gas. Burns hive of diseased bee colony or sterilizes hive, using caustic soda solution. Uncaps harvested honeycombs and extracts honey. Arranges with buyers for

sale of honey. May cultivate bees to produce bee colonies and queen bees for sale and be designated Bee Producer (agriculture); Queen Producer (agriculture).
GOE: 03.01.02 STRENGTH: H GED: R3 M3 L3 SVP: 7 DLU: 81

413.161-014   REPTILE FARMER (agriculture)
Breeds and raises reptiles for exhibition, preservation, meat, venom, and skins: Buys or captures reptiles, such as snakes and tortoises and keeps them in cages that simulate their natural habitat. Feeds and waters animals according to appropriate schedule for species. Examines reptile for signs of illness, injury or parasites, and administers prescribed treatment. Cleans animal pens, using rake and hose. Records breeding data. Kills reptiles and sells meat and skins. Extracts venom from live snakes. May specialize in raising rattlesnakes and be designated Rattlesnake Farmer (agriculture).
GOE: 03.01.02 STRENGTH: L GED: R4 M3 L4 SVP: 6 DLU: 77

413.161-018   WORM GROWER (agriculture) alternate titles: fish-worm grower
Breeds and raises earthworms for sale as fishing bait, garden soil conditioners, and food for exotic fish and animals: Mixes sand, loam, and organic materials to make growing media for worms, fills growing tubs with media and adds water. Plants mature worms in growing media for breeding stock, spreads food materials over surface of media and covers it with burlap. Inspects food supply and moisture of growing media and adds water and food to maintain optimum breeding conditions for worms. Shovels worm-laden media onto screen and shakes screen to remove worms. Places specified number of worms into sales container and scoops required amount of growing media into container to sustain worms. Sells earthworms to buyers. May dry worms under heat lamps and grind and package them for sale as tropical fish food.
GOE: 03.01.02 STRENGTH: M GED: R4 M3 L3 SVP: 6 DLU: 77

413.687-010   WORM PICKER (agriculture) alternate titles: fish-bait picker
Gathers worms to be used as fish bait: Walks about grassy areas, such as gardens, parks, and golf courses, after dark and picks up earthworms (commonly called dew worms and night crawlers). Sprinkles chlorinated water on lawn to cause worms to come to surface, and locates worms by use of lantern or flashlight. Sorts worms and packs them in containers for shipment.
GOE: 03.04.01 STRENGTH: L GED: R2 M1 L1 SVP: 1 DLU: 77

413.687-014   WORM-FARM LABORER (agriculture) alternate titles: worm-bed attendant; worm raiser
Mixes sand, loam, and specified organic materials to make growing media for breeding earthworms. Dumps media into growing tubs to breed earthworms, and waters and fertilizes media during breeding and growing period. Shovels worm-laden media onto screen, and shakes screen to separate worms. Counts earthworms, sorts them according to size, and packs them in containers.
GOE: 03.04.01 STRENGTH: M GED: R2 M1 L1 SVP: 1 DLU: 77

413.687-018   BEE WORKER (agriculture)
Attends bee colony to produce queen bees: Fits bar containing cell cups grafted with bee larvae into notched hive frame to prepare frame for placement in cell building hive in which bees form queen cells on cup base. Blows smoke into hive to quiet bees, using smoke producing device. Reads grafting date, opens hive, and inserts frame in sequence by date. Pulls out queen cell frame of specified age and places frame in incubator to continue maturation process. Opens hive and pours sugar on tops of frames to feed bees. Mixes and kneads specified types and quantities of ingredients to make bee candy. Presses piece of candy into end of queen shipping cage to provide food for queen and workers during shipping. May construct shipping cages. May select and collect queen bees meeting specified criteria for shipping.
GOE: 03.04.01 STRENGTH: M GED: R2 M1 L1 SVP: 2 DLU: 86

418   ANIMAL SERVICE OCCUPATIONS

This group includes occupations concerned with furnishing services in support of breeding, raising, caring for animals, and collecting their products.

418.137-010   SUPERVISOR, LABORATORY ANIMAL FACILITY (agriculture)
Supervises and coordinates activities of workers involved in operations of animal research facility: Plans budget and arranges purchase of items, such as animal feed, medicines, and research instruments. Advises workers regarding requirements of research projects and requirements for compliance with federal guidelines for operation of research facility. Instructs workers regarding procedures, such as feeding and cleaning schedules and compilation of data for research reports. Monitors care and health of animals. Reviews work of personnel to verify accuracy of research and reports and to determine established procedures are followed.
GOE: 02.04.02 STRENGTH: L GED: R4 M3 L4 SVP: 7 DLU: 86

418.137-014   SUPERVISOR, RESEARCH KENNEL (agriculture)
Supervises and coordinates activities of workers engaged in caring for domestic animals in research kennel: Directs and assists workers in maintaining kennel in prescribed condition and in feeding and caring for animals in conformance with research study requirements. Monitors progress of studies, such as animal food palatability and drug effectiveness tests, to verify adherence to study guidelines. Prepares activity charts to assist subordinates in performing

duties. Observes animals to detect signs of illness or injury and notifies designated personnel of unusual conditions. Compiles research study reports from log entries to prepare data for use by researchers, using calculator.
GOE: 03.02.01 STRENGTH: M GED: R3 M3 L3 SVP: 4 DLU: 86

418.381-010   HORSESHOER (agriculture) alternate titles: plater
Selects aluminum and steel shoes (plates) and fits, shapes, and nails shoes to animals' hooves: Removes worn or defective shoe from hoof, using nail snippers and pincers. Examines hoof to detect bruises and cracks and to determine trimming required. Trims and shapes hoof, using knife and snippers. Measures hoof, using calipers and steel tape. Selects aluminum or steel shoe from stock, according to hoof measurements and animal usage. Places leather pad, sponge, or oakum-pine tar mixture on bruised or cracked hoof for protection. Shapes shoe to fit hoof, using swage, forge, and hammer. Nails shoe to hoof and files hoof flush with shoe. May forge steel bar into shoe. May drive shop truck to work site.
GOE: 03.03.02 STRENGTH: M GED: R3 M2 L2 SVP: 6 DLU: 77

418.384-010   ARTIFICIAL INSEMINATOR (agriculture) alternate titles: inseminator
Injects prepared bull semen into vagina of cows to breed them: Observes animal in heat to detect approach of estrus. Selects semen specimen according to breeding chart and pours semen into breeding syringe. Cleans cow's vulva with soap, water, and antiseptic solution. Inserts nozzle of syringe into vagina and depresses syringe plunger to inject seminal fluid. Maintains log of semen specimens used and cows bred. May exercise animal to induce or hasten estrus.
GOE: 03.04.05 STRENGTH: M GED: R3 M3 L2 SVP: 3 DLU: 77

418.384-014   ARTIFICIAL-BREEDING TECHNICIAN (agriculture) alternate titles: breeding technician
Collects and packages bull semen for artificial insemination of cows: Attaches rubber collecting sheath to genital organ of tethered bull, and stimulates animal's organ to excite ejaculation. Examines semen, using microscope, to determine density and motility of gametes, and dilutes semen with prescribed diluents according to formulas. Transfers required amount of semen to container, using titration tube, and labels it with identifying data, such as date taken, source, quality, and concentration, and records similar data on file cards. Packs container of semen in dry ice or liquid nitrogen for freezing and storage or shipment. May inseminate cows [ARTIFICIAL INSEMINATOR (agriculture)].
GOE: 03.02.04 STRENGTH: L GED: R3 M3 L2 SVP: 6 DLU: 77

418.674-010   DOG GROOMER (personal ser.) alternate titles: dog beautician; dog-hair clipper
Combs, clips, trims, and shapes dogs' coats to groom dogs, using knowledge of canine characteristics and grooming techniques and styles: Reads written or receives oral instructions to determine clipping pattern desired. Places dog on grooming table and fits grooming collar on dog to hold animal to table. Studies proportions of dog to determine most appropriate cutting pattern to achieve desired style. Clips dog's hair according to determined pattern, using electric clippers, comb, and barber's shears. Combs and shapes dog's coat. Talks to dog or uses other techniques to calm animal.
GOE: 03.03.02 STRENGTH: M GED: R3 M2 L3 SVP: 4 DLU: 77

418.677-010   DOG BATHER (personal ser.)
Bathes dogs in preparation for grooming: Combs and cuts out heavy mats from dog's coat, using barber shears and steel comb. Brushes fur to remove dead skin, using dog brush. Draws bath water and regulates temperature. Washes dog, using perfumed soap or shampoo and handbrush and repeats process until dog is clean. Dries dog, using towel and electric drier. Cleans animals' quarters. May trim and shape dog's coat and clip toenails, using scissors and clippers.
GOE: 03.03.02 STRENGTH: L GED: R3 M2 L2 SVP: 2 DLU: 77

419   ANIMAL FARMING OCCUPATIONS, N.E.C.

This group includes occupations, not elsewhere classified, concerned with animal farming and related activities.

419.224-010   HORSE TRAINER (agriculture; amuse. & rec.)
Trains horses for riding, show, work, or racing: Feeds, exercises, grooms, and talks to horses to accustom them to human voice and contact. Talks to horses to calm and encourage them to follow lead, or standstill when hitched or groomed. Places tack or harness on horse to accustom horse to feel of equipment. Mounts and rides saddle horse to condition horse to respond to oral, spur, or rein command, according to knowledge of horse's temperament and riding technique. Hitches draft horse to wagon, sledge, or other horse drawn equipment and conditions horse to perform in single or multiple hitch, using rein and oral commands. Trains horses for show competition according to prescribed standards for gaits, form, manners, and performance, using knowledge of characteristics of different breeds and operating routines of horse shows. Retrains horses to break habits, such as kicking, bolting, and resisting bridling and grooming. Usually specializes in conditioning and developing horses of one breed only, or in training horses for one type of riding, driving, racing, or show activity. May train horses for racing, utilizing knowledge of training methods to plan training, according to peculiarities of each horse and instructs JOCKEY (amuse. & rec.) 153.244-010 on how to handle specific horse during race and

be designated Racehorse Trainer (amuse. & rec.). May train horses or other equines to carry pack loads and work as part of pack train. May arrange for mating of stallions and mares, and assist mares during foaling. May train horses as independent operator and advise owners on purchase of horses.
GOE: 03.03.01 STRENGTH: M GED: R3 M2 L2 SVP: 7 DLU: 77

42   MISCELLANEOUS AGRICULTURAL AND RELATED OCCUPATIONS

This division includes occupations concerned with activities which are not specifically related to either plant or animal agricultural activities or which may be concerned with a combination of both.

421   GENERAL FARMING OCCUPATIONS

This group includes occupations concerned with combined plant and animal farming.

421.161-010 FARMER, GENERAL (agriculture)
Raises both crops and livestock: Determines kinds and amounts of crops to be grown and livestock to be bred, according to market conditions, weather, and size and location of farm. Selects and purchases seed, fertilizer, farm machinery, livestock, and feed, and assumes responsibility for sale of crop and livestock products. Hires and directs workers engaged in planting, cultivating, and harvesting crops, such as corn, peas, potatoes, strawberries, apples, peanuts, and tobacco, and to raise livestock, such as cattle, sheep, swine, horses, and poultry. Performs various duties of farm workers, depending on size and nature of farm, including setting up and operating farm machinery.
GOE: 03.01.01 STRENGTH: H GED: R4 M4 L4 SVP: 7 DLU: 77

421.683-010 FARMWORKER, GENERAL I (agriculture) alternate titles: hired worker
Drives trucks and tractors and performs variety of animal and crop raising duties as directed on general farm: Plows, harrows, and fertilizes soil, and cultivates, sprays, and harvests crops, using variety of tractor-drawn machinery [FARM-MACHINE OPERATOR (agriculture)]. Cares for livestock and poultry, observing general condition and administering simple medications to animals and fowls. Hauls feed to livestock during grass shortage and winter months. Operates, repairs, and maintains implements and mechanical equipment, such as tractors, gang plows, ensilage cutters, hay balers, cottonpickers, and milking machines. Repairs farm buildings, fences, and other structures. May irrigate crops. May haul livestock and products to market [TRUCK DRIVER, HEAVY (any industry); TRUCK DRIVER, LIGHT (any industry)]. Usually works year-round and may oversee casual and seasonal help during planting and harvesting.
GOE: 03.04.01 STRENGTH: H GED: R3 M2 L3 SVP: 5 DLU: 77

421.687-010 FARMWORKER, GENERAL II (agriculture) alternate titles: chore tender; farm laborer
Performs variety of manual, animal-and-crop-raising tasks on general farm under close supervision: Feeds and waters cattle, poultry, and pets. Cleans barns, stables, pens, and kennels, using rake, shovel, water, and other cleaning materials. Digs seedlings, such as tobacco plants, strawberries, tomatoes, and orchard trees, using hoe, and transplants them by hand. Shovels earth to clear irrigation ditches and opens sluice gates to irrigate crops. Cleans plows, combines, and tractors, using scraper and broom. Picks, cuts, or pulls fruits and vegetables to harvest crop. Stacks loose hay, using pitchfork, or pitches hay into automatic baling machine. Stacks bales of hay and bucks them onto wagon or truck, using handhook.
GOE: 03.04.01 STRENGTH: H GED: R2 M1 L1 SVP: 2 DLU: 77

429   MISCELLANEOUS AGRICULTURAL AND RELATED OCCUPATIONS, N.E.C.

This group includes occupations, not elsewhere classified, concerned with miscellaneous agricultural and related occupations.

429.387-010 COTTON CLASSER (agriculture; textile) alternate titles: cotton grader
Classifies cotton according to grade, staple length, and character, employing knowledge of cotton fiber and standards for various grades as established by U.S. Department of Agriculture: Examines cotton sample to detect variations in color; foreign matter, such as pieces of bolls, leaves, or twigs; undeveloped seeds, sand, and dust; and preparation defects, such as gin-cut fibers and neps. Pulls layer of fibers from cotton sample with fingers to form rectangular tuft, places tuft on black background, and estimates or measures staple length, using cotton-stapling rule. Determines character (strength, uniformity, and cohesive quality) of fibers by pulling sample tuft apart between fingers, observing effort expanded in breaking sample, fineness of fibers, and drag as fibers cling to each other. Classifies fibers according to standards for various grades. May examine fibers through microscope to determine maturity and spirality of fibers. Records grade on bale identification tag and bale number and grade on shipping, receiving, or sales sheet.
GOE: 06.01.05 STRENGTH: L GED: R4 M3 L3 SVP: 7 DLU: 77

429.587-010 COTTON CLASSER AIDE (agriculture)
Performs any combination of following duties to assist COTTON CLASSER (agriculture; textile) 429.387-010: Records grades called out by COTTON

CLASSER (agriculture; textile) on sample classification certificates and related documents. Summarizes and tabulates classification results, using specified numeric symbols. Assembles classification certificates and other records for mailing to growers, government officials, and other designated recipients. Carries cotton samples to and from storage and grading areas. May assist in testing cotton samples.
GOE: 06.03.02 STRENGTH: L GED: R2 M1 L2 SVP: 2 DLU: 86

429.685-010 GINNER (agriculture)
Tends variety of machines, such as dryers, cleaners, gin stands, and linters, that dry, clean, and separate cotton lint from seed and waste material: Slides hand into seed chutes and removes accumulations of seed. Observes saw ribs in gin stand and linter screens to detect clogging. Removes cotton manually or using ginstick. Opens gas supply valve and pushes alarm switch to warn workers that machinery is starting. Pushes switches to start separator, vacuum, and trash fans; seed augers; linters; cleaners; and other auxillary equipment. Turns control knobs on automatic dryers to ignite fire and set drying temperature. Ascertains seed-handling instructions from seed tags, pulls ropes to open gates, allowing seeds to be deposited in hoppers according to instructions, and resets automatic seed-weighing counter. Pulls ropes to open suction gates and start suction that controls flow of cotton through equipment. Listens to sounds of running machinery, observes flow of seeds and cotton, feels cotton sample, and sniffs air to detect equipment malfunction and maladjustment and burning cotton. Stops machine and removes obstructions, adjusts dryer temperature, and regulates cotton feed to correct malfunctions, achieve optimum drying of cotton, and maintain maximum ginning capacity of machines. Closes suction gates after last bale of order has been ginned. Records seed weight and bale weight on report form. Periodically replaces worn and defective parts on machines. Lubricates motors, bearings, and other friction surfaces. May be identified with machines tended or with work performed, such as linting, cleaning, drying, and ginning.
GOE: 05.12.07 STRENGTH: L GED: R3 M1 L2 SVP: 4 DLU: 81

429.685-014 THRESHER, BROOMCORN (agriculture)
Tends machine that threshes and bales broomcorn straw: Cuts string or rubber band binding from sheaves of broomcorn straw, using knife, and feeds straw into threshing machine to remove seeds. Off bears straw from discharge end of threshing machine and drops straw into bucket to align straw. Hands bucket of aligned broomcorn straws to PRESS FEEDER, BROOMCORN (agriculture) who places straws in compression chamber of hydraulic press. Closes compression chamber and starts hydraulic press to compress broomcorn straws into bale. Ties wire around bale and pushes bale from chamber.
GOE: 03.04.01 STRENGTH: L GED: R2 M1 L1 SVP: 2 DLU: 77

429.686-010 PRESS FEEDER, BROOMCORN (agriculture)
Feeds hydraulic press that bales broomcorn straw: Places broomcorn in compression chamber of hydraulic press. Aligns stalks of straw in chamber to ensure that straws are not broken when compressed. Signals THRESHER, BROOMCORN (agriculture) to bale broomcorn straw.
GOE: 03.04.01 STRENGTH: L GED: R2 M1 L1 SVP: 2 DLU: 77

44   FISHERY AND RELATED OCCUPATIONS

This division includes occupations concerned with seeding, cultivating, transplanting, stocking, catching, or gathering aquatic life of any kind or their remains.

441   NET, SEINE, AND TRAP FISHERS

This group includes occupations concerned with catching or gathering aquatic animal life by use of such equipment as nets, traps, and pots.

441.132-010 BOATSWAIN, OTTER TRAWLER (fishing & hunt.)
Supervises and coordinates activities of fishing vessel crew engaged in deploying, retrieving, and repairing otter trawl net to catch fish, and operates winches to launch, tow, haul, hoist, and dump net: Confers with CAPTAIN, FISHING VESSEL (fishing & hunt.) 197.133-010 or MATE, FISHING VESSEL (fishing & hunt.) 197.133-018 to ascertain specified fishing depth, terrain of ocean floor, and location of fish concentrations, and selects required otter trawl net and other fishing gear accordingly. Directs crew in attachment of floats, weights, otter boards (net guides), and other gear to trawl net preparatory to net deployment. Directs lowering of net over side of vessel, and moves winch controls to release otter boards and tow cables into sea. Observes action of otter boards to ensure that net is tangle free and in desired position, and moves winch controls to maintain even alignment and designated depth of net behind vessel, according to markings on tow cables. Monitors tension on tow cables during tow and moves winch controls as necessary to free net when snagged on obstructions, such as rough bottom, rock pinnacles, or sunken ships. Moves winch controls to haul filled trawl net from sea bottom to ship's stern, and directs crew to specified stations for retrieval of net and dumping of fish onto deck. Trains and directs crew in maintenance of fishing gear, such as reinforcing or replacing frayed or missing sections of trawl net and splicing frayed or weakened tow cables.
GOE: 03.04.03 STRENGTH: H GED: R4 M2 L3 SVP: 7 DLU: 86

441.683-010 SKIFF OPERATOR (fishing & hunt.)
Operates seiner skiff to hold one end of purse seine in place while purse seiner circles school of fish to set net. Holds purse seine away from ship during

pursing and brailing operations. May splash water with pole, on opposite side of school away from purse seiner, to prevent fish from escaping as fish are encircled by purse seine. May locate schools of fish sighted by other fishers.
GOE: 03.04.03 STRENGTH: H GED: R3 M1 L2 SVP: 4 DLU: 77

441.684-010 FISHER, NET (fishing & hunt.)

Catches finfish, shellfish, and other marine life alone or as crewmember on shore or aboard fishing vessel, using equipment such as dip, diver, gill, hoop, lampara, pound, trap, reef, trammel, and trawl nets; purse seine; and haul, drag, or beach seine: Inserts and attaches hoops, rods, poles, ropes, floats, weights, beam runners, otter boards, and cables to form, reinforce, position, set, tow, and anchor net. Attaches flags and lights to buoys to identify net location. Puts net into water and anchors or tows net according to kind of net used, location of fishing area, and method of fishing. Hauls net to boat or ashore manually or using winch. Empties catch from net, using dip net, brail, buckets, hydraulic pump, and conveyor, and by lifting net, using block and tackle, and dumping catch. Stows catch in hold and containers, or transfers catch to base ship or buy boat. Fishing with some types of nets may be illegal in some states. May ride in skiff and hold end of net, as base ship discharges net, to surround school of fish or to pull net ends and trap fish. May sort and clean fish. May repair fishing nets and gear. May act as lookout or observe instruments to sight schools of fish. May be designated according to kind of net used as Fisher, Dip Net (fishing & hunt.); Fisher, Diver Net (fishing & hunt.); Fisher, Gill Net (fishing & hunt.); Fisher, Hoop Net (fishing & hunt.). May be designated: Fisher, Haul, Drag, Or Beach Seine (fishing & hunt.); Fisher, Lampara Net (fishing & hunt.); Fisher, Pound Net or Trap (fishing & hunt.); Fisher, Purse Seine (fishing & hunt.); Fisher, Reef Net (fishing & hunt.); Fisher, Trammel Net (fishing & hunt.); Fisher, Trawl Net (fishing & hunt.).
GOE: 03.04.03 STRENGTH: H GED: R2 M1 L1 SVP: 4 DLU: 77

441.684-014 FISHER, POT (fishing & hunt.)

Fishes for marine life, including crab, eel, or lobster, using pots (cages with funnel-shaped net openings): Ties marker float to line, attaches line to pot, fastens bait inside pot, and lowers pot into water. Hooks marker float with pole and pulls up pot. Reaches through hinged door of pot to remove catch or dumps catch on deck. Measures catch with fixed gauge to ensure compliance with legal size. Places legal catch in container and tosses illegal catch overboard. Places peg in hinge of claws to prevent lobsters, in container, from killing each other. May rig and lower dredge (rake scoop with bag net attached), drag dredge behind boat to gather marine life from water bottom, and hoist it to deck by hand or using block and tackle. May be designated according to type of marine life fished for as Fisher, Crab (fishing & hunt.); Fisher, Eel (fishing & hunt.); Fisher, Lobster (fishing & hunt.). May work alone or as member of crew.
GOE: 03.04.03 STRENGTH: V GED: R2 M1 L1 SVP: 2 DLU: 77

441.684-018 FISHER, TERRAPIN (fishing & hunt.)

Catches terrapins by stretching net across marsh, creek, or river and routing terrapins downstream or with tide into net. May pole skiff among grassy waters and catch terrapins with hand net. May catch terrapins by hand while wading in mud and probing with stick.
GOE: 03.04.03 STRENGTH: H GED: R2 M1 L1 SVP: 2 DLU: 77

441.684-022 FISHER, WEIR (fishing & hunt.) alternate titles: fisher, trap

Constructs weirs of brush or netting to catch fish: Drives poles and stakes in channels at points of land extending into water, between islands, or in rapids to form circular or heart-shaped enclosure. Fastens stringers and weaves brush or netting horizontally between posts and stakes. Constructs lead of brush to deflect fish into trap. Removes fish from weir with purse seine. This method of fishing is considered illegal in some states when navigation and conservation are obstructed.
GOE: 03.04.03 STRENGTH: H GED: R2 M1 L1 SVP: 4 DLU: 77

442 LINE FISHERS

This group includes occupations concerned with catching aquatic animal life by means of baited, hooked, and entangling lines.

442.684-010 FISHER, LINE (fishing & hunt.) alternate titles: fisher

Catches fish and other marine life with hooks and lines, working alone or as member of crew: Lays out line and attaches hooks, bait, sinkers, and various anchors, floats, and swivels, depending on quarry sought. Puts line in water, and holds, anchors, or trolls (tows) line to catch fish. Hauls line onto boat deck or ashore by hand, reel, or winch, and removes catch. Stows catch in hold or boxes and packs catch in ice. May hit fish with club to stun it before removing it from hook. May fish with gaff to assist in hauling fish from water. May slit fish, remove viscera, and wash cavity to clean fish for storage. May steer vessel in fishing area. When fishing with line held in hand, is designated Fisher, Hand Line (fishing & hunt.). When fishing with fixed line equipped with hooks hung at intervals on line, is designated according to whether line is trawl (anchored in water at both ends) as Fisher, Trawl Line (fishing & hunt.); or trot (reaching across stream or from one bank) as Fisher, Trot Line (fishing & hunt.). When fishing with line that is trolled, is designated Fisher, Troll Line (fishing & hunt.).

GOE: 03.04.03 STRENGTH: M GED: R2 M1 L1 SVP: 3 DLU: 77

443 FISHERS, MISCELLANEOUS EQUIPMENT

This group includes occupations concerned with catching and gathering aquatic animal life by means of equipment other than that used in Groups 441 and 442.

443.664-010 FISHER, DIVING (fishing & hunt.)

Gathers or harvests marine life, such as sponges, abalone, pearl oysters, and geoducks from sea bottom, wearing wet suit and scuba gear, or diving suit with air line extending to surface: Climbs overboard or is lowered into water from boat by lifeline. Picks up pearl oysters; tears sponges from sea bottom; pries abalone from rocks, using bar; and flushes geoducks from sand, using air gun connected to air compressor on boat. Places catch in bag or basket and tugs on line to have catch pulled to boat, or surfaces and empties catch on boat or in container. Signals other workers to extend or retract air lines. May monitor air lines and operate air compressor as alternating member of diving crew. May be designated according to quarry sought as Abalone Diver (fishing & hunt.); Geoduck Diver (fishing & hunt.); Pearl Diver (fishing & hunt.); Sponge Diver (fishing & hunt.).
GOE: 03.04.03 STRENGTH: H GED: R3 M2 L2 SVP: 4 DLU: 77

443.684-010 FISHER, SPEAR (fishing & hunt.) alternate titles: harpooner, fish; spearer

Catches fish, such as eels, salmon, and swordfish, using barbed spear: Spears fish from platform built in stream or on river bank or from fishing vessel, using harpoon attached to buoy by rope, and allows fish to tire. Hoists fish from water, using gaff. Kills swordfish with club, rifle, or gaff. May be designated according to gear used as Fisher, Eel Spear (fishing & hunt.); Gaffer (fishing & hunt.); Harpooner (fishing & hunt.); or according to quarry sought as Fisher, Swordfish (fishing & hunt.).
GOE: 03.04.03 STRENGTH: H GED: R2 M1 L1 SVP: 4 DLU: 77

446 AQUATIC LIFE CULTIVATION AND RELATED OCCUPATIONS

This group includes occupations concerned with such activities as breeding, caring for, planting, transplanting, harvesting, or transferring (stocking with) aquatic animals or plant life. Includes developing and maintaining the subsistence environment of such life.

446.133-010 SUPERVISOR, SHELLFISH FARMING (fishing & hunt.)

Supervises and coordinates activities of workers engaged in planting, cultivating, and harvesting shellfish: Confers with manager to determine time and place of seed planting, cultivating, feeding, and harvesting shellfish. Plans work schedules according to tidal levels, and availability of personnel and equipment. Inspects beds and ponds to ascertain the quality of seed distribution, adequacy of cultivation, and completeness of harvesting, and directs workers to correct deviations and irregularities. Oversees maintenance of planting, cultivating, and harvesting equipment, *tidal pens,* and shellfish beds. Trains worker to drive or operate equipment, and in methods and techniques of shellfish farming. Performs other duties as described under SUPERVISOR (any industry) Master Title. May assign workers to guard pens and beds against encroachment. May record planting and harvesting data, and keep workers' time records. May supervise workers engaged in farming a specific type of shellfish and be designated Supervisor, Clam-Bed (fishing & hunt.); Supervisor, Oyster Farm (fishing & hunt.); Supervisor, Shrimp Pond (fishing & hunt.).
GOE: 03.02.01 STRENGTH: M GED: R4 M2 L3 SVP: 6 DLU: 77

446.134-010 SUPERVISOR, FISH HATCHERY (fishing & hunt.)

Supervises and coordinates activities of workers engaged in trapping and spawning fish, incubating eggs, and rearing fry in fish hatchery: Assigns workers in collecting, fertilizing and incubating of spawn, and transferring of fingerlings to rearing ponds and tanks. Oversees treatment and rearing of fingerlings. Observes appearance and actions of developing fish to detect diseases, and specifies medications to be added to food and water. Coordinates work schedule and directs workers to feed, sort, and transfer fish to designated ponds, streams, or commercial holding tanks. Trains workers in methods of spawning and rearing fish. Records number and type of fish reared, released, or sold. Performs other duties as described under SUPERVISOR (any industry) Master Title. May supervise workers engaged in rearing food fish or tropical and exotic fish and be designated Supervisor, Commercial Fish Hatchery (fishing & hunt.).
GOE: 03.02.01 STRENGTH: M GED: R4 M2 L3 SVP: 7 DLU: 77

446.161-010 FISH FARMER (fishing & hunt.)

Spawns and raises fish for commercial purposes: Strips eggs from female fish and places eggs in moist pans. Adds milt stripped from male fish to fertilize eggs. Fills hatchery trays with fertilized eggs and places trays in incubation troughs. Turns valves and places baffles in troughs to adjust volume, depth, velocity, and temperature of water. Transfers fingerlings to rearing ponds. Feeds high protein foods or cereal with vitamins and minerals to fingerlings to induce growth to size desired for commercial use. Arranges with buyers for sale of fish. Removes fish from pond, using dip net. Counts and weighs fish. Loads fish into tank truck, or dresses and packs in ice for shipment. May perform

standard tests on water samples to determine oxygen content. May be designated according to kind of fish raised as Trout Farmer (fishing & hunt.).
GOE: 03.01.02 STRENGTH: M GED: R4 M1 L2 SVP: 6 DLU: 77

446.161-014 SHELLFISH GROWER (fishing & hunt.) alternate titles: oyster culturist

Cultivates and harvests beds of shellfish, such as clams and oysters: Lays out and stakes tide flats (ground beneath shallow water near shoreline). Piles up stone, poles, and mud, using farm tractor and hand implements to make dikes to control water drainage at low tide. Removes debris by hand and levels soil with tractor and harrow. Sows spat by hand or with shovel or sets out strings or baskets of shells onto which spat attaches. Covers seeded area with mixture of sand and broken shells or transfers seeded strings or baskets to growing area. Rigs net or star mop (mop of heavy rope yarn) and drags it over bed behind power boat to entangle and remove shellfish predators, such as crabs and starfish. Walks about bed at low tide, and scoops or digs shellfish and piles them onto barge or mud sled, using pitchfork or shovel. Packs shellfish, according to market specifications, in containers and returns small ones to bed. Poles barge to wharf at high tide or pulls it, using boat. Drags mud sled from bed, using tractor. May pour oil around bed and spread oil-treated sand over bed with shovel to form chemical barrier to shellfish predators. May reach from boat with rake-tongs and grope for shellfish by moving handles to open and close tongs. May supervise workers who cultivate and harvest bed. May negotiate with buyers for sale of crop. May be designated according to type of shellfish grown as Clam Grower (fishing & hunt.); Oyster Grower (fishing & hunt.).
GOE: 03.01.02 STRENGTH: M GED: R4 M1 L2 SVP: 6 DLU: 77

446.663-010 SHELLFISH DREDGE OPERATOR (fishing & hunt.) alternate titles: shellfish harvester

Drives and operates mechanical or hydraulic dredge to cultivate, transplant, and harvest marine life, such as oysters, clams, and sea grass: Steers dredge to designated area, using navigational aids, such as compass and landmarks, and knowledge of tides, or is towed by other vessel. Fastens water pressure hoses, lifting and towing cables, and dredge baskets to dredge, using handtools. Primes pumps and adjusts angle of water jets and conveyor, to prepare for dredging. Activates dredge engine and lowers dredge baskets or hydraulic dredger to sea bottom, using hoisting boom and winch. Activates hydraulic dredge impeller pumps and conveyor and drags hydraulic dredger or dredge baskets along sea bottom to scoop or flush shellfish from beds. Inspects contents dumped from dredges onto deck to determine depth of cut into sea bottom, and adjusts water pressure or angle of basket blade to attain depth of cut desired. Observes flow of shellfish on conveyor and stops conveyor to prevent or clear jamming. Observes and listens to operation of equipment to detect malfunction and makes adjustments and minor repairs to correct operational defects. Attaches cutting blades or harrows to dredge and lowers to specified distance above or on sea bottom and steers dredge in diminishing circles to cultivate shellfish beds or cut sea grass. May record date, harvest area, and yield in logbook. May direct helpers in sorting of clams. May be designated according to type of dredge operated as Hydraulic Dredge Operator (fishing & hunt.); Self-Propelled Dredge Operator (fishing & hunt.); or kind of shellfish harvested as Clam Dredge Operator (fishing & hunt.); Oyster Dredge Operator (fishing & hunt.).
GOE: 03.04.03 STRENGTH: H GED: R3 M2 L2 SVP: 5 DLU: 77

446.684-010 FISH HATCHERY WORKER (fishing & hunt.) alternate titles: fish hatchery assistant; fish hatchery attendant

Performs any combination of following tasks to trap and spawn game fish, incubate eggs, and rear fry in fish hatchery: Secures net on both banks of river to divert fish to holding pond. Catches ripened fish from holding pond with hand net and squeezes or slits bellies of female fish to release eggs in pail. Squeezes bellies of male fish to force milt over eggs, and stirs with rubber-gloved hand to fertilize eggs. Fills hatchery trays with fertilized eggs and places trays in incubation troughs. Turns valves and places baffles in troughs to adjust volume, depth, velocity, and temperature of water. Inspects eggs and picks out dead, infertile, and off-color eggs, using suction syringe. Sorts fish according to size, coloring, and species and transfers fingerlings to rearing ponds or tanks, using buckets or tank truck. Scatters food over surface of water by hand or activates blower that automatically scatters food over water to feed fish. Observes appearance and actions of developing fish to detect diseases, and adds medications to food and water as instructed by superior. Transfers mature fish to rivers and lakes, using tank truck. Records field data and prepares reports of hatchery activities. Drains and cleans ponds and troughs, using brushes, chemicals, and water. Makes minor repairs to hatchery equipment, paints buildings, and maintains grounds. May spawn and rear food fish or tropical and exotic fish for commercial use. May mark migrating fish with liquid nitrogen, using hand-operated branding device.
GOE: 03.04.03 STRENGTH: M GED: R3 M1 L2 SVP: 5 DLU: 77

446.684-014 SHELLFISH-BED WORKER (fishing & hunt.) alternate titles: bed worker

Cultivates and harvests shellfish by performing any combination of following duties: Loads marking stakes on barge, and moves barge to shellfish bed. Drives stakes into mud in pattern specified by SHELLFISH GROWER (fishing & hunt.), using sledgehammer. Sows spat by scattering it within staked enclosure. Covers seeded area with mixture of sand and broken shells of shellfish onto which spat attaches, using shovel. Wades in shellfish bed and digs or rakes for shellfish, using rake, fork, and spade. Treads in water and feels for shellfish

with bare feet, gathers shellfish, and drops them into container. Reaches from boat with rake-tongs and gropes for shellfish by moving handles to open and close tongs. Drags brail rod (pipe with series of hooks attached) behind power-boat to pull shellfish from mud. Rigs and lowers dredge into shellfish bed from mast and boom of powerboat, using block and tackle. Hoists dredge and pulls dump ring to empty catch. Picks out market-size shellfish from catch, and replants smaller ones. Packs and ices marketable shellfish in containers for shipment. Unloads loose shellfish from boat, using shovel. May be designated according to type of shellfish bed worked as Clam-Bed Worker (fishing & hunt.); Oyster-Bed Worker (fishing & hunt.); shellfish harvested as Fisher, Clam (fishing & hunt.); Fisher, Oyster (fishing & hunt.); or task performed as Clam Digger (fishing & hunt.); Oyster Unloader (fishing & hunt.). May be designated: Clam Tonger (fishing & hunt.); Clam Treader (fishing & hunt.); Fisher, Mussel (fishing & hunt.); Fisher, Quahog (fishing & hunt.); Fisher, Scallop (fishing & hunt.); Oyster Dredger (fishing & hunt.); Oyster Picker (fishing & hunt.); Oyster Tonger (fishing & hunt.); Oyster Worker (fishing & hunt.); Scallop Dredger (fishing & hunt.); Scallop Raker (fishing & hunt.).
GOE: 03.04.03 STRENGTH: H GED: R2 M1 L1 SVP: 3 DLU: 77

446.684-018 SOFT CRAB SHEDDER (fishing & hunt.)

Raises soft-shell crabs for food markets by catching crabs from sea and retaining them in tanks until they molt: Catches crabs, using lines [FISHER, LINE (fishing & hunt.)] or pots [FISHER, POT (fishing & hunt.)]. Sorts crabs according to stages of shell development and dumps them into open tanks containing sea water. Starts pumps to aerate water and maintain constant flow of sea water through tanks. Observes crabs to ascertain when they begin to shed their brittle outer shell. Holds shell being shed, when necessary, to assist emerging crab that gets hung in shell during molting. Gathers freshly emerged soft-shell crabs and places them in containers for shipment to market.
GOE: 03.04.03 STRENGTH: M GED: R2 M1 L1 SVP: 4 DLU: 77

446.687-010 CLAM SORTER (fishing & hunt.)

Removes marketable clams from conveyor belt or from pile on deck of clam-harvesting dredge and deposits them in containers. Dumps clams from containers onto worktable or deck, and sorts and packs them in containers for shipping according to species. May assist SHELLFISH DREDGE OPERATOR (fishing & hunt.) in adjustment, repair, and maintenance of dredge and conveyor equipment, using handtools.
GOE: 03.04.03 STRENGTH: H GED: R2 M1 L2 SVP: 2 DLU: 77

446.687-014 LABORER, AQUATIC LIFE (fishing & hunt.)

Performs any combination of following tasks related to cultivating, growing, and harvesting or gathering shellfish, finfish, amphibians, and other marine life: Stakes or fences ponds and growing areas following specified pattern to lay out planting bed. Sows spat on sea bottom and covers with sand and shell mixture. Patrols shrimp ponds and *tidal pens* on foot or by motorboat to detect presence of predators. Transfers finfish from tanks to rearing ponds, using dip net. Scatters food over growing area by hand or using blower. Wades in water or drives boat to harvest area. Collects marine life, using gill net, brail, shovel, or tongs. Rigs and lowers dredge baskets, using block and tackle, and raises to empty catch. Picks out marketable marine life and places in container, returning illegal catch to sea. Packs and ices catch for shipment. Unloads catch from boat deck, using conveyor, basket, or shovel. Strings empty oyster shells (used for growing-media) on wire or places in basket. Cleans ponds and tanks, and repairs screens, retaining walls, and fences. Removes debris, seaweed, and predators from water to maintain growing area. May be designated according to type of marine life worked as Clam-Bed Laborer (fishing & hunt.); Fish Hatchery Laborer (fishing & hunt.); Oyster-Bed Laborer (fishing & hunt.); Shrimp Pond Laborer (fishing & hunt.).
GOE: 03.04.03 STRENGTH: H GED: R2 M1 L1 SVP: 2 DLU: 77

447 SPONGE AND SEAWEED GATHERERS

This group includes occupations concerned with gathering sponge and seaweed by any means not involving the use of underwater breathing equipment.

447.684-010 SPONGE HOOKER (fishing & hunt.) alternate titles: fisher, sponge hooking; hooker

Gathers sponges from sea bottom, using pronged hook attached to end of pole, wading or using boat: Sights sponge, using water glass (bucket or tube with transparent bottom), inserts hook into base of sponge, and pulls hook to tear sponge from its attachment. Lifts hook and removes sponge.
GOE: 03.04.03 STRENGTH: L GED: R2 M1 L1 SVP: 2 DLU: 77

447.687-010 DULSER (fishing & hunt.)

Gathers dulse from rocks at low tide and spreads it on beach to dry.
GOE: 03.04.03 STRENGTH: L GED: R1 M1 L1 SVP: 2 DLU: 77

447.687-014 IRISH-MOSS BLEACHER (fishing & hunt.)

Bleaches Irish moss, gathered by IRISH-MOSS GATHERER (fishing & hunt.), by pouring buckets of salt water over moss in tubs. Spreads moss along beach to dry and bleach.
GOE: 03.04.03 STRENGTH: L GED: R2 M1 L1 SVP: 2 DLU: 77

447.687-018 IRISH-MOSS GATHERER (fishing & hunt.)

Gathers Irish moss from rocks by hand or by use of rake, and hauls it into boat. Transfers moss to beach where it is washed and bleached by IRISH-MOSS BLEACHER (fishing & hunt.).

GOE: 03.04.03 STRENGTH: L GED: R1 M1 L1 SVP: 2 DLU: 77

447.687-022 KELP CUTTER (fishing & hunt.)
Gathers kelp from sea bottom, using mower (cutter equipped with oscillating knives): Lowers mower into water from kelp-harvesting boat, and starts mower to cut kelp. Attaches grabhook of winch to kelp after kelp is dropped into bow of boat during harvesting so that kelp can be pulled back to keep load evenly distributed as kelp accumulates in boat.
GOE: 03.04.03 STRENGTH: H GED: R2 M1 L1 SVP: 2 DLU: 77

447.687-026 SPONGE CLIPPER (fishing & hunt.; wholesale tr.)
Cleans sponges of foreign particles, such as shells and coral fragments, and sorts sponges according to size for packing: Clips torn or irregular parts from sponge, with shears, measures size of sponge with go-not-go gauge, and tosses sponge into specified pile according to size. May cut sponge into specified size, using serrated knife.
GOE: 03.04.03 STRENGTH: L GED: R2 M1 L1 SVP: 2 DLU: 77

449 FISHERY AND RELATED OCCUPATIONS, N.E.C.

This group includes occupations, not elsewhere classified, concerned with fishery and related occupations.

449.664-010 NET REPAIRER (fishing & hunt.) alternate titles: rigger; web worker
Assembles and repairs nets on shore and aboard ship: Assembles, ties, and adjusts various webbing material, floats, weights, rings, and ropes to make gill nets, purse seines, *reef nets*, and trawls, using knife and twine-filled bobbin shuttle. Hoists net into ship's rigging to dry after fishing operations, using block and tackle, and repairs holes and tears in webbing. Gives direction to workers engaged in taking down nets. May retrieve lost nets from water. May participate in fishing [FISHER, NET (fishing & hunt.)].
GOE: 05.10.01 STRENGTH: H GED: R3 M1 L2 SVP: 6 DLU: 77

449.667-010 DECKHAND, FISHING VESSEL (fishing & hunt.)
Performs any combination of following duties aboard fishing vessel: Stands lookout, steering, and engine-room watches. Attaches nets, slings, hooks, and other lifting devices to cables, booms, and hoists. Loads equipment and supplies aboard vessel by hand or using hoisting equipment. Signals other workers to move, hoist, and position loads. Rows boats and dinghies and operates skiffs to transport fishers, divers, and sponge hookers and to tow and position nets. Attaches accessories, such as floats, weights, and markers to nets and lines. Pulls and guides nets and lines onto vessel. Removes fish from nets and hooks. Sorts and cleans marine life and returns undesirable and illegal catch to sea. Places catch in containers and stows in hold and covers with salt and ice. Washes deck, conveyors, knives and other equipment, using brush, detergent, and water. Lubricates, adjusts, and makes minor repairs to engines and equipment. Secures and removes vessel's docking lines to and from docks and other vessels. May be designated according to type of vessel worked as Deckhand, Clam Dredge (fishing & hunt.); Deckhand, Crab Boat (fishing & hunt.); Deckhand, Oyster Dredge (fishing & hunt.); Deckhand, Shrimp Boat (fishing & hunt.); Deckhand, Sponge Boat (fishing & hunt.); Deckhand, Tuna Boat (fishing & hunt.).
GOE: 03.04.03 STRENGTH: H GED: R2 M1 L1 SVP: 3 DLU: 77

449.674-010 AQUARIST (amuse. & rec.) alternate titles: aquarium tank attendant
Attends fish and other aquatic life in aquarium exhibits: Prepares food and feeds fish according to schedule. Cleans tanks and removes algae from tank windows. Attends to aquatic plants and decorations in displays. Collects and compares water samples to color-coded chart for acid analysis and monitors thermometers to ascertain water temperature. Adjusts thermostat and adds chemicals to water to maintain specified water conditions. Observes fish to detect disease and injuries, reports condition to supervisor, and treats fish according to instructions. May fire sedation gun and assist crew expedition members in collection of aquatic life.
GOE: 03.03.02 STRENGTH: L GED: R3 M2 L2 SVP: 4 DLU: 77

449.687-010 OYSTER FLOATER (fishing & hunt.)
Spreads freshly harvested oysters in shallow barge or float so constructed that water flows over oysters to afford temporary oyster storage. Oysters taken from beds exposed to sewage are usually floated in water of specified degree of salinity as designated by health authorities until oysters are free of impurities.
GOE: 03.04.03 STRENGTH: L GED: R1 M1 L1 SVP: 1 DLU: 77

45 FORESTRY OCCUPATIONS

This division includes occupations concerned with developing, maintaining, cultivating, and protecting forests, forest tracts and woodlands, and harvesting their products. Cultivating ornamental trees, shrubs, and flowers is included in Group 405.

451 TREE FARMING AND RELATED OCCUPATIONS

This group includes occupations concerned with raising tree seedlings for reforestation purposes; and planting, pruning, and harvesting Christmas trees.

Planting of tree seedlings in forested areas and woodlands is included in Group 452.

451.137-010 FOREST NURSERY SUPERVISOR (forestry)
Supervises and coordinates activities of workers engaged in planting, cultivating, and harvesting seedling forest trees and grading, bundling, baling, or otherwise packing trees for storage or shipment at forest nursery. Performs duties as described under SUPERVISOR (any industry) Master Title.
GOE: 03.02.02 STRENGTH: L GED: R4 M3 L3 SVP: 6 DLU: 77

451.137-014 SUPERVISOR, CHRISTMAS-TREE FARM (forestry) alternate titles: crew boss
Supervises and coordinates activities of workers engaged in planting, shearing, thinning, and harvesting Christmas trees on company-owned or leased land tracts: Tours land tracts to ascertain conditions and estimate work-hour requirements to plant, cultivate, or harvest trees. Confers with management to report conditions of lands and crops, recommend actions to be taken, and obtain instructions regarding variety and number of trees per acre to plant, cultural practices to apply, and harvesting date and location. Trains workers in planting, shearing, or harvesting trees. Performs duties as described under SUPERVISOR (any industry) Master Title.
GOE: 03.02.01 STRENGTH: L GED: R3 M2 L2 SVP: 5 DLU: 77

451.687-010 CHRISTMAS-TREE FARM WORKER (forestry)
Plants, cultivates, and harvests evergreen trees on Christmas-tree farm: Removes brush, ferns, and other growth from planting area, using mattock and brush-hook. Plants seedlings, using mattock or dibble [TREE PLANTER (forestry)]. Scatters fertilizer pellets over planted areas by hand. Shears tops and limb tips from trees, using machete and pruning shears, to control growth, increase limb density, and improve shape. Selects trees for cutting according to markings or size, specie, and grade, and fells trees, using ax or chain saw. Drags cut trees from cutting area, and loads trees onto trucks. May be designated according to seasonal task performed.
GOE: 03.04.01 STRENGTH: H GED: R1 M1 L1 SVP: 2 DLU: 77

451.687-014 CHRISTMAS-TREE GRADER (forestry)
Grades and tags trees in sorting yard of Christmas tree farm: Gauges height of tree, using marked increments on conveyor belt. Turns tree, examines limbs and foliage for color and growth pattern, and determines grade according to standards chart. Staples color-coded grade tags to tree limbs, using hand stapler.
GOE: 03.04.04 STRENGTH: M GED: R2 M1 L1 SVP: 3 DLU: 77

451.687-018 SEEDLING PULLER (forestry) alternate titles: tree puller
Harvests tree seedlings in forest nursery: Walks along seedling tree rows, stoops, and pulls clumps of seedlings from loosened soil. Knocks clumps together to dislodge soil and loosen roots, and places seedlings in field trays.
GOE: 03.04.02 STRENGTH: M GED: R1 M1 L1 SVP: 1 DLU: 77

451.687-022 SEEDLING SORTER (forestry) alternate titles: tree sorter
Sorts tree seedlings in forest nursery: Removes seedlings from field trays, separates them, and compares root formation, stem development, and foliage condition with standards chart and verbal instructions. Discards substandard seedlings and places remainder on conveyor for baling.
GOE: 03.04.02 STRENGTH: L GED: R1 M1 L1 SVP: 2 DLU: 77

452 FOREST CONSERVATION OCCUPATIONS

This group includes occupations concerned with planting tree seedlings; pruning and thinning trees to improve quality of stand; locating and combating fires, insects, pests, and diseases harmful to trees; and controlling erosion and leaching of forest soil.

452.134-010 SMOKE JUMPER SUPERVISOR (forestry)
Supervises and coordinates activities of airborne fire-fighting crews engaged in extinguishing forest fires: Dispatches crews according to reported size, location, and conditions of fires. Directs loading of fire suppression equipment into aircraft and parachuting of equipment to crews on ground. Maintains aerial observation and radio communication with crews at fire scene to determine equipment and work force requirements, learn of any casualties, and inform crews and base camp of changing conditions. Parachutes to major fire locations and directs suppression activities. Explains and demonstrates parachute jumping, fire suppression, aerial observation, and radio communications to workers. Performs duties as described under SUPERVISOR (any industry) Master Title.
GOE: 04.02.04 STRENGTH: V GED: R3 M2 L3 SVP: 8 DLU: 77

452.167-010 FIRE WARDEN (forestry)
Administers fire prevention programs and enforces governmental fire regulations throughout assigned forest and logging areas: Inspects logging areas and forest tracts for fire hazards, such as accumulated wastes, hazardous storage or mishandling of fuels and solvents, defective engine exhaust systems, and unshielded electrical equipment. Examines and inventories water supplies and firefighting equipment, such as axes, firehoses, pumps, buckets, and chemical fire extinguishers to determine condition, amount, adequacy, and placement of materials with respect to governmental regulations and company rules. Prepares reports of conditions observed, issues directives and instructions for correcting violations, and reinspects areas to verify compliance. Directs maintenance and repair of firefighting tools and equipment and requisitions new equipment and materials to replace expended, lost, and broken items or add to inventory as

required. Restricts public access and recreational use of forest lands during critical fire season. Gives directions to crew section on fireline during forest fire. May direct FIRE RANGERS (forestry).
GOE: 04.01.02 STRENGTH: L GED: R5 M3 L3 SVP: 7 DLU: 77

452.364-010 FORESTER AIDE (forestry) alternate titles: forest technician

Compiles data pertaining to size, content, condition, and other characteristics of forest tracts, under direction of FORESTER (profess. & kin.) 040.061-034; and leads workers in forest propagation, fire prevention and suppression, and facilities maintenance: Traverses forest in designated pattern to gather basic forest data, such as topographical features, species and population of trees, wood units available for harvest, disease and insect damage, tree seedling mortality, and conditions constituting fire danger. Marks trees of specified specie, condition, and size for thinning or logging. Collects and records data from instruments, such as rain gauge, thermometer, stream-flow recorder, and soil moisture gauge. Holds stadia rod, clears survey line, measures distances, records survey data, and performs related duties to assist in surveying property lines, timber sale boundaries, and road and recreation sites. Trains and leads conservation workers in seasonal activities, such as planting tree seedlings, collecting seed cones, suppressing fires, cleaning and maintaining recreational facilities, and clearing fire breaks and access roads. Gives instructions to visitors of forest, and enforces camping, vehicle use, fire building, sanitation, and other forest regulations.
GOE: 03.02.02 STRENGTH: M GED: R4 M3 L3 SVP: 6 DLU: 82

452.364-014 SMOKE JUMPER (forestry)

Parachutes from airplane into forest inaccessible by ground to suppress forest fires: Jumps from airplane near scene of fire, pulls rip cord when clear of plane, and pulls shroud lines to guide direction of fall toward clear landing area. Orients self in relation to fire, using compass and map, and collects supplies and equipment dropped by parachute. Ascertains best method for attacking fire and communicates plan to airplane or base camp with two-way radio. Fells trees, digs trenches, and extinguishes flames and embers to suppress fire, using ax, chain saw, shovel, and hand or engine-driven water or chemical pumps. May pack parachutes [PARACHUTE RIGGER (air trans.)].
GOE: 04.02.04 STRENGTH: V GED: R3 M2 L2 SVP: 6 DLU: 77

452.367-010 FIRE LOOKOUT (forestry) alternate titles: watcher, lookout tower

Locates and reports forest fires and weather phenomena from remote fire-lookout station: Maintains surveillance from station to detect evidence of fires and observe weather conditions. Locates fires on area map, using azimuth sighter and known landmarks, estimates size and characteristics of fire, and reports findings to base camp by radio or telephone. Observes instruments and reports daily meterological data, such as temperature, relative humidity, wind direction and velocity, and type of cloud formations. Relays messages from base camp, mobile units, and law enforcement and governmental agencies relating to weather forecasts, fire hazard conditions, emergencies, accidents, and location of crews and personnel. Explains state and federal laws, timber company policies, fire hazard conditions, and fire prevention methods to visitors of forest. Maintains records and logbooks.
GOE: 07.04.05 STRENGTH: L GED: R3 M2 L3 SVP: 5 DLU: 77

452.367-014 FIRE RANGER (forestry)

Patrols assigned area of forest to locate and report fires and hazardous conditions and to ensure compliance with fire regulations by travelers and campers: Hikes or drives to vista points to scan for fires and unusual or dangerous conditions. Reports findings and receives and relays emergency calls, using telephone or two-way radio. Visits camping sites to inspect activities of campers and ensure compliance with forest use and fire regulations. Gives instructions regarding sanitation, fire, and related forest regulations. Extinguishes smaller fires with portable extinguisher, shovel, and ax. Serves as crew leader for larger fires. Renders assistance or first aid to lost or injured persons. Participates in search for lost travelers or campers.
GOE: 04.02.02 STRENGTH: M GED: R3 M2 L3 SVP: 4 DLU: 77

452.687-010 FOREST WORKER (forestry)

Performs variety of tasks to reforest and protect timber tracts and maintain forest facilities, such as roads and campsites: Plants tree seedlings in specified pattern, using mattock, planting hoe, or dibble. Cuts out diseased, weak, or undesirable trees, and prunes limbs of young trees to deter knot growth, using handsaw, powersaw, and pruning tools. Fells trees, clears brush from fire breaks, and extinguishes flames and embers to suppress forest fires, using chain saw, shovel, and engine-driven or hand pumps. Clears and piles brush, limbs, and other debris from roadsides, fire trails, and camping areas, using ax, mattock, or brush hook. Sprays or injects trees, brush, and weeds with herbicides, using hand or powered sprayers or tree injector tool. Erects signs and fences, using posthole digger, shovel, tamper, or other handtools. Replenishes firewood and other supplies, and cleans kitchens, rest rooms, and campsites or recreational facilities. Holds measuring tape or survey rod, carries and sets stakes, clears brush from sighting line, and performs related tasks to assist forest survey crew.
GOE: 03.04.02 STRENGTH: H GED: R2 M1 L1 SVP: 2 DLU: 77

452.687-014 FOREST-FIRE FIGHTER (forestry) alternate titles: fire crew worker; smoke eater

Suppresses forest fires, working alone or as member of crew: Fells trees, cuts and clears brush, digs trenches, and extinguishes flames and embers to contain or suppress fire, using ax, chain saw, shovel, and hand- or engine-driven water pumps. Patrols burned area after fire to watch for hot spots that may restart fire. When leading and directing fire-fighting activities of a crew of workers, may be designated Suppression-Crew Leader (forestry).
GOE: 03.04.02 STRENGTH: H GED: R2 M1 L1 SVP: 2 DLU: 77

452.687-018 TREE PLANTER (forestry)

Plants seedling trees to reforest timber lands or Christmas tree farms: Digs planting hole at predetermined spaced interval, using mattock-like tool or dibble. Places seedling in hole and packs soil around plant, using foot or planting tool.
GOE: 03.04.02 STRENGTH: H GED: R1 M1 L1 SVP: 1 DLU: 77

453 OCCUPATIONS IN HARVESTING FOREST PRODUCTS, EXCEPT LOGGING

This group includes occupations concerned with gathering from forests and woodlands such products as ferns, mistletoe, barks, moss, seed cones, gums, resins, saps, and wild nuts and berries.

453.687-010 FOREST-PRODUCTS GATHERER (agriculture; forestry)

Gathers decorative greens, medicinal plants and barks, tree cones, moss, or other wild plant life from forest by hand or using handtools, such as pruning shears, knife, or shovel. Bundles or sacks products and delivers them to buyer. May climb trees to reach cones and boughs, using climbing belt and climbing spurs. May sort gathered plant life by size or species. May be designated according to product gathered as Cascara-Bark Cutter (forestry); Decorative Greens Cutter (forestry); Medicinal-Plant Picker (agriculture); Moss Picker (agriculture); Seed-Cone Picker (forestry).
GOE: 03.04.02 STRENGTH: M GED: R2 M1 L1 SVP: 2 DLU: 77

453.687-014 LABORER, TREE TAPPING (agriculture; forestry)

Performs any combination of following tasks to collect sugar, oleoresin, or other tree sap: Cuts or bores tap in face of tree, using auger, ax, hack (hook-shaped tool) or other handtool. Inserts spout or trough into tap and hangs or nails receptacle under tap. Dumps filled receptacles into collection barrel, tank, or similar container and transports to central collection point. May gather scrape (hardened gum) at end of season, using hand scraper. May rake leaves and other debris to clear trees for tapping and lessen fire hazard.
GOE: 03.04.02 STRENGTH: M GED: R1 M1 L1 SVP: 2 DLU: 77

454 LOGGING AND RELATED OCCUPATIONS

This group includes occupations concerned with felling trees and cutting them into logs or products such as cordwood, shakes, firewood, and posts, using chain saws, axes, wedges, and related tools. Occupations in cutting Christmas trees are included in Group 451. Occupations in yarding and loading logs by machine are included in Division 92.

454.134-010 SUPERVISOR, FELLING-BUCKING (logging) alternate titles: powersaw supervisor; saw boss; timber supervisor

Supervises and coordinates activities of workers engaged in felling trees, trimming off limbs, and sawing felled trees into logs: Specifies log lengths to be cut, trees to be left, stump height, and cutting sequence. Trains workers in felling and bucking techniques and safety practices. Gives instructions to workers in felling trees with unusual or dangerous characteristics. May supervise TREE-SHEAR OPERATORS (logging). Performs other duties as described under SUPERVISOR (any industry) Master Title.
GOE: 03.04.02 STRENGTH: L GED: R4 M2 L3 SVP: 7 DLU: 77

454.384-010 FALLER I (logging) alternate titles: chopper

Fells timber trees, applying knowledge of tree characteristics and cutting techniques to control direction of fall and minimize tree damage: Appraises tree for characteristics, such as twists, rot, and heavy limb growth, and gauges amount and direction of lean, using ax as plumb bob. Determines position, direction, and depth of cuts to be made and placement of wedges or jacks. Clears brush and debris from work area and escape route, and cuts saplings and other trees from falling path, using ax and chain saw. Scores cutting lines with ax, saws undercut along scored lines with chain saw, and knocks slabs from cuts with ax. Saws back-cuts, leaving sufficient sound wood to control direction of fall. Inserts jack or drives wedges behind saw to prevent binding of saw and start tree falling. Stops saw engine as tree tips, pulls cutting bar from cut, and runs to predetermined location to avoid injury from falling limbs and flying debris. May work on piecework basis and be designated Busheler (logging). May cut trees into log lengths [BUCKER (logging)]. Fallers of small timber (generally under 18 inches in diameter) are classified as FALLER (logging) II.
GOE: 03.04.02 STRENGTH: H GED: R3 M2 L2 SVP: 6 DLU: 77

454.683-010 TREE-SHEAR OPERATOR (logging) alternate titles: feller operator

Drives and operates logging tractor equipped with frontal hydraulic shear to fell trees: Maneuvers tractor to position jaws of shear around tree bole, and activates shear to cut and fell tree. May control hydraulic tree clamp and boom to lift, swing, and bunch sheared trees and be designated Feller-Buncher Operator (logging).
GOE: 03.04.02 STRENGTH: M GED: R3 M1 L1 SVP: 4 DLU: 77

454.684-010 BUCKER (logging)

Saws felled trees into lengths: Places supporting limbs or poles under felled tree to avoid splitting underside and to prevent log from rolling. Cuts pre-

viously marked tree into logs, using power chain saw and ax. Drives wedges into cut behind saw blade to prevent binding saw. May cut limbs from felled trees. May mark felled tree for cutting into log lengths to obtain maximum value [LOG MARKER (logging)].
GOE: 03.04.02 STRENGTH: H GED: R2 M1 L1 SVP: 3 DLU: 77

454.684-014 FALLER II (logging) alternate titles: stumper-feller
Fells trees, applying specified cutting procedures to control direction of fall: Clears brush from work area and escape route, and cuts saplings and other trees from falling path, using ax and chain saw. Saws or chops undercut in bole of tree to fix designated direction of fall, using chain saw and ax, and saws opposite side (back cut) to fell tree. Drives wedges behind saw with mall to tip tree and prevent binding of saw. May cut limbs from tree. May cut tree into log lengths. May tag trees in unsafe condition with high visibility ribbon. Workers are classified as FALLER (logging) I where adherence to standards of minimum tree damage are of prime importance and considerable judgment is exercised in determining cutting techniques.
GOE: 03.04.02 STRENGTH: H GED: R2 M1 L1 SVP: 3 DLU: 77

454.684-018 LOGGER, ALL-ROUND (logging)
Harvests timber trees, performing combination of following tasks: Fells trees in specified direction, removes limbs and top, and measures and cuts tree into log lengths, using chain saw, wedges, and ax. Secures cables to logs and drives tractor or horses to skid logs to landing. Loads logs onto trucks by hand or using winch. May drive truck to haul logs to mill.
GOE: 03.04.02 STRENGTH: H GED: R2 M2 L1 SVP: 4 DLU: 78

454.684-022 RIVER (logging)
Rives (splits) logs or wooden blocks into bolts, pickets, posts, shakes, or stakes, using handtools, such as ax wedges, sledgehammer, froe, and mallet: Drives wedge into log with ax and sledgehammer to split log along grain to form posts or bolts. Positions froe on block according to grain and thickness of specified product and pounds it into block with mallet to start cut. Pulls froe handle up or down to pry and split pieces from block. May fell trees, using chain saw [FALLER (logging) II] and cut logs into desired lengths [BUCKER (logging)]. May be designated according to product cut as Rail Splitter (logging); Shake Splitter (logging); Shingle-Bolt Cutter (logging); Stave-Block Splitter (logging).
GOE: 03.04.02 STRENGTH: H GED: R2 M1 L1 SVP: 2 DLU: 77

454.684-026 TREE CUTTER (agriculture; logging)
Fells trees of specified size and specie, trims limbs from tree, and cuts tree into lengths for firewood, fence posts, or pulpwood, using ax, measuring tool and chain saw. Splits logs, using ax, wedges, and maul. May stack wood in rick or cord lots. May load wood onto trucks. May be designated Fence-Post Cutter (agriculture); Firewood Cutter (logging); Pulpwood Cutter (logging).
GOE: 03.04.02 STRENGTH: H GED: R2 M1 L1 SVP: 3 DLU: 77

454.687-010 CHAIN SAW OPERATOR (chemical; logging; millwork-plywood)
Trims limbs, tops, and roots from trees, and saws logs to predetermined lengths, using chain saw, preparatory to removal from forest or processing into wood products. May measure and mark logs for sawing. May be designated according to activity performed as LIMBER (logging). For related classifications involving judgment in determining cutting techniques, see BUCKER (logging); FALLER (logging) II; and TREE CUTTER (agriculture; logging).
GOE: 03.04.02 STRENGTH: H GED: R2 M1 L1 SVP: 2 DLU: 77

454.687-014 LABORER, TANBARK (logging) alternate titles: tanbark peeler
Harvests tanbark, performing any combination of following tasks: Cuts limbs from felled trees, using chain saw or ax. Cuts rings and slits in bark, and strips bark from tree, using spud or ax. Stacks bark in ricks (piles), bark-side down.
GOE: 03.04.02 STRENGTH: M GED: R2 M1 L1 SVP: 3 DLU: 77

454.687-018 LOG MARKER (logging; millwork-plywood)
Measures and marks logs or felled trees for cutting into sawlogs, pulpwood, or *veneer blocks:* Inspects felled tree or log to determine waste. Marks cutting locations to obtain maximum yield of standard lengths, using measuring rod or tape and marking chalk or crayon. May record log dimensions.
GOE: 05.07.06 STRENGTH: M GED: R3 M2 L1 SVP: 3 DLU: 77

455 LOG GRADING, SCALING, SORTING, RAFTING, AND RELATED OCCUPATIONS

This group includes occupations concerned with determining the volume and condition of logs; and segregating, rafting, or similarly preparing them for storage or shipment.

455.134-010 SUPERVISOR, LOG SORTING (logging; millwork-plywood)
Supervises and coordinates activities of workers engaged in unloading, scaling, grading, and sorting logs in log boom or sorting yard: Designates storage location for each category of log grade, specie, and size. Oversees scaling and grading activities to verify adherence to industry or company standards. Trains workers in log scaling, grading, and marking standards. Coordinates selection and movement of logs from storage areas according to transportation schedules or production requirements of wood products plants. May supervise raft building and loading of trucks and railcars for log shipment. Performs duties as de-

scribed under SUPERVISOR (any industry) Master Title. May supervise sorting activities in log boom and be designated Boom Supervisor (logging).
GOE: 03.04.02 STRENGTH: L GED: R3 M2 L3 SVP: 7 DLU: 77

455.367-010 LOG GRADER (logging; saw. & plan.)
Grades logs in sorting yard, millpond, or log deck according to industry or company standards: Measures diameter and length of log, using scale stick, steel tape, or other measuring aid, and determines total volume, using conversion table [LOG SCALER (logging; millwork-plywood; paper & pulp; saw. & plan.)]. Jabs log with metal end of scale stick and inspects log to ascertain conditions or defects, such as sound or water-soaked wood, splits, broken ends, rotten areas, twists, and curves. Evaluates log's characteristics and determines grade according to established criteria. Paints identification mark of specified color on log to identify grade and species, using paint spray can, or calls out grade to LOG MARKER (logging). Estimates and deducts volume of waste wood from total volume, and records volume by grade in tally book.
GOE: 05.07.06 STRENGTH: L GED: R3 M3 L2 SVP: 6 DLU: 77

455.487-010 LOG SCALER (logging; millwork-plywood; paper & pulp; saw. & plan.)
Estimates marketable content of logs or pulpwood: Measures dimensions of each log or entire loads of pulpwood, using scale stick, tape measure, or other measuring device. Determines total board feet, cordage, or other wood unit, using conversion table. Inspects logs or pulpwood for rot, knots, and other defects, deducts estimated waste from total volume, and records results. May identify logs of substandard or special grade for return to shipper or transfer to other processes. May weigh log trucks before and after unloading, and record weight data and supplier. May tend conveyor chain that moves logs to and from scaling station. May be designated according to work location as Deck Scaler (saw. & plan.); Landing Scaler (logging); Pond Scaler (paper & pulp; saw. & plan.); or item scaled as Pulpwood Scaler (paper & pulp).
GOE: 05.07.06 STRENGTH: L GED: R3 M3 L2 SVP: 5 DLU: 79

455.664-010 RAFTER (logging)
Assembles floating logs into rafts for towing to mill: Bores holes in boom sticks (side poles of raft), and swifters (cross poles or ribs) with power-driven auger, and threads chain or cable through holes to form raft frame. Signals LOG SORTER (logging) to push logs between frame members and maneuvers them into position with pike pole, or signals boat operator to push log bundles into raft. Binds logs into rafts with chain or cable and fastens binder with cable clamp or clevis. May unload logs from railroad cars and log trucks.
GOE: 03.04.02 STRENGTH: H GED: R2 M1 L1 SVP: 3 DLU: 77

455.684-010 LOG SORTER (logging)
Sorts logs in boom according to species, size, and owners' markings: Separates logs, floats them into designated bays with pike pole, and closes bay with chain or cable. Opens bay and maneuvers logs into designated rafting or mill storage area. May unload logs from railroad cars and log trucks. May operate motorboat to move logs. May assemble log rafts [RAFTER (logging)]. May brand logs with owners' markings [LOG MARKER (logging)].
GOE: 03.04.02 STRENGTH: H GED: R3 M1 L1 SVP: 3 DLU: 77

455.687-010 LOG MARKER (logging) alternate titles: marker
Marks logs in river or pond to designate ownership, cutting origin, species, or intended use, using any of following methods: (1) Brands each end of log with hammer or ax having raised characters on head. (2) Paints mark on ends of log, using spray can. (3) Chops or saws mark in bark near end of log.
GOE: 03.04.02 STRENGTH: M GED: R2 M1 L1 SVP: 2 DLU: 77

459 FORESTRY OCCUPATIONS, N.E.C.

This group includes occupations, not elsewhere classified, concerned with forestry and harvesting forest products.

459.133-010 SUPERVISOR, LOGGING (logging) alternate titles: yarding supervisor
Supervises and coordinates activities of workers engaged in felling and bucking trees, skidding logs from forest, and loading logs on trucks: Trains workers in felling and bucking trees, operation of tractors and loading machines, yarding and loading techniques, and safety regulations. Performs duties as described under SUPERVISOR (any industry) Master Title. When logging activities are confined to one side of timber stand or tract, may be designated Side Boss (logging).
GOE: 03.02.02 STRENGTH: L GED: R4 M2 L3 SVP: 7 DLU: 77

459.137-010 WOODS BOSS (logging) alternate titles: woods overseer
Supervises and coordinates activities of workers engaged in pulling, blasting, chopping, and transporting stumps, used in destructive distillation process for obtaining crude turpentine. Performs duties as described under SUPERVISOR (any industry) Master Title.
GOE: 03.02.02 STRENGTH: L GED: R4 M2 L3 SVP: 7 DLU: 77

459.387-010 CRUISER (forestry; logging) alternate titles: timber cruiser
Cruises forest land to estimate volume of marketable timber and collect data concerning forest conditions for appraisal, sales, administration, logging, land use, and forest management planning: Traverses forest area on foot in established pattern and applies sampling technique. Sights over scale stick to estimate height and diameter of each tree in sample. Estimates loss of marketable

volume due to defects, such as rot and bends in tree, and computes quantity of useable wood in each tree. Logs cruise data and prepares summary report of timber types, sizes, condition, and outstanding features of area, such as existing roads, streams, lakes, and communication facilities. May mark trees with spray paint to denote trail, boundary, or for cutting. May be designated Chief Cruiser (forestry) when leading a crew.
GOE: 03.02.02 STRENGTH: M GED: R4 M3 L3 SVP: 7 DLU: 77

459.687-010 LABORER, BRUSH CLEARING (any industry) alternate titles: brusher; swamper
Cuts trees, brush, and other growth, using chain saw, ax, brush-hook, and other handtools to clear land for construction, forestry, logging or agriculture activities, to remove infestation, or to control growth along utility, highway, or railroad right-of-way. May pile brush for burning or load onto trucks. May feed brush into shredding or chipping machine.
GOE: 03.04.02 STRENGTH: H GED: R1 M1 L1 SVP: 2 DLU: 77

46 HUNTING, TRAPPING, AND RELATED OCCUPATIONS

This division includes occupations concerned with searching for and taking, dead or alive, wild birds and animals, including seal, walrus, otter, and whales.

461 HUNTING AND TRAPPING OCCUPATIONS

This group includes occupations concerned with taking wild or pest animals and birds, dead or alive, by means of weapons, poisons, nets, and traps.

461.134-010 EXPEDITION SUPERVISOR (fishing & hunt.)
Supervises and coordinates activities of workers engaged in hunting for and capturing sea mammals for research and display: Confers with management to ascertain kind and number of animals to be captured, time and location of hunt, and mode of travel. Determines personnel, food, equipment and other supply requirements for hunt and capture of animals. Inspects equipment for adequacy and condition. Arranges for repair services and requisitions needed supplies. Maintains and repairs, or supervises maintenance and repair of equipment. Assigns workers to activities, such as mending nets and attaching floats and packing and loading food and material in carrier. Scouts ocean beaches and rookeries and stands watch on boat to locate mammals. Coordinates activities, such as catching mammals, on-site container construction, and in-transit mammal care. Performs other duties described under SUPERVISOR (any industry) Master Title.
GOE: 03.04.03 STRENGTH: V GED: R4 M2 L3 SVP: 6 DLU: 77

461.661-010 PREDATORY-ANIMAL HUNTER (fishing & hunt.) alternate titles: bounty hunter; forestry hunter
Hunts, traps, and kills predatory animals to collect bounty: Hunts quarry, using dogs, and shoots animals. Traps or poisons animals depending on environs and habits of animals sought. Removes designated parts, such as ears or tail from slain animals, using knife, to present as evidence of kill for bounty. May skin animals and treat pelts for marketing. May train dogs for hunting. May be designated according to animal hunted as Cougar Hunter (fishing & hunt.); Coyote Hunter (fishing & hunt.); Wolf Hunter (fishing & hunt.).
GOE: 03.04.03 STRENGTH: H GED: R3 M1 L1 SVP: 5 DLU: 77

461.664-010 UNDERWATER HUNTER-TRAPPER (fishing & hunt.) alternate titles: hunter, skin diver
Collects and captures sea life specimens, such as finfish, shellfish, and mammals working individually or as member of crew, using skin-diving equipment: Dives or walks into sea and swims underwater to scout terrain and reach work area. Twists, cuts, and tears specimens, such as abalone, starfish, or sponge from surface to which attached, and places specimens in container. Catches finfish and shellfish, using net. Signals boat crew to hoist container or net to surface. Places nets underwater to capture sea mammals, such as whales, porpoises, and dolphins. Stands watch to observe behavior of captured mammals. Swims in, around, and under nets to free captive and other quarry caught in net and to prevent injury, escape, or drowning. Restrains mammal with arms or nets, and rigs net or sling under catch to permit hoisting without bodily injury.
GOE: 03.04.03 STRENGTH: V GED: R4 M2 L3 SVP: 5 DLU: 77

461.684-010 SEALER (fishing & hunt.) alternate titles: fisher, seal
Kills seals for pelts, using clubs: Rounds up droves of bachelor seals resting or sleeping on beach adjacent to, but distinct from, rookery, using pole to prod them and keep them together. Drives male seals inland to killing grounds, and sorts droves into pods. Kills male seals that are within specified age and size limits, by striking them on head with club, after allowing others to escape. Severs skin around head and flippers of dead seal, using knife, pins its skull to ground with metal bar, and pulls off seal's skin from head to tail. Loads pelts onto trucks for transportation to plant for cleaning and curing. Washes pelts in sea water. Scrapes fat and blubber from pelts, using hand scraper. Cures pelts in salt or brine, sprinkles boric acid on skin side of pelt to prevent bacterial development, and packs and salts pelts in barrels for shipment and further processing. May be designated according to specific task performed as Seal Driver (fishing & hunt.); Seal Killer (fishing & hunt.); Seal Skinner (fishing & hunt.). Sealing operations are controlled by the United States Fish and Wildlife Service.
GOE: 03.04.03 STRENGTH: M GED: R2 M2 L1 SVP: 2 DLU: 77

461.684-014 TRAPPER, ANIMAL (fishing & hunt.) alternate titles: fur trapper
Traps animals for pelts, live sale, bounty, or to relocate them in other areas: Sets traps with bait, scent, or camouflage, and in patterns according to size, species, habits, and environs of animal sought or according to reason for trapping. Patrols trapline to remove catch and reset or relocate traps. Clubs or drowns trapped fur-bearing animals to prevent damage to pelts. Skins animals, using knife, and stretches pelts on frames to be cured. Scrapes or skives skin-side of pelt with knife to remove fat and flesh, and rubs skin with salt to dry and preserve it. Sorts pelts according to species, color, and quality. Removes parts, such as ears or tail, from predatory animals and presents them as evidence of kill for bounty [PREDATORY-ANIMAL HUNTER (fishing & hunt.)]. May be designated according to animal trapped as Beaver Trapper (fishing & hunt.); Muskrat Trapper (fishing & hunt.).
GOE: 03.04.03 STRENGTH: H GED: R3 M2 L2 SVP: 5 DLU: 77

461.684-018 TRAPPER, BIRD (fishing & hunt.)
Traps birds to serve as brood stock, or for exhibition, extermination, identification, or relocation: Selects and sets traps, nets, or cages according to size, habits, and habitat of bird and reasons for trapping. Walks about to drive quarry toward traps or net or patrols trap-line periodically to inspect setting. Releases quarry from trap or net and transfers it to cage. Kills birds or secures identification tag to bird and releases it. May locate and flush ground birds into nets, using dogs.
GOE: 03.04.03 STRENGTH: M GED: R3 M2 L2 SVP: 4 DLU: 77

5 PROCESSING OCCUPATIONS

This category includes occupations concerned with refining, mixing, compounding, chemically treating, heat treating, or similarly working materials and products. Knowledge of a process and adherence to formulas or other specifications are required in some degree. Vats, stills, ovens, furnaces, mixing machines, crushers, grinders, and related equipment or machines are usually involved.

50   OCCUPATIONS IN PROCESSING OF METAL

This division includes occupations concerned with molding, casting, coating, conditioning, or otherwise processing metal. Foundry occupations are included in Division 51.

500   ELECTROPLATING OCCUPATIONS

This group includes occupations concerned with covering the surfaces of objects by electro-deposition or electrolysis.

500.131-010 SUPERVISOR (electroplating) alternate titles: plater supervisor

Supervises and coordinates activities of workers engaged in cleaning, racking, plating, and polishing of metal or plastic objects: Selects equipment, such as hooks, plating barrels or tanks, and racks, according to quantity, size, and type of objects to be plated. Verifies types of plating metals and solutions, length of immersion period, and amount of electric current flowing through solutions, following plating specifications. Assigns tasks to workers and processes paperwork, such as timecards and supply, production and personnel reports. Resolves personnel problems and expedites production bottlenecks to meet deadlines and production schedules. Inspects plated surfaces of objects to detect defects, such as rough spots, thin plating, and unpolished areas. Collects and labels samples of plating solutions for laboratory analysis. Examines equipment, such as plating tanks, polishers, and racks, and notifies maintenance department of needed repairs. May analyze plating solutions to verify conformance to specifications, performing variety of tests, such as specific gravity and titration tests. May measure thickness of plating on metal objects, using micrometer, to verify conformance to specifications. May be designated according to specific process supervised as Supervisor, Anodizing (electroplating); Supervisor, Electrolytic Tinning (nonfer. metal). Performs other duties as described under SUPERVISOR (any industry) Master Title.
GOE: 06.02.01 STRENGTH: L GED: R4 M3 L4 SVP: 7 DLU: 77

500.132-010 SUPERVISOR, SHEET MANUFACTURING (smelt. & refin.)

Supervises and coordinates activities of workers engaged in making copper starting sheets by electrolysis. Performs duties as described under SUPERVISOR (any industry) Master Title.
GOE: 06.02.01 STRENGTH: L GED: R4 M3 L3 SVP: 7 DLU: 77

500.134-010 SUPERVISOR, MATRIX (recording)

Supervises and coordinates activities of workers engaged in electroplating, stripping, finishing, and inspecting metal phonograph record matrices. Requisitions processing materials, such as chemicals, wiping cloths, and polishing compounds. Confers with workers' representatives to resolve grievances. Trains workers in processing functions. Performs duties as described under SUPERVISOR (any industry) Master Title.
GOE: 06.02.01 STRENGTH: L GED: R4 M3 L3 SVP: 6 DLU: 77

500.287-010 INSPECTOR, PLATING (electroplating) alternate titles: sample tester

Inspects plated surfaces of metal or plastic objects visually or using chemical or electrical tests: Examines part for defects, such as uneven coating or scratches. Applies chemicals to or immerses object in test solution and observes reaction or measures dissolving time. Turns on electrical current and reads gauge to measure plating thickness. Attaches magnet to metal part and reads gauge to measure magnet pull to determine plating thickness. Compares readings with specifications and returns defective objects for rework. May test samples of electrolytic solutions.
GOE: 06.03.01 STRENGTH: M GED: R3 M3 L3 SVP: 3 DLU: 77

500.362-010 ELECTROGALVANIZING-MACHINE OPERATOR (electroplating)

Sets up and operates continuous multistrand electrogalvanizing and heat-treating machine to coat steel strip or wire with zinc, according to written specifications: Mixes chemical solutions, using formulas. Fills cleaning, pickling, galvanizing, and waxing tanks. Charges furnace with gas or coal to prepare for galvanizing process. Inserts wire reels and feeds wire into machine. Moves controls on rheostats and generators to regulate movement of wire strand between reels, plating tanks, and coils, to obtain specified thickness of coating. Adjusts controls to regulate temperature of leadpot, cleaners, picklers, and plating tanks. Performs chemical solution tests, such as titration tests, wire hardness tests, dip coating tests, and welding tests, to determine conformance to specifications. Readjusts controls based on findings. Records test results. Examines coating, washing, and alignment of wire strands visually and using micrometers to compare finished strands with specifications. Resets and changes combs when changing width and number of strands. Replaces anodes and recharges leadpot at specified intervals.
GOE: 06.02.21 STRENGTH: H GED: R4 M3 L3 SVP: 6 DLU: 77

500.362-014 PLATER, BARREL (electroplating) alternate titles: barrel-line operator; drum plater; plater, machine; tumbler plater

Operates barrel plating equipment to coat metal objects electrolytically with metal to build up, protect, or decorate surfaces: Places metal objects in mesh container and immerses objects in cleaning solutions. Places objects in perforated or mesh barrel of plating equipment and clamps door in barrel opening. Turns handle to lower barrel into plating solution and to close electrical contacts. Starts rotation of barrel. Starts flow of electric current through plating solution that decomposes plating metal at anode and deposits metal coating on objects in barrel. Stops flow of current after specified time and removes objects. Places objects in mesh container and immerses objects in rinsing solutions. Dries plated objects, using centrifugal drier or tumbler filled with sawdust. Tests solutions, using hydrometer, and adds chemicals to maintain specified concentrations.
GOE: 06.02.21 STRENGTH: M GED: R3 M3 L3 SVP: 5 DLU: 77

500.380-010 PLATER (electroplating) alternate titles: electroplater; plating-tank operator

Sets up and controls plating equipment to coat metal objects electrolytically with chromium, copper, cadmium, or other metal to provide protective or decorative surfaces or to build up worn surfaces according to specifications: Reads work order to determine size and composition of object to be plated; type concentration and temperature of plating solution; type and thickness and location of specified plating metal; and amount of electrical current and time required to complete plating process. Immerses object in cleaning and rinsing baths [METAL-CLEANER, IMMERSION (any industry)]. Suspends object, such as part or mold, from cathode rod (negative terminal) and immerses object in plating solution. Suspends stick or piece of plating metal from anode (positive terminal) and immerses metal in plating solution. Moves controls on rectifier to adjust flow of current through plating solution from anode to cathode and to permit electrodeposition of metal on object. Removes plated object from solution at periodic intervals and observes object to ensure conformance to specifications. Adjusts voltage and amperage based on observation. Examines object visually at end of process to determine thickness of metal deposit or measures thickness, using instruments, such as micrometers or calipers. Grinds, polishes or rinses object in water and dries object to maintain clean even surface. May mix, and test strength of plating solution, using instruments and chemical tests. May measure, mark, and mask areas excluded from plating. May plate small objects, such as nuts or bolts, using motor-driven barrel. May direct other workers performing variety of duties, such as racking, cleaning, or plating objects. May operate electroplating equipment with reverse polarity and be known as Plating Stripper (electroplating). May be designated according to plating materials used as Brass Plater (electroplating); Bronze Plater (electroplating); Cadmium Plater (electroplating); Chromium Plater (electroplating); Copper Plater (electroplating); Gold Plater (electroplating). May be designated: Nickel Plater (electroplating); Plastics Plater (plastic prod.); Silver Plater (electroplating); Tin Plater (electroplating).
GOE: 06.02.21 STRENGTH: M GED: R4 M3 L3 SVP: 7 DLU: 77

500.380-014 PLATER APPRENTICE (electroplating) alternate titles: electroplater apprentice; plating-tank-operator apprentice

Performs duties as described under APPRENTICE (any industry) Master Title.
GOE: 06.02.21 STRENGTH: M GED: R4 M3 L3 SVP: 7 DLU: 77

500.381-010 CYLINDER GRINDER (print. & pub.) alternate titles: grinder and plater

Electroplates rotogravure printing cylinders with coating of copper and grinds plates to specifications, using grinding machines: Immerses cylinder in cleaning bath, using chain hoist. Removes cylinder and places cylinder in copper sulfate plating solution for prescribed period of time to cover cylinder with copper [PLATER (electroplating)]. Removes cylinder from plating vat, rinses in water, and fastens cylinder between centers of grinding machine, using handtools. Selects and fastens abrasive wheel onto spindle of machine. Starts machine and turns handwheels to bring abrasive wheel into contact with surface of cylinder, and to engage automatic feed. Measures dimension of cylinder surfaces during grinding and polishing operation, using micrometers to obtain required precision. Removes finished cylinder from machine and places cylinder in rack.
GOE: 05.10.05 STRENGTH: L GED: R3 M3 L3 SVP: 7 DLU: 77

500.384-010 MATRIX PLATER (recording)

Electroplates phonograph record matrices to form metal replicas of positive and negative recorded surfaces, and to form stamper used in pressing phono-

graph records: Inserts silver-coated lacquer disk (original recording) in rubber masking ring to prevent plating of specified surfaces, such as edges of disk. Hangs disk in tanks containing plating solutions, such as nickel and copper or inserts disk over centering pin of automatic plating tanks to form negative metal master matrix of disk. Observes dials and gauges to ensure solutions and electric current flowing through solutions conform to specifications, and adjusts controls as required. Removes plated disk from tanks after specified time, removes masking ring, washes and dries disk, and routes disk to finishing department for stripping and finishing process by MATRIX WORKER (recording). Washes master matrix after finishing process to prevent adhesion during subsequent plating processes. Plates master matrix to form *mother* matrix and plates mother to form stamper used on record presses, following prescribed plating procedures. May prepare and test plating solutions.
GOE: 06.02.21 STRENGTH: L GED: R3 M2 L2 SVP: 4 DLU: 77

500.384-014   MATRIX-BATH ATTENDANT (recording)
Maintains electrolytic baths in operating condition for plating phonograph record matrices: Draws sample of solution from tanks, using pipette. Tests strength of solution, using hydrometer, and adds specified amounts of metallic salts, acid, or water to solution as needed. Examines anodes for specified size and for position in baths. Activates controls and reads meters to test electrical connections for open or short condition.
GOE: 06.02.21 STRENGTH: M GED: R3 M3 L3 SVP: 5 DLU: 77

500.485-010   ZINC-PLATING-MACHINE OPERATOR (electroplating)
Tends machine that coats wire electrolytically with zinc to protect wire surface from corrosion: Mixes zinc solution according to specified formula and turns valves to fill tank with solution. Threads wire through machine and sets rheostat to regulate flow of current through solution. Starts machine to pull wire through solution. Examines surface of wire for defects, such as bubbles or bare spots, and measures thickness of coating, using micrometer. Adjusts controls to regulate speed of reel and flow of current to coat wire to specified thickness.
GOE: 06.02.21 STRENGTH: M GED: R3 M2 L2 SVP: 4 DLU: 77

500.682-010   ANODIZER (any industry) alternate titles: white-metal corrosion proofer
Controls anodizing equipment to provide corrosion resistant surface to aluminum objects: Selects holding rack according to size, shape, and number of objects to be anodized. Wires or clips objects to anodizing rack and immerses rack in series of cleaning, etching, and rinsing baths. Positions objects in anodizing tank by suspending them from anode. Estimates amount of electric current and time required to anodize material. Turns rheostat to regulate flow of current. Removes objects from tank after specified time, rinses objects, and immerses them in bath of hot water or dichromate solution to seal oxide coating. Hangs objects on racks to air-dry. May immerse objects in dye bath to color them for decorative or identification purposes. May anodize workpiece with corrosion resistant material, using automated equipment that automatically cleans, rinses, and coats.
GOE: 06.02.21 STRENGTH: H GED: R3 M2 L3 SVP: 4 DLU: 77

500.684-010   ELECTROFORMER (electroplating)
Sprays or smears electrically conductive solution onto nonconductive objects, such as baby shoes or plastic molds, or dips objects in solution to prepare objects for electroplating. May electroplate objects [PLATER (electroplating)].
GOE: 06.04.33 STRENGTH: L GED: R2 M1 L1 SVP: 4 DLU: 77

500.684-014   MATRIX WORKER (recording) alternate titles: finisher
Performs any combination of following tasks involved in finishing and inspecting metal phonograph matrices after electroplating processes: Strips (separates) master, *mother*, and stamper matrices, using handtools, files, and knife. Holds matrices against sanding belt or grinding wheel of bench grinder to remove burrs. Punches center hole in stamper and mother matrices, using punch press. Fills offcenter holes with solder, using soldering iron or acetylene torch. Steam cleans and polishes matrices, using brushes, cloths, and polishing compounds. Examines stamper matrices for defects, and weighs matrices to ensure conformance to standards, using scale. Cuts and flares edges of stamper matrices, using press. Marks identifying information on master matrices, using scribe.
GOE: 06.04.24 STRENGTH: L GED: R2 M2 L2 SVP: 2 DLU: 77

500.684-018   PLATE FORMER (elec. equip.)
Forms (treats) storage battery plates for dry charge or wet charge batteries: Positions plates on conductor base of forming tank and burns lead strips to lugs of plates [LEAD BURNER (elec. equip.)]. Inserts separators between positive and negative plates to form element. Places elements in containers and attaches push-on or clamp-type jumpers to connect elements in series. Mixes forming acid solution of prescribed specific gravity. Drains solution from mixing tank into forming tanks or element containers, using hose. Connects posts of units to electrical circuit. Adjusts rheostat to regulate current, using ammeter. Removes formed plates from acid and places plates in water bath to remove electrolyte. Separates positive and negative plates, places plates [in racks, and places racks in driers. Dumps forming acid from element containers and refills containers with finishing acid. Conveys or trucks elements to final charging line.
GOE: 06.02.32 STRENGTH: L GED: R3 M2 L2 SVP: 4 DLU: 77

500.684-022   SILVER SPRAY WORKER (recording)
Sprays surfaces of prerecorded lacquer disks with silver solution to make disks conductive, using spray gun: Positions disk on spindle of turntable in spraying booth. Sprays revolving disk with cleaning solvents to prepare disk for silver coating. Sprays silver solution on revolving surface of disk. May place disk in spray machine that automatically cleans and sprays surface with silver solution.
GOE: 06.04.33 STRENGTH: L GED: R2 M2 L2 SVP: 4 DLU: 77

500.684-026   PLATER, PRINTED CIRCUIT BOARD PANELS (electron. comp.)
Electroplates printed circuit board (PCB) panels with metals, such as copper, tin, gold, nickel, or solder, to resist corrosion, improve electrical conductivity, and facilitate solder connections: Dips panels in cleaning solutions or wipes panels with cloth to clean panels. Clamps panels or rack of panels to overhead bar above tanks to complete electrolytic current. Immerses panels in plating solution. Sets timer for specified plating time and turns on electrical current. Observes meter and turns dial to maintain specified current in plating solution. Removes plated panels and immerses panels in rinsing tank. Examines plated panels for defects. May test thickness of plating, using gauge or test equipment. May tape areas to be excluded from plating, using tape machine. May trim excess material from PCB panels, using shearing machine. May calculate amperage setting, following specified formula. May be designated according to plating material used as Gold Plater (electron. comp.); Nickel Plater (electron. comp.).
GOE: 06.02.21 STRENGTH: H GED: R2 M1 L2 SVP: 3 DLU: 86

500.684-030   PLATER, SEMICONDUCTOR WAFERS AND COMPONENTS (electron. comp.)
Electroplates semiconductor wafers and electronic components, such as copper leads and rectifiers, with metals, such as gold, silver, and lead: Reads processing sheet to determine plating time and specifications. Places components or wafers in basket or fixture, using tweezers, and immerses components or wafers in chemical solution baths for specified time to clean and plate components or wafers. May measure thickness of photoresist and metal on wafer surface, using micrometer, and test electrical circuitry of individual *die* on wafer, using test probe equipment. May measure anode width on wafer surface, using microscope measuring equipment.
GOE: 06.04.19 STRENGTH: L GED: R3 M2 L2 SVP: 3 DLU: 86

500.684-034   PLATER (inst. & app.) alternate titles: electroformer
Plates component parts, such as micromesh screen patterns and electronic tubes, used in medical and laboratory measuring and controlling instruments, using electrolytic plating tank: Positions screen pattern or component part in frame or on rack, and hangs frame or rack in plating tank. Sets switch for specified plating time, and activates electric current to deposit ionized metal on nonprinted area of screen pattern or component part. Immerses electroformed part in water to rinse off electrolyte, and immerses rinsed part in solvent to dissolve pattern. May measure thickness of electroplating on component part to verify conformance to specifications, using micrometer.
GOE: 06.02.32 STRENGTH: L GED: R3 M2 L2 SVP: 5 DLU: 89

500.685-010   ETCHER, ELECTROLYTIC (cutlery-hrdwr.) alternate titles: etcher
Tends equipment that electrolytically etches markings, such as insignias, trademarks, and part numbers on metal articles: Turns switches on power control unit to allow flow of electric current through electrolytic solution in tank. Positions workpiece on stencil and against contact strip to complete electric circuit. Places workpiece in electrolytic solution that etches stencil markings on metal. Removes workpiece from solution, after specified time, and sprays workpiece with water to remove acid. Immerses workpiece in rust preventive solution.
GOE: 06.04.10 STRENGTH: L GED: R2 M2 L2 SVP: 2 DLU: 77

500.685-014   PLATING EQUIPMENT TENDER (electroplating) alternate titles: electroplater, automatic; plater production
Tends automatic equipment that conveys objects through series of cleaning, rinsing, and electrolytic plating solutions to plate objects with metallic coating: Starts equipment and regulates flow of electricity through plating solution and immersion time of objects in solutions, according to specifications. Monitors automatic plating process to ensure conformance to standards. Adds water or other materials to maintain specified mixture and level of cleaning, rinsing, and plating solutions. Observes temperature gauges and adjusts controls to maintain specified temperatures of cleaning and rinsing solutions. Lubricates moving parts of plating conveyor. Cleans plating and cleaning tanks. May test plating solution, using hydrometer and litmus paper, or obtain random sample of plating solutions for laboratory analysis. May replace anodes and cathodes in plating equipment. May fasten objects onto hooks or racks, or place objects into containers or onto conveyor attached to plating equipment. May start and monitor computerized plating process. May manually immerse objects into plating or rinsing solutions.
GOE: 06.04.21 STRENGTH: M GED: R2 M2 L2 SVP: 3 DLU: 88

500.686-010   LABORER, ELECTROPLATING (electroplating) alternate titles: electroplater helper; plater helper; plating-department helper
Performs any combination of following tasks to load and unload electroplating equipment or to assist PLATER (electroplating) 500.380-010: Fastens metal workpieces to devices, such as hooks, racks, and cathode bars, or loads workpieces in baskets or barrels. Immerses workpieces in series of cleaning, plating, pickling, and rinsing tanks, following timed cycle, manually or using

hoist. Carries workpieces between conveyors that move workpieces through electroplating processes. Sets temperature dials of tanks to prescribed level. Flips switch to activate electroplating process in tanks. Removes workpieces from hooks, racks, bars, baskets, or barrels, and examines workpieces for plating defects, such as rough spots and thin plating. Dries plated workpieces in oven, centrifugal drier, or sawdust-filled container. Packs workpieces in boxes or cartons for shipment [PACKAGER, HAND (any industry) 920.587-018]. Drains solutions from and cleans and refills tanks. Removes buildup of plating metal from racks, using hammer or compressed-air vibrator, and coats racks with shellac. Replaces damaged or worn equipment parts. May be designated according to task performed as Cleaner (electroplating); Rack Cleaner (electroplating); Racker (electroplating); Sawdust Drier (electroplating).
GOE: 06.04.21 STRENGTH: H GED: R2 M2 L2 SVP: 2 DLU: 88

500.687-010 PLATE-TAKE-OUT WORKER (elec. equip.)
Removes storage-battery plates from forming tanks preparatory to further processing. Submerges negative plates in water-filled tank truck to prevent excessive oxidation. Stacks positive plates in dry tank. May push loaded tank trucks to washing and drying room.
GOE: 06.04.24 STRENGTH: M GED: R2 M1 L1 SVP: 2 DLU: 77

501 DIP PLATING OCCUPATIONS

This group includes occupations concerned with covering, without electrolysis, the surfaces of objects with metal coatings by immersing them in molten, liquid, or solute form of the coating metal, or in materials which react with the object surface to form the metal coating.

501.130-010 SUPERVISOR, HOT-DIP-TINNING (steel & rel.)
Supervises and coordinates activities of workers engaged in operating hot-dip-tinning machines to tinplate black-pickled steel sheets, and in classifying and assorting tinplate. Trains workers in set up of machines. Performs duties as described under SUPERVISOR (any industry) Master Title.
GOE: 06.02.01 STRENGTH: M GED: R4 M3 L4 SVP: 8 DLU: 77

501.137-010 SUPERVISOR, HOT-DIP PLATING (galvanizing)
Supervises and coordinates activities of workers engaged in applying corrosion-resistant coatings of zinc, tin, or other metal to variety of metal objects. Monitors gauges to verify operational specifications, such as solution temperature and immersion time. Examines products for even and complete coating. Trains new workers in job duties. Performs duties as described under SUPERVISOR (any industry) Master Title.
GOE: 06.02.01 STRENGTH: L GED: R4 M3 L4 SVP: 7 DLU: 77

501.362-010 COATING-MACHINE OPERATOR (galvanizing)
Sets up and controls automatic hot-dip lines to plate steel sheets with protective coating of metal, such as tin or terne: Reads production schedule to determine setup of lines. Turns screwdown mechanism to set distance between coating brushes and rolls, using handtools. Measures and sets stops and guides on automatic feeder and conveying equipment according to dimensions of product to be coated, using rule and wrenches. Measures and sets temperatures of coating metal and palm-oil pots. Starts conveyor line and moves controls to synchronize speed of line with speed of coating machine that conveys sheets into molten tin covered with palm oil to cause even distribution of tin. Inspects coated product for defects and changes setup to coat sheets to specifications. May be designated according to type of coating as Tinner, Automatic (galvanizing).
GOE: 06.02.10 STRENGTH: M GED: R3 M3 L3 SVP: 7 DLU: 77

501.485-010 WIRE-COATING OPERATOR, METAL (galvanizing) alternate titles: strand galvanizer; wire galvanizer
Tends one or more machines, equipped with series of tanks, that coat wire with corrosion-resistant material, such as tin, zinc, or lead: Lifts and mounts coils of wire on feed reels. Threads end of wire through series of guides, rollers, wipers, and tanks and secures it to rewind reel. Moves levers to heat coating material to molten consistency and set specified temperature of fluxing, cooling, and cleaning baths. Moves controls to start machine, set tension on wire, and adjust speed that wire feeds through tanks. Observes levels of materials in tanks and replenishes material when levels drop below specified point. Measures finished wire to ensure uniformity of coverage, using micrometer. Adjusts machine settings to regulate thickness of coating, according to specifications. Welds coils of wire together, using butt-welder, to maintain continuous wire coating operation. May be designated according to type of coating material applied as Lead Coater (galvanizing); Wire Tinner (galvanizing).
GOE: 06.04.21 STRENGTH: M GED: R2 M1 L1 SVP: 2 DLU: 77

501.685-010 PLATER, HOT DIP (galvanizing) alternate titles: galvanizing dipper; pot runner
Tends equipment to coat iron and steel products with corrosion-resistant molten nonferrous metal: Suspends metal objects, such as pails, shelving, nuts and bolts, and structural steel from conveyor hooks or places them in wire baskets. Immerses objects in chemical solution to clean surface of scale and foreign matter. Lowers objects into tank of ammonium chloride or other flux to protect surface from oxidation and facilitate coating. Dips objects into tank of molten metal to coat objects, using hoist or conveyor. Removes objects from tanks after specified time. Places objects, such as nuts and bolts, in centrifuge and starts machine to cool objects and remove excessive coating. Places objects,

such as shelving and structural steel, into water tank or transfers them to storage area to cool. Smooths coating, using wire brush and file. Inspects objects for even and complete coating and returns defective objects for reprocessing. Scoops dross from tank, using long-handled scoop, pours dross into molds, and weighs molded dross. Turns valves to regulate temperature in dipping tank. Adds coating metal and chemicals to maintain specified levels and mixtures in cleaning, dipping, and fluxing tanks. May be designated according to type of coating applied as Galvanizer, Zinc (galvanizing); Tin Dipper (galvanizing).
GOE: 06.04.21 STRENGTH: H GED: R2 M1 L1 SVP: 4 DLU: 77

501.685-014 TINNING-EQUIPMENT TENDER (elec. equip.)
Tends equipment that coats preassembled groups of contact springs for relays and switches: Secures springs with screws, using foot-controlled pneumatic screwdriver. Loads multispring subassemblies on conveyor of equipment that coats terminals of subassemblies with tin. Loads solder bars and flux solution into equipment, and sets thermostat to control temperature of tinning solution.
GOE: 06.04.21 STRENGTH: L GED: R1 M1 L1 SVP: 2 DLU: 77

501.685-018 BLACK OXIDE COATING EQUIPMENT TENDER (electron. comp.) alternate titles: black oxide operator
Tends computerized equipment that applies black oxide coating to printed circuit board (PCB) panels to prevent electrical contact between layers and to aid adhesion of layers of multilayer PCBs: Loads PCB panels into racks and positions racks under equipment crane. Pushes button to activate crane that automatically lifts racks of panels and immerses racks into series of tanks that coat panels with black oxide. Measures temperature of solutions with pyrometer and turns equipment knobs and valves to adjust temperature and regulate liquid volume. Places panels in oven to dry.
GOE: 06.04.21 STRENGTH: M GED: R2 M2 L2 SVP: 2 DLU: 86

501.685-022 ELECTROLESS PLATER, PRINTED CIRCUIT BOARD PANELS (electron. comp.) alternate titles: deposition operator
Tends electroless plating equipment that immerses printed circuit board (PCB) panels into series of chemical tanks to clean, rinse, and deposit metal plating on panels to improve electrical conductivity and facilitate solder connections in production of PCBs: Turns valves to fill tanks with solutions to specified levels. Loads panels onto dipping racks and attaches racks to bar, hoist, overhead crane, or holding fixture. Sets timer for deposition cycle. Keys data into computer keyboard, presses buttons or pulls levers to activate equipment that moves racks of panels through tanks, or lowers racks into tanks manually. Observes gauges and adjusts valves on tanks to maintain required temperature. Removes PCB upon completion of deposition cycle. May compute length of deposition cycle, using calculator. May add chemicals to tanks. May be designated according to type of coating applied as Copper Deposition Operator (electron. comp.).
GOE: 06.04.21 STRENGTH: H GED: R2 M2 L2 SVP: 2 DLU: 86

502 MELTING, POURING, CASTING, AND RELATED OCCUPATIONS

This group includes occupations concerned with heating metal to change it from a solid to a liquid state, pouring it into a mold or other receptacle and allowing or causing it to solidify.

502.130-010 SUPERVISOR, CASTING-AND-PASTING (elec. equip.)
Coordinates processes, supervises workers, and sets up machines used to manufacture storage-battery grids and plates: Coordinates hand and machine operations, such as lead melting, casting and trimming, paste mixing, grid pasting and drying, and inspection. Sets up machines, such as trimming press and pasting machines. Adjusts stops, guides, blades and rollers, and changes molds. Inspects in-process or finished parts, such as grids, connectors, and wet and dry plates to determine conformance to specifications. Observes gauges, thermometers, temperature controls, and operation of machines and equipment to detect malfunctions and directs or makes changes to correct defects. Reports mechanical breakdowns to maintenance department. Performs other duties as described under SUPERVISOR (any industry) Master Title. May be designated according to operation supervised as Supervisor, Grid-Casting-And-Pasting (elec. equip.); Supervisor, Plate Pasting (elec. equip.).
GOE: 06.01.01 STRENGTH: L GED: R4 M3 L3 SVP: 7 DLU: 77

502.362-010 SHOT DROPPER (ordnance)
Controls kettles at top of shot tower to melt scrap shot, pure lead, and lead alloys and drops mixture through perforated pans down tower to form shot for shotgun shells: Computes in pigs and pounds, amounts of pure lead and lead alloys, containing various percentages of antimony, required to produce mixture of specified antimony content. Notifies MATERIAL HANDLER (any industry) type and quantity of pigs to load onto conveyor. Starts conveyor and turns wheel or moves lever to regulate feed rate of lead pigs and scrap shot into kettle. Observes pyrometers and turns knobs to adjust kettle temperature, according to specifications. Positions specified *shot pan, spreader pan, and cup* in fixture beneath kettle spout. Turns crank to regulate molten metal flow from kettle into cup. Observes falling pellets to detect defects, such as irregular shot size, clogged holes in shot pan, and impurities in lead. Adjusts flow of lead to increase or decrease size of pellets. Adjusts kettle temperature to burn out impurities. Removes pans and dips pans in kettle to melt clogged lead from perforations prior to reuse. Shakes shot samples through gauging sieve and esti-

mates production of specified shot size from percentage of pellets passing through sieve.
GOE: 06.02.10 STRENGTH: M GED: R3 M3 L3 SVP: 6 DLU: 77

502.381-010 CASTER (jewelry-silver.) alternate titles: molder; slush caster

Casts jewelry pieces and ornamental figures for trophies and placques from molten lead or zinc: Melts zinc or lead alloy bars in kettle. Assembles sections of mold and secures mold with C-clamp. Pours molten metal into mold, using hand ladle. Disassembles mold after specified time and knocks sand from casting, using mallet. Places jewelry piece or figure in tray to cool.
GOE: 06.02.24 STRENGTH: M GED: R3 M2 L2 SVP: 6 DLU: 77

502.381-014 MOLDER, PUNCH (aircraft mfg.) alternate titles: molder; molder, closed molds

Casts male dies (punches) used in stamping aircraft parts from sheet metal: Operates hoist to position female dies on foundry floor [MONORAIL CRANE OPERATOR (any industry) 921.663-042]. Clamps metal and plywood strips around die to form mold. Shapes mold to specified contours with sand, using trowel and related tools. Tilts melting pot or uses ladle to pour molten alloy (aluminum, lead, zinc) into sand mold. Places metal jig with anchor bolts attached, or similar insert setup, over mold and into molten metal in prescribed manner to attach anchor bolts to punch. May smooth dies. May preheat dies, using blowtorch or other equipment. May apply parting compound to dies. May operate furnaces and ovens.
GOE: 06.02.24 STRENGTH: M GED: R4 M3 L3 SVP: 7 DLU: 88

502.382-010 BULLET-SLUG-CASTING-MACHINE OPERATOR (ordnance) alternate titles: machine-casting operator and adjuster

Operates machine to cast slugs for subsequent swaging into small arms ammunition bullets: Slides lead pigs and scrap into melting kettle, turns valves to control fuel-air mixture to furnace and coolant water flow to molds, and starts pump that forces molten metal through pipes to casting wheels adjacent to kettle. Starts machine and observes water on heated molds to determine when water sizzles, indicating specified temperature of molds for production casting. Examines slugs for such defects as fins, out of miter (halves not matching), partial formation, and pits. Adjusts machine controls and replaces worn and warped molds to correct malformation of slugs, using handtools. Examines molds, using straightedge and light, to detect incomplete closure and warpage, and straightens warped molds, using hand-powered press.
GOE: 06.02.10 STRENGTH: H GED: R3 M2 L2 SVP: 5 DLU: 77

502.382-014 FLUOROSCOPE OPERATOR (nonfer. metal)

Operates fluoroscope to inspect metal castings for hidden defects, such as excessive porosity and subsurface cracks: Aligns castings on table, lowers fluorescent screen over castings, and starts machine. Turns dials to adjust fluorescent penetration depth according to density of metal. Examines reflections of castings on illuminated lid to locate defects. Realigns castings for cross-sectional views, adjusting dials to new focus points. Rejects castings not conforming to plant specifications and places castings aside for salvaging. Notifies superior of findings. Records number of castings inspected and rejected, using automatic counter. Submits minometer pencil worn on person to supervisory personnel for reading to ascertain amount of stray radiation escaping from fluoroscope. May inspect casting for defects, using magnetic testing machine [INSPECTOR, MAGNETIC PARTICLE AND PENETRANT (any industry) 709.364-010].
GOE: 06.03.01 STRENGTH: L GED: R3 M3 L3 SVP: 5 DLU: 77

502.384-010 PEWTER CASTER (jewelry-silver.)

Casts pewter alloy to form parts for goblets, candlesticks, and other pewterware: Places pewter ingots into cauldron and turns controls to heat cauldron to specified temperature. Stirs molten alloy and skims off impurities, using skimmer. Sands inside of mold parts to remove glaze residue, using emery cloth; applies new glaze, using paint brush; and sets mold parts aside to dry. Assembles mold, wraps mold in heat-resistant cloth, and ladles molten alloy into mold opening. Manually rotates mold to distribute alloy in mold and prevent formation of air pockets. Strikes mold to separate dried casting from mold, using knocker. Repeats casting process until specified number of parts are cast. Trims gates and sharp joints from cast parts, using bandsaw. Carries trimmed castings to storage area. Periodically weighs and mixes alloy ingredients according to formulas and knowledge of ingredient chemical qualities, heats mixture to specified temperature, and fills molds to form ingots from which parts are cast. May cast items, using other equipment, such as temporary molds or casting machines.
GOE: 06.02.24 STRENGTH: H GED: R3 M2 L2 SVP: 6 DLU: 86

502.482-010 CASTER (nonfer. metal)

Operates gas-fired furnace to melt nonferrous metal, such as aluminum, magnesium, and zinc, and pours molten metal into molds to form castings of items, such as kitchen utensils, laundry equipment, metal furniture, and power mower housings: Weighs specified amounts of ingots or scrap and loads metal into furnace. Turns valve to regulate temperature in furnace. Verifies specified pouring temperature of molten metal, using pyrometer. Positions and clamps specified mold in holding device. Dips hand ladle into furnace pot and pours molten metal into mold. Observes light on preset timing gauge which indicates metal in mold has solidified. Removes casting from mold with handtools, and examines casting for defects, such as cracks, chips, and missing metal. May transport ladle from furnace to pouring station, using jib or monorail crane.

GOE: 06.02.10 STRENGTH: M GED: R2 M2 L2 SVP: 3 DLU: 77

502.482-014 CASTING-MACHINE OPERATOR, AUTOMATIC (elec. equip.) alternate titles: parts-casting-machine operator

Operates one or more automatic single- or multiple-mold casting machines to mold storage battery parts, such as grids, connectors, and posts: Loads lead bars or shovels pig lead and scrap lead into melting kettle. Ignites burners and sets controls to melt lead and heat molds to specified temperature. Smokes or coats mold with compound to prevent sticking, using acetylene torch or spray gun. Aligns and adjusts mold halves to ensure casting of grids according to specified thickness, using handtools. Turns valves to control flow of lead to ladles and water to mold-cooling sprays. Starts machine that automatically pours specified amount of lead from ladle into mold. Inspects parts ejected from molds to detect defects or discolorations, and measures and weighs grids, using fixed gauges and scale, to ensure conformance to thickness and weight specifications. Adjusts temperatures of lead and molds and flow of lead or water to correct defects. Removes lead adhering to mold, using brush or scraper. Skims dross from molten lead, using hand ladle. May operate single-mold machine equipped with press that automatically trims grids. May repair pipe connections and stitch or replace conveyor belt, using handtools. May change or adjust molds.
GOE: 06.02.10 STRENGTH: M GED: R3 M2 L2 SVP: 4 DLU: 77

502.482-018 ROTOR CASTING-MACHINE OPERATOR (elec. equip.) alternate titles: die-casting machine operator

Sets up and operates die press, using demountable dies (dies with interchangeable parts) to cast motor and generator rotors: Stacks rotor core laminations [LAMINATION ASSEMBLER (elec. equip.)] and mounts them over keyed mandrel secured to die base of casting machine. Verifies skew of core slots, using fixed gauge and places die shell and top plate over assembly and secures with C-clamp. Loads aluminum bar stock into pot-type furnace. Observes thermocouple dial and turns gas valve to regulate temperature of molten metal. Lines cylinder pot with asbestos strips and disk to prevent chilling. Pours specified amount of molten aluminum into cylinder, using hand ladle. Loads die and lamination assembly into press cavity and closes door. Pulls levers to activate die rams that force molten aluminum through and around laminations and eject cast rotor from press cylinder. Removes and stamps rotor with identifying data.
GOE: 06.02.10 STRENGTH: H GED: R3 M2 L2 SVP: 5 DLU: 77

502.664-010 BLAST-FURNACE KEEPER (steel & rel.)

Taps blast furnace to fill ladles with molten metal: Drills taphole preparatory to tapping, using power hand drill. Positions splasher plate in front of taphole to prevent splashing of metal when furnace is tapped. Guides point of oxygen lance into drilled taphole to tap furnace. Opens gates and shutters to direct flow of molten iron onto runners and into ladles. Plugs taphole after ladles are filled, using mud gun. Assists other workers in breaking up and removing slag from runners, relining runners with sand, clay, and refractory mixture, and drying relined runners. Repairs or replaces defective tuyeres, blowpipes, and boshplates in furnace, using handtools.
GOE: 06.04.10 STRENGTH: H GED: R3 M2 L2 SVP: 6 DLU: 77

502.664-014 STEEL POURER (steel & rel.) alternate titles: caster

Pours molten metal into molds to form ingots: Examines molds to ensure that they are clean, smooth, and coated. Signals OVERHEAD CRANE OPERATOR (any industry) 921.663-010 to position pouring nozzle of ladle over molds. Pulls lever to lift ladle stopper and allow molten steel to flow into ingot molds to specified height. Replaces defective stoppers, using handtools, sledges, and bars. Signals STEEL-POURER HELPER (steel & rel.) during steel pouring operation to obtain sample of steel for analysis, spray water on filled molds, and cap molds. Removes solidified steel or slag from pouring nozzle, using long bar or oxygen burner.
GOE: 06.02.24 STRENGTH: M GED: R3 M2 L2 SVP: 6 DLU: 77

502.664-018 STEEL-POURER HELPER (steel & rel.)

Assists STEEL POURER (steel & rel.) in pouring molten metal into molds: Places equipment, such as shovels, water hose, and boards on pouring platform. Counts molds and caps to ensure specified number for pouring operation. Measures and marks molds to indicate specified filling heights, using tape and chalk. Weighs specified additives, and transports additives to pouring platform, using wheelbarrow. Shovels additives into molds to prevent metal from boiling and forming air bubbles inside ingot. Signals OVERHEAD CRANE OPERATOR (any industry) 921.663-010 to position hot-tops (covers) or steel plates on filled molds to retard cooling of steel. Pours sample of molten steel into test mold for laboratory analysis. Sprays mold covers with water to cool covers. Signals OVERHEAD CRANE OPERATOR (any industry) to remove covers from molds after steel has solidified. Removes bricks from ladles that require relining and sets stopper assemblies and nozzles in relined ladles, using bars, sledge, and handtools. Performs other duties as described under HELPER (any industry) Master Title.
GOE: 06.02.24 STRENGTH: M GED: R2 M2 L2 SVP: 5 DLU: 77

502.682-010 BULLET-CASTING OPERATOR (ordnance)

Controls automatic equipment to melt and cast lead into cylindrical billets, and extrude billets into wire for making bullets and cores used in small arms ammunition: Starts electric furnace, observes gauges, and turns rheostat to maintain specified temperature and pressure. Charges furnace with lead pigs and scrap of specified alloy, using conveyor and elevating platform. Skims

dross from molten lead with skimming ladle. Turns wheel to adjust flow of molten lead into mold. Adjusts stroke of billet extractor mechanism, installs extruding dies, and regulates ram speed and flow of water coolant, using handtools. Threads extruded wire over pulleys into slug-forming machines or through guide pipes to be coiled in drums. Verifies wire size with snap gauges to ensure conformity to specifications.
GOE: 06.02.10 STRENGTH: H GED: R3 M2 L2 SVP: 4 DLU: 77

502.682-014 CASTING-MACHINE OPERATOR (nonfer. metal)
Sets up and operates continuous casting machine to produce tubes and rods: Threads graphite die into bottom of crucible that holds molten metal during casting process. Places water jacket around die and connects waterlines. Inserts metal bar (starting tip) through die into crucible to form weld with molten metal. Inserts metal extension rod through driving rollers and threads rod to starting tip. Regulates speed of rollers to draw extension rod, starting tip, and molten metal through die in continuous casting process.
GOE: 06.02.10 STRENGTH: M GED: R3 M2 L2 SVP: 4 DLU: 77

502.682-018 CENTRIFUGAL-CASTING-MACHINE OPERATOR (jewelry-silver.) alternate titles: caster
Operates one or more centrifugal-casting machines to cast metal parts of costume jewelry: Dusts inside of rubber mold with chalkdust compound to facilitate flow of metal during casting and prevent mold from burning. Fits halves of molds together and places them on mold setting. Places disks under mold to adjust working pressure. Positions metal-pressure plate on mold to level mold on machine. Sets dial for specified pressure and speed of rotation, closes lid, and starts machine. Pours molten metal through funnel into machine, using ladle. Stops machine and removes mold. Separates halves of mold to remove casting, using pliers. May cast wax models of jewelry.
GOE: 06.02.10 STRENGTH: L GED: R3 M2 L2 SVP: 5 DLU: 77

502.684-010 LEAD CASTER (elec. equip.) alternate titles: parts caster, hand
Casts lead storage battery parts, such as grids, connectors, posts, and straps: Installs specified type and size mold on bed of machine, using handtools. Loads lead bars or shovels pig lead or scrap lead into melting kettle. Ignites burner and sets controls to melt and heat lead to casting temperature. Coats or smokes faces of mold to prevent sticking, using spray gun or acetylene torch. Dips ladle into molten metal and pours metal into mold. Moves lever or strikes knock-out pins with mallet to open mold and release parts. Inspects parts for cracks, flash, or faulty molding, and adjusts temperature of kettle to correct defects. Trims edges of parts, using hand scraper or pedal-operated power shear. Cleans mold, using brush. May change mold inserts and adjust knock-out pins, using handtools and depth gauge. May position and manually hold one half of mold against other half, pour metal into mold, and separate mold parts and loosen castings, using soft mallet. May pour lead into molds held in radial arms of machine that brings molds to worker and discharges castings onto table. May sort and weigh parts. May be designated according to part cast as Grid Caster (elec. equip.).
GOE: 06.04.10 STRENGTH: L GED: R2 M2 L2 SVP: 3 DLU: 77

502.684-014 MILL HELPER (nonfer. metal) alternate titles: lead-sheet cutter
Mixes specified ingredients with molten lead, pours lead into molds, and cuts lead slabs to specified dimensions: Charges kettle with materials for melting, using shovel. Guides crane-supported mixer into kettle, and mixes contents in kettle. Opens valve permitting molten metal to flow into mold to form slab. Skims surface of bath to remove impurities, using skimming board. Marks cutting lines on lead sheet, using chalk, steel square, and tape measure, after ROLLING-MILL OPERATOR (nonfer. metal) has rolled slabs into sheets of specified thickness. Guides power-driven knife along chalklines to cut sheets to specified size. Cuts smaller sheets, using portable electric saw or slitting machine. May melt solidified metal in outlet pipes, using gas torch.
GOE: 06.04.24 STRENGTH: H GED: R2 M2 L2 SVP: 3 DLU: 77

502.684-018 MOLD SETTER (elec. equip.) alternate titles: casting-machine adjuster
Positions and aligns molds used for hand or machine casting lead parts, such as grids, battery posts, and straps: Positions and secures mold on bed of machine, using handtools. Adjusts timing mechanism to coordinate flow of lead and coolant to molds. May oversee workers engaged in hand or machine casting.
GOE: 06.04.32 STRENGTH: M GED: R3 M3 L3 SVP: 3 DLU: 77

502.684-022 NEEDLE LEADER (button & notion) alternate titles: needle molder
Casts needle or thread guide assemblies for use in knitting machines: Selects size and type of mold according to instructions. Positions needles or thread guides into mold slots with fingers and closes mold preparatory to casting process. Ladles molten lead into mold opening to form casting around parts. Removes assembly from mold, using pliers. Cuts excess lead from assembly and smooths rough edges, using knife, saw, and electric grinder. May align needles or thread guides, using gauges, hammer, and pliers.
GOE: 06.04.32 STRENGTH: L GED: R2 M2 L2 SVP: 2 DLU: 77

502.685-010 MOLDER, LEAD INGOT (ordnance)
Tends furnace to melt lead-antimony pigs and scrap, and ladles molten metal into molds: Slides pigs into furnace pot, allowing oil fumes to burn off melting

metal to avoid accumulation of explosive oil vapor-air mixture. Stirs molten metal, skims dross from surface, and ladles metal into ingot molds. Turns valves to control flow of coolant water to molds. Inverts molds, when metal is solidified, and knocks ingots loose.
GOE: 06.04.10 STRENGTH: H GED: R2 M2 L2 SVP: 2 DLU: 77

502.685-014 REMELTER (elec. equip.; machinery mfg.; print. & pub.)
Tends furnace that melts scrap metal and casts it into pigs (bars or ingots) for reuse: Regulates furnace controls to attain specified temperature. Shovels scrap metal into furnace. Skims dross (scum) from molten metal, using ladle. Turns valve and allows molten metal to run into molds to form pigs. Removes cooled pigs from mold and stacks pigs in storage area.
GOE: 06.04.10 STRENGTH: M GED: R2 M2 L2 SVP: 2 DLU: 77

502.686-010 CASTING-MACHINE-OPERATOR HELPER (elec. equip.) alternate titles: grid-casting-machine-operator helper
Assists CASTING-MACHINE OPERATOR, AUTOMATIC (elec. equip.) in molding storage battery grids performing such tasks as removing grids from machine rails, counting grids, and stacking grids on dollies. Performs other duties as described under HELPER (any industry) Master Title.
GOE: 06.04.10 STRENGTH: M GED: R2 M1 L1 SVP: 2 DLU: 77

502.687-010 BLAST-FURNACE-KEEPER HELPER (steel & rel.)
Assists BLAST-FURNACE KEEPER (steel & rel.) in tapping blast furnace: Breaks slag from casting equipment, such as slag runners, iron troughs, gates, and dams, using bars, hammers, and shovels. Relines runners, troughs, gates, and dams with refractory materials, such as fireclay, sand, and coal dust. Cleans and loads clay gun for plugging taphole. Removes obstructions in runners during casting operations, using tong bar. Obtains sample of molten iron during cast, with spoon and pours sample into test mold. Assists in changing tuyeres, coolers, cinder notches, and blowpipes on blast furnace, using handtools. Cleans dust, debris, and solidified metal from blast furnace and casting area. Performs other duties as described under HELPER (any industry) Master Title.
GOE: 06.04.10 STRENGTH: H GED: R2 M2 L2 SVP: 3 DLU: 77

502.687-014 BUSHER (nonmet. min.)
Pours molten lead into center of grinding wheels to form bushing: Lights blowtorch under pot to melt lead. Positions grinding wheels on table with shaft or spindle protruding through center of wheel. Fills area around shaft with molten lead to form bushing. Cuts excess lead from around edge of bushing, using mallet, chisel, and power reamer.
GOE: 06.04.32 STRENGTH: H GED: R2 M1 L1 SVP: 2 DLU: 77

502.687-018 LEAD-CASTER HELPER (elec. equip.)
Performs any combination of following duties pertaining to casting of lead storage battery parts: Inspects cast storage-battery parts, such as lead washers, lugs, connectors, straps, and trimmed grids for holes, warps, discoloration, or other defects, and segregates rejects for salvage. Cleans excess lead (fins, flashings, and burs) from parts, using handtools. Stacks acceptable grids and sorts other parts according to type. Shovels pig and scrap lead into melting kettle. Skims dross from molten metal, using ladle. May tally number and type of rejects. May be designated according to part processed as Casting Inspector (elec. equip.); Grid Inspector (elec. equip.); or task performed as Lead-Supply Worker (elec. equip.).
GOE: 06.04.24 STRENGTH: L GED: R2 M1 L1 SVP: 2 DLU: 77

503 PICKLING, CLEANING, DEGREASING, AND RELATED OCCUPATIONS

This group includes occupations concerned with removing coatings of grease, scale, tarnish, oxide, etc., from metal objects to obtain a clean surface. Cleaning is usually accomplished by subjecting the metal objects to acid baths.

503.137-010 SUPERVISOR, SANDBLASTER (ship-boat mfg.)
Supervises and coordinates activities of workers engaged in sandblasting surfaces of ships in drydock and shop equipment: Confers with planning personnel to ensure requisition of equipment and materials. Inspects work to ensure conformance to prescribed standards. Trains new workers. Performs other duties as described under SUPERVISOR (any industry) Master Title.
GOE: 05.12.01 STRENGTH: L GED: R4 M3 L3 SVP: 7 DLU: 77

503.362-010 PICKLER, CONTINUOUS PICKLING LINE (any industry) alternate titles: cleaner operator; continuous-dryout operator; pickler operator; strip cleaner
Sets up and controls continuous pickling or electrolytic-cleaning line to remove dirt, oil, and scale from coils of brass, copper, or steel strip and wire: Turns valve to add acid to processing tanks and shovels inhibitor into tanks to obtain baths of specified acid concentration. Installs and adjusts guides, pinch and leveler rolls, and side shears on processing line, according to specified dimensions of coils to be cleaned, using handtools. Moves controls to regulate speed of coil through line, to shear coil on each side of weld or stitch, and to remove coil from upcoiler machine. Verifies dimensions of pickled coils, using micrometer and measuring tapes. Examines surface of coils to verify removal of dirt, oil, and scale. Tests solution concentration in baths, using titration test equipment, and adjusts processing line controls to ensure conformance to specifications. May be designated according to type of line controlled as Electrolytic De-Scaler (any industry).
GOE: 06.02.10 STRENGTH: M GED: R3 M3 L2 SVP: 6 DLU: 78

503.362-014 SHOTBLAST-EQUIPMENT OPERATOR (foundry)

Operates equipment to clean dirt, scale, and core materials from steel castings with blasts of steel shot: Presses control panel buttons to adjust equipment settings for manual or automatic operations, length of cycle, sequence and timing of various operations, and position of oscillator. Moves control to activate tow-mechanism drive to transport trolley loaded with castings into shotblast chamber, and watches operation to ensure that hydraulic doors close completely, trolley and oscillator positions are correct, and that air turbine and shotblast wheels start in sequence. Monitors control panel dials and listens to equipment operations to detect jams or malfunctions. Stops equipment to clear jams, replace fallen castings, reposition oscillator, and adjust hydraulic equipment. Notifies machine repairer when unable to correct malfunction. Greases equipment, maintains hydraulic fluid levels, and performs minor maintenance, using grease gun and handtools.
GOE: 06.02.10 STRENGTH: H GED: R3 M2 L3 SVP: 5 DLU: 86

503.684-010 CLEANER (ordnance)

Cleans and prepares subassemblies of pistols, rifles, shotguns, and revolvers for bluing: Disassembles components, such as barrel and ratchet, trigger and hammer, trigger guard, and back strap. Blows out particles remaining after sand blasting, using airhose. Places parts in rack or wire basket and immerses parts in degreasing tank to remove oil and dirt. Mixes alcohol and whitening powder and rubs resultant paste onto gun parts to facilitate bluing. Wires parts together and attaches them to immersing rod. Blows excess solution from blued parts with airhose. Inspects parts for nicks, scratches, clearness of trademark, and cleanness. Reassembles subassemblies, using screwdriver. May pour specified amount of chemical solution (acid) into degreasing tanks.
GOE: 06.04.39 STRENGTH: L GED: R2 M1 L1 SVP: 3 DLU: 77

503.685-010 COATER (business ser.)

Tends equipment that cleans, coats, and dries baking pans: Mixes cleaning and glazing solutions according to formula or uses premixed solutions. Places pans in baskets and immerses baskets in stripping and soaking tanks to remove glaze and corrosion. Fills spray reservoirs with cleaning and glazing solutions. Removes pans from tanks and places pans on conveyor that carries pans through sprays that wash and coat surfaces with glazing solution to reduce need for greasing and to protect them against rust. Turns nozzles to adjust direction and pressure of sprays. Transfers pans to ovens that dry coating. Turns knobs to adjust oven temperature according to chart. Removes pans from oven and examines surfaces to detect defects, such as warpage and uneven coating. Tends hydraulic press to straighten warped pans. May tend overhead hoist to immerse and transfer pans to and from tanks, conveyors, and ovens. May load and unload pans from trucks, using handtruck.
GOE: 06.04.21 STRENGTH: M GED: R3 M2 L2 SVP: 4 DLU: 77

503.685-014 DIP-LUBE OPERATOR (ordnance)

Tends tanks to clean lead bullets and coat bullets with wax: Scoops bullets into perforated drum and immerses bullets in solvent to remove chips and grease. Immerses bullets into molten wax. Presses buttons on portable control box to rotate drum. Empties coated bullets onto conveyor belt, closes cover of blower, and starts blower to dry wax and draw off solvent fumes. Examines bullets for defects, such as malformations, gouges, dents, or blunted ends. Discards defective bullets. Starts conveyor to dump bullets that conform to standards into tote boxes. Tests coating solution, using hydrometer, and adds solvent or wax to maintain specified viscosity.
GOE: 06.04.21 STRENGTH: H GED: R2 M1 L1 SVP: 2 DLU: 77

503.685-018 DRIFTER (steel & rel.) alternate titles: drifting-machine operator

Tends drifting machine that removes scale from inner surfaces of pipe: Installs specified drift mandrel in machine, using handtools, and inserts pipe into head of machine. Moves controls to tighten pneumatic grip that holds pipe in position, and to move mandrel in and out of pipe to loosen scale.
GOE: 06.04.02 STRENGTH: M GED: R2 M2 L1 SVP: 3 DLU: 77

503.685-022 FLAME DEGREASER (automotive ser.)

Tends oven and auxiliary equipment that burn away grease from used automobile parts preparatory to rebuilding: Ignites gas jets in degreasing oven. Starts machine conveyor and hangs or places grease-coated parts on moving conveyor that carries them through oven and deposits them in collecting basket. Shuts off machine when basket is full. Removes deposited soot and other foreign matter from parts, after parts have cooled, using rotating power brush.
GOE: 06.04.39 STRENGTH: M GED: R1 M1 L1 SVP: 2 DLU: 77

503.685-026 FURNACE-AND-WASH-EQUIPMENT OPERATOR (ordnance) alternate titles: continuous-washer operator

Tends equipment that cleans and dries metal cartridge parts: Loads parts into hopper by hand or using hoist. Moves switches to start conveyor system and rotate open end tumbling barrels that remove oil, scale, and dirt from cartridge parts. Turns steam and water valves and reads gauges to regulate temperature and level of cleaning solutions in tanks and to regulate temperature in drying drum. Adds chemicals, such as acids and detergents, to maintain solutions at specified concentrations. Examines parts at ejection chute to ensure parts are cleaned and dried according to specifications. May operate electric tier-lift truck to position containers filled with parts on platform above feed hopper. May tumble parts in metal-drawing (lubricating) solution prior to drying process.
GOE: 06.04.10 STRENGTH: M GED: R2 M2 L2 SVP: 2 DLU: 77

503.685-030 METAL-CLEANER, IMMERSION (any industry) alternate titles: acid dipper; cleaner; galvanizer; grease remover; neutralizer; pickler; pickling operator; pickling-tank operator; power washer; process treater

Tends equipment that chemically cleans grease, scale, dirt, and other foreign matter from metal objects to prepare them for processes, such as electroplating and galvanizing: Removes shavings, dirt, and rust spots from objects, using airhose, file, or sandpaper. Loads objects on conveyor which carries them through series of chemical and rinsing baths, or places objects on racks or in containers and immerses objects in chemical and rinsing solutions, manually or using hoist. Moves controls to start conveyor and to regulate temperature of solution or conveyor speed. Maintains consistency of cleaning solutions by adding specified amount of chemical to solutions. Drains, cleans, and refills tanks with chemicals. May dry objects, using dryer. May examine cleaned objects to ensure conformance to standards. May be known as Degreaser (any industry); or may be designated according to type of cleaning equipment as Ultrasonic Cleaner (any industry).
GOE: 06.04.39 STRENGTH: M GED: R2 M2 L1 SVP: 2 DLU: 86

503.685-034 METAL-WASHING-MACHINE OPERATOR (svc. ind. mach.)

Tends machine that washes, rustproofs, and dries metal parts used in air-conditioners: Turns valves to activate spray washers. Reads dial instruments and turns valves to adjust pressure. Observes machine operation and loads conveyor line hooks with parts which are then degreased, rinsed, coated with rustproof film, and dried in oven. Tests solutions in tanks by placing few drops in test tubes or pipettes, applying chemical reagents and observing reaction of test sample. Strengthens or dilutes solution as necessary. May perform same tasks on parts used in manufacture of oil burners.
GOE: 06.04.21 STRENGTH: M GED: R2 M2 L2 SVP: 2 DLU: 77

503.685-038 SANDBLAST OPERATOR (ordnance)

Tends automatic sandblasting machine that cleans grease, oil, and grit from fragmentation-bomb cavities: Rolls bomb off conveyor into machine cabinet. Closes door and sets automatic timer at starting position. Pushes button to release pressurized sand stream into bomb cavity. Stops machine when timer indicates completion of sandblasting. Opens cabinet and removes bomb.
GOE: 06.04.02 STRENGTH: M GED: R2 M2 L1 SVP: 3 DLU: 77

503.685-042 SANDBLAST-OR-SHOTBLAST-EQUIPMENT TENDER (any industry) alternate titles: bead blasting machine tender; shot-blast tender

Performs any combination of following tasks to tend equipment that cleans dirt, scale, and other materials from metal objects with blast of abrasive, such as steel shot, sand, steel grit, or glass beads: Dumps or shovels objects into tumbler and starts tumbler that exposes surfaces of objects to blast of abrasive and tumbling action. Stacks objects on racks, places racks in chamber, and starts blast of abrasive. Places objects on moving conveyor that carries objects under blast of abrasive. Adjusts controls on equipment to regulate pressure and amount of abrasive blast. Pours or shovels abrasive material into feed hopper to replenish supply. May tend equipment to harden or strengthen surface of metal parts and be designated Shot-Peen Operator (any industry).
GOE: 05.12.18 STRENGTH: M GED: R2 M2 L1 SVP: 2 DLU: 87

503.685-046 STRIP-TANK TENDER (ordnance) alternate titles: enthone solder stripper

Tends electrolytic stripping tank to remove excess silver solder from brazed areas of shotgun barrels: Loads barrels in rack and immerses rack in hot cleaning solution and rinsing baths, to remove grease and dirt. Lowers rack into electrolytic tank filled with sodium cyanide solution, using chain hoist. Connects positive charge (anode) to rack and turns valves to regulate temperature and level of liquid in tank. Turns controls to set timing cycle and to regulate flow of current through solution. Returns barrels containing excess solder to tanks for additional treatment. Dips barrels in rinsing tank and immerses them in oil bath to impart rustproof coating. Tests strength of cleaning and stripping solutions, using hydrometer, and adds chemicals to solution to maintain specified concentrations.
GOE: 06.04.10 STRENGTH: M GED: R2 M2 L1 SVP: 3 DLU: 77

503.686-010 PICKLER HELPER, CONTINUOUS PICKLING LINE (any industry) alternate titles: continuous-dryout-operator helper

Assists PICKLER, CONTINUOUS PICKLING LINE (any industry) 503.362-010 in cleaning coils of metal strips and wire: Sets specified spacing between scale-breaking and straightening rolls and adjusts wipers, brushes, and feed guides, using handtools. Places metal coil on feed-out reel manually or with hoist and feeds leading edge of coil into rollers. Moves controls to lock trailing edge of processed coil to leading edge of coil on feed-out reel to form continuous workpiece. Stacks processed coils on skids. Performs other duties as described under HELPER (any industry) Master Title.
GOE: 06.02.21 STRENGTH: M GED: R2 M2 L2 SVP: 3 DLU: 78

503.687-010 SANDBLASTER (any industry) alternate titles: abrasive-blasting equipment operator

Abrades surfaces of metal or hard-composition objects to remove adhering scale, sand, paint, grease, tar, rust, and dirt, and to impart specified finish, using abrasive-blasting equipment: Shovels or pours abrasives, such as sand, grit, or shot of specified grade into machine hopper. Masks specified areas of object to protect from abrading action. Loads parts on racks in enclosed rooms, into

tumbling barrels, or into cabinets. Turns valves on equipment to regulate pressure and composition of abrasive mixture flowing through nozzle or into tumbling barrel. Starts equipment that directs blast or flow of abrasive-laden compressed air, gas, or liquid over surface of parts. Manually directs nozzle over surface of large parts or inserts arms through glove-fitted cabinet openings and manipulates small parts under nozzle for specified interval. May examine finished parts to ensure conformance to specifications. May be designated by type of equipment or abrasive used as Cabinet-Abrasive Sandblaster (any industry); Shotblaster (any industry).
GOE: 05.12.18 STRENGTH: M GED: R2 M2 L1 SVP: 2 DLU: 87

504 HEAT-TREATING OCCUPATIONS

This group includes occupations concerned with subjecting metal to heat, cold, or chemicals to relieve or redistribute stresses and affect such characteristics as hardness, flexibility, and ductility.

504.131-010 HEAT-TREAT SUPERVISOR (heat treating) alternate titles: heat treater, head; supervisor, hardening; supervisor, heat treating

Supervises and coordinates activities of workers engaged in hardening, tempering, annealing, and other heat-treating processes to condition metal workpieces and products, applying knowledge of heat-treating processes and properties and structure of metals. Conducts metallurgical analyses on metal samples and machine tools. Estimates, requisitions, and inspects materials. Confers with other supervisory personnel to coordinate activities of individual departments. Confers with workers' representatives to resolve grievances. Trains workers. Performs other duties as described under SUPERVISOR (any industry) Master Title.
GOE: 06.01.01 STRENGTH: L GED: R4 M3 L3 SVP: 7 DLU: 77

504.281-010 HEAT-TREAT INSPECTOR (heat treating)

Inspects parts and assemblies before and after heat-treating for conformance to specifications: Examines parts for cleanliness and previous inspection clearances. Reads control dials, such as pyrometer, at periodic intervals to ensure specified temperatures, and soaking and cooling times are maintained. Examines processed parts for conformance to specifications, using handtools and precision measuring instruments. Stamps approved items and writes rejection notices and rework orders on parts not meeting specifications. May operate equipment to determine hardness of parts and thermal treatment required to process parts, following blueprint specifications [HARDNESS INSPECTOR (heat treating)].
GOE: 06.01.05 STRENGTH: L GED: R4 M3 L3 SVP: 7 DLU: 77

504.360-010 FLAME-ANNEALING-MACHINE SETTER (heat treating)

Sets up battery of machines that anneal sidewalls of metal cartridge and shell cases preparatory to further processing: Lights gas burners and turns valves to regulate flow of gas and coolant water. Starts conveyors and dial feeder plates, and turns setscrews in burner nozzles to direct flames which anneal specific area of cartridge case. Replaces worn dial-feed, burner and conveyor parts, using handtools. Instructs new workers in machine operation. Observes color and area of dullness of annealed cases to determine flame temperature and coverage of cases. Crushes random samples between fingers to determine degree of annealing attained. May test cases for hardness [HARDNESS INSPECTOR (heat treating)] and examine cases to determine grain size of metal, using microscope.
GOE: 06.01.02 STRENGTH: L GED: R4 M3 L3 SVP: 6 DLU: 77

504.380-010 FLAME-HARDENING-MACHINE SETTER (heat treating)

Sets up flame-hardening machines for FLAME-HARDENING-MACHINE OPERATORS (heat treating) according to metallurgical work order specifications, utilizing knowledge of heat-treating methods and metal properties: Positions fixture for holding workpiece and fastens fixture to machine, using wrenches. Mounts workpiece in fixture, on arbor, or between centers of machine. Estimates flame temperature and heating time cycle based on degree of hardness required and metal to be treated. Moves controls to light burners and adjust flame of oxyacetylene, propane, or other gas to prescribed temperature, judging temperature by flame color. Starts automatic feeding or rotating mechanism that moves part through hardening flame. Tests hardness of sample part [HARDNESS INSPECTOR (heat treating)]. Adjusts automatic feeding or rotating mechanism and flame temperature until sample parts meet specifications.
GOE: 06.01.02 STRENGTH: M GED: R4 M3 L3 SVP: 7 DLU: 77

504.380-014 INDUCTION-MACHINE SETTER (heat treating)

Sets up variety of induction machines for INDUCTION-MACHINE OPERATORS (heat treating) to heattreat metal objects according to specifications: Reads work order to determine size and grade of workpiece to be processed. Determines frequency of current, time cycle, and induction heating coil to be used for each job, using knowledge of induction machines, heat-treating methods, and properties of metals. Positions and fastens induction coil and fixture on machine, using wrenches. Adjusts controls to set frequency of current and automatic timer judging from color whether pan is heated to specified temperature. Positions and fastens part in fixture and starts machine to heattreat sample part. Tests hardness of sample [HARDNESS INSPECTOR (heat treating)]. Adjusts frequency of current, automatic timer, and fixture on machine until sample meets specifications. May operate induction machine as part of regular duties.
GOE: 06.01.02 STRENGTH: M GED: R3 M3 L3 SVP: 7 DLU: 77

504.382-010 HARDENER (clock & watch)

Controls furnace to harden, anneal, or temper watch parts: Presses button to admit gas mixture, forcing air out of furnace and burning mixture at entrance to prevent discoloration of parts and to maintain carbon content in parts. Places parts in metal basket or cylinder and inserts parts into furnace at specified temperature. Advises on furnace temperatures and heat-treating time periods, and recommends procedures to produce desired hardness. Quenches pieces with air or oil. May cover parts with charcoal to prevent rapid heating causing discoloration of parts. May insert thermocouple into furnace and connect thermocouple to recorder.
GOE: 06.02.10 STRENGTH: H GED: R4 M3 L3 SVP: 6 DLU: 77

504.382-014 HEAT TREATER I (heat treating)

Controls heat-treating furnaces, baths and quenching equipment to alter physical and chemical properties of metal objects, using specifications and methods of controlled heating and cooling, such as hardening, tempering, annealing, case-hardening, and normalizing: Determines temperature and time of heating cycle, and type and temperature of baths and quenching medium to attain specified hardness, toughness, and ductility of parts, using standard heat-treating charts, and utilizing knowledge of heat-treating methods, equipment, and properties of metals. Adjusts furnace controls and observes pyrometer to bring furnace to prescribed temperature. Loads parts into furnace. Removes parts after prescribed time and quenches parts in water, oil, brine, or other bath, or allows parts to cool in air. May test hardness of parts [HARDNESS INSPECTOR (heat treating)]. May set up and operate die-quenching machine to prevent parts from warping. May set up and operate electronic induction equipment to heat objects [INDUCTION-MACHINE SETTER (heat treating)]. May align warped fuel elements, containing radioactive uranium, using hydraulic ram straightener.
GOE: 06.02.10 STRENGTH: M GED: R4 M3 L3 SVP: 7 DLU: 77

504.382-018 HEAT-TREATER APPRENTICE (heat treating)

Performs duties as described under APPRENTICE (any industry) Master Title.
GOE: 06.02.10 STRENGTH: M GED: R4 M3 L3 SVP: 7 DLU: 77

504.387-010 HARDNESS INSPECTOR (heat treating)

Tests metal objects to determine their degree of hardness, using hardness testing equipment: Positions workpiece on anvil of testing machine and turns controls to press steel ball or diamond point against surface of piece or to allow diamond-pointed hammer fall on surface to be tested. Measures diameter of indentation caused by steel balls, using microscope, or reads scale on test equipment that indicates depth of penetration of ball or diamond point, or calibrated height of hammer rebound. Reads hardness number from calibrated scale on equipment or converts scale reading to hardness number, using formula or conversion chart. Important variables may be indicated by trade names of equipment used. May cut cross section of sample part and examine part under microscope to determine hardness depth.
GOE: 06.03.01 STRENGTH: M GED: R3 M3 L2 SVP: 4 DLU: 77

504.485-010 RIVET HEATER (heat treating)

Tends furnace that heats rivets to specified temperature: Places specified rivets in gas, oil, or coke furnace, or between electrodes in electric furnace. Turns knobs to regulate heat or current of furnace. Removes rivets from furnace when color indicates rivets are heated to specified temperature and throws rivets to RIVETER HELPER (any industry), using tongs. May tend portable coke furnace to heat rivets in field. May be designated according to type of furnace tended as Rivet Heater, Electric (heat treating); Rivet Heater, Gas (heat treating).
GOE: 05.12.10 STRENGTH: M GED: R3 M2 L2 SVP: 4 DLU: 77

504.665-010 SLAB-DEPILER OPERATOR (steel & rel.) alternate titles: table and slab depiler

Tends equipment that transfers steel slabs from conveyor onto charging table of reheating furnace: Moves controls to transfer slab from conveyor onto depiler. Measures slab for conformance to specifications, using tape, and compares identifying marks on slab with information on charging schedule. Pushes levers to lower depiler table and cause pushoff arm of depiler to push slab onto charging table. Assists furnace crew in cleaning bottom of furnace and hearth and in positioning slabs in furnace.
GOE: 06.04.10 STRENGTH: M GED: R3 M2 L2 SVP: 4 DLU: 77

504.665-014 CHARGER OPERATOR (steel & rel.) alternate titles: charger; pusher

Tends charging mechanism that moves steel shapes, such as blooms, billets, and slabs, in specified sequence, through soaking-pit furnace: Signals CHARGER-OPERATOR HELPER (steel & rel.) 504.686-010 or OVERHEAD CRANE OPERATOR (any industry) 921.663-010 to position steel on furnace skids. Moves levers on control panel to position skid on entry bed, open furnace door, and start pusher arm that pushes steel into furnace. Observes inside of furnace, projected on television screen, and moves controls to spot steel in specified locations. Moves controls to discharge steel onto mill rollers. Records quantity of steel charged and discharged. Assists other workers in cleaning furnace bottoms and repairing or replacing defective equipment, using handtools.
GOE: 06.04.10 STRENGTH: L GED: R3 M2 L2 SVP: 4 DLU: 78

504.682-010 ANNEALER (heat treating) alternate titles: normalizer

Controls furnace to relieve internal stresses in metal objects and to soften and refine grain structure: Reads production schedule to determine processing se-

quence and furnace temperatures for objects to be processed. Turns furnace controls and observes gauges to prepare furnace for annealing process. Charges objects directly onto furnace bed, or packs objects into section of furnace or tubes sealed with clay to prevent oxidation. Reduces heat and allows objects to cool in furnace, or removes objects from furnace to cool in open air. May operate continuous furnace through which objects are passed by means of reels and conveyors and be designated Continuous-Annealing Furnace Operator (heat treating). May anneal wire and be designated Pot Annealer (heat treating).
GOE: 06.02.10 STRENGTH: M GED: R3 M2 L1 SVP: 4 DLU: 78

504.682-014 CASE HARDENER (heat treating) alternate titles: carbonizer; carburizer

Controls furnace to harden surface of steel objects, using any of following methods: (1) Places objects in wire basket and immerses them in heated chemical bath, such as sodium cyanide. (2) Packs objects in metal boxes filled with carbonaceous material, such as coke, coal, bone charcoal, or barium carbonate, and charges boxes into furnace. (3) Charges objects into furnace and opens valves to circulate carbon-rich gas, such as methane, around objects during heating process. Removes objects from bath or furnace and quenches objects in oil, water, or brine, or allows objects to cool to predetermined temperature before quenching, depending on metal properties specified. May be designated according to article case-hardened as Die Case Hardener (heat treating); or by process used as Cyanide Furnace Operator (heat treating).
GOE: 06.02.10 STRENGTH: M GED: R3 M3 L2 SVP: 4 DLU: 77

504.682-018 HEAT TREATER II (heat treating)

Controls one or more furnaces to heat treat metal objects according to specifications: Places parts in racks, trays, or baskets, and places objects on conveyor or loads objects directly into furnace. Adjusts furnace temperature and observes pyrometer to heat metal to prescribed temperature. Sets speed of conveyor for prescribed time cycle, or records removal time of parts to ensure objects attain specified temperature for a specified time. Removes parts after prescribed time and quenches parts in water, oil, or other bath, or allows parts to cool in air. May test hardness of parts [HARDNESS INSPECTOR (heat treating)]. May feed die-quenching machine to prevent parts from warping. May degrease or remove scale from parts. May draw wire or sheet metal through furnace and attach metal to winding mechanism that pulls metal through furnace.
GOE: 06.02.10 STRENGTH: M GED: R3 M3 L2 SVP: 4 DLU: 77

504.682-022 HEAT-TREATING BLUER (heat treating) alternate titles: dulite-machine bluer

Operates gas furnace that heats metal gun parts to rustproof and impart decorative nonreflecting blue finish: Sprays parts with steam to remove grease, grit, and dirt. Places parts in barrel of gas furnace and covers parts with mixture of bone chips and whale or pine tar oil. Closes furnace door and moves lever to rotate barrel. Turns gas valves and observes pyrometer to regulate temperature of furnace. Opens door after furnace cools, and pulls lever to tilt barrel and dump contents into sieve. Sifts parts from bone mixture and quenches parts in oil. Blows oil and chips from blued parts, using airhose. Examines parts to ensure shade and color conform to specifications, utilizing knowledge of heat-treating methods and metal properties.
GOE: 06.02.10 STRENGTH: M GED: R3 M3 L3 SVP: 4 DLU: 77

504.682-026 TEMPERER (heat treating)

Controls furnace to reheat previously quenched and hardened metal objects, and quenches them in brine, water, oil, or molten lead to remove quenching strains and brittleness and to impart toughness to metal.
GOE: 06.02.10 STRENGTH: M GED: R3 M3 L2 SVP: 4 DLU: 77

504.685-010 BASE-DRAW OPERATOR (ordnance)

Tends electric furnace that anneals base sections of hardened projectile bodies to facilitate subsequent machining operations: Lifts projectile from conveyor with tongs and fits projectile in holder on machine table. Pushes switch to activate mechanism that elevates table and thrusts projectile base into furnace unit. Observes dial indicator and presses button to maintain flow of current according to specifications. Removes projectile when table descends automatically. Quenches projectile base in water.
GOE: 06.04.10 STRENGTH: M GED: R3 M2 L2 SVP: 3 DLU: 77

504.685-014 FLAME-HARDENING-MACHINE OPERATOR (heat treating) alternate titles: gas-anneal feeder

Tends flame-hardening machine, according to set procedures, to case-harden metal objects: Positions and fastens part in fixture, on arbor, or between centers of machine. Presses buttons on control panel to light burners that direct flame against part and start automatic feeding or spinning mechanism. Observes machine operation and removes finished part. May anneal metal cartridge or shell cases and be designated Flame-Annealing-Machine Operator (heat treating).
GOE: 06.04.10 STRENGTH: M GED: R2 M2 L1 SVP: 2 DLU: 77

504.685-018 HEAT-TREATER HELPER (heat treating) alternate titles: bluing-oven tender; draw-furnace tender; furnace feeder; furnace loader; heat-treat puller; tempering-kiln tender

Assists HEAT TREATER (heat treating) I or HEAT TREATER (heat treating) II in annealing, hardening, or tempering metal objects by performing any combination of the following duties: Cleans foreign matter, such as scale, rust, or grease, from metal objects, using solvents, wire brushes, scrapers, or hammer and chisel. Hangs parts on racks, hooks, or fixture, or places them on hand-

trucks or conveyors, and charges them into furnace manually or using hoist. Adjusts controls to maintain specified temperature in furnace. Immerses objects in chemical bath or places objects in containers and packs carbonaceous material around them. Quenches heated objects in liquid, such as oil or water. Marks identification on parts. Performs other duties as described under HELPER (any industry) Master Title.
GOE: 06.04.10 STRENGTH: M GED: R2 M2 L2 SVP: 2 DLU: 77

504.685-022 INDUCTION-MACHINE OPERATOR (heat treating) alternate titles: electronic induction hardener

Tends electronic induction machine, according to set procedures, to harden, braze, or anneal metal objects: Positions and fastens part in fixture of machine. Presses button on control panel to start electric current flowing through induction coil for prescribed time. May load automatic machine by dumping parts into hopper. May test parts for hardness, using preset hardness testing equipment, and stamp heat treatment identification mark on casting, using hammer and punch.
GOE: 06.04.10 STRENGTH: M GED: R2 M2 L1 SVP: 2 DLU: 77

504.685-026 PRODUCTION HARDENER (heat treating) alternate titles: carbonizer; case hardener

Tends battery of molten carbonizing salt bath or ammonia-methane furnaces that case harden steel objects, such as buckles, screws, wrenches, and bicycle crank cups: Loads objects by hand into wire basket attached to steel-rod handle. Immerses basket into chemical bath inside furnace pot or into ammonia-methane furnace. Scoops salt into furnace pots to maintain bath level or opens valves to inject gases into furnace, and sets timer. Removes basket from furnace at end of heating cycle and dumps objects into mesh container submerged in tank of quenching oil. May lift container from quenching tank and dip container in rinse water. Dumps objects into box or tray. May signal forklift operator to deposit or extract containers of objects into and from furnaces and quenching and rinse tanks.
GOE: 06.04.10 STRENGTH: H GED: R2 M2 L2 SVP: 3 DLU: 77

504.685-030 REEL-BLADE-BENDER FURNACE TENDER (agric. equip.)

Tends gas oven that heats lawnmower blades preparatory to bending: Places cold blade on furnace apron and presses pedal to raise furnace door. Positions blade in slotted rack on furnace bed, using tongs. Removes blade from furnace after specified time. Lubricates bending machine, using grease gun.
GOE: 06.04.10 STRENGTH: L GED: R1 M1 L1 SVP: 2 DLU: 77

504.686-010 CHARGER-OPERATOR HELPER (steel & rel.)

Assists CHARGER OPERATOR (steel & rel.) in moving steel blooms, billets, and slabs through soaking-pit furnace: Straightens steel on furnace skids and roller conveyor, using bar. Places separators between steel shapes and marks identifying information on shapes. May cut, transport and store trial bars in bins. Performs other duties as described under HELPER (any industry) Master Title.
GOE: 06.04.10 STRENGTH: M GED: R1 M1 L1 SVP: 2 DLU: 77

504.686-014 FURNACE HELPER (heat treating)

Performs any combination of following tasks near heat-treat furnace: Transfers metal slabs, plates, sheets, and fabricated forms from tables and conveyors to furnace cars and trays, using hoist, handtruck, tractor or by hand. Loads and unloads material from heat-treating, and process-chamber furnaces. Feeds metal into straightening rolls. Breaks lumps of sludge from furnace pots, using airhammer, and shovels sludge into crushing machine. Cuts, identifies, and marks samples, using shear and crayon. Verifies dimensions with tape and micrometer. Separates scrap for remelt according to marking. May feed metal rods from coils into furnace, using hoist, and wind rods into coils as rods emerge from furnace, using winding mechanism.
GOE: 06.04.10 STRENGTH: M GED: R2 M2 L1 SVP: 2 DLU: 77

504.686-018 HARDENER HELPER (clock & watch)

Assists HARDENER (clock & watch) in hardening and tempering watch parts, maintaining flow of work into and out of department, and cleaning and packaging finished work. Performs other duties as described under HELPER (any industry) Master Title.
GOE: 05.09.01 STRENGTH: H GED: R1 M1 L1 SVP: 2 DLU: 77

504.686-022 HEAT TREATER (electron. comp.)

Feeds and off bears furnace that heats semiconductor wafers to relieve stress caused by sawing and to stabilize resistivity: Transfers wafers from storage container to quartz *boat*. Places boat on conveyor belt that automatically moves wafers through furnace. Removes boat from conveyor belt at furnace exit. Transfers wafers from boat to storage container after cooling. Records production information on work order.
GOE: 06.04.19 STRENGTH: L GED: R1 M1 L1 SVP: 1 DLU: 86

504.687-010 ANNEALER (jewelry-silver.) alternate titles: heat treater

Heat treats jewelry fittings to soften fittings for further processing, using electric or gas furnace: Sets automatic controls to specified temperature. Fills steel tray with fittings and places fittings in oven, using tongs. Removes tray after specified time and immerses fittings in water. May clean oxide and scale from fittings by immersing fittings in chemical and water baths. May heat treat ingots, using Bunsen burner or torch, and immerse ingots in alcohol to restore ingot malleability. May open and close gas valves, ignite and extinguish gas flames, and set time clock alarm for heating and cooling periods.

GOE: 06.04.10 STRENGTH: L GED: R2 M1 L1 SVP: 2 DLU: 77

505 METAL SPRAYING, COATING, AND RELATED OCCUPATIONS

This group includes occupations concerned with covering the surfaces of objects with metal or an accretion of metal and adjuncts in molten or semimolten form usually by brushing, spraying, immersing, or coating processes.

505.130-010 SUPERVISOR, METALIZING (any industry)

Supervises and coordinates activities of workers engaged in spraying protective metal coatings on metal to prevent corrosion and to build up surfaces of worn or damaged metal parts: Analyzes work orders, workpieces, and blueprints to determine process, materials, and sequence of operations required to coat metal. Sets up machine tools and metal spray guns to perform special or experimental operations. Trains workers in operation of equipment. Examines finished pieces for conformity to specifications. Directs workers in processes, such as degreasing, sandblasting, welding and brazing, metal spraying, and machining. Inspects malfunctioning of machines and equipment to determine need for repair. Performs other duties as described under SUPERVISOR (any industry) Master Title.
GOE: 06.02.01 STRENGTH: L GED: R4 M4 L4 SVP: 8 DLU: 77

505.130-014 SUPERVISOR, VACUUM METALIZING (any industry)

Supervises and coordinates activities of workers engaged in vacuum metalizing of glass, plastic, or metal objects, applying knowledge of vacuum metalizing processes, equipment, and procedures: Computes time and pressure specifications for VACUUM-METALIZER OPERATORS (any industry). Observes operations to detect malfunction. Sets up and operates equipment to perform experimental work. Trains workers in operation of equipment. May insert filaments into holders on rack, fill oil tanks of pumps, and examine gauges for malfunction to prepare vacuum metalizing equipment for operation. May position spray nozzles and turn knobs to synchronize conveyor speed, electric-eye action, and temperature and blower action of drying oven to set up automatic spray-painting equipment. May repair and maintain tools and machinery. Performs other duties as described under SUPERVISOR (any industry) Master Title.
GOE: 06.01.01 STRENGTH: M GED: R4 M3 L3 SVP: 7 DLU: 77

505.380-010 METAL SPRAYER, MACHINED PARTS (any industry) alternate titles: flame-spray operator; metalizer, machined parts; metal-spray operator

Sets up and operates flame-spray equipment and machine tools to build up worn parts, such as crankshafts, motor shafts, clutch plates, and piston rods, and to salvage defective machined parts, according to specifications: Washes object with solvents, or heats object with torch or in furnace to remove impurities, such as grease or paint. Operates machines, such as engine lathes and external grinders, to undercut or groove surface of object. Cleans and roughens surface of object in sand or shotblast cabinet [CABINET-ABRASIVE SANDBLASTER (any industry) 503.687-010] or by electrobonding process. Preheats object for spraying, using oxyacetylene torch or metalizing gun. Sprays metal or other material on object by either of following methods: (1) Positions and clamps metalizing gun to engine lathe carriage. Selects nozzle to accommodate size of wire to be sprayed and screws nozzle into place on metalizing gun. Inserts wire to be sprayed into rear of gun and through feed rollers and nozzle. Connects hoses from gun to air compressor and tanks of oxygen and fuel gas, such as acetylene. Turns knobs to synchronize speed of wire feed, air pressure, flow of oxygen and fuel indicated on dials to specifications computed from data charts. Installs gears in lathe and turns knobs to synchronize rotating speed of chuck and movement of carriage with rate of spray to achieve specified coating on workpiece. Ignites gases to melt wire and presses button or trigger to release compressed air which atomizes and sprays molten metal onto workpiece. (2) Pours specified powder of metal or other material, such as ceramics, into hopper mounted on metalizing gun. Selects nozzle according to type of powder to be used and screws nozzle into place on gun. Turns dials and valves to synchronize feeding rate of powder and flow of oxygen and fuel gas, according to type of powder used. Ignites gases and presses button or trigger to start flow of powder which is atomized and sprayed onto workpiece. Heats object with torch or in heat-treating furnace to fuse coatings, and cools object slowly to prevent cracking. Measures object, using measuring instruments, such as micrometers, gauges, and calipers, to determine conformance to specifications. Operates portable metalizing gun to fill cracks, holes, and apply coating to restore flat or irregular surfaces of machined, forged, or cast objects to original dimensions. May operate machines, such as engine lathes, turret lathes, or precision grinders, to machine-coat objects to original specifications. May spray protective coatings of corrosion-resistant metal onto metal objects. May tend portable air compressors, sandblasting guns, and set up metalizing gun on lathes in customers' plants to repair damaged, worn, or improperly machined parts. May be designated according to type of metalizing equipment used as Thermospray Operator (any industry).
GOE: 06.01.03 STRENGTH: M GED: R4 M3 L3 SVP: 6 DLU: 77

505.382-010 METAL-SPRAYING-MACHINE OPERATOR, AUTOMATIC I (any industry) alternate titles: flame-spraying-machine operator, automatic; metalizing-machine operator, automatic

Sets up and operates metal spraying machine to bond protective or decorative coatings to metal objects: Positions workpieces into holding fixtures of con-veyor. Attaches nozzle onto spray gun and positions gun at specified distance from workpiece. Connects hoses from gun to air compressor and fuel tanks. Threads end from roll of specified wire through gun. Turns knobs and levers to synchronize speed of wire feed, air pressure, and specified flow of oxygen and fuel. Turns knobs and installs gears to set conveyor speed and holding device. Ignites gun to melt emerging wire at nozzle and presses button or turns handle to release compressed air which atomizes and sprays molten metal onto surface of workpiece. Inspects workpieces for coating defects and removes finished pieces from conveyor. May install gears to accommodate larger workpieces. May operate sandblasting equipment to roughen and clean surface of workpieces [SANDBLASTER (any industry)]. May preheat workpieces in oven. May be designated according to type of equipment used as Metal-Spraying-Machine Operator, Crucible Gun (any industry).
GOE: 06.02.21 STRENGTH: M GED: R4 M3 L2 SVP: 7 DLU: 77

505.382-014 WELDING-ROD COATER (elec. equip.)

Controls variety of machines to mix, dip, grind and bake flux onto electric welding rods: Operates bandsaw to cut welding rod stock to specified length. Pours flux ingredients into mixing machine and starts machine. Measures specific gravity of flux mixture, using hydrometer. Pours flux into hydraulic dipping machine. Places rods in dip holding rack and turns end bolt to secure rods, using wrench. Slides rack into dipping machine and adjusts temperature and humidity gauges, according to work order specifications. Removes and places dipped rods on drying rack to dry. Operates grinding machine to remove excess flux from coated rod tips. Bakes coated rods in drying oven for specified period of time. Operates marking machine to print identification code on rods as specified. Cleans equipment, using water hose and scraper.
GOE: 06.02.21 STRENGTH: H GED: R3 M3 L2 SVP: 6 DLU: 77

505.482-010 PASTING-MACHINE OPERATOR (elec. equip.) alternate titles: grid-pasting-machine operator

Operates pasting machine and dryer to apply specified amount of lead-oxide paste onto grids used in making storage battery plates: Stacks grids or multiple-grid panels on bench or in automatic feeding device. Adjusts shoes (guides) on pasting machine to size of grid, using handtools. Adjusts scraper blade (wiper) and roller, according to thickness specified for plate, using wrenches. Hoists carts of paste into position near machine and shovels paste into hopper. Starts machine that automatically feeds grids or manually places grids between shoes. Weighs wet plates on scale and changes elevation of scraper to produce plate of specified weight. Installs device (pyramid) in machine that prevents pasting of center strip of panels and determines width of plates. Sets temperature of dryer. Cleans machine. Changes conveyor belts or cheesecloth cover on roller, using handtools. May tend machine that breaks finished double-grid plates into single units. May segregate defective plates, stack acceptable plates in box, and set aside for curing period. May clean edges and lugs of plates, using wire brush. May mix lead-oxide powders, water, and acids into paste.
GOE: 06.02.18 STRENGTH: L GED: R3 M2 L2 SVP: 4 DLU: 77

505.682-010 SPRAYER OPERATOR (smelt. & refin.)

Controls metal spraying machine and melting furnace to coat carbon anodes with molten aluminum for use in reducing pots: Sets furnace temperature control dial at desired level and checks level of molten aluminum in furnace. Adjusts flow of compressed air through spray nozzle and hydraulic tilt of furnace and turntable. Presses button on control panel to move monorail trolley holding anode assembly onto turntable of spray machine. Starts hydraulic system that lowers turntable and anode to bottom of spray pit. Starts flow of compressed air through nozzle that sprays specified amount of molten metal onto rotating anode. Repositions furnace in original position, stops equipment, and hoists anode assembly onto monorail conveyor for movement to loading station. Cleans aluminum overspray from sides and bottom of pit and places residue in container for reuse. Skims slag from molten aluminum in furnace to remove impurities.
GOE: 06.02.10 STRENGTH: L GED: R3 M2 L2 SVP: 3 DLU: 77

505.684-010 ELECTROLESS PLATER (any industry)

Coats small steel valve parts, crystal slices used in making semiconductors, or related materials with nickel plate, using nonelectric dipping process: Fills dip tank with nickel salt solution and sets controls to maintain specified temperature. Fills basket with parts to be plated or mounts slides bearing crystal slices on holding fixture, and lowers materials into plating tank. Determines time parts remain in bath, using knowledge of process and thickness of plating desired. Removes parts when process is completed. Gauges parts frequently with micrometers to see that specified tolerances are maintained. Adds plating solution or refills tanks, as necessary, to complete plating process. May immerse materials in leaching or cleaning solution preparatory to plating.
GOE: 06.04.33 STRENGTH: M GED: R2 M2 L2 SVP: 3 DLU: 77

505.684-014 METAL SPRAYER, PRODUCTION (any industry)

Sprays variety of objects, such as valves, clutch plates, and cylinder linings, on production basis, to coat them with specified thickness of metal: Cleans and roughens surface of object in sand or shotblast cabinet [CABINET-ABRASIVE SANDBLASTER (any industry)]. Fastens objects in fixture or between bench centers. Preheats object for spraying, using oxyacetylene torch or metalizing gun. Moves controls to set specified rate of wire feed and flow of oxygen and fuel gases through metalizing gun. Ignites gases to melt wire and presses button or trigger to release compressed air which atomizes and sprays molten metal onto workpiece. Manually directs spray over object to apply coating of speci-

fied thickness. May spray metal objects with soft solder preparatory to assembly and be designated Solder Sprayer (any industry).
GOE: 06.04.33 STRENGTH: M GED: R2 M2 L2 SVP: 3 DLU: 77

505.685-010 BROWNING PROCESSOR (ordnance)
Tends equipment that imparts decorative bluing or brown-black color, and hard, corrosion resistant surface to gun barrels: Mixes solution of acids and metallic salts, according to formula. Places barrels on conveyor that passes through coloring tanks, electrical drying, and preheating oven into steam chamber where controlled temperature and humidity promote oxidation. Rinses barrels in boiling water and holds them against wire or fiber brush wheel to remove loose rust particles and produce satin finish. Repeats rusting and brushing cycle until color of barrel conforms to specified standards. Swabs browned barrels with rust-preventing oil, using rag or sponge.
GOE: 06.04.10 STRENGTH: M GED: R2 M2 L2 SVP: 3 DLU: 77

505.685-014 METAL-SPRAYING-MACHINE OPERATOR, AUTOMATIC II (any industry) alternate titles: sprayer
Tends automatic or semiautomatic metal spraying machine that bonds protective or decorative coatings to metal objects, such as clutch plates and valves, on production basis: Loads objects on conveyor or places them in fixture. Sets controls on panel to regulate such functions as conveyor speed, rate of wire or powder feed, flow of compressed air and fuel gas, and starting and stopping of spray. Starts machine and observes operation to detect malfunctioning of equipment.
GOE: 06.04.21 STRENGTH: M GED: R2 M2 L2 SVP: 2 DLU: 77

505.685-018 VACUUM-METALIZER OPERATOR (any industry) alternate titles: vapor coater
Tends vacuum metalizing equipment that deposits decorative or protective coating of specified metal on metal, glass, or plastic objects: Hooks or clamps articles onto rack. Positions pieces of coating metal over heating filament on rack. Positions rack in vacuum chamber, manually or using hoist. May plug in electrical connection or filaments. Connects gear to motorized jig that rotates rack inside chamber. Closes door and turns handles to seal chamber. Turns handwheel and starts pump to remove air from chamber. Starts booster and high vacuum pumps, and observes dials to obtain specified state of vacuum in chamber. Pushes button to heat filament which vaporizes coating metal and deposits it as film on objects on rack. Turns off electric current after specified time and turns handwheel to permit air to enter chamber. Opens door, removes rack, and lifts coated objects onto truck or dolly.
GOE: 06.04.21 STRENGTH: M GED: R2 M2 L2 SVP: 3 DLU: 77

509 OCCUPATIONS IN PROCESSING OF METAL, N.E.C.

This group includes occupations, not elsewhere classified, concerned with molding, casting, coating, conditioning, or otherwise processing metal.

509.130-010 SUPERVISOR, POWDERED METAL (nonfer. metal; steel & rel.)
Supervises and coordinates activities of workers engaged in mixing and pressing metal powders, and in sintering, coining, impregnating, and inspecting powdered metal products, applying knowledge of powdered metal properties, press and furnace operation, and sintering and impregnating processes. Trains workers in setup of machines and equipment. May set up briquetting and coining presses and sintering furnaces. Performs duties as described under SUPERVISOR (any industry) Master Title.
GOE: 06.02.01 STRENGTH: L GED: R4 M3 L3 SVP: 7 DLU: 77

509.130-014 SUPERVISOR, POWER-REACTOR (chemical)
Supervises and coordinates activities of workers engaged in controlling nuclear reactors to produce plutonium and steam: Observes panel control board indicators to ensure operation of reactors conforms to government and company safety regulations. Analyzes instrumentation data to determine equipment adjustments. Trains new workers. Performs other duties as described under SUPERVISOR (any industry) Master Title.
GOE: 06.01.01 STRENGTH: L GED: R4 M3 L3 SVP: 7 DLU: 77

509.132-010 SUPERVISOR, SOAKING PITS (steel & rel.)
Supervises and coordinates activities of workers engaged in heating and soaking steel ingots preparatory to rolling in blooming and slabbing mills: Prepares schedule for charging and drawing steel into and from preheating and soaking pits. Directs workers in charging ingots into pits and in heating and drawing operations. Inspects furnaces and equipment to determine necessary maintenance. Trains workers in mill operations. Performs other duties as described under SUPERVISOR (any industry) Master Title.
GOE: 06.04.01 STRENGTH: M GED: R4 M3 L3 SVP: 8 DLU: 77

509.362-010 MIXER OPERATOR, HOT METAL (steel & rel.)
Operates machine to mix various charges of molten metal and maintain metal at specified temperature for use in converters and furnaces: Moves controls to raise lid of mixer and signals OVERHEAD CRANE OPERATOR (any industry) 921.663-010 to pour metal from transfer ladle into mixer. Turns controls to adjust fuel and air mixture to mixer burners to maintain specified temperature in mixer, and to rotate arm that mixes molten metal. Signals OVERHEAD CRANE OPERATOR (any industry) to position ladle for receiving molten metal from mixer for delivery to converters or furnaces. Moves controls to tilt

mixer and fill ladle. Inserts long-handled spoon in ladle to obtain sample of molten metal and pours sample into mold for laboratory analysis. Repairs mixer lining, using refractory materials and handtools.
GOE: 06.02.10 STRENGTH: L GED: R3 M2 L2 SVP: 5 DLU: 77

509.382-010 COATER OPERATOR (any industry)
Operates roll-coating machine and auxiliary equipment to coat coils of sheet metal, flat metal blanks, or fabricated metal parts with paint, vinyl plastic, or adhesive film: Positions coiled metal strip on mandrel of feed reel or places metal blanks onto feed carriage of machine. Feeds coils of sheet metal into take-up rolls of stitching machine. Starts stitching machine that staples strips together to form endless metal strip. Turns control dials of machines to regulate speed of metal strip, temperature of drying ovens, and flow of chemicals that maintain specified viscosity of solutions in cleaning tanks. Mixes paint or coating solution to specified viscosity and starts equipment to pump mixture into machine reservoir. Turns setscrews to adjust distance between coating rollers that control thickness of coating. Measures thickness of coating to test viscosity, using wet film gauge. Starts pump that fills printing machine reservoir. Adjusts printing cylinder that prints designs on painted metal strip and hydraulic pressure valve of laminating machine that applies plastic vinyl or adhesives to heated metal strip. Turns valve to control spray of water in quenching process that tempers paint, adhesives, or plastic vinyl. Presses pedal of shear machine to cut metal strips. Pushes reel lever to rewind coated metal strip into coil. Examines coated metal workpieces for defects, such as air bubbles or uncoated surfaces.
GOE: 06.02.21 STRENGTH: M GED: R3 M3 L2 SVP: 6 DLU: 77

509.382-014 DENTAL-AMALGAM PROCESSOR (nonfer. metal) alternate titles: special-machine operator
Operates machines to process dental-amalgam and tests amalgam with interferometer: Anneals ingot of tin, copper, and silver to obtain specified molecular characteristics [ANNEALER (heat treating)]. Cuts ingot into chips of uniform size, using engine lathe. Pours chips into hopper of grinder and starts machine to grind chips into microgranules of specified size. Loads granules into elutriator and turns valve to regulate flow of water that forces granules through sieves to separate granules, according to size. Loads moist granules in drying machine or oven. Mixes specimen quantity of alloy with mercury, using amalgamator machine or mortar and pestle, and packs mixture into mold. Removes amalgam from mold and places amalgam between glass panels of instrument. Counts black bands appearing within circle of instrument and informs supervisor of number of bands.
GOE: 06.02.09 STRENGTH: M GED: R3 M2 L2 SVP: 4 DLU: 77

509.384-010 CASE PREPARER-AND-LINER (ordnance)
Cleans rocket-motor cases and lines them with heat-resistant coatings by performing any combination of following tasks: Moves motor cases through various process stations of building, using hoist and conveyor system. Attaches and removes special handling devices (handling rings) on motor cases, using wrenches and other handtools or portable power tools. Immerses case in chemical bath for specified period to remove protective coatings or contaminants. Wipes solution from inside of case, using cloth. Removes chemical film from surface of case, using sandblasting equipment [SANDBLASTER (any industry)]. Paints outside of motor case, using spray gun. Bakes motor case in drying oven. Lowers motor case onto bed of lining machine. Connects turntable to end of motor case, using wrenches. Starts machine which rotates case and sprays heat-resistant material on inside of case. Examines coating for voids or other defects. Conveys lined motor case to curing oven. Observes recording instrument charts on control panel of curing oven to verify specified temperatures and curing time. Lowers cured cases onto skids and covers ends with paper and gummed tape.
GOE: 06.02.24 STRENGTH: L GED: R3 M2 L2 SVP: 4 DLU: 77

509.462-010 ALODIZE-MACHINE OPERATOR (nonfer. metal)
Sets up and operates machine that coats flat sheet or coiled metal to specified color and finish: Mixes *alodize* solution in tank of machine, according to formula. Places container of solution sample under test tube and reads gauge to determine solution concentration. Sets up machine rolls and guides, using handtools and micrometer. Turns dial and observes gauge to heat solution to specified temperature. Operates hoist to place sheets on machine feed carriage or to lift coil onto machine spindle. Feeds sheets or end of coil into machine rolls. Adjusts controls to maintain machine speed and temperature of solution to obtain specified color and coverage of metal.
GOE: 06.02.10 STRENGTH: M GED: R3 M3 L2 SVP: 5 DLU: 77

509.485-010 COMPOUND MIXER (tinware) alternate titles: coating mixer
Tends agitator machines that mix compounds used to line and coat tin cans: Measures and pours specified amounts of concentrates and solvents into barrel of solution, using measuring can. Lowers agitator into barrel and starts machine to mix solution. Tests viscosity of solution with viscosimeter and adds solvent or concentrates to obtain specified consistency. Starts pump that forces mix from barrel into storage tank and through feed lines into coating machine reservoirs. Raises and stacks barrels on racks, using chain hoist, and transports them to mixing room with handtrucks. Keeps stock control records.
GOE: 06.04.11 STRENGTH: H GED: R3 M2 L2 SVP: 4 DLU: 77

509.485-014 SHOT POLISHER AND INSPECTOR (ordnance)
Tends equipment in shot tower that segregates, routes, blends, and polishes shot (lead pellets) used in shotgun shells: Starts bucket elevator that conveys

newly formed pellets to shot tower and into screening drums that remove oversize and undersize pellets. Turns crank to adjust angle of glass plates over which screened shot is rolled to remove out-of-round pellets, using graduated measuring stick to verify pitch. Pulls levers and chains to direct flow of shot into sieves, polishing barrel, and storage bins, or into scrap bin for remelting. Connects Y-pipe between specified bins and polishing barrel, starts barrel rotating, and opens bin valves to blend full and off-size shot by flowing shot together in Y-pipe. Weighs sample of mixed shot at designated intervals and counts total number of pellets in sample, using pellet counting plate. Measures size of pellets, using pellet measuring stick, and counts number of each size to determine average size. Rolls pellets under dial micrometer to ascertain roundness of pellets. Turns valves by trial and error to obtain shot blend that conforms to specifications. Records results of tests.
GOE: 06.04.02 STRENGTH: L GED: R2 M2 L2 SVP: 3 DLU: 77

509.565-010 KILN OPERATOR (steel & rel.)
Tends battery of rotary kilns that heat minerals, such as lime, chrome ore, and manganese, preparatory to mixing minerals with molten metal to form steel: Signals OVERHEAD CRANE OPERATOR (any industry) 921.663-010 to deliver specified type and amount of material to kiln feedbox. Pushes switches to start kiln rotating and conveyors feeding materials from feedbox to kiln. Ignites burners under kiln and moves controls to attain specified temperature in kiln. Pulls lever to dump heated material into steel box on platform scale. Weighs and records weight, type, and amount of material heated.
GOE: 06.04.10 STRENGTH: M GED: R2 M2 L2 SVP: 3 DLU: 77

509.566-010 MIXER OPERATOR HELPER, HOT METAL (steel & rel.)
Assists MIXER OPERATOR, HOT METAL (steel & rel.) 509.362-010 to mix molten metal: Attaches electrical connections to torpedo-ladle car and pushes controls to tilt car and pour metal into hot-metal transfer ladle. Signals OVERHEAD CRANE OPERATOR (any industry) 921.663-010 to pour molten iron from ladle into mixer. Records tare weight of torpedo-ladle car. Knocks solidified slag from pouring spout and rim of hot-metal ladle, using hammer and bar. Performs other duties as described under HELPER (any industry) Master Title.
GOE: 06.04.10 STRENGTH: M GED: R2 M2 L2 SVP: 2 DLU: 77

509.584-010 TEST PREPARER (nonfer. metal; steel & rel.) alternate titles: sampler; steel sampler; test assembler; test carrier
Collects samples of materials, such as scrap iron and ore, and products, such as metal sheets, rails, tubes, and bars, and prepares samples for physical analysis, using grinders, crushers, drill press, power saws and milling machine. Identifies samples and routes samples to laboratory for analysis. Records test data and type and amount of samples tested.
GOE: 06.04.02 STRENGTH: M GED: R2 M2 L2 SVP: 4 DLU: 77

509.666-010 COMPOUND-COATING-MACHINE OFFBEARER (tinware) alternate titles: end packer
Removes tin can ends from discharge rack of coating machine: Inspects rubber base coating compound on can ends and ring-pull for conformity to specifications. Notifies PUNCH-PRESS SETTER (any industry) of machine jam or defects in can ends. Packs ends in cartons or paper bags and places containers on pallet.
GOE: 06.04.21 STRENGTH: M GED: R2 M1 L1 SVP: 2 DLU: 77

509.684-010 ENAMELER (plumbing-heat.) alternate titles: enamel drier
Sprays finish coat of enamel onto cast-iron sanitary units, such as bathtubs and sinks and bakes unit to provide permanent finish: Wheels units into furnace for preheating, using steel fork mounted on overhead conveyor. Observes color of unit through window in furnace to determine when desired temperature has been reached. Removes unit from furnace and sprays powdered enamel over it, using pneumatic gun. Returns unit to furnace to fuse and glaze enamel, repeating heating and enameling process until unit is coated without discolorations, blisters, or pinholes.
GOE: 06.04.33 STRENGTH: L GED: R3 M2 L2 SVP: 5 DLU: 77

509.685-010 ALODIZE-MACHINE HELPER (nonfer. metal)
Tends machine that rewinds metal coils processed by ALODIZE-MACHINE OPERATOR (nonfer. metal) and assists in coating metal sheets and coils: Places cardboard core on rewinding arbor and starts end of coil around core. Pulls levers to start rewinder. Cuts material to specified lengths, using hand shear. Tapes loose end and removes coil from rewinder, using hoist. Lifts sheets from discharge end of machine and stacks finished sheets onto skid. Places coil on unwinding equipment and threads coil end through machine, preparatory to alodizing process. Performs other duties as described under HELPER (any industry) Master Title.
GOE: 06.04.02 STRENGTH: M GED: R2 M2 L2 SVP: 3 DLU: 77

509.685-014 BRANNER-MACHINE TENDER (galvanizing)
Tends equipment that applies bran or mixture of sawdust and lime to tin plate surfaces to remove palm oil from plates: Moves controls and valves to regulate speed of conveyor and feed mechanism and adjust flow of soda ash solution to wash unit. Observes operation to detect faulty feeding of plates into units that brush plate surfaces with bran and wash residue from plates. Replenishes exhausting supply of bran in hopper. Inspects plates to ensure removal of palm oil from plates.
GOE: 06.04.39 STRENGTH: M GED: R3 M2 L2 SVP: 4 DLU: 77

509.685-018 BURNING-PLANT OPERATOR (ordnance)
Tends furnace that heats scrapped small arms ammunition to explode powder and reclaim lead and brass: Pulls trucks of tote boxes from storage area to fur-

nace hoppers. Scoops or dumps primers or loaded cartridges into hopper. Shovels exploded primers from furnace floor or skims cartridge and bullet cases from surface of molten lead, using skimming tool, and deposits them in containers, according to type of metal. Ladles molten lead from furnace pot into pig molds. Carries cooled pigs to storage area and stacks them on skids. May burn waste powder in open pit by dumping it onto wood fire, using remote-control trolley.
GOE: 05.12.10 STRENGTH: H GED: R2 M1 L1 SVP: 2 DLU: 77

509.685-022 CERAMIC COATER, MACHINE (any industry) alternate titles: ceramic plater
Tends machine that coats metal objects with ceramic material: Places workpiece on rack, observing reflection in mirror below rack to determine when surface to be coated is exposed. Closes machine door and presses button to start rack revolving and initiate coating cycle. Observes gauges and turns valves to maintain specified flow through coating nozzle. Fills reservoir with ceramic material and turns valves on hydrogen supply tanks to maintain flow of gas to machine. Removes coated parts, blows away excess material with airhose, and places in container.
GOE: 06.04.21 STRENGTH: M GED: R2 M2 L1 SVP: 2 DLU: 77

509.685-026 GETTERING-FILAMENT-MACHINE OPERATOR (light. fix.) alternate titles: getterer; getter operator
Tends machine that sprays or dips tungsten wires with chemical (getter) used to burn off residual air and moisture in electric light bulbs: Fills receptacle of machine with getter. Starts machine that sprays or dips getter onto tungsten filaments. Observes application of getter to ensure uniformity and to prevent distortion. May weigh specified quantity of filaments and calculate number, using slide rule and known weight of single unit. May place tray with coated filaments in oven to dry.
GOE: 06.04.21 STRENGTH: L GED: R2 M2 L1 SVP: 3 DLU: 77

509.685-030 IMPREGNATOR (nonfer. metal; steel & rel.)
Tends vacuum or pressure tank that impregnates powdered-metal parts with lubricating oil or molten plastic: Pours impregnating material into tank. Sets controls of heating unit to attain specified temperature of solution. Places containers of parts in tank and closes cover. Observes gauge and turns valves to attain specified pressure or vacuum in tank. Closes valves after specified time, and removes finished parts from tank.
GOE: 06.04.10 STRENGTH: M GED: R2 M2 L2 SVP: 2 DLU: 77

509.685-034 LACQUER-DIPPING-MACHINE OPERATOR (button & notion)
Tends battery of machines that dip metal buttons, buckles, and related parts into lacquer: Pours lacquer into tank to indicated level. Hangs racks of parts over lacquer tank, and starts machine that automatically dips buckles into lacquer and raises them over tank to drip dry. Lifts racks from machine to handtruck and transports racks into drying oven.
GOE: 06.04.21 STRENGTH: M GED: R2 M2 L1 SVP: 2 DLU: 77

509.685-038 LUBRICATING-MACHINE TENDER (ordnance)
Tends tumbling machine that sprays small arms cartridge parts with lubricating solution and dries them preparatory to drawing operations: Empties containers of parts into hopper, manually or using electric hoist. Turns handwheel to regulate spray of lubricating solution. Reads gauges and adjusts steam valves or electrical controls to maintain specified drying temperature within drum. Positions empty container at discharge chute to receive dried parts and removes filled container, using handtruck.
GOE: 06.04.21 STRENGTH: M GED: R2 M2 L1 SVP: 2 DLU: 77

509.685-042 LUBRICATOR-GRANULATOR (nonfer. metal; steel & rel.)
Tends machines that lubricate, granulate, and pelletize metallic powder: Pours specified amount of powder and lubricants into mixing machine. Starts machine that mixes powder with lubricants for specified length of time. Pours mixture into trays and places mixture in drying ovens. Dumps lubricated and dried powder into hopper of granulator-screener machine. Starts machine that granulates and screens powder. Pours screened powder into jars. Dumps specified amounts of lubricated and screened powder in glass pellet-rolling jars and screws covers on jars. Places jars on rack of rolling machine and starts machine that forms powder into pellets. Separates pellets according to size and places them in jars.
GOE: 06.04.10 STRENGTH: L GED: R2 M2 L1 SVP: 2 DLU: 77

509.685-046 SCRAP BALLER (nonfer. metal; steel & rel.)
Tends machine that winds metal scrap into balls for salvage: Hooks end of scrap onto reel of machine, using hook or handtool. Starts machine that rotates reel and winds scrap into ball of specified size. Turns lever to eject wound ball from machine. Signals OVERHEAD CRANE OPERATOR (any industry) 921.663-010 to lower sling, and hooks ball onto sling for removal from work area. Ties ball with wire to prevent unraveling. May grade scrap according to alloy content. May turn reel, manually to wind scrap. May cut scrap metal, using power shear. May weigh scrap metal, using floor scale.
GOE: 06.04.02 STRENGTH: M GED: R2 M1 LI SVP: 3 DLU: 77

509.685-050 SCRAP HANDLER (any industry)
Tends machines, such as baling machine, centrifugal separator, and oil purifier to salvage metal parts and cutting oil: Loads and moves barrels or crates of metal chips, shavings, or clippings from machining operations, using handtruck. Dumps metal scrap into baling machine and activates machine to com-

press scrap into bales. Binds bales of metal scrap with wire or metal strapping. Shovels scrap in spinner bucket. Clamps covers, sets timer, adjusts sump pump and oil line valves, and flips switches to start automatic cycle of centrifugal machine that spins metal scrap to separate cutting oil from scrap. Starts centrifugal oil purifier that filters foreign matter from used cutting oil to make oil reusable. Disassembles rejected devices and materials, such as thermostats, valves, conduit, and connectors, using handtools, arbor press, vises, and power hacksaw. Sorts parts according to type of metal or part. Weighs bales and barrels of scrap metal and ties identification tags on scrap. May oversee and demonstrate salvaging procedures to other SCRAP HANDLERS (any industry).
GOE: 06.04.09 STRENGTH: H GED: R3 M2 L2 SVP: 3 DLU: 77

509.685-054 TANK TENDER (smelt. & refin.)
Tends equipment that refines silver in electrolysis tank: Suspends silver anodes contained in canvas bags, between stainless-steel cathodes held on rack. Aligns and spaces anodes to prevent dislodging by mechanical scrapers. Swabs cathodes with oil to facilitate removal of deposited silver. Lowers rack of electrodes into tank and fills tank with silver nitrate electrolyte. Connects and starts wooden scrapers that scrape deposited silver from cathode. Scrapes remaining silver from cathode with knife and opens bottom of rack to empty silver into box. Removes bags containing depleted anodes and black mud. Examines bags for holes and broken frames and replaces defective parts. May mix acid and silver to prepare electrolyte solution, following standard formula.
GOE: 06.04.10 STRENGTH: M GED: R3 M2 L2 SVP: 5 DLU: 77

509.686-014 PASTING-MACHINE OFFBEARER (elec. equip.)
Removes battery plates from discharge conveyor of automatic equipment on which twin battery grids are pasted, dried, and broken apart into single grids: Removes and discards grids having defects such as bent, cracked, or unevenly pasted plates. Stacks specified number of finished plates on rack or dolly. Records number and type of rejected plates.
GOE: 06.04.09 STRENGTH: L GED: R1 M1 L1 SVP: 2 DLU: 77

509.686-018 SCRAP SORTER (nonfer. metal) alternate titles: picker
Sorts scrap metal and removes foreign matter preparatory to use in recasting: Shovels metal scrap onto conveyor leading to magnetic drum that removes iron and steel pieces. Removes contaminating nonferrous metals, manually. May sift scrap to remove excess dirt and rust, using wire sifting tray. May remove inserts from defective castings, using gas torch, tongs, and pliers, and be designated Salvager, Inserts (nonfer. metal).
GOE: 05.12.03 STRENGTH: M GED: R2 M1 L1 SVP: 2 DLU: 77

509.687-010 BOTTOM MAKER (steel & rel.)
Relines bottoms of ingot-soaking pits with coke dust to retard formation of oxide scale on hot ingots: Digs out molten metal, slag scale, and cinder from bottoms of pits, using flat-pointed bar, and scrapes debris into ladle. Shovels coke dust into pit, using bar to level bottom surface. May change crane tong bits, using sledgehammer.
GOE: 06.04.40 STRENGTH: M GED: R2 M1 L1 SVP: 3 DLU: 77

509.687-014 PORCELAIN-ENAMEL LABORER (any industry) alternate titles: check-and-transfer beader
Performs any combination of following tasks, usually on conveyor line, in porcelain enameling process: Brushes or scrapes dry porcelain from holes and designated areas of workpiece, using powered or hand brushes and scraping tools. Inspects enameled workpiece and sands workpiece to remove dirt, blisters, and lumps. Brushes porcelain into nicks. Marks workpiece to indicate routing for further repair or processing. Removes excess enamel from dipped parts with cloth, finger, or suction hose. Marks workpiece with production number, unit number, or other code. Loads or unloads workpieces from conveyor line. Cleans workpiece with solvent and hangs workpiece on rack to dry preparatory to dipping in enamel. May immerse workpiece in porcelain enamel solution. May transport workpiece to work or storage areas, using handtruck.
GOE: 06.04.33 STRENGTH: M GED: R1 M1 L1 SVP: 2 DLU: 77

509.687-018 STRINGER (jewelry-silver.)
Strings jewelry articles on wire or hangs articles on racks preparatory to further processing, such as soldering, cleaning, plating, or stripping, and carries to machine operator. May clean machines. May be designated according to specific operation performed as Stringer-Up, Soldering Machine (jewelry-silver.).
GOE: 06.04.34 STRENGTH: L GED: R1 M1 L1 SVP: 1 DLU: 77

509.687-022 WEIGHER, ALLOY (nonfer. metal) alternate titles: charge-gang weigher
Sorts and weighs nonferrous scrap metal and ingots for furnace charges: Separates grades and types of alloys by color or shape of casting and shovels metal into handtrucks. Selects scrap and ingots for furnace charge, according to specifications. Takes sample of furnace melts for laboratory analysis, observes metal in diecasting holding pots and finished castings, or reads label to verify use of specified alloys. May unload box cars of alloy materials. May operate lift truck to transport materials. May charge furnaces with alloy materials.
GOE: 06.03.02 STRENGTH: M GED: R2 M1 L2 SVP: 3 DLU: 77

509.687-026 LABORER, GENERAL (steel & rel.)
Performs any combination of following tasks to assist workers engaged in production of iron and steel: Feeds and off bears equipment, such as conveyors, pilers, and loaders, to charge furnaces, transport hot metal to rollers, and store finished products. Bundles and ties metal rods, sheets, and wire, using banding machine and handtools. Attaches crane hooks, slings, or cradles to material for

moving by OVERHEAD CRANE OPERATOR (any industry) 921.663-010. Transports material to and from production stations, using handtruck. Feeds material, such as ganister, magnesite, and limestone into crushers to prepare additives for molten metal. Grinds defects, such as burrs, seams, and scratches from rolled steel, using portable grinder. Sweeps scale from work area and empties dust bins, using wheelbarrow, broom, and shovel. Breaks up manganese and scrap metal to facilitate handling, using sledge and pneumatic hammer. Marks identification numbers on steel billets, using chalk. Verifies dimension of products, using fixed gauge. Wipes grease and oil from machinery with rags and solvent. May be designated Conveyor Feeder (steel & rel.); Crusher Feeder (steel & rel.); Loading Checker (steel & rel.); Marker (steel & rel.); Racker (steel & rel.); Scrap Breaker (steel & rel.).
GOE: 06.04.40 STRENGTH: H GED: R2 M1 L1 SVP: 3 DLU: 78

51 ORE REFINING AND FOUNDRY OCCUPATIONS

This division includes occupations concerned with reducing, smelting, refining, or alloying metalliferous extracted ore, ore concentrate, pig, or scrap; and casting ingots, shapes for further processing, and finished metal products in a foundry.

510 MIXING AND RELATED OCCUPATIONS

This group includes occupations concerned with combining mineral ore with solvents or other amalgams to produce a single mass or compound.

510.465-010 CARBIDE-POWDER PROCESSOR (machine shop)
Tends machine and ovens to mix and dry ingredients used to fabricate carbide cutting-tool inserts, following work orders and charts: Reads work order to determine amount and grade of carbide specified. Computes amounts of ingredients required, using charts. Scoops ingredients from canisters, and weighs ingredients on scale to obtain specified amounts. Pours ingredients into cylindrical-tumbler mixing machine, starts tumbler, and stops it after specified time. Pours mixed ingredients into pans, and places them in decarbonizing oven to dry and burn off impurities. Removes pans from oven, adds other ingredients, and sifts mixture through screen to obtain powder of even consistency. Cleans equipment after each batch.
GOE: 06.02.10 STRENGTH: H GED: R3 M2 L2 SVP: 5 DLU: 77

510.465-014 SLURRY-CONTROL TENDER (smelt. & refin.)
Tends ball mill and auxiliary equipment that grind bauxite and mix it with materials to form slurry: Computes amounts of bauxite, starch, and liquor in specified proportion, using weightometer. Turns valves on ball mill to grind bauxite. Turns valves on pumps to release liquor and starch from storage bins and to mix them with bauxite to form slurry. Starts pumps to transfer slurry to digester feed tanks. Opens and closes valves to pump sodium sulfide solution into slurry. Lubricates valves with grease gun, and adjusts packing glands to prevent leaks.
GOE: 06.02.10 STRENGTH: M GED: R3 M2 L2 SVP: 5 DLU: 77

510.685-010 DUST MIXER (smelt. & refin.)
Tends machines that mix flue dust and milk of lime to facilitate reprocessing in copper smelter: Starts screw conveyor and opens valves and hopper gate to start flow of lime solution and flue dust into mixer. Starts mixer, observes mixture for consistency, and adjusts flow rate to attain specified consistency. Stops flow of ingredients into mixing tank, and draws sample for laboratory analysis. Starts pump to transfer mix to filtering process. Cleans mixer after each batch. Records number of mixes, test results, and amount mixed on production forms.
GOE: 06.04.10 STRENGTH: L GED: R3 M2 L1 SVP: 4 DLU: 77

510.685-014 MIX-HOUSE TENDER (smelt. & refin.)
Tends machine that mixes sintered lead or zinc ore with materials, such as pulverized coal and coke, salt, water, skimmings, and chemical solutions preparatory to smelting: Starts rotary-drum or paddle-type mixing machine. Squeezes handful of mixture to lump and crumbles it to determine consistency and moisture content of mixture. Turns valves to add water or chemical solution to mixture. May scoop samples of mixed ore into bucket for laboratory analysis. May be designated according to type of mixer tended as Mixing-Pan Tender (smelt. & refin.).
GOE: 06.04.10 STRENGTH: L GED: R2 M1 L1 SVP: 3 DLU: 77

510.685-018 MIXER (nonfer. metal; steel & rel.) alternate titles: blender
Tends mixing machines that blend batches of powdered metal, according to specifications: Weighs out specified amounts of materials, using scales. Dumps powders into mixing machine, such as tumbling-barrel or paddle-type mixer, and starts motor. Stops motor after specified time, and dumps mixture into containers.
GOE: 06.04.10 STRENGTH: M GED: R2 M2 L2 SVP: 3 DLU: 77

510.685-022 PUG-MILL OPERATOR (smelt. & refin.) alternate titles: mixer tender
Tends pug mill that mixes preheated magnesia and carbon with hot asphalt to form viscous mixture for use in making pellets: Moves lever to open slide gate at outlet of heating chamber to permit heated mixture of magnesia and carbon to flow into pug mill. Opens and regulates valves to control flow of hot asphalt into mill. Opens valves to feed mixture into hoppers of briquetting machine.

GOE: 06.04.10 STRENGTH: L GED: R3 M1 L2 SVP: 4 DLU: 77

510.685-026 SINTER-MACHINE OPERATOR (smelt. & refin.; steel & rel.)

Tends sintering machine and auxiliary equipment, such as conveyors, pug mill, and suction fan, to produce sinter cake from finely ground iron ore, lead, coke, and flue dust: Turns gas valve of sintering machine and ignites burner with torch. Moves controls on panelboard to start equipment. Signals SINTER FEEDER (steel & rel.) to feed pug mill conveyor specified amounts of sinter material. Feels mixture processed by pug mill to determine moisture content. Moves controls to regulate water supply to pug mill to attain specified moisture in mixture. Examines sinter cake produced by sintering machine and moves controls of machine to produce cake to specifications. Chips sinter material from chutes and spouts of machine, using bar and hammer. Records weight and type of materials used.

GOE: 06.04.10 STRENGTH: M GED: R3 M1 L1 SVP: 5 DLU: 77

510.685-030 SLIME-PLANT OPERATOR I (smelt. & refin.)

Tends agitation tanks that mix copper ore slime and acid solution preparatory to precipitation of copper: Turns valves to regulate flow of slime and sulfuric acid from storage tanks into agitation tanks. Tests samples of solution for alkalinity or acidity, using filter paper, or by means of titration. Combines samples of solution from various stages of process for laboratory analysis. May dry, grind, or screen combined sample.

GOE: 06.04.10 STRENGTH: L GED: R3 M2 L1 SVP: 6 DLU: 77

511 SEPARATING, FILTERING, AND RELATED OCCUPATIONS

This group includes occupations concerned with setting apart desirable materials in ore or concentrate by such means as forcing or drawing it through filtering devices by suction or pressure, sifting, straining, squeezing, centrifugal force, flotation, leaching, amalgamation, electrolysis, distillation, precipitation, or agitating devices.

511.130-010 ALUMINA-PLANT SUPERVISOR (smelt. & refin.) alternate titles: line supervisor; shift adjuster

Supervises and coordinates activities of workers engaged in extracting alumina from bauxite: Calculates feed rates of raw materials, using formulas and chemical analysis reports. Inspects machines and equipment. Performs other duties as described under SUPERVISOR (any industry) Master Title.

GOE: 06.02.01 STRENGTH: M GED: R4 M3 L3 SVP: 8 DLU: 77

511.132-010 PRECIPITATOR SUPERVISOR (smelt. & refin.; steel & rel.)

Supervises and coordinates activities of workers engaged in operating electrostatic dust precipitators to control emission of air pollutants or to salvage usable dust from flue: Inspects precipitators in service to determine adjustments required, and out-of-service precipitators for need of maintenance and repair. Trains new workers in adjusting operation and *rapping,* and explains plant layout, working procedures, and safety regulations. May notify air and water pollution-control personnel when operating difficulties cause deviations from pollution standards. May be designated according to type of precipitation as Stack Supervisor (smelt. & refin.). Performs other duties as described under SUPERVISOR (any industry) Master Title.

GOE: 05.10.02 STRENGTH: L GED: R3 M2 L2 SVP: 5 DLU: 77

511.135-010 FILTER-PLANT SUPERVISOR (smelt. & refin.)

Supervises and coordinates activities of workers engaged in tending machines and equipment, such as screens, settlers, flotation cells, thickeners, or filterers, to process ore concentrate and slurry: Inspects machines, equipment, and conveyor systems to detect mechanical defects or malfunctions, and assigns workers to make repairs or adjustments. Observes workers to ensure compliance with safety regulations. Instructs new employees in machine and equipment operation. May be designated according to process supervised as Dewatering-Filtering Supervisor (smelt. & refin.); Flotation Supervisor (smelt. & refin.); Screen Supervisor (smelt. & refin.). Performs other duties as described under SUPERVISOR (any industry) Master Title.

GOE: 06.04.01 STRENGTH: L GED: R4 M3 L3 SVP: 6 DLU: 77

511.382-010 TUNGSTEN REFINER (smelt. & refin.) alternate titles: chemical operator

Controls chemical-processing equipment to recover tungsten oxide from ground concentrated ore: Starts conveyor to fill reactor tank with ore. Turns valves to pump specified quantity of hydrochloric acid into tank and to admit steam into tank jacket. Observes temperature gauge and adjusts valves to maintain acid solution at specified temperature for specified time. Fills tank with water to wash slurry, and drains waste-bearing water. Turns valve to pour slurry into caustic tank. Precipitates impurities, such as chlorides and oxides, by adding ammonia and sulfuric acid to solution. Filters solution into holding tank to remove precipitate. Adds specified amount of hydrochloric acid to tank to crystallize solution. Dries tungsten oxide crystals by pumping them through filter or centrifuge.

GOE: 06.02.10 STRENGTH: M GED: R3 M2 L2 SVP: 5 DLU: 77

511.385-010 ZINC-CHLORIDE OPERATOR (smelt. & refin.)

Tends equipment that separates zinc chloride from slag: Breaks up slag, using sledgehammer. Loads slag into water-filled tank, using hoist. Agitates so-lution to dissolve zinc chloride from slag, using airhose. Determines specific gravity and acidity of solution, using hydrometer and chemical reagents. Pumps impurities from solution through filters. Samples solution and observes its color to determine need for additional reagents and agitation. Pumps treated solution to tank cars or drums. Cleans sediment from equipment, using shovel and water hose, and replaces filter cloths.

GOE: 06.02.10 STRENGTH: M GED: R3 M2 L2 SVP: 4 DLU: 77

511.462-010 CONCENTRATOR OPERATOR (smelt. & refin.)

Controls machines and equipment from instrumented control board to scrub, condition, float, classify, and convey phosphate rock for use in fertilizer and phosphoric acid: Monitors recording instruments, gauges, panel lights, and other indicators, and listens for warning signal to verify conformance to plant standards. Turns screws and knobs on control board to adjust flow of reagents, airflow, phosphate-rock feed rate, and conveyor belts. Observes flotation tanks to determine amount of sand clinging to rock, cyclones to detect presence of solids, and classifiers to detect wobble in or uneven feed rate of screw. Reports belt weight, amount and evenness of feed rate, waterflow amount, and specific density of slurry to mine, using telephone. Weighs samples from scrubber and conditioner to determine that amount of reagents in tank meets specifications. Reviews laboratory test results and makes adjustments required on control board. Inspects machines and equipment for potential and actual hazards, wear, leaks, and mechanical malfunctions requiring maintenance. Collects samples at various stage of operation for laboratory analysis. Records instrument readings, process conditions, and other operating data in shift log. Manually regulates or shuts down equipment as directed by supervisor. May assist in making mechanical repairs to machines and equipment during shutdown. May tag samples collected for laboratory analysis.

GOE: 06.02.11 STRENGTH: L GED: R4 M3 L3 SVP: 7 DLU: 77

511.465-010 TOP-PRECIPITATOR OPERATOR (smelt. & refin.)

Tends battery of tanks that precipitate aluminum hydroxide from rich liquor: Schedules filling, seeding, and emptying of precipitator tanks. Opens feedline valves to fill tanks to designated levels with liquor and alumina seed slurry. Adjusts valves to regulate rate of filling precipitators and to maintain specified level in green-liquor tanks. Opens feedline valves to admit measured quantities of aluminum hydrate seed particles into precipitators. Turns valves to agitate mixture with compressed air. Turns valves to control flow of liquor to tanks of secondary thickness. Weighs sample of mixture in flask on platform scale. Reads charts and graphs to determine amount of slurry or liquor required to obtain specified consistency. Signals BOTTOM-PRECIPITATOR OPERATOR (smelt. & refin.) to pump mixture from tanks. Records sequence of operations on forms. May lubricate valves and adjust packing glands to prevent leaks.

GOE: 06.02.10 STRENGTH: M GED: R3 M1 L2 SVP: 4 DLU: 77

511.482-010 CONTROL OPERATOR (smelt. & refin.)

Controls temperature, chemical composition, and level of cryolite baths in reduction pots to smelt aluminum oxide into aluminum: Breaks off sample piece of crust formed on bath surface, and grinds it into powder, using roll crusher. Routes sample to laboratory for analysis. Dips out sample of solution and pours it into containers, using ladle. Drops chemicals into sample and notes resultant color. Adds specified amounts of chemicals and alloys to bath, according to color shade of sample, to maintain solution at specified level and composition. Measures current flow and voltage between electrical connections on pots, using meters, and computes voltage drop between connections. Measures temperature of bath, heat exchangers, and heat-control pipes, using pyrometer, and turns rheostat to regulate temperature. Verifies specified distance between electrodes, using measuring rod. Measures depth of bath, and computes amount of aluminum available for tapping. Records tests made, amount of chemicals and alloys added to bath, and amount of aluminum tapped from pots.

GOE: 06.02.10 STRENGTH: L GED: R3 M2 L3 SVP: 5 DLU: 77

511.482-014 CRYOLITE-RECOVERY OPERATOR (smelt. & refin.)

Operates machines to recover cryolite from scrap potlining: Sets mill gauge to specified feed rate and adjusts air volume, according to screen analysis from laboratory. Sets hearth rheostats and heat controller to specified temperature, and turns valves to adjust rate of flow of steam and oil to burners. Starts system of conveyors, grinder, roaster, mixer equipment, cooling and exhaust fans, and burners. Moves levers to regulate flow of materials, and adjusts valve to control volume of liquor. Turns valve to drain spent liquor and lime hydrate to *causticizer* tanks. Makes titration test, records results, and sends samples to laboratory. Observes gauges, indicators, thermometers, and controls to ensure conformity to specifications.

GOE: 06.02.10 STRENGTH: L GED: R3 M2 L2 SVP: 5 DLU: 77

511.482-018 DUST-COLLECTOR OPERATOR (smelt. & refin.) alternate titles: dust operator

Operates battery of electrical precipitators to collect metallic dust particles from fumes of smelting ore: Observes ammeters and voltmeters and moves panel controls to regulate flow of electric current to precipitators according to type of ore being smelted, or according to amount of draft, moisture content of dust, and color of stack emission. Switches off electric current. Replaces broken wire in precipitators, using pliers. May turn valves to spray acid and water into chambers to oxidize dust particles. May pull levers to actuate airhammers that knock dust from electrodes.

GOE: 06.04.19 STRENGTH: L GED: R3 M1 L1 SVP: 3 DLU: 77

511.485-010 MOLYBDENUM-STEAMER OPERATOR (smelt. & refin.)

Tends equipment that removes reagent from molybdenum ore concentrate: Installs different-size orifices to regulate flow of solids and liquids into vats.

Adjusts steam valve to maintain concentrate at specified steaming point. Draws sample to determine alkalinity of concentrate, using titration test. Regulates flow of lime solution into vats according to alkalinity test readings to neutralize acids. Weighs sample and compares it with standard chart to determine percentage of solids in concentrate. Inserts airhose into vats to clear clogged outlets.
GOE: 06.02.10 STRENGTH: L GED: R3 M2 L2 SVP: 4 DLU: 77

511.485-014 THICKENER OPERATOR (smelt. & refin.)
Tends thickeners that separate waste solids from ore solutions or water, preparatory to recovery of metal or disposal of waste: Turns valves to regulate flow of mixture into thickeners. Inserts indicator into mixture to measure sludge level. Observes operation of equipment, overflow of concentrated metal solution, and flow of sludge from tank. Breaks up sedimentation in troughs with wooden paddle. Prepares sample of sludge for chemical analysis by weighing sample, adding acid to facilitate settling of solids, and reducing amount of sample to desired proportion in splitter. May titrate sample and compare resultant color with standard chart to test overflow solution for metallic content. May add chemicals to soften water in tanks. May fill out forms for scale readings and details of malfunctions. May be designated according to kind of materials separated as Red-Mud Thickener Operator (smelt. & refin.); Tailing-Thickener Operator (smelt. & refin.).
GOE: 06.04.10 STRENGTH: L GED: R3 M1 L2 SVP: 4 DLU: 77

511.562-010 CLASSIFIER OPERATOR (smelt. & refin.) alternate titles: hydrate-thickener operator; tray thickener operator
Operates classifier units to separate coarse and fine precipitated alumina particles from liquor: Regulates valves on settling trays of hydroseparators to draw fine particles from top and coarse particles from bottom of trays. Adjusts valves to wash liquor from coarse particles in classifier unit. Pumps fine hydrate from underflow of tray thickeners to storage tank for use in precipitating more alumina, and pumps coarse particles to storage tanks to await further processing. Lubricates valves and adjusts packing glands to prevent leaks. May open and close valves and start and stop pumps to circulate cleaning solutions through process lines. May keep log of operations.
GOE: 06.04.10 STRENGTH: M GED: R3 M2 L2 SVP: 5 DLU: 77

511.565-010 DEWATERER OPERATOR (smelt. & refin.) alternate titles: kiln-head house operator
Tends dewatering machines that filter moist solid aluminum hydroxide from coarse slurry: Turns valves to regulate flow of slurry and wash water to dewaterers and to admit solids to kilns, according to temperature readings, alumina-quality reports, and discharge rates given by KILN OPERATOR (smelt. & refin.). Adjusts valves to maintain supply of water for vacuum pumps, wash water, and water-cooled bearings. Regulates valves in cooperation with other operators to obtain balancing levels in filtrate tanks, hydrate storage tanks, and hydrate storage overflow tanks. Lubricates valves and adjusts packing glands to prevent leaks. Changes automatic recording charts in machines. Records tank levels and density readings of hydrate in log. May tend dust-recovery system.
GOE: 06.04.10 STRENGTH: M GED: R3 M1 L2 SVP: 5 DLU: 77

511.565-014 DRIER TENDER (smelt. & refin.) alternate titles: drier operator; rotary-drier operator
Tends oil-fired, rotary, magnetic drier that removes oil and iron from aluminum-scrap turnings: Ignites burner, and adjusts mixture of oil and air to obtain desired temperature. Starts drier, and turns on current to remove iron magnetically. Signals workers to load scrap into drier, and regulates rate of feed in accordance with oil content of scrap. Places wheelbarrow at discharge end of drier to receive processed turnings. Weighs filled wheelbarrow, records weight, and dumps load onto pile.
GOE: 06.04.10 STRENGTH: M GED: R3 M2 L2 SVP: 4 DLU: 77

511.565-018 IRON-LAUNDER OPERATOR (smelt. & refin.)
Tends iron launders that precipitate copper from solution: Signals OVERHEAD CRANE OPERATOR (any industry) 921.663-010 to load launders with shredded tin cans (iron). Starts pumps and turns valves to regulate flow of solution through series of launders to ensure maximum precipitation of copper. Measures copper content of solution at various stages of processing by titration tests. Adds iron to launders to maintain maximum recovery of copper. Excavates precipitated copper from launders and cleans tanks. Keeps record of titration tests.
GOE: 06.04.10 STRENGTH: L GED: R3 M1 L2 SVP: 4 DLU: 77

511.582-010 LEACHER (smelt. & refin.)
Controls equipment to leach out metal from ore in solution: Weighs sample of solution and evaporates moisture from it, using heater. Reweighs sample to determine percentage of solid material in solution. Siphons water from solution to obtain specified concentration, following chart. Turns valves to feed chemicals, such as cyanide or acid, into tank of ground ore or filtered slime. Starts mechanical agitators and observes percolation of solution to ascertain dissolution of ore. Tests solution with hydrometer to determine degree of ore concentration. Obtains sample of solution for laboratory analysis. May supervise workers in loading and excavating leaching tanks. May tend filtering machine to separate fluids from metal. May tend pumps to force ground ore and solution into or from tanks. May lubricate equipment and clean tank with water hose. May heat solution in tank with steam and add premeasured amounts of solid materials, such as manganese. May be designated according to ore leached as Molybdenum-Leaching-Plant Operator (smelt. & refin.).
GOE: 06.02.10 STRENGTH: L GED: R3 M2 L2 SVP: 5 DLU: 77

511.585-010 HYDRATE-CONTROL TENDER (smelt. & refin.)
Tends equipment that pumps aluminum hydrate from secondary thickeners through wash tanks to storage tanks: Turns valves to regulate amount of hydrate flowing into thickeners and washing tanks to maintain specified density of hydrate. Adjusts valves and pumps to transfer hydrate from secondary thickeners through wash tanks into seed storage tanks. Tests sample of hydrate to determine its density, using hydrometer. Lubricates valves and adjusts packing glands to prevent leaks. Keeps operating log.
GOE: 06.04.10 STRENGTH: M GED: R3 M1 L2 SVP: 4 DLU: 77

511.586-010 TOP-PRECIPITATOR-OPERATOR HELPER (smelt. & refin.)
Assists TOP-PRECIPITATOR OPERATOR (smelt. & refin.) in precipitating aluminum hydroxide from rich liquor: Opens valves and starts pumps to fill precipitators according to schedule and to add specified seed charges to tanks as directed, using levelometer to determine amount of seed added. Raises and lowers circulating lines, using electric hoist. Drops metal weights from tops of tanks to break scale and crust formations in empty tanks. Lubricates valves and adjusts packing glands to prevent leaks. Examines precipitator tanks for adequate circulation and empty tanks for cleanliness. Performs other duties as described under HELPER (any industry) Master Title.
GOE: 06.04.10 STRENGTH: M GED: R2 M1 L1 SVP: 2 DLU: 77

511.662-010 CLARIFIER OPERATOR (smelt. & refin.)
Controls equipment that separates mud from alumina liquor and recovers soda from mud: Pumps thickened mud to washers and turns valves to regulate flow of water into washers. Turns valves to release specified amount of mud into washers to maintain sludge balance. Turns valves to pump sediments from washer into earthen thickeners. Opens valves to introduce starch into mud settlement and to regulate flow of milk of lime at specified rates. Lubricates valves and adjusts packing glands, using grease guns and wrench.
GOE: 06.04.10 STRENGTH: M GED: R3 M2 L2 SVP: 4 DLU: 77

511.664-010 BOTTOM-PRECIPITATOR OPERATOR (smelt. & refin.)
Empties slurry from precipitator tanks as directed by TOP-PRECIPITATOR OPERATOR (smelt. & refin.): Starts and stops pumps to transfer slurry to thickener tanks. Adjusts valves to control rate of discharge of slurry and to maintain required level of mixture in equalizer tanks. Removes barrel flanges, using handtools. Cleans precipitator barrels and screen boxes, using hose and cleanup tools. Cleans airline of precipitator tank, using metal rod. Lubricates valves and adjusts packing glands to prevent leaks.
GOE: 06.04.10 STRENGTH: M GED: R2 M1 L2 SVP: 4 DLU: 77

511.667-010 CLARIFIER-OPERATOR HELPER (smelt. & refin.)
Assists CLARIFIER OPERATOR (smelt. & refin.) in separating mud from alumina liquor and in recovering soda from mud: Turns valves to flush lines. Turns valves to divert flow of alumina liquor through standby equipment as directed by CLARIFIER OPERATOR (smelt. & refin.). Reads tank gauge and records sludge levels of mud settlers and washers. Takes sample of mud sediments and weighs it to determine density. Lubricates valves and adjusts packing glands to prevent leaks, using grease gun and wrench. Cleans screen boxes. Performs other duties as described under HELPER (any industry) Master Title.
GOE: 06.04.10 STRENGTH: M GED: R2 M1 L1 SVP: 3 DLU: 77

511.667-014 COLOR TESTER (smelt. & refin.)
Collects and tests samples of copper-ore slurries: Draws samples from processing tanks or vats at specified times and locations, and labels containers with identifying data. Weighs samples, compares color against chart, and measures acidity or alkalinity, using pH meter. Records test results on product-control forms. Observes equipment during rounds to detect malfunctions, and notifies FILTER-PLANT SUPERVISOR (smelt. & refin.) of irregularities.
GOE: 06.03.01 STRENGTH: L GED: R3 M1 L2 SVP: 3 DLU: 77

511.682-010 DUST COLLECTOR, ORE CRUSHING (smelt. & refin.)
Operates dust-collecting equipment in crushing department of copper refinery to recover dust from ore: Starts feed conveyors, suction fans, impellers, and electrodes, and moves controls to regulate dampers, equalizing ports, and water eliminators. Turns valves to fill and maintain level of water in tanks. Observes operation of equipment and filling of collected dust in hoppers to ensure efficient operation. Inspects and cleans water eliminators, impellers, hopper walls, air chambers, fan housings and wheels, safety switches, and water-level control devices, using water and airhose. Removes and cleans strainers in waterlines. Adjusts and tightens belts on motors or pulley wheels to maintain tension, using handtools. Lubricates motors and exhaust bearings.
GOE: 06.02.10 STRENGTH: M GED: R3 M1 L2 SVP: 3 DLU: 77

511.685-010 AMALGAMATOR (smelt. & refin.)
Tends equipment that separates gold or silver from ground ore by mercury amalgamation process, using either of following methods: (1) Turns valves or opens gates to regulate flow of ore and water over mercury-coated plates. Adjusts angle of plates to facilitate collection of amalgam. Scrapes accumulated amalgam from plates and coats plates with mercury. (2) Turns valves or opens gates to charge ground ore and mercury into rotating-type barrels or agitating-type tanks. Starts equipment and observes accumulation of amalgam. Discharges or drains barrel or tank to recover gold or silver amalgam.
GOE: 06.04.10 STRENGTH: L GED: R3 M1 L1 SVP: 3 DLU: 77

511.685-014 CLASSIFIER TENDER (smelt. & refin.)
Tends equipment that separates crushed ore into sands (coarse particles) and slimes (fine particles), preparatory to concentration of metal: Starts equipment,

and regulates flow of crushed ore, water, and flotation reagent into classifiers which separate coarse particles by raking mechanism or swirling action of water while fine particles are carried off in overflow. Observes meter indicating alkalinity of slime, and adds lime solution, as necessary. Removes sand to prevent clogging by flushing or pulling lever on classifier to dump it. May lubricate machines. May replace defective parts, using handtools. May be designated according to type of classifier used as Cone-Classifier Tender (smelt. & refin.).
GOE: 06.04.10 STRENGTH: L GED: R3 M1 L2 SVP: 4 DLU: 77

511.685-018   CONDENSER-TUBE TENDER (smelt. & refin.)
Tends battery of condenser tubes in which gaseous mercury is condensed into liquid mercury: Places water-filled buckets at base of each tube to collect liquid mercury. Removes buckets as mercury accumulates, pours off water, and strains mercury into steel flask. Pours mixture of water, mercury, and dust onto sloping table, adds quicklime, and stirs mixture with hoe to separate remaining mercury from sediment.
GOE: 06.04.10 STRENGTH: H GED: R2 M1 L1 SVP: 2 DLU: 77

511.685-022   DUST-COLLECTOR ATTENDANT (mine & quarry)
Tends equipment that washes taconite ore dust collected from air: Starts dust collection equipment and turns valves to adjust pressure to required level as indicated by manometer. Examines parts of dust collector, such as pipes, nozzles, strainers, and collection surfaces, for pluggings, breaks, leaks, and residue. Closes water valves and stops pumps to permit cleaning and repairing of equipment. Washes residue from collection surfaces, pumps, hoppers, and fans, using water hose. Turns threaded water nozzles into fittings to change type of nozzle or to replace defective ones. Removes mesh strainers and cleans them, using airhose. Tightens glands on pumps and valves, using wrenches. May record gauge readings. May tend equipment that extracts carbon dust from air.
GOE: 06.04.09 STRENGTH: L GED: R3 M1 L1 SVP: 3 DLU: 77

511.685-026   FLOTATION TENDER (smelt. & refin.)
Tends flotation machines that separate metals from gangue of ore: Turns valves to regulate flow of pulp and reagents into cells. Turns valves to introduce compressed air into cells to agitate mixture and to promote froth that carries metallic particles to surface of liquid and deposits them through side opening of cell into launders. May tend cells that are agitated either mechanically or by air, or combination of both. May lubricate and repair machines. May be designated according to metal separated as Copper-Flotation Operator (smelt. & refin.); Molybdenum-Flotation Operator (smelt. & refin.).
GOE: 06.04.10 STRENGTH: L GED: R3 M1 L1 SVP: 4 DLU: 77

511.685-030   KETTLE TENDER II (smelt. & refin.)
Tends gas-fired kettle that removes gold, silver, and copper from black mud: Shovels mud into kettle, and turns valve to admit acid until mud is covered. Rakes mud to dissolve gold and silver. Ladles solution into water-filled settling tank to precipitate gold and silver compounds. Removes precipitates and adds reagents to change their chemical composition. Heats precipitates in cupola furnace to extract gold and silver. Ladles remaining mud into tank filled with water and admits steam to dissolve copper.
GOE: 06.04.10 STRENGTH: M GED: R3 M1 L2 SVP: 4 DLU: 77

511.685-034   KETTLE TENDER, PLATINUM AND PALLADIUM (smelt. & refin.)
Tends gas-fired evaporator that recovers gold, platinum, and palladium from electrolyte used in gold-refining tanks: Adds liquid and gaseous reagents to electrolyte and heats it in evaporator to precipitate metals. Separates each precipitate from solution, using porcelain filters. Heats platinum and palladium precipitates in crucible furnaces to make *sponge*. Breaks up sponge preparatory to shipment, using pliers.
GOE: 06.04.10 STRENGTH: M GED: R3 M1 L2 SVP: 4 DLU: 77

511.685-038   PRECIPITATOR I (smelt. & refin.)
Tends equipment that precipitates gold or silver from cyanide solution: Packs zinc shavings into compartments of zinc boxes. Regulates flow of solution through boxes where gold or silver precipitates on zinc. Shuts off flow of solution and turns on water. Agitates shavings to remove precipitate. Pulls plugs and draws off slime (precipitate and water) from boxes. Treats slime with sulfuric acid. Turns slime solution into filter press that filters solution and removes precipitate residue. Washes precipitate with water under pressure, and dries it with compressed air.
GOE: 06.04.10 STRENGTH: L GED: R3 M1 L1 SVP: 4 DLU: 77

511.685-042   PRECIPITATOR II (smelt. & refin.)
Tends tanks that precipitate uranium oxide from solution of uranium nitrate: Moves pump controls and turns valves to regulate flow of uranium nitrate solution into precipitation tank. Starts tank agitator and turns valve to feed specified amount of ammonia into tank. Dumps specified amount of magnesium oxide from bags into tank. Turns off agitator after specified period to allow uranium oxide to settle. Pumps tank underflow to automatic drier and tank overflow to thickener.
GOE: 06.04.10 STRENGTH: M GED: R3 M1 L2 SVP: 4 DLU: 77

511.685-046   REAGENT TENDER (smelt. & refin.)
Tends mechanical agitator that mixes chemicals for use in separating metallic particles from ore gangue: Turns valves to pour specified amounts of chemical solutions from storage tanks into mixing tank. Weighs chemical compounds on scales, and dumps chemicals into mixing tanks, using forklift truck. Starts agitator to blend mixture. Turns valves on pumps to transfer mixture to storage tank.

May weigh steel rods and balls and transport them to mills, using air-powered dinkey engine. May open chute door of storage tank to charge ball mills.
GOE: 06.04.10 STRENGTH: L GED: R3 M1 L1 SVP: 4 DLU: 77

511.685-050   SCREEN OPERATOR (smelt. & refin.)
Tends series of vibrating screens that separate crushed ore or stone according to size: Pushes controls to start screens vibrating and move ore on conveyors or belts. Pulls levers to discharge crushed ore from conveyor or chute onto vibrating screens. Clears screen holes clogged with oversize ore, using bar. Removes clogged screens, using wrenches, and cleans them with compressed air. May tend conveyor belts and process ore through crushers [CRUSHER TENDER (smelt. & refin.)]. May obtain ore samples, using mechanical sampler, hand sieve, or splitter. May tend screens that separate phosphate rock from matrix and be designated Feed-Preparation Operator (mine & quarry).
GOE: 06.04.08 STRENGTH: M GED: R3 M1 L2 SVP: 4 DLU: 77

511.685-054   SLIME-PLANT OPERATOR II (smelt. & refin.)
Tends equipment, such as grinders, leachers, filters, pressers, and evaporators that recover gold, silver, selenium, and other minerals from impurities: Grinds impure slag or ore in ball mill, and mixes slag with water to form slurry. Turns valves and starts pumps to force mixture into leaching tanks. Starts agitators and adds chemicals to leach combined solutions. Starts pumps to force leached solution into settling tanks, and installs orifices to control rate of flow of sediment and liquids to and from settling tanks to remove liquid. Feeds settled solution through rotary-drum filters, and presses filtered slime in press [FILTER-PRESS OPERATOR (any industry)]. Boils selenium residue to remove moisture for barreling. Obtains and weighs samples of slimes during process, using container and platform scales, and delivers samples to laboratory for analysis. Drains and cleans tanks, wire screens, inflow pipes, and equipment with water hose. May be designated according to mineral recovered as Selenium-Plant Operator (smelt. & refin.).
GOE: 06.04.12 STRENGTH: L GED: R3 M1 L2 SVP: 4 DLU: 77

511.685-058   SLIME-PLANT-OPERATOR HELPER (smelt. & refin.)
Assists SLIME-PLANT OPERATOR (smelt. & refin.) II in separating ore concentrate from slurry: Turns valves to regulate flow of liquids into tank. Observes operation of filters and notifies SLIME-PLANT OPERATOR (smelt. & refin.) II of malfunctions. Replaces worn filters, using handtools. Lubricates valves and adjusts packing glands. May record operating data in log. May tend overhead bridge crane to transport filters and equipment. Performs other duties as described under HELPER (any industry) Master Title.
GOE: 06.04.10 STRENGTH: M GED: R2 M1 L1 SVP: 3 DLU: 77

511.685-062   TABLE TENDER (smelt. & refin.)
Tends concentrating tables that separate valuable metals from gangue of ore and scrap: Turns valves to regulate flow of pulp onto tables. Regulates speed of reciprocating tables to effect maximum separation and recovery of metals. Adjusts slope of tables to establish line of separation between ore and gangue and between valuable metal and scrap. Repairs tables, and adjusts and lubricates driving mechanism. May be designated according to materials processed as Table Tender, Sludge (smelt. & refin.).
GOE: 06.04.10 STRENGTH: M GED: R3 M1 L1 SVP: 4 DLU: 77

511.685-066   TROMMEL TENDER (smelt. & refin.)
Tends trommel (revolving drumlike sieve) that washes copper precipitate from scrap iron: Starts previously loaded trommel and turns on water sprays. Pumps precipitated copper and water mixture into settling tank. Shovels spilled scrap iron back into tank. Lubricates trommel bearings, and washes copper from equipment with water hose. May line bottom of railroad car with precut wooden boards preparatory to loading car with copper.
GOE: 06.04.10 STRENGTH: M GED: R2 M1 L1 SVP: 2 DLU: 77

511.686-010   REAGENT TENDER HELPER (smelt. & refin.)
Assists REAGENT TENDER (smelt. & refin.) in separating metallic particles from gangue of ore: Connects air line and line from storage tank to tank car, using handtools. Turns valves to release air pressure into lines, and observes connections for leaks. Turns valves to pump chemical solutions, such as chlorine, caustic soda, and fuel oils, from tank cars into storage tanks. May weigh steel rods and balls and transport them to mills, using air-powered dinkey engine. Performs other duties as described under HELPER (any industry) Master Title.
GOE: 06.04.10 STRENGTH: M GED: R2 M1 L1 SVP: 2 DLU: 77

511.687-010   BLANKET WASHER (smelt. & refin.)
Cleans flannel blankets over which mixture of finely ground gold ore and cyanide solution from grinding mills is passed to collect free particles of gold not dissolved by cyanide: Collects blankets from frames at outflow point of mills. Washes blankets in pans of weak cyanide solution to dislodge gold particles so they may be collected in amalgamation process. Replaces blankets on frames after washing.
GOE: 06.04.27 STRENGTH: M GED: R2 M1 L1 SVP: 2 DLU: 77

511.687-014   DUST COLLECTOR-TREATER (smelt. & refin.) alternate titles: rapper
Assists DUST-COLLECTOR OPERATOR (smelt. & refin.) in collecting metallic dust particles from fumes of smelting copper ore: Pushes switches to shut off electric current to precipitators, and observes amount of dust accumulated on electrode pipes and plates. Pulls levers to start hammers that knock dust from electrodes into collecting chambers. Opens chamber doors and blows

down dust remaining in chamber, using airhose. Replaces broken wires in precipitators, using pliers. Turns valves to add acid solution and water to chambers to cool and treat fumes. Performs other duties as described under HELPER (any industry) Master Title. May be designated as Acid Conditioner (smelt. & refin.); Cottrell Blower (smelt. & refin.).
GOE: 06.04.09 STRENGTH: M GED: R2 M1 L1 SVP: 3 DLU: 77

511.687-018 FLOTATION-TENDER HELPER (smelt. & refin.)
Scrapes caked waste material from sides of flotation cells, and washes cells with water. May ream out air passages of agitators, using steel rod. May collect samples of pulp and concentrate at prescribed intervals for analysis. May assist in dismantling and repair of equipment. May record details of operating conditions in log.
GOE: 06.04.34 STRENGTH: M GED: R1 M1 L1 SVP: 1 DLU: 77

511.687-022 SKIMMER, REVERBERATORY (smelt. & refin.)
Skims slag from surface of copper being refined in reverberatory furnace: Signals OVERHEAD CRANE OPERATOR (any industry) 921.663-010 to lower pan, and positions it in front of slag tapping hole. Inserts wood pole through door in side of furnace, working pole back and forth to push slag toward front of furnace. Drags slag from surface of copper into pan, using steel hoe. Inserts compressed-air line through furnace opening, and turns valve to force air through molten metal to oxidize impurities. May shovel coke over surface of skimmed metal to prevent excess oxidation.
GOE: 06.04.34 STRENGTH: M GED: R2 M1 L1 SVP: 3 DLU: 77

511.687-026 TAILINGS-DAM LABORER (smelt. & refin.)
Directs waste ore materials through pipelines into tailings basin: Opens and closes spigots to regulate flow of tailings. Connects hoses to spigots and adds pipes to lengthen discharge lines, using wrenches. Distributes tailings evenly in basin to form dam of waste materials. Digs ditches with shovel to drain water.
GOE: 06.04.34 STRENGTH: H GED: R2 M1 L1 SVP: 2 DLU: 77

512 MELTING OCCUPATIONS

This group includes occupations concerned with heating ore concentrate or metal to change it from solid to liquid for such purposes as compounding with other materials, refining, and preparing for casting.

512.130-010 REDUCTION-PLANT SUPERVISOR (smelt. & refin.)
Supervises and coordinates activities of workers engaged in operation and maintenance of aluminum-reduction pots. Performs duties as described under SUPERVISOR (any industry) Master Title.
GOE: 06.04.01 STRENGTH: L GED: R4 M3 L3 SVP: 7 DLU: 77

512.132-010 MELTER SUPERVISOR (steel & rel.)
Supervises and coordinates activities of workers engaged in operating open-hearth, electric-arc, or oxygen furnaces to produce steel: Directs workers in charging furnace with specified raw material and in taking temperature tests of molten metal. Observes color of molten metal through cobalt-blue glasses, and orders changes in furnace temperature. Coordinates charging and melting with molding and pouring operations. Performs other duties as described under SUPERVISOR (any industry) Master Title. May be designated according to type of furnace as Melter Supervisor, Electric-Arc Furnace (steel & rel.); Melter Supervisor, Open-Hearth Furnace (steel & rel.); Melter Supervisor, Oxygen Furnace (steel & rel.).
GOE: 06.04.01 STRENGTH: L GED: R4 M3 L3 SVP: 7 DLU: 77

512.132-014 RECLAMATION SUPERVISOR (nonfer. metal)
Supervises and coordinates activities of workers engaged in melting reclaimed dross and scalpings, casting molten scrap into ingots, and alloying aluminum with metals, such as copper, nickel, and iron. Inspects condition (paper-covered, dirty, glass-mixed) and type of incoming scrap to determine melting process, and records information on planning chart. Confers with other departments to determine alloys to be used and priority of casting. Performs duties as described under SUPERVISOR (any industry) Master Title.
GOE: 06.04.01 STRENGTH: L GED: R4 M2 L3 SVP: 7 DLU: 77

512.132-018 REMELT-FURNACE EXPEDITER (nonfer. metal)
Supervises and coordinates activities of workers engaged in tapping remelt furnaces, and in fluxing aluminum alloy preparatory to casting: Directs workers in tapping of aluminum alloy from remelt furnaces into ladles and in introducing chlorine gas into ladles to flux molten alloys. Directs OVERHEAD CRANE OPERATOR (any industry) 921.663-010 in moving ladles from tapping position to casting units. Records temperature and time of tapping furnaces and of fluxing ladles. May supervise workers engaged in collecting and weighing charges of aluminum and other metals for melting into alloys and be designated Metal Expediter (nonfer. metal). Performs other duties as described under SUPERVISOR (any industry) Master Title.
GOE: 06.04.01 STRENGTH: M GED: R4 M2 L3 SVP: 7 DLU: 77

512.132-022 SUPERVISOR, BLAST FURNACE (smelt. & refin.)
Supervises and coordinates activities of workers engaged in controlling blast furnaces to smelt concentrates of lead ore preparatory to refining it. Performs duties as described under SUPERVISOR (any industry) Master Title.
GOE: 06.04.01 STRENGTH: L GED: R4 M3 L3 SVP: 7 DLU: 77

512.135-010 POT-ROOM SUPERVISOR (smelt. & refin.)
Supervises and coordinates activities of workers engaged in tending reduction pots to smelt aluminum oxide into aluminum: Observes gas flames, warning lights, and voltmeters on pots to verify specified voltage input. Signals POT TENDER (smelt. & refin.) to raise and lower anode to restore pot to normal operation. Performs other duties as described under SUPERVISOR (any industry) Master Title.
GOE: 06.04.01 STRENGTH: L GED: R4 M3 L3 SVP: 7 DLU: 77

512.362-010 FIRST HELPER (steel & rel.) alternate titles: melter assistant; open-hearth-furnace operator
Operates open-hearth furnaces to produce specified types of steel: Examines raw materials for conformance to specifications. Signals CHARGING-MACHINE OPERATOR (steel & rel.) to place materials in furnace. Turns fuel, air, and steam controls to adjust fuel mixtures and draft. Moves levers to circulate gas throughout furnace to distribute heat and prevent burning out of furnace walls. Signals OVERHEAD CRANE OPERATOR (any industry) 921.663-010 to pour molten metal in furnace. Obtains sample of metal, using long-handled spoon, and pours sample into test mold. Tests sample for carbon content, using carbon analyzer. Moves controls to open furnace doors, and shovels additives, such as fluorspar, lime, and alloys, into furnace to obtain specified type of steel. Determines temperature of metal, using thermocouple. Observes color of molten metal through cobalt-blue glasses to determine when to tap furnace and notifies MELTER SUPERVISOR (steel & rel.). Directs crew in tapping furnace and adding specified additives to ladle. Records operational data on forms. Examines furnace to determine repairs needed, and directs crew in repairing furnace walls and flooring.
GOE: 06.02.10 STRENGTH: H GED: R3 M2 L2 SVP: 6 DLU: 77

512.362-014 FURNACE OPERATOR (nonfer. metal; smelt. & refin.)
Controls furnace to refine or melt nonferrous ore or metal to specifications: Sets furnace controls to regulate flow of air, gas, oil, or current to heat metal to specified temperature. Observes color, fluidity of molten bath, and appearance of metal on bar, to estimate temperature, or measures temperature, using pyrometer. Inserts end of green pole into furnace to prevent oxidation of copper. Adds reagents to remove impurities, according to type of metal processed. Skims slag with rabble, dross hoe, or ladle. Opens blowers to force air through tuyeres to agitate bath, and stirs bath with wooden pole or iron rod to release oxygen. Seals taphole with fire clay and firebrick. Turns handwheel or moves lever to tilt or turn furnace and taps metal into pots for removal to other furnaces [TAPPER (nonfer. metal; smelt. & refin.)]. Lifts and transfers ladles of melt, using hoist. Sprays dore or silver crystals with water, and dries them with vacuum drier prior to melting. Samples materials and sends samples to laboratory for analysis [RAW SAMPLER (smelt. & refin.)]. Sprays molds with bone ash to prevent metal from adhering to mold. May replace defective parts or clean equipment. May operate puncher to clear tuyere holes and allow air to pass through molten copper in converters to burn off impurities. May be designated according to type of furnace operated or product processed.
GOE: 06.02.10 STRENGTH: M GED: R4 M2 L2 SVP: 5 DLU: 77

512.362-018 FURNACE OPERATOR (foundry; steel & rel.) alternate titles: air-furnace operator; caster, investment casting; pit-furnace melter; rotary-furnace operator
Controls gas, oil, coal, electric-arc, or electric induction furnace to melt metal prior to casting: Weighs out specified amounts of metal ingots and scrap metal, and charges metal into furnace by hand, using hoist, or by directing crane operator to charge furnace. Loads molten metal into furnace, using transfer ladle. Turns valves to regulate injection of fuel and air into furnace, or moves controls to regulate flow of electricity and water coolant through electrodes to heat furnace to specified temperature. Observes color of metal and instruments, such as voltmeter, ammeter, wattmeter, and pyrometer, and adjusts controls to maintain specified temperature. Sprinkles fluxing agent over surface of molten metal to bring impurities to surface, forming layer of slag. Skims off slag, using strainer. Removes crucible containing molten metal from furnace, using hoist, moves levers to tilt crucible or open crucible door, or breaks clay plug to pour metal into ladle for transportation to molds. Removes test sample of molten metal from crucible, using hand ladle, and pours it into mold. Records data from each melt on form. Positions new electrodes over worn electrodes in electric-arc furnace, using overhead crane, and screws electrodes together, using chain wrench. May transport crucible or ladle to pouring station and pour metal into molds. May be designated according to type of furnace operated as Electric-Arc-Furnace Operator (foundry; smelt. & refin.; steel & rel.); Furnace Operator, Oil Or Gas (foundry); Induction-Furnace Operator (foundry); Tilting-Furnace Operator, Oil Or Gas (foundry).
GOE: 06.02.10 STRENGTH: M GED: R3 M2 L3 SVP: 5 DLU: 77

512.382-010 OXYGEN-FURNACE OPERATOR (steel & rel.)
Operates oxygen furnace and auxiliary equipment from pulpit to produce specified types of steel: Moves controls to position furnace for charging operation. Observes temperature gauges and recorders, and moves controls to position oxygen lance and regulate flow of oxygen through lance onto charge. Sets weight indicator gauge according to specified amount of additives to be added to charge. Starts automatic weighing machine that releases additives, such as fluorspar, lime, and alloys, from bins onto conveyor leading to chute over furnace. Moves lever to release additives from chute into furnace. Moves controls to adjust position of oxygen lance in furnace, regulate oxygen flow, or adjust hood draft when sparking or slopping of charge occurs or furnace overheats. Moves controls to position transfer car, carrying ladle and slag pots, under taphole and to tilt furnace for tapping operation. Records operation data.
GOE: 06.02.10 STRENGTH: M GED: R3 M2 L2 SVP: 5 DLU: 77

512.382-014 STOVE TENDER (steel & rel.) alternate titles: hot blaster

Operates battery of gas-fired stoves to supply heated airblast to blast furnace: Turns gas valves and ignites burners in combustion chamber of stove, using torch. Observes temperature records, and moves controls to close gas and chimney valves when heat inside stove reaches specified temperature. Opens valves on stove allowing air from blowing engine to pass through hot-blast stove into furnace. Adjusts stove controls to maintain specified temperature of airblast. Alternates operation among stoves in battery to provide continuous blast of hot air. Cleans carbon and dirt from flues to prevent internal explosions. Inspects cooling and washing equipment for leaks. Assists furnace crew in casting hot metal and flushing slag from furnace.
GOE: 06.02.10 STRENGTH: L GED: R3 M1 L2 SVP: 5 DLU: 77

512.382-018 TIN RECOVERY WORKER (smelt. & refin.)

Controls scruff and burn-off furnaces and auxiliary equipment to reclaim tin or terne from coating pots, tinplate, and used electrolytic anodes: Washes scruff with hose to remove flux. Starts crushing machine, and shovels scruff into machine to reduce scruff to uniform size. Charges scruff into furnace, and ignites gas burner with torch. Adjusts heat controls to obtain specified temperature for reclaiming metal from scruff. Breaks up lumps in scruff, using rake and hoe. Turns valves to tap furnace and allow reclaimed metal to flow into iron kettle or melting pot. Heats kettle, and skims foreign metal from top, using ladle. Adds specified amounts of tin or lead in producing terne. Pours metal into pig or electrolytic anode molds. Weighs and records amount of recovered metal. Marks weight on pigs, and stores pigs in warehouse.
GOE: 06.02.10 STRENGTH: H GED: R3 M2 L2 SVP: 4 DLU: 77

512.467-010 POTLINE MONITOR (smelt. & refin.)

Tests electrical circuitry and measures temperature and depth level of materials in aluminum reduction pots: Places contact rods of voltmeter against anode of reduction pot and against lining (cathode) of next pot on line to obtain voltage reading of pot circuit. Records meter reading, repeats test on next pot, and deducts reading from previous reading to determine any power loss. Repeats test on each succeeding pot to obtain and record power loss at each point along potline. Removes concrete sections of floor, using overhead hoist, to expose electrical circuits. Places prongs of millivoltmeter on ground and electrical connections to measure amount of positive and negative charges entering pot. Inspects electrical connections, firebrick lining, and wiring to detect damaged, worn, or broken parts, and notifies POT-ROOM SUPERVISOR (smelt. & refin.) of discrepancies. Breaks hole in pot crust with crowbar, and inserts thermocouple to measure temperature of contents. Measures depth of contents, using measuring rod, and records temperature and depth on control form. Dips ladle into pot to remove sample of aluminum for laboratory analysis, and pours sample into mold. Records test readings, voltage loss, temperatures, and depth levels on master control form, and submits it to POT-ROOM SUPERVISOR (smelt. & refin.).
GOE: 06.03.01 STRENGTH: M GED: R3 M2 L2 SVP: 4 DLU: 77

512.487-010 METAL CONTROL WORKER (foundry)

Weighs alloy, shot, or strips of metal to obtain specified amounts required by FURNACE OPERATOR (foundry; steel & rel.), using platform scale: Cuts bar stock to specified lengths, using power saw. Stamps code on bar to indicate alloy and heat number. Places pelletized metal in barrels. Records weight and kind of metals issued in logbook. Delivers specified metal to FURNACE OPERATOR (foundry; steel & rel.), using handtruck or industrial truck. May verify incoming metal shipments against invoice, store metal, and maintain inventory of metal on hand.
GOE: 06.03.01 STRENGTH: M GED: R3 M2 L2 SVP: 3 DLU: 77

512.662-010 CUPOLA TENDER (foundry) alternate titles: furnace tender

Controls cupola furnace to melt and refine iron, scrap metal, and other additives to produce gray iron castings: Closes and props door in bottom of cupola. Shovels sand into cupola and tamps sand to form wedge-shaped layer on cupola bottom sloping toward taphole. Kindles fire, using gas torch, to ignite coke bed in cupola, and starts and sets speed of blowers that supply air to cupola. Signals CUPOLA CHARGER (foundry) 512.686-010 to begin charging metal, coke, and limestone into cupola. Reads gauges indicating temperature of molten metal in cupola and amount of air flowing into and out of cupola, and adjusts controls accordingly. Taps molten metal from cupola. Estimates, from color of slag draining from surface of molten metal, physical properties of metal being melted. Pulls prop from bottom doors of cupola, when shutting down furnace, to allow residual materials to drop out. May charge layer of excelsior, rags, and wood over sand bed to protect cupola from initial charge of coke and to ignite fuel.
GOE: 06.02.10 STRENGTH: M GED: R3 M2 L2 SVP: 4 DLU: 77

512.666-010 FURNACE HELPER (nonfer. metal; smelt. & refin.)

Assists FURNACE OPERATOR (nonfer. metal; smelt. & refin.) by performing any combination of following duties: Seals furnace opening with fire clay and firebrick, using paddle and shovel. Charges furnace with materials, such as scrap, ore, flux, reagents, slimes, oxides, pellets, or coke, by moving levers to open bin or hopper gates, by shoveling, or by signaling FURNACE CHARGER (nonfer. metal; smelt. & refin.) or OVERHEAD CRANE OPERATOR (any industry) 921.663-010 to load furnace. Turns valves to force air through tuyeres into molten metal to oxidize impurities. Observes gauges and manipulates controls on panel to admit nitrogen to prevent igniting of magnesium. Stirs molten metal with green poles to prevent copper from oxidizing.

Skims slag from molten metal, using bar, rabble, or ladle. Cleans slag from tuyeres to let air flow, using bar, hammer, or pneumatic drill. Signals OVERHEAD CRANE OPERATOR (any industry), or uses electric hoist, to position ladles or buckets near furnace, and moves levers to tilt furnace into pouring position. Scrapes and chips slag, solidified metal, furnace lining, and residue from furnace, using hammer, chisel, and scraper. Breaks condensers and defective retorts with sledgehammer for removal to crusher. Raps flues and dust catchers with bar to remove dust. Performs other duties as described under HELPER (any industry) Master Title.
GOE: 06.04.10 STRENGTH: H GED: R2 M1 L1 SVP: 2 DLU: 77

512.667-010 TEMPERATURE REGULATOR, PYROMETER (foundry) alternate titles: fire regulator

Tests temperature of molten metal for conformance to pouring specifications, using optical or thermocouple pyrometers: Advises CUPOLA TENDER (foundry) or furnace operator when temperature reading varies from specifications. Records temperature reading on standard form.
GOE: 06.03.02 STRENGTH: L GED: R2 M2 L2 SVP: 2 DLU: 77

512.683-010 CHARGING-MACHINE OPERATOR (steel & rel.) alternate titles: charger; furnace-charging-machine operator; poker-in; pusher runner

Controls charging machine to charge open-hearth furnaces with materials, such as limestone, pig iron, and metal scrap: Moves controls to engage arm of charging machine in slot of charging box. Pushes levers to position charging machine at door of furnace, to thrust box through door, and to rotate arm, dumping contents of box on furnace floor. Withdraws empty box, disengages arm, and moves to next furnace to repeat process. May charge furnace with molten metal and be designated Hot-Metal Charger (steel & rel.).
GOE: 06.02.10 STRENGTH: L GED: R3 M1 L1 SVP: 5 DLU: 77

512.684-010 SECOND HELPER (steel & rel.) alternate titles: open-hearth-furnace-operator helper

Assists FIRST HELPER (steel & rel.) to melt and cast iron and steel in open-hearth furnaces: Cleans furnace tapholes, using scraper and oxygen lance. Closes furnace tapholes with pipe, chrome ore, dolomite, or magnesite to prevent loss of molten metal, and relines steel runners. Weighs additives, such as fluorspar, lime, and manganese, and trucks them to furnace areas. Shovels refractory materials into furnace. Assists crew in slagging or flushing furnace. Starts furnace by igniting gas, using torch. Performs other duties as described under HELPER (any industry) Master Title.
GOE: 06.04.10 STRENGTH: H GED: R2 M1 L1 SVP: 3 DLU: 77

512.684-014 FURNACE CHARGER (nonfer. metal; smelt. & refin.; steel & rel.) alternate titles: fettler

Performs any combination of following tasks to charge smelting furnaces with aluminum scrap and ingots, and other nonferrous metals, as well as ore, coke, flux, and other materials: Moves levers to open and close furnace doors and to pour specified materials into furnace. Moves controls of charging machine to lift, insert, and dump materials into furnace, or shovels materials into furnace, using hood shovel. Draws samples of molten metal from furnace for laboratory analysis. Reviews laboratory report to determine that smelting is within specified standards, and computes types and amounts of materials to add to furnace to correct smelting, using calculator. Rakes dross or flux from furnace, using skimming tool. Maintains production records of materials charged into furnace. May weigh out specified amounts of materials to be charged into furnace, using scale. May operate industrial dump or lift truck to transport, hoist, and dump scrap or refined aluminum into charging machine or furnace. May operate bucket loader to hoist, convey, and dump aluminum ore, coke, and flux into hopper of smelting furnace.
GOE: 06.02.10 STRENGTH: M GED: R3 M2 L2 SVP: 4 DLU: 78

512.685-010 FURNACE TENDER (foundry; nonfer. metal) alternate titles: remelt operator

Tends furnace that remelts nonferrous alloyed metals used in diecasting process: Shovels specified proportions of scrap metal and ingots into furnace. Sprinkles fluxing compound on molten metal to bring impurities to surface. Skims slag from surface of molten metal, using hand strainer. May transfer molten metal from furnace to bull ladle, using hand ladle. May convey molten metal in bull ladle along overhead monorail, and pour metal into retainer of diecasting machine. May pour molten metal into sand molds, using power hoist. May clean furnaces and equipment.
GOE: 06.04.10 STRENGTH: H GED: R2 M1 L1 SVP: 3 DLU: 77

512.685-014 NOZZLE TENDER (nonfer. metal)

Tends equipment that produces aluminum powder from molten aluminum: Installs ceramic tube in furnace and positions air nozzle and power collection duct as specified. Taps furnace to allow molten aluminum to flow through ceramic tube where it is transformed into powder by blast from air nozzle and blown into powder collection duct. Observes flow of metal and adjusts air nozzle to regulate fineness of powder. Sifts powder sample through series of sieves and weighs contents remaining in each sieve to estimate quantity of each grade of powder.
GOE: 06.04.10 STRENGTH: M GED: R2 M1 L2 SVP: 3 DLU: 77

512.685-018 POT TENDER (smelt. & refin.) alternate titles: pot puncher

Tends battery of reduction pots that smelt aluminum oxide into aluminum: Adds specified amounts of oxide to pots from overhead hopper, at designated

time intervals, and rakes oxide over crust formed by cooling of bath. Observes gas flames breaking through crust, and rakes oxide or pieces of crust over flames to prevent damage to anode. Watches warning lights and notes color of electrolyte (solution), and breaks up crust to add oxide to bath, using crowbar or pneumatic crust-breaking machine. Stirs bath to eliminate gas, using rake. Observes instruments and turns rheostat, or repositions anode in bath, to increase or decrease current flow and regulate temperature of solution. May train workers in operation of reduction pots.
GOE: 06.04.10 STRENGTH: M GED: R3 M1 L1 SVP: 3 DLU: 77

512.685-022 RECLAMATION KETTLE TENDER, METAL (smelt. & refin.)
Tends melting kettle to remelt metal scrap, dross, and skimmings to recover lead, cadmium, zinc, or other nonferrous metals and cast it into pig molds for reuse: Charges kettle manually or using shovel or hoist. Ignites burner to melt and heat metal. Observes thermometer or color of molten metal and adjusts temperature control or turns valve to adjust fuel supply to obtain pour temperature. Stirs and skims molten metal, using bar and skimming tool. Drains, ladles, or pumps metal into molds.
GOE: 06.04.10 STRENGTH: M GED: R2 M1 L1 SVP: 3 DLU: 77

512.686-010 CUPOLA CHARGER (foundry) alternate titles: cupola stocker
Charges scrap iron or pig iron, coke, and limestone (flux) into cupola in which iron is melted to make castings: Determines quantities and types of materials to be charged, following work orders or verbal instructions from CUPOLA TENDER (foundry). Shovels materials into wheelbarrow. Weighs net contents and wheels materials to charging door of cupola. Dumps iron, coke, and limestone through charging door so that charge in cupola is in alternate layers. May operate power-driven hopper, conveyor, or crane to transfer materials from storage bins to cupola. May weigh out materials or load materials from preweighed piles onto conveyor that charges cupola.
GOE: 06.04.10 STRENGTH: M GED: R2 M1 L2 SVP: 2 DLU: 77

512.687-010 CONDENSER SETTER (smelt. & refin.)
Places condenser on plate supports in front of retort in zinc furnace to collect and condense zinc vapor created by heating ore in retort: Charges retort with mixture of ore and coal, using skip-loader. Lifts and positions condenser in front of retort, using tongs. Seals joint between retort and condenser by spreading finely ground and dampened mixture of coal and loam to prevent escape of zinc vapor. Banks mouth of condenser with mixture of coal and ore or waste material to prevent zinc from overflowing while allowing combustion gases to escape.
GOE: 06.04.10 STRENGTH: M GED: R2 M1 L1 SVP: 2 DLU: 77

512.687-014 THIRD HELPER (steel & rel.) alternate titles: open-hearth-furnace laborer
Performs any combination of following duties involved in operation of open-hearth furnaces: Moves controls to open and close furnace doors. Removes molten metal in low spots or pockets of furnace floor, using *air lance*. Shovels refractory materials onto furnace bottom. Transports additives from bins to furnace. Shovels additives into furnace and ladle. Cleans and reams furnace taphole and pries solidified metal from pouring spout, using reaming rod and bar. Sprays slag with water, using hose. Maintains tools and equipment required for furnace operations. Cleans charging floor and furnace areas.
GOE: 06.04.10 STRENGTH: H GED: R2 M1 L1 SVP: 3 DLU: 77

513 ROASTING OCCUPATIONS

This group includes occupations concerned with heating ore and concentrates in calciners, furnaces, or kilns to remove moisture or to drive off impurities.

513.132-010 CONVERTER SUPERVISOR (smelt. & refin.)
Supervises and coordinates activities of workers engaged in operating converter furnaces to produce metallic copper from copper matte, or in mixing, roasting, or drying copper concentrate prior to smelting operation: Monitors processing to verify conformance to specifications. Inspects equipment to detect malfunctions or defects and assigns worker to make repairs or adjustments. Demonstrates operation and maintenance of machines and equipment to new workers, and explains plant layout, processing techniques, and safety regulations to orient new workers. May be designated according to operation supervised as Roaster Supervisor (smelt. & refin.). Performs duties as described under SUPERVISOR (any industry) Master Title.
GOE: 06.04.01 STRENGTH: L GED: R4 M3 L3 SVP: 6 DLU: 77

513.362-010 CALCINER OPERATOR (mine & quarry; smelt. & refin.)
Controls calciners and allied equipment from instrumented panelboard to heat ore slurry, dry slurry, and drive off impurities: Monitors recording instruments, flowmeters, panel lights, and other indicators, and listens for warning signals on panel to operate calciner, conveyor system, and allied equipment. Turns screws and knobs on panelboard to control feed rate, temperature, and conveying of ore. Examines calcined ore to determine, by color, that it meets company specifications. Confers with other departments to adjust steam, water, and fuel supply, using telephone or radio. Confers with supervisor to report equipment failure or malfunction, and to resolve problems in process changes. Maintains record of steam, water, and fuel used during shift. Records process changes, malfunctions, and other actions in shift log and operator's sheet. Examines

calciners and allied equipment, such as conveyor belts and chutes, blowers, pumps, compressors, and power lines, waterlines, and air lines, for wear or defects. Periodically cleans calciner, working as member of team, and using air-hammer, water hose, pick, shovel, and wheelbarrow. When drying copper ore, may be designated Reactor Operator (smelt. & refin.).
GOE: 06.02.10 STRENGTH: L GED: R3 M2 L2 SVP: 6 DLU: 77

513.462-010 FURNACE OPERATOR (smelt. & refin.)
Operates furnace to remove moisture, arsenic, or sulfur from ore: Charges top hearth of roaster with ore, regulating rate of charge by means of chute door. Determines speed with which roaster is being charged by weighing sample of charge ore obtained over measured interval of time. Starts rabbles (automatic rakes) that scrape hearth beds continually and move ore from one hearth to next lower one. Regulates draft and temperature of roaster by adjusting dampers and gas pressure. Replaces rabble arms by detaching arm from shaft with bar and removing it with hoist. Replaces defective rabble teeth. Directs workers in removing incrustations from hearth beds. Removes samples of roasted ore for laboratory analysis. May clean arms and rabbles with scrapers and iron bars. May determine oxide content of dried ore by titrating specified amount of flakes and calculating percentage. May replace defective parts and clean equipment.
GOE: 06.02.10 STRENGTH: M GED: R3 M2 L2 SVP: 4 DLU: 77

513.565-010 KILN OPERATOR (smelt. & refin.)
Tends battery of rotary kilns in which hydrated alumina is calcined: Moves levers and switches to start kilns and regulate their speed. Adjusts controls to regulate temperature, pressure, and rate of flow of oil, gas, air, flue gases, and steam vapor. Directs DEWATERER OPERATOR (smelt. & refin.) in regulating flow of hydrated alumina into kilns. Turns valves to adjust water supply to cooler coils, kiln trunnions, and water-cooled bearings. Inspects kilns, carriages, and drive mechanisms for signs of faulty operation or overheating. Keeps log of operational data, such as air temperature and oil or gas pressure. May lubricate valves and adjust packing glands to prevent leaks. May tend air slides and bucket elevators to convey alumina to storage bins.
GOE: 06.02.10 STRENGTH: L GED: R3 M1 L2 SVP: 4 DLU: 77

513.587-010 KILN-OPERATOR HELPER (smelt. & refin.) alternate titles: calcination helper
Assists KILN OPERATOR (smelt. & refin.) in calcining hydrated alumina in rotary kilns: Moves controls to direct flow of alumina through standby equipment. Lubricates valves with grease guns. Adjusts packing glands to prevent leaks, using handtools. Cleans coolers, using *air lance*. Observes flow of alumina through kilns, inspects equipment, and reports defects or malfunctions to KILN OPERATOR (smelt. & refin.). Takes sample of alumina in bucket for laboratory analysis. Records weights of alumina stored. Performs other duties as described under HELPER (any industry) Master Title.
GOE: 06.04.10 STRENGTH: M GED: R2 M1 L1 SVP: 3 DLU: 77

513.667-010 CALCINER-OPERATOR HELPER (mine & quarry; smelt. & refin.)
Records machine and equipment readings in shift log at specified intervals, examines machines and equipment for malfunctions, and draws composite samples of ore at various stages of processing for laboratory testing: Reads gauges and records water and oil levels, temperatures, and pressures at specified intervals. Examines motors for leaks or hot bearings, conveyor belts for buildup or spillage, belt rollers for squeaks that indicate wear or belt misalignment, oil level in sight glasses, and exhaust fans for dirt and dust buildup. Turns handle to reposition filter on fluidizing blower. Dips sample of ore into bucket or jar at various stages of processing to collect composite sample for laboratory analysis. Notifies CALCINER OPERATOR (mine & quarry; smelt. & refin.) of machine and equipment malfunctions.
GOE: 06.04.10 STRENGTH: L GED: R3 M1 L1 SVP: 4 DLU: 77

513.682-010 ROTARY-KILN OPERATOR (smelt. & refin.)
Operates rotary kiln in which cinnabar (mercuric sulfide ore) is volatilized to obtain free mercury: Ignites oil burner and turns fuel and air flow valves to heat kiln to specified temperature. Sets controls to regulate conveyor speed and rotation of kiln. Observes gauges and flow of ore into kiln and turns controls to maintain temperature and amount of ore in kiln. Lubricates and repairs kiln and equipment.
GOE: 06.04.10 STRENGTH: M GED: R3 M2 L2 SVP: 4 DLU: 77

513.685-010 SINTER FEEDER (steel & rel.)
Tends table-feeding equipment that regulates flow of finely ground iron ore, coke, and flue dust from storage bins onto sintering machine conveyors: Starts table feeder and conveyor and adjusts rheostats to regulate speed of vibrating feeders. Moves controls to regulate opening of feed gate according to rate of flow of material onto conveyor. Observes equipment to detect malfunctions. Clears clogged chutes or feed gates, using bar and shovel. Fills sample box with material on conveyor, weighs sample, and records weight. Reads weightometer scale and records weights of material being processed.
GOE: 06.04.10 STRENGTH: M GED: R3 M2 L2 SVP: 4 DLU: 77

514 POURING AND CASTING OCCUPATIONS

This group includes occupations concerned with pouring, injecting, centrifuging, or pressing molten or powdered metal into a mold or other receptacle, and permitting or causing it to solidify.

514.130-010 PERMANENT-MOLD SUPERVISOR (foundry; nonfer. metal)

Supervises and coordinates activities of workers engaged in producing nonferrous metal castings by permanent-mold process: Verifies setup of permanent-mold casting machines. Consults with LAY-OUT INSPECTOR (machine shop) 600.281-014 to check layout of castings and to determine cause of casting defects, such as core shift, mold shift, or pouring termperature. Initiates changes in mold and core alignment, pouring temperature, or timing cycle of casting machine to correct defects. Trains new workers in departmental or job procedures. May perform minor maintenance on permanent-mold casting machines. Performs other duties as described under SUPERVISOR (any industry) Master Title.
GOE: 06.01.01 STRENGTH: M GED: R4 M3 L3 SVP: 7 DLU: 77

514.130-014 SUPERVISOR, DIE CASTING (foundry; smelt. & refin.)

Supervises and coordinates activities of workers engaged in setting up and operating diecasting machines, applying knowledge of diecasting process and properties of molten metal: Reads work orders to determine type of diecasting machines to be used. Initiates changes in timing of casting cycle, lubrication of dies, cooking of dies, or spacing between dies to correct defects in castings. Trains new workers in job duties. May supervise operation of melting furnaces and trim presses. May adjust thermostats to control temperatures of molten metal. May set up diecasting machines for workers. May be required to have experience with specific materials or type of machine. Performs duties as described under SUPERVISOR (any industry) Master Title.
GOE: 06.01.01 STRENGTH: L GED: R4 M3 L3 SVP: 7 DLU: 77

514.131-010 INSPECTOR, CHIEF (foundry)

Supervises and coordinates activities of workers engaged in inspecting and measuring metal castings: Lays out reference points on sample castings and verifies dimensions against blueprints [LAY-OUT INSPECTOR (machine shop) 600.281-014]. Inspects rejected castings for defects, such as blowholes, cracks, and rough spots, to determine repairs required to salvage castings. May weigh and count castings, and record inspection data on standard form. Performs other duties as described under SUPERVISOR (any industry) Master Title.
GOE: 06.02.01 STRENGTH: M GED: R4 M3 L3 SVP: 7 DLU: 77

514.134-010 TAPPER SUPERVISOR (smelt. & refin.)

Supervises and coordinates activities of workers engaged in tapping molten aluminum from reduction pots: Inserts metal rod into pots and inspects coating deposited on rod to determine amount of metal to tap. Moves hand controls to raise and lower anode and to control voltage drop in pot during tapping. Records pot number on outside of crucible, using chalk. Performs other duties as described under SUPERVISOR (any industry) Master Title.
GOE: 06.04.01 STRENGTH: L GED: R4 M3 L3 SVP: 7 DLU: 77

514.137-010 SUPERVISOR, PIG-MACHINE (steel & rel.)

Supervises and coordinates activities of workers engaged in casting molten iron into pigs, and in cleaning blast furnace area, pig machine, and slag pits. Coordinates movement of materials into and out of department. Performs duties as described under SUPERVISOR (any industry) Master Title.
GOE: 06.02.01 STRENGTH: M GED: R4 M2 L3 SVP: 6 DLU: 77

514.137-014 SUPERVISOR, PIT-AND-AUXILIARIES (steel & rel.)

Supervises and coordinates activities of workers engaged in preparing equipment for tapping furnace, teeming (pouring) molten steel in molds, and stripping and weighing ingots. Performs duties as described under SUPERVISOR (any industry) Master Title.
GOE: 06.04.01 STRENGTH: L GED: R3 M2 L3 SVP: 6 DLU: 77

514.360-010 DIE-CASTING-MACHINE SETTER (foundry)

Sets up diecasting machines that cast parts, such as automobile trim, carburetor housings, and motor parts from nonferrous metals, such as zinc, aluminum, or magnesium: Lifts specified die sections into machine, using chain fall or hoist. Secures die sections in position and adjusts stroke of ram, using handtools. Connects water hoses to cooling system of die. Preheats die sections with torch or electric heater. Turns valves and sets dials to regulate flow of water circulating through die, timing cycle, and operating speed of machine, based on size and structure of part to be cast and type and temperature of metal being used. Starts machine to produce sample casting, and examines casting to verify setup. May clean diecasting machines, using high-pressure steam hose and detergent. May perform maintenance on machine or dies, such as replacing pipelines or hoses, lubricating machine, or replacing ejector pins in dies. May verify machine setups and adjust malfunctioning machines and be designated Die-Casting-Machine Maintainer (foundry). May dismantle dies for repair by DIE MAKER, STAMPING (machine shop).
GOE: 06.01.02 STRENGTH: M GED: R4 M3 L3 SVP: 7 DLU: 77

514.362-010 PIG-MACHINE OPERATOR (steel & rel.) alternate titles: mold-car operator

Operates pig machine to pour molten iron into molds to cast pig iron: Starts conveyor that positions mold under spout of pig-machine ladle. Moves controls to tilt ladle, allowing molten iron to flow into mold. Observes filling operation to detect sticking of molten iron to inside of molds, and signals LIME MIXER TENDER (steel & rel.) to spray additional lime on walls of molds. Performs maintenance, such as relining iron runners, repairing pig machine chains, and replacing broken molds, using handtools, bars, and jib crane.
GOE: 06.02.10 STRENGTH: H GED: R3 M2 L2 SVP: 5 DLU: 77

514.382-010 DIE-CASTING-MACHINE OPERATOR I (foundry)

Sets up and operates diecasting machine to cast parts, such as automobile trim, carburetor housings, and motor parts from nonferrous metals, such as zinc, aluminum, or magnesium: Lifts specified die sections into machine, using chain fall or hoist. Bolts die section in position and adjusts stroke of ram, using handtools. Connects water hose to cooling system of die. Preheats die sections with torch or electric heater. Turns valves and sets dial to regulate flow of water circulating through die and to control speed of machine, based on size and structure of part being cast and type and temperature of metal being used. Blows metal fragments from die surfaces, using airhose, and brushes lubricant into die cavity and onto plunger. Hand ladles molten metal into chamber of machine when operating cold-chamber machine. Pushes button to close and lock dies and activate plunger that forces molten metal into the die cavities. Removes casting after dies open automatically, using pliers or tongs. Inspects casting for defects. May inspect castings, using fixed gauges. May dip castings in water to cool them. May load metal ingots into melting furnace, and transfer molten metal to heated reservoir of diecasting machine, using hand ladle.
GOE: 06.02.10 STRENGTH: M GED: R3 M2 L2 SVP: 5 DLU: 77

514.562-010 CENTRIFUGAL-CASTING-MACHINE OPERATOR III (foundry)

Operates centrifugal casting machine to cast artillery barrels: Grinds rough spots from inside of mold with grinding wheel mounted on end of long rod. Fills pits on inside surface of mold with refractory material. Fits refractory stoppers into ends of mold. Mounts pouring box, which serves as funnel for pouring melt from furnace into mold, on special frame at breech end of mold and fits spout of box through hole in stopper. Starts machine rotating at specified speed. Directs OVERHEAD CRANE OPERATOR (any industry) 921.663-010 in positioning portable furnace containing melt for pouring, and pushes electric controls to tilt furnace and pour melt into pouring box. Forces casting from mold, using hydraulic ram. Observes instruments and records data, such as temperature of mold before and after pouring and time required to complete pour. May operate machine from control board and be designated Casting-Machine-Control-Board Operator (foundry).
GOE: 06.02.10 STRENGTH: M GED: R3 M2 L2 SVP: 6 DLU: 77

514.567-010 MOLD WORKER (steel & rel.)

Removes steel ingots from molds after casting, and prepares molds for additional castings: Signals OVERHEAD CRANE OPERATOR (any industry) 921.663-010 to lift mold, and knocks out ingot, using handtools and sledge. Marks casting code on ingot with paint or chalk. Examines mold and supporting plates for dirt, cracks, or breaks, and removes dirt and metal particles, using scraper, wire brush, and airhose. Mixes mold wash according to formula, and coats mold, using spray gun; or signals OVERHEAD CRANE OPERATOR (any industry) to dip mold in tar tank.
GOE: 06.04.32 STRENGTH: M GED: R2 M1 L1 SVP: 3 DLU: 77

514.582-010 VACUUM CASTER (foundry)

Operates vacuum casting machine to produce molten metal and pour castings of high density: Removes ceramic mold from preheat oven, using tongs, and places it on lift in lower air lock of machine. Closes and clamps air-lock door. Inserts premeasured metal charge into upper air lock. Starts pumps to create specified vacuum in air locks. Pulls levers that cause ram to push charge into melting pot in vacuum chamber. Turns on current and adjusts temperature controls of furnace. Determines when molten metal is ready to pour by observing color through glass-covered opening, or by measuring temperature of molten metal with pyrometer. Moves controls that cause lift to raise mold from lower air lock to vacuum chamber. Pulls lever that causes furnace to invert and pour molten metal into mold.
GOE: 06.02.10 STRENGTH: M GED: R2 M1 L2 SVP: 5 DLU: 77

514.584-010 INGOT HEADER (nonfer. metal; smelt. & refin.) alternate titles: billet header; casting header; header

Pours molten, nonferrous metals into solidifying ingots to compensate for shrinkage that occurs when ingots cool in their molds: Dumps specified amount of metal and flux into pot of gas- or oil-fired furnace. Reads temperature indicators and adjusts furnace flame to melt heading metal. Adds metal to molds to compensate for shrinkage, using ladle. Stencils identifying characters on top of solidified ingots, using special hammer tool. Opens mold and removes ingot, using tongs.
GOE: 06.04.10 STRENGTH: M GED: R3 M1 L1 SVP: 4 DLU: 77

514.662-010 CASTING OPERATOR (nonfer. metal)

Controls pouring station in which aluminum and aluminum alloys are cast into ingots: Regulates flow of molten metal from ladle or directly from melting furnace into trough feeding casting molds of casting unit. Regulates flow of metal from trough into molds by adjusting screw valves at bottom of trough. Controls cooling conditions of casting unit by maintaining constant level of metal in molds and regulating series of valves to spray water against molds to produce ingots of uniform crystalline structure. Signals OVERHEAD CRANE OPERATOR (any industry) 921.663-010 to remove ingots.
GOE: 06.02.10 STRENGTH: M GED: R3 M2 L2 SVP: 5 DLU: 77

514.664-010 CUPOLA TAPPER (foundry)

Draws molten metal from cupola into ladles for pouring into molds to make castings: Signals OVERHEAD CRANE OPERATOR (any industry) 921.663-010 or POURER, METAL (foundry) to place ladle under cupola spout. Withdraws bott (clay plug) from taphole, using long iron rod, and allows molten

metal to flow into ladle. Inserts new plug on end of rod when ladle is full. Molds clay plugs by hand and affixes them to rods.
GOE: 06.04.10 STRENGTH: M GED: R2 M2 L2 SVP: 2 DLU: 77

514.664-014 TAPPER (nonfer. metal; smelt. & refin.)
Taps refining furnaces or reduction pots by one of following methods to pour molten slag or nonferrous metal, such as copper or aluminum, into molds, crucibles, or ladles: (1) Punches clay plug from taphole, using steel rod, to allow molten metal to flow into molds. Molds clay plugs and inserts them into taphole to stop flow of metal, using rod, or builds clay-retaining wall over taphole. Chips or burns away solidified slag and metal from taphole, using chisel-edged bar, oxygen lance, or by short-circuiting current from *bus bar* to taphole with steel rod. (2) Signals OVERHEAD CRANE OPERATOR (any industry) 921.663-010 to place pouring crucible near pot. Breaks hole in crust of electrolytic bath, using crowbar. Clamps siphon lid on crucible, and inserts other end of siphon into hole. Attaches airhose to siphon, and turns valve to siphon molten metal into crucible. Lowers anode into bath, using pulley to maintain its position beneath bath surface.
GOE: 06.04.10 STRENGTH: H GED: R2 M1 L1 SVP: 2 DLU: 77

514.667-010 CASTING-WHEEL-OPERATOR HELPER (smelt. & refin.)
Removes castings from molds by performing any combination of following duties: Brushes and sprays empty molds with water and bone ash or clay to prevent castings from sticking to mold. Chips and removes surplus bone ash, using chipping hammer and vacuum hose. Turns valves to adjust water sprays to cool molds or to loosen and drop castings from inverted molds. Pries castings from molds, using bar. Attaches crane hooks to lugs and signals OVERHEAD CRANE OPERATOR (any industry) 921.663-010 to lift casting from mold. May mix water, bone ash, or clay to specified consistency for coating molds.
GOE: 06.04.32 STRENGTH: M GED: R2 M1 L1 SVP: 2 DLU: 77

514.667-014 PIG-MACHINE-OPERATOR HELPER (steel & rel.)
Assists PIG-MACHINE OPERATOR (steel & rel.) to cast pig iron: Observes pouring operations and signals PIG-MACHINE OPERATOR (steel & rel.) to stop flow of metal from ladle when molds overflow or mechanical malfunction occurs. Knocks pieces of iron and slag from ladle lips, pouring spout, or iron runners, using pole. Cleans slag and iron from pouring equipment and pig machine, using bars and sledges. Performs other duties as described under HELPER (any industry) Master Title.
GOE: 06.04.10 STRENGTH: H GED: R2 M1 L1 SVP: 3 DLU: 77

514.667-018 SPOUT WORKER (smelt. & refin.)
Directs pouring of slag from ladle through spout into reverberatory furnace used for smelting: Raises furnace door, using lever or air hoist. Guides OVERHEAD CRANE OPERATOR (any industry) 921.663-010 by signal horn and lights in positioning ladle over spout and pouring slag. Sprays water on inner walls of spout to remove encrusted slag, or pries slag loose with iron bar. Shovels slag into car or furnace. Patches cracks in spout with moist clay, smoothing surface with hand or shovel. Scatters slurry of silica and clay evenly over inner surface of spout to decrease slag-crust during pouring operation. May guide DINKEY OPERATOR (any industry) into position over furnace, using hand signals. May record amount of slag dumped into furnace on analysis sheet.
GOE: 06.04.10 STRENGTH: M GED: R2 M1 L1 SVP: 2 DLU: 77

514.682-010 CASTING-WHEEL OPERATOR (smelt. & refin.) alternate titles: pourer
Operates rotating casting wheel to pour molten nonferrous metal, such as copper, lead, or aluminum into molds to form ingots: Moves control lever to rotate wheel and position mold under pouring spout of kettle or furnace. Pulls lever to remove stopper from bottom of kettle or to tilt ladle to allow metal to flow into mold. Rotates wheel to spot successive molds under spout. Observes process to ensure that castings are dumped and that molds are returned to starting position. May spray empty molds with coating to prevent metal from sticking to mold [CASTING-WHEEL-OPERATOR HELPER (smelt. & refin.)]. May skim slag or dross from metal in furnace with rake or hoe [FURNACE HELPER (nonfer. metal; smelt. & refin.)]. May divert stream of metal into bucket, using hose, to obtain samples for laboratory. May operate pump to force lead from kettle into mold. May skim impurities, using spatula or spoon, and solidify molten lead by regulating flow of water in water-cooled mold. May observe furnace gauge to verify that temperature of molten metal meets specifications. May change pouring spout, using chain hoist and handtools. May operate casting-wheel machine that advances molds automatically at predetermined rate.
GOE: 06.02.10 STRENGTH: L GED: R3 M2 L2 SVP: 4 DLU: 77

514.682-014 PRESS OPERATOR, CARBON BLOCKS (smelt. & refin.)
Operates press that forms carbon paste into anodes used in metal-reduction pots: Pushes panel buttons to activate hopper, chain conveyor, cooling chamber belt, and power rolls. Turns valve to regulate flow of water to carbon cooling chamber. Observes signal light on hopper which indicates hopper is filled and paste is discharged into mold. Starts mechanical vibrator to pack mix in mold. Moves levers to synchronize rotation of index table with dropping of ram to press mix into blocks. Adjusts ram stroke to press carbon block to specified size, using wrench. Stops press when warning light indicates malfunction or when mold is overheated. Removes rejects from conveyor, using pneumatic ram.
GOE: 06.02.18 STRENGTH: L GED: R3 M1 L1 SVP: 4 DLU: 77

514.684-010 CASTER (smelt. & refin.) alternate titles: metal pourer
Casts nonferrous metal into pigs and transports them to storage, using handtools and forklift: Secures hook to eye on bottom of crucible and signals OVERHEAD CRANE OPERATOR (any industry) 921.663-010 to position crucible and pour metal into stationary molds. Turns handwheel and moves levers to regulate flow of metal from furnace into conveyor molds. Skims slag from surface of pigs into dross buggy, using dross hoe, metal rake, or carbon stick. Installs and changes stencils in automatic stenciler, or stamps identifying information on pigs with hammer and die. Removes pigs from mold, using crowbar, or sets pins and hooks chain for crane to lift pigs from molds. Shovels scrap metal into buggy for return to furnace. Moves pigs to storage area, using forklift. Inserts fire clay on end of rod into taphole to seal furnace.
GOE: 06.04.24 STRENGTH: M GED: R2 M1 L1 SVP: 4 DLU: 77

514.684-014 LADLE POURER (smelt. & refin.)
Casts refined lead into molds moving along conveyor belt: Connects pipelines from kettle to ladle, and preheats pipes, valves, and ladle with gas burner to prevent hardening of metal. Controls flow of metal into ladle, and pours lead into molds by tilting ladle. Skims oxide from surface of metal in molds.
GOE: 06.04.32 STRENGTH: M GED: R2 M1 L1 SVP: 4 DLU: 77

514.684-018 NOZZLE-AND-SLEEVE WORKER (nonfer. metal)
Removes, replaces, and adjusts nozzles and cylinders (sleeves) of diecasting machines: Disconnects and removes gooseneck (spout) from gooseneck machine, using wrenches, chain falls, and hoist. Knocks nozzle loose with bar and hammer. Drives replacement nozzle into gooseneck. Reinstalls gooseneck in metal pot, aligning nozzle with gate according to scale measurements. Removes plunger from sleeve of cold-shot machine, using wrenches, and pushes defective sleeve from machine. Installs new sleeve by inserting holding pin, making screw adjustments, and taking scale measurements. Periodically inspects nozzle and sleeve adjustments along machine line. Assists other workers in adjusting, installing, and removing diecasting machine nozzles and cylinders. Keeps records of sleeve and nozzle adjustments and replacements. May replace movable gooseneck setup with new parts.
GOE: 06.04.24 STRENGTH: M GED: R2 M1 L1 SVP: 3 DLU: 77

514.684-022 POURER, METAL (foundry) alternate titles: ladle handler
Pours molten metal from ladle into molds to produce metal castings: Tilts ladle or opens pouring spout by turning handwheel or moving levers to pour metal into sand molds. Skims slag off molten metal, using strainer device, or tilts ladle to dump out slag. May move ladle from cupola or furnace to work station, manually or using overhead monorail or chain fall. May be designated according to type of ladle used as Pourer, Buggy Ladle (foundry); Pourer, Bull Ladle (foundry); Pourer, Crane Ladle (foundry); Pourer, Crucible (foundry).
GOE: 06.04.10 STRENGTH: H GED: R2 M1 L1 SVP: 2 DLU: 77

514.685-010 CENTRIFUGAL-CASTING-MACHINE OPERATOR I (foundry)
Tends centrifugal casting machine that casts tubular metal products, such as pipes, brakedrums, or bushings: Lays specified mold on spinning mechanism. Brushes dirt and metal fragments from inside of mold. Places and fastens cover on ends of mold. Preheats mold with torch. Starts machine and sprays insulation on inside surface of rotating mold. Pours molten metal into mold, using hand ladle. Allows mold to spin for specified time to solidify metal against mold walls. Unfastens mold cover and removes casting, using tongs or hydraulic ram. May set machine controls to rotate mold at specified speed.
GOE: 06.04.10 STRENGTH: H GED: R3 M1 L1 SVP: 3 DLU: 77

514.685-014 CENTRIFUGAL-CASTING-MACHINE OPERATOR II (foundry)
Tends one station on indexing-type centrifugal casting machine, performing any combination of following tasks involved in casting metal: Removes dirt and metal fragments from mold, using brush, water, or airhose. Fastens cover on end of mold. Starts mold rotating, and sprays insulation on inside surface of mold. Pours specified amount of metal into mold, using hand or crane ladle. Moves levers on tilting furnace to control flow of metal into pouring ladle. Removes cover on end of mold, and pulls casting from mold, using tongs. May be designated according to task performed as Dumper, Mold Cleaner (foundry); Puller (foundry); Sprayer (foundry).
GOE: 06.04.10 STRENGTH: M GED: R2 M1 L1 SVP: 3 DLU: 77

514.685-018 DIE-CASTING-MACHINE OPERATOR II (foundry)
Tends diecasting machine that casts parts, such as automobile trim, carburetor housings, and motor parts from nonferrous metals, such as zinc, aluminum, or magnesium: Turns valves to regulate flow of water circulating through dies. Blows metal fragments from die surfaces, using airhose, and brushes lubricant over die cavity and plunger. Ladles molten metal into chamber by hand when using cold chamber machine. Pushes button to close and lock dies and activate plunger that forces molten metal into die cavities. Removes casting after dies open automatically, using tongs or pliers. Inspects casting for defects, such as cracks or bubbles. May measure casting, using fixed gauges. May dip castings in water to cool. May regulate speed of machine.
GOE: 06.04.10 STRENGTH: M GED: R2 M1 L1 SVP: 2 DLU: 77

514.685-022 LIME MIXER TENDER (steel & rel.)
Tends mixing machine that mixes lime and water, and sprays mixture on interior of molds to prevent cast iron from sticking to molds: Shovels lime into mixing machine, starts machine, and opens valve to allow water to enter ma-

chine to obtain mixture of specified consistency. Cleans molds, using airhose. Starts pump of spray gun, and sprays molds. Observes coating on molds, and adjusts spray gun and consistency of mixture to obtain specified coating. Sprays water on molds containing molten iron to cool metal, using hose. Removes stuck pigs from molds, using bar.
GOE: 06.04.10 STRENGTH: M GED: R2 M1 L1 SVP: 3 DLU: 77

514.685-026 TUBE-CLEANING OPERATOR (foundry)
Tends machine that extracts core pipe from interior of tubular castings: Strikes end of core pipe with sledge to loosen baked sand between casting and core pipe. Inserts end of core pipe through holding block and secures pipe between jaws set on dolly. Starts machine that pushes and pulls dolly along tracks, pulling out core pipe while casting strikes against holding block. Cleans casting, using airhose and wire brush.
GOE: 06.04.02 STRENGTH: M GED: R2 M1 L1 SVP: 2 DLU: 77

514.687-010 CASTING INSPECTOR (foundry) alternate titles: casting tester; final inspector; soft-iron inspector
Inspects metal castings for dimensional accuracy and surface defects: Measures dimensions of casting, using fixed gauges. Examines casting for defects, such as cracks and blowholes. Separates and marks defective castings according to salvage operation required. May chip surplus metal from casting, using hammer and chisel. May tap casting with hammer to determine from sound if casting has been heattreated or to detect defects, such as cracks or thin walls.
GOE: 06.03.02 STRENGTH: L GED: R2 M2 L2 SVP: 3 DLU: 77

514.687-014 CASTING-HOUSE WORKER (nonfer. metal)
Assists aluminum foundry workers by performing variety of manual tasks: Skims dross from furnaces. Loads handtrucks with ingots or sorted scrap. May sort and weigh metal, charge furnaces, and transport metal. May mark heat number on billets. May operate tier-lift truck to transport materials.
GOE: 06.04.24 STRENGTH: H GED: R2 M1 L1 SVP: 2 DLU: 77

514.687-018 CASTING-OPERATOR HELPER (nonfer. metal)
Assists CASTING OPERATOR (nonfer. metal) in casting aluminum alloys into ingots: Places distributing trough between furnace taphole and mold. Positions baffle plates, screens, and control pins in trough, using handtools. Takes sample of molten metal for subsequent analysis. Skims dross off molten aluminum in holding furnace, using drag rake. Inserts thermocouple into mold and records temperature of ingot. Examines ingot for cracks, using reflectoscope. Stencils identification numbers on ingots. Hooks cable to ingot for removal by OVERHEAD CRANE OPERATOR (any industry) 921.663-010. Performs other duties as described under HELPER (any industry) Master Title.
GOE: 06.04.10 STRENGTH: M GED: R2 M1 L2 SVP: 3 DLU: 77

515 CRUSHING AND GRINDING OCCUPATIONS

This group includes occupations concerned with reducing ore or concentrate to granules, grits, powder, paste, or pulp, or otherwise changing it from larger to smaller particles by such means as compression, smashing, cutting, grinding, or any combination of these methods.

515.130-010 MILL SUPERVISOR (smelt. & refin.) alternate titles: supervisor, grinding; supervisor, ore dressing
Supervises and coordinates activities of workers engaged in crushing, grinding, and concentrating ore preparatory to further processing or shipment: Observes meters, gauges, recording instruments, and operation of machines and equipment to detect malfunctions, faulty operation by worker, or need for repairs. Orders adjustments and repairs to restore machines and equipment to production specifications. Directs dismantling, and inspects parts to determine cause of malfunction or breakdown. Demonstrates and explains machine operation and processes to new workers. May determine time, duration, and sequence of utilizing ore from silos, and rates of extraction to attain blend of ore specified on work order. Performs duties as described under SUPERVISOR (any industry) Master Title.
GOE: 06.02.01 STRENGTH: L GED: R4 M3 L3 SVP: 7 DLU: 77

515.132-010 CRUSHER SUPERVISOR (smelt. & refin.)
Supervises and coordinates activities of workers engaged in transporting, crushing, and storing ore, skimmings, and other residue. Trains workers in operation of equipment. Performs duties as described under SUPERVISOR (any industry) Master Title.
GOE: 06.02.01 STRENGTH: L GED: R4 M3 L3 SVP: 7 DLU: 77

515.382-010 GRINDING-MILL OPERATOR (mine & quarry; smelt. & refin.)
Operates panelboard to control machinery and equipment, such as conveyor belts, vibrating feeders, rod and ball mills, centrifugal separators, distributors, magnetic separators, and pumps, to grind ore and scrap metal and to separate iron particles from gangue: Sets and adjusts automatic controls on panel to regulate feed flow of conveyors, flow of lubricant to rod and ball mill bearings, and flow of water to mills and separators. Starts grinding and separating machinery and equipment. Observes lights, dials, and gauges, and turns levers or pushes buttons on panel to adjust operating conditions, such as temperature of mill bearings, amount of electric current flowing through mill drive motors, and rate of ore and scrap metal flowing from feeder conveyors. Records number of machinery breakdowns and repairs, number of rods and balls charged into mills, and amount of ore and scrap metal processed. May pass hand magnet

over sludge to determine extent of separation of iron particles from gangue by magnetic separators.
GOE: 06.04.08 STRENGTH: L GED: R3 M2 L2 SVP: 6 DLU: 77

515.567-010 WEIGHER-AND-CRUSHER (smelt. & refin.)
Weighs and crushes zinc ore and other materials, using platform scale, crusher, and handtools: Signals OVERHEAD CRANE OPERATOR (any industry) 921.663-010 to lower loaded bucket of zinc ore onto platform scale. Balances scale beam. Records weight of materials and signals OVERHEAD CRANE OPERATOR (any industry) to dump them into crusher. Starts vibrating screens that crush ore and separate it according to size. Shovels unscreened ore back into crusher. Scoops samples of ore from conveyor belt for laboratory analysis. Opens bin gate to fill bucket with sintered ore. Levels ore in bucket, using bar and shovel. Signals OVERHEAD CRANE OPERATOR (any industry) to remove filled bucket and to replace it with empty one. Moves empty or filled buckets on cars about yard and plant, using power-driven winch.
GOE: 06.04.08 STRENGTH: M GED: R3 M1 L1 SVP: 4 DLU: 77

515.585-010 SCALE-RECLAMATION TENDER (smelt. & refin.)
Tends conveying and grinding equipment that reclaims aluminum-hydrate scale: Moves controls to regulate conveyor flow of hydrate scale to hammer mill and rodmill. Turns valves to add plant liquor to rodmill to maintain specified slurry density. Clears hoppers, pan feeders, and conveying equipment of accumulated materials, using bar, hammer, or shovel. Cleans conveyors, idlers, and pulleys, using scrapers and cleaning tools. Turns valves and starts pumps to switch product flow through auxiliary units. Catches product samples. Keeps operating log. Lubricates valves and adjusts packing glands to prevent leaks:
GOE: 06.04.10 STRENGTH: M GED: R3 M1 L1 SVP: 4 DLU: 77

515.685-010 BATCH MAKER (nonfer. metal; steel & rel.)
Tends equipment that mills and recovers powdered metal used in powder metallurgy: Pours specified amount of powder into ball mill. Screws covers on drum and straps drum to ball mill machine rack. Starts motor that rotates drum to grind powder by tumbling action of metal balls. Inserts filter bag and sieve in centrifuge drum. Opens water valve to flush milled powder from mill through sieve and filter bag into centrifuge. Starts centrifuge that separates water from powder. Pours extracted powder into trays for drying. Charges ball mill with additional balls as specified.
GOE: 06.04.10 STRENGTH: L GED: R2 M1 L1 SVP: 2 DLU: 77

515.685-014 CRUSHER TENDER (smelt. & refin.) alternate titles: ore crusher
Tends machine that breaks ore, skimmings, furnace residue, clay pieces, potroom butts, or green carbon scrap into smaller sizes for further processing: Starts crusher. Regulates flow of materials into crusher from conveyors, chutes, or bins. Prods large lumps with bar to force them through crusher. Breaks oversize lumps with sledgehammer. Maintains uniform flow of crushed materials to screens or roll crushers for further sizing by controlling movement of conveyor belt or feeder. Cleans, lubricates, and makes minor repairs to crusher. May remove scrap wood or iron by hand or with an electromagnet. May operate vibrating screens to separate materials within size ranges. May select samples of materials, using shovel or mechanical sampler. May tend control panel to monitor crushing machines that clean anode assemblies and be designated Anode-Assembly Cleaner (smelt. & refin.) I.
GOE: 06.04.08 STRENGTH: M GED: R3 M1 L1 SVP: 3 DLU: 77

515.685-018 STAMPING-MILL TENDER (smelt. & refin.)
Tends stamping mills that crush ore to specified fineness: Turns valve to regulate flow of ore and water over plates beneath stamps. Examines crushed ore at outflow of mill to determine degree of fineness. Adjusts raising and dropping sequence of stamps. Replaces broken stamps, plates, and shafts.
GOE: 06.04.02 STRENGTH: L GED: R2 M1 L1 SVP: 3 DLU: 77

515.686-010 BATTERY-WRECKER OPERATOR (nonfer. metal)
Loads conveyor of battery-crushing machine: Lifts batteries from stockpile. Loads conveyor of machine that crushes batteries and separates plastic, metal, and lead-bearing acid. Listens for machine jams and other malfunctions. Dislodges jams, using metal bar or air compressor. Notifies designated worker of major malfunctions. May operate industrial truck to move pallets of batteries from storage area to work area.
GOE: 06.04.40 STRENGTH: V GED: R2 M1 L1 SVP: 2 DLU: 86

515.687-010 HAMMER-MILL OPERATOR (smelt. & refin.) alternate titles: shredder operator
Prepares iron and steel machine-tool cuttings for use in making ferrosilicon by selecting scraps of desired thickness and breaking them up in hammer mill.
GOE: 06.04.24 STRENGTH: M GED: R2 M1 L1 SVP: 3 DLU: 77

518 MOLDERS, COREMAKERS, AND RELATED OCCUPATIONS

This group includes occupations concerned with making molds or cores to be used in casting metal in foundries.

518.361-010 MOLDER (aircraft mfg.; concrete prod.; foundry) alternate titles: sand molder
Forms sand molds to fabricate metal castings, using patterns or match plates, flasks, handtools and power tools, following instructions and applying knowl-

edge of variables, such as metal characteristics, molding sand, pattern contours, and pouring procedures: Places flask and drag onto *molding board* and positions pattern inside drag. Sprinkles or sprays parting agent onto pattern and flask, to facilitate removal of pattern from mold, and positions reinforcing wire in flask. Sifts sand over pattern, using riddle, and compacts sand around pattern contours. Shovels and packs sand into flask, using hand or pneumatic ramming tools. Inverts drag, positions cope half of pattern and flask onto drag, and repeats sand molding operation to imbed pattern into cope. Lifts cope from drag and removes pattern. Cuts runner and sprue hole into mold and repairs damaged impressions, using handtools, such as slick, trowel, spoon, and sprue cutter. Positions specified cores into drag and reassembles cope and drag. Moves and positions workpieces, such as flasks, patterns, and bottom boards, using overhead crane, or signals OVERHEAD CRANE OPERATOR (any industry) 921.663-010 to move and position workpieces. Pours molten metal into mold, manually or using crane ladle, or directs POURER, METAL (foundry) 514.684-022 to fill mold. May form and assemble slab cores around pattern to reinforce mold, using handtools and glue. May operate ovens or furnaces to melt, skim, and flux metal. May form molds at bench and be designated Molder, Bench (concrete prod.; foundry) or form molds on floor and be designated Molder, Floor (foundry).
GOE: 06.01.04 STRENGTH: M GED: R4 M3 L3 SVP: 6 DLU: 87

518.361-014 MOLDER APPRENTICE (aircraft mfg.; concrete prod.; foundry) alternate titles: sand-molder apprentice
Performs duties as described under APPRENTICE (any industry) Master Title.
GOE: 06.01.04 STRENGTH: M GED: R4 M3 L3 SVP: 6 DLU: 77

518.361-018 MOLDER, SWEEP (foundry) alternate titles: floor molder, sweep method
Makes molds, using sweep method which is adaptable only in cases where required casting is symmetrical: Assembles drag, flask, bottom plate, and spindle (projects through center of flask). Shovel sand into flask, and compacts it by hand ramming. Attaches sweep (board with bottom edge cut to shape corresponding to casting surface) and rotates it about spindle, until mold impression (usually convex) is swept (scraped) to desired shape. Places cope flask on drag, and shovels and compacts sand over drag mold which serves as pattern for cope mold. Removes cope mold. Scrapes drag mold with smaller sweep to reduce size of mold. Smooths and shapes mold surface, using slick and trowel. Assembles mold sections for pouring. When making parts of large floor or pit mold, usually rectangular in shape, with sides parallel and same impressions running full length of part of mold, draws sweep back and forth along guides to scrape out desired impressions.
GOE: 06.01.04 STRENGTH: M GED: R4 M3 L3 SVP: 7 DLU: 77

518.380-010 SETTER, MOLDING-AND-COREMAKING MACHINES (foundry) alternate titles: pattern setter
Sets up and adjusts molding and coremaking machines, such as roll-over, squeeze, coremaking, and shell molding: Obtains specified pattern, moves pattern to work station manually or using hoist, and bolts it to bed of mold or core forming machine, using wrenches. Adjusts stops, height of squeeze or rollover mechanism, and height of sand hopper according to size of pattern or core, using handtools. Adjusts timing cycle of machines to specified settings. Replaces worn parts, such as air lines, gaslines, gaskets, and core box vents, using handtools.
GOE: 06.01.02 STRENGTH: M GED: R3 M2 L2 SVP: 4 DLU: 77

518.381-010 BENCH-MOLDER APPRENTICE (jewelry-silver.) alternate titles: sand-caster apprentice
Performs duties as described under APPRENTICE (any industry) Master Title.
GOE: 06.01.04 STRENGTH: L GED: R4 M3 L3 SVP: 7 DLU: 77

518.381-014 COREMAKER (foundry) alternate titles: coremaker, experimental
Makes sand cores used in molds to form holes or hollows in metal castings: Cleans core box with blast of compressed air. Dusts parting sand over inside of core box to facilitate removal of finished core. Partially fills core box with sand by pulling cord that releases sand from overhead chute or by using hands or shovel. Compacts sand in core box, using hands, hand rammer, and air rammer. Bends reinforcing wires by hand, and inserts them in sand. Fills core box and rams sand in tightly. Inverts core box onto metal plate, and lifts box from sand core. Patches cracked or chipped places on core and smooths core surfaces, using spoon and trowel. May bake cores to harden them. May assemble cores. May work at bench making small cores and be designated Coremaker, Bench (foundry); or make large cores on floor of foundry and be designated Coremaker, Floor (foundry).
GOE: 06.01.04 STRENGTH: M GED: R3 M2 L2 SVP: 5 DLU: 77

518.381-018 COREMAKER APPRENTICE (foundry)
Performs duties as described under APPRENTICE (any industry) Master Title.
GOE: 06.01.04 STRENGTH: M GED: R3 M2 L2 SVP: 5 DLU: 77

518.381-022 MOLDER, BENCH (jewelry-silver.) alternate titles: sand caster
Casts metal molds to form jewelry articles: Forms plaster mold of model. Builds sand mold in flask, using plaster mold as pattern. Places flask in furnace

or heats flask with blowtorch to dry and harden sand mold. Removes plaster mold from flask. Melts metal in crucible or furnace, and pours molten metal into channel of sand mold to cast metal mold. Opens flask and removes metal mold when metal has hardened, using pliers or tongs.
GOE: 06.01.04 STRENGTH: L GED: R4 M3 L3 SVP: 7 DLU: 77

518.484-010 PLASTER MOLDER II (foundry)
Forms plaster molds, used to make metal castings, using molder's handtools, patterns, and flasks: Mixes plaster powder and water according to specified formula. Places cope and drag on molding table. Places drag half of pattern in drag. Pours liquid plaster into drag, removes excess plaster, using straightedge, and allows mold to harden. Assembles cope half of pattern to drag half of pattern in mold. Places cope on drag and makes depressions in plaster around drag pattern to ensure accurate joining of mold halves for casting. Brushes parting agent on surfaces of mold, pattern, and flask, and pours liquid plaster into cope. Separates cope and drag after specified time and removes pattern. Repairs cracks and broken edges of mold, using molder's handtools, such as spoon, trowel, and slick. May cut gates and risers in mold after mold is baked. May position cores in drag and assemble mold. May pour molten metal into molds, using hand ladle. Makes plaster cores by pouring plaster in core box and clamping box shut. May cast plaster molds from rubber molds, spraying parting agent on mold face and pouring plaster into drag and cope.
GOE: 06.02.30 STRENGTH: M GED: R3 M1 L2 SVP: 4 DLU: 77

518.664-010 MOLD MAKER (smelt. & refin.)
Forms molds used in casting copper: Assembles metal casting frame on flat car, using wrench. Seals frame with fire clay, using trowel, and sprays interior of frame and core with bone ash to prevent adherence of molten metal to core. Pushes car under pouring spout of ladle. Moves lever to tilt ladle of molten copper and fill frame to indicated level. Pulls lever to lower core, attached to hydraulic press ram, to imbed core in molten copper. Turns valve to circulate water through core to solidify copper. Withdraws core when mold cools, dismantles frame, and removes mold.
GOE: 06.04.32 STRENGTH: M GED: R2 M1 L2 SVP: 4 DLU: 77

518.682-010 MACHINE MOLDER (foundry) alternate titles: machine line molder
Operates molding machine to form sand molds used in production of metal castings: Assembles flask, pattern, and *follow board* on molding table of machine. Sifts sand over pattern, using riddle, and feels flask with sand by opening hopper or using shovel. Packs sand around pattern contours, using ramming tool or pneumatic hammer. Starts machine that compacts sand in flask to form mold. Cuts pouring spout and vents in mold, using sprue cutter and wire. Lifts cope half of flask off drag half and removes pattern. Cleans cavity of mold, using airhose. Positions cores in drag, and assembles cope and drag. May set cores in mold cavity. May install pattern on bed of machine, and adjust pressure of ram. May be designated by machine operated as Machine Molder, Roll-Over (foundry); Machine Molder, Squeeze (foundry); or product molded as Molder, Fitting (foundry).
GOE: 06.04.32 STRENGTH: M GED: R3 M2 L2 SVP: 4 DLU: 77

518.683-010 SAND-SLINGER OPERATOR (foundry)
Controls sand-slinging machine to pack sand in mold flask: Engages controls to move machine along tracks and to position impeller head over flask. Starts machine, and moves controls to guide impeller head back and forth to direct flow of sand into flask. Cleans and oils machine. May replace worn parts in impeller head, using handtools.
GOE: 06.04.08 STRENGTH: L GED: R2 M1 L1 SVP: 3 DLU: 77

518.684-010 CORE SETTER (foundry)
Positions cores in drag of sand mold. Examines mold and cores for defects, such as cracks and broken surfaces, before mold is closed. Verifies spacing between mold and cores, using gauges. May assist in closing mold. May operate hoist to move and position large cores. May assemble groups of cores in fixture of automatic core-setting machine.
GOE: 06.04.32 STRENGTH: M GED: R2 M1 L1 SVP: 2 DLU: 77

518.684-014 COREMAKER, PIPE (foundry)
Makes clay cores around which ferrous and nonferrous pipe is cast: Clamps rod in bench vises so that it can be rotated. Wraps rod with paper, straw, or jute, tying it firmly in place with twine. Mixes mud, sand, and loam to form clay. Spreads clay over wrapping, adding molasses to make mixture cohesive and working coating by hand so that it is smooth and even. Spreads core blacking over core and places it in drying oven for specified time. Removes dried core and applies second coating to bring core to specified diameter. Spreads blacking on core and returns it to oven for final drying.
GOE: 06.04.32 STRENGTH: M GED: R2 M1 L1 SVP: 3 DLU: 77

518.684-018 MOLD CLOSER (foundry) alternate titles: core mounter; core setter; finish molder; flask fitter; mold finisher
Cleans and assembles foundry molds to prepare them for pouring: Cleans inside surface of sand molds with airhose. Positions cores in drags. Thrusts rod into ventholes to remove obstructions. Fits and clamps cope and drag together to form flask. Places runner cup over pouring hole. May patch and smooth damaged portions of mold, using spoon or trowel. May assist in pouring metal into molds. May remove castings from molds.
GOE: 06.04.32 STRENGTH: H GED: R2 M1 L1 SVP: 3 DLU: 77

518.684-022 WAX-PATTERN ASSEMBLER (foundry)
Assembles wax components of patterns used in lost-wax casting process: Melts edges of wax components, using heated knife, and manually positions

and joins components. Repairs surface defects of patterns, such as holes and indentions, and smooths and seals joints, using wax and heated knife.
GOE: 06.02.24 STRENGTH: M GED: R2 M1 L1 SVP: 2 DLU: 77

518.684-026 WAX-PATTERN REPAIRER (foundry) alternate titles: in-spector
Repairs wax patterns used in lost-wax casting process: Inspects patterns for defects, such as cracks, seams, broken edges, and excess wax. Seals cracks, seams, and joints, removes excess wax, and builds up damaged edges, using wax and heated knife.
GOE: 06.02.24 STRENGTH: L GED: R2 M1 L1 SVP: 2 DLU: 77

518.685-010 CORE-OVEN TENDER (foundry)
Tends baking oven that hardens and strengthens green sand cores used in casting metal: Loads cores on racks, trays, or carts, and pushes them into oven. Lights gas- or oil-fired furnace and turns valves to obtain specified temperature; or sets thermostat and closes switch to heat element in electric furnace. Closes oven door and allows cores to bake for specified time. Opens oven door and removes cores. May adjust baffle plates that direct flow of heat in oven.
GOE: 06.04.17 STRENGTH: M GED: R2 M1 L2 SVP: 2 DLU: 77

518.685-014 COREMAKER, MACHINE I (foundry) alternate titles: core stripper
Tends turnover draw-type coremaking machine that makes sand cores for use in casting metal: Clamps core box over die on front table of machine, and part-ly fills core box with sand from overhead chute, or by using hands or shovel. Depresses pedal to open compressed-air valve that causes table to rise and fall with series of jolts, to compress sand in box. Positions reinforcing wires in sand, fills box with sand, and repeats jolting. Tamps sand into core box with hand or pneumatic tool. Removes excess sand from top of core box with hands or straightedge and clamps metal plate to top of box. Pulls lever to roll front table over and deposit box top down on rear table. Pushes rear table down to withdraw core from core box and lifts core from machine.
GOE: 06.04.08 STRENGTH: M GED: R2 M1 L2 SVP: 3 DLU: 77

518.685-018 COREMAKER, MACHINE II (foundry) alternate titles: tube coremaker
Tends conveyor-screw coremaking machine that extrudes sand cores having uniform cross section: Installs specified core tube and conveyor screw in ma-chine, using handtools. Shovels sand into hopper, and tamps it down by hand. Positions core plate at opening of core tube, and starts motor-driven or hand-operated conveyor screw which forces sand through core tube and onto core plate. Cuts core at core tube opening when core fills plate. May tend oven to bake cores. Cuts baked cores to specified lengths with saw.
GOE: 06.04.08 STRENGTH: M GED: R2 M1 L2 SVP: 2 DLU: 77

518.685-022 COREMAKER, MACHINE III (foundry) alternate titles: core-blower operator
Tends blower-type coremaking machine to produce sand cores: Removes sand and particles of dirt from pattern with compressed air or brush. Places core box over pattern on bed of machine. Pulls lever or depresses pedal to blow and compact sand in core box. Places plate or drier on top of core box and turns box over. Lifts core box from core and lifts core from machine. May po-sition reinforcing wires in core box before blowing in sand. May perform only one of above operations on revolving, multiple station, blower-type coremaking machine. May tend automatic blower-type coremaking machine and clean, glue, and rack cores as they are ejected from machine. May tend machine equipped with double core box and glue and clean cores from one box while machine forms and cures cores in other core box.
GOE: 06.04.08 STRENGTH: M GED: R2 M1 L2 SVP: 2 DLU: 77

518.685-026 SHELL MOLDER (foundry)
Tends machine that makes shell molds used to produce metal castings: Starts machine that automatically forms and cures shell. Strips cured shell halves from machine and positions shell half on fixture of mold-closing machine. Brushes glue around edges of each shell half. Positions remaining shell half on top of lower half and activates ram that exerts pressure on shell until glue has set. May glue and assemble shell halves by hand. May clamp, wire, or bolt shell halves to-gether. May bolt pattern and core box to bed of machine. May produce cores on shell making machine and be designated Shell Coremaker (foundry).
GOE: 06.04.17 STRENGTH: H GED: R2 M1 L2 SVP: 2 DLU: 77

518.685-030 SHELL-MOLD-BONDING-MACHINE OPERATOR (found-ry) alternate titles: bonder; bonding-machine operator; shell mold bonder
Tends machine that bonds cope and drag together to form completed shell mold: Turns dials of shell-mold bonding machine to heat upper pressure plate and set pressure stroke of ram as specified. Positions drag onto lower pressure plate of machine. Fills vibrator pan with bonding agent, and pushes button to sift bonding agent onto edge of drag. Positions cope on drag, and pushes button or pulls lever which pushes hot plate onto cope to heat and compress cope to drag. Knocks out sprue holes with iron rod. Directs airhose onto mold to blow out loose sand. May tend machine that automatically releases pressure after specified period of time. May assemble cores to drag and cope.
GOE: 06.04.08 STRENGTH: M GED: R2 M1 L1 SVP: 2 DLU: 77

518.687-010 CORE CHECKER (foundry) alternate titles: core inspector
Verifies dimensions and shapes of cores for conformance to specifications, using straightedge, gauges, and calipers: Places cores in fixtures, manually or

using hoist. Moves straightedge along surface of cores to verify contours. Veri-fies dimensions, using gauges and calipers. Records tally of inspections on standard forms. May file high spots from cores. May repair defects, such as cracks and broken edges. May clean flask from cores, using wire scrapers or files. May inspect molds and be designated Mold Checker (foundry).
GOE: 06.03.02 STRENGTH: L GED: R2 M2 L2 SVP: 3 DLU: 77

518.687-014 FOUNDRY LABORER, COREROOM (foundry) alternate ti-tles: core fitter; coremaker helper; core paster
Performs any combination of following tasks involved in coremaking: Pastes core sections together to form completed core. Brushes, dips, or sprays solution, such as graphite, on cores to produce smooth finish. Carries and loads cores into oven. Piles cores on racks for drying. Carries sand to coreroom. Forms core reinforcing rods and wires into specified shape by hand or by machine. Pulls wires and rods from finished castings, using pliers, hammer and chisel, and special hooks. Dresses cores, using handtools or power tools, such as files, scrapers, and grinding wheel. May fill cracks in surface of core with putty or patching sand, using putty knife.
GOE: 06.04.32 STRENGTH: M GED: R2 M1 L1 SVP: 2 DLU: 77

518.687-018 MOLD-MAKER HELPER (smelt. & refin.)
Assists MOLD MAKER (smelt. & refin.) in forming molds used in casting copper: Measures and marks pouring level on insides of mold to obtain castings of specified weights, using rules or gauges. Sprays inner surface of iron plugs with lampblack to prevent copper from adhering to them. Fastens plug in bot-tom of mold with locking pin. Sprays molds with steam or hot water to heat them to specified casting temperature. Cleans splashed copper from mold car, using hammer and chisel. Performs other duties as described under HELPER (any industry) Master Title.
GOE: 06.04.32 STRENGTH: M GED: R2 M1 L1 SVP: 3 DLU: 77

518.687-022 WAX-PATTERN COATER (foundry) alternate titles: dipper
Covers wax foundry patterns with coating compound to form shell mold used in lost-wax casting process: Dips pattern in suspension of silica sand and chem-ical binder. Coats pattern by sifting materials, such as sand or aluminum oxide, onto pattern; or places patterns in tumbling barrel, containing short fibers, to strengthen coating. Repeats coatings as specified to form shell. Examines pat-tern for evenness of coating. Places coated pattern clusters on cart and pushes cart into drying room, or places shell molds on conveyor of tunnel oven to dry mold interiors. May place patterns in steam-pressure vessel to melt pattern wax from shell.
GOE: 06.04.32 STRENGTH: M GED: R2 M1 L1 SVP: 2 DLU: 77

519 ORE REFINING AND FOUNDRY OCCUPATIONS, N.E.C.

This group includes occupations, not elsewhere classified, concerned with re-fining ore, ore concentrate, pig, or scrap metal, and casting metal in foundries.

519.130-010 CELL-FEED-DEPARTMENT SUPERVISOR (smelt. & refin.)
Supervises and coordinates activities of workers engaged in concentrating, flaking, and drying magnesium chloride preparatory to obtaining magnesium by electrolysis. Performs duties as described under SUPERVISOR (any industry) Master Title.
GOE: 06.02.01 STRENGTH: L GED: R4 M3 L3 SVP: 7 DLU: 77

519.130-014 SAMPLER, HEAD (smelt. & refin.)
Supervises and coordinates activities of workers engaged in crushing, drying, screening, and testing samples of ores preparatory to assaying them. Performs duties as described under SUPERVISOR (any industry) Master Title.
GOE: 06.04.01 STRENGTH: L GED: R4 M3 L3 SVP: 7 DLU: 77

519.130-018 SUPERVISOR, LEAD REFINERY (smelt. & refin.)
Supervises and coordinates activities of workers engaged in refining lead, casting it into ingots, and preparing ingots for shipment. Performs duties as de-scribed under SUPERVISOR (any industry) Master Title.
GOE: 06.01.01 STRENGTH: L GED: R4 M3 L3 SVP: 8 DLU: 77

519.130-022 SUPERVISOR, REVERBERATORY FURNACE (smelt. & refin.)
Supervises and coordinates activities of workers engaged in operating rever-beratory furnaces and casting machines to smelt and cast copper: Observes gauges and color of flames in furnace and adjusts valves to ensure combustion of fuels. Regulates furnace dampers to maintain specified temperatures. Ob-serves color and surface characteristics of bath to determine pouring tempera-tures and oxygen content of copper. Inspects operation of casting wheels to en-sure uniform product. Performs other duties as described under SUPERVISOR (any industry) Master Title.
GOE: 06.04.01 STRENGTH: L GED: R4 M3 L3 SVP: 8 DLU: 77

519.130-026 SUPERVISOR, SINTERING PLANT (smelt. & refin.)
Supervises and coordinates activities of workers engaged in moving, mixing, sintering, and crushing ore concentrates to remove impurities preparatory to smelting process. May supervise workers engaged in calcining phosphate rock and be designated Supervisor, Calcining (smelt. & refin.). Peforms duties as de-scribed under SUPERVISOR (any industry) Master Title.
GOE: 06.02.01 STRENGTH: L GED: R4 M3 L3 SVP: 8 DLU: 77

519.130-030 SUPERVISOR, URANIUM PROCESSING (smelt. & refin.)
Supervises and coordinates activities of workers engaged in processing uranium ore to recover uranium oxide. Trains workers in setup and operation of equipment. Performs other duties as described under SUPERVISOR (any industry) Master Title.
GOE: 06.01.01 STRENGTH: L GED: R4 M3 L3 SVP: 8 DLU: 77

519.131-010 FOUNDRY SUPERVISOR (foundry)
Supervises and coordinates activities of workers engaged in making cores and molds, in charging, operating, and tapping furnaces, in pouring molten metal into molds, and in chipping, grinding, and sandblasting castings: Examines materials and products at various stages of processing for conformance to specifications. Observes machines and equipment for malfunction and orders adjustments or repairs, or directs workers to make adjustments or repairs. Trains workers in foundry processes and in operation of machines and equipment. Performs other duties as described under SUPERVISOR (any industry) Master Title. May be designated according to part of process supervised as Casting Supervisor (foundry); Coremaking Supervisor (foundry); Cupola-Melting Supervisor (foundry); Finishing Supervisor (foundry); Mold-Making Supervisor (foundry); Shell-Core-And-Molding Supervisor (foundry); Wax-Room Supervisor (foundry).
GOE: 06.01.01 STRENGTH: M GED: R4 M3 L3 SVP: 7 DLU: 77

519.131-014 MILL-LABOR SUPERVISOR (smelt. & refin.)
Supervises and coordinates activities of workers engaged in maintaining ball mills, classifiers, flotation machines, and other ore-dressing equipment, and in cleaning offices, rest rooms, and work areas. Performs other duties as described under SUPERVISOR (any industry) Master Title.
GOE: 06.04.01 STRENGTH: L GED: R4 M3 L3 SVP: 7 DLU: 77

519.132-010 SUPERVISOR, BLAST FURNACE (steel & rel.) alternate titles: blower, blast furnace
Supervises and coordinates activities of workers engaged in operation of blast furnace to produce molten pig iron: Directs workers in charging furnace with specified amounts of raw materials, such as iron ore, coke, and limestone. Observes color of molten metal through tuyeres, or reads pyrometer and orders changes in furnace temperature and pressure. Estimates amounts of ferrosilicon, manganese, and phosphorous to add to molten metal to obtain specified type of pig iron. Directs workers in flushing and tapping furnace and in positioning ladles to receive molten metal. Observes color of molten metal flowing in runners during casting operations to determine quality of iron. Performs other duties as described under SUPERVISOR (any industry) Master Title.
GOE: 06.04.01 STRENGTH: L GED: R4 M3 L3 SVP: 6 DLU: 77

519.132-014 SUPERVISOR, BLAST-FURNACE-AUXILIARIES (steel & rel.)
Supervises and coordinates activities of workers engaged in unloading, crushing, screening, blending, and sintering iron ore. Directs workers in stockpiling materials, such as sinter cake, manganese, and limestone for blast furnace operations. Trains workers in operation of equipment. Performs duties as described under SUPERVISOR (any industry) Master Title.
GOE: 06.04.01 STRENGTH: L GED: R4 M3 L3 SVP: 6 DLU: 77

519.132-018 SUPERVISOR, CELL OPERATION (smelt. & refin.)
Supervises and coordinates activities of workers engaged in electrolytic refining of magnesium and in making hydrochloric acid from chlorine freed during refining process. Performs duties as described under SUPERVISOR (any industry) Master Title.
GOE: 06.02.01 STRENGTH: L GED: R4 M3 L3 SVP: 7 DLU: 77

519.132-022 SUPERVISOR, SOLDER MAKING (nonfer. metal)
Supervises and coordinates activities of workers engaged in refining scrap solder and tin and lead alloy with refined scrap to make solder: Directs workers in weighing tin, lead, and scrap solder and in refining operations. Molds and weighs test piece to compute ratio of tin and lead in refined metal. Computes amounts of tin, lead, and refined solder to be used in making solder according to formula. Directs workers in melting and mixing metals in melting pot, molding solder, weighing, recording weights, and packing. Performs other duties as described under SUPERVISOR (any industry) Master Title.
GOE: 06.04.01 STRENGTH: L GED: R4 M3 L3 SVP: 6 DLU: 77

519.134-010 POT-LINING SUPERVISOR (smelt. & refin.)
Supervises and coordinates activities of workers engaged in relining aluminum-reduction pots with carbon paste to form cathode. Inspects work to verify conformance to standards. Trains new workers in job duties. Performs duties as described under SUPERVISOR (any industry) Master Title.
GOE: 06.04.01 STRENGTH: L GED: R4 M3 L3 SVP: 7 DLU: 77

519.137-010 SUPERVISOR, MOLD YARD (steel & rel.)
Supervises and coordinates activities of workers engaged in cleaning and coating molds used to cast steel ingots, and in relining and repairing mold covers (hot tops). Performs other duties as described under SUPERVISOR (any industry) Master Title.
GOE: 06.04.01 STRENGTH: L GED: R4 M3 L3 SVP: 7 DLU: 77

519.137-014 SUPERVISOR, SCRAP PREPARATION (steel & rel.)
Supervises and coordinates activities of workers engaged in various duties, such as unloading scrap material from cars, sorting different grades of scrap into piles, burning or shearing scrap to charging-box size, and handling and

storing ingots. Performs duties as described under SUPERVISOR (any industry) Master Title.
GOE: 06.04.01 STRENGTH: M GED: R4 M3 L3 SVP: 6 DLU: 77

519.362-010 NICKEL-PLANT OPERATOR (smelt. & refin.)
Controls electrolysis tanks to purify electrolyte used in copper refining by removing copper, arsenic, and nickel: Places lead anodes and copper cathode starting sheets in tanks and turns valves to fill tanks with impure electrolyte. Switches on current and starts circulation pumps to remove copper from solution and deposit it onto cathode. Pumps solution into high-voltage tank system to deposit arsenic on cathodes. Pumps electrolyte from high-voltage tanks into evaporators that concentrate solution to specified specific gravity. Turns valves to drain condensed solution into settling tanks and to recover acid after nickel sulfate has settled.
GOE: 06.02.10 STRENGTH: M GED: R3 M2 L2 SVP: 6 DLU: 77

519.362-014 TANK-HOUSE OPERATOR (smelt. & refin.)
Controls equipment to purify copper by electrorefining: Signals MONORAIL CRANE OPERATOR (any industry) to lower impure copper anodes into tank filled with electrolyte. Immerses copper starter sheets (cathodes) into tank. Passes steel rod between electrodes to break off lumps which might cause short circuit and to verify specified clearance between electrodes. Examines, cleans, and tightens electrical connections, using steel wool and handtools. Turns on electrical current, and verifies voltage, using voltmeter. Measures density of electrolyte, using hydrometer. Observes deposition of copper on cathodes, and signals MONORAIL CRANE OPERATOR (any industry) to remove coated cathodes and depleted anodes from tank after specified time. Inspects tanks for defects, such as loose connections, leaks, deteriorated suspension bars and fittings, clogged floats, and drainage connections. Repairs or replaces parts, or notifies maintenance department. May cover lead sheets with primary coat of copper to make cathodes and be designated Starting-Sheet-Tank Operator (smelt. & refin.). May operate equipment that purifies copper through electrolysis without anodes and be designated Electro-Winning Operator (smelt. & refin.).
GOE: 06.02.10 STRENGTH: M GED: R3 M2 L2 SVP: 6 DLU: 77

519.387-010 MANOMETER TECHNICIAN (smelt. & refin.)
Tests pulverized material and computes specific gravity, using manometer tube: Collects mill samples, weighs specified amount of pulverized material, and pours it into cylinder and taps powder into compact mass. Raises mercury level in left side of manometer tube by pumping air into right side, using hand pump. Inserts cylinder of pulverized material into top of left tube. Releases air pressure from right side and times drop of mercury level in left side, using stopwatch. Computes specific surface of material, using standard algebraic formula. Reports below-standard reading to mill operator. May test milled sample of aluminum alloy to identify metals in sample and be designated Quantometer Operator (smelt. & refin.).
GOE: 06.03.01 STRENGTH: L GED: R3 M2 L2 SVP: 3 DLU: 77

519.484-010 CARNALLITE-PLANT OPERATOR (smelt. & refin.)
Mixes ingredients to prepare carnallite flux used in refining magnesium: Weighs carnallite ingredients according to formula. Mixes ingredients on concrete floor, using shovel. Melts mixture in furnace crucible. Tilts furnace with handwheel to pour molten carnallite into cooling pans. Pulverizes solidified carnallite in grinding mill and shovels powder into metal drums.
GOE: 06.02.18 STRENGTH: M GED: R2 M1 L2 SVP: 4 DLU: 77

519.484-014 RAW SAMPLER (smelt. & refin.) alternate titles: sample carrier
Collects and prepares laboratory samples of metal-bearing ores, refined metals, and other materials, such as coke, cryolite, slag, scrap, or flue dust, by any combination of following methods: (1) Collects samples of crushed ore, concentrates, or other material from conveyors, storage bins, carloads, or refining equipment, using sample containers or diverting mechanisms on conveyors or chutes. Grinds materials, using grinder mill. Weighs, dries, and reweighs material, using scales and oven, and computes moisture content. Sifts material through screen to remove oversized particles. Places sample in labeled containers, flasks, or bags for laboratory analysis. (2) Takes samples of molten metal from furnaces or casting stations, using ladle and wafer mold. Stamps or marks identifying information on cast wafer for delivery to laboratory. (3) Cuts samples of metal sheet or plate, using shears or punch. Saws sample sections from metal castings, plate, or rod for metallurgical analysis, using circular saw. Smooths cut surfaces of metal with grinder and sandpaper. Etches samples in acid to expose crystalline structure for spectrographic analysis. Drills holes in castings to obtain shavings for laboratory analysis. Stamps or labels samples for identification.
GOE: 02.04.01 STRENGTH: L GED: R3 M1 L1 SVP: 4 DLU: 77

519.485-010 GRINDER-MILL OPERATOR (smelt. & refin.)
Tends ball mill that grinds ore and classifier that separates coarse from fine particles: Turns pump valves and moves conveyor-control levers to feed soda ash, starch, lime, water, ore, and other materials into ball mill to make slurry. Adds chemical reagent to slurry that causes fine particles to float and enables classifier to separate fine from coarse particles and to return coarse ones to mill for regrinding. Obtains sample of slurry in bucket from mill and classifier. Weighs sample and calculates density of mixture or titrates sample to measure alkalinity. May examine ore tactually or observe its color to ascertain size of particles. May set automatic device to regulate amount of ore passing on conveyor belt to ball mill.

GOE: 06.02.08 STRENGTH: L GED: R3 M1 L1 SVP: 4 DLU: 77

519.485-014 RECOVERY-OPERATOR HELPER (smelt. & refin.)

Assists RECOVERY OPERATOR (smelt. & refin.) in operating kiln, ball mill, and conveyor system to recover soluble soda and alumina from waste materials: Moves controls to adjust feeds to rotary kiln and ball mill and to regulate operation of dust-collection equipment. Reads and records tank levels and slurry and soda ash temperatures. Collects and weighs batches of slurry to determine density. Measures oxygen content of flue gases, using gas analyzer. Keeps operating log. Turns valves to supply water to kiln trunnions and water-cooled bearings. Lubricates valves and adjusts packing glands to prevent leaks. Cleans cooler grates, using handtools. Performs other duties as described under HELPER (any industry) Master Title.

GOE: 06.04.10 STRENGTH: M GED: R2 M1 L2 SVP: 3 DLU: 77

519.565-010 DIGESTION OPERATOR (smelt. & refin.)

Tends battery of digester vessels that dissolve bauxite in plant liquor: Turns valves on pumps to transfer liquor and bauxite slurry through heaters into digester vessels. Turns valves to inject milk of lime into vessels. Adjusts pumps and valves to circulate cleaning solution through process lines. Collects samples of slurry and alumina solution for laboratory analysis. Keeps log of operations.

GOE: 06.04.10 STRENGTH: H GED: R2 M1 L1 SVP: 3 DLU: 77

519.565-014 TANK-HOUSE-OPERATOR HELPER (smelt. & refin.)

Assists TANK-HOUSE OPERATOR (smelt. & refin.) in setting up electrolytic copper-refining tanks by performing any combination of following duties: Cuts, strips, and trims copper sheets from starting blanks, using knife, pincers, and power shear. Places sheets in machine to clean and coat them with oil solution. Cinches or rivets loop strips to sheets, using looping machine. Straightens starter sheet blanks, using paddle or sledgehammer. Lifts and hangs starter sheets on electrical suspension bars in tanks. Guides MONORAIL CRANE OPERATOR (any industry) in positioning or removing anodes and coated starting plates. Scrapes and flushes out tanks, using scraping tools and water hose. May be designated according to function performed as Grease-Machine Worker (smelt. & refin.); Looper (smelt. & refin.); Sheet Hanger (smelt. & refin.); Stripper (smelt. & refin.). Performs other duties as described under HELPER (any industry) Master Title.

GOE: 06.04.10 STRENGTH: H GED: R2 M1 L2 SVP: 3 DLU: 77

519.582-010 RECOVERY OPERATOR (smelt. & refin.)

Operates rotary kiln, ball mill, and conveying equipment to recover soluble soda and alumina from waste materials: Moves lever and switch controls to start and regulate rotation speed of kiln. Moves controls to maintain specified temperatures throughout kiln and feed rate of kiln. Catches samples of slurry clinker from kiln, and observes discharge of slurry at sample points to ensure specified burning. Moves controls of cooling air fan, cooler exhaust fan, and air dampers to adjust temperature of grate cooler and airflows to burners. Moves controls and adjusts feed valves to start conveyor and bucket elevator system and to transport calcined clinker, bauxite, and soda ash into ball mill. Regulates valves and pumps to transfer slurry from ball mill into digestion tanks and to supply water to kiln trunnions and water-cooled bearings. Keeps operating log. Replaces charts in automatic recording devices.

GOE: 06.02.10 STRENGTH: M GED: R3 M2 L2 SVP: 5 DLU: 77

519.585-010 HARDNESS TESTER (mine & quarry)

Tends tumble drums, screens, and balance scales to test hardness of baked taconite pellets: Reads schedule to obtain specifications, such as furnace from which pellets are to be drawn and time of withdrawal, and notifies sampling personnel to prepare sample pellets. Pours sample over screen, and weighs screened pellets on balance scale. Dumps pellets into drum, and starts drum rotating for specified number of turns. Screens tumbled pellets, and weighs them to determine weight loss from tumbling. Reads conversion chart to obtain hardness number. Records hardness number of samples tested. May clean work area, using broom, shovel, and water hose.

GOE: 06.03.02 STRENGTH: L GED: R3 M2 L2 SVP: 3 DLU: 77

519.585-014 MUD BOSS (smelt. & refin.)

Tends machines that drain, filter, dry, crush, and package slime from electrolytic tanks, preparatory to recovery of valuable metals, such as gold, silver, platinum, and vanadium: Pulls lever to drain and filter slime from electrolytic tanks into storage tank. Drains slime into machine to subject it to heat and pressure to remove moisture. Starts conveyor to transport dry slime to automatic grinder machine. Observes flow of slime from grinder into container. Weighs container, and marks weight on container and tally sheet. Inspects tanks for leaks and other defects. Collects samples of liquids for analysis. May tend machine which dries and presses slime into cakes for shipment. May transfer electrolyte from one tank to another by passing it through intermediate steam-heated tank, offsetting evaporation by adding hot water. May smooth surface of starting sheets with sandpaper to remove pits and scratches.

GOE: 06.04.10 STRENGTH: M GED: R3 M2 L2 SVP: 4 DLU: 77

519.585-018 SAMPLE TESTER-GRINDER (mine & quarry)

Tends crushers, ovens, and screens to test samples of ore: Starts crusher to pulverize ore. Removes ore from crusher and places it in oven to dry. Sends portion of sample to laboratory for chemical analysis. Places sample in vibrator containing magnets and water. Starts vibrator to separate magnetic content of ore from impurities. Drains water from vibrator and weighs magnetic remainder. Pours ore sample through series of vibrating screens of different size open-

ings to separate ore samples. Weighs and records each size of ore. Records number of tests performed. May collect ore samples from various sites in plant or mine, and record origin of samples. May perform chemical sedimentation or hardness tests on samples.

GOE: 05.12.07 STRENGTH: L GED: R3 M2 L2 SVP: 4 DLU: 77

519.663-010 DOOR-MACHINE OPERATOR (steel & rel.)

Operates machine equipped with door jack and coke guide to remove doors from discharge end of coke ovens and guide discharged coke from oven to quenching car: Drives machine along rails to designated oven. Moves levers to hook machine arm onto door and remove it from oven, and to position frame which guides discharged coke from oven into quenching cars. Signals PUSHER OPERATOR (steel & rel.) to discharge coke from oven. Cleans fire clay and tars from door and jamb, using chisel bar. Gathers dry clay and residue with shovel and wheelbarrow, and dumps it into hopper. Replaces door. May manually hook coke-guide hangers to oven and drop apron to oven sill. May steam clean door machine.

GOE: 06.04.12 STRENGTH: M GED: R3 M2 L2 SVP: 3 DLU: 77

519.663-014 HOT-CAR OPERATOR (steel & rel.)

Drives electric car to haul hot coke from oven to quenching station and wharf: Positions dumpcar coupled to electric car below coke guide on designated oven. Signals PUSHER OPERATOR (steel & rel.) to discharge coke. Moves car forward to distribute coke evenly in car. Transports coke to quenching station, and starts equipment that sprays hot coke with measured amount of water. Moves car to wharf, and turns air valve to open gates on car and dump coke on wharf. Cleans cab and cab windows, using cleaning agents, broom, and brushes.

GOE: 06.04.40 STRENGTH: L GED: R2 M1 L2 SVP: 3 DLU: 77

519.663-018 PUSHER OPERATOR (steel & rel.)

Operates pusher machine which runs on rails at base of coke ovens, to push hot coke from ovens: Drives pusher to designated oven. Moves levers to open door arm to oven door and to remove it from oven, and to position ram. Starts ram at signal from worker on discharge side of oven to push coke out of oven. Withdraws ram and replaces door in oven. Moves leveling bar back and forth through opening near top of oven to level fresh charge of coal. Signals LARRY OPERATOR (steel & rel.) to recharge oven. Cleans pusher, using steam hose.

GOE: 06.04.12 STRENGTH: L GED: R2 M1 L2 SVP: 3 DLU: 77

519.664-010 ASSEMBLY CLEANER (smelt. & refin.)

Removes pot crust and carbon from spent anode assemblies, and cast-iron thimbles from contact rods, using crushing press, handtools, and power tools: Secures anode assembly to vibrating table, using hydraulic shaft and clamps. Depresses pedal to activate vibration that shakes loose pot crust (cryolite), and breaks crust remaining on anode, using airhammer. Sorts scrap aluminum from crust, and throws scrap in barrel. Removes anode assembly from table. Pushes pot crust from table into hopper of automatic crusher to prepare crust for reuse. Observes machine and clears jams in hopper. Breaks carbon or pot crust from contact rods, using hammer or airhammer. Observes automatic thimble press that crushes and cracks cast-iron thimble formed around rod, and stops machine when malfunction occurs. Examines assemblies on conveyor to detect damaged rods, and removes assemblies that need repair. Removes cast iron reclaimed from rods for transfer to reduction furnace for remelting. May be designated according to operation performed as Anode-Assembly Cleaner (smelt. & refin.) II; Thimble-Press Operator (smelt. & refin.).

GOE: 06.04.24 STRENGTH: H GED: R3 M2 L2 SVP: 3 DLU: 77

519.664-014 POT LINER (smelt. & refin.)

Relines pots and rebuilds continuous anodes used in reduction of aluminum by performing any combination of following duties: Replaces spacers, shunts, risers, brackets, straps, supports, and collector bars in pots, using wrenches. Attaches cables to pot superstructure and signals OVERHEAD CRANE OPERATOR (any industry) 921.663-010 to lift it from pot. Blows dust from top of anode, using air gun. Cuts metal sheet to size, using shears or pneumatic cutter, bends it around stub of anode, and rivets it to casing. Roughens top of stub, using fork, and pours carbon paste into form to build up anode to specified height. Pours water into pot to loosen material. Digs burned-out lining, insulation ore, bath material, and brick from interior of pot, using digger or jackhammer. Lays brick base on pot floor and signals OVERHEAD CRANE OPERATOR (any industry) to dump carbon mix into pot. Lines walls and floor with mix to specified depth, and tamps mix into cracks, using pneumatic hammer. Reforms shell cavity with insulating board, masonite, plywood, or sheet metal. Removes steel shell for repair, using hoist.

GOE: 05.10.01 STRENGTH: H GED: R3 M1 L2 SVP: 4 DLU: 77

519.665-010 GRANULATOR TENDER (steel & rel.) alternate titles: slag expander

Tends granulator machine that expands blast-furnace slag for use as building or insulating material: Signals OVERHEAD CRANE OPERATOR (any industry) 921.663-010 to position iron runners that carry slag from furnace to granulator machine. Opens gate of furnace to allow slag from furnace to flow onto runners, and turns water, air, and steam valves to spray slag in granulator. Positions container under discharge chute of granulator to receive expanded slag, using car puller. Starts conveyor that carries expanded slag from granulator to discharge chute. Stops equipment and clears slag from runners, granulator, and conveyor, using iron bar. Lubricates equipment, using grease gun and oilcan.

GOE: 06.04.10 STRENGTH: M GED: R2 M1 L1 SVP: 4 DLU: 77

519.665-014 STANDPIPE TENDER (steel & rel.)

Tends equipment that regulates flow of byproduct gases in coke-oven standpipes preparatory to discharging or charging oven: Moves controls to regulate flow of gases to collecting main, to open standpipes and oven charging holes, clear oven and standpipe of gases, and control flow of ammonia liquor and steam during charging. Sweeps spillage into charging holes. Cleans top of ovens, using broom and shovel. Clears standpipe, nozzles, and charging holes, using chisel bar and drill. Pokes coal from hoppers on charging car, using bar. May hook chains to oven doors and use winch to raise or lower doors. May loosen, unplug, and move tar in main, using bar [CHASER, TAR (steel & rel.)].

GOE: 06.04.12 STRENGTH: M GED: R2 M1 L1 SVP: 2 DLU: 77

519.665-018 WET-PLANT OPERATOR (smelt. & refin.)

Tends equipment that recovers cadmium, lead sulfate, and zinc oxide from dust collected in precipitators: Signals OVERHEAD CRANE OPERATOR (any industry) 921.663-010 to dump dust into tank from which it is processed through series of sulfating tanks to precipitate and wash lead sulfate and cadmium. Pumps washed liquor to another tank for treatment prior to recovery of zinc oxide. Prepares lime solution and mixes it with zinc oxide liquor. Titrates samples or tests solution for acidity and specific gravity, using hydrometer. Distills cadmium in retort furnace.

GOE: 06.04.10 STRENGTH: L GED: R3 M2 L2 SVP: 4 DLU: 77

519.667-010 CARBON SETTER (smelt. & refin.)

Replaces carbon anodes of electrolytic cells used in processing aluminum or magnesium: Disconnects anode assembly from connector arm, using wrenches. Signals OVERHEAD CRANE OPERATOR (any industry) 921.663-010 to lift burned anodes from pot and lower new anode assembly into pot. Cleans connector arms, using sandblast hose. Fastens anode rod to connector arm, and adjusts assembly to suspend anode in bath. Breaks burnt carbon block from steel stubs, using sledgehammer, and unbolts steel stubs from copper rods, using wrench. Shovels broken carbon into boxes, and loads rods and stubs on trailers for removal.

GOE: 06.04.34 STRENGTH: H GED: R3 M1 L1 SVP: 3 DLU: 77

519.667-014 LABORER, SOLDER MAKING (nonfer. metal)

Performs any combination of tasks involved in melting, refining, and pouring solder: Shovels scrap into furnace melting pots and adjusts fuel valves to regulate melting. Skims off dross with ladle. Plunges sieve box filled with potatoes to bottom of molten metal so that steam from charring potatoes agitates metal and brings additional dross to top. Skims off remaining dross. Ladles refined metal from pots to molds. Removes cooled metal from molds and places it on handtruck. Mixes tin, lead, or refined scrap solder in melting pots, as directed by SUPERVISOR, SOLDER MAKING (nonfer. metal). Ladles new solder into pig molds or into troughs of solder-making table. May cut bars into short lengths. Ties bars into bundles and packs bundles for shipment or storage. May charge lead and tin pigs into furnace melting pots, by hand or using overhead power hoist. May weigh pigs preparatory to charging furnace, using scale. May level machine that converts molten lead-tin alloys into powdered metal to process solder cream and be designated Solder Cream Maker (nonfer. metal).

GOE: 06.04.24 STRENGTH: M GED: R2 M1 L1 SVP: 3 DLU: 77

519.683-010 DROSS SKIMMER (smelt. & refin.)

Operates overhead crane to control perforated metal basket to skim dross from molten lead and to transfer lead from blast furnace to heated kettle: Moves levers to lower basket and skim off dross into barrel for salvage. Attaches electrically powered pump to kettle and starts pump to transfer molten lead into kettle. Starts powered stirrer that agitates lead. Skims off sulfide dross into barrel, using crane. Moves containers to salvage bin, using handtruck.

GOE: 06.04.10 STRENGTH: H GED: R2 M1 L1 SVP: 4 DLU: 77

519.683-014 LARRY OPERATOR (steel & rel.) alternate titles: charger-car operator; charging-car operator; gas tender

Operates larry (electric charging-car) to charge coal into coke ovens: Weighs empty larry on scale to obtain tare weight. Opens chutes of storage bin to dump specified weight of coal into hoppers on larry. Drives larry to ovens, and moves controls to position hoppers over open charging holes. Pushes levers to drop thimbles (sleeves) into charging holes and to open slides in hoppers. Pokes bar through opening in hopper to force coal into oven. Records oven number, battery, date, mix of coal, and shift. May move controls to lower and raise porcupine in open standpipe to clean walls. May signal PUSHER OPERATOR (steel & rel.) to level coal in oven.

GOE: 06.04.40 STRENGTH: M GED: R2 M1 L2 SVP: 3 DLU: 77

519.684-010 LADLE LINER (foundry; smelt. & refin.) alternate titles: ladle cleaner; ladle patcher

Repairs and relines ladles used to transport and pour molten metals: Chips slag from interior lining of ladle, using hammer and chisel. Mixes sand, clay, and water, using shovel to form refractory clay mud. Patches lining where cracked or worn by covering lining with refractory clay and tamping it in place. Chips out entire lining when beyond repair, using hammer and chisel. Relines ladle with refractory clay, using trowel. Dries and bakes new lining by placing inverted ladle over burner, building fire in ladle, or by using blowtorch. Relines and shapes pouring spouts of ladles with fire clay. May reline ladles with refractory brick. May make stoppers for stopper-type ladle. May brush graphite facing on lining.

GOE: 06.02.30 STRENGTH: M GED: R2 M1 L1 SVP: 3 DLU: 77

519.684-014 LEAF COVERER (smelt. & refin.)

Cleans and re-covers leaves of aluminum-ore filtering units, using overhead bridge crane and handtools: Opens filter units and removes filter leaves, using crane. Strips worn covers from filter leaves, using knife and wire cutters. Transports filter leaves from filter units into cleaning vats, using crane. Cleans discharge neck of leaves, and swabs them with graphite paste. Covers cleaned filter leaves with cloth, and replaces leaves in filter units, using crane.

GOE: 06.04.39 STRENGTH: M GED: R2 M1 L1 SVP: 3 DLU: 77

519.684-018 MOLD DRESSER (any industry) alternate titles: mold repairer

Removes residue, blemishes, corrosion, and similar defects from interior of molds, using handtools and power tools: Inspects interior surfaces of molds to locate pits and holes. Positions molds for work, using hoist. Repairs defects, using hammers, drills, chisels, routers, or grinding wheel. Smooths interior of mold, using file, buffing wheel, emery paper, or steelwool. May add metal to or remove metal from plates, rings, and molds, using welding equipment and files. May reassemble molds after repairing. May be designated according to type of mold repaired as Glass-Mold Repairer (glass mfg.).

GOE: 06.04.24 STRENGTH: M GED: R2 M1 L1 SVP: 4 DLU: 77

519.684-022 STOPPER MAKER (steel & rel.) alternate titles: stopper-rod maker

Assembles refractory stoppers used to plug pouring nozzles of steel ladles: Mixes specified amount of refractory mortar powder with water, using trowel or hoe. Fastens stopper head to rod with metal pin. Spreads mortar on rod, using trowel, and slides brick sleeves over rod to form refractory jacket. Tightens locknuts holding assembly together, using wrench. Spreads mortar on jacket to seal sleeve joints. Hoists stopper and rod assembly on drying rack and pushes rack in oven to dry mortar. Pulls rack from oven and pushes it to storage area.

GOE: 06.04.30 STRENGTH: H GED: R2 M1 L1 SVP: 3 DLU: 77

519.684-026 TOOL REPAIRER (smelt. & refin.)

Repairs worn and damaged equipment and tools used by workers engaged in electrolytic refining of copper: Examines rubber boots and gloves and fills them with water to detect holes. Mends holes with rubber patches. Mends leaky metal buckets by soldering holes. Grinds dull tools, such as picks, shovels, and scoops, using electrically powered emery wheel. Replaces handles, hose, and other defective parts of tools and equipment. Issues new or repaired replacements.

GOE: 06.02.32 STRENGTH: L GED: R3 M1 L1 SVP: 5 DLU: 77

519.685-010 BRIQUETTING-MACHINE OPERATOR (smelt. & refin.) alternate titles: pellet-press operator

Tends equipment to dry, mix, and compress copper fines into briquettes for use by smelter: Starts belt conveyors that automatically feed mixture from wetbin hopper to heated rotary dryer. Turns valve to set burner at specified temperature. Tests moisture content of mixture by feeling with fingers. Pulls lever to open discharge gate of heating chamber to admit mixture into pug mill. Opens valve to add binding solution to obtain mixture of required consistency. Turns valve to feed mixture into press to form briquettes. Oils and greases equipment, using oilcan and grease gun.

GOE: 06.04.10 STRENGTH: L GED: R2 M1 L1 SVP: 3 DLU: 77

519.685-014 GROUT-MACHINE TENDER (smelt. & refin.)

Tends machine that forces mortar into spaces between firebrick and steel shell of taconite ore furnace: Inspects furnace to detect discoloration spots which indicate flaws in firebrick inner wall of furnace. Shovels grout into reservoir of machine. Attaches airhose to compressed air system and grout hose to nipple on shell of furnace with wrench. Starts machine and observes pressure gauge to determine when space is filled. Caps nipple welded onto furnace shell, using wrench. May mix mortar, using electrically driven paddle wheel. May dismantle and clean grout machine and equipment, using wrenches, water, and airhoses.

GOE: 06.04.10 STRENGTH: M GED: R2 M1 L1 SVP: 2 DLU: 77

519.685-018 KETTLE OPERATOR (smelt. & refin.)

Tends oil-fired kettles that melt and fume antimony to make antimony oxide: Charges antimony crystals into melting kettle with hoist, and fires burners. Regulates temperature according to thermometer readings and color and appearance of metal. Skims slag from surface of kettle. Connects trough from melting to fuming kettle, and pours metal into trough by tilting kettle. Heats metal to specified temperature to vaporize antimony which is drawn to baghouse and condensed as oxide dust. Fills buggy with antimony oxide from hoppers, and weighs filled buggy on floor scale. Empties buggy onto conveyor leading to rotating drum in which oxides from different charges are blended. Transfers blended dust to conveyor leading to automatic bagging machine. Determines antimony content by casting sample into rod of specified size, weighing it, and referring to standard chart.

GOE: 06.04.10 STRENGTH: M GED: R3 M2 L2 SVP: 4 DLU: 77

519.685-022 KETTLE TENDER I (smelt. & refin.)

Tends series of oil-fired kettles that refine lead: Charges kettle with lead in molten or pig form, and fires kettle. Adds specified type and amount of reagent and agitates mixture to cause impurities, such as antimony, arsenic, bismuth, and tin to form into dross. Skims dross off mixture, using ladle, shovel, or per-

forated dipper. Throws zinc bricks into kettle and agitates mixture to desilverize lead. Skims crust of silver and gold content into basket of press, and compresses dross with air-driven ram. Pumps lead through reaction cylinder while chlorine is admitted to form zinc chloride slag. Skims slag after completion of reaction as indicated by color of slag and molten metal. Pours metal into molds or dips samples into cold water to prepare them for laboratory analysis. May hook pot to crane and signal OVERHEAD CRANE OPERATOR (any industry) 921.663-010 to transfer lead from one kettle to another. May crystallize zinc in water-cooled vacuum tank to remove zinc from desilverized lead. May produce antimony crystals from antimonial lead by mixing prescribed reagents with molten metal in kettle, by skimming dross, and by cooling bath to specified temperature. May be known according to specific duty performed as Desilverizer (smelt. & refin.).
GOE: 06.04.10 STRENGTH: M GED: R3 M1 L2 SVP: 4 DLU: 77

519.685-026 MUD-MILL TENDER (smelt. & refin.)
Tends mill that mixes flue dust with water to settle it for shipment: Opens bin outlet allowing dust to fall into mixing mill. Dislodges banked dust in bin by hammering sides. Starts mill and opens valve of water spray. Opens door of mill allowing moistened dust to fall onto conveyor belt leading to railroad car. May distribute mixture evenly in car, using shovel.
GOE: 06.04.10 STRENGTH: M GED: R2 M1 L2 SVP: 3 DLU: 77

519.685-030 ROD-MILL TENDER (cement; smelt. & refin.) alternate titles: regrind mill operator
Tends rod mills that grind ore, clinkers, and rock into fine particles: Starts mill and feed conveyors. Turns valves to feed lime, water, starch, soda ash, and other materials into mill to make slurry. Pushes button to start screw conveyor that separates coarse particles from slurry and returns them to mill for regrinding. Obtains sample of ore or slurry in bucket for laboratory analysis. Weighs sample on balance scales to determine density of slurry. Turns valves to feed water into mill to obtain specified density of slurry. Replaces worn rods in mill, using electric hoist. May record operating time of rod mills and levels of materials in storage bins.
GOE: 06.04.08 STRENGTH: L GED: R2 M1 L1 SVP: 2 DLU: 77

519.686-010 LABORER, GENERAL (nonfer. metal)
Performs any combination of tasks to aid other workers in production of nonferrous metal products: Transfers metal scrap from work areas to storage areas, using handtruck, and records quantity and type of scrap transferred. Dumps scrap metal into crusher that reduces bulk of metal. Shovels metal scrap onto furnace conveyor to dry scrap preparatory to melting. Dumps paste oil or fat into drum, adds water, and mixes solution, using steam hose, to prepare lubricant used in drawing tubes and rods. Examines metal products for defects, such as dents, cracks, and scratches. Taps dents from products, using mallet. Feeds metal castings into automatic finishing machine that performs operations, such as reaming, stamping, and cleaning. Scrapes carbon, dirt, and metal particles from interior surface of casting molds. May be known according to specific duties performed as Chip-Crusher Operator (nonfer. metal); Chip Drier (nonfer. metal); Inspector (nonfer. metal) II; General Scrap Worker (nonfer. metal); Soap Worker (nonfer. metal).
GOE: 06.04.10 STRENGTH: H GED: R2 M1 L1 SVP: 2 DLU: 77

519.687-010 CELL PLASTERER (smelt. & refin.)
Seals opening around carbon anode, where it protrudes through cover of magnesium refining cell, to prevent leakage of chlorine gas and to secure anode in position. Applies mixture of asbestos fiber or pulp and water or oil, using trowel.
GOE: 06.04.34 STRENGTH: L GED: R2 M1 L1 SVP: 3 DLU: 77

519.687-014 DUST PULLER (smelt. & refin.) alternate titles: flue-dust laborer
Rakes or scrapes flue dust from converter flues or hoppers into larry cars or screw conveyors for shipment to furnaces. Breaks up packed dust with bar or pole, and hammers sides of hopper with mallet or bar to dislodge contents. May drive larry car to furnace, and dump load into furnace. May scrape dust into collecting hoppers. May measure depth of dust in flue, using sounding chain.
GOE: 06.04.39 STRENGTH: H GED: R2 M1 L1 SVP: 2 DLU: 77

519.687-018 FLUX-TUBE ATTENDANT (nonfer. metal; smelt. & refin.)
Mixes flux for graphite tubes and replaces tubes and chemical supply tanks on aluminum remelt furnaces: Mixes silicon aluminum paint solution (flux) and dips ends of new graphite tubes into solution to coat them. Transports tubes and tanks of chlorine and nitrogen to furnaces, using handtruck. Turns valves to shut off flow of chlorine and removes tubes from furnace, using handtools. Discards broken tubes and installs new ones. Cleans usable tubes, using wire brush, and installs them to specified depth. Installs replacement tanks of chlorine and nitrogen on furnace, using handtools, and adjusts valves until tank pressure and flowmeters reach specifications. Records amounts of chemicals and tubes used for each furnace. Tours furnace area to verify readings of pressure and flowmeter gauges and makes required adjustments.
GOE: 06.04.10 STRENGTH: M GED: R3 M1 L2 SVP: 3 DLU: 77

519.687-022 FOUNDRY WORKER, GENERAL (foundry)
Performs any combination of following tasks in foundry concerned with melting metal, pouring metal into molds, removing castings from molds, dressing castings, moving foundry materials, and cleaning equipment and work areas: Moves sand, castings, flasks, or other materials about foundry by hand, using wheelbarrow or cart, or by loading them onto conveyor. Assembles flasks, using wrench, bolts, and tap screws. Waters and mixes sand, shovels sand into flasks, and compacts sand in flasks, using ramming tool. Sprays binder on surface of sand molds and dries surface with blowtorch. Fits together, clamps, and unclamps cope and drag on production line. Weighs out specified amounts of materials for furnace charge, and loads charge into melting furnace. Skims slag from surface of molten metal, using scoop. Carries or pushes ladles of molten metal on monorail and pours metal into molds. Installs and removes steel jackets and bands used to hold snap molds together during casting. Breaks sand mold from finished casting, using bar or hammer. Sorts castings into pairs or groups for assembly. Pulls reinforcing wires from castings. Directs high pressure stream of water onto castings to clean castings and remove cores. Cleans castings, patterns, and flasks, using wire brush. Removes gates, sprues, and other projections from castings with sledge, pneumatic hammer, power shear, or power hacksaw. Breaks up used sand molds with bar, shovels sand into drying oven and sand-mixing machine, and sifts sand through motor-driven screen for reuse in new molds. Breaks up slag, using hammer, and shovels it into buckets for removal to dump. Chips out worn cupola and ladle linings, using bar. Prepares plaster and relines ladle. Sweeps and cleans work areas. May be designated according to worker assisted or according to duty performed as Casting Carrier (foundry); Casting Sorter (foundry); Cupola-Tender Helper (foundry); Flask Carrier (foundry); Jacket Changer (foundry); Ladle-Liner Helper (foundry). May be designated: Ladle Pusher (foundry); Mold Clamper (foundry); Mold-Closer Helper (foundry); Molder Helper (foundry); Molder Helper, Machine (foundry); Mold Stacker (foundry); Pattern Carrier (foundry); Pattern Cleaner (foundry); Sand-Screener Operator (foundry); Sand Shoveler (foundry); Sand Wheeler (foundry); Shake-Out Worker (foundry); Skimmer (foundry); Slag Worker (foundry); Sprue Knocker (foundry).
GOE: 06.04.32 STRENGTH: H GED: R2 M1 L1 SVP: 2 DLU: 77

519.687-026 LABORER, GENERAL (smelt. & refin.)
Performs any combination of following tasks as directed by workers engaged in crushing, sampling, smelting, refining, loading, and moving ore and other materials, and cleaning machines and equipment: Loads and unloads material from freight cars or trucks, manually or using hoist, conveyor, or handtruck. Sifts and screens materials, using screen and shovel. Fills sacks or barrels with materials, such as arsenic, nickel, and selenium. Weighs materials, such as ore and scrap. Shovels scrap into trucks and storage bins or sorts and stacks scrap. Segregates and stacks castings, using tongs or hoist, and marks or stamps identifying codes on castings. Flushes mud and sludge from cooling and circulating tanks, using water hose and scrapers. Removes arsenic from kitchens, using cable-drawn scrapers. Empties slag pans from furnace, using hoist. Brushes cores with oil to prevent cores from cracking. Hooks and unhooks charge boxes and scrap trucks, to and from overhead crane. Cleans work area and delivers samples to laboratory for analysis. May remove scrap metal and wood from conveyors that feed machines. May spray firebrick with clay solution to reduce corrosive and abrasive action.
GOE: 06.04.40 STRENGTH: H GED: R2 M1 L1 SVP: 2 DLU: 77

519.687-030 MACHINE-CASTINGS PLASTERER (foundry)
Caulks machine castings, using putty knife or trowel: Measures out required amount of metallic plaster, and mixes it into paste of specified consistency. Applies paste to surface of machine castings, filling cracks and blowholes and leveling rough spots, using putty knife or small trowel. Allows putty to dry and sands plaster to smooth surface.
GOE: 06.04.33 STRENGTH: L GED: R2 M1 L1 SVP: 2 DLU: 77

519.687-034 RODDING-ANODE WORKER (smelt. & refin.)
Renews carbon anode assemblies used in electrolytic processing of aluminum by performing any combination of following duties: Removes carbon blocks from conveyor, using hoist. Feeds steel stubs on conveyor through bath solution to coat them with graphite. Positions pouring ring and steel stub on carbon block. Tilts crucible to pour molten iron around stub to cast it to block. Bolts copper rod to stub, using wrench. Loads anode assemblies onto trailer for removal to potroom, using hoist. Unbolts copper rod from steel stub embedded in disintegrated block. Places stub in hydraulic press and pulls lever to break off unused portions of block. Cleans and straightens stubs and rods, using chipping gun, disc grinder, and straightening hammer. Chips iron splashings from poured blocks, using chisel and hammer. Pushes buttons and pulls levers to activate and switch conveyors to move blocks or assemblies through assembly process.
GOE: 06.04.34 STRENGTH: H GED: R2 M1 L1 SVP: 3 DLU: 77

519.687-038 STOPPER-MAKER HELPER (steel & rel.)
Assists STOPPER MAKER (steel & rel.) in assembling refractory stoppers: Places steel rod in vise and bends it to specified shape, using sledgehammer. Mixes cement and fire clay with water to form refractory mortar. Carries materials, such as rods, stopper heads, and sleeves, to work area. Performs other duties as described under HELPER (any industry) Master Title.
GOE: 06.04.30 STRENGTH: H GED: R2 M1 L1 SVP: 2 DLU: 77

519.687-042 TEST WORKER (foundry)
Obtains sample of molten metal from each furnace heat, using hand ladle or glass tube: Dips hand ladle or inserts glass tube into pouring ladle, before molds are poured. Pours molten metal into sand mold or allows it to solidify in glass tube. Breaks or drills solidified metal to obtain test sample, using ham-

mer or drill press. Marks sample according to heat from which sample was taken.
GOE: 06.04.24 STRENGTH: L GED: R1 M1 L1 SVP: 2 DLU: 77

52 OCCUPATIONS IN PROCESSING OF FOOD, TOBACCO, AND RELATED PRODUCTS

This division includes occupations concerned with preparing food, tobacco, and related products for commercial use. Includes manufacturing phases after harvesting and prior to marketing. Such activities as slaughtering livestock, blending cheeses, fermenting alcohol, and smoking hams are included in this division. Marking and packaging occupations are included here when they occur at the end of a production process.

520 MIXING, COMPOUNDING, BLENDING, KNEADING, SHAPING, AND RELATED OCCUPATIONS

This group includes occupations concerned with combining and mingling various materials to produce a single mass or compound and working an object or material by pressure and configuration to shape it or effect its texture and consistency.

520.132-010 BLENDING SUPERVISOR (grain-feed mills)
Supervises and coordinates activities of workers engaged in blending various grades of flour into blends and mixing blends with cooking ingredients to prepare self-rising flour and premixes: Confers with plant management and other supervisors to plan daily production and coordinate blending department activities with other departments. Inventories storage bins and packaging hoppers to determine priority of blends and availability of grades for blending. Trains new workers. Turns knobs on blending equipment to set blending meters for scheduled grades of flour to be produced. Performs other duties as described under SUPERVISOR (any industry) Master Title.
GOE: 06.04.01 STRENGTH: L GED: R4 M3 L3 SVP: 6 DLU: 77

520.132-014 SUPERVISOR, COMPRESSED YEAST (food prep., nec)
Supervises and coordinates activities of workers engaged in pressing, mixing, and packaging bakers yeast: Trains workers in operation of machines. Examines and feels yeast throughout process for color, consistency, and sharpness of breaking edge. Observes progress of yeast through filter pressing, mixing, extruding, and packaging operations to ensure continuous workflow, conformity to specifications, and sanitary conditions. Prepares and submits requisitions for materials and supplies. Performs other duties as described under SUPERVISOR (any industry) Master Title.
GOE: 06.02.01 STRENGTH: L GED: R4 M3 L3 SVP: 7 DLU: 77

520.136-010 BLENDING SUPERVISOR (tobacco)
Supervises and coordinates activities of workers engaged in feeding tobacco leaves onto blending conveyor: Plans daily work schedules based on analysis of work orders and inventory of tobacco in storage area. Assigns workers to feed tobacco of different grades into conveyor to achieve specified blend. Instructs individual workers to adjust rate of feeding based on hourly poundage and blending report. Compiles reports to show daily production and departmental labor cost by grade. Confers with plant officials and other supervisors to coordinate flow of tobacco through department. Trains new workers. Performs other duties as described under SUPERVISOR (any industry) Master Title.
GOE: 06.04.01 STRENGTH: L GED: R4 M3 L3 SVP: 5 DLU: 77

520.137-010 SUPERVISOR, LUMP ROOM (tobacco) alternate titles: supervisor, rolling room
Supervises and coordinates activities of workers engaged in molding lumps, plugs, or twists of chewing tobacco: Reads production schedules for information, such as quantity of plugs or twists and type of blend and wrapper leaf specified. Computes amount of filler and wrapper leaf required for production. Examines plugs and twists to detect variations from standards. Schedules cleaning and repairing of lump-making machines to avoid interruptions of production. Coordinates receipt of tobacco from casing and drying department and transfer of plugs to shipping department. Performs other duties as described under SUPERVISOR (any industry) Master Title.
GOE: 06.04.01 STRENGTH: L GED: R4 M3 L2 SVP: 7 DLU: 77

520.361-010 HONEY GRADER-AND-BLENDER (food prep., nec) alternate titles: honey liquefier
Grades honey according to type, color, bouquet, and moisture content, and blends various grades to obtain uniform product: Compares samples of liquid honey lots with standard samples for color and bouquet, and ascertains moisture content, using refractometer. Calculates amount of various types of honey for mixing to produce product of uniform color, clarity, and bouquet. Directs other workers in dumping and blending of various honey lots in warming chamber. May grade and mark honeycomb sections according to government regulations.
GOE: 06.01.04 STRENGTH: S GED: R4 M3 L3 SVP: 6 DLU: 77

520.362-010 BULK-PLANT OPERATOR (sugar & conf.)
Controls equipment in bulk sugar plant to load and unload sugar and to blend sugar syrups according to formula: Signals drivers or engineers by hand to give

directions in positioning trucks and railroad cars for unloading. Positions conveyors and attaches unloading hoses and pipes to truck and railroad cars. Opens conveyor gate and pipe valves and starts pumps, blowers, and conveyors to unload sugar from vehicle and to transport it to storage bins. Starts pumps and agitators to transport and mix specified amounts of water, corn syrup, and sugar in blending tanks. Dumps bags of diatomaceous earth into blend and pumps mixture through filter to remove impurities. Tests syrup to measure acid, yeast, and soluble sugar content, using pH meter and refractometer. Keeps records of test results, weight of sugar received and shipped, amount and type of syrup blended, and percentage of wasted materials. May weigh truck before and after loading. May tend steam boiler to supply steampower to plant equipment [BOILER OPERATOR (any industry)].
GOE: 06.02.15 STRENGTH: L GED: R4 M3 L3 SVP: 5 DLU: 77

520.362-014 DRY-STARCH OPERATOR (grain-feed mills)
Operates machines and equipment to mix cornstarch blends: Signals STARCH-TREATING ASSISTANT (grain-feed mills) to admit starch suspension into mixing and storage tanks, and to dump measured amount of chemicals into mixing tanks to prepare chemical solutions. Reads meters and turns valves to admit chemical solutions into blending tank. Manipulates switches and turns valves to regulate heaters and agitators that mix solutions, and to pump starch mixtures into blending and filter tanks. Receives or draws samples of product and performs standard tests to ascertain if acidity, alkalinity, and viscosity conform to specifications, using hydrometer and other test equipment. Records quantity and kind of chemicals used. Inspects equipment and observes gauges, thermometers, and meters to maintain efficient production. May direct workers engaged in regulating filters, shakers, centrifugal driers, and related equipment to produce dry starch products.
GOE: 06.02.15 STRENGTH: H GED: R3 M2 L3 SVP: 7 DLU: 77

520.382-010 CISTERN-ROOM OPERATOR (beverage) alternate titles: cistern-room working supervisor; subwarehouse supervisor
Controls regauging equipment from panelboard to reduce proof of newly distilled liquor in cistern tank before barreling: Reads charts to ascertain proof of liquor to be regauged, number of gallons to be regauged, and number of gallons of deionized water required to produce liquor of specified proof. Pumps specified number of gallons of liquor and deionized water into cistern tank. Opens valves to admit compressed air and agitate mixture. Reads thermometer and alcohol-proof hydrometer during process and compares readings with standard gauging manual to determine final proof of liquor. Pumps liquor into filling tanks for barreling or into railroad tank cars for shipment.
GOE: 06.02.15 STRENGTH: L GED: R3 M2 L3 SVP: 4 DLU: 77

520.382-014 LIQUID-SUGAR MELTER (sugar & conf.)
Controls equipment to blend granulated sugar and water to produce liquid sucrose of specified concentration: Reads job order to ascertain type and amount of liquid sucrose specified. Opens water and steam valves to fill tank and heat water to specified temperature. Reads chart to ascertain amount of sugar required for producing liquid sucrose of specified concentration. Starts pneumatic conveyors and opens valves to fill hopper with specified amount of sugar. Opens hopper gate to feed sugar into heated water. Starts agitators to mix liquid sucrose in tank for specified period. Closes steam valve and allows liquid to cool. Pumps liquid sucrose from mixing tank to specified storage tank. Records operating data in station log. Takes samples of liquid sucrose produced for laboratory analysis.
GOE: 06.02.15 STRENGTH: L GED: R3 M2 L2 SVP: 4 DLU: 77

520.384-010 BENCH HAND (bakery products) alternate titles: baker, bench; dough molder, hand
Forms dough for bread, buns, and other bakery products: Rolls dough to desired thickness with rolling pin or guides dough through rolling machine. Sprinkles flour on dough and workbench to prevent dough from sticking. Kneads dough to eliminate gases formed by yeast. Cuts dough into pieces with knife or handcutter. Adds spices, fruits, or seeds when making special rolls or breads. Weighs pieces on scales and keeps record of production. Places dough in baking pans. May cut dough into bun divisions by machine. May form dough into special shapes and add fillings or flavorings.
GOE: 06.02.28 STRENGTH: M GED: R3 M2 L2 SVP: 6 DLU: 77

520.385-010 MIXER, WHIPPED TOPPING (food prep., nec)
Tends machines that mix and blend ingredients to make whipped topping for use on desserts: Weighs prescribed amounts of raw materials, such as oil, water, sugar, and caustics. Adjusts thermostat for specified temperature in mixers and pumps or dumps ingredients into tank of mixer. Admits prescribed quantities of water and other ingredients into mixing tank at specified intervals. Tests solution for specified acidity, using pH meter. Pumps mixture into blending tank and adds flavoring prior to pasteurization.
GOE: 06.04.15 STRENGTH: M GED: R2 M2 L2 SVP: 3 DLU: 77

520.387-010 BLENDER (tobacco) alternate titles: granulating blender; leaf blender
Selects various grades and kinds of tobacco, to produce specific blend, according to formula and knowledge of tobacco characteristics: Removes leaves or hands of tobacco from hogsheads or bins, sorting tobacco according to texture, color, variety, and locality grown. Feeds specified amount of various grades and types of tobacco onto conveyor, or places tobacco in baskets, boxes, or piles for processing.
GOE: 06.03.01 STRENGTH: L GED: R3 M2 L2 SVP: 4 DLU: 77

520.462-010 DOUGH-MIXER OPERATOR (bakery products) alternate titles: control-panel operator

Controls semiautomatic equipment, from control panel, to blend ingredients for bread and deposit specified quantity of dough in baking pans: Notifies other workers to admit broth into feedlines and to start loading specified size pans onto conveyor. Turns handwheel to adjust conveyor guides to size of pans. Starts flour sifter, premixer that blends ingredients, and developer that kneads dough, working from remote control panel. Observes dials and recording instruments to verify temperature of broth, viscosity of dough, and speed of mixing units. Feels dough emerging from developer to ascertain that consistency meets plant standard. Turns developer speed control to specified setting and starts divider blades that pinch off and drop dough into pans passing on conveyor. Turns handwheel and control bar to adjust discharge aperture above divider blades so that dough is uniformly shaped and deposited in center of pan. Weighs sample pieces of dough and turns divider speed handle to regulate amount of dough deposited in pans. Records temperatures, viscosity, and feed rate from instrument readings.
GOE: 06.02.15 STRENGTH: L GED: R3 M1 L3 SVP: 5 DLU: 77

520.485-010 FLOUR MIXER (grain-feed mills) alternate titles: mixer-and-scaler; mixer operator

Tends machine that mixes flour and ingredients, such as buttermilk solids, phosphate, salt, soda, and sugar, to produce self-rising or other premixed flour: Dumps specified amount of flour into mixer or turns dial to convey measured amount into mixer. Weighs and dumps other ingredients, such as buttermilk solids, phosphate, soda, and sugar, according to formula, and starts machine. May record amount of ingredients in each batch. May be designated according to type of flour mixed as Self-Rising-Flour Mixer (grain-feed mills).
GOE: 06.04.15 STRENGTH: H GED: R2 M2 L2 SVP: 2 DLU: 77

520.485-014 GRAIN MIXER (grain-feed mills) alternate titles: grain blender

Tends equipment to mix grain for milling into blended flour: Starts belt conveyor and adjusts valve controls on automatic feeders to regulate proportions of specified grades of grain flowing from storage tanks onto conveyor. Starts conveyors to transfer grain to milling department. May inspect grain for smut, rust, or other contamination. May find weight of minimum test bushel by filling standard measure with grain and recording weight.
GOE: 06.04.15 STRENGTH: L GED: R2 M1 L1 SVP: 2 DLU: 77

520.485-018 MINCEMEAT MAKER (can. & preserv.)

Tends equipment to mix ingredients used in preparing mincemeat: Weighs and measures ingredients, such as raisins, currants, ground orange peels, salt, spices, and hot water, using platform scale and measuring containers. Dumps ingredients from measuring containers into kettle and activates agitator to mix ingredients for specified period of time. Turns valve to permit ingredients to flow from kettle into cooling trough preparatory to canning.
GOE: 06.04.15 STRENGTH: M GED: R3 M2 L2 SVP: 3 DLU: 77

520.485-022 REFINED-SYRUP OPERATOR (sugar & conf.)

Tends equipment that blends, inverts, and cools edible sugar syrups according to production schedules: Opens valves and starts pumps to move specified amounts of syrups and inverting materials from storage to mixing tanks. Calculates proportions of ingredients when blending syrups other than standard. Conducts light tests to determine viscosity and color of syrup, using refractometer and polariscope. Bottles samples of products for laboratory analysis. Opens valves to route and distribute syrups to tank cars or trucks. Maintains production and distribution records.
GOE: 06.02.15 STRENGTH: M GED: R3 M3 L3 SVP: 4 DLU: 77

520.485-026 SYRUP MAKER (beverage) alternate titles: cooker, syrup; sauce maker

Tends equipment to mix ingredients that produce syrups used in canned fruits and preserves, flavorings, frozen novelty confections, or non-alcoholic beverages: Determines amounts of ingredients, such as sugar, water, and flavoring, required for specified quantity of syrup of designated specific gravity, using sugar concentration and dilution charts. Opens valve to admit liquid sugar and water into mixer, or dumps crystalline sugar into mixer and admits water. Adds flavoring ingredients and starts mixer to make syrup. Opens valve to admit steam into jacket of mixer to invert sugar, eliminate air, and sterilize syrup. Tests syrup for sugar content, using hydrometer or refractometer. Pumps syrup to storage tank. May filter syrup to remove impurities and be designated Syrup Filterer (beverage). May blend raw syrups and be designated Syrup Blender (beverage).
GOE: 06.02.15 STRENGTH: M GED: R3 M2 L3 SVP: 4 DLU: 77

520.485-030 STARCHMAKER (grain-feed mills)

Tends equipment to separate starch from ground potatoes, and adds chemicals to resulting solution to produce starch of specified purity: Flushes shaker screen containing ground potatoes, using water hose, to remove foreign matter and form crude starch suspension. Turns valves to admit suspension and water to settling and rewash tanks in which impurities rise to surface, forming scum. Turns valves to transfer scum (brown starch) to starch tables and settling tanks until all white starch has been separated. Drains salvaged starch into vat, starts agitator, and adds equal volume of water to form white starch suspension prior to drying. Determines acidity, viscosity, and bacteria content of suspension, using pH meter and viscometer. Adds measured amounts of specified chemicals to further purify and preserve product.

GOE: 06.04.15 STRENGTH: L GED: R3 M2 L3 SVP: 3 DLU: 77

520.487-010 CHEESE BLENDER (dairy products)

Prepares charts of quantities, grades, and types of cheese required for blending to make cheese products: Feels, tastes, smells, and observes cheese for firmness, mellowness, acidity, and color, and selects cheese products for specified blend. Calculates quantities of cheese required for each batch, according to formula, and records quantities, grades, and types on chart. Compares laboratory reports with specifications and alters calculations to achieve specified body, texture, flavor, moisture, fat, acidity, and salt in finished product.
GOE: 06.01.04 STRENGTH: L GED: R4 M4 L3 SVP: 6 DLU: 77

520.487-014 FORMULA-ROOM WORKER (dairy products)

Prepares, bottles, and sterilizes infant formulas: Weighs or measures and mixes specified quantities of ingredients, such as evaporated, condensed, or powdered milk, food supplements, sugar product, soy product, and prepared meat base, using scales, graduated measures, spoons, and electric blender. Computes number of calories per fluid ounce of formula from information on labels of ingredients, and records information on gummed label and places on bottles. Pours formula into bottles, seals with nipple, protector cap, and collar, and places in autoclave for prescribed length of time to sterilize, or affixes hermetically sealed protector caps and places in commercial retort for sterilization and cooling. Removes sterilized bottles from autoclave and stores in refrigerator or removes bottles from retort after cooling process and packages for delivery. Washes and sterilizes empty bottles and unused nipples and caps. May be known according to specific duties performed as Formula Bottler (dairy products); Formula Maker (dairy products).
GOE: 05.10.08 STRENGTH: L GED: R2 M2 L2 SVP: 3 DLU: 77

520.487-018 PANTRY WORKER (sugar & conf.)

Assembles, weighs, and measures candy ingredients, such as egg whites and butter, according to formula: Selects batch formula cards in accordance with type of batch scheduled. Weighs dry ingredients on scales and pours liquid ingredients into graduated containers. Attaches formula card and identifying batch number to containers of measured ingredients for use by CANDY MAKERS (sugar & conf.). Keeps record of batches produced. May weigh ingredients, such as nuts, flavoring, extracts, condiments, and shortening that are not metered mechanically.
GOE: 06.04.28 STRENGTH: L GED: R3 M2 L2 SVP: 3 DLU: 77

520.565-010 CHURNER (oils & grease) alternate titles: picker-box operator

Tends one or more machines that churn processed shortening and margarine to obtain specified viscosity of mixture: Observes flow of stock in churner to avoid spilling. Adjusts valves to control and direct overflow into reprocessing tank. Starts machine to churn mixture, stops machine when specified viscosity is obtained, and opens valves and starts pump to transfer mixture. Adjusts governor to regulate speed of pump that transfers product into packaging machines. Collects and weighs sample of shortening at prescribed intervals to determine amount of nitrogen gas or air content in batch, using balance scale. Notifies VOTATOR-MACHINE OPERATOR (meat products; oils & grease) to add or delete nitrogen gas, according to weight standards. Adjusts valves to keep specified temperature in churner. Observes pressure and temperature gauges, and records readings. Cleans equipment and lines, using pressurized steam and nitrogen gas.
GOE: 06.04.15 STRENGTH: L GED: R2 M1 L1 SVP: 2 DLU: 77

520.585-010 BLENDER (bakery products) alternate titles: bolter; flour mixer; mill operator

Tends machine that blends flour: Loads pallets with sacks of specified flour and transports them to blending machine, using truck. Dumps flour from sacks into machine hoppers. Holds sack over suction bag-cleaning device to remove remaining flour dust. Starts blender and turns dials to regulate speed of screw conveyors that mix flour in prescribed ratios. Records weights of flours blended.
GOE: 06.04.15 STRENGTH: H GED: R1 M1 L1 SVP: 2 DLU: 77

520.585-014 BROTH MIXER (bakery products) alternate titles: broth setter

Tends flour sifter and vats to mix fermenting, oxidizing, and shortening solutions, according to formula: Dumps flour from bins into sifting machine, using mechanical tipping apparatus or power chain hoist. Opens valve, meters specified amount of water into fermenting vats, and adjusts thermostat to heat water to specified temperature. Measures or weighs yeast food, milk solids, salt, sugar, and enrichment ingredients, according to formula, and dumps ingredients into vats. Starts vat agitators and adds yeast at specified period to ferment solution. Opens valves and starts pumps to run solution through heat regulator to dough-mixing machine. Measures specified amounts of oxidizing solution and liquid shortening and dumps them into holding tanks. Keeps record of time and temperature readings.
GOE: 06.04.15 STRENGTH: H GED: R3 M2 L2 SVP: 4 DLU: 77

520.585-018 COOLER TENDER (sugar & conf.)

Tends mixing tanks and cooling equipment that blend unslacked lime with molasses for extraction of sugar and monosodium glutamate: Turns valves and starts conveyor to fill cooler vat with specified amount of molasses and lime. Starts agitator and cooling system. Reads dials and gauges on panel control board to ascertain temperature, alkalinity, and density of mixture, and turns

valves to obtain specified mixture. Opens valves and starts pump to pump mixture to filter station. Records data, such as volume of lime and molasses used, temperature, alkalinity, and density on report form. May be designated according to machine operated as Vortex Operator (sugar & conf.).
GOE: 06.04.15 STRENGTH: M GED: R2 M1 L1 SVP: 4 DLU: 77

520.585-022 LIQUID-SUGAR FORTIFIER (sugar & conf.)
Tends mixing tanks to fortify sugar liquid extracted from beets with concentrated sugar liquids to obtain standard sugar liquor: Starts pumps and mixing tank agitators and opens valves to fill mixing tank with thin sugar juice and concentrated sugar liquid. Tests density of sugar liquor, using hydrometer. Pumps liquids into tank until specified density of liquor is obtained. Takes sample of liquor for laboratory analysis. Records operational data.
GOE: 06.04.15 STRENGTH: L GED: R2 M2 L2 SVP: 4 DLU: 77

520.585-026 SPICE MIXER (food prep., nec) alternate titles: spice blender
Tends mixing machine that blends spices: Weighs out each variety of spice required and pours or shovels them into hopper of machine. Starts machine to mix spices to specified consistency. Pulls lever to tilt machine and dump mix into container or storage bin. May sift spices before mixing, using mechanical sifter. May compare color of mixture with standard color chart to ensure color meets specifications. When mixing tea, may be designated Tea Blender (food prep., nec).
GOE: 06.04.15 STRENGTH: H GED: R2 M1 L1 SVP: 2 DLU: 77

520.587-010 PRETZEL TWISTER (bakery products)
Twists round strips of dough to form into pretzels: Picks piece of dough from conveyor and holds one end between thumb and forefinger of each hand. Flips dough into loop, and crosses and presses ends to outer circumference. Arranges pretzels on tray for baking. Records number of pretzels twisted.
GOE: 06.04.28 STRENGTH: L GED: R1 M1 L1 SVP: 2 DLU: 77

520.662-010 NOODLE-PRESS OPERATOR (food prep., nec)
Operates machine to blend ingredients, and knead, extrude, and cut dough used to make noodles: Installs specified die in press, using handtools. Adjusts press rollers to regulate thickness of dough, using micrometer and handtool. Dumps premeasured quantity of eggs into tub, sets meter, and turns spigot to admit prescribed amount of water. Starts beater to mix eggs and water for specified time. Starts pumps to transfer mixture to mixing unit of press. Opens hopper to admit flour into mixing unit and starts press to process mixture. Turns screw to set speed of knives to cut product to specified length. Patrols drying chambers and observes temperature and humidity readings recorded on charts for variation in drying procedure. Reports chart deviations to production manager. Records type of product, date, and time of entry and discharge of product from drying chambers.
GOE: 06.02.15 STRENGTH: M GED: R3 M3 L2 SVP: 6 DLU: 77

520.665-010 MINGLER OPERATOR (sugar & conf.)
Tends minglers that mix raw sugar and affination (syrup) to prepare raw magma of specified density: Starts mingler and signals MELT-HOUSE DRAG OPERATOR (sugar & conf.), using bell, to start flow of sugar to minglers. Turns valve to start flow of affination into minglers. Regulates speed of mingler and controls flow of affination to maintain magma at specified density and level in receiving tanks.
GOE: 06.04.15 STRENGTH: M GED: R2 M1 L1 SVP: 3 DLU: 77

520.665-014 MIXING-MACHINE OPERATOR (food prep., nec)
Tends machine that mixes compressed yeast with oils and whiteners preparatory to extrusion and packing: Signals worker to fill mixer with specified amount of compressed yeast. Pours specified quantity of cutting oils and whitening agents into yeast and starts agitators to mix ingredients for specified time. Observes and feels mixed yeast to determine its consistency and pours specified amount of water into yeast to achieve required consistency. Starts screw conveyor to transfer yeast to extruders.
GOE: 06.04.15 STRENGTH: M GED: R2 M1 L1 SVP: 2 DLU: 77

520.665-018 STARCH-TREATING ASSISTANT (grain-feed mills)
Tends mixing and blending tanks, and auxiliary equipment to assist in preparing starch blends from raw starch suspensions: Dumps specified amount of chemicals into mixing tank to prepare chemical solutions. Observes signals from DRY-STARCH OPERATOR (grain-feed mills) and pushes or pulls switches, and turns valves to start pumps, heaters, and agitators, and to admit raw starch and chemical solutions into blending tanks. Draws samples of mixtures for testing. Monitors thermometers, meters, and gauges, to ensure that filters, shakers, centrifugals, and driers are operating efficiently. Reports equipment malfunctioning to DRY-STARCH OPERATOR (grain-feed mills).
GOE: 06.04.15 STRENGTH: H GED: R3 M2 L2 SVP: 4 DLU: 77

520.682-010 BLENDING-PLANT OPERATOR (oils & grease)
Controls equipment to weigh and mix vegetable oils for products, such as salad oils, shortening, and margarine, according to formula: Opens valves to pump oils from storage tanks to scale tank. Weighs oils and pumps specified quantity of each oil into blending tank. Draws off sample of mixed oil and examines it for texture and color. Sends sample to laboratory for chemical analysis. Turns valves to make adjustments to blending process according to results of tests. Pumps mixed oil to storage tanks.
GOE: 06.02.15 STRENGTH: L GED: R3 M3 L2 SVP: 5 DLU: 77

520.682-014 CENTER-MACHINE OPERATOR (sugar & conf.) alternate titles: casting-machine operator; extruding-machine operator
Sets up and operates machine that extrudes soft candy, such as fondant, to form centers of specified size and shape for bonbons and chocolates: Inserts die plate in machine and tightens thumbscrews to secure plate. Examines and feels candy for specified consistency. Dumps candy into machine hopper. Starts machine that automatically feeds candy through openings in die plate and cuts off and deposits formed pieces on conveyor, or moves control to force candy through openings in die plate and moves wires that cut extruded candy to specified thickness. Weighs formed pieces at random to determine adherence to specifications. Adjusts wire or knife that cuts extruded candy to specified dimensions. When making cream centers to be coated with chocolate, may synchronize speed of center machine with enrobing machine. May be designated by product formed as Fondant-Puff Maker (sugar & conf.); Marshmallow Runner (sugar & conf.).
GOE: 06.02.15 STRENGTH: M GED: R3 M2 L2 SVP: 5 DLU: 77

520.682-018 EXTRUDER OPERATOR (grain-feed mills)
Operates dough-mixing and -extruding press to produce cereal products in form of letters, pellets, or other shapes: Cleans and installs perforated metal disk, containing openings of various shapes, in mixer. Attaches blade, using wrench, that sweeps around disk, shearing off extruded dough as it is forced through holes. Moves controls to set temperature of water, start flow of flour, water, and other ingredients into mixer, and regulate pressure forcing dough through extrusion die to maintain specified moisture content, color, and consistency of dough. May operate extruding press only, when mixing is performed by another worker. May be designated by form of extruded product as Pellet Operator (grain-feed mills).
GOE: 06.02.15 STRENGTH: L GED: R3 M2 L2 SVP: 5 DLU: 77

520.682-022 GUM-SCORING-MACHINE OPERATOR (sugar & conf.) alternate titles: gum-rolling-machine tender
Operates one or more machines that roll chewing gum into sheets and score (partially cut) sheets to specified size: Turns handwheels to adjust rollers, knives, and scoring blades on machine to regulate thickness of sheet gum and depth of scoring, according to specifications, using ruler. Starts scoring machine and flow of gum from mixer into hopper of machine. Measures width, length, and thickness of scored sheets to ensure conformance to specifications, using ruler. Examines sheets for scoring defects and completeness of sugar coating. May give directions to other workers engaged in loading and unloading scoring machine and coating gum with sugar.
GOE: 06.02.15 STRENGTH: M GED: R3 M2 L1 SVP: 5 DLU: 77

520.682-026 MOLDING-MACHINE OPERATOR (sugar & conf.) alternate titles: mogul operator
Sets up and operates machine to mold soft candies, such as gumdrops, orange slices, and jellies: Installs *mold-printing board* in machine and tightens thumbscrews or inserts wedges to secure it. Observes thermometer and turns steam valve to maintain specified temperature in candy-melting hopper. Opens valve or starts pump to fill hopper of depositing unit with fluid candy. Starts machine and turns handwheels to synchronize flow of candy from depositing spouts with speed of mold board as it passes beneath spouts for filling. Weighs formed candy for adherence to specifications and regulates spouts to increase or decrease flow accordingly.
GOE: 06.02.15 STRENGTH: L GED: R3 M2 L3 SVP: 6 DLU: 77

520.682-030 SPINNER (sugar & conf.) alternate titles: batch-roller operator; hard-candy spinner; stick-candy puller; stick spinner
Operates machine that rolls or spins hot plastic candy into rope-like strip ready for cutting: Kneads hot candy into cylindrical shape on steam-jacketed pouring plate with gloved hands. Turns water and steam valves to regulate temperature of plate. Actuates heating unit of batch roller and starts machine. Lifts candy from pouring plate and feeds candy between machine rollers. Pushes lever to reverse action of rollers to stretch and compact candy to required size strip. May feed strip, discharged from batch roller, into cutting machine. May make specified types of hard candy, performing combination of duties, such as flavoring or coloring batch; spreading soft-center mixture, such as peanut butter, jam, or paste onto partially set candy; pulling candy prior to rolling and spinning [CANDY PULLER (sugar & conf.)]; or applying varicolored candy strips along cylinder to achieve mottled effect. May control battery of machines that automatically pump soft centers into candy, roll or spin candy, size rope candy, cut it to specified size, and pass it through cooling conveyor for wrapping and packing. When preparing rolls of jelly-centered coconut candy, may be designated Coconut-Jelly Roller (sugar & conf.).
GOE: 06.04.15 STRENGTH: M GED: R3 M2 L2 SVP: 6 DLU: 77

520.682-034 CRACKER-AND-COOKIE-MACHINE OPERATOR (bakery products) alternate titles: machine captain
Operates machine to roll dough into sheets and to form crackers or cookies, preparatory to baking: Turns crank to adjust space between rollers. Selects and installs stamping or extruding die unit in machine, using wrench. Pushes trough of dough to machine and shovels dough into hopper or dumps it into hopper, using hoist. Starts machine and inserts end of dough from hopper into roller. Observes operation and removes malformed cookies or crackers. Verifies weight of samples against standards, using balance scale. Scoops such ingredients as salt, sugar, and nuts into hoppers located along conveyor belt. May be designated according to machine operated as Bar-Machine Operator (bakery

products); Drop-Machine Operator (bakery products); Rotary-Machine Operator (bakery products); or according to product formed as Fig-Bar-Machine Operator (bakery products); Matzo-Forming-Machine Operator (bakery products).
GOE: 06.02.15 STRENGTH: M GED: R3 M2 L2 SVP: 5 DLU: 78

520.684-010 ALMOND-PASTE MOLDER (sugar & conf.) alternate titles: marzipan molder

Colors, kneads, and forms almond paste into decorative shapes, such as fruits and flowers: Adds specified amount of coloring to batch of almond paste and kneads it to distribute coloring uniformly. Rolls paste into sheets or cuts pieces from lump of paste and molds into decorative shapes, using fingers. May affix trimmings, such as artificial leaves and stalks, and form designs, using fingers or pronged instrument. May paint molded products with edible coloring, using brush.
GOE: 06.04.32 STRENGTH: L GED: R2 M1 L2 SVP: 5 DLU: 77

520.684-014 ROLLER I (sugar & conf.) alternate titles: candy mixer; candy roller; center maker, hand; slab worker; stick roller

Kneads soft candy into rolls, cuts rolls into slices, and shapes slices into centers for bonbons or other candies: Dusts worktable with powdered sugar to prevent adherence of candy to table. Kneads slab of soft candy into roll and cuts roll into slices of specified size. Shapes slices to form centers for coated candies. May dump rolls of candy into hopper of machine that automatically cuts and shapes centers, or feed rolls into machine that slices them into loaf-shaped sections.
GOE: 06.04.28 STRENGTH: M GED: R3 M2 L2 SVP: 3 DLU: 77

520.685-010 BATTER MIXER (bakery products) alternate titles: mixing-machine attendant

Tends machine that mixes ingredients to produce batter for cakes and other bakery products: Positions mixing bowl under mixer and attaches water hose. Selects and installs beater in mixer, according to type of batter being produced. Observes meter and moves lever to admit specified amount of water into bowl. Dumps preweighed ingredients into bowl. Starts machine, turns cranks, and sets dials to regulate speed and mixing time. Feels texture of batter to judge desired consistency. Weighs batch of batter to ensure conformance to weight specifications. May mix dough. May be designated according to type of batter mixed as Cake-Batter Mixer (bakery products); Doughnut-Batter Mixer (bakery products); Wafer-Batter-Mixer (bakery products).
GOE: 06.04.15 STRENGTH: L GED: R3 M2 L2 SVP: 4 DLU: 77

520.685-014 BATTER MIXER (food prep., nec) alternate titles: batch mixer

Tends machine that mixes ingredients to prepare batter for ice cream cones: Dumps required number of sacks of sifted flour into mixer. Measures or weighs out specified amounts of other ingredients, such as sugar, coloring, water, and baking soda and pours them into mixer. Starts mixer and opens valve to transfer batter from mixer to storage tanks.
GOE: 06.04.15 STRENGTH: H GED: R2 M2 L2 SVP: 2 DLU: 77

520.685-018 BLENDER-MACHINE OPERATOR (oils & grease)

Tends blending machine that mixes salt with coarse-grained margarine to produce finished product: Weighs specified amount of kneaded margarine and shovels it into open top of blender. Adds specified amount of salt. Starts paddle of blender to mix ingredients. Tips mixing bowl and shovels margarine into handtrucks.
GOE: 06.04.15 STRENGTH: M GED: R2 M1 L1 SVP: 2 DLU: 77

520.685-022 BLENDER, SNUFF (tobacco)

Tends machine that blends cut leaf tobacco, toasted tobacco stems, and sweetener preparatory to being ground into snuff: Hauls tubs filled with tobacco or stems to work area. Raises side of tub and rakes tobacco and stems into hopper of blending machine. Weighs and dumps specified amount of sweetener into hopper. Starts machine and regulates speed of conveyor.
GOE: 06.04.15 STRENGTH: L GED: R2 M1 L1 SVP: 2 DLU: 77

520.685-026 BLENDING-LINE ATTENDANT (tobacco)

Tends conveyors and machines that blend various types and varieties of tobacco with domestic blends of tobacco: Starts conveyors to move continuous flow of tobacco under blenders (revolving spikes) to feeders that add specified types of tobacco, through ordering cylinder, overflow scales, and onto final blending belt. Sets timers to control blending and feeding speeds and sets flow scales to control amount of tobacco fed, following specifications. Forks specified tobacco into feeder at intervals, to obtain desired blend. Observes flow of tobacco and operation of conveyors and machines to ensure efficient operation. Records weight of each lot processed. May be designated according to type of tobacco processed as Turkish-Line Attendant (tobacco); Virginia-Line Attendant (tobacco).
GOE: 06.04.15 STRENGTH: M GED: R2 M1 L1 SVP: 3 DLU: 77

520.685-030 BLENDING-TANK TENDER (beverage; can. & preserv.) alternate titles: blender; blending-kettle tender

Tends equipment to blend citrus fruit juices: Opens valves to permit juices to flow from extractor machines to holding tanks. Fills blending tanks with required amounts of specified juices. Turns on mechanical agitators in blending tanks to mix contents, and pumps mixture to deoiling and pasteurizing machines.
GOE: 06.04.15 STRENGTH: H GED: R2 M1 L2 SVP: 2 DLU: 77

520.685-034 BRINE-MIXER OPERATOR, AUTOMATIC (can. & preserv.)

Tends machine that mixes water and salt to prepare brine solution for use in preserving or separating food products: Turns valves to transfer solution from mixing machine to storage or separator tanks. Tests specific gravity of solution with hydrometer and adds water or salt to bring solution to specified density. May clean machinery and equipment, using steam hose, soap, and brushes.
GOE: 06.04.15 STRENGTH: L GED: R2 M1 L1 SVP: 2 DLU: 77

520.685-038 CAKE FORMER (oils & grease) alternate titles: former; former puller

Tends machine that forms cooked oilseed meats into cakes prior to oil extraction: Places cloth on cake-forming tray and presses lever or pedal to position charging buggy (hopper) over tray. Releases oilseed onto tray and folds ends of cloth over oilseed meats. Lowers head (metal block) into position over tray containing meats, and pulls lever to raise tray against head and form oilseed meats into cake.
GOE: 06.04.15 STRENGTH: L GED: R2 M1 L1 SVP: 2 DLU: 77

520.685-042 CAKE STRIPPER (oils & grease)

Tends machine that removes cloth wrapper from pressed cottonseed cake: Inserts end of cloth in which cottonseed cake is wrapped into slotted shaft of cake-stripping machine. Presses pedal to revolve shaft that strips cloth from cake. Places cake onto conveyor for further processing.
GOE: 06.04.19 STRENGTH: M GED: R2 M1 L1 SVP: 2 DLU: 77

520.685-046 CANDY PULLER (sugar & conf.) alternate titles: hard-candy batch-mixer

Tends candy-pulling machine or kneads candy by hand to impart specified flavor, color, and consistency to candy preparatory to spinning and cutting: Kneads and pulls batch of candy. Adds specified amount of coloring and flavoring agents and continues kneading until coloring and flavoring are uniformly distributed and candy feels hardened enough to withstand machine pulling. Hangs kneaded ribbon of candy on hooks of pulling machine and starts machine that pulls candy until it feels sufficiently hardened to retain specified consistency after spinning and cutting. May be designated according to candy pulled as Taffy Puller (sugar & conf.).
GOE: 06.04.15 STRENGTH: M GED: R3 M2 L2 SVP: 5 DLU: 77

520.685-050 CANDY-MAKER HELPER (sugar & conf.) alternate titles: candy-cooker helper; whipper-beater

Tends candy making machines that mix candy ingredients: Weighs, measures, mixes, and dumps specified ingredients into cooking utensils. Opens discharge valve, and starts pumps or tilts cooker or kettle to pour cooked candy onto tables or into beaters. May form soft candies by spreading candy onto cooling and warming slabs, cut candy by hand or with machine knife, cast candy in starch or rubber molds, or by machine that extrudes candy. May form hard candies by hand or machine-pulling or spinning. Washes kettles, cookers, machines, and equipment after each batch. Performs other duties as described under HELPER (any industry) Master Title. May be designated according to type of candy mixed or cooked as Caramel-Candy-Maker Helper (sugar & conf.); Nougat-Candy-Maker Helper (sugar & conf.).
GOE: 06.04.15 STRENGTH: M GED: R3 M2 L1 SVP: 4 DLU: 77

520.685-054 CASING-FLUID TENDER (tobacco) alternate titles: flavoring maker

Tends vats, tanks, and pumps to mix, store, and transfer flavoring ingredients for use in making casing fluid: Pumps liquid from tank car to holding tanks and from holding tanks into vats for mixing. Adds specified amount of powdered flavoring to liquid in vat and admits steam to vat to blend liquid and powdered ingredients. Pumps mixture into aging tanks or to casing machine storage tanks.
GOE: 06.04.15 STRENGTH: M GED: R2 M1 L1 SVP: 3 DLU: 77

520.685-058 CASTING-MACHINE OPERATOR (dairy products)

Tends machine that forms, cools, and cuts process cheese into slices of specified size and weight: Places forming die into manifold of cheese hopper. Starts refrigerant pump and observes thermometer to cool conveyor to specified temperature. Starts and sets speed of cheese pump which forces cheese through openings in manifold to form ribbons of cheese of specified width and thickness. Threads ribbons of cooled cheese through stacking rolls which pile them on top of each other. Observes lighted panel buttons which indicate off-weight cheese stacks going through automatic cutter, weigher, and counter. Alters speed of cheese pump or presses button to automatically reset speed of conveyor to obtain specified weight cheese. Places cheese stack on scale to test accuracy of automatic weigher. Stops machine to clear jams.
GOE: 06.04.15 STRENGTH: H GED: R2 M2 L1 SVP: 3 DLU: 77

520.685-062 CASTING-MACHINE OPERATOR (sugar & conf.)

Tends machine that forms sugar decorations for cakes: Fills machine hopper with prepared sugar mixture. Places sheet of paper on machine bed under die. Turns handwheel on machine to force mixture through die to form decorations on paper sheet. Places filled sheet on rack for transfer to packing department.
GOE: 06.04.15 STRENGTH: L GED: R2 M1 L1 SVP: 2 DLU: 77

520.685-066 CHOPPING-MACHINE OPERATOR (meat products)

Tends machine that chops and mixes ground meat into emulsion for use in making such products as bologna, meat loaves, sausages, and wieners: Dumps

337

ground meat and premixed seasonings into chopping machine, using fork or hoist, or pulls lever to raise hopper and turns valve to feed meat trimmings into chopping machine. Pours designated amount of premixed seasonings and water or ice into chopping machine to season, moisten, and obtain specified temperature of mixture. Starts machine to mix emulsion to specified consistency. Stops machine and pulls lever to lower center core of mixing bowl and discharge emulsion into pan or truck. Scrapes emulsion from bowl. May push truck filled with emulsion to stuffing machine. May grind meat [MEAT GRINDER (meat products)]. May add ingredients, such as pickles, olives, and pimentos to emulsion.
GOE: 06.04.15 STRENGTH: M GED: R2 M1 L1 SVP: 4 DLU: 77

520.685-070   CHURN OPERATOR, MARGARINE (oils & grease)
   Tends equipment that mixes and churns ingredients to produce margarine: Turns valves to admit preweighed ingredients, such as milk, water, and oil, into mixing vat. Weighs or measures additives, such as emulsifier, preservatives, salt, and vitamins, according to formula, using scale or graduate. Dumps additives into mixing vat. Starts agitator that blends and emulsifies ingredients. Observes temperature gauge and adjusts steam valve to maintain specified temperature in vat. Stops agitator after specified period of time, and turns valve to transfer ingredients to cooling unit. May pasteurize milk [PASTEURIZER (oils & grease)]. May harden emulsion [VOTATOR-MACHINE OPERATOR (meat products); oils & grease)]. May test milk for acidity. May disassemble and clean stock lines, and change filtering apparatus. May mix ingredients for vegetable shortening and be designated Shortening Mixer (oils & grease).
GOE: 06.04.15 STRENGTH: M GED: R2 M2 L2 SVP: 2 DLU: 77

520.685-074   COCOA-POWDER-MIXER OPERATOR (sugar & conf.)
   Tends machine that mixes dry ingredients to make cocoa blends and dairy powder mixes: Weighs out specified amounts of ingredients, such as sugar, powdered milk, and cocoa, according to formula, and dumps ingredients into mixing machine. Starts machine that mixes ingredients for specified length of time. Opens machine valve and starts conveyor to transfer mixed batch to storage. Collects sample of completed mix for laboratory analysis. May add ingredients and remix batch, according to laboratory recommendation. May be designated according to product mixed as Dairy-Powder-Mixer Operator (sugar & conf.). May tend panel-controlled conveyorized system that transfers measured amounts of ingredients from respective bins to continuous mixing machine and be designated Quick-Mixer Operator (sugar & conf.).
GOE: 06.04.15 STRENGTH: M GED: R3 M2 L2 SVP: 4 DLU: 77

520.685-078   CONFECTIONERY-DROPS-MACHINE   OPERATOR (sugar & conf.)
   Tends one or more machines that extrude chocolate or nonchocolate confectionery mixture through die plate onto conveyor to form such products as stars, chips, or sheets: Attaches specified die plate to machine, using handtools. Starts machine and observes action to ensure that confection is forming according to standards. May clamp metal bar to bed of conveyor to form mixture into sheets. May be designated according to design of product as Chocolate-Drops-Machine Operator (sugar & conf.).
GOE: 06.04.15 STRENGTH: L GED: R1 M1 L1 SVP: 2 DLU: 77

520.685-082   COOKER, CASING (tobacco) alternate titles: flavor maker
   Tends heated vats to mix and cook tobacco casing fluid ingredients: Admits steam into jacket of vat. Dumps solid ingredients into vat and pours liquids from pail or turns valve to admit liquids, following written or oral instructions. Starts agitator in vat or stirs mixture with paddle to mix ingredients and prevent them from boiling over. Starts pump or removes bung from bottom of vat, after mixture is cooked into syrup, to transfer casing fluid to storage tanks. May measure specific gravity of fluid, using hydrometer, and add water, according to consistency of mix. May weigh or measure cooked ingredients.
GOE: 06.04.15 STRENGTH: M GED: R2 M1 L1 SVP: 3 DLU: 77

520.685-086   DIVIDING-MACHINE OPERATOR (bakery products) alternate titles: roll-dough divider; roll-machine operator
   Tends machines that automatically divide, round, proof, and shape dough into units of specified size and weight, according to work order, preparatory to baking: Presses buttons and turns dials or handcranks to start machines and to adjust capacity of dividing compartments and speed of feeding conveyor on dividing machine. Weighs units of dough, using balance scale, and adjusts machine when units vary from standard. Scoops flour or starch into sifters which automatically dust units of dough to prevent sticking. Observes progress of units of dough through machines that automatically round, proof, and shape dough. Turns rheostats to control speed of proofing and molding machine conveyors. Inspects shaped units of dough as they are ejected into pans from molding machine and discards misshapen units. May place dough in pans by hand, position pans in racks, and push racks to holding area for proofing. May fill reservoir of automatic feeding device with seeds, such as sesame, caraway, and poppy seeds, when processing buns. May be designated according to machine tended as Molding-Machine Operator (bakery products).
GOE: 06.04.15 STRENGTH: L GED: R3 M1 L1 SVP: 3 DLU: 79

520.685-090   DOUGH-BRAKE-MACHINE OPERATOR (bakery products)
   Tends machine that kneads dough to desired texture: Sprinkles roller and catching apron of machine with flour to keep dough from sticking. Starts machine and turns handwheels to adjust distance between rollers. Cuts off lump of dough in trough and inserts dough between rollers. Catches dough as it ex-

trudes from machine and reinserts it at different angles until texture reaches desired consistency.
GOE: 06.04.15 STRENGTH: M GED: R2 M1 L1 SVP: 3 DLU: 77

520.685-094   FEED BLENDER (grain-feed mills)
   Tends agitator tubs that blend ingredients used in making stock feed: Turns valves to admit measured amounts of materials, such as bran, gluten, and steep water into tubs, and starts paddle agitators. Feels sample of mixture to determine if feed consistency meets plant standard. Pulls lever to open sliding gate and drain mixture from tubs.
GOE: 06.04.15 STRENGTH: M GED: R2 M1 L1 SVP: 2 DLU: 77

520.685-098   FEED MIXER (grain-feed mills) alternate titles: batch-mixer operator; feeder operator; mash-feed-mixer operator
   Tends machines that mix stock or poultry feed according to formula and conveys it to packing machine or storage: Dumps specified number of sacks of meal, mash, grain, and meat scrap into machine hopper, or presses buttons on control panel to transfer individual ingredients from separate bins to batch scale hopper until specified weight of each ingredient is obtained. Weighs additives, such as minerals and vitamins, and dumps them into hopper. Starts machine to mix ingredients, and starts elevators and conveyors to transfer feed to storage tanks or packing machine hoppers. May match color of mix with standard sample by adjusting automatic feeder controls to regulate amount of ingredient in mix. May adjust nozzles, rheostat, or steam controls to spray heated molasses onto feed. May record weight of feed mixed or ingredients used. May be designated according to type of feed mixed as Dairy-Feed-Mixing Operator (grain-feed mills); Poultry-Feed-Mixer Operator (grain-feed mills); or according to ingredient mixed with feed as Limer (grain-feed mills); Molasses-Feed Mixer (grain-feed mills). May tend machines that automatically weigh out specified amounts of mash and grain prior to mixing with ingredients and be designated Feeder Operator, Automatic (grain-feed mills).
GOE: 06.04.15 STRENGTH: H GED: R2 M2 L2 SVP: 2 DLU: 77

520.685-102   FLAKING-ROLL OPERATOR (grain-feed mills) alternate titles: flake-or-shred-roll operator; roll operator
   Tends machine containing rolls that form cooked grain into flakes, shredded biscuits, or other shapes to produce cereal products: Moves controls to start pairs of rollers rotating and to convey cooked grain to roll feeders. Turns dials and handwheels to adjust pressure of rollers to maintain specified thickness and consistency of formed product, as indicated by feel and visual inspection, and to control rate of feed of grain through feeding mechanism. Replaces worn knives used to scrape formed grain from roller surface, using handtools.
GOE: 06.04.15 STRENGTH: L GED: R3 M1 L1 SVP: 3 DLU: 77

520.685-106   FLOUR BLENDER (grain-feed mills) alternate titles: blender
   Tends machines that blend and sift flour, and conveyors that carry flour between machines: Starts screw conveyors or turns valves on feed chutes to transfer flour from storage bins to mixing machine, or dumps designated bags of flour into hopper of machine. Starts machine to mix flour and pulls lever to open gate and allow blended flour to flow from machine. Starts separator that sifts mixed flour to remove lumps. Starts conveyors that transfer blended and sifted flour to packing machine.
GOE: 06.04.15 STRENGTH: H GED: R2 M1 L1 SVP: 3 DLU: 77

520.685-110   GREEN-COFFEE BLENDER (food prep., nec) alternate titles: coffee blender
   Tends machines that blend various grades of green coffee beans: Transfers sacks of specified grades of green coffee beans to dumping chute, using handtruck. Empties beans onto chute. Starts machine that mixes coffee beans. Pulls levers to dump mixed coffee beans into elevators that convey them to cleaning and storage areas.
GOE: 06.04.15 STRENGTH: H GED: R2 M1 L2 SVP: 2 DLU: 77

520.685-114   ICING MIXER (bakery products) alternate titles: filler mixer
   Tends equipment that mixes ingredients for icing or filling bakery products: Weighs and measures ingredients, such as sugar, chocolate, food coloring, and pulped or ground fruit or nuts, according to recipe. Dumps ingredients into mixing bowl. Selects and installs beater arms in mixing machine, using wrench. Turns dials and pushes buttons to set mixing time, temperature, and speed to start machine. Pours measured amount of water from container into mixing bowl, and adds additional ingredients, as necessary, during mixing cycle to ensure that icing or filling meets company standards. Observes and feels texture of mix to determine when desired consistency has been obtained. May cook some types of icings or fillings in steam-jacketed kettles. May mix meringue for pie topping. May be designated according to product mixed or cooked as Cooker, Pie Filling (bakery products); Fruit Mixer (bakery products); Pie-Filling Mixer (bakery products).
GOE: 06.04.15 STRENGTH: H GED: R3 M1 L2 SVP: 3 DLU: 78

520.685-118   KETTLE TENDER (sugar & conf.)
   Tends machine that mixes chewing gum base with powdered sugar: Places spout of vibrating hopper, containing powdered sugar, in top of mixing machine and starts vibrator and mixer. Places container on scale under spout of centrifuge machine and opens valve to allow specified amount of gum base to fill container. Positions container over mixer and opens discharge valve to allow gum base to flow into mixer. Dumps gum requiring reprocessing into mixer to mix with new batch. May substitute glucose syrup for powdered sugar.

GOE: 06.04.15 STRENGTH: H GED: R2 M1 L1 SVP: 2 DLU: 77

520.685-122 LOZENGE-DOUGH MIXER (sugar & conf.)

Tends machine that mixes formulated ingredients, such as sugar, syrup, and flavoring to make dough for candy lozenges: Weighs and measures ingredients according to formula, and dumps specified quantity of ingredients into trough of mixing machine. Starts machine that kneads and mixes ingredients, forming dough. Examines and feels mixture for specified consistency and to determine need for additional ground sugar or other ingredients. Scoops lozenge mixture onto tray for further processing. May be designated according to product mixed as Kiss Mixer (sugar & conf.); Mint-Lozenge Mixer (sugar & conf.).
GOE: 06.04.15 STRENGTH: H GED: R2 M2 L2 SVP: 4 DLU: 77

520.685-130 MASH GRINDER (dairy products)

Tends mill and agitating vat that grind and mix flour and malt with water, to make malted milk mash: Turns water valve to fill vat and starts grinder and agitator. Transfers flour and malt from storage silo by moving microswitch controls to deposit specified amounts through automatic scale hopper into mill or by placing counters on meters and starting conveyors that carry measured amounts through grinder into vat. Observes ammeter, and grain and water meters to detect deviations from specifications, and moves levers to alter grain and water flow. Pumps mash to mash kettles. May heat mash by mixing steam with water.
GOE: 06.04.15 STRENGTH: H GED: R2 M2 L2 SVP: 2 DLU: 77

520.685-134 MILL FEEDER (grain-feed mills)

Tends machine that mixes meat scraps, used in poultry feed, into uniform mixture: Starts machine and opens slide gate in hopper to feed scraps into machine. Observes meter and adjusts slide gates in feed hopper to regulate flow of material into machine.
GOE: 06.04.15 STRENGTH: M GED: R1 M1 L1 SVP: 2 DLU: 77

520.685-138 MIXER (food prep., nec)

Tends automatic grinding and blending machine to prepare condiments, such as dry and liquid salad dressing mixes, spaghetti sauce mix, garlic spread, and seasoning salts: Weighs out and measures ingredients, such as spices, oils, cheese, and salt. Dumps ingredients into hopper of machine and turns valve to admit specified amounts of liquid ingredients into hopper. Moves controls to adjust speed of grinding rollers. Sets thermostats to maintain specified temperature. Starts machine to mix ingredients for predetermined period. May transfer ingredients from storage to work area, using lift truck.
GOE: 06.04.15 STRENGTH: M GED: R2 M2 L1 SVP: 3 DLU: 77

520.685-142 MIXER OPERATOR II (chemical)

Tends machine that mixes specified amounts of additives and raw salt to fortify salt products, such as table salt, salt tablets, and block salt: Weighs out specified amounts of additives, such as potassium iodide, magnesium carbonate, garlic, and spices, using scale, and dumps them into drum of mixer. Starts automatic weighing machine that weighs out prescribed amount of salt. Moves levers to transfer salt from scales to mixing drum and starts mixer. Pushes lever to open bottom of mixer and discharge mixed product into packing bins or into feed hopper of tablet compressor. May tend vibrating screens to size salt crystals. May be designated according to product for which salt is mixed as Mixer Operator, Raw Salt (chemical); Mixer Operator, Tablets (chemical); Mixer Operator, Vacuum-Pan Salt (chemical).
GOE: 06.04.15 STRENGTH: H GED: R2 M1 L1 SVP: 2 DLU: 77

520.685-146 MIXER OPERATOR (beverage)

Tends mixer to produce powdered drink or food: Weighs and measures ingredients according to formula and pours them into mixers, or starts conveyor to move premeasured ingredients into mixer. Starts mixer to mix ingredients for specified time. Compares color of mixture with color chart to ensure product color meets specifications. Moves lever to dump mixture into container or onto conveyor. May be designated according to product mixed as Gelatin-Powder Mixer (beverage); Soft-Drink-Powder Mixer (beverage).
GOE: 06.04.15 STRENGTH: L GED: R2 M2 L1 SVP: 3 DLU: 77

520.685-150 MIXER OPERATOR (sugar & conf.) alternate titles: five-roll-refiner batch mixer

Tends machine that mixes such ingredients as chocolate liquor, sugar, powdered milk, and cocoa butter preparatory to making sweet chocolate: Weighs and dumps dry ingredients into mixing machine by hand, hydraulic lift, or conveyor equipped with automatic scale. Observes meters and turns valves to admit measured amounts of liquids into mixer. Observes thermometer and sets thermostat to heat mixer to specified temperature. Starts mixer. Examines mixture to ensure that consistency conforms to standards. Starts conveyor to transfer finished batch to refining machine. May tend automatic sugar grinders or pulverizers [SUGAR GRINDER (sugar & conf.)]. May be designated according to type of mixer used as Melangeur Operator (sugar & conf.).
GOE: 06.04.15 STRENGTH: H GED: R2 M2 L1 SVP: 3 DLU: 77

520.685-154 MIXER-AND-BLENDER (food prep., nec)

Tends machine that mixes and blends food ingredients to produce such products as mayonnaise, mustard and salad dressing, and spices, according to formula: Weighs such ingredients as eggs, salt, spices, and sugar, using scale or weighing hopper. Dumps ingredients into mixing machine. Turns valves to permit measured amounts of such liquids as oil, water, or vinegar to flow from tanks into mixing machine. Starts machine and observes mixing to ensure thorough blending. Starts pumps to transfer contents of mixer to containers, filling

machines, or storage tanks. May grind dry ingredients, using grinding machine. May be designated according to product mixed as Egg-And-Spice Mixer (food prep., nec); Mayonnaise Mixer (food prep., nec); Mustard Mixer (food prep., nec).
GOE: 06.04.15 STRENGTH: H GED: R3 M2 L2 SVP: 4 DLU: 77

520.685-158 MIXER, CHILI POWDER (food prep., nec)

Tends machine that mixes chili powder with other spice ingredients for use as seasoning: Measures and weighs out specified quantities of ground chili peppers, garlic, salt, and other ingredients and dumps them into hopper of mixing machine. Adjusts controls to regulate steam pressure in jacket of mixer and starts machine. Compares sample of mixture with standard sample to ensure that mixture meets color and texture specifications.
GOE: 06.04.15 STRENGTH: H GED: R2 M2 L1 SVP: 3 DLU: 77

520.685-162 MIXER, DRY-FOOD PRODUCTS (food prep., nec)

Tends machine that mixes, blends, or kneads ingredients to make dry-food products, such as baking powder, gelatin desserts, pie thickeners, and ice cream powders: Weighs or measures ingredients and dumps them into mixer or opens valve to admit specified amounts of each ingredient into mixer from storage hopper. Admits steam or coolant into jacket of mixer and sets thermostat to maintain temperature in mixer at specified level. Regulates mixing time and speed for mixing, blending, or kneading, and starts machine. May perform acidity tests, using pH meter or may submit samples to laboratory. May add additional ingredients and remix batch on basis of test results or laboratory recommendation. May start conveyor to transfer dry-food product to next process. May be designated according to food product mixed as Baking-Powder Mixer (food prep., nec).
GOE: 06.04.15 STRENGTH: H GED: R2 M1 L2 SVP: 3 DLU: 77

520.685-166 MIXING-MACHINE OPERATOR (can. & preserv.)

Tends machine that mixes food ingredients for subsequent processing, canning, or freezing: Loads hopper of mixer with premeasured quantities of ingredients by hand, conveyor, bucket hoist, or by opening valves. Starts mixer and observes operation to ensure thorough blending. Pulls lever to tilt and empty mixer or uses scoop to empty mixture into chute, hopper, or container. May weigh out and measure ingredients, using platform scale and measuring containers. May observe and control conveyors and filling machines in processing line to ensure continuous operation.
GOE: 06.04.15 STRENGTH: H GED: R1 M1 L1 SVP: 2 DLU: 77

520.685-170 MIXING-TANK OPERATOR (oils & grease)

Tends equipment that mixes ingredients for use in producing margarine: Turns valve to admit liquid ingredients, such as water or milk, into mixing vat. Dips measuring stick into vat and closes valve when liquid reaches specified level. Weighs specified quantities of dry ingredients, such as salt and powdered milk, and empties ingredients into vat. Starts agitator to mix liquid and powdered ingredients for specified time. Turns valve to empty mixed ingredients from vat for further processing.
GOE: 06.04.15 STRENGTH: H GED: R2 M1 L2 SVP: 2 DLU: 77

520.685-174 MOLDER, MEAT (meat products)

Tends stuffing machine that fills molds with meat emulsion to form meat loaves: Slides mold under discharge nozzle of stuffing machine and moves lever to discharge emulsion into mold. Removes filled molds and places them on racks for further processing. May fill molds with meat cuts or whole pieces of meat by hand or using compressed air plunger and be designated Hand Molder, Meat (meat products). May stuff bologna and canadian bacon into casings by hand. May close ends of filled casings with metal clip and by tying with string.
GOE: 06.04.15 STRENGTH: M GED: R2 M1 L1 SVP: 2 DLU: 77

520.685-178 PELLET-MILL OPERATOR (grain-feed mills) alternate titles: feed-and-pellet operator

Tends machine that presses ingredients into feed pellets for poultry and stock feed: Turns steam valves to regulate temperature of machine. Observes ammeter and turns valves to regulate flow of material to machine. May adjust nozzles to regulate flow of molasses into ingredients and turn steam valves to regulate temperature of molasses. May adjust flow of air to cool pellets in cooler. May tend bucket elevator equipment to transfer pellets to storage. May adjust rollers to crush pelletized feed into crumbles. May mix poultry or stock feed preparatory to pelletizing [FEED MIXER (grain-feed mills)].
GOE: 06.04.15 STRENGTH: L GED: R2 M1 L1 SVP: 2 DLU: 77

520.685-182 PRESS OPERATOR, MEAT (meat products)

Tends machine that presses such meats as bacon slabs, beef cuts, hams, and hog butts, into shape to facilitate slicing or packing: Positions meat on table of pressing machine and depresses pedal or pulls lever to lower ram onto meat that compresses meat into shape. Removes meat from machine and places in container, or on conveyor for transfer to slicing machine. May tend slicing machine [SLICING-MACHINE OPERATOR (dairy products; meat products)]. May be designated according to cut of meat pressed as Butt Presser (meat products); Ham Molder (meat products).
GOE: 06.04.15 STRENGTH: M GED: R1 M1 L1 SVP: 2 DLU: 77

520.685-186 PRESS TENDER (food prep., nec)

Tends battery of presses that automatically mix ingredients, and knead and extrude dough for use in making macaroni products: Installs specified dies in presses, using handtools. Sets automatic weighing device. Opens valves to

admit prescribed ingredients into mixing unit and turns dials that control rate of flow of material through processing units. Starts machines that trim and rack extruded strands of long goods over drying sticks (rods) and convey them into preliminary drying chamber, or extrude short goods onto conveyor chutes leading to series of driers. Observes presses in operation to ensure progressive movement of mixture. Regulates speed of press to control product quantity. Observes color of dough and feels its consistency to determine, from knowledge and experience, if product conforms to standard. May be designated according to type press product as Press Tender, Long Goods (food prep., nec); Press Tender, Short Goods (food prep., nec).
GOE: 06.02.15 STRENGTH: H GED: R3 M1 L1 SVP: 4 DLU: 77

520.685-190 PRETZEL-TWISTING-MACHINE OPERATOR (bakery products)
Tends machine that automatically rolls, cuts to size, and twists dough to form pretzels and conveys them to oven: Turns knobs to adjust machine to roll and cut dough to specified thickness and length. Loads dough into machine hopper and starts machine. Observes processing of dough through machine to detect broken or misformed pretzels. Stops machine to clear jams. May be designated according to type of pretzel formed as Pretzel-Stick-Machine Operator (bakery products).
GOE: 06.04.15 STRENGTH: L GED: R2 M1 L1 SVP: 2 DLU: 77

520.685-194 RELISH BLENDER (can. & preserv.) alternate titles: relish maker
Tends machine that blends diced pickles with other ingredients to make relish: Weighs out specified quantity of diced pickles in barrel, using floor scales, and dumps pickles into blending tank, using automatic hoist. Pumps cooked mixture of sugar, syrup, spices, and preservatives into blending tank. Starts agitator in blending tank and observes process to ensure thorough blending. Opens valve to transfer relish to bin for packing.
GOE: 06.04.15 M GED: R2 M1 L1 SVP: 3 DLU: 77

520.685-198 ROLLING-MACHINE OPERATOR (sugar & conf.) alternate titles: candy-rolling-machine operator; cut-roll-machine operator; roller operator
Tends machine that rolls slabs of candy to specified thickness prior to cutting: Turns handwheel to adjust clearance of rollers to accommodate thickness of slab without binding. Starts machine and feeds slab of candy between rollers. Reverses rollers to return candy for removal. Readjusts rollers and continues operation until candy is rolled to specified thickness.
GOE: 06.04.15 STRENGTH: M GED: R2 M1 L1 SVP: 3 DLU: 77

520.685-202 SAUSAGE MAKER (meat products)
Tends machine that mixes ingredients, such as ground meat and condiments, to make sausage, according to formula: Weighs ingredients and dumps them into mixing machine. Starts machine that mixes ingredients. Empties mixed ingredients into containers. May grind meat. May fill casings with bulk sausage [BULK-SAUSAGE-STUFFING-MACHINE OPERATOR (meat products)].
GOE: 06.04.15 STRENGTH: M GED: R2 M1 L2 SVP: 2 DLU: 77

520.685-206 SAUSAGE MIXER (meat products)
Tends machine that mixes ground meat and condiments to make bulk sausage: Shovels meat into bowl of mixing machine and adds specified amounts of seasonings. Starts machine, observes thermometer, and adds water or ice to bowl to regulate temperature of mixture. Moves lever to tilt mixing bowl and empty contents into cart. Scrapes meat from bowl and mixing paddles.
GOE: 06.04.15 STRENGTH: H GED: R2 M1 L2 SVP: 3 DLU: 77

520.685-210 STUFFER (meat products) alternate titles: sausage stuffer
Tends equipment that forces meat emulsion into casings to make meat products, such as linked sausages, frankfurters, and wieners: Lifts lid from compression cylinder and shovels meat emulsion into cylinder. Tamps emulsion with shovel to remove air pockets and replaces lid. Turns valve to admit compressed air into cylinder. Slides casing over discharge nozzle and moves lever to discharge emulsion into casing. Ties knot in end of filled casing, or seals casing with clipping device to prevent loss of emulsion. May tend machine that automatically fills, links, and ties casings with wire band. May feed filled casing into linking machine. May tend stuffing machine that fills casings with bulk sausage and be designated Bulk-Sausage-Stuffing-Machine Operator (meat products).
GOE: 06.04.15 STRENGTH: M GED: R2 M1 L1 SVP: 2 DLU: 77

520.685-214 SWEET-GOODS-MACHINE OPERATOR (bakery products) alternate titles: bench hand, machine; dough sheeter
Tends machine that automatically rolls (sheets), curls, and cuts sweet goods into specified size and weight preparatory to making rolls, coffee cake, and other sweet goods: Fills dispensing units of machine with such ingredients as oil, cinnamon, and sugar. Adjusts valve to control sprinkling of ingredients on dough and starts machine. Picks up dough from pan and sprinkles with flour. Places dough on conveyor that feeds into sheeting rolls. Observes progress of dough rolling, and stops machine to correct malfunctions. May roll dough by repeated hand feeding through machine to obtain desired consistency.
GOE: 06.04.15 STRENGTH: M GED: R2 M1 L1 SVP: 3 DLU: 77

520.685-218 TRAY-CASTING-MACHINE OPERATOR (dairy products)
Tends conveyor-type casting machine that pumps process cheese into molds to form slices of specified size and weight: Places paper interleaves in dispenser and presses button to signal for cheese to be dropped into hopper. Starts ma-

chine that automatically pumps measured amounts of cheese onto interleaves in trays, and spreads cheese into slices of specified size. Observes weight-indicator light and moves lever to regulate amount of cheese deposited in tray. Straightens interleaves, replaces clogged dispenser, or feeder needle, scrapes cheese from tamper and vacuum openings in tray, and removes malformed slices.
GOE: 06.04.15 STRENGTH: L GED: R2 M1 L1 SVP: 2 DLU: 77

520.685-222 TUMBLER TENDER (food prep., nec)
Tends machine to season potato chips, corn chips, or similar food products: Dumps food products into drum of machine and starts machine that rotates drum. Scoops seasoning from barrel, using measuring cup, and sifts seasoning onto food product in drum. Stops machine after specified time and tilts drum to dump material into container, onto conveyor, or into hopper of bagging machine.
GOE: 06.04.15 STRENGTH: L GED: R1 M1 L1 SVP: 2 DLU: 77

520.685-226 UNLEAVENED-DOUGH MIXER (bakery products)
Tends five-position mixing machine to mix unleavened dough ingredients, such as flour, eggs, salt, and water in production of matzoh products: Pushes mixing pot onto roller platform and positions pot under automatic filling and weighing devices. Flips switch and turns controls to fill mixing pot with dough ingredients. Observes scale indicators to determine when specified amounts of ingredients have been added. Dumps premeasured pail of condiments into mixing pot. Pushes pot from roller platform onto platform of mixing machine. Depresses button to move platform to each of five mixing positions and to simultaneously agitate mixing fork in mixing pot. Depresses foot pedal to uncradle mixing pot from final position, lifts and pulls pot onto roller platform, and pushes pot onto elevator for conveying to dough-dumping station. Observes machine and auxiliary automatic pot-washing system, and stops machine and notifies supervisor when malfunctions occur. Cleans mixer cover, using brush and airhose, and unscrews mixing fork from spindle for cleaning by other worker.
GOE: 06.04.15 STRENGTH: L GED: R2 M1 L1 SVP: 2 DLU: 77

520.685-230 MIXER OPERATOR, SNACK FOODS (food prep., nec)
Tends numerically controlled equipment that automatically mixes oil, water, and mixture of grain products to make dough used in production of snack foods: Reads chart to determine time intervals and sequence for adding oil and water and length of mixing cycle. Pulls knobs to activate control panel and observes lights and dials to verify that panel is functioning. Inspects sections of mixing equipment, such as agitator blades, drum of mixer, and feed hopper to verify that equipment is clean. Adds emulsifier and contents of oil drum into reservoir prior to mixing process, using air-powered pump. Selects and pushes wheeled container of preweighed mixture of grain products or dough scrap into automatic locking device of mixer elevator. Presses specified buttons on control panel to purge air from oil and water lines, open drum door of mixer, raise and dump contents of container into mixer, and activate mixer. Observes digital timer and presses buttons at specified intervals to add predetermined amounts of oil and water, stop mixing process, and dispense dough onto conveyor for further processing. Observes oil and water pipes during mixing process to ensure that oil and water are flowing into mixer. Feels dough on conveyor to detect defects, such as excessively dry, moist, or lumpy dough. Scoops cup of dough from initial batch of mix for quality assurance testing. Notifies supervisor of dough not meeting mixing standards and of equipment malfunction.
GOE: 06.04.15 STRENGTH: M GED: R2 M1 L1 SVP: 2 DLU: 86

520.685-234 DOUGH MIXER (bakery products) alternate titles: mixing-machine attendant
Tends machines and equipment that automatically mix ingredients to make straight and sponge (yeast) doughs according to formula: Moves controls and turns valves to adjust metering devices that weigh, measure, sift, and convey water, flour, and shortening into mixer, and that measure and dump yeast, vitamins, yeast food, sugar, salt, and other ingredients into mixing machine. Turns knobs or dials to set mixing cycle time and maintain temperature of dough. Starts machine. Feels dough for desired consistency. Positions wheeled dough trough in front of mixer, opens mixer door, and starts mixer to rotate blades and dumps dough into trough. Pushes troughs of sponge dough into room to ferment for specified time. Dumps raised sponge dough into mixer, using hoist, and adds ingredients to complete mixture. Records number of batches mixed. May weigh and measure ingredients which are manually fed into mixer. May dump all ingredients into mixer by hand. May be designated according to type of dough mixed as Bread-Dough Mixer (bakery products); Cookie Mixer (bakery products); Dog-Food Mixer (bakery products); Doughnut-Dough Mixer (bakery products); Pastry Mixer (bakery products); Pie-Crust Mixer (bakery products). May be designated: Cracker-Dough Mixer (bakery products); Pretzel-Dough Mixer (bakery products); Sweet-Dough Mixer (bakery products).
GOE: 06.02.15 STRENGTH: H GED: R3 M3 L3 SVP: 5 DLU: 78

520.686-010 BALL-MACHINE OPERATOR (sugar & conf.) alternate titles: ball-rolling-machine operator; candy roller
Feeds automatic rolling machine that forms pliable candy into shapes, such as balls or disks: Applies colored candy strips onto outside of candy roll to form stripes. Places bulk candy on heated canvas belt. Rolls candy into ropelike shape. Starts machine. Feeds rolled candy into machine that cuts, rolls, cools, and drops shaped candy onto conveyor leading to wrapping department.
GOE: 06.04.15 STRENGTH: L GED: R1 M1 L1 SVP: 2 DLU: 77

520.686-014 DESSERT-CUP-MACHINE FEEDER (bakery products)
Feeds freshly baked wafers into machine that forms dessert cups: Positions and holds wafer over male die. Withdraws hand as female die forces wafer over male die to form dessert cup.
GOE: 06.04.15 STRENGTH: L GED: R1 M1 L1 SVP: 2 DLU: 77

520.686-018 FEED-MIXER HELPER (grain-feed mills) alternate titles: feeder loader; hopper loader; mixer-machine feeder
Assists FEED MIXER (grain-feed mills) to prepare stock and poultry feed: Dumps sacks of wheat, corn, or other ingredients into hopper of mixing machine. Stirs ingredients in hopper, using paddle to facilitate flow into mixer. Performs other duties as described under HELPER (any industry) Master Title.
GOE: 06.04.15 STRENGTH: H GED: R1 M1 L1 SVP: 2 DLU: 77

520.686-022 FLOUR-BLENDER HELPER (grain-feed mills) alternate titles: blender helper; bolter helper; flour-mixer helper
Fills hopper of blending machine with flour to assist FLOUR BLENDER (grain-feed mills): Moves sacks of flour from storeroom to blending machine, using handtruck, forklift, or electric hoist. Cuts sacks open and dumps contents into hopper of machine, or turns hand screws or moves levers to adjust gate openings of overhead storage bins to release specified amounts of flour into blender hopper. Performs other duties as described under HELPER (any industry) Master Title.
GOE: 06.04.15 STRENGTH: H GED: R1 M1 L1 SVP: 2 DLU: 77

520.686-026 GLUCOSE-AND-SYRUP WEIGHER (sugar & conf.)
Weighs specified amounts of glucose and flavoring syrup for use in making chewing gum: Places container on wheeled scale and positions container under glucose tap. Fills container with specified weight of glucose. Adds syrup to glucose until prescribed weight of combined ingredients is reached. Pours ingredients into mixing machine.
GOE: 06.04.28 STRENGTH: H GED: R1 M1 L1 SVP: 2 DLU: 77

520.686-030 MOLDING-MACHINE-OPERATOR HELPER (sugar & conf.) alternate titles: mogul feeder; stack puller
Feeds candy-filled starch molding trays onto conveyor or into feed rack of machine that empties trays, removes starch from candy, and deposits candy on trays or conveyor for packing and shipment. Positions trays under machine to receive molded candy. Stacks filled trays and transfers them to drying area, using handtruck. May dump trays of candy into hopper of machine that shakes starch from candy and be designated Starch Dumper (sugar & conf.).
GOE: 06.04.15 STRENGTH: M GED: R1 M1 L1 SVP: 2 DLU: 77

520.686-034 PLUG SHAPER, MACHINE (tobacco)
Feeds lumps of tobacco into shape cells of automatic press that compresses lumps into plugs of chewing tobacco.
GOE: 06.04.15 STRENGTH: H GED: R1 M1 L1 SVP: 2 DLU: 77

520.686-038 TAMALE-MACHINE FEEDER (food prep., nec)
Feeds machine that automatically encases ground meat mixture with cornmeal mixture to form tamales: Fills respective hoppers with cornmeal and ground meat mixture and presses button to start machine. Removes formed tamales from conveyor, wraps tamales in corn husks, and packs them in plastic containers.
GOE: 06.04.15 STRENGTH: L GED: R1 M1 L1 SVP: 2 DLU: 77

520.687-010 BLENDER LABORER (tobacco)
Moves leaf tobacco loaded on dollies to blending line from storage room in tobacco processing plant: Observes workers feeding tobacco onto blending conveyor to determine when supply of tobacco needs replenishing. Reads grade on card above worker and locates same grade in storage area. Pulls dolly loaded with tobacco from storage into position along blending line, using hook. Unties burlap sheet wrapped around tobacco, using pliers. Removes sheets and dollies from work area.
GOE: 06.04.40 STRENGTH: V GED: R1 M1 L1 SVP: 1 DLU: 77

520.687-014 BLINTZE ROLLER (food prep., nec) alternate titles: cheese-pancake roller
Fills precut sheets of egg dough with cheese, folds ends over filling, and rolls lengthwise to make blintzes (rolled cheese pancakes). Places blintzes on conveyor leading to packer.
GOE: 06.04.28 STRENGTH: M GED: R1 M1 L1 SVP: 2 DLU: 77

520.687-018 CANDY MOLDER, HAND (sugar & conf.) alternate titles: molder, hand; novelty-candy maker; paste worker
Pours liquid candy into chilled molds to form solid candy figures, such as animals or Christmas trees: Dumps or pours candy into warming pan and turns dial to heat product to pouring temperature. Stirs candy to facilitate melting and pours it into chilled mold. Taps or tilts mold to distribute candy uniformly throughout mold. Opens mold when candy has congealed and removes figure. May be designated by type of candy molded as Chocolate Molder (sugar & conf.).
GOE: 06.04.28 STRENGTH: L GED: R2 M1 L1 SVP: 3 DLU: 77

520.687-022 CANDY SPREADER (sugar & conf.) alternate titles: candy-maker helper
Pours and spreads batches of cooked candy, such as fudge, caramel, or toffee, in pans or trays, or onto temperature-controlled slabs preparatory to cutting: Covers pan, tray, or slab with wax paper, dusts lined pan with powdered sugar, or greases with shortening to prevent sticking. Spreads candy to specified thickness, using spatula or roller. May cut candy into sections, using knife, for use by CUTTING-MACHINE OPERATOR (sugar & conf.) or set cutter frames into candy to slice it into individual sections. May roughen surface with scraper to simulate homemade candy or sprinkle chopped nuts or fruit over candy to decorate it. When spreading and cutting bar candy, may be designated Candy Maker, Bar (sugar & conf.).
GOE: 06.04.28 STRENGTH: M GED: R1 M1 L1 SVP: 2 DLU: 77

520.687-026 CASING-MATERIAL WEIGHER (tobacco) alternate titles: casing mixer; top flavor attendant
Weighs and measures ingredients used in making casing fluid, according to formula, using scales and measuring cans. Adds or removes ingredients until specified amount is obtained and dumps or pours ingredients into cooking vats. Opens containers in which ingredients are stored. May assist COOKER, CASING (tobacco) in cooking ingredients.
GOE: 06.04.28 STRENGTH: H GED: R2 M1 L2 SVP: 2 DLU: 77

520.687-030 FILLER MIXER (tobacco) alternate titles: filler blender; scrap preparer
Mixes various types of cigar filler or plug filler tobacco: Weighs out specified amounts of each type of tobacco and dumps tobacco on floor. Forks tobacco leaves together to obtain uniform mix. Forks mixed leaves into storage bin. May fill bags with blended filler tobacco. May be designated according to type of filler tobacco mixed as Seed And Havana-Scrap Preparer (tobacco).
GOE: 06.04.28 STRENGTH: L GED: R1 M1 L1 SVP: 2 DLU: 77

520.687-034 FOOD MIXER (grain-feed mills)
Mixes specified amounts of liquid and solid ingredients together to make bird foods. Packs product into molds or containers.
GOE: 06.04.28 STRENGTH: M GED: R2 M2 L2 SVP: 2 DLU: 77

520.687-038 GUM PULLER (sugar & conf.)
Conveys lump chewing gum from mixer and dumps gum into hopper of machine that rolls and scores gum sheets: Positions cart under door of mixer. Sprinkles sugar by hand over interior surfaces of cart to prevent gum from sticking. Tilts mixing machine and opens door. Pulls quantity of gum from mixer, cuts it with knife, and drops gum into cart. Pushes cart into position over hopper of scoring machine. Tilts rear of cart to dump gum into hopper, using electric hoist.
GOE: 06.04.15 STRENGTH: M GED: R2 M1 L1 SVP: 2 DLU: 77

520.687-042 HOP WEIGHER (beverage)
Weighs hops used in brewing beer: Selects bale of prescribed hops from storage area in hop room and transports bale to work area, using handtruck. Opens burlap wrapping of bale, using knife. Breaks bale into chunks and throws chunks into basket on platform scale. Fills basket to prescribed number of pounds. Wheels filled baskets to brew kettles.
GOE: 06.03.02 STRENGTH: M GED: R2 M1 L2 SVP: 3 DLU: 77

520.687-046 MEXICAN FOOD MAKER, HAND (food prep., nec)
Performs any combination of following tasks concerned with preparing and packaging Mexican ready-to-serve or frozen foods: Places portions of cooked foods on tortilla. Rolls or folds tortilla over seasoned ground meat, bean, or cheese mixture to form Mexican food item. May garnish food with cheese, peppers, olives, and other condiments. May wrap tortilla around mixture to form characteristic shape and be known as Burrito Maker (food prep., nec). May fill taco shell with meat and be known as Taco Maker (food prep., nec). May encase cheese or meat mixture in tortilla and be known as Enchilada Maker (food prep., nec). May spoon sauce and meat mixture onto tortilla shaped cornmeal dough and wrap product in corn husk or paper and be known as Tamale Maker (food prep., nec).
GOE: 06.04.28 STRENGTH: L GED: R2 M1 L1 SVP: 2 DLU: 77

520.687-050 PLUG SHAPER, HAND (tobacco) alternate titles: shape hand
Compresses lumps of tobacco into plugs of chewing tobacco in hand shapes, performing any combination of following tasks: Greases sinkers to prevent lumps from sticking, using cloth saturated with liquid paraffin or petrolatum. Places sinkers and frames into shape boxes and fills frame cells with specified number of lumps. Positions filled shape box under ram of hydraulic press and turns valve to lower ram onto shapes that compress lumps into plugs. Removes shape boxes from press and sinkers and frames from shape box. Knocks plugs from frame cells, using rake or metal bar. Stacks plugs on table for further processing. Cleans tin plates in washing machine or with cloth and water.
GOE: 06.04.28 STRENGTH: M GED: R1 M1 L1 SVP: 3 DLU: 77

520.687-054 SEASONING MIXER (meat products) alternate titles: spice mixer
Weighs and mixes seasonings, such as salt, pepper, and sage, according to formula, for use in making sausage: Mixes ingredients by hand or in machine. Dumps mixture into containers and attaches tags or marks containers with identifying information. May grind whole peppers in grinding machine. May cube eggs, pimientos, and pickles, by placing them on cutter screen and lowering press to force them through cutters. May peel and cut onions, using knife. May clip one end of meat casings with clipping tool, and stamp date and code on casings and sausage containers, using rubber stamp.
GOE: 06.04.28 STRENGTH: M GED: R2 M1 L2 SVP: 2 DLU: 77

520.687-058 SYRUP-MIXER ASSISTANT (grain-feed mills)
Empties sacks of ingredients, such as cane and beet sugar, into mixing vats preparatory to making table syrups. Carries containers and materials and cleans vats, using steam hose, as instructed by SYRUP MIXER (grain-feed mills).

GOE: 06.04.40 STRENGTH: V GED: R1 M1 L1 SVP: 2 DLU: 77

520.687-062 SPICE MIXER (can. & preserv.)
Weighs and mixes seasonings and other ingredients to prepare spice mixes, according to formula, for use in flavoring canned food products: Weighs specified ingredients, such as spices, salt, and flour, using scales. Mixes ingredients, using mixing machine, spatula, or portable mixer. Fills containers to specified weight with mix for use in canning process.
GOE: 06.04.28 STRENGTH: L GED: R2 M2 L2 SVP: 2 DLU: 77

520.687-066 BLENDING-TANK TENDER HELPER (can. & preserv.)
Assists BLENDING-TANK TENDER (beverage; can. & preserv.) 520.685-030 by directing filling of holding tanks and performing related duties: Pulls latch of lid-locking hinge or clips metal band holding lid on barrel of juice concentrate, using clippers, to remove lid from barrel. Signals INDUSTRIAL-TRUCK OPERATOR (any industry) 921.683-050 by hand to guide lifting and positioning of barrel adjacent to opening of holding tank. Manually holds barrel in contact with tank opening as barrel is tilted to dump juice concentrate into tank. Sprays inside of barrel to wash remaining concentrate into tank, using hose. Turns valve of holding tank as directed by BLENDING-TANK TENDER (beverage; can. & preserv.) to open flow of concentrate into blending tank and to fill blending tank to specified capacity. Cleans residue and film from equipment and floors following processing, using waterhose, cleaning solution, brushes, and rags.
GOE: 06.04.40 STRENGTH: L GED: R2 M1 L1 SVP: 2 DLU: 86

521   SEPARATING, CRUSHING, MILLING, CHOPPING, GRINDING, AND RELATED OCCUPATIONS

This group includes occupations concerned with setting apart materials in a mixture by filtering, sifting, straining, squeezing, precipitation, centrifugal pressure, or agitation, and breaking materials and reducing them to smaller size by compression, chipping, and smashing.

521.130-010 MILLER SUPERVISOR (grain-feed mills) alternate titles: miller, first; miller, head; mill operator
Supervises and coordinates activities of workers engaged in cleaning and grinding grain and in bolting flour to ensure milling, according to specifications. Feels flour during processing and adjusts grinding rolls and other equipment to mill product to specifications. Performs duties as described under SUPERVISOR (any industry) Master Title.
GOE: 06.02.01 STRENGTH: L GED: R4 M2 L3 SVP: 7 DLU: 77

521.130-014 SUPERVISOR, POWDERED SUGAR (sugar & conf.)
Supervises and coordinates activities of workers engaged in pulverizing and packing powdered sugar. Inspects pulverizing station to verify that grinders are not overheating, load on electrical system is within specified limits, and dust collector system is operative. Performs duties as described under SUPERVISOR (any industry) Master Title.
GOE: 06.02.01 STRENGTH: L GED: R4 M3 L3 SVP: 7 DLU: 77

521.131-010 SUPERVISOR, RICE MILLING (grain-feed mills)
Supervises and coordinates activities of workers engaged in milling rice: Reviews instructions covering grade and amount of rice to be milled, and plans operations accordingly. Issues instructions for adjusting shelling-stones, rice hullers, rice-cleaning machine, rice grader, rice polishing equipment, reel, scalping machine and other milling machinery. Observes milling process, examines rice, and issues instructions for adjustment of machinery to maintain quality and quantity of product. May inspect and repair machinery. May plan installation of machinery. Performs duties as described under SUPERVISOR (any industry) Master Title.
GOE: 06.02.01 STRENGTH: L GED: R4 M2 L3 SVP: 6 DLU: 77

521.132-010 MILL PLATFORM SUPERVISOR (sugar & conf.)
Supervises and coordinates activities of workers engaged in grinding sugarcane in series of crusher mills to extract juice: Signals workers to regulate speed of conveyors and crusher rollers. Pries cane loose from between rollers to break up jams, using wooden pole. Adjusts tension of rollers to ensure total extraction of juice. Performs other duties as described under SUPERVISOR (any industry) Master Title.
GOE: 06.02.15 STRENGTH: M GED: R4 M2 L3 SVP: 7 DLU: 77

521.132-014 SUPERVISOR, THRESHING DEPARTMENT (tobacco)
Supervises and coordinates activities of workers in threshing department of tobacco processing plant: Pushes buttons on control panels to start conveyors and machines. Observes threshing machine units to detect jams and defective machine operations. Removes clogged tobacco, using metal rod or hand, or diverts flow of tobacco to another processing line until jams have been corrected. Feels tobacco to determine moisture content and turns valves to regulate flow of steam and water into ordering machine [ORDERING-MACHINE OPERATOR (tobacco)]. Keeps payroll timecards for subordinates. Performs other duties as described under SUPERVISOR (any industry) Master Title.
GOE: 06.02.01 STRENGTH: L GED: R4 M2 L3 SVP: 5 DLU: 77

521.137-010 SUPERVISOR, PICKING (tobacco)
Supervises and coordinates activities of workers engaged in removing off-color tobacco, stem particles, and foreign matter from tobacco as it moves along belt conveyors: Observes conveyors to detect malfunctioning. Observes activities of workers picking green and dark tobacco, stem particles, and foreign matter, such as string, dirt, and paper from tobacco to ensure that tobacco is processed, according to instructions. Notifies maintenance department of major breakdowns. Turns knob and moves lever to adjust feed chutes and equalize distribution of tobacco on conveyors. Performs other duties as described under SUPERVISOR (any industry) Master Title.
GOE: 06.04.01 STRENGTH: L GED: R4 M3 L3 SVP: 7 DLU: 77

521.362-010 CONTINUOUS-ABSORPTION-PROCESS   OPERATOR (sugar & conf.)
Controls continuous absorption process equipment to remove coloring from sugar beet juice and gas regenerating furnace to reactivate carbon (burn out impurities): Starts conveyors and elevators to fill absorption tank with activated carbon. Opens valves and starts pumps to force sugar juice through carbon in tank. Observes gauges and recorder readings on panelboard and adjusts controls to obtain constant flow of juice through tank. Draws sample of juice and observes color for conformance to specifications. Diverts flow of juice through standby tank when color of juice does not meet specifications. Moves controls on panelboard to admit fuel and air into regenerating furnace, and presses button that automatically ignites fire in furnace. Starts conveyors and feeders to convey carbon from tank into furnace that removes impurities in carbon. Reads gauges and recorders and adjusts controls to regulate furnace temperature, fuel-air ratio, and feed rate of carbon into furnace. Records operating data in station log.
GOE: 06.02.15 STRENGTH: L GED: R3 M2 L2 SVP: 4 DLU: 77

521.362-014 MILLER, DISTILLERY (beverage)
Controls equipment to clean and grind whole grain for use in production of distilled liquors: Inspects carloads of whole grain to detect presence of harmful insects, such as weevils and grain beetles. Collects sample of grain from each carload for laboratory analysis. Records number of boxcar from which each sample is taken. Pumps whole grain from boxcars to storage tanks or hopper of cleaning machine, using air-conveyor chutes. Starts automatic cleaning machine that blows and sifts foreign particles, such as dirt, twigs, and stones from whole grain and conveys clean grain to storage tank for further processing. Pumps clean grain from storage tank into hopper balanced on scale and records weight of grain before dumping into grinding machine. Starts grinding machine, and regulates flow of grain from hopper. Pumps ground meal from grinding machine into scale-hopper to compute and record difference in weight of grain before and after grinding. Pumps ground meal into meal tank for further processing. Signals MILLER HELPER, DISTILLERY (beverage) to connect air-conveyor chutes to pumps and storage tanks, clean or change screens on cleaning machine, stop and start pumps, conveyors, and machines, and lubricate moving parts of machines and equipment. Makes minor repairs and adjustments to pumps, air-conveyor chutes, and machines. May be designated according to specific duties as Grain Miller (beverage); Grain-Cleaner-And-Transfer Operator (beverage).
GOE: 06.02.15 STRENGTH: M GED: R3 M3 L2 SVP: 4 DLU: 77

521.362-018 REFINERY OPERATOR (grain-feed mills) alternate titles: control board operator, sugar refining
Controls refinery equipment to produce sugar and sugar products from starch: Reads dials, meters, and gauges, and moves controls to adjust and regulate treating time, temperature, rate of flow and density of sugar liquors through filter and evaporator units. Monitors panelboard to detect and correct equipment malfunctioning. Records processing, control, and other production data in log. Directs REFINERY OPERATOR, ASSISTANT (grain-feed mills) and FILTER TENDER (grain-feed mills) when emergency operation of equipment is manually required, or in operational assignments.
GOE: 06.02.15 STRENGTH: L GED: R4 M3 L3 SVP: 7 DLU: 77

521.365-010 CHAR-FILTER OPERATOR (sugar & conf.)
Tends bone-char filters to remove soluble impurities and nonsugars from sugar-liquor solutions: Directs CHAR-FILTER-OPERATOR HELPER (sugar & conf.) in filling filter tanks with bone-char and liquor. Inspects installations to ensure that hoses are connected to specified manifold pipe. Posts data on blackboard relating to filter operations, such as starting and ending time and quality of liquor being filtered, filters broken down for char regeneration, and filters being washed to recover sugar in char. Notifies other stations when changing filter hookups to ensure flow of specified liquor. Directs helper in removing filter heads, poking filters to break up layers of diatomaceous earth, and changing manifold setups to ensure continuation of refining.
GOE: 06.02.15 STRENGTH: L GED: R3 M2 L2 SVP: 5 DLU: 77

521.382-010 EVAPORATOR OPERATOR (can. & preserv.; dairy products; sugar & conf.)
Controls evaporating equipment to concentrate suspensions and solutions to specified degree in vacuum tanks or pans: Pumps liquid into evaporator tank or vacuum pan. Moves switches to start vacuum pumps and maintain specified pressure. Turns valves to admit steam into evaporator chest, coils, tubes, or jackets and regulate steam input to maintain specified temperature. Tests concentration of evaporated solution, using refractometer and hydrometer, and adjusts feeds, temperatures, and pressure accordingly. Pumps concentrated liquid to storage. May tend auxiliary equipment, such as settling tanks, preheating tanks, condensers, and cooling equipment. May supervise workers weighing and mixing batches to predetermined formulas. May pump batch through sterilizer.

May control chiller to reduce temperature of fresh citrus juice. May be designated according to material evaporated as Evaporator Operator, Molasses (can. & preserv.); Tomato-Paste Maker (can. & preserv.).
GOE: 06.02.15 STRENGTH: L GED: R3 M2 L2 SVP: 5 DLU: 78

521.382-014 SEPARATOR OPERATOR (grain-feed mills)
Operates flotation machine to remove germs (embryos) from cracked grain, and tests product to ensure conformance with standards: Determines specific gravity of cracked grain suspension, using hydrometer. Turns valves to add grain or water to attain specified density. Starts machine that agitates suspension and permits oil-laden germs to rise to surface. Adds liquid of specified density that causes germs to float and tests residue for presence of germs. Makes iodine titration on fluid and suspension leaving germ separator, computes sulfur dioxide content from amount of iodine added, and records test findings. May turn valves to regulate flow of materials to other processes, as directed. May operate shakers to remove bran and other fibers from starch suspension.
GOE: 06.02.15 STRENGTH: L GED: R2 M2 L2 SVP: 4 DLU: 77

521.385-010 CRACKING-AND-FANNING-MACHINE OPERATOR (sugar & conf.) alternate titles: cracker-fanner operator
Tends one or more cracking and fanning machines that shell and crack cocoa beans and separate shells from nibs (cracked beans) preparatory to further processing: Starts machine rollers and blowers that shell and crack beans and starts conveyors that carry off shells and transfer nibs to treating drum. Turns handwheels to adjust roller pressure so that resultant nibs are of specified size. Moves handles to adjust air supply to blower to ensure thorough separation of shells from nibs. Observes thermometer and turns cold water valve to cool conveyor carrying beans from roaster to cracking fanning machine. May grind nibs to obtain liquid chocolate of specified consistency [LIQUOR-GRINDING-MILL OPERATOR (sugar & conf.)].
GOE: 06.04.15 STRENGTH: M GED: R2 M1 L1 SVP: 3 DLU: 77

521.462-010 REFINERY OPERATOR, ASSISTANT (grain-feed mills)
Controls semiautomatic refinery equipment to convert starch into liquid sugars and concentrate sugars to specific density: Controls pumps and flow of materials through converters, neutralizers, and evaporators, as instructed. Operates equipment manually during breakdowns [CONVERTER OPERATOR (grain-feed mills); NEUTRALIZER (grain-feed mills)]. Observes instruments to detect equipment malfunctions and reports readings to REFINERY OPERATOR (grain-feed mills). Observes equipment to detect and correct fluid leakage or spillage. Tests sample of product to verify specific gravity, acid strength, and filtration, using hydrometer and other standard test equipment. Adds acids or alkalies to neutralize converted sugar liquors, and verifies concentration, using pH meter.
GOE: 06.02.15 STRENGTH: L GED: R3 M2 L2 SVP: 6 DLU: 77

521.565-010 LIQUOR-BRIDGE OPERATOR (sugar & conf.) alternate titles: liquor-gallery operator; liquor runner
Tends equipment to regulate flow of liquor (sugar solution) from char filters to receiving tanks, as scheduled: Opens valves and starts pumps to maintain flow of liquor into specified storage tank. Places weir box (flow box) under outlet pipe from filter with flow box outlet over gutter leading to tank inlet. Changes position of weir, in accordance with notices from CHAR-FILTER OPERATOR (sugar & conf.), as prescribed by schedules, or when tests of salt content, densities, and purities indicate change in quality of liquor. Regulates flow of soft liquor bypass to attain specified color and purity of soft-sugar liquor (brown sugar). Records hourly readings of soft-liquor flow and purities. Directs LIQUOR-BRIDGE-OPERATOR HELPER (sugar & conf.) in regulating flow and routing of sweetwater and wash waters from char filters. Keeps record of filter operations. Takes samples of liquors for laboratory analysis.
GOE: 06.04.15 STRENGTH: M GED: R2 M1 L1 SVP: 3 DLU: 77

521.565-014 MASH-FILTER OPERATOR (beverage) alternate titles: filter-press operator; mash-filter-press operator
Tends filter machine to clarify and separate wort from mash: Observes pressure gauges and turns valves to permit and regulate flow of mash to filter. Starts pump to recirculate wort through filter until sample reveals desired clarity. Turns valve on signal from KETTLE OPERATOR (beverage) to sparge (sprinkle) mash residue with hot water to obtain maximum amount of wort. Measures and records specific gravity of wort with hydrometer and tallies number of barrels obtained from mash. Turns valve to allow flow of cold water to cool mash residue and filter. May be designated according to type of filter equipment as Lautertub Tender (beverage).
GOE: 06.04.15 STRENGTH: L GED: R1 M1 L1 SVP: 2 DLU: 77

521.565-018 SOFT-SUGAR OPERATOR, HEAD (sugar & conf.)
Tends centrifuging and screening equipment that separate brown sugar crystals from syrup and sifts crystals to obtain powdered sugar: Sets spinning, washing, and steam cycles on automatic centrifuges, and resets cycles as necessary to attain specified color and quality of sugar. Turns valves to regulate temperature and levels in mixers, surge hoppers, and supply bins. Gives directions to workers packing sugar in bulk bags. Ensures that containers are weighed, coded, and sealed according to specifications. Keeps production records, and prepares reports as specified.
GOE: 06.02.15 STRENGTH: M GED: R3 M2 L3 SVP: 4 DLU: 77

521.582-010 SILICA-FILTER OPERATOR (beverage) alternate titles: filter-machine operator
Operates silica-filtering machine to remove protein and yeast particles from beer: Positions filter screens between frames and lowers screens into filter tank,

using power winch. Fills mixing tank with specified amounts of silica and water. Starts agitator that mixes water and silica, and starts pump to transfer mixture into filter tank and coat screens. Turns calibrated carbon dioxide air valve to pressurize tank. Starts pump that transfers beer from storage tank through filter screens to strain protein and yeast particles from beer. Drains off sample of beer and examines it for clarity. Starts pump to transfer filtered beer to bottle-house storage tank or to lager cellars for carbonation. Removes screens from tank, using power winch, and rinses screens with water, using hose. Records number of barrels and type of beer filtered on production records.
GOE: 06.02.15 STRENGTH: M GED: R3 M1 L1 SVP: 4 DLU: 77

521.585-010 CENTRIFUGAL-STATION OPERATOR, AUTOMATIC (sugar & conf.)
Tends battery of automatic batch-type, recycling centrifugals that separate sugar crystals from mother liquor (syrup): Sets timing of cycles on control board, according to type and consistency of syrup being processed. Turns switches on control panel to start centrifugals and regulate flow of solution. Observes colored panel lights, dials, and continuous graphs, and adjusts controls to maintain specified temperature, pressure, and cycling and recycling operations. Adjusts timers or controls as necessary to obtain specified operating conditions. Observes progress of solution through loading, washing, spin drying, and dumping processes to detect faulty operation of equipment. Records operational data.
GOE: 06.02.15 STRENGTH: L GED: R3 M2 L2 SVP: 5 DLU: 77

521.585-014 MILLER (beverage)
Tends milling machine that grinds malted barley and cereals, such as corn and rice, for use in making brew mash: Starts preset milling machine and conveyor. Pulls chain to open slide gate on storage bin and drop grain onto conveyor for transfer to machine. Weighs milled grain, using scale hopper or machine. Records weight and type of product milled.
GOE: 06.04.15 STRENGTH: L GED: R1 M1 L1 SVP: 2 DLU: 77

521.585-018 POWDER-MILL OPERATOR (sugar & conf.)
Tends powder-mill pulverizer that grinds granular sugar into fondant or powdered sugar: Starts powder mill, conveyors, dust collectors, and humidifying equipment to ready station for operations. Opens valves to admit and regulate flow of sugar into pulverizer. Adjusts controls to compensate for changes and fluctuations in production. Dissolves specified amounts of sugar in water and spins solution in centrifugal device to determine starch percentage. Regulates starch flow to bring percentage within specified limits and prevent powder from caking. Dissolves other samples to test them for grist. Cleans dust lines, scrolls, and chutes and clears hopper and elevator blockades. Observes dials and gauges to ascertain that grinders are not overloaded or overheated. Inspects chains, belts, and scrolls for signs of wear. Keeps records of tests and production. May be designated according to type of sugar pulverized as Powdered-Sugar-Pulverizer Operator (sugar & conf.); or equipment operated as Fondant-Machine Operator (sugar & conf.).
GOE: 06.04.15 STRENGTH: H GED: R2 M2 L2 SVP: 4 DLU: 77

521.662-010 MILLER, WET PROCESS (grain-feed mills)
Operates fuss and impact mills to crack and grind steeped or degerminated grain, such as corn or milo, to facilitate separation of starch, bran, and gluten: Turns handwheels and moves levers to regulate pinch of buhrs and to control flow of grain through gates. Opens valve to start flow of liquid starch into mill to flush buhrs. Feels ground grain to ascertain if specified degree of fineness is attained. Signals millhouse workers to ensure continuous flow of materials to and from grinding mill. May disassemble mill to install new buhrs, using wrenches and hoist.
GOE: 06.02.15 STRENGTH: L GED: R3 M2 L3 SVP: 7 DLU: 77

521.665-010 CHAR-FILTER-TANK TENDER, HEAD (grain-feed mills)
Tends char filter tanks that remove undesirable colloids from glucose and corn syrup: Signals FILTER-TANK-TENDER HELPER, HEAD (grain-feed mills) to fill tanks with char (activated carbon) and turn valves to start flow of syrup from storage. Couples flexible pipe to filters to transfer solution to and from filters, or signals FILTER-TANK-TENDER HELPER, HEAD (grain-feed mills) to couple pipe. Collects sample of solution to examine color and measure density, using hydrometer. Reads thermometers and directs workers to turn steam valves to maintain specified temperature. Directs workers engaged in washing activated carbon and informs CHAR PULLER (grain-feed mills; sugar & conf.) when to remove char.
GOE: 06.02.15 STRENGTH: L GED: R3 M2 L2 SVP: 4 DLU: 77

521.665-014 EXTRACTOR-MACHINE OPERATOR (can. & preserv.)
Tends machines that extract juice from citrus fruit: Starts machines, observes fruit rolling down chutes, and clears jams by prodding fruit with stick. Inspects machine for proper functioning. Examines refuse to determine whether maximum amount of juice had been extracted. Notifies supervisor of needed adjustments or faulty machine operation. Stops machines when signal indicates juice tanks are filled. Lubricates and cleans machines. May make minor adjustments to machines. May change reamer heads for different fruit sizes.
GOE: 06.04.15 STRENGTH: L GED: R1 M1 L1 SVP: 2 DLU: 77

521.665-018 FILTER-PRESS TENDER, HEAD (grain-feed mills)
Tends filter presses that remove solids, such as carbon, proteins, and *filtracell*, from solution to produce glucose syrup of standard color and clarity: Turns valves to control flow of material through press. Folds and jams edges

of filter cloths between plates to seal leaks in press, using sharp-edged tool. Observes gauges for increased pressure which indicate need for cleaning presses, and notifies PRESS PULLERS (grain-feed mills) when cleaning is required. Starts agitator and pumps that transfer filtrate into tank. Washes filter cloths in washing machine. May add activated carbon to tank to decolorize filtrate. May tend vacuum or cloth filter press that removes water from corn tailings used in preparing stock feed and be known as Press Tender, Head, Feed House (grain-feed mills).
GOE: 06.04.15 STRENGTH: M GED: R2 M1 L1 SVP: 3 DLU: 77

521.665-022 RICE CLEANING MACHINE TENDER (grain-feed mills)
Tends battery of machines that clean rough grain preparatory to milling, and mill, brush, grade, and polish grain: Starts machines, such as shelling stones, grain hullers, paddy separators, grain brush, grain cleaning machine, and grain polisher. Turns wheels to adjust feeder equipment of machines. Turns valves to regulate flow of compressed air into machines to blow chaff and dust from grain. Examines grain during processing to ensure that production and quality standards are met. Adjusts machines. Opens gates on feed pipes to route grain to designated milling machines. Performs maintenance duties, such as scraping sieves in machine with stick to remove dirt, straw, or other foreign material, lubricating equipment, and tightening belts, bolts, and nuts, using mechanics handtools. Gauges height of grain in storage tank, using tape measure. Converts measurement to number of bushels in bin, using conversion chart.
GOE: 06.04.15 STRENGTH: L GED: R3 M1 L1 SVP: 3 DLU: 77

521.665-026 SIEVE-GRADER TENDER (can. & preserv.)
Tends battery of rotary or oscillating screens that segregate vegetables, such as peas and beets, according to size: Starts motors to activate screens and observes peas passing over screens to prevent clogging and overflow. Observes signal and opens hopper gate to permit peas of specified size and grade to drop into whitening trough for decolorization.
GOE: 06.04.15 STRENGTH: L GED: R2 M1 L1 SVP: 2 DLU: 77

521.682-010 CENTRIFUGAL OPERATOR (grain-feed mills; sugar & conf.)
Operates centrifugal machines to separate and wash molasses and mother liquor (syrup) from sugar crystals: Opens gate allowing sugar mass to flow into centrifuge basket. Starts centrifuge that automatically passes through cycles of spinning off mother liquor, washing off molasses, and spinning off washwater. Lifts plate covering bottom of basket, positions cutting arm over sugar and starts machine to cut sugar crystals from inside basket. Washes centrifuge, using hose. May be designated by type of sugar processed as Soft-Sugar Cutter (sugar & conf.); White-Sugar Centrifugal Operator (sugar & conf.); or purpose of operation as Cubelet-Centrifugal Operator (sugar & conf.); Low-Raw-Sugar Cutter (sugar & conf.); Melt-House Centrifugal Operator (sugar & conf.); Remelt-Centrifugal Operator (sugar & conf.); Remelt-Sugar Cutter (sugar & conf.).
GOE: 06.02.15 STRENGTH: M GED: R3 M2 L2 SVP: 3 DLU: 77

521.682-014 COCOA-PRESS OPERATOR (sugar & conf.)
Operates one or more hydraulic cocoa presses that remove specified amounts of cocoa butter (natural oil of cocoa bean) from chocolate liquor: Starts pump to remove liquor from storage to steam-heated tanks. Observes thermometers and sets thermostat to heat liquor to specified temperature. Sets pressure gauge and stroke of ram on cocoa press, according to specifications, using handtools. Starts press to activate ram that automatically fills pots with chocolate liquor, extrudes specified amounts of cocoa butter into holding tank, and ejects cocoa cakes onto conveyor. Records weight of cocoa butter as indicated on scale-equipped holding tank. May start pump to move cocoa butter into storage tank through filters or centrifugal separator to remove cocoa residue [COCOA-BUTTER-FILTER OPERATOR (sugar & conf.)]. May fill pots, remove and stack cocoa cakes, and install steel and fiber separator pads by hand when machine is nonautomatic.
GOE: 06.02.15 STRENGTH: L GED: R3 M2 L2 SVP: 4 DLU: 77

521.682-018 FILTER OPERATOR (grain-feed mills)
Operates filter machine to separate contaminants from cornstarch and controls temperature and specific gravity of starch suspension fed to filters: Turns valves to admit water to dilute starch suspension in standardization tank, until hydrometer indicates specific gravity of solution conforms to specifications. Starts pumps and turns valves to transfer starch suspension between filter and tanks, and to regulate flow of wash water to filter spray nozzles. Reads thermometers and turns steam valves to heat tank coils and maintain specified temperature of water. Assists in changing filter cloths, and repairs or replaces broken filter strings. May flush soiled filter cloths, using hose. May insert wires into filter nozzles to clear clogging. May standardize starch suspensions in batch tanks after filtering [BATCH-TANK CONTROLLER (grain-feed mills)].
GOE: 06.02.15 STRENGTH: L GED: R3 M2 L2 SVP: 5 DLU: 77

521.682-022 FLAKE MILLER, WHEAT AND OATS (grain-feed mills) alternate titles: cereal miller
Operates drier, huller, separator, steel cutter, cooker, and flake roller machines to produce wheat and oats flakes, according to specifications: Adjusts slides in chutes and turns valves to regulate flow of grain to machines. Adjusts flow of air to dry grain and feels grain to determine hulling capability. Observes hulling process and adjusts speed of machines that remove and separate hulls from oats. Turns valves to regulate temperature and moisture in cooker, and adjusts tension on flaking-machine rolls, according to hardness and size of grain.

GOE: 06.02.15 STRENGTH: L GED: R3 M2 L3 SVP: 5 DLU: 77

521.682-026 GRINDER OPERATOR (grain-feed mills) alternate titles: feed miller; gristmiller; mill operator; roller-mill operator
Operates bank of roll grinders to grind grain into meal or flour: Opens and closes slides in spouts to route grain to various grinders and sifters. Turns wheels to adjust pressure of grinding rollers for each break (passage of grain between rollers), according to grain size and hardness, and adjusts feed chutes to regulate flow of grain to rollers. Inspects product and sifts out chaff to determine percentage of yield. Adjusts rollers to maintain maximum yield. Replaces worn grinding rollers, using handtools. May sift and bolt meal or flour. May clean and temper grain prior to grinding. May direct workers who drain and temper grain and bolt meal or flour. May be designated according to grain milled as Corn Miller (grain-feed mills). May operate burr mills instead of roll grinders to grind grain and be designated Burr-Mill Operator (grain-feed mills).
GOE: 06.02.15 STRENGTH: M GED: R3 M1 L2 SVP: 7 DLU: 77

521.682-030 HULLER OPERATOR (grain-feed mills)
Operates machines to clean rice and remove hulls from rice preparatory to milling: Starts machinery, such as rice cleaner, reel, shelling stones, rice huller, and conveyor. Adjusts gate in spout to regulate flow of rice into reel. Observes cleaning and hulling processes, feels rice, and adjusts machinery to ensure rice is processed in accordance with specifications. Performs related duties, such as lubricating equipment and repairing machinery. May keep production reports. May direct workers in storage of graded rice.
GOE: 06.02.15 STRENGTH: L GED: R3 M1 L1 SVP: 5 DLU: 77

521.682-034 REFINING-MACHINE OPERATOR (sugar & conf.) alternate titles: chocolate-finisher operator; chocolate finisher; chocolate refiner; chocolate-refining roller
Operates refining machines equipped with rollers to grind chocolate paste in accordance with specifications: Starts conveyor to feed chocolate into refiner hoppers. Feels consistency of chocolate in hoppers to determine grinding required. Turns handwheels on machine to adjust clearance between rollers. Opens hopper and starts machine that feeds chocolate between rollers of refining machine. Observes thermometer or feels rollers and turns water valves to obtain specified temperature of rollers. Examines, feels, and tastes ground chocolate paste to ascertain if color, texture, and taste meet standards. Collects sample of paste for laboratory analysis. May observe flowmeters and turn valves to measure out cocoa butter, vegetable oil, and other ingredients, according to formula, and to fortify chocolate in mixing tanks. May scoop refined chocolate paste into wheeled troughs or barrels. May weigh and transport barrels to cold storage rooms, using handtruck.
GOE: 06.02.15 STRENGTH: L GED: R3 M2 L2 SVP: 6 DLU: 77

521.682-038 SHRIMP-PEELING-MACHINE OPERATOR (can. & preserv.)
Sets up and operates peeling machine to behead and peel shrimp preparatory to canning or freezing: Spaces peeling rolls on machine, according to size of shrimp to be processed and adjusts holding rack bars to intermesh between rolls, using wrenches. Turns thumbscrews to adjust spring tension on holding rack bars, according to shrimp size and turns valves to start water flow over rolls. Starts machine and feed conveyor and spreads shrimp over feed pan at head of rolls to ensure even distribution, using wooden rake. Examines samples of peeled shrimp to ensure conformance with standards. Adjusts roll spacing and holding for tension as required. Dismantles and cleans machine with high-pressure stream from water hose. May sterilize machine parts by directing hot water or live steam over them with hose.
GOE: 06.02.15 STRENGTH: M GED: R3 M1 L2 SVP: 5 DLU: 77

521.685-010 ALMOND HULLER (can. & preserv.)
Tends machine that removes hulls and foreign matter from almonds: Starts machine and dumps almonds into hopper of machine. Moves levers to control flow of almonds from hopper to machine that agitates screens or cylinders to remove hulls from almonds. Turns valve to regulate pressure and directional flow of air that separates loose hulls, twigs and foreign matter from nuts. Observes almonds as they pass on conveyor belt from machine to ascertain that hulls are removed. Changes screens or adjusts cylinders of machine to accommodate different varieties of almonds, using wrench. May sew sacks of almonds. May nail covers on crates filled with hulled almonds.
GOE: 06.04.15 STRENGTH: H GED: R2 M1 L1 SVP: 2 DLU: 77

521.685-014 ALMOND-BLANCHER OPERATOR (can. & preserv.)
Tends almond-blanching machine that removes skins from almonds: Turns valves to fill kettle of machine with water and to admit steam into heating chamber of kettle. Observes steam pressure and water temperature gauges, and turns valves to regulate steam pressure and water temperature, according to specifications. Actuates machine to start flow of almonds into kettle. Turns handwheel to adjust rollers that squeeze skins from almonds. Observes blanched (skinned) almonds as they emerge from blanching machine and makes necessary adjustments to machine to ensure that skins are removed.
GOE: 06.04.15 STRENGTH: L GED: R2 M1 L1 SVP: 2 DLU: 77

521.685-018 ALMOND-CUTTING-MACHINE TENDER (can. & preserv.)
Tends machine that dices, halves, slices, or slivers almond meats: Installs specified cutting blades, using handtools. Actuates machine to start flow of almond meats into machine. Examines cut almond meats to check for conform-

ance with cutting specifications. Adjusts cutting blades as required. Inserts different blades into machine to accommodate various sizes of almonds. Sharpens blades with file or *bench grinder*. May be designated according to function of machine tended as Dicer-Machine Operator (can. & preserv.); Halver-Machine Operator (can. & preserv.); Slicer-Machine Operator (can. & preserv.); Sliver-Machine Operator (can. & preserv.).
GOE: 06.04.15 STRENGTH: L GED: R2 M1 L1 SVP: 3 DLU: 77

521.685-022 BATCH-TANK CONTROLLER (grain-feed mills)
Tends equipment to maintain specific gravity of starch suspensions emerging from filter machines and starch-flushing system, and transfers solution for conversion into sugar and glucose: Dips sample from breaker tank and tests for specific gravity, using hydrometer. Turns valves to return suspension for reflushing if density does not meet standards. Starts tank agitators to prevent starch from settling. Turns valves and starts pumps to transfer solution to storage tanks.
GOE: 06.04.15 STRENGTH: L GED: R2 M1 L1 SVP: 3 DLU: 77

521.685-026 BLEACHER, LARD (meat products; oils & grease) alternate titles: lard maker
Tends equipment that bleaches and filters unrefined lard or edible oil: Starts pumps to draw unrefined material from storage tank into bleaching kettle. Dumps prescribed amount of fuller's earth into kettle to absorb impurities in material. Starts agitators to mix materials. Turns valves to allow steam or cool water to circulate through bleacher coils to heat or cool material to specified temperature. Draws sample of material for laboratory analysis. Dumps additional fuller's earth in kettle as directed. Inserts new filter cloths on filter plates. Starts pumps to draw material from bleaching kettle and force it through filter-press. Starts pumps to drain bleached and filtered material from filter-press tank into storage tank.
GOE: 06.04.15 STRENGTH: M GED: R2 M1 L1 SVP: 2 DLU: 77

521.685-030 BOLTER (grain-feed mills) alternate titles: sifter operator
Tends banks of sifting and purifying machines that separate fine flour from coarse flour or middlings: Opens spouts and adjusts feed slides to route flour to machines and to regulate flow across sifters without overloading. Feels sifted flour to detect uneven texture that indicates breaks in screens. Pulls screen frames from machine to locate and replace broken screens. Records weights of flour grades produced as indicated on automatic scales. May collect flour samples periodically for laboratory testing. May perform color tests of flour, comparing color of various batches to maintain quality of milled product. May be designated according to machine tended as Purifier (grain-feed mills).
GOE: 06.04.15 STRENGTH: L GED: R2 M1 L1 SVP: 3 DLU: 77

521.685-034 BREAKING-MACHINE OPERATOR (sugar & conf.) alternate titles: breaker operator; cutting-machine operator
Tends machine that breaks scored sheets of chewing gum into tablet size pieces. Starts machine and empties trays of scored gum sheets into revolving drum of machine. Inserts wire mesh basket into opening of machine to collect and withdraw gum tablets.
GOE: 06.04.15 STRENGTH: M GED: R2 M1 L1 SVP: 2 DLU: 77

521.685-038 BRINE-TANK-SEPARATOR OPERATOR (can. & preserv.)
Tends gravity-fed brine-filled tanks that separate young, tender vegetables, such as peas and lima beans, from more matured vegetables: Turns valve to add solution to tank and maintain specified level. Pushes vegetables down chute to prevent clogging, as vegetables emerge from tank. Cleans tank and work area, using scraper and water hose. May mix brine solution [BRINE-MIXER OPERATOR, AUTOMATIC (can. & preserv.)].
GOE: 06.04.15 STRENGTH: L GED: R1 M1 L1 SVP: 2 DLU: 77

521.685-042 CENTRIFUGE OPERATOR (dairy products)
Tends centrifuge machines that refine liquid wort for use in making malted milk: Assembles and attaches bowl, rings, and cover onto centrifuge, using hoist and handtools. Starts machine, observes tachometer, and adjusts controls to regulate speed. Starts pumps, turns valves, and observes gauges to convey wort through machine at specified pressure. Regulates clarity of wort by observing color and turning valves to alter pressure flow. Removes solids from machine with wooden paddle. Cleans machine with water.
GOE: 06.04.15 STRENGTH: H GED: R2 M2 L2 SVP: 2 DLU: 77

521.685-046 CENTRIFUGE OPERATOR (grain-feed mills)
Tends centrifugal separator and flotation cells that separate starch from gluten in processing milled grain: Observes recording instruments, turns valves, and moves levers to obtain specified temperatures, specific gravities, and air, water, and product flow rates in centrifuges and flotation cells. Inspects, cleans, and lubricates equipment. Observes gauges and turns valves to maintain level of wash and dilution waters in supply tanks.
GOE: 06.04.15 STRENGTH: L GED: R2 M2 L2 SVP: 3 DLU: 77

521.685-050 CENTRIFUGE OPERATOR (oils & grease)
Tends centrifuge machines to remove solid impurities and water from animal and vegetable oils: Turns valves to admit steam to jackets of machines. Starts pumps and opens valves to feed oil to machines and to transfer oil to receiving tanks. Observes gauges on machines to determine when temperature is within prescribed range. May rub oil between fingers to detect grit and reprocess oil that does not meet company standards. May open valves to pump oil through one or more settling tanks to separate water from oil. May clean centrifuge and settling tanks. Does not utilize heat when processing essential oils, such as citrus oils, due to volatility of these oils.

GOE: 06.04.15 STRENGTH: L GED: R2 M2 L1 SVP: 3 DLU: 77

521.685-054 CLARIFIER (grain-feed mills; oils & grease)
Tends equipment that removes sediment and moisture to purify oleo stock: Turns steam valve to heat clarifying tank. Positions strainers across filling vents of tank. Turns valve to start flow of oleo stock through strainers and into tank. Removes foreign material from surface of hot oleo stack, using skimmer. Observes gauges and adjusts steam valves to keep oleo stock heated to specified temperature.
GOE: 06.04.15 STRENGTH: L GED: R2 M1 L1 SVP: 2 DLU: 77

521.685-058 CLARIFIER (beverage)
Tends machine that clarifies wine prior to filtering: Starts pump to transfer fermented wine from settling cask to clarifying tank. Spreads chemicals over surface of wine to aid in clarification, and starts agitator to mix ingredients for specified period of time. Stops agitator to allow suspended matter to settle. Starts pumps to transfer clarified wine to filtering tank. May fumigate empty wine casks with bottled gas and burn sulfur sticks in casks to kill bacteria.
GOE: 06.04.15 STRENGTH: L GED: R2 M1 L2 SVP: 3 DLU: 77

521.685-062 CLEAN-RICE GRADER AND REEL TENDER (grain-feed mills)
Tends machines that clean, grade, and polish rice: Turns wheels of feeder box to regulate amount of rice on cleaning screen. Adjusts air valve to regulate air draft that removes dust and straw from rice on screen. Regulates air suction in aspirator that cools rice and removes bran. Observes rice passing through reels that separate brewer's rice (broken grains) from rice screenings (larger broken grains) and head rice (whole grains). Adjusts rice grader to ensure required separation of rice screenings from head rice. Tends machine that mixes water and corn syrup used as rice polish. Opens outlet in mixer to permit polish to flow into auger mixer and polish rice.
GOE: 06.03.02 STRENGTH: L GED: R2 M1 L1 SVP: 3 DLU: 77

521.685-066 COCOA-BEAN CLEANER (sugar & conf.) alternate titles: bean dumper
Tends machine that removes from cocoa beans, such foreign materials as stones, string and dirt: Selects bags of cocoa beans, according to instructions and transfers them to hopper of machine, using handtruck; or presses button to start conveyors that move beans from silo to hopper. Opens bags with knife and dumps beans into machine hopper. Positions conveyor spout to direct cleaned beans to specified silo for storage. Starts conveyors and machine that carry beans through air-cleaning system to remove foreign matter. Observes cleaning process to detect machine malfunction or material overflow. Removes and stacks sacks of dirt from discharge spout of air-cleaning system. Examines silo to verify conveyance of specified type of bean.
GOE: 06.04.15 STRENGTH: M GED: R2 M1 L1 SVP: 2 DLU: 77

521.685-070 COCOA-BUTTER-FILTER OPERATOR (sugar & conf.)
Tends press that separates residue from cocoa butter: Reads pressure gauge and starts pump that forces unrefined cocoa butter through filter screen to separate residue from oil and transfers refined cocoa butter to storage. Unclamps door of filter to remove screen and gain access to interior of machine. Flushes and removes residue from screen and filter interior, using scraper and water hose. May treat cocoa butter with prescribed amounts of charcoal and clay to deodorize cocoa butter in treatment tank and filter press. May tend centrifuge to separate cocoa butter from residue and be designated Centrifugal Separator (sugar & conf.).
GOE: 06.04.15 STRENGTH: M GED: R2 M1 L1 SVP: 2 DLU: 77

521.685-074 COCOA-ROOM OPERATOR (sugar & conf.) alternate titles: cocoa-mill operator
Tends automatic equipment and machinery that pulverizes cocoa cakes into powder of specified fineness and weighs and bags cocoa powders: Starts conveyors to move cocoa cakes through rollers of crusher into hammer mill for grinding into powder, through cooling chamber, and into air classification system which separates powder, according to density. Feels cocoa to ascertain fineness and collects sample for laboratory analysis. Fastens bag to holding tank outlet and pushes button to discharge specified amount of cocoa into bag through automatic weighing device. Verifies weight of filled bags, using scale. Closes bag and stacks bag on skids. May move cocoa cakes from storage area preparatory to dumping into hopper of crusher, using pallets and handtruck.
GOE: 06.04.15 STRENGTH: H GED: R2 M1 L1 SVP: 3 DLU: 77

521.685-078 COFFEE GRINDER (food prep., nec) alternate titles: granulizing-machine operator
Tends machines that grind coffee beans to specified fineness: Pulls lever or adjusts control to regulate flow of coffee beans into grinding machines. Starts machines and turns dials or moves levers to adjust grinding rollers. May control conveyors that carry ground coffee to storage bins.
GOE: 06.04.15 STRENGTH: L GED: R1 M1 L1 SVP: 2 DLU: 77

521.685-082 CORN GRINDER (food prep., nec)
Tends grinding machine that hulls cooked corn and grinds it into masa (cornmeal dough) for use in production of products, such as tortillas and corn chips: Scoops cooked corn into hopper of grinding machine or attaches pipe to outlet on soaking vat and starts pump to transfer corn from holding vat through washer and onto conveyor that carries corn into hopper of grinder. Starts grinder. Feels masa to determine consistency of grind, and adjusts grinding stones when necessary.

GOE: 06.04.15 STRENGTH: M GED: R2 M1 L1 SVP: 3 DLU: 77

521.685-086 CORN-GRINDER OPERATOR, AUTOMATIC (grain-feed mills)

Tends semiautomatic machine that crushes and rolls cooked corn into dough for use in various prepared food products: Starts machine and moves controls to set speed of grinder screws and clearance of spreader rollers to produce dough of specified texture and thickness. Fingers handful of dough to verify texture and fineness of grind. Moves controls to synchronize conveyor speed with machine action, maintaining dough supply at efficient level for production of food products by other workers.
GOE: 06.04.15 STRENGTH: L GED: R2 M1 L1 SVP: 2 DLU: 77

521.685-090 CRUSHER OPERATOR (sugar & conf.) alternate titles: carrier operator

Tends series of multiple roller mills that grind sugarcane to extract sugar juice. Moves levers to feed shredded sugarcane into mills.
GOE: 06.04.15 STRENGTH: M GED: R2 M1 L1 SVP: 3 DLU: 77

521.685-094 CRUSHING-MACHINE OPERATOR (beverage) alternate titles: grape crusher

Tends machine that crushes grapes to form must (juice, pulp, and skins of grape) for use in making wine: Starts machine and regulates rate of flow of grapes into crusher. Opens outlet valves to drain must into fermenting tanks. Starts refuse conveyor that removes stems from machine. Removes debris from crusher reservoir (sump) and outlets. Cleans and lubricates machine.
GOE: 06.04.15 STRENGTH: L GED: R1 M1 L1 SVP: 2 DLU: 77

521.685-098 CUTTER, FROZEN MEAT (can. & preserv.)

Tends machine that cuts frozen meats, such as fish, poultry, and beef into pieces preparatory to grinding: Dumps cartons of food product onto cutting table. Starts machine and positions meat in front of pusher. Starts automatic pusher or turns handwheel to push meat into cutter, and to regulate thickness of cut. May record weight of meat cut.
GOE: 06.04.15 STRENGTH: H GED: R2 M1 L1 SVP: 2 DLU: 77

521.685-102 CUTTING-MACHINE OPERATOR (sugar & conf.) alternate titles: candy cutter, machine; cutter, machine; slicing-machine feeder; stripper-machine operator

Tends machine that cuts candy, such as caramel, nougat, or fudge, in pieces or strips of specified size: Cuts slab of candy into sections, using knife. Selects cutting disks, mounted on shaft, according to specified width of cut, and installs cutting disks in machine. Places candy on conveyor that carries it under rotating disks for cutting into strips. Repositions cut strips on conveyor or feeds strips against knife so that slicing occurs at right angle to first cut, forming square or oblong pieces of candy suitable for shipment or further processing. Weighs random samples to ensure conformity of product with size and weight specifications. Dusts candy with flour or starch to prevent sticking. May tend machine equipped with two cutting heads, and device that changes feed angle so that candy is automatically sliced into strips and cut into pieces of specified size and shape. May be designated according to candy processed as Caramel Cutter, Machine (sugar & conf.); Mint-Machine Operator (sugar & conf.); Nougat Cutter, Machine (sugar & conf.).
GOE: 06.02.15 STRENGTH: M GED: R3 M1 L2 SVP: 4 DLU: 77

521.685-106 DETHISTLER OPERATOR (can. & preserv.)

Tends flotation cleaner that removes materials, such as pod fragments, leaves, or thistles from peas and other vegetables preparatory to canning or freezing: Mixes emulsion solution with water, according to standard formula. Turns valves to fill supply and separator tanks, and pretreater with water, and starts heater, pretreater pump, and recovery reel. Starts separator pump and pours emulsion and oil into air inlet pipe. Pulls lever to allow vegetables to flow into separator tank which floats foreign material out over recovery reel screen. May weigh sample of cleaned peas and compute weight loss.
GOE: 06.04.15 STRENGTH: M GED: R3 M1 L2 SVP: 3 DLU: 77

521.685-110 DRIED FRUIT WASHER (food prep., nec)

Tends machine that washes dried fruit, such as apricots, figs, prunes, and raisins preparatory to canning, packaging, or making specialty foods, such as mincemeat and chutney: Dumps fruit into hopper of machine. Starts machine that rotates fruit rapidly in water to remove dirt and automatically ejects fruit onto receiving tray. May inspect washed fruit and remove foreign matter. May be designated according to dried fruit washed as Apricot Washer (food prep., nec); Fig Washer (food prep., nec); Prune Washer (food prep., nec); Raisin Washer (food prep., nec).
GOE: 06.04.15 STRENGTH: L GED: R1 M1 L1 SVP: 2 DLU: 77

521.685-114 EGG-BREAKING-MACHINE OPERATOR (can. & preserv.)

Tends machine that breaks eggs and separates yolk from white of egg: Starts machine that automatically breaks eggs and dumps contents into individual cups. Observes eggs for specified yolk and white color, quality, and clarity. Trips cup lever to drop inferior yolk or white before cups enter separator trays. Stops machine to remove contaminated cups.
GOE: 06.04.15 STRENGTH: L GED: R1 M1 L1 SVP: 2 DLU: 77

521.685-118 EXTRACTOR OPERATOR (beverage)

Tends centrifuge or power-driven press that extracts moisture from residue of fermented mash after distillation: Pumps residue from storage tanks into centrifuge, or through filter screens and into power-driven press, that separates solids from liquids and extracts moisture from residue solids. Starts conveyor or blower system that transfers residue solids to rotary drier for further processing. Cleans and sterilizes equipment, using steam cleaning apparatus and alkali solutions. May maintain and repair equipment, using handtools. May be designated according to equipment tended as Centrifuge Operator (beverage); Press Operator (beverage).
GOE: 06.04.15 STRENGTH: L GED: R2 M1 L2 SVP: 3 DLU: 77

521.685-122 FEED GRINDER (grain-feed mills)

Tends machines that grind, cut, crimp, shell, or roll grain, hay, corncobs, chaff, and screenings for stock and poultry feed: Opens chute to regulate flow of grain into machine or pitches hay and corncobs into machine hopper. Starts machine and adjusts control to regulate speed, according to fineness of grind specified. May tend separator that cleans grain prior to grinding or to sift ground grain. May start conveyors and elevators to transfer processed feed to storage or packing machine bins. May fill sacks and weigh them on platform scale. May be designated according to machine tended as Corn-Cutter Operator (grain-feed mills); Corn-Sheller Operator (grain-feed mills); Crimper Operator (grain-feed mills); Crusher-Machine Operator (grain-feed mills); Hammer-Mill Operator (grain-feed mills); Rolled-Oats-Mill Operator (grain-feed mills).
GOE: 06.04.15 STRENGTH: M GED: R2 M1 L1 SVP: 2 DLU: 77

521.685-126 FILTER OPERATOR (beverage; sugar & conf.)

Tends filtering machines that separate liquids from slurry and remove impurities: Starts filter, and turns valves to circulate slurry through filtering machines to recover liquids from slurry. Moves controls to regulate speed of drum rotation and turns valves to regulate vacuum pressure that forces slurry through liquid. Observes discharge of filter cake from drum and adjusts controls to regulate speed of drum rotation. May remove and replace filter cloths and clean drums or plates. May tend equipment that filters, dionizes, and cools bulk wine.
GOE: 06.04.15 STRENGTH: M GED: R2 M1 L1 SVP: 3 DLU: 77

521.685-130 FILTER-PRESS TENDER (beverage)

Tends screw-type filter press that removes tartrates from wine or produces sheen on wine prior to bottling: Covers filter plates with cloth pads and turns handwheel to close press. Starts press and turns valves to admit wine through filters. Starts pumps to transfer filtered wine to storage tanks or bottling room. Replaces filter pads.
GOE: 06.04.15 STRENGTH: M GED: R2 M1 L1 SVP: 2 DLU: 77

521.685-134 FILTER-TANK-TENDER HELPER, HEAD (grain-feed mills)

Tends filter tank that separates undesirable solids from glucose and dextrose under direction of CHAR-FILTER-TANK TENDER, HEAD (grain-feed mills): Couples pipe to filters and turns valves to control flow of solution from storage. Removes filter head, using wrench. Inserts charging spout into opening of filter and pulls lever of sliding gate to admit char (activated carbon) into filter. Replaces filter head, using wrench.
GOE: 06.04.15 STRENGTH: M GED: R2 M1 L1 SVP: 2 DLU: 77

521.685-138 FILTERING-MACHINE TENDER (grain-feed mills)

Tends filtering machines that separate cornstarch from undesirable protein solids: Tends machine and turns valves to admit starch suspension from tank through filters and to control flow of wash water to filter spray nozzles. Observes thermometers and turns steam valves to maintain specified temperature of water in tank. Controls flow of water into standardization tanks to regulate specific gravity of starch suspension, according to instructions from FILTER OPERATOR (grain-feed mills). Changes damaged filter cloths and flushes soiled cloths, using hose. Inserts wire into holes of spray nozzles to prevent clogging.
GOE: 06.04.15 STRENGTH: L GED: R2 M2 L1 SVP: 3 DLU: 77

521.685-142 FINISHER OPERATOR (can. & preserv.)

Tends filtering equipment that separates skins and seeds from tomato sauce, chile sauce, and catsup, prior to packaging: Installs specified screens in filtering equipment, using handtools. Places refuse drums under tank outlet to receive skins and seeds. Starts agitating paddles that force sauce through filter screens to separate skins and seeds from liquid. Dips ladle into sauce tank to obtain sample for examination. Examines sauce for consistency and presence of skins and seeds that indicate clogged or damaged filter screens. Changes damaged screens, using handtools. Starts pump to transfer filtered sauce to holding tanks.
GOE: 06.04.15 STRENGTH: M GED: R2 M1 L1 SVP: 2 DLU: 77

521.685-146 FRUIT-PRESS OPERATOR (beverage; can. & preserv.)

Tends power press that extracts juice from fruit: Positions empty filter bags between sections of press, or places frame equipped with filter cloth (blanket) on press cart. Pulls lever or turns valve to release fruit from hopper or pipeline into bag openings or onto filter cloth. Seals tops of filled bags, using metal clamps; or spreads fruit evenly over filter cloth, folds corners of cloth to cover fruit, removes forming frame, and pushes cart loaded with fruit into press. Starts press. Removes filter bags or pulls cart from press and dumps fruit pulp residue into container. May start pump to transfer juice to storage tanks. May perform duties as member of crew.
GOE: 06.04.15 STRENGTH: H GED: R1 M1 L1 SVP: 2 DLU: 77

521.685-150 GLUTEN-SETTLING TENDER (grain-feed mills)

Tends settling tanks that separate gluten from water: Turns valves to discharge gluten and water from starch tables into tank. Turns and adjusts inlet

and outlet valves to maintain constant level in tank until water has drained from settled grain. Starts pump that transfers gluten to *plate press*. Pushes remaining gluten from tank, using squeegee, and cleans tank, using hose.
GOE: 06.04.15 STRENGTH: H GED: R1 M1 L1 SVP: 2 DLU: 77

521.685-154 GRADER TENDER (agriculture)
Tends machines that clean and grade seed corn: Starts machines and opens chute gate to permit corn to flow through series of vibrating screens. Adjusts chute slides to regulate flow of corn to reciprocating screens and revolving cylinders that separate corn kernels, according to width, thickness, and length. Examines graded kernels for uniformity, using test screen. Replaces defective screens and cylinders.
GOE: 03.04.01 STRENGTH: M GED: R2 M1 L1 SVP: 3 DLU: 77

521.685-158 GRANULATING-MACHINE OPERATOR (tobacco) alternate titles: granulator operator
Tends machine that cuts tobacco into granular form and screens dust and coarse particles from granulated tobacco: Starts conveyor, cutting knives, fans, and screens. Shovels tobacco into hopper and shoves tobacco between feed rolls of machine that carry tobacco under cutting knives. Observes screening process and removes foreign material left in screened tobacco. Places boxes or trucks at discharge end of machine to catch granulated tobacco.
GOE: 06.04.15 STRENGTH: M GED: R2 M1 L1 SVP: 2 DLU: 77

521.685-162 GRATED-CHEESE MAKER (dairy products) alternate titles: grating-machine operator
Tends grinding, drying, and cooling equipment to make grated cheese: Starts grater, drying drums or drying chamber, heater, blowers, cooling cones, and hammer mill. Dumps cheese blocks into feedbox of grater, and starts ram that pushes cheese against grating wheel. Tests sample of grated cheese for moisture content, using moisture meter, and turns handles or valves to alter conveyor speed or flow of hot air in drier to obtain specified moisture content. Observes gauges on cooling chambers and milling hammers, and notifies supervisor of deviation from specifications.
GOE: 06.04.15 STRENGTH: M GED: R2 M2 L2 SVP: 3 DLU: 77

521.685-166 GRINDER OPERATOR (grain-feed mills)
Tends grinding mills that process baked or dried bulk cereal products prior to packaging: Starts grinder and opens chute gate on hopper to direct bulk cereal between grinding rolls. Sifts handful of ground and graded cereal through set of screens to determine whether cereal has been ground to specified size. Moves levers to adjust roll clearance in grinder to produce cereal comparable to that of screened sample. Cleans and replaces clogged or worn screens.
GOE: 06.04.15 STRENGTH: L GED: R2 M1 L1 SVP: 2 DLU: 77

521.685-170 HASHER OPERATOR (meat products) alternate titles: mincing-machine operator
Tends machine that chops (hashes) and rinses entrails, fat, and other condemned or inedible parts of carcasses preparatory to rendering: Starts hasher machine and feeds meat onto machine conveyor or into hopper by hand or using pitchfork or shovel. Turns valves to admit water into revolving drum of washer that rinses chopped meat. Dismantles and cleans machine, using wrench and water hose. May cut up whole carcasses, using cleaver. May chill pieces of fat with ice before hashing.
GOE: 06.04.15 STRENGTH: H GED: R2 M1 L1 SVP: 2 DLU: 77

521.685-174 HONEY EXTRACTOR (food prep., nec)
Tends machine that extracts liquid honey from combs: Places decapped honeycombs in baskets of honey-extracting machine and closes cover. Sets clock for specified time cycle and starts extractor machine to pump honey from honeycombs to drums for storage. Stops machine when time bell rings. Removes emptied honeycombs from machine and places them in vacant supers. May cut caps from honeycombs [HONEYCOMB DECAPPER (food prep., nec)].
GOE: 06.04.15 STRENGTH: M GED: R1 M1 L1 SVP: 2 DLU: 77

521.685-178 HOP STRAINER (beverage) alternate titles: hop separator
Tends machine and equipment to strain hops (used in flavoring beer) from hot wort: Turns valves and starts pumps to transfer wort from brew kettle, through straining machine, and into hot wort storage tank. Starts conveyor which disposes of hops removed from wort. Turns intake and outlet valves to control rate of straining. Observes flowmeters and pressure gauges to determine if equipment is malfunctioning. Inspects strained wort through portholes and sight glasses to ascertain if hops have been removed. Cleans interior and exterior of straining machine with water hose.
GOE: 06.04.15 STRENGTH: L GED: R2 M1 L1 SVP: 2 DLU: 77

521.685-182 HOPPER ATTENDANT (sugar & conf.)
Tends equipment that distributes and screens sugar: Opens hopper gates, and starts, reverses, or stops feed scrolls to distribute sugar to bulk systems and packing station. Adjusts feed of sugar to rotating screens that separate sugar crystals, according to size. Collects samples of grists for laboratory analysis.
GOE: 06.04.40 STRENGTH: M GED: R2 M1 L1 SVP: 2 DLU: 77

521.685-186 HOT-WORT SETTLER (beverage)
Tends equipment to fill tanks with hot wort and permit solids to settle before transferring to cooling machine: Opens valves to admit hot wort from hop strainer to storage tank. Taps (drains) filled tanks after solids have settled. Turns valves, sets float line, and pulls bottom plug to drain wort into cooling line. Climbs into empty settling tank to scrub inside and remove residue, using

hose and brush. May read gauges and record amount of hot wort received in tanks.
GOE: 06.04.15 STRENGTH: L GED: R1 M1 L1 SVP: 2 DLU: 77

521.685-190 ION EXCHANGE OPERATOR (beverage)
Tends equipment that removes chemical salts from wine: Starts pump and opens valves to circulate wine through column of synthetic resin crystals to absorb potassium ions from wine. Opens valve to admit water into column to backflush accumulated sediment. Opens valve and starts pump to circulate acid or brine solution through column to regenerate resin crystals. Notifies maintenance engineer of equipment malfunction.
GOE: 06.04.15 STRENGTH: L GED: R2 M1 L1 SVP: 2 DLU: 77

521.685-194 LABORATORY MILLER (grain-feed mills)
Tends machines that clean and grind samples of grain to obtain flour samples for testing: Pours grain into machines to remove chaff, dirt, undesirable seeds, and determine moisture content. Dumps cleaned grain into mill hopper to grind wheat into flour. Dumps flour into machine to sift it into standard flour samples. Dumps samples in container and records identifying data for laboratory information. May perform chemical tests on grain and flour samples.
GOE: 06.04.15 STRENGTH: L GED: R2 M1 L1 SVP: 3 DLU: 77

521.685-198 LINTER TENDER (oils & grease) alternate titles: ginner; linter
Tends battery of linter machines that remove linters (bits of cotton fibers adhering to cottonseed) before seed is crushed and pressed to extract oil: Starts flow of seed into machine. Observes and feels seeds that flow from machine to ensure removal of linters. Turns thumbscrews to regulate pressure of seed against saws. Removes setscrews with wrench and moves shaft holding brushes closer to saws to maintain efficient cleaning operation. May assist LINTER-SAW SHARPENER (oils & grease) to remove saw cylinder for sharpening.
GOE: 06.04.19 STRENGTH: M GED: R2 M1 L1 SVP: 3 DLU: 77

521.685-202 LIQUOR-GRINDING-MILL OPERATOR (sugar & conf.) alternate titles: cocoa-milling-machine operator
Tends one or more grinding mills that grind nibs (cracked cocoa beans) or preground nibs of cocoa bean paste to obtain liquid chocolate of specified consistency: Starts machine and opens slide gate of hopper to release nibs, or turns valve to permit paste to flow through grinding stones. Observes ammeter on machine to determine amount of current produced by friction of grinding stone, and moves handles to adjust clearance between stones. Feels and tastes liquor to ascertain if texture conforms to standards. Draws sample for laboratory analysis. Pumps liquor to storage tanks. May pregrind nibs into paste-like consistency.
GOE: 06.04.15 STRENGTH: L GED: R2 M1 L1 SVP: 3 DLU: 77

521.685-206 LYE-PEEL OPERATOR (can. & preserv.)
Tends machine that removes skins of fruits and vegetables and outer membrane of peeled citrus fruits: Turns valves to admit steam to heat lye solution in tank and to regulate lye and water sprays. Starts conveyor to carry fruit or vegetables through machine. Observes and feels fruit or vegetable emerging from machine to determine if immersion time is sufficient to ensure removal of skin or membrane. May load conveyor by hand. May prepare lye solution by dumping lye chips into tank of heated water. May scald products to loosen skin or peel and be designated Scalder (can. & preserv.).
GOE: 06.04.15 STRENGTH: L GED: R1 M1 L1 SVP: 2 DLU: 77

521.685-210 MEAL-GRINDER TENDER (grain-feed mills) alternate titles: roller tender
Tends machines that grind grain between rollers: Observes flow of grain between grinding rollers. Adjusts slides to regulate flow of grain to rollers and turns hand screws to regulate space between rollers, under direction of GRINDER OPERATOR (grain-feed mills). Pulls lever to spring rolls apart when grain stops flowing, to prevent damage to rollers. May start conveyor that transports grain from storage area to grinding machines. May lubricate machines. May obtain sample of ground grain for testing.
GOE: 06.04.15 STRENGTH: L GED: R1 M1 L1 SVP: 2 DLU: 77

521.685-214 MEAT GRINDER (meat products)
Tends machine that grinds meat for use in making such products as bologna, meat loaves, and sausages: Pushes truck of cut meat from cooler room to grinding machine. Selects and inserts grinding plate in machine for specified particle size. Shovels meat into machine hopper, using fork, and positions truck under discharge spout. Starts machine. May cut chunks of meat into smaller pieces, using power operated cleaver or slicer. May select and weigh meat in cooler room for grinding.
GOE: 06.04.15 STRENGTH: H GED: R1 M1 L1 SVP: 2 DLU: 77

521.685-218 MEAT-GRADING-MACHINE OPERATOR (can. & preserv.)
Tends grading machine that sorts almond meats, according to size: Loosens turnbuckles to open grading machine, using wrench, and inserts circular grading screens into drum of machine. Closes drum of machine, and turns knob to regulate air pressure, according to specifications. Starts flow of almond meats into machine, and starts machine that sorts almond meats by shaking action that causes smaller almond meats to drop through holes on screens and larger almond meats to run off top of screen onto conveyor belts. Observes almond meats on screen to ensure that they are sorted as required. Tightens or loosens bolt on spindle of machine to adjust shaking action of grading screen to sort almond meats as specified.

GOE: 06.04.15 STRENGTH: M GED: R2 M1 L1 SVP: 2 DLU: 77

521.685-222 MILK-POWDER GRINDER (dairy products) alternate titles: malted-milk mixer
Tends equipment that mills and sifts milk powders: Fastens specified screen in sifter, using handtools, and starts hammer mill, vibrating sifter, and tank agitator. Starts conveyor that transfers coarse, dried powder from sifter to hammer mill. Turns crank to move motor belt and alter speed of hammer mill to obtain specified consistency. Starts pneumatic vacuum blower to convey ground powder through sifter to storage tank. Fills bags or barrels with powder [PACKAGER, MACHINE (any industry)].
GOE: 06.04.15 STRENGTH: H GED: R1 M1 L1 SVP: 2 DLU: 77

521.685-226 MILL OPERATOR (grain-feed mills)
Tends mills that grind stockfeed: Turns gate valves on feed chute to regulate flow of materials into mills. Starts mills and turns handwheel to adjust distance between rollers to attain desired fineness of grind. Feels sample of product to verify fineness of grind.
GOE: 06.04.15 STRENGTH: L GED: R1 M1 L1 SVP: 2 DLU: 77

521.685-230 MONITOR-AND-STORAGE-BIN TENDER (grain-feed mills) alternate titles: storage-bin adjuster
Tends machine that blows chaff and foreign material from rice and regulates flow of rice to designated storage bins: Starts machine and turns control valve to regulate flow of rice from storage bin to feeder box. Opens valve to release compressed air into machine to blow chaff and foreign material from rice as it passes over sieves. Pulls out slide on top of storage bin to allow rice to flow into bin. Scrapes sieves in machine with stick to remove dirt, straw, and other foreign material. Lubricates equipment and tightens belts, nuts, and bolts.
GOE: 06.04.15 STRENGTH: L GED: R1 M1 L1 SVP: 2 DLU: 77

521.685-234 NUT GRINDER (can. & preserv.)
Tends machine that grinds nut meats into meal: Turns thumbscrew or handwheels to adjust distance between grinding rollers. Fills machine hopper with almond meats, and starts machine. Places container at discharge end of machine to catch emerging nut meal. Inspects sample of ground nut meal for fineness of grind, and adjusts rollers when necessary to ensure that nut meats are ground to specifications. May start vacuum hose to remove foreign matter from nut meats. May be designated according to type of nut ground as Almond Grinder (can. & preserv.).
GOE: 06.04.15 STRENGTH: L GED: R1 M1 L1 SVP: 2 DLU: 77

521.685-238 NUT-SORTER OPERATOR (can. & preserv.) alternate titles: electric-sorting-machine operator
Tends machine that separates whole nut meats from those that are chipped, broken, or wormy: Turns dials to specified settings to separate nut meats. Connects calibrator to dials to verify settings. Starts machine and observes rejected nut meats to ascertain whether machine is functioning efficiently. Examines dial settings of machine periodically, using calibrator, and adjusts dials when necessary.
GOE: 06.04.15 STRENGTH: L GED: R2 M1 L1 SVP: 3 DLU: 77

521.685-242 OILSEED-MEAT PRESSER (oils & grease) alternate titles: charger; cottonseed-meat presser; pan shaker; pan shoveler; pan shover
Tends hydraulic press that extracts oil from cloth-covered cakes of oilseed meat: Lifts cakes from cake-forming tray, using metal pan (blade), shoves cakes into compartments of press, and withdraws empty pan. Turns handwheel to raise hydraulic ram that presses cakes to extract oil from cake.
GOE: 06.04.19 STRENGTH: M GED: R1 M1 L1 SVP: 2 DLU: 77

521.685-246 PEANUT BLANCHER (can. & preserv.) alternate titles: blanching-machine operator
Tends blanching machine that removes skins from shelled peanuts: Starts machine and pours peanuts into machine hopper. Inspects peanuts as they fall from machine onto moving belt and picks out foreign matter, unblanched peanuts, and peanuts that fail to meet production specifications. May sack blanched peanuts [PACKAGER, HAND (any industry)]. May tend sorting machine that electronically locates and removes unblanched peanuts.
GOE: 06.04.15 STRENGTH: H GED: R1 M1 L1 SVP: 2 DLU: 77

521.685-250 POTATO-PEELING-MACHINE OPERATOR (food prep., nec)
Tends machine that washes and peels potatoes: Loads potatoes into hopper of machine by hand or by use of hoist. Starts machine and equipment that cuts oversized potatoes in half and conveys potatoes through washing and peeling units. Observes operation of machine to prevent jamming and ensure that potato skins are removed. In batch-type machine, adjusts timing device to control stay of potatoes in pot containing abrasive disk. In continuous-type machine, pushes lever to regulate flow of potatoes over abrasive rollers to control amount of skin removed. Inspects peeled potatoes, passing on conveyor belt, and discards rotten potatoes. Cuts up oversized potatoes and removes unsuitable parts, using knife.
GOE: 06.04.15 STRENGTH: M GED: R2 M1 L1 SVP: 2 DLU: 77

521.685-254 PROCESSOR, GRAIN (grain-feed mills) alternate titles: grain cleaner; smutter
Tends grain separating, washing, and scouring machines that remove foreign matter, such as dirt, smut, and rust, from grain preparatory to milling: Adjusts

slides in bin spouts and starts elevators to route grain from storage bins to machines. Turns valves to regulate water temperature and water level in washer, to adjust air suction to remove dust from separators, and to regulate flow of air through drier. Turns wingnuts to adjust angle of separator screens, according to grain flow and amount of refuse. Hooks bag under end of screen to catch refuse. Starts machines to process grain and observes flow entering machines to prevent overloading. Examines processed grain to verify cleanliness. Pounds chutes with mallet to dislodge clogged grain. May tend separating equipment only and be designated Separator Tender (grain-feed mills) I.
GOE: 06.04.15 STRENGTH: L GED: R2 M1 L1 SVP: 2 DLU: 77

521.685-258 PULP-PRESS TENDER (sugar & conf.)
Tends presses and auxiliary equipment that extract water from beet pulp, and mix pulp with molasses to produce animal fodder: Starts conveyors, elevator, and presses. Places gates on conveyor belts to divert pulp into automatic presses. Opens valve on molasses tank to mix molasses and pulp. Adjusts presses, valves, and flow of pulp to obtain pulp and molasses mixture with specified moisture content. Takes samples of pulp before pressing, and of pulp and molasses mixture for laboratory analysis.
GOE: 06.04.15 STRENGTH: L GED: R2 M1 L1 SVP: 3 DLU: 77

521.685-262 PULPER TENDER (can. & preserv.) alternate titles: extract operator
Tends machine that extracts juice, and separates seeds and pulp from fresh and precooked fruits, berries, and tomatoes: Places containers under discharge outlets of pulping machine to receive juice, seeds, and pulp. Starts equipment to pump or convey material through machines or dumps fruit, berries, or vegetables in machine hopper. Observes passage of juice flowing from discharge outlet to ensure that juice is free of pulp and seeds. Removes filled containers from discharge outlets. Replaces damaged or clogged filter screen, using handtools. May adjust paddles in machine, using wrench. May add measured amounts of salt to tomato juice. May heat berries in open kettle prior to processing in pulping machine. May clean and sterilize machine, using steam hose. May be designated according to product pulped as Tomato-Pulper Operator (can. & preserv.).
GOE: 06.04.15 STRENGTH: M GED: R1 M1 L1 SVP: 2 DLU: 77

521.685-266 PULVERIZER (meat products)
Tends grinding mill that grinds dried flake albumen into granules: Starts grinder mill and opens chute gate on machine hopper to direct flake albumen between grinder rolls. Fills hopper with flake albumen, using scoop. Examines granules and adjusts machine roller settings as required, using handtools, to ensure albumen is ground to specified size.
GOE: 06.04.15 STRENGTH: M GED: R1 M1 L1 SVP: 2 DLU: 77

521.685-270 RIDDLER OPERATOR (tobacco) alternate titles: tobacco cleaner; tobacco-sieve operator
Tends screening device (riddle) to separate coarse pieces of tobacco from cut tobacco: Starts riddle and observes conveyor feeding tobacco into riddle from cutting machine. Scrapes off coarse tobacco left on flat screen and returns tobacco to cutting machine. Replaces filled boxes of sifted tobacco with empty boxes. May brush tobacco from clogged screens. May be designated according to type of tobacco processed as Granulated-Tobacco Screener (tobacco); Shorts Sifter (tobacco); Tobacco-Scrap Sifter (tobacco).
GOE: 06.04.15 STRENGTH: M GED: R1 M1 L1 SVP: 2 DLU: 77

521.685-274 ROUGH-RICE TENDER (grain-feed mills)
Tends battery of machines that mill and brush cleaned rough rice: Starts machines, such as shelling stones, rice hullers, paddy separator, and rice brush. Turns feed controls to regulate flow of rice into series of machines that automatically hull rice, separate hulled from unhulled rice, brush dust from hulled rice, and blow off bran. Examines rice visually and tactually, and adjusts machines to ensure standard product. Inspects machines to ensure efficient milling. Lubricates machines and makes minor repairs.
GOE: 06.04.15 STRENGTH: L GED: R2 M1 L1 SVP: 3 DLU: 77

521.685-278 ROUTING-EQUIPMENT TENDER (grain-feed mills)
Tends equipment that routes rice to milling machines: Opens feed pipes to route rice for each lot to designated milling machines. Turns wheels, bolts, and moves levers to adjust grading machines to obtain specified proportions of broken and whole grain rice in lot being milled. Performs maintenance on mill machinery.
GOE: 06.04.40 STRENGTH: M GED: R2 M2 L1 SVP: 3 DLU: 77

521.685-282 SCREEN-ROOM OPERATOR (sugar & conf.)
Tends machines that separate sugar crystals, according to grain size: Observes machine vibrating screens to ascertain that sugar is flowing. Cleans screens with brush and regulates vibrations of screens to maintain flow. Changes screens by disconnecting sleeves, removing wing nuts, and hoisting cover, using block and tackle. Takes sample of screened sugar for laboratory analysis. Tightens machine parts loosened by vibration, using handtools.
GOE: 06.04.15 STRENGTH: M GED: R2 M1 L1 SVP: 3 DLU: 77

521.685-286 SEPARATOR OPERATOR, SHELLFISH MEATS (can. & preserv.)
Tends machine that separates shell particles and sand from shellfish meats, by water and air agitation, preparatory to blanching and canning or freezing: Turns valves to admit water and air to separator vat as shelled meats are dumped into it from peeling machine or by another worker. Adjusts air volume

and operating time according to bulk and cleanliness of meats in vat. Moves floating meats to conveyor by hand, or by using wooden paddle. Drains vat to remove shells and sand from bottom.
GOE: 06.04.15 STRENGTH: M GED: R2 M1 L1 SVP: 2 DLU: 77

521.685-290 SEPARATOR TENDER II (grain-feed mills)
Tends reels or shakers that separate and remove bran, gluten, or other insolubles from starch suspension: Starts reels or shakers. Turns valves to admit and regulate flow of liquid suspension to separators. Starts conveyor that carries off insolubles separated from suspension. Tests specific gravity of liquid starch to ascertain if separation meets standards, using hydrometer. Cleans shakers or reels with caustic solution and water hose. Replaces worn or broken bearings, springs, and other parts, using handtools. May tend driers to dehydrate brans.
GOE: 06.04.15 STRENGTH: M GED: R2 M1 L1 SVP: 3 DLU: 77

521.685-294 SHELLER II (can. & preserv.)
Tends nut-cracking machine that cracks shells of nuts and separates broken shells from nut meat: Starts machine and turns handwheels to adjust cylinders or rollers and control flow of nuts into machine. Observes cracked nuts emerging from machine to ascertain that they are cracked and separated from shells.
GOE: 06.04.15 STRENGTH: H GED: R1 M1 L1 SVP: 2 DLU: 77

521.685-298 SLICE-PLUG-CUTTER OPERATOR (tobacco) alternate titles: cheese cutter; slice-cutting-machine operator; tobacco cutter
Tends slicing machine that cuts plugs (cheeses) of tobacco into slice-plug smoking tobacco: Arranges plugs in even piles on cutting board. Starts machine and tightens setscrew to feed plugs under reciprocating knife. Holds cut slices together in form of plugs from which slices are cut, using stick. Slides sliced tobacco onto tray. Replaces dull knife blade, using wrench.
GOE: 06.04.15 STRENGTH: L GED: R2 M1 L1 SVP: 2 DLU: 77

521.685-302 SLICING-MACHINE OPERATOR (bakery products)
Tends machine that slices bread, cakes, and other bakery products: Positions and tightens cutting blades and adjusts guides to accommodate size of product to be sliced, using wrench. Starts machine. Places product on conveyor and monitors slicing action of machine. Removes sliced products from machine conveyor and places them on conveyor leading to wrappers. May tend machines that wrap and pack bakery products [PACKAGER, MACHINE (any industry) 920.685-078]. May be designated according to machine tended as Band-Saw Operator, Cake Cutting (bakery products); or according to product sliced as Bread Slicer, Machine (bakery products); Cake Cutter, Machine (bakery products); Wafer Cutter (bakery products).
GOE: 06.04.15 STRENGTH: L GED: R2 M1 L1 SVP: 2 DLU: 78

521.685-306 SLICING-MACHINE OPERATOR (dairy products; meat products)
Tends one or more machines that automatically slice food products, such as cheese or meat for packaging: Threads roll of interleaf paper into machine. Turns screws to adjust guides on machine for size of food slab, using wrench. Places slab of food on feeder bed. Presses levers to clamp chunk to bed and start feeder. Turns dials to set number and thickness of slices in each stack. Presses switch to start rotating slicer with synchronized devices that cut, count, interleaf, and stack slices of food. Weighs stack and turns dial to regulate thickness of slices to achieve prescribed weight. Removes and replaces imperfect slice with one from spare pile. Places sliced stack on packaging conveyor.
GOE: 06.04.15 STRENGTH: M GED: R2 M1 L1 SVP: 2 DLU: 77

521.685-310 SMOKING-TOBACCO-CUTTER OPERATOR (tobacco) alternate titles: tobacco cutter
Tends machine that cuts cakes of pressed tobacco (cheeses), into granular form for smoking tobacco: Places cake of tobacco on bed of machine and pushes cake between corrugated feed rollers. Catches cut tobacco on tray and feeds ends of slices between rollers, keeping slices in line. Changes dull knife blades, using wrench. Cleans machine, using steam hose.
GOE: 06.04.15 STRENGTH: L GED: R2 M1 L1 SVP: 2 DLU: 77

521.685-314 SNUFF GRINDER AND SCREENER (tobacco)
Tends machines that pulverize chopped tobacco into snuff and sift snuff through screens to remove oversized particles: Presses button to start hammer mill and observes operation of machine to ensure that tobacco is being pulverized into snuff, according to company specifications. Pushes lever to start screener vibrating to sift pulverized snuff. Picks up and rubs handful of snuff between hands to verify that oversized particles have been removed. Adjusts hammer mill or changes filter on screener as needed, using handtools. Observes flow of snuff through screw-type conveyor to ensure that sufficient amount of snuff is fed to packing machine from screener.
GOE: 06.04.15 STRENGTH: L GED: R2 M1 L1 SVP: 4 DLU: 77

521.685-318 SORTING-MACHINE OPERATOR (can. & preserv.) alternate titles: grading-machine feeder; sizing-machine operator; sorting-machine attendant
Tends automatic-sorting machine that separates fruits, vegetables, shrimp, or pickles, according to sizes: Places baskets, tubs, or crates beneath discharge outlets of machine. Starts machine and dumps boxes of fruit or vegetables in feed chute or opens supply chute to feed material into machine. Removes full containers from discharge outlets and replaces them with empty ones. Cleans, oils, and greases machine, using oilcan or grease gun. May post identifying information on containers.

GOE: 06.04.15 STRENGTH: H GED: R2 M1 L1 SVP: 2 DLU: 77

521.685-322 SPICE CLEANER (food prep., nec)
Tends machine that removes foreign matter, such as rocks, mold, and insects, from spices: Dumps spices into machine hopper. Attaches empty bag to discharge end of machine and starts machine. Inspects cleaned spices to verify that foreign matter is removed. May sew ends of filled bags, using power-sewing machine.
GOE: 06.04.15 STRENGTH: H GED: R2 M1 L1 SVP: 2 DLU: 77

521.685-326 SPICE MILLER (food prep., nec) alternate titles: spice grinder; spice-grinding-mill operator
Tends machines that grind spices, such as cinnamon and chili pepper: Opens storage hopper gate to fill hammer or rolling-type grinding mill with spice. Moves lever to control spice feed and places containers under sifting screen or discharge spout. Examines crushed spices to verify consistency of grind. Cleans or replaces rollers, sifters, and other machine parts. May be designated according to spice ground as Chili-Pepper Grinder (food prep., nec); Cinnamon Grinder (food prep., nec); or according to type of grinding machine tended as Spice Miller, Hammer Mill (food prep., nec); Spice Miller, Rolling Mill (food prep., nec).
GOE: 06.04.15 STRENGTH: H GED: R2 M1 L1 SVP: 3 DLU: 77

521.685-330 STEM-ROLLER-OR-CRUSHER OPERATOR (tobacco) alternate titles: crusher operator; roller operator
Tends machine that flattens tobacco stems or stems and veins of tobacco leaves: Starts conveyor that feeds tobacco to rollers of machine and forks tobacco onto conveyor. Regulates flow of steam and water to moisten tobacco and clean and cool rollers. May remove flattened leaves from machine and stack leaves in pile or fork flattened stems into hogsheads.
GOE: 06.04.15 STRENGTH: M GED: R1 M1 L1 SVP: 2 DLU: 77

521.685-334 STEMMER, MACHINE (tobacco) alternate titles: stripping-and-booking-machine operator; tobacco stemmer, machine; tobacco-stripping-machine operator; wrapper-stemmer operator
Tends machine that removes stems from leaves of tobacco and arranges stemmed leaves into books: Starts machine and feeds leaf between rollers. Removes stacks of stripped leaves and ties leaves together. Separates leaves according to books of right or left halves. Dumps stems from machine into cans. May be designated according to type of tobacco stemmed as Binder Stripper, Machine (tobacco); Wrapper Stripper (tobacco).
GOE: 06.04.15 STRENGTH: L GED: R1 M1 L1 SVP: 2 DLU: 77

521.685-338 STRIP-CUTTING-MACHINE OPERATOR (tobacco) alternate titles: shredding-machine operator; tobacco cutter
Tends machine that cuts tobacco into shreds for use in making cigarettes: Starts feeders, ordering drum, conveyors, and cutting machine. Observes operation of conveyors and cutting machine and pulls lever to regulate flow of tobacco on conveyor to prevent jamming. May tighten bolts that hold knives, or may change knives, using wrench and screwdriver, and maintain record of knives used.
GOE: 06.04.15 STRENGTH: L GED: R1 M1 L1 SVP: 2 DLU: 77

521.685-342 STRIPPER-CUTTER, MACHINE (food prep., nec) alternate titles: sawyer
Tends machines equipped with guillotine knives or bandsaw, stick pusher, and deheader, that automatically strip, dehead, and cut macaroni long goods to specified length: Starts elevator to position rack of dried macaroni beside machine. Pulls machine arm that lifts drying stick (rod) of macaroni from rack onto chain conveyor that feeds it onto machine bed. Starts deheading hammer, stick pusher, and knives, and feeds macaroni onto packaging conveyor. Starts machine that automatically strips and dehooks macaroni, and passes it through preset bandsaw to cut product into specified lengths for packaging. Removes cut macaroni from trough and places in box on packaging conveyor line.
GOE: 06.04.15 STRENGTH: L GED: R2 M1 L1 SVP: 2 DLU: 77

521.685-346 SUGAR GRINDER (sugar & conf.)
Tends machine that grinds granulated sugar into powdered sugar: Turns handwheel to set spacing between grinding rollers or stones, or installs gratings in drum of grinding machine to obtain specified degree of fineness. Starts machine and empties bags of granulated sugar into hopper. Observes grinding and discharging process to verify pulverization of sugar to specified fineness and discharge of sugar through air-leg into bags. Removes filled bags from air-leg onto pallet and replaces them with empty bags.
GOE: 06.04.15 STRENGTH: H GED: R2 M1 L1 SVP: 3 DLU: 77

521.685-350 SUGAR PRESSER (grain-feed mills)
Tends press that removes corn-sugar hydrol from crystallized cakes of sugar. Places cakes in press and turns handwheels to compress cakes and squeeze out hydrol. Releases pressure and removes slabs.
GOE: 06.04.15 STRENGTH: M GED: R1 M1 L1 SVP: 2 DLU: 77

521.685-354 SUGAR-CHIPPER-MACHINE OPERATOR (grain-feed mills) alternate titles: sugar grinder
Tends machine that chips cakes of sugar into pieces: Lifts cakes of sugar onto table of machine having rotating wheel equipped with knives. Starts machine and pushes sugar cakes against wheel that chips cakes into pieces.
GOE: 06.04.15 STRENGTH: H GED: R1 M1 L1 SVP: 2 DLU: 77

521.685-358 SWEET-POTATO DISINTEGRATOR (can. & preserv.)
Tends machine that grinds sweet potatoes into semifluid state to facilitate cooking process: Starts machine and turns handwheel to admit water into discharge chute of conveyor and into machine to lubricate potatoes during grinding process. Starts conveyor that moves potatoes from hopper into chute feeding grinding machine. Observes level of semifluid potatoes fed into receptacle and stops grinding process when receptacle is full. Clears potato jam-ups on conveyor, using rod.
GOE: 06.04.15 STRENGTH: M GED: R2 M1 L1 SVP: 2 DLU: 77

521.685-362 THRESHING-MACHINE OPERATOR (tobacco) alternate titles: stem-cleaning-machine feeder; stem-threshing-machine operator
Tends threshing machine that strips leaf particles from tobacco stems: Starts motor that rotates spike-studded drums or vibrates screen. Forks dried stems onto feed conveyor or opens chute gate to drop tobacco onto feed conveyor. Removes filled catching bag, empties bag into bin or sack, and replaces bag on machine. Removes matted stems from spikes of drum.
GOE: 06.04.15 STRENGTH: L GED: R2 M1 L1 SVP: 2 DLU: 77

521.685-366 TIPPLE TENDER (grain-feed mills)
Tends tipple to dump casings loaded with dried corn starch onto conveyor: Lowers casing into tipple, using hoist. Turns handwheel to dump starch into hopper above moving conveyor, and opens hopper gate to deposit starch uniformly on conveyor.
GOE: 06.04.40 STRENGTH: H GED: R1 M1 L1 SVP: 2 DLU: 77

521.685-370 WINERY WORKER (beverage)
Performs any combination of following tasks involved in winemaking: Lifts bulk grapes or dried pomace onto conveyor leading to crusher, disintegrator, or de-alcoholizer still, using pitchfork. Connects portable pumps between tanks and turns valves to pump wine and alcohol from fermenting and fortifying tanks to tanks that cool wine to prevent further fermentation. Pumps chilled wine into clarifying tanks and adds prescribed chemicals to wine. Starts agitator that mixes solution to induce sedimentation of wine particles. Pumps clarified wines through filtering tanks into tank to obtain blended wine. Pumps wine through pasteurizer to prevent wine spoilage. Pumps pasteurized wine through filtering device to collect sediment and precipitates and into tanks in bottling room. Tends press that separates juice from pomace and starts conveyor that transports pomace to disintegrating machine. Starts disintegrating machine and de-alcoholizer steam still that salvages alcohol from pomace, and starts conveyor that transports residue to storage. Cleans and sterilizes fermenting and fortifying tanks and railroad tank cars, using airhose and soda ash.
GOE: 06.04.15 STRENGTH: M GED: R3 M1 L1 SVP: 3 DLU: 77

521.685-374 WINTERIZER (oils & grease) alternate titles: oil winterizer
Tends equipment that strains stearin from vegetable oils, such as soybean, corn, and cottonseed to produce salad oil: Turns valves to admit oil to chilling tank and to circulate refrigerant through tank coils for specified time to solidify stearin. Opens filter valves and adjusts air pressure to force oil through filters and trap suspended stearin.
GOE: 06.04.15 STRENGTH: L GED: R2 M1 L1 SVP: 2 DLU: 77

521.685-378 DEBONER, PET FOOD (can. & preserv.)
Tends deboning-grinder machine that separates flesh from bones to make boneless ground pet food: Positions and secures hopper, screw, and disk assemblies in deboning-grinder machine housings, using wrench, and depresses buttons to activate machine and conveyor. Observes volume of meat parts moving on conveyor into hopper, and adds or removes parts, using shovel, and spreads parts in hopper, using stick, to ensure steady supply of parts to machine. Picks bones and similar matter from parts on conveyor to assist in separating process. Observes processing and adjusts disk assembly when required to maintain specified consistency and volume of ground parts, using ratchet lever. Shovels separated bones and foreign matter into disposal drum. Cleans machine and work area, using hose, brush, and shovel.
GOE: 06.04.15 STRENGTH: M GED: R2 M1 L2 SVP: 2 DLU: 86

521.685-382 FLAVORING OIL FILTERER (beverage)
Tends filtering equipment that removes wax from citrus oil used to make flavoring: Selects formula card according to work order specifications and pours oil and other ingredients into mixing tank. Inserts clean filter pad into filter pump and attaches hoses from mixing tank to filter in prescribed order. Depresses button to activate pump that moves mixture from mixing tank through filtering mechanism to filter and clarify oil. Opens valve of holding tank to collect sample of filtered oil and refilters oil when sample does not meet clarity and color standards. At end of processing, opens valve of holding tank to draw filtered oil into containers. Maintains records of kinds and quantities of materials used and amount of oil processed.
GOE: 06.04.15 STRENGTH: H GED: R2 M1 L2 SVP: 4 DLU: 86

521.685-386 SCALING MACHINE OPERATOR (can. & preserv.)
Tends machine that removes scales from fish: Turns valve to start spray of water over spiked rollers of scaling machine. Pushes buttons to start and stop conveyor that feeds fish from holding tank into tray at feeding end of machine and to start scaling machine. Feeds fish onto conveyor that moves fish through spiked rollers that remove scales from sides of fish, and that dumps fish into containers.
GOE: 06.04.15 STRENGTH: L GED: R1 M1 L1 SVP: 2 DLU: 86

521.686-010 BOLTER HELPER (grain-feed mills)
Assists BOLTER (grain-feed mills) in tending flour sifting and purifying machines: Opens slides in chutes and starts elevators to route flour between sifters, purifiers, and grinding machines. Observes flour to ensure flow through specified chutes and machines. Pounds on chutes with mallet to keep flour flowing. Brushes cloth sieves in sifters and purifiers to prevent clogging. May adjust flow of water onto belt to temper grain for milling. Performs other duties as described under HELPER (any industry) Master Title.
GOE: 06.04.15 STRENGTH: L GED: R2 M1 L1 SVP: 2 DLU: 77

521.686-014 CAKE PULLER (oils & grease) alternate titles: knocker
Removes cottonseed cakes from hydraulic presses after extraction of oil: Pulls lever or turns handwheel to release pressure on ram. Knocks cake loose and moves it to edge of press, using metal rod. Places cakes on table for removal of press cloth.
GOE: 06.04.19 STRENGTH: H GED: R1 M1 L1 SVP: 2 DLU: 77

521.686-018 CHICLE-GRINDER FEEDER (sugar & conf.)
Feeds chicle and gum bases into grinding machine, preparatory to making chewing gum: Loads blocks of chicle or other gum bases onto conveyor of grinding machine, using electric hoist or lift truck. Starts machine and places empty containers under discharge spout to catch ground ingredients. Shovels ground material into barrels on platform scale until specified weight is obtained. May dump salvage gum into grinding machine and be designated Salvage Grinder (sugar & conf.).
GOE: 06.04.15 STRENGTH: M GED: R2 M1 L1 SVP: 2 DLU: 77

521.686-022 COTTON PULLER (oils & grease)
Removes rolls of linters (cotton lint cleaned from cottonseed) from takeup rolls of linter machine. Places empty roll onto brackets of machine and threads end of material onto roll. Moves rolls of linters to baling room, using handtruck.
GOE: 06.04.19 STRENGTH: L GED: R1 M1 L1 SVP: 1 DLU: 77

521.686-026 CUSTOM-FEED-MILL-OPERATOR HELPER (grain-feed mills)
Assists CUSTOM-FEED-MILL OPERATOR (grain-feed mills) in milling grain and feed to customer specifications. Sacks mill products, loads them on truck, and delivers products to customer. Performs other duties as described under HELPER (any industry) Master Title.
GOE: 06.04.15 STRENGTH: H GED: R1 M1 L1 SVP: 2 DLU: 77

521.686-030 CUT-IN WORKER (grain-feed mills)
Opens sacks of rough (uncleaned) rice, using knife, and empties rice into hopper, preparatory to cleaning and storing of rice in bins. Piles empty sacks on handtruck and removes sacks to warehouse.
GOE: 06.04.40 STRENGTH: H GED: R1 M1 L1 SVP: 1 DLU: 77

521.686-034 FISH-MACHINE FEEDER (can. & preserv.)
Feeds cleaned fish into machines that bone, skin, or cut and pack fish sections into can: Inspects fish to ensure that color, odor, and texture meet standards. Places fish on feed conveyor of machine. May start machines and pull levers to regulate feed conveyor speed. May be designated according to machine fed as Filling-Machine Feeder (can. & preserv.); Fish-Boning-Machine Feeder (can. & preserv.); Fish-Cutting-Machine Operator (can. & preserv.); Fish-Skinning-Machine Feeder (can. & preserv.); or according to activity performed as Fish Flipper (can. & preserv.); Fish Straightener (can. & preserv.).
GOE: 06.04.15 STRENGTH: M GED: R2 M1 L1 SVP: 2 DLU: 77

521.686-038 FLUMER (grain-feed mills)
Feeds potatoes into flume (trough) that carries them to washing machine: Removes board covering flume to allow potatoes to fall from stockpile. Scoops potatoes from edges of pile, using wheelbarrow, and dumps them into flume. Adjusts headgates to regulate flow of potatoes into flume.
GOE: 06.04.39 STRENGTH: M GED: R1 M1 L1 SVP: 1 DLU: 77

521.686-042 FLUMER II (sugar & conf.) alternate titles: beet flumer
Fills flumes (troughs) with sugar beets, performing any combination of following duties: Trips lever on gondola loaded with beets, or removes sideboards on storage bin allowing beets to spill into flume. Prods beets with bar to maintain continuous flow of beets. Washes gondola or storage bin, using water hose. Dumps truckloads of beets into hopper and feeds beets onto conveyor leading to flume or storage bins. Removes leaves, stems, and trash from flume, using shovel or pitchfork. Loads rocks extracted from flume onto dump truck.
GOE: 06.04.39 STRENGTH: L GED: R1 M1 L1 SVP: 1 DLU: 77

521.686-046 NUT CHOPPER (can. & preserv.; food prep., nec; sugar & conf.)
Feeds machine that chops nuts: Places container under discharge outlet of chopping machine, scoops nuts into hopper of machine and starts machine. Empties container of chopped nuts as they emerge from machine into trays, sacks, or containers for further processing. May place trays of nuts in steam cabinet for softening, and slice nuts, using slicing machine.
GOE: 06.04.15 STRENGTH: L GED: R1 M1 L1 SVP: 2 DLU: 77

521.686-050 PROCESSOR HELPER (grain-feed mills)
Assists PROCESSOR, GRAIN (grain-feed mills) in tending machines and equipment that clean, scour, and separate grain. Regulates flow of grain to machines. Relieves stoppages. Adjusts machines. Performs other duties as described under HELPER (any industry) Master Title.

GOE: 06.04.15 STRENGTH: H GED: R1 M1 L1 SVP: 2 DLU: 77

521.686-054 SLICE-PLUG-CUTTER-OPERATOR HELPER (tobacco) alternate titles: slice-cutting-machine-operator helper

Assists SLICE-PLUG-CUTTER OPERATOR (tobacco) to cut plugs of tobacco (cheeses), into slice-plug smoking tobacco. Performs other duties as described under HELPER (any industry) Master Title.
GOE: 06.04.15 STRENGTH: L GED: R1 M1 L1 SVP: 2 DLU: 77

521.687-010 ALMOND BLANCHER, HAND (can. & preserv.)

Observes blanched (skinned) almonds on conveyor belt emerging from blanching machine and removes almonds with skins missed by machine. Rubs or squeezes almonds between fingers to remove skins. May rub or squeeze skins from almonds that have been immersed in hot water and dumped into trays.
GOE: 06.04.28 STRENGTH: S GED: R1 M1 L1 SVP: 1 DLU: 77

521.687-014 BINDER CUTTER, HAND (tobacco) alternate titles: filler-leaf cutter, long

Cuts leaf tobacco used to bind bunches to specified size. Places tobacco leaf on cutting table against guides and lowers knife blade to cut leaf. Moves guides to obtain cut of specific size.
GOE: 06.04.28 STRENGTH: L GED: R1 M1 L1 SVP: 2 DLU: 77

521.687-018 BINDER SELECTOR (tobacco) alternate titles: binder sorter

Inspects leaves of tobacco before and after stripping to determine whether leaves are suitable for use as binders: Inspects each leaf for holes and tears. Places leaves to be used as binders in bundle for stripping and discards defective leaves. Removes defective leaves from books and places books of perfect leaves in container. May sprinkle water on books that appear dry.
GOE: 06.03.02 STRENGTH: L GED: R2 M1 L1 SVP: 2 DLU: 77

521.687-022 BONE PICKER (can. & preserv.)

Examines shellfish meats under ultraviolet light and removes pieces of shell, preparatory to canning: Places tray of shelled meats on table, or observes meats passing on conveyor under ultraviolet generators that cause shell particles to glow. Turns and stirs meats by hand to view all sides and picks out and discards bits of shell, viscera, and foreign matter.
GOE: 06.04.28 STRENGTH: L GED: R1 M1 L1 SVP: 1 DLU: 77

521.687-026 BUNCH TRIMMER, MOLD (tobacco)

Draws knife along ends of cigar molds to cut off excess tobacco protruding from molds. Loads trimmed molds onto truck for removal to rolling department.
GOE: 06.04.28 STRENGTH: L GED: R1 M1 L1 SVP: 1 DLU: 77

521.687-030 CHAR PULLER (grain-feed mills; sugar & conf.)

Removes contaminated char (activated carbon) from corn syrup filters for reclaiming: Positions receiving platform at discharge gate of filter to unload used char. Removes nuts to open discharge gate, using wrench. Loosens and pulls char onto receiving platform and into chute to conveyor. Sweeps filters to remove remaining char. Arranges and smooths blankets that cover bottom plates of filter. Replaces gate and tightens nuts evenly to prevent warp and leakage. Cleans char from platform and floor.
GOE: 06.04.39 STRENGTH: H GED: R2 M1 L1 SVP: 2 DLU: 77

521.687-034 CHAR-FILTER-OPERATOR HELPER (sugar & conf.)

Prepares char filter tanks for sugar-liquor filtration: Attaches hoses between filters and manifold, using wrenches. Removes filter covers, using block and tackle. Positions char chutes and starts conveyors to fill empty filters. Attaches hose from manifold to weir box for mixing liquor with char while filling. Covers filters after filling. Opens air vents to purge air from filled filters. Cleans hoses and drip pans.
GOE: 06.04.39 STRENGTH: H GED: R2 M1 L1 SVP: 3 DLU: 77

521.687-038 DRIP-BOX TENDER (grain-feed mills)

Positions spout of portable tank containing starch solution over series of boxes lined with cloth and opens valve to fill each box. Inverts boxes after water has drained through cloth to remove solid starch cakes, or scoops out starch with shovel, and places product on handtruck for transfer to kiln. May move levers controlling flow of starch into steel casings and hang casings on hooks of overhead conveyor leading to kiln and be designated Starch Presser (grain-feed mills).
GOE: 06.04.15 STRENGTH: M GED: R1 M1 L1 SVP: 1 DLU: 77

521.687-042 EGG BREAKER (any industry)

Separates yolk and glair (white) of eggs for use in food products: Strikes eggs against bar, allows contents to fall into bowl, and throws empty shells into receptacle. Smells broken eggs to detect spoiled ones and dumps them in waste container. Pours broken eggs from bowl over egg-separating device. Pulls lever to retain yolk and to allow white to fall into cup below. May be designated according to specialization as Egg Smeller (any industry).
GOE: 06.04.28 STRENGTH: L GED: R1 M1 L1 SVP: 2 DLU: 77

521.687-046 FILLER SPREADER (tobacco)

Separates individual leaves from pads of tobacco leaves pressed together in shipping. Arranges leaves in rows on screen racks. Assists other workers in carrying and lifting screen racks to storage racks.
GOE: 06.04.28 STRENGTH: M GED: R1 M1 L1 SVP: 1 DLU: 77

521.687-050 FILTER CHANGER (beverage)

Replaces soiled filter cakes in beer filter, using handtools. Disassembles filter press and separates plates (frames) to remove old filter pads. Positions clean cakes between plates and reassembles filter.

GOE: 06.04.15 STRENGTH: M GED: R1 M1 L1 SVP: 2 DLU: 77

521.687-054 FILTER-SCREEN CLEANER (beverage)

Cleans filter screens used in diatomaceous-silica filtering machine: Disassembles screens from frame by hand or using wrenches. Flushes residue from screens with water hose or immerses and boils screens in tanks of boiling water. Cleans and reassembles screens and frames, using brushes and handtools. Cleans working area and equipment, using mops and brooms.
GOE: 06.04.39 STRENGTH: M GED: R2 M1 L1 SVP: 2 DLU: 77

521.687-058 FISH CHOPPER, GANG KNIFE (can. & preserv.)

Positions fish on cutting table and pulls *gang knife* handle to cut fish into several lengths for packing into cans. May load and distribute trays of cut fish to packers.
GOE: 06.04.28 STRENGTH: M GED: R1 M1 L1 SVP: 2 DLU: 77

521.687-062 FISH-LIVER SORTER (can. & preserv.; fishing & hunt.)

Sorts fish livers, according to species of fish and size, shape, color, and texture of liver: Cuts liver from viscera, using knife, and places liver in specified tub. Discards diseased, spoiled, and poor quality livers. May clean and fillet fish [FISH CLEANER (can. & preserv.; fishing & hunt.)].
GOE: 06.04.28 STRENGTH: M GED: R2 M1 L1 SVP: 2 DLU: 77

521.687-066 FRUIT CUTTER (sugar & conf.)

Cuts dried, fresh, candied, or crystallized fruit into cubes or pieces for candy fillings and for garnishing iced candies, using knife. When opening, pitting, and chopping dates, is designated Date Puller (sugar & conf.).
GOE: 06.04.28 STRENGTH: L GED: R1 M1 L1 SVP: 1 DLU: 77

521.687-070 HONEYCOMB DECAPPER (food prep., nec) alternate titles: comb capper

Cuts caps from commercial honeycombs with hand or motor-driven knife, preparatory to extracting honey: Breaks propolis (beeglue) seals with scraper, and lifts frame of honeycomb from super. Moves honeycomb frame into oscillating knife, or cuts caps from frame, using hand knife. Trims superfluous wax from wooden parts with knife and places frame in stand. May place frames of honeycomb in extractor [HONEY EXTRACTOR (food prep., nec)].
GOE: 06.04.28 STRENGTH: H GED: R2 M1 L1 SVP: 3 DLU: 77

521.687-074 LABORER, SYRUP MACHINE (grain-feed mills)

Collects rejected cans of corn syrup and pours contents into strainer that removes impurities. Cleans work area and reservoir of filling machines, using water, brushes, and mop. Carries cans and supplies to machines.
GOE: 06.04.39 STRENGTH: H GED: R1 M1 L1 SVP: 1 DLU: 77

521.687-078 LIQUOR-BRIDGE-OPERATOR HELPER (sugar & conf.)

Routes flow of wash water from char filter as directed by LIQUOR-BRIDGE OPERATOR (sugar & conf.): Prepares filter-record board, showing filters to be filled with liquor. Ties clean pockets on filter discharge nipple to prevent splashing in weir boxes. Changes weir boxes to divert flow of sweetwater (wash water from filter containing sugar) or waste water to specified tanks or bays, noting changes on filter record board. Tests water for density to ascertain sugar content, using hydrometer. Bottles samples of liquor and sweetwater for laboratory analysis. Washes weir boxes and keeps work station in sanitary condition.
GOE: 06.04.15 STRENGTH: M GED: R2 M1 L1 SVP: 3 DLU: 77

521.687-082 MILLER HELPER, DISTILLERY (beverage) alternate titles: grain-miller helper

Assists MILLER, DISTILLERY (beverage) to clean and grind grain into meal for use in distillation of distilled liquors: Adjusts grain and meal discharge chutes on storage tanks. Removes covers from storage tanks to admit grain and meal. Changes vibrating screens on cleaning machines, using handtools. Places empty grain sacks over discharge ends of cleaning machines to collect dust and refuse. Assists MILLER, DISTILLERY (beverage) to make minor repairs to pumps, air-conveyor chutes, and machines. Performs other duties as described under HELPER (any industry) Master Title.
GOE: 06.04.15 STRENGTH: M GED: R2 M1 L1 SVP: 3 DLU: 77

521.687-086 NUT SORTER (can. & preserv.) alternate titles: hull sorter; nut picker; nut sifter; picking-belt operator

Removes defective nuts and foreign matter from bulk nut meats: Observes nut meats on conveyor belt, and picks out broken, shriveled, or wormy nuts and foreign matter, such as leaves and rocks. Places defective nuts and foreign matter into containers. May be designated according to kind of nut meat sorted as Almond Sorter (can. & preserv.); Peanut Sorter (can. & preserv.).
GOE: 06.03.02 STRENGTH: S GED: R1 M1 L1 SVP: 2 DLU: 77

521.687-090 NUT STEAMER (can. & preserv.) alternate titles: steamer operator

Immerses nuts in hot water to soften shells to facilitate shelling process: Turns valve to fill vat or kettle with water. Starts heaters and sets temperature gauge to maintain required temperature. Places nuts, such as almonds, pecans, or walnuts, into wire basket, and lowers basket into vat of hot water, using hoist. Removes basket from vat after specified time.
GOE: 06.04.28 STRENGTH: H GED: R2 M1 L1 SVP: 2 DLU: 77

521.687-094 PEELED-POTATO INSPECTOR (food prep., nec) alternate titles: potato spotter

Inspects peeled potatoes, passing on conveyor belt. Picks out rotten potatoes. Cuts out unsuitable parts and halves over-sized potatoes, using knife.

GOE: 06.03.02 STRENGTH: L GED: R1 M1 L1 SVP: 2 DLU: 77

521.687-098 PICKER (tobacco) alternate titles: lamina searcher; scrap picker; searcher

Removes stems, offcolor tobacco, and foreign material, such as strings, dirt, and paper from tobacco as it moves along conveyor to ensure clean and uniform product. May drop pickings into bags attached to conveyor frame, according to whether pickings are dark tobacco, green tobacco, tobacco with stems, or foreign material. May be designated according to type of tobacco processed as Filler Picker (tobacco); Scrap Sorter (tobacco).

GOE: 06.03.02 STRENGTH: L GED: R1 M1 L1 SVP: 2 DLU: 77

521.687-102 PICKING-TABLE WORKER (sugar & conf.)

Picks stems, stones, metal, or wood not eliminated by trash-picking machine from conveyor to prevent damage to beet knives. May trim tops from beets to prevent clogging of knives in slicers.

GOE: 06.03.02 STRENGTH: L GED: R1 M1 L1 SVP: 1 DLU: 77

521.687-106 SAUSAGE-MEAT TRIMMER (meat products) alternate titles: beef trimmer; lard trimmer; piece-meat trimmer; piece trimmer; retrimmer

Prepares meat for use in making ground and smoked meat products, such as sausage and bologna: Obtains specified meat from stock and carries to cutting table. Cuts and trims meat from bone and dices meat, using knife, cleaver, and bandsaw. Weighs meat on platform scale and places in tubs. Tags each tub for weight and contents. May grind meat.

GOE: 06.04.28 STRENGTH: H GED: R2 M2 L1 SVP: 2 DLU: 77

521.687-110 SHAKER (tobacco) alternate titles: bundle shaker; filler opener; filler shaker; hand shaker; tobacco shaker

Shakes hands of cured tobacco to separate, straighten, and expose leaves to air and remove dirt. Places loosened tobacco on table or conveyor for further processing. May be designated according to type of leaf processed as Frog Shaker (tobacco); Wrapper Opener (tobacco).

GOE: 06.04.28 STRENGTH: L GED: R1 M1 L1 SVP: 1 DLU: 77

521.687-114 SHAKER WASHER (grain-feed mills)

Flushes shaker tables and reel panels, using hose, to remove material that clogs mesh and prevents effective separation of starch from bran and gluten. Sponges and rinses back of fabric with detergent solution and water. Removes and installs repaired frames, using wrench and screwdriver, under direction of SHAKER REPAIRER (grain-feed mills).

GOE: 06.04.39 STRENGTH: M GED: R2 M1 L1 SVP: 2 DLU: 77

521.687-118 SHELLER I (can. & preserv.) alternate titles: huller operator

Cracks nuts, such as pecans, brazil nuts, and walnuts, using vise. Picks out nut meats and drops meat in container.

GOE: 06.04.28 STRENGTH: L GED: R1 M1 L1 SVP: 1 DLU: 77

521.687-122 SHELLFISH SHUCKER (can. & preserv.) alternate titles: shucker

Shucks fresh or steamed shellfish, such as oysters, clams, or scallops (bivalves), preparatory to canning, freezing, or fresh packing: Holds shellfish firmly or against block and forces shucking knife between halves of shell at hinge juncture. Twists knife to sever muscles holding shell closed and pries open. Cuts shellfish from shell, flips it into container, and discards shell. May break off edges of shells before shucking, using hatchet. May be designated according to shellfish shucked as Clam Shucker (can. & preserv.); Oyster Shucker (can. & preserv.); Scallop Shucker (can. & preserv.).

GOE: 06.04.28 STRENGTH: L GED: R2 M1 L1 SVP: 3 DLU: 77

521.687-126 SKIN LIFTER, BACON (meat products)

Cuts slit in flank end of bacon slab between meat and skin, using knife, so that slab may be inserted into derinding machine.

GOE: 06.04.28 STRENGTH: M GED: R1 M1 L1 SVP: 1 DLU: 77

521.687-130 SKULL GRINDER (meat products) alternate titles: head-bone grinder; turbinated-bone grinder

Picks up split and brained hog head and holds nasal passages against revolving emery wheel to clean out dirt. Removes dirt from ear passages. Throws hog head in container.

GOE: 06.04.39 STRENGTH: L GED: R1 M1 L1 SVP: 2 DLU: 77

521.687-134 STEMMER, HAND (tobacco) alternate titles: filler stemmer, hand; leaf stemmer, hand; sprigger; tobacco stripper, hand; wrapper stemmer, hand

Removes stems from tobacco leaves to prepare tobacco for use as filler, binder, or wrapper for cigars, plug, or twist chewing tobacco: Strips leaf from stem, starting at tip end of leaf. Spreads and stacks wrapper leaves in piles, keeping leaves separated into left- and right-hand books. Places filler tobacco and stems in box or can. May be designated according to tobacco stripped as Binder Stripper, Hand (tobacco); Scrap Stripper, Hand (tobacco); Wrapper Stripper, Hand (tobacco).

GOE: 06.04.28 STRENGTH: L GED: R1 M1 L1 SVP: 2 DLU: 77

521.687-138 TABLE HAND (tobacco)

Forks tobacco from bin onto cutting-machine supply table to supply SMOKING-TOBACCO-CUTTER OPERATOR (tobacco).

GOE: 06.04.40 STRENGTH: L GED: R1 M1 L1 SVP: 2 DLU: 77

522 CULTURING, MELTING, FERMENTING, DISTILLING, SATURATING, PICKLING, AGING, AND RELATED OCCUPATIONS

This group includes occupations concerned with growing bacteria or other microorganisms in materials; liquefying solid materials by means of heat; breaking down complex molecules in organic compounds by the introduction of a ferment such as yeast; heating a mixture to separate the more volatile from the less volatile parts and then cooling and condensing the resulting vapor to produce a nearly pure or refined substance; soaking thoroughly, filling, charging, or treating a substance with another so that no more can be taken up; preserving and flavoring materials or products by immersing, coating, or injecting them with preservatives; and subjecting materials or products to the effects of time.

522.130-010 SUPERVISOR, MELT HOUSE (sugar & conf.)

Supervises and coordinates activities of workers engaged in washing, centrifuging, and melting bulk raw sugar: Reads production schedule and consults with SUPERVISOR, FILTRATION (sugar & conf.) to ascertain quantity of liquor required. Calculates melting rates of raw sugar, using standard formula. Moves controls to set timing cycles on centrifuges and start machinery, such as elevators, scrolls, and pumps. Inspects process stations to verify that equipment and machinery are operating as specified. Performs other duties as described under SUPERVISOR (any industry) Master Title. May supervise workers engaged in reclaiming contaminated sugars and syrups and be designated Supervisor, Remelt (sugar & conf.).

GOE: 06.01.01 STRENGTH: L GED: R4 M3 L3 SVP: 7 DLU: 77

522.131-010 DISTILLING-DEPARTMENT SUPERVISOR (beverage)

Supervises and coordinates activities of workers engaged in distilling liquors, such as gin, brandy, and whiskey: Verifies specified amount and proof of distilled liquor produced. Directs workers in preparing and storing ingredients, such as sour beer. Prepares flavoring ingredients used in distilling gin. Reviews distillation records to verify adherence to specified formula. Inspects operating condition of stills and auxiliary equipment. Performs other duties as described under SUPERVISOR (any industry) Master Title.

GOE: 06.02.01 STRENGTH: L GED: R4 M3 L4 SVP: 7 DLU: 77

522.132-010 SUPERVISOR, MALT HOUSE (beverage)

Supervises and coordinates activities of workers engaged in producing malt from barley: Adjusts controls on steeping tanks, germinating tanks, and drying kilns, following readings on recording charts. Coordinates steeping, germinating, and drying operations and evaluates operations against quality control laboratory reports. Performs other duties as described under SUPERVISOR (any industry) Master Title.

GOE: 06.01.01 STRENGTH: L GED: R4 M3 L4 SVP: 7 DLU: 77

522.134-010 SUPERVISOR, BRINEYARD (can. & preserv.)

Supervises and coordinates activities of workers engaged in receiving and brining food products, such as cucumbers, peppers, onions, and cauliflower, preparatory to further processing, utilizing knowledge of federal, state, and company standards: Studies weekly production schedule to ascertain quantity and type of products to be processed, and reviews status charts for individual tanks to determine availability of brined products for processing. Instructs workers to move or store products from or into tanks, according to production requirements. Maintains record of transactions for each tank on chart. Performs other duties as described under SUPERVISOR (any industry) Master Title.

GOE: 06.02.01 STRENGTH: H GED: R4 M3 L3 SVP: 7 DLU: 77

522.264-010 TRAINING TECHNICIAN (can. & preserv.)

Trains and directs workers in methods of processing fish roe: Teaches FISH ROE PROCESSOR (can. & preserv.) 522.687-046 characteristics, such as color, maturity, and outer appearance of membrane of egg skeins (membrane-enclosed ovaries, tissue, and fish roe) to enable worker to recognize skeins of different species, appearance of unacceptable skeins, and commercial grades of skeins. Demonstrates packing procedures, such as method of lining boxes, placement patterns of processed skeins in boxes, and amount of salt to apply to each layer. Directs workers to change brine solution used to preserve skeins and sets timer that controls processing times of skeins in brining vats. Retrains workers as necessary. Sorts, salts, grades, and packs skeins of fish roe [FISH ROE TECHNICIAN (can. & preserv.) 522.384-010]. Tests processed egg skeins for nitrate content, using prepared chemical kit, comparison charts, and following kit instructions. May direct activities of other workers.

GOE: 06.04.15 STRENGTH: M GED: R3 M2 L2 SVP: 6 DLU: 86

522.362-010 YEAST DISTILLER (beverage) alternate titles: yeast maker

Controls equipment to prepare mixture of mash and yeast for use in manufacture of distilled liquors: Weighs specified quantities of rye and malt meal, depending upon amount of yeast required, and dumps them into yeast tub (cooker) filled with specified amount of water. Opens valves to admit steam that circulates through coil pipes in tub and cooks mixture. Starts revolving blades in tub to agitate mixture as it cooks. Observes temperature gauges and increases or decreases steam pressure to maintain constant temperature as mash cooks. Pours yeast culture into cooked mash and mixes mash with revolving blades. Stops revolving blades when mash and yeast are thoroughly mixed. Tests mash

to determine temperature and specific gravity (proof), using thermometer and hydrometer, and records results. Observes gauges and increases or decreases steam to ensure that mash ferments at constant temperature. Notifies FERMENTATION OPERATOR (beverage) when mash is ready to be pumped into fermentation tank. Removes sample of mash for laboratory analysis.
GOE: 06.02.15 STRENGTH: L GED: R3 M2 L3 SVP: 4 DLU: 77

522.382-010 COTTAGE-CHEESE MAKER (dairy products)

Controls equipment to make cottage cheese from milk: Washes cheese vat and tools with sterilizing solution and rinse water. Turns valves and observes meters to convey specified amounts of milk and culture into vat. May add rennet to coagulate milk, and dye to tint curd. Turns steam and water valves and observes thermometer and clock to heat milk for specified time and at specified temperature to incubate culture. Starts agitator in vat and stirs ingredients, using paddle. Tests sample of whey for acidity and cuts curd with knife to allow seepage of whey. Observes thermometer and adjusts steam and water valves to cook curd at slowly increasing temperature. Feels and breaks sample of curd to determine when it is sufficiently cooked. Turns cold water and drain valves or sprays curd with chlorinated water to wash curd and remove whey. When making baker's cheese, drains uncooked whole curd from vat into porous bags to remove whey and dumps curd into blending machine to distribute residual moisture. When making creamed cottage cheese, adds cream and stirs with paddle or starts agitator. Records processing steps. May taste cheese for salt and acid content. May pasteurize milk. May make culture.
GOE: 06.02.15 STRENGTH: M GED: R3 M2 L3 SVP: 4 DLU: 77

522.382-014 FERMENTATION OPERATOR (beverage)

Controls fermentation process of sweet or sour mash inoculated with yeast to produce fermented mash for use in distillation of distilled liquors: Pumps specified number of gallons of cooked mash and yeast into fermentation tank, simultaneously, to ensure that mash and yeast are thoroughly mixed together. Opens valves to admit specified number of gallons of water into mixture, according to formula. Opens valves to circulate steam through coil pipes in tank to heat mixture to prescribed temperature. Turns valves to admit and control air pressure that agitates mixture as it ferments or to accelerate chemical reaction of yeast. Observes gauges or dials to ascertain that prescribed temperature and gas pressure are remaining constant in tank. Tests mash at prescribed intervals to determine temperature and specific gravity (proof), using thermometer and alcohol-proof hydrometer. Compares test results with standard charts to determine when mixture is fully cooked. Regulates steam, air, and gas pressure in tank to ensure that chemical reaction of yeast and fermentation process is taking place, according to formula. Pumps sour mash into cistern tank, preparatory to distilling. Cleans tanks by rinsing them with water.
GOE: 06.02.15 STRENGTH: M GED: R4 M2 L3 SVP: 5 DLU: 77

522.382-018 LIQUOR BLENDER (beverage) alternate titles: filter operator

Controls equipment to regauge, filter, rectify, blend, and verify proof of whiskeys and other distilled liquors, preparatory to bottling: Pumps specified number of gallons of whiskey and deionized water into regauging tanks (reducing tanks) and agitates mixture with compressed air to reduce proof of barreled whiskey. Measures temperature, using thermometer, and specific gravity, using alcohol-proof hydrometer, and compares readings with tables from standard gauging manuals to determine proof of mixture. Pumps regauged whiskey into cooling tank and opens valves to circulate cold water through coil pipes in tank to reduce whiskey to specified temperature before filtering. Starts filter press to remove impurities from distilled liquor, and adjusts valves to control vacuum pressure in press and to regulate flow of liquor through press. Observes dials and gauges to ascertain that temperature and pressure remain constant during filtering process. Pumps different proofs of whiskeys into agitating tank, adds specified amount of deionized water, and agitates mixture to blend whiskeys. Mixes flavorings and other ingredients, according to formula, into mixing tank with specified number of gallons of spirits, such as gin or vodka, and adjusts valves to control temperature and compressed air to produce brandies, cordials, and fortified beverages. May specialize in one phase of processing and be designated according to duties performed as Rectifying Attendant (beverage); Whiskey Filterer (beverage); Whiskey-Proof Reader (beverage); Whiskey-Regauger (beverage).
GOE: 06.02.15 STRENGTH: L GED: R4 M3 L3 SVP: 6 DLU: 77

522.382-022 MASH-TUB-COOKER OPERATOR (beverage) alternate titles: cooker

Controls equipment to cook grain meal to prepare mash for fermentation process prior to distillation into alcohol, gin, or whiskey: Fills cooker with water and opens valves to admit steam that circulates through pipes in vat and heats water to specified temperature. Pumps ground meal from meal tank into hopper, balanced on scale, to weigh specified amount and turns handwheels to regulate flow of meal into cooker. Starts revolving blades in cooker to agitate mixture as it cooks. Observes temperature gauges to ascertain temperature of mixture in cooker and turns valves to increase or decrease temperature. Cooks mash for specified time and pumps cooked mash into cooling tub. Pumps cooled mash into fermenting tank. Opens valves to admit compressed air, through perforated pipes at bottom of fermenting tank, to keep meal in suspension as it flows from cooling tub into fermenting tank.
GOE: 06.02.15 STRENGTH: M GED: R4 M2 L3 SVP: 5 DLU: 77

522.382-026 STILL OPERATOR II (beverage) alternate titles: beer-still runner compounder; still runner

Controls still from central control board, to distill brandy, gin, vodka, or whiskey: Adjusts valves to control temperature and rate of flow of distilling materials through still and auxiliary equipment, such as stripping column, rectifier, condenser, and *tribox*. Observes gauges, dials, and charts to ensure that temperature and rate of flow of distillants are maintained according to formula, so that specified proof of distilled liquor is obtained. Ascertains temperature and specific gravity of liquor, using thermometer and hydrometer, and compares readings with standard gauging manual to determine proof of distilled liquor. Draws sample of distilled liquor for laboratory analysis. Pumps distilled liquor from tribox into cistern tank to be *regauged*. May be designated according to type of liquor distilled as Still Operator, Brandy (beverage); Still Operator, Gin (beverage); Still Operator, Whiskey (beverage).
GOE: 06.02.15 STRENGTH: L GED: R4 M4 L3 SVP: 6 DLU: 77

522.382-030 STILL OPERATOR I (beverage)

Controls still that produces high-proof alcohol from fermented wine: Records temperature, pressure, flow gauge and meter readings. Sets and adjusts controls to regulate and maintain specified temperature and pressure of unit. Turns valves to regulate flow of alcohol through unit and into storage tanks. Records amount of time consumed during distilling process. Collects alcohol samples for laboratory analysis.
GOE: 06.02.15 STRENGTH: L GED: R3 M2 L3 SVP: 5 DLU: 77

522.382-034 SUGAR BOILER (sugar & conf.)

Controls vacuum pan sugar boilers to concentrate sugar liquor and grow sugar crystals to specified size: Starts vacuum pump, and opens valves to admit specified amounts of liquor and steam into vacuum pan, and water into condenser unit. Observes boiling of liquor through sight glasses. Adjusts valves to maintain specified temperatures and pressures and obtain supersaturated solution without carmelizing sugar. Opens valve to shock solution with panseed (powdered sugar) and start formation of sugar crystals. Obtains samples of solution, using proofstick, and observes grain size under microscope to determine when crystals have grown to specified size. Opens pan-feed valve to control growth of crystals. Samples solution to ensure that sugar crystals remain at specified sizes as pan fills. Closes pan-feed valve when pan is filled and continues boiling until solution reaches specified concentration of sugar-crystals and massecuite. Turns valves to stop boiling and to break vacuum seal on pan. Turns valve to dump sugar into mixing tank or crystallizer. Washes and steams pan after dumping strike to remove sugar remaining on coils or calandria. Records strike on station log. May be designated according to type of liquor boiled as Soft-Sugar Boiler (sugar & conf.); White-Sugar Boiler (sugar & conf.); or according to stage in process as High-Raw-Sugar Boiler (sugar & conf.); Remelt-Sugar Boiler (sugar & conf.).
GOE: 06.02.15 STRENGTH: L GED: R3 M2 L3 SVP: 6 DLU: 77

522.382-038 VINEGAR MAKER (food prep., nec)

Controls equipment to produce vinegar: Starts pumps and opens valves to charge generators and concentrators with specified volume of vinegar starter, water, alcohol, and coolant. Monitors air and temperature gauges and flowmeters and adjusts thermostats, valves, and dials to maintain prescribed generating and concentrating conditions for strength of vinegar being processed. Turns valves to regulate rate and volume of solution through filter tank and to transfer solution to storage or shipping tank. Tests vinegar samples for grain content (strength), using pH meter and hydrometer. Records test results and air temperature readings on process control cards.
GOE: 06.02.15 STRENGTH: M GED: R3 M2 L3 SVP: 4 DLU: 77

522.384-010 FISH ROE TECHNICIAN (can. & preserv.)

Sorts, grades, and packs egg skeins containing fish roe: Examines egg skeins (membrane-enclosed ovaries, tissue, and fish roe) for unacceptable conditions, such as immaturity, bruises, or blood saturation. Discards unacceptable skeins and places acceptable skeins in containers for weighing and to await further processing. Dissolves specified salts in water, following brining formula; tests specific gravity of solution, using hydrometer; and pours brining solution into agitation vat. Flips switches to start vat agitators, pours preweighed amount of egg skeins into vat, and turns knob on timer to set brining cycle. Feels skeins for firmness and texture to determine effect of brine on skeins. Removes processed skeins from vat, using wooden-handled seine, and places skeins in container to drain. Tests brine in vat, using hydrometer, and adds specified salts when required to maintain salinity of brining solution at specified level. Examines, grades, and separates processed egg skeins, according to factors such as color, length, and width, utilizing product experience. Selects boxes marked for prescribed grade of egg skeins, places plastic sheets across bottom of boxes as liner, and sprinkles salt over liners prior to packing skeins. Positions layers of skeins in boxes to ensure preservation and seasoning in boxes. Weighs boxes on scales after packing, and adds or removes skeins to obtain specified weight. Folds plastic liner over filled boxes, positions lids on boxes, and stacks packed boxes for storage during aging process.
GOE: 06.02.28 STRENGTH: M GED: R3 M2 L2 SVP: 6 DLU: 86

522.465-010 STEEP TENDER (grain-feed mills)

Tends steep tanks to soften corn and other grains preparatory to grinding: Opens hatch and chute gate leading to steep tank, and signals GRAIN RECEIVER (grain-feed mills) to load tank with grain. Turns valves and starts pumps to fill tank with steep-water to specified level. Observes thermometers

and opens steam valves to heat tank to specified temperature. Tests specific gravity of water in tanks, using hydrometer, to determine when steeping process is complete. Records data, such as number of batches and bushels steeped, length of steeping cycle, and temperature and specific gravity of each batch. May prepare grinding schedules to facilitate production. May operate sulfur burner to regulate sulfuric acid concentration in steep water, millhouse, and starch wash water. May work as member of team and be designated according to position as Bottom Steep Tender (grain-feed mills); Top Steep Tender (grain-feed mills).
GOE: 06.04.15 STRENGTH: L GED: R3 M2 L2 SVP: 4 DLU: 77

522.482-010   MASHER (beverage)
Operates cooker and mashing tub to cook and combine cereal, such as corn or rice, and malt to produce wort: Opens slide gate on scale hopper to fill cooker and tub with measured amounts of malt and cereal. Starts pumps and turns valves to admit hot water into cooker and tub. Starts power-rakes that mix cereal and water in cooker, and malt and water in tub. Ignites burners to cook cereal and mash over controlled cooking cycle. Turns outlet valve on cooker and starts pump that transfers cereal mash to tub. Turns valve that admits steam into tub to heat mash to specified temperature. Starts power-rake that mixes mash. Adds iodine to sample of mash and examines color to determine degree of saccharization. Turns outlet valve to transfer cooked mash to filter press or lautertub. Washes mashing tub and cooker, using high-pressure water hoses and cleaning solutions. Records mash temperature, steam pressure, and degree of saccharization.
GOE: 06.02.15 STRENGTH: L GED: R3 M2 L3 SVP: 4 DLU: 77

522.485-010   PICKLING SOLUTION MAKER (meat products)
Tends machine that mixes pickling solution for use in curing meats: Weighs specified amount of dry ingredients, such as phosphate and nitrate, on scale, according to written specifications. Turns valve to fill vat of mixing machine with water, and dumps dry ingredients into vat. Presses button to activate machine agitator that mixes ingredients and turns valve to admit brine solution into vat. Tests mixed solution for saline content, using salinometer, and turns valve to stop flow of brine solution into vat when specified saline content is obtained. Turns drain valve or presses pump button to drain or pump mixed pickling solution from vat into storage tank for use in curing process. May turn steam valve to heat solution to specified temperature. May weigh specified amounts of ingredients to prepare dry-cure mix and mix ingredients, using ladle or electric mixer. May observe meat color to determine degree of cure.
GOE: 06.04.15 STRENGTH: H GED: R2 M2 SVP: 3 DLU: 77

522.584-010   OLIVE BRINE TESTER (can. & preserv.) alternate titles: storage brine worker; storage laborer
Tests brine in olive barrels, maintains salinity of specified level, and inspects olives for evidence of spoilage: Knocks bung from barrel, using mallet. Siphons sample of solution from cask and reads indicator level, using hydrometer, to measure solution salinity. Replaces solution or adds water or salt to maintain brine salinity at specified level. Feels, smells, and visually examines olives to detect spoilage, wrinkling, and discoloration. Reseals barrel with bung, using mallet. May add vinegar or lactic acid to solution to retard spoilage.
GOE: 06.03.02 STRENGTH: L GED: R2 M2 L2 SVP: 3 DLU: 77

522.585-014   GERMINATION WORKER (beverage)
Tends equipment that controls temperature and humidity in rotating drums or compartments in which barley is germinated to produce malt: Starts fans that force and circulate moist, heated air into drums or compartments. Moves damper counterweights or lowers handle to adjust and obtain specified temperature and humidity. Adds water to drum, using metered hose, or starts screw-type mixing machine equipped with water sprayer to ensure uniformity of germination. Removes sample of germinated barley from drum or compartment for laboratory analysis. Records such data concerned with malting cycle as air and water temperature and humidity content.
GOE: 06.02.15 STRENGTH: M GED: R3 M2 L2 SVP: 5 DLU: 77

522.587-010   CARBONATION TESTER (beverage)
Measures and records volume of carbon dioxide in storage tanks during carbonation of beer, and purity of carbon dioxide present in beer after fermentation: Connects test apparatus to tank test cocks on storage tanks during carbonation of beer. Reads electronic meter on test apparatus and records meter readings that indicate volume of carbon dioxide, or amount of carbonation, present in beer. Observes calibrated tube of testing instrument attached to tank test cocks after fermentation of beer, and records readings that indicate percentage of oxygen or purity in carbon dioxide content of beer.
GOE: 06.03.02 STRENGTH: L GED: R3 M2 L2 SVP: 2 DLU: 77

522.662-010   RECEIVER, FERMENTING CELLARS (beverage)
Operates pumps that add yeast to wort, following standard instructions: Turns spigot to drain yeast from pressurized yeast tub into yeast wagon, or starts pump to transfer yeast from storage tank to yeast brink (pressurized tank that pumps measured amounts of yeast to starting tank). Connects wort and starting tank lines. Signals PUMPER, BREWERY (beverage) or starts pump to transfer wort from storage to starting tanks. Mixes yeast and wort, using paddle and connects wagon and wort lines, or opens valve on brink tank to transfer yeast mixture or yeast to wort in starting tank. Observes flow dials and pressure gauges to ensure that specified ratio of yeast to wort is maintained. Opens starting tank valve to obtain sample for laboratory analysis. May pump pure yeast culture, prepared by YEAST-CULTURE DEVELOPER (beverage), from sterile

barrels through successive yeast culture tanks to permit further cultivation of yeast prior to adding it to wort and be designated Culture-Room Worker (beverage).
GOE: 06.02.15 STRENGTH: M GED: R3 M2 L2 SVP: 4 DLU: 77

522.662-014   REDRYING-MACHINE OPERATOR (tobacco) alternate titles: tobacco drying-machine operator
Operates redrying machine to dry, cool, and moisten tobacco for packing or further processing: Starts flow of steam or hot air into drying units and steam and water in ordering section. Starts fan that circulates hot air in drying units and conveyor that carries tobacco through drying unit, cooling section, and ordering section. Observes air pressure gauges, humidity and temperature charts, or thermometer to determine whether specified amount of heat, steam, or air pressure is maintained. Feels tobacco to determine moisture content and regulates flow of hot air, steam, and water to correct deviations from standard. May remove sample leaves of tobacco from machine for moisture content measurement.
GOE: 06.02.15 STRENGTH: L GED: R3 M2 L2 SVP: 5 DLU: 77

522.665-010   FILTER TENDER (grain-feed mills)
Tends rotary vacuum and drum or leaf pressure filters that purify liquid sugars: Turns valves to control flow of materials through filters during semiautomatic or manual operation of equipment, as instructed. Observes liquid sugar flowing through filters to detect cloudiness and turns valves to regulate flow, recirculate filtrate, or bypass filter for cleaning. Moves levers to raise filter covers and cleans filter, using hot water hose.
GOE: 06.04.15 STRENGTH: L GED: R3 M1 L2 SVP: 4 DLU: 77

522.665-014   YEAST PUSHER (beverage)
Tends equipment to transfer surplus yeast from fermenting cellar to storage tanks in yeast drying plant: Couples hose between yeast tank and flow lines, using wrench. Opens valves on line to effect uninterrupted flow. Notifies yeast plant to prepare to receive yeast. Opens gravity-feed outlet valve to permit yeast to drop into storage tanks. Climbs into tank to spray yeast residue with water and pushes it to outlet to complete transfer, using water hose and paddle.
GOE: 06.04.15 STRENGTH: M GED: R2 M1 L1 SVP: 2 DLU: 77

522.667-010   LIQUOR INSPECTOR (beverage) alternate titles: content checker
Examines filled bottles of distilled liquor to detect imperfections or breaks in glass or foreign particles within bottle: Removes bottle from conveyor line, places it in front of strong light, and examines it to detect imperfections in glass or foreign particles within bottle. Informs CONTAINER WASHER, MACHINE (any industry) to stop machine when foreign particles are detected within bottles. May be designated according to type of liquor inspected as Gin Inspector (beverage); Whiskey Inspector (beverage).
GOE: 06.03.02 STRENGTH: L GED: R2 M1 L1 SVP: 2 DLU: 77

522.682-010   KETTLE OPERATOR (beverage)
Controls equipment to cook grain mash and boil resulting liquor (wort) with hops to flavor it preparatory to fermentation, following written or oral specifications: Mixes and cooks specified amounts of malt, corn, and rice in water, maintaining temperatures for designated periods of time. Turns valves to transfer mash to lautertub to strain and extract wort, and to control flow of wort from lautertub to brew kettle. Adds specified amounts of hops to wort in brew kettle and cooks mixture [KETTLE TENDER (beverage)]. Drains wort through hop-extractor into hot-wort tank and starts pump to transfer wort to cooler. May add hop extract to mixture in brew kettle.
GOE: 06.02.15 STRENGTH: L GED: R3 M2 L3 SVP: 4 DLU: 77

522.682-014   ORDERING-MACHINE OPERATOR (tobacco) alternate titles: conditioning-machine operator; ordering-box operator; steam-box tender; steamer
Operates *ordering machine* to moisten tobacco preparatory to processing: Starts machine and conveyor and turns valve to start flow of steam into chamber. Observes gauge to determine whether specified amount of steam pressure is maintained. Feels tobacco leaves to determine moisture content and regulates flow of steam, hot air, or water so that tobacco will be pliable and easily processed. Observes flow of tobacco from machine onto conveyor or into tubs or boxes. Regulates speed of conveyor. May feed tobacco onto conveyor of ordering machine.
GOE: 06.02.15 STRENGTH: L GED: R3 M2 L2 SVP: 4 DLU: 77

522.684-010   PICKLER (can. & preserv.) alternate titles: pickle maker; pickle processor
Pickles prepared food products in preservative or flavoring solutions: Mixes ingredients, such as salt, vinegar, or sugar in barrels, vats, or tanks, according to formula, to make pickling or flavoring brine. Dumps product, such as vegetables, fruit, fish, fish eggs, or meat into solution to soak for specified time. May pack product into barrels in layers, covering each layer with preservative compound. May remove contents from containers by hand or with dip net. May be designated according to product pickled as Fish Pickler (can. & preserv.); Gherkin Pickler (can. & preserv.); Pepper Pickler (can. & preserv.); Sweet-Pickled-Fruit Maker (can. & preserv.); Sweet-Pickle Maker (can. & preserv.).
GOE: 06.04.28 STRENGTH: H GED: R2 M2 L2 SVP: 3 DLU: 78

522.685-010   BLENDING-MACHINE OPERATOR (dairy products)
Tends machine that rinses and dries cottage cheese and blends it with cream to produce cream-style cottage cheese: Inserts plastic liner in tub, sprays liner

interior with sterilizing fluid, and slides tub under machine discharge outlet. Signals COTTAGE-CHEESE MAKER (dairy products) to pump cottage cheese to machine. Presses switches and turns water valve to start machine that spreads cottage cheese into even layer, sprays cheese with refrigerated water to cool and rinse it, and squeezes cheese dry under pressure belt. Feels dried cheese to determine if specified amount of water is removed, and adjusts pressure belt, as required, using wrenches. Starts pump and turns valve to control flow of cream from refrigerated tank to auger that blends cream with cottage cheese. Observes texture of creamed cottage cheese and adjusts valve to maintain cream content at specified level. Tastes cottage cheese and reports off-flavors to management. Stops machine and closes filled tub. Blends cream and salt according to formula, using mixer, and pumps cream to refrigerated tank.
GOE: 06.04.15 STRENGTH: M GED: R3 M2 L2 SVP: 3 DLU: 77

522.685-014 BREWERY CELLAR WORKER (beverage)
Tends equipment that cools and adds yeast to wort to produce beer: Starts pumps and turns valves to control flow of refrigerant through cooler coils, to regulate flow of hot wort from tank through cooler into starting tank, and to admit specified amounts of air into wort [COOLING-MACHINE OPERATOR (beverage)]. Turns valves to add yeast to wort and to transfer wort to fermenting tanks [RECEIVER, FERMENTING CELLARS (beverage)].
GOE: 06.04.15 STRENGTH: M GED: R2 M1 L1 SVP: 2 DLU: 77

522.685-018 BRINE MAKER I (can. & preserv.) alternate titles: pickling-solution maker
Tends steam cooker to prepare brines and pickling solutions used for preserving food products: Opens valve to admit required amount of water into steam cooker, observing water gauge or designated mark on cooker. Pours salt or other ingredients, such as vinegar, alum, tumeric, sugar, and flavoring, into water, using measuring container. Mixes ingredients in kettle, using paddle. Admits steam into jacket of cooker and allows solution to boil for specified length of time. Observes temperature gauge and regulates heat to maintain boiling temperature. Tests solution for salt and other preserving content, using salinometer or hydrometer. Adds water, salt, or other ingredients until prescribed specific gravity is attained. Pumps solution to brine vat or holding tank for aging and curing.
GOE: 06.04.15 STRENGTH: M GED: R2 M2 L2 SVP: 3 DLU: 77

522.685-022 BRINE MAKER II (can. & preserv.)
Tends equipment that mixes brine solution of specified sulfur-dioxide concentration in vat to bleach and preserve cherries prior to processing them into maraschino cherries: Turns valve and observes volume indicators to fill vat with specified volume of water. Screws hose coupling on outlet valve of sulfur-dioxide gas container, using wrench, and lowers other end of hose into water. Reads chart and gauges and opens valve to admit specified amount of gas into vat to obtain solution of specified concentration. Draws sample of brine solution from vat and tests it for volumetric concentration, using test equipment and reagents, such as starch and iodine. May add lime, according to formula, and in proportion to volume of brine and ripeness of cherries to provide firming agent. Mixes lime in solution, using paddle. May pump brine from vat into plastic-lined bins filled with cherries.
GOE: 06.04.15 STRENGTH: M GED: R2 M2 L1 SVP: 4 DLU: 77

522.685-026 CARBONATION EQUIPMENT TENDER (beverage)
Tends equipment to regulate flow of carbon dioxide into beer lines and tanks to carbonate beer: Observes volume meters and pressure gauges and turns valves to admit specified amounts of carbon dioxide at specified pressures into tanks and lines. Observes beer through sight glasses and adjusts flow and pressure of carbon dioxide to control turbulence.
GOE: 06.04.15 STRENGTH: L GED: R3 M2 L2 SVP: 3 DLU: 77

522.685-030 CASING-MACHINE OPERATOR (tobacco) alternate titles: flavoring-machine operator; overshot operator; tobacco flavorer
Tends machine that applies flavoring or *casing fluid* to chewing or smoking tobacco, by either of following methods: (1) Starts machine, pours fluid into trough of machine. Forks or shovels tobacco into hopper or onto conveyor that carries tobacco through revolving drum immersed in fluid or under spraying device. (2) Turns valves and starts pumps to transfer fluid from storage tank to spray tank and to spray fluid on tobacco passing under sprayer on conveyor or fed into revolving drum. Opens valve to admit steam into jacket of spray tank to heat fluid to specified temperature. May remove excess fluid from tobacco [WRINGER OPERATOR (tobacco) 522.685-106]. May tend grinders that grind menthol crystals and add menthol to casing fluid.
GOE: 06.04.15 STRENGTH: L GED: R2 M2 L2 SVP: 3 DLU: 77

522.685-034 CORN COOKER (food prep., nec)
Tends equipment that cooks corn in steam cooking vat or kettle to soften corn preparatory to grinding into products, such as masa (cornmeal dough), for use in making corn chips and tortillas: Dumps prescribed quantities of ingredients, such as shelled corn, water, and lime, into cooking vat, and sets controls to admit steam into jacket of vat. Adjusts cooking temperature and starts equipment that automatically cooks and stirs ingredients. Drains corn into tank of water, after specified cooking time, for cooling and soaking preparatory to hulling and grinding by CORN GRINDER (food prep., nec).
GOE: 06.04.15 STRENGTH: H GED: R2 M2 L2 SVP: 2 DLU: 77

522.685-038 CURING-BIN OPERATOR (grain-feed mills)
Tends moistening drums of curing bins that spread moisture uniformly through cooked grain prior to or after being shaped into breakfast cereal, such

as flakes or shredded biscuits: Opens gate in conveyor duct to deflect incoming grain into first bin. Closes gate when bin is full, records time, and repeats filling operation with next bin. Pulls lever to dump grain onto conveyor as specified curing time is completed for each bin. Dislodges remaining grain from bin, using pole. May tend bins and cooling towers that cool toasted grain to specified temperature for packaging by starting fan and turning water valves as grain moves through equipment and moving lever to direct grain into chutes of filling machines.
GOE: 06.04.15 STRENGTH: H GED: R2 M2 L2 SVP: 3 DLU: 77

522.685-042 DE-ALCOHOLIZER (beverage)
Tends distilling equipment that removes alcohol from beer to convert it to near-beer: Turns valves to admit water to condensers. Starts impellers and vacuum pumps, and opens beer inlet valve. Observes meters, and steam-pressure and vacuum gauges, and turns valves to make adjustments required to draw off vaporized and condensed alcohol and return other gases to solution. Starts pump to transfer solution (near-beer) to storage tank or rack room. Inspects hoses, pipes, tanks, and connections for leaks and cleans equipment by flushing with water.
GOE: 06.04.15 STRENGTH: L GED: R2 M2 L2 SVP: 3 DLU: 77

522.685-046 DEODORIZER (chemical)
Tends distilling equipment and filter presses that deodorize processed oils used in manufacture of margarine, shortening, and other edible products: Turns valves to admit steam to heat oils to specified temperature. Pours or dumps specified chemicals into hopper, using standard measuring container. Maintains specified pressure and vacuum to remove fatty acids and gases from oil.
GOE: 06.04.15 STRENGTH: M GED: R2 M2 L2 SVP: 3 DLU: 77

522.685-050 DORR OPERATOR (sugar & conf.)
Tends processing equipment that separates organic colloidal matter from carbonated raw sugar beet liquor, and purifies liquor prior to refining into granulated sugar: Opens valves and starts pump to fill settling tank with liquor and adds specified amounts of lime or milk of lime solution. Sets controls to maintain specified temperature of lime-liquor solution to aid in precipitation process. Takes sample of liquor from tank and tests for purity, using refractometer. Opens valves and pumps liquor to process storage tanks and lime sludge to filter station. Washes remaining sludge from bottom of settling tank. Records data, such as amount of liquor processed and refractometer readings on batches, in station log.
GOE: 06.04.15 STRENGTH: L GED: R2 M2 L2 SVP: 3 DLU: 77

522.685-054 DROPPER, FERMENTING CELLAR (beverage)
Tends pumps to transfer pitched wort from starter tank to fermenting tank: Observes yeast in *pitched wort* to verify yeast development and collects samples of beer in early fermentation stages for laboratory analysis. Skims brown yeast from beer surface, using paddle. Fastens and clamps hose terminals to connect lines from starter to fermenting tank, using wrenches. Turns valves to open line to transfer pitched wort by gravity feed into fermenting tank. Pumps caustic soda solutions through transfer lines to clean interior.
GOE: 06.04.15 STRENGTH: M GED: R2 M1 L2 SVP: 2 DLU: 77

522.685-058 DRUM LOADER AND UNLOADER (beverage)
Tends revolving drums in which barley is germinated under controlled temperature and humidity to produce malt: Couples drum spout to steeping tanks or to base of screw conveyors containing steeped barley. Turns valve or pulls lever to drop barley into drum or starts conveyor that empties barley into drum. Starts rotation of drum that mixes barley to promote uniformity of growth and temperature. Stops drum, following oral instructions. Unlocks and opens slide door, and starts drum rotating to dump barley onto conveyor. Crawls into drum and scrapes walls, using metal hook to remove barley. Washes drum with water, using high-pressure hose. May stand in pit under revolving drum and pull barley from drum, using metal hook.
GOE: 06.04.15 STRENGTH: H GED: R2 M1 L1 SVP: 2 DLU: 77

522.685-062 FERMENTER, WINE (beverage)
Tends tanks that convert (ferment) crushed fruit or must into wines by either of following methods: (1) Dumps or shovels specified amounts of crushed fruits into wine tanks and starts pump to admit premeasured amounts of syrup. Turns valve to admit compressed air into tank and allows mash to ferment for specified period of time. (2) Pours and dumps specified amount of chemicals and yeast into tank containing must to prevent bacteria growth and induce fermentation. Starts pump to circulate must to enrich color and flavor of wine. Starts pump to circulate must through heat exchanger as required to prolong fermentation, according to temperature readings. Turns valve to admit compressed air into must when producing sparkling burgundy and champagne. Starts pump to transfer fermented mash or wine into storage tanks. May pump fermented wine through filter equipment to remove sediment. May meter out specified amounts of sugar and water into automatic mixing tank to produce syrup. May be designated according to type of wine produced as Fermenter, Champagne (beverage).
GOE: 06.04.15 STRENGTH: L GED: R3 M2 L3 SVP: 4 DLU: 77

522.685-066 FISH SMOKER (can. & preserv.)
Tends smoke chamber in which fish are cured: Removes salt-cured fish from barrels and hangs fish on racks. Places racks of fish in washing tank, and turns valve to regulate fresh water flow. Lifts racks of fish from tanks and places racks in smoke chamber. Fills hopper of chamber with wood chips and turns

on burner. Turns wheel to regulate amount of smoke entering chamber. Examines color and texture of fish to ensure that curing has proceeded according to specifications. Removes and stacks cured fish on trays for packaging.
GOE: 06.04.15 STRENGTH: H GED: R2 M1 L2 SVP: 3 DLU: 77

522.685-070 HONEY PROCESSOR (food prep., nec) alternate titles: pasteurizer

Tends equipment that pasteurizes and filters liquid honey, and seeds honey with crystals to make crystallized honey for use as food spread: Turns valve to admit honey from blending tanks to pasteurizer, and to adjust and control pasteurizing temperature. Installs pads in filter press and turns handcrank to tighten pads. Starts pumps and adjusts pressure to force honey through filter and transfer honey to bottling machine or cooling vats. Pours container of honey crystals into vat of liquid honey and mixes it with paddle or electric stirring rod to induce controlled crystallization. May bottle honey.
GOE: 06.04.15 STRENGTH: L GED: R2 M1 L1 SVP: 3 DLU: 77

522.685-074 MALT-HOUSE OPERATOR (beverage)

Tends equipment to germinate barley to make malt: Fills tank with water, weighs barley conveyed into beam scale hopper, and drops barley into tank to steep for predetermined period. Starts conveyors to load rotating drums or compartments with steeped barley. Regulates temperature and humidity in closed drums or open compartments to achieve maximum germination of barley. Moves discharge chute to spread germinated barley evenly over kiln floor for drying. Starts furnaces to heat kilns to specified temperature to dry malt (germinated barley). Starts conveyors to move dried malt successively through cleaning, separating, and grading machines.
GOE: 06.04.15 STRENGTH: M GED: R2 M2 L2 SVP: 3 DLU: 77

522.685-078 MOLASSES PREPARER (food prep., nec) alternate titles: mash-floor operator

Tends equipment to process molasses wort for use in production of baker's yeast: Turns valve to admit molasses into weigh tank. Observes scale and pumps measured molasses into heating tank. Adds specified amounts of water and chemicals to molasses to precipitate impurities. Starts mixing unit and opens valves to allow steam to circulate in coils of tank to heat molasses to specified temperature. Mixes diatomaceous earth with water and pours specified amount of mixture into tank to clarify molasses. Pumps filter solution through filter to precoat screens. Pumps molasses through filter to settling tank to remove impurities from molasses. Measures sludge level in settling tank, using depth gauge, and opens valve to decant molasses. Observes level indicators and pumps specified amount of cane molasses to mix with beet molasses in holding tank.
GOE: 06.04.15 STRENGTH: M GED: R3 M2 L2 SVP: 3 DLU: 77

522.685-082 NEUTRALIZER (grain-feed mills)

Tends equipment that neutralizes acid in glucose (converted starch): Weighs prescribed amount of soda ash on scales and dissolves soda ash in water. Pours measured amount of *filtracell* into neutralizer tank. Turns valves to admit soda ash solution into tank to neutralize acid. Obtains sample from tank, and holds sample against light to detect formation of precipitate. Adds additional soda ash if precipitate is not readily forming. Adds acid to tank of starch to begin hydrolysis of starch into glucose.
GOE: 06.04.15 STRENGTH: L GED: R3 M2 L2 SVP: 3 DLU: 77

522.685-086 PICKLE PUMPER (meat products) alternate titles: injection-machine operator; pickle-water-pump operator; vein pumper

Tends machine that automatically injects meat with curing solution: Adjusts height of injection needles and width of conveyor guides, using wrenches. Turns valves to regulate flow and pressure of curing solution in pumping system. Starts machine and conveyor. Places meat on conveyor that pulls meat under machine injection needle which forces measured amount of curing solution into meat, and dumps treated piece into cart. Weighs meat before and after injection to ensure that specified amount of solution has been injected. May lift treated meat from conveyor, using handhook, and drop it into tank. May inject curing solution into meat, using hand pump, and be designated Pumper, Hand (meat products).
GOE: 06.04.15 STRENGTH: M GED: R2 M2 L2 SVP: 3 DLU: 77

522.685-090 SEED-YEAST OPERATOR (food prep., nec) alternate titles: pure-culture operator; yeast-culture operator

Tends series of tanks to inoculate molasses wort with pure yeast culture to produce seed yeast for use in production of baker's yeast: Pours molasses wort and chemicals into tank, according to formula, and adds yeast culture from flask. Observes thermometer on tank and opens valves to allow water to circulate in coils of tank to maintain specified temperature. Pumps air into tank to aerate yeast. Tests specific gravity of yeast, using hydrometer, and tests acidity of yeast, using pH meter. Adds required chemicals to adjust acidity when necessary. Pumps wort to successive tanks as yeast growth progresses. Submits samples of wort to laboratory for analysis.
GOE: 06.04.15 STRENGTH: L GED: R3 M2 L2 SVP: 3 DLU: 77

522.685-094 STEAM-CONDITIONER OPERATOR (tobacco)

Tends equipment that injects steam into opened hogsheads of tobacco to order tobacco prior to further processing: Slips end of perforated metal tube over holder of hydraulic press, pushes hogshead under tube, and presses button to activate mechanism that pushes tube into center of tobacco. Presses button to release tube and raise press. Pulls hogshead from bed of press, throws canvas

cover over top of hogshead, pushes hogshead into steam chamber, and connects flexible hose to end of tube protruding from top of hogshead. Presses buttons to lower door to seal chamber and to activate steam. Turns knobs to build up steam pressure and to activate air pressure that forces steam through air vents of tube into tobacco. Sets timer and observes light that signals when tobacco has been conditioned to specifications. Flips switch to activate exhaust mechanism that removes steam from chamber. Presses button to raise door. Pulls hogshead from chamber and removes tube from hogshead, using overhead chain hoist. Pushes hogshead to feeder conveyor.
GOE: 06.04.15 STRENGTH: H GED: R2 M1 L1 SVP: 2 DLU: 77

522.685-098 STILL OPERATOR (agriculture; can. & preserv.)

Tends batch stills and related equipment to separate and condense vitamins or oils from fruits or mint hay: Pumps or pours specified quantities of liquids into still. Observes thermostat and sets controls on instrument panel to maintain specified temperatures throughout distillation cycle and to control condensation. Draws samples of distillant for laboratory analysis. Observes color of distillant to determine when distillation is completed. Records operating data, such as weight, yield of product, gauge readings, and number of batches distilled.
GOE: 06.04.15 STRENGTH: M GED: R3 M1 L2 SVP: 4 DLU: 77

522.685-102 VACUUM-CONDITIONER OPERATOR (tobacco) alternate titles: steam-pressure-chamber operator

Tends vacuum conditioner (steam-pressure chamber) that moistens opened hogsheads of tobacco for further processing: Opens chamber door and pushes hogsheads of tobacco into chamber or starts hydraulic lift that moves hogsheads into chamber. Closes chamber door, starts vacuum pump, and turns valve to admit steam into chamber. Observes gauges and dials on control panel to determine when temperature and air, steam, and vacuum pressure reach specified levels to force steam through tobacco. Removes hogsheads from chamber.
GOE: 06.04.15 STRENGTH: H GED: R3 M2 L2 SVP: 3 DLU: 77

522.685-106 WRINGER OPERATOR (tobacco) alternate titles: casing-wringer operator; wrapper dipper

Tends machine that saturates tobacco leaves with *casing fluid* and removes excess fluid from leaves: Admits fluid to vat. Starts conveyor that feeds leaves through fluid and to wringer rolls of machine, or dumps leaves into vat, allows leaves to absorb moisture for specified time, and feeds moistened leaves between wringer rolls. Removes clogged leaves from rollers, using stick. Cleans rollers and vat, using steam and airhose.
GOE: 06.04.15 STRENGTH: H GED: R2 M1 L1 SVP: 2 DLU: 77

522.685-110 YEAST-FERMENTATION ATTENDANT (food prep., nec)

Tends fermentation tanks to propagate yeast in molasses wort: Opens valves to admit specified amounts of seed yeast and molasses wort into tanks. Dumps, pours, or meters measured quantities of nitrogen and phosphate to supplement diet of yeast. Pumps air into tank to aerate wort. Sets thermostat to maintain prescribed temperature levels in fermentation tanks. Tests wort for acidity, using pH meter, and adds specified chemicals to maintain required acidity. Adds additional wort and chemicals to tank, as yeast concentration increases, to facilitate yeast growth. Pumps wort with yeast cream (concentrated yeast suspension) to yeast-separating department.
GOE: 06.04.15 STRENGTH: L GED: R2 M2 L2 SVP: 3 DLU: 77

522.685-114 BARLEY STEEPER (beverage) alternate titles: steeper

Tends steeping tank that saturates barley with water preparatory to germination: Moves lever to open slide gate of weighing tank. Dumps barley into tank and weighs out specified amount. Turns handle to open and load barley into steeping tank. Turns water and air valves to fill steeping tank with water, remove chaff, and aerate barley. Reads and copies water and air temperature data to maintain record of steeping cycle. Drains and refills tank during cycle. Turns handles to open steeping tank and dumps steeped barley onto conveyor. May tend equipment to germinate barley [GERMINATION WORKER (beverage) 522.585-014].
GOE: 06.04.15 STRENGTH: M GED: R2 M2 L2 SVP: 2 DLU: 78

522.686-010 CHIP WASHER (beverage)

Shovels beechwood chips (used to impart flavor to beer) from fermenting tank into cart. Pushes cart into automatic washer and starts washer. Removes cart from washer and shovels washed chips onto floor of fermenting tank.
GOE: 06.04.39 STRENGTH: H GED: R1 M1 L1 SVP: 2 DLU: 77

522.686-014 GENERAL HELPER (food prep., nec) alternate titles: fermenter helper; yeast stacker

Dumps chemical nutrients into yeast fermentation tanks to supplement diet of yeast cells. Takes samples of wort from tank for laboratory analysis. Cleans fermentation tanks, using steam and water. Transfers ingredients, materials, and finished products to production, storage, and shipping area, using handtrucks.
GOE: 06.04.40 STRENGTH: M GED: R1 M1 L1 SVP: 2 DLU: 77

522.687-010 BARREL FILLER I (beverage) alternate titles: checker

Fills metal or wooden containers with distilled liquors, preparatory to aging: Rolls metal drum or wooden barrel, with bunghole side up, under spigot attached to storage tank. Inserts spigot nozzle into bunghole of container and opens valve to fill container with whiskey, gin, or vodka. Removes spigot nozzle from filled container when spigot has shut off automatically. Hammers bung into bunghole of barrel or screws threaded metal bung into bunghole of metal drum, using wrench. Rolls filled container aside for storing. When filling metal drums only, may be known as Drum Filler (beverage).

GOE: 06.04.36 STRENGTH: H GED: R1 M1 L1 SVP: 2 DLU: 77

522.687-014 BRINER (can. & preserv.) alternate titles: dipper, fish

Immerses fresh fish fillets in brine solution to condition them for wrapping or freezing: Places fish fillets in wire basket and submerges basket in salt and water solution for specified time. Removes basket from brine tank and dumps fillets on conveyor belt.
GOE: 06.04.28 STRENGTH: H GED: R1 M1 L1 SVP: 2 DLU: 77

522.687-018 BULKER (tobacco)

Fills *bulking cell* with stemmed and cased tobacco: Directs conveyor tube into cell and spreads tobacco in cell, using handfork. Positions hydraulic press over tobacco and pulls lever to activate press to pack tobacco into bulk for fermentation.
GOE: 06.04.28 STRENGTH: L GED: R1 M1 L1 SVP: 2 DLU: 77

522.687-022 FILLER ROOM ATTENDANT (tobacco)

Spreads filler tobacco leaves on trays after conditioning (wetting) to allow air to circulate between leaves. Feels leaves to determine moisture content and empties trays into boxes or cans when leaves are at stage specified for processing. May fill cans with tobacco [CAN FILLER (tobacco)]. May moisten tobacco [LEAF CONDITIONER (tobacco)].
GOE: 06.04.28 STRENGTH: M GED: R1 M1 L1 SVP: 2 DLU: 77

522.687-026 LEAF CONDITIONER (tobacco) alternate titles: casing wetter; tobacco conditioner; tobacco curer; tobacco dipper

Moistens (conditions or cases) hands of tobacco to make leaves pliable for processing: Removes hands from receiving box and dips them into water or sprays water over leaves. Stacks leaves, stem down, on drainboard and covers leaves with cloth or paper. May pack drained leaves in cases and transfer cases to steam or humidifier room, using handtruck. May mix various grades and types of tobacco prior to conditioning. May be designated according to type of tobacco as Binder Caser (tobacco); Wrapper Caser (tobacco). May feel tobacco leaves from steam room and moisten butts and tops of hands that are too dry and be designated Cigar-Tobacco Rehandler (tobacco).
GOE: 06.04.28 STRENGTH: M GED: R1 M1 L1 SVP: 2 DLU: 77

522.687-030 LEAF-CONDITIONER HELPER (tobacco) alternate titles: caser helper

Assists LEAF CONDITIONER (tobacco) to condition tobacco leaves. Performs other duties as described under HELPER (any industry) Master Title.
GOE: 06.04.28 STRENGTH: M GED: R1 M1 L1 SVP: 2 DLU: 77

522.687-034 PICKLER (meat products) alternate titles: curing packer; green-meat packer; vat overhauler; vat packer

Loads cuts of meat into pickling vats or barrels to cure meat preparatory to smoking: Packs and arranges meat in vats or barrels by hand or with meat hook to ensure maximum saturation. Turns valves to admit curing solution into vats or pours in solution by hand. Covers vat or barrel to keep meat protected and submerged in solution. Sticks trier (hook) into meat and smells trier to determine degree of curing. Opens valves or pulls bungs to drain vats and barrels, and removes cured meat for further processing. Dumps frozen meat in water tank to defrost it preparatory to curing. May roll barrels to rearrange meat and ensure maximum saturation. May flush or blow marrow from ham bones. May clean vats with water and steam hoses.
GOE: 06.04.28 STRENGTH: M GED: R2 M1 L1 SVP: 2 DLU: 77

522.687-038 TURNER (can. & preserv.) alternate titles: box turner

Rearranges containers of fruit stacked in tiers in ripening room to expose all fruit equally to room temperature during ripening period. May truck fruit in and out of ripening room.
GOE: 06.04.40 STRENGTH: M GED: R1 M1 L1 SVP: 2 DLU: 77

522.687-042 WRAPPER-HANDS SPRAYER (tobacco) alternate titles: tobacco sprayer

Moistens hands of tobacco wrapper leaves with water, using spraygun, to make leaves pliable for processing. Feels leaves to determine whether moisture content is within prescribed limits. Weighs specified amounts of leaves and places leaves in containers for untier. Records amounts of wrapper and binder leaves used in making cigars.
GOE: 06.04.28 STRENGTH: L GED: R2 M2 L1 SVP: 2 DLU: 77

522.687-046 FISH ROE PROCESSOR (can. & preserv.)

Performs any combination of following tasks concerned with cannery processing of fish roe: Presses headless fish against work surface to ascertain sex of fish by presence or absence of milt. Inserts hand into body cavity of female fish, feels along ventral area of body to locate vent, and cups hand to remove viscera and egg skeins (membrane-enclosed ovaries, tissue, and fish roe). Separates viscera and organs from egg skeins by hand. Discards viscera and organs and places egg skeins in baskets for weighing. Weighs baskets containing egg skeins, using scales, and records totals on tally sheets. Dumps basket of egg skeins on work surface, and examines egg skeins for imperfections, such as blood saturation, immature eggs, and torn membranes. Separates egg skeins, according to size and species of fish. Places acceptable egg skeins in containers for reweighing. Rinses containers of egg skeins with water, using water hose, and dips containers in mild saline solution to rinse egg skeins prior to brining. Works under direction of FISH ROE TECHNICIAN (can. & preserv.) 522.384-010 to fill brining tanks, dump egg skeins into tanks, remove processed egg skeins, and pack egg skeins for shipment, following prescribed procedures. May slit underside of fish before removing egg skeins, using knife.

GOE: 06.04.28 STRENGTH: M GED: R2 M1 L1 SVP: 2 DLU: 86

523 HEATING, RENDERING, MELTING, DRYING, COOLING, FREEZING, AND RELATED OCCUPATIONS

This group includes occupations concerned with subjecting materials or products to heat and cold for a specific purpose, such as removing moisture or fat content, or preserving and storing them by refrigeration.

523.131-010 TESTING AND ANALYSIS DEPARTMENT SUPERVISOR (can. & preserv.)

Supervises and coordinates activities of workers engaged in sorting and packing nuts, and inspects sampling of nuts to estimate percentage that will be marketable from each delivery: Selects random sample of nuts from each delivery, places sample in containers, and attaches identification tag to container. Places nuts in drier to remove specified percentage of moisture. Weighs nuts before and after drying and records weight lost. Places nuts on perforated plate through which nuts pass into separate containers, according to size. Cracks nuts and examines them for blanks, worms, and shriveled centers. Segregates salable nuts, weighs nuts, and records percentage of marketable products. May explain procedures for estimating percentage of marketable products to growers. Performs other duties as describeed under SUPERVISOR (any industry) Master Title.
GOE: 06.01.01 STRENGTH: L GED: R4 M3 L4 SVP: 7 DLU: 77

523.132-010 SUPERVISOR, CHAR HOUSE (sugar & conf.)

Supervises and coordinates activities of workers engaged in regenerating bone-char, charcoal, and diatomaceous earth used as filtering media for sugar liquor: Orders emptying of filters, and transferring of char between char-house by CHAR PULLER (grain-feed mills; sugar & conf.) and other workers. Directs kiln operator in maintaining specified temperature in kiln and flow-rate of material through kiln. Performs other duties as described under SUPERVISOR (any industry) Master Title.
GOE: 06.02.01 STRENGTH: L GED: R4 M3 L3 SVP: 7 DLU: 77

523.137-010 SUPERVISOR, ICE HOUSE (food prep., nec)

Supervises and coordinates activities of workers engaged in filling cans, sucking cores, and pulling and dumping cans in ice plant. Performs duties as described under SUPERVISOR (any industry) Master Title.
GOE: 06.02.01 STRENGTH: L GED: R4 M2 L2 SVP: 7 DLU: 77

523.362-010 COCOA-BEAN ROASTER I (sugar & conf.)

Operates one or more roasters to remove moisture and impart specified color and flavor to cocoa beans: Adjusts thermostat and fuel valve to heat roasters to specified temperature. Observes temperature chart to ascertain heat pattern of roaster. Pulls handle to open hopper and drop beans into roaster. Starts roaster cylinder rotating to roast beans evenly. Examines sample of beans for color, dryness, or brittleness after specified roasting cycle, and tastes bean to judge if flavor conforms to standard. Adjusts roaster flame and dampers to control circulation of hot air on basis of evaluation of sample. Pulls handle when desired degree of roasting is reached to discharge beans onto conveyor that transfers beans to cracking and fanning machine. Records amounts of beans roasted. May tend bean-cleaning machine.
GOE: 06.02.15 STRENGTH: L GED: R3 M1 L1 SVP: 7 DLU: 77

523.362-014 DRIER OPERATOR (food prep., nec)

Controls equipment that dries macaroni according to laboratory specifications: Turns dials and opens steam valves on panelboard to regulate temperature, humidity, and drying time in preliminary, secondary, and final drying chambers, according to outside atmospheric conditions, specific product requirements, and drying stage. Enters chambers and feels macaroni to determine if product is drying according to specifications, relying upon knowledge and experience. Opens chamber hatch to admit cool air and adjusts controls to change drying speed at particular drying stages to comply with laboratory recommendation or to meet changing atmospheric conditions. Regulates temperature and humidity in pressroom to maintain required atmospheric conditions. Evaluates quality of dried macaroni on basis of color.
GOE: 06.02.15 STRENGTH: L GED: R4 M2 L3 SVP: 7 DLU: 77

523.380-010 COCOA-BEAN ROASTER II (sugar & conf.)

Sets up and operates such equipment as continuous roaster, cracker and fanner, dryer, and grinder, to process cocoa beans to make chocolate liquor: Turns gas valves and electric switches to start and heat roaster. Sets thermostat and rheostat to control temperature of roaster and speed of rotation. Starts conveyor to transfer specified type and amount of beans from storage to roaster. Examines sample of beans for color, tastes beans for flavor, and crumbles beans to determine moisture content. Adjusts temperature and speed of roaster in accordance with findings. Starts cracking and fanning machine to break and remove husks from roasted cocoa beans [CRACKING-AND-FANNING-MACHINE OPERATOR (sugar & conf.)]. Observes nibs (cracked roasted cocoa beans) and shells to evaluate husking process, and adjusts machine accordingly. Opens slide gate on fanner to convey nibs scheduled for dutch processing [DRIER OPERATOR (sugar & conf.)]. Starts agitator to mix beans in treating tank for specified time. Opens tank gate to release beans for conveying to dryer. Starts gas-fired dryer, sets rheostat, and feels beans for dryness. Starts conveyor to move dried beans to roaster for roasting or to grinding machine

[LIQUOR-GRINDING-MILL OPERATOR (sugar & conf.)]. Turns valve to pump chocolate liquor to storage tanks. Patrols area to observe coordination of machine and equipment to ensure orderly flow of material at specified rates.
GOE: 06.01.03 STRENGTH: L GED: R4 M2 L3 SVP: 7 DLU: 77

523.382-010 GUNNER (grain-feed mills) alternate titles: cereal popper; shooter

Controls guns (pressure cylinders) to expand or puff whole grain to produce breakfast cereal: Presses button to admit grain and water to electric- or gas-heated cylinder. Clamps lid in place and starts cylinder rotating. Turns valves and moves controls to regulate air pressure and temperature in cylinder to obtain product having puffed kernels of specified size, color, and uniformity. Removes lid after specified time, causing grain to expand as it escapes from cylinder. Examines and feels product to determine need for adjustments in process conditions.
GOE: 06.02.15 STRENGTH: L GED: R2 M2 L2 SVP: 2 DLU: 77

523.382-014 MAPLE-SYRUP MAKER (food prep., nec)

Controls equipment to produce maple syrup: Transfers maple sap to evaporator pan placed on stove, allowing product to flow through various compartments of evaporator. Pours additional sap into evaporator as needed to maintain uniform temperature. Transfers syrup to heated finishing pan when level of product in evaporator indicates evaporation is complete. Tests syrup for prescribed consistency by adding quantity of syrup to cold water and observing appearance. Filters evaporated syrup through cloths or other filtration media. Pours syrup into containers or molds for storage, use, or sale. May boil, stir, and evaporate syrup to form variety of maple products, such as maple sugar, wax, butter, or candy, depending on processing temperature and time, and be designated Maple-Products Maker (food prep., nec).
GOE: 06.02.15 STRENGTH: L GED: R3 M2 L2 SVP: 5 DLU: 77

523.382-018 MELTER OPERATOR (sugar & conf.)

Operates heating and mixing equipment (melters) that reclaims uncrystallized sugar from molasses and softens molasses adhering to sugar crystals: Starts pumps, turns valves to start flow of molasses, and starts conveyor that dumps sugar crystals into melting tanks. Turns steam valves to maintain specified temperature, and starts agitators. Observes dials on panelboard and adjusts controls to maintain specified temperature, steam pressure, and density of mixture. Tests mixture for alkalinity, using pH meter, and posts data, such as test results, temperature, and density of mixture on report form. May mix and store milk of lime solution. May add milk of lime to mixture to obtain specified alkalinity. May pump liquors to char house for filtration. May clean pump screens, using hose and water.
GOE: 06.02.15 STRENGTH: M GED: R3 M2 L2 SVP: 4 DLU: 77

523.382-022 PROCESSOR, INSTANT POTATO (food prep., nec)

Controls equipment to process potatoes into instant potato granules: Reads laboratory reports to stay apprised of laboratory test results of potato samples taken during processing. Observes lights, gauges, and meters on panelboard controls to determine temperature readings of equipment, such as precoolers, precoolers, cookers, and driers. Turns dials on panelboard to maintain operating temperature ranges as required to meet company standards. Flips switches and presses buttons on panelboard to start potato processing equipment, such as feed screws, mixers, cookers, and granule driers. Walks through processing areas and observes product consistency and product level in equipment, such as feed screws and cookers. Turns equipment controls on panelboard to adjust temperatures of cookers or airflow through driers, utilizing knowledge of product processing. Listens for alarms that indicate malfunctions of processing units and takes required steps, such as shutting down equipment and notifying supervisor. Records shift activities in log.
GOE: 06.02.15 STRENGTH: L GED: R3 M2 L2 SVP: 3 DLU: 86

523.385-010 PRESSURE-TANK OPERATOR (chemical)

Tends steam pressure tanks to extract glue from bones: Opens valve to admit steam into tank of bones, and observing gauges, adjusts pressure according to specifications. Shuts off steam and releases pressure after required period, and drains glue liquor into storage tank. Measures density and temperature of liquor, and records hydrometer and thermometer readings on control sheet. Weighs out specified amount of zinc sulfate preservative and adds it to glue in storage tank.
GOE: 06.04.19 STRENGTH: L GED: R2 M1 L1 SVP: 3 DLU: 77

523.562-010 DIFFUSER OPERATOR (sugar & conf.)

Operates automatic multicell diffuser to extract sugar juice from beet slices: Starts diffuser and auxiliary equipment, such as beet slicers, conveyors, and automatic weighing scales. Observes dials and turns controls to regulate flow of beets and water into diffuser, speed of agitators, and temperature of liquid in cells. Reads laboratory report to determine sugar content of beets, and adjusts controls to obtain maximum amount of sugar juice. Examines diffuser cells to determine if screens are clear, and that liquid levels are maintained at specified height. Reads control panel dials and automatic indicators, and records operating data, such as tonnage of beets sliced and diffused, and tonnage of water required to diffuse beet slices.
GOE: 06.02.15 STRENGTH: L GED: R3 M2 L3 SVP: 4 DLU: 77

523.585-010 BUTTER LIQUEFIER (oils & grease) alternate titles: butter melter

Tends equipment that melts and pasteurizes butter for use in fortifying and flavoring margarine: Opens valves to admit steam to heat chambers of liquefier

and pasteurizer to prescribed temperatures. Places butter blocks on revolving table and starts liquefier to melt and deposit liquified butter into receiving tank. Pumps melted butter through pasteurizer and preset cooling unit into holding tank. Weighs and adds prescribed ingredients to complete batch. Dismantles piping, using handtools. Flushes lines, and cleans tanks and equipment, using solvents and water. Maintains operating log and temperature charts.
GOE: 06.04.15 STRENGTH: M GED: R2 M2 L2 SVP: 3 DLU: 77

523.585-014 CHILLER TENDER (meat products)

Tends immersion vats and cooling equipment that chill dressed chickens to prevent spoilage: Starts water pumps, agitators, ice feeders, and conveyors and turns valves to control rate of flow and temperature of water circulating through chilling vats. Observes flow of ice through troughs that feed conveyor and dislodges caked ice with mallet. Reads gauges and thermometers to verify temperatures in chilling vats and cooler. Activates mechanical rakes to regulate flow of ice from storage bins to vats. Records temperatures on report form.
GOE: 06.04.15 STRENGTH: L GED: R2 M2 L2 SVP: 3 DLU: 77

523.585-018 CRYSTALLIZER OPERATOR (sugar & conf.)

Tends crystallizers that agitate mixture of crystallized sugar and massecuite (molasses) while it cools to prevent solidification and to allow sugar crystals to grow: Opens valves on signal from SUGAR BOILER (sugar & conf.) to permit strike to flow into mixing tanks. Starts agitators to prevent sugar crystals and massecuite from separating. Turns valves to maintain level, temperature, and consistency of sugar mass in crystallizers. Steams out empty crystallizers to remove and recover hard sugar adhering to agitators, tank sides, and piping. Maintains records, such as equipment power and temperature readings and disposition of sugar strikes.
GOE: 06.04.15 STRENGTH: L GED: R2 M2 L2 SVP: 3 DLU: 77

523.585-022 DRIER, LONG GOODS (food prep., nec) alternate titles: long-goods drier

Tends battery of preset, final drying chambers that automatically dry macaroni long goods: Pushes rack of macaroni into drying chambers and starts drying cycle. Observes hydrometer on chamber and removes rack of dried macaroni after completion of drying cycle. Records date and time of drying process on tag and fastens tag to rack. Pushes rack to storage area.
GOE: 06.04.15 STRENGTH: H GED: R2 M2 L2 SVP: 2 DLU: 77

523.585-026 PASTEURIZER (oils & grease)

Tends equipment that pasteurizes, incubates, and blends sweet or sour milk for use in manufacture of margarine: Opens valve to pump prescribed amount of water into tank and adds preweighed powdered milk or opens valve to pump fresh milk or reconstituted powdered milk into tank. Starts agitator. Turns steam valve to heat batch to designated temperature for specified period of time. Admits water into cooling system to reduce heat of batch to storage temperature. Adds specified culture of mixture to produce batch of sour milk. Pumps sweet and sour milk mixture into mixing tank preparatory to churning. Records number of batches produced. May clean and sterilize tank and auxiliary equipment, using steel wool, detergent, and caustic soda solution.
GOE: 06.04.15 STRENGTH: M GED: R3 M2 L2 SVP: 2 DLU: 77

523.585-030 PULP-DRIER FIRER (sugar & conf.)

Tends drum-type rotary driers and heating kilns, from central control station, to remove moisture from beet pulp and molasses mixture being processed into cattle fodder: Moves controls to admit fuel and air into kiln and ignite fire in kiln. Adjusts controls to obtain specified temperature in drier drum. Starts scrolls, elevators, and belt conveyors. Observes panelboard gauges and automatic recorder readings and moves controls to regulate drier temperature and rotation speed of drier drum according to moisture content of pulp-molasses mixture. Feels processed pulp to ensure that drying process meets specifications. Takes readings from conveyor scale to ascertain tonnage of fodder produced. Records production and operating data in station log. Collects samples of cattle fodder produced for laboratory analysis.
GOE: 06.04.15 STRENGTH: L GED: R2 M2 L2 SVP: 3 DLU: 77

523.585-034 ROASTER, GRAIN (grain-feed mills)

Tends equipment that roasts whole or milled grain to specified color or hardness preparatory to processing into cereal: Lights gas jets under drum or pan and sets temperature regulator at specified setting. Moves controls to transfer grain to drum or pan and start agitator that prevents sticking of grain to sides of vessel. Shovels grain from outer edge of pan to center to ensure uniform agitation of batch. Pushes grain from pan, using scoop, or pulls lever to dump grain onto conveyor after specified time, or determines removal time by matching color of roasted grain with color of standard sample. Records temperature reading and roasting time of batch. May start conveyor to move roasted grain to cooling pan and agitate grain with rake as blower forces air through perforated bottom of pan.
GOE: 06.04.15 STRENGTH: L GED: R3 M2 L2 SVP: 4 DLU: 77

523.587-010 DRIER, SHORT GOODS (food prep., nec)

Observes meters and gauges to ensure that drying process of macaroni short goods proceeds as scheduled: Patrols drying room and reads instruments and charts that control and record automatic drying process in preliminary, secondary, and final drying chambers. Reports deviations from specified chart trackings. Fills hydrometer wells with water. Dumps specified quantities of vitamins into press hopper, and reads meter to ensure required vitamin feed rate. Prepares report of drying operations and number of vitamin hoppers filled. May relieve PRESS TENDER (food prep., nec).

GOE: 06.03.02 STRENGTH: L GED: R2 M2 L2 SVP: 3 DLU: 77

523.587-014 DRYING-ROOM ATTENDANT (tobacco)

Loads stripped or unstripped tobacco on racks in drying room and remoistens tobacco to increase pliability for use in making cigars: Places trays of tobacco on racks and removes them after specified time. Sprays leaves with water, using hose, and stacks trays. Places moistened leaves in containers for cigar making after specified time. Weighs and records weight of tobacco processed.
GOE: 06.04.28 STRENGTH: L GED: R2 M1 L1 SVP: 2 DLU: 77

523.662-010 BONE-CHAR KILN OPERATOR (grain-feed mills) alternate titles: head kiln operator

Controls kilns to reclaim char (activated carbon) used in filtering corn syrups: Turns valve to admit gas to kilns. Specifies to BONE-CHAR KILN TENDER (chemical) temperature to maintain in kiln. Reads pyrometers to verify temperature. Observes operation of char conveyors to prevent spillage. Collects and replaces temperature-recording graphs. Patches flues, plugs up retorts, and replaces broken or worn parts in kiln.
GOE: 06.02.15 STRENGTH: L GED: R3 M2 L3 SVP: 4 DLU: 77

523.665-010 SUGAR DRIER (grain-feed mills)

Tends steam-heated rotary drier that dehydrates sugar products: Starts drier revolving and adjusts gates on ducts to prevent overloading and incomplete drying. Observes flow of materials through elevators and conveyors to prevent jamming or spillage. Signals CRYSTALLIZER OPERATOR (grain-feed mills) and CENTRIFUGAL OPERATOR (grain-feed mills; sugar & conf.) in synchronizing flow of materials to rate of intake at drier. Dumps sugar dust from collector into melting tanks and adds water to reclaim sugar lost during process. Cleans equipment with steam, hot water, and hose.
GOE: 06.04.15 STRENGTH: M GED: R2 M1 L1 SVP: 3 DLU: 77

523.666-010 COCOA-BEAN-ROASTER HELPER (sugar & conf.) alternate titles: roaster helper

Assists COCOA-BEAN ROASTER (sugar & conf.) I and COCOA-BEAN ROASTER (sugar & conf.) II to process cocoa beans preparatory to making cocoa, chocolate, or other cocoa products: Receives signal to charge and discharge cocoa beans from roasting ovens. Observes thermometers and clock and notifies supervisor of deviations from specific temperature or roasting cycle. Starts conveyors to move cocoa bean shells from cracker and fanner to shell cleaning machines or to transfer cleaned nibs (cracked roasted cocoa beans) to treating drums. Examines shells for presence of nibs and dumps shells into cracker and fanner machine to recover nibs. May tend cleaning machine [COCOA-BEAN CLEANER (sugar & conf.)]. May mix potassium solution used in processing cocoa beans to make dutch process chocolate. Performs other duties as described under HELPER (any industry) Master Title.
GOE: 06.04.15 STRENGTH: M GED: R2 M2 L1 SVP: 2 DLU: 77

523.682-010 CHOCOLATE TEMPERER (sugar & conf.) alternate titles: tempering-machine operator

Controls water-jacketed kettles or automatic equipment that tempers chocolate preparatory to molding or coating operations: Starts pumps to transfer specified quantity of chocolate from storage tanks or dumps block chocolate into tempering kettles. Observes thermometer and turns valves to admit water or steam into jacket of kettle and to alternately heat and cool chocolate, according to temperature time chart specifications. Starts agitators and scrapers to mix chocolate in tank. Tests viscosity of chocolate with viscosimeter, and adds cocoa butter and lecithin as required. Pumps chocolate from tempering kettle through water-cooled column when using automatic tempering equipment. Sets thermometer dial to regulate temperature of chocolate to achieve specified temper.
GOE: 06.02.15 STRENGTH: L GED: R3 M2 L2 SVP: 5 DLU: 77

523.682-014 COFFEE ROASTER (food prep., nec)

Controls gas fired roasters to remove moisture from coffee beans: Weighs batch of coffee beans in scale-hopper, and opens chute to allow beans to flow into roasting oven. Observes thermometer and adjusts controls to maintain required temperature. Compares color of roasting beans in oven with standard to estimate roasting time. Opens discharge gate to dump roasted beans into cooling tray. Starts machine that blows air through beans to cool them. Records amounts, types, and blends of coffee beans roasted.
GOE: 06.02.15 STRENGTH: L GED: R3 M2 L2 SVP: 5 DLU: 77

523.682-018 DEXTRINE MIXER (grain-feed mills)

Controls operation of steam-jacketed cooker that heats mixture of starch and acid to make dextrine paste: Opens gate on overhead chute or shovels starch into cooker. Adds specified amount of acid to start starch conversion process. Turns valves to admit steam into jacket of cooker. Starts agitator to stir cooking starch. Observes process to determine when conversion to dextrine is made and turns valve to transfer dextrine to storage tanks or drums.
GOE: 06.02.15 STRENGTH: L GED: R3 M2 L2 SVP: 4 DLU: 77

523.682-022 DRIER OPERATOR (can. & preserv.; dairy products) alternate titles: powder operator

Controls vacuum-drying equipment to convert egg or milk liquids into powder of specified moisture content: Couples spray unit between pipeline and drier, using wrench. Places charts in temperature and vacuum recorders. Starts gas-fired drier, vacuum pump, and circulating fan, and adjusts dampers. Turns controls and observes gauges to obtain specified temperature and vacuum pressure in dryer. Starts pump and turns valves to spray liquid into heated vacuum chamber where milk droplets are dried into powder. Tests dried powder conveyed out of drier, using meter. Observes interior of chamber walls for burned scale which indicates excessive temperature. Adjusts temperature of dryer and amount of liquid sprayed into dryer to obtain specified moisture content and eliminate scale which appears as sediment in powder. Places container on scale under outlet of drying equipment to fill container with specified amount of powder. May be designated according to product dried as Buttermilk-Drier Operator (dairy products); Yolk Spray Drier (can. & preserv.).
GOE: 06.02.15 STRENGTH: M GED: R2 M2 L3 SVP: 4 DLU: 77

523.682-026 DRUM DRIER (grain-feed mills)

Operates steam-heated drum drier in vacuum tank to dry liquid cereal mixture to specified consistency: Adjusts temperature regulator of vacuum tank to specified setting. Starts vacuum pump and revolving drum in vacuum tank. Turns valve to raise level of liquid in pan beneath drum, causing thin film of liquid to dry as it contacts rotating drum. Turns valve and moves controls to regulate drum temperature and speed and level of liquid in pan to attain specified color and consistency of dried cereal. Installs scraping blade that peels dried cereal from drum into handtruck, using wrench. Opens vacuum chamber and removes loaded handtruck. Pushes truck onto scale, records weight, and trips lever to dump contents into hopper.
GOE: 06.02.15 STRENGTH: M GED: R3 M2 L2 SVP: 4 DLU: 77

523.682-030 KILN OPERATOR, MALT HOUSE (beverage)

Controls gas-fired furnace that heats malt drying kilns: Pushes ignition switch and turns gas valve to light furnace. Observes temperature gauge or recording charts, and adjusts gas valves, dampers, and speeds of draft and exhaust fans to maintain specified temperature in kiln. May move levers that tip floor sections of kiln to drop dried malt into storage hopper. May open and control slide gate of storage hopper dispensing malt to cleaning machine.
GOE: 06.02.15 STRENGTH: M GED: R3 M2 L2 SVP: 4 DLU: 77

523.682-034 PERCOLATOR OPERATOR (grain-feed mills)

Operates percolating equipment to produce liquid mixture of water, grain, and other ingredients according to formula, as part of cereal-manufacturing process: Starts agitator and turns valves to draw premeasured amounts of milled grain, water, and other ingredients into percolating vessel. Sets temperature regulator of vessel at specified setting. Turns valve at bottom of tank to draw off liquid percolate into storage tanks. Tests sample of percolate, using hydrometer, to determine concentration of liquid filter bed and turns valve to shut off percolate flowing to storage tanks when hydrometer indicates ingredients in filter bed are exhausted. Pulls lever to dump spent grain mixture into handtruck.
GOE: 06.02.15 STRENGTH: L GED: R3 M2 L2 SVP: 4 DLU: 77

523.682-038 TOBACCO CURER (agriculture)

Controls heating equipment in tobacco barns to cure tobacco: Starts coal or wood fire in furnace, lights oil or gas burner, or turns on electric furnace to heat barn. Regulates temperature and draft controls, depending on type of tobacco and weather conditions, until leaves are yellowed. Observes color and moisture content of leaves to determine when to increase heat and regulate draft controls to dry leaves and stems. When bulk curing barns (tobacco leaves packed in metal racks and cured by forced air heat) are used, starts and regulates fan speed to control movement of air and heat through tobacco leaves.
GOE: 06.02.15 STRENGTH: M GED: R3 M1 L1 SVP: 3 DLU: 77

523.685-010 BATCH FREEZER (dairy products)

Tends batch freezer that freezes liquid ice cream mix to semisolid consistency: Measures specified amounts of ice cream mix, color, and flavor, using graduate, and dumps ingredients into freezer barrel. Starts beaters and refrigerating unit. Observes clock and ammeter for specified reading denoting end of freezing cycle and turns valve to start flow of frozen mix into containers. Places fixture which ripples ice cream into valve outlet, and stirs syrups into ice cream with spoon or adds candies, fruit, and nuts to make various varieties of ice cream. Places containers of mix in hardening cabinet. Washes and sterilizes equipment, using cleansing solution, brushes, and hot water.
GOE: 06.04.15 STRENGTH: H GED: R2 M1 L1 SVP: 2 DLU: 77

523.685-014 BLANCHING-MACHINE OPERATOR (can. & preserv.)

Tends machine that blanches fruits and vegetables preparatory to canning and preserving: Observes gauges, sets dials, and turns valves to fill machine with water and admit steam and to regulate temperature and blanching time. Starts machine, and conveyor or pump to feed product to and from machine. Feels and visually examines blanched product to determine adequacy of softening or color setting. May fill and weigh containers of blanched product, using shovel and platform scale. May feed paste products, such as spaghetti or noodles into machine by hand.
GOE: 06.04.15 STRENGTH: M GED: R2 M2 L2 SVP: 3 DLU: 77

523.685-018 CHILLING-HOOD OPERATOR (meat products)

Tends machine that chills cased chickens and chicken parts preparatory to storage in refrigerated holding rooms: Monitors thermometers and carbon dioxide gas pressure gauges, and turns regulating valve controls to adjust flow of gas refrigerant into cartons.
GOE: 06.04.15 STRENGTH: M GED: R1 M1 L1 SVP: 2 DLU: 77

523.685-022 CHOCOLATE TEMPERER (bakery products; grain-feed mills) alternate titles: chocolate maker; chocolate-mixer operator

Tends jacketed kettles to temper chocolate used for coating baked products: Breaks slabs of prepared chocolate into pieces and dumps pieces into kettle.

Turns valves to adjust kettle heat to specified temperature to melt chocolate. Starts agitator. Opens water valve to cool mixture to desired consistency. Opens valve to drain mixture into container and dumps chocolate into enrobing machine tank. May mix cocoa butter with melted chocolate for use as filling. May process grain to form gluten and be designated Premix Operator, Concentrate (grain-feed mills).
GOE: 06.04.15 STRENGTH: M GED: R2 M1 L1 SVP: 3 DLU: 77

523.685-026 COFFEE ROASTER, CONTINUOUS PROCESS (food prep., nec)
Tends coffee roaster equipped with rotating cylinder through which green coffee beans flow in continuous stream for roasting. Moves controls to regulate speed of cylinder rotation, rate of flow of beans, and temperature of oven for each coffee blend, according to specifications. May tend machine that grinds coffee beans [COFFEE GRINDER (food prep., nec)].
GOE: 06.04.15 STRENGTH: L GED: R2 M2 L2 SVP: 3 DLU: 77

523.685-030 COOK-BOX FILLER (meat products)
Tends steam-jacketed tank in which flesh is removed from bones of animals: Lowers basket of bones into water-filled cooking tank, using hoist. Opens and regulates steam valves to heat water to specified temperature. Removes basket of cleaned bones from tank with hoist.
GOE: 06.04.15 STRENGTH: M GED: R2 M1 L1 SVP: 2 DLU: 77

523.685-034 COOKER, MEAL (oils & grease) alternate titles: cooker; heater tender; meal cook; meal temperer
Tends steam cooker that breaks down oil cells and controls moisture content of corn, soybeans, cottonseed, linseed meal (meats) or fish, prior to extraction of oil: Turns valves to regulate steam pressure inside cooker or steam jacket and to maintain temperature within specified range. Observes conveyor feeding material to cooker or climbs to top of cooker to determine that material is feeding continuously. May scoop handful of material from entry or discharge point of cooker and examine or feel material to determine how much steam should be added. May record steam pressure and temperature readings at specified intervals. May tend machine to crush meats for processing. May tend cake-forming machine to shape cottonseed meats for pressing [CAKE FORMER (oils & grease)].
GOE: 06.04.15 STRENGTH: L GED: R2 M2 L1 SVP: 3 DLU: 77

523.685-038 COOLER TENDER (grain-feed mills)
Tends equipment that cools corn sugar syrup and transfers syrup to storage tanks: Observes thermometer and turns valves to regulate flow of cold water through cooling coils, and to start flow of syrup over coils. Starts pump to transfer cooled syrup to storage tanks. Draws samples to test for Baume (specific gravity), sulfur dioxide, acidity, and alkalinity.
GOE: 06.04.15 STRENGTH: L GED: R2 M2 L1 SVP: 2 DLU: 77

523.685-042 COOLING-MACHINE OPERATOR (beverage) alternate titles: cooler operator
Tends equipment that cools and transfers wort to starting tank preparatory to fermenting: Turns valves to control flow of refrigerant through cooler coils. Starts pumps and opens valves to draw hot wort from tank through cooler and into starting tank. Monitors pressure gauges, flowmeters, thermometers, and temperature recorders, and turns valves to control rate of flow and temperature of wort passing through cooling machine. Observes flowmeter and opens valves to admit specified amounts of air into wort. Opens valves to circulate solutions through wort coils to clean and sterilize lines.
GOE: 06.04.15 STRENGTH: L GED: R2 M1 L1 SVP: 2 DLU: 77

523.685-046 COOLING-PAN TENDER (can. & preserv.)
Tends equipment that cools preserves and fruit concentrate: Turns valve to admit water into jacket of cooling pan to cool preserves and fruit concentrate. Skims foam from top of preserves, using ladle. Stirs preserves or fruit concentrate with paddle to prevent coagulation and to allow even cooling. Observes thickening and starts pump, or opens dump valve, to transfer preserves or fruit concentrate from cooling pan to holding tank or filling machine when desired consistency is reached. May determine sugar content of preserves or fruit concentrate, using refractometer, and record results. May add sugar or water to preserves or fruit concentrate, according to formula, to bring sugar content up to standard. May start fan above cooling pan to aid cooling.
GOE: 06.04.15 STRENGTH: L GED: R2 M1 L1 SVP: 2 DLU: 77

523.685-050 CRYSTALLIZER OPERATOR (grain-feed mills)
Tends cooling tank and crystallizer that starts crystallization of liquid sugar: Turns valves and starts pumps to fill cooling tank with liquid sugar and regulate flow of cold water through cooling coils until specified temperature is attained. Turns wing nut to release tension on outlet door of crystallizer and pushes lever to raise door. Knocks out sugar plug to allow sugar to flow to centrifugals. Measures depth of sugar in crystallizer to ensure that small amount of sugar remains to start crystallization of next batch.
GOE: 06.04.15 STRENGTH: M GED: R2 M2 L2 SVP: 3 DLU: 77

523.685-054 DEHYDRATOR TENDER (can. & preserv.)
Tends sulfur and drying chambers to bleach and dehydrate fruit: Starts conveyors to load trays with fruit, and levels fruit in trays to ensure thorough processing. Pushes loaded cart into sulfurizing chamber and lights burner to generate fumes. Moves cart from sulfurizing chamber into drying chamber to dehydrate fruit. Observes gauges, and regulates and maintains specified temperature and humidity in drying chambers. Feels and observes fruit during dehydrating

process to ascertain firmness and color in accordance with standards. Pulls cart from heating chamber. May record drying time of each load.
GOE: 06.04.15 STRENGTH: H GED: R2 M2 L2 SVP: 3 DLU: 77

523.685-058 DRIER ATTENDANT (can. & preserv.; grain-feed mills) alternate titles: dehydrator; steam drier
Tends rotary driers that remove moisture from materials, such as corn germs, alfalfa, and shredded sweet potatoes: Turns valves to admit steam through lines or fuel to furnace to heat drier. Observes gauges to verify drier temperature. Turns valves to regulate steam pressure or starts blower of furnace to regulate temperature of drier. Examines and feels discharged material or observes gauges to determine that moisture content of material conforms to standard. Turns handwheel or valve to control rate of speed and amount of material conveyed into drier. Starts blower to remove material from drier. May direct workers engaged in shredding potatoes and sacking dried material. May be designated according to material dried as Germ Drier (grain-feed mills); or method of heating drier as Fire Drier (grain-feed mills). May tend attrition and hammer mills [MILL OPERATOR (grain-feed mills)] in addition to rotary drier to prepare stock feed from bran and gluten and be designated Feed-Drier Tender (grain-feed mills).
GOE: 06.04.15 STRENGTH: L GED: R2 M1 L1 SVP: 3 DLU: 77

523.685-062 DRIER OPERATOR (can. & preserv.) alternate titles: flaker operator
Tends steam-heated drying machine that removes moisture from cooked potatoes preparatory to grinding into flour: Rakes uniform coating of cooked potato mash deposited from auger-type conveyor over heated revolving cylinder to remove moisture. May tend drying equipment that recovers starch byproduct from gluten wash.
GOE: 06.04.15 STRENGTH: M GED: R1 M1 L1 SVP: 2 DLU: 77

523.685-066 DRIER TENDER (can. & preserv.) alternate titles: nut-dehydrator operator
Tends machines that dehydrate nuts: Starts heater and sets thermostat to control air temperature. Starts blower system that forces warm air through nuts to dry them, improve storage qualities, and prepare them for further processing. Starts conveyor to move nuts into machine for dehydration. Tests dryness of nuts by feeling or by using moisture indicator. Attaches sack to discharge end of machine to catch dried nuts, or starts conveyor system that transfers dried nuts to storage bin. May sew sack, using needle and twine. May be designated according to kind of nut dehydrated as Walnut-Dehydrator Operator (can. & preserv.).
GOE: 06.04.15 STRENGTH: M GED: R2 M1 L1 SVP: 3 DLU: 77

523.685-070 DRIER TENDER (grain-feed mills)
Tends drying equipment to reduce moisture content of cooked grain to specified degree of dehydration for cereal products: Adjusts steam valves to regulate temperature and pressure of drier to specified levels. Turns valve or adjusts gate on conveyor to regulate amount of cereal entering drier. Turns handcrank to adjust speed of conveyor through drier. Visually and tactually inspects dried grain and collects samples throughout drying process to determine moisture content of grain. May turn valve and push button to start granulators and picker rolls that break lumps in cooked grain prior to or after drying.
GOE: 06.04.15 STRENGTH: L GED: R2 M2 L2 SVP: 3 DLU: 77

523.685-074 DRIER TENDER I (oils & grease)
Tends rotary drier that removes moisture from fish scrap preparatory to grinding scrap into meal: Starts drier and conveyors that feed fish scrap into drier and move dried material to storage area. Observes gauges and turns valves to regulate steam pressure and to keep temperature within prescribed range.
GOE: 06.04.15 STRENGTH: L GED: R1 M1 L1 SVP: 2 DLU: 77

523.685-078 FIRER, KILN (sugar & conf.)
Tends battery of char-kilns that revivify char used in filtration of liquor: Starts fires and regulates gas and air pressure in kilns and flow of char through heat exchanges to control temperature. Observes inside of kiln through peep-hole to detect wall defects and char leakages. Examines and adjusts equipment, such as char-draw mechanisms, emergency stop alarms, remote control switches, and water-sprays on char-conveyors.
GOE: 06.04.15 STRENGTH: L GED: R2 M1 L1 SVP: 3 DLU: 77

523.685-082 FREEZER TUNNEL OPERATOR (can. & preserv.)
Tends freeze tunnel to quick-freeze food products: Pushes switches to start and control speed of conveyorized screen that conveys food product through tunnel that flash freezes food as it passes. Turns valves to adjust temperature in tunnel and monitors temperature and pressure gauges to ensure conformance to company specifications. Patrols tunnel to observe progress of vegetables to ensure freezing and to detect machinery malfunctions. Scrapes conveyor to remove excess ice or frost from conveyor and to break vegetables loose from conveyor to prevent accumulation, using hands and handtools. Breaks excess ice from tunnel outlet to facilitate conveyorized frozen food off bearing. Notifies supervisor of machinery malfunctions. May tend machine that deposits breading onto food products [BREADING MACHINE TENDER (can. & preserv.)].
GOE: 06.04.15 STRENGTH: L GED: R3 M1 L2 SVP: 3 DLU: 77

523.685-086 GRAIN DRIER (beverage) alternate titles: spent-grain dryer
Tends steam or gas-fired drum to dry grain or yeast: Starts dryer, turns steam valve, or lights gas burner and observes thermometers and pressure gauges to

heat dryer to operating temperatures. Opens valve or starts screw conveyor and vacuum pump to convey wet grain through heated drum and into discharge hopper. Observes feeder gauge and turns valve or moves rheostat lever to adjust flow of yeast or grain to capacity of dryer. Feels dried grain or yeast to judge moisture content or measures with moisture meter. Adjusts valves to vary heat of dryer and grain and yeast flow to change moisture content to specifications. When drying grain, attaches cloth bag to discharge hopper. Weighs filled bag and seams top of bag, using portable sewing machine.
GOE: 06.04.15 STRENGTH: H GED: R2 M2 L2 SVP: 2 DLU: 77

523.685-090 GRAIN-DRIER OPERATOR (grain-feed mills)
Tends grain-drying machines that reduce moisture content of grain: Reviews data concerning moisture content of grain to be dried. Moves levers to regulate gate on feed hopper and flow of grain through drier. Observes temperature recorders and turns valves to regulate flow of steam pressure or gas to heat driers to specified temperature. May observe conveyors transferring grain from storage bin and control flow of grain into feed hopper. May test grain to ensure moisture content standards are being met, using moisture meter or standard oil-distillation test. May be designated according to grain dried as Rice-Drier Operator (grain-feed mills).
GOE: 06.04.15 STRENGTH: L GED: R2 M2 L2 SVP: 3 DLU: 77

523.685-094 GRAIN-WAFER-MACHINE OPERATOR (bakery products)
Tends machines that soak, form, and bake whole grains of wheat or rice into wafers: Dumps sacks of grain into soaking tank. Turns valve to regulate flow of water into tank, and starts tank revolving. Turns off water after specified soaking period and starts air blower to dry grain. Pushes lever to empty tank, and starts screw conveyor that moves grain into feed hopper of baking machine. Lights gas burners to heat crushing and baking rollers. Starts machine that flattens and bakes grains into solid sheets. Turns valve to adjust temperature of rollers depending on color and texture of extruded sheet of wafers. Fills salting hopper, using hand scoop.
GOE: 06.04.15 STRENGTH: H GED: R2 M1 L2 SVP: 3 DLU: 77

523.685-098 GRANULATOR OPERATOR (sugar & conf.) alternate titles: sugar drier
Tends rotary-type kiln that dries sugar to specified moisture content: Starts equipment, such as scrolls, and conveyors. Turns valve to admit steam into heating coils, and starts fan that blows air around steam coils in drum. Opens gate on feed scroll to admit sugar to drum. Observes instruments to ascertain that temperatures and humidity in drums are within specified limits. Adjusts gate or speed of feed scroll and amount of steam pressure in coils to control temperature, luster, and grist of sugar. Keeps records of station operations. Takes samples of sugar for laboratory analysis. Clears blockages in scrolls and magnetic screens, using mallet or brush.
GOE: 06.04.15 STRENGTH: L GED: R2 M1 L1 SVP: 3 DLU: 77

523.685-102 ICE MAKER (food prep., nec)
Tends refrigerating equipment that freezes water into ice, performing any combination of following tasks: Opens valves to fill containers with specified amounts of water, and lowers containers into freezing tanks, using hoist. Inserts air bubbler into containers and starts agitator in freezing tank to ensure uniform freezing. Siphons or pumps water containing foreign matter from centers of partially frozen ice blocks, using suction pump, and refills container with fresh water. Flushes surfaces of ice blocks with hose. Removes container from tank, using hoist, and immerses it in warm water or places it in steam bath to free ice from container sides. Positions cans on *dumping pivot* and pushes buttons to tilt pivot and dump ice onto conveyor or platform. Adds prescribed amounts of materials into mixing vats and starts agitator to mix brine solution for freezing tanks. May turn valves to regulate compressors and condensers. When performing specific duty, may be known as Can Filler (food prep., nec); Dumper (food prep., nec); Ice Puller (food prep., nec).
GOE: 06.04.15 STRENGTH: H GED: R2 M1 L2 SVP: 3 DLU: 77

523.685-106 INSTANTIZER OPERATOR (dairy products)
Tends hydrating and drying equipment to make instant dairy products, using either of following methods: (1) Turns valves, starts fans, and observes thermometers and gauges to heat drying chamber to specified temperature and supply steam to hydrating jets. Starts conveyors and shaker screen. Turns dial to transfer powder from feeder hopper through steam spray, drying chamber, and vibrating screen into storage hopper. Turns steam valves and feeder dial to adjust temperature or powder flow to maintain specified moisture content. (2) Starts pumps, turns valves, and observes meter to spray water into hydrator at specified rate. Starts blower to push powder from storage hopper, through water spray, and onto conveyor leading to dryer and sizing rolls. Turns valve and observes thermometer to maintain specified temperature in dryer. Positions sizing rolls on conveyor, using wrench, to crumble dried powder to specified size. Examines and feels powder for moisture and charring.
GOE: 06.04.15 STRENGTH: L GED: R2 M2 L1 SVP: 3 DLU: 77

523.685-110 PASTEURIZER (beverage; can. & preserv.)
Tends machine that pasteurizes bottled or canned food products or beverages: Starts water spray or steam in pasteurizer and starts conveyor that moves bottles or cans through machine. Observes water or steam temperature gauge to ensure constancy of temperature or notifies quality control laboratory of deviations. Pushes pasteurized bottles or cans from machine table onto conveyor by hand or with metal bar to prevent jamming. Removes broken bottles from conveyor.
GOE: 06.04.15 STRENGTH: L GED: R2 M2 L1 SVP: 2 DLU: 77

523.685-114 STERILIZER OPERATOR (dairy products)
Tends conveyor line enclosed in series of circular chambers to cook canned milk to sterilize and change viscosity and color of milk: Turns steam, water, and hot air valves and observes gauges to adjust temperature of heating, cooking, cooling, and drying chambers. Observes panel lights for machine failure and stops conveyor to remove jammed cans. Observes filled sealed cans moving through chambers and removes dented cans or sample test cans. Opens sample can and dips spoon into sterilized milk to observe grain (texture), viscosity, and color. May alter cooking temperature or add measured amount of calcium or phosphate to milk batch to obtain specified grain and viscosity.
GOE: 06.04.15 STRENGTH: L GED: R2 M2 L2 SVP: 3 DLU: 77

523.685-118 TOBACCO-DRIER OPERATOR (tobacco) alternate titles: drying-oven tender
Tends driers that remove moisture from leaf and processed tobacco: Starts driers (rotating drums) and turns valves to admit steam to heat coils of driers or opens valves on gas burners and sets thermostat. Periodically feels tobacco to determine dryness and regulates heat to dry tobacco within specified limits. May record readings of humidigraphs and thermometers on chart. May feed tobacco into drier. May be designated according to types of tobacco dried as Snuff Drier (tobacco); Tobacco-Stem-Drier Operator (tobacco). May tend driers that impart distinctive flavor (toast) to tobacco and be designated Toaster Operator (tobacco).
GOE: 06.04.15 STRENGTH: L GED: R2 M2 L2 SVP: 2 DLU: 77

523.685-122 VACUUM DRIER OPERATOR (can. & preserv.)
Tends vacuum drier system to dehydrate prebleached and preevaporated fruit in evaporating plant: Loads fruit-filled trays onto drier shelves and closes and seals doors. Turns switches and dials to start heater and set temperature and timing for preheating system's circulating water. Turns switches and dials in prescribed sequence to activate timer, water pumps, and condenser and to put system on automatic cycle. Turns hand-valve to break vacuum at end of cycle, sets timer, and allows fruit to cool. Removes filled trays from drier and turns and pulls trays across bin-mounted scraper to remove dehydrated fruit. Listens for sounds that indicate malfunctions, and notifies supervisor of malfunctions that fail to respond to specified corrective actions.
GOE: 06.04.15 STRENGTH: H GED: R3 M1 L2 SVP: 2 DLU: 77

523.685-126 WINE PASTEURIZER (beverage)
Tends tanks used to pasteurize fermented wine: Meters out specified quantities of wine into tanks and turns steam valves to admit heat. Observes thermometer readings and gauges of tanks to ensure heating of wine at required temperature for specified time to effect pasteurization. Starts pumps to transfer wine from pasteurizing tanks to storage tanks.
GOE: 06.04.15 STRENGTH: L GED: R2 M2 L1 SVP: 3 DLU: 77

523.687-010 COFFEE-ROASTER HELPER (food prep., nec)
Assists COFFEE ROASTER (food prep., nec) to roast green coffee beans: Picks over green coffee, discarding black and dead coffee beans, to prepare coffee for roasting. May weigh and pack ground coffee. Performs other duties as described under HELPER (any industry) Master Title.
GOE: 06.04.28 STRENGTH: L GED: R1 M1 L1 SVP: 2 DLU: 77

523.687-014 FISH DRIER (can. & preserv.) alternate titles: fish flaker; flaker; flaker tender
Dries fish, such as salmon, cod, herring, or sardines: Hangs fish on racks or poles, or places them in trays. Sets racks, poles, or trays in drying room or oven.
GOE: 06.04.28 STRENGTH: H GED: R1 M1 L1 SVP: 2 DLU: 77

523.687-018 KILN LOADER (beverage)
Spreads germinated barley or green hops on kiln floor to dry: Holds and directs swing chute to discharge and spread barley or hops evenly over floor. Levels barley or hops, using fork. Loosens lock bolts to tip holding-kiln floor screens and drop barley or hops onto next drying floor or into storage hopper or pushes product into lower bin, using scraper. May clean and scrub malthouse floors.
GOE: 06.04.40 STRENGTH: M GED: R1 M1 L1 SVP: 2 DLU: 77

523.687-022 FREEZING-ROOM WORKER (can. & preserv.)
Moves racks of food packages into and out of freezing room: Wheels portable racks filled with food packages and fresh meat into freezing room for freezing. Records identifying data, such as brand name, package sizes, and time of entry in freezing room. Feels packages after specified time to test solidity of freeze. Notifies supervisor when specified quotas are filled, and when temperature fluctuates, or outside air leaks into freezing compartments. Pulls racks from freezing room with power winch when wheels are frozen.
GOE: 06.04.40 STRENGTH: H GED: R2 M1 L1 SVP: 2 DLU: 78

524 COATING, ICING, DECORATING, AND RELATED OCCUPATIONS

This group includes occupations concerned with applying coverings, fillings, sprays, and decoration to products or components to complete assembly, affect flavor and appearance, improve baking and keeping qualities, and serve as identification.

524.381-010 CAKE DECORATOR (bakery products) alternate titles: pastry decorator
Decorates cakes and pastries with designs, using icing bag or handmade paper cone: Trims uneven surfaces of cake or cuts and shapes cake to required

size, using knife. Spreads icing between layers and on surfaces of cake, using spatula. Tints white icing with food coloring. Inserts die of specific design into tip of bag or paper cone and fills bag or cone with colored icing. Squeezes bag to eject icing while moving bag with free-arm writing motions to form design on cake. Forms decorations on *flower nail* and transfers decorations to cake, using spatula. May mix icing.
GOE: 05.05.17 STRENGTH: L GED: R3 M2 L2 SVP: 6 DLU: 77

524.381-014 DECORATOR (dairy products)
   Molds and decorates ice cream confections according to order: Packs ice cream into metal molds shaped as flowers, fruit, animals, cake, or pie, using spoon, knife, or spatula. Presses mold halves together and places mold in hardening cabinet. Immerses hardened molds in water, pries molds open and removes confection, using knife. Whips cream, sugar, and dye by hand or in machine beater to make whipped cream of specified color and consistency. Folds parchment paper into cone shape, places metal extrusion tip into bottom of cone and fills cone with whipped cream. Presses tube and moves tube over confection to create designs and figures, such as leaves, flowers, wreaths, or letters to decorate confection as indicated on order. Holds confection under stencil in tray and covers confection with whipped cream, using spatula, or with dye to form wording, using spray gun. May place paper, plastic or metal decorations on confection.
GOE: 01.06.03 STRENGTH: L GED: R4 M3 L3 SVP: 6 DLU: 77

524.382-010 COATING-MACHINE OPERATOR (sugar & conf.) alternate titles: candy polisher; coater; finisher; glazer; glosser; pan operator; polisher
   Operates machine to coat items, such as candy, nuts, and chewing gum tablets, with syrup, wax coloring matter, or other material to provide specified finish or polish: Dumps product into pan and starts pan revolving. Pours specified quantity of syrup over whirling candy or other product, and passes hands through batch to spread syrup uniformly. Turns steam valve and observes thermometer to regulate pan temperature, according to changes in atmospheric conditions, or when hard coatings have been specified. Examines and feels product to determine adequacy of coating, and applies successive charges of syrup until specified coating thickness is attained. Adds flavoring and coloring ingredients in final coating, as specified. May mix together and apply emulsified or dry ingredients, such as gum solution, cornstarch, and powdered sugar to product. May transfer contents to polishing pans and add specified ingredients to polish coating. May set temperature controls and start blower to dry syrup. May be designated according to product coated or polished as Almond-Pan Finisher (sugar & conf.); Chocolate-Peanut Coating-Machine Operator (sugar & conf.); Gum Coater (sugar & conf.).
GOE: 06.02.15 STRENGTH: M GED: R3 M2 L2 SVP: 6 DLU: 77

524.382-014 ENROBING-MACHINE OPERATOR (bakery products; sugar & conf.)
   Controls machines and equipment to enrobe (coat) confectionery or bakery products with melted chocolate or other coating and to cool enrobed products preparatory to packing: Turns switches and valves on central control panel and pushes levers to start machine and conveyor that transfer candy or other products over prebottoming device to coat bases, under flow pan to receive coating, past air nozzle to blow off surplus coating, over trimming device to wipe drippings from enrobed pieces, and through cooling tunnel to packing area. Weighs coated products at random to ensure specified thickness of coating and examines products for conformity to solidification, gloss, and uniformity of coating. Adjusts air blower, trimming rod, and flow of coating to correct product deviations. Turns switches and valves to adjust steam and water flow in jacketed supply tank, belt speed, and temperature of cooling tunnel in accordance with findings. May adjust automatic decorating device on machines so equipped to produce hand-dipped effect on coated product. May be designated according to coating material as Chocolate-Machine Operator (bakery products; sugar & conf.).
GOE: 06.02.15 STRENGTH: L GED: R3 M1 L2 SVP: 6 DLU: 77

524.565-010 TROLLEY OPERATOR (bakery products)
   Tends trolley conveyors that convey icing-dipped cookies to cool and solidify them preparatory to packaging: Transports cookies and bowls of icing to other workers in trolley room, using handtruck. Weighs icing on scales, records weights, and dumps contents of bowl into reservoirs. Starts trolley conveyors and turns knob on rheostat to regulate its speed. Turns valve in steam line or starts ventilating fans to adjust temperature of trolley room.
GOE: 06.04.40 STRENGTH: M GED: R1 M1 L1 SVP: 2 DLU: 77

524.665-010 SANDING-MACHINE OPERATOR (sugar & conf.)
   Tends equipment that applies coating of sugar to candy, such as gumdrops and orange slices: Dumps sanding sugar into hopper of rotating cylinder. Turns steam valve and starts conveyor that carries candy through steam bath for heating and moistening, and into cylinder for application of sugar coating. Examines sugared candy as it emerges on conveyor and adjusts flow of steam and sugar to correct imperfections in coating. Notifies other workers to remove malformed or improperly coated candies.
GOE: 06.04.15 STRENGTH: M GED: R1 M1 L1 SVP: 2 DLU: 77

524.682-010 DEPOSITING-MACHINE OPERATOR (bakery products) alternate titles: filling-machine operator; marshmallow-machine worker; spreading-machine operator
   Operates machine to deposit filling, such as icing, marshmallow, or peanut butter on cookies or crackers: Installs specified nozzles in machine, using

wrench. Starts pump to load machine hopper with filling. Starts conveyor to position cookies under nozzles. Turns valve to deposit specified amount of filling on cookies. Pulls lever to feed product under refrigerated roller to spread filling over cookies. Wipes filling from roller, using wet cloth. Verifies weight of cookies on scale. May place pans or sheets of cookies under nozzles. May mix ingredients for filling.
GOE: 06.02.15 STRENGTH: M GED: R3 M1 L2 SVP: 4 DLU: 77

524.684-010 CANDY DIPPER, HAND (sugar & conf.)
   Dips candy centers, fruit, or nuts into coatings to coat, decorate, and identify product: Scoops liquid coating material onto slab of heated dipping table and kneads material, such as chocolate, fondant, or icing to attain specified consistency. Drops candy into mass and swirls candy about until thoroughly coated, using fingers or fork. Removes candy and marks identifying design or symbol on top, using fingers or fork, to identify type of center or brand. May decorate top of candy with nuts, coconut, or other garnishment. May mix coating ingredients and dip candy into vat containing coating material, regulating vat temperature to maintain specified consistency. May pour liquid chocolate into molds to form figures [CANDY MOLDER, HAND (sugar & conf.)]. May be designated according to type of center dipped as Bonbon Dipper (sugar & conf.); Cherry Dipper (sugar & conf.); Cream Dipper (sugar & conf.); Pecan-Mallow Dipper (sugar & conf.); or according to type of coating as Chocolate Coater (sugar & conf.); Icing Coater (sugar & conf.).
GOE: 06.04.28 STRENGTH: L GED: R2 M1 L1 SVP: 4 DLU: 77

524.684-014 DECORATOR (bakery products; sugar & conf.) alternate titles: decorator, hand; ornamenter
   Decorates confectionery products with chocolate, colored icings, or pastry cream: Screws nozzle of specified size and shape into outlet of decorating bag. Fills bag with icing, chocolate, or pastry cream. Squeezes bag to force material through nozzle, forming decorations, such as lines, letters, figures, or flowers. May mix, cook, and color decorating material. May spread material with brush, fingers, pronged instrument, or spatula. May fill molds with icing to form decorations, such as bells, birds, and bootees. May be designated according to product decorated as Candy Decorator (sugar & conf.).
GOE: 06.04.28 STRENGTH: L GED: R2 M1 L1 SVP: 3 DLU: 77

524.684-018 ENROBING-MACHINE CORDER (sugar & conf.) alternate titles: decorator, hand; streaker; stringer; stroker
   Marks top surface of coated candies with identifying or decorative stroke to simulate hand-dipped appearance: Dips fingers in semiliquid chocolate or other coating and marks candies with diagonal line, bead, or other design as candies emerge from enrobing (coating) machine on conveyor. May mark tops of candies with symbol to identify type of center or flavor of candy.
GOE: 06.04.28 STRENGTH: L GED: R2 M1 L1 SVP: 4 DLU: 77

524.684-022 ICER, HAND (bakery products) alternate titles: decorator; finisher; froster; icing spreader
   Covers baked goods with icing, frosting, or glaze by hand: Spreads icing evenly over surface of solid baked goods, using spatula. Builds up layer cakes by spreading icing or filling between layers and then icing outer surface. Applies glaze or thin icings to sweet rolls, fruit cake, speciality breads, and other items, using brush. May sprinkle chocolate chips, shredded coconut, chopped nuts, or other decorative materials over baked goods. May mix icings. May pack iced products in cartons. May be designated according to product iced as Bread Icer (bakery products); Cake Icer (bakery products); Doughnut Icer (bakery products); Pie Icer (bakery products); Roll Icer (bakery products).
GOE: 06.04.28 STRENGTH: L GED: R2 M1 L1 SVP: 3 DLU: 77

524.685-010 BREADING MACHINE TENDER (can. & preserv.)
   Tends machine that covers food products with breading material: Opens bag and dumps breading material into breading machine hopper. Turns valve to regulate flow of breading material onto food products on conveyor passing beneath hopper. Observes machine to detect malfunction. Cleans machine and conveyor with water.
GOE: 06.04.15 STRENGTH: M GED: R1 M1 L1 SVP: 2 DLU: 77

524.685-014 CHEESE SPRAYER (sugar & conf.)
   Tends equipment that coats popcorn or similar food product with melted cheese: Dumps salt into hopper of salt-sprinkling device. Measures out specified quantity of cheese and coconut oil into thermostatically controlled melting and mixing kettle. Starts conveyor to admit popcorn to rotating drum. Starts drum rotating and pump that forces melted cheese through spray nozzle onto popcorn. Places container at discharge end of drum to receive coated popcorn. Transfers filled containers to packing room, using handtruck.
GOE: 06.04.15 STRENGTH: L GED: R1 M1 L1 SVP: 2 DLU: 77

524.685-018 COATING OPERATOR (grain-feed mills)
   Tends coating and drying equipment that coats cereal products, such as flakes or puffed grain, with syrup, vitamin mixture, or other liquid: Lights gas burners or turns steam valve to attain specified temperature in drier and syrup storage tank. Starts revolving drum and conveyors that feed cereal product into drum and through drier. Pumps liquid from storage tank to perforated spraying pipe in drum. Adjusts speed of conveyor and drum to coat cereal to specified thickness, indicated by feel and color inspection.
GOE: 06.04.15 STRENGTH: L GED: R2 M1 L1 SVP: 3 DLU: 77

524.685-022 CRACKER SPRAYER (bakery products)
   Tends machine that sprays crackers with oil to impart color and prevent drying out: Pours oil into reservoir, using pail. Adjusts steam valve to heat oil to

specified temperature. Starts machine and turns valves to regulate spray of oil on crackers. Feeds crackers onto conveyor. Weighs sampling of crackers to measure amount of oil being applied.
GOE: 06.04.15 STRENGTH: L GED: R1 M1 L1 SVP: 2 DLU: 77

524.685-026 ENROBING-MACHINE OPERATOR (bakery products) alternate titles: chocolate-coating-machine operator; enrober
Tends equipment that melts and sprays chocolate on cookies or crackers to enrobe (cover) them: Fills machine hopper with chocolate, using buckets or conveyor. Turns valve to regulate temperature of tank to melt and facilitate flow of chocolate, according to thermometer reading. Starts machine to spray chocolate on cookies or crackers. Observes cookies emerging from machine to ensure adequate coating. May melt and temper chocolate [CHOCOLATE TEMPERER (bakery products; grain-feed mills)].
GOE: 06.04.15 STRENGTH: M GED: R2 M1 L1 SVP: 2 DLU: 77

524.685-030 FILLING MACHINE TENDER (bakery products)
Tends machine that automatically injects cream filling into snack-size cakes: Starts pump to fill machine hopper with filling. Presses button to activate conveyor that conveys cakes under nozzles that automatically inject filling into cakes. Observes cakes being filled to ascertain that cream is injected into center of cakes in prescribed portions. Observes action of automatic dumping device at end of conveyor to ensure that all cakes in pan are dumped onto another conveyor which routes them for packaging. Cleans residual filling from machine hopper and nozzles. May turn hand valves to regulate pressurized flow and quantities of cream filling injected into cakes. May collect and weigh measured amounts of aerated filling to ensure conformance with gravity specifications. May remove, discard, and keep tally of unacceptable cakes.
GOE: 06.04.15 STRENGTH: L GED: R2 M1 L2 SVP: 3 DLU: 77

524.685-034 ICER, MACHINE (bakery products) alternate titles: finisher, machine; froster, machine; icing-machine operator
Tends machine that coats baked products with premixed icing: Loads machine hopper with icing, using scoop. Starts machine and places products to be iced on conveyor. Turns valve on hopper to regulate flow of icing. May be designated according to product iced as Bread Icer, Machine (bakery products); Cake Icer, Machine (bakery products); Doughnut Icer, Machine (bakery products); Pie Icer, Machine (bakery products); Roll Icer, Machine (bakery products).
GOE: 06.04.15 STRENGTH: M GED: R2 M1 L1 SVP: 3 DLU: 77

524.685-038 MEXICAN-FOOD-MACHINE TENDER (food prep., nec)
Tends machine that automatically dispenses cheese onto tortillas to form enchiladas or ground meat onto taco shells to form tacos: Fills vat with meat or cheese mixture and turns control knobs to regulate flow of filling through dispenser mechanism. Presses button to convey tortillas or taco shells under dispenser mechanism. Periodically weighs sample product, using scale, and turns knob to adjust dispenser flow to maintain specified weight of product.
GOE: 06.04.15 STRENGTH: L GED: R2 M1 L1 SVP: 2 DLU: 77

524.686-010 ENROBING-MACHINE FEEDER (sugar & conf.) alternate titles: candy feeder; candy separator, enrobing; enrober tender
Arranges candy centers on conveyor leading to enrobing (coating) machine according to specified feeding sequence: Selects assorted centers from boxes or trays and places them in rows on conveyor belt to conform to individual box or layer arrangement. Removes malformed or broken centers and places them in salvage box.
GOE: 06.04.15 STRENGTH: L GED: R2 M1 L1 SVP: 2 DLU: 77

524.686-014 NOVELTY WORKER (dairy products) alternate titles: cone chocolate dipper; cone racker; sticker
Performs any combination of following tasks to make ice cream novelties, such as pies, cake rolls, cones, and vari-colored packs: Ladles fruit sauce over ice cream pie. Places layer of cake roll on tray and sets tray on conveyor. Cuts continuous ribbon of ice cream deposited on cake, using knife. Rolls up cake. Places roll in slicing machine and pulls lever to cut and eject slices onto packing table. Rotates transparent containers under nozzle that fills containers with vari-colored ice cream. Places cones, cups, pie plates, and other containers into dispenser of automatic filling machines.
GOE: 06.04.28 STRENGTH: L GED: R2 M1 L1 SVP: 2 DLU: 77

524.687-010 CHERRY CUTTER (can. & preserv.)
Cuts candied cherries into halves for use in decorating cakes, using sharp hand knife. May assist in the packing department as directed.
GOE: 06.04.28 STRENGTH: L GED: R1 M1 L1 SVP: 1 DLU: 77

524.687-014 GARNISHER (sugar & conf.)
Garnishes candy and fills dried or pitted fruit, such as prunes, dates, peaches, and figs, with nuts to make confections: Places nuts on top or presses them into candy or fruit items. Rolls candy in chopped or ground nut meats to coat product. May be designated according to task performed as Fruit Stuffer (sugar & conf.); Roller (sugar & conf.) II.
GOE: 06.04.28 STRENGTH: L GED: R1 M1 L1 SVP: 1 DLU: 77

524.687-018 RACKER (bakery products)
Loads wire racks with cookies, crackers, and wafers preparatory to their being dipped in icing: Removes wire rack from overhead trolley conveyor and places products on rack. Lifts and hooks rack to conveyor. May impale products on pins of wire rack and be designated Sticker (bakery products).

GOE: 06.04.28 STRENGTH: L GED: R1 M1 L1 SVP: 1 DLU: 77

524.687-022 BAKERY WORKER, CONVEYOR LINE (bakery products)
Performs any combination of following tasks in preparation of cakes along conveyor line: Reads production schedule or receives instructions regarding bakery products that require filling and icing. Inspects cakes moving along conveyor to detect defects and removes defective cakes from conveyor to reject bins. Positions cakes on conveyor for application of filling or icing by machine, observes filling or icing application to ensure uniform coverage, and places additional cake layers on coated layers, depending on number of cake layers in product. Observes cakes moving under automatic topping shaker and cake cutting machine to ensure uniform topping application and cutting. Smooths iced edges of cake, using spatula, and moves decorating tool over top of designated cakes to apply specified appearance. Notifies supervisor of malfunctions.
GOE: 06.04.28 STRENGTH: L GED: R1 M1 L1 SVP: 2 DLU: 86

525 SLAUGHTERING, BREAKING, CURING, AND RELATED OCCUPATIONS

This group includes occupations concerned with killing animals for use as food or byproducts, cutting up carcasses, and preserving and flavoring food, and related products by salting or smoking them.

525.131-010 SUPERVISOR, ABATTOIR (meat products)
Supervises and coordinates activities of workers engaged in slaughtering, skinning, and dressing cattle, hogs, and sheep on killing floor of abattoir: Directs and trains workers in use of knife, air-knife, saws, and other handtools. Inspects meat for specified color and texture to verify conformity to government regulations. Sets control timer to regulate conveyors according to production schedules. Performs other duties as described under SUPERVISOR (any industry) Master Title.
GOE: 06.02.01 STRENGTH: L GED: R4 M2 L2 SVP: 7 DLU: 77

525.131-014 SUPERVISOR, CUTTING AND BONING (meat products)
Supervises and coordinates activities of workers engaged in cutting cattle, sheep or swine carcasses into standard cuts, removing bones and trimming excess fat from cuts, and preparing special cuts for marketing: Instructs new employees in cutting carcasses and preparing special cuts. Examines cuts of meat to determine if quality standards are met. Directs COOLER ROOM WORKER (meat products) in selection of carcasses to be processed. Performs other duties as described under SUPERVISOR (any industry) Master Title.
GOE: 06.02.01 STRENGTH: L GED: R4 M2 L2 SVP: 7 DLU: 77

525.132-010 SUPERVISOR, CURED MEATS (meat products)
Supervises and coordinates activities of workers engaged in curing and smoking meats, such as bacon and hams, following formulas for pickling meats and specifications for operating smokeroom equipment: Trains workers in operation of equipment. Mixes dry and liquid pickling mixtures [PICKLING SOLUTION MAKER (meat products)]. Controls smokeroom equipment to smoke meat [SMOKER (meat products)]. Observes dial indicators and recording instruments to verify specified operating conditions of smokerooms and to detect machine and equipment malfunctions. Observes color and appearance of meats and feels meats to verify quality. Performs other duties as described under SUPERVISOR (any industry) Master Title.
GOE: 06.02.01 STRENGTH: L GED: R4 M2 L2 SVP: 6 DLU: 77

525.132-014 SUPERVISOR, TANK HOUSE (meat products)
Supervises and coordinates activities of workers engaged in processing slaughtering-and-meat-packing byproducts, such as tallow, hides, and cracklings (residual solids from extracting tallow from bone, trimmings, and viscera): Trains new employees in operation of equipment. Observes meters and dials to verify specified pressures and temperatures at various process stages. Moves controls to regulate equipment and correct equipment malfunctions. May supervise trimming and packing of offal products, such as tongues, livers, and tails. May assist in purchase of hides and sales of offal products. Performs other duties as described under SUPERVISOR (any industry) Master Title.
GOE: 06.02.01 STRENGTH: L GED: R4 M2 L2 SVP: 7 DLU: 77

525.134-010 SUPERVISOR, FISH PROCESSING (can. & preserv.)
Supervises and coordinates activities of workers engaged in cleaning, eviscerating and preparing fish for packing or canning: Trains workers to clean, eviscerate or prepare fish for packing or canning. Inspects fish at various stages of processing to determine if company standards are being met. Performs other duties as prescribed under SUPERVISOR (any industry) Master Title.
GOE: 06.04.01 STRENGTH: M GED: R4 M2 L2 SVP: 7 DLU: 77

525.134-014 SUPERVISOR, POULTRY PROCESSING (meat products)
Supervises and coordinates activities of workers engaged in slaughtering, dressing, and packing poultry: Trains new workers in slaughtering, dressing, and packing duties. Observes and evaluates performance of workers to ensure conformance to processing standards. May substitute for line workers in emergencies. Performs other duties as described under SUPERVISOR (any industry) Master Title.
GOE: 06.04.01 STRENGTH: L GED: R4 M2 L2 SVP: 7 DLU: 77

525.361-010 SLAUGHTERER, RELIGIOUS RITUAL (meat products)
Slaughters cattle, calves, and sheep as prescribed by religious law, and examines parts of carcasses to determine whether carcasses meet standards estab-

lished by specific religion: Sharpens knife on whetstone or sharpening steel and washes knife. Cuts throat of animal, using single stroke. Inspects carcass and internal organs to verify absence of diseases. May inspect and bid for animals at auction. May offer ritual prayers while slaughtering animal. May inflate lungs with air to determine whether lungs are punctured. May mark carcasses of animals that meet religious standards. May butcher meat for marketing. May be required to hold license issued by religious organization. May be designated according to specific religious group, such as Islamic Butcher (meat products), Shactor (meat products), Halal Butcher (meat products), Kosher Cutter And Searcher (meat products), or Shochet (meat products).
GOE: 06.03.01 STRENGTH: M GED: R3 M2 L2 SVP: 5 DLU: 86

525.381-010 BUTCHER APPRENTICE (meat products) alternate titles: slaughter-and-butcher apprentice
Performs duties as described under APPRENTICE (any industry) Master Title.
GOE: 06.02.28 STRENGTH: H GED: R3 M2 L2 SVP: 6 DLU: 77

525.381-014 BUTCHER, ALL-ROUND (meat products)
Performs slaughtering and butchering tasks in small slaughtering and meat packing establishment, using cutting tools, such as cleaver, knife, and saw: Stuns animals prior to slaughtering [STUNNER, ANIMAL (meat products)]. Shackles hind legs of animals, such as cattle, sheep, and hogs, to raise them for slaughtering or skinning [SHACKLER (meat products)]. Severs jugular vein to drain blood and facilitate slaughtering [STICKER, ANIMAL (meat products)]. Trims head meat and otherwise severs or removes parts of animal heads or skulls [HEAD TRIMMER (meat products)]. Saws, splits, or scribes slaughtered animals to reduce carcass [CARCASS SPLITTER (meat products)]. Slits open, eviscerates, and trims carcasses of slaughtered animals. Cuts, trims, skins, sorts, and washes viscera of slaughtered animals to separate edible portions from offal [OFFAL SEPARATOR (meat products)]. Washes carcasses [WASHER, CARCASS (meat products)]. Wraps muslin cloth about dressed animal carcasses or sides to enhance appearance and protect meat [SHROUDER (meat products)]. Shaves hog carcasses [SHAVER (meat products)]. Trims and cleans animal hides, using knife [HIDE TRIMMER (meat products; oils & grease)]. Cuts bones from standard cuts of meat, such as chucks, hams, loins, plates, rounds, and shanks, to prepare meat for marketing [BONER, MEAT (meat products)]. Examines, weighs, and sorts fresh pork cuts [GRADER, GREEN MEAT (meat products)]. Skins sections of animals or whole animals, such as cattle, sheep, and hogs [SKINNER (meat products)]. Works in small slaughtering and meat packing establishment. May prepare meats for smoking [SMOKED MEAT PREPARER (meat products)]. May cut and wrap meat. May salt (cure) and trim hides [HIDE HANDLER (meat products; oils & grease)].
GOE: 06.02.28 STRENGTH: H GED: R3 M2 L2 SVP: 6 DLU: 77

525.387-010 GRADER, MEAT (meat products)
Examines animal carcasses to determine grade in terms of sales value: Examines carcasses suspended from stationary hooks or hooks attached to overhead conveyor to determine grade based on age, sex, shape, thickness of meat, quantity and distribution of fat, color, texture, and marbling of lean meat. Attaches grade identification tag to carcass. May estimate weight of carcass or observe dial of automatic weighing scale to determine weight of carcass. May be designated according to carcass graded as Beef Grader (meat products); Hog Grader (meat products); Sheep Or Calf Grader (meat products).
GOE: 06.03.01 STRENGTH: L GED: R3 M2 L1 SVP: 5 DLU: 77

525.587-010 SHROUDER (meat products) alternate titles: bagger
Covers dressed animal carcasses with muslin to protect meat during storage or shipment: Trims ragged edges of flesh from carcass, using knife. Soaks muslin in brine solution and drapes wet muslin around suspended carcass. Pins muslin to carcass, using skewers. Slides carcass along conveyor and onto scale, and records weight. Pushes carcass to conveyor leading to storage or shipping areas. May wash carcass, using water hose.
GOE: 06.04.38 STRENGTH: M GED: R1 M1 L1 SVP: 2 DLU: 77

525.587-014 SMOKED MEAT PREPARER (meat products)
Prepares meats for smoking, performing any combination of following tasks: Soaks meat in water or brine and washes and scrapes encrusted salt, slime, grease, excess moisture, and discoloration from meat. Weighs meat and stamps or presses inspection labels, weight, or symbols on meat by hand or using branding iron. Ties cord through small end of hams and shoulders to form hanging loop. Encases meat in stockinets (cloth bags) to preserve shape of meat during smoking. Places metal hanging devices on racks, and hangs slabs of bacon on hooks of devices. Hangs meat products on tree racks suspended from conveyor and starts conveyor to move products to smokeroom. May strip stockinets from meat. May trim and bone hams. May be known according to task performed as Bagger, Meat (meat products); Comber (meat products); Hanger, Meat (meat products); Scraper, Meat (meat products); Soaker, Meat (meat products); Tier, Meat (meat products); Tree Loader, Meat (meat products); Washer, Meat (meat products).
GOE: 06.04.28 STRENGTH: H GED: R1 M1 L1 SVP: 2 DLU: 77

525.664-010 MEAT DRESSER (agriculture) alternate titles: farm butcher
Butchers livestock, such as hogs, sheep, and cattle, in private slaughter house or on customer's premises: Kills animals, using rifle and sticker knife. Raises carcass from floor, using hoist. Skins animal with skinning knife and cleans carcass with brush and water. Cuts carcass for packing, smoking, freezing, and salting, according to knowledge of meat cutting and customer's specifications, using saw, knives, and cleaver. May wrap meat. May grind meat into sausage.

GOE: 03.04.05 STRENGTH: M GED: R3 M2 L2 SVP: 6 DLU: 77

525.682-010 SMOKER (meat products) alternate titles: meat smoker; smokehouse attendant
Controls battery of smoke chambers in which meats, such as bacon, hams, meat loaf, sausage, shoulders, and wieners are cooked and cured: Loads racks and cages, suspended from overhead conveyor, with meat products and filled molds, and pushes racks into smokehouse for cooking and curing. Shovels sawdust into hopper of smoker and lights burner to ignite sawdust. Starts electric blower to admit air and blow smoke into curing chambers. Observes gauges, turns steam valves, and adjusts ventilators and dampers to regulate temperature, humidity, and density of smoke to control cooking and curing process. Inspects meat for color, feels meat for firmness, and inserts thermometer into meat to ascertain progress of cooking and curing. Opens water valve to spray and chill meat. Removes cooked and cured meat and empties molds. Places meat loaves on racks and returns them to smokehouse for further smoking and drying. Pushes racks of cured meat to chill room. May stuff meat loaves into plastic casings, using horn (funnel-shaped tube). May record weight and amount of meat cured. May steam-clean smoke chambers and heating coils, and remove ash.
GOE: 06.02.15 STRENGTH: H GED: R3 M2 L1 SVP: 4 DLU: 77

525.684-010 BONER, MEAT (meat products) alternate titles: ribber
Cuts bones from standard cuts of meat, such as chucks, hams, loins, plates, rounds, and shanks to prepare meat for packing and marketing, using knife and meat hook: Inserts knife in meat around bones to separate meat, fat, or tissue. Pulls and twists bones loose from meat. Cuts and trims such meat cuts as butts, hams, flanks, and shoulders to shape meat and remove fat and defects. Trims meat from bones and ribs. May pull bones and skin from cooked pigs feet, and cut out toe bones and nails. May be designated according to cut of meat boned as Blade Boner (meat products); Chuck Boner (meat products); Ham Boner (meat products); or type of animal boned as Beef Boner (meat products); Hog Ribber (meat products); Sheep Boner (meat products). May be designated: Loin Boner (meat products); Plate Boner (meat products); Rib Boner (meat products); Round Boner (meat products); Shank Boner (meat products); Shoulder Boner (meat products).
GOE: 06.04.28 STRENGTH: M GED: R2 M1 L2 SVP: 4 DLU: 77

525.684-014 BUTCHER, FISH (can. & preserv.)
Butchers eviscerated frozen, fresh, and salted fish for marketing or further processing: Dumps containers of fish into fresh water tank for cleaning. Places cleaned fish on table or bench. Trims off fins and tails, removes skin, and cuts fish into pieces of specified size, using knife or bandsaw. Sorts pieces according to color and texture.
GOE: 06.04.28 STRENGTH: H GED: R1 M1 L1 SVP: 2 DLU: 77

525.684-018 CARCASS SPLITTER (meat products)
Performs any combination of following tasks involved in dismembering and cutting up hog, veal, beef, and other animal carcasses to facilitate handling preparatory to marketing or further processing, using knife, cleavers, hand and power saws, and other cutting tools: Saws or cuts through pelvic area of animal, and splits belly to expose and remove viscera. Splits suspended carcass in half lengthwise along backbone of beef sides, and smooths and shapes beef with paddle. Saws ribs along interior of hog carcasses to facilitate removal of loins and ribs. Cuts, cleaves, or saws carcass sections to sever forequarters, hindquarters, shoulders, rumps, legs, and other parts. Saws trimmed bones, such as skulls, ribs, and legs, into pieces preparatory to processing into byproducts. May be known according to type or part of animal cut as Aitchbone Breaker (meat products); Beef Ribber (meat products); Bone Sawyer (meat products); Breast Sawyer (meat products); Ham Sawyer (meat products); Hog Sawyer (meat products). May be designated: Rump Sawyer (meat products); Shoulder Sawyer (meat products); Side Splitter (meat products).
GOE: 06.04.28 STRENGTH: M GED: R2 M2 L1 SVP: 3 DLU: 77

525.684-022 CRAB BUTCHER (can. & preserv.) alternate titles: crab backer
Butchers live crabs preparatory to canning: Grips crab with both hands and impales it on stationary spike. Twists, pulls, and detaches crab body from back, leaving back on knife. Wipes off gills and viscera and tosses crab body in vat of water. Pulls crab back from knife and discards it.
GOE: 06.04.28 STRENGTH: M GED: R1 M1 L1 SVP: 2 DLU: 77

525.684-026 FINAL-DRESSING CUTTER (meat products)
Cuts out defective portions of dressed animal carcasses, following established procedures: Trims or skins carcass to remove residual blood, fat, hair, ragged edges, and overscalded skin, using knife. Cuts condemned parts, such as broken bones and bruised flesh, from carcass under direction of government inspector, using knife, cleaver and saw. May cut up condemned animals for rendering. May be designated according to work area as Final-Rail Cutter (meat products); Retaining-Room Cutter (meat products).
GOE: 06.04.28 STRENGTH: M GED: R3 M1 L1 SVP: 4 DLU: 77

525.684-030 FISH CLEANER (can. & preserv.; fishing & hunt.) alternate titles: dress-gang worker; fish cutter; fish dresser
Cleans fish aboard ship or ashore, performing any combination of following tasks, alone or as member of crew: Scrapes scales from fish with knife. Cuts or rips fish from vent to throat with knife, and tears out viscera and gills. Cuts off head of fish with knife, drops head in tub, and slides fish along table to

next worker. Washes blood from abdominal cavity by dropping fish in tub of water or by use of hose, and removes discolored membrane from abdomen lining with knife, spoon, scraper, glove, or piece of burlap. Cuts gashes along sides of fish to facilitate salt penetration during curing. Cuts fish behind gill slits, draws knife along backbone and ribs to free fillet (boneless portion of flesh), lays fillet skinside down on table, and draws knife laterally between skin and flesh to remove skin. Slices flesh from bones in fletches (longitudinal quarter sections) for further processing into boneless slices of fish. Unloads catch from fishing vessels [LABORER, WHARF (can. & preserv.) 922.687-062]. May pack fish in containers. May remove slime from fish preparatory to canning and be designated Slimer (can. & preserv.; fishing & hunt.). May clean, dress, wrap, label, and store fish for guests at resort establishments and be designated Fish Housekeeper (hotel & rest.). May fillet fish and be designated Fish Filleter (can. & preserv.; fishing & hunt.).
GOE: 06.04.28 STRENGTH: M GED: R1 M1 L1 SVP: 2 DLU: 78

525.684-034 HEAD TRIMMER (meat products) alternate titles: head boner; templer, head
Trims meat, glands, and organs from carcass heads for use in making meat products or processing for medicinal use or byproducts, performing any combination of following tasks: Places head on table or in holding hooks and trims skin and meat from jaw, jowls, and skull with knife. Cuts fat from lean meat and drops it into containers. Inserts knife into mouth cavity to cut and remove tongue. Trims fat, ragged edges, veins, and bruises from tongue. Cuts and pulls hog snout from head, using knife and snout-pulling machine. Pulls jaw from skull, using jaw pulling machine, bar, or chisel. Places skull on block and splits it with automatic splitter or cleaver. Removes brains, pituitary gland, and other parts, and places them in separate trays. Removes horns from head, using shears. May be known according to duty performed as Brain Picker (meat products); Chiseler, Head (meat products); Jawbone Breaker (meat products); Jowl Trimmer (meat products); Snout Puller (meat products); Splitter, Head (meat products); Temple-Meat Cutter (meat products); Tongue Cutter (meat products).
GOE: 06.04.28 STRENGTH: M GED: R2 M1 L1 SVP: 3 DLU: 77

525.684-038 OFFAL SEPARATOR (meat products)
Separates edible portions of animal viscera from offal, performing any combination of following tasks: Cuts away such organs and glands from adjoining tissue as heart, sweetbreads, stomach, spleen, gall bladder, liver, and thyroid, using knife. Skins outer tissue of bung gut with fingers. Washes parts and places them in containers. Cuts off ends of oxtails and trims loose tissues, using knife and rotary brush. Trims excess fat and tissue from muscles, intestines, and organs, using knife. Separates membrane from gullet and windpipe, inner lining from stomach, and small intestines from large. Flushes intestines and bladders with water hose and squeezes them to remove water, slime, and foreign matter. Weighs and sorts viscera, according to condition, and discards diseased or damaged parts. Bleaches casings (intestines) by soaking them in salt solution. Stamps plant identification number on edible organs, using rubber stamp. Brands tails and tongues with electric iron. May tend machine that washes viscera and flesh parts. May grind meat. May be known according to functions performed or part of viscera processed as Beef-Pluck Trimmer (meat products); Bladder Trimmer (meat products); Bung Grader (meat products); Casing Puller (meat products); Liver Trimmer (meat products); Lung Splitter (meat products); Viscera Washer (meat products).
GOE: 06.04.28 STRENGTH: L GED: R2 M1 L1 SVP: 2 DLU: 77

525.684-042 POULTRY KILLER (meat products) alternate titles: sticker
Severs jugular vein with knife to slaughter suspended fowl passing on overhead conveyor.
GOE: 06.04.28 STRENGTH: L GED: R1 M1 L1 SVP: 2 DLU: 77

525.684-046 SKINNER (meat products)
Skins sections of animals or whole animals, such as cattle, sheep, and hogs, performing any combination of following tasks as member of a crew: Slits skin on head of carcass, and pulls and cuts connective tissue until head and neck are exposed, using knife. Severs head from carcass of animal, using knife and cleaver and places it on racks for inspection. Trims meat or fat from head skins. Slits remaining hide on carcass from breastbone to crotch. Pulls, cuts, and forces hand between hide and carcass to break connective tissue and separate it from neck, sides, shoulders, flanks, back, and tail of suspended carcass. Breaks and severs legs at knee joint, and removes such parts as dew claws, bungs, tails, and genital organs. Raises cattle from floor, using hoist, and pulls hide off carcass by hand or using pinchers. Severs and exposes gullet and windpipe on small stock, using knife, and ties gullet to prevent leakage of fluid when viscera is removed. Slits womb of cattle with knife to remove slunk (unborn calf). Shackles neck of slunk and pulls off skin, using winch. May saw brisket bone on cattle. May skin pork, using drawknife. May be designated according to kind of animal or portion of carcass skinned as Backer (meat products); Calf Skinner (meat products); Cattle Header (meat products); Slunk Skinner (meat products); Leg Skinner (meat products); Shoulder Puncher (meat products); Small-Stock Facer (meat products). May be designated: Cattle Dropper And Pritcher (meat products).
GOE: 06.04.28 STRENGTH: M GED: R2 M2 L1 SVP: 2 DLU: 77

525.684-050 STICKER, ANIMAL (meat products)
Severs jugular vein of previously stunned animals with knife to prepare animals for butchering: Positions neck of animal suspended from overhead rail or shackled on table for sticking. Thrusts knife into throat of animal and twists

blade to locate and sever jugular vein. May shackle and suspend animal before sticking [SHACKLER (meat products)]. May sever head and remove skin with knife, after blood has drained. May be designated according to animal killed as Calf Sticker (meat products); Cattle Sticker (meat products); Hog Sticker (meat products); Sheep Sticker (meat products).
GOE: 06.04.28 STRENGTH: M GED: R2 M2 L1 SVP: 3 DLU: 77

525.684-054 TRIMMER, MEAT (meat products)
Trims fat, skin, tendons, tissues, and ragged edges from meat cuts, such as loins, spareribs, butts, hams, rounds, sirloins, fillets, and chops, using meathook and knife: Trims meat and fat from bones and places trimmings and bones in separate containers. Trims fatback from hog bellies and cuts bellies into specified shapes, using knife. Feeds bacon bellies through rolls to flatten bellies to prescribed thickness. May wash or scrape dirt and blood from meat. May be designated according to section of meat trimmed as Belly Trimmer (meat products); Butt Trimmer (meat products); Fatback Trimmer (meat products); Loin Trimmer (meat products); Spareribs Trimmer (meat products).
GOE: 06.04.28 STRENGTH: M GED: R1 M1 L1 SVP: 2 DLU: 77

525.684-058 TURKEY-ROLL MAKER (meat products)
Cuts, bones, and sews parts of eviscerated turkeys together to form turkey roll, using knife and needle and thread: Cuts legs, wings, thighs, and whole skin from turkey and sews together wing holes in carcass. Cuts breast meat from bones and sews two portions of meat together. Rolls meat, places roll on opened turkey skin, overlaps skin on meat, and sews ends together to form roll.
GOE: 06.04.28 STRENGTH: L GED: R2 M1 L1 SVP: 2 DLU: 77

525.685-010 BAND-SAW OPERATOR (meat products)
Tends electrically powered bandsaw that cuts portions from hams to prepare hams for smoking, curing, or packing processes: Lifts ham from meat tank onto saw table, using meat hook. Presses button to start saw and adjusts saw gauges according to size of ham. Pushes and guides ham into saw blade by hand or with wooden device to cut shank from ham or to remove tip from shank. Pushes sawed meat onto conveyor for further processing. May tend bandsaw that cuts poultry into serving pieces for packaging.
GOE: 06.04.15 STRENGTH: M GED: R2 M1 L1 SVP: 2 DLU: 77

525.685-014 CASING-RUNNING-MACHINE TENDER (meat products) alternate titles: casing runner; shirring tender
Tends machine that gathers casings into short lengths on horns (metal nozzles of sausage-stuffing machine) to facilitate stuffing of casings with emulsified meat: Places reel of flattened casings on holder of gathering machine. Threads casing between feed rollers, onto tube, and onto take-up reel. Starts machine that automatically expands and rounds casings. Cuts rounded casings from reel into specified lengths, using cutting attachment on machine. Places horn over water pipe, fits casing over end of horn, and turns valve to flow water through pipe and into casing to facilitate gathering of casing on horn. Places horn between two cone-shaped rollers which force and gather casing lengths over horn. Removes loaded horn and places horn in container.
GOE: 06.04.15 STRENGTH: L GED: R1 M1 L1 SVP: 2 DLU: 77

525.685-018 DEHAIRING-MACHINE TENDER (meat products)
Tends equipment that dehairs slaughtered hogs preparatory to dressing: Turns steam and water valves to fill scalding tank with water and heat it to specified temperature. Starts machine conveyors, and releases hogs shackled to overhead rail to drop them into tank by tripping lever on shackle or prying shackle loose with steel bar. Pushes hogs through vat and into dehairing machine, using pole, or hooks hog's leg to conveyor chain that pulls hog through tank and dehairing machine. May cut slit in leg to expose tendon for hooking to conveyor chain. Opens exit door of machine and pulls carcass onto conveyor. May be known according to specific task performed as Dropper, Dehairing Machine (meat products); Feed-in Tender, Dehairing Machine (meat products); Pull-Through Hooker (meat products); Scalder (meat products).
GOE: 06.04.15 STRENGTH: M GED: R2 M2 L1 SVP: 3 DLU: 77

525.685-022 HIDE PULLER (meat products)
Tends machine that pulls hides from carcass: Pulls lever to position clamps on each side of carcass. Places ends of hide previously separated from carcass into clamps and pulls lever to lock hide in place. Starts machine that forces carcass forward, tearing off hide. Rips brisket open to expose viscera, using portable power saw.
GOE: 06.04.15 STRENGTH: M GED: R2 M1 L1 SVP: 2 DLU: 77

525.685-026 POULTRY-PICKING MACHINE TENDER (meat products)
Tends machines that scald, remove feathers, singe, and wash slaughtered poultry preparatory to eviscerating and disjointing: Adjusts clearance between revolving brushes of machine to achieve maximum feather removal without bruising or tearing skin of poultry. Scans poultry emerging from picking machines to determine if poultry are scalded to specifications and turns steam valves to increase or decrease temperature levels.
GOE: 06.04.15 STRENGTH: L GED: R2 M1 L1 SVP: 2 DLU: 77

525.685-030 SKIN-PEELING-MACHINE OPERATOR (meat products)
Tends machine that removes cellophane or plastic covering from smoked meat products, such as link-sausages, frankfurters, and wieners, to produce skinless variety: Turns setscrews to adjust skinning mechanism according to size of product. Starts machine and feeds strand of linked-meat into machine. Peels remaining fragments of covering from product, using knife.
GOE: 06.04.15 STRENGTH: L GED: R2 M1 L1 SVP: 2 DLU: 77

525.686-010 CASING CLEANER (meat products)
Feeds animal intestines into machine rollers that prepares them for use as sausage casings: Soaks intestines in vats of warm water to loosen waste matter and deposits. Separates soaked intestines and removes loosened matter. Feeds intestines between crushing and finishing rolls that strip (squeezes out) lime, fat, and mucus, and roll casing into shape. Measures and ties casings into bundles, and packs bundles in salt for shipment. Unpacks cured casings and soaks them for subsequent processing into sausage casings. May clean and flush animal stomachs for use as casings. May adjust tension on machine rollers. May be designated according to function performed as Casing Packer (meat products); Casing Soaker (meat products); or machine tended as Casing-Machine Operator (meat products).
GOE: 06.04.15 STRENGTH: L GED: R2 M1 L1 SVP: 2 DLU: 77

525.686-014 CONVEYOR LOADER II (meat products)
Guides dehaired hogs from stationary rail to moving chain conveyor. Lifts first stop bar to allow specified number of dehaired hogs to roll along suspended rail to second stop bar and then lowers bar. Lifts second stop bar and pushes specified number of hogs into moving chain conveyor. May remove empty gambrels (hog-suspended attachments) from hogs and place them on return conveyor. May be designated according to type of conveyor loaded as Cooler-Conveyor Loader (meat products).
GOE: 06.04.40 STRENGTH: L GED: R2 M1 L1 SVP: 2 DLU: 77

525.686-018 HEAD-MACHINE FEEDER (meat products)
Feeds machines that automatically pull snouts or jawbones from hog heads and split heads to prepare meat for further processing: Cuts jawbone joints and sides and front of snout to prepare parts for pulling process, using knife. Positions and holds head on bed of automatic machines to pull snout or jawbone from head or to split head in half. May trim cheek meat from head with knife subsequent to removal of jawbone.
GOE: 06.04.15 STRENGTH: L GED: R2 M1 L1 SVP: 2 DLU: 77

525.686-022 SKINNING-MACHINE FEEDER (meat products)
Feeds machine that skins pork pieces, such as fatbacks, jowls, hams, and bacon, preparatory to curing: Turns crank to raise or lower knife according to thickness of meat. Places unskinned piece on conveyor that moves it under machine knife that skins meat. Trims remaining skin fragments with knife. May skin pork by hand, using drawknife.
GOE: 06.04.15 STRENGTH: M GED: R2 M1 L1 SVP: 2 DLU: 77

525.687-010 ANIMAL EVISCERATOR (meat products) alternate titles: gutter
Eviscerates cattle, hogs, lambs, and small animals, performing any combination of following tasks: Slits body cavity of carcass, reaches inside abdominal cavity and cuts membranes holding intestines. Inserts spiral rod in gullet to sever gullet and windpipe from other neck tissue. Cuts bung from intestines and ties intestines, bladder, bung, and gullet to prevent leakage of contents. Pulls intestines from carcass, trims off fat, and dumps them into gut truck or conveyor pan. Cuts out glands, ovaries, sweetbreads, liver, heart, lungs, kidneys, spleen, and spermatic cord, places them on conveyor, in containers, or throws them down chute. Cuts bruises, blemishes, and ragged tissue from carcass. Cuts skin from tail to shoulders to bisect carcass. Severs head from carcass. May wash viscera and carcass, using hose. Patches leaks in intestines, using skewer. May break and bind hoofs of lambs or sheep. May be designated according to function performed as Bruise Trimmer (meat products); Leak Patcher (meat products); Weasand Rodder (meat products); or part of animal eviscerated as Belly Opener (meat products); Bung Dropper (meat products); Bung-Gut Tier (meat products). May be designated: Caul-Fat Puller (meat products); Gut Puller (meat products); Gut Sorter (meat products); Leaf-Fat Scraper (meat products); Rabbit Dresser (meat products).
GOE: 06.04.28 STRENGTH: M GED: R2 M2 L1 SVP: 3 DLU: 77

525.687-014 CASING SPLITTER (meat products)
Slits cured intestines lengthwise, using knife. Presses intestines flat and stacks them in piles for subsequent production of surgical sutures and violin and tennis racket strings.
GOE: 06.04.28 STRENGTH: L GED: R1 M1 L1 SVP: 1 DLU: 77

525.687-018 CONVEYOR LOADER I (meat products)
Pulls spreads (metal rods inserted in breast of hog halves to separate parts and allow circulation of air) from breast of suspended hog halves preparatory to storage in cooling room. Drops spreads into barrel. Pushes halves along overhead monorail to chain conveyor which carries halves into cooler. May count and record number of halves processed.
GOE: 06.04.40 STRENGTH: H GED: R1 M1 L1 SVP: 2 DLU: 77

525.687-022 COOLER ROOM WORKER (meat products)
Stores and prepares dressed meat for further processing or shipment, performing any combination of tasks in cooler room of slaughtering plant: Examines carcasses to determine condition of meat, such as hardness, softness, and oiliness prior to cutting. Records information on inspection tag. Weighs carcass on conveyor scale and records weight on production sheet. Trims excess fat from meat, using knife. Cuts carcasses into quarters, using knife and meat saw. Stamps predetermined grade on meat, using rubber stamp, and attaches date tags. Brands carcasses and meat products with electric iron. Pushes carcasses, or meat cuts, suspended from conveyor, from killing and dressing floor to cooler room or between departments. Separates cuts of meat according to weight,

and grade. Pushes truck, filled with pieces of meat, glands, and organs, into cooling room and places them in pans or hangs them on racks. Transports containers of tallow to cooler room and other departments, using handtruck. Carries meat from shipping platform and loads it into delivery truck. Places trolleys on conveyor rails, and cleans and greases rails. Washes floor and containers with hose and shovels fresh sawdust onto floor. May shroud carcasses [SHROUDER (meat products)].
GOE: 06.04.28 STRENGTH: H GED: R2 M2 L1 SVP: 2 DLU: 77

525.687-026 DRY CURER (meat products) alternate titles: salter
Cures meat products, such as pork, ham, bacon, or casings preparatory to smoking: Pushes sacks of such materials as sugar, sodium nitrate, and salt to curing room, using handtruck or cart. Weighs out specified amounts of materials and mixes them by hand or in mixing machine. Packs and arranges meat in boxes, vats, tierces, or piles, and sprinkles mixture over each layer. Sweeps excess mixture from meat with broom. Rearranges layers after specified time to circulate air around meat. Dips ham hocks in brine solution, sprinkles soda on them, and hangs them on rack for curing. May be designated according to product cured as Belly Packer (meat products); Casing Salter (meat products); Ham-Hock Mopper (meat products); Salt-Bellies Overhauler (meat products).
GOE: 06.04.28 STRENGTH: H GED: R2 M1 L1 SVP: 2 DLU: 77

525.687-030 GAMBRELER (meat products) alternate titles: hanger-off
Hangs animal carcasses on overhead rail preparatory to dressing: Slits skin to expose tendons in hind ankles, using knife, and inserts *gamb stick* (hooked metal or wooden rod) between tendon and ankle bone to spread legs. Hooks gamb stick to trolley on overhead rail and pushes carcasses to next work station. Cuts flesh between toes of carcass and removes toenails.
GOE: 06.04.28 STRENGTH: M GED: R1 M1 L1 SVP: 2 DLU: 77

525.687-034 GAMBRELER HELPER (meat products)
Supplies GAMBRELER (meat products) with *gamb sticks* and moves animal carcasses to dressing stations: Removes gamb sticks from overhead conveyor and stacks them for use by GAMBRELER (meat products). Places trolley (two-wheeled device equipped with hanger to which gamb sticks are hooked) onto overhead conveyor rail so that carcasses can be hung. Positions animal carcasses on table or overhead conveyor. Pushes carcass on overhead rail to various dressing stations. May slit leg tendons on carcass, using knife, to facilitate insertion of gamb sticks.
GOE: 06.04.28 STRENGTH: M GED: R1 M1 L1 SVP: 2 DLU: 77

525.687-038 HIDE HANDLER (meat products; oils & grease) alternate titles: hide selector; pelt salter; salt spreader
Salts (cures) and trims hides to prepare hides for storage or shipment, performing any combination of following tasks: Spreads hides, flesh side up, in layers on pile. Shovels and spreads salt over each layer of hides to preserve (cure) hides. Drags cured hides from pile and strikes hide against table to remove caked salt or sweeps salt from hides, using broom. Trims ears, ragged edges, snout skin, tail, and excess flesh from hide, using knife. Folds hides, flesh side inward, and ties cord around bundle. May scan hides for defects, such as holes and brandmarks. May be designated according to duty performed as Hide Salter (meat products; oils & grease); Hide Shaker (meat products; oils & grease); Hide Spreader (meat products).
GOE: 06.04.27 STRENGTH: H GED: R2 M1 L1 SVP: 2 DLU: 77

525.687-042 HIDE INSPECTOR (meat products) alternate titles: green-hide inspector; hide grader; pelt inspector
Inspects animal hides, pelts, and slunk (unborn animal) skins for blemishes and grades them according to condition, size, and weight: Spreads hides, pelts, or skins on floor and examines or probes them with wooden skewer to detect defects, such as grub holes, cuts, brands, and residual meat and fat to determine grade. Outlines defective areas on diagram. Records grade of hide on tag according to condition, size, and weight, and attaches tag to hide. May trim excess fat from flesh, and cut off snout, ears, and tail, using knife. May place hides in curing vat. May remove pituitary gland from split sheep skull, using knife. May weigh hides on platform scale. May record number and types of grades of hides on production sheets.
GOE: 06.03.02 STRENGTH: M GED: R2 M1 L2 SVP: 3 DLU: 77

525.687-046 HIDE TRIMMER (meat products; oils & grease) alternate titles: beamer; selector
Trims and cleans animal hides, using knife: Places hide on table and cuts off superfluous fat, flesh, ragged edges, and parts, such as ears, snout, skin, and tail. Spreads hide on floor, skin side up, to prepare them for inspection. May separate hides according to size, weight, and condition. May be designated according to animal hide trimmed as Calfskin Trimmer (meat products); Cow Trimmer (meat products); Pigskin Trimmer (meat products).
GOE: 06.04.39 STRENGTH: M GED: R2 M1 L1 SVP: 3 DLU: 77

525.687-050 NECK SKEWER (meat products) alternate titles: neck pinner
Pushes skewer into neck meat of suspended beef halves to pin flabby meat together after head has been removed. May roll shrouded carcass with handtool to give it a smooth appearance.
GOE: 06.04.28 STRENGTH: L GED: R1 M1 L1 SVP: 2 DLU: 77

525.687-054 OFFAL ICER, POULTRY (meat products)
Shovels ice into chicken offal (waste parts) container to cool waste and retard spoilage. Loads and removes containers, using handtruck. May tend baling machine to bale wet feathers.

GOE: 06.04.40 STRENGTH: H GED: R1 M1 L1 SVP: 1 DLU: 77

525.687-058 ORDER RUNNER (meat products)
Prepares smoked meat for packing and further processing, performing any combination of following duties: Removes specified smoked meats from bins and racks, and places them on conveyor leading to packing room. Wipes salt and moisture from smoked hams. Inserts hooks in smoked meats and hangs them on racks for further processing.
GOE: 06.04.40 STRENGTH: M GED: R1 M1 L1 SVP: 2 DLU: 77

525.687-062 PAINTER, DEPILATORY (meat products)
Prepares sheep pelts for removal of wool: Positions pelt on table, hair side down, and brushes depilatory solution on pelt to loosen wool. Folds pelt and hangs it on hook to dry. Loads handtruck with dried pelts and pushes it to WOOL PULLER (leather mfg.; meat products).
GOE: 06.04.27 STRENGTH: M GED: R1 M1 L1 SVP: 1 DLU: 77

525.687-066 POULTRY BONER (meat products)
Cuts, scrapes and pulls meat from cooked poultry carcasses, using fingers and boning knife: Pulls wings and drumsticks from carcasses. Cuts along each side of breast plate, using knife, and peels meat from breast, using hands. Pulls and scrapes meat from rest of carcass, using knife and hands. Segregates light and dark meat into separate piles. Discards wastes, such as skin, bones, and gristle, into waste containers.
GOE: 06.04.28 STRENGTH: L GED: R1 M1 L1 SVP: 2 DLU: 77

525.687-070 POULTRY DRESSER (agriculture; meat products) alternate titles: tipper
Slaughters and dresses fowl in preparation for marketing, performing any combination of following tasks: Chops off bird's head or slits bird's throat to slaughter bird, using knife. Hangs bird by feet to drain blood. Dips bird into scalding water to loosen feathers. Holds bird against projecting rubber fingers of rotating drum to remove feathers. Cuts bird open, removes viscera, and washes bird and giblets. May pluck chickens by hand. May be designated according to type of fowl dressed as Chicken Dresser (meat products); Turkey Dresser (meat products). May be known according to specific duties performed as Poultry Picker (meat products); Poultry Scalder (meat products).
GOE: 06.04.28 STRENGTH: L GED: R1 M1 L1 SVP: 2 DLU: 77

525.687-074 POULTRY EVISCERATOR (meat products)
Butchers and processes poultry performing any combination of following tasks: Severs legs at first joint, using knife, and drops legs into container. Slits breast skin, removes crop, and places crop on conveyor. Removes oil sack and slits abdominal wall with knife. Grasps carcass with hands, opens abdominal cavity, and pulls out viscera. Separates and washes liver, heart, and viscera and drops them into trays. Cuts around anus to remove remaining viscera and drops it onto conveyor. Holds gizzard over machine rollers to remove skin and drops it into washer. Trims fat from giblet meat with knife and places meat and fat in trays. May be designated according to part of poultry processed as Foot Cutter (meat products); Gizzard-Skin Remover (meat products); or kind of poultry cleaned as Chicken Cleaner (meat products); Turkey Cleaner (meat products).
GOE: 06.04.28 STRENGTH: L GED: R1 M1 L1 SVP: 2 DLU: 77

525.687-078 POULTRY HANGER (meat products)
Shackles and suspends live or slaughtered poultry from conveyor for killing, scalding, removal of feathers or cleaning. Removes live poultry from shipping crates, or picks up slaughtered birds from platforms and chilling vats and hangs them by feet, neck, or wings on shackles of conveyor.
GOE: 06.04.28 STRENGTH: M GED: R1 M1 L1 SVP: 1 DLU: 77

525.687-082 POULTRY-DRESSING WORKER (meat products)
Weighs, wraps, and prepares poultry for shipment or storage, performing any combination of following tasks: Loads dressed poultry into carts in layers, and shovels ice between layers to prevent spoilage. Pushes filled cart to and from cold storage room. Wraps dressed poultry in paper and packs it in shipping container. Weighs poultry and marks weight on container. May shovel ice into cooling machines. May load trucks. May wrap heads of poultry in paper. May remove crops with knife and sew eviscerated poultry, using needle and twine. May hang or stack cases of dressed poultry in cold storage room.
GOE: 06.04.38 STRENGTH: H GED: R1 M1 L1 SVP: 2 DLU: 77

525.687-086 SHACKLER (meat products) alternate titles: hanger
Chains hind legs of stunned animals, such as cattle, sheep, and hogs, to hoist or conveyor that suspends animals for slaughtering process. May place trolley hooks or *gamb stick* in leg tendon of animal to raise them.
GOE: 06.04.40 STRENGTH: M GED: R1 M1 L1 SVP: 2 DLU: 77

525.687-090 SHACTOR HELPER (meat products)
Lifts head of animal suspended from conveyor to facilitate examining and throat-cutting by official as prescribed by Jewish law. Pushes animal over bleeding trough after cut has been made.
GOE: 06.04.28 STRENGTH: M GED: R1 M1 L1 SVP: 2 DLU: 77

525.687-094 SHAVER (meat products)
Removes hair and dirt from hog carcasses preparatory to further processing or marketing, performing any combination of following tasks: Shaves and scrapes suspended carcasses to remove dirt and hair, using knife and scraper. Pulls off toenails, using hook. Pulls lever to dip suspended hog into resin tank and peels off hardened resin to remove hair. Applies hot resin with brush to remove remaining hair. May remove eyelids, feet, and bruised areas with knife.

May slit ankle joints for insertion of gambrel sticks for hanging carcass prior to shaving. May be designated according to specific activity performed as Resin Worker (meat products); Toe Puller (meat products).
GOE: 06.04.28 STRENGTH: L GED: R2 M1 L1 SVP: 2 DLU: 77

525.687-098 SINGER (meat products)
Singes hair from carcasses of suspended hogs to prepare them for further processing, using torch. Inserts end of butcher's steel in nostril of hog to remove hair. May be designated according to part of hog singed as Hog-Head Singer (meat products).
GOE: 06.04.28 STRENGTH: L GED: R2 M1 L1 SVP: 2 DLU: 77

525.687-102 SKIN GRADER (meat products) alternate titles: skin bundler
Transfers hog-back skins from vat to grading table and measures size and length of skin on graduated grading board. Separates skins according to size.
GOE: 06.03.02 STRENGTH: M GED: R2 M1 L2 SVP: 2 DLU: 77

525.687-106 SLUNK-SKIN CURER (meat products)
Cures slunk (unborn calf) skins in vat of brine solution: Turns valve to fill vat with water and adds salt. Places slunk skins in vat and stirs them with pole to ensure complete curing. Removes cured skins from vat and rolls them into ball or places them in barrel for shipment.
GOE: 06.04.34 STRENGTH: M GED: R2 M1 L1 SVP: 2 DLU: 77

525.687-110 STEAMER (meat products)
Sprays steam on suspended hog carcasses to remove hair and dirt (scurf).
GOE: 06.04.39 STRENGTH: L GED: R1 M1 L1 SVP: 1 DLU: 77

525.687-114 STUNNER, ANIMAL (meat products)
Stuns animals, such as cattle, hogs, sheep, or goats, preparatory to slaughtering: Opens gate to allow animal to enter knocking pen or chute. Moves levers to close squeezing mechanism that immobilizes animal. Stuns animal by striking it on forehead with sledgehammer, pneumatic hammer, or cartridge-firing stunning device; by shooting it in head; or by placing electric shocking device against head of animal. Pulls levers to tilt floor of pen and slide animal onto killing floor, or onto conveyors leading to sticking and shackling tables. May stick, shackle, and suspend animals from overhead conveyors or rails [SHACKLER (meat products); STICKER, ANIMAL (meat products)]. May assist in driving animals into knocking pen or chute.
GOE: 06.04.28 STRENGTH: M GED: R1 M1 L1 SVP: 2 DLU: 77

525.687-118 TIER (meat products) alternate titles: roast tier
Rolls and ties cuts of meat to form roasts: Places cut of meat on table and rolls meat into circular shape. Forces skewer threaded with twine through roll of meat at various points to hold roll in place. Knots and cuts twine.
GOE: 06.04.28 STRENGTH: L GED: R1 M1 L1 SVP: 2 DLU: 77

525.687-122 WASHER, CARCASS (meat products)
Sprays suspended animal carcasses with water hose to wash off blood and dirt and pushes carcass along overhead rail to next work station. May brush or scrape off foreign matter. May shroud carcass [SHROUDER (meat products)].
GOE: 06.04.39 STRENGTH: M GED: R1 M1 L1 SVP: 1 DLU: 77

525.687-126 CRAB MEAT PROCESSOR (can. & preserv.) alternate titles: crab picker
Performs any combination of following tasks in processing crab meat for canning, freezing, or packing: Separates claws from crabs, positions claws in metal holder used to facilitate breaking claw shells, and breaks shells of claws and crabs, using knife or metal rod. Picks meat from shells, using knife and fingers. Feels meat for presence of shell and removes shell pieces by hand. Inspects meat for discoloration and discards meat not meeting company requirements. Places meat in containers for further processing. Gathers filled containers of meat, places containers on scale, and adds or removes meat from containers to obtain specified weight. Closes lids of containers, places containers in cartons, and seals cartons. May disjoint legs and body of large crabs, using power saw, and be known as Sawyer (can. & preserv.). May remove crab meat from smaller ends of leg segments, using pedal-controlled air jet, and be known as Blower (can. & preserv.).
GOE: 06.04.28 STRENGTH: L GED: R1 M1 L1 SVP: 2 DLU: 86

526 COOKING AND BAKING OCCUPATIONS, N.E.C.

This group includes occupations, not elsewhere classified, concerned with treating components or products with heat to affect such characteristics as flavor, color, edibility, consistency, and texture.

526.131-010 BAKERY SUPERVISOR (bakery products)
Supervises and coordinates activities of workers engaged in mixing, dividing, molding, and proofing of dough, and in baking, slicing, and wrapping of bread, pastries, and other bakery products: Examines dough and batter for specified consistency. Reads charts of fermentation room and ovens to verify specified humidity and temperature. Oversees operation of automatic machinery, such as rounding, curling, icing, slicing, and wrapping machines to ensure maintenance of specified quality standards and production schedules. Sets up and adjusts wrapping and slicing machines. Trains new workers. Performs other duties as described under SUPERVISOR (any industry) Master Title. May be designated according to product as Bread Supervisor (bakery products); Cake Supervisor (bakery products).

GOE: 06.01.01 STRENGTH: M GED: R4 M3 L3 SVP: 8 DLU: 78

526.134-010 COOK, MEXICAN FOOD (food prep., nec)
Supervises and coordinates activities of workers engaged in preparing, cooking, portioning, and packaging ready-to-serve Mexican food specialties, such as chili, tamales, enchiladas, and tacos (seasoned chili beans wrapped in tortillas): Requisitions ingredients, such as meat, olives, chili, garlic, and spices from storeroom. Directs activities of workers engaged in feeding and tending grinding and mixing machines, rolling, cutting, and baking tortillas, and stirring and tending food in cooking vessels. Tastes foods to determine that they meet seasoning specifications. Supervises workers engaged in portioning and packaging foods. Frequently performs duties of workers supervised. May be designated according to food cooked as Cook, Chili (food prep., nec); Cook, Enchilada (food prep., nec); Cook, Taco (food prep., nec); Cook, Tamale (food prep., nec); Cook, Tortilla (food prep., nec).
GOE: 06.01.01 STRENGTH: M GED: R4 M2 L3 SVP: 7 DLU: 77

526.137-010 POTATO-CHIP-PROCESSING SUPERVISOR (food prep., nec)
Supervises and coordinates activities of workers engaged in peeling and slicing potatoes, frying potato slices, and inspecting fried potato chips: Examines incoming shipments of potatoes to detect rotten and diseased potatoes. Tests sample of potatoes in container of water to determine solidity content (degree of solidity) of potatoes, using Nicholson hydrometer (instrument used to measure specific gravity of a solid). Inserts thermometer into potato to determine temperature of potato shipment. Routes sample of potatoes from each shipment to POTATO-CHIP FRIER (food prep., nec). Rejects or accepts potato shipment based on color and crispness of fried chips, number of defective potatoes in shipment, and solidity content and temperature of potatoes. Inspects potato chips to verify conformance to standards. Inventories and requisitions supplies. Performs other duties as described under SUPERVISOR (any industry) Master Title.
GOE: 06.02.01 STRENGTH: L GED: R4 M3 L3 SVP: 6 DLU: 77

526.381-010 BAKER (bakery products)
Mixes and bakes ingredients according to recipes to produce breads, pastries, and other baked goods: Measures flour, sugar, shortening, and other ingredients to prepare batters, doughs, fillings, and icings, using scale and graduated containers [DOUGH MIXER (bakery products) 520.685-234]. Dumps ingredients into mixing-machine bowl or steam kettle to mix or cook ingredients according to specifications. Rolls, cuts, and shapes dough to form sweet rolls, piecrust, tarts, cookies, and related products preparatory to baking. Places dough in pans, molds, or on sheets and bakes in oven or on grill. Observes color of products being baked and turns thermostat or other controls to adjust oven temperature. Applies glaze, icing, or other topping to baked goods, using spatula or brush. May specialize in baking one type of product, such as breads, rolls, pies, or cakes. May decorate cakes [CAKE DECORATOR (bakery products) 524.381-010]. May develop new recipes for cakes and icings.
GOE: 06.02.15 STRENGTH: H GED: R3 M2 L2 SVP: 7 DLU: 80

526.381-014 BAKER APPRENTICE (bakery products)
Performs duties as described under APPRENTICE (any industry) Master Title.
GOE: 06.02.15 STRENGTH: H GED: R3 M2 L2 SVP: 7 DLU: 77

526.381-018 BAKER, TEST (grain-feed mills) alternate titles: baker, laboratory; flour tester
Bakes loaves of bread to verify adherence of blended flour to specifications: Weighs equal portions of test flour and standard flour. Mixes flour and other ingredients and makes batch of dough from each flour. Records mixing formula and observes water absorption and kneading qualities of each batch to ensure that flour conforms to specifications. Places loaves in oven. Examines and compares baked loaves for uniformity of color and texture. Weighs each loaf and records weights. May prepare written reports of findings.
GOE: 06.02.15 STRENGTH: L GED: R3 M2 L2 SVP: 6 DLU: 77

526.381-022 CAKE TESTER (grain-feed mills)
Bakes samples of premixes, such as cake, biscuit, muffin and pancake to test batch prior to packaging: Mixes ingredients and bakes in oven. Examines baked cake for color, texture, and density. Records findings on worksheet and determines if cake passes standards. Issues approval slip for batch meeting standards. Notifies plant chemist if batch does not meet standards. May test ingredients to determine cause of cake failure.
GOE: 06.02.15 STRENGTH: L GED: R3 M2 L2 SVP: 6 DLU: 77

526.381-026 COOK, KETTLE (beverage; can. & preserv.; grain-feed mills) alternate titles: cook; cooker; cook, pressure
Cooks fruits, vegetables, meats, condiments, or fish products, preparatory to canning or extraction of byproducts, using cooking equipment: Weighs or measures ingredients according to recipe, using scale or graduated container. Loads ingredients into kettle or pressure cooker. Observes thermometer and gauges, turns valve to admit steam to pressure cookers or lights gas burner to heat and cook contents of kettles. Stirs mixture in kettle to blend and prevent scorching of contents, using hand or power-driven paddles. Observes cooking process or tests batch liquor with viscosimeter or hydrometer to verify viscosity or specific gravity and to ascertain completeness of cooking process. Starts pump, opens valve, or tilts or scoops contents of kettle into container to unload cooked contents. May test batch for sugar content, using refractometer. May mix ingredi-

ents prior to cooking. May be designated according to material cooked as Cook, Fish Eggs (can. & preserv.); Cook, Fruit (can. & preserv.); Cook, Jelly (can. & preserv.); Cook, Juice (can. & preserv.); Cook, Sauce (can. & preserv.); Cook, Starch (can. & preserv.). May be designated: Cook, Mayonnaise (can. & preserv.); Cook, Pickled Meat (can. & preserv.); Cook, Preserve (can. & preserv.); Cook, Seafood (can. & preserv.); Cook, Spaghetti (can. & preserv.); Cook, Vegetable (can. & preserv.).
GOE: 06.01.04 STRENGTH: M GED: R3 M2 L2 SVP: 6 DLU: 77

526.382-010 CONCHE OPERATOR (sugar & conf.) alternate titles: conche loader and unloader
Operates conche machine to heat and agitate refined chocolate mass with cocoa butter to enrich color, flavor, and texture: Pumps specified amount of chocolate mixture into steam-heated stationary tank or rotary drum. Meters out specified amount of such ingredients as cocoa butter or flavorings. Turns steam valves and adjusts thermostat to heat contents of tank or drum to specified temperature. Pushes lever to start agitators and rotate drum. Pushes levers to change rate of agitation, drum rotation, and temperature, following specified time cycles. Observes and tastes mixture to evaluate conformity to standard and sends sample to laboratory for analysis. Adjusts temperature, agitation speed and timing cycle, and adds ingredients, such as cocoa butter and lecithin, according to laboratory findings. Pumps mixture to storage tank.
GOE: 06.02.15 STRENGTH: M GED: R3 M2 L2 SVP: 4 DLU: 77

526.382-014 CONFECTIONERY COOKER (sugar & conf.)
Controls open-fire or steam-jacketed kettles or batch or continuous pressure cookers to cook candy, gum, or other confectionery ingredients according to formula: Weighs or measures ingredients, such as sugar, corn syrup, butter, and gum base, and adds them to cooking utensil. Starts agitators to mix ingredients. Turns valve to admit steam and sets pressure gauge and thermostat to cook ingredients at specified temperature. Feels batch for specified consistency and verifies percentage of sugar in syrup, using refractometer or hydrometer. Adjusts steam valve and heating element accordingly. Opens discharge valve and starts pump or tilts cooker or kettle to pour or dump confection into beaters or onto cooling belts or tables. May partially cook batch in open kettle and pump it into pressure cooker. May beat or knead confection to attain specified consistency, as determined by color and texture. May shovel fondant into remelt kettles and add measured amounts of flavoring and coloring. May be designated according to type of confectionery cooked as Bonbon-Cream Warmer (sugar & conf.); Crystal-Syrup Maker (sugar & conf.); Coconut Cooker (sugar & conf.); Fondant Cooker (sugar & conf.); Gum Maker (sugar & conf.); or equipment used as Vacuum-Cooker Operator (sugar & conf.). May be designated: Icing Maker (sugar & conf.); King Maker (sugar & conf.); Marshmallow Maker (sugar & conf.).
GOE: 06.02.15 STRENGTH: M GED: R4 M2 L3 SVP: 7 DLU: 77

526.382-018 CONVERTER OPERATOR (grain-feed mills)
Controls converter to change starch into glucose or corn syrup, and tests products to verify purity (specified dextrose content): Turns valves to admit steam and water into converter. Introduces starch into converter so that cooking occurs as starch is added. Detects from sound of cooking process formation of paste, and adds acid, as necessary, to reduce viscosity. Closes converter and turns valve to attain specified pressure. Draws off samples, and makes standard iodine and alcohol titration tests. Turns valves to blow syrup into tank when tests indicate conversion is complete.
GOE: 06.02.15 STRENGTH: L GED: R3 M2 L1 SVP: 4 DLU: 77

526.382-022 MOLASSES AND CARAMEL OPERATOR (grain-feed mills)
Controls equipment to cook liquid sugar to produce caramel coloring or molasses: Turns valves to fill vessels with liquid sugar and adds specified amounts of salts or caustic solution. Observes thermometers and gauges and turns valves to regulate steam pressure and cooking temperature in vessels. Draws samples of material and performs standard tests to ascertain acid content and specific gravity, and to verify color, using pH meter, hydrometer, and colorimeter. Records test results. Turns valves or starts pumps to transfer material to evaporator feed tanks, filter supply tanks, or to storage or tank cars. May tend filters to remove undesirable solids from caramel coloring.
GOE: 06.02.15 STRENGTH: H GED: R3 M2 L3 SVP: 4 DLU: 77

526.382-026 STEAM-OVEN OPERATOR (can. & preserv.) alternate titles: parboiler; steamer operator
Operates steam oven to parboil tuna fish loins preparatory to canning: Pushes racks of fish loins into oven chamber, and spaces racks to ensure free circulation of heat throughout oven. Closes oven doors and turns handwheel to secure and seal doors. Turns valves to admit steam into oven, observes temperature and pressure gauges, and adjusts valve settings to maintain temperature and pressure for specified time. Turns off heat, opens oven, and pulls racks of fish to cooling area.
GOE: 06.02.15 STRENGTH: M GED: R2 M1 L1 SVP: 3 DLU: 77

526.485-010 WORT EXTRACTOR (dairy products) alternate titles: malted-milk masher
Tends kettles and separating machines that cook mash and separate resulting liquid (wort): Assembles piping and starts pump or turns valve to start flow of mash from grinder to kettles. Places time and temperature chart in automatic recorder. Starts sweep to stir mash. Turns valve to admit steam into cooking kettle, observes pressure gauge, thermometer, and clock, and cooks mash for

specified time at specified temperature. Drops iodine on mash sample and observes resulting color to determine if mash is sufficiently cooked. Records time and number of batches run. Turns valves to pump mash through centrifuge and vibrating filter to remove wort. Turns sparging valve to spray water over spent grain to recover remaining wort. Observes ammeter, thermometer, water and mash flowmeters and adjusts valves and pump pressure to prevent overloading of separating machines. Cleans kettles, piping, centrifuges, filters, and clarifiers. May pump spent grain through roller press to remove wort. May operate centrifuge to remove nonsoluble solids from wort. May push control panel button that automatically sets temperature.
GOE: 06.04.15 STRENGTH: H GED: R3 M1 L1 SVP: 3 DLU: 77

526.585-010 OVEN OPERATOR (grain-feed mills) alternate titles: flake-miller helper
Tends ovens and related equipment that toast cereal products, such as flakes, biscuits, and pellets: Lights gas burners and moves control levers to attain specified temperature in ovens. Starts conveyors that move cereal through oven. Inspects and feels cereal emerging from oven to determine whether specified color, blister, and consistency is maintained. Adjusts gas control lever, speed of conveyors, and opens or closes doors on side of oven. Pushes lever to direct unsuitable cereal into feed bin. Records bulk and production rate of product, noting time it takes to fill container, and weight of container.
GOE: 06.04.15 STRENGTH: L GED: R2 M1 L1 SVP: 3 DLU: 77

526.665-010 COOKER, PROCESS CHEESE (dairy products) alternate titles: cook blender
Tends vat to cook blended cheeses or cheese curd and other ingredients to make process cheese: Starts agitator and signals for cheese to be dropped into vat. Turns steam valve and observes thermometer to heat vat to specified temperature. Measures or weighs out prescribed ingredients, such as sodium citrate, disodium phosphate, and cream, using scale and measuring glass. Dumps ingredients into vat. Cooks mixture at specified temperature for specified time or observes consistency of mixture to determine when it is cooked to specifications. Pulls lever to drain cheese into hopper or bucket. May pump cheese through viscolizer to achieve finer texture. May mix unheated cheese or cheese curd and other ingredients to make cold pack cheese or creamed cheese and be designated Cream-Cheese Maker (dairy products).
GOE: 06.04.15 STRENGTH: M GED: R3 M2 L2 SVP: 3 DLU: 77

526.665-014 KETTLE TENDER (beverage)
Tends brewing kettle that boils wort and hops preparatory to making beer: Opens valve and starts pump to transfer wort from filter tank to brewing kettle, or signals MASH-FILTER OPERATOR (beverage) to pump wort from filter tank into brewing kettle. Turns valve to admit steam into kettle steam jacket to boil wort. Dumps hops into boiling wort. Observes dials and gauges and adjusts controls to maintain specified pressure and temperature. Tests sample of wort from kettle for specific gravity, using hydrometer. Signals HOP STRAINER (beverage) or opens valve and starts pump to transfer unfiltered beer into hop-straining tank. Tallies and records barrels of wort processed. Cleans and rinses kettle, using high-pressure water hose.
GOE: 06.04.15 STRENGTH: L GED: R2 M1 L1 SVP: 2 DLU: 77

526.682-010 BATTER SCALER (bakery products) alternate titles: batter depositor; depositing-machine operator; divider; scaling-machine operator
Operates machine that deposits measured amount of batter into baking pans as pans pass on conveyor: Dumps batter from mixing bowl into machine hopper, using hoist. Attaches depositing dies to machine and tightens, using wrench. Adjusts gauge on hopper to measure specified amount of batter. Weighs filled pans on balance scale to ensure conformity to standards. Removes filled pans from machine and places on racks. May be designated according to type of batter used as Cake-Batter Scaler (bakery products).
GOE: 06.02.15 STRENGTH: L GED: R3 M2 L2 SVP: 4 DLU: 77

526.682-014 COOK, DOG-AND-CAT FOOD (meat products)
Controls battery of steam-jacketed kettles that cook ingredients for preparation of dog and cat foods: Dumps or pours premeasured amounts of water and ground meat into kettles. Starts agitator to mix ingredients. Opens steam valve and observes thermometer reading to heat contents and to maintain specified temperature. Dumps specified amounts of seasoning, chemical solution, and grain into mixture at designated intervals. Opens valves to allow mixtures to circulate through other kettles. Observes mixture for required viscosity and closes valves upon completion of cooking cycle. Starts pumps to transfer contents from kettles to tank of filling machines.
GOE: 06.02.15 STRENGTH: M GED: R3 M2 L2 SVP: 4 DLU: 77

526.682-018 COOK, SYRUP MAKER (beverage)
Operates equipment to mix and cook ingredients to produce flavoring extracts and syrup: Scans formula sheet to determine proportion of ingredients required, such as sugar, water, and flavoring. Pushes buttons to admit automatically metered ingredients into blending tank and to activate mixer. Observes mixture to ensure that color and consistency conform to company specifications. Pushes buttons to pump mixture to cooking kettle. Opens valves to admit steam into pressure cooker to invert sugar, eliminate air, and sterilize syrup. Observes gauges and adjusts valves to regulate temperature and pressure while cooking mixture. Presses switch to activate paddles to stir mixture and prevent scorching. Tests batch to determine viscosity or specific gravity and sugar content, using viscometer, hydrometer, and refractometer. Presses switches to acti-

vate equipment to filter impurities and pump syrup into holding tanks. Maintains production records.
GOE: 06.02.15 STRENGTH: M GED: R3 M2 L2 SVP: 4 DLU: 77

526.682-022 DOUGHNUT-MACHINE OPERATOR (bakery products) alternate titles: cruller maker, machine; doughnut-cooking-machine operator; fried-cake maker
Operates machine that shapes and fries doughnuts: Slides block of ejectors (cutters) into machine and tightens them, using wingnuts. Turns switch to heat frying tank to desired temperature. Mixes prepared ingredients with specified amount of water in mixing machine to form batter. Dumps batter into doughnut machine hopper, using chain hoist. Turns and adjusts valves to control air pressure for ejecting batter into frying tank and to regulate size of doughnuts, temperature and feed of grease, and speed of conveyor. Starts machine and observes color and verifies weight of doughnuts to ensure conformity to standards. Dismantles doughnut ejectors for cleaning. May melt and temper chocolate [CHOCOLATE TEMPERER (bakery products; grain-feed mills)].
GOE: 06.02.15 STRENGTH: L GED: R3 M2 L3 SVP: 4 DLU: 77

526.682-026 MALT ROASTER (beverage)
Controls gas-fired ovens to roast barley malt: Observes temperature gauges, and turns gas valves and ignition switches to start and heat ovens to specified temperatures. Opens slide gate of hopper to dump malt into oven. Sets timer to control roasting cycle. Shuts off ovens and opens water valves to drench roasted malt at end of cycle. Dumps malt in cooler tubs and pushes to cleaning machine. Starts conveyor that lifts and dumps malt into cleaning machine. Opens gate and valves to drop malt into storage bins for bagging.
GOE: 06.02.15 STRENGTH: M GED: R3 M2 L2 SVP: 4 DLU: 77

526.682-034 RETORT OPERATOR (can. & preserv.)
Controls retort chamber (steam pressure cooker) to cook canned foods according to specifications: Pushes trucks or lowers baskets using hoist, or presses buttons to start conveyorized flow of canned foods into chamber of retort. Closes retort door or lid, and turns wheels or moves levers to seal chamber. Observes dials and thermometers, and turns valves to admit steam to retort, and control temperature, pressure, and cooking time. Turns valves to release steam and admit cooling water into chamber to prevent overcooking at end of cooking cycle. May open retort and move basket of canned food to cooling trough, using hoist. May record items such as retort number, can size and grade designation, cooking time, and number of pounds pressure on canning report.
GOE: 06.02.15 STRENGTH: H GED: R3 M1 L1 SVP: 5 DLU: 77

526.684-010 DOUGHNUT MAKER (bakery products) alternate titles: baker, doughnut; cruller maker
Mixes, forms, and fries dough to produce doughnuts, according to work order: Dumps prepared doughnut mix into mixing-machine bowl, adds water and dehydrated eggs, and starts mixer. Turns switch on heating unit of frying tank and sets thermostat at specified temperature. Dumps dough from mixing bowl into hopper of doughnut cutter. Sets lever to control amount of dough that doughnut cutter will portion to frying tank. Moves cutter machine back and forth over frying tank and depresses trigger to eject individual doughnuts into hot cooking oil. Turns doughnuts over in tank, using stick. Lifts wire tray of fried doughnuts from tank and places it in glazing tank. Slides trough containing glazing syrup over doughnuts. May glaze doughnuts, using hand dipper. May roll dough with rolling pin and form doughnuts with hand cutter. May lower wire tray of uncooked doughnuts into fryer, using hooks. May tend automatic equipment that mixes, cuts, and fries doughnuts. May weigh cut dough and fried doughnuts to verify weight specifications, and adjust controls of equipment accordingly when weights vary from standards.
GOE: 06.02.28 STRENGTH: M GED: R3 M1 L1 SVP: 4 DLU: 78

526.684-014 LUMPIA WRAPPER MAKER (food prep., nec)
Mixes and fries dough to prepare *lumpia* wrappers in establishment processing Philippine food specialties: Mixes premeasured ingredients by hand to prepare dough. Kneads dough to required consistency. Places griddle on stove to heat griddle. Shapes and spreads, by hand, specified amount of dough on heated griddle to cook and form lumpia wrappers. Removes cooked lumpia wrappers from griddle, using fingers, and stores wrappers for further processing or packaging. Periodically returns dough to freezer to maintain dough consistency. Cleans equipment and work area.
GOE: 05.10.08 STRENGTH: H GED: R2 M1 L1 SVP: 2 DLU: 86

526.685-010 COOK (meat products)
Tends equipment that bakes, boils, and deep-fat fries meats, such as ham, beef, liver, pork, sausage, tongues, and tripe, to prepare them for further processing: Turns valves to admit water or cooking oil into vat, and steam to heating vat. Observes gauge and turns valves to maintain specified temperature in vat. Loads vat with mesh bags, wire cages, metal molds, and sealed cans containing uncooked meat. Lifts cuts of meat from truck and loads them into vat. Suspends link sausages on holding fixtures in vat. Turns valve to drain vat, removes cooked meats, and places them on racks or in carts. Spreads sugar or honey over top of hams and places hams and other meat items in baking oven. May garnish hams with cherries and pineapple slices. May add gelatin and other ingredients, such as olives, pickles, and pimientos, to cooked meat and mix them by hand or in machine. Pours mixture into molds to form gelatinized meat loaf. May stuff meat loaves into plastic casings, using horn (funnel-shaped tube). May cook products, such as chili, souse, and head cheese. May remove bones and fat from cooked meat, using knife. May grind meat, using grinding machine.

369

GOE: 06.04.15 STRENGTH: H GED: R3 M1 L1 SVP: 3 DLU: 77

526.685-014 COOK, FRY, DEEP FAT (can. & preserv.; hotel & rest.)
Tends deep-fat cookers to fry meats, vegetables, or fish in cooking oil: Empties containers or opens valves to fill cookers with oil. Sets thermostat to heat oil to specified temperature. Empties containers of meat, vegetable, or fish into metal basket and immerses basket into vat manually or by hoist. Sets timer. Observes color at end of frying time to determine conformity to standards and extends frying time accordingly. Removes basket from cooker, drains it, and dumps contents onto tray. May dip foods into batter or dye before frying. May specialize in a particular food product for canning or freezing or may fry variety of foods for immediate consumption.
GOE: 06.04.15 STRENGTH: M GED: R2 M1 L1 SVP: 2 DLU: 77

526.685-018 COOK, VACUUM KETTLE (can. & preserv.)
Tends vacuum cooker and open kettle to cook fruit and berries preparatory to making jams and jellies: Observes thermometer, turns rheostat and steam valve, or pushes switch or lights burner to heat vacuum cooker and open kettle to specified temperature. Turns valve to transfer contents of kettle into vacuum cooker. Observes refractometer on vacuum cooker to determine sugar content and adds ingredients according to formula. Places container under discharge outlet of distillation jacket of cooker to reclaim esters. Opens valve or starts pump to transfer contents of vacuum cooker to holding tank or filling machine.
GOE: 06.04.15 STRENGTH: L GED: R2 M1 L1 SVP: 2 DLU: 77

526.685-022 COOKER (grain-feed mills)
Tends steam-heated pressure cookers to cook cracked and tempered grain for further processing into cereal products: Presses button to load first cooker with measured amount of grain and liquid flavor. Clamps lid of cooker in place, using wrench. Moves dials and turns valves to attain specified temperature and pressure in cooker. Removes lid of cooker and dumps cooked grain onto conveyor after determining that grain has reached specified color and consistency. Records cooking time and number of batches prepared. May start automatic equipment that admits steam, rotates cooker, and stops cooker after specified time.
GOE: 06.04.15 STRENGTH: L GED: R2 M1 L2 SVP: 3 DLU: 77

526.685-026 CORN POPPER (sugar & conf.) alternate titles: popcorn maker; popped-corn oven attendant
Tends one or more gas ovens to pop corn: Lights ovens and starts rotating cone- or drum-shaped perforated oven. Dumps measured amount of corn into oven. Places container at discharge end of oven to receive popcorn or starts conveyor to carry corn through screen to remove unpopped kernels. Moves lever to reverse rotation of oven and to dump unpopped kernels into container beneath oven. When popping corn by wet method, pushes level to release measured amount of oil into unpopped corn in stationary oven. May prepare syrup and coat popcorn to make popcorn candy [POPCORN-CANDY MAKER (sugar & conf.)].
GOE: 06.04.15 STRENGTH: H GED: R1 M1 L1 SVP: 2 DLU: 77

526.685-030 OVEN TENDER (bakery products)
Tends stationary or rotary hearth oven that bakes bread, pastries, and other bakery products: Places pans of unbaked goods on blade of long-handled paddle (peel). Opens oven door and slides loaded peel into oven. Jerks paddle from under pans to deposit them on hearth. Observes gauges and turns valves to regulate heat and humidity of oven. Notes color of products during baking to ensure uniformity of finished products. Removes baked goods from oven with peel, and places them on tiered racks. Flips switch to position hearth for loading and unloading when tending rotary hearth oven. May place bagels into kettle of boiling water, remove bagels from kettle, using ladle, and sprinkle bagels with seasoning prior to placing bagels in oven. May be designated according to type of oven tended or product baked as Oven Tender, Bagels (bakery products); Peel Oven Tender (bakery products); Rotary-Peel Oven Tender (bakery products).
GOE: 06.04.15 STRENGTH: M GED: R3 M1 L1 SVP: 4 DLU: 79

526.685-034 PAN GREASER, MACHINE (bakery products)
Tends machine that automatically coats inside surfaces of baking pans with grease: Places container of grease alongside machine and inserts suction pipe into container. Starts machine. Adjusts gauge to regulate spray of grease. Removes greased pans from machine conveyor and places pans on second conveyor for transfer to batter depositing machine, or stacks pans on racks. May be designated according to type of pans greased as Bread-Pan Greaser (bakery products); Cake-Pan Greaser (bakery products).
GOE: 06.04.21 STRENGTH: L GED: R1 M1 L1 SVP: 2 DLU: 77

526.685-038 PIE MAKER, MACHINE (bakery products)
Performs any combination of following duties on pie-machine conveyor line: Loads dough into hopper of pie-dough scaling machine. Turns hand lever to adjust scaling cylinder of machine to produce lumps of dough of prescribed size. Removes lumps of dough deposited from scaling machine and places them in dough-rolling-machine hopper. Turns hand lever to adjust rollers of machine to produce dough disks of desired thickness, catches dough emerging from first set of rollers, and drops dough into second set of rollers. Catches dough emerging from rolling machine and places it in piepan as it moves on conveyor. Dumps pie filling from container into hopper of filling machine, using hoist. Observes pies being filled and adjusts mechanism to regulate feed of filling or fills pies by hand. Catches dough emerging from rolling machine and places

it over filled pies. Perforates pie covers to identify filling, using hand stamp. Inserts pan containing pie in pie-crimping machine and depresses pedal to crimp and seal perimeter of pie. Trims excess dough from pie with knife. May be designated according to phase of operation performed as Pie Bottomer (bakery products); Pie-Crimping-Machine Operator (bakery products); Pie-Dough Roller (bakery products); Pie Filler (bakery products); Pie Topper (bakery products).
GOE: 06.04.15 STRENGTH: M GED: R3 M1 L1 SVP: 4 DLU: 77

526.685-042 POPCORN-CANDY MAKER (sugar & conf.)
Tends equipment to cook and mix syrup with popcorn, forming popcorn candy: Weighs, measures, adds, stirs, and cooks ingredients, such as corn syrup, butter, and water in open-fire cooker or steam-jacketed kettle according to formula and specified procedure. Dumps popped corn into bowl of mixing machine or other container. Pours syrup over corn and starts agitator to mix corn and syrup for specified time or until coating is complete. May tend molding press to form popcorn novelties or shapes, such as balls or fritters (disks).
GOE: 06.04.15 STRENGTH: L GED: R2 M2 L1 SVP: 3 DLU: 77

526.685-046 POTATO-CHIP FRIER (food prep., nec) alternate titles: cooker, chip; potato-chip cooker machine
Tends machine that washes, slices, fries, and salts potatoes to make potato chips: Opens valve to pump preheated cooking oil into cooking vats. Fills salt hopper. Adjusts burner controls to maintain specified temperature in cooking vats. Turns valves to rinse potato slices, and moves levers to control rate of flow of potato slices into cooking vats. Stirs potato slices to ensure uniform cooking, using paddle or by use of automatic reciprocating rakes. Observes color of cooked potato chips as they emerge onto conveyors from cooking vats. Replaces worn blades on slicing heads, using handtools. May cook potatoes by lowering wire basket of sliced potatoes into vat of cooking oil.
GOE: 06.04.15 STRENGTH: L GED: R2 M1 L1 SVP: 3 DLU: 77

526.685-050 POTATO-PANCAKE FRIER (food prep., nec)
Tends machine that deep-fries potato pancakes in oil, preparatory to freezing and packaging: Dumps potato batter into hopper of machine that automatically forms and fries pancakes. Turns valve to add specified amount of frying oil into machine. Inspects fried pancakes on conveyor to verify specified size and color.
GOE: 06.04.15 STRENGTH: M GED: R2 M1 L1 SVP: 2 DLU: 77

526.685-054 PRETZEL COOKER (bakery products)
Tends oven that automatically cooks, salts, bakes, and dries pretzels: Lights oven and sets thermostats of cooker, oven, and kiln at specified temperature. Dumps specified amount of salt, soda, and water into hoppers of oven. Turns valve to sprinkle salt and to allow soda solution to drain continuously into cooking pit of oven. Observes progress of uncooked pretzels moving on conveyor into oven, and straightens pretzels, using wire hooked rod. Tastes baked pretzels, observes their color, and adjusts speed of conveyor or temperature of cooker, oven, and kiln to ensure pretzels conform to color and taste standards. May place unbaked pretzels on oven conveyor by inverting boards loaded with pretzels.
GOE: 06.04.15 STRENGTH: M GED: R2 M1 L1 SVP: 3 DLU: 77

526.685-058 THERMOSCREW OPERATOR (can. & preserv.)
Tends machine that precooks meat products preparatory to canning: Starts machines and conveyors, and loads meat into grinder to be ground and fed into cooker. Observes temperature gauge and color of meat during cooking process, and turns valve or adjusts rheostat to maintain specified temperature for prescribed cooking time. Turns valves to permit flow of cooking fluid into machine and from machine into filtering tanks.
GOE: 06.04.15 STRENGTH: H GED: R2 M1 L1 SVP: 3 DLU: 77

526.685-062 TRIPE COOKER (meat products)
Tends equipment that cooks tripe to tenderize it preparatory to further processing: Dumps tripe into scalding vat to remove outer skin. Turns valve to admit water and steam into cooking vat and transfers tripe into vat by hand or using pitchfork. Observes gauge and regulates valves to maintain specified temperature in vat. Removes cooked tripe from vat after specified length of time and places it in trays or on racks for chilling. May cook tongue.
GOE: 06.04.15 STRENGTH: M GED: R2 M1 L1 SVP: 2 DLU: 77

526.685-066 WAFER-MACHINE OPERATOR (bakery products) alternate titles: waffle baker; waffle-machine operator
Tends machines that automatically deposit and bake batter in molds to form wafers: Lights gas burners to heat baking molds. Fills hopper of machine with batter. Starts machine and turns setscrew to regulate amount of batter deposited in mold. Turns thermostat to adjust temperature of baking molds. Observes color of baked wafers being ejected onto conveyor to detect defects. May be designated according to type of wafer made as Sugar-Wafer-Machine Operator (bakery products). May tend machine that also rolls batter into shape of cones prior to baking and be designated Cone Baker, Machine (bakery products).
GOE: 06.04.15 STRENGTH: L GED: R2 M1 L1 SVP: 3 DLU: 77

526.685-070 OVEN OPERATOR, AUTOMATIC (bakery products) alternate titles: baker operator, automatic
Tends automatic reel or conveyor type oven that bakes bread, pastries, and other bakery products: Reads work order to determine quantity and type products to be baked. Turns dials and valves to set operation speed of conveyor, baking time, and temperature controls of baking unit. Presses buttons to start

equipment, and observes gauges to maintain heat according to specifications. Observes filled baking pans entering oven to determine whether pans are filled to standard, spacing between pans is sufficient to prevent pans jamming together, and speed of pans entering oven is specified speed to control baking time of product in oven. Observes color of baking product to detect burning or over baking and to verify uniformity of finished products. Adjusts controls according to procedure or notifies supervisor when conditions require equipment adjustments. May load and unload ovens. May be designated according to type of oven controlled as Conveyorized Oven Tender (bakery products); Reel Oven Tender (bakery products). May tend mixing machine and auxiliary equipment that automatically mixes, shapes, and bakes batter to form fortune cookies and be designated Fortune Cookie Maker (bakery products).
GOE: 06.04.15 STRENGTH: L GED: R3 M2 L2 SVP: 3 DLU: 78

526.686-010 BAKER HELPER (bakery products)
Performs any combination of following tasks in production of baked goods: Moves and distributes bakery supplies and products in and around production area of bakery, using handtrucks, dollies, troughs, and rack trucks. Weighs and measures ingredients, such as sugar, flour, yeast, syrup, and dough. Lifts and dumps containers of materials to help load and unload machines, bins, hoppers, racks, and ovens. Feeds lumps or sheets of dough into hopper or between rolls of machine. Cleans equipment, using brushes, cleanser, and water. Greases, lines, or dusts pans or boards preparatory to receiving product for baking. May cut, turn, or twist dough into specified products and fill baking pans with dough. May observe and rearrange baked products on conveyor before products enter slicing machine. May tend equipment that dumps baked bread from pans onto conveyor for further processing. May push racks of bakery products into designated areas to await further processing. May be designated according to worker assisted as Batter-Mixer Helper (bakery products); or according to machine operator assisted as Cracker-And-Cookie-Machine Operator Helper (bakery products); Doughnut-Machine-Operator Helper (bakery products); Cookie-Mixer Helper (bakery products); Dividing-Machine-Operator Helper (bakery products); Dough-Mixer Helper (bakery products); Ingredient-Scaler Helper (bakery products).
GOE: 06.04.15 STRENGTH: H GED: R2 M1 L1 SVP: 2 DLU: 86

526.687-010 POTATO-CHIP SORTER (food prep., nec)
Observes potato chips on conveyor and removes chips that are burned, discolored, or broken.
GOE: 06.03.02 STRENGTH: L GED: R1 M1 L1 SVP: 1 DLU: 77

526.687-014 STARCHMAKER (sugar & conf.) alternate titles: candy-starch-mold printer; printer
Makes starch molds in which gum or jelly candy is formed, using manual press: Fills trays with starch and levels filled trays, using straightedge implement. Slides molding plate into press and secures it with thumbscrews. Pushes starch-filled tray under molding plate and pulls lever to press plate into starch, forming mold cavities. May tend machine that automatically empties molded candy from trays, refills them with starch, and reprints mold cavities [MOLDING-MACHINE-OPERATOR HELPER (sugar & conf.)].
GOE: 06.04.28 STRENGTH: L GED: R2 M1 L1 SVP: 3 DLU: 77

529   OCCUPATIONS IN PROCESSING OF FOOD, TOBACCO, AND RELATED PRODUCTS, N.E.C.

This group includes occupations, not elsewhere classified, concerned with processing food, tobacco, and related products.

529.130-010 SUPERVISOR, CANDY (sugar & conf.)
Supervises and coordinates activities of workers engaged in cooking, forming, coating, wrapping, and packing candy: Trains workers in setting up and operating machines, such as depositors, enrobers, and cutters. Inspects candy to verify specified size, shape, solidification, gloss, and weight. Performs other duties as described under SUPERVISOR (any industry) Master Title. May be designated according to operation as Supervisor, Enrobing (sugar & conf.); or type of candy as Supervisor, Hard Candy (sugar & conf.).
GOE: 06.02.01 STRENGTH: L GED: R4 M2 L3 SVP: 7 DLU: 77

529.130-014 SUPERVISOR, CHOCOLATE-AND-COCOA PROCESSING (sugar & conf.)
Supervises and coordinates activities of workers engaged in producing and packaging chocolate and cocoa products: Designates quantities and types of beans to clean, roast, blend, alkalize, and grind to make chocolate liquor. Indicates time sequence, quantity, type of chocolate liquor, and formulas to use to make cocoa and coatings. Trains workers in setting up and adjusting machines and equipment to achieve standards and correct malfunctions. Reviews laboratory reports on quality control of products in process, such as shell content of nibs, fat content of cocoa powder, viscosity of coatings, and moisture content of alkalized beans. Reads thermometers and pressure gauges on storage tanks and pipelines to verify specified temperature of liquids to prevent solidification. Oversees roasting of cocoa beans for adherence to flavor, taste, moisture content, and color standards. Inspects nibs for shell content and fineness of cracking. Inspects grinding of nibs for specified fineness of chocolate liquor. Tests liquor for fineness. Directs mixing, refining, tempering, conching, and molding operations to make sweet chocolate and coatings. Inspects products for specified viscosity, texture, color, and taste. Directs workers engaged in insect and rodent control and in cleaning production and storage areas. Performs other duties as described under SUPERVISOR (any industry) Master Title.

GOE: 06.01.01 STRENGTH: L GED: R4 M3 L3 SVP: 8 DLU: 77

529.130-018 SUPERVISOR, COFFEE (food prep., nec)
Supervises and coordinates activities of workers engaged in grinding, blending, roasting, and packaging of coffee. Requisitions supplies. Sets up machines, such as grinders and filling machines. Performs duties as described under SUPERVISOR (any industry) Master Title.
GOE: 06.02.01 STRENGTH: L GED: R4 M2 L3 SVP: 7 DLU: 77

529.130-022 SUPERVISOR, FILTRATION (sugar & conf.)
Supervises and coordinates activities of workers engaged in filtering, clarifying, and storing sugar liquors, slurries, and sweetwaters. Observes automatic recording devices to verify specified temperature, density and alkalinity of liquors, slurries, and sweetwaters. Performs duties as described under SUPERVISOR (any industry) Master Title.
GOE: 06.02.01 STRENGTH: L GED: R4 M2 L3 SVP: 7 DLU: 77

529.130-026 SUPERVISOR, NUT PROCESSING (can. & preserv.)
Supervises and coordinates activites of workers engaged in cracking, sorting, blanching, cutting, grinding, roasting, packing, and shipping nuts: Sets up and repairs nut-processing machines, such as nut-cracking machine, meat grading machine, or nut-cutting machines. Observes operation of machines to detect malfunctions or to detect worn parts. Inspects nuts to verify conformance with plant standards. May install and service showcases in retail stores to display nut products. Performs other duties as described under SUPERVISOR (any industry) Master Title.
GOE: 06.02.01 STRENGTH: M GED: R4 M2 L3 SVP: 7 DLU: 77

529.130-030 SUPERVISOR, PULP HOUSE (sugar & conf.)
Supervises and coordinates activities of pulp-house workers engaged in processing sugar-beet pulp into cattle fodder: Consults with SUPERVISOR, BEET END (sugar & conf.) to ascertain tonnage of beets being processed, and schedules number of driers and presses required to handle pulp. Adjusts automatic presses to press water from pulp. Moves controls to start equipment, such as elevators, scrolls, and conveyors, and to regulate flow of molasses into mingler scroll. Observes gauges and automatic recorders to verify specified temperatures in driers. Directs workers in clearing blockades and cleaning spillages. Performs other duties as described under SUPERVISOR (any industry) Master Title.
GOE: 06.02.01 STRENGTH: M GED: R4 M2 L3 SVP: 7 DLU: 77

529.130-034 SUPERVISOR, REFINING (sugar & conf.) alternate titles: sugar-end supervisor
Supervises and coordinates activities of workers engaged in storing and distributing liquors and syrups, and in boiling, crystalizing, and drying sugar. Reads records and gauges to verify that equipment is operating according to standards. Performs duties as described under SUPERVISOR (any industry) Master Title.
GOE: 06.01.01 STRENGTH: L GED: R4 M2 L3 SVP: 7 DLU: 77

529.130-038 SUPERVISOR, SOFT SUGAR (sugar & conf.)
Supervises and coordinates activities of workers engaged in centrifuging, screening, distributing, and packing brown sugar: Sets timing on centrifuge cycles to control color of product. Orders packing machine operators to set up machines. Turns valves and opens gates to distribute sugar to packing station. Directs workers in washing equipment when changing color of pack. Performs other duties as described under SUPERVISOR (any industry) Master Title.
GOE: 06.02.01 STRENGTH: M GED: R4 M2 L3 SVP: 7 DLU: 77

529.130-042 SUPERVISOR, WHITE SUGAR (sugar & conf.) alternate titles: centrifugal supervisor
Supervises and coordinates activities of workers engaged in centrifuging, granulating, and storing sugar: Sets timing controls on centrifuges for spinning, washing, and predrying cycles. Observes operation of equipment and temperature and flowmeters to verify specified flow of product between stations. Performs other duties as described under SUPERVISOR (any industry) Master Title.
GOE: 06.02.01 STRENGTH: L GED: R4 M2 L3 SVP: 7 DLU: 77

529.131-010 CELLAR SUPERVISOR (beverage)
Supervises and coordinates activities of workers engaged in operation of winery cellars: Directs workers in crushing grapes, fermenting and fortifying juice, finishing and aging wine, operating portable pumps to transfer wine, and racking wine (filtering). Inspects fermentation tanks for cleanliness and operation of valves and other accessories. Orders filling of tanks and adds yeast culture to must in tanks to promote fermentation. Turns valves to circulate ferment through heat exchangers or other devices to maintain vintage at specified temperature. Observes gauges and records readings. Performs other duties as described under SUPERVISOR (any industry) Master Title.
GOE: 06.02.01 STRENGTH: M GED: R4 M2 L3 SVP: 8 DLU: 77

529.131-014 SUPERVISOR, DAIRY PROCESSING (dairy products)
Supervises and coordinates activities of workers engaged in producing dairy products, such as milk, butter, cheese, and evaporated milk in liquid, solid, or powdered form: Directs workers in receiving and testing milk and in operations, such as pasteurizing, separating, evaporating, drying, cooling, and storing dairy products. Feels, tastes, and smells cheese samples to determine types of cheeses required for specified blend. Examines samples of evaporated milk, orders changes in cooking temperature, and adds measured amounts of calcium or phosphate to milk to obtain specified texture and viscosity. May add specified

amount of lactic ferment cultures to pasteurized milk to develop starter for sour dairy products, such as buttermilk, cheese, or sour cream. Performs other duties as described under SUPERVISOR (any industry) Master Title. May be designated according to type of product as Butter Production Supervisor (dairy products); Cheese Production Supervisor (dairy products); Instant-Powder Supervisor (dairy products); or according to process as Pasteurizing Supervisor (dairy products).
GOE: 06.02.01 STRENGTH: L GED: R4 M3 L3 SVP: 7 DLU: 77

529.132-010 CUSTOM-FEED-MILL OPERATOR (grain-feed mills)
  Supervises and coordinates activities of workers in operation of feed mill that grinds grain and mixes feed to customer's specifications. May operate grinders and auxiliary equipment to grind and mix feed. May compute charges and collect payment. May purchase supplies and equipment and keep financial records. May manage commercial feed store in conjunction with mill to sell grain, stock feed, fertilizer, and other products to retail trade. Performs other duties as described under SUPERVISOR (any industry) Master Title.
GOE: 05.12.01 STRENGTH: L GED: R4 M2 L3 SVP: 7 DLU: 77

529.132-014 PLANT SUPERVISOR (grain-feed mills)
  Supervises and coordinates activities of workers engaged in drying, shelling, grading, and bagging hybrid seed corn: Regulates valves to maintain specified temperature of drying room. Periodically inspects and samples corn during various stages of processing for accuracy of operation, and for germination and purity. Tags and stores bagged grain. Performs other duties as described under SUPERVISOR (any industry) Master Title.
GOE: 06.01.01 STRENGTH: L GED: R4 M2 L3 SVP: 7 DLU: 77

529.132-018 SUPERVISOR, BEET END (sugar & conf.)
  Supervises and coordinates activities of workers engaged in extracting sugar juice from sugar beets, processing juice into sugar liquor, and processing beet pulp into cattle fodder: Reads production schedules and beet delivery reports and assigns workers to such duties as fluming and washing beets, controlling equipment to slice and extract juice from beets, and processing juice through carbonation, filtration, and evaporation stages to obtain standard sugar liquor. Reads automatic recording devices and gauges and operating logs at various stations to ascertain that juice is being extracted and processed into standard sugar liquor, according to prescribed procedures, and that standard liquor meets density and concentration requirements. Prepares production and employee time reports. Directs workers in repairing and overhauling processing equipment during slack periods. Performs other duties as described under SUPERVISOR (any industry) Master Title.
GOE: 06.02.01 STRENGTH: L GED: R4 M3 L3 SVP: 7 DLU: 77

529.132-022 SUPERVISOR, BOTTLE-HOUSE CLEANERS (beverage)
  Supervises and coordinates activities of workers engaged in cleaning bottle house, and bottling equipment and machines: Trains workers in operation of equipment. Observes draining, dismantling, and cleaning of machines, such as bottle washing, can dumping, case unloading, filling, labeling, and pasteurizing machines. Examines machines for conformance to cleanliness criteria and standards. Reads gauges and thermometers on pasteurizing and bottle washing machines to verify specified operating temperatures. Performs other duties as described under SUPERVISOR (any industry) Master Title.
GOE: 06.02.01 STRENGTH: L GED: R4 M3 L3 SVP: 7 DLU: 77

529.132-026 SUPERVISOR, BREW HOUSE (beverage)
  Supervises and coordinates activities of workers in brewhouse of malt liquor establishment: Trains workers in operation of equipment. Inspects and evaluates milling, mashing, brewing, and cooling operations to determine conformance to laboratory report specifications and established production procedures. Observes time, temperature, and pressure recording charts on machines and compares readings with work order specifications. Conducts iodine tests of mash and specific gravity tests of malt to determine completeness of mashing operations. Performs other duties as described under SUPERVISOR (any industry) Master Title.
GOE: 06.02.01 STRENGTH: L GED: R4 M2 L3 SVP: 8 DLU: 77

529.132-030 SUPERVISOR, CEREAL (grain-feed mills)
  Supervises and coordinates activities of workers engaged in processing and packaging grains for cereal or animal feed products, according to knowledge of plant operations, processing machinery, and equipment: Directs experienced workers to instruct new workers in operation of grinders, cookers, driers, flaking rolls, ovens, frosting and packaging equipment. Evaluates performance of new workers for understanding of equipment and duties. Visually and tactually inspects grain mill products in process for conformance to plant standards. Reads laboratory tests results to verify specified moisture content of products. Directs workers to supply packaging lines with cartons, shipping cases, and other packaging materials. Investigates and directs repair of malfunctioning equipment based on knowledge of equipment and process. Maintains time and production records. May perform processing tasks in worker's absence. Performs other duties as described under SUPERVISOR (any industry) Master Title.
GOE: 06.02.01 STRENGTH: L GED: R4 M2 L4 SVP: 7 DLU: 77

529.132-034 SUPERVISOR, CIGAR-MAKING MACHINE (tobacco)
  Supervises and coordinates activities of workers engaged in operating cigar-making machines: Weighs and measures cigars to ensure conformance to standards. Adjusts machines and notifies MAINTENANCE MECHANIC (any indus-

try) of machine malfunction. Trains workers in machine operation. Performs other duties as described under SUPERVISOR (any industry) Master Title.
GOE: 06.02.01 STRENGTH: L GED: R4 M2 L3 SVP: 7 DLU: 77

529.132-038 SUPERVISOR, COOK ROOM (can. & preserv.)
  Supervises and coordinates activities of workers engaged in brining, syruping, lidding, or capping containers of food products. Controls temperature of atmospheric (conveyor-type) cooking machines. Performs duties as described under SUPERVISOR (any industry) Master Title.
GOE: 06.02.01 STRENGTH: L GED: R4 M2 L3 SVP: 7 DLU: 77

529.132-042 SUPERVISOR, DRIED YEAST (food prep., nec)
  Supervises and coordinates activities of workers engaged in extruding, drying, milling, inspecting, and packaging dried yeast: Observes temperature and humidity controls on conveyor belt-type drier for adherence to specifications. Reviews laboratory reports and inspects dried and milled yeast for specified fineness. Examines packaged yeast at various stages and directs workers to adjust malfunctioning machines. Inspects equipment and machine to ensure adherence to sanitary specifications. Trains workers in machine and equipment operations. Performs other duties as described under SUPERVISOR (any industry) Master Title.
GOE: 06.02.01 STRENGTH: L GED: R4 M3 L4 SVP: 7 DLU: 77

529.132-046 SUPERVISOR, DRY-STARCH (grain-feed mills)
  Supervises and coordinates activities of workers engaged in treating raw-starch suspensions with chemical solutions, such as acids and alkalies, and in operating pumps, heating units, agitators, filters, shakers, centrifugal separators, and driers to produce variety of dry-starch products: Reads thermometers, instrument-control meters, dials, and gauges to verify specified processing procedures. Operates equipment, adjusting valves, levers, and switches to control flow of product, temperatures, moisture content, and other characteristics. Trains workers in operation of equipment. Performs other duties as described under SUPERVISOR (any industry) Master Title.
GOE: 06.02.01 STRENGTH: L GED: R4 M2 L3 SVP: 7 DLU: 77

529.132-050 SUPERVISOR, FEED HOUSE (grain-feed mills)
  Supervises and coordinates activities of workers engaged in grinding and drying byproducts of starch (bran and gluten) in preparation of stock food: Trains workers in operation of equipment. Examines machinery, valves, pumps, and conveyors to detect malfunctions resulting in leakage, spillage, overflow, and choke-up. Reads laboratory test reports to verify specified chemical characteristics, such as protein content of product. Performs other duties as described under SUPERVISOR (any industry) Master Title.
GOE: 06.02.01 STRENGTH: L GED: R4 M2 L3 SVP: 8 DLU: 77

529.132-054 SUPERVISOR, FEED MILL (grain-feed mills)
  Supervises and coordinates activities of workers engaged in grinding, screening, and mixing stock and poultry feed from grain and other ingredients according to specifications: Directs grinding of feed materials, such as grain, alfalfa, and corn cobs in hammer mills, or attrition mills, or roll grinders and mixing of ground feed with malt, mash, molasses, salt, soda, vitamins, and other ingredients, according to formula. Oversees cooking, cooling, and pelletizing of feed. May supervise packing of feed and storage and shipment of feed products. Performs other duties as described under SUPERVISOR (any industry) Master Title. May be designated according to type of feed as Poultry Feed Supervisor (grain-feed mills).
GOE: 06.01.01 STRENGTH: L GED: R3 M3 L3 SVP: 7 DLU: 77

529.132-058 SUPERVISOR, FERMENTING CELLARS (beverage)
  Supervises and coordinates activities of workers engaged in fermenting liquid wort: Moves controls of refrigeration equipment to maintain specified temperatures in cellar. Observes time, temperature, and pressure recording charts on fermenting tanks and compares with job order specifications. Directs workers in yeast pitching, fermenting, and pumping operations to ensure conformance to specified production procedures. May test specific gravity of wort. Performs other duties as described under SUPERVISOR (any industry) Master Title.
GOE: 06.02.01 STRENGTH: L GED: R4 M2 L3 SVP: 7 DLU: 77

529.132-062 SUPERVISOR, GRAIN AND YEAST PLANTS (beverage)
  Supervises and coordinates activities of workers engaged in drying, bagging, and loading spent brew mash grains and surplus fermenting yeast: Coordinates drying, bagging, and car-loading operations and requisitions materials to meet daily production schedules. Measures moisture content of grain and yeast, using hygrometer. Moves controls of drying machine to regulate moisture content of grains and yeast. Marks or specifies railroad cars to be loaded with bagged or bulk grain. Performs other duties as described under SUPERVISOR (any industry) Master Title.
GOE: 06.02.01 STRENGTH: L GED: R4 M3 L3 SVP: 7 DLU: 77

529.132-066 SUPERVISOR, LIQUID YEAST (food prep., nec)
  Supervises and coordinates activities of workers engaged in production of yeast cream used in manufacture of bakers' yeast and food yeast: Trains workers in machine and equipment operation. Observes production operations and reviews laboratory results of liquid yeast. Inspects equipment to ensure adherence to sanitary specifications. Performs other duties as described under SUPERVISOR (any industry) Master Title.
GOE: 06.02.01 STRENGTH: L GED: R4 M3 L3 SVP: 7 DLU: 77

529.132-070 SUPERVISOR, MALTED MILK (dairy products)
  Supervises workers engaged in making, bottling, and packaging malted milk powder: Assigns production runs to operators of mashing, evaporating, drying,

blending, filling, and casing machines. Tours department to observe machines, production records, and automatic recording charts for specified temperature, pressure, liquid level, and machine setting. Trains workers in operation of masher, centrifuge, separator, evaporator, drum drier, blender, filler and packager machines, and auger, roller, or vacuum conveyor systems. Examines materials and transporting equipment of suppliers for unsanitary conditions to prevent processing of substandard powder. May rerun laboratory test for such quality factors as moisture or sediment in malted milk powder. Performs other duties as described under SUPERVISOR (any industry) Master Title.
GOE: 06.02.01 STRENGTH: M GED: R4 M2 L3 SVP: 7 DLU: 77

529.132-074 SUPERVISOR, MILL HOUSE (grain-feed mills)
Supervises and coordinates activities of workers engaged in processing grain for use in manufacturing starch, sugar, and feed products: Directs workers in softening and expanding grain kernels in acid solution (steep-water), grinding grain in mills, and in separating elements, such as starch and gluten from milled grain. Feels milled grain to determine fineness of grind. Performs other duties as described under SUPERVISOR (any industry) Master Title.
GOE: 06.02.01 STRENGTH: L GED: R4 M3 L3 SVP: 7 DLU: 77

529.132-078 SUPERVISOR, NUTRITIONAL YEAST (food prep., nec)
Supervises and coordinates activities of workers engaged in pasteurizing and drying yeast cream and milling and packing yeast for use as food: Examines dried yeast sheet for color and thickness and milled yeast for fineness. Trains workers in equipment and machine operation and adjustment. Inspects equipment and machines to ensure adherence to sanitary specifications. Performs other duties as described under SUPERVISOR (any industry) Master Title.
GOE: 06.02.01 STRENGTH: L GED: R4 M3 L4 SVP: 7 DLU: 77

529.132-082 SUPERVISOR, SOAKERS (beverage)
Supervises and coordinates activities of workers engaged in washing beer bottles: Trains workers in operation of machines. Examines soaked bottles for cleanliness. Reads gauges to verify temperature of soda solution in machines, and directs workers to regulate strength of solution. Performs other duties as described under SUPERVISOR (any industry) Master Title.
GOE: 06.04.01 STRENGTH: L GED: R4 M2 L3 SVP: 6 DLU: 77

529.132-086 SUPERVISOR, STEFFEN HOUSE (sugar & conf.)
Supervises and coordinates activities of workers in processing sugar-beet molasses, and in operating kilns to produce lime and carbon-dioxide gas used for carbonation of raw sugar-beet juice. Directs workers in diluting molasses, mixing lime with solution, and recovering hot and cold saccharate cake and filtrate from filter presses. Performs other duties as described under SUPERVISOR (any industry) Master Title.
GOE: 06.02.01 STRENGTH: L GED: R4 M3 L3 SVP: 8 DLU: 77

529.132-090 SUPERVISOR, SUGAR HOUSE (grain-feed mills)
Supervises and coordinates activities of workers engaged in cooling, crystalizing, separating, and drying sugar liquors to produce granular sugar: Reads instrument-control meters, thermometers, and gauges to verify specified processing procedures. Examines valves, pumps, and conveyors to detect malfunctions resulting in leakage, spillage, overflow, or choke-up. Trains workers in operation of equipment. Supervises workers engaged in production of caramel color, molasses, and other related products from liquid sugar. Performs other duties as described under SUPERVISOR (any industry) Master Title.
GOE: 06.02.01 STRENGTH: L GED: R4 M2 L3 SVP: 8 DLU: 77

529.132-094 SUPERVISOR, SUGAR REFINERY (grain-feed mills)
Supervises and coordinates activities of workers engaged in converting liquid starch to liquid sugars: Trains workers in operation of equipment. Reads instrument dials in control room of automatic plant, and thermometers, meters, and gauges at stations in plant to verify specified processing procedures. Examines valves, pumps, and conveyors to detect malfunctions resulting in leakage, spillage, overflow, or choke-up. Performs other duties as described under SUPERVISOR (any industry) Master Title.
GOE: 06.01.01 STRENGTH: L GED: R4 M2 L3 SVP: 8 DLU: 77

529.132-098 SUPERVISOR, TANK STORAGE (beverage) alternate titles: supervisor, finishing department
Supervises and coordinates activities of workers engaged in processing, storing, and aging beer: Inspects beer for clarity and color to determine need for aging, filtering, blending, carbonating, and storing. Moves controls of refrigeration equipment to maintain specified temperatures in tank-storage department. May conduct alcoholic content, carbonization, and specific gravity tests to determine conformance of beer to laboratory and production specifications, using hydrometer and other test apparatus. Performs other duties as described under SUPERVISOR (any industry) Master Title.
GOE: 05.02.07 STRENGTH: L GED: R4 M2 L3 SVP: 8 DLU: 77

529.132-102 SUPERVISOR, TEA AND SPICE (food prep., nec)
Supervises and coordinates activities of workers engaged in receiving, processing, packaging, and storing dry food products, tea, and spices used in food preparations, such as gelatin desserts, soups, and liquid extracts: Mixes ingredients for liquid extracts and flavoring, following formula. Requisitions materials. Trains workers in machine operations. Performs other duties as described under SUPERVISOR (any industry) Master Title.
GOE: 06.02.01 STRENGTH: L GED: R4 M3 L3 SVP: 7 DLU: 77

529.132-106 SUPERVISOR, WASH HOUSE (beverage)
Supervises and coordinates activities of workers engaged in washing, pitching, and repairing metal beer kegs and barrels: Trains workers in machine oper-

ation. Adjusts keg washing and pitching machines. Observes temperature gauges and turns steam valve to maintain specified operating temperatures and speeds. Examines cleaned and pitched kegs for conformance to specifications. Performs other duties as described under SUPERVISOR (any industry) Master Title.
GOE: 06.02.01 STRENGTH: L GED: R4 M2 L3 SVP: 7 DLU: 77

529.132-110 SUPERVISOR (food prep., nec)
Supervises and coordinates activities of workers engaged in mixing, pressing, and drying macaroni products: Confers with supervisor of previous shift and management to determine production needs, such as changes of press dies, production rate increases, or changes in dryer temperatures as recommended by quality control personnel. Informs workers of production changes, and monitors control panels of mixing, pressing, and drying machines and equipment to determine whether control settings meet company specifications. Observes products in various stages of process to determine whether products meet requirements for size, color, texture, and smoothness; and reads temperature and humidity charts, drying chamber charts, and entries in daily reports to determine compliance with company standards. Informs workers involved with specific steps in process to bring products into compliance with standards. Performs other duties as described under SUPERVISOR (any industry) Master Title. May be designated according to process supervised as Supervisor, Long Goods (food prep., nec); Supervisor, Short Goods (food prep., nec).
GOE: 06.02.01 STRENGTH: L GED: R3 M2 L2 SVP: 6 DLU: 86

529.135-010 COOKING, CASING, AND DRYING SUPERVISOR (tobacco)
Supervises and coordinates activities of workers engaged in cooking *casing fluid*, and casing and drying tobacco for further processing into chewing tobacco. Trains new workers in machine operation. Performs duties as described under SUPERVISOR (any industry) Master Title.
GOE: 06.02.01 STRENGTH: L GED: R4 M3 L3 SVP: 7 DLU: 77

529.135-014 SUPERVISOR, CURED-MEAT PACKING (meat products)
Supervises and coordinates activities of workers engaged in wrapping and packing sausages, sliced bacon, sides of bacon, and ham: Trains workers in tending skin-peeling machine and other equipment. Directs workers on bacon line in activities, such as molding sides of bacon, slicing and weighing bacon, and inserting bacon into packages. Directs workers on sausage line in activities, such as peeling sausages (removing skins) by hand or machine, inserting sausages in containers, hand or machine wrapping sausage container, and packaging containers of sausage in cartons for shipment. Inspects cured meats for specified color and texture to verify quality of product. Performs other duties as described under SUPERVISOR (any industry) Master Title.
GOE: 06.04.01 STRENGTH: L GED: R4 M2 L2 SVP: 7 DLU: 77

529.137-010 PREPARATION SUPERVISOR (can. & preserv.)
Supervises and coordinates activities of workers engaged in receiving, sorting, preparing, and processing food products, such as fruits, vegetables, and fish, for canning or freezing. Performs duties as described under SUPERVISOR (any industry) Master Title. May be designated according to type of preserving process as Preparation Supervisor, Canning (can. & preserv.); Preparation Supervisor, Freezing (can. & preserv.).
GOE: 06.02.01 STRENGTH: L GED: R4 M2 L3 SVP: 7 DLU: 78

529.137-014 SANITARIAN (any industry) alternate titles: sanitation supervisor
Supervises and coordinates activities of workers engaged in duties concerned with sanitation programs in food processing establishment: Inspects products and equipment for conformity to federal and state sanitation laws and plant standards. Directs food handlers and production personnel in sanitary and pest-control procedures. Directs cleaning of equipment and work areas. Inspects premises for unsanitary practices and conditions. Examines incoming shipments of food ingredients for foreign matter, such as insects, poisons, or dirt, and gathers samples of ingredients for laboratory analysis. Confers with management and production personnel on sanitation problems, and recommends changes in equipment, plant layout, lighting, ventilation, or work practices to improve sanitation standards and purity of product. Compiles required reports regarding regular inspections, sanitation violations, and steps taken to resolve deficiencies. Routes reports to designated plant personnel. Performs other duties as described under SUPERVISOR (any industry) Master Title. May be designated according to type of establishment as Supervisor, Bakery Sanitation (bakery products); Supervisor, Dairy Sanitation (dairy products).
GOE: 11.10.03 STRENGTH: L GED: R4 M2 L3 SVP: 7 DLU: 79

529.137-018 SUGAR-REPROCESS OPERATOR, HEAD (sugar & conf.)
Supervises and coordinates activities of workers engaged in reprocessing damaged refined sugars: Directs workers opening bales and cases and inspecting cartons and pockets. Oversees repacking of undamaged containers in cases and bales, and ensures specified code-marks are stamped on containers. Directs workers dumping damaged sugar into barrels and hoppers and conveying containers to remelt hoppers. Directs worker tending metal-detecting equipment that locates and removes metallic objects from damaged sugar. Oversees return of bulk sugar from trucks to remelt station. Keeps records, such as amounts of sugar processed, labor costs, and inventories.
GOE: 06.02.01 STRENGTH: L GED: R3 M2 L3 SVP: 6 DLU: 77

529.137-022 SUPERINTENDENT, GRAIN ELEVATOR (beverage; grain-feed mills)
Supervises and coordinates activities of workers engaged in unloading, loading, storing, cleaning, and blending of grain for milling and shipment: Inspects

sample of grain from incoming shipment to verify variety of grain with invoice and route to designated storage bin according to variety and protein content of grain. Prepares switching orders for guidance of train crews in moving grain cars to unloading pits according to mill requirements. Observes unloading and transportation of grain by bucket elevators and conveyors to storage tanks. Inspects grain to determine cleaning requirements and directs processing of grain to prepare grain for milling. Performs other duties as described under SUPERVISOR (any industry) Master Title.
GOE: 06.01.01 STRENGTH: L GED: R4 M3 L4 SVP: 6 DLU: 77

529.137-026 SUPERVISOR (tobacco)
Supervises and coordinates activities of workers engaged in making or packing cigarettes or cigars: Inspects cigars, cigarettes, and filters to determine that length, circumference, firmness, printing of brand name, and gluing are according to specifications. Observes machine operations to detect defective operation and product. Schedules and coordinates work activities within cigar or cigarette making or packing lines and with other supervisors to maintain established production standards. Performs other duties as described under SUPERVISOR (any industry) Master Title. May be designated according to department supervised as Supervisor, Cigar Processing (tobacco); Supervisor, Cigarette-Filter Making Department (tobacco); Supervisor, Cigarette-Making Department (tobacco); Supervisor, Cigarette-Packing Department (tobacco).
GOE: 06.02.01 STRENGTH: L GED: R4 M2 L3 SVP: 7 DLU: 78

529.137-030 SUPERVISOR (oils & grease)
Supervises and coordinates activities of workers engaged in processing oils, vegetables, and nuts, such as cottonseed, linseed, peanuts, palm kernels, and castor beans, used in manufacture of margarine, shortening, and other edible oils: Observes gauges and determines cooking time and temperature, according to equipment used and material to be processed, to ensure maintenance of quality and quantity standards. Calculates, according to formula, adjustments to be made if laboratory analysis shows batch to be substandard. Maintains production records and prepares reports for cost and production departments. Patrols department to observe automatic equipment, such as hullers, separators, and crushing rolls, to ensure efficient operation. May determine scrap reprocessing operations, according to condition of scrap, quality control specifications, and legal requirements. May weigh random samples of margarine prints, using scale, to verify weight of prints against specifications and examine packaged product to verify brand names and code numbers against order. May direct workers in refining and bleaching edible oils and be known as Refinery Supervisor (oils & grease). May direct workers in packaging operations and be known as Packaging Supervisor (oils & grease). May perform other duties as described under SUPERVISOR (any industry) Master Title.
GOE: 06.01.01 STRENGTH: L GED: R4 M3 L3 SVP: 7 DLU: 77

529.137-034 SUPERVISOR, CIGAR TOBACCO PROCESSING (tobacco)
Supervises and coordinates activities of workers engaged in receiving, sorting, sizing, conditioning, *mulling*, and packing tobacco used in manufacture of cigars. Examines tobacco to determine suitability of leaves for processing into wrapper or filler. Trains new workers in equipment operation and work processes. Performs other duties as described under SUPERVISOR (any industry) Master Title.
GOE: 06.02.01 STRENGTH: L GED: R4 M2 L2 SVP: 6 DLU: 77

529.137-038 SUPERVISOR, CURING ROOM (tobacco)
Supervises and coordinates activities of workers engaged in blending, aging, and fermenting tobacco strips and stems in production of cigars, chewing tobacco, or snuff: Reads production schedules for information, such as quantity of stems, and strip tobacco, amounts of water and *casing fluid*, and aging time specified. Computes amount of tobacco strips and stems required to maintain production. Analyzes thermometer readings of piles of tobacco to determine stages of fermentation, and schedules turning or transfer of tobacco cures. Coordinates receipt of tobacco from supplier and transfer to drying department. Performs other duties as described under SUPERVISOR (any industry) Master Title.
GOE: 06.02.01 STRENGTH: L GED: R4 M3 L3 SVP: 7 DLU: 77

529.137-042 SUPERVISOR, EGG PROCESSING (can. & preserv.; wholesale tr.) alternate titles: egg room supervisor
Supervises and coordinates activities of workers engaged in processing eggs for shipment and storage: Schedules processing according to type of eggs ordered, delivery date, availability of eggs, and capacity of machines. Informs MATERIAL HANDLERS (any industry) of number of cases to pack. Verifies counting of eggs, preparation of receipts, and movement of eggs, according to company standards. Directs workers in government and company sanitation regulations. Inspects appearance and work methods of EGG CANDLER (any industry) and EGG BREAKER (any industry) for conformance to sanitation regulations. Repairs or adjusts machinery. Performs other duties as defined under SUPERVISOR (any industry) Master Title.
GOE: 06.01.01 STRENGTH: L GED: R4 M3 L3 SVP: 7 DLU: 77

529.137-046 SUPERVISOR, FRUIT GRADING (wholesale tr.)
Supervises and coordinates activities of workers engaged in grading fruits: Trains employees in grading methods, detection of defective or improperly colored fruit, and other factors affecting standards. Assigns workers to positions at grading belt. Observes workers to correct discrepancies and ensure that graded fruit meets specified standards. May interview and recommend hiring of new employees. Performs other duties as described under SUPERVISOR (any industry) Master Title.

GOE: 06.03.02 STRENGTH: L GED: R4 M2 L3 SVP: 6 DLU: 77

529.137-050 SUPERVISOR, MAPLE PRODUCTS (food prep., nec)
Supervises and coordinates activities of workers engaged in boiling, stirring, molding, and packing maple products, such as maple sugar and syrup. Inspects product for conformance to prescribed standards of purity and appearance. Performs other duties as described under SUPERVISOR (any industry) Master Title.
GOE: 06.02.01 STRENGTH: L GED: R4 M3 L3 SVP: 6 DLU: 77

529.137-054 SUPERVISOR, READY-MIXED FOOD PREPARATION (food prep., nec)
Supervises and coordinates activities of workers engaged in processing ready-mixed food preparations: Requisitions ingredients from warehouse and prescribes mixing sequence. Inspects ingredients and product to ensure conformance to company specifications and ensures that samples are taken of each batch mixed for quality control purposes. Maintains record of ingredients used and batches mixed. Trains new workers. Performs duties as described under SUPERVISOR (any industry) Master Title.
GOE: 06.04.01 STRENGTH: L GED: R4 M3 L3 SVP: 5 DLU: 77

529.137-058 SUPERVISOR, SYRUP SHED (sugar & conf.)
Supervises and coordinates activities of workers engaged in blending edible sugar syrups, cleaning storage facilities and vehicle tanks, and filtering, pasteurizing and pumping syrups into tank trucks and railroad tank cars. Performs other duties as described under SUPERVISOR (any industry) Master Title.
GOE: 06.02.01 STRENGTH: L GED: R4 M3 L3 SVP: 6 DLU: 77

529.137-062 SUPERVISOR, SPECIALTY FOOD PRODUCTS (can. & preserv.; meat products)
Supervises and coordinates activities of workers engaged in mixing, cooking, molding, and packaging speciality food products, such as frankfurters, chili, sausage, and fish roe: Reads production schedule to determine work procedures, supplies to be requisitioned, personnel requirements, and processing equipment to be used. Assigns workers to work stations and issues instructions concerning formulas to follow and work procedures. Coordinates flow of work between work stations. Keeps production and timecard records. Performs other duties as described under SUPERVISOR (any industry) Master Title. May supervise workers engaged in processing fish roe and be designated Supervisor, Roe Processing (can. & preserv.).
GOE: 06.02.01 STRENGTH: L GED: R4 M3 L4 SVP: 8 DLU: 78

529.137-066 SUPERVISOR, WHIPPED TOPPING (dairy products)
Supervises and coordinates activities of workers engaged in processing and packing whipped topping: Observes operations of equipment, such as versators, colloid mills, pasteurizers, cooling tanks, and homogenizers to verify conformance of whipped topping with quality and quantity standards. Performs other duties as described under SUPERVISOR (any industry) Master Title.
GOE: 06.02.01 STRENGTH: L GED: R4 M2 L3 SVP: 7 DLU: 77

529.137-070 SUPERVISOR, YARD (beverage)
Supervises and coordinates activities of workers engaged in blocking and icing loaded freight cars, manufacturing ice, and cleaning brewery yards: Trains workers. Maintains specified amount of ice in storage. Spots cars for workers to ice and block. Directs movement of freight cars in yard. Performs other duties as described under SUPERVISOR (any industry) Master Title.
GOE: 06.04.01 STRENGTH: L GED: R4 M2 L2 SVP: 8 DLU: 77

529.137-074 SUPERVISOR, INSPECTION (sugar & conf.)
Supervises and coordinates activities of workers engaged in inspecting chewing gum to ensure product conformance to processing standards: Reads production schedule and assigns duties to workers. Observes inspection process to detect defective operations. Reviews inspection reports to determine type and cause of product deviations from company standards. Periodically reads instructions on batch cards to ensure ingredients meet formula specifications. Performs other duties as described under SUPERVISOR (any industry) Master Title.
GOE: 06.02.01 STRENGTH: L GED: R4 M3 L3 SVP: 7 DLU: 86

529.137-078 SUPERVISOR, INSTANT POTATO PROCESSING (food prep., nec)
Supervises and coordinates activities of workers engaged in cooking, blending, screening, and drying instant potato granules: Reviews shift specifications with supervisor to determine production goals, additives to be mixed with potato granules, and schedule for cleaning machinery. Reviews shift logs to ascertain production delays encountered, such as machinery breakdown, production lines involved, and action taken. Completes shift reports, and submits reports to management. Instructs workers to fill storage tanks with instant potato granules according to type of granules produced, type of additives mixed with granules, and tank capacity. Approves employee requests for vacation and forwards leave forms to personnel department. Requests personnel department to provide substitute workers when regular workers are absent. Performs other duties as described under SUPERVISOR (any industry) Master Title.
GOE: 06.02.01 STRENGTH: L GED: R4 M3 L3 SVP: 7 DLU: 86

529.137-082 SUPERVISOR, PROCESSING (sugar & conf.)
Supervises and coordinates activities of workers engaged in processing raw ingredients into chewing gum: Coordinates washing, melting, blending, mixing, and cooking of ingredients; rolling and scoring of gum into sheets; and coating of sheets with powdered sugar. Trains new workers in operation of equipment.

Maintains inventory records and requisitions ingredients as necessary to meet production schedules. Inspects and weighs ingredients to maintain establishment standards. Confers with SUPERVISOR (sugar & conf.) 920.137-018 to coordinate activities between departments. Performs other duties as described under SUPERVISOR (any industry) Master Title.
GOE: 06.02.01 STRENGTH: L GED: R4 M3 L3 SVP: 7 DLU: 86

529.167-010 FRUIT COORDINATOR (can. & preserv.) alternate titles: metal mover
Coordinates flow of materials through departments of citrus-fruit processing plant. Observes processing procedures and informs workers to speed up, slow down, or temporarily cease operations to maintain even flow of fruit through plant.
GOE: 05.09.02 STRENGTH: L GED: R4 M3 L3 SVP: 5 DLU: 77

529.281-010 TASTER (food prep., nec)
Tastes samples of food or beverages to determine palatability of product or to prepare blending formulas: Cooks or brews small lots of beverages or other food products and tastes product to determine grade, approximate market value, or acceptability to consumer tastes. Writes blending formulas for guidance of workers who prepare food products in commercial quantities. May purchase food products. May be designated according to product tasted as Coffee Taster (food prep., nec); Tea Taster (food prep., nec).
GOE: 06.01.05 STRENGTH: L GED: R4 M3 L4 SVP: 7 DLU: 77

529.361-010 ALMOND-PASTE MIXER (sugar & conf.) alternate titles: marzipan maker
Mixes and cooks blanched, ground, and refined almonds with sugar solution to make marzipan (almond paste) for candy centers. Dumps ingredients into steam-jacketed rotating cooker. Transfers cooked batch to water-cooled kettle. May operate refining machine to reduce particle size of cooked batch.
GOE: 06.01.04 STRENGTH: M GED: R4 M2 L3 SVP: 8 DLU: 77

529.361-014 CANDY MAKER (sugar & conf.) alternate titles: batch maker; boiler; confectioner; cook, candy
Mixes and cooks candy ingredients by following, modifying, or formulating recipes to produce product of specified flavor, texture, and color: Cooks ingredients [CONFECTIONERY COOKER (sugar & conf.)] at specified temperatures in open-fire or steam-jacketed kettles or in batch or continuous pressure cookers. Casts candy by hand, using molds and funnel, or tends machine that casts candy in starch or rubber molds [DEPOSITING-MACHINE OPERATOR (sugar & conf.)]. Spreads candy onto cooling and heating slabs. Kneads and machine-pulls candy [CANDY PULLER (sugar & conf.)]. Spins or rolls candy into strips ready for cutting [SPINNER (sugar & conf.)]. Examines, feels, and tastes product to evaluate color, texture, and flavor. Adds ingredients or modifies cooking and forming operations as needed. May direct CANDY-MAKER HELPERS (sugar & conf.). May be designated according to type of candy produced as Caramel-Candy Maker (sugar & conf.); Coconut-Candy Maker (sugar & conf.); Fudge-Candy Maker (sugar & conf.); Hard-Candy Maker (sugar & conf.); Nougat-Candy Maker (sugar & conf.); Taffy-Candy Maker (sugar & conf.).
GOE: 06.02.28 STRENGTH: M GED: R4 M3 L4 SVP: 7 DLU: 77

529.361-018 CHEESEMAKER (dairy products) alternate titles: cheese cooker
Cooks milk and specified ingredients to make cheese, according to formula: Pasteurizes and separates milk to obtain prescribed butterfat content. Turns valves to fill vat with milk and heat milk to specified temperature. Dumps measured amounts of dye and starter into milk. Starts agitator to mix ingredients. Tests sample of milk for acidity and allows agitator to mix ingredients until specified level of acidity is reached. Dumps and mixes measured amount of rennet into milk. Stops agitator to allow milk to coagulate into curd. Pulls curd knives through curd or separates curd with hand scoop to release whey. Observes thermometer, adjusts steam valve, and starts agitator to stir and cook curd at prescribed temperature for specified time. Squeezes and stretches sample of curd with fingers and extends cooking time to achieve desired firmness or texture. Gives directions to CHEESEMAKER HELPER (dairy products) or other workers to make curd, drain whey from curd, add ingredients, such as seasonings, or mold, pack, cut, pile, mill, dump, and press curd into specified shapes. Directs other workers who immerse cheese in brine or roll cheese in dry salt, pierce or smear cheese with cultured wash to develop mold growth, and place or turn cheese blocks on shelves to cure cheese. Tastes, smells, feels, and observes sample plug of cheese for quality. Records amounts of ingredients used, test results, and time cycles. Makes variations in time cycles and ingredients used for succeeding batches. Dumps specified culture into milk or whey in pasteurizer to make bulk starter. May be required to hold state cheesemaker's license.
GOE: 06.01.04 STRENGTH: L GED: R4 M3 L4 SVP: 7 DLU: 77

529.362-010 BUTTERMAKER (dairy products)
Controls equipment to make grades of butter by either of following methods: (1) Butter churn method: Connects sanitary pipe between cream storage vat and churn. Starts pump to convey sterile solution through equipment and to admit measured amount of pasteurized cream into churn, and starts churn. Observes separation of buttermilk from butter and pumps buttermilk from churn. Opens churn and sprays butter with chlorinated water to remove residue buttermilk. Compares butter with color chart and adds coloring to meet specifications. Tests butter for moisture, salt content, and consistency, using testing apparatus,

and achieves specified consistency by adding or removing water. Examines, smells, and tastes butter to grade it according to prescribed standard. (2) Butter chilling method: Pasteurizes and separates cream to obtain butter oil, and tests butter oil in standardizing vat for butter fat, moisture, salt content, and acidity, using testing apparatus. Adds water, alkali, and coloring to butter oil to achieve specified grade, and starts agitator to mix ingredients. Turns valves and observes gauges to regulate temperature and flow of water, refrigerant, and butter oil through chilling vat. Smells, tastes, and feels sample to grade butter emerging from chilling vat. May be designated according to equipment operated as Butter-Chilling Equipment Operator (dairy products); Butter Churner (dairy products).
GOE: 06.02.15 STRENGTH: H GED: R3 M3 L2 SVP: 6 DLU: 77

529.362-014 DRY-STARCH OPERATOR, AUTOMATIC (grain-feed mills)
Controls equipment that produces dry starch products from raw starch, and tests product for adherence to specifications: Dumps bags of chemicals into mixing tanks, and turns valves to admit fluids to prepare slurries for treating raw starch. Regulates material flow, and starts and controls pumps, heaters, agitators, shakers, filters, driers, and related equipment, following standard procedures. Monitors gauges and recording instruments to ensure standard operating conditions. Directs other workers in operating equipment in event of malfunction. Obtains samples of product at various stages of process to test for viscosity, acidity, and specific gravity, using viscometer, pH meter, and hydrometer. Records instrument readings and other data on daily log.
GOE: 06.02.15 STRENGTH: M GED: R3 M2 L2 SVP: 7 DLU: 77

529.367-010 CIGARETTE-AND-FILTER CHIEF INSPECTOR (tobacco)
Examines plain or filter-tipped cigarettes or filters to ensure that quality of product conforms to standards: Inspects cigarettes or filters produced to detect imperfections, such as loose ends, stems, stemholes, defective glue lines, and defectively attached filters. Examines cigarettes, attached filters, and filters rejected by CIGARETTE-MAKING-MACHINE CATCHER (tobacco) and CIGARETTE INSPECTOR (tobacco) and discards inferior products. Notifies CIGARETTE-MAKING-MACHINE OPERATOR (tobacco) of deviations from standards. Records number of cigarettes found with defects and compiles summary production sheets. Verifies and totals figures posted by CIGARETTE INSPECTOR (tobacco).
GOE: 06.03.01 STRENGTH: L GED: R3 M2 SVP: 5 DLU: 77

529.367-014 HOGSHEAD INSPECTOR (tobacco)
Examines hogsheads and bales of tobacco after ordering process to determine whether temperature and quality of tobacco conform to standards: Places thermometer in tobacco and records temperature of each lot. Inspects tobacco for damage. Removes damaged tobacco, weighs, and records amount damaged. Notifies supervisor when temperature or condition of tobacco does not meet standards. Verifies weight of hogsheads and bales against checksheet.
GOE: 06.03.01 STRENGTH: L GED: R3 M2 L2 SVP: 4 DLU: 77

529.367-018 QUALITY-CONTROL INSPECTOR (bakery products)
Weighs and tests cookies and crackers for conformance to quality and weight standards: Gathers random packages of cookies or crackers from each conveyor line and weighs packages on platform scale to verify weight specifications. Adds crumbled crackers to chemical solution to ascertain level of acidity or alkalinity, using pH meter, or compares color of solution with color chart. Records weight of crackers or cookies, and places crumbs in drier. Turns on drying unit for specified time to remove moisture from crumbs. Weighs dried crumbs to ascertain moisture content. Records results of tests in record book and reports variations from weight standards. May verify weight of individual packages during packing process.
GOE: 06.03.01 STRENGTH: L GED: R3 M2 L2 SVP: 4 DLU: 77

529.367-022 QUALITY-CONTROL TECHNICIAN (beverage)
Compiles taste preference data on whiskeys for use by laboratory personnel as aid to developing improved methods of producing and storing distilled liquors: Requests samples of whiskey from warehouse or bottling workers for tasting and laboratory analysis, according to brand of whiskey and serial numbers of barrels from which samples are to be taken. Records proof and weight of whiskey and date whiskey was placed in storage. Schedules designated persons to taste various brands of standard quality whiskey and brand to be bottled. Fills glasses with whiskeys for tasting by panel members. Prepares reports indicating number of like and unlike comparisons, date sample tasting was made, brand of whiskey, and serial numbers of barrels from which sample was taken, and submits information to laboratory. Attaches labels to bottles of whiskey samples and routes bottles to laboratory for analysis.
GOE: 05.09.02 STRENGTH: L GED: R3 M3 L2 SVP: 5 DLU: 77

529.367-026 ROUGH-RICE GRADER (grain-feed mills)
Grades unhulled rice visually as it is unloaded from freight cars or trucks, and directs workers in storage of rice according to grade: Obtains samples from each carload or truckload, using probe. Examines samples and determines grade of each load according to amount of damaged grains and grass seed content. Directs workers in conveying rice to storage bins to ensure that each grade is stored separately. Records amount and grade of rice received.
GOE: 06.03.01 STRENGTH: L GED: R3 M2 L2 SVP: 5 DLU: 77

529.367-030 YIELD-LOSS INSPECTOR (grain-feed mills)
Inspects operating condition of machinery and equipment used in manufacture of stock feed, starch, sugar, and liquid sugar products to detect potential

sources for loss of product: Examines valves, pipe connections, conveyors, pumps, and equipment assemblies for potential malfunction and cause of leakage, spillage, overflow, and excessive dusting. Takes samples from process streams, such as wash water and waste disposal lines, to laboratory for test of product content. Prepares periodic reports of inspection findings. Participates in special studies, such as grain moisture and sewer sampling surveys, reviews new sampling methods and procedures, and makes suggestions to improve yield loss inspection procedures.
GOE: 06.03.01 STRENGTH: L GED: R4 M3 L3 SVP: 5 DLU: 77

529.367-034 QUALITY CONTROL INSPECTOR (sugar & conf.)
Inspects bagging, storage, and shipping facilities for conformance to company sanitation and safety standards in beet sugar refinery: Monitors indicator lights and weighs randomly selected sugar bags from packaging line conveyor to verify accuracy of automatic weighing equipment. Pulls lever to adjust fill rate of equipment when sample bags are over or under specified weight. Inspects boxcars for cleanliness and to ascertain valves and hatches are closed and sealed. Obtains sugar samples from bulk car for laboratory analysis, using probe. Inspects warehouse areas to detect unsafe or unsanitary conditions, such as lubricants on walkways and cracks in storage bins. Informs designated person of conditions requiring immediate repair, such as unsanitary condition of boxcars and warehouse areas. Completes reports that indicate condition of boxcars, warehouse area, and incoming shipments of brown sugar and starch.
GOE: 06.03.01 STRENGTH: H GED: R3 M2 L2 SVP: 7 DLU: 86

529.381-010 COMPOUNDER, FLAVORINGS (beverage)
Compounds natural or synthetic flavorings from liquid and solid ingredients, according to formula: Selects prescribed ingredients and measures or weighs ingredients, using English or metric measures and balance scales. Determines mixing sequence, in kettles, placed on floor scales, or in weigh tanks, based on knowledge of temperature effects, and solubility and miscibility properties of specific ingredients. Stirs mixture with paddle or uses agitator. Homogenizes material to prevent separation of substances, using homogenizing device. Maintains record of batches prepared.
GOE: 06.02.28 STRENGTH: M GED: R4 M2 L3 SVP: 6 DLU: 77

529.382-010 BUTTERMAKER, CONTINUOUS CHURN (dairy products)
Operates continuous churn to produce butter of specified grade and quality, and performs quality control tests: Starts agitator of salt injector and fills tank of injector with salt solution. Turns valve control and starts pump to move cream from storage tank to churn. Presses switches to start beater and extruders of churn, and adjusts controls while monitoring gauge and ammeter to regulate churn speed. Connects salt injector tube to extruder of churn and starts salt injector pump. Raises or lowers nozzle to adjust height of buttermilk drainpipe to control level of buttermilk in extruder, using wrenches. Observes butter granules dropping from beater section to ensure that beater is operating efficiently. Removes sample of butter from discharge of churn and performs standardized tests for moisture, butterfat, and color content. Tastes butter to detect undesirable flavors and to ensure required salt level. Rubs sample of butter between thumb and finger to determine if texture meets specifications. Turns control knobs to adjust speed of beater, speed of salt pump, height of buttermilk discharge pipe, or adds vegetable color to salt solution to ensure butter meets specifications. Observes and listens to churn to detect possible malfunctions, such as leaks or plugging, and reports malfunctions or undesirable taste to supervisor. Mixes salt and water, according to formula, to maintain stock of solution. Records production and test data on record sheet.
GOE: 06.02.15 STRENGTH: M GED: R3 M2 L3 SVP: 3 DLU: 77

529.382-014 CHOCOLATE-PRODUCTION-MACHINE OPERATOR (sugar & conf.) alternate titles: general utility machine operator
Operates any of following machines and equipment to relieve regular operators engaged in processing cocoa beans into chocolate liquor and in producing cocoa powder and sweet chocolate, according to formula: Controls roaster that roasts cocoa beans to develop specified color and flavor and reduces moisture content of beans [COCOA-BEAN ROASTER (sugar & conf.) I; COCOA-BEAN ROASTER (sugar & conf.) II]. Tends mill to grind nibs (cracked cocoa beans) into liquid chocolate of specified fineness [LIQUOR-GRINDING-MILL OPERATOR (sugar & conf.)]. Tends hydraulic press to extract cocoa butter from chocolate liquor, and operates cocoa room machinery and equipment to grind and pulverize cocoa cakes into cocoa powder [COCOA-PRESS OPERATOR (sugar & conf.); COCOA-ROOM OPERATOR (sugar & conf.)]. Mixes ingredients, such as chocolate liquor, sugar, and powdered milk to make sweet chocolate [MIXER OPERATOR (sugar & conf.)]. Operates refining machine to grind chocolate paste to specified consistency [REFINING-MACHINE OPERATOR (sugar & conf.)]. Operates tempering equipment to control temperature of chocolate in cooling process before molding [CHOCOLATE TEMPERER (bakery products; grain-feed mills)]. May tend molding machines, pressure cookers, and dryers. May assist in supervising and training production line workers.
GOE: 06.02.15 STRENGTH: H GED: R4 M3 L3 SVP: 6 DLU: 77

529.382-018 DAIRY-PROCESSING-EQUIPMENT OPERATOR (dairy products)
Operates continuous flow or vat-type equipment to process milk, cream, and other dairy products, following specified methods and formulas: Connects pipes between vats and processing equipment. Assembles fittings, valves, bowls, plates, disks, impeller shaft, and other parts to equipment with wrench to prepare for operation. Turns valves to pump sterilizing solution and rinse water through pipes and equipment and spray vats with atomizer. Starts pumps and equipment, observes temperature and pressure gauges, and opens valves on continuous flow equipment to force milk through centrifuge to separate cream from milk, through homogenizer to produce specified emulsion, and through filter to remove sediment. Turns valves to admit steam and water into pipes to pasteurize milk and to circulate refrigerant through coils to cool milk. Starts pump and agitator, observes pressure and temperature gauges, and opens valves on vat equipment to fill, stir, and steam-heat milk in vat. Pumps or pours specified amounts of liquid or powder ingredients, such as skim milk, lactic culture, stabilizer, neutralizer, and vitamins into vat to make dairy products, such as buttermilk, chocolate milk, or ice cream mix. Tests product for acidity at various stages of processing. Records specified time, temperature, pressure, and volume readings. May be designated according to process performed as Byproducts Maker (dairy products); Clarifier Operator (dairy products); Cooler Operator (dairy products); Homogenizer Operator (dairy products); Mix Maker (dairy products); Pasteurizer Operator (dairy products); Separator Operator (dairy products). May be required to hold license from State Board of Health or local government unit.
GOE: 06.02.15 STRENGTH: H GED: R4 M2 L3 SVP: 5 DLU: 77

529.382-022 GELATIN MAKER, UTILITY (chemical)
Performs any combination of following duties to relieve other workers in producing gelatin or glue from animal stock (skins, splits, fleshings, and trimmings): Tends equipment to wash animal stock used to make gelatin and glue [WASH-MILL OPERATOR (chemical)] and lime vats to loosen hair and open pores of stock [LIMER (chemical; leather mfg.)]. Tends equipment to cook stock for broth [COOK (chemical)], and operates evaporator to dehydrate broth to concentrate gelatin contents [EVAPORATOR OPERATOR (chemical) I]. Tends press to filter impurities from gelatin or glue [FILTER-PRESS OPERATOR (any industry)]. Tends equipment to spread gelatin or glue into sheets for drying [SPREADING-MACHINE OPERATOR (chemical)] and equipment that grinds, weighs, and packages gelatin or glue [GLUE-MILL OPERATOR (chemical)].
GOE: 06.02.18 STRENGTH: M GED: R3 M1 L2 SVP: 6 DLU: 77

529.382-026 HYDROGENATION OPERATOR (oils & grease) alternate titles: clarifier
Controls equipment to process base oils used in manufacture of margarine and shortening: Starts pumps to move premeasured batches of refined oils or fats into converter vessel. Turns valves to adjust rate of flow of hydrogen, steam, air, and water into converter, and weighs and adds specified amounts of catalytic agents and other chemicals to harden batch of oils or fats, as required. Tests samples of batch to ensure that hardness of product is in accordance with specifications, using refractometer. Pumps hardened oils through filter press to remove catalyst and attaches lines to transfer filtered oil to blending vessel. Starts pump to add specified amounts of blending oils to blending vessel and turns valves to heat and blend oils for required amount of time. Observes temperature and pressure gauges, and turns valves to make adjustment when necessary. Pumps finished oils through filter press to holding tank. May be designated according to equipment controlled as Blender (oils & grease); Hardener (oils & grease).
GOE: 06.02.15 STRENGTH: M GED: R3 M2 L2 SVP: 4 DLU: 77

529.382-030 IRISH-MOSS OPERATOR (chemical) alternate titles: drying-machine operator; weed-cooking operator
Operates centrifugal separator, pressure cooker, drum drier, hammer mill, and air separator to process Irish moss (carrageen) into powdered stabilizer used in food processing: Pumps boiled mixture from holding tank into centrifugal separator and starts machine to separate moss from mixture. Pumps mixture from centrifuge to pressure cooker. Weighs out and adds specified amounts of powdered ingredients. Turns steam valve and observes pressure gauges on pressure cooker to cook mixture for specified time. Pumps mixture to drier and turns valve to heat drier to prescribed temperature and reduce product to solid form. Starts screw conveyor to carry mixture out of drier through hammer mill and air separator to pulverize and deosit product in containers for storage. May draw sample of product and perform tests, using meters, or submit sample for testing.
GOE: 06.02.11 STRENGTH: M GED: R3 M2 L1 SVP: 5 DLU: 77

529.385-010 NOODLE MAKER (food prep., nec)
Tends series of machines that mix, knead, roll, and cut dough to make noodles: Weighs and measures specified ingredients according to standard formulas, and dumps them into mixing machine. Moves lever to empty mixed ingredients into kneading machine. Feeds kneaded dough into rolling machine that forms dough into sheet and winds sheet into roll. Turns knob to regulate roller clearance and dusts rolled sheet with cornstarch. Inserts end of sheet into feed rollers of cutting machine that slits sheet into strands. Slides rod under emerging strands to drape strands over rod. Pulls lever to cut strands to specified length and hangs filled rod on rack. Pushes rack into drying room, and sets thermostat to specified temperature. Feels and observes consistency of product throughout operation to control quality and processing time. May cut noodles into packaging lengths, using knife. May weigh and wrap noodles in cellophane or pack them in cartons.
GOE: 06.04.15 STRENGTH: H GED: R2 M1 L2 SVP: 3 DLU: 77

529.387-010 CHEESE GRADER (dairy products)
Evaluates and grades body, texture, flavor, and color of natural cheese: Pushes trier into cheese to obtain sample plug. Smells and tastes cheese for

odor, acidity, and flavor. Examines cheese with fingers to determine firmness and texture. Observes cheese for color, shape, size, finish, and surface blemishes. Records weight, grade, and identifying data. Must hold state or federal license. May buy cheese and assist with production problems.
GOE: 06.03.01 STRENGTH: L GED: R3 M2 L2 SVP: 5 DLU: 77

529.387-014 CIGARETTE TESTER (tobacco) alternate titles: tester operator

Tests cigarettes and cellophane wrappers to ensure that products conform to company standards, according to following methods: (1) Feeds sample from cigarette-making machine into hopper of weight recorder that tallies weight of each cigarette and totals number of each weight. Computes average weight of cigarettes in sample and compares average weight with standard to determine deviations. (2) Slits cigarette paper, dumps tobacco into container, and places container in electric moisture meter to obtain moisture content [MOISTURE-METER OPERATOR (tobacco) 529.687-162]. (3) Weighs tobacco from specified number of cigarettes and places tobacco in agitator equipped with series of screens to separate shreds according to size. Weighs separate tobacco and determines percentage of each size of shreds in single cigarette, using conversion table. (4) Removes cellophane wrapper from cigarette pack and tests resistance to air by slipping wrapper over suction device of instrument that draws air through wrapper and indicates amount of airflow. Records test finding, date, and machine number from which samples were taken.
GOE: 06.03.01 STRENGTH: L GED: R3 M3 L3 SVP: 5 DLU: 77

529.387-018 FRUIT-BUYING GRADER (can. & preserv.; wholesale tr.) alternate titles: fruit inspector; platform inspector

Examines, sorts, and grades sample fruit from load at receiving point: Takes random samples from load, weighs sample and containers, and calculates net weight and tare of total load. Sorts sample fruit by grade and size, according to company or government specifications. Weighs each portion of sample and calculates percentage of each size and grade in total load. Issues grade ticket or receipt for load.
GOE: 06.03.01 STRENGTH: M GED: R3 M3 L2 SVP: 3 DLU: 77

529.387-022 GAUGER (beverage)

Tests wine samples for alcohol content, acidity, and sugar content, using hydrometer, thermometer, and other laboratory equipment: Collects samples of wine from tanks for tests. Immerses hydrometer and thermometer in wine sample and compares readings with gauging manual to determine alcohol content. Pours specified amount of wine in glass cylinder and inserts hydrometer to determine sugar content. Measures sample for acid content, using chemicals and gauges. Examines sample for quality of color. Drafts charts and writes test reports.
GOE: 06.03.01 STRENGTH: L GED: R3 M2 L2 SVP: 5 DLU: 77

529.387-026 INSPECTOR, GRAIN MILL PRODUCTS (grain-feed mills) alternate titles: inspector technician

Weighs packaged cereal, feed, and flour products to verify weights and examines packages for adequacy of labeling, stamping, sewing, or sealing: Records weights on report form. Tests scales for accuracy, using standard weights, and adjusts scales. Compares sample of mixed feed with standard sample to verify adequacy of mixing or pelletizing process. Obtains and labels samples of flour grades produced and delivers them to laboratory. May review laboratory analysis of flour samples. May verify production reports with report of quantity of packed products received in warehouse and trace reason for discrepancies.
GOE: 06.03.01 STRENGTH: M GED: R3 M2 L2 SVP: 3 DLU: 77

529.387-030 QUALITY-CONTROL TECHNICIAN (can. & preserv.; food prep., nec)

Inspects raw materials and finished products, and tests and adjusts packaging or canning equipment during processing of foods, such as corn chips, vegetables, and breaded shrimp: Inspects, tests, weighs, tastes, and smells raw materials and finished products to determine such information as spoilage, whether cans, packages, or jars have vacuum seal, pH content of specified products, and weight of sample products, using equipment such as vacuum gauge, pH meter, and weight scale. Determines that oil, salt, and moisture content of raw materials or finished products meet company standards, using thermometer, pyrometer, and conductivity tester. Places standard weights on balance mechanism to determine accuracy of equipment packaging scales, and adjusts regulating mechanism of scales when necessary, using handtools. Reads temperature indicator on heat-sealing equipment, and turns knobs to adjust controls for intensity of heat required to seal packages, cans, or jars. Records inspection data, writes reports, and notifies supervisor of irregularities. May assign lot numbers to products and record product information, such as cooking time, date, and equipment pressure settings, to maintain log of operation, according to company requirement.
GOE: 06.03.01 STRENGTH: L GED: R3 M2 L3 SVP: 4 DLU: 78

529.387-034 SAMPLER (oils & grease)

Collects samples of oilseeds, such as soybean, cottonseed, and safflower, and tests for splits, foreign matter, and moisture: Dips probe into oilseeds to secure sample. Weighs and sifts sample to separate whole beans, splits, and foreign matter. Weighs splits and foreign matter to determine percentage of each in sample. Weighs whole beans to determine number of pounds per bushel. Tests sample, using moisture meter, to determine moisture content.
GOE: 06.03.01 STRENGTH: L GED: R3 M2 L2 SVP: 4 DLU: 77

529.462-010 SYRUP MIXER (grain-feed mills)

Controls steam-heated vats to heat and mix syrup ingredients, according to formula: Computes and weighs specified amounts of ingredients, such as corn, beet, and cane syrups and flavoring, and directs SYRUP-MIXER ASSISTANT (grain-feed mills) to dump ingredients into mixing vats. Starts pumps and agitators to admit steam into heating coils and transfer ingredients to vat filled with measured amount of corn syrup. Reads thermometers and turns steam valve to maintain mixture at specified temperature. Collects sample of syrup and tests to determine specific gravity, using hydrometer. Starts pumps to transfer batch to storage tanks. Inspects vats after cleaning by SYRUP-MIXER ASSISTANT (grain-feed mills) to ensure that fermentable residue is removed. May clean vats.
GOE: 06.02.15 STRENGTH: M GED: R3 M2 L3 SVP: 5 DLU: 77

529.467-010 TIP-LENGTH CHECKER (tobacco) alternate titles: tip tester

Measures length of tips cut from tobacco leaves and records data pertaining to sample: Gathers tip samples from conveyor belts and places samples in tip-length measuring boxes, according to length of tips. Counts tips of each length and records number and length. Submits tip-length report to supervisor at specified intervals.
GOE: 06.03.01 STRENGTH: L GED: R3 M3 L2 SVP: 3 DLU: 77

529.482-010 FREEZER OPERATOR (dairy products) alternate titles: freezer; ice-cream freezer

Operates one or more continuous freezers and other equipment to freeze ice cream mix into semisolid consistency: Weighs or measures powder and liquid ingredients, such as flavoring, or fruit puree, using graduate, and dumps ingredients into flavor vat. Starts agitator to blend contents. Starts pumps and turns valves to force mix into freezer barrels, admit refrigerant into freezer coils, and inject air into mix. Starts beater, scraper, and expeller blades to mix contents with air and prevent adherence of mixture to barrel walls. Observes ammeter and pressure gauge and adjusts controls to obtain specified freezing temperature, air pressure, and machine speed. Fills hopper of fruit feeder with candy bits, fruit, and nuts, using scoop, or pours syrups into holder of rippling pump. Sets controls according to freezer speed to feed or ripple ingredients evenly into ice cream expelled from freezer. Opens valve to transfer contents to filling machine that pumps ice cream into cartons, cups, and cones, or molds for pies, rolls, and tarts. Places novelty dies in filler head that separates flavors and forms center designs or rosettes in packaged product. Weighs package and adjusts freezer air valve or switch on filler head to obtain specified amount of product in each container. Assembles pipes, fittings, and equipment for operation, using wrench. Sprays equipment with sterilizing solution.
GOE: 06.02.15 STRENGTH: L GED: R3 M2 L2 SVP: 5 DLU: 77

529.482-014 NOVELTY MAKER I (dairy products) alternate titles: novelty dipper

Operates machines and equipment to freeze, cut, harden, and wrap stickless ice cream novelties: Turns valve and sets thermostat to circulate refrigerant and maintain specified temperature in hardening box. Inserts forming fixtures in nozzles of ice cream feedlines that extrude specified shape of ice cream ribbon for bar, doughnut, patty, or roll shaped novelty. Starts pumps and turns steam and water valves to fill and heat chocolate coating in enrobing tank to specified temperature. Starts machines that cut extruded ice cream ribbon into measured portions, deposit them on conveyor pallets moving through hardening box, and under chocolate coating spray, and envelope them in wrappers. Measures cut portions of ice cream, using gauge, and adjusts freezer air intake to obtain specified thickness of mixture. Observes fallen bars in hardening box or their position on pallets and turns controls to synchronize conveyor with freezer speed, and change hardening temperature or freezer pressure. Replaces wire over posts of cutter arm to repair broken cutter. Tends automatic wrapping machine [PACKAGER, MACHINE (any industry)]. Brushes pallets, using bristle brush to remove frost. Cleans machines.
GOE: 06.02.15 STRENGTH: L GED: R3 M2 L2 SVP: 4 DLU: 77

529.482-018 NOVELTY MAKER II (dairy products)

Operates machines and equipment to mold and freeze ice cream, fruit juice, or syrup stick novelties: Positions molds on machine, using hoist or places mold pans on conveyor. Attaches single or double extrusion valves to filler head with handtools. Observes gauges, turns valves, and starts pumps, to regulate temperatures of solutions in brine, wash, rinse, and chocolate dip tanks, and pressure in pneumatic power lines. Places sticks in dispensers of inserting machine and positions sticks over mold. Loads bags or cartons into dispensers or wrapping paper onto spindle and adjusts guides and controls on packaging machine [CARTON-FORMING-MACHINE OPERATOR (any industry); PACKAGER, MACHINE (any industry)]. Starts machines that freeze, coat, wrap, and eject novelties onto packing table. Inserts depth gauge into molds to measure fill and turns dial to obtain prescribed level. Weighs novelty and turns dial to adjust freezer speed or air intake to obtain specified thickness of mixture. Removes jammed sticks from dispensing slots, using pliers or picks.
GOE: 06.02.15 STRENGTH: L GED: R3 M2 L2 SVP: 5 DLU: 77

529.482-022 SYRUP MAKER (sugar & conf.)

Controls equipment, such as mixing kettles, pumps, pressure cooker, and homogenizer to make chocolate and other flavored syrups, according to formula: Weighs and dumps ingredients, such as cocoa powder, milk solids, and sugar into mixing kettle. Admits metered amounts of invert sugar syrup, whole milk,

cocoa butter, and chocolate. Starts agitators to mix batch for specified time and pumps mixture into pressure cooker. Observes gauges and thermometer and adjusts steam valves to control pressure cooker. Examines batch to detect lumps, and pumps mixture through homogenizer to ensure uniform consistency. Collects sample for laboratory analysis.
GOE: 06.02.15 STRENGTH: L GED: R3 M2 L2 SVP: 5 DLU: 77

529.484-010 STEAK SAUCE MAKER (can. & preserv.)
Prepares and cans mushroom steak sauce, using mixing, filling, and canning machines: Weighs ingredients, such as flour, chicken fat, starch, and seasoning, and dumps them into agitator partly filled with water. Closes kettle and cooks to proper consistency. Adds sliced mushrooms and continues cooking for specified time. Opens valve to permit flow of sauce to filling machine and starts automatic can filler and canning machines. Keeps hopper supplied with lids.
GOE: 06.02.28 STRENGTH: M GED: R3 M2 L3 SVP: 3 DLU: 77

529.485-010 BARREL FILLER (grain-feed mills)
Tends equipment to transfer glucose from refinery to cooling equipment and storage tanks or to load tank cars and drums preparatory to shipment: Starts vat agitator, and turns valves to admit water to cooling coils and transfer glucose from refinery to cooling vat. Starts pump to transfer cooled glucose to storage tank or tank cars. Removes bung cap of drum and examines interior for cleanliness. Positions drum on rack and turns spigot to fill drum with glucose. Screws bung cap to seal filled drums, using wrench. Weighs drums before and after filling, and stencils tare, gross, and net weight on drums. Obtains sample of glucose from vat for laboratory analysis.
GOE: 06.04.15 STRENGTH: H GED: R2 M2 L1 SVP: 2 DLU: 77

529.485-014 BLOW-UP OPERATOR (sugar & conf.)
Tends equipment that mixes diatomaceous earth, milk of lime, and acid with liquors and syrups to form slurry for filtration process: Turns valves to regulate flow of slurries through series of blow-up tanks, and to maintain temperature, content level, and air agitation in tanks. Adds milk of lime or phosphoric acid to slurry to obtain specified alkalinity. Tests slurries for density, using refractometer, and adds liquor or diatomaceous earth to maintain specified density. Tests samples of slurries to ascertain that specified purification is occurring. Records operating data on forms or blackboard. Prepares phosphoric acid solutions of specified concentration for use in filtration process. Cleans blocked lines and blow-ups.
GOE: 06.04.15 STRENGTH: M GED: R3 M2 L3 SVP: 3 DLU: 77

529.485-018 DRIER, BELT CONVEYOR (food prep., nec)
Tends equipment that extrudes and dries compressed yeast to make bakers' active dry yeast: Dumps compressed yeast into hopper of extruding machine. Observes temperature indicator and moisture gauges on drier, and sets controls to maintain prescribed temperature and humidity in drier. Starts extruder that forms yeast into noodles and deposits them onto conveyor belt that carries yeast noodles through drier. Collects yeast samples from conveyor at specified locations in drier, submits samples to laboratory for analysis, and adjusts temperature and humidity of drier on basis of laboratory report. Connects mill to hopper outlet to grind dried yeast to specified fineness. Opens outlet of drier or mill hopper to fill containers. Weighs containers and records weight. Transfers containers to storage, using lift truck.
GOE: 06.04.15 STRENGTH: M GED: R3 M1 L2 SVP: 3 DLU: 77

529.485-022 MATURITY CHECKER (can. & preserv.)
Tends machine that mashes peas and registers force required to crush them to ascertain hardness (maturity) and grades peas: Fills measured pail with pea sample and weighs sample, using scale. Washes and cleans sample to remove debris, such as thistles and weeds, reweighs sample, and calculates percentage of waste per load of peas based on sample. Pours pea sample into top of size grader and counts number of peas in each grade level to calculate percentage of each grade of pea in crop. Dumps cleaned peas on grid of machine and closes cover. Starts motor to rotate disks of grid which mash peas and simultaneously registers force required on dial. Repeats test on second sample from same pan and records dial readings. Records average force required to mash peas, which determines quality of product. Inserts slip showing quality into container.
GOE: 06.03.01 STRENGTH: L GED: R3 M3 L2 SVP: 2 DLU: 77

529.485-026 WEIGH-TANK OPERATOR (oils & grease) alternate titles: scale-tank operator
Tends equipment to weigh oils and other ingredients used in making margarine or shortening, following standard formulas: Starts pump, and turns valve to admit ingredients into scale tank until specified weight has been reached. Positions weights on scale bar to weigh additives or smaller batches of ingredients. Records weights of ingredients. Turns valves to empty weighed ingredients from scale tanks into mixing vat for blending. May turn valve to admit air into scale tanks to agitate and mix ingredients.
GOE: 06.03.02 STRENGTH: L GED: R3 M2 L2 SVP: 3 DLU: 77

529.486-010 NUT-PROCESS HELPER (can. & preserv.) alternate titles: cooker helper
Performs any combination of following duties concerned with processing nuts: Stirs nuts being boiled in water to soften shells preparatory to cracking, using paddle. Dumps softened nuts into hoppers or onto conveyors leading to cracking and packing machines. Changes nut-cracking barrels on machines, using handtools. Mixes, weighs, and pours nuts into containers. Cleans working

areas, machines, and equipment. Moves materials, supplies, and nuts between work areas, using dollies and handtrucks. May be concerned with specific phase of nut processing and be designated Nut-Roaster Helper (can. & preserv.).
GOE: 06.04.15 STRENGTH: H GED: R1 M1 L1 SVP: 2 DLU: 77

529.487-010 SPECIAL TESTER (tobacco)
Tests tobacco samples from various stages of processing to determine conformance to quality standards: Obtains tobacco samples from various processing areas to ensure representative sampling. Conducts tests to determine characteristics of tobacco batch, such as stem length, percentage of lamina, stem, and foreign matter content, using scales, laboratory equipment, and calculator.
GOE: 06.03.01 STRENGTH: L GED: R3 M3 L3 SVP: 3 DLU: 77

529.565-010 SUGAR CONTROLLER (sugar & conf.)
Tends equipment to screen, blend, and convey granulated and confectioner's sugar to packing room and storage bins: Installs separation screens in machines according to size of sugar crystals specified. Tests sugars for color and grist. Blends sugars according to specifications. Starts pneumatic conveyors and regulates speed to convey blended sugar to packing units or storage bins. Gives directions to workers in screening, blending, and routing of sugar. Keeps records of sugar on hand. Inspects equipment and reports malfunction to superior. May repair torn screens.
GOE: 06.04.15 STRENGTH: M GED: R2 M2 L2 SVP: 3 DLU: 77

529.567-010 CIGARETTE INSPECTOR (tobacco) alternate titles: catching inspector; cigarette examiner; cigarette-making examiner
Inspects cigarettes to determine quality of cigarette-making machine output: Collects and examines samples from each machine for defective printing, filling, sealing, and cutting. Places twenty cigarettes in tray gauge to verify dimensions. Verifies position of brand name printed on wrapper, using gauge. Weighs cigarettes to determine conformance to standard and records weight and hour of weighing. Notifies CIGARETTE-MAKING-MACHINE OPERATOR (tobacco) of deviations from standards.
GOE: 06.03.02 STRENGTH: L GED: R2 M1 L2 SVP: 3 DLU: 77

529.567-014 MARKER, COMPANY (tobacco) alternate titles: embossing clerk
Inspects tobacco purchased by company at auction warehouse for quality and uniformity of grade and identifies each basket of tobacco: Pulls handful of tobacco from pile and inspects tobacco for damage, mixed color, and grades. Embosses company name over price marked on warehouse ticket to prevent alteration, using hand-embossing machine, or copies ticket and attaches duplicate to basket.
GOE: 05.09.03 STRENGTH: L GED: R2 M1 L1 SVP: 3 DLU: 77

529.582-010 CARBONATION EQUIPMENT OPERATOR (sugar & conf.)
Controls carbonation and sulfitation equipment to purify and bleach sugar solution: Reads alkalinity indicator and turns knob on instrument control panel or hand valves on tanks to regulate flow of sulfur dioxide gas, carbon dioxide gas, lime, milk of lime, saccharate slurry, or sugar beet juice into carbonation tanks. Draws, filters, and tests for alkalinity, solutions taken from carbonation tanks, using phenolphthalein and dilute hydrochloric acid. Records results of tests on form.
GOE: 06.02.15 STRENGTH: L GED: R4 M3 L3 SVP: 6 DLU: 77

529.582-014 FLASH-DRIER OPERATOR (grain-feed mills)
Operates flash-drier and semiautomatic equipment to produce stockfeed or starch products from milled grain: Turns handwheels to regulate fineness of grind in processing stockfeed through attrition or hammer mill. Starts pumps and turns valves to regulate moisture content and flow of material through filters, shakers, and centrifugal separators to process starch products. Observes and reads instruments, such as thermometers and gauges to monitor process. Listens for alarm that indicates excessive temperature in drier. Turns valves to regulate gas burners and adjust drier temperature and flow of materials. Feels sample of product to determine dryness. Inspects conveyor system to prevent or correct jams. Keeps record of instrument readings and processing conditions. May manually operate equipment in event of emergency.
GOE: 06.02.15 STRENGTH: L GED: R4 M2 L3 SVP: 7 DLU: 77

529.585-010 CHEESE CUTTER (dairy products)
Tends machine that cuts blocks of cheese into pieces of specified shape and size: Examines cheese for defects in color, texture, and body. Bolts specified cutting head to machine, using wrench, adjusts stops on cutting table, and turns wheels to position cutting wires. Places block on table, and moves lever to lower cutting head or raise table to cut cheese. Weighs cut cheese, places pieces on conveyor, and records amount cut. May measure cheese with ruler and cut with hand cutter. May trim rind, mold, or sediment from cheese, using knife.
GOE: 06.04.15 STRENGTH: M GED: R2 M1 L1 SVP: 2 DLU: 77

529.585-014 TANK TENDER (sugar & conf.)
Tends equipment that distributes syrups, molasses, sludges, and sweet waters for further processing or into storage tanks: Starts pump to move liquid to tank or to transfer liquid to processing stations. Regulates amount of steam and air in tanks to maintain temperature and density of solutions. Adds milk of lime to liquid to maintain specified alkalinity. Records data concerning purity, density, and routing of tank contents. Drains and cleans lines and screen pots to prevent caking or contamination of liquor. Delivers samples of solutions to laboratory for analysis. May be designated according to tanks operated as Receiv-

ing-Tank Operator (sugar & conf.); Remelt-Pan-Tank Operator (sugar & conf.); White-Sugar-Pan-Tank Operator (sugar & conf.); White-Sugar-Syrup Operator (sugar & conf.).
GOE: 06.04.15 STRENGTH: M GED: R3 M2 L2 SVP: 3 DLU: 77

529.587-010 BOTTLE GAUGER (beverage) alternate titles: gauger
Measures quantity and temperature of whiskey in bottles as they are filled by bottle-filling machine: Removes, at random, filled bottle of whiskey from conveyor, empties contents into graduated cylinder and records scale reading indicating fluid ounces. Inserts thermometer and hydrometer into cylinder to measure temperature and proof of whiskey and records results of test. Compares readings with charts indicating desired company standards to ensure that high quality of product is maintained during bottling process. Pours contents of cylinder back into bottle and places bottle on conveyor for labeling. Records size of bottle being filled, serial numbers, and brand of whiskey.
GOE: 06.03.02 STRENGTH: L GED: R3 M2 L2 SVP: 3 DLU: 77

529.587-014 SAUSAGE INSPECTOR (meat products) alternate titles: frankfurter inspector
Inspects frankfurters, wieners, or link sausages for uniformity of length and firmness of stuffing. Records number and weight of product.
GOE: 06.03.02 STRENGTH: L GED: R1 M1 L1 SVP: 2 DLU: 77

529.587-018 SCRAP SEPARATOR (food prep., nec)
Separates macaroni scraps recovered from presses and packaging areas, according to type and condition, for disposal, remilling, or for sale as hog or poultry feed: Collects scraps dropped from processing and packaging equipment and sorts scrap into barrels for reprocessing, according to type of scrap (wet or dry), and dirt content. Removes trimmings from batch drier and dumps trimmings into barrels designated for remilling. Moves filled barrels to designated areas and replaces empty barrels in processing departments. Records amount and type of scrap recovered and its disposition.
GOE: 06.03.02 STRENGTH: L GED: R1 M1 L1 SVP: 2 DLU: 77

529.587-022 TOBACCO-SAMPLE PULLER (tobacco) alternate titles: moisture-test puller; sample puller; test puller
Obtains and grinds samples of tobacco leaves used in making moisture tests: Pulls leaves from hands of tobacco at discharge end of redrying machine or extracts sample of tobacco strips (stems removed) from hogsheads or shipping cartons, using electric auger. Feeds sample into grinder. Pours ground tobacco into container, places container in tumbler, starts tumbler to mix ground sample, and labels container showing date, machine, hogshead number, grade, and time collected. May only extract and label samples for grinding and be designated Sample Driller (tobacco).
GOE: 06.04.28 STRENGTH: L GED: R2 M1 L1 SVP: 2 DLU: 77

529.665-010 FRUIT-GRADER OPERATOR (agriculture; wholesale tr.)
Tends machine that grades fruit according to size: Changes chains and other driving gear according to type of fruit. Directs workers engaged in loading of elevator belt and removal of graded fruit. Cleans and lubricates chains, bearings, and machine gears, using rags and grease gun. Repairs, replaces, and adjusts malfunctioning parts of machine.
GOE: 06.04.15 STRENGTH: L GED: R2 M1 L1 SVP: 2 DLU: 77

529.665-014 WASHROOM OPERATOR (sugar & conf.)
Tends beet washing equipment and elevators that clean sugar beets preparatory to slicing: Starts elevators and washing equipment, and turns valves to regulate water flow through washing vat. Signals FLUMER (sugar & conf.) I to adjust flow of beets in flume, using telephone. Turns valves to drain water from washing vat. Cleans debris from vat, using water hose.
GOE: 06.04.15 STRENGTH: S GED: R2 M1 L1 SVP: 2 DLU: 77

529.665-018 WET-AND-DRY-SUGAR-BIN OPERATOR (sugar & conf.)
Tends equipment, such as elevators, drags, and scrolls, that conveys wet sugar to granulator scrolls, and dry sugar to separator screens: Signals GRANULATOR OPERATOR (sugar & conf.) with bell signal to stop granulator when content of wet-sugar bins is low or dry-sugar bins are congested. Washes equipment with hose and directs sweetwater (wash water containing sugar) into recovery system. Shuts off flow of sugar to each bin periodically to prevent caking and hardening of sugar in bins and conveying equipment. Refills bin after emptying.
GOE: 06.04.15 STRENGTH: M GED: R2 M1 L1 SVP: 3 DLU: 77

529.665-022 YEAST-CUTTING-AND-WRAPPING-MACHINE OPERATOR (food prep., nec) alternate titles: yeast-cake cutter
Tends machines that compress and extrude bulk yeast into continuous bars, cut bars into cakes of specified size, and wrap and heat-seal cakes: Signals worker to fill hopper of extruder with yeast. Positions and threads roll of paper, plastic film, or foil through roller guide of wrapping mechanism, and starts machines. Removes yeast cakes from conveyor emerging from cutter and feeds cakes into wrapping machine, discarding cracked or malformed cakes. Observes cutting and wrapping operation to detect jamming or twisted wrapping. Packs wrapped yeast cakes in cartons.
GOE: 06.04.15 STRENGTH: L GED: R2 M1 L1 SVP: 2 DLU: 77

529.666-010 CATCHER, FILTER TIP (tobacco) alternate titles: catcher, plug
Off bears and examines cigarette filter plugs (tips) discharged from cigarette filter-making machine: Picks up double handful of plugs and examines them for defects in cutting, gluing, size, and filling. Inspects both ends of plugs and places plugs in tray. Removes defective plugs from tray. Notifies CIGARETTE-FILTER-MAKING-MACHINE OPERATOR (tobacco) of defective product.
GOE: 06.04.15 STRENGTH: L GED: R2 M2 L2 SVP: 2 DLU: 77

529.666-014 CIGARETTE-MAKING-MACHINE CATCHER (tobacco) alternate titles: cigarette and assembly-machine inspector; making-machine catcher
Off bears and examines cigarettes discharged from cigarette-making machine and places them in cigarette tray preparatory to packaging: Picks up double handful of cigarettes from conveyor and observes cigarettes to detect defective gluing, filling, and printing of brand name. Places cigarettes in tray and pushes cigarettes against back of tray to even edges, using hand or paddle. Places defective cigarettes in separate container. Periodically inserts 20 cigarettes in tray gauge to verify length, circumference, and location of brand name. Notifies CIGARETTE-FILTER-MAKING-MACHINE OPERATOR (tobacco) of machine malfunction.
GOE: 06.04.15 STRENGTH: S GED: R2 M1 L2 SVP: 2 DLU: 77

529.667-010 INSPECTOR, FILTER TIP (tobacco) alternate titles: inspector, plug seam
Inspects cigarette filter plugs (tips) to detect imperfections: Removes plugs from conveyor of filter-making machine and examines plugs for dirt and irregularities in size, firmness, sealing, and cut. Tears paper from plug and examines filter material for defects. Measures and examines plug seams, using magnifying glass with graduated scale. Records findings on chart. Notifies CIGARETTE-FILTER-MAKING-MACHINE OPERATOR (tobacco) or MACHINE ADJUSTER (tobacco) of deviations from specifications. Tests air draft of filter rods, using draft-resistence meter.
GOE: 06.03.02 STRENGTH: L GED: R2 M2 L2 SVP: 3 DLU: 77

529.667-014 MASH-FILTER-CLOTH CHANGER (beverage) alternate titles: cloth changer
Removes and replaces filter cloth in mash filter, working as member of team: Unscrews and removes backplate of filter. Slides cloth-covered plates out of filter to drop spent grains on conveyor. Pulls wet cloths off plates and throws cloths into disposal chute. Moves racks of clean cloths to filter, using electric hoist. Positions and fits cloths over plates and replaces plates. Washes inside and outside of filter, using hose.
GOE: 06.04.15 STRENGTH: M GED: R1 M1 L1 SVP: 2 DLU: 77

529.682-010 CENTRIFUGE OPERATOR (sugar & conf.) alternate titles: drier operator
Controls centrifuge machine to melt, mix, and filter chicle for use in manufacturing chewing gum: Weighs specified amounts of ingredients and moves ingredients to machine, using handtruck. Loads ground chicle into steam-jacketed cooker of centrifuge according to prescribed time sequence. Reads gauges and turns air pressure and steam valves to maintain specified temperature and pressure in cooker and to control melting of chicle. Starts pumps that force melted chicle through strainers that filter out impurities and pump chicle into receiving tank. Cleans strainers and filters to remove collected impurities. Lubricates and makes minor repairs to equipment.
GOE: 06.02.15 STRENGTH: M GED: R3 M2 L2 SVP: 4 DLU: 77

529.682-014 CHEESEMAKER HELPER (dairy products)
Operates dairy processing equipment and performs following tasks to assist CHEESEMAKER (dairy products) in making cheese: Separates and pasteurizes milk, using dairy processing equipment. Starts pump, turns valves, and observes gauges to fill cheese vats with specified amount of milk and maintain specified temperature in vats. Dumps dye and starter into milk. Starts agitator to mix ingredients. Dumps rennet into vat to coagulate milk into curd. Dumps, presses, and salts curd. Pierces, washes, and turns cheese blocks to cure cheese. Operates washing machine and extractor to clean and dry cloths. Performs other duties as described under HELPER (any industry) Master Title.
GOE: 06.02.15 STRENGTH: M GED: R3 M2 L2 SVP: 6 DLU: 77

529.682-018 DEPOSITING-MACHINE OPERATOR (sugar & conf.) alternate titles: first helper; starch crab
Operates machine that deposits metered amount of fluid candy in molds, on trays or mats, or directly on conveyor: Opens valve or starts pump to fill hopper of machine. Observes thermometer and adjusts steam supply to maintain specified temperature in steam-jacketed machine hopper. Turns handwheel to regulate flow of candy from depositing spout. Positions trays, molds, or mats on conveyor leading to machine. Turns handwheel to synchronize piston stroke of depositor with speed of conveyor belt. Weighs formed candy and adjusts pouring spouts to regulate specified amount of candy deposited. May manually feed trays, molds or mats into machine. May prepare starch molds [STARCHMAKER (sugar & conf.)]. May be designated according to candy formed as Mint-Wafer Depositor (sugar & conf.).
GOE: 06.02.15 STRENGTH: L GED: R3 M2 L2 SVP: 5 DLU: 77

529.682-022 DRIER OPERATOR (sugar & conf.)
Controls equipment, such as mixing and treating tanks, incubator (pasteurizer), and drier, to alkalize nibs (cracked roasted cocoa beans) for dutch process chocolate: Mixes measured amounts of water with potash in mixing tank to prepare alkali solution. Turns thermostat, rheostat, valves, and switches to control pasteurization process in incubator, temperature of drier, processing time cycles, and speed of conveyor carrying nibs and other materials to and

379

from equipment. Immerses measured amounts of nibs in alkali solution in treating tank and allows tank to rotate for specified time. Releases treated nibs onto conveyor or through slide gate to admit into storage bins or to pasteurizer for specified time. Discharges pasteurized nibs onto conveyor to carry material through drier. Collects samples of dried nibs for laboratory analysis. May move and position portable incubator, using electric truck. May pregrind nibs preparatory to making chocolate liquor [LIQUOR-GRINDING-MILL OPERATOR (sugar & conf.)].
GOE: 06.02.15 STRENGTH: M GED: R4 M2 L3 SVP: 5 DLU: 77

529.682-026 LOZENGE MAKER (sugar & conf.)
Operates machine that rolls dough into sheets, and embosses and cuts dough into candy lozenges: Positions and secures cutting and embossing dies in place, using wrench. Adjusts ram stroke of cutting die to synchronize it with speed of dough rollers and discharge conveyor. Turns handwheel to adjust clearance between rollers. Dumps lozenge dough into hopper and starts machine. Sprinkles cornstarch onto dough to prevent sticking to rollers and dies. Examines and weighs formed lozenges for conformity to size, shape, and weight specifications, and readjusts roller speed and clearance to meet product standards. May adjust printer bars on machines to print or emboss designs on lozenges before cutting.
GOE: 06.02.15 STRENGTH: H GED: R3 M1 L2 SVP: 5 DLU: 77

529.682-030 SILO OPERATOR (tobacco)
Controls panelboard to convey stemmed and redried tobacco from redrying machines into silos (interim storage) and to packing machines: Pushes buttons to start conveyors in specified sequence, according to daily production schedule. Observes dials and gauges to route stemmed and redried tobacco from redrying machines, through silo, and into packing machines. Observes panel lights for indication of malfunction and adjusts conveyors to regulate feed of tobacco into and out of silos.
GOE: 06.02.15 STRENGTH: L GED: R3 M2 L2 SVP: 4 DLU: 77

529.682-034 WHIPPED-TOPPING FINISHER (oils & grease)
Operates equipment to process ingredients, such as oil, emulsifier, stabilizer, liquid sugar, and flavorings into whipped topping: Turns valves and starts pump to transfer mixed batch through equipment, such as blending tank, versator, pasteurizer, homogenizer, and colloid mill and into storage tank. Adjusts colloid mill to reduce liquid particles to specified emulsion size. Observes gauges and adjusts valves to control temperature and pressure when pasteurizing, homogenizing, and cooling product. Observes gauge on storage tank to ensure maintenance of specified stock level. Turns valve to blanket product with carbon dioxide to prevent contamination. Cleans equipment, using water, solvents, and brushes.
GOE: 06.02.15 STRENGTH: L GED: R3 M2 L2 SVP: 5 DLU: 77

529.682-038 EGG PASTEURIZER (agriculture)
Controls and monitors equipment that pasteurizes liquid egg product: Connects pipes between holding tanks and processing equipment and assembles equipment parts, such as fittings and valves, using wrench. Turns control to set timer for pumping cycle, records starting time on processing record, and adjusts temperature controls to bring temperatures to specified level. Places container under discharge outlet to collect initial flow of water and liquid egg product through equipment. Turns valves to admit liquid egg product from holding tank into collection pot and to start pump that propels product and water through equipment. Turns bypass valve to direct flow into discharge containers until mix of water and egg product reaches desired density. Turns valve to shut off bypass and to direct liquid egg product to containerization room. Monitors product flow and adjusts controls to maintain temperature and pressure at specified levels. Turns bypass valve to shut off flow to containerization room when mixture thins. Drains remaining flow into discharge containers.
GOE: 06.02.15 STRENGTH: M GED: R3 M2 L3 SVP: 4 DLU: 86

529.684-010 FROZEN PIE MAKER (can. & preserv.)
Measures specified amounts of ingredients, such as precooked meats, vegetables, fruits, or sauce, into dough-lined pie plate, and covers ingredients with prerolled pie crust topping in preparation for freezing: Manually bones meats. Weighs specified amount of meat, vegetable, or fruit pieces and places them in pie plate. Adds specified ingredients, such as sugar, spices, or sauce, to fill pie plate. Covers pie with prerolled pie crust and crimps edges, using hand crimping device. Dips brush in egg yolk mixture and spreads mixture over pie crust. Places pie in refrigerator to dry egg topping. Removes dried pies, packs pies in boxes, and stacks boxes in freezer.
GOE: 06.04.28 STRENGTH: M GED: R2 M1 L1 SVP: 2 DLU: 77

529.684-014 INGREDIENT SCALER (bakery products; dairy products) alternate titles: ingredient mixer
Measures ingredients according to formula for bakery, dairy, and confectionery batches: Reads daily production schedules and selects formula cards for desired batches. Weighs dry ingredients on scales or pours liquid ingredients into graduated containers. Places assembled ingredients for each batch with identifying batch number on conveyor or handtruck or dumps batches in mixing bowl or machine. Records number of batches prepared.
GOE: 06.04.28 STRENGTH: M GED: R3 M2 L3 SVP: 2 DLU: 78

529.684-018 SIEVE MAKER (grain-feed mills)
Makes and repairs sieves used in flour sifting machines, using handtools: Tacks cotton cloth lining onto frame and stretches and staples wire screen across bottom. Places free-moving cloth pads in frame. Stretches and tacks silk cloth across top of frame. Tacks strips of cotton flannel around outer sides of frame so sieve fits snugly into machine. Removes and replaces defective parts of damaged sieves. May be designated according to function as Sieve Repairer (grain-feed mills).
GOE: 06.04.25 STRENGTH: M GED: R2 M1 L1 SVP: 2 DLU: 77

529.685-010 AUTO ROLLER (tobacco)
Tends machine that automatically rolls cigars and cheroots: Starts machine and positions wrapper leaf on die of machine. Pulls handle that lowers knife and cuts wrapper leaf in shape of die. Feeds cut wrapper leaves into machine along with bunches.
GOE: 06.04.15 STRENGTH: L GED: R2 M1 L1 SVP: 2 DLU: 77

529.685-014 AUTOMATIC LUMP MAKING MACHINE TENDER (tobacco)
Tends machine that automatically presses and slices cased (tobacco with flavoring added), shredded tobacco into lumps of chewing tobacco: Turns knobs to adjust speed of machine conveyor according to brand, grade, and weight of cased tobacco. Starts machine and observes operation to detect malfunctions, such as jam-ups or uneven flow of tobacco entering machine. Stops machine to remove tobacco caught between pressing rollers or weighing unit. Weighs random lumps to verify accuracy of reject weighing unit, using scale. Turns knob to adjust weighing unit as necessary to maintain standard weight of lumps. Replenishes containers with alcohol solution that is automatically sprayed on machine rollers and conveyor to prevent sticking of cased tobacco. Cleans machine.
GOE: 06.04.15 STRENGTH: L GED: R2 M1 L2 SVP: 2 DLU: 77

529.685-018 BINDER LAYER (tobacco)
Tends unit of fresh-work cigar machine that cuts binder leaves: Starts machine. Flattens binder leaf and lays it on suction plate die. Repositions leaf on die as machine cuts and removes portions. Brushes leaf scraps into box.
GOE: 06.04.15 STRENGTH: L GED: R2 M1 L1 SVP: 2 DLU: 77

529.685-022 BLENDER-CONVEYOR OPERATOR (dairy products)
Tends machines that automatically grind, sift, weigh, blend, and convey milk powders to instantizing and filling vats: Slides specified screens into grinder, opens chutes on conveyor, and dumps blended powder into vat. Weighs ingredients, such as potash, salt, soda, and vitamins, according to formula, and dumps them into blending machine. Starts machines that automatically grind and screen chunks of dried milk, weigh and blend powder with other ingredients, and convey blended powder to instantizing or filling vats. May weigh prescribed amount of liquid lecithin and pump into blending vat. May operate power lift truck to move material.
GOE: 06.04.15 STRENGTH: H GED: R2 M1 L2 SVP: 2 DLU: 77

529.685-026 BOTTLED-BEVERAGE INSPECTOR (beverage) alternate titles: beverage-inspection-machine tender; bottle inspector
Tends beverage inspection machine, equipped with photoelectric cell, that automatically detects and rejects filled beverage bottles containing solid impurities: Starts conveyor that conveys bottles filled with alcoholic or nonalcoholic beverages through inspection machine. Removes rejected bottles from reject tray and examines contents of bottles in front of inspection light to verify presence of solid impurities. Drops bottles containing impurities in refuge container for disposal. Observes bottles on conveyor to detect jamming or bottle defects, such as chips and cracks. Drops defective bottles in refuse container for disposal. Removes fallen or other bottles blocking feed or discharge openings of inspection machine and replaces bottles on conveyor. Periodically places test bottle in feed opening of inspection machine and examines reject tray for bottle to ensure that machine is operative.
GOE: 06.03.02 STRENGTH: L GED: R2 M1 L2 SVP: 3 DLU: 77

529.685-030 BRINE-TANK TENDER (dairy products) alternate titles: pusher; putter-in
Tends equipment to make frozen stick confections, performing any combination of following tasks: Positions mold pan under filler spouts and presses pedal to fill pan with ice cream, fruit juice, or syrup mix. Places tray against machine and pushes levers to insert and lock sticks in tray slots. Places tray over mold pan and presses switch or pushes pans to move them over brine tank to freeze ingredient onto sticks. Dips frozen mold pans into water to defrost and removes tray of stick bars. Dips tray of frozen bars into chocolate and places tray on conveyor leading to chill tunnel. Fills dispensers of bagging machine, positions tray over bagging chutes, and pulls lever to drop bars into bags. Turns valves, controls, and switches to alter level of mix in molds, flow of ingredients into filler hopper and chocolate tank, or temperature of chocolate or brine. May test brine content, using hydrometer and add salt to maintain prescribed strength. May mix flavor, sugar, and water to make flavored ice mixes. May fill dispensers and remove jammed sticks from automatic stick machines. May be designated according to work performed as Mold Filler (dairy products); Mold Remover (dairy products); Stick Inserter (dairy products).
GOE: 06.04.15 STRENGTH: M GED: R2 M1 L1 SVP: 2 DLU: 77

529.685-034 BULKER, CUT TOBACCO (tobacco)
Tends chutes and raking machine to feed and spread tobacco evenly into bulks: Opens chute to direct flow of tobacco into bulks and starts rake. Adjusts angle of rake to spread tobacco evenly in bulks.
GOE: 06.04.15 STRENGTH: L GED: R1 M1 L1 SVP: 2 DLU: 77

529.685-038 BUNCH MAKER, MACHINE (tobacco) alternate titles: bunch-breaker-machine operator; buncher, machine; short-filler-bunch-machine operator

Tends machine that rolls cigar filler and binder leaves into bunches: Places binder on rubberized fabric apron (breaker) of machine, and pulls lever of hopper to distribute filler on binder, or manually distributes filler. Presses pedal of machine that rolls tobacco into cigar shape. Removes bunch from machine and applies glue to edge of binder to secure binder. Places bunches in molds for compressing or in machine that wraps them in wrapper leaves to form complete cigar. May be designated according to type of tobacco used in forming bunches as Scrap-Bunch Maker (tobacco).
GOE: 06.04.15 STRENGTH: L GED: R2 M1 L1 SVP: 2 DLU: 77

529.685-042 BUTT MAKER (tobacco)

Tends machine that forms scrap and binder leaf tobacco into cigar-like roll and cuts roll into butts (slices) of chewing tobacco: Starts machine and dumps scrap into hopper of machine. Feeds binder leaf into machine that wraps leaf around scrap into roll and conveys roll under cutting knives. Places box or basket at discharge end of machine to catch butts.
GOE: 06.04.15 STRENGTH: L GED: R2 M1 L1 SVP: 2 DLU: 77

529.685-046 CAN-CONVEYOR FEEDER (food prep., nec)

Tends machine that automatically feeds empty coffee cans onto conveyors leading to filling machines: Presses button to activate machine-lift mechanism that raises stacked cans and transfers them onto mechanical conveyor. Observes passing cans and removes defective ones. May place cans on sloping metal runway leading to conveyors to feed cans onto conveyors from freight cars. May transfer cans from containers onto belt or chain conveyor.
GOE: 06.04.40 STRENGTH: L GED: R2 M1 L1 SVP: 2 DLU: 77

529.685-050 CHAR-CONVEYOR TENDER (sugar & conf.)

Tends conveyor-belt system to distribute wet char from filters to drying hoppers and dried char from driers or bins to filters: Starts conveyor system under filter being emptied, and positions gate on belt over designated hopper to divert char from belt into hopper. Rakes char from one hopper to another to keep hoppers full. Starts shaker machine that distributes dried char from hopper or bins onto conveyor for transmission to filters. Inspects and cleans drier screens and pots. Sweeps and weighs char dust from dust-cooler room. May be designated according to conditon of char as Wet-Char Conveyor Tender (sugar & conf.); or location of job as Char Conveyor Tender, Cellar (sugar & conf.).
GOE: 06.04.40 STRENGTH: M GED: R2 M1 L1 SVP: 2 DLU: 77

529.685-054 CHOCOLATE MOLDER, MACHINE (sugar & conf.)

Tends machine and equipment that deposit tempered chocolate into molds to form bars, blocks, and assorted figures: Opens valves to draw chocolate from tempering kettle or automatic tempering equipment into water-jacketed depositor of molding machine. Observes thermometer and turns valves to admit and circulate water in jacket to maintain specified temperature of chocolate in depositor. Adjusts piston stroke of depositor that forces measured amounts of chocolate into conveyorized molds, using handtools. Turns handwheel to adjust speed of conveyor. Starts machine. Weighs filled molds to ensure that weight of chocolate casts meet specifications. Observes thermometer and turns thermostat and valve to control temperature in cooling tunnel. Observes action of machine to ensure that molds do not jam. May temper chocolate [CHOCOLATE TEMPERER (bakery products; grain-feed mills)].
GOE: 06.04.15 STRENGTH: L GED: R3 M2 L2 SVP: 4 DLU: 77

529.685-058 CIGAR-HEAD PIERCER (tobacco) alternate titles: cigar-head holer; cigar-head pegger; cigar-head perforator; cigar-head puncher; cigar-head stringer

Pierces draft holes in ends of cigars. Holds cigar in guide of machine and presses pedal that forces revolving pin into cigar, or manually pushes pin into cigar to pierce draft holes in ends of cigars.
GOE: 06.04.28 STRENGTH: S GED: R2 M1 L1 SVP: 2 DLU: 77

529.685-062 CIGARETTE-FILTER-MAKING-MACHINE OPERATOR (tobacco) alternate titles: plug-making operator

Tends machine that wraps and cuts cigarette filter plugs (tips): Installs rolls of filter material (fiber) and tissue paper on spindles of machine and threads ends between rollers. Starts machine and observes machine operation, product, and gauges to detect malfunction. Turns setscrew or handwheel to adjust feed mechanism and cutting knives. Repairs or replaces worn, damaged, or broken parts, such as pulley belts and cutting knives, using handtools. Removes and replaces empty paste cylinders. Supplies CATCHER, FILTER TIPS (tobacco) with empty cardboard trays and removes filled trays onto pallet.
GOE: 06.04.15 STRENGTH: L GED: R2 M1 L1 SVP: 3 DLU: 77

529.685-066 CIGARETTE-MAKING-MACHINE OPERATOR (tobacco) alternate titles: cigarette and assembly machine operator; making-machine operator, filter

Tends cigarette-making machine that encases tobacco in continuous paper roll and cuts cigarettes from roll: Places roll of cigarette paper on spindle. Sets monogram-printing device to print brand name on paper at specified position, using wrenches. Regulates flow of shredded tobacco to ensure that cigarette contains specified amount of tobacco. Fills ink and glue reservoirs. Threads cigarette paper between guide rolls and adjusts friction tension on holding spindles, using wrench. Starts machine and observes operation. Reports malfunction to MACHINE ADJUSTER (tobacco). Cleans paper scraps and waste materials

from machine, using brush. Places coil of tipping material on spindle and fills hopper with filters when making filter-, cork-, straw-, or ivory-tipped cigarettes. Replaces full catching trays. May be designated according to type of cigarette as Filter-Cigarette-Making-Machine Operator (tobacco).
GOE: 06.04.15 STRENGTH: M GED: R3 M1 L1 SVP: 3 DLU: 77

529.685-070 COLORER, CITRUS FRUIT (wholesale tr.)

Tends equipment to subject citrus fruits to ethylene gas to destroy chlorophyll and produce fruit of natural appearance: Ascertains from supervisor time, humidity, and amount of gas to be used for each lot of fruit stored in coloring room. Observes gauges and dials and manipulates controls to steam-heat room, to pump gas throughout room, and to keep specified humidity.
GOE: 06.04.15 STRENGTH: L GED: R2 M1 L1 SVP: 2 DLU: 77

529.685-074 CONTAINER WASHER, MACHINE (any industry)

Tends machine that cleans and sterilizes containers, such as barrels, fruit juice bottles, milk cans, and baking pans: Moves controls to fill washing and sterilizing tanks with water and steam, and to regulate temperature in cleaning tank. Dumps specified amounts of chemicals into cleaning tank. Loads containers on conveyor that carries containers through cleaning and sterilizing operations. Examines containers for cleanliness and defects, such as dents and cracks. Cleans and lubricates equipment. May manually clean containers prior to machine cleaning, using sponge or brush. May be designated according to type of container washed as Barrel Washer, Machine (any industry); Bottle Washer, Machine (any industry) I; Can Washer, Machine (any industry).
GOE: 06.04.39 STRENGTH: M GED: R2 M1 L1 SVP: 2 DLU: 77

529.685-078 CORN-PRESS OPERATOR (food prep., nec)

Tends machine that shapes and cooks dough to make tortillas and corn chips: Kneads masa (cornmeal dough) into loaves as masa emerges from corn-grinding machine and places masa into hopper of shaping machine. Starts machine to flatten dough between rollers, cut it into shape, and convey shaped dough through baking oven to make tortillas, or frying tank to make corn chips. Inspects cooked tortillas or corn chips for color, size, and textural quality. Observes cooking temperature and regulates conveying speed as required. May be designated according to product made as Corn-Chip Maker (food prep., nec); Tortilla Maker (food prep., nec).
GOE: 06.04.15 STRENGTH: M GED: R2 M1 L1 SVP: 3 DLU: 77

529.685-082 CUTTER (food prep., nec)

Tends bandsaw or cut-off saw to cut macaroni products, such as spaghetti and noodles, into packaging lengths: Slides strands of macaroni product from drying stick onto table and presses curved ends to break strands in half. Gathers strands into bunches and positions them against saw guide. Starts saw, cuts product into specified lengths, and packs them in carton. May tend hydraulic knife to cut products.
GOE: 06.04.15 STRENGTH: L GED: R1 M1 L1 SVP: 2 DLU: 77

529.685-086 DECAY-CONTROL OPERATOR (wholesale tr.)

Tends machine that pumps gas to retard decay of fresh fruits and vegetables during storage and shipment: Loads machine with chlorine and salt. Starts machine that pumps gas into storage space or freight car. Periodically tests concentration of gas, using comparometer, and adjusts flow accordingly. Stops machine when specified time has elapsed and blows gas from storage area or freight car.
GOE: 06.04.15 STRENGTH: L GED: R2 M1 L1 SVP: 2 DLU: 77

529.685-090 DEFECTIVE-CIGARETTE SLITTER (tobacco) alternate titles: ripper operator; slitting-machine feeder

Tends machine that cuts paper from defective cigarettes to reclaim tobacco: Attaches hoisting bar to tub of cigarettes. Starts machine and pulls rope to hoist tub and dump cigarettes into hopper that feeds cigarettes under cutting knives and onto separator (vibrating screen) that separates paper from tobacco.
GOE: 06.04.15 STRENGTH: M GED: R2 M1 L1 SVP: 2 DLU: 77

529.685-094 DEOILING-MACHINE AND PASTEURIZING-MACHINE OPERATOR (beverage)

Tends machines that extract and pasteurize oils from citrus fruit juices: Starts machines, and turns steam valves to heat juice. Observes steam gauges and thermometers and adjusts controls to keep temperature and pressure within specified limits. Notifies supervisor of malfunctioning machines. Washes machines.
GOE: 06.04.15 STRENGTH: L GED: R1 M1 L1 SVP: 2 DLU: 77

529.685-098 DRIER OPERATOR, DRUM (food prep., nec)

Tends machines that dry and grind liquid food products, such as chocolate, malt, milk, or yeast: Turns valve to control flow of steam to heat drier to operating temperature and observes thermometer and pressure gauge to ensure that specified temperature and pressure are maintained. Installs cutting blades and screens in mill. Starts drier and turns valve to regulate material flow between heated revolving drums. Observes thickness and color of dried material sheet emerging from drums to determine moisture content of material. Turns screws to adjust drum speed and thickness of sheet to ensure that required dryness of material is attained. Turns screws to adjust knife that scrapes material off drum. Starts conveyor that carries dried material into mill. Places container at outlet of mill to catch dry, ground product. May be designated according to material dried and ground as Yeast-Drier Operator, Drum (food prep., nec).
GOE: 06.04.15 STRENGTH: L GED: R2 M1 L2 SVP: 2 DLU: 77

529.685-102 DUMPING-MACHINE OPERATOR (can. & preserv.; wholesale tr.)

Tends dumping machine that automatically grips, tilts, and dumps boxes of fruit or other produce into flue or onto conveyor leading to washing vat, and returns empty boxes. May start and stop conveyor to control flow of fruit. May oil, grease, and make minor adjustments to machine. May clear box jams and restart machine.
GOE: 06.04.40 STRENGTH: L GED: R1 M1 L1 SVP: 2 DLU: 77

529.685-106 EXPELLER OPERATOR (grain-feed mills; oils & grease) alternate titles: corn-oil extractor; roll operator

Tends machine that flattens and dries oilseed, such as soybean, cottonseed, and corn, and presses it to extract oil: Turns handwheels to adjust distance between rollers that flatten oilseed. Starts rollers and turns gate valve to admit oilseed. Observes rolling process to ensure that pressure of rollers on oilseed is not sufficient to extract oil. Turns control of heat drier to specified temperature, and opens chute to admit flattened oilseed to drier. Turns steam valves of heat cooker to cook dried oilseed. Turns handwheels to adjust roller pressure of oil expeller. Feels samples of expelled oilseed to determine that sufficient quantity of oil has been removed. May tend attrition mill that breaks up dehydrated oilseed [MILL OPERATOR (grain-feed mills)]. May tend filter press to filter oil [PRESS TENDER, HEAD, FEED HOUSE (grain-feed mills)]. May be designated according to process phase as Crusher Tender (oils & grease); Drier Tender (oils & grease) II; Oil-Expeller (grain-feed mills; oils & grease).
GOE: 06.04.15 STRENGTH: M GED: R2 M1 L1 SVP: 4 DLU: 77

529.685-110 FILLER SHREDDER, MACHINE (tobacco) alternate titles: filler sifter, machine; scrap cutter, machine; shredded-filler-cutter operator

Tends machine that cuts tobacco leaves into shreds and cleans shredded tobacco for use as cigar filler: Spreads tobacco evenly on conveyor feed belt or dumps tobacco into hopper of machine. Starts machine. Scrapes tobacco from revolving knife of machine. Replaces filled receptacles under filler chute and foreign matter chutes.
GOE: 06.04.15 STRENGTH: M GED: R2 M1 L1 SVP: 3 DLU: 77

529.685-114 FILTER TENDER, JELLY (can. & preserv.)

Tends control panel that regulates flow of fruit juices through filtering system and cooks juices preparatory to processing into jelly: Depresses button to regulate flow of juice from storage tank, through filter system, into cooking kettle. Turns valves to open supply lines to add specified amount of sugar into kettle and activates heating controls to cool mixture. Turns valves on centrifugal pump to transfer juice from kettles to receiving tanks for processing into jelly.
GOE: 06.04.15 STRENGTH: L GED: R3 M2 L1 SVP: 3 DLU: 77

529.685-118 FISH CLEANER MACHINE TENDER (can. & preserv.)

Tends machine that removes heads, fins, viscera, and tails from fish preparatory to canning: Starts machine and conveyor system. Positions fish on feed table and aligns head with cutting knife. Places beheaded fish in machine feed trough and pushes tail into teeth of fish cleaning machine. Pulls lever to regulate speed of conveyors. May replace worn knives, using handtools.
GOE: 06.04.15 STRENGTH: M GED: R2 M1 L1 SVP: 2 DLU: 77

529.685-122 FISH-CAKE MAKER (food prep., nec)

Tends machines and equipment that grind, mix, form, and cook raw fish to make fishcakes: Skins and bones fish, using knife. Places boned fish in grinding machine that grinds fish into paste. Dumps paste in mixing machine and adds specified amounts of ingredients, such as flour, water, and spices. Feeds mixed ingredients into extrusion machine that forms and places fishcakes onto conveyor for transfer to automatic deep-fry cooker, freezing tunnel, and packaging machine. May cook cakes in steam cooker or fries cakes in oil. May wrap cooked fishcakes in wax paper.
GOE: 06.04.15 STRENGTH: L GED: R2 M1 L1 SVP: 4 DLU: 77

529.685-126 FLAVOR EXTRACTOR (grain-feed mills)

Tends equipment that extracts cereal flavoring from mixture of malt, sugar, salt, water, and other ingredients: Opens valve to fill mixing tank with water. Dumps specified amount of malt into hopper, from which it is fed through crimping rolls and into mixing tank. Starts agitator revolving in tank. Opens valve admitting steam to tank jacket or lights gas burners to maintain specified temperature of mix for prescribed time. Turns valve to drain liquid into flavor tank. Dumps sugar, salt, and other ingredients into tank according to formula, and turns valve to pump mixture to storage tank. Removes spent mash from mixing tank, using hoe, and dumps it into feed trough.
GOE: 06.04.15 STRENGTH: M GED: R2 M1 L1 SVP: 3 DLU: 77

529.685-130 FLAVOR ROOM WORKER (dairy products)

Tends equipment, such as blenders, roasters and grinders, and performs any combination of following tasks to prepare ice cream flavoring, coloring, and nut and fruit mixtures: Weighs or measures specified quantities of ingredients, such as syrup, sugar, water, butter, fruit pulp, fruit juice, salt, dye, and gelatin, using graduate. Dumps ingredients into blending vat. Turns valve and starts agitator to heat and blend contents for specified period. Opens valve to start flow of blend to storage vat, or moves it to processing unit, using handtruck. Fills hopper of nut grinder and turns knob to adjust teeth for desired grind. Dumps ground nuts into roaster and adjusts burner to roast them. Dumps prepared fruits into sieve to remove juice. Observes ingredients and removes foreign

matter. Sprays containers and equipment with sterilizing solution to clean them. Maintains inventory of supplies.
GOE: 06.04.15 STRENGTH: H GED: R3 M2 L3 SVP: 4 DLU: 77

529.685-134 FRUIT-BAR MAKER (sugar & conf.)

Tends machine that grinds dried fruit preparatory to making natural fruit confections: Dumps mixed dried fruit, such as raisins, dates, figs, and prunes, into machine hopper and starts grinder. Places container at machine discharge outlet to receive ground fruit. Removes filled container and molds ground fruit into circular shape by hand. Cuts molded fruit into equal bars, using hand held cutting wheel. Places bars onto tray preparatory to coconut coating.
GOE: 06.04.15 STRENGTH: L GED: R2 M1 L1 SVP: 2 DLU: 77

529.685-138 HAM-ROLLING-MACHINE OPERATOR (meat products)

Tends machine that winds binding around boned hams: Threads binding string through winding shaft and starts machine. Impales boned ham on spiked pilot. Pushes lever to engage winding shaft with pilot and steps on treadle to wind string spirally around ham. Holds ham between hands during winding to maintain its round shape. Stops machine, cuts and ties string, and removes bound ham.
GOE: 06.04.15 STRENGTH: L GED: R1 M1 L1 SVP: 2 DLU: 77

529.685-142 HORSERADISH MAKER (can. & preserv.) alternate titles: horseradish grinder

Tends machines and equipment to wash, grind, mix, and bottle horseradish: Starts machine to wash horseradish roots. Dumps washed roots on floor. Holds root against rotating wire brush to remove skin and blemishes. Places container under discharge outlet of grinder, starts machine manually, and feeds roots into grinder hopper. Turns valve to fill mixing machine with vinegar to specified level. Dumps ground horseradish into mixer and starts machine. Tilts mixer, or ladles out mixed horseradish into containers. Loads horseradish into hopper of filling machine, and starts machine. Holds jars under filling spout that deposits measured amount of horseradish in jar. Manually caps and labels jars. May dump horseradish roots into washing machine.
GOE: 06.04.15 STRENGTH: L GED: R2 M1 L1 SVP: 2 DLU: 77

529.685-146 ICE CREAM FREEZER ASSISTANT (dairy products) alternate titles: freezer assistant

Assists FREEZER OPERATOR (dairy products) to freeze and package ice cream, performing any combination of following tasks: Pours cans of fruit into sieve to separate juice. Places cans of chocolate coating into hot water vat, pushes barrel into mechanical heating unit, or adds specified amount of water to chocolate to increase its fluidity. Measures specified kinds and amounts of ingredients, such as ice cream mix, flavor, and color. Starts pump, or dumps ingredients into flavor-mix tanks to maintain continuous flow of mix into freezer. Adjusts guides or controls of automatic carton forming, filling, and wrapping machines. Shapes and feeds carton blanks, bottoms, and rims into carton forming machine [CARTON-FORMING-MACHINE OPERATOR (any industry)]. Holds bulk carton under filler head or places it on mechanical filling platform to fill carton with ice cream. Weighs carton. May mix ingredients, such as fruit juice, color, water, flavor, sugar, citric acid, and stabilizers to make mix for frozen ice confections. When tending flavor tanks, may be known as Flavor-Tank Tender (dairy products). Performs other duties as described under HELPER (any industry) Master Title.
GOE: 06.04.15 STRENGTH: M GED: R2 M1 L1 SVP: 2 DLU: 77

529.685-150 ICE CUTTER (food prep., nec)

Tends machines that crush, shave, cut, or cube ice: Pulls blocks of ice into working area with tongs, and breaks ice into chunks, using ice pick or pronged bar. Feeds ice into hoppers of crushing or shaving machines. Places bag under discharge chute and pulls lever to fill bag with crushed or shaved ice. Ties wire around bag, marks weight on bag, and slides bag into storage room. Cuts blocks of ice to specified size, using handsaw, power saw, or heated shearblade. Pushes sections of ice over series of rotating saws that cut it into layers, rows, and cubes. May be designated according to work performed as Cube Cutter (food prep., nec); Ice Crusher (any industry).
GOE: 06.04.15 STRENGTH: H GED: R1 M1 L1 SVP: 2 DLU: 77

529.685-154 LABORER, STARCH FACTORY (grain-feed mills)

Tends equipment, such as grinders and mixers, and performs any combination of following tasks to convert vegetables and grain, such as potatoes, corn, and wheat, into starch: Transports grain or vegetable from storage, using lift truck, opens sacks, and dumps materials into chute or conveyor leading to grinding mill. Tends hammermill that removes foreign matter and grinds grain or vegetable into particles to form starch paste. Turns valves and starts pumps and paddle agitators to transfer starch solution to settling vat, flush impurities from surface of solution, using water hose, drain water, and mix fresh water with settled starch. Adds and mixes chemicals to starch milk as directed. Starts pump, centrifuges, and driers to remove excess moisture from white (purified) starch. Fills and weighs bags of dried starch and transports bags to storage, using lift or handtruck. May be designated Door Slinger (grain-feed mills) when opening and closing lever-actuated doors of starch kiln.
GOE: 06.04.15 STRENGTH: H GED: R2 M1 L1 SVP: 3 DLU: 77

529.685-158 LARD REFINER (meat products; oils & grease)

Tends equipment that cooks animal fat, and filters and bleaches oil: Cooks fat in steam-jacketed kettle. Turns valve to admit rendered oil to agitator tank. Starts agitator, and turns valve to heat tank. Dumps specified amount of fuller's

earth (bleaching agent) into tank. Turns valves to transfer oil through filter drums into storage tank. May add preservative solution to lard in mixing tank and press button to blend ingredients. May be designated according to material handled as Oleo-Hasher-And-Renderer (oils & grease).
GOE: 06.04.15 STRENGTH: M GED: R2 M1 L1 SVP: 3 DLU: 77

529.685-162   LINKING-MACHINE OPERATOR (meat products)
Tends one or more machines that automatically tie stuffed casings into links to form meat products, such as frankfurters, sausages, and wieners: Threads string into tying mechanism of machine and turns screws to regulate length of links. Starts machine and feeds end of stuffed casing into machine. Hangs string of linked casings on racks or rods for transfer to smokeroom.
GOE: 06.04.15 STRENGTH: L GED: R2 M1 L1 SVP: 2 DLU: 77

529.685-166   MEAT BLENDER (can. & preserv.)
Tends machinery that grinds and mixes frozen meat with water according to formula for use in baby food: Opens cartons of specified weight meat and places specified weight into automatic dumping mechanism of grinder. Turns valves and presses buttons to start grinder, conveyor, mixing machine, and pump that grind and blend meat with specified amount of water, and transfer mixture to storage tanks. Observes conveyor to prevent jamming and rakes meat from jammed conveyor into mixing machine. Occassionally weighs, cuts, and adds additional chunks of meat into grinder to meet batch weight specifications, using platform scale and electric bandsaw. Records batches processed.
GOE: 06.04.15 STRENGTH: H GED: R2 M2 L2 SVP: 2 DLU: 77

529.685-170   MOISTURE-MACHINE TENDER (tobacco)
Tends moisture-machine that automatically moistens filler tobacco preparatory to processing: Pushes button to start automatic machine which forces prongs through boxes of tobacco to release preset amount of steam. Observes gauges to ensure that specified amount of steam pressure is maintained. Stops machine and notifies supervisor of machine malfunctions.
GOE: 06.04.15 STRENGTH: L GED: R2 M1 L1 SVP: 2 DLU: 77

529.685-174   NUT ROASTER (can. & preserv.) alternate titles: cooker; oven roaster; roaster
Tends equipment that roasts, blanches, and cleans shelled nuts: Sets temperature and time controls on oven for roasting process. Fills trays with nuts by hand and places trays in oven, or dumps nuts into feeder bin of screen conveyorized cooker or rotary drum in oven. Removes sample of nuts from oven, using spoon, compares nuts with color standard, and adjusts time and temperature controls of oven to ensure specified roasting. Removes specified number of trays of roasted nuts from oven for further processing, or pulls lever to empty roasted nuts from rotary oven into bin. Smooths out nuts in bin, using rake. Pushes bin over forced draft air vent to cool nuts. Tilts bin by hand or by hoist to dump cooled nuts into hopper of machines that remove skins, sprouts, stones, shell particles, and dirt, and starts machine. May immerse and roast nuts in hot oil bath. May coat nuts with liquid gum arabic prior to roasting to provide adhesive surface for salt. May sprinkle nuts with salt, garlic, cheese, or other seasonings by hand or by using automatic equipment. May pack nuts in bags or sacks. May be designated according to kind of nut roasted as Almond Roaster (can. & preserv.); Peanut Roaster (can. & preserv.); or according to whether oil is used as Dry Roaster (can. & preserv.); Wet Roaster (can. & preserv.).
GOE: 06.04.15 STRENGTH: H GED: R2 M2 L2 SVP: 3 DLU: 77

529.685-178   PEANUT-BUTTER MAKER (can. & preserv.; food prep., nec)
Tends machines that make peanut butter: Opens valves to fill mixing chamber with roasted nuts, and adds specified amounts of salt, sugar, and homogenizing ingredients. Observes gauges to determine if temperature in mixing chamber is within specified limits. Turns dial to regulate speed of pumps which force mixture through grinding chambers. Opens valves to allow mixture to flow from one grinding chamber to another to obtain specified texture, and transfer ground mixture into cooling mixer. May tend automatic equipment that roasts nuts, fills, labels, and caps containers, and packs containers in shipping cartons.
GOE: 06.04.15 STRENGTH: M GED: R2 M1 L1 SVP: 4 DLU: 77

529.685-182   PLUG-CUTTING-MACHINE OPERATOR (tobacco) alternate titles: plug-cutter; plug-cutting-and-wrapping-machine operator
Tends machine that cuts plugs of chewing or smoking tobacco into plugs of specified size for retailing: Loads plugs into hopper that discharges plugs onto conveyor leading to knives. Starts flow of flavoring onto knives or wipes knives with cloth dipped in flavoring to lubricate cutters. May scrape cutting knives with blade to remove tobacco particles. May tend cellophane-wrapping machine in tandem with cutter. May pack plugs in cartons manually.
GOE: 06.04.15 STRENGTH: L GED: R1 M1 L1 SVP: 2 DLU: 77

529.685-186   PLUG-OVERWRAP-MACHINE TENDER (tobacco)
Tends machine that wraps lumps of chewing tobacco in *homogenized leaf* prior to further processing: Mounts roll of homogenized leaf on holding rod of machine and guides leaf through rollers and under cutter. Pours glue into container. Starts machine and observes operation of machine to detect malfunctions. Stops machine when malfunction or jam-up occurs, and removes lump end leaf from machine to clear jam-up. Sprays machine parts with alcohol to prevent tobacco sticking and notifies mechanic when machine requires adjustment or repair.

GOE: 06.04.15 STRENGTH: M GED: R2 M1 L2 SVP: 3 DLU: 77

529.685-190   PRESERVATIVE FILLER, MACHINE (can. & preserv.) alternate titles: syruper
Tends machine that automatically dispenses brine, oil, salt, or syrup into containers of food products prior to lidding or capping: Starts machine and turns valves to allow flow of solution. Feeds or guides containers onto conveyor that carries containers under dispensing nozzles. Observes filling operation and adjusts flow of solution or material to optimum volume. Removes broken jars from conveyor and deposits jars in waste receptacles. May fill machine reservoirs with dry salt, oil, brine, or sugar solution as required. May be designated according to solution used as Briner, Machine (can. & preserv.); Oil Dispenser (can. & preserv.); Syruper, Machine (can. & preserv.).
GOE: 06.04.15 STRENGTH: L GED: R2 M1 L2 SVP: 3 DLU: 77

529.685-194   RAW-JUICE WEIGHER (sugar & conf.)
Tends equipment that automatically weighs specified amount of raw sugarcane juice to fill processing tanks: Opens valves to admit juice and lime solution. Adds chemicals to solution to remove impurities. Takes samples of juice for laboratory analysis. Washes tanks, using water hose.
GOE: 06.04.15 STRENGTH: L GED: R1 M1 L1 SVP: 2 DLU: 77

529.685-198   REFINING-MACHINE OPERATOR (oils & grease)
Tends machine that refines crude oils, such as soybean, cottonseed, and peanut: Turns valve to pump oil and caustic solution from storage tanks into machine tanks as specified. Starts machine to separate caustic from oil by centrifugal force. Sets thermostat, observes gauges, and regulates valves to maintain prescribed temperature in wash and dryer tanks. Turns valves to pump mixtures to wash and dryer tank to remove byproducts with water, and impurities with heat. Turns valve to pump refined oil to storage tanks. Cleans bowls, using water and steam. May test samples of crude and refined oil to determine specific gravity and free fatty acid content, using hydrometer and refractometer. May be designated according to type of machine tended as Sharples-Machine Operator (oils & grease).
GOE: 06.04.15 STRENGTH: L GED: R3 M2 L2 SVP: 3 DLU: 77

529.685-202   RENDERING-EQUIPMENT TENDER (meat products)
Tends equipment, such as cooking tanks, expellers or presses, driers, grinders, auxiliary pumps, and conveyors to render and process offal for use as plant and animal foods, performing any combination of following tasks: Opens valves and starts pumps and conveyors to move materials through rendering process. Observes temperature gauges and rate of flow and condition of materials passing through cookers, expellers, and grinders, and adjusts valves and rate of flow. Shovels or dumps guts, bones, and other inedible or condemned parts of slaughtered animals into chute leading to grinder and cooking tanks. Drains oil from surface of cooked offal and opens tank discharge to drop cooked material into trough leading to expellers. Starts grinding and screening equipment to pulverize and sift tankage, cracklings, and cooked blood for sacking. Hangs sack on discharge hopper of screening equipment and opens gate to discharge specified amount of material into sack. Ties or sews mouth of sack. May be known according to specific work performed as Cooker And Presser (meat products); Crackling-Press Operator (meat products); Oil-Expeller (meat products); Press Operator (meat products); Tallow Pumper (meat products); Tankage-Grinder Operator (meat products); Tank Charger (meat products).
GOE: 06.04.15 STRENGTH: M GED: R3 M2 L2 SVP: 3 DLU: 77

529.685-206   RESERVE OPERATOR (tobacco)
Relieves workers on fresh-work cigar machine: Feeds filler tobacco to machine [FILLER FEEDER (tobacco)]. Tends unit of machine that cuts and feeds binder leaves [BINDER LAYER (tobacco)]. Tends unit that cuts and feeds wrappers [WRAPPER LAYER (tobacco)]. Inspects finished cigars [FRESH-WORK INSPECTOR (tobacco)].
GOE: 06.04.15 STRENGTH: L GED: R2 M1 L1 SVP: 3 DLU: 77

529.685-210   SANDWICH-MACHINE OPERATOR (dairy products)
Tends machine that forms and wraps ice cream sandwiches: Attaches tube lines from freezer machine to ice cream forming head, using wrench. Assembles dispenser trays, wafer extruders, sandwich pusher, paper tucker, and elevator table to form sandwich of specified size. Threads roll of wrapping paper from spindle through guide rolls to wrapping box. Turns tension screws to obtain desired size wrapper. Starts machine and turns valve to start flow of ice cream from freezer through forming head past wafer extruders. Observes formed ice cream ribbon as it is automatically enclosed with wafers, cut at specified intervals, and wrapped. Turns valve and stops machine to remove jammed or defectively formed and wrapped sandwiches. Turns handwheel or presses jogging button to alter position of elevator table or wrapping paper to correct jam. May replace worn electrical or mechanical parts.
GOE: 06.04.15 STRENGTH: L GED: R2 M1 L2 SVP: 2 DLU: 77

529.685-214   SHELLFISH-PROCESSING-MACHINE TENDER (can. & preserv.)
Tends washing, blanching, steaming, brining, peeling, or shucking machine that prepares shellfish for canning, freezing, or fresh packing: Opens valves to admit water, steam, or air under pressure into machine vats, and adds specified quantities of additives, such as salt or food coloring. Lowers baskets of shellfish into vats by hand or hoist, or pushes cars of shellfish into steamer chamber. Closes door of steamer chamber, clamps fasteners over edges of door, and turns wing nuts to secure door. Starts conveyors that move product through machines

or into weighing carts. May turn screws to adjust tension of peeler, using wrench. May tend machines that slice, grind, and tenderize clam meat. May be designated according to machine tended as Clam-Shucking-Machine Tender (can. & preserv.); Shrimp-Peeling-Machine Tender (can. & preserv.); or by shellfish processed as Clam Steamer (can. & preserv.); Crab Steamer (can. & preserv.); Oyster Washer (can. & preserv.); Shrimp Blancher (can. & preserv.).
GOE: 06.04.15 STRENGTH: H GED: R2 M1 L1 SVP: 2 DLU: 78

529.685-218   SPICE FUMIGATOR (food prep., nec)
Tends equipment that fumigates incoming shipments of spices to kill insects: Stacks sacks, boxes, and cartons of spices in fumigating tank; or moves loaded pallet into fumigating room, using handtruck. Starts exhaust pump or opens valve on carbon dioxide pressure cylinder to remove or force air from fumigating tank or room. Pours specified quantities of liquid fumigants, such as ethylene oxide, into container in fumigating tank; or opens valve on pressure cylinder to admit specified amounts of gaseous fumigant into tank or room. Opens ventilating valves and starts vacuum pump or blower to remove fumigants after specified time. Removes spices from fumigating tank or room. May be required to hold fumigator's license issued by local health department.
GOE: 06.04.15 STRENGTH: H GED: R3 M2 L2 SVP: 2 DLU: 77

529.685-222   SPREADER OPERATOR, AUTOMATIC (tobacco) alternate titles: strip feeder
Tends machine that spreads tobacco evenly onto conveyor belt. Places saratoga filled with tobacco on hydraulic lift and starts machine. Pulls lever to hoist saratoga and dump tobacco into hopper of machine where prong-studded shaft fluffs tobacco and spreads tobacco evenly onto conveyor belt. Cleans tobacco from prongs of shaft.
GOE: 06.04.40 STRENGTH: M GED: R1 M1 L1 SVP: 2 DLU: 77

529.685-226   STEAMER (beverage) alternate titles: soaker-soda worker; soda worker
Tends equipment to maintain caustic soda solution and water levels and temperatures in bottle-washing machine: Observes thermometers and gauges, and turns valves to heat soda solution and water to specified temperatures and fill compartments of bottle-washing machine to specified levels. Collects sample of soda solution for laboratory analysis. Opens valve to allow used soda solution to drain into reclaiming tank. May maintain water and temperature levels in pasteurizer and label machines.
GOE: 06.04.39 STRENGTH: L GED: R2 M1 L1 SVP: 2 DLU: 77

529.685-230   STEM-DRYER MAINTAINER (tobacco)
Cleans redrying machines and keeps tobacco-stem offal removed from shaker-screen: Pulls dust pans from redryers and empties pans into box. Blows dust and fine scrap from under machines and work area, using airhose. Pushes full boxes of offal from shaker-screen to collecting point and replaces full box with empty one. Beats dust from canvas dust-collecting tubes, using wooden stick.
GOE: 06.04.39 STRENGTH: M GED: R1 M1 L1 SVP: 2 DLU: 77

529.685-234   SUCKER-MACHINE OPERATOR (sugar & conf.) alternate titles: lollypop-machine operator; lollypop maker
Tends machine that automatically forms lollypops of specified shape on ends of wooden sticks: Turns steam valve to heat candy hopper or rollers of candy-spinning unit. Pours candy into machine hopper and fills receptacle with sucker sticks. Monitors and adjusts machine to prevent jamming.
GOE: 06.04.15 STRENGTH: M GED: R1 M1 L1 SVP: 3 DLU: 77

529.685-238   TABLET-MACHINE OPERATOR (dairy products)
Tends machine that compresses malted milk powder into tablets: Dumps powder into hopper, using scoop, and starts machine. Moves hopper lever to deposit specified amount of powder into forming dies in machine table. Examines tablets to determine thickness and hardness, and turns wheel to adjust positions of forming dies and punch dies in machine head.
GOE: 06.04.15 STRENGTH: L GED: R2 M1 L1 SVP: 2 DLU: 77

529.685-242   TANK PUMPER, PANELBOARD (beverage)
Tends central control panelboard, connected to series of pumps and hose lines, to transfer whiskeys from storage tanks to bottling tanks: Connects hose lines from panelboard to series of electric pumps with lines connected to storage tanks and bottling tanks. Starts pumps and turns valves on panelboard to transfer and regulate flow of whiskey from storage tank to bottling tank. Reads meters on panelboard to ascertain when tanks are filled. Turns valves on panelboard to admit compressed air through valves and hose lines to clear excess whiskey from lines. Collects whiskey samples for laboratory analysis.
GOE: 06.04.15 STRENGTH: M GED: R2 M1 L1 SVP: 3 DLU: 77

529.685-246   TAPPER (beverage) alternate titles: dropper; dropper, tank storage
Tends equipment that taps (drains) beer storage tanks to maintain continuous flow of beer to filtering machine: Couples hose lines to pumps, tanks, and filtering machine. Observes meters and turns valves on gas tank to admit specified amounts of carbon dioxide into storage tank to create effervescence in beer, and to apply external pressure on tank to counteract internal stress. Observes gauge to determine when to turn valves to switch from empty to full tank. Opens valve to release counter pressure on empty tanks and uncouples hoses.
GOE: 06.04.15 STRENGTH: L GED: R2 M2 L1 SVP: 2 DLU: 77

529.685-250   VOTATOR-MACHINE OPERATOR (meat products; oils & grease)
Tends one or more machines that cool liquid margarine, lard, or shortening, and knead solidified material preparatory to packaging: Starts kneading unit of machine. Opens valve to admit liquid material to cooling unit that solidifies it and to transfer solids to kneading unit that imparts smooth texture. Observes gauges and adjusts controls to keep specified temperature and pressure of material in cooling and kneading units. Turns valves to regulate flow of processed material into hoppers of packaging machine. May clean lines and equipment, using pressurized steam and nitrogen gas.
GOE: 06.04.15 STRENGTH: L GED: R2 M1 L1 SVP: 3 DLU: 77

529.685-254   WASH-HOUSE WORKER (beverage)
Tends equipment to clean and spray interiors of aluminum or steel beer barrels or kegs, performing any combination of following tasks: Tends drilling machine to remove plastic or wood cork from bunghole. Lifts barrel onto conveyor for transfer to washing or pitching machine. Tends washing or pitching machine that cleans or coats barrels with pitch. Observes gauges and thermometers and turns valves to maintain temperatures at specified operating levels. Dumps bags of pitch into machine pots. Screws metal plugs into tap and bungholes. Unscrews plugs from pitched barrels, wipes holes with rags to remove excess pitch, and hammers cork into taphole. Inserts light into barrel and inspects interior surfaces for dents, holes, dirt, and completeness of pitch coverage. Loads and unloads conveyors. Stacks barrels on floor.
GOE: 06.04.39 STRENGTH: M GED: R2 M1 L1 SVP: 2 DLU: 77

529.685-258   WASHER, AGRICULTURAL PRODUCE (agriculture; can. & preserv.; sugar & conf.; wholesale tr.)
Tends machine that washes raw fruits or vegetables, preparatory to processing, canning, freezing, or packing: Opens valve to fill machine with water and adds prescribed cleaning agents. Dumps raw fruits or vegetables into machine hopper and starts conveyor that carries produce through machine. Drains, cleans, and refills machine at designated intervals. May lubricate machine and make minor repairs. When operating washer with waxing unit attached, may be designated Washing-And-Waxing-Machine Operator (agriculture; can. & preserv.; wholesale tr.). May be designated according to commodity washed as Apple Washer (agriculture; can. & preserv.; wholesale tr.); Carrot Washer (agriculture; can. & preserv.; wholesale tr.); Orange Washer (agriculture; can. & preserv.; wholesale tr.).
GOE: 06.04.39 STRENGTH: L GED: R1 M1 L1 SVP: 2 DLU: 77

529.685-262   WHEAT CLEANER (grain-feed mills) alternate titles: bump-grader operator
Tends equipment that cleans, moisturizes, and cracks wheat for cereal products, preparatory to cooking: Starts conveyors to transfer wheat from storage to vibrating screens in grading and cleaning units. Sets thermostat at specified temperature to heat water used to wash grain and increase moisture content to designated value. Turns valves and moves controls to regulate flow of water and grain through washer and soaking bin and to transfer grain to grinder rolls for cracking. Observes process to correct conveyor jamming and to open plugged holes in separator screens.
GOE: 06.04.15 STRENGTH: L GED: R2 M1 L1 SVP: 3 DLU: 77

529.685-266   WRAPPER LAYER (tobacco) alternate titles: fresh-work wrapper-layer; long-filler-cigar roller, machine
Tends unit of fresh-work cigar machine that cuts wrapper leaf and wraps leaf around bunch: Spreads wrapper leaf over die of machine. Presses pedal to lower knife that cuts leaf. Releases pedal to raise knife and start mechanism that removes cut leaf and wraps it around bunch. Pastes portion of leaf over holes or tears to patch wrapper leaves.
GOE: 06.04.15 STRENGTH: L GED: R2 M1 L2 SVP: 3 DLU: 77

529.685-270   WRAPPER-LAYER-AND-EXAMINER, SOFT WORK (tobacco) alternate titles: scrap-filler-cigar roller, machine; shredded-filler cigar-maker, machine; shredded-filler-machine wrapper-layer; soft-work-cigar-machine operator
Tends soft-work cigar machine (turret machine) that rolls wrapper tobacco leaves around bunches to make cigars: Lays wrapper leaf on die of machine and presses treadle to lower knife that cuts leaf and to activate mechanism that draws cut leaf into machine and rolls leaf around bunch. Inspects finished cigars for defects as cigars emerge from machine. Pastes portions of leaf over holes or tears in wrappers. Discards defective cigars that cannot be repaired. Works in conjunction with BUNCH MAKER, MACHINE (tobacco) who supplies bunches to machine.
GOE: 06.04.15 STRENGTH: L GED: R1 M1 L1 SVP: 2 DLU: 77

529.685-274   X-RAY INSPECTOR (can. & preserv.; tobacco) alternate titles: fluoroscope operator
Inspects packaged tobacco products or jars of baby food to detect foreign matter, using x-ray equipment: Activates equipment and conveyor. Observes shadows cast on fluorescent screen by package or jar passing in front of x ray which indicates presence of foreign matter, such as sticks, stems, metal, or dirt. Removes defective packages or jars.
GOE: 06.03.02 STRENGTH: L GED: R2 M1 L1 SVP: 2 DLU: 77

529.685-278   YEAST WASHER (food prep., nec)
Tends equipment that washes, pasteurizes, and cools yeast cream (concentrated yeast suspension) used in manufacture of baker's yeast and yeast food: Opens valve to pump yeast cream into tank, and adds water to yeast cream to remove traces of wort adhering to yeast cells. Pumps yeast cream and wash water to storage tank preparatory to centrifugal separation. Turns valves to admit steam into jacket of pasteurizer and circulate brine through cooling

coils of cooler. Pumps yeast cream, that has been washed and separated from wash water, to pasteurizer and through cooling equipment to storage tank. Tests cream for acidity, using pH meter, and adds necessary chemicals to attain required acidity level.
GOE: 06.04.15 STRENGTH: L GED: R3 M2 L3 SVP: 2 DLU: 77

529.685-282 CAN-FILLING-AND-CLOSING-MACHINE TENDER (can. & preserv.)
Tends machines that automatically wash, fill, and seal cans in cannery: Pushes buttons and levers on control panel to start machines and monitors machine operations to verify that can washer, can food and liquid filler, can sealer, and conveyor mechanisms function in prescribed sequence. Observes cans leaving machines to detect defects, such as overfilled cans or misaligned lids. Pushes buttons to stop machines when machines malfunction, and notifies MAINTENANCE MECHANIC (any industry) 638.281-014 of detected defects.
GOE: 06.04.15 STRENGTH: L GED: R2 M1 L1 SVP: 2 DLU: 86

529.685-286 CIGAR-WRAPPER TENDER, AUTOMATIC (tobacco)
Tends machines that automatically encase tobacco filler in layers of *homogenized leaf* tobacco to form cigars: Places rolls of homogenized leaf on spindles and guides leaf through tension guides and rollers of machine. Starts machine that automatically wraps filler with binder, mouth end of cigar with reinforcing band, and bunch with wrapper leaf to form cigar. Observes machine operation to detect malfunctions. Turns setscrews to adjust feed rate and stops, and clears machine when jam-up occurs. Examines cigars discharged from machine for defects, such as holes, tears, and insufficient filler, and for conformity to size specifications. Loads inspected cigars into storage containers.
GOE: 06.04.15 STRENGTH: L GED: R2 M1 L2 SVP: 2 DLU: 86

529.685-290 COOK, SOYBEAN SPECIALTIES (food prep., nec)
Tends equipment that processes soybeans to make soymilk, tofu, tempeh, and related products: Pours specified quantity of presoaked soybeans into mill hopper and depresses button to start grinding of beans and flow of bean mash into steam-jacketed cooker. Adds specified amount of water to mash and stirs mash to prevent burns and boilovers, using paddle. Sprays cooker exterior with water to maintain temperature in acceptable range. At end of prescribed time, turns valve to allow mash to flow into filter-lined hydraulic press tub. Depresses controls to actuate press that expresses soymilk from mash and pumps milk into vats. Heats and injects additives into soymilk to form curd, using syringe, skims off and discards surface residue, using ladle, and places weights on curd to express whey from curd to form tofu. Adds flavorings and stabilizers to soymilk and cooks and freezes mix, using steam cooker and freezing machine, to make soy ice cream. Cooks whole soybeans, mixes tempeh mold with cooked rice to make tempeh starter, and mixes incubated starter with cooked soybeans to form tempeh. Fills packaging containers with product, following prescribed procedures. May blend and cook bean mash or processed soy products with other ingredients to prepare ready-to-eat packaged foods. May be designated according to product prepared as Soyfreeze Operator (food prep., nec); Tempeh Maker (food prep., nec); Tofu Maker (food prep., nec).
GOE: 06.04.15 STRENGTH: M GED: R2 M1 L2 SVP: 2 DLU: 86

529.686-010 BUNDLES HANGER (tobacco) alternate titles: hands hanger
Hangs bundles of tobacco on sticks moving on chain conveyor to redrying machine: Removes bundles from table and observes color shade. Spreads leaves of bundle to form opening and hangs bundle on stick conveying bundles of similar color shade. May shake bundles that have been packed in hogsheads to loosen leaves prior to hanging bundles on stick [SHAKER (tobacco)].
GOE: 06.04.40 STRENGTH: L GED: R1 M1 L1 SVP: 1 DLU: 77

529.686-014 CANNERY WORKER (can. & preserv.)
Performs any combination of following duties to can, freeze, preserve, or pack food products: Dumps or places food products in hopper, on sorting table, or on conveyor. Sorts or grades products according to size, color, or quality. Feeds products into processing equipment, such as washing, refrigerating, peeling, coring, pitting, trimming, grinding, dicing, cooking, or slicing machines. Trims, peels, and slices products with knife or paring tool. Feeds empty containers onto conveyor or forming machines. Fills containers, using scoop or filling form, or packs by hand [PACKAGER, HAND (any industry) 920.587-018]. Counts, weighs, or tallies processed items according to specifications. Inspects and weighs filled containers to ensure product conforms to quality and weight standards. Places filled containers on trays, racks, or into boxes. Loads, moves, or stacks containers by hand or handtruck, and cleans glass jar containers, using airhose. May be designated according to work performed as Dumper (can. & preserv.); Peeler (can. & preserv.); Sorter (can. &preserv.); Trimmer (can. & preserv.).
GOE: 06.04.15 STRENGTH: L GED: R2 M2 L2 SVP: 2 DLU: 78

529.686-018 CIGARETTE-MAKING-MACHINE-HOPPER FEEDER (tobacco)
Pushes box truck filled with cigarette tobacco to cigarette-making machine, and feeds double handful of tobacco into hopper.
GOE: 06.04.15 STRENGTH: M GED: R1 M1 L1 SVP: 2 DLU: 77

529.686-022 CUTLET MAKER, PORK (meat products)
Feeds machine that shreds and presses pork into cutlets: Cuts strips of pork into pieces, using knife. Dumps cut meat into feed hopper of machine that automatically shreds meat, presses shredded meat into cutlets, and stacks cutlets on waxed paper dividers. Weighs and packs cutlets into cardboard carton on weighing scales, according to work ticket specifications. Seals carton, using pneumatic staple gun.
GOE: 06.04.15 STRENGTH: M GED: R1 M1 L1 SVP: 2 DLU: 77

529.686-026 DAIRY HELPER (dairy products)
Performs any combination of following tasks in dairy: Scrubs bottles, pipes, fittings, and machines with cleaning solution, using brush. Attaches pipes and fittings to machines, using wrenches. Examines canned milk for dirt and odor, and dumps milk into receiving tank. Dumps milk, cream, butter, cottage cheese, and powdered milk into machine hoppers. Starts and stops machines and equipment. Cuts butter and cottage cheese, using knives. Wraps butter prints in foil or parchment and seals them with hot iron. Packs bulk butter into cartons. Pulls lever on hopper to fill cartons or bags with powdered milk. Weighs containers on scale. Places bottles, cartons, and packages into container, and moves to storage, using handtruck. Dumps empty bottles, cases, and cans onto conveyor for transfer to receiving, washing, or filling stations. May be designated according to product handled as Buttermaker Helper (dairy products); or stage of treatment as Pasteurizer Helper (dairy products).
GOE: 06.04.40 STRENGTH: H GED: R2 M1 L1 SVP: 2 DLU: 77

529.686-030 EGG WASHER, MACHINE (agriculture; wholesale tr.)
Feeds eggs into machine that removes earth, straw, and other residue from egg surface prior to shipment: Places eggs in saucer-like holder that carries eggs into machine where rotating brushes or water sprays remove residue. Removes cleaned eggs from discharge trough of machine and packs eggs in cases for shipment.
GOE: 06.04.39 STRENGTH: L GED: R1 M1 L1 SVP: 1 DLU: 77

529.686-034 FACTORY HELPER (sugar & conf.) alternate titles: general utility helper
Feeds candy processing and packaging machines and performs any combination of following tasks in candy manufacturing establishment, working individually or as interchangeable member of crew: Feeds one or more candy processing or packaging machines. Off bears, separates, counts, or culls finished or unfinished confectionery items and ingredients. Transfers molds, trays of candy, and supplies between storage, processing, and packing areas, using dolly or handtruck. Fills bags with bulk items, inserts toys or prizes in containers, and packs, labels, or wraps cartons for shipment. Assembles or forms confectionery items on assembly line or table, performing duties, such as pressing candy onto wafers to make candy waffles, and sprinkling sugar onto gum candy prior to cutting. Empties, cleans, or brushes molds, trays, utensils, containers, and equipment used in cooking, forming, and cooling candy. May be designated according to equipment fed as Raisin-Separator Operator (sugar & conf.); worker assisted as Coating-Machine Helper (sugar & conf.); material or product handled as Scrapper (sugar & conf.); or specific task as Steamer, Gum Candy (sugar & conf.); Vanilla-Chocolate-Coin Counter (sugar & conf.). When filling trays or vats with melted chocolate, fondant, or icing to facilitate work of hand dippers, is designated Table Filler (sugar & conf.). May be designated: Candy-Bar-Core Inspector (sugar & conf.); Candy Catcher (sugar & conf.); Candy Separator, Hard (sugar & conf.); Candy-Spreader Helper (sugar & conf.); Candy-Waffle Assembler (sugar & conf.); Caramel-Cutter Helper (sugar & conf.); Cut-Roll-Machine Offbearer (sugar & conf.); Cutting-Machine-Operator Helper (sugar & conf.); Lozenge-Maker Helper (sugar & conf.); Marshmallow Packer (sugar & conf.); Pan Washer, Hand (sugar & conf.); Sanding-Machine Operator Helper (sugar & conf.); Syrup Crystallizer (sugar & conf.); Spinner Helper (sugar & conf.); Sugar-Coating Hand (sugar & conf.); Toy Sorter (sugar & conf.).
GOE: 06.04.15 STRENGTH: M GED: R1 M1 L1 SVP: 2 DLU: 77

529.686-038 FEEDER-CATCHER, TOBACCO (tobacco) alternate titles: chute feeder; conveyor feeder; hopper feeder
Feeds or off bears tobacco leaves, bundles, or strips to or from processing machine: Loads tobacco onto conveyor or into chutes or hoppers with hands, pitchfork, or shovel, or dumps tobacco from tubs or hampers onto conveyor, using hoist or hydraulic lift. Places containers at discharge end of conveyor to catch tobacco. Pushes containers onto scales. Starts and stops conveyors. May spray tobacco leaves with water to moisten tobacco for further processing. May be designated according to task performed as Packing-Machine Feeder (tobacco); Rack Loader (tobacco) II.
GOE: 06.04.40 STRENGTH: H GED: R1 M1 L1 SVP: 2 DLU: 77

529.686-042 FILLER FEEDER (tobacco)
Feeds filler tobacco into fresh-work cigar machine: Places filler tobacco in slot on conveyor of machine. Feels tobacco in slot to determine whether sufficient filler tobacco for cigar is in slot.
GOE: 06.04.15 STRENGTH: L GED: R1 M1 L1 SVP: 2 DLU: 77

529.686-046 GENERAL HELPER (sugar & conf.)
Feeds, weighs, mixes, and transports ingredients and performs any combination of following tasks to assist other workers in processing chocolate and cocoa products: Moves ingredients from storage to production area, using handtruck. Weighs and mixes ingredients under supervision of MIXER OPERATOR (sugar & conf.) and SYRUP MAKER (sugar & conf.). Removes and stacks cocoa cakes from cocoa press machine, and transports them to storage area. Positions filled mold pans on belt conveyor moving through cooling tunnel. Feeds chocolate sheets into shaker and hammer mill that break sheets into bits.
GOE: 06.04.40 STRENGTH: H GED: R1 M1 L1 SVP: 2 DLU: 77

529.686-050 LABORER, CHEESEMAKING (dairy products)
Makes and cures cheese, performing any combination of following tasks: Cuts curd with knife or harp or separates curd with scoop to release whey and

firm curd. Pushes curd to back of vat or center of kettle with rake. Inserts strainer in vat or kettle outlet, assembles pipe or hose, and turns valve to drain whey. Pulls dip cloth (cheesecloth) through kettle to remove curd, or banks curd to side of vat with hands or rake to drain residual whey and mat curd. Stretches matted curd in hot water, using paddle, and cuts, weighs, and hand molds resulting elastic curd to make Italian cheeses. Cuts matted curd into measured slabs, piles slabs into banks, and turns them over periodically to obtain specified acidity and moisture. Feeds slabs into mill that cuts curd into cubes. Spreads specified amount of salt over cubes. Scoops, weighs, and dumps curd into assembled cheese hoops (perforated forms) with bucket. Places hoops in automatic press, turns screw of wooden handpress or places and turns filled molds on wheying table to remove whey and shape cheese. Dumps molded cheese into brine tank and turns it periodically or wets and rolls cheese in salt bed to flavor cheese and develop rind. Hangs cheese in rope basket or places, turns, and raises cheese to varying shelf levels in temperature controlled or smoked room to develop flavor, texture, eye formation and body, and to dry cheese surface. Pierces cheese or smears with cultured wash to promote mold growth. Wipes surface with grease or oil to soften rind and stop mold growth. Stamps cheese with date, vat, and company number. Wraps cheese in foil and places in wood or paper box. May be designated according to working area as Brine-Room Laborer (dairy products); Cellar Laborer (dairy products).
GOE: 06.04.28 STRENGTH: M GED: R2 M1 L1 SVP: 2 DLU: 77

529.686-054 LABORER, PIE BAKERY (bakery products)
Feeds automatic fruit peeling, coring, and slicing machine and performs any combination of duties involved in preprocessing fruit to be used in making pies and other bakery products: Feeds automatic machine that peels, cores, and slices fruit. Fills containers with sliced fruit from discharge conveyor or bin. Examines fruit and discards spoiled or damaged pieces. Manually loads and unloads trucks and transports material to and from storage area, using handtruck. Cleans machines and work areas, using broom, mop, brush, scraper, and rags.
GOE: 06.04.15 STRENGTH: M GED: R2 M1 L1 SVP: 2 DLU: 77

529.686-062 LONG-GOODS HELPER, MACHINE (food prep., nec) alternate titles: spaghetti press helper
Feeds and off bears macaroni containers on and off macaroni press, drier conveyors, and stick-handling equipment: Lays empty sticks (macaroni holders) on stick filler-feeder machine. Aligns out-of-line sticks moving along drier conveyor. Lifts sticks filled with moist macaroni into drier racks. Pushes racks into drying chambers. Fills, carries, and sets boxes of macaroni trimmings on drier shelves. Cleans and lubricates press and conveyor parts. May assist PRESS TENDER (food prep., nec) to install and remove macaroni press parts such as screw feeders, tubes and dies.
GOE: 06.04.15 STRENGTH: M GED: R2 M1 L1 SVP: 2 DLU: 77

529.686-066 PRESS MACHINE FEEDER (tobacco)
Feeds cigars into pressing machine that heats and presses cigars into square shape preparatory to banding and cellophaning. Removes cigars from handtruck and places cigars onto feed device of pressing machine.
GOE: 06.04.15 STRENGTH: L GED: R1 M1 L1 SVP: 2 DLU: 77

529.686-070 PRODUCTION HELPER (can. & preserv.; food prep., nec) alternate titles: general production worker
Feeds machine hoppers with ingredients, transports and packs finished products, and performs any combination of following tasks in food processing and packaging establishment: Dumps prepared ingredients into hoppers of grinding and mixing machines. Transfers finished products and raw materials about plant and warehouse, using handtruck. Stacks processed food in warehouse and coolers. Packs food products in paper bags and boxes. Loads packaging machines with bags, cans, and jars. Verifies weights of filled containers emerging from packaging machines. Removes foreign material from food on conveyor belts. Sprinkles grated cheese and other flavoring on foods.
GOE: 06.04.15 STRENGTH: M GED: R2 M1 L1 SVP: 2 DLU: 77

529.686-074 RACK LOADER I (tobacco) alternate titles: stick feeder
Removes sticks on which tobacco hands have been hung from conveyor of hanging machine and loads them on racks or onto conveyor leading to tobacco-drying machine. Pushes filled rack from work area and replaces with empty rack.
GOE: 06.04.40 STRENGTH: H GED: R1 M1 L1 SVP: 2 DLU: 77

529.686-078 RAW-CHEESE WORKER (dairy products)
Cuts out or scrapes mold, wax, and sediment to prepare natural cheese for packaging or making into process cheese by performing any combination of following tasks in cheese processing department of a dairy: Removes covers and wrappers from cheese, using knife, and dumps blocks of specified cheese from containers onto conveyor. Positions cheese block in conveyor cradle to expose desired surface and digs into plug holes or openings with knife. Removes mold, wax, and sediment from cheese surface, using handscraper or buffing wheel. Cuts cheese blocks into equal portions, using power wire cutter, power knife cutter, or wire. Places pieces of cheeses on truck, and weighs batch to obtain specified amounts for each cook. Dumps cut pieces of cheese into machine that grinds and transports it to next work station.
GOE: 06.04.28 STRENGTH: H GED: R2 M1 L1 SVP: 2 DLU: 77

529.686-082 STEAK TENDERIZER, MACHINE (meat products)
Feeds steaks into machine to tenderize meat. Places tenderized meat on paper separators and stacks them in piles for packaging.

GOE: 06.04.15 STRENGTH: L GED: R1 M1 L1 SVP: 2 DLU: 77

529.686-086 UTILITY WORKER (sugar & conf.)
Feeds machines that apply sugar coating and score (partially cut) sheets of chewing gum, preparatory to separating them into sticks, performing any combination of following tasks: Fills hopper of machine that automatically coats gum with powdered sugar to add flavor and prevent gum from sticking to rollers of scoring machine. Sprinkles sugar by hand on sheets of gum that are inadequately coated. Inspects sheets of gum for surface or scoring imperfections and removes defective sheets for reprocessing. Stacks empty trays on conveyor assembly that automatically fills trays with sheets of scored gum and stacks filled trays.
GOE: 06.04.15 STRENGTH: L GED: R2 M1 L1 SVP: 2 DLU: 77

529.687-010 BASKET FILLER (can. & preserv.)
Removes sealed cans or jars of food products from conveyor and dumps or stacks them in metal basket. May load basket in layers, using hydraulic mechanism to lower each layer to table level. May move baskets within plant or through cooling tank, using trucks or hoist.
GOE: 06.04.40 STRENGTH: L GED: R1 M1 L1 SVP: 1 DLU: 77

529.687-014 BIN CLEANER (beverage; grain-feed mills)
Scrapes, scours, and fumigates interior of grain bins: Climbs into grain bin or lowers self into bin on scaffolding or bucket seat, using block and tackle. Cleans interior of bin, using hand scrapers and brushes. Sprays interior of bin with insecticides and rodent deterrents or poisons, using spray gun. Closes bins for specified length of time. Airs bin and marks it for use. Places rodent traps and powders in designated areas in elevator. Maintains inventory of insecticides and rodent control supplies.
GOE: 06.04.39 STRENGTH: M GED: R1 M1 L1 SVP: 2 DLU: 77

529.687-018 BOX-TRUCK WASHER (meat products)
Cleans box-trucks (four-wheeled handtruck) used to move or store meat, grease, oleo, or inedible fat, using scrapers, wire brushes, handbrushes, steam, water, and detergent. May clean offal trays with water spray and rags and lubricate handtrucks with paraffin oil, using spray gun.
GOE: 06.04.39 STRENGTH: M GED: R1 M1 L1 SVP: 1 DLU: 77

529.687-022 BULK FILLER (can. & preserv.)
Fills wooden tubs, barrels, or containers with processed food products and covers with preservatives to preserve contents: Dumps food into barrel, tub, or container, and adds prescribed amounts of preservatives, such as salt, sugar, brine, syrup, or vinegar. Covers container with lid, waxed paper, or plastic. May weigh contents of container. May apply labels to outer surface of container. May be designated according to container filled as Barrel Filler (can. & preserv.); or product treated as Cabbage Salter (can. & preserv.).
GOE: 06.04.28 STRENGTH: H GED: R2 M1 L2 SVP: 3 DLU: 77

529.687-026 CASING GRADER (meat products) alternate titles: casing inspector; casing sorter; casing tester
Inspects and grades animal casings used as sausage skins: Removes casings from soaking tank. Cleans and inflates casing, using air or water hose. Places inflated casing between grading pegs to determine size. Squeezes casing to detect changes in circumference, damaged sections, or slime. Cuts out damaged sections, warts, and other blemishes, using knife. Places casings in rack or container according to size or condition of casing. May measure and cut casings to length. May pack and salt casings for shipment or reclaim cured casings for use.
GOE: 06.03.02 STRENGTH: L GED: R2 M1 L1 SVP: 2 DLU: 77

529.687-030 CASING SEWER (meat products) alternate titles: bung sewer
Sews sections of animal intestine to form casings for lunch meat and specialty meat products: Positions edges of dried intestines together, places strips of paper (liners) over intestines, and slides them under presser foot of sewing machine. Starts machine, and stitches edges of liner and end of intestines to form casings. Maintains count of casings sewed for company records. May inspect and grade casings [CASING GRADER (meat products)].
GOE: 06.04.28 STRENGTH: L GED: R2 M1 L1 SVP: 2 DLU: 77

529.687-034 CASING TIER (meat products) alternate titles: stuffed-casing tier
Closes ends of empty and filled meat casings with metal clips and string preparatory to hanging them for smoking or cooking: Attaches metal clip to one end of empty casing, using clipping tool. Twists open end of filled casing and ties it with string leaving loop for hanging. Cuts off excess string and casing, using scissors or knife. May be designated according to type of meat cased as Bulk-Sausage-Casing Tier-Off (meat products); Canadian-Bacon Tier (meat products); Hog Stomach Preparer (meat products). May tie lacing cord at regular intervals around bologna sausage to brace and support casing and be designated Bologna Lacer (meat products); or lace rolled ham and be designated Rolled-Ham Lacer (meat products).
GOE: 06.04.28 STRENGTH: L GED: R1 M1 L1 SVP: 1 DLU: 77

529.687-038 CHAR-DUST CLEANER AND SALVAGER (sugar & conf.)
Cleans floors and equipment, and performs following duties in char-house: Cleans and collects char dust from floors, pump basins, pipelines, and tank tops. Observes operating machinery, such as char-draw mechanisms, spreaders, and char-collectors, for blockades or malfunctioning, and reports irregularities

to superiors. Fills sacks with salvaged char dust and sews, weighs, and stores sacks. Obtains samples of char and takes them to laboratory for analysis. Delivers requisitions, runs errands, and supplies filter blankets and wedges to other workers.
GOE: 06.04.40 STRENGTH: H GED: R2 M1 L1 SVP: 2 DLU: 77

529.687-042 CIGAR INSPECTOR (tobacco) alternate titles: cigar-packing examiner; final cigar and box examiner
Inspects cigars for imperfections and verifies quality of packing and labeling: Examines cigars for size, shape, and imperfections in wrappers. Replaces defective cigars in boxes. Examines banded and cellophane-wrapped cigars to determine whether bands are positioned and cellophane is applied according to standards. Observes boxes of cigars to determine whether label is in specified position. May open lid of box to inspect cigars and close and nail lid onto box after inspection, using handtool.
GOE: 06.03.02 STRENGTH: L GED: R1 M1 L1 SVP: 2 DLU: 77

529.687-046 COFFEE WEIGHER (food prep., nec)
Weighs sacks of specified varieties of coffee and dumps coffee into chute leading to coffee-cleaning or blending machines. May record sack weights.
GOE: 06.03.02 STRENGTH: H GED: R1 M1 L1 SVP: 1 DLU: 77

529.687-050 COOK HELPER (can. & preserv.)
Assists COOK, KETTLE (beverage; can. & preserv.; grain-feed mills) to cook food products, such as juices, meats, fruits, or preserves, preparatory to canning or preserving, performing any combination of following duties: Weighs or measures ingredients, such as sugar, salt, meat, lard, berries, or fruit, according to formula, using platform scale, weighing hopper, and measuring containers. Transfers materials to cooking area by hand or handtruck. Turns valves to admit steam to kettle-heating jacket, and dumps ingredients into kettle to precook or melt them. Cleans cooking kettles and containers, using water and pressurized steam. May stir contents of cooking kettle with paddle and skim off foam or foreign materials, using ladle or spoon. May stack and tally containers. May be designated according to food product being processed as Cook Helper, Fruit (can. & preserv.); Cook Helper, Juice (can. & preserv.); Cook Helper, Meat (can. & preserv.); Cook Helper, Preserves (can. & preserv.). Performs other duties as described under HELPER (any industry) Master Title.
GOE: 06.04.28 STRENGTH: M GED: R2 M2 L2 SVP: 3 DLU: 77

529.687-054 COOKER CLEANER (can. & preserv.) alternate titles: coil cleaner
Cleans coils and inside surfaces of steam kettles used for cooking foods: Climbs inside of kettle and scrubs coils and interior surface of kettle, using cleanser, steel wool, and soap. Opens drain valve at bottom of kettle and sprays water over interior of kettle to flush soap, steel wool, cleanser, and food particles through drain.
GOE: 06.04.39 STRENGTH: M GED: R1 M1 L1 SVP: 2 DLU: 77

529.687-058 DEFLECTOR OPERATOR (beverage) alternate titles: lights inspector; wine-bottle inspector
Inspects bottled beer or wine for foreign matter and defective bottles: Examines contents of bottles for foreign matter, such as dirt and barrel or tank sediment, and bottles for defects, such as cracks, damaged caps or corks, and nicks. Observes bottles on conveyor belt passing in front of light and reflecting mirror or lighted frosted glass box or holds bottles up to unshielded light bulb, to examine bottle and content. Stores rejected or defective bottles in containers for disposal.
GOE: 06.03.02 STRENGTH: L GED: R2 M1 L1 SVP: 2 DLU: 77

529.687-062 DIE CLEANER (food prep., nec)
Cleans dies used to extrude dough to form macaroni: Unbolts and removes dies from presses, using wrench and screwdriver, and places dies in tub of water to soften dough residue. Adjusts die-washing-machine platform to accommodate shape of die, positions die on platform, and turns faucet to force jets of water through dies. Scrapes dough residue from die holes, using handtool. Replaces dies on press or places dies on storage shelves. May inspect dies on presses for cleanliness or damage. May verify alignment of die pins, using preset gauge. May record location and condition of dies.
GOE: 06.04.39 STRENGTH: H GED: R2 M1 L2 SVP: 3 DLU: 77

529.687-066 DISTILLERY WORKER, GENERAL (beverage)
Cleans, transports and applies identifying data on steel drums in liquor distilling plant, performing any combination of following duties: Cleans interior of metal drums, using steam-cleaning apparatus, or interiors of barrels by rinsing them with water and alcohol. Stencils identifying information on barrelheads, using paint brush or spray gun to paint over cut-out stencils, or cuts identifying information on barrelheads, using metal dies and mallet. Paints or scrapes heads of used barrels to remove identifying information. Removes bungs from drums, using wrench or chisel and hammer. Rolls barrels into position for filling. Empties barrels or drums filled with liquor into dumping trough. Stamps serial numbers on barrelheads, using hand-stamping machine. Empties cartons of empty whiskey bottles on conveyor belt for filling. Stacks cartons filled with whiskey bottles. Repairs damaged cartons, using adhesive tape to cover tears and rips in cartons. Removes metal sealing rings from improperly labeled whiskey bottles preparatory to removal of labels. May be known according to specific work performed as Barrel Cutter (beverage); Barrel Roller (beverage); Barrel Scraper (beverage); Bung Remover (beverage); Carton Repairer (beverage); Drum Cleaner (beverage); Drum Sealer (beverage); Dumper (beverage).

GOE: 06.04.40 STRENGTH: H GED: R2 M1 L1 SVP: 2 DLU: 77
529.687-070 DISTRIBUTOR-CLEANER (tobacco) alternate titles: floor hand
Cleans production department in tobacco processing plant and distributes tobacco to workers: Sweeps floors [CLEANER, INDUSTRIAL (any industry)]. Sorts stems from waste and puts stems in bin. Conveys tobacco to workers, using handtruck [MATERIAL HANDLER (any industry)]. Stacks tie-bands into tray and distributes tie-bands to workers.
GOE: 06.04.40 STRENGTH: H GED: R1 M1 L1 SVP: 1 DLU: 77

529.687-074 EGG CANDLER (any industry)
Inspects eggs to ascertain quality and fitness for consumption or incubation, according to prescribed standards: Observes eggs moving on conveyor over light, or holds eggs before shielded light or rolls them over lighted glass plate to render egg translucent. Observes shell color and texture, and internal characteristics, such as streaks, shadings, discolorations, size and position of yolk, and size of air cell. Places spoiled and substandard eggs in cases. Packs salable eggs in cartons or releases them on conveyor belt for packing by other workers. May break substandard eggs in container for further processing. May grade eggs according to size, shape, color, and weight and be designated Egg Grader (any industry).
GOE: 06.03.01 STRENGTH: L GED: R2 M1 L1 SVP: 2 DLU: 77

529.687-078 FILLER-SHREDDER HELPER (tobacco) alternate titles: filler-shredding-machine loader; filler-sifter helper
Assists FILLER SHREDDER, MACHINE (tobacco) to cut tobacco leaves into shreds and clean shredded tobacco for use as cigar filler. Performs other duties as described under HELPER (any industry) Master Title.
GOE: 06.04.28 STRENGTH: M GED: R1 M1 L1 SVP: 2 DLU: 77

529.687-082 FISH-BIN TENDER (can. & preserv.)
Opens chute gates to release fish into various bins according to species, and onto conveyor for transfer to cleaning machine. Expedites flow of fish, using wooden rake, hoe, or water hose. Shovels chipped ice into bins to preserve fish. Sorts fish according to species and size, and discards spoiled or damaged fish.
GOE: 06.04.28 STRENGTH: M GED: R2 M1 L1 SVP: 2 DLU: 77

529.687-086 FISH-EGG PACKER (can. & preserv.) alternate titles: bait packer
Cleans and packs fish eggs for commercial purposes: Rubs clusters of eggs over screen to separate eggs according to size. Dumps eggs into vat of cleaning solution to remove blood and into barrel of brine to cure eggs. Shovels processed eggs into containers for shipment, or fills jars with eggs, using scoop. Works as member of crew. May prepare curing and cleaning solutions, according to formula.
GOE: 06.04.28 STRENGTH: M GED: R1 M1 L1 SVP: 2 DLU: 77

529.687-090 FRESH-WORK INSPECTOR (tobacco) alternate titles: racker; selector; table inspector
Inspects cigars from fresh-work cigar machine to determine conformance to standards: Weighs random bundles of cigars to determine whether cigars are of prescribed weight and notifies SUPERVISOR, CIGAR-MAKING MACHINE (tobacco) when weight is not standard. Inspects cigars for broken tobacco wrappers, soft spots, defective patches, and variations from standard length and discards defective cigars. May place full boxes of perfect cigars in case.
GOE: 06.03.02 STRENGTH: L GED: R2 M2 L2 SVP: 3 DLU: 77

529.687-094 GENERAL HELPER (oils & grease)
Performs any combination of duties, such as carrying supplies to work area, forming cartons for packing, feeding cans onto conveyor, removing scrap, cleaning work area, and reclaiming oil stock from damaged containers. Dumps containers into steam tub, covers tub with canvas, and opens valve to introduce heat to melt and reclaim contents. Cleans work area using brooms, mops, and detergents.
GOE: 06.04.40 STRENGTH: M GED: R1 M1 L1 SVP: 2 DLU: 77

529.687-098 GRADER (can. & preserv.)
Examines, classifies, and separates seafood according to size, quality, color, condition, or species at receiving station or on conveyor line. May record grade on ticket and attach ticket to filled container. May be designated according to product graded as Clam Grader (can. & preserv.); Fish Grader (can. & preserv.).
GOE: 06.03.02 STRENGTH: L GED: R2 M1 L2 SVP: 3 DLU: 78

529.687-102 GRADER, DRESSED POULTRY (meat products)
Examines and grades dressed poultry: Removes dressed poultry from conveyor, and examines color of skin, feels poultry for prescence of bruises, deformities, and pin feathers, and grades accordingly for quality and size. Sorts poultry into specified containers according to grade. May weigh filled containers and record weight of each grade of poultry.
GOE: 06.03.02 STRENGTH: L GED: R2 M1 L2 SVP: 3 DLU: 77

529.687-106 GRADER, GREEN MEAT (meat products) alternate titles: fresh-meat grader; pickling grader
Inspects and sorts pork cuts, such as hams, shoulders, bellies, and fatbacks, preparatory to curing: Examines and feels meat for defects, such as bruises, thickness of skin, shape, and broken leg bones. Segregates pork cuts not meeting standards. Weighs and segregates cuts according to weight and size. May

push thermometer into meat to ascertain if it is too cold for processing. May stamp government inspection seal on approved lean shoulders, using rubber stamp.
GOE: 06.03.02 STRENGTH: L GED: R2 M1 L2 SVP: 3 DLU: 77

529.687-110 GRAIN PICKER (grain-feed mills)
Separates and weighs samples of grain preparatory to grading: Pours grain sample into hopper of sample divider and pulls lever to allow grain to fall through divider into two receptacles. Removes and weighs specific amount of grain from each receptacle to obtain representative but reduced sample. Pours sample into cleaning mill (dockage tester) or through sieve of standard mesh to remove foreign matter. Smells and examines sample to determine if grain is sour or musty, or to detect damage from excessive heat or moisture. Pours grain sample into standard quart kettle, weighs sample, and reads conversion chart to obtain weight per bushel. Separates damaged, weathered, soil-stained, and undeveloped grain from grain with no defects and places grain in separate containers. May remove grain sample from incoming shipments.
GOE: 06.03.02 STRENGTH: L GED: R2 M2 L2 SVP: 2 DLU: 77

529.687-114 INSPECTOR (sugar & conf.)
Inspects candy or chewing gum in containers or on conveyor to ensure that it is formed, coated, cupped, wrapped, or packed according to plant standards: Weighs containers [WEIGHER, PRODUCTION (any industry) 929.687-062]. Rewraps, recups, rearranges, or replaces pieces not meeting standards. May stamp date of inspection on boxes or return them to packing department with reason for rejection. May pack boxes in shipping cartons.
GOE: 06.03.02 STRENGTH: L GED: R2 M1 L2 SVP: 2 DLU: 77

529.687-118 INSPECTOR, CANNED FOOD RECONDITIONING (can. & preserv.) alternate titles: smeller
Smells opened cans of food products as they pass on conveyor to detect · spoilage as indicated by odor. Sets aside rejected cans of food for disposal.
GOE: 06.03.02 STRENGTH: L GED: R2 M1 L2 SVP: 4 DLU: 77

529.687-122 KISS SETTER, HAND (sugar & conf.) alternate titles: seafoam-kiss maker
Picks up quantity of candy with fork and rolls and shapes it against spatula to shape candy kisses. Places formed kisses on wax paper or tray to harden.
GOE: 06.04.28 STRENGTH: L GED: R1 M1 L1 SVP: 4 DLU: 77

529.687-126 KOSHER INSPECTOR (dairy products)
Observes milking of cows to ensure compliance with Jewish dietary laws governing collection and storage of milk prior to processing and sale.
GOE: 06.03.02 STRENGTH: L GED: R3 M1 L1 SVP: 2 DLU: 77

529.687-130 LABORER (meat products)
Performs any combination of following tasks in slaughtering and meat packing establishment: Holds meat while it is being cut. Straightens and washes carcasses or parts on conveyor lines. Distributes meat to various work areas for further processing, using cart. Scrapes excess meat from surfaces of filled casings, such as sausages and bologna, and hangs them on conveyor racks. Pushes conveyor racks, hanging attachments, and meat carts, to various departments. Unloads smoked meats from conveyor racks and weighs, stamps, and tags them. Removes empty trolleys from overhead rail and places them in chute or onto other rails. Trucks empty ham molds to washing machines for cleaning process. Loads meat onto conveyor racks, carts, worktables, or trucks, using hook. Transports offal (carcass waste) from killing floor to rendering room and dumps offal into tankage cookers. Weighs and sacks rendered inedible offal. Fills ice trucks, using shovel. Stacks cartons of meat products on pallets or trucks and moves load to shipping or storage areas, using hand or power operated truck. Pushes meat through spray cabinet to wash meat. Washes equipment and utensils, using water hose and spray cabinet. Sweeps and washes railroad refrigeration cars. May cut specific parts such as hooves or tendons, using knife.
GOE: 06.04.40 STRENGTH: H GED: R2 M1 L1 SVP: 2 DLU: 77

529.687-134 LEAF SORTER (tobacco) alternate titles: selector; wrapperleaf inspector
Sorts tobacco leaves according to color and condition for use as cigar wrappers or binders: Selects leaves without obvious defects from bundle and lays them on booker bench (curved-top stand over which leaves are draped). Examines leaves for color variations, tears, tar spots, tight grain, and size under specifications. Places leaves not suitable for wrapper in separate pile. Folds wrapper leaves into bundles for stripping.
GOE: 06.03.02 STRENGTH: L GED: R2 M1 L1 SVP: 2 DLU: 77

529.687-138 LEAF TIER (tobacco)
Ties tobacco leaves in hands (bundles) to facilitate processing: Selects loose leaves for hand and arranges leaves with butt ends together. Winds tie leaf around butts and pulls end of tie leaf into hand.
GOE: 06.04.28 STRENGTH: S GED: R1 M1 L1 SVP: 1 DLU: 77

529.687-142 LEAF-SIZE PICKER (tobacco) alternate titles: hands-size sorter
Sorts hands of tobacco according to size. Places hands of same size leaves on conveyor leading to ordering machine.
GOE: 06.03.02 STRENGTH: L GED: R1 M1 L1 SVP: 2 DLU: 77

529.687-146 LIGHTOUT EXAMINER (beverage)
Examines interior and exterior of washed tanks, metal barrels, or kegs for cleanliness and to detect corrosion. Crawls into tank or inserts light through

bunghole to examine interior of container. Removes corroded and dirty barrels or kegs from conveyor.
GOE: 06.03.02 STRENGTH: L GED: R2 M1 L2 SVP: 3 DLU: 77

529.687-150 LINKER (meat products) alternate titles: roper; sausage linker
Twists and ties casings filled with sausage to form links of specified length: Ties one end of stuffed sausage casing with twine to prevent contents from spilling out. Presses casing between thumb and index finger at length specified. Twists casing at pressed section to form link. Twirls remaining length of stuffed casing to make additional links. Ties ends of stuffed casings to make longer string of links. Drapes sausages over rack for subsequent processing. Cuts casings to remove defective parts or to separate links, using cutting tool. May retie ends. May hold stomachs or casings during filling by SAUSAGE MAKER (meat products) and tie ends.
GOE: 06.04.28 STRENGTH: M GED: R2 M1 L1 SVP: 3 DLU: 77

529.687-154 MAT SEWER (oils & grease)
Repairs mats used in pressing oil from linseed: Cuts worn or damaged sections from mats, using knife. Stitches useable mat strips together and reinforces borders to make new mats, using sewing machine.
GOE: 06.04.27 STRENGTH: L GED: R2 M1 L1 SVP: 2 DLU: 77

529.687-158 MELT-HOUSE DRAG OPERATOR (sugar & conf.)
Regulates flow of raw-sugar box to drags (conveyors) and elevators: Starts drags. Lifts slide on raw-sugar box to allow sugar to fall on drags. Breaks up sugar lumps in box, using scraper. Shifts slides to rotate drawing of sugar from box and to prevent caking and buildups. Draws samples of raw sugar for laboratory analysis. Opens or closes slides to increase or decrease flow of sugar. Removes sugar strings from drag, scrolls, and grates and throws strings in waste container.
GOE: 06.04.40 STRENGTH: M GED: R2 M1 L1 SVP: 3 DLU: 77

529.687-162 MOISTURE-METER OPERATOR (tobacco) alternate titles: tag-meter operator
Tests moisture content of tobacco in various stages of processing by either of following methods: (1) Places tobacco sample in electrical moisture meter and turns on current. Observes meter indicator and compares reading with conversion chart to determine moisture content. Records date, time, temperature, moisture content, and meter reading for each sample tested. (2) Weighs sample of tobacco and places sample in oven. Removes and weighs sample after specified time. Compares difference in weights with conversion chart to determine moisture content.
GOE: 06.03.02 STRENGTH: L GED: R2 M2 L2 SVP: 2 DLU: 77

529.687-166 ODD BUNDLE WORKER (tobacco)
Aligns tips of leaves, fed onto conveyor by other workers, against guide rail of conveyor to ensure tips will be cut to uniform length by power knife.
GOE: 06.04.15 STRENGTH: L GED: R1 M1 L1 SVP: 2 DLU: 77

529.687-170 PRESS PULLER (grain-feed mills)
Removes filter cloths from filter presses to unload separated solids used for making stock feed: Opens press and inserts prying tool between plates to free filter cloths or turns wheel to release ram holding filter frames together. Pulls cloths loaded with solids from press and shakes material onto conveyor or scrapes residue into pans with a spatula. Replaces clean cloths between plates and closes press. Shovels solids from pans into containers for further processing. Turns valve to move hydraulic ram against plates and hold cloths in position. May cut new filter cloths or papers. Usually works as member of team.
GOE: 06.04.15 STRENGTH: H GED: R1 M1 L1 SVP: 2 DLU: 77

529.687-174 SALVAGE INSPECTOR (can. & preserv.)
Inspects and sorts returned canned and bottled food products for possible salvage of contents: Opens containers by hand or with opening devices and inspects containers and contents for defects such as leaking or mislabeled containers, or defective wrapping. Sets aside salvaged cans and bottles. Pours useable contents of defective cans or bottles into bulk containers. Discards rejected contents and containers into waste containers. Routes inspected materials to appropriate filling, packaging, and waste disposal points. May repackage salvaged cans and bottles. May wash glass containers.
GOE: 06.03.02 STRENGTH: L GED: R2 M1 L1 SVP: 3 DLU: 77

529.687-178 SAMPLER (beverage) alternate titles: sampler, pickup
Collects samples of grain, mash, or wort, and alcoholic beverages in various stages of processing for laboratory analysis: Dips, scoops, or siphons samples into laboratory containers and labels containers to identify sample. Records information such as sampling station and time, or brewer name and location on forms or journals. Loads sample containers on handtruck and pushes handtruck to laboratory area.
GOE: 06.04.40 STRENGTH: L GED: R2 M2 L2 SVP: 2 DLU: 77

529.687-182 SHREDDED-FILLER HOPPER-FEEDER (tobacco)
Shovels filler tobacco into hoppers of cigar-making machines and bunchmaking machines. Transfers boxes or cases of shredded filler tobacco to machines, manually or using handtruck.
GOE: 06.04.28 STRENGTH: M GED: R2 M1 L1 SVP: 2 DLU: 77

529.687-186 SORTER, AGRICULTURAL PRODUCE (agriculture; can. & preserv.; wholesale tr.) alternate titles: sorter, food products
Sorts agricultural produce, such as bulbs, fruits, nuts, and vegetables: Segregates produce on conveyor belt or table, working as crewmember, according

to grade, color, and size, and places produce in containers or on designated conveyors. Discards cull (inferior or defective) items and foreign matter. Bunches, ties, and trims produce, such as asparagus, carrots, celery, and radishes. Picks out choice produce to be used as cappers (top layers on marketing containers). Packs produce in boxes, barrels, baskets, or crates for storage or shipment [PACKER, AGRICULTURAL PRODUCE (agriculture) 920.687-134]. May be designated according to work performed as Apple Sorter (agriculture; can. & preserv.; wholesale tr.); Asparagus Grader And Buncher (agriculture); Capper Picker (agriculture; wholesale tr.); Citrus-Fruit-Packing Grader (agriculture; wholesale tr.); Cull Grader (agriculture; wholesale tr.); Potato Grader (agriculture; wholesale tr.). May be designated: Asparagus Sorter (agriculture; can. & preserv.; wholesale tr.); Banana Grader (agriculture; wholesale tr.); Bulb Sorter (agriculture); Cherry Sorter (agriculture; can. & preserv.; wholesale tr.); Cranberry Sorter (agriculture; wholesale tr.); Fig Sorter (agriculture; can. & preserv.; wholesale tr.); Flower Grader (agriculture); Fruit Sorter (agriculture; can. & preserv.; wholesale tr.); Hop Sorter (agriculture); Nut Sorter (agriculture); Peach Sorter (agriculture; can. & preserv.; wholesale tr.); Potato Sorter (agriculture; wholesale tr.); Seed Sorter (agriculture); Tomato Grader (wholesale tr.); Vegetable Sorter (agriculture; can. & preserv.; wholesale tr.); Mushroom Sorter-Grader (can. & preserv.); Trimmer-Sorter (can. & preserv.); Sorter-Grader (can. & preserv.); Raspberry Checker (can. & preserv.).
GOE: 03.04.01 STRENGTH: L GED: R1 M1 L1 SVP: 2 DLU: 81

529.687-190 STONE CLEANER (beverage) alternate titles: carbonating-stone cleaner
Cleans or replaces stones in carbonating-stone assembly used to introduce carbon dioxide into tanks of beer: Carries stone to work area. Climbs into aging tank and disassembles frame and stone assembly, using handtools. Examines stone to detect faults or breaks. Scrubs stone, using brush and cleaners. Reassembles stone in frame. Discards faulty stones.
GOE: 06.04.39 STRENGTH: L GED: R2 M1 L1 SVP: 2 DLU: 77

529.687-194 SUCTION-PLATE-CARRIER CLEANER (tobacco) alternate titles: carrier blower; carrier washer
Cleans perforated suction plates of cigar-making machines: Turns thumbscrews to remove plates. Scrubs plates, using scrub brush and water. Immerses plates in boiling water to loosen dirt in airholes and blows out dirt, using airhose.
GOE: 06.04.39 STRENGTH: L GED: R2 M1 L1 SVP: 2 DLU: 77

529.687-198 SUMATRA OPENER (tobacco)
Removes hands of Sumatra tobacco from case or bale, shakes tobacco, removes broken leaves, and piles hands in stacks according to moisture content.
GOE: 06.04.28 STRENGTH: L GED: R1 M1 L1 SVP: 2 DLU: 77

529.687-202 TEMPERATURE INSPECTOR (meat products)
Inspects temperature readings of meat coolers for conformance to standards: Tours coolers periodically and compares temperature readings of each cooler with charts. Adjusts expansion valves in coolers to maintain specified temperature in each cooler.
GOE: 06.03.02 STRENGTH: L GED: R2 M1 L2 SVP: 3 DLU: 77

529.687-206 TROLLEY CLEANER (meat products)
Cleans trolleys used to move animal carcasses along overhead rail, in vats or tanks filled with solution: Turns water and steam valves to fill and heat cleaning vats or tanks. Dumps caustic soda and detergents into tank and stirs mixture with paddle. Pushes rack of trolleys to tank and lowers each trolley into solution, or immerses rack into solution, using hoist. Removes trolleys from solution and rinses them in hot water spray. Lubricates trolley wheels.
GOE: 06.04.39 STRENGTH: M GED: R1 M1 L1 SVP: 2 DLU: 77

529.687-210 WASHER (grain-feed mills) alternate titles: flusher
Washes and removes starch deposits from starch tables by flushing table with stream of water: Directs water hose over starch table to wash film of gluten from starch deposits. Plugs line to gluten tank at end of table and raises tailboard to allow starch deposit to flow to flushing tank. Turns valve to admit strong stream of water into starch table that loosens and flushes starch deposits into flushing tank.
GOE: 06.04.39 STRENGTH: M GED: R2 M1 L1 SVP: 2 DLU: 77

529.687-214 WASHROOM CLEANER (sugar & conf.)
Cleans beet washroom in sugar beet refinery: Removes beet tails, mud, stones, and trash from washer pit, using shovel. Removes debris from area of washroom, using wheelbarrow, pitchfork, and shovel. Washes floors, using hose.
GOE: 06.04.39 STRENGTH: M GED: R1 M1 L1 SVP: 2 DLU: 77

529.687-218 WRAPPER SELECTOR (tobacco) alternate titles: wrapper sizer; wrapper sorter
Selects perfect wrappers from books (halved leaves, bundled after stripping) and sorts wrappers according to size and color: Unties book and separates half leaves. Inspects wrapper leaves for holes or tears and discards imperfect leaves. Piles wrappers in stacks according to size and color. Wipes water-moistened sponge over top leaves of stack to prevent drying. Packs wrappers of like size and color into bundles and places bundles into containers.
GOE: 06.03.02 STRENGTH: L GED: R2 M1 L1 SVP: 3 DLU: 77

529.687-222 WRAPPING MACHINE HELPER (tobacco)
Mounts tobacco leaf and replenishes glue supply in plug-overwrap machine and assists PLUG-OVERWRAP-MACHINE TENDER (tobacco) to tend machine that wraps lumps of chewing tobacco in *homogenized leaf:* Mounts roll of homogenized tobacco leaf on overwrap machine and guides end of roll between machine rollers and under cutter. Pours glue into machine glue container to replenish supply reservoir. Pushes wire through hole of glue container to assure free flow of glue. Observes wrapping operation and removes defectively wrapped lumps from machine discharge conveyor. Wets down belts of machine, using rag, to prevent lumps from sticking to belt. Performs other duties as described under HELPER (any industry) Master Title.
GOE: 06.04.28 STRENGTH: M GED: R1 M1 L1 SVP: 2 DLU: 77

529.687-226 INSPECTOR, PROCESSING (sugar & conf.)
Examines, weighs, and measures sheets and strips of unwrapped, finished chewing gum to ensure conformity to specifications and standards: Examines trays of rolled and scored gum to verify that finished gum is free of caked sugar, indentations, and foreign matter. Inspects gum surface for uniformity of sugar coating and for prescribed scoring and trimming. Weighs and measures thickness and length of gum strips, using scale, micrometer, and length gauge. Notifies supervisory personnel of deviations from prescribed standards.
GOE: 06.03.02 STRENGTH: L GED: R3 M2 L2 SVP: 4 DLU: 86

529.687-230 LABORER, SHELLFISH PROCESSING (can. & preserv.)
Performs any combination of following tasks concerned with fresh packing, canning, freezing, or smoking shellfish: Transports shellfish, shellfish meats, cans, or cases to work area manually, or using wheeled hopper, handtruck, or power hoist. Loads conveyors, hoppers, or handtrucks with product, cans, or cases. Spreads shellfish on conveyor, drenches them with water, and removes foreign matter. Weighs shellfish or shellfish meat, using scales. Records weight of product on standard form. Sorts shellfish according to size, and trims off unusable portions, using knife or scissors. Packs shellfish meat in jars, cans, or boxes, and packs containers in crushed ice to fresh pack. Cleans conveyors, machines, and work areas, using high pressure hose spray. May feed cans and lids into lidding machine [PACKAGER, MACHINE (any industry) 920.685-078]. May be designated according to work performed as Shellfish Checker (can & preserv.); Shellfish Packer (can. & preserv.); Shellfish Sorter (can. & preserv.); Shellfish Weigher (can. & preserv.).
GOE: 06.04.40 STRENGTH: H GED: R2 M1 L1 SVP: 2 DLU: 78

53 OCCUPATIONS IN PROCESSING OF PAPER AND RELATED MATERIALS

This division includes occupations concerned with the manufacture of paper and products made from paper. Includes converting wood, other cellulosic materials, and rags into pulp.

530 GRINDING, BEATING, AND MIXING OCCUPATIONS

This group includes occupations concerned with reducing logs, straw, rags, and similar cellulosic materials to chips, dust, powder, paste, pulp, or other smaller particles by means of compression, grinding, or agitation; and combining and mingling materials to produce a single mass or compound.

530.132-010 COATING-MIXER SUPERVISOR (paper & pulp)
Supervises and coordinates activities of workers engaged in blending and mixing materials used to make coating for paper and related products: Reads production order to determine type and quantity of coating needed. Plans mixing sequence and orders raw materials from stockroom. Assigns job duties to workers and supervises weighing and mixing of materials. Tests each batch of coating for specific gravity, consistency, and color. Directs routing of coating mix to paper machines or storage tanks. Keeps daily production records. Instructs new workers in use of machinery and safety procedures. Performs other duties as described under SUPERVISOR (any industry) Master Title.
GOE: 06.04.01 STRENGTH: L GED: R4 M3 L4 SVP: 7 DLU: 77

530.132-014 SUPERVISOR, BEATER ROOM (paper & pulp) alternate titles: beater, head
Supervises and coordinates activities of workers engaged in beating and refining pulp to prepare furnish for processing into paper: Calculates volume or weight of ingredients, such as pulp, fillers, size, alum, and dyes, using formulas and laboratory analyses of ingredient concentrations. Orders charging of beater vats with ingredients, beater roll adjustment, and time of beating. Examines pulp samples and reviews laboratory reports to determine when beating process is completed. Compares sample of paper produced with specifications or standard paper and orders changes in beating procedure to produce paper to specified standards. Performs other duties as described under SUPERVISOR (any industry) Master Title.
GOE: 06.02.01 STRENGTH: L GED: R4 M4 L4 SVP: 7 DLU: 77

530.132-018 SUPERVISOR, WOOD ROOM (paper & pulp) alternate titles: wood-mill supervisor; wood-preparation supervisor
Supervises and coordinates activities of workers engaged in debarking, sawing, cleaning, and chipping logs to make wood chips for use as pulp: Schedules production of chips according to quantity and species of wood required by digesters. Plans routing of wood through mill according to species of wood. Inspects chips, and adjusts cutter knives to ensure chips are cut to specified standards. Performs other duties as described under SUPERVISOR (any industry) Master Title.

GOE: 06.02.01 STRENGTH: L GED: R4 M3 L4 SVP: 7 DLU: 78

530.132-022 WOOD GRINDER, HEAD (paper & pulp) alternate titles: ground-wood supervisor; supervisor, groundwood mill

Supervises and coordinates activities of workers engaged in grinding logs and wood blocks into pulp: Directs workers in feeding and adjusting machines to obtain pulp of specified consistency. Observes grinders, examines pulp for length and thickness of fiber, and reads laboratory reports on pulp consistency to determine need for sharpening grindstone or machine adjustment. Installs sharpening burr in stone-dressing lathe, using wrench. Moves controls to feed burr against revolving stone to dress and sharpen stone. Replaces worn stone, using hoist and handtools. Performs other duties as described under SUPERVISOR (any industry) Master Title.

GOE: 06.02.01 STRENGTH: L GED: R4 M2 L3 SVP: 6 DLU: 77

530.261-010 COLOR DEVELOPER (paper & pulp)

Develops formulas for paper-coloring dye and prepares directions for mixing dye with pulp to produce colored paper to specifications or customer's sample: Determines composition of color sample, using spectrophotometer. Mixes pulp with water, size, filler, and other ingredients to make sample furnish of type and quality of paper specified. Weighs and mixes pigments to prepare dye, and mixes dye with furnish. Pours furnish on screen to make handsheet sample. Compares color of handsheet with color sample, visually or with spectrophotometer. Calculates weights and proportions of pigments and other materials required to make production batch of dye and prepares formulas and mixing directions for COATING-MIXER TENDER (paper & pulp). Prepares directions for BEATER ENGINEER (paper & pulp; tex. prod., nec) for mixing dye with furnish. Prepares spectrophotometer charts on dye materials. Observes procedures of production staff in mixing dye with furnish and reviews laboratory reports to investigate causes of substandard colored paper. Consults with and advises production staff regarding technical problems in mixing colors and making colored paper to improve formulas and improve production methods.

GOE: 02.04.01 STRENGTH: L GED: R4 M4 L4 SVP: 7 DLU: 77

530.382-010 PULP-REFINER OPERATOR (paper & pulp)

Operates battery of machines to refine pulp and shorten fibers as pulp flows continuously through machines to prepare pulp for papermaking: Turns handwheels to adjust distance between bedplate and rotor knives to obtain specified fineness of fibers. Starts machines and pumps to regulate flow of pulp from beater chests through refining machines to paper machine chest. Examines pulp, reviews laboratory test reports, and adjusts machines to ensure that pulp meets specifications. May change bedplates and rotor knives, using handtools. May clean interior of storage chests, using water hose.

GOE: 06.02.14 STRENGTH: M GED: R3 M3 L2 SVP: 4 DLU: 78

530.384-010 MIXER HELPER (concrete prod.) alternate titles: puddler

Performs following duties to facilitate making wallboard (plasterboard): Puddles plaster slurry discharged from mixing machine, using puddling stick, and spreads it evenly for feeding into machine that combines slurry and paper into wallboard. Observes flow and squeezes flexible discharge nozzle (boot) of mixing machine to prevent formation of lumps in slurry. Scrapes hardened slurry from edge guides and smoothing bars. Scoops sample of slurry in cylinder, weighs it, and sets sample aside for specified period to determine consistency (slump). Places sample under testing needle that drops from specified height and indicates on dial depth of penetration to determine hardness (set) of core. Records test results and reports defects to supervisor. Clears jams on wallboard machine and cleans work area. Participates in splicing paper and in repairing wallboard and mixing machines.

GOE: 06.04.34 STRENGTH: L GED: R2 M1 L1 SVP: 2 DLU: 77

530.582-010 PULPER, SYNTHETIC SOIL BLOCKS (paper & pulp)

Operates hydrapulper and batch reactor to blend woodpulp, plastic binders, and liquid fertilizers into slurry for use in molding synthetic soil blocks: Fills hydrapulper tank with water, adds woodpulp and measured amounts of chemicals, and starts agitator. Observes and records temperature, pressure, and time interval of agitation cycle. Pumps cooled pulp slurry to reactor tank and flushes hydrapulper tank with water. Starts reactor, adjusts temperature and pressure controls, and adds measured amounts of liquid fertilizers and plastic binders. Tests acidity of solution by titration and adds ingredients as needed to attain prescribed level. Pumps mixed slurry to storage tank for further processing. Flushes reactor tank with water.

GOE: 06.02.14 STRENGTH: H GED: R3 M3 L2 SVP: 4 DLU: 77

530.662-010 BEATER ENGINEER (paper & pulp; tex. prod., nec) alternate titles: beater operator

Controls beater engines and related equipment to process furnish for making paper, roofing felt, and related products: Starts pumps and adjusts valves to regulate flow of specified amount of slush pulp into vat. Starts engines and adjusts beater rolls to obtain specified degree of pulp fineness and hydration. Examines furnish for specified consistency and size of fibers. Dips sample from vat for laboratory testing. Starts pumps to transfer furnish to storage chests. May operate machine to refine pulp. May make *freeness* and acidity tests. May calculate volume and weight of furnish ingredients from technical control formulas. May mix and cook dyes for furnish. May control operation of battery of beaters and be designated Beater, Lead (paper & pulp; tex. prod., nec).

GOE: 06.02.18 STRENGTH: M GED: R3 M3 L2 SVP: 5 DLU: 78

530.662-014 WOOD GRINDER OPERATOR (paper & pulp)

Operates machines to grind logs or wood blocks into fibers used in making paper pulp, using one of following methods: (1) Opens slide gate, tosses wood into grinder pocket, and moves lever to actuate hydraulic piston that presses wood against revolving grindstones. (2) Adjusts panel controls to regulate conveyor system that feeds wood to hopper of grinder machines. Straightens wood in machine pocket or hopper to prevent jams, using *picaroon*. Turns valves to regulate spray of water to cool grindstones and to control consistency of pulp. Turns handwheel to raise or lower dam to control flow of pulp from discharge end of machine. Observes temperature gauge and color of pulp for evidence of burns caused by dull or broken grindstones and notifies WOOD GRINDER, HEAD (paper & pulp) 530.132-022 of defects. May be designated according to type of machine operated as Pocket-Grinder Operator (paper & pulp); Ring-Grinder Operator (paper & pulp).

GOE: 06.02.14 STRENGTH: M GED: R3 M2 L2 SVP: 5 DLU: 77

530.665-010 BEATER-ENGINEER HELPER (paper & pulp; tex. prod., nec) alternate titles: beater-operator helper

Tends beaters and vats that prepare furnish for making paper, roofing felt, and related products: Turns valves to charge vats with specified amounts of slush pulp, fillers, size, and liquid chemicals. Weighs and dumps dry ingredients into vat according to formula. Dips furnish sample from vat for laboratory testing. Removes plug of vat to dump furnish into beater chest or starts pump to transfer furnish from vat to storage. Observes vat and beater operation and notifies BEATER ENGINEER (tex. prod., nec; paper & pulp) 530.662-010 of malfunction. Cleans vat with water and hose and scrapes out adhering matter. May truck materials from storage. May weigh, mix, and cook dyes. May chip rust, scale, and other deposits from machine rolls, using airhammer. May truck sheet pulp and other materials from stockroom.

GOE: 06.04.19 STRENGTH: M GED: R2 M2 L2 SVP: 2 DLU: 78

530.665-014 RAG-CUTTING-MACHINE TENDER (paper & pulp; tex. prod., nec)

Tends rag-cutting machine that cuts rags to specified size preparatory to processing into paper, roofing felt, or related products: Presses buttons to actuate conveyor, cutters, and blowers. Observes movement of rags along conveyor to detect clogging or malfunctioning machine. Stops machine at sound of warning buzzer and removes clogged rags, using iron pry. Reports mechanical defects to supervisor. Lubricates, adjusts, and replaces worn blades of machine. May record amount of rags cut on daily production record.

GOE: 06.04.05 STRENGTH: M GED: R2 M2 L1 SVP: 2 DLU: 77

530.666-010 RAG-CUTTING-MACHINE FEEDER (paper & pulp; tex. prod., nec) alternate titles: cutter operator

Feeds machine that cuts rags to size for cooking, bleaching, and defibering prior to making paper, roofing felt, or related products: Places rags on apron of machine and pushes them into feeder roll or loads rags onto conveyor leading to machine. Examines cut rags for size and notifies supervisor if machine knives need adjusting or sharpening. May loosen setscrews with wrench and remove knives. May clean dirt and dust from dust compartment and work area.

GOE: 06.04.05 STRENGTH: L GED: R2 M1 L1 SVP: 2 DLU: 77

530.682-010 PULP GRINDER AND BLENDER (paper & pulp; wood prod., nec)

Operates machines to grind cooked wood chips into pulp and blend pulp with other specified ingredients in manufacture of wallboard: Turns handwheel to adjust grinding-plate settings. Starts machines and adjusts panel controls to maintain level in pulp and water chests and regulate flow of chips through grinding machines. Observes charts, dials, and gauges; and adjusts levers, valves, and panel controls to regulate flow of specified amounts of pulp, alum, wax, asphalt, and starch into blending machine. May weigh samples of wet and dry pulp on scales and calculate moisture content. May test pulp for *freeness, fineness, density, and breakage*. May record production and test data.

GOE: 06.02.14 STRENGTH: L GED: R3 M2 L2 SVP: 6 DLU: 77

530.685-010 COATING-MIXER TENDER (paper & pulp) alternate titles: clay mixer

Tends machine that mixes and strains filling and coating materials for paper: Weighs and dumps specified quantities of materials, such as clay, soda ash, titanium dioxide, lithopone, or gypsum, into hopper of mixing machine. Turns valve to admit metered volume of water into mixing machine and starts machine that mixes ingredients. Starts pumps that force mixture through straining screens and into storage tanks. Lifts screens from machine and washes screens with water hose. May deliver sacks of materials to mixer, using handtruck or forklift truck. May weigh and add specified quantities of color pigments to mixture. May plan mixing according to paper production orders.

GOE: 06.04.14 STRENGTH: H GED: R2 M2 L2 SVP: 2 DLU: 77

530.685-014 PULPER (paper & pulp; tex. prod., nec) alternate titles: slusher operator

Tends machine that reduces broke or dry pulp sheets to pulp or slurry for use in making paper, wallboard, or related products: Dumps broke or pulp sheets onto conveyor or into vat to fill pulper machine. Pushes buttons and turns valves to admit water, ink removing solution, and steam that softens material to specified consistency. Starts beating machine that reduces material to pulp. Observes and monitors material, dials, or charts to ensure specified consistency of pulp. Opens discharge gate or starts pump to dump or transport pulp to storage or to other processes. May catch pulp in broke boxes and push boxes to beater engines. May push cart loads of broke from paper machines to pulper. May be designated according to material reduced as Broke-Beater Tender (paper & pulp; tex. prod., nec); or according to type of machine used as Hydropulper (paper & pulp).

GOE: 06.04.14 STRENGTH: M GED: R2 M2 L1 SVP: 2 DLU: 81

530.686-010   BEATER-AND-PULPER FEEDER (paper & pulp; tex. prod., nec)

Feeds scrap paper or wood chips into beater tanks for grinding into furnish used in making paper, roofing felt, or related products: Conveys bales of scrap paper, fillers, starch, and chemicals to beater room, using forklift truck or hand-truck. Opens bales and dumps paper and fillers into beater tanks. Observes scrap paper and discards plastic or other insoluble items into trash bin. Stacks bales of scrap paper and sacks of chemicals onto conveyor of pulper machine, using forklift truck. Sweeps and cleans work area. May open valves to drain furnish from beater tanks into storage units. May clean equipment screens, blades, and interior surfaces, using brushes, broom, and cleaning solutions.
GOE: 06.04.14 STRENGTH: M GED: R2 M1 L1 SVP: 2 DLU: 77

530.686-014   LOADER, MAGAZINE GRINDER (paper & pulp) alternate titles: magazine loader

Loads pulp logs or wood blocks into magazines of grinder that reduces them to fibers used in making paper: Lifts and places logs into magazines, using lumber hooks or *picaroon* to align logs and avoid jams. Cuts oversized logs to desired length, using cutoff saw.
GOE: 06.04.14 STRENGTH: H GED: R2 M1 L1 SVP: 2 DLU: 77

530.686-018   WASTE-PAPER-HAMMERMILL OPERATOR (paper & pulp)

Feeds waste paper into machine that cuts paper into small pieces for use as building insulation. Fills sack with cut paper.
GOE: 06.04.14 STRENGTH: L GED: R1 M1 L1 SVP: 1 DLU: 77

530.687-010   RAG INSPECTOR (paper & pulp) alternate titles: inspector, rag sorting

Examines rags to verify that they have been sorted according to color, quality, type, and condition, and that foreign matter, such as clips, buttons, and elastic, has been removed. Weighs rags and records weight. Trucks rags to cutting machines.
GOE: 06.03.02 STRENGTH: L GED: R2 M2 L1 SVP: 2 DLU: 77

532   COOKING AND DRYING OCCUPATIONS

This group includes occupations concerned with removing moisture from paper and related materials by exposing them to heat or air or placing them in a vacuum, and cooking materials at specific temperatures for varied intervals to effect their composition, consistency, or texture.

532.362-010   DIGESTER OPERATOR (paper & pulp; paper goods) alternate titles: cook; digester cook

Operates battery of stationary or rotary steam digesters to cook wood chips with soda ash or acid to make pulp for use in manufacture of paper and insulation board: Signals DIGESTER-OPERATOR HELPER (paper & pulp; paper goods) 532.686-010 to charge digesters with specified amounts of chips and chemicals. Turns valves or moves panel controls to admit steam into digesters, to raise temperature and pressure within specified limits, and to start rotary digesters. Monitors temperature, flow, and pressure gauges and charts to ensure that chips are cooked according to specifications. Tests samples of digester liquid by titration or standard color chart to determine completion of cooking process. Opens valves of stationary digester to blow cooked pulp into pit, or pulls lever to tip rotary digester and dump contents. Compiles production records. May be designated according to process as Cooker, Soda (paper & pulp; paper goods); Cooker, Sulfate (paper & pulp; paper goods); Cooker, Sulfite (paper & pulp; paper goods).
GOE: 06.02.14 STRENGTH: L GED: R3 M3 L3 SVP: 6 DLU: 78

532.585-010   MATRIX-DRIER TENDER (paper & pulp)

Tends cylinder drier that dries sheets of matrix paper: Sets controls of drier to regulate temperature and speed of cylinder and position of belt. Starts drier and feeds wet sheets between revolving cylinder and belt. Observes gauges and feels dried sheets for moisture content, and adjusts controls to achieve specified dryness. Gauges thickness of fiberboard and matrix mats, using micrometer calipers. Sorts and records mats according to thickness and stacks them on skids.
GOE: 06.04.14 STRENGTH: M GED: R2 M2 L2 SVP: 3 DLU: 77

532.685-010   BACK TENDER, INSULATION BOARD (wood prod., nec) alternate titles: pulp drier

Tends oven drier at back end of pulp-making machine that removes moisture from pulp sheets: Observes gauges and charts, and turns valves to regulate flow of steam and control oven temperature. Aligns sheets on conveyor to prevent jams. Regulates speed of conveyor to ensure that dried sheets conform to moisture content specifications.
GOE: 06.04.14 STRENGTH: L GED: R2 M1 L1 SVP: 2 DLU: 77

532.685-014   COOKER TENDER (paper & pulp)

Tends cooker that cooks logs for processing into pulp: Bolts bottom of cooker in place. Opens gate of loading chute and guides logs into cooker with pike pole. Turns valve to fill cooker with steam to cook wood for specified period. Unbolts bottom of cooker and loads logs onto handtruck.
GOE: 06.04.14 STRENGTH: M GED: R2 M1 L1 SVP: 3 DLU: 77

532.685-018   EVAPORATOR OPERATOR (paper & pulp)

Tends evaporator that condenses sulfite and black liquor to prepare them for recovery furnace: Adjusts controls and turns valves of evaporator to regulate flow and temperature of liquor to dehydrate liquor to specified density. Tests sample of liquor concentrate, using hydrometer and thermometer, to determine density. Cleans evaporator chambers, using steam hose.
GOE: 06.04.11 STRENGTH: L GED: R2 M2 L1 SVP: 2 DLU: 77

532.685-022   MOISTURE-CONDITIONER OPERATOR (paper & pulp)

Tends machine that threads continuous sheet of paper through moisture-conditioning cabinet to dampen paper: Turns valves to regulate flow of air, steam, and water in cabinet to control temperature and moisture. Places roll of paper on reel stand, using hoist, and wraps end of paper around threader bar. Starts machine that automatically threads paper between feed and tension rolls in cabinet. Wraps end of dampened paper sheet on core shaft of rewinder reel. Adjusts tension of paper by adding or removing weights on chain.
GOE: 06.04.14 STRENGTH: M GED: R2 M2 L1 SVP: 4 DLU: 77

532.685-026   PULP-PRESS TENDER (paper & pulp) alternate titles: hydraulic-press tender

Tends hydraulic press that removes moisture from fiberboard, laps, or sheets of wet pulp: Pushes loaded truck under hydraulic pressing plate and starts machine to lower ram and press water from pulp. Pulls truck away from press and pushes it to baling area. May stack layers of laps or sheets on handtruck, placing wire mesh or fiber mats between layers to facilitate pressing water from stock.
GOE: 06.04.14 STRENGTH: H GED: R2 M1 L2 SVP: 3 DLU: 77

532.686-010   DIGESTER-OPERATOR HELPER (paper & pulp; paper goods) alternate titles: cook helper; digester-cook helper; pulp-making-plant operator

Feeds wood chips and soda ash or acid into digester that processes wood chips into pulp: Unbolts and removes digester cover, using wrench and chain hoist. Lowers feed pipe into digester, using hoist, and pushes button or turns handwheel to load digester with wood chips. Pushes control panel button or turns valve to admit specified quantities of soda ash or acid into digester. Replaces and bolts cover. May remove cover and blow steam from digester at completion of cooking cycle. May tend conveyors that convey chips to hopper or cooked pulp to storage bins. May open valves to blow cooked pulp into pit. May pull lever to dump cooked pulp from rotary digester. May draw and deliver pulp sample to laboratory for analysis.
GOE: 06.04.18 STRENGTH: L GED: R2 M2 L1 SVP: 2 DLU: 78

532.686-014   PAPER-CONE-DRYING-MACHINE OPERATOR (paper goods)

Dumps paper cones treated with solution of turpentine and beeswax into drying cabinet and starts fan. Rakes cones from cabinet after specified drying time.
GOE: 06.04.14 STRENGTH: L GED: R1 M1 L1 SVP: 1 DLU: 77

532.687-010   LABEL DRIER (recording)

Dries phonograph labels in oven for use by record-press section: Obtains specified labels from stock and spreads them on drying racks of oven. Turns dial of automatic timer to start drying cycle. Removes dried labels from racks and separates labels by title. Stacks labels on warming plates near record presses, according to production schedule. Collects, sorts, and returns unused labels to storage at end of shift.
GOE: 06.04.34 STRENGTH: L GED: R2 M1 L1 SVP: 2 DLU: 77

533   COOLING, BLEACHING, SCREENING, WASHING, AND RELATED OCCUPATIONS

This group includes occupations concerned with cleaning materials with water, making them cooler, whitening them by use of chlorine gas or other bleaching agents, and separating finer from coarser parts by use of a screen.

533.362-010   BLEACHER, PULP (paper & pulp)

Controls equipment to bleach pulp: Starts pumps and adjusts controls to regulate flow of pulp to chlorination towers, bleaching and soaking tanks, and pulp washers, according to specified bleaching sequence. Opens valves to allow metered flow of such chemicals as liquid and gaseous chlorine, sulfur dioxide gas, caustic soda, hypochlorite, and peroxide into pulp, according to bleaching specifications. Starts agitators to mix pulp and chemicals. Tends cylinder washers to wash soluble impurities and excess bleach from pulp after each bleaching operation. Adjusts controls to ensure that pulp bleaching meets specifications, according to laboratory test reports. Starts equipment to pump bleached pulp to storage. May make titration tests. May test whiteness of pulp, using *reflectance meter*. May tend decker machines that thicken pulp. May be designated according to pulp-making process as Bleacher, Groundwood Pulp (paper & pulp); Bleacher, Kraft Pulp (paper & pulp); Bleacher, Sulfite Pulp (paper & pulp).
GOE: 06.02.14 STRENGTH: M GED: R3 M3 L3 SVP: 5 DLU: 78

533.665-010   BLOW-PIT OPERATOR (paper & pulp)

Tends blow pits that wash pulp to remove cooking acid: Covers blow pit floor with specified amount of water, using hose, and clamps shut doors and hatches to prepare blow pit for receiving cooked pulp. Turns wheel, as signaled by DIGESTER OPERATOR (concrete prod.; paper & pulp), to open digester outlet valve and blow cooked pulp under pressure into blow pit. Opens valve to drain spent cooking liquor and water from pulp in blow pit. Opens water faucet or sprays pulp with water from high-pressure hose to wash cooking liquor from pulp and flush pulp from blow pit into receiving chests. Dips pulp sample from pit for testing in laboratory.

GOE: 06.04.14 STRENGTH: M GED: R2 M1 L1 SVP: 3 DLU: 77

533.682-010 DECKER OPERATOR (paper & pulp) alternate titles: rotary-filter operator

Operates decker or rotary filter machines to remove water from pulp stock and reduce stock to specified consistency for bleaching or beating: Turns valves to regulate flow of pulp stock into machine vat. Starts machine and adjusts controls to regulate speed of cylindrical screen in vat. Turns valve to adjust suction in cylinder to deposit pulp on screen at specified rate and remove white water through meshes of screen. Turns handwheels or pulls lever to adjust press roll against screen to obtain pulp of specified consistency. Pulls lever to adjust blade that scrapes pulp from screen into storage chest. May tend flat or rotary screens to remove coarse fibers from pulp.
GOE: 06.02.14 STRENGTH: L GED: R3 M2 L2 SVP: 4 DLU: 77

533.685-010 BLEACH-BOILER FILLER (paper & pulp) alternate titles: bleach-boiler packer; filler

Tends rotary bleach boiler that cleans and bleaches rags used in making paper: Charges boiler with rags, chemicals, and water. Fastens boiler cover, starts rotary motor, and turns steam valve to clean and bleach rags in boiler for specified length of time. Opens valves to reduce steam pressure and drain liquid from boiler. May pack boiler with alternate layers of rags and dry chemicals. May mix chemicals.
GOE: 06.04.14 STRENGTH: L GED: R2 M2 L1 SVP: 2 DLU: 77

533.685-014 BROWN-STOCK WASHER (paper & pulp)

Tends machines that wash cooking liquor from pulp: Starts machines and pumps, and turns valves to regulate spray from water jets and flow of pulp through washer to remove cooking liquor. Opens drains to dispose of wash water or transfer wash water to recovery storage tank. May tend flat or centrifugal screens that remove knots or uncooked chips from pulp.
GOE: 06.04.14 STRENGTH: L GED: R2 M2 L1 SVP: 2 DLU: 77

533.685-018 SAVE-ALL OPERATOR (paper & pulp)

Tends machine that salvages woodpulp suspended in white water: Opens valves or starts pumps to regulate flow of white water and glue size into vat causing pulp to flocculate (form fluffy mass) for easier removal. Starts cylinder of machine revolving to remove pulp from water. Turns valve to adjust vacuum in cylinder to remove water from pulp deposited on screen. Pulls levers to adjust blade that scrapes pulp from cylinder into receiving chest. Starts pumps to transport recovered pulp and residue of white water containing fillers, dyes, and chemicals to storage chests. Cleans machine and pipelines with brushes and chemical solution.
GOE: 06.04.14 STRENGTH: L GED: R2 M1 L1 SVP: 2 DLU: 77

533.685-022 SCREEN TENDER (paper & pulp) alternate titles: screen-room operator

Tends knotters, rifflers, and centrifugal and flat screens that remove knots, sand, coarse fibers, and uncooked chips from cooked woodpulp: Starts machine and turns valves to adjust flow of pulp and water into screening machine at specified consistency, or sets automatic consistency regulator. Adjusts water sprays to wash pulp through screens and refuse into receiving chests. Examines and feels usable (fine) fibers and screened-out material to detect inefficient cleaning and loss of stock, and adjusts flow of pulp stock and water accordingly. Replaces defective screen plates, using handtools. Cleans screen plates and flow boxes with water hose. Washes and scrapes sand deposits from rifflers. May tend washers to wash cooking liquor from pulp [DECKER OPERATOR (paper & pulp)]. May be designated according to type of machine tended as Centrifugal-Screen Tender (paper & pulp); Riffler Tender (paper & pulp); Rod-Machine Operator (paper & pulp).
GOE: 06.04.18 STRENGTH: M GED: R3 M2 L1 SVP: 4 DLU: 77

533.685-026 SCREEN TENDER, CHIPS (paper & pulp)

Tends rotary or shaker screens that remove slivers, sawdust, dirt, knots, and oversized chips from wood chips used for paper pulp: Starts conveyors to move wood chips from storage to screens and to transfer cleaned chips to designated bins. Starts screens and blower to clean chips and adjusts feeding mechanism on screens to prevent overloading. Cleans screens with airhose and brush after each run. Oils machine and conveyors. May tend rechipping machine to reduce size of oversize chips.
GOE: 06.04.03 STRENGTH: M GED: R2 M1 L1 SVP: 3 DLU: 77

533.685-030 THRASHER FEEDER (paper & pulp) alternate titles: rag-willow operator

Tends thrasher (dusting machine) that removes dust and lime from rags: Starts machine and feeds rags into machine hopper. Removes dust receiver from machine, dumps dust, and cleans machine.
GOE: 06.04.05 STRENGTH: L GED: R2 M1 L1 SVP: 2 DLU: 77

533.685-034 WASHER ENGINEER (paper & pulp)

Tends equipment that bleaches and washes cooked rags used in making paper: Turns valve to fill vat with water. Dumps specified quantities of chlorine, lime, and alum into vat to prepare bleaching solution. Places rags in solution to bleach them for specified length of time. Turns valve to drain solution from vat. Sets controls to regulate flow of water into vat to wash bleach solution from rags. Starts roller to pick up and eject dirty water from vat. Turns valve to drain wash water from vat. Removes rags from vat and places them in seasoning bin.
GOE: 06.04.14 STRENGTH: L GED: R2 M2 L1 SVP: 3 DLU: 77

533.686-010 BLOW-PIT HELPER (paper & pulp)

Assists BLOW-PIT OPERATOR (paper & pulp) in washing pulp to remove cooking acid: Pulls lever to close blow pit drain covers. Dumps pulp from digester into blow pit. Turns handwheel to open drain valves that permit gravity drainage of cooking liquor into recovery vat or sewers. Flushes residual pulp from blow pit, using high-pressure water hose. Cleans work area, using broom, hose, and shovel. Performs other duties as described under HELPER (any industry) Master Title.
GOE: 06.04.14 STRENGTH: M GED: R2 M1 L1 SVP: 2 DLU: 77

533.686-014 WASHER-ENGINEER HELPER (paper & pulp)

Assists WASHER ENGINEER (paper & pulp) in bleaching and washing cooked rags used in making paper: Removes covers from boiler, using hoist and wrenches. Positions stock boxes under boiler openings to receive cooked rags. Removes rags stuck in boiler, using metal hook. Pushes loaded boxes to washer and dumps rags into washer, using hoist. Turns valves to emit rags from machine after completion of wash cycle and conveys material to designated area of plant for further processing. Records rag type and time of wash cycle on production sheet. Cleans equipment and work area. Performs other duties as described under HELPER (any industry) Master Title.
GOE: 06.04.14 STRENGTH: M GED: R2 M1 L1 SVP: 2 DLU: 77

533.687-010 SCREEN-TENDER HELPER (paper & pulp) alternate titles: screen washer

Assists SCREEN TENDER (paper & pulp) in removing impurities and uncooked chips from cooked woodpulp: Turns valve to activate pump that fills defoamer tank. Washes clogged masses of fibers and impurities from screen plates, using water hose. Washes and scrapes sand and sludge from rifflers and flow boxes. Draws and spreads pulp sample in sheet mold. Observes sample against light, and notifies SCREEN TENDER (paper & pulp) when sample fails to meet cleaning specifications. May remove and replace screen plates, using handtools. Performs other duties as described under HELPER (any industry) Master Title.
GOE: 06.04.14 STRENGTH: M GED: R2 M1 L1 SVP: 2 DLU: 77

534 CALENDERING, SIZING, COATING, AND RELATED OCCUPATIONS

This group includes occupations concerned with imparting a desired finish or ensuring uniform thickness in paper by pressure applied with rollers; applying a thin pasty substance such as glue, starch, or resin to paper to glaze it, act as a filler, or otherwise treat the surface; and brushing a layer of mineral over paper and then drying it as a preliminary step to calendering.

534.130-010 SUPERVISOR, COATING (photo. appar.)

Supervises and coordinates activities of workers engaged in operating coating machines to sensitize blueprint and photographic paper: Sets up machine and adjusts roller speed and drying temperature. Reads gauges and graphs and inspects control mechanisms to verify machine setup. Adds chemical ingredients, such as solvents and neutralizing agents, to solution as specified by quality control test reports. Performs other duties as described under SUPERVISOR (any industry) Master Title.
GOE: 06.02.01 STRENGTH: L GED: R4 M3 L3 SVP: 7 DLU: 77

534.132-010 SUPERVISOR, CALENDERING (paper & pulp)

Supervises and coordinates activities of workers engaged in operating calender machines to impart specified gloss and finish to surface of paper: Assigns duties to workers, according to production orders and knowledge of machine capacities. Inspects finish of paper for adherence to specifications. Trains workers in operation of machines. Maintains production, quality control, and personnel records. Performs other duties as described under SUPERVISOR (any industry) Master Title.
GOE: 06.02.04 STRENGTH: L GED: R4 M3 L4 SVP: 8 DLU: 77

534.132-014 SUPERVISOR, PAPER COATING (paper & pulp; paper goods)

Supervises and coordinates activities of workers engaged in operating machines to coat, laminate, or impregnate paper and related materials with substances such as wax, resins, starches, or polyethylene: Confers with customers and company officials to obtain order specifications. Prepares work schedules and assigns duties to workers. Analyzes production reports and maintains production records. Trains workers. May operate coating machines during absences of regular workers. Performs other duties as described under SUPERVISOR (any industry) Master Title.
GOE: 06.02.01 STRENGTH: L GED: R4 M3 L4 SVP: 8 DLU: 78

534.137-010 SUPERVISOR, CARBON-PAPER-COATING (pen & pencil)

Supervises and coordinates activities of workers engaged in manufacturing carbon paper and inked ribbons, and processing printed forms into multicopy business forms and teletype rolls: Reads work orders and production schedules to determine processing sequence. Prepares time and cost estimates and other production reports. Assigns duties and interprets company policy to workers. Performs other duties as described under SUPERVISOR (any industry) Master Title.
GOE: 06.02.01 STRENGTH: L GED: R4 M3 L4 SVP: 7 DLU: 77

534.380-010 CARBON-PAPER-COATING-MACHINE SETTER (pen & pencil)

Sets up and adjusts battery of machines that pass paper or plastic sheeting between series of rolls to coat it with inked wax-oil preparation to make carbon

paper: Selects and installs specified rolls, such as printing (to print specified wording and design on back of paper), applicator, wiper, hot, and cold rolls, using wrenches. Wipes rolls with cloth and solvent to remove dirt and excess wax. Turns valves to admit steam and cold water into hot and cold rolls. Observes gauges and adjusts valves to regulate temperature of rolls and heat of wax in reservoir pan. Measures thickness of material to be coated, using micrometers, to determine that weight is as ordered. Observes paper as it passes over and around rolls, and turns nuts to adjust positions of rolls to remove wrinkles. Measures thickness of coated paper with micrometers, and adjusts distance between applicator and wiper rolls to produce coating of specified thickness. Assists CARBON-COATER-MACHINE OPERATOR (pen & pencil) in installing and removing rolls of material and in cutting jammed paper from rolls.
GOE: 06.01.02 STRENGTH: H GED: R3 M3 L3 SVP: 5 DLU: 77

534.482-010 WAXING-MACHINE OPERATOR (paper goods) alternate titles: sheeter-waxer operator; wax-coating-machine tender; waxer operator
Operates machines to coat paper or cardboard container blanks with wax or paraffin: Mounts paper roll on machine feedrack by hand or using chain hoist, or loads blanks on stacking mechanism. Fills tank with wax chunks or paraffin blocks, and turns valves to regulate temperature and melt material. Starts machine and adjusts controls to regulate machine feed, temperature of wax, paraffin, cooling rolls, or cold water bath, and tension of paper feed or stacking mechanism. Weighs standard-size paper sheets before and after coating and calculates weight of wax, or measures thickness of coated blanks with automatic micrometer, to verify that coating meets specifications. Examines blanks for uneven paraffin distribution, bubbles, spots, or other imperfections. May be designated according to type of product coated as Carton-Waxing-Machine Operator (paper goods).
GOE: 06.02.14 STRENGTH: H GED: R3 M3 L2 SVP: 5 DLU: 77

534.565-010 OVEN TENDER (ordnance)
Tends series of drying and humidifying ovens and waxing tanks that waterproof and condition paper tubes preparatory to processing into shotgun shells: Turns valves and pushes buttons to heat oven, admit water and liquid wax into tanks, and start cooling fans. Observes temperature, humidity, and steam pressure charts and gauges, and adjusts equipment accordingly. Notifies maintenance workers of equipment malfunction. Lifts baskets of die-sized tubes into monorail carriers at sizing machines. Pushes loaded carriers into polymerizing oven to harden linseed-oil coating and into humidifying oven to soften paper for subsequent machining. Immerses carriers in molten wax to waterproof tube interiors, using hoist. Empties carriers into steam-heated tumbler to remove excess wax from tubes. Records types and quantities of tubes processed.
GOE: 06.04.14 STRENGTH: H GED: R2 M2 L1 SVP: 2 DLU: 77

534.582-010 PAPER-COATING-MACHINE OPERATOR (photo. appar.) alternate titles: coater; sensitizer
Operates machine to coat paper with chemical solution or emulsion to produce paper for graphic duplicating or photographic printmaking: Fills coating troughs with specified chemicals. Mounts paper roll on machine spindle, using hoist or lift truck. Threads paper through coating rollers and drying chamber. Adjusts screws on roller shaft to regulate machine speed and paper tension, using handtools. Adjusts temperature in drying chamber to regulate drying of paper. Examines and feels surface of coated paper emerging from machine for streaks, discoloration, and adequate moisture content. Cuts paper with knife to obtain sample for laboratory testing. Records gauge and graph readings and production data. May be designated according to type of coating applied as Blueprint-Paper-Coating-Machine Operator (photo. appar.); Photographic-Paper-Coating-Machine Operator (photo. appar.).
GOE: 06.02.14 STRENGTH: L GED: R3 M3 L2 SVP: 5 DLU: 77

534.662-010 BACK TENDER, PAPER MACHINE (paper & pulp) alternate titles: second hand, paper machine
Operates drier, calender, and winding sections of fourdrinier or cylinder-type papermaking machines to produce paper and wind it onto rolls: Threads continuous sheet of paper through carrier, drier, and calender rolls by hand. Observes charts and gauges, and turns valves to adjust steam pressure, temperature of drier and calender rolls, and hot air blowing into continuous sheet. Turns wheels to adjust tension on rolls and control running speed of sheet. Inspects sheet for defects, such as dirt, slime spots, holes, and wrinkles, and marks defective portions for removal at rewinding section. Directs workers engaged in winding, slitting, weighing, wrapping, and stenciling paper rolls. May operate size tub or spray paper with steam, water, or dyes to obtain specified finish. May operate drying section only to produce rolls or sheets of dry pulp and be designated Back Tender, Pulp Drier (paper & pulp). May be designated according to type of machine as Back Tender, Cylinder (paper & pulp); Back Tender, Fourdrinier (paper & pulp).
GOE: 06.02.14 STRENGTH: M GED: R3 M3 L3 SVP: 6 DLU: 78

534.665-010 SCREEN TENDER (paper & pulp; wood prod., nec)
Tends filter-screen unit at wet end of fourdrinier machine that makes paper, sheet pulp, or insulation board from pulp stock: Adjusts guides to prevent wet felt from running off machine, using wrench. Turns valves to regulate flow of water and pulp onto filter screens as requested by FOURDRINIER-MACHINE OPERATOR (paper & pulp; paper goods). Scrapes residue from screens with hand rake. Observes pickup of pulp from cylinder screens by carrier mat and

formation of continuous sheets to detect defects in paper, such as breaks, slivers, dirt, and slime spots. Notifies FOURDRINIER-MACHINE OPERATOR (paper & pulp; paper goods) of paper defects and machine malfunctions.
GOE: 06.04.14 STRENGTH: L GED: R2 M1 L2 SVP: 3 DLU: 77

534.682-010 AIR-DRIER-MACHINE OPERATOR (paper & pulp) alternate titles: continuous-loft operator
Controls equipment to size (coat) and dry paper: Positions paper roll on feedrack, using hoist. Threads paper through size tank and press and drier rolls, and secures it to winding reel. Starts equipment and adjusts controls to regulate speed of winding reel, temperature of drier rolls, and temperature of air rising from ducts to obtain specified finish. Examines paper during winding for uniformity of finish and defects, such as wrinkles and tears, and flags defective sections for removal. May operate slitter and winder machine to slit and rewind paper into smaller rolls [SLITTING-MACHINE OPERATOR (any industry) I]. May operate machine to cut paper into specified sizes [CUTTER OPERATOR (any industry)].
GOE: 06.02.14 STRENGTH: M GED: R3 M2 L2 SVP: 5 DLU: 77

534.682-014 CARBON-COATER-MACHINE OPERATOR (pen & pencil) alternate titles: coater, carbon paper
Operates machine that coats paper or plastic sheeting with inked wax-oil preparation to make carbon paper: Dips hot solution from storage vat, using pail, and pours solution into pans of machine. Installs roll of paper on machine and threads roll through series of rollers that roll coating on paper, imprint back of paper with identifying data, and chill coating to harden it. Observes gauges and turns steam and cold water valves to regulate temperatures of rolls. Starts machine and observes paper to detect defects, such as tears, slits, holes, and light spots, blurred or incomplete printing, and lack of sheen in coating that indicates need for replenishing ink supply. Turns nuts to adjust tension of roll to prevent wrinkles in paper. Measures thickness of coated paper, using micrometer, to verify that specified quantity of coating is being applied. Cuts jammed paper from rolls and machine, using knife and shears. Cleans rolls and machine parts with solvent and cloths.
GOE: 06.02.21 STRENGTH: H GED: R3 M2 L2 SVP: 3 DLU: 77

534.682-018 COATING-MACHINE OPERATOR (paper & pulp; paper goods) alternate titles: grounding-machine operator; paper coater
Operates machine to glaze or impregnate paper with size or coating mixtures: Adjusts spreader rollers and aligns or fastens brushes or scraper blade in machine, using handtools, to spread coating to specified depth on paper. Loads paper roll on machine feedrack, using hoist, and threads paper through spreader, pressure, and drying rolls. Turns valve to admit specified coating mixture into machine tank. Starts machine and observes paper to detect wrinkles, breaks, and uneven coating. Turns handwheels or levers to adjust tension of paper and pressure of rollers. May measure depth of coating, using micrometer. May be designated according to coating material used as Clay-Coating-Machine Tender (paper & pulp; paper goods); Varnisher-Plasticoater (fabrication, nec). May coat printed wallpaper with plastic solution to waterproof it and be designated Waterproof-Coating-Machine Tender (paper goods).
GOE: 06.02.14 STRENGTH: M GED: R3 M2 L2 SVP: 4 DLU: 77

534.682-022 COATING-MACHINE OPERATOR, HARDBOARD (paper goods; wood prod., nec) alternate titles: paint-coating-machine operator
Operates machine to spray paint and print surface finish on hardboard sheets: Fills hoppers of machine with ready-mixed paint. Starts machine and moves controls to regulate spraying action, specified tension of rollers, and temperature of infrared drying lamps. Tests density of paint, using viscometer. May tend machine that coats unfinished insulation board with talc to prevent sticking during subsequent pressing and be designated High-Density-Talc-Coater Operator (wood prod., nec).
GOE: 06.02.14 STRENGTH: M GED: R3 M2 L2 SVP: 5 DLU: 77

534.682-026 COMBINER OPERATOR (paper & pulp; paper goods) alternate titles: combiner-sheet operator; hot-melt-machine operator; laminating-machine operator; paster operator; solid-fiber-paster operator
Sets up and operates machine to combine two or more continuous sheets of material, such as paper, paperboard, foil, and plastic film, to form such laminated products as building paper, fiberboard, wallboard, or material from which metallic yarn is slit: Mounts rolls of materials in machine, using hoist. Threads materials over and under guide rollers (one sheet over adhesive roller), around cooling drum, and to rewinder core. Starts pumps to transfer adhesive solution from storage tanks to machine. Starts machine, observes gauges, and adjusts controls to maintain temperature and pressure of rollers, temperature of adhesive, filling of cooling drum, functioning of doctor blade, and speed of machine. Inspects samples of laminated products for defects, such as wrinkles and thick spots. May test specific gravity of adhesive solution, using hydrometer. May attach ends of new material to material in machine with tape. May set up and operate machine to extrude polyethylene film, combine film with paper or aluminum foil, and print design on processed laminated paper used for wrapping materials and be designated Polyethylene Combiner (paper goods).
GOE: 06.02.09 STRENGTH: M GED: R3 M2 L2 SVP: 4 DLU: 78

534.682-030 CREPING-MACHINE OPERATOR (paper goods) alternate titles: crinkling-machine operator
Operates machine to crinkle smooth-surfaced paper to form crepe paper: Mounts stock roll on machine, using chain hoist. Regulates flow of glue or lam-

inate to pans and steam to drying cylinders. Starts machine and threads sheet through glue pan, feed rolls, creping (crinkling) roll and blade, rolls that remove excess glue or laminate, drying cylinders, tension rolls, and onto rewinding rolls. Moves controls to bring creping blade in contact with moving paper to crinkle paper, and adjusts temperature of steam-heated rolls, tension of paper, and pressure of rolls to prevent tearing or folding of paper. Cuts paper, using knife, and removes roll of crepe paper when required amount has been wound. May operate machine equipped with cylinder press that simultaneously prints and laminates surface of paper in addition to creping process and be designated Crepe-Laminator Operator (paper goods).
GOE: 06.02.14 STRENGTH: M GED: R3 M2 L2 SVP: 3 DLU: 77

534.682-034   STRAP-MACHINE OPERATOR (paper goods) alternate titles: strap-making-machine operator
Operates strapping machine to glue, compress, and dry multiple strands of twisted fiber yarn to form straps used for packaging: Hangs cones of yarn on creel and empty spool on winder. Turns valves to fill glue troughs. Opens steam valves and observes thermometer to heat glue and drying cans to specified temperature. Adjusts distance between dies to specified measurements, using handtools. Threads strands through tension device, glue bath, compression dies, infrared tacking lamps, around drying can, and through roller and counter to spool. Starts equipment and inspects finished strapping for strand separation, thickness, and width, visually or using gauges. Cuts out faulty areas and splices cut ends together. Replaces full spools on winder. Observes creel, replaces emptying cones, and splices ends. Repairs breaks in yarn by splicing ends. Tags and marks full spools for identification.
GOE: 06.02.05 STRENGTH: L GED: R3 M2 L2 SVP: 4 DLU: 77

534.682-038   SUPERCALENDER OPERATOR (paper & pulp)
Operates supercalender machine to impart specified gloss and finish to surface of paper: Positions roll of paper on machine reel stand, using hoist. Fastens collar and alignment guides on shaft to secure roll, using wrench. Threads paper around feed, calender, and tension rolls, and wraps end of paper around core shaft of rewinder roll. Observes gauge and turns valve to control temperature by regulating flow of steam to calender rolls. Turns handwheels to control tension of paper and pressure of rolls. Inspects paper for dirt, slime spots, wrinkles, and compactness of winding. Splices breaks in paper with glue or splicing paper, and seals splices with heated flatiron. Tests paper samples for gloss and finish, using glarimeter. Holds sandpaper against revolving rolls to remove lint and dirt.
GOE: 06.02.04 STRENGTH: L GED: R3 M2 L2 SVP: 5 DLU: 77

534.685-010   DAMPENER OPERATOR (paper & pulp)
Tends machine that dampens rolls of paper prior to calendering: Inserts steel shaft in core of roll and positions roll on machine frame, using hoist. Aligns roll on shaft and fastens collar to shaft to secure alignment, using rule and wrench. Turns valve to regulate flow of water into tank and starts machine. Threads paper through feed and tension rolls and wraps end of paper around rewinding roll. Turns handwheels to adjust tension and friction rolls. Turns switch to start rotary brush that throws spray of water from tank onto underside of paper. Pounds paper with wooden club to prevent loose winding on roll. Observes feeding, spraying, and winding of paper for excess moisture and loose winding, and makes adjustments. Loads rewound roll onto dolly, using hoist, and pushes it away from machine.
GOE: 06.04.14 STRENGTH: M GED: R2 M2 L1 SVP: 2 DLU: 77

534.685-014   FRICTION-PAINT-MACHINE TENDER (fabrication, nec)
Tends equipment that applies and dries strip of friction paint (striking material) on cards of matchbook covers and matchbox slides: Loads stack of cards into machine feed magazine. Observes machine feed to prevent jam of cards on conveyor. Inspects friction paint coverage for specified thickness of application, and adjusts friction paint feedwheels, using handtools. Removes paper dust and dirt from revolving feedwheels with knife. Fills machine reservoir with friction paint. Turns steam valves and reads gauge to maintain specified temperature in conveyor-drier.
GOE: 06.04.21 STRENGTH: H GED: R2 M2 L1 SVP: 2 DLU: 77

534.685-018   OILING-MACHINE OPERATOR (paper & pulp; paper goods)
Tends machine that immerses hardboard sheets in oil to impart smooth finish and cuts sheets to size preparatory to tempering: Adjusts position of saws to cut sheets to specified length and width. Observes gauge and turns steam valve to fill oil reservoir and maintain oil at prescribed temperature. Starts feed conveyors, saws, and automatic sheet-stacking mechanism. Feeds uncoated sheets into machine and pulls table saw across end of each sheet before coating to remove irregular edges. Observes sheets for presence of coating flaws, scratches, and oil droplets on surface. Grades hardboard sheets according to defects and size. Places board beneath each stack of oiled sheets and inverts top sheet to protect surfaces against marring during storage or further processing. Keeps records of rejected hardboard sheets for shift log.
GOE: 06.04.14 STRENGTH: H GED: R2 M1 L1 SVP: 2 DLU: 77

534.685-022   PAPER COATER (paper & pulp; paper goods)
Tends machine that dyes paper to specified color: Pours prepared dye solution into machine receptacle. Loads roll of paper in machine. Pulls lever to start device that applies color solution to paper. Observes paper as it passes through machine to detect blemishes, streaks, or other defects. Replenishes dye solution and loads machine with paper when depleted.

GOE: 06.04.14 STRENGTH: L GED: R2 M1 L1 SVP: 3 DLU: 77

534.685-026   PARAFFIN-MACHINE OPERATOR (paper goods)
Tends machine that sprays fiber can lids or paperboard box blanks with paraffin wax to make items moistureproof or airtight: Fills machine reservoir with paraffin chunks and opens steam valve to heat and liquefy paraffin. Places items into machine that automatically sprays melted paraffin wax on inner surfaces as items pass under nozzle. Examines sprayed items to ensure uniformity of coating. Stacks finished items on trays or handcart for removal to storage area. May keep daily production records.
GOE: 06.04.21 STRENGTH: L GED: R2 M1 L1 SVP: 2 DLU: 77

534.685-030   VARNISHING-MACHINE OPERATOR (print. & pub.)
Tends machine that coats paper decals with varnish: Mixes varnish according to formula and fills machine reservoir. Starts and feeds sheets of paper decals between rollers that coat them with varnish.
GOE: 06.04.21 STRENGTH: L GED: R2 M2 L1 SVP: 2 DLU: 77

534.685-034   WET-END HELPER (wood prod., nec)
Tends wet end of machine that cuts and paints wallboard, as directed by FOURDRINIER-MACHINE OPERATOR (paper & pulp; paper goods): Turns valve to regulate flow of paint onto wet board. Turns handwheel to adjust cutters. Guides end of wet-board mat from pressure rolls onto tipple rolls at start of each new run. Observes wet-board panels and pulls lever to drop defective boards into recovery box. Sharpens and cleans cutter as it rotates. Removes and replaces screens and pressure rolls, using hoist and handtools. May weigh sample of wet board, dry sample in electric retort, and compute moisture loss and estimated density, using standard conversion tables or slide rule. May measure thickness of board, using calipers. May record production data in logbook.
GOE: 06.04.14 STRENGTH: L GED: R2 M2 L2 SVP: 2 DLU: 77

534.686-010   PAPER-PROCESSING-MACHINE HELPER (paper & pulp; paper goods)
Mounts rolls of paper on machines, such as combiner, coating machine, and waxing machine, and performs related duties to assist machine operators: Inserts metal shaft through core of paper roll, positions roll on machine feedrack, using hoist, and clamps shaft in bearings. Shoves core on rewind shaft and positions shaft in machine rewind rack. Assists operator in threading paper through machine, and starts end of paper around rewind core. Splices breaks in paper, using tape and hot iron. Removes rewound roll from machine with hoist, and pulls shaft from core by hand. Performs other duties as described under HELPER (any industry) Master Title. May stack cardboard container blanks and return blanks to operator for further processing of untreated sides of blanks. May examine coating of blanks for imperfections and notify operator when imperfections occur. May be designated according to worker assisted, as Coating-Machine-Operator Helper (paper & pulp; paper goods); Combiner-Operator Helper (paper & pulp; paper goods); Supercalender-Operator Helper (paper & pulp); Waxing-Machine-Operator Helper (paper goods).
GOE: 06.04.14 STRENGTH: H GED: R2 M1 L1 SVP: 2 DLU: 81

534.687-010   CONE TREATER (paper goods)
Treats paper cones with mixture of turpentine and beeswax: Combines specified amounts of turpentine and beeswax in vat and adjusts controls to heat mixture to specified temperature. Fills wire basket with paper cones and lowers basket into heated mixture until thoroughly saturated (treated). Raises basket, drains mixture from cones, and sets basket aside for transfer to drying cabinet.
GOE: 06.04.14 STRENGTH: M GED: R2 M1 L1 SVP: 2 DLU: 77

534.687-014   CREPING-MACHINE-OPERATOR HELPER (paper goods)
Assists CREPING-MACHINE OPERATOR (paper goods) in forming crepe paper: Trucks paper rolls to machine and storage areas. Weighs finished rolls and cleans working area. Performs other duties as described under HELPER (any industry) Master Title.
GOE: 06.04.40 STRENGTH: H GED: R2 M2 L1 SVP: 2 DLU: 77

535   FORMING OCCUPATIONS, N.E.C.

This group includes occupations, not elsewhere classified, concerned with imparting a desired shape to paper and related material.

535.482-010   WAD-COMPRESSOR OPERATOR-ADJUSTER (ordnance) alternate titles: compressor operator-adjuster
Operates battery of compressor machines and drying ovens to press and dry cardboard-fiber and wood-flour slurry to form filler wads for shotgun shells: Turns valves to fill compressor jackets with slurry and to heat drying ovens. Starts feed tank agitator, wad compressors, and conveyors. Observes molded wads emerging from compressor punches to detect concave tops indicating fouled punch tip. Unbolts punch tube and cleans accumulated slurry from tip, using compressed air or water. Replaces bent or broken punches, tubes, knock-off fingers, and transfer plates, using handtools. Weighs specified number of dried wads from each batch of slurry on grain scale, and computes quantity of water needed to produce wads of specified weight. Measures thickness of wads, using dial gauge, and adjusts spacing between top and bottom punches to change wad thickness, using micrometers, feeler gauges, and precision gauge blocks. Washes accumulation of slurry from machine. May operate and adjust battery of stationary pneumatic compressors that press slurry into holed wads for further compressing into base wads and be designated Base-Wad Operator-Adjuster (ordnance).

GOE: 06.02.18 STRENGTH: L GED: R3 M3 L2 SVP: 4 DLU: 77

535.685-010 PLATE WORKER (paper & pulp) alternate titles: composition-board-press operator; high-density-press operator; hot-press operator

Tends steam-heated hydraulic press which compresses paper and cardboard to form insulation board: Positions preformed cardboard and paper on bed of press. Starts press to lower ram, and turns steam valve to bond paper and cardboard together. Closes valve, raises ram, and removes finished board from press. May tend semiautomatic press that forms insulation panels and transfers them to trimming and painting machines, monitoring temperature and pressure gauges to maintain press conditions within plant standards. May measure thickness of pressed board, using micrometer, to determine conformity of product to specifications.
GOE: 06.04.04 STRENGTH: M GED: R2 M2 L2 SVP: 2 DLU: 77

539   OCCUPATIONS IN PROCESSING OF PAPER AND RELATED MATERIALS, N.E.C.

This group includes occupations, not elsewhere classified, concerned with effecting the composition, texture, shape, color, consistency, and finish of paper and related materials.

539.130-010 SUPERVISOR, HARDBOARD (wood prod., nec)

Supervises and coordinates activities of workers engaged in cutting peeler log cores into chips, grinding chips into pulp, and pressing pulp into insulation board or hardboard: Observes various processing operation and reads dials and charts to verify conformance of products to specifications. Inspects and tests samples of chips, mat, and hardboard for water absorption, resin and wax content, internal bond, modulus rupture, weight, and dimensions, using laboratory equipment. Trains and assign tasks to new workers. Performs other duties as described under SUPERVISOR (any industry) Master Title.
GOE: 06.02.01 STRENGTH: L GED: R4 M3 L4 SVP: 7 DLU: 77

539.130-014 SUPERVISOR, WET ROOM (paper & pulp)

Supervises and coordinates activities of workers engaged in screening, pressing, sheet-forming, and baling pulp used in making paper: Trains workers in operation of equipment. Reads dirt and moisture test reports and orders adjustments made to machinery to obtain pulp of specified quality. Performs other duties as described under SUPERVISOR (any industry) Master Title.
GOE: 06.02.01 STRENGTH: L GED: R4 M4 L3 SVP: 8 DLU: 77

539.131-010 SUPERVISOR, WET END (wood prod., nec)

Supervises and coordinates activities of workers engaged in cooking and processing wood chips to form pulp, and in processing pulp to form hardboard or insulation board. Performs duties as described under SUPERVISOR (any industry) Master Title.
GOE: 06.02.01 STRENGTH: L GED: R4 M3 L3 SVP: 7 DLU: 77

539.132-010 SUPERVISOR, PAPER MACHINE (paper & pulp)

Supervises and coordinates activities of workers engaged in operating paper-making machines to make cardboard, paper, and pulp sheets from pulp stock, and winding and cutting paper sheets: Directs workers in installing wet and dry felts and wire-mesh belts in machine, and in threading paper through feed, press, drier, and calender rolls. Observes consistency of pulp and reads laboratory reports of moisture, caliber, and oil tests to verify conformation of product to quality control specifications. Supervises workers in requisitioning, repairing, and maintaining wire-mesh belts, wet and dry felts, and machine accessories and parts. Performs other duties as described under SUPERVISOR (any industry) Master Title. May be designated according to machines operated by workers supervised as Fourdrinier-Paper-Machine Supervisor (paper & pulp); or according to product as Superintendent, Board Mill (paper & pulp).
GOE: 06.02.01 STRENGTH: L GED: R4 M3 L3 SVP: 7 DLU: 78

539.132-014 SUPERVISOR, PULP PLANT (paper & pulp)

Supervises and coordinates activities of workers engaged in cooking, bleaching, and screening pulp and in making cooking and bleaching liquors to prepare pulp for use in making paper: Trains workers in operation of equipment. Reads laboratory reports and observes cooking, bleaching, screening, and liquor-making operations to verify that specified procedures are followed and that products meet specifications. Observes level of pulp in storage chests, and directs workers in routing pulp from bleachers to chests, to ensure that pulp of specified quantity and quality is available for delivery to papermaking machines. Inspects equipment, such as pumps and digester shells, for leaks and worn bearings, and schedules shutdown of equipment for maintenance and repair. Performs other duties as described under SUPERVISOR (any industry) Master Title. May be designated according to activities of workers supervised as Supervisor, Bleach Plant (paper & pulp).
GOE: 06.01.01 STRENGTH: L GED: R4 M4 L4 SVP: 8 DLU: 78

539.132-018 SUPERVISOR, REPULPING (paper & pulp) alternate titles: head-stock operator

Supervises and coordinates activities of workers engaged in repulping, refining, and adding colors and clays to ground woodpulp and broke: Reads production order to determine operating sequence, type and length of fibers to use, and specified amounts and mixture of colors and clays. Directs flow of materials to meet production schedules. Compares laboratory test results with production specifications and confers with department supervisors to ensure that

pulp meets quality control standards. Directs training of new workers, and instructs them in safety procedures. Initiates promotions within department. Performs other duties as described under SUPERVISOR (any industry) Master Title.
GOE: 06.02.01 STRENGTH: L GED: R4 M3 L4 SVP: 8 DLU: 77

539.134-010 SUPERVISOR, PAPER TESTING (paper & pulp; paper goods)

Supervises and coordinates activities of workers engaged in testing paper and pulp products, and in calibrating and maintaining related equipment: Assigns duties to workers and instructs them on new test procedures. Confers with company officials to develop new products and resolve customer complaints. Analyzes test reports to verify product adherence to company standards. Performs other duties as described under SUPERVISOR (any industry) Master Title.
GOE: 06.02.01 STRENGTH: L GED: R4 M4 L4 SVP: 8 DLU: 77

539.137-010 SUPERVISOR, RAG ROOM (paper & pulp)

Supervises and coordinates activities of workers engaged in sorting, cutting, cooking, and bleaching rags for use in making paper. Performs duties as described under SUPERVISOR (any industry) Master Title.
GOE: 06.04.01 STRENGTH: L GED: R3 M3 L3 SVP: 5 DLU: 77

539.137-014 PRODUCTION SUPERVISOR (nonmet. min.)

Supervises workers engaged in tending machines that process and package recycled newspapers into cellulose insulation: Observes sorting, equipment loading, processing, and packaging operations for conformance to establishment specifications. Performs other duties as described under SUPERVISOR (any industry) Master Title.
GOE: 06.02.01 STRENGTH: L GED: R4 M3 L4 SVP: 6 DLU: 86

539.362-010 CYLINDER-MACHINE OPERATOR (paper & pulp; wood prod., nec)

Operates cylinder-type machine to make paper, cardboard stock, insulation board, or pulp sheets according to specifications: Turns valves to start flow of water and specific types of pulp stock into designated cylinder vats. Starts machine and turns handwheels and valves or adjusts panel controls to regulate flow of stock onto wire mesh of revolving pickup cylinders and onto wet felt mats on which continuous sheets of product are formed. Inspects machine products, reviews laboratory reports, and observes machine operations to determine causes of defects in paper. Regulates and coordinates stock flow, speed of pickup cylinders and wet felts, and water removal by vacuum action of cylinders and by pressure of rolls on pulp mat, according to type of stock and specified kind, grade, weight, and moisture content of product. Directs workers engaged in replacing felts, threading sheets through drier rolls, slitting and cutting sheets to specified dimensions, and winding sheets onto roll. May be designated according to product made as Cylinder-Machine Operator, Pulp Drier (paper & pulp).
GOE: 06.02.18 STRENGTH: L GED: R3 M2 L3 SVP: 6 DLU: 77

539.362-014 FOURDRINIER-MACHINE OPERATOR (paper & pulp; paper goods) alternate titles: paper-machine operator

Operates wet end of fourdrinier machine to make paper, sheet pulp, or insulation board from pulp stock: Turns valves and pushes buttons, flips switches, or moves levers of control panel to start flow of pulp stock into machine headbox and flow of white water to dilute pulp stock. Starts machine and turns wheel to adjust flow of stock onto wire-mesh belt on which paper or other product is formed. Observes formation of product and removal of water, and inspects samples of completed product. Adjusts volume and speed of stock flow, speed and pitch of wire belt, frequency and amplitude of belt shake, water removal by suction boxes and rolls, and pressure of rolls on pulp mats, according to type of pulp stock and kind, grade, and weight of product specified. Tends auxiliary equipment, such as agitators, pumps, and filters. Gives instructions to BACK TENDER, PAPER MACHINE (paper & pulp) 534.662-010 in operating machines that dry, size, calender, wind, or cut paper or paper products. Replaces or directs workers engaged in replacing wire belts and drying-roll felts. Adjusts, cleans, repairs, and replaces rolls and other machine parts, using handtools. May install and adjust dandy roll to impress watermark on paper. May install and adjust paint roll to paint surface of insulation board.
GOE: 06.02.14 STRENGTH: M GED: R3 M2 L3 SVP: 6 DLU: 81

539.362-018 SLURRY MIXER (ordnance)

Operates attrition mill, hydrabeater, and related equipment to produce slurry for subsequent processing into shotgun shell wads: Feeds bagasse and scrap paper into attrition mill that shreds material. Turns handwheel to adjust hydrabeater blades according to slurry consistency specified, and adjusts timer for prescribed cycle. Weighs and measures specified quantities of milled material, wood flour, starch, and dyes, according to formula, and dumps ingredients into hydrabeater in prescribed sequence, using lift truck. Drains unabsorbed water from measured quantity of slurry into graduated cup to determine slurry *freeness* and adjusts beating time and water content of next batch accordingly to maintain uniform consistency of batches. Starts pump to transfer slurry into dilution tank, starts agitator in tank, and admits metered amount of water to dilute slurry to specified consistency. Pumps slurry into holding tank and signals WAD-COMPRESSOR OPERATOR-ADJUSTER (ordnance) to start molding machine.
GOE: 06.02.18 STRENGTH: M GED: R3 M2 L2 SVP: 4 DLU: 77

539.364-010 PULP-AND-PAPER TESTER (paper & pulp)

Tests samples of each batch of pulp and run of paper, using standard testing equipment and chemical analyses to control quality and uniformity of products:

Measures acidity of pulp, using pH meter. Measures weight, thickness, and bulk of standard paper sample, using micrometer and scales. Determines liquor content of pulp, using standard chemical analyses. Makes hand sheet from pulp, using wire screen, press, and drying oven. Counts dirt specks in unit area of sheet, using microscope. Tests hand sheet and paper samples for bursting, tearing, and folding strength, using specified test equipment. Measures brightness of hand sheet and paper, using *reflectance meter* and compares color with standard colors. Records test data and prepares report for machine operators. May be designated according to product tested as Paper Tester (paper & pulp); Pulp Tester (paper & pulp); or according to processing stage as Dry-End Tester (paper & pulp); Wet-End Tester (paper & pulp).
GOE: 06.03.01 STRENGTH: L GED: R3 M3 L3 SVP: 5 DLU: 78

539.367-010 FINAL INSPECTOR, PAPER (paper & pulp) alternate titles: head paper tester

Inspects paper rolls and reviews reports on production to maintain quality control: Compares test report with specifications for indication of substandard production. Examines paper rolls to verify test reports indicating substandard production, and orders rejection of paper not meeting specifications. Evaluates previous tests and machine detail records to determine corrective action. Notifies FOURDRINIER-MACHINE OPERATOR (paper & pulp; paper goods) of machine adjustments required to produce paper of specified quality. Compiles test records of paper produced by each machine to maintain quality control of future production. Reviews work of other inspectors for adherence to prescribed procedures. Schedules testing of products to verify their conformance to customer specifications.
GOE: 06.03.01 STRENGTH: L GED: R3 M3 L3 SVP: 5 DLU: 77

539.367-014 WATER-QUALITY TESTER (paper & pulp)

Reviews data from meters, recorders, and sampler, and inspects equipment in mill to ensure compliance with government standards: Records readings from plant measuring devices, such as recorders and meters. Removes and replaces record charts. Computes effluent flow from chart for sampling period. Collects waste water samples, using sample bottle. Submits samples to laboratory for testing. Writes report on findings. Observes operation of mill effluent system to determine areas of abnormal pulp spills, leaks, or defects in piping. Inspects machine sampling and measuring devices to determine source of problem or if equipment is malfunctioning. Reviews sampling and operational reports to ensure that results are within limits of water quality standards. Conducts tests, such as pH and dissolved oxygen, to ascertain effluent levels. Notifies supervisor of excessive fluctuation in waterflow or major breakdown in equipment. Records findings on daily logsheet.
GOE: 05.07.04 STRENGTH: L GED: R3 M3 L3 SVP: 5 DLU: 77

539.387-010 CHIP TESTER (paper & pulp)

Tests samples of purchased wood chips, used in making pulp, to determine moisture content and quality: Observes dumping of chips into receiving pit and starts conveyor that transfers chips to screening and storage areas. Draws measured sample from conveyor, places chips in drying oven for specified period of time, and records dry weight to determine weight loss. Places additional sample of chips in pilot screen to separate unsuitable wood, such as sawdust, slivers, and oversized chunks. Removes bark from acceptable portion, reweighs sample, and records data on chip quality form. Sweeps and cleans work area. May test samples for acidity and *freeness,* using standard testing equipment.
GOE: 06.03.01 STRENGTH: L GED: R3 M3 L2 SVP: 3 DLU: 77

539.482-010 CALENDER OPERATOR, INSULATION BOARD (wood prod., nec)

Operates machines in tandem to press rough insulation board into specified caliper (thickness), calender (iron) it into smooth finish, and paint and dry it: Pumps paint from portable tank into machine well. Turns handwheel to space paint rolls and control specified paint spread on board. Starts machines and turns valves to start flow of steam and regulate temperature in calender rolls and paint-drying oven. Weighs unpainted and painted sample boards to calculate amount of paint adherence. Observes processing to ensure that finished boards meet quality control specifications.
GOE: 06.02.09 STRENGTH: L GED: R3 M2 L1 SVP: 4 DLU: 77

539.485-010 WEIGHT TESTER (paper & pulp)

Tends machine that records variations in weight along sample strip of paper or other material: Inserts end of sample strip into testing machine to obtain reading on graph of basic weight of sample. Turns dial to bring weight indicator to center line on graph to calibrate machine for weight of material tested. Starts feed rolls that carry sample strip through machine to record variations in weight of material on graph. Calculates percentage of variation in material weight, using formula or chart. Fills machine ink reservoir, using dropper.
GOE: 06.03.01 STRENGTH: S GED: R3 M3 L3 SVP: 2 DLU: 77

539.487-010 INSPECTOR, FIBROUS WALLBOARD (wood prod., nec)

Inspects each phase of processing in manufacture of hardboard, insulation board, and acoustical tile to ensure conformity to specifications: Weighs samples of wet and dry chips, pulp, and board; and calculates moisture content. Tests tensile strength of products, using breakage tester. Examines boards for oil spots, scratches, scuffs, broken flanges, and lug marks. Compares acoustical tile with template for location of drilled holes and cleanness of cut. Measures sample boards, using tape and square frame. Examines flanges for depth and sharpness of cut, using measuring device. Tags and records offgrade products. May conduct titration tests to determine acidity of pulp.

GOE: 06.03.01 STRENGTH: L GED: R3 M3 L2 SVP: 4 DLU: 77

539.562-010 HIGH-DENSITY FINISHING OPERATOR (wood prod., nec)

Sets up and operates trimming and coating machines to cut, bevel, and paint sheets of insulation board emerging from forming press: Adjusts position and angle of saws to cut and bevel stock according to plant specifications for each type of board, using wrenches. Cleans and adjusts clearance of paint brushes on coating machine to apply uniform coat without brush streaks and foreign matter in paint. Moves controls to start flow of paint to brushes and to regulate drying and cooling temperature of coating machine to prevent coating irregularities, scorching of paint, fire, and explosion. Observes trimming and coating operations and regulates speed of feed conveyor, transfer mechanisms, and discharge conveyor to prevent jamming, faulty coating, and ragged or irregularly beveled edges. Culls boards not meeting appearance or dimensional standards. Reports equipment malfunctions. Cleans paint lines and reservoir, using solvent and brushes. Records production output and number of rejected boards in shift log. May set up and operate machines to trim, coat, and pack insulation tile and direct activities of tile inspecting and packing crew and be designated Tile-Machine Operator (wood prod., nec).
GOE: 06.02.18 STRENGTH: M GED: R3 M2 L2 SVP: 3 DLU: 77

539.565-010 VULCANIZED-FIBER-UNIT OPERATOR (paper goods)

Tends machine that compresses and vulcanizes layers of paper or related materials into homogeneous sheets: Reads job order to determine type and thickness of fiber sheets to be made. Inserts metal shafts through core of paper roll, and mounts roll onto machine, using hoist. Tightens holding collars on feed roll shaft to adjust tension on paper roll. Sets counter to record number of layers of paper needed to obtain desired thickness. Threads paper under guide bar, through acid immersion tank, and over calender rolls. Starts machine and observes compressing and vulcanizing process, adjusting tension of paper rolls as needed. Cuts vulcanized sheet from roll, using knife. Directs removal of vulcanized sheets from machine and immersion of sheets into leaching vats for specified period. Maintains production records.
GOE: 06.02.04 STRENGTH: M GED: R3 M3 L3 SVP: 5 DLU: 77

539.587-010 LABORER, RAGS (paper & pulp) alternate titles: apron operator

Performs any combination of following tasks involved in preparing rags for use in making paper: Cuts material, such as clips, buttons, and elastic from rags, using hand shears or automatic circular knife. Removes dusted rags from conveyor of thrasher (dusting machine), weighs and records weight of rags, and trucks them to cutting machine. Removes cover from bleach boiler, allowing rags to fall into stock cars. Marks cars according to grade and type of rags and pushes cars to washing machines. Removes washed rags from drainer (seasoning bin), places them in stock cars, and pushes cars to beater room. May be designated according to work performed as Bleach-Boiler Puller (paper & pulp); Cutter (paper & pulp); Stock Pitcher (paper & pulp).
GOE: 06.04.40 STRENGTH: L GED: R2 M1 L1 SVP: 2 DLU: 77

539.667-010 CONTROL INSPECTOR (paper & pulp; wood prod., nec)

Inspects pulpwood construction board, such as ceiling tiles, insulation panels, and siding, for conformity to appearance and dimensional standards and packing and labeling specifications: Examines materials for surface defects, such as flaws in paint, excess or insufficient glue on laminated panels or joints, warped panels, and ragged edges. Verifies thickness, size, and squareness of boards or panels, using calipers, carpenter's square, and rule. Starts circular saw to cut samples from finished products for testing flame resistance, strength, and insulation qualities by control laboratory. Notifies supervisor or equipment operators when board does not meet specifications to facilitate control adjustments. Prepares reports of defects discovered, origin of defects, shift production, and number of rejects for quality control personnel. Examines packing materials and observes packing activities to ensure that customer and plant specifications are met and that products are appropriately labeled for shipment. Notifies supervisor to direct destruction, reprocessing, or repacking of faulty shipments. May perform standard quality control tests on products, using prescribed laboratory equipment and procedures. May be designated according to product inspected as Siding-Coreboard Inspector (paper & pulp; wood prod., nec); or according to work area assigned as Coating-Line Checker (paper & pulp; wood prod., nec).
GOE: 06.03.02 STRENGTH: L GED: R3 M2 L2 SVP: 4 DLU: 77

539.685-010 COATER OPERATOR, INSULATION BOARD (wood prod., nec)

Tends machine that automatically smooths and paints flanges of acoustical tile: Starts machine. Turns dial to control temperature of pressing irons. Adjusts pressure of irons to obtain smooth finish on flanges. Adjusts rollers, using wrench, to control amount of paint applied to flanges as tile moves on conveyor. Observes processing and makes necessary adjustments.
GOE: 06.04.21 STRENGTH: L GED: R2 M2 L1 SVP: 2 DLU: 77

539.685-014 IMPREGNATION OPERATOR (paper goods)

Tends machines that impregnate fiber tubing, pipe, or conduit with pitch: Loads items into treatment tank with hoist and closes tank lid. Presses button to start pumps that circulate pitch in tank. Turns valves and observes gauges to control vacuum pressure and temperature. Records instrument readings at designated intervals. Removes impregnated tubes from treatment tank and places them in water tank to cool, using hoist.

GOE: 06.04.09 STRENGTH: L GED: R2 M1 L2 SVP: 3 DLU: 77

539.685-018 MOLDING-MACHINE TENDER (paper & pulp)

Tends molding machine that casts articles, such as pots, cups, trays, and synthetic soil blocks from pulp slurry: Opens valve to admit water into pulp-mixing vat. Weighs and dumps specified amounts of scrap paper, rosin, wax, and other binders into vat. Transfers mixed slurry to storage tank or slurry tank. Activates forming heads to dip molds into slurry tank. Monitors operation of vacuum suction that fills forms or molds. Weighs amount of slurry gathered in random molds to ensure quality control. Adjusts timers to control curing and drying cycles. Observes pickup die which removes cured articles from forming heads or molds. Cleans residue from molds, using water hose. May tend machine that forms fiber pipe or conduit around mandrels of specified sizes and be designated Forming-Machine Operator (paper & pulp).
GOE: 06.04.09 STRENGTH: M GED: R2 M2 L1 SVP: 3 DLU: 77

539.685-022 PUMP-PRESS OPERATOR (paper & pulp)

Tends equipment that forms wet pulp into bales according to specifications: Turns valves to regulate flow of pulp slush from main supply line to pulp machine headbox. Starts equipment, such as vacuum and water pumps, mix tank agitator, cyclone drier and fluffer, shredder disks, screw conveyor, and compressor, to mix, dry, shred, and bale pulp of specified moisture content. Examines pulp for specified consistency and adjusts panel controls to correct inconsistency.
GOE: 06.04.14 STRENGTH: L GED: R3 M2 L2 SVP: 4 DLU: 77

539.685-026 SCREEN HANDLER (paper & pulp)

Tends equipment that loads and unloads press and humidifier unit that press and treat hardboard, performing any combination of following tasks: Starts conveyor to transfer unpressed mats of woodpulp to automatic press loader. Aligns shelves of press loader with opening in press, and moves controls to transfer mat to pressing screen or metal plate on press bed. Moves controls to align press unloader with press discharge and to activate tongs that grasp pressing screen or plate to pull hardboard from press onto unloader shelves. Lowers unloader and retracts tongs. Moves humidifier transfer car to press unloader and starts hydraulic mechanism that aligns openings in car with shelves of unloader. Starts unloader rollers that transfer pressed hardboard sheets onto humidifier car. Pushes car to humidifier, and activates piston that transfers car to humidifier. Unloads humidifier car after it is automatically discharged from humidifier by aligning rollers of unloading device with car and feeding boards between rollers that pile boards for packing. Assists HUMIDIFIER OPERATOR (concrete prod.) to remove pressing screens manually from press and transfer them to dolly. Examines screens for damage or defects and marks faulty screens, using crayon. Transfers usable screens to press loader for reuse.
GOE: 06.04.14 STRENGTH: H GED: R2 M1 L1 SVP: 2 DLU: 77

539.685-030 WET-MACHINE TENDER (paper & pulp) alternate titles: lap-machine tender; pulp-machine operator

Tends battery of machines that form continuous sheets of pulp from woodpulp slush: Starts machines and turns valves to regulate flow of slush pulp into machine vat. Turns handwheels to adjust feed cylinders in vat, pressure of press rolls, and tension on pickup felt to produce pulp sheet of specified moisture content. Cuts and folds continuous sheet into laps and loads laps onto skid or handtruck. May install cutters to cut sheets to specified dimensions.
GOE: 06.04.14 STRENGTH: L GED: R2 M2 L2 SVP: 3 DLU: 77

539.686-010 CUTTER, WET MACHINE (paper & pulp) alternate titles: roll skinner; sheet taker; skinner; web-machine tender; wet-press tender

Cuts and folds continuous pulpwood sheet into laps as it emerges from wet-machine cutter rolls, using lap cutter (pointed wooden stick) or power-cutting bar. Piles laps on rack truck or conveyor for transfer to hydraulic press, inserting wire-mesh screen between each lap. May compress pile of laps in hydraulic press to remove specific amount of moisture. May assist in threading pulp sheet through press rolls and in other duties.
GOE: 06.04.14 STRENGTH: M GED: R2 M1 L1 SVP: 2 DLU: 77

539.687-010 WINDER HELPER (paper & pulp)

Performs any combination of following tasks in papermaking: Places cardboard roll core on steel shaft, and positions shaft on winding reel, using hoist. Threads paper through drier and calender rolls, and wraps end around roll core. Observes paper winding on roll, and flags defects with colored chalk mark or by inserting paper strip in roll. Lifts full rolls from winding reel onto dolly, using hoist, and pushes them to finishing area. Turns valves to spray steam, air, and water on paper in preparation for calendering. Pulls broke from drier and calender rolls. Cleans calender rolls, using hand scraper, solvent, and rags. Turns handwheel to adjust tension on paper. Assists MACHINE-CLOTHING REPLACER (paper & pulp) 629.361-010 in changing papermaking machine clothing, such as wire-mesh belts and wet and dry felts. Oils and greases machine. Cleans wire-mesh belt, wet felt, and machine frame, using water hose, airhose, soap, brushes, and rags. May inflate shaft designed to grip inside of roll core and prevent slipping of paper while winding. May push rolls of paper into position on scales for weighing and mark rolls of paper for shipment, using stencil and stencil brush.

GOE: 06.04.14 STRENGTH: H GED: R2 M2 L1 SVP: 3 DLU: 82

54 OCCUPATIONS IN PROCESSING OF PETROLEUM, COAL, NATURAL AND MANUFACTURED GAS, AND RELATED PRODUCTS

This division includes occupations concerned with the post-extraction phases involved in preparing for commercial use the products of oil shales, oil and gas wells, and coal mines. Includes preparing and refining petroleum and recovering refinery byproducts; manufacturing asphalt and tar paving mixtures and blocks and asphalt felts and coatings; preparing and manufacturing gaseous, liquid, and solid fuels including coke, coke-oven byproducts, and commercial gas; and processing tars for the chemical industry. Occupations concerned with treating wood are included in Division 56.

540 MIXING AND BLENDING OCCUPATIONS

This group includes occupations concerned with combining and mingling materials to produce a single mass.

540.382-010 COMPOUNDER (petrol. refin.)

Controls equipment to blend specified oils and additives to obtain oils possessing specified characteristics: Reads specifications to determine batch characteristics and type and weight of ingredients to be used. Selects and weighs industrial, automotive, and special lubricating oils, and additives, such as antioxidants, corrosion inhibitors, detergents, dispersants, pour-point depressants, foam inhibitors, and viscosity-index improvers. Turns valves and pours ingredients to fill mixer and pump containers. Starts equipment and adjusts temperature, time, and speed controls to blend ingredients, adding additional ingredients during blending cycle as specified. Records type and quantity of materials used.
GOE: 06.02.12 STRENGTH: L GED: R3 M3 L3 SVP: 7 DLU: 77

540.462-010 BLENDER (petrol. refin.) alternate titles: gasoline finisher; lead blender

Controls equipment to blend straight run or natural gasoline with chemicals, tetra-ethyl leads, and light distillates of crude oil to produce commercial fuel, according to formula: Reads blending schedules to determine specified components and quantities to be blended. Turns controls to open valves and starts pumps or notifies STILL-PUMP OPERATOR (petrol. refin.) to transfer gasoline to blending tanks. Computes amount of additives or sets weighing machine that automatically weighs quantities of additives in ratio to quantity of gasoline. Turns handwheels to open valves and spray jets to admit and circulate specified quantities of gasolines, additives, and chemicals in mixing tanks. Moves controls of pumps, agitators, and mixers to blend mixture mechanically or with air agitation. Observes temperature gauges and turns valves to regulate and maintain specified temperature in tanks. Draws sample of mixture for laboratory analysis. Repeats blending process as required by laboratory recommendations, or starts pumps to draw off blended gasoline to storage tanks or leading racks. Opens valves to draw off chemical and lead residue. Records quantity blended and materials used. May lubricate, adjust, and repair pumps, agitators, and mixers. May test products [TESTER (petrol. refin.)]. May operate control panels utilizing electronic computers and controls, to blend products in pipelines (inline blending). May be designated according to type of additive as Ethyl Blender (petrol. refin.). May blend asphalt with petroleum products to improve their quality, viscosity, and performance and be designated Asphalt Blender (petrol. refin.).
GOE: 06.02.12 STRENGTH: L GED: R3 M3 L2 SVP: 6 DLU: 77

540.585-010 MIXER OPERATOR, CARBON PASTE (elec. equip.; smelt. & refin.)

Tends machines that mix ground coke, coal, anode butts, and pitch into carbon paste and press paste into anodes or electrodes: Sets automatic scale and steam regulator to specified weight and pressure. Opens hopper valves to load specified amounts of coke, coal, butts, and pitch scales into batch car. Starts equipment and charges mixer with mixing ingredients. Turns valve to admit liquid pitch into mixer. Records charging and discharging time of mixer. Periodically inspects system to verify consistency of carbon paste and dimensions of anodes or electrodes emerging from press. Records data for each batch processed. May lubricate and perform minor repair on machines. May tend machine that grinds material for electrodes [GRINDER, CARBON PLANT (smelt. & refin.)]. May tend machines, using panelboard, and be designated Carbon-Paste-Mixer Operator, Panelboard (elec. equip.; smelt. & refin.).
GOE: 06.04.19 STRENGTH: L GED: R2 M2 L2 SVP: 4 DLU: 77

540.686-010 COMPOUNDER HELPER (petrol. refin.)

Assists COMPOUNDER (petrol. refin.) in blending oils: Gauges supply of oil in tanks. Segregates and dumps barrels of oil into respective tanks. Takes samples of blended oil to laboratory for analysis. Loads and unloads tank cars [LOADER (any industry) I]. Performs other duties as described under HELPER (any industry) Master Title.
GOE: 06.04.12 STRENGTH: M GED: R2 M2 L2 SVP: 2 DLU: 77

540.687-010 SEAL MIXER (elec. equip.) alternate titles: seal-mixing operator

Mixes ingredients according to formula to compound seal used to attach covers to storage-battery containers: Weighs specified amounts of ingredients,

using gram scale, and dumps ingredients into pail. Starts mechanical mixer. Lifts pail manually to sink mixer blades into ingredients. Determines when ingredients are mixed and lowers pail. Pours mixture into metal cylinders for use in hydraulic extrusion press. Cleans equipment, using water and brushes. May adjust and clean extrusion press, using handtools, brushes, and water. May carry covers and seal to extrusion press.
GOE: 06.04.34 STRENGTH: L GED: R2 M2 L2 SVP: 2 DLU: 77

541 FILTERING, STRAINING, AND SEPARATING OCCUPATIONS

This group includes occupations concerned with separating desirable materials by means of filtering, straining, sifting, squeezing, centrifugal force, or agitating devices.

541.362-010 DESULFURIZER OPERATOR (steel & rel.) alternate titles: gas desulfurizer
Controls equipment, such as vats, thionizer tower, absorbing tower, and autoclave, arranged in series to recover sulfur from coke-oven gas: Turns valve to admit coke-oven gas into absorbing tower. Starts pumps that force solution containing arsenic compound and soda ash through tower. Pumps resulting foul solution into thionizer tower, and admits compressed air to precipitate sulfur and form froth which overflows into tank. Filters slurry [FILTER OPERATOR (any industry)], and washes salts from caked sulfur. Melts sulfur in autoclave, and casts it into pans. Determines alkalinity of absorbing solution by titration tests, and directs helper to add soda ash or arsenic compound. Observes meters and gauges to control temperature of solution. Punches dirt from holes in absorbing tower sprays with bar, and lubricates equipment.
GOE: 06.02.11 STRENGTH: M GED: R4 M3 L2 SVP: 6 DLU: 77

541.362-014 PUMP OPERATOR, BYPRODUCTS (steel & rel.) alternate titles: pump tender; tar-and-ammonia pump operator
Operates equipment to cool, condense, and separate tar and ammonia from coke-oven gas and pump separated substances to specified locations: Turns valves to transfer materials from collecting mains through cooler, scrubbers, and *decanter*. Starts pumps, reads gauges and thermometers, and adjusts valves to regulate temperatures, pressures, and rate of flow of gas, tar, ammonia liquor, and water. Observes flow of tar from decanter and manually adjusts seal to alter level of interface between tar and liquor and regulate liquor settling time. Pumps gas to next process, tar to storage tanks, and liquor to collecting mains or to liquor storage tanks. Records temperature, pressures, and amount of tar and liquor pumped. Repairs pipes, using handtools. Turns valves to bypass equipment requiring repair or cleaning. May flush interior of coils with hot ammonia liquor to remove tar. May adjust and lubricate floats, valves, and other equipment, using handtools and lubricating equipment.
GOE: 06.02.17 STRENGTH: L GED: R3 M2 L2 SVP: 5 DLU: 77

541.382-010 COAL WASHER (mine & quarry) alternate titles: coal-washer tender; wash-box operator; washer operator
Operates equipment to size and wash coal for shipment or further processing: Starts equipment, such as launders, tables, shakers, sizing screens, and conveyors. Regulates flow of coal and water to separate coal from slate, rock, and other foreign material and transfers cleaned and sized coal to loading chutes or storage. Observes equipment, gauges, and indicator lights and adjusts equipment to ensure maximum cleanliness of product. May lubricate and repair equipment and replace parts, using handtools. May test refuse samples to determine coal content, using scales to weigh material precipitated from sample by chemical reaction.
GOE: 06.02.18 STRENGTH: L GED: R3 M2 L2 SVP: 5 DLU: 77

541.382-014 CRUDE-OIL TREATER (petrol. & gas) alternate titles: dehydrator operator; production operator; pumper; treater
Operates chemical, electrical, and centrifugal oil-treatment units to remove sediment and water from crude oil before transporting oil by pipeline to refineries: Opens valves and starts pumps to pump oil from storage tanks to treating units. Opens valves to mix specified chemicals with oil, and adjusts controls to heat mixture to specified temperature. Starts centrifugal machines that break up oil and water emulsions and drain off water. Opens valves and starts pumps to transfer oil into settling tanks where sediment is precipitated from oil. Tests sample in gravity- or centrifugal-separation machine to determine content of oil specified for pipeline transportation. Pumps treated oil into pipelines leading to refinery. Cleans and lubricates motors, pumps, and other moving parts of units. Records data, such as volume of oil treated, operating temperatures of units, and test results. May operate pumps at oil well sites [OIL PUMPER (petrol. & gas)]. May tend treating-plant equipment to remove impurities from natural gas [GAS TREATER (any industry)].
GOE: 06.02.12 STRENGTH: L GED: R3 M3 L3 SVP: 5 DLU: 77

541.585-010 CENTRIFUGE-SEPARATOR TENDER (nonfer. metal)
Tends centrifuge separator that purifies used coolant oils from rolling mill machines: Opens valves and starts pumps to transfer oil from machine pit tanks to holding tank. Pulls control levers to add specific amounts of sulfuric acid and water to oil. Opens valves to allow mixture to flow through centrifuge and back to pit tanks of machine. Orders supplies of oil and acid from storeroom and keeps records of solutions used. Delivers samples of purified oil to laboratory. Replaces filters in centrifuge and cleans centrifuge disks, using wire brush and rags.

GOE: 06.04.12 STRENGTH: L GED: R2 M2 L2 SVP: 4 DLU: 77

541.665-010 SHAKER TENDER (steel & rel.) alternate titles: shaker operator
Tends shaking screen and conveyor that screen coke to specified size and load it into bins: Estimates amount of coke needed in bins. Starts conveyors and screens, and signals COKE LOADER (steel & rel.) to unload contents. Turns handwheel to adjust vibration rate of screen. Lubricates screen eccentrics and conveyors, using grease gun and oilcan. Patches screens, and assists in changing vibrator coils and splicing belts, using handtools. Cleans walks and floors, using broom and shovel.
GOE: 06.04.12 STRENGTH: L GED: R2 M2 L1 SVP: 3 DLU: 77

541.682-010 PARAFFIN-PLANT OPERATOR (petrol. refin.) alternate titles: wax pumper
Operates filter presses to separate oil of paraffin distillate from paraffin wax: Installs filter plates, using handtools, and turns handwheel to adjust hydraulic ram pressure. Starts pump that force chilled distillate into filter plates. Starts machine to activate hydraulic rams that squeeze oil from distillate as wax solidifies. Observes oil pressed from filter plates, and adjusts ram pressure to extract maximum amount of oil from wax. Scrapes accumulated wax from filter plates into spiral conveyor that carries it to melting pan. Turns valve to regulate flow of steam into melting pan to heat wax. Starts pump to return salvaged distillate from tank to filter press for reprocessing. May be designated according to phase of processing as Leak Operator, Paraffin Plant (petrol. refin.); Press Operator, Paraffin Plant (petrol. refin.).
GOE: 06.02.12 STRENGTH: L GED: R3 M2 L2 SVP: 5 DLU: 77

541.685-010 HEAVY-MEDIA OPERATOR (mine & quarry)
Tends gravity device that separates coal from refuse: Tests solution in tank for specific gravity, adds pulverized magnetite, and starts oscillating rake to maintain constant density. Opens chute gate to admit coal into tank. Observes coal as it floats over weir onto conveyor. Opens gate to draw off refuse that was raked into discharge chute. Recovers magnetite, drawn off with coal and refuse, from filtering device, using shovel and wheelbarrow.
GOE: 06.04.08 STRENGTH: M GED: R2 M1 L1 SVP: 3 DLU: 77

541.685-014 LEAD RECOVERER, CONTINUOUS-NAPHTHA-TREATING PLANT (petrol. refin.)
Tends centrifuge machine to separate lead compound, used in treating gasoline, from treating solution: Starts pumps to force treating solution into cylinder of centrifuge. Starts machine and allows cylinder to revolve until cake of lead compound has separated from solution. Stops machine, if batch-type centrifuge is used, and scrapes cake from cylinder into barrel, or if continuous-type centrifuge is used, starts steam pumps to force cake and liquid from cylinder into tanks as separation progresses.
GOE: 06.04.12 STRENGTH: M GED: R3 M2 L2 SVP: 4 DLU: 77

542 DISTILLING, SUBLIMING, AND CARBONIZING OCCUPATIONS

This group includes occupations concerned with removing or obtaining gases, condensations, or residue in stills, ovens, or retorts. Includes liquefying and then distilling natural gases.

542.130-010 SUPERVISOR, NATURAL-GAS PLANT (petrol. refin.) alternate titles: plant supervisor
Supervises and coordinates activities of oil field workers operating equipment, such as compressors, boilers, pumps, and dehydration vessels, to remove sediment and water from crude oil, extract natural gas, and separate natural gasoline from gas by means of heat, pressure, and chemical action. Orders flow cycles, pressures, and temperatures of petroleum to be maintained according to process involved and properties of petroleum being processed. Performs other duties as described under SUPERVISOR (any industry) Master Title.
GOE: 05.06.04 STRENGTH: L GED: R4 M3 L4 SVP: 8 DLU: 77

542.130-014 SUPERVISOR, TAR DISTILLATION (chemical)
Supervises and coordinates activities of workers engaged in operation of stills to distill crude oil, produce pitch, and to recover naphthalene-bearing oils and creosote oils. Trains workers in operation of equipment. Analyzes laboratory reports and test results of materials, and orders process changes as required. Performs duties as described under SUPERVISOR (any industry) Master Title.
GOE: 06.01.01 STRENGTH: L GED: R4 M3 L4 SVP: 7 DLU: 77

542.132-010 SUPERVISOR, BYPRODUCTS (steel & rel.)
Supervises and coordinates activities of workers engaged in processing coke-oven gas to obtain byproducts: Directs workers in separating ammonia and tar from gas, scrubbing gas to obtain light-oil, and recovering and refining benzol, toluol, and xylol from light-oil. Studies production reports and orders changes in temperature and circulation rates to produce product of specified quality. Trains new workers. Performs other duties as described under SUPERVISOR (any industry) Master Title.
GOE: 06.04.01 STRENGTH: L GED: R4 M3 L4 SVP: 7 DLU: 77

542.132-014 SUPERVISOR, OVENS (steel & rel.)
Supervises and coordinates activities of workers engaged in carbonizing coal to obtain coke and byproducts. Assigns duties to workers according to production schedules. Examines machinery, equipment, and finished coke and directs

changes in process to promote efficiency and produce product of specified quality. Trains new workers. Performs other duties as described under SUPERVISOR (any industry) Master Title.
GOE: 06.04.01 STRENGTH: L GED: R4 M3 L4 SVP: 8 DLU: 77

542.362-010 HEATER II (steel & rel.)
Controls ovens to carbonize coal according to coking schedules: Removes flue caps, using hook, and determines temperature in flue and condition of nozzles by observing color of flame and using optical pyrometer. Determines type of gases in flue, using gas analyzer. Reads gauges and turns valves to regulate flow of fuel gas and air and maintain specified temperatures in flues. Observes gauges and adjusts weights on governor to maintain specified gas pressure in collecting main. Cleans plugged gas nozzles, using poker. Inspects airflow and gas-reversing mechanisms, and adjusts or repairs equipment, using handtools. Inspects finished coke visually or with pyrometers for temperature and quality, as it is pushed from oven, and adjusts temperature of oven accordingly. Prepares daily reports from gauges and pyrometer readings, noting changes in pressure or temperature. Repairs ovens, using handtools and spray gun.
GOE: 06.02.17 STRENGTH: M GED: R3 M2 L2 SVP: 6 DLU: 77

542.362-014 REFINERY OPERATOR HELPER (petrol. refin.)
Assists REFINERY OPERATOR (petrol. refin.) in distillation and processing of crude and refined oil: Patrols area and inspects equipment, such as furnaces, distilling units, lines, and pumps, to detect malfunctions and leakage. Reads flowmeters and temperature and pressure gauges, and records data. Adjusts control instruments and dampers on oil burners to maintain specified firing conditions. Reports operating condition of units to REFINERY OPERATOR (petrol. refin.). Turns valves and switches as directed to regulate temperature, pressure, and flow rate of product; to direct flow of product to other units; to maintain specified levels of oil in tanks and towers; and to start, stop, and regulate equipment, such as pumps, compressors, and blowers. Draws samples of product from tanks and towers for laboratory testing. Gauges product in tanks and operates pumps and agitators to mix product or load it into storage tanks. Lubricates, cleans, and repairs equipment. May change recording charts and ink pens. May be designated according to type of processing unit or department as Absorption-Plant-Operator Helper (petrol. refin.); Purification-Operator Helper (petrol. refin.); Refinery Operator Helper, Cracking Unit (petrol. refin.); Refinery Operator Helper, Crude Unit (petrol. refin.). Performs other duties as described under HELPER (any industry) Master Title.
GOE: 06.02.12 STRENGTH: L GED: R3 M2 L2 SVP: 6 DLU: 77

542.562-010 FURNACE OPERATOR (petrol. refin.)
Controls operation of burners to maintain temperature in furnaces of petroleum-processing units according to specifications: Observes temperature, pressure, and flow gauges to verify operating conditions of units, and records data. Starts furnace and turns valves and switches to increase or decrease flow of fuel oil or gas to burner and still to regulate temperature according to processing schedule. Throws switches to place burner on automatic control. Examines furnace to detect overheating of walls and tubes, and leakage of still bottoms or oil tubes. Observes flame distribution and combustion conditions in furnace, color of burner flame, and gas issuing from stack, and moves air damper control to correct combustion conditions and stop flame impingements. Reports irregularities in operation to REFINERY OPERATOR (petrol. refin.). May remove and clean burners, using handtools, brusher, solvent, or steam. May change recording charts [CHART CHANGER (clerical)].
GOE: 06.02.12 STRENGTH: M GED: R3 M2 L2 SVP: 6 DLU: 77

542.567-010 COKE INSPECTOR (steel & rel.)
Inspects hot coke pushed from ovens and quenched coke passing on conveyor for color, texture, quality, and size: Notifies supervisor to adjust crusher for size of coke specified. Picks irregularly sized and insufficiently carbonized coke from belt and tosses it into reject hopper. Places samples in containers for laboratory testing. Records car number, carrier, tonnage, and grade of coke of each shipment. Observes conveyor belts for breaks and pulled-out lacings and notifies maintenance department.
GOE: 06.03.02 STRENGTH: L GED: R3 M2 L2 SVP: 4 DLU: 77

542.665-010 OVEN-HEATER HELPER (steel & rel.) alternate titles: heater helper
Assists HEATER (steel & rel.) II in carbonizing coal: Turns handwheel to open and close decarbonizing caps which admit air to flues to burn carbon from gas and air nozzles. Observes pressure gauges, and notifies HEATER (steel & rel.) II if pressure varies from specified limits. Reads pyrometer to determine oven wall temperature. Cleans carbon from plugged nozzles, using poker, and replaces broken nozzles, using handtools. Turns handwheel in emergency to operate automatic reversing machinery. Cleans and lubricates equipment. Performs other duties as described under HELPER (any industry) Master Title.
GOE: 06.04.12 STRENGTH: M GED: R2 M2 L2 SVP: 3 DLU: 77

542.667-010 WHARF TENDER (steel & rel.)
Signals HOT-CAR OPERATOR (steel & rel.) to dump coke onto wharf. Quenches hot spots in dumped coke, using water hose, to prevent burning of conveyor belt. Pushes and pulls lever gates to control flow of coke from wharf onto conveyor belt. Shovels spilled coke onto conveyor.
GOE: 06.04.12 STRENGTH: H GED: R1 M1 L1 SVP: 2 DLU: 77

542.685-010 PLANT OPERATOR, CHANNEL PROCESS (chemical)
Tends series of burners, located in channel-process burner buildings (hot houses), that produce carbon black by contact of gas flame with collecting channels, from which deposited carbon is scraped: Turns valves to regulate flow of gas or mixture of gas and oil to burners to produce flames that deposit carbon black on channels (flat surfaces). Turns handwheel to bring channels into contact with flame. Opens and closes doors at sides and ends of burner building to regulate draft and compensate for changes in atmospheric conditions, air-fuel mixtures, draft, and fuel consumption. Observes, through building ports, accumulation of carbon black, automatic scraping of accumulation from channel, and flow of carbon black through conveyors to detect malfunction of burners and scrapers and to verify production rate.
GOE: 06.04.19 STRENGTH: L GED: R3 M2 L2 SVP: 2 DLU: 77

542.685-014 SUBLIMER (chemical)
Tends equipment that sublimates (refines by vaporization) crude salicylic acid derived from coal tar: Weighs specified amount of salicylic acid and dumps it onto conveyor leading to sublimation unit. Starts fans that circulate heated air in unit to promote vaporization of salicylic acid. Starts pump to draw salicylic-acid vapor through filters into condenser tanks where salicylic acid recrystallizes. Keeps daily production records.
GOE: 06.04.11 STRENGTH: L GED: R2 M2 L1 SVP: 3 DLU: 77

542.685-018 UNIT OPERATOR (chemical) alternate titles: plant-operator helper
Tends equipment in furnace-process plant that produces carbon black by partial combustion of crude oil, natural gas, or mixture of both: Starts individual units, such as reactors (furnaces), quenchers, precipitators, cyclones (grit collectors), pumps, compressors, and conveyors. Turns valves to regulate flow of water in quencher, feed rate of fuel and air, and movement of accumulated carbon black through equipment, as directed by PLANT OPERATOR, FURNACE PROCESS (chemical). Observes gauges and meters to verify specified temperature, pressure, and flow rates of materials. Opens inspection ports and observes flow of product through conveyors to detect jamming.
GOE: 06.04.19 STRENGTH: L GED: R3 M2 L1 SVP: 3 DLU: 77

543 DRYING, HEATING, AND MELTING OCCUPATIONS

This group includes occupations concerned with subjecting materials to heat in order to warm, melt, dry, char, purify, or concentrate them.

543.362-010 OIL BOILER (tex. prod., nec)
Controls kettles to boil oil to specified viscosity for use in making coated textile material: Pumps oil into kettle. Lights burner with torch and monitors burners and temperature gauges to ensure that specified oil temperature is maintained. Adds chemicals to facilitate drying when coating is applied to cloth, and stirs mixture, using paddle. Draws sample of oil and feels oil with fingers to estimate viscosity. Marks oil temperature and time of reading on chart for laboratory use. Pumps oil to and from kettle through water-cooled coils to maintain specified temperature and viscosity. Collects sample of oil for laboratory viscosity verification. Pumps oil to storage tank. Records amount of oil used and amount remaining in tanks.
GOE: 06.02.18 STRENGTH: H GED: R3 M3 L2 SVP: 5 DLU: 77

543.382-010 DRIER OPERATOR (utilities)
Operates battery of driers that remove moisture from coal to facilitate pulverization: Pulls chain to open gate and allow coal to enter drier. Opens dampers to admit hot gas and permit exit of cool gas. Adjusts dampers to regulate amount of gas applied to coal, observing thermometers to ensure adherence to drying specifications. Controls fan on draft line to regulate force of draft. Pulls chain to open gate at bottom of drier, upon completion of drying process, to transfer coal to pulverizer. Cleans drier by removing doors and prying or knocking off coal clinging to sides of drier on supply and exit lines.
GOE: 06.02.08 STRENGTH: M GED: R3 M2 L2 SVP: 4 DLU: 77

543.562-010 CARBON-FURNACE OPERATOR (smelt. & refin.)
Operates pit furnace to bake carbon-block anodes (electrodes) to remove volatile matter and increase electrical conductivity: Lights burner and adjusts fuel and water valves, manifold damper, and head covers to regulate temperature in furnace. Observes gauges and records water and fuel pressures. Measures flue and pit temperatures, using optical pyrometer. Inspects and maintains pumps, motors, fans, gas scrubber system, and pipelines. Signals CARBON-FURNACE-OPERATOR HELPER (smelt. & refin.) to prepare alternate pits for furnace changeover to maintain baking schedule.
GOE: 06.02.18 STRENGTH: L GED: R3 M2 L2 SVP: 5 DLU: 77

543.664-010 CARBON-FURNACE-OPERATOR HELPER (smelt. & refin.)
Assists CARBON-FURNACE OPERATOR (smelt. & refin.) in baking carbon anodes in pit furnaces: Disconnects water and fuel lines from equipment after baking cycle. Hooks cable to portable burner, blower, and exhaust manifold, and signals OVERHEAD CRANE OPERATOR (any industry) 921.663-010 to lift equipment from fired pit and lower it into alternate pit. Replaces gas main covers, flue lids, and port plates on vacated pit. Cleans and installs cloth dustbags and vaporizer in headwall and burner respectively, and connects water and fuel hoses, using handtools. Fills expansion joints, flue cracks, gas connections, and pitholes with mortar or coke, using trowel and shovel. Dumps and spreads coke on pit, using overhead hoist and shovel. Regulates dampers and turns valves on fuel lines as directed. Performs other duties as described under HELPER (any industry) Master Title.

GOE: 06.04.19 STRENGTH: M GED: R3 M2 L2 SVP: 3 DLU: 77

543.666-010 FURNACE WORKER (elec. equip.)

Loads green electrodes in gas or electric furnaces, packs them with insulating materials for firing, and cools and unloads them after processing, working as member of furnace crew: Dumps, levels, and tamps mixture of coke, sand, and sawdust on furnace bed. Attaches sling to individual electrodes, and signals OVERHEAD CRANE OPERATOR (any industry) 921.663-010 in positioning electrodes in furnace. Spreads coke over each layer of electrodes and tamps coke between electrodes to insulate them until specified number and layers of electrodes are loaded. Spreads insulating mixture uniformly over top of charge. Positions brick side blocks on side of furnace with aid of crane operator. Signals crane operator in hoisting *bus bars* into place on electric furnace, and bolts bars to feeders and to furnace terminals. Removes bus bars and side blocks after processing (graphitizing or baking) and pokes hole in insulating mix to observe color of electrodes. Refills and tamps insulating mix in hole to prevent oxidation if charge is cooking too rapidly; or rakes, hoes, or shovels insulating mix from charge and quenches charge with water to speed cooling. Shovels mixture into pile for reprocessing. Attaches sling to processed electrodes and signals crane operator to remove them from furnace. Cleans residue from electrodes, using airhose. May be designated according to duty performed as Furnace Cooler (elec. equip.); Furnace Loader (elec. equip.); Furnace Packer (elec. equip.); Furnace Unloader (elec. equip.).

GOE: 06.04.19 STRENGTH: M GED: R2 M2 L2 SVP: 2 DLU: 77

543.682-010 COKE BURNER (steel & rel.)

Controls beehive coke ovens in which coal is carbonized to produce coke of specified quality: Turns valves to maintain specified temperature in oven and control rate of formation of coke. Measures temperature of melting coal in each oven with optical pyrometer. Determines when coke is ready for drawing, according to color and length of flame in oven.

GOE: 06.02.17 STRENGTH: M GED: R3 M3 L2 SVP: 5 DLU: 77

543.682-014 DRIER OPERATOR (mine & quarry) alternate titles: coal-drier operator; furnace operator; kiln operator

Controls one or more furnaces or kilns and auxiliary drying equipment to dry coal or ore before or after washing, milling, or pelletizing: Fires furnace or kiln, observes gauges, and adjusts controls to maintain specified temperature. Starts conveyor that feeds materials into drying equipment. Observes operation to detect plugging of equipment, and dislodges material, using crowbar. Observes color of materials to determine moisture content, and adjusts temperature or drying time. Cleans and repairs equipment. May shovel in additives. May weigh and compare samples. May keep production records.

GOE: 06.02.18 STRENGTH: L GED: R3 M2 L2 SVP: 4 DLU: 77

543.682-018 FURNACE OPERATOR (elec. equip.)

Controls continuous-feed gas, oil, or electric ovens to harden coated electric welding rods: Turns controls to light burners, open steam valves, and start blowers and conveyor lines. Dumps ink into pot and turns positioning screws on ink rolls to mark rods. Observes gauges and adjusts controls to maintain specified conveyor speed and heat and humidity in each baking zone. Observes coated welding rod to detect tool wear or coating flaws and reports findings to supervisor.

GOE: 06.04.10 STRENGTH: L GED: R3 M2 L2 SVP: 3 DLU: 77

543.682-022 PARAFFIN-PLANT-SWEATER OPERATOR (petrol. refin.) alternate titles: sweater operator

Operates sweater tank to separate liquid from slack wax (processed paraffin distillate): Pumps charge of slack wax into sweater tank. Opens valves to circulate cold water through sweater to cool slack wax. Opens and closes steam valves and reads temperature gauges to sweat (heat) cooled wax at specified temperature levels for specified periods. Turns valves to divert cuts (waxes of different boiling points and specific gravities) to storage tank after completion of each run. Takes samples and observes melting point of each cut at regular intervals. Opens valves to admit steam into sweater tank to melt wax residue when run is completed. Drains melted wax residue from sweater into storage tank.

GOE: 06.02.12 STRENGTH: L GED: R3 M2 L2 SVP: 4 DLU: 77

543.682-026 STILL OPERATOR (build. mat., nec)

Controls equipment that heats asphalt to specified temperature and viscosity for use in manufacture of roofing materials: Starts pumps that fill tanks with asphalt, and turns wheels and valves to regulate temperature and steam pressure. Actuates air compressor to force air bubbles through liquid asphalt, creating chemical reaction that raises asphalt melting point. Observes and adjusts dials and gauges to maintain specified temperature, pressure, and depth of asphalt in tanks. Starts discharge pumps, and turns valves to direct flow of heated asphalt into plant and storage tanks.

GOE: 06.02.18 STRENGTH: L GED: R3 M2 L2 SVP: 5 DLU: 77

543.684-010 QUALITY-CONTROL TESTER (fabrication, nec)

Tests charcoal briquettes at end of processing to verify conformance to specifications: Removes bag of briquettes from packaging line periodically and carries briquettes to testing laboratory. Grinds specified quantity of briquettes, using hand grinder, places grounds into moisture-testing equipment, and observes moisture meter to determine moisture content of sample. Saturates stacked briquettes with fire-starter fluid, ignites briquettes, and observes burning characteristics of briquettes and time required for white ash to form over bri-

quette surfaces. Places prescribed number of briquettes in burner pot, ignites briquettes, and observes heat sensor dial to determine temperature released by burning briquettes. Weighs briquettes. Records test results on test report forms.

GOE: 06.03.02 STRENGTH: L GED: R3 M2 L3 SVP: 3 DLU: 86

543.685-010 BULLET-LUBRICANT MIXER (ordnance)

Tends steam-heated kettle that melts wax and other ingredients to make compound for lubricating lead bullets: Weighs specified amounts of ingredients and loads them into kettle. Turns valve to regulate heat and stirs mixture with wooden paddle. Drains melted compound from kettle into molds. Empties cooled molds and stores cakes in bins. Conveys compound to production departments to fill requisitions, using handtruck.

GOE: 06.04.19 STRENGTH: M GED: R2 M2 L1 SVP: 2 DLU: 77

543.685-014 DRIER TENDER (fabrication, nec) alternate titles: drier attendant

Tends drying equipment that removes moisture from fuel briquettes to harden them after shaping: Turns steam valves and observes gauges to regulate temperature and humidity in drying chamber. Presses button to start hot-air blowers to dehydrate briquettes. Turns handwheel to control speed and amount of material passing through drying chamber. Examines and feels samples to determine if briquettes meet hardness standards. Observes dial on moisture-checking machine to verify dryness.

GOE: 06.04.12 STRENGTH: L GED: R2 M2 L2 SVP: 3 DLU: 77

543.685-018 OVEN TENDER (elec. equip.)

Tends gas or electric furnaces that bake carbon rods, such as those used for commutator brushes, resistors, and switches, to harden them: Inserts carbon rods into ceramic containers and loads containers into furnaces. Regulates furnace temperature by turning gas valves or electric controls according to specifications. Shuts off heat after specified time. Unloads furnace after cooling.

GOE: 06.04.19 STRENGTH: M GED: R2 M2 L2 SVP: 3 DLU: 77

543.685-022 THAW-SHED HEATER TENDER (steel & rel.)

Tends heating units that thaw frozen materials, such as coal and coke, in railroad cars: Pushes buttons to start fuel-feed pumps, heater, and exhaust and air-volume fans. Lights oil burner, and opens valve of fuel line to heating unit in shed where cars are placed. Lubricates and adjusts equipment, such as pump and fan bearings. Cleans working area and equipment with airhose.

GOE: 06.04.12 STRENGTH: M GED: R2 M2 L1 SVP: 4 DLU: 77

543.687-010 COKE DRAWER, HAND (steel & rel.)

Performs any combination of following duties involved in emptying coke oven: Scrapes coke from coke oven, using iron rod (scraper). Forks coke onto conveyor that dumps coke in railroad cars. Picks foreign matter, such as slate and slag, from coke on conveyor. May fork coke into wheelbarrow and push wheelbarrow to railroad cars. May apply brakes or place car-stop to hold railroad cars under coke-pushing machine. May place firebrick doors in oven door-frame, using overhead hoist, to close oven. May seal doors of ovens, using firebricks and loam.

GOE: 05.12.03 STRENGTH: M GED: R1 M1 L1 SVP: 2 DLU: 77

543.687-014 OVEN DAUBER (steel & rel.) alternate titles: dauber; luter; paster

Performs any combination of following tasks involved in sealing coke-oven doors with lute (mud made from clay, coke dust or ashes, and water) to prevent escape of gases during baking of coal: Shovels mud into mud carrier and transfers mud pails to ovens. Chips old clay, carbon, and residue from doorway of oven, using chisel bar. Seals crack around oven door with mud, using trowel and tamping bar. Shovels dry clay into dry-clay box on pusher or into wheelbarrow. Shovels excess mud, oven spillage, and coal from working area. Opens and closes chuckhole door, using handwheel and lever. May open oven, using bar, and manually position coke guide in doorway. May signal LARRY OPERATOR (steel & rel.) to charge oven. May push buttons to move electric mud car.

GOE: 06.04.30 STRENGTH: M GED: R2 M1 L1 SVP: 2 DLU: 77

544 GRINDING AND CRUSHING OCCUPATIONS

This group includes occupations concerned with reducing materials to smaller particles, such as granules, grits, powder, or paste, by means of compression, smashing, cutting, or a combination of these.

544.565-010 GRINDER, CARBON PLANT (smelt. & refin.)

Tends machine that grinds and blends coke according to specifications: Sets mill gauge to specified fineness of grind. Starts conveyors and screening and grinding equipment. Moves gate levers to regulate flow of raw coke into machine, and processed coke to mixer or packing-material hopper. Turns valve to regulate moisture content of material. Opens gauge valves to fill buckets under hopper spouts, attaches crane cable to buckets, and signals RIGGER (any industry) to remove them. Weighs materials at specified intervals, using platform scales, and records data. Observes operation to ensure continuity of flow and to detect malfunctioning. May tend machine that mixes materials for electrodes [MIXER OPERATOR, CARBON PASTE (elec. equip.; smelt. & refin.)].

GOE: 06.04.12 STRENGTH: M GED: R3 M2 L1 SVP: 4 DLU: 77

544.582-010 CRUSHER-AND-BLENDER OPERATOR (steel & rel.) alternate titles: pulverizer operator

Operates machines and equipment to crush and blend coal of various compositions to obtain specified mixture used in producing coke: Turns valve to

admit oil to mixer. Starts hammer mill, mixer, and conveyor equipped with harrow disks. Moves lever to adjust blade on feed tables to deliver coal to mixer. Observes operation of machines to detect malfunctioning, clogging, and unevenness of flow. Frees clogged coal by striking side of hopper with mallet. Adjusts or replaces screens and hammers in mill, using handtools. Observes meters, gauges, and thermometer, and records temperature, oil consumption, tonnage mixed, and operating time. Cleans work areas, using broom. May open valves and start pumps to unload oil trucks. May test pulverized coal for conformance to specifications. May crush specific composition of coal (without blending) and be designated Coal-Pulverizer Operator (any industry).
GOE: 06.02.08 STRENGTH: M GED: R3 M2 L2 SVP: 4 DLU: 77

544.585-010 MIX-CRUSHER OPERATOR (elec. equip.)
Tends mechanical crusher to crush and screen, for reuse, insulating mixture from electrical furnaces in which carbon is graphitized: Breaks mixture to size with pick. Shovels mixture into hopper of crusher. Starts crusher and conveyor belts that carry crushed and screened mixture to storage bins. Marks bins as to types of mixture stored. Adjusts and cleans conveyors and screen vibrators.
GOE: 06.04.09 STRENGTH: M GED: R2 M1 L1 SVP: 2 DLU: 77

544.662-010 COKE-CRUSHER OPERATOR (steel & rel.)
Operates crushers, conveyors, and screens to produce crushed coke of various sizes: Moves levers and buttons to activate equipment. Pushes belt conveyor into position to load or unload hoppers, railroad gondolas, and trucks. Pushes buttons to adjust stops on conveyor to deflect and regulate flow of coke into crusher, screens, or storage bins. Observes operation of equipment to detect malfunctions and prevent clogging. Notifies supervisor of needed repairs. Shovels coke back onto conveyor belt.
GOE: 06.02.08 STRENGTH: M GED: R3 M2 L1 SVP: 4 DLU: 77

544.665-010 MILL-AND-COAL-TRANSPORT OPERATOR (utilities) alternate titles: coal-transport-and-mill operator; mill operator
Tends equipment that pulverizes coal and conveys it to storage bins or boiler feed hoppers: Signals DRIER OPERATOR (utilities) to send dried coal to mill, and closes switch to set mill in operation. Moves levers to adjust automatic mechanism that controls feed rate of coal into pulverizing mill. Tends conveyors or pneumatic bulk-conveyor system to move pulverized coal to storage bins or boiler feed hoppers. Cleans, oils, and makes minor adjustments to machinery.
GOE: 06.04.08 STRENGTH: L GED: R2 M2 L2 SVP: 3 DLU: 77

544.685-010 BREAKER TENDER (steel & rel.)
Tends machine that breaks coal into lumps of specified size preparatory to pulverizing: Starts steel drum containing coal revolving to tumble, break, and pass coal through perforations in drum. Starts conveyors to transfer coal to and from breaker machine. Observes flow of material on conveyor to detect and remove foreign material and clear jams. Removes metal from pocket of magnetic separator. Lubricates breaker machine with grease gun and oilcan. Cleans work area, using shovel and broom. May assist with repair work.
GOE: 06.04.12 STRENGTH: L GED: R2 M1 L1 SVP: 3 DLU: 77

546 REACTING OCCUPATIONS, N.E.C.

This group includes occupations, not elsewhere classified, concerned with changing the chemical composition of petroleum, coal, natural and manufactured gas, and related products.

546.382-010 CONTROL-PANEL OPERATOR (petrol. refin.) alternate titles: operator, control room
Operates control panel to regulate temperature, pressure, rate of flow, and tank level in petroleum refining, processing, and treating units and petro-chemical units, according to process schedules: Observes instruments and meters to verify specified conditions and records readings. Moves and adjusts dials, switches, valves, and levers on control panel to regulate and coordinate process variables, such as flows, temperatures, pressures, vacuum, time, catalyst, and chemicals as specified. Reports malfunctioning equipment to REFINERY OPERATOR (petrol. refin.). Records results of laboratory analyses. May test products for chemical characteristics and color, or send them to laboratory for analysis. May change recording charts and ink pens [CHART CHANGER (clerical)]. May operate auxiliary equipment to assist in distilling or treating operations. May be designated according to type of unit or process as Control-Panel Operator, Cracking Unit (petrol. refin.); Control-Panel Operator, Crude Unit (petrol. refin.); Control-Panel Operator, Polymerization Unit (petrol. refin.); Control Panel Operator, Solvent-Treating Unit (petrol. refin.).
GOE: 06.02.12 STRENGTH: L GED: R3 M3 L2 SVP: 7 DLU: 77

546.385-010 GAS TREATER (any industry)
Tends automatically controlled treating plant, consisting of *absorption towers*, actifiers, heat exchangers, pumps, and other auxiliary devices, that removes unwanted components and renders gas suitable for use as fuel: Observes gauges and meters to ascertain operating conditions and adjusts valves and controls accordingly. Performs chemical tests on treating materials. Adds chemicals to treating system as required. Observes safety precautions to prevent fires and explosions.

GOE: 06.02.12 STRENGTH: L GED: R3 M3 L2 SVP: 4 DLU: 77

549 OCCUPATIONS IN PROCESSING OF PETROLEUM, COAL, NATURAL AND MANUFACTURED GAS, AND RELATED PRODUCTS, N.E.C.

This group includes occupations, not elsewhere classified, concerned with preparing for commercial use the products of oil shales, oil and gas wells, and coal mines.

549.130-010 SUPERVISOR, TOWER (petrol. refin.)
Supervises and coordinates activities of workers engaged in operation of stills and related units, such as absorbers, debutanizers, catalyst hoppers, reboilers, heat and vapor exchangers, desalters, clay towers, stabilizers, furnaces, strippers, and desulfurizers, in which crude oil and resultant distillates are processed to separate and recover various petroleum products: Confers with laboratory personnel to plan production schedules and to determine temperatures, pressures, rates of flow, and tank levels required for control of process. Directs refining operations in assigned units through REFINERY OPERATOR (petrol. refin.). Reviews recording-instrument and flowmeter charts, logsheets, and laboratory analysis reports to verify control of process. Performs other duties as described under SUPERVISOR (any industry) Master Title.
GOE: 06.01.01 STRENGTH: L GED: R4 M3 L4 SVP: 7 DLU: 77

549.131-010 SUPERVISOR, NATURAL-GAS-FIELD PROCESSING (petrol. & gas; pipe lines)
Supervises and coordinates activities of workers engaged in sampling and testing natural gas, and controlling processing equipment at oil field installations: Directs workers in inspection of storage tanks, regulators, traps, and dehydration plants. Orders sample taking and field testing to determine specific gravity, vapor and hydrocarbon content, and other properties of gas and to verify suitability of boiler water used in gas processing equipment. Confers with workers to resolve operational problems. Revises field maps to show locations of gas processing and control equipment. Trains new workers. Performs other duties as described under SUPERVISOR (any industry) Master Title.
GOE: 06.01.01 STRENGTH: L GED: R4 M3 L3 SVP: 7 DLU: 77

549.132-010 GREASE MAKER, HEAD (petrol. refin.) alternate titles: supervisor, grease making
Supervises and coordinates activities of GREASE MAKERS (petrol. refin.) engaged in producing various grades of lubricating grease, performing duties as described under SUPERVISOR (any industry) Master Title.
GOE: 06.04.01 STRENGTH: L GED: R4 M4 L4 SVP: 8 DLU: 77

549.132-014 SUPERVISOR III (fabrication, nec)
Supervises and coordinates activities of workers engaged in drying, pulverizing, mixing, and pressing ingredients used to produce fuel briquettes: Feels fuel mixture to estimate moisture content. Observes reading on hygrometer to determine humidity of atmosphere, and specified temperature for drier and flow rate of material. Inspects finished product and takes sample for pressure test. Specifies changes in percentage of binder to bring product to specified quality level. Trains new workers. Performs other duties as described under SUPERVISOR (any industry) Master Title.
GOE: 06.04.01 STRENGTH: L GED: R4 M3 L3 SVP: 7 DLU: 77

549.132-018 SUPERVISOR, COAL HANDLING (steel & rel.)
Supervises and coordinates activities of workers engaged in unloading, stacking, reclaiming, crushing, and blending coal and delivering coal to ovens. Trains workers in operation of equipment. Performs duties as described under SUPERVISOR (any industry) Master Title.
GOE: 06.04.01 STRENGTH: L GED: R4 M3 L3 SVP: 7 DLU: 77

549.132-022 SUPERVISOR, COKE HANDLING (steel & rel.)
Supervises and coordinates activities of workers engaged in quenching, conveying, sizing, inspecting, storing, and loading coke, and repairing machinery and equipment. Trains workers in operation of equipment. Performs duties as described under SUPERVISOR (any industry) Master Title.
GOE: 06.04.01 STRENGTH: L GED: R4 M3 L3 SVP: 8 DLU: 77

549.132-026 SUPERVISOR, PASTE PLANT (steel & rel.)
Supervises and coordinates activities of workers engaged in grinding, mixing, and baking coke and pitch to produce carbon anodes: Reviews production schedules and confers with supervisory staff to plan shift operation of paste plant and bakeshop. Assigns duties to workers according to production schedules and demonstrates safe and efficient use of equipment. Inspects machinery and equipment to verify conformance to production standards. Prepares time, attendance, and production reports. Performs other duties as described under SUPERVISOR (any industry) Master Title.
GOE: 06.02.01 STRENGTH: L GED: R4 M3 L4 SVP: 7 DLU: 77

549.132-030 SUPERVISOR, PURIFICATION (petrol. refin.) alternate titles: chief operator, hydroformer; chief operator; extraction supervisor; fractionation operator, head; fractionation supervisor
Supervises and coordinates activities of workers engaged in operating superfractionation towers, absorbers, stabiliziers, rerun towers, naphtha-

desulfurizing units, caustic-wash units, separators, catalytic reactors, furnaces, stripper towers, and auxiliary equipment, such as pumps, engines, and compressors to separate light naphtha blends from crude naphtha, compound hydroformates from light naphtha, and extract products, such as benzene, toluene, and xylene from hydroformates: Coordinates operation of various units in system, according to run sheets, test books, order books, logbooks, gauge sheets, and pumping reports. Observes recording-instrument charts, flowmeters, and gauges to verify specified temperatures, pressures, flow rates, and liquid levels. Correlates instrument readings and test results to diagnose process malfunctions. Inspects equipment and cathodic-protection system to detect defects and malfunctions, such as excessive wear, overheating, and leaks. Directs workers in spraying catalyst beds with steam to regenerate catalyst. Trains workers in procedures for correcting malfunctions in equipment. Prepares bills of lading and manifests, inspects tank cars and tank trucks for cleanliness, and directs loading of cars and trucks to ship product. May be designated according to product as Supervisor, Benzene-Refining (petrol. refin.). Performs other duties as described under SUPERVISOR (any industry) Master Title.
GOE: 06.01.01 STRENGTH: L GED: R4 M4 L4 SVP: 7 DLU: 77

549.132-034 SUPERVISOR, TREATING AND PUMPING (petrol. refin.) alternate titles: treating and pumping supervisor
Supervises and coordinates activities of workers engaged in treating petroleum products with chemicals, steam, water, or air to remove sulfur and other impurities, in blending products to specification, and in pumping products to storage tanks, loading racks, and other processing units: Inspects treating and pumping units to verify specified temperatures and pressures. Reads logsheets, gauging records, and laboratory test reports to verify conformity of product to production schedules and specifications. Trains new workers. Performs other duties as described under SUPERVISOR (any industry) Master Title.
GOE: 06.01.01 STRENGTH: L GED: R4 M3 L4 SVP: 8 DLU: 77

549.137-010 SUPERVISOR, CARBON ELECTRODES (steel & rel.)
Supervises and coordinates activities of workers engaged in extruding, baking, graphitizing, and preparing graphite electrodes for shipment: Gives instructions to workers concerning formulas and amounts of materials to use, and type and size of electrodes to extrude, bake, graphitize, or prepare for shipment. Performs other duties as described under SUPERVISOR (any industry) Master Title. May be designated according to department as Supervisor, Baking (steel & rel.); Supervisor, Extrusion (steel & rel.); Supervisor, Graphite (steel & rel.).
GOE: 06.02.01 STRENGTH: L GED: R4 M3 L4 SVP: 6 DLU: 77

549.137-014 SUPERVISOR, PREPARATION PLANT (mine & quarry) alternate titles: breaker boss; tipple supervisor; washery boss
Supervises and coordinates activities of workers engaged in crushing, sizing, cleaning, treating, or loading coal, stone, or other minerals at tipple or preparation plant: Receives daily reports of quantity and grade of materials to be loaded into railroad cars or trucks. Transmits loading orders to equipment operators and loading crew. Observes activities of workers to ensure that impurities and materials of unspecified size are extracted. Directs operation of crushers, pumps, and furnaces, and assists workers with faulty equipment. Inspects processing and loading equipment and schedules necessary maintenance. Computes daily production from weight of loaded cars or trucks. Performs other duties as described under SUPERVISOR (any industry) Master Title.
GOE: 06.01.01 STRENGTH: L GED: R4 M3 L3 SVP: 7 DLU: 77

549.137-018 SUPERVISOR, SPECIALTY PLANT (petrol. refin.) alternate titles: loading supervisor
Supervises and coordinates activities of workers engaged in blending, compounding, packing, loading, and shipping special petroleum products, such as asphalt paints, paint primer, mastics, and lighter fluid: Confers with department heads to coordinate work of department with sales, billing, and other refinery activities. Plans blending schedules to maintain stock of standard products and computes blends from standard formulas. Writes shipping orders for loading tank cars and trucks. Performs other duties as described under SUPERVISOR (any industry) Master Title.
GOE: 06.01.01 STRENGTH: L GED: R4 M4 L4 SVP: 7 DLU: 77

549.260-010 REFINERY OPERATOR (petrol. refin.)
Analyzes specifications and controls continuous operation of petroleum refining and processing units to produce products, such as gasoline, kerosene, and fuel and lubricating oils, by such methods as distillation, absorption, extraction, adsorption, thermal and catalytic cracking and reforming, polymerization, isomerization, coking, visbreaking, and alkylation: Reads processing schedules, operating logs, test results of oil samples, and laboratory recommendations to determine changes in equipment controls required to produce specified quantity and quality of product. Moves and sets controls, such as knobs, valves, switches, levers, and index arms, on control panels to control process variables, such as flows, temperatures, pressures, vacuum, time, catalyst, and chemicals, by automatic regulation and remote control of processing units, such as heaters, furnaces, compressors, exchangers, reactors, quenchers, stabilizers, fractionators, rechargers, absorbers, strippers, debutanizers, stills, and towers [CONTROL-PANEL OPERATOR (petrol. refin.)]. Moves controls to regulate valves, pumps, compressors, and auxiliary equipment to direct flow of product. Reads temperature and pressure gauges and flowmeters, records readings, and compiles operating records. Determines malfunctioning units by observing control instruments, such as meters and gauges, or by automatic warning signals, such as lights and sounding of horns. Inspects equipment to determine location and

nature of malfunction, such as leaks, breakages, and faulty valves. Determines need for schedules and performs repair and maintenance of equipment. Patrols unit to verify safe and efficient operating conditions. May sample liquids and gases [SAMPLER (petrol. refin.)] and test products for chemical characteristics and color [TESTER (petrol. refin.)]. May inspect and adjust furnaces, heaters, and damper controls. May lubricate equipment. May clean interior of processing units by circulating chemicals and solvents through them. May treat products [TREATER (petrol. refin.)]. May control activities of several processing units operated in conjunction. May be designated according to process involved or plant operated as Absorption Plant Operator (petrol. refin.); Purification Operator (petrol. refin.); Refinery Operator, Cracking Unit (petrol. refin.); Refinery Operator, Polymerization Plant (petrol. refin.); Refinery Operator, Reforming Unit (petrol. refin.); Refinery Operator, Visbreaking (petrol. refin.). May be designated: Refinery Operator, Alkylation (petrol. refin.); Refinery Operator, Coking (petrol. refin.); Refinery Operator, Crude Unit (petrol. refin.); Refinery Operator, Gas Plant (petrol. refin.); Refinery Operator, Light-Ends Recovery (petrol. refin.); Refinery Operator, Vapor Recovery Unit (petrol. refin.).
GOE: 06.01.03 STRENGTH: L GED: R4 M3 L3 SVP: 8 DLU: 77

549.261-010 MECHANICAL INSPECTOR (petrol. refin.) alternate titles: inspector
Inspects processing and storage tanks, pipelines and fittings, stills, towers, and pumping units for defects, following specified inspection procedures: Examines mechanical installations, instrumentation, valves, and fittings for defects, such as cracks, corrosion, and leaks. Measures thickness of tank walls, tower walls, and pipelines, using calipers and electronic instruments, to determine extent of corrosive damage. Drills test holes in tank and tower walls to take samples of corrosive deposits and verify extent of damage. Installs probes and other instruments in tanks and towers to obtain samples of corrosive deposits and to measure rate of corrosion. Computes rate of corrosion from laboratory analysis of probe samples, using mathematical tables and charts. Reports need for immediate repairs to mechanical department. Prepares inspection reports to indicate nature of repairs and replacements required and to specify safe limits of temperature and pressure to follow pending repair of unit. Inspects construction and installation of new mechanical equipment for conformity to specifications. May inspect operating condition of firefighting equipment. May be designated according to equipment inspected as Still And Tank Inspector (petrol. refin.).
GOE: 05.07.01 STRENGTH: L GED: R4 M3 L3 SVP: 7 DLU: 77

549.360-010 PUMPER (petrol. refin.)
Controls pumps and manifold systems to circulate crude, semiprocessed, and finished petroleum products, water, and chemical solutions through processing, storage, and shipping departments of refinery, according to schedules: Reads operating schedules or instructions from DISPATCHER, OIL (petrol. & gas; petrol. refin.; pipe lines). Plans movement of products through lines to processing, storage, and shipping units, utilizing knowledge of interconnections and capacities of pipelines, valve manifolds, pumps, and tankage. Synchronizes activities with other pumphouses to ensure continuous flow of products and minimum of contamination between products. Starts battery of pumps, observes pressure meters and flowmeters, and turns valves to regulate pumping speeds according to schedules. Turns handwheels to open line valves and direct flow of product. Signals STILL-PUMP OPERATOR (petrol. refin.); PUMPER HELPERS (petrol. refin.); and GAUGERS (petrol. & gas; petrol. refin.; pipe lines) by telephone or radio to operate pumps in designated units, to open and close pipeline and tank valves, and to gauge, sample, and determine temperature of tank contents. Records operating data, such as products and quantities pumped, stocks used, gauging results, and operating time. May blend oils and gasolines [BLENDER (petrol. refin.)]. May repair pumps, lines, and auxiliary equipment.
GOE: 06.02.12 STRENGTH: M GED: R4 M3 L3 SVP: 6 DLU: 77

549.362-010 STILL-PUMP OPERATOR (petrol. refin.) alternate titles: process pumper; pump operator
Operates steam- or electric-driven pumps to circulate crude, semiprocessed, and finished petroleum products, water, and chemical solutions through processing, storage, and shipping departments of refinery, according to work orders: Starts pumps in specified units, observes flowmeters and pressure meters, and turns valves and switches to change pumping rates, as directed by PUMPER (petrol. refin.). Turns handwheels to open or close tank and pipeline valves to direct flow of products to specified destinations. Observes operation of pumping equipment to detect malfunctioning and leakage. Lubricates cocks, valves, joints, and pumps, using oilcan and grease gun. Tightens bolts and screws to adjust and repair equipment, using handtools. Gauges contents of tank, using gauging tape. May record operating data, such as products and quantities pumped, stocks used, gauging results, and operating time. May remove sample from tank and test it for specific gravity and color. May repair and overhaul pumps [PUMP SERVICER (any industry)]. May blend oils or gasolines [BLENDER (petrol. refin.)]. May communicate with PUMPER (petrol. refin.) by radio or telephone to send and receive pumping and gauging information. May be designated according to specialty as Cooling-Tower Operator (petrol. refin.).
GOE: 06.02.12 STRENGTH: M GED: R3 M3 L2 SVP: 5 DLU: 77

549.362-014 TREATER (petrol. refin.) alternate titles: treating-plant operator
Controls continuous-treating or batch-treating equipment to process petroleum products, such as gasoline, kerosene, and lubricating oils, with chemicals, sol-
m

vents, steam, clay, and hydrogen to remove impurities and to improve color, odor, and stability, according to specifications: Moves and sets levers, switches, dials, and handwheels to admit products and treating agents to processing units in specified ratio; to direct flow of products through treating stages, such as mixing, precipitating, and neutralizing; and to regulate temperatures, pressures, and circulation rates of treating equipment. Observes temperature gauges, pressure gauges, and flowmeters; records readings; and compiles operating records. Patrols unit to detect malfunctions and leaks. Opens bleeder valves to sample products and tests them for chemical characteristics, specific gravity, and color, or sends sample to laboratory for analysis. Reprocesses products or pumps them to storage tanks, according to test results and laboratory recommendations. Opens valves to drain sludge from units. May repair and lubricate equipment. May treat products, using hydrogen-catalytic process. May operate refrigerating equipment [REFRIGERATING ENGINEER (any industry)]. May add dyes or fortifying chemicals to product [BLENDER (petrol. refin.)]. May be designated according to product treated as Crude-Oil Treater (petrol. refin.); Wax Treater (petrol. refin.); treating agent used as Acid Treater (petrol. refin.); Hydrogen Treater (petrol. refin.); plant operated as Clay-Plant Treater (petrol. refin.); Naphtha-Plant Treater (petrol. refin.); Solvent-Plant Treater (petrol. refin.); or type of operation as Batch-Unit Treater (petrol. refin.).
GOE: 06.02.12 STRENGTH: L GED: R4 M3 L3 SVP: 7 DLU: 77

549.364-010 TESTER, COMPRESSED GASES (chemical) alternate titles: compressed-gas tester; gas tester
Tests compressed gases for moisture content, purity, ratio of gases in mixture, and cylinder pressure, using standard testing equipment and following specified procedures: Drains gas samples from tanks, or rolls cylinders to test station. Adjusts test equipment, such as volumetric moisture tester, burette, conductometer, and pressure gauges, according to type or mixture of gases as shown on chart. Records test procedures and results in log. Prepares and places identifying tags on cylinders or tanks. Notifies supervisor of deviations from specifications. May test accuracy of calibrations on pressure gauges, using dead-weight tester. May mix gases according to customer specifications. May vaporize liquid gases and fill tube trailers. May measure percentage of carbon monoxide in truck cabs, using automatic gas-metering device or by spraying chemical from syringe into atmosphere and matching degree of discoloration against color chart.
GOE: 06.03.01 STRENGTH: M GED: R3 M3 L2 SVP: 3 DLU: 77

549.367-010 INSPECTOR (build. mat., nec)
Tests samples of composition shingles and rolls of coated roofing felt for conformance to specifications: Weighs bundles of shingles and rolls of roofing felt to verify gross weight with label weight, and records data on production report. Examines surface of shingles for uniformity of color, and feels slate to determine that slate is evenly distributed. Cuts strips from shingles, using knife, and actuates scratch tester to determine if slate is embedded to specifications. Calculates percentage of slate loss after scratch test, using balance scales, and notifies COATER, SLATE (build. mat., nec) of results. Measures shingles as they pass on conveyor, using tape rule. May test material samples for porosity, time required for saturation, and light-relfective characteristics, using specified test equipment.
GOE: 06.03.01 STRENGTH: M GED: R3 M2 L2 SVP: 5 DLU: 77

549.382-010 NATURAL-GAS-TREATING-UNIT OPERATOR (petrol. & gas)
Operates automatically controlled natural-gas treating unit in oil field to render gas suitable for fuel and for pipeline transportation: Opens valves to admit gas and specified chemicals into treating vessel where moisture is absorbed and impurities removed. Adjusts controls of auxiliary equipment, such as pumps, heating coils, and cooling tower. Reads temperature and pressure gauges, and adjusts controls to keep heat and pressure at level of maximum efficiency within safe operating limits. Performs routine tests or delivers samples to laboratory to determine qualities of gas, such as Btu value, flame candlepower, and specific gravity, and proportions of elements, such as methane, propane, and natural gasoline. Drains samples of boiler water from treating unit for laboratory analysis. Adds specified chemicals to water to keep heating and cooling systems in working order. May adjust and repair gas meters and governors, using handtools [METER REPAIRER (any industry)]. May change charts on meters equipped with automatic recorders. May advise and assist workers repairing gas meters, regulators (governors), and other control instruments.
GOE: 06.02.12 STRENGTH: L GED: R3 M3 L2 SVP: 6 DLU: 77

549.382-014 OIL-RECOVERY-UNIT OPERATOR (petrol. refin.)
Controls processing equipment to separate recoverable oil from refinery sewage system: Starts pumps, observes flowmeters and pressure meters, and turns valves to regulate directional flow of oil, water, solids, chemicals, and air, according to operating procedures. Turns handwheels to control skimming devices that collect *sprung oil* from reservoirs of separation units. Opens valves on steam heat-exchanger to raise temperature of skimmed oil to treating temperature. Mixes and blends caustic cleansing and demulsifying chemicals into oil to remove impurities and water. Turns valves to pump reclaimed oil to storage tanks, solids to disposal unit, and water to oxidation ponds or to separator unit for recycling. Records amount of oil reclaimed, amount of water or impurities removed, and specified data concerning operating condition of processing equipment.
GOE: 06.02.12 STRENGTH: H GED: R3 M3 L2 SVP: 3 DLU: 77

549.382-018 WASH-OIL-PUMP OPERATOR (steel & rel.) alternate titles: light-oil operator; wash-oil-cooler operator
Operates variety of pumps and auxiliary equipment, following standard procedures to extract light oil (crude benzol) from coke-oven gas: Turns valves and starts pumps to admit gas and wash oil to still and steam to heating coil. Reads gauges and thermometers and regulates pumps to control temperature, pressure, and rate of flow of materials. Pumps washed gas to processing station or storage. Admits steam to coil to separate light oil from wash oil. Pumps light oil to benzol plant or storage and wash oil through heat exchangers and coolers for reuse in system. Drains water and sludge from tanks. Cleans gaugelines, gauge glasses, and decanters. Records oil and water temperatures, and quantity of light oil extracted.
GOE: 06.02.17 STRENGTH: L GED: R3 M3 L2 SVP: 5 DLU: 77

549.387-010 CARGO INSPECTOR (petrol. refin.; pipe lines)
Inspects crude and refined petroleum before and after transfer from terminal tanks to ship tanks, to determine if it meets prescribed standards: Lowers sample container into ship tanks to obtain sample of oil residue and into terminal tanks to sample oil, or opens bleeder valves on pipelines to obtain sample. Determines amount and type of bottom sediment, water, and foreign substance present in oil sample, using centrifugal tester and following standard formulas. Lowers thermometer into tanks to obtain temperature reading, and determines quantity of oil in ship tanks, using calibrated tape and conversion tables. Records test results. Turns valves to close tanks, inspects valves for leaks, and clamps seal around valves to secure tank contents. Prepares, verifies, and examines cargo ladings, oil transportation records, and export records. May direct BOAT LOADER (water trans.) I in taking samples and assist in loading and unloading oil. May lubricate and adjust valves, using grease gun, oilcan, and handtools.
GOE: 05.07.05 STRENGTH: L GED: R3 M3 L2 SVP: 5 DLU: 77

549.585-010 ACETYLENE-PLANT OPERATOR (chemical)
Tends generating equipment that processes calcium-carbide crystals and water into acetylene gas: Turns valves, level gauge, and thermostat to raise and heat water to prescribed level and temperature in generator. Dumps specified quantity of calcium-carbide crystals into hopper, bolts in cover, and starts generator. Opens hopper gate and starts vibrator that sifts crystals into generator. Records amount of time consumed during operation and cylinder shipping data. May tend compressor. May ascertain level of acidity or alkalinity of gas with litmus paper, and test filled cylinders for leaks by brushing on chemical solution. May fill cylinders with compressed gas [CYLINDER FILLER (chemical)].
GOE: 06.04.11 STRENGTH: H GED: R2 M2 L2 SVP: 3 DLU: 77

549.587-010 COMPRESSED-GAS-PLANT WORKER (chemical)
Performs any combination of following tasks in establishment making compressed and liquefied gas: Loads cylinders or ton containers on vehicles, using handtruck or chain hoist, and records type and quantity of cylinders. Examines returned cylinders for surface defects, such as dents, cracks, and burns, and rolls cylinders to designated work area. Removes valves and installs reconditioned valves on cylinders, using wrenches. Connects exhaust manifold to cylinders and turns valve to draw off residual gas. Bounces or hammers cylinders to loosen rust and scale, and inserts water, steam, and air nozzles and turns valves to clean and dry cylinders. Tests filled cylinders for leaks by brushing or spraying chemical solution around valve. Weighs filled cylinders on platform scale and records weight. Screws protection cap over valve and ties warning and identification tags on cylinder. Wraps cakes of dry ice in paper and stores them in icehouse. May clean cylinder exteriors with wire brush. May place cylinders on heating rack to expand gas to ensure complete removal. May be known according to work performed as Blow-Off Worker (chemical); Cylinder Handler (chemical); Cylinder Valver (chemical); Hoist-Cylinder Loader (chemical); Ice Handler (chemical); Valve Steamer (chemical). May be designated: Cylinder Checker (chemical); Cylinder Devalver (chemical); Cylinder Steamer (chemical); Ton-Container Shipper (chemical).
GOE: 06.04.40 STRENGTH: M GED: R2 M2 L2 SVP: 2 DLU: 77

549.587-014 SAMPLER (petrol. refin.) alternate titles: laboratory sampler
Collects samples of petroleum products from various parts of refinery for laboratory analysis, using sample container: Samples contents of tank cars, processing units, stills, and pipelines by lowering sample container into contents at various depths, or by opening bleeder valves to release flow of products into container. Collects samples taken by other workers. Pours samples from containers into sample bottles and ties identification tags to bottles or marks identifying information on them. Delivers samples to laboratory for analysis. May convey messages between laboratory and processing units. May collect samples of other materials for laboratory analysis.
GOE: 06.04.40 STRENGTH: L GED: R2 M2 L1 SVP: 3 DLU: 77

549.587-018 SAMPLER (elec. equip.)
Digs, weighs, and prepares ground samples of coal and pitch, used in making carbon electrodes, for laboratory testing: Digs sample from designated area, using shovel or sampling stick. Places sample into containers and labels or writes identifying information on containers. Weighs, crushes, screens, and reweighs materials in laboratory to prepare sample for testing. Records information pertaining to size distribution of respective materials.
GOE: 05.12.07 STRENGTH: L GED: R2 M2 L1 SVP: 2 DLU: 77

549.662-010 BRIQUETTE-MACHINE OPERATOR (fabrication, nec) alternate titles: briquette molder; molding-machine operator
Operates machines and equipment to dehydrate, pulverize, mix, and mold ingredients to produce fuel briquettes: Shovels or empties sacks of materials into

hoppers or bins, or starts elevator-conveyors. Turns valves, handwheels, or rheostats to move and control flow of fuels, water, and dry or liquid binders to machines. Starts conveyors, rotary drier, mixers, pulverizer, mixing augers, and compressing machines. Inspects briquettes and adjusts flow of materials to produce briquettes of specified dimensions. Removes and replaces broken bolts and worn shafts, using handtools. Lubricates machinery or directs oiling of equipment. May be designated according to type of briquette produced as Barbecue-Briquette-Machine Operator (fabrication, nec); Charcoal-Briquette-Machine Operator (fabrication, nec); Coal-Briquette-Machine Operator (fabrication, nec).
GOE: 06.02.17 STRENGTH: M GED: R3 M2 L2 SVP: 4 DLU: 77

549.665-010   ACETYLENE-CYLINDER-PACKING MIXER (chemical)
Tends mixing machine, autoclave, and drier to mix, pack, solidify, and dry asbestos, dirt, charcoal, lime, water, and other ingredients to form absorbent packing for compressed acetylene gas: Meters out water and powdered ingredients, and dumps them into mixer. Starts agitator to mix ingredients for specified period of time. Opens chute to transfer mixture to vibrator. Clamps cylinders to vibrator, and connects funnels and packing rods to cylinders. Starts vibrator and rods that sift and pack mixture into cylinders. Weighs cylinders to ascertain amount of mixture packed. Rolls cylinders into autoclave, and turns valve to specified pressure level to solidify packing. Rolls cylinders into drier, and turns thermostat to heat cylinders. Installs valves and safety plugs on cylinders, and places them on scale. Connects acetone feedlines to cylinders, using handtools, and turns valves to fill cylinders with acetone, according to specifications.
GOE: 06.04.19 STRENGTH: M GED: R2 M2 L2 SVP: 2 DLU: 77

549.682-010   GREASE MAKER (petrol. refin.)
Controls gas- or steam-heated kettles to produce various grades of lubricating grease: Pours specified quantities of ingredients, such as melted fats, mineral oils, and soda or lime base, into kettle, and starts agitator to stir mixture to required consistency. Adjusts kettle temperature controls to form basic soap from mixture. Turns off heat and adds water, dye, and various mineral oils to soap in designated proportions for emulsification. Stirs and reheats mixture to produce grease of required texture.
GOE: 06.04.12 STRENGTH: M GED: R3 M2 L3 SVP: 5 DLU: 77

549.684-010   PUMPER HELPER (petrol. refin.)
Assists STILL-PUMP OPERATOR (petrol. refin.) and PUMPER (petrol. refin.) in pumping crude, semiprocessed, and finished petroleum products, water, and chemical solutions through processing, storage, and shipping departments of refinery: Turns valves and switches to start and regulate operation of pumping units. Turns handwheels to open and close pipeline and tankage valves to direct flow of product to destination. Inspects pumps, lines, and tankage valves for leaks and malfunctioning. Lubricates valves and pumps. Tightens connections, using wrenches. Gauges contents of tanks, using tape gauge or automatic remote-controlled gauging equipment. Takes temperature readings by lowering thermometer into tank. Draws samples of product by lowering sample container into tank or by opening bleeder valves on pipelines to draw sample. Loads barges and tank cars. May make specific gravity and color tests. May clean equipment. May use radio or telephone to communicate with PUMPER (petrol. refin.). May blend and dye gasolines, using standardized formulas, and prepare blending report. Performs other duties as described under HELPER (any industry) Master Title.
GOE: 06.04.12 STRENGTH: M GED: R2 M2 L2 SVP: 3 DLU: 77

549.685-010   AIR-TABLE OPERATOR (mine & quarry)
Tends pneumatic coal-cleaning table that blows coal dust, sulfur, and other impurities from coal as it passes through preparation plant: Starts machine and adjusts valve to regulate air pressure. Observes coal as it passes over cleaning table and removes oversized lumps, rocks, or foreign matter. Adjusts and lubricates mechanical parts of machine, using handtools, grease gun, and oilcan.
GOE: 06.04.08 STRENGTH: L GED: R2 M1 L1 SVP: 2 DLU: 77

549.685-014   GRAPHITE PAN-DRIER TENDER (nonmet. min.)
Tends vacuum-filter dewaterer and gas-fired pan-drier to prepare flake graphite from mill slurry: Starts pumps, filter, and drag mechanism on pan-drier. Lights gas burners on drier with torch and turns valves to regulate temperature as judged by color of flame. Turns valves to admit graphite slurry into dewaterer which extracts water (by means of vacuum exerted through rotating filter paddles) and discharges damp graphite onto pan of drier. Judges degree of dryness of graphite as drag mechanism moves it along length of drier pan. Adjusts drying rate by regulating input rate of graphite slurry into dewaterer. Removes filter paddles and replaces filter cloths (socks), using mechanic's handtools.
GOE: 06.04.19 STRENGTH: L GED: R2 M2 L1 SVP: 4 DLU: 77

549.685-018   MOLDER, WAX (petrol. refin.)
Tends equipment that molds wax recovered from processed petroleum into cakes: Turns valves to fill molds with hot wax. Moves controls to circulate chilling fluid through molds, solidifying wax. Removes wax cakes from molds.
GOE: 06.04.12 STRENGTH: M GED: R2 M2 L1 SVP: 4 DLU: 77

549.685-022   REELER (build. mat., nec) alternate titles: roll winder; winder operator
Tends machine that winds asphalt-coated roofing felt into rolls of specified length and width: Threads felt through feed rollers and inserts end in takeup reel. Starts machine that automatically weighs and ejects completed roll after

specified weight has been wound. Depresses pedal to activate knife that severs roll from continuous feed after specified weight has been attained. May change gears to vary size and weight of rolls, using handtools.
GOE: 06.04.09 STRENGTH: H GED: R2 M2 L1 SVP: 3 DLU: 77

549.685-026   SCREENER-AND-BLENDER OPERATOR (steel & rel.) alternate titles: graphite-mill operator
Tends screening and blending machine that removes rocks and twigs from coarse coke and mixes it with fine-ground coke to produce blended mix used to pack carbon electrodes in graphite furnaces: Shovels or dumps coarse coke onto vibrating screens. Starts screens that separate rocks, twigs, and other materials from coke. Starts conveyors that carry sifted coke from screening area and fine-ground coke from storage bins to top of blending tanks and dumps them into tanks. Starts blender blades that mix coke. Turns valves to release blended mix from blending tanks into storage tanks for removal to graphite furnaces.
GOE: 06.04.12 STRENGTH: H GED: R2 M2 L2 SVP: 2 DLU: 77

549.685-030   TREATER HELPER (petrol. refin.)
Assists TREATER (petrol. refin.) in processing petroleum products, such as gasoline, kerosene, oils, and wax, with chemicals, steam, water, or air to remove impurities, such as sulfur: Examines pipelines and valves for leaks. Turns valves to charge equipment with product to be treated and to draw off water and spent chemicals after treatment and separation. Adds treating chemicals, such as sulfur and litharge, to product by turning valves or by dumping chemicals directly into equipment. Lubricates, adjusts, and performs minor maintenance on equipment and machinery as directed. May regulate pump speeds to control circulation of solution and product through unit. May gauge tanks with calibrated rod or tape to determine quantity of content [GAUGER (petrol. & gas; petrol. refin.; pipe lines)]. May make chemical, specific gravity, and color tests of product and treating solution to determine process conditions. May draw samples of product for laboratory analysis. Performs other duties as described under HELPER (any industry) Master Title.
GOE: 06.04.12 STRENGTH: M GED: R2 M2 L2 SVP: 4 DLU: 77

549.685-034   WASH-OIL-PUMP OPERATOR HELPER (steel & rel.)
Assists WASH-OIL-PUMP OPERATOR (steel & rel.) in extracting light oil (crude benzol) from coke-oven gas: Opens valves and starts equipment. Reads gauges and records data as directed. Cleans coils, equipment, and work areas, using hose, water, cleaning agents, and broom. Performs other duties as described under HELPER (any industry) Master Title.
GOE: 06.04.12 STRENGTH: L GED: R2 M2 L2 SVP: 3 DLU: 77

549.685-038   WAX MOLDER (foundry; jewelry-silver.)
Tends semiautomatic wax-molding machine that produces wax patterns used in lost-wax casting process: Sprays interior surface of die with parting agent. Places die against stops in bed of machine and starts machine that forces melted wax into die by injection or centrifugal process. Loosens pattern from die, using airhose. Removes pattern from die and inspects it for defects. Cleans excess wax from pattern, using knife. May pour melted wax into holding cup of machine. May be designated according to molding process used as Centrifugal-Wax Molder (foundry; jewelry-silver.); Injection-Wax Molder (foundry; jewelry-silver.).
GOE: 06.04.09 STRENGTH: L GED: R2 M1 L2 SVP: 2 DLU: 77

549.685-042   UTILITY OPERATOR III (chemical)
Tends pumps that refill air and hydrogen purification filters with water and solutions to maintain operating levels: Reads gauges to check levels of water, liquid nitrogen, and caustic solution in air and hydrogen purification filters. Starts pumps that refill purification filters with water or other solutions to maintain specified levels. Cleans and changes filters of air and hydrogen driers. Records pressure and temperature readings of compressors, filters, and driers.
GOE: 06.04.11 STRENGTH: M GED: R2 M1 L1 SVP: 3 DLU: 86

549.686-010   BRIQUETTE-MACHINE-OPERATOR   HELPER   (fabrication, nec)
Assists BRIQUETTE-MACHINE OPERATOR (fabrication, nec) in dehydrating, pulverizing, mixing, and molding ingredients to produce fuel briquettes: Inserts suction hose into opening in top of tank trucks and starts motor to transfer powdered charcoal, coal, or coke from truck to storage. Shovels or dumps sacked briquette ingredients in hoppers. Scrapes ingredients from drying oven with scraper and shovels ingredients onto conveyor. Pounds on conveyor pipes with hammer or woodblock to loosen clogged material. Lubricates machines and removes and installs machine parts as directed by BRIQUETTE-MACHINE OPERATOR (fabrication, nec).
GOE: 06.04.12 STRENGTH: H GED: R2 M1 L1 SVP: 2 DLU: 77

549.686-014   FELT HANGER (build. mat., nec) alternate titles: dry-talc racker
Installs rolls of untreated roofing felt on feedrack and prepares roll for continuous asphalt-saturating process with aid of another worker: Inserts spindle in mandrel, pushes roll onto feedrack, and secures holding devices over spindle ends. Cuts away roll covering, using knife, threads end of felt through rollers, and splices end to end of previous roll with tape and hot iron. Inspects felt as roll unwinds and repairs defects, such as holes and tears, using tape and iron.
GOE: 06.04.19 STRENGTH: H GED: R2 M2 L2 SVP: 2 DLU: 77

549.687-010   CHASER, TAR (steel & rel.) alternate titles: tar chaser; tar runner
Removes tar, pitch, and carbon accumulated in coke-collecting mains, using chisel bar: Lifts plugs from collecting main, using hook. Places disk over

plughole and shoves chisel bar through center hole of disk. Twists bar to pry tar from walls of main. Removes tar and pitch from traps, using spooning bar. Sweeps and cleans area. Cleans spray nozzles of collecting mains, using wire-cleaning tool. May apply steam to loosen residue from walls of collecting mains.
GOE: 06.04.39 STRENGTH: M GED: R1 M1 L1 SVP: 2 DLU: 77

549.687-014 HOTHOUSE WORKER (chemical)
Replaces burner tips, gas pipe, and carbon-collecting channels (flat surfaces) in hothouses (burner enclosures) used to produce carbon black by channel process, using wrenches and pipe-fitting tools. Cleans carbon dust from equipment and work area, using brooms and brushes.
GOE: 06.04.34 STRENGTH: M GED: R2 M2 L2 SVP: 2 DLU: 77

549.687-018 LABORER, PETROLEUM REFINERY (petrol. refin.) alternate titles: process helper
Performs any combination of following tasks in refinery: Digs ditches, builds dikes and levees, and fills holes with earth, rock, sand, and asphalt gravels, using pick and shovel. Smooths ground surfaces and roadways, using hand tamper. Cleans refining equipment. Removes debris from roadways and work areas, and sprays and hoes weeds. Shovels sand and gravel off vehicles and dumps or shovels cement and sand into mixers. Mixes and pours cement and transports cement to forms with wheelbarrow. Unloads materials, such as tools, equipment, sacks of cement, sand, catalyst, salt, and lime, and oil barrels from freight cars and trucks, manually or with handtruck; and stacks barrels and sacks for storage. Uncrates equipment and parts, such as fractionating or treating towers and bubble trays, using pry bar and hammer; and installs bubble caps, using wrenches. Rips open sacks and dumps chemicals and catalysts into mixing, treating, or storage tanks. Dopes pipelines to prevent corrosion, using doping pot and tar. Changes hoist cables, and rigs chain hoists, rope blocks, power winches, and gin poles used to move or raise equipment. Skims oil from cooling water in water boxes. May be designated according to section of refinery in which work is performed as Laborer, Filter Plant (petrol. refin.).
GOE: 05.12.03 STRENGTH: H GED: R2 M1 L1 SVP: 3 DLU: 77

549.687-022 MUD-MIXER HELPER (steel & rel.)
Shovels clay, cinders, coke dust, and refuse scraped from oven doors into wheelbarrow, and transfers materials to MUD-MIXER OPERATOR (smelt. & refin.; steel & rel.) for mixing and eventual use in sealing coke-oven doors. Unloads mixed mud from trucks at mud distribution stations, using shovel and wheelbarrow. May clean coke-oven doors and standpipes, using rags.
GOE: 06.04.30 STRENGTH: H GED: R1 M1 L1 SVP: 2 DLU: 77

55 OCCUPATIONS IN PROCESSING OF CHEMICALS, PLASTICS, SYNTHETICS, RUBBER, PAINT, AND RELATED PRODUCTS

This division includes occupations concerned with manufacturing basic chemicals, such as acids, alkalies, salts, and organic chemicals; chemical products to be used in further manufacture, such as synthetic organic fibers, synthetic rubber, dry colors, and pigments; finished chemical products to be used as materials in other industries, such as paints, fertilizers, and explosives; plastics powders, granules, pellets, liquids; plastics sheets, blocks, rods, tubes, and laminations; and rubber-stock shapes and objects from natural, synthetic, or reclaimed rubber.

550 MIXING AND BLENDING OCCUPATIONS

This group includes occupations concerned with combining, mingling, or thoroughly fusing materials to produce a single mass or compound or to achieve a desired quality of texture, color, or similar characteristic.

550.131-010 COSMETICS SUPERVISOR (pharmaceut.)
Supervises and coordinates activities of workers engaged in producing liquid, powder, and cream cosmetics: Observes operation of machines to detect malfunctions and directs workers to replace defective parts, such as micro-sifters, mixer brushes, and screens. Blends color bases, following formulas. Examines liquid filterings for clarity and color prior to storage. Examines product for conformance to specifications. Performs other duties as described under SUPERVISOR (any industry) Master Title.
GOE: 06.01.01 STRENGTH: L GED: R4 M3 L3 SVP: 7 DLU: 77

550.132-010 SUPERVISOR II (chemical)
Supervises and coordinates activities of workers engaged in mixing and packaging chemicals for use in insecticides, fungicides, herbicides and soil fumigants, utilizing knowledge of chemicals and machine operations: Records on batch card quantity and type chemicals required to obtain mixture, using chart. Draws sample from mixing tank, using syringe, and tests dissolvability of liquid in water to determine that product meets specifications. Observes workers to ensure products are processed according to specifications. Trains new workers in methods and techniques of chemical mixing. Performs other duties as described under SUPERVISOR (any industry) Master Title.
GOE: 06.01.01 STRENGTH: L GED: R4 M2 L3 SVP: 6 DLU: 77

550.132-014 SUPERVISOR, FISH BAIT PROCESSING (toy-sport equip.)
Supervises and coordinates activities of workers engaged in mixing, canning, labeling, and packing paste fish bait: Inspects mixture during processing to ensure conformance to specifications in color, scent, and consistency. Changes formula ingredients or mixing process to ensure adherence to standards. Observes machine operations to determine that product meets quality standards. Trains workers in machine operation and process methods. Performs other duties as described under SUPERVISOR (any industry) Master Title.
GOE: 06.02.01 STRENGTH: L GED: R4 M2 L3 SVP: 7 DLU: 77

550.135-010 SUPERVISOR, COLOR-PASTE MIXING (textile)
Supervises and coordinates activities of workers engaged in mixing colors for use in printing textiles: Schedules mixing of colors to correspond with production schedule and issues formulas to workers. Compares color smears and printed samples with standard color swatches to determine if mixed colors meet specifications. Alters formulas if colors on printed sample do not match colors on sample swatch, utilizing knowledge of colors and printing requirements. Examines surplus color returned from printshop and schedules its use in other formulas. Inventories and requisitions supplies, such as base colors, starch, oils, and chemicals. Trains workers in operation of machines and equipment. Performs other duties as described under SUPERVISOR (any industry) Master Title.
GOE: 06.02.01 STRENGTH: L GED: R4 M3 L3 SVP: 7 DLU: 77

550.135-014 MIXING SUPERVISOR (plastic prod.)
Supervises and coordinates activities of workers engaged in mixing plastic resins, color pigments, and additives for use in machine molding of plastic items: Reviews production records for each molding machine to determine amount of plastic mixture used and whether amount available is sufficient to fill existing orders, and notifies production control personnel of findings. Determines amount of virgin plastic needed to combine with reground material and reformulates mixing order to meet production requirements. Examines samples of rejected products to determine cause of defect and recommends corrective action, based on knowledge of ingredients and molding machine operations. Trains new employees. Confers with management and subordinates to resolve production problems. Performs other duties as described under SUPERVISOR (any industry) Master Title.
GOE: 06.02.01 STRENGTH: L GED: R4 M3 L3 SVP: 5 DLU: 86

550.137-010 SUPERVISOR, COMPOUNDING-AND-FINISHING (chemical)
Supervises and coordinates activities of workers engaged in compounding, weighing, and packaging of sulfonated oils, esters, stearates, and industrial soaps: Directs workers in compounding ingredients, using knowledge of chemical properties and reactions of ingredients. Reviews cumulative weight charts and examines compounds in process to detect discrepancies in weight, odor, clarity, and color. Designates type and size of container for packaging, according to product. Reviews laboratory analysis of samples and orders changes in process specifications, according to knowledge of chemical processes, ingredient characteristics, and experience with specific products. Performs other duties as described under SUPERVISOR (any industry) Master Title.
GOE: 06.01.01 STRENGTH: L GED: R4 M3 L3 SVP: 8 DLU: 77

550.137-014 SUPERVISOR, PASTE MIXING (chemical)
Supervises and coordinates activities of workers engaged in mixing ingredients of pastes used to form cores or to line cans of dry cells. Computes amounts of ingredients required from work orders and formulas. Performs other duties as described under SUPERVISOR (any industry) Master Title.
GOE: 06.04.01 STRENGTH: L GED: R4 M3 L3 SVP: 6 DLU: 77

550.137-018 SUPERVISOR, SHIPPING (chemical)
Supervises and coordinates activities of workers engaged in milling, blending, bagging, and shipping dry glue: Directs workers in moving and assembling prescribed amounts and kinds of glue for blending and shipment. Inspects assembled items and verifies amounts to ensure compliance with specifications. Directs worker to blend ingredients for specified period of time. Performs other duties as described under SUPERVISOR (any industry) Master Title.
GOE: 06.04.01 STRENGTH: L GED: R4 M2 L3 SVP: 7 DLU: 77

550.362-010 FROTHING-MACHINE OPERATOR (rubber goods)
Operates *frothing machine* to mix air with latex for use in making foam rubber products: Observes gauges and turns valves to regulate flow of latex and air into frothing tank. Starts agitators in frothing tank to mix air with latex. Weighs out specified quantity of mixed latex and compares with formula to determine density of latex. Drains latex from frothing tank to holding tanks. Signals POURER (rubber goods) when latex is ready for molds. Regulates temperature and spray pumps in preconditioning chamber to heat and coat molds in preparation for loading.
GOE: 06.02.13 STRENGTH: L GED: R3 M2 L2 SVP: 5 DLU: 77

550.381-010 COLOR MATCHER (leather mfg.; plastic-synth.; tex. prod., nec)
Mixes pigments or color concentrate to formulate coloring solutions used in dyeing leather or coated fabrics: Compares sample of desired color with standard color specifications to determine pigments required. Weighs and mixes pigments or concentrate with thinning and drying solutions until mixture matches sample. Dyes piece of leather or coated fabric and compares it with sample to verify color. May examine color of dispersed pigment, using color-checking lamps. May weigh, add, and mix ingredients to correct color discrepancy. Records specifications necessary to produce desired color.
GOE: 06.02.32 STRENGTH: M GED: R3 M2 L3 SVP: 5 DLU: 77

550.381-014 TINTER (paint & varnish) alternate titles: color matcher; color shader; finish mixer; paint tinter; shader

Mixes pigments or base colors with paints, enamels, or lacquers to match standard or sample colors, following formulas and standard color samples: Starts agitator in tank filled with basic paint product. Pours pigments or base colors from containers and dumps specified amounts into tank to color basic product. Smears sample of batch on glass or paper, using spatula or brush, and compares sample with standard color, using colorimeter. Repeats operation to attain specified shade. Records ingredients added on batch ticket. Ladles sample into container, writes identifying data on container, and submits sample to laboratory for final color, gloss, weight, and viscosity tests. May add materials to thin batch [THINNER (paint & varnish) 550.585-038]. May remove foreign matter from batch, using centrifuge [CENTRIFUGE OPERATOR (paint & varnish) 551.685-034]. May weigh sample and calculate weight per gallon. May determine specific gravity, using hydrometer. May test for viscosity, using viscometer. May be designated according to product colored as Enamel Shader (paint & varnish); Lacquer Shader (paint & varnish); Latex-Paint Shader (paint & varnish); Oil-Paint Shader (paint & varnish).
GOE: 06.02.11 STRENGTH: M GED: R3 M2 L3 SVP: 6 DLU: 78

550.382-010 COLOR MAKER (chemical)

Controls equipment to make dyes from coal tar derivatives: Measures coal tar derivatives, using balance scale or graduated container, dumps them and required amounts of sodium salt of nitrous acid with hydrochloric acid into vat of water, and starts agitator to make chromogen (dye-forming substance). Adds ice to chromogen to maintain temperature at prescribed level. Dips litmus paper into chromogen to determine its acidity. Adds required amounts of auxochromes (salt-forming materials) to chromogen to strike (form) dye. Tests acidity of dye, using pH meter, and corrects variances from standard by adding specified acid or alkali to dye.
GOE: 06.02.11 STRENGTH: M GED: R3 M2 L2 SVP: 5 DLU: 77

550.382-014 COLOR MAKER (tex. prod., nec)

Operates machines to mix or grind daub, printing ink color, and color pigments, for artificial leather: Calculates batch size according to roll yardage to be coated. Weighs and measures, according to formula, components, such as ball mill mix, color pigments, and oils to attain colors and specified consistency. Moves components to agitator or ball mill mixers and roll grinders for processing, using handtruck. Dumps ingredients into and starts machines that grind and mix them. Collects color sample and compares it with color standard. Adds ingredients, such as white, clear, or colored pigments, or thinner to correct color discrepancies. Prepares new color batches when drum content in inventory storage is low. Lifts and moves drums, using portable air-operated hydraulic hoist. May be designated according to operation performed as Ball-Mill Mixer (tex. prod., nec); Daub-Color Matcher (tex. prod., nec); Daub-Color Mixer (tex. prod., nec); Grinding Operator (tex. prod., nec); Print-Color Matcher (tex. prod., nec); Print-Color Mixer (tex. prod., nec).
GOE: 06.02.11 STRENGTH: M GED: R3 M2 L3 SVP: 5 DLU: 77

550.382-018 MIXER OPERATOR I (chemical) alternate titles: blender operator; mixing-house operator

Controls mixing machine and auxiliary equipment to blend ingredients for explosives, such as dynamite, smokeless powder, and solid-propellant rocket fuel: Weighs out and charges specified quantities of solid materials into mixer, or feeds preweighed materials into mixing chamber. Meters prescribed quantities of liquid chemical agents, such as nitroglycerin, wetting agents, catalysts, or solvents into machine. Starts mixer to blend ingredients for specified time or until prescribed reaction occurs. Tilts mixer to discharge contents, moves dump lever, or shovels materials into containers for storage, shipment, or further processing. May compute quantities of chemical agents required for batch of given size, according to formula. May tend auxiliary equipment units, such as dissolving tanks, oven, or vibrating screens, to prepare or further process materials before or after mixing. When blending ingredients for pyrotechnic tracer shells, is designated Composition Mixer (chemical). When mixing nitroglycerin and dry ingredients to produce dynamite, regulating mixer speed and ingredients according to grade and type of dynamite specified, is designated Dope Mixer (chemical).
GOE: 06.02.18 STRENGTH: H GED: R3 M2 L2 SVP: 4 DLU: 77

550.382-022 MIXING-MACHINE OPERATOR (any industry)

Operates mixing machine to blend ingredients into compounds for processing: Loads ingredients into mixing machine hopper from conveyor, scales, or handtrucks, or directs other workers in performing this task. Starts machine and adjusts valves to admit steam or cooling fluids to steam jacket or devices in mixing chamber to aid in blending and densifying mixture. Operates machine until mixture reaches desired consistency, and turns lever to unload mixture into container, conveyor, or mill for sheeting. May operate auxiliary equipment to break up, grind, dry mix, or otherwise prepare mixture for final processing. May tend automatic mixing machine. May be designated according to trade name of machine.
GOE: 06.02.13 STRENGTH: H GED: R3 M2 L2 SVP: 4 DLU: 78

550.382-026 OPERATOR, CATALYST CONCENTRATION (plastic-synth.)

Controls equipment, such as dissolving and mixing drums, catalyst chillers, heat exchangers, filters, moisturizer, vacuum strippers, pumps, and auxiliary equipment to dissolve and blend catalytic agents with isobutylene extract, and mix additive chemicals used to slurry butyl polymers: Empties catalyst from drums into dissolving drum to maintain specified concentration. Turns valves and instrument control dials on units and control panel to maintain required temperatures, pressures, and flow rates. Starts pumps that blend catalyst and feed stock in specified proportions and circulate catalyst through moisturizer, chillers, filters, and vacuum strippers. Weighs solid chemicals in required batches. Starts mixing tanks to blend additive chemicals used to slurry butane polymers. Pumps additives to storage drums. Turns valves or lowers liter bottle into vessels to take samples for laboratory tests. Gauges storage tanks. Records meter and gauge readings, quantities of chemicals used, and other operating information.
GOE: 06.02.13 STRENGTH: H GED: R3 M2 L2 SVP: 5 DLU: 77

550.382-030 ROOF-CEMENT-AND-PAINT MAKER (build. mat., nec; nonmet. min.)

Operates one or more mixing machines to combine tar, asbestos fiber, asphalt, or similar ingredients to make roof coating and cement: Starts mixing machine and pump and opens line valve to admit asphalt into mixing machine. Observes indicator or measuring stick and stops asphalt flow when specified amount has entered mixing machine. Dumps specified ingredients through weil into mixing tank or starts conveyor and dumps ingredients onto conveyor leading to mixing machine. Reads ammeter to determine consistency of mixture and adds materials as needed, or visually determines when mixture has attained consistency and stops mixing machine. Draws off sample of mixture for laboratory testing. Turns lock bolts to open lines between mixing tank and storage tank, using wrench. Keeps record of batch made, including deviations from written formula.
GOE: 06.02.18 STRENGTH: H GED: R3 M2 L2 SVP: 5 DLU: 77

550.382-034 SOLUTIONS OPERATOR (plastic-synth.)

Controls equipment to blend butadiene-styrene latexes together with processing oils, stabilizers, and other additives to produce various kinds of synthetic rubber according to formulas: Turns valves to connect pipelines from storage tanks to blending tanks or weigh tanks. Starts pumps and agitators. Turns valves to discharge blended materials from tanks into streams for coagulation. Pumps latex into blending tanks to obtain specified mixtures. Gauges tank or observes markings on side of tank to verify specified volumes of each type of latex. Observes dials and pumps specified amounts of additive materials into weigh tanks. Discharges additives into blending tanks. Takes samples of blends for laboratory testing. Records blend data in logs.
GOE: 06.02.13 STRENGTH: L GED: R3 M2 L2 SVP: 5 DLU: 77

550.485-010 CHEMICAL MIXER (photofinishing)

Tends machine that mixes specified chemicals and liquids according to formula to prepare solutions for use in processing exposed film: Opens valves and starts pumps to transfer specified amount and type of liquid from storage tank into mixing tanks. Weighs specified chemicals on scale and dumps chemicals into mixing tank. Activates mixing tank agitators and sets timer to mix ingredients for specified period of time. Observes gauge readings on mixing tank and adjusts temperature and flowmeter controls when readings vary from established norms. Obtains sample of solution in tube and tests for acidity or alkalinity, using pH meter. Submits sample of solution to laboratory for analysis, reviews analysis, and adds required amounts of chemicals to attain solution of specified standard. Opens valves and pumps solution into storage tank. May recover silver or other chemical solid from used solution by electrolysis, using reclamation tank, or by chemical precipitation, using centrifuge.
GOE: 06.02.11 STRENGTH: H GED: R3 M2 L2 SVP: 6 DLU: 77

550.485-018 PAINT MIXER, MACHINE (any industry)

Tends paint-mixing machines that mix paint, lacquer, and stain: Attaches powered mixer to barrels of unmixed paint and starts mixer to stir paint for specified time to obtain specified consistency. Computes amounts and weights of paint, lacquer, solvent, or thinner required from standard formula, and pours specified amounts into mixing machine. Starts mixer and allows it to run for prescribed time to attain specified viscosity and color. Measures viscosity, using viscosimeter and stop watch. May pump paint from central pumping station to spray booths. May filter paint or pyroxylin to remove impurities. May maintain record of paint issued and inventory of supplies on hand.
GOE: 06.04.11 STRENGTH: H GED: R2 M1 L1 SVP: 3 DLU: 77

550.485-022 POWDER BLENDER AND POURER (chemical)

Tends equipment that blends various types of propellent powders used in manufacture of small arms ammunition: Examines and verifies powder with identifying data on container and type of powder specified on work order. Pours powder from containers into partitioned hopper and turns knob to adjust rate of flow from hopper compartments according to powder blend proportions. Verifies accuracy of hopper adjustment by drawing powder sample from each hopper compartment, using stopwatch to time flow, and weighing samples and calculating rate of flow; or by starting agitator that shakes powders into blending tube, separating blended powders according to grain size, using sieve, and weighing each size. Readjusts hopper controls as indicated by rate-of-flow or sieve test until powder proportions match specifications. Replaces full containers of blended powder under discharge tube. May fill small containers with powder by hand.
GOE: 06.04.11 STRENGTH: M GED: R2 M2 L2 SVP: 3 DLU: 77

550.485-026 PULVERIZING-AND-SIFTING OPERATOR (chemical)

Tends mechanical equipment, such as jaw crusher, disintegrator, ball mill, swing hammer mill, agitator sifter, and silk screen shakers that pulverize and

sift ingredients of propellant and priming powders preparatory to blending: Feeds raw material into machine or hopper, using hands or scoop. Adjusts machines to reduce material to granules of desired size by turning screw, using spanner wrench, to adjust space between reciprocating crusher jaws, or turning rheostat to regulate vibrator speed controlling rate of flow into disintegrator, or changing number of balls or hammers in mills, depending on type of machine used. Tends agitator-sifter to sift pulverized ingredients to obtain granules within specified grain size in desired proportions. Sends sample to laboratory and computes quantity of individual grain size to be added or screened out to bring blend to acceptable proportions. Changes screens, using wrench, to produce desired size granules. Pours sifted material into drum and rolls drum on floor to blend material. Tends shaker machine to sift pulverized glass through silk screen for blending in priming mixture. May hand blend priming compounds.
GOE: 06.02.18 STRENGTH: H GED: R3 M2 L2 SVP: 4 DLU: 77

550.564-010 METAL-BONDING CRIB ATTENDANT (chemical)
Mixes, stores, and issues metal bonding adhesives for use by workers assembling metal parts for aircraft, missile and space vehicles, marine craft, or trailer parts: Measures and weighs ingredients according to formula to obtain specified weight and proportion, using scales, balances, and graduated vessels. Dumps ingredients into machine, and starts machine that mixes ingredients into adhesives. Removes adhesives from machine and stores them in bins. Requisitions ingredients, issues adhesives to workers, and keeps records of disposition of materials.
GOE: 06.02.32 STRENGTH: M GED: R3 M2 L2 SVP: 4 DLU: 77

550.565-010 PRIMER-POWDER BLENDER, DRY (ordnance)
Tends equipment that blends and screens dry explosive powders in cloth, cone-shaped mixing and screening device to make primer powder for center-fire cartridges: Selects and carries predetermined quantities of ingredients from storage magazines and dryhouse to mixing house. Positions containers in specified order on dumping shelf of mixing device. Moves dump arm by remote control from behind cement wall to empty containers in mixing bag. Turns mixing crank specified number of times to move bag center up and down to blend powders, observing operations in mirrors set at angles. Pours blended powder into rubber containers, marks with identifying data, and carries them to storage magazines. Washes equipment and premises to prevent accumulation of explosive dust. Mends and replaces torn mixing bags, using needle and thread. Repairs screens and attaches bags to wall of mixing cylinder, using special lacing and tying technique. May blend wet mixtures [PRIMER-POWDER BLENDER, WET (chemical)].
GOE: 06.04.11 STRENGTH: L GED: R2 M1 L2 SVP: 3 DLU: 77

550.582-010 PRIMER-POWDER BLENDER, WET (chemical)
Controls mixing kettles to blend explosive ingredients and produce wet priming mixture used in rim-fire cartridges: Carries prescribed quantities of dry powder, ground glass, liquid gum, and other ingredients from storage house to control house. Measures and mixes specified amounts of ingredients in rubber basin, using rubber spatula. Carries initial mixture to isolated mixing house and scoops it into mixing machine. Returns to control house and starts mixer, using switch on control panel. Stops mixer at designated intervals to add ingredients and to examine mixture to detect degree of dryness, adding water as required to prevent ignition of mixture during blending. Scoops blended mixture into rubber containers (boats), marks boats with identifying data, and carries them to storage house. Washes equipment and premises to prevent accumulation of explosive material. May prepare ingredients for blending.
GOE: 06.02.18 STRENGTH: L GED: R3 M2 L2 SVP: 4 DLU: 77

550.582-014 WEIGHER-BULKER (chemical)
Operates battery of agitator-equipped tanks to blend base perfume fragrances for use in items, such as soaps, perfumes, and insecticides: Rolls drums or trays of solid material into heating chamber to melt and prepare for bulking. Sets thermostat to prescribed temperature and leaves drums in chamber for specified period. Starts blower to cool chamber. Pushes materials to bulking area. Rolls trays of containers or drums of liquid material to bulking tanks. Dumps or pumps specified quantities into tanks. Starts agitators in tanks and allows materials to blend for specified periods. Examines materials in tanks for impurities and to determine if color conforms to standard. Places empty drum on preset floor scale. Attaches filter press hoses to outlet on blending tank and to drum intake spout. Opens valve to drain material from tank through filter press to drum. Sets thermostat at prescribed temperature and dumps flaked or crystallized material into steam-jacketed kettle to melt. Ties filter cloth on discharge spout, and turns spigot to drain material into bucket. Dumps material from bucket into casting trays and allows to cool until congealed. Removes congealed cubes or slabs from casting trays, using wooden mallet, and stores in plastic lined containers. Draws off samples from each bulked lot and labels it for laboratory files. Seals containers. Stencils lot numbers on drums or affixes labels to bottles and cans. Maintains record of bulking operations. Transports drums and other containers on trays or handtrucks to storage room. Cleans tanks, filter presses, and other equipment, using solvents, hoses, and brushes. May add prescribed chemicals to bulked materials to neutralize acid or control color. May blend materials by stirring with paddle.
GOE: 06.02.11 STRENGTH: H GED: R3 M2 L2 SVP: 5 DLU: 77

550.584-010 FLUX MIXER (chemical)
Mixes soldering flux, and supplies soldering or welding machines with flux and solder: Mixes flux in crock or vat according to formula, using paddle. Tests

consistency of flux with hydrometer. Carries or trucks flux or solder to machines. Cleans reservoirs of spent or stale flux, using solvent. Keeps records of solder and flux consumed and salvaged.
GOE: 06.04.34 STRENGTH: M GED: R3 M1 L1 SVP: 4 DLU: 77

550.584-014 SAMPLE-COLOR MAKER (paint & varnish)
Mixes color samples from standard pigments and production pigments, for subsequent comparison of color characteristics, to ensure conformity of production pigments with standard pigments: Weighs out specified amounts of standard and production pigments and places them on glass plates or in beakers. Mixes pigments with specified vehicle, such as water or oil to form color samples, using spatula. Smears samples on paper and rubs samples with paint scraper or glass rod. Writes identifying data on color sample sheets and submits sheets to supervisor for evaluation.
GOE: 06.04.34 STRENGTH: L GED: R2 M1 L1 SVP: 2 DLU: 77

550.585-010 BINDER TECHNICIAN (glass mfg.)
Tends machine that mixes binder fluid used in production of fiberglass sliver or mats: Weighs and measures ingredients according to formula and pours or dumps ingredients into mixing vats. Turns valve to start flow of water and steam into vats and starts portable or power mixer to agitate ingredients for specified time. Observes temperature charts and thermometers to determine if specified temperature is maintained. Turns valve to increase flow of steam or water to regulate temperature of mixture or notifies supervisor of excessive temperatures. Dips beaker into vat to obtain sample of binder fluid and delivers sample to testing room. Obtains test results and adds ingredients according to instructions or turns valve to start flow of binder fluid into specified circulatory tank. Cleans mixing vats, mixers, and other equipment, using water and cloths. Records number of batches mixed, ingredients used, gallons mixed, gallons lost, and net gallons mixed for inventory and production records.
GOE: 06.04.11 STRENGTH: M GED: R3 M2 L2 SVP: 3 DLU: 77

550.585-014 CELLOPHANE-BATH MIXER (plastic-synth.)
Tends equipment to mix and transfer acid bath that coagulates viscose solution into cellophane: Starts pumps and evaporators to mix bath ingredients, such as acid, softener, and bleach, according to specifications, and to transfer bath solution to storage tanks. Observes indicators and controlling instruments and turns valves to regulate flow rate, temperature, and pressure of solution in pipelines and evaporators. Tests acidity of bath, using pH meter, or draws sample for laboratory analysis. Maintains record of bath temperature, acidity, and operating conditions of equipment.
GOE: 06.04.13 STRENGTH: L GED: R3 M2 L2 SVP: 3 DLU: 77

550.585-018 CHEMICAL MIXER (textile)
Tends equipment that mixes chemicals for use in bleaching, cleaning, desizing, latexing, mercerizing, and finishing canvas goods, carpets and rugs, felt goods, and textile yarns and fabrics: Weighs or measures quantities of ingredients, such as peroxide, silica, caustic, solvents, emulsions, resins, starches, and detergents, following formula, and pours them into mixing tank. Turns valves to admit water into tank up to mark on tank wall. Starts mixer and allows solution to mix for specified period of time. Turns valve to transfer solution from mixing tank to storage tank. Tests solutions in storage tanks with hydrometer, viscosimeter, or by titration to detect variations from standards and adds appropriate ingredients to restore solution to standard strength. Records test results, batches of solutions mixed, and chemicals used in each batch for production and inventory purposes. May inject steam into solution to dissolve ingredients or cook solution to specified consistency. May be designated according to solution mixed as Acid-Bath Mixer (textile); Ammonia-Solution Preparer (textile); Caustic Mixer (textile); Gum Mixer (textile); Latex Compounder (textile); Size Maker (textile); Soap Mixer (textile); Waterproofing Mixer (textile).
GOE: 06.04.11 STRENGTH: M GED: R3 M2 L2 SVP: 4 DLU: 77

550.585-022 COATING OPERATOR (chemical)
Tends battery of mixing vessels that mix chemical solutions with process catalysts to apply chemical coating, such as alumina: Starts pump to admit coating solution to automatic measuring tank and to transfer solution from measuring tank to coating vessel. Starts agitator to mix solution. Draws sample from coating vessel, using dipstick, and tests for specified balance between acidity and alkalinity, using pH meter. Turns valve to add solutions to coating vessel until required balance is achieved. Stops agitator and pumps mixture to storage tanks after specified mixing time. Records processing time and pH reading on operating record.
GOE: 06.04.11 STRENGTH: L GED: R3 M1 L2 SVP: 4 DLU: 77

550.585-026 LIME-SLUDGE MIXER (paper & pulp)
Tends agitator tanks that mix chemicals with lime sludge to produce filler used in finishing paper: Adjusts valves to control flow of sludge through filter screen into agitator tank. Adds acid and alum, and starts agitator to stir mixture. Tests alkalinity of mixture by titration test, and adds acid or alum as necessary. Weighs specified samples of sludge and compares them with standard chart to determine density. Screens sludge sample through wire mesh to detect presence of foreign matter. Records test results and quantities of sludge processed.
GOE: 06.04.11 STRENGTH: M GED: R2 M1 L1 SVP: 3 DLU: 77

550.585-030 NITRATING-ACID MIXER (chemical)
Tends mixing tanks and auxiliary equipment to combine acids or other specified liquid ingredients to produce solutions for manufacturing explosives, such

as nitroglycerin, tetryl, and TNT: Pumps specified liquids through metering or weighing tanks into mixing tank. Starts tank agitator to mix ingredients for specified time. Draws samples of product for laboratory analysis and transfers additional ingredients to tank until product meets plant standard. Pumps mixed product to storage, tank cars, or other processing units. May turn steam or coolant valves to heat or cool product during mixing, maintaining temperature in equipment within prescribed limits as indicated by tank thermometer. May maintain records of mixing time, gauge readings, and number of batches produced per shift log. May be designated according to product produced as Ammonium-Nitrate Neutralizer (chemical); Dimethylaniline-Sulfator Operator (chemical).
GOE: 06.04.11 STRENGTH: L GED: R3 M2 L2 SVP: 5 DLU: 77

550.585-034 PASTE MIXER (chemical)
Tends mixing machine or mulling mill that mixes lead oxide powders, water, and acid into paste for storage-battery grids: Measures or weighs specified amounts of oxide, water, and acid, using barrels, buckets, or measuring tanks. Dumps barrels of oxide into mixer or into pit equipped with bucket elevator and conveyor leading to mixer. Starts mixer and turns valves to add specified amount of water and acid to oxide. Tests sample of paste for temperature, solidity, and density, using probe thermometer, penetrometer, and gram scale and records results. Dumps mixture into cart and pushes or pulls cart to pasting machine. Records batch weight and starting and withdrawal time. Cleans machine, using water and brush. May tend equipment to heat and mix ingredients of liquid paste and be designated Paste Mixer, Liquid (elec. equip.).
GOE: 06.04.11 STRENGTH: M GED: R2 M1 L1 SVP: 3 DLU: 77

550.585-038 THINNER (paint & varnish)
Tends equipment to mix specified amounts of liquid and powdered ingredients, such as oils, solvents, lead salts, and resins, with paint products, such as paint pigment and paste, varnish, and stain, to thin products: Weighs ingredients, using scales, and dumps into mixer. Turns valves on storage tanks to admit specified liquids into mixer, and starts power agitator to blend ingredients. Starts pump to transfer batch to storage tank or clarifying machine. Writes identifying code on tanks and records quantities and types of ingredients added to batch. May be designated according to mixture thinned as Bulk-Pigment Reducer (paint & varnish); Paste Thinner (paint & varnish); Stain Maker (paint & varnish); Varnish Thinner (paint & varnish).
GOE: 06.04.11 STRENGTH: H GED: R3 M2 L2 SVP: 3 DLU: 77

550.585-042 TRACER-POWDER BLENDER (chemical)
Tends machines and equipment that prepare and blend dry and liquid chemicals to produce flammable mixtures of specified composition for igniter, subigniter, and tracer powders used in tracer bullets: Weighs and measures amounts of ingredients in pounds, ounces, and drams, according to chart, using bench scale and beakers. Tends remote-controlled tumbling barrels to blend chemicals, adding ingredients in designated sequence at timed intervals; steam-heated oven to dry ingredients; and remote-controlled ball mill to pulverize dried ingredients, adding required number of rubber balls to achieve prescribed degree of pulverization. Sifts powder through silk screen by hand. Pours finished mixes into rubber pouches, marks with identifying data, and carries them to storage magazines. Brushes, washes, and hoses equipment and premises to prevent dangerous accumulation of powder.
GOE: 06.04.11 STRENGTH: M GED: R3 M2 L2 SVP: 3 DLU: 77

550.585-046 WAX BLENDER (fabrication, nec)
Tends equipment to color wax used in candles: Weighs and dumps wax into kettles, according to specifications. Turns valves to circulate steam through jackets or turns thermostat knob to heat wax to specified temperature. Turns valve or starts pumps to transfer molten wax to tanks and kettles and adds prescribed dye to color wax. Pours wax into molds to form sample candles and examines candles to ensure compliance with specifications. Records quantities and types of wax used.
GOE: 06.04.19 STRENGTH: H GED: R3 M1 L2 SVP: 3 DLU: 77

550.586-010 BLENDER HELPER (plastic prod.; plastic-synth.)
Transports materials from storage areas, using handtruck: Weighs materials on platform scales and records weights. Loads materials in bags or in tubs on conveyor to transport them to blending machine. Raises and transports drums of liquid ingredients, such as oils, using hoist. Empties drums, using bung-wrench, and turns valves to admit liquid ingredients into tanks. Opens sacks with knife and empties dry materials, such as clay, carbon black, or glass filler, into blending machine. May press buttons to start agitator. Performs other duties as described under HELPER (any industry) Master Title.
GOE: 06.04.40 STRENGTH: H GED: R2 M1 L1 SVP: 2 DLU: 77

550.587-010 MAKE-UP OPERATOR HELPER (chemical)
Weighs dry chemicals in batches, records weights on process sheets, and transfers materials to mixing area, using handtruck. May collect samples of solutions for laboratory tests. May clean tanks, process lines, hoppers, and other equipment.
GOE: 06.03.02 STRENGTH: L GED: R2 M1 L2 SVP: 3 DLU: 77

550.587-014 SAMPLE COLLECTOR (chemical)
Mixes fertilizer samples preparatory to laboratory analysis: Collects material from storage bin, railroad car, or bagging area, using auger or shovel. Dumps material onto mixing table. Blends material, using shovel, paddle, or hands. Pours blended sample into container, writes identifying information, such as

material, date, and sample number, on label and attaches label to container. Collects samples of granulated fertilizer during various stages of processing, pours sample through riffle (separator) to mix and reduce amount to representative sample, and sends sample to laboratory for analysis.
GOE: 06.04.17 STRENGTH: L GED: R2 M1 L1 SVP: 2 DLU: 77

550.662-010 BLEACH-LIQUOR MAKER (paper & pulp)
Controls chemical reaction vats and mixing equipment to compound pulp bleaching solution, following specifications: Starts conveyor and opens valve to dump specified quantities of lime or sodium hydroxide and water into mixing tank to make lime slurry. Starts pump and turns valve to start flow of chlorine and lime slurry to chlorinating tanks. Adjusts controls to regulate temperature of solution to prevent adverse chemical reactions. Starts mixing machine in tank to mix bleaching solution. Sprinkles indicator solution on top of mixture in tank or makes titration test to determine completion of chemical reaction. Starts pumps to transfer bleach solution to storage. May control reaction cells and *absorption tower* in which chlorine dioxide bleaching gas is formed from calcium chlorate and sulfurous acid. May operate conveyor to remove bulk lime from railroad cars to storage bins. May connect pipe and hose lines to tank cars containing chlorine gas.
GOE: 06.02.14 STRENGTH: L GED: R3 M2 L2 SVP: 5 DLU: 77

550.663-010 FORMULA WEIGHER (rubber goods)
Operates tram car, suspended from monorail, beneath overhead storage bins to collect and weigh powdered chemicals in weighing bin, according to laboratory formulas, and empties assembled ingredients into chute of mixer: Moves levers to drive electrically powered car from one bin to another and to raise accordionlike mouth of weighing bin to mouth of storage bin. Pulls lever to drop chemical from storage into weighing bin and observes scale until weight specified is reached. Moves car and repeats weighing until each specified ingredient is added. Scoops from barrels, and weighs and adds by hand, quantities of chemicals too small or too rarely used to warrant storing in bins. Positions bottom of weighing bin over mixer chute, and on all-clear-light from MIXING-MACHINE OPERATOR (any industry), depresses pedal to drop accumulated chemicals into mixer chute. Confers with MIXING-MACHINE OPERATOR (any industry) to discuss changes in chemicals or quantities specified.
GOE: 06.04.11 STRENGTH: L GED: R2 M1 L2 SVP: 3 DLU: 77

550.665-010 BLENDER II (chemical)
Tends equipment that blends batches of smokeless powder to obtain final product having uniform ballistic properties: Moves levers in control room to activate rotation equipment or to transfer powder repeatedly between top and bottom bins to effect thorough mixing. Opens vent in bottom bin to dump powder into containers or buggies for storage, shipment, or further processing. May add or remove powders in rotating blender barrels, using hand scoop, to adjust mixture or remove sample. When tending machine equipped with toothed rotors to blend powder, is designated Macerator Operator (chemical). May be designated according to kind of powder blended as Tetryl-Blender Operator (chemical).
GOE: 06.04.11 STRENGTH: H GED: R3 M2 L2 SVP: 4 DLU: 77

550.665-014 COMPOSITION MIXER (fabrication, nec)
Tends mixers that blend ingredients for use in production of hard-surface floor covering: Positions charge chute on mixer and signals worker to charge machine with preweighed ingredients. Pulls lever to close mixer, starts mixing mechanism, and sets steam and temperature controls. Examines color and consistency of mix to determine whether ingredients are blended according to specifications. Starts machine drive to discharge mix into sheet mill or shovels mix into container. May pull lever of hydraulic dump cylinder to discharge mix into bucket of lift truck.
GOE: 06.04.19 STRENGTH: M GED: R3 M1 L2 SVP: 4 DLU: 77

550.665-018 FERTILIZER MIXER (chemical)
Tends machine that mixes nitrogen, phosphate, and potash to produce fertilizer: Pulls lever to feed dry materials from storage hopper into mixer. Observes gauges and turns valves to admit specified amounts of liquids, such as ammonia and sulfuric acid, into mixer. Stops mixer after specified time and turns handwheel or pulls lever to dump batch onto conveyor.
GOE: 06.04.11 STRENGTH: L GED: R2 M1 L1 SVP: 2 DLU: 77

550.665-022 MOTTLER OPERATOR (fabrication, nec)
Tends mottling machines that blend prescribed color mixes to achieve specified patterns or shade combinations for finished hard-surface floor covering: Selects specified mix from storage area and moves mix to charging station, using handtruck. Divides panned mix into portions, according to formula, weighs fractional quantities on balance scale, and dumps them into hopper of machine. Weighs filler, whiting, and other material as specified, using floor scale, and dumps them into hopper. Sets timer on mottler for prescribed cycle, or examines mix periodically to determine when desired mottle has been achieved. Shovels mottled mix into trucks for delivery to storage area.
GOE: 06.04.11 STRENGTH: H GED: R2 M1 L1 SVP: 3 DLU: 77

550.682-010 SIZE MAKER (paper & pulp)
Operates equipment to cook and mix materials, such as starch, casein, resin, chemicals, and fillers, according to formula to make size for pulp paper: Turns valves to fill cooking vats with metered volumes of liquid ingredients and dumps specified amounts of solid ingredients into vats according to formula. Turns steam valves or adjusts burner to maintain specified temperature in vats for cooking starch, resin, or casein with water, lime, and chemicals. Opens

drain valve or starts pump to transfer cooked material to mixing machine, dumps specified weights of alum, lithopone, clay, or titanium dioxide into machine, and starts machine to mix ingredients for specified length of time. Adds chemicals to mixture, according to specification, to prevent decomposition. Drains or pumps size to specified storage tanks.
GOE: 06.04.14 STRENGTH: H GED: R3 M2 L2 SVP: 5 DLU: 77

550.682-014 TANNING-SOLUTION MAKER (chemical)
Controls series of vats that boil tanbark, quebracho, chemicals, and water to prepare tanning solution: Weighs specified amounts of materials on scale and dumps them into vat. Opens valves to admit water and steam into vat. Adjusts steam valve to maintain solution at specified temperature. Tests sample of solution for specific gravity, using hydrometer. Adds materials to solution to obtain solution of specified gravity. Starts pump to transfer solution from vat to storage tank. May grind bark or wood, using grinding machine.
GOE: 06.04.11 STRENGTH: M GED: R3 M1 L2 SVP: 5 DLU: 77

550.684-010 COAGULATING-BATH MIXER (plastic-synth.)
Prepares coagulating bath used to transform cellulose slurry into rayon filaments, according to formula or proportion chart and process specifications: Measures prescribed types and quantities of bath ingredients, depending on forming process used in plant. Dumps or pumps ingredients, such as caustic soda or sulfuric acid, sodium sulfate, zinc sulfate, and glucose into mixing tank for transfer to trough containing water into which slurry is extruded. Tests acidity or alkalinity of bath at specified intervals, using pH meter, and adds additional ingredients to maintain solution at prescribed standard. May be designated Acid-Correction Hand (plastic-synth.) in plants producing rayon by viscose process.
GOE: 06.04.11 STRENGTH: M GED: R3 M2 L2 SVP: 4 DLU: 77

550.684-014 DYE WEIGHER (any industry) alternate titles: chemical weigher; color weigher; drug-room clerk; dye maker; dyer assistant
Mixes dyes and chemicals for use in dyeing products, such as fabrics, hosiery, and yarns: Weighs out quantities of powdered or liquid dyes and chemicals, following formula sheet. Pours dyes and chemicals into pail or mixing tank and turns valve to admit water into tank or pail up to mark on container wall. Stirs ingredients with paddle and injects steam into solution to dissolve dye. Dumps contents of pail into supply tank or turns valves to transfer dye solution from mixing tank to supply tanks in dye room. Inventories dyes and chemicals and notifies DYER, SUPERVISOR (knitting; tex. prod., nec; textile) 582.131-014 as supplies are needed. May be designated according to dye mixed as Indigo Mixer (textile).
GOE: 06.04.34 STRENGTH: H GED: R3 M2 L2 SVP: 3 DLU: 81

550.684-018 PAINT MIXER, HAND (any industry)
Mixes stains, paints, and other coatings for use in painting according to formulas: Pours pigments, paint paste, vehicle, and thinner into can. Stirs mixture with paddle. Compares mixed liquid with desired color sample to ensure that it matches. May blend colors to obtain desired shades. May test specific gravity of mixture, using hydrometer. When mixing colors for spray painting, may be designated Spray Blender (any industry).
GOE: 06.04.34 STRENGTH: L GED: R2 M1 L1 SVP: 3 DLU: 77

550.684-022 PRIMING-POWDER-PREMIX BLENDER (chemical)
Weighs and blends powdered ingredients to form priming mixtures for small arms ammunition: Weighs specified amounts of pulverized and sifted ingredients and filters them by hand in prescribed order through silk screen onto blending paper. Lifts each corner of paper and pulls slowly toward diagonally opposite corner to fold and blend powder until examination of color shade indicates blending is accomplished. Pours mixture from paper into cardboard containers and marks containers with identifying data.
GOE: 06.04.34 STRENGTH: L GED: R2 M1 L2 SVP: 3 DLU: 77

550.684-026 SILVER-SOLUTION MIXER (chemical)
Mixes silver solution for spraying lacquer disks (original recording): Measures prescribed quantities of premixed silver solution and combines with distilled water. Tests mixed solution for conformity to standards, using laboratory test equipment. Deposits mixture in containers or spray tanks. May analyze plating solutions for conformity to standards.
GOE: 06.04.34 STRENGTH: L GED: R3 M2 L2 SVP: 3 DLU: 77

550.685-010 BATCH MIXER (soap & rel.)
Tends mixer that compounds cleaning powder: Opens valves to admit specified quantities of ingredients into mixer or weighs and dumps ingredients into mixer, using scale. Presses button or moves lever to activate mixer that blends ingredients for designated time. Stops machine and opens valve to discharge cleaning powder into storage bins. May draw sample of blended ingredients for laboratory analysis. May keep production log.
GOE: 06.04.19 STRENGTH: M GED: R2 M1 L1 SVP: 3 DLU: 77

550.685-014 BLENDER I (chemical)
Tends machine that blends batches of flushed colors derived from coal tar hydrocarbons: Dumps specified flushed pigments or dyes into tub of machine, using hoist. Adds specified chemicals to batch according to product specifications. Starts agitator to mix ingredients for specified time. Turns valves to pump blended pigments or dyes into storage tanks or drums.
GOE: 06.04.11 STRENGTH: M GED: R2 M1 L1 SVP: 2 DLU: 77

550.685-018 BRINE MAKER I (chemical)
Tends tanks, filters, and auxiliary equipment that produce brine solution for use in electrolytic cells: Pumps water through salt beds or starts conveyor

bringing salt from storage area for dissolution in water, producing mixture of specified salt content. Admits salt water and specified amounts of liquid chemicals, such as caustic soda or acid, to mixing tank to produce brine solution meeting plant standard. Pumps solution to settling tank to settle out impurities and through sand-bed filters for final purification. Draws sample of brine for laboratory analysis to test density, salt content, and acidity, using hydrometer, salinometer, and pH meter. Turns valves to transfer brine to electrolytic cells and maintain brine at specified levels in supply lines, tanks, and cells. May dump materials into brine to adjust chemical composition to plant standard, using titration test to determine strength of solution. May pump water through resin and carbon beds to demineralize it. May tend heat exchanger to maintain temperature of brine within specified limits. When pumping brine through filters only, is designated Brine Purifier (chemical).
GOE: 06.04.11 STRENGTH: M GED: R3 M2 L2 SVP: 3 DLU: 77

550.685-022 CD-MIXER (rubber reclaim.)
Tends machine that mixes ground scrap rubber with pigments, caustics, and oils to prepare rubber for devulcanization: Pulls slide on gravity chute or shovels scrap rubber into weigh hopper. Pulls lever to dump scrap rubber from weigh hopper into mixer. Measures and weighs pigments, caustics, and oils according to formula, and dumps or drains them into mixer. Starts machine that mixes materials for specified time. Pulls lever to release mixture from machine into pans. Lifts pans onto heater cars by hand or with hoist. Signals worker to move pans of mixed stock into heaters. May tend cracker mill that grinds scrap rubber into particles [GRINDER (rubber goods; rubber reclaim.)]. May unload heaters and dump devulcanized scrap rubber from pans. May line pans with waxed paper or sprinkle with pulverized soapstone to prevent rubber from sticking.
GOE: 06.04.13 STRENGTH: M GED: R2 M1 L1 SVP: 3 DLU: 77

550.685-026 CEMENT MIXER (rubber goods; rubber tire)
Tends machine that mixes synthetic or natural rubber with solvents and chemicals to produce liquid rubber cement: Weighs and measures specified amounts of rubber, chemicals, and solvents, according to mixing instructions. Breaks down full batch formulas into partial batches and samples. Presses buttons to activate electrically driven paddles that stir mixture, or stirs mixture by hand, using paddle. Opens petcock of mixer to discharge cement into cans, or opens pipeline valves to transfer cement. Records types of cement mixtures and production of each.
GOE: 06.04.13 STRENGTH: H GED: R2 M1 L2 SVP: 3 DLU: 77

550.685-030 CHEMICAL PREPARER (chemical; electron. comp.)
Tends equipment that compounds ingredients into chemical solutions used as adhesive or conductive coatings for electron tubes: Weighs and measures specified type and quantity of liquid and powdered ingredients. Pours, dumps, or pumps ingredients into mixing equipment. Starts equipment that compounds chemical ingredients and deionized water into chemical solutions, such as frit or conductive graphite. Tests mixture for conformance to prescribed standards, using testing devices, such as pH meter, resistivity meter, titration apparatus, colorimeter, thermometer, and viscometer. Pours compounded product into containers for application to tube seams, funnel, or ceramic parts by other workers.
GOE: 06.04.11 STRENGTH: L GED: R3 M3 L3 SVP: 4 DLU: 88

550.685-034 CHURN TENDER (plastic-synth.)
Tends rotary mixer that blends aged alkali-cellulose crumbs with carbon disulfide to form cellulose xanthate for further processing into cellophane or rayon: Couples pipe to mixer to admit specified amount of carbon disulfide to churn (mixer chamber) filled with alkali-cellulose crumbs by other workers. Starts drum rotating, observes gauges, and moves or sets controls to maintain temperature of churn and length of mixing cycle within plant specifications. Stops machine and turns valve to expel excess gas remaining in drum. Opens hatch and dumps cellulose xanthate into cart or machine hopper for further processing. Scrapes interior of drum, using putty knife or scraper, to remove product residue before preparation of next batch. May tend continuous process equipment and be designated Disulfurizer Tender (plastic-synth.). May blend cellulose xanthate and caustic soda and be designated Tank Worker (plastic-synth.).
GOE: 06.04.13 STRENGTH: L GED: R3 M2 L2 SVP: 3 DLU: 77

550.685-038 COLOR-PASTE MIXER (textile)
Tends machine to mix color paste for use in printing textiles: Measures out specified amounts of base colors and thickener, using calibrated ladles and spoons. Mixes ingredients in tub, using power mixer, and observes mixture to determine when ingredients have combined. Smears sample of printing paste on cloth and submits sample smear to COLORIST (profess. & kin.) for comparison with color standard. Adds base colors to mixture when advised by COLORIST (profess. & kin.). May strain color paste through cloth to remove lumps. May convey tubs of color to printing machine, using handtruck.
GOE: 06.04.11 STRENGTH: M GED: R3 M2 L2 SVP: 3 DLU: 77

550.685-042 COMPOUND FINISHER (chemical)
Tends mixing machine to finish mixing of matchhead compound to produce mixture of specified viscosity: Lifts kettles of compounds from cart onto mixer with hoist. Starts mixer and pours dye solution into compound. Sets thermostat or opens valve to admit steam into jacket around kettle to heat compound if specified, and verifies temperature with thermometer. Fills graduated dipper with compound and times flow of compound from dipper with stopwatch to test viscosity. Adds specified ingredient according to test results until viscosity is correct.

GOE: 06.04.11 STRENGTH: M GED: R2 M1 L1 SVP: 3 DLU: 77

550.685-046 COMPOUNDER (pharmaceut.; soap & rel.)

Tends mixer tanks and compounding kettle that mix and compound tinctures, perfumery solutions, color solutions, essential oils, and aromatic synthetics for use in manufacture of creams, perfumes, soaps, and powders: Weighs out specified types and quantities of liquid or solid ingredients in balance scale or scale tank, according to formula. Drains solution from scale tank into strainer pan to filter foreign particles. Dumps or pumps solution into compounding kettle that automatically washes it with alcohol to remove odors or adjusts valves and observes thermostat to heat solution as specified. Pumps solution into mixer tank that blends it for specified time, and through filter press for further purification. Drains sample for laboratory analysis. May test solution for color. May grind ingredients, such as castor bags or vanilla beans, using machine or hand grinder.

GOE: 06.04.11 STRENGTH: H GED: R3 M2 L2 SVP: 4 DLU: 77

550.685-050 COMPOUNDER (chemical)

Tends machines that grind and mix ingredients, such as glue, dyes, water, chemicals, and resins, according to specifications, to produce compounds used in heads and striking surfaces of kitchen, penny, and book matches: Dumps chemicals, dyes, and other ingredients into sifting and grinding machines and starts machines to sift and grind ingredients, according to specifications. Dumps or pours specified quantities of ingredients into mixing machine and starts machine to mix ingredients, according to specifications. Measures viscosity of ingredients, using viscometer. May submit sample to laboratory for testing.

GOE: 06.04.11 STRENGTH: H GED: R2 M1 L1 SVP: 3 DLU: 77

550.685-054 CRUTCHER (soap & rel.)

Tends machines that mix specified quantities and types of liquid, powder, and paste ingredients to form slurry for processing into soap products, such as bars, flakes, chips, and granules: Pulls slide from discharge chute of hopper to admit preweighed dry materials into tank, or shovels preweighed solid ingredients into tank. Opens valves to add specified amount of water, paste, or steam. Starts agitator to mix materials for prescribed period of time. Observes gauge and adjusts valves to maintain specified temperature. Weighs and dumps specified additional ingredients or adjusts scale tank and pumps in additional ingredients. Turns valve to pump completed batch to booster tank, or shovels completed batch into wheelbarrow. Draws sample of slurry for laboratory analysis. Records number of batches mixed.

GOE: 06.04.19 STRENGTH: M GED: R3 M2 L2 SVP: 4 DLU: 77

550.685-058 DUSTLESS OPERATOR (chemical)

Tends machine that mixes powdered carbon black with water or binding agents in rotating drum to form pellets: Starts machine and turns valves to admit and regulate flow of water or binding agents into mixing drum. Examines and feels samples of product to verify that pellet size and moisture content meet specified standards. Opens inspection ports and observes conveyor system to detect jamming.

GOE: 06.04.19 STRENGTH: L GED: R3 M1 L2 SVP: 3 DLU: 77

550.685-062 GLUE MIXER (any industry)

Tends agitator tanks that mix ingredients to produce chemical compounds, such as sealants, adhesives, fillers, and linoleum paste: Weighs and measures ingredients, such as casein, clay, flour, glue powder and gelatin, lignin, resins, and liquid catalysts or water, following prescribed formula, and dumps, pours, pumps, or scoops ingredients into machine, tank, or kettle. Pushes button to start agitators that blend ingredients. Observes mixing process and adds ingredients according to specifications. Manipulates controls to drain mixture from tanks or kettles. May draw product sample for laboratory analysis. May cook mixture, using steam-jacketed kettle. May manually mix compounds. May mark identifying information on containers. May record amount of product mixed. May be designated according to product mixed as Sealant Mixer (aircraft mfg.).

GOE: 06.04.19 STRENGTH: H GED: R3 M2 L2 SVP: 3 DLU: 87

550.685-066 GROUND MIXER (chemical)

Tends agitator and auxiliary equipment to mix pigments according to specifications for use in ground coating and coloring on wallpaper: Measures and mixes ingredients in electric agitator to make sizing compounds. Dumps bags of powdered clay into mixing vat, and turns valves to add water. Starts pump to transport specified quantity of sizing compound from drum into mixing vat, and starts agitator. Loosens lumps of clay from sides of vat during mixing process, using paddle. Moves drums of base solution about work area, using handtruck.

GOE: 06.04.11 STRENGTH: H GED: R2 M1 L1 SVP: 2 DLU: 77

550.685-070 INSECTICIDE MIXER (chemical)

Tends machine and equipment that mix liquid and dry ingredients according to formula to produce insecticides, pesticides, and fungicides: Weighs, measures, or turns valves to admit specified quantities and type of ingredients into mixer. Starts mixer to blend ingredients. Turns valve, pulls lever, or presses button to transfer mixture to storage tank or filling machine. Records quantity and type of ingredients mixed. May draw sample of product for laboratory testing.

GOE: 06.04.11 STRENGTH: H GED: R2 M1 L1 SVP: 2 DLU: 77

550.685-074 MIXER I (tex. prod., nec)

Tends agitator tanks, portable mixing machines, and related equipment to produce compounds for coating and waterproofing fabrics: Measures and

weighs materials, such as oils, pigments, plasticizers, resins, stabilizers, fillers, color concentrate, and water according to formula. Trucks drums of ingredients to mixers and dumps them into mixing chamber, using hoist, tilt, or by hand. Starts mixer to blend ingredients. Drains ingredients into storage tanks, buckets, or drums. Scrapes and cleans mixers, using hand scraper and solvents. May pump specified amounts of liquid plasticizer into supply containers or mixing chamber, as directed.

GOE: 06.04.11 STRENGTH: H GED: R3 M2 L1 SVP: 3 DLU: 77

550.685-078 MIXER (paint & varnish) alternate titles: batch mixer; blender; dispersion mixer

Tends mixing machines that blend solid and liquid ingredients to make products, such as paints, lacquers, putty, paint pigments, and binders, following formula: Turns valves or sets pump meters to admit specified amounts of liquids, such as oils, solvents, and water into mixer. Weighs and dumps specified amounts of dry ingredients, such as plastic flash, color concentrates, and resins into mixer, as indicated on batch ticket, or dumps preweighed ingredients into tank. Pushes or pulls tank to dispersion mixing machine. Depresses pedal to lower mixing blades into tank and presses button to start blades revolving to mix and disperse ingredients. Turns valves to drain batch through hoses into pebble or ball mill or into holding tank. Draws sample from batch for laboratory test and adds ingredients to mixture as specified by laboratory. May clean equipment, using rags, solvent, and scraper. May be designated according to product mixed as Glass Enamel Mixer (paint & varnish); Lacquer Blender (paint & varnish); Paint Maker (paint & varnish); Paste Mixer (paint & varnish); Pigment Mixer (paint & varnish); Putty Maker (paint & varnish).

GOE: 06.04.11 STRENGTH: H GED: R3 M1 L2 SVP: 3 DLU: 78

550.685-082 MIXER OPERATOR (chemical; electron. comp.) alternate titles: blender

Tends mixing machine that blends liquid and solid materials into chemical solutions and slurries used in manufacturing various products: Transfers materials to work area, using handtruck or forklift. Weighs materials according to formula or proportion tables, dumps materials into mixing chamber, and starts machine to mix materials. Examines or feels mixture, or observes gauges or timer to determine when mixing is completed, and stops machine. Dumps or shovels material from mixing chamber onto conveyor or into containers for storage, shipment, or further processing, or turns valves or starts pumps to transfer mixed materials to designated processing areas. May test sample to ensure material meets specifications. May tend auxiliary equipment, such as grinders or driers, to prepare ingredients or process product.

GOE: 06.04.11 STRENGTH: H GED: R2 M2 L2 SVP: 3 DLU: 86

550.685-086 MIXER, FOAM RUBBER (rubber goods)

Tends machine that mixes foam rubber particles with liquid latex and discharges mixture into molds to make products, such as cushions and mattresses: Opens storage bin chute to transfer ground particles to barrel. Weighs barrel, adds or removes foam rubber particles to obtain specified weight, and dumps material into mixing machine. Weighs and pours specified amount of latex into machine and starts machine that mixes ingredients. Places mold under discharge spout of machine and fills mold with mixture. May grind foam rubber, using powered grinding machine. May tend hydraulic press that cures filled molds to form cushions and mattresses [MOLDER, FOAM RUBBER (rubber goods)].

GOE: 06.04.13 STRENGTH: M GED: R2 M1 L1 SVP: 2 DLU: 77

550.685-090 MIXING-MACHINE TENDER (chemical; pharmaceut.)

Tends mixing machines, agitator tanks, kettles, roller mills, and related equipment to compound and process ingredients according to formula to make powdered, liquid, paste, or cream chemical products: Weighs ingredients and dumps, pours, pumps, or shovels them into machine, tank, or kettle. Turns controls to achieve specified temperature. Starts agitator to mix ingredients for specified time. Adds ingredients as specified during mixing cycle. Tests solution for specific gravity, viscosity, or acidity, using testing devices, or submits sample to laboratory. May cook mixture, using steam-jacketed kettle. May pump mixture through homogenizer to prepare emulsions or through filter press to remove impurities. May connect waterlines between deionizer, filter press, and vapor and storage tanks to purify water for use in products. May drain product into other machine units or into storage tanks. May be designated according to type of product mixed as Chemical Mixer (pharmaceut.); Cream Maker (pharmaceut.); Dental-Cream Maker (pharmaceut.); Dye Mixer (photo. appar.); Liquid Compounder (pharmaceut.) II; Ointment-Mill Tender (pharmaceut.). May be designated: Perfume And Toilet Water Maker (pharmaceut.); Powder Compounder (pharmaceut.); Powder Mixer (chemical); Roller-Mill Tender (pharmaceut.); Rouge Mixer (pharmaceut.).

GOE: 06.04.11 STRENGTH: H GED: R3 M2 L2 SVP: 4 DLU: 77

550.685-094 PEARL-GLUE OPERATOR (chemical)

Tends equipment that converts liquor glue into pearl glue (pearl-like bits): Opens valve to fill tank with gasoline. Starts refrigerant-circulating pumps to cool gasoline to required temperature. Pumps liquor glue through pearler-head tubes that deposit drops of glue into refrigerated gasoline to form pearl glue.

GOE: 06.04.19 STRENGTH: L GED: R2 M1 L1 SVP: 3 DLU: 77

550.685-098 POWERHOUSE HELPER (chemical)

Tends mixing machine to blend phosphate, soda ash, lime, and other water-conditioning agents for use as binding agent for making carbon black: Starts pumps to transport ingredients into blending tanks. Starts mixing machine to blend ingredients. Starts pumps to transport mixture to storage tanks feeding

furnace boilers of carbon manufacturing plant. Keeps log of gauge readings, such as water temperature and level in boilers and storage tanks.
GOE: 06.04.19 STRENGTH: M GED: R2 M1 L1 SVP: 3 DLU: 77

550.685-102 RUBBER-MILL TENDER (plastic-synth.; rubber goods; rubber reclaim.; rubber tire)

Tends rubber milling machine to mix, blend, knead, or refine scrap, crude, synthetic, or precompounded rubber for further processing: Starts machine and turns valves on steam and cold waterlines to regulate temperature of rolls. Lays rubber slabs between rolls of mill. Cuts stock with knife, rolls it into bundle, and feeds stock back into mill until rubber reaches specified consistency. Sets adjustable knives against mill roll to cut continuous strip as rubber emerges from mill and feeds strip onto conveyor that carries strip to calenders or extruders, Adjusts clearance between mill rolls, using wrench. May wash or crack crude rubber by passing it through corrugated mill rolls and water spray. May weigh and measure liquid and dry chemicals and add them to rubber during kneading process. May be designated according to specialized operation performed as Mill Tender, Break-Down (rubber goods; rubber tire); Mill Tender, Warm-Up (rubber goods; rubber tire); Mill Tender, Washing (rubber goods; rubber tire); Mix-Mill Tender (rubber goods; rubber tire); Slab-Off Mill Tender (rubber goods; rubber tire).
GOE: 06.04.13 STRENGTH: H GED: R2 M2 L2 SVP: 3 DLU: 77

550.685-106 SEASONING MIXER (chemical)

Tends equipment that mixes various pigments, lacquers, or chemicals used to color, coat, clean, or soften hides or skins: Pours specified ingredients into rotary mixing drum or mixing vat, according to formula. Moves lever to rotate drum, or lowers automatic mixing paddle into vat and moves switch to actuate paddle. Opens door of drum or tips vat to pour mixture into buckets. Delivers buckets to other workers, using handtruck. May be designated according to product mixed as Degreasing-Solution Mixer (chemical); Finishing-Compound Mixer (chemical); Pigment And Lacquer Mixer (chemical).
GOE: 06.04.11 STRENGTH: L GED: R2 M2 L2 SVP: 3 DLU: 77

550.685-110 SWEEPING-COMPOUND BLENDER (chemical)

Tends machine that mixes ingredients, such as dye, oil, sand, sawdust, and water to make sweeping compound: Measures or weighs out ingredients according to formula. Dumps or pours ingredients into mixer. Starts tumbler and mixes ingredients for specified time. Turns valve to drain mixture into barrels. Weighs barrel on floor scale to determine weight. May clean mixers, scales, kettles, and work area, using rags and solvent. May pack and seal products in wooden cases and label cases and barrels.
GOE: 06.04.11 STRENGTH: H GED: R2 M1 L2 SVP: 3 DLU: 77

550.685-114 TETRYL-DISSOLVER OPERATOR (chemical)

Tends equipment to dissolve crude tetryl in heated benzene for manufacture of explosives: Starts pump to transport benzene in weighing tank and turns valve to transfer it to dissolving tank. Admits steam to outer jacket of dissolving tank to heat solvent. Weighs out raw tetryl on scale and scoops it into tank with heated solvent. Starts agitator to mix solution for prescribed time. Turns valve to transfer solution to crystallizer for recovery of solvent.
GOE: 06.04.11 STRENGTH: L GED: R3 M1 L2 SVP: 3 DLU: 77

550.685-118 TUMBLER OPERATOR (chemical)

Tends tumbling machine that blends ingredients of pyrotechnic powder for use in signal flares: Pours roughly mixed ingredients into tumbler. Closes door of tumbler, and starts tumbling machine to blend ingredients for specified period of time. Scoops blended mixture into container.
GOE: 06.04.11 STRENGTH: M GED: R2 M1 L1 SVP: 2 DLU: 77

550.685-122 WEIGHER AND MIXER (chemical)

Tends machines that mix ingredients, such as pigments, resins, varnishes, solvents, and oils to produce ink or ink paste: Reads specifications to determine type and quantity of ingredients to be mixed. Starts pumps to tranport preweighed liquid ingredients from storage tanks into containers. Weighs specified amounts of pigments and adds them to containers. Dumps contents of containers into rotary mixer, using hoist, or moves container onto bed of mixer and turns wheel that lowers mixing blades into containers. Starts motor to mix ingredients for predetermined time. Draws sample or scoops sample of solution for laboratory analysis. Adds ingredients as directed by laboratory, or extends mixing period to attain prescribed consistency. Scoops or pumps ink or ink paste to holding tanks or into containers. May heat solvents in kettle or with steam coil to remove chill before adding pigments.
GOE: 06.04.11 STRENGTH: H GED: R2 M1 L1 SVP: 4 DLU: 77

550.685-126 WET MIXER (chemical)

Tends machine that mixes ground phosphate with sulfuric acid to produce superphosphate: Pulls levers to open storage tank or hopper and admit materials into weighing hopper of machine. Pulls lever to open bottom of weighing hopper and dump materials into mixer. Tests sulfuric acid to determine if strength and temperature meet specifications, using hydrometer and thermometer. Starts mixer and blends materials for specified time. Pulls lever to dump mixed materials into storage pit. Records weight of materials mixed.
GOE: 06.04.11 STRENGTH: L GED: R2 M1 L1 SVP: 2 DLU: 77

550.685-130 MATERIAL MIXER (plastic prod.)

Tends drum-tumbling machine that mixes ingredients, such as resins, color pigments, and additives, for use in fabrication of plastic cosmetic packaging: Lines drum with plastic bag. Presses control to activate hopper that automati-

cally fills drum with specified ingredients, or dumps measured ingredients into drum according to formula, using hand scoop and scale. Conveys filled drum to tumbling machine, using handtruck. Mounts and secures drum in holding device of machine, turns knob to set timing control, and presses button to actuate drum-tumbling action. Removes drum from machine at end of cycle and conveys drum to specified production machine, using handtruck.
GOE: 06.04.13 STRENGTH: V GED: R2 M2 L2 SVP: 2 DLU: 86

550.685-134 MIXING-MACHINE OPERATOR (plastic prod.; plastic-synth.)

Tends machines that mix chemical ingredients, such as resins, plasticizers, solvents, and coloring matter with filler to produce plastics materials: Weighs, measures, and combines ingredients according to formula, and dumps or pours ingredients into mixer. Turns valves to pump liquid ingredients into mixer. Starts agitator to mix batch for specified time. Turns wheel or valves, opens gates, or presses switch to tilt mixer to discharge compound into containers, storage tanks, or hoses. Posts operating information in log. May wash equipment, using hose and brushes. May turn steam and water valves and observe gauges to regulate temperature of mix. May dry material in atmospheric drier. May be designated according to operation performed as Blender (plastic prod.; plastic-synth.); Color Mixer (plastic prod.; plastic-synth.); Resin Compounder, Batch Lot (plastic-synth.); Solution Mixer (plastic-synth.).
GOE: 06.04.13 STRENGTH: M GED: R3 M2 L2 SVP: 4 DLU: 78

550.686-010 BATCH TRUCKER (rubber reclaim.)

Feeds specified quantities and types of ground devulcanized scrap rubber into mix mill to prepare batch for processing: Shovels mixture into monorail bucket or pushtruck, and dumps mixture into designated chute or onto feed conveyor of mix mill. Records batches produced. May drive scooptruck to transport mixture. May add specified pigments to mixture when blending.
GOE: 06.04.13 STRENGTH: M GED: R1 M1 L1 SVP: 2 DLU: 77

550.686-014 COMPOUND FILLER (chemical)

Feeds supply of compounds and dope in tanks at dip conveyors for forming and treating heads of kitchen, penny, and book matches: Dips compounds from kettle into respective feed containers that automatically maintain tank level. Mixes specified solution of glyoxal and water, that hardens formed matchhead, and pours solution into dope tank. Removes and replaces dirty screens in dip tanks. Verifies level and temperature of paraffin in dip tanks. Pushes kettle trucks to and from compound room and dip area.
GOE: 06.04.11 STRENGTH: H GED: R1 M1 L1 SVP: 2 DLU: 77

550.686-018 CRUTCHER HELPER (soap & rel.)

Weighs and dumps specified dry materials into feeder hopper of crutcher equipment, that forms slurry for processing into soap powder: Opens valves of supply tanks and waterlines to add prescribed liquid and paste. Mixes dye according to specifications and dumps dye into batch. Changes and cleans strainers. Sweeps and cleans work area.
GOE: 06.04.19 STRENGTH: H GED: R2 M1 L1 SVP: 2 DLU: 77

550.686-022 GLAZING OPERATOR, BLACK POWDER (chemical)

Feeds grain powder, graphite, and other materials into glazing barrels: Dumps specified amounts of graphite, grain powder, and other ingredients into mechanically rotated glazing barrels that smooth out and lubricate powder. Opens barrel door to discharge contents into containers. May time rotation (glazing) period, using watch.
GOE: 06.04.19 STRENGTH: H GED: R3 M1 L1 SVP: 4 DLU: 77

550.686-026 MIXER HELPER (build. mat., nec)

Dumps asphalt resin chunks into heating kettle to liquefy resin used as binding sealer in asphalt shingles. Chops resin into pieces, using ax, and feeds pieces into kettle. Lifts screen on return flow trough and removes foreign matter from screen by hand.
GOE: 06.04.19 STRENGTH: L GED: R1 M1 L1 SVP: 2 DLU: 77

550.686-030 MIXING-MACHINE FEEDER (chemical)

Feeds dry chemical ingredients used in manufacture of fertilizer and insecticides into mixing machine. Empties hoppers or sacks of specified ingredients into machine or elevator bucket, using forklift truck or by hand. May start elevator to empty buckets into machine.
GOE: 06.04.11 STRENGTH: H GED: R1 M1 L1 SVP: 2 DLU: 77

550.686-034 MOTTLER-MACHINE FEEDER (fabrication, nec)

Dumps color mix into hoppers of designated color-depositing machines: Scoops mix from bins and dumps it into hopper. Adds specified ingredients as directed. Breaks up lumpy color in feedlines, using long-handled stick. Cleans roller blades, using scraper.
GOE: 06.04.19 STRENGTH: H GED: R2 M1 L1 SVP: 2 DLU: 77

550.686-038 ROOF-CEMENT-AND-PAINT-MAKER HELPER (build. mat., nec; nonmet. min.)

Assists ROOF-CEMENT-AND-PAINT MAKER (nonmet. min.) in making roof cement: Weighs sacks filled with materials to make roof cement and paint and dumps contents from sacks onto conveyor leading to mixing machine. Places cans under spigot of mixing machine. Performs other duties as described under HELPER (any industry) Master Title.
GOE: 06.04.11 STRENGTH: H GED: R1 M1 L1 SVP: 2 DLU: 77

550.687-010 CHEMICAL-COMPOUNDER HELPER (chemical)

Shovels specified chemicals into tank of heated water to dissolve chemicals preparatory to charging mixing kettle that produces optical brightener (organic

white dye) for soaps and fabrics. Moves drums of chemicals to work area, using handtruck. May read work orders to determine type and amount of chemicals to add to kettle. May be designated according to material produced as Optical-Brightener-Maker Helper (chemical).
GOE: 06.04.11 STRENGTH: M GED: R2 M1 L1 SVP: 2 DLU: 77

550.687-014 COLOR STRAINER (textile)
Assists COLOR-PASTE MIXER (textile) in mixing color for use in printing textiles: Strains mixed colors through vacuum or other straining device to remove lumps and foreign matter. Carries colors to and from mixing area. Cleans working area and mixing equipment, using water hose. May mix colors. Performs other duties as described under HELPER (any industry) Master Title.
GOE: 06.04.16 STRENGTH: H GED: R1 M1 L1 SVP: 2 DLU: 77

550.687-018 DYE-WEIGHER HELPER (any industry)
Assists DYE WEIGHER (any industry) in mixing dyes and chemicals for use in dyeing textile yarns and fabrics: Opens steam valve to heat dye solution. Stirs solution with paddle to dissolve dye. Dumps contents of mixing pails into or turns valve to transfer dye solution to supply tanks in dyeing department in response to light signal or to request over speaker system. Moves barrels of dye and chemicals to dye room, using handtruck. Cleans mixing tanks and work area, using waterhose. Performs other duties as described under HELPER (any industry) Master Title.
GOE: 06.04.34 STRENGTH: M GED: R2 M1 L1 SVP: 2 DLU: 77

551 FILTERING, STRAINING, AND SEPARATING OCCUPATIONS

This group includes occupations concerned with separating desirable materials by means of filtering, precipitating, straining, sifting, squeezing, centrifugal force, or agitating devices.

551.130-010 SUPERVISOR, PROCESSING (chemical)
Supervises and coordinates activities of workers engaged in conveying, washing, screening, packaging, or storing reclaimed or stockpiled salt: Reads production schedule to verify type and amount of salt to be processed. Inspects conveyor system and equipment, such as vibrating feeder screens, conveyor junction feeders, and automatic conveyor scales, for evidence of malfunctioning. Trains workers in operation of equipment. Coordinates flow of salt to processing stations to prevent production delays. Maintains production records and prepares reports on department activities. Performs other duties as described under SUPERVISOR (any industry) Master Title.
GOE: 06.04.01 STRENGTH: L GED: R4 M3 L3 SVP: 7 DLU: 77

551.362-010 PURIFICATION OPERATOR II (chemical) alternate titles: gas-scrubber operator
Controls gas-scrubbing and related equipment to remove impurities from gases: Observes temperature, flow, pressure gauges, and liquid-level indicators and moves controls to effect operating equilibrium in equipment, according to plant procedure and correlation of instrument readings. Observes gas-scrubbing fluid through sight glasses to determine process efficiency, indicated by color and flow rate of fluid. Turns valves to maintain brine in brine scrubber at specified strength and regulate temperature of hot water in scrubber jacket, according to indicated efficiency of scrubbing fluid. Inspects pumps, motors, valves, and related equipment and replaces packing in column scrubbers and nitrogen-drying columns at specified intervals with acid, calcium chloride, or brine. Draws samples of gases and fluids for laboratory analysis. Maintains log of gauge readings and results of laboratory analyses. Directs activities of PURIFICATION-OPERATOR HELPER (chemical) 551.465-010.
GOE: 06.02.11 STRENGTH: L GED: R4 M2 L3 SVP: 7 DLU: 77

551.365-010 STRAINER TENDER (rubber reclaim.) alternate titles: fabric-separator operator; strainer-mill operator; tuber operator
Tends machines that screen foreign material from ground, devulcanized scrap rubber: Opens chute on feed conveyors or shovels scrap rubber into hopper of strainer. Starts machine that forces scrap rubber through strainer screen. Regulates speed of machine and conveyors to prevent jamming of stock. Discharges strained scrap rubber onto conveyors for transfer to refining mills, or onto handtrucks for transfer to storage. Feels strainer, and opens water valves to prevent overheating of machine and scorching of rubber. Observes rubber for color and appearance and feels strained rubber to ensure that foreign material is removed. Cleans clogged strainer screens, using scraper and solvent, or replaces clogged and worn strainer screens, using handtools. Signals drying and milling department workers to maintain specified flow of scrap rubber through strainers. May dump bags of soapstone in discharge chute to facilitate movement of stock through screen conveyor. May tend magnetic device to facilitate removal of metal from rubber. May fill containers with screened rubber to specified weight and keep record of production.
GOE: 06.02.07 STRENGTH: L GED: R2 M1 L2 SVP: 4 DLU: 77

551.382-010 ABSORPTION OPERATOR (chemical) alternate titles: saturator
Controls equipment that absorbs gases and liquids into water or other solvents to produce chemicals, such as hydrochloric acid or ammonium hydroxide: Starts pumps, turns valves, and observes flowmeters to control concentration, flow, temperature, and quantity of coolant, gas, liquid, and absorbing liquor

through cooling and absorption towers. Turns valves to regulate feed of solution produced and rate of steam to purge boilers and condensers to separate impurities from solution and obtain product of designated strength and specific gravity. Draws sample and tests specific quality and acidity, using hydrometer and pH meter, or submits sample to laboratory for analysis. Pumps solution between equipment and storage tanks or tank cars. Maintains log of instrument readings, test results, and shift production. May be designated according to solution produced as Ammonium-Hydroxide Operator (chemical); Aqua-Ammonia Operator (chemical); Hydrochloric-Acid Operator (chemical).
GOE: 06.02.11 STRENGTH: L GED: R3 M2 L2 SVP: 5 DLU: 77

551.465-010 PURIFICATION-OPERATOR HELPER (chemical)
Tends gas scrubbing and related equipment that removes impurities from gases, as directed by PURIFICATION OPERATOR (chemical) II: Loads brine saturators and nitrogen-drying columns with lump calcium chloride. Mixes hydrosulfate solutions used in process, according to proportion chart or oral directions. Observes gauges to determine gas pressures throughout system, computes and records drops in pressure, and ascertains from data obtained optimum time to shut down and clean equipment for efficient operation. Draws samples of acids, brine, and gases from equipment units for laboratory analysis and determines specific gravity of brine, using hydrometer. Drains liquid from nitrogen driers. Assists operator in maintaining operating log of gauge and instrument readings.
GOE: 06.02.11 STRENGTH: L GED: R3 M2 L2 SVP: 4 DLU: 77

551.485-010 WATER-TREATMENT-PLANT OPERATOR (chemical)
Tends water plant equipment that scrubs and purifies gases from smelting furnaces: Starts pumps and fans in scrubber towers and turns valves to regulate flow of water through nozzles. Pulls lever to open car bottom to unload lime from hopper cars into storage tanks. Knocks on bottom of hopper with pry bar or uses portable vibrator to loosen lime remaining in car. Dumps specified number of sacks of sulfate, hydroxide, and fluoride into mixer machines. Starts conveyors to transport mixed chemicals and lime to reactor tanks that make reagent solution. Observes control panel, records readings, and calculates solution temperatures, scrubber fan loads, and flow of treatment solutions, using charts and graphs. Changes basket screens in reactor tanks, using chain hoist, and cleans screens with water or steam. Collects samples of treatment solutions and sludge for laboratory analysis. Measures acidity or alkalinity of clarifier overflow to determine efficiency of impurity recovery, using pH meter.
GOE: 06.02.11 STRENGTH: L GED: R3 M2 L2 SVP: 4 DLU: 77

551.562-010 FILTRATION OPERATOR, POLYETHYLENE CATALYST (chemical)
Controls rotary-leaf filters and such auxiliary equipment as centrifuges, pumps, compressors, heat exchangers, and conveyors, to remove process catalyst from polyethylene products: Starts pumps, centrifuges, and compressors. Observes gauges and chart recorders; turns valves; and sets automatic control instruments to regulate temperatures, pressures, flow-rates, and liquid levels within plant specifications, and to transfer materials between units to ensure efficient removal of catalyst. Directs other workers engaged in tending pumps, compressors, and centrifuges and in making manual adjustments to equipment to maintain required process conditions. Moves manual and automatic controls to switch filters into and out of service for replacement of diatomaceous-earth coating. Records instrument readings and laboratory test results in operating log. Inspects equipment for malfunctions, wear, and leaks, reporting need for repairs to maintenance personnel.
GOE: 06.02.11 STRENGTH: L GED: R3 M2 L2 SVP: 5 DLU: 77

551.582-010 HYDRAULIC-STRAINER OPERATOR (plastic-synth.) alternate titles: filter operator
Operates hydraulic filter machine to remove foreign matter from plastics material: Cuts plastics dough into slabs, using knife, or rolls material into lump and packs it into cylinder. Selects and installs wire and cloth strainers and die heads in machine, according to type and form of material, using handtools. Adjusts controls of hydraulic ram, according to pressure gauge reading, and starts machine to force material through strainers. Cleans strainers, die head, and machine cylinder, using brushes, scrapers, and solvents. Records amounts and type of dough strained.
GOE: 06.02.13 STRENGTH: M GED: R3 M1 L2 SVP: 5 DLU: 77

551.585-010 FILTER-TANK OPERATOR (chemical)
Tends filter that cleans detergent used in toothpaste: Starts pumps that transfer toothpaste-detergent slurry to filter tank, and turns valve on vacuum line to draw liquid from slurry. Turns valves on feed lines to wash residual toothpaste detergent with specified solvent fluid. Shovels caked detergent into drum and clamps on lid. Weighs drum and records weight. Moves drum to storage area, using handtruck. Starts pumps to force filtrate liquid down through filter to stills to recover solvent. May record production data in log.
GOE: 06.04.11 STRENGTH: M GED: R2 M1 L1 SVP: 2 DLU: 77

551.585-014 MERCURY PURIFIER (chemical)
Tends continuous-process equipment that purifies mercury recovered from electrolytic cells: Turns compressed air and water valves to start flow of mercury through acid bath and purification towers that remove contaminants from mercury. Drains purified mercury into storage tank. Refills purifying towers with mercurous nitrate purifying agent and verifies specific gravity of nitrate, using hydrometer, to ensure efficient purification. Cleans and flushes towers, using water hose. Records weight of mercury purified during shift.

GOE: 06.04.11 STRENGTH: M GED: R2 M2 L1 SVP: 4 DLU: 77

551.585-018 PAN HELPER (chemical)
Tends equipment, such as filters, settlers, and thickeners, to assist in concentrating chemical solution: Turns valves and starts pumps to start flow of liquids from storage tanks through series of pans. Dumps sacks of chemicals into processing units. Patrols area to detect leaks and malfunctioning of equipment. Records data, such as temperature and pressure readings, and monitors gauges and recording charts to ensure safe operating conditions. Draws sample of product and tests for specific gravity, using hydrometer. Opens valves to drain and flush salt accumulations from pans and lines. Repacks pumps and valves and repairs equipment by adjusting or replacing parts, using handtools. Performs other duties as described under HELPER (any industry) Master Title.
GOE: 06.04.11 STRENGTH: H GED: R3 M1 L2 SVP: 4 DLU: 77

551.585-022 ROTARY-CUTTER OPERATOR (rubber goods)
Tends machine that pulverizes scrap fabric into flock (powder): Cuts wire from bale of scrap, using wirecutters. Starts machine and dumps and spreads scrap on conveyor that moves scrap to rotary knives turning within fixed knives that pulverize scrap. Clamps sack over blower pipe and opens valve to fill sack with flock. Pushes plunger that forces pneumatic tamper into sack to compress flock. Closes top and sews filled sack, using needle and twine. Weighs filled sack and records weight on production record and tag.
GOE: 06.04.05 STRENGTH: H GED: R1 M1 L1 SVP: 2 DLU: 77

551.665-010 NAPHTHALENE OPERATOR (steel & rel.)
Tends equipment that separates naphthalene from chemical drain oil used to wash coke-oven gas or tar distillate: Starts pumps to remove drain oil from scrubbing tower to collecting tank where naphthalene settles and crystallizes as oil cools. Opens drain valves or starts pumps to remove oil from pans to storage tanks. Dumps crystals into centrifuge to remove remaining oil [CENTRIFUGAL-DRIER OPERATOR (chemical)]. Dumps or shovels crystallized naphthalene into steam-heated tank to melt and further purify crystals. Draws sample from melting tank for laboratory analysis. Starts pumps to transfer naphthalene into storage tanks or railroad tank cars. May be designated according to work performed as Drier Tender Naphthalene (steel & rel.).
GOE: 06.04.11 STRENGTH: M GED: R2 M1 L1 SVP: 3 DLU: 77

551.666-010 PITCH WORKER (optical goods)
Dumps salvaged pitch into heated filtering kettle that filters pitch for reuse in blocking lens blanks: Opens valve to drain filtered pitch into cooling troughs and breaks up solidified pitch with hand tamper. Loads pitch into containers and delivers to BLOCKING-MACHINE TENDER (optical goods).
GOE: 06.04.19 STRENGTH: L GED: R1 M1 L1 SVP: 2 DLU: 77

551.682-010 BENZENE-WASHER OPERATOR (chemical; steel & rel.) alternate titles: acid-wash operator; agitator operator; benzene operator; benzol operator
Controls agitator tank to wash (mix) benzol, benzene, toluene, and xylene with sulfuric acid and caustic soda to remove impurities: Turns valves and starts pumps to charge agitator vessel with specified amount of benzol or derivatives. Drains measured quantity of acid into vessel and starts agitator to mix contents for specified time. Stops agitator to allow acid and sludge to settle. Draws sample of washed product for laboratory colorimetry test to determine need for further washing. Opens valve, using wrench, to drain excess acid and sludge, adds caustic soda solution to neutralize remaining acid, and measures alkalinity, using standard titration test. Adds water, agitates mixture to wash out traces of caustic, and drains off water after contents have settled. Pumps washed benzol or derivatives into storage tank. Turns valves to admit steam to sludge kettle, solidifying sludge. Lifts kettle cover, using chain hoist, and removes sludge from kettle. May distill washed benzol in batch still [BATCH-STILL OPERATOR (chemical) I]. May remove impurities from crude ethylbenzene by adding lime and water and agitating mixture.
GOE: 06.02.11 STRENGTH: L GED: R3 M2 L3 SVP: 5 DLU: 77

551.685-010 BAND TUMBLER (rubber goods)
Tends tumbler that removes water from rubberbands: Carries tote box of bands from band-cutting machine and dumps bands into tumbler. Starts mechanism that rotates bands for specified time to remove moisture from bands. Removes and carries bands to bundling and boxing machines.
GOE: 06.04.07 STRENGTH: M GED: R1 M1 L1 SVP: 2 DLU: 77

551.685-014 BOILING-TUB OPERATOR (chemical) alternate titles: washing-tub operator
Tends tanks in which crude tetryl explosive or nitrocellulose is boiled and washed to remove acids and impurities: Admits batch of crude tetryl slurry to boiling tank. Starts tank agitators and turns valve to admit steam to tank jacket to boil slurry for specified time. Pumps off water after material has settled. Pumps fresh water through tank to wash tetryl and flush away impurities. When boiling nitrocellulose, admits acid to tub and boils contents for specified time, adds neutralizing agent, and repeats process until all nitrocellulose impurities are removed. May test acidity of solution, using hydrometer or titration test. When boiling tetryl, is designated Tetryl-Boiling-Tub Operator (chemical).
GOE: 06.04.11 STRENGTH: L GED: R2 M1 L1 SVP: 2 DLU: 77

551.685-018 BONE-COOKING OPERATOR (chemical)
Tends steam-heated vats that extract gelatin from crushed bone: Turns valve to introduce steam that heats vat filled with crushed bone. Adds water to vat and dumps in specified amounts of ingredients that hasten extraction of gelatin. Drains vat and signals other workers to remove bone residue from vat.

GOE: 06.04.19 STRENGTH: L GED: R3 M1 L2 SVP: 3 DLU: 77

551.685-022 CATALYST-RECOVERY OPERATOR (chemical)
Tends filter presses, evaporators, dissolvers, and precipitators that recover and recondition catalysts used in manufacturing styrene and edible oils: Starts pump and opens feed and discharge valves to transfer used catalyst from processing equipment into tank for reconditioning. Observes meters and gauges, and turns valves to maintain prescribed rate of flow, temperature, and pressure of compressed hydrogen, steam, and acid in filter or reconditioning tank. Weighs and adds specified amounts of neutralizer and filter aid. Pumps batch to filter press to change catalyst into cake form for recovery. Turns valves to regulate feed and temperature of filtrate in evaporating tank for recovery of remaining catalyst. Removes catalyst residue from tank and filter plates, using shovel and scraper.
GOE: 06.04.11 STRENGTH: H GED: R3 M2 L2 SVP: 3 DLU: 77

551.685-026 CENTRIFUGAL-DRIER OPERATOR (chemical) alternate titles: centrifuge operator
Tends centrifugal drier that removes water or other liquids from slurries: Inserts filter cloth and screen in basket of centrifugal drum. Lowers bell-shaped cover over outlet in bottom of basket if unit is bottom-discharge type and shovels, pours, or pumps slurry into basket. Closes lid if unit is top-discharge type. Starts basket revolving and moves control to regulate speed, according to specifications. Lifts bell, lowers blade to cut crystallized cake from walls of basket, and pushes centrifuged mass through outlet into containers or onto conveyor, using paddle. May release trap door, start pumps, or shovel material from basket to unload drier. May turn steam or fuel valves to heat drier basket or drum to maintain centrifuged material at specified temperature while drying. When drying and discharging salt, may be designated Salt Cutter (chemical).
GOE: 06.04.11 STRENGTH: M GED: R3 M1 L1 SVP: 4 DLU: 77

551.685-030 CENTRIFUGE OPERATOR (soap & rel.) alternate titles: salt operator
Tends centrifuge and auxiliary equipment that washes and dries slurry solution, formed during making of soap, to recover glycerin-free salt: Tests sample of slurry from decantation tank for salt content and to determine rate of flow of solution into centrifuge hopper, using testing instruments, such as hydrometer. Turns valve to run slurry into centrifuge and presses switch to start machine. Observes gauges to verify rate of flow and adjusts thermostat to regulate temperature of water in centrifuge. Opens valves to fill drums or silo with salt flakes. Turns valve to discharge liquid into holding tanks. May dissolve salt in liquid to make brine and perform specific gravity test, using hydrometer.
GOE: 06.04.19 STRENGTH: L GED: R2 M1 L1 SVP: 2 DLU: 77

551.685-034 CENTRIFUGE OPERATOR (paint & varnish)
Tends centrifuge that removes impurities from varnishes and lacquers: Positions filter cloth on supply tank of centrifuge. Starts pump to transfer product from cooling tank, through filter, into containers or supply tank. Starts centrifuge and opens discharge valve to transfer filtered material from centrifuge into portable tank. Adjusts controls to regulate flow of material through lines and tanks. May start pumps to transfer liquids from portable tank to storage tank. Disassembles centrifuge and pump, using handtools and cleans equipment with solvents. Pumps liquids to filter press if further filtration is specified. May be designated according to material filtered as Lacquer Filterer (paint & varnish); Varnish Filterer (paint & varnish) I.
GOE: 06.04.11 STRENGTH: H GED: R2 M1 L1 SVP: 2 DLU: 77

551.685-038 CENTRIFUGE-SEPARATOR OPERATOR (chemical)
Tends centrifuge to separate grease from liquid glue: Admits glue liquor from bone-cooking tank into centrifuge machine and starts machine. Drains grease and glue into separate storage tanks. Disassembles and cleans equipment.
GOE: 06.04.11 STRENGTH: L GED: R2 M1 L1 SVP: 2 DLU: 77

551.685-042 CHILLER OPERATOR (chemical)
Tends chiller and centrifugal drier that crystallize diluted caustic soda solution and remove liquid from crystallized product: Starts pump to transfer caustic soda solution and water into dilution tank and determines specific gravity of diluted solution, using hydrometer. Pumps solution through refrigerating unit and into chiller. Observes consistency of crystallized slurry flowing from chiller to centrifuge, and turns valves to regulate feed rate and maintain slurry at specified consistency. Tends centrifugal drier [DRIER OPERATOR (chemical) III] to remove liquid component of slurry. May turn valve to heat centrifuge unit if machine is so equipped. Inspects feed and outlet pipes of equipment and flushes lines, using hose, to prevent clogging.
GOE: 06.04.11 STRENGTH: L GED: R2 M1 L2 SVP: 3 DLU: 77

551.685-046 DEHYDRATING-PRESS OPERATOR (chemical; plastic-synth.)
Tends press that removes water from nitrocellulose used in manufacturing smokeless powder and pyroxylin for use in plastics: Pours specified amount of nitrocellulose into bottom cylinder of dehydrating press. Presses button or opens water valve to force plunger down onto bottom cylinder. Pumps alcohol into lower cylinder and through wet nitrocellulose to displace water. Removes cakes of water-free nitrocellulose and places them on handtruck for removal.
GOE: 06.04.11 STRENGTH: M GED: R2 M1 L2 SVP: 2 DLU: 77

551.685-050 DUST-COLLECTOR OPERATOR (soap & rel.)
Tends equipment, such as scrubbing towers and centrifugal pumps, that recover powder from spray-tower exhaust gas and prevent air pollution: Starts fan

to draw air and accumulated dust from spray tower into scrubbing tower. Starts steam pump to wet powder, causing it to flow down baffle plates to bottom of tower. Opens valve to permit recovered powder to flow into storage tank for reuse. Pumps recovered powder from storage tank to crutcher machine for reprocessing. Records spray-tower exhaust temperatures and gas pressures on chart.
GOE: 06.04.19 STRENGTH: L GED: R2 M1 L1 SVP: 3 DLU: 77

551.685-054 EXTRACTOR OPERATOR (chemical; oils & grease)
Tends steam pressure tanks that extract grease from cracklings: Adjusts temperature and pressure of tank filled with cracklings. Starts pumps to transfer specified solvent into tank to dissolve cracklings. Opens valve to transfer extracted grease to still. Takes sample of grease from still and inspects for clarity.
GOE: 06.04.19 STRENGTH: H GED: R2 M1 L1 SVP: 2 DLU: 77

551.685-058 EXTRACTOR OPERATOR (pharmaceut.)
Tends equipment that heats and mixes solvent with ground leafy plant to separate products, such as chlorophyll: Weighs specified amount of ground plant matter, such as alfalfa, and dumps it into steam-jacketed tank. Starts pumps to transfer specified amount of solvent into tank. Starts agitator that mixes solvent with plant matter to dissolve usable constituents. Observes thermometer and opens valve to regulate admission of steam to jacket and to maintain tank heat at prescribed temperature. Connects siphon hose and starts vacuum pump to transfer liquid products to collecting barrel, or to other departments for further processing or storage. May record production data in log. Opens tank outlet to dump residue into waste container.
GOE: 06.04.11 STRENGTH: M GED: R2 M2 L2 SVP: 3 DLU: 77

551.685-062 EXTRACTOR OPERATOR, SOLVENT PROCESS (chemical) alternate titles: solvent-plant operator
Tends solvent extraction equipment that extracts oil from rice bran, soybeans, and cottonseeds: Observes temperature and steam pressure gauges, flowmeters and ammeters, and turns valves or handwheels to regulate temperature and flow of material in equipment within specified limits. Tests samples of material for conformity to plant standards, using scales, moisture meter, and hydrometer, or by titration. Records indicator readings and test results. May clean filter plates of extractor.
GOE: 06.04.11 STRENGTH: L GED: R2 M1 L1 SVP: 2 DLU: 77

551.685-066 EXTRACTOR-AND-WRINGER OPERATOR (chemical)
Tends equipment that extracts salicylic acid from sodium salicylate solution by precipitation and dries salicylic acid by centrifugal force: Opens valves to pump sodium salicylate solution and required amount of sulfuric acid into extractor columns that absorb phenol from solution and cause precipitation of salicylic acid crystals. Opens steam valves to heat extractors to specified temperature to increase rate of precipitation of salicylic acid. Pumps off solution of sulfuric acid and phenol, and pumps slurry of salicylic acid through cooler to centrifugal drier. Tends centrifugal drier that forces out water to dry salicylic acid. Removes salicylic acid from drier and places acid into containers, using scraper and shovel.
GOE: 06.04.11 STRENGTH: L GED: R2 M1 L1 SVP: 2 DLU: 77

551.685-070 FAT-PURIFICATION WORKER (oils & grease) alternate titles: acidulator
Tends acidulation tanks and auxiliary equipment that separate undesirable compounds from oils: Turns valves to fill tanks with basic materials and to admit prescribed amounts of sulfuric acid and caustic. Starts agitator that mixes and separates ingredients. Starts pumps or opens drain valve to transfer separated material into storage tanks. May draw sample to test for pH volume, using titration test.
GOE: 06.04.11 STRENGTH: L GED: R3 M1 L2 SVP: 3 DLU: 77

551.685-074 FILTER HELPER (chemical)
Tends filter that removes excess water from activated carbon slurry, preparatory to drying, for variety of industrial and consumer applications: Moves lever to transfer carbon slurry from discharge chute onto revolving filter cloth. Raises and lowers spreader gate to spread carbon uniformly over surface of filter cloth. Dumps bags of processed carbon onto conveyor leading to shipping or storage area. Monitors vacuum gauge on filter and observes color of wash water to detect leaks in cloth. Scrapes carbon from surface of cloth, using wood paddle, to examine for leaks and other damage or wear. Flushes filter cloth with water hose preparatory to changing cloths.
GOE: 06.04.19 STRENGTH: M GED: R2 M1 L1 SVP: 2 DLU: 77

551.685-078 FILTER OPERATOR (any industry) alternate titles: sludge-filter operator; vacuum-filter operator
Tends rotary drum-filters that separate slurries into liquid and filter cake (insoluble material): Couples flexible hose or pipe to vat, starts pump, and turns valves to regulate flow of slurry to filter tanks. Adjusts controls to regulate rotation speed of drums. Turns valve to regulate pressure that forces slurry through filter, separating filter cake from liquid. Observes discharge to ensure that scrapers are removing filter cake from drum. May tend thickeners, washing sprays, settlers, or related equipment. May draw sample for laboratory analysis. May be known according to trade name of machine.
GOE: 06.04.19 STRENGTH: M GED: R2 M1 L1 SVP: 2 DLU: 77

551.685-082 FILTER-PRESS OPERATOR (any industry)
Tends filter plate press that removes impurities or moisture from slurries and chemical solution: Covers filter plates with cloth, canvas, or paper. Opens valve

to admit liquid ingredients into tank, dumps specified dry ingredients into tank, and starts agitator to mix ingredients and form slurry. Starts pump to transfer slurry from mixing tank to filter plate press. Opens pressure valves to force slurry through plates to remove impurities and moisture. Turns gear wheel to release tension of plates at completion of cycle. When filtering to obtain liquid product, dislodges solid material from plates and cleans frames, screens, and filters, using scraper, steam, or compressed airhose. When filtering to obtain solid product, cuts mixture from frames with knife and loads materials on drying trays. May draw samples for laboratory analysis. May be designated according to product filtered as Pigment Presser (chemical); Plate-and-Frame-Filter Operator (any industry); Resin Filterer (paint & varnish); Varnish Filterer (paint & varnish) II.
GOE: 06.04.11 STRENGTH: H GED: R2 M1 L1 SVP: 3 DLU: 81

551.685-086 GREASE-REFINER OPERATOR (oils & grease)
Tends kettle that refines grease according to specifications: Moves lever to admit grease into kettle and opens valve to admit steam into grease to control boiling. Draws off sample of grease and inspects it for clarity. Starts pump to add required amounts of acid to kettle and boils grease with acid until grease reaches specified clarity. Closes steam valve and allows water and impurities to settle to bottom of kettle. Opens valve to drain off water and impurities. Closes drain valve, opens steam valve, and starts pump to fill kettle with water. Boils mixture for specified amount of time to wash out acid and remaining impurities. Opens drain valve to drain off water and impurities. Pumps grease to storage tanks.
GOE: 06.04.19 STRENGTH: L GED: R2 M1 L1 SVP: 3 DLU: 77

551.685-090 LEACHER (paper & pulp)
Tends leach tanks that recover soda ash from black ash: Opens valve to admit water or weak liquor (soda ash) solution into leach tanks containing black ash. Starts agitators to stir mixture and dissolve soda ash. Withdraws samples of resultant solution and tests for concentration of soda ash, using hydrometer. Starts pump to circulate water or soda ash through leach tanks and into storage tanks until test samples contain specified concentration of soda ash. Shovels black ash into leach tanks as supply in tank becomes exhausted. Opens drain to remove insoluble charcoal residue from leach tanks after completion of recovery process.
GOE: 06.04.11 STRENGTH: L GED: R2 M1 L1 SVP: 3 DLU: 77

551.685-094 LYE TREATER (chemical; soap & rel.)
Tends heated kettle and filter press in which lye is treated with chemicals to remove undesirable properties in glycerine purification process: Starts pump to transfer premeasured lye into kettle, starts agitator to mix batch, and turns steam valve to heat kettle to prescribed temperature. Dumps specified amounts of dry chemicals or pumps liquid chemicals into kettle to attain product of specified concentration. Inspects batch sample for clarity and submits sample laboratory for testing. Regulates chemical concentration of batch, following laboratory report. Pumps batch through filter press to remove materials precipitated during treatment. Cleans filter press and replaces filter cloths, using handtools. Records kettle temperature, agitation and treating time, and amount of chemicals used in process.
GOE: 06.04.11 STRENGTH: M GED: R3 M2 L2 SVP: 3 DLU: 77

551.685-098 MERCURY WASHER (chemical) alternate titles: mercury recoverer
Tends equipment that recovers and reconditions mercury used in electrolytic cells: Sweeps, shovels, and dumps mercury-bearing material onto vibrating screen that separates mercury. Flushes screen with water, using hose, and drains off water into settling tank, forming sludge. Ladles contaminated mercury and sludge into reclaiming kettle and turns valves to admit acid and steam to separate foreign matter from mercury. Drains mercury into flask. May break used cell anodes to salvage porcelain insulators and copper posts, using hammer. May tend concentrating table to remove mercury residue from scrap material for recovery. May weigh flasks of recovered mercury for inventory records.
GOE: 06.04.11 STRENGTH: H GED: R2 M1 L1 SVP: 3 DLU: 77

551.685-102 NITROGLYCERIN-SEPARATOR OPERATOR (chemical) alternate titles: separator
Tends gravity separator to separate nitroglycerin from spent acids, preparatory to washing, neutralizing, and processing into explosives: Turns petcock to transfer mixture of spent acids and nitroglycerin from batch nitrator to separator. Turns petcock to drain acids from nitroglycerin into trough leading to spent-acid storage. Observes liquid flowing from spigot and moves trough to discharge product into wash tank when color change indicates nitroglycerin is flowing from separator. Observes tank thermometer to detect accumulation of heat that could cause decomposition and explosion and turns valves to regulate heat to prevent explosion or decomposition. May move control to dump tank contents into water-filled vat if temperature increase indicates explosion may be imminent. May wash and neutralize nitroglycerin [NITROGLYCERIN NEUTRALIZER (chemical)].
GOE: 06.02.18 STRENGTH: L GED: R3 M1 L1 SVP: 4 DLU: 77

551.685-106 POACHER OPERATOR (chemical) alternate titles: pulp-screen operator
Tends tanks that remove acidity, impurities, and inadequately processed material from nitrocellulose, used in manufacturing chemical and explosive products: Pumps nitrocellulose into poacher tubs (tanks) fitted with steam coils or steampipes. Turns valves to admit water and steam to boil mixture for specified

time. Tends shaker screen and vacuum filter to wash nitrocellulose. Takes samples to laboratory for analysis. Reads laboratory reports and adjusts blends to meet specifications. Loads blender tubs with measured amount of different types of nitrocellulose to blend products according to specifications.
GOE: 06.02.18 STRENGTH: L GED: R3 M1 L2 SVP: 4 DLU: 77

551.685-110 PRECIPITATE WASHER (chemical)
Tends filters and related equipment to wash and filter catalytic chemicals used in manufacturing styrene and butadiene: Starts pump to force water into and out of tanks containing precipitate. Titrates sample of wash water to determine when solution is neutralized. Pumps precipitate into slurry tank and wash water to filter press to separate contaminants and recover usable products. Transfers containers of filtered solutions to storage or further processing, using hoist or handtruck.
GOE: 06.04.11 STRENGTH: M GED: R3 M1 L1 SVP: 3 DLU: 77

551.685-114 PRESS OPERATOR (oils & grease)
Tends hydraulic press to extract grease and tallow from cooked offal, bone, and meat scraps: Opens storage chute gate to start flow of material into press basket or shovels material from vat into basket, and places steel plate over each layer until basket is full. Pulls press-head over basket and pulls lever to raise hydraulic ram that presses grease and tallow from cooked material. Removes crackling cakes and plates from basket and dumps cakes into conveyor chute.
GOE: 06.04.19 STRENGTH: H GED: R2 M1 L1 SVP: 2 DLU: 77

551.685-118 PRESS OPERATOR II (chemical)
Tends hydraulic press that squeezes liquid from crystallized chemical products and compacts material to facilitate melting: Shovels crystallized material into basket of press and positions metal disks in layers throughout material in basket. Moves levers to raise basket against plunger, squeezing liquid from crystals and compressing crystals into round, layer-like blocks. Dumps blocks into heated tank and turns steam valves to melt blocks. Starts pumps to transfer resulting liquid for further processing.
GOE: 06.04.11 STRENGTH: M GED: R2 M1 L1 SVP: 2 DLU: 77

551.685-122 PURIFICATION OPERATOR I (chemical)
Tends equipment that separates hydrocarbons from coal tar derivatives: Opens valves and starts pump to transfer slurry of hydrocarbons into tank containing organic solvent. Adjusts steam valves to heat solution to specified temperature. Opens water valves to cool solution and promote crystallization of hydrocarbon. Pumps solvent into reclaim tanks, and pumps slurry or hydrocarbon crystals to centrifugal drier. Starts centrifugal drier to remove remaining solvent from hydrocarbon crystals. Discharges hydrocarbon into loading hopper. Records production data in log. May be designated according to specific hydrocarbon processed as Anthracene Operator (chemical). May tend equipment that clarifies creosol derived from coal tar and be designated Clarification Operator (chemical).
GOE: 06.04.12 STRENGTH: M GED: R3 M2 L2 SVP: 2 DLU: 77

551.685-126 SALT WASHER (chemical)
Tends machine that removes dirt and other foreign particles from salt prior to storage or processing into commercial products: Starts conveyor that transfers required quantity of salt into tank of water to prepare saline solution of specified density. Turns valve to admit cleaning solution into machine. Observes operation to detect equipment malfunction and to ensure that salt meets standards of cleanliness. Pumps dirty solution into tank and adds soda ash and lime to cause dirt and foreign matter to precipitate and settle. Draws sample of clean solution for laboratory analysis. May be designated according to stage of treatment at which salt is cleaned as Salt Washer, Harvesting Station (chemical); Salt Washer, Processing Station (chemical).
GOE: 06.04.11 STRENGTH: L GED: R3 M1 L2 SVP: 4 DLU: 77

551.685-130 SCREEN OPERATOR (chemical) alternate titles: shaker-screen operator; vibrating-screen operator
Tends vibrating or oscillating shaker screens that separate solids from liquids or sift powdered chemical materials into particles of specified size: Starts action of screens. Turns valves, starts conveyors, or moves chute vanes to control flow of materials to screens according to type of material to be screened. Sifts sample of sized product through laboratory test screens to determine if particle size meets specifications and records results. Changes screen mesh or cloths as directed and repairs equipment, using handtools. Cleans screens, using brushes and liquid cleaning agents. May tend related equipment, such as grinding mills, conveyors, and container-filling units. May examine materials to detect impurities that could contaminate product or damage screens.
GOE: 06.04.11 STRENGTH: L GED: R2 M1 L1 SVP: 3 DLU: 77

551.685-134 SODA DIALYZER (plastic-synth.)
Tends tanks that recover caustic soda from solutions used in viscose rayon production: Turns valves to admit impure soda solution to outside section of tank and water to inside section, effecting absorption of soda into water by osmosis through cloth membrane separating sections. Turns valves to regulate discharge of resulting pure soda and intake of impure soda, according to level of solution in tank sections.
GOE: 06.04.13 STRENGTH: L GED: R3 M1 L2 SVP: 4 DLU: 77

551.685-138 STEEPING-PRESS TENDER (plastic-synth.) alternate titles: caustic-room attendant
Tends open tank that impregnates (steeps) sheets of woodpulp with caustic soda for use in rayon production: Positions rectangular sheets of pulp between

perforated separator plates, using tongs. Turns valves to admit caustic solution and steam into tank. Drains tank after specified steeping time. Presses button to activate hydraulic ram that presses excess caustic from steeped sheets and discharges sheets into shredder.
GOE: 06.04.18 STRENGTH: L GED: R2 M1 L2 SVP: 3 DLU: 77

551.685-142 SULFATE DRIER-MACHINE OPERATOR (steel & rel.)
Tends equipment that cleans and dries ammonium sulfate crystals: Pushes crystals from drain table into trough. Opens trough gate to discharge crystals into drier. Starts centrifuge to separate crystals of ammonium sulfate from acid and tar. Washes remaining impurities from crystals with hot water, using hose. Resumes spinning of centrifuge to complete drying. May neutralize acid in sulfate crystals with ammonia liquor.
GOE: 06.04.11 STRENGTH: L GED: R2 M1 L1 SVP: 4 DLU: 77

551.685-146 TETRYL-SCREEN OPERATOR (chemical)
Tends shaker screen to remove lumps from dried tetryl explosive: Transfers trays of dried tetryl to screening area, using handtruck. Starts motor that activates shaker screen to separate tetryl powder from lumps. Dumps tetryl from trays into feed hopper of screen. Lines catch boxes with wax paper, and positions boxes beneath discharge spout of screen to receive screened tetryl powder. Weighs filled boxes and stacks on handtruck for transfer to storage. Carries containers of tetryl lumps to distillation equipment for reprocessing.
GOE: 06.04.11 STRENGTH: M GED: R2 M1 L2 SVP: 2 DLU: 77

551.685-150 VACUUM-PAN OPERATOR I (chemical)
Tends vacuum pan to wash and dry crystallized tetryl powder for further processing into explosives: Opens release valve to transfer tetryl from crystallizer to vacuum pan. Fills pan with warm water and turns suction valve to draw off liquid and dissolved impurities, leaving powder to settle in felt bag. Shovels and scrapes powder into tub on handtruck. May scrape powder into trays and place trays in drying chambers.
GOE: 06.04.11 STRENGTH: M GED: R2 M1 L2 SVP: 2 DLU: 77

551.685-154 VACUUM-PAN OPERATOR II (chemical)
Tends equipment that removes excess acid from nitrated crude tetryl explosive, preparatory to further processing: Opens valve to load vacuum pan with tetryl slurry. Turns steam jet to draw off excess acid. Shovels and scrapes remaining moist powder from pan, grids, and filter cloth; and flushes it with water hose down into funnel leading to washing tubs. May neutralize acid water from subsequent washing operations. May shovel specified amounts of lime into hopper of lime feeder that neutralizes acid water from subsequent washing operations.
GOE: 06.04.11 STRENGTH: L GED: R2 M1 L2 SVP: 3 DLU: 77

551.685-158 WAX BLEACHER (chemical) alternate titles: beeswax bleacher
Tends vats and filter presses to bleach wax used in candlemaking: Measures and dumps specified chemicals and wax into vats and turns thermostat knob to prescribed temperature to liquefy wax. Packs granulated charcoal on sides of filter press and starts pump to circulate molten wax through press. Stops pump after specified time and drains sample for laboratory analysis. Turns valves or starts pumps to transfer wax from press to tanks. Records types and quantities of wax used.
GOE: 06.04.11 STRENGTH: H GED: R3 M1 L2 SVP: 3 DLU: 77

551.685-162 WRINGER OPERATOR (chemical) alternate titles: tetryl-wringer operator
Tends centrifugal wringer to remove acid or water remaining in nitrocellulose after processing: Starts pumps to convey partially processed nitrocellulose slurry to wringer basket. Moves control to regulate speed of wringer throughout process, as instructed. Stops wringer after specified time and loosens nitrocellulose from walls, using scraper or fork, Opens discharge gate and pushes nitrocellulose through aperture into water immersion bowl to convey slurry to next operation, or hopper to be packed into containers. When removing water from nitrocellulose, may be designated Poacher-Wringer Operator (chemical). May take samples of nitrocellulose for laboratory analysis.
GOE: 06.04.11 STRENGTH: M GED: R2 M1 L1 SVP: 2 DLU: 77

551.686-010 BEAD PICKER (rubber reclaim.)
Picks bead wires from ground rubber tires as they pass on conveyor from grinding machine and drops them in container or on conveyor for removal to scrap area.
GOE: 06.04.29 STRENGTH: L GED: R1 M1 L1 SVP: 1 DLU: 77

551.686-014 EXTRACTOR LOADER AND UNLOADER (chemical)
Feeds conveyor and loads bones into tank of machine that extracts grease. Closes tank and seals cover. Rakes bones from tank after extraction process. Removes burlap filter from bottom of tank and washes and replaces filter.
GOE: 06.04.19 STRENGTH: L GED: R2 M1 L1 SVP: 2 DLU: 77

551.686-018 HOPPER FEEDER (oils & grease) alternate titles: grease-press helper
Rakes cooked offal or tankage from cookers or from platform near press into hopper of hydraulic press used to extract grease. Cleans working area and scrubs floors, using cleaning agents and brushes. May rake crackling residue from extractor tanks onto conveyor and start pump to transfer solvent to extractor tanks to dissolve crackling and be designated Extractor Puller (oils & grease).

GOE: 06.04.19 STRENGTH: M GED: R1 M1 L1 SVP: 2 DLU: 77

551.687-010 BONE PICKER (chemical)
Picks bones from offal as it passes on conveyor belt and tosses bones onto conveyor.
GOE: 06.04.34 STRENGTH: L GED: R1 M1 L1 SVP: 1 DLU: 77

551.687-014 BRINE MAKER II (chemical)
Weighs and adds specified quantities of chemicals to brine to purify solution preparatory to further treatment and refining of salt: Weighs chemicals, such as soda ash and lime, using scale, and pours them into brine tank. Removes residue from tank, using water hose and pumps. Dissolves specified tonnage of unprocessed salt in water to produce brine.
GOE: 06.04.11 STRENGTH: L GED: R2 M1 L1 SVP: 3 DLU: 77

551.687-018 DYNAMITE RECLAIMER (chemical) alternate titles: warehouse operator
Screens dynamite sweepings and broken cartridge shells to reclaim usable dynamite: Shovels floor sweepings and broken shells from powder buggy onto brass screen, using wooden shovel. Picks out foreign matter, such as paper and wood splinters, sifts explosive material from broken or malformed cartridges, and discards debris. Rubs dynamite through screen, using gloved hand. Shovels or dumps reclaimed dynamite into powder buggy for reprocessing.
GOE: 06.04.34 STRENGTH: H GED: R2 M1 L1 SVP: 2 DLU: 77

551.687-022 LABORER, COOK HOUSE (chemical)
Performs any combination of following duties to process stock (animal skins, splits, fleshings, and trimmings) for use in making glue or gelatin: Moves stock to kettle upon signal from COOK (chemical), using handtruck, and dumps stock into kettle. Turns valve to fill kettle with water to submerge stock. Skims grease from surface of water in kettle, using skimmer. Cleans kettle, using shovel, brushes, and water. Packs bottom of kettle with excelsior used to filter broth drained from kettle.
GOE: 06.04.34 STRENGTH: H GED: R1 M1 L1 SVP: 2 DLU: 77

551.687-026 NAPHTHALENE-OPERATOR HELPER (steel & rel.)
Assists NAPHTHALENE OPERATOR (steel & rel.) in separating naphthalene from chemical drain oil used to wash coke-oven gas or tar distillants: Shovels crystallized naphthalene from cooling pans into wheelbarrow. Breaks up large pieces of naphthalene, and transports material to centrifugal drier. Performs other duties as described under HELPER (any industry) Master Title.
GOE: 06.04.34 STRENGTH: H GED: R1 M1 L1 SVP: 2 DLU: 77

551.687-030 SIFTER (pharmaceut.)
Sifts residue from tablet processing machines to salvage usable tablets and powder for reprocessing: Selects sieve according to size tablet being processed. Dumps residue from pail into sieve and picks out foreign matter and usable tablets. Places tablets in container and discards foreign matter. Shakes sieve to sift powder onto paper and pours powder into container. Weighs residue and records weight and identifying information on worksheet.
GOE: 06.04.34 STRENGTH: L GED: R2 M1 L1 SVP: 2 DLU: 77

551.687-034 SODA-ROOM OPERATOR (plastic-synth.) alternate titles: mercerizer; soaking-room operator; steeping-press operator
Guides sheets of woodpulp, used in rayon production, as they are lowered mechanically into steeping presses or vats of caustic soda and pressed to remove excess alkali. May weigh specified number of sheets, using scales. May convey woodpulp to steeping machine, using handtruck.
GOE: 06.04.19 STRENGTH: M GED: R1 M1 L1 SVP: 2 DLU: 77

552 DISTILLING OCCUPATIONS

This group includes occupations concerned with heating a mixture to vaporize the more volatile parts and separate them from the less volatile, and then cooling and condensing the vapor to produce a nearly pure or refined substance.

552.132-010 SHIFT SUPERINTENDENT, CAUSTIC CRESYLATE (chemical)
Supervises and coordinates activities of workers engaged in treating and distilling caustic cresylate to produce variety of cresol products: Observes recording-instrument charts, flowmeters, and gauges to verify process conditions. Correlates instrument readings and test results to diagnose malfunctions in process. Trains workers in procedures for correcting machine malfunctions and in specifications for process changes. Inspects equipment for mechanical defects and malfunctions, such as leaks and excessive wear. Performs other duties as described under SUPERVISOR (any industry) Master Title.
GOE: 06.02.11 STRENGTH: L GED: R4 M3 L3 SVP: 8 DLU: 77

552.362-010 MONOMER-PURIFICATION OPERATOR (chemical)
Controls caustic-wash purification units to remove chemical inhibitors from butadiene and styrene monomers to prevent spontaneous polymerization during storage and transit: Starts pumps and injectors to recycle caustic solution through wash tank and mix liquid monomer with caustic solution. Reads gauges and laboratory analysis reports and adjusts controls to regulate mixing and separating of purified monomer and caustic solution containing inhibitor, according to plant standard. Drains caustic solution from wash tank and piping system and pumps cleaning solution through system to remove impurities.
GOE: 06.02.11 STRENGTH: L GED: R3 M2 L2 SVP: 5 DLU: 77

552.362-014 OXYGEN-PLANT OPERATOR (chemical)
Controls fractionating columns, compressors, purifying towers, heat exchangers, and related equipment to extract nitrogen and oxygen from air for industrial and therapeutic use: Turns valves in specified sequence to control flow of air through series of units that compress and liquefy it, remove carbon dioxide and impurities, and separate resulting product into nitrogen and oxygen. Observes pressure, temperature, level, and flow gauges to ensure standard operation. Tests oxygen for purity and moisture content at various stages of process, using burette and moisture meter. Adjusts equipment according to test results and knowledge of process and equipment. Opens valves to transfer liquid or gaseous oxygen through heat exchanger to cool air, to heat and vaporize liquid oxygen, and to store gaseous or liquid oxygen in storage tanks at specified temperature and pressure. Turns valves to transfer compressed oxygen to storage cylinders. Cleans and repairs equipment, such as replacing defective valves and removing carbon from valves, using handtools. Records gauge readings and test results. May open valves to convey hot nitrogen through alternate batteries of driers to remove moisture. May clean and refill drier with activated alumina. May operate equipment to extract, compress, and liquefy hydrogen from natural gas and be designated Liquid-Hydrogen-Plant Operator (chemical).
GOE: 06.02.11 STRENGTH: L GED: R3 M3 L3 SVP: 4 DLU: 78

552.362-018 RECOVERY OPERATOR (paper & pulp)
Controls evaporators, furnaces, and dissolving tanks to recover sodium compounds from chemicals spent in paper manufacturing processes: Patrols area around recovery units, observing recording devices and indicators on panelboards, flow of chemicals through units, and color of flame in furnaces to detect variations in pressure and temperature of evaporators, determine solid content of evaporated liquor, and detect incomplete burning of liquor in furnace. Turns rheostats to regulate pressure and temperature of evaporators, temperature and rate that liquor is sprayed into furnaces, and rate that molten sodium compounds are transferred from furnace to dissolving tanks. Tests solution at various stages of processing for specific gravity and titration, using testing devices. Adjusts and resets control instrument proportional bands on control board. Records meter readings at specified intervals on progress chart.
GOE: 06.02.11 STRENGTH: L GED: R4 M3 L3 SVP: 5 DLU: 77

552.362-022 STILL OPERATOR, BATCH OR CONTINUOUS (chemical) alternate titles: purification operator; rectifying operator
Controls batch stills or continuous stills and auxiliary equipment from instrumented control board or other control station to separate and condense liquids having close volatilization points, maintaining process control according to instrument readings, test results, and knowledge of equipment and procedure: Reads charge sheet to determine types and quantities of materials to be distilled, specified sequence of operations, and control settings for attainment of prescribed fractionation. Starts pumps and turns valves to admit volatile liquids into still. Observes pressure and temperature gauges and moves controls to specified settings to attain volatilization rate consistent with efficient and safe operation, according to knowledge of process and equipment. Moves controls to maintain specified operating equilibrium in condensers and still auxiliaries, and to set reflux rate for recycling maxium portion of distillate through equipment consistent with efficient operation. Draws sample of product for laboratory analysis, or performs standard refractometric, boiling-range, colorimetric, titration, or specific quantity analyses to determine effectiveness of distillation. Turns valves and starts pumps to route distilled fractions to receiving tanks according to correlation of data from laboratory tests or observation of product color. Records data computed from instrument readings and test results, such as weight of product and yield. May direct activities of other workers who assist in operation of stills and auxiliary equipment. May be designated according to distilled product as Alcohol-Still Operator (chemical). May be designated according to type of still operated as Batch-Still Operator (chemical) II; Continuous-Still Operator (chemical).
GOE: 06.02.11 STRENGTH: L GED: R4 M3 L3 SVP: 6 DLU: 77

552.382-010 PYRIDINE OPERATOR (steel & rel.) alternate titles: pyridine-recovery operator
Controls equipment, such as washers, rectifiers, condensers, and mixing tanks arranged in series to recover pyridine sulfate from tar oils: Prepares solutions of diluted sulfuric acid and sodium carbonate to specified concentration by adding water. Pumps solutions into system to dissolve pyridine and neutralize acids. Starts pumps to circulate batch through system, observing gauges and other instruments. Removes tarry compounds dissolved in pyridine sulfate solution by rectifying (boiling) solution with steam. Samples products for analysis, and interprets results and makes adjustments to control quantity and quality of product according to laboratory report. Inspects equipment, and steams out lines, changes charts, lubricates equipment, and makes minor repairs and adjustments.
GOE: 06.02.11 STRENGTH: M GED: R3 M3 L3 SVP: 6 DLU: 77

552.462-010 DISTILLATION OPERATOR (chemical) alternate titles: purification operator
Operates batch or continuous still to separate intermediate products or impurities from coal tar compounds: Charges still and starts flow of coal tar compound through still units. Turns control valves and observes recording instruments and gauges to attain temperatures, material flow rate, pressure, or vacuum specified for distillation of designated product. May compute variances between laboratory analysis and product specifications, using prescribed formula to determine temperature and flow-rate adjustments. May observe gauges or use measuring rod to verify quantities of chemical materials in feed and hold tanks of still unit. May direct activities of helpers. May be designated according to product distilled as Naphthalene-Still Operator (chemical); Tar-Heater Operator (chemical).

GOE: 06.02.18 STRENGTH: M GED: R4 M3 L3 SVP: 6 DLU: 77

552.682-010 DISTILLER I (chemical) alternate titles: refining-still operator; still tender

Operates stills to refine crude wood turpentine obtained by destructive distillation and steam distillation process: Regulates flow of crude wood turpentine into stills and regulates steam used to heat stills. Observes progress of stills and at specified time during process diverts distilled products (wood turpentine, pine oils, resin oils) into tanks.
GOE: 06.04.11 STRENGTH: L GED: R3 M2 L2 SVP: 5 DLU: 77

552.682-014 DISTILLER II (chemical)

Controls continuous still equipment to distill pine oleoresin into oil of turpentine and rosin: Turns valves to transfer heated oleoresin from melting vats into cleaning, filtering, and washing tanks to clean, filter, and wash trash, foreign matter, and other impurities from resin preparatory to distillation. Pours specified amounts of oxalic acid into tanks to facilitate cleansing process, using graduated cylinder. Drains impurities from wash tanks and starts pump that forces resin into still. Turns valve to circulate water through steam jackets. Observes temperature gauge and turns valve to regulate heat to specified temperature to condense turpentine vapors. Turns valve to drain rosin from still. Observes sample of distillate for clarity and separation of turpentine from oleoresin to determine completion of distillation. Occasionally replaces filters in tank and cleans tank as necessary.
GOE: 06.02.11 STRENGTH: L GED: R3 M2 L2 SVP: 4 DLU: 77

552.682-018 EXTRACTOR OPERATOR (chemical) alternate titles: digester operator

Operates digesters in steam distillation process to extract crude turpentine from wood: Regulates flow of steam through digesters. Gives directions to EXTRACTOR-OPERATOR HELPER (chemical) engaged in filling digesters with wood chips and dumping spent wood from digester.
GOE: 06.04.18 STRENGTH: L GED: R3 M2 L2 SVP: 5 DLU: 77

552.685-010 ACETONE-RECOVERY WORKER (plastic-synth.)

Tends equipment to recover acetone, used in acetate rayon manufacture, from vapor produced by dry spinning (forming) of rayon filaments: Turns valves to admit vaporized acetone from spinning units to recovery system and to maintain cooling coils in condenser at specified temperature for efficient acetone recovery. May pump recovered acetone to storage tanks or recirculate it to mixing machines in which cellulose acetate flakes are dissolved to form spinning solution.
GOE: 06.04.11 STRENGTH: L GED: R2 M1 L2 SVP: 3 DLU: 77

552.685-014 BATCH-STILL OPERATOR I (chemical) alternate titles: distiller

Tends batch stills to separate, by distillation, liquids having divergent volatilization temperatures: Pours specified types and quantities of materials into still. Observes thermostat and sets controls on instrument panel to maintain specified volatilization temperatures throughout distillation cycle and to control condensation of components. Draws samples of distilled liquids for laboratory analysis or performs refractometric or other tests, using standard procedure and equipment. Observes color of distillate to determine when distillate is completed. Records operating data, such as weight, yield of products, gauge readings, and number of batches distilled. May tend continuous-flow vacuum still. May be designated according to product distilled or formed as Ammonia-Still Operator (chemical); Crystallizer Operator (chemical) II; Degreasing-Solution Reclaimer (chemical); Glycerin Operator (soap & rel.).
GOE: 06.04.11 STRENGTH: L GED: R3 M2 L2 SVP: 4 DLU: 77

552.685-018 BATH-MIX OPERATOR (plastic-synth.)

Tends still that purifies solvents used in processing plastics: Screws drain valves into chemical drums and lifts drum onto rack, using hoist. Dumps contaminated solvents into still, and turns steam valve to vaporize impurities and reclaim solvents. Cleans empty drums, using brush and solvent and moves them to storage on handtruck.
GOE: 06.04.11 STRENGTH: H GED: R2 M1 L1 SVP: 2 DLU: 77

552.685-022 RETORT-CONDENSER ATTENDANT (chemical)

Tends retort vapor condensers used in destructive distillation of wood: Starts pump that discharges contents of receiving tanks into settling tanks. Caulks doors of retort if leak occurs. Turns valves on gasline or oil line to supply fuel to burners or to to control temperature in retort.
GOE: 06.04.19 STRENGTH: L GED: R3 M2 L2 SVP: 3 DLU: 77

552.685-026 STILL TENDER (any industry)

Tends flash-type still that reclaims or separates liquids, such as solvents, through volatilization and condensation: Starts pump to draw liquid into tank and allows impurities to settle. Turns valve to transfer liquids into still. Observes temperature gauge and adjusts valve to heat liquid to specified temperature and vaporize liquid in tank. Turns valve to circulate water through tank jackets to condense vapors. Observes distillate for clarity, through pipeline viewer. May be designated according to liquid recovered as Solvent Recoverer (plastic-synth.).
GOE: 06.04.19 STRENGTH: L GED: R3 M2 L2 SVP: 3 DLU: 77

552.685-030 STILL-OPERATOR HELPER (chemical)

Tends distillation units and auxiliary equipment to separate volatile chemical compounds into specified components, performing combination of following tasks under direction of equipment operator: Turns valves and starts pumps as directed. Records temperature, pressure, and flow indicator readings. Measures liquid in tanks, using gauging rod or tape, and draws samples for laboratory analysis. Inspects pipes for leaks. Moves controls to start semiautomatic still auxiliaries, such as heat exchangers, stripping columns, vaporizers, flash tanks, and condensers, and to maintain specified operating equilibrium in equipment as directed. Assists STILL OPERATOR, BATCH OR CONTINUOUS (chemical) in transferring equipment and materials. Cleans equipment, using hose, brushes, and scrapers. May tend machine to produce gas leak detectant odorants and be designated Second Operator (chemical).
GOE: 06.04.11 STRENGTH: H GED: R3 M2 L2 SVP: 3 DLU: 77

552.686-010 EXTRACTOR-OPERATOR HELPER (chemical)

Feeds wood chips into digesters used in steam distillation process for extracting crude turpentine: Seals cover to opening at bottom of digester. Starts conveyor to fill digester with wood chips through charging hole at top. Seals cover to charging hole. Removes cover on hole at top of digester to dump spent wood from digester at end of extraction process.
GOE: 06.04.18 STRENGTH: M GED: R2 M1 L1 SVP: 2 DLU: 77

552.687-010 DISTILLATION-OPERATOR HELPER (chemical)

Starts pump to transfer coal tar distillates to storage or processing tanks. Dips measuring rod into tanks to verify quantities of distillates in tanks. Moves neutralizing chemicals to work area preparatory to charging of still, using handtruck.
GOE: 06.04.40 STRENGTH: M GED: R2 M1 L1 SVP: 2 DLU: 77

553 HEATING, BAKING, DRYING, SEASONING, MELTING, AND HEAT-TREATING OCCUPATIONS

This group includes occupations concerned with removing moisture from material by exposure to heat, air, vacuum, or desiccants; exposing material to heat to facilitate its processing by others, liquefy solids or gases, change chemical composition, effect texture and consistency, or remove solvents or other undesirable components.

553.132-010 SUPERVISOR, GREASE REFINING (oils & grease)

Supervises and coordinates activities of workers engaged in extracting and refining grease produced by cooking glue stock and in converting tankage to fertilizer: Estimates weight and type of tankage or grease in process and specifies amount of acid to be used. Examines refined grease to ensure specified level of clarity. Directs blending of grease according to formula and loading of grease into tank cars. Records amounts of grease refined, blended and shipped, amounts of acid used, and moisture content of each batch of fertilizer. Trains workers in operation of cookers. Performs other duties as described under SUPERVISOR (any industry) Master Title.
GOE: 06.02.01 STRENGTH: L GED: R4 M3 L3 SVP: 7 DLU: 77

553.362-010 BELT-PRESS OPERATOR I (rubber goods)

Sets up and operates single- or double-deck platen curing press to cure transmission or conveyor belting: Gives directions to workers engaged in setting up press according to specified width of belt, pressure, temperature, and curing time. Positions guide stops in press to accommodate height of belt to be cured. Inspects sections of press for conformity to specifications and verifies temperature and time settings. Observes machine operation to detect malfunction. Signals OVERHEAD CRANE OPERATOR (any industry) 921.663-010 to lift and position belt rolls in work area.
GOE: 06.02.13 STRENGTH: H GED: R3 M2 L2 SVP: 5 DLU: 77

553.362-014 AUTOCLAVE OPERATOR (aircraft mfg.) alternate titles: bonding equipment operator

Sets up and operates autoclaves and auxiliary equipment to cure and bond metallic and nonmetallic aircraft parts and assemblies according to specifications: Reads and interprets shop orders and authorization documents to determine bonding process specifications. Selects parts and assemblies for simultaneous bonding, based on similarity of processing requirements and autoclave capacity. Arranges jigs and fixtures containing parts and assemblies on bonding racks and positions racks in autoclave, manually or using equipment, such as hoist, forklift, or tow. Inspects general condition of parts and assemblies, examines positioning of parts and assemblies in jigs and fixtures, and verifies that vacuum bag installation conforms to specifications prior to bonding. Connects thermocouples and vacuum lines to fittings on jigs and fixtures and inside autoclave. Adjusts manual controls or enters commands in computerized control panel to regulate and activate autoclave power supply, cooling system, vacuum, heat, and pressure gauges and recorders, and to close interlocking autoclave doors. Monitors instruments, switches, and recorders and listens for warning signals during autoclave operation to ensure conformance to specifications, and modifies or aborts process as required. Maintains manual or computerized autoclave processing records. Operates curing ovens and presses with heated platens [METAL-BONDING PRESS OPERATOR (aircraft mfg.) 553.382-026] to cure and bond parts. Suggests methods or procedures for improved operations to supervision or liaison personnel. Discusses loading, unloading, and operation of autoclaves and auxiliary equipment with other operators and workers to ensure safety of individuals working in and around high-pressure autoclaves. May calibrate autoclave system components.

GOE: 06.02.18 STRENGTH: M GED: R4 M3 L3 SVP: 6 DLU: 88

553.364-010 SAMPLE TESTER (chemical)
Tests samples of phosphoric acid, according to prescribed standards, to determine chemical and physical characteristics of acid for purposes of quality control, process control, and conformity to specifications: Mixes specified amounts of processed acid with control chemicals in flask, shakes flask to mix them, pours solution into container of colorimeter to determine strength of acid, and records results of test. Determines specific gravity of acid in slurry, using water vacuum equipment and hydrometer, and records results of test. Determines specific gravity of final product, using hydrometer, and records results of reading. Notifies operators of changes in their processes that affect quality of final product. Bottles and labels samples taken at various stages of processing for laboratory analysis. Cleans laboratory and equipment after each test run and at end of shift.
GOE: 02.04.01 STRENGTH: L GED: R3 M2 L3 SVP: 5 DLU: 77

553.382-010 AUTOCLAVE OPERATOR I (chemical)
Controls autoclave (high-pressure tank) to process liquid, solid, and gaseous ingredients into chemical products according to specifications: Reads production schedule to determine product, ingredients, temperature, pressure, and duration of process. Turns valves to load liquid ingredients into tank. Weighs out and dumps solid ingredients and catalyst into equipment, and turns steam and coolant valves to heat mixture to specified temperature. Turns valves to displace accumulated gases to avoid explosion. Closes vent to seal autoclave. Sets dials to control pressure and flow of gaseous material through mixture. Opens vent to admit product into load tank. Connects drain line from load tank to filter press, using handtools, and starts pumps to force product through press to separate catalyst. Drains product into drum and starts pumps to transfer catalyst to load tank for reuse. May test samples of materials produced, using refractometer or other standard test equipment, to ensure attainment of specified product.
GOE: 06.02.11 STRENGTH: H GED: R3 M2 L2 SVP: 5 DLU: 77

553.382-014 BOILER (soap & rel.)
Controls kettles to boil soap ingredients, such as lye, resin, palm oil, and tallow, to specified consistency: Opens valves to fill kettle with ingredients in specified amounts, and weighs and dumps ingredients in kettle, using scale. Opens steam valve to heat kettle to specified temperature. Observes boiling rate, reads temperature gauges, and turns valves to maintain temperature within critical limits. Boils ingredient for specified time and draws and tests sample for consistency, specific gravity, and chemical content, using laboratory equipment, such as hydrometer. Starts pumps and opens valves to transfer mixture to storage tanks. May stir ingredients with paddle.
GOE: 06.02.18 STRENGTH: L GED: R4 M3 L3 SVP: 7 DLU: 77

553.382-018 EVAPORATOR OPERATOR I (chemical) alternate titles: multiple-effect evaporator operator; vacuum-pan operator
Controls single-stage or multiple-effect evaporators to concentrate chemical solutions to specified density by evaporation: Starts pumps and turns valves to admit liquid solution, steam, and cooling water into system. Observes temperature, pressure, and vacuum gauge readings and adjusts pumps to conform to specifications. Turns feed valves to regulate flow of solution through system and to obtain specified concentration. Tests solution pumped from last effect, using hydrometer, to ascertain that solution is concentrated to specified density. Observes manometers and looks through sight glass to ensure that steam vapors are not carried to next effect with solution. Tests steam condensate with reagents to detect contaminated solution. May control equipment from instrumented control board. May tend equipment, such as preheaters, thickeners, settlers, and filters, that prepare solution for evaporation. May clean evaporator shell and tube nest with chemical to remove scale. May operate multiple-effect unit as one or more single evaporators.
GOE: 06.02.11 STRENGTH: L GED: R4 M3 L3 SVP: 6 DLU: 77

553.382-022 VARNISH MAKER (paint & varnish) alternate titles: varnish blender; varnish cooker; varnish melter
Controls equipment to melt, cook, and mix ingredients, such as gums, oils, turpentine, and naphtha, for use in manufacture of varnishes: Weighs gum and dumps it into gum pot or agitator tank over burner. Pours in oil, as gum becomes liquid, and adjusts burner controls to regulate heat. Controls burners to cook mixture for specified time. Starts pump to transfer varnish base and thinner into reducing tank. Starts agitator to mix base and thinner for specified time. Fills test tube with varnish and compares viscosity with standard sample, or delivers test tube to laboratory for test. Pumps varnish through filter press to remove sediment from varnish.
GOE: 06.02.11 STRENGTH: M GED: R3 M2 L2 SVP: 5 DLU: 77

553.382-026 METAL-BONDING PRESS OPERATOR (aircraft mfg.) alternate titles: platen operator, metal bond
Sets up and operates hydraulic press equipped with heated platens to bond metal aircraft and space vehicle parts and assemblies: Reads blueprints and shop orders to determine areas of parts to be joined, amount of bonding agent to apply, and temperature and pressure required. Examines parts or assemblies for surface defects and positions parts on machine bed, using jigs or fixtures. Applies adhesives to surfaces to be bonded. Installs thermocouple leads to machine, using handtools. Starts machine and adjusts controls to regulate pressure, heat, and curing time. May assemble parts prior to aligning them in machine. May operate autoclaves and ovens to cure and bond parts and assemblies [AUTOCLAVE OPERATOR (aircraft mfg.) 553.362-014].

GOE: 06.02.02 STRENGTH: M GED: R3 M2 L2 SVP: 5 DLU: 87

553.385-014 PRIMER EXPEDITOR AND DRIER (chemical)
Tends vacuum tank that dries priming mixture, and dries and stores loaded cartridge primers and primed rim-fire cartridge cases: Transfers trays or boards filled with explosive primers or cases from loading room to steam-heated dryhouse, using shockproof cart. Places filled trays in numbered racks or bins. Reads gauges and turns valves to control temperature in dryhouse. Collects primers and cases from storage to fill requisitions and keeps perpetual inventory. Loads primers on screen trays of vacuum tank and starts vacuum pump, steam heat, and fans that force-dry priming mixture when requisitions do not permit sufficient time for air drying. May deliver primers and cases to production departments and record date, lot number, and grade.
GOE: 06.04.11 STRENGTH: L GED: R2 M1 L2 SVP: 3 DLU: 77

553.462-010 FLASH-DRIER OPERATOR (chemical)
Controls flash-drier furnace and auxiliary equipment to remove water from activated carbon slurry, for use in industrial and consumer applications: Tests specific gravity of carbon slurry in agitator tank, using hydrometer, and draws sample for acidity testing by WASH OPERATOR (chemical). Admits water and dumps prescribed amount of caustic into slurry tank to bring density and acidity readings to prescribed standard. Turns valve to heat slurry to specified temperature and starts pumps to transfer slurry to vacuum drum filter. Adjusts gate leading to paddle mixer to regulate flow of slurry to furnace. Sets automatic controls to maintain furnace temperature at plant standard. Moves switches and turns valves to regulate furnace blowers and cyclone filters that control flow and discharge dried carbon. Directs activities of workers engaged in tending filter and carbon-bagging machines. Weighs carbon samples taken from furnace discharge spouts and computes percentage of moisture removed, using standard formula. Keeps log of gauge readings and test results. Verifies setup of scraper blade on filter drum for efficient operation. May turn fuel valves to regulate furnace conditions in manually controlled units, according to specifications.
GOE: 06.02.18 STRENGTH: M GED: R3 M2 L2 SVP: 4 DLU: 77

553.482-010 AGER OPERATOR (plastic-synth.)
Controls continuous process equipment to age alkali cellulose for use in cellophane manufacture: Takes wet and dry-bulb temperature readings in air ducts through which cellulose will pass on conveyor and calculates humidity in ducts, using graphs. Reads instruction tables to determine setting of conveyor screws and belts under existing humidity conditions. Turns screws to adjust conveyor speed to regulate length of aging cycle, and to set humidistat that maintains specified humidity in ducts. Records operating data.
GOE: 06.02.13 STRENGTH: L GED: R3 M2 L2 SVP: 5 DLU: 77

553.486-010 CALCINE FURNACE LOADER (paint & varnish)
Performs variety of duties to assist CALCINE-FURNACE TENDER (paint & varnish) in baking pigments to bring out color: Scoops dry blend of pigments from drums into clay saggers (pigment containers) and stacks saggers on bed of kiln. Positions kiln bed on hydraulic lift, using forklift. Moves controls of hydraulic lift to raise kiln bed into overhead kiln and secures bed in kiln. Removes bed from kiln on signal from CALCINE-FURNACE TENDER (paint & varnish) and empties saggers of calcined pigments into drum. Weighs and tags drum and moves it to storage area, using handtruck. May load saggers of dry blend onto revolving track of circular kiln for continuous-calcination process. Performs other duties as described under HELPER (any industry) Master Title.
GOE: 06.04.11 STRENGTH: H GED: R1 M1 L1 SVP: 2 DLU: 77

553.582-010 DRIER OPERATOR II (chemical) alternate titles: tunnel-drier operator
Operates atmospheric tunnel driers that heat liquids or slurries to remove water or other volatile liquids: Moves controls to regulate preheaters, fans, and conveyor belts or other material feeding mechanisms to maintain continuous operation. Turns steam valves and sets automatic temperature controls to attain specified drying temperature. Observes temperature charts and conveyors to correct equipment malfunctions and jamming of feed or discharge conveyors. Examines and feels materials for moisture content or obtains sample for laboratory moisture analysis, and readjusts equipment controls to attain specified product. Stops drier units in sequence as material feed is exhausted. Records data, such as type and quantity of material dried and drying time. May tend continuous pan driers that automatically transfer materials through drier in pans on conveyor chains, and dumps dried contents after drying. May tend or feed auxiliary equipment, such as grinding mills and baling machines that process dried product. May be designated according to type of drier as Continuous-Conveyor-Screen Drier (chemical).
GOE: 06.02.11 STRENGTH: L GED: R3 M2 L2 SVP: 4 DLU: 77

553.582-014 POT FIRER (chemical)
Controls heated pots to dehydrate concentrated caustic solution, according to operating procedures: Starts pumps and opens valves to admit specified quantity of caustic solution to pots. Reads pressure and flowmeters and charts, and turns valves to control flow of caustic liquor to prevent overflow in pots. Observes boiling rate and temperature recorders and turns valves or sets thermostat to maintain pot temperature within specified limits. Records flow, pressure, and temperature readings in operating log. May perform chemical tests on caustic and add reagents to facilitate production of standard product. May tend machine that flakes caustic soda [FLAKER OPERATOR (chemical; smelt. & refin.)]. May fire oil or gas furnaces under direction of STATIONARY ENGINEER (any industry).

GOE: 06.02.11 STRENGTH: L GED: R3 M2 L2 SVP: 5 DLU: 77

553.585-010 DEBUBBLIZER (plastic-synth.)
Tends high-pressure heating equipment that removes internal solvent bubbles from nitrocellulose rod stock: Loads precut rods into cylinder chamber. Turns valves to fill cylinder with hot water and admit steam into cylinder jacket. Observes gauges and turns valves to regulate temperature and pressure. Turns valves to drain water, reduce pressure, and refill cylinder with coolant to set softened and compressed stock. Drains coolant from cylinder and removes debubblized rods from cylinder chamber. Records number and type of rods processed.
GOE: 06.04.13 STRENGTH: M GED: R2 M1 L1 SVP: 3 DLU: 77

553.585-014 DRY-HOUSE ATTENDANT (chemical)
Tends drying room in which pyrotechnics (fireworks) are cured, dried, or stored: Stores trays of pyrotechnics on racks according to date of processing. Observes room thermometers and moves controls of blower heater to keep drying room temperature within prescribed limits. Issues stored pyrotechnics to workers according to date of processing or removes materials at expiration of specified period and stores them in metal containers for further processing.
GOE: 06.04.11 STRENGTH: M GED: R2 M1 L1 SVP: 3 DLU: 77

553.585-018 DRYING-ROOM ATTENDANT (soap & rel.) alternate titles: drier tender
Tends equipment in steam-heated drying room that dries and hardens bar soap: Pushes racks of soap into and out of room according to prescribed schedule. Turns and adjusts steam valves to heat and maintain room at specified temperature. Starts electric dolly that moves soap racks through drying chamber. Records number of racks processed.
GOE: 06.04.19 STRENGTH: M GED: R1 M1 L1 SVP: 2 DLU: 77

553.585-022 THERMAL MOLDER (rubber goods) alternate titles: heater tender
Tends steam heaters or presses that shape and cure rubber floor mats: Positions sheets of precut calendered rubber on molds. Turns valve to activate vacuum fixtures that draw and hold rubber against contours of mold. Examines molds to ascertain that rubber sheet covers mold and smooths out wrinkles. Removes excess rubber from mold, using knife or roller. Pushes switch to close press and move heater carriage into heater. Turns valve to admit steam and sets timer for specified curing time. Strips cured mats from mold. Examines mats for defects, such as discoloration, misforming, blisters, and cracks. Marks defective mats for repair and places them on skids.
GOE: 06.04.13 STRENGTH: M GED: R2 M1 L2 SVP: 3 DLU: 77

553.585-026 TUMBLER OPERATOR (rubber goods)
Tends tumblers that dry, treat, and screen latex prophylactics preparatory to testing: Weighs and keeps each batch separate. Dumps batch into drying, treating, and screening tumblers, following specified sequence. Adds treating agents, such as oil emulsion, cornmeal, and lycopodium to treating tumbler for finishing. Dumps finished batch into container and identifies batch with date, time, type, and number, and sets batch aside for testing. Records temperature and humidity gauge readings, treating agents used, and number of batches tumbled.
GOE: 06.04.13 STRENGTH: M GED: R2 M1 L1 SVP: 2 DLU: 77

553.665-010 BELT-PRESS OPERATOR II (rubber goods)
Tends section of single- or double-deck platen press to cure rubber transmission and conveyor belting under direction of BELT-PRESS OPERATOR (rubber goods) I 553.362-010, working as crewmember: Positions guide stops in press to cure belting to specified thickness and width. Sprays press with solution to prevent adherence to belt during cure. Helps crew pull belt from roll onto press. Lifts empty roll shell onto *windup rack* and adjusts guides and speed of windup as belt goes onto roll after cure. Adjusts knives to trim rind from belt. May guide belt over pricker roll prior to going into windup after cure. May signal OVERHEAD CRANE OPERATOR (any industry) 921.663-010 to lift and position belt rolls from windup rack to storage area.
GOE: 06.04.13 STRENGTH: H GED: R2 M1 L1 SVP: 3 DLU: 77

553.665-014 BLACK-MILL OPERATOR (chemical)
Tends furnace and shaker screens to produce boneblack animal charcoal from ground bones: Turns dial on control panel to start feed of ground bones to furnace and turns handwheel to adjust oscillating speed of shaker screens to maintain uninterrupted production. Observes recording thermometer to verify specified temperature in furnace. Inspects conveyors, vibrating feeders, and shaker screens for clogging or malfunction. Tightens drive belts, using wrenches and other handtools. Gives directions to other workers in spreading boneblack over cooling floor and in loading cooled boneblack onto conveyors.
GOE: 06.04.19 STRENGTH: L GED: R3 M2 L2 SVP: 4 DLU: 77

553.665-018 COOK (chemical) alternate titles: extractor; hide-cooking operator
Tends equipment that cooks animal stock (animal skins, splits, fleshings, and trimmings) used to make glue or gelatin: Signals workers to fill kettle with stock. Turns valve to allow water to flow into kettle to submerge stock. Starts heaters and adjusts temperature. Cooks stock for prescribed period of time and tests sample of broth for specific gravity, using hydrometer. Compares hydrometer readings with readings on conversion tables to determine approximate amount of glue or gelatin that batch will produce. Drains broth from vat to storage tank, refills kettle with water, and cooks stock several times at progressively higher temperatures. May stir stock in kettle, using wooden paddles. May

tend equipment to wash stock prior to cooking [WASH-MILL OPERATOR (chemical)].
GOE: 06.04.19 STRENGTH: L GED: R3 M2 L2 SVP: 3 DLU: 77

553.665-022 COOKER TENDER (oils & grease)
Tends cookers that melt grease and tallow from offal, bone, and meat: Turns valves to admit steam to cooker (steam-jacketed tank equipped with revolving, power-driven paddles for agitating material) until indicator on steam pressure gauge reaches specified point. Turns handwheel or lifts lever to open discharge gate of cooker when light indicates material is ready for further processing. Starts (reverses) agitator paddles that force cooked material into vat or conveyor hopper. Signals COOKER LOADER (oils & grease) or OVERHEAD CRANE OPERATOR (any industry) 921.663-010 to refill cooker. May shovel cooked material from vat into conveyor hopper. May load cookers. May pull material from cooker, using hoe.
GOE: 06.04.19 STRENGTH: H GED: R2 M1 L1 SVP: 2 DLU: 77

553.665-026 DRIER OPERATOR I (chemical) alternate titles: atmospheric-drier tender; dry-room operator
Tends cabinet or room-type driers that heat liquids or slurries to remove water or other volatile liquid components: Shovels or dumps materials into pans and places them on drier shelves, in racks, or on wheeled trucks that are pushed into drier. Observes thermometer and humidity gauge, turns steam or fuel valves, and moves controls to maintain temperature, humidity, and air circulation in drier, according to specifications. Shuts down drier at end of drying cycle or on notification by control laboratory. Unloads driers or notifies other workers to remove dried material. May weigh dried materials and fill bags or other containers. May feel materials to ascertain dryness.
GOE: 06.04.11 STRENGTH: H GED: R2 M1 L1 SVP: 3 DLU: 77

553.665-030 DRUM-DRIER OPERATOR (chemical)
Tends drum drier that dries activated carbon sludge, used in variety of industrial and consumer applications: Sets drier controls and starts sludge pumps and agitators to dry product that meets prescribed standard. Turns valves to increase water content of sludge to prevent caking, according to hydrometer readings supplied by other workers.
GOE: 06.04.19 STRENGTH: L GED: R2 M1 L1 SVP: 3 DLU: 77

553.665-034 FIRER HELPER (paper & pulp)
Tends equipment that burns condensed black liquor into black ash: Turns valves to regulate spray of black liquor into cyclone drier and flow of air through drier to dry black liquor to specified concentration. Determines moisture content of liquor, using moisture testing equipment. As directed, turns rheostat to adjust mechanism in mixing tank to feed salt cake into black liquor prior to burning. Turns valves as directed to channel steam into evaporators or into main line. Pushes *steam lance* through boiler tubes or turns crank that rotates steam jets through boiler to blow out soot and sludge. Scrapes sludge from interior of furnace, using scraper and rake.
GOE: 06.04.14 STRENGTH: L GED: R2 M1 L1 SVP: 2 DLU: 77

553.665-038 HEATER TENDER (rubber goods; rubber reclaim.; rubber tire) alternate titles: curer; rubber curer; vulcanizer operator
Tends equipment, such as cylindrical ovens, horizontal pot heaters, tunnel driers, or atmospheric heaters that shrink, cure, or remove moisture from natural or synthetic rubber materials or products: Loads or feeds rubber materials or products, such as sheets of raw rubber, devulcanized scrap rubber, rubber coated fabric, or rubber products into oven, using trays, racks, handtrucks, or conveyors. May lift fabric rolls onto *letoff rack* of heater, using hoist, and thread fabric between feed rollers and onto *takeup roll*. May turn controls to regulate speed and amount of materials conveyed through heated chamber. Turns heater valves to admit steam or regulate temperature and to admit ammonia when specified. May start blowers to circulate air. Removes product or material from oven after specified time. May be designated according to product dried as Drier (rubber goods); Drier Operator (rubber reclaim.); Drier Tender (rubber goods).
GOE: 06.04.13 STRENGTH: M GED: R2 M1 L2 SVP: 2 DLU: 77

553.665-042 PLASTICS-SEASONER OPERATOR (plastic-synth.)
Tends dry houses, cell driers, or drying ovens that remove solvent and contaminants from plastics materials: Observes temperature and moisture gauges and turns controls to control drying process. Unloads driers or notifies workers to unload ovens.
GOE: 06.04.13 STRENGTH: M GED: R2 M1 L1 SVP: 2 DLU: 77

553.665-046 STEAM-PRESS TENDER I (rubber goods)
Tends press that cures rubber transmission and conveyor belting, as directed by BELT-PRESS OPERATOR (rubber goods) I, working as crewmember: Turns valves to obtain specified pressure and temperature, and sets timers on section of press. Verifies pressure, temperature, and timers on other sections of press, and notifies STEAM-PRESS TENDER (rubber goods) II of findings. Pulls belt into press from *letoff rack*. Moves levers to open press. Participates in rolling belt onto *windup rack* after cure.
GOE: 06.04.13 STRENGTH: H GED: R2 M1 L1 SVP: 4 DLU: 77

553.665-050 STEAM-PRESS TENDER II (rubber goods)
Performs following duties to prepare press for curing transmission and conveyor belting, working as crewmember: Turns pressure valves, adjusts temperature controls, and sets timers on press sections, following directions of

STEAM-PRESS TENDER (rubber goods) I. Pulls levers to open and close press. Positions shells in *windup rack* and guides cured belt onto roll. *GOE: 06.04.13 STRENGTH: M GED: R2 M1 L1 SVP: 3 DLU: 77*

553.665-054 TRAY-DRIER OPERATOR (chemical)
Tends tray drier and drum filter that dries and filters activated carbon sludge used in variety of industrial and consumer applications: Turns dials and observes temperature and moisture gauges to control drying process. Pushes empty trays onto roller conveyor for filling with sludge and transferring filled trays to drier chamber in wheeled cage.
GOE: 06.04.19 STRENGTH: M GED: R2 M1 L1 SVP: 3 DLU: 77

553.682-010 BLACK-ASH-BURNER OPERATOR (paper & pulp)
Controls furnace in which condensed black liquor is burned to black ash for use in recovering sodium compounds: Turns rheostat control to adjust mechanism in mixing tank to feed specified quantities of salt cake into black liquor. Turns valves and air intake ports to regulate spray of liquor and air into furnace, according to combustion charts, to ensure complete combustion of organic matter. Starts conveyor to carry molten black ash from taphole of furnace to water dissolving tank in which green liquor is formed, or opens furnace port allowing ash to flow directly into dissolving tank. Starts motor to pump green liquor into settling tank. Adjusts valves to channel steam generated by furnace through liquor evaporators or into main steam line. Cleans liquor pipes, using steam and rod, and scrapes residue from furnace interior.
GOE: 06.02.14 STRENGTH: L GED: R3 M2 L2 SVP: 4 DLU: 77

553.682-014 CURER, FOAM RUBBER (rubber goods)
Operates conveyorized curing unit from control panel to process latex mixture into foam rubber sheeting: Starts pump to transfer latex and air into mixing tank to obtain latex of specified density. Weighs sample of latex in measuring cup to determine if density meets specifications. Pumps specified compounds into mixing tank with latex and starts agitators that mix ingredients. Starts belt conveyor and turns setscrews to adjust scraper bars for dimensions specified for rubber sheeting. Turns dial to regulate heat in curing ovens. Pumps latex mixture onto belt conveyor that carries it under scraper bars and through curing ovens. Verifies dimensions of cured rubber sheeting with rule.
GOE: 06.02.13 STRENGTH: L GED: R3 M2 L2 SVP: 4 DLU: 77

553.682-018 EVAPORATOR OPERATOR II (chemical)
Operates evaporator to separate turpentine oils from rosin: Regulates valves and pump controls to pump specified amount of crude turpentine to evaporator. Regulates valves and pump controls to draw off vapors from evaporator, leaving rosin as residue.
GOE: 06.02.18 STRENGTH: L GED: R3 M1 L2 SVP: 4 DLU: 77

553.682-022 REDUCTION-FURNACE OPERATOR (chemical) alternate titles: catalyst operator
Operates reduction furnaces and equipment to produce catalyst used in manufacture of margarine and shortening: Scoops powder into rotating reduction furnace that feeds it into mixing tank containing premeasured amount of oils. Observes gauges and regulates heating and mixing controls to ensure processing according to standards. Turns valves to pump finished product into holding tank. Opens valve to fill containers with catalyst. Keeps log of operations.
GOE: 06.02.15 STRENGTH: L GED: R3 M2 L2 SVP: 4 DLU: 77

553.682-026 V-BELT CURER (rubber goods)
Operates automatic presses to cure rubber V-belts: Hoists uncured belts from storage rack arm, using lifting device and slides belts over collapsible curing drum. Aligns belts in individual V-shaped rings of drum, and pushes button to expand first drum segment. Realigns belts in rings and expands last segment. Brushes soap solution on air bag of drum-curing retainer and pushes button to insert loaded drum into retainer. Observes gauges and adjusts pressure and temperature valves and regulator arms to maintain specified curing conditions. Slides carrying device under belts where segments automatically break down when drum slides from retainer after cure. Forces carrying device between belts and stationary segment of drum to break belts loose. Lifts cured belts and slides belts onto rack arm. Changes drums and retainers, using hoist and handtools.
GOE: 06.02.13 STRENGTH: M GED: R3 M2 L2 SVP: 4 DLU: 77

553.684-010 HEAT WELDER, PLASTICS (plastic prod.) alternate titles: welder, plastic
Fuses together plastic sheets, using hot-air gun to melt and join edges of sheets: Cuts sheets to be joined to form smooth edges, using knife. Sands edges, using power sander, to form V-joint. Places plastic rod in V-joint and activates hot-air gun to melt rod, causing mass to fill V-joint and join edges of sheets.
GOE: 06.04.31 STRENGTH: M GED: R2 M2 L1 SVP: 3 DLU: 77

553.684-014 NITROCELLULOSE OPERATOR (chemical)
Screens and dries nitrocellulose to prepare it for use in making dynamite: Shovels nitrocellulose from drum onto nonsparking screen, using wooden shovel. Rubs nitrocellulose through screen by hand to remove foreign material. Spreads screened material on trays and places trays in drying chamber. Starts blower and tests drying material periodically, using moisture meter, to ensure that moisture content of nitrocellulose meets specifications. Scrapes dried material into fiber drums for delivery to dynamite mix house.
GOE: 06.04.34 STRENGTH: H GED: R3 M1 L1 SVP: 4 DLU: 77

553.685-010 AMMONIUM-NITRATE CRYSTALLIZER (chemical)
Tends equipment that evaporates ammonium nitrate solution to form crystals used in making dynamite: Starts pump to move specified quantities of ammonium nitrate solution from storage tank to weighing tank. Opens valve to drain weighed solution into heated tub. Starts agitator to mix solution as water evaporates and turn material as it crystallizes. Weighs out and pours specified quantities of chemicals into tub to prevent hardening of ammonium nitrate and to ensure uniform crystallization, indicated by visual inspection. Opens gate in side of tub to transfer crystals to storage barrels.
GOE: 06.02.18 STRENGTH: M GED: R3 M2 L2 SVP: 4 DLU: 77

553.685-014 BAGGER (plastic prod.) alternate titles: vacuum-forming-machine operator
Tends heating and vacuum equipment to cure preformed plastic parts: Positions part in plastic bag and seals bag with hot iron. Inserts vacuum tube in bag and seals bag around tube with tape. Places part on cart, connects vacuum line to tube to remove air from bag, and smooths bag around part with brush to ensure complete vacuum. Pushes cart into curing oven or places part in autoclave. Sets oven controls or turns air-pressure valve of autoclave, as specified, to cure part. Removes part and cuts away plastic bag, using knife. May form part by positioning plastic sheet and mold in plastic bag, heating sheet under lamps, and forcing conformation of sheet to mold by vacuum pressure of bag. May impregnate fabric with plastic resins and cut fabric into strips for use in laminating preformed part.
GOE: 06.04.13 STRENGTH: H GED: R2 M1 L1 SVP: 3 DLU: 77

553.685-018 BONE-CHAR KILN TENDER (chemical)
Tends gas-fired kiln to reclaim char (activated carbon) used in filtering corn syrups: Observes thermometers and turns gas valves to heat and maintain specified temperatures in kiln. Starts conveyors that transfer char to and from kiln. Dumps sacks of char into kiln to replenish supply lost during firing process.
GOE: 06.04.19 STRENGTH: M GED: R2 M1 L1 SVP: 2 DLU: 77

553.685-022 BONE-DRIER OPERATOR (chemical) alternate titles: bone drier; dry-box operator; glue-bone drier
Empties bone cooking tanks and tends oven that dries bones from which glue has been extracted: Opens bottom of bone cooking tank. Starts feed mechanism and rotary paddles of oven. Places rod into top of cooking tank and pushes bones through opening of tank bottom into feed mechanism of oven. When bones are dried, presses button to stop rotary action of paddle in oven. Moves lever and locking device to release oven door. Presses button to actuate paddles inside oven that push dried bones from oven into bags or onto cart. Loads filled bag onto handtruck and pushes truck or cart to storage area. May turn dials to regulate temperature of oven. May bag, weigh, and close bags containing dried bones.
GOE: 06.04.19 STRENGTH: M GED: R2 M1 L1 SVP: 2 DLU: 77

553.685-026 CADMIUM-LIQUOR MAKER (paint & varnish) alternate titles: liquor maker
Tends equipment that makes cadmium sulfate used in making pigments for paints and enamels. Shovels cadmium *moss* into tank of boiling water and sulfuric acid to form cadmium liquor. Tests liquor solution for acid and foreign content, as specified by laboratory.
GOE: 06.04.11 STRENGTH: H GED: R2 M1 L1 SVP: 2 DLU: 77

553.685-030 CALCINE-FURNACE TENDER (paint & varnish) alternate titles: kiln operator
Tends kiln that develops color of pigments used in making paints and glass enamels: Moves controls to set automatic heat regulator that maintains specified temperature in kiln. Adjusts gas burners in kiln, using handtools, and lights pilot flames and burners. Raises kiln bed or signals CALCINE FURNACE LOADER (paint & varnish) to raise kiln bed, containing pigments, into kiln and to remove bed from kiln after specified time. May fill and empty saggers (pigment containers) [CALCINE FURNACE LOADER (paint & varnish)]. May tend crusher that breaks calcined chunks of pigment into smaller particles. May tend auxiliary equipment, such as coaler, conveyor systems, pump, and rotary vacuum filter.
GOE: 06.04.11 STRENGTH: H GED: R2 M1 L1 SVP: 3 DLU: 77

553.685-034 CONTINUOUS-LINTER-DRIER OPERATOR (chemical)
Tends equipment that fluffs and dries cotton linters or woodpulp for further processing into explosives: Places portion of linters or woodpulp on revolving rollers that feed it into cylinder equipped with picking spikes. Inspects fluffed material for presence of impurities and fluffy appearance as it is discharged into drier. Moves controls to maintain temperature of hot-air oven at plant standard and to regulate speed of drier conveyor for efficient drying. When tending separate picking and drying units, may be designated according to unit tended as Cotton-Picker Operator (chemical); Linter-Drier Operator (chemical).
GOE: 06.04.19 STRENGTH: M GED: R2 M1 L1 SVP: 2 DLU: 77

553.685-038 CURING-OVEN TENDER (chemical)
Tends ovens that cure fuels loaded (cast) into rocket-motor cases: Observes recording instrument charts and dials of timing devices to verify required temperatures and curing-cycle times. Turns valves to switch from automatic-instrument controls to manual control of steam-supply valves to regulate temperature.
GOE: 06.04.11 STRENGTH: L GED: R3 M1 L1 SVP: 4 DLU: 77

553.685-042 DRIER OPERATOR (chemical; pharmaceut.) alternate titles: drum-drier operator; vacuum-drum-drier operator
Tends vacuum drum driers that heat liquid compounds to form caked or powdered chemical products: Connects tube from feed inlet to drum containing liquid to be dried. Turns steam and coolant valves and observes thermometer to

420

regulate temperature of steam-jacketed drum enclosed in vacuum chamber, according to specifications. Starts pump and observes vacuum gauge to maintain prescribed vacuum in chamber. Starts revolving drum that dries liquid as it splashes against heated drum, forming caked or powdered product that is removed from surface of drum by scraper blade. Observes and feels dried product, periodically submits sample for laboratory moisture analysis, and adjusts drying temperature and vacuum if product does not meet plant standards. Records drying time of batch, gauge readings, and amount or weight of materials dried. May set scraper blade at specified distance from drum, using handtools. May fill containers with dried materials, weigh containers, and tag containers for shipment or storage.
GOE: 06.04.11 STRENGTH: M GED: R3 M2 L2 SVP: 3 DLU: 77

553.685-046   DRIER OPERATOR II (plastic-synth.)
Tends equipment, such as centrifuge and rotary drier, that removes moisture and recovers plastic resin from slurry: Observes gauges, turns valves, and starts pumps to regulate flow of slurry from storage tank to centrifuge. Starts centrifuge to separate resin from slurry and observes flow of partially dried resins into rotary drier. Observes gauges and turns valves to regulate flow of hot air and maintain specified temperature in drier. May tend pneumatic conveyor that carries dried resin into storage silos. May measure level of stored materials in silo, using calibrated plumbline.
GOE: 06.04.13 STRENGTH: L GED: R2 M1 L1 SVP: 2 DLU: 77

553.685-050   DRIER OPERATOR III (chemical) alternate titles: calciner operator; rotary-drier operator
Tends batch or continuous rotary driers that remove moisture from solid chemical materials: Dumps or shovels materials into batch drier chamber, or starts feed conveyors of continuous drier. Starts drying chamber rotating. Admits steam or hot air to drying chamber until specified heat is attained, as indicated by temperature chart recorders and gauges. Opens vacuum valves to withdraw accumulated vapors where materials require drying at subatmospheric pressure. Stops rotation of drying chamber to dump dried materials, or starts discharge conveyor to empty contents of chamber and transfer dried product to storage, packaging, or further processing. May tend auxiliary equipment, such as condensers and vacuum pumps. Records operating data in equipment log, such as temperatures, pressures, drying time, and hourly production. May feed discharged materials for specified dryness. May submit samples to control laboratory for moisture analysis. May regulate drier temperature, and speed of conveyors and rotary chamber, according to knowledge of process and material being dried.
GOE: 06.04.11 STRENGTH: M GED: R3 M2 L2 SVP: 5 DLU: 77

553.685-054   DRIER OPERATOR IV (chemical) alternate titles: spray drier
Tends spray driers that evaporate water from slurries, forming caked or powdered product: Pumps slurry to atomizer nozzle in drier and regulates spray of slurry as instructed. Observes temperature recorders and adjusts valves, controls, and dampers to heat or cool and direct air through drier to evaporate water or solidify slurry. Observes discharge conveyor for malfunctions or jamming to maintain uninterrupted flow of dried materials to storage. Rakes out accumulated cake or powder remaining in drier, and clears clogged lines, using length of wire. May place empty drums under discharge end of spray tower to be filled with specified amount of powdered emulsifier. May tend auxiliary equipment, such as cyclone filters and scrubbing tower to refine product or recover usable materials.
GOE: 06.04.11 STRENGTH: M GED: R3 M2 L2 SVP: 4 DLU: 77

553.685-058   DRIER-OPERATOR HELPER (chemical) alternate titles: laborer, glue drying
Assists DRIER OPERATOR (chemical) VI in drying glutinous material, such as gelatin and glue. Starts equipment and turns valves as directed. Moves glutinous material to drier, using handtruck. Performs other duties as described under HELPER (any industry) Master Title.
GOE: 06.04.19 STRENGTH: M GED: R1 M1 L1 SVP: 2 DLU: 77

553.685-062   FIRE-HOSE CURER (rubber goods)
Tends steam-heating equipment that cures rubber in jacketed firehose: Lifts precut lengths of specified rubber tubing and braided fabric hose jacket onto table. Dusts rubber tubing with soapstone to prevent tubing from sticking to jacket. Turns crank to wind tubing onto stock wheel. Aligns jacket with mechanical threading device and clamps threading fixture to end of rubber tubing. Starts winch that pulls tubing into jacket. Lifts and clamps ends of jacketed hose to fixtures on steam lines. Presses hose into curing cavities on table that hold hose in flattened position when curing. Observes gauges and turns valve to inject steam into hose at specified temperature and pressure for curing. Places cured hose on storage rack.
GOE: 06.04.13 STRENGTH: H GED: R2 M1 L1 SVP: 2 DLU: 77

553.685-066   FIRER, RETORT (chemical)
Tends burners supplying heat to retorts (reaction vessels) to facilitate heating of materials to produce chemical products: Moves controls to regulate flow of gas or oil to burners to maintain temperature of retorts at specified reading. Cleans and repairs retorts, using handtools, scrapers, brushes, and cleaning agents.
GOE: 06.04.11 STRENGTH: L GED: R2 M1 L1 SVP: 3 DLU: 77

553.685-070   KETTLE WORKER (soap & rel.)
Tends kettles that boil soap ingredients: Opens valves to admit alkali, fat, tallow, lye, and steam into kettles: Observes temperature gauges and rate of

boiling and turns valves to regulate temperatures. Draws samples and delivers them to laboratory. Adds soda and water, according to instructions, to bring mixture to specifications, using scoop and hose. Opens valves to drain off glycerine, water, and sludge. May stir soap solutions with wooden paddle to promote blending.
GOE: 06.02.18 STRENGTH: M GED: R3 M2 L2 SVP: 4 DLU: 77

553.685-074   LIME-SLUDGE KILN OPERATOR (paper & pulp)
Tends gas- or oil-fired kiln that burns lime sludge to recover lime: Turns panel controls to adjust burner and flow of sludge into kiln according to temperature gauges. Starts conveyor that carries lime from kiln to hopper of slaking machine. May tend washers and filters that remove cooking liquor from sludge before it is burned.
GOE: 06.04.11 STRENGTH: L GED: R2 M1 L1 SVP: 2 DLU: 77

553.685-078   MILLED-RUBBER TENDER (rubber goods; rubber tire)
Tends conveyor, and spraying and drying unit that cools and dries milled rubber stock: Monitors flow of rubber stock as it drops from mixer through batch-off mill onto conveyor. Removes stock adhering to mill rollers with long-handled scraper and frees stock if it piles up on conveyor. Adjusts conveyor speed and turns valves to regulate water spray and airflow that cools and dries stock.
GOE: 06.04.13 STRENGTH: M GED: R2 M1 L1 SVP: 2 DLU: 77

553.685-082   OVEN TENDER (paint & varnish) alternate titles: baker, paint; enamel burner; kiln tender
Tends oven that bakes freshly painted furniture parts to harden finish: Starts equipment to heat oven to prescribed temperature. Pushes truckload of dipped or sprayed pieces into heated oven, hangs pieces on hooks suspended from overhead trolley, or places pieces on conveyor belt and regulates speed of belt through oven in accordance with temperature of oven and size of pieces. Allows pieces to bake for specified length of time and removes finished articles from oven.
GOE: 06.04.21 STRENGTH: M GED: R3 M1 L1 SVP: 3 DLU: 77

553.685-086   PIGMENT FURNACE TENDER (chemical)
Tends kiln or furnace that makes pigments from specified chemical ingredients or develops specified colors in pigments or metallic powders for use in making paints, enamels, and varnishes: Weighs or measures specified chemical ingredients and dumps them into furnace hopper, conveyor, blending, pulverizing and sifting machine hoppers, or into clay saggers. Opens chute on hopper or conveyor, or shovels prepared charge into furnace. Positions specified temperature cam into automatic heat control unit, or turns dials to specified setting to regulate temperature, temperature changes, and heating and cooling cycles. Observes control panel of furnace to verify standard functioning of preset furnace. Opens discharge chute, or shovels pigment or powder from furnace. May clean and adjust burners on gas-fired furnaces. May verify color of pigments or powders to standard samples or color chart.
GOE: 06.04.11 STRENGTH: M GED: R3 M2 L2 SVP: 3 DLU: 77

553.685-090   RABBLE-FURNACE TENDER (chemical)
Tends furnace and auxiliary equipment that heat carbon black to reduce sulfur content by starting feed and discharge conveyors, opening fuel and water valves, and lighting burners with rabble (torch on end of iron rod). May tend furnace that dries carbon into granules preparatory to bagging and be designated Granular Operator (chemical).
GOE: 06.04.19 STRENGTH: L GED: R3 M1 L1 SVP: 3 DLU: 77

553.685-094   ROTARY-FURNACE TENDER (chemical)
Tends rotary furnace that roasts sulfur or other materials to liberate gases for use in processing chemical products: Weighs materials to be roasted and scoops or dumps specified quantity into furnace hopper. Starts revolution of furnace, consisting of hollow cylinder mounted between power-driven rollers. Observes thermometer and turns fuel or steam valves to maintain specified temperature in furnace and efficient roasting of materials. Shuts down furnace after roasting is completed and assists other workers in cleaning and preparing furnace for subsequent operation. May adjust and repair furnace, using handtools. When roasting sulfur for use in production of sulfuric acid, is designated Sulfur Burner (chemical).
GOE: 06.04.11 STRENGTH: H GED: R2 M1 L1 SVP: 3 DLU: 77

553.685-098   SOAP-DRIER OPERATOR (soap & rel.) alternate titles: drier-machine hand; flake drier; roll-machine attendant
Tends equipment and machinery that converts viscous soap into flakes and removes excess moisture from flakes: Turns valves to admit refrigerated water into rollers to chill them to specified temperature to harden soap. Opens valve to allow viscous soap to flow from crutcher machine into chamber equipped with chilling rollers. Starts rollers to press soap into sheets. Adjusts flaking knives that cut sheets of soap into flakes. Turns valve to regulate flow of flakes into drier. Turns valves to admit steam to drying cylinders and oven jackets to heat drier to specified temperature. Removes sample of dried flakes and tests for moisture content, using moisture testing apparatus. Adjusts temperatures accordingly. Opens valve to discharge dried flakes onto conveyor belt leading to storage bins. May sharpen flaking knives, using hand file. May tend equipment to convert liquid insecticide into flakes and be designated Flaker Operator (chemical).
GOE: 06.04.19 STRENGTH: L GED: R2 M1 L1 SVP: 2 DLU: 77

553.685-102   TIRE MOLDER (rubber tire) alternate titles: curing finisher; retread-mold operator
Tends retreading mold that vulcanizes camelback (raw rubber tread) onto tire casing and molds tread design: Places air bag of specified size inside tire,

tire-spreading device, and clamps tire into mold. Inflates air bag to specified pressure and heats mold to specified temperature to cook and mold tread. Removes tire after predetermined time and trims loose ends from molded tread, using knife.
GOE: 06.04.13 STRENGTH: H GED: R2 M1 L1 SVP: 3 DLU: 77

553.685-106 VACUUM-DRIER TENDER (chemical) alternate titles: shelf-drier operator
Tends vacuum driers that heat chemical solids to remove water or other liquids: Observes temperature indicators and vacuum gauges and turns steam valves and sets dials to regulate temperature and vacuum pressure in drier as specified. Observes drying material in glass viewer of equipment for conformance with specifications. Collects samples of material for laboratory moisture test. Records gauge readings, type of material dried, weight, and drying time.
GOE: 06.04.11 STRENGTH: L GED: R3 M1 L1 SVP: 4 DLU: 77

553.685-110 WAX-POT TENDER (foundry) alternate titles: melter
Tends melting pots in which wax is melted for use in lost wax casting process: Breaks slabs of wax and deposits them in melting pots. Adjusts thermostat to maintain specified temperature of liquid wax. Dips wax from melting pot, using hand ladle, and pours it into receiving pot. May fill cylinders of wax-injection machines with liquid wax and place cylinders in aging oven for specified period of time.
GOE: 06.04.32 STRENGTH: M GED: R2 M2 L1 SVP: 2 DLU: 77

553.685-114 CADMIUM BURNER (chemical)
Tends furnace and auxiliary equipment that heat cadmium to produce cadmium oxide: Turns handwheel to tilt and lower mouth of crucible for initial loading, and dumps cadmium balls into crucible until scale indicator reaches specified weight. Returns crucible to upright position and turns control to activate automatic pilot that fires furnace. Positions empty drum under oxide collector discharge outlet, clamps discharge cover over drum, and turns switch that starts flow of cadmium oxide from collector into drum. Periodically scrapes molten accumulation from mouth of crucible, using metal rod. Dumps additonal cadmium balls into crucible when indicator falls below prescribed weight, using pipe carrier. Turns switch to stop flow of cadmium oxide when drum is filled. Removes drum from under discharge cover, and closes drum with lid and sealing collar. Weighs drum, records weight on shipping tag, and attaches tag to sealing collar. Periodically scrapes and chips accumulations of cadmium oxide from floor and from crucibles not in use. Sifts scrapings, weighs, and stores solids. Maintains production logs.
GOE: 06.04.11 STRENGTH: H GED: R2 M1 L2 SVP: 2 DLU: 86

553.685-118 DRIER OPERATOR VI (chemical) alternate titles: glue-drier operator; pearl-glue drier
Tends equipment that dries glutinous material, such as gelatin and glue, by either of following methods: (1) Starts pumps to admit glutinous material through coolers to congeal it and through extruders to form noodles. Starts conveyor that moves noodles through series of drying compartments and turns on heaters and fans in compartments. Feels noodles for moisture content and regulates speed of equipment to ensure prescribed degree of dryness. Reads hydrometer to detect excessive moisture in drying compartments and turns on dehumidifier when necessary. (2) Transfers containers of pearl glue (granular forms) or moves frames or trays of sheets of glue or gelatin into drying compartment, using handtruck. Starts heaters and fans in heating compartment. Feels glutinous material for moisture content and regulates temperature in drying compartment when necessary. May tend equipment that spreads glutinous material into sheets for drying [SPREADING-MACHINE OPERATOR (chemical) 559.685-170].
GOE: 06.04.19 STRENGTH: M GED: R3 M1 L1 SVP: 4 DLU: 77

553.686-010 BONE-CHAR OPERATOR (chemical)
Unloads furnace in which ground bones are charred to produce boneblack (animal charcoal): Opens and closes slide gate on bone-char furnace to fill bucket, mounted on dolly, with boneblack. Tilts bucket, assisted by other workers, to discharge contents onto cooling floor. Spreads boneblack over floor to cool, using rake. Shovels cooled boneblack onto conveyor for transfer to storage tanks. May sprinkle water onto material to facilitate cooling. May shovel ground bones into furnace or retort and dump charred product onto storage conveyor, using wheelbarrow, and be designated Retort Feeder, Ground Bone (chemical).
GOE: 06.04.19 STRENGTH: M GED: R2 M1 L1 SVP: 2 DLU: 77

553.686-014 CD-MIXER HELPER (rubber reclaim.) alternate titles: pan-devulcanizer helper
Performs following duties in devulcanizing ground scrap rubber in steam heater: Places pans beside mixer and loads pans with scrap rubber compound. Loads pans onto heater car by hand or hoist and pushes car into heater. Pulls heater cars out of heaters, using electric winch, and dumps or shovels devulcanized rubber into storage bins.
GOE: 06.04.11 STRENGTH: H GED: R1 M1 L1 SVP: 2 DLU: 77

553.686-018 CURING-PRESS OPERATOR (rubber tire)
Feeds and off bears machines that cure (vulcanize) tires, performing any of following duties: Removes foreign matter from molds, using airhose, and sprays molds with dope solution to prevent tire from sticking. Lifts tires from saddle trucks to position them in molds. Pushes switch to inflate air bag to expand tire into closing mold. Lifts cured tires from mold at end of cycle and places

tires on inflating unit to preserve tire shape during cooling period. Lifts tires from inflating unit at end of cooling cycle and loads them onto overhead conveyor.
GOE: 06.04.13 STRENGTH: H GED: R1 M1 L1 SVP: 2 DLU: 77

553.686-022 DECKHAND (chemical)
Dumps oleoresin into hopper of vats that melt resin preparatory to distillation into turpentine and rosin: Rolls filled barrels of oleoresin onto scales to be weighed and rolls weighed barrels to storage area above vats. Upends barrels to dump resin into hopper of melting vats and pushes resin near steam jets of vats with stick to facilitate melting.
GOE: 06.04.11 STRENGTH: H GED: R1 M1 L1 SVP: 2 DLU: 77

553.686-026 DRIER OPERATOR V (chemical)
Feeds wet smokeless powder into equipment that dries powder and removes process solvents, such as acetone, ether, and alcohol: Observes gauges to ascertain that temperature of water is within specified limits. Removes filled containers of dried powder from equipment, using handtruck.
GOE: 06.04.11 STRENGTH: H GED: R2 M1 L1 SVP: 2 DLU: 77

553.686-030 DRIER-OPERATOR HELPER (rubber reclaim.) alternate titles: dry-room helper
Performs following duties to remove moisture from devulcanized scrap rubber: Cleans adhering scrap stock from drier and shaker screens, using handtools and airhose. Dumps bags of soapstone into hopper of mechanical shaker that sifts soapstone to prevent tacky surfaces of stock from adhering to shaker. Opens and closes discharge chutes of drier as instructed. May move dried stock to storage bins on handtrucks.
GOE: 06.04.13 STRENGTH: M GED: R1 M1 L1 SVP: 2 DLU: 77

553.686-034 FRAME FEEDER (chemical)
Positions gelatin-drying frames on conveyor below gelatin-spreading machine to receive sheets of congealed gelatin discharged by machine. Slides loaded frame to elevator which stacks frames on truck. Pushes loaded truck to drying alley.
GOE: 06.04.34 STRENGTH: M GED: R1 M1 L1 SVP: 2 DLU: 77

553.686-038 ROTARY-DRIER FEEDER (chemical) alternate titles: calciner feeder
Feeds crystalline or granular materials to conveyor system or feed hopper of rotary driers for drying: Starts feed conveyor and shovels material onto moving belt, or adjusts controls of conveyor or feed hopper to regulate automatic feed according to instructions from equipment operator. May be designated according to materials fed as Soda-Drier Feeder (chemical); Sulfur Feeder (chemical).
GOE: 06.04.11 STRENGTH: M GED: R2 M1 L1 SVP: 2 DLU: 77

553.686-042 VARNISH-MAKER HELPER (paint & varnish)
Assists VARNISH MAKER (paint & varnish) in manufacturing varnish, performing any combination of following duties: Transfers ingredients, such as gums, resin, turpentine, and oils from storage to work area, using handtruck. Weighs specified amounts of dry materials and shovels them into kettles or vessels. Measures liquids in receptacle and pours them into kettles or supply tanks. Mixes ingredients in kettles with paddle. Cleans kettles and other equipment, using high-pressure hose, solvents, and brushes. Performs other duties as described under HELPER (any industry) Master Title.
GOE: 06.04.11 STRENGTH: H GED: R2 M1 L1 SVP: 2 DLU: 77

553.687-010 DRIER HELPER (chemical)
Performs variety of manual duties in drying and storing chemical materials, as directed: Turns valves to fill sample bottles for laboratory testing. Inspects product through sight glasses at various stages of drying process to detect malfunctions. Inspects equipment and piping for leaks or malfunctions. Notifies equipment operator or supervisor of unusual conditions. Lowers gauge tape into storage towers to facilitate inventory and production control. Records gauge readings on operating record. Cleans equipment, using hose and water. May be designated according to type of drier as Spray-Drier-Operator Helper (chemical).
GOE: 06.04.11 STRENGTH: L GED: R2 M1 L1 SVP: 2 DLU: 77

553.687-014 FURNACE HELPER (chemical)
Observes flow of sawdust on conveyors leading to carbon-producing furnace and adjusts feed gates as necessary to maintain uniform flow. Positions sample cans under carbon-discharge spouts of furnace tubes and opens spouts to fill bottles for laboratory analysis, timing sampling with interval timer. Weighs and labels containers. Clears jams in feed and discharge conveyors, using rod.
GOE: 06.04.34 STRENGTH: L GED: R2 M1 L1 SVP: 2 DLU: 77

554 COATING, CALENDERING, LAMINATING, AND FINISHING OCCUPATIONS

This group includes occupations concerned with imparting a desired finish or ensuring uniform thickness in materials by pressure applied with rollers; forming or pressing materials into thin sheets or layers and then adding them to other materials; covering materials and objects with a layer of another material for such purposes as preserving or decorating them; adding a desired surface effect to materials and objects; and removing blemishes from them.

554.137-010 FINISHING SUPERVISOR, PLASTIC SHEETS (plastic-synth.)
Supervises and coordinates activities of workers engaged in polishing surfaces of plastic sheets to remove scratches, masking sheets preparatory to ship-

ment, and weighing and tagging sheets. Performs other duties as described under SUPERVISOR (any industry) Master Title.
GOE: 06.04.01 STRENGTH: L GED: R3 M2 L2 SVP: 6 DLU: 77

554.137-014 SUPERVISOR, COATING (plastic-synth.)

Supervises and coordinates activities of workers engaged in operating equipment to coat cellophane with solvents, resins, plasticizers, or wax to moistureproof cellophane. Directs workers in maintenance and cleaning of coating towers, bath mixers, driers, and solvent recovery equipment. Performs other duties as described under SUPERVISOR (any industry) Master Title.
GOE: 06.02.01 STRENGTH: L GED: R4 M3 L3 SVP: 7 DLU: 77

554.362-010 CALENDER OPERATOR (rubber goods; rubber tire) alternate titles: spreader machine tender

Operates machine, alone or as member of crew, to coat, impregnate, imprint, or form rubber sheeting or rubberized fabric: Turns steam valves to regulate heat or rolls, judging heat by action of rubber and by feeling rolls with hand. Turns handwheels or capstan bar to adjust distance between rolls. Verifies thickness of calendered material, using gauges. Threads fabric or rubber sheeting around and between rollers, through coating reservoirs or water coolant tanks, and onto pickup reel core or takeoff conveyor. Adjusts knives that trim selvage or cut material to specified width by moving knives along bar and turning setscrews, or replaces numbered rack (set) of knives, using wrenches. Adjusts weights on arms of holders so knives will press against rolls and cut through thickness of material processed. Observes calendered material for defects, such as bubbles, lumps, streaks, and pitting, and marks defects. May direct other workers who feed stock, change takeup reels, take off and inspect stamped parts, and place them in books, boards, and frames. May be designated according to material calendered as Calender Operator, Fabric (rubber goods; rubber tire); Calender Operator, Gum Stock (rubber goods; rubber tire).
GOE: 06.02.13 STRENGTH: M GED: R3 M2 L2 SVP: 4 DLU: 77

554.382-010 COATER (pharmaceut.) alternate titles: pill coater; tablet coater

Controls battery of coating machines that apply coatings to pharmaceutical tablets to flavor, color, preserve, add medication, or control disintegration time: Dumps uncoated tablets into rotary pans of machines and starts machine. Pours measured amounts of liquid coatings, such as medicated syrup, dye, and gelatin, onto tablets to form base or successive coats according to formula or production order. When applying enteric coating to control disintegration, pours enteric solution over tablets prior to subcoating. Sprinkles dusting powder onto tablets and stirs them to prevent tablets from sticking together and to produce uniform coating. Examines tablets for defects, such as chips and discoloration, and scrapes coating with fingernail to ascertain dryness. Measures sample tablets, using caliper or micrometer, and weighs them on balance scale to determine adherence to weight and coating-thickness specifications. Dumps coated tablets and measured amount of liquid wax into canvas-lined pan and starts pan revolving to give tablets final glossy coating.
GOE: 06.02.21 STRENGTH: M GED: R3 M2 L2 SVP: 5 DLU: 77

554.382-014 PLASTICS-SPREADING-MACHINE OPERATOR (plastic-synth.)

Operates machinery to spread synthetic resins and glass fibers over continuous sheet of plastics film to prepare materials for subsequent molding: Moves controls to set and regulate width of sheet and to adjust line speeds with flow rate of materials. Moves plungers to start flow of synthetic resin solution through metering device (material buckets). Observes gauges and starts pumps and degassing system on supply tanks to regulate pressure. Inserts thermometer in synthetic resin to verify temperature. Observes tachometers, flowmeters, and gauges to verify specified process conditions.
GOE: 06.02.13 STRENGTH: L GED: R3 M2 L2 SVP: 4 DLU: 77

554.384-010 DYER (chemical)

Mixes coloring solution in tank or kettle, and dyes pearl and plastic buttons to match color of standard button or fabric sample: Weighs powdered dyestuffs according to formula. Pours powder into mixing bowl or pan, adds hot water, and stirs with spoon to form paste. Turns water and steam valves to fill dye kettle to indicated level, and stirs in paste, using paddle or spoon. Immerses wire basket containing buttons in solution. Withdraws sample buttons from solution and compares with standard button or fabric sample, to determine if color matches. Lifts basket from solution when color match is attained, immerses basket in boiling water to rinse excess dye from buttons, and places basket in barrel of centrifugal drying machine. Moves switch to start dryer that spins excess dye from buttons.
GOE: 06.02.32 STRENGTH: L GED: R3 M2 L2 SVP: 3 DLU: 77

554.485-010 BUCKLE-STRAP-DRUM OPERATOR (rubber goods)

Tends machine that coats uncured rubber or rubber-coated fabric strips and winds them on drum to make straps for rubber footwear: Computes number and kind of books required, and keeps production chart. Places strip at back of drum, threads end through guides and cement-filled reservoir, and inserts end in groove of drum to secure it. Turns handwheel to regulate machine speed and starts machine that winds strip onto drum so that each turn abuts and adheres to edge of one previously wound. Stops machine when drum is filled and pulls knife along drum groove and across wound strip to form sheet of strips. Pulls sheet from drum onto cutting table, using stick, and cuts sheets into strips of specified length with knife, using triangular cutting bar as guide. Lifts rows of cut strips with stick and places them in book.

GOE: 06.04.13 STRENGTH: L GED: R2 M1 L1 SVP: 2 DLU: 77

554.485-014 STRAP-FOLDING-MACHINE OPERATOR (rubber goods)

Tends machines that automatically fold uncured rubber strip or coated friction tape over parallel reinforcing cords to form strap material to which buckles, eyelets, or snaps are attached for use on rubber footwear: Calculates from work orders width, length, and quantity of stock to be made and prepares production schedule. Mounts spools of cord on spindles and roll of strip or tape on arbor. Attaches folder to machine bracket by turning thumbscrews or using screwdriver. Cuts end of tape on bias, using scissors, and threads tip and cord through folder. Threads folded strap through paired rollers that press down folded edges. Positions carton at discharge end, starts machine, and runs strap material into carton. May fold and wind strip into rolls for cutting into straps by STRAP-CUTTING-MACHINE OPERATOR (rubber goods), using pedal-operated machine.
GOE: 06.04.07 STRENGTH: L GED: R3 M2 L2 SVP: 2 DLU: 77

554.585-010 CATHODE MAKER (chemical)

Tends tanks and related equipment that coats cathode screens with asbestos for use in electrolytic cells: Opens valve to fill cathode tank with caustic liquor. Weighs out prescribed quantity of asbestos and dumps it into tank. Starts air compressor and opens valve to force asbestos and cell liquor to mixing tank and return it to cathode tank after agitation for specified time. Draws sample of resulting slurry and determines specific gravity, using hydrometer. Positions cathode screen over cathode tank, using crane. Connects vacuum hose to cathode and lowers cathode into tank for asbestos coating, using hoist. Observes vacuum gauge to determine number of dips or immersion time necessary to apply asbestos coating of specified thickness to cathode. Applies asbestos tape to secure cathode rim. Transfers coated cathode to drying area, using crane. Records number of cathodes coated, immersion and drying time, and quantity of materials used. May tin cathode bars, using tinning compound. May cut asbestos paper to size and cover screens and plates with new linings.
GOE: 06.04.21 STRENGTH: H GED: R3 M2 L2 SVP: 4 DLU: 77

554.585-014 COATER OPERATOR (plastic-synth.) alternate titles: dipping-machine operator; impregnating-machine operator

Tends machine that coats continuous sheet of plastic material with synthetic resin solutions to impart special properties, such as heat resistance, impact strength, or waterproofing: Loads roll of material onto unwind stand, using overhead hoist. Threads material through rollers of coating machine, drier unit, and onto winding machine. Sets controls to regulate speed of material feed and amount of coating solution. Sets tension on material by adjusting speed of unwind and windup rolls. Turns valves to regulate steam or turns on infrared lamps to control drier temperature and moisture. Examines material passing through drier and onto windup machine for wrinkles or breaks. Patches breaks, using glue. Maintains log of machine running time and number of rolls processed.
GOE: 06.04.21 STRENGTH: M GED: R3 M1 L2 SVP: 3 DLU: 77

554.586-010 FINISHER (plastic-synth.)

Performs any combination of following duties involved in final processing of plastics sheets: Removes plastics sheets from overhead monorail conveyor, weighs them, and replaces them on conveyor. Moves sheets to various locations, using handtruck. Cuts masking paper to size. Mixes adhesive and transfers it to reservoir of masking machine. Copies identification data, such as size, thickness, and weight on sheets or labels.
GOE: 06.04.40 STRENGTH: M GED: R2 M1 L1 SVP: 2 DLU: 77

554.587-010 ROLL INSPECTOR (plastic-synth.) alternate titles: slit-roll inspector

Examines finished rolls of cellophane for defects and verifies accuracy of roll labels: Observes and feels rolls passing on conveyor to detect flaws, such as wrinkles, streaks, or tears on edges. Measures width and diameter of rolls, using tape rule. Compares identification labels with specifications to prevent errors. Pushes rejected rolls onto table. Records number of rolls processed and number of rolls rejected.
GOE: 06.03.02 STRENGTH: L GED: R2 M2 L2 SVP: 3 DLU: 77

554.662-010 CALENDER OPERATOR, FOUR-ROLL (plastic prod.; rubber goods; rubber tire)

Operates four-roll calender to coat fabric with rubber or produce plastic sheeting and roll sheets to specified thickness: Adjusts automatic control and observes temperature dial to heat calender rolls to specified temperature. Starts machine and adjusts conveyor speed to regulate feeding of stock. Turns adjustment wheels of rollers to specified settings to stretch fabric for calendering. Verifies thickness and width of calendered stock with gauge and ruler. Positions knife to trim edge of calendered fabric. Interprets work orders, assigns duties, and informs crew of processing specifications. May operate equipment from control board.
GOE: 06.02.13 STRENGTH: L GED: R3 M2 L2 SVP: 5 DLU: 77

554.665-010 CALENDER-WIND-UP TENDER (rubber goods; rubber tire) alternate titles: calender helper; roll changer

Tends *windup rack* on *four-roll calender* that winds calendered fabric onto liner rolls: Starts *festoons* that accumulate fabric during roll change, and stops windup rack. Cuts fabric with scissors between machine and full roll and guides fabric into roll on auxiliary rack with aid of CALENDER-WIND-UP HELPER

(rubber goods; rubber tire). Stops festoons, starts windup rack, and moves tension and speed levers to wind new roll. Places full roll onto scale, using hoist. Reads yardage gauge and compares roll weight with standard on yardage chart for conformance to specifications. Notifies CALENDER OPERATOR, FOUR-ROLL (plastic prod.; rubber goods; rubber tire) of weight discrepancies or fabric defects, such as wrinkles and spread cords. May run identification strings into calendered stock as windup proceeds.
GOE: 06.04.07 STRENGTH: M GED: R2 M1 L1 SVP: 2 DLU: 77

554.665-014 LAMINATING-MACHINE TENDER (rubber goods) alternate titles: doubling-machine operator

Tends machine that combines two continuous sheets of material, such as rubber, sponge rubber, fabric, felt, or fleece, working as team member: Transfers rolls of material to and from machine, using handtruck, and lifts or hoists rolls into cradles, using chain hoist. Threads ends of cemented and noncemented materials over feed rollers, between combining rollers, and onto single *takeup roll*. Turns wheels or capstan bolts to set pressure of combining rolls by trial and error to produce complete adhesion of both materials. Starts machine and moves lever to engage clutch and start material winding. Leans against one rotating roll of material to control tension and pulls or feeds edge to align it with other roll, while other worker controls tension and aligns material on opposite end of roll. Stops winding when either feeder roll is empty and cuts off other roll of material to match length, using scissors. Tapes ends of unused material, reads yardage indicator, and marks amount left on roll.
GOE: 06.04.09 STRENGTH: M GED: R2 M1 L2 SVP: 2 DLU: 77

554.682-010 CALENDER-LET-OFF OPERATOR (rubber goods; rubber tire)

Operates letoff, dipping, and drying units of *four-roll calender* to bond rubber to fabric: Positions fabric roll in letoff rack, using hoist, and starts *festoon*. Splices undipped roll to end of roll in process by inserting gum strip between ends and aligning splice in vulcanizer to cure splice. Adjusts guides and pretension rolls to maintain specified width of fabric during dip process. Moves controls on central switch panel to adjust drier temperature, solution level in dip tank, and festoon speed. Notifies CALENDER OPERATOR, FOUR-ROLL (plastic prod.; rubber goods; rubber tire) of material defects or machine malfunction. May mix ingredients in agitator drum according to written specifications to make dip solutions. When operating dip unit independently of calender, tends windup rack [CALENDER-WIND-UP TENDER (rubber goods; rubber tire)] and is designated Dip-Unit Operator (rubber goods; rubber tire).
GOE: 06.02.13 STRENGTH: M GED: R3 M2 L1 SVP: 4 DLU: 77

554.682-014 MASKING-MACHINE OPERATOR (plastic-synth.)

Operates machine to apply cement to masking paper and press coated paper onto surfaces of plastics sheets to provide protection during final processing and shipping: Positions paper roll on mandrel, using chain hoist. Threads paper through machine. Turns valves to fill hoppers with cement from reservoir. Moves levers to set paper cutters and to adjust pressure on squeeze rolls to accommodate size and thickness of plastics sheet. Turns screws to set blades that control amount of cement applied to paper and verifies position of blades, using feeler gauge. Adjusts tension and speed controls to eliminate wrinkling and excessive coating. Maintains production records.
GOE: 06.04.38 STRENGTH: M GED: R3 M2 L2 SVP: 4 DLU: 77

554.682-018 ROLL OPERATOR (plastic-synth.) alternate titles: calender-roll operator; mill-roll operator

Operates roll mill to homogenize and roll plastic compounds into sheeting or slab form: Pushes button to transfer plastic from mixing machine to revolving heated mill rolls. Cuts material with knife and feeds material back through rolls to obtain sheet of specified color, consistency, and thickness. Adjusts slitting knives or starts automatic scraper to strip sheet from rolls. Guides material onto conveyor belt. Observes gauges or feels material and turns steam and water valves to control temperature of rolls. Cleans rolls to prevent contamination of stocks, using wire brush, hand scraper, solvents, and airhose. May adjust roll clearance with hand wrenches.
GOE: 06.02.13 STRENGTH: M GED: R3 M1 L1 SVP: 5 DLU: 77

554.682-022 ROOFING-MACHINE OPERATOR (build. mat., nec)

Operates machine to coat continuous rolls of roofing felt with asphalt, colored slate granules, powdered mica, or tar, to make roll roofing or shingles: Threads felt through or around series of coating rollers. Pulls felt through rollers and adjusts tension. Sets machine controls to gradually increase speed of rollers to specified operating speeds, or pulls levers and turns valves and wheels to synchronize machine speed and flow of coating material. Observes gauge and adjusts rheostat to regulate temperature of coating material in reservoir. Examines felt as it emerges from rollers to ensure that coating material is applied according to specifications. May feel moving felt to determine whether granules are being deposited uniformly and are adhering as specified. May be designated according to type of coating applied as Coater, Asphalt (nonmet. min.); Coater, Slate (nonmet. min.).
GOE: 06.02.18 STRENGTH: L GED: R3 M1 L2 SVP: 4 DLU: 77

554.684-010 CAUSTIC OPERATOR (plastic-synth.)

Immerses plastics sheets into tank containing heated caustic solution to impart finish to sheet surface: Places sheets into tank. Tests water temperature and solution concentration, using thermometer and hydrometer. Turns steam valve to regulate temperature and adds water or caustic solution to maintain specified concentration of solution. Removes sheets from tank after specified time and

places them in rinse tub or under water spray. Stacks rinsed sheets on absorbent cardboard preparatory to drying and inspection.
GOE: 06.04.13 STRENGTH: M GED: R2 M1 L1 SVP: 3 DLU: 77

554.684-014 FOAM DISPENSER (rubber goods)

Sprays padding solution (liquid rubber foam) in formed skins (shaped plastic sheets) with hose to produce automotive padded products, such as dashboards and door panels: Positions cardboard inserts at defroster locations and ignition cluster to prevent buckling during cure. Positions metal reinforcement panels at clusters and edges of product to be cured into skin. Dispenses solution in specified areas of skin and pours solution from cardboard containers around clusters and metal panels to prevent overflow.
GOE: 06.04.32 STRENGTH: M GED: R2 M1 L1 SVP: 3 DLU: 77

554.685-010 BULK-SEALER OPERATOR (plastic-synth.)

Tends automatic, radiant-heat bulk sealer that bonds plastic sheets for fabricating bags: Places lifts (two sheets of plastic film separated by single sheet of paper) alternated with asbestos pads on piston of sealer. Straightens disarranged sheets, using wooden paddle. Starts sealer in which plastic film is bonded as piston slowly travels through heated chamber. Inspects samples of bonded sheets to detect machine malfunction.
GOE: 06.04.02 STRENGTH: L GED: R2 M1 L1 SVP: 2 DLU: 77

554.685-014 COATING-AND-BAKING OPERATOR (any industry)

Tends equipment that automatically applies and bakes enamel or other coating onto fabricated steel products: Fills machine reservoir with coating solution, such as lacquer, enamel, or varnish. Starts conveyor or feed rolls that carry products to be coated and baked, through equipment. Sets heating unit at specified temperature and starts pumps and exhaust fans. Feeds products onto conveyor or between feed rolls that apply coating. Examines products emerging from baking unit for conformance to coating thickness and appearance specifications. May mix coating to prescribed viscosity, using viscometer. May gauge thickness of coating to determine adherence to quality control specifications, using dial indicator. May be designated according to equipment or process employed as Flash-Oven Operator (elec. equip.); Operator, Coating Furnace (cutlery-hrdwr.); or according to product coated as Coating-Machine Operator, Metal Tags And Signs (fabrication, nec).
GOE: 06.04.21 STRENGTH: L GED: R3 M1 L2 SVP: 3 DLU: 77

554.685-018 COMBINING-MACHINE OPERATOR (plastic-synth.)

Tends combining-roll machine that presses and impregnates synthetic resins and glass fibers between continuous sheets of plastics film to form homogenous sheeting of specified thickness preparatory to molding operations: Turns crank to adjust opening between rolls to form sheeting of specified thickness. Verifies width of opening with feeler gauge. Threads plastics film through rolls. Presses switch to start machine and observes flow of materials through machine to detect foreign particles and machine malfunctions. Moves lever to adjust tension on sheeting and to synchronize speed of sheeting with speed of belt.
GOE: 06.04.20 STRENGTH: L GED: R3 M1 L1 SVP: 4 DLU: 77

554.685-022 LINER REROLL TENDER (rubber goods; rubber tire) alternate titles: reroll tender; wrapper rewinder

Tends machine that cleans, smooths, repairs, and rerolls fabric liners for reuse in winding uncured rubber and fabric materials, calendered rubber or rubberized fabric: Positions liner roll in letoff bracket manually or by use of hoist. Starts machine and guides liner through rollers to ensure evenness of liner and removal of wrinkles. Examines liner for adhering rubber particles and torn areas. Scrapes rubber particles from liner with handtool. Sews additional fabric onto liners or repairs defective areas, using sewing machine. May verify weight and length of roll, using scale and yardage gauge.
GOE: 06.04.07 STRENGTH: H GED: R2 M1 L1 SVP: 2 DLU: 77

554.685-026 SIZING-MACHINE OPERATOR (nonmet. min.)

Tends machine that coats cloth, fiber, or paper with glue or other adhesive to prepare material for coating of abrasive: Starts machine and feeds precut blanks into machine, or mounts roll of base material on machine spindles for automatic feed through machine. Pours liquid adhesive into container on machine.
GOE: 06.04.21 STRENGTH: L GED: R2 M1 L1 SVP: 3 DLU: 77

554.685-030 LAMINATOR (wood prod., nec)

Tends laminating machine that bonds decorative material, such as plastic or paper, to face of hardboard panels: Conveys rolls of materials specified in work order from storage area to laminating machine, using forklift truck. Positions roll on machine carriage, using chain hoist. Pulls end of material from roll onto takeup rollers of machine and turns handwheel that moves carriage to align material with panels. Turns dials and moves levers to set machine roller speed, roller pressure, and heating unit temperature, following processing specifications. Turns valve to replenish glue supply. Depresses buttons to start machine. Inspects and measures first panels discharged from machine to verify correct alignment of bonded material on panel, using tape measure. Adjusts controls to correct machine operations such as speed of machine units. Severs material between laminated panels, using cutter, to free panels discharging onto off bearing conveyor. Refills glue reservoir as required. Performs routine maintenance.
GOE: 06.04.34 STRENGTH: L GED: R3 M1 L2 SVP: 3 DLU: 86

554.685-034 PHOTORESIST LAMINATOR, PRINTED CIRCUIT BOARD (electron. comp.) alternate titles: hot roll laminator; laminating machine tender

Tends machine that laminates dry photoresist film to surfaces of panels used in manufacturing printed circuit boards (PCB's): Mounts rolls of photoresist

film and plastic protective film on machine spindles. Threads film through machine rollers and secures film to takeup spindles. Presses button to activate machine. Adjusts controls to regulate speed, temperature, and pressure of laminating rollers. Moves levers and adjusts controls to align panels with edge of film. Feeds panels into roller, or positions panels on conveyor that feeds panels into laminating machine. Observes lamination process, monitors speed and temperature gauges, and adjusts controls to ensure compliance with standards. Removes laminated panels from machine. Cuts excess photoresist and protective plastic film from panel edges, using knife. May tend machine that scrubs, cleans, and dries PCB panels prior to laminating process [SCRUBBER MACHINE TENDER (electron. comp.) 599.685-134]. May examine laminated panels for defects.
GOE: 06.04.09 STRENGTH: M GED: R2 M1 L2 SVP: 2 DLU: 89

554.686-010 CALENDER FEEDER (rubber goods)
Feeds milled rubber stock into rolls of calendering machine to maintain continuous supply: Lifts pig (roll) of rubber stock from warmup mill conveyor and pushes it between horizontal rotating rolls until stock is drawn between and rolled around calender rolls. Turns wheels or capstan bolts to adjust distance between rolls to produce sheeting of specified thickness. May mount roll of backing material, such as sponge rubber, insole mixture, or cloth fabric, in cradle and thread it through rolls for coating with rubber.
GOE: 06.04.13 STRENGTH: H GED: R1 M1 L1 SVP: 2 DLU: 77

554.686-014 CALENDER-LET-OFF HELPER (rubber goods; rubber tire)
Positions fabric rolls and string spools on *letoff rack* and removes empty roll shells from calender machine. Inserts ends of fabric into hot press to splice them. Conveys fabric rolls to and from storage, calender, and production areas, using electric crane hoist or forklift. Cleans dip tank.
GOE: 06.04.40 STRENGTH: H GED: R2 M1 L1 SVP: 2 DLU: 77

554.686-018 CALENDER-OPERATOR HELPER (rubber goods; rubber tire) alternate titles: liner-roll changer; rubber-calender helper; wind-up operator
Performs any of following duties at calendering machine to facilitate coating, imprinting, or forming rubber sheeting or rubberized fabric: Changes fabric rolls and roll shells, using overhead hoist, on *letoff racks* and *windup racks.* Threads material through machine. Observes operation to detect faulty calendering. Sets yardage counter. Turns handwheels, moves lever, or presses buttons on control panel to adjust sheeting tension and windup speed. Prepares and attaches identification tag to calendered roll. May splice uncoated roll to end of roll in process inserting gum strip between ends and vulcanizing in bar splice press. May read yardage gauge and compare weight for conformance to specifications. May relieve CALENDER OPERATOR (rubber goods; rubber tire). Performs other duties as described under HELPER (any industry) Master Title.
GOE: 06.04.13 STRENGTH: H GED: R2 M1 L1 SVP: 2 DLU: 77

554.686-022 CALENDER-WIND-UP HELPER (rubber goods; rubber tire)
Positions liner rolls on windup rack and lowers full calender rolls to floor, using hoist. Cuts roll and starts fabric liner into liner rolls. Trims ragged fabric edges, using scissors. Examines fabric for wrinkles or other defects and tags finished rolls to show weight, yardage, and stock type.
GOE: 06.04.29 STRENGTH: M GED: R1 M1 L1 SVP: 2 DLU: 77

554.687-010 SPREADER (plastic-synth.) alternate titles: impregnator
Impregnates fiberglass matting and other fabric materials with resin compounds for use in laminating plastic products: Places cellophane or wax paper on worktable and spreads resin compounds over sheet evenly with hand spreader. Places precut fabric matting on resin and rolls it with wire-mesh-covered roller to saturate matting. May weigh specified quantities of plastics ingredients on scale and dump them into containers for use in molding plastic products. May pour premixed resins into saturating tank and thread fabric through rollers of impregnating machine to prepare material for laminating. May cut specified patterns from impregnated fabric, using template, hand shears, and knife.
GOE: 06.04.27 STRENGTH: M GED: R2 M1 L1 SVP: 2 DLU: 77

555   GRINDING AND CRUSHING OCCUPATIONS

This group includes occupations concerned with reducing materials to smaller particles, such as granules, grits, powder, or paste, by means of compression, smashing, cutting, or a combination of these.

555.382-010 PULVERIZER-MILL OPERATOR (rubber goods; rubber reclaim.)
Operates machine to prechop and pulverize vulcanized scrap rubber for reuse: Transfers material between storage and work areas on pallet, using forklift truck. Starts prechopper, pulverizer, and connecting conveyor. Places box on scale under discharge hopper of pulverizer to load ground material to specified weight. Loads scrap into prechop hopper, selecting it according to specified type, compound, and color. Examines scrap while loading and removes foreign matter, such as metal, cloth, and plastic. Observes thermometers and dials for room and exhaust temperatures and amperage used. Adjusts speed of conveyor feed to pulverizer to avoid overloading and prevent overheating and burning material. Observes temperature indicators on control panel of water cooling sys-

tem and air vents, turns valve to adjust water flow, and opens ports to increase airflow to cool machine jacket or grinding stock. Examines ground rubber for size and adjusts gap of discharge opening to prevent rubber from passing until ground to desired fineness. Observes magnetic grid at mouth of pulverizer that screens pellets to remove any metal missed on visual inspection. Removes screen and wipes off accumulated metal, using cloth. Folds and tapes filled box top, and marks weight and compound number on box. Posts amount and type of ground rubber processed to production record.
GOE: 06.02.13 STRENGTH: M GED: R3 M2 L2 SVP: 4 DLU: 77

555.565-010 MILL ATTENDANT I (chemical)
Tends system of grinders, crushers, conveyors, vibrating screens, and elevators in salt mill that crush and screen rock salt extracted from mine: Moves switches, levers, and other controls on instrument panels to start and stop equipment. Reads gauges to verify specified operation of equipment. Starts and stops various conveyors to control direction of flow, to store salt of specified size in designated storage bins. Observes and listens to operation of equipment and reports malfunctions to supervisor.
GOE: 05.12.07 STRENGTH: M GED: R3 M1 L1 SVP: 3 DLU: 77

555.585-010 CUTTER OPERATOR (plastic-synth.)
Tends machine that shreds woodpulp to specified size for use as filler in producing plastics materials: Inserts mandrel through core of woodpulp roll and mounts roll on unreeling stand, using overhead hoist. Threads sheet into machine feed rolls and adjusts cutting blade, using handtools. Starts machine and observes discharge of shredded pulp into conveyor system or automatic weigh bin to ascertain conformity to specifications. Cleans dust from equipment, using airhose or brush. Records weight and number of rolls cut. May adjust braking device to prevent bulking or tearing of sheet.
GOE: 06.04.03 STRENGTH: M GED: R3 M1 L1 SVP: 3 DLU: 77

555.665-010 SHREDDER TENDER (chemical)
Tends machine that chops and shreds animal stock (skins, splits, fleshings, and trimmings) used in making glue. Lifts stock from table, places stock on conveyor leading into machine and starts machine. Greases and oils machine. May signal other workers to load stock onto conveyor.
GOE: 06.04.19 STRENGTH: L GED: R2 M1 L1 SVP: 2 DLU: 77

555.682-010 MILLER II (chemical)
Operates mixing, screening, and milling machines to process salt: Installs specified size screens and rollers in milling machine, using handtools to obtain salt crystals of designated sizes. Opens chute to admit salt into milling machine and starts machine. Brushes oversized salt from vibrating screen to prevent clogging. May be designated according to salt product being milled as Miller, Kiln-Dried Salt (chemical).
GOE: 06.02.11 STRENGTH: H GED: R3 M1 L1 SVP: 7 DLU: 77

555.682-014 ROLLER-MILL OPERATOR (paint & varnish) alternate titles: paint grinder, roller mill
Operates mill equipped with rollers to grind paste of premixed ingredients, such as pigments, resins, solvents, oils, and plasticizers, for use in paint, lacquer, and ink: Moves controls to set specified roll spacing and pressure. Starts flow of water through roll cooling system to prevent ignition or discoloration of paste. Adjusts feed gate to regulate flow of paste from hopper onto feeder roll. Secures scraper blade to takeoff roll and bolts chute to scraper blade, allowing paste to flow from roll into thinning and storage tanks or scrapes paste from mill apron into container, using spatula. Tests paste sample for fineness, using grind gauge, or sends sample to laboratory for analysis. Adjusts roll pressure controls to regulate flow of paste during grinding. Cleans equipment, using scrapers and solvents. May pump specified types and quantities of thinners into thinning tank. May blend specified extenders (chemicals that increase bulk of paint) with paste, using portable mixer.
GOE: 06.02.11 STRENGTH: M GED: R3 M2 L2 SVP: 5 DLU: 77

555.682-018 SAND-MILL GRINDER (paint & varnish)
Operates sand mill that grinds premixed paint ingredients to disperse solid ingredients in vehicle: Starts mixer to combine ingredients settled in portable tub. Hangs hose in tub and attaches opposite end to sand mill intake. Turns valve to circulate cooling water through jacket to prevent mill overheating. Presses buttons to start mill agitator and pump. Draws paste sample to test for dispersion, using grind gauge, and adjusts pump speed as indicated by test results. Turns lever to open gate and starts pump to discharge ground mixture from machine. Washes residue from filter screen, using brush and solvent. Starts pump to clean sand mill and hose system, using solvent.
GOE: 06.02.11 STRENGTH: M GED: R3 M1 L2 SVP: 3 DLU: 77

555.682-022 STONE-MILL OPERATOR (paint & varnish) alternate titles: paint grinder, stone mill; stone-grinder operator
Operates mills equipped with grinding stones to grind paint or paint ingredients to specified fineness: Weighs ingredients, such as pigments and oil on scale and dumps them into feed hopper of mill. Starts mill and turns valve to admit steam into mill jacket to heat ingredients. Feels or examines mixture to determine fineness of grind. Turns screws to set clearance between grinding stones to grind ingredients to specified fineness. Opens valve or starts pump to transfer mixture into cooling and storage tanks. Cleans millstones, hoppers, and scrapers, using hot water hose, solvent, and brushes. Replaces worn grinding stones, using handtools and hoist.
GOE: 06.02.11 STRENGTH: H GED: R3 M1 L2 SVP: 3 DLU: 77

555.685-010 BEATER OPERATOR (chemical) alternate titles: pulping-machine operator

Tends machine that cuts strands of nitrocotton or pyrocotton into smaller segments for processing: Pumps nitrocotton slurry to feed tanks, starts beater blades, and opens valves to force slurry against blades. Turns handwheel to adjust speed of blades during operation according to gauge reading and process specifications, to produce uniformly beaten product. Pumps beaten slurry over sieve to remove water. Submits samples of batch to laboratory for approval of product texture. Starts agitators in tub to loosen nitrocotton and pumps it into *poaching* tubs for removal of impurities.
GOE: 06.04.11 STRENGTH: L GED: R2 M1 L1 SVP: 3 DLU: 77

555.685-014 BONE CRUSHER (chemical) alternate titles: glue-bone crusher

Tends machine that crushes animal bones used in manufacturing animal glue: Starts bone crushing machine conveyor that carries bones into crushing machine. Pushes button to start second conveyor that carries crushed bones from machine into cooking tanks for further processing. May tend hydraulic press that extracts grease and glue from cooked bones and be designated Steam-Bone-Press Tender (chemical).
GOE: 06.04.19 STRENGTH: L GED: R2 M1 L1 SVP: 2 DLU: 77

555.685-018 COPRA PROCESSOR (soap & rel.)

Tends battery of machines that grind and filter copra (dried coconut meat) into coconut oil and meal: Turns valves to regulate flow of steam that heats crushing machine to specified temperature. Starts conveyors, crushing machines, and expeller and signals worker to start feeding copra into feed hoppers. Feels ground copra to ensure that texture conforms to specifications. Observes oil flowing from expeller for presence of excess solids, and feels coconut meal to determine if meal contains excessive oil. Observes gauges and clarity of oil leaving filter presses to determine if pressure inside filters is within specified limits. Transfers oil to standby filter presses when clarity or pressure deviates from prescribed standards. Records oil and meal production in log.
GOE: 06.04.19 STRENGTH: L GED: R3 M1 L2 SVP: 3 DLU: 77

555.685-022 CRUSHER TENDER (fabrication, nec) alternate titles: frame-and-scrap crusher; frame crusher; scrap crusher

Tends machine that crushes scrap vinyl, asphalt, and asbestos preparatory to reprocessing into floor tile: Starts continuous flow of scrap material from calender and punch press onto conveyors into crusher. Observes flow of material and regulates speed of feed conveyor. Removes foreign material from conveyor and dislodges jammed material. May grind and screen mottle into various size chips used to produce marbelized effect on hard surface floor coverings.
GOE: 06.04.09 STRENGTH: H GED: R2 M1 L1 SVP: 2 DLU: 77

555.685-026 GRINDER (plastic prod.; plastic-synth.) alternate titles: cutter operator; pulverizer

Tends machine that grinds particles of solid plastics materials to specified size: Starts machine and dumps or shovels plastics into hopper. Observes equipment to detect stoppages. May clean equipment with airhose, scrapers, or brushes. May tend machine that grinds scrap material for reuse and be designated Regrinder Operator (plastic prod.).
GOE: 06.04.02 STRENGTH: H GED: R2 M1 L1 SVP: 2 DLU: 77

555.685-030 GRINDER (rubber goods; rubber reclaim.) alternate titles: chopper and cracker feeder; cracker; hog operator

Tends mill and separating equipment that grinds scrap or devulcanized rubber to reclaim and reprocess rubber: Turns handwheel to adjust clearance between corrugated rollers of machine to accommodate stock. Loads rubber into machine hopper. Starts machine and observes stock to ensure passage through rollers. May use magnetic device to remove metal particles from ground scrap rubber. Moves handtrucks, containing rubber stock, into position for loading. May clean or replace clogged shaker screen that sifts out oversize pieces. May pick bead wires from ground rubber tire scrap [BEAD PICKER (rubber reclaim.)]. May be designated according to type of grinding as Fine Grinder (rubber reclaim.).
GOE: 06.04.07 STRENGTH: H GED: R2 M1 L2 SVP: 2 DLU: 77

555.685-034 GRINDER OPERATOR (chemical) alternate titles: crusher operator; mill operator; pulverizer tender

Tends machine that pulverizes solid or semisolid materials used in manufacturing chemicals and related products: Installs screens of specified type and mesh in machine, using handtools, or starts auxiliary shakers (vibrating screens) that size ground particles. Starts feed conveyors, or shovels or dumps materials into machine hopper. Starts grinder and observes ground product discharged onto conveyors or into containers for impurities, lumps, or improperly sized particles. Cleans machine and conveyors, using airhose, scrapers, and brushes, to prepare equipment for grinding subsequent batches. May shovel ground product into containers for storage, shipment, or further processing. May tend machines that fill bags or drums with product. May weigh containers of materials, record weight, and enter number of containers filled on inventory records. May be designated according to material or product ground as Filtrose Crusher (chemical); Paradichlorobenzene-Machine Operator (chemical).
GOE: 06.04.11 STRENGTH: M GED: R2 M1 L2 SVP: 3 DLU: 78

555.685-038 MILL ATTENDANT II (chemical)

Tends roll mill that crushes and disperses particles of pigment material in batches of viscid organic pigments: Starts roll mill, and scoops or pours batch of viscid organic pigment into hopper of roll mill. Observes distribution of pigment particles on roll of mill, and moves lever to adjust rollers to ensure even grinding and distribution of pigment particles in viscid batch. Places container at discharge end of mill to collect batch. Clamps lid on container to prepare container for shipment. Cleans roll mill, using solvent, brush, and cloth.
GOE: 06.04.11 STRENGTH: M GED: R2 M1 L1 SVP: 2 DLU: 77

555.685-042 PELLET-PRESS OPERATOR (chemical) alternate titles: granulator operator; hydraulic-press operator; mechanical-press operator

Tends hydraulic press and auxiliary equipment that forms, granulates, and sizes calcium chloride prior to use in chemical processing: Starts automatically fed ram press that forms calcium chloride into pellets. Examines pellets ejected from press and turns dials that regulate length of ram stroke and control cooling of press, according to specifications. Tends jaw crusher, granulator, and screens that crush, granulate, and screen calcium chloride to produce granules of specified size. Lubricates and repairs equipment, using handtools. Places drums under chute to fill with finished product for shipment, storage, or further processing.
GOE: 06.04.11 STRENGTH: M GED: R3 M2 L1 SVP: 3 DLU: 77

555.685-046 PULVERIZER (chemical) alternate titles: blender; salicylic-acid blender

Tends machine that pulverizes lumps of salicylic acid: Starts machine and flow of lumps of salicylic acid into machine. Dumps pulverized salicylic into drums. Weighs and seals drums and uses powered handtruck to transport or stack filled drums.
GOE: 06.04.11 STRENGTH: H GED: R2 M1 L1 SVP: 2 DLU: 77

555.685-050 SCRATCHER TENDER (fabrication, nec)

Tends mill equipped with scratcher that granulates color mix for use in hard-surface floor covering: Adjusts roll clearance and speed of scratcher motor to attain required particle size, using handtools. Starts scratch mill, and positions pans under discharge trough to receive granulated mix from scratch mill. Records number of pans filled. Records color and pattern data on tickets and affixes tickets to loaded handtrucks. Pushes handtrucks to storage area. May weigh and add oils or other liquid materials to mix as required. May be designated according to task performed as Color Receiver (fabrication, nec).
GOE: 06.04.09 STRENGTH: H GED: R2 M1 L1 SVP: 3 DLU: 77

555.685-054 SECOND OPERATOR, MILL TENDER (chemical)

Tends roller mill and auxiliary equipment, such as pumps and agitators (reaction vessels) that facilitate production of phosphoric acid by strong-acid process from reaction of sulfuric acid with ground phosphate rock. Pumps acid into tank trucks and loads ground phosphate rock into hopper trucks as directed.
GOE: 06.04.11 STRENGTH: L GED: R3 M1 L1 SVP: 3 DLU: 77

555.685-058 SHREDDER OPERATOR (plastic-synth.)

Tends machine that heats and chops sheets of alkali cellulose into crumbs for use in producing rayon: Opens hatch of machine to accommodate sheets of cellulose dumped into machine by other workers. Closes and secures hatch and starts machine. Turns valves and observes thermometers to maintain temperature of product at plant standard. Stops machine after prescribed time for unloading by other workers.
GOE: 06.04.09 STRENGTH: L GED: R2 M1 L2 SVP: 3 DLU: 77

555.685-062 SOAP GRINDER (soap & rel.) alternate titles: frame stripper and crusher

Tends one or more machines that crush, screen, and pulverize soap solids and chips to form powder: Dumps soap chips into hopper of crusher, using shovel or chain hoist. Starts equipment, observes operations, and stops machines when malfunctions occur. Observes sifting of soap granules in power-driven shaker-screen and removes chunks for further grinding in crusher. Places empty drum or bag under spout of pulverizer to receive soap powder. Removes filled containers to storage area.
GOE: 06.04.19 STRENGTH: H GED: R2 M1 L1 SVP: 2 DLU: 77

555.685-066 WHEEL-MILL OPERATOR (chemical)

Tends grinding mill that crushes powder or explosives ingredients, such as sulfur, saltpeter, and charcoal, used in manufacturing gunpowder: Charges mill with prescribed amounts of ingredients. Starts mill wheel revolving for specified time or until materials are crushed and mixed and rakes or dumps contents into containers for storage or further processing. When tending mill that crushes finished powder to grains of specified size to attain uniform ballistic properties, is designated Graining Operator (chemical). May tend vibrating screens to separate particles of varying sizes.
GOE: 06.04.11 STRENGTH: M GED: R2 M1 L1 SVP: 2 DLU: 77

555.686-010 BLOCK-BREAKER OPERATOR (chemical) alternate titles: digester operator

Feeds equipment that breaks up cakes of dehydrated nitrocellulose to facilitate subsequent mixing and packing processes: Feeds nitrocellulose cakes into hopper of electrically powered cylinder fitted with spikes that break up cakes. Removes nitrocellulose for further processing and packing. May monitor scale to determine when specified amount of smokeless powder is expelled from machine into tub and to turn lever to stop machine.
GOE: 06.04.11 STRENGTH: H GED: R2 M1 L1 SVP: 2 DLU: 77

555.686-014 SOAP CHIPPER (soap & rel.)

Feeds soap bars into machine that reduces them to chips: Starts machine and conveyor belt. Dumps soap bars onto conveyor belt or feeds them into machine

hopper. Observes operation of machine that automatically reduces bars to chips and discharges chips onto conveyor belt or into tray. Routes soap chips by conveyor belt to drying room, or spreads chips evenly in trays and removes them to drying room. May fill boxes with soap flakes or bars of soap.
GOE: 06.04.09 STRENGTH: M GED: R1 M1 L1 SVP: 2 DLU: 77

555.687-010 SCALE OPERATOR (chemical)
Weighs finished glue from crushing units, and dumps it into containers for shipment.
GOE: 06.03.02 STRENGTH: L GED: R2 M1 L2 SVP: 2 DLU: 77

556 CASTING AND MOLDING OCCUPATIONS, N.E.C.

This group includes occupations, not elsewhere classified, concerned with shaping or solidifying molten or powdered materials by pouring, injecting, or pressing them into molds or other receptacles, and allowing or causing them to solidify.

556.130-010 SUPERVISOR, PLASTICS FABRICATION (boot & shoe; inst. & app.; plastic prod.; plastic-synth.)
Supervises and coordinates activities of workers engaged in casting, molding, inspecting, and packaging fabricated plastic products: Sets up and adjusts or oversees set up of machines and equipment used to fabricate products, according to blueprint specifications. Reviews production schedules and assigns work. Inspects products for defects, such as surface flaws, color, flashing, or die marks. Measures product to verify conformance to specifications, using measuring instruments, such as micrometers, vernier calipers, and plug gauges. Observes packaging operations and examines containers to verify conformance to standards. Trains worker in job duties and production techniques. Performs other duties described under SUPERVISOR (any industry) Master Title.
GOE: 06.01.01 STRENGTH: L GED: R4 M3 L4 SVP: 7 DLU: 89

556.130-014 SUPERVISOR, PLASTICS (toy-sport equip.)
Supervises and coordinates activities of workers engaged in manufacturing molded plastic toys and toy parts: Sets up injection-molding machines. Trains workers in operation of machines and assembly methods. Performs other duties as described under SUPERVISOR (any industry) Master Title.
GOE: 06.02.01 STRENGTH: L GED: R4 M3 L3 SVP: 7 DLU: 77

556.130-018 MOLDING SUPERVISOR (plastic prod.)
Supervises and coordinates activities of workers engaged in molding plastic products, applying knowledge of molding machine setup and operating techniques and production machining methods: Reads operating logs to identify inoperative injection or blow molding machines, determines reasons for machine malfunction, and arranges for machine repair. Reviews production schedules and work orders, and assigns duties to workers according to order priorities. Studies quality control reports to identify product defects and directs machine operators to adjust machines to eliminate flaws. Examines molded products from each machine to verify conformance to specifications. Conducts or directs training of new employees in machine operation. Confers with management and other supervisors to resolve production problems. Performs other duties as described under SUPERVISOR (any industry) Master Title.
GOE: 06.02.01 STRENGTH: L GED: R4 M3 L3 SVP: 6 DLU: 89

556.362-010 ARCH-CUSHION-PRESS OPERATOR (rubber goods)
Operates steam-heated conveyor press that molds and vulcanizes uncured sponge rubber to form arch cushions for rubber footwear: Reads work ticket to determine number of molds and blanks required for each style and size cushion. Notifies CALENDER OPERATOR (rubber goods; rubber tire) of stock thickness and DIE CUTTER (any industry) of dies to use and amounts of blanks needed. Selects required number of molds and baskets of blanks and supplies them to workers. Starts conveyor press and turns valves to regulate heat of vulcanizing plates. Turns handwheel to adjust distance between vulcanizing plates and molds, using feeler gauge. Directs workers engaged in positioning blanks in mold cavities and in removing molded cushions. Observes operations and examines finished product for defects, such as lumps, pits, and blisters, and to determine if mold cavities are filled and rubber is completely vulcanized. Operates warming mill to prepare stock for calendering from which blanks are cut for use in cushion press.
GOE: 06.02.13 STRENGTH: M GED: R3 M2 L2 SVP: 4 DLU: 77

556.380-010 MOLD SETTER (inst. & app.; office machines; plastic prod.; recording) alternates titles: die setter; setter, plastics-molding machine
Sets up and adjusts automatic compression, injection, or transfer machines used to mold plastic materials to specified shape, following blueprints, and utilizing knowledge of machine functions: Reads specifications to determine machine setup and prescribed temperature and time settings. Positions, aligns, and secures assembled mold or mold components, and machine accessories, onto machine press bed, according to guide marks, using hoist, power tools, and handtools. Attaches connecting lines, such as air, oil, or water to mold, and adjusts controls to regulate mold temperature. Sets machine controls and turns dials to regulate specified machine forming pressure and plastic curing time in mold. Starts machine to produce sample product. Measures and visually inspects sample product for surface and dimensional defects, using microscope, micrometer, and gauges, and adjusts machine setup to eliminate defects. May

repair and maintain machines and auxiliary equipment, using handtools and power tools. May be designated according to type of machine set up as Compression-Molding-Machine Setter (plastic prod.); Injection-Molding-Machine Setter (plastics prod.).
GOE: 06.01.02 STRENGTH: M GED: R3 M2 L3 SVP: 6 DLU: 89

556.380-014 PREFORM-MACHINE OPERATOR (button & notion)
Sets up and adjusts battery of automatic machines that compress powdered plastics into tablets used in molding plastic buttons: Installs specified dies and punches onto machine holder plate according to tablet size specifications, using wrench. Adjusts stroke of punch according to tablet density specifications. Starts battery of automatic machines that compress powdered plastics into tablets. Breaks sample tablets between fingers to test hardness. Weighs sample lot of tablets to verify density. Adjusts machine controls to eliminate tablet defects.
GOE: 06.01.02 STRENGTH: L GED: R3 M1 L2 SVP: 4 DLU: 77

556.382-014 INJECTION-MOLDING-MACHINE OPERATOR (plastic prod.) alternate titles: injection molder; molder
Sets up and operates injection-molding machines to cast products from thermoplastic materials: Installs dies on machine, according to work order specifications, using clamps, bolts, and handtools. Sets machine controls, regulating molding temperature, volume of plastic, molding pressure and time, according to knowledge of plastics and molding procedures. Dumps premixed plastic powders or pellets into hopper, and starts machine. Pulls lever to close dies and inject plastic into dies to cast part. Removes finished product from dies, using handtools. Trims excess material from part, using knife. May mix thermoplastic materials and coloring pigments in mixing machine, according to formula. May grind scrap plastic into powder for reuse.
GOE: 06.02.13 STRENGTH: M GED: R3 M2 L2 SVP: 5 DLU: 77

556.382-018 POLYSTYRENE-BEAD MOLDER (plastic prod.)
Operates preexpander and continuous molding machine that expands and molds polystyrene beads under heat and pressure, forming bead board: Reads work order to determine resin type and density requirements for bead board production. Shoves intake tube in resin and presses tube into coupling of venturi feed system. Presses buttons and turns valves to activate centrifuge, supply steam, and feed resin to expander. Fills volumetric can with beads and weighs beads to determine density, using balance scale. Compares bead density with production requirements. Reads steam pressure and temperature gauges and turns steam valve or rotates auger disk, adjusting heat and resin feed rate to control bead density. Connects hose of molder feed hopper to aging bin and pushes feed hopper into place to feed molding machine. Turns venturi feed valve, sending air through feeder to draw beads from hopper into molder. Starts molding machine. Guides bead board from molder through rollers of trimmer and saw to start board. Monitors gauges and observes operation of molding machine and equipment to ensure operation according to specifications. Inspects bead board for specified fusion and finish. Turns steam and air valves to adjust heat and bead feed rate to prevent machine overload and to correct flaws in bead board. Records lot number of resin, feed rate, and steam pressure, for various densities and board dimensions. Computes production in board feet to determine output.
GOE: 06.02.13 STRENGTH: M GED: R3 M2 L2 SVP: 4 DLU: 77

556.385-010 CENTRIFUGAL-CASTING-MACHINE TENDER (button & notion)
Tends centrifugal casting machine that casts plastic cylinders used in fabrication of button blanks: Mixes resins and chemicals to form liquid plastic, following formula. Sets timing device which stops machine automatically, and presses button to start centrifugal casting machine. Pours liquid plastic into rotating drum of machine that spreads, hardens, and shapes mixture into cylindrical layer of uniform thickness on wall of drum. Slits cylinder in straight line along length, at end of cycle, using razor, and peels and removes sheet from drum wall. Uncurls and spreads sheet on table and dusts sheet with powder, using mitt, to dry surface. May pour plastic mixture of different color onto semihardened first layer. May tend machine that cuts button blanks from sheet.
GOE: 06.04.19 STRENGTH: M GED: R3 M2 L2 SVP: 3 DLU: 77

556.484-010 SCAGLIOLA MECHANIC (nonmet. min.) alternate titles: imitation-marble mechanic
Molds imitation marble (scagliola) into objects, such as desk sets, penholders, sections of pillars, and interior decorative slabs: Compounds materials in vat according to formula. Pours mixture into molds or on glass-flanged table. Dumps set pieces out of molds. Smooths objects with brick covered with moist emery, rottenstone, or other abrasive. Polishes parts with felt-covered brick. May use acetic acid solution to increase polishing quality of felt and add to luster of polished surface.
GOE: 06.02.30 STRENGTH: H GED: R2 M2 L1 SVP: 5 DLU: 77

556.582-010 PLATE MOLDER (pen & pencil; print. & pub.)
Operates hydraulic press, equipped with steam or electrically heated platens, to cast rubber or plastic matrices and rubber dies or types: Turns dial to set electric thermostat or steam valves to maintain specified temperature in press. Inserts chase containing type into press to heat type to specified temperature, or inserts engraved metal plate into press. Places sheet of hard plastic or similar material on type and allows to heat for prescribed period of time. Pulls lever to impress material into type form to make matrix. Peels matrix from type, places rubber of plastic sheet on matrix and inserts it in press. Places metal strips (bearers) of specified thickness along sides of rubber or plastic and matrix

to limit depth of pressing and determine thickness of die. Repeats heating and casting process to produce rubber die. Trims excess rubber from edges of designs, letters, symbols, and figures, using curved knife. May mix casting compound and water to puttylike consistency, spread compound on mold plate, invert casting plate over type, press compound into type and dry compound in oven. When making rubber dies or type, may be known as Vulcanizer, Rubber Plate (pen & pencil; print. & pub.).
GOE: 06.02.18 STRENGTH: M GED: R3 M2 L2 SVP: 4 DLU: 77

556.585-010 CASTING-ROOM OPERATOR (plastic-synth.) alternate titles: hopper operator

Tends equipment that forces viscose fluid between two adjustable metal bars and into acid bath that coagulates fluid into continuous sheet of cellophane: Reads gauges and observes image on video display screen to ascertain thickness and uniformity of cellophane sheet. Turns clamp nuts, using wrench, to adjust bar gap to produce sheet of specified thickness and uniformity. Turns valves and starts pumps to regulate flow of viscose. Maintains log of operating conditions and output of casting machine.
GOE: 06.04.13 STRENGTH: L GED: R3 M2 L2 SVP: 4 DLU: 77

556.585-014 POLYMERIZATION-OVEN OPERATOR (plastic-synth.) alternate titles: oven attendant

Tends steam oven that heats liquid plastics in glass molds (cells) to form sheets: Examines and removes defective molds from handtrucks. Loads trucks holding molds into ovens and records time molds entered ovens. Turns steam and cold-air valves to maintain specified pressure and temperature in oven. Inserts knife into baked sheet or feels sheet to determine that sheet is baked to specifications.
GOE: 06.04.13 STRENGTH: M GED: R2 M1 L1 SVP: 3 DLU: 77

556.587-010 MOLD PARTER (plastic-synth.) alternate titles: cell stripper, final; parter

Removes plastics sheets from glass molds (cells): Positions mold on stand or table. Inserts wedge between edges of glass plates and pries slates from plastics sheet. Stacks plate glass on rack or trucks. Records weight of plastics sheets. May lower molds into soaking tanks to loosen plastics sheet, using hoist.
GOE: 06.04.40 STRENGTH: M GED: R2 M1 L1 SVP: 2 DLU: 77

556.665-010 CAKE-PRESS OPERATOR (plastic-synth.)

Tends hydraulic presses that compress and bake chipped, rolled, or slabbed plastics materials into cake molds for sheeting: Turns valves to regulate pressures and temperatures in baking and cooling presses. Turns dial indicator arm to set press-cycle time. Pulls hopper lever to fill mold with specified weight of plastics chips. Places platen on top of mold and lifts filled mold to roller conveyor. Pushes baked molds out of heated press, using bar. Pushes filled molds from conveyor and supply rack into baking press. Turns valve to close press. Observes meters and gauges to verify specified temperatures, pressures, and press-cycle times.
GOE: 06.04.13 STRENGTH: H GED: R3 M2 L1 SVP: 4 DLU: 77

556.665-014 CORRUGATOR OPERATOR (plastic-synth.)

Tends machine that pulls thermosetting plastics sheeting materials through preheating oven and forming frames to form sheets to specifications: Turns dials on control panel to regulate specified temperatures in oven and molds. Moves lever to regulate tension on sheeting. Observes gauges to verify temperatures. Observes width and alignment of sheeting to ensure flanging of sides. Positions mold frame laterally in machine to correct alignment. Feels stiffness and consistency of molded sheeting to detect machinery malfunctions. Signals PLASTICS-SPREADING-MACHINE OPERATOR (plastic-synth.) to synchronize feed of materials into molding process. Replaces molds in frame to conform to product specifications. Patches tears in film, using gummed tape.
GOE: 06.04.13 STRENGTH: L GED: R3 M2 L2 SVP: 4 DLU: 77

556.665-018 MOLDER, PIPE COVERING (plastic prod.)

Tends equipment that fuses granulated polystyrene into pipe coverings, used for insulation: Positions funnel into top of mold and dumps or opens chute of overhead hopper to load specified quantities of material. Removes funnel and adjusts stripper plate and cutter rim to ensure molding of material into specified sizes and shapes. Manually locks mold and opens steam valve to admit heat. Observes heat recorder and adjusts valves to attain specified temperature to fuse materials for prescribed period of time. Unlocks mold and removes pipe covering, using hoist. Moves product to storage area, using handtruck. May mold special products, such as toys and games, and be designated Specialty Molder (plastic prod.).
GOE: 06.04.13 STRENGTH: M GED: R2 M1 L1 SVP: 3 DLU: 77

556.682-010 BLOW-MOLDING-MACHINE OPERATOR (plastic prod.)

Sets up and operates blow molding machine to mold plastic products according to specifications: Turns valves to start flow of water and release air pressure to machine. Moves machine controls to set timing unit and temperature of heating unit and start automatic feed mechanism. Adjusts machine mandrel and aligns mandrel with mold chamber, using wrenches. Starts molding machine that automatically feeds material from mixing unit to mandrel and to mold chamber. Closes chamber to mold product under heat and pressure. Removes workpiece from mold after timing device opens mold, and trims excess material from workpiece, using knife or bandsaw. Regrinds excess material and unsatisfactory workpiece for reuse, using grinding machine. May weigh completed workpiece to determine accuracy of machine operation.
GOE: 06.02.13 STRENGTH: L GED: R3 M2 L2 SVP: 3 DLU: 77

556.682-014 COMPRESSION-MOLDING-MACHINE OPERATOR (elec. equip.; plastic prod.)

Sets up and operates compression molding machines to mold plastic and carbon, graphite, or copper powder products according to specifications: Installs dies on press, using clamps, bolts, and handtools, and coats dies with parting agents, according to work order. Sets thermostat to regulate temperature of dies. Weighs premixed compounds and dumps compound into die well, spreads fabric on die and dumps compound over fabric, or fills hoppers of machines that automatically supply compound to dies during machine operation, using scoop. Presses button or pulls lever to activate machines to compress compounds between dies to form and cure specified products. Removes cured products from mold, using handtools and airhose. Observes machine operation and examines products ejected by machines to determine whether products meet specifications, using calipers. Turns pressure control knobs, bolts, and handwheels to adjust machines. May mix catalysts and coloring pigments with plastic compound, using paddle and mixing machine. May operate compression molding machines to form product under pressure only and be designated Cold-Molding-Press Operator (plastic prod.). May be designated Press Operator, Carbon Products (elec. equip.).
GOE: 06.02.13 STRENGTH: H GED: R3 M2 L2 SVP: 5 DLU: 88

556.682-018 PLODDER OPERATOR (soap & rel.) alternate titles: plodding-machine operator

Sets up and operates plodder machine to compress milled soap into bars: Unbolts head of machine and inserts specified plate that shapes and sizes bar. Opens valves to admit steam into heating coils, water to reduce heat caused by friction on compression screw, and create vacuum to draw soap through machine. Unbolts filter cap from machine and changes filter. Starts machine. Inspects compressed bars for specified color, size, and smoothness.
GOE: 06.02.18 STRENGTH: L GED: R3 M1 L2 SVP: 4 DLU: 77

556.682-022 COMPRESSOR (elec. equip.; pharmaceut.)

Sets up and operates machine to compress granulated or powdered ingredients into products, such as medicinal tablets and storage battery pellets: Installs dies in machine and adjusts spring tension and ram pressure of air- or hydraulic-powered press, according to specifications, using handtools. Presses control button to activate machine. Scoops ingredients into hopper or positions canister of powder on top of hopper, using overhead lift. Raises lever to stop machine and collects samples of product, according to established frequency, using tweezers. Examines, weighs, and tests samples for defects, such as surface chips and pits, soft centers, and excessive brittleness, using micrometers, scale, and hardness tester; or determines dimensions of sample to verify machine setup, using calipers, micrometers, and go-not-go gauges. Routes sample to lab for analysis, according to procedure. Adjusts machine pressure and tension to remove product flaws and ensure conformity to product specifications. Records product information, such as scrap quantity, machine number, and ingredients, used to complete work ticket. Places completed work tickets with trays of product awaiting further processing. Removes and cleans dies and compression chambers, using swabs. May only operate machines and notify supervisor or setup personnel of needed adjustments to machines. May pour metal bottom sections of battery and battery pellets into bins of consolidation equipment that operates automatically in conjunction with press machines to insert pellets into cans to form partial assembly of battery. May apply heat to pellets to impart desired color prior to assembly into bottom sections of battery, using torch and asbestos squares. May be designated Compressor, Battery Pellets (elec. equip.).
GOE: 06.02.11 STRENGTH: M GED: R3 M2 L2 SVP: 4 DLU: 87

556.684-010 CELL INSPECTOR (plastic-synth.) alternate titles: mold inspector

Inspects viscous plastics material in plate glass molds (cells) and removes defects preparatory to curing: Examines material through glass sheet to detect defects, such as air bubbles, dirt particles, and other foreign matter. Stands cell on end to elevate bubbles to surface and inserts spatula between molds to remove bubbles and foreign matter from edges. Inserts metal clip into mold, using spatula, and maneuvers clip, using magnet to remove defects from body of cell. May weigh cell on floor scale.
GOE: 06.03.02 STRENGTH: L GED: R2 M1 L1 SVP: 4 DLU: 77

556.684-014 ENCAPSULATOR (aircraft mfg.) alternate titles: molder, resin

Seals and encapsulates magnetic, electrical, electronic, and mechanical components of aircraft and missile parts and assemblies in plastic and other sealant materials, using handtools, power tools, and equipment: Mixes specified amounts of resins, curing agents, and fillers in container, according to formula, using spatula. Cleans parts to be sealed and encapsulated, using solvents, brush, and rags. Positions component parts in molds and pours or injects sealing compound into molds. Places molds in preset oven for specified time to harden mixture around units. Smooths and finishes surfaces of hardened sealing compound, using scratch remover, files, sander, and other work aids. May apply protective coating to component parts by spraying or dipping parts in resin vat. May engrave identifying symbols, letters, and numbers on unit encasement, using pantograph engraving machine. May inspect components prior to sealing and encapsulating, using preset measuring devices. May operate curing equipment. May build temporary molds from metal, putty, plastic, and other materials.

GOE: 06.04.34 STRENGTH: M GED: R3 M2 L2 SVP: 4 DLU: 88

556.684-018 MOLD-FILLING OPERATOR (plastic-synth.) alternate titles: cell pourer; flat-sheet maker

Casts plastics resin monomer in glass molds (cells) to form sheets: Opens feedline to fill scale tank with specified amount of solution and mounts cell on filling table. Moves table lever to hold cell at inclined position and inserts funnel in cell opening. Fills mold with premeasured amount of syrup, using pitcher or hose. Turns valves to control solution flow rate and adjusts angle of cell to avoid formation of air bubbles. Removes funnel and seals mold opening with tape, gasket, or other sealing device. Places cell on rack.
GOE: 06.04.32 STRENGTH: M GED: R2 M1 L1 SVP: 4 DLU: 77

556.684-022 NEEDLE-BAR MOLDER (carpet & rug)

Positions loom needles into slots of mold and pours liquid resins into mold to cast needle bars for use in weaving on looms: Selects type and size mold according to type and size loom needles to be set. Weighs out and mixes resins and hardeners to prepare casting material. Inserts and aligns loom needles into slots of mold, and clamps top onto mold. Pours casting mixture into opening in mold and allows mixture to set for specified time. Removes cast needle bar from mold, using pliers, and smooths rough spots, using steel wool, sandpaper, and electric emery wheel. Breaks up cracked or broken needle bars, using hammer, to salvage reusable loom needles. Hammers out bent places in used loom needles to prepare needles for recasting.
GOE: 06.04.32 STRENGTH: L GED: R2 M1 L1 SVP: 2 DLU: 77

556.684-026 RUBBER MOLDER (fabrication, nec)

Molds rubber display statuettes and models of hands, feet, and heads for attachment to display mannequins: Brushes lubricant onto interior of mold. Pours liquid rubber into mold until full. Pours surplus rubber from mold after shell of rubber has formed on inside of mold. Strips form from mold after rubber has set. Trims edges of form, using knife and smooths surface, using sandpaper.
GOE: 06.02.29 STRENGTH: L GED: R2 M1 L1 SVP: 4 DLU: 77

556.684-030 LOADER-DEMOLDER (furniture)

Casts plastic furniture parts, using molds, furniture stock, and plastic molding compound and gun: Conveys pallets loaded with furniture stock to work site, using industrial truck. Places furniture stock inside specified mold, clamps mold to furniture stock, and places mold onto conveyor. Inserts nozzle of molder gun between mold and furniture stock and dispenses plastic compound into mold around furniture stock to cast plastic furniture parts, such as edge bands. Unclamps and removes cast parts from mold after specified setup time, using chisel and knife.
GOE: 06.04.32 STRENGTH: M GED: R2 M1 L1 SVP: 3 DLU: 86

556.685-010 AIR-BAG CURER (rubber tire)

Tends steam-heated press that molds and cures air bags used in automatic tire curing presses: Weighs slugs of rubber to obtain specified charge. Positions bag core in mold, using hoist. Places charge in mold cavity and presses switch to close press and start curing cycle. Lifts core from mold when curing cycle is completed. Pushes lever to lower hydraulic clamp on core and pulls air bag free, using hoist. Counts and tallies cured air bags. May set automatic timer for specified curing cycle.
GOE: 06.04.13 STRENGTH: M GED: R2 M1 L1 SVP: 2 DLU: 77

556.685-014 BLOCK-PRESS OPERATOR (chemical) alternate titles: powder-press operator

Tends hydraulic press that compresses smokeless powder into block form for further processing: Charges press, using colloidal smokeless powder. Closes compression chamber and opens valves to compress powder. Removes block from chamber. May be designated according to pressing stage as Final-Block-Press Operator (chemical); Preliminary-Block-Press Operator (chemical).
GOE: 06.04.11 STRENGTH: M GED: R2 M1 L1 SVP: 2 DLU: 77

556.685-018 BOWLING-BALL MOLDER (toy-sport equip.)

Tends presses that mold cover material on bowling-ball cores preparatory to steam curing, performing any combination of following duties: (1) Cuts rubber cover stock to approximate size, using knife, and lays specified number of rubber squares in mold half. (2) Positions mold half under press ram and presses button to lower ram into mold to shape rubber. Places bowling-ball core in every other mold with marked, weighted area away from seam. (3) Places cover, mold half on core, and pushes pins through mold flanges to hold halves in position. Places mold into press and presses button to lower ram and to mold cover to core. (4) Pulls *flash* from mold seam and places or pounds brackets onto mold flange to hold mold together during curing. Opens press, pounds pins out of flange, and stacks mold on pallet. May clean cores prior to molding operations, using cabinet sandblast equipment.
GOE: 06.04.13 STRENGTH: M GED: R2 M1 L1 SVP: 3 DLU: 77

556.685-022 COMPRESSION-MOLDING-MACHINE TENDER (plastic prod.) alternate titles: molder; plastic-press molder

Tends compression-molding machines that mold thermosetting plastics into products, such as automobile heater housings, ashtrays, buttons, electronic parts, plastic panels, and dishes: Dumps specified amount of plastic powders or pellets into hopper of machine, or positions pellets or sausage-shaped plastics in mold installed on machine. Starts machine that compresses plastic into mold under heat and pressure, and allows plastic to set for specified time. Removes product from mold and cleans mold, hopper, and bed of machine, using airhose and handtools. May place plastics material on hot grid or in oven to soften it

prior to molding. May weigh prescribed amount of material for molding. May place plastic sheet into machine fixture to fabricate buttons.
GOE: 06.04.13 STRENGTH: L GED: R2 M1 L1 SVP: 2 DLU: 77

556.685-026 COSMETICS PRESSER (pharmaceut.) alternate titles: molder; rouge presser

Tends equipment that compresses powdered cosmetics, such as face powder, eye shadow, or rouge, into cakes or sticks for use in compacts or cylindrical cases by either of following methods: (1) Spreads or brushes glue onto pans set into indentations of mold board. Fills individual molds with powder and pulls handle to force die into molds and compress powder. Positions mold on die of press and starts press that squeezes powder into cakes or sticks. Removes molds and dumps product onto tray to dry. (2) Scoops cosmetic powder into hopper of molding and pressing machine and starts machine. Places molds on conveyor that carries them into machine for automatic filling and pressing. Shakes or brushes loose powder from cosmetic cakes ejected by machine and places them on tray to dry. Discards cakes having irregularities, such as bubbles, indentations, and cracks. Feeds mold pans into glue machine and turns preset valves to spray molds with glue and dry for reuse.
GOE: 06.04.09 STRENGTH: L GED: R2 M1 L1 SVP: 3 DLU: 77

556.685-030 DIPPER (rubber goods)

Tends machine that dips forms into tanks of coagulant or liquid latex to produce rubber goods, such as gloves and balloons: Lifts *form board* from conveyor and fastens form board to machine bed with hinge clamps and slide bolts. Manually inverts bed and moves lever to submerge forms in tank of solution according to specifications. Raises and rocks bed to create movement that dries coagulant or equally distributes and sets latex on forms. Lifts boards to conveyor for next process. Adds solutions to tanks, using dipper to speed drying time or replenish supply to specified level. May tend automatic dipping machine that fabricates artificial rubber gloves. May be designated according to dipping solution used as Coagulant Dipper (rubber goods); Latex Dipper (rubber goods).
GOE: 06.04.13 STRENGTH: M GED: R2 M1 L1 SVP: 2 DLU: 77

556.685-034 DIPPING-MACHINE OPERATOR (rubber goods)

Tends conveyorized machine that dips forms into liquid latex to produce rubber goods, such as balloons, finger cots, and prophylactics: Mixes liquid latex in drums, using electric mixer or wooden paddle. Dips latex from drum into cans, and conveys filled cans on handtruck to machine holding tanks. Pours latex into gravity flow tank to maintain specified tank level. Starts machine that moves forms through various vats, driers, ovens, and rinses in continuous operation to form product. Removes sample of latex goods from form after final dip, weighs it, and adds solution of ammonia or latex to tank when weight does not meet requirements. Changes filters in latex tanks. Replaces dirty, loose, or broken forms on conveyor. Adds water softener to curing tanks. Verifies temperature and humidity on instrument control charts.
GOE: 06.04.13 STRENGTH: M GED: R2 M1 L1 SVP: 3 DLU: 77

556.685-038 INJECTION-MOLDING-MACHINE TENDER (plastic prod.; recording; rubber goods)

Tends injection-molding machines that form plastic or rubber products, such as typewriter keys, phonograph records, and luggage handles: Dumps plastic powder, preformed plastic pellets, or preformed rubber slugs into hopper of molding machine. Starts machine that automatically liquefies pellets, slugs, or powder in heating chamber, injects liquefied material into mold, and ejects molded product. Observes gauges to ensure specified molding temperature and pressure are maintained. Examines molded product for surface defects, such as dents and cracks. May heat plastic material over steamtable or in oven to prepare material for molding. May remove product from mold, using handtools. May trim *flash* from product, using shears or knife. May place product in cold water or position it on cooling fixture to prevent distortion.
GOE: 06.04.10 STRENGTH: L GED: R2 M1 L1 SVP: 2 DLU: 81

556.685-042 MATTING-PRESS TENDER (rubber goods)

Tends press that molds and cures rubber sheeting for use as floor matting: Places roll of calendering rubber sheeting in *letoff rack* using hoist, and unwinds sheeting onto bed of steam-heated curing press. Aligns rubber sheeting with edges of die, and closes press to mold and cure rubber sheeting for specified time. Winds cured rubber matting onto powered spindle. Continues process until roll is completed.
GOE: 06.04.13 STRENGTH: M GED: R2 M1 L1 SVP: 2 DLU: 77

556.685-046 MOLDER, FOAM RUBBER (rubber goods)

Tends hydraulic steam press that heats molds filled with mixture of foam rubber particles and latex (liquid rubber) to form cushions and mattresses: Carries filled mold from mixing machine to table of press. Smooths mixture in mold to distribute it evenly. Positions top cover on mold and places mold on press bed. Turns valve to lower ram against mold that heats and cures mixture. Removes mold, dumps molded product, and places it on storage rack. May grind foam rubber scrap, using electrically powered grinding machine. May mix ground foam rubber particles with latex, using mixing machine, and fill molds with mixture [MIXER, FOAM RUBBER (rubber goods)].
GOE: 06.04.13 STRENGTH: M GED: R2 M1 L1 SVP: 3 DLU: 77

556.685-050 MOLDER, MACHINE (pharmaceut.)

Tends equipment that heats and transfers mixture to conveyorized molds to form drug and toilet products, such as lipsticks and suppositories: Sets thermostat control to specified setting and opens valve to circulate coolant through pipes of mold-cooling chamber. Starts conveyor that carries empty molds into cooling chamber. Turns valve to admit product to reservoir of molding machine, starts agitator, and sets thermostat control to heat product to specified pouring temperature. Starts pump to fill molds as they pass on conveyor. Removes damaged or defective molds and adjusts mold scraper to prevent overflow or underfilling of molds.

GOE: 06.04.11 STRENGTH: M GED: R3 M2 L1 SVP: 4 DLU: 77

556.685-054 PARADICHLOROBENZENE TENDER (chemical) alternate titles: paradi tender; para operator

Tends equipment that cools and solidifies paradichlorobenzene preparatory to storage, shipment, or further processing: Pumps chemical into water-jacketed molds and turns valve to circulate chilled water through jacket and solidify material. Opens valve to admit steam to jacket to loosen crystallized product for removal. May break solidified product into smaller pieces preparatory to crushing, using wooden stick. May tend crusher to granulate product. May fill containers with crushed product and transfer containers to storage or shipping area, using handtruck.

GOE: 06.04.11 STRENGTH: L GED: R2 M1 L1 SVP: 2 DLU: 77

556.685-058 PILLING-MACHINE OPERATOR (plastic prod.; plastic-synth.) alternate titles: biscuit-machine operator; briquetting-machine operator; pelletizer; pellet-machine operator; preform-machine operator; tablet-machine operator

Tends pilling machine that compresses plastics powder into pellets or biscuits of specified weight and shape: Dumps plastics powders into machine hopper, using drum hoist or starts screw conveyor that loads hopper with material from storage bin. Opens gate valve to control flow of powder from hopper into machine. Turns steam valve to regulate temperature of machine according to ammeter gauge, and adjusts die pressure to attain specified hardness of pill. May clean, change, and adjust die. May be designated according to type of machine tended as Rotary Preformer (plastic prod.; plastic-synth.); Single-Stroke Preformer (plastic prod.; plastic-synth.).

GOE: 06.04.13 STRENGTH: H GED: R2 M1 L1 SVP: 4 DLU: 77

556.685-062 POLYSTYRENE-MOLDING-MACHINE TENDER (plastic prod.)

Tends automatic molding machines that mold preexpanded polystyrene beads under heat and pressure into cast foam products: Observes platens and listens to steam exhaust to determine end of molding cycle. Lifts cast foam products, such as balls, coolers, displays, and packing nests, from mold cavities while platens are parting. Presses cycle repeat button to reactivate molding machine, and blows loose beads from mold cavities as platens close, using airhose. Examines castings for post-expansion, fusion, shrinkage, and pits to ensure product meets quality standards. Rubs wire screen along mold parting line on casting to remove *flash*. May wrap advertising label around cooler cover and secure label, using masking tape. May adjust machine knobs to compensate for variations in product, such as moisture content and bead density.

GOE: 06.04.13 STRENGTH: L GED: R2 M1 L1 SVP: 2 DLU: 77

556.685-066 PRESS TENDER (rubber goods; rubber tire; toy-sport equip.) alternate titles: forming-press operator; hydraulic-steam-press operator; molding-press operator

Tends heated presses that mold and cure rubber goods or sports equipment, such as bowling balls, golf and tennis ball covers, and golf ball cores: Moves mold to press, using powered truck or handtruck. Sprays inner surface of mold with lubricant to prevent rubber from sticking. Positions *preform rubber*, half-shells, or cores in mold cavities or on lower die and places upper die over rubber. May insert metal parts in mold cavities to join with rubber during process. Closes mold and pushes it into press or moves lever to raise lift-table. Closes and starts press. Sets timer for specified curing time. Pulls mold from press and strips articles from mold. Tears *flash* ring from edge of workpieces. Removes rind from molds, using airhose and steel wool. May cut preform rubber for molding May be designated according to articles molded as Curer, Acid Drum (rubber goods); Gasket Molder (rubber goods); Golf Ball Molder (toy-sport equip.); Heel Molder (rubber goods); Outsole Molder (rubber goods); Rubber-Heel-And-Sole Press Tender (rubber goods).

GOE: 06.04.19 STRENGTH: M GED: R2 M1 L1 SVP: 2 DLU: 77

556.685-070 RECORD-PRESS TENDER (recording)

Tends automatic steam-hydraulic press that molds plastic compound into phonograph records: Places record labels over top and bottom center pins of press, and places preweighed and heated biscuit (plastic compound) into press mold. Moves lever to close mold and start press on cycle that molds biscuit under pressure and heat to form phonograph record. Removes record at end of cycle, places record onto spindle of edge trimmer, and presses lever to start turntable that rotates record against circular blades to trim *flash* from record edge. Examines record for flaws, such as discoloration and scratches. Retains specified record samples for audio testing. May tend machine that automatically inserts labels and compound into mold, forms record, punches center hole, and trims flash from record edge.

GOE: 06.04.13 STRENGTH: L GED: R2 M1 L1 SVP: 3 DLU: 77

556.685-074 SLUG-PRESS OPERATOR (elec. equip.)

Tends machine that compresses moist welding rod coating mix into cylinder-shaped slugs: Dumps mix into forming chamber of slug press, using forklift. Presses button to close press and activate ram that automatically forms and

ejects slug. Slips cellophane bag over slug or places it in container to prevent crusting or dehydration. Cleans machine, using brush, scraper, and airhose.

GOE: 06.04.19 STRENGTH: M GED: R2 M1 L1 SVP: 2 DLU: 77

556.685-078 STAMPER (chemical) alternate titles: press operator; stamp-press operator

Tends press that compacts deodorant and mothicide crystals into blocks: Bolts dies in press, using handtools. Pours crystals into lower half of press die. Turns handwheel to force upper half of die down and press crystals into block form. Lifts lever to eject block from press.

GOE: 06.04.11 STRENGTH: L GED: R2 M1 L1 SVP: 2 DLU: 77

556.685-082 VACUUM PLASTIC-FORMING-MACHINE OPERATOR (plastic prod.) alternate titles: molder, vacuum

Tends machine that molds thermoplastic sheets into plastic products: Places sheet on top of mold, positions sealing frame around sheet, and fastens frame to rim of mold, using clamps. Pushes button to start machine that heats sheet, draws it into mold to form product, and sprays product with cool water or air to harden product. Removes product from molds and reloads thermoplastic sheet into machine. May trim excessive molding material from products, using knife, scissors, or bandsaw.

GOE: 06.04.13 STRENGTH: L GED: R2 M1 L1 SVP: 2 DLU: 77

556.685-086 BLOW-MOLDING-MACHINE TENDER (toy-sport equip.)

Tends blow molding machine that automatically forms plastic toy parts: Observes continuous operation of automatic molding machine, adjusts plastic flow, and notifies supervisor of machine malfunctions. Removes molded part from conveyor or mold and trims *flash* from part, using knife, hammer, and file. Examines part for defects, such as bubbles, splits, or thin areas, and weighs part on scale to ensure specifications are maintained. Stacks molded parts in boxes for subsequent processing. Throws flash and rejected parts into regrinder machine to be recycled.

GOE: 06.04.13 STRENGTH: L GED: R2 M1 L1 SVP: 2 DLU: 86

556.685-090 CENTRIFUGAL-CASTING-MACHINE TENDER (plastic prod.) alternate titles: molder operator

Tends machine that casts plastic containers: Fills tubs with prescribed amounts of colored thermoplastic powder and zinc compound, using scoop and scale. Positions tubs containing mixture to facilitate loading of molds. Fills molds with specified amount of mixture, closes mold covers, and depresses toggle latches to lock covers in place. Presses buttons to start centrifugal-casting machine that automatically heats, spreads, hardens, and shapes mixture into plastic molds to form refuse containers. Pulls toggle latches to release mold covers and removes covers. Breaks seals that hold plastic containers in molds and removes containers from molds, using handtool. Wipes moisture from inside of molds, using cloth rag. Trims flashing (excess plastic) from containers, using utility knife.

GOE: 06.04.19 STRENGTH: M GED: R1 M1 L1 SVP: 2 DLU: 86

556.686-010 CAKE-PRESS-OPERATOR HELPER (plastic-synth.)

Assists CAKE-PRESS OPERATOR (plastic-synth.) in compressing and baking chipped, rolled, or slabbed plastics materials into cake molds for sheeting: Positions empty molds on platform scales. Spreads plastics chips evenly over mold, using spreader. Pushes molds along roller conveyor from baking press to cooling press. Pushes cooled molds from press onto roller conveyor. Removes platen from mold and pushes it along roller conveyor to storage rack. Removes cake from mold and trims *flash*, using knife. Stacks cakes on pallets. Pushes empty mold along conveyor to scale. Cleans molds and presses, using knife and scraper. Performs other duties as described under HELPER (any industry) Master Title.

GOE: 06.04.13 STRENGTH: H GED: R2 M1 L1 SVP: 2 DLU: 77

556.686-014 CELL STRIPPER (plastic-synth.) alternate titles: mold stripper; stripper, preliminary

Prepares plastics sheets for removal from glass molds (cells), performing any combination of following duties: Pulls materials, such as cellophane, rubber tubing, or tape from cells. Unscrews clamps and pries spacing devices from cells. Sorts rubber tubing according to size and stacks clamps in bin for reuse. Loads cells on conveyor or stacks cells in racks and lowers racks into tank solution, using hoist.

GOE: 06.04.20 STRENGTH: H GED: R2 M1 L1 SVP: 2 DLU: 77

556.686-018 STRIPPER (plastic prod.; rubber goods) alternate titles: mold stripper

Strips molded latex or plastic products, such as masks, puppets, and footwear, from molds, performing any of following methods: (1) Removes mold from conveyor emerging from drying oven and clamps it in holder to secure mold. Trims excess plastic from mold top, using knife. Pries section of workpiece from mold wall, grips workpiece manually or using stripping pliers or *prongs*, and twists and pulls footwear from mold. (2) Dusts talc into molds and removes masks or puppets, using knife. (3) Immerses rack of molds in water tank to cool them, dries molds, using airhose, and pulls masks or puppets from molds, using pliers. Places acceptable items on transfer belt or in box and damaged ones on salvage pile. May clean molds by hand or using steam hose. May be designated according to material used as Stripper, Latex (rubber goods); Stripper, Soft Plastic (plastic prod.).

GOE: 06.04.13 STRENGTH: M GED: R1 M1 L1 SVP: 2 DLU: 77

556.686-022 SUPPOSITORY-MOLDING-MACHINE OPERATOR (pharmaceut.)

Fills jars with suppositories ejected from automatic molding machine, preparatory to capping: Positions empty jar under chute of machine to fill jar with

suppositories ejected from machine that automatically melts, molds. and refrigerates glycerine, forming suppositories. Places filled jar on conveyor that carries jar to capping operation. May assist MOLDER, MACHINE (pharmaceut.) in adjusting mold scraper and replacing damaged or defective molds.
GOE: 06.04.11 STRENGTH: L GED: R1 M1 L1 SVP: 2 DLU: 77

556.687-010 BOWLING-BALL-MOLD ASSEMBLER (toy-sport equip.)

Coats bowling ball molds components with parting agent, installs ball cores, and assembles and seals molds preparatory to filling and curing: Inspects parts to ensure clean and dry condition and applies parting agent, using brush or spray gun. Installs core on support bolt and turns bolt to adjust core to center of mold. Lays yarn gasket in groove around bottom flange, aligns top of mold over bottom, and secures it with thumbscrews or clamps. Places completed mold in rack for filling. May disassemble molds and remove cured balls from molds.
GOE: 06.04.32 STRENGTH: M GED: R2 M1 L1 SVP: 2 DLU: 77

556.687-014 CELL PREPARER (plastic-synth.)

Prepares molds (cells) used in casting liquid plastics materials into sheet form: Inserts wooden or plastic wedges between sides of glass cells to widen cell opening. Folds paper into funnel shape and inserts paper funnel in cell opening to provide passage for liquid plastics. Records identification data on tag and attaches it to cell.
GOE: 06.04.24 STRENGTH: H GED: R2 M1 L1 SVP: 2 DLU: 77

556.687-018 MOLD CLEANER (rubber goods)

Cleans, stores, and distributes molds used to form rubber goods: Conveys molds to presses according to work orders, manually or using handtruck. Sprays molds with steam to remove protective oil or cleaning fluid. Immerses used molds in tank of hot cleaning fluid, manually or using hoist, to loosen adhering rubber particles. Removes rubber particles from mold cavities, using hand or powered wire brush. Brushes oil on mold before storing to prevent rusting. Places mold in storage racks. May sandblast molds to renew surfaces. May repaint identifying data on cleaned molds. May disassemble molds for cleaning and reassemble cleaned molds, using handtools.
GOE: 06.04.39 STRENGTH: H GED: R2 M1 L1 SVP: 2 DLU: 77

556.687-022 MOLDER, TOILET PRODUCTS (pharmaceut.)

Fills molds with heated mixture to form drug and toilet products, such as lipsticks, deodorant, and eyeshadow sticks: Pours or opens valve to admit mixture slowly into mold cavities to avoid forming bubbles. Places mold on chilling plate or in refrigerator, or starts fan to cool and congeal contents. Scrapes excess material from mold, using spatula. May open mold and remove formed product. May insert lipstick cases or other containers into molds to hold and form product. May pump or pour mixture into temperature-controlled kettle prior to molding to heat mixture to pouring temperature. May be designated according to product molded as Lipstick Molder (pharmaceut.); Suppository Molder (pharmaceut.).
GOE: 06.04.11 STRENGTH: L GED: R2 M1 L1 SVP: 3 DLU: 77

556.687-026 POURER (rubber goods)

Fills curing molds with latex to cast foam rubber products by any of following methods: (1) Inserts hose nozzle in opening of closed mold and twists hose clamp to control flow and fill mold with latex, observing when overflow to determine when mold is full. (2) Pulls lever on bottom of mixing bowl to fill mold as mold is carried in position by conveyor. Scoops excess latex from mold, using scraper to prevent overflow during curing. May stir latex in mold, using paddle to remove air bubbles. May feel latex to determine consistency. May manually pour measured amount of latex into dipping tank into which molds are inserted to form coated latex articles.
GOE: 06.04.32 STRENGTH: M GED: R1 M1 L1 SVP: 2 DLU: 77

556.687-030 MOLD FILLER (toy-sport equip.)

Fills bowling ball molds: Lifts mold from supply cart, places mold on holding fixture, and positions filler hole of mold under spigot of resin tank. Turns valve to open spigot and control flow of resin from tank into mold. Turns valve to stop resin flow when mold is filled. Lifts filled mold from holding fixture onto storage cart.
GOE: 06.04.32 STRENGTH: M GED: R1 M1 L1 SVP: 1 DLU: 86

557 EXTRUDING OCCUPATIONS

This group includes occupations concerned with forcing or pulling materials through dies or similar small openings to form a variety of objects, such as plastic rods, tubing, and synthetic fibers.

557.130-010 SUPERVISOR, EXTRUDING DEPARTMENT (plastic prod.)

Supervises and coordinates activities of workers engaged in adjusting and operating machines to extrude and print polyethylene film used in manufacture of bags: Examines polyethylene film from extruding machine for defects and conformance to dimensional specifications. Examines samples from printing machine for clarity and registration of print, color intensity, and discriminations of shading to determine quality of print on film. Trains new workers in operation and setup of machines. May adjust and install replacement parts on machines. Performs other duties as described under SUPERVISOR (any industry) Master Title.
GOE: 06.02.01 STRENGTH: H GED: R4 M3 L3 SVP: 8 DLU: 77

557.130-014 SUPERVISOR, PLASTIC SHEETS (plastic prod.)

Supervises and coordinates activities of workers engaged in extruding plastic sheets: Observes installation of dies, and examines extruded sheets for defects. Trains new workers in machine operation and setup. May diagnose operating difficulties and adjust machine cycles. Performs other duties as described under SUPERVISOR (any industry) Master Title.
GOE: 06.02.01 STRENGTH: M GED: R4 M3 L3 SVP: 7 DLU: 77

557.382-010 EXTRUDER OPERATOR (plastic prod.; plastic-synth.) alternate titles: stuffer, vertical hydraulic; tuber operator

Sets up and operates machine to extrude thermoplastic materials to form tubes, rods, and film according to specifications: Installs dies, machine screws, and sizing rings, using handtools. Couples hose to die holder to circulate steam, water, air, or oil to die. Weighs and mixes pelletized, granular, or powdered themoplastic materials and coloring pigments in tumbling machine according to formula. Fills machine hopper with mixed materials, using conveyor auger, or stuffs rolls of plastic dough into machine cylinders. Starts machine and sets controls to regulate vacuum, air pressure, sizing rings, and temperature; and synchronizes speed of extrusion with pulling rolls. Examines extruded product for defects, such as wrinkles, bubbles, and splits. Measures extruded articles for conformance to specifications, using micrometers, calipers, and gauges; and adjusts speed and weight controls or turns hot and cold water, air, oil, or steam valves to obtain product of specified dimensions. Tests physical properties of product with acid-bath tester, burst tester, and impact tester. May reel extruded product into rolls of specified length and weight [EXTRUDER-OPERATOR HELPER (plastic prod.; plastic-synth.)].
GOE: 06.02.13 STRENGTH: M GED: R3 M2 L2 SVP: 5 DLU: 77

557.382-014 WINK-CUTTER OPERATOR (rubber goods)

Sets up and operates machines to extrude uncured rubber into continuous strip and to cut strip into specified lengths and weight for molding rubber footwear outsoles: Installs dies on tube machine, turns steam valve to heat die and screw chamber, feeds milled rubber chunks into machine hopper, and starts machine to force rubber through die to form continuous strip [TUBER-MACHINE OPERATOR (rubber goods; rubber tire)]. Threads extruded strip through coldwater tank and holddown bars, and between feeder belts to cutter. Turns wheel to adjust feed speed to length of blank cut. Starts machine and measures and weighs sample blank, using ruler and scale, for conformance to specifications. Removes cut pieces from discharge belt and places them on trays.
GOE: 06.02.07 STRENGTH: L GED: R3 M2 L2 SVP: 4 DLU: 77

557.564-010 EXTRUDER-OPERATOR HELPER (plastic prod.; plastic-synth.)

Assists EXTRUDER OPERATOR (plastic prod.; plastic-synth.) in extruding thermoplastic materials to form tubes, rods, and film: Tapes end of extruded article to reel spindle and starts machine that winds material onto revolving spindle. Measures extruded article with measuring wheel and cuts it to specified length, using saw or knife. Removes roll or coil from spindle, weighs roll, and records length and weight of roll on shipping tag. Saws scrap tubes and rods into lengths for grinding in hammer mill, using bandsaw. Starts hammer mill and feeds sawed scrap into mill to grind it for reprocessing. May mix thermoplastic materials and pigments, according to formula, for feeding extrusion machine. Performs other duties as described under HELPER (any industry) Master Title.
GOE: 06.04.13 STRENGTH: H GED: R2 M2 L1 SVP: 2 DLU: 77

557.564-014 PUMP TESTER (plastic-synth.)

Verifies adjustment of pumps used to force cellulose solution through spinnerettes, forming rayon, to ensure that pump speed conforms with plant specifications for prescribed weight of yarn: Turns valve to transfer measured amount of solution to container and times flow, using stopwatch. Weighs container and solution and records findings.
GOE: 06.03.02 STRENGTH: L GED: R3 M2 L2 SVP: 4 DLU: 77

557.565-010 EXTRUDING-MACHINE OPERATOR (tex. prod., nec)

Tends machine that extrudes continuous synthetic filaments from resins to be used in making twine: Pours resin into loading drum of machine, and pours buckets of color resin into hopper of machine. Cleans extruding die or installs new die in machine. Observes thermostat heat-control unit and notifies engineer of deviations from prescribed temperature. Notifies supervisor when extruded filaments fail to meet specified standards for thickness and color. Tends tumbling machine that rotates drums of resin to mix different colors of resins before they are poured into extruder.
GOE: 06.04.13 STRENGTH: H GED: R2 M1 L1 SVP: 3 DLU: 77

557.565-014 SYNTHETIC-FILAMENT EXTRUDER (plastic-synth.)

Tends machines and auxiliary equipment that extrude continuous synthetic filaments from liquid polymer: Starts metering pumps and observes operation of machines and equipment to ensure continuous flow of filaments extruded through spinnerettes and to detect processing defects, such as drips, filament stains or missing, oversized, or fused filaments. Notifies other workers through intercom when defects occur, necessitating interruption of extruding process, to clean spinnerettes. Opens cabinet doors to cut threadlines (multifilaments) away from guides, using scissors. Lowers pan inside cabinet to catch molten filaments until flow of polymer through *packs* is stopped. Presses metering-pump buttons and turns valves to stop flow of polymer. Cuts entangled filaments wrapped around gears of machine, using pliers. Restarts metering pumps, notifies other worker to receive threadlines, pulls extruded filaments together below

spinnerettes to form threadlines, and inserts threadlines through guides to facilitate drawing process on floor below. Observes flow of finish across finish rollers and turns valves to adjust flow to specifications. Occasionally removes polymer deposits from spinnerettes and equipment, using silicone spray, brass chisel, and bronze-wool pad. Wipes finish rollers with cloths and washes finish trays with water when necessary. Marks type of malfunctions on maintenance tag, and attaches tag to machine for subsequent repair.
GOE: 06.04.13 STRENGTH: M GED: R2 M1 L1 SVP: 3 DLU: 77

557.665-010 SYNTHETIC-STAPLE EXTRUDER (plastic-synth.)

Tends machines that form continuous synthetic filaments from liquid polymer and lay tow in cans according to specified pattern: Installs *pack* into machine, using handtools, and turns lever to activate metering pump which controls amount of polymer extruded through pack. Catches extruded filaments in compressed-air gun and threads filaments through guides to capstans. Separates filaments at spinnerette, by hand, inserts cooling tube into spinnerette, and pushes lever to force air through tube to cool filaments. Guides tow over capstans and into device that lays tow into cans according to specified pattern. Observes machine operation, panelboard, gauges, and rotameter to detect machine malfunction. Turns valves and levers to adjust machines as necessary. Cuts windup from capstan. Notifies Polymer Department, using telephone, when color of polymer is not according to specifications.
GOE: 06.04.13 STRENGTH: M GED: R3 M1 L2 SVP: 4 DLU: 77

557.682-010 GRAINING-PRESS OPERATOR (chemical) alternate titles: finishing-powder-press operator; macaroni-press operator; powder-press operator

Sets up and operates hydraulic press to extrude blocks of smokeless powder into strands preparatory to cutting, drying, and bagging: Attaches specified dies to compression cylinder of press with thumbscrews or clamps. Inserts block in compression cylinder and locks cover in place with thumbscrews. Turns ram control valve to extrude powder slowly to avoid explosion. Examines extruded lengths for dirt streaks and malformations. Positions fiber containers under discharge chute of each die hole, and replaces containers as they are filled.
GOE: 06.02.18 STRENGTH: H GED: R2 M1 L1 SVP: 3 DLU: 77

557.684-010 JET HANDLER (plastic-synth.) alternate titles: spinnerette cleaner

Cleans spinnerettes that extrude synthetic fibers: Disassembles *packs* containing spinnerettes. Disassembles spinnerettes, washes them in acid bath, and drys them with compressed air. Inspects holes in cleaned spinnerettes to detect damage or wear. Disassembles, cleans, and reassembles *outflow quench sticks.* May reassemble cleaned spinnerettes, using wrench. May buff surface of spinnerettes, using power buffer. May clean clogged spinnerette holes, using ultrasonic vibrator.
GOE: 06.04.39 STRENGTH: H GED: R2 M1 L1 SVP: 4 DLU: 77

557.684-014 JET WIPER (plastic-synth.)

Wipes jets (spinnerettes) through which filaments of rayon are extruded and ties broken filaments together to facilitate uninterrupted production of acetate rayon: Observes cellulose solution emerging from spinnerettes to detect interruption or narrowing of stream, indicating blockage. Wipes surface of spinnerette with thumb to remove clogged cellulose particles. Catches and ties together strands of rayon if breaks occur in filament. Notifies SPINNER (plastic-synth.) to rethread filaments through machine after repairing breaks or wiping jets. Reports permanently clogged, damaged, or worn jets to maintenance personnel.
GOE: 06.04.27 STRENGTH: L GED: R2 M1 L1 SVP: 2 DLU: 77

557.685-010 CORE EXTRUDER (elec. equip.)

Tends manually operated extrusion press and wirecutter that extrudes and cuts paste (black mix) to form dry-cell battery cores: Loads press hopper with paste and moves lever to start ram that forces paste through die of prescribed diameter onto cutter. Pulls lever to lower wire cutter and cut extruded paste into segments (cores). Tilts cutter to dump cores onto tray.
GOE: 06.04.10 STRENGTH: L GED: R2 M1 L1 SVP: 2 DLU: 77

557.685-014 EXTRUDER TENDER (rubber goods)

Tends machine that extrudes rubber compound to produce strands for use in making elastic yarn: Adjusts valves to regulate and maintain specified flow of rubber compound and size of extruded strand. Separates strands in acid bath with tweezers and places strands on rollers leading to curing oven. Cleans and replaces nozzles. Fills feed tank with liquid-rubber compound.
GOE: 06.04.13 STRENGTH: L GED: R2 M1 L1 SVP: 3 DLU: 77

557.685-018 PROCESSOR (plastic-synth.)

Tends processing (washing, bleaching, and drying) section of machine that extrudes synthetic fiber filaments: Threads continuous filaments through guides and around rollers that carry product through machine, apply washing and bleaching solutions, and dry filaments prior to winding, twisting, or cutting into staple lengths. Observes gauges and moves controls to start and regulate flow of washing and bleaching solutions, applied to moving filament through openings in rollers, and to maintain temperature of drying rollers according to plant standards. Repairs breaks in filaments by tying ends together. In nylon plants, may set temperature of rolls that heat and stretch filaments to impart strength and fuse filaments into tow. May doff bobbins of yarn at end of windup cycle and reset clock device that regulates speed of filament travel according to diameter of bobbin.

GOE: 06.04.13 STRENGTH: L GED: R2 M1 L1 SVP: 3 DLU: 77

557.685-022 SECOND-FLOOR OPERATOR (plastic-synth.)

Tends unit of spinning machine that extrudes synthetic filaments and passes filaments to draw (stretching) machine on floor below: Observes operation of machine to ensure continuous flow of filaments through spinnerettes. Inserts filaments through guides to facilitate drawing process on floor below. Presses buttons and turns valves to stop flow of polymer to clean spinnerettes.
GOE: 06.04.13 STRENGTH: M GED: R2 M1 L1 SVP: 3 DLU: 77

557.685-026 SPINNER (plastic-synth.) alternate titles: spinning operator

Tends machine or machine section that extrudes rayon filaments preparatory to washing, bleaching, drying, and winding resulting yarn onto bobbins or cutting it into staple lengths: Grasps filaments as they are extruded into solidifying bath and brings ends together to form single strand. Passes strand over glass rollers that carry it through machine for subsequent processing. Ties strands together if breaks occur. May thread strands through washing, bleaching, and drying rollers and attach them to takeup bobbins [PROCESSOR (plastic-synth.)]. May gather filaments and throw them into glass funnel, mounted on machine, with quantity of acid that carries filaments into revolving *spinning box.* May remove and replace bobbins as they become filled and reset clock device that controls speed of filament travel according to diameter of bobbin. When repositioning glass funnels after doffing, is known as Funnel Setter (plastic-synth.). May be designated according to type of spinning process as Spinner, Box (plastic-synth.); Spinner, Continuous (plastic-synth.).
GOE: 06.04.13 STRENGTH: L GED: R2 M1 L1 SVP: 3 DLU: 77

557.685-030 SPINNING-BATH PATROLLER (plastic-synth.)

Tends equipment to regulate flow of chemical-bath solution to trough into which cellulose slurry is extruded, forming rayon filaments: Turns valves to transfer slurry from storage tanks to trough containing spinnerettes, maintaining constant level and flow according to gauge readings and plant specifications. May be designated Acid-Bath Tender (plastic-synth.) when performing duties in plants manufacturing rayon by viscose process.
GOE: 06.04.11 STRENGTH: L GED: R2 M1 L2 SVP: 4 DLU: 77

557.685-034 TAKE-UP OPERATOR (plastic-synth.)

Tends machine that applies finish to and winds up newly extruded polyester fibers onto takeup bobbins: Turns valves on vacuum lines to activate aspirators that break and suck up yarn ends during doffing process. Grasps yarn lines at each bobbin position to gather and guide moving yarn to aspirator. Pushes filled bobbins of yarn away from bobbin drive rollers on takeup machine to stop spinning takeup bobbins. Lifts filled bobbins from machine and places bobbins on cart. Places empty bobbins on bobbin shafts of takeup machine. Pushes bobbin shafts with empty bobbins next to spinning drive rollers to power rotation of bobbins preparatory to takeup of yarn on bobbins. Pulls specified lines of yarn down from aspirator over rollers on takeup unit that guide and advance newly extruded yarn and throws yarn ends down against empty, spinning bobbins to takeup lines of bobbins. Separates yarn ends along specified guide notches of machine to facilitate takeup of yarn on separate bobbins. Aligns yarn taken up on bobbin, using wire brush.
GOE: 06.04.13 STRENGTH: M GED: R2 M1 L1 SVP: 3 DLU: 86

558 REACTING OCCUPATIONS, N.E.C.

This group includes occupations, not elsewhere classified, concerned with producing a chemical change in components.

558.130-010 SUPERVISOR, PHOSPHATIC FERTILIZER (chemical)

Supervises and coordinates activities of workers engaged in operation of automatic chemical process equipment to produce granular phosphatic fertilizers from raw chemicals, chemical products, and phosphate rock: Observes recording instruments, panel lights, and other indicators, and listens for warning signals to verify conformity of process conditions to plant standards. Reviews operating records and laboratory test reports to determine specific process conditions and to diagnose malfunctions in equipment. Confers with technical personnel to resolve conditions affecting safety, efficiency, and product quality. Directs workers to manually regulate process equipment or to shut down equipment during emergency situations, using telephone and radio communication systems. Trains workers in new job assignments. Performs other duties as described under SUPERVISOR (any industry) Master Title.
GOE: 06.01.01 STRENGTH: L GED: R4 M3 L3 SVP: 8 DLU: 77

558.132-010 SUPERVISOR, CHEMICAL (plastic-synth.)

Supervises and coordinates activities of workers engaged in converting woodpulp into viscose for use in manufacturing cellophane and rayon: Orders rolls of pressed woodpulp transferred from storage to shredding room. Directs workers in moving controls to regulate caustic treatment of pulp to form alkali cellulose. Sets conveyor speed for specified aging of cellulose traveling through process chambers. Directs operation of equipment that mixes and blends cellulose with chemicals to form viscose. Directs workers in moving controls of valves and pumps to filter viscose and transfer viscose to storage. Trains workers in operation of equipment. Performs other duties as described under SUPERVISOR (any industry) Master Title.
GOE: 06.01.01 STRENGTH: L GED: R4 M3 L3 SVP: 7 DLU: 77

558.132-014 SUPERVISOR, PHOSPHORIC ACID (chemical)

Supervises and coordinates activities of workers engaged in producing phosphoric acid by reaction of sulfuric acid with phosphate rock in continuous

strong-acid process: Directs workers in changes in operating processes, work procedures, and production rates according to production instructions. Observes workers to ensure compliance with safety regulations. Prepares work orders for repair or maintenance of equipment. Trains new employees or assigns trainees to experienced workers to learn job duties. Performs other duties as described under SUPERVISOR (any industry) Master Title.
GOE: 06.04.01 STRENGTH: L GED: R4 M3 L4 SVP: 8 DLU: 77

558.132-018 SUPERVISOR, SULFURIC-ACID PLANT (chemical)
Supervises and coordinates activities of workers engaged in producing sulfuric acid from liquid sulfur by catalytic conversion and absorption methods. Trains new employees in machine operation. Observes meters, charts, and gauges and reviews operating records to verify specified process conditions and to diagnose malfunctions in automatic operation. Performs other duties as described under SUPERVISOR (any industry) Master Title.
GOE: 06.01.01 STRENGTH: L GED: R4 M3 L4 SVP: 8 DLU: 77

558.134-010 SUPERVISOR, BRINE (chemical)
Supervises and coordinates activities of workers engaged in preparing solutions for use in producing chlorine and caustic soda by electrolysis. Performs other duties as described under SUPERVISOR (any industry) Master Title.
GOE: 06.02.01 STRENGTH: M GED: R4 M3 L3 SVP: 7 DLU: 77

558.134-014 SUPERVISOR, CELL ROOM (chemical)
Supervises and coordinates activities of workers engaged in producing chlorine, caustic soda, and caustic potash from brine by electrolysis. Performs other duties as described under SUPERVISOR (any industry) Master Title.
GOE: 06.02.01 STRENGTH: M GED: R4 M3 L3 SVP: 7 DLU: 77

558.134-018 SUPERVISOR, CELL-EFFICIENCY (chemical)
Supervises and coordinates activities of workers engaged in maintenance of electrolytic cells and in drawing off hydrogen and chlorine generated by electrolysis. Performs other duties as described under SUPERVISOR (any industry) Master Title.
GOE: 06.02.01 STRENGTH: M GED: R4 M3 L4 SVP: 7 DLU: 77

558.134-022 SUPERVISOR, HYDROCHLORIC AREA (chemical) alternate titles: hydrochloric-manufacturing supervisor
Supervises and coordinates activities of workers engaged in producing hydrogen chloride from decomposition of salt by sulfuric acid. Performs other duties as described under SUPERVISOR (any industry) Master Title.
GOE: 06.02.01 STRENGTH: M GED: R4 M3 L3 SVP: 7 DLU: 77

558.260-010 CHIEF OPERATOR (chemical)
Controls chemical process equipment from instrumented control board or other control station: Monitors recording instruments, flowmeters, panel lights, and other indicators, and listens for warning signals to verify conformity of process conditions to plant standards of safety and efficiency. Moves control settings or notifies CHEMICAL OPERATOR (chemical) III 559.382-018 or other workers to make control adjustments on equipment units affecting speed of chemical reactions and quality and yield of product, using telephone or intercommunications system. Notifies maintenance, stationary-engineering, and other auxiliary personnel to correct equipment malfunctions and adjust power, steam, water, or air supply as indicated. Confers with technical and supervisory personnel to report or resolve conditions affecting safety, efficiency, and product quality. Interprets chemical reactions visible through sight glasses or on television monitor and reviews laboratory test reports to determine need for process adjustments. Inspects equipment for potential and actual hazards, wear, leaks, and other conditions requiring maintenance or shutdown. Records instrument readings, process conditions, and other operating data in shift log, calculating material requirements or product yield as necessary from standard formulas. Manually regulates or shuts down equipment during emergency situations, as directed by supervisory personnel. May be designated according to product produced as Chief Operator, Ammonium Sulfate (chemical); according to equipment used as Chief Operator, Reformer (chemical); or according to chemical process as Chief Operator, Purification And Reaction (chemical); Chief Operator, Synthesis (chemical).
GOE: 06.01.03 STRENGTH: L GED: R4 M3 L4 SVP: 7 DLU: 78

558.362-010 CATALYTIC-CONVERTER OPERATOR (chemical) alternate titles: catalytic-case operator
Controls catalytic converters to alter chemical composition of liquid or gaseous substances, according to knowledge of process and sequence of operations: Turns valves and starts pumps to admit feed stock to converter units at specified rate, and to recycle unreacted products or byproducts to auxiliary equipment. Moves controls to regulate temperatures, pressures, and reaction time, according to gauge readings, chart recorders, and knowledge of processing requirements, to maintain efficient converter operation within specified limits. Operates or tends auxiliary equipment, such as heaters, scrubbers, vapor compressors, filters, distillation units, condensers, and humidifiers, to prepare or further process materials entering or leaving converters, according to plant operating procedures. Directs activities of CATALYTIC-CONVERTER-OPERATOR HELPER (chemical). Draws samples of materials for laboratory analysis, or tests materials for specified characteristics, using standard gas-analysis procedures and equipment. May introduce inert gas into converters to remove explosive vapors or purge catalyst. May replace catalyst or tend equipment that regenerates catalyst for reuse. May set semiautomatic control system that places equipment units in operating equilibrium, to attain specified products and transfer them for

further processing. May be designated according to materials produced as Acetaldehyde-Converter Operator (chemical); Butadiene-Converter Operator (chemical); Ethylene-Converter Operator (chemical); Ethylene-Plant Operator (chemical); or according to chemical reaction effected as Dehydrogenation-Converter Operator (chemical); Ethylbenzene Hydrogenator (chemical); Ethylbenzene Oxidizer (chemical).
GOE: 06.02.11 STRENGTH: L GED: R3 M2 L2 SVP: 7 DLU: 77

558.362-014 CD-REACTOR OPERATOR, HEAD (chemical)
Controls catalytic reactor to convert monovinylacetylene into unpolymerized constituent of neoprene rubber, according to knowledge of process and sequence of operations: Opens valves to admit water and nitrogen to system, removing air to prevent fires or explosions. Admits specified chemicals to system and observes their color to detect presence of oxygen. Sets valves and controllers to maintain prescribed positive pressure in system. Turns valves to circulate hydrogen chloride solution through gas scrubbers and to pass vaporized monovinylacetylene through solution that removes impurities. Starts reaction system or directs CD-REACTOR OPERATOR (chemical) to start system. Adjusts valves, flowmeters, and automatic controllers to obtain specified equilibrium between gas feeds and to maintain pressures and temperatures within specified limits. Determines adjustments required to avert or correct emergency situations with minimum loss in time and yield. Starts condenser to remove unreacted monovinylacetylene from product. Inspects equipment and arranges for cleaning and repairs. Drains and steam-cleans processing equipment and lines during shutdowns, using steam generator and hose. Draws samples of products for laboratory analysis. Records operational data in log.
GOE: 06.02.11 STRENGTH: M GED: R3 M3 L3 SVP: 7 DLU: 77

558.362-018 SATURATOR OPERATOR (chemical; steel & rel.) alternate titles: ammonium-sulfate operator; sulfate operator
Controls saturator tank and auxiliary equipment to precipitate ammonium sulfate by reaction of ammonia with sulfuric acid: Turns valves to admit sulfuric acid and liquid or gaseous ammonia to saturator until precipitation occurs, and to regulate saturation of solution, using titration test to determine acidity of bath. Observes temperature and pressure gauges to ascertain that process conditions meet plant standards, and turns valves to maintain operating equilibrium within specified range. Notifies supervisor or starts pumps to discharge precipitate onto drain table to settle out crystals, and pumps strained liquor back to bath. Records gauge readings for operating log. May move controls to reheat gas prior to saturation. May tend centrifuge to dry ammonium sulfate. May take samples of product and constituents for laboratory analysis.
GOE: 06.02.11 STRENGTH: L GED: R3 M2 L2 SVP: 5 DLU: 77

558.382-010 ACID EXTRACTOR (steel & rel.)
Controls equipment, such as washers, rectifiers, acid pots, and mixing tanks arranged in series to recover tar acids from coal-tar oils: Starts pumps to circulate oil through equipment, and opens valves at various stages to treat oil with chemicals, carbon dioxide, and steam, according to specified instrument readings. Performs routine tests at different processing stages to determine effectiveness of treatment. Samples products for laboratory analysis, and interprets results of analyses to make adjustments in processing operations and to control quality and quantity of production. Inspects equipment for operating efficiency, lubricates equipment, and makes minor repairs and adjustments.
GOE: 06.02.11 STRENGTH: L GED: R3 M2 L3 SVP: 5 DLU: 77

558.382-014 BURNER OPERATOR (chemical) alternate titles: ammonia operator
Controls converter and auxiliary equipment that combine hydrogen and nitrogen to produce anhydrous ammonia: Lights burner and starts pumps, compressors, scrubbers, and absorption units. Moves controls on panelboard to regulate temperatures of solutions and opens valves to admit heated and purified air and hydrogen into combustion chamber of burner, where nitrogen driven from air combines with hydrogen to form ammonia. Reads instruments, such as thermometers, pressure gauges, and potentiometers. Makes control adjustments according to operating instructions and charts. Pumps fresh solutions into scrubbing and *absorption towers* when readings indicate excessive alkalinity. Records operational data in logbook. May compute percentage of hydrogen and ammonia in burner gases, using standard test procedure.
GOE: 06.02.11 STRENGTH: M GED: R3 M3 L3 SVP: 5 DLU: 77

558.382-018 CAUSTICISER (paper & pulp) alternate titles: caustic-liquor maker
Controls equipment to process green liquor (soda ash solution) and lime into caustic liquor used in cooking woodpulp: Starts pumps and adjusts valves to control flow of water and lime into tank or revolving drum and over screens to remove lumps to make lime slurry of specified density. Adjusts valves to control flow of lime slurry and green liquor into reaction tanks in specified proportions and opens steam valve to heat reaction tank to specified temperature to make caustic cooking liquor. Adjusts controls to pump cooking liquor to settling tank and makes titration tests to determine extent of settling of lime sludge. Turns valves to pump clear liquor to storage tank and lime sludge to sludge tank. May test green liquor and calculate quantity of lime slurry additive. May make titration test to determine concentration of cooking liquor.
GOE: 06.02.11 STRENGTH: L GED: R3 M2 L1 SVP: 4 DLU: 77

558.382-022 CAUSTICISER (chemical) alternate titles: reactor operator
Operates equipment to control chemical reaction of soda ash and milk of lime to make caustic soda: Opens valves and starts pumps to fill dissolving tank

with specified amounts of soda ash and milk of lime. Starts mixer in tank to agitate materials and dissolve solids. Draws sample of mixture from tank and measures its gravity with hydrometer. Opens water valve to dilute mixture and obtain specified concentrations according to type of product. Turns valves and rheostats to adjust feeding of solution to reactor tank. Periodically takes samples of reacting liquor and titrates samples with normal acid to determine concentration of caustic soda being formed. Conducts similar tests and titrations to determine salt content and concentration of various liquors. Clears stopped pipelines and repairs equipment, using handtools.
GOE: 06.02.11 STRENGTH: M GED: R3 M2 L2 SVP: 5 DLU: 77

558.382-026 CELL TENDER (chemical) alternate titles: cell attendant; unit tender
Controls electrolytic cells to produce caustic soda, chlorine, or hydrogen to specified standards from brine (sodium chloride) solution: Regulates brine flow to cells, according to power input and strength of electrolyte. Observes flow through sight glasses; reads gauges, chart recorders, and manometer; and moves controls to regulate level of cell liquor, brine flow, cell pressure, current, and temperatures, within efficient operating limits. Turns valves and starts pumps to maintain specified back pressure on hydrogen and vacuum on chlorine. Observes gauges, turns valves, and starts pumps to tend auxiliary equipment, such as hydrogen scrubbers, water sprayers, condensers, and driers to purify, recover, or further process hydrogen, chlorine, and caustic liquor. Inspects cells, contact bars, pumps, turbines, and hydrogen and caustic outlets to detect overheating, stoppages, and leaks. Opens valves to flush lines and to draw sample of cell liquor. Measures specific gravity of liquor to facilitate process controls using hydrometer. Records data, such as temperatures, flow rate, operating time, and repairs made or needed. May replace glass and rubber tubing, nipples, and assemblies, and clean cell orifices and vents. When operating auxiliary equipment only to recover chlorine or hydrogen gas, may be designated Chlorine-Cell Tender (chemical); Hydrogen-Cell Tender (chemical).
GOE: 06.02.11 STRENGTH: L GED: R3 M2 L3 SVP: 5 DLU: 77

558.382-030 CHLORINATOR OPERATOR (chemical)
Controls equipment in which chemicals or other materials are chlorinated by reaction with chlorine gas: Pumps specified amounts of chemicals to chlorinator. Reads flowmeter and opens valves to regulate flow of chlorine and rate of chlorination reaction. Reads temperature gauges and turns steam and coolant valves to maintain reaction within specified temperature range. Tests sample of product for specific gravity and for boiling or freezing point, using hydrometer and thermometer. Observes color of product to determine when chlorination is completed. Records operating data, such as temperature and pressure in chlorinator and related equipment. May operate auxiliary units, such as vaporizer, filters, stills, and stripping columns. May be designated according to product formed as Bleach Chlorinator (chemical); Sulfur-Chloride Operator (chemical).
GOE: 06.02.11 STRENGTH: L GED: R3 M2 L2 SVP: 5 DLU: 77

558.382-034 CUPROUS-CHLORIDE OPERATOR (chemical) alternate titles: catalyst-manufacturing operator
Controls equipment to produce cuprous chloride, used as catalytic agent in chemical processes: Weighs or measures specified amounts of cuprous powder and other ingredients, and dumps materials into tank. Starts tank agitator and moves controls to heat and agitate ingredients to effect prescribed reaction, and to transfer product to auxiliary equipment for further processing. Tests filtrate for impurities, using standard chemical test equipment and procedure, and draws samples of chloride for laboratory analysis. Operates hydrogen-chloride coolers, condensers, and absorbers [ABSORTION OPERATOR (chemical)] to produce and supply hydrochloric acid to reactor units, using hydrometer to verify that specific gravity is maintained within prescribed limits. Compiles inventory reports of materials used and consumed. May shovel chloride from filter tank into containers for storage or transfer to other processing areas.
GOE: 06.02.11 STRENGTH: M GED: R3 M2 L2 SVP: 4 DLU: 77

558.382-038 KETTLE OPERATOR I (chemical)
Controls heated reaction kettles to process liquid and solid materials into specified chemical products: Turns valves or starts automatic metering pumps that admit specified quantity of liquid materials into kettle. Weighs and dumps or scoops prescribed solid, granular, or powdered ingredients into kettle, according to production sheet. Starts agitator to mix materials for specified time or stirs mixture with paddle. Observes gauges and recording instruments, and adjusts valves and controls to maintain temperature, vacuum pressure, and speed of reaction in kettle within prescribed limits. Draws sample of product for laboratory analysis. May test product for specified characteristics, such as acidity and composition, using standard litmus paper test and pH meter. May observe reaction through porthole in equipment and adjust controls to regulate speed or degree of reaction, according to knowledge of process. May tend auxiliary equipment, such as quench tanks and filter presses, to process resulting product or ingredients used to sustain reaction. May be designated by degree of pressure maintained in kettle as High-Pressure-Kettle Operator (chemical); Low-Pressure-Kettle Operator (chemical).
GOE: 06.02.11 STRENGTH: M GED: R3 M2 L2 SVP: 5 DLU: 77

558.382-042 KETTLE OPERATOR (plastic-synth.) alternate titles: reactor-kettle operator
Controls automatic or semiautomatic equipment to polymerize solutions in reaction kettles to produce synthetic-rubber polymers, such as silicone or neo-

prene, following written specifications: Weighs solid or liquid chemical additives, using balance or floor scale. Dumps ingredients into kettle, using overhead hoist. Turns valves to load kettles with monomer, catalyst, and modifier solutions. Starts agitator and turns steam or water valves to activate and control polymerization. Observes and records dial and gauge readings, and draws and tests samples to determine degree of completion of polymerization. Turns valves to release vacuum and to cool batch to terminate polymerization. Starts pumps to transfer nonreacted materials to rerun tank. Flushes kettle with water and changes filter socks, or cleans kettle, using brushes and cleaning solvents. May remove reactor cover and manually dump catalyst in reactor.
GOE: 06.02.13 STRENGTH: L GED: R3 M2 L2 SVP: 5 DLU: 77

558.382-046 NITRATOR OPERATOR (chemical)
Controls equipment to combine and process acids and specified chemical ingredients to produce explosives, such as nitroglycerin, tetryl, or TNT: Admits specified ingredients, such as mixed acids and toluene compounds, to metering or weighing tanks, and regulates feed to nitrator in specified timing and sequence. Starts agitator to mix ingredients for prescribed time or until settling occurs. Observes temperature and pressure gauges and turns steam and coolant valves to regulate reaction within specified limits to prevent explosion. Transfers batch or specified components to storage tanks or other processing equipment after prescribed time or when visual inspection indicates reaction is completed. Records gauge readings, nitration time, and ingredients consumed in shift log. May be designated according to explosive produced as Nitroglycerin-Nitrator Operator, Batch (chemical); Tetryl-Nitrator Operator (chemical); or according to intermediate materials nitrated as Binitrotoluene Operator (chemical); Mononitrotoluene Operator (chemical). May control continuous-process equipment and be designated Biazzi-Nitrator Operator (chemical).
GOE: 06.02.11 STRENGTH: L GED: R3 M2 L2 SVP: 6 DLU: 77

558.382-050 POLYMERIZATION-KETTLE OPERATOR (plastic-synth.) alternate titles: kettle operator; resin maker; syrup-kettle operator; synthetic-resin operator
Controls reactor vessels to polymerize raw resin materials to form phenolic, acrylic, or polyester resins: Pumps specified amount of raw material into calibrated tank according to formula and transfers materials into reactor. Starts mixers and pumps reagents and catalysts into reactor. Starts circulation and vacuum pumps. Adjusts valves to regulate flow of preheated or cooled fluid around jacket of reactor and to start and regulate polymerization reaction. Adjusts valves to regulate pressure and temperature in reactor. Tests viscosity and pH of resins to determine length of polymerization time, using pH meters and viscosimeters. Turns valves to discharge processed materials from kettles into cooling pans. Records processing time, pressure, temperature, and test results in log; and writes daily reports on amounts of raw materials used and finished product barreled or stored. May dump compounds into polymerized resins to thicken product. May pump polymerized resin from storage tanks to tank trucks or cars for shipment. May cast liquid plastics in molds. May analyze sample of plastics materials to determine clarity, acidity, fusibility, or brittleness, using slide rule, torsion balance, and other testing equipment.
GOE: 06.02.13 STRENGTH: M GED: R4 M3 L3 SVP: 7 DLU: 77

558.382-054 SODA-COLUMN OPERATOR (chemical)
Controls carbonating tower to precipitate sodium bicarbonate crystals from ammoniated brine in Solvay process production of soda ash: Observes temperature, pressure, and flowmeter gauges and adjusts valves and controls to admit ammonia and brine to converter and to regulate process conditions, according to plant procedure. Tests concentration of product, using standard test equipment and procedure, and adjusts temperature in tower to produce sodium bicarbonate crystals of specified size and concentration for efficient filtering, washing, and drying of product, to form soda ash. Flushes feedlines, using steam hose; and replaces gaskets, using handtools. May tend stills and related equipment to produce ammonia for absorption into brine.
GOE: 06.02.11 STRENGTH: L GED: R3 M2 L2 SVP: 4 DLU: 77

558.382-058 WET-MIX OPERATOR (chemical)
Controls premixer and reaction vessels to produce orthophosphate liquor by reaction of phosphoric acid with soda ash: Sets timing device on weigh tank to effect prescribed feed rate of soda ash to premixer. Starts premixer, pumps, exhaust fans, screw conveyors, and bucket elevator in required sequence. Observes flowmeters and turns valves to regulate flow of phosphoric acid and water to premixer as specified. Swings discharge spout over reaction vessel, and starts agitator in vessel to admit and mix product. Turns valve to regulate flow of steam through vessel heating coils to attain reaction, observing thermometer to verify required temperature. Lowers dipstick into tank to obtain sample for laboratory testing. Turns valves to add measured amounts of chemicals, as indicated by laboratory reports, to regulate chemical properties of mixture to specifications. Turns valves and starts pump to transfer finished mixture to spray drier feed tanks.
GOE: 06.02.11 STRENGTH: L GED: R3 M2 L2 SVP: 4 DLU: 77

558.385-010 CD-REACTOR OPERATOR (chemical)
Tends catalytic reactor that converts monovinylacetylene into unpolymerized constituent of neoprene rubber as directed by CD-REACTOR OPERATOR, HEAD (chemical): Moves equipment controls to start and shut down reactor components in sequence as directed. Gauges catalyst level in reactors and patrols area to record instrument readings in operating log. Collects and titrates samples of catalyst to facilitate process adjustments and production of product

meeting specified standards. Starts pumps to discharge and recharge catalyst in reactors and calcium chloride in driers and scrubber towers. Drains and flushes process lines and equipment, using water, steam hoses, and nitrogen-sweeping equipment. Inventories supplies received and consumed.
GOE: 06.02.11 STRENGTH: M GED: R3 M2 L2 SVP: 4 DLU: 77

558.385-014 TOWER HELPER (chemical)
Tends equipment units that generate hydrogen chloride to facilitate process control by ABSORPTION OPERATOR (chemical): Installs chlorine cylinders in chlorinating unit. Starts equipment and pumps to mix metered amount of chlorine with hydrochloric acid from absorption system and to transfer chlorinated acid to feed tanks of stripper still. Draws samples of product for laboratory analysis, or tests sample for specific gravity, acidity, and composition to maintain product specifications, using such instruments as hydrometer and pH meter. Maintains records of tank levels, gauge and instrument readings, and inventory of materials used and produced.
GOE: 06.04.11 STRENGTH: M GED: R3 M2 L2 SVP: 3 DLU: 77

558.482-010 FURNACE OPERATOR (chemical)
Controls continuous-process furnace and related equipment to decompose salt cake, forming hydrogen chloride: Starts salt conveyors or shovels salt cake into furnace; turns valves to fill furnace reaction pot with sulfuric acid from supply tank; and sets burners, dampers, and vents to fire furnace to specified temperature and effect liberation of hydrogen chloride. Computes salt and acid requirements, using instrument readings and formulas, and sets feed scales and timers for continuous operation or manually regulates feed and temperature controls to maintain production in conformity with plant standards. Removes scale from furnace walls and agitates salt cake to maintain efficient production, using scrapers and rake. Starts or regulates speed of salt-removal device to prepare furnace for new charge. Maintains log of shift production, gauge readings, and equipment failures.
GOE: 06.02.11 STRENGTH: M GED: R3 M3 L2 SVP: 4 DLU: 77

558.485-010 CAUSTIC OPERATOR (paper & pulp)
Tends equipment to causticize sodium compounds recovered from paper manufacturing processes: Observes dial indicators, charts, flowmeters, and signal lights on panel to determine level and temperature of solution in reactor tank, rate that chemicals flow into reactor tank, level of lime sludge in settling tanks, and amount of sludge in washers. Starts pumps to control flow of slaked lime and recovered chemicals into reactor tank, causticized solution to storage tanks, and lime sludge through washers to lime kiln, according to specifications. Tests alkalinity of causticized solution by titration, records test results, and computes percentage of caustic in solution, using slide rule.
GOE: 06.02.11 STRENGTH: L GED: R3 M3 L2 SVP: 4 DLU: 77

558.565-010 ACID-PLANT HELPER (chemical)
Tends furnace, absorber, cooler, scrubber, and auxiliary equipment used in producing phosphoric acid by oxidation and hydration of elemental phosphorus: Patrols work area; observes water levels in scrubber, venturi-duct pan, and cooling-tower basin; and reads flowmeter and pressure gauges on phosphorus pump, fans, and blower to verify process conditions. Records or calls readings to operator. Observes flow of cooling water over top and outer walls of furnace to ensure uniform distribution, and notifies operator of malfunction. Takes sample of cooling water for laboratory alkalinity test. Turns valves to transfer acid to specified storage tanks and to start and stop water sprays in absorber, as directed, to control acid strength. Removes and replaces screens and filters, using wrenches. Opens valves to flush phosphorus pump and water-treating equipment with steam and regenerative chemicals.
GOE: 06.04.11 STRENGTH: L GED: R3 M1 L2 SVP: 4 DLU: 77

558.565-014 ELECTRIC-CELL TENDER (chemical)
Tends battery of electric cells (tanks having positive and negative poles) to dissociate chemical elements from solutions: Examines poles and sides of cells for defects, such as corrosion or cracks, and notifies supervisory personnel of findings. Opens valves to fill cells with solutions, and moves controls to start electrolytic process. Observes gauges and indicators on panelboard; and moves controls to maintain specified pressure, temperature, amperage, and voltage in each cell. Presses button to actuate automatic measuring and gas-testing device, and observes gauges that indicate gas volume and dissociation of solution in each cell. Records data in operational log.
GOE: 06.02.11 STRENGTH: M GED: R3 M2 L2 SVP: 4 DLU: 77

558.582-010 PHOSPHORIC-ACID OPERATOR (chemical)
Operates agitators (reaction vessels), vacuum-filtrate system, and allied equipment from instrumented control board to produce phosphoric acid by reaction of sulfuric acid with phosphate rock in continuous strong-acid process: Monitors recording instruments, flowmeters, panel lights, and other indicators, and listens for warning signals to verify conformity of process conditions to plant standards. Starts automatic feed of phosphate rock, water, and sulfuric acid through reaction tanks, vacuum-filtrate system, and pumps. Turns knobs and screws on control board to regulate temperatures, weight, pressures, and flow of materials through system to effect prescribed reaction, according to knowledge of equipment and process. Draws samples of product at specified stages of process for laboratory analysis. Maintains log of gauge readings, shift production, and equipment malfunctions. Patrols area to inspect equipment for leaks and hazards, such as wear and pending malfunction.
GOE: 06.02.11 STRENGTH: L GED: R4 M3 L3 SVP: 7 DLU: 77

558.584-010 CELL TESTER (chemical) alternate titles: anode adjuster
Adjusts anodes on electrolytic cells to regulate voltage, using handtools: Attaches voltmeter wires to cell and millivoltmeter wires to anode and observes

readings to determine adjustments required. Loosens locknut and position nut, using wrenches, to lower anode until specified voltage reading is attained. Records cell voltage readings before and after adjustments and records number of anodes adjusted. May examine and repair defective cells [CELL REPAIRER (chemical)] or notify maintenance personnel of repairs needed. May clean cells and clear clogged feedlines, using scrapers, brushes, and rod. May seal cell leaks, using putty.
GOE: 06.03.02 STRENGTH: L GED: R3 M2 L2 SVP: 4 DLU: 77

558.585-010 CATALYTIC-CONVERTER-OPERATOR HELPER (chemical)
Tends catalytic converters that alter chemical composition of liquid or gaseous substances as directed by CATALYTIC-CONVERTER OPERATOR (chemical): Moves controls to set material feed, temperature, and pressure regulators at specified values. Monitors operation of pumps and auxiliary equipment, such as heat exchangers and absorbers, and moves controls to maintain operating equilibrium in auxiliaries as directed. Assists other workers in changing catalyst in reactor units. Turns valves to purge converters and sets thermostat on catalyst regenerators to rejuvenate spent catalyst. Records instrument readings in operating log. May be designated according to product produced as Butadiene-Converter Helper (chemical); Ethylbenzene-Converter Helper (chemical); Ethylene-Plant Helper (chemical); or according to chemical reaction effected as Dehydrogenation-Converter Helper (chemical).
GOE: 06.04.11 STRENGTH: L GED: R2 M1 L1 SVP: 5 DLU: 77

558.585-018 CONTACT-ACID-PLANT OPERATOR (chemical) alternate titles: regeneration operator; sulfuric-acid-plant operator
Tends automatic equipment that produces sulfuric acid by *contact process:* Turns valves and moves levers to start and stop flow of liquids and gases through converter, heat exchangers, absorber, cooler, and related equipment as indicated. Monitors lights, gauges, and recording instruments on control panel to determine that temperature, steam pressure, and flow of materials through system conform to plant standards. Patrols equipment area and records gauge readings at specified intervals for operating log. Collects sample of product for laboratory analysis and performs tests to determine specific gravity and percentage of sulfuric acid being processed. Periodically examines emission exits to determine that anti-pollution standards are met.
GOE: 06.02.11 STRENGTH: L GED: R3 M2 L2 SVP: 5 DLU: 77

558.585-022 CUPROUS-CHLORIDE HELPER (chemical)
Tends tanks, *absorption tower,* and related equipment that produces cuprous chloride for use as process catalyst, as directed by CUPROUS-CHLORIDE OPERATOR (chemical): Turns valves to transfer materials through auxiliary units, such as coolers, condensers, and absorbers, and to storage tanks. Assists CUPROUS-CHOLORIDE OPERATOR (chemical) in charging reaction tank with powdered copper. Records gauge readings and shift production for operating log. Patrols work area to detect and report malfunctions.
GOE: 06.04.11 STRENGTH: M GED: R2 M1 L2 SVP: 2 DLU: 77

558.585-026 DEVULCANIZER TENDER (rubber reclaim.) alternate titles: devulcanizer operator; digester charger
Tends *devulcanizers* that process ground scrap rubber with chemical compounds under steam pressure to produce *reclaim* rubber: Turns valves and observes gauges to drain specified quantities of materials, such as oil, pigments, and water onto scrap rubber in devulcanizer. Closes and bolts loading hatch to seal devulcanizer. Turns valves and observes gauges to maintain specified operating temperature and release steam pressure when unloading devulcanizer. May attach specified cycle chart to automatic timer. Records production data. May open discharge valve, allowing steam pressure to blow devulcanized rubber into holding tank. May weigh and dump ground scrap rubber into devulcanizers [DEVULCANIZER CHARGER (rubbee reclaim.)]. May tend high-pressure devulcanizer and be designated High-Pressure Devulcanizer Operator (rubber reclaim.).
GOE: 06.04.13 STRENGTH: M GED: R2 M2 L2 SVP: 3 DLU: 77

558.585-030 LEAD-NITRATE PROCESSOR (chemical) alternate titles: lead-shop operator
Tends heated kettle and auxiliary equipment to process molten lead and nitric acid into lead nitrate: Loads lead-melting kettle with lead ingots, using hoist. Turns valves to regulate flow of fuel oil and air, and tends stoker or shovels coal to fire furnace that melts lead in kettle. Ladles molten lead into trough or tips melting kettle to pour molten lead into trough for transfer to vat containing nitric acid where ingredients combine to form lead nitrate. Turns outlet valve to transfer lead nitrate to filter press for removal of impurities [FILTER-PRESS OPERATOR (any industry)]. Tests sample of filtrate for purity by observing color or using litmus paper. Starts pumps to transfer batch to storage tank. Gauges contents of tanks, using calibrated stick, and records quantity on batch card. May ladle molten lead into vats containing cold water to cause solidification into irregular, spongelike shapes, exposing more surface area for faster chemical reaction in subsequent process treatment. May drain off water and shovel solidified sponged lead onto conveyor for further processing.
GOE: 06.04.11 STRENGTH: H GED: R2 M1 L2 SVP: 3 DLU: 77

558.585-034 NEUTRALIZER (soap & rel.)
Tends kettles to neutralize alkaline paste used in preparation of liquid and powdered detergents: Turns valves to charge kettle with specified liquid ingredients, and starts agitator. Observes thermometer and adjusts flow of materials to maintain reaction temperature. Tests sample with meter to ensure neutral

product. Records readings and test results. Tends pumps to maintain supply of liquid ingredients in measuring tanks.
GOE: 06.04.19 STRENGTH: L GED: R2 M2 L2 SVP: 3 DLU: 77

558.585-038 POLYMERIZATION HELPER (plastic-synth.)
Assists POLYMERIZATION-KETTLE OPERATOR (plastic-synth.) in polymerizing raw resin materials to form phenolic, acrylic, and polyester resins: Starts pumps and turns valves to route raw materials into designated reactor vessels. Dumps powdered ingredients and resins into reactors by hand or using hoist. Turns reactor discharge valve to allow material to flow through funnel into drums to fill drums with base and blended resins. Marks product data on drums, using precut stencils, ink, and brushes. Makes new stencils as necessary, using stecil-cutting machine. Transports materials in production area, using handtruck and powered hoists. Taps reactors to obtain test samples for laboratory tests. Starts pumps and opens valves to pump resin from storage tanks into tank trucks or railroad cars for shipment. May tend coolers to reduce temperature of resins after polymerization. Performs other duties as described under HELPER (any industry) Master Title.
GOE: 06.04.13 STRENGTH: M GED: R3 M2 L2 SVP: 4 DLU: 77

558.585-042 TWITCHELL OPERATOR (chemical)
Tends vats in which fats or vegetable and animal oils are processed into glycerin and fatty acid: Pumps specified amount of fat or oil into vat and admits prescribed quantity of sulfuric acid from storage tank. Observes gauges and thermometer and turns steam valves to boil contents of vat. Pumps oil or fat to second vat and adds specified amount of distilled water and Twitchell's reagent. Starts agitator in vat and turns steam valves to boil mixture for prescribed time. Observes mixture through sight glass in pump line and turns valves to transfer fractions of product having different color and density to respective storage tanks. Records shift production, materials used, and heating and agitating time.
GOE: 06.04.11 STRENGTH: L GED: R2 M2 L2 SVP: 3 DLU: 77

558.666-010 DEVULCANIZER CHARGER (rubber reclaim.) alternate titles: weigh and charge worker
Charges ground scrap rubber into *devulcanizers* that process rubber with chemicals and steam: Pulls levers to drop measured amount of rubber into scale hopper. Pushes loaded hopper along monorail and pulls lever to dump contents into machine. Signals DEVULCANIZER TENDER (rubber reclaim.) when machines are loaded. May measure and pour specified pigments, caustics, and oils into devulcanizer. May observe gauges and turn valves to relieve steam pressure in devulcanizer preparatory to unloading and blow devulcanized rubber through tubes into storage bins.
GOE: 06.04.13 STRENGTH: H GED: R2 M1 L1 SVP: 2 DLU: 77

558.682-010 CRACKING-UNIT OPERATOR (plastic-synth.) alternate titles: recovery-unit operator
Operates cracking (recovery) unit of lead pots and condensers to vaporize and condense scrap plastics materials and recover monomer: Unbolts and removes side covers from lead pot, using handtools, and charges it with lead pigs. Adjusts controls of oil burner to melt lead at specified temperature. Sets pressure regulators to supply specified quantity of carbon dioxide to lead pot to eliminate formation of explosive mixture and observes process to detect leaks. Turns screw feed controls to regulate flow of scrap materials into molten lead. Adjusts controls on condensers which automatically recover monomer from solvent and pumps cracked monomer to storage tanks. Dismantles lead pot. Drains lead into molds.
GOE: 06.02.13 STRENGTH: M GED: R3 M2 L2 SVP: 5 DLU: 77

558.682-014 DISSOLVER OPERATOR (chemical)
Controls equipment that dissolves and precipitates chemicals used in manufacturing chemical products, such as butadiene and styrene: Pumps chemical solutions through premeasuring tanks, dissolver tanks, and precipitator tanks, observes thermometers, and turns valves to maintain temperature in tanks within specified limits to dissolve and precipitate solutions. Starts tank agitator to mix solution for prescribed time. Titrates sample of solution and inserts hydrometer to determine acidity and specific gravity of product. Observes flowmeters and turns valves to regulate flow of ingredients through tanks to alter concentration and produce product meeting specified standard. Pumps or drains remaining solutions from precipitate and turns valves to transfer product for further processing, shipment, or storage. When controlling precipitator tanks only, may be designated Precipitator Operator (chemical). When dumping caustic soda cake into dissolving tanks and controlling tanks to produce solution of specified concentration, may be designated Bottom-Liquor Attendant (chemical).
GOE: 06.02.11 STRENGTH: L GED: R3 M2 L2 SVP: 4 DLU: 77

558.682-018 FERMENTATION OPERATOR (chemical) alternate titles: biological-plant operator
Controls fermentation chambers and tanks to produce enzymes from fungal or bacterial growth for use as industrial catalysts: Sprinkles seed from hand container into mixing drum containing culture medium, such as bran, and starts drum revolving for specified time to disperse seed throughout medium. Opens drum to discharge batch into tubs, and shovels batch onto trays. Places trays on racks and pushes them into growing chambers. Sets thermostats, observes pressure gauges and meters, and moves controls to maintain specified atmospheric conditions that promote growth of culture. Examines batch for contamination by smell, touch, or observation, using knowledge of fermentation reactions. Removes trays from chamber after specified time. Dumps contents onto

conveyor that transfers material through delumping machine into portable tanks. Positions tanks under water faucets and opens valves to flush enzymes through sieve. Turns valve to siphon solution through series of portable tanks into head tank. Tests extraction for specific gravity, acidity, and alkalinity, using hydrometer and litmus paper; and adds specified salts, acids, or bases. May start centrifuge to separate solids from product.
GOE: 06.02.11 STRENGTH: M GED: R3 M2 L2 SVP: 5 DLU: 77

558.682-022 RECOVERY OPERATOR (chemical) alternate titles: denitrator operator
Controls distillation equipment to recover sulfuric and nitric acids from residue produced in manufacturing TNT and nitroglycerin: Turns valves and observes gauges and instruments to regulate flow of acids, steam, and water into denitrator tower to liberate nitric fumes, and to effect absorption of fumes in absorption towers for recovering acid of specified concentration. Draws acid samples for laboratory testing and pumps acid to storage tanks after laboratory approval. May determine concentration of acid, using hydrometer.
GOE: 06.04.11 STRENGTH: L GED: R3 M1 L2 SVP: 4 DLU: 77

558.685-010 ACID-POLYMERIZATION OPERATOR (chemical)
Tends batch still and polymerization vessel to distill and polymerize acrylic acid used in production of plastics: Tends laboratory-type batch still to vaporize and condense acrylic acid [BATCH-STILL OPERATOR (chemical) I]. Measures amount of distillate, using burette or gauging rod, and pours distilled acid into water-jacketed polymerization vessel. Heats vessel to prescribed temperature, and adds specified quantity of reagents to effect polymerization. Draws samples of product for laboratory analysis. Turns valves to transfer polymerized acid to storage or processing areas.
GOE: 06.04.11 STRENGTH: M GED: R3 M2 L1 SVP: 3 DLU: 77

558.685-014 BALL-MILL OPERATOR (chemical)
Tends ball mill and auxiliary equipment to produce sodium salicylate for use in production of salicylic acid: Opens valves to transfer specified quantities of sodium hydroxide and phenol solutions to tank, and starts agitators to mix solutions to form mixture of sodium phenate and water. Drains mixture into ball mill (closed metal tank), opens exhaust valve, and starts heaters to evaporate water from sodium phenate. Observes moisture indicators to determine when water has been removed from sodium phenate. Pumps cold water into jacket of ball mill to contract mill walls sufficiently to loosen pulpy sodium phenate. Heats ball mill to specified temperature, increases pressure in ball mill to required level, and pumps carbon dioxide into ball mill to change sodium phenate to sodium salicylate. Opens vents to rid sodium salicylate of excess carbon dioxide. Pumps specified quantity of water into ball mill to dissolve sodium salicylate, and pumps sodium salicylate solution into tanks for further processing into salicylic acid.
GOE: 06.04.11 STRENGTH: L GED: R3 M2 L2 SVP: 3 DLU: 77

558.685-018 BLEACHER OPERATOR (chemical; soap & rel.) alternate titles: cp bleacher operator
Tends tanks in which liquid and solid chemicals are bleached: Pumps specified amounts of liquid materials into tank. Dumps or scoops preweighed solids into feed hopper and starts agitator to mix ingredients for prescribed time. Observes temperature recorder and turns steam valves to maintain mixture at specified temperature. May drain sample of product for laboratory analysis. May pump product to storage tanks or to other equipment for further processing. May record weight of material used and bleaching time.
GOE: 06.04.11 STRENGTH: M GED: R2 M1 L1 SVP: 3 DLU: 77

558.685-022 CELL-TENDER HELPER (chemical) alternate titles: cell-attendant helper
Tends electrolytic cells to produce chlorine, caustic soda, and hydrogen, performing any combination of following tasks under direction of CELL TENDER (chemical): Pulls and positions current jumpers, connects jumper arms on circuits, and throws switches to cut cells out of service. Disconnects brine, gas, and hydrogen lines, using wrenches, to prepare cells for changing; and assists CELL CHANGER (chemical) in positioning cathodes and cell assemblies in place. Reconnects lines and flips switches to return cells to operation. Opens valves to flush lines, adjust and maintain brine flows and levels, and switch flow from brine tanks to bypasses. Draws sample of cell liquor and tests sample for caustic strength, using standard test equipment and chart. Cleans brine lines, using brushes and steam hose; and removes and dips sight glasses, nipples, bushings, elbows, tube assemblies, and rubber tubing in acid, solvent, or water bath to clean them. Examines chlorine lines for cracks, and cleans out orifices and vents. Changes chart recorders.
GOE: 06.04.11 STRENGTH: L GED: R2 M2 L2 SVP: 4 DLU: 77

558.685-026 DE-IONIZER OPERATOR (chemical)
Tends equipment that purifies glycerin by deionization process: Starts pumps to force glycerin slurry through resin beds in series of purification tanks. Observes flowmeters and pressure gauges, and adjusts controls as necessary to meet process standards. Tests slurry for acidity periodically, using litmus paper. Draws samples of purified glycerin for laboratory analysis. Back-flushes tanks with acid solution to regenerate resin, as necessary.
GOE: 06.04.11 STRENGTH: L GED: R3 M2 L2 SVP: 4 DLU: 77

558.685-030 ION-EXCHANGE OPERATOR (smelt. & refin.)
Tends battery of machines that recover uranium from slime (uranium sulfate and waste materials) through ion-exchange process: Regulates pumps to control

flow of slime through machine tanks at specified level. Fills porous baskets in tanks to specified level with uranium collector (synthetic resin beads), using bucket. Starts machine that dips baskets into slime to recover uranium which is deposited on surface of collector through ion-exchange. Drains tanks after specified period of contact time and cleans slime residue from tanks with hose. Refills tanks with nitric acid solution, using pump. Restarts machine to dissolve uranium from surface of collector in nitric acid solution. Starts pumps to move uranium nitrate solution from machine tanks to precipitation tanks.
GOE: 06.04.10 STRENGTH: L GED: R3 M1 L2 SVP: 4 DLU: 77

558.685-034   ION-EXCHANGE OPERATOR (chemical)
Tends equipment that removes metallic salts from gelatin solutions: Opens valves to control flow of hot water through jackets on exchangers (columns) to preheat equipment to prevent premature coagulation of gelatin solution. Connects gelatin-solution hoses to exchangers and pumps gelatin from storage tank through exchangers. Reads gauges to determine pressure in exchangers and adjusts valves as required to maintain specified pressure. Reads dial to determine pH (acid concentration) of solution and adjusts valve that controls flow of acid to maintain pH necessary to convert metallic salts in gelatin solution into acids that are absorbed by synthetic resins contained in exchangers. Pumps gelatin solution from exchangers to storage tank. Mixes solutions of acid and alkali and pumps solution through exchangers to wash metallic salts from synthetic resins and regenerate them. Turns valves to admit condensate that removes excess acid and alkali. Reads dial that indicates pH of regenerating solution and adjusts valves to maintain specified pH.
GOE: 06.04.19 STRENGTH: L GED: R3 M2 L2 SVP: 3 DLU: 77

558.685-038   ION-EXCHANGE OPERATOR (pharmaceut.)
Tends equipment to remove impurities from water used in manufacturing pharmaceuticals and toilet preparations: Starts pumps and turns valves to regulate flow of water into ion-exchanger to remove impurities such as magnesium and calcium. Activates electronic particle-detection devices to indicate level of impurities in treated water and automatically shut down system when impurities reach undesirable level, indicating need to regenerate system. Pumps water through tanks to flush system preparatory to regeneration. Circulates caustic solution through ion-exchanger to remove impurities from synthetic resins. Pumps water through system to rinse resin beds to remove caustic solution. Observes operation of pump units and pipe systems to detect leaks or mechanical defects. May tend water softener and demineralizing units to provide purified water for chemical process systems.
GOE: 06.04.11 STRENGTH: M GED: R3 M2 L2 SVP: 5 DLU: 77

558.685-042   LEAD-OXIDE-MILL TENDER (elec. equip.)
Tends continuous oxide mill and auxiliary equipment that converts pig lead into lead oxide used in manufacture of storage battery paste: Ignites furnace burner and loads pig lead into kettle that automatically melts lead and pours molten lead into machine that shapes lead into balls and discharges balls into storage bin. Rakes specified number of lead balls into mill that converts lead balls into lead oxide powder. Observes temperature and weight gauges, and turns valve to add coolant to mill as needed. Opens chute to release powder into barrel when milling is completed. Weighs and tests powder to determine percentage of oxidation, using reagents, gram scale, and other testing equipment. Reprocesses powder not meeting specifications. Records test results and amount of lead oxide powder milled.
GOE: 06.04.10 STRENGTH: M GED: R2 M2 L1 SVP: 3 DLU: 77

558.685-046   MVA-REACTOR OPERATOR (chemical)
Tends catalytic reactor and auxiliary equipment that produce monovinylacetylene for use in neoprene rubber manufacture, as directed by MVA-REACTOR OPERATOR, HEAD (chemical): Determines specific gravity of brine solution in drier unit, using hydrometer, and turns valve to circulate brine through saturator to maintain strength at plant standard. Weighs prescribed quantities of materials, dumps materials into mixing tanks to prepare brine solution, and opens valve to admit brine to drier as directed. Moves controls to start equipment that removes byproduct solution from drier by continuous flotation. Draws samples of materials as directed and determines acidity, using standard chemical test equipment and procedure. Maintains acidity at specified level in equipment to prevent explosion hazard. Drains and flushes saturators, using steam hose, and refills units with calcium chloride to maintain saturator efficiency.
GOE: 06.04.11 STRENGTH: M GED: R3 M2 L2 SVP: 4 DLU: 77

558.685-050   NITROGLYCERIN NEUTRALIZER (chemical) alternate titles: neutralizer
Tends vats that wash and treat nitroglycerin to neutralize acids remaining from nitrating process in explosives manufacture: Admits warm water to vat of nitroglycerin, and introduces stream of air from bottom of vat to agitate and mix product for specified interval. Turns off water and air to allow mixture to settle and opens drain cock to draw off wash water. Admits prepared aqueous solution of soda ash to vat to neutralize remaining acids, and starts agitating airflow. Tests mixture with litmus or other chemical indicator, rewashes nitroglycerin when it tests neutral, and transfers it to storage or processing areas. May prepare soda-ash solution, according to formula or proportion table.
GOE: 06.04.11 STRENGTH: M GED: R3 M1 L2 SVP: 5 DLU: 77

558.685-054   RED-LEAD BURNER (paint & varnish) alternate titles: oxide-furnace tender
Tends furnaces that convert litharge (yellow- or orange-colored monoxide) and lead tailings into red lead (lead oxide) for use in products, such as storage

batteries, paints, and ceramics: Ignites gas burners in furnace. Reads temperature gauge and adjusts controls to regulate flow of gas to maintain specified furnace temperature. Starts conveyor leading to furnace and dumps specified quantity of litharge or lead tailings onto conveyor. Starts furnace pan rotating to ensure uniform heating of material. Pulls lever to open door in bottom of furnace to drop powdered lead oxide onto conveyor leading to grinder. May test lead oxide, using beaker, acid, balance scale, and electric hotplate.
GOE: 06.04.11 STRENGTH: M GED: R2 M1 L1 SVP: 2 DLU: 77

558.685-058   CHEMICAL RECLAMATION EQUIPMENT OPERATOR (electron. comp.)
Tends equipment that distills printed circuit board (PCB) processing solvents from PCB processing waste solutions and etches gold from PCBs to reclaim gold and solvents: Places gold covered board section in drum and inserts drum in agitation system of rinse tank manually, and presses button to start and stop agitation at specified interval to rinse boards. Removes drum from rinse tank and places drum in agitator system of reclamation tank. Pushes button to start and stop agitator at specified interval to remove gold from boards. Removes drum from reclamation tank and places drum in agitator system of rinse tank. Pushes button to start and stop agitation system at specified interval to rinse boards. Removes drum from rinse tank and places PCBs into barrel. Pushes switch on rinse tank to pump gold solution from tank into empty barrel. Pushes buttons on still to start pumps and equipment that distill PCB processing solvents from solutions. Observes gauges on panel indicating collection barrels are full and presses button to shut off system.
GOE: 06.04.11 STRENGTH: H GED: R2 M1 L2 SVP: 3 DLU: 86

558.685-062   CHEMICAL OPERATOR II (chemical) alternate titles: reactor operator
Tends equipment units or semiautomatic system that processes chemical substances into industrial or consumer products, such as detergents, emulsifiers, salts, bleaching agents, acids, and synthetic resins: Dumps specified amounts of solid materials into heating vessels or blending tanks; and turns valves to feed liquid and gaseous materials through equipment units, or sets controls in specified sequence on control panel to start automatic feed. Turns valves or moves controls to maintain system at specified temperature, pressure, and vacuum levels. Observes chemical reactions; monitors gauges, signals, and recorders; and receives notification from control laboratory, supervisor, or other workers to make specified operating adjustments. Draws samples of products for laboratory analysis. Maintains log of gauge readings and shift production. May perform chemical tests on product to ensure conformance with specifications, using standard test equipment, materials, and procedure. May be designated according to substance processed as Low-Chloride Soda Operator (chemical); Salt-Plant Operator (chemical); Sodium-Methylate Operator (chemical); equipment tended as Styrene-Dehydration-Reactor Operator (chemical); Tower Operator (chemical) II; or reaction produced as Emulsification Operator (oils & grease); Precipitation Equipment Tender (chemical).
GOE: 06.04.11 STRENGTH: M GED: R3 M2 L2 SVP: 4 DLU: 80

558.686-010   FURNACE HELPER (chemical)
Assists FURNACE OPERATOR (chemical) in decomposing salt cake to form hydrogen chloride: Shovels salt cake into furnace on startup. Removes scale from walls of furnace, using handscrapers, and cleans conveyors, salt-cake cooler, and crusher with brushes and handtools. May start motors and move controls as instructed to regulate flow of coolants, action of salt-cake crusher, and speed of conveyors that transfer salt-cake between furnace building and storage towers or bins. May drive tractor to transfer salt cake about plant. Performs other duties as described under HELPER (any industry) Master Title.
GOE: 06.04.11 STRENGTH: H GED: R1 M1 L1 SVP: 2 DLU: 77

558.687-010   BLEACH PACKER (chemical) alternate titles: charger
Starts conveyors that automatically convey slaked lime to chlorinating chamber where it is transformed into bleaching powder. Spreads lime uniformly over chamber floor, using shovel or wood spreader, and rakes spread lime to furrow layer, exposing maximum surface area for chlorination. Shovels bleaching powder through chutes into containers, and closes containers preparatory to storage or shipment.
GOE: 06.04.11 STRENGTH: M GED: R1 M1 L1 SVP: 1 DLU: 77

559   OCCUPATIONS IN PROCESSING OF CHEMICALS, PLASTICS, SYNTHETICS, RUBBER, PAINT, AND RELATED PRODUCTS, N.E.C.

This group includes occupations, not elsewhere classified, concerned with processing chemicals, plastics, synthetics, rubber, paint, and related products.

559.130-010   CHEMICAL-PROCESSING SUPERVISOR (pharmaceut.) alternate titles: synthetic department supervisor
Supervises and coordinates activities of workers engaged in processing organic chemicals, plant and animal tissue, and solvents for use in manufacturing medications. Sets up and operates mixing, drying, pulverization, distillation, filtration, separation, extraction, and crystallization equipment to produce test samples of new products. Performs other duties as described under SUPERVISOR (any industry) Master Title.
GOE: 06.01.01 STRENGTH: M GED: R4 M3 L3 SVP: 8 DLU: 77

559.130-014 SUPERVISOR, FERTILIZER PROCESSING (chemical)
Supervises and coordinates activities of workers engaged in controlling equipment to produce nitric acid from anhydrous ammonia and reprocessing nitric acid to produce solid and liquid fertilizers and fertilizer materials: Directs workers in setting up equipment according to product specifications, using knowledge of equipment functions and chemical processes involved. Observes recording-instrument charts, flowmeters, and gauges to determine processing conditions, and analyzes laboratory test results to verify conformance of product to specifications. Trains workers in operation of equipment. Performs other duties as described under SUPERVISOR (any industry) Master Title.
GOE: 06.02.01 STRENGTH: L GED: R4 M3 L3 SVP: 7 DLU: 77

559.130-018 SUPERVISOR, RECORD PRESS (recording)
Supervises and coordinates activities of workers engaged in pressing, audio-testing, and inspecting phonograph records: Directs workers in setting up record presses. Examines records for defects, such as bubbles and dents and analyzes data compiled in audio-testing to determine cause of defects. Directs workers in changing record compound, ordering new dies, or cleaning dies to correct defects. Adjusts press controls to regulate water and steam pressure or length of process cycle, according to type of record compound. Performs other duties as described under SUPERVISOR (any industry) Master Title.
GOE: 06.02.01 STRENGTH: L GED: R4 M3 L3 SVP: 7 DLU: 77

559.130-022 SUPERVISOR, TILE-AND-MOTTLE (fabrication, nec)
Supervises and coordinates activities of workers engaged in weighing, crushing, and mixing ingredients, and operating machines to manufacture asphalt and vinyl asbestos floor tile: Examines product to identify contaminated, defective, or substandard material. Trains new workers in job duties. Performs other duties as described under SUPERVISOR (any industry) Master Title.
GOE: 06.02.01 STRENGTH: M GED: R4 M3 L3 SVP: 6 DLU: 77

559.131-010 PHARMACEUTICAL-COMPOUNDING SUPERVISOR (pharmaceut.)
Supervises and coordinates activities of workers engaged in compounding inert and active ingredients to produce pharmaceutical products in tablet, granule, ampoule, liquid, powder, and ointment form. Determines processing methods necessary to achieve product of specified standard, using knowledge of chemical reactions and pharmaceutical processing methods and procedures. Performs other duties as described under SUPERVISOR (any industry) Master Title.
GOE: 06.01.01 STRENGTH: L GED: R4 M3 L3 SVP: 7 DLU: 78

559.131-014 QUALITY-CONTROL SUPERVISOR (plastic-synth.)
Supervises and coordinates activities of workers engaged in testing quality of polyethylene sheet and tubular film: Selects and schedules tests to measure factors, such as color intensity, tensile strength, optical distortion, and printability of film, according to job specifications and procedure manuals. Trains new workers in use of test equipment, such as fadometer and burst tester. Reviews new product specifications, and conducts experimental tests for strength, permeability, and other factors, using weights, acid, ink, and other materials to determine quality control procedures necessary to meet new specifications. Prepares reports of experimental test results for use by management personnel. Performs other duties as described under SUPERVISOR (any industry) Master Title.
GOE: 06.02.01 STRENGTH: L GED: R4 M3 L3 SVP: 7 DLU: 77

559.131-018 TNT-LINE SUPERVISOR (chemical)
Supervises and coordinates activities of workers engaged in production of TNT. Directs workers in mixing acids and toluene in nitrators, recovering nitric acid from spent solutions, and packing finished product. Performs other duties as described under SUPERVISOR (any industry) Master Title.
GOE: 06.02.01 STRENGTH: L GED: R4 M3 L3 SVP: 7 DLU: 77

559.132-010 ACID SUPERVISOR (chemical)
Supervises and coordinates activities of workers engaged in operation of equipment to process, store, and mix acids for use in making explosives, such as nitroglycerin, TNT, and dynamite: Trains workers in operation of equipment. Inspects equipment and observes workers to ensure safe work practices. May supervise production of ammonium nitrate crystals and drying of dynamite-filler ingredients. Performs other duties as described under SUPERVISOR (any industry) Master Title.
GOE: 06.02.01 STRENGTH: L GED: R4 M3 L3 SVP: 7 DLU: 77

559.132-014 CALENDER SUPERVISOR (plastic-synth.)
Supervises and coordinates activities of workers engaged in mixing and blending plastics materials according to formulas, screening plastics dough to remove lumps and foreign objects, rolling dough into sheets of specified width and thickness, and inspecting product for conformance to specifications: Trains new employees. Observes meters, gauges, and recording-instrument charts to verify process specifications. Examines product for defects and measures thickness of sheets with micrometer. Performs other duties as described under SUPERVISOR (any industry) Master Title.
GOE: 06.02.01 STRENGTH: L GED: R4 M3 L3 SVP: 7 DLU: 77

559.132-018 CATALYST OPERATOR, CHIEF (chemical) alternate titles: catalyst plant supervisor
Supervises and coordinates activities of workers engaged in operation of equipment, such as impregnators, precipitators, dissolvers, crushers, washers, driers, and reduction furnaces, to prepare catalysts used in production of buta-
diene, styrene, and edible oils: Performs titration tests and takes pH readings of compounds to determine amounts of acids and neutralizers to be added to compounds for conformance to formula specifications. Calculates amount of catalyst produced, using laboratory reports and computations from standards chart. Directs workers pumping nitrogen through furnace lines to release hydrogen to prevent explosions. Trains workers in machine operation. Performs other duties as described under SUPERVISOR (any industry) Master Title.
GOE: 06.01.01 STRENGTH: L GED: R4 M3 L3 SVP: 7 DLU: 77

559.132-022 FINISHING-AREA SUPERVISOR (plastic-synth.)
Supervises and coordinates activities of workers engaged in operating coagulation tanks, vacuum filters, atmospheric driers, hammer mills, calender machine, and cutting, stacking, and wrapping machines to convert synthetic-rubber latex to crumbs (solids) and to prepare rubber for shipment: Observes meters and recording-instrument charts to follow progress of process reactions, verify process specifications, and diagnose malfunction. Inspects operating condition of machinery and equipment and examines product to detect equipment malfunctions. Trains workers in operation of equipment. Performs other duties as described under SUPERVISOR (any industry) Master Title. May supervise workers engaged in coagulation, filtration, and drying activities only and be designated Coagulating-Drying Supervisor (plastic-synth.).
GOE: 06.01.01 STRENGTH: L GED: R4 M3 L3 SVP: 8 DLU: 77

559.132-026 HEAD OPERATOR, SULFIDE (chemical)
Supervises and coordinates activities of workers engaged in tending catalytic reactors, continuous stills, and auxiliary equipment, such as pumps, compressors, heaters, scrubbers, strippers, separators, condensers, and coolers, to produce organic sulfur chemicals from materials, such as sulfur, methane gas, alcohols, and olefins: Trains workers in operation of equipment. Observes flowmeter, gauges, and recording-instrument charts to verify conformity of process with specifications. Examines equipment for malfunctions, such as excessive wear and leaks. Performs other duties as described under SUPERVISOR (any industry) Master Title.
GOE: 06.01.01 STRENGTH: L GED: R4 M3 L3 SVP: 8 DLU: 77

559.132-030 HEATING-AND-BLENDING SUPERVISOR (chemical) alternate titles: mixing-and-dispensing supervisor
Supervises and coordinates activities of workers engaged in heating and mixing chemical ingredients to make cleaning and polishing compounds: Schedules utilization of equipment, such as agitation, blending, and heating kettles and storage tanks, to meet production schedules. Trains workers in operation of equipment. Observes appearance and reaction of chemical ingredients during heating and blending process to detect deviations from standard. Obtains samples of product for quality control laboratory. Performs other duties as described under SUPERVISOR (any industry) Master Title.
GOE: 06.02.01 STRENGTH: L GED: R4 M2 L3 SVP: 8 DLU: 77

559.132-034 MILL SUPERVISOR (nonmet. min.)
Supervises and coordinates activities of workers engaged in grinding ores, separating graphite from sand and other impurities by flotation processes, and drying finished graphite: Reads meters and gauges and observes operating condition of equipment and appearance of product in various stages of process to detect malfunction. Reviews laboratory test results to resolve problems affecting grade and purity of product, and recovery rate from ores. Trains workers in operation of equipment. Performs other duties as described under SUPERVISOR (any industry) Master Title.
GOE: 06.04.01 STRENGTH: L GED: R4 M3 L3 SVP: 7 DLU: 77

559.132-038 NITROGLYCERIN SUPERVISOR (chemical)
Supervises and coordinates activities of workers engaged in nitrating glycerine with nitric acid to make nitroglycerin, separating, washing, and neutralizing operations, and delivering nitroglycerin to dynamite mix house. Trains workers in operating equipment and instructs workers in safety procedures. Performs other duties as described under SUPERVISOR (any industry) Master Title.
GOE: 06.01.01 STRENGTH: L GED: R4 M3 L3 SVP: 7 DLU: 77

559.132-042 PROCESS-AREA SUPERVISOR (plastic-synth.) alternate titles: kettle operator, head; mill operator, head; poly-area supervisor
Supervises and coordinates activities of workers engaged in preparing chemical solutions and in operating purification units, reaction vessels, and driers in polymerization of raw materials, such as synthetic rubber or resin: Plans preparation of chemical solutions and rate of flow of materials through reaction vessels to maintain continuous flow of polymer through process. Observes control-panel instruments to verify conformity of reaction and monomer-recovery process to specifications. Trains workers in operation of equipment. Performs other duties as described under SUPERVISOR (any industry) Master Title. May be designated according to activity of workers supervised as Drier Operator, Head (plastic-synth.); Monomer-Recovery Supervisor (plastic-synth.); Polymerization Supervisor (plastic-synth.).
GOE: 06.01.01 STRENGTH: L GED: R4 M3 L3 SVP: 7 DLU: 77

559.132-046 PRODUCTION SUPERVISOR, ANHYDROUS AMMONIA (chemical)
Supervises and coordinates activities of workers engaged in operating equipment to produce anhydrous ammonia by catalytic-cracking of methane (natural) gas, compressing gas, removing carbon compounds from gas, and combining

(synthesis) hydrogen and nitrogen into liquid (anhydrous) ammonia: Reads operating reports and tests results to evaluate processing operations and production efficiency. Observes recording-instrument charts, meters, and gauges to verify specified temperatures, pressures, flow rates, and material ratios. Correlates variations in instrument readings to diagnose causes of equipment malfunctions. Moves controls to set or adjust automatic equipment to process specifications. Performs other duties as described under SUPERVISOR (any industry) Master Title.
GOE: 06.01.01 STRENGTH: L GED: R4 M3 L3 SVP: 8 DLU: 77

559.132-050 PRODUCTION SUPERVISOR, DEFLUORINATED PHOSPHATE (chemical)
    Supervises and coordinates activities of workers engaged in mixing, curing, calcining, cooling, grinding, and screening powdered phosphate rocks in production of defluorinated phosphate (tricalcium phosphate): Observes meters, gauges, and recording-instrument charts to verify specified process conditions, such as flow rates of materials, process temperatures, and operating speed of calciner and feeders. Turns dials to regulate automatic controls of various processes. Orders changes in weight settings at vibrator-scale feeder, burner setting in calciner, and operating speeds of calciner and feeders, according to production requirements. Inspects process and bagging equipment for malfunctions. Performs other duties as described under SUPERVISOR (any industry) Master Title.
GOE: 06.02.01 STRENGTH: L GED: R4 M3 L3 SVP: 7 DLU: 77

559.132-054 SUPERVISOR I (chemical)
    Supervises and coordinates activities of workers engaged in making organic chemical products: Computes quantities of chemicals required for specific batches, following laboratory formulas. Verifies processing of chemical products at specified checkpoints to ensure that formulas are followed, pressure and temperature specifications are within tolerance, and chemical batches are within standard limits. Trains employees in job duties. May test chemical batches for acidity, alkalinity, and solubility, using standard test equipment. Performs other duties as described under SUPERVISOR (any industry) Master Title. May be designated according to process as Supervisor, Color Making (chemical); Supervisor, Flushing (chemical); Supervisor, Intermediates (chemical).
GOE: 06.01.01 STRENGTH: M GED: R4 M3 L3 SVP: 7 DLU: 77

559.132-058 SUPERVISOR (rubber reclaim.) alternate titles: devulcanizer, head; hog-room supervisor; shipping-room supervisor
    Supervises and coordinates activities of workers engaged in processing scrap rubber into reclaimed rubber: Analyzes production schedules and assigns workers to activities, such as grinding, straining, devulcanizing, drying, refining, and inspecting. Trains employees in work methods and procedures. Inspects reclaimed rubber for conformance to specifications and orders reprocessing if required. Performs other duties as described under SUPERVISOR (any industry) Master Title. May be designated according to activity as Devulcanizer Inspector (rubber reclaim.); Final-Inspection Supervisor (rubber reclaim.); Grinding-Room Inspector (rubber reclaim.); Millroom Supervisor (rubber reclaim.); Rubber-Compounder Supervisor (rubber reclaim.).
GOE: 06.02.01 STRENGTH: L GED: R4 M3 L3 SVP: 6 DLU: 77

559.132-062 SUPERVISOR, ALUM PLANT (chemical)
    Supervises and coordinates activities of workers engaged in producing alum liquor (aluminum sulfate) by continuous process reaction (digestion) of sulfuric acid with powdered bauxite ore: Requisitions bauxite ore from other company plants and schedules required delivery dates. Reads operating reports showing temperature, specific gravity, and flow-rate readings to verify specified process conditions. Inspects equipment for mechanical defects and malfunctions. Trains new employees in operation of equipment. May study technical papers to plan process improvements, and diagrams changes, using drafting instruments. Performs other duties as described under SUPERVISOR (any industry) Master Title.
GOE: 06.02.01 STRENGTH: L GED: R4 M3 L3 SVP: 7 DLU: 77

559.132-066 SUPERVISOR, BONE PLANT (chemical)
    Supervises and coordinates activities of workers engaged in producing boneblack (animal charcoal), bonemeal, bone flour, and grease by extracting, crushing, grinding, screening, and charring bones: Trains new employees in machine operation. Performs other duties as described under SUPERVISOR (any industry) Master Title.
GOE: 06.02.01 STRENGTH: L GED: R4 M3 L3 SVP: 8 DLU: 77

559.132-070 SUPERVISOR, CD-AREA (chemical) alternate titles: cd-manufacturing supervisor
    Supervises and coordinates activities of workers engaged in converting monovinylacetylene to chlorobutadiene (chloroprene) for subsequent polymerization to neoprene rubber. Trains new workers in operation of equipment. Performs other duties as described under SUPERVISOR (any industry) Master Title.
GOE: 06.02.01 STRENGTH: M GED: R4 M3 L4 SVP: 7 DLU: 77

559.132-074 SUPERVISOR, COOK HOUSE (chemical)
    Supervises and coordinates activities of workers engaged in making and dehydrating glue made from skins, splits, fleshings, and trimmings: Directs loading of stock into cooking vats. Estimates amount and type of stock and specified cooking time. Observes operation of filters, evaporators, and driers to ver-

ify maximum production at specified level of quality. Trains new workers. Performs other duties as described under SUPERVISOR (any industry) Master Title.
GOE: 06.02.01 STRENGTH: L GED: R4 M3 L3 SVP: 7 DLU: 77

559.132-078 SUPERVISOR, DEHYDROGENATION (chemical; petrol. refin.) alternate titles: catalyst supervisor; dehydrogenation operator, head
    Supervises and coordinates activities of workers engaged in operation of preheat furnaces, catalytic reactors, quench and stripper towers, absorbers, stabilizer, rerun continuous stills, and auxiliary equipment, such as inert-gas generating system, condensers, heat exchangers, pumps, compressors, and blowers to produce petrochemicals, such as butadiene, styrene, butylene, and ethylbenzene: Trains workers in operation of equipment. Coordinates operation of various units in system to ensure required production yields, referring to run sheets, test books, order books, logbooks, and pumping records. Observes recording-instrument charts, flowmeters, and gauges to verify conformity of temperatures, pressures, flow rates, and liquid levels to process specifications. Correlates instrument readings and test results to diagnose process malfunctions. Inspects equipment and cathodic-protection system to detect defects and malfunctions. May be designated according to product as Butadiene Operator, Chief (chemical; petrol. refin.); Ethylbenzene-Cracking Supervisor (chemical; petrol. refin.); Isobutylene Operator, Chief (chemical); Styrene Operator, Chief (chemical; petrol. refin.). Performs other duties as described under SUPERVISOR (any industry) Master Title.
GOE: 06.01.01 STRENGTH: L GED: R4 M3 L3 SVP: 8 DLU: 77

559.132-082 SUPERVISOR, DRY PASTE (chemical)
    Supervises and coordinates activities of workers engaged in processing mixtures of flour and water, according to formulas, to produce dry wallpaper pastes: Directs workers in mixing slurries (milk), and drying, pulverizing, and packaging pastes. Feels paste flakes and reads test results to detect causes of deviation of product from prescribed quality standards. Trains workers in operation of equipment. Performs other duties as described under SUPERVISOR (any industry) Master Title.
GOE: 06.02.01 STRENGTH: L GED: R4 M2 L3 SVP: 7 DLU: 77

559.132-086 SUPERVISOR, ESTERS-AND-EMULSIFIERS (chemical)
    Supervises and coordinates activities of workers engaged in compounding, blending, and reacting fatty acids and other chemicals to produce industrial esters and emulsifiers: Reads production orders and specifications and plans operating procedures. Assigns workers to duties, such as controlling compounding, reacting, and flaking equipment, and packing finished products. Explains duties to inexperienced workers and assigns them to work with experienced operators during training period. Reads laboratory reports, and orders process equipment changes as necessary to meet quality standards. Performs other duties as described under SUPERVISOR (any industry) Master Title.
GOE: 06.02.01 STRENGTH: L GED: R4 M3 L3 SVP: 7 DLU: 77

559.132-090 SUPERVISOR, FERTILIZER (chemical)
    Supervises and coordinates activities of workers engaged in mixing, weighing, and bagging fertilizer materials: Directs workers in receiving and storing chemicals and other ingredients. Maintains inventory of tools, equipment, and materials in storage. Directs workers in bagging and weighing finished product. Trains workers in operation of equipment. Performs other duties as described under SUPERVISOR (any industry) Master Title.
GOE: 06.04.01 STRENGTH: L GED: R4 M3 L3 SVP: 6 DLU: 77

559.132-094 SUPERVISOR, FURNACE PROCESS (chemical)
    Supervises and coordinates activities of workers engaged in producing various types of carbon black by partial combustion of crude oil or natural gas, or mixtures of both, in furnace-process plants. Interprets process specifications to subordinates according to types of carbon black to be produced. Observes meters and gauges and reviews operating reports to verify control of process. Trains workers in furnace operation. Performs other duties as described under SUPERVISOR (any industry) Master Title.
GOE: 06.02.01 STRENGTH: L GED: R4 M3 L3 SVP: 7 DLU: 77

559.132-098 SUPERVISOR, GLYCERIN (soap & rel.)
    Supervises and coordinates activities of workers engaged in processing oils to produce fatty acids and glycerin: Reads laboratory test reports, analyzes causes of deviation from specifications, and orders changes in time, temperature, or flow rate to bring product into conformance with standards. Demonstrates duties to new workers and assigns experienced operator to work with them during training period. Performs other duties as described under SUPERVISOR (any industry) Master Title.
GOE: 06.02.01 STRENGTH: L GED: R4 M3 L4 SVP: 7 DLU: 77

559.132-102 SUPERVISOR, INSECTICIDE (chemical)
    Supervises and coordinates activities of workers engaged in processing chemical ingredients to produce insecticide: Reads production orders to determine product specifications and raw material requirements. Assigns workers to chemical processing equipment, such as mixing tanks, reaction chambers, condensers, flake-forming cylinders, and milling machines. Issues processing instructions for control variables, such as temperature, pressure, and material flow rate. Reviews laboratory reports and orders equipment adjustments to produce product to quality standards. Trains new workers in operation of equipment. Performs other duties as described under SUPERVISOR (any industry) Master Title.

GOE: 06.02.01 STRENGTH: L GED: R4 M3 L3 SVP: 7 DLU: 77

559.132-106 SUPERVISOR, LIQUEFACTION (chemical)
Supervises and coordinates activities of workers engaged in compressing and liquefying gases, such as oxygen, chlorine, and nitrogen, and in filling tank cars, cylinders, or storage tanks with gases. Trains new workers. Performs duties as described under SUPERVISOR (any industry) Master Title. May be designated according to gas processed as Supervisor, Chlorine-Liquefaction (chemical).
GOE: 06.02.01 STRENGTH: L GED: R4 M3 L3 SVP: 7 DLU: 77

559.132-110 SUPERVISOR, LITHARGE (paint & varnish) alternate titles: furnace-room supervisor
Supervises and coordinates activities of workers engaged in oxidizing, drying, and grinding lead to produce litharge. Trains new workers. Performs other duties as described under SUPERVISOR (any industry) Master Title.
GOE: 06.02.01 STRENGTH: L GED: R4 M3 L3 SVP: 7 DLU: 77

559.132-114 SUPERVISOR, PAINT (paint & varnish)
Supervises and coordinates activities of workers engaged in mixing, grinding, thinning, tinting, cooking, or clarifying pigments and other ingredients used in making paints and related products: Plans production schedules to coordinate departmental activities. Verifies batch tickets for compliance with master formula. Calculates batch quantities to ensure utilization of production capacity. Evaluates laboratory control-test results and tests batches of paint, using equipment such as grind-gauge, colorimeter, and viscometer, to verify adherence to specifications. Trains new workers. Performs other duties as described under SUPERVISOR (any industry) Master Title. May be designated according to activities of workers supervised as Supervisor, Grinding (paint & varnish); Supervisor, Mixing (paint & varnish); Supervisor, Thinning-Tinting (paint & varnish).
GOE: 06.01.01 STRENGTH: L GED: R4 M3 L3 SVP: 7 DLU: 78

559.132-118 SUPERVISOR, PHOSPHORUS PROCESSING (chemical)
Supervises and coordinates activities of workers engaged in oxidation and hydration of elemental phosphorus, mixing soda ash with phosphoric acid to produce disodium phosphates, and drying, calcining, and cooling phosphate mixture to produce sodium tripolyphosphate: Trains employees in operation of equipment. Reviews reports and observes recording-instrument charts, flowmeters, and gauges to verify specified operating conditions of equipment, and to diagnose equipment malfunctions. Inspects equipment to detect mechanical defects and malfunctions. Performs other duties as described under SUPERVISOR (any industry) Master Title.
GOE: 06.02.01 STRENGTH: L GED: R4 M3 L3 SVP: 8 DLU: 77

559.132-122 SUPERVISOR, PIGMENT MAKING (chemical) alternate titles: supervisor, color making
Supervises and coordinates activities of workers engaged in grinding, dispersing, filtering, drying, and mixing chemicals to produce color pigments: Inspects mechanical equipment and pipelines for defects. Adjusts meters, gauges, and automatic controls, and repairs equipment, using handtools. Trains workers in operation of equipment. Performs other duties as described under SUPERVISOR (any industry) Master Title. May be designated according to function as Color Control Supervisor (chemical); Color-Making Supervisor (chemical); Drying-Room Supervisor (chemical); Filter-Press Supervisor (chemical); Grinding-Room Supervisor (chemical).
GOE: 06.02.01 STRENGTH: L GED: R4 M3 L3 SVP: 7 DLU: 77

559.132-126 SUPERVISOR, REFINING (chemical)
Supervises and coordinates activities of workers engaged in refining salt: Reads production schedule to determine product specifications such as type and quantity of salt to be processed, refining sequences, and formulas for mixing salt with additives. Directs workers in mixing, milling, and screening of salt and coordinates flow of finished product to packaging and bulk-loading stations according to shipping schedule. Trains workers in operation of machines and equipment. May direct workers in packaging product. Performs other duties as described under SUPERVISOR (any industry) Master Title.
GOE: 06.01.01 STRENGTH: L GED: R4 M3 L3 SVP: 7 DLU: 77

559.132-130 SUPERVISOR, TOILET-AND-LAUNDRY SOAP (soap & rel.)
Supervises and coordinates activities of workers engaged in manufacture of bar, granular, and liquid soap: Requisitions materials, such as acids, dyes, perfumes, tallow, and packaging materials. Analyzes laboratory reports on in-process materials to determine changes in operating conditions required to resolve processing problems, such as excessive alkalinity or off-color materials. Examines finished product to determine conformance to specifications. Trains workers in machine operations. Performs other duties as described under SUPERVISOR (any industry) Master Title.
GOE: 06.01.01 STRENGTH: L GED: R4 M3 L3 SVP: 7 DLU: 77

559.132-134 SUPERVISOR, VARNISH (paint & varnish) alternate titles: tankroom supervisor
Supervises and coordinates activities of workers engaged in cooking, thinning, filtering, storing, and blending gums, resins, and oils to produce varnish and related products: Plans production schedules to coordinate cooking, thinning, filtering, storing, blending, and filling operations, according to processing time and availability of equipment, materials, personnel, and storage facilities. Converts master-formula quantities to smaller batch amounts, according to departmental production capacity. Reviews test results of viscosity and orders specified thinners to be added to varnish. Trains new workers. Performs other duties as described under SUPERVISOR (any industry) Master Title.
GOE: 06.02.01 STRENGTH: L GED: R4 M3 L3 SVP: 8 DLU: 77

559.132-138 TRANSFER-AND-PUMPHOUSE OPERATOR, CHIEF (chemical) alternate titles: pumphouse operator, chief; terminal supervisor
Supervises and coordinates activities of workers engaged in receiving, storing, and pumping raw chemical materials to production units, and in loading finished products into tank cars and tank trucks: Trains workers in new job assignments. Examines storage tanks, loading racks, and pumping equipment to ensure safe working conditions and to detect mechanical defects and malfunctions, such as hot bearings, excessive wear, and leaks. Observes meters and gauges to verify specified flow rates, temperatures, and pressures. Directs workers in transfer of raw materials from tank cars to specified storage areas, spotting of cars at unloading and loading stations, and loading finished products into tank cars. Performs other duties as described under SUPERVISOR (any industry) Master Title.
GOE: 06.04.01 STRENGTH: L GED: R4 M3 L3 SVP: 7 DLU: 77

559.134-010 QUALITY-CONTROL SUPERVISOR (plastic prod.)
Supervises and coordinates activities of workers engaged in inspecting incoming materials, inprocess molded plastic components, and finished fabricated plastic products to ensure adherence to company quality standards and customer specifications: Draws sketch and writes inspection procedure for each new item to be fabricated, indicating areas to be examined, measuring devices to be used, and maximum and minimum acceptable dimensions. Distributes sketch and procedure to engineering, production control, and inspection work stations. Inspects molded components following first-run production of new item, using gauges and shadow comparator, and advises technician of type of defects noted and need for machine adjustment. Repeats inspection procedure until product meets quality standards and specifications are attained. Confers with customer representative to resolve complaints. Notifies suppliers and subcontractors of reasons for rejection of materials and parts received. Performs other duties as described under SUPERVISOR (any industry) Master Title.
GOE: 06.02.01 STRENGTH: S GED: R4 M2 L4 SVP: 4 DLU: 86

559.134-014 SUPERVISOR, DRYING AND WINDING (plastic-synth.)
Supervises and coordinates activities of workers engaged in drying polyester chips and winding synthetic fibers: Observes machines, equipment, personnel, and work areas to detect potential safety hazards, and enforces company safety rules. Inspects yarn on takeup machines for defects, such as unspecified yarn diameter. Confers with designated supervisory personnel to discuss matters related to takeup of yarn and drying of chips. Summons maintenance personnel to inspect machine for malfunctions or to repair machine. Usually inspects takeup unit at specified intervals to verify conformance to standard of polymer extrusion characteristics and yarn takeup characteristics. Turns valve and thermostat knobs to adjust polymer melt zone of extruders to conform to standard temperature. Prepares reports on areas, such as yarn waste, accidents, employee absenteeism, and work time records. Performs other duties as described under SUPERVISOR (any industry) Master Title.
GOE: 06.02.01 STRENGTH: M GED: R3 M2 L2 SVP: 6 DLU: 86

559.137-010 SALVAGE SUPERVISOR (paint & varnish)
Supervises and coordinates activities of workers engaged in salvaging defective or obsolete paint products: Confers with supervisors of sales, cost, production, and testing departments to determine sales possibilities for nonsalvageable paint, costs of reprocessing salvageable products, and reasons for return of goods by customers. Prepares work instructions and department assignments for reprocessing, reworking, or selling salvaged material. Performs other duties as described under SUPERVISOR (any industry) Master Title.
GOE: 06.01.01 STRENGTH: L GED: R4 M3 L3 SVP: 7 DLU: 77

559.137-014 SUPERVISOR II (rubber goods)
Supervises and coordinates activities of workers engaged in manufacture of rubber goods: Inspects products to ensure adherence to specifications. Performs other duties as described under SUPERVISOR (any industry) Master Title. May be designated according to process involved as Curing Supervisor (rubber goods); Finishing Supervisor (rubber goods); Millroom Supervisor (rubber goods); Rubber-Compounder Supervisor (rubber goods); Stock-Preparation Supervisor (rubber goods).
GOE: 06.02.01 STRENGTH: L GED: R4 M3 L3 SVP: 7 DLU: 77

559.137-018 SUPERVISOR, BLEACH (chemical)
Supervises and coordinates activities of workers engaged in processing lime to produce bleaching powder. Performs duties as described under SUPERVISOR (any industry) Master Title.
GOE: 06.02.01 STRENGTH: M GED: R4 M3 L3 SVP: 7 DLU: 77

559.137-022 SUPERVISOR, CHANNEL PROCESS (chemical)
Supervises and coordinates activities of workers engaged in producing carbon black by channel process [partial combustion of natural gas in burner buildings (hot houses)], pelletizing carbon black in rotating drums, and bagging and shipping carbon black. Performs other duties as described under SUPERVISOR (any industry) Master Title.
GOE: 06.02.01 STRENGTH: L GED: R4 M3 L3 SVP: 7 DLU: 77

559.137-026 SUPERVISOR, EVAPORATOR (chemical)
Supervises and coordinates activities of workers engaged in producing concentrated caustic soda or potash, liquid carbonate of potash, and caustic potash.

Performs other duties as described under SUPERVISOR (any industry) Master Title.
GOE: 06.04.01 STRENGTH: M GED: R4 M3 L4 SVP: 7 DLU: 77

559.137-030 SUPERVISOR, GELATIN PLANT (chemical)
Supervises and coordinates activities of workers engaged in processing skins, splits, and trimmings to produce gelatin: Directs workers engaged in chopping, washing, liming, and cooking of stock, according to procedures specified for type of raw material in process. Estimates weight of stock in vats and specified amount of lime to be used in cooking. Performs other duties as described under SUPERVISOR (any industry) Master Title.
GOE: 06.02.01 STRENGTH: L GED: R4 M3 L3 SVP: 8 DLU: 77

559.137-034 SUPERVISOR, GLUE SPECIALTY (chemical)
Supervises and coordinates activities of workers engaged in making dextrin, casein, polyvinyl, and resin glues: Directs workers in measuring, weighing, and mixing chemicals according to formula, cooking dry glue and various other ingredients, and packaging finished product in steel or fiber drums, or paper cartons. Performs duties as described under SUPERVISOR (any industry) Master Title.
GOE: 06.02.01 STRENGTH: L GED: R4 M3 L3 SVP: 7 DLU: 77

559.137-038 SUPERVISOR, INSPECTION (plastic-synth.) alternate titles: process control supervisor
Supervises and coordinates activities of workers engaged in inspecting and storing rolls of cellophane. Directs workers in work procedures. Performs other duties as described under SUPERVISOR (any industry) Master Title.
GOE: 06.02.01 STRENGTH: L GED: R4 M3 L3 SVP: 7 DLU: 77

559.137-042 SUPERVISOR, PUTTY AND CAULKING (paint & varnish)
Supervises and coordinates activities of workers engaged in manufacturing putty or caulking compound: Selects mixing formula used to produce putty or caulking compound. Removes samples from mixing machine and examines blend of oils and powders. Examines incoming shipments of raw materials to verify compliance with order specifications. Maintains inventory files to record amounts of raw materials and finished products in warehouse. Performs other duties as described under SUPERVISOR (any industry) Master Title.
GOE: 06.02.01 STRENGTH: L GED: R4 M2 L2 SVP: 7 DLU: 77

559.137-046 SUPERVISOR, ROCKET PROPELLANT PLANT (ordnance)
Supervises and coordinates activities of workers engaged in mixing and loading (casting) rocket fuel in rocket motor cases: Reads meters, gauges, and recording-instrument charts to verify process conditions. Inspects rocket motor cases, machinery, and equipment for defects or malfunction. Performs other duties as described under SUPERVISOR (any industry) Master Title.
GOE: 06.02.01 STRENGTH: L GED: R4 M3 L3 SVP: 6 DLU: 77

559.137-050 SUPERVISOR, TANK CLEANING (paint & varnish)
Supervises and coordinates activities of workers engaged in cleaning tanks, vats, kettles, and chutes used in production of paint, varnish, and related products. Performs other duties as described under SUPERVISOR (any industry) Master Title.
GOE: 06.04.01 STRENGTH: L GED: R4 M2 L3 SVP: 6 DLU: 77

559.165-010 CHECKER (chemical)
Coordinates activities of workers engaged in loading, operating, and unloading equipment used in production of nitrocellulose, using signal-light system: Moves switches on control panel to illuminate lights above nitrators and wringers to notify workers to load, start, stop, and unload equipment in specified sequence. Records charging and discharging times to maintain records of nitrating cycle.
GOE: 06.02.11 STRENGTH: L GED: R3 M2 L2 SVP: 5 DLU: 77

559.167-010 CD-STORAGE-AND-MATERIALS-MAKE-UP OPERATOR, HEAD (chemical)
Coordinates activities of workers engaged in preparing chemical solutions used in production of synthetic rubber and in maintaining chlorobutadiene storage system: Schedules weighing of materials and preparation of solutions to maintain adequate flow of ingredient materials. Observes operating procedures and preparation of solutions to ensure that schedules are met and that solutions are prepared according to specifications. Inspects equipment to detect malfunctions and arranges for repairs as necessary. Keeps inventory records of materials received and consumed.
GOE: 06.02.11 STRENGTH: M GED: R4 M3 L3 SVP: 7 DLU: 77

559.361-010 LABORATORY TECHNICIAN, PHARMACEUTICAL (pharmaceut.)
Prepares vaccines, biologicals, and serums for prevention of animal diseases: Inoculates fertilized eggs, broths, or other bacteriological media with organisms. Incubates bacteria for specified period and prepares vaccines and serums by standard laboratory methods. Tests vaccines for sterility and virus inactivity. Prepares standard volumetric solutions and reagents used in testing.
GOE: 02.04.02 STRENGTH: L GED: R5 M4 L4 SVP: 6 DLU: 78

559.362-010 ALUM-PLANT OPERATOR (chemical) alternate titles: alum mixer
Controls equipment to produce alum liquor (aluminum sulfate) in continuous process reaction of sulfuric acid with powdered bauxite: Notifies other workers to unload bauxite from boxcars into hopper of crusher. Starts crusher, mill, and conveyors to replenish storage supply of powdered ore. Observes flowmeters and turns valves to regulate flow of powdered ore, acid, and weak alum liquor into first digester in specified proportions to produce mixture of prescribed specific gravity and through other digesters where chemical reaction occurs and resultant aluminum sulfate liquor is settled and diluted to specified concentration. Tests samples from each digester, using hydrometer and thermometer, to verify specific gravities and temperatures. Turns valves to adjust flow of steam through digester jackets and proportions of materials fed into first digester to regulate temperatures and specific gravities accordingly. Pumps finished alum liquor into storage tank and weak alum liquors into settling tanks (thickeners) for recycling into process. Records temperatures, specific gravities, and flow rates of materials in operating log and level of alum liquor storage tanks on inventory records.
GOE: 06.02.11 STRENGTH: L GED: R3 M2 L2 SVP: 4 DLU: 77

559.362-014 FINISHING-AREA OPERATOR (plastic-synth.)
Controls semiautomatic or automatic machines and equipment, such as blenders, mixers, extruders, pelletizers, pumps, blowers, and conveyors, from control panel to produce pellets from plastic flakes: Moves controls on panel to start and stop equipment, to set timing devices for operating cycles, and to direct flow of materials on conveyor. Observes thermometers, gauges, and meters to verify process conditions. Records readings in logs. Turns valves to regulate temperature, pressures, and rate of flow of materials. Inspects equipment for mechanical defects. Gives directions to workers in blending, mixing, and extruding pelletizing materials, and in repairing machines and equipment.
GOE: 06.02.13 STRENGTH: L GED: R3 M2 L2 SVP: 6 DLU: 77

559.362-018 LIQUEFACTION-PLANT OPERATOR (chemical) alternate titles: chlorine operator; chlorine-plant operator; liquefier; liquid-chlorine operator
Controls equipment to liquefy and compress chlorine gas: Ascertains demand and disposition of product and equipment malfunctioning from logsheet. Adjusts equipment to control temperature, pressure, vacuum, level, and flow rate in refrigerating system and compressors to maintain prescribed flow of gas. Calculates ratio of chlorine to hydrogen, using burette and other testing apparatus, and notifies production workers of deviations from specifications. Meters out sulfuric acid sealant to maintain specified level in compressors, drying towers, and pumps. Records operational and test data, and calculates daily averages of readings on logsheet. May direct workers engaged in filling of cylinders and other containers. May be designated according to specialized equipment controlled as Compressor Operator (chemical) I; Refrigeration Operator (chemical).
GOE: 06.02.12 STRENGTH: L GED: R3 M3 L2 SVP: 4 DLU: 77

559.362-022 MVA-REACTOR OPERATOR, HEAD (chemical)
Controls catalytic reactors and auxiliary equipment to produce monovinylacetylene and to refine, vaporize, and transfer product for use in neoprene rubber manufacture: Starts pumps, reactors, and blowers. Observes gauges and recording instruments and moves controls to regulate flow of gases and liquids, and to maintain temperatures, pressure, and liquid levels in preheaters, reactors, condensers, brine driers, and distillation columns within specified limits. Turns valves to regulate concentration of acid and water in catalyst reactor to maintain efficient operating conditions, according to knowledge of process. Starts pumps to transfer acid to feed and drip tanks and to admit water to packing in acid scrubbing tanks. Cleans reactors, using mechanical reamer. Records gauge readings in operating log. Directs activities of MVA-REACTOR OPERATOR (chemical) in tending equipment and in drawing and testing product samples.
GOE: 06.02.11 STRENGTH: L GED: R3 M3 L3 SVP: 6 DLU: 77

559.362-026 PLANT OPERATOR, FURNACE PROCESS (chemical)
Controls semiautomatic furnaces and auxiliary equipment to produce carbon black by partial combustion of crude oil, natural gas, or mixture of both: Notifies UNIT OPERATORS (chemical) to start or shut down equipment units, such as reactors (furnaces), quenchers, precipitators, cyclones (grit collectors), and filters to maintain efficient production. Monitors pyrometers, recording meters, and other gauges to verify process conditions as indicated by control panel instruments. Turns valves and moves switches on central control panel to regulate temperature, pressure, and flow of fuel and air in reactors, and to transfer accumulated carbon black through auxiliary units to produce carbon black of specified type and grade. Tours plant area to verify that equipment is operating as indicated by central control panel. Records instrument readings in operating log and reports abnormal conditions to supervisory personnel. Gives directions to crew during manual operation of equipment to maintain production or verify accuracy of instrumentiezed controls.
GOE: 06.02.18 STRENGTH: L GED: R3 M2 L3 SVP: 5 DLU: 77

559.362-030 ROLL TENDER (chemical)
Controls equipment to mill flaked adhesive from slurry of flour and water: Turns valves or moves levers or side gates to admit steam into pressure cooker to cook milk (slurry of flour and water). Opens discharge line after specified period, and signals worker to pump milk paste onto heated rollers that dry paste. Adjusts distance between rollers to maintain specified thickness of paste and activates knives that cut paste into flakes. Opens hopper chutes to dump flakes into rotating screen cylinder that sifts flakes and transfers them to storage bins. Measures temperature of milk at specified intervals, using thermometer, and tests viscosity of milk, using viscometer. Determines moisture content of flakes by feeling them or by using moisture meter. Weighs standard cupful of

paste to determine its density and adjusts water and steam valves to regulate density. Inspects equipment to detect malfunctions.
GOE: 06.02.18 STRENGTH: L GED: R3 M2 L2 SVP: 5 DLU: 77

559.362-034 TOWER OPERATOR (soap & rel.)

Controls heated-air tower from control panel to make variety of soap powders by atomizing liquid soap: Starts pumps to regulate flow of oil, steam, air, and perfume to tower or collectors. Observes temperature, pressure, and flowmeter recorders to ensure uniform product. Keeps log of tower operations. Weighs sample, dries it in heated chamber, and reweighs sample to calculate moisture loss and percentage of moisture in powder. Inspects operating units, such as towers, soap-spray storage tanks, scrubbers, collectors, and driers, to ensure all are functioning and to maintain maximum efficiency in powder-producing towers. Gives directions to workers engaged in operating machinery to regulate flow of material and product. May oversee cleaning of towers, strainers, and spray tips. May make such repairs as replacing damaged strainers.
GOE: 06.02.18 STRENGTH: L GED: R3 M3 L3 SVP: 4 DLU: 77

559.364-010 FURNACE-STOCK INSPECTOR (elec. equip.) alternate titles: baked-and-graphite inspector

Determines density and resistance of carbon samples which have been graphitized and inspects graphitized stock after removal from furnace: Marks samples of green stock before graphitization to indicate their position in furnace. Receives samples from FURNACE UNLOADER (elec. equip.) before remaining charge is unloaded. Cleans samples with scraper and steel wool and weighs them. Measures samples in several places with diameter rule to obtain average diameter. Places samples on resistance-testing device, sets meter to allow specified number of amperes to pass through sample, and records readings from millivoltmeter. Calculates average density and average resistance from weight, average diameter, and millivolt reading, using slide rule and formula. When furnace is unloaded, marks pieces with resistance grade number of samples. Inspects cleaned stock for pits, cracks, burrs, and bends. Determines extent of damage from cracks and imperfections, and marks salvageable pieces for cutting to next largest possible size. Directs workers to remove inspected pieces.
GOE: 06.03.01 STRENGTH: L GED: R3 M3 L2 SVP: 4 DLU: 77

559.367-010 QUALITY-CONTROL TESTER (paper goods; plastic-synth.)

Inspects and tests polethylene and cellophane sheets or bags for surface defects, dimensional accuracy, strength, and clearness of print to verify conformance to specifications, and to assist production personnel in solving quality control problems. Inspects sample sheet to detect surface defects, such as bubbles, pattern defects, and haze variations. Measures thickness of sample, using micrometer, and weighs sample to determine compliance to specifications. Tests sample strips in pull-tester machine, impact tester, and stress-flex test machine to determine strength, tenacity, and flexibility. Places adhesive paper on printed section, pulls paper from printed section, and examines adhesive for ink to verify stability of print. Writes inspection and testing reports and confers with production personnel to determine cause of deviations from qualitative standards.
GOE: 06.03.01 STRENGTH: L GED: R3 M2 L3 SVP: 4 DLU: 77

559.381-010 INSPECTOR (plastic prod.; plastic-synth.) alternate titles: customer-return inspector; process inspector

Inspects and tests plastic sheets, rods, tubes, powders, or fabricated articles for uniformity of color, surface defects, hardness, and dimensional accuracy, following plant specifications or blueprints and using measuring instruments and test equipment: Examines surface of product for defects, such as scratches, burns, and discolorations. Positions transparent sheet between light and calibrated screen and observes shadow pattern of sheet projected on screen to determine optical distortion. Verifies weight and dimensions of product, using scales, gauges, calipers, micrometers, and templates. Compares color of product with color standard. Determines hardness and structural strength of product, using acid bath, burst tester, and hardness tester. Records test data, and grades and labels product according to type of defect. May investigate cause of recurring defects and recommend changes in production procedures. May file, buff, or sand product to remove defects.
GOE: 06.03.01 STRENGTH: L GED: R3 M3 L3 SVP: 5 DLU: 77

559.381-014 RUBBER TESTER (rubber goods; rubber tire)

Tests samples of milled rubber compounds and finished rubber goods, using testing devices, and compares gauge readings against prepared standards, such as charts, graphs, and tables, to verify adherence to specifications: Collects samples of rubber from MIXING-MACHINE OPERATOR (any industry) at prescribed intervals. Mixes and blends sample stock on laboratory warmer mill to obtain desired consistency and tests sample for plasticity, using plastometer. Cures uncured rubber samples in heated mold at specified temperature for designated time and tests its hardness, using durometer. Determines density of cured and uncured stock by weighing samples on scale and testing sample in densimeter. Records test results for use by control laboratory.
GOE: 06.01.05 STRENGTH: L GED: R3 M2 L2 SVP: 6 DLU: 77

559.382-010 AMMONIA-STILL OPERATOR (steel & rel.) alternate titles: pump-and-still operator

Operates stills, pumps, and related equipment to extract and refine ammonia from ammonia liquor: Adjusts feed valves to regulate flow of liquor and steam to stills and water to condensers and dephlegmator. Reads thermometers and gauges, adjusts valves, and regulates pumps to maintain specified temperatures

and pressures to boil off waste vapors (foul vent) and ammonia. Pumps ammonia to saturator for mixing with water to produce liquid ammonia, and pumps ammonia to storage tanks. Pumps waste liquor to sewer. Determines amount of ammonia in waste liquor and water, using titration test, and adjusts temperatures and pressures to reduce loss of ammonia. Keeps record of pressures, temperatures, test results, and amount of liquor and steam fed to stills. May produce concentrated ammonia liquor by condensing vapors in water-cooled condensers. Cleans work area, using broom, brushes, and lime.
GOE: 06.02.17 STRENGTH: L GED: R3 M3 L2 SVP: 5 DLU: 77

559.382-014 CATALYST OPERATOR, GASOLINE (chemical)

Controls machines that combine ingredients, such as sodium silicate, sulfuric acid, water, and caustic soda to make catalysts used in manufacture of high-octane gasolines: Dumps dry ingredients into electric mixing vats and turns valves to admit prescribed amounts of liquid ingredients. Observes thermometers and flowmeters, and adjusts gauges to control temperature and amount of flow. Turns valves to allow mixture to flow from mixing vats to vacuum filters to remove excess water. Controls pumps that force mixture through spray-dryers where particles of catalyst are formed, and turns dials on control panel to regulate temperature and speed of spray. Controls pumping of catalyst particles from bottom of dryers to washer-filters for removal of cation and anion impurities. Turns valves to regulate flow of catalyst through hot-air steam dryers and observes temperature and speed of flow to ensure specified drying. May draw off samples of mixture for analysis. May keep records of batches processed.
GOE: 06.02.11 STRENGTH: H GED: R3 M3 L2 SVP: 5 DLU: 77

559.382-018 CHEMICAL OPERATOR III (chemical) alternate titles: reactor operator

Controls equipment units or system that processes chemical substances into specified industrial or consumer products, according to knowledge of operating procedures, chemical reactions, laboratory test results, and correlation of process instrumentation: Reads plant specifications to ascertain product, ingredients, and prescribed modifications of plant procedures. Starts automatic feed of solid or semisolid materials through equipment units, such as heating vessels and mixing tanks; or dumps preweighed ingredients into tanks, hoppers, or onto conveyor. Moves controls to regulate feed of liquids and gases through equipment in specified timing and sequence, or starts automatic feed. Sets up and adjusts indicating and controlling devices, such as gas analyzers, recording calorimeters, and radiographic detecting or gauging instruments to facilitate simultaneous analysis and control of process conditions. Observes gauges, signals, and recording instruments, turns valves, and moves controls to regulate temperatures, pressures, and flow of steam, coolant, and chemical constituents through system to effect prescribed reaction within critical limits, according to knowledge of equipment and process. Draws samples of product at specified stages of synthesis and performs litmus, titration, refractometer, gas-analyses, or other standard tests to determine if reaction is proceeding efficiently and in conformity with plant standards. Observes color or consistency of product through sight glasses, and correlates observations with test results, laboratory analyses, and instrument readings to facilitate regulation of process and production of standardized product. Maintains log of gauge readings, shift production, and equipment malfunctions. May patrol area to inspect equipment for leaks and hazards and to record gauge readings. May direct activities of other workers assisting in control or verification of process. May be designated according to equipment or system controlled as Caustic-Purification Operator (chemical); Gas-Generator Operator (chemical); Lanolin-Plant Operator (pharmaceut.); Sulfonator Operator (chemical); or according to product produced as Alkylation Operator (chemical; petrol. refin.); Ethylene-Oxide Panelboard Operator (chemical); Polymer Operator (plastic-synth.); Sodium-Chlorite Operator (chemical).
GOE: 06.01.03 STRENGTH: M GED: R3 M3 L2 SVP: 7 DLU: 77

559.382-022 GLUE MAKER, BONE (chemical)

Controls pressure, temperature, and water level of cooking tanks, and operates centrifuges and separators, to manufacture animal glue: Admits hot water and steam into cooking tanks containing crushed animal bones, following specifications [BONE-COOKING OPERATOR (chemical)]. Opens valves to drain glue and tallow solutions (grease) into separate vats [PRESSURE-TANK OPERATOR (chemical)]. Starts centrifuge machine that separates animal oils (grease) from glue solution [CENTRIFUGE-SEPARATOR OPERATOR (chemical)]. Cooks glue solution to evaporate water from glue. Reads gauge of hydrometer to determine percentage of glue solid in solution. Disassembles plates of centrifuge, using wrench and hoisting device; and cleans plates, using brush and abrasives. May weigh and add specified amounts of chemical to preserve glue. May direct other workers engaged in cleaning tanks or vats.
GOE: 06.02.18 STRENGTH: M GED: R3 M2 L2 SVP: 5 DLU: 77

559.382-026 GRANULATOR-MACHINE OPERATOR (pharmaceut.) alternate titles: granulator; wet-mix operator

Operates mixing and milling machines to mix and granulate powdered ingredients preparatory to compressing into medicinal tablets: Weighs out and measures ingredients, according to formula and size of batch to be mixed. Starts mixing machine to blend ingredients and adds starch paste, gelatin, or water and alcohol solution to mixture to bind ingredients. Breaks up lumps in mixture, using spatula or mortar and pestle, spreads mixture onto trays, and places trays in oven or steam drier at preset temperature. Removes trays and feels material to ascertain dryness, or tests material with moisture meter to determine whether batch requires additional mixing or drying. Installs cutting blades and screens, using handtools, and operates oscillating or comminuting mill to force

mixture through sieves and produce product of specified fineness. May screen granulated mixture to determine size range of granules. May tend ion-exchange equipment to remove mineral salts from water. May tend tumbling barrel or other equipment to mix binders, flavoring oils, and lubricating agents for use in compounding tablets.
GOE: 06.02.11 STRENGTH: H GED: R3 M2 L2 SVP: 5 DLU: 77

559.382-030 LINSEED-OIL REFINER (oils & grease) alternate titles: refinery operator

Operates equipment that refines raw linseed oil for use in manufacture of paint, lacquers, white lead paste, and high-speed printing ink: Starts pump to transfer raw linseed oil from storage tank into refining tank, and starts agitator paddles. Opens valve to drain settled tar and foreign matter from tank. Opens tank steam valve to heat mixture. Sprays hot water over oil with hose to neutralize acid and allows water to settle. Opens valve to drain water from tank. Starts agitator paddles and adds dry neutralizing ingredients, such as *whiting compound,* powdered magnesia, and common salt. Observes material during refining process to determine if color and consistency meets standards, and removes sample for laboratory tests. Opens valve to permit oil to flow into storage tank. Sets thermostat and steam valve to maintain required temperature in storage tank.
GOE: 06.02.11 STRENGTH: M GED: R3 M2 L2 SVP: 4 DLU: 77

559.382-034 MAKE-UP OPERATOR (chemical) alternate titles: materials-make-up operator; solution-make-up operator

Controls equipment to prepare chemical constituents of synthetic rubber for synthesis by other workers, following formulas and maintaining reactions within prescribed limits: Weighs solid materials according to formula, using scale. Pumps liquid chemicals to metering or weigh tanks. Observes thermometer and recording instruments, and moves heater controls to attain specified temperature in system. Starts agitator and opens valves to regulate admission of chemical agents into mixing tanks in prescribed sequence. Dumps solid materials into tanks to complete reaction. Draws samples of solution for laboratory analysis and titrates sample to determine concentration and facilitate control of materials flow for attainment of product meeting plant standard. Tends auxiliary equipment, such as colloid mills, melt tanks, scrubbers, and homogenizers, to prepare or further process emulsions and dispersions. Regulates flow of rubber constituents to storage or rubber-synthesis areas, according to schedule or indicated plant needs. Maintains records of materials and supplies, shift production, process times and temperatures, and gauge readings for operating log or inventory records. May receive and store materials. May tend tank farm containing liquid chemicals [TANK-FARM ATTENDANT (chemical)]. May clean, inspect, and recharge equipment with materials, such as soda ash or calcium chloride. May be designated according to substance prepared as Emulsion Operator (chemical); Persulfate Make-Up Operator (chemical); or equipment unit operated as Chlorobutadiene-Scrubber Operator (chemical).
GOE: 06.02.11 STRENGTH: M GED: R3 M2 L2 SVP: 5 DLU: 77

559.382-038 NAPHTHA-WASHING-SYSTEM OPERATOR (plastic-synth.)

Controls equipment to purge and wash reactors used in polymerization of isobutylene to produce butyl rubber slurry: Starts pumps and agitators. Turns valves to line up streams for wash cycles and to evacuate slop naphtha and trapped gas. Defrosts frozen valves, using steam hose. Turns pump valves to drain refrigerant from reactor chilling jackets into storage drums, to purge chilling jackets with hot refrigerant, and to flush reactor vessels with hot feed stock and flash tanks with steam. Starts pumps to exhaust gases and vapors through flash tanks. Starts pumps and agitators to wash and rinse reactor vessels with hot naphtha. Admits natural gas under pressure to exhaust naphtha from reactors. Observes control panel to verify temperatures, pressures, and flow rates required to return reactors to service. Records operating data in log.
GOE: 06.02.13 STRENGTH: L GED: R3 M2 L2 SVP: 5 DLU: 77

559.382-042 PHARMACEUTICAL OPERATOR (pharmaceut.) alternate titles: laboratory technician

Controls equipment and tends machines to produce variety of pharmaceutical and toilet products or ingredients, performing any combination of following duties: Weighs and measures out coating ingredients and coats medicinal tablets [COATER (pharmaceut.) 554.382-010]. Tends mixing machine and heated kettles to prepare specified ingredients for ointments, creams, liquid medications, powders, gums, and similar drug products, adding ingredients according to formulas [COMPOUNDER (pharmaceut.; soap & rel.) 550.685-046]. Tends milling and grinding machines that reduce mixtures to designated particle sizes, or grinds materials with mortar and pestle. Prepares granulated products [GRANULATOR-MACHINE OPERATOR (pharmaceut.) 559.382-026]. Tends filter presses, sifting machines, autoclaves, water stills, and related equipment to prepare ingredients for further processing. Operates machine to compress ingredients into tablets [COMPRESSOR (elec. equip.; pharmaceut.) 556.682-022]. Inspects, weighs, and tests hardness of tablets [TABLET TESTER (pharmaceut.) 559.667-010]. May be designated according to substance prepared as Liquid Compounder (pharmaceut.).
GOE: 06.02.11 STRENGTH: M GED: R3 M2 L2 SVP: 5 DLU: 78

559.382-046 PILOT-CONTROL OPERATOR (chemical; plastic-synth.) alternate titles: fine-chemicals operator; laboratory technician; pilot-plant technician; process operator; research-manufacturing operator

Sets up and operates small-scale chemical production equipment under laboratory conditions to test methods and chemical processes for product development, following specifications and guidance from research chemists or engineers: Sets up production equipment, such as reactors, stills, stripping towers, separators, and blending tanks, using mechanics' handtools and portable power tools. Starts pumps and compressors. Turns valves to regulate equipment temperatures, pressures, flow rates, and liquid levels, following process specifications or instructions of technical personnel. Observes meters and gauges to verify process conditions. Performs standard quantitative or qualitative chemical analyses, such as titration, distillation, caustic-insoluble, and color-measurement tests, to verify process conditions and compile research data. Mixes chemical solutions as directed for use in tests. Prepares operating records and reports of test results. May adjust and repair mechanical and electronic testing equipment, using handtools, circuit diagrams, and maintenance manuals.
GOE: 02.04.01 STRENGTH: L GED: R4 M3 L3 SVP: 7 DLU: 77

559.382-050 SHREDDING-FLOOR-EQUIPMENT OPERATOR (plastic-synth.)

Operates shredding and filtering equipment and pumps to process woodpulp into alkali cellulose: Mounts roll of woodpulp sheeting on unwind stand, and inserts end of roll into shredder. Monitors recording and controlling instruments, and presses buttons and turns valves to regulate speed of pumps and flow of materials through caustic treatment and filtering process. Inspects filters and filter presses, and cleans equipment, using water hose. Records production figures. May operate lift truck to convey pulp rolls from storage area to shredding room.
GOE: 06.02.13 STRENGTH: M GED: R3 M2 L2 SVP: 5 DLU: 77

559.382-054 SOAP MAKER (soap & rel.) alternate titles: soap boiler

Controls equipment that produces soap according to formula: Opens valves to charge kettle with prescribed amounts of ingredients. Turns valve to admit steam through bottom of tank to boil and agitate mixture. Observes mixture through opening in top of tank to detect variations of color, consistency, and homogeneity of boiling ingredients. Adds soda or water to mixture as directed by laboratory; or determines degree of alkalinity of caustic soda in mixture, using meter, and adds soda or water as required. Observes color, consistency, and homogeneity of product to determine when boiling and agitating cycle are completed, and allows batch to cool and settle for specified period of time. Raises or lowers pumpline to locate separation level of neat (pure soap) and nigre (residue). Starts pump to transfer neat to designated department. Lowers pump line to bottom of tank to transfer residue to reclaiming tank. May calculate amount of ingredients needed to make various soaps, using formula.
GOE: 06.02.18 STRENGTH: L GED: R3 M2 L3 SVP: 7 DLU: 77

559.384-010 LABORATORY ASSISTANT, CULTURE MEDIA (pharmaceut.) alternate titles: laboratory aide; technical assistant

Prepares culture media used to develop vaccines and toxoids or to conduct chemical, microscopic, and bacteriologic tests: Measures and weighs ingredients, such as food source, chemicals, preservatives, and vitamins, to prepare growth medium, using scales, graduated flasks, syringes, pipettes, and standard formulas. Adjusts controls of equipment, such as pumps, filters, steam kettles, and autoclaves, to obtain uniform consistency of sterile medium. Removes sample of medium from batch and tests sample for consistency, potency, and sterility, according to standardized procedures. Pours medium or adjusts controls on automatic equipment that dispenses medium into containers, such as petri dishes, test tubes, or storage drums. Seals containers and prepares and affixes identification labels to containers. Maintains production and test records. May order supplies. May mix ingredients to prepare stains used in tests.
GOE: 02.04.02 STRENGTH: L GED: R3 M3 L3 SVP: 5 DLU: 86

559.387-010 INSPECTOR IV (ordnance)

Inspects mixing, drying, storage, packaging, and arrangements for transportation of explosives to determine that processing specifications and safety measures are followed: Observes processing of explosive and notes condition of ingredients for qualities, such as dryness, even texture, and absence of solvents. Verifies accuracy of scales used. Observes transfer of powder from shipping containers to cans used to carry powder through loading process. Examines filled cans for specified packing slip and for colored stripe indicating uses for which powder is intended. Inspects plant periodically for adherence to safety regulations and prepares written reports on compliance with such regulations.
GOE: 06.03.01 STRENGTH: L GED: R3 M2 L2 SVP: 5 DLU: 77

559.387-014 INSPECTOR (pharmaceut.)

Inspects pharmaceutical ingredients and products to detect deviations from manufacturing standards: Selects samples of in-process pharmaceutical ingredients, capsules, tablets, and related products for testing, according to prescribed procedures. Weighs samples, using scales, and measures samples, using micrometer. Places specified samples in disintegration baths and observes and times rate of dissolution. Records inspection results on designated forms. Checks incoming purchased pharmaceutical ingredients against invoice to verify conformity of product name, count, and labeling. Carries samples of incoming products to analytical laboratory for quality assurance testing.
GOE: 06.03.02 STRENGTH: L GED: R3 M2 L3 SVP: 4 DLU: 86

559.467-010 TEMPERATURE-CONTROL INSPECTOR (plastic-synth.)

Measures temperature and humidity in vicinity of machine that transforms liquid polymers, cellulose, or other materials into synthetic fibers by dry spinning (forming) process, to detect deviations from plant standards: Takes humidity readings near spinnerettes through which fibers are extruded into air, using

hygrometer or similar humidity gauge. Reads thermometers and temperature-recording charts on machine. Notifies machine operator or other personnel when temperature or humidity conditions are not within specified range, to facilitate equipment adjustments for production of fibers having prescribed characteristics. May compute humidity readings, using wet-bulb and dry-bulb thermometer and standard procedure. May turn valves or move controls to regulate machine or process conditions, according to changes in temperature or humidity.
GOE: 06.03.01 STRENGTH: L GED: R3 M2 L2 SVP: 4 DLU: 77

559.482-010 COMPOSITION-ROLL MAKER AND CUTTER (rubber goods) alternate titles: roll molder
Operates machines to mold and cut composition rubber rollers used to coat or lithograph tinware: Dumps cold rubber in melting reservoir of machine and turns steam valves to melt rubber. Starts agitator to stir melting rubber. Places core of roller in molding chamber of machine, using hoist. Bolts plates on ends of molding chamber, using wrench. Turns air valve to force melted rubber into mold, and turns water valves to cool mold. Removes molded roller and places it in chuck of cutting machine. Installs knives on cutting bar. Positions bar and turns crank to rotate chuck and cut circumference or end of roller. Replaces worn felt coverings on padding rollers. Slips felt jackets over roller core and sews end of felt around roll, using needle. Sorts and stacks rolls in rack. Records number and type of rolls, cores, and materials used, shipped, or received.
GOE: 06.02.07 STRENGTH: M GED: R3 M2 L2 SVP: 4 DLU: 77

559.482-014 PUTTY TINTER-MAKER (paint & varnish)
Sets up and operates machines and equipment to mix, color, and mold putty, according to specifications: Weighs and measures ingredients and dumps them into kettle, using power lift. Lowers agitators into kettle of putty mix and starts them to combine ingredients. Adds colored paste paints to putty mix to tint putty to desired shade. Withdraws sample, prepares smear, and compares it with standards. Lowers suction pump into kettle and pumps mix into molding-machine tank. Sets up and operates molding machine that forms putty into crayon-like applicators. Off bears product from discharge chute to boxes or storage shelves. Records mixing, coloring, and molding time on production records.
GOE: 06.02.18 STRENGTH: M GED: R3 M2 L2 SVP: 5 DLU: 77

559.485-010 WASH-MILL OPERATOR (chemical)
Tends equipment that washes animal stock (animal skins, splits, fleshings, and trimmings) used to make glue and gelatin: Turns valve to start continuous flush of water into tub to wash foreign materials from stock. Turns handwheel to actuate roller that kneads and turns stock in tub. Turns off water and roller after time necessary to reduce foreign material to required level. Drains water from tub and pumps specified amount of acid into tub to kill organisms in stock. Tests concentration of acid-sample in tub, using titration, burette, and pH indicator, and adds acid to tub when necessary. Drains acid from tub after prescribed time and washes stock with water.
GOE: 06.04.19 STRENGTH: M GED: R2 M2 L1 SVP: 3 DLU: 77

559.562-010 DRIER OPERATOR I (plastic-synth.) alternate titles: roper operator
Operates machines to dry hypalon or neoprene rubber solution to form film, to shape film into rope, and to cut rope into chips: Moves controls on panel to start rotating drum drier, pumps, and blowers, and to adjust speeds of roper machine and drier. Observes meters and gauges to verify pressures and temperatures of machines. Moves dials on automatic instruments to set and adjust level of rubber solution in drier and flow of steam through drier. Turns valves to regulate flow of cooling water and temperature in cooling drum. Threads film of rubber from drier through guiding rolls and slots of roper and through automatic cutting machine. Keeps production and storage records. Gives directions to workers in cleaning equipment, weighing, stenciling, and storing articles, filling roper chamber with talc, and in packing finished rubber chips into bags or drums.
GOE: 06.02.13 STRENGTH: L GED: R3 M2 L3 SVP: 6 DLU: 77

559.565-010 CYLINDER FILLER (chemical) alternate titles: charging operator; cylinder loader; drum filler; filler; gas worker; manifold operator; pumper
Tends equipment to fill cylinders and other containers with liquefied or compressed gases: Changes cylinder valves with wrench, or adjusts them to prescribed tension, using torque wrench. Rolls cylinders onto platform scale, or positions cylinders in manifold racks manually or with chain hoist. Connects lines from manifold to cylinders, using wrench. Fills cylinders by any of following methods: (1) Sets pressure gauge to specified reading and listens for buzzer indicating completion of filling. (2) Adjusts valves and observes gauge to fill cylinders to specified pressure. (3) Observes scale indicator to fill cylinders to specified weight. (4) Fills cylinder to excess, rolls cylinder onto scale, and connects exhaust line to release excess gas and attain prescribed gross weight. Sprays or brushes chemical solution onto cylinder valve to test for leaks. Fills out and attaches warning and identification tags or decals, specifying tare and gross weight, cylinder number, type of gas, and date filled, and records data. May test gas for purity, using burette or other testing equipment. May inspect or test empty cylinder [CYLINDER INSPECTOR-AND-TESTER (chemical)]. May evacuate residual gases from cylinders. May test filled cylinders for specified gas pressure by connecting gauge and comparing reading with chart. May tend and maintain generator or compressor in filling process. May be designated according to type of container filled as Ton-Container Filler (chemical); Tube-Trailer Filler (chemical).

GOE: 06.04.12 STRENGTH: H GED: R3 M2 L2 SVP: 3 DLU: 77

559.567-014 WEIGHER AND GRADER (chemical)
Weighs and examines barrels of oleoresin prior to distillation into turpentine and rosin and grades rosin prior to storage: Reads scale to obtain gross weight of barrel of oleoresin. Examines and feels oleoresin to determine color, cleanliness, water content, and age, and estimates turpentine and rosin content and rosin grade that can be produced. Records estimate and weight of barrel on incoming record sheet. Observes distillation process and directs DISTILLER (chemical) II to stop operation of melter or still whenever temporary shortages of oleoresin occur. Draws rosin sample from still and grades sample according to U.S. Government specifications. Records grade and barrel number on grade record form. Directs or assists DECKHAND (chemical) to push barrels of oleoresin or rosin to and from scales, storage area, and distilling equipment, and to dump barrels of oleoresin into hopper of melter.
GOE: 06.03.02 STRENGTH: L GED: R2 M2 L2 SVP: 3 DLU: 77

559.582-010 COAGULATION OPERATOR (plastic-synth.) alternate titles: flocculator operator
Controls equipment, such as coagulation tanks, soap conversion tanks, leach tanks, filters, screens, hammer mills, and pneumatic conveyors to coagulate synthetic rubber latex into rubber crumb slurry and to prepare rubber crumbs for finishing processes: Turns valves, starts feed pumps, and adjusts flow-controlling and proportioning devices in supply lines to control flow of latex and of solutions to creaming and coagulating tanks. Adjusts recirculating pumps to control overflow of creamed latex to coagulating tank and of coagulated slurry to soap conversion tank to convert soap to fatty acid and extract fatty acid. Regulates tank stirring mechanisms to mix contents and controls temperatures and acid concentration by automatic recorder-controllers. Observes appearance of crumbs through sight glasses and regulates operation of filters, shaker screens, and hammer mills to remove moisture from and pelletize rubber crumbs for finishing processes. Records data on coagulation logsheets. May prepare brine, acid, and other solutions used.
GOE: 06.02.13 STRENGTH: L GED: R3 M2 L2 SVP: 5 DLU: 77

559.582-014 SPECIALTIES OPERATOR (chemical)
Controls equipment to prepare chemical solutions to meet customers' small-lot orders or special specifications, performing any combination of following tasks: Starts pumps and agitators. Turns valves to admit and discharge chemicals to and from process vessels and to weigh tanks. Observes scales and stops pumps when required weight is attained. Mixes chemicals, according to proportion tables and prescribed formulas, in reaction vessel, and turns steam valves or sets thermostat to heat vessel to specified temperature. Mixes prepared materials with precipitants to produce slurry in dissolving and precipitating tanks [DISSOLVER OPERATOR (chemical)].
GOE: 06.02.11 STRENGTH: L GED: R3 M3 L2 SVP: 5 DLU: 77

559.584-010 ROLL-TENSION TESTER (plastic-synth.) alternate titles: pull-out operator
Tests rolls of cellophane for conformance with specified winding tension: Slides roll onto shaft of testing frame. Threads film from roll around rewind and tension rollers and turns setscrews to secure cellophane to clip on sliding bar. Turns handwheels to move sliding bar that pulls cellophane predetermined distance from roll and to press tension roller against film to apply specified tension. Reads rule gauge to measure slack in film between rewind roller and sliding bar. Cuts cellophane from roll, using knife. Records number and width of tested roll, amount of tension applied, and degree of slack. May examine cellophane for defects such as discoloration, wrinkles, scratches, and holes.
GOE: 06.03.02 STRENGTH: L GED: R2 M1 L2 SVP: 3 DLU: 77

559.584-014 VARNISH INSPECTOR (paint & varnish)
Inspects and tests sample lots of varnish for conformance to specifications: Pours sample varnish into spray gun reservoir, adjusts nozzle of spray gun, and sprays wood, paper, tile, or steel panels, using knowledge of spray painting techniques to obtain uniform coating on panels. Places panels in oven or under heat lamps to dry varnish. Inspects dried varnish for clearness, cracks, crystallization, and drying qualities. Compares sample color with standard varnish colors to determine adherence to color specifications. Dips strip of indicator paper into sample and observes color change of paper to determine acidity of varnish. Tests viscosity of varnish by comparing flow of sample varnish to flow of standard varnish in test tubes. Weighs sample to determine weight per gallon.
GOE: 06.03.02 STRENGTH: L GED: R2 M2 L1 SVP: 3 DLU: 77

559.585-010 DRY-HOUSE TENDER (ordnance)
Tends equipment that controls moisture content of stored explosive mixtures and their ingredients, used in detonators, primers, and fuses for shells, cartridges, and bombs according to prescribed standards: Scoops chemicals from rubber containers into paper- or cloth-lined trays. Places trays on racks in steam-heated drying or humidified rooms for specified time to dehydrate or moisten chemicals. Observes recording instruments and turns valves to maintain temperature and humidity of rooms within prescribed safety limits. Records storage time to identify material of specified moisture content for further processing. Turns valves to drain explosive material from mixing-room waste collection tank into vat in which it is cooked to render it harmless for disposal. Shovels designated quantity of caustic soda and aluminum chips into vat and closes loading hatch. Turns valves to admit steam into heating coils and sets automatic timer for prescribed cooking period. Drains vat of cooked material

and flushes out sediment. Cleans utensils, floors, and walls, using water hose, to remove accumulations of explosive material in accordance with safety regulations. May screen and blend materials, such as powder, shellac, and ground glass.
GOE: 06.04.11 STRENGTH: L GED: R2 M2 L2 SVP: 2 DLU: 77

559.585-014 GREASE-AND-TALLOW PUMPER (oils & grease)
Tends pumps to transfer grease and tallow from rendering tank to storage tanks, tankcars, and shipping containers: Turns valves and starts pumps to start flow of material; stops flow when material reaches specified level. Observes measuring gauge reading on storage tank or measures material, using measuring rod, and compares reading with conversion chart to determine poundage pumped. Records poundage stored and shipped.
GOE: 06.04.19 STRENGTH: L GED: R2 M1 L1 SVP: 2 DLU: 77

559.585-018 TANKROOM TENDER (plastic-synth.) alternate titles: aging room operator; ripening-room hand; spin-tank tender
Tends tanks in which viscose slurry is aged and blended for use in rayon and cellophane production: Pumps slurry from mixing machines to blending and aging tanks, and from tanks to processing area after specified time. Records aging time for each batch in plant log. May tend tanks in which cellulose (viscose raw material) is aged, by moving controls to maintain tank temperature or room temperature at prescribed level, and be designated Ripening-Room Operator (plastic-synth.).
GOE: 06.04.13 STRENGTH: L GED: R2 M1 L2 SVP: 3 DLU: 77

559.585-022 VACUUM-PAN OPERATOR III (chemical)
Tends evaporators, rotary vacuum filters, kilns, and coolers that purify and remove moisture from brine to make salt: Turns switches and valves to start equipment, pumps, and flow of steam and brine. Lights fires in kiln, using torch. Observes recorders and gauges and adjusts controls to maintain specified temperature. Records salinity, temperature, and vacuum readings. Reports equipment malfunctioning to maintenance department. Removes residue from evaporators by flushing them with water.
GOE: 06.04.11 STRENGTH: L GED: R3 M2 L2 SVP: 3 DLU: 77

559.587-010 ROD-AND-TUBE STRAIGHTENER (plastic-synth.) alternate titles: tube-and-rod straightener
Straightens seasoned thermoplastics rods or tubes by immersing them in hot water and rolling them across flat surface: Turns valve to fill soaking tank with hot water and places rods or tubes into tank to soften them. Removes softened rods or tubes from tank and rolls them across flat table surface to straighten them. Sprays straightened stock with cold water and lays stock on racks. Records number of tubes or rods straightened.
GOE: 06.04.24 STRENGTH: M GED: R2 M1 L1 SVP: 2 DLU: 77

559.662-010 ACID MAKER (paper & pulp)
Controls rotary or spray sulfur furnaces and alkali *absorption towers* to make cooking acid for use in digesting woodpulp: Moves controls and observes gauges to regulate combustion chamber, speed of furnace rotation, and volume of liquid sulfur in furnace to maintain specified temperature and acidity required to produce sulfur dioxide gas. Adjusts valves to regulate flow of water and sulfur dioxide gas through alkali absorption towers according to titration tests to produce cooking acid of specified concentration. Starts pumps to pump acid through filters and to storage tanks. Chips slag from furnace, using chipping bar. May make titration tests of produced acid.
GOE: 06.04.11 STRENGTH: L GED: R3 M2 L2 SVP: 5 DLU: 77

559.662-014 WASH OPERATOR (chemical)
Controls system of tanks to wash and reduce acidity of activated carbon sludge, preparatory to drying, for variety of industrial and consumer applications: Turns valves to regulate flow of acid, carbon sludge, and water through thickener and agitator tanks according to tank-level and specific gravity readings supplied by WASH HELPER (chemical). Draws sample of product in beaker and tests for acidity, using pH meter and standard titration test. Compares level of solution in graduated suction tube with conversion chart to determine acidity of sludge. Turns valve to admit caustic solution to neutralizer tank until acidity level meets prescribed standard. Patrols work area to observe level of carbon in thickener tank and wash solutions in overflow troughs to prevent spills, regulating pump speeds as necessary. Gauges tank levels, using calibrated rod. Keeps records of tank levels and test results for shift log.
GOE: 06.02.18 STRENGTH: L GED: R3 M3 L2 SVP: 5 DLU: 77

559.664-010 NITROGLYCERIN DISTRIBUTOR (chemical)
Distributes nitroglycerin to processing departments of dynamite plant and prepares NITROGLYCERIN NEUTRALIZER (chemical) to release specified amounts of nitroglycerin to storage tanks. Tests acidity of nitroglycerin, using litmus paper. Turns valve to release sodium carbonate solution into nitroglycerin to neutralize excess acid that could cause decomposition of material and explosion. Transfers nitroglycerin from storage tank to lead-lined or stainless steel tanks mounted on wheels. Pushes tanks to mix house or other processing department. Washes tanks between loads with sodium carbonate solution and water, using hose and brush. Fills glass or stainless steel vials with nitroglycerin, using filling spout, and packs vials in boxes.
GOE: 06.04.40 STRENGTH: H GED: R2 M1 L1 SVP: 2 DLU: 77

559.664-014 PILOT-CONTROL-OPERATOR HELPER (chemical; plastic-synth.) alternate titles: pilot-plant-operator helper
Assists PILOT-CONTROL OPERATOR (chemical; plastic-synth.) in testing methods and chemical processes for product development: Climbs absorption,

fractionating, and scrubbing towers to collect samples of solutions or products for laboratory analysis. Performs routine titration, concentration, and gravity tests, using standard test equipment. Adds catalysts, reagents, liquids, or solids to solutions as directed. Reads gauges and charts and records operational data in plant log. Performs other duties as described under HELPER (any industry) Master Title.
GOE: 06.04.11 STRENGTH: M GED: R2 M2 L2 SVP: 5 DLU: 77

559.665-010 BONE-PROCESS OPERATOR (chemical)
Tends equipment that grinds and sifts animal bones to form bonemeal and bone flour: Starts grinder, shaker screens, and conveyors. Turns dials on control panel to synchronize feed of bones into grinder and ground bones into shaker screens that separate bonemeal and bone flour. Adjusts length of rocker arm on vibratory feeders and shaker screens to regulate oscillation speed, using wrenches, to maintain uninterrupted production. Observes ammeter on control panel to detect overloading. Monitors equipment to detect clogging and malfunctions.
GOE: 06.04.09 STRENGTH: L GED: R2 M2 L2 SVP: 4 DLU: 77

559.665-014 DRY-END OPERATOR (plastic-synth.)
Tends dry end of cellophane casting machine that dries and winds continuous sheet of cellophane into rolls: Threads film emerging from washing and coating tanks through heated rollers and starts sheet onto winding core. Turns switch to regulate winding speed and film tension according to specifications. Observes temperature gauge and turns steam valve to maintain specified heat of rollers. Cuts cellophane with knife to stop feed on completed roll and removes roll from winding assembly, using hoist. Signals CASTING-ROOM OPERATOR (plastic-synth.) to request changes in forming speed of cellophane to prevent film breaks or wrinkles during roll changes.
GOE: 06.04.13 STRENGTH: M GED: R3 M2 L2 SVP: 3 DLU: 77

559.665-018 EXTRACTOR-PLANT OPERATOR (chemical; oils & grease)
Tends extractor tanks, distilling and condensing units, and auxiliary equipment that removes grease from bones for further processing: Loads bones into extractor tanks and bolts tank door, using wrench. Turns valves to circulate naphtha and live steam through extractor tanks to dissolve and remove grease from bones. Observes tank thermometer and color of vapor through viewing glass to determine when all grease has been removed. Turns valves to circulate spent naphtha through distilling and condensing units. Starts steam pump to force grease into treating tank. Notifies other workers to start and stop screw conveyor that removes degreased bones from extractor. Closes top valves and opens bottom valves on extractor tanks to flush naphtha from tank for processing subsequent batches of bones.
GOE: 06.02.18 STRENGTH: L GED: R3 M2 L2 SVP: 4 DLU: 77

559.665-022 FORMING-MACHINE OPERATOR (button & notion)
Tends battery of automatic machines that heat and form plastic or nylon filament into spiral, serpentine, or ladder shape for teeth portion of zippers: Mounts reel of filament on machine spindle and threads filament through guides and tension bars into electrically heated device (strip heater). Threads filament between forming dies and through cooling tube to takeup reel. Starts machine and observes filament for loosely formed spiral or tight kinks, indicating variations in temperature, and adjusts rheostat knob to regulate heat. Measures filament for conformance to specified dimensions of height, width, and spacing, using micrometer. Inspects samples of formed filament for height, width, and spacing of teeth, using comparator (shadowgraph), and counts number of teeth in specified length of filament to verify conformance to specifications. Notifies supervisor of machine malfunction.
GOE: 06.02.02 STRENGTH: L GED: R3 M2 L2 SVP: 5 DLU: 77

559.665-026 MIXER I (chemical) alternate titles: formulator
Tends mixing kettles to mix and heat chemical ingredients to make cleaning and polishing compounds according to formula: Weighs or measures specified amounts of ingredients on scale or in measuring containers. Pours or shovels ingredients into mixing kettles. Turns valves to regulate gas flame or steam pressure to maintain specified temperature in kettles. Starts agitator to mix ingredients for specified time. Turns valve to drain mixed ingredients into drums, filler machine, or storage tanks. Cleans mixers, kettles, scales, and work area, using solvent and rags. May mix ingredients in portable mixer. May be designated according to kind of cleaning or polishing product made as Shoe-Dressing Maker (chemical).
GOE: 06.04.11 STRENGTH: M GED: R2 M2 L2 SVP: 4 DLU: 77

559.665-030 PRESS OPERATOR I (chemical) alternate titles: carbon-dioxide operator
Tends equipment that converts liquid carbon dioxide into dry ice: Turns valves to transfer liquid carbon dioxide to batch tank for weighing, and to expansion chamber where snow is formed by sudden release of pressure. Pushes lever of press to lower hydraulic ram that compresses snow into cakes. Pushes cakes onto conveyor that carries them under power saws that cut cakes to specified size and transfers them onto scale. Weighs cakes on scale, records weight, and covers dry ice with paper. Lifts ice into insulated box. Tends booster pumps to fill cylinders with liquid carbon dioxide under pressure. May tend automated system that converts liquid carbon dioxide into dry ice.
GOE: 06.04.19 STRENGTH: L GED: R2 M2 L1 SVP: 3 DLU: 77

559.665-034 SPLASH-LINE OPERATOR (fabrication, nec) alternate titles: marbleizing-machine tender; mottle line operator
Tends equipment that mixes, rolls, cuts, and grinds raw materials into chips used to marbleize vinyl and asphalt asbestos floor tile: Weighs out specified

quantities of materials, such as limestone, resins, and asbestos fibers, and dumps them into hopper of mixer. Starts mixer and adjusts temperature controls to attain specified consistency of material. Dumps materials from mixers onto conveyor that conveys material into calenders that roll materials to prescribed thickness. Presses pedal to activate knife that automatically cuts material into slabs. Loads slabs onto conveyor that moves them through drying oven and dumps them into grinders to form chips.
GOE: 06.04.19 STRENGTH: M GED: R2 M2 L2 SVP: 4 DLU: 77

559.665-038 TANK-FARM ATTENDANT (chemical) alternate titles: transfer-and-pumphouse operator
Tends series of spheres or tanks to store and distribute liquid chemicals for use in production of industrial or consumer products, such as phosphoric acid, synthetic rubber, resins, and solvents: Observes flowmeters and pressure gauges, turns valves, and starts pumps to transfer fluid chemicals to or from specified tanks and to processing areas. Gauges quantity of chemicals in tanks, using calibrated steel tape or rod and conversion tables [GAUGER (petrol. & gas; petrol. refin.; pipe lines)]. Maintains records of materials received and distributed, gauge readings, pumping time, and storage dates. Patrols tank farm area to inspect pumps, motors, valves, piping, and electrical ground-wire connections. Reports leaks, temperature and pressure abnormalities, and other potential hazards. May regulate admission of products through preliminary processing units, such as water-treating and refrigerating units, heat exchangers, and purification and filtration equipment. May draw samples of chemicals for laboratory analysis or perform concentration, acidity, or composition tests, using standard test procedure and equipment. May circulate fluids through weigh tanks to facilitate inventory control or supply processing areas with preweighed ingredients.
GOE: 06.04.11 STRENGTH: M GED: R3 M3 L2 SVP: 4 DLU: 77

559.665-042 WASH HELPER (chemical)
Tends equipment that washes and reduces acidity of activated carbon, preparatory to drying: Turns valves, couples hoses, and starts pumps to circulate carbon sludge through washing and blending tanks in specified timing and sequence. Admits prescribed amount of caustic soda into mixing tank or barrel to produce neutralizing solution of prescribed concentration. Starts agitators in blending tanks and opens valves to admit water, caustic solution, and steam to system as directed by WASH OPERATOR (chemical). Takes samples of carbon sludge and wash solution to determine acidity, using titration test and conversion chart. Determines specific gravity of neutralized solution, using hydrometer, beaker, and siphon, and reports reading to system operator to facilitate process control. Measures depth of carbon sludge in tank, using calibrated rod or suction tube. Pumps washed and neutralized carbon to driers when test results indicate washing is completed. Records tank-level and specific gravity readings in shift log. Flushes tanks and lines with water hose, dismantling piping as necessary to remove caked deposits, using wrenches.
GOE: 06.04.19 STRENGTH: M GED: R3 M2 L2 SVP: 4 DLU: 77

559.666-010 TOWER ATTENDANT (paper & pulp) alternate titles: limerock tower loader
Charges tower with limerock used in preparation of acid for cooking wood chips: Breaks limerock with maul and washes dirt from pieces, using hose. Fills handtrucks with limerock and pushes truck to tower. Starts elevator or bucket conveyor to transport limerock to top of tower and fill tower to specified depth. Closes tower filling hatch and fastens it with clamps. Scrapes slag from tower grate and rakes slag from tower floor, using scraper and rake. May operate scoop truck to transport limerock to tower.
GOE: 06.04.14 STRENGTH: H GED: R2 M1 L1 SVP: 2 DLU: 77

559.667-010 TABLET TESTER (pharmaceut.)
Tests hardness of medicinal tablets to ensure conformity with production specifications, using balance scale and hardness tester: Places sample tablet on scale pan, using tweezers, and records weight. Places tablet in hardness tester, turns screw to raise tablet until it touches pressure rod, and depresses pneumatic foot pedal to squeeze tablet until breakage occurs. Examines and fingers tablets to detect chips and tackiness. Notifies COMPRESSOR (elec. equip.; pharmaceut.) when tablets do not meet weight or hardness specifications. May test tablets, using hand-operated hardness tester. May weigh entire batch of tablets to compare with total weight of ingredients used.
GOE: 06.03.02 STRENGTH: S GED: R2 M2 L2 SVP: 3 DLU: 77

559.667-014 LABORER, GENERAL (plastic-synth.)
Performs any combination of following tasks involved in manufacturing plastics materials, synthetic resins, and synthetic rubber: Transports materials to workers and machines, using hoist or handtruck. Inserts metal core in rolls of plastics film. Tightens clamps on supply racks, using wrenches. Cleans machinery and work area, using vacuum cleaner, brushes, and cleaning solvents. Measures, weighs, and dumps ingredients into mills, kettles, or hoppers. Replaces spools or coils of materials on supply racks or reels. Delivers samples of materials to testing laboratory. Records weights, types, and amounts of materials used, stored, or shipped.
GOE: 06.04.40 STRENGTH: M GED: R2 M1 L1 SVP: 2 DLU: 78

559.682-010 CAPSULE-FILLING-MACHINE OPERATOR (pharmaceut.)
Operates capsulating machine to fill gelatin capsules with medicinal preparations: Scoops empty capsules into loading hopper and scoops medicinal preparation into filling hopper of capsulating machine. Fills capsule rings with empty capsules, uncouples rings, and fills lower half of capsule with powdered or pelletized medicine. Recouples capsule rings and inserts rings into closing and ejecting forks. Depresses pedal to close filled capsules and eject them into receiving container. Polishes capsules, using polishing cloth, and inspects capsules for breakage and defective filling. Weighs specified number of capsules and compares weight with weight specification sheet. May operate capsule branding machine to print establishment name on capsule.
GOE: 06.02.18 STRENGTH: M GED: R3 M2 L2 SVP: 4 DLU: 77

559.682-014 CASTING-AND-CURING OPERATOR (chemical)
Controls equipment to fill rocket motor cases with rocket fuel and to cure rocket fuel: Attaches handling ring or sling to motor case, using handtools or portable power tools. Positions motor cases in casting rig (special jig), using hoist, and tightens holding clamp with wrench. Inserts mandrel (core) inside motor case, using hoist, and tightens clamps on casting rig to hold it in position. Conveys and positions casting can over rig, using hoist, and connects hose to rig. Moves console controls to pump fuel from casting can to motor case. Observes level of fuel in case through closed-circuit television and moves controls to regulate volume of fuel charge. Stops pump and presses hydraulic control to move mandrel into final position in motor case. Lifts motor case onto overhead conveyor, using hoist, and starts conveyor to move motor case into curing oven. Observes recording-instrument charts on control panel of curing oven to verify specified temperatures and curing times.
GOE: 06.02.11 STRENGTH: L GED: R3 M2 L2 SVP: 5 DLU: 77

559.682-018 CHEMICAL COMPOUNDER (chemical)
Controls equipment that processes coal tar hydrocarbons into intermediate compounds for use in manufacture of dyestuffs and pharmaceutical products: Measures coal tar derivatives, using balance scales and volume indicators. Shovels or pumps derivatives into specified containers. Observes recording instruments, and adjusts steam, water, and vacuum valves to regulate temperature and pressure during chemical reactions that produce specified intermediates. Tests acidity of intermediates, using pH indicators. Tests solubility of intermediates in liquids, such as water, alcohol, and chloroform. Adds specified chemicals to intermediates to ensure that they meet requirements. Dumps ice into intermediates to reduce temperature. Pumps intermediates through filter to remove liquid residue. Heats intermediates and circulates vapors through condenser lines to isolate components of intermediates. May be designated according to equipment tended as Kettle Operator (chemical) II; Tub Operator (chemical); process involved as Bromination Equipment Operator (chemical); Sulfonation Equipment Operator (chemical); or material produced as Optical-Brightener Maker (chemical).
GOE: 06.02.18 STRENGTH: M GED: R3 M2 L2 SVP: 4 DLU: 77

559.682-022 FILM-CASTING OPERATOR (plastic-synth.) alternate titles: caster
Controls equipment, such as spray line, oven, conveyor, and winding reel to produce transparent plastic wrapping material from prepared chemical solutions: Opens valves to spray solution from bank of spray nozzles onto moving conveyor. Observes gauges and adjusts controls to regulate oven temperature, spray rate of solution, and conveyor speed to produce sheeting of specified thickness and quality. Examines sheet material and inserts marker in spooled material to indicate defective areas. May control operations from remote-controlled panelboard. May send sample piece of material to laboratory for analysis. May examine thickness and clarity of material, using micrometer and illuminated viewing panel. May operate solvent recovery unit.
GOE: 06.02.13 STRENGTH: M GED: R3 M2 L1 SVP: 4 DLU: 77

559.682-026 FLUSHER (chemical)
Controls equipment to displace water from damp pigments by introducing oil or other liquid into pigment: Shovels batch of damp pigment into tub and starts agitator. Turns valve to admit steam into jacket of tub to heat batch to specified temperature. Adds required quantity of liquid vehicle to displace water in pigment. Tilts tub to drain displaced water from top of batch. Clamps lid on tub and opens vacuum valve to draw remaining water from batch. Collects samples of batch for laboratory analysis. Adds type and quantities of oils and extenders specified by laboratory to bring body, strength, and shade of batch within acceptable limits. Mixes batch for specified time. Drains batch into containers and clamps on lid.
GOE: 06.04.12 STRENGTH: M GED: R3 M2 L2 SVP: 5 DLU: 77

559.682-030 LACQUER MAKER (paint & varnish) alternate titles: lacquer mixer
Operates jar-type grinding mill and mixing machine to produce lacquers and synthetic paints according to formulas and work order specifications: Starts jar mill and portable mixer to grind and mix ingredients. Places ingredients, such as gums, pigments, and thinners in mill. Dumps coloring and lacquer ingredients according to specifications into portable mixing kettle and places kettle under mixer. Takes sample from batch and strains it into can. Uses spray gun to spray test panel. Heats prepared mixture with steam coil, causing wax to rise to top of solution, and then settle to bottom to be drawn off into clean tank. Adds required color for tinting batch to meet plant specifications [TINTER (paint & varnish)].
GOE: 06.04.11 STRENGTH: M GED: R3 M2 L2 SVP: 5 DLU: 77

559.682-034 LATEX-RIBBON-MACHINE OPERATOR (rubber goods)
Operates machine to produce and cure latex ribbon and thread used for such items as elastic and garters: Moves drums of liquid latex and coagulant to dip trays, using hoist. Opens petcock on drums and adjusts flow to regulate level

of coagulant in trays. Positions number of dip belts, according to gauge of finished latex ribbon or thread, over belt spindles. Starts equipment to activate dip belts and conveyor system. Observes belts as they float on top of latex in tray and through coagulant to verify cohesion of latex to dip belts. Observes separation of coagulated ribbon or thread from bottom of dip belt to conveyor carrying ribbon or thread through rinsing and drying areas. Inspects ribbon and thread for such defects as holes and dried coagulant. Threads end of ribbon or thread through guides leading to curing drum. Cuts, weighs, and examines samples, to verify adherence to specifications, using scissors, scale, and gauge. Inspects and sharpens circular knives with stone. When producing thread, may be designated Latex-Thread-Machine Operator (rubber goods); Thread-Machine Operator (rubber goods).
GOE: 06.02.13 STRENGTH: M GED: R3 M2 L2 SVP: 6 DLU: 77

559.682-038 RIPENING-ROOM ATTENDANT (plastic-synth.)
Controls equipment to filter, transfer, and remove bubbles from viscose fluid used in manufacturing rayon or cellophane: Turns valves to transfer viscose from mixing station to filter presses that remove impurities and to vacuum tanks that remove air bubbles. Observes gauges and adjusts controls to maintain specified temperature, pressure, and feed rate in equipment and pipes. May tend tanks to age viscose for specified time before transfer to casting (forming) units [TANKROOM TENDER (plastic-synth.)]. May record aging time, viscose output, and gauge readings. May be designated Viscose-Cellar Attendant (plastic-synth.) in plants producing rayon by viscose process.
GOE: 06.02.13 STRENGTH: L GED: R3 M2 L2 SVP: 4 DLU: 77

559.682-042 RUBBER-MILL OPERATOR (plastic-synth.)
Operates extruders and calender mill to remove moisture from butyl rubber crumbs: Presses buttons on control panel to start conveyors that feed rubber crumbs from drier through extruder and into hot mill. Opens breech-lock head on extruder, using wrenches. Removes foreign matter from equipment, using hot hoe and wooden tamper. Turns handwheel to adjust space between rollers on hot mill to remove moisture and to regulate thickness of product on rollers. Observes color and surface characteristics of rubber to determine degree of dryness. Turns valves on steam lines to maintain temperatures. Turns handwheels to adjust mill knives. Cuts samples of product for laboratory tests and cleans undried rubber from rollers for remilling, using knife. Inspects machinery for lubrication and to detect mechanical malfunction.
GOE: 06.02.13 STRENGTH: L GED: R3 M1 L2 SVP: 5 DLU: 77

559.682-046 SODA-ROOM OPERATOR (beverage)
Controls equipment to make cleaning solution used in beer bottle-washing machines: Dumps specified bags of chemicals into mixing tank and adds measured amount of water. Starts pump that transfers chemical solution to tank containing specified amount of concentrated soda. Observes gauges and turns steam valve to heat solution to specified temperature. Pumps used soda from washing machines into separators and settling and storage tanks to remove solid matter, clarify solution, and store solution. Opens hoppers on settling tanks to dump solid refuse into trucks. Connects hoses and starts pumps to transfer concentrated soda from tank car to storage tanks. Washes separator, settling tanks, and floor, using hose.
GOE: 06.04.11 STRENGTH: M GED: R3 M2 L2 SVP: 4 DLU: 77

559.682-050 SPONGE-PRESS OPERATOR (rubber goods)
Operates combination calendering mill and vulcanizing conveyor that rolls out and cures, in continuous process, sponge rubber sheeting for use gaskets, underlay for carpeting, and insulation for footwear: Turns handwheels and capstan screws to set distance between calender rolls and between vulcanizing plates and conveyor, verifying setting with feeler gauges. Operates calender to produce uncured sponge rubber sheeting [CALENDER OPERATOR (rubber goods; rubber tire)]. Turns rheostat for each vulcanizing plate to designated temperature setting and observes heat indicators. Starts conveyor, when plates reach specified heat, to vulcanize calendered sheeting beneath them. Replaces worn canvas conveyor belts between calendering and vulcanizing units, using portable vulcanizing machine to bond ends. Adjusts tension bars that tighten belt, using wrenches. Mounts roll of underlay backing cloth into cradles, using electric chain hoist. Threads backing cloth (netting) through cement trough and series of rollers that press it onto sponge rubber sheeting, and through drying oven. Adjusts width between calender rolls to increase or decrease thickness of sheeting and adjusts temperatures of vulcanizing plates when there are deviations from specifications in thickness or curing. May operate vulcanizing conveyor without warming mill, calender, or vulcanizing plates that draws, by vacuum pressure, uncured sponge rubber between links of wire mesh that expands and vulcanizes rubber as it passes through heated oven to produce waffle-imprinted underlay on precalendered stocks and be known as Rug-Underlay-Machine Operator (rubber goods).
GOE: 06.02.13 STRENGTH: M GED: R3 M2 L2 SVP: 4 DLU: 77

559.682-054 STERILE-PRODUCTS PROCESSOR (pharmaceut.) alternate titles: compounder, sterile products
Operates water still, mixer, *clarifier,* and filtering unit to process liquid and powder ingredients into sterile medications: Turns valves to admit deionized water and steam to still and circulate water through condenser for distillation. Pours metered or measured amount of distilled water into container, weighs out or dumps preweighed ingredients into water and lowers mixing head into solution to dissolve and mix ingredients. Turns dial on pH meter to standard acidity reading, immerses electrodes in beaker of buffer solution, and adds acid or al-

kali, as specified, to achieve prescribed acidity. Pours mixture into clarifier unit to remove insoluble material. Immerses bacteriological filtering candle in clarified solution, connects tubing between candle and collecting vessel, and starts vacuum pump to draw solution through candle pores to remove bacteria and spores and produce sterile product. May set up ampoule- or vial-filling machine. May operate equipment to produce sterile, deionized water used in sterile medications. May sterilize equipment, using autoclave and disinfectant solution.
GOE: 06.02.18 STRENGTH: H GED: R3 M2 L2 SVP: 5 DLU: 77

559.682-058 STRETCH-MACHINE OPERATOR (plastic prod.)
Operates machine to stretch plastic sheets to specified dimensions: Positions sheet in machine and clamps hydraulic rams to edges of sheet. Sets temperature control and starts blowers to heat sheet. Adjusts stops on hydraulic rams (pullers) and starts machine to stretch sheet to specified dimensions. Removes sheet and places it on table or rack to cool. May cut stretched sheet into pieces of specified size, using bandsaw. May inspect stretched sheet against grid board to locate distortion-free areas.
GOE: 06.02.02 STRENGTH: H GED: R3 M2 L2 SVP: 5 DLU: 77

559.682-062 STRONG-NITRIC OPERATOR (chemical) alternate titles: nitric-acid-concentrator operator; tc operator
Controls equipment to increase strength of nitric acid, used in making TNT and nitroglycerin: Regulates flow of sulfuric acid and weak nitric acid into mixing tank and controls flow of steam, water, air, and mixed acids through dehydrating tower, absorption tower, bleaching tower, still, and condenser to produce concentrated nitric acid meeting plant standard. Monitors thermometers and pressure gauges and adjusts valves to maintain specified temperature and pressure in each unit. Takes samples of product for laboratory analysis or tests acid strength, using pH meter. Records instrument readings in shift log.
GOE: 06.02.18 STRENGTH: L GED: R3 M2 L2 SVP: 4 DLU: 77

559.682-066 UTILITY OPERATOR I (chemical)
Operates or controls stills, compressors, reactors, and related chemical process equipment during rest periods, lunch hour, or emergency, performing duties of regular operators as directed by operators or supervisory personnel. When not relieving equipment operator, performs tasks such as assisting operator in turning valves to control flow of materials, setting equipment controls at specified readings, gauging tank levels, and recharging equipment with fresh catalytic agents. May be designated according to equipment operated or worker relieved as Benzene-Still Utility Operator (chemical); Butadiene-Converter-Utility Operator (chemical); Dehydrogenation-Converter Utility Operator (chemical); Ethylbenzene-Compressor Utility Operator (chemical); Styrene-Continuous-Still Utility Operator (chemical).
GOE: 06.02.11 STRENGTH: M GED: R3 M2 L2 SVP: 5 DLU: 77

559.682-070 SCREEN-MACHINE OPERATOR (tex. prod., nec)
Operates screen machine that folds and bonds edges of vinyl sheets to reinforcing strips and punches holes in strips to form shower curtains: Selects roll of vinyl specified on work order, inserts metal cylinder in roll, positions roll in holding brackets of machine, and turns knobs to secure cylinder. Fills cylinder with air to prevent slippage of roll during machine operation, using airhose. Cuts lead end of vinyl with scissors to straighten end and attaches end to material in machine, using tape. Adjusts guides that fold edges of vinyl and solvent release mechanism that seals folded edges, using handtools. Turns knobs to set heat level of rollers that press and seal folded edges of vinyl. Inserts roll of vinyl reinforcing strip in holder above press of machine, and pushes end of strip onto chain that automatically positions strip for bonding to and reinforcing lead end of vinyl sheet. Pushes button to start machine and measures vinyl in machine to verify width specified on work order, using tape measure. Flips switches to activate feed chains that automatically pull vinyl and reinforcing strip into position under press, and to lower press that cuts, punches holes in, and presses and bonds strips against vinyl to form shower curtains. Observes movement of vinyl through machine and adjusts machine periodically to eliminate detected defects.
GOE: 06.02.13 STRENGTH: H GED: R3 M1 L2 SVP: 5 DLU: 86

559.684-010 PACK-ROOM OPERATOR (plastic-synth.)
Fills spinnerette *packs* (metal cups) with measured amount of treated sand to filter impurities from molten nylon before extrusion into filaments: Examines holes in bottom of pack, using microscope, to detect damaged or clogged openings. Weighs out prescribed amounts and grades of treated sand and pours sand into pack, leveling sand with crescent-shaped tool. Repeats filling and leveling process until specified number of layers have been built up, according to type of nylon to be spun. Disassembles used packs, pours out sand, and washes pack in soapy water to remove burned sand adhering to cup after extrusion of molten nylon.
GOE: 06.04.30 STRENGTH: H GED: R3 M2 L1 SVP: 4 DLU: 77

559.684-018 RUBBER-MOLD MAKER (jewelry-silver.) alternate titles: mold maker
Forms rubber wax injection molds by vulcanizing pieces of rubber around metal sample: Places metal sample into frame and packs raw rubber around sample. Clamps sample, frame, and rubber into vulcanizing machine. Turns on machine, waits specified time, and removes mold from machine. Splits mold into two pieces to remove metal sample, using knife or scalpel. Inspects mold for defects. May form investment molds around wax patterns. May operate centrifugal casting machine. May burn grooves or crevices in mold to correct defects, using soldering gun.

GOE: 06.04.32 STRENGTH: L GED: R2 M1 L1 SVP: 3 DLU: 77

559.684-022 TANK CLEANER (paint & varnish) alternate titles: chipper

Cleans tanks, vats, kettles, and chutes, used in production of paint products: Disconnects pipelines and locks safety devices on agitator switch. Enters tanks and examines condition of interior to determine cleaning method. Connects air-compressor hoses to portable pneumatic chisel and forced-air ventilating equipment. Starts portable electric pump to draw residual liquid from tank. Chips and scrapes caked material from walls, ceiling, agitator, and floor surfaces, using pneumatic chisel or hand scrapers. Shovels scrapings into container and removes container from tank, using hoist. Dumps scrapings into disposal drum and carts drum to refuse area. Scrubs tank surfaces, using brush, water, and solvent. May presoak tank with caustic solution. May haul kettles and chutes to burning area and burn off inflammable residue in vessels.

GOE: 06.04.39 STRENGTH: H GED: R2 M1 L1 SVP: 3 DLU: 77

559.684-026 UTILITY WORKER, MOLDING (plastic prod.)

Performs any combination of following and related tasks in molding department of plastics fabricating establishment: Examines plastic products for defects, such as scratches, *flash*, and discoloration, and discards defective items into reject box. Packs finished products into cartons and affixes content labels. Conveys supplies from storage to work stations, using handtruck. Opens collapsed cartons, folds and seals carton bottoms, using moistened gummed tape, and inserts nesting into cartons. Unloads plastic mixture from machine hoppers into barrels upon completion of job order, affixes identification labels on barrels, and conveys barrels to mixing department. Dumps cleaning solution into hopper and actuates molding machine to purge internal sections of unused plastic mixture. Dismantles hopper and drying unit of machine, using handtools, and cleans internal sections, using rags, cleaning solution, and airhose. Sweeps and mops production floor.

GOE: 06.04.24 STRENGTH: L GED: R3 M1 L2 SVP: 3 DLU: 86

559.684-030 HAT-FINISHING-MATERIALS PREPARER (hat & cap)

Mixes and blends finishing grease and coloring powders used in manufacture of felt hats: Pours specified amounts of ingredients, such as oil and lanolin into blending pot, following formulas and using measuring containers. Places pot on heated range and stirs ingredients to blend mixture, using paddle. Places rolls of greasing or pouncing (smoothing) cloth in processing pan and pours mixture over rolls. Turns knobs to activate oven and places processing pans in oven to heat rolls of cloth in mixture for specified period. Removes pans from oven at end of processing, affixes batch labels to rolls, and carries rolls to specified storage area. Refines dye powders, using powder-refining tumbler machine, and weighs and blends refined powders according to formulas and work order specifications, using scale and automatic mixing machine. Labels and stores blended powders, according to color, in specified storage areas.

GOE: 06.04.34 STRENGTH: M GED: R3 M2 L2 SVP: 5 DLU: 86

559.684-034 UTILITY WORKER, PRODUCTION (pharmaceut.) alternate titles: utility worker, virus

Performs any combination of following duties in production of vaccines or toxoids: Adds chemical solutions, disease virus, or bacteria to and removes culture fluids from glass vessels, using pump. Connects pumping equipment to storage, filtration, formentation, and refrigeration containers to transfer and refrigerate chemical ingredients or to flush containers. Conveys chemical ingredients, disease bacteria, and disease viruses in drums, containers, jars, or vials to and from storage or refrigeration rooms, using handtruck. Carries samples of chemical broth, vaccine, or toxoid to quality control unit. Tends sterilizers, oven, and autoclave that sterilize glassware, instruments, and portable equipment. Washes designated equipment by hand, using brushes, rags, and detergent. Thaws frozen ingredients used in developing vaccines or toxoids, using thawing equipment.

GOE: 06.04.19 STRENGTH: M GED: R3 M2 L3 SVP: 4 DLU: 86

559.685-010 ACID PURIFIER (chemical)

Tends equipment that filters acid liquor from slurry and dehydrates residual materials for further processing: Opens feed valves and starts rotary drum that filters liquor from slurry. Turns valves to transfer residue to dehydration unit. Adjusts controls to regulate temperature, pressure, and speed of material flow as specified to dry residue. Collects samples of acid liquor and residual materials for laboratory analysis. May be designated according to material processed as Phthalic-Acid Purifier (chemical).

GOE: 06.04.11 STRENGTH: L GED: R2 M1 L1 SVP: 3 DLU: 77

559.685-014 ALUMINUM-HYDROXIDE-PROCESS OPERATOR (chemical; pharmaceut.)

Tends steam-jacketed kettles, mixing tanks, filter press, string filter, and related equipment to process ammonia solution and aluminum sulfate into aluminum hydroxide: Meters water into steam-jacketed kettle and sets thermostat at specified temperature. Dumps preweighed bags of aluminum sulfate into kettle, and starts agitator to dissolve ingredient. Meters specified amounts of hot water and ammonia into mixing tank and starts agitator. Pumps aluminum sulfate solution through filter press into heated agitator tank to remove insoluble materials. Pumps ammonia solution to tank with aluminum sulfate solution. Ladles sample of mixture, adds test solution, and observes color reaction to determine degree of precipitation. Adds specified ingredients to mixing tank to complete precipitation, according to results of test. Pumps slurry through string filter to separate aluminum hydroxide from mixture. May replace filtering media and repair equipment, using handtools.

GOE: 06.04.11 STRENGTH: M GED: R3 M2 L2 SVP: 4 DLU: 77

559.685-018 AMPOULE FILLER (pharmaceut.) alternate titles: ampoule filler and sealer

Tends machine that fills ampoules with metered doses of liquid drug products: Starts machine and dumps empty ampoules into hopper or places them on rotating table of machine that automatically positions them for filling. Seals ampoules [AMPOULE SEALER (pharmaceut.)]. May regulate gas flame in ampoule-sealing unit. May inspect [AMPOULE EXAMINER (pharmaceut.)], count, and pack ampoules in cartons for shipment. May place sealed ampoules in wire basket and immerse in dye bath for leak test. May tend machine that steam-washes ampoules preparatory to filling [AMPOULE-WASHING-MACHINE OPERATOR (pharmaceut.)].

GOE: 06.04.19 STRENGTH: L GED: R2 M1 L1 SVP: 2 DLU: 77

559.685-022 AMPOULE-WASHING-MACHINE OPERATOR (pharmaceut.) alternate titles: washing-machine operator

Tends machine that steam-washes ampoules, preparatory to filling: Places ampoules on spokes of rotary table of washing machine. Depresses pedal to move ampoules through steam bath. Removes washed ampoules and places them in holes of perforated tray. Discards chipped or cracked ampoules. May load ampoules into drying ovens and remove after specified time.

GOE: 06.04.39 STRENGTH: L GED: R2 M1 L1 SVP: 2 DLU: 77

559.685-026 BRINE-WELL OPERATOR (chemical) alternate titles: pump operator, brine well

Tends pumps to maintain brine wells at specified levels to ensure adequate salt supply for chemical processes: Turns valves and monitors gauges and water-pressure recorders to maintain level and brine strength of wells within prescribed limits, and to reverse flow of flush wells as directed. Determines specific gravity of salt water in wells, using hydrometer. Determines iodine content of brine, using standard titration test. Monitors automatic pump operation and inspects water supply system to detect broken or frozen lines, stoppages, and leaks. Records brine strength and pressure in system for operating log.

GOE: 06.04.11 STRENGTH: L GED: R3 M2 L2 SVP: 4 DLU: 77

559.685-030 BRIQUETTER OPERATOR (chemical)

Tends machine that automatically forms ore mixture or chemical compounds into briquettes: Shovels mix into feed hopper and pokes out feed chutes, using rod, to prevent jamming of material as it flows to briquetting rollers and to rotary drier. Turns valves to maintain vacuum pressure in drier within specified limits. Pushes down sealing ring to prevent loss of vacuum and transfers briquettes to drums for shipment or storage. Weighs drums, using platform scale, to facilitate compilation of shipping data. Monitors potentiometer on drier and reports unusual fluctuations to maintenance or supervisory personnel. Examines drier feedlines for condition, to detect potential air leaks and loss of vacuum.

GOE: 06.04.11 STRENGTH: M GED: R3 M2 L2 SVP: 3 DLU: 77

559.685-034 CD-STORAGE-AND-MATERIALS MAKE-UP HELPER (chemical)

Tends equipment to prepare basic chemical solutions used in production of synthetic rubber: Opens valves and starts pumps to admit chlorobutadiene into weigh tank. Adds specified ingredients into tank, according to formula. Starts agitator in tank to mix contents. Turns valve to control flow of steam into tank jacket to maintain specified temperature of solution. Mixes persulfate and water in tank according to formula. Pumps prepared solution to processing areas. Records data, such as materials prepared and chemicals used. Pumps brine or nitrogen through chlorobutadiene stored in tanks to prevent spontaneous polymerization. Disassembles and cleans scrubbers, using handtools and steam hose.

GOE: 06.04.11 STRENGTH: M GED: R2 M2 L2 SVP: 4 DLU: 77

559.685-038 COMPRESSOR OPERATOR II (chemical) alternate titles: block-press operator

Tends machine that compresses loose salt into blocks for use as cattle feed supplement: Opens gate to transfer premixed salt from bin to measuring hopper. Starts press that automatically admits measured amount of salt into compression chamber, compresses salt into blocks, and ejects blocks onto chute. Lifts blocks from chute and stacks them on pallet. Cleans machine. May fortify salt by adding and mixing specified amounts of potassium iodide or other fortifiers to salt before it is compressed into blocks.

GOE: 06.04.11 STRENGTH: H GED: R2 M1 L1 SVP: 2 DLU: 77

559.685-042 CRYSTALLIZER OPERATOR I (chemical)

Tends crystallizer to process chemical solution into crystalline form: Pumps specified amounts of materials and solvent or dumps drums of solutions into crystallizer. Starts agitator and pumps coolants into coils of crystallizer. Reads thermometer, observes product, and turns coolant valve to regulate temperature and control rate of crystallization according to specifications. May heat ingredients in crystallizer to prevent premature crystallization. May start centrifuge to separate crystallized substances from solvent [CENTRIFUGAL-DRIER OPERATOR (chemical)].

GOE: 06.04.11 STRENGTH: H GED: R3 M2 L2 SVP: 4 DLU: 77

559.685-046 DOPE-DRY-HOUSE OPERATOR (chemical) alternate titles: dope-house operator helper; dry-house operator

Tends machines that dry, grind, and screen materials, such as sodium nitrate, apricot pits, sulfur, and clay for use in making dynamite: Shovels or dumps materials into drier hopper and adjusts temperature of steam-heated drier to

specified reading. Starts conveyors and elevators that convey materials through drier and grinder. Starts grinder and sifting screens that grind and screen materials and deposit them in bins. May drive scoop tractor to fill drier hopper. May test moisture content of ingredients, using carbide-filled jar and gauge that registers gas produced. May weigh out dried ingredients according to formula, to prepare batches for mixing with nitroglycerin. May be designated according to ingredient treated as Soda-Dry-House Operator (chemical).
GOE: 06.04.19 STRENGTH: M GED: R2 M1 L1 SVP: 2 DLU: 77

559.685-050 DRIER-AND-PULVERIZER TENDER (chemical)
Tends mill that dries and pulverizes pasty chemical materials: Starts mill, turns valves, and observes gauges to regulate temperature and suction as specified. Hoists containers of materials to be milled onto loading platform, using chain fall, and dumps specified quantity of materials into mill. Regulates flow of hot air through mill, according to size of milled batch, and controls speed of suction pump that removes pulverized product after milling and drying.
GOE: 06.04.11 STRENGTH: H GED: R2 M1 L1 SVP: 2 DLU: 77

559.685-054 DUSTING-AND-BRUSHING-MACHINE OPERATOR (rubber goods)
Tends machines that automatically dust uncured sponge rubber sheeting with talc powder to prevent rolled surfaces sticking together or remove excess powder from sheeting: Shovels powder into hopper to load machine for dusting. Mounts roll of sheeting in cradle and threads end between fleece rollers or brushing unit of machine to dust surface with talc or remove excess talc, and wind sheeting onto empty roll. Starts machine, observes feeding of material, and keeps hopper filled with talc, when dusting. Blows dust from operating parts of machine, using airhose.
GOE: 06.04.21 STRENGTH: M GED: R2 M1 L1 SVP: 2 DLU: 77

559.685-058 EFFERVESCENT-SALTS COMPOUNDER (pharmaceut.) alternate titles: process operator
Tends mixing machine, evaporating pans, grinding mills, and drying oven that process powdered ingredients into granulated effervescent salts for use in drug preparations: Dumps prescribed quantity of citric acid crystals into mill and starts machine to grind crystals. Starts mixer and adds ground crystals and specified amount of powdered ingredients to blend for designated time. Sets thermostat to regulate temperature of steam-jacketed evaporator pans, and dumps mixture into pans to heat for specified period and remove moisture. Inserts screen in mill and dumps contents of evaporator pans into machine to granulate to uniform size. Scoops granules into trays. Places trays in drying oven for predetermined time. Dumps or scoops dried granules into hopper or chute for transfer to storage or packaging area. May screen granules to remove particles smaller than specified size, using sieve.
GOE: 06.04.11 STRENGTH: H GED: R3 M2 L2 SVP: 4 DLU: 77

559.685-062 ELECTRODE-CLEANING-MACHINE OPERATOR (elec. equip.)
Tends electrode cleaning machine that scrapes excess carbon from baked or graphitized electrodes: Pushes machine, mounted on rails, to area where electrodes are stacked horizontally on racks and aligns machine with guide bars extending from rack. Blocks wheels to prevent machine from rolling during cleaning process. Moves levers that lower stop bar on machine and allow electrode to roll from rack onto rollers of machine. Starts machine to rotate electrode on rollers and moves lever to lower abrasive belt onto electrode to scrape away excess carbon. Stops machine when scraping is complete and moves lever that raises abrasive belt and ejects cleaned electrode onto rack adjacent to machine. Inspects cleaned electrode to ensure that excess carbon is removed.
GOE: 06.04.09 STRENGTH: H GED: R2 M1 L1 SVP: 2 DLU: 77

559.685-066 FABRIC NORMALIZER (rubber goods) alternate titles: normalizing-equipment tender
Tends equipment that shrinks rubberized fabric sheeting or tubing to increase strength of material: Positions reel of rubberized stock in letoff rack, by hand or using hoist. Adjusts stock guides and tension rollers on machine, using handtools, to accommodate stock. Dumps powdered soapstone in hopper of equipment to dust stock. Moves controls to regulate temperature of water in dip tank and speed of equipment. Threads rubberized fabric stock through machine. Starts equipment that moves stock through water bath, drying compartment, under soapstone dispenser, and onto windup reel.
GOE: 06.04.16 STRENGTH: M GED: R2 M1 L1 SVP: 3 DLU: 77

559.685-070 FERMENTER OPERATOR (pharmaceut.)
Tends fermenting tanks and auxiliary equipment to produce active constituent of antibiotic drug products: Starts agitator fermenting and mixing tanks and adds prescribed quantities of ingredients, such as salt, sugar, and yeast. Turns valves and starts pumps to transfer mixture to fermenting tank and maintain specified temperature in tanks for prescribed time. Opens valves to admit water, liquid seed antibiotic, and foam-preventing oil, according to critical plant specifications. Unbolts lid of fermenter tank and measures level of solution, using dipstick. Turns valves to transfer mixture to crystallization tank for further processing.
GOE: 06.04.11 STRENGTH: L GED: R3 M2 L2 SVP: 4 DLU: 77

559.685-074 FLAKER OPERATOR (chemical; smelt. & refin.) alternate titles: drier-and-evaporator operator; finishing-pan operator; flaking-machine operator; pan operator
Tends drum-flaking machine that solidifies and converts chemical compounds into flakes preparatory to shipment or further processing: Pumps molten mate-

rials or concentrated solutions into feed pan of flaking machine. Moves rheostat and turns valves to regulate speed of revolving flaking drum and flow of coolant to control solidification and thickness of flakes scraped from drum by stationary blade, according to procedure. Scoops samples of flakes into container for laboratory moisture analysis. May dump flakes into bags or drums, weigh, and secure bags with stitching device, or seal drums. May tend auxiliary equipment, such as grinding mills, shaker screens, and loading conveyors. May be designated according to material flaked as Pitch Flaker (chemical); Potash Flaker (chemical); Soda Flaker (chemical).
GOE: 06.04.11 STRENGTH: M GED: R2 M2 L2 SVP: 3 DLU: 77

559.685-078 FOAM-MACHINE OPERATOR (plastic prod.; plastic-synth.)
Tends machine that sprays thermoplastic resins onto conveyor belt to form plastic foam: Pours catalysts and resins into machine hoppers and starts belt conveyor and resin pumps. Turns valves to start spray and synchronize spray with conveyor speed. Cuts solidified foam block to specified length, using handsaw. May cut foam block to specified thickness, using horizontal bandsaw [SAWYER (plastic prod.; plastic-synth.)].
GOE: 06.04.13 STRENGTH: M GED: R2 M1 L1 SVP: 2 DLU: 77

559.685-082 FORMULA WEIGHER (pen & pencil)
Tends mills and mixing machines to prepare ink for typewriter ribbons and oil-wax coating for carbon paper, according to prescribed formulas: Weighs and measures ingredients, following written instructions. Pours ingredients into specified mixing machine, such as mixing mill, ball mill, or agitator. Starts and stops machines. Observes temperature indicators and turns valves to maintain specified heat in mills. Cleans machines and utensils, using solvent and cloth.
GOE: 06.02.18 STRENGTH: M GED: R3 M2 L2 SVP: 4 DLU: 77

559.685-086 FRAME STRIPPER (soap & rel.)
Pushes empty soap frames (open metal tanks with removable sides) under crutcher machine to fill frames with liquid soap, and tends machine that cuts soap into slabs: Opens slide in crutcher to allow soap to pour into and fill frame. Pushes filled frame to hardening area to allow soap to harden for specified time. Moves hardened frame to slabbing machine, using handtruck. Unscrews bolts on frame to remove sides, or connects hoist to frame to lift sides. Pushes soap cake into slabbing machine and presses lever to activate cutting wires that cut soap cakes into slabs. Removes slabs from machine.
GOE: 06.04.19 STRENGTH: M GED: R2 M1 L1 SVP: 2 DLU: 77

559.685-090 FREEZING-MACHINE OPERATOR (pharmaceut.) alternate titles: shell-freezing-machine operator
Tends machine that freezes blood plasma preparatory to hydration or storage: Starts machine that circulates solution of dry ice and alcohol over rollers to chill them. Moves blood plasma from walk-in freezer to freezing machine, using handtruck. Places bottles of blood plasma onto rotating rollers submerged in cold alcohol in machine. Taps revolving bottles with metal wand to accelerate and ensure uniform freezing of plasma, increasing speed of tapping on bottles when crystallization does not occur uniformly. Places bottles of plasma that do not freeze uniformly into reject container and frozen plasma on trays for further processing. Reads thermometer to ascertain that temperature of solution remains constant, according to specifications. May place bottles on rack to drain off alcohol before packing. May tend centrifuge machine that separates plasma from red corpuscles present in whole blood. May tend fractionator machine that breaks down plasma into proteins by centrifugal action.
GOE: 06.04.11 STRENGTH: M GED: R3 M2 L2 SVP: 3 DLU: 77

559.685-094 FUSE MAKER (chemical)
Tends equipment to make fuses for pyrotechnics: Screens black powder to required fineness and pours it into hopper of spinning machine. Threads end of rolls of cotton roving into spindle of spinning machine. Starts machine that automatically spins strands of cotton yarn together and around a train of black powder to make fuses and winds fuses onto bobbins. Stops spinning machine and removes bobbins. Positions filled bobbins in holders of dope trough. Threads fuses over pulleys in dope trough and drying chamber, fastening ends of fuses to reels in drying chamber. Fills trough with dope and regulates temperature of drying chamber. Starts motor to pull fuses through dope and through heated chamber to dry dope-covered fuses and to wind fuses onto reels. Removes reels of dried fuse when automatic counter indicates that specified amount of fuse has been wound onto reel.
GOE: 06.04.19 STRENGTH: M GED: R2 M1 L2 SVP: 3 DLU: 77

559.685-098 GLUE-MILL OPERATOR (chemical) alternate titles: paste-mill operator
Tends line of mills, conveyors, shakers, and filling machine to break, sift, and package dry glue or gelatin: Starts mills, conveyors, and shakers equipped with screens of prescribed mesh size. Opens gate in chute of hopper and drops coarse material into mill. Observes line to detect malfunction or breakdown of machinery as material is milled, sifted, and loaded into tank of filling machine. Stops line when malfunctions occur. Places container below filling machine and clamps spout equipped with scale to container. Opens valve to fill spout to prescribed weight, observing scale. Closes valve and opens slide gate to drop glue into container. Pushes slide gate to close spout and seals container. May stack bags on skid. May use device (levelator) which levels each layer of bags with floor to facilitate stacking.
GOE: 06.04.19 STPENGTH: H GED: R2 M2 L1 SVP: 3 DLU: 77

559.685-102 GOLF-BALL-COVER TREATER (toy-sport equip.) alternate titles: cover treater

Mixes chemicals, dips buckets of golf balls into chemical solutions, and tends machines that tumble balls in solutions to vulcanize, etch, and cure covers preparatory to painting: Pours specified amounts of chemicals and water into dip tanks. Fills dip buckets with balls and lifts bucket into tanks manually or using hoist. Moves bucket through series of dip tanks for specified time in each tank. Empties balls into storage boxes and moves boxes to curing room for specified time. Loads tumblers with balls and opens valves to fill tumbler with water. Measures and pours or pumps in specified amounts and types of chemicals. Runs tumblers for set time, empties solution, and fills and runs tumbler through rinse cycle. Repeats chemical treating and rinse cycles according to curing specifications. Empties balls into buckets and places balls on racks for storage in drying room. May test sample balls for compression [INSPECTOR, GOLF BALL (toy-sport equip.)].
GOE: 06.04.11 STRENGTH: H GED: R2 M2 L2 SVP: 2 DLU: 77

559.685-106 IMPREGNATOR OPERATOR (chemical) alternate titles: catalyst impregnator

Tends tank in which catalytic material is impregnated with liquid chemicals for use in manufacturing butadiene: Weighs specified quantity of catalyst and dumps it into tank containing measured amounts of liquid chemicals. Turns steam valve to heat mixture in tank until boiling occurs, impregnating catalytic material. Determines specific gravity of mixture, using hydrometer, and adds specified types and quantities of reagents to attain prescribed specific gravity.
GOE: 06.04.11 STRENGTH: M GED: R2 M2 L2 SVP: 4 DLU: 77

559.685-110 LABORER, GENERAL (paint & varnish)

Performs any combination of following tasks involved in production of paints and varnishes: Dumps calcined and metallic pigments into hopper of automatic grinder to reduce pigments to powdered form. Spreads layers of cinders and black ash over screen of leach box and opens valve that sprays hot water on box to recover barium sulfide from black ash. Pumps pigment slurries and paints through filters to remove lumps and impurities. Fills cleaning tank with water and caustic and turns steam valve to heat tank. Places equipment to be cleaned, such as pails, chutes, and mixing pans in tank. Removes equipment from cleaning tank after specified time and rinses equipment, using water hose. Unloads drums, barrels, and raw materials from freight cars and trucks, and stacks them in warehouse or work areas. Cleans work areas, using broom, rags, and solvent. May be known according to specific task performed as Black-Ash Worker (paint & varnish); Equipment Cleaner (paint & varnish); Strainer (paint & varnish).
GOE: 06.04.11 STRENGTH: H GED: R2 M1 L1 SVP: 2 DLU: 77

559.685-114 LATEX SPOOLER (rubber goods) alternate titles: spooler, rubber strand

Tends equipment to spool latex thread or wind latex ribbon into rolls: Pushes curing drum to position at spooling or winding equipment and fastens it in place. Attaches latex threads or ribbons from curing drum to spools or roll-winding equipment. Starts equipment that revolves curing drum to unwind goods and activates takeup equipment. Observes operation and adjusts speed of takeup to regulate tension. Straightens bent thread guides and ties broken threads. Removes and wraps filled spools or rolls, and packs them in carton for shipment. Weighs packed carton to determine yardage.
GOE: 06.04.07 STRENGTH: H GED: R2 M1 L1 SVP: 4 DLU: 77

559.685-118 LIME-KILN OPERATOR (paper & pulp) alternate titles: lime slaker

Tends kiln and mixing tanks to recover lime from lime sludge and produce slaked lime from recovered lime: Observes gauges and temperature charts on panel to detect variations in kiln temperature, amount of sludge in kiln, percentage of oxygen in kiln atmosphere, and rate that carbon dioxide is exhausted from kiln. Turns rheostats to regulate amount of sludge fed into kiln according to capacity of kiln. Adjusts dampers to maintain kiln at specified temperature. Turns rheostats to regulate intake fans according to percentage of oxygen in kiln and exhaust fans according to rate that sludge decomposes into quicklime and carbon dioxide. Starts conveyors to move quicklime from storage bins to dissolving tanks that automatically mix quicklime with water to form slaked lime.
GOE: 06.02.18 STRENGTH: L GED: R3 M2 L2 SVP: 4 DLU: 77

559.685-122 LINSEED-OIL-PRESS TENDER (oils & grease) alternate titles: linseed-oil-mill tender

Tends equipment that grinds, cooks, and presses flaxseed to make meal cakes for animal feed, and to obtain oil for use in making products, such as soap, paint, and varnish: Dumps flaxseed into grinding mill and starts mill to grind flaxseed into meal. Empties ground meal into tempering kettle. Turns valves to regulate and maintain specified temperature and moisture content in kettle. Opens valve to dump cooked meal between mats to form cakes. Places mats in hydraulic press. Starts press that lowers ram and presses oil from cakes.
GOE: 06.04.19 STRENGTH: M GED: R2 M2 L1 SVP: 3 DLU: 77

559.685-126 NOODLE-CATALYST MAKER (chemical)

Mixes materials and tends equipment to form kaolin into noodle-like strips, for use as catalyst in production of ethylene from alcohol: Dumps specified amount of kaolin into mixing trough, using wheelbarrow. Adds water until specified consistency is attained and mixes materials, using hoe, until mixture appears suitable for extrusion. Starts pug mill (extruder) and shovels mix into

mill that extrudes kaolin mixture into noodles of specified length and thickness. Places noodles on trays and loads trays into oven or drier for prescribed time. Removes cooked noodles and stacks them in piles for later use.
GOE: 06.04.11 STRENGTH: M GED: R2 M1 L1 SVP: 2 DLU: 77

559.685-130 PIGMENT PROCESSOR (chemical; paint & varnish)

Tends one or more equipment units, such as reaction tanks, bleach tanks, wash tanks, filters, dryers, furnaces, and mills to process pigments, such as titanium, barytes, bentonite, and iron oxide for use in products, such as paint, industrial coating, rubber, plastic, and ink: Pushes buttons on control panel and turns valves to start feed of raw materials, such as ore or scrap metal, into processing equipment. Monitors gauges, dials, and recorders and adjusts equipment controls to maintain temperatures, pressures, and flow of materials according to specifications. May perform chemical tests on product to ensure conformance with specifications, using standard test equipment and procedures.
GOE: 06.04.11 STRENGTH: M GED: R3 M2 L2 SVP: 3 DLU: 77

559.685-134 POWDER-CUTTING OPERATOR (chemical)

Tends machine that cuts strands of smokeless powder into grains of designated size to produce explosives having uniform ballistic properties: Changes gear ratio of machine-feed mechanism to cut grains to specified size. Feeds flexible strands of colloidal powder through guide holes into cutter. Starts flow of liquid coolant, such as alcohol or water, playing on cutting area to prevent outbreak of fire. Empties fiber containers of cut powder into cart.
GOE: 06.04.11 STRENGTH: M GED: R2 M1 L1 SVP: 2 DLU: 77

559.685-138 PRESS OPERATOR (rubber reclaim.) alternate titles: washing-machine operator

Tends equipment that washes and squeezes devulcanized scrap rubber to remove caustic materials used in devulcanization process: Starts pumps or opens chute to feed devulcanized rubber onto vibrating screen conveyor. Turns valves to adjust spray that washes rubber. Observes screen that filters rubber residue from wash water to detect clogging of holes. Opens hopper chute to feed washed material into screw press or between rollers that squeeze out water. Feels pressed material to estimate remaining moisture content and turns handwheels to adjust squeezing action of screw press or dewatering rollers.
GOE: 06.04.13 STRENGTH: L GED: R2 M1 L1 SVP: 3 DLU: 77

559.685-142 PRESSER (soap & rel.) alternate titles: cutter and presser; soap-press feeder

Tends cutting and stamping equipment that cuts bars of soap from logs (long bars of soap) and embosses bars with firm name or trademark: Moves controls to regulate machine speed to maintain uniform movement of soap through plodder (bar-forming machine), cutting and stamping machines, and cooling tower. Examines soap bars for clean-cut form and uniform color and stops equipment when bars are defective, unbolts plodder, and removes accumulated soap from plodder plate. May rub bars under running water to test them for smoothness. Sends sample bars to laboratory for moisture tests. May tend press that presses bars into specified shape.
GOE: 06.04.09 STRENGTH: L GED: R2 M1 L1 SVP: 2 DLU: 77

559.685-146 PRESSROOM WORKER, FAT (oils & grease) alternate titles: filter-press pumper; refiner bleacher

Tends equipment that boils, agitates, bleaches, and cleans tallow: Turns valves to drain specified amount of tallow from storage tank into bleaching tank and to create vacuum inside tank when vacuum bleaching method is used. Moves controls to heat tank with steam and maintain specified temperature. Admits specified amount of carbon (ground charcoal) and diatomaceous earth into bleaching tank and starts agitator. Draws sample from tank and pours it through filter paper, observing its color for conformance to specifications. Adds tallow or diatomaceous earth to tank as required. Opens valves to force tallow by steam pressure through filter press to remove foreign material and into storage tank.
GOE: 06.04.19 STRENGTH: L GED: R2 M1 L1 SVP: 2 DLU: 77

559.685-150 REBRANDER (rubber goods)

Tends revolving wire brush and hot die presses that remove brand from rubber footwear and rebrand footwear for sale under another vendor's name, using either of following methods: (1) Holds footwear with brand against wire brush and buffs off brand. (2) Positions footwear on hot die press and presses pedal to lower ram and hot blanking die on brand to melt brand. Positions debranded footwear on another hot die press equipped with rebranding die, places patch of uncured rubber over brand location on footwear, and depresses pedal to lower ram for preset time to vulcanize patch into brand.
GOE: 06.04.07 STRENGTH: L GED: R2 M1 L1 SVP: 2 DLU: 77

559.685-154 RESTRICTIVE-PREPARATION OPERATOR (ordnance)

Tends mixing machine to prepare materials used in insulation jackets of rocket-engine chambers, and repairs defective jackets: Weighs out and pours specified quantities of chemical ingredients into mixing chamber of colloid mill. Starts mill and moves controls to set automatic timer and maintain specified temperature of mixture. Opens valves to transfer mixed ingredients from mill to storage tanks. Examines and feels insulation jackets for defects, such as breaks and surface flaws. Removes defects, using power grinder, and fills recesses with specified insulation material, using spatula or spray gun. Buffs repaired area, using power buffer.
GOE: 06.04.11 STRENGTH: M GED: R2 M2 L1 SVP: 3 DLU: 77

559.685-158 RUBBER CUTTER (rubber goods; rubber tire)

Tends machine that cuts bales of crude rubber into pieces: Removes wired wooden wrapping or metal straps, using cutters. Loads bale into machine bed,

using electric hoist or pulls bale from chute, using hook. Moves lever to release hydraulic ram that pushes bale through stationary knives. May remove burlap covering from bales and truck them to machine. May push bales onto bed of cutting machine. May pull layers of smoked or crepe rubber apart, using hook.
GOE: 06.04.07 STRENGTH: H GED: R1 M1 L1 SVP: 2 DLU: 77

559.685-162 SCREENER-PERFUMER (soap & rel.)
Tends equipment that screens soap powder and impregnates it with perfume: Adjusts chute slide to regulate flow of powder onto screens over hopper. Adjusts scale tank to weigh out specified amount of perfume. Turns valve to pump perfume through spray jets into powder hopper. Observes level of powder flowing into hopper and diverts powder into drums if specified level is exceeded.
GOE: 06.04.19 STRENGTH: M GED: R2 M1 L1 SVP: 3 DLU: 77

559.685-166 SEPARATOR OPERATOR (chemical)
Tends machine that separates crushed bone from glue liquor: Opens valve to start flow of bone emulsion into basket of separator machine. Starts machine and pumps separated glue liquor into storage tanks. Stops machine and removes basket of crushed bone. Weighs basket and dumps bone into elevator chute.
GOE: 06.04.19 STRENGTH: L GED: R2 M2 L1 SVP: 2 DLU: 77

559.685-170 SPREADING-MACHINE OPERATOR (chemical)
Tends equipment that spreads and cuts glutinous material, such as glue and gelatin, into sheets for drying: Opens valve to allow glutinous material to spread onto conveyor belt or onto tray. Starts conveyor belt to move material through chilling tunnel to congeal, or cuts off material, using knife, when tray is filled. Turns on cooling system in chilling tunnel, observes thickness of congealed material, and regulates flow of material onto conveyor belt to ensure specified thickness. Starts knives that cut congealed material into sheets of specified length and machine that deposits sheets onto drying frames. Stacks drying frames or trays of glutinous material onto handtruck and pushes handtruck to drying compartments. May tend equipment to dry glutinous material [DRIER OPERATOR (chemical) VI].
GOE: 06.04.05 STRENGTH: L GED: R2 M1 L1 SVP: 3 DLU: 77

559.685-174 TUBE-BUILDING-MACHINE OPERATOR (rubber goods)
Tends machine that forms air tubes from rubberized fabric for use in pneumatic airplane de-icers: Examines fabric over light for such defects as holes, tears, and fabric misweaves. Cuts defects from rubberized fabric strip with scissors, and rewinds strip onto reel. Threads specified reels of rubberized fabric and paper gum tape into machine. Fills machine dispenser with powdered soapstone and adjusts machine for specified tube diameter, using handtools. Starts machine that shapes and seals rubberized fabric into tubular form, dusts tubing with soapstone, and winds tubing on reel. Carries loaded reel to storage rack.
GOE: 06.04.05 STRENGTH: L GED: R2 M1 L1 SVP: 3 DLU: 77

559.685-178 TUMBLER-MACHINE OPERATOR (rubber goods)
Tends tumbler machine to break off *flash* from molded rubber products: Loads tumbler with rubber products and sets controls to regulate flow of liquid nitrogen to machine and tumbling time. Starts machine that freezes product to make it brittle and tumbles product to break off flash. Empties contents of tumbler on screening device to separate flash from rubber products.
GOE: 06.04.07 STRENGTH: M GED: R2 M1 L1 SVP: 2 DLU: 77

559.685-182 WASH-TANK TENDER (chemical)
Tends wash tanks and centrifugal wringers to wash and dry nitrated TNT: Starts agitators in wash tank to mix water and TNT received from NITRATOR OPERATOR (chemical). Turns valves to draw off wash water after prescribed washing and settling time and to regulate flow of steam or hot water to tank coils to maintain contents at specified temperature. Admits metered amounts of chemicals to facilitate purification and crystallization of TNT. Opens valves at bottom of tank to drop crystallized TNT through vibrating screen and water spray to form pellets. Pumps pellets from receiving pits to baskets of centrifugal wringers and starts wringers to expel water from pellets. Pulls lever to empty TNT from wringers.
GOE: 06.04.11 STRENGTH: L GED: R2 M2 L2 SVP: 3 DLU: 77

559.685-186 WET-END OPERATOR I (plastic-synth.)
Tends wet end of forming machine that forces viscose fluid between adjustable metal tips (bars) and into acid bath that coagulates fluid into continuous sheets of cellophane: Threads sheet through rollers and smooths moving sheet to remove slack and wrinkles. Performs titration test to determine strength of acid bath solution and adds specified quantity of chemicals to bath to maintain solution strength. Mixes fresh solution according to schedule and formula. Turns valves to drain tanks. Moves waste products to salvage area on handtruck.
GOE: 06.04.13 STRENGTH: M GED: R3 M2 L2 SVP: 4 DLU: 77

559.685-190 WET-END OPERATOR II (plastic-synth.) alternate titles: coagulator
Tends low pressure kettle and auxiliary equipment to coagulate latex particles in thiokol latex suspension: Opens valves and pumps specified amount of latex suspension and water into kettle. Starts agitator and turns steam valve to heat solution to specified temperature. Turns valve to admit acid into solution. Observes processing of solution and coagulation of latex suspension into uniform crumb size. Examines sample to determine clarity of water and turns valves to stop flow of acid into solution. Determines pH of batch, using test papers. Adds alkali to batch to neutralize acid content. Opens outlet valve to transfer suspension to filter or shaker screen for separation of crumb from liquid. May open

water valve to cool solution in kettle prior to transfer. May tend auxiliary equipment to dewater crumbs. May record data from operations in log.
GOE: 06.04.13 STRENGTH: L GED: R2 M2 L1 SVP: 3 DLU: 77

559.686-010 COMPOUND WORKER (recording)
Performs any combination of following tasks in compound room of phonograph record manufacturing plant: Weighs out specified quantities of ingredients, such as lampblack, resins and plastic materials, and dumps them into hopper of mixing machine. Pulls kneaded compound onto rollers of mixing machine, using hook, as material flows from discharge end of machine. Breaks plastic sheeting into sheets of uniform length as it emerges on conveyor from cooling process, and weighs sheets on skids. Removes labels from defective records, using machine, to salvage material for reprocessing. Dumps delabeled records into machine that grinds material into scrap. May be designated according to particular task performed as Breaker Table Worker (recording); Grinder (recording); Roller Hand (recording); Weigher (recording).
GOE: 06.04.13 STRENGTH: M GED: R1 M1 L1 SVP: 2 DLU: 77

559.686-014 DRIER FEEDER (rubber reclaim.)
Feeds devulcanized scrap rubber stock into agitator tanks that wash it to remove caustic substance: Shovels specified amount of stock into tank of water and starts mechanical agitator. Shovels washed stock onto conveyors leading to drier or into dewatering device that squeezes moisture from stock. May adjust dewatering device, using wrench. May pump washed stock into vibrating screen to facilitate removal of moisture.
GOE: 06.04.07 STRENGTH: M GED: R1 M1 L1 SVP: 2 DLU: 77

559.686-018 HOSE-TUBING BACKER (rubber goods) alternate titles: rubber-tubing backer; tube backer
Feeds rubber tubing into machine that cements calendered gum rubber onto tubing to provide adhesive backing for braided fabric covering. May cut and cement gum rubber backing to rubber tubing.
GOE: 06.04.07 STRENGTH: M GED: R2 M1 L1 SVP: 2 DLU: 77

559.686-022 LABORER (pharmaceut.) alternate titles: batcher
Performs any combination of following duties concerned with processing and packaging drug and toilet products: Transfers specified ingredients from storage to production area, using handtruck. Assembles specified ingredients for compounding. Feeds plants, roots, and herbs into machines, such as silage cutters, fanning mills, and washing machines. Loads botanicals into driers. Cuts animal tissue into strips, using saws. Feeds strips into meat grinders. Opens drums and scoops or dumps contents into kettles, tanks, or machine hopper. Removes filled cartons from packaging machine conveyor.
GOE: 06.04.19 STRENGTH: H GED: R2 M1 L2 SVP: 2 DLU: 77

559.686-026 LABORER, GENERAL (rubber goods; rubber reclaim.; rubber tire)
Performs any combination of following tasks involved in production of rubber goods, reclaimed rubber, or rubber tires and tubes: Inserts, dumps, places, or pours materials in or removes materials from rubber processing machines and equipment, manually or using shovels, hoists, conveyors, or special devices. Replaces spools or coils of materials on supply racks or reels of machines. Loads and unloads materials, parts or products onto or from pallets, skids, conveyors, or trucks, manually or using hoists. Transports materials, parts, or products from storage areas to work stations, using handtruck or other conveyances. Arranges, stacks, or places materials, parts, or products into books or bundles for storage or shipping. Cuts materials to specified size and length, using knife, scissors, miter box or cutting machine. Pulls or trims *flash* and excess material from goods, manually or using knife or scissors. Imparts smooth finish or removes foreign matter or rough and uneven edges from goods, using buffing wheels or cutting machines. Fits, assembles, or bolts parts together, using cements, handtools, or mechanical devices. Performs minor repairs to salvage parts, such as cutting out and replacing defective areas, using variety of handtools and work aids. Dusts finished goods with powder, talc, or soapstone to prevent sticking during storage and shipping. Examines goods for obvious defects and imperfections and verifies weight and dimensions of goods, using fixed gauges and scales. Sorts, counts, or marks goods by size, grade, color, or salvageability. Bundles and packs goods in containers for shipping. Washes or cleans adhering stock, grease, dust and foreign matter from machines and equipment with water, solvents, or other cleaning compounds, using rags, brushes, and air or steam hoses.
GOE: 06.04.13 STRENGTH: M GED: R1 M1 L1 SVP: 2 DLU: 77

559.686-030 LABORER, VAT HOUSE (chemical)
Performs any combination of following tasks to process stock (animal skins, splits, fleshings, and trimmings) used to make glue: Loads stock onto conveyor leading to chopper or moves stock, using handtruck, and dumps stock into vat or mill. Gathers stock from vat or mill, using pitchfork, and tosses stock into truck. Cleans mills, vats, and floors, using forks, brushes, and water.
GOE: 06.04.19 STRENGTH: H GED: R1 M1 L1 SVP: 2 DLU: 77

559.686-034 OPENER (rubber goods)
Feeds grooved rubber weather stripping into machine that pulls it along die to force apart sides stuck together during curing.
GOE: 06.04.07 STRENGTH: L GED: R1 M1 L1 SVP: 2 DLU: 77

559.686-038 REDUCTION-FURNACE-OPERATOR HELPER (chemical; oils & grease)
Assists REDUCTION-FURNACE OPERATOR (chemical) or CATALYST OPERATOR, GASOLINE (chemical) in mixing and drying ingredients used to

produce or recondition catalysts: Loads materials into mixing tanks, places pans in driers, and empties dried material into containers on scale. Labels and removes containers to process or storage areas. Performs other duties as described under HELPER (any industry) Master Title.
GOE: 06.04.11 STRENGTH: H GED: R2 M1 L1 SVP: 2 DLU: 77

559.686-042 SLABBER (soap & rel.) alternate titles: cutter, first; cutting-table operator, first; slabbing-machine operator; soap slabber

Feeds soap slabs into machine that cuts slabs into bars: Places slab of soap on cradle of machine. Starts motor or depresses clutch to activate mechanism that forces slab through cutting frame, divides it into bars, and deposits bars in racks at opposite end of cradle. Inspects bars for specified size. Removes scrap soap from cutter and dumps it into hopper for reprocessing. Pushes rack dolly into dryer. May draw cutting wires through soap slab, using hand-powered winch. May be designated according to size or weight of slab cut as Slabber, Light (soap & rel.).
GOE: 06.04.09 STRENGTH: M GED: R1 M1 L1 SVP: 2 DLU: 77

559.687-010 AMPOULE EXAMINER (pharmaceut.)

Examines ampoules filled with liquid drug products for discoloration, flaws in glass, presence of foreign particles, and specified filling level: Holds ampoule against light source and examines it, using magnifying glass or naked eye. Rejects defective ampoules. May hold ampoules alternately against black and white background to facilitate examination. May count and record number of inspected units and place in containers. May seal end of ampoule, using bunsen burner and tweezers [AMPOULE SEALER (pharmaceut.)].
GOE: 06.03.02 STRENGTH: S GED: R2 M1 L2 SVP: 3 DLU: 77

559.687-014 AMPOULE SEALER (pharmaceut.)

Seals ampoules filled with liquid drug products, preparatory to packaging: Rotates neck of ampoule in flame of bunsen burner to melt glass. Grips tip of ampoule, using tweezers, and draws tip away from neck to seal ampoule as glass hardens. Places sealed ampoule in basket for sterilization and inspection. May hold unsealed ampoule against jet of inert gas to displace air. May immerse sealed ampoules in dye bath to test for leaks. May tend machines that steam-wash and fill ampoules.
GOE: 06.04.34 STRENGTH: S GED: R2 M1 L1 SVP: 2 DLU: 77

559.687-018 CASTING-MACHINE-SERVICE OPERATOR (plastic-synth.)

Cleans casting machine and auxiliary equipment, such as pumps and exhaust hood, used in production of cellophane: Pumps solutions from casting machine to storage tanks or into system feeding other casting machines. Dismantles hopper and cleans viscose residue from internal parts, using water hose and airhose. Sprays walls and bottom of tanks with water to flush chemicals and sludge through drainage openings. Scrapes and scrubs tank walls, guide rods, and rollers, using scraper, steel wool, and sandpaper to remove deposits of viscose and other chemicals. Vacuums scrapings from tanks, using portable vacuum cleaner and rinses tanks and fixtures with water to remove remaining debris.
GOE: 06.04.39 STRENGTH: M GED: R2 M1 L1 SVP: 3 DLU: 77

559.687-022 CELL CLEANER (chemical)

Cleans electrolytic cells and cell assemblies, performing any combination of following tasks: Connects hose to water or steam line and flushes cell to clean surfaces. Scrapes assemblies, using handscrapers and wire brushes to remove accumulations of dirt, putty, scale, and encrusted salt. Transfers cathodes to washrack, using wheeled cart and hoist. Flushes cathodes and cathode screens with water to remove asbestos and caustic residue, and transfers cathodes to drying area. Flushes pit sump and recovered asbestos with water. Cleans sight glasses and glass tubing by dipping in acid, solvent, and water. May be designated according to cell equipment cleaned as Cathode Washer (chemical).
GOE: 06.04.39 STRENGTH: H GED: R2 M1 L1 SVP: 2 DLU: 77

559.687-026 CONTACT-ACID-PLANT-OPERATOR HELPER (chemical)

Performs any combination of following duties in production of sulfuric acid: Diverts acid stream from production unit to storage tanks as directed. Inspects machinery and equipment to detect malfunctions, leaks, and spills. Cleans work area around units, using broom and shovel or water hose. Collects samples of product for laboratory testing. Records gauge readings and levels of acid in tanks.
GOE: 06.04.11 STRENGTH: M GED: R2 M1 L1 SVP: 2 DLU: 77

559.687-030 COTTON WASHER (plastic-synth.) alternate titles: cotton cleaner

Dumps cotton linters into tubs for washing and bleaching. May dump washed and bleached linters into wringer unit and be designated Cotton Wringer (plastic-synth.).
GOE: 06.04.39 STRENGTH: H GED: R1 M1 L1 SVP: 1 DLU: 77

559.687-034 EGG PROCESSOR (pharmaceut.) alternate titles: harvester

Removes virus-bearing fluid from fertile chicken eggs for use in manufacturing vaccines, such as influenza vaccine: Saws end off egg, using electric saw, and removes fetal membrane, using tweezers to break sac containing viral fluid. Siphons fluid into sterilized and labeled bottles for further processing. Sterilizes tweezers by dipping them into antiseptic solution after each egg has been harvested.
GOE: 06.04.34 STRENGTH: S GED: R2 M1 L1 SVP: 2 DLU: 77

559.687-038 FILTER CLEANER (plastic-synth.) alternate titles: clarifier; filter changer; filterer

Cleans gum and other sediment from filter that strains viscose or similar cellulose solution before it is spun into filaments for rayon yarn or cast into transparent wrapping material: Removes core or center of filter from its casing. Removes cloth wrappers of core and rewraps it with clean cloth. Replaces other strainers in filters that need cleaning.
GOE: 06.04.39 STRENGTH: M GED: R2 M1 L1 SVP: 2 DLU: 77

559.687-042 FILTER WASHER (chemical) alternate titles: strainer cleaner

Boils, washes, and cleans filters, such as cloth strainers and metal grids used in manufacture of explosives: Soaks filters in solution of boiling water and soap powder or caustic solution. Scrapes and dissolves with acetone any tetryl powder remaining. Hangs cloth filters on drying racks.
GOE: 06.04.39 STRENGTH: M GED: R2 M1 L1 SVP: 2 DLU: 77

559.687-046 FRAME STRIPPER (chemical) alternate titles: stripper

Loosens and removes dry glue or gelatin from drying frames by striking frame with whip or by placing frame upside down on vibrating table. Dumps glue or gelatin into hopper of grinding machine.
GOE: 06.04.19 STRENGTH: M GED: R1 M1 L1 SVP: 1 DLU: 77

559.687-050 LABORER, CHEMICAL PROCESSING (chemical) alternate titles: drum carrier

Performs any combination of following tasks in chemical manufacturing establishment: Fills or empties equipment and containers by pumping, opening valves, scooping, dumping, scraping, or shoveling liquid, gaseous, or solid materials. Weighs materials and writes or stencils identifying information on containers. Fastens caps or covers on container, or screws bungs in place. Transports materials, using handtruck. Cleans stills and other equipment, using detergents, brushes, or scrapers. Loads railroad cars or trucks. Delivers samples to laboratory. Cleans work areas. Prepares materials by pulverizing, milling, crushing, or liquefying. Paints containers, using spray gun. May be known according to task performed as Carboy Filler (chemical); Drum Filler (chemical); Kettle-Room Helper (chemical); Shipping Hand (chemical); Wheeler (chemical).
GOE: 06.04.40 STRENGTH: H GED: R2 M1 L1 SVP: 3 DLU: 80

559.687-054 SKEIN-WINDING OPERATOR (any industry)

Winds skeins of thread used to test effect of dyes, using hand-turned crank: Passes end of thread through guides and attaches it to winding arm. Turns crank to wind thread onto skein. Weighs wound skeins and pulls away excess thread or winds additional turns onto skein to attain specified weight.
GOE: 06.04.27 STRENGTH: L GED: R1 M1 L1 SVP: 1 DLU: 77

559.687-058 SOAP INSPECTOR (soap & rel.)

Inspects bars of toilet soap to ensure conformance to product specifications: Removes soap from conveyor and inspects bar for defects in shape, depth and clarity of embossing, and conformance to color specifications. Rubs fingers lightly over bar to test for smoothness. Places approved bars back on conveyor and places rejected bars into box for reprocessing.
GOE: 06.03.02 STRENGTH: L GED: R2 M1 L1 SVP: 2 DLU: 77

559.687-062 TANK CLEANER (chemical; plastic-synth.) alternate titles: kettle chipper

Cleans storage tanks and glass-lined, high-pressure reaction vessels used in production of copolymer synthetic rubber: Turns vacuum system valves to remove vapors from vessels, and locks electrically driven agitator in position. Steams and ventilates vessels, using steam and airhoses. Removes solidified resin from vessel and cleans inner surfaces and equipment, using sparkproof safety tools, cleaning compounds, and waterhose. May test fumes with explosion meter to determine presence of explosive mixture of gases.
GOE: 06.04.39 STRENGTH: M GED: R2 M1 L1 SVP: 2 DLU: 77

559.687-066 TUBE SORTER (rubber reclaim.) alternate titles: tube depatcher

Scans and feels scrap rubber tubes to identify butyl, synthetic, or natural rubber and sorts them into separate piles. Cuts out cots (valve patches), using knife. Loads sorted tubes into boxes, and weighs boxes on scale. Tags boxes to identify contents and record weight. May cut out valve stems. May bale depatched tubes [BALING-MACHINE TENDER (any industry)]. May cut samples from tubes and test with specified acid to determine if rubber is natural or synthetic.
GOE: 06.03.02 STRENGTH: L GED: R2 M1 L2 SVP: 3 DLU: 77

559.687-070 WEIGHER OPERATOR (chemical) alternate titles: conveyor-weigher operator; cotton-weigher operator

Weighs out specified amounts of dried and fluffed cotton linters prior to nitrating process in manufacture of smokeless powder: Rakes dried cotton linters into weigh cans, removing dust clusters and inadequately processed cotton. Moves weigh cans along overhead monorail to section of rail connected with scales. Adds or removes linters to obtain specified weight. Pushes weigh cans along monorail to drive chain which conveys cans to next operation. May regulate drier temperature and speed of conveyor [CONTINUOUS-LINTER-DRIER OPERATOR (chemical)]. May combine specified amount of acid and preweighed amount of cellulose in dipping pot in which they react chemically to produce nitrocellulose.
GOE: 06.03.02 STRENGTH: L GED: R2 M1 L2 SVP: 3 DLU: 77

559.687-074 INSPECTOR AND HAND PACKAGER (plastic prod.)

Inspects molded plastic products, such as bottle caps or tops, for defects, and packs inspected products into shipping cartons: Visually examines molded prod-

ucts for defects, such as scratches, discoloration, and *flash,* and discards defective products. Packs inspected product in cartons according to customer specifications, and carries cartons to storage area. May attach metal bands to bottle tops prior to packing to form necks for bottles and measure necks to ensure specified length, using gauge.
GOE: 06.03.02 STRENGTH: L GED: R2 M1 L2 SVP: 2 DLU: 86

56 OCCUPATIONS IN PROCESSING OF WOOD AND WOOD PRODUCTS

This division includes occupations concerned with producing wood particles, such as chips, sawdust, and powder, and conglomerates, such as plywood, particle board, and compressed-sawdust fuel logs, from stock, removing moisture from wood; and treating wood with materials, such as preservatives and fire retardants.

560 MIXING AND RELATED OCCUPATIONS

This group includes occupations concerned with mingling wood in pulpy or pasty form to produce a consistent mass of compound for such purposes as making particle board.

560.465-010 CHIP-MIXING-MACHINE OPERATOR (wood prod., nec) alternate titles: chip mixer; glue-mixer operator; glue-plant operator

Tends machine that mixes wood chips and glue preparatory to extruding particle board: Pulls lever to admit dried chips from storage bins into rotary batch mixer. Weighs resin glues and catalyst material according to formula and pours materials into mixer. Verifies moisture content of chips by feeling chips with hand or by weighing sample of chips, drying sample in miniature oven, computing weight of moisture removed, and converting weight to percentage, using mathematical tables. Adds water to mixture if chips are too dry. Notifies DRIER TENDER (concrete prod.) to increase or decrease drier temperature to control moisture content of chips. Pulls lever to discharge mixture into extruder hopper.
GOE: 06.04.14 STRENGTH: L GED: R3 M3 L2 SVP: 3 DLU: 77

560.585-010 MIXING-MACHINE TENDER (wood prod., nec) alternate titles: cork mixer

Tends one or more mixing machines that compound ground cork: Measures ingredients, such as glycerin, glue, resin, and ground cork, according to formula, and shovels or dumps them into machine hopper. Starts machine and opens steam valve to heat and mix ingredients. Observes gauges and adjusts steam and coolant valves to maintain specified temperature and attain standard mixture. May set timer to stop machine automatically. Drains sample of mixture from machine for laboratory analysis. Starts conveyor or places bag over opening and pulls chain that opens chute and dumps mixture onto conveyor or into bag for transfer to storage bins. Records operational data, such as yield, temperature, and time cycle. May be designated according to type of product mixed as Mixing-Machine Tender, Cork Gasket (wood prod., nec); Mixing-Machine Tender, Cork Rod (wood prod., nec).
GOE: 06.04.14 STRENGTH: M GED: R2 M2 L2 SVP: 3 DLU: 77

560.587-010 COMPOUNDER, CORK (wood prod., nec) alternate titles: cork mixer

Measures or weighs ingredients, such as sulfur, zinc oxide, stearic acid, and granulated cork, preparatory to mixing into cork composition material: Scoops or pours ingredients on scale or in graduate and dumps prescribed quantities into containers. Marks or stencils container to identify materials and records quantities and types. Scoops samples from containers and delivers them to laboratory for analysis. Delivers filled containers to mixing machine, using handtruck.
GOE: 06.04.14 STRENGTH: M GED: R2 M2 L2 SVP: 2 DLU: 77

561 WOOD PRESERVING AND RELATED OCCUPATIONS

This group includes occupations concerned with impregnating and covering wood and wood products with substances that prevent decay and rotting.

561.131-010 TREATING-PLANT SUPERVISOR (wood prod., nec)

Supervises and coordinates activities of workers engaged in treating wood products with preserving and fireproofing chemicals: Analyzes production charts, manuals, and customer specifications, and examines types of wood, to determine treatment of wood. Orders treating sequence, type of chemicals used for treatment, temperature and pressure in retort, and length of time wood is to remain in retort. Observes gauges and progression charts to detect malfunctioning equipment; and adjusts controls to regulate temperature, pressure, or level of liquid in retort to correct malfunction. Tests wood borings, using laboratory equipment, to verify specified treating solution and moisture content, retention of preservative, and depth of penetration and concentration of salt. Performs other duties as described under SUPERVISOR (any industry) Master Title. May be designated according to process supervised as Supervisor, Incising (wood prod., nec).
GOE: 06.02.01 STRENGTH: L GED: R4 M3 L3 SVP: 7 DLU: 78

561.362-010 TREATING ENGINEER (wood prod., nec) alternate titles: retort engineer; timber-treating-tank operator; treating-plant operator

Controls one or more cylinder retorts to impregnate wood products, such as railroad ties, piling, telephone poles, and fenceposts, with preserving and fireproofing chemicals: Turns valves to admit treating solution into retort and steam into heating coils. Presses buttons to activate vacuum- and hydraulic-pressure pumps that remove air and steam from retort and force treating solution into pores of wood to accelerate treatment process. Observes gauges and turns valves to maintain specified heat, vacuum and hydraulic pressure, and level of solution in retort during each phase of treatment cycle, according to treating schedule. Pumps treating solution back into storage tank at end of treating cycle. Opens, or signals TREATING-ENGINEER HELPER (wood prod., nec) 561.685-010 to open, retort doors. Heats unseasoned wood in retort to remove moisture preparatory to treating process. May operate locomotive or winch to move tram loads of wood products in and out of retort. May take and test sample borings, using laboratory equipment, to determine if treatment meets customers' specifications or standard chemical-analysis requirements. May be required to hold license.
GOE: 06.02.18 STRENGTH: M GED: R3 M3 L3 SVP: 6 DLU: 78

561.585-010 STAIN APPLICATOR (wood prod., nec)

Tends machine that sprays stain preservative on finished lumber to retard decay and excessive weathering: Empties drums of stain into storage tank and turns valve to combine water with stain at specified ratio. Turns valve to pump staining solution into spray units, and turns dial to adjust spray on lumber passing on conveyor. Examines lumber to determine amount of solution being applied, and adjusts spray units to ensure adequate coverage while preventing excessive waste. Opens valves to switch to alternate tank when solution level is low. Cleans equipment and work area, using airhose, water hoses, and other cleaning aids. Records amount of stain preservative used.
GOE: 06.04.21 STRENGTH: H GED: R2 M2 L2 SVP: 2 DLU: 77

561.587-010 POLE INSPECTOR (wood prod., nec) alternate titles: pole classifier

Inspects poles and piling supplied to plant for defects and classifies them according to size and specifications preparatory to treating process: Examines poles for framing and defects, such as splits and knots. Measures length and diameter of poles. Stamps or writes measurements and symbols on ends of poles. Classifies poles according to size and prepares written report showing size, class, and number of poles ready for treating process.
GOE: 06.03.02 STRENGTH: L GED: R2 M2 L2 SVP: 3 DLU: 77

561.665-010 TANKER (wood prod., nec) alternate titles: dip tanker; platform worker; scaffold worker

Tends open tank to impregnate wood products with preservatives: Signals OVERHEAD CRANE OPERATOR (any industry) 921.663-010 to lift load of material over tank and guides load into tank by hand or with rod, working from elevated platform. Chains tank loads of poles to high rack to prevent toppling. Observes gauges and turns valves to regulate heat and flow of preserving solution in tank. Impregnates sashes, doors, and other millwork products, using hand or power hoist to load and unload tank. May tend vacuum-type dip tank that impregnates wood by pressure.
GOE: 06.04.18 STRENGTH: M GED: R2 M1 L1 SVP: 3 DLU: 77

561.685-010 TREATING-ENGINEER HELPER (wood prod., nec)

Assists TREATING ENGINEER (wood prod., nec) in impregnating wood products with preserving or fireproofing chemicals, performing any combination of following duties: Opens and closes retort door, using pneumatic wrench. Turns steam, vacuum- or hydraulic-pressure, or solution valves in response to signals. Tends pumps to transfer chemicals from railroad cars, trucks, or boat tankers into storage tanks. Drills test-bores in treated or untreated wood, using hand drill. Moves trams loaded with products in and out of retort. Performs other duties as described under HELPER (any industry) Master Title.
GOE: 06.04.18 STRENGTH: M GED: R2 M1 L1 SVP: 2 DLU: 77

561.686-010 LABORER, WOOD-PRESERVING PLANT (wood prod., nec)

Performs any combination of following duties to store, move, treat, and process wood products in wood-preserving plant: Piles wood products, such as ties, piling, poles, and fence posts, on trams, by hand or by use of overhead hoist. Inserts wooden strips to bind and space load, and shapes load to fit cylinder retort. Chains or bolts down tram loads, using wrenches and fasteners. Bolts and unbolts doors of retorts with hand or pneumatic wrench. Pulls loads in and out of retorts, using winch. Drills test-bores in treated or untreated wood with hand drill. Opens and closes valves for operating retort. Loads and unloads wood materials from railroad cars, trucks, and barges. Moves and positions timbers and piling in framing or pole yard. Feeds woodstock into various machines that adz, bore, cut, incise, or peel it; and removes processed material by hand or by use of hoist. Burns identification markings in poles, using branding iron. May be designated according to duties performed as Adzing-and-Boring-Machine Helper (wood prod., nec); Cross-Tie-Tram Loader (wood prod., nec); Tie Handler (wood prod., nec); Wincher (wood prod., nec).
GOE: 06.04.18 STRENGTH: V GED: R2 M1 L1 SVP: 2 DLU: 77

561.687-010 WOOD-POLE TREATER (wood prod., nec)

Treats underground portion of transmission poles with chemical preservative after installation: Digs around base of pole to expose area susceptible to decay,

using pick and shovel. Scrapes dirt and other residue from pole surface and chips away decayed wood, using handtools. Paints dressed area with preservative solution, using brush. Wraps treated portion of pole with waterproof paper, fastening paper with hand stapler. Refills hole and packs earth firmly around base of pole, using shovel.
GOE: 06.04.25 STRENGTH: H GED: R1 M1 L1 SVP: 1 DLU: 77

562 SATURATING, COATING, AND RELATED OCCUPATIONS, N.E.C.

This group includes occupations, not elsewhere classified, concerned with thoroughly soaking, filling, charging, or otherwise treating wood with a variety of substances to the point where no more can be taken up, or covering wood with another substance.

562.485-010 WHITING-MACHINE OPERATOR (wood prod., nec)
Tends machine that coats picture-frame molding with hard, glossy composition as base for painting: Digests measured quantities of glue, rosin, linseed oil, and water in heated gluepot, following work order and specifications. Pours liquid into heated mechanical mixer, adds whiting (powdered chalk), and starts mixer that automatically stops when mixture is of specified consistency. Turns handwheels to adjust tension of feed rollers, using sample strip of stock molding to verify tension. Fills supply chamber of machine with coating mixture and starts machine. Inserts molding stock in guide under rollers that force it through supply chamber. Picks coated stock from chamber and stands it on end until coating has hardened.
GOE: 06.04.21 STRENGTH: M GED: R2 M2 L2 SVP: 4 DLU: 77

562.665-010 LOG COOKER (wood. container) alternate titles: steam-vat tender; wood cooker
Tends steam or hot-water vats that condition logs before cutting into veneer sheets used in making wooden slat baskets and boxes: Hoists logs into vat or onto conveyor that carries them into cooker. Turns valves to maintain steam pressure or water temperature at specified setting. Removes logs or directs their removal after prescribed time, depending on size of logs and kind of wood. May remove bark from logs, using handtools.
GOE: 06.04.18 STRENGTH: M GED: R2 M1 L1 SVP: 2 DLU: 77

562.665-014 STEAM-BOX OPERATOR (woodworking) alternate titles: retort operator; stave steamer; steam-tunnel feeder
Tends retort that steams woodstock to make it pliable: Places stock into retort or loads stock on conveyor or car that conveys material into retort. Turns lever to seal retort door and turns valve to admit steam into retort. Observes pressure gauge and informs SUPERVISOR, MACHINING (woodworking) if pressure varies from standards. Removes steamed stock from retort and conveys stock to succeeding work station. May remove steamed stock from retort and place it in jigs to dry and cool.
GOE: 06.04.18 STRENGTH: M GED: R2 M2 L2 SVP: 2 DLU: 77

562.682-010 HUMIDIFIER OPERATOR (wood prod., nec)
Controls humidifier unit and auxiliary equipment to impart specified moisture content to pressed hardboard sheets or panels: Starts hydraulic elevator to position humidifier car (wheeled buggy) at discharge end of press that forms hardboard and deposits formed sheets or panels in rack of car. Pushes loaded car to humidifier unit and starts hydraulic ram to transfer car to humidifier. Observes gauges, opens valves, and moves controls to regulate moisture, heat, and pressure in humidifier to impart specified moisture content to board. Starts elevator to lower car, automatically ejected from humidifier, to unload and transfer board for tempering. Inspects board for watermarks, scratches, and similar imperfections and rejects substandard units. Removes screens from forming press used to support wet pulp mats for pressing into hardboard. Examines screens for damage and marks faulty screens for repair or disposal. Records number of boards processed and rejected. Labels each lot of hardboard passing inspection to facilitate further processing.
GOE: 06.02.18 STRENGTH: M GED: R3 M2 L2 SVP: 4 DLU: 77

562.685-010 GLUE-SIZE-MACHINE OPERATOR (furniture)
Tends machine that coats wooden furniture panels with glue size and dries panels to raise grain and reveal defects: Mixes sizing solution according to specifications and pours solution in tank. Starts machine and places panels on conveyor that carries them under sizing spray or rollers and through drying cabinet.
GOE: 06.04.21 STRENGTH: M GED: R2 M2 L2 SVP: 2 DLU: 77

562.685-014 IMPREGNATOR (pen & pencil)
Tends equipment that impregnates wooden pencil slats with dye, oil, and wax to color and soften slats: Places bundles of slats in cylinder and closes door. Turns bolts to secure cylinder door, using wrench. Measures out and pours specified amounts of dye, oil, and wax into tank. Turns switches and valves to pump solution from tank into cylinder to impregnate slats for specified time. Pumps solution from cylinder to tank and opens cylinder door. Removes slats from cylinder and places them in drying kiln.
GOE: 06.04.18 STRENGTH: H GED: R2 M2 L2 SVP: 2 DLU: 77

562.685-018 OPERATOR, PREFINISH (millwork-plywood)
Tends machines in tandem that coat surfaces of decorative hardwood-veneer panels with stain, paint, or wax: Mixes stain according to formula, using graduated container, mixing drum, and portable mixer. Connects hoses of coating

machines to containers of stain, paint, and wax. Measures thickness of panels, using steel tape, and turns handcranks to adjust coating machines. Moves controls to activate conveyors and pumps, to set thermostats on heating ovens, and to start sanding, roller-coating, and spray-coating machines. Compares processed panels with sample panel to verify adherence to specifications. Pumps cleaning solution through lines of machines upon completion of process; and replaces worn components, such as rollers, brushes, doctor blades, and sandpaper.
GOE: 06.02.21 STRENGTH: M GED: R3 M2 L2 SVP: 5 DLU: 77

562.685-022 COATER, SMOKING PIPE (fabrication, nec)
Tends machine that sprays and coats interior of smoking pipe bowls with mixture of charcoal, shellac, and alcohol: Pours specified amounts of charcoal, shellac, and alcohol into agitator and mixes solution for specified period to prepare coating solution. Pours solution through filter into tank, replaces tank top, pulls lever to start machine pump, and turns handles to regulate pump pressure to specified setting. Attaches hose and spray nozzle to machine, using wrench and pliers. Reads work ticket to determine shape and size of pipe bowl to be processed. Places corresponding size of collar on machine spray nozzle. Positions and holds pipe bowl on collar, and depresses pedal to spray and coat inside of bowl with coating solution. Places coated pipe bowls in box for storage. Disassembles and cleans spray nozzle and hose, using wrench, pliers, methanol, rag, and brush.
GOE: 06.04.21 STRENGTH: M GED: R2 M2 L2 SVP: 3 DLU: 86

562.686-010 STEAM-TUNNEL FEEDER (saw. & plan.)
Pushes cars, loaded with halved and quartered logs, into steam tunnel that steams and softens fiber of wood before logs are cut into staves.
GOE: 06.04.18 STRENGTH: M GED: R1 M1 L1 SVP: 1 DLU: 77

562.687-010 DYER (woodworking)
Colors handles or other small wooden articles with dissolved dyes: Fills vat with water. Stirs specified amounts of various dyes into water with stick. Dumps articles into vat. Opens valve to release steam into vat and allows liquid in vat to boil for specified time. Drains vat, forks out articles, and loads them into drying and polishing drum.
GOE: 06.04.33 STRENGTH: M GED: R2 M1 L1 SVP: 2 DLU: 77

562.687-014 RESIN COATER (wood prod., nec) alternate titles: coater, hand; cork coater
Coats cork products, such as floats, washers, and gaskets, with liquid resins: Pours premeasured quantities of liquid ingredients into tumbler to prepare coating solution. Dumps cork products into solution to soak. Determines soaking cycle of products, using knowledge gained through experience. Scoops cork products from tumbler, drains off excess solution, using strainer, and dumps them into containers.
GOE: 06.04.33 STRENGTH: L GED: R2 M2 L2 SVP: 2 DLU: 77

563 DRYING, SEASONING, AND RELATED OCCUPATIONS

This group includes occupations concerned with exposing to or treating wood with air, heat, fire, a vacuum, or the like for such purposes as removing moisture, curing, charring, and aging.

563.135-010 SUPERVISOR, DRYING (millwork-plywood)
Supervises and coordinates activities of workers engaged in drying veneer sheets in kilns: Confers with supervisors of subsequent processes to determine grade and amount of veneer sheets required, and schedules production to meet priority orders and production quotas. Measures moisture content of dried veneer, using moisture meter, and adjusts conveyor and blower speeds when deviations from company standards are detected. Instructs and demonstrates methods of work to new employees. Performs other duties as described under SUPERVISOR (any industry) Master Title.
GOE: 06.02.01 STRENGTH: M GED: R4 M3 L3 SVP: 6 DLU: 77

563.137-010 SUPERVISOR, BEEHIVE KILN (chemical)
Supervises and coordinates activities of workers engaged in tending woodburning kilns that produce charcoal at briquette manufacturing establishment: Examines supply of cordwood to determine weight, size, and quality of wood to be loaded into kilns; and instructs workers in loading kilns. Starts fire in kiln fuel boxes, and directs workers to seal doors and adjust flue controls to regulate woodburning process. Supervises removal and transporting of charcoal from kilns to storage or shipping areas. May purchase cordwood from woodcutters at plant site for use in making charcoal. Performs other duties as described under SUPERVISOR (any industry) Master Title.
GOE: 06.02.01 STRENGTH: L GED: R3 M3 L3 SVP: 6 DLU: 78

563.382-010 KILN OPERATOR (woodworking) alternate titles: dry-kiln operator
Controls dry kilns to dry lumber to specified moisture content: Measures moisture content of lumber preparatory to drying, using moisture meter, or cuts, weighs, and places lumber samples in curing oven and reweighs samples periodically as they are drying to determine rate and percentage of moisture reduction. Determines drying cycle and schedule, considering factors such as species, dimensions, and quantity of lumber to be dried, initial moisture content of lumber, or moisture reduction rate of lumber samples. Presses buttons, or turns valves and control knobs to activate, control, and record temperature, humidity,

and ventilation of dry kilns. Reads recording gauges and weighs lumber samples periodically during seasoning process, and readjusts temperature and humidity controls to regulate moisture reduction rate and avoid damage to lumber. Measures moisture content of lumber at completion of drying cycle, using moisture meter, to ensure that specified amount of moisture has been removed. Maintains records of species, dimensions, and footage of lumber dried, and initial and final moisture content of lumber. Changes graphs on pen-graph recorders as required. May direct workers engaged in loading lumber onto kiln cars, placing cars in kilns, and removing dried lumber from kilns.
GOE: 06.02.18 STRENGTH: L GED: R3 M3 L2 SVP: 6 DLU: 78

563.585-010 DRIER TENDER (wood prod., nec)
Tends gas-heated continuous drier that dries wood chips to prescribed moisture content for use in particle board manufacturing: Turns valve and thermostat and presses buttons to ignite gas, set drier temperature, and activate drier, conveyors, and blower fans. Moves controls to synchronize speed of conveyors and blower fans to ensure continuous flow of wood chips from storage hopper through drier and into dry-storage bin. Observes gauges and collects, weighs, and tests sample of dried chips, using scales and electronic moisture tester, to ascertain moisture content of chips. Resets controls to maintain prescribed temperature and humidity, according to test and gauge readings. Records test results in log.
GOE: 06.02.18 STRENGTH: L GED: R3 M2 L2 SVP: 4 DLU: 77

563.662-010 TREATING-PLANT OPERATOR (wood prod., nec)
Controls oven, humidifier unit, and auxiliary equipment to temper pressed hardboard by heat and moisture: Observes gauges and chart recorders on instrument panel and adjusts controls to start fans, set oven temperature, and regulate moisture conditions in humidifier unit according to plant specifications. Tends machine that immerses hardboard sheets in oil to impart smooth finish on both sides. Pushes hardboard sheets to be tempered onto roller conveyor leading from oiling machine to tilting device that dumps sheets into electric transfer cart. Drives loaded cart to oven. Pulls overhead wire to position loaded cart in oven to cure board. Drives cart from oven to humidifier unit after prescribed time and back to tilting device for unloading board after tempering. Starts mechanism that dumps tempered board from cart. Inspects board for defects, such as scratches, streaks, and discoloration. Verifies adherence of board to specifications, using viscometer to determine resilience of sheet to known stress, and coating machine that applies varnish to board surface to test sealing qualities of finish. Delivers samples of tempered board to control laboratory for exhaustive testing. Keeps records of gauge readings, test results, and shift production. Labels ticket attached to each lot of tempered board to facilitate work of inventory control and shipping personnel.
GOE: 06.02.18 STRENGTH: M GED: R3 M2 L2 SVP: 4 DLU: 77

563.682-010 CHARCOAL BURNER, BEEHIVE KILN (chemical) alternate titles: collier; kiln burner
Operates series of beehive kilns to produce charcoal: Places kindling in kiln and starts fire. Seals top of kiln when specified heat is attained, using cement and hand trowel. Observes color of smoke as it issues through draft holes in kiln bottom to ensure burning of charcoal as specified. Opens and closes draft holes, using bricks, to regulate forming of charcoal. Seals draft holes and cracks in kiln with cement to smother fire when charcoal has been formed.
GOE: 06.02.18 STRENGTH: H GED: R3 M2 L2 SVP: 4 DLU: 77

563.685-010 BARK-PRESS OPERATOR (paper & pulp)
Tends hydraulic bark press that squeezes water from pulpwood bark: Starts conveyor and observes wet bark as it passes into hydraulic press. Pushes button to actuate press that squeezes water from bark and emits dried bark onto conveyor leading to boilerroom. Frees bark jammed on conveyor, using rake. Sweeps and cleans work area. May tend rotating cutter that cuts oversized bark to suitable size for feeding into press.
GOE: 06.04.14 STRENGTH: L GED: R2 M1 L1 SVP: 2 DLU: 77

563.685-014 CLOTHESPIN-DRIER OPERATOR (woodworking)
Tends machines that dry and polish clothespins: Loads drum of machine with clothespins and wax blocks. Admits steam into drum and starts its rotation. Stops machine after specified tumbling time. Unloads clothespins when dry.
GOE: 06.04.21 STRENGTH: M GED: R1 M1 L1 SVP: 2 DLU: 77

563.685-018 DRY-HOUSE ATTENDANT (woodworking) alternate titles: wood-stock-blank handler
Tends kiln that conditions wood used for firearms stocks and shaped wooden articles: Examines woodstock ends to determine whether tar or wax coating meets specifications. Dips stock blank ends into vats of tar or wax to prevent splitting during drying. Places stock in oven and turns gas valves to regulate temperature to specified heat. Observes wood blanks to determine whether drying is required. Removes wood blanks to storage sheds. Records storage time and amounts processed, coated, scraped, and rejected.
GOE: 06.04.18 STRENGTH: M GED: R2 M1 L1 SVP: 3 DLU: 77

563.685-022 VENEER DRIER (millwork-plywood) alternate titles: veneer-drier tailer
Tends conveyor-type drier that dries freshly cut veneer sheets to prevent mildewing and discoloration: Turns valves to regulate temperature of drying oven according to thickness and moisture content of veneer. Presses buttons or turns lever or handwheel to regulate speed of conveyor belt or feed rollers. Removes veneer sheets from conveyor belt or rollers as they emerge from drying oven and stacks them on handtruck. May measure moisture content of discharged veneer sheets, using moisture meter, to ensure specified drying. May discard sheets with defects, such as splits, knotholes, or decayed sections. May return incompletely dried veneer to be fed again into drier. May feed machine [VENEER-DRIER FEEDER (millwork-plywood)].
GOE: 06.04.18 STRENGTH: M GED: R2 M1 L1 SVP: 2 DLU: 77

563.685-026 VENEER REDRIER (millwork-plywood) alternate titles: platen-drier operator
Tends platen drier that redries veneer to ensure uniform moisture content before gluing into plywood or furniture parts: Turns valve to admit steam to platens and adjusts pressure control so that specified steam pressure can be applied to heat platens. Inserts veneer between platens and turns handwheel or pulls lever to close platens. Opens platens and removes dried veneer sheets.
GOE: 06.04.18 STRENGTH: M GED: R2 M1 L1 SVP: 2 DLU: 77

563.686-010 STICKER (saw. & plan.)
Pulls reclaimed stickers from conveyors or portable bins and places them in racks of stacking machine. Moves levers on panel to open or lock racks according to number and spacing of stickers required between lumber courses, or places stickers between lumber courses manually.
GOE: 06.04.03 STRENGTH: M GED: R2 M1 L1 SVP: 2 DLU: 77

563.686-014 VENEER-DRIER FEEDER (millwork-plywood)
Feeds freshly cut veneer sheets into drier that dries veneer: Pushes handtruck of veneer into position at loading end of drier. Lifts sheets from top of stack and slides them onto conveyor that conveys sheets into and through drier, using care not to damage edges. May press pedal to activate elevator platform that raises veneer sheets to working level as stack is reduced.
GOE: 06.04.18 STRENGTH: M GED: R1 M1 L1 SVP: 1 DLU: 77

563.686-018 OFFBEARER, PIPE SMOKING MACHINE (fabrication, nec) alternate titles: pipe smoking machine operator
Off bears smoking pipes from smoking machine used to break-in (char) new pipe bowls: Removes pipe bowls from suction tubes of pipe smoking machine. Examines pipes to determine tobacco has been burned and places aside pipes containing unburned tobacco. Empties ashes into water bucket and inspects interior of charred bowls to verify conformance to company standards. Cleans smoker tubes, using wire pipe cleaner.
GOE: 06.04.03 STRENGTH: M GED: R2 M1 L1 SVP: 1 DLU: 86

563.687-010 ANTICHECKING-IRON WORKER (wood prod., nec)
Hammers shaped steel bands into ends of timbers and railroad ties to prevent checking (splitting) while seasoning. May clamp, drill hole, and insert bolt or metal dowel through split timbers or ties to hold split parts together. May be designated according to shape of band as Beegle-Iron Worker (wood prod., nec); C-Iron Worker (wood prod., nec); S-Iron Worker (wood prod., nec).
GOE: 06.04.25 STRENGTH: L GED: R1 M1 L1 SVP: 2 DLU: 77

563.687-014 MOISTURE TESTER (woodworking)
Verifies moisture content of dried lumber, using portable electric moisture meter: Holds meter against ends of lumber or presses electrodes of meter into lumber and reads meter to determine moisture content. Removes and stacks pieces that do not meet specified percentage of moisture content.
GOE: 06.03.02 STRENGTH: L GED: R2 M2 L1 SVP: 2 DLU: 77

564 GRINDING AND CHOPPING OCCUPATIONS, N.E.C.

This group includes occupations, not elsewhere classified, concerned with reducing logs and other wood material to chips, flakes, dust, or powder by means of compression, grinding, cutting, or smashing.

564.132-010 WOOD-CREW SUPERVISOR (chemical; saw. & plan.) alternate titles: supervisor, chipping
Supervises and coordinates activities of workers engaged in reducing scrap wood, stumps, and bark to wood chips or fuel: Inspects machinery, such as *hog mills*, hammer mills, chipping machines, knife grinders, and conveyors, to detect excessive wear or malfunctions, and schedules required maintenance or repair. Inspects processed wood chips to ensure conformance to plant specifications. Trains new workers in operation of machinery. Performs other duties as described under SUPERVISOR (any industry) Master Title.
GOE: 06.02.03 STRENGTH: M GED: R4 M3 L3 SVP: 7 DLU: 77

564.662-010 LOG-CHIPPER OPERATOR (logging) alternate titles: chipper
Operates trailer-mounted grapple-loader and chipping machine to reduce logs and logging waste to wood chips: Controls loading boom and power-grapple attachment to pick up logs and place them on feed conveyor. Adjusts speed and opening of feed rolls according to log diameter, and activates feed rolls that pushes log through chipper unit. Monitors gauges and adjusts speed and opening of feed rolls to prevent equipment strain. Replaces defective chipping knives, using wrenches and feeler gauges. May control opening of debarking spuds (tined rotating drums) that remove bark from log before chipping.
GOE: 06.02.03 STRENGTH: M GED: R3 M1 L2 SVP: 4 DLU: 77

564.682-010 CHIPPING-MACHINE OPERATOR (wood prod., nec)
Operates machine to cut and screen peeler-log cores into chips of specified size: Installs and adjusts cutting knives and reciprocating screens to obtain

chips of specified size, using handtools. Starts machine and conveyors to transfer material between processes and to storage bins. Selects cores according to species and pushes cores onto feed conveyor, using pike pole. Observes chips moving through screens and makes required adjustments. May repair breaks in conveyor belts, using handtools.
GOE: 06.02.03 STRENGTH: M GED: R3 M1 L1 SVP: 5 DLU: 77

564.682-014 FLAKE-CUTTER OPERATOR (wood prod., nec)
Operates one or more machines that cut wood flakes of specified size from slabs, edgings, and core logs: Installs cutting knives, using handtools. Starts machines and discharge conveyors and feeds material into cutters. Observes cutting of flakes and turns dial to regulate speed of cutters and to control thickness of flakes. May operate lift truck to transport slabs, edging, and logs from supply area to machine.
GOE: 06.02.03 STRENGTH: M GED: R3 M2 L2 SVP: 4 DLU: 77

564.682-018 MILLER, WOOD FLOUR (woodworking)
Operates milling machine that pulverizes and sifts sawdust to make wood flour: Reads work order to ascertain quantity and particle size of flour required. Selects screen of specified mesh and places it on bed of reciprocating sifter. Starts hammer mill, conveyors, and sifter, and observes pulverizing and sifting operation. Inspects flour samples to verify adherence to specifications. Empties sifters, conveyors, or mills with handscoop when overloading or jamming occurs. Repairs holes in screens by gluing section of mesh over damaged area or by fastening screen onto frame. May sack flour.
GOE: 06.02.03 STRENGTH: L GED: R3 M2 L2 SVP: 6 DLU: 77

564.684-010 KNIFE SETTER, GRINDER MACHINE (paper & pulp) alternate titles: knife changer
Changes knives used in chipper machines that reduce pulpwood to chips: Dismantles machine, using hooks and chain hoist. Inspects blades, and removes defective blades with handtools. Removes chips collected between blade and disk wheel, using airhose. Bolts new blades in machine, using fixed gauge to obtain accurate setting. Files knife blades.
GOE: 05.10.02 STRENGTH: M GED: R2 M1 L1 SVP: 3 DLU: 77

564.685-010 BREAKER-MACHINE OPERATOR (saw. & plan.; wood prod., nec)
Tends machine, equipped with crushing rollers or hammers, that reduces corkwood, cork waste, or bark to fine particles: Dumps corkwood, waste, or bark into machine hopper or onto conveyor leading to machine. Removes wooden sticks and steel straps to prevent clogging. Starts machine that crushes and grinds material into fine particles and blowers that force ground particles over shaker screens to remove dust and separate ground material into bins, according to particle size. May tend machine equipped with conveyors that convey ground material through driers to remove moisture before segregating particles. May pull bags over bin outlets and open outlets to empty dust and ground cork or bark. May remove and stack filled bags on pallets. May record number of bags and grades of corkwood, waste, or bark processed.
GOE: 06.04.14 STRENGTH: L GED: R2 M1 L1 SVP: 4 DLU: 77

564.685-014 CHIPPER (chemical; paper & pulp; saw. & plan.)
Tends machine that reduces log slabs, stump wood, trimmings, and other scrap wood to chips of uniform size for making paper pulp and charcoal, and for use in wood distilling: Starts conveyor system that feeds wood into hopper of chipping machine. Positions pieces of wood on conveyor, using *picaroon* to prevent congestion and to regulate flow. May replace worn and bent knives, and adjust knives to vary size of chips, using handtools. May examine wood on feed conveyor for conformity to specified standards and remove nonconforming wood. May stop machine when jams or malfunctions occur, and clears machine or conveyor of wood pieces.
GOE: 06.04.03 STRENGTH: M GED: R2 M1 L1 SVP: 2 DLU: 81

564.685-018 HOG TENDER (woodworking)
Tends *hog mill* that grinds scrap wood into chips for use as fuel: Pulls lever to start hog mill and presses button to start conveyors that convey scrap wood to hog mill. Spreads scrap wood evenly across trough of conveyor, using hands, rake, or *picaroon* to regulate flow of wood and prevent damages to hog-mill knives. Stops machine and removes scrap wood lodged in throat of machine when machine becomes clogged. Lubricates hog mill and conveyors, using grease gun and oilcan.
GOE: 06.04.03 STRENGTH: M GED: R2 M1 L1 SVP: 2 DLU: 77

564.686-010 WOOD SCRAP HANDLER (millwork-plywood)
Feeds *hog mill* that grinds wood scraps into chips for use as fuel: Loads container, such as push cart or handcart, with wood scrap, and pushes or pulls container to hog mill. Lifts and throws wood chips from container onto conveyor that feeds hog mill. Spreads wood scraps evenly across conveyor to regulate flow of wood scraps to prevent machine damage or malfunction, such as clogged or damaged mill knives. May assist machine operators in cleaning work area.
GOE: 06.04.03 STRENGTH: H GED: R1 M1 L1 SVP: 2 DLU: 86

564.687-010 CHOPPER (chemical)
Saws and chops pieces of stumps into smaller pieces for feeding into chipper machine.

GOE: 06.04.25 STRENGTH: H GED: R1 M1 L1 SVP: 1 DLU: 77

569 OCCUPATIONS IN PROCESSING OF WOOD AND WOOD PRODUCTS, N.E.C.

This group includes occupations, not elsewhere classified, concerned with processing wood and wood products.

569.130-010 GASKET SUPERVISOR (wood prod., nec)
Supervises and coordinates activities of workers engaged in fabricating and packing cork gaskets: Sets up machines, such as grinder, mixer, and punch press. Observes operation of machines to detect malfunctions and adjusts machines, using handtools and measuring instruments, such as gauges, calipers, and micrometers. Performs other duties as described under SUPERVISOR (any industry) Master Title.
GOE: 06.01.01 STRENGTH: L GED: R4 M3 L3 SVP: 6 DLU: 77

569.132-010 SUPERVISOR, PARTICLEBOARD (wood prod., nec)
Supervises and coordinates activities of workers engaged in manufacturing particleboards: Analyzes work orders to determine quantity, dimensions, and quality of panels to be produced. Plans work schedule according to priority of orders and availability of machinery. Inspects machinery and equipment, reviews machine status reports, and schedules maintenance and part replacements. Inspects consistency of particleboard mixture and finished particleboards for adherence to specifications. Explains and demonstrates job tasks and techniques to new workers. Performs other duties as described under SUPERVISOR (any industry) Master Title.
GOE: 06.02.01 STRENGTH: L GED: R4 M3 L3 SVP: 6 DLU: 81

569.135-010 SUPERVISOR, VENEER (millwork-plywood)
Supervises and coordinates activities of workers engaged in gluing, assembling, and pressing veneer sheets and core boards into plywood panels, employing knowledge of production, products, and personnel practices: Analyzes work orders and route tickets to determine production schedules and type and dimensions of stock to be produced. Computes amounts of stock and supplies required and requisitions materials from storage area. Visually examines, feels, and measures dimensions of stock at various stages of processing, using measuring tape and dial thickness gauge, to determine if company specifications are met. Instructs and demonstrates methods of work to new employees. Confers with supervisory personnel to expedite production. May observe pengraph charts and oil gauges and adjust controls of hot-plate plywood press to regulate hydraulic pressure, temperature, and oil level of press. Performs other duties as described under SUPERVISOR (any industry) Master Title.
GOE: 06.02.01 STRENGTH: L GED: R4 M3 L3 SVP: 6 DLU: 79

569.367-010 TREATING INSPECTOR (wood prod., nec)
Inspects logs and verifies their conformance to specifications before and during processing into poles for use in power line construction: Examines logs at timber-cutting site and selects logs for poles, inspecting each for soundness and size requirements. Tests logs at various times during seasoning period with *megger* to determine when specified seasoning has been attained. Inspects poles after framing to ensure conformance to specifications. Inspects test cores taken from poles during treatment and sends sample cores and treating solution to laboratory for analysis to ascertain that preservative treatment is being applied according to specification. Gives instructions to workers engaged in shipping and handling poles to avoid damage.
GOE: 05.07.06 STRENGTH: L GED: R3 M3 L3 SVP: 3 DLU: 77

569.382-010 LINE TENDER, FLAKEBOARD (wood prod., nec)
Operates machines and conveyors to dry, segregate, and treat wood flakes, form them into mats, and press them into flakeboard panels: Starts machines and regulates flow of resin and wax additives. Adjusts panel controls to regulate speed of conveyors, drying time and temperature, and platen pressure. Adjusts height of leveling-brush to control thickness and consistency of mat prior to pressing into flakeboard. Observes control panel of platen press to determine that panels conform to specifications. Weighs and measures sample panels, using scales, rule, and micrometers.
GOE: 06.02.18 STRENGTH: L GED: R3 M2 L2 SVP: 5 DLU: 77

569.384-010 QUALITY-CONTROL TESTER (wood prod., nec)
Tests samples of wood products to determine fiber content and strength, using test equipment and standardized formula: Gathers samples, such as particleboard and wood shavings, from production areas. Weighs wood shavings before and after drying process and computes weight variances for cost analysis purposes, using scale, calculator, and formula. Conducts pressure and strength tests on particleboard to determine quality control standards, such as moisture content, strength, and resistance, using test equipment. Records test results on company chart.
GOE: 06.03.01 STRENGTH: L GED: R4 M3 L3 SVP: 6 DLU: 86

569.565-010 CREW LEADER, GLUING (millwork-plywood)
Leads workers in gluing, assembling, and pressing veneer sheets into plywood panels, and tends glue mixing tanks: Reads work order to determine quantity, type, and dimensions of veneer sheets needed. Notifies INDUSTRIAL-TRUCK OPERATOR (any industry) 921.683-050 to deliver veneer sheets from storage to gluing area. Observes glue application and panel layering, pressing, and conveying processes to maintain establishment specifications. Assists GLUING-MACHINE OPERATOR, ELECTRONIC (woodwork-

ing) 569.685-050, using wrenches and handtools, in replacement of forms that shape panels to customer specifications. Notifies MAINTENANCE REPAIRER, INDUSTRIAL (any industry) 899.261-014 of machine malfunctions. Dumps measured dry ingredients into glue mixing tanks. Turns valves to admit specified amounts of liquid ingredients and presses button to begin agitators that automatically mix ingredients into glue.
GOE: 06.04.03 STRENGTH: M GED: R3 M3 L3 SVP: 4 DLU: 86

569.662-010 INCISING-MACHINE OPERATOR (wood prod., nec) alternate titles: perforating-machine operator
Operates machine to perforate wood products, such as timbers, ties, or poles, to facilitate penetration of wood preservatives: Installs knife-studded incising rollers in machine and sets roller stops according to size of material being processed, using hand wrenches and pry bar. Turns air valve to regulate pressure on incising rollers and starts machine and conveyor system. Signals other workers to load or move timbers or poles onto conveyor or powered feeding tram. Moves levers or presses pedal to regulate speed of conveyor and opening of incisor rollers to accommodate various size timbers and poles. Examines rollers, knives, bearings, and conveyor mechanisms, and replaces worn or broken parts, using handtools. May operate discharge conveyor with lifting controls to unload poles onto ramp or into water. May operate trim saw to square ends on poles. May brand poles or timbers, using branding hammer. May be designated according to product processed as Pole-Incisor Operator (wood prod., nec); Timber-Incisor Operator (wood prod., nec).
GOE: 06.02.18 STRENGTH: L GED: R3 M2 L2 SVP: 4 DLU: 77

569.682-010 GRINDER, HARDBOARD (wood prod., nec)
Controls steam cooker and grinding machines to reduce wood chips to felt (fiber): Installs and adjusts grinding plates, using rule and handtools. Starts machines and conveyors and regulates steam pressure, cooking temperature, and spray or flow of water, wax, resin, and material. Observes cooking, grinding, and felting of material, pressure and temperature gauges, and flow and moisture charts to ensure that material is processed according to specifications.
GOE: 06.02.18 STRENGTH: M GED: R3 M3 L2 SVP: 6 DLU: 77

569.682-014 PRESS OPERATOR, HARDBOARD (wood prod., nec)
Operates line of machines to form wood fiber mats and to cut and press them into hardboard panels: Installs and adjusts stainless-steel cauls and screens, drive sprockets, chains, rollers, and cutoff saw, using handtools. Starts machine and cutoff saw. Observes gauges and turns valves to regulate water and steam pressure and to control temperature of press. Moves panelboard control switches to adjust pressing time and to synchronize timing of tiered feeding and unloading conveyors with elevator movement of tiered hardboard press. Observes forming of mat, cutting of panels, and pressing of panels into hardboard to ensure product of specified dimension and quality. May ride open elevator and flip end of panel in each tier of press to loosen it from hot pressing plate and facilitate automatic transfer to tiered unloading conveyor. May verify weight of sample panels, using scale.
GOE: 06.02.18 STRENGTH: M GED: R3 M2 L2 SVP: 5 DLU: 77

569.683-010 KILN-TRANSFER OPERATOR (woodworking) alternate titles: transfer operator
Drives electric-powered transfer (flat) car to transfer carloads of lumber between loading, drying, and storage areas, and operates winch to load and unload kilns: Turns rheostat lever to drive transfer car along track to loading platform, and aligns rails (tracks) on transfer car with rails on platform. Hooks winch cable to carload of lumber and pushes and pulls levers to activate winch and pull loaded lumber car onto transfer car. Drives transfer car with carload of lumber to designated dry kiln and aligns transfer car rails with rails into kiln. Hooks cable to lumber car and operates winch to pull lumber car into kiln. Pulls lumber car from kiln when lumber is dry and transfers it to storage or to processing department. May tend stacking machine that stacks and unstacks lumber onto lumber car [STACKER, MACHINE (woodworking)].
GOE: 05.11.04 STRENGTH: M GED: R2 M1 L1 SVP: 3 DLU: 77

569.684-010 LOG PEELER (saw. & plan.)
Peels bark from logs by hand, using two-handled drawknife: Pulls log from storage area and positions log for peeling, using cant hook. Secures log, using log-dog (wedge), and pulls drawknife lengthwise along log to strip bark from log. Rotates log and repeats stripping action until bark is removed from log. Chops branch stumps from log, using hatchet. Stacks stripped logs between spacing boards to facilitate drying of wood. Straps specified number of logs together, using steel banding tape and strapping tools.
GOE: 06.04.25 STRENGTH: V GED: R2 M1 L1 SVP: 2 DLU: 86

569.685-010 ARTIFICIAL-LOG-MACHINE OPERATOR (fabrication, nec; saw. & plan.)
Tends machines that automatically compress sawdust into artificial fuel logs and extrude them onto conveyors: Starts machines. Observes compression marks on finished logs to ensure that logs are compressed according to specifications, and turns thumbscrews to adjust degree of compression. Weighs sample log periodically to verify conformance to standards. May replace sawdust-feeding screws, using screwdriver and wrenches. May add chemicals to sawdust to produce log that burns colored flame.
GOE: 06.04.03 STRENGTH: L GED: R2 M2 L1 SVP: 4 DLU: 77

569.685-014 BENDER, MACHINE (woodworking) alternate titles: bending-press operator
Tends machine equipped with heated molds, platens, or roller that bends woodstock or veneer strips to form wooden parts for products, such as furniture, sports equipment, or musical instruments: Places or clamps steamed or water-soaked woodstock or veneer strips in molds or forms, under roller, or between platens shaped to specified design. Moves lever or presses button or pedal that raises hydraulic lift under molds, closes platens, or forces roller along form, to bend woodstock or veneer strips into specified shape. Removes formed parts from machine after specified period of drying time. May steam woodstock or veneer strips in retort to make them flexible [STEAM-BOX OPERATOR (woodworking)]. May convey processed parts to kiln for further drying or seasoning. May be designated according to article or part formed as Bender (toy-sport equip.); Rib Bender (musical inst.).
GOE: 06.04.03 STRENGTH: M GED: R2 M1 L1 SVP: 3 DLU: 77

569.685-018 CORE FEEDER, PLYWOOD LAYUP LINE (millwork-plywood)
Tends plywood-layup line machine that applies glue to top surfaces of veneer sheets before assembly into plywood panels, working as member of team: Presses pedals to start machine and to activate infeed conveyors that convey stacks of *face sheets, crossbands,* and *core stock* to feed end of machine. Removes face sheets, crossbands, and core stock from respective infeed conveyors and places sheets in specified sequence on machine conveyor that carries sheets past trash gate and through glue curtain to BACK FEEDER, PLYWOOD LAYUP LINE (millwork-plywood) and CORE LAYERS, PLYWOOD LAYUP LINE (millwork-plywood). Presses pedals to open trash gate to remove detected unusable veneer, such as broken or split sheets, from conveyor.
GOE: 06.04.03 STRENGTH: M GED: R2 M1 L1 SVP: 3 DLU: 77

569.685-022 CORE-COMPOSER-MACHINE TENDER (millwork-plywood)
Tends core composer machine that automatically glues salvaged veneer strips together to form continuous sheet, saws continuous sheet in half, and clips sawn sheets to standard length for use as plywood *core stock:* Presses button to start machine. Depresses pedal to convey veneer strips discharged from tenderizer machine onto infeed conveyor of core composer machine. Pushes each strip against wedge-edge detector that detects oblique edges, and positions wedge-shaped veneer strips against oblique edges to form square edges prior to gluing. Observes gluing apparatus that applies continuous melted glue strings across tops of veneer strips to connect strips, and replaces exhausting glue-string spools. Observes machine operations to detect jamming, and reverses machine as necessary to unclog jams. Records production.
GOE: 06.04.03 STRENGTH: M GED: R2 M1 L1 SVP: 3 DLU: 77

569.685-026 CORE-LAYING-MACHINE OPERATOR (millwork-plywood)
Tends machine that automatically lays *face sheets, back sheets,* and *core stock* in sequence and spreads glue on core stock to form plywood panels: Starts machine, observes operation, and turns wheels, valves, and dials to adjust and synchronize conveyors, reach and vacuum of mechanical feed arms, tension on glue-spreading rollers, and to regulate flow of glue. Depresses pedal to control conveyor that moves stacked panels to hot-plate presses.
GOE: 06.04.03 STRENGTH: M GED: R2 M2 L1 SVP: 4 DLU: 77

569.685-030 CORK MOLDER (wood prod., nec)
Performs any combination of following duties, as crewmember, to cast and bake ground cork mixture into slabs: Lubricates mold to prevent mixture from adhering to sides, using spray gun or oil-soaked rags. Weighs and dumps specified quantity of mixture into mold; or opens overhead storage outlet to fill mold with mixture. Lifts and places pressure plate on mold and inserts holding pins to secure plate. Moves mold under hydraulic press, using chain hoist. Presses button to lower ram that exerts pressure on plate and compresses mixture to prescribed density and hardness. Releases ram, pulls holding pins from mold, and pries off pressure plate, using pinchbar. Fastens monorail hoist to mold frame and pushes mold into oven. Observes gauges and moves controls to maintain predetermined oven temperature. Removes mold from oven and cast slab from mold, after specified time. May be designated according to specific task performed as Mold Filler (wood prod., nec); Mold Hoister (wood prod., nec); Mold Sprayer (wood prod., nec).
GOE: 06.04.09 STRENGTH: H GED: R2 M2 L1 SVP: 3 DLU: 77

569.685-034 EDGE-GLUE-MACHINE TENDER (millwork-plywood)
Tends machine that automatically presses glue-coated edges of veneer strips together to form continuous sheet and clips sheets to specified widths: Turns dials and pushes levers to adjust tension of pressure rollers and speed of feed belts. Sets trip lever on clipping unit of machine for width of veneer sheets to be produced, using wrench. Depresses pedal and moves lever that controls conveyor and lift platform to position stack of veneer for feeding into machine. Starts machine. Removes veneer strips from stack and feeds them into machine. Observes pressure gauges and gluing process, and readjusts roller tension if necessary. Removes unglued, torn, or otherwise defective strips for reprocessing or disposal.
GOE: 06.04.03 STRENGTH: M GED: R2 M1 L1 SVP: 2 DLU: 77

569.685-038 EXTRUDER OPERATOR (wood prod., nec)
Tends one or more extruders that form particleboard from wood chips treated with glue: Turns nuts on machine to regulate platens according to thickness specified for boards, using wrenches. Selects ram that corresponds to platen setting and positions ram on machine spindle. Notifies CHIP-MIXING-MACHINE OPERATOR (wood prod., nec) to start flow of charge. Starts ram that forces charge through extruder, forming continuous sheet of particleboard. Alters

space between platens as directed. May be designated according to type of extruder operated as Extruder Operator, Horizontal (wood prod., nec); Extruder Operator, Multiple (wood prod., nec); Extruder Operator, Vertical (wood prod., nec).

GOE: 06.04.19 STRENGTH: L GED: R2 M2 L2 SVP: 2 DLU: 77

569.685-042 GLUE SPREADER, VENEER (millwork-plywood; wood prod., nec) alternate titles: core feeder; glue-spreader operator; veneer gluer

Tends machine that spreads glue on both sides of precut veneer stock (*crossbands* or core boards) or particleboard before assembly into plywood or veneered panels: Turns valve on glue hopper above machine to fill troughs formed between application rollers and doctor rolls. Turns handwheel, crank, or tension screws to space rollers according to thickness of stock. Starts machine, scans stock to detect knotholes or large splits, and discards culls in handcart. Feeds stock between rollers. Observes level of glue in troughs between doctor rolls and rollers, and turns valve to replenish glue when level is low. Periodically feels discharged stock to determine if glue is being spread evenly and if glue coating is sufficient to bond stock in panels, and adjusts rollers to correct defective gluing. Cleans glue from rollers, using hot water or alcohol and brush. May lubricate machine. May mix glue.

GOE: 06.04.03 STRENGTH: L GED: R2 M1 L1 SVP: 3 DLU: 81

569.685-046 GLUING-MACHINE OPERATOR (woodworking)

Tends machine that utilizes pressure and heat to bond preglued boards into panels of specified size: Regulates speed and pressure of rollers and temperature of heating unit, according to type of glue, thickness of wood parts, and density and moisture content of wood. Starts machine, and places preglued boards of combined specified length edge to edge on feed rolls or chain that carry them through machine and curing tunnel. May tend machine with saw attachment that bonds preglued boards into continuous panel and automatically cuts panel into specified lengths and be designated Plycor Operator (woodworking).

GOE: 06.04.03 STRENGTH: H GED: R2 M2 L2 SVP: 3 DLU: 78

569.685-050 GLUING-MACHINE OPERATOR, ELECTRONIC (woodworking) alternate titles: electronic gluer; hot press operator; panel gluer

Tends machine that utilizes pressure and electronic energy to bond preglued wooden parts together: Turns knobs to regulate clamp pressure, intensity of electron emission, and timer according to type of glue, thickness of wooden parts, and density of wood. Adjusts clamps according to size of assemblies to be glued, using wrenches and hammer. Assembles and positions preglued parts in clamp bed of machine, and turns air-pressure valve and presses button to actuate clamp and release flow of electrons through glue joints. Removes assembly from machine, and examines assembly for defective gluing. May apply glue to parts with brush or by running surface of part over wheel set in pot of liquid glue. May mix glue.

GOE: 06.04.03 STRENGTH: M GED: R2 M2 L1 SVP: 4 DLU: 78

569.685-054 HOT-PLATE-PLYWOOD-PRESS OPERATOR (millwork-plywood) alternate titles: hot-plate-press operator; veneer-press operator

Tends hot-plate press that bonds glue-coated veneer sheets together to form plywood: Turns knobs on control panel to set temperature and pressure of press. Turns valves to release steam to heat plates. Lifts and loads veneer panels (assembled glue-coated veneer sheets) and caul boards into press, working in teamwork with LABORER, HOT-PLATE PLYWOOD PRESS (millwork-plywood). Presses button controls to bring plates of press together and subject veneer panels to temperature and pressure that glue and convert them into plywood. Cleans glue from caul boards, using scraper. May rub edges of plates with paraffin to facilitate loading and unloading. May tally number, dimensions, and core thickness of pressed panels on daily pressing report.

GOE: 06.04.03 STRENGTH: H GED: R2 M1 L1 SVP: 3 DLU: 77

569.685-058 HYDRAULIC-PRESS OPERATOR (millwork-plywood) alternate titles: cold-press operator

Tends hydraulic press that bands together layers of veneer sheets and core stock to form plywood or veneered products, such as tabletops and doors: Places clamp rails and backing board in press. Loads stack of assembled layers from conveyor or handtruck into press by hand or by use of hoist. Places backing board and clamp rails on top of stack. Turns handwheels to set pressure specified for material and starts press. Attaches retainer rods to top and bottom clamp rails and tightens turnbuckles on rods to maintain pressure on stack after removal from press. Releases press and removes clamped stack from press bed for drying.

GOE: 06.04.03 STRENGTH: H GED: R2 M1 L2 SVP: 3 DLU: 77

569.685-062 SPLICER OPERATOR (millwork-plywood) alternate titles: veneer splicer

Tends splicing machine that bonds preglued edges of veneer strips together to form larger sheets: Turns dial or handwheel of machine to regulate heat, pressure of rollers, and conveyor speed according to thickness of veneer sheets to be processed. Positions two veneer strips side by side against center guide of machine and feeds them into machine that automatically forces glued edges together and cures edges to bond sheets. Observes bonded sheets to detect defects, such as overlapping or unbonded edges. Adjusts heat, pressure, and speed of machine, or cleans heating bar with scraping tool to correct malfunctions.

Verifies dimensions of veneer sheets against work order, using tape measure. May record footage spliced as indicated by meter on machine. May spray glue on edges of veneer strips prior to bonding, using spray gun. May tend splicing machine that automatically applies glue to edges prior to bonding and be designated Edge Gluer (millwork-plywood).

GOE: 06.04.03 STRENGTH: M GED: R2 M1 L1 SVP: 4 DLU: 78

569.685-066 STACKER, MACHINE (woodworking) alternate titles: lumber-piler operator; stacker; wood piler

Tends machine that stacks or unstacks lumber to load or unload kiln car to level of lumber table: Starts conveyor that carries lumber onto kiln car in layers, drops stickers between layers, or removes dried lumber from car. Straightens lumber on conveyor for even flow onto stack, using handhook. May record data such as thickness, grade, length, and quantity of lumber stacked. May drive kiln car to transfer lumber car to kiln or storage [KILN-TRANSFER OPERATOR (woodworking) 569.683-010]. May tend machine that stacks inspected boards in layers of specified width prior to further processing and be designated Stacker (furniture). When concerned only with unloading kiln cars, may be designated Unstacker (woodworking).

GOE: 06.04.03 STRENGTH: M GED: R2 M1 L1 SVP: 2 DLU: 78

569.685-070 VARNISHER (fabrication, nec)

Applies varnish to stems and bowls of corncob pipes by any combination of following methods: (1) Places pipe bowls on revolving disks of plate that carries them past nozzle of spray gun. (2) Places parts of pipe in tumbling cylinder containing varnish and presses button to start cylinder, coating parts with varnish. (3) Places bowl of pipe on revolving spindle and holds brush against bowl.

GOE: 06.04.21 STRENGTH: L GED: R1 M1 L1 SVP: 2 DLU: 77

569.685-074 VENEER TAPER (millwork-plywood) alternate titles: veneer joiner; veneer-taping-machine operator

Tends machine that joins sheets of veneer with gummed-paper tape: Places pieces of matched veneer or veneer strips edge to edge between machine rollers. Lowers feed rollers that draw veneer through machine and apply moistened tape. Raises feed roller when taping is complete. Replaces reels of tape on spindle and threads tape through machine. Pours water into dispenser. Moves lever or turns handwheel to regulate speed of machine or to set pressure of feed roller according to thickness of veneer. May tend machine that joins sheets of veneer with gummed thread rather than tape.

GOE: 06.04.03 STRENGTH: L GED: R2 M1 L1 SVP: 3 DLU: 77

569.685-078 WOOD-FUEL PELLETIZER (fabrication, nec)

Tends machines and equipment that automatically extrude, pelletize, and cool mixture of ground wood and bark to form wood-fuel pellets: Moves controls to adjust temperature and steam pressure gauges, according to type of wood and bark mixture being processed, regulate conveyor speed, and start machine. Periodically tests samples of extruded mixture for moisture content, using electronic moisture tester, and readjusts steam pressure gauges as required. Listens to machines and equipment and monitors control panel to detect malfunctions and to ensure production flow. Clears jams, using paddle. Removes and replaces worn dies, using wrench and screwdriver. Washes, cleans, lubricates, and greases machines and equipment, using water, detergent, brushes, rags, oilcan, and grease gun. Records control panel readings in operating log.

GOE: 06.04.03 STRENGTH: M GED: R3 M2 L2 SVP: 4 DLU: 86

569.686-010 BACK FEEDER, PLYWOOD LAYUP LINE (millwork-plywood)

Feeds veneer *back sheets* onto conveyor of plywood-layup line machine for subsequent assembly into plywood panels: Pushes button to activate infeed conveyor that conveys stack of back sheets to worker. Removes back sheet from stack and places sheet on conveyor of plywood-layup line machine behind glue-coated *face sheet, crossbands,* and *core stock* placed by CORE FEEDERS, PLYWOOD LAYUP LINE (millwork-plywood), for subsequent assembly into plywood panel by CORE LAYERS, PLYWOOD LAYUP LINE (millwork-plywood). Presses counter control pedal to tally each back sheet placed on conveyor.

GOE: 06.04.40 STRENGTH: M GED: R1 M1 L1 SVP: 2 DLU: 77

569.686-014 CORE LAYER, PLYWOOD LAYUP LINE (millwork-plywood)

Removes glue-coated veneer sheets from conveyor of plywood-layup line machine and stacks them in sequence to form plywood panels, working as member of team: Presses pedals to activate chain conveyor that conveys stack of caul boards to discharge end of machine and to raise lift table to working level to facilitate assembly of plywood panels. Places caul board on lift table to protect surface of *face sheet* in bottom panel. Places preglued face sheets, *crossbands, core stock, and back sheets* in sequence on lift table as they are discharged from machine to form plywood panels. Discards detected unusable sheets, such as broken or split sheets, to prevent assembly of defective panels. Presses pedal and button to lower completed stack of plywood panels to chain conveyor and to convey stack to hot-plate plywood press.

GOE: 06.04.40 STRENGTH: M GED: R2 M1 L1 SVP: 2 DLU: 77

569.686-018 CORK-PRESSING-MACHINE OPERATOR (wood prod., nec)

Positions tubes of ground-cork mixture into slots of machine that compresses material into rods. Removes tubes and places tubes in frame. Pushes and pulls

frame down slide conveyor for subsequent baking and slicing of compressed mixture.
GOE: 06.04.09 STRENGTH: L GED: R1 M1 L1 SVP: 2 DLU: 77

569.686-022 GLUING-MACHINE OFFBEARER (woodworking)

Off bears gluing machine that utilizes pressure and heat to bond preglued woodstock together: Removes glued woodstock emerging from machine and stacks woodstock on handtruck. Stacks defectively glued woodstock on designated conveyor. Stops machine when jams occur in curing tunnel, and removes or assists GLUING-MACHINE OPERATOR (woodworking) in removing jammed stock. Lubricates machine and cleans work area, using grease gun and shovel. Conveys wood chips and sawdust to boilerroom, using wheelbarrow. May record production. May signal GLUING-MACHINE OPERATOR (woodworking) to start machine.
GOE: 06.04.03 STRENGTH: H GED: R2 M1 L1 SVP: 2 DLU: 77

569.686-026 LABORER, HOT-PLATE PLYWOOD PRESS (millwork-plywood)

Performs any combination of following tasks as member of team involved in loading and unloading hot-plate plywood press that bonds glue-coated veneer sheets together to form plywood: Interstacks veneer panels (assembled glue-coated veneer sheets) and caul boards on press dolly and pushes dolly to press. Inserts assembled cauls between press plates and pushes them into press. Pushes cauls from press, using stick, and stacks finished plywood panels and caul boards on separate dollies. Examines pressed panels for surface defects and discards defective panels. Conveys panels to storage area and caul boards to and from cooling area, using handtruck. May be designated according to working position as Hot-Plate Plywood-Press Feeder (millwork-plywood); Hot-Plate Plywood-Press Offbearer (millwork-plywood).
GOE: 06.04.03 STRENGTH: H GED: R2 M1 L1 SVP: 2 DLU: 79

569.686-030 PAD-MACHINE OFFBEARER (saw. & plan.)

Off bears machine that compresses and wraps excelsior into pads used in packing furniture and other products: Removes paper-covered excelsior pads from conveyor and inspects them for torn wrapping and completeness of filling. Tears open defective pads and dumps excelsior on salvage pile. Folds moistened gummed-paper tape over opened ends of acceptable pads to complete sealing of pads and stacks acceptable pads on floor.
GOE: 06.04.09 STRENGTH: L GED: R1 M1 L1 SVP: 1 DLU: 77

569.686-034 RETORT UNLOADER (chemical) alternate titles: charcoal unloader; kiln unloader; retort forker

Unloads retort or kiln after destructive distillation processing or making of charcoal: Pushes loaded cars out of retort or kiln. Rakes charcoal from racks or cars and discards unburned wood. Starts conveyor and shovels charcoal onto conveyor that transfers it into trucks. May drive truck to and from retort or kiln and dumping ramp where charcoal is dumped and bagged.
GOE: 06.04.40 STRENGTH: H GED: R1 M1 L1 SVP: 2 DLU: 77

569.686-038 GLUING-MACHINE FEEDER (woodworking)

Feeds woodstock onto conveyorized glue wheel that applies glue to edges of woodstock preparatory to bonding: Locates specified woodstock in storage area and conveys woodstock to work station. Lifts woodstock pieces from stock in prescribed sequence, following assembly sequence reference marks on woodstock pieces, and loads woodstock onto conveyor that conveys woodstock across glue-applying mechanism. Places final piece in assembly sequence at specified angle on conveyor or marks piece, using pencil, to signal GLUING-MACHINE OPERATOR, ELECTRONIC (woodworking) 569.685-050 or worker bonding woodstock by other methods of end of sequence.
GOE: 06.04.03 STRENGTH: M GED: R2 M1 L1 SVP: 2 DLU: 86

569.686-042 LAMINATING-MACHINE FEEDER (wood prod., nec) alternate titles: board handler

Feeds laminating machine that bonds coating material, such as paper or plastic to hardboard panels: Pulls panel from supply pallet, centers panel on machine feed conveyor, and pushes panel between power rollers of machine that automatically applies coating to panel, bonds material to panel with glue, heat, and pressure, and discharges laminated panel onto off-feed conveyor.
GOE: 06.04.09 STRENGTH: M GED: R1 M1 L1 SVP: 1 DLU: 86

569.686-046 LAMINATING-MACHINE OFFBEARER (wood prod., nec) alternate titles: laminator grader

Off bears laminating machine and inspects and sorts processed products: Depresses buttons to activate off bearing conveyors and to start action of panel edge sanders along sides of conveyors. Turns dial to synchronize off bearing conveyor speed with off bearing rate of laminating machine. Observes laminated panels to detect processing flaws, such as loose corners, damaged edges, or discolorations. Grades panels according to prescribed standards, and routes graded panels onto designated conveyors for delivery to assigned storage areas.
GOE: 06.03.02 STRENGTH: L GED: R2 M1 L2 SVP: 2 DLU: 86

569.686-050 PRESS BREAKER (wood prod., nec)

Unloads pressed hardboard panels from hardboard pressing machine: Pushes buttons that activate elevator platform to facilitate worker access to tiers of hardboard pressing machine. Inspects wood fiber mats to ensure specified position in pressing machine. Breaks seals of pressed hardboard from pressing plates, using pry bar, and activates drive chain motors to eject hardboard panels from press into tiers of unloading machine. Activates conveyor to unload hardboard panels onto panel stacker that stands panels on edge in humidifier cars.

Removes and weighs randomly selected hardboard panels from conveyor belt, and records weights on tally sheet to facilitate quality control. Replaces weighed panels onto conveyor belt. Pushes loaded humidifier carts into humidifier cabinet.
GOE: 06.04.40 STRENGTH: V GED: R2 M1 L1 SVP: 2 DLU: 86

569.686-054 VENEER-TAPING-MACHINE OFFBEARER (millwork-plywood) alternate titles: tape machine tailer

Off bears veneer taping machine: Lifts taped face veneer sheets from discharge bed of veneer taping machine and stacks sheets on storage cart. Hands veneer sheets that are not taped according to specifications to VENEER TAPER (millwork-plywood) 569.685-074 for retaping. Pushes loaded cart from machine to specified processing area.
GOE: 06.04.03 STRENGTH: M GED: R2 M1 L1 SVP: 2 DLU: 86

569.687-010 CLAMP REMOVER (millwork-plywood)

Detaches clamping devices and stacks glued veneer panels after removal from cold press, working as member of team: Loosens turn buckles with metal rod and removes retaining rod attached to rails at top and bottom of stack. Removes top rail from stack and stacks veneer panels and caul boards on separate handtrucks. Pushes handtruck with veneer panels to drying oven or storage area for drying. May separate layers of veneer panels with spacer sticks. May clean glue from caul boards, using scraper. May be known according to specific task performed as Veneer Stacker (millwork-plywood).
GOE: 06.04.40 STRENGTH: M GED: R1 M1 L1 SVP: 2 DLU: 77

569.687-014 LOG WASHER (saw. & plan.)

Washes loose dirt, gravel, or stones from bark of logs being drawn up slip or chute from pond to deck, using high-pressure waterhose (in many mills this work is accomplished by mechanical sprayers).
GOE: 06.04.39 STRENGTH: L GED: R1 M1 L1 SVP: 2 DLU: 77

569.687-018 SCREEN CLEANER (wood prod., nec)

Washes screens and cauls of press machine with caustic soda and water, using brush and hose. Moves parts to and from press machine, using handtruck.
GOE: 06.04.39 STRENGTH: M GED: R1 M1 L1 SVP: 2 DLU: 77

569.687-022 SORTER I (wood prod., nec)

Sorts and stacks cork sheets, used for making cork gaskets, according to size. Examines sheets and rejects those with defects, such as cracks or holes.
GOE: 06.03.02 STRENGTH: L GED: R1 M1 L1 SVP: 2 DLU: 77

569.687-026 WOOD HACKER (fabrication, nec; paper & pulp) alternate titles: block chopper, hand; block hacker; spudder; wood barker

Cuts bark spots, knots, and diseased and decayed portions from logs or wood blocks, using spudder, ax, hatchet, or portable power saw, to prepare wood for further processing. Turns logs and blocks with peavey to expose underside. May straighten logs on conveyor, using pike pole. May load cleaned blocks on conveyors.
GOE: 06.04.25 STRENGTH: M GED: R2 M1 L1 SVP: 3 DLU: 77

569.687-030 QUALITY CONTROL INSPECTOR (furniture; millwork-plywood)

Inspects veneer during processing phases to verify that veneer meets specified quality standards: Reads work cards at processing stations to determine specifications for veneer being processed. Observes clipping and splicing operations and examines veneer sheets to ensure veneer is processed according to company standards. Inspects random sheets of spliced veneer to detect gluing defects and to ensure veneer grain is matched in prescribed manner. Measures length and width of veneer for conformance to specifications, using tape ruler. Tests moisture content of veneer according to wood type, using portable moisture meter. Discards veneer that deviates from specified standards. Observes activities of VENEER GRADER (millwork-plywood) 569.687-034 to ensure that grading of veneer conforms to quality standards. Records inspection data and submits reports to designated personnel.
GOE: 06.03.02 STRENGTH: L GED: R3 M2 L2 SVP: 3 DLU: 86

569.687-034 VENEER GRADER (millwork-plywood)

Inspects sheets or strips of veneer for color, texture of grain, and knots, wormholes, cracks, or unsanded spots. Marks grade on individual sheets on conveyor or on top sheet of stack, according to prescribed standard. Discards unacceptable panels. Records number of sheets inspected by grade on tally sheet. When examining and grading plywood, is known as Plywood-Stock Grader (millwork-plywood).
GOE: 06.03.02 STRENGTH: L GED: R2 M2 L2 SVP: 3 DLU: 78

57 OCCUPATIONS IN PROCESSING OF STONE, CLAY, GLASS, AND RELATED PRODUCTS

This division includes occupations concerned with preparing for market raw materials, such as stone, clay, glass, and sand. Includes abrasive, asbestos, and miscellaneous nonmetallic mineral materials; forming such materials and adjuncts in their plastic or moldable states into stock shapes, parts, and other products; and impregnating, coating, heat treating, and thermal finishing such materials and formed products. Includes fiberglass.

570 CRUSHING, GRINDING, AND MIXING OCCUPATIONS

This group includes occupations concerned with reducing materials to smaller particles by means of compression, cutting, smashing, and combining or mingling materials to produce a single, blended mass. Includes the stirring of molten glass.

570.130-010 SUPERVISOR, CLAY PREPARATION (pottery & porc.)
Supervises and coordinates activities of workers engaged in production of casting slip and plastic clay used in forming pottery and porcelain ware: Gives workers directions in blending, mixing, filtering, and pugging clay. Inspects slip and plastic clay for specified composition, weight, specific gravity, and plasticity. Sets up and adjusts mixing and screen machines, filter-presses, pug mills, pumps, and storage tanks. Performs other duties as described under SUPERVISOR (any industry) Master Title.
GOE: 06.02.01 STRENGTH: L GED: R4 M3 L3 SVP: 8 DLU: 77

570.132-010 CONCRETE-BATCHING AND MIXING-PLANT SUPERVISOR (construction) alternate titles: batch-plant supervisor
Supervises and coordinates activities of workers engaged in transporting and mixing ingredients to make concrete: Directs workers engaged in transferring sand and gravel aggregates by crane or other conveyor from barges and trucks to storage piles or bins. Reads specification sheets to determine sizes of aggregates and proportions of cement and water required for batch of concrete. Signals workers to charge mixing drums with specified amounts of ingredients and discharge mixed concrete into truck or other conveyor. May supervise workers engaged in assembling and dismantling plant at construction site. Performs other duties as described under SUPERVISOR (any industry) Master Title.
GOE: 05.11.01 STRENGTH: L GED: R4 M3 L2 SVP: 7 DLU: 77

570.132-014 MILLING SUPERVISOR (brick & tile)
Supervises and coordinates activities of workers engaged in operating machines to grind, crush, mix, and blend materials to make batches of clay for pressing into clay products. Performs duties as described under SUPERVISOR (any industry) Master Title.
GOE: 06.04.01 STRENGTH: L GED: R4 M3 L2 SVP: 7 DLU: 77

570.132-018 WASHING-AND-SCREENING PLANT SUPERVISOR (construction)
Supervises and coordinates activities of workers engaged in washing, crushing, and screening sand and gravel to produce aggregate of specified size for use as ingredients in making concrete. Directs workers in adjusting equipment and replacing screens to regulate size of aggregate. Performs other duties as described under SUPERVISOR (any industry) Master Title.
GOE: 06.02.01 STRENGTH: M GED: R4 M3 L3 SVP: 7 DLU: 77

570.132-022 SUPERVISOR (brick & tile)
Supervises and coordinates activities of workers engaged in operation of equipment to scrape clay and shale from open pits: Assigns duties and demonstrates methods of work and use of equipment to maintain production schedule and ensure safe operations. Determines needed repairs of pit roadways and of equipment used to scrape, load, and haul clay and shale. May supervise and coordinate activities of workers engaged in crushing, grinding, and screening clay and shale [MILLING SUPERVISOR (brick & tile) 570.132-014]. Performs other duties as described under SUPERVISOR (any industry) Master Title.
GOE: 06.04.01 STRENGTH: L GED: R4 M2 L3 SVP: 6 DLU: 86

570.137-010 SUPERVISOR (mine & quarry)
Supervises and coordinates activities of workers engaged in grinding, drying, mixing, and processing talc and borate: Reviews work orders, invoices, and maintenance schedules to plan production schedules. Examines processed materials to determine if specifications are met. Performs other duties as described under SUPERVISOR (any industry) Master Title.
GOE: 06.02.01 STRENGTH: L GED: R3 M2 L2 SVP: 5 DLU: 77

570.362-010 BULK-STATION OPERATOR (petrol. & gas)
Controls conveyors and blending equipment to mix materials according to specification for use in cementing oil and gas wells: Operates electric-powered winch to spot railroad cars over underground hoppers. Breaks seal and opens bottom-dump doors on car with prybar to unload cement and other materials in hopper. Presses button to start conveyor which transfers materials to storage bins. Pulls levers and presses switches to start and stop conveyors and blending equipment and to open and close discharge gates on storage bins. Empties sacks of additive chemicals into blender hoppers to prepare dry cement mixtures, following formulas. Prepares delivery tickets (call sheets) and weighs trucks and materials as loaded. Records quantities of materials received and issued on inventory control records. Estimates materials in bulk storage bins periodically to verify inventory records. Requisitions materials to replenish stocks.
GOE: 06.04.12 STRENGTH: H GED: R3 M2 L2 SVP: 5 DLU: 77

570.382-010 MILL OPERATOR (brick & tile; pottery & porc.) alternate titles: clay temperer
Operates crushers, mixers, and blenders to grind, mix, and temper clay for use in molding ceramics products: Drives liftscoop tractor to convey clay from storage piles or bins and dumps material on crusher pit grates. Breaks up clay with bar or sledge. Starts crusher, conveyors, elevator, and vibrating screens to grind raw materials to specified size and to transport ground materials to storage bins. Examines screens and clears blockages, using wire brush. Weighs and dumps raw materials into mixing machine, following formula. Starts mixer and turns valve to feed water into mixing machine. Inserts instrument into mixture to measure water content. Discharges mixture onto conveyors leading to blending machine. Starts blending machine that mulls mixture into tempered clay. May be designated according to machine operated as Blender Operator (brick & tile); Crusher Operator (brick & tile); Mixer Operator (brick & tile); or according to kind of materials processed as Clay-Dry-Press-Mixer Operator (brick & tile); Silica-Mixer Operator (brick & tile).
GOE: 06.02.17 STRENGTH: M GED: R3 M2 L1 SVP: 5 DLU: 77

570.382-014 PLASTER MIXER, MACHINE (concrete prod.)
Controls equipment to weigh and mix gypsum with specified proportions of fiber, retarder, perlite, and other additives to make plaster: Starts mixing machine and sets weigh hopper. Engages screw feeder that feeds specified amount of gypsum from storage bin into weigh hopper. Weighs additives according to specifications and dumps them into hopper. Opens gate of hopper to drop ingredients into mixer. Opens mixer gate after specified time to discharge mixed plaster product into packer hopper. May fill bags with mixed plaster.
GOE: 06.02.18 STRENGTH: H GED: R3 M2 L1 SVP: 5 DLU: 77

570.382-018 SUPPLY CONTROLLER (concrete prod.)
Controls grinders, mixers, and conveyors to prepare ingredients for plaster wallboard and feed prepared ingredients into hopper of board machine: Transfers gypsum, flour, potash, soap, lime, and other materials from storage area to supply tanks, using handtruck or powered truck or conveyor. Dumps ingredients into agitator tanks according to formula to mix edge glue and soap solution. Feeds materials, in specified proportions, into machine hopper, by pump line and conveyor. Reads tank dials and flowmeters to determine reserve of materials in tanks and rate of flow of materials into machine hopper. Regulates feeders and pumps, using handtools, to ensure continuous supply of ingredients into hopper. May operate hydropulper to grind and mix paper into pulp slurry for use as additive.
GOE: 06.02.18 STRENGTH: H GED: R4 M2 L2 SVP: 4 DLU: 77

570.482-010 CLAY MAKER (brick & tile; pottery & porc.) alternate titles: blunger-machine operator; clay mixer; clay washer; slip maker; slip mixer; wet mixer
Operates blunger (mixing machine) and auxiliary equipment to blend and mix clay into semiliquid for use in casting ceramic ware: Dumps sacks of clay into conveyor to charge blunger. Turns valve to admit water into blunger. Starts blunger that mixes clay into semiliquid. Stops blunger and places hydrometer in semiliquid to determine specific gravity. Adds water or clay to obtain mixture of specific gravity. Regulates valves to discharge mixture over screens, agitators, and magnets to remove iron or steel in mixture. Removes excess water from mixture with vacuum filter. Washes screens and magnets to remove foreign particles and sludge, using hose. May mix clays according to formula [BATCH MIXER (brick & tile)].
GOE: 06.04.17 STRENGTH: H GED: R3 M2 L2 SVP: 5 DLU: 77

570.484-010 MIXER, DIAMOND POWDER (nonmet. min.)
Combines resin, diamond, and silicone carbide powders to form mixture for use in molding diamond-abrasive grinding wheels, following formulas and using scraper, spatula, plate glass, and gram weight balance: Selects mixing formula from book according to type of wheel to be molded. Weighs ingredients separately on gram weight balance, and dumps ingredients onto plate glass. Mixes powders on plate glass, and dumps mixture into jar, using scraper and spatula. Caps jar, using rolling machine. Removes jar after specified time from machine. Labels jar to identify mixture with type of wheel to be molded.
GOE: 06.04.34 STRENGTH: L GED: R2 M2 L2 SVP: 4 DLU: 77

570.485-010 ABRASIVE MIXER (nonmet. min.) alternate titles: mixer operator
Tends machine that mixes abrasive compounds for use in making polishing and buffing wheels, and hones: Calculates amount of grit, clay, and adhesive required according to formulas. Weighs out ingredients, dumps ingredients into mixing machine, and starts mixing machine. Feels mixture and adds water and resins until specified consistency is attained. Scoops mixed compound into oscillating sieve to screen out lumps and oversized granules. Dumps compound into barrels for further processing. Records quantities of ingredients used in each mix.
GOE: 06.04.19 STRENGTH: H GED: R3 M2 L1 SVP: 4 DLU: 77

570.665-010 DRY-PAN OPERATOR (brick & tile) alternate titles: dry-mill operator
Tends series of dry-pans, screens, and conveyors that grind, sift, and convey dry clay to storage tanks: Signals OVERHEAD CRANE OPERATOR (any industry) 921.663-010 to load clay into hoppers of dry-pans. Turns valve to feed water into pans. Starts equipment that grinds and sifts clay. Starts and regulates speed of conveyors and elevators to transport clay to storage tanks. Removes rocks or other obstructions from dry-pans and screens, using pry bars and wire brushes. Breaks up lumps of clay, using sledgehammer. Observes panel lights for indications of equipment failures. Adjusts, tightens, or replaces wire screens, using handtools.
GOE: 06.04.17 STRENGTH: M GED: R2 M2 L1 SVP: 4 DLU: 77

570.682-010 ABRASIVE GRADER (optical goods)

Operates pebble mill to grind emery, rouge, and other abrasives and separates them according to fineness by water suspension method: Examines abrasive under microscope to determine grinding time required, and grinds abrasive in pebble mill. Turns valve to allow ground particles and water to flow into agitator tank. Presses button to start agitator which stirs particles into suspension. Stops machine and determines by microscopic examination when particles of particular grade have settled below tank outlet. Opens stopcock to allow particles remaining above the outlet to descend into vat. Repeats separation process for other grades, regrinding as required.
GOE: 06.02.09 STRENGTH: M GED: R3 M2 L2 SVP: 4 DLU: 77

570.682-014 PLANT OPERATOR (concrete prod.; construction)

Operates concrete, asphalt, or sand and gravel plant to batch, crush, or segregate materials used in construction: Moves controls on panelboard or control board to heat, dry, and mix ingredients, such as asphalt, sand, stone, and naphtha to produce asphalt paving materials; to weigh and mix aggregate, cement, and water to produce concrete; or to control feeding, crushing, and sifting machinery in sand and gravel plant. Observes gauges, dials, and operation of machinery to ensure conformance to processing specifications. May repair machinery, using handtools, power tools, and welding equipment. May be designated according to type of plant operated as Asphalt-Plant Operator (construction); Concrete-Batch-Plant Operator (concrete prod.; construction); Sand-And-Gravel-Plant Operator (construction); or according to machine function as Crusher Operator (concrete prod.; construction).
GOE: 05.11.02 STRENGTH: M GED: R3 M2 L2 SVP: 4 DLU: 79

570.682-018 SAND MIXER, MACHINE (foundry) alternate titles: sand conditioner, machine; sand mill operator; sand-system operator

Operates machine to mix or recondition molding sand: Weighs out specified amounts of ingredients, such as sand, sea coal, and bonding agents, and shovels them into machine or automatic hopper. Sets dials for specified amounts of water, core oil, and other ingredients that are automatically measured and fed into machine. Turns dials to time mixing cycle of machine. Removes sample of sand and feels sand for consistency. Adjusts controls and adds ingredients to vary mixture according to sampling. May be designated according to purpose for which sand is to be used as Sand-Mill Operator, Core-Sand (foundry); Sand-Mill Operator, Facing-Sand (foundry); Sand-Mill Operator, Molding-Sand (foundry).
GOE: 06.02.10 STRENGTH: M GED: R3 M1 L1 SVP: 4 DLU: 77

570.683-010 DRY-PAN CHARGER (brick & tile) alternate titles: dry-pan feeder

Transports, mixes, and charges specified quantities of clay into dry-pan hoppers, using overhead crane, equipped with clamshell, or lift-scoop tractor: Reads production schedule to determine proportions of various clays needed for scheduled products. Transports specified amounts of clays from storage piles to mixing area and mixes clay by filling clamshell or scoop with clay and dumping clay back on pile. Transports mixed clay to dry-pan and charges it into hoppers. Lubricates equipment, using grease gun and oilcan. May press switches or buttons and turn dials and knobs to start and stop equipment used to pulverize, screen, and convey materials.
GOE: 06.04.40 STRENGTH: M GED: R3 M2 L2 SVP: 5 DLU: 77

570.683-014 SAND-CUTTER OPERATOR (foundry) alternate titles: sand-cutting-machine operator; sand-mixer operator

Controls machine equipped with cutting disks to mix binder and sand, and aerate sand used in construction of foundry molds and cores: Sprays water over sand on foundry floor and adds binder (clay, flour, or molasses) to sand. Starts machine and steers it back and forth through pile to mix water, binder, and sand. Rubs sand through fingers to test cohesiveness of mixture and adds water or binder to sand to obtain desired consistency.
GOE: 06.04.08 STRENGTH: L GED: R2 M1 L1 SVP: 4 DLU: 77

570.685-010 AUXILIARY-EQUIPMENT TENDER (cement) alternate titles: cement mixer; slip mixer; slurry blender; slurry-tank tender

Tends auxiliary equipment such as pumps, motors, and conveyors to supply materials and power to slurry tanks and other equipment to mix cement slurry for kilns: Receives signal from ROTARY-KILN OPERATOR (cement; chemical; mine & quarry). and starts pumps and conveyors to feed raw materials into kiln. Opens valves to fill slurry tanks with specified amounts of water and raw materials or to correct slurry mixture. Starts tank agitators that mix slurry. Greases and oils equipment. May be designated according to equipment tended as Kiln Feeder (cement); Mixer Tender (cement).
GOE: 06.04.17 STRENGTH: M GED: R2 M2 L1 SVP: 3 DLU: 77

570.685-014 CLAY MIXER (brick & tile)

Tends machines and equipment that mix materials, such as clay, iron oxide, magnesium, and water according to formula for use in making brick or ceramic floor tile: Gathers materials specified by work order from storage area and transports materials to scales, using handtruck or industrial truck. Weighs materials, and records weight on batch card. Dumps materials into mixer, using hoist, or shovels materials into mixer. Turns valves to admit specified amount of water into mixer and flips switch or presses button to start mixer. Presses button to discharge mixture from machine or shovels mixture into container.
GOE: 06.04.17 STRENGTH: H GED: R2 M1 L1 SVP: 2 DLU: 79

570.685-018 CRUSHER OPERATOR (concrete prod.)

Tends conveyors and grinders that crush raw gypsum into specified pebble size: Opens storage gates and starts grinders, feeders, and belt conveyors. Observes flow of materials on conveyors. Cleans carriers and removes wedged rock from conveyors and clogged chutes, using scraper and poker. Opens slide gates to allow flow of pebbles into storage bins or trucks. May fill supply chutes with gypsum rock, using tractor equipped with scoop.
GOE: 06.04.08 STRENGTH: H GED: R3 M1 L1 SVP: 2 DLU: 81

570.685-022 CRUSHER TENDER (any industry) alternate titles: crusher operator; primary-crusher operator; roll attendant

Tends any of several types of crushers that size materials, such as coal, rock, salt, clay and shale, or ore for industrial use or for further processing: Moves levers to regulate flow of materials to and from conveyors, chutes, pumps, or storage bins. Starts crusher, and prods, breaks, or discards lumps to prevent plugging, using bar, sledgehammer, or jackhammer. Adjusts equipment, such as screens, conveyors, and fans, to control or vary size or grade of product, or to maintain uniform flow of materials. Cleans and lubricates equipment. May keep record of materials processed.
GOE: 06.04.08 STRENGTH: M GED: R2 M2 L1 SVP: 3 DLU: 78

570.685-026 CULLET CRUSHER-AND-WASHER (glass mfg.) alternate titles: crusher operator; glass crusher; glass pulverizer equipment operator

Tends crushing machine that crushes and washes cullet (waste glass) for use in manufacturing glass: Starts conveyor that transfers cullet from storage to crushing machine. Starts machine and observes its operation to determine whether cullet is ground to specified fineness. Starts water spray to wash crushed cullet. Inspects crushed cullet for foreign matter such as stones, bottle caps and neck rings. Directs flow of crushed cullet to specified bins by color and type of glass. May transfer cullet to and from crusher, using industrial truck. Workers who unload bulk ingredients from railcars and truck and tend crushers. May be designated Batch Unloader (glass mfg.).
GOE: 06.04.08 STRENGTH: M GED: R2 M2 L1 SVP: 2 DLU: 77

570.685-030 HAMMER-MILL OPERATOR (nonmet. min.)

Tends hammer mill that breaks slags, slate, and similar materials into fine pieces: Starts machine and watches rate of feeding into hopper from conveyor or moves gate lever to allow materials to drop into hopper from chute. Oils and cleans machine.
GOE: 06.04.08 STRENGTH: L GED: R2 M1 L1 SVP: 3 DLU: 77

570.685-034 LIME SLAKER (concrete prod.) alternate titles: lime mixer; lime-plant operator; milk-of-lime slaker

Tends rotary slaker or open batch tank that mixes lime and water to make milk of lime (slaked lime) by either of following methods: (1) Regulates automatic feed of lime and water into rotary slaker to obtain continuous production of milk of lime. Tests concentration with hydrometer. (2) Weighs lime and dumps lime into tank. Adds water and starts agitators to dissolve lime. Tests specific gravity of mixture with hydrometer and adds lime or water to obtain specified concentration. Opens drain valve or starts pump to transfer mixture through mesh screens or settling tank into storage tank. May separate coarse and fine lime particles in classifier. May crush or grind limestone in crushing machine or ball mill. May collect samples of lime or waste material for assaying. May test lime solution by titration to determine its concentration. May heat water with steam coils to speed mixing process.
GOE: 06.04.11 STRENGTH: L GED: R2 M2 L1 SVP: 4 DLU: 77

570.685-038 MILLER (mine & quarry) alternate titles: crusher, wet-ground mica

Tends one or more grinding mills to pulverize mica: Fills hopper of mill with mica, using tractor equipped with scoop. Opens hopper gate to start flow of mica into mill and turns valve to admit specified amount of water into mill. Starts mill to grind mica for specified length of time. Feels sample of mixture and adds water to mill to maintain slurry-like consistency. Circulates water through mill at end of grinding cycle to flush ground mica from mill, through intermediate tank, and into settling tank. Shovels oversize mica from bottom of intermediate tank back into mill.
GOE: 06.04.17 STRENGTH: M GED: R2 M1 L1 SVP: 2 DLU: 77

570.685-042 MILLER I (chemical)

Tends mill that pulverizes phosphate rock used in making fertilizer: Starts conveyor that feeds rock to mill. Moves lever of feedgate to increase or decrease amount of rock fed to mill, according to grinding sound or ammeter readings. Applies preservative to belts and lubricates machine.
GOE: 06.04.11 STRENGTH: L GED: R2 M1 L1 SVP: 2 DLU: 77

570.685-046 MILLER (cement) alternate titles: grinder operator

Tends machines that crush, mix, or pulverize materials, such as limestone, shale, oyster shells, clay, iron ore, silica, gypsum, and cement clinkers, used in making cement: Starts mill and conveyors. Observes conveyor system to ensure continuous flow of material. Stops conveyor and removes clogged material, using bar. Opens chute over conveyor to add materials, such as iron, silica, or gypsum, according to specifications. Observes operation of auxiliary equipment, such as cement pumps, air or screen separators, air slides, cement coolers, and dust collectors. Turns valves to regulate water, air, and oil lines on machine, according to laboratory specifications. May regulate feeder mechanism on machines not equipped with automatic regulators. May add moisture to ma-

terials to facilitate flow into machine. May be designated according to type of mill tended as Ball-Mill Operator (cement); Finish-Mill Operator (cement); Hammer-Mill Operator (cement); Miller, Rod-Mill (cement); Pug-Mill Operator (cement); Raw-Finish-Mill Operator (cement); Tube-Mill Operator (cement); Vertical-Mill Operator (cement).
GOE: 06.04.08 STRENGTH: M GED: R2 M1 L1 SVP: 3 DLU: 78

570.685-050 MIXER (nonmet. min.) alternate titles: feeder
Tends mixing machine that blends asbestos fibers and ingredients, such as ground marble, water, cement, and oil to form compounds used in making asbestos products, such as pipe, shingles, and brake linings: Dumps or pours ingredients into mixer in specified proportions. Starts mixer and allows ingredients to mix for specified time. Stops mixer and moves control or turns valve to dump or transfer mixture into storage container. Flushes water through mixer to clean mixing equipment. Records production data.
GOE: 06.04.19 STRENGTH: H GED: R2 M1 L1 SVP: 2 DLU: 77

570.685-054 MIXER (glass mfg.) alternate titles: batch mixer; batch-plant operator; mix-house operator
Tends batch-mixing equipment that blends raw ingredients, such as sand, soda ash, cullet and others for use in making glass or fiberglass yarn, by one of following methods: (1) Weighs specified amounts of ingredients on scale. Dumps ingredients into mixing machine and starts machine to blend ingredients. Pulls lever to unload mass into batch wagon for transport to small-batch, pot furnaces. (2) Monitors and regulates automatic mixing and feeding equipment that supplies blended ingredients to continuous-operation furnace. Sets controls on instrument panel regulating equipment which automatically discharges ingredients onto scales and weighs and blends ingredients in specified ratios. Pushes button to start discharging, weighing, mixing, and feeding equipment. Observes control panel instruments to monitor operations and manually overrides controls in case of malfunction. May weigh trace elements on balance scale, and add them to batch mix. May record batch number, mixer, and other production data. May drive forklift to transport containers of ingredients.
GOE: 06.04.13 STRENGTH: L GED: R2 M1 L1 SVP: 3 DLU: 77

570.685-058 MIXER OPERATOR (concrete prod.)
Tends machine that mixes lime with materials, such as hair and sand, to make plaster and mortar: Starts mixer and loads specified amounts of materials into drum. Pulls lever to dump mixed contents into chute. May weigh materials to be mixed.
GOE: 06.04.11 STRENGTH: L GED: R1 M1 L1 SVP: 2 DLU: 77

570.685-062 MIXER TENDER, BOARD (concrete prod.)
Tends equipment that mixes ingredients to produce slurry (plaster mix) and feeds slurry into rollers for pressing into wallboard or lath: Regulates flow of stucco (dry plaster mix), water, and soap solution into mixing machine in specified proportions. Adjusts glue feed for sealing board edges, using handtools. Observes flow of mix onto wallboard paper and removes lumps from mix, using putty knife. Observes scoring and folding of paper for defects and notifies KNIFE OPERATOR (concrete prod.) of defects found. Tests slurry samples for density, using measuring cup and scale. Inserts weighted needle into slurry and times needle with stopwatch as it settles into slurry to determine setting time of slurry.
GOE: 06.04.19 STRENGTH: L GED: R3 M2 L1 SVP: 4 DLU: 77

570.685-066 MOLDING-MACHINE TENDER (pen & pencil) alternate titles: mixing-and-molding-machine operator
Tends machine that mixes modeling clay ingredients and molds clay for packaging: Fills hopper of machine with modeling compounds and color pigments, according to formula. Moves lever or depresses pedal to start machine that grinds and mixes ingredients. Turns valve to admit mixed clay ingredients into unit of machine that molds clay for packaging.
GOE: 06.04.17 STRENGTH: M GED: R2 M1 L1 SVP: 2 DLU: 77

570.685-070 MUD-MIXER OPERATOR (smelt. & refin.; steel & rel.) alternate titles: mixer operator; mud grinder; mud-mill operator
Tends mixer that makes lute used for sealing oven doors or tap holes in furnaces: Shovels specified amounts of materials, such as sand and clay, into mixing pan. Turns valve to add water, starts machine, and mixes materials with paddle as pan rotates to obtain specified consistency. Shovels lute into transfer truck. May be designated according to material mixed as Adobe-Ball Mixer (smelt. & refin.); Clay Mixer (steel & rel.); or machine used as Wet-Pan Mixer (smelt. & refin.; steel & rel.).
GOE: 06.04.17 STRENGTH: H GED: R2 M1 L1 SVP: 2 DLU: 77

570.685-074 PUG-MILL-OPERATOR HELPER (brick & tile; pottery & porc.) alternate titles: pugger helper
Tends mixing chamber that mixes clay and water to make pugged clay: Loads sacks and cakes of clay from storage area onto truck and pushes truck to pug mill. Dumps clay into mixing chamber of mill. Turns valves to regulate flow of water into mixing chamber. Stacks rolls of pugged clay on truck. May wrap pugged clay in burlap to prevent dehydration. May move clay to molding room, using handtruck.
GOE: 06.04.17 STRENGTH: V GED: R2 M1 L1 SVP: 2 DLU: 77

570.685-078 REFRACTORY MIXER (steel & rel.)
Tends equipment that crushes and mixes materials, such as brick, clay, and refractory mud, to form refractory mortar, used to line interior of furnaces:

Starts crushing machine and shovels materials into hopper. Shovels crushed materials into wheelbarrow and dumps materials into hopper of mulling (mixing) machine. Turns valve to admit water into mulling machine and starts machine. Feels consistency of mixture and adds crushed material or water to obtain mixture of specified consistency. Shovels mixture into mud box for transportation to work area.
GOE: 06.04.08 STRENGTH: H GED: R2 M1 L1 SVP: 3 DLU: 77

570.685-082 ROUGE MIXER (optical goods)
Tends machine that mixes powdered rouge and water to make polishing paste for lens blanks: Dumps specified amount of rouge into mixing tank and meters prescribed amount of water into tank. Starts agitator and allows ingredients to mix for prescribed time. Draws off sample and tests for density, using hydrometer.
GOE: 06.04.19 STRENGTH: M GED: R1 M1 L1 SVP: 2 DLU: 77

570.685-086 SAGGER PREPARER (pottery & porc.) alternate titles: mixer; sagger soak
Tends grinding machine and vat to prepare material to make new saggers: Starts grinding machine and loads machine with broken saggers for grinding into grog. Combines grog, domestic clay, and water in vat and permits material to soak for several days. Tends pug mill to prepare clay for molding into saggers.
GOE: 06.04.17 STRENGTH: M GED: R2 M1 L1 SVP: 3 DLU: 77

570.685-090 SILICA-SPRAY MIXER (smelt. & refin.) alternate titles: slurry-plant operator
Tends machine that grinds and mixes silica and fire clay into slurry for spraying inner surfaces of furnaces: Pulls lever on storage hopper chute to fill mobile equipment box with silica, transports load to mixing unit, releases end gate, and dumps silica into ball mill and mixer. Turns valve to saturate material with water. Starts agitators and shovels fire clay into mixer to mix slurry to specified consistency. Opens valve to drain slurry from mixer into storage tank.
GOE: 06.04.17 STRENGTH: M GED: R2 M1 L1 SVP: 3 DLU: 77

570.685-094 SLATE MIXER (build. mat., nec) alternate titles: blender
Tends machine that mixes multicolored granules of slate for use in surfacing asphalt-coated roofing felt: Adjusts gates on slate chutes, using gauge, and pulls levers to deposit specified proportion of granules of each color onto mixer conveyor. Starts mixer that blends granules and activates discharge conveyor leading to surfacing machine hopper.
GOE: 06.04.08 STRENGTH: L GED: R2 M1 L1 SVP: 2 DLU: 77

570.685-098 GLAZE MAKER (brick & tile; pottery & porc.) alternate titles: frit maker; pulverizer
Tends ball mill that mixes and grinds materials to produce glaze for coating pottery, tile, and porcelain: Weighs materials, such as calcium, carbonate, clay, feldspar, flint, and lead oxide, in specified proportions, using tubs and scale. Dumps materials into mill and pushes button to start mill that pulverizes and mixes glaze ingredients. Turns valve to transfer finished glaze from mill over screens and magnets and into storage jars.
GOE: 06.04.09 STRENGTH: H GED: R3 M2 L1 SVP: 3 DLU: 78

570.686-010 ABRASIVE-GRADER HELPER (optical goods)
Dumps abrasives into pebble mill, connects hose from mill to agitator tank, and shovels graded abrasives from vats.
GOE: 06.04.19 STRENGTH: M GED: R1 M1 L1 SVP: 2 DLU: 77

570.686-014 ABRASIVE-MIXER HELPER (nonmet. min.)
Assists ABRASIVE MIXER (nonmet. min.) in mixing ingredients to form polishing and buffing compounds by performing any of following duties: Dumps specified ingredients in mixing machine. Turns valve to drain finished mix from machine. Transports supplies and products between plant locations, using handtruck. Performs other duties as described under HELPER (any industry) Master Title.
GOE: 06.04.19 STRENGTH: M GED: R2 M1 L1 SVP: 2 DLU: 77

570.686-018 PREPARATION-ROOM WORKER (nonmet. min.) alternate titles: beater
Prepares asbestos, cotton, and synthetic fibers for use in manufacture of asbestos products, performing any combination of following duties: Assembles asbestos, cotton, and synthetic fibers, according to instructions, into lots for blending. Feeds fibers into hopper or chute of duster, hammer mill, picker, or blending machine, using shovel or pitchfork. Opens or closes gates of blower pipes to direct fiber from blending machine into handtrucks and trucks fiber to storage area or production department. Fastens bags under spout of bin and trips lever to fill bags with fiber. May be designated according to task performed as Blending-Machine Feeder (nonmet. min.); Picker Feeder (nonmet. min.); Stock Mixer (nonmet. min.).
GOE: 06.04.19 STRENGTH: M GED: R1 M1 L1 SVP: 2 DLU: 77

570.687-010 BATCH MIXER (brick & tile) alternate titles: clay puddler
Mixes and dumps raw materials, such as silicas or clays, into mixers: Obtains materials from storage area, using shovel, wheelbarrow, or towmotor, and transports material to batching area. Measures specified quantities of materials according to batch cards, using scales or measuring box. Dumps material from sacks onto conveyor leading to mixer or empties bulk material from wheelbarrow into mixer.

GOE: 06.04.17 STRENGTH: H GED: R2 M1 L1 SVP: 2 DLU: 77

571   SEPARATING OCCUPATIONS

This group includes occupations concerned with separating desirable materials from others by means of filtering, sifting, straining, squeezing, centrifugal force, gravitation, precipitation, or agitating devices.

571.685-010 BURNER TENDER (mine & quarry)

Tends furnace that heats perlite to expel volatile material and reduce ore to powder (calcine) for use as insulating material, plaster, and concrete aggregate: Dumps pulverized perlite onto shaker screen that sifts perlite to specified fineness. Starts conveyor that feeds screened material into furnace. Shovels calcined perlite into sack or fills sack by holding it under discharge hopper.
GOE: 06.04.19 STRENGTH: L GED: R2 M1 L1 SVP: 2 DLU: 77

571.685-014 GLAZE HANDLER (brick & tile)

Tends equipment that filters glaze mixtures and conveys glaze to spraying units: Filters aqueous glaze through electromagnetic filters and screens to remove metal particles or other foreign substances, and stores filtered glaze in stone jars. Tests specific gravity of solutions with hydrometer and adds water to obtain solutions of designated specific gravity. Turns valves to transfer glaze to spraying units or to pressure tanks.
GOE: 06.04.17 STRENGTH: M GED: R2 M1 L1 SVP: 4 DLU: 77

572   MELTING OCCUPATIONS

This group includes occupations concerned with subjecting materials to heat to change them from a solid to a liquid state.

572.360-010 FURNACE-COMBUSTION ANALYST (glass mfg.) alternate titles: combustion analyst

Tests temperature of glass melting furnaces and regulates gas and air supply to maintain specified temperature, using any of following methods: (1) Measures temperature of furnace sections, using optical pyrometer. Sights through opening of pyrometer into furnace opening and turns sleeve dial on pyrometer until color of wire filament matches luminosity of flames. Reads dial indicator to obtain millivolt reading and compares reading with temperature chart to determine if temperature is in accordance with specifications. Turns valves to adjust gas-to-air ratio and increase or decrease temperature within refractory. (2) Computes and plots averages of glass temperatures on graph paper from temperature charts, using pencil and template to draw lines and circles. Interprets graph to determine need for temperature adjustment. Turns valve to increase or decrease air and gas supply into burners. (3) Tests gas-to-air ratio of burned atmosphere, using gas analyzer. Inserts hose of gas analyzer into furnace and starts suction pump to withdraw sample of burned atmosphere. Observes dial indicator on analyzer to determine if gas-to-air ratio is in accordance with specifications. Turns valve to adjust gas-to-air ratio and control heat of furnace. Records tests, temperatures, and adjustments in log.
GOE: 06.01.05 STRENGTH: L GED: R4 M3 L3 SVP: 6 DLU: 77

572.382-010 BATCH-AND-FURNACE OPERATOR (glass mfg.) alternate titles: furnace attendant; tank-and-batch operator

Controls automatic equipment to weigh, mix, and melt ingredients to make glass: Adjusts panel controls to transfer specified amounts of ingredients, such as silica sand, soda ash, limestone flurospar, feldspar, borax, clay, and cullet (waste glass) from storage bins to automatic weigh hopper and batch mixer [MIXER (glass mfg.)]. Adjusts panel controls to dump blended mix into furnace. Observes signal lights, dials, and charts, and turns switches to adjust air, fuel, water pressure, and furnace temperature. Turns switch to reverse gas fire from one side of gas-and-air regenerative chambers to other side to equalize heat in furnace. Observes color of molten glass through furnace opening or reads gauges or pyrometer to determine when furnace temperature has reached prescribed level. Collects sample of molten glass for laboratory analysis. Makes adjustments on equipment to correct deviations from specifications. Records batch mixing, glass melting, and production data. May control furnace to melt and fuse premixed ingredients and be designated Tank-Furnace Operator (glass mfg.).
GOE: 06.02.13 STRENGTH: L GED: R4 M3 L3 SVP: 7 DLU: 77

572.685-010 GLASS-FURNACE TENDER (paint & varnish) alternate titles: furnace tender

Tends automatic furnace that makes glass used as flux in production of glass enamel: Weighs out specified chemical ingredients. Shovels ingredients into hopper of conveyor that transports ingredients through automatic blending, pulverizing, and sifting process. Lifts tank with blended mix over hopper of gravity-fed furnace, using hoist, and releases mix from tank into hopper. Observes gauges and adjusts controls of furnace to maintain specified temperature in crucible. Stirs ingredients in hopper of furnace, using glass rod.
GOE: 06.04.13 STRENGTH: H GED: R2 M1 L1 SVP: 2 DLU: 77

572.686-010 CUPOLA CHARGER, INSULATION (nonmet. min.)

Charges cupola furnace with slag, basalt, lime, and silica to produce mineral wool: Weighs and measures portions of coke, slag, basalt, lime, and silica according to formula specified in orders from CUPOLA OPERATOR, INSULATION (concrete prod.). Charges materials into furnace in alternate layers. May use tractor equipped with scoop to move raw materials to storage and conveyors to feed materials to furnace.

GOE: 06.04.19 STRENGTH: M GED: R2 M1 L1 SVP: 3 DLU: 77

573   BAKING, DRYING, AND HEAT-TREATING OCCUPATIONS

This group includes occupations concerned with raising, lowering, or maintaining the temperature of materials to effect their physical composition and facilitate further processing. Includes such activities as firing terra cotta, treating formed glass with heat or cold to relieve or redistribute internal stresses and effect such characteristics as hardness and ductility, and removing liquid and moisture from materials.

573.132-010 BURNING SUPERVISOR (brick & tile) alternate titles: brick burner, head

Supervises and coordinates activities of workers engaged in controlling field, periodic, retort, and tunnel kilns to bake green clay products, such as brick, tile, and sewer pipe. Performs duties as described under SUPERVISOR (any industry) Master Title.
GOE: 06.02.01 STRENGTH: L GED: R4 M3 L2 SVP: 7 DLU: 77

573.362-010 DRY-KILN OPERATOR (brick & tile) alternate titles: drier operator

Controls drying tunnels to condition and dry brick, sewer pipe, roofing tile, and other clay products before treatment in kiln: Reads production schedule to determine humidity and temperature required for size and type of product to be dried. Positions portable blowers in drying aisles to circulate heat and air. Closes tunnel doors and starts blowers and heaters to regulate humidity and temperature within tunnel. Examines products for cracks indicating excessive drying. Reads humidity and temperature gauges, and adjusts speed and dampers on blowers. Directs DRY-KILN OPERATOR HELPER (brick & tile) to cover product with tarpaulin or to flood aisles with water to retard drying process. Records gauge reading in logbook. May patch damaged products, using patching clay and handtools. May control tunnel kiln [TUNNEL-KILN OPERATOR (brick & tile)].
GOE: 06.02.17 STRENGTH: M GED: R3 M2 L1 SVP: 5 DLU: 77

573.382-010 ROTARY-KILN OPERATOR (cement; chemical; mine & quarry) alternate titles: calciner; drier operator; roaster

Controls rotary type kilns and auxiliary equipment, such as conveyors, feeders, and dust collectors, to calcine chemicals, raw ground stone, gypsum, slate, or clay or cement slurry: Lights burners, starts equipment to feed materials, and moves controls to rotate kiln drum, start dust collecting mechanism, and regulate damper. Observes color and shape of flame, monitors gauges, and moves controls to regulate feed of fuel to maintain specified temperature. Records data, such as kiln temperature, fuel consumption, and power consumed. Inspects kiln for accumulation of clinkers and deterioration of lining. May fire tripod-mounted shotgun to blast clinkers from kiln wall. May tend cooler mechanism. May tend grinders and vibrating screens to pulverize and size product prior to calcining.
GOE: 06.02.17 STRENGTH: L GED: R3 M2 L2 SVP: 4 DLU: 77

573.382-014 SPRAY-DRIER OPERATOR (brick & tile)

Operates spray drier to evaporate water from clay slip to form pellets used in production of mosaic quarry, wall and floor tile: Connects hose to ball mill and drier pump, using wrenches, and opens valves. Sets controls on panelboard for specified temperatures and pressure in drier and to route pellets into specified silo. Starts pump and drier and observes dials and gauges and adjusts controls to ensure that specified temperature and pressure are maintained. Draws sample of pellets from drier and measures moisture content, using moisture meter. Records specified processing data.
GOE: 06.02.17 STRENGTH: L GED: R3 M2 L1 SVP: 4 DLU: 77

573.382-018 TUNNEL-KILN OPERATOR (brick & tile)

Controls preheating chamber and tunnel kiln to preheat and bake clay products, such as brick, sewer pipe, mosaic tile, and ceramic and quarry tile: Observes color of fires and reactions of pyrometric cones to increases in temperatures in kiln and reads gauges and automatic recording instruments to verify specified temperatures in kiln. Turns fuel and air valves and opens or closes dampers to adjust temperatures. Pulls loaded kiln car from drier, opens preheater doors, and pushes kiln car into preheater, using car puller or transfer car. Closes preheater doors and starts mechanism that pushes car through preheater. Pulls loaded kiln cars from preheating chamber, opens tunnel kiln doors, and starts mechanism that pushes string of cars through kiln. Removes cars from tunnel kiln and moves them to sorting area, using transfer car. May control kiln equipped with automatic loading and drawing equipment. May control drying tunnel [DRY-KILN OPERATOR (brick & tile) 573.362-010]. May control tunnel kiln equipped with preheating chamber to bake clay products. May be designated according to type of tile burned as Bisque-Tile Burner (brick & tile); Glost-Tile Burner (brick & tile).
GOE: 06.02.17 STRENGTH: M GED: R3 M2 L2 SVP: 5 DLU: 78

573.462-010 LIME-KILN OPERATOR (concrete prod.) alternate titles: kiln firer; lime burner

Controls equipment in which limestone is burned to produce lime or carbon dioxide: Turns panel controls to start flow of materials, fuel, and air, rotation of kiln and speed of conveyors, and to regulate draft and vent mechanisms. Adjusts automatic scale that controls amount of limestone flowing into kiln.

Scoops samples of hot limestone from kiln for chemical analysis, using shovel. Observes material flow, air, temperature, and fuel charts, and oxygen gauges, and makes adjustments to maintain kiln conditions within specified limits. Keeps production records. May be designated according to type kiln operated as Rotary-Kiln Operator (concrete prod.); Vertical-Kiln Operator (concrete prod.).
GOE: 06.02.18 STRENGTH: L GED: R3 M2 L1 SVP: 5 DLU: 77

573.585-010 OVEN TENDER (glass mfg.)
Tends oven to bake cakes of fiberglass sliver for further processing: Scans tubes of sliver for defects, such as soft and unraveled edges, grease spots, and water damaged tubes. Removes defective tubes from truck. Weighs trucks of sliver, deducts tare weight, and records on production records weight of sliver processed. Pushes trucks of sliver onto oven conveyors. Turns time selector to set length of baking cycle according to instructions. Observes temperature charts to determine if specified oven temperature is maintained.
GOE: 06.04.13 STRENGTH: M GED: R2 M2 L2 SVP: 2 DLU: 77

573.662-010 FIRER, KILN (pottery & porc.) alternate titles: kiln burner; kiln operator
Controls kiln to fire greenware, or decorations or glazes on ware, to specified hardness: Gives directions to helper in preparing firebox, building up door, and lighting fires. Determines level and uniformity of oven temperature by observing, through peepholes, changes in shape and color of pyrometric cones, rings, and saggers. Regulates temperature by adjusting drafts and fuel feed. May be designated according to type kiln fired as Firer, Round Kiln (pottery & porc.); Firer, Tunnel Kiln (pottery & porc.); or type of ware fired as Decorating-Kiln Operator (pottery & porc.); Firer, Bisque Kiln (pottery & porc.); Firer, Glost Kiln (pottery & porc.).
GOE: 06.02.18 STRENGTH: M GED: R4 M3 L2 SVP: 5 DLU: 77

573.667-010 KILN DRAWER (pottery & porc.) alternate titles: round-kiln drawer
Removes fired ware, such as china or pottery, from kiln and prepares kiln for reuse: Opens kiln door or removes brick and mortar that seals kiln during firing. Picks up fired ware from tunnel-kiln car, conveyor slabs, or from saggers. Presses ware against abrasive grinding wheel to remove rough spots or marks. Segregates ware according to pattern or design. Cleans interior of kiln. May be designated according to kiln drawn as Bisque-Kiln Drawer (pottery & porc.); Glost-Kiln Drawer (pottery & porc.); Tunnel-Kiln Drawer (pottery & porc.).
GOE: 06.04.17 STRENGTH: M GED: R2 M1 L1 SVP: 2 DLU: 77

573.682-010 KILN BURNER (brick & tile) alternate titles: baker; burner
Controls periodic, field, or retort kilns to bake clay products, such as brick, sewer pipe, clay refractories, and roofing tile: Opens fuel valves and lights gas or oil fire, using oil-soaked stick. Seals kiln door with bricks and daubs brick with clay to prevent loss of heat, using trowel. Observes thermometer and action of pyrometric cones through peepholes, or removes object from kiln with tongs and examines object to determine rate of burning. Turns gas or oil valves and dampers to adjust rate of burning or baking of objects. Closes fuel valves and fireboxes, opens kiln-crown holes, and installs fans to cool objects. May be designated according to type of kiln operated as Dry-Kiln Burner (brick & tile); Field-Kiln Burner (brick & tile); Retort-Kiln Burner (brick & tile); or according to product burned as Brick-Kiln Burner (brick & tile); Roofing-Tile Burner (brick & tile).
GOE: 06.04.17 STRENGTH: M GED: R3 M2 L2 SVP: 5 DLU: 77

573.683-010 STEAM-TANK OPERATOR (nonmet. min.)
Tends autoclave to cure asbestos-cement pipe: Transports specified supplies and empty trays (forms) to forming department, and trays loaded with pipe to curing area, using industrial truck. Loads autoclave with trays of pipe, using industrial truck. Closes autoclave door and inserts safety pin to secure door. Places chart on recording instrument and sets indicator for starting time and curing limits. Opens steam value to build up specified pressure in autoclave. Closes valves, opens exhaust vents and starts fans to reduce steam pressure to specified level and opens autoclave door. Removes cured pipe from autoclave, using industrial truck. Maintains record of production.
GOE: 06.04.16 STRENGTH: M GED: R2 M2 L2 SVP: 4 DLU: 77

573.684-010 KILN-DOOR BUILDER (brick & tile) alternate titles: sealer and stripper
Builds temporary casing doors and seals crown openings in kilns, using handtools: Stacks brick in doorway of kiln. Mixes dirt and water to form mud, and spreads mud over brick to seal opening, using trowel. Climbs on top of kiln and places covers or crown openings over kiln and seals them with mud. Positions and screws burners in openings. Pulls down doors with hook after firing of kiln and removes crown covers to control cooling.
GOE: 05.10.01 STRENGTH: M GED: R2 M1 L1 SVP: 3 DLU: 77

573.684-014 SETTER (brick & tile) alternate titles: kiln setter; kiln stacker
Stacks products, such as blocks, bricks, sewer pipe, and roofing tile in specified patterns on tunnel kiln cars or in periodic kilns for burning: Spaces and levels setting rings on kiln car or in kiln to facilitate circulation of air about products during burning. Spreads sand on floor or setting rings to prevent cohesion of products during burning. Lifts and positions products on setting rings, using air-hoist. Examines products for cracks and measures them for straight-

ness, using straightedge. Discards defective products. May direct SETTER HELPER (brick & tile). May draw products from kiln.
GOE: 06.04.40 STRENGTH: H GED: R2 M2 L1 SVP: 4 DLU: 77

573.685-010 ANNEALER (glass products) alternate titles: firer
Tends gas or electric kiln to affix paint on glass: Ignites and regulates gas burners to heat kiln to prescribed temperature, or regulates thermostat to control temperature of electric kiln. Spreads plaster of paris on metal trays with trowel, roller, or palette knife to form smooth, level bed for glass. Sets sections of glass on trays and positions trays in kilns, using tongs. Observes glass through peepholes in kilns to detect signs of warping, bubbling, cracking, or blistering. Removes trays after specified period of time, and stacks trays for gradual cooling and annealing in lehr.
GOE: 06.04.13 STRENGTH: L GED: R3 M1 L1 SVP: 3 DLU: 77

573.685-014 CLAY ROASTER (petrol. refin.) alternate titles: burner operator; clay burner; earth burner
Tends clay roasting kilns and auxiliary equipment in which clay, used as filter in treating oil, is cleaned and treated for reuse. Adjusts temperature of rotary kilns in which clay is roasted, by regulating valves controlling gas or oil and air supply. Starts, stops, and regulates speed of conveyors and elevators by which used clay is charged into kilns from storage bins. Fires oil-burning or gas-burning steam heater to supply steam for treating clay before it is dumped from filters. Checks weight per cubic foot of clay to determine whether it conforms to requirements, using spring balance. Cleans lumps of fused clay from screens at outlet of kilns. Oils and greases equipment.
GOE: 06.04.17 STRENGTH: M GED: R3 M2 L2 SVP: 4 DLU: 77

573.685-018 GLAZING-MACHINE OPERATOR (glass mfg.) alternate titles: beveler; finisher; tube closing machine operator; tube finishing machine operator
Tends equipment that heats and fire polishes glassware, such as tubes, kitchen utensils, and trays to remove defects, such as rough surfaces, air bubbles, and chips, or to seal tubes: Places tubes on spindles or other glassware on rotating table which carries them into contact with gas flame to melt or fuse glass. Turn valves to regulate polishing flame. Removes articles after heating with tongs.
GOE: 06.04.13 STRENGTH: L GED: R2 M1 L1 SVP: 2 DLU: 77

573.685-022 KILN-OPERATOR HELPER (concrete prod.) alternate titles: kiln-firer helper
Assists LIME-KILN OPERATOR (concrete prod.) to control kiln used in converting limestone into lime: Opens and closes gates on kiln to adjust draft as directed. Observes flow of lime from kiln and removes lumps blocking discharge end of kiln, using bar. Shovels spilled material onto conveyor. Performs other duties as described under HELPER (any industry) Master Title.
GOE: 06.04.11 STRENGTH: M GED: R2 M1 L1 SVP: 2 DLU: 77

573.685-026 LEHR TENDER (glass mfg.) alternate titles: automatic lehr operator; furnace operator; heat treat worker; lehr attendant; lehr operator; lehr stripper
Tends automatic or semiautomatic lehrs that anneal flat glass or glassware to relieve internal stresses or to fuse painted designs on glassware: Observes gauges and turns controls to start exhaust fans, to ignite burners, and to regulate lehr temperatures, speed of lehr conveyors, and draft rates. Observes annealed glass for splits, cracks, breaks, and color that indicate improper lehr settings or for fusing of paint to glass. Loads or unloads glass entering or leaving lehr by hoisting flat glass with vacuum-cupped crane or by manually placing glassware on and removing from lehr conveyor. Packs annealed glass by placing flat glass in crates, using vacuum-cupped crane, or inserting glassware in cartons. Maintains record of glass annealed and packed. May adjust height of lehr entranceway curtain to accommodate containers of specific height. May tend hot- or cold-end spray equipment used to coat glassware with surface hardener. May change conveyor gears to alter speed of conveyor and replace defective burners, using handtools.
GOE: 06.04.13 STRENGTH: M GED: R2 M1 L1 SVP: 3 DLU: 77

573.685-030 LENS HARDENER (optical goods)
Tends electric oven-type machine that hardens lenses used in safety eyeglasses, and tests hardness of lens, using steel-ball drop-test: Measures lens thickness with calipers to determine if lens meets thickness requirements for prescribed hardening. Positions lenses in holding fixture and pushes fixture into electric oven. Sets timer and temperature controls on oven according to chart specifications for prescribed hardness of lens. Removes lenses at end of cooling cycle, or places lenses in airflow to cool. Holds finished lens in polarized light fixture to detect defects produced by hardening. Places lens on bed of droptest fixture and covers lens with cloth or plastic. Places steel ball of specified weight in release mechanism of fixture. Positions mechanism at specified distance from lens and releases ball. Discards broken lenses.
GOE: 06.04.13 STRENGTH: L GED: R2 M2 L1 SVP: 2 DLU: 77

573.685-034 REGENERATOR OPERATOR (sugar & conf.)
Tends furnace driers, and auxiliary equipment that regenerate diatomaceous earth used as filtering medium: Opens valves on storage tank to allow dry earth to mix with mud discharged from filter. Feels mixture and adjusts valves to obtain mixture that can be dried readily. Moves controls to regulate flow of mixture to furnace driers, and temperatures of furnace to ensure specified regeneration. Obtains samples of earth before and after regeneration for lab-

oratory analysis. Turns valves to route regenerated earth to storage bins. Clears blockages in minglers, dust collector hoppers, and mud gauges. Changes and cleans pump screens. May be designated according to material regenerated as Kieselguhr-Regenerator Operator (sugar & conf.).
GOE: 06.04.17 STRENGTH: L GED: R2 M2 L2 SVP: 4 DLU: 77

573.685-038 BURNER (brick & tile)
Tends kilns that fire magnesium materials, such as filter cake and briquettes to remove specified impurities: Observes influx of material into kiln and movement of material through kiln stages to verify that material passes through kiln at prescribed rate. Monitors console dials and gauges and adjusts controls to maintain specified temperatures and other processing parameters. May be designated according to type of kiln tended as Burner, Hearth (brick & tile); Burner, Shaft (brick & tile).
GOE: 06.04.17 STRENGTH: L GED: R2 M1 L1 SVP: 2 DLU: 86

573.685-042 OVEN-PRESS TENDER I (nonmet. min.)
Tends hot press and related equipment that hardens asbestos disc pads for use as brake linings: Positions metal die plate on roller-type conveyor, picks up stack of asbestos disc pads from table, and places individual pads into wells of die plate. Discards broken or defective pads. Pushes filled die plates onto racks of hot press. Starts machine that automatically closes press to heattreat pads for specified time and opens press at end of press cycle. Pulls die plates from press onto conveyor. Removes cured disc pads from die plates, using knockout device that forces pads from plates. Loosens stuck pads with rubber mallet and tosses pads into storage container. Sprays empty die plates with silicone solution, using spray gun, to prevent pads from sticking to plates during heat-treating process.
GOE: 06.04.19 STRENGTH: M GED: R2 M1 L1 SVP: 4 DLU: 86

573.685-046 OVEN-PRESS TENDER II (nonmet. min.)
Tends hot press that hardens asbestos disc pads for use as brake linings: Pushes metal die plate filled with asbestos disc pads onto feed elevator of machine. Presses buttons to open press, move die plates from elevator into press, and close press. Observes timer lights, dials, and pressure gauges on control panel of machine to determine end of press cycle. Presses buttons at end of cycle to simultaneously open press and move cured disc pads from press onto discharge elevator. Pushes die plates from elevator onto roller-type conveyor, using metal rake.
GOE: 06.04.19 STRENGTH: M GED: R2 M1 L1 SVP: 4 DLU: 86

573.686-010 BRAKE-LINING CURER (nonmet. min.)
Feeds and off bears oven that cures and hardens brake linings: Presses switches to ignite burners in oven and start conveyor. Lifts spring-loaded mold onto table and opens mold with pressure device. Places brake lining into mold and releases pressure device to close mold. Places mold containing brake lining on conveyor that moves mold through oven to cure and harden brake lining. Off bears mold from conveyor, removes cured lining from mold, and places lining on rack. Records production data.
GOE: 06.04.19 STRENGTH: L GED: R1 M1 L1 SVP: 2 DLU: 77

573.686-014 FUSING-FURNACE LOADER (optical goods) alternate titles: furnace clerk; picker
Loads and unloads conveyor of furnace that fuses multifocal lens parts: Positions multifocal lens blank and button assemblies, or assembled button parts, on emery disks, places disks on trays, and places filled trays on conveyor that passes through fusing furnace. Removes trays of fused items from end of conveyor and places them in rack to cool. Records production count. May mark identification number on lenses, using marking pen. May observe temperature indicators and inform supervisor of furnace malfunction.
GOE: 06.04.13 STRENGTH: L GED: R2 M1 L1 SVP: 2 DLU: 77

573.686-018 GLASS-VIAL-BENDING-CONVEYOR FEEDER (cutlery-hrdwr.) alternate titles: glass bender
Places glass vials for levels on endless belt conveyor that carries vials through gas heated oven to soften glass and form curve required for centering level bubble: Removes filled box and bundles vials, hole end up, in metal cups. Carries racked cups in tray to filling work station.
GOE: 06.04.13 STRENGTH: L GED: R2 M1 L1 SVP: 2 DLU: 77

573.686-022 HACKER (brick & tile)
Lifts green-clay products, such as brick, roofing tile, or quarry floor tile, from press-conveyor belt, and stacks them in specified pattern on kiln car, drier rack, or pallet. May press button to control movement of conveyor belt.
GOE: 06.04.40 STRENGTH: M GED: R1 M1 L1 SVP: 2 DLU: 77

573.686-026 KILN PLACER (pottery & porc.) alternate titles: kiln setter; sagger filler; setter-in
Places greenware and glazed ware on kiln conveyor for firing: Arranges ware on metal or firebrick slab, using kiln furniture, such as saggers and setter pins, to separate and support ware during firing cycle. Places pyrometric cones, that bend at predetermined temperatures and indicate when desired heat in kiln is reached, on top of ware load. Turns handwheel to move hydraulic ram into contact with slab to convey ware load through kiln. Closes door of kiln. May be designated according to type of kiln loaded as Bisque-Kiln Placer (pottery & porc.); Glost-Kiln Placer (pottery & porc.).
GOE: 06.04.17 STRENGTH: M GED: R2 M1 L1 SVP: 2 DLU: 81

573.687-010 BEDDER (pottery & porc.) alternate titles: claying-up worker; sander-up
Sets greenware in piles with sand and clay between pieces to support and separate them during bisque-kiln firing by either of following methods: (1)

Throws refractory clay mixed with sand between each plate, and after pile is built up, fills in edges with refractory clay, packing and pressing it by hand. (2) Arranges ware in piles with sandy clay between layers. Fills in edges by setting pile on whirler which revolves it before spout forcing fine sand or refractory clay by gravity between plates. Inspects ware and rejects inferior pieces. May build up pile of greenware in saggers, sanding and packing it piece by piece.
GOE: 06.04.30 STRENGTH: M GED: R2 M1 L1 SVP: 3 DLU: 77

573.687-014 DRY-KILN OPERATOR HELPER (brick & tile)
Assists DRY-KILN OPERATOR (brick & tile) in drying clay products in tunnel: Positions fans in drying areas to circulate heated air. Closes or opens tunnel room doors. Covers product with canvas or sacking. Floods aisles with water. Adjusts floor furnace to maintain specified temperature and circulation of heat. Examines products in tunnel for cracks or other defects. Patches damaged products with patching clay, using handtools. Brushes paint sealer or drying agent on product to retard evaporation. Performs other duties as described under HELPER (any industry) Master Title.
GOE: 06.04.17 STRENGTH: M GED: R2 M1 L1 SVP: 3 DLU: 77

573.687-018 KILN CLEANER (concrete prod.)
Cleans bottom of lime kilns and rubberized conveyors. Sweeps, stacks, and removes refuse, using brooms, brushes, and shovels and performs related tasks.
GOE: 06.04.39 STRENGTH: M GED: R2 M1 L1 SVP: 2 DLU: 77

573.687-022 KILN WORKER (pottery & porc.) alternate titles: kiln maintenance laborer
Performs routine tasks concerned with maintenance and repair of kilns under direction of such workers as KILN PLACERS (pottery & porc.) or BRICK-LAYERS (brick & tile).
GOE: 06.04.17 STRENGTH: M GED: R1 M1 L1 SVP: 2 DLU: 77

573.687-026 KILN-BURNER HELPER (brick & tile)
Assists KILN BURNER (brick & tile) 573.682-010 in baking clay products, such as tile, sewer pipe, brick, and refractories, in periodic or tunnel kilns: Pushes loaded kiln cars into kilns and driers, using hydraulic ram. Removes cars from kilns or driers, using car puller. Transports loaded or empty cars from kiln tracks to car siding, sorting, or storage area, using electric-transfer car. Lubricates kiln cars, using grease gun. Opens and closes kiln doors. Tears down kiln doors, using handtools and bars. Separates sand from finished mosaic tiles in saggers, using screening device. Performs other duties as described under HELPER (any industry) Master Title.
GOE: 06.04.17 STRENGTH: M GED: R2 M1 L1 SVP: 3 DLU: 79

573.687-030 SETTER HELPER (brick & tile) alternate titles: kiln-setter helper
Loads and moves clay products on kiln cars into kilns for burning: Places setting rings on floor of kiln cars or periodic kiln according to setting pattern. Moves setting table in kiln and pushes loaded trailer into kiln. Carries defective or rejected pipe from kiln. Clips pipe on kiln cars to secure load. Stacks empty boards and pallets.
GOE: 06.04.40 STRENGTH: H GED: R1 M1 L1 SVP: 2 DLU: 77

573.687-034 SORTER (brick & tile) alternate titles: inspector; yard pipe grader
Sorts burned clay products, such as brick, roofing tile, and sewer pipe, according to form, color, and surface characteristics: Picks up products from kiln car, pallet, or handtruck, and examines products for defects, such as cracks, chipped edges, squareness, and discoloration. Sorts products into piles according to varying degrees of characteristics. Discards unusable products. May stack bricks in specified pattern for banding by machine. May be designated according to product sorted as Brick Sorter (brick & tile); Roofing-Tile Sorter (brick & tile); Sewer-Pipe Sorter (brick & tile).
GOE: 06.03.02 STRENGTH: M GED: R2 M2 L2 SVP: 2 DLU: 78

573.687-038 TILE SORTER (brick & tile) alternate titles: glost tile sorter
Sorts glazed tile according to color shades and defects: Picks up tile from tray, compares it against color shades on color sample board, and sorts it according to shade variations. Examines tile for defects, such as cracks, spots, warping, and dents, and grades it according to quality. Keeps records of tile rejected. May pack tile in cartons.
GOE: 06.03.02 STRENGTH: L GED: R2 M1 L2 SVP: 3 DLU: 77

574 IMPREGNATING, COATING, AND GLAZING OCCUPATIONS

This group includes occupations concerned with impregnating, dip coating, brushing, spraying, rolling, or spreading materials with other substances. Includes uniting filaments of glass or mineral wool batts; silvering mirrors; solidifying asbestos fibers to form brake bands; and covering pottery with glazing sap.

574.130-010 GLAZE SUPERVISOR (brick & tile)
Supervises and coordinates activities of workers engaged in operating frit-furnaces, ball mills, and mixing and spraying machines to make glaze and to spray glaze on brick and tile products. Performs duties as described under SUPERVISOR (any industry) Master Title.
GOE: 06.02.01 STRENGTH: M GED: R4 M2 L2 SVP: 7 DLU: 77

574.132-010 GLAZE SUPERVISOR (pottery & porc.)

Supervises and coordinates activities of workers engaged in applying glaze to bisque or greenware and drying ware prior to firing: Inspects sprayed, dipped, or dried ware for defects in glaze coating and weighs sample ware for conformance to specifications. Verifies viscosity of glaze, using viscometer. Issues instructions or adjusts controls of processing equipment to correct glaze defects. Performs other duties described under SUPERVISOR (any industry) Master Title.
GOE: 06.02.01 STRENGTH: L GED: R4 M3 L2 SVP: 7 DLU: 77

574.132-014 SUPERVISOR, SILVERING DEPARTMENT (glass products)

Supervises and coordinates activities of workers engaged in operating silvering range to manufacture mirrors: Observes washing, silvering, painting, and drying processes, and inspects mirrors for quality. Determines surface temperature of mirrors after drying, using pyrometer. Observes pressure gauges and thermometers on conveyors to verify specified water temperature and air pressures. Turns heat control button to regulate oven temperature. Maintains record of chemicals used in preparing silver and copper solutions. May weigh or examine painted glass sample to determine density of paint. May operate silvering unit of silvering range. Performs other duties as described under SUPERVISOR (any industry) Master Title.
GOE: 06.02.01 STRENGTH: L GED: R4 M2 L2 SVP: 7 DLU: 77

574.134-010 SUPERVISOR, HAND SILVERING (glass products)

Supervises and coordinates activities of workers engaged in washing, silvering and painting by hand, cleaning, and inspecting glass used in manufacture of mirrors: Inspects washed, silvered, and painted glass to detect faulty wash-water or chemical solutions, and uneven paint, silver, or copper coatings. Observes drying-oven thermometer to verify specified oven temperature. Weighs and measures chemical ingredients according to formula to prepare tin, silver, and copper solutions and reducing agents. Pours or combines chemicals in mixing tank, and transfers solution to storage tank. May wash, silver, paint, clean, or polish mirrors. Performs other duties as described under SUPERVISOR (any industry) Master Title.
GOE: 06.02.01 STRENGTH: M GED: R4 M3 L4 SVP: 7 DLU: 77

574.367-010 TILE SHADER (brick & tile) alternate titles: glost-tile shader; shade classifier; tile classifier

Classifies samples of glazed tile according to color shade, and prepares color sample for board for use by TILE SORTER (brick & tile): Selects samples of burned tile and examines tile to determine number of shade variations in each lot. Assigns catalog number for each color variation. Mounts tile samples of each shade on board. Explains range of variations in each shade to TILE SORTER (brick & tile) to ensure uniform sorting of shades.
GOE: 06.03.01 STRENGTH: L GED: R3 M2 L2 SVP: 5 DLU: 77

574.462-010 ABRASIVE-COATING-MACHINE OPERATOR (nonmet. min.)

Sets up and operates machine to coat cloth, fiber, or paper with granules of abrasive material: Positions machine guides and stops on machine bed according to size of base material, using rule or template. Turns screws to adjust valve openings to regulate thickness of abrasive coating sprinkled on base material. Dumps specified abrasive, such as flint, garnet, emery, or corundum into container on machine. Positions flat piece of base material on machine bed and against guides and stops. Starts machine and manually feeds base material through machine. Examines base material for uniformity and thickness of abrasive coating. May operate machine to coat rolls of base material with abrasive granules.
GOE: 06.02.21 STRENGTH: L GED: R3 M2 L1 SVP: 4 DLU: 77

574.484-010 OPTICAL-GLASS SILVERER (optical goods) alternate titles: silverer

Coats optical glass surfaces with silvering solutions to make mirrors used in optical instruments: Cleans glass specimens, using prescribed chemicals, and inspects to detect surface appearance defects. Mixes chemicals according to formula and pours solution into funnels. Positions glass under funnels and starts electric motor to agitate funnels and allow specified quantities of solution to distribute over surface of glass. Electroplates copper backing over silvering by immersing glass in electrolyte and passing electric current through solution according to standard procedure. Places plated glass in electric oven to dry for specified time. Marks outlines of specified dimensions on glass specimen, using milling machine. Removes excess silvering and copper, using hand scraper and solvents.
GOE: 06.04.33 STRENGTH: L GED: R3 M1 L1 SVP: 4 DLU: 77

574.582-010 SILVERING APPLICATOR (glass products)

Sets up and operates silvering range to mix and spray tin, silver, and copper solutions on mirror glass: Weighs or measures chemical ingredients, following formula. Turns valves to admit steam and specified amount of water into mixing vat. Verifies water temperature and pours ingredients into vat. Starts power mixer to mix solutions for specified time. Turns valve to drain solutions into storage tanks. Starts unit of range and turns valves to start flow of solutions into spray heads. Observes silvering process to detect clogged sprays, uneven silver and copper coating, and imperfections, such as streaks and spots, and color of sludge, that indicate impure water or faulty copper and silver mix. Turns valves to regulate air pressure to sprayer and to maintain specified water temperature. Removes spray heads and pipes with wrenches and soaks spray

heads in cleaning fluid. Records batches mixed and chemicals used. May measure and record thickness of silver coating, using gauge.
GOE: 06.02.21 STRENGTH: M GED: R3 M2 L2 SVP: 5 DLU: 77

574.585-010 PAPERHANGER (concrete prod.)

Tends machine that combines paper and plaster to form continuous ribbon of wallboard (plasterboard): Inserts shaft through paper roll, places plates and collars over ends of shaft, and secures collars with wrench. Mounts and aligns rolls of paper in machine racks, using hoist. Threads paper through guides with unsized surface next to plaster. Starts and monitors machine for alignment and defective paper, such as pinholes, rough surface, mill splices, and soiled areas. Stops machine to cut defective paper from roll and splice ends by overlapping them and to splice exhausted paper to new roll. Records identifying number, weight, and amount of paper wasted for each roll.
GOE: 06.04.19 STRENGTH: M GED: R2 M2 L1 SVP: 2 DLU: 77

574.665-010 FIBERGLASS-BONDING-MACHINE TENDER (glass mfg.) alternate titles: bonded-strand operator

Tends waxing machine that bonds several strands of fiberglass yarn into single cord: Places bobbins of yarn on creel of machine and threads yarn through guides, over and under tension bars, through strip heater, wax reservoir, dies, and cooling tank, and laps end of cord around mandrel of winding machine. Places chunks of wax in melting tank and turns valve to admit melted wax into reservoir. Starts machine and observes waxing and winding process to detect broken ends. Ties ends together by hand. Dips thermometer into wax and water or reads temperature gauge on control panel to detect variations from standards. Doffs tubes of bonded cord from machine. Weighs tubes of bonded cord and packs cord in shipping containers. Records weight on labels and production records.
GOE: 06.04.16 STRENGTH: L GED: R2 M2 L2 SVP: 2 DLU: 77

574.667-010 DUST BOX WORKER (build. mat., nec)

Positions swinging conveyor spout over hopper of machine that deposits slate granules on surface of asphalt-coated roofing felt, and notifies SLATE MIXER (build. mat., nec) to start conveyor and flow of slate of specified color. Verifies level of slate in tanks to maintain supply.
GOE: 06.04.34 STRENGTH: L GED: R2 M1 L1 SVP: 2 DLU: 77

574.682-010 FIBERGLASS-MACHINE OPERATOR (glass products)

Operates machine to spray melted glass fibers onto products, such as boat hulls and lawn furniture: Feeds strands of raw fiberglass into machine, monitors gauges, and moves controls to obtain specified temperature, pressure, and flow rate of molten glass through spray jets onto article to be coated. Cleans and adjusts machine, according to maintenance schedule or instructions from supervisor, using handtools and prescribed cleaning agents.
GOE: 06.02.13 STRENGTH: M GED: R3 M2 L1 SVP: 4 DLU: 77

574.682-014 SPRAY-MACHINE OPERATOR (brick & tile; pottery & porc.) alternate titles: sprayer, automatic spray machine

Controls combination drying oven and spray booth equipment that preheats and glazes bisque ware: Lights gas jets of drying ovens that preheat ware to set glaze. Adjusts controls to regulate speed of conveyor. Starts pumps to pump glaze to spray guns. Positions spray guns in booths at required angles, adjusts nozzles, and turns valves controlling air pressure to produce even coating of glaze according to size and shape of ware. Examines glazed ware for cracks, glaze runs, and uneven thickness of glaze. Cleans machine and replaces clogged glaze filters, air lines, and spray nozzles. May coat interior of ware with glaze, using spray gun.
GOE: 06.02.21 STRENGTH: M GED: R3 M2 L1 SVP: 3 DLU: 81

574.684-010 GROUND LAYER (pottery & porc.) alternate titles: duster

Applies powdered glaze to plain or decorated clayware: Dusts dry glaze over portion of ware previously coated with liquid size. Removes excess powder and distributes glaze evenly over sized area, by hand. May smooth and clean ware to be dusted, using sandpaper and sponge.
GOE: 06.04.33 STRENGTH: L GED: R2 M1 L1 SVP: 3 DLU: 77

574.684-014 SILVERER (glass products) alternate titles: mirror silverer

Sprays back of mirror glass with silver or copper solution to coat glass, using spray gun: Turns valve to admit solution and reducing agents into spray gun and sprays surface of glass. Rinses glass with hose before and after application of solution to remove residue. Observes sprayed surface to detect spots, streaks, and residue coloring that indicate faulty mix or reducer burns. Transfers silvered or coppered glass from rack onto conveyor of drying ovens. May clean, polish, and frame mirrors.
GOE: 06.04.33 STRENGTH: M GED: R3 M1 L1 SVP: 3 DLU: 77

574.685-010 COATER, BRAKE LININGS (nonmet. min.)

Tends machine that automatically coats inside of brake lining with adhesive preparatory to bonding lining to brake shoe: Starts machine and conveyor and feeds brake lining into machine to obtain sample for approval by supervisor. Feeds brake linings into machine and observes coating for conformance to specifications as linings are discharged onto conveyor. Places linings with coating defects aside for disposal.
GOE: 06.04.21 STRENGTH: S GED: R2 M1 L2 SVP: 2 DLU: 77

574.685-014 PAINT-SPRAY TENDER (glass products)

Tends paint spraying and drying units of mirror-silvering range that spray and dry paint coatings on silvered glass: Measures paint and thinner, according

to formula, and pours paint into storage tank. Turns valves to start power mixer and flow of paint to spray heads. Pushes button to start spray heads across conveyor, to clear thinner from paint lines, and to spray paint on silvered glass. Observes painting area to detect uneven spray. Reads pressure gauges and turns valves to adjust paint flow and air pressure. Regulates oven temperature as specified. Removes spray nozzles and pipelines with wrenches and cleans equipment, using solvents. Pours paint thinner into paint lines to prevent paint residue from hardening and clogging paint lines. May determine amount of paint applied to glass, comparing sample with factory standard, or weighing glass before and after painting. May disassemble carriage and replace worn or broken parts of spraying unit.
GOE: 06.04.21 STRENGTH: M GED: R3 M2 L1 SVP: 4 DLU: 77

574.686-010 SPRAY-MACHINE LOADER (brick & tile; pottery & porc.)
Feeds or off bears machine operated by SPRAY-MACHINE OPERATOR (brick & tile; pottery & porc.) 574.682-014 that sprays glaze onto bisque tile or pottery ware. Examines sprayed ware and segregates defective pieces.
GOE: 06.04.21 STRENGTH: L GED: R2 M1 L1 SVP: 2 DLU: 78

575 FORMING OCCUPATIONS

This group includes occupations concerned with shaping material by pouring, injecting, blowing, gathering, bending, or pressing it in, upon, or around a mold, die or similar device; forcing or pulling it through dies or rollers; drawing it from an emitting source at rates of speed and temperatures which determine its diameter. Includes baking, drying, and cooling of formed materials when done by the worker who formed them.

575.130-010 PRESS SUPERVISOR (brick & tile)
Supervises and coordinates activities of workers engaged in operating auger presses, friction presses, handpresses, and ram presses to press clay into products, such as brick, tile, and sewer pipe, and in drying products for firing. Performs duties as described under SUPERVISOR (any industry) Master Title.
GOE: 06.02.01 STRENGTH: M GED: R4 M3 L2 SVP: 7 DLU: 78

575.130-014 SUPERVISOR III (nonmet. min.)
Supervises and coordinates activities of workers engaged in molding, curing, and cutting fiberglass pipe coverings: Sets up and adjusts machinery and equipment. Trains new workers in operation of machinery and equipment. Performs other duties as described under SUPERVISOR (any industry) Master Title.
GOE: 06.02.01 STRENGTH: M GED: R3 M2 L2 SVP: 5 DLU: 77

575.130-018 SUPERVISOR, FORMING DEPARTMENT I (glass mfg.)
Supervises and coordinates workers engaged in operating either press-and-blow, blow-and-blow, or spin forming machines and controlling auxiliary equipment, such as forehearths and lehrs, used to form glass bottles, containers, and other glassware: Reviews production schedules to plan job change-overs, to requisition molds and parts from mold department, and to assign workers. Observes machine operations to verify mold pressures and temperatures, plunger pressures, timing of sequences, and size of gob (lump of molten glass), using knowledge of machine operation and product specifications. Inspects formed glassware for surface defects and conformance to specifications for size, shape, and weight, using templates, dial indicators, and scales. May make or assist in making job change-overs by removing and replacing molds, air lines *feeder tubes,* and plungers, and by adjusting gob shears and timing mechanism, using handtools and knowledge of job change-over procedures. May regulate and adjust temperatures and conveyor speeds of annealing lehr. May be designated Supervisor, Bottle Machines (glass mfg.). Performs other duties described under SUPERVISOR (any industry) Master Title.
GOE: 06.02.01 STRENGTH: M GED: R4 M3 L3 SVP: 7 DLU: 77

575.131-010 SUPERVISOR, CONCRETE-STONE FABRICATING (concrete prod.) alternate titles: casting supervisor
Supervises and coordinates activities of workers engaged in casting concrete with granite, quartz, or vitreous porcelain to form structural panels, floor and roof slabs, flower planters, highway dividers, and grave markers. Performs duties as described under SUPERVISOR (any industry) Master Title.
GOE: 06.02.01 STRENGTH: L GED: R4 M3 L2 SVP: 7 DLU: 77

575.131-014 SUPERVISOR, PRECAST AND PRESTRESSED CONCRETE (concrete prod.)
Supervises and coordinates activities of workers engaged in assembly of precut wood and metal forms for molding reinforced concrete slabs and beams, and pouring and finishing of concrete: Lays out and marks measurements for assembly of new forms on prepared molding floor, from blueprints and drawings. Directs workers engaged in bolting or clamping together of forms and tightens bolts to attain prescribed tension on wire or cable reinforcing members, using wrench equipped with torque gauge. Directs workers engaged in mixing, and pouring of concrete into molds. Finishes concrete to impart uniform texture, using trowel, floats, and other handtools or work aids. Releases tension on reinforcing members during drying and curing process, using wrench, to impart slight arc and increase strength of concrete.
GOE: 05.05.01 STRENGTH: M GED: R4 M3 L3 SVP: 7 DLU: 78

575.137-010 DRAWING-KILN SUPERVISOR (glass mfg.)
Supervises and coordinates activities of workers engaged in melting and drawing of glass into sheet form: Reads recorder instruments to verify specified melting-tank temperatures. Observes glass drawing process to ensure glass is drawn to specifications. Determines cause of malfunctioning equipment or defects in glass, and advises DRAWING-KILN OPERATOR (glass mfg.) of action necessary for correction. Performs other duties as described under SUPERVISOR (any industry) Master Title.
GOE: 06.02.01 STRENGTH: L GED: R4 M3 L3 SVP: 5 DLU: 77

575.137-014 SUPERVISOR, WET POUR (concrete prod.)
Supervises and coordinates activities of workers engaged in setting up forms and pouring wet-mix concrete to make water and sewer pipe, manholes, steel wire reinforcing cages, and to repair damaged pipe. May conduct quality control tests on finished products. Performs duties as described under SUPERVISOR (any industry) Master Title.
GOE: 06.02.01 STRENGTH: M GED: R4 M2 L2 SVP: 7 DLU: 77

575.360-010 GLASS-BULB-MACHINE ADJUSTER (glass mfg.)
Sets up and adjusts automatic, multiunit, bulb-forming machines, using handtools, work orders, and measuring devices: Installs fixtures, such as collets, tube feeders, and molds, and attaches fuel, air, and coolant lines to machine, following specifications. Adjusts controls, such as stop guides, setscrews, timing devices, and cams to synchronize machine mechanisms. Regulates temperature control of burner units. Replaces defective parts, such as collets, molds, seals, and fuel, air, and coolant lines. Starts machine to test adjustments and examines product to determine need for readjustments.
GOE: 06.01.02 STRENGTH: M GED: R4 M3 L3 SVP: 6 DLU: 77

575.362-010 DRAWING-KILN OPERATOR (glass mfg.) alternate titles: drawing-machine operator; kiln operator
Operates drawing kiln to process molten glass into continuous sheet of flat glass: Sets rheostat to control speed of rolls on kiln that draw glass sheet of specified thickness, and adjusts setting to maintain thickness, based on gauge or recorder readings during processing. Regulates gas-firing to edges of glass sheet to prevent slippage of sheet from knurl guide wheels. Inspects glass sheet through kiln peephole for defects, such as stones and blisters, as sheet is drawn vertically by rolls. Signals BALCONY WORKER (glass mfg.) to open rolls and allow passage of defective area to prevent break in sheet. Receives gauge readings and positions asbestos pads on sides of cooling jacket in kiln with iron rod to correct irregular thickness in glass sheet. Closes lower roll of drawing kiln to prevent broken sheets of glass from collapsing into kiln. Lights auxiliary gas jets in kiln to heat glass sheet below break and stop run of break. Replaces jacket cooling pads and plugs in kiln with mortar, using trowel.
GOE: 06.02.13 STRENGTH: L GED: R3 M2 L2 SVP: 3 DLU: 77

575.362-014 GLASS-RIBBON-MACHINE OPERATOR (glass mfg.)
Sets up and operates automatic machine to form bulbs and other products from molten glass: Installs molds, forming devices, and orifice plates, following specifications. Positions forming mechanisms between forehearth and lehr. Turns controls to regulate temperatures and pressures in forehearth and forming molds and flow of coolant on rollers. Verifies temperature of molten glass in forehearth, using optical pyrometer. Raises plunger forehearth orifice to start flow of molten glass through machine units. Adjusts rollers to control glass thickness, using handtools and measuring devices. Monitors gauges, such as temperature, pressure, machine speed, and rate of glass flow. Examines for variations from processing standards, using templates and gauges.
GOE: 06.02.13 STRENGTH: L GED: R4 M3 L3 SVP: 7 DLU: 77

575.365-010 GLASS-RIBBON-MACHINE-OPERATOR ASSISTANT (glass mfg.)
Tends intermediate units of machine that forms bulbs and other products from molten glass: Positions turntable at crack-off (breaking) unit and synchronizes motion of hammer with flow of molten glass to separate bulbs from ribbon. Turns controls to regulate machine speed, flow of coolant on molten glass, and temperature in machine units. Aligns glass ribbon in units with wooden pole, following signal from GLASS-RIBBON-MACHINE OPERATOR (glass mfg.). Inspects orifice plates for damage and cleans excess glass from plate, using hammer.
GOE: 06.02.13 STRENGTH: L GED: R3 M2 L3 SVP: 6 DLU: 77

575.380-010 FORMING-MACHINE UPKEEP MECHANIC (glass mfg.) alternate titles: upkeep mechanic
Sets up, adjusts, and repairs automatic glass forming machines, such as press-and-blow, blow-and-blow, and spinning machines, used to form bottles, containers, and other glassware, utilizing knowledge of glass forming machinery: Reads work order to determine which molds, mold components, and machine parts are needed. Removes molds, mold components, and *feeder tubes* from machines, using handtools. Mounts blanking mold and final mold to hanger arms on machine, and installs gob (lump of molten glass) feeder tube leading from forehearth to molds, using handtools. Installs and aligns *neck rings* and press plunger to blanking mold to form neck and mouth of glassware, using handtools. Couples air lines to molds and coolant lines to mold jacket to regulate solidification of glass. Adjusts size of orifice which releases gob from forehearth, and shears cutting gob to control size of gob fed to mold, using handtools. Adjusts *trip buttons* on *timer drum* to set gob feeding, blank molding, final molding, and discharge sequence. Couples gas line to preheating burner under mold to maintain plasticity of glass during molding. Turns controls that regulate air pressures, coolant flows, gas line pressure, and glass temperatures in forehearth to form acceptable products, using knowledge of machine operation and product specifications. Performs test run and inspects glassware to verify setup. Repairs damaged machines by replacing defective parts,

such as cams, hanger arms, or forming components, using handtools. Changes lehr drive gears to control annealing time of glassware in lehr. May be assisted by FORMING-MACHINE OPERATOR (glass mfg.) in setting up machines. May ascertain temperature of gob, using pyrometer.
GOE: 06.01.02 STRENGTH: M GED: R4 M3 L3 SVP: 7 DLU: 77

575.381-010 MOLDER (optical goods)

Molds optical glass into various shaped blanks: Reads work order to determine type and quantity of optical glass to be molded. Changes dies and adjusts length of stroke and pressure of press, and regulates temperature of ovens and die heater according to type of glass to be processed. Places glass pieces in preheating oven to prepare glass for molding. Spreads refractory powder on oven floor to prevent glass from sticking and places preheated glass in oven. Presses glass pieces with paddles to determine readiness for molding and to shape glass to approximate shape of spoon die. Slides glass into spoon die, positions die in press, and depresses foot pedal to lower ram of press to mold glass blank. Removes spoon die from press and drops molded blank onto floor of cooling oven.
GOE: 06.02.30 STRENGTH: M GED: R3 M2 L2 SVP: 6 DLU: 77

575.382-010 BRICK-AND-TILE-MAKING-MACHINE OPERATOR (brick & tile)

Sets up and operates series of machines to mix ingredients, extrude clay mixture, and to cut extruded column into brick and tile products: Turns valves to feed and regulate flow of ingredients into mixing machine and to create vacuum in de-airing machine. Installs die, core, rings, and former in extrusion head, using handtools and measuring instruments. Sets controls on automatic cutoff knives to cut clay column according to job order specifications. Starts machinery. Examines extruded product to detect variations from specified hardness, and turns valves to feed water and oil into pug mill to correct consistency of clay. Replaces knives, reamers, and finishers in automatic finishing units. Records production. May operate individual machine and be designated Auger-Press Operator (brick & tile); Cutter Operator, Brick (brick & tile); Cutter Operator, Tile (brick & tile); Pug Mill Operator (brick & tile; pottery & porc.).
GOE: 06.02.17 STRENGTH: M GED: R3 M2 L2 SVP: 5 DLU: 78

575.382-014 FORMING-MACHINE OPERATOR (glass mfg.) alternate titles: automatic forming machine operator; flow machine operator; glass blower, machine forming

Sets up and operates automatic glass forming machines that either press, blow, or spin gobs (lumps) of molten glass in molds to form bottles, containers, cathode ray tubes, and other glass products: Adjusts shears to cut or plungers to force gobs from forehearth, using handtools. Installs and adjusts *feeder tubes* leading from forehearth to molds to deliver gob to mold, using wrenches. Mounts and bolts blanking molds and final molds to hanger arms on machine, or bolts molder to spinner plates, using handtools. Installs and aligns *neck rings* and press plungers to blanking molds, using wrenches, to form neck and mouths of product. Couples air lines to molds and coolant lines to mold jacket to regulate solidification of formed glass. Couples gas lines to burners under molds to maintain plasticity of glass during forming. Adjusts *trip buttons* on *timer drum* to set gob feeding, blank molding, final molding, and product discharging sequence. Turns controls to regulate air pressure, gas pressure, glass temperatures, and coolant flow. Observes machine operation to maintain sequences and air and fluid volumes, using knowledge of machine operation and product specifications. Frequently swabs molds with graphite solution to prevent glass from sticking to mold, using swab or spray gun. Periodically, visually examines product for surface defects that indicate damaged or scored molds and measures shape, size, and weight of product, using fixed gauges and scales to determine if air pressure, solidification rate, and gob size are correct. May regulate annealing lehrs to cool glass product. May be designated by product formed as Bottle-Machine Operator (glass mfg.). May be called Mold-Press Operator (glass mfg.) if operating press-and-blow machine with indexing turntable.
GOE: 06.02.13 STRENGTH: M GED: R3 M3 L2 SVP: 7 DLU: 77

575.382-018 GLASS-BULB-MACHINE FORMER, TUBULAR STOCK (glass mfg.)

Operates automatic, multiunit machine to form bulbs and other glass products from tubular stock: Loads glass tubes in feed mechanism and clamps collets around rods to secure and position tubular stock for molding process. Observes operation to determine variations from prescribed temperature levels, and turns controls, aims burners, or places and ignites auxiliary burners to adjust temperatures. Turns controls to regulate air pressure or vacuum processing in molds. Adjusts stops and guides that control indexing and positioning of glass rods in machine units to correct alignment or timing of sequence. Swabs molds with lubricant to prevent glass from adhering to mold walls. Replaces defective air and gas lines and tubes, using handtools. Inspects bulbs for color or transparency, size, shape, and wall thickness, using color panels, templates, and dial indicators.
GOE: 06.02.13 STRENGTH: M GED: R3 M2 L3 SVP: 5 DLU: 77

575.382-022 GLASS-ROLLING-MACHINE OPERATOR (glass mfg.)

Sets up and operates automatic machine to roll molten glass into sheets: Positions glass-rolling machine between glass-melting tank and lehr, using power winch. Connects drive chains to rollers and cooling pipes to waterlines, using handtools. Ignites burner to preheat lip (refractory bridge that supports flow of molten glass from furnace to rollers) and raises knife gate on tank orifice to

start flow of molten glass over lip onto rollers. Raises or lowers upper roller to regulate thickness of glass and adjusts rheostat control to regulate machine speed. Examines sheet of glass for defects, such as blisters and surface adhesions. Monitors gauges and recorders and records readings, such as lehr conveyor and machine speeds, water temperatures, and rate of glass flow.
GOE: 06.02.13 STRENGTH: L GED: R3 M2 L3 SVP: 6 DLU: 77

575.382-026 RETORT-OR-CONDENSER PRESS OPERATOR (brick & tile)

Operates mechanical or hydraulic press to mold fire-clay retorts or condensers used in smelting zinc ores: Packs plastic mixture of fire-clay into mold of press and closes mold. Pulls lever to actuate ram which forces clay into all parts of mold. Removes molded retort or condenser from press. Places protective jacket around retort or condenser, and puts it into drying chamber for seasoning.
GOE: 06.02.17 STRENGTH: L GED: R3 M1 L1 SVP: 4 DLU: 77

575.461-010 CONCRETE-STONE FABRICATOR (concrete prod.)

Casts mixture of concrete and aggregate in mold to form plain or decorative structural panels according to specifications and approved samples: Fits wooden sides of mold together and fastens them in place with wood clamps and bolts, using power wrench. Sprays or brushes acid and oil solution on inside of mold to prevent concrete from adhering to mold and to retard setting of concrete. Shovels and spreads mixed concrete and facing aggregate into mold and tamps mix with pneumatic vibrator to distribute facing evenly and to form facing of required thickness. Positions and fastens reinforcing materials, such as steel rods, wire mesh, hanger plates, and hoisting hooks in mold by hand, following specifications, using rule, gauges, wrenches, and wood clamps. Places hoist chain hooks in position on hopper filled with concrete backing mixture and moves controls of hoist to lift and position hopper over mold. Pushes hand lever of hopper to release backing mixture into mold and tamps mixture with pneumatic vibrator. Puddles and levels off casting, using wooden screed, and smooths surface with trowel. Unbolts wood clamps, using power wrench, and removes sides of mold by hand. Inserts overhead crane hooks in hoisting hook and presses hoist control buttons to lift casting and strikes mold, using rubber hammer, to separate casting from mold. Lowers casting onto skids and transports castings to storage area, using hydraulic lift truck. Brushes and scrapes concrete from sides and bottom of mold preparatory to next casting. May cast colored floor and roof slabs, highway dividers, ornamental flower pots, and grave markers.
GOE: 06.02.30 STRENGTH: H GED: R3 M2 L2 SVP: 7 DLU: 77

575.462-010 AUGER PRESS OPERATOR, MANUAL CONTROL (brick & tile)

Operates auger-press to press clay products, such as sewer pipe, drainpipe, and flue tile from tempered clay: Installs and adjusts extrusion dies, cores, rings, formers, and cutoff knives according to type of product, using handtools, calipers, and ring gauge. Moves levers to adjust automatic oilers. Starts press that forms, extrudes, and cuts clay to specified shape and length. Measures product for conformance to specifications, using scale and calipers. May move lever to position extruded tile or pipe column for cutting by DIE TRIPPER (brick & tile). May direct DIE TRIPPER (brick & tile) to change press dies. May be designated according to product pressed as Drain-Tile-Press Operator (brick & tile); Flue-Tile-Press Operator (brick & tile); Sewer-Pipe-Press Operator (brick & tile).
GOE: 06.02.08 STRENGTH: L GED: R3 M2 L2 SVP: 6 DLU: 77

575.565-010 LINING-MACHINE OPERATOR (concrete prod.)

Tends machine that spins steel cylinder as inner surface is coated with concrete mortar to make reinforced concrete pipe: Lifts and rolls cylinder onto belt cradle of machine, using hoist, and aligns hot air blower with cylinder opening. Starts machine which rotates cylinder and signals BUCKET OPERATOR (concrete prod.) to feed mortar into rotating cylinder. Starts blower which vaporizes and removes moisture from mortar as cylinder spins. Stops machine when inner surface of cylinder is lined with layer of mortar. Slides rod through interlocking metal ends of lifting straps and moves cylinder to storage area, using hoist.
GOE: 06.04.21 STRENGTH: L GED: R2 M1 L1 SVP: 2 DLU: 77

575.662-010 DRY-PRESS OPERATOR (brick & tile) alternate titles: molder, machine

Operates machine to press dry tempered clay or silica into brick and other shapes: Selects and installs upper and lower pressing dies, using rule and hand wrenches. Starts machine and observes flow of clay and pressing process. Measures brick with set-limit gauge and turns handwheel to adjust die. Removes bricks from press bed and stacks bricks in specified pattern on kiln car. Signals LABORER, GENERAL (brick & tile) to move loaded car and bring up empty car. May be designated according to material pressed as Clay-Dry-Press Operator (brick & tile); Silica-Dry-Press Operator (brick & tile).
GOE: 06.02.17 STRENGTH: M GED: R3 M2 L2 SVP: 5 DLU: 77

575.662-014 YARDAGE-CONTROL OPERATOR, FORMING (glass mfg.)

Controls temperature of bushings and speed of winders on fiberglass forming machines to maintain specified yardage per pound in sliver: Monitors bushing control panels, temperature charts, and indicators to determine if temperature of furnace bushings, molten glass over bushings, forehearths, and canals meet specifications. Obtains test skein of sliver from TEST-SKEIN WINDER (glass mfg.) and dries skein for specified time in electric furnace. Weighs dried test

Processing Occupations

skein to obtain weight in grams and converts weight to yards per pound to determine deviations from specifications, using yardage conversion chart. Turns digital dial on bushing control panel to regulate temperature of bushings. Tests voltage on compensator units that vary speed of collets (winding rings), using voltage meter. Determines bushing temperature specified for voltage reading from table and turns button to set temperature and regulate speed of collet. Records data, such as shift, crew, date, time of temperature reading, time of yardage reading, type of sliver produced, temperatures, and adjustments made, in yardage control log.
GOE: 06.02.13 STRENGTH: L GED: R3 M3 L3 SVP: 5 DLU: 77

575.664-010 CENTRIFUGAL SPINNER (concrete prod.) alternate titles: feeder operator; spinner, concrete pipe
Performs any combination of following tasks to coat concrete pipe in metal molds: Slides prepared wire mesh cage into mold and secures cage with short lengths of wire. Places cotton rope gasket between flanges along length of split mold. Bolts mold halves together and fastens bell ring and guide wheels into place, using hand and power wrenches. Signals operator of hoist or industrial truck to transfer mold onto wheels of spinning machine. Starts spinning machine and adjusts controls of filling machine to feed wet concrete into spinning mold, to specified level. Increases speed of rotating mold for specified length of time to set concrete. Pushes pole and brush against inside of spinning pipe to finish surface. Signals worker to move mold to curing area or uses chain hoist. Covers mold with plastic tarpaulin and turns on steam to cure concrete. Removes, cleans, and oils mold when concrete is cured, using hand and power wrenches and brushes. May adjust filling machine to accommodate size of pipe, using handtools.
GOE: 06.04.21 STRENGTH: M GED: R2 M1 L1 SVP: 2 DLU: 77

575.665-010 CONCRETE-PIPE-MAKING-MACHINE OPERATOR (concrete prod.)
Tends machine that casts concrete draintile or pipe by either of following methods: (1) Positions metal mold specified for pipe size on floor stand of machine beneath core and spout. Lowers core into mold and pulls overhead tamping bar into position in mold. Starts machine to rotate mold and activate tamping bar. Releases supply of wet concrete from hopper into mold. Trowels concrete at top of filled mold to level off end of pipe. Stops machine for removal of mold by PIPE STRIPPER (concrete prod.). (2) Positions and bolts pallet rings specified for pipe size to turntable and bottom of feed table. Positions and screws packer head on drive shaft. Resets trip lever to adjust feed table height. Starts machine which lowers packer head into mold and conveys supply of concrete to feed table. Rakes concrete from feed table into mold as packer head rises and descends to tamp concrete in mold. Steps on pedal to rotate turntable for automatic removal of filled mold and positioning of empty mold. Feels concrete and signals worker to increase or decrease moisture of mixture. May be designated according to type of product made as Drain-Tile Machine Operator (concrete prod.); or according to type of machine tended as Packerhead-Machine Operator (concrete prod.).
GOE: 06.04.19 STRENGTH: M GED: R2 M1 L1 SVP: 2 DLU: 77

575.665-014 DIE TRIPPER (brick & tile) alternate titles: greaser
Tends machine that cuts extruded tile or pipe clay column to specified lengths: Swabs press die with oil between operations to prevent adhesion of clay. Moves levers in coordination with movements of machine and AUGER PRESS OPERATOR, MANUAL CONTROL (brick & tile) to form bell or socket of pipe and to cut it to size. May change press dies.
GOE: 06.04.17 STRENGTH: M GED: R2 M2 L1 SVP: 2 DLU: 77

575.665-018 SHOT-COAT TENDER (concrete prod.)
Tends machine that coats external surface of rotating steel cylinder with concrete mortar to make reinforced concrete pipe: Pulls lever to open chucks of machine and signals worker to position cylinder between chucks. Closes chucks to secure cylinder for spinning and presses button to rotate cylinder and move it along track at preset rate. Moves lever to regulate flow of mortar from revolving brushes or into space between two parallel moving belts which compress mortar and spray or throw mortar onto exterior of rotating cylinder moving along track. Stops machine, releases chucks, and signals INDUSTRIAL-TRUCK OPERATOR (any industry) to remove mortar coated cylinder to curing area.
GOE: 06.04.21 STRENGTH: L GED: R2 M1 L1 SVP: 2 DLU: 77

575.682-010 FIBERGLASS-DOWEL-DRAWING-MACHINE OPERATOR (plastic prod.) alternate titles: solid-glass-rod-dowel-machine operator
Sets up and operates fiberglass drawing machine to form fiberglass dowels: Mounts specified dies in soak tank and curing tables, using handtools. Sets stop at end of curing table, according to specified length of dowel, and turns switches to start electrical heating units along curing tables. Pours specified amounts of resin and catalyst into mixer, starts mixer, and pours mixture, after specified period, into soak tank. Mounts spools of fiberglass roving on spindles, draws strands through guides into soak tank, and starts ends of resin soaked fibers through preform die. Attaches fiberglass strands to end of previous dowel, or ties strands to wire, and draws fibers through diameter control tube. Starts motor to draw fiberglass through soak tank, preform die, diameter control tubes, and curing oven. Saws off cured dowels at specified length or removes dowels cut by automatic cutoff saw. Observes color and shape of dowels for conformance to standards. Adjusts controls to regulate temperature of oven and drawing speed to obtain conformance to standards.

GOE: 06.04.13 STRENGTH: L GED: R3 M2 L1 SVP: 4 DLU: 77

575.682-014 MOLDING-MACHINE OPERATOR (toy-sport equip.)
Operates press to cast resined glass into glass bows: Cleans molds and applies wax to mold, using swab. Cuts glass from winder reel and places glass into mold to fill mold as specified. Pulls top mold and press down into position. Opens press and removes bow. May keep production records.
GOE: 06.02.18 STRENGTH: M GED: R3 M1 L1 SVP: 4 DLU: 77

575.682-018 PRESS OPERATOR (brick & tile)
Operates machine to press clay into products, such as wall tile, trim tile, and mosaic floor tile: Feels consistency of clay in hopper to determine that mixture meets texture and dampness specifications. Fills feedbox, shaker box, and die cavity with clay. Levels and removes excess clay from die, using cutting stick. Depresses pedal, moves lever, or turns handwheel to lower top die and press out product. Removes product from die and measures thickness, using gauge. Adjusts press to obtain product of specified thickness. Cleans and oils die cavity and adjusts fettling tools on off-bearing belt. May tend automatic hydraulic press that presses clay into products.
GOE: 06.02.08 STRENGTH: M GED: R2 M1 L1 SVP: 3 DLU: 78

575.682-022 RAM-PRESS OPERATOR (pottery & porc.)
Sets up and operates hydraulic ram press to form ware: Positions hydrostone (plaster) die on bed of press, using hoist. Clamps upper and lower halves of die to ram and bed of press. Connects airhose to die. Aligns die, using pins, jacks, and measuring device. Cuts pugged (plastic) clay to specified size and places clay on die face. Presses control to lower ram to shape ware. Depresses pedal to force air through die and release ware from bed of press. Moves control to raise ram and release ware from die. Holds setter under ram to allow ware to drop on setter as it is released. Inspects ware for specified thickness and adjusts position of die if necessary. Sponges die to remove moisture and removes scrap clay, using knife. May turn controls to adjust length and timing of ram stroke according to type ware pressed.
GOE: 06.02.08 STRENGTH: M GED: R3 M2 L1 SVP: 5 DLU: 77

575.683-010 BUCKET OPERATOR (concrete prod.)
Operates track-mounted machine, equipped with traveling pouring bucket, to cast reinforced concrete pipe: Moves lever to position bucket under hopper of cement buggy to receive cement. Pulls levers and turns handwheels to move machine along track, and to pour cement from bucket into rotating metal pipe (can) which acts as a mold and remains as reinforcement. Observes interior of can and withdraws bucket when concrete is level with lip of mold ring. Washes bucket, using water hose.
GOE: 06.04.40 STRENGTH: L GED: R2 M1 L1 SVP: 3 DLU: 77

575.684-010 BATTER-OUT (pottery & porc.) alternate titles: batter
Prepares clay for forming into pottery and porcelain ware by either of following methods: (1) Pulls chunk of clay from large roll or picks up clay slab cut by machine. Centers clay on rotating horizontal wheel and pulls lever to lower tool that flattens clay and forms bat. Throws bat onto jigger mold and pulls lever to lower tool that spreads clay firmly over mold. (2) Shapes clay into ball by hand and throws clay into jolly mold used in making such hollowware as cups and bowls.
GOE: 06.04.30 STRENGTH: M GED: R2 M1 L2 SVP: 4 DLU: 77

575.684-014 CASTER (pottery & porc.) alternate titles: pourer
Casts pottery and porcelain ware in plaster of paris molds: Fills molds with slip (semiliquid clay), using hose from slip supply tank, or bucket. Pours excess slip from molds when accumulation of clay around inside of mold opening indicates clay shell inside mold has built up to specified thickness. Changes position of molds to produce uniform shell thickness of irregularly shaped items. Places molds upside down to drain. Trims excess clay from inside mold opening, opens mold, and removes green casting when experience and observation of shell indicate casting is firm enough to handle. Smooths casting surfaces to remove mold marks, using knives and wet sponge, and places castings on boards to dry. May attach handles [HANDLER (pottery & porc.) 774.684-022].
GOE: 06.02.30 STRENGTH: M GED: R2 M1 L1 SVP: 2 DLU: 81

575.684-018 CASTER (nonmet. min.)
Casts plaster of paris objects, such as ashtrays, piggybanks, lamps, figurines, and statuary, using prepared molds: Assembles sections of prepared mold and secures them together with cord, clamps, or bolts, and nuts. Dumps plaster of paris into container, adds specified amount of water, and stirs mixture to required consistency to make casting, using spatula. Inserts wires and tubing into mold to reinforce casting when necessary. Pours plaster of paris into mold, shakes mold to distribute layer of plaster of paris on inside of mold and pours off excess mixture. Repeats process after each layer hardens until specified thickness of casting is attained. Disassembles mold, fills holes and defects in casting with plaster of paris, and smooths surface of casting, using scraping tool and sandpaper.
GOE: 06.02.30 STRENGTH: H GED: R2 M1 L1 SVP: 4 DLU: 77

575.684-022 CROSSCUTTER, ROLLED GLASS (glass mfg.)
Cuts continuous glass sheet into specified lengths as sheet emerges from drawing or rolling machine and removes defective cross sections, using suspended cutting wheel: Pulls lever to lower cutting wheel. Draws cutting wheel along template across surface of moving glass sheet to divide sheet into specified lengths. Observes sheet for defects, such as scratches, stones, bubbles, and pits, and draws cutting wheel across sheet to remove defective cross sections.

GOE: 06.04.30 STRENGTH: L GED: R2 M1 L2 SVP: 2 DLU: 77

575.684-026 GATHERER (glass mfg.) alternate titles: ball maker
 Dips punty (metal rod used to gather molten glass) or blowpipe into tank furnace to gather gob (lump) of molten glass for further processing: Reads product specifications to determine size of gob of molten glass to be gathered. Immerses head of punty or blowpipe into molten glass in furnace and turns punty or blowpipe to gather gob of molten glass. Twirls punty or blowpipe and blows through blowpipe to maintain gob of molten glass in globular form. Hands punty to PRESSER (glass mfg.) 575.685-074 or blowpipe to GLASS BLOWER (glass mfg.) 772.381-022 for further processing. May twirl gob of molten glass in container of alkali solution or in cavity of wet wooden block to form thin skin on gob of molten glass to prevent punctures in glassware during pressing or blowing. May hold punty in mold while PRESSER (glass mfg.) cuts off required amount of glass. May make head of punty from clay. May reheat gob to retain shape and temperature.
GOE: 06.04.30 STRENGTH: M GED: R2 M1 L2 SVP: 5 DLU: 79

575.684-030 HANDLE MAKER (pottery & porc.)
 Forms handles for clayware by either of following methods: (1) Pours slip (semiliquid clay) into mold. (2) Cuts pugged clay (plastic clay) to specified size, and places into segmented mold. Assembles and presses mold segments together by hand. (3) Opens valve of supply line (hose) and fills mold with slip. Places mold on drying rack. Opens mold and removes hardened handle. Trims and scrapes handles to remove excess clay, using knife. Cleans molds with airhose.
GOE: 06.04.30 STRENGTH: M GED: R2 M1 L1 SVP: 3 DLU: 77

575.684-034 LAUNDRY-TUB MAKER (concrete prod.)
 Forms tubs, using molds: Places wooden bottom section of mold on raised assembly-line track by hand. Sets core in position on bottom mold section and places metal rim around base. Fastens end and side sections of wooden (metal lined) mold together around core and to bottom section, using clamps and bolts. Binds assembled mold sections together with metal band, using ratchet-lever banding device and crimping pliers. Mixes concrete according to standard formula. Dumps concrete into wheelbarrow and pushes it to prepared molds. Shovels wet concrete into mold and tamps concrete, using tamper. Pushes metal drain fitting through wet concrete against core, or places drain fitting in core before shoveling concrete into mold. Smooths top of concrete, using trowel. Disassembles mold from partially cured casting and sprays completed tub with calcimine. May clean and oil mold sections. May crate finished tubs for shipment.
GOE: 06.02.30 STRENGTH: H GED: R3 M2 L2 SVP: 4 DLU: 77

575.684-038 MOLD MAKER, TERRA COTTA (brick & tile)
 Forms plaster molds used to shape terra cotta blocks: Fills wooden form with clay and slides template over clay surface to make model of face, end, and side of block. Brushes oil over hardened model and mixes and pours plaster over model to make mold. Assembles hardened plaster molds of face, ends, and sides, and seals joints with plaster to form block mold.
GOE: 06.04.32 STRENGTH: M GED: R2 M1 L1 SVP: 3 DLU: 77

575.684-042 MOLDER, HAND (brick & tile; elec. equip.)
 Molds odd-shaped brick, pipe, and other refractory products, using hand-molding tools: Kneads gobs of clay or silica mud to form molding mixture. Obtains specified mold from storage, or assembles molds, when necessary according to specifications. Brushes mold cavity with oil or hot wax to prevent casting from sticking to mold. Packs molding mixture into mold and tamps it with hand or automatic tamper. Removes excess mixture from top of mold, using wire or straightedge. Lifts and overturns mold on steel pallet to remove product. Finishes and smooths product, using hand-molding tools. Throws sand on casting to prevent bonding during subsequent firing. Stamps identifying code on product. Cleans and oils used molds. May tend pug mill that mixes clay or silica mud to form molding mixture. May place molds in furnace to cure. May stamp surface of refractory products, prior to curing, to impart specified pattern, using handtool. May embed heater coils wound through ceramic heaters with mud, and bake units to dry mud and be designated Embedder (elec. equip.). May be designated according to product molded as Brick-Molder, Hand (brick & tile); Pipe-Fittings Molder (brick & tile); Pot Maker (brick & tile); Shape-Brick Molder (brick & tile); Tile-Molder, Hand (brick & tile); or according to material used as Adobe Maker (brick & tile); Soft-Mud Molder (brick & tile).
GOE: 06.02.30 STRENGTH: H GED: R3 M1 L1 SVP: 3 DLU: 87

575.684-046 TERRAZZO-TILE MAKER (brick & tile)
 Molds pulverized marble, metallic oxides or pigment, cement, and water in specific pattern to form terrazzo tile: Mixes colored marble and metallic oxides with cement and water to prepare molding mixture. Inserts pattern in mold and applies layer of colored mixture over surface in sections of pattern to form design of tile face. Removes pattern and sprinkles mixture of dry cement and sand on mold to absorb moisture. Fills remainder of mold with wet cement and sand to form tile backing. Draws straightedge across top of mold to remove excess cement. Places block on mold and compresses tile in hydraulic press to obtain smooth surface on tile face. Removes mold from press and separates tile from die. May coat surface of die with oil to prevent tile from adhering to die.
GOE: 06.04.32 STRENGTH: M GED: R2 M1 L1 SVP: 3 DLU: 77

575.684-050 CULTURED-MARBLE-PRODUCTS MAKER (stonework)
 Casts and molds cultured marble products, such as sink basins and wall panels: Calculates amount of material, such as ground marble, resin, and catalyst, needed to make products, utilizing specifications on work order. Weighs materials, using scales, and pours materials into mixing machine. Pours specified amount of material into pail, adds color, and mixes ingredients to impart color to products, using wood paddle. Applies wax to mold sections to facilitate separation of products from molds, using cloth. Assembles cast, using bolts, and attaches sink mold to cast, using clamps. Sprays smoothing agent on mold and cast prior to pouring material. Pours material from mixing machine into cast on vibrating table, and applies colored mix randomly to material to impart marble appearance to product. Positions sink mold on previously cast product, and applies layers of mix by hand to form sinks. Disassembles mold, using handtools, and places products on racks for curing. Trims *flash* from molds, using portable sander or grinding wheel. Polishes surfaces of products to remove blemishes, using pumice and powered polisher.
GOE: 06.02.30 STRENGTH: H GED: R3 M2 L3 SVP: 5 DLU: 86

575.685-010 ABRASIVE-WHEEL MOLDER (nonmet. min.) alternate titles: molder
 Tends hydraulic press that molds synthetic abrasive disks, hones, and grinding wheels: Selects mold parts according to size and thickness of wheel desired, and assembles parts to form mold. Weighs out specified amounts of abrasive compound and adhesive or activates automatic hopper that dumps specified quantity of abrasive mix into pan, pours compound into mold on rotating turntable, and inserts bushings and hubnuts in center of mold to form wheel. Places top plate on mold, positions mold in press, and turns valves and levers to close press and start pressing cycle. Removes pressed wheels from mold and places wheels on bats (plate) for drying in kilns. May stamp or mark code numbers on pressed wheels. May mix grit, resin, and clay to form abrasive compound, using mixing machine. May be designated according to type of abrasive used as Diamond-Wheel Molder (nonmet. min.); Emery-Wheel Molder (nonmet. min.).
GOE: 06.02.18 STRENGTH: M GED: R3 M2 L1 SVP: 4 DLU: 78

575.685-014 BLOCK-MAKING-MACHINE OPERATOR (concrete prod.) alternate titles: block maker
 Tends automatic machine that casts concrete blocks: Starts and stops machine that automatically fills molds, vibrates molds to compact wet concrete, scrapes off excess concrete, and strips finished blocks from molds. Guides hoist to transfer pallets loaded with blocks to curing racks. May assist in setting up machine. May tend machine equipped with automatic off-bearing mechanism. May verify dimensions of formed blocks, using template.
GOE: 06.04.19 STRENGTH: M GED: R2 M2 L1 SVP: 4 DLU: 79

575.685-018 CHALK-EXTRUDING-MACHINE OPERATOR (pen & pencil)
 Tends automatic extruding machine and cutter that extrude and cut to length chalk billets: Loads billet into extrusion die, locks die in place, and starts machine that automatically forces billet through die onto cutting table. Places extruded chalk under cutter and depresses pedal to cut chalk to specified length.
GOE: 06.04.09 STRENGTH: L GED: R2 M1 L1 SVP: 3 DLU: 77

575.685-022 CHALK-MOLDING-MACHINE OPERATOR (pen & pencil)
 Tends machine that mixes and molds ingredients, using molding table, to make writing chalk: Weighs plaster, dyes, and other materials, according to formula. Places material in agitator and starts machine to mix ingredients. Pours mixture on molding table and smooths it over inlaid holes, using paddle. Pushes ejector button to remove hardened chalk from holes. May be designated according to materials molded as Crayon-Molding-Machine Operator (pen & pencil).
GOE: 06.04.19 STRENGTH: L GED: R2 M1 L1 SVP: 3 DLU: 77

575.685-026 DIE PRESSER (pottery & porc.) alternate titles: former; press operator; tube-machine operator
 Tends screw, mechanical, or hydraulic press that forms clay into electrical porcelain ware, such as insulators: Inserts die into bed of press. Pours moist, pulverized clay or ceramic powder into hopper of press. Starts press which deposits clay in die and lowers ram to form ware. Removes formed ware from die cavity and places ware on board for firing. May tend one or more presses that automatically form insulators. May inspect fired products to ensure conformance to specifications, using micrometer, go-not-go gauge, and microscope.
GOE: 06.04.08 STRENGTH: L GED: R3 M2 L1 SVP: 3 DLU: 77

575.685-030 FIBER-MACHINE TENDER (glass mfg.) alternate titles: forming operator; sliver former; sliver handler
 Tends one or more machines that form fiberglass filaments from molten glass and combine filaments into sliver: Pulls fiberglass filaments extruded through *bushing* over sleeve where binding solution is applied and into groove of graphite shoe that binds filaments into single strand of sliver. Passes sliver strand through opening in floor to FLOOR WINDER (textile) on floor below who winds sliver onto tubes. Patrols and observes bushings to detect defects, such as clogged bushings, beads, bead straps, and defective binder applicators. Stops machine and removes beads or bead straps from bushing with wire pick to unclog bushing. Notifies YARDAGE-CONTROL OPERATOR, FORMING (glass mfg.) or FORMING-MACHINE ADJUSTER (glass mfg.) of defective product or machine operation. Turns petcocks to adjust flow of binding fluid to sleeves. May turn rheostat on station to adjust specified temperature in electric furnace where glass is melted. May fill furnace hopper with glass marbles and adjust feed mechanisms so that marbles enter furnace at specified rate. May be designated according to length and fineness of fibers produced as Staple-Fiber-Machine Tender (glass mfg.).

GOE: 06.04.13 STRENGTH: L GED: R3 M1 L1 SVP: 3 DLU: 77

575.685-034 FLOWER-POT-PRESS OPERATOR (pottery & porc.) alternate titles: pot-press operator

Tends power press to form clay flowerpots: Fastens shaping die of specified size and shape on press and adjusts ram travel, using handtools. Throws ball of plastic clay into female die and presses switch to lower shaping die into clay and form pot. Lifts pot from die and places pot on ware board, using tongs.
GOE: 06.04.17 STRENGTH: L GED: R2 M1 L1 SVP: 2 DLU: 77

575.685-038 FORMING-MACHINE TENDER (glass mfg.) alternate titles: bottle-blowing-machine tender; press-and-blow-machine tender

Tends automatic glass forming machines, used to form bottles, containers, and other glassware from molten glass: Turns valves to regulate temperatures of molten glass in forehearth, flow of glass to forming machine, and coolant to solidify glass shape. Lubricates molds with graphite solution to prevent glass sticking to molds, using swab or spray gun. Inspects glassware to ascertain conformance with specifications, using fixed gauges and scales. May correct timing sequence by adjusting *timer drum*. May tend annealing lehr used to control cooling of formed product [LEHR TENDER (glass mfg.)].
GOE: 06.02.08 STRENGTH: M GED: R3 M2 L2 SVP: 4 DLU: 77

575.685-042 HOT-PRESS OPERATOR (nonmet. min.)

Tends hydraulic press that presses fiberglass cutouts into outer sides of grinding wheels: Picks up cloth cutout from supply stack and places it on steam-heated press table. Picks up grinding wheel from supply stack and positions it on cloth cutout. Picks up another cloth cutout and places it on grinding wheel. Presses electric switch to start machine that presses cloth cutouts into sides of wheel between press table and steam-heated plate. Removes grinding wheel from machine and places it on stack of finished workpieces.
GOE: 06.04.08 STRENGTH: M GED: R2 M1 L1 SVP: 3 DLU: 77

575.685-046 HYDRAULIC-BILLET MAKER (pen & pencil)

Tends hydraulic press that forms chalk billets: Scoops mixed ingredients into mold, closes cap, and pulls lever to pressurize ingredients. Releases cap and places billet on table for extrusion. Turns valve to regulate pressure.
GOE: 06.04.19 STRENGTH: L GED: R2 M1 L1 SVP: 3 DLU: 77

575.685-050 LEAD FORMER (pen & pencil) alternate titles: lead presser

Tends hydraulic press that extrudes graphite mixture to form pencil leads: Scoops mixture of clay, graphite, and other materials from pot and pours it into cylinder of machine. Pounds material to compact it in cylinder to eliminate air bubbles, using wooden mallet. Turns valve and observes dial to supply prescribed hydraulic pressure to ram. Starts machine that activates ram to force mixture through extrusion dies. May cut leads into specified lengths after they are extruded, dried, and deposited on machine table, using knife.
GOE: 06.04.19 STRENGTH: L GED: R1 M1 L1 SVP: 2 DLU: 77

575.685-054 LENS-MOLDING-EQUIPMENT OPERATOR (glass mfg.) alternate titles: glass bender; glass sagger; lens molder; punch press operator

Tends molding press or mold heating equipment to form lenses, such as speedometer and instrument faces or automotive lenses, such as taillights from glass rods, sheets, or disks: Forms lenses by either inserting heated glass rods in press mold and activating ram to press shape, or placing glass disks, preformed or cut from sheet, in mold and inserting mold in furnace to melt glass to shape of mold. May place weights on glass in mold to prevent warping during cooling. May preheat glass in oven to improve workability.
GOE: 06.04.13 STRENGTH: L GED: R2 M1 L1 SVP: 2 DLU: 77

575.685-058 MARBLE-MACHINE TENDER (glass mfg.)

Tends machine that automatically forms marbles of varying colors and sizes from molten glass: Adjusts flow of molten glass, temperature of cooling system, and size of automatic cutoff. Starts machine that cuts off glass lumps and drops them between rollers to form spheres.
GOE: 06.04.13 STRENGTH: L GED: R2 M2 L2 SVP: 3 DLU: 77

575.685-062 MOLDER-MACHINE TENDER (nonmet. min.)

Tends machines that heat and mold slurry into pipe and boiler coverings: Presses button on control panel of each molding machine to lower mold and activate hopper that automatically heats slurry, fills molds with slurry, and molds slurry into pipe and boiler coverings. Presses buttons on panels to raise finished moldings from machine and off bears moldings by hand. Discards defective moldings. Scrapes excess slurry from molds, using wooden blocks. Records type and quantity of moldings processed.
GOE: 06.04.17 STRENGTH: H GED: R2 M1 L1 SVP: 2 DLU: 77

575.685-066 MOLDER, FIBERGLASS LUGGAGE (leather prod.)

Tends laminating press that molds fiberglass preforms into luggage cases. Places preform in machine mold and pours specified amount of pigmented bonding solution into center of preform. Starts machine to lower rubber press onto preform and to apply heat and pressure for specified time. Opens gate and removes molded article.
GOE: 06.04.13 STRENGTH: L GED: R2 M1 L1 SVP: 2 DLU: 77

575.685-070 PRESS OPERATOR (mine & quarry)

Tends machine that compresses several plates of built-up mica into single plates of specified thickness: Inserts specified number of mica plates into each compartment of machine. Moves lever to close and seal door to machine compartments. Turns valves to circulate steam through machine to make plates pliable, activate ram that compresses pliable plates together, and to circulate water through machine to cool and harden compressed plates. Removes compressed plates from machine compartments.
GOE: 06.04.08 STRENGTH: L GED: R2 M1 L1 SVP: 3 DLU: 77

575.685-074 PRESSER (glass mfg.)

Tends press mold to cast glassware from molten glass: Cuts gob of molten glass from punty (metal rod used to gather molten glass), using hand shears, and allows gob of molten glass to drop into mold. Adjusts tension spring on mold plunger to regulate plunger pressure, using handtools. Positions mold against preset stops under plunger, pulls lever that lowers plunger into mold forcing molten glass to fill spaces in mold, and withdraws plunger from mold after specified time. Opens mold and removes ware, using pincers.
GOE: 06.04.30 STRENGTH: M GED: R2 M1 L1 SVP: 3 DLU: 77

575.685-078 SYNTHETIC-GEM-PRESS OPERATOR (jewelry-silver.)

Tends automatic press that molds pellets for use as synthetic gems: Installs die in press with handtools and loads hopper with pellets. Starts machine and observes that pellets are pressed into gems of specified size and shape. May mix ingredients from which pellets are made. May assist in polishing finished gems.
GOE: 06.04.02 STRENGTH: L GED: R2 M1 L1 SVP: 2 DLU: 77

575.685-082 TEST-SKEIN WINDER (glass mfg.) alternate titles: frickertron checker

Tends fiberglass forming and winding machines to obtain sample skeins of sliver used in testing yardage per pound: Inserts cord of timing instrument into wall outlet near machine from which sample is taken and releases pedal to start machine. Places arm of timing device against strands of sliver and pushes button to start timer. Stops winder after specified time and removes takeup tube. Removes test skein from tube and hangs skein on board designated for each furnace and *bushing*. Carries skeins to YARDAGE-CONTROL OPERATOR, FORMING (glass mfg.) for testing when sufficient skeins are obtained.
GOE: 06.04.16 STRENGTH: L GED: R3 M2 L3 SVP: 3 DLU: 77

575.686-010 DRY-PRESS-OPERATOR HELPER (brick & tile)

Assists DRY-PRESS OPERATOR (brick & tile) in pressing dry tempered clay or silica into brick or other shapes: Removes pallets loaded with brick and replaces empty pallets in position to receive brick from press. Places loaded pallets in rack of car. Removes defective pallets for repair. Removes bricks from molds, and places bricks on kiln car in specified pattern. Throws sand on bricks to level tiers. Moves rack or kiln cars into position near press and moves loaded cars away from press. Fills hoppers with sand and other material. Cleans press, dies, tables, and press pits, using handtools, shovels, and brooms. Performs other duties as described under HELPER (any industry) Master Title. May be designated according to materials pressed as Clay-Dry-Press Helper (brick & tile); Silica-Dry-Press Helper (brick & tile).
GOE: 06.04.17 STRENGTH: M GED: R1 M1 L1 SVP: 2 DLU: 77

575.686-014 MOLDER HELPER (optical goods) alternate titles: feeder

Feeds optical glass squares into furnace to heat glass to prescribed state of plasticity for molding: Spreads or sprinkles refractory powder on furnace floor or tray, by hand, to prevent adherence of heated glass to floor or tray. Positions glass squares on tray and slides tray into furnace, using paddle, or places squares on slide which automatically feeds squares into furnace and spaces them on furnace floor.
GOE: 06.04.13 STRENGTH: M GED: R1 M1 L1 SVP: 2 DLU: 77

575.686-018 PIN MAKER (pottery & porc.)

Feeds clay into hopper of machine that automatically forms potter pins used to support clayware during firing. Places formed pins in drier. May change die on machine according to size and shape of pins to be formed.
GOE: 06.04.17 STRENGTH: L GED: R2 M1 L1 SVP: 2 DLU: 77

575.687-010 BALCONY WORKER (glass mfg.) alternate titles: platform worker

Performs any combination of following duties to process molten glass into continuous sheet under direction of DRAWING-KILN OPERATOR (glass mfg.): Observes continuous sheet of glass for scratches, breaks, and other blemishes as it passes through rolls of drawing kiln. Wipes foreign matter from rolls and adjusts roll weights to minimize surface defects and breaks in glass. Moves controls to open rolls of drawing kiln when signaled by DRAWING-KILN OPERATOR (glass mfg.) to allow passage of stones and prevent breaks in glass. Opens air jets or draws metal rod across hot sheet of glass to prevent breaks from running. Adjusts slides on air ducts to cool glass and minimize warping. Clears broken glass from rolls. May transport cullet from work area to storage area, using handtruck.
GOE: 06.04.13 STRENGTH: L GED: R2 M1 L1 SVP: 2 DLU: 77

575.687-014 FORMING-MACHINE UPKEEP-MECHANIC HELPER (glass mfg.) alternate titles: mold changer

Assists FORMING-MACHINE UPKEEP MECHANIC (glass mfg.) in setting up and repairing bottle-forming machines and lubricates feeder chutes and molds: Removes and replaces glass-forming molds and components and adjusts shears and orifice rings (furnace channel opening), according to instructions, using handtools. Swabs or brushes feeder chutes and molds with oil or compound to prevent molten glass from sticking. Lubricates machine parts, using oilcan. Transfers molds to and from mold repair shop, using handtruck. Performs other duties as described under HELPER (any industry) Master Title.

GOE: 06.04.13 STRENGTH: M GED: R3 M2 L2 SVP: 3 DLU: 77

575.687-018 LABORER, PRESTRESSED CONCRETE (concrete prod.)
Performs any combination of following duties involved in preparing forms and pouring concrete to make prestressed structural beams: Cleans forms, using hammer, scraper, and brush, and sprays form with oil to prevent adhesion of concrete. Places reinforcing steel cage in form, using power winch. Pushes stressing cables through form, threads ends through guide holes in end plates, and clamps end of cables to plate. Tightens nuts at base of form with power wrench, and inserts spacer bars and locking pins at intervals along top of form to maintain specified dimensions of form. Clamps vibrators in holders on sides of forms. Lays planks on protruding ends of spacer bars to make elevated walkway on both sides of form. Lifts four-wheeled pouring buggy into position on walkway, using winch. Lifts belt conveyor into position between pouring buggy and ready-mix truck with winch and bolts it to truck, using power wrench. Starts conveyor and vibrators. Shovels sample of concrete into cannisters and tests consistency of concrete, using cone-shaped mold and trowel. Pushes pouring buggy along walkway to follow ready-mix truck. Settles concrete at top of form with hand vibrator, and fills low spots with concrete taken from conveyor. Removes forms from cured beams, using handtools, and cuts protruding end of stressing cable, using oxyacetylene torch. Lifts beam, using four-wheeled portable hoist (hoisting buggy), and moves hoist to yarding area by hand or with truck. May prepare forms and cast concrete lintels.
GOE: 06.04.34 STRENGTH: H GED: R1 M1 L1 SVP: 2 DLU: 78

575.687-022 MAT INSPECTOR (concrete prod.)
Examines mat of fiberglass insulation material for defects, picks out spots and foreign matter, and cuts out nonstandard portions: Scans mat for defects as mat passes inspection station of mat machine and picks out grease and binder spots and foreign matter, using knife. Lowers blade to cut thick or thin spots of mat that fail to meet standards. Records defect and mat machine downtime on production records. Aids MAT-MACHINE OPERATOR (concrete prod.) in guiding mat under pressure rollers, over inspection light and slitting knives, and under automatic cutters.
GOE: 06.03.02 STRENGTH: L GED: R3 M2 L2 SVP: 3 DLU: 77

575.687-026 PIPE STRIPPER (concrete prod.)
Moves metal molds containing wet concrete from pipemaking machine to steam-cooking area, using industrial truck or handtruck, and removes mold from concrete: Hooks pickup arms attached to frame of handtruck under lugs on sides of standing metal mold, and lifts and removes filled mold from pipemaking machine. Pushes truck to steam-cooking area and lowers mold to standing position on floor. Unclamps and removes mold halves by hand. Places mold halves around metal bottom stand and snaps clamps shut to reassemble mold. Places empty mold on floor near CONCRETE-PIPE-MAKING-MACHINE OPERATOR (concrete prod.). Shovels spilled concrete into return hopper or floor opening.
GOE: 06.04.40 STRENGTH: M GED: R1 M1 L1 SVP: 2 DLU: 77

575.687-030 PRESS-PIPE INSPECTOR (brick & tile) alternate titles: green-pipe inspector
Examines green sewer pipe for defects: Scans and feels exterior and interior of sewer pipe for blisters, cracks, or hollow areas. Marks unsatisfactory pipe, using chalk. May count rejected pipe sections.
GOE: 06.03.02 STRENGTH: L GED: R3 M2 L2 SVP: 2 DLU: 77

575.687-034 INSPECTOR I (pottery & porc.)
Examines automatically cast toilet bowls for molding defects: Moves toilet bowls from casting and drying area to inspecting area, using handtruck. Examines exterior and interior surfaces of bowls for defects, such as shape distortion, chips, or cracks. Marks defective bowls to indicate type and location of defects, using marking pencil. Applies glaze to specified areas of bowls, using paint brush, to prevent cracking during subsequent finishing. Records number and types of defects on product identification tags for inventory and production records. Places boards on roller conveyor to support bowls, positions bowls on boards, and pushes inspected bowls along conveyor for further finishing. Returns defective bowls to casting area for reworking.
GOE: 06.03.02 STRENGTH: H GED: R2 M1 L1 SVP: 2 DLU: 86

575.687-038 TIP-OUT WORKER (concrete prod.)
Removes concrete pipes from steam-curing chamber, with assistance of another worker, using hydraulic lifting device: Presses button to activate chain mechanism that conveys kiln cars containing cured pipes from curing chamber into position under lifting device. Presses button to activate lifting device that lowers, grips, and lifts pipes from vertical to horizontal position on kiln car. Strikes metal pallets around bell end of pipes to remove pallet from pipes, using sledgehammer. Rolls pipes from kiln cars onto metal rack to facilitate transporting of pipes to storage yard. Removes couplings that join kiln cars, pushes kiln cars onto chain conveyor, and activates conveyor to return cars and pallets to pipe making section.
GOE: 05.12.04 STRENGTH: V GED: R1 M1 L1 SVP: 2 DLU: 86

579 OCCUPATIONS IN PROCESSING OF STONE, CLAY, GLASS, AND RELATED PRODUCTS, N.E.C.

This group includes occupations, not elsewhere classified, concerned with preparing for market such raw materials as stone, clay, glass, and sand.

579.130-010 SUPERVISOR, BOARD MILL (concrete prod.)
Supervises and coordinates activities of workers engaged in operating equipment to mix plaster slurry, and to roll, perforate, mark, cut, and dry plaster wallboard and lath. Directs workers in operation of equipment. Performs duties as described under SUPERVISOR (any industry) Master Title.
GOE: 06.02.01 STRENGTH: L GED: R4 M3 L3 SVP: 8 DLU: 81

579.130-014 SUPERVISOR, CONCRETE BLOCK PLANT (concrete prod.)
Supervises and coordinates activities of workers engaged in mixing concrete, in setting up, maintaining, and operating concrete-block-making machines and equipment, and in curing and storing blocks. Performs duties as described under SUPERVISOR (any industry) Master Title.
GOE: 06.02.01 STRENGTH: L GED: R4 M3 L3 SVP: 7 DLU: 79

579.130-018 SUPERVISOR, CONCRETE PIPE PLANT (concrete prod.)
Supervises and coordinates activities of workers engaged in mixing concrete, setting-up, operating, and maintaining pipe plant machinery and equipment, and steam-curing concrete pipe. Performs duties as described under SUPERVISOR (any industry) Master Title.
GOE: 06.02.01 STRENGTH: L GED: R4 M3 L3 SVP: 7 DLU: 78

579.130-022 SUPERVISOR, FORMING DEPARTMENT II (glass mfg.)
Supervises and coordinates activities of workers engaged in batching, mixing, and melting raw materials to form molten glass, and in extrusion of fiberglass sliver: Observes automatic batching, weighing, and mixing equipment, furnaces, and forming machines to detect malfunctions. Reads charts, gauges, and control panels to verify maintenance of specified air supply, gas to air ratio, and temperatures of furnace and *bushings*. Adjusts or repairs malfunctioning machines and furnaces. Performs other duties as described under SUPERVISOR (any industry) Master Title.
GOE: 06.02.01 STRENGTH: L GED: R4 M3 L3 SVP: 6 DLU: 77

579.131-010 SUPERVISOR, MIRROR MANUFACTURING DEPARTMENT (glass products)
Supervises and coordinates activities of workers engaged in manufacturing mirrors: Mixes solutions for coating mirror glass. Coordinates operation of spray coating machine. Inspects completed mirror glass for bevel or cut to verify quality and quantity specifications. Performs other duties as described under SUPERVISOR (any industry) Master Title.
GOE: 06.02.01 STRENGTH: L GED: R4 M3 L2 SVP: 7 DLU: 77

579.132-010 SUPERVISOR II (nonmet. min.)
Supervises and coordinates activities of workers engaged in manufacturing asbestos automotive brake linings: Reviews production orders to determine material and labor requirements and machine setup. Directs workers to set up, operate, and tend mixers, ovens, extruders, and grinders. Inspects product in various stages of manufacture for conformance to specifications and directs adjustment of machine or change in processing methods as needed. Performs other duties as described under SUPERVISOR (any industry) Master Title.
GOE: 06.01.01 STRENGTH: L GED: R4 M3 L3 SVP: 7 DLU: 77

579.132-014 SUPERVISOR, LIME (concrete prod.)
Supervises and coordinates activities of workers engaged in crushing, burning, grinding, pulverizing, and hydrating limestone to produce hydrated lime for commercial use. Directs workers in operation of equipment. Reviews customer orders and requisitions freight cars or trucks to provide for shipment of product. Performs other duties as described under SUPERVISOR (any industry) Master Title.
GOE: 06.02.01 STRENGTH: L GED: R4 M3 L2 SVP: 8 DLU: 77

579.134-010 SUPERVISOR, INSPECTION (glass mfg.)
Supervises and coordinates activities of workers engaged in inspecting and testing glass products for conformance to specifications: Schedules test and inspection activities, based on production estimates and job change orders. Trains workers in test procedures. Examines samples of glass products for defects, using gauges and micrometers. Reviews test reports and confers with department heads to correct defects revealed by inspection and testing procedures. Requisitions supplies and equipment repair. Performs other duties as described under SUPERVISOR (any industry) Master Title.
GOE: 06.02.01 STRENGTH: L GED: R4 M3 L3 SVP: 6 DLU: 77

579.134-014 SUPERVISOR, EPOXY FABRICATION (brick & tile)
Supervises and coordinates activities of workers engaged in production of clay sewer pipe junction fittings, and assembly of pipe couplings: Observes pipe preparation, epoxy fabrication, ceramic sawing, coupling assembly, and palletizing of products to ensure workers follow prescribed production methods and procedures. Inspects products in all stages of production to detect cracks, pipe distortion, or assemblies which do not meet prescribed standards. Confers with supervisor to resolve personnel or production problems. Trains workers in production tasks and evaluates performance. Moves equipment, supplies, or products, using forklift truck. Performs minor repairs or adjustments to equipment, using handtools. Performs other duties as described under SUPERVISOR (any industry) Master Title.
GOE: 06.02.01 STRENGTH: M GED: R3 M2 L2 SVP: 6 DLU: 86

579.134-018 SUPERVISOR, REFRACTORY PRODUCTS (brick & tile)
Supervises and coordinates activities of workers engaged in production of refractory products, such as brick, slabs, and posts: Trains and observes workers

to ensure job performance meets standards and that safety procedures are followed. Observes operation of machinery and equipment, such as kilns, extruder, and mixing machine, to detect malfunctions. Examines extruded clay and shale columns, cut green brick, and fired brick to detect defects and for adherence to production standards. Maintains record of ingredients used in preparing finishing mixture and requisitions ingredients as needed. May assist workers in setting up, operating, and repairing machinery and equipment in department. Performs other duties as described under SUPERVISOR (any industry) Master Title.
GOE: 06.02.01 STRENGTH: M GED: R3 M2 L3 SVP: 6 DLU: 86

579.137-010 SUPERVISOR (cement)
Supervises and coordinates activities of workers engaged in processing raw materials used in manufacture of cement: Performs duties as described under SUPERVISOR (any industry) Master Title.
GOE: 06.04.01 STRENGTH: L GED: R4 M2 L2 SVP: 7 DLU: 77

579.137-014 SUPERVISOR, ASBESTOS TEXTILE (nonmet. min.)
Coordinates activities and supervises workers engaged in processing asbestos fibers into textile materials performing duties described under SUPERVISOR (any industry) Master Title. May be designated according to process supervised as Cardroom Supervisor (nonmet. min.).
GOE: 06.02.01 STRENGTH: L GED: R4 M3 L2 SVP: 7 DLU: 77

579.137-018 SUPERVISOR, MOLD CLEANING AND STORAGE (glass mfg.)
Supervises and coordinates activities of workers engaged in cleaning and storing cast iron molds and mold parts used to make glass containers: Examines and feels forming pins, *neck rings,* and inner surfaces of molds for scale, scratches, and nicks. Verifies dimensions of molds after cleaning, using go-not-go gauges. Receives mold change orders for production machines, inspects storeroom for specified molds and notifies mold making department of mold shortages. Performs other duties as described under SUPERVISOR (any industry) Master Title.
GOE: 06.04.01 STRENGTH: M GED: R3 M3 L3 SVP: 6 DLU: 77

579.137-022 SUPERVISOR, MOLD-MAKING PLASTICS SHEETS (plastic-synth.) alternate titles: cell-making supervisor, plastics sheets
Supervises and coordinates activities of workers engaged in sanding, washing, inspecting, and assembling plate glass sheets for use as molds (cells) in casting plastic sheets. Performs duties as described under SUPERVISOR (any industry) Master Title.
GOE: 06.04.01 STRENGTH: L GED: R3 M2 L2 SVP: 6 DLU: 77

579.137-026 SUPERVISOR, RECEIVING AND PROCESSING (glass mfg.) alternate titles: shift supervisor, melting; supervisor, furnace; supervisor, furnace room
Supervises and coordinates activities of workers engaged in unloading, storing, mixing, and melting raw materials, such as sand, soda ash, and cullet, to make molten glass for use in making flat glass, glass containers, optical glass, or glass fibers: Directs unloading of hopper cars, storage of ingredients in bins and silos, and examination of ingredients prior to mixing. Schedules mixing and melting of materials to manufacture particular color and composition of glass. Ensures mixtures are blended to specifications, using knowledge of raw ingredient mixtures for type of glass produced. Reads gauges, charts, and dials to determine if fuel consumption rates, air-to-gas ratios, atmospheric conditions, temperatures, and glass levels in furnace are within specified ranges applying knowledge of glass manufacturing or production specifications for kind of glass produced. Adjusts controls or directs subordinates to make corrective adjustments. Records amounts and types of ingredients used and in stock. Performs other duties described under SUPERVISOR (any industry) Master Title. May analyze raw materials and molten glass to determine if they are of acceptable quality. May regulate temperatures of annealing lehrs that control cooling of glass. May regulate homogenizer.
GOE: 06.02.01 STRENGTH: L GED: R4 M3 L3 SVP: 7 DLU: 77

579.137-030 DISPATCHER, CONCRETE PRODUCTS (concrete prod.; construction)
Supervises and coordinates activities of workers engaged in manufacturing concrete products and delivering ready-mix concrete: Quotes prices and receives orders for company products, such as ready-mix concrete, pipes, utility vaults, or septic tanks. Confers with plant production and yard personnel to establish delivery schedules according to factors, such as truck capacities, distances to delivery site, and unloading time. Computes amount of water to be added to each mix of concrete, using moisture meter to determine moisture content of sand and following moisture mix table. Records quantity of sand, cement, gravel, and water required for each mix on loading ticket for use by CONCRETE-BATCH-PLANT OPERATOR (concrete prod.; construction) 570.682-014. Prepares invoices, delivery tickets, and related shipping documents and assigns drivers for scheduled deliveries. Receives cash payments for shipments from drivers and prepares reports of cash and charge sales. Posts transactions to customers' accounts and issues customers account statements to customers. Maintains payroll and driver expense records. Maintains radio contact with drivers to expedite deliveries. Performs other tasks as described under SUPERVISOR (any industry) Master Title. May direct production workers to cast concrete products according to customer specifications. May be designated Dispatcher, Ready-Mix Plant (concrete prod.; construction).

GOE: 07.05.01 STRENGTH: L GED: R4 M3 L3 SVP: 5 DLU: 86

579.364-010 QUALITY CONTROL TECHNICIAN (concrete prod.)
Tests and inspects gypsum and gypsum wallboard during manufacture, using variety of testing devices and procedures to maintain product quality: Collects, measures, and weighs samples of minerals and chemical additives, such as gypsum and vermiculite. Performs tests on samples, using such equipment as ovens and molds, and performs calculations to measure such factors as gypsum purity, particle size, and hardness, applying arithmetic formula. Tests wallboard panels to verify factors, such as adhesion of paper to gypsum, edge hardness, and strength of panels. Observes designated worker performing standard wallboard tests and measurements, reads results, duplicates tests, and compares test results and measurements to verify accuracy of measurement. Collects and records results of sampling and testing to maintain record of product quality. Inspects wallboard at job sites to substantiate customer's claim of product defects. Formulates compensation offers to resolve claims and submits offer to management for approval.
GOE: 06.03.01 STRENGTH: M GED: R3 M3 L3 SVP: 6 DLU: 86

579.367-010 QUALITY-CONTROL INSPECTOR (glass mfg.)
Examines cases of inspected glass containers to determine quality of inspection and packing: Removes sample of glass containers from shipping case and examines containers for defects, such as chips, cracks, and stones. Inspects cases for imperfections in packing, sealing, and printing. Marks rejected lots, using crayon or pencil, and returns defective work to packing department. Records findings on worksheet and computes percentage of defective containers.
GOE: 06.03.01 STRENGTH: L GED: R3 M2 L3 SVP: 3 DLU: 77

579.367-014 QUALITY-CONTROL TECHNICIAN (glass mfg.) alternate titles: technician
Inspects flat glass and compiles defect data based on samples to determine variances from quality standards: Examines samples of flat glass for defects, such as stones, blisters, and cracks. Clamps sample of flat glass on carriage of distortion-analyzing machine, and starts machine. Interprets gauge readings and graphic recordings of machine to determine degree of ream (wavy distortion) in glass. Calculates standard control tolerances for flat glass, using algebraic formulas, plotting curves, and drawing graphs. Records nature and extent of defects for use of production department.
GOE: 06.03.01 STRENGTH: L GED: R3 M3 L3 SVP: 4 DLU: 77

579.380-010 BOARD-MACHINE SET-UP OPERATOR (concrete prod.)
Sets up and adjusts mixers, feeders, rollers, cutters, and other equipment to fabricate wallboard and lath: Sets edging bars, rollers, and scoring cutters to ensure that wallboard produced attains specified width and thickness, using rules, gauges, and handtools. Adjusts paper guides, glue feeders, chamfering wheels, and stenciling machine so that board edges will be smoothly sealed and markings legible and evenly spaced. Regulat s flow of material into mixing machine. Observes machine operations and adjusts setup on basis of factors, such as atmospheric conditions, slurry composition, and line-speed requirements. May test slurry for consistency, using scale and by feeling it.
GOE: 06.01.03 STRENGTH: L GED: R3 M2 L2 SVP: 6 DLU: 77

579.382-010 CALCINER, GYPSUM (concrete prod.)
Controls grinding mills, kettles, and conveyors to grind and dehydrate gypsum rock and transfer gypsum to storage bins or pulverizing machine: Opens storage bin gates to admit rock into grinding mill and starts mill. Feels ground rock to determine consistency and adjusts mill as required to obtain specified consistency. Opens chute to allow ground rock to flow into kettle. Lights fire under kettle. Reads temperature gauge and regulates fuel feed valve to maintain specified temperature inside kettle. Collects sample of calcined gypsum for laboratory analysis. Opens chute after specified time and turns air valve to force calcined gypsum into hot pits for cooling. Starts bucket elevators and conveyors to move gypsum from pits to storage bins or to ball mill for pulverizing. May operate rotary drier to dry gypsum rock before calcination.
GOE: 06.02.18 STRENGTH: L GED: R3 M2 L2 SVP: 4 DLU: 77

579.382-014 CUPOLA OPERATOR, INSULATION (nonmet. min.)
Operates water-cooled cupola furnace and related equipment to melt coke, slag, basalt, lime, and silica into molten mineral, and spins molten mineral into mineral wool fibers: Lights fire in furnace to melt charge. Reads gauges and turns valves to regulate water and steam pressure. Observes melting of ingredients in furnace through porthole, and adjusts airblast on flaming coke bed to control intensity of heat and melting process. Activates spinning wheel. Removes taphole plug to allow molten stream to flow into water-cooled furnace trough, over high-pressure steam jet and into spinning wheel, to be spun into mineral wool fibers. Observes color intensity and flow of molten stream to determine suitability for spinning. Adjusts distance of steam ring and spinning wheel from end of trough to control length of spun fibers. Scrapes residue slag from trough and spinning wheel, using bar and scraper.
GOE: 06.02.10 STRENGTH: H GED: R3 M2 L2 SVP: 6 DLU: 77

579.382-018 KNIFE OPERATOR (concrete prod.)
Sets up and controls equipment to perforate, cut, and stencil plaster wallboard and convey board through kiln: Adjusts perforator and knife according to specifications, using gauge and handtools. Inserts code letters in stenciling drum, using tweezers and fills drum with ink. Adjusts speed of roller and accelerator conveyors according to size of board. Sets speed of kiln conveyor for specified

drying time. Inspects wallboard emerging from drying kiln for unsealed edges and surface blemishes. Removes defective wallboard from conveyor line. Measures and weighs wallboard samples for conformance to specifications, using rule, micrometer, and scale.
GOE: 06.02.09 STRENGTH: M GED: R3 M2 L2 SVP: 5 DLU: 77

579.382-022 BLANKMAKER (glass mfg.)
Operates glass lathe to form glass tubes into glass blanks used in fabrication of laser light conductors: Reads work orders and technical manuals to determine lathe setup procedures, and pushes buttons and turns knobs to adjust lathe gas-injection and temperature controls. Locks glass tube into spindle chuck, using wrench. Trues and flares glass tube, using lathe carriage burner, ruler, and calipers. Attaches chemical spray nozzle to glass tube to coat interior of tube with gases, and inserts auger into tube to remove chemical residue. Lowers and locks spindle shield to form dust-free chamber. Presses keys on keyboard to transmit production specifications to computer and to transfer lathe operation from manual to automatic control for duration of blankmaking process. Observes lathe dials and gauges, computer display panel, and color of flame on lathe carriage burner to verify adherence to manufacturing specifications. Calculates data, such as blank weights, diameters, and densities, using calculator, and enters data on record sheet. Repairs lathe, using wrenches, pliers, and screwdrivers to correct malfunctions.
GOE: 06.02.13 STRENGTH: L GED: R3 M3 L3 SVP: 6 DLU: 86

579.384-010 BRICK TESTER (brick & tile)
Fabricates brick and tile samples and tests samples for conformance to strength specifications: Starts machines that grind, sift, and mix clay. Molds brick and tile samples, using mold, hand rammer, and trowel. Places models in kiln burner and turns switches or valves to heat kiln to specified temperature. Removes samples from kiln and places samples on testing machine supports. Turns handwheel to force bearing plate against samples. Reads gauge to obtain transverse breaking load in pounds per square inch, and records data. Inspects products for size, cracks, and other imperfections, using hammer and notched rule. May test products for strength, using testing machine.
GOE: 06.02.30 STRENGTH: L GED: R2 M2 L1 SVP: 4 DLU: 77

579.384-014 QUALITY TECHNICIAN, FIBERGLASS (glass mfg.) alternate titles: laboratory technician
Tests fiberglass yarn, fibers, or binder solutions at any stage in manufacturing process to determine if standards are met: Weighs samples of fiber and binder solution on balance scales before and after drying in miniature oven and burning in muffle furnace, and computes percentage of binder on fiber and percentage of solids in binder solution, using slide rule or mathematical formula. Examines and tests goods returned by customer or at customer's establishment to detect manufacturing defects or damage incurred in transit and records results for use by quality control and production supervisors.
GOE: 06.03.01 STRENGTH: L GED: R3 M3 L3 SVP: 4 DLU: 77

579.384-018 WARE TESTER (glass mfg.)
Collects, inspects, and tests glassware, such as containers and cathode-ray tubes, for conformance to specifications: Collects samples to be tested and measured, and marks samples and logs with identifying information, such as batch number, machine number, and mold number. Visually inspects glassware for defects, such as striations (stress lines), bubbles, pits, discolorations, incomplete grinding and polishing, and painting flaws, such as chips and smears. Fills containers with water to determine fluid capacity by weighing filled container on scales or pouring contents into graduated cylinder. Verifies size, shape, radius, thickness, weight, eccentricity, and surface flatness, using templates, calipers, micrometers, scales, eccentricity table, surface blocks, wedge blocks, or electronic measuring instruments. Determines annealed quality of glassware by either observing glass through polariscope, measuring wave length of glass color with spectrophotometer, or by examining microsections for annealing striations. Immerses containers in hot or cold water tanks to estimate thermal shock resistance. Determines bursting point of container by either filling container with water and inserting electrically controlled plunger in container to apply pressure, or placing container in pressurized chamber. Cuts glass into wafers and examines glass under microscope to measure micro defects. Records results of tests and deviations from standards and submits to supervisor; notifies supervisor of serious defects, such as failure to withstand thermal shock or defective mold. May set and adjust measuring devices used in laboratory or by SELECTOR (glass mfg.). May compile specifications from new product orders for setting quality control standards. May place sample in test tube, immerse test tube in controlled temperature water, and observe settling point of glass to estimate density of glass. May place container in surface abrader to estimate container scratch resistance. May place container in jaws of calibrated vice to determine horizontal bursting point. May test gob (lump) of molten glass from furnace and forehearth to ensure glass temperatures are within specifications. May pack sample ware for shipment to customer. May perform dimensional measurements at production work stations and be designated Floor Inspector (glass mfg.). May be designated according to article inspected as Bottle Inspector (glass mfg.); Television-Tube Inspector (glass mfg.).
GOE: 06.03.01 STRENGTH: L GED: R3 M3 L3 SVP: 5 DLU: 77

579.387-010 MAT TESTER (nonmet. min.)
Tests mat of fiberglass insulation material to determine if product conforms to specifications: Cuts sample of mat, using knife or razor blade and template, and weighs mat on balance scale. Burns weighed sample in miniature oven to remove binder, weighs burned sample, and computes percentage of binder in sample, using slide rule. Suspends sample of mat in styrene solution and times disintegration of sample to determine solubility of binder. Places sample between plates of thickness gauge and reads dial indicator before and after application of pressure to gauge to determine thickness with or without stress. Records test results on mat-testing record.
GOE: 06.03.01 STRENGTH: L GED: R3 M2 L2 SVP: 3 DLU: 77

579.484-010 SAMPLER (mine & quarry) alternate titles: bucker; coal inspector; hardness tester; materials inspector; ore sampler; tester
Collects samples of coal, ore, crushed stone, aggregate, sand or gravel from railroad cars, conveyors, stockpiles or mines and tests materials for conformance to specifications: Gathers samples from specified locations and transports samples to laboratory. Dumps material into sample divider to reduce volume of sample. Weighs material, using balance scale, and dumps sample into grinding machine to grind and blend sample or into screen testing machine to separate particles by size. Weighs segregated particles collected on each screen and computes percentage of each in total sample. Examines samples for presence of foreign matter and variation from color standard. Compiles reports indicating percentages of materials of specified size. Notifies management when materials do not meet specifications. May weigh, dry, and reweigh samples to determine moisture content of samples. May bag samples for testing at other locations. May perform chemical sedimentation or magnetic separation tests. May perform hardness test on pellets. May plot origin of samples on mine map.
GOE: 02.04.01 STRENGTH: M GED: R3 M2 L1 SVP: 4 DLU: 77

579.584-010 FIBERGLASS-CONTAINER-WINDING OPERATOR (glass products)
Performs any combination of following duties to fabricate fiberglass air containers used in hydraulic systems: Assembles hemispherical mold or mandrel sections of lead alloy to form sphere. Covers sphere with rubber-liner halves and cements halves together. Examines rubber covering for defects. Attaches threaded fittings onto rubber lining at top and bottom of sphere. Inserts shaft through fitting opening into sphere and screws into place, using wrench. Weighs resin and catalyst in specified amounts and mixes them with agitator. Mounts sphere in winding machine and applies resin to surface, using brush. Starts machine that winds fiberglass yarn around sphere. Measures tension of fiberglass using tensiometer, and adjusts tension arm. Removes and weighs fiberglass-covered sphere. Records weight on production sheet. Places covered spheres in electric oven to bake and dry for specified time. Removes and weighs spheres. Mounts spheres on steam unit to melt and remove mold. Turns valve to admit steam into sphere. Turns spigot to discharge molten alloy. Weighs sphere and records weight. Performs hydrostatic tests on completed spherical containers at various pressures. Connects fitting on container to water pipe in safety tank. Turns water valves and starts pump to increase pressure in container to specified level.
GOE: 06.04.13 STRENGTH: M GED: R2 M2 L2 SVP: 4 DLU: 77

579.585-010 SAMPLER-TESTER (nonmet. min.)
Grades samples of asbestos fibers taken from various parts of fiber-manufacturing plant by combining samples and tending machine that agitates known quantity and weight of fibers for specified time. Weighs quantity of fibers deposited on each of four screens in machine to find average weight that determines grade of fibers. Records grade on bags of fibers according to test results. May collect fiber samples from clothing of workers, using portable vacuum device. May monitor noise levels at each work station, using sound level meter.
GOE: 06.03.02 STRENGTH: L GED: R2 M2 L2 SVP: 3 DLU: 77

579.587-010 ROUND-UP-RING HAND (concrete prod.)
Bolts round-up ring sections around steel can (cylinder) to retain circular shape of cylinder during casting of reinforced concrete pipe: Rolls can on raised track into assembly line position, assisted by other workers. Measures and marks length of can to position rings, using gauge and chalk. Braces interior of can near end, using curved blocks and jack. Aligns mold-ring flange over can end and tightens set bolts, using wrench to lock rings in place. Positions and bolts ring halves against can, using jack and wrench. Rolls completed can on track to mortar-lining area.
GOE: 06.04.22 STRENGTH: M GED: R2 M1 L2 SVP: 3 DLU: 77

579.662-010 MAT-MACHINE OPERATOR (nonmet. min.)
Operates range consisting of staple cutters, conveyor, binder and water sprayers, drying oven, pressure rollers, inspection table, and automatic cutting and winding device to produce continuous sheets of fiberglass insulation material: Turns knob on control panel to heat drying oven. Starts range and guides sheet of matted fiberglass under pressure rollers, over inspection table and slitting knives, under cutting blade, and laps end around winding shaft. Patrols work area and observes range units, temperature gauge, and flow of material through range to detect irregular operation of machine and variations from standards. Examines matted sheets for thin spots and foreign matter. Directs STRAND-AND-BINDER CONTROLLER (nonmet. min.) to increase or decrease number of fiberglass sliver ends fed into staple cutters to restore finished product to specified thickness. Adjusts temperature of oven to dry material according to specifications.
GOE: 06.02.09 STRENGTH: L GED: R3 M2 L1 SVP: 4 DLU: 77

579.664-010 CLAY-STRUCTURE BUILDER AND SERVICER (glass mfg.) alternate titles: clay-house worker; refractory specialist
Builds and replaces clay structures that control flow and temperature of molten glass in melting tanks and drawing kilns: Bolts sections of specified wooden

mold together, using wrench, and lines assembled mold with paper to prevent adherence of clay to wooden mold. Dumps and tamps clay in mold, using tamping tool. Disassembles mold and covers clay structure with damp burlap to prevent rapid drying. Cuts, chips, and smooths molded clay to form such structures as floaters, shutoff bars, drawbars, and L-blocks, using square, rule, and handtools. Transfers clay structures to curing ovens, melting tanks, and drawing kilns, using electric forklift truck. Installs clay structure replacements in melting tanks and drawing kilns, using chain hoists and handtools. Cleans out openings of melting tanks, using airhose. May mix clay for structures.
GOE: 05.10.01 STRENGTH: M GED: R3 M2 L2 SVP: 4 DLU: 77

579.664-014 INSPECTOR II (concrete prod.)
Inspects finished concrete building products for flaws, finish, and conformance to dimensional specifications, using blueprints and precision measuring instruments: Compares dimensions of product, such as prestressed concrete building panels, conduit, and beams, with blueprints, using micrometer, calipers, fixed gauges, and rule. Examines products for flaws, such as cracks, warped sections, bent reinforcing rods, and surface or color irregularities. Rejects products not meeting specifications and notifies originating department to repair product or take measures to minimize future irregularities. May cast and crush sample concrete product in hydraulic press to test strength of concrete.
GOE: 06.03.02 STRENGTH: L GED: R3 M2 L3 SVP: 4 DLU: 77

579.665-010 BRAKE-LINING FINISHER, ASBESTOS (nonmet. min.) alternate titles: impregnator operator
Tends tanks that impregnate asbestos lining stock with asphalt solution: Loads vacuum tank with rolls of asbestos lining, using hoist. Turns valves to admit specified quantities of asphalt solution into tank. Turns steam valves to heat tanks, observes temperature control chart, and adjusts coolant valves to maintain temperature within specified limits. Transfers impregnated rolls of asbestos from tank to oven, using hoist. Allows material to heat for specified time to complete impregnating process. Starts blower to dry and exhaust fumes from asbestos. May standardize width and thickness of asbestos lining [CALENDER-MACHINE OPERATOR (nonmet. min.)]. May test impregnated stock to ensure conformance to specifications, using brake-testing machine. May deliver samples to control laboratory. May tend mixing machine to prepare impregnating solution.
GOE: 06.04.19 STRENGTH: M GED: R3 M1 L1 SVP: 3 DLU: 77

579.665-014 LABORER, CONCRETE-MIXING PLANT (construction) alternate titles: concrete-mixer-operator helper; laborer, mixing plant; machine helper; mixer helper; mixer tender; mixing-plant dumper
Performs any combination of following duties in concrete mixing plant: Verifies amount of aggregate in storage bins by visual inspection, and turns swivel head to direct aggregate into specified bin. Tends electrically powered conveyor or pneumatic pump to hoist cement from feeder hopper, railroad car, or transport truck into storage container, such as cement silo. Loosens locking pin, using hammer, to dump cement from cars into storage hopper, prodding cement with pole through trapdoor in car until car is empty. Positions trucks, cars, or buckets under spouts of concrete mixers, batching plants, or hoppers, using hand signals, and moving levers or handwheels to discharge concrete into trucks, cars, or buckets. May haul cement from storage in bulk or bags, emptying, cleaning, and bundling empty bags. May be designated according to duties performed as Aggregate-Conveyor Operator (construction); Bag Shaker (construction); Cement Car Dumper (construction); Cement-Conveyor Operator (construction); Cement Handler (construction); Cement-Sack Breaker (construction). May be designated: Concrete-Bucket Loader (construction); Concrete-Bucket Unloader (construction); Concrete-Conveyor Operator (construction); Concrete-Hopper Operator (construction); Concrete-Mixer Loader, Truck Mounted (construction); Conveyor Tender, Concrete-Mixing Plant (construction); Dumper, Central-Concrete-Mixing Plant (construction); Loft Worker, Concrete-Mixing Plant (construction).
GOE: 05.12.04 STRENGTH: H GED: R2 M1 L1 SVP: 2 DLU: 77

579.665-018 WIRE SETTER (glass mfg.)
Tends machine that unwinds wire netting to be imbedded in sheet glass: Cuts V-shaped point on leading edge of roll, using hand shears, and positions roll on holding frame of machine. Signals coworker to feed end of wire netting into glass-rolling machine. Splices end of depleted roll of netting to lead end of new roll and places new roll in unwinding frame.
GOE: 06.04.02 STRENGTH: L GED: R2 M1 L1 SVP: 2 DLU: 77

579.667-010 LABORER, GENERAL (brick & tile) alternate titles: clean-up worker; yard worker
Performs any combination of following duties involved in manufacturing brick and tile products: Loads articles, such as brick, tiles, and sewer pipe on pallets and transports them to machines, disposal, or storage area, using handtruck. Carries bricks to kilns. Pushes empty kiln cars, drier cars, and mine cars to work areas. Replaces sifting screens in grinding units. Shovels clay-bearing earth into mine cars, couples cars, and signals TRUCK-CRANE OPERATOR (any industry) 921.663-062 to draw loaded cars to mouth of pit mine. Clears weeds, topsoil, roots, and debris from working areas in pit mines. Digs ditches in pit, using shovel. Trims walls and roof of clay tunnel in pits, using shovel. Cleans machines and passage areas of dust and clay residue, using broom and shovel. Smooths dried, unburnt clay blocks, using knife, board, and mallet.
GOE: 06.04.30 STRENGTH: H GED: R1 M1 L1 SVP: 1 DLU: 78

579.682-010 MIXER, WET POUR (concrete prod.) alternate titles: mixer operator
Operates rotary type machine to mix concrete and fills metal molds to make pipe and other concrete products: Pulls trip bar and lever on overhead chutes to fill suspended weighing hoppers and cart with specified weights of sand, gravel, and cement. Pushes cart of cement to mixing machine and tilts cart by hand to dump cement into machine. Turns valve to admit specified quantity of water. Fills mold with sample batch of concrete. Lifts mold from sample and compares diameter of sample with diameter of mold to determine whether consistency of concrete conforms with specifications. Adjusts mixture by adding water, cement, sand, or gravel. Bolts pneumatic vibrator to mold, using hand wrench. Pulls lever to open mixer chute and fill pouring bucket. Positions bucket over mold, using overhead hoist and pulls trip bar to fill mold. Starts vibrator to settle concrete. Pushes concrete remaining on core cover into mold, using hoe. Levels off top of fresh casting, using trowel. Records each batch of concrete produced.
GOE: 06.04.17 STRENGTH: V GED: R3 M2 L1 SVP: 4 DLU: 77

579.684-010 CONCRETE-VAULT MAKER (concrete prod.)
Casts concrete burial vaults: Places vault handles in lid mold, lifts mold sides, and inserts pin to secure mold sides. Pulls lid handles through mold slots and inserts wedge to secure lid handles. Lifts bottom mold sides and secures sides, using pins and hammer. Greases top edge of mold inner core to prevent concrete seepage from mold. Positions concrete bucket over molds, using electric hoist, and pulls lever to empty concrete into molds. Slides pneumatic vibrator into mold socket to settle concrete in molds. Smooths top of concrete, using screed and trowel. Removes pins from bottom mold sides, and pulls sides of bottom mold down, using hammer and pry bar, to separate mold from vault. Pulls lever to relax inner core mold to permit vault removal. Removes securing pin to lower lid mold sides. Scarifies lid surface and applies and stipples finishing cement to decorate lid, using scarifier and brush. Transfers vault bottom and lid to spraying area, using hoist. Sprays vault with asphalt and colored paints to protect and decorate vault. Applies sealing compound to vault lid, using trowels. Hoists vault bottom and lid onto truck. Delivers vault to grave site, and lowers vault into ground.
GOE: 06.04.32 STRENGTH: H GED: R2 M1 L1 SVP: 2 DLU: 77

579.684-014 CRAYON GRADER (mine & quarry)
Inspects talc crayons for defects, sorts crayons according to length, and packs crayons for shipment: Spreads crayons in hands and examines crayons for defects, such as broken, split, or incomplete pieces. Separates crayons into grades according to length and defect. Packs graded crayons in cardboard boxes and places defective crayons in tray. Seals boxed crayons, using tape, and glues label on box.
GOE: 06.03.02 STRENGTH: S GED: R2 M1 L2 SVP: 3 DLU: 77

579.684-018 KILN-FURNITURE CASTER (pottery & porc.)
Fabricates ceramic kiln furniture used to support glazed ware during firing: Weighs domestic clay and grog according to formula. Dumps materials into mixing machine, adds water, and allows machine to run for specified time. Drains grog from container into molds. Removes furniture (setters and pedestals) from mold when dry, finishes funiture with knife and sponge, and places furniture in kiln for firing at specified temperatures. Removes fired pieces from kiln to storage, using handtruck. May cut setters from extruded clay sheets, using specified shape cutters.
GOE: 06.04.17 STRENGTH: M GED: R2 M1 L1 SVP: 4 DLU: 77

579.684-022 MICA-PLATE LAYER, HAND (mine & quarry)
Applies mica splittings to paper or fiberglass cloth to produce mica sheet: Places precut sheet of paper or piece of fiberglass cloth on table and places mica splittings over entire surface so that pieces of mica overlap each other. Brushes silicone varnish over surface, using paint brush, and places sheet on table for drying.
GOE: 06.04.33 STRENGTH: S GED: R2 M1 L1 SVP: 2 DLU: 77

579.684-026 CASTER (brick & tile) alternate titles: castables worker
Mixes slurry, fills molds, and conveys filled molds to drier to cast refractory brick, using mixer, vibrating table, chain hoist, and related equipment: Reads work order to determine product to be cast and bolts specified mold parts together, using impact wrench. Attaches chain hoist to assembled mold and moves mold to vibrating table. Empties premeasured ingredients into mixer according to formula, adds water, and starts mixer. Observes mixture and adds additional water, as required, to achieve prescribed consistency, utilizing acquired experience. Fills bucket with slurry and pours slurry into mold. Presses switch to start vibrating device on table and adds slurry to fill mold as mixture settles during vibration. Draws metal bar across surface of mixture to level casting. Stacks filled molds in drier car, using chain hoist, and pushes loaded car along rail into drier. Sets drier controls to dry castings according to specifications, and pulls drier car from drier at end of cycle. Removes molds from dried products, using impact wrench. Cleans mold parts, using brush.
GOE: 06.04.32 STRENGTH: H GED: R2 M1 L2 SVP: 3 DLU: 86

579.684-030 CUTTER (brick & tile)
Cuts kiln furniture, bricks, or other clay and shale products to specified shape and size, using one of following methods: (1) Adjusts cutting jig of table-mounted handsaw to specified setting, using tape measure and allen wrench. Positions casting in jig and pulls saw blade to cut ware to specifed size. (2) Places pressed ware into table-mounted form. Lowers die or wire cutter onto ware to cut ware into specified shape and size.

GOE: 06.04.30 STRENGTH: M GED: R2 M1 L1 SVP: 2 DLU: 86

579.685-010   DRIER-AND-GRINDER TENDER (mine & quarry) alternate titles: crusher, dry-ground mica

Tends drying cylinder and hammer mill arranged in tandem to dry and pulverize mica: Turns valve to start flow of oil in burner and ignites oil to heat drying-cylinder. Starts machines that tumble mica in heated cylinder and automatically feed dry mica into hammer mill. Examines pulverized mica for discolorations caused by excess heat and for conformance with grinding specifications. Adjusts controls of drying cylinder to regulate temperature and replaces worn hammers to grind mica to specifications, using handtools. Changes screens on discharge chute of hammer mill according to size specified for mica. May fill machine hopper with mica, using tractor equipped with scoop.

GOE: 06.04.08 STRENGTH: L GED: R3 M1 L1 SVP: 4 DLU: 77

579.685-014   FRIT-MIXER-AND-BURNER (brick & tile; pottery & porc.) alternate titles: frit burner

Tends equipment that blends and melts materials, such as clay, flint, and lead oxides, to make glaze: Weighs specified amounts of ingredients on scale according to batch card. Dumps weighed materials into mixing machine. Sets timing device on mixer for specified period and starts mixer. Observes mixture for conformance to coloring specifications. Empties batch from machine into bin and transports bin to frit furnace, using lift truck. Dumps materials into furnace and turns gas and air valves to heat furnace to specified temperature. Shuts off furnace and turns wheel to pour fused mass from furnace into water sump to undergo crystallization. Drains off water and shovels crystals (frit) into bin. Transports bin to storage area, using handtruck.

GOE: 06.04.17 STRENGTH: H GED: R2 M2 L1 SVP: 4 DLU: 77

579.685-018   GLASS-CLEANING-MACHINE TENDER (glass products)

Tends machine that automatically dips, sprays, steams, and dries glass articles, such as instrument lenses and hypodermic syringes. Loads articles into baskets of machine. Presses button to start and stop machine. May mix cleaning solution and test solution for acidity, using hydrometer.

GOE: 06.04.08 STRENGTH: L GED: R2 M1 L1 SVP: 3 DLU: 77

579.685-022   GLASS-WOOL-BLANKET-MACHINE FEEDER (glass products)

Tends machine that laminates and glues paper to glass-wool for use as building insulation material: Feeds rolls of paper into machine. Starts machine and observes operation to ensure that glue spreads evenly and rolls of paper adhere to both sides of glass-wool to form blanket.

GOE: 06.04.09 STRENGTH: L GED: R2 M1 L1 SVP: 3 DLU: 77

579.685-026   MICA-PLATE LAYER (mine & quarry)

Tends machine that forms plates of built-up mica: Turns knob on control panel to set oven temperatures according to specifications. Dumps mica splittings into machine hopper and fills supply tanks with binding solution. Starts machine that distributes mica splittings on conveyor, sprays splittings with binding solution, and dries continuous sheet of mica. Examines mica plates at discharge end of machine to detect variations in thickness. Cuts mica sheets into plates of specified length, using cutter attached to table. Moves controls on hopper to regulate flow of splittings according to thickness of mica plates. Adjusts oven controls to regulate temperature. Notifies supervisor of machine malfunctions.

GOE: 06.04.08 STRENGTH: M GED: R2 M1 L1 SVP: 2 DLU: 77

579.685-030   MOLD POLISHER (glass mfg.) alternate titles: mold cleaner

Tends machines that clean or polish forming molds and components by any of following methods: (1) Starts pumps on vapor-blast machine to circulate water and cleaning compound through hose. Places parts on table and pushes table into machine cabinet. Pushes control lever to start flow of compressed air through hose. Holds and turns parts while directing pressurized stream of water and cleaning compound onto parts to remove dirt, carbon, and scales. Dips parts in oil solution to prevent rusting. (2) Inserts and secures blank mold and plunger into chuck of open-end polishing jack or lathe. Holds emery cloth over rotating plunger or inserts rod, covered with emery cloth, into mold to clean and polish parts. (3) Holds and turns parts against rotating emery wheel. May soak parts in hot cleaning compound or scrape parts, using scraper to loosen or remove scales and carbon. May rub mold surface with oil or kerosene and abrasive stone or wire brush to remove scale, rust, scratches, and dirt. May apply cork or graphite paste coating to mold interiors to prevent adherence of glass to molds during forming operation. May store cleaned molds in storage bins. May transfer molds and mold parts from storage to production area, using handtruck.

GOE: 06.04.39 STRENGTH: H GED: R2 M2 L2 SVP: 3 DLU: 77

579.685-034   NODULIZER (cement) alternate titles: pelletizer

Tends equipment that dries raw ground materials and makes pellets: Starts pelletizer rotating and starts feed and discharge conveyors and traveling grates in preburning-ovens. Turns valves to regulate water sprays in pelletizer and heat in oven. Observes mixing of materials and water to determine if uniform nodules are being formed. Observes feed hopper to ensure uniformity of filling. Regulates feed of materials, rotation of pelletizer, amount of water spray, and heat of oven to ensure pellets are produced to specifications. Opens inspection ports on oven and observes or removes pellets for examination to ensure specified hardness and heat.

GOE: 06.04.19 STRENGTH: L GED: R3 M2 L2 SVP: 3 DLU: 77

579.685-038   PACKER, INSULATION (nonmet. min.)

Tends machine that compresses stack of mineral wool insulation batts and inserts them into bag cover: Starts machine and compressing mechanism. Opens and slides bag cover over form for filling. Pulls lever to operate discharge mechanism and force stack into bag. Slides package onto table for stapling.

GOE: 06.04.09 STRENGTH: M GED: R2 M1 L1 SVP: 2 DLU: 77

579.685-042   PRECAST MOLDER (concrete prod.) alternate titles: precast worker

Tends portable concrete-mixing machine and handcasts ornamental and structural concrete building products, such as blocks, colored tile, simulated-brick facings, fireplace units, and reinforced roof and floor sections: Shovels sand, cement, gravel, or pumice into mixing machine. Adds water and pigments as instructed and starts machine. Dumps mix into wheelbarrow and pushes to casting room. Brushes casting oil on molds to prevent adhesion of concrete. Casts products by any of following methods: (1) Places molds on vibrating table, shovels mix into molds, starts vibrator to settle concrete or pumice, levels surface of mix with wood bar, and carries filled molds to curing racks. (2) Shovels mix into floor molds and sets reinforcing steel rods into mix to cast fireplace, roof, or floor sections. Dismantles forms after concrete has cured, using pry bar and wrench. (3) Places bricks into mold and pours concrete over bricks to form solid block. Sets reinforcing rods in mix and clamps mold shut. Removes forms after blocks are cured by releasing clamps or disassembling mold, using pry bar and wrench. May be designated according to product cast as Brick Veneer Maker (concrete prod.); Cement-Tile Maker (concrete prod.).

GOE: 06.04.19 STRENGTH: H GED: R2 M1 L2 SVP: 3 DLU: 77

579.685-046   ROUGE SIFTER AND MILLER (optical goods) alternate titles: sifter and miller

Tends machines that sift and mill powdered rouge for use in polishing lenses: Loads hopper of sifter with rouge powder and starts machine to separate coarse from fine particles. Fabricates paste for polishing lenses [ROUGE MIXER (optical goods)], using mill to reduce particle size. May fill containers with rouge paste or powder for shipment [PACKAGER, HAND (any industry)].

GOE: 06.04.09 STRENGTH: L GED: R1 M1 L1 SVP: 2 DLU: 77

579.685-050   SILO TENDER (cement) alternate titles: cement-storage worker

Tends stationary pump in pneumatic conveyor system that conveys fine-ground raw materials or finished cement from one bin to another preparatory to further processing: Pushes levers to start pump, air compressor, and other conveying equipment. Observes pressure dials on pump that indicate operating condition of conveyor. Makes minor repairs to pump to correct faulty operation. Oils and greases equipment. May pump bulk cement from unloading bins into tank trucks, railroad cars, and boats [CEMENT LOADER (cement)]. May tend mobile pump.

GOE: 06.04.40 STRENGTH: M GED: R2 M2 L1 SVP: 3 DLU: 77

579.685-054   SILVER STRIPPER, MACHINE (glass products)

Tends machine that removes silver, copper, and paint from defective mirrors: Weighs specified amount of caustic soda and pours into storage tank. Starts conveyor, washer, and drier unit and turns valves to admit water, acid, and caustic soda into spray pipes or tank. Places mirror on conveyor that carries mirror through caustic soda and water sprays, acid tank, and washing and drying units. Reads gauge and turns valve to regulate temperature to prevent soda from boiling over.

GOE: 06.04.39 STRENGTH: H GED: R2 M2 L1 SVP: 2 DLU: 77

579.685-058   BRICK SETTER OPERATOR (brick & tile) alternate titles: stacker operator

Tends machine that cuts columns of extruded clay and shale into brick and stacks layers of brick onto kiln cars for firing: Depresses buttons on panelboard to start conveyor that moves columns of clay and shale from extruder through cutter that cuts column into brick and assembles layer of brick on platform of machine. Depresses button to activate hydraulic pickup head of machine that picks up layer of brick from platform and stacks brick on kiln car. Straightens uneven brick on stack, using hands. Clears jammed conveyor and machine, using metal bar and scraper. Discards broken columns of clay and shale or damaged brick onto conveyor for recycling. Activates control on panelboard to tie (set at right angles) two top layers of brick on kiln car. Replaces broken cutter wires on machine cutter, using handtools. Dusts conveyor, cutter, and pickup head, using airhose. Oils and greases specified parts of machinery, using oilcan and grease gun.

GOE: 06.04.08 STRENGTH: M GED: R3 M1 L2 SVP: 3 DLU: 86

579.685-062   BRICK UNLOADER TENDER (brick & tile)

Tends equipment that automatically unloads brick from kiln cars after firing: Depresses buttons on control panels to activate equipment that moves loaded kiln cars along rails into unloading position, lowers hydraulic pickup head that lifts stacks of brick from kiln car onto conveyor, and conveys brick to subsequent processing area. Depresses buttons to stop equipment when rows of brick are unevenly stacked, damaged bricks are detected, or jamming or other malfunctions occur. Replaces damaged bricks and straightens rows. Removes jammed bricks, using iron bar. May unload stacked bricks from conveyor, using hydraulic ram. May manually remove rows of stacked brick to create tine course (open spaces) to facilitate handling by forklift during packaging.

GOE: 06.04.40 STRENGTH: L GED: R2 M2 L2 SVP: 3 DLU: 86

579.685-066   BRIQUETTE OPERATOR (brick & tile)

Tends vacuum screen that screens magnesium liquor and briquette press equipment that presses screened residue (filter cake) to form briquettes of

periclase (refractory material): Flips control panel switches to start multilevel arrangement of vacuum screen feeder wheel, vacuum screen hearth kiln, and briquette press. Observes vacuum screen feeder wheel to verify that cups positioned on feeder wheel are full of magnesium liquor for emptying onto vacuum screen. Turns dials on control panel to adjust speed of vacuum screen feeder wheel and vacuum screen to control thickness of filter cake, following prescribed procedure. Reads counter on feeder wheel to determine revolutions per hour and records totals in logbook. Moves control knobs to adjust amount of filter cake fed from hearth furnace onto conveyor and into briquette press. Turns knobs to regulate speed and pressure of briquette rollers that form briquettes. Observes indicator lights and gauges on control panels to detect equipment malfunction and notifies supervisor. Records equipment downtime in logbook.
GOE: 06.04.19 STRENGTH: L GED: R3 M1 L1 SVP: 2 DLU: 86

579.685-070 MARKER MACHINE ATTENDANT (glass mfg.)
Tends equipment that automatically detects and marks defects in glass ribbon (continuous sheet of flat glass) on conveyor line in glass manufacturing establishment: Observes indicator lights on equipment to ensure activation of all inspection zones. Activates marker at each inspection zone and observes operation of markers to test marker operation. Draws line across glass ribbon, using chalk, to simulate glass defects, and observes equipment operation to verify inspection process. Replenishes chalk in marker mechanism and sheets of paper beneath glass ribbon. Observes lighted panel to determine frequency of marking, according to company standards, and notifies designated personnel if overmarking or undermarking occurs. Inspects glass from catwalk to ensure defects are marked by machine. Cleans and removes dirt, dust, and broken glass from machine and work area, using broom, shovel, vacuum cleaner, and dust cloths.
GOE: 06.04.08 STRENGTH: L GED: R2 M1 L1 SVP: 3 DLU: 86

579.685-074 MIXER (brick & tile)
Tends machines that dry and mix ingredients, such as clay, chromite, shale, and sand to form finishing mixture used in making brick: Reads batch card and notifies helper to assemble ingredients specified on card. Opens bags and weighs specified quantities of ingredients, using scale and bucket. Pours weighed ingredients into storage bins prior to mixing. Turns knob to set temperature of dryer and pulls lever to start mixer. Shovels or pours ingredients into dryer that automatically dries and feeds ingredients into mixer, and dumps mixture into bin for further processing. Observes operation of machines and notifies supervisor of malfunctions. Oils and greases machinery. Removes caked ingredients from dryer and mixer, using metal bar and scraper.
GOE: 06.04.17 STRENGTH: H GED: R2 M1 L1 SVP: 2 DLU: 86

579.686-014 MAT PACKER (nonmet. min.)
Off bears fiberglass insulation material from discharge end of range and packs material for shipment: Guides end of mat around tube mounted on mandrel of automatic roller. Observes mat as it winds on tube and presses button to lower blade, cutting obvious flaws from mat. Doffs rolls of mats from machine rack, using hoist, and reads scale indicator to determine weight of roll. Packs roll of material in cardboard box, seals box, using gummed tape, and pastes label on container. Records roll number, packer number, roll weight, and number of pieces in roll on label and production record.
GOE: 06.04.38 STRENGTH: M GED: R2 M1 L1 SVP: 2 DLU: 77

579.686-018 MICA-LAMINATING-MACHINE FEEDER (mine & quarry)
Performs following tasks in rotation with other workers to laminate continuous sheet of built-up mica splittings to fiberglass cloth: Places roll of built-up mica, backed with fiberglass cloth, on shaft at feed end of conveyor and feeds roll onto conveyor. Visually inspects built-up mica sheet for thin spots or holes and places mica splittings over defective area to ensure complete coverage. Feeds fiberglass cloth through guides and positions cloth on top of built-up mica sheet as sheet emerges from dip tank containing bonding solution. Spreads bonding solution over top layer of fiberglass cloth, using paint roller. Tapes end of laminated sheet to take-up spool after sheet emerges from curing oven.
GOE: 06.04.19 STRENGTH: L GED: R2 M1 L1 SVP: 2 DLU: 77

579.686-022 MIRROR-MACHINE FEEDER (glass products) alternate titles: conveyor loader
Feeds mirror glass onto conveyor of glass silvering machine or automatic washing and drying machine. Removes silvered or cleaned mirror from conveyor. May examine mirror glass for defects.
GOE: 06.04.21 STRENGTH: H GED: R1 M1 L1 SVP: 2 DLU: 77

579.686-026 OFFBEARER, SEWER PIPE (brick & tile) alternate titles: auger-machine offbearer; turner
Performs any combination of following tasks involved in fabricating sewer or conduit clay pipe: Bends green pipe emerging from press to specified angle. Trims pipe socket edges, using hand or automatic trimmer. Lifts and places pipe on pallet board, wagon, or rack, using overhead hoist or pipe turner. Coats pipe socket with grease, oil, or water to prevent premature drying, using sponge or leather smoother. Sprays inside of pipe with glaze, using spray gun. Places kiln furniture and fittings on pipe to prepare pipe for firing. Moves kiln cars along tracks, using car pulley. Cleans machines, presses, and working area, using broom, shovel, and wheelbarrow. Changes press dies, using sledges, bars, and handtools.
GOE: 06.04.17 STRENGTH: H GED: R1 M1 L1 SVP: 2 DLU: 77

579.686-030 PRESS OFFBEARER (brick & tile)
Unloads pressed clay products from forming press in establishment manufacturing refractory products: Lifts and carries clay products from press to holding rack. Measures product to verify thickness conforms to standards, using calipers. Marks on products, using pencil, and places products on holding rack. Pushes filled holding rack to drying area and empty rack to press area. Cleans press die of clay residue and dust, using handtools and airhose.
GOE: 06.04.30 STRENGTH: H GED: R1 M1 L1 SVP: 1 DLU: 86

579.687-010 BRAKE-LINING-FINISHER HELPER, ASBESTOS (nonmet. min.)
Assists BRAKE-LINING FINISHER, ASBESTOS (nonmet. min.) to finish asbestos brake lining stock: Loads asbestos lining stock into vacuum tanks, using hoist. Cuts brake lining stock into strips, using handsaw, and trims edges of stock, using side-trimming machine. Grinds brake strips to specified thickness, using surface grinder. Shellacs edges of finished brake strip, using brush or spray gun. May dump specified quantities of materials into mixing machine to prepare brake lining impregnating solution. Performs other duties as described under HELPER (any industry) Master Title. May be designated according to duties performed as Cutter, Brake Lining (nonmet. min.); Grinder, Brake Lining (nonmet. min.).
GOE: 06.04.19 STRENGTH: M GED: R2 M1 L1 SVP: 2 DLU: 77

579.687-014 DECORATING INSPECTOR (glass mfg.)
Examines decorated glassware as it emerges from decorating or label-applying machines for decorating defects, such as off-coloring, smears, paint chips, illegible design, and misaligned labels, and for forming defects, such as misshapened glassware: Removes defective ware from conveyor and places ware with decorating defects in cartons or on conveyor for transport to decorating removal station, and discards ware with forming defects in cullet (waste glass) bin. Records number and type of defects and submits report to supervisor. May pack acceptable ware in cartons. May measure dimensions of ware, using fixed gauges and templates. May transfer decorated ware to drying oven.
GOE: 06.03.02 STRENGTH: L GED: R2 M2 L1 SVP: 2 DLU: 77

579.687-018 FLOOR ATTENDANT (glass mfg.) alternate titles: flow floor attendant; turn-out worker
Performs any combination of following tasks in forming department to facilitate manufacturing of glass products, such as bottles, containers, and other glassware: Hauls molds, mold components, and machine parts to and from forming department for job changes, and transports cullet (waste glass) from department to storage area, using forklift or handtruck. Supplies machine operators with graphite solution and swabs used to prevent sticking of glass to molds. Sweeps department, using broom to keep work area clean. Assists machine operators by observing automatic transfer mechanism that moves product from forming machine to annealing lehr to prevent jams, filling lubrication dispenser with oil, blowing debris off machine, using airhose. May adjust speed of annealing lehr. May tend container coating equipment which sprays surface hardening solution on containers. May transfer products to inspection or shipping departments, using forklift. Performs other duties as described under HELPER (any industry) Master Title.
GOE: 06.04.40 STRENGTH: M GED: R2 M1 L1 SVP: 2 DLU: 77

579.687-022 GLASS INSPECTOR (any industry)
Visually inspects plate glass or glass products, including fiberglass, for defects, such as scratches, cracks, chips, holes, or bubbles: Places workpiece on inspection stand or table for examination. Examines workpiece and marks defects. Rejects or classifies pieces for potential use, such as mirrors, glass pane, or furniture tops. Scrapes or washes foreign material from surface, using scraper, sponge, or brush. May clean or polish glass by washing with water or solvent and drying with cloth. May place straightedge over glass plates to determine if plates are warped. May attach identifying label to glassware.
GOE: 06.03.02 STRENGTH: L GED: R2 M1 L2 SVP: 3 DLU: 86

579.687-026 MICA PATCHER (mine & quarry)
Examines continuous sheet of built-up (bonded) mica for thin spots and foreign matter as mica emerges from oven onto inspection table: Patches thin spots, using mica splittings and picks out foreign matter. Removes lengths of built-up mica from delivery end of machine and stacks mica on table.
GOE: 06.03.02 STRENGTH: L GED: R2 M1 L1 SVP: 2 DLU: 77

579.687-030 SELECTOR (glass mfg.) alternate titles: glass-products inspector; inspector, machine-cut glass; inspector-packer, glass container
Inspects finished glassware for conformance to quality standards: Examines glassware for defects, such as cracks, chips, reams (wavy distortions), discolorations, and blisters. Verifies weight and dimensions of glassware, such as height, circumference, thickness, and bottle throat openings, using templates, jigs, micrometers, and fixed gauges; or monitors automatic gauging equipment that measures glassware. Examines glass for annealing defects, using polariscope. Removes glassware to unjam automatic equipment. Throws rejects in cullet (waste glass) bin. May record production, number of rejects, and lehr temperatures. May pack acceptable glassware in cartons, close and seal cartons, and stencil information on carton, using brush and ink. May turn controls to synchronize automatic gauging equipment with conveyor speed.
GOE: 06.03.02 STRENGTH: L GED: R2 M2 L1 SVP: 3 DLU: 77

579.687-034 DISC-PAD KNOCKOUT WORKER (nonmet. min.)
Removes cured asbestos disc brake pads from metal die plates, using knockout device: Positions die plate on roller-type conveyor, removes lid from plate,

and scrapes asbestos residue from lid, using putty knife. Pushes plate onto revolving tray and pulls lever to flip plate over to facilitate knockout of disc pads. Presses button to activate knockout device that forces metal rods into wells of die plate to punch pads from plate. Pushes empty plate along conveyor for subsequent re-use in heat-treating process.
GOE: 06.04.34 STRENGTH: M GED: R2 M1 L1 SVP: 3 DLU: 86

579.687-038 DISC-PAD-PLATE FILLER (nonmet. min.)
Places asbestos disc pads into wells of die plates prior to heat-treating process: Sprays die plate to prevent pads from adhering to plate during heat-treating process, using spray gun and silicone solution. Positions individual pads into wells of die plates and pushes filled plate along roller-type conveyor to oven or hot press. Discards broken or defective pads.
GOE: 06.04.34 STRENGTH: M GED: R2 M1 L1 SVP: 3 DLU: 86

579.687-042 LABORER, CONCRETE PLANT (concrete prod.)
Performs variety of tasks in establishment manufacturing concrete products: Ties strip of cloth around bell of freshly cast concrete pipe to maintain circular shape of bell during curing. Arranges pipe in storage yard and stacks pipe for shipment. Places rubber gaskets on pipe. Stacks concrete blocks on pallets for removal by forklift truck. Feeds concrete blocks into block-breaking machine or abrasive saw to shape blocks. Immerses chimney flue liner sections in sealing compound. Brushes stone facings to remove loose material, applies acid solution, using brush to remove concrete around stones, and washes acid from stone, using water hose. Repairs defects in concrete surfaces, using mortar or grout and trowel, and smooths rough spots, using chisel and abrasive stone. Opens gates of railroad cars to allow materials to flow into storage chutes. Loads, unloads, and moves cement, sand, and gravel to work areas, using wheelbarrow, handtruck, or industrial truck. Cleans yard and plant, using shovel, broom, and water hose, and performs other duties as assigned. May be designated according to specific duties performed as Acid Cutter (concrete prod.); Bell Tier (concrete prod.); Block Breaker (concrete prod.); Block Cuber (concrete prod.); Flue-Lining Dipper (concrete prod.); Rough Patcher (concrete prod.); Yarder (concrete prod.).
GOE: 06.04.40 STRENGTH: H GED: R2 M1 L1 SVP: 2 DLU: 79

58 OCCUPATIONS IN PROCESSING OF LEATHER, TEXTILES, AND RELATED PRODUCTS

This division includes occupations concerned with applying treatment materials and additives to textile, leather, and textile products; subjecting such materials and products to chemicals, heat, mechanical action, cleaning agents, and the like to impart such characteristics as body weight, pliability, size, texture, water resistance, and finish. Includes converting hides and skins into leather.

580 SHAPING, BLOCKING, STRETCHING, AND TENTERING OCCUPATIONS

This group includes occupations concerned with imparting or restoring shape to materials and objects by the use of such devices as blocks, and extending materials to their full extent or to greater size by such devices as tenters (frames for stretching).

580.380-010 FIXER, BOARDING ROOM (knitting)
Sets up and adjusts machines and equipment used to shape and dry hose, using knowledge of machine function and *boarding II* process: Turns valves to admit steam to drying cabinet or boarding forms. Changes *toe boards* or boarding forms according to size of hose being processed, using key and handtools. Observes gauges during boarding and turns valves to increase or decrease steam pressure and temperature of drying chamber or boarding forms, according to type of hose being boarded. Replaces worn or broken parts, such as conveyors, boarding forms, and electric motors, using handtools.
GOE: 06.01.02 STRENGTH: M GED: R4 M2 L3 SVP: 7 DLU: 77

580.485-010 CALENDERING-MACHINE OPERATOR (knitting) alternate titles: calenderer; finisher; folding-machine operator; mangle tender, cloth; rolling-up-machine operator
Tends machine that stretches and sets circular knitted cloth (knit tubing) to uniform width: Turns screws to adjust width of spreader according to specifications. Turns valves to admit steam into steam box that sets stretched cloth. Threads cloth over feed and guide rollers, around spreader, through steam box, and between pressure rolls, and wraps end of cloth around *takeup roll* or guides end through *swing-folding attachment*. Starts machine and observes flow of cloth to detect cloth defects, such as dirt, dye streaks, and holes. Cuts defects from cloth, using shears. Measures width of calendered cloth with hand rule. Cuts calendered cloth with shears or automatic cutter attached to machine and doffs rolls of cloth from machine. May lower top pressure roller to press cloth. May attach identification tag to end of cloth bolt. May tend calender fed from rolls, handtruck, or another machine.
GOE: 06.04.05 STRENGTH: H GED: R2 M1 L2 SVP: 3 DLU: 77

580.682-010 WEFT STRAIGHTENER (textile)
Operates weft straightener that straightens and aligns skewed weft of broad woven fabrics after wet finishing: Observes cloth passing under beam of light to detect skewed weft. Presses buttons to control movement of rollers that hold back leading selvage of skewed cloth and to allow lagging selvage to catch up. May tend finishing machines, such as cloth drier, calender, or *tenter frame*.

GOE: 06.04.16 STRENGTH: L GED: R3 M1 L2 SVP: 4 DLU: 77

580.684-010 BLOCKER, HAND I (hat & cap) alternate titles: blocker, heated metal-forms; felt puller; hat blocker; roper
Shrinks felt cones to size and shapes cones to form unfinished hat bodies: Immerses cone in hot water, places cone in steam cabinet, or holds cone over steam jet, to shrink and soften cone. Positions softened cone over heated headshaped block. Presses and rubs cone to smooth and shape cone by hand or using iron. Ties cord around base of crown and pulls edge of cone over base of block to form brim of hat. Removes cord and block from hat body after drying. May place cones in drying cabinet following blocking process.
GOE: 06.02.27 STRENGTH: L GED: R2 M1 L2 SVP: 3 DLU: 77

580.684-014 BLOCKER, HAND II (hat & cap) alternate titles: cap blocker; hat-blocking operator; strawhat-blocking operator
Presses caps or hats over heated hat blocks, by hand or with electric iron, to shape, smooth, or finish articles by any combination of following methods: (1) Turns dial or handle on metal block to heat block and fits article over block. Presses, pulls, and rubs article by hand to smooth article. (2) Inserts parts of adjustable block into hat or cap and forces wedge between parts to expand parts to fill article. Places article on bed of steam chamber or holds article over steam jet to soften article. Presses article with electric iron before placing in heated drying box. May be designated according to hat blocked as Panama-Hat Blocker (hat & cap); Strawhat Blocker (hat & cap); or according to production stage as Trimming-Department Blocker (hat & cap). When performing final finishing operations in addition to blocking, such as brushing hats and clipping loose threads, may be known as Set-Off Blocker (hat & cap).
GOE: 06.04.27 STRENGTH: L GED: R2 M1 L1 SVP: 2 DLU: 78

580.685-010 BRIM-STRETCHING-MACHINE OPERATOR (hat & cap) alternate titles: brimmer blocker; brimming-machine operator; brim stretcher
Tends machine that stretches lower part of unfinished hat body to form brim: Immerses hat bodies in hot water to soften material preparatory to stretching. Moves lever to adjust angle of metal ribs under hat-shaped block of machine to control specified brim width and crown height. Slips softened hat body onto block and over ribs. Presses button or depresses pedal to raise hat block and start movement of machine fingers that stretch brim. Releases pedal, turns body on block, and repeats stretching operation until brim is formed around entire hat body. Measures width of brim to ensure conformity with specifications, using ruler. Removes hat body from machine and places hat body on rack.
GOE: 06.04.05 STRENGTH: L GED: R2 M1 L1 SVP: 3 DLU: 78

580.685-014 CLOTH DRIER (knitting) alternate titles: cloth spreader; drier tender; drying-machine operator; steaming-machine operator
Tends machine that stretches and dries knitted material: Inserts spreader of specified width into material. Pulls end of material through drying chamber equipped with fans and inserts material between feed rolls of machine. Starts fans which circulate heat and rolls which pull wet material over spreader and through chamber to stretch and dry knitted material.
GOE: 06.04.05 STRENGTH: M GED: R2 M1 L2 SVP: 2 DLU: 77

580.685-018 COLLAR-TURNER OPERATOR (garment) alternate titles: collar-folder operator; collar-shaper operator
Tends machine that reverses partially finished collars on garments, such as ladies' dresses, and flattens seams of collars: Folds collar back along seam and draws folded seam over lower jaw of machine. Depresses pedal that lowers upper jaw of machine to spread seam. Grasps and moves collar back and forth over lower jaw to flatten seam. Releases pedal and removes collar.
GOE: 06.04.05 STRENGTH: L GED: R2 M1 L2 SVP: 2 DLU: 77

580.685-022 COTTON-BALL-MACHINE TENDER (protective dev.)
Tends battery of machines that comb cotton fibers into sliver and form sliver into balls for use as surgical sponges: Positions roll of cotton on carding machine and threads end through rollers. Starts machine that forms sliver. Threads sliver through rollers of machine that forms and ejects balls into bag. Adjusts machine to control size and weight of cotton balls. Sets counter and starts machine. Removes bag when filled with specified number of balls. Folds over flap and seals bag in container. Removes cotton fibers from carding machine, using stripping roller [CARD STRIPPER (textile)].
GOE: 06.02.06 STRENGTH: L GED: R3 M2 L2 SVP: 4 DLU: 77

580.685-026 HAT-BLOCKING-MACHINE OPERATOR I (hat & cap) alternate titles: blocking-machine operator; stamper blocker; steam blocker; tipper; western-felt-hat blocker; wet crown-blocking operator
Saturates felt cones in water and tends machine that stretches felt cones to form hat shapes: Places felt cones in container of hot water or on racks in steam cabinet to condition cones. Removes conditioned cone from water or cabinet and pulls cone onto hat block. Positions hat block on holding device in bed of machine. Presses levers to close machine claws that grasp rim of cone and pull rim outward to form brim. Starts ram that forces block upward into cone to shape crown. Presses lever or depresses pedal to spray water and force air through cone, or pours water over cone to stiffen cone. Releases levers and removes hat from machine. Places hats on wheeled racks. May be designated according to type of hat blocked as Wool-Hat Blocker (hat & cap).
GOE: 06.04.05 STRENGTH: L GED: R2 M1 L1 SVP: 4 DLU: 78

580.685-030 HAT-BLOCKING-MACHINE OPERATOR II (hat & cap)
Tends double-unit hat-blocking machine that shapes white twill Navy hats: Places hat on bottom part of block (mold), pushes block forward, and pulls lever to lower upper part of block over lower section. Opens air valve that inflates rubber lining and presses crown outward against sides of block to shape (block) hat. Moves lever to raise upper section of block, releases air pressure, pulls lower section to starting position, and removes shaped hat. Stacks hats on table.
GOE: 06.04.05 STRENGTH: M GED: R1 M1 L1 SVP: 2 DLU: 77

580.685-034 HOOKING-MACHINE OPERATOR (textile)
Tends machine that tightens twist in skeins of dyed thread: Opens and examines skeins of thread to ensure that thread matches specifications of work order. Hooks one end of skein to upper hook of machine and hooks other end to lower hook on movable beam of machine. Releases clutch that lowers beam and stretches skein. Turns crank that rotates beam and twists skein. Feels skein to determine if twist has been tightened as specified.
GOE: 06.04.05 STRENGTH: M GED: R2 M1 L2 SVP: 3 DLU: 77

580.685-038 HYDRAULIC BLOCKER (hat & cap) alternate titles: hydraulic-press operator; presser
Tends hydraulic press that shapes hats, hatbrims, or crowns: Selects shaping die, according to specifications, and positions die in recess of machine bed. Positions saddle (rubber hat-shaped liner) in die to protect hat during pressing. Pours water into tank of machine and turns valve to regulate level of water in rubber pressing bag, attached to machine ram, according to size of hat to be shaped. Inserts hat, crown down, into die. Moves lever to lower ram and water-filled bag against brim or into crown to press hat, brim, or crown. May be designated according to hat material as Straw-Hat-Hydraulic-Press Operator (hat & cap); according to hat part shaped as Brim Presser (hat & cap) II; Crown Presser (hat & cap); or according to processing stage as Blocking-Machine Operator, Second (hat & cap); Hydraulic-Press Operator, First Pressing (hat & cap). When tending machine that shapes hatbrims between flange (brim-shaped collar) and water-filled bag, is known as Hydraulic-Brim-Flanging-Machine Operator (hat & cap). May be designated: Band-Plating-Machine Operator (hat & cap); Panama-Hat-Hydraulic-Press Operator (hat & cap); Wool-Hat Hydraulicker (hat & cap); Woven-Paper-Hat-Hydraulic-Press Operator Finisher (hat & cap).
GOE: 06.04.09 STRENGTH: L GED: R2 M1 L2 SVP: 3 DLU: 78

580.685-042 MOLDER (hat & cap) alternate titles: brim molder; stamper
Tends machine that presses hat-body material, such as crinoline, paper, or buckram between dies to form hat crowns or cap visors: Places sheets of precut material between layers of wet cardboard or dampens material with sponge to soften material preparatory to pressing. Stretches softened material over heated crown-shaped lower die and depresses pedal, causing upper die to descend and press material into shape of hat crown.
GOE: 06.04.05 STRENGTH: L GED: R2 M1 L1 SVP: 4 DLU: 77

580.685-046 ROLLER OPERATOR (hat & cap)
Tends machine that forms unfinished hat bodies, and separates formed bodies for further processing: Guides sheets of wool or other hat material onto revolving egg-shaped roller that winds material into shape of roller. Presses cutting disk or knife against center of revolving roller or stops machine and severs material with scissors to cut formed material into two hat bodies.
GOE: 06.04.05 STRENGTH: L GED: R2 M1 L2 SVP: 2 DLU: 77

580.685-050 STAKER, MACHINE (leather mfg.)
Tends machine that flexes (stakes) and stretches leather to make leather pliable: Positions leather between rotating belt and jaws of reciprocating arm. Starts machine to reciprocate arm that flexes and stretches leather. Shifts position of leather on belt to flex entire area. Turns wheel to regulate stroke of arm. May tend machine that stretches hide on frames and be designated Stretching-Machine Tender, Frame (leather mfg.).
GOE: 06.04.16 STRENGTH: L GED: R2 M1 L1 SVP: 2 DLU: 77

580.685-054 STRETCHER (hat & cap)
Tends machine that stretches and softens fur pelts that are too hard or rumpled to pass through fur-shaving machine: Depresses pedal to separate power-driven rollers of machine and inserts skin between rollers. Releases pedal and holds skin as corrugated rollers stretch skin, softening it for further processing into hatter's fur.
GOE: 06.04.16 STRENGTH: M GED: R2 M1 L1 SVP: 2 DLU: 77

580.685-058 STRETCHING-MACHINE OPERATOR (tex. prod., nec)
Tends machines that stretch nets and tighten knots by either of following methods: (1) Places end of net over straightening roller and threads net through tension rollers of machine. Turns crank to adjust tension of net. Observes net on trial run to determine tightness of knots. Unfolds and straightens net as net is drawn into machine. (2) Threads holding rods through meshes at each end of net. Places rod in channel of stationary block. Stretches net by hand and places second rod in channel of winch block. Starts electric winch to stretch net to specified tension. May tie and pack nets in cartons for shipment. May attach cork or lead lines on fishing nets. May be designated according to type of machine used as Depth-Stretching-Machine Operator (tex. prod., nec); Vertical-Stretching-Machine Operator (tex. prod., nec).
GOE: 06.04.05 STRENGTH: M GED: R2 M1 L2 SVP: 3 DLU: 77

580.685-062 TIP STRETCHER (hat & cap) alternate titles: tipper; tipping-machine operator
Tends machine that kneads tips of felt hat cones to form and shape crowns of hats: Soaks cones in trough of heated water. Selects hat form according to size specifications, positions form on machine bed, and moves lever to secure form. Pulls soaked cone onto form and depresses pedal to raise form and cone against moving machine fingers that knead tip of cone, stretching cone onto form and shaping crown. Grasps bottom of cone and rotates cone to ensure symmetrical shaping of crown. Removes resulting hat body and pulls it onto hat block to smooth crown and set shape.
GOE: 06.04.05 STRENGTH: L GED: R2 M1 L1 SVP: 2 DLU: 78

580.685-066 TENTER-FRAME OPERATOR (textile) alternate titles: cloth stretcher; drier tender; drying-machine tender; framing-machine tender; hot-frame tender; open-tenter operator; pin-tenter operator; steam-frame operator; tentering-machine operator
Tends *tenter frame* that stretches cloth in width, removes wrinkles, and dries cloth after processes, such as dyeing or finishing: Trucks folded cloth to feed-end of machine or mounts roll of cloth at scray, using hoist. Sews cloth end to leader in machine, using sewing machine. Turns wheel to adjust clips or pins to stretch cloth to specified width. Moves lever to control speed of cloth through drying cabinet, to *swing-folding attachment*. Measures width of cloth emerging from machine, using yardstick. Records yardage clock readings. May replace full trucks with empty ones and ravel seams to separate truck loads of cloth. May tend tenter frame equipped with weft-straightening attachment.
GOE: 06.04.16 STRENGTH: M GED: R2 M1 L2 SVP: 3 DLU: 80

580.687-010 ORIENTAL-RUG STRETCHER (any industry) alternate titles: rug stretcher
Stretches oriental rugs to restore shape of rug and remove wrinkles or misshapen areas of rug: Places rug face down on floor or table. Pulls edges, by hand or using stretching device, and places weights on rug or tacks edges of rug to floor or table. Applies warm sizing solution to back of rug, using brushes, spray gun, or sprinkler. Removes weights or tacks when sizing has dried.
GOE: 06.04.27 STRENGTH: M GED: R2 M1 L2 SVP: 2 DLU: 77

580.687-014 HIDE STRETCHER, HAND (leather mfg.) alternate titles: laborer, drying department
Smooths, stretches, and dries cowhides, using slicker (squeegee-type device) and steam-heated tables, to extend and thin hides for further processing: Carries wet hide from rack to steam-heated table and manually extends and smooths hide on table. Rubs hide with slicker to stretch and smooth hide and to remove excess water. Stretches hides on additional tables and observes steam rising from hides to determine when hides are dry. Loads dry hides onto rack to store hides for further processing. Counts and records number of hides stretched and dried to maintain production record. Cleans steam-heated tables, using water hose and broom.
GOE: 06.04.27 STRENGTH: L GED: R1 M1 L1 SVP: 1 DLU: 86

581 SEPARATING, FILTERING, AND DRYING OCCUPATIONS

This group includes occupations concerned with removing moisture, chemicals, and other substances from materials by draining, straining, squeezing, centrifugal force, gravitation, precipitation, or agitation; and removing moisture by exposure to heat or air.

581.585-010 CARBONIZER (textile)
Tends *range* that reduces and chars vegetable matter in woolen fabrics to facilitate removal of matter: Pushes trucks of cloth into feeding position and sews cloth end to lead cloth, using portable sewing machine. Turns handwheels to adjust width guides and tension devices according to width of cloth. Turns valves to admit water and acid into wet-out and carbonizing troughs. Sets thermostat to control temperature in charring unit. Starts range and turns handwheel to regulate movement of cloth through range, according to weight of fabric. Tests strength of acid solution by titration or with hydrometer. Admits water or acid into carbonizing trough to maintain uniform strength of carbonizing agent. Records titration results or hydrometer readings, style number, and yardage of cloth processed. Cleans lint from filters of charring unit, using vacuum hose.
GOE: 06.04.16 STRENGTH: M GED: R2 M1 L2 SVP: 3 DLU: 77

581.586-010 HEAT CURER (textile)
Loads and unloads oven that cures color in screen-printed textiles: Hangs articles on rack and pushes rack into preheated oven. Removes articles from oven after specified time. Counts and records number of articles cured and packs articles into boxes.
GOE: 06.04.16 STRENGTH: L GED: R2 M1 L1 SVP: 2 DLU: 77

581.685-010 CLOTH SANDER (textile) alternate titles: sander; sanding machine operator
Tends machine that breaks up and softens size, and imparts brushed effect to surface of fabric: Pushes truck or roll of cloth into feeding position and sews end to leader cloth, using portable sewing machine. Turns valve to admit steam into *drying can*. Starts machine that passes cloth around drying can to break up and soften size in fabric, and between emery rollers that abrade surface of fabric to impart brushed effect. Positions handtruck to receive cloth from *swing-folding attachment*.
GOE: 06.04.16 STRENGTH: M GED: R1 M1 L1 SVP: 2 DLU: 77

581.685-014 DRIER (garment)
Tends curing oven that dries and cures finish applied to garments, such as skirts and suits: Hangs garments on hooks of conveyor rack and pushes rack

into oven. Turns knobs to set time, temperature, and humidity controls. Removes garments from oven at end of cycle for further processing.
GOE: 06.04.16 STRENGTH: L GED: R2 M1 L2 SVP: 3 DLU: 77

**581.685-018   DRIER OPERATOR III (plastic-synth.) alternate titles: dry-
ing-machine operator; drying-room operator**
Tends drier in which bobbins or skeins of synthetic yarn are dried prior to finishing: Hangs bobbins or skeins on poles supported by wheeled frames or by continuous chain conveyor. Moves controls to attain specified temperature in dryer and to start chain conveyor if drier is so equipped. May be designated according to article dried as Bobbin Drier (plastic-synth.); Skein Drier (plastic-synth.). May perform duties of WASHER (plastic-synth.) in plants where washing, bleaching, and drying are combined into single operation.
GOE: 06.04.16 STRENGTH: L GED: R2 M1 L1 SVP: 3 DLU: 77

**581.685-022   DRY-CANS OPERATOR (textile) alternate titles: can-drier
operator; cans operator; can tender; cloth-dry-can operator;
drier tender; drying machine tender**
Tends *drying cans* that dry cloth following processes, such as washing, desizing, or finishing: Positions truck of folded cloth at feed-end of machine. Pins cloth end to preceding bolt or sews ends together with sewing machine. Turns valve to admit steam into revolving cans that dry fabric as fabric is drawn around and between cans. Moves lever to regulate speed of revolving cans to adjust drying time according to cloth thickness. Turns wheel to change cloth tension according to type or style of fabric.
GOE: 06.04.16 STRENGTH: M GED: R2 M1 L2 SVP: 2 DLU: 77

**581.685-026   DRYING-MACHINE OPERATOR, PACKAGE YARNS
(textile) alternate titles: drier operator; kier drier; oven-drier
tender; package drier; port drier**
Tends machines that dry packages of dyed or bleached yarn by any of following methods: (1) Removes yarn packages from yarn stand and places them on drying-oven rack. Sets temperature control gauges according to specifications and pushes rack of yarn into drying oven. (2) Positions loaded yarn stand removed from dyeing machine over hot-air port, using power hoist. Sets controls to direct air through holes in yarn stand to dry yarn. (3) Loads stand of yarn into kier, using power hoist. Closes lid and tightens bolts, using wrench. Sets controls to circulate hot air through yarn. Removes dried yarn from drying machine, inspects packages for dyeing defects, and packs packages in cases for storage or shipment. May fasten case with metal band and truck case to warehouse.
GOE: 06.04.16 STRENGTH: M GED: R2 M1 L1 SVP: 2 DLU: 77

**581.685-030   DRYING-MACHINE TENDER (textile) alternate titles: cur-
ing oven tender; tubing drier**
Tends machine that dries cloth without tension to give cloth a soft hand, or cures finish applied to cloth: Positions trucks of cloth at feed end of machine. Laps end of cloth over feed roller or ties end of cloth to leader in machine. Turns knob to set temperature control gauge according to instructions. Moves lever to start machine and regulate speed of cloth through drying cabinet. Manually straightens cloth entering machine to remove wrinkles. Cleans machine, using vacuum hose. May doff cloth from *swing-folding attachment* at delivery end of machine. May mark lot numbers on cloth ends with crayon. May be designated according to type of drying machine as Loop-Drier Operator (textile); Suction-Drum-Drier Operator (textile).
GOE: 06.04.16 STRENGTH: M GED: R2 M1 L2 SVP: 2 DLU: 77

**581.685-034   DRYING-UNIT-FELTING-MACHINE OPERATOR (tex.
prod., nec) alternate titles: continuous-drier operator; drier**
Tends drying chamber that removes moisture from felt strips: Opens steam valves to heat chamber to specified temperature and opens and closes vents in chamber to control ventilation. Attaches leading edge of felt strip to hooks of conveyor and starts machine to draw strip through drying chamber. Clamps leading edge of strip to winding drum as strip emerges from chamber. Cuts strip with knife when specified amount of felt is wound on drum.
GOE: 06.04.16 STRENGTH: L GED: R2 M1 L2 SVP: 4 DLU: 77

**581.685-038   EXTRACTOR OPERATOR (any industry) alternate titles:
centrifugal-extractor operator; clothes wringer; drying-machine tender; extractor; rapid-extractor operator; wringer**
Tends centrifugal extractor that removes surplus moisture or dye from materials, such as wet cloth, garments, knit goods, linens, raw fibers, or yarn: Pushes loaded handtrucks or portable extractor baskets into position at machine or under hoist. Lifts material from handtruck, or raises baskets, using chain or electric hoist to load extractor. Distributes material uniformly in extractor baskets to balance load and reduce vibration. Observes tilt of portable baskets to verify balance when starting extractor. Closes cover and starts machine. Unloads materials into handtruck for transfer to subsequent work station. May unload washing machines. May work with raw cotton and be designated Extractor Tender, Raw Stock (textile). May tend drying machine [TUMBLER OPERATOR (laundry & rel.) 369.685-034]. May tend machine that extracts moisture from cakes of rayon or other synthetic yarn and be designated Cake Wringer (plastic-synth.).
GOE: 06.04.16 STRENGTH: M GED: R2 M1 L1 SVP: 2 DLU: 78

**581.685-042   EXTRACTOR OPERATOR (textile) alternate titles: suction-
machine operator; vacuum-extractor operator**
Tends vacuum extractor that removes excess moisture from washed, bleached, or dyed cloth by either of following methods: (1) Mounts roll of cloth

onto brackets at back of machine. Pins cloth to leader to pass cloth over suction tube and between rollers. Starts vacuum pump and opens drain valve. Regulates roller speed according to thickness of cloth. Places empty truck under *swing-folding attachment* to receive processed cloth and doffs full truck. (2) Mounts roll of cloth, wound on perforated beam, on machine, using hoist. Connects one end of beam to suction tube and turns handwheel to place cap over other end to create vacuum chamber within beam. Starts vacuum pump and opens drain valve to extract moisture. Transfers roll to takeoff brackets, using hoist. Threads end of cloth over rollers and through swing-folding attachment, and straightens cloth feeding into handtruck.
GOE: 06.04.16 STRENGTH: M GED: R2 M1 L2 SVP: 2 DLU: 77

**581.685-046   RAW-STOCK-DRIER TENDER (textile) alternate titles:
fiber-drier operator; stock-drier tender**
Tends machine that completes drying of dyed raw cotton, wool, or synthetic fibers, from which excess liquid has been extracted: Feeds raw stock to conveyor by hand or turns switch to control vacuum pipe through which stock is fed onto conveyor. Moves lever to regulate speed of screen or apron which carries loose fibers through drying cabinet. Sets gauge to control drying temperature. Cleans equipment, using compressed air and steam.
GOE: 06.04.16 STRENGTH: L GED: R2 M1 L1 SVP: 2 DLU: 77

581.685-050   RUG-DRYING-MACHINE OPERATOR (carpet & rug)
Tends machine that dries spools of dyed carpeting: Positions spools of wet material on machine brackets and ties ends to asbestos strips in machine. Turns switches to regulate speed of intake and exhaust blowers and to obtain specified temperature from infrared and gas heat units. Starts machine and observes as carpet emerges from discharge end and winds onto spools to determine if drying meets specifications. Observes gauges and adjusts switches to maintain specified temperature in drying chamber. May run carpet through *swing-folding attachment* as carpet emerges from machine.
GOE: 06.04.16 STRENGTH: L GED: R2 M1 L2 SVP: 3 DLU: 77

**581.685-054   SKEIN-YARN DRIER (textile) alternate titles: drying-ma-
chine operator; steam-drier operator; yarn-dry-room worker**
Tends machine that dries skeins of yarn: Turns valves to set temperature of drying cabinet according to specifications. Starts fans to circulate heat in drying cabinet. Places yarn skeins on conveyor that conveys yarn through cabinet, hangs skeins on drying rack and pushes rack into drying cabinet, or loops skeins over poles and places poles on conveyor that conveys yarn through cabinet. Removes dried skeins of yarn from conveyor, racks, or poles. Shakes tangled skeins of yarn before and after drying to straighten skeins.
GOE: 06.04.16 STRENGTH: M GED: R1 M1 L1 SVP: 2 DLU: 77

581.685-058   STEAM-DRIER TENDER (carpet & rug)
Tends equipment that steams and dries fiber mats to untwist yarns and impart fuller surface to mat: Adjusts steam valves to regulate flow of spray on mats. Pushes button to start conveyor that moves mats through steam and drying cabinets. Loads mats on conveyor and observes thermometers and adjusts controls to maintain specified temperature in cabinets.
GOE: 06.04.16 STRENGTH: H GED: R3 M2 L3 SVP: 5 DLU: 77

581.685-062   TUMBLER TENDER (knitting)
Tends tumbler that dries and fluffs knitted garments or cloth after washing or dyeing: Loads garments or cloth into drum of machine. Turns knob to set temperature gauge and turns timing dial to set length of drying cycle according to type of material. Starts machine. Unloads machine at end of drying cycle. May lap end of cloth over reel and start reel to wind cloth in skein before loading drier. May separate garments according to size, style, and color. May inspect garments to detect color streaks.
GOE: 06.04.16 STRENGTH: M GED: R2 M1 L1 SVP: 2 DLU: 77

581.685-066   VACUUM-DRIER OPERATOR (tex. prod., nec)
Tends vacuum drier that removes moisture from felt pads: Pushes dollies loaded with pads into tunnel of drying chamber. Lifts pads onto drying racks. Closes airtight doors and starts vacuum pumps and electric fans. Opens steam valves to adjust heat of drying chamber to specified temperature. Loads dried pads on dollies for further processing.
GOE: 06.04.16 STRENGTH: M GED: R2 M1 L1 SVP: 4 DLU: 77

**581.685-070   WHIZZER (hat & cap) alternate titles: extractor; whizzer
operator**
Tends machine that spins felt hat bodies to remove excess water: Pulls bodies over hat-shaped holder of machine or places bodies in basket. Presses button or depresses pedal to start holder or basket spinning, removing excess water from bodies. Releases pedal to stop machine and feels hat bodies to ascertain dryness. May soak hat bodies in waterproofing solution.
GOE: 06.04.16 STRENGTH: L GED: R2 M1 L1 SVP: 2 DLU: 77

581.685-074   WINDING-RACK OPERATOR (tex. prod., nec)
Tends equipment in dry room that winds coated fabrics into rolls: Aligns track-mounted *windup rack* with dry room alley to receive coated cloth. Cleans foreign material from water-cooled rollers, using rag, solvent, and scraper. Threads cloth from dry room through rollers, and sews cloth to leader on windup core, using automatic sewing machine. Adjusts control to synchronize winding tension with cloth feed to avoid wrinkles, turned edges, and tears. Places cloth-support sticks on handtruck as sticks arrive from dry room. Notifies supervisor of recurring coating defects. Lifts finished roll from rack onto dolly, using hoist.

GOE: 06.04.16 STRENGTH: M GED: R2 M1 L2 SVP: 3 DLU: 77

581.685-078 FLAT DRIER (tex. prod., nec)
Tends equipment that dries felt strips, assisted by another worker: Removes work ticket from rolls of felt and records on ticket drying time and temperature required to dry felt. Places felt rolls on holding fixture of drying chamber, and turns handcrank to adjust carrier rack of chamber to width of felt. Unrolls felt and attaches edges of entire roll to spikes on both sides of carrier rack, using wooden hammer. Pushes carrier rack with felt into drying chamber, closes chamber door, and turns valves to obtain specified steam pressure and temperature. Presses button to start fan to circulate heat evenly in chamber, and turns dial of timer to set length of drying cycle, according to thickness of felt. Observes gauges to maintain specified chamber temperature and steam pressure. Closes steam valve and opens chamber door to cool drying chamber. Feels felt to ascertain dryness. Rerolls felt for further processing.
GOE: 06.04.16 STRENGTH: M GED: R3 M1 L2 SVP: 4 DLU: 86

581.685-082 DRUM-DRIER OPERATOR (plastic-synth.)
Tends drum-drier that removes moisture from polyester chips prior to processing chips into synthetic fibers: Pushes button and turns lever to start and rotate drum-drier into position for loading. Positions specified number of boxes of polyester chips on hydraulic loader, and pushes button to dump chips into loader bin. Spreads chips evenly in bin while vacuum system sucks chips into drum-drier. Presses button to rotate drum-drier for specified time to dry polyester chips. Opens tops of portable storage bins, using wrench, positions bins underneath unloading spout of drum-drier, using forklift, and opens spout to fill bins with chips, using wrench. Secures tops of bins, and attaches nozzles of nitrogen gas supply to filled bins to maintain chips moisture-free while in bins. Transports bins to storage, using forklift; or places bins on elevator to raise bin to upper floor, removes top of chip silo, lowers bins into silo, using hoist, and opens valves on bins to empty chips into silo for further processing. Obtains chip samples at specified times for chemical analysis. Fills out inventory cards and attaches cards to side of bins. Removes cards when emptying bins, and submits cards to supervisor. Maintains log of drum-drier start-up times, type of chips loaded, and name for plant record.
GOE: 06.04.16 STRENGTH: V GED: R2 M1 L1 SVP: 3 DLU: 86

581.686-010 BLOWER FEEDER, DYED RAW STOCK (textile)
Feeds loose, partly dried textile fibers into pipe through which fibers are blown to drier or storage bin.
GOE: 06.04.40 STRENGTH: H GED: R1 M1 L1 SVP: 2 DLU: 77

581.686-014 DRIER (knitting) alternate titles: drying-machine tender
Feeds and off bears oven drier that dries and sets knitted articles after *boarding II* and dyeing: Dumps articles from bag onto table and arranges articles in stacks. Shakes wrinkles from articles and places articles on conveyor that feeds articles into drier. Off bears conveyor and folds and stacks articles on tray.
GOE: 06.04.16 STRENGTH: L GED: R2 M1 L1 SVP: 2 DLU: 77

581.686-018 DRIER ATTENDANT (garment)
Hangs garments, such as skirts and suits, on hooks suspended from chain conveyor that carries garments through curing oven to dry and cure finish applied to garment. Removes cured garments from conveyor onto rack for further processing.
GOE: 06.04.40 STRENGTH: M GED: R1 M1 L1 SVP: 1 DLU: 77

581.686-022 DRYING-OVEN ATTENDANT (hat & cap) alternate titles: dryer feeder; skin-drying-room attendant
Lays wet, freshly carroted pelts in trays on conveyor chain that carries pelts through heated drying chamber to prepare fur for manufacturing felt hats. May push handtrucks loaded with skins into drying room and lay out skins on drying trays.
GOE: 06.04.16 STRENGTH: M GED: R1 M1 L1 SVP: 1 DLU: 77

581.686-026 DRYING-RACK CHANGER (boot & shoe)
Feeds finished lasted shoes into drying chamber to dry and stiffen leather and shape shoes: Removes lasted shoes from bar racks and places shoes on racks having padded rests. Starts conveyor track and pushes rack of shoes onto moving track that carries rack into drying chamber. Removes rack at other end of chamber after specified time. May set scale to adjust drying room temperature according to hygrometer readings.
GOE: 06.04.05 STRENGTH: L GED: R2 M1 L1 SVP: 2 DLU: 77

581.686-030 DUST-MILL OPERATOR (tex. prod., nec)
Feeds feathers, used in stuffing mattresses, pillows, and cushions, into beating machine that removes dust and dirt from feathers and discharges feathers into bag. Removes filled bag from machine outlet pipe and replaces filled bag with empty bag. May feed feathers into machine that fluffs feathers preparatory to removal of dust and dirt.
GOE: 06.04.39 STRENGTH: M GED: R1 M1 L1 SVP: 1 DLU: 77

581.686-034 FEATHER-DRYING-MACHINE OPERATOR (tex. prod., nec)
Loads feathers, used for stuffing pillows and cushions, into steam-heated drying tank or centrifugal drier to dry feathers after washing. Removes feathers from drier by hand or opens outlet valve.
GOE: 06.04.09 STRENGTH: M GED: R1 M1 L1 SVP: 2 DLU: 77

581.686-038 TRAY DRIER (knitting) alternate titles: drying-machine operator
Tends machine that dries preboarded and dyed hose in perforated trays: Removes folded hose from dye bag and smooths out wrinkles. Places hose into tray of drying machine and pushes filled tray into drying cabinet. Pulls tray from cabinet after hose have dried for specified time. Removes and stacks hose on tray for pairing.
GOE: 06.04.16 STRENGTH: M GED: R1 M1 L1 SVP: 2 DLU: 77

581.686-042 WET-COTTON FEEDER (textile)
Feeds dyed cotton or synthetic raw stock into hopper of extractor that removes liquid by forcing cotton through rollers. Cleans machine, using steam and airhose.
GOE: 06.04.16 STRENGTH: M GED: R1 M1 L1 SVP: 2 DLU: 77

581.687-010 BURLAP SPREADER (tex. prod., nec)
Spreads washed, ripped-open, second-hand burlap bags and washed burlap strips out of doors or hangs articles on racks to dry.
GOE: 06.04.27 STRENGTH: M GED: R1 M1 L1 SVP: 1 DLU: 77

581.687-014 DRYING-ROOM ATTENDANT (hat & cap)
Hangs racks of hat bodies in room for drying. Places rack of hats on hangers and turns switch to activate hot-air blowers. Removes dried hats onto handtruck for further processing.
GOE: 06.04.27 STRENGTH: L GED: R1 M1 L1 SVP: 1 DLU: 77

581.687-018 DRYING-UNIT-FELTING-MACHINE-OPERATOR HELPER (tex. prod., nec) alternate titles: continuous-drier helper
Assists DRYING-UNIT-FELTING-MACHINE OPERATOR (tex. prod., nec) to tend machine that removes moisture from felt strips: Pushes dollies containing filled drums (spools) of wet felt to drying chamber, and clamps drum to spindle of drying equipment. Loads drums of dried felt on dollies, and pushes dollies to designated area for further processing of felt. Performs other duties as described under HELPER (any industry) Master Title.
GOE: 06.04.16 STRENGTH: H GED: R1 M1 L1 SVP: 2 DLU: 77

581.687-022 SPREADER (hat & cap) alternate titles: stretcher and drier
Stretches fur pelts on frames and hangs pelts in hot room for drying after *carroting*, preparatory to removing fur for felt.
GOE: 06.04.27 STRENGTH: M GED: R1 M1 L1 SVP: 1 DLU: 77

582 WASHING, STEAMING, AND SATURATING OCCUPATIONS

This group includes occupations concerned with applying water and steam, and chemical agents to materials; and thoroughly soaking, filling, impregnating, or treating materials with substances to the point where no more can be taken up. Occupations concerned with steaming and saturating materials in order to shrink them are included in Group 587.

582.130-010 SUPERVISOR, GLAZING DEPARTMENT (textile)
Supervises and coordinates activities of workers engaged in applying finishing solution to thread for strength and luster: Directs machine setup, adjustment, and repair activities, and mixing of finishing compounds. Trains new employees and evaluates work performances. Examines thread for excess moisture and firmness of finish. Requisitions machine parts and supplies. Performs other duties as described under SUPERVISOR (any industry) Master Title.
GOE: 06.02.01 STRENGTH: M GED: R4 M3 L3 SVP: 7 DLU: 77

582.131-010 DYE-HOUSE SUPERVISOR (leather mfg.)
Supervises and coordinates activities of workers engaged in bleaching, dyeing, tanning, and washing fur pelts: Prepares bleaching, dyeing, and tanning solutions according to specified formula. Examines processed pelts and reports irregularities in dyeing or tanning process to chemist and management. Sets thermostat to regulate temperature in drying room according to type of pelt. Trains workers. Performs other duties as described under SUPERVISOR (any industry) Master Title. May be designated according to process as Bleaching Supervisor (leather mfg.); Dyeing Supervisor (leather mfg.); Tanning Supervisor (leather mfg.).
GOE: 06.02.01 STRENGTH: L GED: R4 M3 L3 SVP: 7 DLU: 77

582.131-014 DYER, SUPERVISOR (knitting; tex. prod., nec; textile) alternate titles: dye-house supervisor; superintendent, dyeing
Supervises and coordinates activities of workers engaged in dyeing textile goods: Compares customer's sample with standard color cards to identify color. Selects formula sheet which corresponds with standard color card, or prepares formula sheet, employing knowledge of characteristics of dyes, pigments, and resins to produce required properties and shade at lowest cost. Schedules production, according to colors required, processes used, and type of goods, to ensure efficient production in dyeing department. Requisitions dyestuffs and materials needed for each order. Compares dyed products with standards to ensure adherence to specifications. Confers with customers to adjust complaints, and with management to plan production schedule. Trains workers in operation of machines and equipment. May develop new colors and dye samples, employing standard laboratory techniques. Performs other duties as described under SUPERVISOR (any industry) Master Title.
GOE: 05.10.07 STRENGTH: L GED: R4 M3 L4 SVP: 7 DLU: 81

582.132-010 AGING-DEPARTMENT SUPERVISOR (textile)
Supervises and coordinates activities of workers engaged in aging printed cloth: Trains workers in operation of machines and equipment. Requisitions supplies. Confers with other supervisory personnel to coordinate activities of individual departments and advise on safety and housekeeping improvements.

Performs other duties as described under SUPERVISOR (any industry) Master Title.
GOE: 06.02.01 STRENGTH: M GED: R4 M3 L3 SVP: 6 DLU: 77

582.132-014 SOAPING-DEPARTMENT SUPERVISOR (textile)
Supervises and coordinates activities of workers engaged in washing and soaping cloth: Trains workers in operation of machines and equipment. Confers with other supervisory personnel to coordinate activities of individual departments. Performs other duties as described under SUPERVISOR (any industry) Master Title.
GOE: 06.02.01 STRENGTH: L GED: R4 M3 L3 SVP: 6 DLU: 77

582.132-018 SUPERVISOR, TAN ROOM (leather mfg.)
Supervises and coordinates activities of workers engaged in tanning hides. Selects and mixes ingredients, such as chrome solution, bicarbonate of soda, and water to prepare tanning solution, following formula. Trains workers in operation of equipment. Performs other duties as described under SUPERVISOR (any industry) Master Title.
GOE: 06.02.01 STRENGTH: L GED: R4 M3 L3 SVP: 7 DLU: 77

582.132-022 SUPERVISOR, VAT HOUSE (chemical; leather mfg.)
Supervises and coordinates activities of workers engaged in washing, liming, and treating skins, splits, fleshings, and trimmings used in making glue or leather: Directs loading of stock into vats and wash mills. Estimates weight of stock to determine quantity of lime required to treat stock, and directs LIMER (chemical; leather mfg.) to pump specified amount into vats. Examines shredded stock for conformance with specification and returns rejected stock to chopper. Trains workers in operation of equipment. Requisitions lime and acids. Performs other duties as described under SUPERVISOR (any industry) Master Title.
GOE: 06.02.01 STRENGTH: L GED: R4 M3 L3 SVP: 7 DLU: 77

582.261-010 COLOR MATCHER (knitting) alternate titles: dyer assistant
Verifies color of hosiery dye lots against standard and modifies dyeing process on basis of knowledge of dyes and dyeing time: Passes sample hose from each dye lot through steam to fix color. Compares color with master sample and approves lot if color matches standard. Determines dyeing time and weighs out additional dyes or reducing agents for lots not meeting specifications. May assist DYER, SUPERVISOR (knitting; tex. prod., nec; textile) 582.131-014 to schedule dyeing of assembled dye lots and to verify color of new styles against customer's color swatch.
GOE: 06.01.05 STRENGTH: L GED: R3 M2 L3 SVP: 6 DLU: 77

582.362-010 PANELBOARD OPERATOR (textile)
Controls programmed equipment to dye yarn or cloth: Mounts specified cycle-control template (program master) in timing track. Turns crank to align starting point on template with vacuum/electric controls, and temperature tracer with profile cut in top of program master. Transfers dye formula to DYE WEIGHER (any industry) 550.684-014 and verifies quantities mixed. Presses buttons on panelboard to begin fill-cycles in specified machines and notifies DYE WEIGHER (any industry) to transfer dye and chemical solutions to machines when panelboard lights indicate yarn or cloth loading is complete and processing cycle in operation. Observes panelboard lights, gauges, graphs, and dials to determine progress of dyeing cycles and to detect malfunctions. Presses buttons and turns knobs to stop automatic cycle to obtain samples, fill or drain machines, adjust variable limits of machine water-level controls, or to resume processing cycle to include washing and stabilizing dye in yarn or cloth. Tests solutions for acidity or alkalinity strengths, using pH testing equipment, and records results onto formula. Notifies supervisory personnel of malfunctions, variations from processing standards, and completion of processing cycles. Records processing data onto dye formulas. May develop and maintain dye formulas.
GOE: 06.04.16 STRENGTH: L GED: R3 M1 L2 SVP: 4 DLU: 77

582.362-014 DYE AUTOMATION OPERATOR (textile)
Controls and monitors programmed electronic equipment to bleach, dye, and finish cotton and synthetic sewing threads: Confers with operator of dye machines to obtain information needed to process customer orders, and records data, such as number of dyeing machines to be used, production order numbers, and color numbers specified for dye orders. Selects programmed procedures based on knowledge of dyeing processes and familiarity with affinity of dyes to specific thread types, or consults procedural manuals for data. Depresses keys of data-entry unit to enter required data into computer. Observes display screen to verify data entered, to ascertain computer response to instruction entered, and to determine compliance with procedural steps. Depresses keys to edit instructions when necessary and to input answers for primary or alternate steps in procedure. Hangs tags on dye board, during shift, to indicate steps in dyeing process for each machine. Confers with workers to determine reasons for delays in dyeing process, and examines dyeing machines and equipment to ascertain reason for malfunctions. Notifies supervisor of malfunctions, and records reasons for delays in log. Receives instructions from supervisor, such as alteration of dyeing temperature, omission of specific steps in dyeing process, or repetition of specific steps. Keys in dyeing instruction changes. Confers with operator on previous shift to ascertain drying steps to complete dyeing in progress.
GOE: 06.02.16 STRENGTH: L GED: R3 M3 L3 SVP: 5 DLU: 86

582.384-010 DYE-LAB TECHNICIAN (knitting)
Dyes knitted socks and sample cloth, according to dye formulae, using sample dyeing equipment and steam table for verification that products conform to company specifications: Computes quantity of dyes required for machine of specified capacity, using desk calculator and dye formula. Gathers, weighs, measures, and mixes dyes and chemicals, using scales, graduated cylinders, measuring cup, and titration cylinder. Dyes individual socks, using steam table. Flips switches and turns valves and handwheel to prepare sample tub dye bath and adds specified quantities of acid and dye, to achieve required pH level and specifications for dye contrast and color intensity, to prepare sample cloth and sock to be inspected. Presses buttons to activate and deactivate drum of extractor to remove excess moisture from machine and dyed sample cloth. Submits dyed sample to supervisor for inspection.
GOE: 02.04.01 STRENGTH: M GED: R3 M3 L2 SVP: 5 DLU: 86

582.387-010 COLOR CHECKER, ROVING OR YARN (textile) alternate titles: shade-and-quality checker;
Tests dyed roving or yarn to determine fastness of dye and uniformity of color: Winds specified quantity of yarn or roving onto reel and binds sample skein with bleached cloth band. Boils test sample in detergent solution for specified length of time. Dries sample in humidity and temperature controlled drier. Winds dried sample onto sample card and compares test sample with standard sample to detect variations in color. Examines bleached cloth band for bleeding of dyes. Records test results and reports variations from standards to MANAGER, QUALITY CONTROL (profess. & kin.). Files samples according to color and type of material.
GOE: 06.03.01 STRENGTH: L GED: R3 M2 L3 SVP: 3 DLU: 77

582.482-010 COLORER, HIDES AND SKINS (leather mfg.) alternate titles: colorer, machine; dye mixer; dyer and washer; dye weigher; leather colorer
Operates equipment to color and soften hides: Weighs and mixes specified ingredients with water to prepare coloring solution. Pours solution into tray or drum and adds oil (softening agent). Pulls hide through tray until specified color is obtained or places hides in drum and starts machine to tumble hides in solution for specified time. Adds ingredients, such as bicarbonate of soda, formic acid, or oil to solution at specified intervals. May be designated according to specialty as Leather Softener, Drum (leather mfg.).
GOE: 06.02.16 STRENGTH: H GED: R3 M2 L2 SVP: 4 DLU: 77

582.482-014 TANNER, ROTARY DRUM, CONTINUOUS PROCESS (leather mfg.)
Operates rotary drum to remove hair and other solubles from hides or skins and convert hides or skins into leather or glue during continuous process: Loads drum with hides, skins, or other animal stock. Turns valves to admit water and steam to drum. Weighs and mixes specified amounts of lime, salt, and other chemicals in mixing tank or drum, following formula, to prepare liming, deliming, pickling, and tanning solutions used in treating hides or skins. Turns valve to transfer solutions to drum during specified processing cycles. Moves lever to activate drum that cleans, washes, pickles, and tans hides or skins. Replaces solid door of drum with perforated door at specified intervals to filter waste from drum at completion of cycles. Verifies salinity and temperature of solutions, using salinometer and thermometer. Transfers tanning solution to drum and tans hides or skins [TANNING-DRUM OPERATOR (leather mfg.)]. May be designated according to process as Delimer (leather mfg.); Limer (chemical; leather mfg.); Pickler (leather mfg.); Vat Tender (chemical).
GOE: 06.02.16 STRENGTH: H GED: R3 M3 L3 SVP: 5 DLU: 77

582.482-018 TANNING-DRUM OPERATOR (leather mfg.) alternate titles: drum tender; pit tanner; retanner; tanner; tawer
Operates rotary drum containing tanning solution to convert hides and skins into leather, according to specifications: Weighs tanning agents, such as metal salts and sodium formate, following tanning formula. Loads agents and hides or skins into drum. Turns valve to fill drum with water, turns steam valve to heat water to specified temperature. Verifies temperature, using thermometer. Locks drum door and moves lever to rotate drum for specified period of time. Removes drum door, replaces door with grating, and rotates drum to drain tanning solution through grating. May boil sample of tanned hide or skin in water to determine thoroughness of tanning. May be designated according to type of tanning solution used as Bark Tanner (leather mfg.); Chestnut Tanner (leather mfg.); Chrome-Tanning-Drum Operator (leather mfg.); Oak Tanner (leather mfg.); Quebracho Tanner (leather mfg.); Sumac Tanner (leather mfg.).
GOE: 06.02.16 STRENGTH: M GED: R3 M2 L2 SVP: 4 DLU: 77

582.562-010 SLASHER TENDER (textile) alternate titles: sizer
Operates machine to saturate warp yarn with size and wind sized yarn onto *loom beam:* Positions section beams onto creel with aid of another worker, using hoist. Gathers ends of warp together and ties warp to corresponding leaders left in machine from previous run, or when machine is empty, bunches ends together and threads yarn through size pot, around drying cylinders, and onto loom beams. Inserts lease rods between alternate strands of yarn to prevent yarn from sticking together. Lays individual warp ends between teeth of expansion comb for even distribution across loom beam. Turns valves to admit size into vat and steam into drying cylinders. Sets yardage clock to indicate yardage to be wound on loom beam. Starts machine and observes flow of warp through machine to detect breaks and tangles in yarn. Disentangles yarn and ties broken ends with fingers. Feels yarn to verify adherence of size to yarn and ensure that yarn is dry but not burned. Inserts *lease string* in warp yarn and secures yarn ends with tape. Doffs loom beam onto handtruck and replaces with empty beam, using hoist. Records style number, yardage beamed, yarn breaks, and

machine stops. May change temperature control chart on control panel. May clean machine. May process yarn for use on narrow fabric looms and be designated Warp-Spool Slasher (narrow fabrics).
GOE: 06.04.16 STRENGTH: H GED: R3 M2 L3 SVP: 6 DLU: 77

582.582-010 DYE-RANGE OPERATOR, CLOTH (textile) alternate titles: cloth dyer; dye feeder; dyeing-machine feeder; dye-range feeder; front tender

Operates feed-end of *range* to dye and dry cloth in open width: Trucks folded cloth to feed-end of machine or pushes roll of cloth onto brackets at scray. Sews cloth end to leader in machine, using portable sewing machine. Turns handwheel to adjust cloth guides. Turns valves to admit dye to dye pad from mixing tank. Sets thermostats to control temperature of dye in padder and hot air in drying box. Starts machines, observes control panel, and turns knobs to synchronize individual motor speeds. Reads yardage clock and records production, lot numbers, and running time. Turns valve to drain used dye from dye pad. Cleans padder and steambox with water hose. May mix dyes [DYE WEIGHER (any industry)] and add chemicals to dye bath. May be designated according to dye used as Indigo-Vat Tender, Cloth (textile).
GOE: 06.02.16 STRENGTH: M GED: R3 M2 L2 SVP: 4 DLU: 77

582.585-010 AGER OPERATOR (textile)

Tends machine that passes printed or dyed cloth through steam and chemical fumes to develop and fix colors: Measures out and mixes chemicals with water in tank. Trucks cloth to feed-end of ager. Sews end of cloth to leader in machine, using portable sewing machine. Observes cloth entering machine to detect defects, such as holes and grease spots. Examines cloth emerging from machine to detect uneven or incorrect color shade and color runs indicating incorrect adjustment of steam and chemical flow. Turns valves to make adjustments. Pulls cloth having imperfections over edge of truck for later removal and ravels seams to separate lots. Marks aged cloth and records production. Stops machine, cools interior with water, and enters ager to rethread cloth that has torn out. May tear out patch of defective cloth for inspection by CLOTH PRINTER (any industry). May tend machine using steam only and be known as Endless-Steamer Tender (textile).
GOE: 06.04.16 STRENGTH: M GED: R2 M1 L2 SVP: 2 DLU: 77

582.587-010 CHEMICAL-STRENGTH TESTER (textile) alternate titles: chemical checker; titrator

Tests and maintains strength of chemical solutions used in treating cloth: Dips sample of solution from finishing machine and titrates solution against known acid or alkali to determine strength, using burettes and chemical indicator, or tests specific gravity of solution, using hydrometer. Turns valve to admit liquid chemicals or scoops dry chemicals into finishing machine to maintain specified strength. Records test results. May be designated according to chemicals tested as Acid-Strength Inspector (textile); Caustic-Strength Inspector (textile).
GOE: 06.03.02 STRENGTH: L GED: R3 M2 L2 SVP: 2 DLU: 77

582.665-010 CYLINDER BATCHER (textile)

Tends machine that draws cloth through softening solution and winds cloth onto perforated cylinder to prepare cloth for dyeing: Threads cloth from supply truck through softening bath, guides, and rollers to takeup cylinder or sews cloth to leader in machine, using portable sewing machine. Presses button to start machine and observes cloth for defects. Cuts out flaws and sews ends together by hand or with sewing machine. Removes full cylinder from machine, using chain hoist. Records yardage cloth reading onto work ticket. May tend *tenter frame* in tanden with cylinder batcher.
GOE: 06.04.16 STRENGTH: M GED: R2 M1 L2 SVP: 3 DLU: 77

582.665-014 DYE-REEL OPERATOR (textile) alternate titles: beck tender; cloth dyer; dye-beck-reel operator; dye-tub operator; dye-winch operator; piece-dyeing-machine tender; piece-dye worker; vat tender

Tends machine that bleaches or dyes cloth in *rope form*: Hangs cuts of cloth over reel above beck (dye tub). Sews ends of cloth together to form endless rope from each cut of cloth, using portable sewing machine. Sets gauges to control automatic cycle of washing, dyeing, and rinsing as instructed by DYER, SUPERVISOR (knitting; tex. prod., nec; textile) 582.131-014. Notifies DYE WEIGHER (any industry) 550.684-014 to release chemicals and dyes to dye tub. Cuts sample from cloth when dyeing cycle is near end and submits sample to DYER, SUPERVISOR (knitting; tex. prod., nec; textile) to determine if color meets specifications. Ravels seams connecting cloth ends after rinsing is completed. Starts reel to pull cloth out of dye tub. Guides cloth into truck. May unwind cloth from roll by machine so cuts of cloth may be separated for dyeing [ROLLING-DOWN-MACHINE OPERATOR (knitting; textile) 589.685-086]. May be designated according to type of cloth dyed as Knit-Tubing Dyer (textile).
GOE: 06.04.16 STRENGTH: M GED: R2 M1 L2 SVP: 3 DLU: 80

582.665-018 JIGGER (textile) alternate titles: jig operator

Tends dye jig that passes cloth from one roll to another through vat of dye or other solution to scour, bleach, or dye cloth: Mounts roll of cloth on machine, using power hoist. Passes cloth under guide rollers in tank to *takeup roll*. Turns valve to fill tank with water and pours specified quantity of dye into tank or notifies DYE-WEIGHER HELPER (any industry) to release dye solution to dye machine. Sets thermostat to control steam for heating solution. Adds chemicals as instructed by DYER, SUPERVISOR (knitting; tex. prod., nec; tex-

tile) 582.131-014. Starts machine that passes cloth through dye bath or chemical solution, reversing direction of cloth until it has passed through solution specified number of times. Opens valve to drain solution from machine. Fills machine with water and rinses surplus dye from cloth by passing cloth through water as in dyeing. Doffs roll of cloth from dye jig, using power hoist. May weigh and mix dyees.
GOE: 06.04.16 STRENGTH: L GED: R2 M1 L2 SVP: 3 DLU: 77

582.665-022 SATURATION-EQUIPMENT OPERATOR (fabrication, nec) alternate titles: tank operator

Tends equipment that saturates continuous sheet of felt paper with asphalt to serve as carrier or backing for hard-surface floor coverings: Adjusts panelboard controls to pump and maintain specified level of asphalt in tank. Regulates machine to compensate for variations in penetration of saturant, according to visual examination, or as indicated on control panel gauge. Adjusts guides to align felt paper feeding through machine, using handtools. Examines continuous sheet of felt paper to detect tears or breaks as material passes through machine.
GOE: 06.04.19 STRENGTH: L GED: R3 M2 L2 SVP: 4 DLU: 77

582.665-026 SIZING-MACHINE-AND-DRIER OPERATOR (tex. prod., nec)

Tends machine that applies finish to felt or fabrics to increase thickness and bulk of material: Places roll of material in feed holder of machine, threads end through rollers, and attaches material to rewind spindle, or sews end of material to leader in machine. Fills trough with specified sizing and adjusts doctor or fills spray gun tank with specified sizing. Rotates air valve knob to adjust spray of size on fabric. Turns knob to admit steam to drying rolls, positions lever to set speed of machine, and starts machine. May turn knobs to regulate temperature and blowers in drying oven. May be designated according to fabric sized as Burlap-Sizing-Machine Operator (tex. prod., nec).
GOE: 06.04.16 STRENGTH: M GED: R3 M1 L2 SVP: 4 DLU: 77

582.682-010 FINISHING-MACHINE OPERATOR (narrow fabrics)

Operates machines to apply finishing solution to narrow fabrics, such as elastic, labels, ribbon, or tape: Measures and mixes ingredients for finishing solution in storage vat or can, following formula. Turns valve to admit solution to trough of machine or pours or dips solution from can into trough. Ties, pins, or staples ends of fabric to leader in machine or threads ends through rollers (pads) and *drying cans*. Feels finished fabric to determine degree of dryness and turns handwheels or knobs to regulate speed at which fabric passes through machine. Observes fabric finish to determine conformance to standards and turns handwheel or replaces weights to regulate pressure of rollers or drying cans.
GOE: 06.02.16 STRENGTH: M GED: R3 M2 L2 SVP: 4 DLU: 77

582.684-010 PATCH FINISHER (textile)

Collects cloth samples during processing for use in determining conformance to dyeing specifications: Cuts patch from cloth in specified dye becks, using scissors. Bathes samples in saline and water solutions to set dye in cloth and remove excess moisture from cloth. Dries and steams sample, using drier and steamer. Dips sample in caustic or acid solutions to dissolve selected fibers from cloth, using tongs. Staples and submits samples to DYER, SUPERVISOR (knitting; tex. prod., nec; textile) 582.131-014 for analysis.
GOE: 06.04.27 STRENGTH: L GED: R2 M1 L2 SVP: 2 DLU: 77

582.684-014 SPOT CLEANER (garment; knitting) alternate titles: washer

Removes soil from garments, using either of following methods: (1) Examines garment to detect lint, loose threads, and soiled areas. Brushes lint and loose threads from garment. Sponges soiled areas with sponge or cloth saturated with cleaning fluid or soap and water. Removes excess fluid or soap from garment, using damp cloth. Spreads garment on bench or table to dry. (2) Examines garment for soiled area and places garment on buck (padded table) of machine. Depresses pedal to force steam through buck and hose and guides nozzle of hose over soiled area. Releases pedal to stop steam and depresses pedal to circulate hot air through buck and hose to dry garment and prevent formation of cleaning rings. May clean and dry soiled garments, using spray gun. May trim excess material from seams and frayed edges of garment, using scissors. May hang garments on hangers. May attach tags and labels to garments.
GOE: 06.04.27 STRENGTH: L GED: R2 M1 L2 SVP: 3 DLU: 77

582.685-010 BACK WASHER (textile)

Tends machine that washes, rinses, and dries sliver to remove impurities, excess dye, and odors: Places balls of sliver on spindles or floor, or sets cans of sliver at feed-end of machine. *Pieces up* sliver with strand left in machine or inserts end of sliver into machine that draws sliver through washing and rinsing solutions, squeeze rollers, and drying cabinets. Turns valves to regulate circulation of washing and rinsing solutions and to adjust temperature of drying cabinets. Intermingles broken ends of fibers to piece up broken sliver. May insert end of sliver in gilling attachment that blends strands and winds sliver into ball [GILL-BOX TENDER (textile)]. May weigh and pack balls of sliver for shipment. May tend machine with oil spray attachment that conditions fiber for further processing.
GOE: 06.04.16 STRENGTH: H GED: R2 M1 L2 SVP: 2 DLU: 77

582.685-014 BEAM-DYER OPERATOR (textile) alternate titles: cylinder dyer

Tends machine that scours and dyes cloth wound on perforated beam: Loads beam of cloth onto machine carriage, using electric hoist. Pushes carriage into

dyeing chamber and bolts door. Places sample spool of material in miniature pressure chamber to obtain swatches for inspection. May tend open-top vat and be designated Beam Dyer, Recessed Vat (textile).
GOE: 06.04.16 STRENGTH: M GED: R3 M2 L2 SVP: 3 DLU: 77

582.685-018 BLEACH-RANGE OPERATOR (textile)
Tends feed-end of *range* that bleaches, washes, and dries greige cloth preparatory to printing, dyeing, or finishing: Pulls cloth from overhead carrier, positions truck of folded cloth at feed-end of machine, or mounts roll of cloth onto brackets at scray. Sews cloth end to leader in range, using portable sewing machine. Presses button or turns handwheel to set width guide according to width of cloth. Turns valves to control level of chemicals in mangle, washboxes, and peroxide saturator. Turns knobs to adjust pressure on squeeze rollers and to set speed of range as specified for various cloth styles. Observes cloth entering machine to detect bad seams or flaws that might cause tear-outs. Stops range and seams cloth to correct flaws. May thread cloth through range when leader not left in range. May tend range that washes, bleaches, scours, whitens, and dries cloth preparatory to further processing.
GOE: 06.04.16 STRENGTH: M GED: R2 M1 L2 SVP: 3 DLU: 80

582.685-022 BOIL-OFF-MACHINE OPERATOR, CLOTH (textile)
Tends machine that removes dirt, natural gums, and waxes from greige cloth preparatory to further processing: Lifts rolls of cloth to platform at feed-end of machine, using hoist. Inserts rod through center of roll and pushes roll onto machine brackets. Sews end of cloth roll to leader in machine, using portable sewing machine. Turns valves to admit caustic solution and steam to vats. Starts cloth winding from roll on to takeup beam in initial boiloff box and from initial boiloff box onto beams in subsequent boiloff and washboxes. Threads cloth from terminal washbox through squeeze rollers and doffs cloth from *swing-folding attachment*. Records cloth lot number, machine running time, and yardage of cloth processed. May measure distance between colored yarn markers on cloth selvage to determine shrinkage.
GOE: 06.04.16 STRENGTH: M GED: R2 M1 L2 SVP: 2 DLU: 77

582.685-026 CLOTH SHADER (garment; textile)
Examines cloth for uniformity of color, using winding device: Inserts end of cloth roll over top roller of winding device and pins end to guide cloth on bottom roller. Presses button to start rollers, winding cloth around bottom roller. Presses button to stop rollers at intervals and holds swatch against cloth to compare color. Examines roll of cloth for uniformity of color. Marks off-shade portions of cloth, using chalk. May weigh and record cloth weights. May inspect cloth for defects [CLOTH EXAMINER, MACHINE (textile)]. May tend machine that measures length of cloth rolls [CLOTH MEASURER, MACHINE (garment; textile)].
GOE: 06.03.02 STRENGTH: L GED: R2 M1 L2 SVP: 4 DLU: 77

582.685-030 CLOTH-WASHER OPERATOR (textile) alternate titles: washing-machine operator
Tends machines that wash or treat cloth with chemicals preparatory to or after processes, such as bleaching, dyeing, printing, and finishing: Pushes truck of cloth into feeding position or mounts roll of cloth on shaft at feed-end of machine. Sews end of cloth to leader in machine, using portable sewing machine. Turns valves to admit water, detergents, caustic, acids, steam, or other chemicals into washing tanks according to specifications. Starts machine and observes flow of cloth through machine to detect tears in cloth. Stops machine, disentangles tear-outs, and knots selvages of torn cloth by hand. Tests solutions in washing tanks by titration or using litmus paper or hydrometer. Adds water, detergents, or chemicals to washing tanks to dilute or strengthen solutions as indicated by tests. May be designated according to chemicals used in washing tanks as Acid-Washer Operator (textile); Naphthol-Soaping-Machine Operator (textile); according to objective of washing as Cloth Neutralizer (textile); or according to type of cloth as Back-Gray-Cloth Washer (textile). May tend machines consisting of series of tanks that process cloth in open-width or *rope form*. Important variables may be indicated by trade names of machines used.
GOE: 06.04.16 STRENGTH: M GED: R2 M1 L2 SVP: 2 DLU: 77

582.685-034 COLORING-MACHINE OPERATOR (hat & cap) alternate titles: dyer
Tends one or more tumbling vats that dye felt hat bodies: Dumps hat bodies into perforated tumbler. Pours premixed dye powder into vat and turns valves to admit water and steam to fill and heat vat. Starts tumbler revolving to saturate hat bodies with dye. Adds prescribed chemicals to solution to increase penetration and permanency of dye. Removes dyed articles after specified time.
GOE: 06.04.16 STRENGTH: L GED: R3 M2 L2 SVP: 3 DLU: 78

582.685-038 CRABBER (textile)
Tends equipment that permanently fixes warp and filling threads in woolen and worsted cloth to prevent uneven shrinkage during subsequent processing: Sews end of cloth to leader, using portable sewing machine, or threads cloth between rollers and through vats. Wraps end of cloth around *takeup roll* or guides end through *swing-folding attachment* and onto handtruck. Turns valves to admit water to vats and to regulate temperature controls, according to specifications. Turns setscrews to adjust pressure of top roller. Starts machine and turns knobs to regulate flow of cloth through vats of boiling water. May doff machine.
GOE: 06.04.16 STRENGTH: M GED: R3 M1 L2 SVP: 2 DLU: 77

582.685-042 DECATING-MACHINE OPERATOR (textile)
Tends machine that circulates steam through cloth wound on perforated cylinder to develop luster, improve hand, remove wrinkles, and shrink cloth: Turns

handwheels to set guides according to width of cloth, and pressure roll of winding unit according to tension specified. Laps end of cloth and wrapper (protective covering which removes wrinkles and holds cloth under tension) around cylinder or pins cloth to leader. Starts machine to wind cloth and wrapper into single roll. Sets controls to admit steam into rotating cylinder and force steam through cloth roll, and to draw air back through cloth to cool and dry cloth following instructions for style of cloth. Winds cloth and wrapper onto separate rolls, and doffs rolls of cloth, using hoist, or unwinds cloth through *swing-folding attachment*. May tend machine that automatically steams, removes moisture, unwinds, and folds cloth. May press cloth in electric pressing machine. May tend machine that initially draws cloth over steam trough for priming. May tend decator (pressure tank) that finishes cloth and be designated Full-Decator Operator (textile).
GOE: 06.04.16 STRENGTH: M GED: R2 M1 L2 SVP: 2 DLU: 77

582.685-046 DESIZING-MACHINE OPERATOR, HEAD-END (textile) alternate titles: desizing-pad operator; malter operator
Tends feed-end of *range* that removes size from cloth to increase affinity of cloth for dye: Weighs out desizing agent and mixes agent with water in mixing tank, following formula. Turns valves to transfer solution from mixing tank to desizing tubs and to control steam for heating solution. Positions truck of cloth at feed-end of machine, or mounts cloth roll onto brackets at scray. Sews cloth end to leader in machine, using portable sewing machine. Observes flow of cloth through machine to detect flaws, such as holes and torn selvages. Cuts out flaws, using scissors, and sews cloth ends together. Turns knob to adjust cloth guides and speed of range to accommodate changes in styles of cloth.
GOE: 06.04.16 STRENGTH: H GED: R2 M1 L2 SVP: 3 DLU: 77

582.685-050 DRUM ATTENDANT (leather mfg.; tex. prod., nec) alternate titles: breaker-wheel operator; mill attendant; softener; stuffer, machine; temperer; wet-milling-wheel operator
Tends machine equipped with revolving drum containing solutions that clean, dye, tan, or oil hides or rag stock: Places hides in drum or loads rags onto drum conveyor and locks drum door. Turns valves to fill drum with specified solution and water or steam. Moves controls to rotate drum for specified period. Stops drum, unlocks door, removes rags or hides, and loads hides or rags on cart or rack. May be designated according to process as Blacking-Wheel Tender (leather mfg.); Degreasing-Wheel Operator (leather mfg.); Oiling-Machine Operator (leather mfg.; tex. prod., nec); Tanning-Wheel Filler (leather mfg.); Washing-Machine Operator (leather mfg.). May tend machine, without adding solutions, to soften hides by tumbling and be designated Dry-Mill Worker (leather mfg.).
GOE: 06.04.16 STRENGTH: M GED: R1 M1 L1 SVP: 2 DLU: 77

582.685-054 DYE-TANK TENDER (tex. prod., nec) alternate titles: net finisher
Tends treating tank that shrinks, dyes, and resins nets: Mixes dyes and resins in tank according to standard formula or customer specifications, using wood paddle. Turns valves to fill tank with water and heat to specified temperature. Immerses net in tank, using hoist or feed rollers. Observes net to ascertain amount of dye absorbed and measures mesh with ruler to determine degree of shrinkage. Removes net from tank and hangs net in drying room, or feeds net into automatic drier rollers. May dip netting in tar tank. May tie and pack nets in cartons for shipment [PACKAGER, HAND (any industry)].
GOE: 06.04.16 STRENGTH: M GED: R2 M1 L2 SVP: 3 DLU: 77

582.685-058 DYED-YARN OPERATOR (textile)
Tends machine that coats fiberglass sliver with dye: Places supply package on machine platform and threads sliver through guides, over tension bars and dye roller applicator, through traverse guide, and attaches sliver to takeup package. Pours or turns valve to admit dye solution into trough of dye roller applicator. Pushes lever to lower winding head and start machine. Observes flow of sliver through machine to detect breaks in sliver and ties broken sliver by hand. Cuts sliver, using scissors, and doffs packages of dyed sliver from machine.
GOE: 06.04.16 STRENGTH: L GED: R2 M1 L2 SVP: 2 DLU: 77

582.685-062 EXTRACTOR OPERATOR (tex. prod., nec)
Tends machine that neutralizes carbonizing solution in felt and extracts moisture: Lowers felt pads into tank of boiling water, adds acid neutralizing agent, such as soda ash, and turns valve to admit compressed air that agitates water. Transfers pads to electrically rotated basket by hand, starts basket, and directs stream of cold water on rotating pads to rinse pads. Shuts off water, and stops basket when moisture is expelled.
GOE: 06.04.16 STRENGTH: M GED: R2 M1 L2 SVP: 3 DLU: 77

582.685-066 FEATHER WASHER (tex. prod., nec) alternate titles: tumbler-machine operator
Tends machine that washes feathers used in stuffing household goods, such as pillows and cushions: Fills paddle-agitated or tumbler-type washing machine with feathers, soap, chemicals, and water, and starts machine. Opens valve to drain water and to admit clean water into washer to rinse feathers.
GOE: 06.04.19 STRENGTH: L GED: R2 M1 L1 SVP: 2 DLU: 77

582.685-070 FELT-WASHING-MACHINE TENDER (tex. prod., nec)
Tends machine that washes and treats felt with chemical preservatives: Wraps felt around machine spindle or presses button to start rollers that pull felt into machine. Turns valves to admit water, steam, detergents, caustics, and

other chemicals into machine at specified intervals according to specifications. Presses button to start machine washing and treating cycles. Unloads machine with aid of another worker or threads felt through rollers for removal of moisture. May tend machine to dye felt and be designated Felt-Dyeing-Machine Tender (tex. prod., nec).
GOE: 06.04.16 STRENGTH: M GED: R2 M1 L2 SVP: 3 DLU: 79

582.685-074 FUMIGATOR AND STERILIZER (furniture) alternate titles: sterilizer operator
Tends retort or vacuum chamber that fumigates or sterilizes used mattresses: Loads mattresses on dollies and pushes them into chamber. Closes and bolts chamber door. Starts vacuum pump to remove air from chamber. Opens valves to control flow of fumigating or sterilizing gases into chamber, observing gauges and scale readings. Pumps gases from chamber and replaces gases with fresh air. Opens chamber door and removes loaded dollies. May tend fumigating device, used inside chamber, that produces fumes from heated chemicals. May tend oven to sterilize mattresses with hot air.
GOE: 06.04.19 STRENGTH: H GED: R2 M1 L2 SVP: 2 DLU: 77

582.685-078 GARMENT STEAMER (knitting) alternate titles: steam hand
Tends machine that removes wrinkles from knitted garments with steam and hot air: Hangs garments on studs of revolving disk of machine. Starts machine that subjects garments to steam spray and hot air as disk revolves. Removes and stacks steamed garments on table.
GOE: 06.04.05 STRENGTH: L GED: R2 M1 L1 SVP: 2 DLU: 77

582.685-082 GREASER OPERATOR (hat & cap) alternate titles: waxer
Tends machine that applies grease and wax to unfinished felt hat bodies to stiffen and finish felt: Mounts rolls of cloth impregnated with grease and wax on holders of machine and threads cloth under feed rollers, between machine guides, and over applicator pads. Fits hat body over block mounted on arm of machine. Presses lever to start machine that forces body against applicator pads to finish and stiffen body. May be designated according to part of hat body processed as Brim-Greaser Operator (hat & cap); Crown-Greaser Operator (hat & cap).
GOE: 06.04.16 STRENGTH: L GED: R2 M1 L1 SVP: 3 DLU: 77

582.685-086 HAIR-BOILER OPERATOR (leather mfg.)
Tends vats that boils animal hair to curl hair. Turns valves to admit water and steam into vats and to drain water from vats after hair is boiled.
GOE: 06.04.19 STRENGTH: M GED: R2 M1 L2 SVP: 2 DLU: 77

582.685-090 JET-DYEING-MACHINE TENDER (textile)
Tends machine that dyes cloth under pressure: Turns valves to admit water, steam, and chemicals into compartments to specified level. Sews ends of cloth together to form endless rope of cloth, using portable sewing machine. Presses button to activate suction device that draws cloth over machine reel into compartments. Presses button to start automatic washing, dyeing, and rinsing cycles, and observes control panel for faulty machine operation. Reports malfunctions to maintenance personnel. Starts reel to pull cloth from machine at end of processing cycles.
GOE: 06.04.16 STRENGTH: L GED: R2 M1 L2 SVP: 3 DLU: 77

582.685-094 KNIT-GOODS WASHER (knitting)
Tends machine that washes and treats knitted tubular cloth with chemicals following finishing: Joins cloth ends together to form continuous lengths, using sewing machine. Loads cloth in machine compartments and pours specified chemicals in machine trough, using dipper. Presses button and flips switches to start machine and observes dials and gauges for variations from standards. Removes cloth from machine onto handtruck following completion of processing cycles.
GOE: 06.04.16 STRENGTH: H GED: R3 M1 L2 SVP: 4 DLU: 77

582.685-098 OPEN-DEVELOPER OPERATOR (textile)
Tends open-developer machine that develops dye in dyed or printed cloth, removes excess color from cloth, and wets cloth before soaping process: Threads end of roll of cloth through machine rolls. Turns steam valves to heat machine tank and opens valves to admit specified chemicals into tank and to start water spray. Turns handwheels to close wringer rolls and starts machine. Straightens wrinkles in cloth as cloth enters machine. Sews end of new roll of cloth to end in machine during processing, using portable sewing machine. Drains tank of machine after cloth is processed. May mix chemicals in storage tank to develop desired color of cloth.
GOE: 06.04.16 STRENGTH: L GED: R3 M2 L2 SVP: 4 DLU: 77

582.685-102 PACKAGE-DYEING-MACHINE OPERATOR (textile) alternate titles: beam dyer; bleacher; dyeing-machine tender; package dyer
Tends machine that dyes or bleaches yarn wound on perforated beams I, tubes I, or spring coils: Loads package stand or beam of yarn into machine, using power hoist. Closes lid and tightens lid bolts with wrench. Mixes preweighed dye or bleach with water in pail or overflow tank, stirring with paddle. Turns valves to control steam and water flow. Sets controls to pump dye or bleach into machine that automatically processes and rinses yarn at specified temperature and pressure. Adds chemicals during dyeing or bleaching cycle as specified. May load packages of yarn onto perforated spindles of stand and unload machine [DYE-STAND LOADER (textile)]. May weigh dyes according to formula. May tend machine to bleach yarn and be designated Yarn-Bleaching-

Machine Operator (textile). May tend machine to dye raw fibers or tops and be designated Raw-Stock-Dyeing-Machine Tender (textile); Top-Dyeing-Machine Tender (textile).
GOE: 06.02.16 STRENGTH: M GED: R3 M1 L2 SVP: 4 DLU: 77

582.685-106 PADDING-MACHINE OPERATOR (textile) alternate titles: dye-padder operator
Tends padding machine that saturates cloth with dye preparatory to further processing: Positions handtruck of cloth at feed-end of machine or mounts roll of cloth on machine, using power hoist, and threads cloth through rollers, or sews supply end to leader in machine, using portable sewing machine. Sets air pressure gauge to control pressure on squeeze roll and temperature gauge to control temperature of dye. Notifies DYE-WEIGHER HELPER (any industry) to release dye to overflow tank. Turns valves to fill padding tank with dye. Starts machine to pass cloth through dye, between squeeze rolls and onto take-up roll. Doffs roll of cloth from machine, or may feed cloth to set of *drying cans*. Cuts sample of cloth for inspection by DYER, SUPERVISOR (knitting; tex. prod., nec; textile) 582.131-014. May weigh and mix dye and chemicals.
GOE: 06.04.16 STRENGTH: M GED: R2 M1 L1 SVP: 2 DLU: 77

582.685-110 PATCH WASHER (textile) alternate titles: patch developer; sample steamer
Tends miniature equipment that develops color in sample swatches of printed cloth: Places sample in miniature steam cabinet and turns valves to spray chemicals and steam into cabinet for specified period of time. Removes sample swatch from cabinet and washes swatch by hand to remove excess color and chemicals. Squeezes excess water from sample, using wringer, and dries sample over heated drum. Returns sample swatch to CLOTH PRINTER (any industry) for comparison with standards.
GOE: 06.04.16 STRENGTH: L GED: R2 M1 L1 SVP: 2 DLU: 77

582.685-114 ROPE-SILICA-MACHINE OPERATOR (textile)
Tends machine, consisting of series of subdivided tanks, that coats cloth with silicate or other chemical solution to strengthen and fluff cloth: Starts pumps to transfer chemicals and water into mixing tank above machine. Determines specific gravity of solution, using hydrometer, and adds chemicals or water until required specific gravity is attained. Threads end of roll of cloth through guides and squeeze rollers of tanks and over takeup reel at end of tanks. Turns rheostat controls to obtain specified roller speed and tank temperature. Turns valve to admit specified amount of silicate or other chemical solution into tanks. Starts machine and observes cloth as cloth passes through tanks and onto takeup reel.
GOE: 06.04.16 STRENGTH: M GED: R2 M1 L2 SVP: 3 DLU: 77

582.685-118 SATURATOR TENDER (build. mat., nec)
Tends machine that saturates rolls of untreated roofing felt with hot, liquid asphalt: Threads felt through machine rollers and starts machine. Turns wheels and moves levers to regulate machine speed, flow of asphalt, and tension on felt and press rollers. Presses control button to regulate flow of felt to ensure uniform saturation and prevent damage of felt. Tears test pieces from saturated felt to verify specified degree of saturation.
GOE: 06.04.19 STRENGTH: L GED: R3 M1 L2 SVP: 3 DLU: 77

582.685-122 SCRUBBING-MACHINE OPERATOR (tex. prod., nec)
Tends machine that washes and dries twine: Turns valve to admit soap solution to starch pots (tanks) of machine and to admit steam to drying cylinder. Creels machine with bobbins of twine and threads twine through starch pots and drying cylinder. Attaches ends of twine to takeup bobbins. Starts machine and observes movement of twine through machine and onto takeup bobbins to detect malfunctions, such as tangles and breaks. Doffs bobbins of cleaned twine. Scrapes accumulations of dried soap from machine.
GOE: 06.04.05 STRENGTH: M GED: R2 M1 L2 SVP: 3 DLU: 77

582.685-126 SHEEPSKIN PICKLER (meat products) alternate titles: slat pickler
Tends tanks, vats, or drums in which sheepskins are pickled: Turns valves to fill equipment with water. Weighs and dumps specified amounts of lime, salt, detergents, and acid into separate tanks. Throws slats (sheepskins less wool), by hand or using tongs, into lime tank to remove fat and flesh, into detergent tank to remove traces of lime, and into salt and acid tank to pickle slats. Starts agitators in tanks and empties and refills tanks. May perform all processes, using rotating drum, and be designated Pickling-Drum Operator (meat products). May be known according to specific task performed as Lime-Vat Tender (meat products).
GOE: 06.04.16 STRENGTH: M GED: R2 M1 L2 SVP: 2 DLU: 77

582.685-130 SKEIN-YARN DYER (textile) alternate titles: dye-machine tender; kettle tender; pilot; yarn dyer
Tends machines that bleach or dye skeins of yarn: Hangs yarn skeins over perforated rack. Turns valves to fill dye vats with water, and turns knob to set temperature of water according to specifications. Pours chemical softeners and liquid dyes into vats according to formula. Starts machine that rotates skeins periodically and circulates dye through yarn. Dumps dye solution from vats at end of dyeing cycle and circulates rinse water through yarn. Loops several skeins of yarn together to form bundle and removes yarn bundles from perforated racks. Places bundles of yarn into boxes. May load and unload machine, using chain hoist. Important variables may be indicated by trade names or machines used.

GOE: 06.04.16 STRENGTH: M GED: R2 M1 L1 SVP: 3 DLU: 77

582.685-134 SOAKER, HIDES (meat products) alternate titles: hide washer

Tends equipment that washes lamb and sheep pelts: Unloads pelts from trucks, railroad cars, or handcarts. Separates sheep pelts from lamb pelts and segregates pelts with cuts, tears, or blemishes. Turns valve to fill soaking tank with water and dumps specified amount of salt into tank. Throws pelts into tank and starts agitators that wash pelts. Removes pelts from tank by hand or using metal hook. May record number of pelts washed and those found defective.
GOE: 06.04.16 STRENGTH: M GED: R2 M1 L2 SVP: 2 DLU: 77

582.685-138 SPRAY-MACHINE OPERATOR (textile)

Tends machine that sprays finish on cloth to increase thickness and bulk of cloth: Places roll of cloth on holders, by hand or using hoist. Sews end of cloth to leader, using sewing machine mounted on feed-end of spraying machine. Adjusts air pressure control, observes gauges, and turns knob to start flow of finish from tanks through spray apparatus. Adjusts temperature control and observes gauges to regulate heat in gas flame dryer and hot air drying compartments, according to temperature chart. Starts machine and observes cloth passing through spray cabinet to ensure that finish is sprayed evenly on cloth. Stops machine and adjusts air pressure control, nozzles on spray apparatus, or cleans clogged nozzles if finish is not uniform. Measures cloth emerging from drying compartment to detect width shrinkage and adjusts temperature controls as needed. Removes roll of cloth from machine by hand or using hoist, or pushes handtruck from under *swing-folding attachments*. Places empty beam on machine or pushes empty handtruck under swing-folding attachment [BACK TENDER (textile)]. May tend machine equipped with doctor to scrape excess size from material. May pour finish from containers into tanks. May be designated according to finish used as Blow-Machine Tender, Starch Spraying (textile).
GOE: 06.04.16 STRENGTH: L GED: R2 M1 L2 SVP: 2 DLU: 77

582.685-142 STAINING-MACHINE OPERATOR (tex. prod., nec)

Tends machine that dyes twine: Dips dye from barrel into dye pots of machine. Creels machine with bobbins of twine. Threads ends of twine through guides, dividing racks, squeeze rollers, and dye pots, and ties ends of twine to rope that draws twine through finishing rollers. Starts machine until twine is drawn through finishing rollers and then stops machine and attaches ends to takeup bobbins. Starts machine and observes operation for malfunctions, such as tangled and broken twine. Doffs bobbins of dyed twine. Cleans hardened dye from rollers with scraper, and washes dye pots with hot water.
GOE: 06.04.16 STRENGTH: L.GED: R2 M1 L2 SVP: 3 DLU: 77

582.685-146 STEAMER TENDER (textile)

Tends pressurized, steam-heated chambers that age dyed or printed cloth or to set pile fabrics: Pulls cloth over rod of carriage or hooks cloth selvages at intervals on rack hooks to hang cloth in loops on carriages. Pushes cloth carriages or racks into steamer and bolts door, using wrench. Turns valve to admit steam into steaming chamber. Pulls carriages or racks from steamer after specified time.
GOE: 06.04.16 STRENGTH: M GED: R2 M1 L2 SVP: 2 DLU: 77

582.685-150 STEAMING-CABINET TENDER (garment) alternate titles: finishing tunnel operator

Tends steaming cabinet that circulates steam, heat, and air through garments to remove wrinkles and imparts finished appearance. Moves levers to activate conveyors that carry garments through steaming cabinet and to specified work stations following processing cycles.
GOE: 06.04.16 STRENGTH: L GED: R2 M1 L1 SVP: 2 DLU: 77

582.685-154 TIN-WHIZ-MACHINE OPERATOR (textile)

Tends machine that weights silk or rayon cloth with tinning solution: Places cloth into bowl of machine and distributes cloth evenly along sides of bowl. Wraps burlap around cloth to prevent silk from separating. Turns valve to admit compressed air into storage tank to agitate tinning solution. Starts pump to transfer specified amount of solution to bowl of machine. Determines specific gravity of solution, using hydrometer, and pours water or concentrated tinning solution from pail into bowl of machine to bring solution to required specific gravity. Starts machine that slowly rotates bowl to saturate cloth with solution. Opens valve to drain solution from bowl of machine into storage tank and turns rheostat control to increase speed of rotating bowl to extract excess solution from cloth. Removes cloth from machine.
GOE: 06.04.16 STRENGTH: M GED: R3 M2 L2 SVP: 4 DLU: 77

582.685-158 WARP-DYEING-VAT TENDER (textile) alternate titles: continuous-yarn dyeing-machine operator; long-chain-dyeing-machine operator

Tends machine that washes, bleaches, dyes, rinses, and dries warp yarn in *rope form*: Weighs chemicals and dyes, according to formula, and dumps ingredients into mixing tank. Turns valves to admit steam and water into tank, and stirs solution with paddle. Turns valves to release dye mixture into vats. Sets *drying can* thermostat at temperature specified for count of yarn to be dried. Mounts *ball warps* on rack at front of machine, using hoist. Ties yarn to leader to thread machine. Observes yarn passing through units of machine to detect yarn breaks or tangles. Stops machine and untangles snarled yarns or ties broken ends. Compares sample of yarn with standard to determine if dyeing meets specifications, and notifies DYE WEIGHER (any industry) if specifications are not met. Observes level of liquid in vats and adjusts liquid flow to maintain specified level. May be designated according to dye used as Indigo-Vat Tender, Warp (textile); or according to process as Warp-Bleaching-Vat Tender (textile); Warp-Scouring-Vat Tender (textile).
GOE: 06.04.16 STRENGTH: M GED: R2 M1 L2 SVP: 4 DLU: 77

582.685-162 WASHER (plastic-synth.) alternate titles: bleacher; doffer

Tends equipment that flushes rayon yarn with boiling bleach solution to remove spinning-bath residue and bleach product prior to finishing: Removes full cones, bobbins, *cakes*, or skeins of yarn from spinning (forming) machines and places product on wash rack. Turns valves to start flow of bleach water to flush yarn. Replaces empty bobbins or cones on spindles of spinning machines. May hang skeins in tubs of bleach solution and be designated Dipper (plastic-synth.) or in tubs of chemicals and be designated Desulfurizer, Hand (plastic-synth.). May wrap cakes of yarn in cloth to protect cakes during washing, bleaching, steaming, and drying operations or to partially dry cakes after washing [CAKE WRAPPER (plastic-synth.)]. May perform duties of DRIER OPERATOR (plastic-synth.) III in plants where washing, bleaching, and drying are combined into single operation. May be designated according to article washed and bleached as Bobbin Washer (plastic-synth.); Cake Washer (plastic-synth.); Skein Washer (plastic-synth.); Staple Fiber Washer (plastic-synth.). May tend equipment that processes yarn in single operation and be designated Desulfurizer, Machine (plastic-synth.).
GOE: 06.04.16 STRENGTH: M GED: R2 M1 L2 SVP: 3 DLU: 77

582.685-166 WOOL-WASHING-MACHINE OPERATOR (textile)

Tends machine that washes endless ropes of woolen piece goods: Threads cloth over reel, between guides, and through feed rollers. Sews ends of cloth together to form endless rope, using sewing machine or by hand. Turns valves to fill tub with water and to control steam for heating solution. Pours liquid detergents into tub, following specifications. Starts machine that revolves piece goods over reel and through solution for specified period of time. Turns valves to drain solution from tub and to fill tub with rinse water. Ravels seams to separate cloth ends after rinsing, laps end of cloth over reel, and starts reel to transfer cloth from machine to handtruck.
GOE: 06.04.05 STRENGTH: L GED: R2 M1 L1 SVP: 2 DLU: 77

582.685-170 DYE-TUB OPERATOR (knitting) alternate titles: drum-dyeing-machine operator; dyer; tumbler-dyeing-machine operator

Tends machines that dye and finish knitted garments, such as hosiery and sweaters: Turns valves to admit water and steam into machine to specified level. Pours dye, cleaning agents, or finishing chemicals into machine. Turns thermostat and timing device to set temperature and dyeing time, according to formula. Places garments in compartments of machine and starts machine. Periodically examines garments from each dye or finish lot to detect variations from processing standards. Adds dye, reducing agent, or finishing chemicals, according to instructions, if standard is not matched. Drains solution from machine at end of dyeing or finishing cycle. Removes dyed or finished garments to handtruck and labels each lot. May tend extractor [EXTRACTOR OPERATOR (any industry) 581.685-038]. May weigh or measure cleaning agents and chemicals. May be designated according to type of machine used as Paddle-Dyeing-Machine Operator (knitting); Rotary-Drum Dyer (knitting).
GOE: 06.04.16 STRENGTH: M GED: R2 M1 L1 SVP: 3 DLU: 81

582.686-010 DYE-HOUSE WORKER (leather mfg.)

Loads pelts into vats containing solutions to bleach, dye, tan, or clean them. Loads pelts into extractors or drums equipped with paddles to remove excess liquid. Hangs wet pelts over sticks and places them on racks in drying room. Places dried pelts in boxes and trucks pelts to next operation. May stretch skins or replace oils lost in dyeing process.
GOE: 06.04.16 STRENGTH: H GED: R1 M1 L1 SVP: 2 DLU: 77

582.686-014 DYE-REEL-OPERATOR HELPER (textile) alternate titles: dye-room helper; laborer, wash-and-dye house

Assists DYE-REEL OPERATOR (textile) to bleach or dye cloth, performing any combination of following tasks: Mounts cloth rolls on brackets and feeds end of cloth through *swing-folding attachment* of machine that unwinds cloth into handtruck. Hangs end of cloth over winding reel in dye beck (tub) and sews ends together to make continuous loop, using portable sewing machine. Ravels connecting seams after rinsing and guides cloth over doffing reel into handtruck. Turns valves to drain, rinse, and fill tanks with water. Carries chemicals, such as dyes, bleaches, and scouring agents, from mixing room to dye house and pours chemicals into beck. Conveys cloth between departments, using handtruck. Performs other duties as described under HELPER (any industry) Master Title.
GOE: 06.04.16 STRENGTH: H GED: R2 M1 L2 SVP: 2 DLU: 77

582.686-018 RAW-STOCK-MACHINE LOADER (textile)

Fills raw-stock-dyeing or bleaching machine with cotton, wool, or synthetic fiber, preparatory to dyeing or bleaching, and removes stock from machine: Places rack in machine to support stock during processing. Opens bales and dumps or packs armfuls of loose fiber into machine. Closes machine lid and tightens lugs, using handtools. Removes rack of fiber after processing cycle, using power hoist. May dump premeasured amounts of dyes, bleaches, or other chemicals into tanks. May turn valves to admit steam into tubs.
GOE: 06.04.16 STRENGTH: H GED: R1 M1 L1 SVP: 2 DLU: 77

582.686-022 SKEIN-YARN-DYER HELPER (textile)

Assists SKEIN-YARN DYER (textile) in bleaching or dyeing skeins of yarn: Hangs yarn skeins over perforated racks of portable cabinet. Loads yarn into

machine, using chain hoist. Removes dyed yarn from machine. Performs other duties as described under HELPER (any industry) Master Title.
GOE: 06.04.16 STRENGTH: M GED: R2 M1 L1 SVP: 2 DLU: 77

582.686-026 SLASHER-TENDER HELPER (textile) alternate titles: sizer helper
Assists SLASHER TENDER (textile) in coating warp threads with size and winding warp onto *loom beams:* Transfers warp or loom beams to or from machine, using handtruck. Positions beams on creel, using hoist. Assists SLASHER TENDER (textile) to pass warp threads through rollers, size pot, and drying rollers and to insert lease rods. Loosens and removes clamps from end of loom beam, using wrench. Lifts loom beam from slasher onto handtruck, using hoist. May mix and cook size in vats according to formula. May turn valves to control flow of size from vat to size pot on slasher machine. Performs other duties as described under HELPER (any industry) Master Title.
GOE: 06.04.16 STRENGTH: H GED: R2 M1 L2 SVP: 2 DLU: 77

582.686-030 TOP-DYEING-MACHINE LOADER (tex. prod., nec; textile) alternate titles: dye-machine-tender helper; kettle-tender helper
Loads worsted or synthetic tops into kettles for dyeing: Pulls portion of inside fiber to outside so tops will pass over spindles (perforated pipes). Wraps tops in cloth or in bags to hold tops intact during dyeing. Pushes wrapped tops over spindles in kettle. Removes tops after dyeing. May convey tops to and from dye room, using handtruck. May weigh and tag tops before dyeing. May drain solution and rinse excess dye from kettles.
GOE: 06.04.16 STRENGTH: M GED: R2 M1 L1 SVP: 2 DLU: 77

582.686-034 TUBE HANDLER (textile)
Positions and removes hollow rods used to support folds of printed cloth while cloth moves through steaming chamber: Removes rods from conveyor in feeder rack that automatically drops rods into position to support cloth. Removes and places rods emerging from discharge end of steaming chamber onto conveyor belt to be returned to feeder rack.
GOE: 06.04.27 STRENGTH: L GED: R1 M1 L1 SVP: 2 DLU: 77

582.686-038 WARP COILER (textile)
Off bears ropes of yarn from discharge end of yarn mercerizing, dyeing, or drying machine, or from machine that divides *ball warps* into smaller warps: Observes ropes of yarn as ropes coil onto cloth or fold into baskets or cartons to detect breaks or tangles in yarn. Ties broken yarn ends to prevent retangling. Signals machine tender to stop machine if yarn tangles. Ties corners of cloth over coiled yarn and replaces filled cloth or basket. Assists machine tenders in threading and cleaning machine.
GOE: 06.04.16 STRENGTH: M GED: R2 M1 L1 SVP: 2 DLU: 77

582.687-010 BAGGER (knitting)
Counts, folds, and places specified number of undyed hose of same size and style in bag, and ties bag to prepare hose for dyeing. Attaches identifying label to bag.
GOE: 06.04.38 STRENGTH: L GED: R1 M1 L1 SVP: 2 DLU: 81

582.687-014 DYER (button & notion)
Dumps feathers into dye vats and stirs feathers, using stick, to color feathers used as trimmings for ladies' garments. Removes and places feathers in steam-heated drums to dry, using wire scoops. May load feathers in extractor.
GOE: 06.04.19 STRENGTH: L GED: R1 M1 L1 SVP: 2 DLU: 77

582.687-018 FELT-HAT STEAMER (hat & cap)
Steams felt hats to remove shine and nap from hats: Rolls brim down and places inverted hat over steam outlet for removal of shine and nap from felt. Places finished hats on trolley.
GOE: 06.04.27 STRENGTH: L GED: R1 M1 L1 SVP: 1 DLU: 77

582.687-022 SHADE MATCHER (textile) alternate titles: general matcher; stack matcher; strip shader; tear-down matcher
Examines rolls or folded cuts of dyed or printed cloth for variations in color shade, and sorts cloth according to shade, preparatory to shipment. Cuts off-shade portions from cloth with scissors. Stacks identical cuts of cloth together on handtruck. May compare swatches from opposite ends of cloth piece to detect variation of color within piece.
GOE: 06.03.02 STRENGTH: L GED: R2 M1 L2 SVP: 3 DLU: 77

582.687-026 SIZER (textile) alternate titles: starcher
Dumps prepared sizing solution into size box. Immerses yarn skeins in solution for specified period to strengthen threads. Lifts yarn from box onto extractor.
GOE: 06.04.16 STRENGTH: M GED: R2 M1 L1 SVP: 3 DLU: 77

582.687-030 TREATER (any industry) alternate titles: applicator; applier
Coats curtains, drapes, and hangings with chemical solutions to render articles fireproof or flameproof: Immerses article in vat containing chemical solution or sprays solution on article. May mix chemicals. May spray hangings at business establishments. Keeps record of work performed and chemicals used.
GOE: 06.04.33 STRENGTH: M GED: R1 M1 L1 SVP: 2 DLU: 77

583 IRONING, PRESSING, GLAZING, STAKING, CALENDERING, AND EMBOSSING OCCUPATIONS

This group includes occupations concerned with imparting or restoring shape, smoothness, or finish to materials by application of pressure or tension usually accompanied by steam; imparting various effects to materials by running them under the pressure of a series of smooth or engraved rollers or plates; and stretching and softening leather in a staking machine to prevent cohesion of the fibers while drying.

583.132-010 SUPERVISOR, PRESSING DEPARTMENT (garment)
Supervises and coordinates activities of workers engaged in pressing, folding, and packing garments: Trains workers in setting up and operating machines and equipment. Examines articles for finishing defects, such as soils and faulty seaming. Performs other duties as described under SUPERVISOR (any industry) Master Title. May operate pressing machine [PRESSER, MACHINE (any industry)]. May press garments, using hand iron [PRESSER, HAND (any industry)].
GOE: 06.02.01 STRENGTH: L GED: R4 M3 L3 SVP: 7 DLU: 77

583.137-010 SUPERVISOR, PLEATING (tex. prod., nec)
Supervises and coordinates activities of workers engaged in pleating fabric material or unfinished skirts: Assigns pleat patterns and materials to workers. Examines pleated skirts to ensure conformance to standards. Records number of skirts processed by each worker for production and billing records. Performs other duties as described under SUPERVISOR (any industry) Master Title.
GOE: 06.04.01 STRENGTH: L GED: R4 M3 L3 SVP: 8 DLU: 77

583.585-010 CALENDER-MACHINE OPERATOR (nonmet. min.) alternate titles: cloth calender; tape calender; button-breaker operator
Tends takeup machine that presses asbestos cloth, tape, rope, or brake lining to uniform thickness and even finish: Places roll of asbestos material on brackets of machine and threads material through feed rollers, calender rolls, and around *takeup roll.* Turns handwheel or air valve to regulate pressure on calender rolls according to material being pressed. Adjusts thermostat to set specified temperature for rollers. Starts machine and guides material into feed rollers. Measures thickness and width of material, using micrometer and tape measure, and adjusts pressure on rollers so thickness and width of material will conform to specifications. Observes recording control chart and adjusts coolant valves to control temperature of rollers. Removes rolls of material from takeup roll. Records width, yardage, and type of material pressed on work ticket and attaches ticket to roll of material. May examine asbestos material for defects and mend defects, using darning needle. May change rollers, using hoist and handtools. May tend machine that presses wire mesh and asbestos to uniform thickness.
GOE: 06.04.05 STRENGTH: M GED: R2 M2 L2 SVP: 3 DLU: 77

583.682-010 COATING-AND-EMBOSSING-UNIT OPERATOR (tex. prod., nec; textile)
Operates machine to size, coat, and emboss fabrics, such as felt or cloth: Places roll of material onto feed holder of machine. Threads end through tandem arrangement of calender, sizing, coating, embossing, and drier units. Attaches end to rewind spindle. Turns handwheels to admit steam that moistens material and to admit steam into calender rolls to heat rolls. Fills troughs with specified sizing and coating solutions and turns screws to adjust doctors. Turns calibrated dial knobs to adjust airflow and temperature in drying ovens. Positions and locks engraved shells on embossing rolls. Turns screws or inserts shims to adjust pressure of roller on material. Turns knob to synchronize speed of machines and conveyors. Positions feed guides, tightens guides with wrench, and starts machine. Examines sample run to determine conformity to specifications. May place additional rolls of material into feed holders to produce laminated fabrics.
GOE: 06.02.16 STRENGTH: M GED: R3 M2 L2 SVP: 6 DLU: 77

583.684-010 PLEATER, HAND (tex. prod., nec)
Forms in wool, cotton, synthetic, or other cloth fabrics, using pleat patterns: Places opened pleat pattern on table, using iron weights to hold pleats open. Lays fabric on pattern and folds creases in pattern to form pleats. Rolls pattern with fabric inside into cylinder preparatory to steaming process.
GOE: 06.04.27 STRENGTH: L GED: R2 M1 L2 SVP: 3 DLU: 77

583.684-014 WAIST PLEATER (tex. prod., nec)
Forms and tapes unpressed pleats around waist of unfinished skirts: Lays material on pleat pattern and folds in pleats. Presses pattern with steam iron to retain pleats. Removes material and tapes waistline with masking tape to keep pleats in place.
GOE: 06.04.27 STRENGTH: L GED: R2 M1 L2 SVP: 4 DLU: 77

583.685-010 BREAKER-MACHINE TENDER (textile)
Tends machine that removes excess starch or stiffness from dyed or printed cloth: Slides cloth roll onto machine brackets. Threads cloth over and under alternate rollers that have surface of wavy ridges or rollers that are covered with metal buttons. Starts machine and observes operation to detect binding of cloth or machine malfunction. Pushes lever to reverse machine, running cloth through several times until texture meets specifications.
GOE: 06.04.16 STRENGTH: M GED: R2 M1 L2 SVP: 2 DLU: 77

583.685-014 BRIM CURLER (hat & cap)
Tends machine that presses and curls brims of fiber helmets: Inserts crown of helmet in lower die on bed of machine. Pushes button or lever that raises and presses die and helmet against upper die to curl brim. Pulls or presses button lever to lower die and removes helmet. May turn switches and valve controls to start cooling unit in lower die and activate heating element in upper die.

GOE: 06.04.05 STRENGTH: L GED: R2 M1 L1 SVP: 2 DLU: 77

583.685-018 BRIM PRESSER I (hat & cap) alternate titles: brim buster; brimmer; brim plater

Tends machine that presses hat brims to smooth and flatten brims: Selects specified flange (collar) and positions flange over hole in heated machine bed. Inserts hat crown in hole with brim resting on flange. Moves lever to lower machine press against hat brim or raise machine bed, containing hat, against stationary press to curl, smooth, or flatten brim. Removes hat from machine and places on rack. May tend machine equipped with rotary block or inflation device to press hat brims. When tending battery of hydraulic presses to shape straw hat brims, is known as Set-Off-Press Operator (hat & cap).
GOE: 06.04.05 STRENGTH: L GED: R2 M1 L1 SVP: 2 DLU: 78

583.685-022 BRIM-AND-CROWN PRESSER (hat & cap) alternate titles: brim buster; brim setter; crown ironer; ironer

Tends one or more machines that press unfinished hat bodies to smooth and shape hats: Positions inverted hat body in specified size heated form, mounted in bed of press. Pulls lever to lower ram and automatically inflate hat body to shape body and brim against form. Removes and inspects hat for wrinkles and specific shape, and stacks hat on rack. May insert specified shaped block in hat body before lowering ram if press is not equipped with inflation device.
GOE: 06.04.05 STRENGTH: L GED: R2 M1 L1 SVP: 2 DLU: 78

583.685-026 CALENDER OPERATOR (tex. prod., nec; textile) alternate titles: calender tender; roll-calender tender

Tends machine that imparts luster and finish to cloth or felt by pressure of cold or steam-heated rolls: Places roll of cloth or felt on brackets of machine, using hoist, and threads end of cloth between rollers and onto takeup beam. Pulls lever to lower rollers and apply pressure to cloth. Turns screws to position brush that cleans nap of felt goods. Turns dial to set temperature gauge according to specification for style of cloth. Turns handwheel to adjust entering guides according to width of cloth and to regulate tension of cloth. May raise rollers to allow seams or clips to pass. May sew end of new cloth to leader cloth. May tend calender fed directly from another machine or from handtruck.
GOE: 06.04.16 STRENGTH: M GED: R2 M1 L2 SVP: 3 DLU: 77

583.685-030 EMBOSSER (any industry) alternate titles: embossing-calender operator; embossing-machine operator; roller embosser

Tends machine that imparts raised design or finish on cloth, coated fabrics, or plastic sheeting, by means of heat and pressure from engraved steel rollers: Adjusts automatic device that regulates heat, or turns valve to admit steam to rollers. Slides bar through center of material roll and lifts it onto machine feed brackets. Threads material between rollers and laps end onto takeup tube. Starts machine and moves controls to adjust speed, pressure of rollers, and tension of material. Observes material as it passes through machine to prevent seams, rolled selvages, or trash from damaging rollers. May guide material by hand. May verify temperature of roller, using pyrometer. May sew cuts of cloth together, using portable sewing machine. May be designated according to material embossed as Silk-Crepe-Machine Operator (textile). May tend machine that imparts artificial graining, size, trademark, or other designs to sweatbands and be designated Sweatband-Decorating-Machine Operator (hat & cap). Important variables may be indicated by trade names of machine used.
GOE: 06.04.02 STRENGTH: M GED: R2 M1 L2 SVP: 3 DLU: 78

583.685-034 EMBOSSING-MACHINE OPERATOR (tex. prod., nec)

Tends embossing machine that imprints grain or pattern on plastic sheeting for use in manufacture of wall covering and padded automotive components, such as dashboards and door panels: Positions rolls of sheeting in *letoff rack,* using hoist. Threads sheeting through guide rolls and onto core on *windup rack.* Adjusts pressure of embossing roll to imprint design to specified depth without damaging sheeting. Starts machine and observes operation of machine to prevent damage to goods by wrinkling or tearing. May laminate and emboss sheets in single operation.
GOE: 06.04.02 STRENGTH: M GED: R3 M2 L2 SVP: 4 DLU: 77

583.685-038 EMBOSSING-MACHINE-OPERATOR HELPER (plastic-synth.)

Tends embossing machine that imprints designs on plastic sheeting: Turns valves and pulls levers, as directed, to regulate heat and tension of machine. Positions rolls of material in *letoff rack* and *windup racks,* using hoist. Threads material between machine rollers. Moves rolls of material to storage, using handtruck. Feeds machine that grinds scrap.
GOE: 06.04.02 STRENGTH: M GED: R2 M1 L2 SVP: 2 DLU: 77

583.685-042 FOLDING-MACHINE OPERATOR (garment) alternate titles: creaser; creasing-machine operator; crimper; folder

Tends machine that folds and presses garment parts, such as collar bands, pockets, and pocket flaps, to shape and prepare parts for sewing, using either of following methods: (1) Positions part in heated die on bed of machine. Depresses pedal to start machine that automatically lowers upper die onto garment part and into lower die, releases steam from lower die, and moves horizontally sliding plates over edges of part to fold and press part. (2) Inserts edges of garment part through folding device and guides folded edges between heated pressing rollers. May be designated according to part creased as Collar-Band Creaser (garment); Cuff Creaser (garment; knitting); Pocket Creaser (garment; knitting); Pocket-Flap-Creasing-Machine Operator (garment); Shirt Creaser (garment).

GOE: 06.04.05 STRENGTH: L GED: R2 M1 L1 SVP: 2 DLU: 77

583.685-046 FUSING-MACHINE TENDER (garment; knitting)

Tends machine that fuses decorative emblems, monograms, labels, collar stays, and backing material to hose or garment parts: Places applique on hose or garment part or positions backing on garment part and presses button or lever to activate machine that heats and seals articles together. May be designated according to article fused as Collar-Stay-Fuser Tender (garment); Emblem-Fuser Tender (garment; knitting); Label-Fuser Tender (garment).
GOE: 06.04.05 STRENGTH: L GED: R1 M1 L1 SVP: 2 DLU: 77

583.685-050 HAT-LINING BLOCKER (hat & cap)

Tends equipment that presses and smooths hat linings preparatory to installation in hats: Turns hat lining inside-out and fits lining over heated hat block. Smooths and straightens lining and seam, using hands and fingers. Pulls lever to lower pressing form onto lining, or lowers sandfilled cloth bag onto lining to press lining using hoist. Depresses pedal to force steam through perforations in hat block to moisten lining and set press. Raises bag or releases press and removes lining from block. Stacks linings on table according to size. May place linings on hat form for cooling following removal from block.
GOE: 06.04.05 STRENGTH: L GED: R2 M1 L1 SVP: 2 DLU: 77

583.685-054 HYDRAULIC-PRESS OPERATOR (knitting)

Tends hydraulic-pressing machine that smooths wrinkles from folded knitted garments: Opens valves to admit steam to pressing plate. Lays folded garments in tray. Slides tray under plate and onto top of piston of machine. Shifts lever to raise piston and force tray against steam-heated plate to press garments. Pulls tray from under steam plate and removes garments after piston automatically lowers.
GOE: 06.04.05 STRENGTH: L GED: R2 M1 L1 SVP: 2 DLU: 77

583.685-058 HYDRAULIC-PRESS OPERATOR (tex. prod., nec)

Tends hydraulic press that compresses hard felt pads to uniform thickness: Places flat steel spacing bars of desired thickness on edges of anvil to limit stroke of ram. Places felt pads between spacing bars and starts ram to compress felt. Opens valve to admit steam to ram for heating felt to aid in compression. Removes felt pads after ram returns to starting position and places pads on floor to cool. Places cooled pads in boxes. May verify thickness of pads, using gauge.
GOE: 06.04.05 STRENGTH: L GED: R2 M1 L2 SVP: 2 DLU: 77

583.685-062 JACQUARD-TWINE-POLISHER OPERATOR (tex. prod., nec)

Tends machine that polishes hand-starched skeins of jacquard twine: Hangs skeins on pole and stretches skein to specified length. Removes laces that bind skeins and dips skeins into starch barrel. Attaches ends of starched skeins to hook that is rotated by handcrank and turns crank to wring excess starch from skeins. Spreads skeins on rollers of polishing machine and starts machine. Observes operation of machine and spreads strands to prevent bunching.
GOE: 06.04.16 STRENGTH: L GED: R2 M1 L2 SVP: 3 DLU: 77

583.685-066 LEATHER ETCHER (garment)

Tends machine that presses and scorches designs into leather garment parts: Starts roll-turning motor and roll heater. Moves handle of variable electric resistor to adjust heating of upper roll to specified temperature. Turns wing nuts to adjust pressure between rolls and feeds garment parts between rolls.
GOE: 06.04.16 STRENGTH: L GED: R3 M2 L3 SVP: 2 DLU: 77

583.685-070 MANGLER (knitting) alternate titles: ironer; mangle operator, garments; pressing machine operator

Tends machine, consisting of pressing roll and ironing shoe, that shapes and smooths knitted garments: Presses control lever to revolve roll and to engage ironing shoe with revolving roll while machine is heating. Adjusts rheostat to heat ironing shoe and to maintain specified temperature. Disengages heating ironing shoe from roll, stops roll, and spreads garment on roll. Starts roll and reengages ironing shoe to press garment. Removes pressed garment from machine. May be designated according to garment or garment part pressed as Cuff Presser (knitting).
GOE: 06.04.05 STRENGTH: L GED: R2 M1 L2 SVP: 2 DLU: 77

583.685-074 NARROW-FABRIC CALENDERER (narrow fabrics)

Tends calender machine that imparts luster and finish simultaneously to several strands (10-50) of narrow fabrics, such as tape and ribbon: Threads ends around rollers of machine and starts strands into cans, or ties ends to ends in machine. Starts machine and observes strands of fabric entering machine to detect tangled or twisted fabric. Stops machine and straightens fabric. May tend machine equipped with spray (mist) attachment that dampens fabric before fabric enters rollers.
GOE: 06.04.16 STRENGTH: M GED: R2 M1 L1 SVP: 2 DLU: 77

583.685-078 PILLOWCASE TURNER (tex. prod., nec)

Tends machine that turns pillowcases right-side-out and stretches material to remove wrinkles: Turns dials to adjust turner arms according to width of pillowcases and to adjust speed and throw of discharge mechanism. Positions pillowcase on arms and depresses pedal to activate mechanism that inverts pillowcase and discharges article onto rack. May turn pillowcases by hand or using turning stand.
GOE: 06.04.05 STRENGTH: L GED: R2 M1 L1 SVP: 3 DLU: 77

583.685-082 PLEATING-MACHINE OPERATOR (any industry)

Tends one or more machines that fold and press pleats into materials, such as cloth, paper, plastic, or parchment: Turns thumbscrews or levers to adjust

pleating knife according to width specified for pleats and for distance specified between pleats, and to adjust temperature of pressing rollers. Places roll of material on rod at entry end of machine and draws end of fabric through guides, pleating knife, and between heated pressing rollers. Laps end of fabric around *takeup roll* or guides end into box. Starts machine and observes pleating for conformance to specifications. May thread material between layers of paper to prevent heated rollers from scorching material. May tend machine that attaches waxed thread to edges of material to hold pleats in fabric.
GOE: 06.04.05 STRENGTH: L GED: R3 M2 L3 SVP: 4 DLU: 77

583.685-086   PRESS OPERATOR (textile)
Tends machine that steams and presses wrinkles from woolen cloth: Starts press and manually guides cloth into machine and under weighted cylinder which steams material and presses out wrinkles. Turns handwheel to adjust cylinder pressure according to type of cloth processed. Sews end of new material to end of material in press, using sewing machine. Cleans and oils pressing machine.
GOE: 06.04.05 STRENGTH: L GED: R2 M1 L1 SVP: 4 DLU: 77

583.685-090   PRESSER, BUFFING WHEEL (tex. prod., nec)
Tends machine that presses cloth buffing wheels after forming to prepare buffing wheels for sewing: Presses lever to start movement of machine bed toward and away from heated press. Removes and replaces buffing wheels on bed of machine as bed moves forward. Moves lever attached to ratchet wheel to adjust space between bed and press to accommodate wheels of different sizes. May tend press to insert cardboard or wood cores in buffing wheels.
GOE: 06.04.05 STRENGTH: L GED: R2 M1 L1 SVP: 2 DLU: 77

583.685-094   ROLLER-MACHINE OPERATOR (leather mfg.) alternate titles: leather polisher
Tends roller machine that smooths or glazes surface or accentuates natural grain of leather: Positions leather on bed of machine and depresses pedal to lower roller onto leather. Starts machine to move roller over leather. Shifts position of leather under roller to impart specified finish to entire surface. Pulls finished leather from machine table and stacks leather on cart. May be designated according to section of hide rolled as Back Roller (leather mfg.); Belly Roller (leather mfg.); Crop Roller (leather mfg.); according to condition of leather rolled as Dry Roller (leather mfg.); Retanned-Leather Roller (leather mfg.); Wet Roller (leather mfg.); or according to type of machine tended as Glazing-Machine Operator (leather mfg.); Graining-Machine Operator (leather mfg.).
GOE: 06.04.16 STRENGTH: M GED: R2 M1 L2 SVP: 2 DLU: 77

583.685-098   SEAM PRESSER (hat & cap)
Tends machine that presses seams of caps, hats, or millinery: Turns dial to regulate temperature of iron in machine head, according to temperature specifications for type of material to be pressed. Positions seam over ironing form on bed of machine and under feed wheel guide. Depresses pedal to lower heated iron onto seam and feeds material under iron to smooth and flatten seam. May be designated according to section of seam pressed as Half-Section Ironer (hat & cap); Quarter-Section Ironer (hat & cap).
GOE: 06.04.05 STRENGTH: L GED: R2 M1 L1 SVP: 3 DLU: 77

583.685-102   SHAPER AND PRESSER (garment) alternate titles: collar pointer; collar-top turner; cuff-turner-machine operator
Tends machine that shapes and presses garment parts, such as collars and cuffs preparatory to joining parts to garments: Pulls collar or cuff onto shaped metal template of machine. Depresses pedals to open heated plates of machine and move template and garment part between heated plates. Releases pedal to close heated plates against part to shape and press part. Turns thermostatic control to regulate temperature of plates according to type of fabric pressed. May invert clothing parts prior to shaping and pressing [TURNER (any industry)].
GOE: 06.04.05 STRENGTH: L GED: R2 M1 L1 SVP: 2 DLU: 77

583.685-106   STEAM-PRESS TENDER (textile)
Tends machine that passes cloth (usually woolen) between rollers and steam-jacketed enclosure to press and remove wrinkles from cloth: Sews end of cloth to leader in machine, using portable sewing machine. Turns wheel to adjust guides according to width of cloth. Turns thumbscrew to regulate pressure of steam jacket for type of cloth and finish specified. Turns valve to admit steam if cloth is to be dampened before pressing. Observes cloth feeding into machine to detect and remove foreign matter. Places empty truck under *swing-folding attachment* and doffs full truck or removes full rolls from machine brackets, using chain hoist. May measure width of cloth after pressing and turn wheel to adjust spread roller that controls width of finished cloth.
GOE: 06.04.05 STRENGTH: M GED: R2 M1 L2 SVP: 3 DLU: 77

583.685-110   STRAW HAT PRESSER, MACHINE (hat & cap)
Tends machine that presses strawhats to shape and smooths brims and crowns: Selects pressing dies according to specifications, and secures dies in holders of machine bed and ram, using screwdriver. Positions hat over heated lower die in machine bed. Moves lever to lower ram containing heated upper die that shapes and smooths hat. Removes hat and examines for flaws, such as wrinkles and shaping irregularities. May tend hydraulic pressing machine [HYDRAULIC BLOCKER (hat & cap) 580.685-038]. May be designated according to pressing stage as Presser, First (hat & cap); Presser, Second (hat & cap). May moisten hat with steam preparatory to pressing.
GOE: 06.04.09 STRENGTH: L GED: R2 M1 L1 SVP: 2 DLU: 78

583.685-114   STRAW-HAT-PLUNGER OPERATOR (hat & cap) alternate titles: straw-hat presser
Tends plunger press that presses and shapes straw hats to size: Turns valve to admit steam to hollow die. Places hat inside die, crown down. Pulls lever to force ram down on hat. Releases press after specified time and removes pressed hat. May tend two presses simultaneously.
GOE: 06.04.09 STRENGTH: M GED: R2 M1 L2 SVP: 2 DLU: 77

583.685-118   STRIP PRESSER (boot & shoe)
Tends machine that presses and removes wrinkles from leather strips used for shoe findings: Sorts strips according to width and color. Presses button that starts machine and inserts strip between pressing rollers. Guides strips from rollers to distribute strips evenly in container under rollers.
GOE: 06.04.05 STRENGTH: L GED: R1 M1 L1 SVP: 2 DLU: 77

583.685-122   TRIMMING-MACHINE OPERATOR (garment; knitting) alternate titles: winder
Tends machine that presses trimming material and winds material onto spools: Inserts end of trimming between heated rollers and fastens end to take-up spool with tape, pins, or glue. Starts and regulates rotation of machine rollers that press and wind trimming material. Guides and smooths material as material is drawn into rotating rollers to prevent tangling. Turns valve to admit steam into rollers to steam press cloth as required.
GOE: 06.04.05 STRENGTH: L GED: R2 M1 L1 SVP: 2 DLU: 77

583.685-126   YARN-POLISHING-MACHINE OPERATOR (textile) alternate titles: glazer; glazing-machine operator
Tends machine that applies finishing solution to yarn, thread, or twine to add strength and luster to item: Places full spools on spindles of creel, draws thread through finishing compound and drying and brushing units, and laps end onto takeup spools, or ties thread to preceding end. Pours finishing compound into tank to maintain specified level. Ties broken threads. Doffs finished spools and replaces them with empty spools.
GOE: 06.04.16 STRENGTH: M GED: R2 M1 L1 SVP: 2 DLU: 77

583.686-010   BEAD-MACHINE OPERATOR (hat & cap) alternate titles: burring-machine operator; sweatband drummer
Feeds sweatband leather between rollers of machine that embosses decorative line or bead preparatory to sewing into hats: Starts machine and feeds strips of leather against guide and between rollers that impart decorative beading or that emboss leather to simulate turned edge in sweatband.
GOE: 06.04.05 STRENGTH: L GED: R2 M1 L2 SVP: 2 DLU: 77

583.686-014   FUSING-MACHINE FEEDER (garment)
Feeds or off bears machine that fuses backing material to garment parts: Aligns material and garment part on conveyor for feeding into machine that heat seals materials. Removes finished articles from conveyor belt.
GOE: 06.04.05 STRENGTH: L GED: R1 M1 L1 SVP: 1 DLU: 77

583.686-018   GLOVE TURNER AND FORMER, AUTOMATIC (glove & mit.) alternate titles: turner and former, automatic
Feeds or off bears machine that turns, shapes, and presses gloves: Dumps box of gloves into bin over machine. Pulls each glove over *turner tubes* to feed machine. Removes turned, shaped (formed), and pressed glove from conveyor. Examines gloves for defective pressing or punched-out finger tips and pairs gloves without defects.
GOE: 06.04.05 STRENGTH: L GED: R1 M1 L1 SVP: 2 DLU: 77

583.686-022   MANGLE-PRESS CATCHER (textile) alternate titles: mangle doffer
Off bears pressed knitted garments, pillowcases, or other textile products, from rear of mangle-press, and places articles on handtrucks.
GOE: 06.04.05 STRENGTH: L GED. R1 M1 L1 SVP: 2 DLU: 77

583.686-026   OUTSOLE FLEXER (boot & shoe)
Feeds leather outsoles through machine equipped with series of powered rollers that bend outsoles to make leather more flexible. Catches outsoles coming from machine and stacks outsoles on handtruck for further processing. May feed knee blocks through machine.
GOE: 06.04.05 STRENGTH: L GED: R1 M1 L1 SVP: 2 DLU: 77

583.686-030   PRESS FEEDER (knitting; textile) alternate titles: roller-presser operator
Positions cloth or knitted garments on belt conveyor of machine that presses garments through heated rollers to smooth out wrinkles, dry, or preshrink articles. May inspect one side of garment to detect holes and lay defective garment on table for MENDER, KNIT GOODS (garment; knitting).
GOE: 06.04.16 STRENGTH: L GED: R1 M1 L1 SVP: 2 DLU: 77

583.687-010   PRESS HAND (knitting) alternate titles: boarder
Stacks knitted garments between alternate layers of pressing boards to prepare articles for pressing in hydraulic press. Removes garments from between boards after pressing.
GOE: 06.04.27 STRENGTH: L GED: R1 M1 L1 SVP: 2 DLU: 77

584   MERCERIZING, COATING, AND LAMINATING OCCUPATIONS

This group includes occupations concerned with treating material with concentrated caustic soda lye to cause swelling and increase luster; forming or pressing material into thin layers and covering materials and products with a layer or layers of the same or another material for such purposes as building them up, decorating, or preserving them.

584.382-010 COATING-MACHINE OPERATOR I (tex. prod., nec) alternate titles: saturator

Operates machine to coat cloth, paper, or other sheet material used in production of artificial leather and other coated fabrics: Installs uncoated sheeting roll on machine brackets, using hoist, or threads sheeting from calender machine through coating machine rollers onto *takeup roll.* Operates sewing machine to join uncoated roll to end of processed roll, and cuts material at seam after seam passes through coating and drying units. Adjusts doctor blade or roller clearance to produce coating of specified thickness. Starts machine when dryer temperature reaches specified setting. Turns valves to control flow of coating solution onto sheeting, or applies solution to fabric surface, using dipper and bucket. Observes process to prevent slippage of sheeting from width guides and turns guides and moves machine controls to correct such defects as streaks, wrinkles, and turned edges in material being processed. Applies gummed tape to repair holes or tears in sheeting. May be designated according to type of coating applied as Dull-Coat-Mill Operator (tex. prod., nec); Finish-Coat-Mill Operator (tex. prod., nec); First-Coat Operator (tex. prod., nec). May remove coated rolls from machine, using hoist.
GOE: 06.02.21 STRENGTH: M GED: R3 M2 L2 SVP: 5 DLU: 77

584.382-014 QUILTING-MACHINE OPERATOR (tex. prod., nec)

Sets up and operates machine to heat-seal vinyl film to cotton and synthetic filler in specified patterns to produce quilted fabric: Reads work order to determine specifications, such as type of vinyl film and batting (filler), die pattern, and total yardage to be fabricated. Bolts die to underside of machine ram with assistance of other worker, tapes insulating paper to bumper plate of machine, and mounts bumper plate onto machine bed under die. Loads vinyl film and batting onto roller bar with assistance of other worker, using hoist, and lowers roller bar onto machine feed-off winder. Adjusts ram stroke and pull-away arm to specified positions, using wrench. Adjusts thermo-seal unit controls for radio-wave frequency, sealing time, and electrical current, applying knowledge of product specifications and machine operations. Buffs die surfaces to remove burrs, using emery cloth. Adjusts slitter knives to specified width of finished material, using rule and hex key. Pushes buttons to activate machine for trial run, inspects quilted fabric for defects such as die cutting through material, and adjusts control settings to correct defects. Restarts machine and observes feeding, positioning, heat sealing, and winding operations to detect malfunctions. Continuously observes light signal that indicates drainage of residual current from die and machine bed after die-sealing operation. Pushes buttons to stop machine when signal is not emitted and notifies designated personnel. Attaches red tape to fabric to mark defects, such as burns, smudges, and printing errors. Positions and tapes end of quilted fabric emerging from machine onto takeup roller, pushes knob to set automatic yardage counter to zero, and pulls lever to stop winder when specified yardage has been reached. Cuts off material, using knife, tapes material end to roll, and wraps and labels roll, following prescribed procedures. Carries finished rolls to specified storage area.
GOE: 06.02.09 STRENGTH: H GED: R3 M2 L2 SVP: 5 DLU: 86

584.562-010 COATING-MACHINE OPERATOR (carpet & rug; tex. prod., nec) alternate titles: roll-coating-machine operator

Operates machine to coat rolls of woven fiber rugs or felt padding with vinyl or other coatings to prolong life of fiber and retard soiling: Dumps specified amounts of coating ingredients into vat and starts mixer. Turns valve to transfer coating to machine reservoir. Observes thermometers and adjusts electrical controls to maintain specified temperatures in bath and drying compartments. Threads fiber rug material through machine or sews end of new roll to end of preceding roll in machine. Pushes switch to start machine that moves material through coating bath and drying compartments onto rewind roller. Cleans machine and equipment, using water, solvents, brushes, scrapers, and chisel. Prepares production report on rugs coated. May operate machine equipped with automatic sprays to coat rugs or padding.
GOE: 06.02.21 STRENGTH: L GED: R3 M2 L2 SVP: 5 DLU: 77

584.665-010 COATER HELPER (textile)

Assists COATER (textile) in applying rubber or pyroxylin coating to fabric, such as carpeting and upholstery material, and to dry coating: Starts pump to admit solution to trough. Observes cloth to detect faulty coating and covers missed spots, using brush. Turns dials to control temperature of *curing oven* and movement of cloth through *range,* and to adjust *tenter frame* guides. Works as member of team to operate and clean range. Assists in removing full rolls from range. May tend intermediate range units that apply backing to carpeting and be designated Laminating-Machine Operator Helper (textile).
GOE: 06.04.16 STRENGTH: M GED: R2 M1 L2 SVP: 3 DLU: 77

584.665-014 GLUE-SPREADING-MACHINE OPERATOR (leather prod.)

Tends glue spreading machine that applies glue to unfinished side of material, such as leather, imitation leather, fabric, and vinyl: Receives light signals indicating size of material to be glued from CASE FINISHER (leather prod.). Fills reservoir with glue, turns adjustment wheel to regulate flow of glue from rollers, and starts machine. Selects designated size of material and guides material into feed roller which glues and drops material onto conveyor for transfer to coverers. May place wax paper between parts to prevent sticking.

GOE: 06.04.05 STRENGTH: L GED: R2 M1 L1 SVP: 2 DLU: 77

584.665-018 SIZING-MACHINE TENDER (textile)

Tends machine that coats strands of yarn with size to stiffen and strengthen yarn for further processing: Positions yarn bobbins and takeup cylinders on spindles of machine. Threads yarn over fingers of *tension guides,* across size-covered rollers, and around cylinders. Determines tension of yarn strands, using tensiometer. Pulls or releases yarn between tension guide and takeup cylinder to increase or decrease tension. Turns valve to admit size into retaining trough of machine. Observes machine to detect deviation of flow or supply of size from standard and notifies KNITTING-MACHINE FIXER, HEAD (knitting) of malfunction. Observes machine to detect yarn breakage and ties knot or rewraps yarn end around sizing cylinder to repair breaks. Doffs and labels cylinders of sized yarn. May mix size, following formula.
GOE: 06.04.16 STRENGTH: L GED: R2 M2 L2 SVP: 3 DLU: 77

584.682-010 COATER (textile)

Operates *range* consisting of units, such as troughs, pickup roller, *curing oven, and tenter frame,* to apply coatings, such as rubber, pyroxylin, or foam to fabrics, such as carpeting or upholstery material, and to dry coating: Sews end of cloth to leader in machine, using portable sewing machine, or threads end of fabric through rolls of machine. Starts pump to admit solution into trough. Observes operation to detect skewed cloth and pushes buttons to control speed of rollers that hold back or advance selvages to straighten cloth. Measures cloth emerging from tenter frame to determine if cloth has been stretched and dried to specified width. Turns handwheel to adjust distance between tenter chains. Turns switches to regulate speed of machine and temperature of drying cabinet, and turns setscrew to set doctor blade for various cloth styles. Tests viscosity of coating solution with viscosimeter and adds solvent or coating ingredients to bring solution to specifed viscosity. Doffs trucks of dry cloth at *swing-folding attachment.* May operate machine equipped with condenser to recover evaporated solvent. May operate range to apply backing to carpeting. May tend beamer that winds packages of fabric onto beams of continuous length to facilitate further processing.
GOE: 06.02.21 STRENGTH: M GED: R3 M2 L2 SVP: 4 DLU: 80

584.682-014 LAMINATING-MACHINE OPERATOR (knitting; textile) alternate titles: combining-machine operator

Operates *range* to laminate materials, such as cloth, carpeting, felt, and foam rubber: Mounts roll of felt or foam rubber on machine brackets. Pushes truck of cloth into feeding position. Sews cloth and felt or foam rubber to leader using portable sewing machine, or threads layers of materials through range unit guides and rollers. Turns dials and handwheels to adjust blade that spreads predetermined quantity of adhesive onto cloth, regulate heat lamps and speed of laminating rollers, or to adjust *tenter frame* according to width of materials. Turns valve to admit steam into *drying cans* or steam pipes and starts range. Aligns cloth entering machine and observes fabrics to detect wrinkles and holes. Patches holes with masking tape and smooths wrinkles by hand. May apply adhesive to material with trowel or dipper. May work as member of team to guide cloth into range.
GOE: 06.02.09 STRENGTH: M GED: R3 M2 L3 SVP: 5 DLU: 77

584.684-010 LATEXER (carpet & rug)

Applies latex to backs of rugs to secure yarn tufts in backing material, using spray gun, brush, or trowel: Spreads rug, bottom-side-up, over specified frame and hooks edges onto frame spikes. Covers rug with backing material and attaches backing edges to spikes. Sprays or pours and spreads latex onto backing, using spray gun or bucket and trowel. Turns knob and moves levers to set temperature and speed of track-mounted drying machine that traverses frame and dries rug. Removes rug from frame onto table, in roll form, for further processing. May tend machine equipped with rollers, that applies latex to back of carpeting.
GOE: 06.04.33 STRENGTH: M GED: R2 M1 L2 SVP: 3 DLU: 77

584.685-010 CALENDER OPERATOR, ARTIFICIAL LEATHER (tex. prod., nec)

Tends calender machine that compresses cloth and coated cloth sheeting to produce artificial leather fabric: Changes cloth rolls on *letoff rack* and *windup racks,* and threads sheeting through calender rollers with assistance of LABORER, GENERAL (tex. prod., nec). Scrapes surfaces of fiber rollers to remove foreign material. Sews ends of cloth rolls together to form continuous sheet, using sewing machine. Inspects sheeting being calendered to detect turned edges, material defects, or uneven coating. Applies gummed tape to holes, faulty seams, or frayed edges, and smooths wrinkles. Applies soap solution to roller to remove surface depressions, and starts calender to dry rollers by friction. May be designated according to processing stage as Raw-Calender Operator (tex. prod., nec); Second-Calender Operator (tex. prod., nec); Third-Calender Operator (tex. prod., nec).
GOE: 06.04.16 STRENGTH: M GED: R2 M2 L2 SVP: 3 DLU: 77

584.685-014 CLOTH-MERCERIZER OPERATOR (textile) alternate titles: lusterer; mercerizer-machine operator; mercerizer; mercerizing-range controller

Tends machine that adds silk-like luster to cotton cloth and increases strength and affinity of cloth for dyes: Mounts roll of cloth on machine or pulls supply cloth from handtruck or overhead poteyes and sews end to leader in machine, using portable sewing machine. Turns valve to admit caustic into vats and handwheel to adjust *tenter frame* clips to maintain tension on cloth and prevent

shrinkage as cloth passes through soapy-water spray. Sets thermostat to control temperature of caustic bath. Starts machine and observes flow of cloth through machine units to detect holes in cloth and torn selvages. Cuts out defects, using scissors, and seams ends of cloth. Turns knobs on control panel to synchronize motor speeds of machine units. Adds soap to wash bath as suds are depleted.
GOE: 06.04.16 STRENGTH: M GED: R3 M2 L2 SVP: 3 DLU: 77

584.685-018 COATING-MACHINE OPERATOR II (tex. prod., nec)
Tends machine that applies asphalt to textile bag material to waterproof material: Lifts roll of textile bag material, roll of paper dipped in hot asphalt, and roll of clean paper onto machine brackets. Threads ends of rolls with asphalt paper inserted between textile bag material and clean paper through machine guide rolls and fastens ends to winding spindle. Starts machine and observes operation to ensure even winding. Glues ends of new rolls of paper to paper in machine and sews end of new roll of textile bag material to roll in machine, using portable sewing machine. When tending machine that applies glue-backed strips of corrugated paper to burlap or other textile bag material preparatory to fabrication of dustproof bags, is designated Padding-Machine Operator (tex. prod., nec).
GOE: 06.04.16 STRENGTH: M GED: R2 M1 L2 SVP: 2 DLU: 77

584.685-022 FOXING PAINTER (rubber goods)
Tends machine that paints decorative edges or stripes on foxing strips: Fills machine reservoir with latex paint of color specified on work ticket. Hangs foxing strips on stand near machine. Adjusts distance between roller and regulates distance strip can be inserted between rollers to locate stripe as specified. Starts machine for roller to pick up paint, peels foxing strip from board, and positions strip against back guide and between rollers that paint colored stripe. Examines stripe for insufficient or excess paint and misalignment, and adjusts rollers and guide to eliminate defective painting. Places acceptable strips between cloth page of book for use by assemblers.
GOE: 06.04.21 STRENGTH: L GED: R2 M2 L2 SVP: 2 DLU: 77

584.685-026 HAT-STOCK-LAMINATING-MACHINE OPERATOR (hat & cap) alternate titles: combiner; hat-brim-and-crown-laminating operator; ironer; presser
Tends machine that sprays adhesive onto sheets of material and presses material together to form stock for manufacturing hatbrims and crowns: Secures rolls of material, such as cotton, paper, or wool, on holders of machine. Starts machine and inserts ends of sheets between feed rollers that carry materials under spray nozzle for application of adhesive. Aligns edges of coated sheets as sheets pass under heated presser rollers, forming hatbrim and crown stock. Fills machine reservoir with premixed adhesive. Turns bolts to adjust clearance of presser rollers to accommodate thickness of material to be joined, using wrench.
GOE: 06.04.05 STRENGTH: H GED: R2 M1 L2 SVP: 4 DLU: 77

584.685-030 KNIFE-MACHINE OPERATOR (textile) alternate titles: foaming machine operator
Tends machine that applies and smooths stiffening compounds, such as starch, onto cloth: Lifts roll of cloth onto machine brackets. Threads cloth end through machine rollers and dryer and ties leader strap to takeup reel. Lowers doctor and turns setscrews to adjust tension on cloth and set guide devices. Pours compound on cloth directly in front of knife assembly and spreads compound evenly with paddle. Starts and observes operation of machine, and adds compound as needed. Lifts finished roll from takeup reel after cloth has passed through dryer. May tend machine that automatically applies stiffening compound to cloth before cloth is drawn beneath knife.
GOE: 06.04.16 STRENGTH: M GED: R2 M1 L2 SVP: 4 DLU: 77

584.685-034 LAMINATOR (tex. prod., nec)
Tends machine that combines layers of quilted fabric and printed burlap for use in producing decorative pot holders: Presses button to start machine and inserts fabric between rollers of glue spreader that coats fabric with adhesive. Positions burlap over fabric and inserts layers of material between rollers that press and bond fabric and burlap.
GOE: 06.04.05 STRENGTH: L GED: R2 M1 L1 SVP: 3 DLU: 77

584.685-038 LATEXER I (protective dev.)
Tends machine that applies latex coating to reverse sides of surgical elastic supports, such as wrist, knee, and elbow braces, to prevent raveling of threads: Fills machine reservoir with sealant. Inverts support, cuts excess threads, using scissors, and places support on roller. Presses levers and pedals to start machine that applies coating to article. Removes support from machine, reverses support, and drops article in handtruck. May tend machines that wash and dry surgical supports.
GOE: 06.04.16 STRENGTH: L GED: R2 M1 L1 SVP: 3 DLU: 77

584.685-042 MANGLE TENDER (textile) alternate titles: cloth presser; mangler
Tends mangle that wets-out cloth or applies finishing chemicals, such as size starch, synthetic resins, or cellulose derivatives to cloth: Positions trucks of cloth at feed-end of machine and threads cloth through guides, under immersion roll, and through expander attachment and squeeze rolls, or sews end of cloth to leader in machine, using portable sewing machine. Turns valve to admit water, starch, or finishing solution to trough of mangle. Turns handwheel to set pressure of squeeze rollers according to thickness of cloth. Observes flow of cloth through mangle to detect holes and torn selvages. Cuts flaws from

cloth, using scissors, and sews ends of cloth together. May tend machine arranged in tandem with *drying cans, tenter frame* or *curing oven*. May be designated according to fluid used in trough as Starch-Mangle Tender (textile); Water-Mangle Tender (textile).
GOE: 06.04.16 STRENGTH: L GED: R2 M1 L2 SVP: 2 DLU: 77

584.685-046 TARRING-MACHINE OPERATOR (tex. prod., nec)
Tends machine that coats twine with tar to strengthen and waterproof twine: Pours tar into tarpots. Creels machine with bobbins of twine. Removes tarpot roller and threads ends of twine through tarport and strippers and attaches ends to takeup bobbins. Replaces tarpot roller and starts machine. Observes operation to detect malfunctions, such as broken and tangled twine, and to ensure that specified amounts of tension and tar are applied to twine. Doffs tarred bobbins of twine.
GOE: 06.04.16 STRENGTH: L GED: R2 M1 L1 SVP: 3 DLU: 77

584.685-050 WAX-MACHINE OPERATOR (textile)
Tends machines that wax fiberglass yarn under pressure: Positions bobbins of yarn over perforated spindles in waxing kettle and pushes levers to force pressure caps onto bobbins and lower and lock lid onto kettle. Turns valves to start flow of wax from melting tank into reservoir and to regulate steam to maintain specified temperature. Starts automatic waxing cycle and pump that forces wax through spindle onto yarn. Observes thermometer and gauges to determine temperature and level of wax. Removes bobbins of waxed yarn from kettle and places bobbins on cart. Places chunks of wax in melting tank to maintain specified level in reservoir and tank.
GOE: 06.04.16 STRENGTH: L GED: R2 M1 L2 SVP: 3 DLU: 77

584.685-054 YARN-MERCERIZER OPERATOR I (textile) alternate titles: mercerizer-machine operator; mercerizer; skein-mercerizing-machine operator
Tends machine that mercerizes yarn in skein form: Shakes skeins of yarn to remove tangles and loads skeins on roller arms of machine. Starts machine that puts yarn under tension, passes skeins through caustic solution, and rinses skeins. Tests caustic solution, using hydrometer, and adds soda or water to maintain uniform strength as specified. Removes skeins from mercerizer and hangs skeins on rack of tank for neutralizing. Turns valves to start spray of water and neutralizing solution. Tests neutralization, using litmus paper. May weigh and mix caustic and neutralizing solutions according to formula. May extract moisture from yarn [EXTRACTOR OPERATOR (textile)] and dry yarn in steam chamber [SKEIN-YARN DRIER (textile)].
GOE: 06.04.16 STRENGTH: M GED: R2 M1 L1 SVP: 2 DLU: 77

584.685-058 YARN-MERCERIZER OPERATOR II (textile) alternate titles: mercerizer-machine operator; mercerizer
Tends *range* that mercerizes and dries yarn in warp form: Pours caustic soda, acids, and softeners into mixing tanks, according to formula. Turns valves to allow solutions to flow into mercerizing, neutralizing, and finishing vats. Mounts balls of warp yarn in creel, using hoist or lift and aid of YARN-MERCERIZER-OPERATOR HELPER (textile). Ties ends of warp to leader, starts machine, and observes movement of warp through baths to detect breaks or tangles. Pulls broken yarn from vat, using hook, and ties ends. Tests caustic solution, using hydrometer, and adds water or caustic to restore solution to prescribed strength. Adjusts controls to regulate water and drier temperature and speed at which yarn passes through machine, according to yarn type. May tend discharge end of drier and observe yarn passing through *swing-folding attachment* into handtruck, boxes, or cans. May oil and make minor adjustments and repairs to machine.
GOE: 06.04.16 STRENGTH: M GED: R2 M1 L2 SVP: 3 DLU: 77

584.686-010 YARN-MERCERIZER-OPERATOR HELPER (textile)
Assists YARN-MERCERIZER OPERATOR (textile) II in mercerizing yarn, performing any combination of following tasks: Mounts balls of warp yarn in creel, using hoist or lift truck, with aid of operator. Straightens tangled yarn and ties broken ends. Conveys yarn and chemicals to and from storage, using handtruck. Performs other duties as described under HELPER (any industry) Master Title.
GOE: 06.04.16 STRENGTH: M GED: R1 M1 L1 SVP: 2 DLU: 77

584.687-010 LEATHER COATER (leather mfg.) alternate titles: doper; enameler; hand finisher; japanner; leather dresser; load mixer; pourer; seasoner, hand; split-leather mosser; streaker-off, hand; swabber; tannery gummer
Spreads premixed solutions, such as dope, grease, or lacquer, on leather, using applicator, to finish or waterproof leather. Positions coated leather on conveyor belt to move leather through drying oven.
GOE: 06.04.27 STRENGTH: L GED: R1 M1 L1 SVP: 1 DLU: 77

584.687-014 SPRAYER, HAND (leather mfg.) alternate titles: leather pourer; leather sprayer; pourer; stencil sprayer
Sprays solution on tanned hides or skins in preparation for further processing or to finish surface of leather, using spray gun: Fills supply tank with specified solution. Hangs leather on hooks in spray booth or over rack and sprays solution on leather. Examines surface of leather to verify completeness of coverage and places leather on drying rack. May mix dyes and chemicals to attain specified color shading. May bundle parts for further processing. May be designated according to solutions sprayed as Color Sprayer (leather prod.); Dope Sprayer (leather mfg.); Final-Coat Sprayer (leather mfg.); Gum Sprayer (leather mfg.); Oil Sprayer (leather mfg.); Seasoning Sprayer (leather mfg.).

GOE: 06.04.27 STRENGTH: L GED: R1 M1 L1 SVP: 2 DLU: 77

585 SINGEING, CUTTING, SHEARING, SHAVING, AND NAPPING OCCUPATIONS

This group includes occupations concerned with burning, scraping, scratching, and similarly working materials for such purposes as removing undesirable components (lint and hair) from them; smoothing their surfaces; removing desirable components (shearing fur from pelts); severing material into sections to facilitate further processing; and obtaining special effects, such as producing a woolly surface on fabrics by passing them over rollers covered with sharp, thin points, or bristles, which scratch and pull up the fibers.

585.130-010 SUPERVISOR, CORDUROY CUTTING (textile)

Supervises and coordinates activities of workers engaged in cutting floats on *filling pile fabrics:* Examines machines and cloth for cutting defects and directs CUTTING-MACHINE FIXER (textile) to repair or replace defective machine parts. Trains workers in operations, such as cutting floats, sharpening knives, and detecting uncut floats. Performs other duties as described under SUPERVISOR (any industry) Master Title.
GOE: 06.01.01 STRENGTH: M GED: R4 M2 L3 SVP: 6 DLU: 77

585.380-010 CUTTING-MACHINE FIXER (textile)

Sets up and repairs machines that cut floats on *filling pile fabrics,* employing knowledge of machine operation and cutting process: Turns thumbscrews to raise or lower straightedge (metal bar over which cloth passes) so that blades will cut through filling floats without damaging ground cloth, using thickness gauge as guide. Patrols work area and examines cloth and machines to detect operating defects. Replaces worn or broken parts, such as belts, cams, gears, pulleys, and cutting blades, using handtools. May operate grinding machine to sharpen cutting blades. May lubricate machine.
GOE: 06.01.02 STRENGTH: M GED: R4 M3 L3 SVP: 6 DLU: 77

585.565-010 CORDUROY-CUTTER OPERATOR (textile) alternate titles: cutting-machine operator

Tends one or more cutting machines that cut woven races in greige corduroy cloth: Sews end of cloth to leader, using portable sewing machine. Places slotted wire guides under circular cutting blades so blades project into guide slots, and inserts guides into alternate races with fingers. Positions magnetic stop-motion bar that automatically stops machine when guides slip out of cloth races and make contact with bar. Starts machine and observes cloth to detect inferior cutting. Notifies CUTTING-MACHINE FIXER (textile) of inferior cutting resulting from machine malfunction. Withdraws guides at seams, pulls seam through machine, and inserts guides into races behind seam to continue cutting process. Records lot number, piece number, yardage, and production. Doffs cloth from *swing-folding attachment* onto handtruck. Points guide tips and aligns guides, using pliers, whetstone, and emery cloth.
GOE: 06.04.05 STRENGTH: M GED: R2 M1 L2 SVP: 3 DLU: 77

585.665-010 NAPPER TENDER (knitting) alternate titles: fleecer

Tends machine that raises nap on socks to produce woolly appearance: Starts machine and feeds socks into rollers that automatically position socks under revolving wire-covered cylinder for brushing. Removes napped socks from machine. Examines socks to determine if nap has been raised according to specifications and notifies fixer of machine malfunction. May turn handwheel to adjust height of cylinder according to sock thickness.
GOE: 06.04.05 STRENGTH: S GED: R2 M1 L1 SVP: 2 DLU: 77

585.681-010 FLESHER (leather mfg.) alternate titles: fur scraper; hide cleaner; pelt scraper

Scrapes particles of flesh, fat, or protective tissue from skins or pelts to clean and soften them: Scrapes particles off with knife or straddles bench that has vertical knife attached and pulls skin over angled knife to remove excess or precise amount of particles, taking care not to cut into skins. Sharpens cutting edges of knife and bends knife to specified shaving angle, using handtools. May use rotary knife or rotary blade to scrape pelts. May be designated according to kind of pelt scraped as Rabbit Flesher (leather mfg.).
GOE: 06.01.04 STRENGTH: L GED: R3 M1 L2 SVP: 6 DLU: 77

585.681-014 FUR PLUCKER (leather mfg.)

Removes guard hairs (long coarse hairs) from pelts of fur-bearing animals, such as beavers, nutrias, and rabbits, to enhance appearance of finished pelts, using fur plucking device: Wraps forward edge of pelt around rod of movable frame to expose hairs for plucking. Starts device and pushes frame towards rotary head that plucks (cuts off) guard hairs, taking care not to damage shorter hairs in pelt. Wraps remainder of pelt around rod to facilitate complete removal of coarse hairs from pelts. May pluck hairs from pelts, using beaming knife.
GOE: 06.02.27 STRENGTH: L GED: R3 M1 L2 SVP: 6 DLU: 77

585.684-010 TRIMMER, HAND (leather mfg.) alternate titles: bend trimmer; block trimmer; blue-line trimmer; counter-pocket trimmer; edge trimmer; grader; preparer; ripper; snipper; trimmer and sorter; unbundler

Marks cutting lines on hides and trims ragged edges, thin areas, and brand marks from hides, using rule, pattern, knife, and chalk. May be designated according to hide trimmed as Black-Leather Trimmer (leather mfg.); Blue-Split Trimmer (leather mfg.); Lambskin Trimmer (leather mfg.); Lime Trimmer (leather mfg.); Raw-Hide Trimmer (leather mfg.); Wet Trimmer (leather mfg.).

GOE: 06.04.27 STRENGTH: L GED: R1 M1 L1 SVP: 2 DLU: 77

585.685-010 BRIM-POUNCING-MACHINE OPERATOR (hat & cap) alternate titles: brim pouncer; fast-brim pouncer

Tends machine that abrades felt hat brims to smooth brims and remove excess fibers: Positions hat in guide between feed and sanding rollers of machine. Depresses pedal to start machine that forces brim against abrasive cone, removing excess fibers and smoothing brim. Removes hat from machine, inverts, and repositions hat to smooth other side of brim. Feels brim surface to ascertain that specified texture has been attained and removes hat. Turns setscrew to remove and replace sanding cone, using screwdriver. When tending machine that abrades brims by action of sandpaper pads mounted on adjustable arms, is designated Jigger-Brim-Pouncing-Machine Operator (hat & cap).
GOE: 06.04.16 STRENGTH: L GED: R2 M1 L2 SVP: 3 DLU: 78

585.685-014 BUFFER (hat & cap) alternate titles: buffing-machine operator; sander; scratcher; wool-hat-sanding-machine operator

Tends machine that buffs unfinished felt or wool hat bodies to raise, smooth, or polish nap: Secures hat block of specified size in chuck of machine, pulls hat body over block, and starts machine. Depresses pedal to rotate block and force hat body against rotating felt, sandpaper, or sharkskin-covered buffing wheels to raise nap or smooth and polish body. Releases pedal to stop machine when buffing is completed and removes body from block. Turns hat body inside out and replaces body on block to buff inside surfaces. May be designated according to type of machine tended as Brim Buffer (hat & cap); Crown Buffer (hat & cap); Hat Buffer, Automatic (hat & cap).
GOE: 06.04.05 STRENGTH: L GED: R2 M1 L1 SVP: 2 DLU: 78

585.685-018 BUFFER, MACHINE (leather mfg.) alternate titles: buffing-wheel operator; burnisher; buzzle buffer; leather sander

Tends machine that buffs hides to specified finish: Turns setscrews to regulate distance between rollers, according to thickness of hide. Inserts hide between rollers and starts machine. Holds half of hide while rollers buff surface of other half. Repeats buffing operation on unbuffed portion of hide. May be designated according to hide buffed as Black-Leather Buffer (leather mfg.); White-Kid Buffer (leather mfg.). May tend machine equipped with abrasive covered rollers that form nap on surface of leather and be designated Sueding-Wheel Operator (leather mfg.).
GOE: 06.04.16 STRENGTH: L GED: R2 M1 L1 SVP: 3 DLU: 77

585.685-022 CHINCHILLA-MACHINE OPERATOR (textile) alternate titles: curling-machine operator; whirling-machine operator

Tends machine that curls pile of fabric to simulate natural fur: Positions truck of cloth at feed-end of machine. Sews cloth to leader in machine, using portable sewing machine. Turns knob to raise or lower curling brushes according to depth of pile. Straightens cloth to remove wrinkles before cloth passes under rotating brushes. Feels curled pile to detect knotting of fibers caused by brushes being out of adjustment. Notifies supervisor when knots are found. Cleans accumulated fibers from brushes, using hook. Ravels seam to separate roll at end of piece. Pulls or lifts roll onto truck. May replace defective brushes, using handtools.
GOE: 06.04.16 STRENGTH: M GED: R2 M1 L2 SVP: 2 DLU: 77

585.685-026 CLOTH TRIMMER, MACHINE (textile) alternate titles: shear tender

Tends machine equipped with rotary blades that trim loose threads from selvage of cloth: Segregates cloth according to type and width. Turns wheel to set width and *tension guides* on machine for each batch. Inserts rod into center of cloth roll and lifts roll onto machine brackets. Sews cloth end to leader in machine, using portable sewing machine. Observes cloth feeding into scray or over inspection board to detect torn selvages, holes, or soils, and cuts out torn sections, or identifies defects with adhesive stickers. Ravels seam to separate roll of trimmed cloth and doffs roll, using hoist, or by pushing it onto platform. Starts cloth winding onto new beam or tube. May verify yardage in rolls. May work as member of team to creel and doff cloth rolls.
GOE: 06.04.05 STRENGTH: M GED: R2 M1 L2 SVP: 3 DLU: 77

585.685-030 CONCAVING-MACHINE OPERATOR (boot & shoe)

Tends machine that hollows (concaves) front of shoe heel to specified shape. Inserts heel into holding device of machine. Depresses pedal to start machine that automatically forces heel against revolving cutting blades, hollowing and shaping front of heel.
GOE: 06.04.05 STRENGTH: L GED: R2 M1 L2 SVP: 2 DLU: 77

585.685-034 CORDUROY-BRUSHER OPERATOR (textile)

Tends machine equipped with series of brushing units that raise and set pile of such fabrics as corduroy and velvet: Pushes truck or roll of cloth into feeding position. Sews end of cloth to leader in machine, using portable sewing machine. Turns crank to set width guides according to width of cloth. Starts machine and observes cloth to detect grease spots, holes, or torn selvages as cloth is drawn between rollers and brushes. Turns valve to admit water into trough of wet brushing unit. May doff cloth from *swing-folding attachment* onto handtruck.
GOE: 06.04.16 STRENGTH: M GED: R2 M1 L2 SVP: 2 DLU: 77

585.685-038 CUT-LACE-MACHINE OPERATOR (leather prod.) alternate titles: cutter, machine; leather-stripping-machine operator; tanned-hide-cutter, machine; width stripper

Tends machine that cuts leather into strips (lace) for power-transmission belting, dress belts, or boot laces: Scribes line along edge of tanned hide, using

ruler, chalk, or pencil. Cuts leather along ruled line to square edge, using knife. Turns screws to adjust machine guide to specified width. Starts machine and inserts leather between feed rollers, against machine guide, and under circular knife that cuts leather into strips. Ties strips into bundles for further processing or shipment by hand or using automatic bundling machine. May be designated according to product as Belting Cutter (leather prod.); Boot-Lace Cutter, Machine (leather prod.); Sole-Stock Cutter (leather prod.).
GOE: 06.04.05 STRENGTH: L GED: R2 M1 L2 SVP: 3 DLU: 77

585.685-042 ELECTRIFIER OPERATOR (textile) alternate titles: hummer operator
  Tends machine equipped with heated, fluted roller that separates, polishes, and raises or flattens pile of plush fabrics: Positions truck of cloth at entry end of machine and sews cloth from truck to leader in machine, using portable sewing machine. Turns knob on thermostat to set temperature of cylinder according to specifications. Starts machine and moves lever to set pressure on hydraulic apron that presses cloth against cylinder to raise or flatten pile as specified. Straightens cloth to remove wrinkles before cloth passes between apron and cylinder. Compares finished cloth with standard swatch, and notifies supervisor if cloth varies from standard. Hangs cloth in loops on racks at delivery end of machine to prevent crushing of pile or doffs rolls of fabric when pile has been flattened. Ravels seams to separate cloth pieces. May tend mangle in tandem with machine to apply finish to cloth [MANGLE TENDER (textile)].
GOE: 06.04.16 STRENGTH: M GED: R2 M1 L2 SVP: 3 DLU: 77

585.685-046 FUR-CUTTING-MACHINE OPERATOR (hat & cap) alternate titles: chopper; clipper; cutter; fur-trimming machine operator; pelt shearer; shaver; shearer
  Tends machine that cuts fur from pelts or trims excess fur from hat and cap parts: Turns setscrew to adjust machine guide to accommodate thickness of pelt or fur-covered parts, such as cap linings or ear flaps. Starts machine and feeds articles against machine guide and under feed roller. Removes fur cuttings from machine tray and places items in containers for further processing. Gathers pelts and places pelts in bags for disposal.
GOE: 06.04.05 STRENGTH: L GED: R2 M1 L2 SVP: 2 DLU: 77

585.685-050 GASSER (textile) alternate titles: thread singer
  Tends machine that singes nap or loose fibers from thread: Creels machine with packages of thread. Draws thread from creel, lays individual ends of thread between teeth of expansion combs, pulls thread over gas burner, and loops ends of thread around takeup spools. Turns valve to start flow of gas and lights flame, using spark lighter. Starts machine that automatically swings flame beneath thread and observes flow of thread through machine to detect breaks in thread ends. Stops machine and ties breaks in thread by hand. Doffs spools of singed yarn.
GOE: 06.04.16 STRENGTH: L GED: R2 M1 L2 SVP: 2 DLU: 77

585.685-054 GIG TENDER (textile) alternate titles: gigger
  Tends machine that raises and sets direction of fiber on surface of woolen cloth, imparting soft and lofty hand to cloth: Mounts roll of cloth on shaft at feed-end of machine, using hoist. Sews end of cloth to leader in machine, using portable sewing machine. Turns handwheels to raise or lower contact rollers that press cloth against gigging cylinder to control amount of nap. Turns valves to admit water into wet-out boxes. Starts machine and processes cloth back and forth through machine until nap has been raised according to specifications. Relaxes pressure on contact rollers and processes cloth through machine to set direction of nap. Doffs rolls of cloth from delivery end of machine. May tend machine equipped with steaming roller rather than wet-out boxes and be designated Steam Gigger (textile).
GOE: 06.04.16 STRENGTH: L GED: R2 M1 L2 SVP: 2 DLU: 77

585.685-058 JIGGER-CROWN-POUNCING-MACHINE OPERATOR (hat & cap) alternate titles: crown-finishing-machine operator; crown pouncer; pouncing-machine operator
  Tends semiautomatic machine that abrades hat crowns to remove excess fibers and impart smooth finish: Selects hat block, according to size specifications, and attaches hat block to spindle of machine, using screwdriver. Turns handwheel to adjust tension of sanding belt against surface of hat. Slips hat onto block and moves lever to start machine that sandpapers crown. Feels surface of crown to ascertain smoothness of nap, and stops machine when specified texture is attained. Turns hat inside out and repeats operation to smooth inside of crown. Threads sandpaper from holder over machine guides as sanding belt becomes worn.
GOE: 06.04.16 STRENGTH: L GED: R2 M1 L1 SVP: 3 DLU: 77

585.685-062 LABEL PINKER (narrow fabrics)
  Tends machine equipped with pinking attachment that cuts strips of labeling material into individual labels: Positions roll of material on holder and inserts end in feeding mechanism. Turns dial to set counter for specified number of labels to be cut. Starts machine and observes cut labels to detect cutting defects. Removes defective labels and notifies machine fixer to adjust machine. Packs specified number of labels in box. May tend machine that cuts labels without pinking and be designated Label Cutter (narrow fabrics).
GOE: 06.04.05 STRENGTH: S GED: R2 M1 L1 SVP: 2 DLU: 77

585.685-066 MELLOWING-MACHINE OPERATOR (hat & cap) alternate titles: brim flexer
  Tends machine that flexes hat brims and raises nap to improve pliability and appearance of brim: Starts machine and inserts hat brim between feed rollers

and cloth-covered pads or rollers that bend and rub brim to flex brim and raise nap. May be designated according to type of hat processed as Felt-Hat-Mellowing-Machine Operator (hat & cap).
GOE: 06.04.16 STRENGTH: L GED: R2 M1 L1 SVP: 2 DLU: 78

585.685-070 NAPPER TENDER (tex. prod., nec; textile) alternate titles: brushing operator; napper operator; napper
  Tends machine that raises fibers on surface of cloth to give cloth soft, fluffy texture: Positions truck of folded cloth at entry end of machine or mounts roll of cloth on machine brackets. Sews cloth to leader in napper with surface to be napped contacting napping cylinder. Feeds each lot of cloth through machine for specified number of nappings. Examines and feels cloth to determine that finish conforms to standards. Ravels seams between cloth lots and doffs machine. May mark lot numbers on cloth with crayon. May turn handwheels to change machine speed and adjust cloth tension according to texture of cloth. May be designated according to type of material napped as Silk Brusher (textile); Sueding-Machine Tender (textile).
GOE: 06.04.16 STRENGTH: M GED: R2 M1 L2 SVP: 3 DLU: 77

585.685-074 POUNCING-LATHE OPERATOR (hat & cap) alternate titles: crown pouncer; end-lathe operator; pouncer; pouncer, machine; pouncing-machine operator; turn-machine operator
  Tends machine that abrades hat crowns to impart smooth, finished appearance: Selects specified hat block and installs block on machine. Moves lever to clamp block in place and pulls hat over block. Starts machine that starts block rotating and forces sanding pads, arm, or abrasive wheel against surface of hat to smooth crown and impart specified texture. Removes hat, turns hat inside out, and repeats sanding operation to smooth and finish inside of crown. Removes hat and inspects it for smoothness of finish.
GOE: 06.04.16 STRENGTH: L GED: R2 M1 L2 SVP: 2 DLU: 77

585.685-078 ROLLING-MACHINE OPERATOR (textile) alternate titles: glacing-machine tender
  Tends machine that raises nap on skeins of yarn or thread: Slips specified number of skeins on rollers of machine in belt form. Turns handwheel to adjust tension on skeins. Starts machine and guides skeins with pole to keep skeins centered on rollers. Removes skeins, twists ends of skeins, and places skeins in truck.
GOE: 06.04.16 STRENGTH: M GED: R2 M1 L1 SVP: 2 DLU: 77

585.685-082 ROTARY CUTTER (boot & shoe)
  Tends machine that cuts leather into *blockers:* Installs cutting disks in machine, using wrenches. Places leather on cutting bed, smooths out wrinkles, and positions leather according to shape of piece and pattern of grain. Trims offal from leather, using knife. Starts machine and guides leather over feed roller that forces it against row of revolving disks that cut leather into blockers.
GOE: 06.04.05 STRENGTH: M GED: R2 M1 L2 SVP: 3 DLU: 77

585.685-086 ROUNDING-MACHINE OPERATOR (hat & cap; tex. prod., nec) alternate titles: brim cutter; cutting-machine operator; flange cutter; round-cutter operator; rounder
  Tends machine that cuts frayed edges or excess material from articles, such as hat brims or fabric buffing wheels, or separates hat brims from crowns prior to finishing operations: Measures radius of article, using ruler. Turns setscrews on machine guide to adjust width of cut, according to specifications. Positions edge of article or crown against guide on bed of machine and pulls lever to lower rotary cutting blade onto article. Depresses pedal or pushes button to start machine that rotates article against revolving blade to cut article. May rotate article against cutting blade by hand. May be designated according to material cut as Straw-Hat-Brim-Cutter Operator (hat & cap); Trimmer, Buffing Wheel (tex. prod., nec). May tend machine that rakes and trims buffing wheels simultaneously and be designated Facer, Buffing Wheel (tex. prod., nec).
GOE: 06.04.05 STRENGTH: L GED: R2 M1 L1 SVP: 2 DLU: 78

585.685-090 RUG INSPECTOR (tex. prod., nec)
  Tends machine that cuts rug felt to specified width: Pulls felt from roll on table, examines felt for imperfections, such as light spots and burrs, and removes imperfections using tweezers. Clamps end of felt to winding roll and starts machine that rewinds inspected felt. May set circular cutting knives and cut felt to specified width.
GOE: 06.03.02 STRENGTH: L GED: R2 M1 L1 SVP: 4 DLU: 77

585.685-094 SHAVING-MACHINE OPERATOR (leather mfg.)
  Tends machine that scrapes flesh or hair from pelts, shears wool on sheepskin to specified length, or shaves hides to uniform thickness: Turns handwheel or setscrew to adjust feed roller to specified height. Places pelt or hide on roller and presses pedal to raise roller that feeds hide to clippers or revolving blades. Verifies thickness of hide, using micrometer. May sharpen blades, using honing stone. May be designated according to operation performed as Fleshing-Machine Operator (leather mfg.); Shearing-Machine Operator (leather mfg.); Unhairing-Machine Operator (leather mfg.).
GOE: 06.04.16 STRENGTH: M GED: R2 M1 L2 SVP: 3 DLU: 77

585.685-098 SHEARING-MACHINE FEEDER (leather mfg.) alternate titles: shearer
  Tends machine that shears fur on pelts, such as lamb and beaver, to produce pelts with hair of uniform length, or obtain specific effect: Arranges skin, fur side up, on conveyor belt, feed tray, or cloth covered roll and fastens skin to

pins protruding through cloth. Turns setscrews to adjust clearance between feeding device, conveyor belt, or rollers, according to specifications, using gauge, or type and size of pelt. Starts machine and guides pelt through rollers, equipped with upper rotary blade that shears fur from pelt.
GOE: 06.04.16 STRENGTH: M GED: R2 M1 L2 SVP: 3 DLU: 77

585.685-102 SHEARING-MACHINE OPERATOR (carpet & rug; textile) alternate titles: brusher and shearer; cloth shearer; shear operator

Tends machine that shears nap, loose threads, and knots from cloth or carpet surface to give uniform finish and texture: Mounts roll of cloth on brackets at feed-end of machine, using hoist or by lifting one end at a time. Sews end to leader, using portable sewing machine, or pulls end of cloth over and under several feed rollers, under knife blade roller, over wire point (brush) tension roller, and secures end to takeup beam. Turns crank to regulate knife blade roller to cut nap to specified depth. Starts machine and smooths wrinkles from cloth entering machine, using hands, to prevent blades from cutting into fabric. Raises knife blade roller to permit seams to pass under blades without being cut. Doffs roll of cloth from delivery end of machine. May replace knife blade, lubricate, and clean machine. May convey rolls of cloth to shearing machine.
GOE: 06.04.06 STRENGTH: H GED: R2 M1 L2 SVP: 2 DLU: 77

585.685-106 SINGER (textile)

Tends machine that singes nap or lint from cloth: Sews end of cloth to leader, using portable sewing machine, or threads end through machine rollers. Observes cloth to detect burning as cloth passes over heated plates, rollers, or gas flame, and through wetting-down equipment. Sets thermostat to maintain specified temperature of singeing element and prevent burning of cloth. Turns valve to control water flow to wetting-down equipment. May doff machine, using handtruck.
GOE: 06.04.16 STRENGTH: H GED: R2 M1 L2 SVP: 3 DLU: 77

585.685-110 SKIVER, BLOCKERS (boot & shoe) alternate titles: scarfer

Tends machine that cuts strips of leather to remove defects and bevel ends for use as trimmings: Examines stripping for defects, such as wrinkles, scars, and discolorations. Positions stripping against guide on machine bed. Pushes bed forward to force stripping against circular blade that cuts and bevels stripping.
GOE: 06.04.05 STRENGTH: L GED: R2 M1 L2 SVP: 2 DLU: 77

585.685-114 SPLITTER, MACHINE (boot & shoe; leather prod.) alternate titles: shaver; splitter; stripper

Tends machine that splits leather or shoe parts to reduce parts to uniform thickness or to cut parts into two or more layers, by any of following methods: (1) Feeds part between rollers that force part against blade. (2) Positions part against machine guides and depresses pedal to force splitting blade against part. (3) Holds part against guide and horizontal band-blade. Turns setscrews or handwheels to adjust blade or rollers as specified. Verifies thickness of parts with specifications, using gauge. May sharpen machine blades. May be designated according to parts split as Ball-Point Splitter (boot & shoe); Heel-Cover Splitter (boot & shoe); Heel splitter (boot & shoe); Heel-Top-Lift Splitter (boot & shoe); Insole-And-Outsole Splitter (boot & shoe); Sole Splitter (boot & shoe). May be designated according to machine tended as Band Splitter (boot & shoe).
GOE: 06.04.05 STRENGTH: L GED: R2 M1 L1 SVP: 2 DLU: 77

585.685-118 STRIPPING CUTTER AND WINDER (boot & shoe)

Tends machines that rewind and cut rolls of material, such as cotton, nylon, and plastic into narrow rolls (stripping) for use in shoe ornamentation: Mounts roll of material on spindle and tightens clamps. Slides empty core on winding axle and threads one end of material between pressure rollers and onto winding axle. Sets guide bar and starts machine that winds material onto core. Stops machine when counter indicates yardage specified on work ticket. Applies gummed tape to prevent unwinding. Positions roll on spindle of cutting machine and sets guide according to specifications. Pulls lever that starts machine and forces blade against roll to cut material into stripping.
GOE: 06.04.05 STRENGTH: M GED: R2 M1 L2 SVP: 3 DLU: 77

585.685-122 SWEATBAND SEPARATOR (hat & cap) alternate titles: size cutter; wired-sweatband cutter

Tends machine that separates, or cuts to size, hat sweatbands temporarily joined together to facilitate production: When separating sweatbands, joined by wire and thread, positions joint under blade on machine table. Depresses pedal to lower blade onto wire and thread, separating sweatbands. When cutting sweatbands to size, turns setscrews to adjust spacing of blades according to specifications. Positions sweatband on bed of machine against guides and under blades. Depresses pedal to lower blade, cutting sweatbands. May place sweatbands in containers or tie string around parts.
GOE: 06.04.05 STRENGTH: L GED: R2 M1 L1 SVP: 2 DLU: 77

585.685-126 TRIMMER, MACHINE (leather mfg.) alternate titles: shearer

Tends cutting machine that trims hides for further processing: Places hide on bed of machine. Starts machine and guides hide under blade, or blade through hide. Stacks trimmed hides on pallets.
GOE: 06.04.16 STRENGTH: H GED: R2 M1 L2 SVP: 2 DLU: 77

585.686-010 FEATHER-CUTTING-MACHINE FEEDER (tex. prod., nec)

Feeds feathers, used to stuff pillows, cushions, and mattresses into hopper of machine that cuts feathers into small pieces and discharges feathers into air duct leading to down separator.

GOE: 06.04.09 STRENGTH: M GED: R1 M1 L1 SVP: 1 DLU: 77

585.687-010 BEAMING INSPECTOR (leather mfg.) alternate titles: beam-house inspector; lime hide inspector; scudding inspector; unhairing inspector

Examines hides and skins for flesh and hair after defleshing and dehairing operations. Places rejected hides on pile for reprocessing and defleshed and dehaired hides on cart.
GOE: 06.03.02 STRENGTH: L GED: R2 M1 L2 SVP: 3 DLU: 77

585.687-014 CARPET CUTTER II (carpet & rug)

Cuts specified lengths from continuous roll of carpet, using power cut-off knife or long-handled cutting blade. May cut felt padding to specified lengths and be designated Felt-Pad Cutter (tex. prod., nec).
GOE: 06.04.27 STRENGTH: L GED: R2 M1 L1 SVP: 3 DLU: 77

585.687-018 CLOTH-EDGE SINGER (textile)

Burns loose threads from edges of cloth rolls, using gas torch, and brushes off charred ends.
GOE: 06.04.27 STRENGTH: L GED: R2 M1 L1 SVP: 2 DLU: 77

585.687-022 PATCHER (leather mfg.) alternate titles: cementer; leather patcher; leather repairer

Inspects hides for defects, such as cuts, holes, and scars, and cements leather patch over defect: Examines defects and selects piece of leather that matches defective area in color and texture. Trims patch to size of defective area. Brushes cement on patch and hammers patch over defect, using mallet. Trims edges of patch, using knife and sandpaper. Folds and places hide on truck.
GOE: 06.04.27 STRENGTH: L GED: R2 M1 L2 SVP: 2 DLU: 77

585.687-026 SHADE-CLOTH FINISHER (furniture)

Fastens cloth onto stretching frame and brushes out nap after sizing solution is applied: Places sized cloth on glued surface of frame. Blends size on cloth with brush. Brushes cloth with straight strokes to smooth and lay nap in one direction. Stretches frame and cuts cloth out when dry. Rolls cloth onto rolling rod.
GOE: 06.04.33 STRENGTH: L GED: R2 M1 L2 SVP: 2 DLU: 77

585.687-030 SINGER (narrow fabrics)

Singes edges of rolls of glass tape to remove broken filaments, using lighted torch. Wraps specified number of singed rolls in paper and packs rolls in shipping cartons or stacks rolls in storage.
GOE: 06.04.27 STRENGTH: L GED: R1 M1 L1 SVP: 2 DLU: 77

586 FELTING AND FULLING OCCUPATIONS

This group includes occupations concerned with matting, toughening, and compressing materials into felt fabric by such means as mechanical oscillation, vibration, and compression, and the use of such agents as moisture, chemicals, soap, and heat; and thickening the fabric, decreasing its surface area, and imparting a fibrous cover by the application of soap, alkali, or acid combined with pressure and friction.

586.130-010 SUPERVISOR V (tex. prod., nec)

Supervises and coordinates activities of workers engaged in shrinking and hardening felt: Estimates processing requirements such as amounts of chemicals and length of processing cycles based on knowledge of working characteristics of materials and machine capability. Sets up felt-processing machines, assigns duties to workers, and assists workers in solving work-related problems. Performs other duties as described under SUPERVISOR (any industry) Master Title. May be designated according to process supervised as Supervisor, Felting (tex. prod., nec); Supervisor, Fulling (tex. prod., nec).
GOE: 06.04.01 STRENGTH: M GED: R3 M2 L2 SVP: 6 DLU: 86

586.382-010 FULLING-MACHINE OPERATOR (tex. prod., nec)

Operates fulling machine to shrink and compress felt: Places roll of felt padding in trough of machine containing lubricating agents, such as soap solution. Threads end of felt beneath cam-actuated wooden blocks and onto takeoff reel. Starts machine and pushes felt evenly beneath blocks that pound and flatten felt. Measures rolls for specified thickness with gauge. Turns and inverts pads to ensure uniformity of size and shrinkage.
GOE: 06.02.16 STRENGTH: M GED: R3 M2 L2 SVP: 4 DLU: 77

586.662-010 FELTING-MACHINE OPERATOR (tex. prod., nec) alternate titles: hardening-machine operator; lay-up presser

Operates felting machine to attach reinforcing burlap to felt strips or to compress several layers of felt by means of heat and pressure: Suspends roll of burlap and two *bats* of felt over conveyor belt. Starts conveyor and unrolls felt strips, with burlap strip between felt strips, onto conveyor. Opens steam valves or water sprays to moisten felt passing through steam chamber or beneath sprays. Stops conveyor when bed of hydraulic press is covered by felt strip. Opens steam valves to heat press bed. Starts oscillating hydraulic ram that compresses felt. Laps end of felt bat to ends of other bats to form continuous strip. Plucks foreign matter from felt surfaces with tweezers and spreads loose felt over thin spots to produce uniform products. Straightens layers of stock on press bed to remove wrinkled stock.
GOE: 06.02.05 STRENGTH: M GED: R3 M2 L3 SVP: 4 DLU: 77

586.682-010 FULLER (textile) alternate titles: fulling-mill operator; wet finisher, wool

Operates *fulling mill* to shrink and interlock fibers of woolen cloth by application of moisture, heat, and pressure: Threads cloth through tension guides or

rollers which control shrinkage in width between pressure rollers, and through trap (crimp box) which controls shrinkage in length. Sews ends of cloth together to form endless rope, using portable sewing machine. Turns handwheel to regulate pressure on tension guides and sets air pressure gauge on rollers and trap, following specifications for style of cloth. Turns valves to admit water and soap solution to tub through which cloth passes. Measures distance between markings on cloth to determine when specified shrinkage has been attained. Ravels seam connecting ends of cloth and guides cloth over reel into handtruck.
GOE: 06.02.16 STRENGTH: M GED: R3 M2 L3 SVP: 4 DLU: 77

586.685-010 CARROTING-MACHINE OPERATOR (hat & cap)
Tends machine that applies *carroting* solution to fur pelts to condition fur fibers for manufacturing felt hats: Pours carroting solution of hydrogen peroxides, water, mercury and nitric acid into machine storage tank. Starts machine and turns valve to regulate flow of solution onto applicator brush. Lifts and feeds pelt under rotating brush or between rollers of machine that carrots fur fibers. May mix carroting solution.
GOE: 06.04.16 STRENGTH: L GED: R2 M1 L1 SVP: 2 DLU: 77

586.685-014 CONTINUOUS-CRUSHER OPERATOR (textile)
Tends crushing machine or *fulling mill* that crushes and dusts carbonized vegetable matter from woolen cloth: Starts crushing machine and observes as cloth flows back and forth, to detect tear-outs. Stops machine, disentangles tear-out, and threads cloth through crushing rollers to *swing-folding attachment.* Doffs trucks of cloth from delivery end of machine. Removes waste from dust bins. Threads cloth through pressure rollers of fulling mill and sews cloth ends together to form endless rope, using sewing machine. Starts machine that processes cloth through pressure rollers for specified period of time. Ravels seam at end of cycle, laps end of cloth over reel, and starts reel to transfer cloth from machine to handtruck.
GOE: 06.04.16 STRENGTH: M GED: R2 M1 L1 SVP: 2 DLU: 77

586.685-018 FELT-STRIP FINISHER (tex. prod., nec) alternate titles: microgrinder operator
Tends machine that sands and smooths surface of felt strips to reduce thickness and impart finish: Mounts roll of felt on machine brackets and draws end over and under machine bed and rollers onto takeup spindle. Turns handwheel to adjust clearance between sanding rollers according to specifications. Starts machine and observes felt for discolorations and loose fibers. Verifies thickness of felt, using gauge. Removes finished roll from machine.
GOE: 06.04.16 STRENGTH: H GED: R2 M1 L2 SVP: 3 DLU: 77

586.685-022 FELTMAKER AND WEIGHER (tex. prod., nec)
Prepares samples of felt for use in color matching and control: Mixes and weighs ingredients, and blends components in milling machine. Compresses blended material into felt samples [GARNETTER (furniture; tex. prod., nec)].
GOE: 06.04.16 STRENGTH: L GED: R2 M2 L2 SVP: 3 DLU: 77

586.685-026 HARDENING-MACHINE OPERATOR (hat & cap) alternate titles: hardener;
Tends machine that agitates fur felt hat cones to mat together interlocking fibers and harden cones preparatory to forming into hats: Wraps wet cones in burlap and wrings or places cones in extractor and starts machine to remove excess water. Wraps cones in woolen cloth and places cloth containing cones on rollers of hardening machine. Pulls handle to lower upper rollers onto cones and simultaneously start timed rollers that agitate cones and tighten fibers in tip of cones. Removes cloth containing cones and repeats operation to tighten fibers in brim area of cones. May inspect cones and work fibers into holes and thin spots, using fingers, to repair damaged cones.
GOE: 06.04.16 STRENGTH: L GED: R2 M1 L2 SVP: 3 DLU: 77

586.685-030 HAT-FORMING-MACHINE OPERATOR (hat & cap) alternate titles: cone former; coner; forming-machine operator
Tends hat-forming machine that mats together fur fibers into hat cones: Positions perforated metal cone on revolving turntable of machine that draws fur fiber onto metal cone. Closes doors of machine to preserve vacuum around metal cone. Depresses pedal to start conveyor belt that deposits preweighed amount of fur fiber in dome of machine. Observes fur flow onto cone and opens doors at completion of fur dumping cycle. Wraps damp cloth around felt cone and places metal cover over cloth. Carries cone from machine turntable to platform of sinker. Depresses pedal that lowers cone into heated water to strengthen fiber cohesion. Releases pedal to raise cone from sinker and removes cone. Removes cover, cloth, and felt cone from perforated cone. May tend machine that converts sheets of woolen fiber to form hat cones and be designated Wool-Hat-Forming-Machine Tender (hat & cap).
GOE: 06.04.16 STRENGTH: M GED: R3 M2 L2 SVP: 3 DLU: 78

586.685-034 SHRINKING-MACHINE OPERATOR (hat & cap) alternate titles: bumper-machine operator; sizer; starter; stumper
Tends machine that kneads fur (felt hat) cones to interlock fibers and shrink cones by either of following methods: (1) Positions cones on belt that moves cones beneath water sprinkler pipes, between rollers, and onto second belt that returns cones to worker. Measures cones, using ruler. Repeats process until cone has shrunk to size specified. (2) Places cones in machine cylinder and turns handle to fill cylinder with hot water, or pours acid-water solution into tank. Starts agitators that knead and tumble cones to interlock fibers and shrink cone. Measures cones, using ruler. Repeats process until cone has shrunk to specified size. May stretch cones to specified sizes, using wire frame.

GOE: 06.04.16 STRENGTH: L GED: R2 M1 L2 SVP: 3 DLU: 78

586.685-038 TESTING-MACHINE OPERATOR (tex. prod., nec) alternate titles: felt finisher
Tends machine that tests hard felt sheets for uniformity of thickness: Turns setscrews to set recorder dials and feed rollers for specific thickness of felt. Starts machine and guides felt between feed rollers. Observes recording dials to ascertain that felt thickness registers within allowable limits and rejects sheets not meeting specifications. Labels piles of accepted and rejected sheets. May reduce thickness of sheets, using drum-type sanding machine.
GOE: 06.03.02 STRENGTH: L GED: R3 M2 L3 SVP: 4 DLU: 77

586.686-010 CARROTING-MACHINE OFFBEARER (hat & cap)
Off bears pelts from *carroting* machine onto handtrucks for further processing in manufacture of felt hats.
GOE: 06.04.16 STRENGTH: L GED: R1 M1 L1 SVP: 1 DLU: 77

586.686-014 FELTING-MACHINE-OPERATOR HELPER (tex. prod., nec) alternate titles: hardening-machine-operator helper
Assists FELTING-MACHINE OPERATOR (tex. prod., nec) to attach reinforcing burlap to felt strips or to compress layers of felt: Lifts *bats* of felt into place at end of conveyor. Smooths wrinkles from felt, and plucks foreign matter from felt, using tweezers. Laps ends of felt bats with ends of successive bats to form continuous strips of padding. Performs other duties as described under HELPER (any industry) Master Title.
GOE: 06.04.05 STRENGTH: M GED: R1 M1 L1 SVP: 2 DLU: 77

586.686-018 HAT-FORMING-MACHINE FEEDER (hat & cap) alternate titles: cone-machine feeder; feeder; fur feeder; fur weigher
Weighs out fur fibers for use in making hats, and spreads fibers on conveyor leading to hat-forming machine: Weighs out specified quantity of fur required to form each hat, using scale. Spreads fibers on belt conveyor leading to feed gate of hat-forming machine, and moves lever to raise gate and dump fibers into machine. Stops conveyor after fur is dumped into machine.
GOE: 06.04.05 STRENGTH: L GED: R2 M1 L2 SVP: 2 DLU: 77

586.686-022 MACHINE HELPER (tex. prod., nec) alternate titles: general worker
Performs any combination of following tasks in machine manufacturing of felt goods: Cuts felt from feed rolls and removes rolls of processed material from machine. Marks length of finished felt on tag attached to roll. Lifts and positions rolls of base material and *bats* into feed holders of machine. Hand sews or glues together roll ends to form continuous feed through machine. Transfers materials by handtruck or dolly from discharge end of one machine to feed end of next. Picks up scraps of material around machine and throws scraps into bins or hoppers. Fills pans on machines with sizing inks. Measures and dumps spray solution ingredients in mixing vats according to specifications. Removes foreign particles from scoured and blended stock. Lifts felt rolls from conveyors, and stacks and bundles finished felt rolls to prepare rolls for shipment or stock. May assist operators to set up machine. May be designated by specific activity performed as Bat Carrier (tex. prod., nec); or according to machine operated as Box Feeder (tex. prod., nec); Cloth-Printer Helper (tex. prod., nec); Garnett-Machine-Operator Helper (tex. prod., nec); Needle-Loom-Operator Helper (tex. prod., nec); Sizing-Machine-And-Drier-Operator Helper (tex. prod., nec). May be designated: Coater Helper (tex. prod., nec); Die-Cutting-Machine-Operator Helper, Automatic (tex. prod., nec); Picking-Machine-Operator Helper (tex. prod., nec).
GOE: 06.04.05 STRENGTH: M GED: R2 M1 L1 SVP: 2 DLU: 79

586.687-010 FELT CARBONIZER (tex. prod., nec)
Removes vegetable matter from felt by immersion in sulfuric acid solution: Mixes specified amount of sulfuric acid and warm water in carbonizing vat, and immerses felt in vat, using chain hoist. Soaks felt for period of time dependent on thickness of material. Periodically tests solution strength, using hydrometer. Adds acid as required. Removes and suspends felt over vat to drain.
GOE: 06.04.16 STRENGTH: M GED: R2 M1 L2 SVP: 3 DLU: 77

587 BRUSHING AND SHRINKING OCCUPATIONS

This group includes occupations concerned with going over materials with a brush to remove such undesirables as lint and loose thread, to improve appearance, or to align nap; and reducing the size of materials by such methods as saturating, spraying, and steaming.

587.384-010 CLOTH-SHRINKING TESTER (textile) alternate titles: wash-test checker
Tests cloth sample to determine potential shrinkage of sample in order to establish shrinking machine settings, and to verify effectiveness of shrinking process: Marks cloth sample at measured intervals, using template. Loads samples into washing drum and adds detergents. Starts machine that automatically washes and rinses samples and extracts excess water. Removes samples from machine at end of washing cycle and presses samples, using flatbed ironer. Measures distance between markings on cloth, using yardstick, and computes average shrinkage of length and width. Converts amount of shrinkage into machine settings, using conversion tables. Records measurements, cloth lot and style number, and machine settings on work ticket for use by CLOTH-SHRINKING-MACHINE OPERATOR (textile). Cuts samples from cloth after shrinking and tests cloth to verify that material meets shrinkage specifications.

GOE: 06.03.01 STRENGTH: L GED: R3 M2 L3 SVP: 3 DLU: 77

587.585-010 AUTOCLAVE OPERATOR (knitting)

Tends autoclave that steamsets hosiery or knitted garments into permanent shape: Stacks articles on machine trays, smooths wrinkles by hand, and pushes trays into autoclave. Turns thumbscrews to seal machine door and presses buttons to start automatic steaming cycle. Removes steamed articles from autoclave at end of steaming cycle and inserts them into bags for further processing. Trucks bagged articles to storage area. Records number of articles steamed and bagged.

GOE: 06.04.05 STRENGTH: M GED: R2 M1 L2 SVP: 2 DLU: 77

587.682-010 AUTOCLAVE OPERATOR (textile)

Controls autoclave to preshrink and preset yarn: Pushes racks of yarn inside autoclave and clamps door shut. Regulates time and temperature controls according to written instructions. Presses buttons to start pump that creates vacuum in autoclave chamber and turns valves to admit steam. Observes gauges and pneumatic controller graphs to ascertain that specified pressure, temperature, and vacuum are maintained to ensure conditioning of yarn according to specifications and to prevent collapse of autoclave. Closes valves and starts vacuum pump to remove moisture at end of steaming chamber. Opens door and removes processed yarn from autoclave to storage, using handtruck. Weighs yarn and records amount of yarn processed. May tend machine that automatically draws yarn into autoclave, seals doors, and discharges yarn at end of steaming cycle.

GOE: 06.04.16 STRENGTH: H GED: R3 M2 L2 SVP: 4 DLU: 79

587.685-010 BRUSH OPERATOR (textile) alternate titles: steam-brush operator

Tends machine that brushes foreign matter, such as lint, strings, and loose fibers from cloth: Pins or sews end of cloth to leader. Turns screws to adjust cloth tension and pressure of brushes. Starts machine and observes operation to detect imcomplete cleaning. Cleans and oils machine. May tend brushing machine with steaming attachment that sets cloth nap.

GOE: 06.04.05 STRENGTH: L GED: R2 M1 L1 SVP: 2 DLU: 77

587.685-014 BRUSHER, MACHINE (hat & cap)

Tends machine that brushes fur pelts to straighten and fluff hairs preparatory to shearing fur for manufacturing felt hats: Starts machine and depresses pedal to move powered brush away from stationary rest on which pelts are placed for brushing. Positions pelt on rest and releases pedal to force moving brush against pelt, straightening and fluffing hairs. Piles furs for shearing by other workers.

GOE: 06.04.16 STRENGTH: M GED: R2 M1 L1 SVP: 2 DLU: 77

587.685-018 CLOTH-SHRINKING-MACHINE OPERATOR (textile) alternate titles: cloth shrinker; cloth sponger; cold-water machine operator; padding-machine operator; presetter operator; shrinker; sponger; water sponger; woolen-suiting shrinker

Tends machine that shrinks woven or knitted cloth to predetermined size: Mounts roll of cloth on machine, using chain hoist. Threads end of cloth through tension bars, guide and feed rollers, and through shrinking elements. Observes flow of cloth through machine onto *takeup roll,* or guides cloth onto shrinking elements to prevent wrinkles and uneven winding, or sets speed of elements according to shrinkage-control guide for various cloth styles. Turns valves or moves switch control to regulate flow of water or steam. May measure cloth width, using yardstick. May tend equipment that preshrinks woolen suiting fabric and be designated Soaker (textile). May sew, using portable sewing machine, or pin cut of cloth to cloth in machine. May doff rolls of shrunken cloth. May tend machine not equipped with water vat and be designated Steam-Pan Sponger (textile). Important variables may be indicated by processes or trade names of machines used.

GOE: 06.04.16 STRENGTH: M GED: R2 M1 L2 SVP: 3 DLU: 77

587.685-022 CONDITIONER TENDER (textile) alternate titles: conditioning-room worker; steam conditioner, filling; steamer; yarn conditioner

Tends steaming cabinet that conditions (sets twist or preshrinks) yarn with steam: Loads trays or racks of yarn on handtruck and pushes yarn into machine. Turns knobs to set time, temperature, and humidity controls, according to specifications. Turns valve to admit steam into cabinet. Removes yarn from conditioner at end of steaming cycle. May separate yarn according to size and grade. May inspect yarn for twist set and shrinkage. May record information, such as processing temperature, weight, or type of yarn on work ticket. May tend machine equipped with conveyor that moves yarn through machine.

GOE: 06.04.16 STRENGTH: M GED: R2 M1 L1 SVP: 3 DLU: 77

587.685-026 DUSTER (hat & cap)

Tends equipment that removes dust, fur particles, and lint from felt hats after pouncing operations, using any of following methods: Selects hat block, according to specifications. Turns screw to secure block on spindle, and slips hat over block. (1) Depresses pedal to start compressor that creates vacuum in slots of hat block and moves hat over slots to remove undesirable matter. (2) Depresses pedal to start hat and block rotating. Presses trigger on pneumatic gun to direct air over hat surface or holds brush against hat surface to dust hat. (3) Depresses pedal to move hat mounted on rotating block against rotating brush. Stops compressor or rotating block, turns hat inside out, and repeats dusting operation on

inside of hat. May be designated according to method used as Hat Brusher, Machine (hat & cap).

GOE: 06.04.05 STRENGTH: L GED: R2 M1 L1 SVP: 2 DLU: 78

587.685-030 STRIKE-OUT-MACHINE OPERATOR (textile) alternate titles: tiger-machine operator

Tends machine that flattens pile of fabrics preparatory to dyeing or printing or to raise, soften, and fluff pile after wet-finishing processes: Positions truck of material at entry end of machine and sews end of cloth to leader in machine, using portable sewing machine. Presses button to set carding or brushing rollers according to finish specified. Starts machine and observes flow of cloth through machine to detect wrinkles, holes, and cloth seams. Smooths wrinkles by hand. Moves lever to lower cloth from rollers as holes and seams pass through machine. Doffs cloth from *swing-folding attachment.* May tend machine arranged in tandem with other finishing equipment.

GOE: 06.04.16 STRENGTH: L GED: R2 M1 L2 SVP: 2 DLU: 77

587.686-010 CLOTH-SHRINKING-MACHINE-OPERATOR HELPER (textile)

Assists CLOTH-SHRINKING-MACHINE OPERATOR (textile) in shrinking cloth: Pushes handtruck of rolled or folded cloth to machine and mounts roll on bracket of machine, using hoist. Threads ends of cloth through guides, rollers, and shrinking elements. Smooths folds of cloth being discharged into handtruck or removes rolls, using hoist. Performs other duties as described under HELPER (any industry) Master Title. May sew ends of new cuts to cloth already in machine. Important variables may be indicated by processes or trade names of machines used.

GOE: 06.04.16 STRENGTH: L GED: R1 M1 L1 SVP: 2 DLU: 77

587.687-010 CANVAS SHRINKER (textile)

Soaks canvas in water to shrink and prepare canvas for use in garment manufacturing: Unrolls bolt of canvas and folds canvas in shrinking tank. Turns valve to admit water into tank, soaking canvas for specified periods of time. Lifts canvas from tank after shrinking and hangs canvas in loops from bars for drying or delivers canvas to other workers.

GOE: 06.04.27 STRENGTH: H GED: R1 M1 L1 SVP: 2 DLU: 77

589 OCCUPATIONS IN PROCESSING OF LEATHER, TEXTILES, AND RELATED PRODUCTS, N.E.C.

This group includes occupations, not elsewhere classified, concerned with processing leather, textiles, and related products.

589.130-010 CLOTH FINISHER (carpet & rug; textile) alternate titles: finishing supervisor

Supervises and coordinates activities of workers engaged in finishing cloth, carpets, rugs, and other fabrics: Schedules finishing of cloth or carpeting according to color, width, and type of finish, to maintain efficient operation. Selects standard formulas that meet customer specifications or uses knowledge of finish ingredients and application methods to develop new formulas. Writes mixing instructions for use by CHEMICAL MIXER (textile). Writes work orders for supervisors indicating specified finish, style, and yardage of cloth or carpeting to be processed. Examines cloth or carpeting to verify that finish meets specifications. Inventories and orders chemicals and supplies from purchasing department. Trains workers in setup, repair, and operation of *ranges,* machines, and equipment. Performs other duties as described under SUPERVISOR (any industry) Master Title. May be designated according to department supervised or process involved as Carpet-Finishing Supervisor (carpet & rug); Cloth-Bleaching Supervisor (textile); Cloth-Brushing-And-Sueding Supervisor (textile); Cloth-Laminating Supervisor (textile); Cloth-Mercerizing Supervisor (textile); Cloth-Napping Supervisor (textile); Cloth-Shearing Supervisor (textile); Cloth-Shrinking Supervisor (textile).

GOE: 05.09.02 STRENGTH: L GED: R4 M3 L4 SVP: 7 DLU: 77

589.130-014 FABRIC-COATING SUPERVISOR (tex. prod., nec) alternate titles: felt-coating-and-mixing supervisor

Supervises and coordinates activities of workers engaged in finishing coated fabrics, artificial leather, and felt: Sets up machines to make experimental samples, observes operation of machines to detect malfunction, and adjusts machines, using handtools. Trains workers in operation of machines and equipment. Inspects work of operators to verify coating weights, printing samples, and embossing imprints. Directs delivery of goods to cutting or shipping department. Performs other duties as described under SUPERVISOR (any industry) Master Title. May be designated according to process involved as Calender Supervisor (tex. prod., nec); Coating Supervisor (tex. prod., nec); Felt-Finishing Supervisor (tex. prod., nec); Mixing Supervisor (tex. prod., nec); Printing Supervisor (tex. prod., nec); Trimming Supervisor (tex. prod., nec).

GOE: 06.01.01 STRENGTH: L GED: R4 M3 L3 SVP: 8 DLU: 79

589.130-018 SUPERVISOR, FINISHING ROOM (leather mfg.)

Supervises and coordinates activities of workers engaged in buffing, brushing, coloring, embossing, and spraying leather. Moves controls to adjust embossing, finishing, and rolling machines. Performs other duties as described under SUPERVISOR (any industry) Master Title.

GOE: 06.02.01 STRENGTH: L GED: R4 M3 L3 SVP: 7 DLU: 77

589.130-022 SUPERVISOR, FUR DRESSING (leather mfg.)

Supervises and coordinates activities of FUR-FLOOR WORKER (leather mfg.) and FUR DRESSER (leather mfg.) engaged in fleshing, plucking, shear-

ing, and shaving fur pelts to prepare pelts for manufacturing: Examines pelts during dressing process to determine cleanliness and suppleness of skins and softness and sheen of hair of furs. Trains workers in setting up and operating machines and equipment. Performs other duties as described under SUPERVISOR (any industry) Master Title. May be designated according to operation supervised as Supervisor, Fleshing (leather mfg.); Supervisor, Fur-Floor Worker (leather mfg.); Supervisor, Shearing (leather mfg.).
GOE: 06.01.01 STRENGTH: L GED: R4 M3 L3 SVP: 7 DLU: 77

589.130-026 SUPERVISOR, MILL (tex. prod., nec)
Supervises and coordinates activities of workers engaged in cleaning, drying, and grading hemp fiber: Trains workers in machine setup and operating. Examines hemp fiber for defects. Performs other duties as described under SUPERVISOR (any industry) Master Title.
GOE: 06.04.01 STRENGTH: L GED: R4 M2 L3 SVP: 7 DLU: 77

589.130-030 SUPERVISOR, SPLIT LEATHER DEPARTMENT (leather mfg.)
Supervises and coordinates activities of workers engaged in sorting, splitting, shaving, pasting, and drying leather. Sets up and adjusts machines. Requisitions supplies. Performs other duties as described under SUPERVISOR (any industry) Master Title. May be designated according to activities supervised as Supervisor, Buffing-And-Pasting (leather mfg.); Supervisor, Drying-And-Softening (leather mfg.); Supervisor, Hanging-And-Trimming (leather mfg.); Supervisor, Shaving-And-Splitting (leather mfg.).
GOE: 06.02.01 STRENGTH: L GED: R3 M2 L3 SVP: 6 DLU: 77

589.132-010 SUPERVISOR VI (tex. prod., nec)
Supervises and coordinates activities of workers engaged in sorting, cleaning, cutting, garnetting, and packaging waste textile fibers, threads, and rags for use as batting, padding, and wiping rags: Spaces knives on delivery end of *garnett machine* according to width specified for batting. Weighs samples and adjust weight mechanisms on machines to meet processing specifications. Trains employees in operating and cleaning of machines. Requisitions materials and machine parts. Performs other duties as described under SUPERVISOR (any industry) Master Title.
GOE: 06.02.01 STRENGTH: M GED: R4 M3 L3 SVP: 7 DLU: 77

589.132-014 SUPERVISOR, SPLIT AND DRUM ROOM (leather mfg.)
Supervises and coordinates activities of workers engaged in coloring, drying, and setting (smoothing grain) hides. Trains workers in operation of machines. Requisitions materials. Performs other duties as described under SUPERVISOR (any industry) Master Title.
GOE: 06.02.01 STRENGTH: L GED: R4 M3 L3 SVP: 7 DLU: 77

589.134-010 SUPERVISOR, BEAM DEPARTMENT (leather mfg.)
Supervises and coordinates activities of workers engaged in trimming flesh, liming hair, and washing tanned hides. Performs other duties as described under SUPERVISOR (any industry) Master Title.
GOE: 06.04.01 STRENGTH: L GED: R4 M3 L3 SVP: 7 DLU: 77

589.135-010 SUPERVISOR, PRODUCTION (tex. prod., nec)
Supervises and coordinates activities of workers engaged in washing, drying, separating, and crushing feathers used in stuffing housefurnishing goods, such as pillows and cushions: Reviews production schedule and assigns work duties. Demonstrates operation of machines and equipment. Performs other duties as described under SUPERVISOR (any industry) Master Title.
GOE: 06.04.01 STRENGTH: L GED: R4 M3 L3 SVP: 7 DLU: 77

589.137-010 SUPERVISOR, PACKING ROOM (leather mfg.)
Supervises and coordinates activities of workers engaged in inspecting, measuring, and wrapping finished leather. Requisitions materials. Performs other duties as described under SUPERVISOR (any industry) Master Title.
GOE: 06.02.01 STRENGTH: L GED: R4 M2 L3 SVP: 7 DLU: 77

589.360-010 BONDING-MACHINE SETTER (textile)
Sets up and adjusts machines that bond, stretch, and apply finishing solution to thread to improve sewing quality: Changes charts in control boxes for recording temperature and viscosity strength and turns knob to set temperature control at specified level on oven unit. Turns handles on roller units to adjust speeds of front and back rollers and verifies revolutions (settings), using tachometer. Turns crank to adjust builder motion on takeup rack to facilitate uniform winding of thread on reels. Operates machine for test run to verify adjustments and to obtain thread samples. Conducts standard tests on samples to determine breaking strength, elongation, and weight of thread, using tensile-testing machine, skein winder, and grain scales. Posts results onto quality control reports. Maintains record of samples and customer orders processed. Changes felt covers on rollers and wipers and replaces worn or broken guides and tapes, using handtools. Lubricates machines, using oilcan.
GOE: 06.01.02 STRENGTH: M GED: R3 M2 L3 SVP: 5 DLU: 77

589.361-010 FUR DRESSER (leather mfg.) alternate titles: tanner
Tans and dresses pelts to improve luster and beauty or restore natural appearance of pelts: Prepares tanning and washing solutions according to formulas and places pelts in vats or revolving drums containing solution to clean, soften, and preserve pelts. Removes long coarse hair from pelts and evens length of underlying fur, using beaming knife and shaving knife [FUR PLUCKER (leather mfg.)]. Removes particles of flesh and fat from pelts and skins, using hand and powered knives determined by thickness and weight of pelt. Examines

skins to detect defects, such as spaces, improper scraping, and tears. Records defect and sorts furs according to grade. May oil and clip pelts.
GOE: 06.01.04 STRENGTH: M GED: R3 M2 L3 SVP: 7 DLU: 77

589.384-010 PRODUCT TESTER, FIBERGLASS (textile) alternate titles: roving technician
Tests fiberglass products, such as bonded cord, insulation mats, roving, and staple lengths to determine if products conform to specifications: Determines breaking strength of bonded cord by mounting sample on arms of testing machine and moving machine controls that apply force necessary to rupture sample. Weighs insulation mat, bonded cord, or roving on balance scales before and after drying and computes percentage of moisture, wax binder, and solids in sample, using slide rule. Observes machines in operation to detect worn equipment, irregular roving packages, or dull cutters. Examines products for defects, such as dirt, frayed ends, clumps in mats, discolorations, and variation in number of ends. Measures staple lengths to verify conformance to standards, using ruler. Tests speed of machine spindles, using tachometer. Records tests results on quality control records and notifies production supervisors, machine repairer, and workers when machine operation, material, or products vary from standards. May perform physical tests to determine yarn porosity, diameter, or denier.
GOE: 06.03.01 STRENGTH: L GED: R3 M2 L3 SVP: 5 DLU: 77

589.387-010 INSPECTOR AND SORTER (leather mfg.) alternate titles: assortor; bend sorter; grader; hefter; hide sorter; leather sorter; passer
Inspects and sorts processed material, such as hides, skins, or leather: Examines material for defects, such as brand marks, cuts, and scars, and trims defects from material, using shears. Verifies thickness of material, using gauge. Sorts material according to qualities, such as color, size, and thickness. Returns defective material for reprocessing. May be designated according to material sorted as Blue-Leather Sorter (leather mfg.); Patent-Leather Sorter (leather mfg.); Russet-Leather Sorter (leather mfg.).
GOE: 06.03.01 STRENGTH: L GED: R3 M2 L3 SVP: 4 DLU: 77

589.387-014 WOOL SORTER (textile)
Sorts and grades wool according to length of fiber, color, and degree of fineness, utilizing sight, touch, experience, and established specifications: Shakes or spreads fleece over screen-topped table to remove dust. Picks out foreign matter, such as burrs, sticks, strings, and cinders. Breaks fleece into pieces and inspects and sorts pieces according to quality.
GOE: 06.03.01 STRENGTH: L GED: R4 M2 L3 SVP: 6 DLU: 77

589.387-018 WOOL-AND-PELT GRADER (meat products) alternate titles: slat grader
Inspects sheep and lamb pelts to determine condition of pelts and grade of wool: Examines and feels wool to determine color, texture, and length, and sorts pelts or loose wool into grades for pulling or drying. Inspects pickled slats (sheep skins) for cuts, tears, blemishes, and skin quality, and stacks pelts in piles according to grade. May record quantity and grades of wool or pelts inspected.
GOE: 06.03.01 STRENGTH: M GED: R3 M2 L2 SVP: 4 DLU: 77

589.387-022 INSPECTOR, FINISHING (tex. prod., nec)
Inspects finished felt for processing flaws, such as random thickness, grease spots, and dye marks, and grades felt, following grading specifications: Places roll of felt onto holding fixture at end of glass-top inspection table, assisted by another worker. Threads front end of felt strip between hold-down bar and table. Activates fluorescent light inside table and sets table gauges to measure length, width, and thickness of felt. Feeds felt onto takeup roller that pulls felt across lighted table. Depresses button to activate takeup roller. Examines felt for lint, grease spots, discolorations, and dye marks. Reads thickness and width gauges to verify conformity to specifications. Depresses button to stop takeup roller when felt meets length specification. Cuts felt from roll and weighs felt piece to detect deviation from prescribed weight. Marks ticket and attaches ticket to portion of felt that needs to be reworked or discarded. Records thickness, width, length, and weight of felt on mill ticket. Grades felt according to grading specifications.
GOE: 06.03.02 STRENGTH: M GED: R3 M2 L2 SVP: 5 DLU: 86

589.464-010 COLOR MIXER (furniture)
Mixes size and paint for use in manufacture of window-shade cloth: Mixes, cooks, and stirs size with paddle in steam heated pot. Tests mixture with hydrometer and thermometer and adds hot or cold water to obtain specified specific gravity. Mixes specified amounts of paint paste, oil, and turpentine, using portable electric mixer. Directs SHADE-CLOTH FINISHER (furniture) in such processes as paint spraying and shade cloth sewing.
GOE: 06.04.34 STRENGTH: L GED: R2 M2 L2 SVP: 3 DLU: 77

589.485-010 PAD-EXTRACTOR TENDER (knitting) alternate titles: extractor; processor
Tends machine that untwists and extracts water or chemicals from knit tubing after bleaching, washing, and dyeing, and applies finish to tubing preparatory to drying: Positions containers of wet knit tubing on turntable of machine. Turns thumbscrews to adjust width of spreader, according to specifications. Threads tubing through tension rollers and around spreader, and ties end of tubing to *leader*. Turns handwheel to regulate pressure on squeeze rollers. Turns valve to admit finishing solution into trough of machine. Starts machine and

observes operation to detect twists in knit tubing. Revolves turntable from which tubing is fed to untwist tubing. Measures width of tubing with hand rule to verify conformance to standards. Doffs tubing from *swing-folding attachment.* May mix finishing solution, following formula.
GOE: 06.04.16 STRENGTH: L GED: R2 M1 L2 SVP: 3 DLU: 77

589.487-010 WEIGHT-YARDAGE CHECKER (textile)
Computes weight per yard of cloth and compares computations with information on style card to determine conformance of cloth to weight standards: Reads ticket attached to cloth rolls for information, such as style, weight, and yardage. Computes weight per yard, using slide rule. Compares results with information on style card to detect variations from standards. Routes cloth that varies from standards to CLOTH MEASURER, MACHINE (garment; textile) for verification of measurement. Reports variations to supervisor. Records weight, yardage, weight per yard, and style number on production sheet. Marks identifying information on cloth.
GOE: 06.03.01 STRENGTH: L GED: R3 M3 L3 SVP: 3 DLU: 77

589.562-010 CLOTH-FINISHING-RANGE OPERATOR, CHIEF (textile) alternate titles: finishing range supervisor; range operator
Controls *range* consisting of units, such as chemical or dye pads, washboxes, steamboxes, J-boxes, *tenter frames, curing ovens,* and *drying cans* to desize, bleach, dye, or finish cloth and other textile goods: Lines up cloth to be processed according to priority, style, and width. Gives directions to CLOTH FEEDER (textile); CLOTH-FINISHING-RANGE TENDER (textile); and BACK TENDER (textile) engaged in tending range units to ensure that desizing, bleaching, dyeing, or other finishing processes conform to specifications. Tests chemical solutions by titration or with hydrometer to detect variation in strength and notifies mixing department to add required quantity of chemicals or water according to test results and specifications. Observes control panel and equipment to detect faulty operation and adjusts controls to synchronize motor-driven rollers. Records test results, style numbers, and yardage of cloth processed. May inspect cloth. May be designated according to process controlled as Cloth-Bleaching-Range Operator, Chief (textile); Cloth-Desizing-Range Operator, Chief (textile); Cloth-Dyeing-Range Operator, Chief (textile).
GOE: 06.04.16 STRENGTH: M GED: R3 M2 L3 SVP: 5 DLU: 77

589.662-010 SCOURING-TRAIN OPERATOR (carpet & rug; textile) alternate titles: scouring-machine operator
Operates scouring train (series of tanks or bowls) to wash, rinse, and dry raw wool preparatory to dyeing or carding: Turns valves to start continuous flow of water, detergent, and acid into bowls. Reads thermometer and turns steam valves to heat wash and rinse solutions to specified operating temperature. Starts machine that feeds raw wool from hopper into washbowl and activates rakes that move wool through bowls to squeeze rolls and rinse bowl. Patrols scouring train to detect choke-up at squeeze rolls and removes jammed fibers by hand. Observes sudsing in washbowls and turns valve to increase or decrease concentration of detergent. Tests acidity of solution in finishing bowl by titration. Turns valve to control flow of acid to maintain specified concentration. Starts fans that circulate hot air in drier. Feels wool delivered from drier and adjusts thermostatic control if wool is not dry. Drains and cleans machine. May feed raw wool into scouring machine hopper. May direct activities of team workers and be designated Scouring-Train Operator, Chief (carpet & rug; textile).
GOE: 06.02.18 STRENGTH: M GED: R3 M2 L3 SVP: 4 DLU: 77

589.662-014 TIRE-FABRIC-IMPREGNATING-RANGE OPERATOR, CHIEF (tex. prod., nec)
Controls *range* to stretch and shrink sheets of tire fabric and reduce fabric elasticity: Turns valves and pushes buttons to start range, admit flow of steam, water, and finishing solutions to range units, and to regulate machine speeds and fabric tension. Records information, such as fabric yardage processed, temperature readings, fabric tensions, machine speeds, and delays caused by range malfunctions.
GOE: 06.02.16 STRENGTH: M GED: R3 M2 L2 SVP: 5 DLU: 77

589.665-010 BONDING-MACHINE TENDER (textile)
Tends machine that bonds, stretches, and applies finishing solution to synthetic thread to improve sewing quality: Places supply packages in creel. Draws ends from packages over, through, and around machine units, guides, and rollers, and attaches ends to takeup reels. Turns valves and taps to transfer bonding and finishing solutions to bath units. Observes operation to detect breaks or *lap-ups.* Cuts tangles with knife and rethreads ends through machine units. Observes temperature and viscosity control charts for variations from standards. Adds chemicals to strengthen or dilute solutions or resets temperature indicator (control). Verifies roller speeds, using tachometer, and turns handle on roller units to adjust speeds. Reports malfunctions to BONDING-MACHINE SETTER (textile). Removes full packages from takeup rack and pushes yarn to storage area.
GOE: 06.04.16 STRENGTH: M GED: R3 M2 L2 SVP: 4 DLU: 77

589.665-014 CLOTH-FINISHING-RANGE OPERATOR (textile) alternate titles: backfiller; finishing-range operator; starcher-and-tenter-range feeder; treater
Tends feed-end of *range* that applies size, starch, water-repellent, wrinkle resistant, or other chemical finishes to cloth, stretches cloth to specified width, and dries finished cloth: Positions truck of folded cloth at feed-end of machine or inserts rod through cloth roll and pushes roll onto brackets. Sews cloth end

to leader in machine, using portable sewing machine. Turns valve to permit flow of finish to trough under mangle. Turns handwheels and knobs to control temperature of *drying cans* and movement of cloth through range, and to adjust width and tension guides. Observes cloth entering machine to detect flaws, such as holes and torn selvages. Cuts out flaws, using scissors. When back-filling cloth with starch, positions doctor at specified angle to scrape excess starch from cloth. Cleans and greases machines. May be designated according to type of finish applied as Back Sizer (textile); Waterproofing-Machine Operator (textile).
GOE: 06.04.16 STRENGTH: M GED: R2 M2 L2 SVP: 2 DLU: 77

589.684-010 RAKER, BUFFING WHEEL (tex. prod., nec)
Tests fabric buffing wheels to determine resistance to pressure and straightens edges of fabric, using metal rod: Mounts stack of buffing wheels on shaft in cabinet and closes cabinet door. Presses button to rotate buffing wheels. Rakes edges of revolving buffing wheels with slanted edge of rod through opening in cabinet. Removes wheels having frayed edges.
GOE: 06.03.02 STRENGTH: L GED: R2 M1 L2 SVP: 3 DLU: 77

589.685-010 BOARDING-MACHINE OPERATOR (knitting) alternate titles: boarder; boarder, machine
Tends machine that shapes and dries hose before or after dyeing process, using either of following methods: (1) Pulls hose over leg-shaped forms of machine, aligns toe and heel with form, and pulls welt down to specified point on forms. Presses button or depresses pedal to start conveyor that carries filled set of forms into drying chamber and removes finished set from chamber. Strips shaped hose from boarding forms. (2) Depresses pedal to start circular conveyor that carries forms through drying chamber and automatic stripping mechanism. Pulls and aligns hose over forms as conveyor moves forms in front of worker. Periodically feels surface of forms for roughness to determine need for waxing. May replace *toe boards* of boarding forms, using key. May turn valves to increase or decrease steam pressure and temperature of drying chamber according to type of hose being boarded. May be designated according to process as Preboarder (knitting). May tend machine that shapes, dyes, and dries hosiery and be designated Dye-Boarding-Machine Operator (knitting).
GOE: 06.04.16 STRENGTH: L GED: R2 M1 L2 SVP: 3 DLU: 81

589.685-014 BREAKER-UP-MACHINE OPERATOR (hat & cap) alternate titles: breaker-up
Tends machine that agitates hats after blocking to render material soft and pliable: Places hats in chamber of machine and starts rotation of paddle arms that toss hats about until material becomes pliable. Stops machine after specified time and removes hats for further processing.
GOE: 06.04.16 STRENGTH: L GED: R1 M1 L1 SVP: 2 DLU: 77

589.685-018 BURN-OUT TENDER, LACE (tex. prod., nec)
Tends machine that burns out (dissolves) connecting threads in knitted lace to separate lace into individual bands: Loads beams of lace onto rack. Pushes rack into machine chamber and bolts door, using wrench. Turns valve to transfer acid solution from still to machine. Presses button to start rotation of lace in acid bath that dissolves connecting threads. Removes lace from machine for further processing. May tend still to reclaim solvents for reuse [STILL TENDER (any industry)].
GOE: 06.04.16 STRENGTH: M GED: R2 M1 L2 SVP: 3 DLU: 77

589.685-022 CLOTH MEASURER, MACHINE (garment; textile) alternate titles: measurer, machine; measuring percher-and-inspector
Tends machine that measures cloth preparatory to or after dyeing and finishing: Threads cloth from supply truck, bale, or roll through feeder rollers, and laps end around *takeup roll* of machine or guides cloth through *swing-folding attachment.* Turns knob to set yardage meter to zero. Starts machine and straightens cloth that becomes twisted entering machine. Stops machine and records yardage of cloth as indicated by meter. May compare meter reading with yardage on manufacturer's tag and record difference. May weigh cloth and record weight.
GOE: 06.03.02 STRENGTH: L GED: R2 M1 L2 SVP: 3 DLU: 77

589.685-026 CLOTH-FINISHING-RANGE TENDER (textile)
Tends intermediate units of cloth or other textile goods desizing, bleaching, dyeing, or finishing *ranges,* such as washboxes, *tenter frame, drying cans, and curing ovens:* Turns valves to admit steam, water, and chemicals to washboxes and chemical troughs. Patrols area between entry and terminal units to detect faulty operation of equipment. Turns knobs to adjust temperature in drying and curing units and to regulate speed of motor-driven rollers, according to specifications. Reports grease spots, holes, and tears in cloth to operator of range. Disentangles tear-outs, rethreads unit, and sews torn cloth, using portable sewing machine. May mix chemicals or dyes. May test strength of chemical solutions by titration or with hydrometer. May be designated according to process as Cloth-Bleaching-Range Tender (textile); Cloth-Desizing-Range Tender (textile); Cloth-Dyeing-Range Tender (textile); Tire-Fabric-Impregnating-Range Tender (tex. prod., nec).
GOE: 06.04.16 STRENGTH: H GED: R3 M1 L2 SVP: 3 DLU: 77

589.685-030 DETACKER (knitting; textile)
Tends machine that removes tacking stitches from selvages of fabric and opens fabric to full width after wet processing: Clips tacking stitches with knife and ravels out length of stitching by hand. Feeds end of fabric over beating

roller and through takeoff rollers and *swing-folding attachment*. Laps end of raveled stitching around reel and starts machine that ravels out stitching and opens cloth to full width. Guides cloth from swing-folding attachment into handtruck. May sew end of cloth to end of cloth in machine to form continuous strip, using sewing machine.
GOE: 06.04.05 STRENGTH: M GED: R1 M1 L1 SVP: 2 DLU: 77

589.685-034 DRUMMER (hat & cap) alternate titles: softener
Tends revolving drum that tumbles fur pelts in moist sawdust and fuller's earth to soften pelts and clean fur used in making felt hats: Opens bales of skins, using knife or wirecutter. Shovels sawdust and fuller's earth into drum, pours water onto sawdust and fuller's earth, and stirs with shovel until sawdust and fuller's earth are saturated. Dumps skins into drum and starts drum revolving for specified time or until skins appear sufficiently clean and soft for further processing. May shake sawdust and fuller's earth from pelts [SHAKER (hat & cap)].
GOE: 06.04.16 STRENGTH: M GED: R1 M1 L1 SVP: 2 DLU: 77

589.685-038 DRY CLEANER (knitting)
Tends cleaning machine and drier that clean and dry knitted garments: Examines garment for soil and determines type of soil. Lays garment on cleaning board with spotted surface exposed. Applies soap solvent to spot with brush and removes excess soap with towel. Opens valve to admit cleaning fluid to tank of washing machine. Lays spotted garment in machine and starts machine. Stops machine after specified time, and removes and places garment in drier. Removes garment from drier and hangs garment on hook in clothes room. Turns fan on in clothes room to drive cleaning fluid fumes from clothes. Removes garment from clothes room.
GOE: 06.04.16 STRENGTH: L GED: R2 M1 L1 SVP: 2 DLU: 77

589.685-042 DYER HELPER (hat & cap)
Tends equipment that bleaches and dries articles: Mixes bleaching solution, according to formula or instructions. Immerses material to be bleached in tub or vat containing solution and removes after specified time. Tends centrifugal extractor to remove excess bleach and dry articles [EXTRACTOR OPERATOR (any industry)].
GOE: 06.04.16 STRENGTH: L GED: R2 M2 L2 SVP: 2 DLU: 77

589.685-046 EDGE STAINER I (leather prod.)
Tends machine that applies decorative ink stain to edges of leather articles, such as coin purses and wallets: Fills reservoir of staining device and turns knob to activate flow of stain into nozzle. Places edge of article against nozzle and moves edge along nozzle for application of stain. Wipes smears from article, using rag and solvent. Places article on revolving table for drying.
GOE: 06.04.21 STRENGTH: L GED: R2 M1 L1 SVP: 3 DLU: 77

589.685-050 FEATHER MIXER (tex. prod., nec)
Tends mixing machine that mixes feathers for use in stuffing household goods, such as pillows, and cushions: Weighs specified amounts of various grades of feathers and dumps feathers into mixing machine. Attaches bags to discharge chutes of machine and starts pump which sucks blended feathers into bags. May mix feathers, using pitchfork. May sew tops of filled bags. May attach identifying tags.
GOE: 06.04.09 STRENGTH: M GED: R2 M1 L1 SVP: 2 DLU: 77

589.685-054 FEATHER SEPARATOR (tex. prod., nec)
Tends equipment that separates down from feathers and separates feathers according to quality: Dumps sacks of feathers of mixed grade into separator by hand. Turns wheels to adjust height of separator walls. Starts blower system to circulate feathers up and over separator walls, heavier or lower grades of which pass over first or lowest walls while lighter or premium grades pass over higher walls. Turns off blowers to allow feathers to settle to floor of bins and sweeps them into sacks. May add chemicals to separator during process to sterilize feathers. When operating machine to remove pin feathers or quills from down, may be designated Pin-Feather-Machine Operator (tex. prod., nec); Quill-Picking-Machine Operator (tex. prod., nec).
GOE: 06.04.09 STRENGTH: L GED: R2 M1 L1 SVP: 3 DLU: 77

589.685-058 FOLDING-MACHINE OPERATOR (knitting; textile) alternate titles: dry folder, cloth; folder operator; layer-up
Tends machine that smooths and folds knitted tubing as tubing unwinds from rolls: Puts roll of tubing on turning rod of machine. Threads end of tubing over supporting rolls of machine, through steam rolls, and through feed rolls which pull tubing over spreader and through steam rolls. Turns crank to adjust height of folding table located under rolls. Starts machine and observes as tubing travels through rolls which move back and forth on carriage and deposit tubing in folds onto table. Removes folded tubing from table and places tubing in boxes. May weigh tubing and record weight.
GOE: 06.04.05 STRENGTH: M GED: R2 M1 L2 SVP: 2 DLU: 77

589.685-062 HAT FINISHER (hat & cap) alternate titles: body finisher
Tends machines that finish felt hat bodies, performing any combination of following tasks: Tends machine that buffs or sands hat bodies to smooth or polish surface [BUFFER (hat & cap); POUNCING-LATHE OPERATOR (hat & cap)]. Tends machine that applies grease and wax to hat body to finish and stiffen body [GREASER OPERATOR (hat & cap)]. Tends machine that trims brim to specified width [ROUNDING-MACHINE OPERATOR (hat & cap; tex. prod., nec)]. Rubs hat to remove surplus fur fibers and smooth surface of hat, using sandpaper. Rubs coloring powder onto hat bodies, using powder-filled

cloth bag, or sprays powder onto hat with compressed-air gun. Presses hat brim to smooth and shape brim, using hand iron. May be designated according to part processed as Crown Finisher (hat & cap); or type of hat processed as Wool-Hat Finisher (hat & cap).
GOE: 06.04.16 STRENGTH: L GED: R2 M2 L2 SVP: 4 DLU: 77

589.685-066 LAUNDRY-MACHINE TENDER (tex. prod., nec)
Tends machines that bleach, dye, and dry bedspreads: Places bedspreads into paddle-dyeing machine and adds chemicals, such as caustic, soap, bleach, dye, and salt, at designated intervals during dyeing cycle to bleach and dye bedspreads. Places dyed bedspreads into ram or centrifugal extractor and starts extractor to remove excess water from spreads [EXTRACTOR OPERATOR (any industry)]. Places bedspreads into tumble drier and starts drier to dry and fluff spreads.
GOE: 06.04.16 STRENGTH: M GED: R2 M1 L1 SVP: 3 DLU: 77

589.685-070 MEASURING-MACHINE OPERATOR (leather mfg.) alternate titles: hide-measuring-machine operator; measurer
Tends machine that measures square footage of finished leather: Sets automatic counter at zero. Starts machine and feeds leather between rollers that carry it under measuring wheels connected to dial. Reads dial and chalks number of square feet onto surface of leather. May tie leather pieces into bundles for shipment.
GOE: 06.03.02 STRENGTH: L GED: R1 M1 L1 SVP: 2 DLU: 77

589.685-074 PLEATER (textile) alternate titles: bin piler; plaiter
Tends machine that guides cloth in *rope form* into storage bins or processing tanks in pleat-like folds to prevent tangling during subsequent removal: Threads cloth through poteyes, over rollers, through sleeve of pleating mechanism, and into bin or tank. Starts machine and turns knob to adjust pleating device so that cloth piles in even layers. May guide cloth with wooden stick or by hand. May sew ends of cloth together, using portable sewing machine. May be designated according to process as Sour-Bleaching Pleater (textile).
GOE: 06.04.16 STRENGTH: M GED: R1 M1 L1 SVP: 2 DLU: 77

589.685-078 PULLER, MACHINE (leather mfg.)
Tends machine that stretches, softens, and cleans pelts: Places pelt on slanted board and depresses pedal to elevate board into contact with rotating roller. Holds and guides pelt under roller as machine stretches and softens pelt and removes undesired flesh from skin side.
GOE: 06.04.16 STRENGTH: L GED: R1 M1 L1 SVP: 2 DLU: 77

589.685-082 RENOVATOR-MACHINE OPERATOR (tex. prod., nec) alternate titles: feather renovator; sterilizer
Tends automatic machine that cleans, sterilizes, and dries feathers used to stuff cushions, and pillows: Dumps sacks of feathers on floor and removes foreign matter. Starts machine and loads feathers to be cleaned and sterilized with steam and dried with hot air into hopper of machine. Opens air valve to blow feathers into storage bins. May weigh specified amount of feathers prior to loading machine.
GOE: 06.04.19 STRENGTH: H GED: R1 M1 L1 SVP: 2 DLU: 77

589.685-086 ROLLING-DOWN-MACHINE OPERATOR (knitting; textile) alternate titles: pleating-machine operator; swing-folding-machine operator
Tends machine that unwinds cloth from rolls and discharges it into loose or folded form to facilitate further processing: Inserts metal rod through roll of cloth and lifts cloth into feeding position. Sews end of cloth roll to cloth in machine, using portable sewing machine. Positions truck under delivery roller or *swing-folding attachment* and starts machine. Pushes loaded trucks from area. May observe cloth to detect defective seams and resew seams to prevent raveling.
GOE: 06.04.05 STRENGTH: H GED: R2 M1 L2 SVP: 2 DLU: 77

589.685-090 SCUTCHER TENDER (textile) alternate titles: cloth opener, hand
Tends machine that opens cloth to full width after cloth is processed in *rope form*: Sews end of cloth to leader, using portable sewing machine, or threads cloth through guides and rollers, over beaters that revolve against direction of cloth to cause cloth to open and over scrimp rail that stretches and smooths cloth. Starts machine and observes cloth passing over beaters to ensure cloth is opened to full width. Scutcher is usually in tandem with other machines, such as vacuum extractor, mangle, or detacker.
GOE: 06.04.16 STRENGTH: M GED: R2 M1 L1 SVP: 2 DLU: 77

589.685-094 SHAKER (hat & cap)
Tends shaker that removes sawdust from fur pelts that have been tumbled with sawdust in skin-softening drum: Places pelts in wire-mesh cylinder of shaker and starts machine. Removes skins after specified time or when sawdust has been removed and piles skins for processing of fur into felt hats.
GOE: 06.04.16 STRENGTH: M GED: R1 M1 L1 SVP: 2 DLU: 77

589.685-098 WRINGER-MACHINE OPERATOR (leather mfg.; tex. prod., nec) alternate titles: extractor operator; extract wringer; putter-out, machine; roll-press operator; setter, machine; striker-out, machine; wringer and setter
Tends machine that removes moisture or wrinkles from felt sheets or hides: Places material between rollers of machine and depresses pedal that rotates lower roller against upper roller to press moisture or smooth wrinkles from ma-

terial. Releases pedal to separate rollers and stop machine. Removes material from rollers and places material on cart. May move controls to adjust rollers according to thickness of material. May be designated according to section of leather processed as Belly Wringer (leather mfg.); Crop-Setting-Out-Machine Operator (leather mfg.); or according to type of leather processed as Blue-Leather Setter (leather mfg.); Colored-Leather Setter (leather mfg.). May sponge water on hides before rolling to ensure uniformity of moisture content and be designated Sponger (leather mfg.).
GOE: 06.04.16 STRENGTH: M GED: R1 M1 L1 SVP: 2 DLU: 77

589.685-102 YARN-TEXTURING-MACHINE OPERATOR (plastic-synth.) alternate titles: crimping-machine operator
Tends machine that crimps thermoplastic yarn to increase bulk, add elasticity, and provide yarn with a soft hand: Places supply packages on spindles and threads yarn ends through guides, feed rolls, and into *crimping attachments*. Pulls yarn ends from stuffer boxes of crimping attachments, using wire hook, threads ends through guides, and attaches ends to takeup packages. Observes flow of yarn through machine to detect breaks in yarn and signal lights to detect variations in temperature of crimping attachments. Ties broken yarn ends by hand or with knotter and reports malfunction of machine to MACHINE FIXER (textile). Stops winding unit and doffs full package. May wrap yarn packages in paper and pack packages in shipping containers. Important variables may be indicated by trade name of yarn produced.
GOE: 06.04.16 STRENGTH: L GED: R2 M1 L2 SVP: 3 DLU: 77

589.686-010 BACK TENDER (textile) alternate titles: cloth drier; desizing-machine offbearer; drying-machine receiver; drying-machine tender; frame catcher; swing tender; take-away attendant; tentering-machine off-bearer
Off bears from delivery end of *range* or machine that dyes, finishes, washes, treats, or dries cloth or other textile goods: Observes as cloth winds onto rolls or passes through *swing-folding attachment* into trucks and notifies supervisor of obvious flaws. Measures cloth with ruler and feels cloth discharging from *drying cans or tenter frame* to verify that cloth meets specifications for width and dryness. Moves lever to lower blade that cuts cloth at seams or ravels seams connecting lengths to remove cloth from machine. Pushes roll of cloth onto platform or lifts roll from machine brackets, using hoist. Places *tube* on winding shaft and starts cloth winding on tube. Replaces filled truck at swing-folding attachment with empty truck to receive folded cloth. May wrap cloth roll with burlap. May regulate heat of drying cans and flow of water into washboxes by turning valves. May be designated according to type of machine as Cloth-Bleaching-Range Back-Tender (textile); Cloth-Finishing-Range Back-Tender (textile); Cloth-Washer Back-Tender (textile); Drying-Machine Back-Tender (knitting; textile); Dyeing-Machine Back-Tender (textile); Tenter-Frame Back-Tender (textile). May be designated: Cloth-Mercerizer Back-Tender (textile); Desizing-Machine Back-Tender (textile); Dry-Cans Back-Tender (textile); Mangle Back-Tender (textile); Mangle Catcher (textile); Singer Back-Tender (textile); Soaping-Machine Back-Tender (textile); Tire-Fabric-Impregnating-Range Back-Tender (tex. prod., nec); White-Washer Piler (textile).
GOE: 06.04.16 STRENGTH: M GED: R2 M1 L2 SVP: 2 DLU: 77

589.686-014 CLOTH FEEDER (textile) alternate titles: range feeder
Feeds cloth into any of various textile finishing machines: Aligns trucks or rolls of cloth to be processed through machine according to priority, style, and width. Positions truck at feed end of machine or mounts roll of cloth onto brackets at scray. Sews end of cloth to leader, using portable sewing machine. Straightens cloth as it enters machine. May assist machine operator to thread cloth through machine. May be designated according to machine fed as Finishing-Range Feeder (textile); Mercerizing-Range Feeder (textile); Tenter-Frame Feeder (textile).
GOE: 06.04.16 STRENGTH: H GED: R1 M1 L1 SVP: 2 DLU: 77

589.686-018 FEATHER-CURLING-MACHINE OPERATOR (tex. prod., nec) alternate titles: crushing-mill operator; feather-crushing-machine operator
Feeds feathers, used to stuff cushions, and pillows, into hopper of machine that curls (crushes) feathers to prevent quills from protruding through ticking of finished product.
GOE: 06.04.09 STRENGTH: M GED: R1 M1 L1 SVP: 1 DLU: 77

589.686-022 FUR-FLOOR WORKER (leather mfg.) alternate titles: floorworker
Cleans and dresses pelts, performing any combination of following tasks: Cuts pelts on belly side from neck to tail with knife to facilitate further handling. Feeds pelts into cylinder of combing machine that untangles hair. Loads, starts, stops, and unloads *beating machine* to remove loose hair and foreign matter from pelts. Brushes grease onto skin side of pelts to restore oils removed in dyeing and tanning processes, or loads pelts and grease into revolving drum for specified time. Loads pelts and sawdust into revolving drum to tumble pelts in sawdust to dry, clean, and soften them. Stops drum after specified interval and transfers pelts to revolving cage to remove sawdust from pelts. Pulls skin of pelt back and forth over edge of metal bar, or slips uncut pelt over tongue of spreading device to stretch, open pores, and soften skin of pelt. Trims furs with scissors to even length of hairs. May be designated according to specialized task performed or machine tended as Beating-Machine Operator (leather mfg.); Comber (leather mfg.); Cutter (leather mfg.); Drummer (leather mfg.); Fur Clipper (leather mfg.); Fur Puller (leather mfg.); Fur Stretcher (leather mfg.); Greaser (leather mfg.).

GOE: 06.04.16 STRENGTH: M GED: R1 M1 L1 SVP: 2 DLU: 77

589.686-026 LABORER, GENERAL (leather mfg.) alternate titles: blue-line hanger; cellar hand; department helper; roustabout; toggler
Performs any combination of following duties in various sections of tannery, such as drying department, beam house, hide house, or tan house: Cuts cord from hide bundles and spreads hides on floor for processing. Dumps tannery refuse, such as skin and fat, in bin and covers refuse with lime to prevent putrefaction. Covers fleshy side of hides with lime solution to prevent putrefaction of hides. Applies solvent to wool of sheepskin to remove painted brands, using rag and brush. Hangs hides in steam room and turns valve to admit steam that loosens hair and wool on hides. Moves steamed hides to dehairing machine or manually pulls loosened wool from hides. Collects hair after dehairing operation and dumps hair into washing machine. Shovels washed hair into centrifugal drier or onto screen over steam coils to remove moisture. Punches holes in hides, using awl or punch press, to facilitate tying hides into bundles for tanning. Counts and ties specified number of hides into bundles. Dumps hides into drums or vats containing various chemical solutions that dehair, delime, or preserve hides. Dampens hides with water in preparation for oiling. Pastes or clips wet hides on frames to prevent wrinkling and slides frames into drying tunnel. Removes dry hides from frames and stacks hides on cart. Feeds and off bears machines that clean and smooth finished hides by pressing, brushing, or vacuuming. Cleans vats, tanks, and drums of lime, tanbark, and refuse and scrubs walls and floors of tannery, using brushes, scrapers, and solvents. Sprays disinfectant in trucks or freight cars used to haul hides to tannery. May be assigned to specific section of tannery and be designated Laborer, Beam House (leather mfg.); Laborer, Drying Department (leather mfg.); Laborer, Hide House (leather mfg.); Laborer, Tan House (leather mfg.).
GOE: 06.04.27 STRENGTH: M GED: R2 M1 L1 SVP: 2 DLU: 77

589.686-030 OPENER II (hat & cap)
Feeds rabbit skins over revolving cutting wheel of machine that slits pelt along belly, opening skin for further processing into hatters' fur. May cut off ears, tail, and feet of rabbit, using knife.
GOE: 06.04.16 STRENGTH: L GED: R1 M1 L1 SVP: 2 DLU: 77

589.686-034 PACKAGE CRIMPER (textile) alternate titles: crimping-machine operator
Feeds machine that rounds edges of thread packages so that dye will penetrate thread uniformly.
GOE: 06.04.16 STRENGTH: M GED: R1 M1 L1 SVP: 2 DLU: 77

589.686-038 RUG-INSPECTOR HELPER (tex. prod., nec)
Assists RUG INSPECTOR (tex. prod., nec) in examination of felt rug pads: Examines felt and points out imperfections. Straightens material to ensure even rewinding. Helps lift finished roll to wrapping machine. Places pipe or bar in winding rack, and starts new roll of padding. Helps RUG INSPECTOR (tex. prod., nec) cut material to specified length. Performs other duties as described under HELPER (any industry) Master Title.
GOE: 06.03.02 STRENGTH: M GED: R1 M1 L1 SVP: 2 DLU: 77

589.686-042 SOCK BOARDER (knitting) alternate titles: boarder, hand; boarder; boarder, steam; boarder tender
Feeds and off bears *boarding II* equipment that shapes and dries knitted socks: Pulls socks over leg-shaped boarding forms, aligns toe and heel with form, and smooths out wrinkles in leg. Strips shaped socks from forms and stacks socks on tray for further processing. May turn valves to increase or decrease steam pressure and temperature of boarding forms according to type of socks being boarded.
GOE: 06.04.16 STRENGTH: L GED: R2 M1 L1 SVP: 2 DLU: 77

589.686-046 TAKER-OFF, HEMP FIBER (tex. prod., nec) alternate titles: taker-off
Removes hemp fibers from conveyor of machines that dry or scutch fibers: Places hemp on table or another conveyor, or coils hemp for next operation. May be designated according to type of machine from which hemp is removed as Taker-Off, Braker Machine (tex. prod., nec); Taker-Off, Drying Kiln (tex. prod., nec); Taker-Off, Scutcher Machine (tex. prod., nec).
GOE: 06.04.16 STRENGTH: M GED: R1 M1 L1 SVP: 1 DLU: 77

589.686-050 TOBACCO-CLOTH RECLAIMER (tex. prod., nec)
Feeds or off bears machine that vacuums foreign matter from reclaimed tobacco cloth (cheesecloth) and cuts cloth into specified lengths for use as disposable wiping rags: Pushes bales of cloth into feeding position and places end of cloth on roller conveyor that conveys cloth through machine. Removes cut lengths of cloth from delivery end of machine and ties lengths into bundles. Deposits bundles in container.
GOE: 06.04.05 STRENGTH: M GED: R2 M1 L1 SVP: 2 DLU: 77

589.687-010 CAKE WRAPPER (plastic-synth.)
Wraps cakes of rayon yarn in cloth to protect threads during steaming, washing, and drying processes. May perform duties of WASHER (plastic-synth.).
GOE: 06.04.38 STRENGTH: M GED: R1 M1 L1 SVP: 2 DLU: 77

589.687-014 CLOTH FOLDER, HAND (tex. prod., nec; textile) alternate titles: book folder; folder, hand; hand-booked folder and stitcher; maker-up, folding
Folds cloth by hand to facilitate wrapping, packing, or further processing: Unreels cloth from bolt onto table. Examines cloth for defects, such as faulty

dyeing, printing, or finishing. Folds fabric into halves, aligns edges, and matches pattern of fabric. Laps cloth at specified intervals to fold into pile. Binds folded cloth, using rope. Records lot number and disposition of goods folded on production sheet. May trim ends of cloth, using scissors. May staple or pin edges of cloth together. May work as member of team to fold broad woven goods. May be designated according to goods folded as Bedspread Folder (tex. prod., nec); Blanket Folder (tex. prod., nec); Dishcloth Folder (tex. prod., nec); Pillowcase Folder (tex. prod., nec); Sheet Folder (tex. prod., nec); Towel Folder (tex. prod., nec); Washcloth Folder (tex. prod., nec).
GOE: 06.04.27 STRENGTH: L GED: R2 M1 L2 SVP: 2 DLU: 77

589.687-018 DIPPER (knitting; textile)
Fills machine trough with adhesive for use in laminating cloth: Pushes barrel of adhesive from storage area to machine, using handtruck. Positions barrel on platform and places tray between barrel and trough. Dips adhesive into tray to maintain adequate supply in trough for laminating process.
GOE: 06.04.27 STRENGTH: M GED: R1 M1 L1 SVP: 2 DLU: 77

589.687-022 FABRIC-LAY-OUT WORKER (textile)
Lays out and folds bolts of fabrics, such as silk and rayon, preparatory to moire processing, dyeing, and other processing: Determines if cloth should be folded by hand or machine, according to type of processing to be done or specifications, and lays aside bolts to be folded by machine. Folds remaining bolts end-to-end as specified. Records data, such as customer's number, lot number, piece number, yardage, date, color, style, and process specified, for each bolt. May fold finished bolts of fabrics.
GOE: 06.04.27 STRENGTH: L GED: R2 M1 L2 SVP: 2 DLU: 77

589.687-026 LABORER, GENERAL (tex. prod., nec)
Performs any combination of following duties in manufacture of coated fabrics: Measures width of rolls of material, identifies rolls with color code card, and weighs rolls before and after coating processes. Conveys rolls of material, engraved printing or embossing rolls, and drums of daub and print color to and from machine, using dollies. Lifts rolls to *letoff rack* and *windup racks*, using hoist. Joins ends of material rolls with automatic sewing machine or tape. Observes material at windup rack and notifies operator of processing defects. Starts rolls onto core, changes knives, and threads material into machine. Scrapes and cleans equipment, removes scrap, and sweeps area. Keeps supply of rags and roll cores. May be designated according to operators assisted as Calender-Operator Helper (tex. prod., nec); Cloth-Printing-Machine-Operator Helper (tex. prod., nec); Coating-Machine-Operator Helper (tex. prod., nec); Embossing-Machine-Operator Helper (tex. prod., nec); Winding-Rack-Operator Helper (tex. prod., nec).
GOE: 06.04.05 STRENGTH: M GED: R1 M1 L1 SVP: 2 DLU: 77

589.687-030 PAD MAKER (textile) alternate titles: padder
Prepares sample pads of textile fibers by hand for use in comparing textile batch color with standard: Cards fibers received from dyeing process, using brush, and dries fibers in oven. Weighs dried fibers, mats specified weight into pads, and washes and dries pads. Cuts excess fibers from pads, using scissors. Attaches identification tags to pads. May blend different colored fibers to determine quantity of each color required to make specified shade.
GOE: 06.04.27 STRENGTH: M GED: R2 M1 L2 SVP: 3 DLU: 77

589.687-034 STAINER (leather prod.) alternate titles: applier; color finisher; smearer
Applies liquid dye or stain to leather articles, such as belts, gloves, and pocketbooks, to cover blemishes and color edges, gussets, and seams of assembled articles, using brushes, daubers, and swabs.
GOE: 06.04.27 STRENGTH: L GED: R2 M1 L1 SVP: 2 DLU: 77

589.687-038 STIFFENER (hat & cap) alternate titles: dipper; machine sizer; sizer; sizing brusher; sizing sponger; smearer; spray-gun sizer
Applies sizing solution, such as gelatin, glue, lacquer, paint, or shellac to hat or hat parts to stiffen, waterproof, or impart finish to hat: Pours premixed solutions into container or thins solution, following work order specifications. Applies solution to hat or hat parts by any combination of following tasks. Brushes or sponges solution onto articles; dips articles into tub of solution; sprays solution onto article, using spray gun; inserts parts between solution-coated rollers of machine. Places articles on holder of machine that spins articles to remove surplus liquid. Hangs articles on pegs or on holders of conveyor belt that carries articles through drying room to complete drying and stiffening operation. May be designated according to hat or hat part stiffened as Brim Stiffener (hat & cap); Panama-Hat Smearer (hat & cap); Strawhat Sizer (hat & cap); or according to solution used in sizing article as Lacquer Sizer (hat & cap); Varnisher (hat & cap). When reapplying sizing solution to article to cover thin spots in original coating, may be known as Retouching Operator (hat & cap).
GOE: 06.04.27 STRENGTH: L GED: R2 M1 L1 SVP: 3 DLU: 78

589.687-042 TUBE CLEANER (textile)
Removes cloth covers from dye tubes or springs to prepare tubes for reuse: Cuts cover with knife or holds tube against revolving emery wheel. Pulls cover from tube by hand.
GOE: 06.04.27 STRENGTH: L GED: R1 M1 L1 SVP: 2 DLU: 77

589.687-046 TUBE COVERER (textile)
Covers dye tubes with cloth tubing to prevent yarn damage during dyeing process: Mounts tubes on prongs of covering device and slides tubing over tubes. Removes tubes from device and tucks excess tubing into ends of tubes. Sorts defective dye tubes for repair or disposal. May cut tubing into specified lengths, using electric cutting wheel.
GOE: 06.04.27 STRENGTH: L GED: R1 M1 L1 SVP: 2 DLU: 77

589.687-050 WOOL PULLER (leather mfg.; meat products)
Removes wool from sheep pelts and sorts wool into bins: Holds pelt against angled table and pulls wool from pelt. Examines and grades wool according to color, texture, and length. Places wool in designated containers. Scrapes remaining wool from pelt, using scraping stick. Cuts off brand marks and wool around head and feet with shears. Places stripped pelts on racks or truck. May grade pelts before pulling.
GOE: 06.03.02 STRENGTH: L GED: R2 M1 L2 SVP: 3 DLU: 77

589.687-054 WOOL-FLEECE GRADER (agriculture)
Examines and sorts wool fleece according to quality: Lifts unprocessed fleece to estimate approximate weight of fleece after processing. Separates locks of fleece and examines fibers for length, diameter, elasticity, and color to determine quality of fleece. Examines fleece and separates locks to determine presence of dirt, manure, straw, stains, and moisture. Separates and places fleece in containers and marks wool grade on container according to government standards for quality.
GOE: 06.03.02 STRENGTH: L GED: R3 M3 L3 SVP: 4 DLU: 77

589.687-058 SHAKER (knitting)
Shakes out, aligns, and folds surgical hose following wet processing to prepare hose for wrinkle-free drying in nit house: Empties bag of hose on worktable, unrolls bundle of hose, and extends hose on worktable. Pulls and aligns heels, toes, and toe openings of hose, and lifts, extends, and smooths hose to dewrinkle and flatten edges and folds of hose legs. Lifts and shakes hose of specified styles, and slaps thigh pouches of hose against front edge of worktable to dewrinkle hose. Turns and straightens elastic welts inserted during bundling, bagging, or wet processing. Opens and flattens panel seams to prepare hose for drying in conformity with quality standards. Stacks specified quantity of hose on storage tray, and completes and attaches work ticket to tray. Shakes, aligns, and folds leotards to prevent setting of wrinkles. Stores irregular hose or panty hose in specified storage areas. Inspects, mends, or pairs hose or panty hose, following processing specifications.
GOE: 06.04.35 STRENGTH: L GED: R2 M1 L1 SVP: 2 DLU: 86

589.687-062 DYE-STAND LOADER (textile) alternate titles: carrier loader; package-dye-stand loader
Stacks yarn packages on spindles of dye stand, preparatory to dyeing in *package-dyeing machine*. Screws cap on top of each spindle to secure packages during dyeing. Loads dye stands, or beams when yarn is wound on beams, into machine, using power hoist. Closes and bolts machine lid, using wrench. Removes dyed yarn from machine and positions dye-stand in storage or holding area prior to unloading dye-stand, using power hoist. Records weight of loaded dye stands or beams. May use compressing device to load dye stand. May feel packages to determine dryness prior to unloading dye-stand.
GOE: 06.04.16 STRENGTH: M GED: R1 M1 L1 SVP: 2 DLU: 80

59   PROCESSING OCCUPATIONS, N.E.C.

This division includes occupations, not elsewhere classified, concerned with processing materials and products.

590   OCCUPATIONS IN PROCESSING PRODUCTS FROM ASSORTED MATERIALS

This group includes occupations concerned with producing singular products by means of mixing, heating, saturating, distilling, melting, and similarly working two or more different materials.

590.130-010 SUPERVISOR, ELECTRONICS PROCESSING (electron. comp.)
Supervises and coordinates activities of workers engaged in processing electronic components and parts, such as printed circuit boards (PCB's), electron tubes, and semiconductor devices: Examines product for conformance to specifications and quality standards, applying knowledge of manufacturing processes. Demonstrates methods and trains workers in sequence of processing tasks and operation and control of machines and equipment. Maintains records and prepares cost, yield, breakage, and maintenance reports, manually or using computer terminal. Inventories and requisitions tools, equipment, and supplies for department activities. Performs other tasks as described under SUPERVISOR (any industry) Master Title. May perform tasks of subordinates, such as machine and equipment setup, adjustment, and repair. May be designated according to product or department as Supervisor, Capacitor Processing (electron. comp.); Supervisor, Electron Tube Processing (electron. comp.); Supervisor, Integrated Circuit Manufacturing (electron. comp.); Supervisor, Printed Circuit Board Processing (electron. comp.); Supervisor, Process Testing (electron. comp.); Supervisor, Semiconductor Wafer Manufacturing (electron. comp.).
GOE: 06.01.01 STRENGTH: L GED: R4 M3 L3 SVP: 7 DLU: 88

590.130-014 SUPERVISOR, INSULATION (nonmet. min.)
Supervises and coordinates activities of workers engaged in melting, and spinning slag and flux into mineral wool for use in forming granulated wool,

batts, and felts. Repairs and adjusts malfunctioning machines and equipment, using handtools. Performs other duties as described under SUPERVISOR (any industry) Master Title.
GOE: 06.02.01 STRENGTH: L GED: R4 M3 L4 SVP: 8 DLU: 77

590.130-018 SUPERVISOR, ROOFING PLANT (build. mat., nec)
Supervises and coordinates activities of workers engaged in saturating, coating, and winding roofing felt to fabricate composition shingles and roll roofing. Assists workers with faulty equipment. Sets up machines for workers. Performs other duties as described under SUPERVISOR (any industry) Master Title. May be designated according to unit or function as Shingle-Machine Supervisor (build. mat., nec).
GOE: 06.02.01 STRENGTH: M GED: R4 M3 L4 SVP: 7 DLU: 77

590.131-010 PORCELAIN-ENAMELING SUPERVISOR (any industry)
Supervises and coordinates activities of workers engaged in preparing and applying porcelain enamel to surface of products, such as electric washers, refrigerators, and automobile mufflers, applying knowledge of metal pickling, pulverizing and mixing of porcelain ingredients, and application, drying, and baking of porcelain enamel: Computes amount of ingredients required to obtain porcelain mixtures of specified color and consistency, following standard formulas. Examines pickled surface of product and orders changes in pickling solution to ensure suitability of surface for porcelainizing. Inspects finished product and moves controls to regulate furnace temperatures and conveyor speeds to ensure fusion of porcelain finish. Performs other duties as described under SUPERVISOR (any industry) Master Title.
GOE: 06.02.01 STRENGTH: L GED: R4 M3 L3 SVP: 7 DLU: 77

590.132-010 SUPERVISOR, CANDLE MAKING (fabrication, nec)
Supervises and coordinates activities of workers engaged in dipping, molding, cutting, and packing candles: Verifies percentage of specified ingredients used to blend molten wax, using plant standards or customer's specifications. Observes molten wax to detect irregularities in color and consistency. Trains workers in machine operation. Requisitions materials. Performs other duties as described under SUPERVISOR (any industry) Master Title.
GOE: 06.02.01 STRENGTH: L GED: R4 M3 L3 SVP: 7 DLU: 77

590.134-010 SUPERVISOR, PIPE JOINTS (brick & tile)
Supervises and coordinates activities of workers engaged in molding plastic seal joints on ends of clay sewer pipes: Inspects finished work for conformance to specifications. Trains workers in performance of duties, such as pouring sealants into molds and trimming excess materials from joints. Performs other duties as described under SUPERVISOR (any industry) Master Title.
GOE: 06.02.02 STRENGTH: L GED: R4 M3 L4 SVP: 7 DLU: 77

590.262-010 CRYSTAL GROWING TECHNICIAN (electron. comp.)
Analyzes processing procedures and equipment functions to identify and resolve problems in growing semiconductor crystals, utilizing knowledge of crystal growing, and trains other workers to grow crystals: Observes furnace operation and crystal growth and reads logbook entries to identify deviations from specifications and procedures, and advises CRYSTAL GROWER (electron. comp.) 590.382-014 on techniques to adjust furnace controls to alter crystal growth to meet company specifications. Demonstrates and explains crystal growing procedures to train CRYSTAL GROWER (electron. comp.) and to improve worker's crystal growing techniques. Inspects furnaces for gas leaks, diagnoses equipment malfunctions, and requests equipment repairs. Sets up and operates furnaces in absence of CRYSTAL GROWER (electron. comp.).
GOE: 06.02.18 STRENGTH: M GED: R4 M3 L3 SVP: 6 DLU: 86

590.262-014 TEST TECHNICIAN, SEMICONDUCTOR PROCESSING EQUIPMENT (electron. comp.)
Operates machines and equipment used in production of semiconductor wafers, such as alignment equipment, automatic developer, and diffusion furnaces, and tests processed wafers to evaluate performance of machines and equipment: Operates machines and equipment to process test wafer. Inspects and measures test wafer, using electronic measuring equipment and microscope, to determine that machines and equipment are processing wafers according to company specifications. Records test results in logbooks. Discusses production problems with workers. Analyzes test results, using engineering specifications and calculator, and writes report on equipment repair or re-calibration recommendations and on operator procedure violations.
GOE: 06.01.05 STRENGTH: L GED: R4 M3 L4 SVP: 7 DLU: 86

590.282-010 EPITAXIAL REACTOR TECHNICIAN (electron. comp.)
Sets up and operates computer-controlled epitaxial reactor to grow layer of semiconductor material on wafer surface, following written specifications: Removes semiconductor wafers from tray, using vacuum wand, and cleans wafers, using blow-off wand. Positions wafers on carousel and aligns carousel on baseplate of reactor. Enters processing data into computer to start rotation of baseplate and to activate vacuum pump and epitaxial growth process program. Observes display screen to monitor epitaxial growth process. Inspects wafers for defects, such as scratches, growths, and pits, and calculates defects per square inch, using calculator. Measures thickness and bow (warp) of wafer and thickness and photo-luminescence of epitaxial layer, using gauges and test equipment. Calculates surface area of wafer surface, using calculator. Inscribes line on wafer, using metal scribe, and breaks off section (light bar sample) of wafer. Cuts line on light bar sample to isolate *die*, using wafer saw, and measures brightness of die, using probe tester. Constructs sheet metal housing and

installs and repairs electrical wiring, water and gas lines, switches, and gauges on reactor following oral instructions, blueprints, and specifications, using handtools and power tools. Checks replacement gas cylinder for leaks before installing on reactor, using leak detector. Connects reactor to computer, using handtools and power tools. Enters information into computer, using keyboard, to activate program to clean reactor, and cleans and replaces reactor accessories, such as bell jar and carousel. Maintains production records.
GOE: 06.02.18 STRENGTH: M GED: R4 M4 L4 SVP: 6 DLU: 88

590.362-010 FORMING-PROCESS WORKER (elec. equip.) alternate titles: process attendant
Controls generating equipment and maintains specific gravity of acid to form (treat) and charge battery plates and cells, and inspects activities of workers at each station along line: Reads meters on generator and moves controls to adjust voltage and amperage to specified levels. Observes generator brushes to detect arcing and adjusts brushes, using handtools. Inspects polarity arrangement of batteries on forming trucks to ensure conformance to instructions. Ascertains charging rate of batteries periodically, using voltmeter. Turns valves to drain specified amounts of acid and water into mixing tank and ascertains specific gravity of solution, using hydrometer and thermometer. Adds water or acid to obtain specified concentration. Observes activities of workers filling cells with acid, stacking batteries on forming trucks, attaching and stripping connectors, treating (forming) plates, dumping acid from batteries, washing and drying plates, testing elements, inserting elements in containers (battery boxes) and charging batteries, and reports deviations to supervisor.
GOE: 06.02.11 STRENGTH: L GED: R3 M3 L3 SVP: 5 DLU: 77

590.362-014 IMPREGNATING-MACHINE OPERATOR (metal prod., nec) alternate titles: asphalt-machine operator
Sets up and operates machine to saturate wire-reinforced paper, used as plaster lath, with oil, wax, or asphalt: Loads wire-reinforced paper roll onto unreeling stand, using power hoist or crane. Threads paper through saturating rolls of machine and drier rollers and attaches end of paper to rewinding reel. Fills machine tank with saturating liquid, using monorail crane. Adjusts valves of gas burners and turns setscrews to regulate steam pressure, temperature, and flow of impregnating liquid. Starts machine and regulates pressure of saturating roll, rumbler rolls, speed of machine feed, and tension of rewinder, using handtools. Removes treated paper roll from rewinder, using power hoist. Seals paper roll, using gummed tape.
GOE: 06.02.18 STRENGTH: M GED: R3 M2 L2 SVP: 4 DLU: 77

590.362-018 GROUP LEADER, SEMICONDUCTOR PROCESSING (electron. comp.) alternate titles: production aide
Assists SUPERVISOR, ELECTRONICS PROCESSING (electron. comp.) 590.130-010 in coordinating and monitoring activities of workers engaged in fabricating electronic devices (components), such as integrated circuits, transistors, and diodes, on semiconductor wafers, utilizing knowledge of semiconductor processing equipment and processing procedures: Receives and answers questions from workers pertaining to production processes or equipment operation. Monitors and expedites flow of materials within production area. Notifies maintenance workers of equipment malfunctions. Tends or operates machines or equipment on production line to substitute for absentee workers. Maintains product workflow records. Trains workers in equipment operation and in processing and safety procedures. May inspect processed wafers, using microscope, to detect processing defects.
GOE: 06.02.18 STRENGTH: L GED: R3 M2 L2 SVP: 7 DLU: 86

590.362-022 MICROELECTRONICS TECHNICIAN (electron. comp.)
Operates variety of semiconductor processing, testing, and assembly equipment to assist engineering staff in development and fabrication of prototype, custom-designed, electronic circuitry chips in research laboratory, using knowledge of microelectronic processing equipment, procedures, and specifications: Operates equipment to convert integrated circuit layout designs into working photo masks; clean, coat, bake, align, expose, develop, and cure photoresist on wafers; grow layers of dielectric, metal, and semiconductor material on masked areas of wafers; clean, etch, or remove materials on areas not covered by photoresist; and implant chemicals to selective areas of wafer substrate to alter substrate electrical characteristics. Operates various test equipment to verify product conformance to processing and company specifications. Operates equipment to assemble, dice, clean, mount, bond, and package integrated circuit devices. May perform some assembly and packaging operations manually. May assist in interpretation and evaluation of processing data and in preparation of related reports. May assist in technical writing of semiconductor processing specifications.
GOE: 06.01.03 STRENGTH: L GED: R4 M4 L3 SVP: 6 DLU: 86

590.364-010 LEAD WORKER, WAFER PRODUCTION (electron. comp.)
Assists supervisor in coordinating activities of workers engaged in abrading, cleaning, etching, heattreating, testing, inspecting, sawing, and other processes in manufacturing semiconductor wafers, utilizing knowledge of equipment, procedures, and specifications for wafer manufacture: Assigns workers to work stations to meet production requirements. Interprets process specifications for workers. Monitors production and adjusts work assignments, supply of material, and machine operation when necessary. Transports materials between production and storage areas. Repairs various machines, using handtools and power tools. Refers extensive machine repairs to maintenance personnel. Confers with supervisor to receive instructions and exchange production information. Tests

random samples of silicon wafers, using various test equipment, to verify wafers meet specifications. Periodically recalibrates test equipment. Trains workers in equipment operation. May perform duties of absent workers to maintain production.
GOE: 06.02.01 STRENGTH: M GED: R3 M2 L3 SVP: 6 DLU: 86

590.365-010 IRON-PLASTIC BULLET MAKER (ordnance)
Tends machines that mix, mold, and bake iron powder and plastic to form spatterless bullets for small arms ammunition: Measures, weighs, and pours specified quantities of iron powder, plastic crystals, and solvent into steam-heated mixing machine to coat each particle of iron powder with adhesive plastic. Starts machine. Observes dials, indicators, and gauges, and turns valves to regulate and maintain prescribed heat and pressure during designated mixing period. Opens hatch in mixer bottom to dump dried, coated iron powder onto shaker screen that removes clinkers. Signals INDUSTRIAL-TRUCK OPERATOR (any industry) 921.683-050 to move cans of sifted powder and to lift them to platform above bullet molding press. Scoops powder from can and sifts it through screen to remove oversize particles and to fill hopper of bullet molding machine. Starts machine that compresses iron powder in molds to form bullets. Examines bullets for malformation and replaces worn punches and dies, using handtools. Regulates conveyor speed and electric oven temperature by pressing buttons and switches to bake and cool bullets. Measures sample bullets, using dial indicator and fixed gauges. Tests samples for hardness, using special device that measures force required to break off bullet nose. Rebakes rejected bullets to reduce diameter or increase hardness to meet specifications.
GOE: 06.04.10 STRENGTH: H GED: R3 M2 L3 SVP: 3 DLU: 77

590.367-010 INSPECTOR II (fabrication, nec)
Inspects hard-surface floor covering for pattern and color defects and grades it according to quality: Participates as crewmember to mount roll of finished floor covering on unwind stand. Signals ROLL-UP-GUIDER OPERATOR (fabrication, nec) 590.685-050 to start machine that pulls hard surface floor covering across cutting table. Examines material for flaws as it unwinds onto table. Marks defective areas with tape or cuts flag into material, depending upon length of defective area. Signals ROLL-UP-GUIDER OPERATOR (fabrication, nec) to cut defective sections from acceptable material. Resets counter after each split. Grades floor covering, based on knowledge of company standards. Removes sample of material for laboratory test. May measure thickness of materials to ensure compliance with specifications, using micrometer or snap gauge. May be designated according to floor covering inspected as Rug Inspector (fabrication, nec); Tile Inspector (fabrication, nec); Wide-Piece-Goods Inspector (fabrication, nec).
GOE: 06.03.01 STRENGTH: L GED: R3 M2 L2 SVP: 5 DLU: 77

590.382-010 OPERATOR, AUTOMATED PROCESS (electron. comp.)
Operates mechanical units of automated production machinery to produce deposited carbon resistors for use in electronic equipment: Turns valves to admit methane and nitrogen gases into carbon-coating furnace and sets furnace temperature for computer control according to work order. Presses buttons and turns valves to start vacuum pump of terminating chambers and set rate for back-filling chambers with argon gas, preparatory to *sputtering* gold contacts on carbonized ceramic cores. Sets thermostats to heat curing oven of encapsulating machine and water vat of air-leak detection unit to specified temperatures. Turns valve to spray water over resistors emerging from curing oven. Observes temperature gauges, pressure gauges, and machine operation to detect mechanical failures in automated machinery. Notifies MAINTENANCE MECHANIC (any industry) 638.281-014 of machinery malfunction.
GOE: 06.02.18 STRENGTH: M GED: R3 M3 L3 SVP: 4 DLU: 87

590.382-014 CRYSTAL GROWER (comm. equip.; electron. comp.) alternate titles: crystal growing furnace operator
Sets up and operates furnaces to grow semiconductor crystals from materials, such as silicon, quartz, or gallium arsenide: Loads furnace with seed crystal, dopant, and crystal growing materials, such as polysilicon, quartz, gallium arsenide, or *remelt*. Reads work order and adjusts furnace controls to regulate operating conditions, such as power level, temperature, vacuum, and rotation speed, according to crystal growing specifications. Monitors meltdown of growing material and crystal growth, and adjusts furnace controls. Shuts down furnace and unloads crystal ingot after cooling. May clean inside furnace, using vacuum cleaner and cleaning supplies, and replace furnace liner and other parts. May weigh and crop crystal ingot, slice sample wafer, measure and test ingot for resistivity, and determine *crystal orientation* [INSPECTOR, CRYSTAL (electron. comp.) 726.684-054]. May operate computer controls to regulate furnace conditions.
GOE: 06.02.18 STRENGTH: M GED: R3 M2 L3 SVP: 5 DLU: 86

590.382-018 EPITAXIAL REACTOR OPERATOR (electron. comp.)
Controls and monitors operation of epitaxial reactor to deposit layer of semiconductor material, such as gallium arsenide or silicon, onto semiconductor wafer surface in production of electronic components, such as transistors, diodes, and integrated circuits, and tests sample processed wafers to evaluate epitaxial layer properties, such as thickness and resistivity, using testing equipment: Cleans semiconductor wafers, using cleaning equipment such as chemical baths and automatic wafer cleaners, to prepare wafers for deposit of epitaxial layer. Places wafers on wafer holder (suspector), using tweezers or vacuum wand, to load reactor. Pushes buttons, flips switches, turns dials, and observes gauges to set and adjust reactor temperature and gas pressure to specified levels

and to start reactor cycle. Monitors temperature and gas gauges during processing cycle and turns dials to adjust temperature and gas levels. Tests epitaxial layer on wafers, using testing equipment, to evaluate thickness and resistivity of layer. Records production data in logbook and processing documents. Cleans and maintains equipment and work area. May compute production statistics, using calculator.
GOE: 06.02.18 STRENGTH: L GED: R3 M3 L3 SVP: 4 DLU: 86

590.382-022 ION IMPLANT MACHINE OPERATOR (electron. comp.)
Operates ion implanting machine to implant semiconductor wafers with gases, such as arsenic, boron, or phosphorus, to implant electrical properties in wafers: Turns valves, flips switches, and presses buttons to start and regulate flow of gases into implant machine. Places semiconductor wafers in holders, such as carousel, wheels, or *boats,* using tweezers. Places loaded holder in machine and secures clamps. Presses buttons to start feeding and implanting process. Monitors gas gauges and meters and turns dials to adjust gases, following specifications, if required. Maintains processing reports. May test semiconductor wafers, using test equipment, to verify that voltage, current, and resistivity of implantation meet company specifications.
GOE: 06.02.18 STRENGTH: L GED: R3 M3 L3 SVP: 4 DLU: 86

590.384-010 CHARGE PREPARATION TECHNICIAN (electron. comp.)
Prepares ampoule containing charge (specified amounts of materials for crystal growing process) to grow gallium arsenide crystal ingot in crystal growing furnace: Cleans ampoules, plugs, and *boats,* using etch tanks and sandblasting equipment. Operates saw to cut *remelt* into sections of specified size. Immerses remelt into etch tank to remove contaminants, and dries remelt in oven. Measures and weighs specified amounts of crystal growing material, such as seed, seed powder, remelt, and dopant, and loads material into boat and ampoule, following prescribed procedure. Attaches ampoule to diffusion pump to remove air from ampoule, and seals ampoule, using blowtorch. Transports sealed ampoule to holding rack in furnace room for further processing by CRYSTAL GROWER (electron. comp.) 590.382-014. Records production information.
GOE: 06.02.32 STRENGTH: L GED: R2 M2 L2 SVP: 4 DLU: 86

590.384-014 PRODUCTION TECHNICIAN, SEMICONDUCTOR PROCESSING EQUIPMENT (electron. comp.)
Cleans and maintains wafer processing machines and equipment and mixes chemical solutions, following production specifications: Reads work orders and specifications to determine machines and equipment requiring replenishment of chemical solutions. Measures and mixes chemical solutions, using graduated beakers and funnels. Pours chemical solutions into wafer processing machine tanks to replenish machine supplies. Cleans furnace accessories, such as quartz tubes and stainless steel tubing, using chemical solutions. Removes broken quartzware and wafers from furnace and vacuums interior of furnace. Cleans processing machines and equipment, using cleaning solvent and cloth. Removes and replaces empty machine and equipment gas tanks. Measures furnace temperatures, using thermal rod or thermocouple, and turns knobs on furnace control panel to adjust temperature. May re-stock storage shelves and work station with supplies, such as chemicals, alcohol, and rubber gloves. May maintain log records of machine and equipment processing readings.
GOE: 05.09.01 STRENGTH: V GED: R3 M2 L2 SVP: 5 DLU: 86

590.464-010 PROCESSOR, SOLID PROPELLANT (chemical) alternate titles: chemical operator; process operator
Performs combination of following duties to produce solid-propellant rocket fuel, prepare rocket motor cases for inserting propellant, cast and cure propellant, install propellant and ignition components in motor case, prepare assembly for static testing, and pack assembly for shipment: Blends fuel ingredients and tends roller mill that grinds mixture to uniform consistency from remote control instrument panel, viewing operations on television monitor. Lowers motor case into degreasing pit filled with solvent, using hoist. Transfers case to sandblasting cabinet and starts compressor to sandblast unit, removing rust and scale. Paints motor case, using spray gun. Weighs out prescribed ingredients for insulating interior of case and starts agitator in mixing tank to blend ingredients to desired consistency. Sprays insulating liner onto case interior, using spray gun. Hoists case into oven to cure lining preparatory to inserting propellant. Fills fuel transfer can with propellant mixture, according to prescribed safety procedures, bolts lid onto can, and starts vibrator to remove air bubbles from mixture. Transfers filled can to casting area, using lift truck. Brushes mold-releasing lubricant onto casting core to facilitate removal of propellant after curing. Positions motor case in rack or pit and aligns casting core in case, using gauge and following markings on case interior. Couples safety hose to valve in lid of transfer can and turns air valves to force propellant into case. Bolts hydraulic jack to retainer ring of case and turns valve from behind safety barrier to force core into position, using system of mirrors to regulate movement of core. Slips plastic bag and metal cap over assembly and transfers filled case to curing oven. Sets automatic temperature controls of oven according to critical specifications for each type of propellant and size of motor. Removes casting core from propellant after prescribed curing time, using hydraulic jack, and trims excess propellant from rim of case, using remote controlled air-powered knives. Secures retaining collars, exhaust nozzle, ignition cable, and igniter motor in motor case, using torque and impact wrenches, to ensure alignment of all components. Hoists motor onto cradle of scale and records weight. Determines center of gravity of assembly, using centering devices and standard formula. Stencils identity and motor specifications on case, using stencil and roller. Prepares assemblies for static testing by transferring units to and from tem-

perature-controlled rooms, securing them to test stand, recording test instrument readings, and disassembling faulty units for inspection. Slides completed assemblies into pressurized shipping containers, using hoist and aligning devices to prevent damage during shipment. Seals container, using gaskets, bolts, tape, resilient packing, and moisture-absorbing agents. May be known as Mold-Release Worker (chemical); Rocket-Assembly Operator (chemical). When casting smaller fuel elements in molds to produce free-standing grain (fuel element), wrapping grain in inhibitor sheath to control rate of burning, and manually loading grain into motor case or container, is designated Technical Operator, Grain Preparation (chemical).
GOE: 06.02.32 STRENGTH: M GED: R3 M3 L3 SVP: 4 DLU: 77

590.487-010 COLOR WEIGHER (fabrication, nec) alternate titles: pigment weigher
Weighs pigments for use in production of hard-surface floor covering: Reviews pattern schedule to determine colors required. Moves bags of designated pigments from storage area to scales, using handtruck. Weighs prescribed pigments, dumps pigment into container, and marks container to indicate sequence in which color should be charged into mixer.
GOE: 06.03.02 STRENGTH: L GED: R3 M2 L3 SVP: 4 DLU: 77

590.662-010 CONTROLS OPERATOR, MOLDED GOODS (fabrication, nec)
Controls processing of molded hard-surface floor covering on table and in consolidating presses: Starts mechanism that moves carrier (backing) over table and starts color-depositing cycles. Pushes lever to move goods from repair table into flat-bed presses that consolidate carrier and color mix into molded hard-surface floor covering. Observes table operations from control booth to detect equipment malfunction or signals from table crew, and stops table movement to allow STRICKLER ATTENDANT (fabrication, nec) to make adjustments. Reads specifications to determine length of goods required for stoving and affixes register slip on material, at point determined, to guide stoving workers.
GOE: 06.02.18 STRENGTH: L GED: R3 M2 L3 SVP: 5 DLU: 77

590.662-014 MECHANICAL OXIDIZER (fabrication, nec)
Controls one or more units of oxidizing equipment to process oils for use in production of hard-surface floor covering: Turns valves to charge prescribed amount of ingredients into equipment, according to formula. Adjusts valves to regulate air supply, as specified, to obtain oxidation. Sets heat controls to maintain prescribed temperature during oxidizing cycle. Tests viscosity of mixture, using viscometer. Observes color of batch during process to determine completion of oxidation, using knowledge gained from previous experience. Opens bottom door to discharge material from oxidizer or starts pumps to remove material for further processing.
GOE: 06.02.18 STRENGTH: M GED: R3 M3 L3 SVP: 5 DLU: 77

590.662-018 MIXING-ROLL OPERATOR (fabrication, nec)
Controls mixing machine to blend asphalt paste of two or more colors to form marbleized asphalt tile: Starts machine and turns valves to heat rollers to specified temperature, or until surface of rollers feels hot enough to melt and mix asphalt. Shovels or feeds asphalt paste of prescribed colors between rollers until mixing appears complete. Signals other workers to cut off and catch marbleized material emerging from machine, and directs helpers who assist in mixing, rolling, and cutting product.
GOE: 06.04.19 STRENGTH: M GED: R3 M2 L3 SVP: 4 DLU: 77

590.662-022 STOVE-CARRIAGE OPERATOR (fabrication, nec)
Operates stove carriage to form bight (top bend) in floor covering and to feed floor covering into curing stoves, working as member of team: Turns crank to position carriage over batten irons. Adjusts controls to form bight and dip (lower curve). Places cone (hollow cylinder) in curve of dip to prevent kinks and sticking. Places spacing strips of prescribed material over batten irons to form cushion for additional layer of floor covering. Marks or labels sections for sampling. May be designated according to tasks performed as Bight Maker (fabrication, nec); Carriage Feeder (fabrication, nec).
GOE: 06.02.18 STRENGTH: M GED: R3 M2 L2 SVP: 4 DLU: 77

590.665-010 OVEN OPERATOR (fabrication, nec)
Tends oven that dries saturated or coated paper felt for use as base or carrier for hard-surface floor covering: Adjusts panel controls to regulate feed of material and temperature of oven. Examines material for paint streaks. Cleans paint-application unit, using spatula or scraper. Observes material for defective splices, tears, and faulty guide alignment.
GOE: 06.04.14 STRENGTH: L GED: R2 M1 L2 SVP: 3 DLU: 77

590.665-014 PRESS-MACHINE OPERATOR (fabrication, nec)
Tends machine that presses sheets of floor covering onto felt base: Positions roll of felt on machine spindle, using hoist. Turns steam valves to adjust temperature of roller presses of machine. Places sheets of covering on top of felt, and starts machine that presses materials together to form designs. Inspects sheets of floor covering emerging from rollers of machine, and discards defective sheets. May adjust rollers to maintain specified thickness of floor covering, using handtools.
GOE: 06.04.19 STRENGTH: M GED: R2 M2 L2 SVP: 2 DLU: 77

590.665-018 WINDER OPERATOR (fabrication, nec) alternate titles: roll-up operator
Tends winding machine that rolls lengths of floor covering between various stages of processing, working as member of crew: Removes spindle from dolly

and positions spindle in winding machine, using power hoist. Pulls end of floor covering sheet through winder and secures sheet to empty spindle, using tape. Starts machine, and regulates speed of winder to maintain even winding. Adjusts tension rolls on machine and sets yardage counter, using handtools. Examines material for pinholes, using magnifying glass. Stops machine when splices reach winder, indicating end of roll. Tears or cuts spliced section, tapes end of sheet to prevent unwinding, and removes full spindle of floor covering from machine. Records locations of pinholes and other imperfections on card and attaches card to full spindle. May stop machine during winding and cut out designated defective sections of floor covering.
GOE: 06.04.09 STRENGTH: H GED: R2 M1 L1 SVP: 2 DLU: 77

590.667-010 STOVE-BOTTOM WORKER (fabrication, nec)
Removes cones (hollow cylinders) from dips (lower curves) in floor covering hanging in curing stoves and replaces cones with larger ones to prevent faces of floor covering from sticking together. Signals STOVE-CARRIAGE OPERATOR (fabrication, nec) at top of stoves to adjust length of dips to effect required spacing. Covers floor of stove with paper to prevent dip from touching floor. Attaches identifying tag to each dip according to length.
GOE: 06.04.19 STRENGTH: L GED: R2 M1 L2 SVP: 2 DLU: 77

590.682-010 CALENDER OPERATOR (fabrication, nec)
Operates calender machine to roll and compress asphalt or asbestos into sheeting to produce floor tile: Sets thermostat to specified temperature and turns valves to admit coolant. Observes temperature-recording chart and adjusts controls to maintain heat of rollers within specified limits. Regulates speed of conveyors that move asphalt or asbestos to calender. May regulate flow of marbleizing chips and wax onto sheet of asphalt or asbestos to attain specified pattern.
GOE: 06.02.18 STRENGTH: L GED: R3 M2 L3 SVP: 4 DLU: 77

590.684-010 CERAMIC CAPACITOR PROCESSOR (electron. comp.)
Performs any combination of following tasks to process substrate, electrode, and termination materials to form monolithic ceramic capacitors: Reviews work orders and production schedules to determine processing specifications. Deposits layer of dielectric ceramic material on thermoplastic sheets, using tape casting equipment. Cuts cast sheets into ceramic wafers. Verifies and sorts wafers according to thickness and quality, using thickness gauge and magnifying device. Deposits electrode material onto wafers, using silk screen printing machine. Heats and compresses stacks of imprinted, ceramic wafers to form laminates, using laminating press. Cuts laminate into chips, using bench-mounted cutting equipment or automatic cutter. Loads chips onto boat and fires chips in kiln to fuse laminated material. Applies conductive termination material to specified edges of ceramic chips, manually or using automatic dipping equipment. Fuses conductive termination material to ceramic chip, using automatic oven. Polishes fused chip, using tumbler. Solders lead wires to ceramic chip, manually or using automatic soldering machine. Encases capacitors in epoxy material.
GOE: 06.04.08 STRENGTH: L GED: R2 M2 L2 SVP: 3 DLU: 80

590.684-014 ELECTRONIC-COMPONENT PROCESSOR (electron. comp.)
Performs any combination of following tasks to process materials into finished or semifinished electronic components: Reads work orders, formulas, and processing charts, and receives verbal instructions to determine specifications and sequence of operations. Weighs or measures specified ingredients and binding agents, using scales and graduates. Mixes and grinds material, using manual or automatic machines and equipment. Loads, unloads, monitors operation, and adjusts controls of various processing machines and equipment that bake, diffuse, cast, x ray, cut, polish, coat, plate, silk-screen, and perform similar operations to prepare, combine, or change structure of materials to produce compositions with specific electronic properties. Cleans materials as required prior to processing operations, using solvents. Inspects, measures, and tests components according to specifications, using measuring instruments and test equipment. Encloses components in housings. Stamps or etches identifying information on finished component. Counts, sorts, and weighs processed items. Maintains manual or computerized records of production and inspection data. May be designated according to duties performed as Baker; Beads (electron. comp.); Firer (electron. comp.); Pellet-Preparation Operator (electron. comp.); Preforming-Machine Operator (electron. comp.); Vacuum-Evaporation Operator (electron. comp.); Weight-Count Operator (electron. comp.). Assembly of processed materials, parts, and components is covered under ELECTRONICS ASSEMBLER (electron. comp.) 726.684-018 and ELECTRONICS ASSEMBLER, DEVELOPMENTAL (electron. comp.) 726.261-010.
GOE: 06.04.19 STRENGTH: L GED: R2 M2 L2 SVP: 3 DLU: 88

590.684-018 ETCHED-CIRCUIT PROCESSOR (electron. comp.)
Performs any combination of following tasks to print and etch conductive patterns on copper-faced plastic, fiberglass, or epoxy board to fabricate printed circuit boards (PCB's): Cuts board to designated size, using sheet metal shears, following written or verbal instructions. Sands board and either places board in vapor degreaser or immerses board in chemical solution to clean and remove oxides and other contaminants. Sprays or brushes light-sensitive enamel on copper surface and places board in whirler machine to spread enamel evenly, or tends machine that flows light-sensitive resist over board. Laminates light-sensitive dry film to board, using heat and pressure equipment. Exposes board and circuit negative to light in contact printer for specified period of time to transfer

image of circuit to board. Immerses exposed board in solution to develop acid-resistant circuit pattern on surface. Compares board to sample to verify development of pattern. Applies acid resist over sections of pattern not developed, using brush. Immerses board in acid or tends etching machine to etch conductive pattern on copper surface. Immerses board in solution to dissolve enamel. Drills holes in board, using drill press, following work sample, drawing, and diagrams. Installs hardware, such as brackets, eyelets, and terminals, using eyelet machine and hand arbors. Reduces circuit artwork prior to printing onto board, using reduction camera. Prints conductive pattern onto board, using silkscreen printing device. Fabricates PCB used as prototype of production model.
GOE: 06.02.32 STRENGTH: L GED: R3 M3 L3 SVP: 4 DLU: 87

590.684-022 SEMICONDUCTOR PROCESSOR (electron. comp.)
Performs any combination of following tasks to process materials used in manufacture of electronic semiconductors: Saws, breaks, cleans, and weighs semiconductor materials to prepare materials for crystal growing. Forms seed crystal for crystal growing, using x-ray equipment, drill, and sanding machine. Loads semiconductor material, seed crystal, and dopant into crystal growing furnace and monitors furnace to grow crystal ingot of specified characteristics. Grinds ingot to attain specified diameter and cylindricity, using grinding machine. Locates crystal axis of ingot, using x-ray equipment, and grinds *flat* on ingot. Saws ingot into wafers, using power saw. Etches, laps, polishes, and heat treats wafers to produce wafers of specified thickness and finish, using etching equipment, lapping and polishing machines, and furnace. Cleans materials, seed crystals, ingots, and wafers, using cleaning, etching, and sandblasting equipment. Inspects materials, ingots, and wafers for surface defects. Measures dimensions of ingots and wafers, using precision measuring instruments. Tests electrical characteristics of materials, ingots, and wafers, using electrical test equipment.
GOE: 06.04.32 STRENGTH: M GED: R2 M2 L2 SVP: 3 DLU: 86

590.684-026 ETCHER-STRIPPER, SEMICONDUCTOR WAFERS (electron. comp.)
Immerses semiconductor wafers in series of chemical baths to etch circuitry patterns into or to strip excess photoresist from wafer surfaces: Places semiconductor wafers in containers, such as boats or cassettes, using vacuum wand or tweezers. Immerses loaded containers in series of chemical and water baths to etch circuitry patterns into or strip excess photoresist from wafer surfaces. Places loaded container into air or spin dryer and pushes buttons to activate drying cycle. May visually inspect etched and stripped wafer, using microscope, to detect scratches, contaminants, and to verify conformance to specifications. May tend plasma (gas) etch machine to etch circuitry patterns into wafer surfaces. May clean and maintain chemical baths.
GOE: 06.04.19 STRENGTH: M GED: R2 M1 L2 SVP: 2 DLU: 88

590.684-030 MATERIAL PREPARATION WORKER (electron. comp.)
Performs any combination of following tasks involved in cleaning, sorting, breaking, weighing, and packaging chunks of silicon for crystal growing: Sandblasts chunks of silicon or immerses chunks in cleaning tanks to remove contaminants. Breaks chunks of silicon into pieces of specified size, using hammer. Tests and sorts silicon pieces according to resistivity type and level, using resistivity device or meter. Weighs out specified amounts of silicon to prepare charges (specified amounts of materials) for crystal growing process, loads silicon into charge can, and records identifying information on label of charge can. May transport charges to crystal growing department.
GOE: 06.03.02 STRENGTH: M GED: R2 M2 L2 SVP: 4 DLU: 86

590.684-034 PHOTO MASK CLEANER (electron. comp.)
Performs any combination of following tasks to clean production photo mask plates used in fabrication of semiconductor devices: Reads specifications sheet to verify type of photo mask plate and number of production runs for each plate. Marks number of production runs on border of each photo mask plate, using diamond scribe. Immerses photo mask plates into series of chemical baths to strip photoresist from photo mask. Places photo mask plates in chamber of specified cleaning machine and starts machine that automatically cleans and dries photo mask plates. Places photo mask plates in chamber of coating machine and starts machine that automatically deposits specified coating onto photo mask. Monitors operation of machines. Inspects photo mask plates for defects or insufficient cleaning, using microscope. Records process and inspection information in logbook.
GOE: 06.04.34 STRENGTH: L GED: R2 M1 L2 SVP: 2 DLU: 86

590.684-038 POLYSILICON PREPARATION WORKER (electron. comp.)
Performs any combination of following tasks to prepare polysilicon for crystal growing process: Operates drilling machine to remove core sample from polysilicon rod for evaluation. Breaks polysilicon rod into chunks, using hammer. Removes tungsten filament from chunks, using circular saw or drill. Immerses polysilicon chunks into series of vats containing chemical solutions to remove contaminants, using steel basket and hoist. Breaks chunks of polysilicon into pieces, using hammer, to prepare polysilicon for meltdown in crystal growing process. Records production information.
GOE: 06.04.19 STRENGTH: V GED: R2 M2 L2 SVP: 2 DLU: 86

590.684-042 INTEGRATED CIRCUIT FABRICATOR (electron. comp.) alternate titles: wafer fab operator
Performs any combination of following tasks to fabricate integrated circuits on semiconductor wafers according to written specifications: Loads semiconductor wafers into processing containers for processing or into inspection equipment, using tweezers or vacuum wand. Cleans and dries photo masks and semiconductor wafers to remove contaminants, using cleaning and drying equipment. Inspects photo masks and wafers for defects, such as scratches, using microscope, magnifying lens, or computer-aided inspection equipment. Deposits layer of photoresist solution on wafers, using automated equipment. Aligns photo mask pattern on photoresist layer, exposes pattern to ultraviolet light, and develops pattern, using specialized equipment. Alters electrical nature of wafer layers according to photo mask patterns to form integrated circuits on wafers, using equipment, such as acid baths, diffusion furnaces, ion implant equipment, and metallization equipment. Removes photoresist from wafers, using stripping chemicals and equipment. Inspects and measures circuitry for conformance to pattern specifications, using microscope with measuring attachment. Tests functioning of circuitry, using electronic test equipment and standard procedures.
GOE: 06.04.34 STRENGTH: L GED: R3 M2 L2 SVP: 3 DLU: 90

590.685-010 BACKING-IN-MACHINE TENDER (fabrication, nec)
Tends machine that feeds molded floor covering into stove for heat-treating: Positions roll of floor covering on spindle of machine, using power hoist. Threads floor covering through rollers and attaches cable that pulls floor covering into stove. Presses foot brake to control feed of material. Removes empty spindle from stand, replaces it with full roll, and attaches material to end of previous roll.
GOE: 06.04.19 STRENGTH: H GED: R2 M1 L1 SVP: 2 DLU: 77

590.685-014 COATING-MACHINE OPERATOR (fabrication, nec) alternate titles: coater
Tends machine that coats asphalt-impregnated felt paper with paint to seal in asphalt and prevent discoloration of light-colored enamels used for finishing: Mounts roll of paper on machine spindle and feeds end of roll through machine or splices end to roll in machine. Fills hoppers with paint. Starts machine that coats paper with paint and observes operation and rewinding of paper in *festoon* ovens for drying. Adjusts oven controls to maintain specified temperature for drying coated paper. Removes paper rewound on rolls from oven when dried.
GOE: 06.04.21 STRENGTH: M GED: R3 M2 L3 SVP: 4 DLU: 77

590.685-018 DIAMOND BLENDER (cutlery-hrdwr.)
Tends mixing machine that blends metal powders with diamonds and powered press that presses metal powder and mixed diamond powder onto bottom surface of mold cavity: Weighs and dumps ingredients into mixing machine. Starts machine that blends metal powder with diamonds. Removes mixture from machine and distributes portions to mold loaders. Requisitions graphite molds and punches. Pours metal powder onto backing cavity of mold and mixed diamond powder onto front of mold cavity, and places mold on table of powered press. Starts machine that presses powders onto bottom surface of mold cavity. Removes mold from press and inserts separation plates between center surfaces of molds. Glues molds together. Records number of molds filled from each diamond batch. Removes excess particles from induction-fired molds.
GOE: 06.04.19 STRENGTH: M GED: R2 M2 L2 SVP: 4 DLU: 77

590.685-022 DIPPER (fabrication, nec) alternate titles: gauger
Tends equipment that applies inflammable tips to kitchen, penny, and book matches: Raises or lowers conveyor or dip roll in tank. Turns handwheel to adjust machine to immerse matches to specified depth in matchhead compound. Sets thermostat or reads thermometer in compound dip tank and turns steam and cold water valves to regulate compound temperature and viscosity. Compares size of matchheads passing on conveyor with drawings of acceptable matchheads and cuts unacceptable matches from conveyor, using long-handled push knife. Drains and washes dip tanks to remove thickened compound. May replenish compounds and paraffin in dip tank [COMPOUND FILLER (chemical)]. May replace worn or bent cutter blades that trim wood matches, using handtools. May tend automatic machine that cuts rolls of cardboard into strips and apply inflammable material to matchheads and be designated Strip-Machine Tender (fabrication, nec).
GOE: 06.04.21 STRENGTH: M GED: R2 M1 L2 SVP: 3 DLU: 77

590.685-026 DRY-CHARGE-PROCESS ATTENDANT (elec. equip.)
Tends equipment that washes, treats, and dries formed dry-charge battery plates: Turns valve to drain water into bath compartment. Mixes solutions, according to specifications, in measuring tank and drains solutions into other compartments. Ignites oven burner and starts blower. Observes thermometer and gauges and adjusts temperature control and valves to maintain specified temperature and pressure in dryer. Starts and regulates speed of conveyor that conveys batteries through bath, solutions, and dryer. Determines oxygen content of gas in oven, using testing device and adjusts airflow to reduce oxidation of plates. Transfers batteries from forming department to machine, using handtruck. Strips connectors from batteries and loads batteries into racks in water bath. Loads containers (battery boxes) from pallet to handtruck at discharge end of machine. Unloads batteries from dryer and tests each battery for moisture content, using resistance meter. Segregates damp batteries and inserts dry batteries in containers according to specified polarity. Transfers batteries to final assembly area, using handtruck. May tend conveyor-equipped drying compartment that dries battery plates and be designated Plate-Drying-Machine Tender (elec. equip.).
GOE: 06.04.19 STRENGTH: M GED: R3 M2 L2 SVP: 4 DLU: 77

590.685-034 FIRER (jewelry-silver.) alternate titles: baker; kiln operator
Tends electric oven that fuses enamel onto metal jewelry parts: Sets controls to heat oven to specified temperature. Places tray or rack containing jewelry

parts, on which liquid or powder enamel has been applied, in oven. Removes tray or rack from oven after prescribed period, using tongs, and allows enameled parts to cool. May determine when settings are sufficiently heated by observing color of enamel. May anneal jewelry parts by heating them in oven to soften metal preparatory to forming and shaping them.
GOE: 06.04.21 STRENGTH: L GED: R2 M1 L2 SVP: 3 DLU: 77

590.685-038 HEEL SPRAYER, MACHINE (boot & shoe) alternate titles: sprayer
Tends machine that sprays wood or plastic heels with lacquer for preservative and decorative effect: Pours lacquer into dispenser. Turns valve to adjust spray mechanism and seats heel on spindle. Activates revolving spindle and spray mechanism to spray lacquer on heel. Examines heel to determine coverage. Adds thinning solution to lacquer as needed. Loads finished heels on rack to dry. May spray leather heels with wax.
GOE: 06.04.21 STRENGTH: L GED: R2 M1 L2 SVP: 3 DLU: 77

590.685-042 IRONER (button & notion) alternate titles: zipper ironer
Tends machine that removes wrinkles from plastic or nylon zippers: Mounts reel of continuous chain zipper onto payoff spindle and turns steam valve to heat grooved irons. Depresses pedal to separate irons and positions chain between irons with nylon or plastic filament in groove. Releases pedal to close irons and starts machine.
GOE: 06.04.02 STRENGTH: L GED: R2 M1 L1 SVP: 2 DLU: 77

590.685-046 JEWELRY COATER (jewelry-silver.)
Tends equipment that coats jewelry parts with powdered enamel: Places jewelry on racks, rods, or in wire trays, and sprays jewelry with agar solution for subsequent application of powdered enamel on metal, using spray gun. Fills hopper of machine with specified shade of powdered enamel. Places rods or racks on conveyor and starts vibrating machine that shakes powder onto parts passing under opening. Dries enamel-coated parts in oven preparatory to firing them at high temperature.
GOE: 06.04.21 STRENGTH: L GED: R2 M1 L2 SVP: 2 DLU: 77

590.685-050 ROLL-UP-GUIDER OPERATOR (fabrication, nec)
Tends equipment that moves hard-surface floor covering over inspection table, trims selvage edges, and rolls up inspected material, working as member of crew: Starts machine that pulls hard-surface floor covering across cutting table and onto roll-up spindle. Sets selvage knives on both sides of table to cut specified width from edge of material. Scans floor covering through mirrors for inspection marks, and stops equipment to cut out defective area, using linoleum knife. Guides floor covering under knives to make specified lengthwise split of defective area from material.
GOE: 06.04.09 STRENGTH: M GED: R2 M1 L1 SVP: 4 DLU: 77

590.685-054 WAD IMPREGNATOR (ordnance)
Tends tumbling barrels that impregnate shotgun-shell filler wads with wax to seal propellant charge against moisture and facilitate ejection of wad when shell is fired: Weighs and dumps specified quantity of wads and wax into steam-heated barrel. Stops barrel at end of prescribed time and examines wads for color shade indicating sufficient impregnation. Weighs specified number of impregnated wads and compares with weight of equal number of dry wads, using chart, to confirm that correct amount of wax has been absorbed.
GOE: 06.04.14 STRENGTH: M GED: R2 M1 L2 SVP: 2 DLU: 77

590.685-058 WAD LUBRICATOR (ordnance) alternate titles: bar-gauger and lubricator tender
Tends batteries of automatic machines that tumble wads for shotgun shells to remove feathery edges, gauge thickness, and lubricate circumference with wax: Fills tumbling barrel with wads from overhead hopper and starts tumbler rotating. Examines wads after estimated time to verify that edges are smooth. Starts machines that reject too thick or too thin wads and replaces filled barrels under accepted and rejected chutes. Dumps accepted wads into pneumatic conveyor that carries them to lubricator hopper. Turns steam valves to liquefy and regulate flow of wax over lubricating plate. Starts feeder plate to arrange wads flat-side-up and feed them between roller and lubricating plate that coats sides with wax. Weighs designated number of wads at prescribed intervals before and after lubricating to determine amount of wax applied. Clears jammed wads, using wire hook.
GOE: 06.04.14 STRENGTH: M GED: R2 M1 L2 SVP: 2 DLU: 77

590.685-062 CLEANING MACHINE TENDER, SEMICONDUCTOR WAFERS (electron. comp.)
Tends equipment that chemically cleans semiconductor wafers used in manufacture of semiconductor components, such as transistors, diodes, and integrated circuits: Places specified program card into cleaning equipment. Places wafers in cleaning trays, using tweezers. Loads trays into cleaning equipment. Pours cleaning solutions, such as hydrogen peroxide, sulfuric acid, and hydrochloric acid into specified tank of cleaning equipment. Presses buttons to activate cleaning cycle. Removes semiconductor wafers from trays, using tweezers. Visually inspects semiconductor wafers for blemishes. Maintains production reports.
GOE: 06.04.39 STRENGTH: L GED: R2 M2 L2 SVP: 2 DLU: 86

590.685-066 COATING EQUIPMENT OPERATOR, PRINTED CIRCUIT BOARDS (electron. comp.)
Tends automated equipment that applies photosensitive coating of masking ink to printed circuit board (PCB) panels to facilitate development of circuit design on boards in fabrication of PCBs: Pushes buttons and switches to start heater, conveyor, and coating equipment. Measures conveyor travel time of sample panel, using stopwatch, and weighs sample panel, using digital scale, to ensure that specifications are met. Turns dials to adjust conveyor speed and to add or delete masking ink in solution, as needed. Feeds panels onto conveyor of automated equipment that cleans, heats, and applies masking ink to panels. Removes panels from unloading rack upon completion of coating process and dries panels in oven. Records production data.
GOE: 06.04.19 STRENGTH: M GED: R2 M2 L2 SVP: 3 DLU: 86

590.685-070 DIFFUSION FURNACE OPERATOR, SEMICONDUCTOR WAFERS (electron. comp.)
Tends furnaces that diffuse chemicals into semiconductor wafer surface to alter electrical characteristics of wafer or to protect wafer surfaces: Places semiconductor wafers in containers, such as *boat* or cassette, using vacuum wand or tweezers. Places loaded container on furnace loader, such as conveyor, track, sled, or tube. Pushes button to advance wafer containers into furnace or pushes wafer container into furnace tube, using quartz rod. Pushes buttons or keys commands on control panel keyboard to activate furnace diffusion cycle. Observes gauges and meters to verify that furnace gases and temperature meet specifications. Maintains production records. Turns dials to adjust furnace gases and temperature, if required. May clean semiconductor wafers, using cleaning equipment, to remove contaminants prior to diffusion. May test and inspect wafer, using testing equipment, to measure resistivity and thickness.
GOE: 06.04.19 STRENGTH: L GED: R2 M2 L2 SVP: 4 DLU: 86

590.685-074 ETCH OPERATOR, SEMICONDUCTOR WAFERS (electron. comp.)
Tends etch machine and equipment that remove metal and photoresist and etches electronic circuitry into metallized substrate of wafer surface, according to processing specifications: Places wafers in boats, using tweezers or vacuum wand. Places boats in etch machine or equipment. Turns dials, sets timer and gauges on equipment, or presses buttons on machine to activate etch cycle to etch or remove materials from wafer surface, such as metal or photoresist. Inspects wafer to verify that wafers are not over-etched and that photoresist has been removed, using microscope. May measure specified dimensions of wafers, using microscope measuring attachment. May manually immerse loaded boats into chemical solution baths to etch circuitry into wafer surface.
GOE: 06.04.19 STRENGTH: L GED: R2 M1 L2 SVP: 2 DLU: 88

590.685-078 ETCHER (electron. comp.) alternate titles: wafer etcher
Tends etching equipment that reduces thickness of semiconductor wafers: Transfers wafers from storage container to chemical-resistant *boat*. Monitors control panel of etching equipment to verify that etching solution temperatures meet processing specifications. Immerses boat of wafers into series of sinks containing etching solutions and water rinses and sets timers. Measures wafer thickness before and after etching, using thickness gauge, and calculates wafer thickness removed by etching. Tends machine that rinses and dries etched wafers. Records production details on work order. Replaces etching and rinsing solutions in equipment and cleans work area. May measure wafer flatness, using flatness gauge. May measure diameter of semiconductor crystals, using micrometer, and tend etching equipment that reduces crystal diameter. May calculate etching time based on thickness of material to be removed from wafers on crystals.
GOE: 06.04.19 STRENGTH: M GED: R2 M2 L2 SVP: 2 DLU: 86

590.685-082 STRIPPER-ETCHER, PRINTED CIRCUIT BOARDS (electron. comp.)
Tends equipment that strips photoresist film and etches layers of copper laminate from exposed surface of printed circuit board (PCB) panels leaving unexposed areas to form conductive circuitry pattern: Reads process specifications and adjusts equipment controls to regulate conveyor speed, spray intensity, and solution strengths and temperatures. Positions copper panels coated with photoresist on conveyor that carries panels through series of processing units, such as sprayers, rinsers, scrubbers, and dryers. Starts and monitors equipment that chemically strips photoresist and excess copper from exposed areas of PCB panels leaving unexposed copper to form circuitry pattern. Observes equipment operation, gauges, and meters to detect malfunctions or variance from specifications. Visually examines sample boards during and after processing for conformance to specifications. Notifies supervisor of equipment malfunction or substandard etching quality. Reroutes panels through processing units to complete stripping or etching process. May periodically change or adjust chemicals and solutions. May test acid solution, using pH meter. May manually immerse panels into processing tanks. May inspect circuitry pattern on panels, using microscope. May be identified according to process involved and be designated Etcher, Printed Circuit Boards (electron. comp.); Stripper, Printed Circuit Boards (electron. comp.).
GOE: 06.04.19 STRENGTH: M GED: R2 M2 L2 SVP: 3 DLU: 88

590.685-086 METALLIZATION EQUIPMENT TENDER, SEMICONDUCTORS (comm. equip.; electron. comp.; inst. & app.)
Tends equipment that deposits layer of metal on semiconductor surfaces to provide electrical contact between circuit components: Places semiconductors, such as silicon wafers, crystal units, or fiber optic microchannel plates, in container, using vacuum wand or tweezers. Cleans semiconductors to remove contaminants prior to metal deposition, using chemical baths or automatic cleaning

equipment. Loads semiconductors into metallization equipment holders, using vacuum wand or tweezers. Places loaded holders and specified metals in chamber of equipment that deposits layer of metal, such as aluminum, gold, or platinum, on semiconductor surfaces, by *sputtering* or evaporation process. Manipulates equipment controls that start and adjust metallization process, following processing specifications. Measures electrical conductivity and thickness of metal layer on processed semiconductors, using test equipment. Maintains chemicals and metals for equipment. May tend equipment that deposits insulating layer of glass onto semiconductor wafer surfaces and be designated Glass Deposition Tender (electron. comp.).
GOE: 06.04.19 STRENGTH: L GED: R3 M2 L2 SVP: 3 DLU: 88

590.685-090 CURING OVEN ATTENDANT (aircraft mfg.; electron. comp.)
Tends electric ovens that cure electronic and aircraft parts, such as printed circuit boards and composite structures and assemblies: Reads work order to determine process specifications for parts to be cured. Loads parts in oven. Pushes button on oven to start curing cycle. Observes control panel indicators, such as gauges, dials, and recorders, to monitor oven operation. Unloads parts at end of curing cycle. Records processing information in curing log. Cleans oven and work area. May operate material handling equipment to load, unload, and transport parts. May adjust controls to regulate processing time and temperature.
GOE: 06.04.19 STRENGTH: M GED: R2 M1 L1 SVP: 2 DLU: 86

590.685-094 PLASMA ETCHER, PRINTED CIRCUIT BOARDS (electron. comp.)
Tends plasma equipment that dry etches unprotected copper from substrate boards or panels to form circuit patterns on printed circuit boards (PCBs): Hangs boards or panels on racks in plasma tank and locks door. Adjusts controls, according to process specifications, to set time, wattage, and percentage of oxygen and nitrogen gases in plasma tank. Pushes button to activate equipment that automatically plasma-etches excess copper from boards or panels to form circuit pattern. Removes boards or panels after processing and inspects boards for completeness of etching process, using microscope. May tend computer-controlled plasma etch equipment that automatically computes and adjusts control settings for time, wattage, and gas content based on data entered, such as quantity of boards and lot number.
GOE: 06.04.19 STRENGTH: L GED: R3 M2 L2 SVP: 4 DLU: 86

590.685-098 ROOFING-MACHINE TENDER (nonmet. min.)
Tends machine that cools and dries coatings applied to roofing material prior to cutting process: Reads work schedule to determine type, amount, and color of roofing material to be processed. Selects machine attachments, such as paint rollers or embosser, depending on material to be processed, and places attachments in designated slots on machine. Places hoses connected to paint tank on machine into paint barrels to circulate paint through tank, or turns handwheel to lower embosser that presses design onto roofing material. Flips switches, turns dials, or pushes buttons to activate pumps that recycle paint, to circulate water to spray system and cooling drums, to raise or lower rollers to flatten and smooth granules on roofing material, to control length of roofing material in cooling or drying sections, and to start hot or cool air blowers. Patrols cooling section of machine to detect sand stuck on rollers or cooling drums, and scrapes off sand to prevent puncture damage to roofing material, using scraper. Observes hand signals of other workers and adjusts speed of rollers, temperature of air, or distance between rollers in drying section of machine, depending on type of signal. Rethreads roofing material through machine after break, assisted by other workers.
GOE: 06.04.09 STRENGTH: L GED: R2 M1 L1 SVP: 3 DLU: 86

590.685-102 WAFER CLEANER (electron. comp.)
Tends equipment that cleans surface of semiconductor wafers after slicing or polishing: Reviews work orders to determine processing steps. Sets temperature controls on automatic chemical cleaning machine or sinks of chemical cleaning station. Places containers of semiconductor wafers into drum of cleaning machine or into heated sinks of solutions in cleaning station to remove dust, oil, wax, slurry, or debris from surface of wafers. May load containers of wafers into scrubbing machine that brushes and sprays contaminants from wafers and dries wafers. May tend machine that dries wafers.
GOE: 06.04.19 STRENGTH: L GED: R2 M2 L2 SVP: 2 DLU: 86

590.686-010 COATING-MACHINE-OPERATOR HELPER (fabrication, nec) alternate titles: loop tender
Mounts roll of asphalt-impregnated felt paper on machine that paints paper to make floor covering: Observes paint level in pans to ensure that prescribed amount is pumped into pans to cover rolls. Examines impregnated felt paper to detect tears. Notifies COATING-MACHINE OPERATOR (fabrication, nec) of discrepancies. Removes painted floor covering from machine.
GOE: 06.04.21 STRENGTH: M GED: R2 M1 L1 SVP: 2 DLU: 77

590.686-014 GUIDER (fabrication, nec)
Guides material used in production of hard-surface floor covering, through rollers to and from processing equipment: Pushes end of material into rollers that convey material through saturation, coating, consolidation, or curing processes. Observes material in passage to detect unevenness or misalignment with marginal markings on roller guides. Pulls material into line manually or turns wheel of mechanical guiding device to straighten material. May be designated according to phase of operation or type of material being processed as Carrier

Guider (fabrication, nec); Dip Guider, Stoves (fabrication, nec); Roll Guider, Mold Goods (fabrication, nec); Side Guider (fabrication, nec).
GOE: 06.04.40 STRENGTH: M GED: R1 M1 L1 SVP: 2 DLU: 77

590.687-010 LABORER (fabrication, nec)
Performs any combination of following tasks in candlemaking plant: Rethreads molds in casting machines with wick material from spools. Mixes batches of colored wax, according to established formulas. Cleans wax reservoir, vats, and processing equipment, using water, soap, and detergents. Loads and unloads trucks. Carries or handtrucks materials, products, and equipment to workers or warehouse.
GOE: 06.04.34 STRENGTH: H GED: R2 M1 L1 SVP: 2 DLU: 77

590.687-014 PLASTIC-JOINT MAKER (brick & tile)
Casts plastic joints for sewer pipe in joint mold: Removes dirt, dust, or grease from pipe, using airhose, rags, and solvent. Examines pipe for straightness, chips, or cracks. Brushes adhesive on end of pipe. Loads pipe on conveyor, using air hoist. Positions joint mold on pipe. Lifts container and pours plastic materials into mold. Places pipe on conveyor leading to curing oven. Removes cured pipe from conveyor at discharge end of oven. Trims excess plastic from joint, using knife.
GOE: 06.04.32 STRENGTH: H GED: R2 M1 L1 SVP: 3 DLU: 77

590.687-018 RACK LOADER (fabrication, nec)
Loads felt-base floor coverings onto racks of oven for drying. Strings pull-in cable and clamp through drying oven rack. Fastens clamp to end of floor covering emerging from printing machine, and pulls floor covering onto oven rack. Removes clamp and pull-in cable upon filling of loading rack.
GOE: 06.04.40 STRENGTH: M GED: R1 M1 L1 SVP: 1 DLU: 77

590.687-022 RUG CUTTER (fabrication, nec)
Cuts specified lengths of floor covering from spindle of rolling machine, using knife.
GOE: 06.04.24 STRENGTH: M GED: R1 M1 L1 SVP: 1 DLU: 77

599 MISCELLANEOUS PROCESSING OCCUPATIONS, N.E.C.

This group includes miscellaneous occupations, not elsewhere classified, concerned with processing materials and products.

599.132-010 SUPERVISOR, TUMBLERS (ordnance) alternate titles: wash-barrel leader
Supervises and coordinates activities of TUMBLER OPERATORS (any industry) engaged in removing scale, burrs, or grease from gun or cartridge parts. Mixes acid solutions in tank according to formula. May experiment with new formulas for abrasives and cleansing materials to be used in tumbling barrels. Performs other duties as described under SUPERVISOR (any industry) Master Title.
GOE: 06.02.01 STRENGTH: L GED: R4 M3 L3 SVP: 7 DLU: 77

599.137-010 SUPERINTENDENT, SEED MILL (agriculture)
Supervises and coordinates activities of workers engaged in drying, cleaning, sorting, treating, and packaging seeds in seed processing plant: Observes and feels incoming seed shipments to determine cleaning and drying requirements, utilizing knowledge of seed characteristics and processing standards. Instructs and monitors workers in use of equipment that sifts debris from seeds, removes moisture from seeds, scrapes off outer layers of seed cover, and sorts seeds according to weight and size. Oversees treatment of seeds with specified chemicals to fill customer orders. Assists and directs workers in loading, unloading, and conveying seeds in warehouse and processing area, using forklift, and in boxing seeds for storage or shipment. Performs routine equipment maintenance, such as lubrication and replacement of parts.
GOE: 06.02.01 STRENGTH: M GED: R3 M2 L3 SVP: 6 DLU: 86

599.382-010 PAINT-SPRAYER OPERATOR, AUTOMATIC (any industry) alternate titles: spray-machine operator
Sets up and operates painting and drying units along conveyor line to coat metal, plastic, ceramic, and wood products with lacquer, paint, varnish, enamel, oil, or rustproofing material: Places or racks workpieces on conveyor. Turns valve to regulate water shield spray. Starts pumps to mix chemicals and paints, to fill tanks, and to control viscosity, adding prescribed amounts or proportions of paints, thinner, and chemicals to mixture. Screws specified nozzles into spray guns and positions nozzles to direct spray onto workpiece. Lights ovens, turns knobs, and observes gauges on control panel to set specified temperature and air circulation in oven, to synchronize speed of conveyor with action of spray guns and ovens, and to regulate air pressure in spray guns that atomize spray. Determines flow and viscosity of paints and quality of coating visually or by use of viscometer. May spray coated product with salt solution for prescribed time to determine resistance to corrosion. May be designated according to coating applied as Bonderite Operator (any industry); Control Operator, Flow Coat (elec. equip.); or according to article coated as Gunstock-Spray-Unit Adjuster (ordnance).
GOE: 06.02.21 STRENGTH: M GED: R3 M2 L3 SVP: 5 DLU: 77

599.382-014 EXHAUST EQUIPMENT OPERATOR (electron. comp.) alternate titles: exhaust operator
Sets up and controls exhaust equipment to remove gases and impurities from electron and cathode ray tubes, following procedure manuals, work orders, and

specifications: Reads production schedules and procedure manuals to determine tube specifications and operational sequence. Calculates equipment control settings, applying standard formulas to determine power, temperature, and vacuum, according to tube size and type. Sets controls on power supplies, ovens, and pumps according to calculations. Observes meters, gauges, and recording instruments during operation, and adjusts controls to ensure tubes are exhausted as specified. Troubleshoots exhaust equipment to locate malfunction when tubes fail to exhaust. Repairs faulty exhaust equipment, or notifies maintenance department of faulty equipment. May test and inspect tubes for leaks, using leak detection equipment. May set up and operate aging equipment to stabilize electrical properties of tube. May be designated according to type of equipment operated as Rotary Pump Operator (electron. comp.).
GOE: 06.01.03 STRENGTH: M GED: R4 M4 L4 SVP: 6 DLU: 89

599.585-010 STERILIZER (medical ser.; pharmaceut.; protective dev.) alternate titles: autoclave operator
Tends autoclave that sterilizes drug products, containers, supplies, instruments, and equipment: Places articles in autoclave manually or by use of electric hoist. Secures door or lid, turns dials to adjust temperature and pressure, and opens steam valve. Shuts off steam and removes sterilized articles after specified time. Records time and temperature setting and gauge readings. May wrap supplies and instruments in paper or cloth preparatory to sterilizing.
GOE: 06.04.19 STRENGTH: L GED: R3 M2 L3 SVP: 3 DLU: 77

599.665-010 SEED-CLEANER OPERATOR (agriculture; oils & grease) alternate titles: seed cleaner; seed-cleaning-machine operator
Tends machines that remove foreign matter from grass seed, grain, or cottonseed: Starts machines and turns handwheel to regulate flow of material into machines. Brushes cleaning screens, using wire brush to prevent clogging. Empties trash bags attached to machines.
GOE: 06.04.09 STRENGTH: L GED: R2 M1 L1 SVP: 2 DLU: 77

599.682-010 PAINTER, ELECTROSTATIC (any industry) alternate titles: electronic paint operator
Operates cone, disk, or nozzle-type electro-static painting equipment to spray negatively charged paint particles onto positively charged workpieces: Moves switches and dials to start flow current and to activate conveyor and paint spraying equipment. Turns valves and observes guages to set pressure and to control flow of paint to each spray station. Adjusts thermostat to maintain specified temperature in paint tanks. Inspects painted units for runs, sags, and unpainted areas. Readjusts pressure valves to control direction and pattern of spray and to correct flaws in coating. Cleans paint from ceiling and walls of booth, conveyor hooks or grid, and from disks, cones, spray heads, and hoses, using solvent and brush. May hand-spray parts to cover unpainted areas or apply rust preventative. May mix paint according to specifications, using viscometer to regulate consistency according to changes in atmospheric conditions.
GOE: 06.02.21 STRENGTH: L GED: R3 M2 L3 SVP: 4 DLU: 77

599.682-014 IMPREGNATOR AND DRIER (elec. equip.; electron. comp.)
Controls equipment such as tanks, vats, ovens, and retorts, to impregnate, dry, or bake insulating, preserving, sealing, or other materials into or onto electrical or electronic components, according to specifications: Reads work orders to determine process specifications and priorities. Loads components into or onto devices, such as racks, arbors, and baskets, manually or using hoist. Manipulates controls to start and stop equipment, such as impregnating tanks, vacuum tanks, and drying and curing ovens, and to regulate processing factors, such as flow of fluids into vats or tanks, vacuum pressure, temperature, and processing time. Monitors equipment to ensure conformance to processing specifications, and records processing information. May operate molding press to encase components in protective compounds. May examine processed components for defects. May trim excess material from components. May clean component parts prior to processing. May spray protective or other coating onto surface of components, using spray gun. May weigh or melt ingredients and mix compounds. May transport components to other areas of plant. May be designated according to processing material or activity involved as Drying-Equipment Operator (elec. equip.); Impregnator, Carbon Products (electron. comp.); Impregnator, Electrolytic Capacitors (electron. comp.); Wax Impregnator (electron. comp.).
GOE: 06.02.18 STRENGTH: M GED: R3 M2 L3 SVP: 5 DLU: 87

599.684-010 EQUIPMENT CLEANER (any industry) alternate titles: night cleaner
Cleans and sterilizes machinery, utensils, and equipment used to process or store products, such as chemicals, paint, food, or beverages: Turns valves to drain machines or tanks and disconnects pipes, using wrenches. Sprays machines, tanks, and conveyors with water to loosen and remove dirt or other foreign matter. Scrubs machines, tanks, tables, pans, bowls, compartments, and conveyors, using brushes, rags, cleaning preparations, and diluted acids. Rinses articles with water, and dries them with compressed air. Scrubs floors and walls, using brushes, rags, and diluted acids. Connects hoses and lines to pump and starts pump to circulate cleaning and sterilizing solution through hoses and lines. Scrubs interior of disconnected pipes, valves, spigots, gauges, and meters, using spiral brushes. Mixes cleaning solutions and diluted acids, according to formula. Draws off samples of cleaning solutions from mixing tanks for laboratory analysis. May replace defective sections of metal coils and lines, using handtools, soldering iron, and pipe couplings. May lubricate machinery. May be designated according to equipment cleaned as Beer-Coil Cleaner (any indus-

try); Lard-Tub Washer (meat products); Line Cleaner (beverage; dairy products); Pipe Washer (dairy products). May sterilize equipment and be designated Equipment Sterilizer (dairy products).
GOE: 06.04.39 STRENGTH: H GED: R2 M1 L2 SVP: 2 DLU: 80

599.684-014 SAMPLER (steel & rel.)
Collects samples of materials, such as benzol, coal, coke, sewer water, sulfate, and tar, and prepares them for laboratory analysis: Shovels coal into crusher to grind samples for analysis. Drops weighed sample of coke from drop-door bucket to steelplate, shakes shattered coke through screen of specified mesh and weighs and records weights of large and small sized coke. Weighs sample, dries it in oven, and reweighs sample of quenched coke to determine moisture content. Identifies type and source of sample on container label. May be designated according to source of sample as Sampler, Ovens (steel & rel.).
GOE: 06.03.02 STRENGTH: L GED: R2 M2 L2 SVP: 3 DLU: 77

599.685-014 BRAN MIXER (grain-feed mills)
Tends machine that mixes specified amounts of wheat and rye middlings with sawdust for use in cleaning tinplate and terneplate: Attaches empty sacks to discharge section of machine, starts machine, and dumps ingredients into hopper. Removes filled sacks and sews tops, using needle and twine. Weighs sacks and trucks them to storage area.
GOE: 06.04.19 STRENGTH: H GED: R2 M1 L1 SVP: 2 DLU: 77

599.685-018 CENTRIFUGE OPERATOR, PLASMA PROCESSING (medical ser.; pharmaceut.)
Tends centrifuges which separate plasma from whole blood for extraction of plasma: Packs plastic bags containing freshly drawn whole blood (whole blood units) into designated containers in centrifuge. Fastens centrifuge cover and depresses switch to activate centrifuge mechanism. Removes centrifuged whole blood units after designated time, examines each to confirm separation of plasma from whole blood, and places each whole blood unit in plasma extractor, positioning holes at top of plastic bag on metal prongs. Inserts plastic tube of transfer unit into each whole blood unit and observes process as plasma is extracted from upper portion of plastic bag into bottle, to make certain that no red blood cells are drawn into plasma bottle. Seals off bottle and returns plasma bottle to rack. Removes blood unit from holder and gives to nursing personnel for return to donor. Marks each plasma bottle with blood group as indicated on plastic bag to assure separation of blood groups and prevent cross-contamination of blood groups during fractionation. Stores filled bottles of plasma in freezer. Cleans centrifuges and work area.
GOE: 06.04.11 STRENGTH: L GED: R2 M2 L2 SVP: 2 DLU: 77

599.685-022 DEFINER (button & notion)
Tends battery of machines that tumble metal or plastic buttons in wire mesh barrels to remove mold flash (fins) or rough edges: Loads barrel with buttons. Pours specified amounts of cleaning compound into barrel. Bolts on lid and starts machine to rotate barrel and tumble buttons for specified length of time. Shakes sifter to separate buttons from cleaning compound and shot (ball bearings).
GOE: 06.04.10 STRENGTH: M GED: R2 M1 L1 SVP: 2 DLU: 77

599.685-026 DIPPER (any industry) alternate titles: dip painter; impregnator
Tends dipping tanks and auxiliary equipment that immerse and coat articles with liquids, such as paint, molten tin, latex, stain, or asphalt: Moves controls to maintain temperature, flow, and composition of liquid. Coats articles, using any of following methods: (1) Loads conveyor or transfer rack that automatically dips articles; (2) Loads wire basket and starts power hoist to lift and dip basket; (3) Dips articles in liquid. Removes excess coating, using rag or brush. May test quality of liquid, using chemically treated paper, color charts, or other devices. Adds coating solution according to test results or specifications. May tend centrifugal drier that dries coating and removes excess. May be designated according to coating applied as Asphalt Coater (elec. equip.); Enamel Dipper (any industry); Porcelain Slusher (any industry); Varnish Dipper (furniture); or according to article dipped as Broom-Handle Dipper (fabrication, nec); Painter, Spring (furniture; metal prod., nec). May be designated: Bluer (ordnance); Bonderizer (auto. mfg.); Clay-Products Glazer (elec. equip.); Paint Dipper (any industry); Rust Proofer (auto. mfg.); Screen-Frame Enameler (struct. metal); Stain Dipper (furniture); Tinner Operator, Connecting Rods (auto. mfg.); Vinyl Dipper (rubber goods).
GOE: 06.04.21 STRENGTH: M GED: R2 M1 L1 SVP: 2 DLU: 80

599.685-030 DIPPER AND BAKER (any industry) alternate titles: impregnating-tank operator
Dips assembled electrical equipment components into materials, such as varnish, enamel, or asphalt to insulate wires and coils and tends oven that dries dipped components: Pours dipping solution into vat and measures consistency with hydrometer, adding thinner to control density. Sets vat thermostat at prescribed temperature. Hangs or bolts components to be dipped, such as armatures or transformers, on racks, lifts them manually or by use of hand-operated hoist, and immerses them in vat for prescribed time. Removes components and places them on racks to drain. Sets oven temperature controls and places dipped units in oven to bake and dry for specified time. May clean and coat electrical leads by dipping them in molten solder. May paint armatures and field coils, using brush, or pour insulating compound over coils. May be designated according to unit impregnated as Armature Varnisher (any industry); Field-Coil Enameler (any industry).

GOE: 06.04.21 STRENGTH: M GED: R2 M1 L1 SVP: 2 DLU: 77

599.685-034 DYER (fabrication, nec)

Tends equipment that dyes broomcorn used in making brooms: Turns valve to admit water to dye vat and measures and pours dyestuff into vat, according to instructions or color of fiber. Immerses and turns bundles of fiber in dye solution to permeate broomcorn to impart color, using pitchfork. Places fibers on drain rack. May trim fiber stalks, using clippers.

GOE: 06.04.19 STRENGTH: M GED: R2 M2 L2 SVP: 2 DLU: 77

599.685-038 FILTER WASHER AND PRESSER (beverage; chemical) alternate titles: filter-pulp washer

Tends equipment that cleans and reshapes cotton, silk, or woodpulp used as filtering material in filter press to filter liquids, such as alcoholic beverages, gelatin, and glue: Removes dirty filter cakes from filter press, using handtools. Transfers filter cakes from filter press, using handtruck, and drops filter cakes into prebreaker machine that reduces filter cakes to loose, wet pulp. Pumps wet pulp to washing machine. Opens valves to admit and circulate water or steam in washer. Opens screen-covered drain in bottom of washer and continues washing pulp until drain-water runs clear. Pumps clean pulp to storage tank. Opens valve to move pulp from storage tank into hydraulic press. Starts hydraulic press that squeezes water from pulp and forms pulp into filter cake. Removes clean filter cake from hydraulic press, and transfers clean filter cake to filter press, using handtruck. Washes filter press plates, using hose and hot water. Installs filter cake into filter press, using handtools.

GOE: 06.04.19 STRENGTH: L GED: R2 M1 L2 SVP: 2 DLU: 77

599.685-042 FILTER-PRESS TENDER (beverage; chemical)

Tends filter press that filters liquors, such as gelatin, glue, and malt beverages: Turns valves to open lines, and pumps liquor through cotton, silk, or woodpulp filter. Inspects filtered liquors for specified degree of clarity. Recirculates cloudy liquor through filter until clear, or connects line to fresh filter press. Reads gauges that indicate pressure in lines and turns valves to maintain specified pressure. Turns valves to transfer clear liquor to specified department. May clean filter by backwashing it with water. May add *chill-proof* enzymes to filter when filtering beer.

GOE: 06.04.19 STRENGTH: L GED: R2 M1 L2 SVP: 3 DLU: 77

599.685-046 IMPREGNATING-TANK OPERATOR (any industry) alternate titles: coating-machine operator; insulating-machine operator; paint-coating-machine operator; sizing-machine operator

Tends machines that coat continuous rolls of wire, strips, or sheets with wax, paint, rubber, asphalt, or other coating material: Places roll of material onto feed spindle of machine. Threads end through feed and guide rolls into dipping vat or onto transfer roll and through drying oven and attaches it to rewind spindle. Fills boxes or vats with coating solution, such as asphalt or liquid rubber. May sew, crimp, or staple ends of material to form continuous roll. May be designated according to impregnating material used as Enamel-Machine Operator (elec. equip.); Varnishing-Machine Operator (elec. equip.); Waxing-Machine Operator (elec. equip.).

GOE: 06.04.21 STRENGTH: M GED: R3 M2 L2 SVP: 4 DLU: 77

599.685-050 IMPREGNATOR-AND-DRIER HELPER (elec. equip.; light. fix.) alternate titles: impregnating helper

Assists IMPREGNATOR AND DRIER (elec. equip.) in impregnating electrical products, such as capacitors, coils, and stators, performing any of the following duties: Loads capacitors into ovens, using hoist, and connects filler pipe of each capacitor to pipes of vacuum system. Turns valves to start and stop vacuum and regulates control equipment during impregnation process under supervision of IMPREGNATOR AND DRIER (elec. equip.). Reads vacuum gauges and capacitance bridge to determine degree of vacuum and capacitance and records or reports readings to IMPREGNATOR AND DRIER (elec. equip.). Cleans ovens and work areas, using solvent and brushes. Performs other duties as described under HELPER (any industry) Master Title.

GOE: 06.04.19 STRENGTH: M GED: R2 M1 L2 SVP: 3 DLU: 77

599.685-054 LACQUERER (plastic prod.)

Tends automatic equipment that sprays fabricated plastic articles with lacquer: Pours premixed lacquer into machine reservoir. Places fabricated plastics articles into enclosed spray booth, closes door, and moves lever to activate spraying equipment. Releases lever after articles appear thoroughly coated.

GOE: 06.04.21 STRENGTH: M GED: R2 M1 L1 SVP: 3 DLU: 77

599.685-058 MILL OPERATOR (any industry)

Tends one or more mills that grind materials, such as rock, ore, ingredients for food, drugs, and chemicals with steel, stone, or ceramic balls or rods: Pushes lever or adds balls to mill as needed or specified. Dumps material or opens flow gate to load mill. Secures cover plate. Starts and runs mill for specified time depending on size of load, grindability of material, and required fineness. Removes cover plate, attaches grid, and starts mill to discharge contents. When operating continuous ball mills, regulates inflow of materials and observes outflow to ensure attainment of specified product. May tend mill utilizing vacuum or other pressure. May tend steam-jacketed mill that heats materials during processing. May use mill to mix materials for wet or dry grinding. May keep production records. May be designated according to grinding agent as Ball-Mill Operator (any industry); Pebble-Mill Operator (chemical; paint & varnish); Rod-Mill Operator (any industry); or according to powder ground as Barytes Grinder (paint & varnish).

GOE: 06.04.10 STRENGTH: M GED: R2 M1 L2 SVP: 3 DLU: 78

599.685-062 OXIDIZED-FINISH PLATER (any industry) alternate titles: plater helper

Tends oxidizing tank that produces dark, lusterless, decorative finish on surface of metal articles, such as door lock parts, buttons, buckles, and small-arm parts: Places containers of workpieces in tank of oxidizing solution for specified time. Dips articles in successive baths to neutralize oxidation. May start tumbling barrel to dry oxidized pieces in sawdust [TUMBLER OPERATOR (any industry)]. May mix chemical solutions according to formula. May tend degreasing tank to clean workpieces before oxidizing.

GOE: 06.04.10 STRENGTH: M GED: R2 M1 L2 SVP: 2 DLU: 77

599.685-066 PAINT-LINE OPERATOR (toy-sport equip.)

Tends equipment that cleans, dips, and sprays toy parts: Mixes paint and thinner of specified color and viscosity, and pours solutions into dipping tanks or containers of electrostatic spraying unit. Adjusts controls of cleaning solution tanks for specified temperature, conveyor controls for rate of movement, and sprayer controls for rate of spray and voltage as indicated by dials. Observes conveyor line until parts run is finished, and changes paint color to meet requirements.

GOE: 06.04.21 STRENGTH: M GED: R2 M1 L2 SVP: 3 DLU: 77

599.685-070 PAINTER, TUMBLING BARREL (any industry) alternate titles: barrel painter

Tends tumbling barrel-painting machine that coats articles of porous materials, such as wooden shoe tree turnings or toy parts, with coating materials, such as paint, varnish, or lacquer: Places parts into tumbling barrel. Mixes coating material and thinner as specified and pours over parts in barrel. Starts barrel rotating to impart coating material on articles while heated air is blown through barrel to dry articles. Stops rotation of barrel, examines articles for uniformity of coating, adds more paint as required, and restarts rotation. Unloads barrel, breaking apart any articles that are stuck together.

GOE: 06.04.21 STRENGTH: M GED: R3 M2 L2 SVP: 3 DLU: 77

599.685-074 PAINTING-MACHINE OPERATOR (any industry) alternate titles: spray-machine operator

Tends machine equipped with compressed-air spray nozzles that coat products or materials with oil, paint, lacquer, varnish, shellac, or rustproofing agents: Pours premixed paint or lacquer into reservoir of machine and couples hose to spray nozzles. Moves sleeve on nozzles to attain specified spraying pressure and turns thumbscrew to direct nozzles toward articles or materials to be coated. Places articles or material onto conveyor or onto transfer table that carries them between spray nozzles. May mix paints with thinner solution according to formula. May regulate temperature of coating solution. May remove articles or materials from conveyor belt and place articles or materials in drying racks or container. May be designated according to coating applied as Lacquer Coater (plastic prod.); Oiling-Machine Operator (steel & rel.); Spray-Painter, Machine (wood prod., nec).

GOE: 06.04.21 STRENGTH: M GED: R2 M1 L2 SVP: 3 DLU: 81

599.685-078 POLISHER (button & notion)

Tends equipment that polishes casein, plastic, or shell buttons: Places buttons in tumbling barrel filled with powdered pumice stone and water, or caustic soda solution. Starts tumbling barrel revolving which causes abrasive to remove tool marks from buttons and to round edges. Dumps buttons from tumbling barrel into open barrel and covers them with hot water. Starts barrel revolving and places specified quantities of sulfuric and hydrochloric acids in barrel to polish buttons. Places buttons in barrel of dry sawdust or ground corncobs to remove residue of acid and give luster to buttons. May tend machines that tumble pearl buttons in bleaching solutions to lighten color.

GOE: 06.04.09 STRENGTH: M GED: R2 M1 L2 SVP: 2 DLU: 77

599.685-082 SCREENER OPERATOR (any industry) alternate titles: separator-machine operator

Tends machine that segregates particles of dry materials, such as sand, powdered minerals, feed, resins, and chemicals, into batches of uniform size by sifting through one or more oscillating screens: Bolts or clamps screen of specified mesh to frame, using handtools. Pours or shovels specified quantities of material into hoppers or onto feed conveyor of machine, manually or using hoist or lift truck. Positions takeoff conveyor, bins, or drums under screens to receive sifted material. Throws switch to activate takeoff conveyor or removes full containers manually or using hoist or truck. May measure or weigh and maintain records of material sifted. May lubricate machine and conveyors.

GOE: 06.04.09 STRENGTH: M GED: R2 M1 L2 SVP: 2 DLU: 77

599.685-086 SHREDDER TENDER, PEAT (agriculture)

Tends equipment that grinds and bags peat moss: Dumps peat moss into shredder that removes foreign matter, using tractor. Observes graph on gas furnace that dries peat moss and adjusts thermostat to maintain specified temperature. Inspects equipment to detect jams and mechanical breakdowns in equipment which cools and grinds peat moss. Observes and feels ground peat moss to determine its consistency. Stops equipment to clear jams and make minor adjustments to fans, blowers, and hammer mill, using handtools. Attaches bag to spout of filling machine and pulls lever to start machine that fills bag to specified weight. Removes bag and places it in loading zone. Loads filled bags on handtruck and transfers them to storage area.

GOE: 03.04.01 STRENGTH: H GED: R2 M2 L2 SVP: 2 DLU: 77

599.685-090   SPRAY-MACHINE TENDER (tinware)

Tends battery of machines that spray protective coating of lacquer inside cans: Adjusts lever to center spraying nozzle in can-holding pocket. Starts machine and observes spraying process as cans revolve on holding turret. Pulls cans from discharge line and inspects coating for conformity to specifications. Stops machine and removes jammed cans manually or with tongs. Cleans excess lacquer from spray nozzle and machine, using solvent and brush. May adjust machine and spraying mechanism, using wrenches. May regulate oven temperature to ensure uniform drying. May mix lacquer spray solution, according to formula, and fill machine reservoirs.
GOE: 06.04.21 STRENGTH: L GED: R3 M2 L2 SVP: 4 DLU: 77

599.685-094   SPRAYER, MACHINE (leather mfg.) alternate titles: blackener; blacking-machine operator; spray-machine operator

Tends machine that sprays solution, such as pigment or lacquer onto leather pieces to finish leather: Places leather pieces on conveyor that carries pieces under spray to coat leather with finishing solution. Turns valves to regulate pressure of compressed air in spray tanks and flow of solution through spray nozzles. Pushes button to control movement of conveyor and moves lever to start and stop rotation of sprayer.
GOE: 06.04.21 STRENGTH: M GED: R2 M1 L2 SVP: 2 DLU: 77

599.685-098   TUBBER (jewelry-silver.)

Tends one or more tumbling machines containing steel shot, soap, and water, that clean and polish jewelry articles preparatory to further processing: Loads machine with jewelry articles. Bolts lid on machine and starts machine that tumbles and rotates articles in cleaning solution for specified length of time. Places articles in sawdust box for drying. Cleans sawdust from articles, using airhose.
GOE: 06.04.02 STRENGTH: L GED: R2 M1 L2 SVP: 2 DLU: 77

599.685-102   TUBE COATER (metal prod., nec)

Tends semiautomatic machine that applies paint to collapsible metal tubes, for packaging drug and toilet products, glue, and similar items: Starts machine and positions unpainted tubes on spindles of revolving transfer table that automatically carries tubes against paint rollers. Removes painted tubes and places tubes on pegs of conveyor leading to drying oven.
GOE: 06.04.21 STRENGTH: L GED: R2 M1 L1 SVP: 2 DLU: 77

599.685-106   TUMBLER (clock & watch)

Tends tumbling machine that deburrs, smooths, and burnishes watch parts: Dumps specified abrasive powder, stones, or metal balls, in machine. Starts machine that cleans and burnishes parts. Rinses tumbled parts and dips them into oil to prevent rusting. Places parts in heated centrifuge to dry.
GOE: 06.04.02 STRENGTH: L GED: R2 M1 L2 SVP: 2 DLU: 77

599.685-110   TUMBLER OPERATOR (any industry)

Tends one or more tumbling barrels that smooth, polish, and clean articles, such as castings, tools, metal parts, jewelry, or porcelain ware: Loads tumbler with parts and specified amounts of cleaning compound or abrasive materials, such as pebbles, sand, shot, and sawdust, using shovel, hand scoop, or powered hoist. May pour specified amount of liquids, such as water, benzene, or kerosene into tumbler. Bolts cover and starts machine to rotate barrel and tumble parts for specified length of time. Tips barrel to pour contents into container or unloads barrel manually. Separates parts from abrasive materials or picks out parts, using hands or magnet.
GOE: 06.04.09 STRENGTH: M GED: R2 M1 L2 SVP: 2 DLU: 77

599.685-114   WASHER, MACHINE (any industry)

Tends machine that washes flat objects, such as plate glass, plastic sheets, or metal: Places workpiece into movable bed of machine or between pinch rolls. Turns valves and observes gauges to set specified flow of water or steam from jets in machine. Starts machine that moves workpiece by action of conveyor or pinch rolls into bath tank through spray of washing water, or steam under rotating brush and through spray of rinse water. Examines workpiece and removes remaining foreign matter, using hand scraper, brush, or sponge. May measure or weigh out and pour specified quantity of soap or detergent into wash water.
GOE: 06.04.39 STRENGTH: M GED: R2 M1 L2 SVP: 2 DLU: 77

599.685-118   WASHING-MACHINE OPERATOR (any industry)

Tends machines that wash and dry manufactured articles or their components, such as rubber gloves, pen and mechanical pencil barrels and lens blanks: Dumps detergent into machine. Places objects or racks of objects in washing machine. Sets controls to regulate length of cycle and water temperature as specified. Starts washing machine. Removes objects and places them in drying machine. Starts drying machine. Removes objects from machine when dry. May tend machine that rinses articles.
GOE: 06.04.39 STRENGTH: M GED: R2 M1 L2 SVP: 2 DLU: 77

599.685-122   WATER TENDER (any industry)

Tends pumps that maintain level of water in boilers: Reads boiler gauges to ascertain need for water. Opens valves and starts boiler-feed water pumps to supply water, or adjusts controls to start pumps automatically when water level reaches specified point. Observes operation of pumps to detect malfunctions. Tests water to determine suitability for boiler use or obtains sample for laboratory analysis. Adds specified chemical to condition boiler water. May clean boilers. May tend evaporator to purify water.
GOE: 05.12.06 STRENGTH: L GED: R2 M2 L2 SVP: 4 DLU: 77

599.685-126   SEED PELLETER (agriculture)

Tends equipment that applies coating to agricultural seeds and separates coated seeds according to size specifications to allow for uniform planting: Dumps seeds into rotary drum and presses buttons to start drum rotation. Adds water, powder, and glue for specified period, using spray guns and scoop and following work order specifications. Stops drum and scoops coated seeds (pellets) from drum, dumps pellets into electric sizing mill or onto manual sizing screen to remove undersized pellets. Returns undersized pellets to drums for additional coating. Dumps and spreads pellets on trays in drying tunnel for drying. Repeats sizing procedure for dried pellets to ensure that pellets meet sizing specifications. Fills pails with pellets specified on shipping order, using scoop, covers pails with lids, and places pails on pallet for shipment. Cleans interior and exterior of drums and work area, using brushes, rags, mop, detergent, and water.
GOE: 06.04.21 STRENGTH: L GED: R2 M1 L2 SVP: 2 DLU: 86

599.685-130   PAINT STRIPPER (petrol. refin.)

Tends equipment that strips paint from steel drums preparatory to repainting: Turns valves to start flow of paint-removing solvent and steam to outlets in respective sections of cleaning equipment. Starts pump that re-circulates solvent, and conveyor that carries drums through paint stripping process. Observes drums passing through paint stripping section, and adjusts speed of conveyor to obtain maximum efficiency during stripping process. Inspects drums to determine whether additional stripping is required, and recycles drums needing more stripping.
GOE: 06.04.39 STRENGTH: H GED: R3 M1 L1 SVP: 5 DLU: 86

599.685-134   SCRUBBER MACHINE TENDER (electron. comp.)

Tends machine that scrubs, cleans, and dries surface of printed circuit board (PCB) panels during manufacturing processes: Loads PCB panels onto conveyor that carries panels through scrubbing (abrading or sanding), cleaning, and drying cycles of machine. Adjusts machine controls to regulate pressure of scrubbing mechanisms, fluid levels, and conveyor speed. Observes gauges and examines processed panels to detect machine malfunctions and conformance to processing specifications. Removes and stacks cleaned PCBs from discharge end of machine. May clean and maintain scrubbing machine. May be designated by type of panels processed as Inner-Layer Scrubber Tender (electron. comp.). May be designated according to point in production when scrubbing occurs as Final Cleaner (electron. comp.).
GOE: 06.04.39 STRENGTH: M GED: R2 M1 L2 SVP: 2 DLU: 88

599.686-010   MILL-OPERATOR HELPER (any industry)

Performs any combination of following duties to assist MILL OPERATOR (any industry): Feeds raw materials to mill, using conveyor belt. Shovels spillage back onto belt. Breaks lumps of incoming raw material, using double jack, to facilitate passage through grizzly before entry into crusher. Opens hatch and drains slurry from mill, using electric vibrator or shaking screen to sift foreign particles from slurry. Places trays of slurry in drying ovens for specified time. Dumps dried slurry into drums. Moves drums to storage area, using handtruck. Lubricates mill and auxiliary equipment. Washes ball mills and cleans work area. Performs other duties as described under HELPER (any industry) Master Title.
GOE: 06.04.19 STRENGTH: M GED: R1 M1 L1 SVP: 2 DLU: 77

599.686-014   SPRAY-UNIT FEEDER (any industry) alternate titles: machine sprayer

Feeds manufactured articles or parts onto conveyor or feed mechanism that carries them through paint dipping and spraying operations. May be designated according to coating applied as Lacquerer (button & notion); or according to article sprayed as Gunstock-Spray-Unit Feeder (ordnance); Sprayer, Light Bulbs (light. fix.); or according to mechanism fed as Hook Loader (toy-sport equip.).
GOE: 06.04.21 STRENGTH: L GED: R2 M1 L1 SVP: 2 DLU: 77

599.687-010   BALLOON DIPPER (rubber goods) alternate titles: soaper

Dips balloons in vats of dye and soap solutions to color and polish them: Pours specified dyes into dye box receptacles. Immerses dye spreader (handled top from which spikes protrude) in dye box and passes it over tank of running water to form crisscross colored pattern of swirls on water. Lifts form pan (pan of molded balloons) from curing oven and places it on tank rack with molds immersed in dye water to form varicolored swirling pattern on balloons. Transfers pan to draining rack. Dips specified form pans in soap solution to impart glossy appearance to balloons and places them on conveyor, preparatory to stripping from molds.
GOE: 06.04.27 STRENGTH: M GED: R2 M1 L1 SVP: 2 DLU: 77

599.687-014   BOOKER (rubber goods; rubber tire)

Places strips of rubberized fabric or rubber between layers of cloth attached to *board*, forming books, or places rubber on trays of handtruck to prevent sticking together and to facilitate transportation.
GOE: 06.04.40 STRENGTH: L GED: R1 M1 L1 SVP: 1 DLU: 77

599.687-018   LEAD HANDLER (ordnance)

Performs any combination of following duties in shot tower to facilitate production of small arms ammunition: Unloads lead pigs from freight car and conveys and stacks them, using electric forklift truck. Loads specified proportions of lead and antimony-lead pigs onto conveyor, using electric hoist. Opens and closes valves, using metal hook, to direct conveyor flow of scrap shot to designated storage bins at top of shot tower. Lights fires under lead melting kettles

and dross converter. Dumps or shovels scrap lead or dross into kettles or converter. Skims dross from molten lead, using skimming ladle. Removes dross from converter, using rake and hoe.
GOE: 06.04.40 STRENGTH: H GED: R2 M1 L1 SVP: 3 DLU: 77

599.687-022   NET WASHER (rubber goods)
Washes stainless steel electronic testing nets to remove printing ink and dust: Immerses nets in soapy water and cleans nets, using handbrush. Inspects nets for broken links or snags and sets aside defective nets. Hangs nets on rack and starts fan to dry them.
GOE: 06.04.39 STRENGTH: L GED: R1 M1 L1 SVP: 2 DLU: 77

599.687-026   SIPHON OPERATOR (medical ser.; pharmaceut.) alternate titles: laboratory assistant; pooling operator
Siphons human blood plasma into pooling bottles for processing or storage: Removes cap from donor bottle and punctures stopper with needle. Connects vacuum pump to donor and pool bottles, using sterile glass and rubber tubing. Opens vacuum valve to siphon plasma into pooling bottle. Draws off and labels sample from each pool bottle. May introduce sterile, compressed air into pool bottles to transfer plasma to individual containers.
GOE: 02.04.02 STRENGTH: L GED: R2 M1 L1 SVP: 2 DLU: 77

599.687-030   WASHER (any industry) alternate titles: cleaner
Washes metal, glass, rubber, or plastic objects: Sprays objects with sprayer nozzle or immerses objects in washing and rinsing solutions to remove debris, manually or using baskets or conveyor. Dries objects, using cloth, airhose, or drying oven. May manually dislodge debris from objects, using brush or hand held power scrubber. May fill vats with water to specified level. May pour specified quantity of soap or chemicals into water or other solutions. May be designated according to object washed as Brush Washer (textile); Tub Washer (textile); Ware Washer (pottery & porc.).

GOE: 06.04.39 STRENGTH: M GED: R2 M1 L1 SVP: 2 DLU: 88

599.687-034   DRUM CLEANER (petrol. refin.) alternate titles: drum chainer
Cleans rust, scale, and other residue from interiors of empty steel drums, using one of following methods: (1) Inserts lighted rod through bunghole of drum to inspect drum interior for rust or residue, and selects chain of length and weight required to clean drum. Threads one end of chain through bunghole into drum, secures other end of chain to drum, using wire, and positions drum on power roller device. Depresses button to start rollers that tumble drum until chain dislodges matter. (2) Inserts steam nozzle into drum, pushes control to activate steam, and shakes nozzle about inside of drum to dislodge residue with blasts of steam. Draws out loose materials, using vacuum. Dries steam condensate, using warm-air hose.
GOE: 06.04.39 STRENGTH: H GED: R2 M1 L1 SVP: 2 DLU: 86

599.687-038   DRUM TESTER (petrol. refin.)
Inspects empty steel drums to detect leaks, using airhose and immersion tank: Fills immersion tank to designated level, using hose. Pulls drum from conveyor and screws bung into bunghole of drum, using wrench. Presses airhose nozzle onto valve of bung to release air into drum and monitors airhose gauge to raise pressure in drum to specified level. Lifts pressurized drum into tank and depresses pedal to actuate sprocket wheel of tank assembly that forces drum under water. Observes water to detect bubbles that indicate drum leak. Returns drum to surface, marks leak with waterproof crayon, and sets drum aside for repair. Replaces bung and gasket of drums not requiring repair and pushes drums onto conveyor.
GOE: 06.03.02 STRENGTH: H GED: R2 M1 L1 SVP: 2 DLU: 86

6 MACHINE TRADES OCCUPATIONS

This category includes occupations concerned with the operation of machines that cut, bore, mill, abrade, print, and similarly work such materials as metal, paper, wood, plastics, and stone. A worker's relationship to the machine is of primary importance. The more complicated jobs require an understanding of machine functions, blueprint reading, making mathematical computations, and exercising judgment to attain conformance to specifications. In less complicated jobs, eye and hand coordination may be the most significant factor. Installation, assembly, repair, and maintenance of machines and mechanical equipment and weaving, knitting, spinning, and similarly working textiles are included.

60   METAL MACHINING OCCUPATIONS

This division includes occupations concerned with shaping metal parts or products through the use of cutting tools, with or without removing excess material from stock or objects, primarily by such means as cutting, boring, milling, broaching, turning, sawing, abrading, and planing. Includes laying out, job setting, repairing, maintaining, calibrating, fitting, and assembling. The machining of nonmetallic materials is also included when the methods and machine tools commonly applied to the machining of metal are used. Occupations primarily concerned with the machining of clay, glass, and related materials are included in Division 67.

600   MACHINISTS AND RELATED OCCUPATIONS

This group includes occupations concerned with shaping metal parts by milling, turning, planing, abrading, boring, chipping, sawing, and shaving, using a variety of metalworking machines. Includes laying out, job setting, fitting, assembling, and repairing. The machining of nonmetallic materials, except wood, is also included when the methods and machine tools commonly applied to the machining of metal are used. Occupations primarily concerned with machine shop tools are included in Group 601 and machining gears in Group 602.

600.130-010   MACHINE-SHOP SUPERVISOR, TOOL (machine shop)

Supervises and coordinates activities of workers engaged in custom-machining metallic and nonmetallic workpieces to produce, maintain, or repair parts for machines, molds, and equipment, applying knowledge of machine shop procedures, variety of machine-tool setup and operating techniques, metal and plastic properties, and custom-machining methods. May supervise workers in related processes, such as forming, welding, inspecting, testing, or assembling. Performs duties as described under SUPERVISOR (any industry) Master Title.
GOE: 05.05.07 STRENGTH: M GED: R4 M4 L4 SVP: 8 DLU: 89

600.131-014   SALVAGE ENGINEER (machinery mfg.)

Supervises and coordinates activities of workers engaged in reworking rejected ball bearings: Disassembles and inspects races, faceways, cups, cones, retainers, and bearings. Diagnoses imperfections, such as parts not within tolerance, scratches, burrs, rust, or dirt and determines if part can be reworked or should be rejected. Assigns bearings to assistants to be reworked, advises them on problems involving bearing salvage, and trains workers in principles and practices of salvaging rejects. Inspects reworked bearings and components, using special go-not-go gauges, calipers, and micrometers. May operate lathes to turn, bore, face, and polish raceways, and perform related operations to rework bearings.
GOE: 06.01.01 STRENGTH: M GED: R4 M4 L3 SVP: 7 DLU: 77

600.260-014   EXPERIMENTAL MECHANIC (motor-bicycles) alternate titles: development mechanic

Sets up and operates variety of machines to fabricate experimental motorcycles or components to meet operating and endurance standards required by blueprints, sketches, or oral instructions: Assembles motorcycle or components, using handtools. Positions and clamps motorcycle on test rack. Attaches test equipment, such as tachometers, thermocouples, pressure and strain gauges, flow and velocity meters, to motorcycles, using handtools. Operates motorcycle at specified speeds and loads, and records meter and instrument readings on test records form. Disassembles motorcycle and analyzes cause of defect in components, such as exhaust system, frame, hydraulic fork, spring, or wheels, using handtools or power tools, calipers, micrometers, gauges, and other measuring instruments. Operates drill press, engine lathe, milling machine, or other machines to fabricate experimental motorcycle parts for testing, and secures test equipment to motorcycle, using jigs & fixtures. Test rides motorcycle to verify performance and durability of motorcycle components. Compiles and submits report to engineering department to show results of tests and recommendations for design or material changes.
GOE: 05.05.09 STRENGTH: M GED: R4 M4 L3 SVP: 8 DLU: 77

600.260-018   MODEL MAKER, FIREARMS (ordnance) alternate titles: sample maker

Sets up and operates metalworking machines to cut, shape, and fit parts to fabricate prototypes or modify existing models of small arms for use as production models, analyzing specifications and determining procedures according to knowledge of metal machining and layout: Lays out design of new parts on steel stock according to blueprints and scale drawings. Determines fixtures,

tooling, and sequence of machining operations to fabricate parts. Sets up and operates metalworking machines to cut, shape, and fit parts [MACHINIST (machine shop)]. Files, grinds, burnishes, and polishes parts to obtain smooth movements [FILER, FINISH (ordnance)]. Verifies conformance of machined workpiece to specifications, using sine bars, verniers, calipers, and micrometers. Records data for use of TOOL MAKER (machine shop) and TOOL DESIGNER (profess. & kin.) in establishing operating standards and machinery procedures. May test fire prototypic arms.
GOE: 05.05.07 STRENGTH: M GED: R4 M4 L3 SVP: 8 DLU: 77

600.260-022   MACHINIST, EXPERIMENTAL (machine shop) alternate titles: prototype machinist

Sets up and operates machine tools, and fits and assembles parts to fabricate tools, mechanisms, and machines for experimental purposes, such as solving problems relative to materials, tools, work-holding arrangements, machine settings, product specifications, and fabrication methods for production process, applying knowledge of mechanics, shop mathematics, metal properties, layout, and machining procedures: Consults with engineer and other personnel regarding product information, such as design, capacity and purpose, and types of material to be used to fabricate product. Analyzes written specifications, drawings, rough sketches, and verbal instructions to plan layout and determine sequence of operations. Selects metal stock and lays out design according to dimensions computed from scale drawings [LAY-OUT WORKER (any industry) I 809.281-010]. Designs fixtures, tooling, and experimental parts to meet special engineering needs. Sets up and operates metalworking machine tools, such as lathe, milling machine, shaper, or grinder to machine parts to specifications, and verifies conformance of parts to specifications, using measuring instruments [TOOL-MACHINE SET-UP OPERATOR (machine shop) 601.280-054]. Tests experimental models under simulated operating conditions for such purposes as development, standardization, and feasibility of design. Installs parts and materials, such as sheet metal covering, hydraulic systems, electrical wiring, lubricants, and batteries into machines and mechanisms. Evaluates experimental procedures and recommends changes or modifications for efficiency and adaptability to setup and production. May establish work procedures for fabricating new structural products, using variety of metalworking machines. May fabricate molds and *power press* dies to produce plastic parts and stamp metal parts. May perform heat-treating and heliarc welding. May train workers in setup and operation of machine tools.
GOE: 05.05.07 STRENGTH: H GED: R4 M4 L3 SVP: 8 DLU: 88

600.261-010   ASSEMBLER, STEAM-AND-GAS TURBINE (engine-turbine) alternate titles: leadman, turbine assembly

Fits and assembles machined parts and castings to erect steam and gas turbines according to drawings and specifications, using machine tools, power tools, handtools, and measuring instruments: Erects, levels, and aligns vertical supports for bedplates of steam turbines, using levels, transit, and *master straightedge*. Lays out work for other assemblers on *thrust end*, oil tank, and cylinder assemblies, following specified assembly procedure. Chips, grinds, bores, and drills machined parts and castings, using portable grinders, boring bar, and lapping disk. Levels and aligns high and low pressure cylinders, oil tank, thrust end assembly, and exhaust assembly, using pin gauges. Scribes foundation holes, lays out offset marks, and directs machine operator to drill foundation holes. Shrink-fits spindle blade rings, diaphragm rings, dummy rings, ring gears, sleeves, couplings, and bushings on shafts to build turbine spindles, using portable gas heating unit. Measures clearance and alignment of spindle to cylinder, using micrometers and calipers. Adjusts spindle bearing pads or moves blade rings to obtain specified clearances. Starts auxiliary oil pump to flush oil piping and bearings. Starts turbine and measures balance of spindle, using vibroscope. Observes functioning of unit and instruments to adjust alignment and clearances and to assure operation according to specifications. Repairs worn and damaged turbines.
GOE: 05.05.07 STRENGTH: M GED: R4 M3 L3 SVP: 8 DLU: 77

600.280-010   INSTRUMENT MAKER (any industry) alternate titles: mechanical technician; parts mechanic; precision-instrument and tool maker; precision-mechanical-instrument maker

Fabricates, modifies, or repairs mechanical instruments or mechanical assemblies of electrical or electronic instruments, such as chronometric timing devices, barographs, thermostats, seismographs, and servomechanisms, applying knowledge of mechanics, metal properties, shop mathematics, and machining procedures and using machine tools, welding and heat-treating equipment, pre-

cision measuring instruments, and handtools: Measures, marks, and scribes stock, such as silver, nickel, platinum, steel, ivory, and plastic, following blueprints and engineering sketches, and using square, rule, and scribe to lay out workpiece for machining [LAY-OUT WORKER (machine shop)]. Sets up and operates machine tools, such as lathes, drill presses, punch presses, milling machines, grinders, brakes, and *lapping* and polishing machines, to machine parts to specifications [MACHINIST (machine shop)]. Anneals and tempers metal parts [HEAT TREATER (heat treating) I]. Assembles parts in jig and brazes or welds. Fits and installs precision components, such as timing devices, springs, balance mechanisms, and gear trains, in housing, using jeweler's lathe, tweezers, loupe, and handtools. Verifies dimensions of parts and installation of components, using measuring instruments, such as micrometer, calipers, and electronic gauges. Coats assembled instrument with protective finish, such as lacquer or enamel, using spray gun. May install wiring and electrical components to specifications. May set up and operate machines to fabricate dies for punch presses [DIE MAKER, BENCH, STAMPING (machine shop)]. May be designated according to product assembled.
GOE: 05.05.11 STRENGTH: M GED: R4 M4 L3 SVP: 7 DLU: 77

600.280-014 INSTRUMENT-MAKER AND REPAIRER (petrol. & gas)
Sets up and operates machine tools to remodel electrical and electronic instruments used in electrical logging, gun perforating, sub-surface surveying, and other oil, gas, or borehole prospecting, testing and servicing operations, following engineering orders and specifications and applying knowledge of electronics, mechanics, metal properties, shop mathematics, and machining procedures: Measures, marks, and scribes dimensions of parts to be made on metal or plastic stock, using layout tools, such as rule, square, or scribe [LAY-OUT WORKER (machine shop)]. Machines parts to specifications, using machine tools, such as lathes, drill presses, and grinders [MACHINIST (machine shop)]. Assembles fabricated mechanical parts and such purchased parts as pulleys, springs, and dials, using bolts, screws, tweezers, wrenches, and screwdrivers [INSTRUMENT MAKER (any industry)]. Installs electrical and electronic parts, such as sockets, switches, and rheostats, in chassis. Connects circuit components, such as tubes, coils, and switches, using wire strippers and soldering iron and following circuit diagrams. Tests instruments to determine conformance to specifications, using equipment, such as voltmeters and ohmmeters. May be designated according to product remodeled or repaired.
GOE: 05.05.10 STRENGTH: L GED: R4 M4 L2 SVP: 7 DLU: 77

600.280-018 INSTRUMENT-MAKER APPRENTICE (any industry) alternate titles: precision-mechanical-instrument-maker apprentice
Performs duties as described under APPRENTICE (any industry) Master Title.
GOE: 05.05.11 STRENGTH: M GED: R4 M4 L3 SVP: 7 DLU: 77

600.280-022 MACHINIST (machine shop) alternate titles: machinist, first-class; machinist, general
Sets up and operates conventional, special-purpose, and numerical control (NC) machines and machining centers to fabricate metallic and nonmetallic parts, and fits and assembles machined parts into complete units, applying knowledge of machine shop theory and procedures, shop mathematics, machinability of materials, and layout techniques: Studies blueprints, sketches, drawings, manuals, specifications, or sample part to determine dimensions and tolerances of finished workpiece, sequence of operations, and setup requirements. Measures, marks, and scribes dimensions and reference points on material or workpiece as guides for subsequent machining [LAY-OUT WORKER (machine shop) 600.281-018]. Selects, aligns, and secures holding fixtures, cutting tools, attachments, accessories, and materials on machines, such as mills, lathes, jig borers, grinders, and shapers. Calculates and sets controls to regulate machining factors, such as speed, feed, coolant flow, and depth and angle of cut, or enters commands to retrieve, input, or edit computerized machine control media. Starts and observes machine operation to detect malfunctions or out-of-tolerance machining, and adjusts machine controls or control media as required. Verifies conformance of finished workpiece to specifications, using precision measuring instruments. Sets up and operates machine on trial run to verify accuracy of machine settings or programmed control data. Fits and assembles parts into complete assembly, using jigs, fixtures, surface plate, surface table, handtools, and power tools. Verifies dimensions and alignment of assembly, using measuring instruments, such as micrometers, height gauges, and gauge blocks. May install machined replacement parts in mechanisms, machines, and equipment, and test operation of unit to ensure functionality and performance. May operate welding equipment to cut or weld parts. May develop specifications from general description and draw sketch of part or product to be fabricated. May confer with engineers, production personnel, programmers, or others to resolve machining or assembly problems. May specialize in setting up and operating NC machines and machining centers and be designated Numerical Control Machine Machinist (machine shop); or set up and operate NC machines linked to automated storage, retrieval, and moving devices and be designated Flexible Machining System Machinist (machine shop).
GOE: 05.05.07 STRENGTH: M GED: R4 M4 L4 SVP: 7 DLU: '89

600.280-026 MACHINIST APPRENTICE (machine shop) alternate titles: machine-shop apprentice
Performs duties as described under APPRENTICE (any industry) Master Title.
GOE: 05.05.07 STRENGTH: M GED: R4 M4 L4 SVP: 7 DLU: 77

600.280-030 MACHINIST APPRENTICE, AUTOMOTIVE (automotive ser.)
Performs duties as described under APPRENTICE (any industry) Master Title.
GOE: 05.05.07 STRENGTH: M GED: R4 M3 L3 SVP: 7 DLU: 77

600.280-034 MACHINIST, AUTOMOTIVE (automotive ser.)
Sets up and operates variety of general or specialized metalworking machines to repair automotive engine parts or auxiliary units, such as transmission, differential, springs, or brakes, applying knowledge of mechanics, shop mathematics, metal properties, and machine procedures: Operates lathe to machine water-pump castings, piston heads, valves, and other automotive parts. Clamps piston in carriage of piston-grinding-and-turning machine to grind piston heads to fit cylinders. Adjusts grinding wheel to make cut of specified depth. Clamps valves in position on grinding wheel to grind seating surfaces of valves, moving levers to achieve required depth of cut. Operates boring machine to machine internal surfaces of cylinders in engine block. Cleans parts, before and after machining, in agitator-type cleaning tank to remove grease, rust stains, and foreign matters. Operates lathe, boring, or honing machine to refinish internal surfaces of bearings and connecting rods. Verifies dimensions, using measuring instruments, such as micrometers, calipers, and height gauges to ensure adherence to tolerance specifications. May grind metal surfaces of engine block or other parts, using portable or *bench grinders*. May spray worn or gouges parts with molten aluminum, zinc, or other metal to build up parts [METAL SPRAYER, MACHINED PARTS (any industry)]. May examine parts for fractures, using magnaflux test equipment. May repair cracks in engine head and other vehicle parts with arc or gas welding equipment. May operate drum lathe to resurface brake drums. May repair and resurface leaf and coil springs, axles, king pins, bushings, and universal joints.
GOE: 05.05.07 STRENGTH: M GED: R4 M3 L3 SVP: 7 DLU: 77

600.280-042 MAINTENANCE MACHINIST (machine shop) alternate titles: machine repairer; machinist, general maintenance; shop mechanic
Sets up and operates variety of machine tools, and fits and assembles parts to fabricate or repair machine tools and maintain industrial machines, applying knowledge of mechanics, shop mathematics, metal properties, layout, and machining procedures: Observes and listens to operating machines or equipment to diagnose machine malfunction and determine need for adjustment or repair. Studies blueprints, sketches, machine parts or specifications to determine type and dimensions of metal stock required. Measures, marks, and scribes dimensions and reference points on metal stock surfaces, using such measuring and marking devices as calibrated ruler, micrometer, caliper, and scriber [LAY-OUT WORKER (machine shop) 600.281-018]. Dismantles machine or equipment, using handtools or power tools, to examine parts for defect or to remove defective part. Replaces defective part with new part or repairs or reproduces part from various kinds of metal stock, using handtools, such as scraper, file, and drill, and machine tools, such as lathe, milling machine, shaper, borer, and grinder [MACHINIST (machine shop) 600.280-022]. Assembles and test operates machine to verify correction of malfunction. Maintains and lubricates machine tools and equipment. May weld parts, using arc or gas welding equipment. May repair or replace faulty wiring, switches, or relays.
GOE: 05.05.07 STRENGTH: M GED: R4 M4 L3 SVP: 7 DLU: 86

600.280-046 PATTERNMAKER APPRENTICE, METAL (foundry)
Performs duties as described under APPRENTICE (any industry) Master Title.
GOE: 05.05.07 STRENGTH: M GED: R4 M4 L3 SVP: 8 DLU: 77

600.280-050 PATTERNMAKER, METAL (foundry)
Lays out, mills, drills, turns, grinds, fits, and assembles castings and parts to make metal foundry patterns, core boxes, and match plates, using handtools and machine tools, and analyzing specifications, according to knowledge of patternmaking methods: Studies blueprint of part to be cast, computes dimensions, and plans sequence of operations. Measures, marks, and scribes layout on castings [LAY-OUT WORKER (machine shop)]. Sets up and operates machine tools, such as milling machines, lathes, drill presses, and grinders, to machine castings to specifications [TOOL-MACHINE SET-UP OPERATOR (machine shop)]. Assembles pattern, using handtools, and bolts, screws, or other fasteners. Cleans and hand finishes workpiece, using emery cloth, files, scrapers, and powered hand grinders. Verifies conformance of machined pattern to blueprint specifications, using templates and measuring instruments, such as scale, calipers, and micrometers. May make templates for layout and inspection [TEMPLATE MAKER (any industry)]. May operate welding equipment in assembling pattern [WELDER, COMBINATION (welding)].
GOE: 05.05.07 STRENGTH: M GED: R4 M4 L3 SVP: 8 DLU: 77

600.280-054 SAMPLE MAKER, APPLIANCES (house. appl.; light. fix.) alternate titles: model maker
Sets up and operates machines to construct complete working models of new or redesigned household electrical appliances, such as fans, heaters, and hair driers: Lays out and fabricates metal and plastic parts, using handtools and machine tools. Devises and constructs own tools, dies, molds, jigs, and fixtures, or modifies existing tools and equipment [TOOL-AND-DIE MAKER (machine shop)]. Assembles mechanical and electrical parts, and installs wiring circuits.
GOE: 05.05.07 STRENGTH: L GED: R4 M3 L3 SVP: 8 DLU: 77

600.281-010 FLUID-POWER MECHANIC (any industry)
Fabricates, assembles, services, maintains, repairs, and tests fluid power equipment, such as power steering units, and components, following blueprints,

schematics, or drawings, using handtools, power tools, and testing devices and applying knowledge of hydraulic, pneumatic, and electrical principles: Analyzes blueprints, schematics, diagrams, and drawings to determine fabrication specifications. Sets up and operates milling machines, lathes, shapers, grinders, drill presses, and welders to make precision parts. Verifies conformance to specifications, using instruments, such as micrometers, verniers, and calipers. Assembles fluid power components, such as pumps, cylinders, valves, reservoirs, motors, accumulators, filters, and controls, using handtools and holding devices. Connects unit to test equipment, and analyzes and records data, such as fluid pressure, flow measure, and power loss due to friction and parts wear. Recommends modifications in unit and in test procedures, instrumentation, or setup, based on analysis of test results.
GOE: 05.05.07 STRENGTH: L GED: R4 M4 L3 SVP: 7 DLU: 77

600.281-014 LAY-OUT INSPECTOR (machine shop) alternate titles: inspector, rough castings; lay-out worker
Inspects castings, forgings, or wax patterns of castings for conformance to blueprints by laying out reference lines and points, and measuring dimensions, using surface plate, precision measuring instruments, and layout procedures: Analyzes blueprint and examines casting to determine reference points for layout. Applies blue pigment or whitewash to layout surface on casting, using rag or brush. Positions casting on surface plate, using parallel bars, angle plates, dial indicator, gauge blocks, V-blocks, shims, and vernier height gauge, to establish reference points for measuring. Computes layout dimensions relative to reference points, using shop mathematics. Marks and scribes reference lines and points on casting and measures dimensions, using instruments, such as micrometer, protractor, combination square, vernier height gauge, and *layout machine*. Records location and extent of defect in rejected casting. May inspect metal equipment used in production of casting to determine source of error.
GOE: 06.01.05 STRENGTH: M GED: R4 M4 L3 SVP: 6 DLU: 77

600.281-018 LAY-OUT WORKER (machine shop)
Lays out metal stock or workpieces, such as castings, plates, or machine parts, to indicate location, dimensions, and tolerances necessary for further processing, such as machining, welding, or assembly, analyzing specifications and computing dimensions according to knowledge of product, subsequent processing, shop mathematics, and layout procedures: Studies blueprint, sketch, model, or other specifications and plans layout. Examines workpiece and verifies such requirements as dimensions and squareness, using rule, square, and straightedge. Lifts and positions workpiece in relation to surface plate manually or with hoist, using such work aids as shims, parallel blocks, and angle plates. Verifies position with measuring instruments, such as gauge blocks, height gauges, and dial indicators. Determines reference points and computes layout dimensions. Sets indicators on height gauge, protractor, or *layout machine* to computed dimensions, or projects dimensions by setting indicators to specified locations on model and moving instrument or machine so that indicators bear on corresponding locations on workpiece. Indents layout points, using prick punch, center punch, and hammer. Marks or scribes layout lines, using handtools and work aids, such as surface gauge, straightedge, compasses, templates, and scriber. Marks such data as dimensions, instructions, and part identification on workpiece. Works to tolerances as close as plus 0.001 inch. May position model in parallel relationship to workpiece. May apply pigment to layout surfaces, using paint brush. May inspect machined parts to verify conformance to specifications. May add dimensional details to blueprints or prepare dimensional drawings to be followed by other workers. May layout sheet metal or plate steel, applying specialized knowledge of sheet metal layout geometry [SHEET-METAL LAY-OUT WORKER (any industry)].
GOE: 05.05.07 STRENGTH: M GED: R4 M4 L3 SVP: 7 DLU: 77

600.281-022 MACHINE BUILDER (machinery mfg.; machine tools) alternate titles: assembler, special machine; bench hand; fitter; machinist, bench; vise hand
Fits and assembles components according to assembly blueprints, manuals, engineering memos, sketches, and knowledge of machine construction to construct, rebuild, and repair machines and equipment, using handtools and power tools: Analyzes assembly blueprint and specifications manual, and plans machine building operations. Verifies conformance of parts to stock list and blueprints, using measuring instruments, such as calipers, gauges, and micrometers. Lays out hole locations and drills and taps holes on parts for assembly. Aligns components for assembly, manually or with hoist, and bolts, screws, dowels, welds, or rivets parts together, using handtools, rivet gun, and welding equipment, or arranges for assembly by welder and electrician. Brushes blue pigment on parts and mates them to detect high spots on surfaces. Removes high spots, and smooths surfaces, using chisels, scrapers, files, and powered hand grinder [SCRAPER, HAND (machine shop)]. Verifies alignment and tolerances of moving parts, using measuring instruments, such as dial indicators and thickness gauges. Tests operation of assembly by hand. Assembles, sets up, and operates machine to verify functioning, machine capabilities, and conformance to customer's specifications. May form and fasten piping, fixtures, and attachments required to service machine with air, water, and oil. May install wiring and electrical components to specifications. May work as member of team on limited part of fabrication process. May set up and operate metalworking machines to shape parts [TOOL-MACHINE SET-UP OPERATOR (machine shop)]. May be designated according to type of machine or machine component as Fixture Builder (machinery mfg.).
GOE: 05.05.09 STRENGTH: M GED: R4 M4 L3 SVP: 7 DLU: 77

600.360-010 MACHINE TRY-OUT SETTER (machine tools) alternate titles: detail maker and fitter
Sets up prototype metalworking machines, such as lathe, milling machine, or forging press to verify conformance to operating specifications, according to knowledge of inspection and machining techniques, tools and processes: Examines electrical components, such as electrical timers, relays, and switches, to ensure adequate functioning of automatic cycles. Compares rotary table *indexing*, when present, to specifications. Inspects fixture alignment, machine table movement, and position of cutting tools, using instruments, such as dial indicators, height setting devices annd gauges. Installs dies or tool holders and tools, following blueprints, and using handtools and measuring instruments. Sets controls to regulate speed of feed, depth of cut, or length of ram stroke, according to type of machine being tested. Operates machine to obtain sample workpiece. Verifies conformance of workpiece to specifications, using measuring instruments, such as calipers, micrometers, and gauges. Determines cause of malfunction from inspection data. Repairs electrical and mechanical components and reports electronic malfunction to supervisor. Records operational data, such as pressure readings, length of stroke, feeds, and speeds, for customer use. May demonstrate setup and operation for customer personnel. May be designated according to type of machine as Honing-Machine Try-Out Setter (machine tools).
GOE: 06.01.05 STRENGTH: M GED: R4 M4 L3 SVP: 7 DLU: 77

600.360-014 MACHINE SETTER (machine shop) alternate titles: machinist, job setter
Sets up and adjusts machine tools, such as lathes, milling machines, boring machines, drills and punch presses, grinders, gear hobbers, and plastic molding machines for other workers, such as PRODUCTION-MACHINE TENDERS (machine shop) 609.685-018, according to specifications and tooling instructions, applying knowledge of machining methods: Reads blueprint or job order for product specifications, such as dimensions and tolerances, and tooling instructions, such as feed rate, cutting speed, depth of cut, fixtures, and cutting tools to be used. Installs and adjusts holding device and fastens specified cutting and shaping tools in position to enable operator to produce finished workpiece to specifications, using handtools, such as wrenches, screwdrivers, and pliers. Selects and sets speed and feed of machine according to type of operation and specified material and finish. Starts machine to obtain first-run workpiece and verifies dimensional tolerances, using micrometers, gauges, and templates. Changes worn cutting tools and adjusts operation of machine, such as cutting speed, feed rate, or depth of cut, when required. May replace parts on machines, such as bearings, filters, wiring, and switches, using handtools. May instruct operators or other workers in machine setup and operation. May set up machines and equipment other than machine tools, such as welding machine and flame cutting equipment.
GOE: 06.01.02 STRENGTH: M GED: R4 M4 L3 SVP: 7 DLU: 86

600.380-010 FIXTURE MAKER (light. fix.)
Sets up and operates metal-working machines to machine workpieces, and fabricate electrical lighting fixture prototypes, such as floor and wall lamps and hanging fixtures, according to specifications: Examines drawings or blueprints to ascertain number and finished dimensions of parts required. Sets up and operates lathes to spin [SPINNER, HYDRAULIC (any industry)] or turn [ENGINE-LATHE SET-UP OPERATOR (machine shop)] ferrous or nonferrous metal, according to specifications. Cuts and shapes sheet metal [MACHINE OPERATOR (any industry) I 616.380-018]. Heats and bends metal to shape fixture parts [ORNAMENTAL-METAL WORKER (metal prod., nec)]. Verifies conformance of parts to specification, using rule, micrometer, square, and protractor. Solders, brazes, and welds parts, using welding and brazing equipment. Attaches glass parts, sockets, and wires to metal parts to form fixture, using handtools. May be designated according to type of fixture fabricated as Chandelier Maker (light. fix.).
GOE: 05.05.07 STRENGTH: L GED: R4 M3 L3 SVP: 7 DLU: 77

600.380-018 MACHINE SET-UP OPERATOR (machine shop) alternate titles: machine operator, all around; machine operator, general; machine specialist; machinist
Sets up and operates machine tools, such as lathes, milling machines, boring machines, and grinders, to machine metallic and nonmetallic workpieces according to specifications, tooling instructions, and standard charts, applying knowledge of machining methods: Reads blueprint or job order for product specifications, such as dimensions and tolerances, and tooling instructions, such as fixtures, feed rates, cutting speeds, depth of cut, and determines sequence of operations. Selects, positions, and secures tool in toolholder (chuck, collet, or toolpost). Positions and secures workpiece in holding device, machine table, chuck, centers, or fixtures, using clamps and wrenches. Moves controls to position tool and workpiece in relation to each other, and to set specified feeds, speeds, and depth of cut. Sets up fixture or feeding device, starts machine, and turns handwheel to feed tool to workpiece or vice versa, and engages feed. Turns valve handle to direct flow of coolant or cutting oil against tool and workpiece. Observes operation of machine and verifies conformance of machined workpiece to specifications, using measuring instruments, such as fixed gauges, calipers, and micrometers. Operates bench grinder to sharpen tools. May set up and operate machines and equipment other than machine tools, such as welding machines and flame-cutting equipment.
GOE: 06.01.03 STRENGTH: M GED: R4 M4 L3 SVP: 6 DLU: 89

600.380-022 MACHINE SETTER (clock & watch)
Sets up variety of metalworking machines to cut, drill, bore, abrade, mill, and assemble clock, watch, and timer parts, according to specifications and

tooling instructions, applying knowledge of metal machining methods: Confers with supervisor and studies blueprints and operation sheet to determine parts or assemblies to be processed. Installs dies, holding devices, and tools, such as cams, gears, chucks, cutters, and drills, using handtools. Operates machine to fabricate sample parts or assemblies and verifies conformance of workpiece to specifications visually and using gauges, such as micrometer, go-not-go, and calipers. Demonstrates operation of machine to workers. Observes machine operation for malfunctions, and notifies supervisor when machine repair or overhaul is required. Adjusts and makes minor machine repairs as required. May repair cams. May teach new operators to operate machine and maintain setup. May tend machines to meet production demands. May operate semiautomatic or hand operated machine to produce low production or experimental parts. May be designated according to type of machine set up as Machine Setter, Automatic (clock & watch); Machine Setter, Hand (clock & watch); Machine Setter, Semiautomatic (clock & watch). Important variables may be designated by brand name of machine used.
GOE: 06.01.02 STRENGTH: M GED: R4 M4 L3 SVP: 7 DLU: 77

600.380-026   TURBINE-BLADE ASSEMBLER (engine-turbine)
Fabricates blade structure of steam and gas turbines according to specifications and drawings, using machine tools, handtools, and measuring devices: Positions blades on bench to form sections, or positions and secures disc on positioner. Measures tenon location on blades with dial indicator and selects two blades with equal tenons for end blades of section. Sets up and operates milling machines and pedestal grinders to grind and mill blade roots to obtain specified section lengths, radial alignment, and root contact. Inserts blades into grooves of spindle, cylinder, or fixture (for section blading) and pounds metal caulking into groove to tighten blades. Operates grinders and metal saw to shape cylinder blade locking device, spindle filler pieces, and wedges from metal stock. Fits locking device to pocket of blade and smooths surfaces, using chalk, files, and abrasive paper. Drills, reams, and taps locking items, such as cylinder locks, spindle filler pieces, seals, and wedges, using drill press, and fastens them to blade by peening or inserting setscrew. Fits shroud over blade ends and peens blade tenon to round edges of rivets, using hammer and capping tool or pneumatic hammer. Measures head of rivet for specified clearance, using measuring tool. Grinds shroud end of each blade section to obtain specified clearance between shrouds, using pedestal grinder. May roll, cut, and chamfer shroud.
GOE: 06.01.03 STRENGTH: M GED: R4 M3 L3 SVP: 6 DLU: 77

601   TOOLMAKERS AND RELATED OCCUPATIONS

This group includes occupations concerned with the entire scope of constructing, repairing, maintaining, and calibrating machine-shop tools, jigs, fixtures, instruments, and metal-forming dies.

601.130-010   TOOL-AND-DIE SUPERVISOR (machine shop)
Supervises and coordinates activities of workers engaged in production and repair of metalworking dies, jigs, fixtures, gauges, and cutting tools, applying knowledge of machining and tool and die construction. Performs other duties as described under SUPERVISOR (any industry) Master Title.
GOE: 05.05.07 STRENGTH: L GED: R4 M4 L3 SVP: 8 DLU: 77

601.260-010   TOOL-AND-DIE MAKER (machine shop)
Analyzes specifications, lays out metal stock, sets up and operates machine tools, and fits and assembles parts to fabricate and repair metalworking dies, cutting tools, jigs and fixtures, gauges, and machinists' handtools, applying knowledge of tool and die design and construction, shop mathematics, metal properties, and layout, machining, and assembly procedures: Studies specifications, such as blueprints, sketches, models, or descriptions, and visualizes product to determine materials required and machines to be used to fabricate parts. Computes dimensions, plans layout, and determines assembly method and sequence of operations. Measures, marks, and scribes metal stock for machining [LAY-OUT WORKER (machine shop) 600.281-018]. Sets up and operates machine tools, such as lathes, milling machine, shaper, and grinder, to machine parts, and verifies conformance of machined parts to specifications [TOOL-MACHINE SET-UP OPERATOR (machine shop) 601.280-054]. Lifts machined parts manually or using hoist, and positions and secures parts on surface plate or worktable, using devices, such as vises, V-blocks, and angle plates. Smooths flat and contoured surfaces, using scrapers, abrasive stones, and power grinders, and fits and assembles parts together and into assemblies and mechanisms, using handtools. Verifies dimensions, alignments, and clearances, using measuring instruments, such as dial indicators, gauge blocks, thickness gauges, and micrometers. Heat-treats tools or parts [HEAT TREATER (heat treating) II 504.682-018]. May connect wiring and hydraulic lines to install electrical and hydraulic components. May examine standard or previously used dies, tools, and jigs and fixtures, and recommend design modifications regarding construction and function of part. May develop specifications from general descriptions for specialty tools and draw or sketch design of product. May specialize in repair work and be designated Tool-And-Die Repairer (machine shop).
GOE: 05.05.07 STRENGTH: M GED: R4 M4 L4 SVP: 8 DLU: 89

601.260-014   TOOL-AND-DIE-MAKER APPRENTICE (machine shop)
Performs duties as described under APPRENTICE (any industry) Master Title.
GOE: 05.05.07 STRENGTH: M GED: R4 M4 L4 SVP: 8 DLU: 77

601.261-010   INSPECTOR, SET-UP AND LAY-OUT (machine shop)
Develops gauging setup and surface plate layout procedures, draws patterns and templates, and inspects variety of parts and tools, to provide inspection devices and fixtures for use in machining or assembly, using blueprints, formulas, trigonometry, and precision measuring instruments: Analyzes inspection problem by comparing part with blueprints or sketches, and devises procedures necessary to measure specified dimensions. Lays out part on surface plate or positions in gauging setup to verify dimensions, using master gauges, *indexing* head, gauge blocks, comparators, verniers, micrometers, and indicators. Develops and draws patterns and templates used to measure curves and angles. Tests surface finish of machined parts, using profilameter. Tests hardness of metal parts [HARDNESS INSPECTOR (heat treating)]. Analyzes defective parts to determine reasons for dimensional variations, such as faulty machining, or assembly procedures, setup, tools, or fixtures. Recommends corrective procedures to design, methods, process, or production engineering departments. Inspects machining or assembly fixtures, tools, or gauges, and suggests replacement or use of new equipment. May approve parts not within specified dimension tolerances. May change allowable tolerances specified on blueprint.
GOE: 05.05.07 STRENGTH: L GED: R4 M4 L4 SVP: 8 DLU: 77

601.280-010   DIE MAKER, STAMPING (machine shop) alternate titles: body-die maker
Lays out, machines, fits, assembles, and finishes metal castings and parts to make and repair metal stamping dies, analyzing specifications and applying knowledge of die design and construction: Studies blueprints of product and die, prototype products, and die models. Visualizes structure and function of die and plans operations, applying knowledge of shop mathematics, machining and assembly methods, properties of sheet metal under pressure, and metal-forming presses. Measures, marks, and scribes castings and stock for machining. Sets up and operates machine tools, such as lathe, milling machine, *radial drill press*, shaper, and grinder, to machine parts to specifications, and verifies conformance of machined parts to specifications [TOOL-MACHINE SET-UP OPERATOR (machine shop)]. Lifts machined parts manually or using hoist, and positions them on worktable or surface plate for assembly. Shapes, smooths, and fits flat and contoured surfaces of die members and parts, using handtools, such as stones, files, and powered grinders [DIE FINISHER (machine shop)]. Verifies dimensions, clearances, and alignment of members and parts in die, using dial indicators, gauge blocks, thickness gauges, and micrometers. Dowels and bolts parts together, using handtools, such as hammers and wrenches. Connects wiring and hydraulic lines to install electric and hydraulic components. Fits and assembles components for mechanical action within die. May operate power press, perform final shaping and smoothing operations on die in press, and inspect sheet metal product, to complete tryout of die [DIE-TRY-OUT WORKER, STAMPING (machine shop)]. May only repair dies and be designated Die Repairer, Stamping (machine shop).
GOE: 05.05.07 STRENGTH: M GED: R4 M4 L4 SVP: 8 DLU: 77

601.280-014   DIE MAKER, TRIM (machine shop) alternate titles: trim die maker; trimmer maker
Lays out, machines, assembles, and finishes metal stock to make dies that trim excess metal *flash* from forged metal parts, following blueprints and applying knowledge of die design and construction, shop mathematics, and metal properties: Analyzes blueprint of part or die and plans sequence of operations. Measures and scribes metal stock to layout design of die. Sets up and operates variety of machine tools, such as shaper, vertical turret lathe, and engine lathe to machine die parts [TOOL-MACHINE SET-UP OPERATOR (machine shop)]. Bolts and dowels die parts to assemble die, using handtools, such as power grinder, scrapers, files, and emery cloth to fit die parts and to obtain specified dimensions and contours. Inspects assembled die with sample part and measuring instruments, such as calipers, micrometers, and height gauges to verify conformance to specifications. May make dies containing mechanical or hydraulic components. May make dies that trim flash diecastings. May make templates to verify dimensions [TEMPLATE MAKER, EXTRUSION DIE (machine shop)]. May make tools to form die parts [TOOL MAKER (machine shop)]. May repair dies and be designated Die Repairer, Trimmer Dies (machine shop).
GOE: 05.05.07 STRENGTH: M GED: R4 M4 L3 SVP: 7 DLU: 77

601.280-018   DIE MAKER, WIRE DRAWING (machine shop)
Lays out, machines, and finishes metal, carbide, and diamond parts to make and repair wiredrawing dies, analyzing specifications and applying knowledge of metal properties, shop mathematics, and wiredrawing die construction: Studies specifications, such as blueprints, sketches, and standard charts, and visualizes shape of die. Computes die dimensions and plans sequence of operations. Measures, marks, and scribes metal stock to lay out for machining [LAY-OUT WORKER (machine shop)]. Sets up and operates machine tools, such as lathes, milling machines, and grinders, to machine die parts [TOOL-MACHINE SET-UP OPERATOR (machine shop)]. Polishes die bores by *lapping* manually or using die-finishing machines, applying progressively finer grades of diamond dust compound. Inspects die for defects, such as cracks and scratches, using loupe or microscope. Pulls wire or rod through die bore manually or using wiredrawing machine. Measures wire or rod, using measuring instruments such as micrometer, vernier gauge, or protractor, to verify conformance of die bore to specifications. May design and make tools, jigs, and fixtures. May be designated according to type of die made or repaired as Carbide-Die Maker (machine shop); Diamond-Die Maker (machine shop).

GOE: 05.05.07.STRENGTH: M GED: R4 M4 L3 SVP: 7 DLU: 77

601.280-022 DIE SINKER (machine shop) alternate titles: forging-die sinker

Lays out, machines, and finishes impression cavities in die blocks to produce forging dies, following blueprints and applying knowledge of diesinking: Analyzes blueprint of part or die and plans sequence of operations. Measures and marks die block to lay out designs of cavities. Sets up and operates variety of machine tools, such as shaper, vertical turret lathe, and engine lathe to machine cavities in die block [TOOL-MACHINE SET-UP OPERATOR (machine shop)]. Obtains specified dimensions, contours, and finish of die cavities, using tools, such as power grinder, scrapers, files, and emery cloth. Inspects die cavities, using templates and measuring instruments, such as calipers, micrometers, and height gauges to verify conformance to specifications. May develop die design from blueprint of part, using knowledge of machining and forging processes. May make templates to verify dimensions of cavities [TEMPLATE MAKER, EXTRUSION DIE (machine shop)]. May make and inspect sample lead or plaster cast of part to verify fit of die members and basic shape of part. May repair forging dies and be designated Die Repairer, Forging (machine shop). May set up and operate machines to plane surfaces and edges of forging dies and be known as Edger Machine Setter (machine shop).
GOE: 05.05.07 STRENGTH: M GED: R4 M3 L3 SVP: 7 DLU: 77

601.280-030 MOLD MAKER, DIE-CASTING AND PLASTIC MOLDING (machine shop) alternate titles: die-cast-die maker; mold maker, plastic molds

Lays out, machines, fits, assembles, and finishes metal parts to make and repair dies for diecasting of metal products and metal molds for injection or compression molding of plastic or glass products, analyzing specifications, and applying knowledge of die and mold design and construction: Studies blueprints of product and die or mold, and computes specifications, applying knowledge of shop mathematics and metal diecasting or plastic or glass molding processes and machinery. Plans sequence of operations, visualizing shape of die or mold in reverse of product. Measures, marks, and scribes metal stock to lay out for machining [LAY-OUT WORKER (machine shop)]. Gives machining specifications to TOOL-MACHINE SET-UP OPERATORS (machine shop) or sets up and operates machines, such as horizontal boring mill, engine lathe, profile milling machine, and pantograph machine to machine outer dimensions and contoured cavity of die or mold [TOOL-MACHINE SET-UP OPERATOR (machine shop); PANTOGRAPH-MACHINE SET-UP OPERATOR (machine shop)]. Grinds, files, and sands parts, using files, emery cloth, and powered grinders, to fit parts for assembly and to smooth and finish cavity. Assembles die or mold, using handtools. Verifies dimensions, using calipers, *planer gauges,* and dial indicators. May repair molds and be designated Mold Repairer, Die-Casting And Plastic Molding (machine shop).
GOE: 05.05.07 STRENGTH: H GED: R4 M3 L3 SVP: 7 DLU: 77

601.280-034 TAP-AND-DIE-MAKER TECHNICIAN (clock & watch)

Sets up and operates machines, such as watchmaker's lathe, bench miller, and tap grinder to make taps and dies used in manufacture of watch screws and taps: Makes master taps following blueprints and working to pitch (thread) tolerance of 0.00002 inch and outside diameter tolerance of 0.0001 inch. Threads master dies, using master taps. Makes working taps and dies from master taps and dies, using variety of semiautomatic machine tools. Laps, mills, spots, etches, drills, and taps die blanks, using variety of abrasives, bench machines, and precision gauges. Anneals and hardens dies, utilizing knowledge of heat-treating operations.
GOE: 05.05.07 STRENGTH: L GED: R4 M3 L3 SVP: 8 DLU: 77

601.280-038 TEMPLATE MAKER, EXTRUSION DIE (machine shop)

Lays out sheet or plate steel, and sets up and operates machine tools to make templates (replicas of cross sections of products to be extruded) used in manufacture of extrusion dies: Analyzes blueprints to determine product specifications and plans operations, applying knowledge of template making, extrusion of nonferrous metals, shop mathematics and sheet metalwork. Applies copper sulfate solution to surface of steel plate, using cloth or brush. Computes dimensions, and measures and scribes outline of product cross section on steel. Saws, files, and operates drill press, arbor press, band-sawing machine, filing machine, and vertical milling machine to drill, saw, shape, and smooth workpiece to layout lines [TOOL-MACHINE SET-UP OPERATOR (machine shop)]. Verifies conformance of template to specifications, using measuring instruments, such as micrometers, calipers, and protractors. May operate bench grinder to grind standard files to shape for particular operation.
GOE: 05.05.07 STRENGTH: M GED: R4 M4 L4 SVP: 7 DLU: 77

601.280-042 TOOL MAKER (machine shop)

Analyzes variety of specifications, lays out metal stock, sets up and operates machine tools, and fits and assembles parts to fabricate or repair cutting tools, jigs, fixtures, gauges, or machinists' handtools, applying knowledge of tool design, shop mathematics, metal properties, and layout, machining, and assembly procedures: Studies specifications, such as blueprints, sketches, or tool description, and plans sequence of operations. Measures, marks, and scribes metal stock to lay out workpieces for machining [LAY-OUT WORKER (machine shop) 600.281-018]. Sets up and operates machine tools, such as lathe, milling machine, shaper, and grinder, to machine parts to specifications, and verifies conformance of machined parts to specifications [TOOL-MACHINE SET-UP OPERATOR (machine shop) 601.280-054]. Positions and secures parts on sur-

face plate or worktable, using devices such as vises, V-blocks, and angle plates. Fits and assembles parts into assemblies or mechanisms, using handtools. Verifies dimensions and alignment, using measuring instruments such as micrometers, height gauges, and gauge blocks. Examines standard tools and modifies tools as required. Develops specifications from general descriptions and draws or sketches tool to be fabricated, using drafting tools or computer and software programs. May heattreat tools or parts [HEAT TREATER (heat treating) II 504.682-018]. May be designated according to special materials used as Carbide-Tool Maker (clock & watch); Diamond-Tool Maker (clock & watch). May only repair tools and be designated Tool Repairer (machine shop).
GOE: 05.05.07 STRENGTH: M GED: R4 M4 L3 SVP: 7 DLU: 88

601.280-054 TOOL-MACHINE SET-UP OPERATOR (machine shop) alternate titles: machine-tool operator, general; machinist; set-up-operator, tool

Sets up and operates variety of machine tools, such as *radial drill press,* lathes, milling machines, shapers, and grinders, to machine metal workpieces, such as patterns and machine, tool, or die parts, usually on custom basis. Analyzes specifications and determines tooling, applying knowledge of metal properties, machining, and shop mathematics: Studies blueprint or layout on workpiece to visualize machining required, and plans sequence of operations. Selects method of holding workpiece. Lifts workpiece manually or using hoist, and positions and secures it to holding device, such as machine table, chuck, centers, or fixture, using wrenches and aids, such as shims, parallel blocks, planter gauges, and clamps. Verifies workpiece position, using instruments, such as surface gauges, height gauges, and dial indicator. Selects feed rate, cutting speed, depth of cut, and cutting tool (bar tool, rotary cutter, or abrasive wheel) for each operation, according to knowledge of metal properties, machining, and shop mathematics. Positions and secures tool in toolholder (chuck, collet, or toolpost). Moves controls to position tool and workpiece in relation to each other, and to set feeds, speeds, and depth of cut. Starts machine, turns handwheel to feed tool in workpiece or vice versa, and engages automatic feeding device. Turns valve handle to start flow of coolant against tool and workpiece. Observes operation and regulates tool position and action. Verifies conformance of machined workpiece to specifications, using instruments, such as micrometers, gauges, and gauge blocks. May measure, mark, and scribe workpiece to lay out for machining [LAY-OUT WORKER (machine shop) 600.281-018]. May devise ways of clamping workpieces and make special jigs and fixtures as needed. May work on nonmetallic materials. May operate bench grinder or cutter grinding machine to sharpen tools [TOOL-GRINDER OPERATOR (machine shop) 603.280-038].
GOE: 05.05.07 STRENGTH: M GED: R4 M4 L3 SVP: 7 DLU: 89

601.280-058 TOOL-MAKER APPRENTICE (machine shop)

Performs duties as described under APPRENTICE (any industry) Master Title.
GOE: 05.05.07 STRENGTH: M GED: R4 M4 L3 SVP: 7 DLU: 77

601.281-010 DIE MAKER, BENCH, STAMPING (machine shop) alternate titles: bench die maker; die maker; stamping-die maker, bench

Lays out, fits, and assembles castings and metal parts to make and repair stamping dies, analyzing specifications according to knowledge of shop mathematics, die construction, and properties of sheet metal under pressure: Studies blueprints of die and product, die models, templates, and prototype parts and visualizes shape, mechanical structure, and operation of die. Computes dimensions, plans machining, layout, and assembly operations. Measures, marks, and scribes metal stock for machining by other workers. Operates drill press to drill and tap holes in parts for assembly. Lifts machined parts manually or with hoist, and positions them for assembly on worktable or surface plate. Smooths flat and contoured surfaces and fits parts to each other, using handtools, such as abrasive stones, files, and power grinder. Verifies dimensions, alignments, and clearances, using dial indicators, gauge blocks, thickness gauges, and micrometers. Dowels and bolts parts together, using handtools, such as hammers and wrenches. Works to tolerances as close as 0.0005 inch. May fit and assemble cam-operated mechanisms for lateral movement of part of die. May connect wiring and hydraulic lines to install electric and hydraulic components. May dismantle die and repair or replace parts. May make multistation *progressive dies* and be designated Progressive-Die Maker (machine shop).
GOE: 05.05.07 STRENGTH: M GED: R4 M4 L4 SVP: 7 DLU: 77

601.281-014 DIE-TRY-OUT WORKER, STAMPING (machine shop)

Tests, shapes, and smooths stamping die, using tryout power press and abrading handtools, until die members impart specified characteristics to sheet metal product: Studies blueprint of die and model of part, applying knowledge of die construction and flowing properties of metal under pressure. Installs die in press. Applies blue pigment to one die member and orange to other, and intermittently operates press through part of cycle to press die members together. Observes pigment markings to locate high spots. Secures press, using blocks, to prevent premature closing, climbs into open press, and uses powered hand grinder and handtools, such as scrapers, files, and abrasive stones, to remove high spots and shape and smooth die surface to conform to other die member. Adjusts press to allow for thickness of sheet metal workpiece and inserts model part. Repeatedly operates press. Observes markings on model part, and performs shaping and smoothing operations accordingly. Inserts sheet metal blank, operates press, and inspects and compares stamped workpiece with model part and customer's specifications, using measuring devices and checking fixture.

May operate power shear to cut blank [SHEAR OPERATOR (any industry) II]. May consult with superiors and other workers to solve metal forming problems. *GOE: 05.05.09 STRENGTH: H GED: R4 M3 L3 SVP: 7 DLU: 77*

601.281-018 INSPECTOR, GAUGE AND INSTRUMENT (machine shop) alternate titles: gauge checker
Inspects and adjusts gauges, measuring instruments, and testing equipment for conformance to blueprint specifications: Verifies accuracy of gauges and measuring instruments, such as dial indicators, fixed gauges, height gauges, and electrical and functional gauges, using master gauges or master parts. Examines gauges or measuring instruments for wear or adjustment. Disassembles inaccurate or worn gauges and measuring instruments with handtools. Inspects parts for wear, warping, or other defects. Verifies dimensions of parts against blueprint specifications, using gauge blocks, micrometer, vernier height gauge, sine bar, bevel protractor, and optical comparator. Measures surface flatness and finish, using optical flats and profilameter. Computes unspecified dimensions and other data, using shop mathematics and trigonometry. Laps corroded or pitted surfaces. Reassembles gauge and adjusts stops and levers to specified settings. Inspects accuracy of new gauges and instruments for conformance to blueprint specifications before they are released for production use.
GOE: 06.01.05 STRENGTH: M GED: R4 M4 L3 SVP: 7 DLU: 77

601.281-022 INSPECTOR, TOOL (machine shop) alternate titles: precision inspector; surface-plate inspector; tool-and-die inspector; tool-and-gauge inspector; tooling inspector
Inspects, tests, and adjusts new and reworked tools, dies, gauges, jigs, and fixtures, for conformance to specifications, such as dimensions, tolerances, and hardness, applying knowledge of tool and die design, shop mathematics, and machining and testing procedures, using precision measuring instruments, testing equipment, and handtools: Computes angles, radii, and other unspecified dimensions of workpiece, using algebra, geometry, and trigonometry. Positions workpiece on surface plate and lays out reference points and center lines on parts [LAY-OUT WORKER (machine shop) 600.281-018]. Measures angular dimensions, radii, contours, clearances, thread lead, and other specifications, using precision measuring instruments, such as micrometer, gauge blocks, dial indicators, height gauges, level protractors, and optical comparators. Tests units for fit of moving parts and mechanical functioning. Tests parts for hardness, using hardness testing equipment [HARDNESS INSPECTOR (heat treating) 504.387-010]. Inspects, adjusts, and verifies accuracy of gauges and measuring instruments for conformance to specifications [INSPECTOR, GAUGE AND INSTRUMENT (machine shop) 601.281-018]. Examines defective parts to determine cause of defect and recommends changes or modifications. Determines salvageability of defective items, utilizing knowledge of material and machining costs. Measures surface finish of part, using profilometer. Inspects first run parts and assemblies. Writes report regarding inspection and testing results. May draw enlarged part details for use on optical comparator. May use laser-equipped measuring instruments. May inspect parts for flaws or internal fissures, using ultrasonic equipment or fluorescent lights. May test gauges used in manufacture and assembly of watches, using measuring devices and microscope, and be designated Gauge Controller (clock & watch).
GOE: 05.07.01 STRENGTH: M GED: R4 M4 L4 SVP: 8 DLU: 88

601.281-026 TOOL MAKER, BENCH (machine shop)
Lays out, fits, and assembles parts to make and repair cutting tools, jigs, fixtures, gauges, or machinists' handtools, analyzing specifications according to knowledge of tool designs, shop mathematics, machining, and layout and assembly procedures: Studies blueprint to determine machining to be done and plans layout and assembly. Measures, marks, and scribes metal stock to lay out for machining by other workers [LAY-OUT WORKER (machine shop) 600.281-018]. Operates drill press to drill and tap holes in parts [DRILL-PRESS SET-UP OPERATOR, SINGLE SPINDLE (machine shop) 606.682-018]. Smooths and scrapes parts to fit, using handtools such as files and scrapers. Positions and secures parts on surface plate with devices such as V-blocks, vises, and angle plates. Assembles parts into product, using tools such as wrenches, hammers, and tweezers, and verifies dimensions and alignments, using measuring instruments such as micrometers, height gauges, and gauge blocks. May set up and operate surface grinder [GRINDER OPERATOR, SURFACE, TOOL (machine shop) 603.280-014] to grind surface of parts. May test assembled mechanism. May be designated according to specialized function as Tool Repairer, Bench (machine shop); or according to product made as Gauge Maker (machine shop); Jig-And-Fixture Maker (machine shop).
GOE: 05.05.07 STRENGTH: M GED: R4 M3 L3 SVP: 7 DLU: 77

601.281-030 TOOL AND FIXTURE REPAIRER (auto. mfg.)
Replaces and adjusts tools and fixtures of production machines and components of transfer systems in industrial establishment, using handtools and precision-measuring instruments, following specifications and blueprints, and applying knowledge of hydraulics, pneumatics, and machine programming and maintenance: Observes production machines, such as punch and drill presses, milling machines, lathes and robotic equipment, to detect malfunctions, need for adjustment and alignment, or replacement of worn or broken tools and fixtures. Removes, replaces, adjusts, and aligns components of machines and equipment, such as production fixtures, programmable machines (robots), and conveyors and transfer devices (workpiece shuttle mechanisms), using precision-measuring instruments and handtools. Enters instructions on *programmable controller* or *robot controller*, to adjust speed, motion and alignment of programmable machines, applying knowledge of machine programming and operations and pro-

duction processes. Repairs and calibrates electronic measuring gauges, using electrical test equipment, master gauges, and handtools. Operates machines to verify that repairs, adjustments, and alignments have corrected problems and that machines function according to specifications. Disassembles, cleans, and polishes machine components. Informs supervisor of machine malfunctions requiring repair by other maintenance workers, such as ELECTRICIAN, MAINTENANCE (any industry) 829.261-018. May set up and operate machine tools, such as lathes, mills, and surface grinders, to repair worn or broken production tools and fixtures.
GOE: 05.05.09 STRENGTH: M GED: R4 M4 L4 SVP: 7 DLU: 90

601.380-010 CARBIDE OPERATOR (machine shop) alternate titles: carbide grinder
Fabricates tungsten-carbide cutting tips for use on lathes, planers, milling machines, and other metalworking tools, using mechanical or hydraulic press, furnaces, cutting and grinding wheels, and precision-measuring instruments: Weighs cobalt, carbon, tungsten, titanium, and other powdered metals on balance scale to obtain specified molding mixture. Pours mixture from pans into molds or into hoppers for automatic feeding into molds in press. Turns valves on press to compress mixture into billet. Removes billet from press. Sets automatic feed, time, and temperature controls on sintering furnace. Feeds billets into furnace to fuse metals together. Removes billets from furnace and cuts and grinds them into cutting tips, using diamond cutting wheel and electric grinding wheel. Measures cutting edges of tips to ensure attainment of specified tolerances, using gauges, rulers, micrometers, and protractors. Sets pyrometer controls of heat-treating furnace, and feeds cutting tips into furnace to harden them. May regrind cutting tips and remeasure for conformance to specifications.
GOE: 05.05.07 STRENGTH: M GED: R4 M4 L3 SVP: 6 DLU: 77

601.381-010 DIE FINISHER (machine shop) alternate titles: die fitter
Grinds, files, sands, and polishes surfaces of metalworking die members to specified shape and smoothness and inspects dies for conformity to wood, plastic, or plaster die models or prototype parts: Lifts and positions die member on bench manually or with hoist. Studies blueprints, die models, and prototype parts, and compares them with die member to ascertain contours. Verifies dimensions and radii, using micrometers, dial indicators, and calipers. Brushes blue pigment on ridged and grooved surface of rough-milled die member, and grinds down ridges with powered hand grinder until only traces of blue pigment remain. Brushes contrasting pigments on die member and prototype part, die model, or corresponding die member, and presses them together, manually or with press. Observes pattern of pigments where surfaces have made contact, and grinds and files high spots until die member conforms to specified contour. Polishes die member, using hand stones. Inspects smoothness and contour conformity visually and tactually. May be designated according to part finished as Punch Finisher (machine shop).
GOE: 05.05.07 STRENGTH: M GED: R4 M3 L3 SVP: 7 DLU: 77

601.381-014 DIE MAKER (jewelry-silver.) alternate titles: die cutter; hub cutter
Fabricates set of dies for use in forming and shaping metal jewelry blanks, following drawings or blueprints and using variety of metalworking machines and engraver's handtools: Brushes blue dye on surface of steel block workpiece. Measures, locates, and marks center of block with cross-lines, using divider and drafter's pencil. Copies design, freehand, from sample drawing or blueprint, maintaining size specifications. Scribes along drawn line, using scribe. Measures finished design for conformance to specifications, using calipers and gauges. Positions workpiece in vise and cuts out lines of design. Chips and cuts away excess metal to complete design, using metalworking machines and handtools. Verifies dimensions of workpiece, using calipers and gauges. Hardens and tempers steel block and drives it into another block of soft steel or plastic to form sunken design, using press, or sends it to machine shop for processing. Engraves other half of die by pounding thin sheets of metal into completed half. May engrave lettering and designs into dies, using pantograph machine. May cut out, shape, and harden upper steel die (forcer) used to stamp out jewelry articles and be known as Forcer Maker (jewelry-silver.).
GOE: 05.05.07 STRENGTH: M GED: R4 M3 L3 SVP: 7 DLU: 77

601.381-018 DIE POLISHER (nonfer. metal)
Polishes and resurfaces bores and cavities of wire drawing dies to specified size and angles, using hand laps or various die polishing machines, tools, and diamond cutting pastes: Cleans dies by immersing them in tank with water, detergent, and agitating pebbles or sonic cleaner. Inspects worn dies to ascertain extent of wear, using loupe, steel gauge pins, and micrometer. Laps die surfaces to specified dimensions as it revolves in *lapping* machine or on bench lathe, using cotton swabs and progressively finer diamond pastes; or resurfaces and polishes die, using polishing machine and diamond pastes. Inspects die for cracks and smoothness of finish, using loupe or microscope, and measures diameter of die openings for conformance to specifications, using steel gauge pins and micrometer. May resurface and clean dies, using powered drill, grinder, or files and other handtools.
GOE: 05.05.07 STRENGTH: L GED: R3 M3 L2 SVP: 6 DLU: 77

601.381-022 DIE-MAKER APPRENTICE (jewelry-silver.) alternate titles: die-cutter apprentice; hub-cutter apprentice
Performs duties as described under APPRENTICE (any industry) Master Title.
GOE: 05.05.07 STRENGTH: M GED: R4 M3 L3 SVP: 7 DLU: 77

601.381-026 PLASTIC TOOL MAKER (machine shop)

Molds and assembles plastic tools, such as gauges, jigs, templates, and fixtures, following blueprints: Spreads layers of glass cloth on molds or forms and brushes each layer with plastic to build plastic tool following configuration of mold. Pries cured plastic tool from mold with prying tool. Calculates, from blueprints, location of guide and reference lines and holes for tools. Measures and marks location of lines and holes on tools, using calipers, micrometers, and protractors. Drills holes in tools, using drill press, and forces bushings into holes, using arbor press or hammer. Assembles tools by laminating them with glass cloth and resin. Verifies alignment and dimensions of assembly, using calipers, height gauges, gram scale, and sight level. Trims excess material from tool parts with power grinder. Fills space between adjoining parts with plastic. May build wood frame to support and maintain alignment of complex tools, using carpenter's handtools. May laminate tools to frame.
GOE: 06.01.04 STRENGTH: M GED: R4 M3 L3 SVP: 7 DLU: 77

601.381-030 PLASTIC-FIXTURE BUILDER (machine shop) alternate titles: model maker, plastic

Fabricates precision plastic checking fixtures used to determine accuracy of stamped metal parts: Casts plastic reproduction from model of part [PLASTIC DUPLICATOR (machine tools)]. Lays out reference lines on cast as guides in assembling, fitting, and trimming operations, using height gauges, surface plates, squares, protractors, and other measuring instruments. Cuts and trims casts following reference lines, using files, saws, planes, and other handtools. Assembles casts with glue, bolts, and other fasteners. Fits and fastens metal inserts into fixture at specified points to increase strength or accuracy. Verifies dimensions of completed fixture for conformance to specifications, using templates and measuring instruments. May fabricate metal inserts used in fixture, using powered saws, powered grinder, and files.
GOE: 05.05.07 STRENGTH: M GED: R4 M3 L3 SVP: 7 DLU: 77

601.381-034 SAW MAKER (cutlery-hrdwr.) alternate titles: saw mechanic

Fabricates blades for bandsaws, circular saws, and jigsaws from steel blanks or band stock, following work order specifications and using handtools, machine tools, and knowledge of metal characteristics: Selects blank or band stock, according to size, type, and operating requirements of blade. Hammers dents, kinks, and twists from blank or band stock. Operates power roller to straighten blade and stretch (roll) blade to specified temper. Installs specified serrating dies in punch press and operates press to cut teeth in blade. Sharpens and sets blade teeth, using power grinder and swaging machine. Operates butt welding machine to join ends of bandsaw blade. May operate surface grinder to grind blanks to specified thickness. May heat-treat saws to relieve internal stress and temper blade [HEAT TREATER (heat treating) I]. May specialize in tempering and aligning blades and be designated Sawsmith (cutlery-hrdwr.).
GOE: 05.05.07 STRENGTH: L GED: R4 M4 L3 SVP: 6 DLU: 77

601.381-038 TEMPLATE MAKER (any industry)

Designs and fabricates templates of assorted materials, such as metal, fiberglass, wood, and plastic, for laying out reference points and dimensions on metal plates, sheets, tubes, and structural shapes used for fabricating, welding, and assembling structural metal products or dies: Plans and develops layout according to blueprints, work orders, tool planning orders, mockups, or sample parts, applying knowledge of trigonometry, product design, and properties of metal. Lays out design onto template material, using instruments, such as compass, protractor, dividers, and ruler, and marks shape and reference points, using scriber, pencil, chalk, and punch. Cuts, trims, drills, reams, files, shapes, and forms templates, using handtools, power tools, and fabricating machines, such as bandsaw, drill press, jointer, punch press, and shear. Nails, glues, screws, bolts, solders, or welds component parts to assemble templates. Marks job numbers, file codes, dimensions, layout, and fabricating instructions on templates. Repairs and reworks templates. May construct jigs and fixtures for fabricating machine operations [TOOL MAKER, BENCH (machine shop) 601.281-026].
GOE: 06.01.04 STRENGTH: M GED: R4 M4 L3 SVP: 7 DLU: 88

601.381-042 DIE MAKER, ELECTRONIC (machine shop)

Lays out, machines, fits, and assembles metal parts to fabricate electronic (heat-sealing) dies used to form plastic products, working from blueprints or drawings and using milling machine, tools, and precision instruments: Studies blueprints, drawings, and specifications to plan machine operations applying knowledge of metal properties and machine shop math. Selects and positions brass or steel stock on milling table, by hand or using hoist. Sets up and operates milling machine to machine channels of specified width and depth in stock to form electrodes. Measures, marks, and cuts electrodes to specified sizes, using rule, scribe, and cutoff knife. Sets aside electrodes for further processing by other workers. Positions completed electrodes on die board template to locate reference points for lugs and die parts, and marks reference points, using hammer and punch. Drills and taps holes in aluminum plate that serves as base for die, using power drill with tapping attachment, and mounts dies to base with screws, using screwdriver. Operates milling machine to reduce electrode altitude from die bottom to top of electrodes, working to tolerances of plus or minus .001 inch. Measures dies to verify conformance to specifications, using vernier gauge, micrometer, and ruler.
GOE: 05.05.07 STRENGTH: M GED: R4 M3 L2 SVP: 7 DLU: 86

601.482-010 PROFILE-GRINDER TECHNICIAN (clock & watch)

Sets up and operates grinding equipment to grind precision cutting tools and dies from tungsten carbide and high-speed steel, working from blueprints and to tolerances of 0.0001 inch: Plans and lays out work and sets up equipment, using variety of precision measuring devices and machine attachments and fixtures. Grinds tools and dies to prescribed dimensions by turning handwheels or adjusting controls to feed work against grinders. Measures dimensions with precision gauges. Removes, dresses, and installs emery, diamond-impregnated, and diamond-charged cast-iron grinding wheels.
GOE: 05.05.07 STRENGTH: L GED: R3 M3 L3 SVP: 6 DLU: 77

601.682-010 TOOL DRESSER (any industry) alternate titles: drill-sharpener operator

Operates compressed-air or steam-driven machine to sharpen large drills, such as rock drills, used in construction, mining, quarrying, and well-drilling: Places cutting end of drill in forge to heat cutting edge to increase malleability. Inserts heated drill into die space on machine. Starts hammering action of die to shape cutting edge of drill. Stops machine and removes edged drill. Tempers drill by heating it in forge and quenching it in water, brine, or oil.
GOE: 06.04.02 STRENGTH: M GED: R3 M2 L2 SVP: 5 DLU: 77

602 GEAR MACHINING OCCUPATIONS

This group includes occupations concerned with shaping metal gears by any combination of milling, turning, planing, abrading, boring, chipping, sawing, or shaving.

602.280-010 GEAR-CUTTING-MACHINE SET-UP OPERATOR, TOOL (machine shop) alternate titles: gear cutter; gear shaper; tool-room gear-machine operator

Sets up and operates variety of gear-cutting machines, such as gear shapers, hobs, and generators to machine spline, *rack*, or gear teeth on metal blanks, analyzing specifications according to knowledge of gear designs, shop mathematics, and gear machining procedures: Studies blueprint to visualize machining required, and plans sequence of operations. Selects machine and method of holding workpiece. Computes machine settings from gear specifications. Positions and secures workpiece to cutting angle on arbor, in chuck or other holding device, using wrenches. Selects, positions, and secures cutters in toolhead, in spindle, or on arbor. Sets feed rates and rotation speeds of cutters and workpiece in relation to each other by selecting and mounting gears, cams, or templates, or by moving levers. Moves controls to set cutting speeds and depth of stroke and cut for reciprocating cutters, and to position tool and workpiece in relation to each other. May select and mount guides to impart twisting motion to spindle for cutting helical gears. Starts machine, turns valve handle to start flow of coolant against cutter and workpiece. Verifies conformance of machined gear to specifications, using gear *measuring wires, involute checker*, master gears, optical comparator (shadowgraph), and other special gear inspection equipment. May operate broaching machine to broach internal splines or gears [BROACHING-MACHINE SET-UP OPERATOR (machine shop) 605.382-010]. May work on nonmetallic materials. May be required to have experience with particular gear type, material, or size, type, or trade name of machine.
GOE: 06.01.03 STRENGTH: M GED: R4 M4 L3 SVP: 7 DLU: 77

602.360-010 GRINDER SET-UP OPERATOR, GEAR, TOOL (machine shop) alternate titles: gear-and-spline grinder

Sets up and operates precision gear grinding machine with special *indexing* equipment to grind master and precision gears, usually on custom basis, analyzing specifications and selecting tooling according to knowledge of gear grinding procedures: Studies blueprints and machining instructions to determine grinding operations and to plan sequence of operations. Computes machine indexing ratios and cam dimensions for specified spacing and contour of gear teeth, using shop mathematics. Selects index plate, cams, grinding wheel, feed rates, grinding speed, and depth of cut, according to computations, gear specifications, and knowledge of gear design, metal properties, and abrasives. Positions and secures index plate, cams, and grinding wheel in machine, using wrenches and measuring devices. Sets up automatic dressing device to dress wheel to specified profile. Moves controls to set synchronized rotation speeds and feed rates. Positions and secures workpiece on mandrel between centers or in chuck, and turns handwheels to position workpiece and wheel, verifying positions with thickness gauges, dial indicators, and micrometers. Turns valve handle and directs flow of coolant against wheel and workpiece. Moves controls to index workpiece and feed wheel to workpiece, adjusting depth of cut in part by sight and feel. Verifies dimensions of ground workpiece for conformance to specifications, using gear *measuring wires and involute checker*. May grind nonmetallic materials. May be required to have experience with particular type of gear, precision level, or type or trade name of machine.
GOE: 06.01.03 STRENGTH: L GED: R4 M3 L3 SVP: 7 DLU: 77

602.362-010 GEAR INSPECTOR (machine shop)

Sets up and operates gear inspection equipment to measure curvature of gear tooth, distance between teeth, concentricity of gear, profile and surface dimensions, surface finish, and material hardness of production and prototype gears, utilizing knowledge of gear inspection techniques and procedures: Reads blueprints or specifications to determine dimensions and tolerances. Mounts master gears on testing machine, attaches recording instrument leads and styluses to gear, and starts machine to calibrate machine instruments. Mounts and secures gear on spindle or arbor of machine, sets instrument stylus on gears, and turns instrument dials to zero. Starts machine and reads instrument dials to determine

dimensions of gear, and compares readings to specifications. Measures profile and surface dimensions of gear, using optical comparator and micrometer, vernier gauges, and sine blocks. Measures surface finish, using profilameter. Measures material hardness, using hardness gauge. Recommends corrections on gear forming machine setup to eliminate defects. Maintains records of gears tested and measured. May lay out and mark drill holes, keyways, and gear tooth profile on blanks, using measuring devices and marking tools. May check gear-forming machine setup, using master gears.
GOE: 06.03.01 STRENGTH: M GED: R4 M3 L3 SVP: 6 DLU: 77

602.362-014 GEAR-SORTING-AND-INSPECTING MACHINE OPERA-TOR (machine shop) alternate titles: gear-coding machine operator

Sets up and operates gear inspecting and sorting machines to measure gears for deviations from dimensional specifications and to test mesh of gears with master (inspection) gears: Positions gear in spindle and moves controls to engage it with master gear. Rotates gear and observes mating with master gear and listens for sounds indicating defective gear. Marks gear with ink or attaches tracing stylus to gear to locate and highlight wear points. Color codes gears to enable other workers to match gears having similar deviations. May file burrs or highspots on gears. May test mesh and accuracy of finished transmission gears and be designated Gear Roller (machine shop).
GOE: 06.03.01 STRENGTH: L GED: R3 M3 L2 SVP: 4 DLU: 77

602.380-010 GEAR-CUTTING-MACHINE SET-UP OPERATOR (machine shop) alternate titles: all-around-gear-machine operator; gear cutter; gear-machine operator, general

Sets up and operates two or more types of gear-cutting and finishing machines, such as gear shapers, hobs, honers and lappers, and generators, to machine spline or gear teeth on metal blanks according to machining instructions and knowledge of gear types and gear machining: Reads blueprint or job order to determine gear dimensions and specifications, fixture and cutter to use, and machine settings. Secures and positions cutters in toolhead, on spindle, or on arbor, and bolts fixtures on machine. Mounts gears, cams, or templates, or moves levers to set feed rates and rotation speeds of cutters and workpiece in relation to each other. Positions and secures workpiece to specified cutting angle on arbor, in chuck, or in fixture, using wrenches. Starts machine, turns valve handle, and directs flow of coolant against tool and workpiece. Verifies conformance to specifications, using micrometers, gear *measuring wires,* master gears, and special gear inspection equipment. May set cutting speeds and depth of stroke and cut for reciprocating cutters. May mount guides to control twisting motion of spindle for cutting helical gears. May compute gear dimensions and machine settings, applying knowledge of shop mathematics and gear design. May machine nonmetallic materials. May be required to have experience with custom or production work, or with particular material, product, or size, type, or trade name of machine.
GOE: 06.01.03 STRENGTH: M GED: R4 M3 L3 SVP: 6 DLU: 77

602.382-010 GEAR HOBBER SET-UP OPERATOR (machine shop) alternate titles: hobbing-machine operator

Sets up and operates one or more gear *hobbing* machines to machine splines or gear teeth on metal blanks according to specifications, machining instructions, and knowledge of gear hobbing procedures: Reads machining instructions or blueprints to determine machine settings, fixtures and hobs to use, and gear specifications, such as dimensions and tolerances. Clamps workpiece in fixture or presses it on arbor and mounts arbor between centers. Positions and secures specified hob on arbor in relation to workpiece, using wrenches. Moves levers or mounts gears in machine to set feed rates and rotation speeds of hob and workpiece following machining instructions. Turns handwheel to feed hob to workpiece or vice versa, and engages automatic feed. Turns valve handle and directs flow of coolant against hob and workpiece. Verifies conformance of hobbed gears to specifications, using micrometers, gear *measuring wires,* master gears, and *involute checker.* May compute data, such as gear dimensions and machine settings, applying knowledge of shop mathematics. May machine plastic or other nonmetallic materials. May be required to have experience with custom or production work, or with particular material, product, or size, type, or trade name of machine.
GOE: 06.03.01 STRENGTH: M GED: R3 M3 L3 SVP: 5 DLU: 77

602.382-014 GEAR-GENERATOR SET-UP OPERATOR, SPIRAL BEVEL (machine shop) alternate titles: curved-tooth-gear-generator operator; gleason-gear generator; hypoid-gear generator; spiral-gear generator

Sets up and operates one or more spiral-bevel *gear generating* machines to cut and shape spiral or hypoid teeth on metal bevel-gear blanks according to specifications, machining instructions, and knowledge of gear types and generating procedures: Reads blueprint or machining instructions to determine gear type, dimensions, and number of teeth, and machine settings and cutter to be used. Clamps workpiece in fixture or presses it on arbor, and positions it to cutting angle. Positions and secures cutter on spindle in relation to workpiece, using wrenches and turning handwheels. Moves levers to set cutter and workpiece rotation speeds in relation to each other. Mounts gears, cams, or templates in machine to control *indexing* of workpiece and rolling motion of cutter. Starts machine, turns valve handle, and directs flow of coolant against cutter and workpiece. Verifies conformance of machined gear to specifications, using micrometers, master gears, and special gear inspection equipment. May compute data, such as gear dimensions and machine settings, applying knowl-

edge of shop mathematics. May machine plastics or other nonmetallic materials. May be required to have experience with custom or production work, or with particular material, product, or size, type, or trade name of machine.
GOE: 06.02.02 STRENGTH: M GED: R3 M3 L3 SVP: 5 DLU: 77

602.382-018 GEAR-GENERATOR SET-UP OPERATOR, STRAIGHT BEVEL (machine shop) alternate titles: bevel-gear-generator operator; generator operator, straight-bevel gear; straight-tooth-gear-generator operator

Sets up and operates one or more straight-tooth bevel-gear generating machines to cut and shape straight teeth on metal bevel-gear blanks, according to machining instructions and knowledge of *gear generating* procedures: Reads blueprint or machining instructions to determine machine settings, fixtures and cutters to use, and gear type, dimensions, tolerances, and number of teeth to be generated. Mounts workpiece on arbor and positions it to cutting angle. Positions and clamps two cutters in toolheads, and positions cutter cradle to specified angle, using wrenches. Mounts gears and cams in machine to control rotation speed and *indexing* of workpiece, cutting speed, and rolling motion of cutter cradle. Starts machine, turns valve handle, and directs flow of coolant against reciprocating cutters and workpiece. Verifies conformance of machined gear to specifications, using micrometers, master gears, and special gear inspection equipment. May compute such data as gear dimensions and machine settings, applying knowledge of shop mathematics. May machine plastics or other nonmetallic materials. May be required to have experience with custom or production work, or with particular material, product, or size, type, or trade name of machine.
GOE: 06.02.02 STRENGTH: M GED: R3 M3 L3 SVP: 5 DLU: 77

602.382-022 GEAR-MILLING-MACHINE SET-UP OPERATOR (machine shop) alternate titles: milling-machine operator, gear

Sets up and operates one or more gear milling machines to machine splines or gear teeth on metal blanks, according to machining instructions and knowledge of gear milling procedures: Reads blueprints or machining instructions to determine machine settings, fixtures and milling tools to use, and gear specifications, such as dimensions and tolerances. Clamps workpiece in fixture or presses it onto arbor. Positions and secures cutter on spindle in relation to workpiece, using wrenches. Moves levers or mounts gears in machine to set feed rates and rotation speeds of cutter and workpiece in relation to each other. Starts machine, turns valve handle, and directs flow of coolant against cutter and workpiece. Verifies conformance of machined gears to specifications, using micrometers, gear *measuring wires,* and special gear inspection equipment. May compute data, such as gear dimensions and machine settings, applying knowledge of shop mathematics. May machine plastics or other nonmetallic materials. May be required to have experience with custom or production work, or with particular material, product, or size, type, or trade name of machine.
GOE: 06.02.02 STRENGTH: M GED: R3 M3 L3 SVP: 5 DLU: 77

602.382-026 GEAR-SHAPER SET-UP OPERATOR (machine shop)

Sets up and operates one or more gear shaping machines to machine splines or gear teeth in metal blanks, according to machining instructions and knowledge of gear types and gear shaping procedures: Reads machining instructions or blueprints to determine machine settings, holding fixtures and cutters to use, and gear type, dimensions, tolerances, and number of teeth to be cut and shaped. Clamps workpiece in fixture or presses it on arbor. Positions and secures specified cutter on spindle in relation to workpiece and sets length of stroke, using wrenches. Moves levers or mounts gears in machine to set feed rates, cutting speeds, and rotation speeds of cutter and workpiece, according to machining instructions. Turns valve handle and directs flow of coolant against cutter and workpiece. Verifies conformance of machined gears to specifications, using micrometers, master gears, gear *measuring wires,* and special gear inspection equipment. May mount guides to control twisting motion of spindle for cutting helical gears. May compute data, such as gear dimensions and machine settings, applying knowledge of shop mathematics. May machine plastics or other nonmetallic materials. May be required to have experience with custom or production work or with particular material, product, or size, type, or trade name of machine.
GOE: 06.02.02 STRENGTH: M GED: R3 M3 L3 SVP: 5 DLU: 77

602.382-030 GEAR-SHAVER SET-UP OPERATOR (machine shop)

Sets up and operates one or more gear-shaving machines that utilize gashed, gear-shaped cutting tools to shape and smooth gear teeth or to correct distortions remaining from roughing (gear-cutting) operation, following machining instructions and knowledge of gear-shaving methods: Reads blueprints or machining instructions to determine machine settings, fixtures and cutterheads to use, and gear dimensions and tolerances. Presses gear on arbor and mounts it between centers, using handtools. Mounts cutter on cutterhead. Moves controls to set feed rates, cutting speeds, reciprocating action, and angles of cutter and gear. Turns handwheel to feed gear to cutter. Verifies conformance to specifications, using micrometers, *measuring wires,* and *involute checker.* May compute gear dimensions and machine settings, applying knowledge of shop mathematics and gear formulas. May work on nonmetallic gears. May be required to have experience with custom or production work, or with particular material, kind of gear, or machine of particular type or trade name.
GOE: 06.01.03 STRENGTH: M GED: R3 M3 L3 SVP: 6 DLU: 77

602.382-034 GRINDER, GEAR (machine shop) alternate titles: gear-grinding-machine operator; gear-tooth-grinding-machine operator

Sets up and operates one or more gear grinding machines to grind surfaces of splines or gear teeth, following machining instructions and applying knowledge of gear grinding techniques: Reads blueprint or machining instructions to determine fixtures and grinding wheel to use, machine settings, and gear dimensions and tolerances. Clamps workpiece in chuck or fixture, or presses it on arbor and mounts between centers. Positions and secures wheel on arbor in relation to workpiece, using wrenches. Moves levers or mounts gears in machine to set feed rates and rotation speeds of wheel and workpiece in relation to each other. Turns handwheels to feed wheel to workpiece or vice versa, and to index workpiece, and engages automatic feeding and *indexing* device. Turns valve and directs flow of coolant against wheel and workpiece. Sets up and operates wheel dressing device to dress and true abrasive wheel. Verifies conformance to specifications, using micrometers, gear *measuring wires, and involute checker.* May compute data, such as gear dimensions and machine settings, applying knowledge of shop mathematics. May work on nonmetallic materials. May be required to have experience with custom or production work or with particular material, gear type, or size, type, or trade name of machine.
GOE: 06.02.02 STRENGTH: M GED: R3 M3 L3 SVP: 5 DLU: 77

602.482-010 GEAR-LAPPING-MACHINE OPERATOR (machine shop) alternate titles: gear finisher; gear nicker; gear-tooth-lapping-machine operator

Sets up and operates gear-lapping machine to lap gears according to specifications, machining instructions, standard charts, and knowledge of gear *lapping* procedures: Reads blueprint or instructions to determine gear dimensions, tolerances, and number of gears to be lapped, and machining instructions for lapping speeds and pressures, work-holding fixtures, and spindle angles to be used. Positions and secures pairs or trains of gears on spindles, using fixture and wrenches. Moves controls to set spindle angles, lapping speeds, tool pressure, and length of cycle. Brushes or sprays *lapping compound* on gears. Starts machine, examines gear contact area, and moves handwheels to adjust action of gears. Inspects lapped gears for conformance to specifications, using knowledge of gear design and surface finishing. May inspect finish and mechanical action of gears with gear inspection equipment. May be required to have experience with particular type of gear or machine. May lap gears against each other metal-to-metal without lapping compound and be designated Gear Burnisher (machine shop).
GOE: 06.02.02 STRENGTH: M GED: R3 M3 L3 SVP: 5 DLU: 77

602.685-010 GEAR-CUTTING-MACHINE OPERATOR, PRODUCTION (machine shop) alternate titles: hob mill operator; production-gear cutter

Tends one or more previously set up gear-cutting machines, such as gear shapers, hobbers, finishers, and generators, to machine spline or gear teeth on metal blanks: Positions and secures workpiece on arbor, or in chuck, fixture, or automatic feeding mechanism. Starts machine and flow of coolant and observes operation. Adjusts machine stops and changes worn cutter, using wrenches. Verifies conformance to specifications, using fixed gauges, micrometers, and preset dial indicators. May machine plastics or other nonmetallic materials. May be required to have experience with particular material, product, or size, type, or trade name of machine.
GOE: 06.04.02 STRENGTH: M GED: R2 M2 L2 SVP: 3 DLU: 77

603 ABRADING OCCUPATIONS

This group includes occupations concerned with smoothing, polishing, sharpening, or cutting through or into metal objects by the wearing away action of abrasives. The smoothing, polishing, sharpening, or shaping of nonmetallic materials, except wood, are also included when the methods and machine tools commonly applied to the machining of metal are used.

603.130-010 SUPERVISOR, GRINDING (any industry)

Supervises and coordinates activities of workers engaged in grinding metal objects to specifications, applying knowledge of metal properties, abrasives, and grinding procedures. May set up machines. May train new workers. Performs duties described under SUPERVISOR (any industry) Master Title.
GOE: 06.02.01 STRENGTH: M GED: R4 M3 L3 SVP: 7 DLU: 77

603.137-010 FILING-AND-POLISHING SUPERVISOR (ordnance)

Supervises and coordinates activities of workers engaged in filing, burring, tumbling, sandblasting, and polishing small arms, such as rifles and machine guns. Performs duties as described under SUPERVISOR (any industry) Master Title.
GOE: 06.02.01 STRENGTH: M GED: R4 M4 L4 SVP: 7 DLU: 77

603.260-010 GRINDER SET-UP OPERATOR, THREAD TOOL (machine shop) alternate titles: precision-thread-grinder operator; thread-grinder, tool

Sets up and operates thread-grinding machine to grind internal or external threads on metal objects, such as worm gears and leadscrews, on custom basis, analyzing specifications and selecting tooling according to knowledge of thread grinding procedures: Studies blueprint to visualize grinding to be done and plans sequence of operations. Selects and computes machine settings, such as positioning angles, rotation speeds, feed rates, and gear ratios, using knowledge

of shop mathematics. Selects grinding wheel, gears, and cams, using knowledge of thread types, metal properties, and abrasives, and installs them, using wrenches. Positions and secures workpiece between centers or in chuck jaws. Sets trip stops along calibrated rack to limit workpiece travel and activate wheel withdrawal. Adjusts device to dress wheel to computed angles, and to set for automatic dressing during operation. Moves controls to adjust, start, and control operation of machine. Verifies conformance of ground workpieces to specifications, using such measuring devices as thread *measuring wires*, dial indicator, gauge blocks, and optical comparator (shadowgraph). May be required to have experience with particular type of thread, kind of computation, or level of precision, or with machine of particular type or trade name.
GOE: 06.01.03 STRENGTH: M GED: R4 M4 L3 SVP: 7 DLU: 77

603.280-010 GRINDER OPERATOR, EXTERNAL, TOOL (machine shop) alternate titles: cylindrical grinder, tool; external-cylindrical-grinder operator; external grinder, tool; grinder, hand; outer-diameter grinder, tool; precision grinder, external

Sets up and operates external grinding machines to grind external cylindrical and tapered surfaces of rotating metal workpieces, such as tool, die, and machine parts, usually for limited runs, analyzing blueprints and specifications and selecting tooling according to knowledge of external grinding procedures: Studies blueprint or layout on workpiece to visualize grinding to be done and plans sequence of operations. Selects grinding wheel, according to knowledge of metal properties and abrasives, and mounts wheel on spindle. Dresses wheel manually or with preset dressing device. Moves controls and reads dials to set angle of workpiece to grinding wheel. Positions and secures workpiece between centers, on magnetic chuck, or in chuck jaws, using wrenches. Selects and sets grinding wheel speed, work surface speed, and travel rate of powered table. Positions and tightens stops to set depth of grinding wheel cut and stroke of worktable. Moves controls to feed wheel to workpiece manually or automatically. Turns valve handle and directs flow of coolant against wheel and workpiece. Verifies dimensions of ground workpiece for conformance to specifications, using such measuring instruments as micrometers, dial indicators, and gauge blocks. May dress grinding wheel to specified profile for contour grinding, using special fixtures and tools. May grind nonmetallic materials. May operate tracer attachment to duplicate contours from templates or models. May be required to have experience with particular material, product, or precision level, or with machine of particular size, type, or trade name. May set up machines for other workers. May be designated according to type of machine operated as Roll Grinder Operator (machine shop).
GOE: 06.01.03 STRENGTH: M GED: R4 M3 L3 SVP: 7 DLU: 78

603.280-014 GRINDER OPERATOR, SURFACE, TOOL (machine shop) alternate titles: grinder, hand; precision grinder, surface; rotary-surface grinder; surface grinder; surface-grinding-machine hand

Sets up and operates surface grinding machines with horizontal or vertical spindle and reciprocating or rotating table to grind flat or contoured surfaces of metal workpieces, such as tool, die, and machine parts, usually for limited runs, analyzing specifications and selecting tooling according to knowledge of surface grinding procedures: Studies blueprint or layout on workpiece to visualize grinding to be done and plans sequence of operations. Positions and secures workpiece on magnetic chuck, in holding fixture, or directly to machine table. Selects grinding wheel, grinding speeds, and feed rates for each operation according to knowledge of metal properties and abrasives, and mounts wheel on spindle. Moves device to dress wheel. Moves controls and reads dials to set rotation speeds and feed rates. Positions and tightens stops to limit table travel. Moves controls to feed workpiece to wheel or vice versa. Turns valve handle and directs flow of coolant against wheel and workpiece. Verifies dimensions of ground workpiece for conformance to specifications, using such measuring instruments as micrometers, comparators, dial indicators, gauge blocks, and load test equipment. May dress grinding wheel to specified profile for contour grinding, using special fixtures and tools. May grind nonmetallic materials, such as plastics. May operate tracer attachment to duplicate contours from templates or models. May be required to have experience with particular material, product, or precision level, or with machine of particular size, type, or trade name.
GOE: 06.01.03 STRENGTH: M GED: R4 M3 L3 SVP: 7 DLU: 77

603.280-018 GRINDER OPERATOR, TOOL (machine shop) alternate titles: precision grinder

Sets up and operates variety of grinding machines, such as external, internal, and surface grinders, to grind metal workpieces, such as machine parts, dies, or tools, according to knowledge of grinding procedures: Studies blueprint or layout on workpiece to visualize grinding to be done, and plans sequence of operations. Selects grinding wheel, applying knowledge of abrasives and metal properties, and secures it on spindle, using wrench. Dresses wheel with dressing device. Lifts workpiece manually or with hoist, and positions and secures workpiece to holding device, using wrenches and clamps. Selects feed rates, grinding speeds, depth of cuts, and grinding wheel of size, shape, and grade for each operation, applying knowledge of metal properties, abrasives, product specifications, and shop mathematics. Positions and tightens stops to limit travel of workpieces or grinding wheel. Moves controls to position wheel and workpiece in relation to each other, and to set feed, speed, and depth of cut. Starts machine, turns handwheel to feed grinding wheel to workpiece or vice

versa, and engages power feeding device. Turns valve handle and directs flow of coolant against wheel and workpiece. Observes operation and adjusts position and action of wheel and workpiece. Verifies dimensions of ground workpieces for conformance to specifications, using measuring instruments, such as templates, micrometers, dial indicators, and gauge blocks. Works to tolerances of plus or minus 0.0001 inch. May measure, mark, and scribe workpiece to lay it out for grinding [LAY-OUT WORKER (machine shop) 600.281-018]. May dress grinding wheels to complex profiles, using special fixtures and tools. May grind nonmetallic materials, such as plastics. May operate tracer attachment to duplicate contours from templates or models. May be required to have specialized experience with particular materials, product, or precision level or with machine of particular size, type, or trade name.
GOE: 06.01.03 STRENGTH: M GED: R4 M4 L3 SVP: 7 DLU: 77

603.280-022 GRINDER SET-UP OPERATOR, INTERNAL (machine shop) alternate titles: grinder, hand; inner-diameter grinder, tool; internal grinder, tool; internal-grinding-machine hand; internal-grinding-machine operator; precision grinder

Sets up and operates internal grinding machines to grind internal cylindrical and tapered surfaces of rotating metal workpieces, such as tool, die, and machine parts, usually for limited runs, analyzing blueprints and specifications and selecting tooling according to knowledge of internal grinding procedures: Studies blueprint or layout on workpiece to visualize grinding to be done and plans sequence of operations. Selects grinding wheel, according to knowledge of metal properties and abrasives, and mounts wheel on spindle. Moves controls and reads dial to set angle of workpiece to grinding wheel, following product specifications. Dresses wheel manually or with preset device. Positions and secures workpiece on faceplate, magnetic chuck, or in chuck jaws, using wrenches. Selects and sets grinding wheel speed, work surface speed, and workpiece table travel rate, according to knowledge of metal properties and abrasives. Positions and tightens stops to set depth of grinding wheel cut and stroke of workpiece table. Moves controls to feed wheel to workpiece manually and automatically. Turns valve handle and directs flow of coolant against wheel and workpiece. Verifies dimensions of ground workpiece for conformance to specifications, using such measuring instruments as micrometers, dial indicators, and gauge blocks. May dress grinding wheel to specified profile for contour grinding, using special fixtures and tools. May grind nonmetallic materials, such as plastics. May operate tracer attachment to duplicate contours from templates or models. May be required to have experience with particular material, product, or precision level, or with machine of particular type or trade name.
GOE: 06.01.03 STRENGTH: M GED: R4 M3 L3 SVP: 7 DLU: 78

603.280-026 GRINDER SET-UP OPERATOR, JIG (machine shop) alternate titles: jig grinder; jig-grinding-machine operator; precision jig grinder

Sets up and operates jig grinding machine to locate and precision-grind holes and contours in metal objects, such as tool, die, and machine parts, on custom basis, analyzing blueprints and specifications and selecting tooling according to knowledge of jig grinding procedures: Studies blueprint, layout on workpiece, or written or oral specifications to visualize grinding to be done and plans sequence of operations. Computes and sketches hole and contour dimensions and locations in relation to base reference points and lines. Positions and secures workpiece on machine table, and turns handwheels to move table and workpiece to computed position under spindle center, verifying each step with dial indicator. Selects grinding wheel, grinding speeds, and feed rates for each operation according to knowledge of metal properties and abrasives, and mounts wheel on spindle. Moves controls and reads dials to set grinding speed, feed rate, spindle angle for taper grinding, diameter of *planetary action,* and limits of automatic reciprocating wheel feed. Dresses wheel manually or with preset dressing device. Moves controls to feed wheel into hole and against surface of workpiece. Verifies hole locations and dimensions for conformance to specifications, using measuring instruments, such as dial indicator, gauge blocks, and *telescoping gauges.* May be required to have experience with particular material, product, precision level, or with machine of particular type or trade name.
GOE: 06.01.03 STRENGTH: L GED: R4 M4 L3 SVP: 7 DLU: 77

603.280-030 GRINDER SET-UP OPERATOR, UNIVERSAL (machine shop) alternate titles: precision grinder, universal; universal grinder, tool

Sets up and operates combination external- and internal- (universal) grinding machine to grind external and internal cylindrical and tapered surface of rotating workpieces, such as tool, die, and machine parts, usually for limited runs, analyzing blueprints and specifications and selecting tooling according to knowledge of external and internal grinding procedures: Studies blueprint or layout on workpiece to visualize grinding to be done and plans sequence of operations. Selects grinding wheel, according to knowledge of metal properties and abrasives, and mounts wheel on spindle. Dresses wheel manually or with preset dressing device. Moves controls and reads dials to set rotation speeds and feed rates. Positions and tightens stops or cams to limit travel of workpiece or wheel. Moves controls to feed grinding wheel to workpiece or vice versa manually or automatically. Turns valve handle and directs flow of coolant against wheel and workpiece. Verifies dimensions of ground workpiece, using such measuring instruments as micrometers, dial indicators, gauge blocks, and optical comparator. May dress grinding wheel to specified profile, using special fixtures and tools. May grind nonmetallic materials, such as plastics. May oper-

ate tracer attachment to duplicate contours from templates or models. May be required to have experience with particular material, product, or precision level, or with machine of particular type or trade name.
GOE: 06.01.03 STRENGTH: M GED: R4 M4 L3 SVP: 7 DLU: 77

603.280-034 JOB SETTER, HONING (machine shop)

Sets up horizontal or vertical honing machines for HONING-MACHINE OPERATORS, PRODUCTION (machine shop) engaged in production honing of metal objects: Reads blueprint to select tooling and plans sequence of operations. Selects and secures tool in spindle, using wrenches. Positions workpiece in fixture or on machine table, securing it with clamps and wrenches, and verifies positions with instruments, such as surface gauges and dial indicators. Selects feed rate, honing tool rotation speed, and depth of cut, according to knowledge of metal properties and abrasives. Moves contros to position tool in relation to workpiece and to set feed rate and spindle speed. Positions and tightens stops, using wrench, to control length of honing tool stroke. Starts machine and turns handwheels to feed tool to workpiece. Measures first-run workpiece for conformance to specifications, using micrometers and fixed gauges. May instruct new workers in machine operation.
GOE: 06.01.02 STRENGTH: M GED: R4 M3 L3 SVP: 6 DLU: 77

603.280-038 TOOL-GRINDER OPERATOR (machine shop) alternate titles: cutter grinder; cutter-grinder operator; grinder operator; tool dresser; tool grinder; tool-grinding-machine operator; tool sharpener

Sets up and operates grinding machines, such as surface and universal, carbide, drill, and tool-and-cutter grinders, to sharpen cutting tools to specifications, using blueprints, job orders, and knowledge of abrasives and metal properties: Reviews blueprints and job orders to plan production sequence. Selects grinding wheel of shape and grade and attaches to spindle, using wrenches. Positions and secures cutting tool on machine table, using magnetic chuck or holding fixture, or mounts tool on arbor and clamps between centers. Turns handwheels to position table or spindle to obtain specified taper and bevel on edges of cutting tools. Moves controls to set cutting tool rotation speed, feed rate, and grinding wheel rotation speed. Starts machine and turns wheel or engages feed to move workpiece to grinding wheel. Measures sharpened cutting tools to verify conformance to specifications, using fixed gauges, micrometers, calipers, optical comparators, and surface gauges. Dresses abrasive wheel to change cutting action or shape. May grind special *form tools,* involving special setups and wheel dressing. May analyze specifications and select tooling to be used on production jobs. May design, modify, or make special tools according to specifications or tooling requirements. May braze or solder carbide tips to cutting tools. May be required to have specialized experience with particular type of cutting tool sharpened or machine operated and be designated Broach Grinder (machine shop); Drill Sharpener (machine shop); Hob Grinder (machine shop).
GOE: 06.01.03 STRENGTH: M GED: R4 M3 L3 SVP: 7 DLU: 77

603.360-010 BUFFING-LINE SET-UP WORKER (any industry)

Sets up buffing line to buff metal parts, such as automobile trim or hardware, to specified finish, following work order and using knowledge of metals, abrasives, and finishing techniques: Reads work order to determine part to be buffed. Selects holding fixtures and bolts them to drive mechanism. Selects buffs and positions and attaches them to spindles, using knowledge of buffing operations to determine type of buffs, angle of contact, and pressure against workpiece. Sets timers to control speed of *indexing,* according to size and material of workpiece and to control application of lubricant and abrasive. Examines finish of first piece through buffing line for conformance to specifications. Adjusts setup to achieve specified finish. May change speed of buffing wheels by varying ratio of drive pulleys.
GOE: 06.01.02 STRENGTH: M GED: R3 M2 L2 SVP: 5 DLU: 77

603.380-010 GRINDER MACHINE SETTER (machine shop)

Sets up metal-grinding machines, such as external, internal, surface, and centerless grinders, for GRINDER OPERATORS, PRODUCTION (machine shop) 603.685-062, according to specifications, tooling instructions, standard charts, and knowledge of grinding procedures, and operates machine to grind first-run workpiece: Reads from blueprint and job order product specifications for dimensions, tolerances, and number of parts to be ground and tooling instructions, such as speeds, feed rates, holding fixtures, and grinding wheels to be used. Mounts grinding wheels on spindles with wrenches. Dresses wheels to specifications, using dressing devices. Moves controls to set specified grinding speeds, feed rates, and angle of grinding wheel to workpiece or vice versa. Positions and tightens cams to control depth of cut and length of stroke. Lifts and positions workpieces manually or with hoist, and secures them on machine tables, faceplates, or magnetic chucks, in chuck jaws, or between centers, using wrenches and clamps. Starts machine, moves controls to adjust machine settings, and observes operation. Verifies first-run products for conformance to specifications, using such measuring instruments as micrometers, calipers, and preset gauges. May feed machine by hand. May direct flow of coolant over cutting area. May measure workpiece prior to grinding to determine amount of material to be removed. May be required to have experience with particular material, product, or precision level, or machine of particular size, type, or trade name.
GOE: 06.01.02 STRENGTH: M GED: R4 M3 L3 SVP: 6 DLU: 77

603.382-010 BUFFING-MACHINE OPERATOR (any industry)

Sets up and operates semiautomatic buffing machine to buff parts, such as automobile trim or hardware to specified finish: Reads work order to determine

parts to be buffed and setup procedure. Selects holding fixture and bolts it to feed arm. Slides spacers between buffs on spindle to set spacing. Measures and sets angle of feed arm to control position of workpiece against buff, according to specifications or using knowledge of machine operation. Sets length of traverse and stroke of feed arm by adjusting air cylinder and setting stops. Starts buff revolving and clamps workpiece in fixture. Presses button to feed workpiece against buff. Removes buffed part from fixture and examines it to ensure that surface coloration meets specifications. Adjusts angle, feed, or traverse of machine to achieve specified finish.
GOE: 06.02.02 STRENGTH: L GED: R3 M2 L2 SVP: 4 DLU: 77

603.382-014 GRINDER SET-UP OPERATOR, CENTERLESS (machine shop) alternate titles: centerless-grinding-machine operator
Sets up and operates one or more centerless grinding machines to grind external or internal cylindrical or tapered surfaces of metal workpieces to blueprint specifications, following tooling instructions and standard charts and applying knowledge of grinding procedures: Reads blueprint and job order for product specifications, such as dimensions, tolerances, and number of parts to be ground, and tooling instructions, such as grinding speeds, feed rates, holding fixtures, and grinding wheels to be used. Mounts grinding wheel and regulating wheel on spindles with wrenches. Dresses wheels to specifications, using dressing device. Moves controls to set specified grinding speeds, feed rates, and spacing between wheel faces. Positions and secures work rest at specified height, using wrenches. Lifts and positions workpiece manually or with hoist, and secures it between wheels and on work rest. Starts machine and observes operation. Verifies dimensions of ground workpiece for conformance to specifications, using measuring instruments, such as micrometers, calipers, and preset gauges. Changes worn grinding wheels, using wrenches. May set up automatic work-feeding device. May grind nonmetallic materials. May be required to have experience with custom or production work or with particular material, product, or precision level, or with machine of particular size, type, or trade name.
GOE: 06.02.02 STRENGTH: M GED: R3 M3 L3 SVP: 5 DLU: 77

603.382-018 HONING-MACHINE SET-UP OPERATOR (machine shop) alternate titles: hone operator; honing-machine operator
Sets up and operates one or more vertical or horizontal honing machines to hone internal or external surfaces of objects, such as cylinders, bearings, and connecting rods to specifications, following tooling instructions, standard charts, and honing procedures: Reads blueprint and job order for product specifications, such as dimensions, tolerances, and number of parts to be honed, speeds, feed rates, work-holding fixtures, and honing tools to be used. Positions and secures fixtures on machine table, using squares, steel rules, micrometers, and wrenches. Lifts workpiece manually or with hoist and positions and secures fixture with clamps and wrenches. Inserts and tightens specified tool in spindle. Moves controls to set tool-feed rate and spindle speed. Sets stops with wrench to control length of stroke and depth of cut. Starts machine and turns handwheels or engages automatic mechanism to feed and oscillate tool along workpiece surface. Turns valve handle to direct flow of coolant against tool and workpiece. Measures honed workpiece for conformance to specifications, using measuring instruments, such as preset gauges, micrometers, calipers, and comparators. May be required to have experience with custom or production work, or with particular material or product, or with machine of particular size, type, or trade name, and be designated accordingly.
GOE: 06.02.02 STRENGTH: M GED: R3 M2 L2 SVP: 5 DLU: 77

603.382-022 HONING-MACHINE SET-UP OPERATOR, TOOL (machine shop) alternate titles: honing-machine operator, tool; job honer; precision-honing-machine operator
Sets up and operates vertical or horizontal honing machine to hone internal or external surfaces of metal objects, such as prototype cylinders, bearings, or connecting rods, usually on custom basis, analyzing specifications and selecting tooling according to knowledge of honing procedures: Studies blueprint to visualize honing to be done and plans sequence of operations. Positions workpiece in fixture or on machine table, and secures it with clamps and wrenches, verifying positions with instruments, such as surface gauges and dial indicators. Selects feed rate, honing speed, depth of cut, and honing tool for each operation, according to knowledge of metal properties, abrasives, and shop mathematics. Positions and secures tool in spindle. Moves controls to position tool in relation to workpiece and to set feed rate and spindle speed. Turns nut on tool or sets automatic mechanism to expand tool to selected diameter. Positions and tightens stops with wrench to control length of stroke. Starts machine and turns handwheels to feed tool to workpiece. Engages automatic mechanism to feed tool along workpiece with oscillating action. Turns valve handle and directs flow of coolant against tool and workpiece. Measures honed workpiece for conformance to specifications, using electromechanical limit gauges, surface gauges, micrometers, and *telescoping gauges*. May use special optical inspection equipment. May replace worn honing stones. May be required to have experience with particular material or product or with machine of particular size, type, or trade name and be designated accordingly.
GOE: 06.02.02 STRENGTH: M GED: R4 M3 L3 SVP: 6 DLU: 77

603.382-026 LAPPING-MACHINE SET-UP OPERATOR (machine shop)
Sets up and operates *lapping* machines to lap surfaces of flat, cylindrical, or spherical objects or of adjacent mechanical parts to specified finish or dimensions, following specifications, tooling instructions, and standard charts, applying knowledge of lapping procedures: Reads blueprint or job order for product

specifications, such as dimensions, tolerances, and number of parts to be lapped, tooling instructions, such as lapping speeds and pressures, work-holding fixtures, and laps to be used. Mounts laps on spindles with wrenches. Positions and secures workpieces in fixture or on machine table. Moves controls to set lapping speeds, tool pressure, and length of cycle and to guide action of laps against workpieces or workpieces against each other. Starts machine and brushes or sprays *lapping compound* on laps and workpieces. Inspects lapped workpiece for conformance to specifications, using instruments, such as comparator, flatness gauges, and surface plates. May be assisted by MACHINE SETTER (machine shop) 600.360-014 in setting up machine. May operate machine equipped with abrasive wheels instead of metal laps. May be required to have experience with custom or production work, with particular material or product, or with machine of particular type or trade name and be designated accordingly.
GOE: 06.02.02 STRENGTH: M GED: R3 M2 L2 SVP: 6 DLU: 77

603.382-030 PRINTING-ROLLER POLISHER (machine shop)
Operates polishing lathe to reduce circumference of printing rollers to specifications and remove defects, such as turning and polishing lines, high spots, and scratches: Mounts roller on mandrel of lathe, using hoist. Measures circumference of roller at several points to locate irregular spots, using girth tape. Examines surface of roller for defects. Depresses pedal to raise water vat and starts lathe to rotate roller in vat. Polishes roller by either of following methods: (1) Moves polishing stone back and forth across length of roller, changing from coarse to finer grades of stone to impart acceptably smooth finish. (2) Mounts flat stone on spindle of polishing head, starts oscillation of stone, and lowers stone onto surface of rotating roller. Moves lever to engage gear that moves machine head back and forth over surface of roller. Changes stones on machine head to impart final polish. Examines polished rollers for rough spots, pinholes, and scratches. Rubs scratches and rough spots with burnishing tool to finish roller. Verifies circumference of polished roller, using girth tape. Cleans roller before and after polishing, using cloth, water, and detergents or cleaning solution.
GOE: 06.02.09 STRENGTH: H GED: R3 M2 L2 SVP: 6 DLU: 77

603.382-034 GRINDER SET-UP OPERATOR (machine shop)
Sets up and operates grinding machines to grind threads on metal objects, such as screws, bolts, and micrometer spindles, and to grind internal and external surfaces of metal workpieces to specifications, following tooling instructions, standard charts, blueprints, and job orders, applying knowledge of grinding procedures: Reads blueprint and job order for product specifications, such as dimensions, tolerances, and number of parts to be ground, and tooling instructions, such as grinding speeds, feed rates, holding fixtures, and grinding wheel to be used. Mounts wheel on spindle, using wrenches. Dresses wheel to specifications, using dressing device. Sets machine controls to specified grinding speeds, feed rates, and angle of wheel. Positions and tightens cams and stops to control depth of cut and length of stroke. Lifts and positions workpiece, manually or using hoist, and secures workpiece on faceplate or magnetic chuck, in fixture or chuck, or directly to machine table. Starts machine and activates controls to feed wheel against workpiece or vice versa, or engages automatic feeding device. Verifies dimensions of finished workpiece for conformance to specifications, using measuring instruments, such as micrometers, calipers, preset gauges, load test equipment, thread *measuring wires*, and thread gauges. Changes worn grinding wheel, using wrenches. May place workpiece in hopper or fixture of automatic feeding device. May grind nonmetallic materials. May be required to have experience with custom or production work or with specific type of machine, material, product, or precision level and be designated Grinder Set-Up Operator, External (machine shop); Grinder Set-Up Operator, Internal (machine shop); Grinder Set-Up Operator, Surface (machine shop); Grinder Set-Up Operator, Thread (machine shop).
GOE: 06.02.02 STRENGTH: M GED: R3 M3 L3 SVP: 6 DLU: 86

603.382-038 KNIFE GRINDER (machine shop) alternate titles: cutterhead sharpener; tool grinder
Sets up and operates grinding machines to shape and sharpen planer knives and woodworking machine cutters according to specifications: Positions and secures workpiece or sheet stock, template, and machine accessories onto machine, using handtools. Turns handwheels to set travel and pressure of cutterhead or knife stock across or against grinding wheel to shape or sharpen workpiece. Starts machine and observes grinding operation to verify conformance to specifications. May cut out plastic templates used to fabricate knives and cutterheads. May hone cutting edge of ground knives, using whetstone and oil. May cut and grind silicon carbide jointing stones to match pattern of knives. May select and install grinding wheels on machine, using handtools, applying knowledge of product specifications and abrasives. May manipulate blade across grinding wheel by hand. May turn valve to control flow of coolant. May sharpen or shape knives and saw blades, using handtools. May sharpen bits and boring tool [BIT SHARPENER (any industry) 603.685-026].
GOE: 06.02.02 STRENGTH: M GED: R3 M2 L3 SVP: 5 DLU: 78

603.482-010 DEBURRER, STRIP (clock & watch)
Sets up and operates multiple stage deburring machine to smooth edges and set (establish) width of mainspring strip: Threads strip from feeding roll through deburring cutters to winding roll, aligning cutters and adjusting cutters for specified width. Makes trial run, cuts off piece of deburred strip, examines piece under microscope, and adjusts cutters to correct deficiencies in operation. Adjusts and sharpens cutters on diamond wheel, using mechanic's tools. Works to tolerances of 0.0005 inch.

GOE: 06.02.02 STRENGTH: L GED: R3 M2 L2 SVP: 6 DLU: 77

603.482-030 GRINDER I (clock & watch) alternate titles: grinder, watch parts

Operates grinding machine to grind blocked watch parts to size: Places blocks on magnetic chuck and regulates feed and depth of grinding wheel cut to grind parts to specified thickness, working to tolerances of 0.0005 to 0.0001 inch. Removes blocks to measure thickness with upright gauge to ensure conformance to specifications. Dresses chuck by running grinding wheel across chuck slowly. Laps part for finish after grinding by putting blocks, parts side down, under pressure pads of *lapping* machine, putting oil and emery on lapping surface, and setting timer for specified time.
GOE: 06.02.02 STRENGTH: L GED: R3 M2 L2 SVP: 5 DLU: 77

603.482-034 HONING-MACHINE OPERATOR, PRODUCTION (machine shop) alternate titles: cylinder honer; honer; honing-machine operator, semiautomatic; production-honing-machine operator

Operates honing machines to hone internal or external surfaces of metal parts, such as cylinders, bearings, and connecting rods to specifications, usually on production basis: Obtains such information as dimensions, tolerances, and number of parts in run from job order and instructions of MACHINE-SHOP SUPERVISOR, PRODUCTION (machine shop) or JOB SETTER, HONING (machine shop). Lifts workpiece manually or with hoist and secures it in fixture. Starts machine and turns handwheels or engages automatic mechanism to feed tool to workpiece. Moves controls to adjust feed rate, spindle speed, length of stroke, and depth of cut. Measures finished workpiece with instruments, such as calipers, fixed gauges, and micrometers. Changes worn tools, using wrenches. May read blueprints. May assist JOB SETTER, HONING (machine shop) to set up machine. May be required to have experience with particular material, or product, with machine of particular size, type, or trade name, and be designated accordingly.
GOE: 06.02.02 STRENGTH: M GED: R3 M2 L2 SVP: 4 DLU: 77

603.664-010 TOOL GRINDER II (any industry) alternate titles: tool sharpener

Sharpens and smooths cutting edge of tools, such as axes, chisels, drills, picks, and straight cutting blades, using abrasive wheel: Presses button to start abrasive wheel. Positions and holds cutting edge of tool against machine guide and abrasive wheel to sharpen and smooth tool edge. Immerses tool in oil to cool edge. Repositions and holds tool edge against guide and abrasive wheel to further sharpen and smooth edge. May heat tools and immerse them in brine, oil, or water to harden them. May remove burrs from ground edges of tools, using whetstone. May sharpen and reduce diameter of circular cutting blades. May be designated according to kind of tool sharpened as Ax Sharpener (any industry); Chisel Grinder (any industry); Knife And Spur Grinder (saw. & plan.); Knife Grinder (any industry).
GOE: 06.02.01 STRENGTH: M GED: R2 M1 L1 SVP: 3 DLU: 77

603.665-010 BUFFING-MACHINE TENDER (any industry)

Tends automatic buffing machine that buffs parts, such as automobile hardware or trim: Loads parts on holding fixture of revolving table that is preset for regular *indexing* and starts machine. Removes buffed parts and examines them for surface defects. Places buffed parts into shallow tray and covers them with cardboard separators. Informs BUFFER (any industry) I or BUFFING-LINE SET-UP WORKER (any industry) of buffing defects. May maintain count of buffed parts and parts which do not meet specifications.
GOE: 06.04.02 STRENGTH: L GED: R2 M1 L1 SVP: 2 DLU: 77

603.682-010 BUFFING-MACHINE OPERATOR, SILVERWARE (jewelry-silver.)

Sets up and operates battery of machines that automatically buff shells for silver-plated hollowware, such as bowls, tea sets, vegetable dishes, and gravy boats, to remove scratches and pressmarks and impart smooth finish for subsequent plating: Selects buffing wheel of size and shape to match workpiece and bolts it to stationary drive shaft. Selects jig to match exterior or interior shape of workpiece and bolts it to chuck on lathe arbor. Clamps workpiece in jig and turns stop nuts to position assembly against buffing wheel. Turns knobs of timing device to regulate buffing time according to kind and thickness of metal and surface area to be buffed. Starts machine and holds stick of compound to wheel to coat wheel with abrasive. Observes operation and removes workpiece when machine stops at end of timed cycle.
GOE: 06.02.02 STRENGTH: M GED: R3 M2 L2 SVP: 4 DLU: 77

603.682-018 LINTER-SAW SHARPENER (oils & grease) alternate titles: saw filer; sharpener

Operates saw machine to sharpen cylinders of circular saws used in linter machines: Removes saw cylinders from linter machine and mounts cylinder in feeding head of sharpening machine. Examines saw blades to determine amount of cut necessary to sharpen them. Turns handwheels to set cutting control to specified depth of cut for saw teeth, and to adjust space between cutting tools. Starts machine and observes operation.
GOE: 06.02.02 STRENGTH: L GED: R3 M3 L2 SVP: 4 DLU: 77

603.682-022 MIRROR-FINISHING-MACHINE OPERATOR (jewelry-silver.) alternate titles: buffing-machine operator, semiautomatic; polishing-machine operator, semiautomatic

Sets up and operates one or more semiautomatic machines to buff silver or stainless steel flatware between cloth or felt rolls to impart mirrorlike finish:

Mounts buffing rolls in machine holders, using wrenches. Turns adjustment wheel and observes pressure dial to set distance between rolls. Turns setscrews and stop nuts to adjust motion of machine table. Starts rollers, turns valve, and depresses pedal to spray buffing compound across rolls or pulls bar-mounted stick of compound across them. Squeezes handles to open jaws of holding fixture and grip ends of workpieces racked in position on racking table. Inserts and locks fixture in sleeves of machine table, with blades, tines, bowls, or handles of workpieces inserted between buffing rolls. Starts machine that closes rolls on workpieces, rocks machine bed up and down and side to side to ensure complete buffing, separates rolls, and retracts machine bed after completion of preset time cycle. Inspects luster of workpieces and adjusts pressure of rolls or changes rolls to buff flatware to desired finish. May position workpieces in racks on racking table. May dump buffed flatware from racks onto conveyor for inspection. May dip ends of workpieces in buffing paste.
GOE: 06.02.02 STRENGTH: L GED: R3 M2 L2 SVP: 4 DLU: 77

603.682-026 POLISHING-MACHINE OPERATOR (any industry)

Sets up and operates belt sanding machine to polish flat metal surfaces, such as small arms parts and metal strips: Pushes button to lower drive wheel and installs abrasive belt of specified grit, using wrenches. Places metal part on conveyor belt and turns knobs to raise conveyor and bring workpiece into contact with polishing belt. Turns valves to regulate flow of coolant onto polishing belt and starts machine. Examines first run part to determine conformance of finish to specifications and adjusts height of conveyor as indicated to achieve specified finish. Replaces worn polishing belts, fills coolant tank, and cleans collection tank, using handtools, to maintain machine in operating condition.
GOE: 06.02.02 STRENGTH: M GED: R3 M2 L2 SVP: 4 DLU: 88

603.682-030 DRILL-BIT SHARPENER (electron. comp.) alternate titles: drill sharpener

Sets up and operates drill-sharpening machine (sharpener) to sharpen drill bits used in numerically controlled drill for fabricating printed circuit boards (PCBs): Reads work order to determine number and size of drill bits to be sharpened. Inserts drill bits into cleaning machine, point-side down, that automatically starts brushes rotating to clean and remove debris from dull bits. Removes drill bit from cleaning machine and measures bit to verify specified size, using micrometer. Selects corresponding size bushing (brass sleeve) and mounts bushing into chuck of sharpener, using handtools. Inserts drill bit in chuck of sharpener and activates table that moves chuck and bit assembly through rotating abrading wheels to sharpen both sides of drill bit. Flips switch to release chuck and and drill bit and removes bit. Observes sharpened bits under optical microscope to detect defects, such as chips or breaks. Discards defective drill bits. Places sharpened drill bits in box, point-end up. May clean sharpener.
GOE: 06.04.02 STRENGTH: L GED: R3 M2 L2 SVP: 3 DLU: 77

603.685-010 BAND-REAMER-MACHINE OPERATOR (nonfer. metal)

Tends pneumatic reaming machine that removes burrs from inner surface of copper bands: Selects reaming fixture (steel spring having cutting edge around outer surface of each coil) of desired size, and secures it in place. Fastens metal trough in place and aligns copper bands in trough. Opens compressed air line and starts machine that pushes reaming fixture through bands. Removes bands by sliding hooked metal bar through reamed holes.
GOE: 06.04.02 STRENGTH: M GED: R2 M1 L1 SVP: 3 DLU: 77

603.685-014 BARREL POLISHER, INSIDE (ordnance) alternate titles: inside polisher

Tends single-spindle, horizontal machine that smooths and polishes shotgun barrel bores: Clamps barrel in holding fixture and secures polishing rod in machine headstock. Wraps emery cloth on rod tip to form polishing tool. Starts machine and turns wheel to feed rotating polishing rod through barrel. Varies rate of feed according to resistance sensed through wheel. Pushes tow-tipped cleaning rod through polished barrel and sights through bore to inspect finish for defects.
GOE: 06.04.02 STRENGTH: L GED: R2 M1 L1 SVP: 3 DLU: 77

603.685-022 BEVEL POLISHER (clock & watch)

Tends single-or-multiple-holder polishing machines that polish beveled edges on rachet and winding wheels or endstone caps: Mounts wheels on rubber heads or endstone caps over pins protruding from holder face. Applies compounds to product or polishing laps. Positions lap over product or vice versa. Starts machine and sets timer for specified polishing period. Loads next set of holders. Inspects products for conformance to specifications. Imparts finish to wheels with cast-iron lap and polishes finish with lead-tin lap.
GOE: 06.02.02 STRENGTH: L GED: R2 M2 L2 SVP: 3 DLU: 77

603.685-026 BIT SHARPENER (any industry) alternate titles: bit grinder

Sharpens boring tools, such as bits and router cutters, using oilstone, and *bench grinder* with tool-holding adapters: Inserts bit into collet of tool adapter, and turns handwheels to adjust relative angle of bit axis and grinding wheel surface, according to specifications. Starts bench grinder, and turns handwheels to move bit against grinding wheel, and turns bit to sharpen each cutting edge. Rubs bit on oilstone by hand to smooth edges and complete sharpening. May file auger spurs to sharpen them. May sharpen cutlery and small shop tools.
GOE: 06.04.02 STRENGTH: M GED: R2 M1 L1 SVP: 3 DLU: 77

603.685-030 BIT-SHARPENER OPERATOR (mine & quarry) alternate titles: bit grinder

Tends bit-sharpening machine to shape and sharpen detachable bits of mining equipment: Inserts bits into clamps of power-driven revolving drum and fastens

them in place, using wrench. Turns handwheel to move bit against grinding wheels and to turn bit to sharpen cutting and reduce it to gauge size. Lubricates sharpening machine and changes worn grinding wheels, using handtools.
GOE: 05.12.02 STRENGTH: M GED: R2 M1 L1 SVP: 2 DLU: 77

603.685-034 BOTTOM POLISHER (elec. equip.)
Tends machine, equipped with power-driven wire brush, that polishes bottoms of metal dry cell battery containers (cans): Dumps box of cans into tray on bed of machine. Presses cans into tray to level bottoms. Start rapidly rotating brush. Grasps handle on tray and slides tray back and forth to bring bottoms into contact with brush. Inspects can bottoms to ensure cleanliness. Withdraws tray and inverts it over box to dump cans.
GOE: 06.04.02 STRENGTH: L GED: R2 M1 L1 SVP: 2 DLU: 77

603.685-038 BRUSH POLISHER (clock & watch)
Tends machine that bevels watch screwheads or polishes cap jewel plates: Secures watch part, shellacked onto surface of metal blocks, in holding fixture and starts machine that presses block of parts against rotating brush to bevel edges of slot or outside diameter of screwheads. Spreads abrasive mixture over brush and sets automatic timer to polish plates for specified period.
GOE: 06.04.02 STRENGTH: S GED: R2 M1 L1 SVP: 3 DLU: 77

603.685-042 BURNISHER (clock & watch)
Tends machine that grinds center-pinion pivots, shoulders, and similar watch parts to specifications: Inserts pivots into chuck or collet of machine, using fingers or tweezers, and starts machine. Removes product when machine stops and measures part for conformance to specifications, using gauge. May clean and oil machine and change machine belts as needed.
GOE: 06.04.02 STRENGTH: L GED: R2 M1 L1 SVP: 2 DLU: 77

603.685-046 BURRER, MACHINE (clock & watch) alternate titles: burring-machine operator
Tends machine that removes burrs from watch pinions and similar timing-device parts: Inserts part in deburring-machine chuck or collet and adjusts levers or depresses pedals to feed part against tool that grinds burrs. Examines parts to ensure removal of burrs.
GOE: 06.04.02 STRENGTH: L GED: R2 M1 L1 SVP: 2 DLU: 77

603.685-050 DEBURRER (button & notion) alternate titles: wire-brushing-machine operator
Tends battery of automatic deburring machines that remove rough edges from metal slide-fastener links attached to tape: Positions carton of stringer (one side of fastener chain) behind machine and threads end through guides, tension bars, and under wire brushes to pickup drum. Starts machine and observes passage of stringer through rotating brushes onto receiving drum. Examines brushed stringer to verify smoothness of surface. Notifies supervisor of machine malfunctioning.
GOE: 06.04.02 STRENGTH: L GED: R2 M1 L1 SVP: 2 DLU: 77

603.685-054 FLAT POLISHER (clock & watch) alternate titles: lap polisher
Tends machine that rough and finish polishes flat watch parts in successive operations: Applies polishing agent to *lap 1* surface. Positions blocked parts face down on lap under tripod holder, turns on air pressure which forces tripod against blocks, and adjusts machine to polish specified time. When machine automatically stops, removes blocks, cleans polished surfaces with tissue and cleansing agent, and inspects parts for scratches and blemishes. Verifies thickness of parts with micrometer, and reruns substandard parts. Refaces surface of lap on automatic turning machine.
GOE: 06.02.02 STRENGTH: L GED: R2 M1 L1 SVP: 4 DLU: 77

603.685-058 GRINDER OPERATOR, AUTOMATIC (cutlery-hrdwr.) alternate titles: grinder-and-honer operator, automatic
Tends machine that grinds and hones blades and blade edges of articles, such as razors, knives, and garden tools: Loads blades in machine hopper or positions blades in holding fixture. Starts machine that automatically feeds blades to abrasive wheel or belt. Verifies dimensions of blades and keenness of blade edges, using fixed gauges.
GOE: 06.04.02 STRENGTH: L GED: R2 M1 L1 SVP: 2 DLU: 77

603.685-062 GRINDING MACHINE TENDER (machine shop) alternate titles: production grinder
Tends grinding machines that grind internal and external surfaces of metal workpieces to specifications: Starts machine, places workpiece in holding fixture or hopper, and engages automatic feeding device. Observes machine operation, and removes and inspects finished workpiece to verify conformance to specifications, using measuring instruments, such as preset gauges, calipers, micrometers, and load test equipment. Replaces worn grinding wheel, using handtools. Dresses wheel, using preset dressing device. May move controls to adjust depth of wheel cut, angle between workpiece and grinding wheel, wheel rotation speed, and feed rate. May grind nonmetallic workpieces. May prepare production records. May be designated Centerless-Grinder Tender (machine shop); Double-Spindle-Disk Grinder Tender, Spring End (metal prod., nec); External-Grinder Tender (machine shop); Internal-Grinder Tender (machine shop); Knife Glazer (jewelry-silver.); Surface-Grinder Tender (machine shop).
GOE: 06.04.02 STRENGTH: M GED: R3 M2 L2 SVP: 3 DLU: 87

603.685-066 GRINDER, LAP (clock & watch)
Tends *lapping* machine that grinds flat watch parts to specified thickness: Secures parts, shellacked onto surface of metal blocks, to holding fixture that ro-

tates blocks on surface of revolving wheel. Spreads oil and abrasive powder over wheel, and adjusts automatic timer to permit grinding for specified period. Tests thickness of parts with micrometer. Removes parts from block, using brush and cleaning solution, and cleans parts by dipping them into series of cleaning solutions. Resurfaces lapping wheel, using automatic turning machine.
GOE: 06.04.02 STRENGTH: L GED: R2 M1 L1 SVP: 3 DLU: 77

603.685-070 LAPPING-MACHINE OPERATOR, PRODUCTION (machine shop) alternate titles: micromatic-hone operator
Tends one or more *lapping* machines to lap surfaces of metal objects to specifications, usually on production basis: Starts machine and places workpieces in machine or engages automatic feeding mechanism. Measures lapped workpieces for conformance to specifications, using instruments, such as preset comparators and surface plate. May move controls to adjust lapping speeds, tool pressure, and length of machine cycle. May assist MACHINE SETTER (machine shop) in setting up machine. May be required to have experience with particular material or product or with machine of particular type of trade name and be designated Barrel Lapper (ordnance).
GOE: 06.04.02 STRENGTH: M GED: R2 M2 L2 SVP: 3 DLU: 77

603.685-074 SHOT-GRINDER OPERATOR (ordnance)
Tends machine that grinds and polishes steel pellets to specified diameter for use as BB shot in air guns: Scoops pellets into feed hopper and starts machine. Turns valve to control coolant flow and adds scouring powder to hasten abrasive action. Measures ejected shot at machine discharge chute to verify size, using gauges, and turns handwheel to adjust pressure plates that increase or decrease size of shot.
GOE: 06.04.02 STRENGTH: M GED: R2 M1 L2 SVP: 2 DLU: 77

603.685-078 SNAILER (clock & watch)
Tends machine that automatically polishes watch crown and ratchet wheels and inscribes decorative snailed (spiral or volute-shaped) lines on them: Places wheel in rotating chuck of machine. Brushes abrasive mixture onto metal lap and starts machine that automatically polishes and snails wheels.
GOE: 06.04.02 STRENGTH: L GED: R2 M1 L1 SVP: 2 DLU: 77

603.685-082 STONER AND POLISHER, BEVEL FACE (clock & watch) alternate titles: screwhead stoner and polisher
Tends machine that stones and polishes bevel face (outside periphery) of screwheads: Inserts screws in spring chuck. Swings stoning face into position against rotating heads and holds it in place until pilot bulb lights, indicating heads are stoned to size. Turns stoning face away and swings polishing lap into position against rotating heads to impart finish to bevel faces. Removes finished screws from chucks.
GOE: 06.04.02 STRENGTH: L GED: R2 M1 L1 SVP: 3 DLU: 77

603.686-010 POLISHING-MACHINE-OPERATOR HELPER (any industry)
Feeds metal parts into automatic polishing machine, and transfers polished parts from conveyor to trays. Adds coolant to reservoir of polishing machine, and removes abrasive sludge from collection tank. Assists POLISHING-MACHINE OPERATOR (any industry) 603.682-026 in changing abrasive belts.
GOE: 06.04.02 STRENGTH: M GED: R2 M1 L1 SVP: 2 DLU: 77

603.686-014 DEBURRER, PRINTED CIRCUIT BOARD PANELS (electron. comp.)
Feeds and off bears machine that automatically cleans and removes burrs from panels for production of printed circuit boards (PCBs): Loads panels into automatic feeder device that conveys panels into deburring machine. Flips switch or presses button to start deburring machine that automatically cleans and deburrs panels. Removes cleaned and deburred panels from machine and examines panels for scratches. Records production data. May turn crank to adjust pressure of steel brushes that deburr panels. May buff scratches on panels, using hand buffer. May replace machine filter, using wrench.
GOE: 06.04.09 STRENGTH: H GED: R1 M1 L1 SVP: 2 DLU: 86

604 TURNING OCCUPATIONS

This group includes occupations concerned with shaping metal by the paring or chipping action of rigid cutting tools applied to metal rotating in a lathe. The shaping of nonmetallic materials, except wood, is also included when the methods and machine tools commonly applied to the machining of metal are used.

604.130-010 SUPERVISOR, ROLL SHOP (steel & rel.)
Supervises and coordinates activities of workers engaged in grinding, turning, and shot blasting mill rolls to specified surface finish and in repairing roll set bearings of mill rolls used in shaping steel in rolling mills: Reviews job orders, studies blueprint specifications, and inspects rolls to plan shop work. Schedules shop operations and daily work loads, considering such factors as mill rolling schedules, amount of turning, grinding, and shot blasting required to dress rolls, and available workers. Assigns workers to duties, explains work requirements, and issues blueprints and templates for performing work. Inspects work in progress and completed work for conformance to specifications and shop standards. Prepares production and progress reports. Inspects roll shop equipment and arranges for maintenance and repair work. Initiates changes in work methods to improve worker performance and production efficiency. Trains workers in operation of shop machines and equipment. Keeps production and time records. Requisitions materials and supplies.

GOE: 06.02.01 STRENGTH: L GED: R4 M3 L3 SVP: 7 DLU: 77

604.260-010 SCREW-MACHINE SET-UP OPERATOR, SWISS-TYPE (clock & watch) alternate titles: automatic-screw-machine setter, swiss-type

Sets up swiss-type automatic screw-machines to perform series of machining operations, such as boring, threading, and facing metal wire, rod, or bar stock to specifications, to produce small, accurately turned parts for clocks, watches, and other timing devices: Studies blueprint and layout sheet to determine machining to be done, dimensions of parts, and permissible tolerances, and plans sequence of operations. Visualizes movements of machine parts, workpieces, and tools in each operation in relation to others and decides on station and timing of each operation to assure efficient use of tools and time. Selects cutting speeds, feed rates, depth of cuts and cutting tools to be used on basis of experience and knowledge of metal properties and shop mathematics, or by referring to tables, charts, or instructions on layout sheet. Installs stock feed pushers, collets, and bushings, using wrenches. Inserts stock into stock feed mechanism and sets stock stop to control length of stock fed. Installs spindle speed and feed change gears to obtain required spindle speeds and tool feeds. Installs cams that control movement of stock and tools. Mounts cutting tools in toolholders and mounts them on machine, using wrenches, verifying their position with gauges and other measuring instruments. Cranks machine through cycle, stopping machine and adjusting tool positions and machine controls to allow for such factors as timing and clearance between moving parts. Starts machine, observes operation, and verifies conformance of first-run and sample workpieces to specifications, using such instruments as micrometers, calipers, limit gauges, and scales. Replaces worn tools. May operate *bench grinder* or cutter-grinding machine to sharpen tools. May set up and operate machine to machine first-run workpiece only. May be required to have experience with particular product, or machine of particular size, type, or trade name.
GOE: 06.01.03 STRENGTH: M GED: R4 M3 L3 SVP: 7 DLU: 77

604.280-010 ENGINE-LATHE SET-UP OPERATOR, TOOL (machine shop) alternate titles: precision-lathe operator; tool-room-lathe operator; tracer-lathe set-up operator

Sets up and operates engine lathe to perform machining, such as turning, *facing,* boring, and threading on rotating metal castings, forgings, and bar stock, to machine tool, die, or machine parts, analyzing specifications and deciding on tooling according to knowledge of metal properties and lathe operation: Studies blueprint or layout on workpiece to visualize machining to be done, and plans sequence of operations. Selects method of holding workpiece according to its size and shape and installs holding fixtures, such as chuck jaws, collets, arbors, and mandrels, to headstock or tailstock, using clamps or wrenches. Lifts workpiece manually or with hoist, and positions and secures it in holding fixture or between centers, using clamps and wrenches, and verifying position with measuring instruments, such as calipers, height gauges, and dial indicators. Selects feed rate, cutting speed, depth of cut, and cutting tool for each operation, according to knowledge of metal properties and shop mathematics. Positions and secures cutting tool in tool holder on cross-slide or tailstock. Moves controls to set cutting speed and feed rate and to position tool in relation to workpiece. Starts machine and turns handwheels to feed tool to and along workpiece, or engages automatic feed. Turns valve handle and directs flow of coolant against tool and workpiece. Verifies conformance of machined workpiece to specifications, using measuring instruments, such as micrometer, calipers, and depth gauges. May operate large engine lathe to machine large objects, such as ship propeller shafts, and be designated Lathe Set-Up Operator, Large (machine shop). May offset position of tailstock to machine tapered surfaces. May mount gears, move levers, and engage threading dial to machine threads, using knowledge of thread cutting. May machine teeth on cutting tools, or duplicate contours from templates or models, using *relieving* or tracing attachments. May operate *bench grinder* to sharpen tools. May work on nonmetallic materials, such as plastics. May be required to have specialized experience with particular materials, product, precision level, machining process or size, type, or trade name of machine.
GOE: 06.01.03 STRENGTH: M GED: R4 M4 L4 SVP: 7 DLU: 77

604.280-014 SCREW-MACHINE SET-UP OPERATOR, MULTIPLE SPINDLE (machine shop) alternate titles: automatic-screw-machine operator; bar-machine operator, multiple spindle; screw-machine operator; screw-machine setter

Sets up and operates one or more multiple-spindle lathe-type screw machines equipped with automatic *indexing* and feeding mechanisms to perform turning, boring, threading, and *facing* operations on metal bar stock on custom basis, analyzing specifications and deciding on tooling according to knowledge of screw-machine operations: Studies blueprint, visualizes machining to be done, dimensions of parts and permissible tolerances, and plans sequence of operations. Visualizes movements of machine parts, workpieces, and tools in each operation in relation to others, and decides on station and timing of each operation to assure efficient use of tools and time. Selects cutting speeds, feed rates, depth of cuts, and cutting tools to be used on basis of experience and knowledge of metal properties and shop mathematics. Installs collets, bushings, and stock pushers in stock-feeding mechanism, using wrenches and screwdrivers. Installs and adjusts cams, gears, and stops to control stock and tool movements at each station. Positions and secures tools in tool holders, verifying positions with gauges and other measuring instruments. Moves controls to set cutting speeds and feed rates. Cranks machine through cycle, stopping machine and ad-

justing tool positions and machine controls to allow for such factors as timing, clearance between moving parts, and chip removal. Starts machine, observes operation, and verifies conformance to specifications of first-run and sample workpieces, using such instruments as plug and ring gauges, calipers, and micrometers. Replaces worn tools. May operate *bench grinder* or cutter-grinding machine to sharpen tools. May machine plastics or other nonmetallic materials. May set up and operate single-spindle screw machine. May be required to have experience with particular material or product or machine of particular size, type, or trade name. May set up machines for other workers.
GOE: 06.01.03 STRENGTH: M GED: R4 M3 L3 SVP: 8 DLU: 77

604.280-018 SCREW-MACHINE SET-UP OPERATOR, SINGLE SPINDLE (machine shop) alternate titles: automatic-screw-machine operator; bar-machine operator, single spindle

Sets up and operates one or more single-spindle lathe-type screw machines equipped with automatic feeding and tool-indexing mechanisms to perform turning, boring, threading, and *facing* operations on metal bar stock on custom basis, analyzing specifications and deciding on tooling according to knowledge of screw machine operations: Studies blueprint to visualize machining to be done, dimensions of parts and permissible tolerances, and plans sequence of operations. Selects cutting speeds, feed rates, depth of cuts, and cutting tools to be used on basis of knowledge of metal properties and shop mathematics. Installs collets, bushings, and stock pushers in stock-feeding mechanism, using wrenches and screwdrivers, and loads with bar stock manually or with hoist. Installs and adjusts cams, gears, and stops to control stock and tool movements. Positions and secures tools in tool holders, verifying positions with gauges and other measuring instruments. Moves controls to set cutting speeds and feed rates. Starts machine, observes operations, and verifies conformance of first-run and sample workpieces to specifications, using such instruments as plug and ring gauges, calipers, and micrometers. Replaces worn tools. May operate *bench grinder* or cutter-grinding machine to sharpen tools. May machine plastics or other nonmetallic materials. May be required to have experience with particular material or product or machine of particular size, type, or trade name, and be designated accordingly. May set up machines for other workers.
GOE: 06.01.03 STRENGTH: M GED: R4 M3 L3 SVP: 7 DLU: 77

604.280-022 TURRET-LATHE SET-UP OPERATOR, TOOL (machine shop)

Sets up and operates turret lathe to perform series of machining operations, such as turning, *facing,* boring, and tapping, on metal workpieces, such as machine, tool, or die parts, analyzing specifications and deciding on tooling, applying knowledge of metal properties, shop mathematics, and turret-lathe operations: Studies blueprint to visualize machining to be done, and plans sequence of operations. Selects and installs work-holding fixtures on machine, such as collets, faceplates, two-jaw chuck, or specially-shaped holding devices, and positions and secures workpiece in holding fixture, using wrenches. Selects cutting speed, tool feed rate, depth of cut, and cutting tools for each operation, according to knowledge of metal properties and shop mathematics. Positions and secures tools in toolholders at each station of turret and cross-slide toolpost, and positions tools in relation to workpiece. Moves stops, cams, or levers to control rotation of workpiece and feeding of tools. Turns handwheels to feed tools to and along workpiece and to *indexing* toolholders between operations, or engages feeding and indexing mechanisms. Turns valve to direct flow of coolant, against tool and workpiece. Verifies conformance of machined workpiece to specifications, using measuring instruments, such as gauges, calipers, and micrometer. May sharpen tools with *bench grinder.* May operate tracing attachment to duplicate profile of template or model on workpiece. May work on nonmetallic materials, such as plastics. May be required to have specialized experience with particular material, product, precision level, machining process, or size, type, or trade name of lathe. May be designated according to whether lathe is primarily equipped to machine bar stock fed through headstock of screw machine as Screw-Machine Set-Up Operator, Tool (machine shop); or workpiece held in chuck (chucking machine) as Chucking-Machine Set-Up Operator, Tool (machine shop). May be designated according to type of lathe as Turret-Lathe Set-Up Operator, Tool, Vertical (machine shop).
GOE: 06.01.03 STRENGTH: M GED: R4 M4 L4 SVP: 7 DLU: 77

604.360-010 SETTER, AUTOMATIC-SPINNING LATHE (any industry)

Sets up automatic spinning lathe to spin (form) shaped articles from sheet or plate metal as specified by blueprints and computed from data charts: Bolts specified spinning chuck to headstock spindle and follow block to tailstock, using handtools or power tools. Positions, aligns, and bolts specified circular forming tool on hydraulic carriage according to diameter and thickness of metal disk, using such measuring tools as calipers, micrometers, and verniers. Turns control knobs to set speed of lathe and feed speed of carriage according to chart. Makes trial run and measures dimensions of first piece for conformance to blueprint specifications. May set up automatic spinning lathe equipped with special forming tools to shape, trim, or form knurls or beads on workpiece and be designated Setter, Automatic-Spinning-And-Beading-Lathe (any industry).
GOE: 06.01.02 STRENGTH: M GED: R4 M3 L3 SVP: 6 DLU: 77

604.362-010 LATHE OPERATOR, NUMERICAL CONTROL (machine shop)

Sets up and operates numerically controlled horizontal lathe to perform machining operations, such as turning, boring, *facing,* and threading parts, such as castings, forgings, and bar stock: Reads process sheets, blueprints, and sketches of part to determine machining to be done, dimensional specifications,

set up, and operating requirements. Inserts beginning point of tape in reading head of control unit. Mounts workpiece between centers, in chuck, or to faceplate, manually or using hoist. Selects and installs preset tooling in tool posts, turrets or *indexing* heads, and automatic-tool-change magazine, in sequence specified on process sheet. Depresses buttons, toggles, or sets tape and starts machining operation. Observes numerical displays on control panel and compares with data on process sheet to verify dimensional adjustments, feed rates, and speeds of machining cuts. Turns dials and switches to override tape control and correct machine performance, applying practical knowledge of lathe operation. Inspects first-run piece and spot-checks succeeding pieces for conformance to specifications, using micrometers and precision *dial* gauges. Studies job packet and organizes materials for next run during automatic tape-controlled cycles to shorten changeover time. May set tools before positioning them in lathe, using precision gauges and instruments. May set up and operate another machine tool during tape-controlled machining cycles. May machine nonmetallic materials. May be designated by type of lathe operated as Engine Lathe Operator, Numerical Control (machine shop); Turret Lathe Operator, Numerical Control (machine shop).
GOE: 06.01.03 STRENGTH: M GED: R4 M3 L3 SVP: 6 DLU: 77

604.380-010 CHUCKING-MACHINE SET-UP OPERATOR (machine shop) alternate titles: chucking-lathe operator

Sets up and operates one or more single- or multiple-spindle horizontal chucking machines (lathes) to perform series of machining operations, such as turning, boring, threading, and *facing,* on metal workpieces, such as castings, forgings and bar stock, according to specifications, tooling instructions, standard charts, and knowledge of turning procedures: Reads blueprint, job order, tooling instructions, or standard charts to determine product specifications, work-holding arrangement, cutting speeds, feed rates, and cutting tools to be used. Attaches specified chuck or chuck jaws to headstock, using wrenches. Moves controls, cams, and stops to set rotation speeds and feed rates and to control tool and workpiece movement for specified operations. Lifts workpiece manually or using hoist, and positions and secures it in chuck. Turns handwheels to position tools in relation to workpiece. Turns valve handle and directs flow of coolant against tools and workpiece. Starts machine, and moves controls to adjust positions and movements of tools during machine operation. Verifies conformance of turned workpieces to specifications, using measuring instruments, such as micrometers, calipers, and fixed gauges. May be required to decide on station and timing of each operation to assure efficient use of tools and time. May set up automatic device to feed workpieces to machine. May compute such data as dimensions, rotation speeds, and feed rates, using knowledge of shop mathematics and metal properties. Important variations are custom or production work; size or trade name of machine operated; types of metals or products machined; or work site (plant or job shop). May set up machines for other workers.
GOE: 06.01.03 STRENGTH: M GED: R4 M4 L4 SVP: 6 DLU: 77

604.380-014 CHUCKING-MACHINE SET-UP OPERATOR, MULTIPLE SPINDLE, VERTICAL (machine shop)

Sets up and operates one or more multiple-spindle vertical chucking machines (lathes) to perform series of machining operations, such as turning, boring, threading, and *facing* on metal workpieces, such as castings, forgings, and bar stock, according to specifications, tooling instructions, standard charts, and knowledge of turning procedures: Reads blueprint, job order, tooling instructions, and standard charts to determine product specifications, work-holding arrangement, and cutting speeds, feed rates, and cutting tools to be used. Visualizes movements of machine parts, workpieces, and tools in each operation in relation to others, and decides on station and timing of each operation to assure efficient use of tools and time. Installs specified chucks or holding fixtures on headstocks, and places and secures workpiece in holding device. Positions and secures tools and toolholders to toolheads. Moves controls, stops, and cams to set specified rotation speeds and feed rates, and to control timing and action of tools at each station. Starts machine, turns valve handle, and directs flow of coolant against tools and workpieces. Stops machine and verifies conformance of workpiece to specifications after initial machining operation, using fixed gauges, calipers, and micrometers. May compute such data as dimensions, rotation speeds, feed rates, tool setting angles, and machining times, using knowledge of shop mathematics and metal properties. May work on nonmetallic materials, such as plastics. May set up and operate machine to machine first-run workpiece only and be designated Chucking-Machine Setter, Multiple Spindle, Vertical (machine shop). May be required to have experience with particular material or product, or with machine of particular size, type, or trade name and be designated accordingly.
GOE: 06.01.03 STRENGTH: M GED: R4 M4 L4 SVP: 6 DLU: 77

604.380-018 ENGINE-LATHE SET-UP OPERATOR (machine shop) alternate titles: bench-lathe operator

Sets up and operates engine lathes to machine metallic and nonmetallic workpieces according to specifications, tooling instructions, and standard charts, applying knowledge of machining methods: Reads blueprint or job order for specifications, such as dimensions and tolerances, tooling instructions on holding devices, feed rates, cutting speeds, depth of cuts, and cutting tools. Positions and secures workpiece in holders, using wrenches. Lifts workpiece manually or with hoist, and positions and secures workpiece in holding device, machine table, chuck, centers, or fixture, using clamps and wrenches. Sets specified rotation speed, feed rate, and depth of cut, and positions tool in relation to

workpiece. Starts machine, turns handwheels to feed tool to workpiece, and engages feed. Turns valve handle to direct flow of coolant against tool and workpiece. Observes cutting action of machine to detect excessive wear or malfunction. Verifies conformance of machined workpiece to specifications, using micrometers, calipers, and fixed gauges. May scribe reference lines on workpiece, using scale, or template and scriber, to lay out interrelated surfaces, lengths, and depths of cut. May compute unspecified dimensions and machine settings, using knowledge of metal properties and shop mathematics. May set up tracing attachment that guides cutting tool to follow movement of tracing stylus along template to duplicate template profile on turned workpiece and be designated Tracing-Lathe Set-Up Operator (machine shop). May be required to have experience with custom or production work, or with particular material, product, level of precision, or size, type, or trade name of machine.
GOE: 06.01.03 STRENGTH: M GED: R4 M4 L3 SVP: 6 DLU: 86

604.380-022 SCREW-MACHINE SET-UP OPERATOR (machine shop) alternate titles: automatic-screw-machine operator; bar-machine operator; screw-machine operator

Sets up and operates single- or multiple-spindle lathe-type screw machines equipped with automatic *indexing* and feeding mechanisms to machine metal bar stock, following specifications and tooling instructions and applying knowledge of screw machine operations: Reads blueprint or job order for product specifications, such as dimensions, tolerances, number of parts to be machined, and tooling instructions, such as cutting speeds, feed rates, depth of cuts, and cutting tools to be used. Positions and secures specified collets, bushings, and stock pushers onto stock-feeding mechanism, using wrenches and screwdrivers, and loads bar stock into feeding mechanism, manually or using hoist. Installs and adjusts specified cams, gears, and stops to control stock and tool movements at each station. Positions and secures tools in toolholders, verifying positions with gauges and other measuring instruments. Sets cutting speeds and feed rates. Moves controls to cycle machine through settings, stopping machine and adjusting tool positions and machine controls to allow for operating factors, such as timing, clearance between moving parts, and chip removal. Starts machine, observes operation, and inspects first-run and sample workpiece to ensure machining conforms to specifications, using measuring instruments, such as plug and ring gauges, calipers, and micrometers. Replaces worn tools. May operate *bench grinder* to sharpen tools. May machine nonmetallic materials. May be required to have experience with particular material or product or machine of particular size, type, or trade name. May set up machines for other workers.
GOE: 06.01.03 STRENGTH: M GED: R3 M3 L3 SVP: 6 DLU: 88

604.380-026 TURRET-LATHE SET-UP OPERATOR (machine shop)

Sets up and operates turret lathes to perform series of machining operations, such as turning, boring, threading, and *facing,* on metal workpieces, such as castings, forgings, and bar stock, according to specifications, tooling instructions, standard charts, and knowledge of turning procedures: Reads blueprint, job order, tooling instructions, and standard charts for such specifications as dimensions, tolerances, and tooling instructions, such as type of holding fixtures, cutting speeds, feed rates, and cutting tools to be used. Positions and secures tools in toolholders on turret and cross-slide, using wrenches. Moves controls to set specified rotation speeds, feed rates, and depth of cuts. Positions and secures workpiece in chuck or to faceplate, using wrenches. *Indexes* turret and adjusts positions of tools at each station in relation to workpiece to assure clearance between moving parts and machining of specified dimensions and tolerances. Observes operation and indexes turret between operations. Verifies conformance of machined workpieces to specifications, using micrometers, calipers, and fixed gauges. Turns valve and directs flow of coolant against tool and workpiece. May compute such data as dimensions, rotation speeds, feed rates, and machining times, using knowledge of shop mathematics and metal properties. May work on nonmetallic materials, such as plastics. May be required to have experience with custom or production work or with particular material, product, level of precision, or machine of size, type, or trade name.
GOE: 06.01.03 STRENGTH: M GED: R4 M4 L4 SVP: 6 DLU: 77

604.382-010 SCREW-MACHINE OPERATOR, MULTIPLE SPINDLE (machine shop) alternate titles: bar-machine operator, multiple spindle

Operates one or more previously set up multiple-spindle screw machines equipped with automatic *indexing* and feeding mechanism to perform series of machining operations on metal bar stock, following specifications: Reads blueprint and job order for such information as dimensions, tolerances, and number of workpieces to be machined. Examines machine to become familiar with tooling setup. Loads stock into feeding mechanism. Starts machine and observes operation. Verifies conformance of sample workpieces to specifications, using preset gauges, micrometers and dial indicators. Replaces worn tools. Adjusts machine controls and changes tool settings to keep dimensions within specified tolerances. May operate *bench grinder* or cutter-grinding machine to sharpen tools [TOOL-GRINDER OPERATOR (machine shop)]. May machine plastics or other nonmetallic materials. May operate single-spindle screw machine [SCREW-MACHINE OPERATOR, SINGLE SPINDLE (machine shop)]. May be required to have experience with particular material or product or machine of particular size, type, or trade name.
GOE: 06.02.02 STRENGTH: M GED: R3 M2 L2 SVP: 6 DLU: 77

604.382-014 SCREW-MACHINE OPERATOR, SINGLE SPINDLE (machine shop) alternate titles: bar-machine operator, single spindle

Operates one or more previously set up single-spindle screw machines (type of lathe) equipped with automatic *indexing* and feeding mechanisms to perform series of machining operations on metal bar stock, following specifications: Reads blueprint and job order for such information as dimensions, tolerances, and number of workpieces to be machined. Examines machine to become familiar with tooling setup. Loads stock into feeding mechanism manually or with hoist. Starts machine and observes operation. Verifies conformance of sample workpieces to specifications, using preset gauges, micrometers or dial indicators. Adjusts machine controls and changes tool settings to keep dimensions within specified tolerances. Replaces worn tools. May operate *bench grinder* or cutter-grinding machine to sharpen tools [TOOL-GRINDER OPERATOR (machine shop)]. May machine plastics or other nonmetallic materials. May be required to have experience with particular material or product or machine of particular size, type, or trade name. Differs from SCREW-MACHINE OPERATOR, PRODUCTION (machine shop) in that this work is characterized by variety, with shorter runs and less repetition.
GOE: 06.02.02 STRENGTH: M GED: R3 M2 L2 SVP: 5 DLU: 77

604.666-010 THREADING-MACHINE FEEDER, AUTOMATIC I (machine shop)

Feeds cylindrical stock into one or more threading machines: Shovels, dumps, or inserts material in hopper or feedrack of machine that automatically threads stock. Carries or wheels filled and empty containers, such as buckets and wheelbarrows, to and from machine. Notifies THREADING-MACHINE SETTER (machine shop) of machine malfunctions. May fill tanks of lubricating oil, clean machine and work area.
GOE: 06.04.02 STRENGTH: H GED: R2 M1 L1 SVP: 2 DLU: 77

604.682-010 SCREW-MACHINE OPERATOR, SWISS-TYPE (clock & watch)

Operates one or more previously set up automatic screw machines to perform series of machining operations, such as boring, threading, and facing metal bar, rod, or wire stock to specifications to produce parts for clocks, watches, and other timing devices: Reads specifications to determine dimensions, tolerances, and number of parts required. Loads specified stock into feeding mechanism. Pushes starting button, and moves clutch lever to start machine and engage gears. Observes machine operation and verifies conformance of workpiece to specifications, using measuring instruments, such as micrometers, calipers, scales, and go-not-go gauges. Makes adjustments to tool and toolholders, stock and guide tensions, and operating speed and lubricant flow to maintain machine setup, using handtools. May operate *bench grinder* to reshape or sharpen edges of cutting tools.
GOE: 06.02.02 STRENGTH: L GED: R3 M3 L2 SVP: 6 DLU: 77

604.682-014 THREADING-MACHINE OPERATOR (machine shop)

Sets up and operates single- or multiple-spindle threading machine to thread and chamfer cylindrical stock according to specifications: Selects, installs, and adjusts threading die, die cutters, chamfering tools, feed grips, pressure tripping mechanism, cams, gears and pulleys, using screwdrivers and wrenches. Lifts precut stock manually or with hoist and positions and secures stock in chuck jaws. Starts machine and moves handwheel or lever to alternately feed stock on each spindle. Verifies dimensions of workpieces with specifications, using fixed gauges and scale. May sharpen die cutters on grinding wheel. May be designated by type of stock threaded as Bolt-Threading-Machine Operator (machine shop); Nipple-Machine Operator (machine shop); Pipe-Threading-Machine Operator (machine shop).
GOE: 06.02.02 STRENGTH: M GED: R3 M3 L3 SVP: 5 DLU: 77

604.685-010 BALANCE RECESSER (clock & watch)

Tends semiautomatic turning machine to cut recess in watch balance wheel: Fits center hole of balance wheel over pin protruding from face of quill (removable headstock), using tweezers. Fits holding ring over wheel and depresses pedal to clamp ring in place. Depresses pedal to start machine. Observes machine operation to detect malfunction. Lifts recessed wheel from pin, using tweezers, when machine automatically stops at end of cycle. Verifies contour of recess, using go-not-go gauge, depth of recess, using upright gauge, and quality of cut, using jeweler's loupe.
GOE: 06.04.24 STRENGTH: L GED: R2 M1 L1 SVP: 3 DLU: 77

604.685-014 FACING-MACHINE OPERATOR (clock & watch)

Tends one or more single- or multiple-spindle lathe-type machines to cut and finish watch parts, such as watch plates, balance wheels, and bridges to specified thickness and surface finish: Depresses pedal to open chuck or nest to clamp piece in place, or fits hole of piece over pin projecting from face of quill, exercising care to seat parts to prevent damage to diamond cutting edge. Starts machine and turns handwheels to move cutting edge into position and across face of part or move machine controls to start machine and engage cutting tool to automatically face parts to specifications. Removes piece at end of facing cut and checks thickness with precision gauges to determine that dimensions and finish meet specifications and shop standards. Notifies supervisor if parts do not meet specifications, of machine malfunctions, and of need for cutter replacement. May change and adjust cutting tools.
GOE: 06.04.02 STRENGTH: L GED: R2 M1 L1 SVP: 3 DLU: 77

604.685-018 KNURLING-MACHINE OPERATOR (ordnance)

Tends band-seating machine that roughens grooves (band seats) of artillery shells so that brass or copper bands affixed by BANDING-MACHINE OPERATOR (ordnance) will secure shell and rotate it when fired: Positions shell in chuck of lathe and tightens chuck, using wrench. Moves machine controls to start shell rotating and engage feed of knurling tool. Presses and releases pedal when band seat is sufficiently scored and removes processed shell from chuck.
GOE: 06.04.02 STRENGTH: M GED: R2 M2 L2 SVP: 3 DLU: 77

604.685-022 LAP CUTTER-TRUER OPERATOR (optical goods)

Tends truing machine that *mills* and recuts surfaces of metal lap used in grinding and polishing eyeglass lenses to specified curvature: Holds lap against rotating brush to remove marks indicating number of times lap was used. Set scale indicators of truing machine, according to dioptric power indicated by numbers on lap, and clamps lap in chuck of machine. Starts machine and positions cutting blade against surface of lap, or engages automatic feed mechanism which reciprocates lap against cutting blade to shave and true surface of lap. Removes lap from machine chuck, and measures it for conformance to specifications, using template. Grooves surface of lap to retain abrasive on surface edges of lap, by hand or machine, to remove roughness caused by cutting, *truing I,* and grooving operations. Occasionally sharpens cutting blade, using grinder.
GOE: 06.04.02 STRENGTH: L GED: R2 M1 L1 SVP: 2 DLU: 77

604.685-026 LATHE TENDER (machine shop) alternate titles: automatic-lathe tender; engine-lathe tender; turret-lathe tender

Tends lathes, such as turret lathes, engine lathes, and chucking machines (lathes) that cut, shape, drill, bore, thread, or face metal workpieces according to specifications: Lifts workpiece, manually or using hoist, and positions and secures workpiece between lathe centers, in chuck, or in holding fixture, using wrenches and clamps, or positions workpiece in automatic loading mechanism. Starts machine and turns handwheels to feed tools to workpiece or engages automatic feed. Turns valve to control flow of coolant against tool and workpiece. Observes machining operation to detect malfunction or excessive tool wear. Verifies that machined workpiece conforms to specifications, using thread, plug, and fixed gauges, dial indicators, calipers, and micrometers. Changes worn tools, using wrenches. May machine plastic or other nonmetallic materials. May be designated by type of machine as Knurling-Machine Tender (pen & pencil); Tapper (clock & watch) I.
GOE: 06.04.02 STRENGTH: M GED: R2 M2 L2 SVP: 3 DLU: 81

604.685-030 RIM-TURNING FINISHER (clock & watch)

Tends semiautomatic lathes that face and chamfer rim, cut diameter to size, and impart finish on watch balance wheels: Places balance wheel on locating pin in nest of quill, heats quill nest, wheel, and shellac stick to melt and apply shellac, using Bunsen burner. Places quill in holder of semiautomatic shellacking machine and presses button to start machine that heats and melts shellac. Presses wheel into nest and cools shellac to secure wheel in position. Places and clamps quill in lathe, exercising care to seat parts to prevent damage to diamond cutters. Presses button to start and run lathe through machining cycle. Removes quill from lathe, heats nest and removes wheel, exercising care to prevent damage to wheel. Places wheel in alcohol to dissolve and remove shellac. Examines finish and gauges outside diameter of wheels to ensure specifications are met, using loupe and micrometer or fine gauge. Removes old shellac from quill, using Bunsen burner and brass wiping tool. Lubricates and cleans quill and machine as needed.
GOE: 06.04.02 STRENGTH: L GED: R2 M1 L1 SVP: 3 DLU: 77

604.685-034 SCREW-MACHINE TENDER (machine shop) alternate titles: bar-machine operator, production

Tends single- or multiple-spindle screw machines equipped with automatic *indexing* and feeding mechanisms that drill, turn, bore, thread, tap, and face metal bar stock according to specifications: Loads bar stock into feeding mechanism. Starts machine, engages feeds, and observes machine operation. Changes worn cutting tools, using wrenches. Removes sample workpiece from machine and inspects workpiece to verify conformance to specifications, using instruments, such as preset comparator, ring and screw pinch gauges, calipers, and micrometer. Moves controls to adjust machine operation. May sharpen tools, using bench grinder. May machine plastic or other nonmetallic materials.
GOE: 06.04.02 STRENGTH: M GED: R2 M2 L2 SVP: 3 DLU: 81

604.685-038 THREADING-MACHINE OPERATOR (ordnance)

Tends planetary-type, threading-cutting machine that cuts interior and exterior threads in artillery shells, so that fittings, such as fuse caps, can be attached: Turns setscrews to secure position and depth of thread and to adapt compressed-air holding chuck to material. Positions shell in machine and tightens chuck. Closes switch to activate cutting tools. Presses levers to stop cutting tools and release chuck. Inspects shells, using fixed gauges.
GOE: 06.04.02 STRENGTH: L GED: R2 M1 L2 SVP: 4 DLU: 77

604.685-042 TURRET-LATHE OPERATOR, TUMBLE TAILSTOCK (clock & watch)

Tends turret lathe to spot, drill, finish-recess, and rough-post watch barrel bridges: Places bridge in nest of quill and turns clamping ring to tighten bridge in place. Depresses pedal to start machine. Feeds spotter, drill, and hollow mill in order against bridge by pressing *indexing* button which clicks each into working position. Loosens clamping ring and removes completed bridges. Verifies dimensions of post and thickness of recess with precision plug and indicator gauges.
GOE: 06.04.02 STRENGTH: L GED: R2 M1 L1 SVP: 3 DLU: 77

604.686-010 WIRE THREADER (clock & watch)

Threads fine wire on automatic wire-threading machine for further processing into watch screws.

GOE: 06.02.02 STRENGTH: L GED: R2 M1 L1 SVP: 2 DLU: 77

605   MILLING, SHAPING, AND PLANING OCCUPATIONS

This group includes occupations concerned with shaping metal by the action of revolving, multiple-tooth cutters; rigid, single-edge cutters; or linear, single-pass, multiple-tooth cutters. Excess material is removed by milling, broaching, shaping, or planing to produce flat or profiled surfaces, grooves, splines, keyways, and slots. Includes shaping, without removal of excess material, by raising burrs, or by shaving strands from stock. The milling, broaching, shaping, or planing of nonmetallic materials, except wood, are also included when the methods and machine tools commonly applied to the machining of metal are used.

605.280-010 MILLING-MACHINE SET-UP OPERATOR I (machine shop)

Sets up and operates variety of milling machines to mill flat or curved surfaces on metal workpieces, such as machine, tool, or die parts, analyzing specifications, and selecting tooling, according to knowledge of milling procedures: Studies blueprints or layout on workpiece to determine sequence of operations and finished dimensions of workpiece. Lifts and positions workpiece on machine table manually or with hoist, and secures it, using clamps, bolts, or fixtures. Selects feed rate, cutting speed, depth of cut, and milling cutter, applying knowledge of metal properties and shop mathematics. Mounts milling cutter in spindle, and positions cutter and workpiece in relation to each other. Verifies alignment of workpiece, using measuring instruments, such as dial indicator and thickness gauge. Turns handwheel to feed workpiece to cutter or vice versa. Turns valve handle to start flow of coolant or lubricant on work area, starts machine, and engages automatic feed. May compute *indexing* ratios and set up and operate dividing head to index workpiece for such operations as milling helical cuts. May mount different tool in place of cutter and perform other operations, such as drilling and boring. May set up and operate attachments, such as *pantograph mechanism* to duplicate contours from models or profiles from templates, or universal head to mill at angles. May mill nonmetallic materials.

GOE: 06.01.03 STRENGTH: M GED: R4 M4 L3 SVP: 7 DLU: 77

605.280-014 PROFILING-MACHINE SET-UP OPERATOR I (machine shop) alternate titles: cam-milling-machine operator; die-sinking-machine operator; profiler

Sets up and operates milling machine equipped with built-in or attached tracing mechanism that guides cutting tool in parallel relationship to stylus that moves along three-dimensional model or two-dimensional template to mill contour of model or profile of template on metal workpieces: Studies blueprint, layout on workpieces, and template or model to determine tooling, sequence of operations, and finished dimensions of workpiece. Positions and secures workpiece and model or template parallel to each other on machine bed or angle plate, using height gauges, parallel blocks, sine bars, steel rule, wrenches, and clamps. Moves handwheel to position cutting tool on workpiece in specified relation to stylus on model or template. Observes operation and makes adjustments to ensure conformance of milled workpiece to specifications. Verifies conformance of workpiece, using dial and surface gauges, templates, calipers, and micrometers. May turn lever to start flow of coolant on machining area. May mill plastics or other nonmetallic materials.

GOE: 06.02.02 STRENGTH: M GED: R4 M3 L3 SVP: 7 DLU: 77

605.280-018 PROFILING-MACHINE SET-UP OPERATOR, TOOL (machine shop) alternate titles: duplicating-machine operator; tracer-controlled-milling-machine operator; milling-machine operator; milling-planer operator; slab-miller operator

Sets up and operates various types of tracer-controlled profile milling machines to mill duplicates of template or model contour on metal workpieces, such as cams, metalworking dies, aircraft parts, and automobile prototype parts, determining tooling according to knowledge of profiling procedures: Studies blueprint, dimensioned sketch, or layout on workpiece to visualize milling required and plans sequence of operations. Lifts and positions workpiece on machine bed manually or using hoist. Secures workpiece and template or model on angle plates or machine table, using clamps, wrenches, and such devices as height and *planer gauges,* parallel blocks, shims, and screwjacks. Selects cutting speeds, depth of cut, cutting tool, and corresponding tracing stylus. Positions and secures cutter and stylus in respective spindles. Turns switches or dials to set feed and speed and to position cutter and stylus at reference points on workpiece and template or model allowing for tool pressure, die clearance, and amount of stock to be left for subsequent removal. Engages feeding mechanism. Observes machining operation and adjusts cutter position, cutting speed, and feed rate to ensure that workpiece conforms to specifications. Verifies conformance of milled workpiece to specifications, using gauges, calipers, and micrometers. May work on nonmetallic materials. May make cutters and styluses. May inspect workpiece on *projection (shadow) comparator machine* to determine if profiled cuts align with projected drawing.

GOE: 06.01.03 STRENGTH: M GED: R4 M4 L3 SVP: 7 DLU: 77

605.282-010 MILLING-MACHINE SET-UP OPERATOR II (machine shop)

Sets up and operates milling machine to mill flat or curved surfaces on metal workpieces, such as machine, tool, or die parts, analyzing specifications and selecting tooling, according to knowledge of milling procedures: Studies blueprints or layout on workpiece to determine sequence of operations and finished dimensions of workpiece. Lifts and positions workpiece on machine table manually or with hoist, and secures it, using clamps, bolts, and fixtures. Selects feed rate, cutting speed, depth of cut, and milling cutter, applying knowledge of metal properties and shop mathematics. Mounts milling cutter in spindle, and positions cutter and workpiece in relation to each other. Verifies alignment of workpiece, using measuring instruments, such as dial indicator and thickness gauge. Turns handwheel to feed workpiece to cutter or vice versa. Turns valve handle to start flow of coolant or lubricant on work area, starts machine, and engages automatic feed. Periodically adjusts machine controls to achieve specified tolerances. May compute *indexing* ratios and set up and operate dividing head to index workpiece for such operations as milling helical cuts. May mount different tool in place of cutter and perform other operations, such as drilling and boring. May set up and operate attachments, such as *pantograph mechanisms* to duplicate contours from models or profiles from templates, or universal head to mill at angles. May work on nonmetallic materials. May set up machines for other workers.

GOE: 06.02.02 STRENGTH: M GED: R4 M4 L3 SVP: 7 DLU: 77

605.282-014 PLANER SET-UP OPERATOR, TOOL (machine shop)

Sets up and operates planers that reciprocate workpieces against stationary bar tools to plane and groove large metal workpieces, such as castings for metalworking dies and machine ways, analyzing specifications and selecting tooling according to knowledge of machine planing procedures: Studies blueprint or layout on workpiece to visualize planing to be done, or marks layout on workpiece with scribe, and plans sequence of operations. Selects method of holding workpiece so that entire surface to be planed will remain parallel to table during planing operation. Lifts workpiece manually or with hoist, and positions and secures it on table, using shims, parallel blocks, clamps, and wrenches. Verifies workpiece position with gauges, rule, square, or other instrument. Selects and mounts cutting tools on railhead or side head. Selects and sets cutting speed, length of stroke, and depth of cut, according to knowledge of metal properties and shop mathematics. Sets stops to limit length of stroke and to actuate table reversing mechanism. Moves controls to position tool in relation to workpiece. Starts table reciprocation, turns handwheels to feed tool to or across workpiece between cuts, and engages feed. Observes operation and verifies conformance of planed workpiece to specifications within tolerances to plus or minus 0.001 inch, using measuring instruments, such as surface gauge, *planer gauge,* and micrometer. May operate *bench grinder* to sharpen tools. May turn valve handle and direct flow of coolant or lubricant against tool and workpiece. May set up and operate milling attachment instead of rail or side head tool [PLANER-TYPE-MILLING-MACHINE SET-UP OPERATOR (machine shop) 605.282-018]. May plane or mill nonmetallic materials. May set up and operate rotary planer which reciprocates cutting tool against workpiece mounted on rotating machine bed and be designated Rotary Planer Set-Up Operator (machine shop).

GOE: 06.02.02 STRENGTH: H GED: R4 M3 L3 SVP: 7 DLU: 77

605.282-018 PLANER-TYPE-MILLING-MACHINE SET-UP OPERATOR (machine shop)

Sets up and operates planer-type milling machine that moves workpiece back and forth against rigidly held rotating cutters to mill workpieces, such as castings and machine parts, according to knowledge of planer-mill operating procedures: Studies blueprints or layout on workpiece to determine machine set-up, and sequence of machining operations. Lifts workpiece, using hoist, to position on machine bed. Secures workpiece in holding fixture, using wrenches, and verifies position, using gauges, calipers, or square. Selects cutting tool and mounts it in spindle, using handtools. Adjusts controls to set feed rate, speed of cutting tool, and depth of cut. Turns controls to position cutting tool relative to workpiece, starts machine, and engages automatic feed. Observes operation, stops machine to change cutting tool, and adjust controls. Verifies conformance of workpiece to finished specifications, using precision measuring instruments. Removes workpiece from machine bed.

GOE: 06.02.02 STRENGTH: M GED: R4 M3 L3 SVP: 7 DLU: 77

605.360-010 ROUTER SET-UP OPERATOR, NUMERICAL CONTROL (machine shop)

Sets up and operates multiaxis, numerically controlled routing machine to cut and shape metallic and nonmetallic workpieces: Selects and positions workpiece on machine bed. Threads perforated or magnetic tape through read head. Inserts precision indicator in machine chuck, and depresses switches to jog chuck into contact with workpiece, synchronize tape and tool, and record setup point. Retracts chuck, and loads and secures first preset cutting tool and holder. Starts machine and observes operation. Compares numerical data displays with specifications on operation sheets, and uses scales, gauges, and micrometer to verify machining operations. Removes and replaces cutting tool when worn or damaged or when new cutting tool is specified by operation sheets. Assembles and presets cutting tools at bench during tape-controlled machining to reduce machine downtime. Repositions workpiece for intermediate setups when specified on operation sheets, and removes and replaces workpiece at end of machining cycle. Verifies new tapes by starting machine and observing operation to detect

errors, plotting two-dimensional movement with recording stylus, or by machining sample workpiece and inspecting each cut, using precision gauges.
GOE: 06.01.03 STRENGTH: M GED: R4 M3 L3 SVP: 6 DLU: 77

605.380-010 MILLING-MACHINE SET-UP OPERATOR, NUMERICAL CONTROL (machine shop)

Sets up and operates multiaxis numerical-control milling machine to mill surfaces of metallic and nonmetallic workpieces according to specifications and tooling instructions, applying knowledge of machining methods: Threads perforated or magnetic tape through read-head in control console, or enters commands into control panel, to retrieve preprogrammed machine data from mainframe computer. Inserts precision indicator in machine spindle, and depresses switches to jog spindle into contact with workpiece, synchronize tape and tool, and record setup point. Retracts spindle and loads and secures first preset tool and holder. Starts machine and observes cutting operation. Compares numerical data display with specifications on operations sheet. Assembles and presets tooling for next operation during automated cycle to reduce machine downtime. Replaces milling tools with drilling and boring tools at specified change points to reduce or eliminate subsequent machining of workpiece on another machine. May operate machine on preliminary dry run before machining first part to detect errors in tape or computer program. May be designated according to make, trademark, or configuration of machine, characteristics of control system, or type of product as Contour-Path Tape-Mill Operator (machine shop); Planer-Type Milling-Machine Operator, Numerical Control (machine shop); Profile-Mill Operator, Tape Control (machine shop); Tape Control Skin-or-Spar-Mill Operator (machine shop); Tape Keller Operator (machine shop).
GOE: 06.01.03 STRENGTH: M GED: R3 M3 L3 SVP: 6 DLU: 87

605.382-010 BROACHING-MACHINE SET-UP OPERATOR (machine shop)

Sets up and operates one or more broaching machines to broach internal or external cylindrical or flat surfaces of metal workpieces according to specifications, tooling instructions, standard charts, and knowledge of broaching: Reads blueprint, job order, or specifications to determine dimensions and tolerances, and tooling instructions, such as holding fixtures, cutting speed, and cutting tools (broaches) to be used. Lifts workpiece manually or with hoist and positions and secures it in fixture. Installs broach or ram, using wrenches. Moves controls to set specified depth of cut and ram speed, and to start ram that pushes or pulls broach along surface of work. Pulls lever to start flow of coolant or lubricant on work area. Verifies conformance of broached workpiece to specifications, using measuring instruments, such as fixed gauges, calipers, and micrometers. May broach nonmetallic materials. May change worn broaches, using handtools.
GOE: 06.02.02 STRENGTH: M GED: R3 M3 L2 SVP: 4 DLU: 77

605.382-014 ENGRAVER, TIRE MOLD (machine shop) alternate titles: skid-machine operator

Sets up and operates cam-controlled tread-engraving (skid) machine to mill tread designs in metal molds for rubber tires, according to specifications: Examines work order or receives verbal instruction to ascertain cams, gearing ratio, and templates to be used. Lifts mold half with hoist and secures it in workholding fixture on machine. Mounts specified cutting tool in machine spindle. Positions and secures drum cam (grooved cylinder) corresponding to specified tread design number in machine, using wrenches. Rotates mold in fixture to align specified design location on mark with mark and design number on fixture corresponding to mounted cam. Moves controls to position tool in relation to mold and starts machine. Turns handwheel and simultaneously exerts pressure on hand lever to traverse pin against cam and tool against mold to mill (engrave) tread pattern in mold, adjusting action according to movement and resistance sensed by hands on controls. Mounts systematically varied sequence of cams which produce tread pattern of minimum tire noise. Verifies engraved mold for conformance to specifications, using precision measuring instruments such as micrometers, calipers, and dial indicators. May setup and operate engraving machine equipped with template tracing stylus and be designated Tire Mold Engraver, Numerical Control (machine shop).
GOE: 06.02.02 STRENGTH: M GED: R3 M3 L2 SVP: 5 DLU: 77

605.382-018 KEYSEATING-MACHINE SET-UP OPERATOR (machine shop)

Sets up and operates keyseating machine (vertical shaper) to cut keyseats in metal workpieces, such as wheels and gears, according to specifications: Reads blueprint or job order to determine dimensions and tolerances of workpiece, and tooling instructions, such as holding fixtures, cutting speeds, depth of cut, and cutting tools to be used. Measures workpiece and scribes guidelines for cutting keyseat, using steel rule and scriber. Mounts specified tool on ram. Lifts workpiece manually or with hoist, and aligns it with cutting tool. Secures workpiece in fixture or to post on machine table, using clamps and wrenches. Moves controls to set specified ram speed, length of stroke, and feed rate. Turns handwheel to feed reciprocating tool to workpiece until depth of cut conforms to specifications, or engages automatic feeding device. Verifies conformance of machined workpiece to specifications, using fixed gauges, calipers, and micrometers. Turns handwheel or adjustment screw to tilt table to cut tapered keyseats.
GOE: 06.02.02 STRENGTH: M GED: R3 M3 L2 SVP: 4 DLU: 77

605.382-022 PANTOGRAPH-MACHINE SET-UP OPERATOR (machine shop)

Sets up and operates pantograph-milling machine to mill contoured two-dimensional profiles and three-dimensional cavities in metal parts of such products as dies and molds for metal diecasting and plastic molding, duplicating contour of template or model to specified scale: Studies blueprint, workpiece, and template or model, and plans operations. Positions and secures workpiece and model or template in relation to each other on machine, using work aids and handtools, such as clamps, parallel blocks, and wrenches. Selects tracing stylus, cutting tool, and cutting speed, according to operation to be performed and knowledge of metal properties and machining methods. Mounts stylus and tool, using handtools. Turns controls to set cutting speed and dimensional ratio of model to workpiece, and starts machine. Grasps knob and moves stylus back and forth against template or model, causing similar action of tool against workpiece. Watches tool, feels action and resistance of tool through hand on knob, and manually controls cutting action in response to these stimuli. Verifies conformance of machined workpiece to specifications, using templates and measuring instruments, such as micrometers, dial indicators, and gauges. May make templates or cutting tools for own use.
GOE: 06.02.02 STRENGTH: M GED: R3 M3 L3 SVP: 7 DLU: 77

605.382-026 PROFILING-MACHINE SET-UP OPERATOR II (machine shop) alternate titles: cam-milling-machine operator; die-sinking-machine operator; profiler

Sets up and operates profile milling machine equipped with built-in or attached tracing mechanism that guides cutting tool in parallel relationship to stylus to mill two-dimensional scale profiles from models, according to specifications: Examines layout or workpiece, blueprints, and work order to ascertain type of tooling required and finished dimensions of workpiece. Positions and secures workpiece and template or model on machine table, using clamp, vise, blocks, measuring instruments, and wrenches. Selects and inserts specified stylus and cutting tool, using handtools. Starts machine, turns controls to change speed of cutting tool, directional movement of stylus, and automatic feed rate to ensure conformance of milled workpiece to specifications. Verifies conformance of workpiece, using dial and surface gauges, templates, calipers, and micrometers. Removes milled workpiece and template or model from machine table. May mill nonmetallic materials. May turn lever to start flow of coolant or lubricant on machining area. May manually move stylus to mill workpiece.
GOE: 06.02.02 STRENGTH: M GED: R3 M2 L2 SVP: 5 DLU: 77

605.382-030 ROTARY-HEAD-MILLING-MACHINE SET-UP OPERATOR (machine shop)

Sets up and operates vertical milling machine with spindle mounted within larger rotary head so that rotating cutter can move anywhere within given circle to mill complex shapes, such as arcs and tangents, without changing position of workpiece or machine table. Computes dimensions of shapes to be milled and successive positions of cutter in relation to rotary head, using knowledge of shop mathematics. Moves controls to position and move cutter in computed directions to mill specified shapes.
GOE: 06.02.02 STRENGTH: M GED: R4 M3 L3 SVP: 7 DLU: 77

605.382-034 ROUTER OPERATOR (any industry)

Sets up and operates routers, such as pin, horizontal, and radial arm, to cut, trim, slot, scarf, chamfer, profile, and shape metallic and nonmetallic materials, parts, castings, and tooling, according to specifications and knowledge of machine routing procedures: Reads work order, tooling instructions, blueprints, sketches, or other specifications to determine machining information, such as material needed, sequence of operations, quantity, tolerances, and dimensions of finished parts. Installs machine accessories, such as pins, collars, cutting tools, blocks, templates, and router boards, using handtools and power tools. Positions and secures parts or materials on machine, using bolts, clamps, or other fasteners. Adjusts controls to regulate speed of cutting tool, depth of cut, and flow of air, coolant, and lubricant. Starts machine and guides material against cutting tool or cutting tool against material. Verifies conformance of finished workpiece to specified tolerances, using precision measuring instruments. Observes machine operation and reports malfunctions to supervisor. May engage automatic feed of material. May record production output. May mark reference points on workpiece. May use milling cutters in router to shape parts. May operate specific type router and be designated Router Operator, Pin (aircraft mfg.) or Router Operator, Radial (aircraft mfg.).
GOE: 06.02.02 STRENGTH: M GED: R3 M3 L3 SVP: 6 DLU: 88

605.382-038 SHAPER SET-UP OPERATOR, TOOL (machine shop) alternate titles: shaper machine hand; shaper operator; shaping-machine operator

Sets up and operates one or more shapers that reciprocate bar tool against stationary workpiece to plane, shape, or groove metal workpieces, such as machine, tool, or die parts, according to specifications and knowledge of shaping operations: Studies blueprint, dimensioned sketch, or layout on workpiece, and plans sequence of operations. Positions and secures workpiece in vise or directly on machine table, manually or with hoist, using clamps or holding fixture. Verifies position with such instruments as dial indicator, thickness gauges, and surface gauge. Selects cutting speed, length of stroke, depth of cut, and cutting tool to be used, according to knowledge of metal properties and shop mathematics. Positions and secures cutting tool in toolpost. Turns handwheels to position tool and workpiece in relation to each other and to feed reciprocating tool to workpiece, or engages automatic feed. Verifies conformance of shaped workpiece to specifications within prescribed tolerances, using micrometers, calipers, and gauge blocks. Turns valve handle to direct flow of coolant against tool and workpiece. May shape contours by intermittently turning handwheel to feed tool to curved layout line while watching cutting action.

May compute angles and manipulate controls to tilt table or toolhead of universal shaper for angular or taper shaping. May sharpen tools, using *bench grinder*. May shape nonmetallic materials. May record production output.
GOE: 06.02.02 STRENGTH: M GED: R4 M3 L3 SVP: 6 DLU: 77

605.382-042 THREAD-MILLING-MACHINE SET-UP OPERATOR (machine shop)
Sets up and operates thread-milling machine to mill threads on external and internal surfaces of metal workpieces, applying knowledge of thread types and thread-milling methods: Studies blueprints, charts, drawings, and work orders to determine pitch and depth of thread, and type of tooling specified. Lifts workpiece to fixture and bolts or clamps it in place, using handtools. Selects and inserts cutting tool in machine spindle. Sets and adjusts speed of cutting tool and feed rate of workpiece. Positions cutting tool and workpiece to computed angles, and installs gears, cams, and stops to control multiple movements of workpiece and cutting tool. Starts machine and inspects workpiece during and on completion of milling operation, using measuring instruments, such as thread gauge and thread *measuring wires*. Removes milled workpiece from fixture. May compute thread dimensions, using standard formulas.
GOE: 06.02.02 STRENGTH: M GED: R3 M3 L2 SVP: 6 DLU: 77

605.382-046 NUMERICAL-CONTROL ROUTER OPERATOR (aircraft mfg.; electron. comp.)
Sets up and operates numerical control router machine to rout (cut) parts, such as individual printed circuit boards (PCB's) from printed circuit panels or metal workpieces from sheet metal stock: Reviews setup instructions and specifications. Loads control media into computer console or enters commands to retrieve programmed control data. Selects and installs specified cutting tools into machine spindle or magazine. Positions and secures materials onto *indexing* table of machine. Enters commands to activate machine that automatically aligns indexing table and panels or metal stock under tool spindle and routs or notches materials, according to programmed instructions. Monitors machine operation and display readouts to detect malfunction. Measures dimensions of finished parts to verify conformance to specifications, using precision measuring instruments. Notifies supervisor of machine malfunction or when parts do not conform to specifications. Cleans machine, using solvent, rag, and airhose. May perform maintenance and replace worn or damaged cutting tools, using handtools.
GOE: 06.02.09 STRENGTH: M GED: R3 M2 L2 SVP: 4 DLU: 88

605.482-010 STEEL-WOOL-MACHINE OPERATOR (nonmet. min.)
Sets up and operates machine that automatically shaves steel wires to form steel wool: Installs specified cutting tools in machine toolholder, using handtools. Turns controls to adjust speed and depth of cut according to cutting specifications. Starts machine and threads wire stock through automatic feed mechanism. Places cut ribbons of wire (steel wool) on machine rollers which carry them to catch basin. Ties broken ribbons. Replaces worn tools to maintain product quality. May operate steel wool balling, padding, and polyethylene extruding machines to produce soap-impregnated steel wool pads and polyethylene foam-backed, soap-impregnated steel wool pads.
GOE: 06.02.02 STRENGTH: L GED: R3 M3 L3 SVP: 5 DLU: 77

605.682-010 BARREL-RIB MATTING-MACHINE OPERATOR (ordnance)
Sets up and operates planer-type machine to cut matting (knurling) on *sighting ribs* of shotguns to improve appearance and reduce glare: Attaches holding fixtures and matting tools on machine and clamps rib, or barrel with rib attached, in fixture, using handtools. Depresses lever to position cutting tool in relation to rib, and starts machine which moves rib under stationary tool. Maintains even pressure on lever to obtain smooth cut. Turns adjustment knob after each pass to increase depth of cut. Removes rib from holding fixture. May shim fixture to level workpiece. May hone surface of rib to remove burs.
GOE: 06.02.02 STRENGTH: M GED: R3 M2 L2 SVP: 4 DLU: 77

605.682-014 BROACHING-MACHINE OPERATOR, PRODUCTION (machine shop) alternate titles: broach operator; production broacher
Operates one or more previously setup broaching machines to broach internal or external surfaces of metal workpieces to specifications, on production basis: Examines blueprints or work order to determine finished specifications of workpiece. Lifts workpiece manually or using hoist, and places and secures it in holding fixture, using handtools. Starts machine, observes operation, and verifies conformance of broached workpieces to specifications, using measuring instruments, such as fixed gauges, calipers, and micrometers. Moves controls to adjust cutting speeds. Changes worn broaches. May aid MACHINE SETTER (machine shop) 600.360-014 in setting up machine. May place workpiece on spindle of revolving turntable which automatically feeds broached workpiece to power conveyor.
GOE: 06.02.02 STRENGTH: M GED: R3 M2 L2 SVP: 4 DLU: 77

605.682-022 SCALPER OPERATOR (nonfer. metal) alternate titles: scalp-machine operator
Sets up and operates scalper (milling) machine to mill defects from surfaces of ingot to prepare it for rolling: Adjusts scalper blades to depth of cut required and positions holding jaws to width of ingot, using handwheel, setscrews, and handtools. Lifts ingot from skid to entry table, using hoist. Starts lifting table that positions ingot in jaws of machine carriage. Starts machine to make first cut. Releases ingot from carriage, inverts ingot, using roller manipulators, and

repositions it in carriage for second cut, using button controls. Cleans machine lubricant from scalped ingot with squeegee. Stacks scalped ingots on skid. May record weight of ingot on production form.
GOE: 06.02.02 STRENGTH: M GED: R3 M2 L2 SVP: 4 DLU: 77

605.682-026 TOOTH CUTTER, ESCAPE WHEEL (clock & watch)
Sets up and operates semiautomatic tooth-cutting machine to shape teeth on watch escape wheels: Positions stack of blanks on arbor, inserts and locks arbor in machine spindle, and starts machine which automatically stops at end of cycle. Removes wheel from machine and verifies dimensions of wheel diameters in ring go-not-go gauge. Examines wheel under toolmaker's microscope and compares its blown-up shadow with scale drawing on projector screen to determine if wheel conforms to specified tolerances. Adjusts machine, using handtools, to correct for size and dimensions until parts are within tolerances, or to accommodate different size wheels. May operate bank of milling machines. May be designated according to type of wheel cut as Tooth Cutter, Contact Wheel (clock & watch).
GOE: 06.02.02 STRENGTH: L GED: R3 M2 L2 SVP: 4 DLU: 77

605.682-030 WHEEL CUTTER (clock & watch)
Operates machine to cut teeth in clock and watch wheels: Clamps wheel blank in chuck of dividing head of machine. Mounts and adjusts cutting tools of specified sizes in turret. Starts motor, causing turret to rotate tool that cuts out groove in wheel. Turns turret to successively blank and cut groove to specified depth and width, using different sized tools. Verifies depth and width of cut, using precision gauges, and quality of cut, using jeweler's loupe.
GOE: 06.02.02 STRENGTH: L GED: R3 M2 L2 SVP: 5 DLU: 77

605.682-034 ROUTER, PRINTED CIRCUIT BOARDS (electron. comp.)
Operates routing machine to cut and shape individual printed circuit boards (PCB's) according to specifications: Positions and secures PCB's between dies or on templates. Positions secured PCB on router platform to align connector edges with machine cutter. Adjusts cutter spindle, using wrenches, and installs cutter of specified size on spindle. Flips switch to activate routing machine. Turns calibrated dials on routing machines to specified markings on dials to adjust milling dimensions of router. Manually guides edges of board against cutter to rout connector edges. Measures dimensions of board, using vernier calipers, to verify that board is routed according to specifications. Separates dies or removes template from PCB. May operate shearing machine to separate PCB from panels. May operate slotting machine to mill slots in PCB's.
GOE: 06.02.02 STRENGTH: L GED: R3 M1 L2 SVP: 4 DLU: 86

605.685-010 BARREL RIFLER (ordnance) alternate titles: barrel-rifler operator
Tends battery of machines that cut spiral grooves into bores of artillery and small arms weapons by either of following methods: (1) Inserts barrel in collet of machine and button in hole of push rod attachment on machine. Starts machine to rotate barrel and feed it over button to impress grooves in bore. (2) Locks broach or hook cutter in drawing head and barrel in *indexing* head of broaching machine, using wrenches. Moves levers to regulate automatic feed and to cut rifling to specified depth and twist. Cleans bore, using cleaning rod and patch, and examines bore for burrs and scratches. Measures rifling for conformance to specifications, using dial and depth gauges. May be designated according to type of rifling tool used as Barrel Rifler, Broach (ordnance); Barrel Rifler, Button (ordnance); Barrel Rifler, Hook (ordnance).
GOE: 06.04.02 STRENGTH: L GED: R2 M1 L2 SVP: 3 DLU: 77

605.685-014 FILE CUTTER (cutlery-hrdwr.)
Tends machine that forms burrs (teeth) on surface of file blanks: Adjusts cutting tool in reciprocating arm of machine to obtain burrs of specified height. Positions blank in jig geared to reciprocating arm for automatic burr spacing. Starts machine that automatically feeds blanks to cutting tool.
GOE: 06.04.02 STRENGTH: L GED: R3 M2 L2 SVP: 4 DLU: 77

605.685-018 HOOKING-MACHINE OPERATOR (clock & watch)
Tends battery of automatic hooking machines that mill hooks (recess on edge of which end of mainspring is secured) in barrel arbors: Loads sleevelike feeding magazines with arbors, using tweezers. Inserts magazine in machine and engages power. Verifies depth of specified number of hooks by measuring diameter of arbor including hook as well as diameter in recess adjacent to hook. Makes adjustments to machine, such as turning setscrews to change depth of hook.
GOE: 06.04.02 STRENGTH: L GED: R2 M1 L1 SVP: 3 DLU: 77

605.685-022 JEWEL STRIPPER (clock & watch)
Tends automatic machine that cuts jewel settings to specified thickness and bevels corners. Places hopper in automatic feed. Measures thickness of stripped settings with dial indicator, and inspects finished work for appearance.
GOE: 06.04.02 STRENGTH: L GED: R2 M1 L2 SVP: 2 DLU: 77

605.685-026 LEVER MILLER (clock & watch)
Tends milling machine that cuts edges of watch levers: Pulls handle to clamp levers in special machine fitting. Turns controls to bring work into contact with cutting tool. Pulls handle to release clamp, and removes milled levers. Verifies conformity of levers to specifications, using gauge.
GOE: 06.04.02 STRENGTH: L GED: R2 M1 L2 SVP: 2 DLU: 77

605.685-030 MILLING-MACHINE TENDER (machine shop)
Tends milling machines that mill surfaces of metal workpieces according to specifications: Positions and secures workpiece in fixture or feeding device.

Starts machine, and turns handwheel to feed workpiece to cutter or vice versa, or engages automatic feeding mechanism. Turns valve handle to direct flow of coolant against cutter and workpiece. Observes machine operation, and removes and inspects machined workpiece to verify conformance to specifications, using instruments, such as gauges, calipers, micrometers, and templates. May change worn cutters, using wrenches. Records production output. May tend machine that mills workpiece according to programmed cycle. May turn controls to adjust feed rate of workpiece or speed of cutting tool. May mill nonmetallic materials.
GOE: 06.04.02 STRENGTH: M GED: R2 M2 L2 SVP: 3 DLU: 86

605.685-034   PLANING-MACHINE OPERATOR (clock & watch)
Tends semiautomatic planing machine that cuts off excess metal and imparts smooth surface to such watch parts as balance cocks and train bridges: Places single part in chuck of machine, depresses pedal to close chuck, trips starting handle, and observes machine which planes piece and ejects it from chuck at end of cycle. Measures thickness of parts with dial indicator.
GOE: 06.04.02 STRENGTH: L GED: R2 M1 L1 SVP: 3 DLU: 77

605.685-038   PROFILING-MACHINE OPERATOR (clock & watch) alternate titles: recessing-machine operator
Tends battery of previously set-up profiling machines that trace templates to cut recesses in watch plates and chamfer edges, undercutting metal to form partially hidden recesses, in watch parts, such as pillar plates and train bridges: Blows metal shavings and dust from work plate, using air compressor. Fits blanks over protruding pins of chuck or in nest of work plate and pulls lever to clamp them in place. Starts machine and loads second machine while first is operating. Depresses pedal to eject workpiece or directs air blast to blow workpiece into catch pan after machine stops at end of cycle. Verifies thickness of metal below recess, and contour of recess, using jeweler's loupe and precision gauges. Important variables may be indicated by trade name of machine used.
GOE: 06.04.02 STRENGTH: L GED: R2 M1 L1 SVP: 2 DLU: 77

605.685-042   SCRIBING-MACHINE OPERATOR (cutlery-hrdwr.)
Tends machine that inscribes graduations in metal surface of measuring tools, such as carpenter's steel squares and rules, and machinist's scales: Slides workpiece into spring clamp on machine carriage. Starts machine that scribes graduations along length of tool by automatic *indexing* of multiple scribing points or cutters. Removes scribed tool at end of cycle and examines and compares it with master scale to verify legibility and accuracy of graduations.
GOE: 06.04.02 STRENGTH: L GED: R2 M2 L2 SVP: 2 DLU: 77

605.685-046   SQUARING-MACHINE OPERATOR (clock & watch)
Tends battery of automatic squaring machines that mill (file) flat round sides of engaging portions of winding stems and barrel arbors: Loads sleevelike feeding magazines with stems or barrels, using tweezers. Inserts magazine in machine and starts machine. Inspects parts, using loupe, to see that square is centered on stem (sides are milled flat leaving rounded corners). Gauges squares in go-not-go gauge.
GOE: 06.04.02 STRENGTH: L GED: R2 M1 L1 SVP: 2 DLU: 77

605.685-050   TOOTH CUTTER (clock & watch)
Tends battery of semiautomatic milling machines to cut teeth in clock and watch parts, such as barrels, pinions, wheels, and clutches: Slides stack of wheel or pinion blanks on fluted arbor, clamps on holding collar, inserts arbor into machine chuck, and clamps in place, using pedal, or opens work holder and inserts barrel or pinion blanks into holder, using tweezers. Pushes lever to start machine which automatically indexes and cuts teeth around periphery of blanks. Loads remaining machines. Removes arbor or individually machined parts from milling machine which automatically stops at end of cycle. Verifies shapes of tooth and quality of cut, using jeweler's loupe, thickness of tooth, using jaw gauge, outside diameter of part, using go-not-go gauge, and length of part, using upright gauge. May adjust machine when machined product does not conform to standards. May clamp arbor in machine chuck manually. May be designated according to type of machine used as Tooth Cutter, Hobbing Machine (clock & watch); or according to type of tooth cut as Tooth Cutter, Clutch (clock & watch); Tooth Cutter, Pinion (clock & watch); Tooth Cutter, Spur (clock & watch).
GOE: 06.04.02 STRENGTH: L GED: R2 M2 L2 SVP: 3 DLU: 77

605.685-054   ROUTER MACHINE OPERATOR (plastic prod.)
Tends routing machine that trims edges of plastic drafting scales: Places and secures router tool in chuck. Places and clamps scale on holding pin of routing machine conveyor belt. Starts machine and observes movement of scale under router. Removes trimmed scale from conveyor and inspects completed work to maintain establishment standards. May tend routing machine that re-routes graduation lines removed accidentally during previous operations and be known as Rework Machine Operator (plastic prod.).
GOE: 06.04.02 STRENGTH: L GED: R2 M1 L1 SVP: 2 DLU: 86

606   BORING OCCUPATIONS

This group includes occupations concerned with piercing metal by means of rotary cutting tools advanced into the material in the direction of the tool's axis to make, enlarge, or thread holes. The piercing of nonmetallic materials, except wood, is also included when the methods and machine tools commonly applied to the machining of metal are used.

606.280-010   BORING-MACHINE SET-UP OPERATOR, JIG (machine shop) alternate titles: jig-borer
Sets up and operates jig borer to perform machining operations, such as boring, drilling, reaming, and *counterboring* holes in metal workpieces, such as jigs, fixtures, gauges, and dies, according to specifications, applying knowledge of metal properties, tooling, and precision machining: Studies machining instructions, such as job order, blueprint, process sheet, or layout on workpiece to determine dimensional and finish specifications, sequence of operation, setup, and tooling requirements. Lifts workpiece either manually or with hoist onto machine table. Positions and secures workpiece on table with bolts, clamps, shims, or other holding devices, using machinist's handtools. Verifies parallelism of reference lines on workpiece to axis of table motion, using dial indicator mounted in spindle. Establishes zero reference point on workpiece, such as at intersection of two edges or over hole location. Turns handwheel to adjust machine table to align spindle over point, using dial indicator. Sets table-position dial at zero; measures all machining locations from this zero point. Selects and sets cutting speeds, feed rates, depth of cut, and cutting tool according to machining instructions or knowledge of metal properties. Installs tool in spindle. Turns handwheels to lower tool to workpiece and engages automatic feed. Turns valve and directs flow of coolant or cutting oil over cutting area. Verifies location and dimensions of holes, using measuring instruments, such as dial indicator, gauge blocks, *telescoping gauge* and internal micrometer. Works to tolerances as close as plus or minus 0.0001 inch. May work only from blueprint. May lay out reference lines and machining locations on workpiece, according to blueprint, using layout tools, such as rule, divider, and scriber, applying knowledge of shop mathematics and layout techniques. May fasten workpiece in holding fixture mounted on machine table or clamp jig or template in position on workpiece. May operate machine manually throughout first piece operation to verify accuracy of setup. May sharpen tools on *bench grinder*.
GOE: 06.01.03 STRENGTH: M GED: R4 M4 L3 SVP: 7 DLU: 77

606.280-014   BORING-MILL SET-UP OPERATOR, HORIZONTAL (machine shop) alternate titles: horizontal-boring-drilling-and-milling-machine operator; horizontal-boring-mill operator
Sets up and operates horizontal boring, drilling, and milling machine to perform machining operations, such as milling, drilling, boring, and reaming metal workpieces, such as machine, tool, or die parts, analyzing specifications and deciding on tooling according to knowledge of shop mathematics, metal properties, and machining procedures: Studies machining instructions, such as job order, blueprint, process sheet, or layout on workpiece to determine machining required, sequence of operation, tooling, feed, and speed rate, applying knowledge of materials and machining. Lifts workpiece either manually or with crane or hoist onto machine table or directs MONORAIL CRANE OPERATOR (any industry) to put workpiece on machine table. Positions and secures workpiece to table or angle plate, using clamps, shims, and parallel blocks and verifies position with such instruments as dial indicators, gauge blocks, and height gauges. Selects and mounts tool in spindle. Moves controls to set feeds, speeds, and depth of cut, and to position tool and workpiece in relation to each other, verifying position visually, with instruments, such as thickness gauge, and by reading dials. Starts machine and observes operation, making one or more trial passes with manual control before engaging feed. Verifies dimensions of machined workpiece with such measuring instruments as micrometers, *telescoping gauges*, vernier calipers, and dial indicators. Works to tolerance of plus or minus 0.001 inch. May use precision positioning devices, such as dial indicators mounted on machine troughs with standard length rods and work to tolerance as close as plus or minus 0.0001 inch. May operate tracing attachment to duplicate contours from templates or models. May operate machine with automatic positioning controls. May lay out reference lines and machining locations on workpiece, according to blueprints, using layout tools, such as rule, divider, and scriber, applying knowledge of shop mathematics and layout techniques. May operate *bench grinder* to sharpen tools. May set up and operate vertical boring mill and be designated Boring-Mill Set-Up Operator, Vertical (machine shop). Important variations may be indicated by trade names of machine used.
GOE: 06.01.03 STRENGTH: M GED: R4 M4 L3 SVP: 7 DLU: 77

606.362-010   DRILL-PRESS OPERATOR, NUMERICAL CONTROL (machine shop)
Sets up and operates numerically controlled drill press that automatically performs machining operations such as drilling, reaming, countersinking, *spot-facing,* and tapping of holes in metal workpieces, according to specifications, setup instructions, and knowledge of machining: Studies blueprints or setup instructions to determine dimensional specifications, setup requirements, and setup procedure. Installs workpiece holders, such as blocks, risers, and clamps, on *indexing* table of machine, using machinist handtools. Lifts workpiece manually or with hoist and positions and secures it on machine table or in holding fixture with clamps and bolts. Installs cutting tools in tool magazine, turret, or spindle of machine. Inserts programmed tape or punched card in tape or card reader of control unit. Actuates machine that automatically positions indexing table containing workpiece under spindle, selects tool, and machines part according to programmed instructions. Stops machine after trial run and inspects machined workpiece to ensure conformance to blueprint specifications, using fixed gauges, dial indicators, micrometers, and calipers. Monitors machine operation and display panel of control unit for indications of malfunction. Notifies supervisor if machined workpiece does not conform to specifications or if machine malfunctions. May make manual adjustments, such as aligning workpiece on machine table, changing cutting tools, or setting cutting speed, feed rates, and

depth of cut. May occasionally operate machine in semiautomatic mode by setting selector switch and manually dialing in data according to oral or written instructions to machine relatively simple pieces.
GOE: 06.02.02 STRENGTH: M GED: R3 M3 L3 SVP: 6 DLU: 77

606.380-010 DRILL-PRESS SET-UP OPERATOR, MULTIPLE SPINDLE (machine shop) alternate titles: gang-drill-press operator; multiple-spindle-drilling-machine operator

Sets up and operates multiple-spindle drilling machine to perform simultaneously or in sequence machining operations, such as drilling, reaming, countersinking, *spot-facing,* and tapping of holes in metal workpieces, according to specifications, tooling instructions, standard charts, and knowledge of machining procedures: Reads blueprint or job order for product specifications, such as hole locations and dimensions, and tooling instructions, such as drilling jigs, holding fixtures, feed rates, cutting speeds, and cutting tools to be used. Places workpiece in fixture or positions it on machine table, and secures it with clamps. Mounts cutting tools in spindle. Positions and secures specified drilling jig and moves controls and positions spindles to align tools with guide bushings in jig. Sets stops to control depth of cut. Moves controls to set cutting speeds and feed rates, and regulate flow of coolant. Engages power feed and observes machine operation. Periodically verifies conformance of machined work to specifications, using such measuring instruments as calipers, micrometers, and fixed gauges. May machine plastics or other nonmetallic materials. May tilt table or spindles to machine holes at specified angles.
GOE: 06.01.03 STRENGTH: M GED: R4 M4 L3 SVP: 6 DLU: 77

606.380-014 DRILL-PRESS SET-UP OPERATOR, RADIAL (machine shop)

Sets up and operates *radial drill press* to perform drilling and other machining operations, such as boring, reaming, and tapping holes in metal workpieces, such as castings, forgings, and weldments, according to specifications, machining instructions, and knowledge of machining: Studies specifications and machining instructions, such as job order, blueprint, process sheet, or layout on workpiece, to determine hole locations and size and setup requirements, including tooling, feed rates, and cutting speeds. Plans sequence of operation, determines suitable work holding arrangement, and fastens holding fixture or jig on machine base to hold workpiece and guide cutting tool. Lifts workpiece manually or with hoist and positions and secures it on machine base or in fixture or jig with clamps and bolts. Verifies position with surface gauges and height gauges. Selects cutting tool, installs it in machine spindle, and moves controls to set cutting speeds and feed rates, according to machining instructions or knowledge of metal properties. Operates controls to swing radial arm over workpiece, position cutting tool over hole center location, engage power feed, and to advance tool into workpiece. Turns valve handle to start flow of cutting oil and coolant against cutting tool and workpiece. Observes machining operation and periodically verifies conformance of machined workpiece to specifications, using measuring instruments, such as *telescoping gauges,* dial indicators, and micrometers. May measure, mark, and scribe reference lines and hole locations on workpiece, according to blueprint, using layout tools, such as rule, divider, and scriber, applying knowledge of shop mathematics and layout techniques. May operate universal-type machine, computing and setting angles of tilting spindle. May work on nonmetallic materials. May sharpen cutting tools, using *bench grinder.*
GOE: 06.01.03 STRENGTH: M GED: R4 M4 L3 SVP: 6 DLU: 77

606.380-018 DRILL-PRESS SET-UP OPERATOR, RADIAL, TOOL (machine shop)

Sets up and operates *radial drill press* to perform drilling and other machining operations, such as boring, reaming, and tapping of holes in metal workpieces, such as machine, tool, or die parts, usually on custom basis, analyzing specifications and deciding on tooling according to knowledge of machining: Studies blueprint or layout on workpiece and plans sequence of operations. Selects method of holding workpiece. Positions and secures workpiece onto machine table, using such devices as shims, blocks, and *planer gauges.* Verifies position with surface gauges and height gauges. Selects cutting speeds, feed rates, and tool for each operation, according to knowledge of metal properties and shop mathematics. Positions and secures tool in spindle. Swings radial arm and moves controls to position spindle and tool along arm over hole center location, to set feeds and speeds, to feed tool in workpiece, and to engage feed. Turns valve handle to direct flow of coolant or cutting oil against tool and workpiece. Observes operation and regulates tool position and action. Verifies hole location and dimensions, using measuring instruments, such as *telescoping gauges,* micrometers, and dial indicators. May measure, mark, and scribe workpiece. May operate universal-type machine, computing and setting angles of tilting spindle. May work on nonmetallic materials. May operate *bench grinder* to sharpen tools.
GOE: 06.01.03 STRENGTH: M GED: R4 M4 L3 SVP: 6 DLU: 77

606.382-010 DRILLER-AND-REAMER, AUTOMATIC (musical inst.)

Operates automatic reamer to ream and mill drilled holes in clarinet posts: Secures reaming tool in chuck of machine. Positions hole over reamer and reams as specified. Secures mill shaft in machine chuck. Mounts mill on end of mill shaft. Mills clarinet post flat on each side of reamed hole to specified tolerances. Verifies milling with go-not-go gauge.
GOE: 06.02.02 STRENGTH: L GED: R3 M2 L2 SVP: 4 DLU: 77

606.382-014 JIG-BORING MACHINE OPERATOR, NUMERICAL CONTROL (machine shop)

Sets up and operates numerically controlled jig-boring machine to perform machining operations, such as boring, drilling and counter-sinking holes in metal workpieces according to specifications and setup instructions, applying knowledge of metal properties and machining methods: Studies blueprints and setup instructions to determine machining required, dimensional specifications, and work procedures and methods. Installs work-holding devices, such as blocks and clamps on *indexing* table of machine, using handtools. Lifts workpiece manually or with hoist and positions and secures it on machine table or in holding device. Inserts cutting tool in spindle of machine. Inserts punched card or loads perforated or magnetic tape containing programmed instructions into reader of control unit. Pushes button to zero indexing table and console at established locating point. Sets conventional cams, stops, and dial-type switches on machine head as indicated on setup instructions if machine spindle is not under numerical control. Actuates machine that automatically positions indexing table containing workpiece under spindle and machines part according to programmed instructions. Inspects and measures dimensions of machined workpiece to verify conformance to specifications and shop standards, using precision measuring instruments, such as precision gauges, dial indicators, micrometers, and calipers. Monitors machine operation and display panel of control unit for indications of malfunctions. Notifies supervisor if machined workpiece does not conform to specifications or if machine malfunctions. May make manual adjustments, such as setting cutting speed, feed rate, and depth of cut. May operate machine in semiautomatic mode by setting selector switch and manually dialing in data according to oral or written instructions to machine relatively simple pieces. May operate machine as inspection machine in manner similar to normal operations by inserting precision measuring instrument in spindle and moving machine through cycle under automatic or manual mode to indicate deviations from prescribed tolerances.
GOE: 06.02.02 STRENGTH: M GED: R4 M4 L3 SVP: 7 DLU: 77

606.382-018 NUMERICAL-CONTROL DRILL OPERATOR, PRINTED CIRCUIT BOARDS (electron. comp.)

Sets up and operates numerical-control drilling machine to drill holes into printed circuit boards (PCB's): Reviews setup instructions and specifications. Loads control media containing programmed commands into control console of machine or enters commands to retrieve programmed control data. Attaches depth collars to drill bits and measures bit depth, using depth gauge, to verify specified drill bit cutting depth. Measures drill bit sizes, using micrometer, and installs specified drill bits in tool magazine of machine. Positions and secures PCB's to *indexing* table of machine. Enters commands to activate machine that automatically aligns indexing table and printed circuit boards under spindle, selects drill bit, and drills holes of specified dimension, location, and sequence into PCB's. Monitors machine operation and display readouts to detect malfunctions. Compares display data to specifications and notifies supervisor of machine malfunctions. Inspects and measures drilled PCB's to verify conformance to specifications, using measuring devices, such as micrometer, plug gauges, and test board. Performs machine adjustments and maintenance, such as setting speed and feed rates, cleaning machine parts, and replacing worn or damaged drill bits, using handtools.
GOE: 06.02.09 STRENGTH: L GED: R3 M3 L3 SVP: 4 DLU: 88

606.382-022 BORING-MACHINE OPERATOR (machine shop)

Sets up and operates boring machines to bore, drill, tap, spot face, groove, mill, or ream metal workpieces according to specifications, tooling instructions, and standard charts, applying knowledge of boring procedures and machining methods: Reads blueprint or job order for product specifications, such as hole locations and dimensions, and tooling instructions, such as fixtures, feed rates, cutting speeds, and cutting tools to be used. Positions and secures cutting tool in toolholder, and toolholder in spindle. Lifts and positions workpiece, manually or using hoist, and secures workpiece in machine table fixture, using wrenches and clamps. Moves controls to position tool in relation to workpiece, and to set feed rate, cutting speed, and depth of cut. Starts machine, moves controls to feed tool against workpiece, or to engage automatic feeding device. Turns valve handle to direct flow of coolant onto cutting area. Observes machine operation, and removes and inspects machined workpiece to verify conformance to specifications, using instruments, such as fixed and air gauges, calipers, and micrometers. May compute cutting speeds, feed rates, and dimensions, using standard charts and shop mathematics.
GOE: 06.02.02 STRENGTH: M GED: R3 M3 L3 SVP: 6 DLU: 88

606.382-026 ROBOTIC MACHINE OPERATOR (aircraft mfg.) alternate titles: industrial robot operator

Sets up and operates industrial robot to drill, countersink, and counterbore metallic and nonmetallic workpieces used to manufacture aircraft parts or tooling, according to specifications and preprogrammed machine control instructions: Reads work order and specifications to determine prescribed setup and operation. Mounts and positions workpiece on locating pins of holding fixture adjacent to robot, manually or using hoist, and aligns and secures workpiece on holding fixture, using template, bolts, handtools, and power tools. Installs specified type and size drill bits in *end effectors* and places end effectors in holding station adjacent to robot. Loads cassette tape of machine instructions into machine controller or enters commands to retrieve preprogrammed instructions from mainframe computer. Pushes button or enters commands to activate robot that automatically retrieves and secures designated end effector on robot

arm and positions arm for drilling. Operates robot to drill holes in test specimen and measures holes for conformance to specifications, using measuring instruments. Obtains written approval of test specimen from quality control inspector. Enters commands to start robot, observes robotic operation, and monitors screen of machine controller for malfunctions and error messages. Changes worn drill bits or adjusts machine according to error message instructions. Inspects finished workpiece for conformance to specifications. Notifies supervisor of numerical control programming problems. Cleans parts, tools, and fixtures, using solvents and rags. May drill holes in parts manually, using drill motor. May perform machine maintenance. May set up and operate robot to perform additional machine operations, such as sealing and fastener installation, to join component parts into complete assembly and be designated Assembly Line Robot Operator (aircraft mfg.).
GOE: 06.02.09 STRENGTH: M GED: R3 M2 L3 SVP: 5 DLU: 88

606.682-014 DRILL-PRESS OPERATOR (machine shop) alternate titles: production-drilling-machine operator
Operates previously set up drilling machines, such as single- or multiple-spindle drill presses to drill, ream, countersink, spot face, or tap holes in metal or nonmetal workpieces according to specifications: Lifts workpiece manually or with hoist, and positions and secures it on machine table in drilling jig or holding fixture. Moves machine controls to feed tools into workpiece, and engages automatic feed. Observes machine operation, and verifies conformance of drilled workpiece to specifications, using fixed gauges, calipers, and micrometers. Changes worn cutting tools, using wrenches. Moves controls to adjust cutting speeds, feed rates, and depth of cut. May assist MACHINE SETTER (machine shop) 600.360-014 in setting up machine. May sharpen cutting tools, using *bench grinder*. May perform minor assembly, such as fastening parts with nuts, bolts, and screws, using power tools and handtools. May be designated according to product as Barrel Reamer (ordnance); or function of machine as Reamer Operator (machine shop); Tapper Operator (machine shop).
GOE: 06.02.02 STRENGTH: M GED: R3 M2 L2 SVP: 3 DLU: 77

606.682-018 DRILL-PRESS SET-UP OPERATOR, SINGLE SPINDLE (machine shop)
Sets up and operates single-spindle drill press to perform such machining operations as drilling, countersinking, *spot-facing*, and tapping holes in metal workpieces, according to specifications, using tooling instructions, standard charts, and knowledge of machining procedures: Reads blueprint or job order and tooling instructions for specifications, such as hole locations and size, feed rates, cutting speeds, and cutting tools to be used. Secures specified tool in spindle. Lifts workpiece manually or with hoist, places it in fixture or jig or on machine table, and secures it with clamps or holds it in position under spindle. Moves controls to set cutting speed, feed rate, and depth of cut. Engages power or automatic feed or manually operates feed lever to feed tool to specified depth in workpiece. Turns valve handle to start flow of coolant against tool and workpiece or dips tool in cutting oil prior to mounting. Verifies conformance of machined workpieces to specifications, using such measuring instruments as calipers, micrometers, and fixed gauges. May position and secure drilling jig to guide cutting tool. May tilt table or spindle to machine holes at specified angles. May work on nonmetallic materials. May measure, mark, scribe, and center punch workpieces to mark hole locations.
GOE: 06.02.02 STRENGTH: M GED: R3 M3 L2 SVP: 4 DLU: 77

606.682-022 TAPPER OPERATOR (nut & bolt)
Sets up and operates one or more automatic tapping machines to cut internal threads in nut blanks: Installs specified tap in spindle, using wrench and rule. Fills feed hopper with nut blanks and starts machine. Measures threaded nuts with gauge and changes worn taps to maintain specified tolerances. May set up machines for other workers to operate.
GOE: 06.02.02 STRENGTH: M GED: R3 M3 L3 SVP: 4 DLU: 77

606.685-010 BORING-MACHINE OPERATOR, PRODUCTION (machine shop)
Tends previously set up single- or multiple-spindle boring machines to perform machining operations, such as boring, *counterboring,* and *facing* metal workpieces on production basis: Lifts workpiece manually or with hoist and clamps it in holding fixtures. Moves machine controls to feed tool into workpiece and engage feed. Observes machine operation and verifies conformance of bored workpiece to specifications, using measuring instruments, such as fixed gauges, calipers, and micrometers. Changes worn tools, using wrenches. May move controls to adjust cutting speeds, feed rates, and depth of cut. May aid MACHINE SETTER (machine shop) 600.360-014 in setting up machine. May bore or drill plastics or other nonmetallic materials.
GOE: 06.04.02 STRENGTH: M GED: R2 M2 L2 SVP: 3 DLU: 77

606.685-014 CHAMFERING-MACHINE OPERATOR I (ordnance)
Tends battery of machines that flare mouths of shell cases to facilitate insertion of bullets: Lubricates and starts each machine and starts flow of compressed air to cool chamfering tools. Observes cases sliding down feed and discharge tubes, repositioning any that are out of order. Observes cutting tools in operation to ensure proper functioning and replaces, sharpens, and resets them as necessary. Examines samples from each machine for burrs, ragged edges, or scratches and determines that dimensions are within prescribed tolerances, using variety of gauges and measuring tools.
GOE: 06.04.02 STRENGTH: L GED: R3 M2 L2 SVP: 3 DLU: 77

606.685-018 CHAMFERING-MACHINE OPERATOR II (ordnance)
Tends automatic screw machine that bevels outside edges of mouth of tracer bullets before they are charged with powder. Observes machine in operation for

malfunctioning and stops machine when bullets are improperly fed, machined, or ejected.
GOE: 06.04.02 STRENGTH: L GED: R2 M1 L1 SVP: 2 DLU: 77

606.685-022 CHOKE REAMER (ordnance)
Tends machine to ream muzzle end of shotgun barrels to choke bores that control spread of pellets during firing: Reams to specified distances within barrel bore with rough, finish, and margin (choke) reamers. Visually examines and measures inside of barrel after reaming to ensure that barrel has been reamed to specified length and diameter, using plug and dial gauges.
GOE: 06.04.02 STRENGTH: L GED: R2 M1 L1 SVP: 3 DLU: 77

606.685-026 DRILL PRESS TENDER (machine shop)
Tends single- or multiple-spindle drill presses that drill, tap, ream, or countersink holes in metal workpieces according to specifications: Lifts workpiece manually, or using hoist, and positions and secures workpiece in drilling jig or fixture on machine table, using clamps and wrenches. Starts machine and feeds workpiece to cutter or vice versa, or engages automatic feeding mechanism. Turns valve to direct flow of coolant and cutting oils over cutting area. Observes operation and releases lever or turns handwheel to raise cutting tool from workpiece when machining is completed. Inspects or measures machined workpiece for conformance to specifications and shop standards, using instruments, such as fixed, plug, depth, and thread gauges, calipers, micrometers, and templates. Changes worn cutting tools, using wrenches. May machine plastics or other nonmetallic materials.
GOE: 06.04.02 STRENGTH: M GED: R2 M2 L2 SVP: 3 DLU: 86

606.685-030 DRILLING-MACHINE OPERATOR, AUTOMATIC (clock & watch)
Tends one or more semiautomatic machines that perform machining operations, such as drilling, boring, tapping, and chamfering holes in clock or watch parts, such as balance wheels, watch plates, and bridges: Positions and clamps part to machine table under cutting tool or inserts part in machine nest, chuck, or over positioning pins in spindle. Depresses pedal or moves controls to start machine that automatically machines part to specifications. Removes part from machine at completion of cycle or activates control that ejects part from machine. Inspects and measures part for conformance to specifications, using loupe and fixed gauges. Changes and replaces worn or broken tools. Cleans metal chips from machine with brush or airhose. Notifies supervisor when machine malfunctions. May tend battery of one kind of machine which may be set up to perform one or several different operations. Workers may be designated according to machine tended or operation performed as Balance-Wheel-Screw-Hole Driller (clock & watch); Boring-Machine Operator (clock & watch); Chamfering-Machine Operator (clock & watch); Reamer (clock & watch); Tapping-Machine Operator, Automatic (clock & watch).
GOE: 06.04.02 STRENGTH: L GED: R2 M1 L1 SVP: 3 DLU: 77

606.685-034 REAMING-MACHINE TENDER (nonfer. metal)
Tends machine that reams and chamfers brass and copper tubing and rods to smooth inside edges of tubing and to remove burrs and sharp edges from ends of tubing and rods: Positions and fastens cutting tool in toolholder and installs funnel-shaped sleeve on machine through which tubing or rod is guided. Starts machine and inserts tubing or rod in sleeve to ream part way through tube or chamfer end of tube or rod. Reverses tube or rod to ream or chamfer opposite end. Changes cutting tool as required, using allen wrench. May pack tubing and rods into cartons.
GOE: 06.04.02 STRENGTH: M GED: R2 M1 L1 SVP: 2 DLU: 77

607 SAWING OCCUPATIONS

This group includes occupations concerned with severing or shaping metal by the reciprocal or rotary cutting action of a serrated or abrasive-edged blade or disk which wears out a kerf. The severing or shaping of nonmetallic materials, except wood, is also included when the methods and machine tools commonly applied to the machining of metal are used.

607.382-010 CONTOUR-BAND-SAW OPERATOR, VERTICAL (machine shop)
Sets up and operates vertical contour-band saw to cut straight, curved, irregular, or internal patterns in metal or plastic stock, according to specifications, utilizing knowledge of sawing techniques: Reads work order or blueprints to locate cutting layout lines on stock, to determine dimensions and tolerances, and to determine metal to be cut, type of blade to be used, blade tension, cutting speed, feed rate, table angle, and positions of table stops and guides. Relieves saw blade support and drive-wheel tension, using handtools. Places saw blade over wheels and resets tension to change blade and adjust tension. Turns controls to set prescribed cutting speed, feed rate, and table angle. Loosens table stops and guides, using handtools, and positions them to align and secure workpiece. Places stock on cutting table, either manually or using hoist, and clamps it into position. Cuts saw blade, threads it through hole drilled in stock, welds blade together, using butt-welding attachment, and files weld smooth to cut internal pattern in stock. Starts saw and manually guides stock along layout lines to cut pattern, or engages automatic feed to cut straight line. Turns control to start airflow to blow metal cuttings away from kerf. Verifies conformance to specifications, using ruler, calipers, fixed gauges, templates, and micrometers. May make precision cuts, using magnifier to see layout lines. May calculate and mark layout lines, according to product specifications. May be re-

quired to have experience with particular product or size, type or trade name of machine.

GOE: 06.02.02 STRENGTH: M GED: R3 M3 L2 SVP: 4 DLU: 77

607.382-014 SAW OPERATOR (aircraft mfg.)

Sets up and operates power saws to cut, slot, groove, miter, and trim metallic and nonmetallic workpieces according to specifications: Selects and installs blade on machine, using handtools. Sets controls to adjust speed, feed rate, and blade tensions. Positions guides, stops, holding blocks, or other fixtures to secure and direct workpiece, using handtools and measuring devices. Scribes reference lines on material as guide for sawing operations, according to blueprints, templates, sample parts, or specifications. Mounts workpiece in holding device, manually or using hoist. Operates saw to cut along scribed lines. Verifies dimensions of finished workpiece, using measuring devices. May weld and anneal saw blades.

GOE: 06.02.02 STRENGTH: M GED: R3 M2 L2 SVP: 4 DLU: 87

607.682-010 CUT-OFF-SAW OPERATOR, METAL (machine shop) alternate titles: band-saw operator; circular-saw operator; hack-saw operator; power-saw operator

Sets up and operates metal-sawing machines, such as hacksaw, bandsaw, circular saw, friction saw, and rubber-disk saw to cut metal stock to dimensions: Reads job order for specifications, such as material, type, and size of stock, and dimensions to be cut. Obtains and transfers stock to machine, manually or with hoist. Installs saw blade and sets blade tension and cutting speed for specified operation. Sets saw blade angle to obtain desired angle cuts, using wrench. Sets stops and guides to control dimension of cut, using steel rule and wrenches. Positions and secures stock against stops or in feeding device. Turns valve to start flow of coolant against cutting area. Starts machine and observes operation. Measures work for conformance to specifications, using rule. Marks identifying data on workpiece. Replaces defective cutting blade or wheel, using handtools. May be required to have experience with custom or production work or with particular material, product, size of workpiece, or type or trade name of machine and be designated accordingly.

GOE: 06.02.02 STRENGTH: M GED: R3 M2 L2 SVP: 4 DLU: 77

607.682-014 PROFILE TRIMMER (jewelry-silver.)

Operates scroll saw or jigsawing-and-nibbling machine to cut or trim hollowware items, such as trays, platters and vegetable dishes into specified shape, performing any combination of following tasks: Marks guidelines on workpiece by tracing from template or sample hollowware, using pencil or scribe. Selects jigsaw or scroll saw blade according to intricacy of outline and gauge of metal, and mounts in drive spindle, using wrench. Starts machine and manually guides workpiece under blade along cutting line to cut workpiece to specified shape or along edge of ornamentation to trim flash from molded items. Removes saw blade and installs nibbling punches in spindle and bed of machine. Turns thumbscrew to adjust depth of stroke to thickness of metal. Starts machine and guides edge of workpiece between reciprocating punches to smooth and trim along edges of mounts (decorative) trim attached after jigsawing by SILVERWARE ASSEMBLER (jewelry-silver.). May file burrs and rough edges from workpiece.

GOE: 06.02.02 STRENGTH: L GED: R3 M2 L2 SVP: 4 DLU: 77

607.685-010 CUT-OFF SAW TENDER, METAL (machine shop)

Tends band or circular saw to cut, miter or groove bar, tube, or sheet metal stock to specified dimensions or shape: Places stock on table or in automatic feed mechanism. Pulls lever or depresses pedal to lower saw blade and cut stock to size or shape. Removes cut stock from table and stacks for removal. May stamp identifying marks on stock, using die and hammer. May work as member of team when cutting structural beams. May assist in changing saw blades and setting table stops and guides.

GOE: 06.04.02 STRENGTH: M GED: R2 M2 L2 SVP: 2 DLU: 77

607.685-014 DEBRIDGING-MACHINE OPERATOR (nonfer. metal)

Tends debridging machine (circular saw) that cuts metal bridge from bottom length of cement-filled aluminum extrusions used in manufacturing windows and doors: Installs cutting blades in machine, using wrenches. Turns controls to set machine cutting speed, blade height, and feed roller position. Places extrusions on intake conveyor and guides extrusions into contact with feed roller for automatic cutting. Removes cut extrusion from off-feed conveyor, and examines exposed cement along cut to detect overlapping metal. Adjusts machine settings to remove metal according to company standards. Stacks extrusions on cart and places cardboard sections between layers.

GOE: 06.04.02 STRENGTH: M GED: R2 M1 L2 SVP: 3 DLU: 86

607.686-010 MAGNESIUM-MILL OPERATOR (nonfer. metal)

Feeds magnesium bar stock into milling machine for grinding into powder: Saws bar stock into sections, places sections in jig of milling machine, and turns handwheel to feed sections to milling cutter. Collects cuttings with air suction hose and dumps them into grinding mill. Cleans magnesium scrap from equipment and work area to eliminate fire hazard.

GOE: 06.04.02 STRENGTH: M GED: R2 M1 L1 SVP: 2 DLU: 77

609 METAL MACHINING OCCUPATIONS, N.E.C.

This group includes occupations, not elsewhere classified, concerned with shaping metal parts or products by removing excess material from stock or ob-

jects. Removing excess material from nonmetallic materials, except wood, is also included when the methods and machine tools commonly applied to the machining of metal are used.

609.130-010 MACHINE-SHOP SUPERVISOR, PRODUCTION (machine shop)

Supervises and coordinates activities of workers engaged in production machining of metallic or nonmetallic workpieces, applying knowledge of machine shop procedures, machine tool setup and operating techniques, and production machining methods. May repair machine tools. Performs duties as described under SUPERVISOR (any industry) Master Title.

GOE: 06.01.01 STRENGTH: L GED: R4 M4 L3 SVP: 8 DLU: 86

609.130-014 SCREW SUPERVISOR (clock & watch)

Supervises and coordinates activities of workers engaged in fabricating watch screws. Performs duties as described under SUPERVISOR (any industry) Master Title.

GOE: 06.02.01 STRENGTH: L GED: R4 M3 L3 SVP: 7 DLU: 77

609.130-018 SUPERVISOR (plumbing-heat.)

Supervises and coordinates activities of workers engaged in polishing, plating, machining, and assembling plumbing fixtures. Sets up and operates machine shop equipment, such as drill press, lathe, and punch press, to fabricate fixtures. Performs duties as described under SUPERVISOR (any industry) Master Title.

GOE: 06.01.01 STRENGTH: L GED: R4 M4 L4 SVP: 7 DLU: 77

609.130-022 SUPERVISOR, AUTOMATIC MACHINES (clock & watch)

Supervises and coordinates activities of workers engaged in setting up automatic machines to drill, ream, tap, chamfer, knurl, countersink, and perform other operations, to make watch parts, such as balance staffs, pinions, pallet arbors, and winding stems. Performs duties as described under SUPERVISOR (any industry) Master Title.

GOE: 06.01.01 STRENGTH: L GED: R4 M3 L3 SVP: 7 DLU: 77

609.130-026 WATCH MANUFACTURING SUPERVISOR (clock & watch)

Supervises and coordinates activities of workers engaged in watch manufacture or assembly, such as hairspring manufacture, balance assembly, or dial manufacture, applying knowledge of watch manufacturing: Computes labor and machine requirements based on work schedules, and assigns work accordingly. Sets up machines [MACHINE SETTER (clock & watch)] and instructs personnel in machine operation. Compares product with blueprint or other specifications, and makes or directs changes in setup to keep product within specified tolerances. Performs duties as described under SUPERVISOR (any industry) Master Title. May supervise workers who are responsible for particular operation or phase of watch assembly or parts manufacture. May be designated according to operations supervised as Watch Balance Assembly Manufacturing Supervisor (clock & watch); Watch Hairspring Manufacturing Supervisor (clock & watch); Watch Metal Dial Manufacturing Supervisor (clock & watch).

GOE: 06.01.01 STRENGTH: L GED: R4 M3 L3 SVP: 7 DLU: 77

609.131-010 INSPECTION SUPERVISOR (machine shop) alternate titles: inspector, chief; quality-control supervisor

Supervises and coordinates activities of workers engaged in inspecting materials, tools, workpieces, and products, such as metal stock, cutting tools, gauges, machine parts, and assembled units for conformance to specifications, products, inspection instruments, and procedures. May compute relative production and repair costs to determine salvageability of rejected products. Performs other duties as described under SUPERVISOR (any industry) Master Title.

GOE: 06.01.01 STRENGTH: L GED: R4 M4 L4 SVP: 8 DLU: 77

609.131-014 SUPERVISOR, MOLD MAKING (glass mfg.)

Supervises and coordinates activities of workers engaged in making and repairing cast iron molds used to produce bottles and other glass containers: Refers to machine shop blueprints and specification charts in manual to determine maximum allowable dimensions for basic type container specified by customer. Studies bottle design designated by customer and estimates glass shrinkage to calculate loss in capacity due to design. Computes dimensional corrections for molds to retain designated glass distribution and bottle capacity. Examines bottles having such defects as improper glass distribution, ridges, and rough surfaces, to determine if defects are due to mold or faulty production equipment. Receives mold change orders, and issues instructions for delivery of molds to bottle-making machines. Performs other duties as described under SUPERVISOR (any industry) Master Title.

GOE: 06.01.01 STRENGTH: L GED: R4 M4 L4 SVP: 8 DLU: 77

609.131-018 SUPERVISOR, MOLD SHOP (glass mfg.)

Supervises and coordinates activities of workers engaged in machining metal castings used in molding glassware: Pours sulfur mix into rough casting to obtain plastic model of object to be molded. Verifies dimensions of model against blueprint, using micrometers and calipers, to determine machining operations required to prepare casting for use as mold. May operate wood lathe to turn patterns for bottle molds. Performs other duties as described under SUPERVISOR (any industry) Master Title.

GOE: 05.05.07 STRENGTH: L GED: R4 M4 L4 SVP: 8 DLU: 77

609.132-010 SLAB-CONDITIONER SUPERVISOR (nonfer. metal)

Supervises and coordinates activities of workers engaged in scalping, sawing, and surfacing of slabs with aluminum to condition aluminum-alloy slabs for

rolling, utilizing knowledge of machining, and conditioning processes and techniques. Performs duties as described under SUPERVISOR (any industry) Master Title.
GOE: 06.02.01 STRENGTH: L GED: R3 M3 L2 SVP: 6 DLU: 77

609.260-010 GUNSMITH, BALLISTICS LABORATORY (ordnance)
Sets up and operates variety of metalworking machines to repair and alter guns and gun parts, and develops designs for special devices used in testing small arms ammunition: Develops designs and fabricates gauges, holding fixtures, and testing equipment, such as gun-holding and target-changing devices, cartridge-slicing fixtures, and special test barrels. May measure velocity of projectiles [CHRONOGRAPH OPERATOR (ordnance)].
GOE: 05.05.07 STRENGTH: M GED: R4 M4 L4 SVP: 8 DLU: 77

609.262-010 TOOL PROGRAMMER, NUMERICAL CONTROL (electron. comp.) alternate titles: programmer operator, numerical control; soft tooling technician
Operates optical programming (digitizing) equipment to generate numerical control (NC) tape program used to control NC machine tools that drill, mill, rout, or notch printed circuit boards (PCB's): Analyzes drawings, specifications, and phototool (photographic film copy of printed circuit pattern) to determine program input data, such as hole sizes, tool sizes, reference points, and direction of machine cutting paths, and calculates data, such as starting point coordinates (location), size of panels or boards, and number of boards per panel. Draws machine tool paths on phototool, using colored markers and following guidelines for tool speed and efficiency, to prepare phototool for use as tool programming aid. Aligns and secures phototool on reference table of optical programmer. Observes enlarger scope of programmer that projects image of circuit board pattern from phototool. Moves reference table, following previously marked paths, to align phototool circuit pattern holes with reference marks on enlarger scope. Depresses pedal or pushes button of programmer to enter coordinates of hole locations into program memory. Repeats process for each hole location on phototool to enter NC machine instructions, such as hole locations, machine paths, and reference points. Keys in additional instructions, such as tool size, machine feed and speed rates, and starting point coordinates, basing entries on specifications, calculations, and knowledge of machine capabilities and programming techniques. Types commands on keyboard to generate NC tape. Observes trial run of NC machine to verify tape program accuracy. Revises NC tape program to eliminate instruction errors. May operate NC machine tools on production basis.
GOE: 05.01.06 STRENGTH: S GED: R3 M3 L3 SVP: 5 DLU: 86

609.280-010 TRIM-MACHINE ADJUSTER (ordnance) alternate titles: shell-trim tool setter
Sets up battery of machines that trim small arms cartridge cases and artillery shell cases to specified length: Installs cutters and adjusts stops and cams to regulate machine stroke and synchronize movements of feeding, cutting, and ejection mechanisms, using handtools. Sharpens dulled cutters and polishes scratched punches, using *bench grinder*, speed lathe, and emery cloth. Removes housings, guards, feed tubes, chutes, tool holders, and other accessories to replace worn or broken parts, such as springs, bushings, and push-rods. May straighten bent punches and machine parts, using hammer and anvil.
GOE: 06.01.02 STRENGTH: M GED: R3 M2 L3 SVP: 5 DLU: 77

609.360-010 NUMERICAL CONTROL MACHINE SET-UP OPERATOR (machine shop)
Sets up and operates numerical control machines or machining centers to perform various machine functions, such as cutting, drilling, milling, reaming, boring, and broaching of metallic and nonmetallic workpieces, utilizing knowledge of machine tool capabilities, machinability of materials, and shop math: Reads and interprets blueprints, planning sheets, sketches, and related technical data to determine tooling requirements, setup procedures, control settings, and machining methods and sequences. Mounts, aligns, and secures tooling, attachments, and workpiece on machine. Selects and installs cutting tools in machine spindle. Loads control media, such as tape, card, or disk, in machine controller or enters commands to retrieve preprogrammed instructions from data base. Calculates and sets machine controls to position spindle in relationship to workpiece and to regulate factors, such as cutting depth, speed, feed, and coolant flow. Starts machine and monitors displays and machine operation to detect malfunctions. Stops machine to change cutting tools and setup according to required machining sequence or to measure parts for conformance to blueprint specifications, using precision measuring instruments. Enters commands or manually adjusts machine controls to correct malfunctions or out-of-tolerance machining. Operates machine manually to perform nonautomated functions and when automatic programming is faulty or machine malfunctions. Discusses control media errors with supervisor or programming personnel to resolve problems. May clean machine, tooling, and parts. May perform machine maintenance.
GOE: 06.01.03 STRENGTH: M GED: R4 M4 L3 SVP: 6 DLU: 89

609.361-010 INSPECTOR, FLOOR (machine shop)
Inspects machined workpieces and assemblies at assembly, inspection, or machining station to ensure conformance to specifications: Reads blueprints or engineering specifications to obtain product information, such as specified material, surface finish, and dimensions. Compares surface finish of workpiece to finish on set of standard blocks making fingertip touch comparison to ensure production of specified surface finish. Measures dimensions, such as length,

height, and distance, between reference points, using precision instruments, such as micrometers, calipers, dial indicator, and snap gauge, to ensure product meets specifications. Locates reference point on part and measures dimensions, such as angle, arc, and radii, using combinations of aids, such as surface plates, parallel bars, angle plates, gauge blocks, V-blocks, sine bars, and precision measuring instruments. Reports findings to INSPECTION SUPERVISOR (machine shop). May inspect first run parts. May set up and try out inspection equipment to ensure accuracy. May substitute known values, such as dimensions from blueprints into standard formulas and solve for unknown quantities, using knowledge of algebra, trigonometry, or geometry to determine dimensions not specified in blueprints. May test hardness of workpiece surface, using hardness testing machine. May be designated according to type of product inspected as Propeller Inspector (ship-boat mfg.); Turbine Inspector (engine-turbine).
GOE: 05.07.01 STRENGTH: M GED: R3 M3 L3 SVP: 6 DLU: 77

609.362-010 NUMERICAL CONTROL MACHINE OPERATOR (machine shop)
Sets up and operates numerical control machine to cut, shape, or form metal workpieces to specifications: Reviews setup sheet and specifications to determine setup procedure, machining sequence, and dimensions of finished workpiece. Attaches fixture to machine bed and positions and secures workpiece in fixture according to setup instructions, using clamps, bolts, handtools, power tools, and measuring instruments, such as rule and calipers. Assembles cutting tools in toolholders and positions toolholders in machine spindles as specified, using handtools, or inserts cutting tools in specified machine magazines. Loads control media, such as disk, tape, or punch card, in machine control console or enters commands to retrieve preprogrammed machine instructions from data base. Manipulates controls and enters commands to index cutting tool to specified *set point* and to start machine. Observes and listens to machine operation to detect malfunctions, such as worn or damaged cutting tools. Changes cutting tools and location of workpiece during machining process as specified in setup instructions. Measures workpiece for conformance to specifications, using measuring instruments, such as micrometers, dial indicators, and gauges. Notifies supervisor of discrepancies. May adjust machine feed and speed and change cutters to machine parts according to specifications when automatic programming is faulty or machine malfunctions. May machine materials other than metal, such as composites, plastic, and rubber.
GOE: 06.02.02 STRENGTH: M GED: R3 M3 L3 SVP: 5 DLU: 77

609.380-010 ELECTRICAL-DISCHARGE-MACHINE SET-UP OPERATOR (machine shop)
Sets up and operates one or more electrical-discharge machines to shape metal workpieces to specifications, following standard charts and manuals, and applying knowledge of *electrical-discharge machining* processes and methods, electric currents and circuitry, metal properties, and shop mathematics: Examines blueprint of product and plans operations. Positions and secures workpiece on machine table with clamps, vise, or fixture. Positions and secures electrode in holder on surface plate, verifying concentricity, alignment, and depth, using measuring instruments, such as calipers and dial indicators. Mounts electrode and holder on machine spindle, using vernier dials on machine to verify alignment of electrode and workpiece. Positions gauge blocks, dial indicator, and spindle stop on machine so that descending electrode will stop at specified depth when indicator feeler point touches gauge blocks. Turns valve to adjust flow of dielectric coolant over electrode and workpiece or to immerse them in circulating bath. Turns controls to adjust machine setting, such as voltage, current, frequency, and electrode feed rate, according to information on charts or knowledge of electrical discharge machining procedures. Starts machine and observes beginning of operation. May move controls to rotate electrode or workpiece. May inspect completed workpiece visually and with templates and other measuring instruments. May compute settings from specifications and knowledge of machine capacities. May give TOOL MAKER (machine shop) 601.280-042 specifications, such as allowances between blueprint dimensions and dimensions of electrode to be made. Important variables may be indicated by trade names of machine used.
GOE: 06.01.03 STRENGTH: L GED: R4 M4 L4 SVP: 7 DLU: 77

609.380-014 THREADING-MACHINE SETTER (machine shop)
Sets up single- or multiple-spindle threading machines to thread and cut, ream, or chamfer cylindrical stock according to order specifications, threading charts, and knowledge of threading procedures: Compiles dimensions of stock, sequence of machining operations, and type and size of thread from charts and specifications. Installs specified feed grips, rotating dies, die cutters (chasers), cutting and reaming or chamfering tool, using micrometers, gauges, and handtools. Installs cams, gears, pulleys, pressure tripping mechanism, and adjusts speed control knobs to synchronize transfer and ejection of stock with machine action. Operates machine to evaluate its performance. Verifies dimensions of workpieces with specifications, using fixed gauges and scale. Sharpens die cutters on grinding wheel. May set up manually operated threading machine [THREADING-MACHINE OPERATOR (machine shop)].
GOE: 06.01.02 STRENGTH: M GED: R4 M3 L3 SVP: 6 DLU: 77

609.462-010 BALANCING-MACHINE OPERATOR (any industry)
Operates dynamic balance machine to locate points of imbalance on parts, such as spindles, impeller wheels, armatures, rotors, and steam engine flywheels, and balances parts by removing excess metal, using handtools and power tools, or adding metal, using soldering and welding equipment: Signals crane operator to position workpiece on machine pedestals. Slides drive belt

over shaft of workpiece or moves drive wheel against workpiece to connect power source that rotates workpiece. Starts machine to rotate workpiece at specified speed. Moves controls of machine to locate points of imbalance indicated by light beam from strobe lamp on identification marks of workpiece, position of wave crest of trace pattern on oscilloscope screen, or readings on wattmeter and protractor dial. Computes amount of weight to be added to or removed from workpiece, or changes size and location of test weight until zero reading is indicated on ammeter. Drills, grinds, chips, or files metal from heavy side, or welds, solders, or rivets metal pieces to light side to correct imbalance, using power drills and grinders, hand file, and soldering and welding equipment.
GOE: 06.02.02 STRENGTH: M GED: R3 M2 L2 SVP: 6 DLU: 77

609.482-010   ELECTRICAL-DISCHARGE-MACHINE   OPERATOR, PRODUCTION (machine shop)
Operates one or more electrical-discharge machines to shape metal workpieces to specifications, following standard charts: Obtains from job order or verbal instructions such information as electrode to be used, depth setting, and number of workpieces or cavities to be shaped. Mounts specified electrode in preset holder on spindle. Positions and secures workpiece on machine table or places it in fixture. Moves controls to align electrode and workpiece and to set electrode feed rate, depth limit, and electric current. Starts machine, turns on flow of dielectric coolant, and observes operation. May inspect work visually or with measuring instruments.
GOE: 06.02.02 STRENGTH: M GED: R3 M2 L2 SVP: 4 DLU: 77

609.482-014   STRAIGHT-PIN-MAKING-MACHINE OPERATOR (button & notion) alternate titles: pinmaker
Operates battery of automatic machines that straighten, cut off, head, and sharpen wire to form straight (common) pins: Places coil of wire on pedestal stand and threads end of wire through machine to heading dies. Adjusts straightening rolls, feeding arm, and stop to diameter and length of wire, using wrenches. Starts machine and measures sampling of first pins for conformance to specifications, such as length, head diameter, and angle of point to shank, using micrometers and fixed gauges. Replaces dull cutters or point-grinding bars, using handtools, such as wrenches, screwdrivers, and pliers. Mounts dies in bench lathe and removes burrs and repolishes head cavity, using stick dipped in polishing paste. Empties pin-filled catch pails into tote trays.
GOE: 06.02.02 STRENGTH: H GED: R3 M3 L3 SVP: 5 DLU: 77

609.682-010   AUTOMATIC-WHEEL-LINE OPERATOR (machine shop)
Controls series of machines to machine cast railroad car wheels to specifications: Changes chucks, boring bar, and cutting tools according to specifications on production orders, using handtools. Pushes buttons on console panel to start machines that perform threading, flanging, boring, inspecting, and other operations to finish wheels. Observes action of machines and transfer stations to detect malfunctions. Examines machined surfaces of wheels at specified stations to detect defective cutting tools.
GOE: 06.02.02 STRENGTH: M GED: R3 M3 L3 SVP: 6 DLU: 77

609.682-014   COLLET MAKER (clock & watch)
Operates three-stage collet making machine to cut and chamfer outside diameters of watch collets, face them to specified thickness, drill hairspring hole, and saw slot in collet: Feeds collet into machine and starts machine. Removes collets by hand, verifies finished collet dimensions, using precision gauges, and makes minor adjustments to machine to keep product within required tolerances.
GOE: 06.02.02 STRENGTH: L GED: R3 M2 L2 SVP: 5 DLU: 77

609.682-018   CROOK OPERATOR (musical inst.)
Operates machine to cut and deburr brass wind instrument tubes, and controls equipment to anneal tubes: Sets length gauge of saw and pushes tubes into rotating blade to cut tubes to specified length. Inserts burring tool into chuck of turning lathe and holds tube ends against rotating burring tool to remove burs. Places tubes in oven or on sprockets of wheel that revolves between two torches to anneal tubes for ease of bending. May fill tube with pitch to facilitate bending tube manually around forming block. Places tube in oven to melt pitch for removal from tube. May place tube in balling-out mold and push steel balls through tube to size part or remove wrinkles.
GOE: 06.02.02 STRENGTH: L GED: R3 M2 L3 SVP: 4 DLU: 77

609.682-022   MACHINE   OPERATOR,   CENTRIFUGAL-CONTROL SWITCHES (elec. equip.) alternate titles: governor assembler
Operates machines, such as lathe and drill press, to machine centrifugal switch assemblies for electric motors, performing any combination of following duties: Positions switch bore and hub cylinder in fixture on hydraulic press. Starts press to lower ram and force hub into switch bore. Clamps assembly to bed of drill press and starts press to ream bore of hub cylinder to specified size. Verifies diameter of bore, using plug gauge. Mounts switch assembly to lathe and inserts specified cutting tool in tool holder. Sets cutting tool to specified depth of cut, using micrometer. Starts lathe to cut outside diameter of switch, to cut slot in contact surface, or to remove rivet heads and burs. Verifies diameter of switch or depth of slot, using micrometer or plug gauge. Mounts switch to test motor. Starts motor and turns control spring setscrew, observing tachometer, until switch opens at specified revolutions per minute. Inserts mandrel in bore of switch assembly and mounts assembly in test stand. Rotates mandrel and observes assembly for static balance. Drills metal from

rivet heads or solders additional metal onto heads to balance switch assemblies. Mounts assembly to lathe and adjusts dial indicator to specified setting. Starts lathe and observes dial indicator to test balance of assembly.
GOE: 06.02.02 STRENGTH: L GED: R3 M2 L2 SVP: 6 DLU: 77

609.682-026   NICKING-MACHINE OPERATOR (cutlery-hrdwr.) alternate titles: nick setter
Sets up and operates machine that notches identification nicks in cutting die edge: Grinds burrs from cutting edge of die, using abrasive wheel. Obtains nicking tools specified on template. Bolts tools to machine bed, using wrench. Heats cutting edge of die to soften metal, using acetylene torch. Positions heated die edge between nicking tools. Pulls lever to close tools that notch identification nicks in die edge.
GOE: 06.02.02 STRENGTH: L GED: R3 M2 L2 SVP: 5 DLU: 77

609.682-030   SCREWMAKER, AUTOMATIC (clock & watch)
Operates machine to automatically shape and cut wire stock to form watch screws: Inserts wire in machine and starts machine that turns head and shank to specified size to form screw, threads and cuts screw to specified length, and slots head. Measures thread and length of finished screw under loupe to determine if it meets specifications, using pitch gauge and upright gauge. Maintains machine adjustment to keep product within specifications.
GOE: 06.02.02 STRENGTH: L GED: R3 M2 L2 SVP: 5 DLU: 77

609.684-010   INSPECTOR, GENERAL (any industry) alternate titles: bench inspector; parts inspector; gauger
Inspects materials and products, such as sheet stock, auto body or engine parts, dental instruments, machine shop parts, and metal castings, for conformance to specifications, using fixed or preset measuring instruments: Examines material or product for surface defects, such as cracks, pits, and incomplete welds. Compares product with parts list or sample model to ensure completion of assembly. Verifies specified dimensions of product or material, using inspection equipment, such as fixed gauges, templates, and preset vernier height gauges, and dial indicator. Rejects defective parts, and marks type of defect on part, container of parts, or inspection tag. May test parts for hardness, using hardness tester [HARDNESS INSPECTOR (heat treating) 504.387-010]. May test products for structural defects, such as leaks and internal cracks, using water pressure tests [HYDRO-PNEUMATIC TESTER (any industry) 862.687-018]. May test mechanisms for clearance and freedom of movement. May be designated Inspector, Filters (auto. mfg.).
GOE: 06.03.02 STRENGTH: L GED: R3 M2 L2 SVP: 4 DLU: 86

609.684-014   LABORER, GENERAL (machine shop)
Performs any combination of following tasks to assist in machine shop activities: Loads and unloads materials, parts, or products onto or from pallets, skids, conveyors, or trucks manually or using hoist. Delivers metal parts or stock to designated work areas for machining, using electric pallet mover, hoist, or overhead crane. Lifts metal part or stock onto machine, manually or using hoist, and secures it on machine table, in chuck, or holding fixture, using wrenches, to assist in setting up machine. Feeds metal parts or stock into automatic metalworking machines and removes machined part from machine after prescribed period of time or at end of machining cycle. Adds coolant to reservoirs of machines and lubricates machine parts and ways, using grease gun and oilcan. Reclaims cutting and lubricating oils from machines by pumping oil from machine reservoir into barrel, dumping oil from barrel into centrifugal separator that removes metal chips and dirt from oil, and drains clean oil from separator into containers. Removes metal chips and shavings from surfaces of machines, using rag or airhose, and wipes surfaces of machines with rag to remove excess oil. Cleans around work areas, using broom and shovel. Separates metal shavings, chips, and scrap materials from trash and places them in bins for resale. May remove burrs or excess metal from machined parts, using files, sandpaper, emery cloth, or grinding machine. May be designated by specific task performed as Brass Reclaimer (machine shop); Gear Cleaner (machine shop); Oil Extractor (machine shop); Sorter (machine shop); Threading-Machine Feeder, Automatic (machine shop) II; Tool Marker (machine shop).
GOE: 06.04.39 STRENGTH: H GED: R2 M1 L1 SVP: 2 DLU: 77

609.685-010   BALL SORTER (machinery mfg.)
Tends machine that sorts metal balls according to size, roundness, or surface defects, such as nicks, scratches, or dents: Adjusts settings on control panel, sets graduated opening on gauge slide, or selects and installs gauging screen in barrel of machine through which balls drop into containers according to variation from specified dimensions. Loads balls into feed hopper, and starts machine that automatically sorts standard size, oversize, undersize, and defective balls into separate pockets or containers. May visually examine or measure sample balls from each container, using micrometer or fixed gauge and label containers, according to quality and quantity of sorted balls. May weigh balls on balance scale and record weight and grades on work ticket.
GOE: 06.04.02 STRENGTH: M GED: R2 M1 L1 SVP: 2 DLU: 77

609.685-014   ENGRAVER, AUTOMATIC (clock & watch)
Tends battery of automatic engraving machines that inscribe numerals and words on watch parts: Loads paddle manually with specified watch parts. Inserts paddle into machine and pulls lever to automatically secure paddle in position for scribing. Presses button to start machine operation and initiate engraving cycle. Inspects finished pieces to detect engraving faults, such as skips, incorrectly located engraving, and irregular cut, using loupe and location gauge.
GOE: 06.04.02 STRENGTH: L GED: R2 M1 L1 SVP: 2 DLU: 77

609.685-018 PRODUCTION MACHINE TENDER (machine shop) alternate titles: machine shop production worker; robotic machine tender, production

Tends one or more machine tools, special-purpose machines, or industrial robots to machine metal workpieces to specifications on production basis: Lifts workpiece manually or using hoist and secures workpiece in fixture or loads automatic feeding device. Starts machine, engages feed, and observes operation. Inspects and measures machined workpieces to verify conformance to specifications, using instruments, such as preset comparator, fixed gauges, calipers, micrometer, or microscope. May move machine controls and guides to adjust machine. May replace worn machine accessories, such as cutting tools or brushes. May add coolant to machine reservoir and turn valve to start flow of coolant. May file, sand, or shape machined parts, using handtools and power tools. May clean machined parts, using degreasing tank or solvent and rags. May machine plastics or other nonmetals. May tend machines and equipment other than machine tools.
GOE: 06.04.02 STRENGTH: M GED: R2 M2 L2 SVP: 3 DLU: 89

609.685-022 TRANSFER-MACHINE OPERATOR (machine shop)

Tends transfer machine consisting of series of stations connected by transfer mechanisms that transfer, position, and secure workpieces and perform machining operations, such as drilling, boring, tapping, and milling on metal workpieces, such as castings and forgings: Lifts workpiece manually or with hoist, and places on holding device, such as pallet. Pushes pallet along track into clamping station, and starts mechanisms to clamp workpiece on pallet and transfer to first work station. Inspects machined workpieces for surface defects and verifies conformance to specifications, using measuring instruments, such as fixed gauges and checking fixtures. Changes tools when panel lights indicate that tool is worn or broken, using wrenches. Moves bar to lift derailed pallets back into position. Notifies supervisor if panel lights indicate machine failure or serious malfunctioning.
GOE: 06.04.02 STRENGTH: M GED: R3 M2 L2 SVP: 3 DLU: 77

609.685-026 TRIM-MACHINE OPERATOR (ordnance) alternate titles: cut-off-machine operator; shell-trim operator; trim and burr operator

Tends battery of machines that trim small arms cartridge cases, bullet jacket blanks, or artillery shell cases to specified length: Loads small arms cartridge cases or bullet jacket blanks into hopper of automatic machine or positions artillery shell cases by hand in feeding device of trim machine. Turns stop nuts and setscrews, using handtools, to adjust chuck and feed punch to cut blanks to specified length. Starts machine and observes operation of feeding, cutting, and ejection mechanisms to detect malfunction. Extracts jammed pieces, using fingers or wire hook. Examines trimmed pieces for such defects as dents, burrs, or scratches. Verifies conformity to specified dimensions, using fixed gauges. Sharpens cutters on *bench grinder*.
GOE: 06.04.02 STRENGTH: M GED: R2 M1 L1 SVP: 3 DLU: 77

61 METALWORKING OCCUPATIONS, N.E.C.

This division includes occupations, not elsewhere classified, concerned with shaping and conditioning metal by rolling, forging, extruding, drawing out, punching, shearing, blanking, and pressworking. The punching, shearing, blanking, and pressworking of nonmetallic materials, except wood, are also included when the methods and machine tools commonly applied to the working of metal are used.

610 HAMMER FORGING OCCUPATIONS

This group includes occupations concerned with heating metal in a forge and hammering it into desired shape with a hand or power hammer (includes drop forging).

610.362-010 DROPHAMMER OPERATOR (aircraft mfg.; forging) alternate titles: blacksmith, hammer operator

Sets up and operates closed-die drophammer to forge metal parts according to specifications, using measuring instruments and handtools: Informs HEATER (forging) 619.682-022 of forging specifications, such as specified quantity and temperature setting. Aligns and bolts specified dies to machine ram and anvil, using scale, rule, square, feeler gauges, shims, and handtools. Positions workpiece onto lower die and depresses pedal to activate ram that repeatedly strikes and forces metal workpiece into die impression. Moves workpiece through series of dies to attain specified detail. May plan work procedures, select tooling, and operate drophammer to form experimental or developmental parts. May turn knobs to regulate conveyor speed and feed that automatically carries heated stock from furnace, places stock on anvil, and removes finished workpiece. May forge unheated metal. May set stops or turn handles to set specified striking force of ram. May trim flash from finished forging. May operate hammer to compress finished forgings to specified tolerances and be designated Restrike Hammer Operator (forging). May be designated according to type of hammer operated as Board Drophammer Operator (forging); Impact Hammer Operator (forging); Steam Hammer Operator (forging).
GOE: 06.02.02 STRENGTH: H GED: R3 M3 L3 SVP: 6 DLU: 87

610.381-010 BLACKSMITH (forging) alternate titles: anvil smith

Forges and repairs variety of metal articles, such as tongs, edged tools, hooks, chains, machine and structural components, and agricultural implements

as specified by work orders, diagrams, or sample parts: Heats metal stock in blacksmith's forge or furnace [HEATER (forging)]. Hammers stock into specified size and shape on blacksmith's anvil or positions stock on anvil of power hammer and depresses pedal to hammer stock with varying force and rapidity. Forge-welds metal parts by heating and hammering them together. Devises jigs and fixtures, forges special handtools, such as hammers or chisels, and sets up form blocks. Tempers or anneals forged articles [HEAT TREATER (heat treating) I]. May record type of repair or fabrication of tools or machine components performed during work shift to maintain daily activity report and records. May cut, assemble, and weld metal parts, using arc or acetylene welding equipment [WELDER, COMBINATION (welding)]. May repair farm machinery and be designated Blacksmith, Farm (agriculture). May be designated according to articles forged as Special-Trackwork Blacksmith (r.r. trans.); Tool-Dresser (forging).
GOE: 05.05.06 STRENGTH: H GED: R4 M3 L2 SVP: 7 DLU: 77

610.381-014 BLACKSMITH APPRENTICE (forging)

Performs duties as described under APPRENTICE (any industry) Master Title.
GOE: 05.05.06 STRENGTH: H GED: R4 M3 L2 SVP: 7 DLU: 77

610.684-010 BLACKSMITH HELPER (forging) alternate titles: striker

Assists BLACKSMITH (forging) in forging metal articles: Obtains equipment, such as stop blocks and hammer dies from toolroom. Cuts metal to predetermined size, using saw. Lights furnace and turns control valves to regulate temperature. Lifts metal parts from furnace with tongs and places parts on anvil or under power hammer. Strikes parts with sledge as BLACKSMITH (forging) positions parts over forming dies set in anvil. Grinds surfaces of finished parts, using portable and stationary power grinders. May sweep floor and remove debris from work area. Performs other duties as described under HELPER (any industry) Master Title.
GOE: 05.12.10 STRENGTH: M GED: R2 M1 L1 SVP: 4 DLU: 77

610.684-014 SPRING SALVAGE WORKER (metal prod., nec)

Reshapes defective spring leaves, using furnace and power hammer: Places leaf in furnace to heat it to specified color. Removes leaf from furnace and positions it on bed of power hammer. Starts machine to pound leaf into specified shape and verifies shape of leaf, using template. Tempers leaf by immersing it in oil bath for specified time.
GOE: 06.04.02 STRENGTH: M GED: R2 M1 L1 SVP: 4 DLU: 77

611 PRESS FORGING OCCUPATIONS

This group includes occupations concerned with heating metal in a forge and shaping it by means of a press.

611.482-010 FORGING-PRESS OPERATOR I (forging) alternate titles: die-machine operator; forging-machine operator

Sets up and operates closed-die power press to produce metal forgings, following work order specifications, using measuring instruments and handtools: Aligns and bolts specified dies on ram and anvil of press, using rule, square, shims, feelers, and handtools. Turns knobs to set pressure and depth of ram stroke. Pulls workpiece from furnace, when color of workpiece indicates forging temperature, and positions workpiece on lower die, using tongs. Depresses treadle or pulls lever to lower ram that compresses metal to shape of die impressions. May move workpiece through series of dies for progressively finer detail.
GOE: 06.02.02 STRENGTH: H GED: R3 M2 L2 SVP: 5 DLU: 77

611.482-014 ROLLER-MACHINE OPERATOR (metal prod., nec) alternate titles: roller operator

Operates machine to flatten and taper heated ends of spring leaf blanks to specified dimensions: Installs dies in upper and lower plates of press and adjusts pressure of rollers, using wrenches and gauges. Heats end of spring blank in furnace and places it on stationary die plate. Pulls lever to flatten end to specified width. Holds compressed end between cam-shaped rollers that grip and taper end to specified thickness.
GOE: 06.02.02 STRENGTH: M GED: R3 M2 L1 SVP: 4 DLU: 77

611.662-010 UPSETTER (forging)

Sets up and operates closed-die forging machine equipped with horizontal ram and gripping die to expand end of hot metal bar stock: Aligns and bolts specified dies and cams in machine, using rule, square, and wrenches. Pulls stock from furnace when color indicates forging temperature and inserts stock in gripping die against stop gauge, using tongs or hoist. Presses pedal to close gripping die on stock and to advance ram, squeezing end of metal into gripping die cavity. Moves workpiece through series of dies to shape stock progressively to specifications. Verifies dimensions of forged piece, using set gauges. May set up and operate closed-die forging machine to expand end of cold metal.
GOE: 06.02.02 STRENGTH: H GED: R3 M2 L2 SVP: 5 DLU: 78

611.682-010 STEEL-SHOT-HEADER OPERATOR (ordnance)

Sets up and operates battery of machines to cold forge BB shot for air rifles from coils of steel wire: Aligns die halves that form ball on end of wire, using handtools. Turns setscrews and stop nuts to adjust and synchronize cutoff tool, ram stroke, and feeder arm. Threads wire through straightening rollers and feeding mechanism into ram head. Starts machine and observes operation to detect malfunction. Measures shot for conformance to specified tolerances, using micrometer. Sharpens and shapes cutoff tool, using *bench grinder*.

GOE: 06.02.02 STRENGTH: M GED: R3 M1 L2 SVP: 4 DLU: 77

611.682-014 AUTOMATIC CASTING-FORGING MACHINE OPERA-TOR (forging)

Controls and monitors operation of automatic casting-forging machine to cast, forge, and trim nonferrous molten metal into finished forgings: Starts hydraulic pumps and sets timers and heater controls. Turns automatic controls, such as shot weight and pouring speed, to set sequence of operation. Notifies forklift operator to pour molten metal into container. Pours molten metal into preform mold, using ladle, and starts manual operation for trial run. Activates automatic pouring device to fill mold, and depresses controls to initiate automatic casting and forging operations. Observes indexing mechanism that moves casting through sequence of operations, such as die press, quenching, and trimming. Observes castings and forgings for imperfections, such as discolorations and distortions. Realigns dies, castings, or forgings to correct out-of-tolerance conditions. Observes lights on control panel to detect machine malfunctions and corrects conditions causing malfunctions, such as clogged filters and sticking valves.

GOE: 06.02.10 STRENGTH: L GED: R4 M2 L3 SVP: 5 DLU: 86

611.685-010 FORGING-PRESS OPERATOR II (forging) alternate titles: press hand; press operator

Tends closed-die power press that produces metal forgings: Pulls workpiece from furnace, when color of workpiece indicates forging temperature, and positions it on lower die, using tongs. Moves controls to lower ram that compresses metal to shape of die impressions. May move workpiece through series of dies for progressively finer detail. May tend press to emboss designs on metal or compress and smooth surface of metal blanks or rough forgings and be designated Coining-Press Operator (forging). May tend press that twists forging to form journals and counterweights on crankshafts to specified degree of eccentricity and be designated Twisting-Press Operator (forging).

GOE: 06.04.02 STRENGTH: H GED: R2 M2 L2 SVP: 2 DLU: 77

611.685-014 HYDRAULIC OPERATOR (nonfer. metal) alternate titles: hydraulic-corrugating-machine operator

Tends hydraulic corrugating machine that corrugates metal tubes used in making bellows: Moves controls of machine to expand corrugating plates and position spacers between plates. Places tube in opening of plates. Pulls levers to close cradle, remove spacers, and pump water into tube forcing tube walls to conform to shape of corrugated plates.

GOE: 06.04.02 STRENGTH: M GED: R2 M1 L1 SVP: 3 DLU: 77

612 FORGING OCCUPATIONS, N.E.C.

This group includes occupations, not elsewhere classified, concerned with shaping and conditioning metal. Includes shaping without benefit of heat by such means as machines equipped with rollers.

612.130-010 SPIKEMAKING SUPERVISOR (steel & rel.)

Supervises and coordinates activities of workers engaged in forging boat or track spikes from hot steel rods: Coordinates setting up of forge machines with set-up worker to ensure machines forge products of specified size. Installs dies and adjusts guide stops in automatic forging machines, using wrenches, hammer, and pry bar. Verifies dimensions of spikes, using gauges and rule. Observes size, shape, and color of heated spikes and adjusts dies and guide stops to ensure production of spikes to manufacturing standards. Repairs machines and conveyor system and replaces worn or broken parts, using wrenches, sledgehammer, pry bar, and chain hoist. Performs other duties as described under SUPERVISOR (any industry) Master Title.

GOE: 06.01.01 STRENGTH: M GED: R3 M2 L1 SVP: 7 DLU: 77

612.131-010 FORGE-SHOP SUPERVISOR (forging) alternate titles: blacksmith supervisor

Supervises and coordinates activities of workers engaged in heating, forging, and inspecting metal workpieces and products: Plans and coordinates sequence of operations within forge shop. Inspects dies, machines, and work in process to detect malfunctions, and orders corrective action. Trains new workers in job duties. Performs other duties as described under SUPERVISOR (any industry) Master Title. May set up machines for experimental runs. May be designated according to department as Hammer-Shop Supervisor (forging); Inspection Supervisor (forging).

GOE: 06.01.01 STRENGTH: M GED: R4 M3 L3 SVP: 8 DLU: 78

612.260-010 FASTENER TECHNOLOGIST (nut & bolt)

Sets up and operates variety of machines to head, trim, drill, and tap metal stock to fabricate machine tools and form metal parts and fasteners, such as screws, bolts, and nuts, according to blueprint specifications and using precision measuring devices, machinist manuals, and handtools: Reads and interprets blueprints to determine specified tolerances and sequence of operations to be used in machining metal parts. Selects and installs cutting tools in machines, using handtools. Selects cutting speeds, depth of cut, and adjusts guides, using handtools. Installs workpiece in vise, marks layout, and verifies dimensions, using precision gauges and machinist manuals. Operates machines to tool specified parts and inspects parts to ensure conformity to blueprint specifications, using gauges and applying knowledge of fractions and decimals. Sharpens cutting tools and drill bits, using bench grinders.

GOE: 06.02.02 STRENGTH: H GED: R4 M3 L3 SVP: 7 DLU: 86

612.261-010 INSPECTOR (forging)

Inspects forgings for conformance to specifications, following blueprints and using measuring instruments, and determines cause of defects by applying knowledge of metal characteristics and forging methods: Verifies dimensions of forgings, using measuring instruments, such as calipers, gauges, and rules. Examines forgings to detect surface defects, such as scale, laps, and cracks. Informs supervisor of defects and their probable cause. May stop production and order variations in forging methods, such as change in heating temperature, modification of ram stroke, or realignment of dies to correct defects. May read job order to determine if all specified operations, such as heat-treating, cleaning, and machining have been performed. May straighten warped forgings [STRAIGHTENING-PRESS OPERATOR (any industry) II 617.482-026]. May test hardness of forgings [HARDNESS INSPECTOR (heat treating) 504.387-010]. May inspect metal forgings for internal flaws, using ultrasonic inspection equipment. May inspect raw stock. May inspect hot forgings before completion and be designated Inspector, Hot Forgings (forging).

GOE: 06.01.05 STRENGTH: M GED: R4 M3 L3 SVP: 6 DLU: 78

612.360-010 DIE SETTER (forging)

Sets up forging machines, such as forging presses, coining presses, drophammers, forging rolls, and upsetters, following blueprint, work order, and data-chart specifications, and using handtools and measuring instruments, such as rules, squares, and gauges: Aligns and bolts specified dies to ram and anvil of presses and hammers. Installs impression and gripping dies and synchronizing cams on upsetting machines. Sets and bolts roll dies into self-positioning slots or dogs on roll shafts of forging rolls. Aligns and bolts positioning fixtures and stops, and turns handles or knobs to synchronize conveyor speed with forging-machining action and heating cycle of furnace. Starts machine and inspects work to verify conformance of die setup to specifications. May be designated according to machine set up as Drophammer Setter-Up (forging); Forging Press Setter-Up (forging); Upsetter Setter-Up (forging).

GOE: 06.01.02 STRENGTH: M GED: R4 M3 L3 SVP: 7 DLU: 77

612.361-010 HEAVY FORGER (forging)

Shapes heated metal stock into forgings on power hammer or press equipped with open dies, applying knowledge of forging techniques and physical properties of metal, following work order, diagrams, or specifications, and using measuring instruments and handtools: Aligns and bolts dies into ram and anvil of machine, using rule, square, gauges, and handtools. Observes color of metal in furnace to determine forging temperature and signals HEATER (forging) to pull metal from furnace. Directs LEVER TENDER (forging) to start machine and regulate action of hammer or press, and directs HEAVY-FORGER HELPER (forging) or MANIPULATOR OPERATOR (forging) to position and turn metal on anvil of machine. Verifies dimensions of forging, using rule and calipers. May forge cold metal. May be designated according to forging equipment as Hammersmith (forging); Press Smith (forging).

GOE: 06.02.02 STRENGTH: M GED: R4 M4 L3 SVP: 8 DLU: 77

612.384-010 INSPECTOR, COLD WORKING (ordnance)

Inspects dimensions of cannon barrels before and after cold-working, following specifications and using measuring instruments: Measures outside and inside diameter of barrel at specified points before and after cold working, using micrometer and star gauge. Examines gun bore for cracks and flaws, using optical device to see down gun barrel. Records inspection data and recommendations for disposition of barrel.

GOE: 06.03.01 STRENGTH: M GED: R3 M3 L3 SVP: 4 DLU: 77

612.462-010 MULTI-OPERATION-MACHINE OPERATOR (any industry)

Sets up and operates machine that automatically performs multioperations, such as roll-threading, heading (upsetting), slotting, slitting, or shearing to form chain or produce fasteners, such as bolts and rivets, from hot or cold metal rod or wire: Selects, installs, and aligns dies, rolls, cutting tools, guides, and stops to set up machine, using handtools and measuring instruments. Sets controls to synchronize machine actions for various operations on workpiece in specified sequence. Positions coil of metal wire or rod on feed spindle and threads it through straightening rolls into feed mechanism; or inserts end of heated rod into feed mechanism. Starts machine to produce sample product and measures for conformance with specifications, using measuring instruments. Adjusts settings of dies on controls, as required, to obtain product meeting specifications and quality standards. Starts machine to begin production and observes machine operations for evidence of malfunction and products for defects. May be designated according to type of product produced, as Bolt-Machine Operator (nut & bolt); Chain-Forming-Machine Operator (forging); Rivet Maker (nut & bolt). May be known according to whether metal is heated or cold forged, as Cold-Header Operator (forging); Hot-Header Operator (forging).

GOE: 06.01.03 STRENGTH: L GED: R3 M3 L2 SVP: 6 DLU: 77

612.462-014 NUT FORMER (nut & bolt)

Sets up and operates one or more automatic machines to shear, form, and punch nut blanks from hot or cold metal bar or coiled stock: Installs punching and shearing dies in machine, using wrenches, rule, hammer, and gauges. Threads end of coiled stock from feeder reel through straightening rolls and against stop in machine, or aligns bar stock between dies by hand or using tongs for hot bar stock. Starts machine and observes feeding operation, or feeds bar stock against dies. Measures nut blanks with gauges and adjusts dies to maintain specified dimensions. May regulate electric induction or gas furnace

to heat stock. May set up machine for PRODUCTION-MACHINE TENDER (nut & bolt).
GOE: 06.02.02 STRENGTH: M GED: R3 M3 L2 SVP: 5 DLU: 77

612.662-010 SPIKE-MACHINE OPERATOR (steel & rel.)
Sets up and operates machine to forge boat and track spikes from heated steel rods: Installs and adjusts forging hammer, squeezing dies, and stop guides, according to specifications, using rule and handtools. Adjusts temperature controls of furnace in which rods are heated depending on color of heated rod. Moves lever or depresses pedal to discharge malformed spikes and waste end of rod into receptacle. Grasps spike with tongs, observes shape of head, and measures spike with gauge to ensure that it conforms to specifications. Directs SPIKE-MACHINE FEEDER (steel & rel.) when setting up equipment. May replace and repair worn and broken parts of machine and conveyor system.
GOE: 06.02.02 STRENGTH: M GED: R3 M2 L1 SVP: 7 DLU: 77

612.666-010 SPIKE-MACHINE FEEDER (steel & rel.)
Feeds heated steel rods into machine that forges spikes: Signals SPIKE-MACHINE HEATER (steel & rel.) to shove end of heated rod through open end of furnace. Grasps rod with tongs and shoves it onto feed rollers of machine. Observes color of rods and notifies SPIKE-MACHINE OPERATOR (steel & rel.) if furnace temperature requires adjustment. Assists in installing dies and adjusting guide stops, using handtools.
GOE: 06.04.02 STRENGTH: M GED: R2 M1 L1 SVP: 2 DLU: 77

612.682-010 BUCKSHOT-SWAGE OPERATOR (ordnance)
Sets up and operates battery of machines to press lead slugs into buckshot for shotgun ammunition: Removes and replaces dies, punches, and die blocks, and adjusts knockout pins, feed fingers, and stops, using handtools. Fills hoppers with lead slugs from scoop or tote box. Starts machines and measures diameters of swaged shot samples, using shot gauge, and weighs them on balance scale to determine conformance to specifications. Rolls shot under dial micrometer to verify roundness. Turns bolts, setscrews, and stop nuts to adjust position of punches and dies by trial and error to produce acceptable shot.
GOE: 06.02.02 STRENGTH: H GED: R3 M2 L2 SVP: 4 DLU: 77

612.682-014 FORGING-ROLL OPERATOR (forging) alternate titles: roll forger; rolling-machine operator
Sets up and operates roll-forging machine to taper, shape, or reduce metal bar stock as specified by work order: Bolts two semicylindrical dies on opposing roll shafts of machine, using wrenches. Positions and bolts limit stops on machine, using rule, scale, and handtools. Pulls workpiece from furnace, when color indicates forging temperature, and places it on worktable, using tongs. Pushes workpiece into open segment of dies and depresses pedal to rotate dies that grasp workpiece in circular grooves and pull it between power-driven rolls bearing contoured dies to shape workpiece. Moves workpiece through progressively smaller grooves on dies to forge it to specified shape. Verifies dimensions, using gauge or scale. May use roll-forging machine that automatically tapers, shapes, or reduces metal bar stock and be designated Rotary-Swaging-Machine Operator (forging).
GOE: 06.02.02 STRENGTH: H GED: R3 M2 L2 SVP: 4 DLU: 77

612.683-010 MANIPULATOR OPERATOR (forging) alternate titles: charging manipulator
Operates manipulator to transport metal stock from furnace and position and turn it on anvil of forging press or hammer: Moves levers and pedals to guide manipulator along floor or on overhead rails to furnace. Moves levers on control box to grasp workpiece with jaws mounted on arm extending from manipulator cab, and transports workpiece to press or hammer. Moves controls of arm to turn and position workpiece on anvil as it is being shaped, following signals of HEAVY FORGER (forging).
GOE: 06.04.02 STRENGTH: L GED: R2 M2 L2 SVP: 5 DLU: 77

612.684-010 UTILITY WORKER, FORGE (forging)
Performs any combination of following tasks in forging plant: Moves workpieces from furnace to hammer anvil, using tongs or hoist. Opens and closes electrically controlled furnace doors to assist steel press crew. Positions and turns workpieces and work aids during forging by HEAVY FORGER (forging). Removes scale from anvil, using broom and airhose. Cleans work area with broom and shovel and cleans machine parts, using rag and solvent. Replaces forge crew tools in specified racks. May assist in installing dies used in forging operations. May cut material to specified size with handsaw, and smooth parts with *bench grinder* to assist BLACKSMITH (forging). May remove cracks in ingots, billets, or forgings, using swing grinder.
GOE: 05.12.10 STRENGTH: M GED: R2 M1 L1 SVP: 2 DLU: 77

612.685-010 LEVER TENDER (forging)
Tends power hammer or power press that forges metal stock: Moves levers, upon signal from HEAVY FORGER (forging), to control force and frequency of hammer blows, or ram pressure, to shape forging. May be designated according to equipment tended as Forging-Press Lever Tender (forging); Hammer Driver (forging).
GOE: 06.04.02 STRENGTH: M GED: R2 M1 L1 SVP: 4 DLU: 77

612.685-014 SPRING TESTER I (metal prod., nec)
Tends power press that tests resiliency of spiral springs and that compresses them to specified length: Positions spring over mandrel of press table and places metal plate over end of spring. Pulls lever that forces plunger of machine against plate to compress spring. Measures compressed length of spring, using

micrometers, calipers, and gauges. Releases press and measures uncompressed length of spring. Inserts metal wedge between spring coils and taps spring with mallet to adjust spring to specified length and pitch.
GOE: 06.03.02 STRENGTH: L GED: R3 M2 L2 SVP: 4 DLU: 77

612.687-010 HEAT READER (forging)
Compares glow inside forge shop furnace with color intensity chart to determine internal temperature of furnace, using pyrometer: Looks through pyrometer into furnace and compares intensity of light generated by furnace with chart depicting color at various temperatures to determine internal furnace temperature. Informs specified forging personnel of observed temperature to permit designated adjustments to furnace controls, maintenance work, and production rescheduling.
GOE: 06.03.02 STRENGTH: L GED: R2 M2 L2 SVP: 3 DLU: 77

612.687-014 HEAVY-FORGER HELPER (forging)
Assists HEAVY FORGER (forging) in shaping hot metal on power hammer or press equipped with open dies, working as member of crew: Pulls workpiece from furnace with tongs and positions and turns it on hammer anvil. Removes scale from metal and anvil during forging, using compressed air or broom. May assist in forging unheated metal. May be designated according to worker assisted as Hammersmith Helper (forging); Press-Smith Helper (forging). Performs other duties as described under HELPER (any industry) Master Title.
GOE: 05.12.10 STRENGTH: H GED: R2 M1 L1 SVP: 3 DLU: 77

613 SHEET AND BAR ROLLING OCCUPATIONS

This group includes occupations concerned with shaping, reducing the cross sectional area, and elongating metal pieces by passing them between smooth-surfaced or circumferentially grooved rotating rolls which exert a continuous compressive force. Includes rolling wire from billets and rods.

613.130-010 SUPERVISOR, BLOOMING MILL (steel & rel.)
Supervises and coordinates activities of workers engaged in rolling heated ingots into steel shapes, such as blooms, billets, and slabs, and in shearing shapes to specified lengths. Trains workers in setting up mill. Performs duties as described under SUPERVISOR (any industry) Master Title.
GOE: 06.02.01 STRENGTH: M GED: R4 M4 L3 SVP: 7 DLU: 77

613.130-014 SUPERVISOR, MERCHANT-MILL ROLLING AND FINISHING (steel & rel.) alternate titles: roller, merchant mill
Supervises and coordinates activities of workers engaged in operation of merchant mill to roll products, such as bars, flats, and skelp from billets and slabs: Reads rolling order to plan setup of roll stands. Directs workers in building and installing rolling stands and equipment on rolling line, and setting draft (space between rolls) for each roll stand. Observes operation of mill, inspects product during rolling operation, and orders adjustments in mill equipment and changes in conveyor speeds for drawing billets or slabs from furnace. Performs other duties as described under SUPERVISOR (any industry) Master Title.
GOE: 06.02.01 STRENGTH: M GED: R4 M3 L3 SVP: 7 DLU: 77

613.130-018 SUPERVISOR, STRUCTURAL ROLLING-AND-FINISHING (steel & rel.) alternate titles: roller, structural mill
Supervises and coordinates activities of workers engaged in setting up and operating structural mills to roll slabs, billets, plates, and structural shapes, such as angles, beams, and channels from blooms or beam blanks: Reads production schedule and rolling orders to plan setup of rolls, tables, and beds required for processing product. Directs workers in dismantling and setting up roll stands and auxiliary equipment. Specifies number of passes for each product, regulation of draft, and shaping to be performed during each pass. Inspects rolled product for conformance to specifications, and orders adjustment of roll screws and changes in rolling temperature. Performs other duties as described under SUPERVISOR (any industry) Master Title. May supervise workers engaged in rolling slabs into plates and be designated Roller, Plate Mill (steel & rel.).
GOE: 06.01.01 STRENGTH: M GED: R4 M3 L4 SVP: 8 DLU: 78

613.132-010 SUPERVISOR, HOT-STRIP MILL (steel & rel.)
Supervises and coordinates activities of workers engaged in heating, rolling, coiling, loading, and shipping hot-strip coils: Reads production schedule for type of products to be rolled, and to plan rolling temperature, mill setup, and sequence of charging slabs into furnace. Inspects mill equipment, such as furnaces, run-out tables, conveyors, and pilers for malfunctions. Performs other duties as described under SUPERVISOR (any industry) Master Title.
GOE: 06.02.01 STRENGTH: L GED: R4 M3 L3 SVP: 7 DLU: 78

613.360-010 ROLL-FORMING-MACHINE SET-UP MECHANIC (any industry)
Sets up machine to form longitudinal bends, beads, rolls, or embossed designs into sheet metal strips by drawing strips through one or more sets of roller dies to fabricate such items as molding trim, or weatherstrip: Bolts specified dies onto spindles. Positions spindles to align male and female dies and adjust dies and drive rolls to thickness of metal strip. May turn knobs or install gears to set speed of machine and synchronize action of cutting die or shear blade with action of machine to cut stock to specified length. Directs flow of coolant onto workpiece or fills oilcups. Turns machine over to ROLL-FORMING-MACHINE OPERATOR (any industry) 617.685-034 II.
GOE: 06.01.02 STRENGTH: M GED: R4 M3 L2 SVP: 6 DLU: 77

613.360-014 ROLL-TUBE SETTER (steel & rel.) alternate titles: roll setter; roll setter, pipe mill

Installs and adjusts rolls on sizing, forming, and welding mill to produce pipe or tube of specified outside diameter, following job specifications and using handtools: Reads mill schedule to determine size of product to be produced. Selects rolls and installs rolls on mill, using handtools. Signals OVERHEAD CRANE OPERATOR (any industry) 921.663-010 to remove previous sizing mill from rolling line and position replacement mill on line. Sets and adjusts bolts to position rolls on mill, using wrenches and bars. Sets controls to regulate speed of mill. Measures outside diameter of product to determine conformance to specifications, using calipers. Adjusts rolls on mill to obtain product of specified dimensions, using handtools. Disassembles sizing mills removed from rolling line and stores parts.
GOE: 06.01.02 STRENGTH: M GED: R3 M2 L1 SVP: 6 DLU: 77

613.360-018 TIN ROLLER, HOT MILL (steel & rel.)

Sets up and operates roughing and finishing roll train to reduce steel slabs to strips and sheets, using knowledge of rolling practices and steel properties: Calculates draft for each roll stand and plans rolling sequence from rolling schedule. Installs and adjusts equipment, such as rolls, guides, scale breakers, shears, and coilers, in mill train, using handtools. Observes steel passing through finish rolls for specified straigthness, flatness, and finish. Observes gauges to verify specified electric load and temperature. Moves controls to adjust electric load, speed of mill, and tension between rollers to equalize mill load and obtain product of specified finish and dimensions. Inspects product for defects, using x-ray gauge. Directs crew in roll changes, removal of cobbles from rolling line, and polishing rolls.
GOE: 06.01.03 STRENGTH: M GED: R4 M3 L3 SVP: 7 DLU: 77

613.361-010 GUIDE SETTER (steel & rel.)

Installs and adjusts rolls, passes, and guides on stands of rolling mill, according to job specifications, using handtools: Determines installation procedure from rolling specifications, product dimensions, and section of mill to be used for rolling product. Assembles roll stands, using hammers, wedges, wrenches, and pry bars. Installs and adjusts guides on stands to control passage of product through roll passes, using handtools. Disassembles previously installed roll stands on mill and installs and aligns new roll stands, using blocks and wedges. Sorts and stores rollers and guides from disassembled stands. Observes guides during rolling to determine if they are functioning according to specifications and adjusts guides to obtain specified performance. May assist other workers in disassembling and removing stands from rolling line. May sort and store rolls, guides, and guards removed from rolling line.
GOE: 06.01.02 STRENGTH: M GED: R3 M2 L2 SVP: 6 DLU: 77

613.362-010 HEATER I (steel & rel.)

Controls gas or oil fired soaking pit or reheating furnaces to heat sheets, blooms, billets, and slabs to specified rolling temperature: Ignites furnace burners with torch, and turns valves to regulate flow of fuel and air to burners. Signals CHARGER OPERATOR (steel & rel.) 504.665-014 to charge steel into furnace. Reads dials and gauges, observes color of steel in furnace, and adjusts controls to maintain specified temperature in furnace. May assist workers in repairing, replacing, or adjusting furnace equipment and burners, using handtools.
GOE: 06.02.10 STRENGTH: L GED: R3 M2 L2 SVP: 6 DLU: 78

613.362-014 ROLLER, PRIMARY MILL (steel & rel.)

Operates primary mill to roll hot steel ingots into blooms, slabs, billets, or beam blanks, following rolling orders and using knowledge of steel properties and rolling practices: Reads rolling order to determine setup, rolling sequences, number of passes required, and draft (space between rolls) for each pass. Sets clearances on guides and rolls, using wrenches and measuring instruments, and starts mill to roll sample ingot. Measures sample for conformance to dimensional specifications, using calipers, tape, and level. Moves levers to regulate draft, as shown by dial indicator, and to control movement of conveyors, water sprays, and mill tables for each pass. Signals soaking pit personnel for ingots as needed. Observes color of ingot to determine if specified rolling temperature has been attained. Gives directions to workers in duties, such as changing rolls, regulating speed of conveyors, and turning ingot, to obtain product of specified size, shape, and quality. May be designated according to type of mill operated as Roller, Billet Mill (steel & rel.); Roller, Blooming Mill (steel & rel.); Roller, Slabbing Mill (steel & rel.).
GOE: 06.02.10 STRENGTH: M GED: R4 M3 L4 SVP: 7 DLU: 78

613.362-018 ROUGHER (steel & rel.) alternate titles: bulldogger

Operates roughing mill roll stands to reduce steel billets, blooms, and slabs to specified dimensions, using knowledge of rolling practices and steel properties: Reads rolling order to determine setup specifications. Installs rolling equipment, such as roll stands, guides, bar turners, and repeaters on rolling line, using handtools, bars, levers, and sledges. Moves controls to set specified draft between rolls at each stand. Observes color of heated steel to determine rolling temperature and starts roughing stands. Examines product passing through mill for surface defects, such as scratches and cracks. Verifies specified gauge of product after each pass, using calipers. Gives directions to mill crew in readjusting roll draft and realigning guides. May set up and monitor computerized roughing roll stands. May be designated according to type of mill operated as Rougher, Bar Mill (steel & rel.); Rougher, Hot-Strip Mill (steel & rel.); Rougher, Merchant Mill (steel & rel.).
GOE: 06.02.02 STRENGTH: L GED: R3 M3 L3 SVP: 7 DLU: 78

613.362-022 SPEED OPERATOR (steel & rel.)

Operates equipment from pulpit of rolling mill to start, stop, and regulate speed of rolls, rollers, conveyors, and edgers to reduce gauge of steel slabs and billets: Turns master switch and motor-breaker switches to build up voltage of mill motors. Moves levers and switches to set specified roll speeds at each roll stand and signals furnace crew to release slab or billet onto entry conveyor. Observes gauges, tachometers, and product being rolled to determine if specified roll speed, motor load, and tension on product is being maintained. Adjusts controls to regulate rolling speed, to prevent looping, warping, or stretching of product as gauge and temperature of product is reduced and roll draft is changed. Stops motors or shut down mill for repairs or roll changes. May assist other workers in making roll changes, and in repairing, replacing, or adjusting roll line equipment, using handtools.
GOE: 06.02.10 STRENGTH: L GED: R3 M3 L2 SVP: 6 DLU: 77

613.382-010 COILER OPERATOR (steel & rel.)

Operates equipment to wind steel strip into coils as strip emerges from rolling mill or continuous annealing, pickling, or tempering lines: Moves controls to synchronize coiling machine speed and action of machine guides, gates, and rolls with feed tables and conveyors. Examines strip surface for scale, weld defects, and specified oil coating. Verifies specified width and gauge of strip, using measuring tape and micrometer. Cuts strip into specified lengths, cuts defects from strip, and cuts excess metal from welds, using power shear and weld notcher. Moves controls to transfer coils onto conveyor for automatic bundling and piling. May assist mill crew in making roll changes and in adjusting or replacing equipment on rolling line, using handtools.
GOE: 06.02.02 STRENGTH: L GED: R3 M1 L1 SVP: 6 DLU: 78

613.382-014 FINISHER (steel & rel.)

Sets up and operates roll stands in finishing mill to roll steel objects, such as strip, bars, and flats, to specified gauge, shape, and finish: Reads rolling order to determine setup specifications. Installs guides on stands, using wrenches, bars, and sledge. Grinds guides to obtain specified fit, using portable power grinder. Moves controls and observes dial indicators and gauges to set roll draft, adjust guides, and align material with mill rolls. Observes material leaving leading stand and adjusts controls to obtain specified flatness and straightness, and to eliminate defects, such as cracks and scratches. Catches steel as it leaves leaf rolls, using hand tongs, and feeds it into finishing stand, or starts carriage that automatically feeds steel into finish rolls. Adjusts roll draft when bell signal indicates material is being rolled off gauge. Assists crew in roll changes and removing cobbles from mill. May remove scratches and polish roll surface, using polishing stone and electric buffer. May be designated according to type of product finished as Finisher, Cold Rolling (steel & rel.); Finisher, Hot Strip (steel & rel.); Finisher, Merchant Products (steel & rel.); Finisher, Plate (steel & rel.).
GOE: 06.02.02 STRENGTH: M GED: R3 M2 L2 SVP: 6 DLU: 77

613.382-018 SCREWDOWN OPERATOR (steel & rel.) alternate titles: finisher; screwdown

Operates electric-screwdown mechanism on rolling mill to set draft (space between rolls) for reducing slabs, ingots, or billets to specified dimensions, using knowledge of rolling practices and steel properties: Reads rolling order for dimensions, properties, and temperature of product to be rolled. Determines, from experience, number of passes and amount of reduction on each pass required to reduce product to specifications. Moves controls to set rolls for each pass, according to draft reading on dial indicator. Performs other duties, such as assisting in roll changes and repairing or adjusting mill equipment. May calibrate dial of screwdown setting with x-ray reading.
GOE: 06.02.02 STRENGTH: M GED: R3 M2 L2 SVP: 5 DLU: 77

613.462-014 FURNACE OPERATOR (nonfer. metal) alternate titles: soaking-pit operator

Operates furnace to heat aluminum slabs and fabricated forms to specified temperature for rolling or processing: Sets furnace controls to regulate temperatures and heating time. Starts conveyors and opens furnace doors to admit slabs, plate, sheet, and coil, or signals OVERHEAD CRANE OPERATOR (any industry) 921.663-010 to uncover soaking pits and lower ingots into them. Observes pyrometer and adjusts rheostat controls to maintain temperature between specified limits. Measures temperature of product to determine necessity for adjusting furnace temperature or timing cycle, using thermal instruments and charts. Removes material from furnace, using crane, or signals OVERHEAD CRANE OPERATOR (any industry) to transfer it to next station. Records time and production data.
GOE: 06.02.10 STRENGTH: L GED: R3 M3 L2 SVP: 5 DLU: 77

613.462-018 ROLLING-MILL OPERATOR (nonfer. metal)

Sets up and operates hot or cold rolling mill to reduce or form nonferrous metal into plate, sheet, foil, flatwire, and rod of specified dimensions: Adjusts rollers, buffs, and guides according to size and dimensions of workpiece, using screwdowns, micrometer, steel tape, and handtools. Turns valves and observes gauges to regulate flow, temperature, and solution of roll lubricants and metal coolants. Starts entry or rolloff tables that feed metal to and from rolls. Threads sheet or rod through rolls for further reduction, or signals ROLLING-MILL-OPERATOR HELPER (nonfer. metal) 613.685-026 to feed separate sheets or rods through rolls. Controls speed of rolling mill and roll tables to synchronize flow of metal with tandem operations, using signals or communications system. Measures width and gauge of rolled metal, using linear tape and depth gauge

and adjusts rolls to form metal to specifications. Observes rolling operation to detect curling, splitting, or buckling of metal. May change rolls on rolling machine, using chain or power hoist. May be designated according to type of mill operated as Tandem-Mill Operator (nonfer. metal); or condition of metal rolled as Cold-Mill Operator (nonfer. metal); Hot-Mill Operator (nonfer. metal).
GOE: 06.01.03 STRENGTH: L GED: R3 M2 L1 SVP: 6 DLU: 77

613.482-014　PIERCING-MACHINE OPERATOR (nonfer. metal) alternate titles: piercer operator

Sets up and operates piercing machine to shape metal tubes from billets or enlarge inside diameter of shells according to job order or blueprints: Selects, positions, and adjusts piercing rolls, which rotate and shape outside of tube, using hoists, wrenches, measuring instruments, and knowledge of metal properties. Attaches specified piercing point to arbor to form and control size of internal diameter of tube. Adjusts feed guides, stops, tailstock, and arbor rings according to size of workpiece, using handtools. Moves levers to control movement of heated billet as it advances through rolls and over piercing point. Measures finished workpiece to verify conformance to specifications, using calipers, fixed gauges, and micrometers. May be specified by employer according to experience with particular material worked or machine operated.
GOE: 06.02.02 STRENGTH: M GED: R3 M2 L2 SVP: 5 DLU: 77

613.662-010　ROLLING ATTENDANT (steel & rel.)

Controls equipment from central console to operate rolling mill which reduces steel into products of specified size, shape, and gauge: Selects prepunched schedule cards for section to be rolled according to specifications and feeds into card reader. Activates card reader memory bank (push-button) which reads and interprets schedule card information and stores data in storage unit for response to electronic signal in rolling cycle. Sets selector switches of console for automatic operation of electronic equipment, roll stands, and auxiliary equipment. Moves console controls to advance steel from approach table to mill entry table and through complete rolling cycle automatically, to reduce steel products to specified shape, size, and gauge. Observes, from control pulpit, rolling irregularities in ingot, such as pipe, split end, or heat loss, and notifies other worker through intercom system to shear defective parts. Observes rolling operations, dial and colored light indicators, and other gauges, and manipulates control levers and switches to adjust roll draft, alignment, or mill speed to correct rolling and tolerance deviations or drift. Stops automated mill and chages to manual control operations on breakdown or failure of electronic or mill equipment. Assists mill crew in setup, roll change, maintenance, and adjustment of mill and auxiliary equipment during manual operation of rolling mill. May make adjustments or minor repairs to electronic control equipment or devices. May move electrical control levers in pulpit to operate mill tables, scale breakers, and broadsiding mill screwdown when mill operates under manual control.
GOE: 06.01.03 STRENGTH: L GED: R4 M3 L3 SVP: 6 DLU: 77

613.662-014　ROUGHER OPERATOR (steel & rel.)

Operates roughing mill stands under direction of ROUGHER (steel & rel.) to reduce steel billets, blooms, or slabs to specified dimensions: Starts roughing rolls and auxiliary equipment, such as conveyor tables, scalebreaker, and water sprays. Signals CHARGER OPERATOR (steel & rel.) to discharge metal object from furnace preparatory to rolling. Moves controls to position metal on conveyor and guide it into rolls. Adjusts controls to regulate scalebreaker and water sprays that remove scale from metal. Installs guides in roughing stands and removes cobbles from rolling line. May assist other workers to change rolls, drag scrap, and pull spanners when mill is down.
GOE: 06.02.02 STRENGTH: M GED: R3 M2 L2 SVP: 5 DLU: 77

613.662-018　COLD-MILL OPERATOR (steel & rel.)

Sets up and operates rolling mill to flatten, temper, and reduce gauge of steel strip, following rolling orders and using measuring instruments: Reads rolling order to determine setup and work sequence. Calculates draft (space between rolls) and roll speed for each mill stand to roll strip to specified dimensions and temper. Turns controls to adjust roll speed, draft, and tension of strip between reels of coiling mechanism. Installs guides, guards, and cooling equipment in stands, using handtools. Starts mill to roll test strip and adjusts roll screws, hydraulic sprays, and mill speeds. Moves controls to start production rolling of steel strip. Examines steel for surface defects, such as cracks and scratches. Verifies dimensions of steel for conformance to specifications, using micrometers, thickness gauges, and measuring tape. Directs other workers in changing rolls, operating mill equipment, removing coils, and banding and loading strip steel. May be designated according to type of mill operated as Reversing-Mill Roller (steel & rel.); Tandem-Mill Roller (steel & rel.). May operate mill to temper steel strip and be designated Temper-Mill Roller (steel & rel.).
GOE: 06.02.10 STRENGTH: M GED: R4 M3 L3 SVP: 7 DLU: 78

613.662-022　STRAIGHTENING-ROLL OPERATOR (any industry) alternate titles: straightening-machine operator

Operates rolling machine to straighten warped or bent metal plates, bars, or sheets: Threads workpiece between rolls of machine manually or with crane. Turns handwheels or nuts to adjust tension between one or more sets of aligned drive and adjustment rolls. Pulls lever to move workpiece through rolls of machine. Hammers or pries workpiece into alignment, using hammer or pry bar. Examines work for straightness, using straightedge and plumb bob. Inserts shims under bulges and repeats process to straighten workpiece to specifications. May be designated by product straightened as Bar-Straightening-Machine

Operator (any industry); Plate Roller (any industry); Wire-Straightening-Machine Operator (any industry).
GOE: 06.02.02 STRENGTH: M GED: R3 M1 L1 SVP: 4 DLU: 78

613.667-010　LINER ASSEMBLER (nonfer. metal)

Attaches metal liners to scalped ingots preparatory to rolling into clad sheet or plate: Positions ingot on cladding conveyor, using hoist. Cleans scalped ingot with solvent and rags. Selects specified liners from stack and straps them to both sides of ingot, using wire and banding machine. Tack-welds liners to ingot, using electric or gas welding equipment. Cuts wire straps with wirecutter and signals OVERHEAD CRANE OPERATOR (any industry) 921.663-010 to remove lined ingot. May interlay clad ingots with wood spacers.
GOE: 06.04.31 STRENGTH: M GED: R2 M1 L1 SVP: 3 DLU: 77

613.667-014　MILL HAND, PLATE MILL (steel & rel.)

Verifies width of first plate rolled on roughing mill, using width gauge: Sets gauge for specified width. Places gauge on first plate rolled to determine conformance to specifications and signals mill operator to continue rolling process. Moves steam-jet controls and throws salt on plates to loosen scale during rolling operation. Removes scale from plates and work area with scraper and shovel.
GOE: 06.04.10 STRENGTH: M GED: R2 M1 L1 SVP: 4 DLU: 77

613.682-010　MANIPULATOR (steel & rel.)

Operates manipulator and entry guide mechanism from pulpit of rolling mill to position ingots or blooms for entry into rolls of mill: Moves levers to transfer ingot from entrance table onto entrance conveyor, and to align side guards that guide ingot into rolls. Pushes controls that cause fingers of manipulator to turn ingot after each pass. Assists rolling mill crew in roll changes and repairs, using handtools.
GOE: 06.02.10 STRENGTH: L GED: R3 M2 L2 SVP: 5 DLU: 78

613.682-014　REELING-MACHINE OPERATOR (steel & rel.) alternate titles: reeler operator

Sets up and operates reeling machine to round out and burnish inside and outside surfaces of seamless steel tubes: Sets distance betweeen rolls according to size of pipe shell and positions mandrel support bar between rolls. Installs specified plug on mandrel. Moves controls to push tube along conveyor, through stationary guides, and into rotating rolls that force tube over mandrel. Turns handwheel to maintain roll pressure on pipe shell to smooth surfaces and round out tube to specified diameter.
GOE: 06.02.02 STRENGTH: M GED: R3 M2 L1 SVP: 5 DLU: 77

613.682-018　ROLLER (jewelry-silver.)

Operates rolling machine to roll ingots into metal strips for use in stamping out jewelry blanks: Positions ingot between pressure rollers. Turns handwheel and observes calibrated scale indicator to set distance between rollers. Moves lever to start machine, and readjusts pressure rollers as needed to reduce ingots to strips of specified thickness. Verifies thickness of strips, using micrometer. May anneal ingot to soften for further rolling.
GOE: 06.02.02 STRENGTH: L GED: R3 M3 L2 SVP: 4 DLU: 77

613.682-022　STRIP ROLLER (metal prod., nec) alternate titles: finish roller

Sets up and operates rolling mill to reduce dimensions of cold strip metal preparatory to processing metal into springs: Clamps roll of strip metal on reel stand and threads end of strip through series of machine guides and pressure rolls. Turns screws to adjust pressure of rollers or presses buttons to regulate reduction of strip to specified gauge. Starts machine, and moves lever to control rate of feed and tension of strip through mill. Stops machine and measures thickness of strip, using micrometer or by observing automatic gauge indicator. Resets roll pressure to reduce strip to specified thickness. May reshape and reduce steel wire.
GOE: 06.02.02 STRENGTH: M GED: R3 M3 L2 SVP: 4 DLU: 77

613.682-026　TABLE OPERATOR (nonfer. metal; steel & rel.)

Operates traveling and stationary tables to feed heated or cold steel or nonferrous blooms, billets, and slabs to rolls for successive passes through roll stands: Moves levers to position tilting and trailing tables in front or rear of roll stand and align steel with roll guides preparatory to feeding steel into rolls. Starts table rollers that feed steel into rolls for specified number of passes. Aids other workers in making roll changes and adjusting equipment. May be designated according to type of table operated as Approach-Table Operator (nonfer. metal; steel & rel.); Delivery-Table Operator (nonfer. metal; steel & rel.); Tilting-Table Operator (steel & rel.); Transfer-Table Operator (steel & rel.).
GOE: 06.04.02 STRENGTH: L GED: R3 M2 L1 SVP: 5 DLU: 78

613.682-030　MILL OPERATOR, ROLLS (any industry)

Sets up and operates rolling mill to form sheet metal sections of various types, gauges, and lengths from coils of sheet steel according to blueprints or other specifications: Verifies gauge and size of raw material against specifications, using tape measure and gauge. Positions and secures stock-coil on payout mandrel and adjusts cone-brake, using handtools. Spaces and adjusts mill rolls and fits shims on shafts according to specifications, using gauges, rules, and handtools. Sets trigger mechanism which actuates cut-off die to specified length by setting and tightening setscrews. Feeds end of coil onto guide table and actuates shear to square end of coil. Actuates controls on panel to thread lead end of coil through mill. Inspects first piece for variation from rolling or

length specifications and makes necessary adjustments to mill. Starts mill for automatic operation and controls speed from control panel. Adjusts valves to control flow of coolant on metal and observes operation of lubrication system. Patrols mill to detect jamming. Inspects raw material or finished product visually or by measurement for variation from specified quality standards. Records mill production on schedule sheet. May train new mill operators.
GOE: 06.02.02 STRENGTH: M GED: R3 M3 L2 SVP: 4 DLU: 78

613.685-010 COILER (nonfer. metal; steel & rel.) alternate titles: coiler operator; slitting-machine coiler
Tends coiler that winds metal strips, sheets, or wire into coils as they emerge from rolling mills, slitters, or other machines: Adjusts coiler guides and rollers according to size of workpiece, using handtools. Starts machine which automatically winds metal onto reels and observes operation to prevent jams, uneven winding, or wrinkles. Regulates tension of coiler to prevent tearing or stretching of metal. Inspects surface of metal for stains, dirt, scratches, and other defects. Binds finished coils to prevent uncoiling. May move controls to activate hydraulic pusher arm and tilt table to transfer coil onto skid or conveyor. May be designated by employer according to experience with particular type of machine, or product coiled.
GOE: 06.04.02 STRENGTH: L GED: R2 M1 L1 SVP: 4 DLU: 78

613.685-014 HEATER HELPER (steel & rel.)
Assists HEATER (steel & rel.) I 613.362-010 in heating steel to specified rolling temperature in soaking-pit furnaces: Ignites furnace burners, using torch. Turns valves and dampers of furnace. Records meter readings of furnace. Performs other duties as described under HELPER (any industry) Master Title.
GOE: 05.12.10 STRENGTH: M GED: R2 M2 L2 SVP: 4 DLU: 78

613.685-018 PIERCING-MILL OPERATOR (steel & rel.)
Tends equipment that pierces steel billets lengthwise preparatory to making seamless tubing: Moves levers to drop hot billet from conveyor into trough and ram it along trough into rollers which force center of billet into piercing mandrel. Moves controls to withdraw piercing mandrel from billet and drop billet on conveyor for further processing.
GOE: 06.04.02 STRENGTH: M GED: R2 M2 L2 SVP: 3 DLU: 77

613.685-022 ROLLER-LEVELER OPERATOR (steel & rel.)
Tends machine that removes wrinkles and creases from tinplate or blackplate: Starts machine and feeds sheets of tinplate into rolls. Examines plates for flatness and adjusts rollers as required, using handtools. Cleans equipment and work area.
GOE: 06.04.02 STRENGTH: M GED: R2 M1 L1 SVP: 2 DLU: 77

613.685-026 ROLLING-MILL-OPERATOR HELPER (nonfer. metal)
Performs following duties in rolling nonferrous metal ingots and bars into plates, sheets, rods, and coils: Guides or turns metal rods or ingots on conveyors or tables to, from, and through rolls of rod rolling machines, using tongs or automatic handling devices. Feeds sheets or plates into carriage or table of rolling machines. Cuts jagged edges from sheet, using hand or machine shears and flattens leading edge of sheet with mallet or machine flattener. Tends equipment to return metal to entry side of mill for rerolling, to feed or off bear coils of metal, to hoist coil on machine spindle, pierce coil to raise end of coil and extend it into rollers of mill, and to remove rolled coil from machine. Clears cobbles (jams), using pry bar, and adjusts guides, using handtools. Observes rolled metal for defects, such as tears and cracks. Performs other duties as described under HELPER (any industry) Master Title.
GOE: 06.04.10 STRENGTH: M GED: R2 M1 L1 SVP: 3 DLU: 78

613.685-030 TUBING-MACHINE OPERATOR (nonfer. metal; steel & rel.)
Tends machine that rolls metal ribbon into coils and solders seams of coils to form conduit tubing: Mounts reel of brass, copper, or steel ribbon and reel of soldering wire on machine. Feeds metal ribbon and soldering wire into machine. Starts machine that pulls metal ribbon through series of dies to form coil, joins flanged edges of coil, and solders seams of tubing. Removes empty reels from machine.
GOE: 06.04.02 STRENGTH: M GED: R2 M1 L1 SVP: 4 DLU: 77

613.685-034 BED OPERATOR (steel & rel.) alternate titles: hotbed operator; hotbed transfer operator
Tends equipment that transfers rolled steel shapes, such as blooms, billets, rails, and pipe from processing lines to cooling beds: Presses controls to raise roll stop, start conveyor, and position material opposite specified cooling bed. Pulls levers to start pusher straightedge and dog-chain (series of projections) that shoves material off conveyor line onto cooling bed. Moves controls of dog-chain to pull cooled material from bed onto cradle or transfer car. Records number and type of object cooled. May assist other workers in making roll and hot saw blade changes and in repairing, replacing, or adjusting mill equipment.
GOE: 06.02.10 STRENGTH: L GED: R3 M2 L1 SVP: 4 DLU: 78

613.686-010 CATCHER (steel & rel.) alternate titles: strander
Guides hot steel shapes, such as bars, rods, and sheets, from one set of rolls to another: Catches end of hot steel with tongs as it comes through first set of rolls and feeds end into next set of rolls. May set and adjust repeaters, guides, and rollers, using handtools.
GOE: 06.04.02 STRENGTH: M GED: R2 M1 L1 SVP: 3 DLU: 77

613.687-010 PLUGGER (steel & rel.) alternate titles: rolling-mill plugger
Replaces plugs used to form inside diameter of seamless tubing in rolling mill machines: Screws specified plug on end of rolling-mill mandrel with tongs

or positions plug in trough of rolling mill, using hoist, preparatory to forming tube. Removes hot plug with tongs or hoist after tube has been rolled. Immerses hot plug in bosh tank for cooling. Moves controls to charge and discharge pipe shells from reheating furnace.
GOE: 06.04.02 STRENGTH: M GED: R2 M2 L2 SVP: 2 DLU: 77

614 EXTRUDING AND DRAWING OCCUPATIONS

This group includes occupations concerned with producing rods, tubes, and various solid and hollow sections by forcing hot metal through a die by such means as rams.

614.132-010 SUPERVISOR, DRAWING (nonfer. metal; steel & rel.)
Supervises and coordinates activities of workers engaged in drawing wire, rods, and tubes from metal stock, applying knowledge of drawing machines and properties of metal: Examines and verifies dimensions of product to determine if specifications are adhered to during production, using gauges or micrometer. Instructs new workers in machine operations. Performs duties as described under SUPERVISOR (any industry) Master Title. May direct workers in straightening and cutoff processes. May set up or assist workers in setting up machines. May be designated according to product drawn as Rod-Drawing Supervisor (nonfer. metal; steel & rel.); Tube-Drawing Supervisor (nonfer. metal; steel & rel.); Wire-Drawing Supervisor (nonfer. metal; steel & rel.).
GOE: 06.04.01 STRENGTH: L GED: R4 M3 L3 SVP: 7 DLU: 77

614.132-014 SUPERVISOR, EXTRUSION (forging) alternate titles: extrusion press supervisor; metal extrusion supervisor
Supervises and coordinates activities of workers engaged in forming nonferrous metal from billets in extrusion presses, applying knowledge of extrusion press operation and properties of metals under heat and pressure. Directs installation of specified dies and other tooling in extrusion presses. Examines sampling of products for adherence to specifications. Trains new workers. Performs duties as described under SUPERVISOR (any industry) Master Title. May set up presses for workers. May be required to have experience with specified products, type of press, or materials, such as radioactive uranium.
GOE: 06.02.02 STRENGTH: L GED: R4 M3 L3 SVP: 7 DLU: 77

614.380-010 EXTRUSION-PRESS ADJUSTER (elec. equip.)
Sets up extrusion press to extrude carbon rods or welding rods and coat core (wire) with metallic paste: Selects coating (extruding) nozzles, spacers, and wire guides, according to diameter and length of rod. Positions, aligns, and bolts abrasive brush, coating nozzles, spacers, marking wheels, and wire guides to machine, using handtools to set up machine to form rods of specified size and length. Pulls lever or presses button to set conveyor speed and extruding pressure. Starts machine that automatically coats wire to form rod of specified diameter and cuts it to specified length. Examines sample piece for splits in coating or burrs on cut ends. Measures diameter of rod and concentricity of coating with fixed gauges. Turns screws to adjust wire guides, spacers, and brushes to eliminate splits and burrs. Varies extrusion pressure or speed of conveyor, or repositions coating nozzle to vary diameter of rod and maintain concentricity of coating around wire.
GOE: 06.01.02 STRENGTH: M GED: R3 M3 L2 SVP: 5 DLU: 77

614.382-010 WIRE DRAWER (nonfer. metal) alternate titles: wire-draw operator
Sets up and operates one or more wiredrawing machines to draw round or fancy-shaped wire or rod through one or series of dies to reduce its cross-sectional dimension, applying knowledge of working properties of metal and wiredrawing: Studies specifications and determines setup procedures. Positions and secures specified dies in dieholders, using handtools. Lifts coil of wire onto feed reel, tapers end, and threads it through dies. Secures end of wire in jaws of drawing block or onto spool which rotates and pulls wire through dies. Coats wire with lubricant to facilitate drawing and starts machine. Inspects and measures drawn wire to verify conformance to specified shape, size, or electrical resistance, using measuring instruments, such as wire gauges, micrometers, and resistance testers. Cuts defective sections from wire, using wire cutters. Replaces worn dies, using handtools. Records production. May feed wire through electrodes of annealing unit to soften work-hardened wire. May weld ends of separate coils together to increase their length, using welding equipment. May be designated according to experience with particular size and shape of wire drawn or material worked on as Coarse-Wire Drawer (nonfer. metal); Fine-Wire Drawer (nonfer. metal). Important variations may also be indicated by trade name of machine used.
GOE: 06.02.02 STRENGTH: H GED: R3 M2 L1 SVP: 4 DLU: 77

614.382-014 WIRE DRAWER (clock & watch)
Operates wire drawing machine to reduce watch spring wire from round to rectangular cross section and improve its physical properties: Reads job instruction which specifies size, number of passes, and amount of reduction on each pass of wire through series of wire drawing dies. Sets adjustable (flat) die for first pass by turning setscrews on which divisions are shown. Threads wire from feeding roll through adjustable die and round die (ring-shaped to control wire width) and attaches end to winding roll. Starts machine and observes operation to ascertain if drawing is proceeding as specified and makes adjustments to obtain required wire tension, using handtools. Stops machine when all wire has passed through dies. Switches wound roll to feeding position and bare roll to winding position, adjusts die for next pass, and repeats until wire is drawn

to size specified. Records production. May examine wire for defects, such as scratches or cracks, using eye loupe.
GOE: 06.02.02 STRENGTH: L GED: R3 M2 L2 SVP: 4 DLU: 77

614.382-018 WIRE DRAWING MACHINE OPERATOR (inst. & app.; jewelry-silver.)
Operates wire drawing machine to shape or emboss wire used in dental work and costume jewelry: Reviews work orders and selects shaping, reducing, or embossing roller dies according to specifications. Positions roller die in machine that shapes, reduces, or embosses wire, such as gold, silver, or copper, to form dental or jewelry wire. Turns setscrews to secure roller die in machine. Inserts wire into machine feed mechanism, starts machine, and monitors machine operation. Measures wire thickness to verify conformance to specifications, using micrometer. Installs progressively smaller dies in machine and repeats operation until wire diameter meets specifications. May measure physical properties of wire, such as tensile strength and bend set, and calculate elongation data, using test instruments and calculator. May record production information, manually or using computer.
GOE: 06.02.02 STRENGTH: M GED: R3 M2 L2 SVP: 4 DLU: 90

614.482-010 DRAW-BENCH OPERATOR (nonfer. metal; steel & rel.)
Operates drawbench to draw metal rods into specified shape and diameter: Positions and secures specified die in diehead, using handtools. Moves levers to set drawing speed according to type and size of material drawn. Inserts pointed end of rod through die and into holding jaws on dolly. Moves control to pull rod through die. Examines surface of finished workpiece for defects, such as pits and scratches. Measures rod to verify conformance to specifications, using template and rule. Replaces worn dies when rod varies from specifications, using handtools. May coat workpiece with lubricant, or engage automatic lubricating mechanism to facilitate drawing. May actuate shearing mechanism to cut rods to specified length. May be specified by employer according to experience with particular type or trade name of machine, or by type of material drawn.
GOE: 06.02.02 STRENGTH: H GED: R3 M1 L2 SVP: 4 DLU: 77

614.482-014 EXTRUDER OPERATOR (forging) alternate titles: extrusion-press operator
Sets up and operates extrusion press to shape hot billets into products, such as bars, tubing, structural shapes, and rods: Installs dies, mandrels, containers, heating coils, press tools, extrusion heads, and run-out bridging in press, according to size and type of product, using handtools. Removes billet from furnace when color indicates specified temperature and guides it along extrusion press conveyor onto press bed, and into billet container, using tongs. Starts ram that spreads billet into container and forces it through press. Regulates rate of extrusion to prevent metal rupture and adherence of metal to container walls. Starts press run-out table and butt shears to guide extrusion from press, and to trim flash. Pulls extrusion along conveyor to racking table. Sprays die with lubricant and caustic, and oils blocks and mandrels. Records data, such as crew time, number of billets used, and items processed. May operate extrusion press equipped with furnace that ejects hot billets into press chamber for ram to force through die. May set up and operate extrusion press to shape hot, radioactive uranium fuel elements.
GOE: 06.02.02 STRENGTH: M GED: R3 M2 L2 SVP: 5 DLU: 77

614.482-018 EXTRUSION-PRESS OPERATOR I (elec. equip.)
Sets up and operates extrusion press and equipment to extrude and apply flux to wire and to brake, mark, and cut coated wire to form welding rods: Selects, positions, aligns, and bolts specified coating (extruding) nozzle, spacers, wire guides, abrasive brushes, cutters, and marking wheels, to machine, using handtools. Places slugs of compressed flux into feeding chamber on welding rod extrusion head. Places boxes of specified wire core on tilter and pulls lever to dump wire into feeder. Starts machine and observes movement of wire through machine to detect malfunctions. Examines completed welding rods for cracks, voids, scores, or scuffs, and measures rods with fixed gauges to determine diameter and concentricity of flux coating. Presses buttons to alter pressure of ram in feed action or speed wire feeder and turns screws to adjust coating nozzle or to position wire guides, spacers, and brushes to eliminate splits, scores, and burs. May adjust controls to maintain specified temperature in ovens. May assist in repair of machine and equipment. May sort rods according to length.
GOE: 06.02.18 STRENGTH: L GED: R3 M3 L2 SVP: 5 DLU: 77

614.586-010 WIRE CHARGER (elec. equip.)
Feeds wire and slugs of fluxing material into extrusion press that coats welding electrodes: Selects wire cores of specified size, places box of cores on tilter, and pulls lever to dump cores in wire feeder hopper, or selects spool of specified size wire and places spool on mandrel for threading through extrusion machine. Removes crustations or trims slugs (compressed flux) to size of extrusion machine cylinder, using knife. Places slugs into feeding chamber of machine. Assists other workers to clear machine of jammed rods. Records production data.
GOE: 06.04.21 STRENGTH: H GED: R2 M2 L2 SVP: 2 DLU: 77

614.682-010 DRAW-BENCH OPERATOR (any industry)
Operates extrusion machine to form flat metal strips into tubular, channel, angular, or other shapes. Positions and bolts or clamps single or multiple dies on bed of press, using handtools. Loads coil of strip metal on spindle of machine. Feeds strip between dies, and locks front end of strip in gripping jaws

or dog of power carriage. Turns handwheels to close and tighten dies on metal strip and starts machine. Stops machine after metal is formed and removes piece from between dies. Cuts formed piece into specified lengths, using electric saw, and verifies conformity of piece to specifications, using micrometers and calipers. Clears dies of loose burrs with blast of compressed air. May straighten sheet metal parts.
GOE: 06.02.02 STRENGTH: M GED: R4 M3 L3 SVP: 5 DLU: 77

614.684-010 BILLET ASSEMBLER (chemical)
Assembles uranium fuel elements for subsequent extrusion in atomic fuel plant: Reads production schedule to ascertain number and size of uranium fuel elements to be assembled and percentage of uranium to be used in each fuel element. Places components, such as copper and zirconium sleeves, uranium billets, and end plates in basket, and immerses filled basket in chemical and rinsing solutions to clean grease, dirt, scale, and other foreign matter from components, using crane. Transfers baskets of components to drier, using crane, and starts blower unit that circulates air to remove moisture from components. Conveys components to assembly table, using crane. Positions components together in specified relationship to form fuel element subassembly. Secures subassembly on rotating base of welding equipment, and welds sections to seal assembly, using argon-gas welding equipment. Connects sealed fuel element valve to pump and activates pump to create vacuum in fuel element to prevent oxidation of element during extrusion process. Connects fuel element to helium leak detector and observes dial readings to detect deviations from standards for each element. Rewelds and retests defective fuel elements.
GOE: 06.02.22 STRENGTH: M GED: R3 M2 L2 SVP: 4 DLU: 77

614.684-014 TESTER OPERATOR (nonfer. metal) alternate titles: breaker operator; nicker and breaker
Breaks extruded tubes and rods by one or more of following methods and inspects exposed surface for defects, such as bubbles beneath skin of metal resulting from too rapid extrusion: (1) Nicks workpiece, using file or saw, and breaks workpiece at nick by bending back and forth. (2) Saws off piece of tube and holds on table under cone-shaped expander of hydraulic breaker. Starts mechanism to raise table, forcing tube over expander to split sides of tube. (3) Loads coiled rod onto coil tester and pulls end of rod to straighten it. Places end of rod in channel of tester and starts mechanism oscillating to fracture rod. (4) Places rod in machine and actuates wedge to partially cut rod. Twists and bends rod to break off test piece. Examines ends or interior of rods and tubes for bubbles and cuts off defective sections, using circular saw or automatic shears. Gathers and sorts scrap materials according to type of metal. Positions rods and tubes on table of circular saw or shearing machine and cuts them to length. Important variables may be indicated by trade names of machines used or workpiece tested.
GOE: 06.03.02 STRENGTH: M GED: R2 M2 L2 SVP: 3 DLU: 77

614.685-010 EXTRUDING-PRESS OPERATOR (ordnance)
Tends machine that presses lead ingots or billets through extrusion die to form slugs or lead wire for processing into bullets or cores used in jacketed bullets: Swabs mouth of press with grease and positions ingot or billet beneath ram. Starts motor and presses lever to lower ram that forces lead through die and between wheels that cut lead wire into slugs or wraps extruded wire on spool. Removes catch box when full of slugs or filled spool. May verify weight of slug on scales to ascertain that production specifications are maintained.
GOE: 06.04.02 STRENGTH: H GED: R2 M2 L2 SVP: 4 DLU: 77

614.685-014 EXTRUSION-PRESS OPERATOR II (elec. equip.)
Tends machine that coats wire with flux and marks and cuts wire into specified lengths to produce welding electrodes: Starts machine and observes as cores are automatically conveyed through wire feeder, coating nozzle in extrusion head, and past abrasive brushes, cutters, and marking wheels. Examines welding rods for cracks, voids, scores, or scuffs. Presses buttons to alter pressure of ram in feeding cylinder or speed of wire feeder to correct defects in formation of rods. May measure welding rods with fixed gauge and turn screws to adjust coating nozzle to obtain specified diameter and concentricity of rod. May adjust abrasive brushes that remove flux from ends and center of coated rod at cutting point. May adjust controls to maintain specified temperature when extruding carbon rods.
GOE: 06.04.21 STRENGTH: L GED: R2 M2 L2 SVP: 2 DLU: 77

614.685-018 REDUCING-MACHINE OPERATOR (optical goods)
Tends machine that reduces diameter of temple wire (used in eye glass frames) and temple shouldered joints. Inserts wire between dies mounted in chuck. Starts machine that hammers wire in dies to uniform size as chuck revolves.
GOE: 06.04.02 STRENGTH: L GED: R1 M1 L1 SVP: 2 DLU: 77

614.685-022 TUBE DRAWER (nonfer. metal; steel & rel.) alternate titles: draw-bench operator; seamless-tube drawer
Tends tube drawing machine that shapes and forms metal tubing of specified internal and external diameters: Positions and fastens specified drawing die in diehead and plug die on plug rod, using handtools. Centers plug die in opening of drawing die. Loads tube over plug rod manually, or activates automatic loading mechanism. Places tapered end of tube in contact with dies of machine that automatically pulls tube through dies. Examines finished tubing for defects, such as scratches, pits, and cracks, and measures cross-sectional dimensions with fixed gauges and micrometers to verify conformance to specifications. May taper end of tubing [LATHE TENDER (machine shop) 604.685-026]. May operate controls to start machine carriage that grips and pulls tubing through

die. May be required to have experience with particular metal, or type and trade name of machine.
GOE: 06.04.02 STRENGTH: M GED: R2 M1 L1 SVP: 3 DLU: 77

614.685-026 WIRE-DRAWING-MACHINE TENDER (nonfer. metal)
Tends machines that weld ends of wire together to form continuous coil and draw wire through dies to reduce wire to specified diameter: Lifts reels of wire onto spindle of floor stand, manually, or using hoist. Welds ends of wire together, using welding machine. Smooths weld to diameter of wire, using abrasive cloth. Threads wire around tension rollers, and through reducing dies, and fastens end of wire to spindle. Starts machine that draws wire through dies and around takeup reel. May verify diameter of drawn wire, using micrometer. May record production.
GOE: 06.04.02 STRENGTH: M GED: R2 M1 L2 SVP: 3 DLU: 77

614.686-010 DRAW-BENCH-OPERATOR HELPER (nonfer. metal; steel & rel.) alternate titles: push-bench-operator helper; tube-draw helper
Assists DRAW-BENCH OPERATOR (nonfer. metal; steel & rel.) in drawing metal tubes or rods by performing various duties according to set procedure: Lifts die and plug onto machine. Rolls or lifts workpieces onto machine table manually or using hoist. Swabs or brushes lubricant on workpiece to facilitate drawing. Piles drawn workpieces according to specified procedure, and attaches tubes to crane, using straps and hooks. Performs other duties as described under HELPER (any industry) Master Title.
GOE: 06.04.40 STRENGTH: H GED: R2 M1 L1 SVP: 2 DLU: 77

614.686-014 TESTER-OPERATOR HELPER (nonfer. metal)
Assists TESTER OPERATOR (nonfer. metal) in cutting and breaking ends of rods and tubes to expose cross-sectional surface for inspection: Feeds end of workpiece into cutting mechanism, manually or with hoist. Piles workpieces in designated areas. Salvages scrap materials and examines surface of workpiece for defects, such as pits and scratches, and bubbles beneath surface of workpiece. Performs other duties as described under HELPER (any industry) Master Title.
GOE: 06.04.02 STRENGTH: H GED: R2 M1 L1 SVP: 2 DLU: 77

615   PUNCHING AND SHEARING OCCUPATIONS

This group includes occupations concerned with perforating (punching) metal by means of dies and punches; and cutting or shearing metal by the action of keen-edged cutting tools. Punching and shearing of nonmetallic materials, except wood, are also included when the methods and machine tools commonly applied to the working of metal are used.

615.130-010 PRESS-HAND SUPERVISOR (jewelry-silver.) alternate titles: power-press supervisor; tool setter
Supervises and coordinates activities of workers engaged in shaping and cutting rings, ring blanks, and jewelry findings, utilizing knowledge of power-press setup and product specifications. Sets up tools and machines. Examines fabricated articles for defects. Performs other duties as described under SUPERVISOR (any industry) Master Title.
GOE: 06.02.02 STRENGTH: L GED: R4 M3 L3 SVP: 7 DLU: 77

615.130-014 SUPERVISOR (cutlery-hrdwr.)
Supervises and coordinates activities of workers engaged in manufacturing tools, such as chisels, screwdrivers, planes, levels, miter boxes, bit braces, and garden shears: Sets up and adjusts machines, such as punch press, riveting machine, lathe, grinders, milling machines, and welding machines based on knowledge of machine capacities and properties of materials, such as metal, wood, plastic, and glass. Verifies dimensions of parts, using micrometers, vernier calipers, height gauges, thread gauges, depth gauges, and fixed gauges. Adjusts machines when parts fail to meet specifications. Performs other duties as described under SUPERVISOR (any industry) Master Title.
GOE: 06.02.01 STRENGTH: H GED: R4 M3 L3 SVP: 7 DLU: 77

615.132-010 SUPERVISOR, SHEARING (any industry)
Supervises and coordinates activities of workers engaged in cutting, punching, shearing, and slitting metal sheets or metal strips: Plans and coordinates sequence of operations. Directs workers in machine setup. Observes workers and machines to detect errors or malfunctions and orders corrective actions. Examines sample products for adherence to specifications. Trains new workers. Performs duties as described under SUPERVISOR (any industry) Master Title. May verify weight and quantity of items produced.
GOE: 06.01.01 STRENGTH: M GED: R4 M3 L3 SVP: 7 DLU: 77

615.280-010 SLITTER SERVICE AND SETTER (tinware)
Sets up and repairs machines that automatically cut tinplate sheets into specified size: Installs and aligns disc cutters on machine spindle, following blueprints or work orders and using handtools. Tests and adjusts feed mechanism and synchronizes feeder with machine cutting speed, using gauge and handtools. Diagnoses cause of machine malfunction and dismantles machine to gain access to and remove defective parts, using handtools and power tools. Examines parts for defects, such as excessive wear, cracks, and broken gears. Repairs or replaces defective parts, adjusts, and aligns parts to specified tolerances, using gauges, handtools, and power tools. Starts machine to test performance and examines first run products to ensure they conform to specifications. Removes jammed metal, using tongs and probes. Lubricates and cleans machine.

GOE: 06.01.02 STRENGTH: M GED: R4 M3 L3 SVP: 6 DLU: 77

615.380-010 SHEAR SETTER (any industry)
Sets up power shear to cut metal sheet, plate, or bar stock according to work card or blueprint specifications: Lays out cutting lines on metal stock according to work order, using ruler and square, to obtain maximum number of pieces from stock. Sets stops, guides, rake (angle) and pressure of blade on machine, using wrenches, rule, built-in gauge, or template. Measures dimensions of first piece for conformance to specifications, using rule and square, or has piece approved by inspector. Turns machine over to SHEAR OPERATOR (any industry) II. May install fixtures to shear, trim, or bevel workpiece.
GOE: 06.01.02 STRENGTH: M GED: R4 M3 L4 SVP: 6 DLU: 77

615.382-010 PUNCH-PRESS OPERATOR I (any industry)
Sets up and operates power press to trim, punch, shape, notch, draw, or crimp metal, composite, or plastic stock: Assembles, installs, and aligns dies in press according to specifications, using feelers, shims, templates, bolts, clamps, and wrenches. Adjusts ram stroke to specified length. Positions workpiece against fixtures or stops on machine bed or on die. Starts press and observes operation to detect misalignment or malfunction. Inspects workpieces for conformance to specifications, visually or using gauges or templates, and adjusts machine to correct errors. May clean and lubricate machines. May be designated according to type of machine as Multiple-Punch-Press Operator (any industry) I; or by function of machine as Draw-Press Operator (any industry); Forming-Press Operator (any industry) I; Straightening-Press Operator (any industry) I; Stretching-Press Operator (any industry).
GOE: 06.02.02 STRENGTH: M GED: R3 M2 L2 SVP: 5 DLU: 88

615.482-010 ANGLE SHEAR OPERATOR (any industry)
Sets up and operates shearing machine equipped with sets of cutting dies or blades to shear structural shapes, such as angles, channels, and Z-bars to specified length or bevel: Aligns and locks selected blades into opening of machine, using rule, gauge, shims, feelers, and wrench. Sets guide stop to specified distance from shearing die, using tape measure and wrench. Positions workpiece on shearing die and against guide stop. Starts machine to activate cams which force blades to shear metal, or depresses pedal, causing shearing die ram to descend and cut workpiece to specified length. May set up shear with single set of blades to cut bars or rounds.
GOE: 06.02.02 STRENGTH: H GED: R3 M2 L2 SVP: 3 DLU: 77

615.482-014 DUPLICATOR-PUNCH OPERATOR (any industry)
Sets up and operates duplicator punch which follows tracer track on template and punches, blanks, and notches metal plates, sheets, and structural shapes: Positions and clamps track template onto template table of machine. Inserts, aligns, and locks specified punches and dies in ram and bed of machine, using hammer, shims, feelers, micrometers, and setscrews. Places workpiece on carriage of machine manually or by using jib or crane. Aligns workpiece to scale on machine and clamps it to carriage. Sets end and side stops to position successive pieces. Positions tracer arm onto track templates and turns handwheels to move carriage along track to punching stations. Pulls lever to activate punch. Positions punch or die over layout marks on jobs for which no template has been made. Inspects work to verify location of holes, using scale, compass, and plug gauges.
GOE: 06.02.02 STRENGTH: H GED: R4 M3 L3 SVP: 5 DLU: 77

615.482-018 IRONWORKER-MACHINE OPERATOR (any industry)
Sets up and operates machine equipped with separate sections that cut-to-length, punch, and notch or trim structural shapes and plates: Positions specified punch and die set and turns pressure screws to lock them in ram and bed of machine to set up punching section. Positions specified cutting blades into cutting slot, and notching dies or shear blades into ram and bed of machine, and turns pressure or clamp screws to lock them in place to set up cut-off, and trimming-and-notching sections of machine. Measures workpiece with rule or tape, or traces from template to locate holes or cutting lines as specified by work order, and marks them with scribe, soapstone, or centerpunch. Pulls lever to engage power to section used. Positions workpiece into cutting slot, or under punch, die, or trim blade, and aligns punch or blade with layout marks. Pulls lever or depresses pedal to activate machine. Sets stops or positions guide jigs to specified point on built-in scale when several pieces are worked. May tend different sections of machine.
GOE: 06.02.02 STRENGTH: H GED: R3 M2 L2 SVP: 4 DLU: 77

615.482-026 PUNCH-PRESS OPERATOR, AUTOMATIC (any industry)
Sets up and operates power press that automatically feeds bars, structural metal, blanks, or continuous roll of sheet metal into position under ram: Installs specified dies in press, using gauges and handtools. Adjusts ram stroke of press, using handtools. Turns knobs or installs gears to synchronize action of feed bar or pinch rollers with feed and takeoff conveyor and automatic action of ram. Positions and clamps feed guides. Threads metal strip from play-out reel through pinch rollers, or loads hopper or conveyor with metal blanks. May operate machine to crimp, punch, and cut metal foil used in fabricating radiator cores.
GOE: 06.02.02 STRENGTH: H GED: R3 M3 L2 SVP: 5 DLU: 77

615.482-030 ROTARY-SHEAR OPERATOR (any industry) alternate titles: circular-shear operator; ring-shear operator
Operates machine equipped with opposing circular blades (one mounted above other) to shear metal plates and sheets to specified circular and curved

dimensions: Turns thumbscrew to adjust distance between cutters to thickness of metal, using feeler gauge, scale, or pattern. Positions and clamps workpiece to turntable and sets specified distance between center point of workpiece and cutting blades, using template or sliding scale on machine. Starts rotating action of cutters and turntable to cut metal. Lifts and aligns workpiece between cutting blades manually or by hoist and guides it along layout lines to cut irregular shapes. May lay out lines onto workpiece, using compass, or trace from template. May turn handwheel which tilts machine table or install fixture to cut specified bevel on workpiece.
GOE: 06.02.02 STRENGTH: H GED: R3 M2 L2 SVP: 4 DLU: 77

615.482-038   TURRET-PUNCH-PRESS OPERATOR (any industry) alternate titles: multi-punch operator
Operates turret punch press to punch holes or layout marks in metal sheets, plates, strips, or bars, following charts which list machine settings for each cut: Inserts, aligns, and locks punches and dies in turret, using hammer, shims, feelers, micrometers, and setscrews. Places workpiece on table manually or by using crane. Aligns workpiece to scale and end gauge on machine and clamps it to machine table. Pushes button to turn turret to specified punch and die. Turns cranks to set indicator to specified dimension on forward and lateral machine scale. Presses pedal to activate punch. Repeats operation for each machine setting specified on charts. Positions center punch from turret to touch plate and turns crank to scratch layout lines. May compute punch charts from blueprints, using square, scale, and applying knowledge of shop mathematics. May punch holes in nonmetallic materials.
GOE: 06.02.02 STRENGTH: H GED: R4 M3 L3 SVP: 5 DLU: 77

615.662-010   SLITTING-MACHINE OPERATOR II (any industry)
Sets up and operates slitting machine to cut sheet metal into strips of specified widths: Selects, cleans, and installs spacers and cutters on arbors, and hones cutters with oilstone to remove nicks. Presses button to lower arbor until cutters mesh, and measures clearance with feeler gauge. Inserts spacers to adjust spacing to specified tolerance. Signals OVERHEAD CRANE OPERATOR (any industry) 921.663-010 to lift metal roll to play-out reel or places roll on reel, using overhead chain hoist. Threads sheeting through slitter and verifies dimensions of cut to specifications, using rule. Secures strips on recoiler, adjusts guides and roller tension with handcrank, and starts machine. Observes slitting and rewinding operation and examines cut strips for flatness, holes, burrs on edges, and surface defects. May oil and clean machine. May feed sheet metal between rotating shear rolls. May install rubber sleeves over spacers to provide gripping surface for rollers and to facilitate movement of material being slit. May operate panel to control specific units of equipment, such as feeder unit.
GOE: 06.02.02 STRENGTH: M GED: R3 M2 L2 SVP: 5 DLU: 78

615.682-010   FLYING-SHEAR OPERATOR (steel & rel.)
Sets up and operates mill equipment, such as flying shear, guides, and crop or entry gates, to cut steel products to specified lengths: Reads production schedule to determine setup or adjustment of equipment. Installs knives in shear and guides on roll stands, using handtools and sledge. Turns rheostats to adjust cutting action of shear according to specified length of product. Starts shear and moves controls to raise and lower pinch rolls, adjusts guides, and opens and closes shear gates. Assists other workers in roll changes and in removing cobbles (waste steel) from rolling line.
GOE: 06.02.02 STRENGTH: M GED: R3 M3 L2 SVP: 5 DLU: 78

615.682-014   PUNCH-PRESS OPERATOR III (any industry)
Operates power press equipped with punch to notch or punch metal or plastic plates, sheets, or structural shapes: Positions, aligns, and clamps specified punch and die set into ram and bed of machine, using feelers, gauges, shims, rule, or template. Turns handwheel or installs shims to set depth of stroke. Lifts workpiece onto machine bed or roller table, manually or by using jib or crane. Positions layout marks on workpiece between punch and die. Positions and clamps guide stops to run successive pieces. Starts ram to drive punch through workpiece. May operate machine equipped with two or more punch and die sets. May trace layout marks or workpiece from template. May be designated according to function of machine as Notching-Press Operator (any industry).
GOE: 06.02.02 STRENGTH: H GED: R3 M2 L2 SVP: 4 DLU: 78

615.682-018   SHEAR OPERATOR I (any industry) alternate titles: plate-shear operator; power-shear operator
Sets up and operates power shear to cut metal objects, such as plates, sheets, slabs, billets, or bars to specified dimensions and angle: Turns handwheels to adjust rake (angle) and pressure of blade. Positions and clamps stops and side guides to set length and angle of cut, using rule, built-in gauges, or template. Lifts workpiece manually or by hoist or crane to machine bed or roller table and positions it against side guide and end stops. Starts machine which clamps workpiece and lowers blade to cut metal. Lays out cutting lines on metal, using rule, square, or template when shearing single pieces. May tilt bed, blade, or install fixtures to shear, bevel, or trim fabricated items. May set up and operate shear on production line in which shear is fed by conveyor, such as automobile frame line or rolling mill. May operate portable shear to cut sheet metal. May inspect work, using tape, compass, gauge, template, or micrometer to verify dimensions. May be designated by type of shear as Gate-Shear Operator (any industry) II; or by application of shear as Square-Shear Operator (any industry) I; Staple-Shear Operator (steel & rel.). May operate shear that automatically shears to uniform length metal sheets, plates, or structural shapes fed into ma-

chine by continuous coil or conveyor and be designated Shear Operator, Automatic (any industry) I.
GOE: 06.02.02 STRENGTH: H GED: R3 M2 L2 SVP: 4 DLU: 78

615.685-010   BURRING-MACHINE OPERATOR (nut & bolt)
Tends semiautomatic machine that removes burrs from hot-forged nut blanks: Shovels nuts into tray that feeds machine. Starts machine. Picks up nut blanks discharged from hopper onto table and positions nuts, burr side up, in channel that gravity feeds nuts into burring cutters. Inspects nut blanks for burrs and readjusts cutters to ensure that burrs are removed.
GOE: 06.04.02 STRENGTH: M GED: R2 M1 L2 SVP: 2 DLU: 77

615.685-014   CLEARANCE CUTTER (clock & watch)
Threads wire through rollers of automatic press that punches out clearances (excess metal) from flat steel wire leaving continuous strip of watch hands. May punch out feed holes (holes in wire strip that permit feeding of wire into machines at a fixed rate).
GOE: 06.04.02 STRENGTH: S GED: R2 M1 L1 SVP: 2 DLU: 77

615.685-018   CUP-TRIMMING-MACHINE OPERATOR (ordnance)
Tends speed lathe to perform cutting-off operation on aluminum cups to be used as component parts of projectile and bomb fuses: Inserts blank cup into revolving spring collet in headstock of machine, using jig. Removes jig, causing collet to secure cup. Depresses pedal to bring cutting tool in contact with revolving cup and cut it to specified length. Removes cup from machine.
GOE: 06.04.02 STRENGTH: L GED: R2 M1 L1 SVP: 2 DLU: 77

615.685-022   CUT-OFF-MACHINE OPERATOR (ordnance)
Tends battery of automatic machines that cut lead wire into slugs to be swaged into bullets or bullet cores for small arms ammunition: Positions drum of wire at rear of machine and threads wire over pulleys and through guides and pull rollers to cutter. Adjusts stroke of cutoff knife to vary length of slugs, using screwdriver and wrench. Starts machine and observes operation for malfunction. Weighs sample slugs on scales to verify conformance to specifications. Empties and replaces slug catch box.
GOE: 06.04.02 STRENGTH: M GED: R2 M1 L1 SVP: 2 DLU: 77

615.685-026   NIBBLER OPERATOR (any industry)
Tends machine that cuts metal plates, sheets, or structural shapes into specified radial or irregular shapes by action of reciprocating cutting knives or punches: Positions and clamps specified cutter or punch into ram and bed of machine. Turns thumbscrews to adjust depth of stroke to thickness of metal. Turns handwheel to set specified distance between cutter or punch and center point of turntable or fixtures, using built-in scale or rule. Clamps guide and drive rollers over workpiece. Depresses pedal which activates ram and feed rollers to cut or punch along radius. Guides workpiece manually along cutting lines or template to cut irregular shapes. May lay out guidelines onto workpiece by tracing from template. Mat drill center hole into workpiece, using portable drill. May bevel edges of steel plates, using portable pneumatic nibbler.
GOE: 06.04.02 STRENGTH: M GED: R2 M2 L2 SVP: 3 DLU: 77

615.685-030   PUNCH-PRESS OPERATOR II (any industry)
Tends one or more power presses that trim, punch, shape, notch, draw, or crimp metal, composite materials, or plastic stock between preset dies: Places workpiece against fixtures or stops on machine bed and under machine die, or threads roll of metal into jig. Starts press and monitors machine operation to detect misalignment or malfunction. Inspects parts visually, or with fixed gauges to verify conformance to specifications or to detect fabrication defects. May be designated according to product machined as Sprue-Cutting-Press Operator (foundry); or function of machine as Forming-Press Operator (any industry) II; Trimming-Press Operator (forging); or according to type of press operated as Multiple-Punch-Press Operator (any industry) II.
GOE: 06.04.02 STRENGTH: M GED: R2 M1 L2 SVP: 3 DLU: 86

615.685-034   SHEAR OPERATOR II (any industry) alternate titles: power-shear operator
Tends power shear that cuts metal objects, such as sheets, plates, billets or bars, to specified length: Lifts workpiece manually, or by hoist or crane, to machine bed or roller table. Positions workpiece against side guides and end stops or aligns layout lines under shear blade. Starts machine that clamps workpiece and lowers blade to cut metal. May tend shear on production line where shear is fed by conveyor, such as automobile frame line or rolling mill. May position stops according to calibrated gauge on machine to shear to length such items as scrap, billets, or reinforcing rods. May verify size of sheared items, using tape measurer, caliper, or template. May shear metal to specified circular or curved dimensions. May be designated by type of shear as Alligator-Shear Operator (any industry); Gate-Shear Operator (any industry) I; or by application of shear as Hot-Billet-Shear Operator (smelt. & refin.; steel & rel.); Scrap-Shear Operator (any industry); Square-Shear Operator (any industry) II.
GOE: 06.04.02 STRENGTH: H GED: R2 M2 L2 SVP: 4 DLU: 79

615.685-038   STRIP-METAL-PUNCH-AND-STRAIGHTENER OPERATOR (wood. container)
Tends machine that straightens coiled strip metal, cuts it into strips of specified length, and punches holes in strips: Hangs coiled metal on spindle between guides of machine. Inserts end of metal between feed rolls of machine. Starts machine that feeds strip through straightening rolls under punching and trimming dies that cut strip to specified length and punch holes in it.
GOE: 06.04.02 STRENGTH: M GED: R2 M1 L1 SVP: 3 DLU: 77

615.685-042 TURRET-PUNCH-PRESS OPERATOR, TAPE-CONTROL (any industry)

Tends tape-controlled turret or hydraulic-powered punch press that automatically positions *indexing* table, selects punch, and punches holes, or layout marks in metal sheets, plates, strips, or bars: Positions and clamps workpiece against fixtures or to specified point on built-in scale. Threads tape through electronic reader to specified position. Starts machine and observes operation. May verify first piece, using rule and plug gauges. May open chucks, using wrench to replace worn or broken punches and dies.
GOE: 06.04.02 STRENGTH: H GED: R2 M2 L2 SVP: 3 DLU: 77

615.685-046 CUTTER-MACHINE TENDER (electron. comp.) alternate titles: shearer, printed circuit boards

Tends machine that cuts copper or aluminum laminated fiberglass sheets, hardboard, and cardboard backers for production of printed circuit boards (PCBs): Reads work orders to determine type, size, and quantity of PCB materials to be cut. Adjusts guides on machine to regulate width of cut, using ruler or following calibrated scale on machine bed. Positions and aligns sheets against guides, and depresses pedal to activate blade that cuts material. Adjusts guides and repositions material to trim or square edges to specifications. Records production data. May mount material on spindle of machine that automatically feeds material onto bed of machine for cutting. May tend pinning machine that inserts metal pins into laminated boards and related backing material prior to drilling operation. May replace machine blades, using handtools. May bake cut boards in oven to remove excess moisture. May clean machines.
GOE: 06.04.09 STRENGTH: M GED: R2 M2 L2 SVP: 2 DLU: 86

615.687-010 HELPER, SHEAR OPERATOR (steel & rel.) alternate titles: sidehand

Assists side shear crew to move, position, and hold hot-rolled steel plate for shearing operations, using push bar and plate wrench: Pushes steel plate over caster bed equipped with goose neck rollers to align plate under knife blade, using long handle push bar. Positions and holds steel plate on shear block to prevent movement during shearing operation, using plate wrench. Assists crew in charging shear knife blade, using handtools. May lubricate knife blade and shear table, using oilcan.
GOE: 06.04.24 STRENGTH: H GED: R2 M1 L1 SVP: 3 DLU: 86

616 FABRICATING MACHINE OCCUPATIONS

This group includes occupations concerned with shaping, fitting, and assembling metal parts. Shaping, fitting, and assembling of nonmetallic parts, except wooden, are also included when the methods and machine tools commonly applied to the fabrication of metal are used.

616.130-010 SUPERVISOR (nut & bolt)

Supervises and coordinates activities of workers engaged in forging, trimming, thread rolling, and tapping of metal stock to produce nuts, bolts, screws, or other fasteners. Trains workers in machine operations. Performs duties as described under SUPERVISOR (any industry) Master Title. May design tools. May set up and repair machines. May inspect finished products for conformance to specifications.
GOE: 06.02.01 STRENGTH: L GED: R4 M3 L3 SVP: 7 DLU: 77

616.130-014 SUPERVISOR, SPECIALTY MANUFACTURING (steel & rel.)

Supervises and coordinates activities of workers engaged in cutting, leveling, shearing, threading, and punching steel products, such as bars, rounds, pipe, plate, and strip to specified patterns or shapes. Trains workers in operation of shears, and pipe cutting and threading machines. Performs other duties as described under SUPERVISOR (any industry) Master Title.
GOE: 06.02.01 STRENGTH: M GED: R4 M3 L3 SVP: 7 DLU: 77

616.130-018 SUPERVISOR, SPRING PRODUCTION (metal prod., nec)

Supervises and coordinates activities of workers engaged in shearing, punching, forming, tempering, assembling, coiling, peening, and painting springs. Trains workers in operation of equipment. Performs duties as described under SUPERVISOR (any industry) Master Title. May be designated according to activities of workers supervised as Supervisor, Forming And Tempering (metal prod., nec); Supervisor, Leaf-Spring Fabrication (metal prod., nec); Supervisor, Leaf-Spring Repair (metal prod., nec).
GOE: 06.02.01 STRENGTH: L GED: R4 M3 L3 SVP: 8 DLU: 77

616.130-022 SUPERVISOR, STEEL DIVISION (furniture)

Supervises and coordinates activities of workers engaged in spinning and assembling wire coils to form mattress innersprings and bedspring units. Directs production workers and machine maintenance personnel in setting up and adjusting equipment, such as coiling, crimping, and wire-border forming machines. Performs other duties as described under SUPERVISOR (any industry) Master Title. May set up machines. May be designated by department as Coil-Machine Supervisor (furniture); Spring-Assembler Supervisor (furniture).
GOE: 06.02.01 STRENGTH: L GED: R4 M3 L3 SVP: 7 DLU: 77

616.260-010 EMBOSSING TOOLSETTER (ordnance)

Sets up and adjusts machines that roll grooves or knurls into shotgun shell caps preparatory to joining cap to shell body.
GOE: 06.01.02 STRENGTH: L GED: R4 M3 L2 SVP: 6 DLU: 77

616.260-014 MULTI-OPERATION-FORMING-MACHINE SETTER (any industry)

Sets up automatic multiple-operation machines to perform any combination of bending, punching, roll forming, beading, cutting, flanging, shearing, seaming and welding, soldering, or clinching to fabricate metal parts, such as rims, molding, cans, tubing, and housing: Sets stops and guides. Installs and aligns forming and drive rolls, roller dies, punching, notching, and cutting dies and rams, shears, or saw blades. Installs electrodes and adjusts voltage to set up welding or soldering unit. Installs coil of tinplate for presses. Adjusts speed controls to synchronize action of rolls, cutoff, welding unit, drive rolls, conveyor, or transfer machine. Greases and oils machinery, using grease gun, oilcan and brush. Operates machines for test run to verify setup. Turns machine over to MULTI-OPERATION-FORMING-MACHINE OPERATOR (any industry) II. May set up mechanized line of machines which operate in tandem. May repair malfunctioning machines. May be designated by function of machines as Production Mechanic, Tin Cans (tinware); Rim-Riller Setter (auto. mfg.); Tubing-Mill Setter (any industry).
GOE: 06.01.02 STRENGTH: M GED: R4 M3 L3 SVP: 7 DLU: 77

616.260-018 SPRING COILING MACHINE SETTER (metal prod., nec)

Sets up automatic spring coiling machines to fabricate compression and extension springs from steel wire, according to blueprints and setup charts: Reviews blueprint to determine setup procedures to follow, machine attachments required, and stock to use, or obtains details from setup charts. Selects machine attachments, such as taper cams, wire size block, coiling point, pitch tool, and cutting tool, according to blueprint or setup chart, and installs them on machine. Verifies wire diameter with micrometer caliper and threads wire through drive rollers and machine guides. Sets cams, turnbuckle, and pitch tool to control spring dimensions. Makes trial run and measures sample product for conformance to specifications, using gauges and micrometers. Adjusts machine to attain specified tolerances and releases machine to SPRING COILER (metal prod., nec) with oral instructions concerning its operation. Grinds cams and pitch tool to maintain their dimensions. May recommend blueprint changes. May make tool attachments, such as coiling point, cams, forming tools, and cut-off tools if not in stock.
GOE: 06.01.02 STRENGTH: L GED: R4 M4 L3 SVP: 7 DLU: 77

616.260-022 TORSION SPRING COILING MACHINE SETTER (metal prod., nec)

Sets up torsion spring coiling machines, according to blueprints and setup charts, to fabricate torsion springs from round wire: Reviews blueprint to determine setup procedures to follow, machine attachments required, and material specifications for new part, or obtains details from setup chart for repeat orders. Requests delivery of specified stock from stockroom to work area. Selects machine attachments, such as arbors, cams, and feed mechanism, according to blueprint or setup chart, and installs them on machine. Verifies wire diameter, using micrometer caliper, and mounts wire on reel stand and threads end through feed mechanism. Sets arbor cam to control pitch of spring. Makes trial run and measures sample for conformance to specifications, using micrometers and gauges. Adjusts machine to attain specified tolerances and releases machine to SPRING COILER (metal prod., nec) with oral instructions concerning its operation. Grinds machine parts, such as cams and arbor, to maintain dimensions. Recommends blueprint changes to resolve production problems.
GOE: 06.01.02 STRENGTH: L GED: R4 M4 L3 SVP: 7 DLU: 77

616.280-010 SPRING MAKER (metal prod., nec)

Sets up and operates variety of machines to fabricate small lots or samples of coiled compression, extension, and torsion springs, and other wire forms from steel wire or strip, following blueprints, drawings, and setup charts: Selects machine tools, such as arbor, grooved tool, and pitch tool, and installs them on lathe winder. Operates lathe winders to form coiled flat and wire springs [LATHE WINDER (metal prod., nec)]. Crimps and trues coiled springs and bends wire and flat forms to specified shape, using handtools, vise, and forming plates. Operates forming presses to form spring washers and flat metal products from flat stock. Measures products for conformance to specifications, using calipers, micrometers, and other gauges. Places pan of springs in gas-fired oven or places individual springs in molten lead bath for heat treating and removes springs after specified period of time to air or water cool. Recommends changes in blueprints, in machine setup, type of metal, and methods and procedures operations for making products. Makes spring-machine attachments and tools not in stock [TOOL MAKER (machine shop)].
GOE: 06.01.03 STRENGTH: M GED: R4 M3 L3 SVP: 7 DLU: 77

616.360-010 BODY-MAKER-MACHINE SETTER (tinware)

Sets up battery of automatic machines that form tin-can bodies: Lights and tends gas burners under soldering vats and adjusts thermostats to regulate temperature of molten solder in machines. Tests air pressure of vacuum feed cups with gauge. Starts machine and observes operation to detect malfunctioning. Inspects can bodies and adjusts machine action until bodies conform with specifications. Adjusts machines for change to different sizes of can bodies. Maintains supply of bar solder in melting reservoirs and adjusts thermostat regulators to regulate flow of molten solder into machine. Adjusts equipment and replaces defective regulator units, using handtools. May repair malfunctioning machines.
GOE: 06.01.02 STRENGTH: L GED: R3 M2 L2 SVP: 6 DLU: 77

616.360-014 LOOM SETTER, WIRE WEAVING (metal prod., nec)

Sets up power looms to weave wire into screening and cloth to size, mesh, and weave patterns specified by work orders, diagrams, and data charts, apply-

ing knowledge of machine function, principles of mechanics and shop mathematics: Selects functional machine parts, such as reeds, heddles, and shuttle, according to wire specified and aligns and bolts them to machine. Selects, positions, and installs cams, shuttle thrower, and gears and turns speed control knobs to synchronize action of machine to produce size and pattern of weave specified, using precision measuring instruments and handtools. Turn knobs to adjust electric eye control which automatically stops machine when specified run is completed, shuttle or warp wire runs out, or wire breaks. Threads wire from back beam through heddles and reeds to cloth roll, and install bobbins in shuttle. Starts machine and makes trial runs. Inspects sample, visually and using gauges and readjusts machine to correct malfunction. May replace or repair broken parts of machine. May tend bobbin-winding machine to wind bobbins for installation in loom. May be designated by product specialty as Loom Setter, Fourdrinier (metal prod., nec).
GOE: 06.01.02 STRENGTH: M GED: R4 M3 L3 SVP: 7 DLU: 77

616.360-022 MACHINE SETTER (any industry)
Sets up various metal fabricating machines, such as brakes, shears, punch presses, bending and straightening machines, to cut, bend, and straighten metal as specified by layout, work order blueprints, and templates: Positions, aligns, and bolts dies, blades, bedplates, cushion pins, and stops, using shims and measuring tools, such as squares, straightedges, rules, micrometers, gauges, feelers, templates, and handtools. Adjusts flow of lubricants, pressure and depth of stroke, or feed of material, applying knowledge of thickness and properties of metal or according to standard specifications. Makes trial runs and measures workpiece for conformance to specifications. Instructs operator in special handling techniques. Clears jams and corrects malfunction of machines. Reports need for machine repairs to supervisor. Dismantles setups. May sharpen shear blades, drills, on cutting tools. May set up drill presses, flame cutting, and welding machines. May set up automatic or multipurpose machines. May specialize in setup of single type of machine and be designated accordingly as Brake Machine Setter (any industry). May set up machines common to sheet metal operations and be designated Machine Setter, Sheet Metal (any industry).
GOE: 06.01.02 STRENGTH: M GED: R4 M3 L3 SVP: 6 DLU: 77

616.360-026 MULTI-OPERATION-FORMING-MACHINE OPERATOR I (any industry)
Sets up and operates automatic multiple-operation machine to perform any combination of bending, punching, roll forming, beading, cutting and welding, soldering, or clinching of metal to fabricate items, such as rims, molding, cams, tubing, and housings specified by blueprint or work orders: Installs and aligns roller dies, drive and forming rolls, punch, notching or forming dies, shear or saw blades, and electrodes, using rules, vernier gauges, square, shims, and handtools. Sets side guides and stops. Turns knobs to regulate voltage of resistance welding equipment and synchronize speed of feed rolls, conveyor, or transfer machine with action of roller dies, forming rolls, punch or shear rams, and welding unit. Places roll of sheet or strip metal or wire onto feedrack and threads end through machine or into drive rolls, or metal blanks or bars onto conveyor, into hopper, or against guides to feed machine. Starts machine. Verifies dimension of finished product visually or using micrometers, calipers, or gauges. May remove finished parts from machine. May operate mechanized line of machines working in tandem. May be designated by function of machine as Tubing-Mill Operator (any industry) II. May set up and operate multioperation forming machine to make pipe from continuous steel coil and be designated Welder, Pipe Making (steel & rel.).
GOE: 06.01.03 STRENGTH: M GED: R4 M3 L3 SVP: 6 DLU: 77

616.360-030 SHOTGUN-SHELL-ASSEMBLY-MACHINE ADJUSTER (ordnance) alternate titles: assembly-machine tool setter; heading-and-priming tool setter
Sets up automatic machines to assemble shotgun shells for loading with powder and shot: Removes, replaces, and adjusts tools and parts, such as punches, dies, pins, dials, spindles, plungers, and hoppers, using handtools and gauges. Turns setscrews and stop nuts to adjust machine coiling and pressing mechanisms. Dismantles hoppers, feed tubes, and feed and press mechanisms to extract jammed components. Notifies MAINTENANCE MECHANIC (any industry) to make major replacements or repairs.
GOE: 06.01.02 STRENGTH: L GED: R3 M2 L2 SVP: 4 DLU: 77

616.360-034 STRAIGHT-LINE-PRESS SETTER (ordnance) alternate titles: assembly-machine tool setter; tracer-bullet assembly-machine tool setter
Sets up machines to shape noses of brass or steel bullet jackets and assemble jacketed bullets for small arms cartridges: Installs punches and dies, feed pipes, magazines, guides, pins, and bushings to accommodate size bullets to be processed, using handtools. Turns setscrews and stop nuts to regulate automatic feeding, transporting, pressing, and ejecting mechanisms, and to adjust microswitches. Operates machine and examines assembled bullets for defects, such as dents, scratches, or malformations, and verifies conformance to specified dimensions, using gauges. Operates speed lathe and bench grinder to reshape or polish punches and dies. Replaces worn or broken machine parts, such as springs, pins, die bolts, screws, and washers. Gives instructions to new workers in machine operation and use of gauges.
GOE: 06.01.02 STRENGTH: M GED: R3 M2 L2 SVP: 4 DLU: 77

616.361-010 SPRING INSPECTOR I (metal prod., nec)
Inspects and tests leaf-springs for conformance to specifications: Verifies curvature of leaf, using template. Tests leaf in load tester by inserting springs into apparatus equipped with gauge that registers amount of leaf distortion to determine if springs meet load requirements. Discards defective leaves. Tends machine that bombards steel shot against leaf spring and measures indentations in leaf, using curvature gauge. Records test results for quality control purposes. Observes spring assembly operations to ensure parts are assembled according to specifications. Discusses with supervisor changes in machine setup or assembly operations to improve product or simplify operations. Stops machine to inspect and test faulty productions and changes or aligns dies, using machinist's tools.
GOE: 06.01.05 STRENGTH: L GED: R4 M3 L3 SVP: 7 DLU: 77

616.362-010 FABRIC-MACHINE OPERATOR I (furniture) alternate titles: link-wire-fabric-machine operator
Sets up and operates link wire fabric machine to form linked wire mesh for flat bedsprings from stock wire, using work orders, knowledge of machine operation, and bending characteristics of wire: Studies work orders to determine dimensions and type of wire mesh required. Selects tool and die elements from standardized stock or requests TOOL-AND-DIE MAKER (machine shop) to fabricate necessary elements. Positions and fastens tool and die elements and cams into required arrangement in machine to cut and bend stock wire by action of sliding rams in coordinated sequence. Places coils of wire on two reels, using forklift. Feeds wire through drive wheels and between dies of slides, using handtools. Starts machine to form and link together lengthwise and crosswise lengths to produce fabric of specified dimensions. Inspects sample, using template and rule. Adjusts setup to correct dimensions of wire fabric. Gives directions to FABRIC-MACHINE OPERATORS (furniture) II.
GOE: 06.02.02 STRENGTH: M GED: R3 M3 L3 SVP: 6 DLU: 77

616.380-010 FOUR-SLIDE-MACHINE SETTER (any industry)
Sets up various sizes and types of multiple-operation slide forming machines to automatically punch, cut, and bend metal strips or wire to fabricate parts, such as clips, brackets, and hairpins, as specified by blueprints and setup charts: Selects and installs cams, center post, and ram slide, and computes feed length position of cams and dies, applying knowledge of geometry and product dimensions. Aligns and bolts cams to shaft, slides to machine bed, and progressive dies to stationary shoes and cam actuated slides, using micrometers, gauges, feelers, rules, and handtools. Adjusts position of cams to synchronize action of rams, cutters, and drive rolls that feed stock. Turns flywheel by hand to produce sample part, and compares part with specifications, using fixed gauges, micrometer, and calipers. Readjusts position of dies and cams to achieve specified shape and dimension. Turns machine over to FOUR-SLIDE-MACHINE OPERATOR (any industry) II. May sharpen and repair dies, using engine lathes, milling machines, precision grinders, hand files, and scrapers.
GOE: 06.01.02 STRENGTH: M GED: R3 M3 L3 SVP: 6 DLU: 77

616.380-014 JOB SETTER (electron. comp.)
Sets up and adjusts machines, such as grid formers or spade-winding machines, used to fabricate parts for electron tubes: Reads work order or receives verbal instructions regarding machine setup. Installs specified parts, such as gears, cams, ratchets, cutters, and guides in machine. Sets control mechanisms that regulate functions, such as feed rate, spindle speed, air pressure, and wire tension. Loads, positions, and aligns wire or other fabrication material on feed mechanisms. Starts machine and observes operation to detect malfunction. Examines and measures sample part, using magnifying device and measuring instruments, such as balance scale, ruler, and micrometer, to ensure part meets specifications or to determine cause of defect. May maintain and repair machinery. May sharpen tools, using grinder or polishing equipment.
GOE: 06.01.02 STRENGTH: L GED: R3 M3 L3 SVP: 5 DLU: 88

616.380-018 MACHINE OPERATOR I (any industry) alternate titles: fabricating-machine operator
Sets up and operates metal fabricating machines, such as brakes, rolls, shears, saws, and presses, to cut, bend, straighten, and form metal plates, sheets, and structural shapes according to blueprints and specifications: Reads and interprets blueprints, engineering specifications, and shop orders to determine machine setup, production methods, and sequence of operation. Selects, positions, and secures dies, blades, cutters, and fixtures onto machine, using rule, square, shims, templates, handtools, and built-in gauges. Positions and clamps stops, guides, and turntables. Adjusts controls to set and regulate machining factors, such as pressure and depth of ram stroke, adjustment rolls, blade angle, and machine speed. Locates and marks bending or cutting lines and reference points on workpiece, using instruments, such as rule and compass, or by tracing from templates. Positions workpiece against stops and guides or aligns layout marks with dies or cutting blades manually or using hoist. Starts machine and observes machine operation to reposition workpiece, change dies, or adjust machine settings for multiple or successive passes. Inspects or measures work, using rule, gauges, and templates. May operate machines to fabricate nonmetallic materials, such as composites or plastics. May set up and operate sheet-metal fabricating machines only and be designated Sheet-Metal-Fabricating-Machine Operator (any industry).
GOE: 06.01.03 STRENGTH: M GED: R3 M3 L3 SVP: 6 DLU: 87

616.382-010 BARBED-WIRE-MACHINE OPERATOR (metal prod., nec)
Operates machine that automatically twists sharp barbs between strands of wire to form barbed-wire fencing materials: Mounts reels of smooth wire on feedrack of machine, using hoist. Butt-welds end of feed wire to wire in machines, and to repair breaks in wire. Starts machine and observes counter on

machine to verify required length of barbed wire on roll. Stops machine and removes pin to drop roll of barbed wire to floor. Cuts wire with cutter. Attaches name tag to roll and places it on pallet. Adjusts machine.
GOE: 06.02.02 STRENGTH: M GED: R3 M1 L1 SVP: 5 DLU: 77

616.382-014 WIRE WEAVER, CLOTH (metal prod., nec) alternate titles: wire weaver
Sets up and operates power loom to weave wire cloth for products, such as industrial cloths, filters, sieves, or strainers: Reviews specifications to determine quantity, type, and size wire required. Lifts spools of wire, and places them on spindles of creel. Verifies specified size of wire, using micrometer. Fastens wire ends to back beam of loom. Starts beam motor to wind and transfer wire from creel to beam. Threads warp wires individually through heddles, between teeth of comb, and fastens ends to roller. Adjusts spring of loom to required tension, using wrench. Inserts bobbin in shuttle, fastens shoot wire end to roller and pushes switch to start loom. Observes loom operation to detect faulty weaving and wire breaks. Reweaves and ties broken wires, using pick and magnifying glass. Counts mesh of woven cloth to ensure that specifications are met, using pick and counting glass. Removes roll of finished cloth from loom, using electric powered lift. May wind bobbins while loom is in operation. May cut off strip of wire cloth, using scissors or shears for quality control inspection prior to start of production. May maintain records of production and non-repairable cloth defects.
GOE: 06.02.02 STRENGTH: M GED: R3 M2 L2 SVP: 7 DLU: 77

616.382-018 TYPING-ELEMENT-MACHINE OPERATOR (office machines)
Sets up, controls, and monitors machine that automatically assembles component parts, such as caps, shims, levers, and springs, to fabricate *typing elements* used in electric typewriters: Reads work order and engineering specifications to determine components needed for assembly. Loads parts into hoppers of automatic feed mechanism of machine. Flips switches on control panel to start machine. Observes panel lights and machine operation to detect malfunctions and ensure prescribed sequence of operation. Fills grease containers on machine and maintains supply of parts in feed mechanism. Inspects assembled typing element to detect defects, such as mislocated springs, chipped characters, and insufficient grease. Adjusts and calibrates machine to adapt machine to processing requirements, following specified procedures and using handtools.
GOE: 06.01.03 STRENGTH: L GED: R3 M3 L3 SVP: 6 DLU: 86

616.460-010 NAIL-MAKING-MACHINE SETTER (steel & rel.) alternate titles: nail-machine operator
Sets up battery of machines that automatically cut and shape coiled wire to make nails of specified sizes: Installs and secures die plates and nail-point cutting knives, and positions feeding mechanism, according to work order specifications, using handtools. Mounts coil of wire on rod and threads wire through straightening rollers, feeding mechanism, and into slots of die plates. Tightens roller bolts to secure wire, using wrench, and turns flywheel to produce sample nail. Measures nail with split gauge or micrometer, and inspects nail for flaws, such as chips and distortions. Starts machine and observes operation to ensure product meets specifications. May set up and maintain battery of machines that automatically cut coiled wire and simultaneously attach nailheads to cut wire to form tacks of specified size. May supervise NAIL-MAKING-MACHINE TENDERS (steel & rel.).
GOE: 06.01.02 STRENGTH: M GED: R3 M2 L3 SVP: 6 DLU: 77

616.482-010 SAFETY-PIN-ASSEMBLING-MACHINE OPERATOR (button & notion)
Operates battery of automatic machines to twist coil in pointed length of wire and form and attach caps and guards to wire to form safety pins: Installs cutting and forming dies in machine according to size of pin specified, using handtools. Lifts reels of cap and guard metal strip onto feed-reel holders, and locks spring clamps to secure reels. Scoops pointed wires into gravity feed hopper and starts machine. Observes operation to detect jamming of mechanisms and extracts jammed pin parts, using pick, screwdriver, and pliers. Measures sample of completed pins for conformance to specifications, such as length, diameter of wire, size of spring coil, and width of pin, using micrometers and fixed gauges. Examines pins for malformation of caps or guards and opens and closes pins to test operation. Adjusts guides, tension bars, cams, feeder arms, and stops, and synchronizes moving parts of machine to correct malfunctions. Replaces broken or worn cutting and forming dies, using machinist's handtools.
GOE: 06.02.02 STRENGTH: H GED: R3 M2 L2 SVP: 5 DLU: 77

616.484-010 TRUER (metal prod., nec)
Trues coiled precision springs and tests springs for conformance to specifications: Places set of springs over mandrel, places metal bar over springs, and pushes against bar to compress springs to specified length. Positions spring over template or between poles of electronic spring checker to detect variation from standard spring length. Places spring on flat surface, and measures squareness of end, using gauge. Inserts wedge between coils and taps wedge with mallet to even pitch between coils and adjust length of spring.
GOE: 06.03.02 STRENGTH: L GED: R2 M2 L2 SVP: 4 DLU: 77

616.485-010 BENCH WORKER (metal prod., nec)
Tends machines that wind, shape, or finish coiled and flat springs or wire forms to specifications: Positions metal or wire blanks or coiled spring on jig press. Depresses pedal to lower shaping die that stamps out spring forms, or crimps, hooks, or loops ends of coiled springs. Presses and turns spring ends

against rotating abrasive wheel to remove burs. Drills and taps holes in flat springs, using single-spindle drill press. Feeds wire through guides and onto mandrel of lathe-type automatic coil-winding machine that coils series of springs on mandrel. Cuts lead-in wire, using handcutters, and removes mandrel. Slides loop of flat metal stock over arbor of power-driven spring winder and starts machine to wind metal around arbor to form coiled-flat springs. Places retaining ring over wound spring to prevent unwinding. Measures springs for conformance to specifications, using gauges and micrometers. Inserts springs into holding device of double-disk grinder and places holding device between grinding wheels. Starts machine that automatically grinds spring ends. Removes springs. May be designated according to task performed as Automatic-Coil-Winding-Machine Operator (metal prod., nec); Double-End-Production Grinder (metal prod., nec).
GOE: 06.04.02 STRENGTH: L GED: R2 M2 L2 SVP: 3 DLU: 77

616.485-014 SPRING COILER (metal prod., nec) alternate titles: coil-machine operator
Tends machine that automatically coils compression, extension, and torsion springs from round and flat wire, following verbal instructions: Examines wire stock with micrometer to ensure conformance to specifications. Threads end of stock through feed rollers, around arbor, and under cutting tool. Starts machine that automatically winds, cuts, and ejects springs. Measures springs for conformance to specifications, using micrometers and gauges. Verifies action of springs under pressure by compressing springs under specified load in spring testing machine. Notifies machine setter when machine malfunctions. May sharpen cut-off tool and remove coiling marks from coiling point and pitch tool, using *bench grinder*.
GOE: 06.04.02 STRENGTH: M GED: R2 M1 L1 SVP: 3 DLU: 77

616.582-010 FENCE-MAKING MACHINE OPERATOR (metal prod., nec)
Operates machine that forms wire mesh fencing: Places rolls of wire onto spools and joins wire ends, using acetylene torch. Selects mesh die, according to wire size. Bolts die on weaving spindle of machine and draws wire through die to specified height, according to work ticket specifications. Turns setscrew to adjust automatic wirecutter, using wrench. Pushes buttons on control panel to start oil pump, machine motor, and automatic shutoff device. Pulls lever to start machine. Observes machine counter and removes rolls of fencing following length specifications on work ticket. Records number of fabricated rolls on work card. May move rolls to galvanizing department, using handtruck. May use electric butt welder to join wire ends.
GOE: 06.02.02 STRENGTH: M GED: R3 M2 L1 SVP: 4 DLU: 77

616.662-010 HYDRAULIC PRESS OPERATOR (construction)
Operates horizontal arbor press to disassemble and assemble press-fitted crawler track links for construction equipment, such as cranes, power shovels, and tractors: Hooks hoist line in sling and directs other workers engaged in placing and removing crawler tracks on conveyor. Removes or tightens bolts fastening track pads to track links, using pneumatic or electric impact wrench. Examines chart to select specified insert jaws (holding fixture for pins and bushings) and disassembly and assembly rams. Inserts rams in press sockets, using wrench. Moves levers to position track over insert jaws, and to advance or retract rams that press pins and bushing into sockets on track links. Directs other workers engaged in removing or positioning track pads, track links, pins, and bushings in press insert jaws. Operates press to disassemble and reassemble track, and to replace worn or damaged pins and bushings.
GOE: 06.02.20 STRENGTH: M GED: R3 M1 L1 SVP: 4 DLU: 77

616.665-010 TENSIONING-MACHINE OPERATOR (concrete prod.)
Tends machine that pulls and spaces reinforcing wire as it is wound around steel cylinder to make prestressed core for fabricating concrete pipe: Pulls wire through machine rollers and clamps to end of cylinder for subsequent welding. Signals WINDING-MACHINE OPERATOR (concrete prod.) to start machine that rotates cylinder. Observes dial indicator and pulls lever on tensioning machine to apply specified tension to wire during winding. Signals WINDING-MACHINE OPERATOR (concrete prod.) to stop rotation of cylinder after specified number of turns of wire. Maintains tension on wire until WELDER, ARC (welding) welds it to cylinder. May tend machine that pulls and spaces reinforcing wire by hydraulic power to make prestressed core for fabricating concrete beams.
GOE: 06.04.02 STRENGTH: L GED: R2 M1 L1 SVP: 3 DLU: 77

616.681-010 WEAVER, BENCH LOOM (metal prod., nec)
Forms wire screens used for partitions, draining racks, and window guards, using bench loom: Reviews specifications to determine quantity, type and size wire required, and obtains wire from storage area. Measures and cuts wire to specified lengths, using ruler and wire cutters. Inserts ends of warp wires in heddles and positions and secures opposite ends on bench with heavy iron bar. Depresses pedal to raise and lower alternate warp wires. Slides *shoot wire* between warp wires and pulls it into position manually. Measures position of shoot wire with ruler to ensure specified and even spacing. Depresses pedal to reverse warp wires, secure inserted shoot wire, and prepare for next shoot wire. Removes finished screen from bench loom and stacks it for pickup. May measure diameter of wire, using micrometer, to verify size of wire. May operate machine that cuts and crimps wires used in weaving wire screens. May trim edges of finished flat wire screens, using power shears.
GOE: 06.02.02 STRENGTH: M GED: R3 M2 L2 SVP: 5 DLU: 77

616.682-010   ARBOR-PRESS OPERATOR I (any industry) alternate titles: floor-press operator

Sets up and operates arbor press to press-fit parts, such as bearings, linings, armatures, or wheels to housings or shafts: Installs specified holding fixtures and dies on press, using rule, gauges, and handtools. Positions workpiece on press bed under ram, manually or using hoist. Moves controls to lower ram that presses part onto shaft or into housing. May mix white lead and apply it to parts as necessary, using brush, and remove scale, rust, burrs, and excess white lead, using files, wire brush, and rags. May be designated according to parts assembled as Bearing-Press-Machine Operator (railroad equip.); Cylinder-Block-Hole Reliner (automotive ser.); Wheel-Press Operator (railroad equip.).
GOE: 06.02.20 STRENGTH: M GED: R3 M1 L1 SVP: 3 DLU: 77

616.682-014   BALE-TIE-MACHINE OPERATOR (metal prod., nec) alternate titles: wire-loop-machine operator

Sets up and operates wirecutting and straightening machine, equipped with forming attachment, to form wire ties for tying bales of paper, hay, or other material: Adjusts driving and straightening rollers, forming attachment, and jaws of holding device, using handtools. Turns crank to adjust feed of driving rollers for specified length of bale tie. Inserts wire between driving and straightening rollers and starts machine that automatically cuts, forms, and ejects specified number of bale ties in bundle onto rack for wrapping. Wraps bundle by hand or uses machine wrapping device. May set counter that records number of ties formed. May stack finished ties in storage area.
GOE: 06.02.02 STRENGTH: M GED: R2 M1 L1 SVP: 4 DLU: 77

616.682-018   CAGE MAKER, MACHINE (concrete prod.)

Sets up and operates machine to fabricate steel cages used for reinforcing concrete pipe: Bolts lagging plates of specified size to expandable mandrel of machine to form drum for shaping and sizing cage. Threads wire from spindle through tensioning rollers and feeder arm of machine. Tack-welds ends of wire to bell-end of lagging plate and pulls lever to expand mandrel. Turns wheel on tensioner to regulate pressure on wire. Starts mandrel rotating as wire is fed through tensioning rollers on carriage which moves along track to space wire as it winds. Tack-welds wire to end of drum on completion of run and cuts wire with welding torch. Pulls lever to move welding and grounding wheels into position to hold rod in place and to form circuit for welding. Starts welding wheel to weld rod and wire at points of intersection. Breaks tack weld at ends of wire, using hammer and pulls lever to retract mandrel and loosen cage. Pulls cage from shaft by hand or aid of pneumatic winch.
GOE: 06.02.02 STRENGTH: L GED: R3 M1 L1 SVP: 6 DLU: 77

616.682-022   CRIMPING-MACHINE OPERATOR (any industry)

Sets up and operates machine to crimp wire to specified shape: Bolts specified crimping wheels into machine jaws, using wrench. Threads end of coiled wire through straightening and feed rollers into wire shaping machine. Starts machine and crimps sample wire of specified type. Measures sample, using micrometers and gauges, and changes crimping wheels or adjusts tension of machine until crimp meets specifications. May place shaped wire in rack. May be designated according to product worked on as Zig-Zag-Spring-Machine Operator (metal prod., nec).
GOE: 06.02.02 STRENGTH: L GED: R3 M2 L2 SVP: 5 DLU: 77

616.682-026   KICK-PRESS OPERATOR I (any industry) alternate titles: assembler, press operator; bench-press operator

Sets up and operates power press to assemble metal, plastic, rubber, or glass products by crimping, shaping, locking, staking, or press fitting: Installs specified dies on machine bed and ram, using measuring instruments and handtools. Positions and clamps holding fixtures to machine bed, using sample workpiece, template, rule, and gauge. Adjusts setscrews to regulate stroke of ram. Aligns parts between dies or positions them against fixtures on machine. Moves controls to lower ram that bends, clinches, or forces parts together. May operate machine to separate parts. May set up and operate machine to punch, cut, face, chamfer, or compress parts preparatory to assembly. May install gears and cams to synchronize action of multiple ram, feed, and positioning action of automatic presses.
GOE: 06.02.20 STRENGTH: L GED: R3 M2 L2 SVP: 4 DLU: 77

616.682-030   NAIL-ASSEMBLY-MACHINE OPERATOR (steel & rel.)

Operates machine to assemble and weld loose nails to pierced metal ribbon: Transports loose nails and metal ribbon from storage areas to machine. Threads pierced strip of metal through machine. Adjusts mechanical and electrical parts of machine to obtain specified feeds and speeds. Starts machine that assembles and welds nails to metal ribbon. Fills cooling tank with rust inhibitor and other liquids. Closes nail assembly cartons, using stapling gun. May operate machine to assemble and weld loose nails to wire.
GOE: 06.02.20 STRENGTH: M GED: R3 M2 L2 SVP: 4 DLU: 77

616.682-034   STRANDING-MACHINE OPERATOR (elec. equip.; light. fix.; metal prod., nec; nonfer. metal) alternates titles: cable-machine operator; cabling-machine operator; strander operator; strand-machine operator

Sets up and operates rotating cylindrical-shaped stranding machine to fabricate wire rope or electric cable: Places spools of wire of specified gauges into cradles, using electric hoist, and locks spool in place, using metal pin. Positions takeup spool onto shaft and adjusts travel of distributor to width of spool. Threads wires through holes on inside edge of machine and through twisting head and coils it around capstan, using blueprints or stranded wire as guide.

Nails or hooks stranded wire onto takeup spool. Adjusts gears for specified direction of twist and speed of capstan, using wrenches. Starts machine. Pours grease into grease pot, and opens valve to lubricate strands. Adjusts clutch to regulate speed of makeup spool shaft. Observes machine to detect malfunctioning. Cuts wire when specified footage has been wound and wraps end with wire, by hand or using mechanical wrapping tool. May butt-weld ends of disjointed wires. When operating stranding machine equipped with closing (finishing) attachments to prevent unraveling when rope is cut, is known as Closer (metal prod., nec). May work with fine wire to produce twisted electric-light cord and be designated Strand Buncher, Fine Wire (light. fix.).
GOE: 06.02.02 STRENGTH: M GED: R3 M2 L2 SVP: 4 DLU: 77

616.685-010   CHAIN-TESTING-MACHINE OPERATOR (forging)

Tends machine that tests strength of chains: Adjusts chain-holding jaws on machine to accommodate size of chain. Sets scale dial to specified pounds to regulate pulling power of machine. Positions chain in machine jaws and starts machine. Examines and gauges chain to detect broken or stretched links. May check chain for free operation, roll chain into coil, and place chain in crate.
GOE: 06.03.02 STRENGTH: L GED: R2 M1 L2 SVP: 4 DLU: 77

616.685-014   CLINCHING-MACHINE OPERATOR (elec. equip.)

Tends reel-fed machine that clinches (crimps) metal terminals or solderless connectors to electrical wires: Positions wire ends in fixture. Steps on switch to start machine that automatically cuts off terminal from continuous strip and clinches terminal to wires. May strip rubber insulation off wire cord to expose wire, using pliers or pedal-operated stripping machine. May take wires to shelves and distribute them in sections according to wire and terminal types.
GOE: 06.04.20 STRENGTH: L GED: R2 M1 L1 SVP: 2 DLU: 77

616.685-018   COIL ASSEMBLER, MACHINE (furniture) alternate titles: automatic-coil-machine operator; coil tier; finisher

Tends machine that joins coil with helical springs to form assemblies for innerspring mattresses, chairs, sofas, and automobile seats: Places coil springs in channels on machine table. Inserts end of helical spring in feeder that rotates and moves spring toward coils. Depresses pedal to start feeder and guides helical spring so that spring joins top edges of coils. Inserts spring in feeder and positions spring to secure bottom edges of coils. Pushes index bar against row of joined coils, or moves button or lever to activate bar that moves coils forward. Inserts coils in channels to form additional row. Removes completed spring assembly from machine or pulls release lever to eject assembly. Adjusts machine and relieves snagging or jamming, using handtools.
GOE: 06.04.20 STRENGTH: M GED: R2 M1 L1 SVP: 4 DLU: 77

616.685-022   FABRIC-MACHINE OPERATOR II (furniture) alternate titles: link-fabric-machine operator; link-wire-fabric-machine tender

Tends automatic machines that cut, bend, and couple wire links to form mesh mattress supports (fabrics) for cots, folding beds, and other furniture: Mounts two spools of wire on machine racks and threads ends into feed rollers that form lengthwise and crosswise spring links. Starts machine and allows machine to operate until desired length of wire mesh has been fabricated. Inspects emerging fabric and replaces missing or defective links, using wire snippers and pliers. Adjusts cams and setscrews of machine to correct malfunctions, using handtools.
GOE: 06.04.02 STRENGTH: M GED: R2 M1 L1 SVP: 3 DLU: 77

616.685-026   HEDDLE-MACHINE OPERATOR (machinery mfg.)

Tends machine that cuts and shapes wire to form metal heddles for textile machinery: Mounts roll of wire on feeder mechanism and threads wire end through guides into machine. Starts machine and observes feed of wire into machine where wire is cut, swaged, and polished. Inspects finished heddles for specified dimensions, using gauges.
GOE: 06.04.02 STRENGTH: M GED: R2 M1 L1 SVP: 3 DLU: 77

616.685-030   KNITTER, WIRE MESH (metal prod., nec) alternate titles: knitting-machine operator

Tends bank of machines that automatically knit strands of wire to form mesh tubing: Places spool of wire on frame of machine and inserts flyer spindle in top hole of spool. Threads wire through guide on flyer, through pulley of rotating frame, around and under hooks of knitting needles and fastens end to tube roller. Slides guide of belt sideways to engage pulley and start machine. Observes machine to detect faulty knitting and wire breaks. Measures width of mesh tube with ruler to ensure conformance to specifications. Stops machine to rethread and tie broken wires, replace spools of wire and remove rolls of mesh tubing. Notifies supervisor of repairs or adjustments needed. Obtains specified size and type of wire from storeroom. Stacks rolls of mesh tubing for pickup. Sprays wire with oil, soap suds or other lubricant to reduce friction.
GOE: 06.04.02 STRENGTH: M GED: R2 M2 L2 SVP: 2 DLU: 77

616.685-034   LOAD TESTER (metal prod., nec)

Tends load-testing machine to test coiled or leaf springs for conformance with load requirements: Positions spring on bed of machine. Turns hand gauges or positions block gauges to regulate travel of flattening ram. Pulls lever to lower ram and compress spring under specified load. Measures contraction of spring, using gauges. Rejects springs which do not contract specified distance. May measure spring dimensions, using micrometers, calipers, protractor, and plug gauges.
GOE: 06.03.02 STRENGTH: L GED: R2 M2 L2 SVP: 3 DLU: 77

616.685-038 METAL-SPONGE-MAKING-MACHINE OPERATOR (nonfer. metal)

Tends machine that makes metal sponges (scouring pads): Places spool of wire on spindle and threads end of wire around tension rollers and around winding spindle. Installs and threads additional spools of wire according to type of sponge to be made. Presses button to start machine that twists, curls, and winds wire around spindle to form sponge. Cuts wire when sponge has been formed. Removes sponge from spindle and pulls and pats sponge to specified shape. Packs sponges in cartons or bags.
GOE: 06.04.02 STRENGTH: M GED: R2 M1 L1 SVP: 3 DLU: 77

616.685-042 MULTI-OPERATION-FORMING-MACHINE OPERATOR II (any industry) alternate titles: forming-mill operator; roll-mill operator

Tends automatic multiple-operation machine that performs any combination of bending, punching, roll forming, beading, cutting and welding, soldering, or clinching of metal to fabricate items, such as rims, molding, panels, cans, tubing, and housings: Places roll of metal sheet, strip, or wire onto feedrack and threads end into drive rolls or through machine. Positions metal blanks manually into feed rolls, or feeds blanks into hopper or onto feed conveyor. Starts machine, observes operation, and verifies finished product visually or by using fixed gauges. May tighten bolts or turn knobs or handwheels to specified points on scale or dial to reset and maintain original setup of machine. May tend one or more work stations of mechanized line of machines operating in tandem. May tend slitting machine to cut body blanks from sheet metal and form seam cans. May be designated by function of machine as Body Maker (tinware); Tubing-Mill Operator (any industry) I.
GOE: 06.04.02 STRENGTH: M GED: R2 M1 L1 SVP: 2 DLU: 77

616.685-046 PAPERBACK-MACHINE OPERATOR (metal prod., nec) alternate titles: weaving-machine operator

Tends machine that stitches paperbacking to wire fabric used as floor and wall plaster lath: Loads paper roll and wire fabric onto unreeling stand, using hoist. Threads paper and wire fabric through guides, feed rollers, machine, and rewinder. Loads stitch wire of specified gauge onto reel and threads end into feed rollers. Adjusts machine to regulate length of stitch on fabric, using handtools. Adjusts cutters and crimping bar of machine to cut and bend protruding end of thread so that wire hooks on to fabric edge. Starts machine to stitch paperbacking to wire fabric. Removes reinforced wire fabric from rewinder, using hoist. Splices wire fabric rolls to specified length, using handtools.
GOE: 06.04.09 STRENGTH: L GED: R2 M1 L1 SVP: 3 DLU: 77

616.685-050 POCKET-MACHINE OPERATOR (furniture) alternate titles: pocketed-spring-machine operator

Tends one or more machines that automatically spin wire coils and sew them into cloth pockets to form units for mattress innersprings: Mounts spools of wire, fabric, and cotton thread on machine spindles. Inserts wire and fabric ends into machine guides and lead rollers, and threads machine needles. Starts machine and folds chain of pocketed coils as it emerges on conveyor. Removes springs at regular intervals and places under plunger of stationary dial gauge to ensure uniformity. Turns regulating wheel to adjust wire cutter for specified coil length. Turns setscrew on sewing machine to regulate thread tension.
GOE: 06.04.20 STRENGTH: L GED: R2 M1 L1 SVP: 3 DLU: 77

616.685-054 RIVETER (light. fix.)

Tends machine that joins flexible upright arms of desk lamps to metal bases: Clamps flexible arm in vise of machine and positions hole in lamp base over flexible arm. Depresses pedal, causing hammer of machine to repeatedly strike flexible arm to flatten and expand arm, securing arm to lamp base.
GOE: 06.04.20 STRENGTH: L GED: R2 M1 L1 SVP: 2 DLU: 77

616.685-058 RIVETING-MACHINE OPERATOR (furniture) alternate titles: machine riveter; rivet-hammer-machine operator

Tends machine that rivets metal furniture parts together: Aligns predrilled holes in parts and inserts rivets into holes. Positions and holds parts on die in machine bed. Depresses pedal or pulls lever to lower ram and die hammer that flattens shank, expanding shank and joining parts. May rivet together slide and cross bars to form cradles for holding file drawers in cabinets and be designated Cradle-Slide Maker (furniture).
GOE: 06.04.20 STRENGTH: M GED: R2 M1 L1 SVP: 2 DLU: 77

616.685-062 SCROLL-MACHINE OPERATOR (struct. metal)

Tends machine that forms metal stock, such as bars, rods, squares, tubing, and wire, into coils or ornamental scrolls: Positions and clamps specified scroll (die) into bed of machine. Threads workpiece through drag roll and clamps roll to center of die. Starts machine that turns die to draw workpiece along contour of die as vertical rod pushes workpiece into center of die, forming scroll or coil. May tend power shear or cutoff saw to cut stock to specified length. May insert leather strip along edge of die to protect finish of workpiece. May bend workpieces along edge of die manually.
GOE: 06.04.02 STRENGTH: M GED: R2 M1 L1 SVP: 2 DLU: 77

616.685-066 SLAT TWISTER (furniture)

Tends machine that shapes right-angle twist in ends of metal bed slats: Starts motor and places end of slat in machine. Depresses pedal that causes machine to twist slat and automatically stop when cycle is completed. Removes twisted end of slat from machine, reverses it, and twists other end.

GOE: 06.04.02 STRENGTH: M GED: R1 M1 L1 SVP: 2 DLU: 77

616.685-070 SPIRAL SPRING WINDER (metal prod., nec) alternate titles: recoil spring winder

Tends machine which coils light gauge metal strips or wire around rotating spindle to form springs used in clocks, watches, and instruments: Threads end of specified length of wire or strip along fixed peg or between guide blocks or rolls and through slot of spindle. Starts machine to rotate spindle that winds wire into coil. Examines coil for conformance with specifications. May tend machine that automatically threads wire through guides and into slot of spindle. May feed automatic shear or punch cutter to cut wire or strip to specified length. May record number of springs wound. May specialize in coiling hairsprings and be designated Hairspring Winder (metal prod., nec).
GOE: 06.04.02 STRENGTH: L GED: R2 M1 L1 SVP: 3 DLU: 77

616.685-074 SPIRAL WEAVER (metal prod., nec)

Tends automatic machines that coil, cut, and interlace wire into spiral-weave screen: Threads and pulls wire through pulling and coiling dies of machines and secures end around coiling die, using pliers. Adjusts distance between dies and speeds of wire feed and pulling-die rotation, according to size of wire and type of spiral weave, using handtools. Starts machines, monitors automatic operation and wire supply, and occasionally measures length of weave to verify conformance to specifications, using gauge. Stops machines when screens of specified length are woven.
GOE: 06.04.02 STRENGTH: L GED: R2 M2 L2 SVP: 3 DLU: 77

616.685-078 SWAGER OPERATOR (pen & pencil)

Tends machine that shapes tubular metal stock to form points or magazines for mechanical pencils: Positions precut stock into holding device of machine and flips switch to start machine that rotates stock. Flips another switch to move rotating holding device horizontally into set of forging dies to shape tube into points or magazines for mechanical pencils.
GOE: 06.04.02 STRENGTH: L GED: R2 M1 L1 SVP: 2 DLU: 77

616.685-082 SWEEP-PRESS OPERATOR (clock & watch)

Tends sweep press that cuts recesses, smooths rough spots, and rounds corners on watch plates and bridges: Positions plate or bridge over protruding pins of chuck. Moves controls that feed cutting head to plate or bridge. May verify dimensions of specified number of parts, using precision plug and indicator gauge. May replace worn or dull bits.
GOE: 06.04.02 STRENGTH: L GED: R2 M1 L1 SVP: 2 DLU: 77

616.685-086 WIRE COINER (button & notion)

Tends battery of machines that make scoop (slider-fastener chain part) impressions on roll of wire: Mounts roll of wire on spindle, threads wire end through machine and around spindle, and starts machine. Examines processed wire with microscope and micrometer to verify that impressions are aligned and pitched to specifications. Notifies supervisor of machine malfunctioning. Splices together ends of wire when breaks occur.
GOE: 06.04.02 STRENGTH: M GED: R2 M1 L1 SVP: 3 DLU: 77

616.685-090 ZIPPER CUTTER (button & notion)

Tends machine that cuts zippers of specified length from continuous strip and removes chain links from end of zipper to accommodate attachment of stops: Positions zipper strip against guide on machine bed or threads end of chain through guides and under blade and punch. Adjusts stop on calibrated scale to obtain specified length and aligns end of strip with stop. Depresses pedal that lowers blade and punch onto strip, cutting zippers for garments to specified length and removing chain links from end of zipper for attachment of stops. May tend machine that cuts zippers to specified length only.
GOE: 06.04.02 STRENGTH: L GED: R2 M1 L1 SVP: 2 DLU: 77

616.687-010 STRANDING-MACHINE-OPERATOR HELPER (nonfer. metal) alternate titles: cable-mill helper

Performs following duties to fabricate wire into cable: Positions spools of wire on spindle of winding reel, using hoist. Turns handwheel or manually removes release rod to release shaft preparatory to installing takeup spool onto reel jack. May remove unused wire from spools with spool stripper. Performs other duties as described under HELPER (any industry) Master Title.
GOE: 06.04.02 STRENGTH: H GED: R2 M1 L1 SVP: 2 DLU: 77

616.687-014 WIRE-WEAVER HELPER (metal prod., nec) alternate titles: loom helper

Assists WIRE WEAVER, CLOTH (metal prod., nec) in weaving wire cloth or screening: Transports beams, magazines, wire stock, and machine parts to looms. Attaches wire from spools to warp beam, threads *warp wire* through heddles and reeds of machine, and ties sections of warp wire together. Removes beams of finished screen or cloth from looms and transports them to stockroom or finishing department, using hoist, truck, conveyor, or dolly. Removes spools and bobbins from automatic spooling machines and racks them onto magazines. May thread warp wires individually through heddles, between teeth of reed, and fasten ends to roller. Performs other duties as described under HELPER (any industry) Master Title.
GOE: 06.04.02 STRENGTH: H GED: R2 M1 L1 SVP: 3 DLU: 77

617 FORMING OCCUPATIONS, N.E.C.

This group includes occupations, not elsewhere classified, concerned with shaping metal by the application of machine pressure.

617.130-010 SUPERVISOR (struct. metal)

Supervises and coordinates activities of workers engaged in coating, embossing, roll forming, and packaging aluminum house siding: Determines material and personnel requirements to meet specified production and coordinates work schedules to ensure efficient operations. Patrols work area to observe workers and machinery to ensure compliance with established work procedures. Examines sample workpieces to determine conformance with specifications, using blueprints and charts. Establishes quality standards for evaluation of products by inspectors. Assists workers in adjustment or repair of machines or equipment. Performs other duties as described under SUPERVISOR (any industry) Master Title.
GOE: 06.02.01 STRENGTH: L GED: R4 M3 L4 SVP: 6 DLU: 77

617.130-014 SUPERVISOR, FENCE MANUFACTURE (metal prod., nec)

Supervises and coordinates activities of workers engaged in operating machines that form steel wire into chain link fence mesh: Reads work ticket to determine material required to fill job orders. Patrols work area to ensure workers and machines meet production goals and product specifications. Confers with other supervisors to coordinate production. Trains new workers to operate, adjust, and lubricate fence making machines. Assists workers by setting up machines to meet production requirements. Performs other duties as described under SUPERVISOR (any industry) Master Title.
GOE: 06.01.01 STRENGTH: L GED: R4 M2 L2 SVP: 6 DLU: 77

617.260-010 PRESS OPERATOR, HEAVY DUTY (any industry) alternate titles: bending-press operator; hydraulic-press operator; toggle-press operator

Sets up and operates heavy-duty power press to bend, form, stretch, and straighten metal plates, metal extrusions, formed sheet metal, structural shapes, forgings, and weldments as specified by blueprints, layout, and templates: Plans sequence of operations, applying knowledge of physical properties of metal. Measures and sights along workpiece, using tape, rule, straightedge, and transit, to mark reference lines. Selects and positions flat, V-block, radius, or special purpose die sets into ram and bed of machine, using jib or crane. Aligns and bolts dies to ram and bed of machine, using gauges, templates, feelers, shims, and wrenches. Turns handwheel or levers to set depth and pressure of ram stroke. Preheats workpiece in furnace, using hand torch. Lifts and positions workpiece between dies of machine, using jib or crane and sledge. Starts machine to lower ram which bends or straightens workpiece between dies. Repositions workpiece and changes dies when making multiple or successive passes. Hand forms or finishes workpiece, using hand sledge and anvil. Grinds out burrs and sharp edges, using portable grinder. Inspects and marks job number on finished workpiece. May bend or straighten cold metal. May set dies to punch and blank heavy metal. May operate horizontal power press to bend or straighten long pieces of bar stock or structural shapes. May operate press equipped with two or more rams to bend angles or flanges or bend to radius by successive passes; or operate multiple acting hydraulic press to perform deep progressive and reverse draw operations of sheet metal. May be designated according to type press operated as Bulldozer Operator (any industry) II; Stretch-Press Operator (any industry); or according to shape product produced as Dishing-Machine Operator (any industry).
GOE: 06.02.02 STRENGTH: H GED: R3 M2 L2 SVP: 7 DLU: 77

617.280-010 SHOT-PEENING OPERATOR (aircraft mfg.)

Sets up and operates shot-peening equipment to shallow form and improve stress tolerance of flight vehicle metal surfaces, according to specifications: Reads and interprets blueprints, sketches, work orders, and other documentation to determine layout of specific areas to be shot-peened, sequence of operations, and finish specifications. Lays out and marks areas to be shot-peened on test specimen or part, using measuring and marking instruments, or fits template over part, scribes pattern, and peels away masking compound to expose areas to be treated. Mounts part on jig, rotary table, or in shot-peening cabinet. Fills hopper with specific size and type shot. Sets up, operates, and adjusts shot-peening equipment to achieve specified contour on test specimen or part. Measures and checks test specimen or part to verify conformance to specifications and to determine required equipment adjustments, using measuring instruments, templates, and fixtures. Records data on equipment settings and adjustments, such as feed rate, nozzle angles and oscillation, number and size of nozzles required, shot size, and air or vacuum pressure settings, to be used for subsequent operation and to develop numerical control programming data. Loads control media, such as computer tape, in control console of equipment, or enters commands to retrieve control instructions from computer data base to operate equipment automatically. Observes operation of equipment to detect malfunctions. Peels masking material from completed part, and cleans part with solutions to remove adhering scale and particles.
GOE: 06.02.02 STRENGTH: M GED: R4 M3 L4 SVP: 6 DLU: 87

617.360-010 BRAKE OPERATOR I (any industry) alternate titles: power-brake operator; press-brake operator

Sets up and operates power brake to bend, notch, punch, form rolls, arc, or straighten metal plates or sheet metal and structural shapes to blueprint or sketch specifications: Selects, positions, and aligns dies in machine ram and bed, using shims, rule, square, or templates. Turns setscrews or bolts to fasten clamp bar that holds dies in position. Turns adjustment screws to set specified pressure of ram and clearance between dies to thickness of metal, as indicated by calibrated scale or feelers. Lays out or details layout on work stock from blueprints or templates. Positions workpiece manually or with crane, to align layout marks to dies. Starts machine to lower ram or depresses pedal to activate ram that bends or cuts metal. Sets stops on machine bed and repositions stock to run successive shapes, or to perform multiple operations. Verifies dimensions of workpiece, using template or scale. May preheat metal in furnace or by using oxyacetylene torch. May grind laps or burrs from edges of workpiece, using portable grinder. May devise and build temporary dies. May operate apron brake which bends metal by forcing metal between movable apron and horizontal bending bar. May be designated according to type material processed as Brake Operator, Sheet Metal (any industry) I; or according to special operations required to process thick metal as Brake Operator, Heavy Duty (any industry).
GOE: 06.02.02 STRENGTH: H GED: R3 M3 L3 SVP: 6 DLU: 80

617.360-014 SWAGING-MACHINE ADJUSTER (ordnance) alternate titles: bullet-swaging-machine adjuster; swage toolsetter

Sets up automatic swaging machines that press lead wire or lead slugs into bullets or into cores for jacketed bullets: Positions and aligns forming die and punch in machine. Changes length and rate of punch and adjusts automatic feed and ejection mechanisms, using handtools and gauges. Starts machine to obtain sample bullets or cores. Examines finished product for defects, such as malformed nose or heel, nicks, and scratches, and determines cause. Verifies profile and dimensions, using fixed gauges. Weighs samples on balance scale to ascertain conformance to specifications. Operates speed lathe and polishing jack to reshape and polish worn punches and polishes dies by hand, using emery cloth. Gives instructions to new workers in machine operation and inspection.
GOE: 06.01.02 STRENGTH: M GED: R3 M2 L3 SVP: 6 DLU: 77

617.380-010 KICK PRESS SETTER (button & notion) alternate titles: tool setter

Sets up and adjusts battery of foot-powered presses that shape and assemble metal buckles, buttons, and parts: Obtains specified die and punch from rack according to size and shape of product. Installs die and punch in machine and adjusts stroke of press ram, using wrenches. Test-operates machine, and examines test-run product for defects, such as malformation, misalignment, dents, burrs, and scratches. Measures product to verify dimensions, using micrometer.
GOE: 06.01.02 STRENGTH: L GED: R3 M2 L3 SVP: 5 DLU: 77

617.382-010 TUBE BENDER, BRASS-WIND INSTRUMENTS (musical inst.)

Sets up and operates hydraulic press to bend tubes used in making brass-wind instruments: Fastens bending die onto press, using wrenches and screwdriver. Fits tube into revolving lateral die, using gauge to align center of tube under descending die. Starts press to lower overhead die and bend tube. Verifies accuracy of bend, using template. May cut tube to specified length, using table saw. May fill tube with lead to prevent wrinkling during bending. May bend tube around forming blocks manually. May press steel balls through tube or hammer pitch-filled tube to remove wrinkles.
GOE: 06.02.02 STRENGTH: M GED: R3 M2 L2 SVP: 4 DLU: 77

617.382-014 HAMMER OPERATOR (aircraft mfg.) alternate titles: planishing-hammer operator; power-hammer operator

Operates reciprocating power hammer to smooth and shape sheet metal used in manufacturing aircraft and aerospace products according to specifications: Reads blueprints and work orders to determine machine setup. Installs dies in machine according to surface contours, size, and thickness and hardness of metal to be shaped. Adjusts drive arm to regulate striking force of hammer. Applies lubricants to surfaces of metal and dies to prevent marring. Starts machine motor and depresses pedal to start action of hammer. Moves metal under hammer to attain specified shape. Observes metal during shaping to detect wrinkles and other defects. Compares finished part with template or sample part to verify conformance to specifications. Shapes part partially formed by machine to specified dimensions, using handtools. Trims excess materials from edges of parts, using shears. May push weighted roller over metal to smooth surfaces.
GOE: 06.02.02 STRENGTH: M GED: R3 M2 L2 SVP: 5 DLU: 87

617.480-010 JOB SETTER, SPLINE-ROLLING MACHINE (machine shop)

Sets up automatic spline roll-forming machines to cold-form splines on gear shafts according to machine setup instructions and knowledge of operational capabilities of machine, using handtools and gauges: Places shims to position die-racks (used to form teeth on splines by pressure-rolling action) at specified height and verifies position with micrometer. Turns knob to adjust vernier gauges and obtain specified spacing of die mounts. Places die-racks in mounts and clamps racks in position. Places spline blank between machine centers and positions machine tailstock to accommodate length of workpiece. Starts and cycles machine to verify operation specified. Inspects trial run splines for conformance to specifications, using micrometer and gauges. Adjusts machine to correct faulty setup if splines do not meet specifications. May set up roll-forming machines to cold-form threads on gear shaft and be designated Job Setter, Thread-Rolling Machine (machine shop).
GOE: 06.01.02 STRENGTH: M GED: R3 M2 L3 SVP: 5 DLU: 77

617.480-014 PRESS SETTER (nonfer. metal; steel & rel.)

Sets up mechanical and hydraulic presses to produce powdered-metal parts, such as bearings, gears, filters, and rings according to blueprints and specifications, using handtools: Installs, positions, and aligns dies in press bed. Adjusts stroke of ram and punches to specified depth of fill and injection stroke, using handtools, and opens supply hopper valves to regulate flow of powder. Starts

machine to produce sample parts for inspection. Measures dimensions of and weighs parts to ensure parts meet specifications, using micrometer and balance scale. May set up sintering furnace. May mix powders [MIXER (nonfer. metal; steel & rel.)].
GOE: 06.01.02 STRENGTH: M GED: R3 M2 L2 SVP: 5 DLU: 77

617.482-010 BENDING-MACHINE OPERATOR I (any industry)
Sets up and operates machine to bend metal structural shapes, such as bars, rods, angles, pipes, and tubes, to angle or contour specified by work order, drawings, templates, or layout: Selects and bolts holding clamp, die block, and guide clamp to machine. Positions and clamps end stops on machine to set specified location of bend. Inserts or screws plug stops into guide wheel to set specified degree of bend. Positions workpiece against end stop. Locks holding clamp and guide clamp onto workpiece. Lubricates workpiece with oil. Starts turntable that draws workpiece through guide clamp around die block until stopped by plug stops or until dial indicator points to specified degree of bend. May slide mandrel into tubing instead of using guide clamp. May preheat workpiece, using hand torch or heating furnace. May use hand-powered bending machine for short runs. May fill tubes or pipe with sand, resin, or lead to prevent wrinkling or collapsing during bending operation. May heat tube, using torch, and manually bend tube or pipe around forming blocks. May flare tube ends, using tube flarer and cut or trim metal stock to length, using power shears or saws. May be designated according to type of stock bent as Pipe-Bending-Machine Operator (construction); Rod-Bending-Machine Operator (any industry) I; Tube-Bending-Machine Operator (any industry) I.
GOE: 06.02.02 STRENGTH: M GED: R3 M2 L2 SVP: 5 DLU: 77

617.482-014 FORMING-ROLL OPERATOR I (any industry)
Sets up and operates rolling machine to straighten, knurl, or form contours in surfaces of metal cylinders and rings as specified by blueprints, templates, and work orders: Selects male and female rolling dies or rolling dies and *forming chuck* from data charts to form specified contour. Positions, aligns, and bolts dies or die and forming chuck onto parallel spindles of machine. Positions workpiece over inner dies or forming chuck. Positions and clamps end guides or clamps workpiece to forming chuck. Starts machine to activate inner drive roll or chuck. Moves lever to press outer roll on workpiece to shape workpiece to specified contour. Verifies contour, using rule or template. May operate machine equipped with vertical table to tilt and force workpiece at angle to plane of opposing rolls to expand outer edge or form flanges to specified shape. May operate machine equipped with multiple sets of opposing rolls which expand and shrink diameter of workpiece to form contours. May move lever to position slitting knife to trim edge of workpiece. May be designated according to type of rolling machine operated as Beading-Machine Operator (any industry) I; Forming-Roll Operator, Heavy Duty (any industry).
GOE: 06.02.02 STRENGTH: H GED: R3 M2 L2 SVP: 4 DLU: 77

617.482-018 ROLL-FORMING-MACHINE OPERATOR I (any industry)
Sets up and operates machine to form longitudinal bends, rolls, beads, or embossed design onto sheet metal strips by action of two or more roller dies to fabricate items, such as molding, trim, weatherstrip, and structural shapes specified by work order or diagram: Bolts specified roller dies and drives rolls onto spindles. Positions spindles to align male and female roller dies and adjusts rolls to thickness of metal, using feelers, rule, shims, gauges, and handtools. Sets side guides. Turns knobs to set footage meter and control which stops machine or activates automatic shear when specified length of strips has been run. Lifts coils of metal onto feedrack, manually or by hoist, and threads end into feed roll. Directs flow of coolant onto rolls or fills oilcups. Starts machine, observes operation, and verifies dimensions of finished products, using micrometers, gauges, and rule. Threads end of formed stock onto rewind spindle and cuts it to specified length, using hand shears, or removes finished pieces from machine bed. May butt-weld ends of coil together to form continuous feed. May feed precut strips of metal into machine. May turn knobs or install gears to adjust speed of machine. May verify coolant levels in machine and oil and grease moving parts as specified.
GOE: 06.02.02 STRENGTH: M GED: R3 M3 L3 SVP: 5 DLU: 77

617.482-022 SPRING FORMER, MACHINE (metal prod., nec) alternate titles: spring bender; submarine operator
Sets up and operates machine to form leaf-type spring leaves: Installs upper and lower dies in machine, following leaf spring, using handtools. Positions heated leaf blank onto lower die, using tongs. Depresses pedal or pulls lever to force dies together, forming curved leaf. Immerses leaf in quenching oil for cooling and hardening if machine does not perform this function automatically. May heat leaf blanks in furnace and form them by hand.
GOE: 06.02.02 STRENGTH: M GED: R3 M2 L1 SVP: 4 DLU: 77

617.482-026 STRAIGHTENING-PRESS OPERATOR II (any industry) alternate titles: straightener
Operates power press equipped with pressure blocks or dies to straighten warped or bent metal objects, such as plates, structural castings, shapes, forgings, and shafts to specified dimensions: Examines workpiece to locate defects, using such devices as straightedge, deflection gauge, template, and square. Positions and locks specified pressure blocks, or die, into ram of machine, or positions shims under high spots of workpiece. Lifts and positions workpiece into bed of machine manually or using jib or crane. Starts ram which presses out bent or high spots of workpiece. Reexamines and repositions workpiece, changing shims for each pass until workpiece conforms with specifications. May turn

levers or handwheels to adjust depth and pressure of ram. May preheat metal, using heating furnace or hand torch and clean dies between pressings, using compressed air, oil, and brush. May tend machine equipped with preset dies to bend metal to specified shapes. May grind rough edges from finished workpiece, using portable hand grinder. May be designated according to part straightened as Barrel Straightener (ordnance) II; Crankshaft Straightener (auto. mfg.); Gear Straightener (auto. mfg.); or according to type press operated as Gag-Press Straightener (steel & rel.).
GOE: 06.02.02 STRENGTH: M GED: R3 M2 L1 SVP: 5 DLU: 77

617.585-010 SWAGING-MACHINE OPERATOR (ordnance) alternate titles: bullet-swaging-machine operator; forming-machine operator
Tends battery of automatic swaging machines that form lead wire or slugs into bullets or cores for jacketed bullets: Threads lead wire from reel over take-up pulleys and through feed mechanism and between forming wheels, or fills machine hopper with cylindrical lead slugs. Starts machine and observes feeding, forming, and ejecting mechanisms to detect malfunction. Examines finished pieces for malformation and scratches. Verifies weight, contour, and dimensions, using balance scale and fixed gauges. Mixes oil and kerosene in prescribed proportion and fills machine wells to lubricate lead wire or slugs. Notifies SWAGING-MACHINE ADJUSTER (ordnance) of machine malfunction. May make minor adjustments, such as replacing worn dies, using handtools.
GOE: 06.04.02 STRENGTH: M GED: R2 M1 L1 SVP: 2 DLU: 77

617.665-010 NAIL-MAKING-MACHINE TENDER (steel & rel.)
Tends machines that automatically cut and shape wire to make nails of specified size: Mounts coil of wire on rod, and threads wire through straightening rollers and feeding mechanism into slots of die plates. Tightens roller bolts to regulate feed of wire, using wrench. Starts machine. Inspects nails for such flaws as chips and distortions. Measures sample nail, using split gauge or micrometer, and notifies NAIL-MAKING-MACHINE SETTER (steel & rel.) of deviations from specifications. Records production data. May tend machines that automatically cut coiled wire and attach tackheads to form tacks of specified size. May tend machine that bends and cuts wire to form spokes for tricycle wheels and be designated Spoke Maker (toy-sport equip.).
GOE: 06.04.02 STRENGTH: M GED: R2 M1 L1 SVP: 2 DLU: 77

617.682-010 BARREL-DEDENTING-MACHINE OPERATOR (beverage) alternate titles: dedenter
Operates machine to remove dents from metal barrels: Positions barrel on lower die of machine, aligning bunghole under water spout of machine. Turns side dies of machine to align contour of dies with contour of barrel ends. Presses switch that closes side, top, and bottom dies around barrel. Pumps water into barrel, forcing walls of barrel against dies and removing dents. Stops pump and opens dies after specified water pressure has been attained. Examines surfaces of barrel to verify smoothness. Pushes barrel from lower die onto conveyor. May drain de-dented barrels, pressurize barrels with air, and place barrel in water tank to detect leaks.
GOE: 06.04.02 STRENGTH: M GED: R2 M1 L1 SVP: 4 DLU: 77

617.682-018 HOBBING-PRESS OPERATOR (any industry)
Operates hydraulic press that forces hard steel hob into soft steel block to form molding die: Receives premarked soft steel block and specified hob from set-up worker. Places block in retainer ring of press and positions hob on block. Places plug block over hob to hold hob in alignment. Turns handwheel to raise ram which holds block and hob in place. Starts pumps to build up prescribed hydraulic pressure. Pulls lever to exert pressure on ram which embeds hob in soft block to specified depth, forming impression die. Removes block manually and clamps it in vise. Taps block with hammer to loosen hob and removes it from block. Inspects die for defects, such as rips or flaws, using magnifying glasses.
GOE: 06.02.02 STRENGTH: L GED: R3 M1 L1 SVP: 4 DLU: 77

617.682-022 SETTER, COLD-ROLLING MACHINE (machine shop)
Sets up and operates single- or double-die gear roll-forming machines to rough and finish roll-forming of gears, according to design information and machine operating instructions: Mounts and centers forming dies on opposing die spindle heads, using handtools. Sets stops to control traversing of die spindle head to predetermined operating position. Adjusts each die spindle to form gears as specified and adjusts and locks phase adjustor to obtain designated rotational timing of dies with gear teeth on workpiece. Positions arbor on machine to form gears of specified diameter. Adjusts speed of arbor motor with speed of dies to ensure clash-free engagement of dies with workpiece. Mounts gear blank on arbor and starts machine to produce trial run gear to verify setup of machine. Feels and inspects gear to detect defects, such as burrs, using gauges and micrometers. Adjusts machine to correct faulty machine setup if gears do not meet specifications. Pushes buttons to start automatic operation of machine and monitors forming of gears.
GOE: 06.02.02 STRENGTH: M GED: R4 M3 L3 SVP: 7 DLU: 77

617.685-010 BENDING-MACHINE OPERATOR II (any industry)
Tends machine that bends metal structural shapes, such as bars, strips, rods, angles, and tubes to specified angle or contour: Positions workpiece against end stops. Locks holding clamp and guide clamp onto workpiece. Lubricates workpiece with oil. Pulls lever or depresses pedal to activate turntable which draws workpiece through guide clamp and around die block until stopped by plug stops. May slide mandrel into tubing instead of using guide clamp. May

use hand-powered bending machine. May perform such fabricating tasks as flaring tube ends, using tube flarer, or cutting metal stock to length, using power shears or saws. May attach specified die to machine, using wrench. May be designated according to type of stock bent as Rod-Bending-Machine Operator (any industry) II; Tube-Bending-Machine Operator (any industry) II; or type of machine tended as Two-Stage, Steel-Bender Annealer (toy-sport equip.).
GOE: 06.04.02 STRENGTH: M GED: R2 M1 L1 SVP: 3 DLU: 78

617.685-014 CORNER FORMER (wood. container)
Tends machine that forms angle iron used in making wood boxes: Shifts lever to start machine. Positions and holds metal strip on die of machine as V-shaped periphery of roller attached to ram passes over metal, pressing metal into shape of angle iron. Removes angle iron from machine.
GOE: 06.04.02 STRENGTH: L GED: R2 M1 L1 SVP: 3 DLU: 77

617.685-018 EMBOSSING-MACHINE OPERATOR (nonfer. metal)
Tends machine that embosses designs on sheet metal: Positions embossing roll of specified design and size in machine and adjusts roll clearance and tension, width of feed table, and roll guides according to dimensions of sheet metal, using hoist, gauges, and handtools. Starts machine and feeds sheets into roll or places coil of metal on unwind spindle and threads coil end through machine onto rewinder. Measures depth of embossed design, using micrometer and adjusts machine roll to meet specifications.
GOE: 06.04.02 STRENGTH: M GED: R2 M2 L2 SVP: 4 DLU: 77

617.685-022 EXPANDING MACHINE OPERATOR (steel & rel.) alternate titles: belling machine operator
Tends machine that expands pipe ends to specified diameter by one of following methods: (1) Starts machine that rotates pipe against die to expand end of pipe. (2) Places pipe in expanding machine and starts machine that forces mandrels into end to expand pipe to specified diameter. (3) Starts machine that inserts and expands cylindrical element within pipe to enlarge pipe to specified diameter. Pushes pipe along conveyor rolls to expander block. Verifies dimensions of pipe end with ring or plug gauge. Important variables may be indicated by trade names of machine used.
GOE: 06.04.02 STRENGTH: M GED: R2 M2 L2 SVP: 3 DLU: 77

617.685-026 POWER-PRESS TENDER (any industry)
Tends power press that cuts, punches, or stamps various size articles from sheets or blocks of materials: Bolts or clamps specified die to machine. Positions or clamps sheet or block of material on machine bed or in holding fixture to obtain maximum cuts from each sheet. Starts machine and depresses pedal or moves lever that rotates or forces cutting die through sheet or block to obtain article of specified size and shape. May tend machine that automatically feeds and positions material under die for cutting. May examine parts for defects, visually or using measuring gauges, and discards parts not meeting specifications. May be designated according to type of machine tended as Blanking-Machine Operator (any industry); Punch-Press Operator (any industry) IV; Stamping-Press Operator (any industry).
GOE: 06.04.02 STRENGTH: M GED: R2 M1 L2 SVP: 3 DLU: 89

617.685-030 RIPPER (furniture)
Tends flaring machine that assembles display stands consisting of tube with disk attached to either end: Inserts end of tube through hole in disk, sets tube in jig on machine table, and starts machine. Depresses pedal to raise table and force upper end of tube against rotating flaring tool to hold disk on tube. May glue felt over outside faces of disks.
GOE: 06.04.20 STRENGTH: L GED: R2 M1 L1 SVP: 2 DLU: 77

617.685-034 ROLL-FORMING-MACHINE OPERATOR II (any industry)
Tends machine that forms longitudinal bends, rolls, beads, or embosses designs onto sheet metal strips to form items, such as molding, structural shapes, and weatherstripping: Bolts specified roller dies onto prepositioned spindles. Loads coils of strip onto feedrack. Turns knob to set footage meter and control which stops machine, or activates automatic shear. Threads end of coil into feed rolls. Starts machine to form and cut strip to specified length. Removes bundles of cut and finished pieces from machine bed. Inspects finished pieces visually or using fixed gauge. May weld together ends of feed coils to form continuous feed, using automatic butt welder.
GOE: 06.04.02 STRENGTH: M GED: R2 M1 L1 SVP: 2 DLU: 77

617.685-038 SINTERING-PRESS OPERATOR (nonfer. metal; steel & rel.) alternate titles: briquette-press operator; coining-press operator; compact-press operator
Tends mechanical or hydraulic presses which compress metal powders into parts, such as bearings, gears, filters, and rings, and coin them to specified size: Pours metal powder into hopper. Starts press, observes operation, and notifies PRESS SETTER (nonfer. metal; steel & rel.) of malfunctions. Examines finished part for nicks, burrs, and cracks. Weighs parts on scale and measures dimensions, using micrometers or fixed gauges, to ensure conformance to specifications. May adjust shuttle mechanism to regulate amount of powder in part. Places finished parts on tray or in stock pan. May write identifying information, such as mix number, number of parts, and date, on tag and attach it to tray or pan. Feeds parts into coining press to correct distortions created in sinking process. Removes parts from press and inspects them for burrs or other imperfections. Places parts on tray or in stock pan. May tend forming presses that fabricate clockwork parts from powdered metal.

GOE: 06.04.10 STRENGTH: L GED: R2 M2 L2 SVP: 2 DLU: 77

617.685-042 SWAGE TENDER (ordnance)
Tends swage machine that chokes (reduces) inside diameter of muzzle end of shotgun barrel to enable pellets or shot to concentrate when gun is fired: Inserts and clamps shotgun barrel into holding device and starts machine that exerts contraction pressure on end of barrel to reduce inside diameter of barrel. Measures diameter of barrel bore, using dial gauge to verify that choke of barrel meets specification.
GOE: 06.04.02 STRENGTH: L GED: R2 M1 L1 SVP: 2 DLU: 77

617.686-010 HOOP COILER (wood. container) alternate titles: hoop-rolls operator
Feeds flat strips of hoop steel, in which rivet holes have been punched, into rolls of machine to form barrel hoops.
GOE: 06.04.02 STRENGTH: M GED: R1 M1 L1 SVP: 2 DLU: 77

619 MISCELLANEOUS METALWORKING OCCUPATIONS, N.E.C.

This group includes occupations, not elsewhere classified, concerned with shaping and conditioning metal by such means as rolling, forging, extruding, blanking, and pressworking. The blanking and pressworking of nonmetallic materials, except wooden, are also included when the methods and machine tools commonly applied to the working of metal are used.

619.130-010 HYDRAULIC-PRESSURE-AUTO-FRETTAGE-MACHINE-OPERATOR SUPERVISOR (ordnance) alternate titles: cold-working supervisor
Supervises and coordinates activities of workers engaged in setting up and operating hydraulic-pressure-auto-frettage machines to cold-work interior of artillery barrels. Performs duties as described under SUPERVISOR (any industry) Master Title.
GOE: 06.02.02 STRENGTH: L GED: R4 M3 L4 SVP: 7 DLU: 77

619.130-014 SUPERVISOR, ALUMINUM FABRICATION (ship-boat mfg.)
Supervises and coordinates activities of workers engaged in fabricating aluminum sheets in preparation for assembly into boats: Trains new workers in performance of tasks, such as stretching, shearing, and trimming aluminum sheets. Inspects work in progress to ensure adherance to company standards. Confers with other supervisors to coordinate interdepartmental workflow. Performs other duties as described under SUPERVISOR (any industry) Master Title.
GOE: 06.02.01 STRENGTH: M GED: R4 M3 L3 SVP: 8 DLU: 77

619.130-018 SUPERVISOR, COLD ROLLING (steel & rel.)
Supervises and coordinates activities of workers engaged in pickling, annealing, cold and temper rolling, and slitting and shearing steel strip or plate: Reads rolling order and production schedule for processing specifications for each unit. Inspects material from each unit for conformance to metallurgical and customer specifications. Determines adjustments required to correct defects noted and directs workers in adjusting machines and equipment to fabricate items meeting specifications. Trains new workers. Performs other duties as described under SUPERVISOR (any industry) Master Title. May supervise pickling and annealing operations only and be designated Supervisor, Cleaning And Annealing (steel & rel.).
GOE: 06.02.01 STRENGTH: L GED: R4 M3 L3 SVP: 6 DLU: 78

619.130-022 SUPERVISOR, CONTINUOUS-WELD-PIPE MILL (steel & rel.) alternate titles: rolling supervisor; continuous-pipe mill
Supervises and coordinates activities of workers engaged in heating, forming, and welding flat steel strips (skelp) to produce butt-welded pipe by continuous welding process. Examines pipe for conformance to dimensional specifications, using gauge and measuring tape. Records production. Performs duties as described under SUPERVISOR (any industry) Master Title.
GOE: 06.02.01 STRENGTH: M GED: R4 M3 L3 SVP: 8 DLU: 77

619.130-026 SUPERVISOR, HOT-WOUND SPRING PRODUCTION (metal prod., nec) alternate titles: supervisor, coil springs
Supervises and coordinates activities of workers engaged in pointing, coiling, and load testing hot-wound springs. Trains workers in operation of equipment. Inspects springs for conformance to specified tension and dimensions, using tension-testing machine and gauges. Performs other duties as described under SUPERVISOR (any industry) Master Title.
GOE: 06.02.01 STRENGTH: L GED: R4 M3 L3 SVP: 8 DLU: 77

619.130-030 SUPERVISOR, LINE (any industry) alternate titles: machine supervisor
Supervises workers engaged in layout and machine operating to fabricate structural, wire, or sheet metal products, applying knowledge of layout, product design, machine functions, capacities, and output potential: Requisitions material required to meet production goals. Examines items produced to determine if items meet specifications. Trains new workers. Performs other duties as described under SUPERVISOR (any industry) Master Title. May be designated by department or operation as Lay-Out Supervisor (any industry); Machine-Operations Supervisor (any industry); Metal-Spinning Supervisor (any industry); Punch-Press Supervisor (any industry); Roll-Forming Supervisor (any industry); or product produced as Supervisor, Metal Furniture Fabrication (furniture).

GOE: 06.02.01 STRENGTH: L GED: R4 M2 L3 SVP: 8 DLU: 77

619.130-034 SUPERVISOR, MACHINE SETTER (any industry)
Supervises and coordinates activities of workers engaged in fabrication of structural metal products, applying knowledge of layout, product design, machine setup, capacities and output, fitting, and welding procedures: Analyzes work orders, workpiece, and blueprints to determine process, materials, machines, tooling, and sequence of operation. Assigns tasks to workers, and specifies methods of coordinating workflow to meet production schedules. Sets up machines, such as bending machines, spot welders, punch presses, drill presses, and brakes. Instructs workers in operation of machines. Inspects finished pieces visually and using precision measuring devices as rules, gauges, squares, and micrometers. Supervises such processes as fabricating, welding, stock handling, and assembling. Investigates malfunction of machines and equipment to determine need for repair. Performs other duties as described under SUPERVISOR (any industry) Master Title.
GOE: 05.05.06 STRENGTH: L GED: R4 M3 L4 SVP: 8 DLU: 77

619.130-038 SUPERVISOR, PIPE FINISHING (steel & rel.) alternate titles: finishing supervisor, weld-pipe continuous
Supervises and coordinates activities of workers engaged in straightening, facing, testing, cutting, and threading steel pipe, and in coating and bundling pipe for shipment. Inspects finished pipe for conformance to specifications, using micrometer, calipers, and gauges. Directs changes in machine set-ups when product fails to meet specifications. Trains new workers. Performs duties as described under SUPERVISOR (any industry) Master Title.
GOE: 06.01.01 STRENGTH: M GED: R4 M3 L3 SVP: 7 DLU: 77

619.130-042 SUPERVISOR, PUNCH-AND-ASSEMBLY DEPARTMENT (elec. equip.) alternate titles: core-assembly supervisor
Supervises and coordinates activities of workers engaged in fabricating and assembling laminations for rotor and stator cores. Trains workers in operation of slitting machines, power shear, punch press, and welding and brazing equipment. Performs duties as described under SUPERVISOR (any industry) Master Title.
GOE: 06.02.01 STRENGTH: L GED: R4 M3 L4 SVP: 7 DLU: 77

619.130-046 SUPERVISOR (comm. equip.)
Supervises and coordinates activities of workers engaged in fabrication of sheet metal chassis, cabinet components, and assemblies in television manufacturing facility: Reviews work orders to ascertain production goals and sequence of operations. Confers with members of management staff to arrange for assignment of workers required to meet production demands. Observes workers performing duties, reviews production reports, and confers with quality control personnel to evaluate work performance. Explains and demonstrates machine setup and inspection procedures to new workers. Assigns experienced workers to assist in training new workers. Conducts periodic inventories, and directs preparation of purchase orders according to company policy. Performs duties described under SUPERVISOR (any industry) Master Title.
GOE: 06.02.01 STRENGTH: M GED: R4 M3 L3 SVP: 7 DLU: 86

619.131-010 MACHINING-AND-ASSEMBLY SUPERVISOR (elec. equip.) alternate titles: supervisor, floor assembly
Supervises and coordinates activities of workers engaged in machining and assembling electric motors, generators, and control and switch gear apparatus: Directs placement of parts, such as stator core, rotor core, field yoke, or panelboard on machining or assembly floor to coordinate machine operation and assembly. Inspects machined parts and assembled units for conformance to specifications, using micrometers and other measuring instruments. May supervise workers engaged only in assembling or in machining electric motors, generators, and control and switch gear apparatus. Performs other duties as described under SUPERVISOR (any industry) Master Title.
GOE: 06.01.01 STRENGTH: L GED: R4 M2 L3 SVP: 5 DLU: 77

619.131-014 SHOP SUPERVISOR (struct. metal)
Supervises and coordinates activities of workers engaged in fabricating of products from pipe, such as trellises, playground equipment, cattle truck frames, hunting stands, and wire fence gates: Studies assembly diagrams to lay out work for pipe products. Measures and cuts pipe to length on pipe-cutting machine. Bends pipe around blocks and forms to shape it according to specification. Clamps pipe in position, and welds joints to assemble products [WELDER, COMBINATION (welding)]. Instructs workers to chip and paint pipe joints. Supervises workers engaged in fabricating and assembling gates. Counts and records quantities of fence building material, supplies, and tools taken from yard. Performs other duties as described under SUPERVISOR (any industry) Master Title.
GOE: 05.10.01 STRENGTH: M GED: R4 M3 L3 SVP: 7 DLU: 77

619.131-018 SHRINK-PIT SUPERVISOR (ordnance)
Supervises and coordinates activities of workers engaged in shrinking hoops, liners, breech rings, and tubes of heavy cannons. Calculates heating time required to shrink object according to diameter of parts and composition of steel. Performs other duties as described under SUPERVISOR (any industry) Master Title.
GOE: 06.02.01 STRENGTH: L GED: R4 M4 L3 SVP: 7 DLU: 77

619.132-010 LEAD-SECTION SUPERVISOR (ordnance)
Supervises and coordinates activities of workers engaged in extruding lead ingots into wire, swaging wire into cartridge components, such as bullet slugs and point fillers, and recasting scrap into ingots. Assists workers in adjusting equipment. Trains new workers. Performs other duties as described under SUPERVISOR (any industry) Master Title.
GOE: 06.02.10 STRENGTH: L GED: R4 M3 L3 SVP: 8 DLU: 77

619.132-014 SHEET-MILL SUPERVISOR (nonfer. metal)
Supervises and coordinates activities of workers engaged in rolling nonferrous ingots into sheets and in stretching, cutting, and coiling sheets to specifications: Verifies dimensions of sheets and coils, using gauge, calipers, and tape measure. Examines sheets for defects, such as scratches, dents, and wrinkles. Performs other duties as described under SUPERVISOR (any industry) Master Title. May be designated according to process as Cold-Mill Supervisor (nonfer. metal); Hot-Mill Supervisor (nonfer. metal).
GOE: 06.02.01 STRENGTH: L GED: R3 M2 L2 SVP: 7 DLU: 77

619.132-018 SHELL-SHOP SUPERVISOR (ordnance)
Supervises and coordinates activities of workers engaged in machining metal into finished shell cases. Organizes production line, determines placing of machines, and plans flow of materials. Oversees workers engaged in maintenance of equipment. Trains new workers. Performs other duties as described under SUPERVISOR (any industry) Master Title.
GOE: 06.02.01 STRENGTH: L GED: R4 M3 L2 SVP: 8 DLU: 77

619.132-022 STRUCTURAL-MILL SUPERVISOR (nonfer. metal)
Supervises and coordinates activities of workers engaged in tempering, sawing, and cleaning metal preparatory to production of aluminum-alloy structural forms, performing duties as described under SUPERVISOR (any industry) Master Title.
GOE: 06.02.01 STRENGTH: L GED: R4 M2 L3 SVP: 6 DLU: 77

619.132-026 SUPERVISOR, FINISHING-AND-SHIPPING (steel & rel.)
Supervises and coordinates activities of workers engaged in shearing, inspecting, and leveling steel sheet and plate to specified dimensions, and in storing and shipping finished sheet and plate. Gives workers directions in setting up machines to fabricate material meeting customer requirements and examines material for conformance to specifications. Trains new employees. Performs duties as described under SUPERVISOR (any industry) Master Title.
GOE: 06.01.01 STRENGTH: M GED: R4 M3 L3 SVP: 6 DLU: 77

619.132-030 SUPERVISOR, PLATE HEATING, ROLLING, AND FINISHING (steel & rel.)
Supervises and coordinates activities of workers engaged in charging and heating slabs in reheating furnaces, rolling slabs into plates, and in laying out and cutting plates to specified sizes. Trains workers in operation of furnace. Inspects finished plates for conformance to job order specifications. Performs duties as described under SUPERVISOR (any industry) Master Title.
GOE: 06.02.01 STRENGTH: M GED: R4 M3 L3 SVP: 8 DLU: 77

619.134-010 SUPERVISOR, CONDITIONING YARD (steel & rel.)
Supervises and coordinates activities of workers engaged in grinding, scarfing, or chipping defects from blooms, billets, or slabs preparatory to rolling. Directs crane operators in moving steel to and from conditioning yard. Performs duties as described under SUPERVISOR (any industry) Master Title.
GOE: 06.04.01 STRENGTH: M GED: R3 M2 L2 SVP: 8 DLU: 77

619.137-010 MACHINE-ADJUSTER LEADER (ordnance) alternate titles: adjuster leader
Supervises and coordinates activities of workers engaged in one phase of producing cartridges and shells. Performs duties as described under SUPERVISOR (any industry) Master Title. May be designated according to process supervised as Machine-Adjuster Leader, Bullet Assembly (ordnance); Machine-Adjuster Leader, Cannelure And Finish (ordnance); Machine-Adjuster Leader, Case Trim (ordnance); Machine-Adjuster Leader, Primer Assembly (ordnance).
GOE: 06.02.01 STRENGTH: L GED: R4 M3 L3 SVP: 8 DLU: 77

619.260-010 ORNAMENTAL-METAL-WORKER APPRENTICE (metal prod., nec) alternate titles: art-metal-worker apprentice; ornamental-metal-fabricator apprentice
Performs duties as described under APPRENTICE (any industry) Master Title.
GOE: 05.05.06 STRENGTH: M GED: R4 M3 L3 SVP: 8 DLU: 77

619.260-014 ORNAMENTAL-METAL WORKER (metal prod., nec) alternate titles: art-metal worker
Sets up and operates variety of machines and equipment to fabricate ornamental metal products, such as light fixtures, church statuary, lamps, plaques, and metal artwork, following sketches, artistic and architectural drawings, models, written descriptions, and photographs: Interprets data to select materials, lay out reference points, and develop sequence of operations. Operates metal fabricating machines, such as shears, saws, brakes, bending machines, and punch and forming presses, to cut stock to size and bend stock to shape. Heats pieces in forge to working temperature, as indicated by color. Bends, twists, and hammers hot or cold workpieces to achieve specified shape and ornamental imprints, using jigs, scroll iron, twisting fork, vise, and selected peening hammers. Operates machine tools to turn, drill, and mill metal to specified dimensions. Hammers and peens sheets of metal to form designs, such as flowers or leaves. Chases castings to finish metal statuary and plaques. Welds, forge welds, brazes, solders, rivets, or bolts components together to assemble workpiece. Grinds, buffs, and polishes surface to desired finish. Fabricates or forges special

jigs, tools, and peening hammers. May sculpture plaster patterns for ornamental castings. May hand paint finished items. May install finished product. May specialize in fabricating religious artwork and be known as Ecclesiastical-Art-Metal Worker (jewelry-silver.; metal prod., nec).
GOE: 05.05.06 STRENGTH: M GED: R4 M3 L3 SVP: 8 DLU: 77

619.261-010 INSPECTOR, METAL FABRICATING (any industry) alternate titles: plate-and-weld inspector; plate-shop inspector; structural inspector
Inspects materials received, finished products, and work in process of fabrication into metal products to ensure conformance with work orders and diagrammatic and template specifications: Measures centerlines and reference points to verify initial and assembly layout and machine setup, using layout plate, templates, squares, straightedge, feelers, tape, transit, and plumblines. Verifies physical properties and size of materials, such as plates, sheets, structural shapes, castings, forgings, dies, fixtures, and work produced by fabricating machines, using magnaflux machine, surface plate, hardness testing equipment, gauges, and micrometers. Verifies hole size, using plug gauge. Examines finished products for rough edges, cracks, and appearance. Marks parts for acceptance or rejection. Makes reports to suggest changes in dies, fixtures, and materials used. Reports inspection results. Makes sketches and recommends procedure for special salvage or scrapping operations. May inspect material for internal defects, using x-ray and ultrasonic test equipment. May specialize in single phase of inspection and be designated Lay-Out Inspector (any industry); Machine-Operations Inspector (any industry); Template Inspector (any industry).
GOE: 06.01.05 STRENGTH: L GED: R4 M4 L4 SVP: 7 DLU: 77

619.280-010 NEEDLEMAKER (button & notion)
Sets up and operates variety of machines to make latch and spring needles for use in manufacture of knitted or sewn goods: Selects dies, jigs, and fixtures working from blueprints. Machines hook, shank (holding device), and slot in needle, grinds needle including point, and mills jack to hold spring needle in place. May grind rivet to contour designed to lock latch of needle in place.
GOE: 06.01.03 STRENGTH: M GED: R4 M4 L3 SVP: 6 DLU: 77

619.280-018 SPRING-MANUFACTURING SET-UP TECHNICIAN (clock & watch)
Sets up and operates variety of metalworking machines to fabricate special-alloy spring wire for watches: Prepares and melts charge of molten metal in vessel (converter) to change form of metal. Sets up equipment and casts, rolls, draws, heattreats, and performs allied metalworking operations, using equipment, such as forging hammer, rolling mill, butt welder, strip-grinding machine, and heat-treating furnace. Diagnoses and corrects malfunctioning of equipment and machinery and makes replacement parts, using machinist's tools and equipment. Works to close metallurgical and dimensional tolerances.
GOE: 06.01.03 STRENGTH: L GED: R4 M4 L4 SVP: 7 DLU: 77

619.281-010 CASTING REPAIRER (any industry)
Repairs broken or cracked castings and forgings, using special cold process requiring no welding: Calculates factors, such as size, depth, and position of fracture, and tensile strength and distribution of stress and strain in material. Employs combination of holding and locking devices to make repair, using airhammers, air drills, air grinders, punches, and strippers to insert holding and locking devices in casting and to smooth finish. May fabricate special angle heads for airhammer, air grinder, and air drill, using blacksmith tools and anvil.
GOE: 05.10.01 STRENGTH: M GED: R3 M3 L3 SVP: 6 DLU: 77

619.361-010 FORMER, HAND (any industry)
Bends and straightens cold and hot metal plates, bars, structural shapes, and weldments to angles, curves, or flanges as specified by drawings, layouts, and templates, using form blocks, fixtures forming bars, sledge, power hammer and portable grinders: Lays out reference points onto workpiece and form blocks, using tape, compass, radius bar and applying knowledge of geometry, effects of heat, and physical properties of metal. Sets up and bolts or clamps fixtures, dies, and forming bars to form block to outline specified contour. Heats metal, using furnace or hand torch. Lifts, positions, aligns, and clamps or bolts workpiece to form block of fixture, using tongs or hoist. Bends workpiece, using bar or by hammering with sledge or mallet. Straightens out warps or bumps by hammering against face block or by heating with hand torch. Chips, trims, and grinds edges to specified contour, using chipping hammer and portable and stand grinder. Verifies size of workpiece, using ruler or template. May operate hand-powered machines, such as roll, brake, or bender. May be designated by product formed as Tool Bender, Hand (any industry).
GOE: 05.05.06 STRENGTH: M GED: R4 M3 L3 SVP: 7 DLU: 77

619.361-014 METAL FABRICATOR (any industry)
Fabricates and assembles structural metal products, such as framework or shells for machinery, ovens, tanks, stacks, and metal parts for buildings and bridges according to job order, verbal instructions, and blueprints: Develops layout and plans sequence of operations, applying knowledge of trigonometry, stock allowances for thickness, machine and welding shrinkage, and physical properties of metal. Locates and marks bending and cutting lines onto workpiece. Sets up and operates fabricating machines, such as brakes, rolls, shears, flame cutters, and drill presses [MACHINE OPERATOR (any industry) I 616.380-018]. Hammers, chips, and grinds workpiece to cut, bend, and straighten metal. Preheats workpieces, using hand torch or furnace. Positions, aligns, fits, and welds together parts [WELDER-FITTER (welding) 819.361-010]. Designs and constructs templates and fixtures. Verifies conformance of

workpiece to specifications, using square, ruler, and measuring tape. May fabricate and assemble sheet metal products. May set up and operate machine tools associated with fabricating shops, such as radial drill press, end mill, and edge planer.
GOE: 05.05.06 STRENGTH: H GED: R4 M4 L3 SVP: 7 DLU: 77

619.361-018 METAL-FABRICATOR APPRENTICE (any industry) alternate titles: ironworker apprentice, shop; structural-metal-fabricator apprentice
Performs duties as described under APPRENTICE (any industry) Master Title.
GOE: 05.05.06 STRENGTH: H GED: R4 M4 L3 SVP: 7 DLU: 77

619.362-010 FLANGING-ROLL OPERATOR (any industry)
Operates machine to roll specified flanges on metal disks and dished heads: Selects and bolts fixture onto free moving ram and powered turntable. Lifts and centers workpiece onto block or fixture on turntable, using hoist, sledge, rule, and tape. Pulls lever to lower ram onto workpiece, clamping it onto turntable. Selects and bolts rollers to spindles of machine, with edge of workpiece between rollers. Turns handwheel to adjust rollers to thickness and curvature of metal and to exert bending pressure. Starts machine which rotates edge of workpiece through rollers. Readjusts curvature and bending pressure to form specified flange on workpiece. Verifies curve of flange, using template.
GOE: 06.02.02 STRENGTH: M GED: R3 M2 L2 SVP: 6 DLU: 77

619.362-014 ROLL OPERATOR I (any industry) alternate titles: bending-roll operator; roll former
Operates rolling machine to bend metal plates, sheets, or bars into arcs, cylinders, or cones, using blueprints, templates, and knowledge of geometry and physical properties of metal to set up machine and plan sequence of operations: Pulls lever to lift upper roll, and positions workpiece into machine manually, or using crane. Lowers rolls and turns nuts or handwheel to lock roll into machine, and to adjust to thickness of metal if operating block (pinch) roll. Turns handwheel to adjust roll to set degree of curvature of initial pass. Starts machine and sets feed speed of workpiece back and forth between rolls. Adjusts roll between each pass to form workpiece into specified shape. Hammers workpiece to align it between rolls. Measures arcs with template. May set adjustment roll at angle to form conical shapes. May adjust roll to straighten warped or bent bars or plates [STRAIGHTENING-ROLL OPERATOR (any industry)]. May preheat metal, using hand torch or heating furnace. May prebend heavy metal or bars, using bull press or bulldozer [BULLDOZER OPERATOR (any industry) I]. May operate horizontal or vertical roll-forming machine to straighten or bend angles, bars, or channels into rings or arcs and be designated Angle-Roll Operator (any industry). May operate rolling machine to bend sheet metal to specified curvature and be designated Roll Operator, Sheet Metal (any industry). May operate vertical roll machine and adjust elevation of roller tables to support workpiece and be designated Vertical-Roll Operator (any industry).
GOE: 05.05.06 STRENGTH: M GED: R4 M3 L3 SVP: 7 DLU: 77

619.362-018 SPINNER, HAND (any industry) alternate titles: spinning-lathe operator
Sets up and operates spinning lathe to spin (form) shaped articles from sheet or plate metal, using blueprints and knowledge of physical properties of metal: Bolts specified spinning chuck to headstock spindle and follow block to tailstock, using handtools or power tools. Clamps metal disk to chuck by turning handwheel that forces follow block against disk. Secures steady rest fixture on cross-slide. Starts machine and coats outside of rotating disk with spinning compound. Positions, holds, and moves long-handled compound lever tool against disk, using steady rest as fulcrum point, to apply required pressure to form disk over and into shape of spinning chuck. Varies amount and location of pressure on disk according to type of metal, shape of spinning chuck, speed of lathe, and temperature and thickness of metal disk. Replaces steady rest with bar tool attachment, turns handwheel to set bar tool and cut off excess metal from workpiece. Verifies dimension of finished article with steel rule and diameter tape. May form wood spinning chucks by turning on lathe.
GOE: 06.02.02 STRENGTH: M GED: R3 M3 L3 SVP: 7 DLU: 77

619.362-022 SPINNER, HYDRAULIC (any industry) alternate titles: spinning-lathe-operator, hydraulic
Sets up and operates spinning lathe equipped with hydraulically controlled forming tools to spin (form) shaped articles from sheet or plate metal, compiling specifications from blueprints and knowledge of physical properties of metal: Lifts specified spinning chuck to machine spindle, manually or with power hoist, and bolts chuck in place, using handtools or power tools. Clamps metal disk to spinning disk. Starts machine and coats rotating disk with spinning compound. Turns valve to set pressure applied to disk according to type of metal, shape of spinning chuck, speed of lathe, and thickness of metal disk. Moves feed pump levers that hydraulically control pressure applied by forming tool, reads pressure gauges to determine amount of pressure applied, and guides tool against disk to form disk over and into shape of spinning chuck. Resets position of forming tool on steady rest to form disk into shape. Replaces forming tool with cutting tool to trim excess metal from shaped part. Verifies dimension of finished article with verniers.
GOE: 06.02.02 STRENGTH: H GED: R4 M3 L3 SVP: 6 DLU: 77

619.364-010 INSPECTOR I (nonfer. metal)
Inspects nonferrous metals and products, such as ingots, rods, sheets, plates, extrusions, and forgings, and records variations from standards and customer

specifications: Verifies dimensions, using measuring instruments, such as ruler, micrometer, and vernier calipers. Examines metal for defects, such as scratches, wrinkles, inclusions, and discolorations, and outlines defective areas, using chalk. Tests hardness of metal [HARDNESS INSPECTOR (heat treating)]. Records variations from dimensional specifications, type of defect, and test results. Reports inspection results to machine operators or supervisor. Inspects packaged material and products for conformance with packing, labeling, and shipping procedures. May band and stencil containers as specified by shipping documents. May obtain samples of metal for laboratory analysis.
GOE: 06.03.01 STRENGTH: L GED: R3 M3 L3 SVP: 6 DLU: 77

619.365-010 PRODUCTION-MACHINE TENDER (nut & bolt)
Tends one or more automatic machines to head, trim, roll-thread, slot, or tap metal stock to produce nuts, bolts, or other fasteners: Feeds machine by filling hoppers or loading coiled steel on reel and threading end of coil through feed rolls. Starts machine and observes operation. Measures parts, using rule or fixed gauge, to determine conformance to specifications. Frees stock jammed in feed mechanism, using rod. Stops machine and notifies supervisor when machine malfunctions or parts do not conform to specifications. Installs and adjusts cutting tools on machine, using wrench and rule. May be designated according to type of machine tended as Tapping-Machine Operator, Automatic (nut & bolt).
GOE: 06.04.02 STRENGTH: M GED: R2 M2 L2 SVP: 2 DLU: 77

619.380-010 HIGH-ENERGY-FORMING EQUIPMENT OPERATOR (aircraft mfg.)
Sets up and operates high energy (explosion) forming machine and associated equipment to shape metallic materials and parts used in manufacturing aeronautical and aerospace products, following operational procedures, blueprints, sketches, and specifications: Reviews instructions to plan work procedure. Trims or assists other workers in trimming preformed part to approximate shape of specified die, using handtools and power tools. Positions part against die and seals edges, using sealing compound. Evacuates air between part and die, using vacuum pump, and submerges part and die into water of forming tank. Prepares and assembles explosive charge and positions charge in forming tank. Detonates charge which forces part into shape of die. Removes part from tank, and examines part for defects.
GOE: 06.01.03 STRENGTH: M GED: R4 M3 L3 SVP: 6 DLU: 87

619.380-014 PUNCH-PRESS SETTER (any industry)
Sets up and installs dies into power presses to punch, notch, cut blanks, form or draw metal plates, strips, sheets, or blanks: Positions, aligns, and locks specified dies into machine ram and bed. Sets stops, guides, or installs jigs or fixtures for positioning workpiece. Adjusts depth and pressure of stroke. Operates press machine to verify functioning of dies. Examines stamped out metal parts to detect malfunctioning machine and defect in dies. May sharpen dies, using grinding machine. May assemble, align, and install progressive dies. May set up automatic punch presses.
GOE: 06.01.02 STRENGTH: M GED: R3 M2 L3 SVP: 6 DLU: 80

619.380-018 SPRING REPAIRER, HAND (automotive ser.) alternate titles: automobile-spring repairer
Sets up and operates forging and shop equipment to repair leaf-type springs used in automotive vehicles: Raises vehicle body, using jack, and removes defective spring. Removes defective leaves from spring, using handtools. Measures broken leaves and cuts out replacement leaf blanks from steel stock, using flame cutter or power shear. Presses ends of main-leaf blank against disk of *bench grinder* to bevel blank according to size of eyes to be formed. Drills or punches bolt holes in blanks, using drill or punch press. Places ends of main-leaf blank in furnace to soften ends and shapes ends of blank into eyes, using eye-forming tool. Reheats leaves and arches them to required specifications, using peen hammer. Quenches spring leaves in oil to temper them according to specifications. Places graphite-impregnated lining between leaves to prevent friction. Bolts and clips leaves together and forces bushings into spring eyes, using bushing press.
GOE: 05.05.06 STRENGTH: M GED: R4 M3 L3 SVP: 7 DLU: 77

619.381-010 INSPECTOR (steel & rel.) alternate titles: product inspector; steel inspector
Inspects steel products, such as blooms, bars, sheets, castings, and strips, for conformity to customer specifications, using measuring instruments: Examines product for flatness, straightness, and defects, such as cracks, slivers, or scars. Marks defective areas with chalk or paint. Verifies dimensions of product, using micrometers, gauges, tapes, and templates. Conducts hardness and heat resistance tests, using upset hammers, hardness testing machines, and heating furnaces. Rejects or regrades products not meeting specifications. Prepares reports covering materials scrapped or salvaged. May use ultrasonic equipment to detect internal and surface defects. May be designated by product inspected as Axle Inspector (steel & rel.); Billet Inspector (steel & rel.); Cold-Mill Inspector (steel & rel.); Finishing Inspector (steel & rel.); Hot-Roll Inspector (steel & rel.); Hot-Strip-Mill Inspector (steel & rel.). May be designated: Plate Inspector (steel & rel.); Rail Inspector (steel & rel.); Tubing Inspector (steel & rel.); Wheel Inspector (steel & rel.).
GOE: 06.03.01 STRENGTH: L GED: R3 M3 L3 SVP: 6 DLU: 78

619.381-014 EDDY-CURRENT INSPECTOR (steel & rel.)
Inspects stainless steel tubes for conformance to customer specifications, using eddy current testing equipment: Reads work order to determine tube tolerance specifications required by customer and type of electric inspection coil to use for tube inspecting. Positions and secures specified inspection coil in coil holder, and turns cranks to align rollers on which tubes pass through coil for inspection. Turns knobs to activate testing equipment. Observes pattern on CRT (cathode ray tube) screen and turns knobs to calibrate equipment settings in accordance with customer specifications, using knowledge of equipment operation and experience. Selects sample tube with known defects and passes it through coil to test equipment settings. Listens for defect detection alarm, depresses button to stop rollers, and observes patterns on CRT screen to ensure that equipment signals and reflects known defects in sample tube. Positions tubes to be inspected on rollers, marks locations of detected defects on rejected tubes with marker, and places defective tubes aside. Periodically cycles sample tube through coil to verify standard operation of equipment. Records information, such as control settings and number of tubes tested, on inspection and production reports. Cuts through defective sections of tubing or rubs nicks on tubing to expose internal or remove surface defects, using abrasive saw and paper.
GOE: 06.03.01 STRENGTH: M GED: R3 M2 L3 SVP: 4 DLU: 86

619.382-010 BULLET-GROOVING-SIZING-AND-LUBRICATING-MACHINE OPERATOR (ordnance)
Sets up and operates battery of hopper-fed machines to automatically groove or knurl, die-size, and lubricate bullets for small arms ammunition: Installs and adjusts grooving segments, lubricating and sizing die, feedpipes, and feeding mechanism, using handtools. Turns crank to withdraw plunger from cylinder and inserts wax stick lubricant which is force fed to lubricating die. Adjusts rheostat to heat and soften wax electrically in die box. Fills hopper with bullets and starts machine. Measures work samples to verify location and depth of grooves, and length and diameter of bullets, according to specifications, using fixed gauges. Inspects bullets to ensure that grooves are filled with lubricant. Turns stop nuts and setscrews to adjust machine by trial and error to produce acceptable bullets. Observes grooving and feeding mechanisms for jams. Removes jammed bullets, using fingers or wire pick.
GOE: 06.02.02 STRENGTH: H GED: R3 M2 L2 SVP: 4 DLU: 77

619.382-014 FITTINGS FINISHER (plumbing-heat.) alternate titles: lead fabricator
Operates lathe to form lead plumbing fittings to specified shape and diameter: Mounts lead pipe over mandrel on lathe. Starts lathe and presses special handtool against end of pipe, or turns handwheel to advance turret on which special tools are mounted to stretch and bend pipe against rounded end of mandrel to form traps of various sizes. Reduces or expands diameter of lead pipe openings by holding tool against outside or inside surface of rotating pipe. Inserts iron ring inside of expanded pipe or outside of reduced pipe. Rolls edge of pipe end over ring to hold it in place. May solder brass ferrule over end of lead bend to seal junction. May heat threaded brass ring and press reduced opening of pipe over ring to fuse them.
GOE: 06.02.02 STRENGTH: L GED: R3 M2 L2 SVP: 4 DLU: 77

619.382-018 FOUR-SLIDE-MACHINE OPERATOR I (any industry) alternate titles: multiple-slide operator; slide-forming-machine operator
Sets up and operates one or more slide-forming machines to automatically punch, cut, and form metal strips and wire by action of opposing rams to fabricate parts, such as spring washers, brackets, and clips, specified by sketches, blueprints, and setup charts: Selects cams, forming tools, and dies according to setup charts. Aligns and bolts specified cams to shaft, slides to bed, and forming tools and dies to slides using knowledge of machine operations, product dimensions, vernier calipers, micrometers, and gauges. Threads stock through stock straighteners and adjusts cams to synchronize action of slides that feed, cut off, and form part. Turns flywheel by hand to produce sample part and compares sample with specifications, using fixed gauges, micrometer, and calipers. Readjusts machine to achieve specified product dimensions. Starts machine and observes operation periodically gauging parts for conformance to specifications. Removes, replaces, and labels trays of finished parts when specified number have been produced. May inspect parts for defects, using shadowgraph. May weld ends of coils together, using butt-welding machine, to form continuous length of feed.
GOE: 06.02.02 STRENGTH: M GED: R4 M3 L3 SVP: 5 DLU: 77

619.382-022 TYPE-ROLLING-MACHINE OPERATOR (office machines)
Sets up and operates machines to roll and press-forge characters onto steel blanks to form typewriter type: Installs and aligns roller jaws, and blank-holding, letter-forming, and trimming dies, using handtools. Fills hopper with blanks and starts machine. Measures type samples for centrality, curvature, and height of characters, using fixture gauge, eye loupe, and shadowgraph or calibrated microscope. Compares measurements against type on chart and turns setscrews and shims tooling to align dies and type that conform to specifications. May hand feed machine by positioning blank in holding die in rotating table. May pry rolled type from holding die, using knife.
GOE: 06.02.02 STRENGTH: L GED: R3 M2 L1 SVP: 4 DLU: 77

619.387-010 SALVAGE WORKER (nonfer. metal)
Sorts and inspects metal rejected by inspection and mill departments for purpose of salvage: Receives and records numbers of rejected metals. Examines metal for defects, such as surface blemishes, flatness, straightness, or dimensional irregularities according to specifications, using rule, micrometer, and vernier gauges. Identifies and marks portion of metal to be salvaged. Routes salvageable metal to next operation and rejected metal to scrap department. May

inspect other specified steel products, such as bars and sheets, for conformance to dimensional specifications and quality standards.
GOE: 06.03.01 STRENGTH: M GED: R3 M2 L2 SVP: 4 DLU: 77

619.462-010 ROLL-THREADER OPERATOR (nut & bolt)
Sets up and operates one or more automatic machines to roll-thread hot or cold forged bolt blanks, according to work orders: Installs specified roll-threading dies in machine, using wrenches and rule. Adjusts distance between roll-threading dies to set pressure of threading dies on bolt shank, using rule and following product specifications. Fills feed mechanism with stock, or feeds bolt blanks by hand and starts machine. Measures bolts with micrometer, thread gauge, or rule, and adjusts dies and stops to maintain specified dimensions. May signal operator of crane to fill feed hoppers with stock. May set up machine for PRODUCTION-MACHINE TENDER (nut & bolt).
GOE: 06.02.02 STRENGTH: M GED: R3 M2 L2 SVP: 5 DLU: 77

619.462-014 TRIMMER OPERATOR (nut & bolt)
Sets up and operates one or more automatic machines to reduce shanks of forged bolt blanks preparatory to thread rolling, and to trim excess metal from bolt-blank heads: Installs dies in machine, using wrenches, rule, and pry bar. Visually sets ram stroke by turning adjusting screw of ram-stroke-controlling arm. Synchronizes knock-out pin with back stroke of ram by turning knock-out pin adjustment screw. Visually adjusts stock transfer arm to feed blanks to transfer finger. Adjusts transfer finger to accommodate stock and centers transfer finger over die opening by turning adjusting screw. Fills feed hopper with bolt blanks and starts machine. Measures shank and head of trial blanks with micrometer or rule and adjusts dies and stops to maintain specified dimensions. May signal worker to fill feed hopper with stock. May set up machine for PRODUCTION-MACHINE TENDER (nut & bolt).
GOE: 06.02.02 STRENGTH: H GED: R3 M2 L2 SVP: 5 DLU: 77

619.482-010 LATHE WINDER (metal prod., nec) alternate titles: coiler
Operates lathe to wind compression, extension, and torsion springs of specified diameter, pitch, and length from wire or bar stock. Lifts roll of stock onto holding device, threads stock through guides, and clamps wire to arbor. Starts machine to revolve arbor until specified number of coils are wound, guiding coils by hand or using pitch tool. Cuts spring from stock, using shears, and reverses arbor direction to remove spring. Measures spring for conformance to specifications, using micrometers and gauges, and adjusts arbor and pitch tool to obtain specified product. Closes ends of springs, using mallet. Squares and flattens spring ends, using grinding machine. May adjust length and pitch of formed springs, using mallet and wedge. May wind wire springs, using hand-powered lathe, and be designated Spring Coiler, Hand (metal prod., nec). May be designated according to product as Flexible-Shaft Winder (metal prod., nec).
GOE: 06.02.02 STRENGTH: L GED: R3 M3 L2 SVP: 4 DLU: 77

619.484-010 ORNAMENTAL-METAL-WORKER HELPER (metal prod., nec) alternate titles: art-metal-worker helper
Assists ORNAMENTAL-METAL WORKER (metal prod., nec) in performing any combination of following tasks: Cuts metal stock to specified size, using shears and saws. Bends or twists stock into specified shape, using handtools, bending jigs, scroll irons, and power brakes. Welds, brazes, forge welds, or bolts components together at designated points. Cleans and builds fire in heating forge. Heats and hammers metal to shape, using specified peening hammers. Grinds and polishes surface of workpieces to specified finish. Performs other duties as described under HELPER (any industry) Master Title.
GOE: 05.12.12 STRENGTH: M GED: R2 M1 L1 SVP: 5 DLU: 77

619.485-010 SPOOL WINDER (nonfer. metal)
Tends machine that winds solder wire onto metal spools: Positions empty spool on machine spindle and secures end of wire to spool. Depresses foot pedal and manually guides wire so that wire winds evenly along revolving spool. Weighs filled spool on scales and adds or removes wire to attain specified weight. Cuts wire with wire snippers and hooks end of wire on rim of spool. Verifies size and type of wire with label on end of spool. May tend machine that winds aluminum wire onto metal spools.
GOE: 06.04.02 STRENGTH: M GED: R2 M1 L1 SVP: 2 DLU: 77

619.485-014 TWISTING-MACHINE OPERATOR (any industry)
Tends machine that twists metal bars, squares, and blades to specified shape: Clamps end of workpiece into stationary holding fixture. Slides carriage, or raises spindle to adjust to length of workpiece and clamps other end of workpiece into chuck or fixture of drive spindle. Starts machine to rotate drive spindle and stops machine after specified number of turns or sets limit switch to stop machine. May install special fixtures and chuck to twist together two or more pieces. Examines finished work for conformance to specifications. May clamp end of workpiece in vise, slide pipe over workpiece to prevent longitudinal warping, and twist workpiece, using pipe wrench or twisting fork.
GOE: 06.04.02 STRENGTH: M GED: R2 M1 L1 SVP: 2 DLU: 77

619.582-010 STRETCHER-LEVELER OPERATOR (nonfer. metal)
Operates machine to stretch metal sheet, strip, or rod to specified length or flatness, or correct extrusion twist and contour defects: Adjusts stretcher blocks to size of metal, using wrench. Lifts and positions material in stationary vise. Measures metal and compares dimensions to those specified to determine stretch required, using micrometer, tape measure, and tolerance tables. Moves controls to clamp metal in stretcher jaws and starts machine to stretch material. Verifies amount of stretch by visual inspection or meter readings attached to

vises. Removes metal and places it on level table to test flatness. Records crew time and production record.
GOE: 06.02.02 STRENGTH: M GED: R3 M2 L2 SVP: 5 DLU: 77

619.662-010 SHRINK-PIT OPERATOR (ordnance) alternate titles: pyrometer operator
Controls shrink-pit furnace to assemble hoops and liners to tubes to form cannon barrels: Positions steel blocks in shrink-pit to form angle for subsequent positioning of tube so that breech end of tube will be at floor level. Cleans and oils contact surfaces of parts with gasoline, oil, and graphite to facilitate assembly. Lowers hoops into furnace, using hoist. Moves furnace controls and observes thermocouple pyrometer and recording potentiometer to heat furnace to specified temperature. Guides cold tube, lowered by crane, through hot hoops in furnace. Turns water valve on cooling ring and lowers ring into furnace, using hoist, to spray hoops and shrink them onto tube. Reheats hoop and tube assembly, guides liner into tube, and regulates water spray to shrink tube onto liner.
GOE: 06.02.10 STRENGTH: M GED: R3 M2 L2 SVP: 5 DLU: 77

619.662-014 SKELP PROCESSOR (steel & rel.) alternate titles: pipe processor
Controls operation of machinery and equipment, such as coil car, uncoiler, rollers, power shears, and hoist, using console, from pulpit in welding mill to form skelp (metal coil) into metal pipe: Receives signal through intercom to begin machine operation. Moves levers and presses buttons on control console to position coil car under overhead hoist and receive supply of skelp. Observes operation of car that transports skelp through series of processing operations, such as uncoiling skelp, rolling coil into sheets, and shearing sheets into specified size prior to welding and forming metal into pipe. Observes operation from pulpit to detect camber (curves in skelp sheet) and machine malfunctions, such as jam-ups. Stops machinery when malfunctions occur and removes sections of cobble (damaged or defective skelp), using acetylene torch. Assists workers in setting up and adjusting machines and equipment, using handtools and measuring instruments. Signals OVERHEAD CRANE OPERATOR (any industry) 921.663-010 to restock or remove skelp and cobble from operating pit.
GOE: 06.02.10 STRENGTH: L GED: R3 M2 L2 SVP: 4 DLU: 86

619.665-010 WINDING-MACHINE OPERATOR (concrete prod.)
Tends electrically powered machine that winds wire, under tension, around rotating steel cylinders to form reinforced cores for concrete pipe: Signals OVERHEAD CRANE OPERATOR (any industry) 921.663-010 to position cylinders between chucks of machine. Pulls levers to engage and secure cylinder in chucks. Signals WELDER, ARC (welding) 810.384-010 to weld end of wire to cylinder. Starts machine to wind wire on cylinder when signaled by TENSIONING-MACHINE OPERATOR (concrete prod.) 616.665-010. Signals WELDER, ARC (welding) to weld ends of wire to cylinder. Pushes levers to release wire from cylinder chucks, and signals INDUSTRIAL-TRUCK OPERATOR (any industry) 921.683-050 to remove cylinder from machine.
GOE: 06.04.02 STRENGTH: L GED: R2 M1 L1 SVP: 2 DLU: 77

619.682-010 BELL SPINNER (musical inst.)
Operates spinning lathe to spin (form) and clean musical instrument bells: Bolts bell-shaped mandrel onto lathe and positions and locks bell on mandrel. Starts bell rotating and positions forming tool in holding device. Holds and moves forming tool along bell, applying pressure to form bell to shape of mandrel. Holds cutting tool against spinning bell to trim bell to size. Removes tarnish and scale from bell, using file, chisel, and emery cloth. Holds scraping tool against bell head to remove excess solder. Holds bead tool against bell to roll edge back, forming bead cavity. May burnish bell with burnishing tool. May insert wire into bead cavity and close cavity with bead tool. May be designated according to instrument as Bell Spinner, Sousaphones (musical inst.).
GOE: 06.02.02 STRENGTH: H GED: R3 M2 L3 SVP: 7 DLU: 77

619.682-014 COUPLING-MACHINE OPERATOR (steel & rel.)
Operates machine to connect metal couplings to pipes: Sets tightening mechanism on machine to correspond to specified numbers of turns. Puts coupling into machine. Starts machine that connects and tightens coupling to pipe. Stops machine and ejects pipe. May tighten couplings manually when machine malfunctions. May keep production records.
GOE: 06.04.20 STRENGTH: M GED: R3 M2 L2 SVP: 4 DLU: 77

619.682-018 FISHING ACCESSORIES MAKER (toy-sport equip.)
Sets up and operates machines to form fishing accessories or accessory parts, performing any combination of following tasks: Sets up and operates power press that cuts out parts, such as fish spear frames, barbed spear tines or fish stringer catches [PUNCH-PRESS OPERATOR (any industry) II]. Starts abrasive wheel and guides barbed end of tine against wheel to sharpen barb [BENCH GRINDER (any industry)]. Joins spear frame and tines together to form head of fish spear, using spot welding machine. Operates machine that bends and cuts wire to form stringer parts. Inserts roll of wire on machine spindle, through guides, and into machine feed. Starts machine that bends and cuts wire to form stringer chain or clips (fasteners). Tends crimping machine that folds metal tip inward against chain or rope to form stringer. Positions preformed hollow metal tip in holding device of machine bed. Inserts end of chain or rope into base of tip. Moves lever to lower machine ram against tip, crimping tip against chain or rope to form fish stringer.
GOE: 06.02.02 STRENGTH: L GED: R3 M2 L2 SVP: 4 DLU: 77

619.682-022 HEATER (forging) alternate titles: furnace operator; furnace tender; hammer heater; heater, furnace; slug-furnace operator

Controls oil, gas, or electrical furnace to heat stock, such as billets, bars, plates and rods, preparatory to forging, following work order specifications: Reads dials and gauges, and turns knobs to regulate flow of fuel or electric current to verify and maintain specified temperature within furnace. Positions stock in furnace, using tongs or chain hoist. Observes color of metal or reads pyrometer to determine when stock reaches forging temperature. Pulls stock from furnace and delivers it to forging press or hammer, using tongs or chain hoist. Usually works as member of hammer, press, or upsetter crew. May place heated workpiece on conveyor for transporting to work area. May turn knobs to synchronize speed of feed and takeoff conveyors of automatic furnace.
GOE: 06.02.02 STRENGTH: H GED: R3 M2 L2 SVP: 4 DLU: 78

619.682-026 HOOP BENDER, TANK (wood. container) alternate titles: hoop-bending-machine operator

Operates hoop-bending machine to bend and shape iron rods into hoops for wooden tanks: Loosens nut of adjusting block and positions roller to obtain specified diameter of hoop. Starts machine and inserts end of rod through feed rollers of machine and over bending roller. Strikes end of rod with wooden maul to start rod over roll. Turns handcrank of feed roller to force rod through machine, bending rod into semicircular or circular shape. Removes bent rod from machine and stacks rod on floor.
GOE: 06.02.02 STRENGTH: M GED: R3 M2 L2 SVP: 3 DLU: 77

619.682-030 HOOP MAKER, MACHINE (wood. container)

Operates machines to make barrel hoops from strap steel: Installs and adjusts rollers, punches, and shear plates in hoop-punch-and-coiler machines, using wrenches. Places roll of strap steel on spindle, inserts end in feed rollers and starts machine. Removes punched and coiled hoops. Aligns holes in ends of coiled hoops on shank of rivets in guide slots of riveting machine. Slides hoop with protruding rivets under reciprocating hammer that flattens rivet shanks. Places hoop over mandrel of hoop-flaring machine and moves leg control to expand jaws that flare hoop to conform to shape of barrel. May be designated according to machine operated as Hoop-Flaring-Machine Operator (wood. container); Hoop-Punch-And-Coiler Operator (wood. container); Hoop-Riveting Machine Operator (wood. container).
GOE: 06.02.02 STRENGTH: M GED: R3 M2 L2 SVP: 4 DLU: 78

619.682-034 HOOP-FLARING-AND-COILING-MACHINE OPERATOR (wood. container) alternate titles: coiler; flarer

Operates hoop-flaring-and-coiling machine to coil and flare strips of hoop steel to fit barrel: Turns setscrews that adjust distance between rolls to obtain specified diameter and flare of hoop, using wrench. Starts machine and feeds end of strip into rolls of machine that coil and flare strip. Removes coiled strip from machine and stacks it on floor.
GOE: 06.02.02 STRENGTH: L GED: R3 M2 L2 SVP: 4 DLU: 77

619.682-038 SAMPLER, FIRST (smelt. & refin.)

Operates machines to form cut of copper ingot into wire samples for metallurgical testing: Smooths lateral sides of sample with emery wheel. Heats sample in furnace to light-red glow. Rolls sample into rod by passing rod through rolling machine. Coils rod and immerses rod in acid bath to remove scale. Tapers end of rod, using hammer. Inserts tapered end through selected steel-wire die, and fastens it to powered clamp. Depresses pedal to draw rod to specified size through series of dies of decreasing diameters. Coils wire to prepare it for metallurgical analysis.
GOE: 06.02.02 STRENGTH: M GED: R4 M2 L3 SVP: 5 DLU: 77

619.682-042 SEAMLESS-TUBE ROLLER (steel & rel.) alternate titles: rotary-bar operator; seamless-tube-mill operator; tube roller

Sets up and operates machine to form seamless tubing from pierced steel billets: Installs series of rollers to form specified outside diameter of tubing. Installs plug onto mandrel to form specified inside diameter of tubing. Starts machine and moves levers to push billet into first set of rollers that force billet over plug and into following series of rollers to reduce or expand billet to tubing of specified dimensions.
GOE: 06.02.02 STRENGTH: M GED: R3 M2 L2 SVP: 5 DLU: 77

619.684-010 FORMER HELPER, HAND (any industry)

Assists FORMER, HAND (any industry) to bend and straighten metal bars, plates, structural shapes, and weldments, performing any combination of following tasks: Transports tools, fixtures, stock, and workpieces manually or by truck. Places metal in furnace or heats metal, using hand torch. Bolts, or clamps fixtures, dies, and shims onto forming block, using hand wrench. Lifts, moves, and clamps workpiece onto forming block or fixture manually or using hoist. Bends workpiece to specified shape, using pry bar, hammer, sledge, or mallet. Measures work to ensure conformance to specifications, using template, rule, or straightedge. Marks or tags identifying information onto finished work. Chips or grinds and trims rough or sharp edges from workpiece, using hand grinder, shears, hack saw, or air chisel. Cleans dirt and grease from tools and equipment. Performs other duties as described under HELPER (any industry) Master Title.
GOE: 06.04.24 STRENGTH: H GED: R2 M1 L1 SVP: 3 DLU: 77

619.685-010 BAND MAKER (agriculture) alternate titles: band splicer

Tends machine that splices pieces of metal banding used to band compressed cotton bales: Overlaps ends of two pieces of banding and positions banding on

bed of splicing machine. Starts machine that automatically folds and crimps metal fasteners around overlapped ends of banding. May bend end of each completed band and attach fastening buckle onto bent end.
GOE: 06.04.02 STRENGTH: L GED: R2 M1 L1 SVP: 2 DLU: 77

619.685-014 BANDING-MACHINE OPERATOR (furniture) alternate titles: bander

Tends machine that presses metal bands into grooved edges of tabletops: Positions tabletop in center of rotary bed of machine. Pushes lever to lower ram that holds tabletop in place. Inserts lip of metal band into grooved edge of tabletop. Starts rotation of machine bed and starts rollers that press band into grooved edges around three sides of tabletop. Lifts tabletop from machine bed and places tabletop in vise. Inserts lip of separate metal band into grooved edge of unbanded side and hammers band into place, using rubber mallet.
GOE: 06.04.20 STRENGTH: L GED: R2 M1 L1 SVP: 2 DLU: 77

619.685-018 BANDING-MACHINE OPERATOR (ordnance)

Tends hydraulic band-seating machine that presses brass or copper rifling bands around shells (projectile bodies): Starts motor. Places shell on machine base, and slides band over nose of shell, pushing or hammering band toward band-groove. Pushes lever to converge retractable jaws around band to force band into groove. Releases lever and turns shell slightly, repeating pressing operation until band is seated. Removes shell from machine.
GOE: 06.04.20 STRENGTH: M GED: R2 M1 L1 SVP: 3 DLU: 77

619.685-022 BOBBIN-WINDER TENDER (glass mfg.)

Tends machine that winds wire onto bobbins, preparatory to formation of wire netting used in reinforcing sheet glass: Threads wire from supply reel through rollers that automatically feed wire to bobbin. Moves lever to start machine and observes operation to ensure uniform winding. Stops machine when wire breaks and splices end to full supply reel, using splicing tool.
GOE: 06.04.02 STRENGTH: H GED: R1 M1 L1 SVP: 2 DLU: 77

619.685-026 BRAKE OPERATOR II (any industry) alternate titles: press-brake operator

Tends power brake that bends, punches, forms, rolls, arcs, or straightens metal sheets, plates, and bars: Positions work manually or with crane against stops, or aligns layout marks to dies. Brushes oil on dies and workpiece. Starts machine to lower ram and shape workpiece. Tightens die nuts to prevent movement of die, using wrenches. Inspects work for conformance to specifications, using rule, square, or templates. Cleans scale or scrap from die with airhose or. brush. May depress pedal to lower ram and shape workpiece. May tend furnace to preheat metal to specified temperatures before bending. May be designated according to material shaped as Brake Operator, Sheet Metal (any industry) II.
GOE: 06.02.02 STRENGTH: M GED: R3 M2 L2 SVP: 4 DLU: 77

619.685-030 COIL-REWIND-MACHINE OPERATOR (nonfer. metal)

Tends machine that rewinds sheet metal coils into compact rolls for shipment: Measures sheet width and thickness, using tape and micrometer. Regulates air valve to raise and lower horizontal and vertical arbor in accordance with width of coil. Places coil on arbor manually or using hoist. Inserts inside end of coil in arbor and starts machine. Observes operation to detect telescoping, or excessive tightness, or coil. Cuts off damaged portions of coil, using shear. Removes and stacks rewound coils. May tend machine that weighs and rewinds sheet metal coils.
GOE: 06.04.02 STRENGTH: M GED: R2 M1 L1 SVP: 2 DLU: 77

619.685-034 DRUM STRAIGHTENER I (any industry) alternate titles: container repairer; dedenter

Tends machine equipped with rolls that removes dents and reforms bodies and chimes (rims) of metal barrels or drums: Slides open end of barrel over cylinder in machine. Pulls lever to lower rolls against barrel. Starts machine that rotates barrel against rolls to reform or straighten side, bead, or chime. Raises rolls and slides barrel off cylinder.
GOE: 06.04.02 STRENGTH: H GED: R2 M1 L1 SVP: 2 DLU: 77

619.685-038 EMBOSSING-MACHINE OPERATOR (ordnance)

Tends battery of machines that automatically roll grooves or knurls on brass shotgun shell heads: Places empty trays under delivery chutes. Moves levers to start machines and flow of caps from hoppers. Clears heads jammed in feed and groove mechanisms, using screwdriver and wire picks. Examines caps for defective trimming, splits, dents, and scratches. Verifies inside and outside diameters of embossed heads at specified intervals, using fixed gauges. Calls HOPPER FEEDER (ordnance) to replenish cap supply and notifies machine repairer of machine malfunction.
GOE: 06.04.02 STRENGTH: L GED: R2 M2 L2 SVP: 2 DLU: 77

619.685-042 ETCHER, MACHINE (cutlery-hrdwr.)

Tends equipment that etches trade name on razor blades: Positions roll of blade steel on etching machine reel and threads steel through feed and etching rollers to cutting die. Fills acid and water fountains that feed etching rollers and wash acid from steel after etching. Lights gas burner in drying chamber and starts machine. Observes discharge of blades into hopper, and stops machine when hopper is full.
GOE: 06.04.02 STRENGTH: M GED: R2 M2 L2 SVP: 4 DLU: 77

619.685-046 FORMING-ROLL OPERATOR II (any industry)

Tends rolling machine that straightens and forms contours in metal sheets, trims and beads edges of metal cylinders and rings, or crimps or seams lids

on container: Positions workpiece over lower die or *forming chuck*. Clamps workpiece to forming chuck or positions workpiece against end stop to hold workpiece in place. Pulls lever to press adjustment dies over workpiece to shape workpiece to contour of dies or forming chuck. May pull lever to lower slitter or knife to trim edges of workpiece and manipulate lever which forces dies against edge of workpiece to bend edge to form bead. May tend machines that automatically feed can ends, seam can ends to can bodies, and test cans for leaks. May be designated by work performed as Beading-Machine Operator (any industry) II; Drum Straightener (any industry) II; Seaming-Machine Operator (tinware).
GOE: 06.04.02 STRENGTH: H GED: R2 M1 L1 SVP: 3 DLU: 77

619.685-050   FOUR-SLIDE-MACHINE OPERATOR II (any industry) alternate titles: multi-slide-machine tender; slide-forming-machine tender
Tends one or more slide-forming machines that automatically feed, punch, cut and form strip metal or wire stock to fabricate parts, such as spring clips, brackets, terminal clips, and hairpins: Threads strip metal or wire through straightening rolls and die sets by turning flywheel by hand and starts machine. Measures sample of finished parts with fixed gauges and examines parts for surface defects or scratches. Shuts off machine and notifies supervisor or machine setter if parts do not meet specifications. May weld ends of two coils together by locking ends in electric-welding device and pulling lever, to form continuous length of stock.
GOE: 06.04.02 STRENGTH: H GED: R2 M2 L2 SVP: 3 DLU: 77

619.685-054   HEAD-GAUGE-UNIT OPERATOR (ordnance)
Tends machines that segregate cartridge cases with oversize and undersize heads: Turns valve to adjust pneumatic conveyor transferring cases from washer-dryer to storage hopper. Raises hopper gate to regulate flow of cases to shaker plate and turns wingnut to adjust spacing of gauge rails. Starts machines to shake cases through specially holed plate that retains cases with oversize heads and feeds cases that pass through holes, nose down, between inclined (gauge) rails to separate cases with undersize heads. Inverts shaker plate periodically to dump cartridge cases with oversize heads. Removes cartridge cases jammed between gauge rails with fingers or wire pick. Lifts barrels of gauged cases from discharge chutes to trucks and pushes barrels to storage.
GOE: 06.04.02 STRENGTH: M GED: R1 M1 L1 SVP: 2 DLU: 77

619.685-058   HEEL-WASHER-STRINGING-MACHINE   OPERATOR (rubber goods)
Tends machine that threads metal washers onto rods for use in machine that molds washers into rubber shoe heels: Fills hopper of machine with washers, using can. Positions rods in machine with one end in slot of revolving disk and other end secured by holder. Starts machine, causing disk to revolve in hopper and magnetically pick up and string washers on rods. Removes filled rods from disk and places rods in box for insertion in washer placing machine. Removes washers facing in wrong direction and reinserts rods in machine for restringing.
GOE: 06.04.20 STRENGTH: L GED: R2 M1 L1 SVP: 2 DLU: 77

619.685-062   MACHINE OPERATOR II (any industry)
Tends fabricating machines, such as cutoff saws, shears, rolls, brakes, presses, forming machines, spinning machines, and punch, that cut, shape, and bend metal plates, sheets, tubes, and structures: Reads job specifications to determine machine adjustments and material requirements. Sets stops or guides to specified length as indicated by scale, rule, or template. Positions workpiece against stops, manually or using hoist, or aligns layout marks with die or blade. Pushes button or depresses pedal to activate machine. Observes machine operation to detect workpiece defects or machine malfunction. Measures workpiece dimensions, using rule, template, or other measuring instruments to determine accuracy of machine operation. Removes burrs, sharp edges, rust, or scale from workpiece, using file, hand grinder, or wire brush. Performs minor machine maintenance, such as oiling machines, dies, or workpieces. Assists machine operators to set up machine, and stack, mark, pack, and transport finished workpieces. May rivet and spot-weld workpieces. May tend machines that fabricate and assemble sheet metal products and be designated Sheet-Metal Production Worker (any industry).
GOE: 06.04.02 STRENGTH: M GED: R2 M1 L2 SVP: 3 DLU: 88

619.685-066   METAL FABRICATOR HELPER (any industry)
Performs any combination of following duties to assist METAL FABRICATOR (any industry) in fabricating and assembling boilers and steel plate vessels, such as tanks and vats: Tends machines, such as drill press, punch press, and boring mill to drill, punch, and ream metal stock for boiler parts. Tends power shears to cut plate to size and shape. Grinds welded joints, seams, and other irregular areas to smooth boiler surfaces, using portable and pedestal grinders. Wraps blanket of spun glass around shell to insulate boiler and tacks blanket to shell surface, using stud welding gun. Operates sandblasting machine to clean tank surfaces prior to painting or coating [SANDBLASTER (any industry)]. Moves and positions materials at work site with help of other workers, using overhead bridge crane or dolly. Removes casing, grates, and grate rigging from boiler prior to repair of boiler and reassembles them after repair, using handtools. Performs other duties described under HELPER (any industry) Master Title.
GOE: 06.04.02 STRENGTH: H GED: R2 M1 L1 SVP: 4 DLU: 77

619.685-070   METALLIC-YARN-SLITTING-MACHINE   OPERATOR (nonfer. metal)
Tends machine that slits rolls of metallic yarn material into narrow yarn widths for use in textile manufacture: Positions narrow roll of laminated metallic material on machine arbor and threads end of material through antistatic pad, circular cutters, tension rollers, and around takeup bobbins. Turns valve to drop oil on antistatic pad. Starts machine and observes flow of material through machine to detect wrinkles and splices in material and breaks in yarn. Cuts out defects, using scissors, and ties broken yarn ends. Doffs full bobbins of metallic yarn from takeup spindles.
GOE: 06.04.02 STRENGTH: L GED: R2 M1 L1 SVP: 3 DLU: 77

619.685-074   REPAIRER, SHOE STICKS (rubber goods)
Tends peening machine to flatten ends of metal pins inserted in holes in shoe sticks (flat iron bars having rows of pins or pegs on which lasts are mounted for carrying): Positions pin in fixture on machine anvil and aligns hole in shoe stick over pin. Depresses pedal to start reciprocating ram that hammers protruding end of pin over securing pin to attach pin to shoe stick. Straightens bent pins in stick by tapping them with hammer, using steel block for backing. Verifies straightness by trial-fitting last onto pins.
GOE: 06.04.02 STRENGTH: M GED: R1 M1 L1 SVP: 2 DLU: 77

619.685-078   ROD-PULLER AND COILER (nonfer. metal)
Tends coiling device that coils hot rod, wire, or tubing from extrusion press or rolling mill: Adjusts coiler reel according to specified size and coil, using handtools. Inserts end of rod, tube, or wire in automatic coiling rack and moves controls to start coiler. Guides straight lengths of rod or tube along table to avoid stretching or kinking material, using tongs. Sets stops on table, using handtools, and cuts workpiece to specified lengths, using circular saw or power shears. Rolls finished lengths into trough for cooling. May stamp grade, alloy mixture, and batch number on each workpiece.
GOE: 06.04.02 STRENGTH: M GED: R2 M1 L1 SVP: 2 DLU: 77

619.685-082   SPINNING-LATHE OPERATOR, AUTOMATIC (any industry)
Tends lathe that spins (forms) shaped articles from sheet or plate metal: Pushes lever to move tailstock, forcing disk against chuck of lathe. Slides hydraulic carriage forward to position circular forming tool against metal disk. Starts machine that presses rotating circular tool against disk to form disk into shape of spinning chuck. Removes finished article and verifies dimensions, using fixed gauge. May tend spinning lathe equipped with knife and beading rolls which trims, or trims and bends, shaped article. May tend spinning lathe to bead and iron smooth finish or form knurls onto drawn articles. May be designated according to operation performed as Automatic-Beading-Lathe Operator (any industry); Rolling-Machine Operator, Automatic (any industry).
GOE: 06.04.02 STRENGTH: L GED: R2 M1 L1 SVP: 2 DLU: 77

619.685-086   WINDING-LATHE OPERATOR (ordnance)
Tends lathe mounted on rails that coils hot iron rods around bodies of fragmentation bombs to increase demolition properties of bombs: Pulls lever to move lathe to mouth of preheating furnace. Lifts bomb from stockpile and clamps it in machine by tightening chuck and tailstock. Pulls red-hot rod from furnace, attaches end to bomb fixture, and hammers portion of rod around bomb, using pulling bar and hammer. Sets coil-spacing gauge. Pushes button to start rotation of bomb in machine. Stops machine when rod is coiled on bomb. Welds end of coil to bomb. Removes bomb from machine, using hoist.
GOE: 06.04.02 STRENGTH: M GED: R2 M1 L1 SVP: 3 DLU: 77

619.685-090   WIRE-WINDING-MACHINE OPERATOR (wood. container)
Tends machine that winds wire on spools for use on wire-bound boxes: Slides empty spool over end of shaft and against winding clutch. Places coil of wire over frame and threads loose end over guide pulley, through hole in post of machine, and between guiding wheels, and attaches it to empty spool. Shifts lever to start and stop shaft rotating and winding wire on spool. Removes spool of wire from machine.
GOE: 06.04.02 STRENGTH: H GED: R2 M1 L1 SVP: 2 DLU: 77

619.685-094   CUT-OFF-MACHINE OPERATOR (steel & rel.)
Tends cutoff machine that automatically cuts sample sections of metal pipes for testing, and bevels, faces, and reams ends of pipes: Reviews pipe specifications to ascertain length of pipes and pressure setting of hydraulic press used for testing pipe sections. Positions pipe stops on machine and beveling, facing, and reaming heads, according to pipe length specified, using handtools. Turns knob on hydraulic press to pressure specified. Pushes button controls to divert pipes to cutoff machine, to cut sample sections of each pipe, and to turn each pipe for beveling, facing, and reaming of pipe ends. Positions sample sections of pipes under hydraulic press, pulls lever to crush pipe sections, and examines sections for broken welds. Cuts additional sample sections of pipes not passing test, repeats test, and either accepts or rejects pipes according to test results. Diverts defective pipes for further processing, and notifies supervisor. Removes pipes that become wedged on conveyor, using cables, chains, and hoist. Maintains tally of work done and oils machine as needed.
GOE: 06.04.02 STRENGTH: M GED: R2 M2 L2 SVP: 3 DLU: 86

619.686-010   AUTOMATIC STACKER (tinware)
Places dollies at discharge end of automatic stacker to catch tin sheets emerging from processing machines. Stops machine and removes sheets jammed in

conveyor. Removes filled dollies. May flip workpieces on opposite side for processing, using mechanical turner. May examine material for defects, grade material, and notify processing machine operator of defects noted.
GOE: 06.04.40 STRENGTH: M GED: R1 M1 L1 SVP: 2 DLU: 77

619.686-014 HOOP-MAKER HELPER, MACHINE (wood. container)
Assists HOOP MAKER, MACHINE (wood. container) to make hoops, performing any combination of following duties: Moves rollers, punches, mandrels, and shear plates and tightens nuts holding them in position. Threads end of strap steel through rollers. Fills rivet box of machine with rivets. Performs other duties as described under HELPER (any industry) Master Title. May be designated according to specific machine operator assisted as Hoop-Flaring-Machine-Operator Helper (wood. container); Hoop-Punch-And-Coiler-Operator Helper (wood. container); Hoop-Riveting-Machine-Operator Helper (wood. container).
GOE: 06.04.02 STRENGTH: M GED: R2 M1 L1 SVP: 2 DLU: 77

619.686-018 HOPPER FEEDER (ordnance)
Feeds brass blanks onto conveyors and into hoppers of machines that form blanks into small arms cartridge cases: Transfers containers of blanks to work area, using handtruck or powered tier-lift truck. Scoops or dumps brass workpieces into feed hoppers of draw presses or onto transfer conveyor leading to other work stations, using hoist. May hoist container to overhead loading platform and along roller conveyor until container is positioned over machine hopper for dumping, using electric hoist or tier-lift truck.
GOE: 06.04.02 STRENGTH: H GED: R1 M1 L1 SVP: 2 DLU: 77

619.686-022 METAL-FABRICATING-SHOP HELPER (any industry) alternate titles: helper, steel fabrication; plate-shop helper; production helper; structural-shop helper
Assists workers engaged in fabrication of structural or sheet metal products, performing any combination of following tasks: Lifts, positions, and removes workpieces from machines to assist in fitting and welding. Holds tape and rods and marks reference points to assist in layout. Loads, stacks, and transports stock, tools, dies, and work in process by hand or truck. Attaches rope or grappling equipment to workpieces to prepare workpiece for moving by crane or jib. Cleans and scrapes metal preparatory to fabricating, welding, painting, or shipping, using scraping tool, abrasive, or placing in solvent bath. Paints metal stocks, using paintbrush. Picks up and trucks scrap from work areas. May be designated by trade as Ironworker Helper, Shop (any industry); Sheet-Metal-Shop Helper (any industry). Performs other duties as described under HELPER (any industry) Master Title.
GOE: 06.04.02 STRENGTH: H GED: R2 M1 L1 SVP: 2 DLU: 78

619.686-026 SPIKE-MACHINE HEATER (steel & rel.)
Heats steel rods in furnace preparatory to forging boat or track spikes: Shoves rods into furnace and spaces them evenly with pry bar to ensure uniform heating. Pushes heated rods from furnace, using cold rod, on signal from SPIKE-MACHINE FEEDER (steel & rel.). May adjust furnace temperature control, clean, and lubricate equipment as specified.
GOE: 06.04.02 STRENGTH: H GED: R2 M1 L1 SVP: 2 DLU: 77

619.686-030 STRETCHER-LEVELER-OPERATOR HELPER (nonfer. metal)
Assists STRETCHER-LEVELER OPERATOR (nonfer. metal) to stretch, flatten, and straighten metal sheet, strip, rod, and extruded forms: Lifts and positions material in vises and moves lever to close clamps. Removes finished product and loads product on saw table, truck, or pallet. May install and adjust stretcher jaws according to size of metal, using wrench. May determine amount of stretch required, using micrometer and tolerance tables. Performs other duties as described under HELPER (any industry) Master Title.
GOE: 06.04.02 STRENGTH: M GED: R2 M1 L1 SVP: 2 DLU: 77

619.686-034 FORGE HELPER (forging) alternate titles: press helper; trim-setter helper
Performs any combination of following tasks to assist workers in forging metal products: Loads bars, billets, or blooms into furnace, using hoist. Transfers workpiece to and from work stations, such as furnace, hammer, and trim press, using tongs or hoist. Removes scale from workpiece and dies, using broom or airhose. Trims excess material from finished parts, using handsaw or bandsaw. Marks material with specified information, using hammer and die. Lifts dies to machine and bolts dies in place, using hoist and wrenches. Loads racks, off bears conveyors, and cleans and lubricates machines. May work as member of crew. Loads radioactive uranium elements into furnace, using hoist. May be designated according to worker assisted as Drop-Hammer-Operator Helper (forging); Extruder-Operator Helper (forging); Heater Helper, Forge (forging); Upsetter Helper (forging); or by work performed as Scale Shooter (forging). Performs other tasks as described under HELPER (any industry) Master Title.
GOE: 06.04.40 STRENGTH: H GED: R2 M1 L1 SVP: 2 DLU: 78

619.687-010 COIL BINDER (nonfer. metal)
Binds coils of sheet aluminum from tandem mill following rolling process: Binds sheet metal coils with steel bands, using hand crimping tools. Pushes controls to tilt coil onto conveyor for removal from mill.
GOE: 06.04.38 STRENGTH: L GED: R2 M1 L1 SVP: 2 DLU: 77

619.687-014 MACHINE HELPER (any industry)
Assists workers in operating metal fabricating machines, performing any of following tasks: Lifts, moves, clamps, and bolts dies and fixtures on machines,

using handtools. Fills tanks and oil cups with lubricants. Helps lift and position workpieces. Brushes or blows dirt from dies, using airhose. Removes workpiece and scrap from machines, using conveyor, pallets or handtruck. Files, grinds, or scrapes sharp edges, burrs, scales, or rust from workpieces, using portable grinder or handtools. Hammers out bent or warped spots in metal. Sorts, marks, or tags finished work. Transports material, using jib or hoist, or signals crane operator to move material. Cleans machine. Compares workpiece with straightedge or template to verify conformance to specifications. May place workpieces into heating furnace or preheat workpieces, using hand torch. May clean dies, using cleaning solution, brushes, and rag. Performs other duties described under HELPER (any industry) Master Title. May be designated according to machine assigned as Bending-Machine-Operator Helper (any industry); Brake-Operator Helper (any industry); Hoop-Punch-Operator Helper (wood. container); Punch-Press-Operator Helper (any industry). May be designated: Roll-Operator Helper (any industry); Shear-Operator Helper (any industry); Slitting-Machine Operator Helper (any industry) II; Straightening-Press-Operator Helper (any industry).
GOE: 06.04.24 STRENGTH: H GED: R2 M1 L1 SVP: 3 DLU: 77

619.687-018 PITCH FILLER (any industry) alternate titles: tube filler
Fills metal tubes with hot pitch or other material to prevent warping during bending operations: Heats pitch in vat and pours it into tubes, using pitcher or ladle. Hangs tubes in heated oven or on rack and heats them with torch to remove pitch. Dips empty tubes into vats of washing and rinsing solutions.
GOE: 05.12.10 STRENGTH: M GED: R2 M1 L1 SVP: 2 DLU: 77

62/63 MECHANICS AND MACHINERY REPAIRERS

This division includes occupations concerned with installing, inspecting, testing, repairing, rebuilding, and maintaining in efficient operating condition all types of engines and a wide variety of mechanical equipment designed for general or specific application in domestic, commercial, industrial, and agricultural activities. Occupations in this division typically require knowledge of the structural and functional characteristics of specific machines or types of machines, and include such tasks as locating and drilling holes, aligning structural and moving parts, and occasionally operating machine tools to remove excess material from semifinished or repaired parts. Occupations concerned with assembling new or rebuilt heavy machines, such as turbines and presses, in machine shop or erection shop, involving close tolerance machining and hand finishing of castings and other machine parts, are included in Division 60. Occupations concerned with machine setup and adjustment only are included in groups covering operation of the same machines.

620 MOTORIZED VEHICLE AND ENGINEERING EQUIPMENT MECHANICS AND REPAIRERS

This group includes occupations concerned with repairing engines and accessories, power trains, suspension systems, and other mechanical units of automobiles, trucks, tractors, buses, and trackless trolleys; graders, bulldozers, cranes, power shovels, portable air-compressors, and other gasoline- or diesel-powered engineering equipment; motorized materials-handling equipment, such as forklifts and lumber carriers; and wheeled or tracked military vehicles, including personnel carriers, self-propelled guns, mobile rocket launchers, and tanks. Ordnance mechanics concerned with military armament are included in Group 632.

620.131-010 SUPERVISOR, ENDLESS TRACK VEHICLE (automotive ser.)
Supervises and coordinates activities of MECHANICS, ENDLESS TRACK VEHICLE (automotive ser.): Determines sequence and assignment of work on basis of work priority, quantity of equipment, and skill of personnel. Inspects work performed to ensure compliance with specifications and time schedules. Interprets specifications, drawings, work orders, technical instructions, and layouts. Coordinates department activities with other departments. Recommends or initiates personnel actions, such as promotions, transfers, discharges, and disciplinary action. Trains new workers. May estimate, requisition, and inspect materials. Performs other duties as described under SUPERVISOR (any industry) Master Title.
GOE: 05.05.09 STRENGTH: L GED: R4 M4 L4 SVP: 7 DLU: 77

620.131-014 SUPERVISOR, GARAGE (automotive ser.) alternate titles: automobile-mechanic supervisor; mechanic, chief; transportation-department supervisor
Supervises and coordinates activities of AUTOMOBILE MECHANICS (automotive ser.) engaged in repairing, adjusting, servicing, and storing motor vehicles in industrial or commercial establishment: Analyzes defective equipment to determine cause of trouble. Inspects and drives repaired vehicles to verify repairs. Trains workers in and demonstrates repair and maintenance of vehicles, using handtools, welding, and grinding equipment. Evaluates performance of workers. Keeps inventory of repair parts and equipment and requisitions replacement stock. Prepares repair reports and vehicle requests. Schedules transporting of passengers or materials to service or storage areas. May supervise workers engaged in inspection and repair of miscellaneous equipment, such as cement mixers and electric trucks. Performs other duties as described under SUPERVISOR (any industry) Master Title.
GOE: 05.05.09 STRENGTH: L GED: R4 M3 L4 SVP: 7 DLU: 77

620.131-018 SUPERVISOR, MOTORCYCLE REPAIR SHOP (automotive ser.)

Supervises and coordinates activities of workers engaged in repairing or replacing engine, frame, electrical system, wheels, or other parts of motorcycle: Analyzes defects in motorcycle to determine feasibility of repairing or replacing worn or defective parts. Trains workers in repair procedures and techniques. Performs duties as described under SUPERVISOR (any industry) Master Title.
GOE: 05.05.09 STRENGTH: L GED: R4 M3 L4 SVP: 8 DLU: 77

620.137-010 TANK AND AMPHIBIAN TRACTOR OPERATIONS CHIEF (military ser.)

Supervises and coordinates activities of workers engaged in operation and maintenance of tanks or amphibian tractors and equipment in combat or training: Instructs personnel in operation of tanks or amphibian tractors and equipment. Inspects equipment to determine need for servicing or repair and directs workers in servicing or repairing vehicles and equipment. Directs loading of personnel and supplies on vehicle. Directs vehicle driver in movement of vehicle in combat situation on land or water. Prepares vehicle journals and worksheets concerning tactical situation.
GOE: 05.10.02 STRENGTH: L GED: R3 M2 L2 SVP: 7 DLU: 77

620.261-010 AUTOMOBILE MECHANIC (automotive ser.) alternate titles: garage mechanic

Repairs and overhauls automobiles, buses, trucks, and other automotive vehicles: Examines vehicle and discusses with customer or AUTOMOBILE-REPAIR-SERVICE ESTIMATOR (automotive ser.); AUTOMOBILE TESTER (automotive ser.); or BUS INSPECTOR (automotive ser.) nature and extent of damage or malfunction. Plans work procedure, using charts, technical manuals, and experience. Raises vehicle, using hydraulic jack or hoist, to gain access to mechanical units bolted to underside of vehicle. Removes unit, such as engine, transmission, or differential, using wrenches and hoist. Disassembles unit and inspects parts for wear, using micrometers, calipers, and thickness gauges. Repairs or replaces parts, such as pistons, rods, gears, valves, and bearings, using mechanic's handtools. Overhauls or replaces carburetors, blowers, generators, distributors, starters, and pumps. Rebuilds parts, such as crankshafts and cylinder blocks, using lathes, shapers, drill presses, and welding equipment. Rewires ignition system, lights, and instrument panel. Relines and adjusts brakes, aligns front end, repairs or replaces shock absorbers, and solders leaks in radiator. Mends damaged body and fenders by hammering out or filling in dents and welding broken parts. Replaces and adjusts headlights, and installs and repairs accessories, such as radios, heaters, mirrors, and windshield wipers. May be designated according to specialty as Automobile Mechanic, Motor (automotive ser.); Bus Mechanic (automotive ser.); Differential Repairer (automotive ser.); Engine-Repair Mechanic, Bus (automotive ser.); Foreign-Car Mechanic (automotive ser.); Truck Mechanic (automotive ser.). May be designated: Compressor Mechanic, Bus (automotive ser.); Drive-Shaft-And-Steering-Post Repairer (automotive ser.); Engine-Head Repairer (automotive ser.); Motor Assembler (automotive ser.).
GOE: 05.05.09 STRENGTH: M GED: R4 M3 L3 SVP: 7 DLU: 77

620.261-012 AUTOMOBILE-MECHANIC APPRENTICE (automotive ser.) alternate titles: automobile-and-truck-mechanic apprentice

Performs duties as described under APPRENTICE (any industry) Master Title.
GOE: 05.05.09 STRENGTH: M GED: R4 M3 L3 SVP:

620.261-014 AUTOMOBILE TESTER (automotive ser.)

Tests and examines automotive vehicles, such as automobiles, buses, and trucks, to determine repairs required: Starts engine of automotive vehicle and listens for sounds indicative of malfunctions. Drives vehicle, noting performance of parts, such as clutch, gears, and brakes. Tests motor timing, cylinder compression, fuel consumption, wheel alignment, and steering, using testing devices. Examines body and fenders of vehicle for scratches and dents. Reports findings to supervisor or customer and recommends repairs required. May examine disassembled engine, differential, or other parts during repair. May be designated according to specialty as Motor Analyst (automotive ser.).
GOE: 05.07.02 STRENGTH: L GED: R4 M3 L3 SVP: 7 DLU: 77

620.261-018 AUTOMOBILE-REPAIR-SERVICE ESTIMATOR (automotive ser.) alternate titles: automobile inspector; collision estimator; manager, service; mechanic, trouble-shooting; sales associate, garage service; service writer

Inspects and tests automobiles and trucks to determine need for and cost of repairs: Determines need for repairs by road test [AUTOMOBILE TESTER (automotive ser.) 620.261-014], by use of mechanical testing devices [BRAKE REPAIRER (automotive ser.) 620.281-026; FRONT-END MECHANIC (automotive ser.) 620.281-038], by questioning customer about vehicle's performance, or by visual inspection of vehicle. Estimates cost of repair and prepares itemized work order, listing costs of parts and labor. May make minor adjustments or repairs, such as brake adjustment, battery cable replacement, or hinge lubrication. May supervise AUTOMOBILE-BODY REPAIRER (automotive ser.) 807.381-010; AUTOMOBILE MECHANIC (automotive ser.) 620.261-010; PAINTER, TRANSPORTATION EQUIPMENT (aircraft mfg.; air trans.; automotive ser.) 845.381-014; and other garage workers. May be designated according to specialty as Truck-Repair-Service Estimator (automotive ser.).
GOE: 05.07.02 STRENGTH: L GED: R4 M3 L3 SVP: 7 DLU: 79

620.261-022 CONSTRUCTION-EQUIPMENT MECHANIC (construction) alternate titles: heavy-equipment mechanic

Analyzes malfunctions and repairs, rebuilds, and maintains construction equipment, such as cranes, power shovels, scrapers, paving machines, motor graders, trench-digging machines, conveyors, bulldozers, dredges, pumps, compressors and pneumatic tools: Operates and inspects machines or equipment to diagnose defects. Dismantles and reassembles equipment, using hoists and handtools. Examines parts for damage or excessive wear, using micrometers and gauges. Replaces defective engines and subassemblies, such as transmissions. Tests overhauled equipment to ensure operating efficiency. Welds broken parts and structural members. May direct workers engaged in cleaning parts and assisting with assembly and disassembly of equipment. May repair, adjust, and maintain mining machinery, such as stripping and loading shovels, drilling and cutting machines, and continuous mining machines, and be designated Mine-Machinery Mechanic (mine & quarry).
GOE: 05.05.09 STRENGTH: M GED: R3 M2 L3 SVP: 7 DLU: 80

620.261-026 ELECTRIC-GOLF-CART REPAIRER (amuse. & rec.; automotive ser.) alternate titles: golf-cart mechanic

Repairs and maintains electric golf carts at golf course or in automotive repair shop, using handtools and electrical testing devices: Determines type of repairs required by reading work orders, talking to cart operator, or test-driving cart. Tests operational performance of motor, using voltmeter, ammeter, and wattmeter. Dismantles motor and repairs or replaces defective parts, such as brushes, armatures, and commutator, using wrenches, pliers, and screwdrivers. Rewires electrical systems, and repairs or replaces electrical accessories, such as horn and headlights. Tests and recharges or replaces batteries. Lubricates moving parts and adjusts brakes and belts. May perform structural repairs to body of cart, seats, and fabric tops. May record parts used and labor time on work order.
GOE: 05.10.03 STRENGTH: M GED: R3 M2 L3 SVP: 5 DLU: 77

620.261-030 AUTOMOBILE-SERVICE-STATION MECHANIC (automotive ser.)

Repairs and services vehicles of service station customers through performance of any of following tasks: Examines vehicles and confers with customers to determine malfunction and repairs desired. Refers customer with major vehicle repairs to garage. Removes and replaces parts of ignition system, such as spark plugs, points, coil, or alternator to complete tune-up or replace malfunctioning part of system, using mechanic's handtools, gauges, and test meters. Turns adjustment screws of carburetor to set idle speed of engine, using screwdriver. Replaces defective chassis parts, such as shock absorbers, balljoint suspension, brakeshoes, and wheel bearings. Services vehicles [AUTOMOBILE-SERVICE-STATION ATTENDANT (automotive ser.) 915.467-010].
GOE: 05.05.09 STRENGTH: M GED: R3 M2 L3 SVP: 5 DLU: 86

620.261-034 AUTOMOTIVE-COOLING-SYSTEM DIAGNOSTIC TECHNICIAN (automotive ser.)

Inspects and tests automotive cooling systems to diagnose malfunctions and estimates cost of repairs: Questions customer and examines cooling system, hoses, and connections to determine nature and extent of malfunctions. Tests and analyzes electrical, vacuum, pressure, and related functions of system components to locate cause of malfunctions, using vacuum tester, pressure tester, voltmeter, and other specialized test equipment and handtools. Compiles estimate of system repair costs and secures customer approval to perform repairs. Occasionally assists AUTOMOBILE-RADIATOR MECHANIC (automotive ser.) 620.381-010 in repair of cooling system components, using mechanic's handtools. Computes parts and labor charges and routes customer bill to office.
GOE: 05.05.09 STRENGTH: M GED: R4 M3 L3 SVP: 7 DLU: 86

620.281-010 AIR-CONDITIONING MECHANIC (automotive ser.) alternate titles: automobile-refrigeration mechanic

Installs and repairs automotive air-conditioning units: Bolts compressor to engine block and installs driving pulley on front end of crankshaft. Places fan belt on pulleys, adjusts tension, and tightens bolts. Bolts evaporator unit under dashboard or in trunk. Welds or bolts mounting brackets to automobile frame. Drills holes through interior panels, threads hoses through holes and connects hoses to compressor, evaporator, and cool-air outlet. Fills compressor with refrigerant and starts unit. Measures compressor pressure to determine efficiency of compressor, using gauge. Listens to operating unit for indications of malfunction. Removes faulty units from vehicles, disassembles them, and replaces worn and broken parts and fluid in unit. Makes electrical connections as required. May specialize in installation of automotive air-conditioning units and be designated Automotive Air-Conditioner Installer (automotive ser.).
GOE: 05.05.09 STRENGTH: M GED: R3 M2 L3 SVP: 6 DLU: 77

620.281-014 AUTOMOTIVE TECHNICIAN, EXHAUST EMISSIONS (government ser.) alternate titles: power equipment mechanic

Conducts and evaluates tests on vehicles to check exhaust emissions: Reviews instructions to determine details of test to be performed. Drives vehicle over dynamometer. Records identifying data. Performs dwell, timing and idle speed tests using gauges, evaluates performance and adjusts performance to manufacturer's specifications. Adjusts dynamometer settings to vehicle specifications and connects instrument sensors to exhaust system. Starts and operates vehicle according to test program, compares performance with specifications and records results. Calibrates, cleans and maintains test equipment and record-

ing devices. May diagnose and repair vehicle malfunctions. May install smog-control device on tested vehicle.
GOE: 05.05.09 STRENGTH: L GED: R4 M2 L3 SVP: 7 DLU: 77

620.281-018 AUTOMOTIVE-MAINTENANCE-EQUIPMENT SERVICER (any industry) alternate titles: automotive-maintenance-equipment repairer; equipment-service engineer; pump-and-tank servicer

Adjusts and repairs automotive repairing, servicing, and testing equipment, using handtools and power tools: Disassembles defective equipment, such as gasoline pumps, air compressors, and dynamometers. Replaces defective parts, using pipe fitting and welding tools. Reassembles, adjusts, and tests repaired equipment. May be required to register with government agency to adjust meters and gauges of fuel and oil pumps serving public. May install new equipment. May specialize in repairing gasoline pumps, lubrication equipment, air compressors, or other type of automotive service equipment.
GOE: 05.05.09 STRENGTH: M GED: R4 M3 L3 SVP: 7 DLU: 77

620.281-026 BRAKE REPAIRER (automotive ser.) alternate titles: brake mechanic; brake-repair mechanic; brakeshoe repairer

Repairs and overhauls brake systems in automobiles, buses, trucks, and other automotive vehicles: Pushes handle of hydraulic jack or pushes hoist control to raise vehicle axle. Removes wheels, using wrenches, wheel puller, and sledgehammer. Replaces defective brakeshoe units or attaches new linings to brakeshoes. Measures brakedrum to determine amount of wear, using feeler gauge. Inserts vacuum gauge into power-brake cylinder, starts engine, and reads gauge to detect brake-line leaks. Repairs or replaces leaky brake cylinders. Repairs or replaces defective air compressor in airbrake systems. Replaces wheel on axle and adjusts drumshoe clearance, using wrench. Fills master brake cylinder with brake fluid, pumps brake pedal, or uses pressure tank, and opens valves on hydraulic brake system to bleed air from brake lines. Closes valves and refills master brake cylinder. May be designated according to specialty as Brake Repairer, Air (automotive ser.); Brake Repairer, Bus (automotive ser.); Brake Repairer, Hydraulic (automotive ser.).
GOE: 05.10.02 STRENGTH: M GED: R3 M3 L3 SVP: 6 DLU: 77

620.281-030 BUS INSPECTOR (automotive ser.) alternate titles: motor-inspection mechanic

Examines and adjusts or repairs engines, chassis, electrical systems, and interior furnishings of buses: Starts engine and listens for indications of malfunctions. Tests engine components, such as carburetors, distributors, radiators, and fuel pumps, to determine causes of malfunctions, using timers, gauges, and other testing devices. Inspects chassis for defects in parts, such as universal joints, drive shaft, and air-suspension units. Inspects electrical systems and equipment [ELECTRICIAN, AUTOMOTIVE (automotive ser.)] and interior furnishings. May be designated according to specialty as Chassis Inspector (automotive ser.); Electrical Inspector (automotive ser.); Engine Inspector (automotive ser.).
GOE: 05.05.09 STRENGTH: M GED: R4 M4 L4 SVP: 7 DLU: 77

620.281-034 CARBURETOR MECHANIC (automotive ser.) alternate titles: carburetor repairer

Repairs and adjusts motor vehicle carburetors: Disassembles carburetors and gasoline filter units, using handtools. Examines parts for defects and tests needle valves with wire gauges and flowmeter. Cleans parts in solvents to remove dirt and gum deposits. Repairs or replaces defective parts. Reassembles carburetor and gasoline filter, and installs them in vehicle. Starts engine and turns adjustment screw to regulate flow of air and gasoline through carburetor, using testing equipment. May operate drill press, lathe, and other power tools to retap jets, ream throttle bodies and chokes, and machine seating surfaces of carburetor housings. May install and repair mechanical devices that convert conventional systems to use of other fuels [VEHICLE-FUEL-SYSTEMS CONVERTER (automotive ser.)].
GOE: 05.10.02 STRENGTH: L GED: R3 M2 L3 SVP: 7 DLU: 77

620.281-038 FRONT-END MECHANIC (automotive ser.) alternate titles: alignment mechanic; axle-and-frame mechanic; chassis mechanic; wheel-alignment mechanic

Aligns wheels, axles, frames, torsion bars, and steering mechanisms of automotive vehicles, such as automobiles, buses, and trucks: Drives automotive vehicle onto wheel alignment rack and tests vehicle for faulty wheel alignment, bent axle, worn ball joints, and bent steering rods, using alignment-testing machine. Straightens axle and steering rods and adjusts shims, tie rods, and joining pins to align wheels, or installs new parts, using handtools. Places wheel on balancing machine to determine where counterweights must be added to balance wheel. Hammers counterweights onto rim of wheel. Installs shock absorbers. Straightens frame, using hydraulic jack, chassis aligner, and acetylene torch.
GOE: 05.10.01 STRENGTH: M GED: R3 M3 L3 SVP: 6 DLU: 79

620.281-042 LOGGING-EQUIPMENT MECHANIC (logging)

Adjusts, maintains, and repairs gasoline-, hydraulic-, and diesel-powered logging equipment and accessories, such as air compressors, cranes, donkey engines, generators, and road graders. May overhaul and repair tractors [TRACTOR MECHANIC (automotive ser.)] and automotive vehicles [AUTOMOBILE MECHANIC (automotive ser.)]. May weld or cut metals, using electric or gas welder [WELDER, COMBINATION (welding)].
GOE: 05.05.09 STRENGTH: V GED: R4 M3 L3 SVP: 7 DLU: 77

620.281-046 MAINTENANCE MECHANIC (construction; petrol. & gas; pipe lines) alternate titles: service engineer; shop mechanic

Inspects, repairs, and maintains functional parts of automotive and mechanical equipment and machinery, such as pumps, compressors, pipe-laying machines, ditchdiggers, trucks, and tractors used in petroleum exploration, on oil fields, in pipeline construction, and in airfield maintenance and pipeline operations, using hoists, handtools, gauges, drills, grinding wheels, and testing devices: Inspects defective equipment and diagnoses malfunctions, using motor analyzers, pressure gauges, chassis charts, and factory manuals. Disassembles and overhauls internal combustion engines, pumps, pump power units, generators, transmissions, clutches, and rear ends, using handtools and hoist. Grinds and reseats valves, using valve-grinding machine. Adjusts brakes, aligns wheels, tightens bolts and screws, and reassembles equipment. Operates equipment to test its functioning. Changes oil, checks batteries, repairs tires and tubes, and lubricates equipment and machinery.
GOE: 05.05.09 STRENGTH: M GED: R4 M3 L3 SVP: 7 DLU: 77

620.281-050 MECHANIC, INDUSTRIAL TRUCK (any industry) alternate titles: truck repairer

Repairs and maintains electric, diesel, and gasoline industrial trucks, following manuals, and using handtools, power tools, and knowledge of electrical, power transmission, brake, and other automotive systems: Reads job order and observes and listens to truck in operation to determine malfunction and to plan work procedures. Installs new ignition systems, aligns front wheels, changes or recharges batteries, and replaces transmissions and other parts, using handtools. Overhauls gas or diesel engines, using mechanic's handtools, welding equipment, standard charts, and hoists. Examines protective guards, loose bolts, and specified safety devices on trucks, and makes adjustments, using handtools. Lubricates moving parts and drives repaired truck to verify conformance to specifications. May fabricate special lifting or towing attachments, hydraulic systems, shields, or other devices according to blueprints or schematic drawings.
GOE: 05.05.09 STRENGTH: M GED: R4 M3 L3 SVP: 7 DLU: 81

620.281-054 MOTORCYCLE REPAIRER (automotive ser.) alternate titles: motorcycle mechanic

Repairs and overhauls motorcycles, motor scooters, and similar motor vehicles: Listens to engine, examines vehicle's frame, and confers with customer to determine nature and extent of malfunction or damage. Connects test panel to engine and measures generator output, ignition timing, and other engine performance indicators. Dismantles engine and repairs or replaces defective parts, such as magneto, carburetor, and generator. Removes cylinder heads, grinds valves, and scrapes off carbon, and replaces defective valves, pistons, cylinders, and rings, using handtools and power tools. Hammers out dents and bends in frame, welds tears and breaks, and reassembles and reinstalls engine. Repairs and adjusts clutch, brakes, and drive chain. Repairs or replaces other motorcycle and motor scooter parts, such as spring fork, headlight, horn, handlebar controls, valve release, gear lever, gasoline and oil tanks, starter, brake lever, and muffler. May specialize in repair of motor scooters and be designated Motor-Scooter Repairer (automotive ser.).
GOE: 05.05.09 STRENGTH: H GED: R3 M3 L3 SVP: 6 DLU: 77

620.281-058 TRACTOR MECHANIC (automotive ser.)

Diagnoses mechanical failures and repairs tractors and tractor components according to manuals, factory specifications, and knowledge of engine performances, using handtools, power tools, and testing instruments: Attaches compression, ignition, and timing test instruments to certain parts of tractor, using clamps and handtools. Starts engine dials and reads meters and gauges of testing equipment to diagnose engine malfunction. Removes and disassembles engine, transmission, and clutches, using hoists, jacks, and mechanic's handtools. Inspects parts for damage, and verifies dimensions and clearances of parts for conformance to factory specifications, using gauges, such as calipers, and micrometers. Replaces or repairs worn or damaged parts. Grinds valves, relines and adjusts brakes, tightens body bolts, aligns wheels, and tunes engine. May weld defective body or frame parts.
GOE: 05.05.09 STRENGTH: M GED: R4 M3 L3 SVP: 7 DLU: 77

620.281-062 TRANSMISSION MECHANIC (automotive ser.)

Repairs manual and automatic transmissions in automobiles, buses, trucks, and other automotive vehicles: Raises automotive vehicle, using jacks or hoists, and removes transmission, using mechanic's handtools. Disassembles transmission unit and replaces broken or worn parts, such as bands, gears, seals, and valves. Adjusts pumps, bands, and gears as required, using wrenches. Installs repaired transmission and fills it with specified fluid. Adjusts operating linkage and tests operation on road. May adjust carburetor. May verify idle speed of motor, using equipment, such as tachometer, making required adjustments. May specialize in repair of automatic transmissions and be designated Automatic-Transmission Mechanic (automotive ser.).
GOE: 05.10.02 STRENGTH: M GED: R3 M3 L3 SVP: 7 DLU: 77

620.281-066 TUNE-UP MECHANIC (automotive ser.)

Tunes automotive vehicle engines to ensure efficient operation: Removes spark plugs, using socket wrench, and tests them, using spark-plug tester. Cleans electrodes in sandblasting machine, sets spark gap with feeler gauge, and replaces or installs new plugs. Inspects distributor breaker points for wear and pits, using feeler gauge, and replaces or resets points. Observes ignition timing, using timing light, and adjusts timing, using handtools. Adjusts carburetor needle setting, using handtools, and verifies adjustment, using instruments,

such as fuel analyzer, vacuum gauge, oscilloscope, and tachometer. Sets valve tappets, using feeler gauge or dial indicator. Replaces defective coils, condensers, and electrical connection. Removes and cleans carburetor and fuel pump. Examines battery and connections and electrical charging and starting circuit. Adjusts, and repairs fan belt, and fuel and water pumps. May tune engine while vehicle runs on rollers connected to dynamometer and be designated Dynamometer Tuner (automotive ser.).
GOE: 05.05.09 STRENGTH: L GED: R4 M3 L3 SVP: 7 DLU: 77

620.281-070 VEHICLE-FUEL-SYSTEMS CONVERTER (automotive ser.)

Converts vehicle fuel systems from gasoline to butane gas operation, using handtools: Dismantles and removes existing gasoline-powered fuel systems from vehicles. Affixes mounting brackets or cradle to rear of vehicle, bolts high pressure butane gas tank to brackets, and installs high pressure vaporizers under hood, using handtools. Attaches butane carburetor and adapter to existing vehicle carburetor, or replaces original carburetor with butane one. Connects water and fuel lines between specified units. Tunes motor to conform to butane performance specifications to obtain maximum power and economy and to meet emission standards. May repair and service operating butane fuel units.
GOE: 05.10.02 STRENGTH: L GED: R3 M2 L3 SVP: 6 DLU: 77

620.364-010 SQUEAK, RATTLE, AND LEAK REPAIRER (automotive ser.)

Drives automobiles of service customers to determine origin of noises and leaks, and repairs or adjusts components to eliminate cause of complaint: Drives vehicle, or accompanies customer on test drive, to listen for rattles, squeaks, or other noises reported by customer, indicating malfunctioning or loose components. Diagnoses cause and determines origin of defect. Makes minor repairs to vehicle, such as tightening muffler and exhaust pipe brackets, loose bolts, and door handles. Reports need for more extensive repairs to AUTOMOBILE MECHANIC (automotive ser.). Sprays site of water leak, identified by customer, using water hose. Repairs leak, using adhesive compound, or replaces faulty rubber or fiber molding on doors and windows, using handtools.
GOE: 05.12.15 STRENGTH: M GED: R2 M2 L2 SVP: 4 DLU: 77

620.381-010 AUTOMOBILE-RADIATOR MECHANIC (automotive ser.) alternate titles: automobile mechanic, radiator; radiator repairer

Repairs cooling systems and fuel tanks in automobiles, buses, trucks, and other automotive vehicles: Pumps water or compressed air through radiator to test it for obstructions or leaks. Flushes radiator with cleaning compound to remove obstructions, such as rust or mineral deposits. Removes radiator core from automobile and cleans it, using rods or boiling water and solvent, or combination of boil out and rod out. Solders leaks in core or tanks, using soldering iron or acetylene torch. Disassembles, repairs, or replaces defective water pump. Replaces faulty thermostats and leaky head gaskets. Installs new cores, hoses, and pumps. Cleans, tests, and repairs fuel tanks.
GOE: 05.10.02 STRENGTH: M GED: R3 M2 L3 SVP: 6 DLU: 77

620.381-014 MECHANIC, ENDLESS TRACK VEHICLE (automotive ser.)

Repairs automotive vehicle chassis assemblies installed on vehicles, such as crawler tractors, half-tracks, scout and reconnaissance cars, and tanks: Removes chassis subassemblies, such as transmissions and crawler treads, using mechanic's handtools, jacks, and cranes. Disassembles units, such as crawler tread blocks and differential unit brake drums. Repairs and replaces worn and damaged parts. Fits parts together and reassembles parts to chassis, making necessary adjustments to ensure proper functioning. Installs parts or subassemblies for special tests as directed. Immerses parts in tanks of solvent or sprays parts with grease solvent to clean parts.
GOE: 05.05.09 STRENGTH: M GED: R4 M3 L3 SVP: 7 DLU: 77

620.381-018 MECHANICAL-UNIT REPAIRER (automotive ser.; railroad equip.)

Repairs, tests, and installs mechanical units, such as fuel and water pumps, control valves, governors, distributors, windshield wiper motors, and door engines on streetcars, trackless trolleys, and buses: Disconnects and removes unit from vehicle, using handtools. Disassembles unit and cleans parts with chemical solution. Inspects parts for wear or damage. Removes foreign particles from unit, using compressed air blower. Repairs, replaces, or adjusts components, such as needles, springs, bolts, relays, and airhoses. Tests air-control valve, air pipes, and airhoses for air leaks. Tests magnetic, hydraulic, and pneumatic control valves that are used to open and close doors and inspects radiator shutters, and other mechanical units on vehicle. Reassembles and installs unit in vehicle. May be designated according to type of mechanical unit repaired as Door-Engine Repairer (automotive ser.; railroad equip.); Windshield-Wiper Repairer (railroad equip.).
GOE: 05.05.09 STRENGTH: M GED: R4 M3 L3 SVP: 7 DLU: 77

620.381-022 REPAIRER, HEAVY (auto. mfg.)

Repairs defective automotive units, such as engines, transmissions, or differentials, in assembled vehicles, using handtools and power tools and applying knowledge of mechanical systems: Reads inspection cards to determine defects in vehicle components. Disassembles and repairs defective units on assembled vehicles or replaces them with different units, using mechanic's handtools and portable power tools. Routes repaired vehicles to testing area for final inspec-

tion. May remove and repair defective units of completed automotive vehicles. May place malfunctioning units on repair stand, using hoist. May be designated according to type of unit repaired as Differential Repairer (auto. mfg.); Engine Repairer (auto. mfg.); Transmission Repairer (auto. mfg.).
GOE: 05.05.09 STRENGTH: H GED: R3 M2 L3 SVP: 6 DLU: 90

620.384-010 MOTORCYCLE TESTER (motor-bicycles)

Inspects and tests motorcycles, performing any combination of following tasks according to standard procedures, using handtools and testing instruments: Mounts motorcycle on test stand. Attaches lead wires of test panel to ignition system of motor and runs motor at various speeds to measure generator output, oil pressure, revolution per minute, and other specified operating characteristics. Compares test instrument readings with operational charts to detect malfunctions. Engages clutch and transmission of motorcycle and listens for sounds denoting malfunction. Records findings on worksheet. Turns adjustment screw on carburetor to regulate idling speed of motor, using screwdriver. Inspects frame and fenders for dents and scratches. Tightens frame nuts and bolts, using handtools. Tests operation of horn and lights. Verifies identification number and optional equipment against data on work order.
GOE: 06.03.01 STRENGTH: M GED: R3 M3 L3 SVP: 5 DLU: 77

620.584-010 SPRING-REPAIRER HELPER, HAND (automotive ser.) alternate titles: spring-fitter helper; spring-maker helper, hand; tear-up worker, spring

Disassembles defective vehicle leaf springs preparatory to repair and assembles repaired leaf springs: Removes center bolt from leaf spring and loosens clips, using handtools. Removes rivets from leaf spring, using punch press or drill. Drills hole in replacement blank for leaf spring, using drill, or punches hole in blank, using punch press. Reassembles leaves for leaf spring, fits keeper on leaves, and fastens with bolts. Records number of leaves in spring, dimensions of leaves, size of connecting bolt, and repairs made.
GOE: 05.12.12 STRENGTH: H GED: R2 M1 L2 SVP: 4 DLU: 77

620.664-010 CONSTRUCTION-EQUIPMENT-MECHANIC HELPER (construction)

Assists CONSTRUCTION-EQUIPMENT MECHANIC (construction) in repairing, assembling, and adjusting construction equipment, such as internal combustion engines, lighting plants, pumps, air compressors, concrete and mortar mixers, concrete vibrators, generators, pneumatic tools, and portable winches. Disassembles and assembles equipment, using mechanic's handtools. Washes parts and tools with cleaning fluids, such as gasoline or naptha. Performs other duties as described under HELPER (any industry) Master Title.
GOE: 05.12.15 STRENGTH: M GED: R2 M1 L2 SVP: 3 DLU: 77

620.664-014 MAINTENANCE MECHANIC HELPER (construction; petrol. & gas; pipe lines) alternate titles: mechanic helper; shop-mechanic helper

Assists MAINTENANCE MECHANIC (construction; petrol. & gas; pipe lines) in repairing and maintaining automotive and mechanical machinery and equipment, such as pumps, compressors, pipelaying machines, ditch-diggers, trucks, and tractors, using jacks, hoists, and handtools: Installs jacks and hoists to raise equipment. Disassembles and assembles equipment, using handtools. Cleans tools and parts with naphtha, gasoline, and other cleaning compounds. Performs other duties as described under HELPER (any industry) Master Title.
GOE: 05.10.02 STRENGTH: H GED: R3 M2 L2 SVP: 5 DLU: 77

620.682-010 BRAKE-DRUM-LATHE OPERATOR (automotive ser.) alternate titles: machinist, brake

Sets up and operates brakedrum lathe to resurface automotive brakedrums, and operates grinding machine to grind brakeshoe linings: Clamps hub and drum on lathe spindle and adjusts cutting tool to machine drum surface. Starts spindle and feeds tool into drum by hand, or adjusts automatic feed mechanism. Measures drum to verify specified dimensions, using calipers, drum gauge, or micrometer. Clamps brakeshoe on grinder and grinds lining to specified arc as determined by new diameter of drum. May replace defective brake cylinders and fill master brake cylinder with brake fluid. May mount wheel on axle and adjust drumshoe clearance.
GOE: 06.02.02 STRENGTH: M GED: R3 M2 L2 SVP: 5 DLU: 77

620.684-010 AUTOMOBILE WRECKER (wholesale tr.) alternate titles: wrecking mechanic

Salvages usable parts from wrecked cars and trucks in auto salvage yard: Dismantles vehicles, using handtools, bolt cutters, and oxyacetylene torch. Cleans parts, using solvents and brush, or vapor-degreasing machine, and stores parts in bins according to condition and part number. Sorts, piles, and loads scrap on railroad cars or trucks. May drive tow-truck. May sell automobile glass, tires, and parts.
GOE: 05.12.15 STRENGTH: H GED: R3 M2 L2 SVP: 4 DLU: 77

620.684-014 AUTOMOBILE-MECHANIC HELPER (automotive ser.) alternate titles: automobile-mechanic assistant; mechanic helper

Assists AUTOMOBILE MECHANIC (automotive ser.) 620.261-010 in repairing automobiles, buses, trucks, and other automotive vehicles: Raises vehicle to specified level, using hydraulic jack. Removes and disassembles unit, such as engine, transmission, or differential, to be repaired, using handtools and power tools. Cleans unit, using prescribed solvent. Lubricates and washes vehicle. Performs other duties as described under HELPER (any industry) Master

Title. May be designated according to specialty of worker assisted as Truck-Mechanic Helper (automotive ser.).
GOE: 05.12.15 STRENGTH: H GED: R2 M1 L2 SVP: 3 DLU: 81

620.684-018 BRAKE ADJUSTER (automotive ser.)
Adjusts hydraulic brakes on automotive vehicles, such as automobiles, buses, and trucks: Observes level of brake fluid in master cylinder of braking system and adds brake fluid to prescribed level. Raises vehicle, using power hoist or jack. Turns toothed wheel on brakeshoe adjustment turnbuckle to set specified distance between brakeshoes and brakedrum, using handtool.
GOE: 05.12.15 STRENGTH: L GED: R2 M2 L2 SVP: 2 DLU: 77

620.684-022 CLUTCH REBUILDER (automotive ser.)
Rebuilds automobile and truck clutches, using handtools and power tools: Immerses clutch assembly in solvent to remove grease and residue. Places assembly into machine that tumbles assembly in abrasive chips to remove rust. Disassembles clutch, using handtools. Grinds and buffs clutch plates and facing, using portable abrasive wheel. Replaces facing on clutch plates, using riveting gun or riveting press. Replaces worn or damaged clutch parts. Reassembles clutch and replaces cover, using handtools.
GOE: 05.10.02 STRENGTH: M GED: R3 M2 L3 SVP: 4 DLU: 77

620.684-026 MOTORCYCLE SUBASSEMBLY REPAIRER (motor-bicycles)
Repairs motorcycle forks, transmissions, or other subassemblies according to specifications, using handtools and power tools: Disassembles unit and examines condition, movement or alignment of parts visually or using gauges. Replaces defective parts, using handtools, arbor press, flexible power press, or power tools. Reassembles and tests unit. May be designated according to place of work as Repairer, Assembly Line (motor-bicycles); or part of motorcycle repaired as Fork Repairer (motor-bicycles); Transmission Repairer (motor-bicycles).
GOE: 05.10.02 STRENGTH: H GED: R3 M2 L2 SVP: 5 DLU: 77

620.684-030 TRACTOR-MECHANIC HELPER (automotive ser.)
Assists TRACTOR MECHANIC (automotive ser.) in repairing tractors and tractor components, using handtools: Installs jacks and hoists to raise equipment and lift dismantled assemblies. Disassembles and assembles tractor parts, using handtools. Cleans tools and parts with naphtha, gasoline, or other cleaning compounds. May wash and lubricate equipment. Performs other duties as described under HELPER (any industry) Master Title.
GOE: 05.12.15 STRENGTH: H GED: R2 M1 L2 SVP: 4 DLU: 77

620.684-034 USED-CAR RENOVATOR (retail trade) alternate titles: used-car conditioner
Renovates used cars for resale at used car lot: Inspects cars for noticeable defects, such as dents, scratches, torn upholstery, and poor mechanical operation. Hammers out dents. Polishes scratches and retouches with enamel. Sews rips and tears in upholstery. Cleans and vacuums interiors. Washes and polishes exteriors. Replaces missing or defective small parts. Performs minor mechanical repairs and adjustments. May inspect cars for compliance with state safety regulations.
GOE: 05.10.04 STRENGTH: M GED: R3 M2 L2 SVP: 4 DLU: 77

620.685-010 BONDER, AUTOMOBILE BRAKES (automotive ser.)
Tends machines that apply adhesive and bond asbestos lining to automobile brakeshoes for installation by BRAKE REPAIRER (automotive ser.): Selects stock lining to fit brakeshoes removed from vehicle. Feeds lining between rollers of machine that applies bonding adhesive. Secures brakeshoes in bonding press after adhesive has set. Positions coated lining on shoe and locks press. Moves lever to activate press that heats and bonds lining to shoe and automatically releases after specified time. Removes bonded shoe from press, using asbestos gloves. May rivet linings to brakeshoes and be designated Riveter, Automobile Brakes (automotive ser.).
GOE: 05.12.10 STRENGTH: L GED: R2 M1 L2 SVP: 3 DLU: 77

621 AIRCRAFT MECHANICS AND REPAIRERS

This group includes occupations concerned with repairing and maintaining aircraft engines and mechanical, pneumatic, hydraulic, and related systems and components of aircraft and missiles.

621.131-010 SUPERCHARGER-REPAIR SUPERVISOR (air trans.)
Supervises and coordinates activities of workers engaged in assembling and repairing aircraft engine and cabin superchargers. Performs duties as described under SUPERVISOR (any industry) Master Title.
GOE: 05.05.09 STRENGTH: L GED: R4 M4 L4 SVP: 7 DLU: 77

621.131-014 SUPERVISOR, AIRCRAFT MAINTENANCE (air trans.)
Supervises and coordinates activities of AIRFRAME-AND-POWER-PLANT MECHANICS (aircraft mfg.; air trans.) 621.281-014 engaged in maintaining and repairing aircraft and aircraft engines: Trains employees in work methods and procedures. Inspects work to maintain specified standards and quality. Requisitions materials and supplies. Must be licensed by Federal Aviation Administration in job occurring in air transportation. May supervise workers engaged in servicing aircraft with fuel, lubricants, and coolants. Performs duties as described under SUPERVISOR (any industry) Master Title.
GOE: 05.05.09 STRENGTH: L GED: R4 M4 L4 SVP: 8 DLU: 77

621.137-010 SUPERVISOR, RECLAMATION (wholesale tr.)
Supervises and coordinates activities of RECLAMATION WORKERS (wholesale tr.) engaged in dismantling wrecked and other decommissioned aircraft: Directs removal of wings, engines, tail assemblies, landing gears, and other aircraft parts. Inspects parts, routing repairable units to repair shops and nonrepairable units to salvage. Compiles reports of reclamation work. May negotiate for sale of aircraft parts reclaimed. Performs other duties as described under SUPERVISOR (any industry) Master Title.
GOE: 05.05.09 STRENGTH: L GED: R4 M3 L3 SVP: 6 DLU: 77

621.221-010 FIELD-SERVICE REPRESENTATIVE (aircraft mfg.) alternate titles: technical specialist, aircraft systems
Advises and trains customer or other personnel in operation, overhaul, and maintenance of company aircraft, applying knowledge of aircraft systems, company specifications, and Federal Aviation Administration inspection procedures and specifications: Conducts investigations to determine source of technical problems. Evaluates results of investigations and recommends corrective action to customer and manufacturing plant. Trains customer or other personnel in operation, overhaul, and maintenance of aircraft. May oversee mechanical and structural repairs. May compile technical data pertaining to changes and improvements. May be required to work in field at permanent station. May be required to be licensed by Federal Aviation Administration in job occurring in air transportation.
GOE: 05.05.09 STRENGTH: L GED: R5 M4 L4 SVP: 7 DLU: 88

621.261-010 AIRPLANE INSPECTOR (air trans.) alternate titles: airplane-and-engine inspector
Examines airframe, engines, and operating equipment to ensure that repairs are made according to specifications, and certifies airworthiness of aircraft: Tests tightness of airframe connections with handtools and employs flashlight and mirror to inspect fit of parts. Signals AIRFRAME-AND-POWER-PLANT MECHANIC (air trans.; aircraft mfg.) to start engine and manipulate aircraft controls. Collects data, such as engine revolutions per minute and fuel and oil pressures, to evaluate engine performance, using tachometer and pressure gauges. Examines assembly, installation, and adjustment of ailerons and rudders to ensure that workmanship and materials conform with Civil Air Regulations, company specifications, and manual procedures. Determines accuracy of installation of components in power plant and hydraulic system with protractor, micrometer, calipers, and gauge to ensure that specified tolerances are met. Signs inspection tag to approve unit, or records reasons for rejecting unit. Logs inspections performed on aircraft. Must hold Airframe and Power Plant Mechanic's License and Inspection Authorization, issued by Federal Aviation Administration. May prepare dismantling schedules for airplanes to be overhauled. May service, repair, and replace airframe components, engines, and operating equipment [AIRFRAME-AND-POWER-PLANT MECHANIC (air trans.; aircraft mfg.)].
GOE: 05.07.02 STRENGTH: L GED: R4 M4 L4 SVP: 8 DLU: 77

621.261-014 ENGINE TESTER (aircraft mfg.; air trans.)
Tests performance of new and overhauled aircraft engines, such as turboprop, turbofan, turbojet, and cylinder-type, and interprets test data: Positions or directs other workers in positioning engine on test stand, using hoist or overhead crane. Connects oil and fuel lines, instruments, controls, and engine accessories, such as generators, magnetos, and fuel injectors, using handtools. Connects testing instruments, such as dynamometers and manometers, to engine. Starts and operates engine for specified time at various speeds. Reads and records test data, such as speed, temperature, oil pressure, fuel consumption, and exhaust pressure. Calculates performance of engine at various speeds, using test data, standard formulas, computer or calculator. Signs off tested engines as ready for service or indicates reasons for rejection based on analysis of test data. Must be licensed by or perform work under licensure of Federal Aviation Administration. May operate computerized test equipment to enter, retrieve, and compute test data and be designated Test Cell Technician (aircraft mfg.).
GOE: 06.01.05 STRENGTH: M GED: R4 M4 L4 SVP: 7 DLU: 88

621.261-018 FLIGHT ENGINEER (air trans.) alternate titles: flight mechanic
Makes preflight, inflight, and postflight inspections, adjustments, and minor repairs to ensure safe and efficient operation of aircraft: Inspects aircraft prior to takeoff for defects, such as fuel or oil leaks and malfunctions in electrical, hydraulic, or pressurization systems, according to preflight checklist. Verifies passenger and cargo distribution and amount of fuel to ensure that weight and balance specifications are met. Monitors control panel to verify aircraft performance, and regulates engine speed according to instructions of AIRPLANE PILOT, COMMERCIAL (air trans.). Makes inflight repairs, such as replacing fuses, adjusting instruments, and freeing jammed flight control cables, using handtools, or takes emergency measures to compensate for failure of equipment, such as autopilot, wing heaters, and electrical and hydraulic systems. Monitors fuel gauges and computes rate of fuel consumption. Keeps log of fuel consumption and engine performance. Records malfunctions which were not corrected during flight and reports needed repairs to ground maintenance personnel. May perform repairs upon completion of flight. Must be licensed by Federal Aviation Administration. May be required to be licensed AIRFRAME-AND-POWER-PLANT MECHANIC (air trans.; aircraft mfg.) or AIRPLANE PILOT, COMMERCIAL (air trans.).
GOE: 05.03.06 STRENGTH: L GED: R4 M4 L4 SVP: 7 DLU: 77

621.261-022 EXPERIMENTAL AIRCRAFT MECHANIC (aircraft mfg.) alternate titles: experimental aircraft and engine mechanic, field and hangar; experimental flight test mechanic; experimental preflight mechanic

Inspects, tests, repairs, maintains, services, and modifies experimental and prototype aircraft, engines, accessories, and components according to governmental, company, and customer requirements: Assembles and installs aircraft electrical, plumbing, mechanical, and structural accessories and components, such as ejection seats, hatch mechanisms, and safety belts, using handtools and power tools. Installs, operates, and adjusts test apparatus, such as recorders, oscillographs, limit switches, inverters, thermocouples, instruments, cameras, timing devices, and photo recorders. Operates aircraft engines and systems, such as hydraulic, air-conditioning, pressurization, fuel, controls, and landing gear, to diagnose malfunctions, using test equipment, such as hydraulic test bench, pressure ratio bench, water injection test cart, and ground power unit. Repairs, adjusts, aligns, and calibrates aircraft systems. Modifies aircraft structure or components following drawings, engineering orders, and other technical publications, as required. Services and maintains gaseous, liquid oxygen, pneumatic, and hydraulic systems on aircraft. May specialize in testing and modifying spacecraft systems and be designated Experimental Mechanic, Spacecraft (aircraft mfg.).
GOE: 05.05.09 STRENGTH: M GED: R4 M3 L4 SVP: 7 DLU: 89

621.281-014 AIRFRAME-AND-POWER-PLANT MECHANIC (aircraft mfg.; air trans.) alternate titles: aircraft mechanic; airplane mechanic

Services, repairs, and overhauls aircraft and aircraft engines to ensure airworthiness: Repairs, replaces, and rebuilds aircraft structures, such as wings and fuselage, and functional components including rigging, surface controls, and plumbing and hydraulic units, using handtools, power tools, machines, and equipment such as shears, sheet metal brakes, welding equipment, rivet gun, and drills. Reads and interprets manufacturers' and airline's maintenance manuals, service bulletins, and other specifications to determine feasibility and method of repairing or replacing malfunctioning or damaged components. Examines engines for cracked cylinders and oil leaks, and listens to operating engine to detect and diagnose malfunctions, such as sticking or burned valves. Inspects turbine blades to detect cracks or breaks. Tests engine operation, using testing equipment such as ignition analyzer, compression checker, distributor timer, and ammeter, to locate source of malfunction. Replaces or repairs worn or damaged components, such as carburetors, alternators, and magnetos, using handtools, gauges, and testing equipment. Removes engine from aircraft, using hoist or forklift truck. Disassembles and inspects parts for wear, warping, or other defects. Repairs or replaces defective engine parts and reassembles and installs engine in aircraft. Adjusts, repairs, or replaces electrical wiring system and aircraft accessories. Performs miscellaneous duties to service aircraft, including flushing crankcase, cleaning screens, greasing moving parts, and checking brakes. May be required to be licensed by Federal Aviation Administration. May service engines and airframe components at line station making repairs, short of overhaul, required to keep aircraft in safe operating condition and be designated Airframe-And-Power-Plant Mechanic, Line Service (air trans.). May service and repair aircraft and engines prior to, during, or after flight to ensure airworthiness, working on flight line of aircraft manufacturing facility, and be designated Aircraft-And-Engine Mechanic, Field-And-Hangar (aircraft mfg.); Flight-Line Mechanic (aircraft mfg.); Mechanic, Field-Service (aircraft mfg.). May specialize in rework, repair, and modification of structural, precision, and functional spare parts and assemblies at manufacturing facility and be designated Spares Rework Mechanic (aircraft mfg.). May specialize in engine repair and be designated Aircraft-Engine Assembler (air trans.); Aircraft-Engine-Cylinder Mechanic (air trans.); Aircraft-Engine Dismantler (air trans.); Aircraft-Engine Installer (air trans.); Aircraft-Engine Mechanic (air trans.); Aircraft-Engine Mechanic, Overhaul (air trans.). May be designated: Carburetor Mechanic (air trans.); Helicopter Mechanic (air trans.); Hydraulic Tester (air trans.); Ignition Specialist (air trans.); Overhaul And Repair Mechanic (aircraft mfg.); Supercharger Mechanic (air trans.).
GOE: 05.05.09 STRENGTH: M GED: R4 M4 L4 SVP: 7 DLU: 88

621.281-018 AIRFRAME-AND-POWER-PLANT-MECHANIC APPRENTICE (air trans.) alternate titles: airplane-mechanic apprentice

Performs duties as described under APPRENTICE (any industry) Master Title.
GOE: 05.05.09 STRENGTH: M GED: R4 M4 L4 SVP: 7 DLU: 77

621.281-030 ROCKET-ENGINE-COMPONENT MECHANIC (aircraft mfg.)

Assembles, tests, and repairs pneumatic, hydraulic, and mechanical components of rocket motors or rocket engines, according to specifications, using handtools, power tools, and precision measuring and testing instruments: Positions parts in jigs and holding fixtures to facilitate assembly. Fits and assembles interrelating precision parts, using handtools. Inspects configuration and dimensions of assemblies, using instruments, such as optical flats, micrometers, calipers, dial indicators, and monolight instruments. Tests assemblies to determine conditions, such as internal leakage, pressure differentials, and cycles of operation, using gauges, meters, and chemicals. Conducts functional tests to determine mechanical performance. Analyzes malfunctions to determine causes, and repairs, adjusts, synchronizes, and calibrates assemblies. May perform welding

and acid etching on various materials. May operate computer to record, analyze, and interpret test data.
GOE: 05.05.09 STRENGTH: M GED: R4 M4 L4 SVP: 7 DLU: 88

621.684-010 AIRFRAME-AND-POWER-PLANT-MECHANIC HELPER (aircraft mfg.; air trans.) alternate titles: airplane-mechanic helper

Assists other workers engaged in servicing, repairing, and overhauling aircraft and aircraft engines, performing any combination of following duties: Replaces batteries, filters, and similar accessories, using mechanic's handtools. Removes inspection plates, cowling, engine covers, floor boards, and related items, to permit access for repair or inspection, and replaces items upon completion of work. Assists AIRFRAME-AND-POWER-PLANT MECHANIC (aircraft mfg.; air trans.) 621.281-014 in dismantling, repairing, overhauling, or replacing parts and assemblies, such as engines, plumbing and hydraulic systems, and aircraft structural sections. Cleans aircraft interior and exterior parts and assemblies with solvents or other cleaning solutions. Inflates tires, fills gasoline tanks and oil reservoirs, and greases aircraft, using grease gun. May assist manufacturing facility flight line personnel in servicing and repairing aircraft prior to flight or customer acceptance and be designated Flight Line Service Attendant (aircraft mfg.). Performs other duties as described under HELPER (any industry) Master Title.
GOE: 05.10.02 STRENGTH: M GED: R3 M2 L2 SVP: 4 DLU: 88

621.684-014 RECLAMATION WORKER (wholesale tr.)

Dismantles wrecked and other decommissioned aircraft and salvages parts and equipment: Removes wings, tails, engines, landing gear, instruments and other repairable parts, using handtools. Dismantles condemned equipment, retaining usable parts. Cleans salvaged parts in solvent and coats with grease or other preservative, using swab, brush, or spray gun.
GOE: 05.12.12 STRENGTH: M GED: R3 M2 L2 SVP: 4 DLU: 77

622 RAIL EQUIPMENT MECHANICS AND REPAIRERS

This group includes occupations concerned with inspecting and repairing surface and subsurface railway equipment.

622.131-010 SUPERVISOR, RAILROAD CAR REPAIR (railroad equip.)

Supervises and coordinates activities of workers engaged in inspecting, dismantling, welding, carpentering, painting, riveting, and testing parts, units, and damaged wood or steel sections of railway cars. May inspect damaged cars and prepare estimate of repair costs. Performs duties as described under SUPERVISOR (any industry) Master Title.
GOE: 05.05.06 STRENGTH: L GED: R4 M3 L4 SVP: 8 DLU: 77

622.131-014 SUPERVISOR, ROUNDHOUSE (railroad equip.)

Supervises and coordinates activities of workers engaged in inspecting, servicing, and repairing railway locomotives such as diesel-electric locomotives and gasoline-powered speeders. Performs duties as described under SUPERVISOR (any industry) Master Title.
GOE: 05.05.09 STRENGTH: L GED: R4 M3 L4 SVP: 8 DLU: 77

622.131-018 SUPERVISOR, WHEEL SHOP (railroad equip.)

Supervises and coordinates activities of workers engaged in repairing, reboring, mounting, dismounting, and turning down railroad car wheel and axle assemblies, according to Federal and American Railroad Association safety specifications. Trains workers. Performs duties as described under SUPERVISOR (any industry) Master Title.
GOE: 05.05.07 STRENGTH: M GED: R4 M3 L4 SVP: 8 DLU: 77

622.137-010 SUPERVISOR, BRAKE REPAIR (r.r. trans.)

Supervises and coordinates activities of workers engaged in maintenance and repair of braking devices on railroad tracks in classification yard: Patrols work area to observe operation and condition of braking device and to note and record defects, such as loose bolts, escaping air, and worn brake shoes. Assigns tasks and plans and coordinates activities of BRAKE REPAIRER, RAILROAD (r.r. trans.) 622.261-010 to maximize work performed and utilization of work force, based on knowledge of worker ability and experience and tasks to be performed. Patrols work sites to resolve problems relative to work and to suggest changes in work procedure to improve efficiency. Examines completed repair of maintenance to ensure conformance to company standards, applying knowledge of operation of braking device and of railroad regulations. Walks throughout yard to detect unsafe conditions or violations of safety rules. Apprises workers of violations to instruct workers in safe work methods and records repeated violations or commendable work methods on specified forms. Maintains records, such as employee timecards, materials used for maintenance and repair of braking device, and summaries of work performed. Performs other duties as described under SUPERVISOR (any industry) Master Title.
GOE: 05.02.02 STRENGTH: L GED: R3 M2 L2 SVP: 7 DLU: 86

622.137-014 SUPERVISOR, CAR AND YARD (r.r. trans.)

Supervises and coordinates activities of workers engaged in repair and maintenance of railroad cars in freight yard, and workers engaged in inspecting incoming and outbound freight cars for malfunctions: Inspects railroad cars and reviews worksheet to determine type and priority of repairs to be performed on cars, such as replacing handholds, couplers, or wheels. Marks side of car, using chalk, to inform workers of work to be performed, such as type of repair,

servicing, or inspection. Requests parts from stockroom needed by workers to repair cars. Assigns workers to repair cars in shop, to perform minor repairs in yard, such as bent grab irons, and to inspect incoming and outbound trains for defects, such as worn brake pads and broken doors. Examines work in progress and completed work to correct faulty work procedures and to ensure that repairs meet specified standards. Patrols work area to observe work methods and ensure compliance with safety regulations. Instructs workers in safe use of equipment in shop and yard. Prepares forms that detail work performed, such as car number, number of staff-hours spent on work, and type of maintenance or repairs performed. Performs other duties as described under SUPERVISOR (any industry) Master Title.
GOE: 05.05.06 STRENGTH: L GED: R3 M2 L2 SVP: 6 DLU: 86

622.261-010 BRAKE REPAIRER, RAILROAD (r.r. trans.)
Repairs and maintains braking devices on railroad tracks leading into yard of terminal to ensure specified performance of braking device, using handtools: Gathers specified tools, such as gauges, grease gun, and handtools, required to complete work assignment, such as greasing fittings or replacing brake shoes. Adjusts and measures distances between brake shoes to specified standards, using handtools, gauge, and steel rule. Removes bolts, screws, and metal plates to access parts of braking device, following blueprints. Examines broken device to isolate defect or verify repairs needed. Removes designated part, places new part in braking device and adjusts fit to ensure accurate placement, working as member of team. Replaces bolts, screws, and metal plates, using hand and pneumatic tools. Inspects braking device for conformance to standards. Greases fittings of braking device to maintain and prevent excessive wear of parts. Loosens and lifts braking device from rail, using handtools and crane, and replaces broken or deteriorated track beams, working as member of team.
GOE: 05.05.09 STRENGTH: V GED: R3 M2 L2 SVP: 6 DLU: 86

622.281-010 LOCOMOTIVE INSPECTOR (railroad equip.) alternate titles: pit inspector
Inspects railroad locomotives in roundhouse or shop to determine extent of wear and needed repairs, using handtools and measuring instruments: Examines firebox, journal boxes, and bearings to detect wear. Taps parts, such as rods, wheels, and bolts with hammer or rawhide mallet and listens to sound to detect ruptures or cracks. Measures wheel flanges with calipers and depth gauge to detect excessive wear or flat spots. Reports defects to SUPERVISOR, ROUNDHOUSE (railroad equip.) or prepares inspection report form.
GOE: 05.07.01 STRENGTH: L GED: R4 M3 L3 SVP: 7 DLU: 77

622.381-010 AIR-VALVE REPAIRER (railroad equip.)
Repairs compressed-air valves, such as triple-air valves, cutoff valves, and retainer valves, using handtools, power tools, and measuring instruments according to specifications: Disassembles valves, using power wrench, and cleans parts with gasoline and airhose. Measures parts, such as gaskets, valve seats, pistons, and slides for conformance to federal and company specifications, using gauges. Scrapes, grinds, and polishes metal contacting surfaces to make surfaces airtight, using rasps and emery polishing cloths. Replaces defective parts and reassembles valves.
GOE: 05.10.02 STRENGTH: L GED: R3 M2 L2 SVP: 6 DLU: 77

622.381-014 CAR REPAIRER (railroad equip.) alternate titles: drop-pit worker; machinist
Repairs and rebuilds railway freight cars, tank cars, or locomotives, following federal and company regulations and specifications and using handtools, power tools, welding equipment, and measuring instruments: Removes and inspects locomotive or car units, such as wheels, truck and brake assemblies, side posts, air cylinders, reservoirs and valves, side and roof sections, and coupler assemblies, using pneumatic hoist and jack, pinch bar, handtools, and cutting torch. Disassembles roller bearings, using jacks, blocks, and frames. Examines bearings, gaskets, and seals for defects, such as scratches, chips, and excessive wear. Replaces defective parts and reassembles roller bearings. Measures diameter of axle wheel seats, using micrometer, and marks dimensions on axle for subsequent boring of wheels to specified press fit dimensions. Repairs wooden sections, such as flooring and interior walls [CARPENTER (construction)]. Repairs or replaces steel sections, such as side posts, rafters, crossties, panels, underframing, and piping, using welding torch, power wrench, and plumber's tools. Assembles repaired or replaced units to rebuild locomotive or car. Positions width gauge between car sides, clamps turnbuckle ends to top of each side, and twists turnbuckle, using wrench, until sides are pressed against gauge to align sides for installation of car ends and crossties. May be designated according to type of car repaired as Tank-Car Repairer (railroad equip.). May be known according to specific tasks performed as Car Straightener (railroad equip.); Wheel Fitter (railroad equip.).
GOE: 05.05.06 STRENGTH: H GED: R4 M3 L3 SVP: 7 DLU: 77

622.381-018 CAR REPAIRER, PULLMAN (r.r. trans.)
Installs and repairs railroad sleeping car equipment, such as plumbing, interior fixtures, windows, steps, and platforms: Fabricates and installs cabinets and other wood fixtures, using carpentry tools. Replaces window glass, using handtools. Repairs damage to metal surfaces and parts, using arc or acetylene welding equipment. Removes mechanical equipment, such as compressors and generators from beneath car for bench repair by other workers.
GOE: 05.10.01 STRENGTH: M GED: R4 M3 L3 SVP: 7 DLU: 77

622.381-022 CAR-REPAIRER APPRENTICE (railroad equip.) alternate titles: machinist apprentice
Performs duties as described under APPRENTICE (any industry) Master Title.

GOE: 05.05.06 STRENGTH: H GED: R4 M3 L3 SVP: 7 DLU: 77

622.381-026 FLOOR-COVERING LAYER (railroad equip.)
Removes worn floor covering from floors of streetcars and lays new floor covering: Sets felt on floor and cuts it around obstructions to fit floor. Applies coat of liquid cement to floor with brush and replaces felt on floor. Sets covering on floor and cuts off correct lengths and shapes. Applies coat of cement to felt and sets floor covering over cemented felt. Tacks edges of covering. Patches linoleum floors in same manner. Heats asphalt with blow torch and applies asphalt to cracks or openings and smooths it to match level of floor, using trowel, to patch asphaltic floors.
GOE: 05.10.01 STRENGTH: M GED: R4 M3 L3 SVP: 7 DLU: 77

622.381-030 MINE-CAR REPAIRER (mine & quarry) alternate titles: pit car repairer; shop blacksmith
Repairs or replaces damaged parts of underground mine cars: Welds, straightens, bolts, rivets, and refits parts, such as axles, wheels, bodies, and couplings, using hoists, jacks, handtools, power tools, and machine shop equipment. Makes new parts, such as body framework and undercarriages, using welding equipment. May examine mine car for defects and be designated Car Inspector (mine & quarry).
GOE: 05.05.06 STRENGTH: H GED: R4 M3 L3 SVP: 7 DLU: 77

622.381-034 RAILROAD WHEELS AND AXLE INSPECTOR (railroad equip.) alternate titles: wheel and axle inspector
Inspects railway car axle and wheel assemblies to determine conformance to Federal and American Railroad Association specifications, using measuring instruments: Verifies diameter of wheel and journal seats on axle, using calipers and micrometers. Measures space between wheels and from center of axle to each wheel, using needle-pointed space gauge, to verify conformance to specifications. Observes hydraulograph pressure-gauge indicator on wheel-pressing machine, as wheels are pressed onto axles, to ensure conformity to ton-pressure tolerances.
GOE: 06.01.05 STRENGTH: L GED: R4 M3 L3 SVP: 6 DLU: 77

622.381-038 SALVAGE INSPECTOR (railroad equip.)
Inspects new and used metal car parts for conformance to company's specifications, using measuring instruments and following blueprints: Examines used metal parts to determine parts salvageable for repair or scrap. Examines broken parts to determine nature and cause of defects. Measures new and used parts to verify specified dimensions and hardness, using micrometer, calipers, scales, and gauges. Forwards parts to laboratory for analysis, shop for repair, or to weighmaster for sale as scrap. Records inspection data, such as parts inspected, types of defects, and disposition of material.
GOE: 06.01.05 STRENGTH: M GED: R4 M3 L3 SVP: 6 DLU: 77

622.382-010 TRIPLE-AIR-VALVE TESTER (railroad equip.) alternate titles: test rack operator
Operates equipment to test various types of triple air valves for conformance to federal and company safety standards: Mounts valve on test frame and connects air supply hoses to valve, using portable power wrench. Moves test panel control levers singly or in combination to open or block air passages into different chambers of valve. Turns lever to inject air into unblocked chambers, reads gauges to determine specified pressure differentials, and to detect leaks, weak springs, and poor fits. Applies soapy water to valve with brush to pinpoint air leaks. Replaces defective parts. Rejects valves that do not meet specifications.
GOE: 05.07.02 STRENGTH: M GED: R3 M3 L3 SVP: 7 DLU: 77

622.684-010 AIR-COMPRESSOR MECHANIC (railroad equip.) alternate titles: compressor repairer
Repairs railroad-car air compressors and compressor motors, following wiring diagrams and using handtools: Disassembles compressor and examines parts for wear or breakage. Cleans parts and installs new piston rings and wrist pins. Replaces worn bearings, armatures, field coils, gears, and pinions in electric motors, following wiring diagram. Reassembles compressor and connects compressor to compressed air and electrical outlets to test operation.
GOE: 05.10.02 STRENGTH: L GED: R3 M3 L3 SVP: 6 DLU: 77

622.684-014 CAR-REPAIRER HELPER (railroad equip.) alternate titles: machinist helper
Assists CAR REPAIRER (railroad equip.) in repairing and rebuilding freight cars, tank cars, or locomotives, performing any combination of following tasks: Threads nuts and bolts and drills metal stock, using hand taps, dies, and drill press. Shears metal sheet and bar stock to specified dimensions. Straightens metal parts, using hammer and sledge. Bolts steel top frames to side frames of car, using power wrench. Rolls axle and wheel assemblies into hydraulic wheel-dismounting machine. Pulls levers to position ram against end of axle and force wheel from wheel seat. Rolls wheel to storage area. Caulks seams of car and fills car with water to detect leaks. Polishes brass trim on car. Repairs or replaces steam and airhoses. Lubricates car. May be known according to specific task performed as Car Tester (railroad equip.); Car-Top Bolter (railroad equip.). Performs other duties as described under HELPER (any industry) Master Title.
GOE: 05.12.12 STRENGTH: M GED: R2 M1 L2 SVP: 4 DLU: 77

622.684-018 SWITCH REPAIRER (r.r. trans.)
Repairs mechanical portion of railway-track switches: Sweeps dirt from switch with broom, and oils parts. Examines switches for worn or broken parts.

Adjusts mechanical parts of pull-chain switches, using handtools. Replaces defective parts, using handtools. May work as member of emergency work crew.
GOE: 05.10.02 STRENGTH: L GED: R3 M2 L2 SVP: 5 DLU: 77

622.684-022 TANK-CAR INSPECTOR (chemical)
Inspects, services, and tests railway tank cars used to transport compressed and liquefied gases: Connects flexible hose from suction line to car and opens valves on car and in blowoff line to facilitate removal of residual gas from used tank cars. Removes safety and flow control valves from car with wrenches, replacing valves with reconditioned ones. Examines car interior for defects and cleanliness, passing light beam into car and viewing it through valve openings or entering car through dome. Washes interior with water and dries with steam. Routes defective cars for repair. Tests tanks for leaks [HYDRO-PNEUMATIC TESTER (any industry)].
GOE: 05.12.12 STRENGTH: M GED: R2 M1 L2 SVP: 4 DLU: 77

623   MARINE MECHANICS AND REPAIRERS

This group includes occupations concerned with repairing mechanical equipment aboard fresh-water and sea-going ships, tugboats, barges, lighters, floating drydocks, and other marine craft and floating structures, and repairing related harbor and dock machinery.

623.131-010 MACHINIST SUPERVISOR, OUTSIDE (ship-boat mfg.)
Supervises and coordinates activities of workers engaged in installation of ship machinery, such as propelling machinery, auxiliary motors and pumps, and steering gear, performing duties as described under SUPERVISOR (any industry) Master Title.
GOE: 05.05.09 STRENGTH: M GED: R4 M3 L3 SVP: 8 DLU: 77

623.131-014 SUPERVISOR, GEAR REPAIR (water trans.)
Supervises and coordinates activities of workers engaged in fabricating, repairing, and supplying equipment used in loading and unloading ships' cargoes: Reviews work orders, inventory and other reports and assigns workers to activities, such as repairing equipment, fabricating special gear, and supplying cargo-handling equipment required for stevedoring operations. Inspects gear for quality of work and conformance to standards. Requisitions materials. Performs other duties as described under SUPERVISOR (any industry) Master Title.
GOE: 05.10.02 STRENGTH: L GED: R4 M3 L3 SVP: 7 DLU: 77

623.261-010 EXPERIMENTAL MECHANIC, OUTBOARD MOTORS (engine-turbine) alternate titles: river tester
Tests, repairs, and rebuilds experimental outboard motors and parts to specified operating efficiency, using machine tools, precision measuring instruments, jigs, and fixtures: Mounts motor to boat and operates boat at various speeds on waterway to conduct operational tests. Observes and records readings on instruments, such as tachometers, monometers, voltmeters, ammeter, and vibration analyzer to measure boat speeds and thrust forces. Analyzes test records and disassembles motor to remove parts needing modification. Operates machine tools, such as lathes, mills, drills, and grinders, to repair or rework parts, such as cams, rods, crankshaft, and propeller.
GOE: 05.05.09 STRENGTH: M GED: R4 M4 L4 SVP: 7 DLU: 77

623.261-014 OUTBOARD-MOTOR TESTER (engine-turbine)
Tests operation of outboard motor in tank and repairs, adjusts, or replaces parts according to specifications and engineering requirements, using measuring instruments and handtools: Lowers motor on test frame into water tank, using chain hoist, and inspects wiring, screws, plugs, and assemblies for missing or broken parts. Starts motor and listens to and inspects it for signs of malfunctioning, such as smoke, excessive vibration, and misfiring. Holds tachometer against turning shaft and reads revolutions per minute. Verifies timing of cam gears, idle gear, and flywheel, using stroboscope. Turns regulating screws on carburetor to adjust idle speed, choke, and high-low speed. Sets starter lock and aligns shift lever shaft with indicated marks for speeds, using gauges, screwdrivers, and wrenches. Measures voltage, amperage, and polarity, using ammeter, voltmeter, and polarity gauge. Idles motor and observes thermometer to determine effectiveness of cooling system. Writes test report to indicate acceptance or reason for rejection of motor. Oils carburetor. Stamps identification number on motor, using hammer and metal stamping equipment. May test specific aspects of engine performance, such as fuel consumption, compression, and power output, and recommend modifications to improve engine performance and be designated Life Tester, Outboard Motors (engine-turbine).
GOE: 06.01.05 STRENGTH: M GED: R4 M3 L3 SVP: 6 DLU: 77

623.281-010 DECK ENGINEER (water trans.)
Repairs and maintains deck machinery, such as cargo winches and anchor windlasses: Operates machinery to determine causes of malfunctioning. Dismantles, repairs, or replaces defective parts, and reassembles machinery, using machinist's handtools, chain hoists, and steel rollers. May maintain ship's plumbing system. May change fuses and lights and overhaul electric motors. Rating must be endorsed by U.S. Coast Guard.
GOE: 05.05.09 STRENGTH: M GED: R4 M3 L3 SVP: 7 DLU: 77

623.281-014 DEEP SUBMERGENCE VEHICLE CREWMEMBER (military ser.)
Services, repairs, and maintains deep submergence vehicle (small noncombatant submarine) and assists DEEP SUBMERGENCE VEHICLE OPERATOR (military ser.) in predive and postdive inspection and operation of vehicle.

Connects high pressure air and oxygen hoses from land based equipment to vehicle. Services vehicle with oil and hydraulic fluid. Connects cables to and charges vehicle's battery. Inspects and replaces seals, gaskets, hoses, tubing, hydraulic motors, pumps, valves, filters, and other specified equipment and components aboard vehicle. Conducts detailed predive and postdive tests of mechanical, life supporting, electrical, and hydraulic systems. May drive vehicle and supervise subordinates.
GOE: 05.10.02 STRENGTH: M GED: R4 M3 L3 SVP: 5 DLU: 77

623.281-018 MACHINIST APPRENTICE, MARINE ENGINE (ship-boat mfg.) alternate titles: marine-engine-installation-and-repairer apprentice
Performs duties as described under APPRENTICE (any industry) Master Title.
GOE: 05.05.09 STRENGTH: M GED: R4 M3 L3 SVP: 7 DLU: 77

623.281-022 MACHINIST APPRENTICE, OUTSIDE (ship-boat mfg.) alternate titles: marine-machinist apprentice; outside-installer apprentice
Performs duties as described under APPRENTICE (any industry) Master Title.
GOE: 05.05.09 STRENGTH: M GED: R4 M3 L3 SVP: 7 DLU: 77

623.281-026 MACHINIST, MARINE ENGINE (ship-boat mfg.) alternate titles: marine-engine mechanic
Installs and repairs gasoline and diesel engines in boats, such as yachts, tugs, and trawlers, following specifications: Positions engine over mounting holes, using chain hoist. Bolts engine to mount and straps fuel tank to cradle, using handtools. Connects fuel, oil, and waterlines to engine. Installs engine controls, propeller shaft, and propeller. Attaches test instruments, such as tachometer and voltmeter to engine. Starts engine and records operating data, such as revolutions per minute, and voltage output. Disassembles defective engines and repairs or replaces damaged parts, using handtools.
GOE: 05.05.09 STRENGTH: M GED: R4 M3 L3 SVP: 7 DLU: 77

623.281-030 MACHINIST, OUTSIDE (ship-boat mfg.) alternate titles: engineer, steam; machinist, installation; marine erector; marine machinist; outfitter; outside-installation machinist
Installs ship machinery, such as propelling machinery, auxiliary motors, pumps, ventilating equipment, and steering gear, working from blueprints and using handtools, calipers, and micrometers. Lays out passage holes on bulkheads, decks, and other surfaces for connections, such as shafting and steam lines. Installs below-deck auxiliaries, such as evaporators, stills, heaters, pumps, condensers, and boilers and connects them to steampipe systems. Tests and inspects installed machinery and equipment during dock and sea trials. May set up and operate such machine shop tools as lathe, boring mill, planer, shaper, slotter, and milling machine to fabricate replacement parts.
GOE: 05.05.09 STRENGTH: M GED: R4 M3 L3 SVP: 7 DLU: 77

623.281-034 MAINTENANCE MECHANIC, ENGINE (water trans.) alternate titles: second assistant engineer; third assistant engineer
Repairs and maintains propulsion engines and other engines and engine parts aboard ship: Examines engine equipment, such as pumps, circulators, condensers, and steering engines to locate malfunctions, and dismantles and repairs defective equipment, using handtools and power tools. Makes engine replacement parts, such as slide valves, stay rods, and bolts, using metalworking machinery. Stands engineroom watch during specified periods, observing gauges to determine that operating conditions, such as temperatures, steam pressure, water and oil levels, and revolutions per minute are within specified ranges. Adjusts controls to maintain specified operating conditions. Records gauge readings in engineering log. Must be licensed by U.S. Coast Guard.
GOE: 05.05.09 STRENGTH: M GED: R3 M3 L3 SVP: 7 DLU: 77

623.281-038 MOTORBOAT MECHANIC (engine-turbine; ship-boat mfg.) alternate titles: boat mechanic
Repairs and adjusts electrical and mechanical equipment of gasoline- or diesel-powered inboard or inboard-outboard boat engines, using handtools, power tools, and electrical testing meters: Starts motor and listens to its sound to determine causes of trouble. Tests motor for conformance to manufacturer's specifications, using electrical testing meters. Dismantles motors, using handtools, and examines parts for defects. Adjusts generator and replaces faulty wiring, using handtools and soldering iron. Installs piston rings, adjusts carburetor, grinds valves, and repairs or replaces reduction gears, and other parts, using lathe, drill press, handtools, and power tools. Examines propeller and propeller shafts and repairs defective parts. Aligns engine to propeller shaft. May operate boat on water to test repairs. May repair only mechanical equipment of engines, such as power-tilt, bilge pumps, or power take-offs. May be designated according to type of engine repaired as Motorboat Mechanic, Inboard (ship-boat mfg.); Motorboat Mechanic, Inboard/Outboard (ship-boat mfg.).
GOE: 05.05.09 STRENGTH: M GED: R4 M3 L3 SVP: 7 DLU: 77

623.281-042 OUTBOARD-MOTOR MECHANIC (engine-turbine; ship-boat mfg.)
Analyzes defects, and adjusts or repairs electrical and mechanical systems of outboard motors: Disassembles and inspects motor for defective parts, using mechanic's handtools and gauges. Replaces parts, such as gears, magneto points, piston rings, and spark plugs, and reassembles engine. Adjusts carbu-

retor mixture and electrical point settings while motor is running in water-filled test tank. May change propeller to increase motor efficiency, based on size and shape of boat hull. May install or repair steering and throttle controls.
GOE: 05.05.09 STRENGTH: H GED: R4 M3 L3 SVP: 7 DLU: 77

623.381-010 GEAR REPAIRER (water trans.)

Fabricates and repairs equipment used in loading and unloading ships' cargoes: Operates power sewing machine to patch and seam canvas hatch tents. Inserts grommets into and attaches ropes to tent. Cuts lumber into specified lengths and constructs cargo boards, using carpenter's handtools and power tools. Splices ropes and cables to make and repair slings and spreaders, using marlin spike and splicing vise. Replaces defective parts of scrapers and clamshells, using wrenches, punches, hammers, and chainfalls. Gathers information as to type of cargo, terminal facilities, and loading and unloading schedule to determine what gear is necessary to perform work. Transports gear to dock by truck. Installs cargo-handling equipment on deck of vessel. Transfers gear from vessel to vessel to obtain greater utilization.
GOE: 05.10.02 STRENGTH: H GED: R3 M2 L3 SVP: 6 DLU: 77

623.684-010 MOTORBOAT-MECHANIC HELPER (engine-turbine; ship-boat mfg.)

Assists MOTORBOAT MECHANIC (engine-turbine; ship-boat mfg.) in repairing gasoline- or diesel-powered motorboats: Removes pumps, generators, and other engine accessories, using handtools. Removes engine head and oil pan to dismantle engine. Removes covers of gear and clutch units or removes entire assemblies as instructed. Washes and cleans disassembled parts. Assists in reassembly of repaired engines. Performs other duties as described under HELPER (any industry) Master Title.
GOE: 05.12.15 STRENGTH: M GED: R2 M1 L2 SVP: 3 DLU: 77

623.687-010 MACHINIST HELPER, OUTSIDE (ship-boat mfg.) alternate titles: machinist helper, marine

Assists MACHINIST, OUTSIDE (ship-boat mfg.) in installing ship machinery, such as motors, pumps, ventilating equipment and steering gear: Drills holes in foundations in specified places for anchoring machinery, using portable, powered drills. Assists in moving and leveling machinery, using portable jacks, as directed. Bolts equipment to deck and attaches fuel, cooling, or lubricating lines as directed, using handtools. Performs other duties as described under HELPER (any industry) Master Title.
GOE: 05.12.15 STRENGTH: H GED: R2 M1 L2 SVP: 3 DLU: 77

624 FARM MECHANICS AND REPAIRERS

This group includes occupations concerned with repairing machinery, equipment, and vehicles used in planting, cultivating, harvesting, moving, processing, and storing plant and animal farm products.

624.131-010 SUPERVISOR, FARM-EQUIPMENT MAINTENANCE (agric. equip.)

Supervises and coordinates activities of workers engaged in repairing and overhauling farm equipment, machinery, and vehicles on farms or in farm-equipment repair shops: Trains workers in vehicle maintenance and repair procedures. Inspects work for compliance with standards. Requisitions replacements parts and supplies. Performs other duties as described under SUPERVISOR (any industry) Master Title.
GOE: 05.05.09 STRENGTH: M GED: R4 M3 L4 SVP: 7 DLU: 77

624.281-010 FARM-EQUIPMENT MECHANIC I (agric. equip.) alternate titles: farm mechanic

Maintains, repairs, and overhauls farm machinery, equipment, and vehicles, such as tractors, harvesters, pumps, tilling equipment, trucks, and other mechanized, electrically powered, or motor-driven equipment, on farms or in farm-equipment repair shops: Examines and listens to machines, motors, gasoline and diesel engines, and equipment for operational defects and dismantles defective units, using handtools. Repairs or replaces defective parts, using handtools and machine tools, such as drill press, lathe, milling machine, woodworking machines, welding equipment, grinders, and saws. Reassembles, adjusts, and lubricates machines and equipment to ensure efficient operation. May install and repair wiring and motors to maintain farm electrical system. May install and repair plumbing systems on farm. May construct and repair buildings and other farm structures. May assemble and erect new farm machinery and equipment. May be designated according to equipment maintained as Viner Mechanic (agric. equip.).
GOE: 05.05.09 STRENGTH: M GED: R4 M3 L3 SVP: 7 DLU: 77

624.281-014 FARM-EQUIPMENT-MECHANIC APPRENTICE (agric. equip.) alternate titles: farm-mechanic apprentice

Performs duties as described under APPRENTICE (any industry) Master Title.
GOE: 05.05.09 STRENGTH: M GED: R4 M3 L3 SVP: 7 DLU: 77

624.361-010 INSPECTOR AND TESTER (agric. equip.) alternate titles: mechanical inspector; tester

Inspects agricultural equipment, such as tractors, combines, and balers for missing, defective, or improperly installed parts and operational malfunctions: Observes operation of equipment being driven around test area or on treadmill to detect defects, such as loose fittings, improper assembly, malfunctioning parts, or faulty controls, as indicated by noise, leaks, or irregularities in braking,

steering, or transmission mechanisms. Aligns power-driven wheels of unit over dynamometer and connects electrical test leads to output terminals. Compares dynamometer readings with specification charts to check unit output. Assigns ASSEMBLY REPAIRER (agric. equip.) to defective equipment, explains defects, and suggests method of repair. Examines equipment for paint defects, incorrect decal application, missing tools, and faulty lights. Records cause and type of defect and repair work performed. May be designated according to type of inspection as Treadmill Inspector (agric. equip.); or type of equipment inspected as Combine Inspector (agric. equip.).
GOE: 06.01.05 STRENGTH: M GED: R4 M3 L3 SVP: 6 DLU: 77

624.361-014 SPRINKLER-IRRIGATION-EQUIPMENT MECHANIC (agric. equip.)

Installs and maintains self-propelled circle-irrigation system on farms according to specifications: Reads work order to ascertain type system to be installed, installation location, and operating specifications. Drives truck to haul tools and equipment to work site. Raises prefabricated sections of irrigator into position, using truck-mounted crane, and connects sections together with precut structural aluminum and bolts. Installs water pipe and sprinkler heads along framework, using pipe-wrenches and couplings. Positions, seals, and secures irrigator to pivot of water supply, using crane, wrenches, and packing compound. Activates irrigator and observes operation to verify synchronization of drive-wheels, and specified distribution and volume of water. Replaces defective water lines, sprinkler heads, and structural members, using pipe threader, tube cutters, welding equipment, and handtools. Tests and replaces electrical wiring and components, using test meter, soldering equipment, and wire strippers. Periodically repacks pivot and lubricates moving parts.
GOE: 05.10.01 STRENGTH: H GED: R4 M2 L3 SVP: 6 DLU: 77

624.381-010 ASSEMBLY REPAIRER (agric. equip.)

Repairs assembly defects of agricultural equipment, such as tractors, hay balers, and combines, using handtools and power tools: Reads inspection reports and examines equipment to determine type and extent of defect. Aligns, adjusts, or replaces parts, such as drive chains, sprockets, housings, and springs, using handtools and pneumatic grinder. Records type and cause of defect.
GOE: 06.02.24 STRENGTH: M GED: R3 M3 L3 SVP: 5 DLU: 77

624.381-014 FARM-EQUIPMENT MECHANIC II (agric. equip.) alternate titles: farm mechanic; field-equipment-maintenance mechanic, farm

Services, adjusts, and makes minor repairs on farm vehicles, machinery, and equipment, such as tractors, trucks, automobiles, harvesters, combines, silo fillers, plows, and similar equipment, using handtools: Observes and examines machinery and parts in operation to detect malfunctioning or defective units. Replaces components, such as carburetors, fuel pumps, generators, ignition points, and spark plugs. Adjusts timing of motors, lubricates, washes, paints, and cleans vehicles and attachments, using handtools. May assist other workers in more complex maintenance tasks, such as overhaul of machinery and equipment, repair and erection of buildings and structures, plumbing repair, and electrical work on farm.
GOE: 05.10.02 STRENGTH: M GED: R3 M2 L3 SVP: 6 DLU: 77

624.381-018 FARM-MACHINERY SET-UP MECHANIC (agric. equip.)

Erects and assembles farm machinery for use in field: Uncrates components at freight station or dealer's warehouse, using crowbar and hammer. Assembles and adjusts machinery according to specifications, using handtools. Oils and greases moving parts. May deliver farm machinery to purchasers.
GOE: 05.05.09 STRENGTH: H GED: R4 M4 L4 SVP: 6 DLU: 77

624.684-010 GREASER (agric. equip.)

Services and maintains farm machinery and equipment: Lubricates and greases tractors and other powered farm machinery and attachments. Fills gasoline tanks and radiators. Changes and inflates tires. Repairs tubes. Couples attachments, such as cultivators and stalk cutter to tractors, and adjusts attachments to till soil at prescribed depth or to perform other operations as indicated.
GOE: 05.12.08 STRENGTH: H GED: R2 M1 L2 SVP: 4 DLU: 77

625 ENGINE, POWER TRANSMISSION, AND RELATED MECHANICS

This group includes occupations concerned with repairing steam engines, except locomotives; reciprocating internal combustion engines; and auxiliary equipment.

625.131-010 ENGINE-TESTING SUPERVISOR (engine-turbine)

Supervises and coordinates activities of workers engaged in final testing of internal combustion engines: Plans and directs training of workers in engine testing procedures. Assigns workers to test engines of different sizes. Specifies type of test to perform, such as dynamometer, full power, variable speed, and variable load. Reviews test results and compares them with specifications. Records engine repairs needed on test rejection tag. Discusses grievances with workers or representatives and prepares report for use by management in resolving problems. Performs other duties as described under SUPERVISOR (any industry) Master Title.
GOE: 06.01.01 STRENGTH: L GED: R4 M4 L4 SVP: 8 DLU: 77

625.131-014 SUPERVISOR, ENGINE-REPAIR (engine-turbine)

Supervises and coordinates activities of ENGINE REPAIRER, SERVICE (engine-turbine) engaged in repairing gasoline and diesel engines in service or

production repair department: Analyzes data on service repair order or test rejection tag to determine nature of repair required. May inspect and test repaired engines. Performs other duties as described under SUPERVISOR (any industry) Master Title.
GOE: 05.05.09 STRENGTH: L GED: R4 M4 L4 SVP: 8 DLU: 77

625.137-010 SUPERVISOR, LOCOMOTIVE (r.r. trans.)
Supervises and coordinates activities of workers engaged in repair and maintenance of railroad locomotives: Reads management and engineering reports of locomotive problems or malfunctions to determine repairs to be made. Assigns duties to workers based on worker abilities and nature of required repairs. Observes progress of work to ensure adherence to prescribed procedures and adherence to company and governmental standards. Directs workers to perform preventive maintenance of locomotive components, such as diesel engine, frame and housing, electrical system, and air brakes. Monitors stock of replacement parts to detect shortages of parts needed for future repair and maintenance, and requisitions needed parts. Examines shop equipment, such as welding machine and engine simulators, to verify that equipment meets safety and performance standards. Notifies specified personnel of shop equipment malfunctions. Patrols work sites to observe methods, to inspect safety equipment, and to ensure compliance with company, union, and governmental regulations. Performs other duties as described under SUPERVISOR (any industry) Master Title.
GOE: 05.05.09 STRENGTH: L GED: R4 M4 L4 SVP: 7 DLU: 86

625.261-010 DIESEL-ENGINE TESTER (engine-turbine)
Analyzes operation of diesel engines and components, such as blowers and compressors to determine performance using engineering specifications and test equipment: Aligns and connects engine to test equipment, such as generator and motor control panel. Connects oil, fuel, and waterlines to engine. Attaches thermocouple wires to various parts of engine and records temperature readings of oil, water, and bearings from pyrometer. Holds tachometer to turning shaft to determine engine revolutions per minute at various governor settings. Measures pressures on compressors and blowers. Replaces defective parts and adjusts settings on injection pumps, timing, fuel racks, and governor, using dial indicator, micrometer, feeler gauges, and handtools. Logs information for engineering and inspection department. May disassemble and repair powerplant engines and perform field service work [ENGINE REPAIRER, SERVICE (engine-turbine)].
GOE: 06.01.05 STRENGTH: M GED: R4 M3 L3 SVP: 7 DLU: 77

625.281-010 DIESEL MECHANIC (any industry)
Repairs and maintains diesel engines used to power machines, such as buses, ships, trucks, railroad trains, electric generators, and construction machinery, using handtools, precision measuring instruments, and machine tools: Diagnoses trouble, disassembles engines, and examines parts for defects and excessive wear. Reconditions and replaces parts, such as pistons, bearings, gears, valves, and bushings, using engine lathes, boring machines, handtools, and precision measuring instruments. May weld and cut parts, using arc-welding and flame cutting equipment. May be designated according to type of diesel engine or equipment repaired as Diesel-Engine Mechanic, Automobile (automotive ser.); Diesel-Engine Mechanic, Bus (automotive ser.); Diesel-Engine Mechanic, Marine (ship-boat mfg.); Diesel-Engine Mechanic, Truck (automotive ser.); Diesel-Mechanic, Construction (construction); Diesel-Mechanic, Farm (agric. equip.); Locomotive Repairer, Diesel (railroad equip.).
GOE: 05.05.09 STRENGTH: H GED: R4 M3 L3 SVP: 7 DLU: 81

625.281-014 DIESEL-MECHANIC APPRENTICE (any industry) alternate titles: diesel-engine-mechanic apprentice
Performs duties as described under APPRENTICE (any industry) Master Title.
GOE: 05.05.09 STRENGTH: H GED: R4 M3 L3 SVP: 7 DLU: 77

625.281-018 ENGINE REPAIRER, SERVICE (engine-turbine)
Repairs internal combustion engines in factory service departments or repair establishments, according to company specification charts, using machine tools, handtools, and measuring instruments: Positions and bolts engine to test stand. Tests engine to determine malfunctions, using instruments, such as vacuum gauge, compression gauge, and exhaust gas analyzer. Disassembles engine and cleans parts, such as cylinder heads, pistons, ring grooves, piston domes, and cylinder sleeves, using cleaning solvent, sand blasting equipment, grinders, and wire brushes. Rebores and hones cylinders, and turns and undercuts armatures according to chart tolerances, using lathes, grinders, boring and honing machines. Repairs, replaces, or adjusts parts, such as valves, valve guides, and tappets, using valve grinding machine, screwdrivers, wrenches, and feeler gauges. Assembles and starts engine and adjusts carburetor and distributor to ensure smooth performance. May test and repair turbo-superchargers [AIR-FRAME-AND-POWER-PLANT MECHANIC (aircraft mfg.; air trans.) 621.281-014].
GOE: 05.05.09 STRENGTH: M GED: R4 M3 L3 SVP: 7 DLU: 77

625.281-022 FUEL-INJECTION SERVICER (any industry)
Rebuilds, tests, and calibrates fuel injection units as used on diesel engines, railroad locomotives, trucks, construction equipment, tractors, and power plants: Studies repair order and disassembles unit to determine cause of malfunction. Refinishes defective parts, using lapping machine to grind and smooth nozzle point and seat. Replaces parts which cannot be refinished. Assembles and calibrates injection pumps, using test equipment. Assembles and tests nozzle assemblies, using test equipment.
GOE: 05.05.09 STRENGTH: M GED: R4 M4 L4 SVP: 6 DLU: 77

625.281-026 GAS-ENGINE REPAIRER (any industry)
Repairs and maintains gas-driven, internal-combustion engines that power electric generators, compressors, and similar equipment, using handtools and precision-measuring devices: Reads operating reports and diagnoses causes of trouble. Disassembles engines and adjusts or replaces parts, using handtools. Verifies clearances and adjustments, using precision-measuring devices. Reassembles engine and listens to engines in action to detect operational difficulties. May repair air or gas compressors.
GOE: 05.05.09 STRENGTH: M GED: R3 M3 L3 SVP: 6 DLU: 77

625.281-030 POWER-SAW MECHANIC (any industry) alternate titles: chain-saw mechanic
Repairs and maintains portable saws powered by internal combustion engines, following manufacturer's repair manuals and using handtools. Disassembles engine and replaces defective parts, such as piston rings, bearings, and timing mechanism. Cleans or replaces fuel lines and adjusts carburetor. Replaces broken links in chain saw or installs new chain. Replaces rotary or reciprocating blades in other saws as indicated.
GOE: 05.05.09 STRENGTH: M GED: R3 M3 L3 SVP: 6 DLU: 77

625.281-034 SMALL-ENGINE MECHANIC (any industry)
Repairs fractional-horsepower gasoline engines used to power lawnmowers, garden tractors, and similar machines, using handtools: Locates causes of trouble, dismantles engines, using handtools, and examines parts for defects. Replaces or repairs parts, such as rings and bearings, using handtools. Cleans and adjusts carburetor and magneto. Starts repaired engines and listens to sounds to test performance. Replaces engines on machine. May be designated according to type of engine repaired as Lawnmower Mechanic (any industry).
GOE: 05.05.09 STRENGTH: M GED: R3 M3 L3 SVP: 6 DLU: 77

625.361-010 DIESEL-ENGINE ERECTOR (engine-turbine) alternate titles: diesel-engine fitter
Positions, fits, and secures engine parts to erect in-line, V-type, or radial diesel engines according to specifications, using machinist's handtools, surface plate, torque wrench, parallel supports, and measuring instruments: Aligns vertical columns over bedplate between A-frames, using transit and levels and secures columns with tie rods to form frame of engine. Positions engine parts and assemblies, such as valve lever assembly, pistons, connecting rods, cylinder liners, cylinder heads, camshaft housing, crankshaft, journals, fuel injection pump, fuel nozzles, and blowers with help of other workers or overhead crane. Reams or hones holes for fitted bolts. Files, scrapes, drills, taps, dowels, and shims parts, such as cylinder liners, keys, and matching parts. Measures clearances and dimensions, using scales, micrometers, combination square, feeler gauge, and dial indicator. Turns screws to adjust fuel rack and governor, using wrenches and screwdriver, and aligns timing marks on crankshaft, camshaft, and flywheel. Installs and connects fuel, lubrication, and cooling piping, using pipe benders, cutters, and threaders. Connects engine to test equipment, such as dynamometer, and runs engine for specified time to test horsepower at designated revolutions per minute. May disassemble engine for shipping.
GOE: 05.05.09 STRENGTH: M GED: R4 M3 L3 SVP: 7 DLU: 77

625.381-010 ENGINE REPAIRER, PRODUCTION (engine-turbine)
Repairs or replaces defective parts of internal combustion engines indicated on test rejection tag, using power tools and handtools: Positions motor in fixture and inspects engine for cracks and missing parts, such as electrical wires and screws. Disassembles motor and repairs or replaces defective parts, such as water pump, carburetor, thermostat, gears, solenoids, magneto, pistons, piston rings, and crankshaft, using wrenches, screwdrivers, and wheel puller. Scrapes, grinds, reams, and retaps parts to obtain specified clearance between parts, using scrapers, stand grinder, taps, reamer, and micrometer. Adjusts points, valves, and spark plugs and verifies gaps, using feeler gauges. Reassembles motor for retest. Records motor number and repairs made.
GOE: 06.01.04 STRENGTH: M GED: R4 M3 L3 SVP: 6 DLU: 77

625.684-010 DIESEL-MECHANIC HELPER (any industry)
Assists DIESEL MECHANIC (any industry) in overhauling and maintaining diesel motors used to operate trucks, generators, and other equipment: Disassembles motor and cleans parts. Obtains parts from stock and hands tools to mechanic. Assists in reassembly, and cleans tools and working area. Performs other duties as described under HELPER (any industry) Master Title.
GOE: 05.12.15 STRENGTH: M GED: R2 M2 L2 SVP: 4 DLU: 77

626 METALWORKING MACHINERY MECHANICS

This group includes occupations concerned with repairing general purpose and specialized metal-cutting, welding, and metal-forming machines, accessories, and related equipment. The repair of general purpose and specialized nonmetallic cutting, welding, and forming machines, accessories, and related equipment is also included when the machines and machine tools repaired are those commonly applied to the working of metal.

626.137-010 SUPERVISOR, WELDING EQUIPMENT REPAIRER (welding)
Supervises and coordinates activities of workers engaged in repairing, maintaining, and programming automated and manual welding machines and equipment in industrial establishment: Confers with engineering, quality control, and supervisory personnel and SUPERINTENDENT, MAINTENANCE (any indus-

try) 189.167-046 to analyze and resolve scheduling, production, and quality control problems. Trains and assists workers in trouble-shooting, maintenance, and repair of robots and automated and manual welding equipment. Directs workers engaged in programming welding robots, *programmable controllers,* and other automated equipment. Maintains parts inventory. Performs other duties as described under SUPERVISOR (any industry) Master Title.
GOE: 05.05.10 STRENGTH: L GED: R4 M4 L4 SVP: 8 DLU: 86

626.261-010 FORGE-SHOP-MACHINE REPAIRER (forging) alternate titles: hammer repairer; power hammer repairer
Repairs and maintains forge shop machinery, such as hammers, forging presses, rolls, upsetters, and furnaces, following blueprints, manufacturer's catalogs, and data chart specifications, using handtools, power tools, and precision measuring instruments, such as micrometer, calipers, rule, square, and gauges: Observes machine in operation to determine malfunction. Disassembles machine, using handtools, and examines parts for defects. Obtains replacement parts from stock or prepares sketches of parts for fabrication in forge shop or machine shop. Welds broken or cracked metal parts. Replaces drophammer boards and adjusts steam, pneumatic, hydraulic, fuel, and blower controls of presses, hammers, and furnaces, using handtools. Fits parts together to reassemble machine, using measuring instruments, files, handtools, and power tools, such as portable drills and grinders. Examines and repairs auxiliary equipment, such as pumps, valves, hoses, and compressors [PUMP SERVICER (any industry)]. Starts machine and observes operation to verify performance. May repair electrical components, such as switches and circuits. May set up machine for other workers. May be designated according to type of machine repaired as Load-Chain Welding-Machine Repairer (forging). May rebuild forging machinery and be designated Machine Rebuilder (forging).
GOE: 05.05.09 STRENGTH: M GED: R4 M3 L3 SVP: 7 DLU: 77

626.261-014 REPAIRER, WELDING SYSTEMS AND EQUIPMENT (welding)
Programs, maintains, and repairs production welding systems and equipment, using handtools, power tools, and test instruments, applying knowledge of welding technology and equipment operation, and following blueprints, specifications, and manufacturers' manuals: Analyzes welding diagrams, blueprints, templates, or other specifications and inspects components to be welded to determine weld program requirements for production welding robots. Presses buttons on *teach pendant* to program travel speeds and positions of robot arm, applying knowledge of robot programming. Presses buttons on *weld controller* to program amperage, pressure, and dwell time of welding gun attached to robot arm, following specifications and applying knowledge of welding technology. Presses buttons on *programmable controller* to coordinate and sequence operations of robots with production line. Inspects welded components and tests strength of welds to verify accuracy of programming, using hammer and applying knowledge gained from experience. Modifies weld program to bring weld quality up to specified standards, using teach pendant and weld controller. Observes and listens to operating robots to detect abnormal movements or sounds. Observes diagnostic lights or codes on video display monitors of programmable controller, *robot controller,* and weld controller to determine nature of malfunction, applying knowledge of diagnostic code and using manufacturers' manuals. Tests electrical and electronic components and circuits of system to determine source of malfunction, using test instruments such as oscilloscopes and voltmeters. Visually inspects printed circuit boards for defects, such as loose or broken pin connections. Replaces defective controller components, such as printed circuit boards, control units, and fuses. Repairs or replaces other system components [REPAIRER, WELDING EQUIPMENT (welding) 626.384-010]. May perform preventive maintenance, such as lubricating parts, changing oil filters, and replenishing fluid levels. May install, set up, adjust, and maintain production welding and brazing machinery, equipment, and devices, such as MIG brazers, press welders, fixtures, shuttles, and safety devices. May rebuild defective parts, such as pressure switches and hydraulic valves. May repair electrical components, such as teach pendants, timers, and control units.
GOE: 05.05.09 STRENGTH: M GED: R4 M4 L4 SVP: 7 DLU: 86

626.361-010 REPAIRER, WELDING, BRAZING, AND BURNING MACHINES (welding)
Repairs and maintains arc, gas, and resistance welding, brazing, and cutting machines, according to blueprints, catalogs, and data charts, applying knowledge of machine repair and welding: Inspects machine and observes operation to detect cause of malfunction. Disassembles machine, using handtools. Selects replacement parts from parts lists and catalogs, or repairs parts, such as hoses, electrode holders, valves, regulators, tubes, transformers, photoelectric cells, automatic wire feeds, bushings, bearings, conveyor links, and gears. Solders loose connections. Rewires electrical circuits. Replaces or repairs worn shafts and cams. Welds cracked or broken frames and housings. Reassembles machine, using handtools, welding and brazing equipment, and measuring instruments. Sets up and starts repaired machine to verify operation. May repair welding equipment [REPAIRER, WELDING EQUIPMENT (welding)]. May be designated by specialty as Repairer, Resistance-Welding Machines (welding).
GOE: 05.05.09 STRENGTH: M GED: R4 M3 L3 SVP: 7 DLU: 77

626.381-010 CASE-FINISHING-MACHINE ADJUSTER (ordnance)
Adjusts and makes minor repairs to lathes and presses used to finish shell cases: Replaces and adjusts cutting tools, using wrenches. Diagnoses causes of malfunction and removes worn or damaged parts, such as springs, cams, and punches, using handtools. May set up presses and lathes.

GOE: 06.01.04 STRENGTH: L GED: R3 M3 L3 SVP: 5 DLU: 77

626.381-014 GAS-WELDING-EQUIPMENT MECHANIC (any industry) alternate titles: apparatus-repair mechanic
Repairs acetylene gas welding equipment, using handtools and metalworking machines: Disassembles parts, such as worn hose, torch tips, torch valves, pressure gauges and regulators. Examines parts and repairs usable ones, using hand files and metalworking machines, such as lathes, drill presses, and grinding wheels. Replaces defective parts with new or rebuilt ones, using handtools.
GOE: 05.05.09 STRENGTH: L GED: R3 M3 L3 SVP: 7 DLU: 77

626.381-018 HYDRAULIC-PRESS SERVICER (ordnance)
Repairs, services, and adjusts hydraulic presses used to extrude wire for swaging into bullet slugs: Operates press to determine cause of defective operation and replaces parts, using handtools, such as wrenches, pliers, and screwdrivers. Removes dies and sets up and adjusts new dies. Fabricates replacement parts from stock materials, using broken parts as patterns.
GOE: 05.05.09 STRENGTH: L GED: R3 M2 L3 SVP: 6 DLU: 77

626.384-010 REPAIRER, WELDING EQUIPMENT (welding)
Repairs welding, burning, and brazing equipment, according to sketches, catalogs, parts lists, and charts: Examines equipment and observes operation to detect malfunction. Dismantles equipment to remove and replace worn or damaged parts, such as regulator diaphragms, torch tips, pressure springs, gauges, pneumatic cylinders, shunts, hoses, cables, and non-consumable electrodes, using handtools. Selects new parts from stock. Screws, solders, or braces parts together to reassemble unit. Tests repaired equipment to ensure specified performance. Dresses and replaces non-consumable electrodes, using grinding and lapping wheel or tip dressing machine. May replace or repair worn or damaged parts of welding and flame cutting machines. May issue supplies, such as electrodes, torch tips, weld rods, and fluxes, to welders. May change tubes and electrodes of resistance-welding machines. May monitor weld current to ensure weld quality. May fabricate steel hangers to support manually operated welding guns.
GOE: 05.10.02 STRENGTH: M GED: R3 M2 L2 SVP: 4 DLU: 86

627 PRINTING AND PUBLISHING MECHANICS AND REPAIRERS

This group includes occupations concerned with maintaining and repairing all types of presses, typecasting and typesetting machines, collators, and related apparatus used in job shops and commercial printing and publishing houses and book binderies, and establishments engaged in printing textiles or plastics.

627.261-010 COMPOSING-ROOM MACHINIST (print. & pub.) alternate titles: printing-equipment mechanic
Maintains in efficient operating condition mechanical, electromechanical, optical, and electronic equipment in newspaper composing room, such as line-and-character-type-casting machines, photographic typesetters, copy cameras and reproduction units, teletypesetter-keyboard converter, proof presses, type-cutting saws, and conveyors. Repairs, cleans, lubricates, and replaces mechanical components and replaces electronic, electromechanical, and optical components, using handtools, power tools, circuit diagrams, and repair manuals. Reports extensive failures in electronics components to supervisor or local service representative of equipment.
GOE: 05.05.09 STRENGTH: H GED: R4 M3 L3 SVP: 8 DLU: 77

627.261-014 MACHINIST APPRENTICE, COMPOSING ROOM (print. & pub.) alternate titles: printing-equipment-mechanic apprentice
Performs duties as described under APPRENTICE (any industry) Master Title.
GOE: 05.05.09 STRENGTH: H GED: R4 M3 L3 SVP: 8 DLU: 77

627.261-018 MACHINIST APPRENTICE, LINOTYPE (print. & pub.) alternate titles: linotype-maintenance-mechanic apprentice
Performs duties as described under APPRENTICE (any industry) Master Title.
GOE: 05.05.09 STRENGTH: H GED: R4 M3 L3 SVP: 7 DLU: 77

627.261-022 MACHINIST, LINOTYPE (print. & pub.)
Adjusts and repairs linotype machines and related equipment, according to maintenance schedule, diagnosis of machine malfunctioning, and manufacturer's service manuals: Inspects machines and operates keyboard to detect potential malfunctions, listening to machine operation for evidence of excessive wear and need for adjustment. Confers with operators of faulty machines to determine nature of malfunction and dismantles suspected components, using handtools. Repairs, straightens, files, or machines worn or defective parts, using handtools and machines, such as drill press, lathe, and grinder. Verifies dimensions of new or repaired parts, using micrometer, feeler gauges, and fixed gauges. Replaces repaired parts or installs new parts to restore machine to operating condition. Cleans parts of machine, such as matrices, magazines, plunger, and spaceband, according to prescribed schedule, using brushes, cloth, and cleaning agents. Lubricates ggrease fittings and moving parts of machine, using grease gun and oilcan. Determines temperature of machine melting pot, using thermometer, to ascertain need for adjustment or repair. May maintain supply of type metal in melting pots. May operate slug-casting machine to form metal bars and strips for securing type during printing. In smaller establishments, may perform duties of LINOTYPE OPERATOR (print. & pub.) 650.582-010.

GOE: 05.05.09 STRENGTH: H GED: R4 M3 L3 SVP: 7 DLU: 77

628 TEXTILE MACHINERY AND EQUIPMENT MECHANICS AND REPAIRERS

This group includes occupations concerned with maintaining and repairing textile machinery used in the preparation of vegetable, animal, or synthetic fibers; producing yarn; weaving or knitting cloth; and producing lace and embroidery; napping, and otherwise finishing fabric; and performing operations, such as slitting or folding preparatory to marketing.

628.261-010 OVERHAULER (textile)

Repairs and rebuilds textile machinery and equipment, using handtools and measuring instruments: Adjusts parts, such as rollers and cylinders, using wrenches and thickness gauges. Aligns and levels spinning, twisting, and *slubber* frames, using straightedge, level, and plumb bob. May install or move machinery. May set up machines. May plumb spindles on spinning or twisting frames.
GOE: 05.05.09 STRENGTH: H GED: R4 M3 L4 SVP: 6 DLU: 78

628.281-010 MACHINE FIXER (carpet & rug) alternate titles: loom fixer

Repairs and maintains fiber-making machinery and equipment, such as slitting, twisting, weaving, and wrapping machines, using handtools, hoists, and precision-measuring instruments: Examines machines and listens to their sounds to locate causes of trouble. Dismantles machines and removes defective parts, using pliers, wrenches, and screwdrivers. Repairs and replaces parts and reassembles machine, using handtools. Affixes special attachments to machines. Sets belts and lubricates machinery and equipment. Moves machine components, using hoists and rollers.
GOE: 06.01.04 STRENGTH: M GED: R4 M3 L4 SVP: 7 DLU: 77

628.381-010 CARD CLOTHIER (textile)

Replaces worn clothing on carding machine cylinders, employing knowledge of machine operation and carding process: Removes worn clothing and aligns, levels, and spaces cylinder evenly on machine frame. Marks cylinder to indicate location of wooden plugs and replaces defective plugs, using handtools. Cleans surface of cylinder with solvent to remove oil and rust. Tapers end of *card clothing fillets* with knife so strips can be wound parallel over circumference of cylinder. Tacks end of fillet to cylinder plugs and guides fillet as fillet is wound onto cylinder, packing each strand tightly against preceding strand. Tacks fillet to cylinder at specified intervals along chalked line. May grind reclothed cylinder.
GOE: 05.10.01 STRENGTH: H GED: R4 M3 L3 SVP: 7 DLU: 77

628.382-010 FLAT CLOTHIER (textile)

Operates machines to replace worn clothing on carding machine flats and to align, grind, and burnish flats: Strips worn clothing from flats, using handtools, and rubs flats with sandpaper to remove rust. Places stripped flat in jig and moves level gauge across length of flat to detect flats that are out of alignment. Straightens bent flats, using lever or hammer. Places flats in milling machine to shape ends of flats to correspond with bends on which flats slide on carding machine. Places flats in jig of rolling press, positions clothing assembly over flats, and starts rolling press that moves over length of flat, shaping and clamping clothing clip to flat. Places clothed flats in bed of grinding machine, lowers grinding head over flats, and starts machine that grinds wire points to uniform length. Removes ground flats from machine after specified length of time, places flats in bed of burnishing machine, and starts burnishing wheel that removes burrs caused by grinding. Dusts rust preventative on reclothed flats, assembles flats in sets, and packs sets in crates. Wraps and seals crates in plastic material and attaches shipping label to crate.
GOE: 06.02.02 STRENGTH: M GED: R3 M2 L3 SVP: 5 DLU: 77

628.382-014 SHEAR-GRINDER OPERATOR (textile)

Sets up and operates machines to sharpen ledger (straightedge) and fly (spiral) blades of cloth-shearing machines: Removes blades from shearing machine, using chain hoist. Mounts and squares ledger blade in jig of grinding machine, using straightedge and level. Turns handwheels to set blade at specified angle and to position grinding stone against blade. Starts machine that automatically moves rotating abrasive stone along edge of ledger blade. Measures blade edge, using micrometer, to determine when thickness is within specified tolerances. Resets machine to grind undercut on ledger blade. Mounts spiral blade in brackets of grinding machine. Turns various wheels to set both ends of blade equidistant from grinding head. Starts machine that rotates abrasive stone and fly blade in opposite directions and moves stone along edge of blade, grinding blade until flaws are removed. Measures diameter of blade with calipers at intervals along surface of blade to detect uneven grinding. Replaces damaged spirals on fly blade, using handtools. Mounts fly blade and ledger blade on lapping rig and starts machine that grinds blades against each other, using emery powder and oil, to finish edges. Boils blades in chemical solution to remove oil and abrasive dust. Applies preservative oil to blades.
GOE: 06.02.02 STRENGTH: M GED: R3 M2 L3 SVP: 6 DLU: 77

628.484-010 REED REPAIRER (textile) alternate titles: reed cleaner; reed maker; reed polisher

Polishes and repairs loom reeds: Cleans lint and gum from reeds, using brush or airhose [HARNESS CLEANER (textile)]. Examines reeds for alignment of wires, rough edges, and breaks. Verifies dents, using micrometers and feeler gauges. Straightens and aligns bent wires, using handtools, and solders broken wires. Smooths and polishes reeds, using pumice, lime, emery cloth, steel wool, and rotating brush, according to condition of reed. Inspects new reeds and stores them with reconditioned reeds according to size. Records receipt and transfer of reeds for perpetual inventory. May replace defective reeds on loom.
GOE: 05.10.02 STRENGTH: M GED: R3 M2 L2 SVP: 5 DLU: 77

628.664-010 OVERHAULER HELPER (textile)

Assists OVERHAULER (textile) 628.261-010 in repairing and rebuilding textile machinery and equipment: Carries or trucks tools, equipment,and parts to work area. Removes, disassembles, assembles, and aligns motors and mechanisms. Cleans parts, machines, and work area, using cloth, solvents, and airhose. Lubricates machines, using grease gun and oilcan. Performs other duties as described under HELPER (any industry) Master Title.
GOE: 05.12.15 STRENGTH: H GED: R2 M1 L2 SVP: 3 DLU: 79

628.682-010 ROLLER COVERER (textile) alternate titles: roller maker; roller-shop worker

Operates buffing machine to recondition drawing, spinning, or roving frame rollers: Cuts worn cot (rubber, cork, or leather covering) from roller arbor and cleans arbor with solvent. Screws arbor guides to handpress and turns knob to adjust press stroke according to length of roller. Dips new cot into water to soften glue. Positions arbor and cot in press and pulls lever to press cot onto arbor. Positions assembled roller between centers on buffing machine carriage. Turns carriage-stop adjustment screw to adjust machine to reduce cot diameter to specified size. Starts machine and turns handwheel to feed revolving roller against buffing wheel. Measures buffed roller with calipers to verify accuracy of diameter and places roller in gauge to ensure that cot is not tapered. Cuts leather to specified size and glues edges to make leather cots. Presses leather cot onto arbor, using arbor press. Presses wooden tool against ends of leather cot as roller turns in lathe to shrink cot onto arbor. Cuts cloth covering and glues it onto *clearer rollers* that clean lint from drawing rollers.
GOE: 06.02.09 STRENGTH: L GED: R3 M2 L2 SVP: 4 DLU: 79

628.684-010 BINDER AND BOX BUILDER (textile) alternate titles: binder fixer

Replaces worn fiber, felt, leather, cork, or asbestos linings on shuttle box and *shuttle binder:* Removes lining by cutting lining with knife and punching out rivets, using hammer and punch. Smooths surface to be recovered, using file and sandpaper. Punches or drills holes in lining to match those in binder or box front, using hand punch or electric drill. Brushes glue on lining and rivets or screws lining to binder or box front, using riveting machine or screwdriver. Places binders and box fronts in vise or clamps to dry. Removes vise or clamps after glue has dried and trims and smooths lining, using knife and sandpaper. May replace linings on other loom parts, such as clutch plates and brake bands.
GOE: 06.04.34 STRENGTH: L GED: R2 M1 L2 SVP: 2 DLU: 77

628.684-014 FRAME BANDER (textile) alternate titles: taper

Replaces broken or worn bands that drive spindles on spinning and twisting frames: Cuts worn leather or cotton band from cylinder with knife. Cuts replacement band of specified length from supply roll. Draws band over cylinder drum and around spindles by hand or with wire hook. Sews or bonds ends together, using portable sewing machine or electric bonding device. Places band around flange of spindles and tension pulley to start spindles. Lubricates spinning frames, using oilcan and grease gun.
GOE: 06.04.34 STRENGTH: M GED: R2 M1 L2 SVP: 3 DLU: 78

628.684-018 NEEDLE STRAIGHTENER (knitting) alternate titles: straightener

Replaces, aligns, and spaces needles or points in needle bar, picot bar, and *welt bar* of knitting machines: Secures bar in jig or vise. Loosens and removes clamping plate, holding needles, or point in bar with screwdriver, and removes broken or worn needles. Positions metal gasket under clamping plate, replaces needles or points, and replaces and tightens clamping plate. Aligns and spaces needles or points, using *space gauge* and pliers. May assist mechanic in aligning machine guide bars and sinkers.
GOE: 06.02.24 STRENGTH: L GED: R3 M2 L2 SVP: 4 DLU: 77

628.684-022 OVERHEAD CLEANER MAINTAINER (textile) alternate titles: traveling cleaner, maintenance

Maintains traveling cleaners that blow dust and lint from production machinery and work area: Examines motor and attachments of cleaner to determine repairs needed. Replaces worn parts, such as blower sleeves. Removes motors requiring major repair and replaces them with new or rebuilt motors, using handtools. Regulates speed of cleaning unit to ensure effective cleaning. Oils and greases parts of cleaner. Cleans motor, blower, sleeves, and monorail, using rags, brushes, and airhose.
GOE: 05.10.01 STRENGTH: L GED: R3 M2 L2 SVP: 3 DLU: 77

628.684-026 SHUTTLE FIXER (textile) alternate titles: shuttle inspector; shuttle repairer

Inspects and repairs wooden and plastic loom shuttles: Examines shuttles for defects, such as splits, knots, and scratches, or determines defect from reading work ticket. Removes metal tips and shuttle edges, using screwdriver. Cleans and polishes metal parts, using abrasive cloth and grinding machine. Smooths rough places on shuttles by hand or using sanding machine. Realigns metal eyes, using screwdriver. Cuts fur, bristles, nylon cord, or other fabrics, using scissors, and glues them to shuttle walls to increase yarn tension. Removes and

replaces shuttles on looms, using wrenches and screwdriver. Measures shuttle exteriors with gauges and rulers to verify dimensions before placing them on loom.
GOE: 06.02.32 STRENGTH: L GED: R3 M2 L3 SVP: 3 DLU: 77

628.684-030 SPINDLE PLUMBER (textile) alternate titles: spindle setter; spindle tester

Straightens and realigns spindles on ring spinning frames: Loosens and tightens spindle nuts with wrench. Places plumb (hollow block of wood) over spindle, and hammers or moves spindle by hand until clearance between block and circumference of opening in ring bar is equal. Starts machine and observes movement of spindles. Inserts shims under bearing collars of spindles that are off-center. May inspect and adjust spindles for horizontal trueness. May overhaul or repair spinning frames.
GOE: 06.02.24 STRENGTH: L GED: R3 M2 L3 SVP: 5 DLU: 77

628.684-034 UTILITY WORKER, ROLLER SHOP (textile)

Reconditions drawing rollers, beams, and other textile machinery parts, performing any combination of following tasks: Replaces defective cots on roller arbors, using compressed air device. Removes worn cloth covering from rollers, using knife and winding device. Cuts cloth covering and glues covering onto rollers. Cleans rollers and other parts, using rags and cleaning solution. Sorts rollers for buffing or covering. Replaces worn felt or other covering on *clearer rollers*. Replaces worn or damaged parts on warp beams, using handtools.
GOE: 05.10.04 STRENGTH: M GED: R3 M2 L2 SVP: 3 DLU: 77

628.684-038 WIRE REPAIRER (carpet & rug)

Examines *pile wires* for defective points and worn areas and repairs defective wires for use on carpet looms: Cuts defective ends or worn sections from wire, using metal snips. Welds corresponding length of metal to pile wire, using spot welder. Traces outline of scalloped pile wires on metal strip, following pattern. Holds wire against electric grinding wheel to smooth weld and to shape wire according to tracing. Stores wires according to size and pattern design.
GOE: 06.04.24 STRENGTH: L GED: R3 M2 L3 SVP: 3 DLU: 77

628.684-042 SPINDLE REPAIRER (textile)

Repairs and maintains pin spindles and refills oil containers on yarn texturing machines: Inspects spindles previously removed from machines for wornout pin shafts and cracked or worn eyelet. Discards spindles with wornout pin shaft. Glues eyelet onto bottom of spindle shaft or inserts cleaned or new pinhead on spindle, using allen wrench, to repair or restore spindle. Cleans spindle, spindle shaft, and inside of pinhead, using cloth and cleaning fluid. Removes empty oil container from machine and fills container with oil from barrel, using hand pump. Replaces container on machine when full. Checks oil level in oil box and fills box with oil, using hand pump.
GOE: 05.12.15 STRENGTH: L GED: R2 M1 L1 SVP: 2 DLU: 86

628.684-046 TEXTURING-MACHINE FIXER (textile)

Repairs yarn texturing machine malfunctions, utilizing knowledge of machine operation: Patrols assigned area to observe cards that indicate malfunctions of specific sections of multiunit machine. Slides cover on suction line behind machine sections with malfunction, breaks yarn, and feeds yarn into suction opening to maintain flow of yarn. Removes unevenly wound packages of yarn, places takeup tube in cradle of machine sections, and observes takeup of yarn onto tubes to determine cause of malfunctions. Feels yarn running from creel through machine sections, such as sensors, rollers, friction units, and guides, to detect excess tension on yarn and replaces defective parts, using handtools. Inspects drive belts on feed rollers and replaces worn belts, using handtools. Observes machine for other defects, such as missing guides and oil leaks. Requisitions replacement parts needed for machine repair. Cleans and removes waste from cutter sensors and friction units. Removes yarn wrapper around feed rolls or power shafts of machine.
GOE: 05.10.02 STRENGTH: M GED: R3 M1 L2 SVP: 4 DLU: 86

628.687-010 FLYER REPAIRER (textile) alternate titles: flyer builder

Cleans, disassembles, and reassembles flyers: Collects damaged, dirty, or rusted flyers from boxes near machines and carries them to worktable. Dumps flyers into tumbler containing cork to clean dirt and rust from them, or uses brush moistened with oil. Removes wire arm from flyer with wrench or places hub under press and depresses pedal to open clamps. Inserts new wires into hub and tightens them, using wrench or press. Drops repaired flyer into chute press or into box. May bend wire arms by positioning flyer under press and depressing pedal. May record number and type of flyers repaired.
GOE: 06.04.06 STRENGTH: L GED: R2 M1 L2 SVP: 3 DLU: 77

628.687-014 SHEAR-GRINDER-OPERATOR HELPER (textile)

Assists SHEAR-GRINDER OPERATOR (textile) in sharpening cloth-shearing machine blades: Removes blades from shearing machines and transports blades to and from grinding area, using handcart. Positions blades in jig or chuck of grinding machines. Hands SHEAR-GRINDER OPERATOR (textile) tools or supplies as directed. Spreads oil and emery powder on blades as blades are being lapped together. Boils sharpened blades in vats to remove oil and abrasive dust. Applies oil preservatives to blades. Performs other duties as described under HELPER (any industry) Master Title.

GOE: 06.04.02 STRENGTH: H GED: R2 M1 L1 SVP: 2 DLU: 77

629 SPECIAL INDUSTRY MACHINERY MECHANICS

This group includes occupations concerned with repairing machines and equipment designed to perform specialized functions in the manufacture of specific products, or to perform particular functions commonly found in an industry or in a group of related industries.

629.131-010 BAKERY-MACHINE-MECHANIC SUPERVISOR (bakery products)

Supervises and coordinates activities of workers engaged in repairing and maintaining bakery machines and equipment: Analyzes service requests and assigns workers to activities, such as dismantling machinery and equipment, installing replacement parts, and testing machinery. Monitors operation of machinery and equipment to ensure conformance to specifications. Performs other duties as described under SUPERVISOR (any industry) Master Title.
GOE: 05.05.09 STRENGTH: M GED: R4 M3 L4 SVP: 7 DLU: 77

629.131-014 OIL-FIELD EQUIPMENT MECHANIC SUPERVISOR (petrol. & gas)

Supervises and coordinates activities of workers engaged in inspecting, dismantling, testing, rebuilding, and storing oil field tools and equipment: Reviews drilling schedules and assigns worker activities. Inspects repaired equipment for conformance to specifications, using precision measuring instruments. Requisitions replacement parts. Performs other duties as described under SUPERVISOR (any industry) Master Title.
GOE: 05.05.09 STRENGTH: L GED: R4 M3 L3 SVP: 8 DLU: 77

629.261-010 LAUNDRY-MACHINE MECHANIC (laundry & rel.)

Repairs and maintains washers, driers, extractors, condensers, pumps, blowers, presses, and other laundry equipment: Operates, examines, and dismantles equipment to diagnose cause of malfunction. Repairs or replaces parts, using handtools and measuring instruments. Replaces components, such as bearings, motors, and microswitches. Replaces faulty sections of pipe, valves, and fittings, using plumbing tools. Dismantles steam traps and removes sediment. Removes faceplate from equipment to clean out dust and lint. Replaces worn or torn aprons, roll covers, and pads on mangles. Lubricates machines and equipment, using grease gun and oilcans. May order spare parts.
GOE: 05.10.02 STRENGTH: M GED: R3 M2 L3 SVP: 6 DLU: 77

629.261-014 MILLER, HEAD, WET PROCESS (grain-feed mills) alternate titles: stonecutter

Analyzes malfunctions, repairs or replaces parts, and dresses buhrstones to maintain grinding mills in operating condition: Aligns and balances stone and grinding wheel, using handtools. Cuts foors (concentric grooves near center of stone) and *cracks* to sharpen stones, using calipers, dividers, and airhammer chisel. Positions stone horizontally in mill, using chain hoist. Inspects mills to determine malfunction or need for repair or reconditioning. Disassembles mill to gain access to worn or damaged parts, replaces shafts and other parts, and rebabbits bearings, using micrometer, scrapers, and handtools.
GOE: 05.05.01 STRENGTH: M GED: R3 M3 L3 SVP: 7 DLU: 77

629.261-018 POWDER-LINE REPAIRER (chemical)

Repairs and adjusts mixing and packing machines used in production of nitroglycerin and dynamite: Washes machines and parts with sodium carbonate or other neutralizing compound prior to and during dismantling to minimize danger of explosion, using brush and rags. Determines cause of equipment malfunction, according to knowledge of machine operation and report of operator or maintenance workers. Dismantles, repairs, and replaces machine parts, using nonsparking handtools. Observes safety regulations while working in explosive areas.
GOE: 05.05.09 STRENGTH: M GED: R4 M3 L3 SVP: 6 DLU: 77

629.261-022 ELECTRONIC-PRODUCTION-LINE-MAINTENANCE MECHANIC (electron. comp.)

Repairs and maintains machines and equipment used in processing and assembling electronic components, such as capacitors, resistors, semiconductor devices and assemblies for television, radio communication, and radar systems, following blueprints, schematic drawings, and other specifications, using handtools, power tools, and test equipment: Confers with operators regarding equipment or machine malfunction. Starts equipment or machine, such as diffusion furnace, wave solderer, or ultrasonic welder, and inspects and tests mechanical, electrical, and electronic units and controls to diagnose malfunction, using test equipment. Reads blueprints and schematic drawings to determine repair procedures. Dismantles machine and disconnects controls, using screwdrivers, wrenches, wire cutters, and other handtools. Removes and repairs or replaces defective units. Assembles and installs equipment, such as shafts, conveyors, wires, tubes, and controls, using handtools and power tools. Adjusts electrical, thermal, and timing elements to meet specifications. Starts repaired or newly installed machines and equipment to verify readiness for operation. Records type of malfunction and repair work performed. Prepares requisitions for material and supplies.
GOE: 06.01.04 STRENGTH: M GED: R4 M4 L4 SVP: 7 DLU: 88

629.280-010 MAINTENANCE MECHANIC (leather mfg.) alternate titles: fitter-up

Sets up, repairs, and adjusts equipment and machines to flesh, split, and spray hides: Disassembles malfunctioning equipment, using handtools, and

welds broken parts [WELDER, GAS (welding)], replaces babbitt in bearings [BABBITTER (machine shop)], or repairs or replaces machine drive belts [BELT REPAIRER (any industry)] to repair equipment. May install blades on machine rollers and be designated Roll Filler (leather mfg.).
GOE: 05.05.09 STRENGTH: H GED: R4 M3 L3 SVP: 6 DLU: 77

629.281-010 BAKERY-MACHINE MECHANIC (bakery products)

Repairs and maintains bakery machinery and equipment, such as ovens, conveyors, and slicing and packaging machines: Examines machines and equipment to locate causes of trouble. Dismantles machines, using wrenches, pliers, and other handtools. Replaces defective parts, adjusts timing gears, sets dies according to specifications, and repairs or replaces belts, conveyor sections, and feeding devices, using handtools, portable electric drills and grinders, and gas and electric welding equipment. Cuts and installs pipe and tubing for gas, water, air, and hydraulic lines, using wrench, cutting die, and threading device. Sharpens and installs cutting blades in slicing machine. Assembles machines. Starts machines and observes gauges and other instruments to ensure adherence to processing standards. Cleans and lubricates equipment, using rags, brushes, and grease gun. May operate machine tools to make or repair parts.
GOE: 05.05.09 STRENGTH: M GED: R4 M3 L3 SVP: 7 DLU: 78

629.281-014 CELLOPHANE-CASTING-MACHINE REPAIRER (plastic prod.)

Repairs and maintains cellophane-forming machines, using handtools: Observes machines in operation and listens for sounds to locate causes of trouble. Dismantles machines and removes defective parts, such as gears, belts, and rollers, using handtools. Replaces broken or worn parts. Lubricates machines.
GOE: 05.05.09 STRENGTH: M GED: R4 M3 L3 SVP: 6 DLU: 77

629.281-018 DAIRY-EQUIPMENT REPAIRER (dairy products)

Repairs and maintains dairy machinery and equipment, such as churns, cream separators and milking machines, using handtools, machine tools, and measuring instruments: Observes and listens to machine in operation to locate causes of trouble. Dismantles machine, using pliers, screwdriver, and wrenches. Replaces or repairs faulty part, using handtools or power tools. Assembles and starts machine to test its operation. Replaces defective wiring, burnt fuses, worn switches, and electric motor parts, and repairs electrical fixtures. Machines worn or new metal parts, using engine lathe, drill press, and other machine tools. Cuts and fuses metals to fabricate metal parts and pipes. Cuts pipe threads and installs and tests gas, steam, water, and air pipes. Fabricates, alters, and installs sheet metal chutes, covers, tubing, containers, and fittings. May affix special attachments, set dies, and repair belts. May operate electric motors, pumps, compressors, and water filters to cool refrigerating rooms.
GOE: 05.05.09 STRENGTH: M GED: R4 M3 L3 SVP: 7 DLU: 77

629.281-026 FORMING-MACHINE ADJUSTER (glass mfg.) alternate titles: forming fixer

Repairs and adjusts fiberglass sliver forming machines, applying knowledge of machine operation: Examines machine parts to determine type of defect. Turns setscrews and nuts to align machine parts. Removes, replaces, and repairs worn or damaged parts, such as spiral traverses, fin coolers, graphite shoes, and binder applicators (sleeves), using handtools. Mounts graphite shoes on shaft and inserts shaft into chuck of turning lathe. Starts lathe and holds crocus cloth against shoes to remove nicks, dirt, and burs. Holds and turns spiral traverse against buffing wheel to smooth and clean traverse. Cleans glass and binder solution from binder applicators, using crocus cloth. Records and maintains production information, such as inventory of parts, and parts cleaned, changed, and adjusted.
GOE: 06.01.04 STRENGTH: M GED: R4 M3 L3 SVP: 5 DLU: 77

629.281-030 MAINTENANCE MECHANIC (grain-feed mills) alternate titles: machine repairer

Inspects, adjusts, and repairs cleaning, grinding, sifting, packaging, sewing, and tying machines and elevator, conveyor, and scale equipment in grain and feed mill: Replaces broken and worn parts, such as gears, bushings, bolts, and needles, using mechanic's handtools. Relines bearings [BABBITTER (machine shop)].
GOE: 05.05.09 STRENGTH: M GED: R4 M3 L3 SVP: 6 DLU: 77

629.281-034 PUMP MECHANIC (paper & pulp)

Repairs pumps of paper making machinery: Examines pumps for malfunctioning and to locate damage or wear, such as blowout packing, misalignment of pump shaft, slippage of drive belt, worn bearings, or need for lubrication. Observes operation of pumps and feels for heat and vibration of parts to detect cause of malfunctioning. Dismantles pumps and performs repairs, such as cleaning impellers, repacking stuffing boxes, tightening glands, and replacing bearings, using handtools.
GOE: 05.05.09 STRENGTH: M GED: R4 M3 L3 SVP: 6 DLU: 77

629.361-010 MACHINE-CLOTHING REPLACER (paper & pulp)

Replaces paper-making machine clothing (conveyor belts) with material, such as canvas, felt, and wire-mesh: Reviews clothing service records of each machine to determine when replacements should be made. Examines clothing for defects, such as worn spots, tears, holes, and rotted areas, and schedules times for change or repair. Lifts feed, tension, press, and drier rolls from machine frame, using hoist, wrench, and pinchbar, assisted by machine crew. Removes lacing from worn canvas and felt belts and unwinds them from machine rolls. Pulls worn continuous wire mesh belt from machine over end of rolls. Threads

canvas and felt belts around rolls and laces ends together or slides and pushes continuous wire mesh belt over end of rolls, into position on machine. Repositions rolls on machine frame and starts machine. Moves levers and turns handwheels to adjust speed and pressure of rolls and tension of clothing. Maintains service record of clothing used. May wash, repair, and store clothing.
GOE: 05.10.02 STRENGTH: M GED: R4 M3 L3 SVP: 7 DLU: 77

629.381-010 FOILING-MACHINE ADJUSTER (ordnance)

Repairs and adjusts machines that stamp out small disks of shellacked paper and press them over open ends of charged primer cups: Adjusts die block so that disks are properly pressed in place. Removes and disassembles die-block assembly for cleaning. Replaces defective parts, such as bent punches and worn rollers. Inspects samples of completed primers. May adjust other machines used in assembly of cartridge primers, such as toggle presses and anvil shakers.
GOE: 06.01.04 STRENGTH: L GED: R3 M2 L3 SVP: 5 DLU: 77

629.381-014 OIL-FIELD EQUIPMENT MECHANIC (petrol. & gas)

Repairs, maintains, and installs oil well drilling machinery and equipment, using handtools and following oral and written work orders: Attaches hoisting cables to pumps, transmissions, diesel engines, and other equipment at drill sites, lashes equipment to trucks for transfer to repair yard, and guides lowering of equipment onto blocks in or near repair shop. Disassembles engines and mechanical units, using hand and power wrenches, screwdrivers, and other handtools. Cleans parts, such as pistons, valves, and parts of transmissions and clutches, using steam hose and detergents. Inspects parts for defects. Installs specified new or reconditioned parts, such as relined brake bands and clutch plates, sprockets, pump cylinders, and other parts of engines and mud pumps. Reassembles complete units. Tests function of pumps and other mechanical units, using auxiliary power. Test-runs engines at various speeds and observes efficiency of operations. Welds broken structures, such as engine mounts, hand rails, machine guards, and pipe racks, using electric and acetylene welding equipment. Paints reconditioned units, using spray gun. Installs repaired equipment at drill sites, observes operations, and readjusts components, as necessary. May maintain, repair, and install machinery and equipment at drill sites and be designated Field Mechanic (petrol. & gas).
GOE: 05.05.09 STRENGTH: M GED: R4 M3 L3 SVP: 6 DLU: 77

629.382-010 MACHINE TESTER (machinery mfg.)

Operates grinding, mixing, and sifting machines to test operational conformance to customer specifications: Selects grinding head and attaches part to grinder. Places material to be ground in hopper, sets speed, starts motor, and examines ground material. Adjusts or replaces grinding heads to obtain specified results. Connects liquid inlet hose to mixer, places material in hopper, and starts mixer. Adjusts paddle deflection, flow controls, and speed as necessary. Measures amount of electrical power used, using ampmeter. Writes report of operations.
GOE: 06.03.01 STRENGTH: M GED: R3 M3 L3 SVP: 4 DLU: 77

629.682-010 ROLL GRINDER (rubber reclaim.) alternate titles: roll-contour grinder

Sets up and operates portable electric grinder to resurface damaged or worn mill rolls used to compress reclaim rubber into slabs: Positions and bolts grinder to holding fixture beside mill. Examines sample slab from mill to determine extent of grinding necessary to resurface rolls. Selects and bolts grinding wheel to grinder, and turns setscrews to align it with roll. Starts grinder and turns travel screw to feed rotating grinding wheel horizontally along roll. Repeats grinding until sample slabs are compressed according to standards. Turns adjustment wheel to close rolls of mill, and spreads abrasive compound over ground area of rolls. Starts mill to polish roll surfaces. Wipes abrasive compound from polished rolls.
GOE: 06.02.02 STRENGTH: M GED: R3 M2 L3 SVP: 5 DLU: 77

629.684-010 CURING-PRESS MAINTAINER (rubber tire)

Maintains tire curing presses in working order: Replaces defective bladders and steam hoses. Saws copper or flexible tubing to specified lengths and attaches fittings to make steam hose. Cleans plugged vent holes in molds, using power drill. May perform preventive maintenance, such as oiling and cleaning. May be designated according to activity performed as Bladder Changer (rubber tire); Mold Changer (rubber tire).
GOE: 05.12.15 STRENGTH: M GED: R2 M2 L2 SVP: 2 DLU: 77

629.684-014 MILLER, HEAD, ASSISTANT, WET PROCESS (grain-feed mills) alternate titles: stonecutter, assistant

Sharpens buhrstones in grain grinding mills under direction of MILLER, HEAD, WET PROCESS (grain-feed mills): Removes bolts holding buhrstones in mill, using wrench, and places stones on workbench, using hoist. Brushes face of stone with broom. Recuts floors (concentric grooves near center of stone) and *cracks* in stone, following original indentations, using air-hammer chisel. Brushes chips from stone, and replaces it in mill.
GOE: 06.04.30 STRENGTH: H GED: R2 M1 L2 SVP: 5 DLU: 77

630 GENERAL INDUSTRY MECHANICS AND REPAIRERS

This group includes occupations concerned with maintenance and repair of a variety of machines and equipment used in various combinations to perform common or specialized functions in the processing and manufacturing industries.

630.131-010 PUMP-SERVICER SUPERVISOR (any industry)

Supervises and coordinates activities of PUMP SERVICERS (any industry) engaged in installing and repairing pumps, such as centrifugal, plunger, and turbine pumps. Trains employees in work methods and procedures. Orders materials and supplies. Inspects installations and repairs of pumps. Performs other duties as described under SUPERVISOR (any industry) Master Title.
GOE: 05.10.02 STRENGTH: L GED: R4 M3 L3 SVP: 7 DLU: 77

630.134-010 ANODE-CREW SUPERVISOR (smelt. & refin.) alternate titles: service-crew supervisor

Supervises and coordinates activities of workers engaged in rebuilding and repairing anodes and cathodes of aluminum-reduction pots. Trains workers in operation of machines and equipment. Observes machine gauges to verify conformance to specifications. Performs duties as described under SUPERVISOR (any industry) Master Title. May supervise workers engaged in adjusting and maintaining electrolytic magnesium refining cells and be designated Supervisor, Cell Maintenance (smelt. & refin.).
GOE: 05.10.02 STRENGTH: L GED: R4 M3 L3 SVP: 7 DLU: 77

630.261-010 MAINTENANCE MECHANIC, COMPRESSED-GAS PLANT (chemical)

Repairs and maintains machinery and equipment used in compressing and liquefying gases, such as compressors, scrubbers, instrument panels, and electrical equipment, following blueprints, schematics, and maintenance manuals, using handtools, welding equipment, and testing instruments: Tests equipment to locate causes of trouble, using standard test meters. Dismantles equipment, using handtools and power tools. Welds, brazes, burns, and solders parts. Repairs and replaces pipes and equipment, using pipefitting tools. Repairs and adjusts instrument control panels, rectifiers, motors, switches, and other electrical equipment. Repacks compressors and pumps. May operate metalworking tools to make and repair parts.
GOE: 05.05.09 STRENGTH: M GED: R4 M3 L3 SVP: 7 DLU: 77

630.261-014 OVEN-EQUIPMENT REPAIRER (steel & rel.)

Maintains coke oven machinery and auxiliary equipment in working condition: Examines or listens to equipment, such as pushers, charging larrys, door removers, coke guides, and mud-handling equipment to detect faulty operation, or worn or damaged parts. Dismantles units and adjusts or replaces defective parts, using bars, airhammers, sledges, chisels, and wrenches. Notifies MAINTENANCE-MECHANIC SUPERVISOR (any industry) of major repairs required, such as replacement of defective bearings or gears and shafts.
GOE: 05.10.01 STRENGTH: M GED: R3 M3 L3 SVP: 6 DLU: 77

630.261-018 REPAIRER I (chemical)

Repairs, adjusts, and installs chemical process equipment, according to knowledge of equipment operation and plant specifications: Observes equipment, such as pumps, compressors, generator, reactors, heat exchangers, filters, grinders, and absorbing towers, in operation or confers with operators to detect and diagnose mechanical defects or malfunction, utilizing knowledge of mechanical function and performance characteristics of equipment. Disassembles equipment, using handtools and portable power tools. Examines parts for defects, such as breakage or excessive wear. Verifies dimensions of parts, using calipers, micrometers, and scales. Sends parts to welding or machine shop for repair or for fabrication of replacement parts. Replaces defective parts and reassembles equipment. Adjusts clearance and timing of control devices to specifications, using pliers, screwdriver, and wrenches. Installs new equipment or modifies existing installations, following blueprints and technical advice of engineers. Directs REPAIRER (chemical) II in performing tasks, such as dismantling and assembling equipment. May be designated according to equipment repaired as Repairer, Evaporator (chemical); Repairer, Pump (chemical); Repairer, Still (chemical).
GOE: 05.10.02 STRENGTH: H GED: R3 M3 L3 SVP: 7 DLU: 77

630.281-010 PNEUMATIC-TOOL REPAIRER (any industry) alternate titles: air-motor repairer; drill doctor

Repairs pneumatic tools and air motors, such as pneumatic hammers, chisels, and reamers, using mechanic's tools: Starts motor or tool and listens to sound to locate cause of trouble. Disassembles motor and repairs or replaces defective gears, pistons, connecting rods, and other parts, using taps, files, reamers, wrenches, and other handtools.
GOE: 05.05.09 STRENGTH: M GED: R4 M3 L3 SVP: 7 DLU: 77

630.281-014 PNEUMATIC-TUBE REPAIRER (any industry)

Repairs and maintains pneumatic-tube carrier system, using handtools and precision-measuring instruments: Locates sources of trouble. Repairs and installs parts, using handtools.
GOE: 05.10.02 STRENGTH: M GED: R3 M3 L3 SVP: 6 DLU: 77

630.281-018 PUMP SERVICER (any industry) alternate titles: pump repairer

Repairs pumps and pump power units, such as centrifugal and plunger-type pumps, and diesel-engine, gasoline-engine, and electric-motor power units, using hoists and handtools: Diagnoses trouble in pumps. Dismantles pumps and repairs or replaces defective parts, using handtools. Reseats and grinds valves. Tests performances of repaired pumps. May wire motor to switchboard and install fuse box. May be designated according to type of pump repaired as Water-Pump Servicer (any industry).
GOE: 05.05.09 STRENGTH: M GED: R3 M3 L3 SVP: 7 DLU: 77

630.281-022 REPAIRER (mine & quarry) alternate titles: mechanic

Lubricates, adjusts, repairs, and inspects machinery used to clean, crush, size, and otherwise prepare coal, limestone, or rock salt for commercial or industrial use, or for further processing. May be designated according to work station as Breaker Repairer (mine & quarry); Preparation-Plant Repairer (mine & quarry); Tipple Repairer (mine & quarry).
GOE: 05.05.09 STRENGTH: M GED: R4 M3 L3 SVP: 6 DLU: 80

630.281-026 REPAIRER (smelt. & refin.)

Repairs machinery and equipment, such as ball mills, filters, crushers, classifiers, flotation machines, conveyor belt systems, thickener tanks, and vibrating screens, used in transporting and processing ore. May be designated according to machinery repaired as Roll Repairer (smelt. & refin.).
GOE: 05.10.02 STRENGTH: M GED: R4 M3 L3 SVP: 7 DLU: 77

630.281-030 RUBBERIZING MECHANIC (any industry)

Repairs and maintains rubber-covered and rubber-lined equipment in pulp mill, such as belting, impellors, pipes, pumps, and valves, using knives, handtools, and pressure vulcanizers: Examines exposed rubberized equipment for flaws and excessive wear. Selects rubber stock according to type of materials and manufacturer's specifications. Dismantles equipment and replaces or repairs damaged parts.
GOE: 05.10.02 STRENGTH: M GED: R4 M3 L3 SVP: 7 DLU: 77

630.281-034 SERVICE MECHANIC, COMPRESSED-GAS EQUIPMENT (chemical)

Inspects, tests, repairs, and installs equipment, such as liquid gas converters and compressors in field installations to supply compressed gas for industrial and therapeutic use: Dismantles, tests, and analyzes malfunctioning equipment, using blueprints, manuals, handtools, and power tools, and tests apparatus to locate defects. Tests, repairs, and adjusts electrical circuits and equipment, such as starters, motors, rectifiers, relays, and heaters, using schematics and handtools and power tools. Solders, brazes, and welds materials to repair and replace copper and steel piping and equipment parts. Records repair work performed and condition of equipment.
GOE: 05.05.09 STRENGTH: M GED: R4 M3 L3 SVP: 7 DLU: 77

630.281-038 TREATMENT-PLANT MECHANIC (waterworks) alternate titles: filtration-plant mechanic; water-treatment-plant mechanic

Maintains and repairs machines and equipment used to process and distribute water for human consumption and industrial use: Dismantles, or partially dismantles electric motors, turbines, pumps, hydraulic valves, chlorinators, limers, meters, gauges, and other equipment, to gain access to or remove faulty parts, using hand and power tools, such as wrenches, screwdrivers, and hoists. Repairs or replaces defective parts. Inspects machines and equipment periodically, lubricating moving parts, or replacing worn parts to prevent breakdown or malfunctioning. May operate plant equipment to process and distribute water [WATER-TREATMENT-PLANT OPERATOR (waterworks)].
GOE: 05.05.09 STRENGTH: M GED: R4 M3 L3 SVP: 6 DLU: 77

630.381-010 CONVEYOR-MAINTENANCE MECHANIC (any industry)

Repairs and adjusts conveyor systems, using handtools: Installs belts in machinery, tightens bolts, adjusts tension rolls, straightens parts, aligns rollers, and replaces defective parts. May install conveyor systems.
GOE: 05.10.02 STRENGTH: M GED: R3 M3 L3 SVP: 6 DLU: 77

630.381-014 DOOR-CLOSER MECHANIC (any industry)

Repairs, services, and installs hydraulic door closers, using machines and handtools: Disassembles closers, using handtools and vise. Immerses parts in solution of caustic soda and water to clean parts. Removes encrusted dirt and rust, using electric rotary wire brush and grinding wheel. Replaces worn or broken parts. Fabricates parts, using lathes, drill presses, shaping and milling machines, and precision measuring instruments, such as micrometers, calipers, and scales. Welds cracked closer casings, using acetylene torch. Fills oil chamber and packs spindle with leather washers. Paints finished door closer.
GOE: 05.10.02 STRENGTH: L GED: R3 M3 L3 SVP: 7 DLU: 77

630.381-018 LEAD OPERATOR (smelt. & refin.)

Tests and repairs ore-crushing and ore-transporting machinery: Starts machines and equipment, such as feeders, jaw crushers, conveyor belts, and suction dust collectors. Observes machines and equipment in operation for defects and malfunctions. Turns valves to regulate flow of water into cooling system. Breaks up clogged ore, using iron bar or pneumatic hammer. Repairs machines and equipment, using handtools.
GOE: 05.05.09 STRENGTH: L GED: R4 M3 L3 SVP: 6 DLU: 77

630.381-022 LUBRICATION-EQUIPMENT SERVICER (any industry)

Repairs and adjusts hand-or power-operated equipment used to lubricate automobiles, trucks, and industrial equipment, using handtools: Dismantles equipment, such as grease guns, air lines, and lubricating pumps. Examines parts for breaks, wear, and dirt. Replaces defective parts. Cleans and assembles equipment.
GOE: 05.10.02 STRENGTH: M GED: R3 M2 L2 SVP: 6 DLU: 77

630.381-026 SPRAY-GUN REPAIRER (any industry)

Repairs and adjusts spray-paint guns and paint-mixing machines, using handtools: Disassembles spray gun, using wrenches. Cleans parts in gasoline or other solvent. Wipes parts dry. Replaces valves, jets, and other worn or broken

parts. Attaches new hose to guns. Turns thumbscrews, nuts, and other controls on gun to adjust jets and nozzles. Repairs agitators of paint-mixing equipment. May mix paints and lacquers, using paddle or electric shaker-agitator, scales, and viscosity cups. May order parts and materials to maintain inventory levels.
GOE: 05.10.02 STRENGTH: L GED: R3 M3 L3 SVP: 7 DLU: 77

630.381-030 VALVE REPAIRER (chemical) alternate titles: cylinder-valve repairer; valve inspector-and-assembler; valve inspector

Rebuilds safety and flow valves used on compressed and liquefied gas cylinders, drums, or railway cars: Disassembles valve, using bench vise and handtools. Inspects components for surface flaws, and defects in stem and threads. Reams valve seats with hand reamer and dresses threads with tap and die. Immerses parts in cleaning solution and reassembles valve. Dips valve in molten lead, using tongs, to prevent leakage. Attaches valve and fusible plug to high-pressure gasline, submerges it in water, and observes for bubbles to test valve and plug for leaks. Melts out defective plugs, scrapes hole clean, and pours in new metal. Records number of valves tested and test results. May attach gauge and open air valve to test filled cylinders for pressure. May brush or spray chemical solution around valves to test filled cylinders for leaks. May fill cylinders [CYLINDER FILLER (chemical)].
GOE: 05.10.02 STRENGTH: M GED: R3 M3 L3 SVP: 6 DLU: 77

630.384-010 FIXTURE REPAIRER-FABRICATOR (any industry)

Fabricates and repairs fixtures, rods, baskets, and hooks used to suspend articles in plating, cleansing, and painting vats, using handtools and portable power tools: Cuts metal stock to size, using handsaws or power saws and forming machines and following working sketches. Bends metal, using vise or hammer. Drills and taps holes, using portable power drill. Bolts or screws parts together, using wrenches and screwdrivers. May braze, solder, or weld parts together.
GOE: 05.10.01 STRENGTH: M GED: R3 M2 L2 SVP: 5 DLU: 77

630.584-010 EQUIPMENT CLEANER-AND-TESTER (smelt. & refin.)

Cleans and repairs aluminum-processing equipment, such as heaters, heat exchangers, evaporators, pipelines, pumps, cooler coils, and filter leaves, using handtools: Removes heads from heaters, evaporators, preheaters, and heat exchangers, using impact wrenches. Mixes acid or caustic with water and inhibiting chemicals to prepare cleaning solutions of specified concentrations. Tests solutions, using acid-testing equipment. Turns valves to circulate cleaning agents through equipment for time indicated by test results. Washes vessels and heaters with water. Removes scale from tubes, using air-powered turbines and drills. Examines vessels or heaters for leaks, and marks defective areas. Reassembles vessels and heaters, using chain falls, block and tackle, impact wrenches, and handtools. Lubricates valves and adjusts packing glands to prevent leaks. May keep records of repairs and test results.
GOE: 06.04.39 STRENGTH: M GED: R3 M2 L2 SVP: 4 DLU: 77

630.664-010 REPAIRER HELPER (smelt. & refin.)

Assists REPAIRER (smelt. & refin.) in repairing machinery and equipment used in processing ore: Cuts out worn parts of conveyor belts, using shears. Draws ends of belt together, using block and tackle, and splices ends with metal fasteners. Loosens sections of machines and equipment, such as turbogenerators, vibrating screens, air compressors, conveyors, crushers, condensers, and boilers, using handtools and electric hoist. Removes worn pipe sections from air, oil, steam, and waterlines, using wrenches and chain hoist. Cleans soot and scale from steam tubes and water-cooling pipes of pressure boilers, using brush and airhose. Performs other duties as described under HELPER (any industry) Master Title.
GOE: 05.12.15 STRENGTH: H GED: R2 M2 L2 SVP: 3 DLU: 77

630.664-014 SCREEN-AND-CYCLONE REPAIRER (mine & quarry)

Repairs sizing screens and cyclones (centrifugal separators) used in processing iron ore, using handtools and chain hoist: Inspects screen panels on vibrating screens and screen cloth on ball mill trommels for wear and damage. Replaces worn screen panels on vibrating screens, using wrenches and hammer. Installs new screen cloth on ball mill trommels, using wrenches and chain hoist. Signals OVERHEAD CRANE OPERATOR (any industry) 921.663-010 to remove and replace cyclones for scheduled maintenance. Measures cyclone parts with rule and tape measure to determine need for replacements. Replaces worn parts, such as feed and shell linings, using wrenches. Cleans spray nozzles and belt scrapers in conveyor belt washing system.
GOE: 05.10.01 STRENGTH: M GED: R3 M2 L2 SVP: 4 DLU: 77

630.664-018 SERVICE-MECHANIC HELPER, COMPRESSED-GAS EQUIPMENT (chemical)

Assists SERVICE MECHANIC, COMPRESSED-GAS EQUIPMENT (chemical) in installing and repairing pumps, tanks, and vaporizers: Cuts and threads pipes, using pipe cutter and dies. Cleans, polishes, and paints surface of parts, using solvent, rags, and spray guns. Performs other duties as described under HELPER (any industry) Master Title.
GOE: 05.12.15 STRENGTH: M GED: R2 M1 L2 SVP: 4 DLU: 77

630.684-010 ANODE REBUILDER (smelt. & refin.)

Rebuilds anodes of aluminum-reduction furnace, performing any combination of following duties: Removes straps (flexible connectors) from bottom channel irons and bolts them onto next level, using wrench. Grinds connector shoes with emery wheel. Pulls pins from anode with hydraulic puller and cleans scale from pins, using sandblast equipment. Replaces studs (pins), using stud driver.

Removes bottom set of channel irons, prior to lowering electrode, and installs new irons on top of pot for rebuilding anode, using jacks, hydraulic squeezer, and wrench. May be designated according to work performed as Channel Rebuilder (smelt. & refin.); Pin Puller (smelt. & refin.); Strap Setter (smelt. & refin.); Stud Driver (smelt. & refin.).
GOE: 05.10.01 STRENGTH: M GED: R3 M2 L2 SVP: 5 DLU: 77

630.684-014 BELT REPAIRER (any industry)

Repairs and replaces canvas, leather, or rubber belts used to drive machinery and convey materials: Examines belts for defects and cuts out defective sections, using knife. Cuts strip of unused belting material, using knife. Clamps metal fasteners to ends of belt, using pincers, or splices ends of belt, using splicing machine. Positions repaired belt on pulleys. Applies dressing compound to belt to prevent slippage. May patch and sew defective areas of belts, using needle and thread. May specialize in repairing conveyor belts and be designated Conveyor-Belt Repairer (any industry).
GOE: 05.12.15 STRENGTH: L GED: R2 M1 L1 SVP: 4 DLU: 77

630.684-018 PUMP INSTALLER (any industry)

Installs and adjusts electric, gasoline, and diesel-driven pumps and blowers, using handtools, power tools, and diagrams: Cuts and threads pipes, ducts, and fittings, using handtools and power tools. Levels and bolts down pump. Connects ducts and drive couplings, and aligns them to minimize friction, using handtools and gauges. Oils and greases moving parts, and adjusts valves to prevent overloading. May recommend repair or adjustment of driving mechanism to improve operation of pumps.
GOE: 05.10.01 STRENGTH: H GED: R3 M2 L3 SVP: 5 DLU: 77

630.684-022 PUMP-SERVICER HELPER (any industry) alternate titles: mechanic helper

Assists PUMP SERVICER (any industry) in repairing pumps, pump power units, and auxiliary equipment: Dismantles pumps, engines, and other machinery, using power hoists and handtools. Hauls pump and engine parts to and from machine shops, using hoisting device. Performs other duties as described under HELPER (any industry) Master Title.
GOE: 05.12.15 STRENGTH: M GED: R2 M1 L2 SVP: 5 DLU: 77

630.684-026 REPAIRER II (chemical)

Maintains, installs, and repairs process equipment in chemical plants, usually working under direction of REPAIRER (chemical) I 630.261-018: Inspects equipment for leaks and defective valves. Tightens flange connections and valves, using wrenches. Replaces driving belts, spray nozzles, gaskets, and packing in equipment and gaskets or seals in pipelines. Lubricates pumps and valves, using grease gun. Grinds and reseals valves, using power grinder. Dismantles and assembles equipment, using wrenches and portable power tools, as directed by REPAIRER (chemical) I to assist in repairs and installations. Cleans dirt and rust from equipment and parts prior to and after repairs are made, using brushes, buffer, and cleaning solutions. May test equipment for leaks, using compressed-nitrogen hose and compressor and vacuum gauge, to detect pressure drops. May assist equipment or process operator in operation or tending of equipment units during emergencies or rest periods.
GOE: 05.10.02 STRENGTH: H GED: R3 M2 L2 SVP: 4 DLU: 81

630.684-030 SCREEN REPAIRER, CRUSHER (mine & quarry)

Repairs rod-screen panels in vibrating screens that divert taconite ore into final crushing stage, using hammers, wrenches, and hydraulic jack: Examines rod-screen panels for worn or damaged rods and liners. Lifts hydraulic jack into place between mounting frame and screen panel. Moves levers on jack to free screen panel from rubber holding flange. Lifts out panel and inserts replacement in holding flange. Taps rod ends with hammer to loosen them from frame and pulls out worn rods. Places frame in alignment jig, inserts new rods in holes, and taps rods with hammer to set them in frame. Replaces worn screen liners, using handtools.
GOE: 05.12.12 STRENGTH: M GED: R3 M2 L2 SVP: 4 DLU: 77

630.684-034 SPRAY-GUN-REPAIRER HELPER (any industry)

Assists SPRAY-GUN REPAIRER (any industry) in repairing and adjusting spray paint guns. Disassembles and cleans spray guns, using handtools, solvent, and rags. Performs other duties as described under HELPER (any industry) Master Title.
GOE: 05.12.15 STRENGTH: M GED: R2 M1 L2 SVP: 3 DLU: 77

630.684-038 WHEEL-AND-CASTER REPAIRER (any industry)

Repairs and maintains wheels and casters on rolling equipment, such as racks and carts. Replaces parts, such as wheels and bearings, using handtools. Oils moving parts.
GOE: 05.12.15 STRENGTH: M GED: R2 M1 L2 SVP: 2 DLU: 77

630.687-010 PULLEY MAINTAINER (mine & quarry)

Oils, greases, and replaces idler rollers or pulleys which support cable used in mine haulage slope. Oils and greases cable.
GOE: 05.12.08 STRENGTH: M GED: R1 M1 L1 SVP: 3 DLU: 77

631   POWERPLANT MECHANICS AND REPAIRERS

This group includes occupations concerned with maintenance and repair of turbogenerators, steam generators, and auxiliary equipment in powerplants, utilizing organic and atomic fuels or waterpower.

631.131-010 POWERHOUSE-MECHANIC SUPERVISOR (utilities)

Supervises and coordinates activities of workers engaged in installing, adjusting, repairing, and maintaining electrical and mechanical parts of hydroelectric turbines, generators, and auxiliary equipment. Trains workers in repair and maintenance procedures. Performs duties as described under SUPERVISOR (any industry) Master Title. May be designated according to type of powerplant in which maintenance is performed as Diesel-Powerplant Supervisor (utilities); Geothermal-Powerplant Supervisor (utilities); Hydroelectric-Powerplant Supervisor (utilities); Nuclear-Powerplant Supervisor (utilities); Steam-Powerplant Supervisor (utilities).
GOE: 05.05.05 STRENGTH: L GED: R4 M4 L4 SVP: 8 DLU: 77

631.261-010 HYDROELECTRIC-MACHINERY MECHANIC (utilities) alternate titles: plant machinist

Repairs and maintains in operating condition mechanical elements of generators, waterwheels, water-inlet and floodgate controls, valves, and piping in hydroelectric generating station. Sets up and operates machine tools to repair or reproduce machine parts and fittings, working from blueprints or defective part.
GOE: 05.10.02 STRENGTH: H GED: R4 M3 L3 SVP: 7 DLU: 77

631.261-014 POWERHOUSE MECHANIC (utilities) alternate titles: station mechanic

Installs, adjusts, maintains, and repairs electrical and mechanical equipment and parts in power-generating station: Installs equipment. Dismantles and overhauls equipment [MILLWRIGHT (any industry) 638.281-018; BOILERMAKER (struct. metal) I 805.261-014]. Dismantles and repairs auxiliary equipment, such as pumps, compressors, and pipe systems [MAINTENANCE REPAIRER, INDUSTRIAL (any industry) 899.261-014]. Assists in conducting acceptance and performance tests on new or existing equipment. Fabricates special tools, rigging equipment, and replacement parts for equipment. May install wiring between machinery, switchboards, and control panels [ELECTRICIAN, MAINTENANCE (any industry) 829.261-018]. May be designated according to type of plant in which maintenance is performed as Diesel-Powerplant Mechanic (utilities); Gas-Turbine-Powerplant Mechanic (utilities); Geothermal-Powerplant Mechanic (utilities); Nuclear-Powerplant Mechanic (utilities); Steam-Generating-Powerplant Mechanic (utilities).
GOE: 05.05.09 STRENGTH: H GED: R4 M3 L3 SVP: 8 DLU: 85

631.261-018 POWERHOUSE-MECHANIC APPRENTICE (utilities) alternate titles: machinist apprentice; station-mechanic apprentice

Performs duties as described under APPRENTICE (any industry) Master Title.
GOE: 05.05.09 STRENGTH: H GED: R4 M3 L3 SVP: 8 DLU: 77

631.364-010 HYDROELECTRIC-MACHINERY-MECHANIC HELPER (utilities)

Assists HYDROELECTRIC-MACHINERY MECHANIC (utilities) in repairing and maintaining mechanical equipment in hydroelectric generating station, performing duties as described under HELPER (any industry) Master Title.
GOE: 05.10.02 STRENGTH: H GED: R3 M2 L3 SVP: 3 DLU: 77

631.684-010 POWERHOUSE-MECHANIC HELPER (utilities) alternate titles: generation-mechanic helper; station mechanic helper

Assists POWERHOUSE MECHANIC (utilities) in maintaining and repairing power-generating equipment: Lubricates automatic recording instruments, changes recording charts, and refills ink containers. Removes instruments from panelboards for repairs, and reinstalls them when repairs are completed, using handtools. Carries or handtrucks tools and equipment to work areas. Removes nuts and bolts from machinery being disassembled for repairs. Holds parts in place for workers performing repair work. Returns tools to toolroom. Constructs scaffolds. Removes rust and scale from inside of boilers, using wire brush. Performs other duties as described under HELPER (any industry) Master Title. May be designated according to plant in which work is performed as Diesel-Powerplant-Mechanic Helper (utilities); Gas-Turbine-Powerplant-Mechanic Helper (utilities); Geothermal-Powerplant-Mechanic Helper (utilities); Nuclear-Powerplant-Mechanic Helper (utilities); Steam-Generating-Powerplant-Mechanic Helper (utilities).
GOE: 05.12.15 STRENGTH: M GED: R3 M2 L3 SVP: 5 DLU: 77

632 ORDNANCE AND ACCESSORIES MECHANICS AND REPAIRERS

This group includes occupations concerned with repairing, modifying, and maintaining in readiness small arms, field artillery, naval weapons, fire-control apparatus, munitions, and related ordnance. Occupations concerned with ordnance fabrication are covered in Groups 694 and 736. Occupations concerned with instruments are covered in Group 711. Occupations concerned with electronic equipment are covered in Groups 722 and 823.

632.131-010 ARTILLERY-MAINTENANCE SUPERVISOR (ordnance)

Supervises and coordinates activities of workers engaged in inspecting, servicing, and repairing artillery weapons. Performs duties as described under SUPERVISOR (any industry) Master Title.
GOE: 05.10.02 STRENGTH: L GED: R4 M4 L4 SVP: 7 DLU: 77

632.261-010 AIRCRAFT-ARMAMENT MECHANIC (government ser.) alternate titles: aircraft armorer

Services armament equipment used on military aircraft: Strips airplanes of removable armament equipment, such as machine guns, synchronizers, and bomb-

release apparatus, using handtools. Disassembles, cleans, oils, and repairs dismantled equipment and nonremovable armament, such as machine-gun mounts and bomb hoists. Inspects electric circuits controlling bomb-release and gun-firing mechanisms, following wiring diagrams. Immerses equipment parts not in use in hot cosmoline to protect parts from rust and stores until needed. Reassembles and remounts equipment. May be designated according to specialty as Bombsight Specialist (government ser.).
GOE: 05.05.10 STRENGTH: M GED: R4 M3 L3 SVP: 6 DLU: 77

632.261-014 FIRE-CONTROL MECHANIC (government ser.) alternate titles: fire-control technician

Services mechanical, electronic, and optical equipment controlling naval guns, following blueprints and diagrams and using handtools and testing devices: Inspects and cleans optical equipment, installing new eyepieces as necessary. Adjusts and lubricates gyroscope. Repairs and replaces parts of motors and remote control equipment, communications equipment, and electronic equipment, using handtools and standard test equipment. Participates in bore-sighting and aligning guns. Tests wiring circuits, following blueprints and diagrams.
GOE: 05.05.11 STRENGTH: M GED: R4 M3 L3 SVP: 6 DLU: 77

632.261-018 ORDNANCE ARTIFICER (government ser.)

Inspects, tests, maintains, stores, and prepares for use ordnance material, such as guns, primers, fuses, shells, mines, bombs, rockets and guided missiles, tanks, chemical, biological, and radiological munitions, and fire-control equipment for weapons: Tests and inspects material for functioning and serviceability, using prescribed gauges and test equipment, and by firing or detonating weapons and munitions. Disassembles, repairs, and reassembles ordnance of all types, using handtools, power tools, and material-handling equipment. Assembles and loads explosive and inert elements to prepare ammunition items for use. Cleans, stores, and maintains ordnance material according to technical manuals. May be designated according to ordnance item involved as Munitions Worker (government ser.); Nuclear Weapons Mechanical Specialist (government ser.); Torpedo Specialist (government ser.). May maintain small arms and artillery and be designated Armorer (government ser.). May deactivate unexploded bombs and mines and be designated Bomb-Disposal Specialist (government ser.).
GOE: 05.10.02 STRENGTH: M GED: R4 M4 L4 SVP: 6 DLU: 77

632.281-010 GUNSMITH (any industry) alternate titles: repairer

Repairs and modifies firearms to blueprint and customer specifications, using handtools and machines, such as grinders, planers, and millers: Fits action and barrel into stock and aligns parts. Installs parts, such as metallic or optical sights, pistol grips, recoil pads, and decorative pieces of firearms, using screws and handtools. Rebores barrels on boring machine to enlarge caliber of bore. Operates broaching machine to cut rifling in barrel of small arms. Installs choke device on shotguns to control shot pattern. Operates machine to grind and polish metal parts. Immerses metal parts in bluing salt bath to impart rust resistant surface and blue color to metal. Fires firearms with proof loads to determine strength characteristics, correct alignment, and assembly of piece. Fabricates wooden stock for guns according to customer specifications. Refinishes wooden stocks for rifles and shotguns by hand sanding and rubbing with special finishing oil and quick-drying lacquer. May lay out plans on paper and calculate bullet-flight arcs, sight positions, and other details to design new guns.
GOE: 05.05.07 STRENGTH: L GED: R4 M3 L3 SVP: 8 DLU: 77

632.360-010 GAUGE-AND-WEIGH-MACHINE ADJUSTER (ordnance)

Sets up machines to measure and weigh loaded cartridges: Turns setscrews and nuts to adjust and synchronize feeding, gauging, weighing, and ejection mechanisms, using handtools, and master cartridge and fixed gauges to verify settings. Starts machine and inspects sample cartridges for conformance to weight and size specifications. Disassembles machine to replace worn or broken parts or to install parts to accommodate specific size or type of cartridge, using handtools. Tags trays of rejected cartridges, indicating reason for rejection, and routes them to other workers for reinspection or salvage. Cleans and lubricates equipment. Gives instructions to new workers for operating machine.
GOE: 06.01.02 STRENGTH: L GED: R3 M2 L3 SVP: 5 DLU: 77

632.360-014 LOADING-MACHINE ADJUSTER (ordnance) alternate titles: cartridge-assembling-machine adjuster

Sets up automatic machine to fill small arms cartridge cases with powder and insert bullets: Installs machine parts, such as shell and bullet dials, carriers, punches, crimping die, and powder charge regulator, to accommodate designated size and type of cartridge to be filled, using handtools. Turns setscrews or nuts to adjust and synchronize mechanisms. Cleans machine and lubricates moving parts. Polishes punches and dies to remove scratches or adhering brass, using *bench grinder* and emery cloth. Disassembles machine or parts to remove jammed cartridges and to replace worn or broken parts. Tests sample of cartridges for pullout of bullets and weighs powder load, using *pull-test machine* and gram scale. Records test results. Gives instructions to new workers in operation of machines and use of gauges.
GOE: 06.01.02 STRENGTH: L GED: R3 M2 L3 SVP: 4 DLU: 77

632.360-018 PRIMER-INSERTING-MACHINE ADJUSTER (ordnance)

Sets up and maintains in operation automatic machines that insert explosive primers in cartridge cases: Installs and adjusts punches, dies, and feed fingers, and regulates feeding and ejection mechanisms, using handtools and gauges. Frees jams and replaces worn or broken parts. Polishes steel punches and feed

fingers to remove burrs, scratches, or adhering brass, using speed lathe and emery cloth. May feed plates or boards of primers into machine hoppers. May instruct new workers in machine operation and use of gauges.
GOE: 06.01.02 STRENGTH: M GED: R3 M2 L3 SVP: 5 DLU: 77

632.380-010 INSPECTING-MACHINE ADJUSTER (ordnance)
Adjusts roller, chain, or belt conveyors that convey small arms ammunition or components past inspectors: Turns stop nuts and setscrews to align tubes, channels, or fingers which transfer workpieces from hopper to carrier, using handtools. Bends and hammers discharge chutes into position. Turns adjustment knob of drive motor or shifting belt to different pulley to change speed of conveyor. Tightens belts by extending tension wheel. Replaces mirrors that enable inspector to see both ends of cartridges. Removes cartridges jammed in feed or discharge channels, using wire tools.
GOE: 06.01.02 STRENGTH: L GED: R3 M2 L3 SVP: 4 DLU: 77

632.380-014 LOADING-UNIT TOOL-SETTER (ordnance)
Sets up series of machines to load plateful of small arms cartridges with powder and bullets: Changes setting screws on eccentric arm of shakers to adjust length of stroke of shaker table according to caliber and style of cartridge and bullet processed. Installs powder volume plate in loading unit and inserts blocks of punches and collets in presses to seat and crimp bullets, using handtools. Turns setscrews, stop nuts, and turnbuckles to adjust, by trial and error, side guides, backstops, conveyor fingers, and stroke of press gates, using height gauges. Distributes plates to each work station according to work requirements. Empties powder from volume plate into tray and weighs it, dividing by number of cartridges in plate to determine if total load and average per cartridge are within weights specified. Changes volume plate for one with larger or smaller cavities until total and average loads meet specifications. Observes unit in operation to detect malfunctioning. Starts machine to load plate of cartridges and sends samples to ballistics laboratory for approval before releasing unit to operating crew.
GOE: 06.01.02 STRENGTH: L GED: R3 M2 L3 SVP: 5 DLU: 77

632.380-018 PRIMER-WATERPROOFING-MACHINE   ADJUSTER (ordnance) alternate titles: lacquer-press adjuster
Sets up dial-feed machine to daub and spray lacquer to base and mouth of cartridge cases to form waterproof seal around primer and bullet: Aligns and adjusts feeding, lacquering, blotting, and ejecting mechanisms, and installs reels of blotting-paper tape, using handtools. Thins lacquer with acetate to desired consistency and pours it into machine reservoirs. Measures drain time of sample mixture to verify conformance to specified viscosity, using electric timer. Drains and flushes reservoirs and feed tubes to prevent clogging, using thinner.
GOE: 06.01.02 STRENGTH: L GED: R3 M2 L3 SVP: 5 DLU: 77

632.380-022 RIM-FIRE-PRIMING TOOL SETTER (ordnance)
Sets up automatic machines to fill head cavity of rim-fire cartridge cases with explosive priming mixture: Installs and aligns knockout pins, primer-spreading punches, and shell-holding blocks, using handtools and gauges. Sets stops and cams to synchronize movements of feeding screws and rolls, shell-holding fingers, and ejection mechanism. Starts machine and examines primed cartridge cases for defects, such as dents, scratches, or unfilled head cavities. Cleans priming mixture from tools and machine bed, using air blast or vacuum hose. Dismantles machine to replace worn or broken parts.
GOE: 06.01.02 STRENGTH: M GED: R3 M3 L3 SVP: 4 DLU: 77

632.380-026 VARNISHING-UNIT TOOL SETTER (ordnance)
Sets up machine to waterproof center-fire cartridges with varnish or lacquer: Selects varnishing plates with pins of specified diameter to accommodate caliber of cartridge to be processed and screws into plate holders. Hammers out and replaces broken, bent, or loose pins. Turns setscrews, stop nuts, and limit pins to adjust height and speed of varnishing machine, using handtools. Mixes varnish or lacquer and thinner in reservoir to obtain waterproofing solution of specified viscosity. Examines samples of varnished cartridges to determine whether coating is sufficient to waterproof them.
GOE: 06.01.02 STRENGTH: L GED: R3 M2 L3 SVP: 3 DLU: 77

632.381-010 GUN SYNCHRONIZER (ordnance)
Adjusts interconnecting control mechanisms of gun to synchronize gun with gunners sight (telescope or range finder) and fire control computer: Lifts gun to work stand, using hoist, and connects electrical and hydraulic lines to power sources. Inserts borescope in muzzle of gun, and telescope and level in breech. Moves controls to level position of gun. Adjusts gunners quadrant to synchronize quadrant with gun at level position. Sets eccentrics within control mechanism in position level with gun and quadrant. Bolts control arm of ballistics computer to sighting adjustment controls. Sights through range finder and moves controls to align cross hairs of range finder on specified target. Looks through borescope in gun to verify alignment of gun bore on target. Adjusts eccentrics, and controls to regulate flow of electrical impulse into control instruments, to align gun and sight on specified target.
GOE: 06.01.04 STRENGTH: M GED: R3 M3 L3 SVP: 5 DLU: 77

632.381-014 INSPECTOR, FIREARMS (ordnance)
Examines working parts of guns used in testing ammunition to determine that they are in satisfactory condition to be used for making tests. Examines bore, cartridge chamber, firing-pin hole, and other parts related to functional operation of gun, using precision measuring instruments. Inspects bore of gun for defects, such as scratches, pits, and corrosion, using illuminated periscope.

Tests operation of gun for satisfactory action. May assist GUNSMITH (any industry) in adjusting test arms.
GOE: 06.01.05 STRENGTH: L GED: R4 M3 L3 SVP: 6 DLU: 77

632.684-010 ORDNANCE-ARTIFICER HELPER (government ser.)
Assist ORDNANCE ARTIFICER (government ser.) in inspecting, maintaining, storing, and preparing for use ordnance material, such as guns, primers, fuses, mines, bombs, rockets, guided missiles, tanks, munitions, and fire-control equipment for weapons. Performs other duties as described under HELPER (any industry) Master Title.
GOE: 05.12.16 STRENGTH: M GED: R2 M2 L2 SVP: 4 DLU: 77

633   BUSINESS AND COMMERCIAL MACHINE REPAIRERS

This group includes occupations concerned with repairing calculating, bookkeeping, addressing, duplicating, and related machines, including both manual and electric typewriters and cash registers. Sales and service occupations are included in Group 275; and electronic data processing equipment is included in Group 722 and Group 823.

633.131-010 OFFICE-MACHINE-SERVICE SUPERVISOR (any industry)
Supervises and coordinates activities of workers engaged in servicing, repairing, and rebuilding office machines, such as calculating, bookkeeping, duplicating machines, and typewriters, in customer's establishment and in repair shop. Trains workers in repairing and servicing procedures. Performs duties as described under SUPERVISOR (any industry) Master Title. May review reports on unserviceable machines and examine them to determine repairs required and to estimate cost of repair. May compute cost of repaired items. When supervising workers in repair shop, may be designated Office-Machine-Repair-Shop Supervisor (any industry).
GOE: 05.05.09 STRENGTH: L GED: R4 M3 L3 SVP: 7 DLU: 77

633.261-010 ASSEMBLY TECHNICIAN (office machines)
Inspects, adjusts, and repairs punched-card office machines, such as interpreters, collators, proof machines for banks, and card punches, using handtools and test equipment: Reads machine assembly specifications, such as charts, blueprints, schematic diagrams, and engineering specifications to determine requirements, such as drive speed, timing of card feed and output, and installation of special features ordered by customer. Operates machine, using prepunched cards, to observe and listen to operation of moving parts, to measure clearances and contact gaps, and to measure voltages and continuity, using voltmeter, ohmmeter, and test lights. Adjusts clearance of moving parts, electrical contact gaps, and alignment of printing units and contact brush units to meet specifications, using tools, such as screwdrivers, wrenches, feeler gauges, and special fixtures. Repairs assembly errors noted by quality control personnel. May install hardware, drill holes, and insert pins to complete assembly prior to final testing of machine. May train workers in assembly operations.
GOE: 06.01.04 STRENGTH: L GED: R4 M3 L3 SVP: 6 DLU: 77

633.261-014 MAIL-PROCESSING-EQUIPMENT MECHANIC (government ser.)
Repairs and maintains mail-processing equipment, such as letter-canceling machines, letter-facing-and-canceling machines, mail-sorting machines, and conveyor systems, following blueprints and schematic diagrams, using handtools, power tools, and electrical testing instruments: Inspects machine to locate causes of trouble, using ammeters, ohmmeters, relay testers, and other testing instruments. Dismantles machine, using handtools and power tools. Repairs wiring circuits and replaces parts, such as relays, resistors, condensers, and rheostats in electrical systems, using handtools. Repairs and replaces parts, such as gears and bearings in mechanical systems, using handtools. Reassembles and starts machines to test performances. Dismantles conveyor systems, using handtools. Repairs or replaces defective parts and reassembles conveyors. May repair hydraulic and pneumatic systems.
GOE: 05.05.09 STRENGTH: M GED: R4 M3 L3 SVP: 6 DLU: 77

633.281-010 CASH-REGISTER SERVICER (any industry) alternate titles: cash-register repairer
Tests and repairs cash registers, using handtools, power tools, and circuit test meters: Examines mechanical assemblies, such as printing mechanisms, counters, and keyboards, for worn or damaged parts, using precision gauges. Replaces defective parts, or reshapes parts on bench lathe or grinder. Tests electrical control units, wiring, and motors, using circuit test equipment. Replaces defective electrical parts, using handtools and welding and soldering equipment. Cleans and oils moving parts. May service adding machines [OFFICE-MACHINE SERVICER (any industry)].
GOE: 05.05.09 STRENGTH: M GED: R4 M3 L3 SVP: 7 DLU: 77

633.281-014 DICTATING-TRANSCRIBING-MACHINE SERVICER (any industry)
Repairs magnetic tape and grooved-tape dictating-transcribing machines, using wiring diagrams, handtools, and electronic testing equipment: Tests machines to isolate defective circuits, using oscilloscope, audioscope, test meters, tube and circuit testers, and referring to wiring diagrams. Replaces faulty parts, such as tubes, transistors, microphones, relays, and resistors, using soldering iron and handtools. Replaces or adjusts mechanical elements, such as playback

mechanisms, remote control switches, and tape reels. Operates repaired machines to test their performances. May operate bench lathe to fabricate shims, bolts, and other similar parts. May be designated according to type of machine repaired as Dictating-Transcribing-Machine Servicer, Grooved Tape (any industry); Dictating-Transcribing-Machine Servicer, Magnetic Tape (any industry). Important variables may be indicated by trade name of machines repaired.
GOE: 05.05.09 STRENGTH: L GED: R4 M3 L3 SVP: 7 DLU: 77

633.281-018 OFFICE-MACHINE SERVICER (any industry) alternate titles: business-machine mechanic; office-equipment mechanic; office-machine inspector

Repairs and services office machines, such as adding, accounting, and calculating machines, and typewriters, using handtools, power tools, micrometers, and welding equipment: Operates machines to test moving parts and to listen to sounds of machines to locate causes of trouble. Disassembles machine and examines parts, such as gears, guides, rollers, and pinions for wear and defects, using micrometers. Repairs, adjusts, or replaces parts, using handtools, power tools, and soldering and welding equipment. Cleans and oils moving parts. May give instructions in operation and care of machines to machine operators. May assemble new machines. May be designated according to machine repaired or serviced as Accounting-Machine Servicer (any industry); Adding-Machine Servicer (any industry); Calculating-Machine Servicer (any industry); Duplicating-Machine Servicer (any industry); Typewriter Servicer (any industry).
GOE: 05.05.09 STRENGTH: L GED: R4 M3 L3 SVP: 7 DLU: 77

633.281-022 OFFICE-MACHINE-SERVICER APPRENTICE (any industry) alternate titles: business-machine-mechanic apprentice

Performs duties as described under APPRENTICE (any industry) Master Title.
GOE: 05.05.09 STRENGTH: L GED: R4 M3 L3 SVP: 7 DLU: 77

633.281-026 SCALE MECHANIC (any industry)

Installs, calibrates, and repairs weighing scales, using handtools, power tools, and standard test weights: Moves scale into position, using hoists and rollers. Inserts shims between scale base and foundation to level scale. Secures scale to foundation, using handtools. Tests scale, using certified weights, and adjusts pivots, dial settings, and pendulums to ensure that weight indication meets legal specifications. Turns setscrews to adjust spring scales. Disassembles scales and repairs or replaces worn or damaged parts, such as pivots and bearings, using *bench grinder*, handtools, and power tools. Straightens, cleans, and repaints structural parts of scale. May install, adjust, and repair electronically controlled scales.
GOE: 05.05.09 STRENGTH: M GED: R4 M3 L3 SVP: 7 DLU: 77

633.281-030 STATISTICAL-MACHINE SERVICER (any industry) alternate titles: customer engineer

Installs and services collators, sorters, and other statistical machines in accordance with graphs and charts, using handtools and precision-measuring instruments: Assembles and installs machines, following timing and wiring charts and using handtools, calipers, micrometers, and other instruments. Starts machines and listens for sounds to locate electrical and mechanical defects. Examines wiring, cards, and printed tape for defects. Dismantles machines and repairs or replaces parts, using handtools. Tightens, loosens, sets, or otherwise adjusts gears, clutches, and electrical connections. May set up machine to obtain particular information by wiring and inserting board in machines and moving switches and levers. May instruct and advise operators of equipment in machine operation and in interpretation of setup charts. May supervise and instruct student servicers.
GOE: 05.05.09 STRENGTH: L GED: R4 M3 L3 SVP: 7 DLU: 77

637 UTILITIES SERVICE MECHANICS AND REPAIRERS

This group includes occupations concerned with installing, maintaining, and repairing mechanical equipment and appliances used to supply heat, conditioned air, refrigeration, water, and related utilities in homes and commercial or industrial establishments.

637.131-010 SUPERVISOR, COOLER SERVICE (svc. ind. mach.) alternate titles: manager, vending department

Supervises and coordinates activities of workers engaged in installation, maintenance, renovation, and repair of vending machines (coolers) dispensing bottled beverages: Orders delivery of coolers to retail locations. Dispatches repairers on service calls to repair or adjust faulty coolers. Instructs and trains new workers. Performs other duties as described under SUPERVISOR (any industry) Master Title.
GOE: 05.10.03 STRENGTH: L GED: R4 M3 L3 SVP: 7 DLU: 77

637.261-010 AIR-CONDITIONING INSTALLER-SERVICER, WINDOW UNIT (construction)

Installs, services, and repairs window air-conditioning units, ranging from 1/2 to 2 tons capacity, in private residences and small establishments: Inspects existing wiring, fuses, or circuit-breaker panels on customer's premises to ensure adequate power supply for operating air-conditioner. Measures window, transom, or other existing openings for air-conditioning unit, using measuring tape or rule, or cuts opening through wall, using mallet and cold chisel. Assembles and positions support brackets in place, using screws, clamps, or other braces, and power tools and handtools. Fills space between window support and edge of opening with caulking compound and filler board. Places air-conditioner on support frame and secures unit in position, leveling unit, using screws, clips, and bolts. Starts unit, adjusts controls, and listens for excessive noise or sounds indicating malfunction. Examines malfunctioning unit for defective parts, utilizing knowledge of mechanical, electrical, and refrigeration theory, to determine cause of malfunction. Dismantles whole or part of unit, as indicated by type of malfunction, and repairs or replaces such parts as switches, relays, fan motors, thermostats, and other components, using handtools and power tools. Replaces filters, lubricates unit, and adjusts controls. Reassembles unit, making necessary adjustments to ensure efficient operation. May give instructions to customer regarding operation and care of unit. May estimate cost of repairs or adjustments. May remove unit from customer's premises for major repairs or overhaul in shop, or for return to manufacturer for extensive repairs. May repair sealed refrigeration units of machines. For installation, service, and repair of central air-conditioning units, see HEATING-AND-AIR-CONDITIONING INSTALLER-SERVICER (construction) 637.261-014.
GOE: 05.05.09 STRENGTH: H GED: R4 M3 L3 SVP: 8 DLU: 77

637.261-014 HEATING-AND-AIR-CONDITIONING INSTALLER-SERVICER (construction) alternate titles: air-conditioning mechanic; environmental-control-system installer-servicer; heating-and-air-conditioning mechanic; heating mechanic

Installs, services, and repairs environmental control systems in residences, department stores, office buildings, and commercial establishments, utilizing knowledge of refrigeration theory, pipefitting, and structural layout: Mounts compressor and condenser units on platform or floor, using handtools, following blueprints or engineering specifications. Fabricates, assembles, and installs ductwork and chassis parts, using portable metalworking tools and welding equipment [DUCT INSTALLER (construction; mfd. bldgs.) 869.664-014]. Installs evaporator unit in chassis or in air duct system, using handtools. Cuts and bends tubing to correct length and shape, using cutting and bending equipment and tools. Cuts and threads pipe, using machine-threading or hand-threading equipment. Joins tubing or pipe to various refrigerating units by means of sleeves, couplings, or unions, and solders joints, using torch, forming complete circuit for refrigerant [PIPE FITTER (construction) 862.281-018]. Installs expansion and discharge valves in circuit. Connects motors, compressors, temperature controls, humidity controls, and circulating-ventilation fans to control panels and connects control panels to power source [ELECTRICIAN (construction) 824.261-010]. Installs air and water filters in completed installation. Injects small amount of refrigerant into compressor to test systems, and adds freon gas to build up prescribed operating pressure. Observes pressure and vacuum gauges and adjusts controls to ensure efficient operation. Tests joints and connections for gas leaks, using gauges or soap-and-water solution. Wraps pipes in insulation batting and secures them in place with cement or wire bands. Replaces defective breaker controls, thermostats, switches, fuses, and electrical wiring to repair installed units, using electrician's handtools and test equipment. May install, repair, and service air-conditioners, ranging from fifteen to twenty tons cooling capacity, in warehouses and factory buildings and be designated Air-Conditioning Mechanic, Industrial (any industry).
GOE: 05.05.09 STRENGTH: M GED: R4 M3 L3 SVP: 7 DLU: 83

637.261-018 GAS-APPLIANCE SERVICER (any industry) alternate titles: appliance servicer; customer servicer

Installs and repairs gas meters, regulators, ranges, heaters, and refrigerators in customer's establishment, using manometer, voltmeter, handtools, and pipe-threading tools: Measures, cuts, and threads pipe and connects it to feeder line and equipment or appliance, using rule, pipe cutter, threader, and wrench. Tests and examines pipelines and equipment to locate leaks and faulty pipe connections and to determine pressure and flow of gas, using manometer, voltmeter, combustible gas indicator, and soap lather. Dismantles meters and regulators, and replaces defective pipes, thermocouples, thermostats, valves, and indicator spindles, using handtools. May assemble new or reconditioned appliances. May collect for monthly bills or overdue payments. May be designated according to appliance serviced as Gas-Refrigerator Servicer (any industry); Gas-Stove Servicer (any industry).
GOE: 05.10.02 STRENGTH: M GED: R4 M3 L3 SVP: 7 DLU: 77

637.261-022 INDUSTRIAL-GAS SERVICER (utilities)

Tests, repairs, and adjusts all types of industrial gas equipment, including control mechanisms, such as thermostats, high-temperature-limit controls, solenoid valves, safety pilots, and various other safety controls actuated by bimetallic expansion, fluid expansion, or thermocouple electric energy. May advise customers on proper installation of equipment. May install or remove large industrial meters, regulators, and related equipment. May read meters [METER READER (utilities; waterworks)].
GOE: 05.05.11 STRENGTH: M GED: R4 M3 L3 SVP: 7 DLU: 77

637.261-026 REFRIGERATION MECHANIC (any industry)

Installs and repairs industrial and commercial refrigerating systems according to blueprints and engineering specifications, using knowledge of refrigeration, structural layout, and function and design of components: Lays out reference points for installation of structural and functional components, using measuring instruments, such as tape, transit, plumb bob, levels, and square. Drills holes and installs mounting brackets and hangers into floor and walls of building. Lifts and aligns components into position, using hoist or block and tackle. Screws, bolts, rivets, welds, and brazes parts to assemble structural and func-

tional components, such as motors, controls, switches, gauges, wiring harnesses, valves, pumps, compressors, condensors, cores, and pipes. Cuts, threads, and connects pipe to functional components and water or power system of premises [PIPE FITTER (construction) 862.281-018]. Pumps specified gas or fluid into system. Starts system, observes operation, reads gauges and instruments, and adjusts mechanisms, such as valves, controls, and pumps to control level of fluid, pressure, and temperature in system. Dismantles malfunctioning systems and tests components, using electrical, mechanical, and pneumatic testing equipment. Replaces or adjusts defective or worn parts to repair systems. May insulate shells and cabinets of systems. May install wiring to connect components to electric power source. May specialize in installing systems and be designated Refrigeration-System Installer (any industry).
GOE: 05.05.09 STRENGTH: H GED: R4 M3 L3 SVP: 8 DLU: 80

637.261-030 SOLAR-ENERGY-SYSTEM INSTALLER (any industry)
Installs and repairs solar-energy systems designed to collect, store, and circulate solar-heated water or other medium for residential, commercial, or industrial use: Locates and marks position of collectors, holding tank, and distribution system on structure, according to specifications and blueprints. Cuts holes in roof, walls, and ceiling to install equipment and plumbing, using power saws and drills. Installs supports and brackets to anchor solar collectors and holding tank, using carpenter's handtools. Cuts, threads, and fits plumbing according to specifications for connecting circulation system, using plumber's handtools. Lays out and connects electrical wiring between controls and pumps according to wiring diagram and knowledge of standard industry practice, using electrician's handtools. Tests electrical circuits and components for continuity, using electrical test equipment. Tests plumbing for leaks, using pressure gauge. Pushes control buttons to activate pumps and observes system to detect malfunctions. Repairs or replaces defective equipment.
GOE: 05.05.09 STRENGTH: H GED: R4 M4 L4 SVP: 7 DLU: 86

637.261-034 AIR AND HYDRONIC BALANCING TECHNICIAN (any industry)
Inspects, tests, adjusts, and *balances* heating, cooling, and ventilating systems in residential, commercial, and industrial buildings, using specialized tools and test equipment, to attain performance standards specified in system design: Studies system blueprints, specifications, and performance data to determine configuration and purpose of system components, such as motors, pumps, fans, switches, ducts, or pipes. Discusses system malfunctions with users to isolate problems. Inspects system to verify system compliance with plans and specifications and to detect malfunctions in system component parts. Adjusts system controls to settings recommended by vendor to prepare to perform tests. Tests performance of air and hydronic systems, using specialized tools and test equipment, such as pitot tube, manometer, anemometer, velometer, tachometer, psychrometer, and thermometer, to isolate problems and determine where adjustments are necessary. Opens or closes louvers in system ductwork or adjusts flow control valves in piping to balance system, using handtools such as pliers, screwdriver, or wrenches. Discusses system operation with users to verify that malfunctions have been corrected.
GOE: 05.05.09 STRENGTH: M GED: R4 M3 L3 SVP: 7 DLU: 86

637.281-010 PUMP ERECTOR (construction) alternate titles: pump installation and servicer
Installs and repairs submerged turbine pumps in waterwells, using rig (truck-mounted hoisting equipment): Drives rig into position adjacent to well. Starts hoisting engine and moves levers and pedals to raise and extend telescoping hoisting mast. Bolts guy wires and struts to mast for support. Threads and tightens pump parts, such as pump bowl, shaft, bearings, tubing, and couplings, using wrenches and chain tongs to assemble pump section. Raises pump section to vertical position and installs section in well casing, using rig loadline and winch. Screws coupling or bolts flange to connect pump base to pipe column. Drives wedges under pump base to align base with pump shaft, centering pump shaft in opening until tube nut or packing container fits without interference, or using dial indicator to verify alignment. Hoists electric motor drive or engine drive gear box into position over pump base and inspects clearance between shaft and hollow spindle of driver to verify alignment of pump shaft. Attaches pressure gauge and orifice meter to pump outlet and pumps air into well to measure static and dynamic water levels and capacity of well. Dismantles pumps to clean, repair, and replace worn or damaged parts. May work in shop to repair various types of pumps, such as centrifugal, plunger, and turbine pumps [PUMP SERVICER (any industry)].
GOE: 05.05.09 STRENGTH: H GED: R4 M3 L3 SVP: 6 DLU: 77

637.281-014 STOKER ERECTOR-AND-SERVICER (any industry) alternate titles: stoker-installation mechanic; cooler servicer
Installs and repairs household, commercial, and industrial automatic coal stokers in furnaces according to specifications, using handtools and welding equipment: Removes plate from side of furnace with screwdriver or wrench or cuts hole in side of furnace with acetylene torch to make opening for entrance of stoker. Places stoker in operating position with feed mechanism projecting through side plate opening or hole in furnace wall and builds up firebrick or clay around it. Installs thermostat in furnace room or other part of building, instrument panel in furnace room, and regulator on boiler or furnace. Connects regulator wires to control panel and stoker wires with control panel wires according to wiring diagram. Replaces fuses, repairs short circuits in wiring, and removes clinkers from furnace bed and pieces of metal from screw conveyor.
GOE: 05.05.09 STRENGTH: H GED: R4 M3 L3 SVP: 7 DLU: 77

637.381-010 EVAPORATIVE-COOLER INSTALLER (any industry)
Repairs and installs cooling units to draw air over moistened pads, using handtools and portable power tools: Disassembles, cleans, and oils parts. Replaces motor bearings, aligns pulleys on motor and blower shafts, and tightens slack in drive belts. Replaces defective wiring. Holds tachometer against revolving centers of blowers and motors to verify specified revolutions per minute. Bolts cooler to window or platform adjacent to window, following layout lines. Cuts and installs plywood or building board to fit vacant window space. Installs electrical outlets and thermostat or humidistat controls. Cuts and connects tubing to cooler and water source. Adjusts rate of water flow. May install cooler on roof and assemble prefabricated sheet metal ducts in attic.
GOE: 05.10.04 STRENGTH: M GED: R3 M3 L3 SVP: 6 DLU: 77

637.381-014 REFRIGERATION UNIT REPAIRER (svc. ind. mach.)
Replaces defective components and reassembles refrigeration units to work orders and blueprint specifications: Studies rejection slips from inspection department or customer's letters and observes functioning of components, such as controls, fan, condenser, evaporator, or compressor to determine need for repair or replacement. Drains oil and pumps gas from unit. Loosens bolts, and melts soldered or brazed seams, to dismantle unit, using handtools and torch. Removes and replaces defective components. Brazes or solders parts to repair defective joints and leaks. Reassembles unit, using measuring instruments, handtools, soldering iron, and hand torch. Routes defective components to salvage department. May adjust unit controls. Records cause of malfunction, repairs, and replacements made.
GOE: 05.10.02 STRENGTH: M GED: R3 M2 L3 SVP: 6 DLU: 77

637.384-010 INDUSTRIAL-GAS-SERVICER HELPER (utilities)
Assists in testing, repairing, and installing gas equipment, domestic gas appliances, and gas meters: Cuts, threads, and joins pipe as directed, using handtools. Brushes soap solution over connections to test for leaks. Positions heavy equipment, using hoist. Performs other duties as described under HELPER (any industry) Master Title.
GOE: 05.10.02 STRENGTH: M GED: R3 M2 L2 SVP: 4 DLU: 77

637.664-010 ENVIRONMENTAL-CONTROL-SYSTEM INSTALLER-SERVICER HELPER (any industry) alternate titles: heating-and-air-conditioning-mechanic helper
Assists workers engaged in installing, repairing, and servicing industrial, commercial, and residential environmental-control systems, performing any combination of following duties: Cuts, punches, flanges, shears, and solders sheet metal ducts and parts, using handtools and portable power tools. Cuts threads and packs pipes. Cements insulation in place over finished piping or tubing. Passes electrical wire through conduit, splices wire connections, and tapes wire. Assembles sheet metal components of prefabricated furnaces, using handtools. Replaces exhausted or defective containers of refrigerant with new refrigerant. Lubricates fans, motors, and control units. Installs air and water units in completed assembly. Performs other duties as described under HELPER (any industry) Master Title. May be designated according to type of equipment serviced as Air-Conditioning-Mechanic Helper, Industrial (any industry).
GOE: 05.10.01 STRENGTH: H GED: R3 M2 L2 SVP: 6 DLU: 77

637.684-010 GAS-APPLIANCE-SERVICER HELPER (any industry) alternate titles: customer-servicer helper; gas-fitter helper
Assists GAS-APPLIANCE SERVICER (any industry) in installing, testing, adjusting, and repairing regulators, ranges, and heaters, in customer's establishments: Transports tools, parts, equipment, and appliances from truck to customer's establishment, using handtruck. Measures, cuts, threads, and connects pipe to feeder line and installed appliance, using pipe cutter, threader, and wrench. Dismantles appliances and replaces defective pipes, thermocouples, thermostats, valves, and spindles, using handtools. Performs other duties as described under HELPER (any industry) Master Title. May be designated according to kind of appliance repaired as Gas-Stove-Servicer Helper (any industry).
GOE: 05.12.15 STRENGTH: H GED: R2 M2 L2 SVP: 4 DLU: 77

637.684-014 QUALITY-CONTROL TECHNICIAN (svc. ind. mach.)
Tests vending, amusement, or other coin-operated machines for operating condition, and adjusts operating components, using handtools: Tests operating cycle of machine, using electrical timer. Tests wiring, using light bulbs to verify circuit continuity. Tests operation of coin-operating-and-return mechanism. Adjusts faulty operating components, using handtools. Rejects units requiring extensive repairs or refinishing. May examine paint finish for blemishes, chips, or other flaws.
GOE: 06.03.02 STRENGTH: L GED: R3 M3 L3 SVP: 3 DLU: 77

637.687-010 AIR-CONDITIONING INSTALLER-SERVICER HELPER, WINDOW UNIT (construction)
Assists AIR-CONDITIONING INSTALLER-SERVICER, WINDOW UNIT (any industry) in repairing, servicing, or installing window-mounted air-conditioning units, performing any combination of following duties: Carries unit from delivery vehicle to work site. Assembles window-support brackets, using handtools. Cuts opening through wall for insertion of unit, using hammer and chisel. Applies caulking compound to excess space between air-conditioner and wall opening. Performs other duties as described under HELPER (any industry) Master Title.
GOE: 05.12.12 STRENGTH: H GED: R2 M1 L2 SVP: 3 DLU: 77

637.687-014 REFRIGERATION-MECHANIC HELPER (any industry)
Assists REFRIGERATION MECHANIC (any industry) in installing, maintaining, and repairing industrial and commercial refrigerating systems: Trans-

ports tools, materials, components, and refuse to and from work area. Lifts or holds parts while REFRIGERATION MECHANIC (any industry) fits, aligns, and fastens them into position. Bolts or unbolts parts, using handtools. May cut and thread pipe to specified length, using pipe cutter, stock, and die. May insulate cabinets and systems. Performs other duties as described under HELPER (any industry) Master Title.
GOE: 05.12.12 STRENGTH: H GED: R2 M1 L2 SVP: 2 DLU: 77

637.687-018 SOLAR-ENERGY-SYSTEM-INSTALLER HELPER (any industry)

Assists SOLAR-ENERGY-SYSTEM INSTALLER (any industry) 637.261-030 in installing and repairing solar-energy systems for residential, commercial, or industrial use: Saws and drills holes in roof and walls for placement of equipment, plumbing, and wiring as directed. Loads and unloads truck. Attaches plumbing and electrical wiring to structure, using handtools. Cuts pipe threads and wraps insulation around pipes. Performs other duties as described under HELPER (any industry) Master Title.
GOE: 05.10.01 STRENGTH: H GED: R2 M2 L2 SVP: 4 DLU: 86

638   MISCELLANEOUS OCCUPATIONS IN MACHINE INSTALLATION AND REPAIR

This group includes occupations which are too broad to classify on the basis of a particular machine or type of machinery.

638.131-010 FUEL-SYSTEM-MAINTENANCE SUPERVISOR (any industry)

Supervises, coordinates activities of, and assists FUEL-SYSTEM-MAINTENANCE WORKERS (any industry) in maintenance and inspection of fuel storage, distribution, and dispensing systems. Determines safety, maintenance, and inspection methods and instructs and directs workers in such procedures. Diagnoses difficult maintenance problems and recurring malfunctions. Performs other duties as described under SUPERVISOR (any industry) Master Title.
GOE: 05.06.03 STRENGTH: L GED: R4 M4 L4 SVP: 7 DLU: 77

638.131-014 MACHINE-ASSEMBLER SUPERVISOR (machinery mfg.)

Supervises and coordinates activities of workers engaged in assembly of machines, equipment, and their subassemblies: Analyzes specifications, such as blueprints, diagrams, and schematics, to determine need for supplies and sequence of operations. Requisitions supplies and coordinates flow of material through department. Trains workers in assembly techniques. Inspects work to ensure conformance to specifications. Performs other duties as described under SUPERVISOR (any industry) Master Title.
GOE: 06.01.01 STRENGTH: L GED: R4 M4 L4 SVP: 8 DLU: 77

638.131-018 MAINTENANCE SUPERVISOR, FIRE-FIGHTING-EQUIPMENT (government ser.)

Supervises and coordinates activities of workers engaged in maintenance and repair of fire-fighting vehicles, equipment, and buildings: Inspects equipment and facilities to determine repair or malfunctioning units and physical structures. Trains workers in equipment repair and structural maintenance, using operating manuals, work orders, and blueprints. Requisitions materials and supplies. Repairs faulty equipment at fire sites, using mechanic's handtools. Performs other duties as described under SUPERVISOR (any industry) Master Title.
GOE: 05.05.09 STRENGTH: M GED: R4 M3 L4 SVP: 8 DLU: 77

638.131-022 MAINTENANCE-MECHANIC SUPERVISOR (any industry) alternate titles: craft supervisor; maintenance advisor; maintenance supervisor

Supervises and coordinates activities of workers engaged in setting up, installing, repairing, and maintaining machinery and equipment, and in fabricating metal parts and tools: Directs workers engaged in repairing and maintaining parts of equipment and machines. Coordinates activities of workers engaged in installation of machinery and equipment. Directs workers in electrical, electronic, mechanical, hydraulic, and pneumatic maintenance and repair of machinery and equipment. Assists workers in diagnosing malfunctions in machinery and equipment based on observation of machinery and applying knowledge from past experience. Directs workers engaged in dismantling, assembling, and installing industrial machinery [MILLWRIGHT SUPERVISOR (any industry) 638.131-030]. Performs other duties as described under SUPERVISOR (any industry) Master Title. May requisition and keep supply of spare parts. May modify programming of robots and related equipment, such as *robot controllers* and *programmable controllers.* May coordinate activities of workers engaged in programming machinery and equipment. May supervise and coordinate activities of workers engaged in making structural repairs to buildings [MAINTENANCE SUPERVISOR (any industry) 891.137-010].
GOE: 05.05.09 STRENGTH: M GED: R4 M4 L4 SVP: 8 DLU: 86

638.131-026 MECHANICAL-MAINTENANCE SUPERVISOR (any industry) alternate titles: maintenance engineer, oil field; shop supervisor

Supervises and coordinates activities of workers engaged in maintaining and repairing mechanical parts of pumps, cranes, compressors, ditch diggers, automobiles, trucks, tractors, pipelaying machines, and similar equipment used in constructing pipelines, transporting oil and other fluids, and in related oil field and construction or airport maintenance activities: Inspects defective equipment

in shop or field to determine extent of wear or damage. Performs other duties as described under SUPERVISOR (any industry) Master Title. May contract repair work. May arrange for sale or purchase of equipment. May supervise workers engaged in repairing company-owned railroad cars. May travel to work sites to supervise and coordinate activities of workers and be designated Traveling-Maintenance Supervisor (any industry).
GOE: 05.05.09 STRENGTH: M GED: R4 M3 L3 SVP: 7 DLU: 80

638.131-030 MILLWRIGHT SUPERVISOR (any industry)

Supervises and coordinates activities of workers engaged in dismantling, moving, assembling, and installing industrial machinery: Measures floor distances with rule to verify foundation layouts. Verifies dimensions of machine parts, using gauges, calipers, and micrometers. Performs other duties as described under SUPERVISOR (any industry) Master Title.
GOE: 05.05.06 STRENGTH: L GED: R4 M4 L4 SVP: 8 DLU: 77

638.131-034 MAINTENANCE SUPERVISOR, MOBILE BATTERY EQUIPMENT (mine & quarry)

Supervises and coordinates activities of workers engaged in maintenance and repair of mobile battery-powered mining equipment: Reviews list of mobile battery-powered equipment needing repairs. Examines defective equipment and equipment batteries to determine malfunctions, using electrical and hydraulic schematics. Assigns personnel to perform repairs. Inspects repaired equipment for conformance to company and federal safety standards. Notifies supervisor when equipment is back in service. Trains new employees. Tests air in mine shafts for presence of methane or lack of oxygen, using hand held testing devices, and notifies shift supervisors of hazards. Observes work area for defective equipment and hazardous electrical conditions, according to federal and state regulations. Completes accident report. Performs other duties as described under SUPERVISOR (any industry) Master Title.
GOE: 05.05.09 STRENGTH: M GED: R3 M3 L3 SVP: 7 DLU: 86

638.261-010 AUTOMATED EQUIPMENT ENGINEER-TECHNICIAN (machinery mfg.) alternate titles: engineer, automated equipment; technician, automated equipment

Installs machinery and equipment used to emboss, die-cut, score, fold, and transfer paper or cardboard stock to form box blanks, knock-down advertising displays, and similar products: Confers with customer's engineering staff to determine layout of equipment, to resolve problems of machine design, and to avoid construction problems in plant. Arranges machine parts according to sequence of assembly and effective use of floor space. Directs workers in positioning equipment, following floor plans and manufacturer's instructions. Assembles and installs electrical and electromechanical components and systems, using handtools, electrical testing instruments, soldering irons, and wiring diagrams. Operates equipment through trial run to verify setup. Adjusts controls and setup of machine for specified type, thickness, and size of stock to be processed, for prescribed sequence of operating stages, and to ensure maximum efficiency. Instructs equipment operators and engineering and maintenance personnel regarding setup, operation, and maintenance of equipment. Repairs and services equipment, following preventive maintenance schedule or upon customer's request. May modify previously installed equipment to ensure compatibility with new units, or install safety devices or attachments to old equipment. May confer with customer's engineers to determine effective methods of programming work for machine processing.
GOE: 05.05.05 STRENGTH: M GED: R4 M4 L4 SVP: 7 DLU: 77

638.261-014 MACHINERY ERECTOR (engine-turbine; machinery mfg.) alternate titles: erector; heavy-machinery assembler

Erects and tests machinery and heavy equipment, such as hydraulic turbines, turbine wheels, jaw stone crushers, industrial surface condensers, flaking machines, valves, and mine hoists, according to blueprints and specifications, using handtools, heating equipment, and measuring instruments: Positions steel beams to support bedplates of machines and equipment. Levels bedplate and establishes centerline, using straightedge, levels, and transit. Signals OVERHEAD CRANE OPERATOR (any industry) 921.663-010 to lower basic assembly unit, such as shaft, shaft casing, frame, or housing unit, to bedplate and aligns unit to centerline. Lays out mounting holes, using measuring instruments and drills holes with power drill. Bolts parts, such as side and deck plates, jaw plates, and journals, to basic assembly unit. Attaches moving parts and subassemblies, such as shafts, rollers, flywheels, runners (water wheels), valves, gates, bearings, and bearing supports, to basic assembly unit, using handtools and power tools. Shrink-fits bushings, sleeves, rings, liners, gears, and wheels to specified items, using portable gas heating equipment. Inserts shims, adjusts tension on nuts and bolts, or positions parts, using handtools and measuring instruments to set specified clearances between moving and stationary parts. Connects power unit to machines, or steam piping to equipment, and tests unit to evaluate its mechanical operation. Replaces defective parts of machine or adjusts clearances and alignment of moving parts. Dismantles machinery and equipment for shipment to installation site.
GOE: 05.05.09 STRENGTH: H GED: R4 M4 L4 SVP: 8 DLU: 77

638.261-018 MANUFACTURER'S SERVICE REPRESENTATIVE (machinery mfg.; machine tools) alternate titles: field engineer; field servicer; service engineer; service representative

Installs and repairs machinery or equipment in customer's establishment, following blueprints and manufacturer's instructions, and utilizing knowledge of mechanical, hydraulic, and electrical machinery: Consults with personnel in en-

gineering department to resolve problems of machine design to avoid construction problems in customer's establishment. Studies blueprints and observes tryout of machine in manufacturer's plant to become familiar with machine operation. Operates machine through trial run at customer's establishment to ensure that quality and rate of production meet specifications, and trains customer's personnel in adjusting, maintaining, and repairing machinery or equipment. Consults with customer about deviations of machine operation from original specifications and explains reasons for changes. Repairs or supervises repair of worn or defective machinery or equipment in customer's plant. May be designated according to type, size, or trade name of machines, tools, or equipment serviced.
GOE: 05.05.09 STRENGTH: M GED: R4 M3 L3 SVP: 8 DLU: 77

638.261-022 PINSETTER MECHANIC, AUTOMATIC (any industry) alternate titles: bowling-pin-machine mechanic

Adjusts and repairs automatic pinsetting bowling machines, following maintenance manuals, schematics, and knowledge of equipment, using handtools, power tools, and testing equipment: Observes operation of machine to determine nature and cause of malfunction. Tests relays, solenoids, transformers, electric motors, and wiring for defects, using continuity tester, ammeter, and voltmeter. Disassembles and replaces or repairs mechanical and electrical components or parts, such as bearings, coils, armatures, and wiring, using handtools. Cleans and lubricates machine. Instructs assistants in locating and repairing minor defects. Directs workers or participates in reconditioning and painting bowling pins. Maintains perpetual inventory of and orders replacements for spare parts.
GOE: 05.10.04 STRENGTH: M GED: R3 M2 L2 SVP: 4 DLU: 77

638.261-026 FIELD SERVICE TECHNICIAN (machinery mfg.) alternate titles: robot technician

Installs, programs, and repairs robots and related equipment, such as *programmable controllers, robot controllers*, end-of-arm tools, conveyors, and parts orienters, applying knowledge of electronics, electrical circuits, mechanics, pneumatics, hydraulics, and programming, using power tools, handtools, and testing instruments and following manuals, schematic diagrams, and blueprints: Reviews work order and related manuals, blueprints, and schematic diagrams to determine tasks to be performed and tools, equipment, and parts needed for installation of repair assignment. Discusses assignment with customer's representative and inspects installation site to verify that electrical supply wires, conduit, switches, and circuit breakers are installed according to specifications. Positions and secures robot and related equipment to floor, assisted by customer's staff, using crane, handtools, and power tools and following manuals and blueprints, or inspects installation site to ensure that robot has been installed according to specifications. Attaches electrical wires to robot controller and programmable controller and connects cables between robot, robot controller, programmable controller, and hydraulic power unit, using handtools. Connects hoses between hydraulic power unit and robot, using handtools. Verifies that electrical power is reaching robot and that voltage is as specified, using testing instruments. Pushes buttons, flips switches, and moves levers to start robot and related equipment to verify that operation is as specified. Programs robot to perform specified tasks, applying knowledge of programming language, using *teach pendant* and keyboard or control panel on robot controller. Modifies program to refine movement of robot, using teach pendant. Observes and listens to robot and related equipment to detect malfunction and repairs or replaces defective parts, using handtools and power tools [MAINTENANCE MECHANIC (any industry) 638.281-014]. Tests electrical components, such as wiring, switches, and relays, using testing instruments, and replaces faulty components, using handtools. Locates and replaces faulty printed circuit boards in robot controller, applying knowledge of circuit board function, using computer display screen on robot controller and following schematic diagram. May train customer's staff in operation of robot and related equipment. May install electric or pneumatic end-of-arm tools on robot. May repair faulty printed circuit boards.
GOE: 05.05.09 STRENGTH: H GED: R4 M4 L4 SVP: 7 DLU: 86

638.261-030 MACHINE REPAIRER, MAINTENANCE (any industry)

Repairs and maintains mechanical and hydraulic components of production machines and equipment, such as metal fabricating machine tools, material handling system, and automated lubrication system, following blueprints and specifications and using handtools, power tools, and precision measuring instruments: Visually inspects and listens to machines and equipment to locate causes of malfunctions. Dismantles machines and equipment to gain access to problem area, using handtools and power tools. Inspects and measures parts to detect wear, misalignment, or other problems. Removes and replaces worn or defective parts of drive mechanism or hydraulic system, using handtools and power tools, and following blueprints, diagrams, and service manuals. Realigns and adjusts components, such as spindles and clutches, using handtools and following diagrams. Locates damaged air and hydraulic pipes on machine, and measures, cuts, threads, and installs new pipe. Starts machines and equipment to test operation following repair. Repairs broken parts, using brazing, soldering, and welding equipment and handtools. May modify computer-controlled motion of robot, applying knowledge of program commands and using *robot controller* and *teach pendant*. May set up and operate metalworking tools, such as lathe, drill press, or grinder, to make or repair parts. May assist MECHANICAL ENGINEER (profess. & kin.) 007.061-014 to modify sketches or computer-generated designs of machine components, such as hydraulic system and

drive mechanism, applying knowledge of shop mathematics, hydraulics, and mechanics, and using computer keyboard and software programs. May work as part of team including such workers as ELECTRICIAN, MAINTENANCE (any industry) 829.261-018; MILLWRIGHT (any industry) 638.281-018; PIPE FITTER (construction) 862.281-022; TOOL MAKER (machine shop) 601.280-042. May be designated according to type of machine repaired as Broaching-Machine Repairer (machine tools); Centerless-Grinding-Machine Adjuster (ordnance); Screw-Machine Adjuster, Automatic (ordnance); Screw-Machine Repairer (machine shop).
GOE: 05.05.09 STRENGTH: H GED: R4 M4 L4 SVP: 7 DLU: 86

638.281-010 FIRE-FIGHTING-EQUIPMENT SPECIALIST (government ser.)

Repairs firefighting vehicles, equipment, buildings, and structures: Inspects vehicles or equipment to determine condition. Repairs vehicles or equipment, using mechanic's tools, precision testing and measuring equipment, and manuals. Orders replacement parts. Repairs and maintains physical structures, using handtools, power tools, blueprints, and wiring diagrams. Estimates repair costs. Keeps records of repairs and cost.
GOE: 05.05.09 STRENGTH: H GED: R4 M3 L4 SVP: 7 DLU: 77

638.281-014 MAINTENANCE MECHANIC (any industry) alternate titles: fixer; machine-maintenance servicer; machine overhauler; machine repairer; mechanical adjuster; repair mechanic; tool-and-machine maintainer

Repairs and maintains, in accordance with diagrams, sketches, operation manuals, and manufacturer's specifications, machinery and mechanical equipment, such as engines, motors, pneumatic tools, conveyor systems, and production machines and equipment, using handtools, power tools, and precision-measuring and testing instruments: Observes mechanical devices in operation and listens to their sounds to locate causes of trouble. Dismantles devices to gain access to and remove defective parts, using hoists, cranes, handtools, and power tools. Examines form and texture of parts to detect imperfections. Inspects used parts to determine changes in dimensional requirements, using rules, calipers, micrometers, and other measuring instruments. Adjusts functional parts of devices and control instruments, using handtools, levels, plumb bobs, and straightedges. Repairs or replaces defective parts, using handtools and power tools. Installs special functional and structural parts in devices, using handtools. Starts devices to test their performance. Lubricates and cleans parts. May set up and operate lathe, drill press, grinder, and other metalworking tools to make and repair parts. May initiate purchase order for parts and machines. May repair electrical equipment. May be designated according to machine repaired as Carton-Forming-Machine Adjuster (any industry); Machine Adjuster (tobacco); Maintenance Mechanic, Record Processing Equipment (recording).
GOE: 05.05.09 STRENGTH: H GED: R4 M4 L3 SVP: 7 DLU: 87

638.281-018 MILLWRIGHT (any industry)

Installs machinery and equipment according to layout plans, blueprints, and other drawings in industrial establishment, using hoists, lift trucks, handtools, and power tools: Reads blueprints and schematic drawings to determine work procedures. Dismantles machines, using hammers, wrenches, crowbars, and other handtools. Moves machinery and equipment, using hoists, dollies, rollers, and trucks. Assembles and installs equipment, such as shafting, conveyors, and tram rails, using handtools and power tools. Constructs foundation for machines, using handtools and building materials, such as wood, cement, and steel. Aligns machines and equipment, using hoists, jacks, handtools, squares, rules, micrometers, and plumb bobs. Assembles machines, and bolts, welds, rivets, or otherwise fastens them to foundation or other structures, using handtools and power tools. May operate engine lathe to grind, file, and turn machine parts to dimensional specifications. May repair and lubricate machines and equipment. May install robot and modify its program, using *teach pendant*. May perform installation and maintenance work as part of team of skilled trades workers.
GOE: 05.05.06 STRENGTH: H GED: R4 M3 L3 SVP: 7 DLU: 86

638.281-022 MILLWRIGHT APPRENTICE (any industry)

Performs duties as described under APPRENTICE (any industry) Master Title.
GOE: 05.05.06 STRENGTH: H GED: R4 M3 L3 SVP: 7 DLU: 77

638.281-026 PARTS SALVAGER (any industry)

Repairs salvable mechanical parts of machines and equipment: Dismantles machinery, equipment, and parts, using handtools, such as hacksaws, files, reamers, wrenches and screwdrivers. Inspects parts to determine salvageability or method of repairing or reworking parts. Sets up and operates metalworking tools, such as engine lathes, milling, drilling, grinding, polishing, and buffing machines to repair parts. Files, taps, reams, bends, and straightens, or uses other methods to recondition parts, using handtools. Verifies dimensions and tolerances, using blueprints, scale, and precision-measuring instruments. May reassemble parts, using handtools and power tools. May direct cleaning, storing, and issuing of reclaimed parts, and packing of usable materials, such as metal sweepings. May arrange for sale of scrap.
GOE: 05.05.09 STRENGTH: M GED: R4 M3 L3 SVP: 7 DLU: 77

638.281-030 HYDRAULIC-RUBBISH-COMPACTOR MECHANIC (sanitary ser.)

Installs and repairs hydraulic rubbish compactors, using tools and equipment: Installs new compactors, utilizing knowledge of electrical wiring and hydraulic-

pneumatic functions and using handtools and power tools. Diagnoses hydraulic and mechanical malfunctions of compactors to determine required repairs. Adjusts, replaces, or repairs faulty hydraulic units, such as pistons, cylinders, and conveyors. Installs or replaces damaged shafts, guards, casings, and metal frame of compactor units, using electric welding, brazing, or soldering equipment and tools. Diagnoses electrical-electronic system malfunction, and replaces or repairs parts, such as electric motors, switches, and starting and stopping units, using knowledge of wiring, wiring diagrams, voltage systems, and electric-electronic components. Loads compactors and parts onto truck, using forklift.
GOE: 05.05.09 STRENGTH: M GED: R4 M3 L3 SVP: 8 DLU: 86

638.281-034 HYDRAULIC REPAIRER (any industry)
Maintains and repairs hydraulic systems of machinery and equipment, such as robots, applying knowledge of hydraulics and mechanics and using handtools: Observes and listens to operating machinery to detect malfunctions. Visually inspects hydraulic lines and components to detect leaks, damage, and wear. Reads pressure gauges to detect abnormal oil pressure and smells to detect overheated oil. Depresses buttons and switches to turn off machinery. Turns valve to release pressure from hydraulic system and disconnects hydraulic supply and return lines, using handtools. Removes and replaces defective accumulator, using handtools. Connects charging assembly to accumulator and fills accumulator bladder with nitrogen gas to recharge accumulator, following manufacturer's specifications. Replaces worn or damaged hydraulic components, such as oil lines, fittings, cylinders, servo-valves, pressure release valves, gaskets, and seals, using handtools. Disassembles hydraulic system and removes and replaces defective actuator, pump bearings, and pump motor, using handtools and hoist. Observes operation of machinery and equipment to verify repair. Performs routine maintenance, such as changing filters, following schedule, using handtools. May observe readout on display screen of *robot controller* to determine nature of system malfunction. May disassemble defective hydraulic components, such as pumps and accumulator, at workbench and rebuilds or repairs components. May install hydraulic oil lines on new machinery and equipment.
GOE: 05.05.09 STRENGTH: H GED: R3 M3 L3 SVP: 7 DLU: 86

638.361-010 MACHINE ASSEMBLER (machinery mfg.)
Assembles machines, equipment, and their subassemblies, such as baling presses, stokers, blowers, compression pumps, and food wrapping machines, according to customer's needs, following blueprints and other written and verbal specifications: Plans assembly procedures, following specifications and using knowledge gained by experience. Removes small quantities of metal, using hand files or portable grinders, to clean parts or to produce close fit between parts. Drills, taps, or reams holes, using drill press or portable drill. Aligns components, and bolts, screws, or rivets them together, using handtools or portable powered tools. Installs moving parts, such as shafts, levers, or bearings, and works them to test free movement. May bend and install pipe for hydraulic systems. May align and mesh gears in gearbox to assemble system of gears. May test or assist in testing operation of completed product.
GOE: 06.02.22 STRENGTH: M GED: R3 M3 L3 SVP: 6 DLU: 77

638.381-010 FUEL-SYSTEM-MAINTENANCE WORKER (any industry) alternate titles: gas-pit specialist
Installs, maintains, repairs, and adjusts pumps, control valves and meters, strainers and filters, water separators, and pipelines of liquid fuel systems for airfields: Makes periodic inspections of units to detect and correct leakage, corrosion, faulty fittings, and malfunction of mechanical units, meters, and gauges, such as fuel hydrants, tank pits, distribution lines, storage tanks, turbines, pumps, and control rooms. Inspects electrical wiring, switches, and controls for safe operating condition, grounding, and adjustment. Repairs, replaces, and adjusts malfunctioning equipment to restore operating condition specified in regulations and repair manuals. Disassembles, adjusts, aligns, and calibrates gauges and meters. Cleans storage tanks, and removes and installs old or new equipment, such as meter and filter installations, pipe systems, pit covers, and vents, to modify existing installations.
GOE: 05.05.09 STRENGTH: H GED: R3 M3 L3 SVP: 7 DLU: 77

638.484-010 MILLWRIGHT HELPER (any industry)
Assists MILLWRIGHT (any industry) in installing, dismantling, and moving machines, conveyors, and other equipment: Erects scaffolding. Nails together forms and mixes cement for machine foundation. Moves materials, using lift truck. Drills holes. Measures, cuts and installs hangers, using handtools and ladders. Installs and dismantles machines and equipment, using crowbars, chain falls, hoists, and wrenches. Performs other duties as described under HELPER (any industry) Master Title.
GOE: 05.12.12 STRENGTH: H GED: R2 M2 L2 SVP: 3 DLU: 77

638.684-010 KNIFE CHANGER (tobacco) alternate titles: knife setter; shredding-machine-knife changer
Replaces dull or worn knives on tobacco shredding machine, using wrench to loosen and tighten bolts that hold knives in position.
GOE: 06.04.15 STRENGTH: L GED: R1 M1 L1 SVP: 2 DLU: 77

638.684-014 KNIFE SETTER (sugar & conf.)
Assembles and installs knife blocks in beet slicing machine: Positions knives on block, aligns knives with cutter bar, using gauge. Bolts knives in place on block, using handtools. Places assembled block on cutter wheel and bolts it in place, using handtools. May order or purchase replacement parts and cutter knives for slicing machines. May remove and disassemble knife blocks preparatory to sharpening.

GOE: 06.01.02 STRENGTH: M GED: R3 M2 L2 SVP: 4 DLU: 77

638.684-018 MAINTENANCE-MECHANIC HELPER (any industry) alternate titles: machine-adjuster helper; repair helper
Assists MAINTENANCE MECHANIC (any industry) 638.281-014 in repairing and maintaining machinery and mechanical equipment: Carries tools and equipment to and from storage and working areas. Holds scaffolding members in place or tightens bolts to erect working platforms about machines. Pulls handles to raise materials and tools to working levels. Loosens bolts to dismantle machinery. Drills and breaks up concrete, using jackhammer. Digs trenches for machinery foundations. Mixes and pours concrete for foundations. Cleans machines with sandpaper, solvent, and wiping rags to prepare surfaces for painting. Oils and greases machines. Performs other duties as described under HELPER (any industry) Master Title.
GOE: 05.12.15 STRENGTH: H GED: R2 M1 L2 SVP: 4 DLU: 88

639 MECHANICS AND MACHINERY REPAIRERS, N.E.C.

This group includes occupations, not elsewhere classified, concerned with inspecting, maintaining, and repairing mechanical equipment.

639.281-010 AVIATION SUPPORT EQUIPMENT REPAIRER (military ser.)
Inspects, maintains, repairs, and modifies aircraft ground equipment, such as M-G (motor generator) sets, air compressors, and test stands: Conducts periodic and special inspections, using test equipment, to detect malfunctions. Tests and operates equipment for output, leakage, and operation in accordance with technical orders to determine serviceability. Disassembles and assembles malfunctioning accessories and components of aerospace ground equipment, such as motor and engine driven generator sets, air compressors, hydraulic-pneumatic sets, air-conditioners, heaters, exhaust and cooling equipment, and test stands. Replaces worn bearings, bushings, shafts, end plates, brushes, springs, coils, armatures, pushrods, valves, exhaust manifolds, tubing, hoses, and defective wiring. Repairs, adjusts, and operates small gas turbine engines.
GOE: 05.10.02 STRENGTH: L GED: R3 M3 L3 SVP: 5 DLU: 77

639.281-014 COIN-MACHINE-SERVICE REPAIRER (svc. ind. mach.) alternate titles: vending-machine repairer
Installs, services, adjusts, and repairs vending, amusement, and other coin-operated machines placed in establishments on concession basis: Assembles machines following specifications, using handtools and power tools. Fills machines with ingredients or products and tests ice making, refrigeration, carbonation, evaporation, dispensing, electrical, and coin-handling systems. Examines defective machines to determine causes of malfunctions. Adjusts and repairs machines, replacing worn or defective electrical or mechanical parts, using handtools, such as screwdrivers, hammers, and pliers. May collect coins from machine and make settlements with concessionaires. May replenish vending machines with gum, candy, or other articles. May be designated according to type of machine serviced as Juke-Box Servicer (business ser.); Pinball-Machine Repairer (business ser.).
GOE: 05.10.02 STRENGTH: M GED: R3 M3 L3 SVP: 5 DLU: 82

639.281-018 SEWING-MACHINE REPAIRER (any industry) alternate titles: sewing-machine adjuster
Repairs and adjusts sewing machines in homes and sewing departments of industrial establishments, using handtools: Turns screws and nuts to adjust machine parts. Regulates length of stroke of needle and horizontal movement of feeding mechanism under needle. Dismantles machines and replaces or repairs broken or worn parts, using handtools. Inspects machines, shafts, and belts. Repairs broken transmission belts. Installs attachments on machines. Initiates orders for new machines or parts. May operate machine tools, such as lathes and drill presses, to make new parts. May be designated according to location in which employed as Fitting-Room Maintenance Mechanic (boot & shoe).
GOE: 05.10.02 STRENGTH: M GED: R3 M3 L3 SVP: 7 DLU: 81

639.281-022 MEDICAL-EQUIPMENT REPAIRER (protective dev.; retail trade) alternate titles: durable medical equipment repairer; wheelchair repairer
Repairs medical equipment, such as manual or powered wheelchairs, hospital beds, and suction equipment, using knowledge of equipment function and handtools: Test operates and examines malfunctioning equipment to determine cause of malfunction. Disassembles and inspects equipment to locate defective components, such as motors, valves, and electrical controls, using test instruments and handtools. Replaces defective parts, and solders, tightens, and aligns parts which have become loose or out of adjustment, using handtools and soldering iron. Cleans, lubricates, and polishes equipment components to restore surface, using solvent, polish, rags, and grease gun. Test operates unit to ensure equipment functions according to manufacturer's specifications. Occasionally installs modified parts, such as respirator equipment or foot rest, onto wheelchairs, according to customer specification, and fills parts orders from customers.
GOE: 05.10.02 STRENGTH: H GED: R3 M2 L3 SVP: 5 DLU: 86

639.681-010 BICYCLE REPAIRER (any industry) alternate titles: bicycle mechanic; cycle repairer
Repairs and services bicycles, using power tools and handtools: Tightens and loosens spokes to align wheels. Disassembles axle to repair coaster brakes and

to adjust and replace defective parts, using handtools. Adjusts cables or replaces worn or damaged parts to repair handbrakes. Installs and adjusts speed and gear mechanisms. Shapes replacement parts, using *bench grinder*. Installs, repairs, and replaces equipment or accessories, such as handle bars, stands, lights, and seats. Paints bicycle frame, using spray gun or brush. Rubs tubes with scraper and places patch over hole to repair tube. May weld broken or cracked frame together, using oxyacetylene torch and welding rods. May assemble and sell new bicycles and accessories.
GOE: 05.10.02 STRENGTH: M GED: R3 M2 L3 SVP: 4 DLU: 77

639.684-010   SEWING-MACHINE-REPAIRER HELPER (any industry)
Assists SEWING-MACHINE REPAIRER (any industry) in repairing household and industrial sewing machines: Lifts machines to work bench and disassembles parts, using wrenches and screwdrivers. Cleans parts, using solvent and rags. Replaces defective parts and reassembles machines. Starts and observes machines in operation to test performances. Uncrates and assembles new machines. Performs other duties as described under HELPER (any industry) Master Title.
GOE: 05.12.15 STRENGTH: M GED: R2 M2 L2 SVP: 4 DLU: 77

64   PAPERWORKING OCCUPATIONS

This division includes occupations concerned with shaping, cutting, scoring, joining, and otherwise machining paper and paper products.

640   PAPER CUTTING, WINDING, AND RELATED OCCUPATIONS

This group includes occupations concerned with cutting multiple sheets of paper, pasteboard, and similar material to specific size; and forming spiral or convolute paper tubing to make such articles as paper containers and covers.

640.132-010   SUPERVISOR, COREMAKER (paper & pulp)
Supervises and coordinates activities of workers engaged in operating machines to spiral-wind continuous cardboard strips to make cores for paper rolls: Orders type of paper and glue to be used, number of strips to be wound, and machine changes required to meet production requirements. Inspects cores for specified length, diameter, and solidity, using rule, calipers, and breakage tester. Directs machine operator in changing speed of traveling cut-off saw, adjusting tension on paper strips, and changing adhesives. Performs other duties as described under SUPERVISOR (any industry) Master Title.
GOE: 06.02.04 STRENGTH: M GED: R4 M3 L3 SVP: 7 DLU: 78

640.360-010   PANEL-MACHINE SETTER (paper goods)
Sets up machine that cuts edges, flaps, notches, or openings in envelope blanks or envelopes: Bolts specified cutting die onto machine ram, using handtools. Turns handwheel to adjust stroke of ram according to depth of die. Turns setscrews to adjust machine guides and stops to accommodate specified size paper stock, using rule and screwdriver. Operates machine for trial run and compares first piece with sample to verify accuracy of machine setup.
GOE: 06.01.02 STRENGTH: L GED: R3 M2 L3 SVP: 6 DLU: 77

640.385-010   RIBBON-HANKING-MACHINE OPERATOR (paper goods)
Tends machine that winds specified lengths of paper ribbon into hanks: Threads ribbon through guides of worktable and hanking machine, fastening end in jaws of machine holder. Starts machine that winds specified yardage over spindle arms to form hank and examines ribbon for missing threads, tears, defective design, or other imperfections. Stops machine and folds seal on creased lines around center of hank to hold ribbon together and prevent unwinding. Removes ribbon from holder, positions it under blade, and releases handle to cut ribbon and hold other end for hanking. Slides hank from spindle arms, packs it in cardboard cartons in specified manner, and inserts identification slip. Adjusts cutting blade and guides to accommodate different widths of ribbon.
GOE: 06.04.04 STRENGTH: L GED: R2 M1 L1 SVP: 2 DLU: 77

640.565-010   PAPER CUTTER (beverage) alternate titles: cutting-machine operator; paper-cutting-machine operator; stamp cutter
Cuts, stores, and issues revenue stamps and labels: Turns hand screws on paper-cutting tool to tighten paper guide that holds sheets of stamps or labels in position. Pulls knife down by hand or steps on treadle that lowers knife to cut sheets. Sharpens knife by rubbing it with abrasive stone. Records number of sheets cut and sequence of serial numbers of revenue stamps. Stocks cut revenue stamps and labels, and issues them on request. May be designated according to type of paper item cut as Revenue-Stamp Cutter (beverage).
GOE: 06.04.04 STRENGTH: L GED: R2 M1 L1 SVP: 2 DLU: 77

640.682-010   CONVOLUTE-TUBE WINDER (paper goods)
Sets up and operates machine to form convolute tubes used for fiber cans or containers: Installs and adjusts winding mandrel, gluing and labeling attachments, and slitting and cutting knives, using handtools. Places roll of paper on machine feedrack and threads paper through gluing, coating, and slitting rollers. Fills glue and paraffin reservoirs, and loads stacks of labels in labeling device or adjusts feeding mechanism. Sets paper feeding timer for specified number of turns. Starts machine and turns wheels and dials to regulate tension on pressure rolls, speed of gluing and coating rollers, temperature of paraffin reservoir, and machine feed speed. Examines cut-labeled tubes for defects, such as mis-

placed or wrinkled labels, uneven or excessive glue and paraffin distribution, and uneven winding of paper strips. May cut labels to specified dimensions, using hand or powered paper cutter. May attach threading or forming fixture to machine that thread end of tube or shape it into box form.
GOE: 06.02.04 STRENGTH: M GED: R3 M2 L2 SVP: 4 DLU: 77

640.682-014   CORE WINDING OPERATOR (paper & pulp)
Controls section of paper machine to wind paper onto core to make jumbo roll of specified dimensions: Positions empty core on machine carriage and tightens support clamps, using hoist and wrench. Tears continuous sheet, using compressed airhose, when roll is filled and blows free end around revolving empty core to start new roll. Removes full roll from machine with hoist. Turns handwheel to regulate tension on paper being wound on new roll. Examines sheet for defects, such as dirt, slime spots, holes, and wrinkles, and marks defective portions with chalk. Periodically runs hand along winding roll of paper to test for tension and to feel for soft spots and lumps. Cleans lint from calender rolls, using hand scraper and cloth.
GOE: 06.02.04 STRENGTH: M GED: R3 M3 L3 SVP: 5 DLU: 78

640.682-018   CUTTING-MACHINE OPERATOR (print. & pub.) alternate titles: cutter operator; finishing machine operator; paper cutter
Sets up and operates machine to cut paper stock and glue from spine of book bodies preparatory to printing, binding, and rebinding: Reviews job sample containing dimensions or specifications to determine page sequence, kind of fold, size of sheet, and amount to trim from spine of book body. Measures from edge of page, using scale, and types instructions on keyboard of computer, pushes buttons to activate computer program, or manually sets cutting guides, clamps, and knives, using wrench, to cut paper or spine to prescribed dimensions. Places book body or stack of paper sheets on bed of machine, rolling or folding oversized sheets as necessary. Fans edges of sheets to prevent adherence of pages. Aligns edges by tapping against paper guide, using hand or stick, to ensure square, true edges. Pushes button, types instructions on keyboard, or pulls lever to activate knife and removes trimming preparatory to next cut. Examines cut stock and spine of book body for trimming imperfections, such as ragged edges and incomplete cuts, and to verify that sheets are cut square and to specified size or cut marks. Removes sheets or book body from machine and stacks on skid. Lubricates machine, changes dull knives, and performs running repairs as needed. Jogs book bodies to align edge or edges against back section of guide or three sections of guide in turn to trim spine (back) or head (top), tail (bottom), and fore (front), pressing buttons or depressing pedal to clamp cut edges at each position [BOOK TRIMMER (print. & pub.) 640.685-010].
GOE: 06.02.04 STRENGTH: H GED: R3 M2 L2 SVP: 4 DLU: 89

640.682-022   SPIRAL-TUBE WINDER (paper goods) alternate titles: winder
Sets up and operates machine to wind continuous strips of paper or cardboard into tubes of specified dimensions and cut tubing to length to form fiber cans, containers, or cores for paper rolls: Installs and adjusts forming mandrels and cutting saw on machine, using handtools. Loads rolls of paper or cardboard on machine feedrack and locks them in place with clamps. Threads paper or cardboard through tension and gluing rollers, fills glue reservoirs, and sets thermostatic control to regulate temperatures of glue. Starts machine and turns wheels to adjust tension on pressure rollers and to synchronize speed of traveling cutoff saw with machine feed speed. Observes tubing for excess glue and open seams and adjusts machine to alter glue deposit and degree of spiral. Removes finished cores and stacks or places them on conveyor for transfer to other work areas. May be designated according to type of product wound as Coremaker (paper goods).
GOE: 06.02.04 STRENGTH: M GED: R3 M2 L2 SVP: 4 DLU: 87

640.685-010   BOOK TRIMMER (print. & pub.) alternate titles: bindery operator; multiple-knife-edge-trimmer operator; shearing-machine operator; trimmer operator, three knife
Tends paper-cutting machine that cuts edges of bound and unbound books, periodicals, catalogs, and directories to specified size for binding and rebinding: Reads instructions on worksheet to ascertain machine setting requirements. Inserts or replaces knives in trimmer and adjusts guides to trim head (top), tail (bottom), and fore (front) edges of book to specified dimensions, and locks sections in place. Starts machine for test run, and examines finished book body to ensure finished sample meets job order specifications and book body sample. Loads book bodies into feed receptacle of machine. Starts machine and observes operation. Examines book bodies to ensure specifications are met. Observes operation of machine during production run. Stops machine when machine malfunctions and adjusts knives and guides as required. Replenishes supply of book bodies periodically. May tend manually operated trimmer, jogging book bodies to align edges and placing book body against three sections of guide in turn to trim three edges of book. Depresses treadle or lever to clamp cut edges at each position. May be required to watch for colored markers between pages that indicate narrow margins and foldouts when positioning edges of book bodies against guides. May stack books as they are trimmed. May operate cutter to cut cardboard, paper, or book covers to specified size. May push cart stacked with books to next work station.
GOE: 06.04.04 STRENGTH: M GED: R2 M1 L1 SVP: 3 DLU: 89

640.685-014   BOOK-JACKET-COVER-MACHINE OPERATOR (paper goods)
Tends machine that combines paper and plastic film to be used as jacket covers for books: Mounts rolls of paper and plastic film on machine holders, using

hoist, and installs roll of adhesive tape on either side of machine. Splices ends of paper, plastic, and tape to ends of previous rolls. Changes rubber stamps on printing roll to print specified data, fills inkpot and glue reservoir, and adjusts forming bar and makes other machine alterations to conform to size specifications. Starts machine, gradually increasing speed by depressing foot lever, and observes machine operation as machine glues paper and plastic film together, cuts it to size, and tapes edges. Measures width and length of finished covers and adjusts machine to obtain specified size. Replenishes stock, clears jams, and makes operating adjustments as required.
GOE: 06.04.09 STRENGTH: L GED: R3 M2 L2 SVP: 3 DLU: 77

640.685-018 CARBON-PAPER INTERLEAFER (pen & pencil) alternate titles: winder
Tends machine that interleafs rolls of carbon and copy paper and winds interleafed paper into rolls of specified length: Reads work order to determine size and type carbon and copy paper to be processed. Places specified rolls of paper on machine spindles, using chain hoist. Threads ends of rolls through feed rollers and paper guides, under edge trimming knives, and laps ends around takeup spindle core. Adjusts paper guides and tension controls, using wrench. Starts machine and observes machine operation to detect wrinkling of paper and uneven winding. Reads footage counter and stops machine when specified footage is wound. Cuts interleafed paper, using knife, and removes roll from machine, using chain hoist. Records size and number of rolls processed on work order.
GOE: 06.04.04 STRENGTH: M GED: R2 M2 L1 SVP: 2 DLU: 77

640.685-022 COMB-MACHINE OPERATOR (fabrication, nec)
Tends one or more machines that cut bookmatch *combs* (blanks) from cardboard rolls: Fastens metal hub to center opening of cardboard roll with handtools and inserts turning shaft in hub. Pushes roll onto let-off rack. Threads cardboard strip into machine through guide and pressure rolls. Adjusts circular cutting knives that slit cardboard to specified width. Turns handwheel to move cutter and punch section of machine forward on track to feed combs into pip conveyor. Starts machine to process combs. Inspects combs for defects, such as insufficient punch pressure and spread, noncuts, and improper width. Adjusts machine with handtools to correct defects.
GOE: 06.04.04 STRENGTH: H GED: R2 M1 L1 SVP: 3 DLU: 77

640.685-026 COMPENSATOR (paper goods)
Tends cutting mechanism of tube-making machine that cuts multiwall tubes: Turns controls to synchronize speed of drawer rolls with speed of stock so cutting mechanism will cut tubes at printed cutoff line.
GOE: 06.04.04 STRENGTH: L GED: R1 M1 L1 SVP: 2 DLU: 77

640.685-030 CORNER CUTTER (paper goods) alternate titles: corner-cutter-machine operator
Tends machine that cuts V-or-L-shape pieces from corners of scored cardboard blanks to facilitate folding and forming boxes or from corners of paper sheets used for covering boxes: Turns wheel to adjust angle and position of guides on machine according to size of sheet or blank and cutting instructions. Positions single or multiple blanks or sheets against guides and depresses pedal to lower blade that cuts out corners. Turns stock to bring each corner into position for cutting and cuts specified number of corners. May be designated according to type of machine used as Double-Corner Cutter (paper goods); Single-Corner Cutter (paper goods).
GOE: 06.04.04 STRENGTH: L GED: R2 M1 L1 SVP: 2 DLU: 79

640.685-034 CUT-OFF-MACHINE OPERATOR (paper goods) alternate titles: paper-tube cutter; paper-tube sawyer; trimming-machine operator; tube cutter
Tends cutting machine that cuts paper tubing to specified lengths: Mounts mandrel of specified size to chuck of machine. Spaces cutters along supporting shaft, using measuring device and wrenches. Adjusts height to which shaft is raised when pedal is depressed to prevent turning knife blades from cutting into mandrel. Slides long tube over mandrel, depresses pedal to raise blades that cut tube to lengths, and removes pieces from mandrel. May tend machine equipped with saw blade to cut tubes.
GOE: 06.04.04 STRENGTH: M GED: R2 M1 L1 SVP: 2 DLU: 87

640.685-038 PANEL-MACHINE OPERATOR (paper goods)
Tends machines that cut edges, flaps, notches, or openings in envelope blanks or envelopes: Positions envelope blanks or envelopes on machine table against guides and stops. Depresses pedal or moves lever to lower ram which forces cutting die through stock to cut edges, flaps, notches, or openings.
GOE: 06.04.04 STRENGTH: L GED: R2 M1 L1 SVP: 2 DLU: 77

640.685-042 PAPER-CORE-MACHINE OPERATOR (paper goods)
Tends machine that winds and seals layers of paper tape around form to make cores for transformer coils: Mounts rolls of glued paper tape in core machine holders. Fills glue moistener reservoir. Turns setscrew and adjusts machine at specified angle for spiral winding. Mounts core form on chuck of machine and wraps end of tape around form. Starts machine that spirally winds and seals layers of paper tape around form and cuts tape when required length is reached. Removes completed cores from machine to stock bins. May oil machine.
GOE: 06.04.04 STRENGTH: L GED: R2 M1 L1 SVP: 2 DLU: 77

640.685-046 PAPER-REEL OPERATOR (paper goods) alternate titles: cord-reel operator; paper reeler; reel cutter; reel operator; sheeter
Tends machine that winds paper or twisted paper cord from rolls onto adjustable reel and cuts it into specified lengths: Fastens roll of paper or cord into

shaft supports. Wraps tape measure around reel and turns handcrank to move horizontal bars in or out to adjust circumference of reel. Removes tape and wraps paper or cord around horizontal bar of reel and secures in place with hooks. Depresses lever or throws switch to start reel, winding paper or cord from roll for specified number of revolutions. Stops machine and cuts through layers of paper or cord along groove in horizontal bar of reel with knife to make individual sheets of paper or pieces of cord. Removes paper from reel to handtruck. Ties cord into bundles. May wrap sheets of paper into bundles preparatory to shipping.
GOE: 06.04.04 STRENGTH: M GED: R2 M2 L1 SVP: 3 DLU: 77

640.685-050 PROCESS-MACHINE OPERATOR (paper goods) alternate titles: gummed-tape-press operator
Tends machine that automatically removes excess curl from gummed or treated paper for winding into rolls: Lifts and positions parent roll of paper on machine support, using hoist. Threads paper through horizontal rollers and guides, over diagonal rollers, and fastens to core on rewind stand. Starts machine, observes operation, and adjusts diagonal and tension rollers according to type of paper processed, using handtools.
GOE: 06.04.04 STRENGTH: M GED: R2 M1 L1 SVP: 3 DLU: 77

640.685-054 REELER (paper goods)
Tends machine that rolls printed wallpaper into reels for further processing: Slides cardboard cylinder over windup shaft and locks shaft in machine, using wrench. Threads wallpaper through machine and onto cardboard cylinder. Starts machine and observes winding until windup shaft is loaded. Rolls completed reel of wallpaper to storage area. May be identified according to type of machine operated.
GOE: 06.04.04 STRENGTH: M GED: R2 M1 L1 SVP: 2 DLU: 77

640.685-058 REWINDER OPERATOR (paper goods) alternate titles: pony winder; rewinder; roll winder
Tends machine that winds paper from one roll to another to form compact rolls of specified footage or diameter prior to cutting: Threads end of parent roll into feeding mechanism of machine and adjusts friction brake by hand to maintain tension of paper. Slides rewind cores (tubes) on shafts and starts machine. Verifies perforations, size, and alignment of rewind rolls. Adjusts machine, using handtools. Removes wound roll from shaft and places it on conveyor. May cut defects from paper and splice cut ends together, using tape.
GOE: 06.04.04 STRENGTH: M GED: R2 M2 L2 SVP: 3 DLU: 78

640.685-062 ROLL RECLAIMER (paper goods)
Tends machine that reprocesses rolls of toilet tissue that do not conform to specifications: Places loosely wound rolls on power-driven spindle which rotates core of roll to tighten paper, or unwinds paper from core for salvage. Glues ends of roll to that of incomplete roll and winds it to specified size. Tears damaged tissue from rolls and splices ends. Holds sandpaper against rotating roll to smooth ends of roll.
GOE: 06.04.04 STRENGTH: L GED: R2 M1 L1 SVP: 2 DLU: 77

640.685-066 ROLL-SLICING-MACHINE TENDER (pen & pencil) alternate titles: inter-fold roll cutter
Tends battery of machines that slice cross sections from rolls of carbon paper or inked plastic sheeting to make narrower rolls: Places roll on arbor of machine and secures paper wrapping around roll with adhesive strip to prevent its unrolling while being sliced. Starts machine, allowing rolls to be rotated against circular knife that slices off narrower rolls. Stops machine and slides sliced rolls from arbor. Examines sides of rolls for ragged or furry edges that show dulling of knife. Places sliced rolls on workbench, places wooden block on top, and pounds with mallet to flatten. Positions flattened roll in fixture of air press, sets plastic spool on center, and pushes buttons causing ram to descend and press spool into roll.
GOE: 06.04.04 STRENGTH: L GED: R2 M1 L1 SVP: 2 DLU: 77

640.685-070 ROLLING-MACHINE OPERATOR (paper goods) alternate titles: embossing-machine-operator helper; wallpaper-embosser helper
Tends machine that winds and cuts wallpaper into rolls of specified lengths: Adjusts guides to accommodate wallpaper of various widths, using wrench. Threads wallpaper through machine and starts machine. Observes wallpaper for tears as it is automatically rolled and cut. Lifts rolls of wallpaper from discharge end of machine and places specified number of rolls into boxes or ties rolls into bundles. May tend embossing machine that imprints paper for rough or textured effect.
GOE: 06.04.04 STRENGTH: M GED: R2 M1 L1 SVP: 2 DLU: 77

640.685-074 ROUND-CORNER-CUTTER OPERATOR (paper goods; print. & pub.)
Tends machine that cuts round corners on paper goods and printed products, such as notebook paper, tablets, pamphlets, and booklets: Reads job ticket to determine number of items to be processed and number and designation of corners to be rounded. Adjusts rounding dies to specified settings, using handtool. Removes stacks of printed products or precounted paper from supply skid and positions and aligns paper, pamphlets, or booklets against guides and backstop of machine. Depresses pedal to activate machine that automatically clamps product onto machine bed and lowers rounding-die that cuts round corners in product. Removes finished products from machine and stacks products on table or pallet. May tend drill-punch machine to drill holes in paper [DRILL-PUNCH

OPERATOR (paper goods; print. & pub.) 649.685-034]. May wrap and label stacks of processed paper [PACKAGER, HAND (any industry) 920.587-018]. May tend machine that automatically wraps and heat shrinks plastic film around product [PACKAGER, MACHINE (any industry) 920.685-078]. May sew gathered and collated signatures by hand to form book [STITCHER, HAND (print. & pub.) 977.684-022].
GOE: 06.04.04 STRENGTH: M GED: R2 M2 L1 SVP: 2 DLU: 89

640.685-078 SLOTTER OPERATOR (paper goods)
Tends machine that cuts slots in paperboard carton and partition blanks: Adjusts slotting and cutting knives in machine according to work order, using measuring tape and wrenches. Loads blanks into machine feed hopper and starts machine. Removes and stacks slotted blanks on pallets for bundling or forming.
GOE: 06.04.04 STRENGTH: M GED: R2 M2 L1 SVP: 3 DLU: 77

640.685-082 TIGHTENING-MACHINE OPERATOR (paper goods)
Tends equipment that tightens loosely coiled fly-catcher tape enclosed in tubes: Pushes loaded tape into revolving tapered steel arbor, fastened to drill press spindle, that winds tape into tight circle. Places tubes on tray for capping by other workers.
GOE: 06.04.04 STRENGTH: L GED: R1 M1 L1 SVP: 2 DLU: 77

640.685-086 TUBE SIZER-AND-CUTTER OPERATOR (ordnance)
Tends machines that die-size and cut paper tubes to specified diameter and lengths preparatory to processing into BB shot containers: Installs and adjusts sizing arbors, dies, cutting rolls, and spacing of pickup fingers, using screwdrivers and wrenches. Starts and observes machines for malfunction. Clears jams and removes scrap paper, using fingers or knife. Measures inside and outside diameters of tubes, using fixed gauges.
GOE: 06.04.04 STRENGTH: M GED: R2 M2 L1 SVP: 3 DLU: 77

640.685-090 BAND-SAW OPERATOR (paper goods)
Tends bandsaw that cuts or slots sheets of paperboard for box blanks or partitions: Reads work order for specifications of box blanks, partitions, or pads. Stacks sheets of paperboard on work surface of bandsaw, squares edges of sheets, and fastens sheets together, using clamps. Marks top sheet of stack according to specifications, using ruler and marking pencil. Presses button to activate bandsaw, and pushes stacks of paperboard against blade, following markings on top sheet to cut out box blanks, partitions, or pads. Places box blanks, partitions, or pads on pallets for further processing.
GOE: 06.04.04 STRENGTH: H GED: R2 M2 L2 SVP: 4 DLU: 86

640.686-010 ROTARY-CUTTER FEEDER (paper & pulp)
Performs any combination of following tasks in slitting paper: Places shaft in core of paper roll, using jack lift. Lifts roll onto feed cutter rack, using hoist, and fastens collars on shaft with wrench to secure roll in position. Positions *layboy* guide stops and stacking paddles to facilitate aligning and stacking sheets, using rule and wrench. May place skids under layboy and remove full skids, using jacklift truck.
GOE: 06.04.04 STRENGTH: M GED: R2 M1 L1 SVP: 2 DLU: 77

640.686-014 SLOTTER-OPERATOR HELPER (paper goods) alternate titles: partition-slotter helper
Assists SLOTTER OPERATOR (paper goods) to operate machine that cuts slots in paperboard carton and partition blanks. Removes slotted blanks from discharge end of machine and stacks them on pallets. Marks stacks with identifying information. Performs other duties as described under HELPER (any industry) Master Title.
GOE: 06.04.26 STRENGTH: M GED: R1 M1 L1 SVP: 2 DLU: 77

640.687-010 ROLL EXAMINER (paper & pulp)
Examines paper winding on reel for defects, such as spots, holes, and wrinkles, and inserts strip of paper in roll to flag defects for removal at cutting and rewinding machine.
GOE: 06.03.02 STRENGTH: L GED: R2 M1 L2 SVP: 2 DLU: 77

640.687-014 SPIRAL-TUBE-WINDER HELPER (paper goods) alternate titles: spiral-winding-machine helper; winder helper
Assists SPIRAL-TUBE WINDER (paper goods) 640.682-022 to fabricate paper cores or tubes: Inspects tubes, ejected from winding machine, for defects, such as excess glue and open seams. Wraps cord around specified number of tubes and ties tubes into bundles. Loads tubes on truck or stacks them on floor. Mounts new reels of paper on machine spindle, using hoist, assists in installing cutting saw and other machine parts, and fills glue reservoir. Performs other duties as described under HELPER (any industry) Master Title.
GOE: 06.04.26 STRENGTH: M GED: R2 M1 L1 SVP: 2 DLU: 78

641 FOLDING, CREASING, SCORING, AND GLUING OCCUPATIONS

This group includes occupations concerned with folding paper, pasteboard, and related materials to desired shapes and angles; creasing the material or cutting part way through it with the aid of scorers; and applying glue or other adhesive substances to it.

641.380-010 ENVELOPE-FOLDING-MACHINE ADJUSTER (paper goods)
Sets up, adjusts, and maintains battery of automatic machines that make envelopes from die-cut blanks or rolls of paper: Installs gears, plungers, and rollers onto machine and turns setscrews to adjust feeding, folding, gumming, sealing, and glassine applying mechanisms according to type and size of envelopes being made, using handtools. Operates machine for trial run and measures dimensions of first piece with rule to ensure conformance to specifications. Observes operation of machines to detect malfunction. Disassembles machines to repair or replace broken or worn parts, using handtools or power tools.
GOE: 06.01.02 STRENGTH: M GED: R3 M2 L2 SVP: 7 DLU: 79

641.562-010 CORRUGATOR OPERATOR (paper goods) alternate titles: corrugated-combining-machine operator
Sets up and operates machine to corrugate and face paperboard to form corrugated paperboard material for containers: Positions rolls of paperboard on machine feedrack, using hydraulic hoist. Threads paperboard through feed, tension, corrugating, and gluing rollers, and fills glue reservoirs. Starts machine and turns dials, wheels, and valves to adjust machine running speed, tension on pressure rolls, temperature of drying belt, and to synchronize speed of feed rolls. Records production data from yardage indicator. May operate machine that corrugates and combines three sheets and be designated Double-Facing-Corrugating-Machine Operator (paper goods); or two sheets and be designated Single-Facing-Corrugating-Machine Operator (paper goods). May operate machine to line paperboard with paper only and be designated Board-Lining-Machine Operator (paper goods).
GOE: 06.02.04 STRENGTH: M GED: R3 M2 L2 SVP: 5 DLU: 77

641.662-010 BOX-SEALING-MACHINE OPERATOR (paper goods)
Sets up and operates machine to spray and dry adhesive onto box blank flaps to make self-sealing boxes: Positions and secures micro-switches in spray chamber to regulate duration of spraying action, according to size of box, using wrench. Adjusts spray unit controls to regulate mixture, intensity, and spread of adhesive on box flaps. Turns crank to position top and side feed guides to hold box blanks in position during spraying and drying process. Opens petcock to start flow of adhesive to spray unit and flips switch to activate conveyor and dryer. Feeds box blanks into machine and observes machine operation to detect malfunction. Adjusts machine controls to correct defective spraying or drying of adhesive.
GOE: 06.02.04 STRENGTH: H GED: R3 M2 L2 SVP: 4 DLU: 77

641.662-014 TUBE-MACHINE OPERATOR (paper goods) alternate titles: tube maker; tube-making-machine operator
Operates machine to automatically form paper into tubing for making bags: Threads paper from parent roll through rollers and guides and tapes end to previous roll. Adjusts guides, folding devices, and cutting blade according to size and thickness of bag to be made, using handtools. Turns valve to regulate flow of glue. Starts machine and observes operation to ensure uniform folding, gluing, cutting, or rewinding of tubing. Adjusts machine to correct malfunctions.
GOE: 06.02.04 STRENGTH: M GED: R3 M2 L2 SVP: 5 DLU: 77

641.682-010 BLANKET-WINDER OPERATOR (paper goods)
Sets up and operates machine to glue together continuous sheets of paper to form sheet of specified width: Positions feed guides, feed rollers, and glue pickup rollers on machine shafts according to job order and turns setscrews to secure guides and rollers in place, using handtools. Slides rolls of paper on unwind shaft and mounts shaft on feed end of machine, using hoist. Fills glue tanks with glue. Threads paper between feed guides, over tension bar, over glue pickup roller, and onto rewind roller. Slides empty core on rewind shaft and positions shaft on rewind roller, using hoist. Turns setscrews to lower or raise guide that presses paper against glue pickup roller to control quantity of glue transferred to paper. Starts machine and adjusts controls to regulate machine feed, glue application, tension of paper, and tension of rewind roller. Inspects paper and rolls for uneven glue application, uneven winding, and other machine malfunctions and verifies width of processed paper, using rule. Removes completed roll from machine, using hoist.
GOE: 06.02.04 STRENGTH: M GED: R3 M2 L2 SVP: 4 DLU: 77

641.682-014 GLUING-MACHINE OPERATOR, AUTOMATIC (print. & pub.)
Sets up and operates machine that automatically glues together specified number of paper sheets, with each sheet protruding equal distance beyond next one, for use as business forms: Moves guides, suction mechanisms, cams, gears, and glue pins to regulate machine according to width and number of sheets glued, and number of places glue is deposited. Loads feeding mechanism with paper sheets, starts machine, and observes spacing and feeding of sheets to ensure that finished assembly meets specifications. Stops machine and removes paper when jams occur.
GOE: 06.02.20 STRENGTH: L GED: R3 M2 L2 SVP: 4 DLU: 77

641.685-010 BENDER, MACHINE (paper goods) alternate titles: bending-machine operator
Tends machine that folds blanks along scored lines to form boxes: Adjusts machine guides and folders for specified size box. Feeds scored and cornered box blanks into machine that folds them.
GOE: 06.04.04 STRENGTH: L GED: R2 M2 L1 SVP: 3 DLU: 77

641.685-014 BOARD-LINER OPERATOR (wood. container)
Tends machine that glues paper lining onto wooden boards for use in manufacture of lined boxes, such as certain types of cigar boxes: Clamps roll of paper on reel of lining machine and threads paper through guide rollers and glue applicator. Adjusts pressure rollers to accommodate thickness of board to

be lined. Starts machine and lays board on conveyor belt to feed mechanism that rolls and presses glued liner paper onto board, cuts off paper at end of board, and drops lined board in stacking bin.
GOE: 06.04.20 STRENGTH: M GED: R2 M1 L1 SVP: 3 DLU: 77

641.685-018 BOX-LINING-MACHINE FEEDER (paper goods)
Tends machine that automatically glues linings to interior of boxes: Mixes glue and water in electrically heated tray of automatic gluing mechanism. Starts machine and conveyor that automatically feeds box to machine. Centers glued lining over opening in metal plate and depresses pedal to lower lining ram through opening to force lining into box.
GOE: 06.04.20 STRENGTH: L GED: R2 M1 L1 SVP: 2 DLU: 77

641.685-022 CARTON-FORMING-MACHINE OPERATOR (any industry)
Tends machine that forms and glues flat blanks or continuous roll of paperboard into finished cartons for packing merchandise: Adjusts forming bars to accommodate size of box to be shaped, using handtools. Fills glue pots with adhesive and positions rollers to dispense glue onto paperboard. Loads feeding magazine with blanks, or mounts roll of paper on machine standard and threads paper to feeding mechanism and starts machine. Observes machine operation to detect malfunction. May load machine with roll of waxed, parchment, or other paper used to line cartons. May mount roll of metal strip to form cutting edge on cartons. May stamp data with handstamp or attach automatic stamping device.
GOE: 06.04.04 STRENGTH: M GED: R2 M1 L1 SVP: 2 DLU: 81

641.685-026 CARTON-FORMING-MACHINE TENDER (paper goods)
Tends one or more machines that automatically cut, glue, and form cartons or caddies from pasteboard rolls for kitchen, penny, and book matches: Rolls pasteboard to machine, positions on letoff rack, and threads end of pasteboard strip into machine. Starts and observes machine operation and corrects malfunctions, such as improper forming, glue flow, or pasteboard tension, using handtools. Observes finished cartons as they drop from forming machine into rotating hopper, then into gravity feed chute, to prevent jamming. May lift tote box of finished cartons and dump cartons into feed hopper.
GOE: 06.04.04 STRENGTH: H GED: R2 M1 L1 SVP: 2 DLU: 77

641.685-030 CHIP-APPLYING-MACHINE TENDER (paint & varnish; print. & pub.) alternate titles: chip applier; mounting-machine operator
Tends machine that cements color samples of coated cut paper (chips) to color card display sheets or folders: Loads specified size, type, and color of chips into feeder racks on machine according to written specifications or sample color card. Fills reservoir with liquid adhesive and stacks printed color card blanks on roller feed of machine. Starts machine and observes cementing of chips on blanks to form color card display sheets or folders. Notifies supervisor of malfunctions, such as poor alignment of chips, jammed paper, or mechanical failures.
GOE: 06.04.04 STRENGTH: M GED: R2 M1 L1 SVP: 3 DLU: 77

641.685-034 COVER STRIPPER (paper goods) alternate titles: box-covering-machine operator; stripping-machine operator; wrapping-machine operator
Tends machine that glues and winds strips of paper around paperboard boxes to form decorative and protective covering: Pours specified amounts of glue and water into glue reservoir. Positions roll of paper on holder and threads end of paper through guides and gluing rollers of machine. Places box on form attached to machine spindle and aligns and presses end of glued paper to side of box. Presses pedal to rotate box to wind paper around box and automatically cut paper after one revolution. Smooths paper on sides of box as it is wound to prevent wrinkling. May turn under excess paper at top and bottom of box.
GOE: 06.04.04 STRENGTH: M GED: R2 M1 L1 SVP: 2 DLU: 77

641.685-038 DOMER (paper goods)
Tends machine that shapes box tops: Sets box top on machine table (anvil) and presses pedal that lowers die onto box top to shape it. May adjust machine and change shaping parts (dies) to accommodate different styles of boxes.
GOE: 06.04.04 STRENGTH: L GED: R2 M1 L1 SVP: 2 DLU: 77

641.685-042 ENDING-MACHINE OPERATOR (paper goods)
Tends machine that glues ends on cardboard boxes or containers: Adjusts box form on machine and stacks ends in machine feedrack. Fills glue reservoir and starts machine. Bends scored blank around box form and presses pedal to position and glue end or ends on box. Stacks boxes on table for wrapping. May be designated according to machine operated as Double-Ending-Machine Operator (paper goods); Single-Ending-Machine Operator (paper goods).
GOE: 06.04.04 STRENGTH: L GED: R2 M1 L1 SVP: 3 DLU: 77

641.685-046 EXTENSION EDGER (paper goods) alternate titles: flanging-machine operator; french-edge operator
Tends machine that glues oversized piece of cardboard (extension piece) to box top or bottom to form decorative protecting edge or flange around box: Loads cardboard pieces into machine feed hopper, fills glue reservoir, and starts machine. Positions formed box on block and presses pedal to activate machine that glues piece onto box. Removes box from machine and stacks on pallet for wrapping.
GOE: 06.04.04 STRENGTH: L GED: R2 M1 L1 SVP: 2 DLU: 77

641.685-050 FOLDING-MACHINE FEEDER (paper goods)
Tends machine that folds paper goods, such as booklets, pamphlets, notebooks, paper sheets, and manila folders: Turns handwheel to adjust folding slot

opening and adjusts backstop according to sample, using rule and wrench. Starts machine and moves lever to engage clutch that activates folding blade and discharge conveyor rolls. Feeds items against backstop of machine, synchronizing feeding with action of folding blade. Removes folded items from discharge table and stacks them on pallets. May rub folded edge with wooden block to crease it. May handfold multiple sheets of paper that exceed machine capacity.
GOE: 06.04.04 STRENGTH: M GED: R2 M1 L1 SVP: 2 DLU: 77

641.685-054 FOUR-CORNER-STAYER-MACHINE OPERATOR (paper goods) alternate titles: quad stayer; staying-machine operator
Tends machine that folds and tapes corners of cardboard box blanks to form containers: Bolts box form to machine ram, using wrench, and adjusts walls of well to correspond to size of box form. Places reels of tape on machine feedrack and threads tape through feed and moisture rolls. Starts machine and loads scored box blanks into automatic feedrack. Examines boxes to detect defects as they are ejected from machine and stacks boxes on pallets or in bins. May tend wrapping machine that glues wrappers onto boxes [WRAPPING-MACHINE OPERATOR (paper goods)].
GOE: 06.04.04 STRENGTH: M GED: R2 M1 L1 SVP: 2 DLU: 77

641.685-058 LINER-MACHINE OPERATOR (paper goods)
Tends machine that glues paper over cardboard container blanks and cuts covered blanks to specified length: Spaces feed and gluing rollers according to dimensions of blanks to be covered and adjusts position of end shears that cut covered blanks to specified length, using handtools. Pours glue into machine reservoir, moves lever to increase or decrease temperature of gluing rollers and threads paper from roll through guide and gluing rollers. Starts machine and feeds cardboard blanks into machine that glues paper over blanks and cuts them to specified length. May mix glue solutions.
GOE: 06.04.04 STRENGTH: L GED: R2 M1 L1 SVP: 3 DLU: 77

641.685-062 PAPER-CONE-MACHINE TENDER (paper goods) alternate titles: body-rolling-machine tender
Tends machine that automatically forms paper *cones* from precut blanks: Loads blanks into feed hopper of machine and fills glue reservoir. Starts machine that forms blanks into cones and glues seams. Inspects paper cones for obvious defects as they are discharged from machine and discards defective cones.
GOE: 06.04.04 STRENGTH: L GED: R2 M1 L1 SVP: 2 DLU: 77

641.685-066 PATCH-MACHINE OPERATOR (paper goods) alternate titles: window-machine operator
Tends machine that glues transparent cellophane or acetate paper over precut windows in envelope or paperboard carton blanks: Replenishes glue reservoir and fills feed chute with precut transparent strips. Loads blanks in automatic feedrack and starts machine, or feeds blanks singly into machine. Removes jammed blanks from rollers, and inspects envelopes or cartons to detect defects in cutting and gluing. May tend machine equipped with roll of transparent material that cuts material into strips before gluing them to envelope or carton blanks.
GOE: 06.04.04 STRENGTH: L GED: R2 M1 L1 SVP: 2 DLU: 77

641.685-070 SCORER (paper goods)
Tends machine that scores cardboard blanks along lines where they are to be folded or cut to form boxes or containers: Positions scoring disks on shaft, according to work order specifications, turns setscrew to secure them in place, and turns wheel to adjust pressure on disks, using handtools. Starts machine and loads blanks into hopper or pushes blanks into scoring roll by hand. Removes scored blanks and stacks them on pallets. May score blanks one direction and be designated Scorer, Single (paper goods); or score blanks two directions and be designated Scorer, Double (paper goods).
GOE: 06.04.04 STRENGTH: M GED: R2 M1 L1 SVP: 2 DLU: 77

641.685-074 SEALING-MACHINE OPERATOR (paper goods)
Tends machine that applies sealing glue, such as dextrin or latex, to envelope flaps and dries them by passing envelopes under heat element: Fills glue reservoir, starts and regulates burners in drying unit, and loads automatic feedrack with envelopes. Observes machine operation and examines envelopes to detect malfunctioning in feeding, gluing, or drying process. Adjusts rollers to regulate glue flow, and turns rheostat to synchronize rate of envelope feed with glue applicator. Removes jammed material from rollers.
GOE: 06.04.21 STRENGTH: L GED: R2 M1 L1 SVP: 2 DLU: 77

641.685-078 SLIDE-MACHINE TENDER (fabrication, nec)
Tends machine that folds and glues paperboard sheets to form match slides, and applies friction paint (striking material): Fills glue and friction paint reservoirs, using dipper. Loads stack of paperboard sheets into feed mechanism and starts machine. Observes completed slides as they pass on conveyor to detect defective folding, gluing, and friction paint application. Adjusts rollers that apply friction paint and glue, using handtools.
GOE: 06.04.04 STRENGTH: L GED: R2 M1 L1 SVP: 2 DLU: 77

641.685-082 SPOOL MAKER (paper goods)
Tends machine that presses glued cardboard tubes and disks to form gift wrap ribbon spools: Places cardboard disk endpieces into slots on sides of machine vise. Dips ends of cardboard tube in glue and places tube between disks in vise. Depresses pedal to press disks and tube together to form spool.

GOE: 06.04.04 STRENGTH: L GED: R1 M1 L1 SVP: 2 DLU: 77

641.685-086   STRING-TOP SEALER (paper goods)
Tends machine that seals string in top of plastic produce bags: Places bag on machine mandrel and positions string on bag with ends under holding clip. Depresses pedal that folds and seals hem around string at top of bag. Removes bag from mandrel and places it in carton. May examine hem for defective sealing.
GOE: 06.04.02 STRENGTH: L GED: R2 M1 L1 SVP: 2 DLU: 77

641.685-090   STRIPPING-MACHINE OPERATOR (paper goods) alternate titles: binder operator
Tends machine that glues fabric strip over back edge of unbound paper products, such as legal tablets, notebooks, and ledger paper: Turns handwheel to adjust machine-head pressure plate to thickness of item being processed. Places roll of gummed tape on reel and threads end through feed guide and rolls. Turns screws to adjust tension springs that bring pressure on tape to facilitate sticking, using wrench and screwdriver. Starts machine and feeds items into machine feed conveyors. Stacks completed product on skids.
GOE: 06.04.04 STRENGTH: L GED: R2 M1 L1 SVP: 2 DLU: 77

641.685-094   VALVING-MACHINE OPERATOR (paper goods)
Tends machine that forms opening (valve) in paper bags through which loose materials, such as cement, sugar, lime, fertilizers, and sand are poured into bag: Positions unsewed paper bag on machine bed between guide arms. Depresses pedal or moves lever to start machine that automatically creases and folds bottom of paper bag to form valve, and discharges it onto conveyor. May tend sleeve machine that automatically cuts and glues strips of paper (sleeves) used to close valves of filled bags [SLEEVER (paper goods)]. May tend machine that forms valve and sews ends of bags and be designated Combination Valving-And-Sewing-Machine Operator (paper goods).
GOE: 06.04.04 STRENGTH: L GED: R2 M1 L1 SVP: 2 DLU: 77

641.685-098   WRAPPING-MACHINE OPERATOR (paper goods) alternate titles: covering-machine operator
Tends wrapping machine that glues wrappers onto box tops or box bottoms by either of following methods: (1) Places box parts on glued wrapper and positions them under plunger of machine. Presses pedal to lower plunger that forces box part and wrapper down past series of brushes that seal wrapper onto box part. (2) Positions box parts onto glued wrappers conveyed by belt that feeds box parts into machine that smooths wrapper around box. May tend four corner stayer machine that folds and tapes corners of cardboard box blanks to form containers [FOUR-CORNER-STAYER-MACHINE OPERATOR (paper goods)]. May tend power shear that cuts sheets of paper to specified dimensions to form wrappers [CUTTING-MACHINE TENDER (any industry)].
GOE: 06.04.04 STRENGTH: M GED: R2 M1 L1 SVP: 2 DLU: 77

641.686-010   BLANKET-WINDER HELPER (paper goods)
Assists BLANKET-WINDER OPERATOR (paper goods) to operate machine to glue together continuous sheets of paper to form sheet of specified width: Slides rolls of paper on unwind shaft and mounts shaft on feed end of machine, using hoist. Slides empty core on rewind shaft and positions shaft on rewind roller, using hoist. Assists operator to thread paper through machine. Fills glue tanks with glue. Removes completed roll from machine, using hoist. Performs other duties as described under HELPER (any industry) Master Title.
GOE: 06.04.04 STRENGTH: M GED: R2 M1 L1 SVP: 2 DLU: 77

641.686-014   CARTON-FORMING-MACHINE HELPER (any industry)
Assists CARTON-FORMING-MACHINE OPERATOR (any industry) to shape, form, and glue flat blanks or continuous roll of cardboard or paperboard into finished cartons: Removes and stacks completed cartons from discharge end of machine. Counts number of completed cartons and compares with production order to verify completion of order. Performs other duties as described under HELPER (any industry) Master Title.
GOE: 06.04.04 STRENGTH: M GED: R2 M1 L1 SVP: 2 DLU: 77

641.686-018   CORRUGATOR-OPERATOR HELPER (paper goods)
Assists CORRUGATOR OPERATOR (paper goods) by performing any combination of following tasks: Inserts spindle through core of roll and adjusts collars to center roll on spindle. Attaches electric hoist hooks to spindle, hoists roll onto machine feedrack, and turns wingnuts to fasten clamps over ends of spindle. Splices end of new roll to end of spent roll, using tape. Mixes starch powder with water to form adhesive, according to formula, and fills glue reservoirs. Performs other tasks as described under HELPER (any industry) Master Title.
GOE: 06.04.26 STRENGTH: H GED: R2 M2 L1 SVP: 2 DLU: 77

641.686-022   LINER-MACHINE-OPERATOR HELPER (paper goods)
Assists LINER-MACHINE OPERATOR (paper goods) in gluing paper over cardboard container blanks: Slides steel shaft through roll of liner paper and secures it in shaft supports of liner machine. Threads liner paper through guide rollers and into feeding mechanism of machine. Keeps adequate supply of cardboard sheets on feeding table and removes lined cardboard sheets from machine. Fills glue reservoir of liner machine with glue. Cleans glue roller and glue pan with solvent solution. May assist in adjusting machine. Performs other duties as described under HELPER (any industry) Master Title.
GOE: 06.04.04 STRENGTH: M GED: R2 M1 L1 SVP: 2 DLU: 77

641.686-026   PAPER-BAG-PRESS OPERATOR (paper goods)
Feeds paper bags into rolls of pressing machine to complete sealing of prepasted seams and bottom folds.

GOE: 06.04.04 STRENGTH: L GED: R1 M1 L1 SVP: 2 DLU: 77

641.686-030   SCORER HELPER (paper goods) alternate titles: scoring-machine-operator helper
Feeds sheets of cardboard or paperboard into guide of scoring machine that scores (creases) sheets used to form box blanks. Removes scored blanks from discharge end of machine and stacks them on pallets. May adjust scoring knives, feed guides, and rollers under specific instructions from SCORER (paper goods). May measure scored blanks for conformity to specifications, using measuring tape.
GOE: 06.04.04 STRENGTH: M GED: R2 M1 L1 SVP: 2 DLU: 77

641.686-034   SLEEVER (paper goods)
Reinforces paper bag openings (valves), performing any of following tasks: Feeds paper sheets into machine that creases paper along one side and deposits glue along creased edge. Opens valved corner with one hand, grasps sleeve with other, and inserts sleeve into valve. Presses bag by hand to refold valve.
GOE: 06.04.04 STRENGTH: L GED: R1 M1 L1 SVP: 2 DLU: 77

641.686-038   TUBE-MACHINE-OPERATOR HELPER (paper goods) alternate titles: tuber helper
Assists TUBE-MACHINE OPERATOR (paper goods) to operate machine that forms paper into tubing for making bags: Inserts shaft into core of parent paper roll, and centers it with steel collars to secure roll, using handtools. Lifts and mounts roll on machine, using electric hoist. Splices end of new roll to previous roll with tape. Assists operator to thread paper through machine and make adjustments to guides, folding devices, and cutter blade. Replenishes glue reservoirs and cleans glue pumps. Counts tubes at start of operation to confirm tally of automatic counter. Performs other duties as described under HELPER (any industry) Master Title.
GOE: 06.04.04 STRENGTH: M GED: R2 M1 L1 SVP: 2 DLU: 77

641.687-010   BOX BENDER (paper goods)
Folds cardboard box blanks along scored lines preparatory to corner staying process. Stacks folded blanks on worktable.
GOE: 06.04.26 STRENGTH: M GED: R1 M1 L1 SVP: 1 DLU: 77

641.687-014   BOX-SEALING INSPECTOR (paper goods)
Inspects band of adhesive on self-sealing box blank flaps to detect irregular width and faulty application: Removes box blanks from discharge end of box-sealing machine. Examines flaps to determine width of adhesive band and feels band to determine thickness of adhesive application. Tests strength of adhesive by sealing sample box blank flaps together and pulling them apart to determine force required to break seal. Notifies BOX-SEALING-MACHINE OPERATOR (paper goods) to stop machine when jamming occurs or to adjust machine controls to correct faulty adhesive application. Counts and stacks inspected boxes on conveyor and pushes stacks down conveyor for bundling.
GOE: 06.03.02 STRENGTH: L GED: R2 M1 L1 SVP: 2 DLU: 77

649   PAPERWORKING OCCUPATIONS, N.E.C.

This group includes occupations, not elsewhere classified, concerned with shaping, cutting, scoring, joining, and otherwise machining paper and paper products.

649.130-010   SUPERVISOR, PAPER PRODUCTS (paper goods)
Supervises and coordinates activities of workers engaged in setting up and operating machines that cut, wind, fold, crease, drill, score, slit, tape, glue, sew, corrugate, and emboss paper and paperboard to form paper products, such as boxes, cartons, bags, napkins, tissue, envelopes, folders, cards, and tablets: Reads work order and schedules production according to machine capacities and customer requirements. Assigns duties to workers according to production schedule. Inspects sample product to ensure conformance to work order specifications. May train new workers. May set up and adjust machines. May inspect machines for malfunction or worn parts. May repair machines. May requisition materials and supplies. May supply workers with production materials. May operate machine in worker's absence. Performs other duties as described under SUPERVISOR (any industry) Master Title.
GOE: 06.02.01 STRENGTH: L GED: R4 M3 L3 SVP: 8 DLU: 79

649.361-010   PATTERNMAKER, ENVELOPE (paper goods)
Draws patterns and prescribes manufacturing specifications for envelopes, compiling required data from customer orders, machine capacities, and knowledge of envelope manufacturing: Computes size, number, and type of paper sheets needed to fill order, using trigonometry, and knowledge of paper sizes and paper cutting machines. Sketches layout and dimensions of envelope on cardboard, using ruler, square, and other drawing instruments. Selects machines, dies, tools, and compiles machine setup data for such operations as paper and die cutting, machine and hand folding, printing, paneling, and attaching fastening devices, utilizing knowledge of machines, tools, and equipment. Determines sequence of manufacturing operations, utilizing knowledge of types and capacities of available machines, and lists such data on layout card.
GOE: 05.03.02 STRENGTH: L GED: R4 M4 L3 SVP: 7 DLU: 77

649.367-010   INSPECTOR, PAPER PRODUCTS (paper goods) alternate titles: bag inspector; quality-control inspector
Inspects paper and paperboard products during corrugating, laminating, printing, cutting, scoring, coating, forming, sealing, and packaging processes to en-

sure adherence to plant quality standards and work orders: Examines product for defects, such as blisters, wrinkles, improper forming and sealing, glue spots, printing overlap, and color distortions. Measures dimensions and thickness of product, using tape measure and automatic micrometer. Weighs coated and uncoated products, calculates weight of coating, and records weight data on inspection report. Tests mullen (burst quality of paper) and crush qualities of paper and paperboard, using mullen and crush tester, and records test results on inspection report. Spot-counts number of articles in bundle or shipping container to verify accuracy. Examines rejects to determine those that can be salvaged and routes unusable material to scrap baler. May be designated according to product inspected as Paper-Bag Inspector (paper goods); Tube Inspector (paper goods); or according to phase of process as Assembly Inspector (paper goods).
GOE: 06.03.01 STRENGTH: L GED: R3 M2 L2 SVP: 5 DLU: 78

649.380-010 MACHINE SET-UP OPERATOR, PAPER GOODS (paper goods)
Sets up and adjusts machines that convert, saw, corrugate, band, wrap, box, stitch, form, or seal paper or paperboard sheets into products, such as toilet tissue, towels, napkins, bags, envelopes, tubing, cartons, wax rolls, and containers, according to specifications, by any combination of following tasks: Adjusts rolls, guides, and chutes to accommodate type of paper or paperboard fed from parent rolls or flat stock from automatic feedracks, using handtools. Measures, spaces, and sets saw blades, cutters, and perforators, according to product specifications, using rule, thumbscrews, and wrenches. Installs printing attachment to machine and makes adjustment for clarity of print. Threads wire through stitching head and synchronizes speed for spacing stitches. Installs or resets cutting dies according to work orders, using handtools. Operates machine for test run to verify adjustments and observes functioning of machine parts, such as gauges, elevator, belts, slip clutches, oil injectors, glue feeders, and electrical devices. Repairs or replaces defective parts. May be designated according to type of machine adjusted as Bag-Machine Set-Up Operator (paper goods); Gluing-Machine Adjuster (paper goods); Stitcher Set-Up Operator, Automatic (paper goods).
GOE: 06.01.02 STRENGTH: M GED: R3 M2 L2 SVP: 7 DLU: 79

649.487-010 INSPECTOR (paper & pulp)
Examines sample of paper sheets for defects according to quality control specifications: Measures dimensions of sheet with rule, folds sheet and aligns edges to verify squareness. Weighs sheet and compares weight with specification for kind and grade of paper. Fans stack of sheets to examine sheets for tears, soil, streaks, and shading and notifies supervisor of defects. Discards defective sheets or marks stack for reprocessing. Writes daily test reports.
GOE: 06.03.01 STRENGTH: L GED: R3 M2 L2 SVP: 3 DLU: 77

649.582-010 PARTITION-ASSEMBLY-MACHINE OPERATOR (any industry)
Operates machine that automatically fits precut cardboard sections together to form complete partitions for cardboard cartons, according to specifications: Installs and adjusts stripper bars, feed dogs, side and finger guides, back stops, and ejector bars on machine table, and receiving fingers and push bars on rotating partition assembling wheel, using rule, gauges, and wrenches. Adjusts timing gear settings to synchronize movement of partition sections from machine table into sections in assembling wheel, using wrench. Fills magazines with partition sections and starts machine. Observes feeding and assembling operations and adjusts machine to form partitions to specifications. Maintains production records.
GOE: 06.02.20 STRENGTH: M GED: R3 M2 L2 SVP: 5 DLU: 77

649.582-014 SIZING-MACHINE OPERATOR (ordnance)
Sets up and operates battery of machines to compress to size and impregnate paper tubes with linseed oil preparatory to processing into shotgun shell bodies: Selects and measures arbors and dies with micrometers and plug gauges to verify specified size. Installs arbors, arbor shanks, collets, dies, and die holders in machine, using handtools. Examines paper tubes for crushed or torn ends, verifies inside diameter periodically, using plug gauge, and dumps tubes into hopper. Turns valve to circulate oil through die holders and starts machine. Observes machine operation and adjusts oil flow that facilitates passage of tubes through sizing dies and impregnates tube exteriors to waterproof and stiffen them. Clears jammed tubes from dies, arbors, and feed channels, and blows out clogged oil lines with airhose. Replaces tube-filled baskets.
GOE: 06.02.18 STRENGTH: H GED: R3 M2 L2 SVP: 4 DLU: 77

649.665-010 SORTING-MACHINE OPERATOR (paper goods)
Inspects sheets of paper for processing defects, using sorting machine: Reads work order and notifies INDUSTRIAL-TRUCK OPERATOR (any industry) to move specified type and quantity of paper from storage area to machine elevator platform. Positions joggers and vacuum feeding mechanism according to size and type of paper, using handtools and ruler. Starts machine and pushes button to raise elevator platform to feed level. Inspects paper sheets moving over machine bed to detect defects and turns lever to eject defective sheets from machine. Notifies INDUSTRIAL-TRUCK OPERATOR (any industry) to remove skids of inspected paper and records production data, such as type paper, time, and quantity inspected.
GOE: 06.03.02 STRENGTH: L GED: R2 M1 L1 SVP: 2 DLU: 77

649.682-010 BOX-FOLDING-MACHINE OPERATOR (paper goods)
Sets up and operates machine to fold corrugated paperboard box blanks and to glue, stitch (staple), or tape edges to form boxes: Installs feed bars and ad-

justs guide assembly and folding mechanism according to box blank dimensions and work order specifications, using handtools. Fills glue reservoir, loads automatic stapler, or threads gummed tape through applicator. Stacks box blanks in feed mechanism, starts machine, and observes automatic feeding and folding of box blanks and gluing, stapling, or taping of edges to detect machine malfunction. Inspects sample completed box to verify conformance to work order specifications and adjusts machine controls to correct variations. May be designated according to type of machine used as Folder-Gluer Operator (paper goods); Folder-Stitcher Operator (paper goods); Folder-Taper Operator (paper goods).
GOE: 06.02.04 STRENGTH: H GED: R3 M2 L2 SVP: 4 DLU: 78

649.682-014 CYLINDER-DIE-MACHINE OPERATOR (paper goods) alternate titles: cutting-and-creasing-machine operator
Operates cylinder press to score and cut paperboard sheets into box or container blanks: Installs specified chase (cutting and scoring die) on flat bed of machine, using handtools. Glues sheet of paperboard on machine cylinder, rotates cylinder by hand to press design of die in sheet, and cuts paperboard from around die impression on sheet, using knife, to form male portion of die. Starts machine and adjusts feed rollers or arms, and adjusts arms on automatic stacker, using handtools. Turns valves to regulate powder (talc) spray on cut-scored sheets. Measures cut-scored blanks to verify cutting and scoring dimensions with work order, using tape measure. May feed odd size paperboard sheets into machine by hand.
GOE: 06.02.04 STRENGTH: H GED: R3 M2 L2 SVP: 5 DLU: 78

649.682-018 DRILL-PRESS OPERATOR, ACOUSTICAL TILE (wood prod., nec)
Sets up and operates automatic horizontal multiple-spindle drill press to drill holes in insulation board to form acoustical tile: Removes machine headplate, using wrench and air hoist. Attaches specified template pattern to chuckplate, using screwdriver. Places drills into chuck, according to template pattern. Removes template and replaces machine headplate. Adjusts feed rolls, using gauge and wrench. Loads automatic feed magazine with tile and starts machine. Examines tile to verify that holes are clean cut and conform to depth and pattern specifications.
GOE: 06.02.09 STRENGTH: L GED: R3 M2 L2 SVP: 5 DLU: 77

649.682-022 EMBOSSER OPERATOR (paper goods) alternate titles: calender operator; roll-embosser operator
Sets up and operates machine to emboss designs on paper and plastics-coated textile and cut materials according to work orders: Positions material and pressure and engraved embossing rolls on machine frame, using hoist. Installs and adjusts cutting disks and fastens collars on shafts to secure rolls, using rule, wrench, and screwdriver. Threads material through rolls and around cutters, adjusts feed guides, and starts machine. Turns air valve to regulate pressure of pressing roll on embossing roll and turns handwheel to adjust tension on material. Observes feeding, embossing, and cutting of material, and makes adjustments. Scrapes dirt from pressing roll and cleans it with solvent. May adjust counterweight device or move lever or clutch to regulate pressure on rolls. May regulate flow of steam into rolls to counteract paper curling and to obtain desired depth of embossing and surface shine on paper. May tend winding machine to wind material onto rolls. May emboss paper between tinted rollers. May feed paper sheets into machine and be designated Sheeter Operator (paper & pulp).
GOE: 06.02.09 STRENGTH: M GED: R3 M2 L2 SVP: 5 DLU: 77

649.682-026 PLATEN-PRESS OPERATOR (paper goods) alternate titles: blanker-press operator
Sets up and operates automatic, platen-type cutting-creasing press to cut rolls of paperboard into carton blanks: Selects, installs, and adjusts specified chase (cutting-creasing die) on press bed, using handtools. Positions and attaches stripping cylinder on roller and turns wheel to adjust tension on rubberized backer roll. Mounts roll of paperboard on machine feed spindle, using hoist, and threads paperboard through feed, tension, and idler rollers. Starts machine and observes operation. Turns dials and wheels to synchronize machine speed with speed of feed rolls and to regulate pressure on feed rolls. Starts conveyor that transports broke to baling machine. Measures cut-scored blanks for conformity to specifications, using tape measure, and examines blanks for defects, such as wrinkles and tears. Adjusts machine to correct defects.
GOE: 06.02.04 STRENGTH: M GED: R3 M2 L2 SVP: 5 DLU: 77

649.682-030 SHELL-MACHINE OPERATOR (chemical) alternate titles: shell-house operator
Sets up and operates machine to make paper cartridge shells for dynamite and impregnate them with paraffin: Positions roll of paper on machine spindle and threads end of paper under shear plate and between rolls. Adjusts bottom crimper, rolls, and shear according to length and diameter of cartridge, using machinist's rule and wrenches. Pours melted paraffin into dispenser and activates heating element. Starts machine and removes formed and impregnated cartridges.
GOE: 06.02.09 STRENGTH: M GED: R3 M2 L1 SVP: 4 DLU: 77

649.682-034 SLITTER-CREASER-SLOTTER OPERATOR (paper goods)
Sets up and operates machine to slot, score, crease, and trim corrugated or plain paperboard sheets to form container blanks: Turns screws and moves picker feed bar and feed table guides to accommodate size of sheets. Positions slitting, scoring, and slotting dies by sliding dieheads along drive shaft over ma-

chine bed to obtain specified size blanks with prescribed depth and location of slots and creases. Stacks and aligns sheets against guide bar on feeder table. Presses lever to start automatic feed. Measures sample with rule to detect deviation in location of slots and creases.
GOE: 06.02.04 STRENGTH: M GED: R2 M2 L2 SVP: 4 DLU: 77

649.682-038 SLITTER-SCORER-CUT-OFF OPERATOR (paper goods)
Sets up and operates machine that slits, scores, and cuts sheets of plain, laminated, or corrugated paperboard to specified dimensions: Positions and fastens scoring and cutting disks on roller, according to specifications, and installs roller in machine, using handtools. Turns wheels to adjust cutter knives, align paper guides on *layboy*, and adjust pressure on slitting and cutting disks. Starts machine and synchronizes speed of traveling cutoff knives with speed of machine feed. Verifies dimensions of cut-scored blanks with work order, using tape rule. May cut samples from sheets for testing. May operate machine that slits and cuts rolls of paper and be designated Slitter-And-Cutter Operator (paper & pulp; paper goods).
GOE: 06.02.04 STRENGTH: H GED: R3 M2 L2 SVP: 5 DLU: 78

649.682-042 TABLET-MAKING-MACHINE OPERATOR (paper goods) alternate titles: packer operator
Sets up and operates machine to cut rolls of paper into sheets and to print lines, glue, and punch holes to make paper tablets: Adjusts feed guides, cutting disks, and punch rams according to work order specifications. Mounts roll of paper on machine, using electric hoist. Threads end of paper through machine and fills ink and glue reservoirs. Starts machine and turns valves to adjust paper tension and flow of glue to paper. Observes machine operation to detect malfunction and inspects finished tablets to verify conformance to specifications. Records production information, such as quantity, type, and size of tablets produced on work order.
GOE: 06.02.04 STRENGTH: M GED: R3 M2 L2 SVP: 4 DLU: 77

649.682-046 TAG-PRESS OPERATOR (paper goods)
Sets up and operates machine to print, cut, and punch holes in paperboard to form paper tags and labels: Reads work order to determine type of setup required. Mounts paperboard roll on machine, using jack, and installs and adjusts specified printing plates onto machine bed, using allen wrench and rule. Mounts roll of reinforcing paperboard onto machine, threads end through stamping section and fills machine hopper with metal reinforcing grommets. Spreads specified color ink onto printing plate, using hand scraper, and fills ink reservoir. Adjusts angle of cutting blade, using allen wrench, and turns valves to adjust timing of cutting blades and punch to specifications. Starts machine and observes machine operation to detect malfunction and inspects completed tags or labels to verify compliance with work order specifications. Removes completed tags or labels from discharge end of machine, stacks specified number of tags into boxes, and stacks boxes on skid. Records production information, such as quantity and type of tags or labels produced on work ticket.
GOE: 06.02.04 STRENGTH: M GED: R3 M2 L1 SVP: 6 DLU: 77

649.685-010 AUTOMATIC-MACHINE ATTENDANT (paper goods) alternate titles: machine assembler
Tends automatic cutting, curling, crimping, capping, labeling, or tubing machines that assemble paper products, such as spools and tubes: Presses pedals, buttons, and switches or turns valves to start and stop machines and auxiliary devices, such as glue heaters, curling heads, and air ejectors. Dumps tubes, caps, labels, covers, spool shields, or paper strips into dispenser, feeds them onto conveyor, or positions them on mandrel. Pours glue into pots. Clears jams. May stack finished product on truck.
GOE: 06.04.04 STRENGTH: M GED: R2 M1 L1 SVP: 2 DLU: 79

649.685-014 BAG-MACHINE OPERATOR (paper goods) alternate titles: bag-making-machine operator
Tends machine that automatically measures, prints, cuts, folds, and glues, or seals plain or wax papers, polyethylene film, or cellophane to form bags: Threads materials from parent roll through guides and rollers to cutters, gluer, printer, folding device, or electric sealer. Starts machine, observes operation, and adjusts machine to ensure uniform shearing, printing, folding, gluing, or sealing of continuous roll of material into finished bags. May insert shaft into core of parent roll and secure with steel collars, using handtools, and mount roll onto machine, using hoist. May be designated according to material processed as Cellophane-Bag-Machine Operator (paper goods); Polyethylene-Bag-Machine Operator (paper goods); Waxed-Bag-Machine Operator (paper goods).
GOE: 06.04.04 STRENGTH: M GED: R2 M1 L1 SVP: 3 DLU: 77

649.685-018 BINDERY WORKER (paper goods)
Tends paperworking machines, such as corner cutter, embosser, scorer, stitcher, taper, gluer, punch press, and plastic index tab machine to fabricate office supplies, such as file folders, file dividers, index cards, and three-ring binders, from paper or paperboard stock: Positions stock against machine guides, starts machine, and depresses pedal to actuate specified machine. Manually folds and creases materials that exceed machine capacity. Collates printed file folders in numerical order to form set. Forms shipping boxes from flattened blanks and glues labels to box tops. Inspects finished product and places specified quantity and type into boxes according to packing instructions.
GOE: 06.04.04 STRENGTH: M GED: R2 M1 L1 SVP: 3 DLU: 77

649.685-022 BOTTOMING-MACHINE OPERATOR (paper goods)
Tends machine that automatically cuts, folds, and glues ends of tubes together to form bottoms in single or multiwall paper bags: Loads paper tubes

into automatic feedrack, fills glue hopper, and starts machine. Observes machine operation, removes material caught in rollers to relieve jams, and spot-verifies processed bags to detect imperfections in cutting, folding, or gluing. Adjusts feed guides, rollers, and glue regulator, using handtools, to ensure conformity to specifications. May tend machine equipped with valving mechanism that automatically forms opening (valve) in top of bag and inserts sleeve in opening.
GOE: 06.04.04 STRENGTH: L GED: R2 M1 L1 SVP: 3 DLU: 77

649.685-026 CORE-CUTTER AND REAMER (paper goods)
Tends machines that cut, ream, and slot paper roll cores made of cardboard, fiber, or metal, according to work order specifications: Installs and aligns cutoff saw, reamer, and slot cutters in machines according to length and diameter of core, using rule and wrench. Starts machines and cuts core to length, using circular saw. Pushes core along feeder trough of reamer to ream out ends. Feeds core into cutters of slotting machine to cut slots in core ends. Inserts metal caps in ends of nonmetal cores to coincide with slots in cores, using hammer. May reclaim defective caps by removing them with cap puller and hammering out dents. May tend machines that cut and slot paper roll cores and be designated Core Cutter (paper & pulp).
GOE: 06.02.09 STRENGTH: M GED: R3 M2 L2 SVP: 4 DLU: 77

649.685-030 COUNTING-MACHINE OPERATOR (paper goods)
Tends machine that counts sheets of paper and inserts marker between sheets at specified interval: Positions skid of paper beside machine counting head, using handtruck. Raises paper at corner, using iron bar, and inserts wedge between skid and paper to fan edge of paper. Secures paper stack to skid, using clamp. Sets counter dial at zero and sets marker interval dial at specified number. Pushes button to move counting head into position against corner of stack and starts machine. Observes machine operation and makes adjustments to counting head to ensure accurate counting.
GOE: 06.04.04 STRENGTH: H GED: R2 M1 L1 SVP: 3 DLU: 77

649.685-034 DRILL-PUNCH OPERATOR (paper goods; print. & pub.)
Tends multiple-spindle drill press that drills holes in paper, such as notebook paper, booklets, envelopes, pamphlets, index cards, and other paper and printed products: Reads job specifications to determine spacing and dimension of holes to be drilled in paper items. Adjusts spacing of drills, positions of backstop and guides according to size of items to be drilled, using handtools. Presses button to start machine. Jogs stack of paper items to straighten and align edges. Positions stacks of paper items against backstop and end guides of machine table. Depresses pedal to raise stock or lower drills to cut holes in paper. Stacks drilled items on pallets. May replace dull drills, using handtools.
GOE: 06.04.04 STRENGTH: M GED: R2 M1 L1 SVP: 2 DLU: 79

649.685-038 EMBOSSING-MACHINE TENDER (paper goods) alternate titles: panel-machine tender
Tends machine that automatically embosses frame-like margin on edge of paper card blanks to form wedding and commercial cards: Loads stack of cards into machine feeder and starts machine. Observes machine operation to detect feeding and embossing malfunction. Inspects completed cards by fanning stacks to detect imperfections, such as dirt spots, dents, and nicks and stacks cards into boxes according to instructions on work ticket.
GOE: 06.04.04 STRENGTH: M GED: R2 M1 L1 SVP: 2 DLU: 77

649.685-042 ENVELOPE-MACHINE OPERATOR (paper goods) alternate titles: envelope-fold operator; folder, machine
Tends machine that forms plain and window envelopes from paper rolls or precut blanks: Loads stack of blanks into rack of feed mechanism or positions roll of paper on machine rack, using hoist, and threads paper (web) through machine. Starts machine and observes progress of blanks and web through cutting, gluing, folding, and drying units. Pushes button to stop machine in case of malfunction. Fans handful of envelopes to inspect them for quality of folding, sealing, and glue application, and packs them in boxes. Counts pack of envelopes periodically to verify accuracy of mechanical counter. Pours glue into machine container to replenish supply. Wipes or washes glue from machine at end of shift. May adjust glue applicator and drying and pressing rolls. May be designated according to type of machine tended as Plunger-Machine Operator (paper goods); Rotary-Envelope-Machine Operator (paper goods); Side-Seam-Envelope-Machine Operator (paper goods). May tend machine that forms envelopes used in cover of books (book pockets) and be designated Book-Pocket-Machine Operator (paper goods).
GOE: 06.04.04 STRENGTH: M GED: R2 M1 L2 SVP: 4 DLU: 79

649.685-046 FOLDING-MACHINE OPERATOR (paper goods) alternate titles: multifold operator
Tends machines that automatically cut continuous rolls of paper into sheets of specified length, and fold and interlock them to form paper towels, toilet tissue, and napkins for dispensers or to package: Threads paper from parent roll through rollers and guides and tapes end to that of previous roll. Installs embossing rolls, and adjusts tucker, gripper, and feed rolls according to grade of paper and work order. Starts machine and observes operation to ensure uniform dispensing of glue, cutting, perforating, and folding of product. Lubricates machine and makes minor repairs, using handtools. May be designated according to type of machine as Double-Fold-Machine Operator (paper goods); Single-Fold-Machine Operator (paper goods); or according to article folded as Folded-Towel-Machine Operator (paper goods); Napkin-Machine Operator (paper goods).

GOE: 06.04.04 STRENGTH: M GED: R3 M2 L2 SVP: 3 DLU: 78

649.685-050 HANDLE-MACHINE OPERATOR (paper goods) alternate titles: paper-cup-handle-machine operator

Tends machine that die-cuts paper cup handles from roll of paper stock and glues handles onto cups: Mounts roll of paper on machine, using hoist. Fills glue reservoir and stacks cups onto machine feeding mechanism. Starts machine and observes machine operation to detect malfunction. Removes stack of finished cups from machine and places them into packing sleeves. Inserts full sleeves in packing carton.
GOE: 06.04.04 STRENGTH: M GED: R2 M1 L1 SVP: 3 DLU: 77

649.685-054 KNOTTING-MACHINE OPERATOR (paper goods)

Tends machine that automatically prints, strings, and knots paper tags: Mounts rolls of string and paper or card stock in machine. Starts machine and examines completed tag to detect machine malfunction. Stops machine to clear jams. Ties finished tags into bundles. May tend machine that automatically threads and fastens string to paper tags and be designated Stringing-Machine Operator (paper goods); or tend machine that threads and fastens wire to paper tags and be designated Wiring-Machine Operator (paper goods).
GOE: 06.04.04 STRENGTH: L GED: R2 M1 L1 SVP: 2 DLU: 77

649.685-058 LACE-PAPER-MACHINE OPERATOR (paper goods)

Tends machine that embosses and pierces paper strips to form lace paper doilies, place mats, and similar decorative articles: Loads roll of paper strip on machine, using chain hoist. Changes dies and cutters on machine and adjusts tension and pressure on feed rolls. Starts machine and inspects sample run for level of embossing, arrangement of piercing, and accuracy of cutoff, and corrects faulty machine.
GOE: 06.04.04 STRENGTH: M GED: R2 M1 L1 SVP: 3 DLU: 77

649.685-062 LAUNDRY-BAG-PUNCH OPERATOR (paper goods)

Tends machine that perforates paper laundry bags and affixes reinforcing paper eyelets: Threads gummed paper over die. Feeds bags singly into machine slot and depresses lever to lower punch that punches hole in bag and cuts out and fastens eyelet around hole. Inserts drawstrings through eyelets and piles finished bags on table for inspection.
GOE: 06.04.04 STRENGTH: L GED: R1 M1 L1 SVP: 2 DLU: 77

649.685-066 LAYBOY TENDER (paper & pulp; paper goods; print. & pub.) alternate titles: jogger operator; sheeter helper

Tends *layboy* that automatically stacks, aligns, and records count of paper sheets at discharge end of paper cutters, printing presses, and ruling and paper-making machines. Inspects sheets as they fall into layboy for defects, such as spots, holes, wrinkles, cockled edges, and dirt, and discards defective sheets. Smooths sheets by hand to eliminate air pockets. Stops and starts machine in emergency. May fan sheets or turn up corners to facilitate inspection. May count sheets and insert tabs to mark off reams if layboy does not have automatic counter and tabber. May align sheets by tapping edges by hand.
GOE: 06.04.04 STRENGTH: L GED: R2 M1 L1 SVP: 2 DLU: 77

649.685-070 MACHINE OPERATOR, GENERAL (paper goods) alternate titles: clasp machine operator; tension machine operator

Tends automatic and semiautomatic machines that punch holes, trim or notch envelope ends, and affix clasps, reinforcing patches, and snap fasteners and string or wire ties to envelopes: Turns screws to adjust guides and stops of machines, such as clasp, eyeletter, patch, tension, and thumb cut to accommodate specified size envelopes, using handtools. Pours clasps, eyelets, snap fasteners, or other envelope parts into machine hoppers and mounts rolls of patching or reinforcing tape on machine spindles. Positions envelopes on feed bed or under operating heads of machines against guides and stops. Depresses hand or foot levers to actuate machines. Removes completed envelopes and packs them in carton or box.
GOE: 06.04.04 STRENGTH: M GED: R2 M1 L1 SVP: 3 DLU: 77

649.685-074 MATCHBOOK ASSEMBLER (fabrication, nec)

Tends machine that automatically cuts, scores, and folds printed paper strips and staples them to matchbook *combs* to form matchbooks: Places roll of matchbook cover strip on machine spindle and threads end through machine. Loads machine magazine with wire staples and starts machine. Inserts matchbook comb strips into slots on feed conveyor that conveys them to stapling unit that fastens cover to comb strip to form matchbook. Observes machine operation to detect malfunction. Removes finished matchbooks from bin and packs specified number into boxes.
GOE: 06.04.04 STRENGTH: M GED: R2 M1 L1 SVP: 3 DLU: 77

649.685-078 PAPER-CUP-MACHINE OPERATOR (paper goods)

Tends machine that automatically forms flat-bottomed paper drinking cups: Loads rolls of bottom and sidewall paper on machine. Threads ends of paper through rollers and forming guides, and starts machine that automatically forms paper into cups and glues seams. Periodically tests samples of cups for leaks. Places specified number of cups in tubes preparatory to packing.
GOE: 06.04.04 STRENGTH: M GED: R2 M1 L1 SVP: 3 DLU: 77

649.685-082 PARTITION-MAKING-MACHINE OPERATOR (paper goods)

Tends machine that cuts interlocking slots or notches in two strips of cardboard and automatically assembles strips at right angles to form multicell partition (divider) for cardboard container: Loads rolls of cardboard into machine

feed reels and threads cardboard through guide rolls. Starts machine and observes operation of feeding, slotting, cutoff, and assembly mechanisms to detect malfunctioning. Examines assembled partitions at discharge chute and verifies conformance to specified dimensions, using go-not-go gauges. Replaces worn slotting punches and dull cutoff blades, using handtools. May assemble slotted strips by hand to form multicell partition for cardboard container.
GOE: 06.04.04 STRENGTH: L GED: R2 M1 L1 SVP: 2 DLU: 77

649.685-086 PATTERNMAKER, ACOUSTICAL TILE (wood prod., nec)

Tends machines that perforate, groove, and blast patterns on insulation board panels to form acoustical tile: Dumps sacks of ground walnut shell into hopper of blaster machine and moves controls to regulate flow of shell into blaster. Adjusts height of saws to control depth of cut, using gauge and wrench. Starts machines and conveyors, and spaces pattern templates on feed conveyor. Feeds panelboards into perforating machine, and observes perforated panels to ensure automatic positioning upon templates. Observes sets of panels and templates as they are conveyed into blaster machine to ensure that specified pattern or decorative design is imprinted upon panels according to template design.
GOE: 06.04.09 STRENGTH: M GED: R3 M2 L1 SVP: 4 DLU: 77

649.685-090 PERFORATING-MACHINE OPERATOR (print. & pub.)

Tends machine that perforates sheets of paper with lines of fine holes to facilitate tearing sheets: Installs perforating disks in machine and sets guides to size of sheet, using handtools. Starts machine and feeds sheets into machine, singly, or keeps feed table supplied with stacks of sheets if machine is fed automatically. Removes perforated sheets as they accumulate on discharge table of machine.
GOE: 06.04.04 STRENGTH: L GED: R2 M1 L1 SVP: 4 DLU: 77

649.685-094 PUNCHBOARD-FILLING-MACHINE OPERATOR (paper goods) alternate titles: stuffing-machine operator

Tends machine that inserts numbered paper cylinders in holes of punchboards: Places printed paper strips in tubular magazine and locks it in filling machine. Presses punchboard over pegs in plate of machine and moves lever to lower blade that cuts paper into strips and raises plate against teeth that stuffs them into punchboard holes.
GOE: 06.04.20 STRENGTH: L GED: R2 M1 L1 SVP: 2 DLU: 77

649.685-098 RING-MAKING-MACHINE OPERATOR (paper goods)

Tends machine that automatically curls and cuts cardboard strips to make rings, such as those used in hat boxes: Mounts rolls of cardboard on machine reel and threads strip through steaming, curling, and cutting devices. Starts machine and gathers and packages ejected rings.
GOE: 06.04.04 STRENGTH: L GED: R2 M1 L1 SVP: 2 DLU: 77

649.685-102 SALVAGE WINDER AND INSPECTOR (paper goods)

Tends rewinder and identifies and cuts out defective sections of tape to salvage rejected rolls of paper tape: Places rubber belt on machine pullup to obtain desired speed ratio. Secures tape roll onto spindle and threads end of tape around takeup roll. Starts machine and observes tape winding onto roll, using knee and foot controls to regulate winding speed. Inspects tape for dry spots, excessive glue, creases, and holes. Cuts out defective areas, using scissors. Presses flat metal bars to each side of rough tape sections to smooth tape surface. Throws defective tape sections into trash bin. Removes tape rolls from machine and places rolls on cart for packing.
GOE: 06.03.02 STRENGTH: L GED: R2 M2 L2 SVP: 3 DLU: 77

649.685-106 SHOT-TUBE-MACHINE TENDER (paper goods)

Tends machines that crimp rolled paper tubes to form caps and press them onto ends of other tubes to make BB shot containers: Starts machines, places tubes on skipped spindles by hand, and removes damaged tubes or scrap paper, using wire hook. Removes completed caps from machine hopper, fills shaker frame with crimped caps from hopper and starts shaker machine to arrange caps crimped-side-down [SHAKER-PLATE OPERATOR (ordnance)]. Examines caps and discards torn, flattened, grease-smeared, or malformed caps. Pushes caps into feeder tray, using T-shape pusher, and hangs loaded tray on gravity-feed station of repairer assembly machine. Notifies machine repairer of malfunction.
GOE: 06.04.04 STRENGTH: L GED: R2 M1 L1 SVP: 2 DLU: 77

649.685-110 STEEL-TIE ADJUSTER, AUTOMATIC (paper goods) alternate titles: tin-tie-machine operator, automatic

Tends machine that automatically cuts steel and paper strips to specified length, covers steel strip with paper, and glues covered steel strip to paper bag for use in sealing. Fills glue pot with paste and loads bags onto machine feed rack.
GOE: 06.04.09 STRENGTH: L GED: R2 M1 L1 SVP: 2 DLU: 77

649.685-114 STITCHER OPERATOR (paper goods) alternate titles: semi-automatic-stitcher operator

Tends machine that stitches (staples) edges of plain and corrugated paperboard box blanks to form boxes: Reads production order to determine number of stitches required, turns gauge to specified setting and starts machine. Folds box blank by hand along scored lines or removes folded box blank from folding machine and feeds blank into machine that stitches edges. Inspects completed boxes for defective stitching and records quantity, style, and grade of boxes in production log.
GOE: 06.04.04 STRENGTH: H GED: R2 M1 L1 SVP: 4 DLU: 77

649.685-118 TAG-MACHINE OPERATOR (paper goods) alternate titles: blanker operator

Tends machine that automatically makes shipping tags and file and index cards: Threads paper stock between guides that pass paper under printing roll, corner cutter, punch, eyeletter, and shears. Turns mechanical counter to zero. Starts machine that prints specified data on tag, trims corners, punches holes in end and reinforces hole with paper or metal eyelets, cuts tag or card to size, and records quantity produced. Examines ejected tags or cards for defects and notifies department supervisor of machine malfunction. Packs specified number of tags or cards in bundles or cartons for shipment. May adjust machine controls to omit specific machine operations when not required.
GOE: 06.04.37 STRENGTH: L GED: R2 M1 L1 SVP: 2 DLU: 77

649.685-122 TAPE-FASTENER-MACHINE OPERATOR (paper goods) alternate titles: tie fastener; tie-tape-machine operator

Tends machine that staples ribbon or string (tape) ties onto flaps of fiber folder: Winds ribbons or string on reel and cuts strands with shears to make lengths of tape according to size of folders [PAPER-REEL OPERATOR (paper goods)]. Adjusts fastening machine guides according to size of folder, using handtools. Fills feed magazine with staples and starts machine. Positions flaps of folders against guides and holds length of tape across envelope flap under machine ram. Depresses pedal to lower ram and staple tape to flap.
GOE: 06.04.04 STRENGTH: L GED: R2 M1 L1 SVP: 2 DLU: 77

649.685-126 TAPER OPERATOR (paper goods) alternate titles: semi-automatic-taper operator

Tends machine that tapes edges of corrugated paperboard box blanks to form boxes: Mounts roll of gummed tape onto machine and threads tape through feed and moisture applicator rollers and under cutoff knife. Turns petcock to start flow of water to applicator tray. Positions and secures cutoff knife microswitch, according to box dimensions, using handtools. Starts machine, folds blank along scored lines, and feeds folded blank into machine that tapes edges to form box. Observes machine operation to detect malfunction and inspects completed boxes to verify tape application according to specifications. Adjusts tape guides, water flow, or cutoff knife to correct faulty tape application.
GOE: 06.04.04 STRENGTH: H GED: R2 M1 L1 SVP: 3 DLU: 77

649.685-130 TABLET-MAKING-MACHINE-OPERATOR HELPER (paper goods)

Tends machine that cuts, rules, punches, binds, and stacks materials to produce looseleaf filler, tablets, and wire bound notebooks: Assists TABLET-MAKING-MACHINE OPERATOR (paper goods) 649.682-042 to set up machine. Presses buttons to activate hydraulic lift that positions rolls of paper in feed position. Pours powdered ink and water into container and mixes ingredients with hand stirrer. Loads backing and cover material on inserter platforms. Inspects finished products to determine required machine adjustments and eliminate machine malfunctions. Notifies MACHINE SET-UP OPERATOR, PAPER GOODS (paper goods) 649.380-010 of unresolved problems.
GOE: 06.04.04 STRENGTH: M GED: R3 M2 L2 SVP: 3 DLU: 86

649.686-010 BAG-MACHINE-OPERATOR HELPER (paper goods)

Assists BAG-MACHINE OPERATOR (paper goods) by feeding paper rolls into machine that automatically prints, cuts, folds, and glues roll of paper, polyethylene film, or cellophane to make finished bags: Inserts shaft into core of parent roll and secures it with steel collars, using handtools. Lifts and mounts roll on machine standard, using electric hoist. Tapes leading end of roll to end of previous roll. Replenishes glue and ink reservoirs. Assists BAG-MACHINE OPERATOR (paper goods) in making repairs and adjustments, using handtools. Performs other duties as described under HELPER (any industry) Master Title.
GOE: 06.04.04 STRENGTH: M GED: R2 M1 L1 SVP: 2 DLU: 77

649.686-014 CARD DECORATOR (print. & pub.)

Tends machine that automatically glues decorative sparkle dust to greeting cards. Feeds greeting cards into machine. Changes dies according to size specified. Refills hoppers of machine with glue and sparkle dust.
GOE: 06.04.04 STRENGTH: L GED: R2 M1 L1 SVP: 2 DLU: 77

649.686-018 CYLINDER-DIE-MACHINE HELPER (paper goods)

Assist CYLINDER-DIE-MACHINE OPERATOR (paper goods) to operate cylinder press to score and cut paperboard sheets into box or container blanks: Obtains cutting die from storage according to work order and assists operator in aligning die on machine cylinder and fastening die to cylinder. Feeds flat paperboard stock into machine that scores and cuts stock to form box or container blanks. Performs other duties as described under HELPER (any industry) Master Title.
GOE: 06.04.04 STRENGTH: H GED: R2 M1 L1 SVP: 2 DLU: 77

649.686-022 FINISHING-MACHINE OPERATOR (paper goods)

Feeds preformed bodies of paper cups into machine that automatically inserts plugs into lower ends to form bottoms, rolls tops to finish edges of cups, and ejects completed cups.
GOE: 06.04.04 STRENGTH: L GED: R1 M1 L1 SVP: 1 DLU: 77

649.686-026 PLATING-MACHINE OPERATOR (paper & pulp) alternate titles: plater

Feeds sheets into plating machine that impresses weave or grain finish into paper: Stacks linen and paper sheets in alternate layers and feeds sheets into rolls of plating machine to impress weave of fabric onto paper.
GOE: 06.04.04 STRENGTH: L GED: R2 M1 L1 SVP: 2 DLU: 77

649.686-030 SLITTER-CREASER-SLOTTER HELPER (paper goods)

Feeds and off bears machine that slots, scores, and creases corrugated or plain paperboard sheets to form container blanks: Aligns sheet against machine guides and feeds sheet into machine feed rolls. Removes completed container blanks from machine and stacks blanks onto skids. May assist SLITTER-CREASER-SLOTTER OPERATOR (paper goods) in setting up machine.
GOE: 06.04.04 STRENGTH: H GED: R2 M1 L1 SVP: 2 DLU: 77

649.687-010 PAPER SORTER AND COUNTER (paper & pulp) alternate titles: inspector and counter; overlooker; sorter

Sorts sheets of paper according to specified grade and examines them for defects, such as tears, cuts, roll marks and slime holes, and discards defective sheets. Counts and stacks acceptable sheets and inserts identification marker between reams. Segregates paper according to customer order and records amount and grade of separate orders.
GOE: 06.03.02 STRENGTH: L GED: R2 M2 L1 SVP: 2 DLU: 77

649.687-014 PAPER-CONE GRADER (paper goods)

Examines paper *cones* emerging from cone-making machines for defects. Places acceptable ones on racks and tosses defective cones in trash receptacle. May examine paper tubes and be designated Paper-Tube Grader (paper goods).
GOE: 06.03.02 STRENGTH: L GED: R2 M1 L1 SVP: 2 DLU: 77

649.687-018 PAPER-PATTERN INSPECTOR (paper goods)

Examines tissue paper patterns for accuracy of cutting, perforating, and numbering.
GOE: 06.03.02 STRENGTH: L GED: R2 M1 L1 SVP: 2 DLU: 77

65   PRINTING OCCUPATIONS

This division includes occupations concerned with reproducing data or designs by mechanical transfer of ink or dye to the surface of materials with the aid of type, plates, rolls, and the like. Includes the preparation of type and plate for machines and mechanical bookbinding.

650   TYPESETTERS AND COMPOSERS

This group includes occupations concerned with assembling and setting type matter for printing by means of typesetting or composing machines. Includes linotype machines which assemble letters into lines and cast strips of type from type metal; monotype machines which compose type matter in separate letters; and phototypesetting machines which assemble and photograph mats of individual characters as a line of type on film or photographic paper. Occupations whose duties include substantial typing tasks concerned with cold type setting of type are included in Group 203.

650.132-010 SUPERVISOR, TYPESETTING (print. & pub.)

Supervises and coordinates activities of workers engaged in machine typesetting: Reads production schedule and plans work assignments according to setup and work load of individual machines. Examines proofs to verify conformance to work order specifications. Periodically verifies status of each job in progress in order to maintain production. Trains workers to operate typesetting machines. May operate typesetting machines as necessary. May coordinate setting of copy into type [COPY CUTTER (print. & pub.)]. May supervise workers engaged in phototypesetting and be designated Supervisor, Photocomposition (print. & pub.). Performs duties as described under SUPERVISOR (any industry) Master Title.
GOE: 07.06.02 STRENGTH: L GED: R4 M3 L3 SVP: 8 DLU: 77

650.582-010 LINOTYPE OPERATOR (print. & pub.) alternate titles: composing-machine operator

Operates machine to cast complete lines of type from type metal and deposit them in galley in composed form for printing: Starts type-casting mechanism and adjusts marginal stops and gauge to regulate length and thickness of lines to be cast. Reads copy and presses keys of keyboard to select matrices of letters from magazine which are assembled into words. Moves lever to cast line and deposit it in galley when line is complete. Transfers lines of type, with copy, to composing or bank table for making proof copy. Sets new lines of type to correct errors as indicated on proofsheet. Places pigs of metal on feed chain of melting pot to replenish supply.
GOE: 07.06.02 STRENGTH: M GED: R4 M2 L3 SVP: 7 DLU: 81

650.582-014 MONOTYPE-KEYBOARD OPERATOR (machinery mfg.; print. & pub.) alternate titles: composing-machine operator; monotype operator

Operates machine to perforate *paper tape* used to control casting type: Clips copy containing instructions to copyholder. Selects and installs bank of keys to make specified size and style of type. Sets and locks scale for indicating spacing of words in line, adjusts line-length indicator, and installs roll of paper strip, threading end of strip through machine. Admits compressed air to machine. Tears strip loose from supply roll, attaches type-casting instructions to reel, and forwards reel for casting type.
GOE: 07.06.02 STRENGTH: L GED: R4 M2 L3 SVP: 6 DLU: 77

650.582-018 PHOTOCOMPOSING-MACHINE OPERATOR (print. & pub.) alternate titles: typesetter

Sets up and operates photocomposing machine to transfer data from perforated or magnetic tape into print on film or photographic paper, using either

of following methods: (1) Loads roll of film or paper in machine magazine. Secures roll of perforated tape on machine reel and threads end of tape through machine feed rollers. Selects type font according to size and face of type specified and positions it on photographic unit. Turns dials to adjust line spacing and light intensity according to size and face of type. Starts machine that automatically prints type onto film or paper according to coded signal on tape. Removes finished copy from magazine for development. (2) Places reel of magnetic tape onto feed spindle of phototypesetting unit. Depresses keys to enter command codes, such as size and style of type, width and length of column, and to activate computer to produce phototypesetting film, phototypesetting paper, or copy of tape. Removes and stacks finished copies from photocopy printing unit. Removes printing unit from machine, drains chemical solution, washes unit, and refills unit with specified developing solution.
GOE: 05.10.05 STRENGTH: L GED: R3 M1 L1 SVP: 6 DLU: 89

650.582-022 PHOTOTYPESETTER OPERATOR (print. & pub.) alternate titles: phototypesetter
Operates keyboard of automatic phototypesetting machine to photographically print type matter onto film or strips of photosensitive paper to prepare positives or paper flats for making printing plates: Loads roll of photosensitive paper or film into camera magazine, positions magazine on machine, and pulls lever to open exposure slot. Starts typesetting mechanism. Turns dial to select lens and regulate gear that controls size (magnification or reproduction) of matrix letter, exposure, and light intensity, or moves selector levers, depresses keys or control buttons to select style and size of type. Depresses keys of keyboard to select *foto mats* for printing onto photopaper or film. Cuts photopaper with knife to separate exposed portion. Removes exposed photopaper or film from magazine for developing. May perform routine maintenance and adjustments on machine, using handtools.
GOE: 07.06.02 STRENGTH: L GED: R4 M2 L3 SVP: 5 DLU: 77

650.682-010 EQUIPMENT MONITOR, PHOTOTYPESETTING (print. & pub.)
Monitors and controls electronic computer system used in phototypesetting: Sets control switches on optical character reader, computer, or phototypesetter. Inserts command codes to integrate and operate equipment according to data requirements specified in mark-up instructions. Selects and loads input and output units with materials for operating equipment. Moves switches to clear system and start operation of equipment. Observes equipment and control panels on consoles for error lights, messages, and machine stoppage or faulty output. Notifies superior of errors or equipment stoppage.
GOE: 05.10.05 STRENGTH: L GED: R3 M1 L2 SVP: 4 DLU: 77

650.685-010 TYPESETTING-MACHINE TENDER (print. & pub.) alternate titles: teletypesetter monitor
Tends and adjusts one or more linecasting machines, equipped with tape converter unit, to produce type composition automatically: Positions spool of punched tape on machine reel. Threads end of tape through feed mechanism of converter unit. Turns control to start unit that sets type automatically as directed by coded signal on punched tape. Transfers lines of type, with copy, to composing or bank table for taking of proof. Adds new pigs of type metal to melting pot to replenish supply. Observes operation of machine to detect malfunction of keyboard, matrix circulation mechanism, tape feeding mechanism or other machine mechanisms, and adjusts their mechanical components, using handtools, or depresses keys on keyboard to clear jamming. Periodically cleans matrices, magazine, and molds. May replace worn parts, such as code bars, keys, and spacebands, using handtools and power tools.
GOE: 05.10.05 STRENGTH: L GED: R3 M1 L2 SVP: 4 DLU: 77

651 PRINTING PRESS OCCUPATIONS

This group includes occupations concerned with producing copies of designs or lettering by transferring ink or pigment on type, plates, or rolls to paper or similar materials by means of a printing press. Includes cylinder presses, offset presses, and platen presses.

651.130-010 SUPERVISOR, PRESS ROOM (print. & pub.)
Supervises and coordinates activities of workers engaged in making ready, operating, and feeding various types of presses used to print newspapers, magazines, books, and other printed matter: Observes press operations and examines printed material to verify conformance with work order specifications. Examines multicolor printed material, using precision instruments, to detect imperfect color tone registration. Performs other duties as described under SUPERVISOR (any industry) Master Title.
GOE: 05.05.13 STRENGTH: L GED: R4 M3 L4 SVP: 8 DLU: 89

651.362-010 CYLINDER-PRESS OPERATOR (print. & pub.) alternate titles: flatbed-press operator; press operator
Makes ready and operates cylinder-type printing press: Verifies size, color, and type of paper and color of ink from job order. Cleans inking rollers with solvent and replaces them in press, using handtools. Adjusts controls to regulate volume of ink. Packs impression cylinder with tissue or folio. Adjusts delivery tapes, and positions and locks form (type setup or plate) on bed or cylinder of press. Directs CYLINDER-PRESS FEEDER (print. & pub.) in adjustment of feed guides, grippers, and elevator, or hand-feeding press. Starts press and runs off proofsheet. Examines proof to determine off-level areas, variation in ink volume, register slippage, indications of offsetting, and color register. Ad-

justs press controls, inking fountains, and automatic feeders, and repacks cylinder with overlay to equalize off-level areas as required. May register forms and mix colors. May make overlay for half-tone shades. May operate cylinder press equipped with cutting attachment or may replace type dies with cutting dies to cut or shape paper or paperboard. May operate more than one press. May be designated according to kind of material printed as Check Imprinter (print. & pub.); Envelope-Press Operator (print. & pub.) I; Label-Press Operator (print. & pub.) I; size of press as Pony-Cylinder-Press Operator (print. & pub.). Important variations may be indicated by trade names of machine used.
GOE: 05.05.13 STRENGTH: M GED: R4 M3 L3 SVP: 7 DLU: 77

651.362-014 CYLINDER-PRESS-OPERATOR APPRENTICE (print. & pub.)
Performs duties as described under APPRENTICE (any industry) Master Title.
GOE: 05.05.13 STRENGTH: M GED: R4 M3 L3 SVP: 7 DLU: 77

651.362-018 PLATEN-PRESS OPERATOR (print. & pub.)
Makes ready and operates platen-type printing press to produce printed material: Determines setup and operating procedures from work order. Inserts type setup or plate in press bed and tightens locking attachment, using wrench. Adjusts inking rollers to obtain even distribution of ink. Regulates ink flow by adjusting thumbscrews on fountain. Starts press and directs PLATEN-PRESS FEEDER (print. & pub.) to feed sheets by hand onto press platen or to place stack of sheets in feed tray if press is equipped with automatic feeding mechanism. Readjusts press during run to obtain specified color registration. May place stack of sheets in feed tray on press equipped with automatic feeding mechanism. May be designated according to type of material printed as Envelope-Press Operator (print. & pub.) II; Label-Press Operator (print. & pub.) II.
GOE: 05.05.13 STRENGTH: L GED: R4 M2 L2 SVP: 7 DLU: 77

651.362-022 PLATEN-PRESS-OPERATOR APPRENTICE (print. & pub.) alternate titles: make-ready apprentice
Performs duties as described under APPRENTICE (any industry) Master Title.
GOE: 05.05.13 STRENGTH: L GED: R4 M2 L2 SVP: 7 DLU: 77

651.362-026 ROTOGRAVURE-PRESS OPERATOR (print. & pub.)
Makes ready and operates rotary-type press that prints illustrative and other subject matter by rotogravure process: Installs engraved copper printing cylinder in press, using handtools. Adjusts doctor (wiper) blade to remove excess ink from surface of printing cylinder. Threads web (roll) of paper or other printing stock through press, adjusting guides and tension bars. Sets focus of electronic scanners on guideline of paper (for multicolor printing) to automatically control color registration. Regulates temperature in web-drying chambers and adjusts automatic cutter at discharge end of press. Inspects material being printed, during production run, and adjusts press as required to produce printed matter to specifications. Directs workers in feeding and unloading press, replenishing ink supply in fountains, cleaning equipment, and other press operations. May operate press equipped to print, cut, and crease paper goods.
GOE: 05.05.13 STRENGTH: M GED: R3 M2 L2 SVP: 7 DLU: 77

651.362-030 WEB-PRESS OPERATOR (print. & pub.)
Makes ready and operates multiunit, web-fed rotary press to print newspapers, books, and periodicals according to written specifications: Locks printing plates on printing cylinder and threads loose end of paper supply roll (web) through and around rollers to cutter and folder. Adjusts compensators to guide paper over rollers and cylinders. Inspects printed sheets visually after registration or position printing and readjusts guides and controls to rectify spacing errors. Adjusts feed controls to rotate cylinder into position where plate locking mechanism is accessible. Unlocks plates and replaces with make-over plates according to directions marked on plate regarding location and time of printing. Rethreads paper through press if web breaks (press stops automatically if web breaks) and readjusts tension rollers. Operates pasting device to splice end of new paper roll to depleted roll. Inspects printed material visually during production and readjusts controls to correct irregular ink distribution, faulty cuts or folds. Replaces cutting blades, worn or damaged ink rolls, and fills ink wells. Cleans, inspects, and lubricates moving parts of press. May supervise and instruct apprentices. May load supply rolls of paper in press at beginning and during run. May be designated Tension Regulator (print. & pub.) when installing paper rolls in press and adjusting controls to regulate tension of paper; or Color-Control Operator (print. & pub.) when adjusting ink controls to secure specified color registration. May operate press from central control console.
GOE: 05.05.13 STRENGTH: M GED: R4 M3 L3 SVP: 7 DLU: 77

651.362-034 WEB-PRESS-OPERATOR APPRENTICE (print. & pub.) alternate titles: newspaper-press-operator apprentice
Performs duties as described under APPRENTICE (any industry) Master Title.
GOE: 05.05.13 STRENGTH: M GED: R4 M3 L3 SVP: 7 DLU: 77

651.382-010 ENGRAVING-PRESS OPERATOR (print. & pub.) alternate titles: die-stamping-press operator
Makes ready and operates press to engrave decorative designs or lettering on announcements, greeting and business cards, letterheads, and related items, following operating procedures outlined on job order: Installs appropriate die and inking rollers on ram, using wrench. Cuts out and fastens paper template to bed of press to maintain flatness of finished cards or sheets. Inserts and adjusts roll

of wiping paper that automatically cleans die between impressions. Thins ink to desired consistency and fills ink fountain. Starts press to obtain proof copy. Examines proof and adjusts press and ink fountain to obtain uniform indentation and color registration. Starts press and feeds cards or sheets to be engraved onto bed of press.
GOE: 05.10.05 STRENGTH: L GED: R4 M2 L3 SVP: 7 DLU: 77

651.382-014   LITHOGRAPH-PRESS OPERATOR, TINWARE (tinware)
Sets up and operates lithograph press to print descriptive material and designs on tinplate: Installs printing plates on machine rolls, using handtools and gauges. Adjusts feed guides, back and side gauges, and rollers with handtools. Mixes colors of paint according to formula and fills paint fountain. Starts machine and makes trial run. Adjusts or changes gears to regulate rate of feed and turns fountain valves to adjust flow of paint. Inspects lithographed plate to ensure that printing is clear and lined-up according to specifications or sample. Examines plates during process and removes defective plates. Observes heat gauges and regulates controls of drying oven to maintain specified heat.
GOE: 06.02.02 STRENGTH: L GED: R3 M2 L2 SVP: 7 DLU: 77

651.382-026   PRINTER, PLASTIC (plastic prod.; tex. prod., nec) alternate titles: flexigraphic printer
Sets up and operates press to print colored designs on rolls of plastic or plastic-coated material: Positions and clamps printing cylinder on press, using handtools. Pours inks into ink pans and threads plastic film through press rolls. Starts press and turns wheels to adjust pickup, transfer, and printing rolls. Turns rheostats to regulate speed and feed of press, and temperature of drying box. Examines printed sheet to detect defects, such as wrinkles, tears, smeared printing, and uneven color distribution. Cleans and oils press. Repairs or replaces broken or worn parts of press, using handtools. May set print on printing cylinder, and blend colored inks, according to job order.
GOE: 06.02.09 STRENGTH: M GED: R3 M1 L2 SVP: 5 DLU: 77

651.382-030   STEEL-DIE PRINTER (print. & pub.) alternate titles: plate printer
Operates printing press to print embossed forms, such as business cards, letterheads, and announcements, from engraved steel plates: Positions plate in plateholder and builds up space beneath plate with cut pieces of fabric material to make slight crimp of printed areas. Glues plate in position. Sets paper guides and adjusts plate-wiping mechanism, using wrenches. Turns on drying lamps over takeoff conveyor and starts press. Engages automatic feed or feeds sheets to press by hand, aligning them against paper guides.
GOE: 05.10.05 STRENGTH: L GED: R3 M2 L2 SVP: 7 DLU: 77

651.382-034   TAB-CARD-PRESS OPERATOR (print. & pub.)
Sets up and operates specially equipped presses to print, perforate, number, and cut data processing cards according to specifications: Installs die in press bed or on press cylinder and tightens locking attachment, using wrench. Mounts paper roll on reel and inserts end into automatic feed mechanism. Tightens or loosens fountain thumbscrew to adjust ink flow. Starts presses and observes operation to detect malfunction. Examines printed cards for conformance to specifications, using line gauge. May record production on logsheet.
GOE: 05.10.05 STRENGTH: L GED: R3 M2 L3 SVP: 5 DLU: 77

651.382-038   TRANSFER OPERATOR (print. & pub.)
Sets up and operates machine to print designs, trademarks, sizes, and other identifying information on continuous roll of paper for use as dry transfers or hot iron patterns: Turns setscrew to secure selected die in machine holder. Slides doctor blade in machine slots and plugs ends of machine trough with paper wads to prevent loss of melted ink. Positions block of dry ink in machine trough and adjusts burner flame to melt ink. Measures lettering or design on die with machinist's scale to determine widths of pressure roller and paper roll required. Installs and secures pressure roller, using wrench. Mounts paper roll in machine and threads end between pressure roller and die, fastening end to winding spindle. Turns handwheel and moves lever to adjust angle of doctor blade, tension of paper, and pressure of roller. Sets automatic counter at zero. Starts machine and observes paper for accuracy of printing. Stops machine when specified number of transfers are printed as indicated by automatic counter. Removes printed roll of transfers and die from machine. Cleans and lubricates machine and die, using solvent and cloths, and makes minor repairs.
GOE: 05.10.05 STRENGTH: L GED: R3 M2 L2 SVP: 4 DLU: 77

651.382-042   OFFSET-PRESS OPERATOR I (print. & pub.) alternate titles: first press operator; lithographic-press operator
Makes ready and operates web or sheet-fed offset printing press to print single and multicolor copy from lithographic plates: Examines job order to determine quantity to be printed, stock specifications, colors, and special printing instructions. Measures plate thickness and inserts packing sheets on plate cylinder to build up plate to printing height and installs and locks plate into position, using handtools, to achieve pressure required for printing. Washes plate to remove protective gum coating. Measures paper thickness and adjusts space between blanket and impression cylinders according to thickness of paper stock. Fills ink and dampening solution fountains and adjusts controls to regulate flow of ink and dampening solution to plate cylinder. Starts press, examines printed copy for ink density, position on paper, and registration, and makes adjustments to press throughout production run to maintain specific registration and color density. Removes and cleans plate and cylinders. May apply packing sheets to blanket cylinder to build up blanket thickness to diameter of plate cylinder. May load paper into feeder or install rolls of paper, make adjustments to feeder

and delivery mechanisms, and unload printed material from delivery mechanism. May lead, give directions to, and monitor work of ASSISTANT PRESS OPERATOR, OFFSET (print. & pub.) 651.685-026; FEEDER (print. & pub.) 651.686-014; JOGGER (print. & pub.) 651.686-018; or ROLL TENDER (print. & pub.) 651.686-022.
GOE: 05.05.13 STRENGTH: L GED: R4 M2 L3 SVP: 8 DLU: 89

651.382-046   OFFSET-PRESS-OPERATOR APPRENTICE (print. & pub.) alternate titles: lithographic-press operator apprentice
Performs duties as described under APPRENTICE (any industry) Master Title.
GOE: 05.05.13 STRENGTH: L GED: R4 M2 L3 SVP: 8 DLU: 77

651.384-010   PLATEN BUILDER-UP (print. & pub.) alternate titles: make-ready worker
Glues paper to back of platen (pressure plate) cover to raise depressed areas of platen cover and reduce clearance between paper and printing head of printing press: Holds platen obliquely to electric light to locate shadowed depressed areas of platen cover, and draws contour rings around depressed areas, using pencil. Cuts out paper to fit within contour lines and cements paper onto back of platen cover to raise depressions in platen cover, using razor blade and paper cement. Examines printed material to detect defects in printing due to platen face cover depressions. Writes requisitions to order supplies.
GOE: 05.10.05 STRENGTH: L GED: R2 M1 L2 SVP: 4 DLU: 77

651.582-010   PROOF-PRESS OPERATOR (print. & pub.) alternate titles: proofer
Makes ready and operates proof press to make proofs of type setup: Places galley of type on bed of press. Depresses pedal to move ink roller over face of type or applies ink, using hand roller. Places sheet of paper on type and depresses pedal or turns crank to pass rollers over paper to obtain proof of type setup. Removes proofsheet from press and delivers it to PROOFREADER (print. & pub.). May print reproduction proofs of type and illustrating cuts on transparent film or glossy paper, to be used in lithographic plate making. May be designated according to type of press operated as Lithographic Proofer (print. & pub.); Offset-Proof-Press Operator (print. & pub.).
GOE: 05.05.13 STRENGTH: M GED: R3 M2 L2 SVP: 5 DLU: 77

651.582-014   LITHOGRAPHIC-PROOFER APPRENTICE (print. & pub.) alternate titles: proofer apprentice
Performs duties as described under APPRENTICE (any industry) Master Title.
GOE: 05.05.13 STRENGTH: M GED: R3 M2 L2 SVP: 5 DLU: 77

651.585-010   ASSISTANT-PRESS OPERATOR (print. & pub.) alternate titles: flexographic-press helper; web-press-operator assistant
Performs any combination of following duties to assist printing press operator to make ready, operate, and maintain roll-fed (web) or sheet-fed, single-or-multicolor flatbed, cylinder, offset, flexographic, or web press: Assists press operator to install paper packing sheets on impression (back-up) cylinder, fasten reinforcing bars to metal printing plates and offset blankets, and install plates and blankets on press cylinders, using handtools and power tools. Adjusts machine parts, such as feed and delivery mechanisms, suction grippers, guides, feed wheels, jogging device, tapes, and cams as directed by press operator, using handtools. Lifts and positions roll of paper in feed mechanism, using chain hoist, or positions skid of unprinted sheets on feed device, using handtruck or electric lift-truck. Removes loaded skid of printed material from stacking mechansim, using handtruck, and replaces with empty skid. Fills fountains with ink paste, using spatula. Tends press in absence of press operator. Observes mechanical operation and indicating gauges, such as ammeter and air pressure gauges to ensure that specified operating levels are maintained and makes specified adjustments or notifies press operator when malfunction occurs. Assists in lubrication of press, using grease gun and oilcan. Assists press operator to remove and replace worn rollers and adjust pressure between rollers, using handtools. Cleans ink and distributing rollers, ink fountains, and printing type, using cleaning solvent, brush, and rags. Cleans press and work area, using vacuum cleaner, brush, and airhose. Keeps daily time, production, and material usage reports. Assists in exposing and developing printing plates. Regulates temperature of gas-fired drying units. May be required to serve apprenticeship.
GOE: 05.05.13 STRENGTH: M GED: R3 M2 L2 SVP: 6 DLU: 90

651.586-010   PRESS HELPER (plastic prod.)
Assists PRINTER, PLASTIC (plastic prod.; tex. prod., nec) in printing designs on plastic material: Inserts spindle through roll of plastic material and adjusts collars to center roll on spindle. Positions spindle on printing press feedrack and clamps it in place. Threads material through press rolls and tapes end to winding roll. Places cardboard core on rewind spindle, tapes end of finished plastic roll to core, and moves controls to rewind specified quantity of printed plastic. Observes plastic during rewinding and marks or cuts out defective portions. Records weight of rolls and amount of plastic on rolls. Washes ink rollers and pan in solvent. Performs other duties as described under HELPER (any industry) Master Title.
GOE: 06.04.02 STRENGTH: H GED: R2 M1 L1 SVP: 2 DLU: 77

651.682-010   FLEXOGRAPHIC-PRESS OPERATOR (paper goods; print. & pub.)
Sets up and operates flexographic printing press to print designs or lettering on rolls of flexible plastic film, paper, and nonabsorbant stock for use in mak-

ing products, such as plastic, paper, or waxed paper bags, and paper drinking cups: Reads job order and mounts specified rubber plate and printing dies on cylinder, installs cylinder on shaft, and secures assembly in bed of press. Fills dye fonts with prescribed inks or dyes. Moves levers to engage dye rolls, adjusting position of cylinder to print two or more colors without overlapping or smearing previously printed area. Inserts shaft through core of paper or plastic roll and secures roll on press in feed position. Splices end of roll to trailer sheet remaining in press, using tape, and turns handwheel to regulate roll tension and feed as directed. Starts press, adjusting speed, tension, and alignment of printing plate as necessary. Cuts sample of printed material from end of printed roll and inspects for imperfections, such as blurred or off-center impressions. Cleans rubber plate, cylinder, and dye fonts, using solvent, and lubricates press as needed, using grease gun. May mix inks or dyes to produce desired colors. May operate press equipped with laminator attachment to print and laminate polyethylene or cellophane sheeting. May operate press that prints, cuts, and folds paper stock to make paper napkins.
GOE: 06.02.09 STRENGTH: M GED: R3 M2 L3 SVP: 4 DLU: 77

651.682-014   OFFSET-DUPLICATING-MACHINE OPERATOR (print. & pub.)
Operates offset duplicating machine to reproduce typeset matter, drawings, graphs, and similar material by photo-offset process: Secures printing plate in offset duplicating machine. Moves controls to set offset duplicating machine for size and thickness of paper, to position printed impression, and to regulate flow of ink and speed of paper feed, according to material to be reproduced. Starts offset duplicating machine and examines printed copy for ink density, position on paper, and registration. Fills ink fountains and makes adjustments to machine throughout production run to maintain fountain solutions, specific registration, and color density. Cleans, greases, and oils offset duplicating machine and components, removes paper jams, and adjusts cylinder pressure to maintain machine in working order.
GOE: 05.10.05 STRENGTH: L GED: R3 M2 L2 SVP: 4 DLU: 89

651.682-018   STRIPER (paper goods)
Operates cylinder press to print color stripes on paper stock used for making paper bags or wrapping paper: Mounts roll of stock paper on unwind shaft, using hoist. Threads paper through rollers of press and onto windup shaft. Fills ink well with specified color of ink. Pushes button to start and stop machine. Observes operation and turns handwheels to adjust tension of paper. May clean inkwell, using alcohol.
GOE: 06.02.04 STRENGTH: L GED: R3 M1 L1 SVP: 5 DLU: 77

651.682-022   TIP PRINTER (hat & cap) alternate titles: lining printer
Sets up and operates cylinder or platen press that prints labels, slogans, trademarks, or trade names onto hat lining material: Inks disk and rollers of press, using brush or sponge. Tightens or loosens inking rollers, using wrench and, regulates flow of ink from reservoir. Arranges type or engraving blocks in chase (holder) according to specifications. Turns setscrews on chase to secure type or engraving, using wrench. Slides chase into channel on bed of press and turns setscrews to lock chase in die plate. Positions lining material against adjustable guides and turns handwheel to align material. Starts press or turns handwheel to print sample of cut or type. Examines impressions on material for alignment and clarity. Starts press and feeds and removes lining material by hand or monitors automatic feed to prevent jamming. May operate several presses to print variety of colors or part of total design onto lining material. May operate platen press equipped with heated die block to imprint data, using goldleaf.
GOE: 06.04.37 STRENGTH: L GED: R3 M2 L2 SVP: 3 DLU: 77

651.685-010   BAG PRINTER (print. & pub.)
Tends rotary printing press that prints data, such as brand name, trademark, content analysis, and weight on paper or textile bags: Inserts specified type into plates or selects previously prepared plates, according to data to be printed on bags, and slides plates into channels or slots on cylinder. Turns setscrews or uses wrench to lock plates onto printing cylinder. Pours specified color ink into ink reservoir. Positions supply of bags on press feed bed. Presses button to start press and moves lever or depresses pedal to activate rotary drum and feed mechanism, and feeds individual bags into press. Removes printed bags from discharge shelf of press and stacks bags in storage area according to data printed on bags. Cleans press, using solvent and rags. May tend press that prints two or more colors.
GOE: 06.04.04 STRENGTH: M GED: R2 M2 L2 SVP: 4 DLU: 77

651.685-014   DESIGN PRINTER, BALLOON (rubber goods)
Tends cylinder press that prints designs and lettering on balloons: Rolls preinflated balloon against printing plate on revolving cylinder press that prints design. Pours ink and solvent in trough of cylinder press and adjusts ink flow. Cleans machine rollers, plates, and troughs with solvent and rag when color changes are specified. May inflate balloon on air nozzle, align and press one or more inked block dies against balloon, deflate balloon, and place balloon in box.
GOE: 06.04.07 STRENGTH: L GED: R2 M1 L1 SVP: 2 DLU: 77

651.685-018   OFFSET-PRESS OPERATOR II (print. & pub.) alternate titles: dial printer
Tends manually controlled offset press that prints lettering on products, such as dial faces and plastic containers: Rolls machine carriage, equipped with pair of clean and inked cylinders, back and forth over press bed to ink engraved

plates or dies and transfer impression to clean cylinder. Positions dial faces or containers in holders in front of engraved plates. Pulls carriage forward so that letters are impressed on clean cylinder and transferred to surface of product. Inspects product for smears, stains, uniform shading, and contrast. Places product on tray and places tray into oven to dry printing ink, or places product on conveyor leading to drying oven. Prints flexible containers on press equipped with airhose; forces air into container with hose to produce solid surface for printing. Periodically washes cylinders with solvent. Spreads ink on cleaned cylinder with spatula. May clean smears and spots from rejects with solvent and reprint them. May change ink, rollers, and die cut to print more than one color.
GOE: 06.04.09 STRENGTH: L GED: R2 M1 L1 SVP: 3 DLU: 77

651.685-022   PLATEN-PRESS FEEDER (print. & pub.)
Tends platen press that prints information onto material, such as paper or cloth, using either of following methods: (1) Places stack of paper in feed tray of automatic feeding mechanism, adjusting height of tray according to height of load. Adjusts guide bars and air pressure controls to regulate force of air in suction feed cups according to size and weigt of paper. Starts press and observes feeding operation. Removes printed sheets from discharge tray. (2) Places piece of cloth or paper against gauge pins on press platen while press head is in upper position. Removes and scans printed material for conformance to standards and inserts new piece after press head descends and returns to upper position. May ink rollers of machine, using putty knife. May be designated according to material printed as Cloth Printer (ordnance).
GOE: 06.04.09 STRENGTH: L GED: R2 M1 L1 SVP: 3 DLU: 77

651.685-026   ASSISTANT PRESS OPERATOR, OFFSET (print. & pub.) alternate titles: offset press operator helper; second press operator; web-press-operator helper, offset
Performs any combination of following tasks to assist OFFSET-PRESS OPERATOR (print. & pub.) I 651.382-042 to make ready, operate, and maintain sheet-fed or web offset printing press: Inserts packing sheets on plate cylinder to build up plate to printing height, fastens reinforcing bars to offset blankets, and installs plates and blankets on press cylinders, using handtools and power tools, to achieve pressure required for printing. Adjusts press machine parts, such as feeder and delivery mechanisms, suction grippers, guides, feed wheels, jogging device, tapes, and cams, as directed by OFFSET-PRESS OPERATOR (print. & pub.) I, using handtools. Positions skid of unprinted sheets on feed device of sheet-fed press, using handtruck or electric lift-truck, or lifts and positions roll of paper in feed mechanism of web press, using chain hoist. Fills ink and dampening solution fountains of press. Observes press operation to detect machine malfunctions and examines printed copy for ink density, position on paper, and registration, and adjusts press or notifies OFFSET-PRESS OPERATOR (print. & pub.) I when malfunction occurs. Removes loaded skid of printed material from stacking mechanism, using handtruck, and replaces loaded skid with empty skid. Assists OFFSET-PRESS OPERATOR (print. & pub.) I to remove and replace worn rollers and adjust pressure between rollers of press, using handtools. Washes press and cleans ink and ink distributing rollers and ink fountains, using ink solvent and cleaning mechanism on press. Keeps daily time, production, and material usage reports. May lead, give directions to, and monitor work of FEEDER (print. & pub.) 651.686-014; JOGGER (print. & pub.) 651.686-018; or ROLL TENDER (print. & pub.) 651.686-022.
GOE: 05.05.13 STRENGTH: M GED: R3 M2 L3 SVP: 7 DLU: 89

651.686-010   CYLINDER-PRESS FEEDER (print. & pub.) alternate titles: cylinder-press-operator helper; flat-bed-press feeder
Feeds blank or partly printed sheets into cylinder press by hand or stacks paper in automatic feeding device: Places pile of paper on feedboard of press and starts press. Lifts and feeds single sheets against feed guides at each rotation of cylinder to manually feed press; or turns setscrews to set side guide, suction feed grippers, and feeding wheels, and stacks paper in elevator of automatically fed press. Removes and stacks printed sheets from discharge board. May assist CYLINDER-PRESS OPERATOR (print. & pub.) in making press ready. May be designated according to type of cylinder press fed as Lithographic-Press Feeder (print. & pub.); Pony-Cylinder-Press Feeder (print. & pub.). May record production as indicated by counter on machine.
GOE: 05.12.19 STRENGTH: H GED: R2 M1 L1 SVP: 3 DLU: 77

651.686-014   FEEDER (print. & pub.)
Stacks sheets of paper into loading tray of sheet-fed offset press or preloading stand adjacent to press: Compares identifying information on paper stock with specifications on work order to verify delivery of specified paper stock. Flexes stack of paper with hands to prevent paper from jamming in press and places stack into loading tray of sheet-fed offset press or preloading stand adjacent to press. Adjusts feeder mechanism on press to correspond with size of paper. May operate mechanical truck to transport boxes of paper to press area. May fill ink fountains and clean press and press components to maintain press in working order.
GOE: 05.12.19 STRENGTH: H GED: R2 M1 L1 SVP: 3 DLU: 89

651.686-018   JOGGER (print. & pub.) alternate titles: press tender; stacker
Removes, flexes, jogs, and stacks printed sheets or folded signatures from discharge unit of web printing press: Removes folded signatures from web press and places signatures on pallet or skid for removal to other area. Removes printed sheets from automatic stacking mechanism of web press, flexes stack

of sheets between hands and taps stack into alignment, using hands and fingers, or places stack on vibrating jogging table and guides stack into precise alignment, and places stack on pallet or skid for removal. May adjust stacking mechanism on press according to paper dimensions. May load and remove rolls of paper on press. May operate mechanical truck to remove paper from press. May clean press and press components to maintain web printing press in working order.
GOE: 06.04.26 STRENGTH: H GED: R2 M1 L1 SVP: 2 DLU: 89

651.686-022 ROLL TENDER (print. & pub.) alternate titles: roll setter
Loads rolls of paper onto automatic splicing unit of web offset printing press: Inspects rolls of paper for blemishes or tears and cuts away damaged area with knife. Rolls paper into loading position on automatic splicer, inserts shaft of automatic splicer through roll core, secures holding chucks of automatic splicer to shaft ends, and threads paper through press components to prepare press for printing. Applies adhesive strip to backup roll and inserts backup roll onto automatic splicing unit of press to prepare paper for automatic splicing. Removes roll of leftover paper from press after automatic splicing. May operate mechanical truck to transport rolls of paper to press area. May clean press and clean and install press components to maintain press in working order.
GOE: 05.12.19 STRENGTH: V GED: R2 M1 L1 SVP: 5 DLU: 90

651.687-010 LITHOGRAPHED-PLATE INSPECTOR (tinware)
Inspects lithographed tinplate for defects, such as ink smears, air bubbles, crooked edges, or imperfect placement of designs. Segregates imperfect sheets and stacks them for further processing.
GOE: 06.03.02 STRENGTH: M GED: R1 M1 L1 SVP: 2 DLU: 77

652   PRINTING MACHINE OCCUPATIONS

This group includes occupations concerned with printing designs or lettering on surfaces of paper, wood, cardboard, or other materials by means of machines other than printing presses.

652.130-010 SUPERVISOR, DECORATING (glass mfg.)
Supervises and coordinates activities of workers engaged in silk-screening stenciled designs on glass or plastic containers or other glassware: Examines product design specifications to verify photographic transfer of design to silk screens, and to select type of machine to be used, silk screen material, coating material, and container style, using knowledge of production silk-screening techniques. Reviews coating tests results to verify color, taper, consistency, clarity, and absorption characteristics of selected coating material. Observes installation and adjustment of silk-screens, squeegees, and container-holding chucks to ensure setup and quality of product. Measures positioning of screens and holding chucks to ensure correct printing location on container. Inspects containers for quality and clarity of design and conformance to specifications. May create and lay out designs and photographically reproduce them on silk screen. May set and adjust drying furnace temperature and conveyor speed controls. May requisition supplies. Performs other duties described under SUPERVISOR (any industry) Master Title.
GOE: 01.06.03 STRENGTH: L GED: R4 M3 L3 SVP: 6 DLU: 77

652.130-014 SUPERVISOR, PRINTING AND STAMPING (jewelry-silver.; leather prod.)
Supervises and coordinates activities of workers engaged in gold stamping and ink printing of designs and identifying data on box linings, plastic boxes, or leather covered instrument and jewelry cases: Sets heat, pressure, and time controls on gold-leaf stamping machine, according to item and type of material to be stamped. Installs stamping dies in chase and locks chase in press. Selects spool of goldleaf or foil, places it on crib and threads it through rollers. Installs printing dies and spacers in platen presses. Installs and adjusts ink rollers to ensure even distribution of ink and fills fountain with specified ink. Adjusts presses during operation to maintain desired printing. Repairs equipment, using handtools. Operates automatic platen press to cut cardboard blanks for use as case linings. Performs other duties as described under SUPERVISOR (any industry) Master Title.
GOE: 06.02.01 STRENGTH: M GED: R4 M2 L3 SVP: 8 DLU: 77

652.130-018 SUPERVISOR, ROLLER PRINTING (textile)
Supervises and coordinates activities of workers engaged in roller-printing of cloth: Analyzes production schedule and work orders and confers with supervisor to determine amount and type of printing specified. Confers with department heads to coordinate printing activities with other departments. Examines setup of printing machines for *printing roller* and color changes to ensure conformity to specifications. Examines printed cloth swatches and compares with standard to determine if specifications are met. Observes work activity and production records to detect variation from standard procedure or lagging production. Directs workers to alter processing methods or sequence of production schedule to correct problems and ensure completion of work by deadlines. Performs other duties as described under SUPERVISOR (any industry) Master Title.
GOE: 06.02.01 STRENGTH: L GED: R4 M2 L3 SVP: 7 DLU: 77

652.132-010 SUPERVISOR, PRINT LINE (furniture) alternate titles: supervisor, engraving
Supervises and coordinates activities of workers engaged in finishing wood or wood composition panels with artificial wood grain print for use in furniture

manufacture: Assigns duties to workers at sanding, filling, coating, and printing stations of panel-printing and drying equipment, according to production priorities. Patrols work areas to detect faulty processing and directs workers to correct substandard products, utilizing knowledge of machine functions and processing standards. Assigns new workers to work with PRINT-LINE OPERATOR (furniture; wood prod., nec) 652.562-010 to learn job duties. Performs other duties as described under SUPERVISOR (any industry) Master Title.
GOE: 06.02.01 STRENGTH: M GED: R4 M3 L3 SVP: 7 DLU: 86

652.137-010 PRODUCTION MANAGER, REPRODUCTION (print. & pub.)
Supervises and coordinates activities of workers engaged in reproduction of special printed matter, such as maps and text books by methods such as offset, handset, or photostatic printing. Performs duties as described under SUPERVISOR (any industry) Master Title.
GOE: 05.10.05 STRENGTH: L GED: R4 M2 L3 SVP: 7 DLU: 77

652.137-014 SUPERVISOR, SCREEN PRINTING (textile)
Supervises and coordinates activities of workers engaged in screen printing cloth: Analyzes production schedules and print orders to determine type and quantity of work to be done, and availability of machinery and personnel. Schedules work according to established priorities. Confers with heads of other departments to ensure coordination of screen printing with activities, such as sample printing, production planning, screenmaking, color mixing, inspecting, and packaging. Analyzes problems encountered in screen printing multicolored patterns onto cloth, such as patterns out of register (alignment), colors offshade, and mechanical malfunctions, and directs workers to correct problems, utilizing knowledge of screen printing techniques. Performs other duties as described under SUPERVISOR (any industry) Master Title.
GOE: 06.02.01 STRENGTH: L GED: R4 M2 L3 SVP: 8 DLU: 77

652.260-010 SECTION LEADER, SCREEN PRINTING (textile) alternate titles: working second hand
Sets up and adjusts automatic screen printing machines for workers engaged in screen printing multicolored designs onto cloth articles: Confers with SUPERVISOR, SCREEN PRINTING (textile) to determine daily production schedule and transmits work instructions to other workers. Analyzes print order to determine settings and adjustments required to set up automatic screen printing machine for specified order. Turns thumbscrews, loosens and tightens bolts, and aligns printing screens, using handtools. Patrols printing area to detect problems, such as mechanical breakdowns or malfunctions, printout of register (alignment), and damaged screens. Adjusts belts, drive assemblies, pneumatic lifting mechanisms, and other machine parts to correct problems, or notifies supervisor of malfunction. Counts and records production in log.
GOE: 06.01.02 STRENGTH: M GED: R4 M2 L3 SVP: 7 DLU: 77

652.380-010 DECORATING-EQUIPMENT SETTER (glass mfg.; glass products)
Sets up manually controlled or automatic decorating equipment that prints designs on glass or plastic containers or ware according to either of following methods: Determines type and color of designs to print on containers from orders. (1) Pushes portable, manually controlled decorating equipment and roller conveyors into position for printing. Centers silk screen and squeegee attachment over container on decorating equipment, using gauge, and bolts screen to holding fixture. Examines containers for paint smears and position of design to determine if equipment needs adjusting. (2) Bolts chucks to conveyor of automatic decorating machine to accommodate containers of specified size. Turns setscrews and bends contacts on trip switches to adjust stroke of automatic decorating machine so designs are printed in designated locations on containers. Inspects decorating equipment, and replaces defective switches, pulleys, fixtures, screws, and bolts, using handtools, and sharpens squeegee blades, using *bench grinder.* May record types of quantities of containers decorated in production log. May mix paints according to formula, using bench mixer.
GOE: 06.01.02 STRENGTH: M GED: R3 M2 L2 SVP: 5 DLU: 77

652.382-010 CLOTH PRINTER (any industry) alternate titles: printer; printing-machine operator
Sets up and operates machine to print designs on materials, such as cloth, fiberglass, plastic sheeting, coated felt, or oilcloth: Turns handwheel to set pressure on *printing rollers,* according to specifications. Turns screws to align register marks on printing rollers with register marks on machine, using allen wrench. Sharpens doctor blade, using file and oilstone, and verifies evenness of blade, using straightedge. Aligns doctor blade against printing roller, using handtools. Dips color from tubs into color boxes to supply printing rollers. Scans cloth leaving machine for printing defects, such as smudges, variations in color shades, and designs that are out of register (alignment). Realigns printing rollers and adjusts position of blanket or back gray cloth to absorb excess color from printing rollers. Records yardage of cloth printed. Coordinates printing activities with activities of workers who feed and doff machine and aid in setting up and cleaning machine. May notify COLORIST (profess. & kin.) 022.161-014 when color shade varies from specifications. May mix own colors. May mount printing rollers on machine for change of pattern [PRINTING-ROLLER HANDLER (textile) 652.385-010]. May position knives specified distance from edge of plastic material to trim excess material from edges. When printing samples of new patterns and novelty designs, is designated Novelty-Printing-Machine Operator (textile) or Proofing-Machine Operator (print. & pub.). May set up and operate cloth printing machine utilizing caustic soda

paste instead of color paste to print designs on cloth which shrink to form plisse and be designated Plisse-Machine Operator (textile).
GOE: 06.02.09 STRENGTH: M GED: R4 M1 L3 SVP: 7 DLU: 77

652.385-010 PRINTING-ROLLER HANDLER (textile) alternate titles: copper-roller handler, printing; mandrel-press hand

Mounts *printing rollers* on cloth printing machine for change of pattern: Inserts mandrel through *printing shell* and positions shell on hydraulic jack, using hoist. Starts jack that presses mandrel into shell to assemble completed roller. Removes used rollers from printing machine and lifts new rollers into position with aid of other workers, using hoist. Removes printing shells from mandrel, using hydraulic jack. Moves used rollers to warehouse for cleaning and storage, using handtruck.
GOE: 06.04.05 STRENGTH: H GED: R2 M1 L1 SVP: 2 DLU: 77

652.462-010 RUBBER-PRINTING-MACHINE OPERATOR (rubber goods) alternate titles: leader, print rubber

Operates machine to print decorative designs on uncured rubber sheeting, used in making footwear: Computes required yardage of each design and type of sheeting compound from work ticket. Selects drum of stock to match order. Pushes A-frame, in which drum of stock is mounted above empty rewind drum, to stop in front of *printing roller* and attaches wheel-mounted motor to axle of rewind drum, using collar and wrench. Selects and installs printing roller engraved with specified design, using wrenches. Fills paint reservoir. Pulls sheeting from wrapper and threads end through rollers onto conveyor belt and attaches wrapper to core of rewind drum. Starts conveyor and rewind motor and observes sheeting for clarity of printing. Turns stopnuts and T-screws to adjust distance between paint transfer and printing rollers to print design clearly and without cutting into stock.
GOE: 06.02.09 STRENGTH: M GED: R3 M2 L1 SVP: 4 DLU: 77

652.567-010 CLOTH-PRINTING INSPECTOR (textile)

Examines cloth during printing process for defects, such as color smears, grease spots, and irregular color shade and register: Observes cloth for printing defects as it emerges from printing machines into handtrucks. Compares cloth patch cut from each truckload of printed cloth with standard to verify color shade and position of design. Reports substandard printing to CLOTH PRINTER (any industry). Records flaws found in each truckload of cloth and lot number on ticket attached to patch cut from fabric.
GOE: 06.03.02 STRENGTH: L GED: R3 M1 L1 SVP: 4 DLU: 77

652.582-010 MARKER (ordnance) alternate titles: gun numberer; piece marker, small arms

Operates presses to imprint serial and parts numbers, trademarks, and insignia on small arms parts: Locks dies in holder on die bed and positions parts, such as gun barrel, slide, receiver, or frame in holding fixture. Starts hydraulic ram, or turns handwheel to impress letter and number dies into surface of part. Stamps parts unsuited for press operations, using punch-dies and mallet. Examines impressions for accuracy and clarity and replaces worn dies. Changes dies after each imprinting when numbering in sequence. Records serial number, model, and caliber of gun for identification purposes. May inspect gun components for external defects.
GOE: 06.02.02 STRENGTH: M GED: R3 M1 L1 SVP: 4 DLU: 77

652.582-014 ROTARY-SCREEN-PRINTING-MACHINE OPERATOR (textile) alternate titles: roller printer

Operates rotary screen-printing machine to print designs on textiles: Mounts screen-printing rollers in specified sequence on machine. Turns knob to set machine speed and adjust pressure of rollers, according to type of design and cloth being printed. Turns valves that automatically admit printing paste into rollers. Starts machine and conveyor belt that carries textile articles under printing rollers. Inspects article being printed to detect colors out of register (alignment). Turns knob to adjust position of rollers so that each color is printed in allotted spaces in design. Removes foreign matter from rollers to prevent irregular flow of printing paste.
GOE: 06.02.06 STRENGTH: M GED: R3 M1 L1 SVP: 4 DLU: 77

652.585-010 PHOTOLETTERING-MACHINE OPERATOR (print. & pub.) alternate titles: typesetter

Tends photolettering machine that photographically prints display type and headings onto film or photographic paper: Secures roll of film or paper in machine magazine. Inserts specified film fonts in machine reel. Turns reel to specified selector mark to position letters to be printed and moves lever to expose specified letter on film or paper. Pushes cutter button to separate finished proofs from roll of film or paper. Removes finished copy from magazine for development.
GOE: 05.12.19 STRENGTH: L GED: R2 M1 L2 SVP: 4 DLU: 77

652.586-010 UTILITY WORKER, CLOTH PRINTING (textile)

Feeds cloth printing machine, off bears drying unit of cloth printing machine, or changes printing machine parts to assist workers engaged in roller printing of cloth, according to one of following methods: (1) Stops scray feed roller when feed roll of cloth is exhausted. Inserts metal rod through new roll of cloth, rolls cloth from dolly into brackets at feed end of printing machine, and clamps rod into brackets. Sews end of cloth from new roll to end of cloth in machine, using portable sewing machine. Restarts scray feed roller. (2) Stops printing machine dryer and ravels seam to separate full takeup cloth roll from cloth in machine. Tucks cloth corners into roll to prevent unwinding. Reads

automatic counter and records yardage on production ticket. Mounts empty takeup rod on machine, wraps end of cloth around rod, and restarts machine. (3) Assists BACK TENDER, CLOTH PRINTING (textile) 652.685-010; GREIGE-CLOTH TENDER, PRINTING (textile) 652.686-018; or PRINTING-ROLLER HANDLER (textile) 652.385-010 in removing and replacing *color boxes, doctors, printing rollers, sieve cloths,* and gears during color or style changeover, using handtools. Washes printing paste from parts, using water hose, solvent, and rags. (4) Pushes handtrucks loaded with rolls of cloth, printing paste, or machine parts to move materials between work stations.
GOE: 06.04.05 STRENGTH: H GED: R2 M1 L1 SVP: 2 DLU: 77

652.662-010 PRINTING-MACHINE OPERATOR, TAPE RULES (cutlery-hrdwr.)

Sets up and operates battery of machines that print graduations and numerals on steel measuring tapes: Wraps strip of rubber ink-blanket on impression wheel and secures strip ends in slots. Mounts printing dies on type-holding wheel, and turns screw clamp to tighten wrap-around wires. Mounts wheel on machine, using electric hoist. Lifts reel of steel tape onto machine spindle and threads tape through machine. Starts machine and observes printing process. Examines tape rule for defects in printing and compares it with master rule to verify its length and accuracy of graduations. Adjusts cams, using handtools, to print tapes of various lengths. Stops machine and notifies supervisor of printing defects.
GOE: 06.02.09 STRENGTH: M GED: R3 M2 L1 SVP: 5 DLU: 77

652.662-014 WALLPAPER PRINTER I (paper goods) alternate titles: surface printer

Sets up and operates machine to print colored patterns on wallpaper: Seats and locks print rollers for designated pattern in specified brackets on machine, using wrench: Threads wallpaper through machine. Turns adjustment screws on drive gears to position print rollers. Adjusts scraper bar and tension on *sieve cloths* with handtool to control quantity and distribution of color solution on wallpaper. Starts machine and observes printed wallpaper for defects, such as color splashes, smears, and misalignment of printed designs.
GOE: 06.02.04 STRENGTH: M GED: R3 M1 L1 SVP: 6 DLU: 77

652.662-018 PRINT-LINE OPERATOR (furniture; wood prod., nec) alternate titles: hardboard panel printer; print-line supervisor

Operates tandem print-line machine to smooth, paint, and print wood grain designs on surface of furniture, composition-wood dimensional panels, or hardboard panels: Confers with supervisor or reads production schedule to determine panels to be processed. Selects printing cylinders according to production schedule and installs cylinders on machine, using hoist and handtools. Gives directions to workers engaged in feeding, inspecting, and removing panels to ensure that sanding, painting, and printing of panels conforms to specifications. Fills reservoir of printing unit with ink or stain. Tests viscosity of paint in painting unit by timing flow of paint through porous container, using watch. Pushes buttons to start individual units, and observes units to detect malfunctions. Turns knobs and handles or pushes buttons to adjust sanding, painting, and printing of panel surfaces. Occasionally assists maintenance personnel in disassembly and reassembly of individual units. Maintains record of ink and paint used. May blend stains to obtain color and viscosity specified by job order. May add catalyst or solvent to paint, utilizing experience, to achieve specified viscosity of paint.
GOE: 06.02.18 STRENGTH: M GED: R3 M2 L2 SVP: 5 DLU: 81

652.665-014 STRICKLER ATTENDANT (fabrication, nec) alternate titles: color-depositing-machine tender

Tends series of color-depositing machines that deposit and brush color mix through stencils to produce patterns on hard-surface floor covering: Observes machines to ensure required laying-on, brushing, and scraping operations in each unit. Signals other worker to stop machines, and adjusts and oils blades, scrapers, and brushes in malfunctioning unit, using handtools and oilcan. Removes mix adhering to plate and cleans out clogged stencils, using brush and scraper. Installs and adjusts stencils for pattern changes. Signals workers to dump colors into machine, according to pattern formula sheet.
GOE: 06.02.09 STRENGTH: L GED: R3 M1 L1 SVP: 4 DLU: 77

652.682-010 BOX PRINTER (any industry) alternate titles: box labeler; box-printing-machine operator; carton-lettering-machine operator; sleeve machine operator

Sets up and operates machine to print trademarks, designs, or identifying data on containers such as cardboard or wooden boxes, performing any combination of following duties: Selects printing plate or type slug, or sets type, according to oral instructions or written job order. Fastens type or printing plate in holding mechanism of machine, using handtools. Fills fountains with ink of required color or colors and adjusts rate of flow of ink with finger screws, or squeezes or spreads ink paste on ink plate or rollers, using ink knife (spatula). Turns setscrews to adjust spacing guides. Feeds or stacks boxes or container pieces in feed hopper of automatic printing machine and removes them from discharge hopper after printing. Places box ends on holding plate and depresses pedal that lowers printing plate onto box end. Scans containers to verify accuracy and clarity of printing. Observes edges of wooden box parts for imperfections, such as split, ragged, or uneven edges, and sets them aside. Removes and cleans type or plate, and ink rollers, using handtools, solvent, and rags. May distribute containers to packaging stations or place containers in storage areas.
GOE: 06.02.09 STRENGTH: L GED: R3 M1 L2 SVP: 3 DLU: 87

652.682-014   EMBOSSOGRAPH OPERATOR (any industry)

Operates press to print embossed display signs: Selects type dies and arranges them on bed of press. Places gummed paper on type, gummed side up, and positions cardboard sign stock on paper. Pulls lever to close press and stamp gummed paper letters into cardboard. Removes sign from press, discards scrap, and touches letters with flatiron to make gummed paper adhere to cardboard. Trims finished sign on papercutter.
GOE: 06.02.09 STRENGTH: L GED: R3 M1 L2 SVP: 4 DLU: 77

652.682-018   SCREEN-PRINTING-MACHINE OPERATOR (textile) alternate titles: automatic-silk-screen printer

Operates automatic screen-printing machine to print multicolor designs on textiles: Mounts screens in specified sequence on machine. Pours printing paste onto screens or fills automatic feed pan. Turns knob to set machine speed and adjusts swing and pressure of squeegees, using handtools, according to type of design and cloth being printed. Starts machine and conveyor belt that carries textile articles under screens. Inspects articles being printed to detect colors out of register (alignment). Turns screws to adjust position of screens so that each color is printed in alloted spaces in design. Removes foreign matter from screens to prevent irregular flow of printing paste. Tapes holes in coated portion of screen if leak develops.
GOE: 06.02.09 STRENGTH: L GED: R3 M1 L1 SVP: 4 DLU: 77

652.682-022   STAMPER, MACHINE (pottery & porc.)

Sets up and operates machine to stamp designs on pottery and porcelain flatware: Clamps ware mold in machine. Observes gauges and moves levers to adjust machine pressure, according to size of ware and pattern to be stamped on ware. Aligns design stamp on bed or head of machine and adjusts guide bars. Stirs premixed ink on pallet and applies ink on stamp with inking pad or fills reservoir of mechanical inking device with color glaze. Positions and clamps ware in head of press, places ware in holding device of stamp fixture, or positions ware over vacuum holding device on bed of press. Positions stamp for transferring design onto ware, using guide bars. Depresses pedal to lower head of press and stamp design on ware. Removes ware from bed of machine. Inspects design and discards ware with defective printing. Rubs ware with abrasive stone to remove ink spots or excess glaze.
GOE: 06.02.08 STRENGTH: L GED: R3 M1 L1 SVP: 4 DLU: 77

652.682-026   STRIPING-MACHINE OPERATOR (nonfer. metal)

Sets up and operates striping machine to ink multicolored identification stripes on insulated wire according to specifications: Installs striping wheels in inking head and fills ink reservoirs. Adjusts footage counter and ink timer. Clamps wire spool on payoff spindle and threads wire around capstan, through inking head, and onto takeup spindle and starts machine. Inspects striped cable for defects and turns setscrews to adjust pressure of striping wheels. Mixes inks in power mixer, following formula, to obtain specified color shades. May thread wire through electric oven to dry ink.
GOE: 06.02.09 STRENGTH: L GED: R3 M1 L1 SVP: 3 DLU: 77

652.682-030   STAMPING-PRESS OPERATOR (any industry) alternate titles: gold-leaf printer; gold marker; gold stamper; hot stamper; leaf stamper; lettering-machine operator; stamper

Operates machine to emboss and imprint designs, lettering, numbers, or product information onto surfaces of material, such as paper, cloth, leather, or plastic, using foil, gold-leaf, coated ribbon, or plastic tape, following specifications: Receives verbal instructions, reads work order sheet, or inserts disk in drive of computer and depresses keys to retrieve job order slip with printing instructions on computer screen. Sets heat, pressure, and time controls, according to material to be stamped. Installs and locks character wheel, embossing die, or stamping die in heated chase of machine. Turns on heating element. Inserts reel of specified material, such as foil, gold-leaf, coated ribbon, or plastic tape in holder or on spindle, and threads end through rollers which feed and guide material under die mounted on ram of machine or places sheet of foil over impression. Positions and aligns workpiece under holding arm in bed of hand fed machine or feed hopper of automatically fed machine in position specified on work order or in illuminated window on computerized machine. Starts machine which lowers ram to heated die or character wheel and ribbon to emboss and imprint workpiece and automatically moves coated ribbon with each stroke of machine. May operate machine to imprint trade names, brand, and grade onto leather sweatbands and be designated Sweatband Printer (hat & cap). When printing titles and designs on book covers, is designated Embosser (print. & pub.). When imprinting identifying information on battery lids or encasements, is designated Embossing-Press Operator (elec. equip.).
GOE: 06.04.09 STRENGTH: L GED: R2 M1 L1 SVP: 3 DLU: 89

652.685-010   BACK TENDER, CLOTH PRINTING (textile)

Tends machine that prints designs on textile fabrics: Pushes cloth roll from handtruck onto rack at back of machine. Sews end of cloth to end of preceding roll, using sewing machine. Starts feed rollers and observes cloth as cloth unwinds into scray to detect cloth pieces sewn into roll face down. Ravels seams, turns face of cloth up, and resews cloth ends. Turns setscrews to adjust width guides and tension devices. Ladles color from buckets into color boxes or turns valve to transfer color from tubs to color boxes. Sews new length of back gray cloth to length in machine. When blanket is used, scoops talcum into hopper where blanket is dusted after passing through washbox. Removes color boxes and doctors and washes *printing rollers,* using brush and water hose, to prevent damage to rollers when printing stops. Assists PRINTING-ROLLER HAN-

DLER (textile) 652.385-010 or GRAY-CLOTH TENDER, PRINTING (textile) 652.686-018 in removing and replacing color boxes, doctors, printing rollers, and gears when changing pattern.
GOE: 06.04.05 STRENGTH: H GED: R2 M1 L1 SVP: 2 DLU: 77

652.685-014   BINDING PRINTER (textile)

Tends machine that prints identifying information on bias binding: Slides rolls of binding on dispenser rod and secures rod into brackets of machine. Fills reservoir of printing machine with ink and inserts presser roller in brackets above *printing roller.* Threads ends of binding from rod over suction guides, between presser and printing rollers and over top guides to takeup rod. Flips switch to start machine that prints identifying data on binding and winds printed binding on takeup rod. Observes printing to detect defects, such as smudges and ink streaks on binding. Cuts smeared binding from roll and staples rolls to prevent unwinding. Slides printed rolls from takeup rod and loads rolls on truck for transporting to drying oven. Loads binding on racks of drying oven and sets automatic timer and temperature control to dry binding. Packs binding in cartons and seals and bands carton, using strapping tool. Writes identifying information on label and attaches label to cartons. Moves cartons of binding to storage area, using handtruck.
GOE: 06.04.05 STRENGTH: M GED: R2 M1 L1 SVP: 2 DLU: 77

652.685-018   CARTON MARKER, MACHINE (boot & shoe; garment) alternate titles: box marker; box stamper, machine; carton stamper

Tends marking machine that prints shoe and garment size, lot, and style numbers on boxes: Positions marking dies by moving fingers (levers) on disk of machine. Removes box cover and places base of box over platen. Depresses pedal or moves lever to lower dies onto end of box and print identifying symbols. May label boxes.
GOE: 06.04.37 STRENGTH: M GED: R2 M1 L1 SVP: 2 DLU: 77

652.685-022   CUTTING-AND-PRINTING-MACHINE OPERATOR (tex. prod., nec) alternate titles: printer

Tends machine that cuts cloth into specified lengths, prints information, such as brand name, contents, and weight on lengths, and folds lengths for use in making bags: Turns dial to specified length number or changes gears with wrench to obtain specified length of cut. Fits crimped edges of printing plate over rods on printing cylinder of machine and tightens setscrews to secure plate to cylinder. Sews end of new cloth roll to end of cloth in machine, using portable sewing machine. Fills ink fountain and starts machine. Verifies location of information on bag length by comparing printed length with order sample. May place folded cloth pieces onto handtruck for removal to sewing department.
GOE: 06.04.05 STRENGTH: H GED: R3 M2 L1 SVP: 3 DLU: 77

652.685-026   DECORATING-MACHINE OPERATOR (glass products)

Tends automatic ceramic-decorating machine that prints single or multicolored pictures or designs on cylindrical glass or plastic containers: Positions precut stainless steel stencils in machine and adjusts roller guides that hold container in place during printing process. Pours premixed paint into ink reservoir. Turns valves to regulate temperature of paint and to regulate flow of paint onto stencil. Smooths paint onto stencil, using flat-bladed knife. Empties cartons of containers onto conveyor that feeds them into machine automatically. Starts machine that rotates container under stencil and ejects printed containers on moving conveyor. Inspects printed containers to ensure that printing is clear and free of smudges.
GOE: 06.04.09 STRENGTH: L GED: R3 M1 L1 SVP: 3 DLU: 77

652.685-034   GLOVE PRINTER (glove & mit.)

Tends printing machine that prints information, such as slogans and trademarks, on gloves: Inserts specified preset type in bar holder of type case, or fits rubber plates over type case. Spreads ink on inking roller, using putty knife. Positions glove or mitten on bed of machine or on conveyor, following markings or guides. Removes printed gloves. Examines printing to detect ink smears and pairs gloves according to quality of printing.
GOE: 06.04.37 STRENGTH: L GED: R2 M1 L1 SVP: 3 DLU: 77

652.685-038   INK PRINTER (jewelry-silver.; leather prod.; plastic prod.)

Tends platen-press that prints designs and identifying data on leather, leatherette, or satin-covered jewelry, watch and instrument cases, and case linings. Cleans and lubricates press.
GOE: 06.04.37 STRENGTH: S GED: R2 M1 L2 SVP: 2 DLU: 77

652.685-042   KEYING-MACHINE OPERATOR (print. & pub.)

Tends keying machine that prints coded data on paper stock used to promote sale of magazines: Ascertains stock and code information to be used. Removes printing head from keying machine, inserts specified type in holder, and replaces head. Adjusts machine for size of stock and loads stock in paper guides on machine table. Starts machine that automatically prints code, and observes operation to determine whether print is legible. Removes processed stock from machine.
GOE: 06.04.37 STRENGTH: L GED: R2 M1 L1 SVP: 2 DLU: 77

652.685-046   MARKING-MACHINE OPERATOR (textile)

Tends machine that prints trademark on back of cloth: Pours printing ink and water into mixing can in proportions specified for cloth style. Starts pump to circulate ink between mixing can and trough under pickup roll. Positions truck of cloth at front of machine and starts cloth feeding over printing roll. Exam-

ines cloth to detect penetration of ink to face of cloth. Turns handwheel to adjust pressure roll that controls amount of ink applied to fabric. Doffs trucks of marked cloth at *swing-folding attachment.*
GOE: 06.04.05 STRENGTH: L GED: R2 M1 L2 SVP: 2 DLU: 77

652.685-050 MARKING-MACHINE OPERATOR (knitting; tex. prod., nec)
Tends machine that prints identifying information, such as brand names, size, and style onto such products as hosiery, knitted garments, or towels: Reads work order to determine color of ink to use and information to print. Pushes lever to move specified stamp keys into position, attaches rubber typing plate to type holder and inserts type holder into slots of printing head, or inserts slugs in chase of printing plate and turns setscrew to lock printing plate in machine. Spreads ink paste on ink roller of machine or clamps tube of ink in automatic ink dispenser. Places article on bed of machine under printing head. Depresses pedal or flips switch to start machine that transfers printed information from inked plate onto article. Stacks printed article onto worktable. Cleans machine, type slugs, type plate and holder, ink plate and rollers, using cleaning solution, cloth, brush, and airhose. May erase misprints, using tissue paper and ink eradicator.
GOE: 06.04.37 STRENGTH: L GED: R2 M1 L1 SVP: 2 DLU: 77

652.685-054 NAME-PLATE STAMPER (any industry)
Tends machine that stamps or embosses identifying data on nameplates for manufactured products, using one of following methods: (1) Assembles dies or aligns type in die block, using setscrews. Positions die block on press bed, lowers ram with handwheel, and feeds blank plates into powered machine or pulls lever to imprint data on blank. (2) Turns wheel to specified character and pulls lever to stamp character on blank. Repeats operation for each character until specified information is embossed on plate. May place nameplate in hinged forming block and close block manually to shape plate to specified curvature.
GOE: 06.04.37 STRENGTH: L GED: R2 M1 L1 SVP: 2 DLU: 77

652.685-058 PRESS FEEDER (tinware)
Tends automatic feeder on press that lithographs tinplate: Cuts bands from pallet load of tinplate, using cutters. Verifies load ticket against production schedule to ensure that specified tinplate is used. Pushes load from roller platform onto feeding hoist. Moves lever to raise load between guides to feeding position. Turns cranks to adjust feeder guides to accommodate size of plate. Observes feeding operation and stops feeder mechanism to remove defective plates. Mixes inks and washes press.
GOE: 06.04.02 STRENGTH: M GED: R2 M1 L1 SVP: 3 DLU: 77

652.685-062 PRINTER (pen & pencil)
Tends machine that prints trademarks, advertisements, and designs on parts of marking devices, such as pens, wooden and mechanical pencils, or felt or fiber tipped markers: Positions and aligns specified printing dies or type in machine head. Places parts, such as casings or caps, in machine hopper or holding device. Presses switch or depresses pedal to start machine that prints characters or designs on parts. Removes parts from machine conveyor or holding device. Inspects printed characters or designs and compares with written specifications. Places parts on rack for drying. May push rack into drying compartment. May pour ink into machine reservoir. May tend machine that prints trademark, size, and code number on ballpoint pen refills.
GOE: 06.04.37 STRENGTH: L GED: R2 M1 L1 SVP: 3 DLU: 77

652.685-066 PRINTER, FLOOR COVERING (fabrication, nec)
Tends machine that automatically prints colors and designs on felt-base floor covering: Places felt paper rolls on machine spindles, using chain hoist. Installs specified printing blocks on presses, using handtools. Pours specified preweighed paint colors into machine troughs. Threads felt paper through rollers and starts machine. Observes felt paper strip passing under paint-filled troughs from which printing blocks are automatically lowered to print pattern onto felt paper.
GOE: 06.04.04 STRENGTH: L GED: R2 M1 L1 SVP: 3 DLU: 77

652.685-070 PRINTER, MACHINE (hat & cap)
Tends machine that prints decorative designs on harvest hats (strawhats) in hat manufacturing establishment: Places specified *printing roller* in machine holding device and turns setscrew to align roller and machine register marks. Pours specified paint into machine reservoirs. Pushes button or pulls lever to start machine. Removes hat from rack and places hat on machine ram. Depresses pedal to raise hat against printing rollers to print design on hat. Releases pedal to lower machine ram and removes hat. Observes printed design for imperfections and places hat on rack to dry or auto oven conveyor.
GOE: 06.04.09 STRENGTH: L GED: R2 M1 L1 SVP: 3 DLU: 77

652.685-074 PRINTING-MACHINE OPERATOR, FOLDING RULES (cutlery-hrdwr.)
Tends machine that prints graduations and numerals on enameled wooden slats used in folding rules, and automatically inserts printed slats in drying racks: Stacks blank slats in magazine of printing machine. Positions empty racks in feed magazine of slat-inserting mechanism. Starts machine and observes printing and racking processes. Examines printed slats for printing defects, and compares them with master rule to verify accuracy of graduations. Stops machine and clears jams in feeding mechanisms, using screwdriver. Replaces broken shearpins, using fingers. Lifts racks of printed slats from machine to handtruck.

GOE: 06.04.03 STRENGTH: L GED: R2 M1 L1 SVP: 2 DLU: 77

652.685-078 ROLLER OPERATOR (toy-sport equip.)
Tends roller-printing machine that colors embossed letters or designs on wooden blocks for games, such as dominoes and anagrams: Adjusts height of machine roller to accommodate block. Positions blocks in racks, and places racks on conveyor belt that feeds them into machine for coloring. Removes blocks from conveyor and stacks them for drying.
GOE: 06.04.21 STRENGTH: L GED: R2 M1 L1 SVP: 2 DLU: 77

652.685-082 STAMPER II (tex. prod., nec)
Tends machine that stencils design onto cloth as outline for tufting: Staples stencil (raised pattern) around stencil cylinder. Lays marking bar (colored paraffin) in holder. Mounts roll of cloth on machine brackets, threads cloth between stencil and marking bar, and laps cloth around takeup roller. Places weights on marking bar to hold bar against cloth. Starts machine that draws cloth between stencil and marking bar, transferring design in paraffin to cloth. Doffs rolls of stenciled cloth from delivery end of machine.
GOE: 06.04.05 STRENGTH: M GED: R2 M1 L1 SVP: 2 DLU: 77

652.685-086 STENCIL-MACHINE OPERATOR (textile)
Tends machine that brushes designs into wet pile of pile fabric: Inserts metal rod through cloth roll and lifts roll into feeding position. Threads cloth over tension rod, between stencil roller with raised design and brushing rollers, and laps around takeup roll, or sews end of cloth roll to cloth in machine, using portable sewing machine. Starts machine, and straightens cloth with hands to remove wrinkles as cloth enters machine. Pushes lever to disengage winding shaft and doffs rolls of stenciled cloth onto handtruck.
GOE: 06.04.06 STRENGTH: M GED: R2 M1 L1 SVP: 3 DLU: 77

652.685-090 STRIKE-OFF-MACHINE OPERATOR (textile) alternate titles: roll tester
Tends strike-off machine that prints cloth with samples of color paste for comparison with color standards prior to production printing: Tapes piece of white cloth on printing drum. Places moist cloth pads between engraved strikes (depressions) on *printing roller* to separate colors being printed. Pours color sample on engraved strikes of roller. Starts strike-off machine to print impression on cloth. Removes printed sample from machine and places cloth in steam press to dry or places cloth in aging machine to develop and fix color. Trims sample, using scissors. Marks identification number on sample and records sample identification data. Washes strike-off roller and doctor, using brush or rag and water. May tend single-roller printing machine that prints cloth samples for use by laboratory.
GOE: 06.04.05 STRENGTH: L GED: R2 M1 L1 SVP: 3 DLU: 77

652.685-094 TICKET PRINTER AND TAGGER (garment)
Tends machine that automatically prints identifying information, such as size, style, and lot number, on tickets, and sews, glues, heat seals, or staples tickets to garments or garment parts: Selects and positions specified type in chase attachment and inserts attachment in machine. Turns knobs to set stationary type or numerical counter of machine in starting position. Places roll of tickets on holder and inserts end of roll into feeding device. Places spool of thread or wire on holder and threads it through machine. Places garment or garment part on machine bed and under needle or stapling device. Pushes lever to start machine that automatically feeds tickets under stamping head, prints information on tickets, and cuts and sews, glues, heat seals, or staples ticket to garment or garment part. May tend machine that prints identifying information on tags or tickets [TICKETER (any industry)]. May be designated according to product labeled as Glove Tagger (glove & mit.).
GOE: 06.04.37 STRENGTH: L GED: R2 M1 L1 SVP: 2 DLU: 77

652.685-098 TICKETER (any industry) alternate titles: label stamper; ticket maker; ticket printer
Tends machine that prints information, such as price, size, style, or color, on identification tags or labeling material: Selects type, according to specifications, and inserts type into machine, using tweezers, or turns dial on machine to move type into printing position. Mounts roll of tags or labeling material on machine brackets and threads end of roll through feeding device. Applies liquid or paste ink to printing rollers or printing pad on machine, using applicator. Flips switch or depresses pedal to start machine that automatically prints information on tags or material. Observes printed tags or material during startup for defects, such as crooked lines, blurred print, or off-centered printing, and turns knobs or repositions printing plate, using handtools, to adjust machine. Removes printed material from delivery end of machine. May turn crank to print information on tags or material. May cut individual labels or tags from rolls of material, using scissors. May tend machine equipped with automatic cutter and counting control that stops machine when specified number of tickets have been printed. May tend machine that threads string through holes in tags or labels [STRINGING-MACHINE OPERATOR (paper goods) 649.685-054]. May tend machine that prints identifying information on tags or tickets and sews tickets to garments or garment parts [TICKET PRINTER AND TAGGER (garment) 652.685-094]. May tend machine that automatically prints identifying information on ticket and pins ticket to articles and be designated Pin-Ticket-Machine Operator (any industry).
GOE: 06.04.37 STRENGTH: L GED: R2 M1 L2 SVP: 3 DLU: 81

652.685-102 WAD-PRINTING-MACHINE OPERATOR (ordnance)
Tends automatic machines that print identifying data on top wad used in shotgun shells: Fills ink reservoir. Selects printing rollers or die set according

to work order and installs them in machine, using handtools. Scoops blank wads from supply trough onto grooved board and shakes board to arrange wads in grooves. Tilts board and slides stacks of wads from grooves into feed tubes. Sets feed tube in machine or fills hopper with blank wads, using scoop. Starts machine and examines wads for clarity of printing. Cleans type, using brush and solvent, or replaces worn dies to obtain clear impression. Weighs containers of printed wads and records amount of each type printed. Loads feed tubes with printed wads, using shaker board, for use in shell-loading machines.
GOE: 06.04.37 STRENGTH: L GED: R2 M1 L1 SVP: 2 DLU: 77

652.685-106   TYPE-PROOF REPRODUCER (machinery mfg.)
Tends phototypesetting machine and photo processor that print and develop proof of phototypesetting type disk in disk manufacturing establishment: Selects roll of programmed tape from file, secures roll onto reel of phototypesetting machine, and threads tape through machine rollers and into reader to prepare machine for automatic operation. Cleans dust and lint from disk and places disk in phototypesetting machine. Depresses keys to enter command codes for projection of type images from type disk onto film cassette in photo unit of machine and onto screen of cathode ray tube. Scans images on screen to detect type defects and notifies SUPERVISOR, TYPE-DISK QUALITY CONTROL (machinery mfg.) 979.137-026 of irregularities. Removes film cassette from machine, places cassette on receiving platform of photo processor, and depresses switch to begin developing cycle. Depresses switch to stop machine when runoff (proofsheet) emerges. Removes disk from phototypesetting machine, and places disk and runoff in specified storage area.
GOE: 05.10.05 STRENGTH: L GED: R2 M1 L2 SVP: 2 DLU: 86

652.685-110   SYMBOL STAMPER, SEMICONDUCTOR PACKAGES (electron. comp.) alternate titles: marker
Tends automatic printing machine that prints identifying symbols and numbers on semiconductor packages: Refills ink or paint reservoir. Inserts printing plate or type block in printing machine. Places semiconductor package on holding fixture in printing machine or places tube containing semiconductor packages in loading device of automatic printing machine. Flips switch or depresses pedal to print symbols and numbers on semiconductor circuit packages. Visually inspects package markings to identify misprints. Cleans and reprints packages, using cleaning solution and cotton swabs. Places printed semiconductor packages in trays. May set type on type block, using tweezers. May place printed packages in oven to dry or set ink.
GOE: 06.04.09 STRENGTH: L GED: R2 M1 L2 SVP: 2 DLU: 86

652.686-010   CLOTH-PRINTER HELPER (any industry)
Feeds and off bears machine that prints cloth: Pushes roll of cloth from handtruck onto rack at back of scray. Sews end of cloth roll to preceding cut of cloth, using sewing machine. Starts feeding rollers that unwind cloth into scray. Positions handtruck beneath *swing-folding attachment* and packs cloth into truck with hands. Tears cloth or ravels seam when truck is filled. May feed and off bear cloth printing machine that utilizes caustic soda instead of color paste to shrink cloth to form plisse and be designated Plisse-Machine Operator Helper (textile).
GOE: 06.04.05 STRENGTH: M GED: R2 M1 L1 SVP: 2 DLU: 77

652.686-014   GRAINER, MACHINE (any industry)
Feeds metal or simulated wood panels, sheets, or strips into machine that prints lines resembling natural wood grain. Holds or moves irregularly shaped pieces against printing roller to impart grainlike appearance. Stacks grained pieces for further processing or assembly into articles, such as television cabinets, automobile dashboards, and office furniture.
GOE: 06.04.02 STRENGTH: M GED: R2 M1 L1 SVP: 2 DLU: 77

652.686-018   GRAY-CLOTH TENDER, PRINTING (textile) alternate titles: gray tender
Feeds back gray cloth into cloth printing machine, and removes printed cloth from delivery end of machine: Trucks rolls of back gray cloth to printing machine, removes burlap wrapping, and sews end of cloth to preceding roll, using sewing machine. Starts feeding rollers that unwind back gray cloth into scray. Positions handtruck beneath *swing-folding attachment* and scans cloth for printing flaws as cloth is folded into truck. Notifies CLOTH PRINTER (any industry) 652.382-010 as flaws occur. Marks lot number on end of each truck of cloth, ravels connecting seam, and replaces full truck with empty truck. Tears sample from each lot of cloth. Assists PRINTING-ROLLER HANDLER (textile) 652.385-010 or BACK TENDER, CLOTH PRINTING (textile) 652.685-010 in removing and replacing color boxes, doctors, *printing rollers*, and gears when changing pattern, and in mounting feedrolls of cloth on printing machine. May truck soiled cloth to BACK-GRAY-CLOTH WASHER (textile) 582.685-030.
GOE: 06.04.05 STRENGTH: H GED: R2 M1 L1 SVP: 2 DLU: 77

652.686-022   LOADER-UNLOADER, SCREEN-PRINTING MACHINE (textile)
Feeds or off bears automatic screen-printing machine that prints designs on textile products, such as towels, sheets, and pillowcases: Positions articles on conveyor belt of machine, following marks on conveyor. Removes printed articles from conveyor at discharge end of machine and places articles over wire, on racks, or on perforated conveyor belt that carries articles through drier. Cleans printing screens, using solvent, water, and rags.
GOE: 06.04.05 STRENGTH: L GED: R2 M1 L1 SVP: 2 DLU: 77

652.686-026   PRINT-LINE FEEDER (furniture)
Feeds furniture composition-wood dimensional panels onto feed conveyor of tandem print-line machines that automatically smooth, paint, and print wood

grain designs on top surfaces of panels: Removes panels, with previously inserted filler blocks, from handtruck and positions panel on feed conveyor so that smooth surface of panel is up and filler blocks support underside of panel.
GOE: 06.04.03 STRENGTH: M GED: R1 M1 L1 SVP: 1 DLU: 77

652.686-030   PRINT-LINE TAILER (furniture)
Removes dimensional furniture panels from discharge conveyor of print-line machines that smooth, paint, and print wood grain designs on top surfaces of panels: Pushes panels along roller conveyor from inspection point to off bearing area and removes panels from conveyor. Scans panels for inspector's marks and stacks defective panels aside. Stacks nondefective panels on handtruck, inserting paper sheets between panels to protect printed surfaces from abrasions.
GOE: 06.04.03 STRENGTH: M GED: R1 M1 L1 SVP: 1 DLU: 77

652.686-034   RAISED PRINTER (print. & pub.) alternate titles: thermograph operator
Feeds cards and stationery (received while ink is still wet after printing) into machine that dusts them with powder that adheres to ink. Feeds dusted stationery through baking equipment to fuse together particles of powder and produce raised effect resembling steel-die or copperplate engraving.
GOE: 06.04.21 STRENGTH: L GED: R1 M1 L1 SVP: 2 DLU: 77

652.686-038   SCREEN-PRINTING-MACHINE-OPERATOR   HELPER (textile)
Performs variety of duties to assist automatic screen-printing machine operator in printing multicolored patterns on textiles: Turns thumbscrews and loosens and tighens bolts, using wrench, to remove, replace, adjust, or align screens in bed of screen printing machine as instructed by machine operator. Pushes new roll of cloth into feed brackets and aligns end of new cloth with end of cloth in machine and sews ends together, using portable sewing machine. Carries stacks of cloth articles, such as towels, washcloths, and bathmats from storage boxes, and stacks articles on shelf for use by workers feeding machine that prints precut cloth articles. Observes operation of printing machine to detect flaws in printing, such as blurs, smears, and color out of register (alignment), and reports problem detected to machine operator. Pours printing paste onto screen as required. Loads and unloads handtrucks, and trucks printing screens and drums of printing paste to and from storage areas.
GOE: 06.02.06 STRENGTH: M GED: R2 M1 L1 SVP: 2 DLU: 77

652.686-042   TOWEL INSPECTOR (textile)
Inspects screen-printed towels for imperfections in print and weave: Pulls or lifts towels from drying rack on conveyor belt emerging from drier. Examines towels for print defects, such as off color, smears, inadequate color penetration, or mismatched pattern, and mill defects, such as picks, tears, broken warp or filling, or soil. Places towels of less than first quality aside and counts and places first quality towels onto wheeled cart or into shipping container. Marks style, quality and quantity on shipping label and attaches label to container, using glue and brush. Carries second quality towels to collection area. Keeps daily time and production reports and submits reports to supervisor.
GOE: 06.03.02 STRENGTH: L GED: R2 M1 L2 SVP: 3 DLU: 77

652.686-046   WARE SERVER (glass mfg.)
Feeds glass containers onto conveyor of machine that prints (stencils) trademarks or labels on them.
GOE: 06.04.37 STRENGTH: M GED: R1 M1 L1 SVP: 2 DLU: 77

652.687-010   CLOTH SPREADER, SCREEN PRINTING (textile)
Spreads cloth on tables in preparation for screen printing and removes cloth from table after printing: Places roll of cloth on unrolling device and pushes cloth along table to unwind it, following markings on table. Pins ends of cloth to table and smooths out wrinkles. Presses cloth against gummed tabletop or pins selvages of cloth to table to prevent slipping. Slides rods under printed cloth and raises it to drying rack. Winds dry cloth onto tube, using handcrank or motor-driven winder.
GOE: 06.04.27 STRENGTH: M GED: R1 M1 L1 SVP: 3 DLU: 77

652.687-014   COLOR DIPPER (textile)
Refills *color boxes* on cloth-printing machine with specified colors, using hand dipper. Typically services machines printing eight to fifteen colors.
GOE: 06.04.16 STRENGTH: M GED: R2 M1 L1 SVP: 2 DLU: 77

652.687-018   FILLER-BLOCK INSERTER-REMOVER (furniture)
Inserts filler (support) blocks into recessed areas on underside of dimensional composition-wood furniture panels to ensure uniform sanding, painting, and printing of wood grain as panels are conveyed through tandem print-line machines, or removes blocks from underside of panels subsequent to processing on print-line machines and pushes panel to PRINT-LINE INSPECTOR (furniture).
GOE: 06.04.25 STRENGTH: M GED: R1 M1 L1 SVP: 1 DLU: 77

652.687-022   PAINT POURER (fabrication, nec)
Pours paint in carriage of machine that prints colors and designs on linoleum rugs. May mix paint to attain required color, using paddle.
GOE: 06.04.34 STRENGTH: M GED: R1 M1 L1 SVP: 1 DLU: 77

652.687-026   PASTER, SCREEN PRINTING (textile) alternate titles: stretcher
Positions (stretches) textile articles, such as towels, bath cloths, blankets, sheets, and pillowcases at designated intervals on gummed-top table to prepare them for screen printing. Smooths wrinkles from articles and presses articles

to table top with hands to prevent slipping. May hang printed articles on line to dry.
GOE: 06.04.27 STRENGTH: L GED: R1 M1 L1 SVP: 2 DLU: 77

652.687-030 PATTERN HAND (woodworking)
Prints patterns on paper strips and glues printed strips to wood or plastic sheets to guide workers engaged in cutting sheets: Covers metal cut of desired pattern with printing ink, using handroller. Places paper strip on lower platen of hand transfer press, and positions inked cut on paper strip. Moves lever to close press and stamp pattern on paper strip. Removes printed strip from press and glues strip to wood or plastic sheet. May nail several sheets together when more than one object is to be cut to same pattern.
GOE: 06.04.27 STRENGTH: L GED: R2 M1 L1 SVP: 3 DLU: 87

652.687-034 PRINT-LINE INSPECTOR (furniture)
Examines furniture composition-wood-dimensional-panels for processing defects on discharge conveyor of tandem print-line machine. Feels and inspects panels to detect defects, such as scratches, blemishes, and discolorations. Marks defective areas with chalk or crayon and pushes panels along conveyor for removal.
GOE: 06.03.02 STRENGTH: L GED: R2 M1 L1 SVP: 2 DLU: 77

652.687-038 PRINTER, FLOOR COVERING, ASSISTANT (fabrication, nec)
Lifts roll of felt paper, using chain hoist, and places roll on spindle of machine that paints designs on roll to make floor covering. Pours specified paint colors into machine troughs.
GOE: 06.04.09 STRENGTH: L GED: R2 M1 L1 SVP: 2 DLU: 77

652.687-042 WALLPAPER INSPECTOR (paper goods) alternate titles: quality-control inspector
Examines rolls of wallpaper for defects, such as discoloration, printing irregularities, streaks, and color splashes, and tests for improper coating or waterproofing: Unrolls portions of wallpaper rolls or hangs rolls on test wall to examine for surface defects and symmetry of printed figures, register of colors, and uniformity of waterproof coating. May inspect new paper stock to detect ripples or other flaws. May inspect sample rolls of wallpaper for printing irregularities before authorizing printing of remaining rolls. May apply specified test chemicals to wallpaper sample to test for washability.
GOE: 06.03.02 STRENGTH: L GED: R2 M1 L1 SVP: 4 DLU: 77

652.687-046 WALLPAPER INSPECTOR AND SHIPPER (paper goods)
Inspects wallpaper for printing defects and prepares wallpaper for shipment: Lifts bolt of wallpaper onto letoff rack. Pulls wallpaper across inspection table and clamps wallpaper to rod on powered *windup rack*. Sets footage meter. Presses foot switch and observes wallpaper for defects, such as color splashes, smudges, and irregular printing as paper is wound onto windup rack. Cuts wallpaper from bolt when specified footage is wound. Wraps rolls of wallpaper with paper covering, and stamps identifying information on rolls. Packs rolls of wallpaper in cartons for shipment or stacks them in storage bins. May compare colors with master swatch to verify color accuracy. May brush excess flock from surface of flocked wallcovering, using soft brush.
GOE: 06.03.02 STRENGTH: L GED: R2 M1 L2 SVP: 3 DLU: 77

652.687-050 WALLPAPER-PRINTER HELPER (paper goods) alternate titles: back tender
Assists WALLPAPER PRINTER (paper goods) I to print wallpaper, performing any combination of following duties: Carries pails of prescribed color solutions to printing machine. Ladles color solutions into specified color trays of machine and maintains supply of color solutions during printing process. Changes color trays and assists WALLPAPER PRINTER (paper goods) I to change print rollers. Washes print rollers and floor area around machine, using water hose. Performs other duties as described under HELPER (any industry) Master Title.
GOE: 06.04.26 STRENGTH: M GED: R2 M1 L1 SVP: 2 DLU: 77

653 BOOKBINDING-MACHINE OPERATORS AND RELATED OCCUPATIONS

This group includes occupations concerned with gathering, folding, sewing, and stapling signatures to form magazines, pamphlets, or books, affixing covers to sewn signatures, compressing books to size, stiffening backs of book bodies with glue, forming joints of book covers and bodies, reinforcing backs of books with fabric strips, gluing cover boards to end sheets, and drying books.

653.131-010 SUPERVISOR, BINDERY (print. & pub.) alternate titles: bindery chief; bookbinder, chief; supervisor; floorleader; section manager
Supervises and coordinates activities of workers engaged in assembling, forming, finishing, covering, and ruling products such as books, pamphlets, periodicals, notebooks, looseleaf binders, tablets, and other printed and published products manually and by machine: Oversees binding or rebinding operations to verify conformance with plant standards. Performs duties as described under SUPERVISOR (any industry) Master Title. May only supervise workers engaged in forming operations, such as folding, cutting, gathering, stitching (stapling), and sewing printed sheets, and be designated Supervisor, Assembly Room (print. & pub.). May only supervise workers engaged in assembling, finishing, and binding sets, folders, and loose leaf binders and be designated Su-

pervisor, Finishing/Binding (print. & pub.). May only supervise workers engaged in setting up and operating machines that draw lines, cut rounded corners, and drill holes in paper products and be designated Supervisor, Ruling (paper goods; print. & pub.).
GOE: 06.02.01 STRENGTH: L GED: R4 M3 L3 SVP: 8 DLU: 89

653.360-010 CASING-IN-LINE SETTER (print. & pub.) alternate titles: machine adjuster
Sets up, according to job order specifications, machines that automatically perform in sequence such operations as rounding and backing, supering (applying strip of reinforcing material to back of book) and lining, casing-in, and pressing to convert gathered signatures (pages) into finished book: Mounts rolls of cloth and paper lining and headbands on machine spindles. Fills glue pot and adjusts flow of glue. Installs and adjusts feed guides, holding clamps, rollers, rounding forms, creasing ram, and other machine parts to accommodate specified size books, using measuring instruments and handtools. Sets thermostatic control and pressure gauge according to thickness of book and amount of pressure to be applied. Turns screws to adjust cutting mechanism to cut linings and headbands to book size. Starts machine to process sample book and verify accuracy of machine setup. Makes adjustments as necessary during production run. May direct activities or perform duties of CASING-IN-LINE FEEDER (print. & pub.) 653.686-010.
GOE: 06.01.02 STRENGTH: L GED: R3 M2 L3 SVP: 8 DLU: 90

653.360-018 BINDERY-MACHINE SETTER (print. & pub.) alternate titles: bindery leadperson
Sets up machine or machines that automatically perform one or more bindery operations, such as folding, cutting, gathering, stitching or gluing, following blueprint or job specifications, and using measuring instruments and handtools: Installs and adjusts machine knives, side guiders, feed guides, holding clamps, pockets, rollers, specified jogging tray at discharge end of machines, and other machine parts to accommodate sheets, signatures, or books of specified size. Turns dials to required graduations to set grippers and gripper feelers according to thickness of signatures or flat sheets being gathered. Secures reel of stitching wire on spindle of stitching heads and threads wire through feeding, cutting, stitch forming, and driving mechanisms. Positions and clamps stitching heads on crossarm to space stitches as specified. Turns thumbscrews and handwheels to adjust length of stitches and tension on creasing blades and folding rollers according to thickness of pages to be stitched or sheet size and number of folds specified. Adjusts cams and other mechanisms to synchronize speed of automatic feeding devices and stitching. Fills glue pot and adjusts flow of glue and speed of conveyors. Starts machines and makes trial runs to verify accuracy of machine setup. Observes operation to detect machine malfunctions and makes adjustments as required. May maintain machinery in operating condition. May train workers to set up, operate, and use automatic bindery machines. May oversee work of BINDERY-MACHINE FEEDER-OFFBEARER (print. & pub.) 653.686-026. May be classified according to name of machine as Folding-Machine Setter (print. & pub.); Gathering-Machine Setter (print. & pub.); Perfect-Binder Setter (print. & pub.); Stitching-Machine Setter (print. & pub.).
GOE: 06.01.02 STRENGTH: L GED: R3 M2 L2 SVP: 8 DLU: 90

653.382-010 FOLDING-MACHINE OPERATOR (print. & pub.) alternate titles: finishing machine operator; folder, machine; folder operator
Sets up and operates machine to automatically fold, slit, and score printed sheets into signatures for binding: Examines work order to determine setup specifications or inserts sample sheet in machine and sets guides to edge of sheet. Adjusts air blasts on feeder to regulate amount of air separating sheets of paper to provide continuous flow of paper through machine. Adjusts conveyor blades or knurled rollers to feed sheet into folding rollers. Turns screws to regulate tension of creasing blades and folding rollers according to thickness of paper and size and number of folds specified, using handtools. Sets slitting knives to slit sheets as specified. Stacks sheets to be folded on conveyor belt of automatic feed. Presses button to activate machine and observes machine operation. Adjusts machine during production run as required. May operate two or more machines. May jog, stack, band, and box folded sheets.
GOE: 06.02.04 STRENGTH: L GED: R3 M2 L2 SVP: 5 DLU: 89

653.382-014 COLLATING-MACHINE OPERATOR (print. & pub.) alternate titles: set-making-machine operator
Sets up and operates collating machine to perform functions such as assembling and perforating, stapling, gluing, folding, or cutting sheets of paper, forms, or signatures in specified sequence to form sets, following job specifications: Turns screws to adjust pockets and guides to accommodate sheets of paper to be collated. Turns dials to required graduations to set grippers and gripper feelers according to thickness of single sheets or signatures being collated, using measuring instruments. Turns knobs, using handtools, to set or adjust air blowers or air suction devices to required position and force to facilitate pickup of individual sheets. Sets *indexing* control to numbered position corresponding to number of sheets to be assembled or sets automatic counter at discharge end of machine. Turns screws to adjust speed of conveyor belt, using handtools, and installs specified jogging tray at discharge end of machine. Threads wire into machine to load stitcher head when sets are to be stapled. Fills glue reservoir and adjusts flow of glue when top edges of sets are to be glued. Flexes and jogs stacks of sheets to ensure sheets are in specified order and to align edges of sheets. Feeds sheets into machine in reverse order (last sheet first) or places stacks of sheets in specified machine pockets. Replenishes

pockets with sheets of paper or signatures throughout production run. Starts machine to verify accuracy of machine setup, following sample, and observes operation of machine throughout production run. Stops, resets, and restarts machine when malfunctions occur. Removes collated products from machine or conveyor belt and stacks products on skid or pallet. Records time spent on specific tasks or number of sets or book bodies collated on daily production sheet. Performs routine maintenance to ensure machine is in working order. May place rolls of paper and carbon paper onto feed spindle of roll-fed machine, using chain hoist. May punch holes in completed sets, using drill punch.
GOE: 06.02.04 STRENGTH: L GED: R3 M2 L3 SVP: 4 DLU: 90

653.662-010 STITCHING-MACHINE OPERATOR (print. & pub.) alternate titles: machine operator; finishing machine operator; stitcher operator

Sets up and operates machine to automatically gather, stitch, and trim folded signatures or flat sheets of paper to form paperbound books, magazines, pamphlets, catalogs, or booklets: Examines work order to determine work instructions. Adjusts feeder pockets to size of folded signatures or flat sheets. Adjusts air pressure pump to separate sheets. Sets stitchers for specified length and thickness of stitch and threads stitching wire into machine. Sets trimmer knives to trim three sides of publication to specified size. Starts machine and makes trial run. Readjusts machine setup if necessary, and regulates machine speed. Takes periodic readings of counter and records number of publications produced or examines samples periodically for defects and records number as indicated on counter to determine when problem occurred. Gives directions to crewmembers engaged in feeding and off bearing activities. May feed and off bear machine. May oil, grease, and clean machine parts and make minor repairs to keep machine in working condition. May be designated according to type of stitching machine operated as Saddle-Stitching-Machine Operator (print. & pub.). May set up and operate machine to apply glue to backs of books prior to trimming and be designated Side-Stitching-Machine Operator (print. & pub.). May set up and operate related stitching machines.
GOE: 06.02.04 STRENGTH: L GED: R3 M1 L2 SVP: 6 DLU: 89

653.667-010 INSPECTOR, PUBLICATIONS (print. & pub.) alternate titles: inspector; quality control inspector

Inspects magazines, periodicals, catalogs, pamphlets, and rebound books for defects, such as loose, torn, or wrinkled pages, missing staples, incorrect bindings, incorrect book cases, and warped laminated paperback covers: Selects copies of publications from machine or table and examines covers and copies for defects, such as ragged edges, torn or wrinkled pages, incomplete cuts, incorrect bindings, incorrect casing material and color, authors, titles, call numbers, dirt and glue on covers, and bubbles in laminated covers. Fans pages to detect defects, such as errors in numbering, duplicate pages, color variation and inaccurate registration, ink smears, cut print, missing inserts, and dirty and wrinkled end papers. Notifies operating personnel of defects. Locates and removes defective copies from conveyor, stacking table, or pallets, and disposes of defective publications according to instructions from supervisory personnel. May clean covers and repair defective books, using cloth, cleaning solvent, and variety of handtools and bindery machines. May examine finished books and compare information on worksheet with work performed on books for accuracy and completeness. May stack books on conveyor or table for shipping. May operate machine to print shipping labels for boxes [ADDRESSING-MACHINE OPERATOR (clerical) 208.582-010].
GOE: 06.03.02 STRENGTH: L GED: R3 M1 L2 SVP: 5 DLU: 89

653.682-010 BOOK-SEWING-MACHINE OPERATOR II (print. & pub.) alternate titles: back sewer

Sets up and operates machine to sew gathered and collated signatures (pages) into book form for binding: Pulls thread through lubrication box, thread guides, and needle to thread machine, and soaks bobbins of thread in water to lubricate thread. Places book under needle, sets presser foot to thickness of book, and turns setscrews to adjust length of stitch. Pushes book under presser foot with back against guide, depresses pedal to activate needle, and sews through length of book. Feeds and sews books in succession until delivery trough is full. Stops machine, cuts threads connecting books, and stacks separated books. May stitch endpapers to top and bottom of signatures. May operate machine equipped with multiple needles. May be known by type of book stitched and be designated Blankbook-Stitching-Machine Operator (print. & pub.) II. May specialize in stitching trimmed or shaved spine of books for rebinding.
GOE: 06.02.04 STRENGTH: L GED: R2 M1 L1 SVP: 4 DLU: 89

653.682-014 COVERING-MACHINE OPERATOR (print. & pub.)

Operates automatic book-covering machine to glue paper covers to wire-stitched books, pamphlets, and catalogs: Adjusts guide, spacing, and tension bars, and glue-distribution device according to size of book, by turning setscrews and handwheels. Fills glue reservoir, and loads feed hoppers of machine with covers and books. Pulls control lever to start machine. Removes finished books from discharge table. May direct other workers in keeping hoppers supplied with covers and books, and in removing and stacking finished books. May operate machine arranged in tandem with other bookbinding machines.
GOE: 06.02.20 STRENGTH: L GED: R3 M2 L1 SVP: 5 DLU: 77

653.682-018 HEAD-BANDER-AND-LINER OPERATOR (print. & pub.)

Sets up and operates machine to glue headbands, paper lining, and superlining to backs of book bodies prior to binding, according to specifications: Reviews work order to determine setup specifications. Sets feed guide

and holding clamps to book size. Installs rolls of cloth, paper lining, and headbands. Sets feeds to cut linings and headbands to book size. Fills glue reservoir and tightens nuts to secure glue rollers, using wrench. Starts machine and runs sample book through machine. Inspects sample to determine if headband and lining are securely attached. Resets feeds, guides, and holding clamps of machine as necessary. Feeds books singly, back down, into machine. Removes books from machine delivery table and stacks them. May fill endpaper feed with endpapers of specified size. May position books singly, back up, in machine, apply glue to back of books, linings, headbands, and endpapers by brushing, feeding between saturated rollers, or holding material against saturated brush, and attach headband, linings, and endpapers to backs of book bodies manually when rebinding books for reuse. May operate machine arranged in tandem with other bookbinding machines.
GOE: 06.02.20 STRENGTH: L GED: R3 M2 L2 SVP: 3 DLU: 89

653.682-022 TINNING-MACHINE SET-UP OPERATOR (print. & pub.)

Sets up and operates automatic machine to fold and clamp metal edging to ends of calender pictures and staples calender to picture: Moves lever to shift gears that adjust speed of feed mechanism. Adjusts metal-forming heads, using hex-head wrench. Turns handcrank to adjust mechanism that inserts hanger loop as metal strip is clamped to top of sheet. Turns handcrank to set cutter that cuts metal strips between sheets after bottom of sheet has been tinned. Manually sets microswitch that activates spray to apply strip of glue that holds calender for stitching. Sets head and side guides of stitcher that staples calender to sheet. Places rolls of metal stripping onto machine, places reel of wire onto stitching device, and pours glue into reservoir. Places stacks of pictures and calenders onto feed tables. Presses button to start machine. Monitors operation of machine, clears jams, and replenishes supplies.
GOE: 06.02.09 STRENGTH: M GED: R3 M1 L2 SVP: 5 DLU: 77

653.685-010 BINDERY WORKER (print. & pub.) alternate titles: bindery operator; table worker

Tends various machines and equipment and performs any combination of following tasks involved in binding books, periodicals, and pamphlets, and assembling related printed materials in accordance with work order specifications: Punches holes in paper sheets, manually or by machine. Creases and compresses signatures prior to affixing covers, using press or by hand. Fastens sheets, signatures, or other printed materials together, using hand or machine stapler, or adjusts or tends machine that inserts wire or plastic binding strips into punched holes to fasten pages and covers together. Feeds covers, signatures, and sheets into various machines for collating, stitching, trimming, folding, ruling, stapling, roughing, *indexing,* gluing, and perforating operations. Removes, stacks, and packs printed material in various stages of completion on pallets as it accumulates on delivery table of machines. Examines stitched, collated, bound, and unbound publications to ascertain that pages are bound in numerical or folio order according to sample copy, and for such defects as imperfect bindings, ink spots, torn, loose, and uneven pages, and loose and uncut threads. Inserts illustrated pages, extra sheets, and collated sets into catalogs, periodicals, directories, pocket portfolios, or looseleaf binders, and inserts sheets and applies labels to envelopes or periodicals by hand or machine. Places paper jackets on acceptable books. Applies gold leaf, silver leaf, or metallic foil lettering or designs on covers, using stamping machine. Applies adhesive tape, mylar strips, and index tabs to sheets by machine. Wraps product in plastic, using shrink-wrapping machine, packs products in boxes, and tapes lids of boxes shut. Records daily production. Cleans work area around machine. May make ready bindery equipment and work stations. May lead, train, and monitor work of less experienced workers.
GOE: 06.04.04 STRENGTH: L GED: R2 M2 L2 SVP: 4 DLU: 89

653.685-014 BOOK-SEWING-MACHINE OPERATOR I (print. & pub.) alternate titles: book sewer; tape-sewing-machine operator

Tends machine that sews sheets of gathered and collated signatures and sews signatures into book form preparatory to binding: Threads needles, adjusts machine bed to width of signatures, sets feed arms for size of signatures, and passes tape through guides, following written instructions. Opens signature and places it over feed arm. Depresses pedal to revolve feed arm, sew signature, and present another arm in feeding position (signature is released from arm after sewing and positioned for sewing to next signature). Places signatures in succession on feed arms, depressing pedal to sew individual signatures and to stitch sewed signatures together. Stops machine when delivery table is full. Cuts stitching holding books together, and stacks separated books. May stitch or fasten endpapers or linings to first and last signatures of books. May stitch signatures and apply glue along binding edge of first and last signatures to reinforce binding of book bodies. May specialize in stitching cut or shaved spine of books preparatory to rebinding for resale or reuse. May be known by type of book stitched and be designated Blankbook-Stitching-Machine Operator (print. & pub.) I.
GOE: 06.02.04 STRENGTH: L GED: R2 M1 L1 SVP: 4 DLU: 90

653.685-018 CASE-MAKING-MACHINE OPERATOR (print. & pub.) alternate titles: caser operator; cover-making-machine operator

Tends machine that glues binder boards and reinforcing strips to covering material, miters corners of covers, and turns edges of covers over boards to assemble book covers: Reads work order to determine adjustment requirements. Turns thumbscrews to adjust feed hopper guides according to size of binder boards and covers, and fills feed hopper with binder boards and covers. Mounts

roll of reinforcing paper onto spindle, or inserts roll into holder, and adjusts cutting blade. Adjusts corner-nicking and mitering blades as specified. Fills glue fountain and turns switch to activate heating element. Adjusts rollers to distribute glue on binder boards and reinforcing strips. Adjusts pressure gauge of roller, according to thickness of binder boards. Starts machine and places covering pieces sequentially onto feeder. Examines finished covers to ensure established standards have been met. Adjusts machine as necessary during production run. Occasionally stirs glue to maintain consistency. May mount roll of headbands on spindle of machine that cuts and glues headbands on each end of reinforcing strip. May position, align, and press binder boards, reinforcing strips, and headbands onto covering material, and turn in corners manually. May slide cover down into machine or push cover between press surfaces of pneumatic-powered machine that folds, creases, and bonds protruding edges of covers over boards and manually rotates cover until all edges have been creased and bonded. May feed covers through rotary press to ensure bonding. May stack finished covers on table.
GOE: 06.04.09 STRENGTH: L GED: R2 M1 L1 SVP: 4 DLU: 90

653.685-022　MAGAZINE REPAIRER (print. & pub.)
Tends saddle-stitching machine to repair salvable magazines, comic books, or catalogs in bindery: Picks up book from supply on worktable, opens book, and places book in tentlike position over fixture of wire-stitching machine. Examines book to determine location of missing stitch (staple), and positions book under stitching head. Depresses pedal to start machine and insert missing stitch. Stacks stitched book on worktable for removal. Examines wrinkled, creased, or dog-eared pages and cover sheets and separates sheets judged to be salvable and discards remainder of sheets. Rolls and bends sheets and smooths with hands and fingers to remove wrinkles and creases. Folds repaired sheets by hand and stacks sheets to be returned to binding machines. Keeps daily production records.
GOE: 06.04.04 STRENGTH: L GED: R2 M1 L2 SVP: 3 DLU: 77

653.685-026　ROUNDING-AND-BACKING-MACHINE OPERATOR (print. & pub.) alternate titles: rounder and backer; rounder
Tends machine that automatically rounds and backs bound signatures and forms grooved hinge space for book covers: Installs rounding form in machine, sets spacing of holding clamps and backing rollers, and adjusts turning of feeder according to size of sample book or work order specifications. Starts machine that automatically rounds and backs test book. Feeds book bodies into feed holder of machine. Examines book bodies for conformance to specifications as book bodies are ejected sequentially from machine onto conveyor belt. Stops machine when malfunctions occur. May adjust machine as necesssary to correct malfunction. May remove and stack rounded and backed books on table. May clamp partially rounded and backed books in press, fan signatures outward, and pound signatures into required curvature manually, using hammer. May tend machine mounted in tandem with other bookbinding machines.
GOE: 06.02.09 STRENGTH: L GED: R3 M2 L2 SVP: 4 DLU: 90

653.685-030　SPIRAL BINDER (paper goods; print. & pub.) alternate titles: insert-machine operator; spiral-bind operator; wire-spiral binder
Tends machine that forms, inserts, trims, and fastens spiral binding in covers of paper goods such as booklets, pamphlets, and notebooks: Measures guides, using ruler, and positions or adjusts guides to accommodate size of sheets to be bound. Tightens setscrews to secure guides in specified position. Starts machine. Positions and holds items to be bound inside guide stops of machine and depresses pedal to form, insert, cut off, and crimp ends of spiral binder. Stacks bound items on skid. Removes broken pieces of wire from machine, using pointed pliers. Removes and replaces damaged covers and backs. May thread wire into machine. May manually start preformed spiral in perforated holes of items to be bound and hold spiral against rubber-covered spindle or wringerlike rollers which twist spiral into remaining perforations.
GOE: 06.04.09 STRENGTH: M GED: R1 M1 L1 SVP: 2 DLU: 86

653.686-010　CASING-IN-LINE FEEDER (print. & pub.) alternate titles: caser-in
Feeds gathered signatures (pages) into machines that automatically perform in sequence such operations as rounding and backing, supering (applying strip of reinforcing material to back of book) and lining, casing-in, and pressing to convert gathered signatures into complete books: Jogs signatures to align edges. Places aligned signatures against guides of feed conveyor. Notifies CASING-IN-LINE SETTER (print. & pub.) of machine malfunction.
GOE: 06.04.04 STRENGTH: L GED: R1 M1 L1 SVP: 2 DLU: 77

653.686-026　BINDERY-MACHINE FEEDER-OFFBEARER (print. & pub.)
Feeds or off bears machines that automatically perform one or more operations to fold and cut printed sheets into signatures, assemble or gather sheets in specified sequence, or wire stitch or glue sheets to form books, magazines, catalogs, and pamphlets: Lifts stacks of sheets, pages, covers, or inserts from supply pallet and jogs stack on machine table to align edges. Flexes stack to ensure sheets are in specified order, following sample, or to admit air between sheets to facilitate suction-cup pickup. Places stacks into specified hoppers, pockets, or against guides on feed conveyor and replenishes stacks as needed. Observes feeding and pickup mechanisms to detect defective pages and removes defective pages from machine. Removes signatures, paperbound books, magazines, catalogs, or pamphlets from discharge conveyor. Observes discharge

mechanism and notifies machine operator or machine setter of jams and excessive defective publications. Places defective publications aside to be salvaged or discarded. May thread wire from feed spool into stitching machine to load stitcher head. May push button to stop machine in case of jams. May count specified number of publications and tie them into bundles or place publications on strapping machine that wraps and seals reinforcing plastic bands around them. May keep daily production records. May be designated according to machine function as Folding-Machine Feeder (print. & pub.); Gathering-Machine Feeder (print. & pub.); Perfect-Binder Feeder-Offbearer (print. & pub.); Saddle-Stitching-Machine Feeder-Offbearer (print. & pub.); Side-Stitching-Machine Feeder-Offbearer (print. & pub.).
GOE: 06.04.04 STRENGTH: L GED: R1 M1 L1 SVP: 2 DLU: 90

653.687-010　COLLATOR (print. & pub.)
Examines gathered book, magazine, and pamphlet bodies to verify order and number of included signatures: Riffles bodies, one section at a time, observing signature figures. Notes omitted, misplaced, or duplicated signatures, and rearranges or inserts sections to correct subject matter. Stacks completed bodies.
GOE: 07.07.03 STRENGTH: L GED: R2 M2 L1 SVP: 2 DLU: 77

654　TYPECASTERS AND RELATED OCCUPATIONS

This group includes occupations concerned with casting and assembling type into equipped form for printing by means of machines that select, cast, cool, and assemble type on sticks.

654.382-010　CASTING-MACHINE OPERATOR (machinery mfg.; print. & pub.) alternate titles: caster operator; monotype caster; type caster
Sets up and operates machine to cast and assemble type for printing: Places reel of controller paper on holder, threads free end around tension and feeding rolls, and attaches it to winding roll. Sets composing stick to length of line specified in casting instructions. Inserts and locks matrix case, designed for specified size of type, in case holder. Locks galley next to stick on bed of machine. Starts machine and admits compressed air to machine (machine automatically selects, casts, cools, and assembles type in stick, being controlled by perforations made in controller paper). Stops machine when galley is full or when strip is completed. Removes and stores controller reel and matrix case. Removes galley and forwards it for proofing.
GOE: 05.10.05 STRENGTH: M GED: R3 M2 L2 SVP: 6 DLU: 77

654.582-010　TYPE-CASTING MACHINE OPERATOR (print. & pub.)
Sets up and operates machine to cast lines of type: Sets up matrices in assembly stick by hand, according to copy for which slugs are to be made. Locks assembly stick containing matrices in groove on top of machine. Starts machine and monitors operation while metal slugs bearing printed characters corresponding to characters on matrices are automatically produced. Removes assembly stick after slugs are made and distributes matrices and slugs in compartments of cases used for storing them until use. May be known by trade name of machine used.
GOE: 05.10.05 STRENGTH: L GED: R3 M2 L2 SVP: 6 DLU: 77

654.687-010　MATRIX INSPECTOR (machinery mfg.)
Examines metal matrices (dies) for defects which are discernible with naked eye.
GOE: 06.03.02 STRENGTH: S GED: R2 M1 L2 SVP: 3 DLU: 77

654.687-014　PAGER (machinery mfg.)
Separates pieces of type after they are removed from type molds. Cleans type and removes burrs, using file. May separate type according to specified quantity of each character and size and face of type.
GOE: 06.04.37 STRENGTH: S GED: R2 M1 L1 SVP: 2 DLU: 77

659　PRINTING OCCUPATIONS, N.E.C.

This group includes occupations, not elsewhere classified, concerned with producing copies of designs or lettering by transferring ink or pigment to paper or other material.

659.360-010　PLATE FINISHER (print. & pub.)
Sets up and operates power cutting tools to trim electrotype or stereotype plates and mounts them on wood or metal blocks, according to specifications, for use in printing press: Operates metal cutting tools, such as saws, plate milling machine, shaving machine, and radial or straight line routing machine, to remove surplus backing from plate, shave and smooth plates to specified thickness, cut out metal from nonprinting areas, and cut plates to size, and bevel edges. Sets plate on surface plate and taps with hammer and block to flatten plate. Rubs face of plate with finisher's rubber or magnesia to determine low and high spots. Taps low spots with punches and hammer to raise and level them to printing height. Operates plate curving machine (slip roll forming machine) that curves plates to fit plate cylinder of rotary printing press. Examines plates with magnifier or microscope to detect flaws in halftone dots and lines and raises, lowers, or repairs imperfections with engraver's handtools. Mounts finished plates on wood or metal blocks, using hammer and nails or thermoplastic adhesive and heat press. May operate hand or power single color proof press to print proof of plate, observing printing quality of plate and conformity of image on copy. May modify plates for other than rotary type presses.

GOE: 05.05.07 STRENGTH: M GED: R4 M2 L2 SVP: 8 DLU: 77

659.381-010 PLATE SETTER, FLEXOGRAPHIC PRESS (print. & pub.)

Prepares cylinders for installation in flexographic printing press according to specifications and diagrams: Measures and cuts brass plate of specified dimensions, using rule and blade-shearer, and bends plate to fit curvature of cylinder, using plate curver. Lifts and places printing cylinder of specified size on proof machine holding-rack. Measures and draws centering lines on cylinder to be used as guides for alignment of plate and dies. Slides formed plate on cylinder, positions plate according to centering lines, and clamps plate in place with tension bands. Trims and bevels rough edges of rubber dies, using knife. Positions dies on cylinder plate, following guide markings and diagrams, and fastens dies to plate with adhesive paper. Applies ink to dies with roller, and operates proof machine to make trial impression on proof paper. Examines proof to detect typographical or compositional errors and to verify quality and registration of print. Measures thickness of mount with micrometer to verify tolerance. Rejects defective dies and remounts or repositions dies to correct errors in original setup until trial impression meets quality standards.

GOE: 06.01.02 STRENGTH: M GED: R3 M3 L3 SVP: 6 DLU: 77

659.382-010 EMBOSSER (print. & pub.)

Sets up and operates machine to emboss gilt or blind (without goldleaf) lettering and designs on book covers, following specifications: Glues embossing plate to copper backing plate and installs backing plate into hot plate of machine. Cuts piece of cardboard to approximate size of plate and places cardboard on machine bed under plate. Starts machine to lower ram and impress cardboard. Cuts surface of cardboard around impression, leaving design or letters raised to increase machine pressure at contact points, using knife, compass, and square, and glues cardboard to bed under plate, adjusting bed so impression and plate are in alignment. Closes switch to heat plate. Sets guides to hold cover in position, and adjusts table height to obtain correct depth of impression. Places cover, with prelaid goldleaf in position, against guides on machine bed and starts machine that lowers ram and stamps goldleaf design or lettering on cover. Removes and stacks embossed covers. Stamps blind lettering or designs on covers in like manner. May perform simple embossing of book covers, using heated handtools.

GOE: 05.10.05 STRENGTH: L GED: R4 M2 L2 SVP: 6 DLU: 90

659.462-010 ELECTROTYPE SERVICER (print. & pub.)

Reviews incoming orders for completeness of customer's instructions and discusses order with customer: Contacts customer by phone or visit to obtain instructions or make suggestions for production of duplicate printing plates. Discusses variations in materials supplied, problems, and delays that arise during production. Verifies condition of plates in stock. Makes black and white proofs of each plate, using proof press, and compares proof with customer's copy and instructions. Inspects outgoing work for compliance with customer's specifications.

GOE: 05.10.05 STRENGTH: L GED: R3 M2 L3 SVP: 3 DLU: 77

659.662-010 PRINTER-SLOTTER OPERATOR (paper goods) alternate titles: cutting-and-creasing-press operator

Operates machine to print and slot container blanks, according to work orders: Selects, installs, and adjusts slotting and perforating knives in machine according to specified dimensions of slot and spacing of perforations, assisted by PRINTER-SLOTTER HELPER (paper goods) 659.686-014. Positions and attaches printing mats to print rollers according to printing order, using hand or air staple gun, wrenches, and tape measure. Fills ink reservoirs with specified colors of ink and turns thumbscrews to adjust flow of ink through fountains. Turns handwheels and pushes buttons or levers to adjust paper guides on machine feed table and automatic stacker, using handtools, and starts machine. Measures printed-slotted blanks to verify machine setup. Examines printed-slotted blanks for even ink distribution, trueness of color, printing flaws, and wrinkles. May operate machine equipped with gluing and folding attachment and be designated Flexo-Folder-Gluer Operator (paper goods).

GOE: 06.02.04 STRENGTH: H GED: R3 M2 L2 SVP: 5 DLU: 78

659.667-010 INKER (print. & pub.)

Compares color of printing ink with sample to ensure adherence to formula or customer specifications: Determines ink viscosity by timing flow from test cup and adds desired amount of solvent to meet viscosity requirements for kind of ink and application. Fills ink reservoirs in presses and adds more solvent to thin ink or uncovers reservoirs to allow evaporation of excess solvent during press run. May fill lubricating cups with oil and grease. May assist press operator to set up printing press.

GOE: 06.03.02 STRENGTH: L GED: R3 M2 L2 SVP: 4 DLU: 77

659.682-010 CUT-AND-PRINT-MACHINE OPERATOR (ordnance)

Sets up and operates battery of one or more types of printing presses to print identifying data on paper sheets that are wound into tubes for shotgun shells: Places type block on press bed, arranges wooden blocks to hold it in desired position, and locks them in place by tightening wedges with key wrench. Wraps and clamps tympan sheet around backing cylinder and fills reservoir with ink, using putty knife. Fills feed tray with paper and turns valve to start suction of feed cups. Starts press and runs proof sheet. Examines it for uniformity of impression, alignment, and spacing, and feels imprint for depth. Builds up tympan for darker impression by inserting sheets of tissue or thicker paper between cylinder and tympan or by cutting and pasting strips over light portions. Mounts paper roll in rear cradle of cut and print machine, using chain hoist, and threads

end through series of rollers to cutoff blade. Selects curved printing plates with desired wording and screws them to printing cylinder. Wraps and clamps tympan sheet around backing cylinder. Runs proof and builds up impression. Examines stock for deviation from color standard by holding it to light and pulling stock through fingers to determine texture. Measures thickness of paper and skived edges, using dial indicator, to periodically verify comformance to specifications. Adjusts guides, pickup fingers, and cylinder and roller alignment by trial and error, by turning setscrews, wingnuts and stopnuts, using handtools. Turns gears to adjust length of cut. Clears jammed paper from mechanism, using fingers or screwdriver.

GOE: 06.02.09 STRENGTH: H GED: R3 M2 L2 SVP: 4 DLU: 77

659.682-014 EMBOSSING-PRESS OPERATOR (print. & pub.) alternate titles: embosser

Sets up and operates press to emboss paper stock, such as labels or stationery: Installs and locks embossed plate in chase and locks chase in bed of press. Mixes embossing composition to puttylike consistency, spreads glue on platen, and applies thin pad of composition over glue. Makes impression of embossing to desired depth in composition on platen, trims off excess, and allows composition to harden. Scrapes high spots on counter die (impressed composition) to prevent it from puncturing paper. Starts press, sets sheets singly in gauge pins, and embosses them, removing and stacking them as embossed.

GOE: 06.02.04 STRENGTH: L GED: R3 M2 L2 SVP: 7 DLU: 77

659.682-018 EMBOSSING-PRESS-OPERATOR APPRENTICE (print. & pub.)

Performs duties as described under APPRENTICE (any industry) Master Title.

GOE: 06.02.04 STRENGTH: L GED: R3 M2 L2 SVP: 7 DLU: 77

659.682-022 RULING-MACHINE SET-UP OPERATOR (paper goods; print. & pub.) alternate titles: disc-ruler operator; head ruler, linoprint ruling machine operator; pen-ruler operator; straight ruling machine operator

Sets up and operates ruling machines to draw lines on tablets, notebooks, looseleaf fillers, and index cards according to specifications: Reads job orders to determine settings. Installs and adjusts machine parts, such as slitting knives, trimming blades, ruling heads, discs or pens, printing reels, belts, and gear, using handtools. Sets guides, feed rollers, punching units, and other machine parts to accommodate size and style of material being produced. Mixes ink compounds, fills ink wells, and turns valves to regulate flow of ink. Places stacks of paper stock on feedboard of machine or installs rolls of paper in roll-fed machine and turns handwheel to adjust cutting mechanism that cuts product to specified length. Sets counter when printing sheets for looseleaf fillers. Starts machine for test run. Examines lines being drawn to detect variations in line width or color tone, and measures dimensions of product, using tape rule, to ensure conformance to specifications. Makes adjustments as required. Starts machine and observes operation of machine during production run. Inserts pieces of cardboard and sheets of printed paper into stacks of lined sheets at specified intervals to provide backs and fronts when making tablets. Stops machine when malfunction occurs, corrects malfunction, or notifies other worker of malfunction. Cleans machine parts, using solvent. May oversee workers in supplying paper stock to machine. May operate roll-fed machine, equipped with paper cutter and two sets of ruling heads or pens to draw horizontal and vertical lines, and be designated L-Type-Ruling-Machine Operator (print. & pub.).

GOE: 06.02.04 STRENGTH: M GED: R3 M2 L2 SVP: 4 DLU: 79

659.682-026 SIGN WRITER, MACHINE (any industry) alternate titles: display-card writer; sign printer

Sets up and operates sign printing machines to print store display cards and signs, according to size and quantity of signs ordered, using either of following methods: (1) Clamps cardboard on base of machine that prints letters one at a time. Pushes lever to position type case over cardboard. Pulls lever to depress plunger that prints letter on cardboard. (2) Chooses type style, positions letters in composing stick, and clamps it on bed of manual platen press that prints sign in one operation. Selects and mixes color of poster paint, and applies paint to type, using roller. Inserts cardboard into holding clamps of press, and pulls carriage to end of press bed. Depresses pedal to lower cylinders against cardboard and type to print sign. May lay out display signs that include photographs or merchandising samples. May use chemicals and heat to produce embossed signs.

GOE: 06.02.09 STRENGTH: L GED: R3 M1 L2 SVP: 4 DLU: 77

659.684-010 DIE MOUNTER (paper goods) alternate titles: plate mounter

Mounts rubber plates (dies) on fiberboard or plastic mats, according to printing order specifications, for use in printing-slotting machines: Lays out and draws outline of box or container on mat, according to specifications, using tape measure and marking pencil. Positions and aligns rubber plates on fiberboard mat, according to markings. Fastens plate on mat, using glue and staple gun. Examines initial run of printed box or container for printing defects, such as overlap and uneven color distribution. Cleans used plates with ink solvent and airhose, and files plates according to printing order number. May requisition new plates.

GOE: 06.02.31 STRENGTH: M GED: R3 M2 L2 SVP: 5 DLU: 78

659.685-014 SAMPLE-BOOK MAKER (paper goods)

Tends machine that cuts wallpaper samples and assembles samples to make sample book: Transfers specified rolls of wallpaper to cutting machine, using

handtruck, and lifts roll onto letoff rack. Threads wallpaper through machine and pushes lever to specified setting for cutting width. Sets type on printing cylinder of machine to print identifying information on wallpaper samples. Turns setscrews to synchronize printing with cutting process and starts machine. Sorts and stacks wallpaper samples on shelves according to code number. Assembles wallpaper samples in specified sequence to make sample book. Trims assembled wallpaper samples with powered shear and staples them together. May be designated according to specific task performed as Sheeter-Machine Operator (paper goods).
GOE: 06.04.04 STRENGTH: M GED: R2 M1 L1 SVP: 2 DLU: 77

659.685-018 SHOTGUN-SHELL-REPRINTING-UNIT OPERATOR (ordnance) alternate titles: shell-reprint operator
    Tends machine that dissolves and wipes defective printing from shotgun shells and reprints them with load information: Pours shells from salvage boxes into deprinting (washing) machine hopper. Inserts felt wipers in wiping wells and shell-holding bushings in feed dial to accommodate gauge shell to be run. Fills solvent and ink reservoirs. Pastes strip of rubber type of specified load data around roller and inserts roller in reprinting machine holder. Starts hopper paddle, drying fan, and deprinting and reprinting mechanisms, and observes machine action for jams. Removes jammed shells, using fingers or wire pick. Examines shells for clarity of print and repositions type strip on roller to center printing on shells.
GOE: 06.04.37 STRENGTH: M GED: R2 M1 L2 SVP: 2 DLU: 77

659.685-022 TRANSFER-MACHINE OPERATOR (knitting; tex. prod., nec) alternate titles: transfer-iron operator
    Tends machine equipped with heated plate that transfers designs or identifying information, such as brand name, style, and size, from transfer paper onto such products as hosiery, towels, and wiping cloths: Selects roll of transfer paper according to work ticket and places roll on reel. Threads transfer paper through feed guides, under heated plate, and onto takeup reel of machine. Turns knob to specified temperature setting to heat transfer iron of machine. Turns setscrews to adjust feed guides of conveyor belt according to specifications. Places article on conveyor belt against guide or positions article on machine bed under transfer iron. Presses button or depresses pedal to start machine that lowers electrically heated iron onto transfer paper to transfer printed data or designs onto article. Examines article to detect deviations from standard and adjust feed guides as necessary or notifies supervisor. Places articles on table or handtruck. May tie specified number of articles in bundle, using string. May clean surface of transfer iron, using sandpaper.
GOE: 06.04.37 STRENGTH: L GED: R2 M1 L2 SVP: 2 DLU: 78

659.685-026 MILL STENCILER (steel & rel.)
    Tends machine that prints identification data on fabricated pipe: Positions and secures type in holder on printing machine, using handtools. Examines test impression to ensure printing of specified information, such as heat and lot numbers; size, gauge, and grade of pipe; and shift and initials of welder. Turns dial on number printer that prints designated consecutive number on each pipe in turn. Monitors and adjusts printer to maintain clarity of print. Cleans printing machine, using solvents and rags.
GOE: 06.04.10 STRENGTH: L GED: R2 M1 L1 SVP: 2 DLU: 86

659.686-014 PRINTER-SLOTTER HELPER (paper goods) alternate titles: creasing-and-cutting-press feeder
    Feeds precut paperboard blanks or sheets into machine that prints, scores, perforates, and slots them for forming into boxes: Loads precut blanks into automatic machine feeder, or positions stacks of paperboard sheets against guides on feed table and inserts each sheet into machine feed rollers. Adjusts scoring, perforating, and slotting disks or knives in machine as directed by PRINTER-SLOTTER OPERATOR (paper goods) 659.662-010, using wrench and tape measure. Fills ink reservoirs with ink of specified color. May off bear machine and stack processed blanks or sheets for further processing. May assist operator of machine equipped with gluing and folding attachment and be designated Flexo-Folder-Gluer-Machine Helper (paper goods).
GOE: 06.04.04 STRENGTH: H GED: R2 M1 L1 SVP: 2 DLU: 78

659.687-010 RACKER (paper goods)
    Hangs wet, freshly printed, or flocked wallcovering on rack to air dry: Slides stick under wallcovering as it emerges from discharge end of silk-screen table or flocking machine. Raises stick to form loop of wallcovering and places stick in specific slots of wooden rack, using care to avoid contact of wet surface with other objects or surfaces.
GOE: 06.04.26 STRENGTH: L GED: R1 M1 L1 SVP: 2 DLU: 77

659.687-014 RACKER, SILK-SCREEN PRINTING (any industry)
    Inspects and racks printed paper or cardboard: Examines printed pieces for smears or uneven color. Places acceptable pieces in rack to dry. Replaces filled racks. Maintains supply of cardboard or paper for printing. Refills printing tray with paint and performs other routine tasks.
GOE: 06.03.02 STRENGTH: L GED: R1 M1 L1 SVP: 2 DLU: 77

66   WOOD MACHINING OCCUPATIONS

    This division includes occupations concerned with shaping wooden parts or products by removing excess material from stock or objects, primarily by such means as cutting, boring, abrading, milling, and planing. Includes laying out,

job setting, repairing, fitting, and assembling. Includes machining cork and corncob pipes.

660   CABINETMAKERS

    This group includes occupations concerned with the complete cycle of cutting, shaping, and assembling prepared parts of complex wood products, such as store fixtures, office equipment, and home furniture. Typical jobs would include operating a variety of machines, such as the bandsaw, jointer, mortiser, tenoner, molder, gainer, and variety machine. Workers who are primarily concerned with one or a limited number of machine phases would be classified according to their specialty.

660.130-010 CABINETMAKER, SUPERVISOR (woodworking)
    Supervises and coordinates activities of CABINETMAKERS (woodworking) engaged in constructing and repairing wooden cabinets and high-grade furniture, performing duties as described under SUPERVISOR (any industry) Master Title.
GOE: 05.05.08 STRENGTH: M GED: R4 M4 L4 SVP: 8 DLU: 77

660.280-010 CABINETMAKER (woodworking)
    Sets up and operates variety of woodworking machines and uses various handtools to fabricate and repair wooden cabinets and high-grade furniture: Studies blueprints or drawings of articles to be constructed or repaired, and plans sequence of cutting or shaping operations to be performed. Marks outline or dimensions of parts on paper or lumber stock, according to blueprint or drawing specifications. Matches materials for color, grain, or texture. Sets up and operates woodworking machines, such as power saws, jointer, mortiser, tenoner, molder, and shaper, to cut and shape parts from woodstock. Trims component parts of joints to ensure snug fit, using handtools, such as planes, chisels, or wood files. Bores holes for insertion of screws or dowels by hand or using boring machine. Glues, fits, and clamps parts and subassemblies together to form complete unit, using clamps or clamping machine. Drives nails or other fasteners into joints at designated places to reinforce joints. Sands and scrapes surfaces and joints of articles to prepare articles for finishing. May repair high-grade articles of furniture. May dip, brush, or spray assembled articles with protective or decorative materials, such as stain, varnish, or paint. May install hardware, such as hinges, catches, and drawer pulls. May repair furniture, equipment, and fixtures and be designated Cabinetmaker, Maintenance (woodworking). May be designated according to products made as Piano-Case Maker (musical inst.). May cut, shape, and assemble wooden parts to construct frames for refrigeration equipment and be designated Refrigerator Cabinetmaker (svc. ind. mach.).
GOE: 05.05.08 STRENGTH: M GED: R4 M4 L3 SVP: 6 DLU: 77

660.280-014 CABINETMAKER APPRENTICE (woodworking)
    Performs duties as described under APPRENTICE (any industry) Master Title.
GOE: 05.05.08 STRENGTH: M GED: R4 M4 L3 SVP: 6 DLU: 77

661   PATTERNMAKERS

    This group includes occupations concerned with laying out, cutting, building, and fashioning wooden patterns. Includes following blueprints to achieve proper dimensions of a pattern, and any combination of gluing, nailing, severing, planing, sanding, and painting. A patternmaker would use a variety of machines, such as bandsaw, circular saw, borer, router, planer, drill press, sander, and shaper.

661.131-010 LOFT WORKER, HEAD (ship-boat mfg.)
    Supervises and coordinates activities of workers engaged in laying out and constructing templates and molds used as patterns and guides for fabrication of structural parts of ship, performing duties as described under SUPERVISOR (any industry) Master Title.
GOE: 05.05.06 STRENGTH: L GED: R4 M4 L3 SVP: 8 DLU: 77

661.137-010 SUPERVISOR, FRAME SAMPLE AND PATTERN (furniture)
    Supervises and coordinates activities of workers engaged in machining and building sample furniture frames and patterns: Analyzes production forms to verify accuracy of figures and to estimate cost factors, such as raw materials and production time, using calculator. Studies blueprints to determine style, type, and dimensions of sample frames and patterns to be fabricated. Directs activities of workers in machining operations. Inspects completed units for compliance with specifications of blueprints and production order, using precision-measuring tools. Initiates changes or adjustments in machine setup or sequence of operations, utilizing knowledge of woodworking and engineering. Performs duties as described under SUPERVISOR (any industry) Master Title.
GOE: 06.02.01 STRENGTH: L GED: R4 M4 L4 SVP: 8 DLU: 86

661.280-010 PATTERNMAKER (furniture)
    Lays out and cuts wooden furniture patterns following blueprints, specifications, or drawings, using handtools and woodworking machines: Consults blueprints, drawings, or written specifications to determine size and shape of pattern and machine setup required to cut pattern to specifications. Draws outline of pattern on stock with drawing instruments or transfers outline to stock by tracing over drawing on woodstock, using pencil. Sets up and operates woodwork-

ing machines, such as bandsaw, variety saw, planer, shaper, borer, lathe, router, or mortiser to cut, shape, and smooth pattern to specified shape. Measures and compares cut pattern with specifications, using rule and caliper. Adjusts woodworking machines to change shape or size of cut pattern to ensure cut stock conforms to drawings and specifications, using various handtools. Marks part number on pattern, using hand stamp or marking pencil, and maintains record of patterns for references. Issues patterns to designated machine operators.
GOE: 05.05.08 STRENGTH: M GED: R4 M4 L4 SVP: 7 DLU: 86

661.281-010 LOFT WORKER (ship-boat mfg.) alternate titles: mold loft worker

Lays out lines of ship to full scale on mold-loft floor and constructs templates and molds to be used as patterns and guides for layout and fabrication of various structural parts of ships: Lays out full-scale portions of ship's plan, working from blueprints and tables of offsets. Marks frame lines and other reference lines on loft floor with marking instrument. Measures dimensions between lines and prepares table of offsets. Compares prepared tables with tables on blueprints. Constructs template, using knowledge of geometric construction, and handtools and woodworking machines, such as crosscut, rip, and bandsaws. Marks templates with identifying data and instructions, such as number of pieces to be made, type, and weight of stock, and location for installation. Constructs full scale wood mockups of ship's parts and sections for use as guide in shaping or positioning parts. May construct wooden plug mold parts, such as hulls, decks, and cabins of fiberglass boats, and be designated Plug Builder (ship-boat mfg.).
GOE: 05.05.08 STRENGTH: L GED: R4 M4 L3 SVP: 7 DLU: 77

661.281-014 LOFT WORKER APPRENTICE (ship-boat mfg.)

Performs duties as described under APPRENTICE (any industry) Master Title.
GOE: 05.05.08 STRENGTH: L GED: R4 M4 L3 SVP: 7 DLU: 77

661.281-018 PATTERNMAKER APPRENTICE, WOOD (foundry)

Performs duties as described under APPRENTICE (any industry) Master Title.
GOE: 05.05.08 STRENGTH: M GED: R4 M4 L3 SVP: 8 DLU: 77

661.281-022 PATTERNMAKER, WOOD (foundry)

Plans, lays out, and constructs wooden unit-or sectional-patterns used in forming sand molds for castings according to blueprint specifications, using handtools and power tools: Lays out pattern on woodstock, dividing pattern into sections according to shape of casting to facilitate removal of pattern from mold, utilizing knowledge of casting techniques, and using marking and measuring devices, such as scriber, shrink rule, and square. Cuts and shapes parts, using bandsaw, lathe, planer, and router. Fits and fastens parts together to form pattern or section, using glue, nails, dowels and screws. Trims, smooths, and shapes surfaces, using handtools, such as plane, drawknife, chisels, and mallets. Assembles sections and verifies dimensions of complete pattern, using templates, straightedges, calipers, and protractors. Glues fillets along interior angles of pattern. Paints pattern in standard code colors to indicate method of assembly. Shellacs, lacquers, or waxes finished pattern. May construct templates for use in shaping irregular curves in pattern [TEMPLATE MAKER (any industry)]. May construct wooden models. May be designated according to type of pattern constructed as Die-Cast Patternmaker (foundry); Die-Lay-Out Worker (foundry). May repair broken or damaged patterns and correct patterns to compensate for defects in castings and be designated Pattern Setter (foundry). I .
GOE: 05.05.08 STRENGTH: M GED: R4 M4 L3 SVP: 8 DLU: 77

661.380-010 MODEL MAKER, WOOD (any industry)

Constructs full-sized and scale wooden precision models of products, such as boats, automobiles, household appliances, aircraft, and machinery, using handtools, measuring instruments, and woodworking machines: Selects wooden stock and marks layout of parts on stock, using precision equipment, such as scriber, square, protractor, surface plates, height gauges, and scales, following blueprint or draft. Cuts and shapes lumber to general outline of part, using woodworking machines, such as bandsaw, lathe, planer, and router, or has stock shaped by SHAPER OPERATOR (woodworking). Assembles wood parts, using dowels, glue, nails, bolts, screws, and other fasteners. Planes, shaves, files, scrapes, and sands model to attain specified shape, using handtools. Verifies dimensions and contours of model during hand forming process, using templates and measuring device. Waxes and polishes finished model. May fabricate work aids, such as scrapers or templates for own use. May construct hardwood hammer form dies used to produce handmade sheet metal parts. May construct plastic duplicates [PLASTIC DUPLICATOR (machine tools)].
GOE: 05.05.08 STRENGTH: M GED: R4 M4 L3 SVP: 7 DLU: 77

661.381-010 HAT-BLOCK MAKER (woodworking) alternate titles: hat-block bench hand

Finishes, shapes, and sizes rough-cut hat blocks: Clamps rough-cut crown block in vise on workbench, and shaves and shapes top of block to specified contour with spokeshave. Removes block from vise and sets in gauge to determine height of crown. Judges crown of block for shape, and marks high spots to be removed. Sands sides of block to shape on curver sander. Measures block with steel tape to ascertain head size. Drives block onto taper chuck turning machine, using mallet. Starts machine and sands rotating block by hand.

GOE: 06.01.04 STRENGTH: L GED: R3 M3 L2 SVP: 6 DLU: 77

662 SANDING OCCUPATIONS

This group includes occupations concerned with smoothing, cleaning, and roughing wood surfaces by means of sandpaper or similar abrasives.

662.132-010 SUPERVISOR, SANDING (woodworking)

Supervises and coordinates activities of workers engaged in sanding wood furniture stock, applying knowledge and experience with specific sanding processes, equipment, and kinds of wood: Computes amount of sanding supplies required, based on production schedules, and requisitions materials. Inspects sanded material for smoothness and to verify conformance to company standards. Trains new workers and assigns workers to work stations. Performs other duties as described under SUPERVISOR (any industry) Master Title.
GOE: 06.02.03 STRENGTH: M GED: R4 M4 L3 SVP: 7 DLU: 77

662.682-010 MOLDING SANDER (woodworking) alternate titles: automatic-mold sander; contour sander

Sets up and operates belt-sanding machine to smooth moldings or contoured surfaces of woodstock: Selects sanding form from stock or builds form, according to pattern, using chisels, mallet, rasps, hammer and nails, and fabric tape. Clamps sanding form to pressure bar above sanding belt, positions specified sanding belt over belt pulleys, and turns handwheels to regulate speed and tension of sanding and feed belts. Starts machine and depresses lever to regulate pressure of sanding form on belt as stock is conveyed beneath belt, or places stock against stops on table and depresses belt against stock with hand-held sanding form. Inspects and feels stock to ascertain smoothness. May sand flat surfaces with hand-held flat form and be designated according to technique as Float Sander (woodworking).
GOE: 06.02.03 STRENGTH: M GED: R3 M2 L1 SVP: 4 DLU: 78

662.682-014 MULTIPLE-DRUM SANDER (woodworking) alternate titles: drum sander

Sets up and operates sanding machine equipped with two or more sandpaper-covered drums to smooth surfaces of flat woodstock: Reads work ticket to ascertain information, such as grade, type, and quantity of woodstock to be sanded, specified thickness of finished pieces, and whether both sides of stock require sanding. Moves specified woodstock to be sanded to feed-end of machine, using handtruck. Wraps specified grades of sandpaper around individual drums, inserts ends of sandpaper in drum slot, and tightens bolts with wrench to close slot and expand drum to produce uniform sanding surface. Turns handwheels or pulls lever to raise or lower individual drums or bed of machine, according to thickness of panels and depth of cut. Presses button to start machine, and turns handwheel to control speed of conveyor, according to grade and type of woodstock to be sanded. Feeds woodstock onto endless belt or between live rolls that carry stock under rotating drums. Feels and examines sanded surfaces and measures thickness of sanded stock with gauge to ensure specified finish and depth of cut. Observes ampere meters and turns handwheels to adjust tension and relieve pressure of individual drums when friction between drums and sanded stock causes excessive heat to drum motors. Replaces sandpaper on drums when dark, wavy streaks are detected on sanded stock. May sand particleboard panels. May be designated according to type of machine operated as Endless-Bed-Drum Sander (woodworking); or according to type of stock sanded as Veneer Sander (woodworking).
GOE: 06.02.03 STRENGTH: M GED: R3 M2 L2 SVP: 4 DLU: 81

662.682-018 STROKE-BELT-SANDER OPERATOR (woodworking)

Operates stroke-belt sanding machine to smooth flat surfaces or edges of wood furniture stock: Turns handwheels to set tension of sanding belt, adjust machine table height, and limit stroke of pressure shoe, according to thickness and length of stock. Presses switch to start sander, and positions woodstock to be sanded on movable table located under sanding belt. Presses lever to lower pressure shoe onto sanding belt and force belt against surface of stock to sand stock. Pushes or pulls table to move stock under belt to smooth entire surface. Feels sanded article to ascertain smoothness. Cleans machine, using airhose and rags. Replaces worn sanding belts. May press belt against stock with pressure blocks to bevel corners and edges of stock or to smooth flat surfaces of ornamental stock.
GOE: 06.02.03 STRENGTH: H GED: R3 M2 L2 SVP: 4 DLU: 79

662.685-010 CORK GRINDER (toy-sport equip.) alternate titles: grinder operator

Tends machine that grinds cork into various shapes, such as semirounds, for shuttlecock bases and handle grips for fishing rods: Starts grinding machine and places workpiece in holding fixture or on arbor. Engages automatic feed or manually feeds cork against grinding drum of machine. May change grinding drums, using wrenches, to grind various shapes.
GOE: 06.04.09 STRENGTH: L GED: R2 M1 L1 SVP: 2 DLU: 77

662.685-014 CYLINDER-SANDER OPERATOR (woodworking)

Tends machine that smooths cylindrical wooden articles by revolving articles against moving abrasive belt: Starts machine and adjusts tension of abrasive belt. Inserts article through collar or pipe, places article on conveyor, or dumps article in hopper to feed it into feed roller or holding guide (track) and against sanding belt. May replace worn sanding belts. May install collar or guide, according to size of stock, using handtools. May be designated according to arti-

cle sanded as Dowel-Sander Operator (woodworking); Handle-Sander Operator (woodworking); Pole-Sander Operator (woodworking); Sander, Wooden Pencils (pen & pencil).
GOE: 06.04.03 STRENGTH: M GED: R2 M1 L1 SVP: 2 DLU: 77

662.685-018 LAST SCOURER (wood prod., nec) alternate titles: last grinder
Tends sanding wheel to smooth wooden shoe lasts to specified finish: Starts sanding machine and holds and turns last against revolving sandpaper-covered wheel to remove specified amount of material and smooth surface of last while retaining original contours. Feels surface of last to ascertain if last is of specified finish and verifies contours, using templates. Replaces worn sandpaper belt on sanding wheel.
GOE: 06.04.25 STRENGTH: L GED: R2 M1 L1 SVP: 4 DLU: 77

662.685-022 SANDING-MACHINE BUFFER (wood prod., nec)
Tends machine that buffs surface of cork sheets, from which outsoles for shoes are cut, to roughen sheets for better adhesion and to remove unevenness: Turns handwheels to set distance between feeder and sander rolls, verifying setting with thickness gauge. Starts machine and feeds sheet sideways through upper rollers that sand, brush, and return finished material through lower rollers on same side for takeoff. Removes worn, and spirally winds new sandpaper onto roll, cuts ends on bias with scissors, and slips metal sleeves over ends to secure paper to roll.
GOE: 06.04.09 STRENGTH: L GED: R2 M1 L1 SVP: 2 DLU: 77

662.685-026 SANDING-MACHINE TENDER (wood prod., nec) alternate titles: grinding operator; polisher and sander
Tends machine that sands and smooths sheets of composition cork to reduce thickness: Turns handwheel to adjust sander to attain specified thickness. Places sheet on feed bed of machine and guides material through rollers to sanding mechanism. Depresses pedal to release pressure of rollers for removal of sheet. Gauges sheets periodically to verify thickness, using ruler, balance scale, and thickness gauge.
GOE: 06.04.09 STRENGTH: L GED: R2 M1 L1 SVP: 2 DLU: 77

662.685-030 SIZING-MACHINE TENDER (pen & pencil) alternate titles: drum sander; end trimmer; trimmer
Tends sanding machine that removes excess glue and lead from wooden pencil blanks: Removes metal clamp from blanks. Places blanks in machine hopper and starts machine. Removes sanded blanks from machine and stacks blanks on cart. May mix and spray coloring on ends of pencil blanks to indicate hardness of pencil lead, using spray gun.
GOE: 06.04.03 STRENGTH: M GED: R2 M1 L1 SVP: 2 DLU: 77

662.685-034 SPEED-BELT-SANDER TENDER (woodworking)
Tends powered belt-sanding machine that sands panels and flat wooden stock: Turns handwheel, moves lever, presses button, or flips switch to adjust clearance between sanding belt and feed bed, according to thickness of stock and depth of cut. Starts machine and inserts end of stock between feed rolls that carry stock through machine. Measures sanded stock to verify specified clearance between sanding belts and feed bed, using gauge, micrometer, or caliper. May replace worn sanding belts. May tend multibelt machine that does rough and finish sanding in tandem.
GOE: 06.04.03 STRENGTH: M GED: R2 M1 L1 SVP: 2 DLU: 81

662.685-038 TURNING-SANDER TENDER (woodworking) alternate titles: sanding-machine tender, automatic
Tends sanding machine that sands cylindrical woodstock by rotating stock against strips of sandpaper backed by sanding brushes: Turns handwheel to space chucks of machine according to length of stock, and aligns feed rest for feeding stock to stock carriers, using wrench. Clamps strips of slitted sandpaper and sanding brushes in position. Pushes button to start machine. Places stock on feed rest for pick up by rotating spindles or positions stocks between chucks manually. Observes and feels stock discharged from machine into receptacle to verify smoothness, or removes stock from chucks manually. Cleans machine with airhose. May move levers to adjust feed carrier and rotating chucks, and to force sanding brushes against stock. May tend sanding machine that removes excess plaster of paris from corncob pipe bowls and be designated Bowl Sander (fabrication, nec).
GOE: 06.04.03 STRENGTH: L GED: R2 M1 L1 SVP: 3 DLU: 78

662.685-042 WOOD-HEEL BACK-LINER (boot & shoe) alternate titles: quirk sander
Tends machine that removes back lines (ridges) from formed wooden heels: Inserts heel in holding device of machine and presses heel against sanding belt or abrasive disk to remove ridges.
GOE: 06.04.03 STRENGTH: L GED: R2 M1 L1 SVP: 2 DLU: 77

662.686-010 END-TOUCHING-MACHINE OPERATOR (wood prod., nec)
Feeds corks into slot or fills hoppers of automatic machines that sandpaper flat surfaces to smooth finish. Observes operating machines to prevent clogging.
GOE: 06.04.09 STRENGTH: L GED: R1 M1 L1 SVP: 1 DLU: 77

662.686-014 MULTIPLE-DRUM-SANDER HELPER (woodworking) alternate titles: drum-sander offbearer
Removes stock as it is discharged from machine and inspects and feels surfaces of stock to determine if stock is sanded to specifications. Places stock

on truck or platform. Counts and records number of pieces sanded. Aids MULTIPLE-DRUM SANDER (woodworking) in replacing worn sandpaper. May feed stock into machine.
GOE: 06.04.03 STRENGTH: M GED: R2 M1 L2 SVP: 2 DLU: 77

663 SHEARING AND SHAVING OCCUPATIONS

This group includes occupations concerned with cutting, slicing, and shaving wood by the action of a keen-edged cutting tool mounted in a machine.

663.132-010 SUPERVISOR, GREEN END DEPARTMENT (millwork-plywood)
Supervises and coordinates activities of workers engaged in peeling veneer strips from logs and clipping veneer strips into sheets of specified sizes: Analyzes work orders to determine quantity, dimensions, and quality of finished plywood panels required by customers. Computes initial log and veneer requirements for each order, allowing for shrinkage, trim work, and waste during processing. Inspects peeled and clipped veneer for dimensional accuracy and to determine if maximum amount of usable veneer is being obtained, using ruler, dial thickness gauge, and tape measure. Directs workers to adjust machines when work does not conform to specifications. Trains new workers in operation of machines. Performs other duties as described under SUPERVISOR (any industry) Master Title. May supervise workers engaged in drying peeled veneer sheets [SUPERVISOR, DRYING (millwork-plywood) 563.135-010].
GOE: 06.02.01 STRENGTH: L GED: R4 M3 L3 SVP: 7 DLU: 78

663.380-010 KNIFE SETTER (saw. & plan.)
Sets up machines to shred woodstock into excelsior of specified thickness: Installs knives and spurs (metal combs that furrow surface of woodstock in front of knives), using wrenches and screwdrivers. Turns setscrews and moves levers to regulate speed of conveyor and depth of cut. May sharpen knives and spurs [KNIVE AND SPUR GRINDER (saw. & plan.)].
GOE: 06.01.02 STRENGTH: L GED: R3 M1 L2 SVP: 4 DLU: 77

663.585-010 CLIPPER, AUTOMATIC (millwork-plywood) alternate titles: defect cutter
Tends air-powered machine that clips continuous sheet of veneer to specified width and to clip out defects: Turns dial to set machine cutting mechanism and starts conveyor that carries veneer under knife. Observes veneer sheet being conveyed to clipper, noting defects, such as knots, cracks, pitch pockets, and rot, and presses button that causes knife to clip out defective portions of veneer to obtain maximum grade. Stacks clipped veneer sheets on skid and marks identification data on top sheet. May replace dull knives, using handtools.
GOE: 06.04.03 STRENGTH: L GED: R2 M1 L1 SVP: 4 DLU: 77

663.682-010 BARKER OPERATOR (millwork-plywood)
Operates barking machine to remove bark, knots, and foreign matter from veneer blocks preparatory to peeling process: Presses buttons to control conveyor system that transfers block from storage deck into position over hydraulic hoist and to raise hoist until block is centered between chucks. Pushes and turns lever to press chucks into ends of block and to start and control rotation speed of block. Pushes lever to lower and control pressure of scraping tool against rotating block and to activate and control horizontal movement until bark is removed. Raises tool, stops block rotation, raises hoist, retracts chucks, and lowers barked block onto conveyor that transfers block to lathe deck. May remove bark, chips, and other material from conveyor and barking machine. May control conveyor that lifts logs from pond onto barker deck.
GOE: 06.04.03 STRENGTH: M GED: R2 M1 L1 SVP: 3 DLU: 77

663.682-014 POLE-PEELING-MACHINE OPERATOR (saw. & plan.; wood prod., nec) alternate titles: pole peeler; pole shaver
Operates machine to peel bark from logs: Moves levers to raise or lower rollers of feed mechanism that moves logs under cutter head of machine. Starts machine and moves levers or turns handwheel to lower knife blades against surface of log and remove bark. Applies pressure to cutting head of machine according to shape and size of log, using lever or handwheel. Sharpens and changes cutting blades of machine, using handtools. May lubricate machine, using oilcan and grease-pump.
GOE: 06.04.03 STRENGTH: L GED: R3 M1 L1 SVP: 3 DLU: 77

663.682-018 VENEER-SLICING-MACHINE OPERATOR (millwork-plywood) alternate titles: straight-slicing-machine operator
Operates machine to slice flitches into veneer strips: Adjusts gears of mechanism that automatically advances flitch specified distance for each slice, using wrench. Places flitch with selected grain pattern side toward knife in machine clamps and tightens clamps, using wrench. Starts machine, verifies thickness of veneer with ruler or caliper, and adjusts feed mechanism. Releases clamps to drop piece too thin for slicing. May cut defects from surface of flitch, using chisel and mallet. May operate circular saw to cut flitches.
GOE: 06.02.03 STRENGTH: M GED: R3 M1 L1 SVP: 3 DLU: 77

663.685-010 BLOCK-SPLITTER OPERATOR (paper & pulp)
Tends machine that splits wood blocks to size, preparatory to grinding: Starts machine and conveyor system. Depresses pedal to stop and start conveyor to move block in front of wedge-shaped splitting ram. Positions one end of block against steel backstop and opposite end in splitting position against ram according to grain, using *picaroon*. Moves lever to force ram against end of block and split block to size. Segregates knots and rotted areas and moves them onto waste conveyor, using picaroon.

GOE: 06.04.03 STRENGTH: M GED: R2 M1 L1 SVP: 3 DLU: 77

663.685-014 EXCELSIOR-MACHINE TENDER (saw. & plan.) alternate titles: excelsior-machine feeder; shredding-machine tender
Tends one or more machines that shred woodstock into excelsior: Presses pedal to open feed rollers and position woodstock. Starts machine that automatically feeds stock to cutters. Stops machine and turns woodstock to expose all surfaces to cutters to obtain maximum amount of excelsior from each log. May change chopper blades when blades become worn.
GOE: 06.04.03 STRENGTH: M GED: R2 M1 L1 SVP: 2 DLU: 77

663.685-018 MOLDING CUTTER (woodworking)
Tends machine that cuts to length and miters ends of molding or shim strips: Slides end-stop against rule to set machine to cut molding of specified length. Slides stock under knife against stop while chopper knife (two blades mounted at right angles) descends automatically to cut molding, or depresses treadle or pulls lever to lower knife that cuts and miters molding. Stacks cut molding on rack. May change chopper blades when blades become worn.
GOE: 06.04.03 STRENGTH: L GED: R2 M1 L1 SVP: 2 DLU: 77

663.685-022 PUNCHER (woodworking)
Tends machine that cuts D-shaped hole in head of wooden handles for tools, such as forks and shovels: Starts machine and withdraws soaked handle from barrel partly filled with steam-heated water. Places head of handle successively in two jigs and under two sets of knives that descend on handle and make rough and finish cuts to form head.
GOE: 06.04.03 STRENGTH: L GED: R2 M1 L1 SVP: 2 DLU: 77

663.685-026 ROUNDING-MACHINE TENDER (pen & pencil) alternate titles: shaping-machine tender
Tends machine that shapes and cuts wooden blanks to form pencils: Places blanks in hopper and starts machine. Removes pencils from bin of machine and places pencils in rack. Ties pencils into bundles. May replace machine cutters according to size and shape of pencil, using wrench. May examine pencils for surface defects, such as nicks and scratches, and measure diameter of pencils, using micrometer.
GOE: 06.04.03 STRENGTH: M GED: R2 M1 L1 SVP: 2 DLU: 77

663.685-030 SHAKE BACKBOARD NOTCHER (saw. & plan.) alternate titles: backer board
Tends machine that notches boards for use as insulation backing on shakes: Inserts insulation board in jig and butts end of board against stop. Presses pedal to lower punch that notches edge of board to provide for circulation of air when board is installed. Removes board from jig and places board on conveyor.
GOE: 06.04.03 STRENGTH: L GED: R2 M1 L1 SVP: 2 DLU: 77

663.685-034 SLICING-MACHINE TENDER (furniture)
Tends machine that slices boards into slats for wood indoor or porch shades: Adjusts guide on machine table to specified width of boards and tightens bolts, using wrench. Starts machine, holds board against guide, and pushes board into blade that slices board into slats.
GOE: 06.04.03 STRENGTH: M GED: R2 M1 L1 SVP: 3 DLU: 77

663.685-038 SPLITTER TENDER (saw. & plan.)
Tends steam or hydraulically powered chisel that splits wooden blocks into bolts used for making shingles or shakes: Positions block on machine table and turns block for splitting, according to grain pattern, knots, and defective sections of block. Moves lever or pedal to raise block against cutter knife or drop chisel on block. Places split blocks or bolts on conveyor.
GOE: 06.04.03 STRENGTH: H GED: R2 M1 L1 SVP: 2 DLU: 78

663.685-042 SPLITTING-MACHINE TENDER (wood prod., nec)
Tends machine that splits slabs or blocks of composition corkboard into sheet of specified thickness: Sets dial gauge or turns handwheels to set rollers at specified distance from each other and from endless belt knife, to cut sheet of prescribed thickness. Places slab or block on roller conveyor that moves it to automatic feeding mechanism or pushes slab or block into roller opening that forces it against knife to cut sheet. Measures sheet with dial indicator or snap gauge and makes machine adjustment to meet thickness specifications. Repositions slab or block for each succeeding cut and stacks sheets. May adjust grinding wheel that sharpens knife, using wrench. May place slabs or blocks and sheets in steam-heated oven to condition them for cutting.
GOE: 06.04.09 STRENGTH: H GED: R2 M1 L1 SVP: 3 DLU: 77

663.685-046 STAVE-MACHINE TENDER (wood. container)
Tends machine that cuts staves or strips for slat baskets from sheets of veneer: Turns nuts, using handtools, to adjust frequency of clipping blade descent onto veneer sheet. Starts conveyor to carry veneer sheets under knife that automatically cuts sheets into staves or strips. Removes staves or strips from machine and examines them for defects and conformance to standards, using ruler.
GOE: 06.04.03 STRENGTH: L GED: R2 M1 L1 SVP: 2 DLU: 77

663.685-050 VENEER CLIPPER (millwork-plywood) alternate titles: drop clipper; dry-clipper tender; veneer cutter; veneer trimmer
Tends drop-knife clipping machine that cuts veneer sheets to specified size and cuts out defective sections: Lifts veneer from cart onto feed table of clipping machine. Examines veneer for defects, such as knots and splits. Positions veneer under drop knife with edge of material at measured distance from knife, using ruler, to obtain cuts of desirable grain pattern and specified width and length that are free of defects. Pushes button, presses pedal, or moves lever to

release knife-locking device and actuate knife. Slides veneer around on table or turns handwheel to reposition veneer after each cut until veneer is clipped to size and free of defects. Stacks clipped veneer on table or handtruck. Records number of sheets in each stack on work ticket or on top sheet of stack. Cleans and lubricates machine, using airhose and grease gun.
GOE: 06.04.03 STRENGTH: M GED: R2 M1 L1 SVP: 4 DLU: 78

663.686-010 BLOCK FEEDER (fabrication, nec)
Feeds wooden blocks into machine that cuts blocks into match sticks: Splits blocks into specified lengths, using hatchet. Places blocks grain up on machine feed table and pushes blocks into feed rollers.
GOE: 06.04.03 STRENGTH: L GED: R2 M1 L1 SVP: 2 DLU: 77

663.686-014 BREAK-OFF WORKER (millwork-plywood)
Off bears and breaks veneer sheets discharged from *rotary lathe* into specified lengths or at points of imperfection, such as holes, splits, and discolorations. Discards waste veneer into handtruck or onto conveyor that carries it to *hog mill* for grinding into fuel wood.
GOE: 06.04.03 STRENGTH: M GED: R2 M1 L1 SVP: 2 DLU: 77

663.686-018 GREEN-CHAIN OFFBEARER (millwork-plywood) alternate titles: clipper offbearer
Removes green veneer sheets from conveyor and stacks sheets on designated carts according to grain pattern and size: Observes veneer sheets to identify grain pattern, size, and quality. Removes veneer sheets from conveyor and stacks sheet on designated carts according to grain pattern. Pushes loaded cart to pickup area.
GOE: 06.04.40 STRENGTH: M GED: R2 M1 L1 SVP: 2 DLU: 77

663.686-022 LATHE SPOTTER (millwork-plywood)
Positions veneer blocks (logs cut to length) between spindles of veneer lathe, using electric hoist: Measures diameter of block to locate and mark center, using ruler. Examines end of log to detect rot, cracks, and splits. Selects chuck of minimum diameter according to size and conditon of block, and places block on lathe spindle. Secures hooks to ends of block, activates hoist to suspend block between lathe chucks, and signals VENEER-LATHE OPERATOR (millwork-plywood; wood. container) to press chucks into block. Removes knots, dirt, and other foreign matter, using ax, steam hose, and pick. May assist in chaining lathe knives. May operate lathe-charging-machine from console to position logs for automatic loading into rotary veneer lathe. May be designated according to type of log peeled as Flitch Hanger (millwork-plywood).
GOE: 06.04.03 STRENGTH: H GED: R2 M1 L1 SVP: 3 DLU: 77

663.686-026 SLICING-MACHINE TENDER (wood prod., nec)
Feeds composition cork sheet into machine that slices sheet to specified widths. Removes and packs sliced products in cartons.
GOE: 06.04.09 STRENGTH: L GED: R1 M1 L1 SVP: 1 DLU: 77

663.686-030 VENEER-CLIPPER HELPER (millwork-plywood)
Assists VENEER CLIPPER (millwork-plywood) in cutting veneer sheets to specified size and cutting out defective portions, performing any combination of following duties: Loads dried veneer sheets on conveyor belt that carries sheets to clipping machine. Positions veneer sheets under clipping blade, following guide marks, to align sheets for clipping edges and to cut sheets to specified width. Stacks clipped veneer sheets on cart and pushes loaded cart to next processing station. Performs other duties described under HELPER (any industry) Master Title.
GOE: 06.04.03 STRENGTH: H GED: R1 M1 L1 SVP: 2 DLU: 77

663.687-010 WOOD INSPECTOR (paper & pulp)
Inspects debarked pulpwood logs used in the manufacture of paper and related materials: Observes logs passing on conveyor to detect completeness of debarking process. Removes partially debarked logs from conveyor and places them in pushcart. Pushes filled cart to feed end of debarker for recycling of logs. Empties contents of cart onto conveyor, pushes cart back to inspection area, and resumes inspection.
GOE: 06.03.02 STRENGTH: L GED: R2 M2 L2 SVP: 2 DLU: 77

664   TURNING OCCUPATIONS

This group includes occupations concerned with shaping wood by the paring or chipping action of rigid cutting tools applied to wood rotating on a lathe.

664.382-010 SWING-TYPE-LATHE OPERATOR (woodworking) alternate titles: automatic-lathe operator; lathe hand; variety-lathe operator
Sets up and operates swing-type (rotary cutting) lathe to cut round and multishaped wood parts in manufacture of furniture: Examines blueprints, drawings, patterns, and specifications to ascertain size and shape of finished product. Selects and installs knives on cutterheads on machine spindle arbor, using template, rule, calipers, and wrenches; or loosens nuts securing end of lathe opposite drive end of arbor, swings support end to side, slides preassembled cutter heads on arbor according to arrangement of knives on cutterheads, and secures cutterheads on arbor and support end of lathe, using handtools. Selects and installs cam on arbor to control rotation and shape of stock to be cut, using wrench. Inserts woodstock between headstock and tailstock and turns crank to clamp stock in position. Starts machine and moves lever to swing rotating stock against rotating knives of cutterhead until shape is completed, or presses switch

GOE: 06.04.23 STRENGTH: M GED: R2 M1 L1 SVP: 2 DLU: 86

665 MILLING AND PLANING OCCUPATIONS

This group includes occupations concerned with cutting a smooth surface on rough woodstock and reducing it to desired thickness by the action of rotating cutting tools mounted on a machine.

665.382-010 CHUCKING-MACHINE OPERATOR (woodworking)

Sets up and operates machine to shape ends of wooden parts to fit into sockets of implements, or into mortises of opposing wooden parts: Selects and installs cutting head, and adjusts knives, guides, and stops, according to size and shape of cuts to be made. Verifies distances of settings and size of stock, using rule and calipers. Clamps stock in feed-yoke or places stock on automatic fixture. Starts machine and turns handwheel to feed stock into cutting head. Withdraws stock when stop is reached. May be designated according to machine operated as Double-End-Chucking-Machine Operator (woodworking).
GOE: 06.02.03 STRENGTH: M GED: R3 M2 L1 SVP: 5 DLU: 77

665.382-014 LOCK-CORNER-MACHINE OPERATOR (woodworking)

Operates routing machine with horizontal spindles to cut matching dovetail or rectangular tenon to form interlocking joints in end of woodstock: Selects, installs, and spaces bits on spindles of machine according to width and number of cuts specified, using rule and wrench and following work ticket. Aligns jigs, guides, and stops to control depth and length of cut, using rule and wrench. Presses button to start machine, inserts stock against sideguide, and depresses pedal to force stock through bits to cut male portion of dovetail. Inserts stock against sideguide and between clamps to cut female dovetail. Fits male and female dovetails together periodically to verify accuracy of cuts, and aligns guides when dovetails do not fit, using wrench. May be designated according to type of joint made as Dovetail-Machine Operator (woodworking).
GOE: 06.02.03 STRENGTH: M GED: R3 M2 L2 SVP: 4 DLU: 78

665.382-018 WOOD-CARVING-MACHINE OPERATOR (woodworking)

Sets up and operates multiple-spindle carving machine to make identical carvings simultaneously on pieces of wooden stock: Examines pattern, stock, and drawings, blueprints, or written instructions to determine knives needed to reproduce pattern on stock to be carved and number of pieces of carved stock needed. Selects, inserts, and locks bits in chuck of cutter spindles, using wrenches. Centers wood blanks between chucks on machine bed and secures blanks by turning handscrews or using wrenches. Inserts and locks *tracer point* in master chuck by turning thumbscrew or lock key. Presses starter buttons to activate cutter spindles to be used. Holds master spindle and moves tracing point over and around contours of pattern to reproduce pattern, as carvings, on blanks. Moves mechanism that turns blanks and pattern for carving on sides or for carving rounded objects, such as chair legs. Removes bits and tracing points after rough cuts are made and installs finish-cutting bits and point to complete carvings, using wrenches. May verify accuracy of carvings against specifications, using caliper, rule, or template. May blow carving chips and dust from carved blanks during carving process, using airhose, to ensure blanks are being cut according to pattern. May sharpen bits, using bench grinder.
GOE: 06.02.03 STRENGTH: M GED: R3 M2 L2 SVP: 4 DLU: 77

665.482-014 MORTISING-MACHINE OPERATOR (woodworking)

Sets up and operates multiple-head mortiser machine to cut mortise slots in woodstock: Selects and installs mortising chisels (cutterheads) or mortise chain saw assembly, according to number and size of mortises to be cut. Turns handcrank or knobs to adjust spacing of cutterheads according to specifications of work order. Lays out and marks cuts to be made on stock, using rule and pencil, or places pattern on machine bed and measures distance between slots in pattern to determine location of mortiser heads. Clamps stock to machine table and adjusts machine table or cutting head for depth of cut. Presses button to start machine and presses pedal to force cutting head into woodstock. Verifies location and depth of mortises, using rule and caliper. May be designated according to type of cutting head used as Chain-Mortiser Operator (woodworking); Chisel-Mortiser Operator (woodworking). May set up and operate machine that automatically spaces and cuts mortises in stiles for insertion of slats to form louvered doors and windows and be designated Louver-Mortiser Operator (saw. & plan.).
GOE: 06.02.03 STRENGTH: M GED: R3 M3 L2 SVP: 4 DLU: 77

665.482-018 TIMBER-SIZER OPERATOR (saw. & plan.) alternate titles: planer operator

Operates planing machine to surface planks and timbers and reduce stock to specified dimensions: Installs cutting heads on machine drive spindles and adjusts blade exposure according to specified depth of cut, using wrenches and gauges. Adjusts feed roll tension and positions fences that guide stock between cutterheads. Starts machine, exhaust blower, and conveyors, and slides timber against guide to align timber on feed rolls. Verifies dimensions of sized stock, using gauge or rule.
GOE: 06.02.03 STRENGTH: M GED: R3 M2 L1 SVP: 4 DLU: 77

665.665-010 ROUGH PLANER TENDER (woodworking)

Tends machine that smooths surface and sizes rough lumber in woodworking establishment: Turns handwheels to adjust cutting depth and feed rate according to thickness and species of lumber to be planed. Presses buttons to start planer and feed conveyor. Depresses pedal to actuate hydraulic load bed that raises lumber stack to level with machine feed conveyor to facilitate loading. Loads boards in consecutive sequence onto feed conveyor that conveys boards through machine planing operation. Periodically attaches sharpening device to planer blade assembly, using wrench, and turns lever to guide abrasive surface of device along blade surface to sharpen blade.
GOE: 06.04.03 STRENGTH: H GED: R3 M3 L2 SVP: 3 DLU: 86

665.682-010 DOWEL-MACHINE OPERATOR (woodworking) alternate titles: dowel-sticker operator

Sets up and operates machine to shape dowel-rod from squared stock: Selects and installs cutting head, and adjusts knives, guides, and feed rolls, according to size and finish of dowel-rod to be cut. Verifies distances of settings and size of stock, using calipers and micrometers. Starts machine and inserts stock between feed rolls that force stock through cutting head. May install cutting heads that cut spirals or longitudinal grooves while rounding stock. May specialize in rounding stock for tool handles and be designated Handle-Rounder Operator (woodworking).
GOE: 06.02.03 STRENGTH: M GED: R3 M2 L1 SVP: 5 DLU: 77

665.682-014 HEADER (wood prod., nec)

Operates machine to scarf end of wooden pipe for fittings: Inserts knives in slots of cutting head and adjusts knives for depth of cut, using steel scale and wrench. Positions pipe on machine bed and turns handwheel to clamp pipe in place. Starts machine and pulls lever to move cutting head over end of pipe to cut scarf. Verifies depth of cut and length of scarf against written specifications and drawings, using steel scale. Removes pipe from machine and rolls pipe onto conveyor.
GOE: 06.02.03 STRENGTH: M GED: R3 M3 L2 SVP: 4 DLU: 77

665.682-018 MOLDER OPERATOR (woodworking)

Sets up and operates molder to plane, shape, and groove woodstock: Reads work ticket and examines pattern shape to determine molder setup procedures and type woodstock to be cut. Selects and installs cutting heads on machine according to pattern to be cut, and inserts and bolts specified knives in slots of cutterheads already in machine, using wrenches and gauges. Positions pattern on molder and turns handwheel to adjust cutting knives flush with pattern. Removes pattern and turns handwheel to adjust guides, pressure bars, and table levels according to depth, position of cuts, and stock dimensions. Starts machine, places stock on feed table, and turns handwheels to press feed rollers against stock for feeding stock through machine; or inserts stock into hopper of automatic feed mechanism that carries stock through machine. Inspects stock being cut to determine defects. Verifies dimensions of cut material, using gauges, rule, or caliper.
GOE: 06.02.03 STRENGTH: M GED: R3 M3 L2 SVP: 5 DLU: 78

665.682-022 PLANER OPERATOR (woodworking) alternate titles: facer operator; planing machine operator

Sets up and operates power-fed facer or planer machine to surface and size woodstock used in furniture production: Selects and installs knives in cutterhead according to work order, using wrenches and gauges. Turns handwheels to adjust table level, pressure bars, and feed rolls according to depth of cut and thickness of stock. Starts planer, and positions woodstock on conveyor or inserts woodstock between feed rolls that carry woodstock through planer. Inspects and feels planed woodstock to verify smoothness of cut and thickness of stock, using gauge and rule. May sharpen cutters on abrasive wheel or stone. May operate circular saw to remove woodstock defects, such as splits and holes, and to square ends of stock prior to processing boards through planer [CUT-OFF-SAW OPERATOR (woodworking) 667.682-022]. May signal co-worker to stop feeding stock into planer when jams occur.
GOE: 06.02.03 STRENGTH: M GED: R3 M2 L2 SVP: 4 DLU: 79

665.682-026 PROFILE-SHAPER OPERATOR, AUTOMATIC (woodworking) alternate titles: rotary profile-shaper operator, automatic

Sets up and operates straight-line or rotary profile shaping machine that automatically follows contours of model or form to shape single or entire edges of wood furniture parts: Selects cutterheads or knives to conform to pattern contour, according to type of cut specified on work order. Installs cutterheads in vertical spindle of machine or inserts and bolts specified knives in slots of cutterheads already in machine, using handtools. Turns handwheel or crank to align knives with contours of model or form. Bolts or clamps model or form to bed of machine, using wrenches or air clamps. Sets stops on straight-line profiling machine and turns crank to adjust air clamps that hold stock in position for cutting. Presses button to start machine and positions stock under clamps and over model or form. Moves controls to actuate mechanism that closes clamps; moves carriage, turntable, or form containing stock against rotating cutters until edges of stock are shaped; returns carriage to starting position; and releases clamps for removal of stock. May turn thumbscrews or handwheel to regulate speed of carriage, turntable, or drive sprocket, according to type of stock and complexity of contours. May compare stock dimensions with pattern to detect cutting defects.
GOE: 06.02.03 STRENGTH: M GED: R3 M2 L1 SVP: 4 DLU: 78

665.682-030 ROUTER OPERATOR (woodworking) alternate titles: routing-machine operator

Sets up and operates single- or multiple-spindle routing machine to cut slots, grooves, designs, or recesses in woodstock: Studies blueprints, drawings, or samples and written specifications to ascertain size, depth, and location of cuts

to be made. Selects and installs router bits in spindle chucks according to specifications, using chuck key. Spaces spindles on shaft at specified intervals, using wrenches, and turns handwheels or sets stops to regulate depth of cut. Clamps stock to jig, inserts pin in guidehole of machine table, and places jig over guide pin, or clamps part to movable table of machine. Starts machine and presses pedal to raise table and feed stock into rotating bits. Moves stock under bits, following guides, lines, or slots in jig, to cut specified slots, designs, grooves, or recesses in stock. Measures dimensions of processed woodstock to verify conformance to specifications, using ruler, gauges, or calipers. May be designated according to machine operated as Multiple-Spindle-Router Operator (woodworking); or according to cut made as Handhole-Machine Operator (wood. container).
GOE: 06.02.03 STRENGTH: M GED: R3 M2 L2 SVP: 4 DLU: 79

665.682-034 SHAPER OPERATOR (woodworking)

Sets up and operates single- or double-spindle shaping machine to cut grooves, rabbets, flutes, or pattern shapes on surface and edges of woodstock: Examines drawings, blueprints, or written orders to determine cutting pattern. Selects, installs, aligns, and adjusts cutterheads, guides, and jigs to make specified cuts and shapes, using handtools. Starts machine and feeds woodstock (with grain of wood) into cutterheads, holding and pressing stock against guide or jig to obtain specified cut. Measures shaped stock to verify conformance to pattern, using rule, calipers, or gauges. May hold and push stock into cutterheads without aid of jig or guide. May sharpen and mount cutting knives in cutterheads, using balance scale, *truing 1* block, emery wheel, and wrench. May be designated according to machine operated as Double-Spindle-Shaper Operator (woodworking). May operate shaper machine to mold panels by cutting away sections along edges of stock and be designated Panel-Raiser Operator (saw. & plan.). May be designated according to parts shaped as Small-Parts-Shaper Operator (woodworking).
GOE: 05.05.08 STRENGTH: M GED: R3 M2 L2 SVP: 5 DLU: 78

665.682-038 VENEER JOINTER (millwork-plywood)

Sets up and operates machine to smooth, square, and apply glue to edges of veneer sheets preparatory to splicing: Turns handwheels to adjust cutter knives, pressure bar, and table or feed bed height to make cuts according to specifications. Pulls lever to adjust conveyor speed, according to length and thickness of veneer. Aligns edges of stack of veneer sheets and pushes stack between pressure bar and conveyor that carries stock over rotating cutting tool and glue wheel. Observes machine and presses pedal to reverse movements of conveyor to relieve jamming. Removes and replaces dull cutter knives, using wrench. May remove sheets and examine edges for evenness and uniform glue application.
GOE: 06.02.03 STRENGTH: M GED: R3 M2 L2 SVP: 4 DLU: 79

665.682-042 JOINTER OPERATOR (woodworking)

Sets up and operates jointer machine to reduce flat furniture woodstock to specified width or to plane, square, smooth, rabbet, or otherwise shape edges of stock so that stock might be joined tightly: Selects and installs knives in cutterhead according to pattern to be cut, using wrenches and gauges. Adjusts and clamps guide in position on machine table, according to width of stock and specified angle of cut. Turns handwheels to adjust table height and to expose cutting knives, according to specified depth of cut and thickness of stock. Starts machine, places stock on machine table against guide, and pushes stock over rotating cutting knives, or inserts stock into automatic feed mechanism that carries stock through machine. Reverses stock and cuts opposite edge. Verifies cuts, angles, and dimensions of stock to ensure conformance with specifications, using gauges, square, rule, or template. May operate machine to square or tongue and groove edges of core stock so that stock may be glued together to form wide boards and be designated Glue-Jointer Operator (woodworking).
GOE: 05.05.08 STRENGTH: M GED: R3 M2 L3 SVP: 4 DLU: 78

665.685-010 BOTTOM-TURNING-LATHE TENDER (wood. container)

Tends machine that shapes tub and bucket bottoms from bottom blanks: Centers blank between faceplates of machine and clamps blank in place, using handwheel. Presses pedal to rotate blank. Feeds cutting bits into rotating stock, by turning handwheel, to cut blank to specified diameter.
GOE: 06.04.03 STRENGTH: L GED: R2 M1 L1 SVP: 3 DLU: 77

665.685-014 END FRAZER (fabrication, nec) alternate titles: stem frazer

Tends machine that tapers ends of wooden stems of smoking pipes for insertion into corncob pipe bowls: Selects frazing head, according to size specifications on work ticket, and inserts frazing head into shaft of machine, using mallet. Starts machine. Grabs stem with pliers and inserts end of stem into frazer head, tapering end to specified dimensions. Verifies dimensions of tapered stem against specifications, using micrometers or slip rings. Turns setscrews to adjust angle of blades in frazer head, using screwdriver. Removes blades from frazer head and sharpens blades, using powered grinding stone.
GOE: 06.04.03 STRENGTH: L GED: R2 M2 L1 SVP: 3 DLU: 77

665.685-018 PLOW-AND-BORING-MACHINE TENDER (woodworking)

Tends machine that cuts grooves and bores holes in window sash stiles for insertion of sash weight cords: Sets stop according to length of stiles and tightens it, using wrench. Starts machine and places woodstock on machine table against guide. Pushes stock over rotating cutter to cut grooves until piece strikes stop. Activates drill to cut hole at end of groove. Stacks completed work on skid.
GOE: 06.04.03 STRENGTH: M GED: R2 M1 L1 SVP: 2 DLU: 77

665.685-022 PLYWOOD-SCARFER TENDER (millwork-plywood) alternate titles: scarfer operator

Tends machine that scarfs ends of plywood panels: Installs knives in rotary cutterhead and adjusts angle of cutter, according to thickness of panel and adjusts guides according to width of panel, using handtools. Positions and clamps panel on machine table and starts machine. Presses pedal to move panel under rotary cutter that scarfs end of panel. Removes scarfed panels from machine and stacks panels on pallets or carts for gluing.
GOE: 06.04.03 STRENGTH: M GED: R2 M1 L1 SVP: 4 DLU: 77

665.685-026 SCOOPING-MACHINE TENDER (furniture) alternate titles: scraper tender; seat scooper, machine

Tends machine to chip out saddle forms in wooden chair seats: Installs cams and cutterheads according to seat contour specified on work ticket. Turns handwheels to set cutterheads for depth of cut. Places chair seat on feed belt that pulls it under cutterheads. Removes chair seat at discharge end of machine. May tend drill that bores holes in scooped seat to permit attachment of chair back.
GOE: 06.04.03 STRENGTH: M GED: R3 M2 L2 SVP: 4 DLU: 77

665.685-030 STAVE JOINTER (wood. container)

Tends machine that smooths, bevels, and tapers edges of wooden barrel staves: Positions stave against guide on machine. Presses pedal to activate mechanism that moves guide forward forcing stave edge against rotating jointer wheel that smooths, bevels, and tapers stave edge.
GOE: 06.04.03 STRENGTH: L GED: R2 M1 L1 SVP: 3 DLU: 77

665.685-034 STOCK CHECKERER II (ordnance) alternate titles: checkering-machine operator; grip checkerer, machine

Tends machine that checkers (series of crosslike grooves) stock or grip of guns for decorative and gripping purposes: Places stock or wooden forepiece of gun in special holding device of machine. Starts machine that cuts checks (similar to knurling) in wood. Inspects checkered portions to ensure that machine is cutting as specified. May adjust checkering machine to correct checkering impression made on gun stocks and forearm, using wrenches.
GOE: 06.04.03 STRENGTH: L GED: R2 M1 L1 SVP: 2 DLU: 77

665.685-038 RODDING MACHINE TENDER (furniture)

Tends machine that cuts spiral grooves in wood dowel-rods and shaves circumference of rod to specified size: Starts rodding machine. Inserts dowel rods into feed trough and between feed rollers of rodding machine that cuts spiral groove in rods and trims diameter of rods to specified size. Observes cutting action of rodding machine and stops machine when malfunctions are noted. Removes spiraled rods from tail end chute and stacks rods on handtruck for removal to subsequent processing. Notifies specified personnel of malfunction of machine.
GOE: 06.04.03 STRENGTH: M GED: R2 M1 L1 SVP: 2 DLU: 86

665.685-042 ROUTER TENDER (furniture)

Tends automatic tape router to cut designs in woodstock: Lifts and positions stock in guides on bed of router. Secures stock to machine bed, using C-clamps. Turns dial to position cutterhead to begin cycle and starts router. Observes router during cycle to detect malfunctions, and notifies specified personnel when malfunctions occur. Blows wood shavings from router stock, using airhose. Unscrews C-clamps and lifts and stacks stock on handtruck.
GOE: 06.04.03 STRENGTH: H GED: R2 M1 L1 SVP: 2 DLU: 86

665.685-046 SHAPING MACHINE TENDER (furniture)

Tends bandsaw and double-spindle shaping machine that cut veneer into curved shapes for use in furniture manufacture: Flips switch and presses buttons to activate machines. Places stack of veneer on bed of bandsaw, positions pattern on top veneer sheet and marks cutting line. Guides stack of veneer against blade of bandsaw to rough-cut veneer. Positions and secures stock of rough-cut veneer on form of double-spindle shaping machine, and guides loaded form between revolving cutterheads, using form as guide, to smooth-cut veneer to shape of pattern.
GOE: 06.04.03 STRENGTH: H GED: R3 M1 L2 SVP: 3 DLU: 86

665.686-010 POLE-PEELING-MACHINE-OPERATOR HELPER (wood prod., nec) alternate titles: pole-peeler helper; pole-shaver helper

Feeds logs into machine that removes bark and unloads peeled logs: Rolls logs from ramp onto dual carriage tram, using peavey or hydraulic jack. Pushes tram to machine and releases carriage bolster to drop butt end of log onto machine feed gears. Fastens peeled end of log to discharge tram, using chain. Trips tram carriage release to unload peeled pole. May square end of pole with power saw. May shave unremoved bark, using chisel or draw knife.
GOE: 06.04.03 STRENGTH: H GED: R1 M1 L1 SVP: 2 DLU: 77

665.686-014 STAVE-PLANER TENDER (saw. & plan.) alternate titles: planer feeder

Feeds machine that smooths concave and convex surfaces of barrel or keg staves. Inserts staves between feed rollers that carry staves between rotating cutters of machine.
GOE: 06.04.03 STRENGTH: L GED: R2 M1 L1 SVP: 2 DLU: 77

665.686-018 VENEER-JOINTER HELPER (millwork-plywood) alternate titles: veneer-glue-jointer feedback; veneer-jointer returner

Turns stack of veneer sheets discharged from veneer-jointing machine and feeds sheets into return channel of machine. Performs duties as described under HELPER (any industry) Master Title.

GOE: 06.04.03 STRENGTH: L GED: R1 M1 L1 SVP: 2 DLU: 77

665.686-022 VENEER-JOINTER OFFBEARER (millwork-plywood)
Off bears jointer machine that smooths, squares, and applies glue to edges of veneer sheets preparatory to splicing: Off bears veneer sheets from discharge end of machine and stacks sheets on worktable. Examines edges of veneer sheets for gluing and stacks sheets requiring more glue onto pallet to be re-fed through jointer machine. Mixes powdered glue with water, using electric mixer, and pours glue into reservoir of jointer machine. May off bear flitches of hardwood veneer from jointer machine and stack flitches on cart.
GOE: 06.04.03 STRENGTH: M GED: R2 M1 L1 SVP: 2 DLU: 77

666 BORING OCCUPATIONS

This group includes occupations concerned with piercing wood by means of rotary cutting tools advanced into the wood in the direction of the tool's axis to make, enlarge, or thread holes.

666.382-010 BORING-MACHINE OPERATOR (woodworking)
Sets up and operates single- or multiple-spindle boring machine to bore holes in wooden parts: Examines blueprints, drawings, samples, or written specifications to ascertain size, type, and setting of boring machine, stops, jigs, and guides to be used. Inserts specified number and size bits in chucks of boring heads according to location specified for holes in stock. Adjusts spindle locations and stops to regulate spacing and depth of bore, using rule or template and wrenches. Turns handwheels to move table and guides to center stock under bits and regulate depth of bore. Starts machine, places wood on table against guides, and moves lever or depresses pedal to activate pneumatic clamps that hold stock in place and to engage wood with rotating bits. Measures location and depth of holes and compares measurements with work order and pattern specifications to verify accuracy of machine setup. Stacks bored material on hand-truck and attaches work ticket where specified. Cleans machine, using airhose and rags. May be designated according to machine operated as Boring-Machine Operator, Double End (woodworking); Boring-Machine Operator, Horizontal (woodworking); Boring-Machine Operator, Vertical (woodworking); Cluster-Bore Operator (woodworking); Gang-Bore Operator (woodworking). May operate boring machine to bore, ream, and countersink bungholes in barrels and be designated Bunghole Borer (wood. container).
GOE: 06.02.03 STRENGTH: M GED: R3 M3 L2 SVP: 4 DLU: 78

666.482-010 PULLEY-MORTISER OPERATOR (woodworking) alternate titles: frame-pulley-mortising-machine operator
Operates boring machine to cut mortises in window jambs for installation of sash weight pulleys: Installs boring bit of specified size in machine chuck and tightens chuck, using wrench. Sets stops and guides on machine carriage according to depth and length of cut, width and length of jamb, and specified location of mortise. Sets jamb in machine carriage against guide and stop, and clamps jamb in place with lever. Starts machine and moves lever to feed jamb into cutter to cut mortise. Measures dimensions and location of cut, using rule.
GOE: 06.02.03 STRENGTH: M GED: R3 M2 L2 SVP: 4 DLU: 77

666.582-010 PREFITTER, DOORS (woodworking)
Operates boring machine to drill holes for latches and locks on doors, and cuts recesses in doors for hinges and locks, using portable router: Places door on worktable and positions template at point indicated on specification sheet or blueprint. Starts and guides router against template. Positions hinge in recess to verify depth of cut. Clamps door to table of boring machine. Positions bits over marks on door indicating location of holes to be bored. Starts machine which indexes cutting heads automatically to bore prescribed holes or pulls cord on lever to lower rotating bit [BORING-MACHINE OPERATOR (woodworking)]. Chisels out wood from recess to prepare it for lock, using wood chisel.
GOE: 06.02.03 STRENGTH: H GED: R3 M2 L2 SVP: 4 DLU: 77

666.684-010 FRAMER (wood prod., nec)
Bores holes in wood structural components, such as trusses, spans, stringers, decking, or fence posts, prior to wood preserving process: Positions wood on blocking of framing floor or guides structural components, suspended from hoist, into position on framing rack, using peavey and working as member of team. Aligns template on top of wood, installs specified bit size in auger, and bores holes of specified diameter in wood, using pneumatic-powered auger, hand auger, or multiple-spindle boring machine. May fabricate template according to work order specifications, using diagrams, measuring tape, square, handtools, and power tools.
GOE: 06.04.25 STRENGTH: M GED: R2 M1 L2 SVP: 3 DLU: 77

666.685-010 STEMHOLE BORER (fabrication, nec)
Tends machine that bores stemhole in corncob-pipe bowls: Places bowl in holding device of machine. Flips switch or presses button to start boring machine and depresses pedal that moves bowl against rotating bit to bore stemhole in pipe bowl. May insert drill bit in chuck of boring machine, according to work ticket, using chuck key. May tend machine that bores stemholes and sands bowl tops and be designated Stemhole-Borer-And-Topper (fabrication, nec).
GOE: 06.04.03 STRENGTH: L GED: R2 M1 L1 SVP: 2 DLU: 78

666.685-014 BORING-MACHINE OPERATOR (furniture)
Tends single- or multiple-spindle boring machine that bores holes in wooden furniture stock: Lifts and places woodstock against preset guides of machine

bed and presses button to start rotating boring bits of previously set up machine. Holds woodstock against guides and presses button to lower rotating bits that bore holes into woodstock. Removes stock from machine and examines workpiece for boring defects, such as splits. May place woodstock in hopper that automatically feeds piece under bits of machine. May cut defects from sections of woodstock prior to boring, using cut-off saw.
GOE: 06.04.03 STRENGTH: M GED: R2 M2 L2 SVP: 2 DLU: 86

667 SAWING OCCUPATIONS

This group includes occupations concerned with severing or shaping wood by the reciprocal or rotary cutting action of a blade which wears out a kerf.

667.137-010 SUPERVISOR, STAVE CUTTING (wood. container)
Supervises and coordinates activities of workers engaged in cutting barrel staves: Coordinates movement of bolts between yard, cutting area, and drying area. Examines staves and bolts to ensure products meet company standards. Directs workers to sharpen saw blades or to adjust cutting of staves to maintain production standards. Examines bolts to detect defects, such as knots and splits. Grades bolts, using factors such as ratio of sapwood to heartwood. Calculates value of bolts and writes pay voucher for purchases. Performs other duties as described under SUPERVISOR (any industry) Master Title.
GOE: 06.02.01 STRENGTH: M GED: R3 M2 L2 SVP: 7 DLU: 86

667.382-010 STOCK GRADER (woodworking)
Appraises and cuts planed lumber to width or length to obtain clear-faced pieces (pieces free from imperfections): Adjusts stops of cutoff saw or ripsaw to required distances. Starts machine and inspects lumber stock for imperfections. Pushes lumber past saw, cutting away undesired parts and cutting acceptable pieces to desired lengths or widths. May be designated according to type of saw used as Cut-Off-Saw Grader (woodworking); Ripsaw Grader (woodworking).
GOE: 06.02.03 STRENGTH: M GED: R3 M2 L2 SVP: 5 DLU: 77

667.482-014 POCKET CUTTER (woodworking) alternate titles: frame-gate-mortiser operator; gate cutter; gate-mortiser operator
Operates machine to cut gates into window jambs to allow for installation and adjustment of sash counterweights after frames are erected: Adjusts distance between saws, using wrench. Positions stops on machine table according to dimensions of jamb and specified location of gate. Places jamb on machine table against stops and clamps jamb in place. Starts machine, and pulls lever to feed stock into circular saws that cut two parallel slits into jamb to form sides of gate. Presses pedal that raises one set of two reciprocating saw blades and lowers another set of two blades to cut slits simultaneously across wood grain on top and bottom of jamb to form ends of gate. Measures completed cuts for accuracy, using rule, and makes machine adjustments. May replace worn saw blades. May operate pocket cutter combined with pulley mortiser and be designated Pocket-And-Pulley-Machine Operator (saw. & plan.).
GOE: 06.02.03 STRENGTH: M GED: R3 M2 L2 SVP: 4 DLU: 77

667.482-018 STOCK CUTTER (saw. & plan.) alternate titles: bill cutter; stock-saw operator; trim sawyer
Operates saws to cut lumber according to customer's order or plant production specifications: Selects lumber of kind and grade specified on work order. Measures and marks lumber according to specifications, using rule and square. Cuts lumber to specified length and width, using crosscut saws [CUT-OFF-SAW OPERATOR (woodworking) I], ripsaws [RIPSAW OPERATOR (woodworking)], or multiple-purpose saws [VARIETY-SAW OPERATOR (woodworking)].
GOE: 06.02.03 STRENGTH: M GED: R3 M2 L2 SVP: 4 DLU: 77

667.485-010 SHINGLE SAWYER (saw. & plan.)
Tends machine that saws wooden blocks into shingles: Places block in machine carriage and adjusts carriage to ensure that shingles are of specified thickness. Starts machine that moves carriage back and forth to feed block into rotating saw to cut shingles. Catches shingles as they fall from saw, grades shingles according to knots, rot, or other defects, and trims off defects with power saw. Sorts trimmed shingles according to grade and tosses shingles into specified containers.
GOE: 06.02.03 STRENGTH: M GED: R3 M1 L1 SVP: 4 DLU: 77

667.662-010 HEAD SAWYER (saw. & plan.) alternate titles: band-log-mill-and-carriage operator; band-sawmill operator
Operates head saw and feed carriage to saw logs into cants or boards: Starts mechanical loader arms that place log on carriage. Sets dogs and adjusts carriage blocks to align log for sawing. Activates carriage that moves log against saw blade. Starts saw to cut log. Observes exposed face of log after first cut to determine grade and size of next cut and adjusts setting of carriage blocks. Starts mechanical log turner that turns log over on carriage for subsequent cuts. May change saw blades. May be designated according to type of saw operated as Band-Head-Saw Operator (saw. & plan.); Circular-Head-Saw Operator (saw. & plan.).
GOE: 06.02.03 STRENGTH: L GED: R3 M2 L1 SVP: 7 DLU: 77

667.662-014 MACHINE-TANK OPERATOR (wood. container) alternate titles: power-saw operator
Operates power saws to cut lumber to specified dimensions for bottom and sides of wooden tanks and cuts out tank bottom from assembled boards: Meas-

ures and marks boards to specified length for tank bottom. Cuts bottom boards, using swinging cutoff saw. Measures and cuts stave lumber to specified length for stave. Gives directions to workers placing and centering bottom assembly on turntable near bandsaw. Turns turntable to move turntable toward band-saw. Starts bandsaw and feeds bottom assembly against blade of saw and revolves turntable to cut assembly along circle marked on assembly by TANK ASSEMBLER (wood. container). Withdraws bottom from saw.
GOE: 06.02.03 STRENGTH: M GED: R3 M2 L2 SVP: 5 DLU: 77

667.682-010 BAND-SCROLL-SAW OPERATOR (woodworking) alternate titles: scroll-saw operator; tilting-head band-sawyer

Operates bandsaw to saw curved or irregular designs on woodstock or to saw thick wooden pieces to size: Turns handwheels to adjust machine bed and set tension on blade between drive and idler wheels of bandsaw. Turns knobs to adjust guide post of blade, according to thickness of stock, and to position friction wheel behind blade to prevent backward movement of blade when cutting stock. Positions jig or attachment on machine bed to cut stock to size, using C-clamps and wrenches. Starts machine and pushes or turns stock against bandsaw blade to cut stock along marked outline or configuration of jig. Removes cut stock and verifies dimensions of stock, using rule, caliper, and pattern. Opens drive and idler wheel covers and turns handwheels to loosen tension on bandsaw blade to replace dull or defective blades. May nail several pieces of woodstock together when one design is to be cut. May position template on woodstock and mark cutting outline on stock, using pencil and template.
GOE: 06.02.03 STRENGTH: L GED: R3 M2 L2 SVP: 5 DLU: 78

667.682-014 BOTTOM-SAW OPERATOR (saw. & plan.)

Operates machine to cut blocks of wood into boards of specified thickness for bottoms of buckets and tubs: Adjusts height of guide for desired thickness of board. Clamps wood in position on feed carriage. Starts saw rotating. Pushes carriage over saw and withdraws carriage cutting off board of specified thickness. Loosens clamp and drops wood down on guide for next cut.
GOE: 06.02.03 STRENGTH: M GED: R3 M1 L1 SVP: 4 DLU: 77

667.682-018 CORNER-TRIMMER OPERATOR (wood. container)

Operates machine to trim corners of lock-corner wooden boxes: Adjusts position of guide rails, using wrench. Starts saw and holds corner of box against guide rails and pushes box into saw, trimming excess material from lock-corner. Piles trimmed boxes on handtruck.
GOE: 06.02.03 STRENGTH: M GED: R3 M1 L1 SVP: 5 DLU: 77

667.682-022 CUT-OFF-SAW OPERATOR I (woodworking) alternate titles: cross-cut-saw operator; trimmer operator

Operates one or more single- or multiple-blade circular saws to cut wood and wood products to specified lengths: Adjusts and secures ends and backstops on saw table, using wrench, or bolts saws to shaft and turns handwheels to space saws and stops, according to specified length of stock. Starts saw and places material to be cut on conveyor belt, drums, or feed chain that feeds stock into saws, or positions workpiece against end stop and under saw, syncronizing action with automatically descending blade, or pushes material on table and cuts wood, depending on type saw, utilizing one of following methods: (1) Pulls lever to swing saw through material. (2) Pushes moveable table past saw. (3) Depresses treadle to raise saw through slot in machine table. (4) Tilts table for angle cut and presses pedal to move saw through workpiece to cut stock. Replaces dull or damaged saw blades and lubricates machine, using wrench and grease gun. May examine material prior to cutting to determine what cuts will remove defects and produce maximum footage. May verify dimensions of stock cut and accuracy of cuts, using rule and square. May be designated according to type of saw used as Double-Cut-Off-Saw Operator (woodworking); Drum-Saw Operator (saw. & plan.); Swinging-Cut-Off-Saw Operator (woodworking); Table-Cut-Off-Saw Operator (woodworking); Tilting-Saw Operator (woodworking); Treadle-Cut-Off-Saw Operator (woodworking). May be designated: Equalizing-Saw Operator (woodworking); Multiple-Cut-Off-Saw Operator (millwork-plywood; wood. container); Timber Cutter (mine & quarry).
GOE: 06.02.03 STRENGTH: M GED: R3 M2 L2 SVP: 4 DLU: 81

667.682-026 EDGER, AUTOMATIC (saw. & plan.)

Operates multiple-blade sawing machine and conveyor system from panel-board to straighten edges of rough lumber and saw lumber into boards of prescribed widths: Starts conveyor to move lumber and scans board as it passes to determine cut that will produce highest quality and grade. Presses panel buttons to space saw blades and trips pedal to start feed rollers leading to saws.
GOE: 06.02.03 STRENGTH: L GED: R3 M2 L1 SVP: 5 DLU: 77

667.682-030 GANG SAWYER (saw. & plan.)

Operates gangsaw or sash-gangsaw to cut lumber from cants: Moves hand and foot levers to shift cants from chain conveyor table to live rolls and align cants with saws. Starts saw and turns handwheels to adjust feed and tension rollers and speed of machine. May adjust saws to vary width of cuts, using handtools. May replace saw blades. May be designated according to type of saw operated as Circular-Gang-Saw Operator (saw. & plan.); Sash-Gang-Saw Operator (saw. & plan.).
GOE: 06.02.03 STRENGTH: L GED: R3 M2 L1 SVP: 5 DLU: 77

667.682-034 HEAD SAWYER, AUTOMATIC (paper & pulp; saw. & plan.) alternate titles: double-cut sawyer

Operates head saw, log carriage, and conveyor system, using panel buttons and hand and foot controls to saw logs into rough cants or boards: Starts con-

veyor that transfers log to log carriage with kicker arms. Activates log turners that turn log, scans log to ascertain best approach for trimming and cutting, and aligns log with saw. Sets specified depth of cut and activates carriage to force log against saw blade to cut board. Scans exposed face of log after first cut to determine grade and size of next cut.
GOE: 06.02.03 STRENGTH: L GED: R3 M2 L1 SVP: 6 DLU: 77

667.682-038 HEADING-SAW OPERATOR (saw. & plan.)

Operates heading saw to cut pieces of heading material from heading bolts: Loosens nut and adjusts guides to thickness of heading material. Stands bolt on end in swing carriage of machine. Moves bolt against guides and clamps bolt with tooth-edged clamp. Starts saw and pushes swing toward saw to cut strips of heading material from bolt. Withdraws swing, removes heading strip, and repeats cuts until bolt is completely sawed.
GOE: 06.02.03 STRENGTH: M GED: R3 M1 L1 SVP: 4 DLU: 77

667.682-042 JIGSAW OPERATOR (woodworking) alternate titles: fret-saw operator; scroll-saw operator

Operates machine equipped with narrow vertically reciprocating saw blade to make irregular external and internal cuts on woodstock: Starts machine and places stock on machine table. Holds and guides stock against saw, following outline marked on stock to make cuts. Detaches saw blade from machine, inserts blade through previously bored hole in stock and reattaches blade to machine, using handtools, to make internal cuts.
GOE: 06.02.03 STRENGTH: M GED: R3 M1 L1 SVP: 4 DLU: 77

667.682-046 PACKAGER, HEAD (saw. & plan.)

Operates double-end trimming machine to saw simultaneously several pieces of lumber to identical lengths: Sets movable saw at specified distance from stationary saw. Stacks lumber in machine and butts ends of lumber against guide block. Moves lever to clamp lumber in machine. Starts saws that cut off ends of lumber. Places sawed lumber on conveyor.
GOE: 06.04.03 STRENGTH: M GED: R2 M1 L1 SVP: 4 DLU: 77

667.682-050 PONY EDGER (saw. & plan.)

Operates multiple-blade sawing machine to straighten edges of rough lumber and cut lumber into boards of prescribed widths: Starts machine. Lays rough board on edger table and spaces saw blades so that board of highest quality will be cut from rough board. Adjusts power-feeding mechanism to thickness of board. Pushes board into feed rollers which force board between saws that straighten edges of board. May replace dull saw blades.
GOE: 06.02.03 STRENGTH: M GED: R3 M2 L1 SVP: 6 DLU: 77

667.682-054 RADIAL-ARM-SAW OPERATOR (woodworking)

Operates circular saw mounted on overhead radial arm to cut boards and other woodstock to specifications: Reads work order or receives instructions from supervisor. Turns crank to raise and lower saw to depth of cut. Turns hand nuts and rotates radial arm and saw arbor to set saw for angle and bevel cuts. Lays material on table and aligns cutting mark under saw blade. Starts saw and pushes or pulls rotating blade against workpiece to make cut. Sets and locks blade at right angles to radial arm and feeds material into saw to rip lumber. May replace saw blade with attachments to shape, rout, groove, mortise, or drill workpiece.
GOE: 06.02.03 STRENGTH: M GED: R3 M1 L2 SVP: 4 DLU: 81

667.682-058 RESAW OPERATOR (woodworking) alternate titles: resaw-machine operator; resawyer; resizer operator; splitter

Operates saws to cut planks, timbers, or boards into boards of lesser thickness according to work orders: Observes lumber on conveyor as lumber approaches saw to determine cut to be made. Turns handwheels or manipulates levers to adjust distance between feed rolls and set saw for thickness of board to be cut. Depresses levers to control speed of saw and feed rolls. Observes automatic feeding of lumber to saw or pushes end of lumber into feed rolls. May replace dull saw blades, using handtools. May be designated according to type of saw used as Band-Resaw Operator (saw. & plan.; wood. container); Circular-Resaw Operator (saw. & plan.; wood. container); Multiple-Resaw Operator (wood container); Horizontal-Resaw Operator (saw & plan.).
GOE: 06.02.03 STRENGTH: H GED: R3 M2 L1 SVP: 6 DLU: 79

667.682-062 RIP-AND-GROOVE-MACHINE OPERATOR (furniture)

Operates machine to rip and cut grooves on curved or irregularly shaped furniture stock in one operation: Turns panel controls to set stops and saws for cutting grooves of specified width and depth. Feeds stock under rollers. Measures first cuts to verify processed part against work order, using rule.
GOE: 06.02.03 STRENGTH: L GED: R3 M2 L1 SVP: 4 DLU: 77

667.682-066 RIPSAW OPERATOR (woodworking) alternate titles: ripsawyer

Operates electrically powered machines equipped with one or more bandsaw or circular saw blades to rip boards along grain or to trim edges of boards, according to work ticket: Turns handwheel, uses wrench and ruler, or positions and secures collars and turns setscrews on saw shaft to adjust ripping and saw guides or distance between saws, according to specified width of boards. Moves levers or turns handwheel to adjust height of saw blade and speed of feed rolls, according to thickness of board. Starts saw, positions board against guide, and slides board into feed rolls or aligns board on feed rolls, using *shadow line* as guide. Verifies accuracy of saw setting and dimensions of lumber stock, using rule. May count pieces of lumber cut to determine when specified quantity has been ripped. May replace saw blades and lubricate machine. May be

designated according to saw operated as Band-Ripsaw Operator (woodworking); Circular-Ripsaw Operator (woodworking); Gang-Ripsaw Operator (woodworking). May operate ripsaws to cut stock so that grain and pattern match adjoining parts and be designated Ripsaw Matcher (woodworking).
GOE: 06.02.03 STRENGTH: M GED: R3 M2 L2 SVP: 4 DLU: 80

667.682-070 SHAKE SAWYER (saw. & plan.)
Operates band ripsaw to cut bolts into shakes: Starts saw and positions bolt on saw table. Pushes and guides bolt through saw so that bolt is cut diagonally to form shakes. Trims edges of shake with saw or saws and grades shake according to length and width. Tosses shake into bin according to grade. May replace saw bands, using handtools.
GOE: 06.02.03 STRENGTH: M GED: R3 M2 L1 SVP: 4 DLU: 77

667.682-074 STAVE-BOLT EQUALIZER (saw. & plan.) alternate titles: equalizer operator; equalizer
Operates equalizer saw to saw barrel-stave bolts into specified lengths with square ends: Adjusts distance between saws. Lays bolt on carriage of equalizer and starts saws. Pushes carriage between saws to trim and square ends of bolts. Withdraws carriage and removes bolts.
GOE: 06.04.03 STRENGTH: M GED: R2 M1 L1 SVP: 4 DLU: 77

667.682-078 STAVE-LOG-CUT-OFF SAW OPERATOR (saw. & plan.) alternate titles: cut-off-saw operator
Operates power saw to cut logs into specified barrel-stave lengths: Rolls log on conveyor or table of saw, using cant hook. Starts conveyor which moves log into position or pushes log along table. Starts saw and lowers saw against or pulls saw through log for each cut to saw log to specified lengths.
GOE: 06.02.03 STRENGTH: H GED: R3 M2 L1 SVP: 4 DLU: 77

667.682-082 STOCK-PATCH SAWYER (woodworking) alternate titles: defect cutter
Operates saw machine to cut out defects in finished woodstock: Inspects board to determine extent of defect and moves lever to adjust saw for length and depth of cut to be made. Places stock on machine table and slides stock under saw blade at point of defect in board. Depresses pedal to lower saw to cut out defect. Releases pedal and pushes board on conveyor for further processing.
GOE: 06.02.03 STRENGTH: M GED: R3 M2 L1 SVP: 4 DLU: 77

667.682-086 VARIETY-SAW OPERATOR (woodworking) alternate titles: combination-saw operator; universal-saw operator
Operates adjustable circular saw to perform such operations as ripsawing, cross cutting, beveling, grooving, and mitering of woodstock: Selects sawing disk according to type of cut specified on work order and bolts disk to machine shaft, using wrench. Turns handwheel or crank to tip machine table to specified angle or to raise table according to specified depth of cut. Positions guides on machine table according to specifications of cut, and turns knobs to set guides or bolts guides in place, using wrench. Starts machine, places woodstock on table against guides, and pushes stock against saw. Measures cut stock with ruler, caliper rule, or square to verify dimensions against specifications. Removes cut stock from machine and maintains production count. May turn handwheels and knobs to adjust machine guide, blade, and table to make additional cuts of woodstock, according to work order. May be designated according to operation performed as Miter Sawyer (woodworking).
GOE: 05.05.08 STRENGTH: M GED: R3 M2 L2 SVP: 5 DLU: 81

667.682-090 LOG-CUT-OFF SAWYER, AUTOMATIC (saw. & plan.)
Operates panelboard of circular saw and conveyor system to saw logs to specified lengths and to move cut logs to other stations for further processing: Starts conveyor belt that transfers log to feed conveyor. Observes log to determine number of usable lengths to be cut, and presses button on panelboard to lower saw that trims and squares log ends. Cuts log to specified lengths by registering length specification on control panel of machine that automatically measures log and lowers saw to cut log when log reaches selected position. Controls discharge conveyor to transfer log to HEAD SAWYER (saw. & plan.) 667.662-010 or GANG SAWYER (saw. & plan.) 667.682-030 according to size and texture of log.
GOE: 06.02.03 STRENGTH: L GED: R3 M2 L2 SVP: 5 DLU: 78

667.682-094 TRIMMER SAWYER (saw. & plan.)
Operates bank of circular saws to cut out defective sections of boards: Reads markings on boards as boards move on conveyor to saws to determine what cuts will produce highest grade. Moves levers (piano-like keys) to raise or lower one or more saws along trimmer bed to cut lumber into lengths and trim out defects. Climbs onto conveyor to lift and remove jammed lumber.
GOE: 06.02.03 STRENGTH: M GED: R3 M2 L1 SVP: 4 DLU: 79

667.685-010 BAND-SAW OPERATOR (wood. container) alternate titles: hogshead head-matcher
Tends bandsaw that cuts headings for barrels, hogsheads, or kegs: Clamps heading mat, boards, or veneer sheet in position on circular table. Loosens nut and sets blade guides according to thickness of heading material. Starts saw and turns table to revolve material against saw, cutting circular headings. Removes headings from table.
GOE: 06.04.03 STRENGTH: H GED: R2 M1 L1 SVP: 2 DLU: 77

667.685-014 BAND-SAW OPERATOR (woodworking)
Tends bandsaw that cuts wooden stock for toys and games: Stacks specified number of pieces of stock on cutting table against preset ripping fence. Pushes

cutting table against saw until stock is severed. Drops cut pieces into tote box. Periodically gauges piece with template to verify accuracy of machine setup.
GOE: 06.04.03 STRENGTH: L GED: R1 M1 L1 SVP: 2 DLU: 77

667.685-018 BEADING SAWYER (fabrication, nec)
Tends beading machine that cuts decorative bead (groove) around edge of smoking pipe bowls: Places bowl of pipe over chuck of machine and turns nut to expand chuck against bowl, using wrench. Pulls lever to position bowl against rotating saw. Turns handwheel to rotate bowl, sawing bead around edge of bowl.
GOE: 06.04.03 STRENGTH: L GED: R2 M1 L1 SVP: 2 DLU: 77

667.685-022 BOLTER (saw. & plan.) alternate titles: bolt sawyer; knee bolter; short-log-bolter operator
Tends circular saw that cuts slabs, edgings, and short logs into pieces suitable for making sawmill byproducts, such as shingles, shakes and laths, or for fuel: Starts conveyor that moves slab, edging, or short log into cutting position against end stop. Starts saw and moves saw to cut pieces according to requirements. May set dogs or wedges to hold slab, ending, or short log in place. May be designated Cut-Off Sawyer, Shingle Mill (saw. & plan.) when cutting pieces used for making shingles. May be designated Scrap Sawyer (saw. & plan.) when cutting scrap lumber for use as fuel.
GOE: 06.04.03 STRENGTH: M GED: R2 M1 L1 SVP: 3 DLU: 78

667.685-026 BUZZSAW OPERATOR (any industry)
Tends circular cutoff saw that custom cuts fireplace and stove fuel wood from random lengths of wood: Places wood on carriage and adjusts guides to specified length. Starts saw and moves carriage past saw to cut wood to length. Advances wood to carriage guides and repeats moving carriage past saw.
GOE: 06.04.03 STRENGTH: H GED: R2 M1 L1 SVP: 3 DLU: 77

667.685-030 COB SAWYER (fabrication, nec)
Tends belt-driven saw that cuts corncobs into specified lengths for bowls of corncob pipes: Pushes lever that engages belt to start saw. Positions cob against stop on table of saw and depresses pedal that advances revolving saw blade, cutting cob to specified length. Places husks and other waste material on conveyor belt for disposal.
GOE: 06.04.09 STRENGTH: L GED: R1 M1 L1 SVP: 2 DLU: 77

667.685-034 CUT-OFF SAWYER, LOG (paper & pulp; saw. & plan.) alternate titles: butt sawyer; deck sawyer; pondsaw operator; timber trimmer
Tends power-driven circular, chain, or drag saw located on deck or at edge of pond to cut logs to standard length: Moves logs in pond into position for sawing, using pike pole. Moves levers to drop dogs to hold log in place. Starts saw and cuts log to required length. May tend circular cutoff saw, mounted on deck, to cut smaller diameter or crooked logs into usable lengths. May replace saw blades.
GOE: 03.04.02 STRENGTH: H GED: R2 M1 L1 SVP: 2 DLU: 77

667.685-038 DOWEL POINTER (woodworking)
Tends machine that cuts dowels from dowel rod, and grooves and points dowels for use: Selects guide sockets according to diameter of stock, and secures sockets in automatic feedhead with locking thumbscrews. Adjusts saws to cut dowels to specified length. Starts machine, and inserts dowel rods in guide sockets to be cut and pointed. May sort and stack finished dowels in rack.
GOE: 06.04.03 STRENGTH: L GED: R2 M1 L1 SVP: 2 DLU: 77

667.685-042 KERFER-MACHINE OPERATOR (furniture)
Tends machine that saws parallel cuts in veneered stock so veneer panels can be bent around corners on furniture: Installs saw blades and adjusts depth of cut. Places veneer stock on jig and feeds stock into machine.
GOE: 06.04.03 STRENGTH: L GED: R2 M1 L1 SVP: 3 DLU: 77

667.685-046 SAWYER, CORK SLABS (wood prod., nec)
Tends bandsaw and circular saw that cuts cork slabs into beveled strips from which heels, with beveled inside edge, are cut: Selects miter jigs according to bevel angle specified and bolts jig onto bandsaw table, using wrench. Starts machine and pushes slab through jig which holds slab at specified angle or pushes slab flat between guides on circular saw tabletop, against rotating blade set at fixed angle, for bevel cut.
GOE: 06.04.09 STRENGTH: L GED: R1 M1 L1 SVP: 2 DLU: 77

667.685-050 SHINGLE TRIMMER (saw. & plan.)
Tends table saw to trim edges and cut defects from shingles: Starts saw and conveyor. Inspects each shingle for defects, such as rot, knots, and faulty grain. Places shingle on saw conveyor and guides shingle through saw. Tosses unusable shingles into waste bin. May replace worn saw blades, using handtools.
GOE: 06.02.02 STRENGTH: L GED: R3 M1 L1 SVP: 4 DLU: 77

667.685-054 SLASHER OPERATOR (paper & pulp; saw. & plan.) alternate titles: slasher sawyer
Tends bank of circular saws that saw logs, slabs, or scrap wood into pieces for fuel or processing into pulp: Starts saws and activates slasher conveyor chains. Straightens moving logs or slabs on conveyor to prevent jamming saws and to maintain uniform spacing, using pike pole.
GOE: 06.04.03 STRENGTH: M GED: R2 M1 L1 SVP: 2 DLU: 77

667.685-058 STAVE-LOG-RIPSAW OPERATOR (saw. & plan.)
Tends power saw that rips logs of specified length into halves or quarters for barrel-stave cutting: Places log, or halved log, on saw carriage or lifts log

to saw table, and starts saw. Shifts lever moving carriage toward saw or pushes log along table to feed log into saw and rip log in half. Moves carriage away from saw and removes sawed pieces.
GOE: 06.04.03 STRENGTH: M GED: R2 M1 L1 SVP: 4 DLU: 77

667.685-062 STAVE-SAW OPERATOR (wood. container) alternate titles: bolt sawyer

Tends stave (hollow cylinder) saw that cuts barrel, keg, tub, and bucket staves from stave bolts: Adjusts guides to attain specified thickness of stave. Lays bolt on carriage and holds bolt against guides. Depresses pedal to start carriage that feeds bolt into stave saw to cut rough staves. Releases pedal to stop carriage and removes stave. Repeats process to produce required number of staves.
GOE: 06.04.03 STRENGTH: M GED: R3 M1 L1 SVP: 4 DLU: 77

667.685-066 TURNING-MACHINE OPERATOR (wood. container) alternate titles: rounding-machine operator; turner-machine operator

Tends machine that rounds and trims assembled blanks for heads of barrels or bottoms of baskets: Adjusts limit of horizontal swing saw to shape blanks of specified size. Centers and clamps blank in chuck of machine. Starts machine and moves feed lever that swings rotating saw against blank and simultaneously starts chuck and blank revolving. Holds saw against revolving blank to trim and shape periphery. Opens jaws of chuck and removes finished head. May remove defects from barrel heading material, using circular saw. May be designated according to part formed as Basket-Bottom-Rounding-Machine Operator (wood. container); Head-Turning-Machine Operator (wood. container).
GOE: 06.04.03 STRENGTH: L GED: R2 M1 L1 SVP: 2 DLU: 77

667.685-070 AUTOMATIC BANDSAW TENDER (furniture)

Tends bandsaw that automatically cuts curved or irregular designs on woodstock or saws stock to size: Compares sample piece of stock with prefabricated templates to select template. Positions and secures template on machine bed, turns dials, and positions stock clamps to set up automatic bandsaw. Places stock on machine bed, pulls lever to clamp stock in position, and presses buttons to activate automatic machine cycle. Pushes lever to release stock clamps, removes cut stock from machine, and stacks stock on handtruck.
GOE: 06.04.03 STRENGTH: M GED: R3 M2 L2 SVP: 4 DLU: 86

667.685-074 CUT-OFF-SAW OPERATOR II (woodworking)

Tends circular saw that saws kiln-dried lumber, rough lumber, or woodstock to standard lengths in sawmills, furniture plants, or woodworking establishments: Examines boards of rough lumber or finished woodstock for defects, such as excessive warping, knots, and cracks, to determine where to cut boards to minimize waste. Pushes boards against stop guides on saw table, and depresses button or pedal to activate saw to cut boards to specified length. Places cut boards on conveyor for further processing. May tend equipment with multiple saws.
GOE: 06.04.03 STRENGTH: M GED: R2 M1 L1 SVP: 2 DLU: 86

667.686-010 CLOTHESPIN-MACHINE OPERATOR (woodworking)

Feeds wooden clothespin blanks into machine that picks up, saws, and flares one end of block. Removes defective stock.
GOE: 06.04.03 STRENGTH: M GED: R1 M1 L1 SVP: 2 DLU: 77

667.686-018 TRIMMER HELPER (saw. & plan.) alternate titles: rebut-machine tail offbearer

Feeds lumber into double-end trimmer and keeps lumber straight into saw blades, working as member of team.
GOE: 06.04.03 STRENGTH: M GED: R2 M1 L1 SVP: 2 DLU: 77

667.686-022 TURNING-MACHINE-OPERATOR HELPER (wood. container)

Assists TURNING-MACHINE OPERATOR (wood. container) in tending machine that rounds and trims assembled blanks for heads of barrels on bottoms of baskets. Performs duties as described under HELPER (any industry) Master Title.
GOE: 06.04.03 STRENGTH: M GED: R2 M1 L1 SVP: 2 DLU: 77

667.687-010 BUZZSAW-OPERATOR HELPER (any industry) alternate titles: cordwood-cutter helper

Assists BUZZSAW OPERATOR (any industry) in cutting logs into suitable lengths for use in stoves and fireplaces: Lifts limbs and trunks onto table of circular saw and holds them steady while they are cut. Throws cut pieces into piles. Lifts sawed pieces and stands pieces on end under blade of hydraulic-powered log splitter. May hold limbs and trunks of fallen trees while they are sawed to length in woods with chain saw. Performs other duties as described under HELPER (any industry) Master Title.
GOE: 06.04.03 STRENGTH: H GED: R1 M1 L1 SVP: 1 DLU: 77

667.687-014 LOG INSPECTOR (saw. & plan.) alternate titles: log culler

Inspects logs, used in manufacture of barrel staves, before they are cut into lengths by STAVE-LOG-CUT-OFF SAW OPERATOR (saw. & plan.) and separates and marks for use in manufacture of barrel-heading material those logs having defects, such as knots, crooks, and checks.
GOE: 03.04.02 STRENGTH: M GED: R2 M1 L1 SVP: 3 DLU: 77

667.687-018 SAWMILL WORKER (saw. & plan.) alternate titles: swamper

Performs any combination of following duties in preparing logs for cutting into lumber and storing cut lumber in sawmill: Unloads logs from trucks or

cars. Rolls logs onto sawmill deck. Examines logs for defects, such as embedded pieces of iron or stone, decayed wood from splits, and marks defects for removal by other workers. Rolls logs from deck onto log or carriage. Rides log carriage of head saw and adjusts position of logs on carriage to cut planks of required thickness. Sorts and guides planks emerging from saw onto roller tables or conveyors for trimming edges. Straightens lumber on moving conveyors. Straightens edges of rough lumber, using saw. Operates and maintains donkey engines. Sharpens and adjusts teeth of woodworking saws. Tends fires in donkey engine. May relieve designated workers engaged in preparing or cutting logs into lumber and be designated Sawmill-Relief Worker (saw. & plan.).
GOE: 06.04.40 STRENGTH: M GED: R3 M1 L1 SVP: 3 DLU: 86

669 WOOD MACHINING OCCUPATIONS, N.E.C.

This group includes occupations, not elsewhere classified, concerned with shaping wooden parts or products by removing excess material from stock or objects.

669.130-010 SUPERVISOR, ASSEMBLY ROOM (furniture)

Supervises and coordinates activities of workers engaged in fabricating wooden shades, venetian blinds, curtain, sash, or traverse rods: Sets up equipment, such as saws, slicing, and wood weaving machines. Verifies conformance of parts to specifications, using gauges, calipers, micrometers, or other measuring instruments. Repairs or requisitions replacement of defective equipment. Trains new workers. Directs workers in operation of equipment. Performs other duties as described under SUPERVISOR (any industry) Master Title.
GOE: 06.02.01 STRENGTH: L GED: R4 M3 L3 SVP: 7 DLU: 77

669.130-014 SUPERVISOR, CUTTING DEPARTMENT (pen & pencil)

Supervises and coordinates activities of workers in cutting department of wooden pencil manufacturing plant: Examines and counts slats, blanks, and pencils for adherence to company standards. Sets up, operates, and adjusts machines, such as disk sanders and rounding machines. Performs other duties as described under SUPERVISOR (any industry) Master Title.
GOE: 06.01.01 STRENGTH: L GED: R4 M2 L3 SVP: 7 DLU: 77

669.130-018 SUPERVISOR, FRAMING MILL (wood prod., nec)

Supervises and coordinates activities of workers engaged in handling, classifying, peeling, trimming, notching and boring, and branding lumber for use as crossties, pilings, bridge timbers, and utility poles: Assigns space in yard for lumber, according to production schedule and type and condition of lumber. Schedules peeling, trimming, adzing, and boring of lumber, according to classification of lumber and length of time in yard. Orders branding of lumber with identification data, such as customer, type of lumber, and date of treatment. Performs other duties as described under SUPERVISOR (any industry) Master title. May be designated according to type of product as Supervisor, Pole Yard (wood prod., nec); Supervisor, Tie Yard (wood prod., nec).
GOE: 06.02.01 STRENGTH: L GED: R4 M2 L2 SVP: 8 DLU: 77

669.130-022 SUPERVISOR, MACHINING (woodworking)

Supervises and coordinates activities of workers engaged in operating variety of woodworking machines to shape wooden parts or products by removing excess material: Analyzes work orders to determine production schedules. Computes amounts of stock and supplies required for operations, based on production schedules, and requisitions materials from storage area. Inspects and measures wood products, using pattern and rule, to verify conformance to company standards. Directs workers in adjusting machines and equipment to repair products which fail to meet standards. Trains new workers in setup and operation of machines. Performs other duties as described under SUPERVISOR (any industry) Master Title. May plan flow of materials through department and develop physical layout of machines according to work orders. May lay out designs on stock to guide workers in machining operations [PATTERN MARKER (woodworking) I 761.381-022]. May be designated according to department supervised as Supervisor, Finish-End (furniture); Supervisor, Rough-End (furniture).
GOE: 05.05.08 STRENGTH: L GED: R4 M3 L3 SVP: 7 DLU: 81

669.130-026 SUPERVISOR, SAWMILL (saw. & plan.)

Supervises and coordinates activities of workers engaged in shaping logs or wood to form rough lumber, shingles, cooperage stock, lathes, and veneer stock: Reads work orders to determine type product to be produced and production schedule. Instructs workers on machine setup to meet production requirements. Inspects material during and after processing to determine that dimensions and grade meet specifications. Directs workers to adjust machine setup or processing procedure to correct defects. Performs duties as described under SUPERVISOR (any industry) Master Title. May inspect, grade, scale, and tally incoming lumber and verify invoices. May compute wood requirements needed to meet production demands. May supervise and coordinate activities of workers engaged in removing bark from logs prior to processing.
GOE: 06.01.01 STRENGTH: M GED: R4 M3 L3 SVP: 7 DLU: 79

669.130-030 SUPERVISOR, SHUTTLE FITTING (woodworking)

Supervises and coordinates activities of workers engaged in cutting and corrugating shuttle chambers, shaping tapered shuttle ends, cutting grooves and slots, and in performing related duties to assemble component parts of wooden shuttles. Sets up machines. Performs duties as described under SUPERVISOR (any industry) Master Title.

GOE: 06.02.01 STRENGTH: L GED: R4 M2 L2 SVP: 7 DLU: 77

669.130-034 SUPERVISOR, SHUTTLE PREPARATION (woodworking)
Supervises and coordinates activities of workers engaged in sawing ends of seasoned wooden blocks, planing surfaces, and boring, scoring, and tapering ends to shape blocks into shuttle blanks. Sets up woodworking machines. Performs other duties as described under SUPERVISOR (any industry) Master Title.
GOE: 06.02.01 STRENGTH: L GED: R4 M2 L2 SVP: 7 DLU: 77

669.130-038 SUPERVISOR, SHUTTLE VENEERING (woodworking)
Supervises and coordinates activities of workers engaged in cutting fiber veneer strips and gluing strips on wooden shuttles. Sets up and operates shearing, shaping, and surfacing machines. Performs duties as described under SUPERVISOR (any industry) Master Title.
GOE: 06.02.01 STRENGTH: L GED: R4 M3 L3 SVP: 7 DLU: 77

669.132-010 SUPERVISOR, SAWING AND ASSEMBLY (furniture)
Supervises and coordinates activities of workers engaged in sawing, shaping, and assembling woodstock to form furniture frames and mock-ups: Reviews production schedules and confers with department head to determine production priorities, availability of equipment and personnel, and processing changes. Examines furniture parts during machining and assembly, and directs workers to change machine setup or work techniques to eliminate defects. Reassigns workers or performs duties of absentee workers. Operates woodworking machines, such as bandsaw, ripsaw, and boring machine to cut woodstock to specifications. Performs other duties as described under SUPERVISOR (any industry) Master Title.
GOE: 06.02.01 STRENGTH: M GED: R4 M3 L3 SVP: 7 DLU: 86

669.137-010 SUPERVISOR, WOOD-CREW (saw. & plan.)
Supervises and coordinates activities of workers engaged in culling, cutting, and loading wood on cars or trucks to be sold for fuel or used at sawmill. Performs duties as described under SUPERVISOR (any industry) Master Title.
GOE: 03.02.02 STRENGTH: L GED: R3 M2 L2 SVP: 6 DLU: 77

669.280-010 MACHINE SETTER (woodworking)
Sets up various types of woodworking machines, such as lathes, molders, planers, routers, sanders, saws, and shapers, for machine tenders and operators: Examines blueprints, drawings, work orders, and patterns to determine size and shape of item to be fabricated, machines to be set up, and sequence of machining operation. Selects and installs required knives, saws, bits, cutterheads, or abrasives on drum, arbor, spindle, or in chuck of machine, using handtools. Positions and attaches or installs guides, patterns, fixtures, or jigs to table or bed of machine with clamps or bolts, and turns handwheels or moves levers to adjust stops, guides, and cutting depths. Cuts or shapes sample and verifies cuts, angles, and dimensions to ensure conformance with specifications, using gauges, calipers, square, rule, or template. Turns handwheels, moves levers, or uses handtools to adjust machine. May reshape or sharpen knives and cutterheads. May be designated according to type of machine set up as Automatic-Lathe Setter (woodworking); Double-End-Tenoner Setter (woodworking); Drum-Sander Setter (woodworking); Molder Setter (woodworking); Planer Setter (woodworking); Tongue-And-Groove-Machine Setter (woodworking). May be designated: Router Setter (woodworking); Sander Setter (woodworking); Shaper Setter (woodworking).
GOE: 06.01.02 STRENGTH: M GED: R3 M3 L3 SVP: 7 DLU: 79

669.360-010 CHECKERING-MACHINE ADJUSTER (ordnance)
Adjusts and maintains semiautomatic checkering machines that cut decorative gripping surfaces on wooden gun stocks and forearms: Bends springs and turns setscrews to adjust stops and cams that regulate length of stroke and depth of cut produced, using handtools. Replaces worn parts, such as microswitches, pulley belts, and motor brushes. May give instructions to new operators [STOCK CHECKERER (ordnance) II] in use of machine.
GOE: 06.01.02 STRENGTH: M GED: R3 M2 L1 SVP: 7 DLU: 77

669.364-010 INSPECTOR, ASSEMBLY (furniture)
Assembles and inspects samples of furniture parts to determine conformity to specifications prior to mass production of parts: Inspects and measures samples of furniture parts to determine conformity to specifications, using ruler, caliper, protractor, and square. Discusses with SUPERVISOR, MACHINING (woodworking) 669.130-022 alternate machine setup to correct defects, utilizing knowledge of wood and woodworking machines. Fits and knocks parts together to form furniture, using mallet. Secures parts together, using clamps. Examines assembled furniture to determine conformity of appearance to finish sketch of furniture. Notifies PRODUCTION SUPERINTENDENT (any industry) 183.117-014 when parts and assembled furniture meet production specifications.
GOE: 06.02.22 STRENGTH: L GED: R3 M2 L2 SVP: 6 DLU: 86

669.380-010 MACHINIST APPRENTICE, WOOD (woodworking)
Performs duties as described under APPRENTICE (any industry) Master Title.
GOE: 05.05.08 STRENGTH: M GED: R3 M3 L3 SVP: 6 DLU: 77

669.380-014 MACHINIST, WOOD (woodworking) alternate titles: woodworking-machine operator
Sets up and operates variety of woodworking machines to surface, cut, and shape lumber, and to fabricate parts for wood products, such as doors, door and window frames, furniture, and sashes, according to specifications: Selects, installs, and adjusts saw blades, cutterheads, boring bits, and sanding belts in respective machines, using handtools and rule. Starts machine and makes trial cut. Operates machines to saw [CUT-OFF-SAW OPERATOR (woodworking) I 667.682-022; RIPSAW OPERATOR (woodworking) 667.682-066; VARIETY-SAW OPERATOR (woodworking) 667.682-086]; to smooth and shape lumber and wood parts [PLANER OPERATOR (woodworking) 665.682-022; SHAPER OPERATOR (woodworking) 665.682-034]; to cut tenons and mortises in woodstock [TENONER OPERATOR (woodworking) 669.382-018; MORTISING-MACHINE OPERATOR (woodworking) 665.482-014]; to bore holes [BORING-MACHINE OPERATOR (woodworking) 666.382-010]; to cut slots, grooves, and designs in woodstock [ROUTER OPERATOR (woodworking) 665.682-030]; and to sand lumber, woodstock, and parts [MOLDING SANDER (woodworking) 662.682-010; CYLINDER-SANDER OPERATOR (woodworking) 662.685-014; SANDER, MACHINE (woodworking) 761.682-014]. Periodically verifies dimensions of parts for adherence to specifications, using gauges and templates. May assemble fabricated parts to make millwork products, such as doors, sashes, and door and window frames. May sharpen machine cutting heads, using handtools and grinder. May be designated according to products as Door Maker (saw. & plan.); Frame Maker (saw. & plan.); Sash Maker (saw. & plan.).
GOE: 05.05.08 STRENGTH: M GED: R3 M3 L3 SVP: 6 DLU: 81

669.380-018 PIPE-AND-TANK FABRICATOR (wood. container)
Sets up and operates machine to cut, croze, slot, shape, and incise materials for prefabricated wooden tanks or pipes: Lays out materials for tank bottoms and clamps material together on platform, using screw clamps. Bolts machine pivot to center of work material and attaches radial-arm bandsaw to pivot, using overhead hoist. Starts saw and removes clamps and sawed pieces as saw moves around radius of tank bottom material. Removes saw, attaches shaper to radial-arm, and bevels outside edges of material. Saws pipe and tank stave material to specified size, using trim saw. Operates straight or curve line crozing machine to bevel or croze end of tank staves that fit into bevel on bottom of tank. Operates stave slotting machine to cut slots in ends of staves. Inserts wood or metal splines in slotted ends of staves by hand. Operates incising machine to incise straight or curved staves and tank pieces for wood preserving treatment. Measures and cuts plates, rafters, trusses, *headers,* center posts and hatches for flat or conical roofs on tanks, using bandsaw, shaper, jointer, drill press, and handtools. Constructs wooden floats and measuring boards for liquid level indicators on tanks. May operate dowel-boring machine. May operate radial shaping machine to form laminated rings for wooden pipe.
GOE: 05.10.01 STRENGTH: M GED: R3 M2 L2 SVP: 7 DLU: 77

669.382-010 DADO OPERATOR (woodworking)
Sets up and operates single- or multiple-blade machine to cut grooves, notches, recesses, rabbets, lap joints, and tenons in wooden parts: Examines drawings, blueprints, or samples and written specifications and selects and installs saws, dado heads, and spacers, using rule and wrenches. Turns handwheels to move guide fence and adjust table height to attain specified location and depth of cut. Starts machine and pushes wooden parts past cutting heads by hand, or inserts parts between feed rolls that carry parts through machine. May be designated according to type of saws used as Warble-Saw Operator (woodworking); or according to part and cut made as Cleat Notcher (wood. container); Partition Notcher (wood. container); Strap Recesser (wood. container).
GOE: 05.05.08 STRENGTH: M GED: R3 M2 L1 SVP: 5 DLU: 77

669.382-014 RAFTER-CUTTING-MACHINE OPERATOR (mfd. bldgs.)
Sets up and operates machine to cut notches and bevels in rafters for precut or prefabricated houses: Determines from specifications or blueprints number and size of rafters to be cut. Selects and installs saws and cutterheads in machine, and adjusts their spacing and depth and angle of cut, using wrenches, rule, and protractor. Positions board on table or carriage of machine and clamps board in place. Starts machine and moves lever to feed board into saws and cutterheads to cut rafter.
GOE: 06.02.03 STRENGTH: H GED: R3 M3 L2 SVP: 4 DLU: 77

669.382-018 TENONER OPERATOR (woodworking)
Sets up and operates single- or double-end machine to cut tenons, or to size, trim, groove, shape, or match ends of woodstock used in furniture manufacture: Examines blueprints, drawings, patterns, or written specifications to determine size, type, and setting of saw blades, cutterheads, cams, and jigs to be used. Selects and installs saw blades, cutters, and accessories in machine, using rule and wrenches. Turns handwheels, presses buttons, and reads gauges; or positions pattern on machine, to space saws and cutterheads, according to length and depth of cut. Positions dogs on conveyor according to width measurement for feeding stock through machine and tightens dogs in place, using wrench. Presses button to start machine, holds stock against guide on machine carriage, and pushes carriage through machine to convey stock between cutters, or places stock against guide and dogs on feed chain which pulls stock through machine. Removes processed stock and verifies dimensions, using rule or template. May turn handwheel during operation of machine to increase or decrease distance between saws and cutterheads and adjust for errors. May be designated according to machine operated as Double-End-Tenoner Operator (woodworking).
GOE: 05.05.08 STRENGTH: M GED: R4 M3 L3 SVP: 5 DLU: 78

669.382-022 MULTI-PURPOSE MACHINE OPERATOR (furniture)
Sets up and operates machine with multiple cutterheads to simultaneously saw, bore, groove, shape, and sand woodstock to form furniture parts: Reads

work ticket to determine machining operations required to form specified furniture parts. Selects, installs, and adjusts blades, bits, cutter knives, and sanding belts, according to specifications, using handtools. Attaches specified forms that hold woodstock during machining operations to automatic carriage holding device of machine, using handtools. Selects and installs punch cards into machine control panel that determine sequence and duration of machining operations. Presses buttons to start machine, positions woodstock in holding forms, and adjusts clamps to secure woodstock in form. Presses button to activate automatic machining cycle. Removes processed parts from holding form and verifies finished dimensions, using steel tape rule, gauges, and calipers. Stacks finished parts in storage area.
GOE: 06.02.03 STRENGTH: M GED: R3 M3 L3 SVP: 6 DLU: 86

669.382-026 TURNING MACHINE SET-UP OPERATOR (fabrication, nec)

Sets up and operates turning machines to shape and bore smoking pipe bowls: Sharpens turning machine cutting knives, using grinding wheel. Inserts and secures knives in cutterhead, using socket wrench. Turns handwheels and moves levers to adjust turning machine carriage stops and cutting depth of machine. Places block in clamp on machine carriage and moves lever to secure block in clamp. Pushes machine carriage handle to move block into cutterhead to shape and bore sample pipe bowl. Examines sample pipe bowl to verify shape and dimension against specifications, using caliper and gauges. Performs other duties as described under BRIAR CUTTER (fabrication, nec) 664.685-010.
GOE: 06.02.03 STRENGTH: M GED: R3 M2 L2 SVP: 4 DLU: 86

669.485-010 POWER-BARKER OPERATOR (paper & pulp; saw. & plan.)

Tends machine that removes bark and dirt from logs by one of following methods: (1) Starts conveyor to move logs from pond to drum of barking machine. Moves lever to activate chains or start drum revolving to tumble logs and knock off bark. Turns valve to regulate water spray that removes chips and dirt from log. Breaks up log jams in drum, using peavey or pike pole and chain hoist. (2) Moves lever to activate kicker arms that kick log into machine cradle. Turns controls that start log rotating between toothed gears that remove bark from log, and regulates and directs pressurized water jet to remove loose bark and dirt. (3) Turns levers to control movement and centering of log in jet ring and to regulate pressure of water jets. Starts conveyors that carry logs from barking machine to saw deck. May be designated according to machine operated as Drum-Barker Operator (paper & pulp); Hydraulic-Barker Operator (paper & pulp; saw. & plan.); Ring-Barker Operator (saw. & plan.).
GOE: 06.04.03 STRENGTH: L GED: R3 M2 L2 SVP: 3 DLU: 77

669.662-010 BOX-BLANK-MACHINE OPERATOR (wood. container) alternate titles: stitching-machine operator

Sets up, adjusts, and operates machine to staple cleats and boards together to assemble box sections: Adds or removes links from chain-feed belt, spaces stops on belt, and spaces stapling heads, according to dimensions of box, using wrench. Mounts spools of wire on machine, threads ends through stapling heads, and starts machine. Directs workers engaged in feeding cleats and boards to machine and removing finished product. May make wirebound box sections, threading binding wire through guides so that staples fasten binding wire to box, and be designated Wire-Bound-Box-Machine Operator (wood. container).
GOE: 06.02.20 STRENGTH: L GED: R3 M2 L2 SVP: 4 DLU: 77

669.662-014 FRAME-TABLE OPERATOR (wood prod., nec) alternate titles: framer; framing-mill operator

Operates machines to frame timbers for utility poles and for structures, such as buildings, bridges, and piers: Lays out timber for cutting operation, according to blueprints, sketches, or work order, using square, ruler, and pencil. Installs dado cutter or adzing knives. Starts motor that adjusts cutter for depth and angle of cut. Signals FRAME-TABLE-OPERATOR HELPER (wood prod., nec) to spot timber on carriage under cutting tool. Starts machine and advances cutter into wood by turning wheel. Marks finished pieces with die-filled hammer or crayon. Changes cutters, using handtools. Makes repairs and lubricates machine. Bores holes in timber, using drill press or portable drill. May specialize in framing utility poles and be designated Pole Framer, Machine (wood prod., nec).
GOE: 06.02.03 STRENGTH: M GED: R3 M2 L2 SVP: 5 DLU: 77

669.662-018 TONGUE-AND-GROOVE-MACHINE OPERATOR (woodworking)

Operates machine that joins woodstock of varying widths to form panels by simultaneously cutting tongue in one piece and groove in other, applying glue, sliding tongue and groove together, and ejecting glued pieces: Adjusts guides, cutters, feed and glue rolls, according to thickness and length of stock, depth of cuts, and dimensions of panel, using handtools. Starts machine and gives directions to feeders who simultaneously feed stock into each end of machine. Inspects joined pieces to detect loose joints and makes machine adjustments to correct operation of machine. Changes worn cutterheads and installs cutterheads, according to type of tongue and groove specified, using handtools. May operate ripsaw to cut panels to specified width. May feed or off bear machine. May select wood pieces of matching grain or color.
GOE: 06.02.03 STRENGTH: M GED: R3 M2 L2 SVP: 5 DLU: 77

669.682-010 ADZING-AND-BORING-MACHINE OPERATOR (wood prod., nec) alternate titles: tie-mill operator

Operates variety of machines to trim, bore, incise, and date stamp railroad ties and utility pole crossarms, preparatory to treating with wood preservatives:

Adjusts stops and guides, and installs dating punches, boring bits, adzing cutters, incising rollers, and knives, according to work order, using rule, wrenches, pry bar, and hammer. Starts machines and conveyor system and observes operation. Removes defective material from conveyor prior to processing operation. Replaces worn or broken drills, adzing cutters, incising knives, and machine parts. May feed ties or crossarms into machine and inspect finished work.
GOE: 06.02.03 STRENGTH: L GED: R3 M2 L3 SVP: 5 DLU: 77

669.682-014 BARREL ASSEMBLER (wood. container)

Controls equipment to assemble wooden barrels, performing any combination of following duties: Positions ends of designated staves in truss hoop to form barrel shell and places shell on conveyor that conveys shell through steam box to make staves pliable. Places shell in hoop driver that forces truss hoop onto end of shell opposite bilge to secure staves in shell. Positions steamed shell over gas burner to form permanent shape of staves. Aligns staves and forces truss rings onto barrel shell, using barrel-assembly machine or vibrator platform, cooper's hammer, and hoop driver. Pulls levers to hold shell in croze cutter and to rotate shell against cutterheads that cut croze and trim ends of barrel shell staves. Removes end truss hoops to facilitate installation of barrelheads, using truss-pulling machine. Positions barrelhead in croze of shell and moves lever to lower cinch ring of machine that forces head into croze; or positions shell and heads in heading machine, hammers heads into place, moves lever to squeeze staves around heads, and place steel hoop into position to secure heads. Starts sander and moves levers to push rotating barrel against sanding belt to smooth exteriors of barrel, or sands exterior of barrel, using hand held belt or disc sander. Installs permanent hoops, using hoop driver. Drills hole in barrel for filling and emptying purposes, using drill press [BUNGHOLE BORER (wood. container) 666.382-010]. Inspects barrels for defects, such as loose staves, cracks, and defective assembly. May be designated according to machine operated as Croze Cutter (wood. container); Head-Up Operator (wood. container); Heater Operator (wood. container); Hoop-Driving-Machine Operator (wood. container); Leveler (wood. container) II; Sander (wood. container). May be designated: Tap-Out Operator (wood. container); Truss Driver (wood. container); Truss Puller (wood. container).
GOE: 06.02.20 STRENGTH: M GED: R3 M2 L2 SVP: 4 DLU: 78

669.682-018 BUCKET TURNER (wood. container) alternate titles: tub turner

Operates bucket-turning machine to smooth and finish outer surfaces of wooden buckets: Clamps bucket between chucks of machine and removes assembling ring from bucket with hammer. Starts machine to rotate bucket. Pushes lever on tool carriage to feed tool along surface of bucket, finishing bucket surface. Smooths surface of bucket, using block covered with sandpaper. Places temporary hoop on bucket and removes it from machine.
GOE: 06.04.03 STRENGTH: M GED: R2 M1 L1 SVP: 4 DLU: 77

669.682-022 CHUCKING-AND-BORING-MACHINE OPERATOR (furniture) alternate titles: chair-post-machine operator

Sets up and operates machine to saw, bore, and round ends of chair posts, rails, and backs: Turns handwheel to adjust space between chucks and saws. Installs cutterheads according to size of stock and angle of cut and spaces boring bits according to specified location of holes, using handtools. Turns knobs to adjust feed stops. Pushes button to start machine. Positions material and depresses pedal to activate mechanism to saw, bore, and shape material or feeds woodstock into machine that automatically clamps, saws, bores, and rounds ends of woodstock. Starts machine and feeds woodstock into machine that automatically clamps and processes it.
GOE: 06.02.03 STRENGTH: M GED: R3 M2 L2 SVP: 4 DLU: 77

669.682-026 CHUCKING-AND-SAWING-MACHINE OPERATOR (woodworking)

Sets up and operates machine to saw woodstock to specified length and to shape ends of stock to fit into mortises (recesses) of opposing wooden parts: Selects knives according to diameter of cut specified on work ticket. Aligns and bolts knives in cutterhead and screws it on spindle, using wrenches. Adjusts angle of table by turning handwheel and bolts or clamps holding jigs to table. Places stock in jig and pushes table containing stock into circular saw to trim end of stock. Pulls table back against stops and depresses pedal to advance cutterhead that shapes end of stock.
GOE: 06.02.03 STRENGTH: L GED: R3 M2 L1 SVP: 4 DLU: 77

669.682-030 CORNER-BRACE-BLOCK-MACHINE OPERATOR (furniture) alternate titles: corner-block cutter

Sets up and operates machine to saw, groove, and drill blocks used to reinforce corners of furniture frames: Sets angle of cutoff saw and installs bit and dado saw, according to work ticket. Places stock on holder and pushes stock into rotating saw to cut end at angle. Lays stock on conveyor belt that carries it into machine that cuts grooves and drills holes.
GOE: 06.02.03 STRENGTH: M GED: R3 M2 L2 SVP: 4 DLU: 77

669.682-034 CROZE-MACHINE OPERATOR (wood. container) alternate titles: crozer

Operates crozer machine to cut croze (groove) in wooden tank staves, into which tank bottom is fitted: Starts machine. Places stave on machine table, aligns mark on stave with cutoff saw blade, and depresses pedal to clamp stave in position. Pulls saw and dado-cutter assembly across stave. Releases pedal and slides stave along machine bench to helper.
GOE: 06.02.03 STRENGTH: L GED: R3 M1 L1 SVP: 4 DLU: 77

669.682-038 DOUBLE-END-TRIMMER-AND-BORING-MACHINE OPERATOR (furniture)

Sets up and operates multiple-spindle boring and trimming machine to bore vertical or horizontal holes and trim or miter ends of stock used in furniture manufacturing: Reads work specifications to determine location, angles, depth, diameter, and number of holes to bore in stock and cuts to be made by saws. Installs specified bits in spindle chucks, using wrench. Adjusts chucks for location specified, using handtools and pattern stock. Attaches holders, jigs, or stops, and adjusts pneumatic clamps with handtools. Removes pattern and starts boring heads and saws. Positions stock under clamps and against stops on machine bed, and depresses pedal or turns automatic cycle lever to activate machine to clamp, bore, trim, and release stock. Periodically verifies accuracy of setup by comparing trimmed and bored stock with pattern stock, using caliper, square, or tape measure. May operate machine that trims or miters only one end of wooden stock and be designated Single-End-Trimming-And-Boring-Machine Operator (woodworking).
GOE: 06.02.03 STRENGTH: M GED: R3 M2 L3 SVP: 4 DLU: 78

669.682-042 DOWEL-INSERTING-MACHINE OPERATOR (woodworking) alternate titles: rail-doweling-machine operator

Sets up and operates machine to bore holes, and glue and insert dowels in ends of door and sash rails: Adjusts stock guides, pressure arms, and glue discharge pipes, and inserts and spaces drills in chucks to accommodate size of rails to be processed, using stock sample, rule, and wrench. Pours glue into machine reservoir, loads dowel hopper, and starts machine. Feeds trial rail into machine and checks spacing of dowels with rule and caliper. Feeds machine by placing stack of rails in rail-feed hopper.
GOE: 06.02.03 STRENGTH: M GED: R2 M1 L1 SVP: 4 DLU: 77

669.682-046 EMBOSSING-MACHINE OPERATOR (wood prod., nec)

Operates machine to indent picture-frame molding with ornamental designs: Installs embossing wheel in machine, using handtools. Turns handwheel to lower wheel over bed of machine to thickness of molding and sets feed guides. Starts machine, places sample piece of molding in guides, and pushes sample under embossing wheel. Inspects embossing on sample and adjusts wheel to correct depth of indentation.
GOE: 06.02.03 STRENGTH: L GED: R3 M2 L2 SVP: 4 DLU: 77

669.682-050 INLETTER (ordnance)

Operates multispindle woodworking machine to rout, mill, drill, and profile recesses in gun stocks to receive metal gun parts, such as barrel, breech, receiver, and trigger: Clamps gunstock blank in fixture on carriage of machine. Turns crank to feed workpiece into series of routing bits, each equipped with tracing pin. Moves dropbar to force tracing pins to follow contours of metal model in designated sequence, so routing tools will cut duplicate recesses in wooden gunstock. Turns crank to feed gunstock into horizontal milling cutter and moves dropbar that controls cutter to round off and smooth routing cuts. Verifies accuracy of cuts by fitting metal gun parts into their respective recesses and using fixed gauges.
GOE: 06.02.03 STRENGTH: L GED: R3 M1 L2 SVP: 4 DLU: 77

669.682-054 LAST TRIMMER (wood prod., nec)

Operates machines to shape and smooth shoe lasts to specified contour and size, performing any combination of following tasks: Cuts lathe centers from last turnings at specified point, using bandsaw or handsaw. Files toe area of last to specified contour outline drawn on bottom of last. Sands toe area with sandpaper or operates sanding machine to attain specified size and finish. Verifies finished size, using templates. Operates sanding machine to sand heel area of last to remove excess material, form heel, and establish specified length of last. Verifies last length, using gauge. Replaces worn sandpaper belts on sanding machines. May draw last bottom outline, using sole pattern and pencil [LAST MARKER (wood prod., nec)]. May specialize on one part of last and be designated Heel Grinder (wood prod., nec); Toe Stripper (wood prod., nec).
GOE: 06.02.03 STRENGTH: M GED: R3 M2 L2 SVP: 3 DLU: 77

669.682-058 NAILING-MACHINE OPERATOR (any industry) alternate titles: box maker; nailer, machine

Sets up and operates machines to drive nails into boards to fasten wood assemblies, such as boxes, furniture frames, crates, and pallets, and to nail lids on boxes: Spaces nail chucks and rails according to specifications and turns setscrews to fasten chucks to rails. Turns wheel to raise or lower table according to size of pieces to be nailed. Fills hopper with nails. Fastens or adjusts stops and jigs on machine table to facilitate positioning of material to be nailed. Starts machine, positions boards on table under chucks, and depresses pedal to drive nails into board. May move levers to control nail feed and turn knobs to position nail setting heads. May be designated according to part nailed as Bottom Nailer (wood. container); Cleat Nailer (wood. container); Frame Nailer (wood. container); Strap Nailer (wood. container); or according to type of machine as Lidding-Machine Operator (any industry).
GOE: 06.02.03 STRENGTH: M GED: R2 M1 L1 SVP: 4 DLU: 77

669.682-062 PLUGGING-MACHINE OPERATOR (woodworking)

Operates machine that routs out defects, such as knots, dents, and holes, in boards, and inserts glue and plugs in cutout areas: Fastens router and plug cutter into machine chucks, using wrench. Fills glue reservoir. Inserts wood slat into machine for plug material. Grasps board and inspects board for defects, such as knots, dents, and blemishes. Starts machine, and inserts defect in board under device holding router and plug cutter. Depresses pedal, causing router to

bore hole, glue injector to inject glue into hole, and plug cutter to cut plug and press it into glued hole. Removes board, wipes off excess glue, and stacks it on pallet on cart.
GOE: 06.02.03 STRENGTH: M GED: R3 M1 L1 SVP: 4 DLU: 77

669.682-066 TIP INSERTER (woodworking)

Operates variety of machines to shape ends of wooden shuttles and attach tips: Squares ends of shuttles, using disk sanding machine. Saws off ends of shuttles, using machine equipped with rotating saw blade. Removes burrs from sawed ends with knife. Bores holes in shuttle ends for insertion of ferrules, using boring machines. Taps steel ferrule into ferrule hole with hammer. Dips corrugated shaft of metal tip in glue and sets tip in hole previously drilled. Forces tip into hole, using arbor press.
GOE: 06.02.09 STRENGTH: M GED: R3 M1 L1 SVP: 4 DLU: 77

669.682-070 UTILITY OPERATOR (saw. & plan.)

Operates and controls barkers, saws, edgers, planers, trimmers, and chippers in sawmill to relieve other operators during rest and meal periods, emergencies, and vacations: Receives assignment to operate specific machine from SUPERVISOR, SAWMILL (saw. & plan.) 669.130-026. Moves levers, turns handwheels, depresses pedals, and pushes console buttons to activate machines and to observe, rotate, and move logs and boards on conveyors and adjustable tables to shape boards for optimum market value. Changes cutting blades, adjusts machines, and clears machine jams, using handtools. Lubricates and cleans machine parts.
GOE: 06.02.03 STRENGTH: M GED: R4 M2 L2 SVP: 6 DLU: 86

669.685-010 BARREL-ASSEMBLER HELPER (wood. container)

Assists BARREL ASSEMBLER (wood. container) to assemble barrels, performing any combination of following duties: Starts gas burner or oven to heat shells (barrels without ends). Removes and replaces machine attachments, such as croze cutter and drill chucks. Replaces worn sanding belts on sander. Performs other duties as described under HELPER (any industry) Master Title. May be designated according to machine operator assisted as Croze-Cutter Helper (wood. container); Head-Up-Operator Helper (wood. container); Heater Operator Helper (wood. container); Hoop-Driving-Machine-Operator Helper (wood. container); Leveler Helper (wood. container); Sander Helper (wood. container); Truss-Driver Helper (wood. container); Truss-Puller Helper (wood. container).
GOE: 06.04.03 STRENGTH: M GED: R2 M1 L2 SVP: 2 DLU: 77

669.685-014 BASKET ASSEMBLER I (wood. container) alternate titles: basket maker

Tends machines that fabricate components of veneer, rattan, reed, and willow baskets of specified size and shape and assembles components, performing any combination of following tasks: Interlaces strips of veneer or other materials to weave basket bottom. Tends machine to shape woven bottom and interlace veneer strips with bottom to form sides. Bends extended ends of bottom perpendicular to matted portion of bottom and places hoop around ends to hold ends in position for weaving ends and sides. Staples rim to basket bottom. Tapers or points ends, using knife, and weaves ends into sides. Nails rims together to hold sides in place. Tends machine that shapes and staples veneer strips to basket rim. Tends basket-cover machine to cut cover mats (woven veneer strips) to size. Tends machine that bends basket cover into arc and staples rim to cover. Stitches or staples reinforcing splints (wood strips) to top edges of mat. Shapes wire in bail-bender to form bails (wire handles). Bends soaked wood strips to form basket handles. Staples wire handles to rim of basket. Tends machine that clamps wood handles to basket. Examines baskets for imperfections and discards defective baskets for repair. May be known according to type or section of basket formed or assembled as Bottom Maker (wood. container); Slat-Basket-Top Maker (wood. container); or machine tended as Handle-Machine Operator (wood. container); Hoop-Coiling-Machine Operator (wood. container); Loop-Machine Operator (wood. container); Mat-Machine Tender (wood. container). May be designated: Basket-Bottom Machine Operator (wood. container); Braider (wood. container); Cover-Machine Operator (wood. container); Cover-Mat-Machine Operator (wood. container); Handle Bender (wood. container); Hamper Maker, Machine (wood. container); Market-Basket Maker (wood. container) I; Stitcher Operator (wood. container); Webb Layer (wood. container).
GOE: 06.04.03 STRENGTH: L GED: R2 M1 L1 SVP: 2 DLU: 78

669.685-018 BLIND-SLAT-STAPLING-MACHINE OPERATOR (woodworking)

Tends machine that drives staples in edges of blind slats and attaches stapled slats to slide rods: Adjusts and sets stop and ratchet, and lays rod in position under stapler head. Places slat under stapler and moves lever to drive staples into slat and hold slat to rod. Ratchet automatically moves rod along until section is completed.
GOE: 06.04.20 STRENGTH: L GED: R2 M1 L1 SVP: 2 DLU: 77

669.685-022 BOTTOM-HOOP DRIVER (wood. container)

Tends machine that drives and tightens bottom hoops on buckets and tubs: Adjusts height of table by adding or removing iron plates from table. Sets bucket or tub on table with bottom up and lays hoop over and around bottom. Centers bucket or tub under driving head of machine and presses on pedal that lowers driving head on hoop, forcing it in place. Releases pedal to raise driving head and removes bucket or tub from machine.
GOE: 06.04.20 STRENGTH: M GED: R2 M1 L1 SVP: 3 DLU: 77

669.685-026 CIRCLE-CUTTING-SAW OPERATOR (wood. container) alternate titles: bottom turner

Tends machine that cuts circular basket bottoms from woodstock and bores holes in bottoms: Positions stock on rotary chuck. Depresses pedal to activate machine that rotates woodstock in opposite direction from rotating drill and cylindrical sawblade to cut woodstock into disk and bore holes in center of disk. Removes wood disk from machine.
GOE: 06.04.03 STRENGTH: L GED: R1 M1 L1 SVP: 2 DLU: 77

669.685-030 CLAMPER (woodworking)

Tends machine that presses partially assembled and glued doors, window sashes, or furniture parts together to complete assembly: Places part on machine table between pressing rails, starts machine, and depresses pedal to squeeze parts together. Positions glued reinforcing blocks to specified locations of assembly, according to instructions, and secures blocks, using pneumatic screwdriver or nailer and stapler. Releases pressure, removes assembly from machine, and stacks assembly on skid or places assembly on conveyor for further processing. May preglue assembly parts and knock parts together, using mallet prior to clamping. May brush glue on parts prior to clamping. May reinforce joints with staples or nails, using pneumatic stapler or hammer. May be designated according to product as Door-Clamp Operator (saw. & plan.); Sash-Clamp Operator (saw. & plan.).
GOE: 06.04.20 STRENGTH: H GED: R2 M1 L1 SVP: 3 DLU: 79

669.685-034 COAT-HANGER-SHAPER-MACHINE OPERATOR (woodworking)

Tends machines that shape and polish unfinished wooden coat hangers: Smooths rough edges on ends of hangers, using rotating sanding disk. Starts automatic shaper and loads machine hopper with hangers. Transfers shaped hangers to polishing machine and places bars of paraffin in machine. Starts machine. Removes filled trays of polished and waxed hangers from polishing machine.
GOE: 06.04.03 STRENGTH: M GED: R2 M1 L1 SVP: 3 DLU: 77

669.685-038 CORE-COMPOSER FEEDER (millwork-plywood) alternate titles: tenderizer tender

Tends machine that trims uneven edges of veneer sheets and tenderizes (indents and breaks wood fibers of) veneer for composing into plywood core sheets: Pushes buttons and pedal to start machine and to raise veneer stack on lift table to feeding height. Aligns uneven edges of veneer sheets on lift table, using *shadow line*, and feeds sheets into machine for trimming and tenderizing. Observes veneer sheets discharged from tenderizer machine onto feed conveyor of core composer machine and slackens feeding pace as necessary to reduce detected pile ups. Observes stacker lift table at discharge end of core composer machine and activates conveyor to remove full stacks and reposition stacker lift table for next stack. Occasionally measures moisture content of veneer prior to tenderizing, using moisture meter, and removes veneer containing excessive moisture for redrying.
GOE: 06.04.03 STRENGTH: M GED: R2 M1 L1 SVP: 3 DLU: 77

669.685-042 CORRUGATED-FASTENER DRIVER (woodworking) alternate titles: corrugator operator; shook splicer; splicer-machine operator; stitcher operator

Tends machine that cuts metal fasteners from corrugated metal stripping and drives fasteners into boards across joints to fasten boards together: Positions spool of corrugated metal stripping onto machine spindles and threads end of stripping between clamps of automatic feed driver-head. Positions and tightens machine driver-head above workpiece joint, using wrench. Starts machine, positions workpiece against machine table stop, and depresses pedal to activate machine driver-head and force fastener into workpiece. May be designated according to parts fastened as Box-Top-Stitching-Machine Operator (wood. container); Door-Frame Assembler, Machine (woodworking).
GOE: 06.04.20 STRENGTH: M GED: R2 M1 L1 SVP: 2 DLU: 77

669.685-046 DOVETAIL-MACHINE OPERATOR (wood. container) alternate titles: bumper operator; forming operator

Tends machine that presses notched ends of boards together to form lock-corner box frame: Turns handwheels to adjust side and end pressure bars according to frame dimension. Positions boards on table and starts machine. Presses pedal to activate pressure bars that force notched ends of boards together, forming lock-corner joints. May dip ends of boards in glue before joining. May melt glue in glue pot.
GOE: 06.04.20 STRENGTH: M GED: R2 M1 L1 SVP: 2 DLU: 77

669.685-050 DOWELING-MACHINE OPERATOR (woodworking) alternate titles: doweler; dowel-setting-machine operator

Tends machine that glues and drives dowel pins into holes in parts of wooden articles preparatory to assembly: Slides stops on machine to align grooves, through which dowels are fed, with holes in wooden part according to work order. Dumps dowel pins into hopper and pours glue into glue reservoir. Turns valve to regulate pressure and amount of glue injected into holes to prevent wood from splitting when dowels are driven into holes. Positions part against stop and depresses pedal to inject glue and drive dowels into holes. Releases pedal and removes wooden part from machine. Secures position of dowels in wooden parts with nails or staples, using pneumatic nail gun or stapler. May mix glue.
GOE: 06.04.20 STRENGTH: M GED: R2 M1 L1 SVP: 3 DLU: 86

669.685-054 END STAPLER (wood. container) alternate titles: end operator

Tends stapling machine that staples battens down center of wire-bound box ends to stiffen and strengthen them: Lays batten in groove of stapler and places end board between guides and on batten. Slides batten and box end onto feed belt of machine. Steps on pedal to operate machine, stapling batten to box end.
GOE: 06.04.20 STRENGTH: L GED: R2 M1 L1 SVP: 3 DLU: 77

669.685-058 FRAME-TABLE-OPERATOR HELPER (wood prod., nec) alternate titles: framing-mill-operator helper

Tends frame table carriage that moves, positions, and holds timbers under radial arm of framing machine to assist FRAME-TABLE OPERATOR (wood prod., nec) to frame timbers: Lifts timbers onto carriage, using air hoist. Pulls levers and turns wheel controls to move carriage and position timbers for cutting. May change saws and cutting tools.
GOE: 06.04.18 STRENGTH: M GED: R2 M2 L1 SVP: 2 DLU: 77

669.685-062 HEADING-MACHINE OPERATOR (pen & pencil) alternate titles: end trimmer

Tends machine that sands excess point from pencil ends and cuts pencils to specified length: Dusts ends of pencils with cornstarch to prevent sticking together. Places pencils in hopper of machine and starts machine. Examines pencils for defects, such as chips in paint and incorrect length. Bundles pencils, using cord, and places bundles on pallet or places pencils in rack and blows wood and lead dust from pencils, using airhose. Replaces worn sandpaper on machine drum. May replace knives in machine, using wrench.
GOE: 06.04.03 STRENGTH: M GED: R2 M1 L1 SVP: 2 DLU: 77

669.685-066 NAILING-MACHINE OPERATOR, AUTOMATIC (any industry)

Tends nailing machine that joins items, such as picture frames, or attaches molding, trimming, carving, scrollwork, or overlay panels to wooden stock: Positions reel of nail wire on spindle of machine and pulls wire through rollers into driving mechanism. Turns knobs or levers to adjust machine to cut nails of specified length. Positions stock parts to be nailed together in specified arrangements on table of machine under driving mechanism. Depresses pedal or button to drive nails into stock. Moves stock as necessary to receive additional nails.
GOE: 06.04.20 STRENGTH: L GED: R2 M2 L1 SVP: 2 DLU: 78

669.685-070 ROOF-TRUSS-MACHINE TENDER (mfd. bldgs.)

Tends machine that automatically joins lumber to fabricate roof trusses used in construction of buildings: Threads stapling wire through staple head of machine and pours glue into machine glue reservoir. Starts machine and feeds pre-cut wood onto machine that glues and staples material together and shears off excess material to form completed roof truss. Removes roof truss from machine and stacks on pallet for further processing.
GOE: 06.04.20 STRENGTH: L GED: R2 M1 L1 SVP: 2 DLU: 77

669.685-074 SLAT-BASKET MAKER, MACHINE (wood. container) alternate titles: basket-factory machine hand; basket-machine operator

Tends machine that staples basket hoops and slats together: Places spools of wire on wire holders and draws wire through machine guides and slots in stapling heads. Inserts end of hoop strips into slots on basket-shaped form and positions veneer stave between stops on form. Depresses pedal to start machine that staples hoop strips and strand of wire to stave and rotates form into position for succeeding staves.
GOE: 06.04.20 STRENGTH: L GED: R2 M1 L1 SVP: 2 DLU: 77

669.685-078 SMOKING-PIPE DRILLER AND THREADER (fabrication, nec)

Tends machine that bores hole and cuts threads in bottom of shankless pipe bowls: Places pipe bowl over chuck of machine and turns nut to expand chuck against bowl, using wrench. Pulls lever to align bowl with drill and turns handwheel to feed bowl into rotating drill. Moves lever to align bowl with circular saw and turns handwheel to rotate bowl beneath saw that cuts threads in bowl.
GOE: 06.04.03 STRENGTH: L GED: R2 M1 L1 SVP: 2 DLU: 77

669.685-082 SQUEEZER OPERATOR (wood. container)

Tends machine that squeezes tongue and groove boards together: Turns handwheels to adjust machine for length, width, and thickness of finished piece. Starts machine. Positions matched boards on feed table from which they are automatically fed into machine that squeezes them together or depresses pedal to activate bars that squeezes them together.
GOE: 06.04.20 STRENGTH: M GED: R2 M1 L1 SVP: 3 DLU: 77

669.685-086 STITCHING-MACHINE OPERATOR (wood. container)

Tends machine that fastens metal channels to hogshead headings: Positions channeled heading on circular table with channel ends against stitching unit. Lowers roller clamps to hold heading in position. Starts machine to revolve table and presses button to stitch channel to heading at uniform intervals. Removes heading from machine.
GOE: 06.04.20 STRENGTH: M GED: R2 M1 L1 SVP: 2 DLU: 77

669.685-090 TIPPLE TENDER (millwork-plywood)

Tends conveyor system that transfers veneer from lathe into holding trays: Starts tipple conveyor, observes action of lathe cutting veneer, and opens trap

to allow waste veneer to flow onto clipper or *hog mill* conveyor. Moves control lever to synchronize tipple conveyor speed with lathe cutting of production veneer and pushes button to align discharge end of tipple conveyor with empty holding tray. Responds to signal that indicates tray is full and separates veneer in tray from veneer sheet by tearing, or with air jets. May assist VENEER-LATHE OPERATOR (millwork-plywood) 664.662-010 in changing lathe knives and in positioning wood between lathe chucks.
GOE: 06.04.40 STRENGTH: L GED: R2 M2 L2 SVP: 2 DLU: 77

669.685-094   TURNER (fabrication, nec)
Tends machine that cuts bowl of smoking pipe from briar block or corncobs and bores hole in bowl: Examines corncobs for chipped edges and cracks and discards defective corncobs. Places block or corncob between machine clamps and moves controls to tighten them. Depresses pedal or moves lever to move block against chucking and coring head that cuts bowl from block and bores hole in briar or corncob bowl. Presses button or pulls lever to release clamps and places bowl in box. May tend machine that automatically saws pipe bowl shanks to specified length, bores holes in shanks, bores airholes in pipe bowls, and inserts metal sleeves in shank holes. May change cutting and boring tool, according to size of bowl, using wrench. May place corncob blanks into feeder that feeds blanks into machine that automatically bores hole in blank. May bore bowls of corncob pipes and be designated Cob Borer (fabrication, nec).
GOE: 06.04.03 STRENGTH: M GED: R2 M1 L1 SVP: 3 DLU: 78

669.685-098   VENEER REPAIRER, MACHINE (millwork-plywood)
Tends machine that cuts defects from veneer sheets and repairs defects by inserting patches in cutout areas: Fills feed chute of machine with veneer patch stock and starts machine. Slides and positions veneer sheet on machine table so that defects, such as knots, holes, and pitch pockets are under head of machine. Depresses pedal to activate head that cuts or punches out defective area and inserts patch. Stacks repaired sheets on skids or slides them onto conveyor. May grade repaired sheets. May be designated according to machine operated as Raimann-Machine Operator (millwork-plywood); Skoog-Machine Operator (millwork-plywood).
GOE: 06.04.03 STRENGTH: L GED: R2 M1 L1 SVP: 2 DLU: 77

669.685-102   GROOVER-AND-STRIPER OPERATOR (wood prod., nec)
Tends machines in tandem that groove, paint, seal, and dry surfaces of hardboard panels: Positions grooving blades and striping wheels according to panel specifications, using handtools and tape measure. Pours paint and sealer into designated reservoirs to supply coating rollers and wheels. Moves controls on console panel to start and synchronize machines. Inspects and feels finished panels, and adjusts controls to conform with production specifications.
GOE: 06.04.03 STRENGTH: L GED: R2 M2 L2 SVP: 2 DLU: 86

669.685-106   PUNCH PRESS OPERATOR (wood prod., nec)
Tends punch press machine that punches holes in hardboard panels to make pegboard panels: Reads work schedule to ascertain production information, such as size, type, and quantity of panels to be processed. Adjusts panel guides on machine table, according to production information, using handtools. Presses buttons to start machine, pulls panels from stack, aligns panels against guides on machine table, and pushes panels against feed rollers of machine. Measures first panel of each stack of hardboards to verify specified measurements, and feels edges of holes in pegboard panels to determine sharpness of punch press. Observes machine operation to detect malfunction of machine parts and notifies supervisor when punch dies need changing or machine malfunctions occur. Lubricates specified sections of machine, using grease gun and oilcan. Bands stacks of pegboards for storage, using steel banding ribbons, clips, and strapping tool.
GOE: 06.04.03 STRENGTH: M GED: R2 M2 L2 SVP: 2 DLU: 86

669.686-010   AUTOMATIC-NAILING-MACHINE FEEDER (woodworking)
Positions door frame parts between chain dogs on conveyor that carries them under driving heads of automatic nailing machine.
GOE: 06.04.03 STRENGTH: L GED: R1 M1 L1 SVP: 2 DLU: 77

669.686-014   BOX-BLANK-MACHINE-OPERATOR HELPER (wood. container)
Assists BOX-BLANK-MACHINE OPERATOR (wood. container) in assembling box sections, performing any combination of following duties: Lays cleats against stops on feed belt of machine. Places boards or slats across cleats held in position by stops. Removes *box blanks* from machine and bends back projecting wire over wood to facilitate handling of blanks. Assists in adding and removing links from chain feed belt and spaces stops and stapling heads. Performs other duties as described under HELPER (any industry) Master Title. May be designated according to duties performed as Board Layer (wood. container); Cleat Layer (wood. container); Wire Bender (wood. container); or type of machine as Wire-Bound-Box-Machine Helper (wood. container).
GOE: 06.04.20 STRENGTH: M GED: R2 M1 L1 SVP: 2 DLU: 77

669.686-018   CHAIN OFFBEARER (saw. & plan.)
Pulls lumber from moving conveyor coming from ripsaw, resaw, planer, trimmer, and grading tables, and slides and stacks lumber on piles, according to grade marked on each piece. May push buttons to start and stop conveyor and deposit waste material onto slasher conveyor for waste recovery. May band stacked lumber to facilitate moving, using banding machine. May be designated according to condition of lumber removed from conveyor as Dry-Chain

Offbearer (saw. & plan.); Green-Chain Offbearer (saw. & plan.); or may be designated according to machine from which lumber is conveyed as Planer-Chain Offbearer (saw. & plan.).
GOE: 06.04.03 STRENGTH: H GED: R2 M1 L1 SVP: 2 DLU: 78

669.686-022   REED-PRESS FEEDER (wood prod., nec)
Feeds reeds into machine that stitches reeds together to make insulation panels of specified dimensions. Trims edges with shears. May remove finished panels from machine and transfer panels to storage areas. May participate in unloading reeds onto work floor.
GOE: 06.04.20 STRENGTH: L GED: R2 M1 L1 SVP: 2 DLU: 77

669.686-026   SLAT-BASKET MAKER HELPER, MACHINE (wood. container)
Assists SLAT-BASKET MAKER, MACHINE (wood. container) in assembly of slat baskets: Positions preformed inside top hoop and basket bottom on basket-shaped form of machine and holds bottom until hoop and bottom are stapled to staves. Removes assembled basket from machine and twists loose ends of wire hoops with handtool to tighten hoops. Performs other duties as described under HELPER (any industry) Master Title.
GOE: 06.04.20 STRENGTH: L GED: R1 M1 L1 SVP: 2 DLU: 77

669.686-030   WOODWORKING-MACHINE FEEDER (woodworking)
Feeds woodstock on conveyors, into hoppers, or between rollers of woodworking machines that cut, saw, sand, bore, or shape woodstock: Conveys woodstock from stock area to woodworking machine, using handcart. Lifts stock from cart and feeds stock onto conveyor, into hopper, or between rollers of machine. Stops machine to remove jammed pieces or make minor adjustments, using handtools. May assist machine operator in setting up machine and in cleaning work area, machines, and equipment. May collect and convey scrap wood from machine areas to *hog mill* and feed scrap into machine. May be designated according to machine fed as Boring-Machine Feeder (woodworking); Flooring-Machine Feeder (saw. & plan.); Molder Feeder (woodworking); Stitcher Feeder (wood. container); Tongue-And-Groove-Machine Feeder (woodworking); or according to product as Shake Feeder (saw. & plan.). May be designated: Adzing-And-Boring-Machine Feeder (wood prod., nec); Box-Blank-Machine Feeder (woodworking); Glue-Jointer Feeder (woodworking); Planer Feeder (woodworking); Resaw Feeder (woodworking); Turner (woodworking).
GOE: 06.04.03 STRENGTH: M GED: R2 M1 L1 SVP: 2 DLU: 78

669.686-034   WOODWORKING-MACHINE OFFBEARER (woodworking) alternate titles: tailer
Off bears material at discharge end of machines that cut, smooth, bore, or shape woodstock: Stacks woodstock aside or loads woodstock on truck, pallet, or conveyor for movement to additional processing stations. May count and examine woodstock to detect manufacturing defects. May reposition woodstock and feed woodstock into machine or back to operator for subsequent processing. May depress pedal to raise or lower conveyor to facilitate stacking. May discard scrap or defective pieces of woodstock into scrap containers or onto conveyor for burning. May place sticks between specified intervals of stacked woodstock to provide air circulation and increase stability of stack. May be designated according to machine assigned as Jointer Offbearer (woodworking); Molder Offbearer (woodworking); Planer Offbearer (woodworking); Saw Offbearer (woodworking); Tenoner Offbearer (woodworking).
GOE: 06.04.03 STRENGTH: M GED: R2 M1 L1 SVP: 2 DLU: 81

669.687-010   CLEAT FEEDER (wood. container) alternate titles: cleat thrower
Positions one or more cleats, used in wood boxes or box shooks, against stop under nailing machine. Carries supply of cleats of specified size from storage area to work station.
GOE: 06.04.40 STRENGTH: L GED: R1 M1 L1 SVP: 2 DLU: 77

669.687-014   DOWEL INSPECTOR (woodworking)
Inspects dowel pins for flaws, such as square ends, knots, or splits, and discards defective dowels.
GOE: 06.03.02 STRENGTH: S GED: R1 M1 L1 SVP: 2 DLU: 77

669.687-018   LUMBER STRAIGHTENER (saw. & plan.) alternate titles: laborer, sawmill; lumber guider
Straightens lumber on conveyor to align lumber for grading, sawing, edging, trimming, sorting, stacking, or for transfer to other conveyors. Clears jammed material, using *picaroon* to permit normal flow of lumber along conveyor. Cleans work area, using broom and shovel. May pile lumber on trucks or pallets. May tend automatic conveyor and sorting machine that sorts lumber for further processing. May be designated according to process involved as Cross-Tie Turner (wood prod., nec); Sorter-Lumber Straightener (saw. & plan.); Stacker-Straightener (saw. & plan.); Trimmer Loader (saw. & plan.); Trimmer Tailer (saw. & plan.).
GOE: 06.04.40 STRENGTH: M GED: R2 M1 L1 SVP: 2 DLU: 79

669.687-022   PICKER (saw. & plan.)
Selects and examines seasoned logs, and loads logs onto skid and machine conveyor for processing into excelsior: Selects seasoned logs, following specifications on work ticket, and examines wood for moisture content, using moisture gauge. Lifts logs onto skid for transportation to cutting machine that cuts logs into log blocks. Lifts log blocks from floor and places them onto conveyor for movement to wood shredding (excelsior) machine.
GOE: 03.04.02 STRENGTH: H GED: R2 M1 L2 SVP: 2 DLU: 77

669.687-026 TIE INSPECTOR (saw. & plan.)

Inspects railroad ties for defects and checks measurement of ties, using tape measure: Examines tie for defects, such as knots, square or round ends, or rot. Measures width of tie, using tape measure. Classifies tie according to width and kind of wood.
GOE: 03.04.02 STRENGTH: H GED: R2 M1 L2 SVP: 2 DLU: 77

669.687-030 GRADER (woodworking) alternate titles: lumber inspector; sizer grader

Inspects and grades milled, rough-sawed, or dimensional stock lumber according to standards: Examines lumber on table, moving belt, chain conveyor, or in racks for defects, such as knots, stains, decay, splits, faulty edges, pitch pockets, wormholes, and defective milling. Grades lumber, using caliper rule, to ensure specified dimensions. Marks lumber to indicate grade and processing instructions, using marker. Tallies pieces of lumber according to grade and board footage. May determine cuts to be made to obtain highest marketable value from material. May remove unsatisfactory pieces from conveyor or table and place pieces on stacks, in bins, or on carts. May scale board footage, using calibrated scale on lumber ruler, and record results. May be designated according to lumber graded as Flooring Grader (saw. & plan.); Green-Lumber Grader (woodworking); or according to location of work as Dock Grader (woodworking); Green-Chain Marker (saw. & plan.); Planer-Mill Grader (saw. & plan.). May review work of other graders and be designated Check Grader (woodworking). May be designated: Dry-Lumber Grader (woodworking); Milled-Lumber Grader (woodworking); Puncher (saw. & plan.); Rough-Lumber Grader (woodworking).
GOE: 06.03.02 STRENGTH: L GED: R3 M2 L2 SVP: 4 DLU: 81

67 OCCUPATIONS IN MACHINING STONE, CLAY, GLASS, AND RELATED MATERIALS

This division includes occupations concerned with shaping stone, clay, and glass parts or products by removing excess material from stock or objects, primarily by such means as cutting, boring, abrading, milling, and planing. Includes laying out, job setting, repairing, fitting, and assembling.

670 STONECUTTERS AND RELATED OCCUPATIONS

This group includes occupations concerned with trimming and surfacing blocks and slabs of stone to desired size, shape, or finish.

670.362-010 GANG SAWYER, STONE (stonework) alternate titles: gang-saw operator;stone sawyer

Sets up and operates one or more gangsaws or reciprocating saws to cut rough blocks of stone into specified dimensions for further processing: Builds bed of timbers on flat car. Aligns and levels stone on bed, using crowbar, sledgehammer, wedges, blocks, and spirit level. Marks dimensions on stone, using straightedge, rule, and crayon. Turns crank or pushes button to activate winch that moves car onto track under saw frame. Moves saw blades along frame, aligning blades with marks on stone; positions blocks (width gauges) between blades; levels blades; and inserts wedges into frame to secure blades to frame. Turns lever to lower saw blades on stone. Starts saws and pump that circulates water and abrasive under reciprocating blades to cut stone. Observes sawing to detect exhausted abrasive supply. Dumps abrasive into abrasive pit to maintain cutting speed. Turns crank to increase or decrease speed of saws according to hardness of stone and uniformity of abrasive flow. Washes stone, using water hose, and verifies width or thickness of cut stone, using rule. Replaces worn saw blades. Signals OVERHEAD CRANE OPERATOR (any industry) 921.663-010 to remove cut slabs from car or saw bed. May operate diamond gangsaw equipped with up to thirty vertically mounted diamond-edged saw blades.
GOE: 06.02.08 STRENGTH: M GED: R3 M2 L1 SVP: 5 DLU: 77

670.384-010 STONE GRADER (stonework) alternate titles: checker;inspector

Inspects, repairs, and grades rough-cut and finished blocks or slabs of stone according to work order specifications: Examines stone block for defects in workmanship and quality, such as cracks, fractures, and scratches. Measures dimensions of block, using tape measure. Cleans fractures and cracks in block with acid and sponge. Fills imperfections with matching colored wax, and polishes patched area, using file, hone, and portable buffer. May select rough blocks from stock for cutting and polishing. May mark code numbers on finished blocks according to work order specifications. May order quarry blocks for cutting and polishing.
GOE: 05.07.01 STRENGTH: H GED: R3 M2 L2 SVP: 6 DLU: 77

670.587-010 STONE LAYOUT MARKER (stonework)

Marks coded instructions on sandstone slabs to specify subsequent processing according to blueprint specifications: Studies blueprint to determine required dimensions of slab and processes needed to finish product. Locates specified slab on conveyor and verifies dimensions, using tape measure. Marks coded instructions on slab to specify processing required, such as radius edge, drip groove, and finished butt joint, using chalk. Records identification number of pieces on form and engraves number on slab edge, using air-powered engraving tool. Pushes slab onto roller conveyor for subsequent processing.

GOE: 06.02.31 STRENGTH: M GED: R3 M2 L1 SVP: 3 DLU: 77

670.685-010 STONE TRIMMER (stonework) alternate titles: slate trimmer

Tends trimming machine fitted with rotary cutting knives or single blade on spring pole to trim rough roofing slate to largest size that slabs will make: Sets notched bar that enables slab to be cut to desired size. Holds irregular slate slab beneath rotating cutting blade to trim edges. Turns slab and trims other edges. Sharpens cutting knives on grinding wheel. May split flagstone along cut line, using hammer and chisel.
GOE: 06.04.08 STRENGTH: M GED: R2 M1 L1 SVP: 3 DLU: 77

673 ABRADING OCCUPATIONS

This group includes occupations concerned with smoothing, polishing, or sharpening stone, clay, or glass by the wearing away action of abrasives on plane or rotary action machine tools.

673.130-010 SUPERVISOR, EDGING (glass products)

Supervises and coordinates activities of workers engaged in edging and beveling of glass and mirrors: Patrols work areas and observes workers to assure conformance to company standards. Trains new workers in duties. Performs other duties as described under SUPERVISOR (any industry) Master Title. May perform routine maintenance on machines. May change or dress grinding wheels. May supervise workers engaged in operation of grooving machine that grinds grooves in glass shelving.
GOE: 06.02.01 STRENGTH: M GED: R3 M2 L2 SVP: 6 DLU: 77

673.364-010 LEAD WORKER, WAFER POLISHING (electron. comp.)

Assists SUPERVISOR, ELECTRONICS PROCESSING (electron. comp.) 590.130-010 in coordinating activities of workers engaged in polishing wafers for use in manufacturing semiconductor devices: Reviews production goals with SUPERVISOR, ELECTRONICS PROCESSING (electron. comp.), prioritizes wafers to be polished, and assigns workers to stations. Monitors production and adjusts work assignments when necessary. Inspects polished wafers and measures wafer thickness, using gauge, to ensure conformance to customer specifications. Trains workers in equipment operation and wafer inspection. Observes workers to ensure compliance with safety rules and production standards. Completes work schedules and daily production reports. May tend polishing machines [POLISHING MACHINE TENDER (electron. comp.) 673.685-094] and demounting machines [WAFER MOUNTER (electron. comp.) 726.685-058] to substitute for workers during worker absence or to relieve bottlenecks in work congested areas.
GOE: 06.02.09 STRENGTH: M GED: R3 M3 L3 SVP: 6 DLU: 86

673.380-010 EDGING-MACHINE SETTER (glass products)

Sets up and adjusts machines that grind and polish edges of glass used in manufacture of mirrors: Turns handwheels to loosen spindle assemblies of horizontal edging machines and turns calibrated gauges and levers to move specified grinding, smoothing, and polishing wheels into processing position and to set spacing between opposed grinding, smoothing, and polishing wheels, according to thickness and width of mirrors. Turns valves to regulate air pressure that forces grinding, smoothing, and polishing wheels against processed surfaces of mirrors. Places trial glass on feed conveyor of machines and observes ammeters to determine load on abrasive wheels and examines ground edge to determine if alignment and cutting depth of wheels are in accordance with specifications. Loosens spindle assemblies and grinding, smoothing, and polishing wheel units, using handwheels and wrenches, and turns setscrews to adjust operating depths of individual wheels. Turns handwheels to adjust edge guides of conveyors to ensure equal grinding, smoothing, and polishing of mirror edges. May set up and adjust machine that automatically drills single holes in mirrors.
GOE: 06.01.02 STRENGTH: M GED: R3 M2 L2 SVP: 5 DLU: 78

673.382-010 SANDBLASTER, STONE (stonework)

Operates sandblasting equipment to cut inscriptions and decorative designs on monumental stone: Dumps abrasive into mixing chamber of sandblasting equipment. Turns valve to admit compressed air into mixing chamber. Selects sandblasting nozzle according to size of lettering or intricacy of design and attaches nozzle to hose leading from mixing chamber. Moves lever or turns valve to jet abrasive through nozzle. Guides nozzle back and forth over stone surface following stencil outline to cut inscription or design in stone. Verifies work by measuring or estimating depth of cut as sandblasting progresses, using rule or employing experience in sandblasting. Removes parts of stencil or adds stencil during blasting to create differences in depth of cuts and intricate designs. May shape (or carve) designs in stone, using sandblasting equipment. May sandblast stone without stencil to produce rough, pitted finish. May operate portable equipment to sandblast letters and designs on stone at cemetery sites. May cut stencils preparatory to sandblasting. May operate machine that automatically moves sandblasting nozzle back and forth over stenciled stone.
GOE: 05.10.01 STRENGTH: M GED: R3 M1 L1 SVP: 6 DLU: 77

673.382-014 SANDBLASTER, STONE APPRENTICE (stonework)

Performs duties as described under APPRENTICE (any industry) Master Title.
GOE: 05.10.01 STRENGTH: M GED: R3 M1 L1 SVP: 6 DLU: 77

673.382-018 STONE POLISHER, MACHINE (stonework)

Sets up and operates machine to grind stone to smooth finish or polish stone to lustrous finish: Selects grinding or polishing wheels according to type of

stone, finish specified, or step in finishing process. Moves arm of machine over wheel and attaches wheel to spindle with bolt or latch. Spreads abrasive or water on stone by hand, or turns valves to circulate abrasive or water on stone. Pushes levers to start machine and guides rotating wheel over surface of stone by hand, observing puddles of water on stone to detect uneven areas. Washes stone, using hose, and changes abrasive or wheel as grinding or polishing progresses to surface stone according to specifications. May grind and polish curved or irregular stone surfaces, using portable polisher [STONE POLISHER, HAND (stonework)]. May fill cracks or imperfections in stone with wax that matches color of stone. May place, align, and level stone on machine bed. May be designated according to type of stone surfaced as Granite Polisher, Machine (stonework); Marble Polisher, Machine (stonework).
GOE: 06.02.08 STRENGTH: M GED: R3 M1 L1 SVP: 6 DLU: 77

673.382-022 STONE POLISHER, MACHINE APPRENTICE (stonework)
Performs duties as described under APPRENTICE (any industry) Master Title.
GOE: 06.02.08 STRENGTH: M GED: R3 M1 L1 SVP: 6 DLU: 77

673.382-026 CRYSTAL GRINDER (electron. comp.)
Operates grinding machine to abrade semiconductor crystal ingot to improve cylindrical shape of ingot and attain specified diameter: Reads work order to determine target diameter of ingot. Measures ingot diameter, using calipers or micrometer, and calculates thickness of material to be removed from ingot and length of grinding time. Positions and secures ingot in trunnions or brackets on grinding machine. Adjusts machine controls for position of grinding tool and speed of grinding. Pushes buttons to activate coolant flow, rotation of ingot, grinding tool, and timer. Measures ingot diameter after grinding and continues grinding to attain specifications for diameter. May change worn grinding tools and other parts and adjust machine, using handtools. May attach graphite pieces to ends of ingot before grinding, using epoxy, and remove graphite and epoxy from ingot after grinding, using radiant oven and solvent. May operate saw to cut sample wafer from ingot for inspection. May perform routine maintenance on grinding machine, such as adding oil and cleaning machine. May operate flat grinding machine to grind *flat* along length of ingot and be designated Crystal Flat Grinder (electron. comp.).
GOE: 06.02.02 STRENGTH: H GED: R3 M2 L2 SVP: 5 DLU: 86

673.662-010 TOP POLISHER (stonework)
Sets up and operates one or more automatic stone polishing machines to polish monument tops: Studies diagram of monument to determine diamond polishing wheel required and attaches wheel to machine, using handtools. Measures length and width of monument top and sets dials to control width and length of travel of polishing head. Moves stone under head of machine and levels stone, using spirit level, wooden blocks and wedges. Positions polishing wheel on top of monument, turns valve to start flow of water, and pulls switch to start polishing wheel. Observes ammeter to determine load on motor and turns dial to adjust current according to reading. Observes operation of machine and adjusts dials and switches to regulate speed of machine and length and width of travel of polishing wheel. Feels stone to determine progress of polishing and rolls stone from under wheel when polishing is completed. Signals OVERHEAD CRANE OPERATOR (any industry) 921.663-010 to pick up stone. Lubricates machine, using grease gun. Inspects inventory of diamond polishing wheels and notifies supervisor when wheels need replacing. May grind sharp edges from monuments, using portable grinding machine.
GOE: 06.02.08 STRENGTH: M GED: R3 M2 L1 SVP: 6 DLU: 77

673.666-010 BELT SANDER, STONE (stonework)
Feeds and off bears automatic belt sanding machine that sands tops of sandstone table and counter tops, assisted by coworker: Pulls cart loaded with sandstone table and counter tops to work area and transfers stone from cart to roller conveyor. Presses button to start sanding machine and pushes stone tops from roller conveyor onto belt conveyor that carries stone under belt sander. Guides stone tops emerging from sanding machine onto roller conveyor. Feels edges of stone to detect rough or uneven areas and sands edges of stone tops, using sandpaper. Pushes stone along roller conveyor for further processing.
GOE: 06.04.08 STRENGTH: V GED: R2 M1 L1 SVP: 2 DLU: 77

673.666-014 STRIPPER (glass mfg.)
Strips sections of ground flat glass from tables: Cuts along joints between sections of flat glass and between glass sections and table edge to break plaster of paris bond, using knife and scraper. Inserts knife blade between table and glass and turns knife blade on edge to separate section of glass from table. Lifts glass from table and inserts flat sheets into individual compartments on truck, or attaches suspended clamps and signals worker on overhead crane to lift glass from table.
GOE: 06.04.08 STRENGTH: L GED: R2 M1 L1 SVP: 2 DLU: 77

673.682-010 AUTOMATIC PATTERN EDGER (glass products)
Sets up and operates pattern edging machine to *pencil edge* pattern (irregularly shaped) mirrors or glass: Turns screws to level arms of machine suction cup platform, using hex wrench. Turns bolts to loosen and extend or retract arms to adjust for size of mirrors or glass being edged, using wrench. Positions workpiece on platform and presses down on workpiece to ensure contact with suction cups and stability of workpiece on platform. Moves calibrated lever mechanism to adjust height of motorized diamond edging wheel. Flips switch and turns valve to start edging machine and flow of water to edging wheel. Depresses pedal to activate suction cups that lock workpiece onto platform.

Grasps hand grips of edging wheel and moves wheel against patterned edges of workpiece to form pencil edge. Feels edge of workpiece to ensure specified smoothness and uniformity. Depresses pedal to disengage suction cups. Removes and carries workpiece from machine and places onto rack.
GOE: 06.02.08 STRENGTH: H GED: R3 M1 L1 SVP: 3 DLU: 77

673.682-014 BEVELING-AND-EDGING-MACHINE OPERATOR (glass mfg.; glass products)
Sets up and operates one or more machines to bevel, *pencil edge,* and polish rectangular glass or mirror edges: Loosens calibrated gauge with wrench and turns gauge to set grinding wheels to cut bevel to close tolerances. Presses buttons and turns handwheels to start flow of coolant (water) and polishing compound (rouge or cerium) onto grinding wheels. Starts machine and places glass or mirrors on conveyor of machine. Observes ammeter to determine grinding load. Turns handwheels to adjust grinding wheels. May move glass from machine and wipe edges to remove polishing compound. Feels edge for smoothness. Rejects defective glass or mirror and readjusts gauge.
GOE: 06.02.08 STRENGTH: M GED: R3 M2 L3 SVP: 4 DLU: 77

673.682-018 EDGER-MACHINE OPERATOR (stonework)
Sets up and operates machine to grind and polish edges and cut drip grooves on underside of sandstone table and counter tops: Reads work instructions written on sandstone slab. Presses buttons and pulls levers on control panel to start diamond saw and specified combination of diamond grinding and polishing wheels. Turns valve to start water flow that cools grinding and polishing wheels and saw blades during operation. Pushes sandstone slab from roller conveyor onto belt conveyor that conveys stone through grinding, polishing, and sawing process. Examines slab to determine if grinding, polishing and sawing conforms to specifications. Reprocesses slabs not meeting specifications. Lubricates machine, using grease gun. Examines diamond grinding, and cutting tools for wear and notifies supervisor of replacement need.
GOE: 06.02.08 STRENGTH: H GED: R2 M1 L1 SVP: 3 DLU: 77

673.682-022 FINISH OPENER, JEWEL HOLE (clock & watch)
Operates jewel-opening machine to smooth and polish jewel holes to size: Mounts wire, on which jewels are strung, in machine, pulls wire taut, and forces sleevelike devices against each end of jewel row to force jewels tightly together. Brushes shellac over jewels and allows them to harden. Starts belt which causes row of jewels to rotate around wire. Pulls diamond-dusted tapered wire back and forth through rotating jewels to enlarge and polish holes. Pulls thicker portion of wire into working position until hole reaches specified diameter. Verifies size of hole on graduated tapered needle. Works to tolerances of 0.0001 inch.
GOE: 06.02.08 STRENGTH: L GED: R3 M2 L1 SVP: 5 DLU: 77

673.682-026 MITER GRINDER OPERATOR (glass mfg.; glass products)
Sets up and operates machine to cut mitered or rectangular grooves in flat glass articles, such as mirrors, counter dividers, or shelves: Installs grinding (cutting) wheels according to specifications, using wrench. Sets guide rails according to width of glass, using ruler and screwdriver. Clamps stop on end of table to hold glass in position. Positions glass against stop and guide rail and starts machine. Turns valve to start flow of coolant against grinding wheel. Depresses pedal to lower wheel to surface of glass. Pushes lever to move glass and table under grinding wheel. Observes grinding process and feels cut to determine if groove is being cut to specified depth. Turns handwheel to adjust weight or pressure of grinding wheel on workpiece.
GOE: 06.02.08 STRENGTH: M GED: R3 M2 L3 SVP: 4 DLU: 77

673.682-030 SLAB GRINDER (stonework)
Operates bridge-like track-mounted machine equipped with horizontally mounted cast iron grinding wheel to level surface of dimension stone used for building purposes and in manufacture of monuments: Turns valve to start and adjust flow of water and abrasive over stone and grinding wheel. Climbs into cab of machine or onto control platform and moves levers to guide abrasive wheel over stone, observing level gauge to detect uneven areas. Observes ammeter to determine resistance against grinding wheel and moves levers or pushes buttons to adjust pressure of wheel against stone and control speed of wheel. May operate machine that oscillates rotating grinding wheel as it traverses slab, using successively finer abrasives to grind and buff stone to mirrorlike finish and be designated SLAB POLISHER (stonework). May operate machine equipped with cast iron wheel set with diamond-impregnated polishing bars to grind (sand) and polish sandstone and be designated Diamond Sander (stonework).
GOE: 06.02.08 STRENGTH: L GED: R3 M1 L1 SVP: 5 DLU: 77

673.685-010 ABRASIVE GRINDER (nonmet. min.)
Tends machine that faces and grinds specified radii on abrasives: Sets machine guides to regulate angle of feed of abrasive to grinder. Places abrasive in fixture and manually feeds abrasive to grinding wheel, or starts machine that automatically feeds abrasive against grinder. Inspects abrasives for conformance to specifications, using fixed gauge and micrometer.
GOE: 06.04.09 STRENGTH: L GED: R3 M1 L1 SVP: 3 DLU: 77

673.685-014 BED RUBBER (stonework)
Tends machine that grinds rough-sawed stone blocks or slabs to smooth surface and specified finish: Positions designated surface of stone on machine bed (rotating circular metal plate), using electric hoist. Dumps abrasive, such as grit, sand, and steel shot into hopper of machine. Starts machine, turns valves, and

opens hopper gate to regulate flow of water and abrasive under stone. Measures block or slab to verify thickness with work order specifications. Removes finished stone from rubbing bed and cleans abrasive from surface, using scraper, brush, and water hose. May place lead or stone weights on block to ensure even abrading of stone.
GOE: 06.02.08 STRENGTH: H GED: R3 M2 L1 SVP: 4 DLU: 77

673.685-018   BEVELER (glass products)
   Tends machine that bevels edges of sheet glass: Starts machine and places glass sheet on edge in feed channel. Removes beveled glass from machine and repeats process to bevel all edges. Verifies width, depth, and angle of bevel, using gauge. Bevels glass of irregular sizes and shapes by hand, using abrasive stone. Stacks beveled glass on pallet or in rack.
GOE: 06.04.08 STRENGTH: M GED: R2 M1 L1 SVP: 3 DLU: 77

673.685-022   BEVELER (nonmet. min.)
   Tends machine that bevels ends of asbestos brake linings: Reads work order to determine quantity, size and type brake linings to be beveled. Moves brake linings to work area, using portable rack. Loosens locknuts and positions machine guides and stop according to specification, using rule, wrench and template. Pushes buttons to start machine and conveyor. Places and holds lining against stop and over grinding wheels to bevel ends of lining. Removes beveled lining from machine and compares with template to determine conformance to specifications. Places lining onto conveyor for conveyance to packaging department. Records number of linings beveled onto work order.
GOE: 06.04.08 STRENGTH: M GED: R2 M1 L1 SVP: 2 DLU: 77

673.685-026   BLOCKER (glass mfg.; glass products)
   Tends machine that polishes (blocks) surface of flat glass for products, such as mirrors and display cases: Positions glass on padded table under felt-covered polishing heads. Pours polishing compound, such as cerium or rouge, on glass surface. Moves lever to lower polishing heads onto glass surface. Pushes and pulls table along guide rails and tracks to bring entire surface of glass into contact with polishing heads or moves polishing heads over glass on stationary table. Raises polishing heads and wipes polishing compound from glass with cloth or sponge. May remove and place glass on conveyor of glass-washing machine.
GOE: 06.04.08 STRENGTH: M GED: R2 M2 L2 SVP: 2 DLU: 77

673.685-030   BLOCKER, AUTOMATIC (glass mfg.; glass products)
   Tends machine that conveys flat glass or mirrors under polishing (blocking) and cleaning heads to polish and clean glass surface: Mixes polishing compound according to formula and pours compound into storage tank. Feeds glass or mirrors onto conveyor of machine. Pushes button to start machine and pulls lever to start flow of polishing compound onto glass or mirror surface. Pushes button to raise or lower polishing heads and cleaning brushes individually or collectively according to size, thickness, and number of glass pieces. May record production.
GOE: 06.04.08 STRENGTH: H GED: R2 M1 L1 SVP: 2 DLU: 77

673.685-034   CIRCLE BEVELER (glass products)
   Tends machines that grind and polish beveled edge of circular-shaped glass for mirrors: Reads work ticket to determine dimension of bevel required. Pulls switch to start suction pump. Holds glass against suction-head (holding device) and depresses pedal to activate suction that holds glass to be beveled. Pushes suction-head assembly toward horizontally mounted grinding wheel and releases locking pin to secure assembly at specified position. Repeats procedure for second suction-head assembly mounted on opposite side of grinding wheel. Pulls switches to start grinding wheel and suction-heads rotating. Turns valves to start flow of water to grinding wheel. Lowers weighted levers that move and hold glass against grinding wheel. Measures depth of bevel periodically, using rule. Removes glass from beveling machine and mounts glass on suction-head of bevel polishing machine. Applies polishing compound to felt polishing wheel, using bristle brush. Lowers weighted lever to position beveled edge of glass against polishing wheel. Wipes bevel with fingers and inspects glass for smoothness.
GOE: 06.04.08 STRENGTH: M GED: R2 M1 L1 SVP: 3 DLU: 77

673.685-038   CIRCLE EDGER (glass products)
   Tends edging machine that automatically *pencil edges* circular mirrors or glass used as table tops: Places template over workpiece and marks center of workpiece, using red pencil. Moves switch levers to start suction pump and circle edging machine and turns valve to start flow of water to edging wheels. Centers workpiece on suction cup of edging machine and depresses pedal to activate suction cup that locks workpiece into place. Raises foot-controlled lever to engage motorized edging wheels to edge of workpiece and presses button to start revolving of workpiece against edging wheels to form pencil edge on workpiece. Observes pencil edging process to ensure specified dimensions and to prevent breakage of workpiece caused by improper setting of motorized edging wheels. Turns bolts to loosen motors, using wrench, and slides motors on tracks to correct setting. Feels edge of mirror or glass to verify smoothness. Removes workpiece from suction cup when edging is complete and places workpiece on rack.
GOE: 06.04.08 STRENGTH: M GED: R2 M1 L1 SVP: 2 DLU: 77

673.685-042   CONVEX-GRINDER OPERATOR (button & notion)
   Tends machine that rounds edges of pearl button blanks and forms convex surface on back of blank: Places blanks face down in automatic chucks of feed

mechanism that forces blanks against abrasive wheel shaped to produce convex surface. May tend convex-grinding machine to form studs on backs of buttons, or to shape button faces. May place single blank in chuck of manually controlled convexing machine and pull on leverage bar to force blank against abrasive wheel.
GOE: 06.04.08 STRENGTH: S GED: R2 M1 L1 SVP: 2 DLU: 77

673.685-046   DIAMOND-POWDER TECHNICIAN (nonmet. min.)
   Tends equipment that pulverizes industrial bort and separates particles into grades of diamond powder: Pours bort into ball mill and starts machine to grind bort. Removes powder from mill and pours it through sieves to separate particles. Pours sifted particles into glass tank containing chemical mixture. Siphons liquid containing particles from tank after specified time into glass jars. Siphons liquid, following settlement of particles, from top of jars. Dumps particles onto table and dries them with infrared lamp. Weighs and bottles powder and labels containers.
GOE: 06.04.08 STRENGTH: M GED: R2 M1 L1 SVP: 3 DLU: 77

673.685-050   ENGRAVER TENDER (glass products)
   Tends multistation glassware cutting machine that engraves designs in sequence on glassware: Presses buttons to start machine and turns valves to start flow of coolant. Places mouth of glassware on *indexing* spindle located between cutting wheels and sets base of ware on rest. Loads and unloads machine in specific sequence to engrave design on outside of ware. Removes and inspects completed ware for defects and places ware in tray. Notifies supervisor of machine malfunction.
GOE: 06.04.08 STRENGTH: L GED: R2 M1 L1 SVP: 3 DLU: 77

673.685-054   FINGER-GRIP-MACHINE OPERATOR (glass products)
   Tends one or more grinding machines that cut finger grips (grooves) in sliding glass doors: Sets guide rails and stops to control length, centering, and depth of cut, using wrenches, setscrews, and measuring tape. Turns valve to start flow of water to grinding wheel, and flips switch to start machine. Positions glass on table against stops and guide rails under cutting wheel and pushes or pulls lever to lower rotating cutting wheel to surface of glass and to raise cutting wheel when groove is ground. May set micro-switch that raises wheel automatically when specified depth of groove is obtained. May install cutting wheels on spindles, using wrench. May dress grinding wheels.
GOE: 06.04.08 STRENGTH: M GED: R3 M2 L1 SVP: 3 DLU: 77

673.685-058   FINISH-MACHINE TENDER (pottery & porc.)
   Tends machine that automatically smooths and cleans edges of ceramic flatware preparatory to firing ware in kiln: Selects rubber cushion rings according to ware being furnished and positions rings on vacuum cradle on machine turntable. Inserts abrasive pads in adjustable arms that press pads against revolving ware and positions sponge belts on rotating machine spindles to clean ware after smoothing. Tightens coupling on water hose to water tank connection and turns valve to start and regulate flow of water onto sponge belts to maintain moisture content of belt. Pushes button to start machine and turns dial to regulate speed of turntable according to size ware being processed. Observes machine operation and product to detect need for machine adjustment. Removes and replaces ware at machine to maintain continuous work flow.
GOE: 06.02.08 STRENGTH: H GED: R3 M1 L1 SVP: 5 DLU: 77

673.685-062   GROOVER (nonmet. min.)
   Tends machine that cuts ventilating (cooling) grooves in asbestos brake linings: Positions tension rollers and guides on machine according to size of brake linings specified on work order, using handcrank, measuring scale, and screwdriver. Turns handwheel to position abrasive grooving wheel for specified depth of cut. Pushes button to start machine and feeds lining into machine and observes lining for surface or grooving defects. Measures depth, width, and position of groove, using template, and adjusts machine as required. Discards linings not meeting specifications and places acceptable linings in rack. Records production data on work order.
GOE: 06.04.09 STRENGTH: L GED: R2 M1 L1 SVP: 2 DLU: 77

673.685-066   LEVEL-VIAL INSIDE GRINDER (cutlery-hrdwr.)
   Tends battery of machines that grind interior walls of glass tubes: Brushes abrasive paste onto abrading rods. Inserts tubes in holders and slides holders over abrading rods. Pushes bar to lower *indexing* wheels onto tube holders and starts machine. Stops machine after specified time and removes tubes and holders. Rinses tubes in water tank to remove compound.
GOE: 06.04.08 STRENGTH: L GED: R2 M1 L1 SVP: 3 DLU: 77

673.685-070   NOTCH GRINDER (glass products)
   Grinds notch in edge of glass dial blank as reference point for assembling, using abrasive grinding wheel: Mounts blank in sliding jig and aligns mark on blank with grinding wheel. Starts machine and pushes jig into rotating wheel. Pulls jig back and removes notched blank.
GOE: 06.04.08 STRENGTH: S GED: R2 M1 L2 SVP: 3 DLU: 77

673.685-074   STONE ROUGHER (optical goods)
   Tends battery of automatic machines that rough grind surfaces of lens blanks: Bolts block with mounted lens to rotating spindle of stone-roughing machine, and releases lever of feed mechanism that places lens block against revolving grindstone. Sets feed mechanism by adjusting setscrew controlling position of spindle. Removes lens block after specified period of time, and inspects lens for conformance to specifications. May turn valve to regulate flow of water over grindstone.

GOE: 06.04.08 STRENGTH: L GED: R3 M1 L1 SVP: 2 DLU: 77

673.685-078 STRAIGHT-LINE EDGER (glass mfg.; glass products)

Tends machine that conveys rectangular glass over grinding and polishing wheels to obtain *pencil edge* and to polish edges: Places glass on grooved conveyor with top edge of glass against guide. Attaches weights to top of glass or pulls lever to lower pressure roller that forces glass against grinding and polishing wheels. Turns handwheel to regulate speed of conveyor according to type of glass. Starts flow of coolant and polishing compound to grinding and polishing wheels. Turns glass to finish other edges and removes glass from machine. Places glass on skid. Observes quality of glass edge to determine need for wheel dressing or adjustment, and lowers or raises wheel by turning nut with wrench; or reads ammeter to determine grinding load and notifies maintenance department to adjust wheels. May wipe polishing compound from edges with cloth. May maintain record of number of pieces edged.
GOE: 06.04.08 STRENGTH: H GED: R2 M2 L2 SVP: 3 DLU: 77

673.685-082 STRIP POLISHER (stonework)

Tends machine to grind and polish slate products, such as flooring, mantels, and coping, to specified thickness and cut grooves in bottom surface of slate to increase adhesion to mortar bed: Selects spacers (width guides) according to distance between grooves and positions saw blades and spacers on machine arbor, using wrench. Turns handwheels to move grinding wheels and blades into grinding and sawing position according to thickness specified for stone and depth of grooves. Places slate strip on conveyor, moves conveyor guides against stone, and tightens guides in position, using wrench. Turns valve to spray water (coolant) on grinding wheels and sawing blades. Starts machine and places slate strips on conveyor that feeds strips between grinding wheels and saw blades of machine. Removes stone from conveyor and places stone on pallet.
GOE: 06.04.08 STRENGTH: M GED: R2 M1 L1 SVP: 2 DLU: 77

673.685-086 DISC-PAD GRINDER (nonmet. min.)

Tends machine that smooths and polishes asbestos disc pads for brake linings: Places disc pads on automatic feed tray of machine. Adjusts grinding head of machine according to specified thickness of polished pads. Starts machine that automatically feeds pads through enclosed grinding and washing units. Observes operation to detect machine malfunctions. Stops machine and clears detected jams. Measures random sample of polished disc pads to determine if pads are ground according to specifications, using caliper. Adjusts grinding mechanism as required, using handtools. Records data, such as production and downtime when machine breakdown occurs.
GOE: 06.04.08 STRENGTH: L GED: R2 M1 L1 SVP: 4 DLU: 86

673.685-094 POLISHING MACHINE TENDER (electron. comp.)

Tends abrading machines that polish or lap surface of semiconductor wafers: Reads work order to determine specifications. Loads wafers or carriers containing wafers onto polishing or lapping machine. Adjusts machine controls or loads programmed control media in machine to regulate pressure, time, and slurry flow. Starts lapping machine that removes saw marks and reduces wafer thickness or starts polishing machine that polishes wafers. Observes machine operation and listens to sounds of belts, cams, and abrading wheel to detect machine malfunctions. Adjusts mechanisms or requests repairs as necessary. Stops machine at prescribed time, removes wafers from machine, and rinses wafers with water to cool wafers and remove slurry. Examines wafers for defects, and measures wafer thickness, using thickness gauge. May clean wafers, using chemical solutions, water, or gases, to remove contaminants from wafer surface. May mount wafers onto carriers. May mix slurry. May tend machine that rounds wafer edges and be designated Edge-Round Tender (electron. comp.). May be designated according to machine tended as Lapping Machine Tender (electron. comp.).
GOE: 06.04.09 STRENGTH: M GED: R3 M2 L2 SVP: 3 DLU: 86

673.685-098 RADIUS CORNER MACHINE OPERATOR (glass products)

Tends machine that grinds and polishes corner edges of flat glass to specified radius: Turns dials to set timer of grinding and polishing wheels to specified settings. Moves lever, turns knob, and presses button to open water valve to start flow of water against grinding wheel, open air pressure valve, and start air pump of machine. Breaks off specified amount of each corner of glass sheets, using glass pliers, positions glass sheets against stops on padded table surface of machine, and presses button to start automatic grinding and polishing cycles of machine. Turns glass sheets to position each corner for processing. Observes and feels corner edges to determine whether reprocessing is necessary. Places processed glass on racks, and separates glass with pieces of cardboard.
GOE: 06.04.08 STRENGTH: H GED: R2 M1 L1 SVP: 2 DLU: 86

673.685-102 WAFER ABRADING MACHINE TENDER (electron. comp.)

Tends abrading machines that roughen surface of semiconductor wafers to distinguish front from back: Adjusts controls to set speed, time, and pressure of abrading belts according to specifications. Loads container of wafers into abrading machine and starts machine that automatically abrades surface of wafer. Removes abraded wafers from machine and inspects wafers to detect abrading defects, such as cracks, using microscope. Replaces worn abrading belts.
GOE: 06.04.09 STRENGTH: L GED: R2 M1 L2 SVP: 2 DLU: 86

673.686-010 BEVELING-AND-EDGING-MACHINE-OPERATOR HELPER (glass mfg.; glass products)

Feeds and off bears automatic edging machines that grind and polish edges of rectangular glass or mirrors: Removes rectangular pieces of glass or mirror

from discharge end of beveling-and-edging machine, turns glass over, and feeds glass onto conveyor of machine to finish other edge. Wipes polishing compound from edge of glass. Places glass or mirror on skid. May work as member of team. May be designated Beveling-Machine-Operator Helper (glass mfg.; glass products); Straightedge-Machine-Operator Helper (glass mfg.; glass products).
GOE: 06.04.08 STRENGTH: H GED: R2 M1 L1 SVP: 2 DLU: 78

673.686-014 BURR GRINDER (optical goods)

Feeds molded lens blanks into automatic burr-grinding machine that removes burrs and sprues, smooths edges, and ejects blanks from machine. Catches blanks ejected from machine and stacks them in trays prior to grinding and polishing. May perform particular phase of operation, such as feeding blanks into machine or catching and stacking ejected blanks.
GOE: 06.04.08 STRENGTH: L GED: R1 M1 L1 SVP: 1 DLU: 77

673.686-018 EDGER-MACHINE HELPER (stonework)

Off bears sandstone slabs from edge-grinding machine and sands edges, using sandpaper-covered block: Pulls sandstone slabs emerging from machine onto turntable and sands edges of slabs, using sandpaper-covered block to smooth irregularities and sharp edges on stone. Pushes slab onto roller conveyor to return slab to edge-grinding machine or onto conveyor for subsequent processing. Lubricates and cleans machine, and cleans work area.
GOE: 06.04.08 STRENGTH: H GED: R2 M1 L1 SVP: 2 DLU: 77

673.686-022 EDGING-MACHINE FEEDER (glass mfg.)

Feeds and regulates machine that smooths edges of automobile window glass.
GOE: 06.04.08 STRENGTH: L GED: R1 M1 L1 SVP: 2 DLU: 77

673.686-026 LAYER (glass mfg.)

Feeds sheets of glass onto conveyor type, plaster-covered table that carries sheets into grinding machine: Climbs onto table and receives glass from workers on floor. Lowers ends simultaneously onto table to avoid cracking sheet. Positions sheets end to end so that edges will not be chipped or glass cracked as glass passes beneath grinding heads. Raises glass and scoops more plaster under edges to level sheets. Pulls roller over glass sheets to settle them in and remove air bubbles from plaster.
GOE: 06.04.08 STRENGTH: L GED: R2 M1 L1 SVP: 2 DLU: 77

673.686-030 DISC-PAD GRINDING MACHINE FEEDER (nonmet. min.)

Feeds asbestos disc pads onto automatic feed platform of grinding machine that polishes pads: Strikes pads against one another to remove excess asbestos particles. Breaks flange from rims of pads by hand and stacks pads onto automatic feed platform of grinding machine.
GOE: 06.04.09 STRENGTH: L GED: R1 M1 L1 SVP: 2 DLU: 86

673.687-010 JOINER (glass mfg.)

Positions and secures sheets of glass on table preparatory to grinding and polishing operations: Dumps quantity of plaster onto table and spreads it, using trowel. Guides sheets of glass, lowered by overhead crane, onto plaster-covered table so that glass sheets lie end to end. Inserts stubs (wooden blocks) between sheets to prevent chipping. Drives wood pegs up through holes along edge of table to prevent glass from shifting or sliding from table. Fills spaces between sheets with plaster to provide continuous smooth surface for grinding and polishing.
GOE: 06.04.30 STRENGTH: L GED: R2 M1 L1 SVP: 2 DLU: 77

674 TURNING OCCUPATIONS

This group includes occupations concerned with shaping materials by the paring or chipping action of rigid cutting tools, or the wearing away action of rotating abrasive wheels, applied to material rotating on a lathe or similar machine.

674.382-010 GLASS-LATHE OPERATOR (electron. comp.)

Operates glass lathe to cut, shape, and seal glass bulbs used in manufacturing electronic tubes, following blueprints, standard procedures, and sample parts: Places glass blanks and tube components in chuck or tailstock of lathe, adjusts and locks parts in lathe manually or depresses pedal of compressed air device that automatically locks parts in lathe. Starts lathe, lights gas-torch heating element, turns valve to regulate flames, according to specified heating rate, and heats glass to working temperature indicated by color. Turns handwheels or pushes lever to control heating of specified areas of glass parts. Depresses pedal to control air blast and holds tools against revolving glass to perform mechanical operations, such as cutting and shaping glass to repair defects. Anneals glass parts, using gas torch. May operate glass lathe to form glass beads on tube components or to seal new glass tubing on necks of rebuilt television or oscilloscope tubes. May fuse glass seal tube and connector pins into side of partially formed vacuum tubes, using gas torch.
GOE: 06.02.08 STRENGTH: M GED: R3 M2 L3 SVP: 4 DLU: 89

674.662-010 STONE-LATHE OPERATOR (stonework) alternate titles: lathe operator; turner

Sets up and operates stonecutting lathe to turn and shape blocks of stone, such as limestone, marble, granite, and sandstone to form columns, pillars, balusters, and other cylindrical building and monumental work: Mounts block of stone between centers of lathe, using hoist. Signals OVERHEAD CRANE OPERATOR (any industry) 921.663-010 to position stone in lathe. Adjusts rough-

ing tool or grinding wheel on carriage and starts machine. Opens water valve and feeds tool or grinding wheel against and along length of rotating stone. Removes roughing tool or wheel and installs finishing tools, using handtools. Measures stone to ensure cutting to specified dimension and contour, using caliper. May knock off corners of rough stone with hammer. May cut intricate designs in stone, using special tools. May sharpen cutting tools. May operate lathe to polish stone objects and be designated Stone-Lathe Polisher (stonework).
GOE: 06.02.08 STRENGTH: H GED: R4 M2 L2 SVP: 7 DLU: 77

674.682-010 FINISHING-MACHINE OPERATOR (nonmet. min.)
Sets up and operates lathe to dress (cut) grinding wheels to specified dimensions and type of surfaces: Positions and fastens grinding wheel in machine chucks, and mounts cutting (abrasive) wheel on machine carriage or traverse mechanism, or inserts and adjusts cutting tool in toolholder. Starts machine and turns wheels to regulate speed of machine and depth and angle of cut depending on type of surface finish desired, width of surface faces, angle between faces, and thickness and diameter of wheel specified. Verifies dimensions of wheel against specifications, using tape measure and calipers.
GOE: 06.02.02 STRENGTH: L GED: R3 M2 L1 SVP: 4 DLU: 77

675 PLANING AND SHAPING OCCUPATIONS, N.E.C.

This group includes occupations concerned with cutting a smooth surface on rough stock and reducing it to desired size by the action of rotating cutting tools; and imparting a particular shape to material.

675.682-010 CONTOUR GRINDER (stonework) alternate titles: profile grinder
Sets up and operates machine with single or multiple grinding wheels to shape building or monumental stone into various designs: Levels and aligns stone on car or machine bed according to design specified for stone, using crowbar, wedges, square, and spirit level. Clamps stone to backstop, securing stone for grinding. Selects template, according to contour of design, and bolts template into position on machine to guide grinding wheel over stone. Turns valve to spray water over wheels and stone. Moves levers to lower grinding wheel against stone and start machine that moves rotating wheel back and forth over stone, following outline of template. Observes ammeter to determine resistance against wheel and moves lever to increase or decrease pressure on wheel. Compares stone with template or scans design marked on stone to determine conformance to specifications. Dresses surface of worn grinding wheels by holding dressing tool against rotating wheel. May rough out contour of stone preparatory to finishing by machine, using chisel, hammer, and pneumatic cutting tools. May operate machine without template to grind flat surface on stone [TOP POLISHER (stonework)]. May operate machine to grind joints or grooves or cut and shape stone moldings, fluted columns, panels, and decorative designs in building or monumental stones.
GOE: 06.02.08 STRENGTH: M GED: R3 M2 L1 SVP: 5 DLU: 77

675.682-014 PLANER OPERATOR (elec. equip.)
Operates machine to plane flat surfaces of carbon or graphite stock to specified thickness and surface finish for use as anodes in electrolytic cells or as brushes in electric motors and generators.
GOE: 06.02.09 STRENGTH: L GED: R3 M2 L2 SVP: 5 DLU: 77

675.682-018 PLANER, STONE (stonework) alternate titles: planing-machine operator
Sets up and operates planing machine to shape, smooth, and square surface of stone blocks and slabs: Positions stone block on machine bed, using hoist, and secures it in place on bed with clamps (dogs). Measures and marks stone, using pattern, tape measure, and marking pencil. Installs and adjusts cutting tool in machine chuck, using wrench, and starts machine. Pulls levers and turns wheels to regulate cutting speed and depth of cut. Cuts specified design by hand in portion of stone that cannot be cut by machine, and smoothes edges of stone, using mallet, chisel, and file. May replace worn or broken parts, using handtools, and lubricate machine.
GOE: 06.02.08 STRENGTH: H GED: R3 M2 L2 SVP: 5 DLU: 77

676 BORING AND PUNCHING OCCUPATIONS

This group includes occupations concerned with piercing material by means of rotary cutting tools or rigid tools advanced into the material to make, enlarge, or thread holes.

676.382-010 DRILL-PRESS OPERATOR, PRINTED CIRCUIT BOARDS (electron. comp.)
Sets up and operates single- or multispindle drill press to bore holes in fiberglass boards used in production of printed circuit boards (PCB's): Studies drill drawing and product specifications to determine hole locations and dimensions, drill speed, and feed rate. Selects and installs bits in spindles, using handtools. Moves controls to set drill speed, feed rate, and depth of cut. Positions board(s) to be drilled over registration pins on machine bed. Views enlarged image of artwork on lighted scope to position and align single-spindle drill and board and depresses pedal or moves lever to operate drill press to bore holes. Positions template on registration pins under stylus of multispindle drill press and

guides stylus that automatically depresses bit to activate drill press to bore holes. May operate single-spindle drill press to bore holes in metal template. May measure hole size, using micrometer gauge. May sand finished boards or template, using sander.
GOE: 06.02.02 STRENGTH: L GED: R3 M2 L2 SVP: 3 DLU: 86

676.462-010 ROUTER OPERATOR (stonework)
Sets up and operates multispindle routing machine to cut sink openings in sandstone countertops and tabletops and to drill holes in synthetic composition board: Reads blueprints to determine location and size of sink openings or holes to be cut. Installs specified router bit in 45- or 90-degree angle spindle chuck, using chuck key. Positions sandstone slab or composition board on machine bed and secures workpiece to bed, using C-clamps. Determines distance from edge of workpiece to opening and distance between holes, and pulls levers, turns handwheel, and presses buttons to position bridge and spindle and to start and lower router bit to drill holes in composition board or route out sink opening. Observes ammeter to determine cutting resistance and lifts lever to reduce speed of drill or movement of bridge or spindle. Turns dial to set automatic control that stops and raises router when specified depth in board has been reached. Removes clamps and pushes workpiece from machine bed. Examines and measures slabs and pegboards to determine adherence to specifications and sands edges of sink opening, using sandpaper. Maintains production records.
GOE: 06.02.08 STRENGTH: H GED: R3 M3 L3 SVP: 3 DLU: 77

676.682-010 DRILL OPERATOR, AUTOMATIC (glass products) alternate titles: driller, multiple spindle
Sets up and operates drilling machine, equipped with vertically opposed hollow drills, that drill holes in glass and mirrors: Reads work ticket to determine size, quantity, and placement of holes to be drilled. Selects specified diamond-tipped hollow drill bits and installs bits in upper and lower spindles, using wrench. Turns knob to adjust depth of bore and rate of ascent and descent at which drill bits enter glass. Measures and clamps guide rail and stops on drill table according to specifications. Turns valve to start flow of coolant and presses button to start electric motor. Positions glass or mirror against stops on drill table. Depresses pedal or presses button to start drilling cycle that automatically clamps glass, drills hole, and releases glass. Repositions glass and repeats drilling procedure until specified number of holes have been drilled. Inspects holes for chips or cracks and verifies placement of holes according to specifications, using ruler. Places mirror or glass on pallet.
GOE: 06.02.08 STRENGTH: H GED: R3 M2 L1 SVP: 4 DLU: 77

676.682-014 STONE DRILLER (stonework) alternate titles: driller
Operates drill to bore holes in blocks or slabs of granite, slate, marble, or sandstone, according to specifications: Places block of stone on machine bed and secures it in position for drilling, using electric hoist, wedges, and wooden blocks. Measures and marks block for drilling, using rule or template and marking pencil. Selects and installs specified bit in drill and starts machine. Pulls lever and turns wheels to regulate speed of machine, flow of water (coolant), and drilling speed. May drill holes in stone, using pneumatic hand drill. May sharpen drill bits, using grindstone. May be designated according to type of machine operated as Drill Operator, Pneumatic (stonework); Radial-Drill Operator (stonework); or according to material drilled as Slate Cutter (stonework).
GOE: 06.02.08 STRENGTH: H GED: R3 M2 L2 SVP: 4 DLU: 77

676.685-010 DRILLER, BRAKE LINING (nonmet. min.)
Tends single or multispindle drill press that drills rivet holes in asbestos brake linings: Places specified brake lining into template, fastens lid to secure lining and positions template under drill. Depresses pedal to lower drill through holes in template and drill holes in lining. Examines lining to detect surface or drilling defects. Discards defective linings and notifies supervisor of faulty material or drill press malfunction. Maintains production records.
GOE: 06.04.08 STRENGTH: L GED: R2 M1 L1 SVP: 2 DLU: 77

676.685-014 DRILLER, MACHINE (glass products)
Tends single-spindle drilling machine that drills holes in glass products, such as panes, mirrors, picture glass, furniture tops, and ornamental glass: Positions pattern on glass and marks glass for drilling, or measures and marks glass, using ruler and crayon. Positions glass on felt-covered table beneath drill, starts drill, and pulls lever to lower drill against glass. Squirts coolant from can onto drill during boring. Raises drill, removes glass, and wipes glass clean with cloth. May sharpen bits, using diamond grinding wheel. May nail or clamp stops to table to hold glass in position.
GOE: 06.04.08 STRENGTH: M GED: R2 M1 L1 SVP: 2 DLU: 77

676.686-010 STONE-DRILLER HELPER (stonework)
Feeds and positions sandstone slabs on bed of drilling machine and off bears drilled slabs: Pushes sandstone slab from roller conveyor onto bed of drilling machine and positions slab against edge stop or places slab into position as directed by STONE DRILLER (stonework). Installs specified size carbide or diamond core drill bits, using handtool. Washes stone chips from drilled slab, using water hose, and pushes slab onto roller conveyor. Knocks cores from core drilled holes, using hammer, and pushes slab along roller conveyor for further processing.
GOE: 06.04.08 STRENGTH: H GED: R1 M1 L1 SVP: 2 DLU: 77

676.686-014 DRILLER AND DEBURRER, REFLECTOR (light. fix.)
Feeds and unloads machine that heats and drills holes in light bulb reflectors for lead wires: Removes and places glass reflectors from cartons onto conveyor

that feeds drilling machine. Removes drilled reflectors from discharge conveyor and places reflectors in tray and carries reflectors to deburrer. Aligns and places reflector holes over deburrer bit that smooths edges of holes. Inspects reflector to ensure that holes conform to specifications. Places reflectors in carton for shipment.
GOE: 06.04.08 STRENGTH: L GED: R2 M1 L1 SVP: 2 DLU: 86

677   CHIPPING, CUTTING, SAWING, AND RELATED OCCUPATIONS

This group includes occupations concerned with shaping material by cutting away flakes or fragments with a hatchet or chisel-like cutting tool, utilizing a percussive power source, and otherwise removing excess material or separating materials with cutting tools.

677.131-010   GLASS-CUT-OFF SUPERVISOR (glass mfg.) alternate titles: supervisor, automatic cutting machines
Supervises and coordinates workers engaged in cutting flat or sheet glass to length from continuous ribbon of glass to facilitate handling or cutting glass to size on automatic or semiautomatic cutting machines: Reviews production schedules to determine cutting dimensions and cutting sequence. Measures length and width of cut glass to ensure cutters are spaced correctly. Gauges thickness of glass with micrometer to ensure that glass thickness is within specifications, and notifies glass drawing or rolling department of measurements. Examines glass for flaws, such as stones, blisters, or cracks, to ensure maintenance of standards. Examines equipment for malfunction and orders repairs, such as change of cutter heads. Performs other duties as described under SUPERVISOR (any industry) Master Title. May perform test runs to ensure cutting program on computerized cutting equipment is correct. May supervise workers packing glass in shipping containers.
GOE: 06.02.01 STRENGTH: L GED: R4 M3 L3 SVP: 7 DLU: 77

677.382-010   BATTING-MACHINE   OPERATOR,   INSULATION (nonmet. min.)
Sets up and operates machine to slit and cut *mineral wool blanket* into batting of specified dimensions and enclose them in paper covering: Installs and adjusts slitting saws, edge cutters, dividers, flange sealing rollers, and paper guide rollers, using rule, wrenches, screwdriver, and hammer, or by turning handwheels and moving levers. Positions paper rolls in upper and lower machine racks, using hoist. Tightens collars on shaft to secure rolls, using wrench. Starts machine and turns wheel to align rolls, and threads paper into feed rollers. Raises and lowers blanket feed table under master roller to control thickness of batting. Stops machine to remove substandard material and make adjustments to correct defects.
GOE: 06.02.09 STRENGTH: M GED: R3 M2 L3 SVP: 5 DLU: 77

677.382-014   SAWYER, OPTICAL GLASS (optical goods)
Operates diamond-studded saw to cut slabs of optical glass into various sizes and shapes for molding into or direct use as blanks for making lenses, prisms, mirrors, and other optical elements for precision instruments: Reads work order or receives oral instructions regarding glass to be cut. Refers to chart to determine size of pieces to be cut for weight specified. Inspects glass for defects, such as bubbles, cracks, or striae, and determines cutting method to obtain maximum number of blanks. Marks cutting lines on glass, using marking pencil. Positions stock on bed of saw and sets guides for depth and width of cut. Starts machine and saws glass following markings. Removes, weighs, and measures glass blank to ensure conformance to specifications. Examines blanks to be molded for chips and sharp edges and removes defects, using grinder. May remove excess stock from cut or molded blanks, using surface grinder.
GOE: 06.02.08 STRENGTH: L GED: R3 M2 L2 SVP: 7 DLU: 77

677.382-018   CRYSTAL SLICER (electron. comp.) alternate titles: crystal cutter; saw operator; wafer slicer
Operates precision saws to slice wafers from semiconductor crystal ingots, such as silicon or gallium arsenide: Attaches mounted crystal to holding fixture of automatic feed on saw, using clamps. Adjusts saw controls to set speed and angle of saw blade, thickness of cut, and angle of holding fixture. Operates saw to cut sample wafer from crystal ingot. Measures *crystal orientation* of sample wafer, using x-ray machine, and measures thickness of sample wafer, using calipers or thickness gauge. Inspects sample wafer for flaws, such as saw marks, chips, bow, and taper. Readjusts saw controls based on measurements and inspection. Starts saw and observes operation of saw to ensure wafers are sliced according to specifications. Removes sliced wafers from saw and cleans wafers in sink or ultrasonic cleaner. May mount crystal ingot to mounting block [CRYSTAL MOUNTER (electron. comp.) 677.687-014]. May be designated according to type of saw operated as V-Block Saw Operator (electron. comp.); Wire Saw Operator (electron. comp.).
GOE: 06.02.09 STRENGTH: M GED: R3 M2 L2 SVP: 4 DLU: 86

677.462-010   CIRCULAR SAWYER, STONE (stonework) alternate titles: cut-off-saw operator; rotary-saw operator
Sets up and operates diamond-or silicon carbide-toothed circular saw to cut blocks of stone into specified dimension: Builds bed of timbers on car preparatory to positioning stone on car. Levels stone on bed, using crowbar, wedges, blocks, rule, and spirit level. Marks dimensions on stone according to diagram, using rule, square, straightedge, and chalked string or crayon. Traces along marks on stone, using chisel and hammer. Turns crank or presses button

to move car under saw frame. Presses buttons to align saw blade with line traced on stone and lower blade to stone. Starts saw and pushes lever to move rotating blade across surface of stone or move stone under blade. Turns valve to circulate water (coolant) or abrasive on blade during cutting. Presses button to lower blade in stone as depth of kerf increases. Inserts bar under stone and lifts it to split stone not severed by blade. Verifies width or thickness of slab, using rule. May set saw for automatic reciprocation. May change blades as depth of kerf increases, using wrench. May attach abrasive grinding wheel to arbor to grind grooves in stone. May set end-stops according to width of cut. May read ammeter to determine resistance against blade and turn crank to adjust blade pressure against stone. May saw products, such as asbestos-cement sheets and pipes or concrete slabs. May be designated according to material cut as Marble-Cutter Operator (stonework); Slate-Cutter Operator (stonework); or according to saw operated as Diamond-Saw Operator (stonework).
GOE: 06.02.08 STRENGTH: M GED: R3 M2 L1 SVP: 4 DLU: 77

677.462-014   WIRE SAWYER (stonework) alternate titles: finishing wire sawyer; single-wire-saw operator; wire-saw operator
Sets up and operates one or more wire saws to cut blocks of stone into specified dimensions: Threads cables through machine pulleys and solders ends of cable together, using silver solder and torch. Builds bed of timbers on car preparatory to positioning stone on car. Signals OVERHEAD CRANE OPERATOR (any industry) 921.663-010 or operates crane to position stone on bed of car. Starts winch that pulls car onto track under sawing cable. Levels stone on timber bed, using crowbar, wedges, blocks, rule, and spirit level. Marks dimensions on stone according to diagram, using rule, square, straightedge, and chalked line. Presses button to lower sawing cable onto stone and moves car to align cable with line marked on stone. Positions abrasive hose on stone, and starts saw and pump that circulate abrasive and water under moving cables that cut stone by dragging abrasive across stone. Observes operation to detect uneven sawing and exhausting supply of abrasive. Tightens pulleys to increase tension on cables to restore even sawing. Dumps abrasive in abrasive pit to maintain cutting speed. Verifies width or thickness of cut stone, using rule. Replaces worn cables. May cut sheet metal pattern of design to be sawed. May drill holes in stone and insert saw cable through hole, using portable drill. May operate vertically mounted wire saw to cut out designs in stone. May be designated according to type of saw operated as Contour Wire Sawyer (stonework); Multiple-Wire Sawyer (stonework).
GOE: 06.02.08 STRENGTH: H GED: R3 M2 L1 SVP: 5 DLU: 77

677.486-010   CIRCULAR-SAWYER HELPER (stonework)
Feeds and off bears diamond circular saw to assist operator to cut slate slabs: Removes slate slab from truck bed and positions slab on machine bed, using electric crane. Measures and marks dimensions on slab, as directed by saw operator, using tape measure and grease pencil. Raises slab from machine bed, using crowbar, and places blocks and wedges under slab to level and support stone during cutting process. Pushes turntable mounted on machine bed to align slab with cutting marks for preliminary cut and each succeeding cut. Examines cut edge of stone for defects, such as splits or fractures. Lifts cut slabs from machine, assisted by operator and places slabs onto pallet. Places waste stone in waste bin or stacks stone for splitting into flagstone. Washes stone chips and dust slabs and work area, using water hose.
GOE: 06.04.08 STRENGTH: H GED: R2 M1 L1 SVP: 3 DLU: 77

677.562-010   GLASS-CUTTING-MACHINE OPERATOR, AUTOMATIC (glass mfg.) alternate titles: finishing-machine operator, automatic; multicut-line operator
Sets up and operates automatic cutting machine that scores and breaks flat glass into standardized sections: Positions trip switches to adjust stroke of cutting bridges for longitudinal and latitudinal scoring of glass. Manually positions sets of cutter heads on bridge or sets controls that position them to score glass into specific dimensions. Turns controls to change height of bridges to adjust depth of scoring cut. Adjusts timing mechanism to synchronize breaker bar to snap glass at score. Starts automatic vacuum-cupped crane that lifts and transfers cut glass. Starts machine to verify setup and to make necessary adjustments. Measures cut glass with tape to verify dimensions and observes glass for irregular breaks and uneven edges. Removes and replaces worn cutter heads, using handtools. Maintains record of production, using counter. May review work order to determine cutting sequence. May direct workers who are members of cutting team. May operate single cut machine.
GOE: 06.02.08 STRENGTH: L GED: R3 M2 L2 SVP: 3 DLU: 77

677.665-010   GLASS-UNLOADING-EQUIPMENT TENDER (glass mfg.) alternate titles: cut-off-machine helper; cut-off-machine unloader
Tends automatic vacuum crane that removes *lites* of glass from cutoff machine conveyor: Turns valves to activate vacuum cups on crane that hold glass during unloading-stacking cycle, and starts crane. Inspects glass for spalls (rough edges) as glass passes on conveyor. Trims spalls from glass with glass-cutting wheel and notifies GLASS-CUTTING-MACHINE OPERATOR, AUTOMATIC (glass mfg.) of glass condition for correction. Stops crane cycle to allow passage of broken or defective glass from conveyor into cullet waste glass chute. Counts glass stacked on turntable, and pushes switch to move turntable to next loading station. May use spotlight to highlight defects in glass. May work as member of team. May load lites on automatic, multicutting machine to cut lites into sections, using automatic vacuum-cupped crane, and be designated Glass-Loading-Equipment Tender (glass mfg.).

GOE: 06.04.08 STRENGTH: L GED: R2 M1 L1 SVP: 2 DLU: 77

677.666-010 SPLITTING-MACHINE-OPERATOR HELPER (stonework)
Feeds and off bears splitting machine that cuts stone slabs for further processing: Signals OVERHEAD CRANE OPERATOR (any industry) 921.663-010 to lower sling, places sling around slab, and signals crane operator to lift and transport slab from layout area to conveyor of splitting machine. Pushes stone slab along roller conveyor onto machine work surface (turntable) and rotates slab to align cutting marks on stone with blade of machine, as directed by operator. Turns stone on work surface of machine for additional cuts. Pushes stone from splitting machine along roller conveyor to holding area. Picks up broken fragments of stone and places them into rubble container, and directs crane operator to lower sling to lift large pieces of rubble for deposit in container. Attaches crane hook to rubble container to facilitate removal to spoil pile. Works as member of team.
GOE: 06.04.08 STRENGTH: H GED: R1 M1 L1 SVP: 2 DLU: 77

677.682-010 HEAD-SAW OPERATOR, INSULATION BOARD (wood prod., nec)
Operates multiple-circular-saw machine that automatically cuts insulation board into panels: Installs and adjusts saws on shaft, using rule and handtools. Starts machine that automatically feeds boards from conveyor into saws. Measures sample panels for conformance to specified dimensions. Inspects cut edge for indications of dulled saw blades. Readjusts or replaces blades.
GOE: 06.02.03 STRENGTH: L GED: R3 M2 L1 SVP: 6 DLU: 77

677.682-014 REFRACTORY-GRINDER OPERATOR (brick & tile)
Operates machines to cut and grind refractory clay blocks to specified dimensions: Measures and scribes cutting lines on block, using ruler and scribe. Lifts block onto bed on cutoff grinder and secures block to bed with holding attachment, using handtools. Turns handwheels to position block under cutting blade. Starts machines that cut block along scribed lines and grind it to specified dimensions. Shapes unmachinable blocks, using chisels, hammers, and hand stones.
GOE: 06.02.08 STRENGTH: M GED: R2 M2 L1 SVP: 2 DLU: 77

677.682-018 SINK CUTTER (stonework)
Operates diamond or carbon silicate saw to cut drain grooves and sink openings in sandstone countertops and smooths and rounds sink openings, using portable sander, metal bar, and sandpaper: Pushes countertop from conveyor onto saw bed and positions top under saw blade. Turns valve to start flow of coolant onto saw blade and pulls trigger to start rotation of saw blade. Lowers saw to stone surface and tightens wing nut to maintain cutting level and pushes saw through slab to cut sink opening, following predrilled holes as guides. Turns slab on bed to cut remaining sides of sink opening. Installs abrasive blade on saw, using wrench, to cut drain grooves in specified slabs. Pushes stone slab into sanding booth and completes cutting of sink openings, using portable, diamond-bladed circular saw. Rounds and smooths sink edges, using portable disc sander, iron bar, and sandpaper.
GOE: 06.04.08 STRENGTH: V GED: R2 M1 L2 SVP: 3 DLU: 77

677.682-022 STONECUTTER, MACHINE (stonework) alternate titles: surfacer operator; surfacing-machine operator
Operates pneumatic surfacing machine to shape and surface stone for building or monumental purposes: Aligns stone with surfacing machine head as stone is lowered on timber or stone bed, and levels stone, using crowbar, hammer, blocks, wedges, and spirit level. Lays out dimensions on stone surface according to diagram, using rule, square, crayon, or chalked line. Chips off stone in excess of stone required for finishing, using hammer and chisels or bull-set (wedge-shaped hammer). Inserts surfacing chisels or bushhammer into surfacing head according to finish specified or task being performed. Turns crank to lower surfacing head onto stone. Turns compressed air valve to activate cutting tool and guides tool over stone surface, following marks on stone and diagram of finished product, to chip fragments from stone surface and work surface down to an even finish. Scans specifications and verifies progress of surfacing, using straightedge, rule, and square. Finishes curved or irregular surfaces, using pneumatic handtools.
GOE: 06.02.08 STRENGTH: M GED: R3 M2 L1 SVP: 6 DLU: 77

677.682-026 TENONER OPERATOR (wood prod., nec)
Sets up and operates machine to cut mortises and tenons in fibrous insulating board and acoustical tile: Installs and adjusts flange, bevel, tongue and groove cutters, holddown rolls, and lug guides, using handtools. Turns wheel to position and adjust width of feed chains to ensure depth and squareness of cuts. Starts machine and automatic feeding conveyor, and observes each phase of processing. Measures sample products for squareness and depth of cuts, using square and jigs.
GOE: 06.02.09 STRENGTH: L GED: R3 M2 L1 SVP: 4 DLU: 77

677.685-010 ABRASIVE SAWYER (nonmet. min.)
Tends machine equipped with circular diamond saw that cuts abrasive sticks and stones for honing machines: Places abrasive bricks (blocks) against guide and clamps bricks onto holding fixture of machine. Starts machine and flow of coolant. Presses button to start feed mechanism that moves brick against diamond saw to cut abrasive sticks of specified dimensions. Measures cut stick, using micrometer. Removes burrs from stick, using file made of same material. May tend diamond saw to trim crust from abrasive brick to expose material for hardness testing.

GOE: 06.04.08 STRENGTH: L GED: R2 M2 L1 SVP: 2 DLU: 77

677.685-014 ASSEMBLER, LAY-UPS (toy-sport equip.)
Tends machine, equipped with circular cutting blade, that assembles fiberglass mats of various weights and textures from rolls into stacks and cuts stacks (lay-ups) to specified length for use in manufacture of skis: Selects color-coded rolls and mounts them on feeder-rack spools in specified order, and threads mats between feed rollers to load machine. Pushes knife trigger-mechanism to designated mark to establish cutting intervals. Starts machine and observes emerging lay-ups to detect tears in cut edges. Lifts lever-control of stone that sharpens blade to restore clean-cutting action during machine operation. Lifts and carries cut lay-ups from off bearing table to storage. Replaces worn-out blade, using hex-wrench.
GOE: 06.04.08 STRENGTH: H GED: R2 M1 L1 SVP: 2 DLU: 77

677.685-018 CARBON CUTTER (elec. equip.)
Tends circular abrasive saw to cut carbon or graphite stock to specified size or bevel: Measures carbon or graphite stock, using rule or micrometers and marks line of cut with rule or scribe. Turns setscrews to adjust guides and stops, according to size of stock. Positions and clamps stock against guides. Starts machine and pushes stock along machine bed through cutting disk.
GOE: 06.02.08 STRENGTH: L GED: R3 M2 L1 SVP: 4 DLU: 77

677.685-022 CRAYON SAWYER (mine & quarry)
Performs any combination of following tasks to cut and shape talc blocks into crayons: Removes block from chute and positions block onto saw bed. Pushes block into saw blade to cut and square edge for slabbing. Feeds squared block onto rotating slotted grate that moves block through multiple blade saw that cuts block into slabs of specified width. Stacks slabs in holding fixture of machine equipped with pneumatic plunger that pushes slab through blades that cut slabs into crayons of specified size, or places slab against guide and pushes slab into saw blade to cut individual crayons from slab. Feeds square crayons into V-shaped groove on grinding machine and pushes crayon between grinding wheels that grind edges and round crayon. Dumps boxes of crayons into bins or chutes for grading.
GOE: 06.04.08 STRENGTH: L GED: R1 M1 L1 SVP: 2 DLU: 77

677.685-026 CUT-OFF-SAW OPERATOR, PIPE BLANKS (nonmet. min.)
Tends machine equipped with multiple abrasive blades that cuts asbestos-cement pipe into blanks in manufacture of pipe couplings: Adjusts and spaces abrasive blades to cut pipe to specified lengths, using wrench. Turns crank to set hydraulic lifters that automatically raise blades that cut pipe. Measures diameter of pipe, using tape measure, and turns handwheel to adjust position of pressure-drive roll according to diameter of pipe being cut. Loads pipe onto feed rack by hand, or using monorail hoist, and rolls pipe into position over cutting blades. Moves lever to lower pressure-drive roll that holds and rotates pipe during cutting process. Presses buttons to start machine that cuts pipe into blanks. Moves lever and pushes button to lift pressure-drive roll and withdraw cutting blades. Moves lever to extend pivoted metal shaft through blanks to lift and remove coupling blanks from machine. Inspects and measures blanks to verify conformity to specifications. Marks identifying information onto blanks, using stencil, paint, and brush, and stacks pipe on steam tray. Records production data.
GOE: 06.04.08 STRENGTH: M GED: R2 M1 L1 SVP: 3 DLU: 77

677.685-030 GLASS CUT-OFF TENDER (glass mfg.) alternate titles: cut-off tender, glass; window-glass cutter off
Tends automatic equipment that burns, scores, and breaks continuous sheet of glass into specific lengths: Turns controls on panel to synchronize cutting heads with rise of vertically drawn glass sheet to score glass into specific dimensions. Pushes or pulls sheet to cap off (break) glass along scored line, and trims knurled edges with glass cutter wheel. Stacks cut glass sheets on rack and throws cullet (waste glass) down chute. Replaces dull cutting wheels on automatic scoring equipment. Periodically measures cut glass length and adjusts cutting heads. May record number of sheets produced per hour. May use vacuum-cupped crane to break off or move cut glass. May work as member of team.
GOE: 06.04.08 STRENGTH: H GED: R2 M2 L2 SVP: 2 DLU: 77

677.685-034 SAMPLE SAWYER (brick & tile)
Tends machine equipped with circular abrasive saw that cuts face from production brick for use as displays or sales sample panels: Sets saw table guides to specified length and width, using machine measuring scale and wrench. Places brick against guides and tightens holding device, using wrench. Starts abrasive saw and pushes table under saw blade and depresses pedal to control depth of cut. Places discard portion of brick into wheelbarrow and stacks cutoff face sample on bench. Carries stack of face samples to next work station and wheels discarded brick to scrap pile. May tend saw that cuts clay sewer pipe to salvage usable pipe from defective pipe and be designated Ceramic Saw, Tender (brick & tile). May tend saw that cuts kiln furniture used to support clay products during firing process and be designated Kiln Furniture, Saw Tender (brick & tile).
GOE: 06.04.08 STRENGTH: L GED: R1 M1 L1 SVP: 2 DLU: 78

677.685-038 SAWYER II (nonmet. min.)
Tends circular saw, equipped with automatic reciprocating or manually operated table, that cuts strip asbestos brake lining into lengths: Positions and bolts

stop on table at length specified on work order, using rule and wrenches. Installs roll of lining on spindle and positions end of lining against stop. Pushes button to start machine and holds lining on machine table that automatically travels under saw blade, or pushes table under saw blade to cut lining. Examines cut lining for defects, such as breaks, cracks, or rough edges, and places acceptable lining on rack or on conveyor. Places defective pieces in discard pile. Records number of linings meeting specifications on work order. May tend battery of automatic saws.
GOE: 06.04.08 STRENGTH: M GED: R2 M1 L1 SVP: 2 DLU: 77

677.685-042   SPLITTER OPERATOR (stonework) alternate titles: jack-hammer-splitter operator; stone splitter
Tends pneumatic chipping machine to split rough slabs of stone: Marks dimensions on stone, according to specifications, using rule and chalk. Lifts guide track onto stone and aligns track with marks on stone. Positions wagon over track, inserts chisel in chuck of airhammer, mounts airhammer on wagon, and lowers chisel into opening in guide track. Presses lever to start airhammer and pushes wagon and airhammer back and forth over guide track to split stone.
GOE: 05.12.13 STRENGTH: H GED: R2 M1 L1 SVP: 2 DLU: 77

677.685-046   SPLITTING-MACHINE OPERATOR (stonework) alternate titles: guillotine cutter
Tends hydraulic machine that cuts stone slabs for further processing: Reads work order to determine dimensions of stone to be cut. Sets end-stops according to dimensions of desired cut, measuring distance from blade with rule, or lays out dimensions on stone, using rule, straightedge, and chalk. Starts conveyor that moves stone over blade and against stops, or directs coworkers to push stone along roller conveyor into cutting position. Depresses pedal to raise turntable of conveyor containing stone slab, and rotates slab manually to align cutting mark with blades or to straighten stone against stops. Presses button to raise blade against stone and moves levers to lower wedges mounted on pressure head against stone. Turns lever or presses button to build up pressure in pressure head, observing gauge to determine when pressure is sufficient to cut stone. Pulls lever to force wedges against stone, splitting stone into specified dimensions. Lowers blade and end-stops, raises pressure head, and starts conveyor to remove stone. May tend machine that cuts granite blocks into paving-blocks (cobblestones) and be designated Paving-Block Cutter (stonework) I.
GOE: 06.04.08 STRENGTH: L GED: R3 M2 L1 SVP: 3 DLU: 77

677.685-050   STONE SPLITTER (concrete prod.) alternate titles: splitter
Tends machine to split concrete stone into building blocks resembling ashlar: Sets end stops according to length or width of cut, measuring distance from blade with rule. Positions block under blade and against stops. Depresses pedal to lower blade and split block. Depresses pedal to raise stops and pushes split blocks into storage hopper.
GOE: 06.04.08 STRENGTH: L GED: R2 M2 L1 SVP: 2 DLU: 77

677.685-054   SAW OPERATOR (brick & tile)
Tends saw that cuts ceramic kiln furniture, such as posts and slabs to specified size: Reads work order to determine size according to customer specifications. Measures product, using tape measure, and marks cutting line with pencil. Positions kiln furniture on worktable and aligns cutting line with saw blade. Pulls switch to activate saw and pushes product against saw blade along cutting line. Stacks cut kiln furniture on storage pallet.
GOE: 06.04.08 STRENGTH: M GED: R2 M1 L1 SVP: 2 DLU: 86

677.686-010   SAWYER I (nonmet. min.)
Feeds machine that automatically cuts and trims asbestos tubes used to insulate pipe: Places tube on feed bed of circular saws that cut tube wall longitudinally and trim tube ends to specified length. Observes feed of tubes through saws and inspects tube for clean cut. Adjusts blades for specified depth and space cut, using wrench.
GOE: 06.04.09 STRENGTH: M GED: R2 M1 L1 SVP: 2 DLU: 77

677.686-014   GLASS-CUTTING-MACHINE FEEDER (glass products) alternate titles: statler operator
Feeds sheet glass into machine that scores and cuts glass to specified size: Positions glass onto feed rollers and against guides to align glass with cutters. Pushes glass into feed end of machine that conveys glass under cutters and cuts glass to specified size.
GOE: 06.04.08 STRENGTH: M GED: R1 M1 L1 SVP: 2 DLU: 86

677.687-010   LOG ROLLER (saw. & plan.) alternate titles: log handler
Performs any combination of following tasks to transfer logs and peeler blocks (logs cut to lathe length) from pond, trucks, or conveyor to log deck, barken deck, or lathe deck: Rolls logs from trucks or conveyor to deck, using peavy, or transfers peeler blocks from pond to barken deck, using electric hoist and conveyor. Arranges logs on deck for feeding logs to saws or positions blocks at lathe or barken deck, using conveyor. Marks center of blocks for lathe chucks, using scale. May attach hoist hooks to blocks and position block between lathe chucks. May move levers to activate mechanism that kicks logs from conveyor to deck. May use ax or pick to remove undesirable material from bark, such as stones or nails.
GOE: 06.04.40 STRENGTH: M GED: R2 M1 L1 SVP: 2 DLU: 77

677.687-014   CRYSTAL MOUNTER (electron. comp.)
Mounts crystal ingot onto mounting block of crystal saw preparatory to slicing semiconductor wafers from ingot: Sorts semiconductor crystal ingots according to size and *crystal orientation*. Mixes resin and hardening agent to form

epoxy adhesive and spreads adhesive on graphite backing, using putty knife. Attaches crystal ingot(s) to adhesive and backing. Mounts crystal ingot attached to graphite backing onto mounting block of crystal saw, using epoxy adhesive. May mount crystal ingot directly onto mounting block, using epoxy as backing and adhesive. May mount crystal ingot to backing and mounting block, using wax.
GOE: 06.04.34 STRENGTH: H GED: R2 M2 L1 SVP: 2 DLU: 86

679   OCCUPATIONS IN MACHINING STONE, CLAY, GLASS, AND RELATED MATERIALS, N.E.C.

This group includes occupations, not elsewhere classified, concerned with shaping materials or products by removing excess material from stock or objects.

679.130-010   SUPERVISOR (stonework)
Supervises and coordinates activities of workers engaged in sawing, planing, grinding, drilling, sandblasting, polishing, finishing, storing, crating, and loading stone used as monuments, stone products, or in building construction. Performs duties as described under SUPERVISOR (any industry) Master Title.
GOE: 05.05.01 STRENGTH: M GED: R4 M3 L4 SVP: 7 DLU: 77

679.130-014   SUPERVISOR, ASBESTOS PIPE (nonmet. min.)
Supervises and coordinates activities of workers engaged in testing, facing, boring, cutting, and grinding asbestos-cement pipe: Directs and assists subordinates in machine setup to ensure conformance of product to specifications. Trains new workers in setup and operation of plant machinery and equipment. Performs duties as described under SUPERVISOR (any industry) Master Title. May supervise workers engaged in fabricating specially designed shapes, such as elbows, bends, Y's, junctions, and S-curves, and be designated Supervisor, Molding (nonmet. min.).
GOE: 06.02.01 STRENGTH: L GED: R4 M3 L2 SVP: 7 DLU: 77

679.130-018   SUPERVISOR, ASBESTOS-CEMENT SHEET (nonmet. min.)
Supervises and coordinates activities of workers engaged in machining and fabricating asbestos-cement sheet products: Inspects and measures products in process of fabrication to ensure conformance to specifications, using rules, templates, and straightedge. Demonstrates methods and procedures for setting up, operating, and adjusting controls of machines to obtain specified operational performance. Trains new workers in work procedures and machine operation. Performs other duties as described under SUPERVISOR (any industry) Master Title.
GOE: 06.02.01 STRENGTH: M GED: R4 M3 L3 SVP: 7 DLU: 77

679.137-010   SUPERVISOR, FINISHING DEPARTMENT (nonmet. min.)
Supervises and coordinates activities of workers engaged in cutting, finishing, wrapping, and packing pipe and boiler covering moldings. Trains new workers. Performs duties as described under SUPERVISOR (any industry) Master Title.
GOE: 06.02.01 STRENGTH: H GED: R3 M2 L2 SVP: 4 DLU: 77

679.137-014   SUPERVISOR, MIRROR FABRICATION (glass products)
Supervises and coordinates activities of workers engaged in beveling, edging, and drilling holes in flat glass or mirrors: Analyzes production orders and assigns duties to workers, using knowledge of capacities of machines and equipment. Confers with other supervisors to coordinate interdepartmental activities. Observes fabrication of glass and mirrors for quality, and measures glass or mirrors to ensure accuracy of dimensions, using measuring tape. Directs workers to adjust machinery when quality or dimensions of glass or mirrors vary from company standards or customer specifications. Prepares requests for machinery repairs and requisitions supplies for department. Performs other duties as described under SUPERVISOR (any industry) Master Title.
GOE: 06.02.01 STRENGTH: M GED: R4 M2 L2 SVP: 7 DLU: 77

679.362-010   CRYSTAL MACHINING COORDINATOR (electron. comp.) alternate titles: machine operator technician
Leads workers engaged in grinding, sawing, flatting, and inspecting crystal ingots used in semiconductor wafer manufacturing under direction of SUPERVISOR, ELECTRONICS PROCESSING (electron. comp.) 590.130-010: Discusses production objectives, work priorities, and workflow progress with SUPERVISOR, ELECTRONICS PROCESSING (electron. comp.). Reviews daily production logs, inventories ingots in each production stage, and assigns tasks to workers according to priorities. Trains new workers in equipment operation, company procedures, and safety practices and observes workers to ensure compliance with rules and policies. Occasionally operates grinding and sawing machines. Inspects crystal ingots for machining defects and machine malfunctions. Performs minor repairs and maintenance on grinding and sawing machines.
GOE: 06.02.09 STRENGTH: H GED: R3 M3 L3 SVP: 6 DLU: 86

679.384-010   SEED CORE OPERATOR (electron. comp.)
Performs following duties to produce seed cores from silicon crystal ingots for use in crystal growing process: Tends saw that cuts ingot into specified lengths. Determines *crystal orientation* of ingot sections, using x-ray equipment, and draws orientation lines on ingot. Positions ingot sections on chuck of drill according to crystal orientation and activates drill that automatically removes seed core from ingot. Grinds seed core to smooth rough edges, using sanding machine, and x rays and marks seed core to indicate crystal orientation. Tends machine that cuts groove in seed core. Cleans seed core to remove contami-

nants, using ultrasonic and etching equipment. Wraps finished crystal in protective paper. Records production information.
GOE: 06.02.09 STRENGTH: M GED: R3 M3 L2 SVP: 5 DLU: 86

679.567-010   STONE GRADER (mine & quarry) alternate titles: measurer
Inspects quarried stone for size and quality, and classifies stone according to standard schedule. Measures dimensions of stone, using rule. Marks measurements and quality classification on stone with chalk. Maintains production record.
GOE: 06.03.02 STRENGTH: L GED: R2 M2 L2 SVP: 4 DLU: 77

679.664-010   BED SETTER (stonework) alternate titles: banker; lumper; setter; stone banker
Aligns dimension stone on bed of timbers preparatory to grinding, polishing, sawing, or chipping: Builds bed of timbers on flatcar or bed of machine. Signals OVERHEAD CRANE OPERATOR (any industry) 921.663-010 to lower stone and guides stone onto timber bed, aligning stone with arm of polishing machine, surfacing machine, or saw. Determines when stone is level, using straightedge and spirit level. Signals crane operator to lift stone, or pries up stone with crowbar and levels stone by inserting or hammering wedges and blocks between stone and timbers. May assist crane operator to position grinding or polishing wheel on stone. May measure and mark blocks for cutting, using rule, straightedge, and crayon. May spread abrasive material over surface of stone. May shovel abrasive material from mill into storage hopper after grinding and polishing processes.
GOE: 05.12.12 STRENGTH: H GED: R2 M1 L1 SVP: 3 DLU: 77

679.665-010   LEVEL-GLASS-FORMING-MACHINE OPERATOR (cutlery-hrdwr.)
Tends battery of automatic machines that flame-cut and form vials for level from glass tubing: Inserts tubing in holder to feed machine. Replenishes tubing and replaces fill catch boxes. Examines formed glasses for defects, such as unclosed bottoms, elongated tops or misshapen vials, and notifies machine adjuster of machine malfunctioning. Removes formed glasses to workbench and files points from glasses to leave opening for filling, using half-round file.
GOE: 06.04.08 STRENGTH: L GED: R2 M1 L1 SVP: 2 DLU: 77

679.682-010   BANDING-MACHINE OPERATOR (pottery & porc.) alternate titles: gold bander, striper
Sets up and operates machine that applies bands of gold, platinum, or color glaze onto rim or surfaces of ceramic ware: Selects chuck to accommodate type of ware to be banded and attaches it to machine. Adjusts band applicator rollers and arm attachments according to width and location of band to be applied on ware. Pours premixed liquid gold or platinum into roller fonts. Positions ware in chuck and starts machine. Removes ware from machine.
GOE: 06.02.08 STRENGTH: L GED: R3 M1 L1 SVP: 4 DLU: 77

679.685-010   MACHINE OPERATOR, CERAMICS (pottery & porc.)
Tends preset automatic, semiautomatic, and manually operated machines to drill, mill, grind, saw, top, head, cut, thread, turn, or groove green technical ceramic pieces for electronic, mechanical, industrial, and other uses: Places pieces on feeder of machines that are preset and automatic. Places pieces in jig or chuck and starts semiautomatic machine. Positions pieces in front of bit or tap, moves piece around for boring, drilling, or tapping operations, and removes piece when machining manually. Inspects piece for defects, such as cracks and chips. Gauges piece on snap gauge or go-not-go gauge and discards defective pieces. Cleans pieces, using airhose and rotating brush. Stacks pieces on tray or handtruck and trucks lot to storage shelves. Records number of machined pieces for production purposes.
GOE: 06.04.08 STRENGTH: L GED: R2 M1 L1 SVP: 3 DLU: 77

679.685-014   PRODUCTION-MACHINE TENDER, GLASS CUTTING-OR-GRINDING (electron. comp.; glass mfg.)
Tends automatic machines that cut, grind, or polish glass products, such as glass tubes or glassware: Reads work orders to determine product specifications. Loads product onto machine holding and feeding devices, and starts machine that cuts, grinds, or polishes glass products. Monitors machine operation to detect malfunctions. Visually inspects parts for defects, such as cracks and chips. Removes finished product from machine after completion of cycle. May replace worn cutters or grinding and polishing wheels, using handtools. May adjust cutter spacing and fixtures to cut tubes to specified lengths. May manually grind, buff, or polish glass surfaces. May pack product for shipping. May clean machine and work area.
GOE: 06.04.08 STRENGTH: M GED: R2 M1 L2 SVP: 2 DLU: 89

679.685-018   THERMAL-SURFACING-MACHINE   OPERATOR (stonework)
Tends machine that applies heat to surface of granite slab, causing surface of granite to flake and chip to impart pebbled texture to face of stone: Positions torch carriage over granite slab on roller-conveyor bed of machine. Turns thumbscrews to adjust trip switches on bridge of machine to set reciprocation limits of torch carriage. Turns knob to start flow of gas to torch and ignites gas. Turns knob to start flow of oxygen to torch and adjust gas-and-oxygen mixture to obtain specified flame. Turns knob to start spray of water to cool stone ahead of and behind flame. Presses button to start torch reciprocating over stone. Observes machine in operation to determine that texture of stone surface is pebbled uniformly. Observes gauges and lights on panel to detect faulty supply of gas, oxygen, water, or compressed air and turns knobs or presses buttons to make adjustments.

GOE: 05.12.10 STRENGTH: L GED: R2 M1 L1 SVP: 2 DLU: 77

679.685-022   TILE GRINDER (brick & tile)
Tends machine that grinds sides of ceramic wall or floor tile to specified size and squares tile preparatory to shipment: Turns crank to adjust spacing between opposed grinding wheels, according to specifications. Starts machine and places ceramic tile into feed device of machine or moves lever to grip and feed tile between grinding wheels. Periodically measures tile to determine conformance to specifications, using rule. Places tile onto bench for packaging.
GOE: 06.04.08 STRENGTH: L GED: R2 M1 L1 SVP: 2 DLU: 77

679.685-026   TURNING-AND-BEADING-MACHINE OPERATOR (button & notion)
Tends series of milling machines to machine crochet needles from bone blanks: Inserts end of blank into chuck of machine. Starts machine, and pushes lever to feed blank along milling cutter to turn it to cylindrical shape. Repeats operation on other machines to form ornamental handle and to cut hook in end of needle. Regulates speed of feed of blank to cutters, according to resistance felt in lever, to avoid burning or breaking blank.
GOE: 06.04.09 STRENGTH: L GED: R2 M1 L2 SVP: 3 DLU: 77

679.686-010   ASBESTOS-SHINGLE   SHEARING-MACHINE   OPERATOR (nonmet. min.) alternate titles: cutter operator, asbestos shingle
Feeds asbestos boards into hopper of power shearing and punching machine that cuts boards into shingles and punches holes in each shingle for installation.
GOE: 06.04.08 STRENGTH: M GED: R1 M1 L1 SVP: 2 DLU: 77

679.687-010   ASBESTOS-SHINGLE INSPECTOR (nonmet. min.)
Inspects asbestos shingles for defects, such as cracks, broken edges, and irregularly punched holes: Scrutinizes shingles to detect defects as they move on conveyor. Removes shingles that fail to meet plant specifications and sorts shingles according to standards for various grades.
GOE: 06.03.02 STRENGTH: S GED: R2 M1 L2 SVP: 3 DLU: 77

68   TEXTILE OCCUPATIONS

This division includes occupations concerned with shaping, joining, spinning, weaving, and otherwise fabricating textiles, textile products, fur, and hair.

680   CARDING, COMBING, DRAWING, AND RELATED OCCUPATIONS

This group includes occupations concerned with opening, separating, paralleling, and intermingling fibers; condensing, doubling, and lengthening them into a continuous, untwisted strand, and crimping fibers and strands.

680.130-010   SUPERVISOR, CARDING (textile)
Supervises and coordinates activities of workers engaged in processing natural and synthetic raw stock into lap sliver and roving for use in yarn spinning, utilizing knowledge of fiber-processing machines: Verifies setup and adjustment of such machines as carding machines and drawing frames, using gauges and handtools. Examines raw stock in storage to determine that specified fibers are available for processing. Inspects products through processing stages to maintain specified standards. Trains workers in operation of machines and equipment and evaluates worker performances. Performs other duties as described under SUPERVISOR (any industry) Master Title. May be designated according to process supervised as Supervisor, Drawing (textile); Supervisor, Opening And Picking (textile); Supervisor, Roving (textile).
GOE: 06.02.01 STRENGTH: M GED: R4 M3 L4 SVP: 7 DLU: 78

680.130-014   SUPERVISOR, MIXING (textile)
Supervises and coordinates activities of workers engaged in blending synthetic fibers and other raw stock for use in yarn preparation: Selects or prepares batch sheets for specified fiber blend, using customer specifications, and directs workers to assemble batches for processing. Inspects machines for malfunctions and directs setup and repair of faulty machines and equipment. Trains workers in operations, such as sorting, weighing, mixing, garnetting, and baling raw stock. Performs other duties as described under SUPERVISOR (any industry) Master Title.
GOE: 06.02.01 STRENGTH: M GED: R4 M3 L3 SVP: 7 DLU: 77

680.135-010   SUPERVISOR, MIXING (tex. prod., nec)
Supervises and coordinates activities of workers engaged in mixing hair for use in producing felt products: Trains workers in operation of machines and in procedures relating to hair types and amounts to be processed. Requisitions materials. Performs other duties as described under SUPERVISOR (any industry) Master Title.
GOE: 06.04.01 STRENGTH: H GED: R4 M2 L3 SVP: 5 DLU: 77

680.367-010   ROVING SIZER (textile)
Weighs roving samples to detect variation in weight produced by tape condensers of woolen carding machines: Positions jackspool of roving in winding position and threads roving ends from spool through guides and takeup roller. Sets yardage counter at specified yardage and turns crank to wind sample of roving. Weighs sample on grain scales and records weight on chart. Plots weight of each end of roving produced by single carding machine on graph paper and compares graph with standard graph to isolate variations in roving. Reports variations from standards to MACHINE FIXER (textile).

GOE: 06.03.01 STRENGTH: L GED: R3 M2 L3 SVP: 4 DLU: 77

680.380-010 CARD GRINDER (nonmet. min.; textile) alternate titles: card fixer; card setter

Grinds wire teeth on drums and flats of carding machines to uniform height, and sets up machines according to specifications and fiber processing standards: Removes fibers adhering to wire teeth of cylinder and doffing drums, using card stripper. Removes belts and disengages gears not needed for grinding operation. Lifts grinding rollers onto brackets above flats and carding and doffing cylinders of machine. Places drive belt between carding machine drive mechanism and grinder rolls, and starts machine. Turns setscrews and listens to sound of grinder to regulate pressure of grinding roller on teeth of drum. Examines and feels teeth to verify that grinding meets specifications. Removes grinding rolls, and brushes emery dust from teeth of cylinder. Adjusts clearances between card rolls and flats to set up machine, using leaf, flat, and pin gauges, and listens for contact of surfaces. Replaces defective parts, using handtools. Cleans and oils machines. May replace worn cloth on cylinders of carding machine [CARD CLOTHIER (textile) 628.381-010]. May remove carding drum and grind drum on separate machine. May direct CARD TENDER (nonmet. min.; textile) 680.685-018 and other cardroom employees in setting up grinding equipment. May be designated according to machine repaired as Napper Grinder (textile).

GOE: 06.01.02 STRENGTH: M GED: R4 M3 L3 SVP: 7 DLU: 78

680.585-010 BATTING-MACHINE OPERATOR (tex. prod., nec; textile)

Tends machine that converts loose textile fibers into batting: Throws or dumps fibers into hopper of machine or moves lever to control automatic feeding by conveyor belt. Lifts roll of finished batting from machine and starts new roll winding onto takeup beam. Weighs and records weight of sample from each roll. Moves weight on lever to control amount of fiber fed into machine and weight of batting produced. May tend picking machine to open and fluff fiber. May cut batting into specified lengths with scissors and roll lengths into bundles. May wrap and pack bundles of batting.

GOE: 06.04.06 STRENGTH: M GED: R2 M1 L1 SVP: 2 DLU: 77

680.585-014 STAPLE-PROCESSING-MACHINE OPERATOR (textile) alternate titles: attenuator

Tends machines that stretch tow, break tow into staple lengths, and crimp resulting sliver: Ties rope of filaments to filaments in machine or threads rope through guides and tension rollers, heating plates, breaking rollers, and crimping device and into receiving can. Observes operation of machines to detect fibers wrapping around rollers and cuts away tangled fibers. Adjusts yardage clock to stop machine when specified amount of fiber is in receiving can. Records production data, and writes identification tickets for cans of sliver. May tend machine that sets crimp in fiber [CRIMP SETTER (textile)].

GOE: 06.04.06 STRENGTH: M GED: R2 M1 L2 SVP: 3 DLU: 77

680.665-014 DRAW-MACHINE OPERATOR (plastic-synth.)

Tends machines that draw out (stretch) continuous synthetic fiber filaments to impart strength and flexibility and combine filaments into tow: Positions can of filaments at machine, places bobbins of filament on spindle and threads filament through rolls, pins, traveler, and onto takeup bobbin or into can, or threads filament directly from spinning machine. Opens valve to admit steam to heat rolls. Inspects tow for conformance to standards. Doffs machine when bobbins or cans are full or when knots, breaks, or tangles occur in filament. May tend tandem units that crimp and dry tow preparatory to cutting tow into staple lengths.

GOE: 06.04.06 STRENGTH: M GED: R2 M1 L1 SVP: 3 DLU: 77

680.665-018 MIDDLE-CARD TENDER (nonmet. min.; textile) alternate titles: alley tender; intermediate-card tender

Tends intermediate carding machines that open, clean, mix, and straighten wool, asbestos, or synthetic fibers and deliver carded stock to finisher card: Patrols area between breaker and finisher cards and observes intermediate carding to detect clogged rollers and breaks in carded web (thin, web-like film of fibers). Stops machine, removes fiber from clogged rollers, and *pieces up* broken web by rolling and twisting fibers between fingers. Signals FINISHER-CARD TENDER (nonmet. min.; textile) to restart carding machines. Oils machine. Cleans machine, using airhose and rake.

GOE: 06.04.06 STRENGTH: L GED: R2 M1 L1 SVP: 2 DLU: 77

680.684-010 CARD GRINDER HELPER (textile)

Assists CARD GRINDER (nonmet. min.; textile) 680.380-010 in setting up and repairing cotton and synthetic fiber carding machines and picking machines: Cleans machines of waste and excess fibers from previous run, using airhose. Inspects machines and machine parts to detect wearing of or damage to parts. Replaces defective parts, such as rollers, belts and gears, using handtools. Adjusts clearance between carding and doffing cylinder and between flats, using leaf, flat, and pen gauges, and listening for contact of surfaces. Adjusts machine parts, such as prefeeders, evenfeeders, and levers, to regulate speed of machine, flow of fiber, and length of lap. Grinds wire teeth of flats and carding and doffing cylinders, using grinding device. Inspects teeth to verify grinding meets specifications. Lubricates wearing surfaces of machine, using oilcan.

GOE: 06.01.02 STRENGTH: V GED: R2 M2 L2 SVP: 3 DLU: 86

680.685-010 BLENDING-MACHINE OPERATOR (textile)

Tends machines that mix textile fibers into uniform blends: Sets sliding counterbalances into position on scale beams of automatic feeders to regulate weight of fiber deposited on conveyor, following lot sheet instructions. Opens chute to feed fibers into machine or deposits armfuls of various types of fiber into hoppers of appropriate feeders, according to blending instructions. Starts machines and observes flow of fiber through mixing picker machines to detect clogged rollers. Stops machines and unclogs rollers by hand. Cleans machines after each lot, using airhose. May mix oil lubricant. May turn valve to regulate flow of oil lubricant onto fiber, according to type of fibers being blended. May tend machines that mix colored wool fibers and be designated Gray Mixing Operator (tex. prod., nec); White Mixing Operator (tex. prod., nec).

GOE: 06.04.06 STRENGTH: M GED: R2 M1 L2 SVP: 3 DLU: 79

680.685-014 CARD STRIPPER (textile)

Tends equipment that removes (strips) accumulated cotton fibers adhering to wire teeth of carding and doffing drums, using any of following methods: (1) Positions stripping roller in brackets of carding machine so that wire teeth of roller project between wire teeth of carding cylinder. Starts machine, allowing stripping roller to revolve rapidly and remove fiber from slowly revolving card cylinder. May use stripping roll hood and suction pipe leading to handtruck to dispose of dust and lint (dustless stripping). (2) Moves lever to position built-in stripping roll so that wire teeth contact teeth of cylinder. Opens suction line to draw away lint collected by roll. (3) Places stripper nozzles of vacuum stripper attachment at side of carding cylinder and doffing drum. Starts machine to move stripper across cylinder, drawing dust into nozzle. May tend carding machines [CARD TENDER (nonmet. min.; textile)]. May assist in grinding card rolls.

GOE: 06.04.06 STRENGTH: M GED: R2 M1 L1 SVP: 3 DLU: 77

680.685-018 CARD TENDER (nonmet. min.; textile) alternate titles: alley tender; card hand; card operator

Tends carding machines that open, clean, and align cotton, asbestos, or other fibers, and convert *laps II* of fibers into sliver: Feeds loose fibers onto feeder apron or into hopper of machine, or mounts lap of fiber on bracket at feed end of machine and threads end of lap through feeder rollers or attaches end to lap in machine by pinching ends together with fingers. Patrols work area and observes machine operation to detect exhausting fiber or lap supply, machine malfunctions, sliver or lap breaks, and full cans of sliver at discharge end of machine. *Pieces up* broken sliver by rolling and twisting ends with fingers. Cleans machine, using brush, waste, and airhose. Replaces full cans of sliver with empty cans. May oil machine. May truck laps from picker room and hang laps on stands of machines. May tend machines that produce sliver from raw stock. May strip cards [CARD STRIPPER (textile) 680.685-014].

GOE: 06.04.09 STRENGTH: M GED: R2 M1 L2 SVP: 3 DLU: 79

680.685-022 CHOPPED-STRAND OPERATOR (textile)

Tends machine that cuts strands of fiberglass sliver into staple lengths: Pulls ends of sliver from creel and feeds sliver into feed rollers of cutter. Observes staple lengths falling from cutters into container on scales to detect defects, such as dirty strands and flared ends. Removes shipping containers from scales as specified weight is attained and seals container with gummed tape. Pastes label on shipping container and places container on pallet. Records weight on production records.

GOE: 06.04.08 STRENGTH: L GED: R2 M1 L2 SVP: 2 DLU: 77

680.685-026 CRIMP SETTER (textile) alternate titles: steam setter

Tends steam-heated machine that sets crimp in synthetic fibers used in high-bulk yarns: Lifts cans of sliver onto loading track of machine, by hand or using hoist. Starts machine that automatically loads, steams, vacuum dries, and unloads sliver. Removes cans of sliver from track on delivery side of machine. Feels sliver to determine if moisture has been removed. Inserts thermometer in can of sliver periodically to verify that fiber is being heated to specified temperature.

GOE: 06.04.06 STRENGTH: M GED: R2 M1 L1 SVP: 3 DLU: 77

680.685-030 CRIMPING-MACHINE OPERATOR (textile)

Tends machine that crimps synthetic fibers to increase bulk and resiliency and to facilitate blending with natural fibers: Turns valves to regulate heat and to control pressure of feed rollers and V-shaped stuffing box according to specifications. Starts machine and feeds sliver between rollers that force fibers through stuffing box where they are compressed and discharges crimped fibers into receiving cans. Observes machine and emerging sliver to detect substandard crimping and adjusts steam heat and pressure of feed rollers and stuffing box accordingly. Doffs and replaces full receiving cans.

GOE: 06.04.09 STRENGTH: M GED: R2 M1 L1 SVP: 3 DLU: 77

680.685-034 DRAW-FRAME TENDER (tex. prod., nec) alternate titles: combing-machine tender

Tends one or more machines that comb, draw, and align sisal and hemp fibers into sliver preparatory to spinning into yarn used in production of rope or twine: Pulls specified number of fiber coils under feed tray of machine, using hook. Places ends of fibers on feed tray and into combing teeth. Starts machine and observes feeding, combing, and coiling operations to ensure that fibers are correctly straightened and blended to form sliver. Pulls coil of sliver from beneath coiling head and slides it to next machine. May weigh and segregate coils according to type and grade.

GOE: 06.04.06 STRENGTH: M GED: R2 M1 L2 SVP: 3 DLU: 77

680.685-038 DRAWING-FRAME TENDER (textile) alternate titles: drawer; drawing tender

Tends drawing frames that combine several strands of sliver into one strand, distributing weight uniformly, and arranging fibers in parallel order: Pulls cans

of sliver to creeling position. Threads end of sliver through guides, stop-motion device, drawing rollers, condenser, and *coiler head*, and into revolving can, or attaches sliver to preceding end by overlapping and twisting ends with fingers. Presses button to start machines, and patrols machines to observe flow of sliver and signal lights indicating machine stoppage caused by sliver break. Repairs breaks in sliver by matting and rolling broken ends together between thumb and fingers. Replaces filled cans of sliver from coiler head with empty cans. Notifies repair personnel of machine malfunctions. Cleans rollers with airhose. May oil machine.
GOE: 06.04.06 STRENGTH: M GED: R2 M1 L2 SVP: 3 DLU: 78

680.685-042 FINISHER-CARD TENDER (nonmet. min.; textile)
Tends finisher carding machine with tape condenser that cleans and straightens wool, asbestos, or synthetic fibers, and condenses fiber into roving: Observes carding and condensing to detect clogged rollers and breaks in roving ends. Laps broken roving ends over spool to resume winding. Removes broken roving ends that have wound on other than specified spools, using fingers. Doffs full spools of roving, places empty spool in winding position, and wraps roving ends around empty spool to continue winding process. Removes fibers from clogged rollers by hand. Cleans machine, using airhose and rake, and oils moving parts. May feed machine by hand when carding asbestos fiber.
GOE: 06.04.06 STRENGTH: M GED: R2 M1 L1 SVP: 2 DLU: 77

680.685-046 FUR-BLOWER OPERATOR (hat & cap) alternate titles: blower; fur blower; fur-blowing-machine attendant; fur-blowing-machine operator; fur mixer
Tends machine that cleans and disentangles fur fibers used in making felt hats: Dumps fur into hopper of machine. Starts machine that forces fibers through sections (chambers) containing air blowers and toothed rollers that clean and disentangle fibers. Feels and examines fibers to determine conformance to quality standards and to detect presence of debris, such as sawdust and particles of pelt, requiring additional passes through machine. Cleans machine and removes debris, using brush, shovel, and compressed-air hose. May weigh and bag specified amounts of fibers. May be designated according to number of sections in fur-blowing unit as Eight-Section Blower (hat & cap); Six-Section Blower (hat & cap).
GOE: 06.04.06 STRENGTH: L GED: R2 M1 L1 SVP: 4 DLU: 77

680.685-050 GARNETT-MACHINE OPERATOR (textile) alternate titles: carder; devil tender; garnetter; garnetting-machine operator; linting-machine operator; waste-machine operator
Tends machine that reduces rags and yarn waste to fiber for reuse: Feeds armfuls of waste into hopper of automatic feeder or opens and closes gates of blower pipes or conveyors when waste feeds from other machines. Starts machine and wraps end of garnetted web around takeup roller to form *lap II* or threads end of condensed web through *coiler head* to form sliver. Observes garnetting to detect clogged rollers or breaks in web. *Pieces up* breaks in web and disentangles clogged rollers by hand. Doffs laps or cans of garnetted material from delivery end of machine. Weighs laps or cans of material and records weight on production records. May tend *garnett machine* equipped with pneumatic conveyors that blow stock into storage bins or subsequent machine hoppers. May tend picking machine [PICKING-MACHINE OPERATOR (any industry)] in tandem with garnett machine.
GOE: 06.04.06 STRENGTH: M GED: R2 M1 L1 SVP: 3 DLU: 77

680.685-054 GARNETTER (furniture; tex. prod., nec) alternate titles: felter; felting-machine operator
Tends machine that garnetts waste yarn and fibers and compresses garnetted fibers into pads of felt, batting, or padding: Moves weight on lever of automatic feeder to control amount of waste material fed into machine and weight of product produced. Spaces knives on either side of delivery end of machine according to width specified for rolls. Turns handwheel to increase or decrease space between compressor roller according to thickness specified for product. Threads end of garnetted material through folding device that spreads layers of material on delivery table preparatory to winding web into rolls.
GOE: 06.04.06 STRENGTH: M GED: R3 M1 L2 SVP: 3 DLU: 77

680.685-058 GILL-BOX TENDER (textile) alternate titles: card-gill tender; gill tender; pin-drafting-machine operator; pin-machine tender
Tends machine that draws out and combines wool, synthetic, or blended sliver and aligns fibers preparatory to further processing: Places balls of sliver on holders or positions cans of sliver at feeding end of machine. Threads sliver through guides, gathering eye, rollers, and under *fallers*. Starts machine and guides sliver into receiving can, or wraps end around spindle that winds it into ball. Observes operation of machine to detect breaks and *pieces up* ends together by hand. Replaces exhausted supply cans or balls of sliver. Doffs can or balls of processed sliver. May weigh cans or balls of sliver and record weight. May weigh sample of sliver to determine quality of sliver produced by machine.
GOE: 06.04.06 STRENGTH: H GED: R2 M1 L1 SVP: 3 DLU: 77

680.685-062 MIXER (hat & cap) alternate titles: blender; devil tender; fur-mixer operator; mixing-machine operator
Tends machine that separates matted fur fibers and blends fibers for use in felt hats: Selects fibers according to quality, type, and weight specifications. Dumps fibers into hopper of machine. Starts machine that forces fibers against teeth of cylinders (picker rollers), that separate matted fibers, and into air-blend-

ing chamber that mixes fibers. Removes blended fibers from machine and places fibers in bags or boxes. Cleans machine, using brush, broom, and airhose. Lubricates machine, using oilcan and grease gun. May sort and weigh waste. May be designated according to type of machine tended as Conical Mixer (hat & cap); Cylindrical Mixer (hat & cap).
GOE: 06.04.06 STRENGTH: L GED: R2 M1 L1 SVP: 3 DLU: 77

680.685-066 MIXING-MACHINE OPERATOR (fabrication, nec) alternate titles: blending-machine operator
Tends machine that cleans, straightens, and blends brush-filling materials, such as horsehair, nylon, vegetable fibers, and plastic filaments: Loosens wingnuts and adjusts conveyor guides to accommodate length of materials to be processed. Removes materials from container according to predetermined sequence and places them on machine conveyor with flag (split) ends together. Moves lever to set specified speed of machine cycle. Starts machine and observes material until blending conforms with prescribed standards. Removes and packs or wraps blended material. Cleans machine, using airhose. May apply antistatic lubricant to material, using brush.
GOE: 06.04.09 STRENGTH: M GED: R2 M1 L1 SVP: 2 DLU: 77

680.685-070 OPENER TENDER (textile) alternate titles: bale-breaker operator; breaker operator; opening-machine tender; stock blender
Tends series of machines in tandem that open, clean, fluff, and mix compressed cotton or synthetic fibers preparatory to picking process: Starts machines and feeds layers of fibers from several bales into machine hoppers to produce uniform blend. Observes processing of fibers and signal lights to detect clogged beaters. Stops machines and pulls fibers from clogged beaters. Cleans and oils machines. May weigh fibers preparatory to feeding machines.
GOE: 06.04.06 STRENGTH: M GED: R2 M1 L1 SVP: 2 DLU: 77

680.685-074 PICKER TENDER (textile) alternate titles: picker
Tends battery of picker machines that break up and clean cotton or synthetic fibers, form them into *lap II*, and wind lap into rolls: Starts machine and pulls cord to open gate of hopper through which cotton tufts feed onto conveyor of machine or hand feeds cotton tufts onto conveyor. Moves levers to regulate weight, length of lap, and speed of machine. Observes and regulates speed of conveyor as conveyor feeds machine to prevent jamming. Inserts metal bar in lap arbor of automatic winding mechanism that winds and ejects lap rolls of specified size. Turns end of lap around lap forming bar by hand, when necessary. Lifts roll of lap from machine, weighs roll of lap, records weight, places roll on portable rack, and removes pin around which lap was wound. Marks lap to identify fiber type, using specified chalk. Cleans and oils machine. May tend machines that open, clean, fluff, and mix cotton or synthetic fibers prior to picking process [OPENER TENDER (textile) 680.685-070].
GOE: 06.04.06 STRENGTH: H GED: R2 M1 L2 SVP: 3 DLU: 78

680.685-078 PICKER-MACHINE OPERATOR (furniture) alternate titles: gin feeder; wooling-machine operator
Tends machine that fluffs and cleans new and used materials, such as cotton, kapok, and sisal used in pads, cushions, and mattresses, performing any combination of following tasks: Moves guide on machine to direct cleaned material into storage bins or *garnett machine*. Opens bales of material, such as cotton and sisal, using wirecutter and knife. Pulls bales apart, starts machine, and feeds specified grades of material into machine hopper. May weigh specified amounts of material according to grades, using platform scales. May tie mattress cover to filling spout and move guide to direct material into it. May be designated according to type of material picked as Cotton Picker (furniture); Excelsior Picker (furniture); Fiber Picker (furniture); Sisal Picker (furniture); Tow Picker (furniture). May tend machine that produces rolls of felt from fluffed and cleaned fiber [GARNETT-MACHINE OPERATOR (textile)].
GOE: 06.04.06 STRENGTH: M GED: R2 M1 L2 SVP: 3 DLU: 77

680.685-082 PICKING-MACHINE OPERATOR (any industry) alternate titles: blender operator; shredder; willower
Tends picking machine that opens or shreds and fluffs raw or used materials, such as wool, kapok, foam rubber, or hair to facilitate further processing: Cuts open bales of raw materials. Starts machine and deposits handfuls of raw material on feeding apron that conveys material into picking or shredding rollers. Observes machine to detect clogged rollers. Stops machine, and strips fiber from rollers, using knife, scissors, or hands. May spray raw material with oil emulsion. May be designated according to material processed as Hair-Picking-Machine Operator (furniture; tex. prod., nec); Tow-Picker Operator (furniture); Wool-Picker Operator (textile).
GOE: 06.04.06 STRENGTH: M GED: R2 M1 L1 SVP: 2 DLU: 77

680.685-086 RIBBON-LAP-MACHINE TENDER (textile) alternate titles: carding doubler; lap-machine tender; lap winder
Tends machines that draw out and combine four to six *laps II* into one of uniform weight and texture preparatory to combing: Places rolls of lap on feed rolls of machine. Threads ends through stop-motion device and rollers, and around takeup spool, or presses end to end of preceding lap. Patrols machines to detect exhausted ends and to observe lights indicating machine stoppage caused by lap break. *Pieces up* broken ends and restarts machine. Turns handle to release roll for doffing. Removes lap from machine and replaces with empty takeup spool.
GOE: 06.04.06 STRENGTH: M GED: R2 M1 L1 SVP: 2 DLU: 77

680.685-090 SILK SPREADER (textile) alternate titles: spreading-machine operator

Tends machine that fluffs and combines silk fibers: Weighs cleaned, raw silk to separate it into small bunches of specified weight. Starts machine and feeds bunches of silk between machine rollers that fluff and combine bunches.
GOE: 06.04.06 STRENGTH: L GED: R2 M1 L1 SVP: 3 DLU: 77

680.685-094 SLIVER-LAP-MACHINE TENDER (textile) alternate titles: carding doubler; lap regulator; lap-winding-machine operator

Tends machines which combine strands of sliver (usually 12 or more) into *lap II* and winds sliver into rolls: Pulls cans of sliver to creeling position. Threads ends of sliver through guides, stop-motion device, and rolls, and onto takeup pin, or attaches end to preceding end by overlapping and twisting sliver with fingers. Patrols machine area to detect exhausted ends and observe lights indicating machine stoppage caused by sliver break. *Pieces up* broken ends. Removes lap and replaces empty pins. May depress pedal to raise roll of lap for doffing or loosen holders by hand. May tend combers [COMBER TENDER (textile) 680.685-118], ribbon lappers [RIBBON-LAP-MACHINE TENDER (textile) 680.685-086], or drawing frames [DRAWING-FRAME TENDER (textile) 680.685-038].
GOE: 06.04.06 STRENGTH: M GED: R2 M1 L1 SVP: 2 DLU: 78

680.685-098 SLUBBER TENDER (textile) alternate titles: roving tender; slubber; slubber hand

Tends *slubber* machines that draw out and loosely twist sliver into roving to strengthen sliver for subsequent drawing and twisting operations: Fastens ends of sliver from full cans to preceding ends by overlapping and twisting ends with fingers, or threads sliver over guide, through rolls and flyers, and onto bobbins. Patrols machines to detect exhausted ends and to observe signal lights indicating machine stoppage caused by sliver breaks. *Pieces up* broken ends by threading sliver through rollers and flyer and twisting sliver to end on bobbin. Doffs bobbin of roving, placing flyers on top of frame and roving in box truck. Sets empty bobbins on spindles, winds end of roving around bobbins, and replaces flyers. Brushes lint and dust from rollers and oils machine. May mark spools of roving with colored chalk to denote weight and texture.
GOE: 06.04.06 STRENGTH: M GED: R2 M1 L2 SVP: 3 DLU: 79

680.685-102 STAPLE CUTTER (textile) alternate titles: chopper feeder; sliver chopper; stock cutter; waste chopper

Tends machine that cuts tow, sliver, or waste fibers into staple lengths preparatory to blending and subsequent processing into yarn: Places cans of sliver or bales of raw stock at feed-end of machine. Cuts bale bands, using hand snips. Places loose fiber on belt which conveys fiber to cutting blades or pulls ends of sliver or tow from cans and guides them into feed rolls at cutter. Examines fiber falling from cutter to detect fusing of fibers due to dull cutting blades. Measures cut fiber with ruler to verify length. Notifies MACHINE FIXER (textile) when cut fiber does not meet specifications. May stock from several bales to blend fibers. May sort loose stock by size and color.
GOE: 06.04.06 STRENGTH: M GED: R2 M1 L1 SVP: 2 DLU: 77

680.685-106 STRAND-AND-BINDER CONTROLLER (nonmet. min.)

Tends feed end of mat-making range that cuts fiberglass sliver into staple lengths and binds staple lengths together to form continuous sheets of fiberglass insulation material: Scoops powdered binder from barrel into hopper of binder sprayer. Gathers specified number of sliver ends from creel and threads ends through guides and rollers into staple cutting units. Observes flow of sliver from creel through staple cutters to verify number of ends being fed into cutters and to detect jam-up of sliver in cutters. Stops cutter and disentangles jam-up, using knife. Drops marker onto conveyor, signifying beginning and end of defective mat. Increases or decreases number of sliver ends fed into cutters as directed by MAT-MACHINE OPERATOR (concrete prod.).
GOE: 06.04.06 STRENGTH: L GED: R2 M1 L1 SVP: 2 DLU: 77

680.685-110 STRETCH-BOX TENDER (textile)

Tends machines that stretch synthetic fibers in sliver or tow form to control elasticity and prevent uneven stretching during subsequent processing: Turns knob to set air pressure control on stretch rolls according to amount of stretch specified. Guides sliver into feed rolls so that it passes over heating element, between stretch rolls, and drops into receiving can. *Pieces up* broken sliver and replaces empty cans. Doffs and weighs cans of stretched sliver. May tend stretch box with crimping and steam-setting attachments.
GOE: 06.04.06 STRENGTH: M GED: R2 M1 L1 SVP: 2 DLU: 77

680.685-114 WASTE-MACHINE TENDER (tex. prod., nec; textile) alternate titles: waste-cotton cleaner; waste duster; willow-machine operator; willow-machine tender

Tends machine that opens, cleans, fluffs, and reduces soft waste yarn, sliver, and roving to fiber for reuse: Spreads armfuls of waste material on feeder apron of machine. Starts machine, and wraps web of processed material around takeup roller or positions truck beneath delivery apron of machine. Observes processing of waste to detect clogged rollers and disentangles rollers by hand. Doffs, laps, or trucks material from delivery end of machine.
GOE: 06.04.06 STRENGTH: M GED: R1 M1 L1 SVP: 2 DLU: 77

680.685-118 COMBER TENDER (textile)

Tends machines that comb *lap II* or sliver to remove short fibers, neps, and dirt and to straighten and align fibers: Lifts lap onto holders or positions cans of sliver at rear of machine. Threads lap or sliver between feeder rollers, combing and drawing rollers, through gathering eyes, *coiler head,* and into cans. *Pieces up* fresh lap or sliver to end of preceding one. Pieces up breaks, and replaces cans of sliver or rolls of lap. Removes full cans of processed sliver from coiler head and pushes cans to designated area to await further processing. Observes signal lights to detect sliver breaks, machine malfunctions, and exhausting cans of unprocessed sliver. Pulls *lap-ups* of fibers from rollers, using hook. May empty bin of waste materials combed out of fibers.
GOE: 06.04.06 STRENGTH: M GED: R2 M1 L1 SVP: 3 DLU: 78

680.686-010 CAN DOFFER (textile) alternate titles: can pusher

Doffs and transfers sliver cans among carding, drawing, and slubbing machines: Pushes or drags full sliver cans from carding to drawing, and from drawing to slubbing machines to maintain workflow. Removes empty cans from drawing and slubbing machines and places them in position for reuse at carding machines. May sweep work area or clean machines. May be designated according to machine area worked as Card Doffer (textile).
GOE: 06.04.40 STRENGTH: M GED: R1 M1 L1 SVP: 2 DLU: 77

680.686-014 FIRST-BREAKER FEEDER (tex. prod., nec)

Feeds fiber, such as hemp or sisal, into machine that breaks up matted bundles, and oils and straightens fibers to form sliver: Places bundles of fibers on machine feed conveyor. Observes sliver emerging from machine and varies rate of feeding to maintain production of uniform sliver of specified weight. Turns valve to start flow of oil that lubricates, softens, and preserves fibers. When feeding armfuls of short hemp fibers into machine, is designated Tow Feeder (tex. prod., nec).
GOE: 06.04.16 STRENGTH: M GED: R1 M1 L1 SVP: 2 DLU: 77

680.686-018 MACHINE FEEDER, RAW STOCK (tex. prod., nec; textile) alternate titles: feeder tender; guillotine operator; hopper feeder; shredder picker

Feeds raw fiber stock into machines that loosen, shred, separate, clean, form nubs, or straighten fibers: Reads work ticket to determine amount and type of stock to be processed. Records amount of materials processed, during work shift. Places fibers on conveyor belt or into machine hopper for processing by machine. Opens and closes gates of belt and pneumatic conveyors on machines fed directly from preceding machines. Loosens material before dumping material into hoppers by pulling fibers apart. Moves stock from storage or other departments to machine, using industrial truck or handtruck. May tend automatic machines and equipment that process fiber stock. May feed polyurethane foam into machines. May feed fiber stock into drum to apply oil to stock prior to further processing. May be designated according to type of machine fed as Carding-Machine Feeder (textile); Garnett Feeder (tex. prod., nec); Nub-Card Tender (textile); Picker Feeder (tex. prod., nec; textile).
GOE: 06.04.16 STRENGTH: H GED: R1 M1 L1 SVP: 2 DLU: 79

680.686-022 WASTE-MACHINE OFFBEARER (tex. prod., nec)

Removes strands of waste cotton that wind around separating cylinder of waste machine, to prevent jams and maintain flow of waste from machine, using wire hook. Carries waste to storage bins.
GOE: 06.04.16 STRENGTH: M GED: R2 M1 L1 SVP: 2 DLU: 77

680.687-010 APRON CLEANER (nonmet. min.) alternate titles: apron scratcher; card-apron cleaner

Cleans dirt or foreign matter from carded asbestos fibers, using wire studded scratchboard.
GOE: 06.04.34 STRENGTH: M GED: R1 M1 L1 SVP: 2 DLU: 77

680.687-014 ROLLER CLEANER (textile) alternate titles: draft-roller picker; frame cleaner; roll picker; top cleaner

Cleans lint and dust from drawing rollers of spinning or roving frames while machines are in operation, using pneumatic *roll picker* or handbrush. Removes roving wound on rollers , using fingers or hook. Feels rubber covered rollers for surface defects, replaces defective rollers, and routes defective rollers for resurfacing. May brush lint and dust from ring rail. May *piece up* roving or yarn breaks.
GOE: 06.04.39 STRENGTH: L GED: R2 M1 L2 SVP: 2 DLU: 79

680.687-018 ROVING-WEIGHT GAUGER (textile)

Weighs roving samples from wool carding machines and adjusts machines to produce roving of specified weight: Measures roving with ruler to obtain sample of specified length. Weighs sample and compares weight with standard chart to detect variations. Moves weight on weight-control lever of carding machine to regulate rate at which raw stock is fed into machine, altering weight of roving produced. May weigh rolls of fibrous web and be designated Web Sizer (textile).
GOE: 06.03.02 STRENGTH: L GED: R2 M1 L2 SVP: 4 DLU: 77

681   TWISTING, BEAMING, WARPING, AND RELATED OCCUPATIONS

This group includes occupations concerned with twisting together yarn, thread, twine, or cordage, to impart such characteristics as strength, texture, resistance, and color tone; collecting the material upon beams or other devices, or gathering it into balls, bulk, coils, or skeins.

681.130-010 SUPERVISOR, PREPARATION DEPARTMENT (textile)

Supervises and coordinates activities of workers engaged in preparation of warp and filling yarn for weaving: Analyzes production schedule to determine

size, type, texture, and quantity of yarn required to meet production demands. Prepares order sheets, warp pattern sheets, and formula sheets and issues them to MATERIAL HANDLER (any industry), to workers tending warping-machines, to CREELER (any industry), and to CHEMICAL MIXER (textile). Schedules changes in machine setups to meet requirements of production schedule, informing workers tending slashers, quilling-machines, and warping-machines of type, size, color, quantity, and number of yarn ends to be wound on quills or loom beams. Examines creel setup of warping machines to detect errors in number of yarn ends and arrangement of yarn in creel, and instructs CREELER (any industry) to alter setup to correspond with warp pattern sheet. Examines on bobbins, quills, or beams to ensure conformance to standards. Trains workers in operation of machines and evaluates work performance. May be designated according to specific process supervised as Supervisor, Drawing-In Department (textile); Supervisor, Slashing Department (textile); Supervisor, Warping Department (textile). Performs other duties as described under SUPERVISOR (any industry) Master Title.
GOE: 06.02.01 STRENGTH: L GED: R4 M3 L3 SVP: 7 DLU: 77

681.130-014 SUPERVISOR, WINDING AND TWISTING DEPARTMENT (textile)
Supervises and coordinates activities of workers engaged in winding yarn or thread from one package to another and in twisting yarn or thread: Reads production schedule to obtain information, such as size, type, texture, quality, and quantity of yarn required to meet production demands. Schedules winding of yarn onto suitable packages for subsequent processes, such as twisting, warping, dyeing, knitting, or weaving. Informs machine tenders of yarn type and size, winding speed, number of ends wound per package, and size of packages. Determines direction and amount of twist to be put into yarn, based on size of yarn, number of ends being plied, twists per inch and direction of twist in single yarn, and ultimate use of yarn. Computes gear size required to effect required twist, using mathematical formulas and tables. Schedules changes in production to meet requirements of production schedule, issuing new instructions to SECTION LEADER AND MACHINE SETTER (textile) 689.260-018. Examines yarn to detect variations from standards. Performs other duties as described under SUPERVISOR (any industry) Master Title. May supervise workers engaged in winding and twisting continuous filament yarns and be designated Supervisor, Throwing Department (textile). May be designated according to specific activity as Supervisor, Twisting Department (textile); Supervisor, Winding Department (textile). May supervise workers engaged in twisting yarn around rubber strands to produce elastic yarn and be designated Supervisor, Rubber Covering (textile).
GOE: 06.01.01 STRENGTH: L GED: R4 M3 L3 SVP: 7 DLU: 80

681.380-014 ROPE-MACHINE SETTER (tex. prod., nec)
Sets up and maintains battery of automatic machines that make hemp rope: Installs and aligns dies and gears to produce specified type and size rope, using handtools. Turns setscrews to adjust machines. May operate and adjust rope-laying machine to make rope.
GOE: 06.01.02 STRENGTH: M GED: R3 M2 L3 SVP: 6 DLU: 77

681.387-010 QUALITY CONTROL CHECKER, TEXTURING PROCESS (textile)
Inspects yarn texturing machines and packages of textured yarn to appraise quality of texturing process: Inspects doff yarn to ensure processing of yarn by texturing machines meets company performance standards. Reads temperature from gauges on thermal unit of texturing machines, records number of malfunctioning thermal units, and calibrates temperature gauges, using thermometer. Monitors spindle speed on texturing machines, using strobe tester, and notifies MACHINE FIXER (textile) 689.260-010 or SUPERVISOR, WINDING AND TWISTING (textile) 681.130-014 of malfunctioning spindle speed. Transports defective yarn package to YARN CLEANER (textile) 681.687-026 for salvaging of yarn. Fabricates needles used by YARN-TEXTURING-MACHINE OPERATOR (textile) I 681.685-158, using handtools.
GOE: 06.03.01 STRENGTH: L GED: R3 M2 L2 SVP: 7 DLU: 86

681.485-010 ROVING WINDER, FIBERGLASS (textile)
Tends machine that winds several strands of fiberglass sliver into a single strand of roving: Gathers strands of fiberglass sliver from creels to form roving, threads roving through guides, and attaches roving to takeup package or laps roving around spindle of winder to form coreless package. Starts machine and observes winding units to detect broken ends and variations in number of ends being wound into roving. Ties broken ends and notifies CREELER (any industry) to increase or decrease ends according to specifications. Observes signal light to determine when package is full. Doffs full packages from machine and packs roving into shipping containers. Weighs roving and records weight on shipping list and production records. Pastes label on container and seals container, using gummed tape. Places containers onto pallet or conveyor. May creel machine [CREELER (any industry)].
GOE: 06.04.06 STRENGTH: H GED: R2 M1 L2 SVP: 3 DLU: 77

681.585-010 BEAMER (textile) alternate titles: dry-slasher tender; rebeamer
Tends machine that winds yarn from several section beams I simultaneously onto single loom beam preparatory to weaving: Positions section beams on creel with aid of BEAMER HELPER (textile), using chain hoist. Lays individual yarn ends from each section beam between dents of reed and teeth of expansion comb, following leases in section warps. Tapes yarn ends to loom

beam or ties groups of yarn ends into knots and inserts knots into slots of loom beam. Turns knob to set yardage clock as specified. Starts machine and observes yarn to detect slubs, breaks, and tangles. Removes slubs with scissors, straightens tangles, and ties broken yarn ends with fingers. Inserts *lease string* in warp yarn and secures yarn ends with tape. Doffs full loom beam onto handtruck and replaces beam with empty beam with aid of BEAMER HELPER (textile), using chain hoist. Records style number, number of yarn breaks, machine stops, and yardage beamed.
GOE: 06.04.06 STRENGTH: M GED: R2 M1 L1 SVP: 3 DLU: 77

681.585-014 BOBBIN WINDER, MACHINE (tex. prod., nec; textile)
Tends machine that transfers yarn, thread, or twine from spools to large bobbins used on knitting and weaving machinery: Mounts spools on spindles over winding arbors of machine. Unwinds length of yarn, thread, or twine from spool and winds onto bobbin. Places bobbin on winding arbor and rotates bobbin to take up slack. Slides thread into eye of winding traveler and starts arbors rotating to wind thread onto bobbins. Observes bobbins as they are winding and cuts thread to remove loaded bobbins. Records number and types of bobbins wound.
GOE: 06.04.06 STRENGTH: M GED: R2 M1 L1 SVP: 2 DLU: 86

681.585-018 SINGE WINDER (textile)
Tends machine that singes lint and fuzz from yarn and winds yarn onto bobbins or *cones:* Places yarn packages on spindles and threads yarn through guides, tension device, slub catcher, heating unit, and grooves of traverse roller. Inserts end of yarn in takeup cone or bobbin and places cone on spindle. Pulls switches to start machine, exhaust fans, and burners. *Pieces up* yarn breaks. Doffs full cones or bobbins and places yarn in handtruck. Records production on work ticket. Cleans rails and burners of machine, using brush, airhose, and cloth.
GOE: 06.04.06 STRENGTH: L GED: R2 M1 L1 SVP: 3 DLU: 77

681.682-010 DRESSER TENDER (textile) alternate titles: thread dresser; warp dresser; warper tender; warping-mill operator
Operates machine to wind yarn from packages onto reel and from reel onto *loom beams* to prepare multiple colored warps for weaving: Moves portable reel into position in front of creel and draws yarn from packages on creel, according to specified pattern. Ties yarn ends into loop and places loop over hook on reel to secure ends for winding. Sets yardage meter to stop machine when specified yardage for section is wound on reel. Inserts *lease strings* in wound section to keep threads in position for weaving. Cuts yarn, using scissors, and places ends under section wound to prevent raveling. Moves reel to front of creel to facilitate winding of additional sections of yarn. Positions loom beam on brackets, using hoist, and secures ends from all sections onto beam. Pulls lever to reverse reel and pushes button to start yarn winding onto beam. Doffs full loom beam, using hoist. Turns valves to fill size box and to regulate temperature in drying cabinet when machine is equipped with slashing attachment. May creel machine.
GOE: 06.02.06 STRENGTH: H GED: R3 M1 L2 SVP: 4 DLU: 77

681.682-014 ROPE-MAKER, ROPEWALK (tex. prod., nec)
Operates track-mounted machine in ropewalk to lay rope-fiber strands into heavy line, such as marine hawser and towline: Lays strands on guide arms parallel to track. Anchors ends of strands to stationary fixture at end of ropewalk. Secures other end of strands in self-propelled machine at opposite end of ropewalk, that lays strands into rope and coils rope onto reel as it moves along track. Moves levers to start machine and to produce specified degree of hardness in rope. Binds ends of finished rope to prevent raveling and removes full reel, using hoist.
GOE: 06.02.09 STRENGTH: H GED: R3 M1 L2 SVP: 4 DLU: 77

681.682-018 RUG SETTER, AXMINSTER (carpet & rug) alternate titles: color-setting-machine operator
Operates machine to wind yarn from short spools onto longer spools in specified color arrangement to prepare yarn for weaving into rugs: Positions spools of yarn on creel as specified by pattern chart. Threads ends of yarn through reeds, tension devices, and guides, as specified by pattern chart. Adjusts tension on thread. Clamps ends to takeup (long) spool. Starts machine and observes winding for yarn tangles and breaks. *Pieces up* broken ends. Stops machine when specified amount of yarn has been wound, cuts yarn with cutting blade, places clamp onto spool to hold yarn in place, and replaces spool with empty one. May be designated according to machine for which yarn is prepared as Rug Setter, Six-Quarter Machine (carpet & rug); Rug Setter, Three-Quarter Machine (carpet & rug). May operate machine to wind yarn onto *loom beams* and be designated Rug Setter, Velvet (carpet & rug).
GOE: 06.02.06 STRENGTH: M GED: R3 M1 L2 SVP: 5 DLU: 77

681.685-010 BALL-WARPER TENDER (textile) alternate titles: baller tender; ball-thread-machine tender; ball winder
Tends warping machine that gathers and winds strands of yarn in rope form into ball form preparatory to mercerizing, dyeing, or bleaching: *Pieces up* ends from supply package to leader to thread machine. Sets yardage counter to record amount of yarn wound and starts machine. Inserts and ties *lease strings* at prescribed intervals. Observes operation to detect yarn breaks. Locates and ties broken ends. Doffs *ball warps*. May tend machine with singeing attachment to remove lint from yarn.
GOE: 06.04.06 STRENGTH: M GED: R2 M1 L1 SVP: 3 DLU: 77

681.685-014 BALLING-MACHINE OPERATOR (textile) alternate titles: ball winder

Tends machine that winds thread, twine, or yarn into balls preparatory to shipping or further processing: Places supply *cones* or spools on creel rack and threads yarn ends through guides and tension device. Pushes core over spindle of machine or wraps end of thread around shaping device of coreless winder. Pulls lever to start machine to wind specified amount of thread. Doffs balls of thread, using knife to cut thread. Inspects balls for defective winding or soiled thread. May insert labels under thread. May place ball on device to crush center and wrap end of thread around center as binder. May pack balls into boxes for shipment.
GOE: 06.04.06 STRENGTH: L GED: R2 M1 L1 SVP: 2 DLU: 77

681.685-018 BEAM-WARPER TENDER, AUTOMATIC (knitting; narrow fabrics; nonmet. min.; textile) alternates titles: beam warper; section beamer; section warper; tricot-warper tender; warper tender

Tends high-speed warpers that automatically wind yarn in parallel sheets onto beams preparatory to dyeing, weaving, or knitting: Examines yarn in creel to ensure that yarn corresponds to warp pattern sheet specifications, for number of yarn ends, arrangement of yarn in creel, yarn size, and color. Requests CREELER (any industry) 689.687-030 to alter creel setup to correspond with warp pattern sheet. Pulls yarn ends from packages mounted on creel, through *drop wires*, and tension, measuring, and spreading devices, and fastens ends to empty warp beam to thread machine. Sets yardage counter to record amount of yarn wound and starts machine. Observes operation to detect yarn breaks which cause machine to stop. Turns beam back to point of break, locates and ties broken ends, and cuts excess yarn, using scissors. Stops machine when specified yardage is wound on beam, cuts yarn, and places gummed tape over ends or loops ends together to secure ends. Doffs full beams and sets in empties [BEAM RACKER (textile) 681.686-010]. May wrap beam with paper. May replace empty yarn packages [CREELER (any industry) 689.687-030].
GOE: 06.04.06 STRENGTH: L GED: R2 M1 L1 SVP: 4 DLU: 80

681.685-022 BOBBIN WINDER, MACHINE (boot & shoe)

Tends machine that winds thread onto bobbins for use on sole-stitching machines: Places bobbins on spindle and inserts spindle into bobbin-winding machine. Wraps thread around first bobbin. Pushes lever to start machine. Holds spindle in place with hand, allows spring to move spindle, and positions next bobbin for winding. Cuts thread between bobbins, using knife. Removes spindle from machine and bobbins from spindle.
GOE: 06.04.05 STRENGTH: L GED: R1 M1 L1 SVP: 2 DLU: 77

681.685-026 BOBBIN WINDER, SEWING MACHINE (textile)

Tends machine with multiple winding units that wind thread onto shuttle bobbins for use on sewing machines: Places empty tube on spindle of winding unit, wraps ends of thread around tube, and cuts off excess thread. Pushes lever to start winding unit which automatically stops when thread breaks or tubes are full. Cuts thread with scissors and removes tube. Removes and discards partially wound bobbins. Measures bobbin periodically, using gauge and turns screws to adjust tension if bobbin is not of specified size.
GOE: 06.04.05 STRENGTH: L GED: R2 M1 L1 SVP: 3 DLU: 77

681.685-030 CARDING-MACHINE OPERATOR (tex. prod., nec)

Tends machine that winds binding, rickrack, and braid on paperboard cards: Clamps card and end of material in machine. Starts machine which makes predetermined number of revolutions to wind specified length of material on card. Cuts end of material with scissors and removes card from machine.
GOE: 06.04.38 STRENGTH: S GED: R1 M1 L1 SVP: 2 DLU: 77

681.685-034 COILER (tex. prod., nec) alternate titles: reeler

Tends machine that winds rope onto reel to form coil: Selects reel according to size of rope and mounts reel on spindle, using wrench. Trims loose strands from end of rope with knife and binds end with tape to prevent unraveling. Ties end of rope to reel and starts machine. Guides rope onto reel to ensure even winding. Stops machine and ties coil with cord to prevent unwinding. Lowers coil onto dolly, using chain hoist. Slides winding reel out of coil. May weigh coils. May splice rope ends.
GOE: 06.04.06 STRENGTH: V GED: R2 M1 L1 SVP: 2 DLU: 77

681.685-038 COVERING-MACHINE OPERATOR (textile) alternate titles: elastic-yarn twister; rubber coverer; rubber-covering-machine operator

Tends covering machine that twists one or more strands of yarn around rubber or synthetic yarn cores to produce elastic yarn: Threads narrow strip (ribbon) of rubber through feed rollers and splitting mechanism, or separates partially cut strands of rubber, or places *cones* of core yarn or rubber thread on holders. Draws ends of core yarn or rubber through guide and hollow spindles, using hook, and laps ends around takeup package. Positions yarn supply packages on spindles, threads ends through guides and tensions, and wraps ends around yarn or rubber core. Observes operation to detect defective twisting caused by taut or slack yarn and turns setscrew to adjust tension. Ties broken ends. Replaces exhausted supply of yarn or rubber and ties ends to ends in machine. Doffs machine and places empty takeup packages on holders. May compare measurements of relaxed and stretched covered rubber, and adjust speed of takeup mechanism that controls rubber tension to ensure stretch of specified length.
GOE: 06.04.09 STRENGTH: M GED: R2 M1 L1 SVP: 3 DLU: 77

681.685-042 COVERING-MACHINE-OPERATOR HELPER (textile) alternate titles: elastic-yarn-twister helper

Observes operation of covering machines to detect defective spindle action: Scrutinizes size and shape of twisting strand blur or places small celluloid sheet in path of whirling traveler to determine if spindles are performing as specified. Stops nonproductive spindles for repair or for replenishment of *cones* of rubber or fiber strands.
GOE: 06.03.02 STRENGTH: L GED: R2 M1 L2 SVP: 3 DLU: 77

681.685-046 DOUBLING-MACHINE OPERATOR (textile) alternate titles: doubler; multiple-tube-winding-machine operator

Tends machine that winds two or more strands of yarn parallel onto bobbin or tube preparatory to twisting: Places supply packages in creel and draws yarn ends through machine guides and tensions onto takeup tube. Starts machine and observes operation to detect yarn breaks, exhausting yarn supply and full packages on takeup tubes. *Pieces up* yarn breaks, using knotter. Replaces supply packages in creel. Doffs full packages.
GOE: 06.04.06 STRENGTH: L GED: R2 M1 L1 SVP: 2 DLU: 77

681.685-050 FLOOR WINDER (textile)

Tends several single-spindle winding frames that wind strands of bonded glass fiber produced on fiber machines onto tubes for further processing: Slips empty tubes on spindles of winding machines, and fastens ends of fiber strand, handed down from floor above by FIBER-MACHINE TENDER (glass mfg.), to each tube. Starts machines. Stops spindles when winding tubes are full, breaks off strand of fiber, and slides full winding tube from spindle. Observes strands being wound and ties together broken fiber ends.
GOE: 06.04.06 STRENGTH: L GED: R3 M1 L2 SVP: 4 DLU: 77

681.685-054 LEASING-MACHINE TENDER (textile)

Tends machine that inserts *lease strings* to keep warp strands separated in specified arrangement to facilitate drawing-in: Positions warp beam in holders, using hoist. Pulls warp ends over lease rod and turns rod to make warp threads taut. Places cone of string on holder and draws string through guides and needle to thread machine. Starts machine that raises and lowers warp threads and inserts string to keep threads in place and prevent tangling. Observes counter on machine to ensure that specified number of warp ends are wound on beam. Removes warp ends from rod, turns warp beam to rewind ends, and secures ends with tape. Removes warp beam from holder, using hoist.
GOE: 06.04.06 STRENGTH: M GED: R2 M1 L1 SVP: 2 DLU: 77

681.685-058 LONG-CHAIN BEAMER (textile) alternate titles: beamer hand; beaming-machine operator; section beamer

Tends machine that winds yarn in chain form from skeins or *ball warps* onto beams in parallel sheets: Laces end of skein around rollers and pulls end through dividers in separate skeins or inserts rod through center of ball warp and lifts warp onto stand for unwinding. Guides end of yarn chain around tension drums and lays individual strands of yarn between teeth of expansion comb. Turns crank to adjust comb to width of beam. Knots section of warp ends and inserts knots in slots of beam to hold yarn for winding. Starts, stops, and controls speed of machine with pedal. Observes yarn to detect slubs and broken or tangled ends; cuts out slubs, using scissors, and ties broken yarn ends with fingers. Inserts *lease strings* at intervals to preserve arrangement of yarn. Secures ends of yarn on beam with gummed tape. May doff beam, using hoist. May be designated according to type of yarn wound as Silk Beamer (textile).
GOE: 06.04.06 STRENGTH: H GED: R2 M1 L1 SVP: 3 DLU: 77

681.685-062 LOOM-WINDER TENDER (textile)

Tends winding units attached to looms that automatically wind yarn onto quills, transfer quills to loom shuttles, and strip bunch yarn from expended quills: Positions yarn packages on machine creel and threads yarn end through guides, tensions, and yarn carrier. Places empty quills in feed tray of winding unit. Patrols aisles between looms to detect malfunctions, such as jammed quills, broken yarn ends, exhausted yarn packages, and unstripped quills in reject tray. Straightens or removes jammed quills, ties broken yarn ends, replaces exhausted yarn packages, strips yarn from rejected quills by hand, and places stripped quills in feed tray. Notifies LOOM FIXER (narrow fabrics; nonmet. min.; textile) of mechanical defects. Important variables may be indicated by trade name of machines used.
GOE: 06.04.06 STRENGTH: L GED: R2 M1 L1 SVP: 2 DLU: 77

681.685-066 PRECISE WINDER (textile)

Tends machine that winds *cones* or tubes of yarn or thread to specified size and lay: Places supply packages in creel and draws yarn ends through machine guides and tensions onto takeup tubes to thread winding units. Turns dial of yardage clock to control amount of yarn wound. Turns gear to set lay, using wrench. Starts machine and observes operation to detect yarn breaks and exhausting supply packages. *Pieces up* broken ends. Doffs yarn when package reaches specified size. May weigh yarn package and remove or wind yarn to bring package to specified weight. May tend machine equipped with troughs to draw yarn or thread through solutions specified by processing instructions.
GOE: 06.04.06 STRENGTH: L GED: R2 M1 L1 SVP: 2 DLU: 80

681.685-070 QUILLER OPERATOR (textile) alternate titles: long-chain-quiller tender; quill-machine tender

Tends quiller that winds strands of yarn from *ball warps* onto bobbins or quills after bleaching, mercerizing, or dyeing: Divides new warp into sections to facilitate handling, using twisting hook or ring to hold yarn parallel. Twists

each new strand to preceding strand in machine with fingers to draw yarn through reed and guides without rethreading. Starts machine and depresses pedal board to control winding speed. Feels warp for tangles and observes yarn for breaks. Stops machine to straighten warp, remove *lease strings,* or thread broken ends through reed and guides. Doffs bobbins or quills from spindles and replaces with empties. Brushes dust and lint from machine and oils spindle bearings.
GOE: 06.04.06 STRENGTH: L GED: R2 M1 L1 SVP: 4 DLU: 77

681.685-074 QUILLING-MACHINE OPERATOR, AUTOMATIC (textile) alternate titles: filling winder; quiller; quiller hand; quiller tender

Tends machine equipped with automatic quill loading and doffing device that winds yarn from *cones* or tubes onto quills for use in loom shuttle: Loads hopper with empty quills by hand or electric hoist. Places supply packages of yarn on holders, according to yarn count, blend, and color of label inside packages, and ties yarn ends from packages to ends in machine and cuts excess yarn at knots with scissors. Observes winding units to detect breaks in yarn. Removes quills when yarn breaks, rethreads yarn through guides, and ties yarn ends. Removes full boxes or pinboards (boards with upright spindles), which receive wound quills ejected by machine, and separates partially filled quills. Keeps production records. May inspect quills for defects, such as broken filament and dirty or damaged yarn. May mark quills of yarn according to style of yarn being processed, using colored chalk.
GOE: 06.04.06 STRENGTH: L GED: R2 M1 L2 SVP: 3 DLU: 80

681.685-078 REELING-MACHINE OPERATOR (textile) alternate titles: reeler; reel tender; skein reeler; skein winder

Tends machine that winds yarn, thread, or textile selvage from bobbins, *cones,* cops, or tubes into skeins for dyeing or shipment: Places supply package of yarn, thread, or selvage on spindles. Threads ends of yarn through guides and wraps or ties them around swift (long collapsible reel). Starts machine and observes yarn for breaks. Stops machine to tie or sew broken ends together and replace exhausted supply packages. Cuts yarn with knife or scissors when specified amount of yarn is reeled, and ties ends of skein together. Laces string through and around skein to prevent tangling. Pulls levers to collapse reel and slides skeins off end of reel or observes automatic discharge to detect tangles. May set dial of revolution counter to measure yardage wound. May tie several skeins into bundle. May be designated according to material wound as Twine-Reeling Machine Operator (tex. prod., nec).
GOE: 06.04.06 STRENGTH: L GED: R2 M1 L1 SVP: 3 DLU: 77

681.685-082 ROPE MAKER, MACHINE (nonmet. min.)

Tends former machine that twists strands of asbestos roving to form *wick,* and rope-twisting machine that twists strands of wick to form rope: Creels spools of asbestos roving or wick on machines and threads material through guides, flyer, and around winding spindles. Starts machines and observes twisting to detect breaks in material. *Pieces up* broken roving ends, or ties broken wick ends. Doffs full package of wick and rope from machines.
GOE: 06.04.06 STRENGTH: L GED: R2 M1 L1 SVP: 3 DLU: 77

681.685-086 ROPE-LAYING-MACHINE OPERATOR (tex. prod., nec) alternate titles: rope-coiling-machine operator; rope-twisting-machine operator

Tends one or more machines that lay (twist) fiber strands or twine into rope and wind rope onto reels: Selects and mounts reels of ready (strands) or twine on machine according to rope size specified, using hoist. Threads strands or twine from reels through guides to twisting mechanism, and splices strands or twine to lead rope attached to reel. Starts machine and monitors operation to detect defective laying or winding of rope. Stops machine when counter shows specified length is wound. Cuts rope with knife and binds coil with cord to prevent unwinding. Hammers pin from end of reel and pulls it from coil. May weigh coils. May install gears and tubes to produce specified types and sizes of rope, using handtools. May burn or cut rough spots from rope, using soldering iron or scissors. May tend machine that forms and twists fiber strands into rope.
GOE: 06.04.06 STRENGTH: M GED: R2 M1 L1 SVP: 3 DLU: 77

681.685-090 RUBBER-THREAD SPOOLER (toy-sport equip.) alternate titles: thread spooler

Tends machine that winds strands of rubber used in golf ball cores onto spools: Pulls strands from container and draws strands along winding area to machine. Runs each strand through separator, wraps ends around spools, and clamps spools to spindles. Holds strands in hand, presses pedal to start spools winding, and feeds and guides strands of rubber from container, along winding area, and to machine. Pulls twisted strands to remove snarls or tangles, and stops machine to untwist knots. Stops machine when length markers reach separators, cuts off strands at marker, removes spools from spindles, and handwraps remainder of strand.
GOE: 06.04.07 STRENGTH: L GED: R2 M1 L1 SVP: 2 DLU: 77

681.685-094 SELVAGE-MACHINE OPERATOR (textile)

Tends machine that winds sheets of selvage yarn onto spools: Positions yarn packages on creel and threads yarn from comb, through guides, stop motions, and expansion comb and laps yarn ends around takeup spool. Starts machine and observes flow of yarn to detect breaks in yarn. Stops machine and *pieces up* broken ends. Doffs full spools of selvage yarn from machine.
GOE: 06.04.06 STRENGTH: L GED: R2 M1 L1 SVP: 2 DLU: 77

681.685-098 SKEIN WINDER (textile) alternate titles: coner; spooler; swift tender

Tends machine that simultaneously winds yarn from skeins onto spools or *cones:* Hangs skeins of yarn on rack and beats out (shakes or pulls) skeins to straighten yarn and facilitate winding. Inspects yarn to detect soil, color spots, or defective twisting and discards faulty skeins. Removes reel (swift) from machine, wraps skein of yarn around reel, and replaces reel. Cuts card holding yarn in place, using scissors. Threads end of yarn through guides and turns it around spool or cone and starts unit winding. *Pieces up* broken ends or ties new skeins with knotter. Observes winding operation and removes cones when full. Sets in empty cones. May be designated according to type of yarn wound as Lastex-Thread Winder (textile).
GOE: 06.04.06 STRENGTH: L GED: R2 M1 L1 SVP: 3 DLU: 77

681.685-102 SKEINER (narrow fabrics) alternate titles: skein winder

Tends machine that winds narrow fabrics, such as tape, into skeins for dyeing or shipment: Draws fabric ends from box, threads each end through traverse guide, and ties end to reel. Turns dial to set yardage counter that stops machine when specified yardage has been wound. Presses pedal to start machine. Laces string through and around each skein to preserve arrangement and prevent tangling. Pulls lever to contract reel, slides skeins to end of reel, and removes skeins.
GOE: 06.04.06 STRENGTH: L GED: R2 M1 L1 SVP: 2 DLU: 77

681.685-106 SPEEDER TENDER (textile) alternate titles: roving-frame tender

Tends machines that draw out, combine, and twist two strands of roving into single strands: Observes machines to detect breaks in roving or nearly exhausted bobbins in creels. Replaces nearly empty bobbins on creels with full bobbins. Stops machine, threads flyer, and *pieces up* broken roving. Removes flyers and doffs bobbins of roving when machine stops automatically. Sets empty bobbins on spindles, replaces flyers, and starts machine.
GOE: 06.04.16 STRENGTH: M GED: R2 M1 L1 SVP: 2 DLU: 77

681.685-110 SPINNING-MACHINE TENDER (tex. prod., nec)

Tends one or more machines that twist combed hemp or sisal fiber or yarn into strands and winds strands onto bobbins: Threads sliver (combed fiber) or yarn through guides to twisting mechanism of spinning machine. Opens safety cover to inspect twisting die, places empty bobbin on spindle, and fastens end of yarn or strand to bobbin. Starts machine and observes operation to detect unsteady flow of material into spinning head, and uneven winding on bobbin.
GOE: 06.04.16 STRENGTH: H GED: R2 M1 L1 SVP: 2 DLU: 77

681.685-114 SPOOLING-MACHINE OPERATOR (tex. prod., nec) alternate titles: spooler; winder; winding-machine operator

Tends machine that winds bias binding, cloth, cording, piping, or tape onto cardboard spools: Clamps spool onto spindle of machine. Starts machine and guides material onto revolving spool by hand. Cuts material with scissors when spool is full. May wrap rolls or spools in paper.
GOE: 06.04.38 STRENGTH: L GED: R1 M1 L1 SVP: 2 DLU: 77

681.685-118 STRAND-FORMING-MACHINE OPERATOR (tex. prod., nec)

Tends machine that forms (twists) rope-fiber yarn into strands preparatory to being laid into rope: Installs specified size tubes that gather and compress yarn preparatory to twisting. Places specified number of full yarn bobbins on creel. Threads yarn ends from bobbins through holes in register plates that align yarn through gathering tubes around capstan that maintains tension on strand, and ties end to reel that revolves to twist and form strand. Stops machine to repair yarn breaks. Removes full reel, using hoist.
GOE: 06.04.06 STRENGTH: H GED: R2 M1 L1 SVP: 3 DLU: 77

681.685-122 THREAD WINDER, AUTOMATIC (textile) alternate titles: spool winder

Tends semiautomatic machine that winds thread from *cones* onto spools or tubes used in sewing machines: Places full cones on rack, and passes threads through guides, tension device, yardage counter, and *drop wires.* Loads tubes or spools into machine hopper. Observes operations of machine to detect breaks or *lap-ups.* Removes spools having winding defects, or *pieces up* broken ends, using knotter. Inspects for defects in winding and color as they are discharged by machine. May verify spool size, using gauge. May pack filled tubes or spools in boxes.
GOE: 06.04.06 STRENGTH: L GED: R2 M1 L1 SVP: 2 DLU: 77

681.685-126 TWISTER (tex. prod., nec)

Tends battery of machines that twists together two or more yarn strands into twine or produce plied yarn for use in rope making: Transfers filled spools of yarn to adjoining twister frame that twists two or more strands together to make twine. Doffs machine and packs filled spools of twine and empty cylinders in cartons. May tend machines that spin roving into yarn preparatory to twisting operation.
GOE: 06.04.06 STRENGTH: L GED: R2 M1 L1 SVP: 3 DLU: 77

681.685-130 TWISTER TENDER (glass mfg.; nonmet. min.; plastic-synth.; textile)

Tends machines that twist together two or more strands of yarn or insert additional twist into single strand of yarn to increase strength, smoothness, and uniformity of yarn: Creels machine with bobbins of yarn [CREELER (any industry) 689.687-030], following work ticket specifications for color and type of

yarn, or notifies change crew of exhausting yarn supply. Pulls ends of yarn over rollers, through *tension guides,* traveler, or flyer, and laps yarn onto takeup spool. Patrols machines to detect yarn breaks and exhausted supply packages. Ties broken ends by hand or with knotter, rethreads stopoffs, and untangles yarn. When twisting fiberglass sliver or yarn, repairs breaks with splicing fluid. May doff takeup packages [DOFFER (textile) 689.686-022] and replace them with empty spools. May tend twisting machine that combines yarn with wire. May record production and worker identification on ticket. May inspect yarn for defective twisting and remove defective takeup packages. May tend machines that produce irregular effects or patterns in yarn by actions of pattern chain or by setup of rolls and be designated Novelty-Twister Tender (textile).
GOE: 06.04.06 STRENGTH: M GED: R2 M1 L2 SVP: 3 DLU: 79

681.685-134   TWISTER TENDER, PAPER (tex. prod., nec) alternate titles: paper twister

Tends single or multiple spindle machine that twists paper strips into twine: Slides roll of paper of specified width onto spindle of machine. Wraps twine leader around spool and threads end through guide and twisting die. Untwists end of leader and splices it to end of paper strip. Starts machine and observes operations to detect uneven twisting and winding of twine. Verifies diameter of twine against specifications, using micrometer; and turns wheel to adjust pressure on twisting die. Cuts twine with cutters and removes filled spool. May thread two or more strands of twine through twisting die to make ply twine.
GOE: 06.04.04 STRENGTH: M GED: R2 M1 L1 SVP: 4 DLU: 77

681.685-138   UPTWISTER TENDER (textile) alternate titles: uptwist spinner

Tends machines that twist single strands of silk or synthetic yarn: Places bobbin in holder and draws yarn from supply package through traverse guide and laps yarn around takeup bobbin. Starts machine and observes operation for yarn breaks. *Pieces up* yarn breaks. Doffs full packages. May fit wire guide onto supply package and thread yarn through guide to retain twist in yarn coming off supply package.
GOE: 06.04.06 STRENGTH: M GED: R2 M1 L1 SVP: 3 DLU: 77

681.685-142   WARP SPOOLER (narrow fabrics; textile) alternate titles: jackspooler; spooler

Tends machine that winds yarn in sheets onto spools used on narrow-fabric looms or dresser machines: Places yarn packages on creel of machine and draws yarn ends through guides and tension devices. Lifts spool onto machine brackets and laps yarn ends around spool. Doffs spool when specified yardage has been wound. When warping glass yarn, repairs yarn breaks with splicing fluid.
GOE: 06.04.06 STRENGTH: M GED: R2 M1 L1 SVP: 3 DLU: 77

681.685-146   WARPER (narrow fabrics)

Tends table-type rotary warping machine that winds warp yarn onto pegs or spools for use in weaving narrow fabrics: Places spool of warp yarn over revolving spindle of machine. Mounts spools on spindles or positions wooden pegs in holes of machine table to produce warp of specified dimensions. Threads warp through eye of spindle and horizontal warping arm attached to spindle, and ties warp to hook holder. Starts machine to rotate warping arm and wind warp around pegs and through hook holder. Places weaving hook in hook holder after each revolution of warping arm to separate warp. Stops machine when specified number of yarn strands have been wound and cuts yarn, using scissors. Turns thumbscrew to secure yarn and hooks in hooks holder. Doffs wound yarn.
GOE: 06.04.06 STRENGTH: M GED: R2 M1 L1 SVP: 4 DLU: 77

681.685-150   WINDER OPERATOR, AUTOMATIC (textile)

Tends automatic yarn-winding machine, equipped with stationary or traveling knotter and traveling winding units that move around machine, to transfer yarn from bobbins to *cones* or tubes: Places bobbins in pockets of feeder magazine and pulls ends of yarn over suction tube opening through which yarn is drawn into knotter. Observes machine operation and signal lights to detect machine malfunctions, exhausting supply packages, full packages of yarn, and tangled yarn. Doffs packages when light indicates package is filled. Replaces tubes or cones on spindles. Laps strands of yarn around cones or tubes to start yarn winding. Presses pedal or button to stop and control speed of machine, according to flow of work. Notifies MACHINE FIXER (textile) 689.260-010 when malfunction occurs.
GOE: 06.04.06 STRENGTH: L GED: R2 M1 L1 SVP: 3 DLU: 79

681.685-154   YARN WINDER (tex. prod., nec; textile) alternate titles: back winder; package winder; rewinder; spooler; winder; winding-machine operator

Tends machine that winds strands of yarn from bobbins, *cakes,* pirns, and other yarn packages into packages specified for further processing, shipment, or storage: Places supply packages on spindles or holders. Threads ends of yarn from each package through guides and tension device and attaches them to takeup package. Moves lever, depresses pedal, or flips switch to start machine. Observes winding units to detect breaks in yarn and ties broken ends by hand or with knotter. Stops machine or winding unit and doffs packages. Inspects yarn for defects. Reports malfunction of machine to MACHINE FIXER (textile) 689.260-010. May weigh yarn package or keep production records. May tend machine that winds yarn through emulsion-filled trough or against paraffin disk to soften or strengthen yarn. May be designated according to package wound or supply package used as Bobbin Winder (textile); Cake Winder (textile); or

according to material wound as Worsted Winder (textile). When winding continuous filament yarn to or from packages used in throwing processes, is known as Redraw Operator (textile). When rewinding tangled or short lengths of yarn, is known as Salvage Winder (textile). Important variables may be indicated by trade names or machines used. May be designated Brass-Bobbin Winder (tex. prod., nec); Cone Spooler (any industry); Cone Winder (textile); Cop Winder (textile); Muff Winder (textile); Piece Hand (textile); Pirn Winder (textile); Quill Winder (narrow fabrics); Spool Winder (textile); Tailing-Machine Operator (textile); Tube Winder (any industry); Twine Winder (tex. prod., nec).
GOE: 06.04.06 STRENGTH: M GED: R2 M1 L2 SVP: 3 DLU: 80

681.685-158   YARN-TEXTURING-MACHINE OPERATOR I (textile)

Tends twisting machine frames equipped with thermal units and *false-twist spindles* to produce stretch yarn: Threads yarn through guides, feed rollers, and heating unit, around entrance wheel of false-twist spindle, through traverse guide, and onto takeup bobbin, utilizing suction lines along path yarn travels, extension rods, and wire threader. Observes signal lights that indicate yarn breaks and malfunction of specified sections of machine. Records information regarding malfunction on flag card and places card on machine unit to signal maintenance crew. Reads doff schedule or uses gauge to determine when packages should be doffed. Doffs full takeup packages.
GOE: 06.04.16 STRENGTH: L GED: R2 M1 L1 SVP: 3 DLU: 79

681.686-010   BEAM RACKER (textile) alternate titles: beam doffer; warp clamper; warp hanger; warp placer; warp trucker 681687010 forming-tube selector

Removes and replaces warp beams on looms, warpers, and slashers. Conveys full and empty beams to and from machine, using handtruck. May place harness assembly attached to new warp yarn with corresponding ends left in loom to facilitate tying-in process. May work as member of team to mount beams on looms.
GOE: 06.04.05 STRENGTH: H GED: R2 M1 L1 SVP: 2 DLU: 77

681.686-014   BEAMER HELPER (textile)

Assists BEAMER (textile) to tend machine that winds yarn from section beams onto *loom beams:* Mounts section beams on creel of beamer, using handtruck and chain hoist. Helps doff and wrap loom beams. Observes warp to detect breaks and ties broken threads. May drive industrial truck to transport beams to and from storage area. Performs other duties as described under HELPER (any industry) Master Title.
GOE: 06.04.06 STRENGTH: M GED: R2 M1 L1 SVP: 2 DLU: 77

681.686-018   SPOOLER OPERATOR, AUTOMATIC (textile)

Feeds and off bears section of spooling machine that ties yarn ends automatically and transfers yarn from bobbins to cheeses: Places starter cheeses (spools containing small amount of yarn) on winding spindles. Places full bobbins in individual magazines of machine. Pulls end of yarn over guides or into suction device of machine to be picked up and tied to end of starter cheese by knotter which travels on track over machine. Doffs full cheeses and places cheeses on trident (three-pronged tray) on handtruck, or into trough located beside machine. May sort bobbins ejected by machine according to amount of yarn on bobbin. May strip defective yarn from bobbins, using knife, or by winding yarn on revolving spindle. May attach pregummed labels to inside of cones to identify cheeses or packages.
GOE: 06.04.06 STRENGTH: L GED: R2 M1 L1 SVP: 2 DLU: 78

681.687-010   END FINDER, FORMING DEPARTMENT (textile)

Examines tubes of fiberglass sliver to detect defects and unwinds defective sliver and short lengths from tube: Removes tubes from monorail conveyor onto table. Examines tubes for defects, such as dirt and grease, and to locate end of sliver. Inserts end of sliver in tube of air suction device to unravel defective portion and short lengths. Breaks excess sliver from tube or cuts sliver, using scissors. Weighs tubes of sliver to determine if weight is within tolerances and places tubes on truck. Tags and places underweight tubes on monorail conveyor.
GOE: 06.03.02 STRENGTH: L GED: R2 M1 L2 SVP: 2 DLU: 77

681.687-014   LOOSE-END FINDER, BOBBIN (knitting)

Observes operation of winding machines to detect loose ends of broken thread and ties them.
GOE: 06.04.27 STRENGTH: L GED: R1 M1 L1 SVP: 2 DLU: 77

681.687-018   THREAD INSPECTOR (plastic-synth.)

Examines synthetic-fiber thread, passing continuously in front of electric light, for such defects as weak spots, lumps, irregular twisting, grease stains, and snags. Rejects lots of thread not meeting plant standard. May inspect washed and dried *cakes* of yarn for loose ends and remove excess thread with scissors and be designated Cake Inspector (plastic-synth.). May grade skeins of yarn by weight or presence of irregularities and be designated Sorter (plastic-synth.).
GOE: 06.03.02 STRENGTH: L GED: R3 M1 L1 SVP: 3 DLU: 77

681.687-022   WARP-YARN SORTER (textile)

Sorts yarn packages into sets of specified numbers to be placed on creel of warper. May convey yarn from storage or other department, using handtruck. May distribute yarn.
GOE: 06.03.02 STRENGTH: L GED: R2 M1 L2 SVP: 2 DLU: 77

681.687-026 YARN CLEANER (tex. prod., nec; textile) alternate titles: bobbin fixer; filling inspector; repairer; tangled-yarn-spool straightener; yarn salvager

Examines packages (or pirns) of wound yarn for defects, such as bruises, cuts, tangles, or soil and removes defective yarn to salvage usable yarn, using one of following methods: (1) Pulls yarn from package by hand. (2) Places yarn in holder, and inserts yarn end in nozzle of vacuum tube that draws defective portion from package. (3) Places defective yarn package on holder and draws yarn end over revolving reel, observing yarn to determine when defective portion is removed. Cuts yarn from reel and segregates yarn according to type. (4) Cleans soiled packages, using cloth and detergent. (5) Cuts through packages, using hooked knife or heated knife. Writes information, such as plant number, worker number, and yarn type on cards and places cards with usable packages. May rewind salvaged yarn by hand or using winding machine.
GOE: 06.03.02 STRENGTH: L GED: R2 M1 L1 SVP: 2 DLU: 79

681.687-030 YARN EXAMINER (glass mfg.; plastic-synth.; textile) alternate titles: cone inspector; filling inspector; finished-yarn examiner; quill inspector; yarn inspector

Inspects yarn for defects prior to shipment or storage: Examines bobbins, *cones,* cops, or tubes of yarn by sight and touch for defects, such as broken threads, cross threads, dirty yarn, and excessively loose or tight winding. Places defective yarn on trays or bobbin carts for reprocessing. Wraps yarn in paper or other material to prevent soiling and damage during shipment or storage. Packs and weighs yarn after inspection. Records amount of yarn packed and number of cones rejected. May stamp shipping carton with identification data. May push loaded racks of yarn into steam cabinet to condition yarn.
GOE: 06.03.02 STRENGTH: M GED: R2 M1 L2 SVP: 3 DLU: 79

682 SPINNING OCCUPATIONS

This group includes occupations concerned with twisting together short fibers to form a continuous length of yarn.

682.130-010 SUPERVISOR, SPINNING (textile)

Supervises and coordinates activities of workers engaged in spinning yarn: Reads production schedule for information, such as quantity of yarn, type of fiber, staple length, yarn size, quality and texture desired, and ultimate use of yarn. Computes draft required to reduce roving to specified yarn size and drafting gear size to effect draft, using mathematical formulas and tables. Determines spacing of drafting rollers according to staple length of fiber. Computes yarn specifications to determine amount of twist to put into yarn. Computes twist gear size, using mathematical formulas and tables. Schedules changes in machine setup to produce yarn according to production schedule, issuing change instructions to SECTION LEADER AND MACHINE SETTER (textile) 689.260-018. Examines yarn to detect variations from standards. Schedules doffing of frames to avoid excessive downtime. Trains new employees. Participates in setup and adjustment of machines and equipment. Performs other duties as described under SUPERVISOR (any industry) Master Title.
GOE: 06.01.01 STRENGTH: L GED: R4 M3 L4 SVP: 7 DLU: 79

682.684-010 ROLLER CHECKER (textile)

Verifies speed of drafting rollers on spinning frames, using tachometer: Presses tachometer button against rollers and observes dial indicator to obtain r.p.m. readings. Examines rollers for surface damage and replaces defective rollers or flags malfunctioning machines. *Pieces up* broken ends. Changes travelers [TRAVELER CHANGER (textile)].
GOE: 06.03.02 STRENGTH: L GED: R2 M1 L1 SVP: 3 DLU: 77

682.685-010 SPINNER, FRAME (nonmet. min.; textile) alternate titles: spinner; spinning-frame tender

Tends spinning frame that draws out and twists roving or sliver into yarn: Patrols work area and observes spinning to detect nearly exhausted supply packages and breaks in yarn, roving, and sliver. *Pieces up* breaks in yarn, roving, and sliver and replaces nearly exhausted supply packages with full packages [CREELER (any industry) 689.687-030]. Twists end of material from supply package to material in machine or threads material from supply package through machine guides and drawing rollers. Brushes yarn or lint from drawing rollers, guides, and rails. Notifies designated personnel of machine malfunction. May doff machine [DOFFER (textile) 689.686-022]. May change travelers [TRAVELER CHANGER (textile) 682.687-010]. May be designated according to machine tended as Spinner, Cap Frame (textile); Spinner, Open-End (textile); Spinner, Ring Frame (textile).
GOE: 06.04.06 STRENGTH: M GED: R2 M1 L2 SVP: 3 DLU: 79

682.685-014 SPINNER, MULE (nonmet. min.; textile)

Tends mule-spinning frame that spins roving into yarn and winds yarn onto bobbins: Creels machine and threads roving through guides, between feed rollers, and onto bobbins. Starts machine and patrols work area to detect breaks in roving. Stops machine and *pieces up* broken roving ends. Turns crank to increase or decrease tension of *faller wires* on yarn according to fullness of bobbins. Doffs full bobbins from machine and replaces them with empty bobbins.
GOE: 06.04.06 STRENGTH: L GED: R2 M1 L1 SVP: 4 DLU: 77

682.687-010 TRAVELER CHANGER (textile)

Changes travelers on ring-spinning frames according to style or size of yarn being processed or at regular intervals because of wear, using fingers, hammer,

or hook. Threads yarn through traveler and restarts machine. May replace supply packages of roving on spinning frame.
GOE: 06.04.06 STRENGTH: L GED: R2 M1 L1 SVP: 2 DLU: 78

683 WEAVERS AND RELATED OCCUPATIONS

This group includes occupations concerned with interlacing two sets of yarn to form a fabric.

683.130-010 FLOOR SUPERVISOR, ENDLESS-BELT-WEAVING DEPARTMENT (narrow fabrics)

Supervises and coordinates activities of workers engaged in weaving narrow fabric products, such as endless belts: Inspects woven material during weaving process to detect loom malfunctions. Adjusts looms to obtain belts of specified pattern. Performs other duties as described under SUPERVISOR (any industry) Master Title.
GOE: 06.04.01 STRENGTH: L GED: R4 M3 L3 SVP: 7 DLU: 77

683.130-014 LOOM-FIXER SUPERVISOR (narrow fabrics) alternate titles: fixer supervisor

Supervises and coordinates activities of workers engaged in operating looms to weave cloth: Sets up loom and adjusts tension and timing of parts, using handtools and following diagrams and manuals. Aligns parts, such as shuttle boxes, race plates, and reeds, using straightedge, level, and square. Replaces defective parts, such as harness straps and shuttles. Performs other duties as described under SUPERVISOR (any industry) Master Title.
GOE: 06.01.01 STRENGTH: M GED: R4 M3 L4 SVP: 7 DLU: 77

683.130-018 WEAVE-ROOM SUPERVISOR (carpet & rug)

Supervises and coordinates activities of workers engaged in weaving and related operations in manufacture of carpets and rugs. Directs warp drawing-in, twisting-in, and repair activities. Performs other duties as described under SUPERVISOR (any industry) Master Title.
GOE: 06.02.01 STRENGTH: L GED: R4 M3 L4 SVP: 7 DLU: 77

683.130-022 WEAVING SUPERVISOR (nonmet. min.; textile)

Supervises and coordinates activities of workers engaged in weaving cloth: Prepares and issues instructions to drawing-in department, indicating harness size, number of harnesses required, type of heddles, number of warp ends per inch, and sequence in which warp ends are to be drawn through harness and reed. Prepares loom change instructions indicating changes in loom shedding, picking, beating-up, warp letoff, and cloth takeup motions according to weaving design. Scans cloth during weaving for defects in yarn, design, and loom setup. Performs other duties as described under SUPERVISOR (any industry) Master Title.
GOE: 06.01.01 STRENGTH: L GED: R4 M3 L4 SVP: 7 DLU: 80

683.132-010 PATTERN-CHAIN MAKER SUPERVISOR (textile)

Supervises and coordinates activities of workers engaged in cutting, lacing, and duplicating pattern cards used to control weaving operations of *jacquard looms:* Analyzes customer orders and design drafts (pattern diagrams) to determine number of pattern chains required to meet production schedule. Directs workers to cut and lace new pattern chains or to duplicate specified patterns. Trains workers in cutting, lacing, and duplicating operations. Performs other duties as described under SUPERVISOR (any industry) Master Title.
GOE: 06.02.01 STRENGTH: L GED: R4 M3 L3 SVP: 7 DLU: 77

683.222-010 INSTRUCTOR, WEAVING (textile)

Teaches workers to operate looms, employing knowledge of weaving techniques: Explains application and utilization of *drawing-in draft.* Identifies and describes functions of loom parts to familiarize trainee with loom. Demonstrates weaving techniques, such as tying weaver's knot, threading shuttle, loading loom magazine or battery, and drawing-in broken warp threads. Examines work of trainees to detect defective weaving and suggests methods to correct defective work. Recommends transfer from trainee status to WEAVER (nonmet. min.; textile) as trainees become proficient.
GOE: 06.02.01 STRENGTH: L GED: R3 M2 L3 SVP: 7 DLU: 77

683.260-010 BRAID-PATTERN SETTER (narrow fabrics) alternate titles: braid maker

Sets up braiding machines to produce braid of specified size, style, or design, according to analysis of samples or pattern-card guides: Studies guide or sample to determine machine settings and size, color, and arrangement of yarn on carrier spindles. Changes gears to set up machine for flat or tubular braid, using handtools. Removes or replaces carrier spindles to alter crossing order of threads. Adjusts let-off motion to control closeness of threads. Replaces weights in carrier spindles or adjusts springs to control thread tension for different styles. Tends machine and examines braid to verify setup. Records settings made for new styles or designs.
GOE: 06.01.02 STRENGTH: L GED: R4 M3 L4 SVP: 7 DLU: 77

683.260-014 CARPET-LOOM FIXER (carpet & rug)

Sets up looms equipped with pile-wire mechanism to weave piled carpeting and repairs looms to ensure production conforms to quality standards, employing knowledge of weaving and loom construction: Inspects loom of woven carpeting to determine adjustments or repairs needed. Repairs or replaces defective parts, using handtools and precision instruments. Changes gears on pile-wire mechanism to alter number of *pile wires* inserted into shed to correspond with

number of picks per inch, following charts. Synchronizes motion of pile wires with motion of lathe, using handtools.
GOE: 06.01.02 STRENGTH: M GED: R4 M3 L3 SVP: 7 DLU: 77

683.260-018 LOOM FIXER (narrow fabrics; nonmet. min.; textile) alternate titles: fixer; loom repairer

Sets up, adjusts, and repairs looms to weave cloth of specified quality and design, using knowledge of loom function and weaving, diagrams, and manuals: Inspects loom or woven cloth to determine adjustments or repairs needed. Repairs or replaces defective parts, such as harness straps and shuttles, and adjusts tension and timing of parts, using handtools. Levels and aligns parts, such as shuttle boxes, race plates, and reeds, to prevent excessive wear, using straightedge, level, and square. May change setup of loom to weave different pattern or different type yarn [LOOM CHANGER (textile) 683.360-010]. May be designated according to type of loom serviced as Dobby-Loom Fixer (textile); Jacquard-Loom Fixer (textile); Narrow-Fabric-Loom Fixer (narrow fabrics); Rapier-Insertion Loom Fixer (textile); Water-Jet Loom Fixer (textile).
GOE: 06.01.02 STRENGTH: M GED: R4 M3 L3 SVP: 7 DLU: 80

683.260-022 SWATCH CHECKER (textile)

Inspects sample cloth swatches for weaving defects and adjusts setup of loom, using knowledge of weaving, to correct cause of defects: Examines loom to detect mistakes in setup, such as defective drawing-in, filling, and warp. Compares swatch of first woven cloth with standard swatch, using pick counter and flashlight equipped with magnifying lens, to detect defects in style, yarn, weaving, or color. Determines adjustments needed to correct defects and makes adjustments or notifies LOOM FIXER (narrow fabrics; nonmet. min.; textile). Examines swatch from cloth woven after adjustments. Records number of swatches examined and defects detected. May boil swatch to remove size to permit examination of threads. May dye swatch or have swatch dyed to ascertain dye retention of threads and to detect weaving defects. May test warp tensions, using tensiometer.
GOE: 06.01.02 STRENGTH: L GED: R4 M3 L3 SVP: 7 DLU: 77

683.360-010 LOOM CHANGER (textile) alternate titles: warp changer

Sets up loom to change pattern of cloth woven, according to work order and supervisor instructions: Removes warp beam, harnesses, *drop wires*, and reed, using handtools. Inspects loom components, such as gears, cams, stop-motion devices, and shuttle-throwing assembly to determine adjustments needed. Repairs defective components and adjusts tension and timing of loom parts, using handtools [LOOM FIXER (narrow fabrics; nonmet. min.; textile) 683.260-018]. Positions full warp beam, harnesses, drop wires, reed, and pattern chain on loom. Levels and aligns shuttle boxes and reed. Ties group of warp ends to cloth beam. *Pieces up* thread breaks. Redraws threads through harness to correct misdraws, using *reed hook*. May clean and oil loom. May remove and replace shuttle-box assembly, using handtools. May repair pattern control device on looms that weave cloth with patterns. May start loom and inspect woven cloth to detect defects [LOOM STARTER (textile) 683.360-014].
GOE: 06.01.02 STRENGTH: M GED: R3 M2 L2 SVP: 7 DLU: 80

683.360-014 LOOM STARTER (textile) alternate titles: starter, weaving; warp starter

Examines loom parts, warp and filling thread, and cloth being woven to ensure that loom is set up to weave specified pattern: Inspects pattern chains, order in which warp threads are drawn through harness assembly, and color of warp and filling thread to detect errors in loom setup. Makes adjustments such as changing pattern chains and redrawing warp threads. Starts loom and examines cloth being woven to detect defects. Determines cause of defective weaving and makes adjustments or notifies LOOM FIXER (narrow fabrics; nonmet. min.; textile). Notifies WEAVER (nonmet. min.; textile) to continue operation of loom after adjustment.
GOE: 06.01.02 STRENGTH: L GED: R4 M2 L3 SVP: 7 DLU: 77

683.380-010 HARNESS BUILDER (textile) alternate titles: harness preparer; harness repairer

Reconditions and prepares *harness frames* for looms preparatory to drawing-in or storage: Inspects and replaces damaged heddles, slide rods, side hooks, and frame hooks. Removes or inserts heddles in harness frame for change in cloth style, according to pattern. Counts, measures with gauge, or connects harness to electric counting machine to determine number of heddles. Spaces heddles in sections between heddle rod hooks. May clean harnesses. May convey harnesses to drawing-in department, using handtruck.
GOE: 06.01.02 STRENGTH: M GED: R4 M2 L3 SVP: 6 DLU: 77

683.381-010 CHAIN BUILDER, LOOM CONTROL (textile) alternate titles: chainer; chain maker, loom control; chain pegger; chain splitter

Assembles pattern chains that control movement of *harness frames* and shuttle boxes during weaving: Arranges rolls and separator tubes on cross bars of links, according to pattern diagram, and connects links, using handtools. May hammer or screw pegs in wooden pattern chain.
GOE: 06.01.04 STRENGTH: L GED: R3 M1 L2 SVP: 5 DLU: 77

683.384-010 PATTERN-LEASE INSPECTOR (textile) alternate titles: misdraw hand

Examines warp threads in loom harness to determine if they are drawn in according to pattern chart: Turns wheel on head of loom to raise *harness frames,* and inspects threads drawn through frames to detect mistakes. Redraws

threads through drop wires, heddle eyes, and reed dents to correct misdraws, using reed hook. May start loom and examine woven cloth for defects caused by misdraws, correct misdraws, and mark defects in cloth, using chalk or thread.
GOE: 06.03.01 STRENGTH: L GED: R3 M1 L1 SVP: 4 DLU: 77

683.487-010 BELTING-AND-WEBBING INSPECTOR (narrow fabrics)

Inspects woven belting and webbing to detect weaving defects and variations from specified size and quality: Counts number of warp and filling threads per square inch, using pick counter. Measures width and gauge of belting, using ruler and calipers. Examines belting for knotted, loose, or broken threads. Rejects belting not meeting specifications.
GOE: 06.03.01 STRENGTH: L GED: R2 M1 L1 SVP: 2 DLU: 77

683.582-010 CARD CUTTER, JACQUARD (narrow fabrics; textile) alternate titles: piano-machine operator

Operates machine to punch holes in *Jacquard loom* pattern cards, following design draft (pattern diagram): Clamps paper design draft to frame on front of machine, and positions blank pattern cards in guide under punches (cutting dies). Places automatic marker in line with first row of design marks. Engages clutch to start punching head. Presses keys that control cutting dies following arrangement of holes indicated on design draft. Compares punched card with pattern to detect cutting errors, and pastes squares of paper over holes punched in error. Numbers cards in consecutive order.
GOE: 06.02.04 STRENGTH: L GED: R3 M1 L2 SVP: 5 DLU: 77

683.662-010 JACQUARD-LOOM WEAVER (textile)

Operates battery of *Jacquard looms* to weave yarn into cloth of intricate design: Observes weaving to detect exhausted filling packages and defects in cloth resulting from worn cards in pattern chain. Pulls out filling to remove defects in cloth. Notifies CARD CHANGER, JACQUARD LOOM (textile) if worn cards are causing weaving defects. Pulls cord to reverse pattern chain and card cylinder so that weaving will resume at place where defect occurred to maintain pattern continuity. Marks or cuts cloth when sufficient yardage has been woven.
GOE: 06.02.06 STRENGTH: L GED: R3 M1 L1 SVP: 5 DLU: 77

683.665-010 WEAVER, NEEDLE LOOM (narrow fabrics) alternate titles: shuttleless-loom weaver

Tends shuttleless looms, equipped with filling-carrier needle, that weave narrow fabrics, such as ribbon, tape, and elastic: Places filling-yarn package on holders and threads ends through guides, tensions, and needle carriers, using hook. Presses button to start looms and patrols area to examine woven fabric for defects and to determine cause of loom stoppage, such as warp or filling breaks. Ties broken warp or filling ends. Notifies LOOM FIXER (narrow fabrics; nonmet. min.; textile) of defective weaving caused by mechanical defects. Cuts or marks fabric when specified yardage has been woven and doffs loom or notifies CLOTH DOFFER (textile). May thread warp yarn through harness to change weave pattern or replace warp [DRAWER-IN, HAND (textile)].
GOE: 06.02.06 STRENGTH: L GED: R3 M1 L2 SVP: 4 DLU: 77

683.680-010 HARNESS PLACER (textile) alternate titles: harness tier; warp hanger; warp tier

Places new harness assembly and *loom beam* in loom to prepare loom to weave different pattern: Unbolts reed and *drop wires,* wires, and unhooks pattern control cords from *harness frames* to release harness assembly in loom. Removes harness assembly and loom beam from loom, using hoist. Bolts screws new reed and drop wires in place on loom. Positions harness frame in loom and connects pattern control cords to frames. Positions loom beam o brackets, using hoist. May level harness frames. May place pattern chain on loom.
GOE: 06.01.02 STRENGTH: M GED: R3 M1 L2 SVP: 4 DLU: 77

683.680-014 HEDDLES TIER, JACQUARD LOOM (narrow fabrics; textile)

Attaches harness parts to head of *Jacquard loom* to prepare pattern control mechanism for weaving process: Ties neck (tail or tug) cords to hooks in head of loom or connects cords with wire link. Draws neck cords through bottom board (holed board) to prevent tangling, and ties neck cords to harness cords which have been threaded through comber board. Places leveling board on loom and reties harness cords to heddles to align heddle eyes. Brushes varnish on cord knots to prevent slipping and clips ends of cord close to knots, using scissors. May draw harness cords through comber board holes in specified order, gathering ends of harness cords in bunches and tying heddles and lingos (small weights) to other ends of cords. May place *drop wires* on warp threads [DROP-WIRE HANGER (textile)].
GOE: 06.01.02 STRENGTH: L GED: R3 M1 L1 SVP: 5 DLU: 77

683.682-010 CARPET WEAVER (carpet & rug)

Operates one or more looms equipped with *pile-wire* mechanism to weave carpeting: Moves lever to open shed and inserts specified number of pile wires through shed in sequence to produce pile. Forces cop of filling into shuttle, using mallet, and inserts shuttle into loom. Places wax in holder to lubricate pile wires as wires enter and are withdrawn from shed. Starts loom and observes weaving to detect exhausted filling packages, mispicks, and irregular cutting of pile. Replaces exhausted filling, inserts pile wires into missed loops, and replaces dull cutting blades. May be designated according to type of carpet woven as Velvet Weaver (carpet & rug).

GOE: 06.02.06 STRENGTH: L GED: R3 M1 L2 SVP: 4 DLU: 77

683.682-014 CARPET WEAVER, JACQUARD LOOM (carpet & rug)
Operates one or more *Jacquard looms* equipped with pile-wire mechanism to weave carpeting of intricate design: Moves lever to open shed, and inserts specified number of *pile wires* through shed in sequence to produce pile. Forces cop of filling into shuttle, using mallet, and inserts shuttle into loom. Places wax in holder to lubricate pile wires as wires enter and are withdrawn from shed. Starts loom and observes weaving to detect exhausted filling packages, mispicks, and irregular cutting of pile. Replaces exhausted filling, inserts pile wires into missed loops, and replaces dull cutting blades. Pulls out filling to remove defects in carpeting. Pulls cord to reverse pattern chain and card cylinder so that weaving will resume at place where defect occurred to maintain pattern continuity. Notifies CARD CHANGER, JACQUARD LOOM (textile) as pattern cards become worn or damaged. May be designated according to type of carpeting woven as Wilton Weaver (carpet & rug).
GOE: 06.02.06 STRENGTH: L GED: R3 M1 L2 SVP: 4 DLU: 77

683.682-018 DRAWING-IN-MACHINE TENDER (textile)
Sets up and operates machine to draw warp threads automatically from warp beam through harness assembly to prepare warp for weaving: Bolts setup stand containing beam and harness assembly to frame of drawing-in machine. Attaches pattern strip to keps (slender wires) that are threaded through heddles to set up machine to draw-in specified pattern. Starts machine and observes operation of automatic threading device to ensure drawing-in according to pattern. Examines drawn warp for mistakes. Corrects misdraws and draws-in selvages, using *reed hook*. Loops warp ends together to prevent ends slipping from harness assembly. Unbolts setup stand and pushes stand from frame of machine. Feeds metal strips into pattern cutting machine, and depresses button to cut holes at designated places. May prepare setup stand for use on machine.
GOE: 06.02.06 STRENGTH: H GED: R3 M1 L2 SVP: 5 DLU: 77

683.682-022 JACQUARD-LOOM WEAVER (narrow fabrics)
Operates battery of *Jacquard looms* to weave multiple widths of intricately designed narrow fabrics, such as labels and ribbon: Observes weaving to detect exhausted filling packages and defects in cloth resulting from worn cards in pattern chain. Replaces exhausted filling packages and notifies CARD CHANGER, JACQUARD LOOM (textile) of worn cards. Pulls out filling to remove defects in weaving. Pulls cord to reverse pattern chain and card cylinder so that weaving will resume at place where defect occurred to maintain pattern continuity. Replaces defective shuttles, tension springs, and shuttle eyes, using handtools. May operate loom equipped with automatic stop motions to stop loom as yarn breaks or after weaving specified number of picks. May draw-in warp yarn [DRAWER-IN, HAND (textile)].
GOE: 06.02.06 STRENGTH: L GED: R3 M1 L2 SVP: 5 DLU: 77

683.682-026 LEVERS-LACE MACHINE OPERATOR (tex. prod., nec) alternate titles: jacquard-lace weaver; lace-machine operator; twisthand
Operates loom, known as Levers-Lace Machine, to weave lace: Throws power rod to start loom and pushes wheel to activate pattern chain. Observes lace being woven to detect weaving defects. Examines loom to determine cause of loom stoppage, such as yarn breaks or mechanical defects. Pulls out broken filling and pushes shuttle through shed to insert new pick. Records number of racks woven and cuts completed lace from loom.
GOE: 06.02.06 STRENGTH: M GED: R3 M1 L2 SVP: 6 DLU: 77

683.682-030 PLUSH WEAVER (textile)
Operates battery of looms to weave plush fabric: Observes fabric being woven to detect weaving defects, such as exhausted filling, yarn breaks, or mechanical defects. Pulls out broken filling and pushes shuttle through shed or pulls yarn through guides for rapier pickup to insert new pick. Replaces exhausted packages with supply packages in creel. Examines cloth for uneven cutting after automatic knife separates double-woven pile fabric. Notifies LOOM FIXER (narrow fabrics; nonmet. min.; textile) 683.260-018 if pile is not cut smoothly; or raises flags on looms to signal breakdown or that cloth needs cutting. Marks or cuts fabric when specified yardage has been woven. Records pick clock readings of assigned looms at beginning and end of shift to maintain plant control form. May be designated according to type of loom operated as Weaver, Rapier-Insertion Loom (textile); Weaver, Wire Loom (textile).
GOE: 06.02.06 STRENGTH: L GED: R3 M1 L2 SVP: 4 DLU: 80

683.682-034 WEAVER (carpet & rug)
Operates power looms equipped with rollers and shuttles adapted for bobbins or cops to weave twisted coir, sisal, or paper yarns to produce items, such as mesh, scrim, and fiber rugs, according to specified color, type, pattern, and size: Positions shuttles and inspects looms for broken strands. Releases brake and pulls lever to start loom. Stops loom when breaks and defective weaving are observed or watches for looms stopped by automatic stop-motion device. Threads warp through guides and heddles, over rollers and wax bars, and ties or splices ends, to repair breaks in warp. Breaks out imperfect strands of filling or turns back roll and removes filling up to defect to repair defects or breaks in filling. Stops loom and replaces empty shuttle. Starts loom and clips off end of filler close to selvage. Clears jams in bobbin-type shuttle by removing bobbin and rewinding snarled yarn or by inserting new bobbin. Inserts full cop into empty shuttles manually while loom is running. Installs specified spools in creel when pattern is changed. Cuts and removes full roll of fabric, and tapes end of fabric (discharging from machine) onto tube, or places fabric end under can-

vas flap and turns roller until fabric is wound tightly onto tube to start new roll, with assistance of CREELER (any industry). May operate loom equipped with three heddles which twist two warp yarns together between each filling yarn to produce leno (open mesh) weave.
GOE: 06.02.06 STRENGTH: M GED: R3 M1 L2 SVP: 5 DLU: 77

683.682-038 WEAVER (nonmet. min.; textile) alternate titles: loom operator; weaver, broadloom
Operates battery of looms to weave yarn into cloth: Observes cloth being woven to detect weaving defects. Removes defects in cloth by cutting and pulling out filling. Adjusts pattern chain to resume weaving. Examines looms to determine cause of loom stoppage, such as warp, filling, harness breaks, or mechanical defects. Ties piece of yarn to broken end and threads yarn through *drop wires*, heddle eyes, and reed dents to repair warp breaks, using *reed hook*. Pulls out broken filling and pushes shuttle through shed to insert new pick and repair filling breaks. Notifies LOOM FIXER (narrow fabrics; nonmet. min.; textile) 683.260-018 of mechanical defects. Marks or cuts cloth when sufficient yardage has been woven and notifies CLOTH DOFFER (textile) 689.686-058. May place quills or bobbins in battery or magazine of loom [BATTERY LOADER (textile) 683.686-010]. May replace empty bobbins in shuttle with full ones on nonautomatic looms [SHUTTLE HAND (textile) 689.686-038]. May tend winding units attached to looms that wind filling onto quills [LOOM-WINDER TENDER (textile) 681.685-062]. May be designated according to type of loom operated as Weaver, Dobby Loom (textile). When weaving samples, is known as Sample Weaver (textile).
GOE: 06.02.06 STRENGTH: L GED: R3 M1 L2 SVP: 4 DLU: 80

683.682-042 WEAVER APPRENTICE (nonmet. min.; textile) alternate titles: loom operator apprentice
Performs duties as described under APPRENTICE (any industry) Master Title.
GOE: 06.02.06 STRENGTH: L GED: R3 M1 L2 SVP: 4 DLU: 77

683.682-046 WEAVER, NARROW FABRICS (narrow fabrics; nonmet. min.)
Operates battery of looms to weave multiple widths of narrow fabric, such as ribbon or tape: Observes weaving to detect exhausted filling packages and replaces exhausted packages with full packages. Replaces defective shuttles, tension springs, and shuttle eyes, using handtools. May operate looms equipped with automatic motions to stop loom as yarn breaks or after weaving specified number of *picks*. May draw-in warp yarn [DRAWER-IN, HAND (textile) 683.684-014]. May tend machine to wind filling [YARN WINDER (tex. prod., nec; textile) 681.685-154]. May be designated according to type of fabric woven as Ribbon Weaver (narrow fabrics); Tape Weaver (narrow fabrics; nonmet. min.).
GOE: 06.02.06 STRENGTH: L GED: R3 M1 L2 SVP: 5 DLU: 77

683.682-050 WEAVER, TIRE CORD (tex. prod., nec)
Operates battery of looms to weave cotton yarn between strands of tire cord to form loosely woven tire cord fabric: Observes fabric being woven to detect weaving defects. Examines looms to determine cause of loom stoppage, such as warp and filling breaks or mechanical defects. Ties piece of yarn to broken end and threads yarn through loom parts to repair warp breaks, using hook. Pulls out broken filling and pushes shuttle throughshed to insert new *pick*. Marks or cuts fabric when sufficient yardage has been woven.
GOE: 06.02.06 STRENGTH: L GED: R3 M1 L1 SVP: 4 DLU: 77

683.684-010 CHAIN REPAIRER (carpet & rug)
Adjusts, changes, and repairs endless chains that carry spools of yarn for weaving on axminster looms: Places chain on frame sprockets, using chain hoist. Inserts or removes links to lengthen or shorten chain, following loom setup specifications and using handtools. Inserts rivets to join end links together to form endless carrier chain. Turns screws and nuts and slides sprockets into slots to adjust chain tension. Replaces defective parts and rebuild chains to specifications.
GOE: 06.02.24 STRENGTH: M GED: R3 M1 L2 SVP: 5 DLU: 77

683.684-014 DRAWER-IN, HAND (textile) alternate titles: drawer; drawing-in hand; draw-in hand; warp drawer
Draws warp yarn through loom parts to arrange warp for weaving specified pattern, following pattern chart: Reads pattern chart to determine information, such as type warp to be drawn, number of *harness frames*, and type of reed required for pattern. Positions warp, harness frames, *drop wires*, and reed on or in proximity of *drawing-in frame* or loom to facilitate drawing-in process. Selects warp yarn according to lease, color, and sequence indicated by pattern chart. Pulls yarn through drop wires, heddle eyes, and reed dents, using *reed hook*. May repair warp yarn on loom when numerous threads are broken [SMASH HAND (narrow fabrics; textile) 683.684-026]. May be handed warp yarn by coworker, during drawing-in process. May be designated according to type of loom on which drawing-in is performed, as Drawer-In, Dobby Loom (textile); Drawer-In, Jacquard Loom (textile); Drawer-In, Plain Loom (textile).
GOE: 06.02.06 STRENGTH: L GED: R3 M1 L2 SVP: 4 DLU: 80

683.684-018 HARNESS PULLER (textile) alternate titles: warp starter
Inspects and adjusts warp ends in loom to ensure accuracy of warp position as specified by warp pattern: Pulls warp ends from reed to verify that each thread is located in harness as specified in pattern and in corresponding slot in reed. Reties warp ends to correct errors and ties warp ends to beam in bunches to prepare warp for weaving.

GOE: 06.03.02 STRENGTH: L GED: R3 M1 L2 SVP: 4 DLU: 77

683.684-022 LEASE-OUT WORKER (textile)
Arranges yarn ends from full *loom beam* with corresponding warp ends in loom preparatory to tying of warp ends and resumption of weaving: Mounts beam in brackets of loom, using jack. Separates alternate ends of new warp and warp left in loom according to lease arrangement and inserts lease rod strands so their position of strands will be maintained. Ties thread to broken end and draws thread through harness to *piece up* breaks. Transfers loom beam to and from loom, using dolly.
GOE: 06.04.27 STRENGTH: H GED: R2 M1 L2 SVP: 3 DLU: 77

683.684-026 SMASH HAND (narrow fabrics; textile)
Repairs warp yarn on loom when numerous threads are broken (breakout): Ties short piece of thread to each end of broken warp yarn and cuts off ends close to knot with scissors. Draws repaired warp yarn through *drop wires,* heddle eyes, and reed dents, using *reed hook.* Picks out filling yarn when defective weaving is observed, using fine metal comb. Starts loom and observes operation to detect defective setup or weaving. May start loom after warp change and repair breaks resulting from knots passing through drop wires, heddle eyes, and reed dents.
GOE: 06.02.27 STRENGTH: L GED: R3 M1 L2 SVP: 3 DLU: 77

683.684-030 WEAVER, HAND LOOM (carpet & rug; textile)
Weaves rugs or woolen cloth, using hand loom: Draws warp yarn through loom parts to arrange warp for weaving specified pattern. Inserts bobbin of filling in shuttle and depresses pedals to start loom. Observes cloth to detect weaving defects, such as broken filling or warp. *Pieces up* broken warp ends. Pulls out broken or defective filling and pushes shuttle through shed to insert new pick. Doffs loom.
GOE: 06.02.27 STRENGTH: M GED: R4 M1 L2 SVP: 6 DLU: 77

683.684-034 WEAVING INSPECTOR (carpet & rug; textile) alternate titles: cloth inspector; loom inspector
Inspects woven fabric during weaving process to detect grease spots and weaving defects, such as broken ends, slubs, and coarse yarn: Patrols work area and scans cloth on loom for defects. Stops loom, ties length of yarn to broken warp yarn, and draws yarn through harness and reed, using *reed hook.* Picks out slubs and coarse yarn, using burling iron, and reweaves cloth, using needle. Marks grease spots and irreparable defects with crayon to indicate yardage allowance. Trims loose threads with scissors.
GOE: 06.02.06 STRENGTH: L GED: R2 M1 L2 SVP: 3 DLU: 77

683.685-010 BRAIDING-MACHINE OPERATOR (narrow fabrics; nonmet. min.) alternate titles: braider tender
Tends battery of machines that braid yarn into flat or tubular narrow fabrics: Creels machine according to work ticket and threads yarn through guides, tensions, braiding point (round or elliptical hole), and tension rollers. Starts machine and laps end around *takeup roll* or places end into receiving can. Observes braiding to detect breaks in yarn and ties or glues broken yarn ends. Doffs full rolls or cans of braided material from machine. May braid jacket around articles, such as rope or wire. May tend yarn rewinding machine [YARN WINDER (tex. prod., nec; textile) 681.685-154].
GOE: 06.04.06 STRENGTH: M GED: R2 M1 L1 SVP: 3 DLU: 77

683.685-014 CARD CHANGER, JACQUARD LOOM (textile) alternate titles: card hanger; jacquard-pattern servicer; pattern changer and repairer; pattern hanger
Changes pattern chain on *Jacquard loom* to alter weave design and replaces worn parts: Cuts lacing connecting first and last cards of pattern chain on loom. Lifts pattern chain from holder brackets onto handtruck and positions new pattern chain in holder. Positions pattern chain over card cylinder of Jacquard head and ties end cards together to form endless chain. Examines pattern chains for worn cards or lacing. Cuts lacing from cards and ties in duplicate cards or new cord.
GOE: 06.04.27 STRENGTH: M GED: R2 M1 L2 SVP: 4 DLU: 77

683.685-018 CARD LACER, JACQUARD (narrow fabrics; textile) alternate titles: lacing-machine operator, jacquard cards
Tends machine that automatically laces Jacquard pattern cards with cord to form pattern chain for use on *Jacquard loom:* Stacks punched pattern cards in sequence or blank cards in automatic feed mechanism or places cards individually on feed belt. Observes machine operation to ensure that cards are spaced evenly and fed singly according to numerical sequence into lacing mechanism. Replenishes spools of lacing cord. May tend machine that duplicates sets of cards [PATTERN DUPLICATOR (textile)]. May number cards according to prescribed sequence, using pencil or hand-numbering device.
GOE: 06.04.06 STRENGTH: L GED: R2 M1 L1 SVP: 2 DLU: 77

683.685-022 DRAWING-IN-MACHINE-TENDER HELPER (textile)
Assists DRAWING-IN-MACHINE TENDER (textile) to tend drawing-in machine: Positions warp beam on brackets of stand, using chain hoist, and hangs *harness frames* in specified order on arms of stand. Attaches reed and *drop wires* to stand, using handtools. Threads heddles eyes with keys (slender wires) that control order in which machine will draw in warp threads. Pushes stand into frame of machine. Removes drawn warp assembly from setup stand and places assembly on handtruck, using chain hoist. Performs other duties as described under HELPER (any industry) Master Title.
GOE: 06.04.05 STRENGTH: H GED: R2 M1 L1 SVP: 4 DLU: 77

683.685-026 PATTERN DUPLICATOR (textile) alternate titles: repeater operator
Tends machine that duplicates sets of pattern cards used to control weaving operations of *Jacquard loom:* Places set of blank cards and set of punched cards into mechanisms that simultaneously feed cards under repeating cylinder where reeler rods locate holes on punched card and activate corresponding punches that punch duplicate holes in blank card. Observes operation of machine to verify accuracy of punching and removes bent or jammed cards. May operate lacing machine to tie punched cards into chain [CARD LACER, JACQUARD (narrow fabrics; textile)].
GOE: 06.04.06 STRENGTH: L GED: R2 M1 L2 SVP: 2 DLU: 77

683.685-030 THREADING-MACHINE TENDER (carpet & rug)
Tends machine that threads axminster loom frames with pile yarn for weaving process: Mounts loom frame and loom spools in machine brackets and aligns frame tubes with machine needle guides. Inserts clamp in holder to lay yarn parallel in guides. Moves lever and presses pedal to lower lock bar and activate needle bar to draw yarn ends through guides and tubes. Examines frame for missed or crossed yarns. Corrects faulty threading, using *reed hook.* Presses lever and button to activate blowers and rotary blade that trims protruding yarn ends from frame tubes. Loads completed assembly onto handtruck for removal to weaving area.
GOE: 06.04.06 STRENGTH: L GED: R2 M1 L1 SVP: 3 DLU: 77

683.685-034 WARP-TYING-MACHINE TENDER (narrow fabrics; textile) alternate titles: knotting-machine operator, portable; knot-tying operator; tying-in-machine operator; warp-tying-machine knotter
Tends portable or stationary automatic warp-tying-in machine that ties warp ends from full warp beam to warp in loom in order to resume weaving without repeating drawing-in process: Reads work order or confers with supervisor to determine looms needing warp-tying-in process. Divides, combs out, straightens, and applies warp softener to ends of warp from full beam and from exhausted beam, and clamps ends in position in tier. Presses button or turns crank to start tying mechanism. Observes and controls tying-in process as machine picks up corresponding strands from warp beam and from *loom beam,* ties strands together, and cuts off excess yarn above knot. Stops machine, corrects misalignment of warp yarn, and releases joined strands from machine. Manually ties ends not tied by machine. May pull warp through *drop wires,* harnesses, and reed so knots will not jam assembly and break when loom is started. May repair tying machine. May doff exhausted warp beams and position full beams prior to warp-tying-in process, using hoist.
GOE: 06.04.06 STRENGTH: M GED: R3 M1 L2 SVP: 4 DLU: 80

683.685-038 WEAVER, AXMINSTER (carpet & rug)
Tends automatic looms simultaneously that weave pile yarn, filling yarn, and warp yarn material to produce carpets and rugs with various colored designs: Starts previously set up loom and observes weaving to detect breaks in yarn and weaving defects. Stops loom, *pieces up* broken ends, and removes filling yarn back to point where defect begins to correct imperfections. Pulls lever to actuate endless chain that moves spools of pile yarn into position for weaving.
GOE: 06.04.06 STRENGTH: M GED: R2 M1 L1 SVP: 4 DLU: 77

683.686-010 BATTERY LOADER (textile) alternate titles: battery filler; battery hand; magazine filler
Loads batteries or magazines of automatic looms with quills or bobbins of filling: Conveys quills or bobbins of filling to loom, using handtruck, and places them in battery or magazine of loom. Draws loose ends of filling through guides and winds ends around thread holder on side of battery or magazine.
GOE: 06.04.06 STRENGTH: L GED: R1 M1 L1 SVP: 2 DLU: 77

683.687-010 DRAWER-IN HELPER, HAND (textile)
Assists DRAWER-IN, HAND (textile) to prepare warp for weaving: Conveys beams of warp from warper, slasher, or storage to *drawing-in frame,* and removes completed draw-in assembly, using handtruck. Assists DRAWER-IN, HAND (textile) to position harness, reed, and *drop wires* on drawing frame, and fastens ends of warp on frame with clamp bar. May place warp beam on brackets of loom, using hoist, and lay ends in position for drawing-in with *reed hook.* Performs other duties as described under HELPER (any industry) Master Title.
GOE: 06.04.05 STRENGTH: M GED: R2 M1 L1 SVP: 2 DLU: 77

683.687-014 DROP-WIRE HANGER (textile) alternate titles: wire dropper
Places *drop wire* on each warp thread in loom to complete drawing-in process for weaving. Job occurs where warp thread is not drawn through eyes of drop wires in drawing-in process.
GOE: 06.04.06 STRENGTH: L GED: R1 M1 L1 SVP: 2 DLU: 77

683.687-018 HANDER-IN (narrow fabrics; textile)
Assists DRAWER-IN, HAND (textile) to draw warp yarn through loom harness and reed: Sits behind harness at *drawing-in frame* or loom, selects warp ends according to lease and places warp ends on *reed hook* held by DRAWER-IN, HAND (textile) who draws ends through heddles and reed. Performs other duties as described under HELPER (any industry) Master Title.
GOE: 06.04.05 STRENGTH: S GED: R2 M1 L1 SVP: 2 DLU: 77

683.687-022 HOOK PULLER (narrow fabrics)
Removes weaving hooks from finished endless belts to prepare belts for inspection. Places hooks in tray.

GOE: 06.04.40 STRENGTH: L GED: R1 M1 L1 SVP: 1 DLU: 77

683.687-026 LINGO CLEANER (textile)

Cleans metal lingos (weighted heddles) used in *Jacquard loom* harness: Cuts harness cords from lingo, using curved, flexible knife, and lays lingos in tray. Places tray of lingos in tub filled with cleaning solution, boils solution to remove dirt and oil from lingos, and rinses lingos in adjoining tub. Places tray of cleaned lingos in drying cabinet. Removes trays from drying cabinet and ties lingos in bunches with cords.

GOE: 06.04.39 STRENGTH: L GED: R2 M1 L1 SVP: 2 DLU: 77

683.687-030 LOOM CHANGEOVER OPERATOR (carpet & rug) alternate titles: changeover operator

Replaces spools of fiber yarn on loom, according to changeover chart for new pattern of woven fiber rug: Removes old spools from spindles of creel places spools on pallet for removal to stockroom. Places new spools of yarn of specified color on spindles and threads individual strands through loom.

GOE: 06.04.05 STRENGTH: L GED: R2 M1 L1 SVP: 3 DLU: 77

683.687-034 WARP-TENSION TESTER (textile) alternate titles: tension checker

Tests and adjusts tension of warp on looms or other textile machines, using tensiometer: Presses arm of tensiometer against several threads of warp and reads gauge. Removes or adds weights, or turns adjustment nut with wrench to adjust tension, according to specifications. May test accuracy of tensiometer with known weights and adjust tensiometer, using screwdriver.

GOE: 06.03.02 STRENGTH: L GED: R2 M1 L2 SVP: 2 DLU: 77

684   HOSIERY KNITTING OCCUPATIONS

This group includes occupations concerned with interlacing a strand of yarn or thread in a series of connected loops to make hosiery.

684.137-010 SUPERVISOR (knitting)

Supervises and coordinates activities of workers engaged in one or more phases of hosiery or sock production, such as knitting, dyeing, finishing, mending, and packaging. May set up and repair machines, such as boarding, looping, or seaming machines. May distribute materials to workers. Performs duties as described under SUPERVISOR (any industry) Master Title. May be designated according to department as Supervisor, Boarding (knitting); Supervisor, Knitting (knitting) I; Supervisor, Looping (knitting) I; Supervisor, Mending (knitting) I; Supervisor, Pairing And Inspecting (knitting); Supervisor, Seaming (knitting); Supervisor, Transferring And Boxing (knitting).

GOE: 06.02.01 STRENGTH: L GED: R4 M3 L3 SVP: 7 DLU: 83

684.384-010 QUALITY-CONTROL TESTER (knitting)

Tests hosiery to verify conformance to plant quality standards or to obtain data for use in establishing quality standards for new styles: Measures overall length, and length of toe, foot, heel, welt, and after welt, with scale. Determines stretch of welt, knee, ankle, and instep, using weighted stretch machine. Tests tensile strength of hose at knee on stretch flex machine. Ascertains number of stitches per inch, using stitch counting machine. Examines samples of hose in production and defective hose returned by purchasers to find knitting, seaming, looping, or dyeing defects, using magnifying glass. Determines cause of defect, basing judgment on knowledge of production methods. Records results of findings.

GOE: 06.03.01 STRENGTH: L GED: R3 M2 L2 SVP: 4 DLU: 77

684.682-010 KNITTING-MACHINE OPERATOR, FULL-FASHIONED HOSIERY, AUTOMATIC (knitting)

Operates knitting machines to knit hose to shape of foot and leg: Places spools of yarn on spindles of machine and threads machine. Places *welt rod* in retaining notch of *welt bar* and turns lever to lower welt bar to knitting position. Pushes yarn carrier into position and turns bar to start machine to knit welt. Hooks draw-off straps from takeup roller to welt rod to hold welt and leg taut during knitting. Turns handwheels to position *picot bar* to knit stitches joining welt to leg of hose and to raise picot and welt bars after welt is knitted. Stops machine and clips loose threads at welt and toe of completed hose, using scissors. Removes welt rods and hose from machine. Counts, bundles, and attaches identifying ticket to hose. Replaces and aligns needles and points of machine, using pliers. May clean and oil machine.

GOE: 06.02.06 STRENGTH: L GED: R3 M2 L1 SVP: 5 DLU: 77

684.682-014 SEWER AND INSPECTOR (knitting)

Inspects seamless hose for knitting defects and operates sewing machine to close openings in toes of hose: Pulls hose over inspection board to turn hose inside out and inspects hose for defects, such as holes, runs, and dropped stitches. Revolves inspection board by hand to inspect both sides of hose. Slides toe portion of hose off end of inspection board and positions toe of hose under presser foot of sewing machine. Presses pedal to start machine and guides toe of hose under needle of machine to close toe. Strips defective hose from inspection board by hand and places hose aside for mending. Pushes hose without defects from left to right off board, where hose is sucked through opening in end of board to turn hose right side out and stack hose in rack. Threads and cleans lint from sewing machine. May examine stitch markings on defective hose to identify malfunctioning knitting machines and flip switch under corresponding machine number on panelboard to stop machine and notify fixer. May attach toe of hose to mechanical device that automatically feeds toe of hose under needle of sewing machine to close toe.

GOE: 06.03.02 STRENGTH: L GED: R3 M1 L1 SVP: 3 DLU: 77

684.684-010 STOCKING INSPECTOR (knitting) alternate titles: grey inspector; inspector and clipper

Inspects unfinished hose or socks for defects and conformance to specifications: Draws hose or socks over inspection board and inspects items for defects, such as holes, runs, torn threads, dropped stitches, and defective looping or seaming. Turns form to inspect both sides of items. Clips loose threads from items, using scissors or electric clipper with suction attachment that removes loose threads. Strips items from board if board is not equipped with automatic turning and stripping device. Sorts items according to type of imperfection. Marks production ticket. May bag first quality items for dyeing. May mark defective area of items for mending, using crayon. May inspect items conveyed by pneumatic tube to inspection station and press control to stop and flag specific machine causing defects in items. May depress pedal to rotate inspection board during inspection of items. May inspect items by hand. Where inspection is performed after each operation, may be designated Knitting Inspector (knitting); Looping Inspector (knitting); Seaming Inspector (knitting). May be designated according to type of item inspected as Sock Examiner (knitting).

GOE: 06.03.02 STRENGTH: L GED: R2 M1 L1 SVP: 3 DLU: 81

684.684-014 SIZER (knitting) alternate titles: length control tester; seamless sizer; size tester

Measures undyed hose to determine if size meets specifications: Pushes stretch measuring devise to machines and collects sample hose from storage bag under ejection chute of each machine. Pulls hose onto closed parallel leg-shaped hydraulic form of stretch measuring device, moves lever to release air into form to spread form and stretch hose, and reads scale device to determine whether hose meets product stretch specifications. Repositions hose on form and repeats process to measure stretch of specified sections of hose, according to procedure. Records results and informs KNITTING-MACHINE FIXER (knitting) 689.260-026 of any machine malfunctions. Adjusts knitting machine to correct minor malfunctions.

GOE: 06.03.02 STRENGTH: L GED: R3 M2 L2 SVP: 4 DLU: 81

684.685-010 SEAMLESS-HOSIERY KNITTER (knitting) alternate titles: knitter; knitting-machine operator, automatic; knitting-machine operator, seamless hosiery; sock-knitting-machine operator

Tends circular knitting machines with automatic pattern controls that knit seamless hose: Places yarn spools on creel; threads and starts machine. Observes operation of machines and notifies KNITTING-MACHINE FIXER (knitting) 689.260-026 of any malfunction. Removes knitted hose from machines. Pulls hose over inspection form or over hand to examine for defects, such as holes, runs, or picks. Classifies hose according to specifications into grades, such as first quality, rejects, and mends. Counts, bundles, ties, and labels each grade of hose. Clips loose or connecting threads on or joining socks, using scissors. May measure overall length of hose, using scale on inspection form. May mark defective portion of hose for HOSIERY MENDER (knitting) 782.684-030, using crayon. May be designated according to type of hose knitted as Sock Knitter (knitting).

GOE: 06.04.06 STRENGTH: L GED: R2 M1 L1 SVP: 3 DLU: 81

684.686-010 CLIPPER, MACHINE (knitting) alternate titles: automatic clipper and stripper; clipper, automatic

Feeds machine that clips threads, turns, and strips hose automatically: Pulls hose over forms that carry hose through machine. May strip hose from forms of machine that is not equipped with turning and stripping device.

GOE: 06.04.06 STRENGTH: L GED: R1 M1 L1 SVP: 2 DLU: 77

684.687-010 PAIRER (knitting) alternate titles: examiner; pairer-inspector

Inspects, grades, and pairs finished surgical hose, panty hose, stockings, leotards, and socks, according to grade, color, size, and length: Spreads hose on pairing table or over inspection forms and examines hose for defects, such as pulls, snags, holes, mends, and dye streaks. Classifies hose into grades, following specifications. Positions graded hose over scale on table to measure overall length and length of toe, foot, heel, and welt. Selects pair of identical hose of same grade and stacks hose on table. Tallies each pair in lot by grade. May be designated according to grade or type hose paired as Pairer, Odds (knitting); Pairer, Substandard (knitting).

GOE: 06.03.02 STRENGTH: L GED: R2 M2 L1 SVP: 3 DLU: 80

684.687-014 REINSPECTOR (knitting) alternate titles: reexaminer

Inspects samples of surgical hose, panty hose, stockings, leotards, and socks of specified styles, or samples previously examined by PAIRERS (knitting) 684.687-010, to ensure that specifications are met. Records findings on each sample, noting quantity and types of defects found and whether sample met specifications. May train and supervise PAIRERS (knitting). May inform supervisors and workers responsible for defective samples.

GOE: 06.03.02 STRENGTH: L GED: R3 M2 L1 SVP: 3 DLU: 81

684.687-022 COLLECTOR (knitting)

Removes collection bags filled with knitted hosiery from knitting machines: Marks work tickets with information, such as style and size of hosiery being knitted on machines, and attaches tickets to machines. Scans collection bags to detect bags filled with hosiery, removes bags from machines, and ties bags, using knitted loops attached to tickets. Places full bags in handcart and attaches empty bags to machines. Pushes handcarts containing full bags to designated area for further processing.

GOE: 06.04.40 STRENGTH: M GED: R2 M1 L1 SVP: 2 DLU: 86

685   KNITTING OCCUPATIONS, EXCEPT HOSIERY

This group includes occupations concerned with interlacing a strand of yarn or thread in a series of connected loops to make a fabric or a knitted product other than hosiery.

685.130-010 SUPERVISOR, KNITTING II (knitting)

Supervises and coordinates activities of workers engaged in knitting fabrics, shaped garments, and other articles from yarn: Schedules changes in machine set up to produce knitted fabric, garment, or article according to production schedules and issues instructions to KNITTING-MACHINE FIXER (knitting). Verifies machine setup and directs repair and adjustment of malfunctioning machines. Directs training of workers in setup and operation of machines and equipment. Examines knitted fabric, garment, or article produced to detect variations from standards. May be designated according to department supervised as Supervisor, Inspecting (knitting); Supervisor, Looping (knitting) II; Supervisor, Mending (knitting) II. Performs other duties as described under SUPERVISOR (any industry) Master Title.

GOE: 06.01.01 STRENGTH: M GED: R4 M3 L3 SVP: 7 DLU: 77

685.360-010 KNITTER MECHANIC (knitting) alternate titles: pattern-and-chain maker

Builds metal chains, consisting of multisize pattern plates, or installs pattern tapes that control operation of *jacquard loom* and link-and-link flat knitting machines and sets up machines to produce specified design in knitted fabric: Obtains specifications for new knitting pattern from supervisor. Studies number, type, and arrangement of stitches in sample and determines arrangement of pattern plates on chains, employing knowledge of machine operation. Connects plates to form chain. Studies sample to determine which perforations in pattern plates are to be covered to produce specified knit and informs JACQUARD-PLATE MAKER (knitting). Installs chains and pattern plates in machine and makes trial run to determine if knitting meets specifications. May make minor repairs to knitting machines.

GOE: 06.01.02 STRENGTH: M GED: R4 M3 L3 SVP: 7 DLU: 77

685.380-010 LINK-AND-LINK-KNITTING-MACHINE   OPERATOR (knitting) alternate titles: knitter, machine; knitting-machine operator, automatic

Sets up and operates battery of automatic, link-type (Jacquard) knitting machines to knit garments of specified pattern and design: Places chains that control operation of machine on machine sprockets. Places cones of yarn on machine spindles and threads end of yarn through machine guides, tension devices, and needle eyes. Turns screws to set carrier stops and adjust stroke of yarn carrier. Pushes lever to separate needle plates of machine and hooks stitches of knitted piece of fabric onto needles to serve as base for knitting. Starts machine and observes operation to detect defective knitting. Ties ends of broken yarn with weaver's knot. Separates needle plates and removes finished fabric from machine.

GOE: 06.01.03 STRENGTH: L GED: R3 M2 L3 SVP: 6 DLU: 77

685.381-010 JACQUARD-PLATE MAKER (knitting) alternate titles: patternmaker

Covers designated perforations of metal pattern plates with metal pieces (snappers) to control operation on needles in automatic knitting machines: Selects and links together specified number of pattern plates or cards to form continuous chain. Arranges snappers over perforations designated by KNITTER MECHANIC (knitting). Aids KNITTER MECHANIC (knitting) to install plates in machine and starts machine for trial run to determine if plates have been prepared as specified. May perforate blank pattern strips to correspond to needle-bed spacing.

GOE: 06.02.23 STRENGTH: L GED: R3 M3 L2 SVP: 5 DLU: 77

685.382-010 SURGICAL-ELASTIC KNITTER, HAND FRAME (protective dev.)

Knits fabric from silk and elastic thread for use in surgical supports, using hand-and-foot-operated knitting machine: Marks width measurements of fabric to be knitted, needles. adjusts machine. Places cones of silk and elastic thread on spindles, and draws thread through machine guides and between needles. Moves levers to activate machine and knit fabric. Depresses pedal of elastic thread-carrier to lay elastic thread between stitches. Passes elastic thread through each end stitch of knitted fabric and knots thread to prevent raveling, using darning needle.

GOE: 06.02.06 STRENGTH: L GED: R4 M2 L1 SVP: 5 DLU: 77

685.665-010 KNITTER, FULL-FASHIONED GARMENT (knitting) alternate titles: transfer knitter

Tends knitting machine that increases and decreases stitches at designated places to knit shaped garment parts onto ribbed cuffs or waist bands: Creels machine and threads yarn through guides, stop-motion devices, and *yarn carriers,* using hook. Positions *transfer bar* containing several ribbed parts over needle bed of machine, pushes stitches from *transfer points* onto machine needles and removes transfer bar. Pulls one ribbed part up to needle eyes and attaches outer edge of rib to hooked bar of *takeup roll.* Starts machine that auto-

matically increases stitches to knit garment part. Turns handle or presses pedal, when machine automatically stops, to activate *narrowing* fingers that cause needles to decrease stitches to shape portions, such as shoulders and neck. Replaces defective needles, using pliers. Notifies KNITTING-MACHINE FIXER (knitting) of machine malfunction.

GOE: 06.04.06 STRENGTH: L GED: R2 M1 L1 SVP: 4 DLU: 77

685.665-014 KNITTING-MACHINE OPERATOR (knitting) alternate titles: knitter; knitter, machine

Tends one or more machines that knit fabrics, garment parts, or other articles from yarn: Creels machine and ties end of yarn to yarn in machine or threads yarn through guides, tension springs, stop-motion devices, and *yarn carrier* or needles, using hook. Starts machine and laps end of tubular or flat knitted goods around *takeup roller.* Observes knitting to detect yarn breaks, exhausted yarn packages, and knitting defects. Ties broken yarn ends, replaces exhausted yarn packages, and notifies KNITTING-MACHINE FIXER (knitting) 689.260-026 of mechanical defects. Cuts knitted fabric, using scissors, and doffs roll of cloth from machine. May mark ticket to indicate number of holes in knitted goods. May replace defective needles, using needle pliers or wrench. May weigh roll of knitted goods and record weight. May oil machine. May be designated according to type of machine tended as Circular Knitter (knitting); Flat Knitter (knitting). May be designated according to type of fabric knitted as Jersey Knitter (knitting); Pile-Fabric Knitter (knitting); Rib-Cloth Knitter (knitting), or garment part as Collar Knitter (knitting); Cuff Knitter (knitting).

GOE: 06.04.06 STRENGTH: M GED: R3 M1 L1 SVP: 3 DLU: 79

685.665-018 WARP-KNITTING-MACHINE OPERATOR (knitting) alternate titles: knitter

Tends battery of warp-knitting machines to knit diverse products, such as tulle, lace, net, fabrics for outer and undergarments, elastic fabric for foundation garments, and carpet material: Patrols knitting area and inspects cloth for defects, such as holes, yarn breaks, and discolorations. Ties broken yarn ends with fingers. Stops machine and notifies supervisor when unable to determine cause of defects. Records number and type of defects. Hand-weaves new threads over and under lease rods, threads yarn through guides, using hook, and ties warp ends with fingers to attach new warp to corresponding threads of old warp. Cuts excess thread from knots, using scissors. May replace defective needles, using hook and wrench. May help position warp beams I on machine and doff rolls of knitted cloth from machine, using chain hoist and handtools. May lubricate machines, using oilcan and brush. May tend machines that knit milanese, raschel, or tricot fabrics and be designated according to machine type as Milanese-Knitting-Machine Operator (knitting); Raschel-Knitting-Machine Operator (knitting); Tricot-Knitting-Machine Operator (knitting).

GOE: 06.02.06 STRENGTH: M GED: R3 M2 L2 SVP: 4 DLU: 77

685.680-010 THREADER (knitting)

Threads warp yarn through needles to prepare warp-knitting machine for knitting: Removes paper covering from warp spools or beam mounted on machine, and turns spools or beams to align yarn ends. Cuts tape holding warp threads at intervals, using scissors. Loops yarn ends over sley points (yarn guides) and pulls ends to front of machine. Draws yarn through open hooks of needles, using threader and *dobber,* and ties ends in bunches to facilitate handling. Starts machine and winds end of cloth on *takeup roll.* Ties broken threads with fingers, and assists in hanging warps and cleaning machine.

GOE: 06.02.27 STRENGTH: L GED: R3 M2 L2 SVP: 5 DLU: 77

685.682-010 CROCHET-MACHINE OPERATOR (knitting) alternate titles: crocheter

Operates machine to crochet trimmings on knitted garments: Selects spools of thread according to specifications, or color of garment, and mounts spools on holder of machine. Threads needle and yarn carrier or looper of machine. Depresses pedal to clamp edge of material under presser foot of machine. Starts machine and guides material under crocheting needle. Stops machine, turns handwheel to raise needle from garment, and cuts threads with scissors.

GOE: 06.02.06 STRENGTH: L GED: R3 M2 L2 SVP: 4 DLU: 77

685.684-010 PATTERN WHEEL MAKER (knitting) alternate titles: pattern puncher; wheel blocker

Installs *needle jacks* in pattern wheels that control operation of needles in circular knitting machines, following pattern chart. Removes top of pattern wheel and inserts jacks in notches of wheel. May paint mark on top of pattern wheels to indicate where pattern begins. May punch out grooves in metal blades and install blades or metal pins in pattern drums and be designated Pattern-Drum Maker (knitting).

GOE: 06.02.27 STRENGTH: L GED: R3 M2 L2 SVP: 5 DLU: 77

685.685-010 KNITTING-MACHINE OPERATOR (tex. prod., nec) alternate titles: loom operator; netting machine operator

Tends knitting machine that makes netting from twine: Adjusts twine guides and tension rollers to conform with width, length, and mesh specification, using handtools and rule. Places spools of twine on machine spindles and inserts wound bobbins in shuttle containers. Threads twine from bobbins and spools through guides and rollers. Starts machine and monitors operation. Stops machine to tie ends of broken twine and to replace empty spools and bobbins. May wind twine on bobbins [YARN WINDER (tex. prod., nec; textile)]. May inspect net and correct defects [NETTING INSPECTOR (tex. prod., nec)].

GOE: 06.04.40 STRENGTH: L GED: R2 M1 L2 SVP: 4 DLU: 77

685.685-014 PATTERN ASSEMBLER (knitting)

Assembles pattern chains that control pattern-forming motion of guide bars (flat metal bars on which yarn guides are attached) on knitting machines: Se-

lects pattern-chain links according to pattern diagram. Marks links according to sequence in chain, using bevel square and scriber. Holds link against electric grinder to bevel end down to marking so link will adjust guide bars smoothly. Inserts connecting pins through holes in links to assemble links that form pattern chain.
GOE: 06.04.06 STRENGTH: L GED: R2 M2 L2 SVP: 3 DLU: 77

685.686-010 FRINGING-MACHINE OPERATOR (knitting) alternate titles: muffler fringer
Feeds knitted mufflers under needle of machine that automatically forms fringes.
GOE: 06.04.06 STRENGTH: L GED: R2 M1 L1 SVP: 2 DLU: 77

685.686-014 KNITTING-MACHINE OPERATOR HELPER (knitting) alternate titles: knitter helper
Assists KNITTING-MACHINE OPERATOR (knitting) to knit cloth: Creels machines and ties yarn ends from each supply cone to yarn ends on exhausted cones. Cuts knitted cloth with shears and doffs cloth rolls from machines. Trucks cloth rolls from knitting area. Replaces broken knitting machine needles, using needle pliers, wrench, and screwdriver. Cleans machine and work area, using airhose, rags, and brooms and performs other duties described under HELPER (any industry) Master Title. May be designated according to worker assisted as Circular-Knitter Helper (knitting); Flat-Knitter Helper (knitting); Tie-Knitter Helper (knitting); Warp-Knitter Helper (knitting).
GOE: 06.04.06 STRENGTH: M GED: R2 M1 L2 SVP: 2 DLU: 77

685.687-010 CLOTH INSPECTOR (knitting) alternate titles: assembler
Examines cloth for knitting defects and rejects cloth not meeting specifications. Measures cloth and sews thread marker into material to indicate length required by specifications. Folds and ties inspected cloth with cord. Records routing information on paper and attaches paper to cloth. May mark knitting defects on cloth with chalk.
GOE: 06.03.02 STRENGTH: L GED: R2 M1 L2 SVP: 4 DLU: 77

685.687-014 CUFF FOLDER (knitting) alternate titles: cuff turner
Folds cuffs preparatory to sewing cuffs to sleeves of knitted garments: Lays flat cuff on table and folds cuff in half or pulls tubular cuff over cone-shaped form and turns cuff half-way back, matching edges. Stacks folded cuffs.
GOE: 06.04.27 STRENGTH: S GED: R1 M1 L1 SVP: 2 DLU: 77

685.687-018 LACE WINDER (tex. prod., nec)
Tends machine that winds lace on cards: Inserts card in machine holder with end of lace next to margin and manually turns card to start winding. Depresses pedal to start machine and control speed, guiding lace across card until specified number of layers are wound. Examines lace for defects during winding and rejects unsatisfactory material.
GOE: 06.04.05 STRENGTH: L GED: R2 M1 L1 SVP: 2 DLU: 77

685.687-022 PATROLLER (knitting)
Patrols knitting area to inspect cloth being knitted on warp or circular knitting machines: Walks continuously between machines and observes cloth for defects, such as yarn breaks, holes, discolorations, and stop marks. Stops machine with hand lever or button and marks defects for WARP-KNITTING-MACHINE OPERATOR (knitting) or CIRCULAR KNITTER (knitting). May tie ends of new warp to corresponding ends of warp in machine. May doff rolls of cloth.
GOE: 06.03.02 STRENGTH: L GED: R2 M1 L2 SVP: 2 DLU: 77

685.687-026 TOPPER (knitting)
Loops stitches of ribbed garment parts on points of *transfer bar* to facilitate transfer of garment part to needles of knitting machine. Cuts several stitches and pulls yarn out by hand to unravel rows of surplus fabric between points and edge of fabric. May assist KNITTER, FULL-FASHIONED GARMENT (knitting) to doff machine.
GOE: 06.04.27 STRENGTH: S GED: R1 M1 L1 SVP: 2 DLU: 77

686 PUNCHING, CUTTING, FORMING, AND RELATED OCCUPATIONS

This group includes occupations concerned with piercing textiles by means of rigid cutting tools advanced into the material to make, enlarge, or thread holes; shaping the material by means of rigid or rotary cutting tools; and otherwise giving shape or form to material.

686.462-010 DIE-CUTTING-MACHINE OPERATOR, AUTOMATIC (tex. prod., nec; textile) alternate titles: die cutter
Operates automatic die-cutting machine to cut various specified shapes from roll of felt: Positions dies into machine, and aligns upper cutting die with surfaces of bed. Inserts shims between die and bed to set specified gap, and locks dies into position, using wrenches. Places rolls of felt in feed holders, turns knobs to synchronize action of feed rolls with ram, and threads end of felt through feed rolls and die bed to takeoff conveyor. Starts machine and inspects sample cuts to determine conformity to specifications. May sew or glue together ends of rolls to form continuous feed. When cutting specified shapes from rolls of foam rubber, may be designated Die-Cutting-Machine Operator, Automatic (rubber goods).
GOE: 06.02.05 STRENGTH: L GED: R3 M1 L2 SVP: 4 DLU: 77

686.585-010 CUTTING-MACHINE OPERATOR (tex. prod., nec) alternate titles: sheet-cutting operator
Tends machine equipped with electric knife or rotary shear that cuts cloth into specified lengths and folds lengths for use in making bags: Places roll of cloth on brackets of machine and threads cloth between feed rollers or sews cloth to leader in machine, using portable sewing machine. Cuts cloth, using either of following methods: (1) Moves slotted bar specified distance from folding bar to obtain length of cut and tightens setscrew to secure bar. Starts machine that moves cloth over slotted bar. Pushes electric knife along slot to cut cloth into lengths. (2) Changes gears of machine, using wrenches, or turns dial to set feeding speed of machine that controls length of cut. Starts machine that automatically cuts cloth into lengths, folds lengths, and deposits folded cloth on catch-bar of machine. Periodically removes folded cloth accumulated on catch-bar and stacks cloth on handtruck. Measures cloth lengths, using rule. Records yardage cut. May be designated according to type of bag cut as Cotton-Bag-Cutting-Machine Operator (tex. prod., nec.); Jute-Bag-Cutting-Machine Operator (tex. prod., nec); Waterproof-Bag-Cutting-Machine Operator (tex. prod., nec).
GOE: 06.04.05 STRENGTH: H GED: R2 M1 L2 SVP: 2 DLU: 77

686.662-010 RUG CUTTER (carpet & rug)
Controls table equipped with electric rotary cutter and other powered equipment to cut rolls of woven fiber rug material to specified lengths: Positions roll in hanger of table, using power hoist. Pulls lever to start power puller that moves material across table or draws carpet along calibrated scale on table by hand. Examines material for flaws and pushes cutter along track to cut out faulty sections. Smooths, squares, and cuts material to make ends even and to avoid waste.
GOE: 06.02.05 STRENGTH: M GED: R3 M1 L2 SVP: 4 DLU: 77

686.682-010 BAND-SAW OPERATOR (tex. prod., nec)
Operates bandsaw to cut felt pads to pattern: Tacks cardboard pattern to pad. Pushes pad against revolving blade, following outline of pattern. Stacks and ties together bundles of finished shapes. Collects scraps for shredding by PICKING-MACHINE OPERATOR (any industry).
GOE: 06.02.05 STRENGTH: M GED: R3 M1 L2 SVP: 4 DLU: 77

686.682-014 BIAS-CUTTING-MACHINE OPERATOR (tex. prod., nec)
Operates machine to cut tubular cloth into narrow widths for use as bias tape or binding: Positions roll of cloth on shaft or truck of flat-folded cloth on stand at feeding end of machine. Places tubes on takeup roller. Turns setscrew to space circular knives on cutting shaft according to width specified for tape. Pulls open end of tubular cloth over arm of machine, under guide bars, through feed rollers, and under rotary knives. Laps ends of bias-cut cloth around tubes. Depresses pedal to start, stop, and control speed of machine and guides cloth under guide bars and through feed rollers to cut cloth on bias. Removes rolls of bias tape or binding from machine. May wrap rolls in paper for storage or shipment.
GOE: 06.02.05 STRENGTH: M GED: R3 M1 L2 SVP: 4 DLU: 77

686.682-018 FELT-CUTTING-MACHINE OPERATOR (tex. prod., nec) alternate titles: power-cutting-machine operator
Operates machine to cut rolls of felt into pieces of specified length and width: Pulls felt from roll onto table, measures specified length, and clamps transverse bar to felt at point where cut is to be made. Clamps circular cutting knives to crossbar at measured intervals to cut or trim felt to specified width. Starts machine and presses foot treadle, when transverse bar reaches cutting-off knife, to cut felt to length. Collects strips cut from edges of felt by circular knives and puts strips in waste baskets for repicking by PICKING-MACHINE OPERATOR (any industry).
GOE: 06.02.05 STRENGTH: M GED: R3 M2 L2 SVP: 4 DLU: 77

686.685-010 CHIN-STRAP CUTTER (hat & cap)
Tends machine that cuts rolls of material to form chinstraps and punches eyelet holes in straps to facilitate attachment to helmets: Positions roll of material, such as fiber, leather, or plastic, on machine spindle. Threads material through feed guide and under blade of machine. Turns setscrews to adjust cutting feed guide to produce strapping cut to specified size. Starts machine that cuts and punches material, forming and perforating chinstraps.
GOE: 06.04.05 STRENGTH: L GED: R2 M1 L1 SVP: 2 DLU: 77

686.685-014 CONTINUOUS PILLOWCASE CUTTER (tex. prod., nec) alternate titles: pillowcase cutter
Tends machine that cuts rolls of tubular cloth into pillowcase lengths: Mounts roll of cloth on rack at entry end of machine. Turns handwheel to set width guides according to width of cloth. Threads end of cloth through width guides and feed rollers. Turns dial to set stroke of rotary knife according to length specified for pillowcases. Starts machine that automatically cuts cloth into pillowcase lengths and blows lengths free from machine. Removes lengths with stains or defective stitching. Places bundles of pillowcase lengths on skid.
GOE: 06.04.05 STRENGTH: M GED: R2 M1 L2 SVP: 3 DLU: 77

686.685-018 CUFF CUTTER (glove & mit.) alternate titles: knit-wrist cutter
Tends battery of machines that cut and fold knit tubing for use as cuffs on gloves: Pushes box of knit tubing from storage to machine, using handtruck. Turns screws on cams that control speed and motion of cutting blade and feeding mechanism to cut tubing to specified length, using handtools. Threads end of tubing through guides and feeder rollers, over spreader arms, and under cutting blade. Starts machine that automatically cuts and folds cuffs. Removes tray or box of cut and folded cuffs from delivery end of machine. Replaces dull cutting blades, using handtools.

GOE: 06.04.05 STRENGTH: M GED: R2 M1 L2 SVP: 3 DLU: 77

686.685-022 CUTTER (tex. prod., nec)

Tends machine that cuts strands of yarn into specified lengths for use as mopheads: Mounts roll of yarn on machine spindle. Sets stops along scale of cutting table according to length and weight specified for mopheads. Threads yarn through machine guides, pulls yarn to stops, and pushes yarn against rotating knife or presses pedal to raise rotating knife through slot in table to cut yarn into lengths. Loops rubberband over ends of each length to prevent ends from tangling. Periodically weighs mopheads to detect variations from specifications and adjusts stops to restore cutting to specifications. May thread sponge-mop yarn through steam cabinet for softening before cutting.
GOE: 06.04.05 STRENGTH: M GED: R2 M1 L2 SVP: 2 DLU: 77

686.685-026 FELT CUTTER (ordnance)

Tends slitting machine that cuts sheets of hair-felt board into strips which are fed into presses that stamp out filler wads for shotgun shells: Turns handwheel to adjust feed rollers to accommodate thickness of sheets to be slit and feed guide bar to specified strip width. Starts machine and pushes sheets against guide bar into feed rollers to obtain desired number of sheets. Measures width and thickness of cut strips to verify conformance to specifications, using ruler and fixed gauge.
GOE: 06.04.05 STRENGTH: L GED: R2 M1 L2 SVP: 2 DLU: 77

686.685-030 FOLDER (narrow fabrics)

Tends machine that cuts canvas to specified widths and folds and presses strips for use as belting: Threads end of canvas roll through cutting mechanism, fold guides, and between pressing rolls. Starts machine and observes processing for defective cutting, folding, or pressing. Cuts folded belting to specified length, using knife, and stacks belting on handtruck.
GOE: 06.04.05 STRENGTH: L GED: R2 M1 L2 SVP: 2 DLU: 77

686.685-034 HANDLE-AND-VENT-MACHINE OPERATOR (furniture)

Tends machine that automatically punches holes and crimps grommets in mattress borders to insert ventilators and attach handles: Slides border into marked position under machine head and depresses pedal to punch holes in boxing (mattress border). Places grommets and ventilating grids over holes and depresses another pedal to crimp grommets and grids into fabric. Inserts handles in grommeted holes.
GOE: 06.04.20 STRENGTH: L GED: R2 M1 L1 SVP: 2 DLU: 77

686.685-038 PERFORATING-MACHINE OPERATOR (hat & cap) alternate titles: clicker-machine operator; crown-perforator operator; eyelet cutter; perforator; perforator operator; punching-machine operator; sweatband perforator

Tends machine that punches holes in hats or hat parts to ventilate or decorate hats or facilitate assembly, utilizing one of following methods: (1) Positions article beneath multiheaded punch on ram of machine; depresses pedals to lower ram and feed guide that automatically moves article across machine bed as punch perforates article. (2) Positions article on mold in machine bed; pushes lever that forces punches, mounted on rams, against article, to punch holes in article. (3) Positions part against machine guide and under punch; depresses and releases pedal to clamp part in place; starts machine that lowers punch onto material to perforate part. May be designated according to type of hat perforated as Helmet-Hat Puncher (hat & cap); or part perforated as Brim Slotter (hat & cap); Helmet-Hat-Sweatband Puncher (hat & cap).
GOE: 06.04.05 STRENGTH: L GED: R2 M1 L2 SVP: 2 DLU: 77

686.685-042 PINKING-MACHINE OPERATOR (boot & shoe; garment) alternate titles: pinker

Tends machine that cuts serrated designs along edges of garment or shoe seams to decorate edges and prevent raveling: Positions raw edge of seam or hem between pressure and pinking rollers of machine. Depresses pedal to start machine. Guides edge between rollers or moves edge against pin guide on machine bed and feeds edge between rollers. May tend machine equipped with lever-type blade to cut sample swatches of cloth.
GOE: 06.04.05 STRENGTH: L GED: R2 M1 L2 SVP: 3 DLU: 77

686.685-046 PREPLEATER (tex. prod., nec)

Tends machine that folds pleats into top of drapery panels and staples folded pleats in position for sewing: Inserts staples in machine. Positions drapery on bed of machine according to marks on machine. Presses button or pedal to start machine that forces material between machine dies to form pleats and staple pleats. May work as member of team when tending machine that forms more than one pleat at a time.
GOE: 06.04.05 STRENGTH: L GED: R3 M1 L2 SVP: 3 DLU: 77

686.685-050 PRESS OPERATOR (protective dev.)

Tends machine that joins and perforates adhesive and felt strips to make corn and bunion plasters: Positions adhesive strip over felt strip fed from spools. Inserts ends of strips into machine and depresses starting pedal.
GOE: 06.04.05 STRENGTH: L GED: R2 M1 L1 SVP: 3 DLU: 77

686.685-054 RIVET-HOLE PUNCHER (garment) alternate titles: rivet-hole-machine operator

Tends machine that punches holes in garments for insertion of reinforcing rivets: Places garment or garment part on bed of machine with section to be punched, such as pocket corner, under punch. Depresses pedal to lower punch and pierce hole in material.

GOE: 06.04.05 STRENGTH: L GED: R2 M1 L1 SVP: 2 DLU: 77

686.685-058 SCALLOP CUTTER, MACHINE (tex. prod., nec)

Tends machine that cuts lengths or belts of embroidered fabric into scalloped strips for use as decorative trimming: Inserts blade in machine head and turns setscrews to raise or lower blade, according to thickness of fabric. Places fabric on machine table, aligns prestitched line on fabric with edge of blade, and sets machine guide according to fabric alignment. Starts machine and observes flow of fabric to detect damage and irregular scalloping as fabric passes under blade. Replaces blade or adjusts height of blade to restore scalloping to specifications. Positions fabric for subsequent runs through machine and repeats process until fabric has been cut into specified number of scalloped strips. Lubricates machine. May sharpen blades.
GOE: 06.04.05 STRENGTH: L GED: R2 M1 L2 SVP: 2 DLU: 77

686.685-062 SHOELACE-TIPPING-MACHINE OPERATOR (narrow fabrics) alternate titles: shoelace tipper; tipping-machine operator, automatic

Tends one or several machines that wrap plastic, fiber, or metal bands at intervals around strands of braid to form tips of shoelaces and cut braid into laces: Sets measuring device to cut laces of specified length, using handtools and rule guide on machine. Threads end of braid through guides and carrier, and around measuring device and feeder wheels, or ties end of braid to braid in machine. Positions container of glue or solvent solution on machine or pours solution into container attached to machine. Places roll of tipping material in holder and draws end through guides and feeder roller of tipping mechanism. Starts machine that feeds braid through gluing, tipping, and cutting mechanisms and drops laces onto racks. Removes laces from rack, picks out defective laces, and ties laces in bundles.
GOE: 06.04.20 STRENGTH: H GED: R2 M1 L1 SVP: 2 DLU: 77

686.685-066 STRIP-CUTTING-MACHINE OPERATOR (textile) alternate titles: slicer; slitter

Tends machine that cuts rolls of textile material into narrow rolls of specified width: Lifts roll of material onto machine bar and hammers wedge into core of roll to secure roll to bar. Turns handwheel to move rotary blade into cutting position, following markings on calibrated scale to obtain specified cutting width. Starts machine that rotates blade and roll in opposite directions. Presses lever to move rotating blade forward and cut through roll of material. Releases lever and positions blade for subsequent cut. Removes narrow rolls of material from machine and stacks rolls on shelf according to width. When cutting rolls of bias material into narrow widths, is designated Bias-Binding Cutter (tex. prod., nec). May be designated according to product cut as Band-Cutting-Machine Operator (garment; knitting); Binding Cutter (garment; textile); Facing-Cutting-Machine Operator (garment); Handkerchief Cutter (textile); Piping-Cutting-Machine Operator (garment); Suspender Cutter (garment); Tape-Cutting-Machine Operator (garment; tex. prod., nec).
GOE: 06.04.05 STRENGTH: H GED: R2 M1 L1 SVP: 2 DLU: 77

686.685-070 TUBULAR-SPLITTING-MACHINE TENDER (knitting)

Tends machine that splits tubular knitted cloth into open-width form: Changes spreader attachments according to width specifications. Positions handtruck under *swing-folding attachment* at delivery-end and starts machine. Guides cloth along cutting line, over spreader, and under circular cutting blade. Observes cloth for defective splitting and reports malfunctions to supervisor.
GOE: 06.04.05 STRENGTH: M GED: R2 M1 L2 SVP: 2 DLU: 77

686.685-074 WELT-TRIMMING-MACHINE OPERATOR (hat & cap) alternate titles: brim-edge trimmer; welt cutter

Tends machine that trims excess welting material from inside edge of hat body or brim: Turns screws to adjust depth of cut of machine blade, using screwdriver. Positions edge of hat body or brim against machine guide and pulls lever to lower presser foot onto material. Depresses pedal to start machine that cuts inside welt of hat body or brim. Removes cut welt from inside edge of hat body.
GOE: 06.04.05 STRENGTH: L GED: R3 M1 L2 SVP: 3 DLU: 77

686.686-010 FELT-TIPPING-MACHINE TENDER (pen & pencil) alternate titles: tipping-machine operator

Feeds machine that shapes felt tips for stencil marking pens: Fills hopper of machine with felt tips and presses switch to start machine that automatically shapes sides and bevels or rounds end of tips for marking pens.
GOE: 06.04.09 STRENGTH: L GED: R1 M1 L1 SVP: 1 DLU: 77

686.686-014 RUG-CUTTER HELPER (carpet & rug)

Feeds fiber material into machine that cuts material into rugs of specified sizes: Pushes handtruck or dolly loaded with rug material to cutting table. Places roll in rack on cutting table. Inserts end of material under pressure roll. Smooths, pulls, and squares material on cutting table. Rolls cut rugs on tubes and places rugs on truck. Pushes trucks to next department.
GOE: 06.04.05 STRENGTH: M GED: R2 M1 L2 SVP: 2 DLU: 77

687 TUFTING OCCUPATIONS

This group includes occupations concerned with inserting tufts or loops of yarn through backing material to produce tufted articles, such as carpets and rugs, without interlacing or interlocking yarn as accomplished in weaving, knitting, and sewing.

687.132-010 SUPERVISOR, TUFTING (carpet & rug)

Supervises and coordinates activities of workers engaged in tufting, finishing, inspecting, and mending carpets and rugs: Analyzes work orders to determine need for supplies and sequence of operation. Coordinates flow of materials to winding, tufting, finishing, and inspecting areas. Trains workers in opeation and adjustment of machines and equipment. Examines carpets and rugs during processing to verify conformance to specifications and to detect defects. Performs other duties as described under SUPERVISOR (any industry) Master Title. May be designated according to department supervised as Supervisor, Broadloom (carpet & rug); Supervisor, Finishing (carpet & rug).
GOE: 06.02.01 STRENGTH: L GED: R4 M3 L4 SVP: 6 DLU: 77

687.464-010 RUG-FRAME MOUNTER (carpet & rug)

Mounts backing material (loosely woven fabric or burlap) on frame to facilitate tufting: Hooks specified backing over frame spikes and clamps metal side bars onto frame to secure material in position for tufting. Moves backing on frame periodically to facilitate completion of tufting process. Measures and marks carpet dimensions on backing, using tape measure and chalk-line reel. May stencil designs on sample backing, using brush and lamp black solution.
GOE: 06.04.27 STRENGTH: H GED: R2 M1 L2 SVP: 3 DLU: 77

687.682-010 FLOWER-MACHINE OPERATOR (tex. prod., nec) alternate titles: flower cheniller

Operates machine to tuft flowered design on articles: Places yarn packages on spindles and draws ends through machine guides, tensions, and needle eyes. Presses knee lever to raise hoop-shaped presser foot, positions material on movable portion of machine bed, and lowers presser foot to hold material taut. Starts machine and turns machine bed to rotate material beneath needles that automatically tuft flower design on material. Observes tufting to detect defects, such as broken yarn and needles. Rethreads machine or replaces damaged needles.
GOE: 06.02.05 STRENGTH: L GED: R3 M1 L2 SVP: 4 DLU: 77

687.682-014 TUFT-MACHINE OPERATOR (carpet & rug; tex. prod., nec) alternate titles: chenille-machine operator; needle-punch operator; overlay operator

Operates machine to tuft designs on articles, such as rugs and bedspreads: Places yarn packages on spindles and draws ends through machine guides, tensions, and needle eyes. Depresses pedal to activate tufting mechanism and guides material under tufting needles, following design specifications. Observes tufting to detect defects, such as broken yarn and needles. Rethreads machine or replaces damaged needles. Rethreads machine needle with specified color of yarn to tuft multicolor design. Workers who tend machines that tuft continuous lengths of cloth are classified under TUFTING-MACHINE OPERATOR (carpet & rug; textile).
GOE: 06.02.05 STRENGTH: L GED: R3 M1 L2 SVP: 4 DLU: 77

687.684-010 RUG HOOKER (carpet & rug)

Tufts yarn through backing material (loosely woven fabric or burlap) to fabricate carpets and rugs, using portable, electric-powered hooking device: Presses trigger of device to start reciprocating action of needle that punches yarn through material to form pile on rug surface. Guides device along stenciled outline on backing material to tuft design in rug according to specifications. Changes yarn color as specified by pattern. May insert missing tufts in rugs. May tuft rugs by hand, using hooked needle, and be designated Rug Hooker, Hand (carpet & rug). When tufting samples, is known as Sample Maker (carpet & rug).
GOE: 06.02.27 STRENGTH: L GED: R3 M1 L2 SVP: 5 DLU: 77

687.684-014 TUFTER (furniture) alternate titles: button tufter; pad tufter; tufter operator

Tufts pads and mattresses with metal pins, using press: Sets pins upright in holders in press bed. Lays pad in place over tops of pins and sets cover form over pad in alignment with pins. Starts motor and pushes lever to press cover form over pad and force pins through pad. Clamps cover form to press bed with hand clamps and raises press head from form. Slips metal washers over projecting ends of pins and spreads and flattens ends of pins over washers, using handtools. Releases clamps and lifts pad from form and press when tufting is complete.
GOE: 06.04.05 STRENGTH: M GED: R2 M1 L1 SVP: 4 DLU: 77

687.685-010 NEEDLE-CONTROL CHENILLER (tex. prod., nec)

Tends tufting machine equipped with pattern roller and solenoids that control machine needles to tuft intricate designs: Selects pattern according to specifications and positions pattern on machine, using handtools. Pulls yarn ends through machine guides, tensions, and needle eyes to thread machine. Draws material under machine needles, through cut-pile mechanism, and laps end around takeup rod. Starts machine and observes operation to detect broken yarn or faulty pile cutting. Rethreads broken yarn or replaces broken needles. Replaces dull knives for cut-pile mechanism, using handtools. Removes dull rolls from machine.
GOE: 06.04.05 STRENGTH: M GED: R3 M2 L2 SVP: 3 DLU: 77

687.685-014 TUFTING-MACHINE OPERATOR (furniture) alternate titles: button-tufting-machine operator

Tends machine that button-tufts mattresses: Adjusts needle stroke and button tying mechanism to thickness of mattress. Fills machine hopper with tufting buttons. Places mattress on movable table of machine and turns wheel to adjust distance between mattress and machine head. Presses button to start machine and moves table laterally, forward, and backward to space tufts as machine head inserts tufts into both sides. May tend machine that automatically moves table and tufts mattress, or semiautomatic machine that requires lever operation for each stroke. May tend machine that tufts with knots. May tuft by hand [TUFTER, HAND (furniture)].
GOE: 06.04.05 STRENGTH: M GED: R2 M1 L2 SVP: 3 DLU: 77

687.685-018 TUFTING-MACHINE OPERATOR (carpet & rug; textile) alternate titles: chenille-machine operator; yardage-tufting-machine operator

Tends multiple-needle machine that tufts material to be used for articles, such as rugs, robes, and bedspreads: Requests CREELER (any industry) to change yarn styles in creel or mounts supply packages on spindles and *pieces up* ends to leaders in yarn guides (plastic tubes). Draws ends through guides leading to machine, using suction device, and threads ends through guides, tensions, *drop wires,* and needle eyes. Places roll of backing material on brackets at entry end of machine, draws backing under machine needles, and attaches end to *takeup roll.* Moves lever that engages or disengages cam wheel to adjust machine to insert tufts in straight or irregular design. Observes tufting to detect yarn breaks and machine malfunctions. Rethreads broken yarn ends and replaces bent or broken needles and hooks (loopers). Replaces dull knives on cut-pile tufting machines, using handtools. Unthreads needles and ties up extra drop wires to adjust machine to accommodate narrower material. Increases or decreases speed of cloth feed and inserts or removes shims between needle plate and machine bed to adjust space between tufts and length of tufts. Workers who operate tufting machines are classified under TUFT-MACHINE OPERATOR (carpet & rug; tex. prod., nec).
GOE: 06.04.05 STRENGTH: M GED: R3 M2 L3 SVP: 3 DLU: 77

687.685-022 TUFTING-MACHINE OPERATOR, SINGLE-NEEDLE (carpet & rug)

Tends single-needle machine that tufts yarn through material to produce rugs: Measures, marks, or traces rug dimensions or outline on backing material (loosely woven fabric or burlap), using tape measure, marking pencil, and rug patterns. Mounts yarn packages on creel spindles and draws ends through guides, tensions, and needle eye. Positions roll of backing on machine brackets at entry end and threads material through feed rollers onto spiked *takeup roll.* Presses buttons and lever to start machine that inserts tufts in singular rows through material. Observes tufting to detect yarn ends and malfunctions. Rethreads broken yarn ends and reports malfunctions to repair personnel. Cuts material with scissors when specified carpeting has been tufted.
GOE: 06.04.05 STRENGTH: L GED: R2 M1 L2 SVP: 3 DLU: 77

689 TEXTILE OCCUPATIONS, N.E.C.

This group includes occupations, not elsewhere classified, concerned with combining, spinning, weaving, knitting, and otherwise working textiles, textile products, fur, and hair.

689.130-010 EMBROIDERY SUPERVISOR (tex. prod., nec) alternate titles: supervisor, production

Supervises and coordinates activities of workers engaged in operating machine to embroider designs on fabric. Sets up and repairs machines. Performs duties as described under SUPERVISOR (any industry) Master Title.
GOE: 06.02.01 STRENGTH: L GED: R4 M3 L4 SVP: 7 DLU: 77

689.130-014 FELT-GOODS SUPERVISOR, NEEDLE PROCESS (tex. prod., nec) alternate titles: kersey-department supervisor

Supervises and coordinates activities of workers engaged in manufacturing needle (punched) felt: Sets up machines to make experimental samples. Observes operation of machines to detect malfunction and adjusts machines, using handtools. Trains new workers. Requisitions materials. Inspects work of operators to verify conformity to specifications. Directs delivery of finished goods to coating or shipping department. Performs other duties as described under SUPERVISOR (any industry) Master Title.
GOE: 06.02.01 STRENGTH: L GED: R4 M3 L3 SVP: 8 DLU: 77

689.130-018 KNITTING-MACHINE FIXER, HEAD (knitting)

Supervises and coordinates activities of KNITTING-MACHINE FIXER (knitting). Verifies setup and adjustment of machines and equipment. Trains workers in operation of machines and assigns work stations. Performs duties as described under SUPERVISOR (any industry) Master Title.
GOE: 06.01.01 STRENGTH: L GED: R4 M3 L4 SVP: 7 DLU: 77

689.130-022 SUPERVISOR, CLOTH WINDING (tex. prod., nec)

Supervises and coordinates activities of workers engaged in winding burlap onto tubes for use in textile bag manufacturing: Requisitions bales of burlap for processing. Trains workers in machine operation. Directs machine adjustments as needed to maintain production level or adjusts machines, using handtools. Performs other duties as described under SUPERVISOR (any industry) Master Title.
GOE: 06.02.01 STRENGTH: L GED: R4 M3 L3 SVP: 6 DLU: 77

689.130-026 SUPERVISOR, ROVING DEPARTMENT (textile)

Supervises and coordinates activities of workers engaged in cutting fiberglass sliver into staple lengths, bonding staple lengths into mats of insulation material, waxing strands of fiberglass yarn together to form cord, dyeing sliver for

tracer yarn, and winding strands of sliver into roving: Examines product and observes processing operations to detect machine malfunctions. Determines cause of malfunction, using knowledge of machines and processes in department. Directs CREELERS (any industry) to increase or decrease number of fiberglass ends fed to staple-cutting machines, mat machines, or winding machines, according to specifications for various products. Trains new workers. Requisitions supplies. Confers with other SUPERVISORS (any industry) Master Title to coordinate activities of individual departments. Performs other duties as described under SUPERVISOR (any industry).
GOE: 06.01.01 STRENGTH: L GED: R4 M3 L3 SVP: 7 DLU: 77

689.130-030   SUPERVISOR, WEAVING (carpet & rug)
Supervises and coordinates activities of workers engaged in creeling, weaving, and rewinding fiber products, such as cloth, rugs, scrim, and binding: Sets up and adjusts looms and winding machines. Directs loom changeover to accommodate new patterns. Inspects in-process and finished materials to ensure attainment of specified levels of quality. Performs other duties as described under SUPERVISOR (any industry) Master Title.
GOE: 06.02.01 STRENGTH: L GED: R4 M3 L3 SVP: 6 DLU: 77

689.130-034   SUPERVISOR, YARN PREPARATION (textile)
Supervises and coordinates activities of workers engaged in processing cotton and synthetic raw stock fibers into yarn, applying knowledge of fiber and yarn types, machines, and any combination of processes, such as picking, carding, combing, drawing, roving, spinning, twisting, spooling, and winding: Confers with other department heads to coordinate activities of different departments, determine processes underway and possible changes in production schedule, and availability of workers for shifts. Examines yarn at various processing stages to detect variations from standards and inspects machines to detect malfunctions and damage to weaving surfaces. Directs repair personnel to alter machine setup or to repair or overhaul processing machines to maintain product standards. May creel and doff machines. May set up, adjust, and repair machines. Performs other duties as described under SUPERVISOR (any industry) Master Title. Supervisors of workers engaged in specific yarn processing activities are classified accordingly [SUPERVISOR, CARDING (textile) 680.130-010; SUPERVISOR, PREPARATION DEPARTMENT (textile) 681.130-010; SUPERVISOR, ROVING DEPARTMENT (textile) 689.130-026; SUPERVISOR, SPINNING (textile) 682.130-010; SUPERVISOR, WINDING AND TWISTING DEPARTMENT (textile) 681.130-014].
GOE: 06.01.01 STRENGTH: L GED: R4 M3 L4 SVP: 7 DLU: 86

689.130-038   SUPERVISOR, SPINNING AND WINDING (plastic-synth.)
Supervises and coordinates activities of workers engaged in spinning and winding synthetic fibers, and sets up takeup machines that wind newly extruded synthetic fibers onto pirns: Observes machines, equipment, personnel, and work areas to detect faulty work habits, and to examine synthetic fibers for conformance to standards. Inspects machine parts cleaned and assembled by designated worker to ensure conformance of parts to standard. Confers with specified supervisory personnel regarding production and possible changes in process, personnel, or machines. Interviews vendors and consults catalogs to obtain information on price and availability of parts and equipment. Prepares and submits purchase orders to designated personnel. Checks level of nitrogen in tanks outside plant and telephones supplier to order more nitrogen to maintain nitrogen at specified level. Develops training manual to be used in training of workers. Times roller and chuck speeds of takeup machines that wind newly extruded synthetic fibers onto pirns, using timing light and stopwatch. Confers with and assists other workers in changing gear ratios of winding drive mechanism, using handtools, according to style of yarn to be processed and setup specifications. Performs other duties as described under SUPERVISOR (any industry) Master Title.
GOE: 06.02.01 STRENGTH: M GED: R4 M2 L3 SVP: 7 DLU: 86

689.132-010   SUPERVISOR, BURLING AND JOINING (textile)
Supervises and coordinates activities of workers engaged in inspecting base cloth for weaving defects, and in manually weaving ends of length of papermaker's felt together to facilitate further processing: Trains workers in burling cloth, hand weaving cloth, and operating sewing machine to join ends together. Reviews production schedules to determine felt type to be joined or base cloth to be inspected. Confers with other supervisors to resolve work problems that slow production. Pulls cloth length over roller and examines cloth for defects, such as mispicks and filling breaks. Pulls defective yarn from cloth and reweaves defective area, using needle, yarn, and scissors. Performs other duties as described under SUPERVISOR (any industry) Master Title.
GOE: 06.02.01 STRENGTH: M GED: R4 M3 L4 SVP: 6 DLU: 86

689.132-014   SUPERVISOR, FIBER-LOCKING (textile)
Supervises and coordinates activities of workers engaged in fiberlocking (needle punching) materials, such as batting and base cloth, to produce papermaker's felt: Reviews production schedule to determine processing priorities. Trains workers in operation of equipment, such as *garnett machines*, blending machines, and fiberlock machines. Patrols work area to ensure processing of fabric is according to specifications. Listens to machines to detect malfunctioning parts and reports malfunction to maintenance personnel. Confers with other supervisory personnel to ensure even flow of work through departments. Performs other duties as described under SUPERVISOR (any industry) Master Title.
GOE: 06.02.01 STRENGTH: L GED: R4 M3 L4 SVP: 6 DLU: 86

689.134-010   CLOTH-GRADER SUPERVISOR (textile)
Supervises and coordinates activities of CLOTH GRADERS (textile) engaged in classifying cloth according to number of defects. Trains workers in inspecting and grading cloth according to company standards. Maintains production records. Performs other duties as described under SUPERVISOR (any industry) Master Title.
GOE: 06.01.01 STRENGTH: L GED: R4 M3 L3 SVP: 7 DLU: 77

689.134-014   SUPERVISOR, LACE TEARING (tex. prod., nec)
Supervises and coordinates activities of workers engaged in separating, inspecting, and winding lace bands: Trains workers in machine operation. Verifies setup and adjustment of machines and equipment. Examines lace to determine first quality products, following standards for various types. Performs other duties as described under SUPERVISOR (any industry) Master Title.
GOE: 06.02.01 STRENGTH: L GED: R4 M3 L3 SVP: 7 DLU: 77

689.134-018   SUPERVISOR, PRODUCT INSPECTION (textile)
Supervises and coordinates activities of workers engaged in inspecting textile products for weaving, printing, and finishing defects: Trains workers in work methods and procedures. Examines malfunctioning machines and requisitions replacement for defective equipment. May supervise packaging of products [PACKAGING SUPERVISOR (any industry)]. Performs other duties as described under SUPERVISOR (any industry) Master Title.
GOE: 06.02.01 STRENGTH: L GED: R4 M2 L3 SVP: 6 DLU: 77

689.134-022   SUPERVISOR, QUILTING (textile)
Supervises and coordinates activities of workers engaged in quilting material used for articles, such as quilts, sleeping bags, and work gloves: Trains workers in operation of machines. Inspects machines to detect malfunctions and notifies SEWING-MACHINE REPAIRER (any industry) of repairs and adjustments. Replaces damaged parts, such as needles and bobbins, using handtools. Performs other duties as described under SUPERVISOR (any industry) Master Title.
GOE: 06.02.01 STRENGTH: M GED: R4 M2 L3 SVP: 6 DLU: 77

689.134-026   SUPERVISOR, LABORATORY (textile)
Supervises and coordinates activities of workers engaged in testing lap, sliver, roving, and yarn for conformance to processing standards and assists workers in performing laboratory tests: Confers with plant personnel to develop testing schedule and to modify processing standards for producing new yarn types requested by customer. Coordinates activities, such as resolving customer complaints of defective yarn, inspecting, calibrating, and maintaining laboratory equipment, and identifying causes of substandard lap, roving, sliver, and yarn. Performs laboratory procedures to test lap, sliver, roving, and yarn for conformance to processing standards, such as evenness of lap and tensile strength of yarn. Performs other duties as described under SUPERVISOR (any industry) Master Title.
GOE: 02.04.01 STRENGTH: M GED: R4 M3 L4 SVP: 6 DLU: 86

689.137-010   SUPERVISOR, SEWING DEPARTMENT (carpet & rug)
Supervises and coordinates activities of workers engaged in winding, braiding, and sewing operations in manufacture of braided rug: Schedules winding of yarn onto suitable packages for braiding process. Issues instructions, such as color of thread and type of stitch to use and size of completed rug. Examines products during fabricating for conformance to customer specifications. Performs other duties as described under SUPERVISOR (any industry) Master Title.
GOE: 06.02.01 STRENGTH: L GED: R4 M3 L3 SVP: 6 DLU: 77

689.137-014   SUPERVISOR, TUBING (textile)
Supervises and coordinates activities of workers engaged in inspecting and winding printed fabric in tubing department: Confers with PRODUCTION PLANNER (profess. & kin.) 012.167-050 and consults work order to determine sequence of cloth styles to process. Directs delivery of specified fabric to work stations. Informs CLOTH EXAMINER, MACHINE (textile) 689.685-038 of quantity of cloth to wind onto tubes and of customer quality specifications. Oversees inspection of cloth being processed to ensure detection of defects, such as wrinkles, seams, and color variations. Submits samples of cloth to COLORIST (profess. & kin.) 022.161-014 for shade matching. Occasionally weighs and labels special orders for shipping. Performs other duties as described under SUPERVISOR (any industry) Master Title.
GOE: 06.02.01 STRENGTH: H GED: R3 M2 L2 SVP: 6 DLU: 86

689.260-010   MACHINE FIXER (textile) alternate titles: fixer; machine repairer
Sets up, and adjusts yarn-manufacturing and processing machines, using charts, oral instructions, and knowledge of machine operation: Changes and adjusts gears, pulleys, rollers, thermal units, *false-twist spindles,* and guides according to type of sliver or yarn processed, type of wind, draft, or number of twists per inch, using handtools. Verifies adjustments, using gauges and instruments, such as voltage and calibrating machines, tensiometer, tachometer, and densimeter. Patrols work area to detect operating defects. Inspects machine to determine cause of faulty operation, utilizing report on defects, and adjusts machine. Replaces worn and broken parts, such as spindles, rollers, guides, gears, pulleys, tape, and belts, using handtools. Lubricates moving parts and wearing surfaces, using oilcan and grease gun. Cleans machines, using airhose, cleaning solution, and rags. May overhaul machines and plumb spindles, following plant schedule. May erect new machines [MILLWRIGHT (any industry) 638.281-

018]. May be designated according to machines maintained as Card Fixer (textile); Comber Fixer (textile); Garnett Fixer (tex. prod., nec); Gill-Box Fixer (textile); Quiller-Machine Fixer (textile); Spinning-Frame Fixer (textile). May be designated: Tufting-Machine Fixer (carpet & rug); Twisting-Frame Fixer (textile); Winder Fixer (textile); Yarn-Texturing Machine Fixer (textile).
GOE: 06.01.02 STRENGTH: M GED: R4 M2 L3 SVP: 6 DLU: 80

689.260-014 QUILTER FIXER (tex. prod., nec)
Sets up, repairs, and adjusts quilting machines, utilizing knowledge of machine construction and function, and charts: Analyzes charts to determine adjustments necessary to effect change in quilting design. Selects cams that will alter movement of machine bed and needle stroke to produce specified design, and installs cams on machine, using wrenches. Synchronizes looper or shuttle motion with needle stroke, using screwdriver. Listens to machine and observes stitching to locate defects in machine operation. Dismantles machine and repairs broken or defective parts, such as motors, bobbins or loopers, needles, and feed dogs. Turns screws to regulate tension on thread, length of needle stroke, and rate of feed, according to type of fabric or thread. Cleans and oils machines.
GOE: 06.01.02 STRENGTH: L GED: R4 M3 L3 SVP: 6 DLU: 77

689.260-018 SECTION LEADER AND MACHINE SETTER (textile)
Sets up, adjusts, and repairs group of textile machines (usually of one type, called section): Transmits orders of SUPERVISOR (any industry) Master Title of section to workers and ensures that orders and safety rules are followed. Patrols section to inspect work for quality and to determine operating condition of machinery. Reads production meters or tickets and records total number of units produced. Examines laboratory sample reports to determine machine adjustments needed to meet company specifications. Adjusts and repairs machines [MACHINE FIXER (textile) 689.260-010]. Trains new workers and assigns workers to stations. May be designated according to section as Section Leader And Machine Setter, Cards (textile); Section Leader And Machine Setter, Drawing And Combers (textile); Section Leader And Machine Setter, Opening And Picking (textile); Section Leader And Machine Setter, Roving Frames (textile); Section Leader And Machine Setter, Spinning (textile); Section Leader And Machine Setter, Winding And Twisting (textile).
GOE: 06.01.02 STRENGTH: M GED: R4 M2 L4 SVP: 6 DLU: 80

689.260-022 SECTION LEADER AND MACHINE SETTER, POLISHING (textile)
Sets up, repairs, and adjusts yarn polishing (glazing) machines: Mixes finishing solutions [CHEMICAL MIXER (textile)]. Separates thread packages according to color and type to prevent faulty mixing of customer orders.
GOE: 06.01.02 STRENGTH: M GED: R3 M3 L3 SVP: 5 DLU: 77

689.260-026 KNITTING-MACHINE FIXER (knitting)
Sets up, adjusts, and repairs knitting machines to knit hose, garments, and cloth according to specifications, using knowledge of machine function: Reads work order and confers with supervisor or engineer to determine knitting machine setup. Inserts cams, links, *buttons,* or *needle jacks* in pattern chain to set up machine to knit hose, garment, or cloth according to pattern design chart. Observes operation of machine and examines knitted material to detect defects. Turns setscrews and handwheels to adjust machine parts, such as gears and cams, and to synchronize *yarn carriers,* needles, dividers, and *sinkers.* Repairs and replaces machine parts, using handtools. Aligns and straightens needles, sinkers, and dividers, using pliers. Cleans and oils machines. May only repair and adjust knitting machines and be designated Line Fixer (knitting).
GOE: 06.01.02 STRENGTH: L GED: R4 M3 L3 SVP: 7 DLU: 81

689.280-010 BOX TENDER (plastic-synth.)
Patrols aisle between rayon-spinning (forming and winding) machines to detect malfunctions. Diagnoses causes of failures. Sets up, adjusts, repairs, or replaces units, using handtools.
GOE: 06.01.02 STRENGTH: M GED: R4 M3 L3 SVP: 6 DLU: 77

689.324-010 INSTRUCTOR (textile)
Instructs workers in operation of textile machines and in product inspection techniques, using knowledge of machines and processes: Plans training schedule to ensure workers achieve standard production in specified time. Demonstrates methods of threading and operating machines, examining product for defects, and grading product according to quality standards. Evaluates worker performances to ensure achievement of production standards and maintains progress reports. Observes machines to detect operation malfunctions and notifies designated personnel. May be designated according to specialty as Instructor, Knitting (textile); Instructor, Looping (textile); Instructor, Product Inspection (textile); Instructor, Creeler (textile); Instructor, Warper (textile).
GOE: 06.02.01 STRENGTH: M GED: R3 M2 L2 SVP: 6 DLU: 79

689.360-010 NEEDLE-LOOM SETTER (tex. prod., nec)
Sets up and adjusts looms that produce needle (punched) felt: Selects specified needle boards and bolts them to holders, using wrenches. Changes driving gears to adjust speed of automatic feed and punching mechanisms, using wrenches or turning knobs. Threads *bat* through needle board, attaches bat to rewind spindle, and starts machine. Makes adjustments to maintain weight specifications, and replaces worn or broken needle boards.
GOE: 06.01.02 STRENGTH: L GED: R3 M2 L3 SVP: 6 DLU: 77

689.362-010 NEEDLE-FELT-MAKING-MACHINE OPERATOR (tex. prod., nec)
Sets up and operates battery of machines in tandem to produce needle (punched) felt products from raw materials: Turns screws to adjust comb and

stripper rolls of *garnett machine* to produce specified *bat I.* Installs specified needle board into needle loom to punch together loose bats into needle (punched) felt. Turns handwheels to adjust tension between steam heated calender rolls which press down nap and firm felt. Turns handwheels to lower circular knives to trim felt to specified width. Fills size tank, positions automatic spray gun, and turns valve handle on airhose to spray size onto felt. Turns knobs to regulate temperature and blower of drying oven. Aligns and bolts cutting dies in ram and bed of automatic diecutting machine to cut felt into specified forms. Turns knobs to synchronize speed of machines and conveyors. Aligns feed guides. Starts machine, observes operations to detect malfunction, and examines work to determine conformity to specifications. Replaces worn needle boards. Sharpens circular knives with hone. May repair needle boards [NEEDLE-BOARD REPAIRER (tex. prod., nec)]. May assist MAINTENANCE MECHANIC (any industry) in repairing machines.
GOE: 06.02.06 STRENGTH: L GED: R3 M2 L3 SVP: 5 DLU: 77

689.364-010 STROBOSCOPE OPERATOR (textile) alternate titles: stroboroma operator; strobotac operator
Verifies speed of spindles and travelers on yarn twisting and spinning frames, using stroboscope, and makes minor adjustments: Turns knob to adjust stroboscope setting to spindle speed specifications. Directs stroboscope light beam onto revolving bobbin. Observes bobbin and traveler to detect illusion of movement indicating variance between spindle speed and speed setting of stroboscope. Turns knob to synchronize stroboscope light oscillations with speed of malfunctioning spindle, and records incorrect spindle speed as shown on stroboscope r.p.m. dial. Makes adjustments, such as tightening screws and removing waste from travelers. Notifies MACHINE FIXER (textile) of machines requiring repairs, such as replacement of spindles and travelers. May use twist-test machine to determine twist (number of turns per inch) in yarn to verify accuracy of machine setup. May test yarn tension, using tensiometer.
GOE: 06.03.01 STRENGTH: L GED: R3 M2 L3 SVP: 5 DLU: 77

689.364-014 PROCESS CONTROLLER (textile)
Verifies performance of yarn texturing machines for conformance to specifications, using test equipment and instruments: Reviews work order to determine machine to be checked and type of inspection required. Inspects machines for threading problems, such as incorrect placement of yarn and opened feed rollers. Measures operation of machine components, such as oil roller, transverse bar, and rotating shaft of feed roll, to measure operation of machine, using counter, speed indicator, and stopwatch. Observes and records factors, such as heat setting and package tube color of yarn. Determines amount of tension on yarn, using tensioner. Examines friction unit to ensure positioning of belt and to identify defects on unit, and measures speed of unit, using stroboscope. Measures level of humidity, using psychrometer. Compiles data of measurements taken of machine and machine operations and compares actual measurement with measurements from specifications book. Notifies specified personnel of deviations from specifications.
GOE: 06.03.01 STRENGTH: L GED: R3 M3 L3 SVP: 4 DLU: 86

689.366-010 HEAD DOFFER (textile)
Leads activities of workers engaged in doffing spinning frames, applying knowledge of yarn types and duration of spinning process: Transmits instructions from supervisor to workers and observes workers to ensure that procedures, rules, and regulations are followed. Reports work rule infractions to supervisory personnel for resolution. Explains and demonstrates doffing techniques to train new employees, and assists workers in resolving problems. Patrols work area to determine frames requiring doffing. Observes taper (buildup) of yarn on bobbins to determine frame doffing priority, utilizing knowledge of yarn types being processed and length of processing cycle. Posts frame numbers on chalkboard to inform workers of doffing schedule. Verifies accuracy of doffing production reports and submits report to supervisory personnel. *Pieces up* yarn breaks detected. Maintains supply of spinning bobbins and doff boxes (attachments for handtrucks) for workers to facilitate doffing of frames. May perform duties of absent workers.
GOE: 06.01.01 STRENGTH: L GED: R3 M2 L3 SVP: 4 DLU: 86

689.380-010 EMBLEM DRAWER-IN (tex. prod., nec) alternate titles: wrapper
Sets up loom preparatory to embroidering emblems on uniforms or other items: Arranges needles according to spacing designated by operator of loom and tightens lock bolt, using wrench. Removes spools of thread from machine spindles and replaces spools with thread of specified weight and color. Wraps (loops) thread around tension bar specified number of times. Guides threads through series of rods and threads needle, using hooked instrument. Pulls out loose ends of thread by hand after several stitches have been made. Repeats operation each time uniform, emblem, or color of thread is changed.
GOE: 06.01.02 STRENGTH: L GED: R3 M2 L3 SVP: 3 DLU: 77

689.382-010 AUTOMATIC-PAD-MAKING-MACHINE OPERATOR (tex. prod., nec) alternate titles: border-machine operator
Sets up and operates battery of machines to produce quilted and laminated padding from batting: Places rolls of batting and burlap base in feed holders of machine. Aligns and threads ends of material through machine. Turns handwheels to heat calender roll. Threads needles of quilting machine that binds batting to base to form padding. Turns air valve that activates stationary spray gun to spray binder to surface of padding. Aligns end of second roll of batting to sprayed surface under pressure roll to form laminated padding. Turns

handwheels to position circular knives that trim padding to specified width. Turns knobs to adjust electric eye controlled mechanism which automatically cuts padding to specified length, drops on layer of gauze, and cuts and laps gauze over pads. Starts spray gun that sizes pad to hold covering in place. Turns knobs to synchronize speed of machine and starts machine. Replaces broken needles. Fills tanks with specified size. Places rolls of narrow reinforcing batting in holder and guides under needles when specified. Sews together burlap and gauze, and laps together batting to form continuous roll.
GOE: 06.02.18 STRENGTH: M GED: R3 M2 L3 SVP: 4 DLU: 77

689.384-010 CLOTH TESTER, QUALITY (textile) alternate titles: laboratory assistant

Determines physical properties of greige and finished cloth, employing standardized tests, equipment, and procedure: Measures width of cloth with ruler. Guides electric knife along markings on cloth to cut fabric samples for testing. Weighs sample on grain scales and converts grain weight into desired units, using mathematical tables. Counts number of warp and filling per unit space, using pick counter. Positions cloth sample between jaws of testing machine and moves machine controls to apply force necessary to rupture sample and determine tensile strength of cloth. Sews across sample, using portable sewing machine, and examines stitching through magnifying lens to detect threads broken by sewing machine needle. Creases sample under controlled conditions and places sample in clamp on crease recovery tester to determine cloth resiliency to creasing. Records test results and reports variation from standards to MANAGER, QUALITY CONTROL (profess. & kin.). In addition, may perform other tests, such as tear test, crimp test, fabric bow test, abrasion test, bursting test, heat transmission test, permeability test, and water repellency test.
GOE: 06.03.01 STRENGTH: L GED: R3 M3 L3 SVP: 4 DLU: 77

689.384-014 LABORATORY TESTER (textile) alternate titles: roving tester, laboratory; yarn tester

Tests textile fibers and yarn at any stage in yarn-manufacturing process to determine conformance to standards: Collects samples from machines, gathers samples from carts, or receives samples at work station. Records information regarding samples on company forms, and identifies samples with tags prior to testing. Computes twists per inch in yarn samples, using formula and readings from twist counter. Feeds yarn, roving, or sliver into evenness tester that detects and records variations in weight on printout sheet. Winds specified length of yarn onto skein winder and removes skeins from winder. Weighs skeins of yarn on balance scale and obtains yarn number (measure of fineness) from dial or chart. Breaks individual strands or skeins of yarn with break tester to determine strength of yarn. Winds yarn on black panel for inspection, compares evenness and number of slubs and neps in yarn with standard photographs, and assigns grade. Weighs fiber sample on balance scale before and after drying and determines percentage of water content (moisture regain) by computation or by consulting chart. Records results of tests, compares results with company standards, and reports variations from standards to lab supervisor or MANAGER, QUALITY CONTROL (profess. & kin.) 012.167-014. Records waste produced by departments. May receive defective yarn returned by customer and test yarn to determine whether company purchased defective materials, defects occurred during company processing, or customer caused defects to occur. May perform standardized chemical tests to determine amount of oil or size in yarn. May be designated according to specialty as Yarn-Weight-And-Strength Tester (textile).
GOE: 06.03.01 STRENGTH: L GED: R3 M3 L3 SVP: 4 DLU: 79

689.387-010 CLOTH GRADER (textile) alternate titles: cloth classer; hand inspector; seconds grader; seconds inspector; table inspector

Classifies cloth into grades according to number of defects: Examines cloth for defects marked in previous inspection and determines whether corrections can be made to restore cloth to standard quality. Cuts defects from cloth with scissors or routes cloth to mending, dyeing, or refinishing department for reprocessing. Classifies cloth that cannot be restored to first quality according to standards for various grades. Records disposition of cloth rehandled. May inform weaving room of repeated imperfections requiring loom adjustments.
GOE: 06.03.01 STRENGTH: L GED: R3 M1 L2 SVP: 5 DLU: 77

689.564-010 CARPET INSPECTOR, FINISHED (carpet & rug)

Examines finished carpeting for weaving or tufting defects, variations in color and finish, soil, and uneven shearing: Pulls carpeting from roll onto floor to facilitate inspection. Walks or crawls over carpeting, feeling and scanning carpeting for defects. Repairs weaving defects and cleans soiled areas or notifies BURLER (carpet & rug; textile) to make repairs. Marks finishing and shearing defects with chalk. Notifies respective departments of defects. Measures length of carpeting or pile height for conformance to specifications, using ruler and tape measure. Records yardage on work ticket. Compares carpeting with standard swatches and grades carpeting according to standards for various grades.
GOE: 06.03.02 STRENGTH: L GED: R3 M1 L2 SVP: 4 DLU: 77

689.582-010 PUNCHER (tex. prod., nec)

Operates punching machine, equipped with pantograph mechanism, to punch pattern designs in rolls of paper or plastic which control stitching operations of automatic embroidery machines: Positions and tacks cartoon (enlarged drawing of pattern) onto pantograph pattern board and mounts roll of paper in holder. Pulls levers to start and to regulate speed of machine, and to move needles

against pattern roll. Guides pantograph pointer over cartoon to activate punching needles that perforate paper roll to form embroidery pattern roll. Marks identifying information on punched roll, using crayon. May place roll of paper in holder. May operate machine equipped with mechanism that simultaneously stitches sample design and punches pattern in paper. May place punched roll in machine that automatically produces copies of design.
GOE: 06.02.09 STRENGTH: L GED: R3 M1 L2 SVP: 4 DLU: 77

689.585-010 BLANKET-CUTTING-MACHINE OPERATOR (tex. prod., nec)

Tends machine that spreads cloth and cuts it into blanket lengths, folds each piece, and stacks folded lengths onto handtruck: Pushes truck of cloth into feeding position and threads cloth through scray, under knife, and into cloth-spreading attachment. Turns thumbscrew to adjust cloth-spreading attachment for specified blanket length. Positions empty truck over hydraulic jack at delivery end of machine and moves lever to elevate truck into receiving position. Releases safety catch from knife and pushes button to start machine. Straightens unevenly piled blankets and adjusts height of truck to facilitate stacking. Records style, color, and number of blanket lengths cut. Works as member of team.
GOE: 06.04.05 STRENGTH: M GED: R2 M1 L2 SVP: 3 DLU: 77

689.585-014 FOLDING-MACHINE OPERATOR (textile) alternate titles: cloth folder, machine; flat-folding-machine operator; folder, machine; hooking-machine operator

Tends machine that folds cloth into uniform lengths preparatory to inspecting, wrapping, or packing: Pushes roll of cloth onto machine brackets and threads cloth through feed rollers, over and under tension rollers, and through slot of folding bar. Inserts end of cloth under clamps on machine tables and sets yardage clock at zero. Starts machine and observes folding to detect seams in cloth. Stops machine and ravels seams with fingers. Depresses pedal to raise clamps, releasing cut of cloth, and removes cloth from machine. Records yardage on production ticket and attaches ticket to cloth. May count folds to determine yardage in each cut of cloth. May be designated according to material folded as Silk Folder (textile).
GOE: 06.04.05 STRENGTH: M GED: R2 M1 L1 SVP: 2 DLU: 77

689.585-018 STRINGING-MACHINE TENDER (tex. prod., nec) alternate titles: clipping, stringing, and turning machine tender

Tends machine that inserts gathering strings in hem of bags and turns bags: Pulls bags joined by connecting threads across feed trough and hooks end bag on feeding apron of machine. Moves lever to start machine that automatically clips joining thread between bags, inserts gathering strings in hems, and turns bags. Removes bags from discharge end of machine, examines bags for stringing flaws, and stacks bags in carton for packing. Places defective bags aside for repair. Draws thread from cones through machine guides and eyes of needles to thread stringing needles. Records number of bags processed.
GOE: 06.04.05 STRENGTH: S GED: R2 M1 L2 SVP: 2 DLU: 77

689.587-010 NUMBERER AND WIRER (textile) alternate titles: card-cutter helper

Numbers punched and laced *Jacquard loom* pattern cards according to prescribed sequence, using pencil or hand numbering device. Wires together series of cards in prescribed sequence to make pattern chain, using handtools.
GOE: 06.04.06 STRENGTH: L GED: R2 M1 L1 SVP: 2 DLU: 77

689.662-010 NEEDLE-LOOM OPERATOR (tex. prod., nec)

Sets up and operates loom with assistance of NEEDLE-LOOM-OPERATOR HELPER (tex. prod., nec) 586.686-022 to produce needle (punched) felt: Selects and bolts specified needle boards to loom holders, according to work order, using wrenches. Installs speed gears or turns knob to synchronize speed of feeder with action of needle board. Threads *bat* through needle board and attaches bat to rewind spindle. Starts machine, watches feed gauge, and stops machine when specified length of felt is produced. Measures thickness and width of felt, using gauge and tape, to ensure product meets specifications. Cuts finished felt from roll with knife or shear. Replaces worn or broken needle boards. May place roll of textile base into feed holder and textile base roll with felt bat to produce textile backed felt. May glue or sew together ends of base to form continuous roll.
GOE: 06.02.06 STRENGTH: M GED: R3 M2 L3 SVP: 5 DLU: 80

689.662-014 STRIPE MATCHER (knitting)

Operates machine to cut, align, and sew stripes parallel in tubular cloth: Turns screw to secure circular cutting blade (horizontal or vertical) in cutting position and adjusts guides according to specified cloth width. Positions cloth at feed-end of machine and threads cloth through machine units onto *swing-folding attachment,* or joins supply end to leader, using portable sewing machine. Starts machine that cuts cloth to open width, aligns stripes parallel, seams edges together, and trims excess cloth from edges. Observes operation for defective cutting, stitching, or misalignment of stripes. Repairs sewing defects, using sewing machine, and reports malfunctions to maintenance personnel. Ravels seams to separate cloth lots and records yardage processed onto cloth ticket.
GOE: 06.02.05 STRENGTH: M GED: R3 M2 L2 SVP: 3 DLU: 77

689.665-010 STRAP BUCKLER, MACHINE (garment)

Tends machine that threads lingerie or foundation garment shoulder strap material through buckle (slide) and link to make adjustable shoulder straps: Places

tubes of buckles and links on machine racks and presses pedal to push buckle and link into holders under vertical threading rod. Positions strap between rod and holders and presses pedal to lower rod that forces material through openings in buckle and link. Loops strap over hook in rod and presses pedal to raise rod that pulls strap back through buckle. Ties specified number of straps into bundle.
GOE: 06.04.05 STRENGTH: S GED: R2 M1 L2 SVP: 3 DLU: 77

689.665-014 THREAD-CUTTER TENDER (tex. prod., nec)
Tends machine that cuts and removes threads which connect designs on machine-embroidered fabrics or bands of knitted lace: Stitches length of embroidered fabric to leader, using stitching machine, or wraps draw threads around takeup bar and inserts ends of bands between stop-motion devices, guides, and rollers. Adjusts clearances, starts machine, and guides fabric so as to break threads. Pulls out loose thread and turns fabric over to repeat operation. Cleans threads from machine, using brush. May be designated according to operation performed as Lace Breaker (tex. prod., nec); Lace Separator (tex. prod., nec); Lace Stripper (tex. prod., nec).
GOE: 06.04.05 STRENGTH: L GED: R3 M1 L2 SVP: 2 DLU: 77

689.665-018 VACUUM-TANK TENDER (textile)
Tends vacuum tanks that collect fiber and lint stripped from carding and other textile machines: Obtains information from CARD STRIPPER (textile) concerning type of fiber stripped to prevent mixing of different fibers. Pulls lever to create vacuum in tank and to relieve vacuum when tank is filled or stripping is completed. Opens door at bottom of tank to dump fiber and lint into handtruck. Pushes handtruck onto scales and records weight.
GOE: 06.04.16 STRENGTH: M GED: R2 M1 L1 SVP: 2 DLU: 77

689.667-010 RUG INSPECTOR I (carpet & rug)
Examines finished fiber rugs for defects: Examines selvage and binding and inspects rug for discolorations, mispicks, loose weaves, creases, dirt, grease, knots, and loose ends. Determines when rugs cannot be repaired and classifies rugs as seconds. Prepares report on flaws and number of rugs in load.
GOE: 06.03.02 STRENGTH: L GED: R2 M1 L2 SVP: 3 DLU: 77

689.682-010 LOOPER (knitting)
Operates *looping machine* to close opening in toe of seamless hose or join knitted garment parts: Pulls lever or depresses pedal to rotate horizontal dial containing looping points and start trimming and seaming mechanism. Places each stitch along *looping line* of garment part or one side of toe over looping points, working against movement of dial. Places stitches of second garment part or side of toe over looping points holding corresponding stitches of first garment part or side of toe. Removes looped articles from dial of machine. Examines looped seams for defects. May mark defects with crayon. May thread machine, using tweezers. When looping contour collars to body of garment, places stitches on looping points in sequence which will curve collar to body of garment. May be designated according to article looped as Garment Looper (knitting); Hosiery Looper (knitting).
GOE: 06.02.06 STRENGTH: L GED: R3 M1 L2 SVP: 4 DLU: 77

689.682-014 NEEDLE-PUNCH-MACHINE OPERATOR (textile)
Operates machine and equipment to *stitch-bond* synthetic fibers to scrim (webbing) to produce nonwoven fabric: Turns dials on control panel to regulate conveyor speeds, feed rate of scrim and fiber stock through machine, roll pressure, and steam in rollers. Adjust compression rollers following thickness specifications. Starts machine and observes operation to detect defects, such as broken needles, folds or lines in webbing, and fabric contamination. Moves mechanism on hopper to regulate flow and weight of fiber stock feeding into machine. Replaces broken needles, using handtools.
GOE: 06.04.05 STRENGTH: L GED: R2 M1 L2 SVP: 3 DLU: 77

689.682-018 SPLICING-MACHINE OPERATOR (tex. prod., nec) alternate titles: splicer
Operates sewing machine to splice (join) ends of partially filled spools of tire cord: Places spools of spliced cord on spindles of machine that winds cord from one spool to another. Pushes and pulls sewing machine along overhead tracks to each machine spindle. Positions ends of cord under sewing head. Depresses pedal to activate machine and splice ends of cord together.
GOE: 06.02.05 STRENGTH: L GED: R2 M1 L1 SVP: 4 DLU: 77

689.682-022 STITCHER (tex. prod., nec)
Operates machine to embroider decorative design on fabric: Positions and tacks pattern sheet onto pantograph drawing board. Pulls levers to engage needle and shuttle rails against cloth and to regulate stitching speed. Depresses pedal to start machine and guides pantograph pointer over pattern. Removes embroidered cloth from machine. Inserts thread, needles, cloth, and backing into embroidery machine frame and applies protective and stiffening solutions to cloth, using brush.
GOE: 06.02.05 STRENGTH: L GED: R3 M2 L2 SVP: 4 DLU: 77

689.684-010 BURLER (carpet & rug; textile) alternate titles: cloth picker; knot picker, cloth; slub picker; string picker
Examines fabric for weaving defects, using power-driven examining machine, and repairs defects, using burling iron (tweezers), needle and thread, tufting device, and scissors: Pulls fabric over rollers, down over inspection board, and wraps cloth end around powered takeup beam or tube. Depresses pedal to start machine that moves fabric over inspection board, and scans and feels fabric for defects, such as burls, slubs, loose threads, mispicks, defective pile or soils.

Stops machine and trims loose threads with scissors and pulls out defective yarn and pile with burling iron. Reweaves mispicks and inserts pile or tufts as specified, using needle or tufting device. Removes soils from carpeting, using brush and cleaning chemicals. May record yardage inspected and repaired. May doff rolls of fabric from machine, using hoist.
GOE: 06.03.02 STRENGTH: L GED: R3 M1 L2 SVP: 3 DLU: 77

689.684-014 DRAWER-IN, STITCH-BONDING MACHINE (textile)
Pulls thread through machine parts to arrange ends for *stitch-bonding*, according to company standards and instructions: Mounts specified spools of thread on spindles and draws ends through guides and stop-motion devices, using hook. Observe threads to ensure ends are positioned as directed.
GOE: 06.04.05 STRENGTH: L GED: R2 M1 L1 SVP: 2 DLU: 77

689.684-018 LEASE PICKER (textile)
Separates sections of tangled threads from salvaged beams to establish lease and strips defective filling from quills: Positions beam onto holding rack, using electric overhead chain hoist. Pulls and cuts knotted sections of yarn to align and separate layers of yarn on beam, using hand shears. Tapes yarn ends to secure alignment on beam prior to establishing lease. Separates alternating strands of yarn between thumb and index finger and places *lease strings* between sheds and repeats process to establish specified lease. Ties lease strings to secure yarn. Wraps protective paper around beam and attaches identifying tag to beam. Removes defective filling from quills [BOBBIN-CLEANING-MACHINE OPERATOR (textile) 689.686-014].
GOE: 06.04.27 STRENGTH: M GED: R3 M1 L2 SVP: 3 DLU: 86

689.685-010 BALL-FRINGE-MACHINE OPERATOR (tex. prod., nec)
Tends machine that automatically cuts bunch of yarn ends, ties ends with wire to loops woven in tape, and winds completed material on spools to form ball fringe.
GOE: 06.04.05 STRENGTH: L GED: R2 M1 L1 SVP: 3 DLU: 77

689.685-014 BLOCKER (narrow fabrics; nonmet. min.)
Tends blocker (winding) machine that winds narrow fabrics, such as tape or braid, into rolls: Moves flange into position on winding shaft to block (even) fabric as fabric winds onto shaft, or guides fabric onto shaft by hand. Depresses pedal to start and control speed of machine. Scans fabric for weaving defects, holes, and soils. Cuts out defects, using scissors. Secures end of roll with staple, gummed tape, or label. Records number of cuts in each roll. May press blocking stick against fabric to hold fabric firm during winding. May wind paper liner between layers of fabric. May tend machine equipped with traverse guide or wind lace onto spools and be designated Spooler (narrow fabrics; tex. prod., nec). May be designated according to material blocked as Ribbon Blocker (narrow fabrics); Tape Winder (narrow fabrics; nonmet. min.).
GOE: 06.04.05 STRENGTH: L GED: R2 M1 L2 SVP: 2 DLU: 77

689.685-018 BOBBIN PRESSER (tex. prod., nec)
Tends hydraulic power press, steam oven, and blowers that shrink threads and temper brass bobbins for use on Levers lace machines: Loads yarn-filled bobbins on fixture posts, fastens cover in place, and positions loaded fixture on press bed. Pulls lever that lowers ram to compress thread and straighten bobbin. Tightens cover nut to prevent expansion when pressure is removed. Sets temperature controls and deposits damp cloths in oven to produce humidity. Places loaded fixture in oven to shrink threads and temper bobbin metal. Removes and cools fixture, using blowers. Removes and delivers bobbins to THREADER (tex. prod., nec).
GOE: 06.04.19 STRENGTH: M GED: R2 M1 L2 SVP: 2 DLU: 77

689.685-022 BOBBIN STRIPPER (tex. prod., nec)
Tends stripper that removes thread residue from brass bobbins to prepare bobbins for rewinding: Loads bobbins on shaft of stripping device and ties thread ends to reel at bottom of stripper. Pulls lever to start device that strips thread from bobbins and winds thread onto reel. Removes bobbins from shaft and holds bobbins in front of light to detect thread particles clinging to base or sides of bobbin. Inserts *searcher* between disks to remove thread particles.
GOE: 06.04.05 STRENGTH: L GED: R2 M1 L1 SVP: 2 DLU: 77

689.685-026 BOUFFANT-CURTAIN-MACHINE TENDER (tex. prod., nec)
Tends automatic sewing machine that fabricates novelty curtains: Mounts rolls of ruffle material on machine holders and threads material through machine guides and under sewing mechanisms. Selects thread according to curtain color and threads machine. Positions curtain panel under sewing mechanisms and depresses pedal that gathers and stitches ruffles to panel and hems curtain top to form rod insert. Observes sewing to detect defective stitching and reports machine malfunctions. Works as member of three person team to fabricate curtains.
GOE: 06.04.05 STRENGTH: L GED: R3 M1 L2 SVP: 4 DLU: 77

689.685-030 BOW-MAKER-MACHINE TENDER, AUTOMATIC (tex. prod., nec)
Tends automatic machine that fabricates decorative bows from ribbons: Turns setscrews to adjust machine according to bow type and size, fills machine hopper with staples. Places roll of ribbon on spindle and draws ribbon through machine guides and rollers. Turns valve to activate pneumatic bow ejection device. Presses button to start machine that forms, staples, and ejects bows.
GOE: 06.04.05 STRENGTH: L GED: R2 M1 L1 SVP: 3 DLU: 77

689.685-034 BUFFING-WHEEL FORMER, AUTOMATIC (tex. prod., nec)

Tends forming machine that folds, gathers, and presses cloth into groove of *lacing* to produce buffing wheels: Lifts roll of cloth on holder or draws end from box and threads it through guides and over steam pipes. Removes front section of winding drum, places lacing on rod in center of rear section, and positions front section on rod at specified distance from rear section. Pulls cloth over drum and centers it over space between drum sections. Secures cloth edges to pins set across drum. Turns valve to admit steam to pipes to soften material. Turns crank to wind specified amount of cloth around drum. Cuts cloth, using hand shears, and pushes drum between jaws of machine. Presses button to activate jaws that fold and gather cloth into space between drums and press gathered edge between points of lacings. Removes laced buffing material when pressing cycle is complete. Turns dial to control length of pressing cycle, according to style of buffing wheel.
GOE: 06.04.16 STRENGTH: M GED: R2 M1 L2 SVP: 2 DLU: 77

689.685-038 CLOTH EXAMINER, MACHINE (textile) alternate titles: cloth inspector; final inspector; inspection-machine tender; percher; perch-machine inspector

Inspects finished or unfinished cloth for weaving or finishing defects, using power-driven examining frame: Pulls fabric over rollers, down over inspection board, and wraps end around takeup beam or tube, or positions supply truck under *swing-folding attachment*. Sets yardage clock at zero and presses button or pedal that starts movement of cloth over inspection board. Scans cloth for defects, such as grease spots, slubs, mispicks, uneven selvages, and irregularities in color. Marks defects with chalk, thread, or adhesive sticker. Records information, such as defects, cloth style, and yardage inspected. May correct reparable defects, such as soils, slubs, or loose ends, using steel pick, scissors, knife, or cleaning solution. May cut irreparable defects from cloth, using scissors, and sew cloth ends together, using needle and thread or sewing machine. May mount and doff rolls of cloth, using hoist. May grade cloth according to quality, using written standards. May cut or tear strip from end of cloth for sample. May count number of picks per inch, using pick counter. May feel cloth to compare texture with that of sample. When reexamining cloth to verify defects marked by other workers, is designated Rechecker (textile). May be designated according to fabric examined as Asbestos-Cloth Inspector (nonmet. min.); Base-Cloth Inspector (carpet & rug); Greige-Goods Examiner (textile); Knitted-Cloth Examiner (knitting); Lace Inspector (knitting). May be designated: Finished-Cloth Examiner (textile); Inspector, Coated Fabrics (tex. prod., nec); Silk Examiner (textile); Tire-Fabric Inspector (tex. prod., nec); Woolens Examiner (textile).
GOE: 06.03.02 STRENGTH: M GED: R3 M2 L2 SVP: 3 DLU: 80

689.685-042 CLOTH REELER (textile) alternate titles: reeling-machine operator

Tends machine that spreads cloth from rope to open form and reels it preparatory to drying or other processing: Positions drum of roped cloth in front of machine. Draws end of cloth from top of drum and ties or stitches end of cloth to cloth in machine. Starts machine and turns drum by hand to ensure that cloth emerges from drum and winds untwisted onto reel.
GOE: 06.04.06 STRENGTH: M GED: R2 M1 L1 SVP: 2 DLU: 77

689.685-046 CLOTH WINDER (textile) alternate titles: cloth beamer; cloth-roll winder; roller; rolling-machine operator; tuber; winding-machine operator

Tends machine that winds cloth from one form to another to facilitate further processing: Threads cloth from supply truck, bale, or roll through guides and rollers to *takeup roll*, tube, or rod, or sews cloth to end of leader in machine, using sewing machine. Turns handwheel to adjust width guides. Starts machine and observes cloth to detect irregular seams and torn selvages. Pushes lever to control tension on cloth and speed of machine. Cuts out flaws and combines several cuts of cloth to form one roll, sewing ends with portable sewing machine. Records yardage clock reading on order ticket. Removes full rolls from machine onto handtruck by hand or using hoist. May wrap cloth roll for storage or shipping [ROLL COVERER, BURLAP (textile) 929.687-042]. May be designated according to process for which cloth is being wound as Boiling-Off Winder (textile); type of material wound as Carpet Winder (carpet & rug); or type of winding machine used as Reeling-And-Tubing-Machine Operator (textile).
GOE: 06.04.06 STRENGTH: M GED: R2 M1 L1 SVP: 2 DLU: 77

689.685-050 CLOTH-DOUBLING-AND-WINDING-MACHINE OPERATOR (textile) alternate titles: doubling-and-rolling-machine operator; doubling-machine operator; wide-cloth folder

Tends machine that folds (lengthwise) and winds cloth around cardboard center or tube for shipment: Mounts roll of finished cloth onto brackets of machine, and threads end through guide rollers and over triangular folding device, or joins ends to form continuous lengths, using sewing machine. Places cardboard center or tube on winding spindles and starts cloth around cardboard center or tube. Starts machine and pulls uneven selvages into alignment as cloth is folded and wound. Turns handwheel to adjust folding attachment. Cuts out seams and defects marked by CLOTH EXAMINER, MACHINE (textile), using scissors or knife. Doffs full rolls when specified yardage has been wound. Feeds paper measuring tape into roll when winding cloth that stretches. May tend machine fed directly from another machine. May paste sticker showing yardage on outside of each bolt. May fold special lots of cloth by hand.

GOE: 06.04.06 STRENGTH: M GED: R2 M1 L1 SVP: 3 DLU: 77

689.685-054 CRUSHER-AND-BINDER OPERATOR (tex. prod., nec)

Tends machine that grooves balls of twine: Inserts wooden peg through ball of polished twine and places peg with ball into machine. Starts machine and holds end of peg while machine presses groove around ball. Stops machine and removes ball. Unwinds length of twine and ties twine around groove in ball to bind twine. Tucks end of twine under binder, using grooved knife.
GOE: 06.04.06 STRENGTH: L GED: R2 M1 L1 SVP: 2 DLU: 77

689.685-058 DRAWSTRING KNOTTER (tex. prod., nec)

Tends machine that automatically knots and cuts cordage to form drawstrings for laundry bags: Mounts spool of cordage on spindle and threads cordage through knotting and cutting mechanisms. Presses button to start machine that knots and cuts cordage into specified lengths. Hangs drawstrings on rack for further processing.
GOE: 06.04.05 STRENGTH: L GED: R2 M1 L1 SVP: 2 DLU: 77

689.685-062 DROP-WIRE ALIGNER (textile)

Tends machine that aligns *drop-wires* used on loom harnesses: Loads drop wires in machine chutes. Turns handwheel to secure electrostatic bar in machine bed. Starts machine and observes operation for clogs. Clears jams, using screwdriver. Removes bar and wires from machine and replaces damaged wires. Slides metal strip through drop wire eyelets to facilitate attachment to loom harness.
GOE: 06.04.06 STRENGTH: L GED: R1 M1 L1 SVP: 2 DLU: 77

689.685-066 FISHING-LINE-WINDING-MACHINE OPERATOR (tex. prod., nec)

Tends machine to wind fishing line onto spools: Places spool of line on spindle. Slides empty spools on shaft of machine. Turns setscrews to hold spools in place. Threads line through machine handle, over blade and onto empty spools. Depresses pedal to start machine and wind line onto spools. Moves machine handle to guide line back and forth across spool.
GOE: 06.04.05 STRENGTH: L GED: R2 M1 L1 SVP: 2 DLU: 77

689.685-070 HEDDLE CLEANER, MACHINE (textile)

Tends machine that brushes lint from heddles in *harness frames*: Positions frame on feeding mechanism and starts machine that draws frame under brushes. Reverses position of frame on mechanism to complete cleaning cycle. Cleans machine and work area, using rags, broom, and airhose.
GOE: 06.04.39 STRENGTH: H GED: R2 M1 L1 SVP: 2 DLU: 77

689.685-074 HELMET COVERER (hat & cap) alternate titles: cloth-covered-helmet puller; cloth coverer; crimping machine operator

Tends machine that presses and joins cloth covering onto fiber helmet bodies, using either or both of following methods: (1) Positions precemented helmet bodies over mold on machine bed. Positions precut cloth over helmet and pulls cloth taut to remove wrinkles, assisted by co-worker. Depresses pedal that raises machine bed to force helmet into heated head of machine, pressing cloth onto crown of helmet. Releases pedal to lower machine bed and removes helmet. Trims excess cloth from edge of helmet brim, using knife or pinking shears. (2) Inserts covered crown of helmet in mold on bed of machine. Depresses pedal that raises machine bed, to force helmet brim into slot of heated head of machine, pressing cloth over rolled edge of helmet to inside of brim. May be designated according to part of helmet covered as Helmet-Brim Coverer (hat & cap); Helmet-Crown Coverer (hat & cap).
GOE: 06.04.20 STRENGTH: L GED: R2 M1 L1 SVP: 3 DLU: 77

689.685-078 HOOKER INSPECTOR (textile) alternate titles: cloth folder, machine; folding-machine operator; hooker operator; measuring-machine tender; yardage-machine operator; yarding-and-folding-machine operator

Examines cloth for weaving or finishing defects, using *hooker machine* that folds cloth into yard lengths: Pushes roll of cloth onto machine brackets and threads cloth through feed rollers, over and under tension rollers, through slot of folding bar, and inserts end of cloth under clamps on machine table. Turns knob to set yardage counter or counts folds to determine yardage of cloth inspected. Depresses pedal to raise clamp, releasing cut of cloth, and removes cloth from machine. May complete folding of cloth by hand.
GOE: 06.03.02 STRENGTH: M GED: R3 M1 L2 SVP: 3 DLU: 77

689.685-082 KAPOK-AND-COTTON-MACHINE OPERATOR (tex. prod., nec)

Tends machines that automatically clean, dry, cut, and separate raw kapok and cotton fibers for use as pillow, cushion, and quilt filler: Removes wire and burlap from bales and pushes material into hopper of machine. Fastens cloth bag to machine outlet pipe and opens air duct to blow material through machine and into bag. Ties filled bag and transports bag to storage area.
GOE: 06.04.16 STRENGTH: M GED: R2 M1 L2 SVP: 2 DLU: 77

689.685-086 LABEL-CUTTING-AND-FOLDING-MACHINE OPERATOR, AUTOMATIC (narrow fabrics)

Tends machine that cuts, folds cut edges, presses, counts, and packs labels in box: Positions roll of labels on holder and inserts end in feeder mechanism. Positions box at discharge end of machine and turns dial to set counter that stops machine when specified number of labels have been processed. Presses lever to start machine and observes labels to detect defective cutting, folding,

or pressing. Removes defective labels and notifies machine fixer to adjust machine. Removes filled box of labels from machine.
GOE: 06.04.05 STRENGTH: L GED: R2 M1 L1 SVP: 2 DLU: 77

689.685-090 NEEDLE-LOOM TENDER (tex. prod., nec)
Tends loom that produces needle (punched) felt: Places roll of felt *bat* into feed holder of loom. Aligns bat on conveyor, threads end of bat through needle bed of loom, and attaches felt to rewind spindle. Starts machine, watches feed gauge, and stops machine when specified length of felt is produced. Cuts felt from roll with shears. May glue or sew together ends of base to form continuous roll. May place roll of textile base into feed holder and align with bat to produce textile backed felt. May replace defective needle boards, using handtools.
GOE: 06.04.06 STRENGTH: L GED: R3 M1 L2 SVP: 3 DLU: 77

689.685-094 PICK-PULLING-MACHINE OPERATOR (textile) alternate titles: float remover; waste filling remover
Tends machine that pulls *false selvages* and waste filling floats from looped pile fabric: Lifts roll of cloth into feeding position and pins end of cloth to leader in machine. Positions false selvage between feed rollers on each side of machine. Starts machine and observes flow of cloth to detect oblique twist due to unequal tension on cloth. Depresses pedal to release tension on leading selvage and allow lagging selvage to catch up. Doffs rolls of cloth and full boxes of filling waste.
GOE: 06.04.06 STRENGTH: M GED: R2 M1 L1 SVP: 2 DLU: 77

689.685-098 PICK-UP OPERATOR (textile)
Inspects greige corduroy or velvet cloth to detect uncut filling floats, and cuts floats, using pickup knife: Positions truck of cloth at entry end of examining frame and pins end of cloth to leader in machine. Depresses pedal to start machine that passes cloth over inspection board, and scans cloth for uncut floats missed by CORDUROY-CUTTER OPERATOR (textile). Inserts point of pickup knife under floats and cuts threads. Doffs cloth from *swing-folding attachment* onto handtruck. Records yardage of cloth inspected.
GOE: 06.03.02 STRENGTH: L GED: R2 M1 L2 SVP: 2 DLU: 77

689.685-102 QUILT STUFFER, MACHINE (tex. prod., nec)
Tends automatic machine that fills (stuffs) quilt, comforter, and sleeping bag covers with padding: Fastens cover, sewn on three sides, over frame that holds cover open, and places padding on movable track. Presses button to activate mechanisms that stuffs and encloses padding in cover. Works as member of team to stuff covers.
GOE: 06.04.05 STRENGTH: L GED: R2 M1 L2 SVP: 2 DLU: 77

689.685-106 QUILTING-MACHINE OPERATOR (glove & mit.; tex. prod., nec) alternate titles: stitcher
Tends one or more automatic, multiple-needle sewing machines that quilt layers of material used to make articles, such as work gloves, quilts, or padding: Places supply packages on thread holders and draws ends through guides, tensions, and needle eyes, using tweezers. Inserts bobbins in shuttle and draws thread through guides and looper eyes. Pulls boxes of flatfolded material into feeding position or mounts rolls of material onto machine with aid of another worker, using chain hoist or electric lift truck. Threads ends of material under yardage counter and needles, and laps end around takeup rod. Starts machine and observes material sewn to detect broken threads, uneven edges or wrinkles, and defective stitching or stitch design. Rethreads needles, straightens edges of material layers, and regulates tension on material or thread, or notifies maintenance department to adjust machine or alter setup. Cuts material when specified yardage has been quilted, using hand shears or electric knife, and doffs roll. Replaces defective or broken needles. Feels needles to detect rough places and smooths rough area, using sandpaper. May unroll bolts of material onto machine table in specified order of layers and draw ends between feeder rollers.
GOE: 06.04.05 STRENGTH: M GED: R3 M1 L2 SVP: 4 DLU: 77

689.685-110 ROLL TURNER (knitting) alternate titles: tube turner; turner; turning-machine operator
Tends machine that turns circular knitted cloth (knit tubing) inside out and winds cloth into rolls: Pulls end of cloth through turning pipe (slotted metal form). Opens and pulls end of cloth over turning pipe and circular spreader. Inserts turned end under feed rollers and laps end around *takeup roll*. Shifts lever to activate feed and winding rollers. May mount roll of tubing on stand and remove turned rolls.
GOE: 06.04.06 STRENGTH: M GED: R1 M1 L1 SVP: 2 DLU: 77

689.685-114 ROLLING-MACHINE TENDER (knitting) alternate titles: batcher tender
Tends machine that spreads knit tubing from *rope form* to full width and winds it into rolls preparatory to further processing: Pulls knit tubing over spreader and wraps end around *takeup roll*. Starts machine and observes cloth to detect splices. Stops machine and separates joined ends, using shears, or by raveling seams with fingers. Lifts roll out of machine.
GOE: 06.04.05 STRENGTH: M GED: R1 M1 L1 SVP: 2 DLU: 77

689.685-118 SEWING-MACHINE OPERATOR, SPECIAL EQUIPMENT (furniture)
Tends machine that automatically stitches designs to decorate mattress covers and to hold padding in place: Places spools of thread on spindles and draws ends through guides, tensions, and needle eyes. Inserts bobbin in shuttle and draws thread through slot in shuttle wall. Clamps covering material and padding

in frame and places frame in rack under sewing head of machine. Bolts pilot pattern plate on platform beneath frame, using wrench. Places pilot or guide bar extending from frame in guide channels of pilot pattern and starts machine. May move pilot or guide bar by hand. May attach framed cover to pulleys that draw it away from machine as cover is stitched, and guide cover under presser foot by hand to stitch design.
GOE: 06.04.05 STRENGTH: L GED: R2 M1 L2 SVP: 2 DLU: 77

689.685-122 SPLICING-MACHINE OPERATOR, AUTOMATIC (tex. prod., nec) alternate titles: automatic-splicing-machine operator
Tends machine that splices (joins) ends of partially filled spools of tire cord and winds cord from one spool to other: Places spools of cord on machine spindles and pulls ends of cord through holding device under needle of sewing machine. Depresses pedal to start sewing machine that automatically sews ends of cord together, cuts thread at end of sewing cycle, and trims excess ends of cord. Removes spliced ends from holding device. Pulls lever to start spindle that winds spliced cord from one spool to another and to turn table, moving succeeding spindles into splicing position. Doffs full spools of cord as table turns complete circle. Mounts cones of thread on machine spindles, ties thread from spindle to thread in machine, and pulls thread through machine guides, tension springs, and needle to thread sewing machine.
GOE: 06.04.05 STRENGTH: L GED: R2 M1 L1 SVP: 2 DLU: 77

689.685-126 STITCH-BONDING-MACHINE TENDER (textile)
Tends machine that *stitch-bonds* fibrous web to produce reinforced nonwoven fabric: Positions *laps II* at feed end of machine and mats supply end to tailing end in machine. Starts machine and observes operation to detect defective stitching, thread breaks, and exhausting laps. Centers lap on feed apron to prevent lap edge from straying from stitching area. *Pieces up* thread breaks. Doffs machine. Cleans and lubricates machine.
GOE: 06.04.05 STRENGTH: M GED: R2 M1 L1 SVP: 3 DLU: 77

689.685-130 SURGICAL-DRESSING MAKER (protective dev.) alternate titles: pad maker
Tends machine that automatically cuts and folds gauze backing around absorbent cotton to form surgical dressings: Starts machine that cuts gauze and absorbent cotton to size, folds gauze around cotton in prescribed manner to form surgical pad, and ejects pad. Examines ejected pads for size, folding of gauze and defects in absorbent cotton. May pack specified quantity of pads in bags or cartons.
GOE: 06.04.05 STRENGTH: L GED: R2 M1 L1 SVP: 2 DLU: 77

689.685-134 TAPE-FOLDING-MACHINE OPERATOR (rubber goods; tex. prod., nec) alternate titles: bias-binding folder
Tends machine that folds, creases, and winds bias binding tape onto spool or reel: Selects folding guide according to width of tape and fastens guide on machine, using screwdriver. Threads tape through folding guide and pressing rolls, and onto takeup reel. Starts machine and observes folding, creasing, and winding of tape.
GOE: 06.04.05 STRENGTH: L GED: R2 M1 L2 SVP: 3 DLU: 77

689.685-138 TAPE-MAKING-MACHINE OPERATOR (tex. prod., nec) alternate titles: string-glue-and-printing-machine operator; twine operator
Tends machine that glues together strands of paper twine to form tape used for tying packages: Places bobbins of twine on creel. Threads ends of twine through guides, glue rollers, and dryer, and fastens tape to reel. Turns drier thermostat knob to regulate temperature. Starts machine and monitors operation to ensure uniform gluing and drying. May adjust printing device to imprint specified data on tape. May adjust guides to regulate width of tape.
GOE: 06.04.04 STRENGTH: L GED: R2 M1 L2 SVP: 3 DLU: 77

689.685-142 TASSEL-MAKING-MACHINE OPERATOR (tex. prod., nec)
Tends automatic machine that makes tassels for use on draperies and tapestries: Inserts braid strip to which tassels will be tied into machine and fills tube in machine with mixture of rayon and cotton. Depresses pedal to start machine. Removes automatically ejected tassels.
GOE: 06.04.05 STRENGTH: L GED: R2 M1 L1 SVP: 2 DLU: 77

689.685-146 TURNING-MACHINE OPERATOR (tex. prod., nec) alternate titles: turner
Tends machines that turn textile bags right side out by either of following methods: (1) Pulls bag over flattened end of pneumatic pipe. Turns valve to start air suction that turns bag. Drops bag between rollers that convey bag to next process. (2) Turns crank to expand or contract jaws and horizontal sticks of machine according to width of bag. Starts machine and pulls open end of bag over jaws of machine that hold bag open while reciprocating sticks invert bag through open end. May straighten and stack turned bags. May be designated according to type of machine tended as Air-Turning-Machine Feeder (tex. prod., nec); Horizontal-Stick-Turning-Machine Operator (tex. prod., nec).
GOE: 06.04.05 STRENGTH: L GED: R2 M1 L1 SVP: 2 DLU: 77

689.685-150 WATCHER, AUTOMAT (tex. prod., nec) alternate titles: automatic embroidery machine tender
Tends machine that automatically embroiders designs on fabric: Threads roll of perforated cardboard that controls stitching operation through guide rollers and attaches end to automatic control mechanism or inserts punched cards in

machine. Aligns pointers on cloth frame with marks on machine chassis to position frame within prescribed stitching action limits. Turns handwheel to make first stitch, observing needle and shuttle action, thread tension, and alignment of stitch. Makes needed adjustments, such as replacing or rethreading needles and inserting new shuttles. Starts machine. May be designated according to product embroidered as Watcher, Automat, Frame Goods (tex. prod., nec); Watcher, Automat, Long Goods (tex. prod., nec).
GOE: 06.04.05 STRENGTH: L GED: R2 M1 L2 SVP: 4 DLU: 77

689.685-154 WATCHER, PANTOGRAPH (tex. prod., nec)
Tends machine that reproduces embroidery designs on fabric: Stretches lengths of fabric on machine or clamps frames of fabric onto machine. Replaces broken needles and threads, threads needles, and locks needles in holders. Aligns pantograph mechanism, starts machine, and observes operation. Marks stitching errors with pins or tape. May pin applique on fabric to obtain variation in design. May fill and replace shuttles.
GOE: 06.04.05 STRENGTH: L GED: R2 M1 L2 SVP: 4 DLU: 77

689.685-158 YARN-TEXTURING-MACHINE OPERATOR II (textile) alternate titles: bulking-machine operator
Tends machine equipped with air-jet chambers through which continuous filament yarn is processed to change texture and increase bulk of yarn: Creels machine and threads yarn ends through machine guides, over feed rollers, air-jet chambers, *tension guides,* and *drop wires.* Loops end of yarn around takeup spool. Turns valve to start compressed air through jets to blow loops into yarn filaments, changing physical structure of yarn. Observes processing of yarn to detect breaks in yarn and filled takeup spools. Ties broken yarn ends. Pulls lever to stop spindle and doffs full package. Important variables may be indicated by trade name of texturing process or machine used.
GOE: 06.04.16 STRENGTH: L GED: R2 M1 L1 SVP: 3 DLU: 77

689.685-162 TOE PUNCHER (knitting)
Tends toe-punching machine that flattens toe seams of knitted seamless socks, and turns socks right-side out: Slides socks over machine mandrel wrong-side out, aligns toe seam of socks across end of mandrel, and moves lever to activate punch that strikes end of mandrel to flatten toe seam of socks. Inserts hand through opening at end of mandrel, and strips socks from mandrel right-side out. Inserts socks into pneumatic tube for collection in bags.
GOE: 06.04.06 STRENGTH: L GED: R2 M1 L1 SVP: 2 DLU: 86

689.685-166 UTILITY TENDER, CARDING (textile) alternate titles: spare hand, carding
Tends any machine in carding department used in converting cotton and synthetic raw stock into laps, sliver, and roving, working as replacement for absent worker: Tends picking machine that cleans and transforms cotton raw stock into laps [PICKER TENDER (textile) 680.685-074]. Tends cotton carding machine that cleans lap and transforms remaining fibers into sliver [CARD TENDER (nonmet. min.; textile) 680.685-018]. Tends breaker and finish drawing frame that draws out and combines sliver into one of uniform size and weight [DRAWING-FRAME TENDER (textile) 680.685-038]. Tends lap winder that combines several slivers into lap roll for use on combing machines [DRAWING-FRAME TENDER (textile) 680.685-038]. Tends synthetic fiber carding machine that opens and transforms raw stock into sliver [CARD TENDER (nonmet. min.; textile) 680.685-018]. Tends combing machine that cleans lap rolls and transforms remaining fibers into sliver [COMBER TENDER (textile) 680.685-118]. Tends roving frame that draws out and slightly twists sliver into roving [SLUBBER TENDER (textile) 680.685-098]. Feeds bobbin-stripping machine that strips excess roving from bobbins.
GOE: 06.04.06 STRENGTH: M GED: R2 M1 L2 SVP: 3 DLU: 86

689.686-010 AUTOMATIC-PAD-MAKING-MACHINE   OPERATOR HELPER (tex. prod., nec) alternate titles: quilting-machine helper
Performs any combination of following tasks in making padding: Carries or trucks *bats I,* burlap, and size to machines, lifts bats to feed holder of machine and fills tanks with size. Laps gauze over pads, using rod. Stamps identification on pads. Removes finished pads or waste from conveyor and places pads or waste in boxes. May assist operators to set up machine.
GOE: 06.04.05 STRENGTH: M GED: R2 M1 L1 SVP: 2 DLU: 77

689.686-014 BOBBIN-CLEANING-MACHINE OPERATOR (textile) alternate titles: bobbin-stripper; cop breaker; quill cleaner; quill-cleaning-machine operator; quill skinner; quill stripper; tailing hand
Feeds machines that strip unused yarn or roving from packages (bobbins, pirns, and quills): Dumps packages in hopper of machine, using chain hoist, or feeds individual packages into machine that strips yarn or roving from packages with knives, brushes, or compressed air. Presses button to start machine. Pushes or pulls packages with rake or rod to regulate flow of packages from hopper onto feed conveyor. Forces jammed packages into position for processing, using handtool, or removes jammed packages from machine. May dump packages into tumbler that removes yarn from packages by agitation, using chain hoist. May transfer cleaned packages to storage area, using handtruck.
GOE: 06.04.06 STRENGTH: M GED: R1 M1 L1 SVP: 2 DLU: 79

689.686-018 CUTTING-MACHINE OFFBEARER (tex. prod., nec)
Removes cut pieces of textile bag material from cutting machine and places material on handtruck. Measures random samples to determine if machine is

cutting material as specified. Stops machine if cutting does not meet specifications and notifies CUTTING-MACHINE OPERATOR (tex. prod., nec). Folds bags if machine is not automatic. May be designated according to type of material handled as Cotton-Bag-Cutting-Machine Offbearer (tex. prod., nec).
GOE: 06.04.05 STRENGTH: L GED: R2 M1 L1 SVP: 2 DLU: 77

689.686-022 DOFFER (textile)
Doffs bobbins of yarn from spindles of spinning, twisting, or roving (slubber) frames: Pushes button to stop machine and depresses pedal to lower ring bar, allowing yarn to wind around base of spindle to facilitate restarting. Removes full bobbins of yarn from machine spindles, deposits yarn in handtruck, and places empty bobbins on spindles of machine. Releases pedal to raise ring bar, starts machine, and *pieces up* breaks in roving or ties breaks in yarn ends. Records information, such as doff time, date, and initials to complete company form. Applies grease or oil to rings, using finger or oilcan. May change travelers [TRAVELER CHANGER (textile) 682.687-010]. May brush waste from machine. May be designated according to machine doffed as Slubber Doffer (textile); Spinning Doffer (textile); Twister Doffer (textile).
GOE: 06.04.06 STRENGTH: M GED: R2 M1 L2 SVP: 2 DLU: 79

689.686-026 FRAME CHANGER (textile) alternate titles: roving changer; slubber-frame changer; speeder-frame changer; spinning-frame changer; twisting-frame changer
Replaces sliver cans or bobbins to change type of sliver, roving, or yarn to be run on slubber, speeder, spinning, or twisting frames. Threads end of sliver, roving, or yarn through rollers and guides of machine. May change gears or travelers on spinning frames.
GOE: 06.04.06 STRENGTH: L GED: R2 M1 L1 SVP: 2 DLU: 77

689.686-030 HAIR-SPINNING-MACHINE OPERATOR (leather mfg.)
Feeds and unloads various machines that winnow, shred, fluff, card, spin, or otherwise process animal hair performing any of following duties: Opens bales of hair and places hair in hopper. Forks hair into hopper by hand. Hand feeds hair rope stock into machine. Unloads bales, mats, rope stock, or other products from machines. Cleans machines and work area.
GOE: 06.04.05 STRENGTH: H GED: R1 M1 L1 SVP: 1 DLU: 77

689.686-034 NEEDLE-PUNCH-MACHINE-OPERATOR HELPER (textile)
Off bears rolls of nonwoven fabric (blanketing) from *stitch-bonding* machine: Observes fabric winding into rolls to detect defects. Cuts defective fabric from roll, using scissors, and joins ends together with needle and thread. Doffs full rolls, using chain hoist.
GOE: 06.04.05 STRENGTH: L GED: R1 M1 L1 SVP: 2 DLU: 77

689.686-038 SHUTTLE HAND (textile) alternate titles: magazine hand; shuttle filler; shuttle threader
Inserts bobbins of filling into shuttles. Threads yarn end through each shuttle eye and loads threaded shuttles into loom magazine. May replenish yarn supply on narrow fabric looms and be designated Quill Changer (narrow fabrics).
GOE: 06.04.06 STRENGTH: L GED: R2 M1 L1 SVP: 2 DLU: 77

689.686-042 STITCH-BONDING-MACHINE-TENDER HELPER (textile)
Creels and doffs *stitch-bonding* machines: Mounts rolls of *bat* on machine supply racks. Reports machine malfunctions to maintenance personnel. Doffs rolls following stitching and weighs and records weight of rolls. Cleans machine area, using airhose.
GOE: 06.04.05 STRENGTH: M GED: R1 M1 L1 SVP: 2 DLU: 77

689.686-046 THREAD-PULLING-MACHINE ATTENDANT (garment)
Feeds and off bears vacuum equipment that removes loose threads from shirts. Inserts collar of shirt in slot of conveyor belt that conveys shirt through cabinet. Removes shirts from conveyor. Folds and stacks shirts in handtruck.
GOE: 06.04.05 STRENGTH: L GED: R1 M1 L1 SVP: 1 DLU: 77

689.686-050 UTILITY WORKER, WOOLEN MILL (textile)
Performs any combination of following duties in weaving, spinning, carding, and finishing departments of woolen mill: Threads or laps cloth between or over rolls of processing equipment, such as washers, dryers, and dye vats. Cuts tacking stitch that secures top and bottom layers of folded cloth with scissors and pulls out threads. Transports wool, yarn, and cloth between operations and departments, using handtruck or hoist. Replaces empty spools with full spools of roving on creel of roving or spinning machines. Cleans machines and floor area of grease, dirt, and lint, using air and vacuum hose, broom, and rags. May be designated according to task performed as Tacking-Stitch Remover (textile).
GOE: 06.04.40 STRENGTH: H GED: R2 M1 L1 SVP: 2 DLU: 77

689.686-054 WASTE CHOPPER (tex. prod., nec)
Feeds or off bears machine that chops waste thread into lengths for use in making wiping rags: Deposits handfuls of loose thread on belt that conveys material to cutting blades. Removes tangles from blades, using scissors or knife. May pack material into containers preparatory to baling. May feed or off bear machine equipped with mechanism that compresses waste into mats following cutting operation.
GOE: 06.04.16 STRENGTH: L GED: R2 M1 L1 SVP: 2 DLU: 77

689.686-058 CLOTH DOFFER (textile) alternate titles: cloth handler; loom doffer; short piece handler
Removes rolls of cloth from looms or knitting machines and trucks cloth to storage: Pulls lever or presses button to stop machine when roll has sufficient

yardage as indicated by yardage clock, mark on cloth, or color-coded card flag. Turns handle to lower roll of cloth, cuts cloth, using scissors, and places cloth roll on handtruck. Places empty takeup beam on bracket of machine, attaches cloth to beam, and restarts machine. Writes identifying information, such as lot and style number, on ticket and attaches ticket to cloth roll. Trucks cloth to storage or inspection department. May weigh and keep record of cloth beams doffed.
GOE: 06.04.06 STRENGTH: H GED: R2 M1 L2 SVP: 2 DLU: 80

689.687-010   BAGGING SALVAGER (textile) alternate titles: sack-cleaning hand
Salvages sacks and bagging used as covering for raw stock fiber: Removes adhering stock fibers from sacks and bagging by hand. Places bagging in sacks or folds and stacks bagging for reuse. May straighten and place metal tie bands in bundles. May dip tie bands in paint for reuse.
GOE: 06.04.38 STRENGTH: L GED: R1 M1 L1 SVP: 1 DLU: 77

689.687-014   BOBBIN CLEANER, HAND (textile) alternate titles: quill cleaner, hand; spool cleaner, hand
Removes unused yarn or roving from bobbins, cones, quills, or spools, using knife and removing yarn with fingers. Separates and places waste yarn in containers according to type. May stack spools in storage racks for reuse.
GOE: 06.04.39 STRENGTH: H GED: R1 M1 L1 SVP: 2 DLU: 77

689.687-018   BUNDLE BREAKER (tex. prod., nec) alternate titles: band cutter; bundle cutter; hands parter
Cuts binding cord from bundles of hemp fiber, using knife. Separates bundle and places fibers on conveyor or table to facilitate feeding operations.
GOE: 06.04.40 STRENGTH: L GED: R1 M1 L1 SVP: 2 DLU: 77

689.687-022   CLOTH EXAMINER, HAND (narrow fabrics) alternate titles: inspector
Inspects narrow woven fabrics, such as labels, ribbon, and tape, to detect defective weaving, color variations, and damaged or soiled fabric: Cuts out defective sections, using hand shears. Ties cut ends together, splices ends with adhesive tape, or secures ends of roll with metal pins, using hammer. May operate sewing machine to sew cut ends together. May measure width of fabric with ruler or guide to determine conformance with standards. May tend winding device (blocker) to wind fabric into rolls [BLOCKER (narrow fabrics; nonmet. min.)].
GOE: 06.03.02 STRENGTH: L GED: R2 M1 L1 SVP: 2 DLU: 77

689.687-026   CLOTH FRAMER (textile) alternate titles: framer
Winds pile fabric onto frames (reel) to prevent crushing of pile during storage or shipment: Places frame on winding brackets of worktable. Turns frame by hand and catches cloth selvages on hooks of frame, spacing cloth around frame in layers. Bolts precut wooden slats to outside of frame, using wrench. Places frame of cloth in box and trucks box to storage area. Works as member of team to frame cloth.
GOE: 06.04.38 STRENGTH: M GED: R2 M1 L1 SVP: 2 DLU: 77

689.687-030   CREELER (textile)
Creels looms, twisters, warpers, tufting, or other textile machines to change style of yarn or to replace exhausted yarn packages: Places yarn packages on spindle of creel, according to supervisor's instructions, color-coded spools, or number on yarn packages. Threads yarn through eyelet plate (yarn guides) or ties yarn ends to ends of yarn from preceeding package to maintain continuous yarn supply. Cuts yarn ends from knots, using scissors, and discards yarn ends in waste container to prevent entanglement of yarn while moving through creel. Removes old yarn from machines before changing to different size or type of yarn. Cleans dust and lint from creel. May repair yarn breaks in creel. May replace yarn packages or spools when faulty yarn appears.
GOE: 06.04.05 STRENGTH: M GED: R2 M1 L1 SVP: 2 DLU: 80

689.687-034   DROP-WIRE BUILDER (textile) alternate titles: drop-wire stringer
Cleans and rebuilds drop wire assemblies: Cleans drop wires with solvent, compressed air, and brushes. Replaces defective drop wires and adds or removes drop wires in assembly, according to specifications. May clean harness frames [HARNESS CLEANER (textile)].
GOE: 06.01.02 STRENGTH: L GED: R2 M1 L1 SVP: 2 DLU: 77

689.687-038   END FINDER, ROVING DEPARTMENT (glass mfg.) alternate titles: creel selector; mat selector; roving selector
Removes tubes from packages of baked fiberglass sliver and locates inside end of coreless package. Unravels portion of sliver to verify location of end and cuts raveled sliver, using scissors, or breaks sliver by hand. May position coreless packages in creels [CREELER (any industry) 689.687-030].
GOE: 06.04.27 STRENGTH: L GED: R2 M1 L1 SVP: 2 DLU: 77

689.687-042   END FINDER, TWISTING DEPARTMENT (textile) alternate titles: twisting-tube selector
Unwinds tubes of fiberglass sliver rejected by TWISTER TENDER (glass mfg.; nonmet. min.; plastic-synth.; textile) to remove short lengths and find end of continuous strand: Holds tube of sliver and inserts end into tube of air suction raveling device. Breaks or cuts excess sliver from tube, using scissors, and places tube on truck.
GOE: 06.04.27 STRENGTH: L GED: R2 M1 L2 SVP: 2 DLU: 77

689.687-046   FRAME HAND (tex. prod., nec)
Performs any combination of following tasks related to embroidering fabric: Carries frames to and from embroidery machines. Installs and removes frames

from machine. Threads needles and changes threads. Replaces empty shuttles. Pins or ties overlapping fabric to frame.
GOE: 06.04.27 STRENGTH: M GED: R1 M1 L1 SVP: 2 DLU: 77

689.687-050   OIL-SPOT WASHER (tex. prod., nec; textile) alternate titles: spot washer
Removes oil and grease spots from cloth by either of following methods: (1)Washes spots from cloth, using handbrush, detergents and water, or prepared chemicals. (2) Dissolves and removes spots from cloth, using spray gun filled with cleaning chemicals. May use illuminated inspection frame to facilitate detection of oil and grease spots. May be designated according to articles cleaned as Pillowcase Cleaner (tex. prod., nec); Sheet Cleaner (tex. prod., nec).
GOE: 06.04.39 STRENGTH: L GED: R2 M1 L1 SVP: 2 DLU: 77

689.687-054   PEGGER, DOBBY LOOMS (narrow fabrics; textile) alternate titles: dobby-loom chain-pegger
Screws or hammers metal pegs into holes of wooden pattern chain that controls weave pattern on dobby loom, following pattern diagram. Removes and relocates pegs with peg wrench or pliers. May replace worn leather on shuttle binders.
GOE: 06.04.06 STRENGTH: L GED: R2 M1 L2 SVP: 2 DLU: 77

689.687-058   PICK REMOVER (textile) alternate titles: thread puller
Removes false selvages and filling floats from looped pile fabric by hand: Lifts roll of cloth onto brackets at end of table and unrolls cloth onto table. Trims false selvage from one edge of cloth, using scissors. Secures trimmed edge of cloth on pins set along edge of table. Pulls false selvage on opposite edge of cloth to remove selvage and floats. Folds and piles cloth on handtruck.
GOE: 06.04.27 STRENGTH: M GED: R1 M1 L1 SVP: 2 DLU: 77

689.687-062   RAW-SILK GRADER (textile)
Inspects raw silk samples to determine if silk meets specified quality standards: Places silk on grading frame. Examines silk, using various lighting effects, and compares shade of silk to standard examples on master panel.
GOE: 06.03.02 STRENGTH: S GED: R3 M2 L2 SVP: 4 DLU: 77

689.687-066   RUG CLEANER (carpet & rug)
Removes grease spots, stains, and similar manufacturing blemishes from rugs, using solvent, such as carbon tetrachloride, and rags, brushes, pads, and sponges. Loads rugs in extractor for drying. Works as member of team to clean and dry rugs.
GOE: 06.02.16 STRENGTH: L GED: R2 M1 L1 SVP: 2 DLU: 77

689.687-070   SHUTTLER (tex. prod., nec)
Threads and replaces shuttles in shuttle rail of embroidery machine to maintain embroidery operation: Inserts thread, needles, cloth, and backing in machine. Inserts and threads prewound bobbins into empty shuttles. Places shuttles into slots of machine shuttle rail to maintain embroidery operation.
GOE: 06.04.06 STRENGTH: L GED: R2 M1 L1 SVP: 2 DLU: 77

689.687-074   SPANNER (tex. prod., nec)
Attaches fabric to frames for installation in embroidery machines: Clips garment piece to top of frame, pulls fabric taut, and clamps or pins overhanging material under frame. Adjusts frame on machine and aligns needles and shuttle rails, using spanner wrench. May pin applique cloth strips over spanned fabric. May cut threads and excess applique material from embroidered garment section before removing pieces from frame. May thread needles, replace depleted bobbins, and cut threads between needles and embroidered fabric.
GOE: 06.04.06 STRENGTH: L GED: R1 M1 L1 SVP: 2 DLU: 77

689.687-078   THREADER (tex. prod., nec)
Assembles and threads brass bobbins into carriages of Levers lace machines: Places yarn-filled bobbin in carriage. Loops bobbin threads over hooked needle and draws thread through carriage eye. Sorts and separates carriages according to spring strength to ensure required placement in machine.
GOE: 06.04.06 STRENGTH: L GED: R2 M1 L1 SVP: 2 DLU: 77

689.687-082   YARN EXAMINER, SKEINS (textile) alternate titles: finished-yarn examiner; skein inspector; yarn inspector
Examines skeins of yarn to detect flaws, such as soils, slubs, breaks, and uneven dyeing or twisting: Shakes skeins to straighten yarn, hangs skeins on rod and spreads and pulls yarn around rod to locate imperfections. Cuts out slubs and ties yarn ends together. Examines winding and tying of skein to determine if skein has been made according to job order. Weighs skein from each lot and records weight. Records number and type of flaws found in each lot of yarn. Knots hank of yarn around several skeins to form bundle and packs bundles into boxes for shipment. May remove soils with cleaning fluid.
GOE: 06.03.02 STRENGTH: L GED: R2 M1 L1 SVP: 3 DLU: 77

689.687-086   YARN SORTER (textile) alternate titles: filling separator; filling sorter and hauler
Sorts yarn according to type, size, weight, blend, and quality for storage or distribution to other departments. May doff winding machines. May convey yarn to storage or other departments, using handtruck. May store yarn in bins.
GOE: 06.03.02 STRENGTH: L GED: R2 M1 L2 SVP: 2 DLU: 77

689.687-090   LAPPER (textile)
Cuts and removes waste yarn entangled around machine parts of yarn texturing machine, using knife: Observes machine positions to ensure yarn ends

are running through automatic cutters and that drop wires are set, and to detect defective cutters or uncut waste yarn left from previous shift. Cuts waste yarn caused by yarn breaks from machine parts, such as feed rollers and takeup packages, using knife. Removes feed rollers to cut waste yarn, and realigns and tightens rollers, using wrench. Sweeps waste yarn from around machines and catwalks, using broom, and deposits yarn in receptacles. Pushes cart loaded with textured yarn to yarn cleaning area. Transports boxes filled with empty color-coded takeup rolls from storage area to machine area, using handtruck.
GOE: 06.04.16 STRENGTH: M GED: R2 M1 L1 SVP: 2 DLU: 86

69   MACHINE TRADES OCCUPATIONS, N.E.C.

This division includes occupations, not elsewhere classified, concerned with feeding, tending, operating, controlling, and setting up machines to work various materials and products.

690   PLASTICS, SYNTHETICS, RUBBER, AND LEATHER WORKING OCCUPATIONS

This group includes occupations concerned with machining plastics materials, synthetic resins, synthetic rubber, cellulosic and manmade organic fibers, and leather, including artificial leather.

690.130-010   SUPERVISOR III (button & notion)
Supervises and coordinates activities of workers engaged in production of buttons: Sets up, repairs, and adjusts machines, using handtools. Examines buttons to ensure conformance to specifications. Trains and assigns workers. Performs other duties as described under SUPERVISOR (any industry) Master Title.
GOE: 06.02.01 STRENGTH: M GED: R3 M2 L3 SVP: 6 DLU: 77

690.130-014   SUPERVISOR, SLITTING-AND-SHIPPING (plastic-synth.)
Supervises and coordinates activities of workers engaged in slitting rolls of plastics sheets into strips, rewinding strips into rolls of specified size, and in packaging, storing and shipping rolls. Trains new employees. Directs workers in setting up slitting machine, and in packaging finished rolls and marking rolls with data, such as lot number and size. Performs duties as described under SUPERVISOR (any industry) Master Title. May supervise workers engaged in packaging and shipping only and be designated Supervisor, Shipping (plastic-synth.).
GOE: 06.02.01 STRENGTH: M GED: R4 M3 L3 SVP: 7 DLU: 77

690.130-018   SUPERVISOR (plastic prod.)
Supervises and coordinates activities of workers engaged in setting up and tending machinery and equipment that punches, stamps, screen-prints, and paints plastic products: Inspects production operations to verify conformance with establishment specifications, using precision measuring instruments and blueprints. Trains new workers. Requisitions materials, supplies, and replacement parts. Repairs machinery and equipment, using power tools and handtools. Performs other duties as described under SUPERVISOR (any industry) Master Title.
GOE: 06.02.01 STRENGTH: L GED: R4 M3 L4 SVP: 6 DLU: 86

690.130-022   SUPERVISOR, FOAM CUTTING (tex. prod., nec)
Supervises and coordinates activities of workers engaged in cutting foam rubber used in manufacture of furniture cushions, and sets up and operates foam cutting machines to cut loaves of foam into specified sizes: Explains and demonstrates work procedures and material saving techniques to new workers. Confers with plant personnel to expedite flow of foam products. Transports loaves of foam to and from machines, using dolly, and positions loaves of foam on table of machine. Turns handwheels, setscrews, and bolts, using handtools, to set stops and position patterns under ram of machine and to set up and operate cutting machines, such as vertical slicing and horizontal slicing machine, to cut loaves of foam into specified sizes. Examines sliced foam to verify product size and conformance to product specifications, using tape measure. Records information on work order, such as date of cut, quantity of products, and time of order. Performs other duties as described under SUPERVISOR (any industry) Master Title.
GOE: 06.02.01 STRENGTH: H GED: R3 M2 L2 SVP: 6 DLU: 86

690.280-010   DEBURRING-AND-TOOLING-MACHINE OPERATOR (office machines)
Sets up and controls operation of computerized deburring and tooling machine to perform series of machining operations, such as drilling, chamfering, and deburring, on ball-shaped plastic *typing element* for use in electric typewriters: Reads blueprints, job order, and tooling instructions to determine cutting tools and sequence of operations. Positions and secures deburring and cutting tools onto holding fixtures of machine, using handtools. Loads plastic elements into feed mechanism of machine. Depresses switch to actuate machine and observes machining operation to detect feeding and tooling malfunctions as typing element is automatically fed through series of tooling stations. Adjusts and changes machine tools to ensure deburring meets company specifications. Repairs or replaces parts, such as cylinders and air lines, using handtools. Inspects machined typing elements at discharge end of machine to ensure conformance to quality specifications, using gauges and microscope. Notifies engineering personnel when corrective action is required. Maintains stock of machined parts and cutting tools.

GOE: 06.01.03 STRENGTH: M GED: R4 M4 L3 SVP: 8 DLU: 86

690.360-010   WAD-BLANKING-PRESS ADJUSTER (ordnance)
Sets up battery of punch presses to stamp out hair-felt and cardboard wads for shotgun shells: Removes, replaces, and adjusts cutters, punches, bushings, dies, ratchets, pawls, web choppers, springs, and chains, using handtools. Turns setscrews and stop nuts to synchronize feeding and punching mechanisms and to position tools. Measures sample wads after each tool change or adjustment to verify specified diameter, using ring gauge. Notifies MAINTENANCE MECHANIC (any industry) when machines, conveyors, or screening barrels require major repairs. Trains new workers in tending machines.
GOE: 06.01.02 STRENGTH: L GED: R3 M2 L2 SVP: 4 DLU: 77

690.362-010   LEAD OPERATOR, AUTOMATIC VULCANIZING (rubber goods)
Operates machine that automatically vulcanizes continuous lengths of rubber hose: Pulls wire protruding from end of hose and bends hose into hook to attach several lengths of hose to provide continuous feed to vulcanizer. Moves controls of machine to specified settings to regulate temperature, pressure, feed rate, and vulcanizing time. Lubricates, adjusts, and makes running repairs to machine, using grease gun, welding equipment, and handtools. Records hose footage processed and vulcanizing time in production log. Transfers filled boxes of vulcanized hose to inspection department, using handtruck.
GOE: 06.02.07 STRENGTH: M GED: R3 M2 L2 SVP: 5 DLU: 77

690.380-010   MACHINE SETTER (button & notion)
Sets up and adjusts automatic machines that shape and drill buttons: Obtains specified button-holding chucks, abrasive wheels, cutting tools, and drill-bits and installs them in machine, using wrenches, screwdrivers, micrometers, and gauges. Adjusts cams to synchronize feeding mechanism with tool action and positions cutting tools in holders to control depth of pattern on button. Selects approximate settings and test-operates machine. Examines and gauges button to determine need for further adjustment. Replaces worn or broken machine accessories, using handtools. May operate *bench grinder* and lathe to sharpen drill bits and cutting tools, and reshape worn button-chucks. May instruct new employees in operating procedures.
GOE: 06.01.02 STRENGTH: M GED: R3 M2 L3 SVP: 5 DLU: 77

690.380-014   MACHINE SETTER-AND-REPAIRER (plastic prod.)
Sets up and repairs variety of plastic fabricating machines that weld and assemble components into plastic products and print decorative logos onto products: Mounts, aligns, and bolts fixtures, dies, and welding heads onto plastic fabricating machines, such as hot-stamping, silk-screening, ultrasonic welding, and automatic assembling and stamping machines, following verbal instructions and using variety of wrenches. Turns knobs or dials to set controls, such as pneumatic stamping pressure, dwell time, conveyor speed, and ram and horizontal stroke of machines. Positions rolls of foil onto feed reels and threads foil around guides onto takeup reels to secure foil on machines. Starts machines to obtain sample products, and examines samples for production defects. Readjusts machine controls or realigns dies or fixtures as necessary to correct detected defects in products, utilizing knowledge and experience of machine operations. Examines moving machine parts during production operations and removes and replaces worn and frayed machine parts as needed to ensure that machines function smoothly. May fabricate replacement dies, using bandsaw, knife, hand file, and drill press.
GOE: 06.01.02 STRENGTH: H GED: R3 M2 L2 SVP: 4 DLU: 86

690.382-010   SHEETER OPERATOR (plastic-synth.) alternate titles: slitter operator
Operates sheeting machine to slice cakes of baked plastics into sheets of uniform thickness: Turns crank to adjust cutting position of knife. Adjusts feed rolls of machine to regulate pressure of cake against knife, using wrenches. Turns steam valves to regulate temperature of heating chamber. Loads cake onto conveyor of machine manually or by using hoist, and starts machine. Observes gauges to verify machine temperatures. Measures thickness of sheets with micrometer. Examines surface of sliced sheets for imperfections and replaces knife, using wrenches. Turns crank to adjust tension on knife. May sharpen knife, using whetstone. May count and record number of sheets cut.
GOE: 06.02.02 STRENGTH: L GED: R3 M2 L2 SVP: 4 DLU: 77

690.382-014   WEATHERSTRIP-MACHINE OPERATOR (rubber goods) alternate titles: windlace-machine operator
Sets up and operates machine to mold and vulcanize sponge rubber beading onto wire mesh strip to form weatherstripping for automobiles: Selects and installs machine parts, such as engraved rolls, rotary gang knives, folding and forming channels, and tubes of specified size and measurement to produce beading of diameter ordered, using wrenches. Mounts reels of canvas carrier strip and wire mesh in creels beneath and above machine table. Threads carrier strip and mesh through rollers, guides, folding channels, and into forming tubes for pick up by metal fingers that carry them through vulcanizing tubes for each row of rubber strip. Turns wingnuts and bolts, using pliers and wrenches, to adjust rollers and guides, to center rubber strip on canvas carrier, to position mesh vertically in crease of imprinted rubber strip at specified depth, and to ensure even folding of carrier canvas around rubber and rubber around bottom half of wire mesh. Adjusts rheostat for each vulcanizing tube to designated setting and observes heat indicators. Starts machine and feeds roll of uncured rubber stock between engraved rolls. Measures sample of imprinted strip for conformance to thickness specifications, using dial micrometer and turns capstan

screws to adjust width between rolls. Adjusts rheostats to maintain vulcanizing heats within allowable degree limits. Calculates length of running time required to produce footage ordered on work ticket. Staples end of supply strip onto leader to replenish carrier strip and wire mesh. Turns wheel of variable speed motor to adjust speed of rollers and metal finger sprockets according to diameter of beading.
GOE: 06.02.09 STRENGTH: M GED: R3 M2 L3 SVP: 4 DLU: 77

690.385-010 PLATEN GRINDER (office machines) alternate titles: grinder; grinding-machine operator
Tends pair of semiautomatic cylindrical grinders that grind typewriter and adding machine rubber platens and feed rollers to specified diameter and finish: Mounts platen between driving head and tailstock and trips lever causing carriage to bear platen against and across grinding wheel for coarse grind and rough finish. Removes platen, mounts it in second machine equipped with finer grit wheel, and grinds platen to specified diameter and desired finish. Examines finished platen for smoothness and for defects in rubber, such as scratches, graining, or holes. Measures platen for conformance to specified diameter, using C-gage. May tend double-bladed cutting device to trim excess rubber from ends of platen. May tend machine that grinds and finishes platens and rollers in single operation.
GOE: 06.04.07 STRENGTH: L GED: R3 M1 L2 SVP: 3 DLU: 77

690.462-010 OUTSOLE CUTTER, AUTOMATIC (rubber goods)
Sets up and operates machine that automatically cuts outsoles for rubber footwear from slabs of uncured rubber or compressed cork: Bolts selected follower (template) on machine and mounts cutting blade in traveler against follower, using handtools. Starts machine and feeds slabs onto conveyor that carries them beneath follower, overlapping ends to form continuous strip. Lifts scrap rubber (web) from cutout outsoles and threads it through rollers that automatically strip it from outsoles and carry it off by conveyor to scrap truck. Calculates from work ticket, number of pairs and books required for each size sole ordered and advises BOOKER (rubber goods; rubber tire), to remove cutout outsoles from other end of conveyor belt. Observes cut outsoles for ragged edges, indicating dulled blade.
GOE: 06.02.09 STRENGTH: M GED: R3 M2 L2 SVP: 4 DLU: 77

690.482-010 SAWYER (plastic prod.; plastic-synth.)
Sets up and operates power-driven circular and abrasive saws and bandsaw to cut plastic sheets, rods, or tubes to specified dimensions: Installs blade in saw and sets guide bars and stops. Positions plastic material on saw table. Starts saw and feeds material to blade. Verifies dimensions of pieces, using micrometer, gauges, and rule. Examines pieces for defects, such as chipped edges and marred surfaces, and sorts defective pieces according to defect. May mark cutting lines on material. May sharpen blade, using abrasive wheel.
GOE: 06.02.02 STRENGTH: M GED: R3 M2 L2 SVP: 5 DLU: 77

690.482-014 TRIMMER (plastic prod.)
Operates machines to finish preformed plastic parts: Trims part to size and shape following template and using power grinder or power saw. Clamps template to part or positions part in jig and slots and drills part, using table or portable router and drill press or power hand drill. Sands edges and rough surfaces of part, using power sander. May trim, shape, and assemble metal or wood components of plastic part. May adjust and repair machines, using handtools.
GOE: 06.02.02 STRENGTH: M GED: R3 M2 L2 SVP: 4 DLU: 77

690.485-010 BAND-SAWING-MACHINE OPERATOR (fabrication, nec) alternate titles: cutter; material cutter
Tends bandsawing machine that cuts pieces of specified shape from sheets of materials, such as fiberglass, foam rubber, or parchment: Positions pattern on material and marks cutting lines. Stacks specified number of sheets and clamps them together. Starts saw and guides stock against blade, following cutting lines. Drills guide holes in stock to mark location for attachment of trim, using power drill.
GOE: 06.04.09 STRENGTH: M GED: R2 M1 L2 SVP: 3 DLU: 77

690.580-010 HIDE SPLITTER (leather mfg.)
Sets up machine to split hides into layers: Turns setscrews on machine table to adjust rollers according to specified thickness of hide, using wrench. Verifies thickness of layers split from hides, using micrometer. Realigns or replaces parts, such as machine belt, knife, and rollers. Reads counter and records number of hides split by SPLITTING-MACHINE FEEDER (leather mfg.).
GOE: 06.02.05 STRENGTH: L GED: R3 M2 L2 SVP: 4 DLU: 77

690.585-010 MILL-ROLL REWINDER (plastic-synth.)
Tends machine that winds cellophane from one roll to another to remove folds, wrinkles, and slack: Positions roll on machine mandrel, using chain hoist, and wraps end of sheet around empty core. Moves controls to regulate machine speed and film tension. Passes hand over moving sheet to remove wrinkles and folds. Cuts defects, such as holes and tears from roll, and splices ends, using tape and hot iron. Removes rewound roll from machine and weighs and places it in rack, using chain hoist. Records number and weight of rolls wound.
GOE: 06.04.02 STRENGTH: M GED: R2 M1 L2 SVP: 4 DLU: 77

690.585-014 MOTTLE-LAY-UP OPERATOR (plastic-synth.) alternate titles: lay-up operator
Tends electric shear-type cutting machine that cuts sheets of plastic materials into specified sizes: Adjusts cutting blade, guides, and stops, using handtools.

Stacks sheets on machine bed and presses control to start machine. Assembles cut pieces in containers or cake-press frame to form specified color combination or configuration. Records amount of materials used and orders completed.
GOE: 06.04.02 STRENGTH: L GED: R2 M2 L2 SVP: 4 DLU: 77

690.662-010 TIRE-REGROOVING-MACHINE OPERATOR (automotive ser.)
Sets up and operates machine to regroove tread surface of pneumatic tires without removing tire from vehicle: Raises front or rear of vehicle, using hydraulic jack. Positions regrooving machine beneath tire and secures in place. Measures depth of usuable tread rubber, using awl. Sets cutting blades of machine to maximum depth consistent with safety. Guides blade to cut desired pattern in tread surface as machine automatically revolves tire. May groove tires by hand [TIRE GROOVER (automotive ser.)].
GOE: 05.12.13 STRENGTH: M GED: R3 M2 L3 SVP: 4 DLU: 77

690.662-014 TUBER-MACHINE OPERATOR (rubber goods; rubber tire) alternate titles: extruder operator
Sets up and operates tuber machine to extrude rubber in specified form: Selects and installs die in machine, using handtools. Turns steam valve or lights gas burner to heat machine to desired temperature. Starts machine, turns dial for specified extrusion speed, and turns die screws to extrude stock of specified size. Feeds rubber stock into machine by hand or conveyor. Verifies dimensions of extruded rubber with gauge, calipers, and ruler. Turns wheels or pulls levers to synchronize conveyor with extruding speed. May be designated according to product extruded as Garden-Hose Tuber-Machine Operator (rubber goods); Inner-Tube Tuber-Machine Operator (rubber tire); Rim-Strip Tuber-Machine Operator (rubber tire); Rubber-Flap Tuber-Machine Operator (rubber tire); Solid-Tire Tuber-Machine Operator (rubber tire); Tread-Tuber-Machine Operator (rubber tire). May cover braided fabric hose with rubber and be designated Covering-Machine Operator (rubber goods).
GOE: 06.02.07 STRENGTH: M GED: R3 M2 L2 SVP: 4 DLU: 77

690.665-010 SLASHER (plastic-synth.) alternate titles: cutter, plastics rolls
Tends equipment that cuts plastic materials to specified lengths: Mounts roll of plastic sheeting material on cutting-machine holding stand, using hoist. Sets cutting guides and moves knife to slice materials being unreeled across table. Examines sheets for defects and scraps and weighs unusable ones.
GOE: 06.04.02 STRENGTH: L GED: R2 M1 L1 SVP: 3 DLU: 77

690.680-010 RUBBER-GOODS CUTTER-FINISHER (rubber goods) alternate titles: rubber-goods finisher
Sets up and operates variety of machines to cut, drill, punch, and grind molded and extruded rubber goods: Changes dies, drills, knives, abrasive wheels, and cutter bars as specified. Adjusts equipment, such as boring machine, tubing cutter, notch cutter, washer cutter, and grinding lathe, using handtools. Positions material, such as molded rubber parts, gaskets, tubing, and office machine rolls, in specified machine and starts machine to bore or punch holes in parts, cut washers from tubing, cut tubing to length, or grind tubing and machine rolls to size. Verifies size of rubber goods with calipers, ruler, plug gauge, and template. Inspects material and rejects defective items. May be designated according to machine operated as Boring-Machine Operator (rubber goods); Cutting-Machine Operator (rubber goods); Lathe Operator (rubber goods); Notch-Machine Operator (rubber goods); or product finished as Gasket Notcher (rubber goods); Roll Grinder (rubber goods); Washer Cutter (rubber goods).
GOE: 06.01.03 STRENGTH: M GED: R3 M2 L3 SVP: 4 DLU: 77

690.682-010 ARCH-CUSHION-SKIVING-MACHINE OPERATOR (rubber goods)
Operates machines to cut arch cushions from sponge rubber sheeting for rubber footwear, using either of following methods: Selects die plate or drum to produce specified size cushions and bolts die in feeder slide or locks die in cradle, using wrenches. Turns setscrews to adjust distance between hold-down roller, belt knife, and plate or drum, verifying clearances, using feeler gauges. (1) Pulls plate length of sheeting from roll, cuts material, using knife, and places sheeting on die plate. Moves lever to open suction valve that draws rubber sheeting into die plate cavities. Depresses pedal causing sheeting on plate to be carried through belt knife to cut cushions flush with plate surface. Returns plate to starting position. Removes excess stock for scrap or turns over salvable stock for second cut. Removes cut out cushion from die cavity and throws into storage box. (2) Mounts roll of sheeting in cradle, threads around hold-down and guide rollers, over rotary die drum and belt knife, and onto takeup reel. Starts automatic machine to cut cushion from sheeting. Positions carton under discharge end of conveyor to catch cushions. Weighs filled cartons to count number of cushions, using conversion chart, and adds or removes cushions to obtain specified amount.
GOE: 06.02.07 STRENGTH: M GED: R3 M2 L2 SVP: 4 DLU: 77

690.682-014 BALL-TRUING-MACHINE OPERATOR (toy-sport equip.)
Sets up and operates battery of ball-truing machines to grind bowling balls spherically to size and smooth them preparatory to finishing and polishing: Installs conical grinding rings on opposing spindles and adjusts clearances and angle of cut, using wrenches and gauges. Places rough cast ball on holding pad between grinding rings and turns valve to start cooling water to flow over ball. Starts machine and moves dial pointer to preset running time cycle on each quadrant of ball. Removes ball from holding pad and gauges it with ring or

calipers and rule to ensure specified size tolerances. May mark imperfections on ball to be drilled and plugged, using crayon.
GOE: 06.02.09 STRENGTH: M GED: R3 M2 L2 SVP: 5 DLU: 77

690.682-018 BED LASTER (boot & shoe) alternate titles: lasting-machine operator, bed; toe and heel laster

Operates *lasting* machine to press and shape toe or heel sections of upper on last: Places upper on last in steamer to soften leather. Removes upper from steamer, places last on *pin jack*, and stretches edges of upper over last, using *lasting tool.* Moves controls to close heel clamp and raise toe or heel into wiping (smoothing) position. Moves controls to cause wipers to press upper edges against insole. May press heated toe iron against upper edges to flatten wiped edges. May trim excess box toe and lining, using knife. May tack upper or counter insole in place to be stitched or to hold edges until cement dries.
GOE: 06.02.05 STRENGTH: L GED: R3 M2 L2 SVP: 5 DLU: 77

690.682-022 BIAS-MACHINE OPERATOR (rubber tire) alternate titles: bias-cutting-machine operator; ply cutter

Operates machine to cut rubberized (calendered) fabric on bias for use as plies or other components in tire construction: Turns thumbscrew or setscrew to adjust measuring arm, protractor, and liner roll to feed and cut fabric according to specified width and angle of bias. Pulls fabric from roll mounted on *letoff rack,* inserts through liner roll, and positions under knife on bias-machine table. Starts machine and adjusts speed of feed and cutting action. Starts conveyor that carries material to SPLICER (rubber tire). Measures plies to verify width and angle, using ruler and protractor. May be designated according to purpose of fabric cut as Band-Bias-Machine Operator (rubber tire); or type of machine as Bias-Cutting-Machine Operator, Vertical (rubber tire).
GOE: 06.02.09 STRENGTH: M GED: R3 M2 L2 SVP: 4 DLU: 77

690.682-026 CUTTER, BARREL DRUM (tex. prod., nec) alternate titles: drum-reel cutter; reel slitter

Operates machine to wind plastic material onto reel and cut wound material into lengths for use in making articles, such as curtains, draperies, and table covers: Positions roll of plastic material on machine brackets, threads end of material through tension rollers, and clamps or tapes material to rod on reel. Turns handwheel or loosens bolts and moves rods to increase or decrease diameter of reel according to length specified for material. Depresses pedal to start, stop, and control speed of machine. Observes material as it winds on reel to detect uneven winding and straightens uneven edges by hand. Stops machine at specified intervals during winding cycle and cuts material on reel by drawing knife through slot in reel rod. Removes lengths of material from reel. May operate machine equipped with knives to slit material in specified widths as it winds.
GOE: 06.02.02 STRENGTH: M GED: R3 M1 L2 SVP: 4 DLU: 77

690.682-030 EMBOSSER (leather mfg.; leather prod.) alternate titles: embossing-machine operator; embossing-press operator; finished-leather presser; plating-press operator; printer; smooth plater

Operates machine to imprint designs on leather or leather articles, such as wallets and key cases: Selects specified embossing plate, bolts plate into chase, and positions and secures chase onto ram of machine. Turns switch or steam valve to heat plate to specified temperature according to type of leather. Pulls lever that lowers ram to impress designs on leather or article. May make bed for embossing plate, using cardboard and paper.
GOE: 06.02.05 STRENGTH: L GED: R3 M2 L3 SVP: 4 DLU: 77

690.682-034 EMBOSSING-PRESS OPERATOR, MOLDED GOODS (fabrication, nec)

Sets up and operates press to emboss designs on molded hard-surface floor covering: Installs press pads and embossing plate on press, using handtools. Places molded hard-surface floor covering in press at designated point on pattern to make crosswise alignement of material with embossng plate and lengthwise alignment with press guidelines. Regulates controls to move material into press and to actuate plate. Examines floor covering after each impression to detect embossing defects. Changes press pads and adjusts temperature and pressing cycle to improve impression. Observes pressure gauges and guide markers as material progresses through press to ensure maintenance of required pressure and alignment.
GOE: 06.02.09 STRENGTH: L GED: R3 M2 L2 SVP: 5 DLU: 77

690.682-038 FOXING-CUTTING-MACHINE OPERATOR, AUTOMATIC (boot & shoe)

Sets up and operates machine that automatically cuts strips of foxing from continuous sheeting of rubber coated fabric and drops them onto conveyor belt for making into books : Pushes A-frame, containing reel of sheeting, and empty takeup reel in front of machine. Attaches castor-mounted driving motor to end of takeup reel shaft, using collar and wrench. Threads sheeting through series of holddown bars and rollers to cutting blades. Adjusts angle of diagonal, scissors-like blades to increase or decrease length of foxing strip according to work ticket specifications. Regulates rate of feed of sheeting to adjust width of strip. Turns valves to drip water onto blades for lubrication and starts machine. Cuts into edge of sheeting on each side, using knife, and pulls off strips of uneven selvages to provide straight even edges to cut foxing. Measures samples of foxing for conformance to length, width, and thickness specifications, using steel tape and dial micrometer. Adjusts machine by trial and error to produce acceptable foxing. Cuts across sheeting and wrapper, using knife, when sufficient quantity of foxing has been booked.

GOE: 06.02.05 STRENGTH: L GED: R3 M2 L2 SVP: 4 DLU: 77

690.682-042 HEEL BREASTER, LEATHER (boot & shoe)

Sets up and operates machine to trim and shape breast of leather heels according to specifications: Sharpens cutting blade on grinding wheel and locks blade to ram of machine with wrench. Turns wheel to adjust cutting stroke of machine to height of heel. Sets lasted shoe on movable *pin jack* and pushes pin jack under or against cutting blade to trim and shape heel. May buff heel to prepare for varnishing.
GOE: 06.02.05 STRENGTH: L GED: R3 M2 L2 SVP: 4 DLU: 77

690.682-046 HEEL-SEAT FITTER, MACHINE (boot & shoe) alternate titles: cutter-in; heel fitter, machine; wood-heel fitter, machine

Sets up and operates machine to cut heel seat of leather sole preparatory to mounting heel: Adjusts guides and stops on machine by using sample wood heel and handtools. Adjusts rotary cutting blade on machine for specified width, depth, and bevel, using wrench and rule. Starts machine and positions shoe between guides. Pushes shoe into machine that makes marginal cut around heel seat to provide snug fit when heel is attached.
GOE: 06.02.05 STRENGTH: L GED: R3 M2 L2 SVP: 4 DLU: 77

690.682-050 HOT-DIE-PRESS OPERATOR (boot & shoe)

Operates press that automatically cuts soles for rubber footwear from slabs of cork or crepe: Selects numbered die plate from storage rack according to size and style numbers on worksheet and places die in preheated oven for designated time. Removes heated dies from oven and slides dies into die holder of press. Switches on current to keep dies hot and starts press and conveyor belt. Positions slab of stock on conveyor belt that carries stock between reciprocating dies and press table to cut soles from slab. Lifts and discards web (scrap stock) from cut out soles. Maintains tally of work performed on report form. May heat dies, replenishing stock according to sequence on work ticket, and be designated Hot-Die Picker (boot & shoe); or may feed slabs and remove web and be designated Hot-Die-Press Feeder (boot & shoe).
GOE: 06.02.09 STRENGTH: L GED: R3 M2 L2 SVP: 4 DLU: 77

690.682-054 ORNAMENTAL-MACHINE OPERATOR (wood prod., nec)

Operates machine to form and attach ornamental putty designs to picture frame moldings: Measures out, heats, and mixes rosin, linseed oil, glue, and water to make putty. Installs specified die roller in machine and adjusts die, guides, and scrapers, using handtools. Pours putty into feed hopper and starts machine. Places molding on feed roller and observes feeding, shaping, and attaching of putty to molding.
GOE: 06.02.09 STRENGTH: L GED: R3 M2 L2 SVP: 4 DLU: 77

690.682-058 PLANISHING-PRESS OPERATOR (plastic-synth.) alternate titles: plastics-sheet-finishing-press operator; press operator; sheet-combining operator; shell-press operator

Operates planishing press to impart finish to plastic sheets: Selects metal plates according to finish desired. Places plastic sheets between metal planishing plates. Slides plates into platens of hydraulic press. Moves controls or inserts circular graph into controlling mechanism of press to heat press to specified temperature and compress plastic sheets between plates. Removes plates from platens after specified time and strips plastic sheets from metal plates, using knife. Examines sheets for defects. Cleans metal plates, using cloths, solvents, or scrapers, or dips plates into vat of hot water, using chain hoist. May adjust heat and pressure controls. May be designated according to purpose of pressing as Sheet Straightener (plastic-synth.).
GOE: 06.02.02 STRENGTH: H GED: R3 M2 L2 SVP: 5 DLU: 77

690.682-062 PRESS OPERATOR (plastic prod.) alternate titles: plate worker

Operates hydraulic press to emboss, laminate, or draw plastic sheets: Clamps sheet to overhead rack and pushes rack into oven to soften sheet for forming. Bolts dies or plates to bed of press and adjusts length of travel of ram arm, using handtools. Positions softened sheet or layers of sheets on press bed and lowers pressure plate to hold sheets in place. Moves controls to lower ram that draws sheet through open die to specified shape, embosses sheet with specified design, or compresses layers of sheets to form laminated plastic board. Turns valves to regulate flow of water or steam through dies or plates to maintain specified forming temperature of plastic. Trims plastic, using shears, power saw, or knife. May be designated according to operation performed as Laminating-Press Operator (plastic prod.); Straightening-Press Operator (plastic prod.).
GOE: 06.02.02 STRENGTH: H GED: R3 M2 L2 SVP: 4 DLU: 77

690.682-066 RING-ROLLING-MACHINE OPERATOR (rubber goods)

Operates machine to roll rings on mouths of balloons prior to curing: Spaces parallel revolving brush arms of machine to correspond with neck size of balloon forms. Turns wheel to adjust height of turntable that holds *form board,* and to align brushes with edge of latex of forms. Pushes machine forward to roll latex on forms into rings.
GOE: 06.02.07 STRENGTH: L GED: R3 M2 L3 SVP: 4 DLU: 77

690.682-070 SOLE-CONFORMING-MACHINE OPERATOR (boot & shoe) alternate titles: archer; molder; outsole or insole molder; sole-molding-machine operator

Operates machine to mold outsoles or insoles to conform to shoe last at shank and arch: Turns thumbscrews or moves lever along calibrated dial to adjust last and size guides to specifications. Sponges grained surface of sole at

arch to soften leather. Positions sole on die and against guides. Pulls lever to lower mold that presses sole against die, shaping arch and shank. Replaces dies and molds when last or shoe sizes change.
GOE: 06.02.05 STRENGTH: L GED: R3 M2 L2 SVP: 4 DLU: 77

690.682-074 SPAGHETTI-MACHINE OPERATOR (plastic prod.) alternate titles: dip-tube assembler, machine
Operates machine to assemble dip tubes and plugs used in plastic squeeze bottles: Places reel of plastic tubing onto spindle and feeds tubing through retaining wheels and channel to edge of razor blade. Loads plugs into bowl on machine. Pushes button to start machine that assembles tubes and plugs and ejects tube assemblies into tote box. Removes filled tote box from machine. Loosens and tightens razor blade holder to return blade to cutting position, using screwdriver. Replaces dull and unusable blades. Inserts dip tube assembly into plastic bottle containing water, and squeezes tube assembly to test for defects. Adjusts machine to correct faulty operation.
GOE: 06.02.20 STRENGTH: M GED: R3 M2 L3 SVP: 4 DLU: 77

690.682-078 STITCHER, SPECIAL MACHINE (boot & shoe) alternate titles: inseamer; stitcher; vamper; welter
Operates stitching machine to perform specific function, such as to reinforce shoe parts or attach buckles: Places specified spool of thread or prewound bobbin on spindle or in shuttle and draws thread through guides, slots, and needles. Aligns parts to be stitched, following seams, edges, or markings. Positions parts under needle and depresses pedal to start machine. Cuts excess threads, using scissors or knife. May guide parts past machine head during stitching cycle. May be designated according to type of stitch used or part stitched as Lockstitcher (boot & shoe); Platform Stitcher (boot & shoe); Plug Stitcher (boot & shoe); Rapid-Outsole Stitcher (boot & shoe); Sole Stitcher (boot & shoe). Important variables may be indicated by trade names of machines used.
GOE: 06.02.05 STRENGTH: L GED: R3 M2 L2 SVP: 4 DLU: 77

690.682-082 STITCHER, STANDARD MACHINE (boot & shoe) alternate titles: closer; fitter; joiner; maker; seamer; sewer; stayer; stitcher; stitching-machine operator
Operates single, double, or multiple-needle stitching machine to join or decorate shoe parts, or to reinforce edges: Selects spool of thread or prewound bobbin, places spool or bobbin on spindle or looper, and draws thread through guides and needles. Aligns parts and presses knee control or pedal to raise presser foot or roller. Positions parts under needle and lowers presser foot or roller. Presses foot or knee control to start machine and guides parts under needle, following seams, edges, or markings, or moves edges of part against guide. Cuts excess thread or material from shoe parts, using scissors or knife. When operating double or multiple-needle machine, may turn setscrew on needle bar and position one or more needles as specified. May be designated according to shoe parts stitched as Back-Seam Stitcher (boot & shoe); Box-Toe Stitcher (boot & shoe). May be designated according to machine operated as Flatbed Stitcher (boot & shoe); Zig-Zag Stitcher (boot & shoe). May be designated according to number of needles in machine operated as Double-Needle Stitcher (boot & shoe); Multiple-Needle Stitcher (boot & shoe); Single-Needle Stitcher (boot & shoe). May be designated: Backstay Stitcher (boot & shoe); Barrer And Tacker (boot & shoe); Binding Stitcher (boot & shoe); Buckle Sewer, Machine (boot & shoe); California Seamer (boot & shoe); Counter-Pocket Sewer (boot & shoe); Cover Maker (boot & shoe); Cut-Out Stitcher (boot & shoe); Edge Stitcher (boot & shoe); Fancy Stitcher (boot & shoe); Flare Stitcher (boot & shoe); Gore Inserter (boot & shoe); Insole Tape Stitcher, UCO (boot & shoe); Label Stitcher (boot & shoe); Lining Closer (boot & shoe); Lining Stitcher (boot & shoe); Lining-Strap Closer (boot & shoe); Lining Vamper (boot & shoe); Neverslip Stitcher (boot & shoe); Postbed Stitcher (boot & shoe); Quarter-Lining Stitcher (boot & shoe); Rand Sewer (boot & shoe); Saddle Stitcher (boot & shoe); Saddle-Lining Stitcher (boot & shoe); Seam-Stay Stitcher (boot & shoe); Shank Stitcher (boot & shoe); Sock-Lining Stitcher (boot & shoe); Stitcher, Utility (boot & shoe); Strap Stitcher (boot & shoe); Tape Stitcher (boot & shoe); Tip Stitcher (boot & shoe); Toe-Lining Closer (boot & shoe); Tongue And Quarter Stitcher (boot & shoe); Tongue-Lining Stitcher (boot & shoe); Tongue Stitcher (boot & shoe); Top Stitcher (boot & shoe); Underlay Stitcher (boot & shoe); Upper Stitcher (boot & shoe); Vamp Stitcher (boot & shoe); Welting Stitcher, Front (boot & shoe); Wrapper Stitcher (boot & shoe).
GOE: 06.02.05 STRENGTH: L GED: R3 M2 L2 SVP: 4 DLU: 81

690.682-086 TRIMMER, MACHINE II (boot & shoe)
Operates machine to trim *flash* from molded rubber heels, soles, or arch cushions or from tops of rubber footwear: Starts machine and positions edge of workpiece on feed roller beneath cutter guard. Holds and turns workpiece against guard, presenting all edges to reciprocating or rotating blade to remove excess material. Depresses pedal to raise guard so that seams will not be jagged or torn. Turns setscrews to adjust height of guard to thickness of material processed and to replace dull blades. May trim heels by setting them on base plate and turning heels by hand against matching circular knives. May be designated according to material trimmed as Cushion Trimmer (boot & shoe); Heel Trimmer (boot & shoe) II; Sole Trimmer (boot & shoe); Top Trimmer (boot & shoe) II.
GOE: 06.02.07 STRENGTH: L GED: R3 M2 L2 SVP: 4 DLU: 77

690.682-090 TRIMMING-MACHINE OPERATOR (button & notion) alternate titles: button broacher
Sets up and operates automatic machine to force steel pins through threadholes of plastic buttons to remove molding *flash*: Selects numbered dial feed-

plate and pin-holding chuck according to size and type of button and installs them in machine, using wrenches. Turns setscrews to align dial plate and pinholder to ensure that pins will be centered in thread-holes of buttons. Pours buttons into hopper, using hand scoop. Observes feeding of buttons into dial pockets and action of pin-driving and ejecting mechanism. Examines buttons for defects and adjusts machine as required. Removes filled containers from beneath ejection chute and places them on bench or handtruck.
GOE: 06.02.02 STRENGTH: M GED: R3 M2 L2 SVP: 4 DLU: 77

690.685-010 ASSEMBLER FOR PULLER-OVER, MACHINE (boot & shoe) alternate titles: counter and upper tacker; machine assembler
Tends machine that tacks shoe parts to last, to prepare shoe upper for further *lasting*: Places counter and tip support (box toe) on rack, immerses rack in liquid cement, and drains excess cement from parts. Inserts precemented parts between lining and upper. Pulls and aligns upper on last. Sets last on *pin jack* of machine. Pushes pin jack and upper into machine that tacks upper to last at heel seam and heel seat.
GOE: 06.04.05 STRENGTH: M GED: R2 M1 L2 SVP: 3 DLU: 77

690.685-014 ASSEMBLY-PRESS OPERATOR (any industry) alternate titles: bench-press operator
Tends hand or power press that shapes or assembles metal, plastic, rubber, or glass parts by crimping, shaping, locking, staking, or press fitting: Aligns workpiece against fixtures under ram as specified. Moves controls to lower ram that shapes parts or presses parts together. May tend machine to separate parts or punch, face, cut, chamfer, or compress parts preparatory to assembly. May tend machine equipped with multiple rams or automatic positioning device. May be designated according to type of press tended as Arbor-Press Operator (any industry) II; Kick-Press Operator (any industry) II; or according to parts assembled as Handle Attacher (any industry); Lens Mounter (optical goods) I.
GOE: 06.04.20 STRENGTH: L GED: R2 M1 L2 SVP: 2 DLU: 86

690.685-018 BACK-STRIP-MACHINE OPERATOR (boot & shoe)
Tends machine that rolls strips of friction tape onto continuous sheeting of uncured rubber stock and cuts assembly into specified widths and lengths to form backstays (backseam reinforcing strips) for rubber footwear: Selects stock and tape of specified color and thickness. Mounts parallel rolls of tape in individual holders and roll of sheeting on machine frame, using hoist. Installs reel in cradle for winding sheeting wrapper and attaches mobile electric motor to drive shaft, using collar and wrenches. Threads sheeting and friction tape around rollers that guide and press materials together. Fastens end of wrapper to reel for rewinding. Starts machine and rewinding motor, and conveyor that pulls assembly under rotary gang knives and under guillotine to slit sheet into strips and cuts strips to length. Winds friction tape around cardboard tubing to form stick, presses stick across row of strips on conveyor, and places strips between cloth leaves to form book. Examines strips for wrinkles and other defects and discards rejects.
GOE: 06.04.07 STRENGTH: L GED: R1 M1 L1 SVP: 2 DLU: 77

690.685-022 BALER (plastic-synth.)
Tends automatic machine that bales rubber pellets: Observes machine compressing, wrapping, and sealing rubber pellets into bales. Reads meters to verify weights of bales. Observes coating mechanism and distribution of dope, talc, or film on bales. Removes wet bales from machines. Examines metal detector and wrapping mechanism for defects. Turns valves and presses button that resets baling operations when automatic controls malfunction. May tend automatic machine that stacks bales on pallets for storage or shipment.
GOE: 06.04.07 STRENGTH: L GED: R2 M1 L2 SVP: 2 DLU: 77

690.685-026 BAND CUTTER (rubber goods)
Tends machine that cuts cured rubber tubing into rubberbands: Changes gears that regulate speed of cutting machine feed rolls, using handtools. Rinses tubing in water to facilitate cutting and guides tubes into feed rolls. Starts machine that cuts tubing into bands and blows bands from machine to conveyor that drops bands into tote box.
GOE: 06.04.07 STRENGTH: M GED: R2 M1 L1 SVP: 3 DLU: 77

690.685-030 BAND-MACHINE OPERATOR (rubber goods)
Tends machine that forms rubber strips into tubing used to produce rubberbands: Sets and adjusts guides, knives, seam hammer, and cement roller on band machine to form and cut tubing to specified length. Lifts and positions roll of rubber stripping on *letoff rack*. Pulls end of rubber strip from roll, places on conveyor, and threads through machine. Starts machine and observes operation. Measures tubing to ensure that specifications are met. Dumps soapstone into blower unit that dusts tubing to prevent sticking.
GOE: 06.04.07 STRENGTH: H GED: R2 M2 L2 SVP: 4 DLU: 77

690.685-034 BOTTOM PRESSER (boot & shoe) alternate titles: bottom ironer; burnisher
Tends bottom-pressing machine that smooths wrinkles from bottom of lasted shoe upper: Turns contour-control dial to adjust shape of heated pressing plate according to specifications stamped on last. Inserts guide jack pin of machine into last, and places lasted shoe on heated pressing plate. Depresses pedal to lower guide jack that presses lasted shoe against pressing plate.
GOE: 06.04.05 STRENGTH: M GED: R2 M1 L2 SVP: 2 DLU: 77

690.685-038 BOWLING-BALL FINISHER (toy-sport equip.) alternate titles: plastic ball buffer; rubber ball finisher
Tends buffing machine that removes scratches and polishes surface of bowling balls: Places ball in holding fixture, pad, or cup of buffer and coats buffing

wheel and pad with abrasive compound. Changes position of ball against revolving wheel to remove grinding and sanding scratches on surface of ball. Removes ball after specified time and holds ball against finish buffing wheel, moving ball with hands to expose all surfaces to wheel. Examines ball for scratches and specified finish. May dress ball with waterproof sandpaper or rubbing compound to remove nicks, pits, and scratches prior to engraving or polishing and be designated Hand Finisher, Bowling Balls (toy-sport equip.).
GOE: 06.04.09 STRENGTH: M GED: R2 M1 L2 SVP: 2 DLU: 78

690.685-042 BRANDING-MACHINE TENDER (rubber goods) alternate titles: machine printer, hose

Tends machine that prints brand name on rubber hose: Bolts specified printing plate on machine fixture. Adjusts guides and feed rollers to accommodate hose, using wrench. Fills feed tank with specified color ink and starts machine. Lifts hose to table by hand or with hoist and starts hose into feed rollers. Examines hose to ensure that printing meets specifications.
GOE: 06.04.07 STRENGTH: M GED: R2 M1 L1 SVP: 3 DLU: 77

690.685-046 BUFFER (boot & shoe) alternate titles: brusher; buffing-machine operator; cuffer; polisher; rasper-machine operator; remover; roughener; ruffer; sander; sander and polisher; scourer

Tends machine that smooths or roughens shoe parts by either of following methods: (1) Holds and presses part against abrasive cylinder that polishes and sands part or against wire roughing wheel to clean and prepare part for cementing. (2) Feeds sole between rubber presser roller and abrasive-covered roller that roughens part for cementing. May feed part into trimming cutter to trim part. May tape parts to protect masked areas during buffing or inking. May grind off rough surfaces from hair side of hides and be designated Hide Buffer (boot & shoe). May be designated according to part buffed, roughened, or sanded as Box-Toe Buffer (boot & shoe). May be designated according to type of material brushed or sanded as Crepe-Sole Scourer (boot & shoe); Crepe-Sole Wire Brusher (boot & shoe). May be designated according to purpose for which part is roughened as Rougher For Cement (boot & shoe). May be designated: Bottom Buffer (boot & shoe); Breast Buffer (boot & shoe); Channel Rougher (boot & shoe); Counter Buffer (boot & shoe); Heel Buffer (boot & shoe); Heel-Emery Buffer (boot & shoe); Heel Sander, Rubber (boot & shoe); Heel-Seat Sander (boot & shoe); Heel Slicker (boot & shoe); Insole Buffer (boot & shoe); Insole Sander (boot & shoe); Joint Sander (boot & shoe); Shank Sander (boot & shoe); Sole Buffer (boot & shoe); Sole Rougher (boot & shoe); Top-Lift Scourer (boot & shoe); Welt Rougher (boot & shoe).
GOE: 06.04.05 STRENGTH: L GED: R2 M1 L1 SVP: 3 DLU: 78

690.685-050 BUFFER, AUTOMATIC (boot & shoe)

Tends pair of automatic machines that grind edges of soles to remove sprues left by molding and roughen edges for foxing: Starts machines. Depresses pedal of first machine to separate toothed feeder wheels. Clamps sole between wheels and against rotating, vertical buffing wheel that grinds excess material from sole edge as feeder wheels automatically turn sole. Observes sole edge after one rotation for complete removal of sprue and removes sole or leaves sole on for second turn. Loads second machine while first is operating and alternates between both.
GOE: 06.04.05 STRENGTH: L GED: R1 M1 L1 SVP: 2 DLU: 77

690.685-054 BUFFER, INFLATED-PAD (boot & shoe)

Tends buffing machine equipped with inflated pad that buffs shoe soles: Presses sole against inflated buffing pad which scours and smooths shank and breast. Removes worn pads, using handtools.
GOE: 06.04.05 STRENGTH: L GED: R2 M1 L1 SVP: 3 DLU: 77

690.685-058 BURNISHER (boot & shoe) alternate titles: brusher; finisher; polisher

Tends machine that waxes and burnishes shoes to protect leather and give smooth finish: Starts burnishing machine and coats revolving burnishing wheel with wax, using wax block. Holds shoe against waxed wheel to apply wax to shoe, then against bristle and cloth brushes to polish. May use hand burnishing tools. May be designated according to part of shoe burnished as Bottom Burnisher (boot & shoe); Heel Burnisher (boot & shoe); Shank Burnisher (boot & shoe); Tip Burnisher (boot & shoe). May hold shoe against corrugated wheel to knurl edge of heel seat to improve appearance and be designated Heel Wheeler (boot & shoe).
GOE: 06.04.05 STRENGTH: L GED: R1 M1 L1 SVP: 3 DLU: 77

690.685-062 BUTTON-DECORATING-MACHINE OPERATOR (button & notion) alternate titles: automatic-fancy-machine operator

Tends automatic machines that cut ornamental designs into face of nonmetallic button blanks: Loads blanks into machine hopper, using hand scoop. Starts machine and observes feeding, cutting, and *indexing* mechanisms. Removes jammed blanks from feed chute, using wire pick. May remove and replace worn cutters and abrasive wheels, using wrenches. May place blanks by hand in chucks of semiautomatic, manually indexed machine. May examine samples for finishing defects.
GOE: 06.04.09 STRENGTH: L GED: R2 M1 L2 SVP: 2 DLU: 77

690.685-066 BUTTON-FACING-MACHINE OPERATOR (button & notion)

Tends battery of automatic machines that drill thread holes and shape surface of nonmetallic button blanks: Loads workpieces into machine hopper, using hand scoop. Starts machine and observes blanks feeding into rotating chucks on transport mechanism that conveys blanks to cutting tools and drills. Stops machine and notifies setup mechanic of malfunction. May hand feed pearl button blanks into machine to ensure that blanks are positioned face-up in chucks. May place single blank in chuck of manually controlled machine and pull on leverage bar to force blank against cutting tool or drill.
GOE: 06.04.09 STRENGTH: L GED: R2 M1 L2 SVP: 2 DLU: 77

690.685-070 CEMENTER AND FOLDER, MACHINE (boot & shoe) alternate titles: french-binding folder; plastic-machine folder; quarter folder; thermo-cementing-folder operator

Tends machine that cements and folds *french binding* or skived edge of shoe uppers to form smooth edge: Moves lever to lower machine head and guides shoe part under head to cement, fold, and press edge of upper. Raises and presses folded edge flat, using awl, to repair rough folds. May depress pedal to lower blades that notch and crease folds on curves. May turn knobs to regulate temperature of heating element and flow of heated plastic cement.
GOE: 06.04.05 STRENGTH: L GED: R2 M1 L2 SVP: 3 DLU: 77

690.685-074 CEMENTER, MACHINE JOINER (boot & shoe) alternate titles: attacher; beater; folding-machine operator; joiner; layer; setter; taper

Tends one of various pressing machines that join precemented shoe parts, performing any of following tasks: Turns setscrew that adjusts distance between pressure rollers, feeds aligned parts between rollers, and observes joining of parts. Positions parts on machine bed and depresses pedal that forces heated presser head against parts to join them. Moves lever that adjusts contour of pad on lower jaw of machine or changes pad, following contour of parts to be joined. Positions parts on pad and depresses pedal that closes jaws to join parts. Positions cemented parts on shoe and places shoe in oven to soften cement. Positions shoe parts on bed of machine and moves lever to start machine that presses and cements parts. May bound toe and shank area of shoe to improve adhesion or waterproofing strip to inner and outer sole parts, using hammer. May brush solvent on precemented parts to soften cement prior to joining parts. May apply cement to parts. May be designated according to parts joined as Insole Coverer (boot & shoe); Insole-Lip Turner (boot & shoe); Platform Presser (boot & shoe); Sole Layer (boot & shoe). May tend machine that uses conveyor-carried air inflated pads to join precemented parts and be designated Compo-Conveyor Operator (boot & shoe). May be designated: Heel Layer (boot & shoe); Insole Taper (boot & shoe); Open-Shank Coverer (boot & shoe); Welt-Sole Layer (boot & shoe).
GOE: 06.04.05 STRENGTH: L GED: R2 M1 L2 SVP: 2 DLU: 77

690.685-078 CENTER-PUNCH OPERATOR (recording)

Tends punch press that punches center holes in phonograph records or stamper: Removes stack of records or stampers from conveyor and places them on machine holder. Positions record in slot over punch die of machine or centers disk under punch die, using calibrated microscope and starts machine. Removes punched record, and simultaneously positions unpunched record in machine or removes and places stamper on sanding spindle for further processing. Places punched records in trays.
GOE: 06.04.02 STRENGTH: L GED: R1 M1 L1 SVP: 2 DLU: 77

690.685-082 CHANNEL OPENER, OUTSOLES (boot & shoe) alternate titles: channel turner

Tends machine that flares slit in preslit edge of shoe outsoles to form channel and facilitate stitching of welt to outsole. Pushes and guides edge of outsole against tapered revolving roller to flare slit.
GOE: 06.04.05 STRENGTH: L GED: R1 M1 L1 SVP: 2 DLU: 77

690.685-086 CHANNELER, INSOLE (boot & shoe) alternate titles: lockstitch channeler; welt-insole channeler

Tends machine that cuts two parallel grooves near edge of insole prior to welting: Positions insole against machine guide. Depresses pedal to raise machine bed against cutting blades that cut grooves (channels) in insole. Adjusts lever to control width of cut, following work ticket. May turn handwheel to regulate speed of cutting blades. May tend machine to bevel outer edge of insole. May channel outsoles and be designated Channeler, Outsole (boot & shoe).
GOE: 06.04.05 STRENGTH: L GED: R2 M1 L2 SVP: 3 DLU: 77

690.685-090 CONTACT-LENS MOLDER (optical goods)

Tends heating equipment and hydraulic casting press that casts plastic contact lenses: Lays separate top and bottom sections of previously set up mold on heated metal block for specified time. Fills lens cavities in heated mold with plastic powder. Aligns guide pins and holes to join top and bottom sections of mold. Places filled mold on bed of press, sets timer, and starts press to lower ram until dial indicates mold sections are under specified pressure. Removes mold from press. Inspects first run of lenses to verify accuracy of lens power, using power determining and optical centering instrument. Reports defects in new molds.
GOE: 06.04.13 STRENGTH: L GED: R2 M2 L2 SVP: 3 DLU: 77

690.685-094 COUNTER CUTTER (boot & shoe) alternate titles: counter maker

Tends machine that cuts counters for shoes from leather, fiberboard, or other materials: Selects materials and cutting dies according to work ticket. Positions leather, sheets of fiberboard, or other material on bed under beam of machine.

Positions die on material to obtain maximum number of parts. Depresses pedal to lower beam onto top of die, cutting out counters.
GOE: 06.04.09 STRENGTH: M GED: R2 M1 L2 SVP: 3 DLU: 77

690.685-098 COUNTER FORMER (boot & shoe) alternate titles: forming-machine operator
Tends forming machine that restores shape to heel counters of finished shoes: Adjusts temperature of forming iron and positions shoe on iron. Depresses pedal that moves presser arms, forcing counter against iron to restore shape to counter. May remove wrinkles, using hand iron. May shape one-piece quarters by similar method and be designated Quarter Former (boot & shoe).
GOE: 06.04.05 STRENGTH: L GED: R2 M1 L2 SVP: 2 DLU: 77

690.685-102 COUNTER MOLDER (boot & shoe)
Tends machine that molds shoe counter into shape of heel: Places counter on head of mold. Regulates temperature of mold as specified for material being used, such as cloth, fiber, or *lumite*. Depresses pedal to exert pressure on mold and form counter. May be designated according to type of counter material as Ciaio-Counter Molder (boot & shoe).
GOE: 06.04.05 STRENGTH: L GED: R3 M1 L2 SVP: 3 DLU: 77

690.685-106 COUNTER ROLLER (boot & shoe)
Tends machine that skives (shaves), corrugates, and waxes precut counters to prepare them for further processing: Stacks counters in feeding device. Presses button to start machine that moves counters under presser rollers and knife blade to shave them to uniform thickness, then under roller that corrugates edges, and applicator that coats counters with wax. May change cutting knives, using wrench.
GOE: 06.04.05 STRENGTH: L GED: R2 M1 L1 SVP: 2 DLU: 77

690.685-110 CUT-OUT-AND-MARKING-MACHINE OPERATOR (boot & shoe)
Tends machine that simultaneously trims leather shoe parts to size, punches perforations, and marks stitching outline: Bolts specified die to ram or bed of machine, using wrench. Brushes ink on roller which marks stitch outline on part. Positions part on machine and presses pedal to start machine. Stacks processed parts.
GOE: 06.04.05 STRENGTH: L GED: R2 M1 L1 SVP: 3 DLU: 77

690.685-114 CUT-OUT-MACHINE OPERATOR (boot & shoe) alternate titles: cut-out-press operator; die-out-machine operator; gang-punch operator; puncher
Tends machine that cuts out decorative designs or ventilating holes in shoe parts by any of following methods: (1) Clips guide plate on machine bed and turns knobs to adjust position. Clamps hammer block or punch in machine head. Aligns part, such as saddle, strap, or vamp on guide plate and starts machine that cuts designs or holes in part. May adjust machine to accelerate reciprocal action of punch or to regulate cutting pressure of head. (2) Positions die plate on machine and clips shoe part on plate. Pushes plate on rails under machine head and starts machine that cuts designs or holes in parts. When operating machine equipped with punch, may be designated Perforator (boot & shoe). May be designated according to part cut as Buckle-Strap Puncher (boot & shoe); Hole Puncher, Strap (boot & shoe); Tip Puncher (boot & shoe).
GOE: 06.04.05 STRENGTH: L GED: R2 M1 L1 SVP: 2 DLU: 77

690.685-118 CUTTER I (fabrication, nec)
Tends machine that automatically cuts cartridges (strips) from continuous sheet of plastic floor covering material emerging from calender machine. Places cartridges, separated by cloths, on buggy for transportation to floor covering press.
GOE: 06.04.02 STRENGTH: L GED: R2 M1 L2 SVP: 2 DLU: 77

690.685-122 CUTTING-MACHINE TENDER (any industry)
Tends power shear that cuts sheets of material, such as paper, pressboard, foil, cardboard, cork, or plastic material to specified dimension for items, such as cartons, wrappers, labels, business forms, or gaskets: Adjusts guides on machine to regulate width of cut according to work order, following calibrated scale on machine bed or using ruler. Positions and aligns sheets against guides and presses lever to clamp sheets to bed of machine prior to cutting. Presses button(s) or moves lever controls to force shear blade through sheets. Adjusts guides and repositions material to trim or square edges to specifications. May change shear blade, using handtools. May be designated according to type of material cut as Cardboard Cutter (any industry); Cutter, Plastic Sheets (plastic prod.; plastic-synth.); Paper Cutter (any industry). May cut material manually, using hand-powered shear, and be designated Paper Cutter, Hand (any industry).
GOE: 06.04.09 STRENGTH: M GED: R3 M2 L2 SVP: 3 DLU: 89

690.685-126 DESKIDDING-MACHINE OPERATOR (boot & shoe)
Tends automatic machine that cuts wavy or zigzag designs in outsoles for rubber footwear to provide nonskid surface: Positions sole on slide carriage under blade and between spring clamps that hold ends of sole to carriage. Starts machine and moves lever to depress cutter that automatically cuts single row to set depth in vertical reciprocating action. Moves lever to raise cutter, depresses pedal to return carriage to starting position, and repeats process to cut additional rows. Releases clamps to replace finished workpiece. Examines depth of cut, using mold mark on sole edge as guide, and raises or lowers blade, using wrench to adjust depth.
GOE: 06.04.07 STRENGTH: L GED: R2 M1 L2 SVP: 2 DLU: 77

690.685-130 DICER OPERATOR (plastic-synth.)
Tends machine that cuts sheets or strands of plastic material into cubes or pellets for packaging: Observes feed of material from cooling unit into machine, and adjusts speed of cutters to cut pellets to specified size. May tend auxiliary equipment, such as tumbler dryer. May bag pellets.
GOE: 06.04.02 STRENGTH: L GED: R2 M1 L1 SVP: 2 DLU: 77

690.685-134 DUAL-HOSE CEMENTER (rubber goods) alternate titles: hose cementer; hose finisher
Tends machine that cements lengths of rubber hose together to form dual hose for use in oxyacetylene torches: Pours rubber cement into machine dispenser and turns valve to regulate flow of cement. Adjusts buffing wheel that smooths sides of hose to be joined. Verifies diameter of hose, using gauge. Threads hose through feed rollers and starts machine. Examines dual hose to ensure that joint is cemented evenly. Ties identification tag on hose. May tend machine that prints brand on hose [BRANDING-MACHINE TENDER (rubber goods)].
GOE: 06.04.07 STRENGTH: L GED: R2 M1 L2 SVP: 2 DLU: 77

690.685-138 EDGE BURNISHER, UPPERS (boot & shoe) alternate titles: edger; upper edger
Tends machine that rolls and presses edges of shoe uppers to smooth and finish edges: Positions edge of shoe upper against guides and under heated burnishing iron. Presses lever to start machine, and guides edge under iron and edge-rolling wheel to roll and press edge of upper.
GOE: 06.04.05 STRENGTH: L GED: R2 M1 L1 SVP: 3 DLU: 77

690.685-142 EDGE GRINDER (plastic prod.)
Tends machine that squares and smooths edges of plastic floor tile: Adjusts guide shoes for squareness, using wrenches and tile gauge. Places stack of tile on table of machine. Taps tiles with mallet to align tile edges against guide shoes. Presses buttons to engage guide shoes and move stack of tile between grinding wheel. Rotates tile on table to grind edges. Places finished tile on conveyor.
GOE: 06.04.02 STRENGTH: L GED: R2 M1 L1 SVP: 3 DLU: 77

690.685-146 EDGE SETTER (boot & shoe) alternate titles: edge burnisher; edge kitter
Tends machine that polishes and shapes edges of heel lifts and shoe soles through vibrating action of heated irons: Selects irons according to thickness of heel lift or sole and clamps them in chuck of machine. Turns dial to heat and regulate temperature of irons, according to work ticket. Pushes lever that rotates chuck to bring heel lift or sole into working position. Presses and guides heel or sole against vibrating iron to burnish edges. May brush, dye, ink, or wax edges. May be designated according to part burnished as Edge Setter, Heel Lift (boot & shoe).
GOE: 06.04.05 STRENGTH: M GED: R2 M1 L2 SVP: 3 DLU: 77

690.685-150 EDGE TRIMMER (boot & shoe) alternate titles: apex trimmer; edge-trimming-machine operator; margin trimmer; outsole trimmer; sole pretrimmer
Tends machine that trims sole and heel edges of lasted shoes to remove excess material and to impart finished appearance: Positions and guides edges against revolving cutter to trim them. May replace cutters or guides, using handtools. May sharpen cutters.
GOE: 06.04.05 STRENGTH: L GED: R2 M1 L1 SVP: 4 DLU: 77

690.685-154 ELECTRIC-SEALING-MACHINE OPERATOR (any industry) alternate titles: bonding-machine operator; dielectric-heat-sealing-machine operator; heat-seal operator; plastic-welding-machine operator
Tends machine that heats and seals precut or predesigned plastic material or film to form book covers, eyeglass cases, baby pants, tubing, and other plastic-coated products: Moves controls on machine to adjust temperature, pressure, and time cycle. Loads feeding mechanism with rolls of plastic material. Aligns edges of continuous plastic strips and guides them into position under electrode. Starts machine and depresses pedal to lower electrode that heats and seals edges of material. Removes product from machine and stacks it in rack or on table. May position plastic strip over article preparatory to heat sealing article.
GOE: 06.04.02 STRENGTH: L GED: R2 M1 L2 SVP: 2 DLU: 77

690.685-158 EMBOSSER (boot & shoe) alternate titles: printer; stamper
Tends machine that imprints trade name or other identifying symbols on shoe parts: Obtains embossed plate specified on work ticket and positions it in heated upper stamping beam of machine. Positions spool of colored embossing ribbon on machine spindle and draws it through guides, under stamping beam, and between feed rollers. Positions shoe part on machine bed. Depresses pedal that lowers stamping beam and embossed plate, pressing colored ribbon against shoe part and imprinting trade name or other symbols on part. May remove embossing ribbon from machine to imprint trade name without color. May be designated according to part stamped as Bottom Stamper (boot & shoe); Sock-Lining And Heel-Pad Embosser (boot & shoe).
GOE: 06.04.05 STRENGTH: L GED: R2 M1 L2 SVP: 2 DLU: 77

690.685-162 FASTENER, MACHINE (boot & shoe) alternate titles: anchor tacker; fastener; nailer; puncher and fastener; puncher; riveter; sewer; stapler; tacker
Tends nailing, slugging, stapling, or tacking machine that attaches shoe parts, such as heel, insole, and shank to partially assembled shoes: Aligns parts on

bed of machine, or positions them under machine head. Depresses pedal that lowers holding device, or holds parts against guide. Depresses pedal or lever that drives fasteners into parts. Fills hopper of nailing or tacking machine, or replaces wire spool on spindle of slugging or stapling machine. May brush cement onto parts prior to joining. May be designated according to part joined as Heeler, Machine (boot & shoe); Insole Tacker (boot & shoe); Ornament Stapler (boot & shoe); Top-Lift Nailer (boot & shoe). May be designated: Bow Stapler (boot & shoe); Buckle Stapler (boot & shoe); Fiber-Heel-Piece Shaper (boot & shoe); Gore Stapler (boot & shoe); Heel-Seat Filler (boot & shoe); Heel-Seat-Flap Stapler (boot & shoe); Nail Welter (boot & shoe); Outsole Tacker (boot & shoe); Platform Stapler (boot & shoe); Rand Tacker (boot & shoe); Shank Stapler (boot & shoe); Sole Stapler, Welt (boot & shoe); Toe Stapler (boot & shoe).
GOE: 06.04.05 STRENGTH: L GED: R2 M1 L2 SVP: 2 DLU: 77

690.685-166 FEATHEREDGER AND REDUCER, MACHINE (boot & shoe) alternate titles: featheredge-machine operator; forepart reducer; outsole beveler; outsole skiver

Tends machine that shaves shank, heel seat, forepart, or edges of shoe outsole to reduce thickness and increase flexibility of outsole by any of following methods: (1) Feeds edge of outsole against guide and between rollers that force edge against machine blade. Turns crank to regulate speed of rollers along curved edges. May depress pedal to separate rollers to accommodate thickness of outsole. (2) Positions specified die rollers on machine shaft. Positions outsoles against guides on machine bed. Depresses pedal that starts rollers that force shank, heel seat, forepart, or edges of outsole against machine blade. Turns handwheel to set cutting gauge according to outsole size. May reduce thickness of insoles at edges. May be designated according to part of outsole reduced or beveled as Heel Reducer (boot & shoe); Shank Beveler (boot & shoe).
GOE: 06.04.05 STRENGTH: L GED: R2 M1 L2 SVP: 2 DLU: 77

690.685-170 FINISHER, MACHINE (plastic prod.)

Tends sanding-and-buffing machine that smooths and polishes surface of plastic sheets to specified finish: Installs sandpaper belt in machine and sets tension of buffer springs to regulate pressure of buffers on sheets, using wrench. Starts machine and feeds sheets into machine. Observes ammeter to verify machine load specified for sanding. Verifies thickness of finished sheets, using dial indicator micrometer. Examines surface of sheets for defects, such as scratches, dull spots, and cracks.
GOE: 06.04.02 STRENGTH: M GED: R2 M2 L2 SVP: 2 DLU: 77

690.685-174 FOLDER, MACHINE (boot & shoe) alternate titles: cover creaser; edge beader; folding-machine operator; wrapper laster

Tends machine that folds precemented edges of shoe parts, such as insoles, platforms, quarters, and vamps to strengthen and smooth edges: Positions part against guide and under presser foot and folding finger, or between rollers of machine. Releases pedal that lowers presser foot, starts machine, and guides part under presser foot and folding finger or between rollers to fold and press edges of part. May repair uneven folds by pressing with hot iron. Important variables may be indicated by trade name of machines used.
GOE: 06.04.05 STRENGTH: L GED: R2 M1 L2 SVP: 3 DLU: 77

690.685-178 FOLDING-MACHINE OPERATOR (leather prod.) alternate titles: gusset folder; zipper-lining folder

Tends machine that folds precemented edges of leather handbag, wallet, coin purse, or key case parts to strengthen and smooth edges: Positions part, such as gusset or zipper lining, against machine guide and under presser foot. Depresses pedal to move part edge against folding bar of machine that forms folded edge.
GOE: 06.04.05 STRENGTH: L GED: R2 M1 L1 SVP: 2 DLU: 77

690.685-182 FORCE-VARIATION EQUIPMENT TENDER (rubber tire)

Tends battery of machines that test or grind tires for conformance to radial balance specifications: Lifts and positions tires in machine. Starts machine that inflates tires and activates sensory roller rotating against tire. Observes panel indicators to determine tires meeting specifications. Places defective tires on conveyor leading to automatic machine that locates and grinds excess rubber from tires. Drops defective tires in scrap truck and stacks balanced tires on shipping pallet.
GOE: 06.03.01 STRENGTH: M GED: R2 M1 L2 SVP: 2 DLU: 77

690.685-186 FOREPART LASTER (boot & shoe) alternate titles: ball laster

Tends *lasting* machine that presses edges of precemented uppers onto insole and shapes forepart section of shoes: Positions last on machine. Moves lever to cause machine pincers to stretch upper, and to cause wipers to press edges of upper onto insole. Presses machine button to release last. Turns handle to reverse pincer grip according to shape of right or left shoe.
GOE: 06.04.05 STRENGTH: L GED: R2 M1 L2 SVP: 2 DLU: 77

690.685-190 FOUNTAIN PEN TURNER (pen & pencil)

Tends multiple-spindle automatic screw machine that bores, turns, or threads plastic or rubber tubing stock to form barrels of pens and pencils: Positions and secures tools in toolholders following job order and verbal instructions, using wrenches. Positions and secures bar stock in chuck. Starts machine and engages automatic feed. Spot checks conformance of completed workpiece to specifications, using dial and fixed gauges.

GOE: 06.04.09 STRENGTH: L GED: R2 M1 L2 SVP: 3 DLU: 77

690.685-194 GRINDING-MACHINE OPERATOR, AUTOMATIC (button & notion) alternate titles: belt back operator

Tends machine that removes bark (rough exterior of pearl-shell) from back of pearl button blanks, and levels back and face of blanks: Places blanks facedown on conveyor belt that feeds blanks between steel plate and abrasive wheel. Inverts blanks by hand, and repeats operation to level faces. May tend machine that inverts blanks automatically. May insert blank in holder of manually controlled machine and pull on leverage bar to force blank against abrasive wheel.
GOE: 06.04.08 STRENGTH: S GED: R2 M1 L2 SVP: 2 DLU: 77

690.685-198 GROOVER AND TURNER (boot & shoe)

Tends machines that cut heel blanks (rough forms) of wood, leather, or fiberboard into heels: Inserts blank in holding device. Pushes heel against revolving knife blades to shape outside of heel. Positions shaped heel in holding device of second machine that hollows out face of heel. May sharpen and insert cutting blades in machines. May be designated according to material grooved or turned as Wooden-Heel Beveler (boot & shoe).
GOE: 06.04.09 STRENGTH: L GED: R2 M1 L2 SVP: 2 DLU: 77

690.685-202 GROOVING-LATHE TENDER (plastic prod.)

Tends lathe-type machine that cuts grooves (knurls) in plastic tubes and cuts tubes to size to form flashlight covers: Slides tubing over mandrel attached to chuck and starts machine. Moves cutting tool against workpiece that knurls tubing and cuts tubing into specified lengths.
GOE: 06.04.02 STRENGTH: L GED: R2 M1 L2 SVP: 2 DLU: 77

690.685-206 HEEL BUILDER, MACHINE (boot & shoe) alternate titles: heel former; lift builder, whole; push-up machine operator

Tends machine that cements, nails, and holds lifts to form heel or heel bases: Inserts and pulls leather or fiberboard lifts through cement-covered rollers of machine according to material, size, and style of heel specified on work ticket. Stacks cement-covered lifts against faceplate (mold) of machine. Places nail in holding device on ram of machine and depresses pedal to start machine that drives nail into stacked lifts and holds heel in conveyor or press until dry. May be designated according to type of heel built as High-Heel Builder (boot & shoe); Low-Heel Builder (boot & shoe). Important variables may be indicated by trade name of machines used.
GOE: 06.04.09 STRENGTH: L GED: R2 M1 L2 SVP: 3 DLU: 77

690.685-210 HEEL COMPRESSOR (boot & shoe) alternate titles: heel molder

Tends machine that compresses heels to give them better wearing quality: Feeds precut heels of leather or composition material into machine and observes operation. May change dies and adjust stroke of ram. May tend machine equipped with blades that trim and shape breast of heel during operation. May compress top lifts and be designated Top-Lift Compressor (boot & shoe).
GOE: 06.04.05 STRENGTH: L GED: R1 M1 L1 SVP: 2 DLU: 77

690.685-214 HEEL GOUGER (boot & shoe)

Tends machine that cuts cavity to form heel seat in heels: Bolts specified cutting disk to machine. Turns setscrews to adjust machine for length and depth of cut. Loads heels into feeding device or positions heel under machine guide and depresses pedal to start machine that cuts gouge in heels and ejects them into storage container. May cut gouge in heel lifts and be designated Heel-Lift Gouger (boot & shoe).
GOE: 06.04.09 STRENGTH: L GED: R2 M1 L2 SVP: 3 DLU: 77

690.685-218 HEEL PRICKER (boot & shoe)

Tends machine that pricks holes in leather heels to facilitate nailing: Selects pricking device according to number of holes to be pricked. Inserts awls of specified size and length through holes in faceplate of device. Positions device in machine and places heel on feed channel. Depresses pedal to start machine that drives awls into heel and pulls them out again.
GOE: 06.04.05 STRENGTH: L GED: R2 M1 L2 SVP: 3 DLU: 77

690.685-222 HEEL SCORER (boot & shoe)

Tends machine that scores insole of shoe to provide guideline for installation of heel and indicate where channel of insole begins: Turns setscrews and moves guides on machine to hold specified insoles. Positions insole against guides and presses switch to start machine that cuts score across heel seat of insole. May make cut in toe of welt insole to prevent puckering when stitched to shoe upper and be designated Insole-Toe-Snipping-Machine Operator (boot & shoe).
GOE: 06.04.05 STRENGTH: L GED: R2 M1 L2 SVP: 2 DLU: 77

690.685-226 HEEL-NAILING-MACHINE OPERATOR (boot & shoe)

Tends nailing machine that attaches wooden or plastic heels to nonleather footwear: Inverts shoe and places heel section over metal rest and against stop guide. Depresses pedal to drive hopper-fed nails automatically around edge of counter into insole to prepare seating for heel. Sets screwhead in hole of machine fixture, holds inverted shoe and heel in assembly position against stop guides, and depresses pedal that presses shoe and heel together and automatically drives screw into heel (pressure turns thread into heel). Pushes knob to load nail-driving device with nails from hoppers, inverts shoe with attached heel over nail holder and against stop guides, and depresses pedal to drive nails automatically into heel.
GOE: 06.04.09 STRENGTH: L GED: R2 M1 L2 SVP: 2 DLU: 77

690.685-230 HEEL-SEAT LASTER, MACHINE (boot & shoe)
Tends *lasting* machine that shapes and attaches heel section edges of upper to insole: Places and holds last on machine spindle. Pulls edges of shoe upper over insole, using *lasting tool*. Depresses pedals that activate wipers that press upper edges against insole and tack drivers that fasten edges onto insole. Turns handwheel to adjust spacing of wipers and tack drivers. May nail down exposed edges and tacks, using hammer. May soften and remove wrinkles from uppers, using hand iron.
GOE: 06.04.05 STRENGTH: L GED: R2 M1 L2 SVP: 3 DLU: 77

690.685-234 INKER, MACHINE (boot & shoe) alternate titles: edge blacker, machine; edge dyer; edge stainer, machine; heel stainer; sole blacker; sole dyer
Tends machine that applies ink or stain to color edges of shoe soles or heels, by any of following methods: (1) Inserts and guides outsole or midsole between pressure roller and ink-covered rollers of machine. (2) Depresses pedal that separates feed rollers; releases pedal that closes and starts rollers that hold and turn sole edge against inked wheel. (3) Positions and guides soles under machine nozzle that applies ink or stain to edge of attached outsole. (4) Positions heel against machine guide and turns heel against revolving brush that applies ink to heel edge. May be designated according to part colored as Heel-Edge Inker, Machine (boot & shoe); Sole-Edge Inker, Machine (boot & shoe).
GOE: 06.04.21 STRENGTH: L GED: R2 M1 L2 SVP: 2 DLU: 77

690.685-238 INSEAM TRIMMER (boot & shoe) alternate titles: inner seamer; inseam-trimming-machine operator; margin trimmer; side trimmer; welt trimmer
Tends machine that trims edges of inseam to remove excess material prior to attachment of midsole or outsole: Turns setscrew that locks reciprocating blade onto machine shaft. Turns knobs that position machine guide. Depresses pedal that withdraws presser device, permitting alignment of excess material with cutting edge of blade. Releases pedal that recoils presser device, forcing excess material under blade. Guides shoe against cutting edge of blade to trim off excess material.
GOE: 06.04.05 STRENGTH: L GED: R2 M1 L2 SVP: 2 DLU: 77

690.685-242 INSOLE BEVELER (boot & shoe)
Tends machine that cuts bevel along channeled stitching lip on top edge of insole: Positions edge of insole under knife. Moves lever to drop knife and pressure foot onto edge of insole and move presser roller against inner surface of channeled lip. Pushes treadle to start machine and guides insole through machine.
GOE: 06.04.05 STRENGTH: L GED: R2 M1 L1 SVP: 2 DLU: 77

690.685-246 INSOLE REINFORCER (boot & shoe) alternate titles: insole-cloth trimmer; insole gemmer; trimmer and reinforcer
Tends machine that presses precemented canvas lining into channel area of insole and trims lining: Positions insole between horizontal disks. Depresses pedal to cause disks to press lining into insole channel, and to cause revolving blade to trim lining flush with insole edge.
GOE: 06.04.05 STRENGTH: L GED: R2 M1 L1 SVP: 3 DLU: 77

690.685-250 JOINT CUTTER, MACHINE (boot & shoe) alternate titles: joiner; jointer, machine; joint maker, machine
Tends jointing machine that trims edge of shoe sole at joint of shank and heel. Positions and guides lasted shoe against cutter that trims sole edge to impart finished appearance at joint.
GOE: 06.04.05 STRENGTH: L GED: R2 M1 L1 SVP: 2 DLU: 77

690.685-254 LACER II (boot & shoe)
Tends machine that laces string through shoe eyelets to close throat prior to *lasting:* Turns knob that adjusts length of string according to specifications. Pushes or pulls lever to adjust distance between protruding needles on machine bed to correspond with eyelet spacing. Positions part on machine bed extending needles through eyelets. Starts machine that laces string through eyelets, and ties and cuts string.
GOE: 06.04.05 STRENGTH: L GED: R2 M1 L2 SVP: 2 DLU: 77

690.685-258 LAMINATOR I (leather prod.)
Tends machine that laminates precemented leather and plastic parts used in making leather products, such as wallets, coin purses, and key cases: Presses button to start conveyor and heating elements. Turns knob to adjust distance between presser rollers. Places aligned parts on conveyor leading to machine that laminates parts. Removes parts from machine and ties parts into bundles for further processing.
GOE: 06.04.05 STRENGTH: S GED: R2 M1 L1 SVP: 2 DLU: 77

690.685-262 LAST SAWYER (wood prod., nec)
Tends variety of saws that cut plastic shoe last forms to specified size and shape: Positions and clamps last form on machine jig. Starts saw and pushes jig against saw to make specified cut on last. Pulls jig from saw, removes last from jig, and places last aside for further processing.
GOE: 06.04.02 STRENGTH: M GED: R2 M1 L1 SVP: 2 DLU. 77

690.685-266 LEATHER-BELT MAKER (leather prod.) alternate titles: belt puncher; cartridge belt puncher; puncher
Tends machines that cut, punch, rivet, or staple parts to leather to make apparel belts: Positions leather in machine. Starts machine, and depresses pedal to cut leather into specified strips for body of belt or belt loops. Places leather strip against guides in stapling or riveting machine or punch press. Depresses pedal to punch buckle or tongue holes in belt, shear and shape belt ends, staple belt loops onto belt, rivet buckle to belt, or attach snap fasteners to join parts. May be designated according to operation performed as Leather-Belt-Loop Cutter (leather prod.); Leather-Belt Puncher (leather prod.); Leather-Belt Shaper (leather prod.); or according to type of belt made as Leather-Cartridge-Belt Maker (leather prod.); Men's Leather-Dress-Belt Maker (leather prod.); Women's Leather-Belt Maker (leather prod.).
GOE: 06.04.05 STRENGTH: L GED: R2 M1 L2 SVP: 3 DLU: 77

690.685-270 LIP CUTTER AND SCORER (boot & shoe)
Tends machine that stamps shoe size and cuts or creases shoe insoles: Installs specified cutting or creasing blade in machine head, using handtools. Turns knob and pushes or pulls slide in groove in machine bed to select shoe size stamp. Positions insole, grain side down, against guide on bed. Depresses pedal that lowers head, cutting or creasing insole to indicate starting and stopping points for subsequent ribbing operations, and forcing insoles against heated size stamp to imprint shoe size.
GOE: 06.04.05 STRENGTH: L GED: R2 M1 L2 SVP: 2 DLU: 77

690.685-274 LIP-OF-SHANK CUTTER (boot & shoe)
Tends machine that cuts lip (inside edge) of shank on insole of shoe to improve flexibility: Adjusts screw to set gauge for size of cut determined on basis of size of insole. Sets insole, inner side up, on machine bed with lip of shank against gauge stop. Depresses lever to activate vertical plunger that makes cuts on insole at lip of shank.
GOE: 06.04.05 STRENGTH: L GED: R2 M1 L1 SVP: 2 DLU: 77

690.685-278 LUMITE INJECTOR (boot & shoe) alternate titles: compound-machine operator; squirt-machine operator
Tends machine that injects *lumite* into counter pocket of shoe to form rigid back: Sets control valve to regulate flow of lumite into counter pocket. Pushes shoe onto injection needle and depresses pedal to inject lumite. Guides back of shoe through rollers to spread lumite within counter pocket. May be designated according to material used to form counter as Ciaio-Lumite Injector (boot & shoe).
GOE: 06.04.05 STRENGTH: L GED: R2 M2 L2 SVP: 2 DLU: 77

690.685-282 MARKER, MACHINE (boot & shoe) alternate titles: machine tracer; stitch marker
Tends marking machine that stamps lines on upper shoe parts to serve as guides for subsequent operations: Selects machine guide and top plates according to work ticket. Positions and attaches guide and top plates on machine. Aligns shoe part in guide plate on machine bed. Depresses pedal that lowers machine head or pulls machine head down to mark lines on part. May mark vamp to indicate where vamp and tip should be joined and be designated Vamp Marker (boot & shoe).
GOE: 06.04.05 STRENGTH: L GED: R2 M1 L2 SVP: 3 DLU: 77

690.685-286 MAT PUNCHER (rubber goods) alternate titles: die-press operator
Tends machine that punches out and trims automobile floor mats from rubber sheeting: Bolts die to ram or seats die on movable table of press. Positions uncured rubber sheeting or cured rubber mats on moveable table or on die. Pushes table under ram of press, and starts machine. Places punched and trimmed mats on skid. May measure and mark guidelines on moveable table.
GOE: 06.04.07 STRENGTH: M GED: R2 M1 L2 SVP: 2 DLU: 77

690.685-290 MOLDED-RUBBER-GOODS CUTTER (rubber goods)
Tends machines that cut and trim cured rubber articles, such as ear plugs, water goggles, and automotive parts, from molded rubber sheets: Positions cutting die and fastens to bed of cutting machine with clamps or bolts. Positions molded rubber sheet over die, feeling with fingers to determine that each article in sheet is evenly aligned with cutting edges of die. Places fiberboard over rubber sheet to prevent damage to die cutting edges from ram. Pushes buttons to lower ram and cut out parts. May be designated according to type of machine used as Hydraulic-Punch-Press Operator (rubber goods); Roller-Die-Cutting-Machine Operator (rubber goods).
GOE: 06.04.07 STRENGTH: M GED: R2 M1 L1 SVP: 2 DLU: 77

690.685-294 MOLDER, LABELS (boot & shoe)
Tends machine that imprints identifying data, such as company name, trademark, or design, onto continuous strip of uncured rubber for labels on rubber footwear: Selects specified die, slides into holder on ram, and locks die in place, using wrench. Mounts roll of strip on spindle, and threads end between feeder rolls and under diehead. Starts machine and observes pressed labels for height of imprint. Stops machine and changes die or adjusts length of ram stroke for clearer imprint. Books finished strip as strip comes from press, cutting strip off at book length, using scissors. Stacks filled book on storage pile.
GOE: 06.04.07 STRENGTH: L GED: R2 M1 L1 SVP: 2 DLU: 77

690.685-298 NICKER (boot & shoe) alternate titles: snipper
Tends machine that nicks curved edges of shoe parts, such as vamps, tongues, quarters, and bindings, to facilitate folding of edges, using either of following methods: (1) Turns machine head to bring designated multiedged die into position. Positions part under die and depresses pedal that forces die downward, nicking edge; or (2) Places part on machine post against guide and presses part against reciprocating knife to nick edge. May be designated according to part nicked as Binding Nicker (boot & shoe).

GOE: 06.04.05 STRENGTH: L GED: R2 M1 L2 SVP: 2 DLU: 77

690.685-302 PAD CUTTER (plastic prod.)
Tends machine that slices foam rubber blocks to specified thickness for use in making chair, cushion, and ironing board pads: Turns handwheel to adjust height of roller conveyor under machine knife according to thickness specifications. Pushes block against knife that slices article from block.
GOE: 06.04.07 STRENGTH: L GED: R2 M1 L2 SVP: 3 DLU: 77

690.685-306 PLUG CUTTER (pen & pencil) alternate titles: cut-off-machine operator
Tends machine that cuts rubber rods or bars into pencil erasers: Adjusts guides on machine to specified length and size of rods or bars to be cut. Starts machine and feeds prescribed colored rods or bars manually into device that feeds them to knives which cut them to specified size. Observes machine operation and spot checks length and size of plugs (erasers), using hand gauge to ensure conformity to specifications.
GOE: 06.04.07 STRENGTH: L GED: R2 M1 L2 SVP: 2 DLU: 77

690.685-310 POINTING-MACHINE OPERATOR (plastic prod.; rubber goods)
Tends machine that rounds points on comb teeth: Starts machine and observes combs being fed into machine for proper positioning, allowing shaping wheels to automatically point teeth.
GOE: 06.04.02 STRENGTH: M GED: R1 M1 L1 SVP: 2 DLU: 77

690.685-314 POUNDER (boot & shoe) alternate titles: jollier
Tends machine that pounds down and buffs edges of leather uppers to provide smooth base for outsole: Starts machine and moves bottom of lasted shoe against wheel that pounds out puckers on edges of upper. Buffs bottom of lasted shoe on emery wheel to provide smooth surface. May be designated according to area of shoe pounded as Bottom Pounder, Cement Shoes (boot & shoe); Heel-Seat Pounder (boot & shoe); Toe Pounder (boot & shoe).
GOE: 06.04.05 STRENGTH: L GED: R2 M1 L1 SVP: 3 DLU: 77

690.685-318 PRESSER (rubber goods)
Tends pneumatic presses that bond and make watertight parts or seams of uncured rubber footwear by either of following methods: (1) Positions last, with partially assembled footwear, between ram and press table or fixture. Depresses pedal to lower ram or raise table and press workpiece around its edges, bonding tacky parts together. (2) Places workpiece between pads. Moves lever to lower upper pad and cover workpiece. Moves lever to pump air from between pads and draw rubber sheeting around surface of workpiece, forcing tacky parts together. Observes gauges and turns valves to maintain required air pressure. Examines workpiece for defects, such as loose edges or misaligned parts.
GOE: 06.04.07 STRENGTH: L GED: R2 M1 L1 SVP: 2 DLU: 77

690.685-322 ROLL CUTTER (rubber goods) alternate titles: lathe operator
Tends lathe that cuts roll of rubberized fabric or gum stock into specified widths: Loads roll of fabric or gum stock on lathe mandrel and starts chuck that revolves stock. Cuts roll of stock by holding knife in slots of guide bar and pressing it against revolving stock. Removes cut roll from mandrel and sorts it into designated boxes.
GOE: 06.04.07 STRENGTH: M GED: R1 M1 L1 SVP: 2 DLU: 77

690.685-326 ROLL-OVER-PRESS OPERATOR (optical goods)
Tends machine that rolls over edge of plastic sunglass frames to secure lenses: Removes frames from heat conveyor and positions in fixture of press. Starts press that rolls over edge of plastic frames to secure lenses. Removes frames and examines for defects, such as cracked or distorted lenses, or cracked frames. Stacks completed frames in rack or places rejected frames in salvage container. Keeps production and rejection records.
GOE: 06.04.02 STRENGTH: L GED: R2 M1 L1 SVP: 2 DLU: 77

690.685-330 ROUGH-AND-TRUEING-MACHINE OPERATOR (toy-sport equip.)
Tends grinding machines that smooth and true bowling balls: Lifts ball onto work bench. Removes excessive molding from ball, using hand power grinder. Places ball between abrasive jaws of grinding machine. Starts machine and observes grinding operation. Stops machine and measures size of ball, using gauge. Removes ball from machine at end of grinding and smoothing cycle, and places ball in rack.
GOE: 06.04.09 STRENGTH: M GED: R2 M1 L1 SVP: 3 DLU: 77

690.685-334 ROUGH-ROUNDER, MACHINE (boot & shoe) alternate titles: forepart rounder; rounder; sole rounder
Tends machine that trims edges of outsole and welt to conform to outline of lasted shoe upper: Adjusts width gauge, following size specifications. Starts machine and depresses pedal that withdraws knife from cutting position. Positions shank or heel seat against machine guide. Releases pedal that forces reciprocating horizontal knife against outsole and welt. Presses and turns outsole and welt against machine guide and cutting edge of knife. Presses control that regulates width of cut at toe, ball, and shank of shoe while edge is being trimmed. May cut channel (groove) in bottom of outsole near edge.
GOE: 06.04.05 STRENGTH: L GED: R2 M1 L2 SVP: 3 DLU: 77

690.685-338 ROUNDER (boot & shoe) alternate titles: insole rounder; sole rounder; sole-rounding-machine operator
Tends machine that trims unfinished shoe soles to pattern size: Selects pattern from stock bin, following work ticket. Positions pattern on machine guide

pins and places sole on pattern. Depresses pedal or pushes lever that clamps sole onto pattern and starts knife blades rotating around outside edge of pattern to cut sole in conformity with pattern. Removes and sharpens blades, using hone.
GOE: 06.04.05 STRENGTH: L GED: R2 M1 L2 SVP: 3 DLU: 77

690.685-342 RUBBER-CUTTING-MACHINE TENDER (rubber goods)
Tends guillotine-type machine that automatically cuts rubber stock into slabs: Starts machine, catches cut slab as it reaches end of conveyor, and throws slab onto pallet. Sprays each layer of slabs with chemical solution to prevent sticking, using hose, and covers layer with canvas sheet. Replaces filled pallet with empty one, using hand-controlled lift truck.
GOE: 06.04.07 STRENGTH: H GED: R2 M1 L1 SVP: 2 DLU: 77

690.685-346 SANDER (toy-sport equip.)
Tends machine that sands and smooths golf club grips, skis, and other sports equipment: Inserts article to be sanded in roller carriage brackets or grip in holding device of machine. Starts machine that automatically feeds article to sanding belt or rotates article against moving abrasive wheel to remove excess stock, paint, and blemishes from article.
GOE: 06.04.09 STRENGTH: L GED: R2 M1 L1 SVP: 2 DLU: 77

690.685-350 SEAM-RUBBING-MACHINE OPERATOR (boot & shoe) alternate titles: counter molder; rubber and pounder; seam roller; shoe hammerer; smoothing-machine operator
Tends machine that smooths and presses seams of shoe parts, such as counters, quarters, and joints of uppers by following methods: (1) Positions part under pounder or roller and guides part while machine pounds or rolls seams flat and smooth. (2) Positions part over or under preheated form and depresses pedal that lowers head of machine over part, pressing part to smooth seam. (3) Positions part on anvil under power hammer and depresses pedal that raises anvil and starts reciprocating hammer, flattening, and smoothing seam. May soften parts, using water-soaked sponge. May be designated according to type of machine operated as Power-Hammer Operator (boot & shoe); Seam-Press Operator (boot & shoe); or according to part of shoe smoothed as Heel-Seam Rubber (boot & shoe); Quarter-Lining Smoother (boot & shoe); Vamp Presser (boot & shoe).
GOE: 06.04.05 STRENGTH: L GED: R2 M1 L1 SVP: 2 DLU: 77

690.685-354 SHAPING-MACHINE OPERATOR (plastic prod.)
Tends machine that cuts spheres, cones, and other shapes from plastic foam blocks: Positions block on machine table and clamps block in holding device. Starts machine and pushes block against curbed blades to cut shapes in block. Removes block from machine and breaks shaped object from block.
GOE: 06.04.02 STRENGTH: L GED: R1 M1 L1 SVP: 2 DLU: 77

690.685-358 SIDE LASTER, CEMENT (boot & shoe)
Tends *lasting* machine that presses edges of precemented uppers onto insole and shapes shank section of shoes: Positions last between machine feed rollers that grip upper edges. Moves last along wiping bar that presses upper edges onto insole. May last entire upper. May remove temporary tacks, using *lasting tool*.
GOE: 06.04.05 STRENGTH: L GED: R2 M1 L1 SVP: 3 DLU: 77

690.685-362 SIDE LASTER, STAPLE (boot & shoe) alternate titles: side stapler; staple laster
Tends *lasting* machine that staples shank section (side) of shoe upper onto insoles and shapes it on shoe last: Places last on *pin jack* and pulls edge of upper over last, using *lasting tool*. Removes last, positions it under machine head, and starts machine that staples edges of upper to insole. May adjust cutterhead to regulate staple length, according to thickness of upper. May tend machine that tacks upper and be designated Side Laster, Tack (boot & shoe).
GOE: 06.04.05 STRENGTH: L GED: R2 M1 L2 SVP: 3 DLU: 77

690.685-366 SIZING-MACHINE TENDER (clock & watch)
Tends machine that cuts grooves in edges of plastic watch crystals: Centers and clamps crystal in rotary holding device. Starts machine and moves cutter blade against rotating crystal to cut grooves in edge of crystal. Removes crystal from machine onto tray.
GOE: 06.04.02 STRENGTH: L GED: R2 M1 L1 SVP: 2 DLU: 77

690.685-370 SKI-TOP TRIMMER (plastic prod.)
Tends machine equipped with cutter attachment that trims plastic layer tops for use in ski manufacturing: Aligns top with guide and clamps top in holding device. Starts machine that trims tops to specified size and shape. Measures width of top for conformance to standards, using caliper.
GOE: 06.04.02 STRENGTH: L GED: R2 M1 L1 SVP: 2 DLU: 77

690.685-374 SKIVER (leather prod.)
Tends machine that bevels edges of leather parts of articles, such as belting, gloves, wallets, cigarette and key cases, and handbags to prepare parts for joining: Turns setscrews to adjust gauge, guide, feed roller, and blade, to regulate angle of bevel. Depresses pedal to start machine. Positions part on bed of machine against gauge and beneath guide. Guides part over feed roller that forces edge of material against blade to skive edge. Sharpens blade, using emery wheel. May pull leather strips across fixed cutting edge to reduce thickness and be designated Skiver, Hand (leather prod.).
GOE: 06.04.05 STRENGTH: L GED: R2 M1 L2 SVP: 4 DLU: 77

690.685-378 SKIVER, MACHINE (boot & shoe; rubber goods) alternate titles: beveler; edge skiver; scarfer; skiving-machine operator
Tends skiving machine that bevels edges of shoe parts to prevent ridges at stitched, cemented, or folded edges: Depresses pedal to start machine. Holds

and guides part against guide and between feed rollers that force edges of part against blade. Turns setscrews to adjust feed rollers, guides, and blade angle to specifications. Verifies width and thickness of beveled edges, using micrometer. May use pedal to regulate speed of rollers along curved, straight, or angled edges of part or to change incline of rollers and alter width and thickness of bevel. May tend machines that roughen edges prior to cementing or skive narrow parts, such as straps and backstraps. May be designated according to parts skived as Skiver, Counter (boot & shoe); Skiver, Tuck (boot & shoe). May be designated: Skiver, Box-Toe (boot & shoe); Skiver, Flare (boot & shoe); Skiver, Heel Tap (boot & shoe); Skiver, Sock Linings (boot & shoe); Skiver, Uppers Or Linings (boot & shoe); Skiver, Welt-End (boot & shoe). Important variables may be indicated by trade names of machines used.
GOE: 06.04.05 STRENGTH: L GED: R2 M1 L2 SVP: 3 DLU: 77

690.685-382   SOLE LEVELER, MACHINE (boot & shoe) alternate titles: beater-out, leveling machine; inseam leveler; leveler; leveling-machine operator; outsole leveler; sole-leveling-machine operator

Tends machine that flattens, shapes, and smooths leather insoles and outsoles: Turns handle to adjust holding device to fit shoe. Positions shoe on *pin jack* and against holding device. Starts machine that forces shoe against presser roller and moves roller back and forth over sole to flatten ridges, bulges, and nicks caused by other operations. May move levers to control motion of roller.
GOE: 06.04.05 STRENGTH: L GED: R2 M1 L2 SVP: 2 DLU: 77

690.685-386   SPLITTING-MACHINE OPERATOR (rubber goods; rubber reclaim.) alternate titles: beadsaw operator; debeader; skiver; slitting-machine operator; trimming-machine operator; turner-splitter-machine operator

Tends machines that cut scrap tires or split rubber sheets for reclaiming rubber: Adjusts guides to accommodate tire size and cut to be made, and installs blades, using handtools. Lifts tire or sheet onto powered holder by hand or with hoist. Starts rollers that force tire or sheet against blade or endless-belt-type saw to split tire or sheet into piles, shear tire into sections, sever bead from tire, trim rubber from carcass, or separate sponge rubber from carpeting. May be designated according to type of cutting performed as Carcass Trimmer (rubber reclaim.); Scrap-Tire Shearer (rubber reclaim.); Tire Debeader (rubber reclaim.).
GOE: 06.04.07 STRENGTH: H GED: R2 M1 L2 SVP: 2 DLU: 77

690.685-390   SPONGE BUFFER (plastic prod.)

Tends machine that buffs edges of household sponges to impart rounded finish: Depresses pedal to open device, inserts sponge between wheel teeth, and releases pedal to clamp sponge in wheels. Starts machine that revolves edge of sponge against buffing wheel to finish and round edges.
GOE: 06.04.02 STRENGTH: L GED: R2 M1 L1 SVP: 3 DLU: 77

690.685-394   SPORT-SHOE-SPIKE ASSEMBLER (boot & shoe)

Tends machine that attaches spikes to sport shoes, such as football or baseball shoes: Positions shoe on bed of drill press and lowers drill to ream holes in shoe sole. Inserts spike stem through outsole from inside of shoe and places washers on protruding stem. Positions shoe on bed of pneumatic ram and lowers ram that clamps and assembles spike to shoe. Repeats operations until specified number of spikes are attached to shoe sole.
GOE: 06.04.05 STRENGTH: L GED: R2 M1 L2 SVP: 3 DLU: 77

690.685-398   STAMPING-MACHINE OPERATOR (boot & shoe) alternate titles: lining stamper; outside marker; upper stamper

Tends marking machine that stamps identifying symbols, such as case number, match number, and size on shoe parts: Turns selector knobs or places metal type on machine head to set specified type symbols. Positions parts on machine bed under head, following machine guide. Depresses pedal to lower heated inked head on shoe part and print symbols.
GOE: 06.04.05 STRENGTH: L GED: R2 M1 L2 SVP: 4 DLU: 77

690.685-402   STRAP-CUTTING-MACHINE OPERATOR (rubber goods)

Tends machine that cuts uncured rubber or rubber-coated fabric strip into specified lengths, for use as leg straps on gaiters and hip boots: Selects cutoff wheel (having X-shaped cutting dies bolted in rim) for severing strap length. Bolts cutoff wheel to drive shaft, positions and bolts backing wheel against it, rim to rim, using wrenches. Mounts roll of strip in holder and threads end through guide and between wheels. Positions carton beneath wheels to catch cut straps. Starts machine, observes and counts mark on cutting wheel as it passes given mark on machine frame, to determine when required number of straps are cut. Arranges cut straps in books for use in assembling boots.
GOE: 06.04.07 STRENGTH: L GED: R2 M1 L2 SVP: 2 DLU: 77

690.685-406   STRING LASTER (boot & shoe) alternate titles: injection molder, outer sole

Tends battery of combination *lasting* and molding machines that mold rubber or plastic outsoles onto fabric, leather, or plastic uppers to make shoes: Positions upper over last with heel centered and even margin of upper around last sole, pulls string in hem tight around sole of last, and ties knot to keep it from slipping. Stretches and hooks upper over pins protruding from heel and instep of last, using claw-tipped end of *lasting tool*, to hold upper in place during molding. Pulls lever to turn last upper to face mold and raise shoe with newly molded sole for stripping. Places uncured rubber blank in mold, depresses pedal to lower last and close sides of mold, and sets automatic timing device for

specified curing time. Strips molded shoe from last and examines sole for discoloration or softness indicative of overcuring or insufficient curing.
GOE: 06.04.09 STRENGTH: M GED: R2 M1 L2 SVP: 2 DLU: 77

690.685-410   TACK PULLER, MACHINE (boot & shoe) alternate titles: nail puller

Tends tack-pulling machine that removes temporary holding tacks from lasted shoes. Pushes lever to start machine. Holds and moves lasted shoe under revolving arm or machine jaws that pull tacks from last and insole or upper.
GOE: 06.04.05 STRENGTH: L GED: R1 M1 L1 SVP: 2 DLU: 77

690.685-414   TAPER, MACHINE (boot & shoe) alternate titles: stayer; taper

Tends machine that applies adhesive tape to reinforce seams of upper shoe parts: Positions part on machine roller. Turns dial to regulate temperature of machine heating element that softens adhesive surface of tape. Depresses pedals that raise part, activate roller, and apply tape. Moves lever to cut adhered tape or uses scissors. Replaces tape roll on machine. May be designated according to part taped as Seam Taper, Machine (boot & shoe); Top Taper, Machine (boot & shoe).
GOE: 06.04.05 STRENGTH: L GED: R2 M1 L2 SVP: 3 DLU: 77

690.685-418   TIP FINISHER (boot & shoe)

Tends multiarmed machine that bevels, burnishes, and perforates edge of toe tip to trim, finish, and decorate edge: Selects perforating punch according to work ticket and locks punch in perforating mechanism. Turns setscrew to adjust angle of beveling blade. Turns dial to regulate temperature of burnishing iron. Positions toe tip on end of rotating machine arm. Depresses pedal to rotate arm that moves tip past beveling blade, perforating mechanism, and automatic unloader. Reloads arms that have completed cycle.
GOE: 06.04.05 STRENGTH: L GED: R2 M1 L2 SVP: 2 DLU: 77

690.685-422   TIRE BUFFER (automotive ser.) alternate titles: buffer

Tends buffing machine that removes rubber from tire body to prepare tire for retreading: Positions tire on holder of machine. Places metal plate against tire and turns bolt to hold plate in place, using wrench. Inflates tire with air. Starts tire rotating and pushes lever that moves tire against abrasive wheel that cuts tread from tire. Turns dial to position buffing wheel against tire. Measures tire to determine size of retreading mold, using tapeline. May apply cement to tire to be retreaded, using brush. May inspect tire casings prior to buffing.
GOE: 05.12.13 STRENGTH: L GED: R3 M2 L2 SVP: 3 DLU: 77

690.685-426   TOE FORMER, STITCHDOWNS (boot & shoe) alternate titles: box-toe flanger, stitchdowns; toe laster, automatic

Tends toe-forming machine that draws leather upper over last to form toe of shoe: Places shoes on steaming rack to soften leather. Selects and clamps specified wiper plates in machine and adjusts plates and shoe holding device to fit size and style of shoe. Positions shoe in holding device. Depresses pedal to cause wiper plates to move forward against toe and slide downward, drawing upper over last to form toe. May insert steel toe cap between layers of leather in upper to form safety shoe box toe.
GOE: 06.04.05 STRENGTH: L GED: R2 M1 L1 SVP: 3 DLU: 77

690.685-430   TOE LASTER, AUTOMATIC (boot & shoe)

Tends *lasting* machine that presses toe section of upper edges onto insole and shapes toe section on last: Clamps specified wipers on machine head and adjusts wiper pressure. Positions toe of last on machine toe plate. Depresses pedal that causes wipers to press edges of upper onto insole for subsequent stitching. Nails anchor tacks in sides of shank and repeats wiper cycle to pull toe wire against toe and anchor it to tacks, to retain shape of toe section until stitched. May press precemented edges onto insole. May place upper in steamer to soften leather prior to lasting. May insert steel toe cap between leather layers to form safety shoe box toe.
GOE: 06.04.05 STRENGTH: L GED: R2 M1 L2 SVP: 3 DLU: 77

690.685-434   TRIMMER, MACHINE I (boot & shoe) alternate titles: shaver; trimmer

Tends machine that trims edges of shoe parts, such as heels, outsoles, or uppers to remove excess material: Turns knobs or setscrews to adjust guides and cutting blade as specified. Holds part against machine guide and presses it against cutter to be trimmed. May depress pedal that raises guide plate to move part into cutter. May be designated according to area or part of shoe trimmed as Heel-Seat Trimmer (boot & shoe); Heel Trimmer (boot & shoe) I; Top-Lift Trimmer (boot & shoe); Top Trimmer (boot & shoe) I. May be designated: Apron Trimmer (boot & shoe); Boot Trimmer (boot & shoe); Cut-Out Worker (boot & shoe); Rolled-Seat Trimmer (boot & shoe); Seat Trimmer (boot & shoe); Upper Trimmer (boot & shoe). Important variables may be indicated by trade names of machines used.
GOE: 06.04.05 STRENGTH: L GED: R2 M1 L1 SVP: 3 DLU: 77

690.685-438   TUBE MOLDER, FIBERGLASS (plastic prod.)

Tends machine that winds fabric and cellophane around mandrel to form fiberglass tubes used in manufacturing articles, such as fiberglass fishing rods or golf club shafts: Moistens edge of resin impregnated fabric with alcohol stick and places edge on steel mandrel. Smooths edge of fabric onto mandrel with hot iron. Rubs iron on sandpaper and silicon treated cloth to clean iron and prevent sticking. Positions mandrel and fabric on heated *rolling table*. Starts machine roller plate which presses and rolls fabric onto mandrel. Attaches cellophane strip diagonally to end of mandrel and hand rolls mandrel on table to

cover fabric, or clamps mandrel into machine, attaches cellophane, and starts machine to wrap cellophane around mandrel. Trims off excess cellophane, using scissors or knife. Wipes air bubbles and excess liquid from wrapped mandrel. Hangs mandrels on curing oven racks. Removes mandrel from cured tube. Places unwrapped end of mandrel through stop, clamps pulling device to end of mandrel and starts machine to pull mandrel out of cured tube. Cleans mandrels, using solvent, sandpaper, or wire brush. Coats mandrels with wax or other parting agents, using paint brush or dips mandrels in tanks. May straighten bent mandrels, using hammer or small press on level block. May be known according to task performed as Mandrel Cleaner (plastic prod.); Mandrel Puller (plastic prod.); Tacker (plastic prod.); Tube Roller (plastic prod.); Wrapper (plastic prod.).
GOE: 06.04.09 STRENGTH: M GED: R2 M1 L2 SVP: 2 DLU: 77

690.685-442 TUBE SPLICER (rubber tire)
Tends machine that splices uncured rubber to form inner tubes for tire: Positions ends of tube in machine and starts machine that butt-splices tube. Lifts tube to hook and places cylinders under fold at each end to prevent creasing of rubber. May cut tube to specified length with hot knife prior to splicing. May punch hole at valve location and secure valve to tube with valve-press machine.
GOE: 06.04.07 STRENGTH: M GED: R2 M1 L1 SVP: 3 DLU: 77

690.685-446 TUBER-MACHINE CUTTER (rubber goods; rubber tire)
Tends machines and auxiliary equipment that cut extruded rubber stock into specified lengths for items, such as tire treads, sidewalls, and other rubber goods: Turns crank and observes dial to adjust automatic cutter frame for specified cutting cycle or turns handwheel to adjust stock stop for specified lengths. Starts machine that cuts rubber as it passes on conveyor or positions stock against stop and pulls rotating blade across stock to cut and bevel ends. Observes passage or treads and sidewalls through automated auxiliary equipment that prints identification numbers on items, glues cushion strip to treads and sidewalls, and weighs items to detect variation from standards. Notifies TUBER-MACHINE OPERATOR (rubber goods; rubber tire) of machine malfunctions and processing defects. Fills reservoirs of printing, gluing, and marking machines. Changes numerals and brushes in printing and gluing machines, using handtools. May cut treads and sidewalls to specified lengths, using shears. May be designated according to product cut as Inner-Tube Cutter (rubber tire); Rubber-Flap Cutter (rubber goods; rubber tire).
GOE: 06.04.07 STRENGTH: L GED: R2 M1 L2 SVP: 2 DLU: 77

690.685-450 V-BELT COVERER (rubber goods) alternate titles: flipping-machine operator
Tends machine that covers machine belts with rubberized fabric: Positions belt on pulleys of machine and raises pulleys to hold belt taut. Positions end of rubberized fabric on guide roll and starts machine that rotates belt and draws fabric through crimping device to cover belt. Cuts end of fabric after one revolution of belt. Presses fabric against belt with fingers and awl. Attaches identification band to each belt.
GOE: 06.04.05 STRENGTH: L GED: R2 M1 L1 SVP: 2 DLU: 77

690.685-454 V-BELT FINISHER (rubber goods)
Tends machines that notch, measure, and brand identifying information on rubber V-belts: Positions belt onto expandable wheel of notching machine. Starts machine that notches inside surface to make belt flexible. Adjusts measuring machine weight tension according to belt-size chart, and positions belt on machine spindles. Pushes lever to rotate spindles that register belt length on gauge and stamp belt with identifying data. Inserts plate in branding machine. Feeds belts into machine to brand belts with identifying information. Ties belts in bundles and hangs bundles on rack. May be designated according to machine tended as Belt Brander (rubber goods); Belt Measurer (rubber goods); Belt Notcher (rubber goods).
GOE: 06.04.07 STRENGTH: L GED: R2 M1 L1 SVP: 3 DLU: 77

690.685-458 V-BELT SKIVER (rubber goods)
' Tends skiving machine that cuts and shapes edges of uncured rubber belts into V-shape: Turns belt inside out and fits belt over machine holding spindles. Turns screws to adjust angle of cutting knives and starts machine to rotate and skive belt. Weighs trim and adjusts knives to meet trim weight specifications. Removes belt from machine, turns belt right side out, and hangs on storage rack.
GOE: 06.04.07 STRENGTH: L GED: R2 M1 L1 SVP: 3 DLU: 77

690.685-462 VULCANIZER (boot & shoe)
Tends machine that vulcanizes synthetic composition outsoles to leather or fabric uppers: Positions upper on heated metal last. Seats precut outsole in cavity of mold and pulls lever to invert last. Starts machine that lowers lasted upper into die cavity and vulcanizes outsole to upper.
GOE: 06.04.13 STRENGTH: L GED: R2 M1 L1 SVP: 2 DLU: 77

690.685-466 VULCANIZING-PRESS OPERATOR (boot & shoe)
Tends machine that joins uppers of cloth sport shoes to rubber soles: Places cloth upper over form and rubber sole in electrically heated mold. Starts machine that unites sole and upper by heat and pressure. Reverses mechanism after specified period of time. Ties shoes together in pairs with shoelaces.
GOE: 06.04.07 STRENGTH: L GED: R2 M1 L1 SVP: 3 DLU: 77

690.685-470 WELT BEATER (boot & shoe) alternate titles: platform beater; slasher; sole beater
Tends machine that shapes and flattens welt of lasted shoe prior to attachment of outsole: Positions shoe on anvil and depresses pedal to start machine.

Guides welt under hammer that shapes and flattens it. Depresses second pedal to start slashing knife that scores toe portion of welt to permit smooth curving of welt at toe. May join shank to insole. May join outsole to shoe.
GOE: 06.04.05 STRENGTH: L GED: R2 M1 L2 SVP: 3 DLU: 77

690.685-474 WELT BUTTER, MACHINE (boot & shoe) alternate titles: rand butter; rand-butting-machine operator
Tends machine that cuts welt strip at heel seat of lasted shoe and tacks welt ends to insole preparatory to bottoming operations: Turns wheel to adjust holding device to fit shoe. Positions shoe on movable *pin jack*. Pushes pin jack under machine head and depresses pedal to start machine that cuts welt strip and tacks welt ends. Fills machine receptacle with tacks. Sharpens cutting blades, using hone.
GOE: 06.04.05 STRENGTH: L GED: R2 M1 L2 SVP: 2 DLU: 77

690.685-478 WELT CUTTER (boot & shoe) alternate titles: welt maker
Tends welt-cutting machine that cuts long narrow leather *blockers* into smaller sections for use as welts: Places ends of heavy paper strip in machine to cover leather strip when placed in cutting position. Positions end of leather strip under paper at point just before paper strip passes over knife, ensuring that edges of leather and paper are flush. Guides paper and leather by hand through cutting area to ensure straight line of feed.
GOE: 06.04.05 STRENGTH: L GED: R2 M1 L1 SVP: 4 DLU: 77

690.685-482 WELT WHEELER (boot & shoe) alternate titles: stitch fudger; stitch wheeler
Tends machine that presses decorative indentations on welt to separate or simulate stitches: Positions shoe against guide on machine bed. Pulls lever to adjust blade for stitch length when separating stitches. Depresses pedal to raise bed, pressing welt against machine head. Holds welt under indenter blade to separate stitches or under heated corrugated wheel that forms simulated stitching. May be designated according to process as Stitch Separator (boot & shoe).
GOE: 06.04.05 STRENGTH: L GED: R2 M1 L2 SVP: 2 DLU: 77

690.685-486 WIDTH STRIPPER (boot & shoe)
Tends machine that cuts series of *blockers* into strips used for shoe trimmings, such as bows and straps: Positions cutting disks and spacers (washers) on arbor and tightens setscrews. Inserts end of blocker series between machine guides and turns bolts to adjust guides to accommodate material. Depresses pedal that starts machine. Measures width of cut strips to verify conformity with specifications, using ruler. Trims imperfections from strips, using scissors. Bundles strips for shipment.
GOE: 06.04.05 STRENGTH: L GED: R2 M1 L2 SVP: 3 DLU: 77

690.685-490 WIRE-WINDING-MACHINE TENDER (rubber goods) alternate titles: wire winder
Tends machine that winds wire around cured rubber hose for reinforcement: Positions spool of specified wire onto *letoff rack,* using hoist, and threads wire through machine. Adjusts machine for specified diameter of hose and pitch of wire spirals, using handtools. Pulls hose onto feed conveyor and positions hose in fixture of machine. Starts machine that winds wire onto hose. Verifies diameter and pitch of wire spirals with caliper and rule. Examines wire to ensure close fit around hose. Cuts wire and crimps ends, using handtools. Coils hose on skid or in packing box for removal to storage or shipping area. May attach coupling hardware to hose [HOSE-COUPLING JOINER (rubber goods)].
GOE: 06.04.09 STRENGTH: H GED: R2 M1 L1 SVP: 2 DLU: 77

690.685-494 STITCHER, TAPE-CONTROLLED MACHINE (boot & shoe)
Tends battery of automatic stitching machines that stitch decorative designs on shoe parts, according to instructions encoded on tape cassettes: Receives bundles of shoe parts with tags that identify instruction cassette and style and color of thread to be used in stitching shoe parts. Places specified spools of thread on spindle of each machine, draws thread through machine guides and needles, and inserts prewound bobbin in shuttle. Positions shoe parts, such as upper or vamp, on holding device of machines, and depresses machine clamps to secure parts on device for stitching. Selects and inserts specified cassette in console of stitching machine, and presses buttons to activate machines that automatically stitch design according to encoded instructions on cassette. Removes shoe parts and examines design to verify conformance to specification.
GOE: 06.04.05 STRENGTH: L GED: R2 M1 L1 SVP: 2 DLU: 86

690.685-498 PLASTIC ROLLER (plastic prod.)
Tends machine that winds drop cloths from precut lengths of plastic: Places end of plastic around takeup cylinder of machine, and overlaps plastic to secure plastic to cylinder. Depresses pedal to activate cylinder and wind plastic onto cylinder. Applies pressure by hand to edge of plastic to ensure evenness of plastic around cylinder. Stops machine, slips rolled plastic drop cloths off cylinder, and folds cloths for further processing. Pushes lever of counter to tally number of drop cloths folded.
GOE: 06.04.02 STRENGTH: L GED: R2 M1 L1 SVP: 1 DLU: 86

690.685-502 ROLLER MAKER (rubber goods)
Tends machine that applies layers of vulcanized rubber onto metal rollers to fabricate or recondition rubber rollers used in industrial machines: Reviews work order to identify type of roller to be covered and type, color, and thickness of vulcanized rubber to be applied onto metal roller. Measures metal roller, using tape measure, to verify dimensions with work order. Transports and mounts roller between holding devices of roller building machine, by hand or

using overhead crane, working as team member. Carries, mounts, and loads roll of vulcanized rubber stock onto feed mechanism of machine. Depresses floor pedals to start feed mechanism and to start building machine that applies layers of vulcanized rubber around metal roller. Observes application of rubber around roller to detect air bubbles. Releases floor pedals to stop application of rubber, punctures air bubbles using knife, and applies pieces of rubber to airholes to seal holes. Measures thickness of rubber application, using calipers. Cuts rubber between roller and feed mechanism, using hot knife, and seals seam to roller, using stitching wheel. Trims rubber that laps over edges of roller, using knife.
GOE: 06.04.07 STRENGTH: M GED: R3 M2 L2 SVP: 3 DLU: 86

690.685-506   SAMPLE MAKER (boot & shoe)
Tends variety of machines that trim, shape, smooth, join, and finish shoe parts to fabricate footwear samples: Reads work order to determine type and style of shoe. Aligns precut components on bed of machine, positions components against machine guides, or feeds components between rollers. Flips switches, pushes buttons, depresses pedals, and moves levers to activate machines. Removes partially assembled component from machine and carries component to next machine in sequence of operation according to specifications. Changes and adjusts guides, cutting blades, buffing wheels, and heating irons, using handtools.
GOE: 06.04.05 STRENGTH: L GED: R3 M2 L2 SVP: 4 DLU: 86

690.685-510   TRADE MARKER (fabrication, nec)
Tends machine that drills hole and presses trademark into hole on stem of smoking pipes: Inserts and secures specified size drill in machine drill chuck, using chuck wrench. Places plastic tape of specified color in die press element of machine and adjusts die pressure, using wrench. Turns knobs to adjust operation speed of moving elements of machine. Presses button to start machine and depresses pedal to activate rotation of machine drum with clamps. Inserts pipe stems in clamps as clamps rotate by work station. Observes operation of machine that drills holes in stem and presses trademark into drilled hole to detect defects. Presses button and depresses pedal to stop machine when defects are noted. Turns handle to align drill and adjust pressure to correct defects.
GOE: 06.04.02 STRENGTH: M GED: R3 M1 L2 SVP: 3 DLU: 86

690.686-010   BEVELING-MACHINE OPERATOR (hat & cap) alternate titles: skiver-machine operator
Feeds sweatband leathers or cap-visor linings between power-driven roller and circular knife to bevel one edge: Starts machine, holds piece against guide, and pushes end between circular knife and roller.
GOE: 06.04.05 STRENGTH: L GED: R1 M1 L1 SVP: 2 DLU: 77

690.686-014   BIAS-MACHINE-OPERATOR HELPER (rubber tire)
Performs following duties in cutting rubberized fabric for tire ply (layer), bead wrapper, and chafer stock: Conveys fabric and liner rolls to machine area, using handtruck or forklift truck. Positions rolls in *letoff rack and windup racks*, using hoist. Threads fabric over guide rolls. Tags filled rolls according to type of stock. May lift cut plies from bias cutter arm to ply splice table. May splice plies by hand for BAND BUILDER (rubber tire).
GOE: 06.04.07 STRENGTH: H GED: R1 M1 L1 SVP: 2 DLU: 77

690.686-018   CEMENTER, MACHINE APPLICATOR (boot & shoe)
Applies cement onto separate shoe parts prior to joining, performing any of following operations: (1) Feeds parts between pressure and cementing rollers of machine and removes cemented parts. (2) Holds part against cement-covered roller or revolving brush that applies cement to part. (3) Feeds parts between rollers that move parts under spray nozzle. (4) Holds parts under machine applicator nozzle. May fill cement reservoir. May join parts together. May be designated according to parts coated as Binding Cementer, French Cord (boot & shoe); Bottom Cementer (boot & shoe) I; Cementer For Folding, Machine (boot & shoe); Channel Cementer, Insole, Machine (boot & shoe); Channel Cementer, Outsole, Machine (boot & shoe); Heel Cementer, Machine (boot & shoe). May be designated: Heel-Lining Paster (boot & shoe); Platform Cementer (boot & shoe); Potdevin Cementer, Machine (boot & shoe); Outsole Cementer, Machine (boot & shoe); Rand Cementer (boot & shoe); Tuck-And-Insole Cementer (boot & shoe); Upper-Lining Cementer (boot & shoe); Welt-Strip Cementer, Machine (boot & shoe).
GOE: 06.04.05 STRENGTH: L GED: R1 M1 L1 SVP: 2 DLU: 77

690.686-022   COATING-MACHINE FEEDER (leather prod.) alternate titles: cementer, machine; glue-machine feeder
Feeds leather or plastic into machine that coats material with waterproof paint or adhesive for use in lining or covering luggage or novelty cases: Covers one side of material with protective leather sheet and feeds material through machine rollers or revolving brush to coat exposed surface.
GOE: 06.04.16 STRENGTH: L GED: R1 M1 L1 SVP: 2 DLU: 77

690.686-026   CRIMPER (rubber goods) alternate titles: binder; hemmer; joiner; seamer
Feeds uncured rubber goods or garments, such as baby pants, through rollers or roller-cutter that crimp or fold over and press edges to reinforce article, or seal edges together and cut off excess material. May simultaneously feed binding tape between rollers that crimp tape to garment edges.
GOE: 06.04.07 STRENGTH: L GED: R1 M1 L1 SVP: 2 DLU: 77

690.686-030   CUTTING-MACHINE-TENDER HELPER (any industry)
Assists CUTTING-MACHINE TENDER (any industry) in cutting sheets of material, such as paper, pressboard, foil, cardboard, cork, or plastic: Positions and clamps material onto machine bed. Removes cut material from machine. Changes blades, using handtools. Performs other duties as described under HELPER (any industry) Master Title.
GOE: 06.04.09 STRENGTH: M GED: R2 M1 L1 SVP: 2 DLU: 77

690.686-034   FOLDING-MACHINE OPERATOR (hat & cap) alternate titles: pugg maker; tube roller; turning-machine operator
Feeds machine that folds and presses pieces or strips of precut material, such as leather or fabric, to form hatbands or sweatbands. Feeds end of material under machine feed guide, into folding device, and between heated rollers to crease folded edges of material.
GOE: 06.04.05 STRENGTH: L GED: R1 M1 L1 SVP: 2 DLU: 77

690.686-038   INJECTION-MOLDING-MACHINE OFFBEARER (pen & pencil)
Removes barrels of fountain pens, ballpoint pens, and mechanical pencils from discharge outlet of injection-molding machine. Inspects barrel for defects. Places completed barrels in container. Opens gate of machine and removes runners from mold and dumps them into grinder.
GOE: 06.04.02 STRENGTH: L GED: R2 M1 L1 SVP: 2 DLU: 77

690.686-042   INJECTION-MOLDING-MACHINE OFFBEARER (musical inst.) alternate titles: gate tender
Removes musical instruments or parts, such as kazoos, fifes, and recorders, from discharge outlet of injection-molding machine. Inspects parts for defects and trims finger holes, using reaming drills.
GOE: 06.04.02 STRENGTH: M GED: R1 M1 L1 SVP: 2 DLU: 77

690.686-046   PLASTIC-DESIGN APPLIER (boot & shoe)
Feeds and off bears rotating machine (merry-go-round) that fuses plastic designs to shoe uppers: Aligns shoe part and design with guides in machine bed. Removes finished article from machine and stacks shoe uppers in bins.
GOE: 06.04.05 STRENGTH: S GED: R1 M1 L1 SVP: 1 DLU: 77

690.686-050   RUBBER-ROLLER GRINDER (pen & pencil)
Feeds automatic grinding machine that smooths surface of rubber rollers in stencil inking device: Positions rubber roller assembly of stencil inker in holding device of grinding machine and starts machine that automatically smooths surface of rubber rollers.
GOE: 06.04.07 STRENGTH: L GED: R1 M1 L1 SVP: 1 DLU: 77

690.686-054   SPLITTING-MACHINE FEEDER (leather mfg.) alternate titles: leather leveler
Feeds hides between rollers of machine that splits hides into layers: Positions hide on feed table and guides it between rollers which force edge of hide against moving knife. Stacks split hides. May cut such imperfections as blemishes or thin spots from hide, using knife. May soak hides in water to soften them preparatory to splitting.
GOE: 06.04.05 STRENGTH: L GED: R1 M1 L1 SVP: 2 DLU: 77

690.686-058   SWEATBAND FLANGER (hat & cap) alternate titles: flanging-machine operator
Feeds hat sweatbands into flanging machine that turns edge of sweatband to fit contour of hat body: Inserts sweatband between rollers and against guide on machine bed. Depresses pedal to start machine. Feeds part into rotating rollers and into slot of guide that turns bottom edge of sweatband. May be designated according to type of sweatband material flanged as Leather Flanger (hat & cap).
GOE: 06.04.05 STRENGTH: L GED: R1 M1 L1 SVP: 2 DLU: 78

690.686-062   SWEATBAND-CUTTING-MACHINE OPERATOR (hat & cap)
Feeds strips or scraps of leather between machine rollers and circular knife that automatically cuts strips to specified length for use as hat sweatbands: Turns handwheel to adjust cutting blade(s) or roller(s) according to sweatband size specified on work order. Flips switch to activate machine, positions leather against cutting blade(s) or roller(s), and pulls lever to secure leather in cutting position. Pulls lever or depresses pedal to activate machine, and observes cutting action of blade(s) to detect dull blade(s). Marks lot number on inside of sweatbands, using marking pencil or chalk. May attach adhesive size label to sweatbands. May inform supervisor of dull cutting blade(s), or replace dull blade(s), using screwdriver.
GOE: 06.04.05 STRENGTH: L GED: R2 M1 L1 SVP: 2 DLU: 78

690.686-066   TOGGLE-PRESS FOLDER-AND-FEEDER (boot & shoe)
Folds uncured, printed and powdered rubber sheeting longitudinally as sheeting is unreeled, and guides folded material beneath dies of toggle press that cut out uppers for gum shoes (rubbers).
GOE: 06.04.05 STRENGTH: S GED: R1 M1 L1 SVP: 2 DLU: 77

690.686-070   TUBER-MACHINE-OPERATOR HELPER (rubber goods; rubber tire)
Assists TUBER-MACHINE OPERATOR (rubber goods; rubber tire) in extruding rubber stock in specified form. Turns bolts to secure dies in machine, using wrenches. Feeds rubber stock into machine by hand or conveyor. May lift braided fabric hose onto turntable for feeding into machine that covers hose with rubber and be designated Covering-Machine-Operator Helper (rubber goods). Performs other duties as described under HELPER (any industry) Master Title.

GOE: 06.04.07 STRENGTH: M GED: R1 M1 L1 SVP: 2 DLU: 77

691   OCCUPATIONS IN FABRICATION OF INSULATED WIRE AND CABLE

This group includes occupations concerned with drawing wire and cable of nonferrous metal from wire bars, rods, or wire, and insulating it.

691.130-010   SUPERVISOR (nonfer. metal)

Supervises and coordinates activities of workers engaged in operations, such as braiding, stranding, and winding, to fabricate insulated wire and cable: Sets up machines for workers. Inspects and tests products for conformance to specifications, using inspection manuals, and testing equipment, such as ohmmeter, wheatstone bridge, and galvanometer. Trains new employees. May verify thickness of insulation, using micrometer, loupe, and graduated microscope. Performs duties as described under SUPERVISOR (any industry) Master Title. May be designated according to activity supervised as Inspection Supervisor (nonfer. metal); Plastic-Tubing-Insulation Supervisor (nonfer. metal).
GOE: 06.01.01 STRENGTH: L GED: R4 M3 L3 SVP: 7 DLU: 77

691.130-014   SUPERVISOR, WIRE-ROPE FABRICATION (metal prod., nec)

Supervises and coordinates activities of workers engaged in spooling and stranding wire rope, and swaging fittings onto rope slings: Sets up spooling, stranding, closing, and swaging machines. Trains workers in operation of machines. Performs other duties as described under SUPERVISOR (any industry) Master Title. May be designated according to activity of workers supervised as Closing Supervisor (metal prod., nec); Inspection Supervisor (metal prod., nec; nonfer. metal); Splicing Supervisor (metal prod., nec); Spooling Supervisor (metal prod., nec); Stranding Supervisor (metal prod., nec); Swaging-And-Plastic Supervisor (metal prod., nec).
GOE: 06.02.01 STRENGTH: L GED: R4 M3 L3 SVP: 7 DLU: 77

691.367-010   INSPECTOR, WIRE (metal prod., nec; nonfer. metal) alternate titles: finished-wire inspector

Inspects and tests coated or uncoated wire for such properties as electrical resistance, hardness, size, cross sectional shape, and tensile strength, to verify their conformance to specifications: Reads written specifications, or receives oral instructions and determines work aids required and inspection procedures. Tests wire for electrical resistance, elongation, and tensile strength, by inserting wire in various testing devices and noting instrument readings. Measures wire for size, using micrometers and fixed gauges. Examines wire for defects, such as pits, scratches, and burnt surfaces. Records test results and informs supervisor when wire varies from specifications. May test wire for defective insulation and resistance to high temperature, using electrical testing equipment and electric heating furnaces. May be designated according to product inspected as Inspector, Wire Rope (metal prod., nec).
GOE: 06.03.01 STRENGTH: L GED: R3 M3 L3 SVP: 5 DLU: 77

691.382-010   EXTRUDING-MACHINE OPERATOR (nonfer. metal) alternate titles: tube-machine operator

Operates extrusion press to encase electric wire and cable in rubber or plastic sheath: Bolts specified dies, guides, and guide holders in extrusion head of press. Clamps roll of rubber strip on spindle of machine and threads strip into hopper-feeder, or fills hopper with plastic chips. Sets temperature control of press according to type of material to be extruded. Loads spool of wire on spindle and threads wire through machine and around takeup reel. Starts machine and adjusts controls to regulate speed of wire travel, pressure of hydraulic ram, and temperature of extrusion die to ensure sheath of uniform thickness. Guides rubber-covered wire through trough of powdered talc or soapstone as it emerges from press to prevent wire from sticking together when spooled. Clamps wire ends in electrodes of electric welder, turns on current, and holds brazing rod against heated wire tips to form continuous wire lengths. May feed wire through pot of molten metal to coat wire with tin prior to sheathing process. May operate machine equipped with wrapping device to wrap tape around wire prior to sheathing. May be designated according to machine operated as Continuous-Vulcanizing-Machine Operator (nonfer. metal); or according to material extruded as Plastic-Extruding-Machine Operator (nonfer. metal).
GOE: 06.02.09 STRENGTH: M GED: R3 M2 L2 SVP: 4 DLU: 77

691.382-014   LEAD-PRESS OPERATOR (nonfer. metal) alternate titles: extruding-press operator; press operator; braider; braider tender

Operates extrusion press to encase electric wire and cable in lead sheath: Bolts die in head of press, fills melting pot with lead, and mounts reel of cable on machine spindle. Threads cable through die and cooling chamber, fastens end to takeup reel, and starts machine. Adjusts controls to regulate speed of cable through machine, temperature and flow of metal, pressure of hydraulic ram, and pressure of water spray in cooling chamber to ensure uniform sheathing of lead on cable. Measures thickness and diameter of sheath with micrometers and calipers to verify conformity to size and surface specifications.
GOE: 06.02.02 STRENGTH: M GED: R3 M2 L2 SVP: 4 DLU: 77

691.387-010   INSPECTOR, INSULATION (nonfer. metal)

Inspects and tests insulated wire and cable for conformance to specifications, using testing instruments, inspection manuals, and blueprints: Measures diameter, wall thickness, concentricity of insulation, and thickness of wire or cable,

using microscope, pin gauges, and micrometer. Attaches weights to cable to test adhesion of insulation to cable. Connects sample to electrical outlet and tests effectiveness of insulation under varying voltages, using such instruments as ohmmeter, wheatstone bridge, and galvanometer. Tests wearability of insulation, using twisting device. Tests breaking strength of wire and cable, using tensile testing machine. Examines and feels surface of braided metal shield surrounding insulation to detect imperfections, and cuts off or interlaces protruding metal strands of shield. Cuts insulation with knife and compares composition of insulation with specifications. Stamps mark of approval or rejection on cable tested.
GOE: 06.03.01 STRENGTH: L GED: R3 M3 L3 SVP: 5 DLU: 77

691.667-010   PNEUMATIC JACKETER (nonfer. metal)

Forces electric cable through rubber jacket (tubing) to insulate cable, using compressed air: Unrolls tubing from reel on truck. Ties leader (cord) to wooden plug of specified dimensions and inserts plug into one end of tubing. Clamps tubing onto compressed-air line and opens valve allowing air to force plug and leader through tubing. Fastens leader to cable end and clamps tubing onto compressed-air line. Scoops powdered talc into hopper connected to air line. Signals worker stationed at opposite end of tubing to pull cable. Turns valve, allowing air to expand tubing and force talc into tubing, as cable is pulled through tubing.
GOE: 06.04.34 STRENGTH: M GED: R1 M1 L1 SVP: 2 DLU: 77

691.682-010   ASBESTOS-WIRE FINISHER (nonfer. metal)

Sets up and operates machine to card asbestos fibers, wrap fibers around electric wire, and impregnate fibers with wax: Loads reels of wire onto machine spindle, threads wire between guides, through taping, carding, impregnating, and cooling units, and fastens wire to takeup reel. Places roll of tape on spindle and inserts end in taping device that folds tape around wire. Places *lap II* of asbestos on carding device that shreds asbestos and cards fibers onto wire in continuous layer. Starts machine. Readjusts controls and replenishes supply of tape and asbestos to ensure uniform coverage of wire.
GOE: 06.02.09 STRENGTH: M GED: R3 M2 L2 SVP: 4 DLU: 77

691.682-014   BRAIDER OPERATOR (nonfer. metal)

Sets up and operates battery of automatic braiding machines that cover electric wire and cable with insulating material, such as cotton yarn, rubber tape, fiberglass, or fine steel, copper, and aluminum strands: Places bobbins of insulating material on machine spindles and threads strands through braiding head according to pattern draft which specifies lay and sequence of braiding. Locks spool of wire to be insulated in payoff spindle; threads wire through machine guides, footage counter, and braiding head; and turns setscrews to control tension of wire. Adjusts traverse attachment to ensure even winding of wire. Starts machine and winds braided wire around capstan and onto takeoff spool. Replaces empty bobbins and ties broken threads. May repair thread breaks, using brush and glue.
GOE: 06.02.09 STRENGTH: L GED: R3 M2 L2 SVP: 5 DLU: 77

691.682-018   INSULATING-MACHINE OPERATOR (nonfer. metal) alternate titles: coat-insulator operator; coat-operator, insulator; wire-taping-machine operator

Operates machine to wind insulating material, such as tape, yarn, and cloth around electric wire and cable: Loads reel of wire onto machine spindle and threads wire between metal and felt cleaning strips, through tank of liquid adhesive, and through taping mechanism. Fastens wire to takeup reel. Winds end of insulating material around wire and starts machine. Observes automatic wrapping of material around wire to detect broken or loose wrapping or uneven winding of wire on reel. Stops machine to repair breaks, adjust guides, and replenish supply of insulating material and liquid adhesive. Forms continuous wire by clamping ends of wire to be joined in electrodes of electric brazing torch, turning on current, and holding filler rod to heated wire ends. Measures wire with micrometer to determine that insulation meets specifications. Wraps paper around full wire reels, attaches identification tag, and lifts reel from machine. May operate machine, equipped with winding device, to wrap protective metal strip over insulation. May thread insulated wire through melted paraffin and polishing wipers to make insulation waterproof. May be designated according to insulating material applied as Paper-Wrapping-Machine Operator (nonfer. metal); Varnish-Cambric-Covering-Machine Operator (nonfer. metal); or type of machine operated as Double-Lay-Winder-And-Paraffin-Unit Operator (nonfer. metal); Tandem-Taping-And-Paper-Wrapping-Machine Operator (nonfer. metal).
GOE: 06.02.09 STRENGTH: M GED: R3 M2 L2 SVP: 4 DLU: 77

691.685-010   ARMORING-MACHINE OPERATOR (nonfer. metal) alternate titles: armored-cable-machine operator; cable armorer; tape armorer

Tends battery of automatic winding machines that wind protective shield of yarn, wire or metal strip into flexible conduit or over insulated wire, such as submarine and underground cable: Starts winding machine and feeds insulated wire into machine and threads protective wire or strip through guides of automatic winding machine. Observes angle of spiral and adjusts guides, using wrench and screwdriver.
GOE: 06.04.09 STRENGTH: M GED: R2 M1 L2 SVP: 2 DLU: 77

691.685-014   LAGGING-MACHINE OPERATOR (nonfer. metal)

Tends machine that fastens wooden slats (lagging) to open reels of lead-covered cable: Fills hopper of machine with lagging and positions reels of steel band on spindles. Mounts cable reel on axle and starts machine that distributes lagging around edge of cable reel and binds lagging with steel banding.

GOE: 06.04.38 STRENGTH: M GED: R2 M1 L1 SVP: 2 DLU: 77

691.685-018 LEAD FORMER (elec. equip.) alternate titles: assembler, flexible leads; former; lead assembler; lead bender

Tends variety of machines that form and assemble electrical wire leads, performing any combination of following tasks: Reads work order to determine information, such as type and sequence of assembly, and color-coded wire to use. Places coil in vise or clamping device of machine and depresses pedal or turns lever to close clamps which shape coil lead. Feeds wire into foot shear to cut wire leads to specified lengths. Scrapes ends of lead wires to remove insulation, using knife and scraper, or adjusts stop guides and feeds wire into pedal-operated wire stripping machine which strips insulation from wires. Dips stripped leads into tinning pot and inserts into wire brush machine to smooth surfaces. Strings specified number of plastic beads or slides cotton sleeving over end of wire to insulate field coil lead. Inserts end of lead wire into bullet press and depresses pedal to automatically position lugs on end of wire and to activate upper die which crimps lugs around end of lead. Wraps cut lengths of insulated wire together, using waxed cord to form cables. Positions lugs on wire leads by hand, prior to inserting assembly in press or crimping machine. May be designated according to task performed as Bead Stringer (elec. equip.); Lead Tinner (elec. equip.); Lugger (elec. equip.); Sleever (elec. equip.); Wire Cutter (elec. equip.); Wire Stripper (elec. equip.).

GOE: 06.04.34 STRENGTH: L GED: R2 M1 L1 SVP: 2 DLU: 81

691.685-022 PAIRING-MACHINE OPERATOR (nonfer. metal)

Tends semiautomatic pairing machines that twist two or more wires together to form insulated telephone or electrical wire, following instructions on production tags: Attaches ends of two wires together; feeds paired wires through guides on bow, around capstan, over guide rollers; and attaches them to takeup reel. Sets counter and presses button to start takeup and pairing motors. Turns adjustment screws to maintain feed and rheostat to maintain running, stopping, and takeup tension. Stops machine to replace empty or filled reels and to check for and repair bare spots in insulation and breaks in wire. Tests paired wires for possible shorts.

GOE: 06.04.09 STRENGTH: M GED: R2 M1 L2 SVP: 3 DLU: 77

691.685-026 SPOOLING-MACHINE OPERATOR (metal prod., nec; nonfer. metal) alternate titles: bobbin winder

Tends machine that winds bare or insulated wire onto spools preparatory to shipment or further processing: Positions empty spool in machine. Threads wire from supply spool or coil through distributor (oscillating guide), *tension guides*, and secures end to empty spool or bobbin and starts machine. Observes machine which automatically winds wire and shuts off when specified amount of wire has been wound. Cuts wire after specified length has been wound, using wirecutters. May butt-weld ends of wire to form continuous strand. May locate and mark defective insulation during winding process, using spark tester. May wind insulation yarn [YARN WINDER (tex. prod., nec; textile)]. May be designated according to product wounnd as Cable Spooler (nonfer. metal).

GOE: 06.04.02 STRENGTH: H GED: R2 M1 L2 SVP: 3 DLU: 77

691.685-030 UTILITY WORKER, EXTRUSION (nonfer. metal)

Performs any combination of following tasks to insulate electric cable: Moves rubber strips from rubber mill to extruder machine, using handtruck. Feeds rubber strips into extruder machine that sheathes cable with rubber insulation. Winds adhesive tape around cable ends to waterproof cable during insulation. Guides sheathed cable onto takeoff reel as cable emerges from extruder. Clamps fittings onto cable ends and lowers reel into autoclave, using hoist. Connects air-pressure hoses and clamps autoclave cover in place. Turns valves to equalize autoclave pressure to prevent distortion of rubber sheath during curing period. Removes reel from autoclave onto payoff spindle of stripping machine. Adjusts slitting knife of stripping machine according to thickness of lead sheathed cable and threads cable beneath knife and spreader attachment. Feels stripped cable for lumps as cable emerges from stripping machine and removes lumps with sandpaper. Keeps log of cable stripped. May be known according to task performed as Reel Tender (nonfer. metal); Spooler And Coiler (nonfer. metal); Tuber Feeder (nonfer. metal).

GOE: 06.04.09 STRENGTH: H GED: R2 M2 L2 SVP: 3 DLU: 77

691.686-010 TWISTING-MACHINE OPERATOR (comm. equip.; elec. equip.)

Feeds two wires into machine that twists wires together to form telephone wire.

GOE: 06.04.09 STRENGTH: L GED: R1 M1 L1 SVP: 2 DLU: 77

691.687-010 PRODUCTION HELPER (nonfer. metal)

Performs any combination of following duties in fabricating and insulating electric wire and cable: Ties pull ropes, attached to cables emerging from extruding machines, onto takeoff reels, and coils cable around reels. Changes machine gears, using wrenches. Unclamps and hoists full reels from braiding, winding, and other fabricating machines, using power hoist. Rolls reels to other work areas or to storeroom. Moves wire, rubber, and other raw materials from storage to work area, using handtruck.

GOE: 06.04.40 STRENGTH: M GED: R1 M1 L1 SVP: 1 DLU: 77

692 OCCUPATIONS IN FABRICATION OF PRODUCTS FROM ASSORTED MATERIALS

This group includes occupations, not elsewhere classified, concerned with fabricating products that are composed of a combination of materials.

692.130-010 BRUSH-FABRICATION SUPERVISOR (fabrication, nec)

Supervises and coordinates activities of workers engaged in fabricating brushes: Schedules utilization of equipment, such as boring and filling, mixing, twisting, and stapling and filling machines to meet production schedule. Sets up boring and filling, stapling and filling, twisting, or other brush making machines to fabricate brushes, such as solid block and twisted-in-wire brushes. Trains workers in operation of machines and equipment. Requisitions and inspects materials. Performs other duties as described under SUPERVISOR (any industry) Master Title.

GOE: 06.02.01 STRENGTH: M GED: R4 M3 L3 SVP: 7 DLU: 78

692.130-014 FINISHING SUPERVISOR (elec. equip.)

Supervises and coordinates activities of workers engaged in operations, such as assembling, cutting, planing, threading, or turning, to make anodes, electrodes, or other carbon products: Studies inspection reports or measures dimensions of finished product to verify conformance to specifications, using calipers, micrometers, or other measuring instruments. Analyzes deviations from specifications and prescribes data to correct machine setup, using knowledge of shop mathematics and machining operations. Inspects machinery to detect malfunction and directs repair or replacement of parts. Performs other duties as described under SUPERVISOR (any industry) Master Title.

GOE: 06.02.01 STRENGTH: L GED: R4 M3 L3 SVP: 7 DLU: 77

692.130-018 SUPERVISOR I (button & notion)

Supervises and coordinates activities of workers engaged in fabricating slide fasteners (zippers) from wire or nylon filament and cloth tape: Examines workpieces for adherence to specifications and quality. Directs workers in machine setup or adjustment. Verifies dimensions of fasteners and parts, using precision instruments and following process sheets, job cards, and blueprints. Trains workers. Requisitions materials. Performs other duties as described under SUPERVISOR (any industry) Master Title.

GOE: 06.02.01 STRENGTH: M GED: R4 M3 L3 SVP: 7 DLU: 77

692.130-022 SUPERVISOR VI (nonmet. min.)

Supervises and coordinates activities of workers engaged in fabricating packing for mechanical equipment, such as engines and compressors: Sets up and adjusts machines, such as shapers, winders, and braiders, using handtools. Trains workers in operation of machines and equipment. Performs other duties as described under SUPERVISOR (any industry) Master Title. May be designated according to process supervised as Supervisor, Braiding (nonmet. min.); Supervisor, Finishing (nonmet. min.).

GOE: 06.01.01 STRENGTH: M GED: R4 M3 L3 SVP: 6 DLU: 77

692.130-026 SUPERVISOR, BROOMMAKING (fabrication, nec)

Supervises and coordinates activities of workers engaged in making brooms: Determines utilization of equipment, such as seeding, clipping, stapling, and winding machines, required to meet production schedules. Sets up and adjusts machines and equipment, using handtools. Trains workers in broom making operations. Requisitions materials and supplies. Performs other duties as described under SUPERVISOR (any industry) Master Title.

GOE: 06.02.01 STRENGTH: M GED: R4 M3 L3 SVP: 6 DLU: 77

692.130-030 SUPERVISOR, PAINT ROLLER COVERS (fabrication, nec)

Supervises and coordinates activities of workers engaged in fabricating paint roller covers: Plans and coordinates utilization of equipment, such as beveling, cut-off, and spiral winding machines to meet production schedule. Sets up and adjusts machines. Trains workers in operation of machines and equipment. Performs duties as described under SUPERVISOR (any industry) Master Title.

GOE: 06.02.01 STRENGTH: L GED: R4 M3 L3 SVP: 7 DLU: 77

692.130-034 SUPERVISOR, TOY PARTS FORMER (toy-sport equip.)

Supervises and coordinates activities of workers engaged in punching and pressing toy parts from metal, plastic, and cardboard material: Sets up and adjusts machines, using handtools. Trains workers in set up and operation of machines and equipment. Performs other duties as described under SUPERVISOR (any industry) Master Title.

GOE: 06.01.01 STRENGTH: L GED: R4 M3 L4 SVP: 7 DLU: 77

692.130-038 SUPERVISOR, KEYMODULE ASSEMBLY (office machines)

Supervises and coordinates activities of workers engaged in assembling components to form modules used in keyboards of electronic computer equipment: Monitors production operations and inspects in-process and completed modules for conformity to specifications. Directs workers in machine setup, adjustment, or repair, using machine blueprints and diagrams and applying knowledge of machine functions. Confers with designated plant personnel to determine corrective action when quality or volume of production does not meet prescribed standard. Performs other duties as described under SUPERVISOR (any industry) Master Title.

GOE: 06.02.01 STRENGTH: L GED: R4 M3 L3 SVP: 7 DLU: 86

692.130-042 SUPERVISOR, SHOP (fabrication, nec)

Supervises and coordinates activities of workers engaged in fabrication of metal paint trays and paint-roller cover frames, applying knowledge of product, machine functions, and properties of metal: Confers with plant personnel to determine customer orders, assign workers to duties, and to determine need for additional workers to meet production requirements. Maintains quantities of materials at each work station. Examines paint-roller cover frames or paint trays

to determine that frames and trays meet specifications. Assists workers in setting up machines, such as ram press, bending press, riveting, and punch press. Performs work activities of subordinate workers to overcome personnel shortages or to relieve workers. Performs other duties as described under SUPERVISOR (any industry) Master Title.
GOE: 06.02.01 STRENGTH: M GED: R3 M3 L3 SVP: 5 DLU: 86

692.132-010 SUPERVISOR IV (nonmet. min.)
Supervises and coordinates activities of workers engaged in fabrication of abrasive products, such as wheels, belts, and rolls: Patrols work area to detect malfunctioning machines. Directs adjustment and repair of faulty machines and equipment. Trains workers. Performs other duties as described under SUPERVISOR (any industry) Master Title.
GOE: 06.02.01 STRENGTH: L GED: R4 M3 L3 SVP: 6 DLU: 77

692.132-014 SUPERVISOR V (nonmet. min.)
Supervises and coordinates activities of workers engaged in cutting abrasive sticks and stones for honing machines: Trains workers to tend machines. Compares color code on abrasive bricks (blocks) and color code on blueprints to ensure conformity to specifications. Inspects cut abrasive sticks for surface defects and measures sticks, using micrometer. Requisitions production and maintenance supplies. Performs duties as described under SUPERVISOR (any industry) Master Title.
GOE: 06.02.01 STRENGTH: L GED: R4 M3 L3 SVP: 6 DLU: 77

692.132-018 SUPERVISOR, SKI PRODUCTION (toy-sport equip.)
Supervises and coordinates activities of workers engaged in fabricating skis: Trains workers in operation of machines and equipment. Requisitions supplies. Examines skis to verify conformance to standards. Performs other duties as described under SUPERVISOR (any industry) Master Title. May be designated according to department or operation supervised as Supervisor, Core Shop (toy-sport equip.); Supervisor, Finishing (toy-sport equip.); Supervisor, Sanding (toy-sport equip.).
GOE: 06.02.09 STRENGTH: L GED: R3 M2 L3 SVP: 6 DLU: 77

692.137-010 SUPERVISOR, PAINTING DEPARTMENT (pen & pencil)
Supervises and coordinates activities of workers in paint department of wooden pencil factory: Orders paint for pencils from laboratory and verifies color of paint against standard color samples. Inspects pencils for evenness of applied coating and surface irregularities, such as nicks or scratches, to determine machine adjustment. Notifies SET-UP MECHANIC (pen & pencil) of needed adjustments on paint machines. Performs other duties as described under SUPERVISOR (any industry) Master Title. May set up and adjust paint machines.
GOE: 06.02.01 STRENGTH: L GED: R4 M3 L3 SVP: 7 DLU: 77

692.137-014 SUPERVISOR I (protective dev.)
Supervises and coordinates activities of workers engaged in fabricating and packaging disposable diapers: Reviews production schedule to determine diaper quantities and sizes to be fabricated during shift. Confers with shift supervisor of previous shift regarding condition of machines and production materials available. Completes requisition forms to request materials needed for diaper fabrication or packaging. Directs workers engaged in fabrication, packaging, and moving packaged diapers to shipping area. Assigns new workers to experienced workers for training. Maintains daily production sheets and quality control checklist of diaper defects for company records. Performs other duties as described under SUPERVISOR (any industry) Master Title.
GOE: 06.04.01 STRENGTH: L GED: R4 M3 L4 SVP: 7 DLU: 86

692.260-010 MACHINE SETTER (nonmet. min.)
Sets up machines to fabricate abrasive products, such as wheels, belts and rolls: Changes and adjusts feed mechanisms, dies, and stop guides according to specifications, using handtools. Starts machine to obtain sample and measures product to verify machine setup, using templates and gauges. Examines product for surface defects and to determine causes. Notifies workers to stop operation of machines that malfunction.
GOE: 06.01.02 STRENGTH: M GED: R3 M3 L3 SVP: 6 DLU: 77

692.360-010 ASSEMBLY-MACHINE-SET-UP MECHANIC (elec. equip.)
Sets up and maintains in operating adjustment machines and equipment, such as capacitor-pack-winding machine, electrode cutter, spot welders, name-plate stamping machine, and induction heating unit: Receives instructions from supervisor regarding size, number, and type of capacitors to be produced. Arranges work benches and assembly lines to facilitate production. Inserts material into feed mechanism of machines and measures distance between points to set stops on machine, using rule. Secures dogs on dials of counting mechanism to indicate stops during winding operations. Installs machine cutting tools and welding electrodes. Adjusts setscrews to obtain tension on holding devices, using handtools. Makes trial run to ensure proper setting and informs operator regarding production requirements and machine operation. Inspects products to locate malfunctions in machine operation.
GOE: 06.01.02 STRENGTH: M GED: R3 M3 L3 SVP: 5 DLU: 77

692.360-014 BRUSH-MACHINE SETTER (fabrication, nec)
Sets up and adjusts machines used to cut materials and fabricate brushes: Changes and adjusts cutting blades, drills, feed mechanisms, and machine speeds according to specifications, using handtools. Verifies adjustments, using fixed gauges. Inspects machines for malfunction and replaces worn or broken parts, using handtools. Lubricates moving parts, using oilcan. May be des-

ignated according to machine maintained as Brush-Fabricating-Machine Setter (fabrication, nec); Brush-Trimming-Machine Setter (fabrication, nec).
GOE: 06.01.02 STRENGTH: M GED: R3 M2 L3 SVP: 5 DLU: 77

692.360-018 FIRESETTER (elec. equip.; electron. comp.; inst. & app.)
Sets up, adjusts, and maintains machines to make flares and stems, seal stems to bulbs, or seal exhaust tubing to bulbs in manufacture of electron tubes and light bulbs: Installs and adjusts specified types and sizes of machine parts, such as cutter, revolving heads, bulb loader, tubing loader, burners, and etching stamp, using handtools. Lights burners and adjusts gas, air, oxygen and hydrogen valves to attain specified cone, color, and density of flames. Starts machine and deposits bulbs, tubing, or other glass parts into hoppers that automatically feed parts into heads of rotating turret, or inserts bulbs and glass parts into sockets of conveyor or molds of rotating turret. Operates machine through trial run and adjusts machine to ensure accuracy of setup. Observes processing operations and inspects sample items for conformance to specifications. Readjusts valves and machine parts to achieve specified standard of product. Maintains machines and replaces faulty parts, using handtools. May operate machine to manufacture production parts.
GOE: 06.01.03 STRENGTH: M GED: R4 M3 L3 SVP: 6 DLU: 89

692.362-010 SET-UP MECHANIC, CROWN ASSEMBLY MACHINE (any industry)
Operates battery of machines that insert and glue cork, paper, plastic or aluminum foil in bottlecap shells: Installs punches and dies in crown assembly machines and adjusts stroke of punches that force lining material into caps. Turns adjustment screws to regulate feed mechanism, rate of glue flow, and heating flame. Starts machine and examines sample caps to verify conformance to specifications. Observes operation of machine to detect and diagnose cause of faulty operations. Disassembles machine and replaces broken or worn parts, using handtools. May repair machine conveyor belts [BELT REPAIRER (any industry)].
GOE: 06.02.20 STRENGTH: L GED: R3 M2 L2 SVP: 5 DLU: 77

692.380-010 SET-UP MECHANIC (pen & pencil)
Sets up and adjusts battery of machines that paint, stamp, tip, or trim wooden pencils: Installs and adjusts feed mechanisms, guide rollers, tracks, machine fittings and attachments, according to size and shape of pencils, using handtools and gauges. Adjusts controls, such as setscrews and cams to synchronize machine mechanisms. Regulates thermostatic controls on heated units of machines. Disassembles machines and replaces worn or defective parts, such as circular knives, grinding wheels, and rollers. Sharpens machine punches and blades, using files and powered emery wheel. Starts machines to test adjustments and examines pencils for defects, such as burns, splintered ends, and nicks to determine needed readjustments. Replaces or repairs defective machine belts. May be designated according to type of machine setup as Set-Up Mechanic, Coating Machines (pen & pencil); Set-Up Mechanic, Heading Machines (pen & pencil); Set-Up Mechanic, Stamping Machines (pen & pencil).
GOE: 06.01.02 STRENGTH: M GED: R4 M3 L3 SVP: 6 DLU: 77

692.380-014 SET-UP MECHANIC, AUTOMATIC LINE (pen & pencil)
Sets up and adjusts battery of automatic machines that groove, sand, insert lead in slats, glue, and press slats together to form wooden pencils.
GOE: 06.01.02 STRENGTH: M GED: R4 M3 L3 SVP: 6 DLU: 77

692.382-010 BALLPOINT-PEN-ASSEMBLY-MACHINE OPERATOR (pen & pencil)
Sets up and operates automatic machine to assemble ballpoint pens: Installs and adjusts feed mechanisms, guide rollers, tracks, fittings, attachments, type, and die according to size and shape of pens and identifying data to be stamped on barrels, using handtools. Loads machine hoppers with parts, such as barrels, ferrules (metal tips), eraser caps, nose cones, and ink cartridges. Fills machine reservoirs with glue and solvent. Mounts roll of printing foil on machine spindle, using wrench.
GOE: 06.02.20 STRENGTH: M GED: R4 M3 L3 SVP: 6 DLU: 77

692.382-014 PLATE STACKER, MACHINE (elec. equip.) alternate titles: plate grouper, machine
Sets up and operates machine to stack (interleaf) separators and positive and negative plates into groups to form storage battery elements: Loads positive and negative plates in magazines of machine. Positions separators in magazine with ribbed side toward positive plate to facilitate passage of sediment. Moves lever to set electric solenoid counter for number of plates specified for group. Turns screws to adjust opening in feeding mechanism (stripper gates), according to plate sizes, using handtools. Starts machine to stack specified number of plates and separators alternately to form group. Clears plate and separator jams and adjusts machine to correct malfunction, using handtools. Places groups on conveyor leading to burning stand. Removes oxide dust from machine, using vacuum cleaner.
GOE: 06.02.20 STRENGTH: L GED: R3 M2 L2 SVP: 4 DLU: 77

692.462-010 CALENDER-ROLL PRESS OPERATOR (machinery mfg.)
Operates hydraulic press to build calender rolls used to make paper and textile imprinting and embossing machinery: Fits flange over end of shaft. Hoists shaft into vertical position on hydraulic press, using crane. Places rings composed of paper, cotton, wool, and corn husks over shaft until shaft is full. Fits top flange onto shaft. Adjusts valves on hydraulic press, and starts pump to build up pressure. Monitors clock and gauges to ensure that pressure is main-

tained. Records weight of material put on shaft, measures length of material being compressed, computes density, and stops press when specified density is reached. Maintains pressure for prescribed time. Releases pressure and adds material to shaft as necessary.
GOE: 06.02.09 STRENGTH: M GED: R3 M3 L2 SVP: 4 DLU: 77

692.482-010 CARBON-AND-GRAPHITE-BRUSH-MACHINE OPERA-TOR (elec. equip.)

Sets up and operates automatic machines to grind, mill, and secure shunt leads to carbon and graphite brushes: Reviews work orders to determine size, type, and number of brushes to be produced. Installs grinding wheels, cutting blades, and tamping tools on machine shafts and turns setscrews to adjust cutting and grinding mechanisms and width guides according to specifications, using handtools. Observes panelboard to detect and remove jammed brushes. Verifies dimensions of brushes, using micrometer, calipers, and ruler. May be designated according to machine operated as Concaving-Machine Operator (elec. equip.); Heading-Machine Operator (elec. equip.); Tamping-Machine Operator (elec. equip.).
GOE: 06.02.09 STRENGTH: M GED: R3 M3 L3 SVP: 4 DLU: 87

692.485-010 STRINGER-MACHINE TENDER (protective dev.)

Tends machine that winds copper wire around plastic cores to produce intrauterine birth control devices: Positions core in winding machine. Starts machine that winds wire around core to fabricate IUD of specified size. Removes IUD from machine and laces thin wire on bottom to facilitate removal by physician. Verifies size of IUD, using preset plug gauge and calipers. Verifies wire tension, using tensiometer, and turns nuts or setscrews to adjust tension. Removes empty spools of copper wire from machine and threads new spools on machine.
GOE: 06.04.09 STRENGTH: L GED: R2 M1 L2 SVP: 2 DLU: 77

692.662-010 DYNAMITE-PACKING-MACHINE OPERATOR (chemical)

Sets up and operates machine to pack dynamite into paper cartridge shells to form sticks: Installs and adjusts tamping sticks and nipple plates in packing machine according to diameter and length of cartridges to be packed, using nonsparking handtools. Starts machine, directs DYNAMITE-PACKING-MACHINE FEEDER (chemical) to fill powder hopper with dynamite, and fills shuttle board (cartridge forming block) with paper cartridge shells. Secures shuttle board in filling position on machine, and scoops dynamite from hopper into box above tamping sticks. Lifts shuttle board of filled cartridges from machine and tends crimping press to finish ends, or passes filled cartridges to DYNAMITE-CARTRIDGE CRIMPER (chemical).
GOE: 06.02.09 STRENGTH: M GED: R3 M2 L3 SVP: 5 DLU: 77

692.662-014 GELATIN-DYNAMITE-PACKING OPERATOR (chemical)

Operates stuffing machine to fill paper dynamite cartridges with gelatin-type dynamite: Installs and adjusts extruding auger and nozzle according to diameter and length of cartridges to be packed. Starts machine and holds end of cartridge to nozzle until filled. Taps bottom of cartridge on bench to settle top level of dynamite, and stands it in frame to be crimped.
GOE: 06.02.09 STRENGTH: M GED: R3 M2 L3 SVP: 5 DLU: 77

692.662-018 WAFER-MACHINE OPERATOR (elec. equip.)

Operates machines to fabricate wafer-type (flat) dry cells: Loads feeding mechanism with materials, such as plastic film, paper, zinc and carbon plates, and silver wax. Starts machine and equipment that cuts piece of plastic film for base of cell, positions and presses zinc plate on plastic film, cuts and places paper cover on zinc plate, drops core (black mix) on plastic film, positions carbon plate on core, deposits sealing compound on carbon plate, covers plate with plastic film, tamps and seals cell and trims edges, and applies silver wax to negative and positive ends. Observes finished cells conveyed past mirror to detect defects. Adjusts machine and equipment for size changes or to correct malfunctions, such as faulty tinning, sealing, and trimming, using handtools. Directs workers extruding black mix cores and feeding cores to machine.
GOE: 06.02.09 STRENGTH: L GED: R3 M2 L2 SVP: 4 DLU: 77

692.662-022 WIRE-WRAPPING-MACHINE OPERATOR (office machines)

Operates automatic wire-wrapping machine to wire panel and plugboard type subassemblies in manufacture of machines, such as computers and punched-card office machines: Reads work orders, wiring diagrams, and blueprints to determine wiring specifications, number of units to be wired, and specified paper tape or punched card deck to use for machine control. Positions specified *paper tape* on spindles or places punched card deck in feed hopper. Mounts unwired panel or plugboard in holding fixture and positions fixture in machine, using wrenches and clamps. Pushes buttons and switches to operate wire-wrapping machine that automatically routes, cuts, and wraps ends of wires around terminal posts to install wiring. Monitors indicator lights, spools of wire, and machine operation to detect machine malfunctions. Notifies supervisor of malfunctions or need for change in machine setup.
GOE: 06.02.09 STRENGTH: L GED: R3 M2 L3 SVP: 4 DLU: 77

692.665-010 BRAIDING-MACHINE TENDER (rubber goods)

Tends battery of machines that braid and cement fabric cord or wire around rubber hose for reinforcement: Threads machine with specified spools of cord, rubber insulation, or wire stock. Notifies BRAIDER SETTER (rubber goods) when change in pitch gear is required. Pulls hose from reel and threads it into braiding machine. Adjusts controls to maintain uniform tension on cord or wire stock. Starts flow of rubber cement into machine and starts machine. Observes operation for defects, such as broken cords and loose braiding. Ties broken cords. Places braided hose on stock rack or coils it in box. May rewind partial spools of cord to make full spool, using electric windup spindle. May tend machine that knits yarn onto rubber hose and be designated Knitting-Machine Tender (rubber goods). May tend one or more looms that weave yarn and wire jacket around hose and be designated Loom Operator (rubber goods).
GOE: 06.04.09 STRENGTH: M GED: R2 M1 L2 SVP: 3 DLU: 77

692.665-014 PUNCH-PRESS OPERATOR (fabrication, nec)

Tends press that automatically punches out blocks of floor tile from sheets of vinyl and asphalt or asbestos material: Starts machine and observes sheet for uniformity of color pattern. Pushes button to release punching ram, allowing defective sections of sheet to pass through and onto scrap conveyor. Feels material to determine its flexibility as it enters machine and notifies CALENDER OPERATOR (fabrication, nec) to adjust temperature of rolls. Stops machine when jams occur and removes damaged floor tile to clear punch press.
GOE: 06.04.09 STRENGTH: M GED: R2 M1 L2 SVP: 2 DLU: 77

692.665-018 DRY-CELL-ASSEMBLY-MACHINE TENDER (elec. equip.)

Tends variety of machines that automatically assemble dry-cell components: Dumps parts and materials, such as top assemblies and electrolyte gel, into hoppers of assembly machines. Places cans (containers) that hold critical parts during assembly operations onto conveyor. Starts machines and conveyor system. Observes operation and movement of units at various stages of assembly to ensure units are assembled according to specifications. Adjusts machines as necessary to correct malfunctions when jam-ups occur. Inspects finished cells to detect defects and missing parts.
GOE: 06.04.20 STRENGTH: H GED: R3 M2 L3 SVP: 4 DLU: 86

692.682-010 ANKLE-PATCH MOLDER (boot & shoe)

Operates electrically heated machine to mold plastic trademark ankle patch onto quarters for sneakers: Pours liquid plastic into feeder tank. Lifts plate cover, equipped with two die openings for simultaneous molding of right and left quarters. Slides dies into holders, tightens screws and replaces plate, using wrench. Starts machine and presses button to blow air through sprue holes in dies to clear openings. Brushes silicone on dies to prevent sticking. Positions right and left quarters over die openings on plate with edges against guide pins. Presses buttons to lower rams onto quarters, inject plastic to fill dies, and mold patches. Examines molded pieces for defects, such as insufficient plastic, lack of adhesion to cloth, discoloration, or unclear imprint, and rejects defective pieces. Cleans adhering plastic from die grooves and sprue holes, using metal pick. Adjusts rheostat to vary heat setting, according to size of die and to correct defects.
GOE: 06.02.02 STRENGTH: L GED: R3 M2 L3 SVP: 4 DLU: 77

692.682-014 BEAD-FORMING-MACHINE OPERATOR (rubber tire)

Sets up and operates machine to coat strands of steel wire with rubber to form beads for use in making pneumatic tires: Installs bead-forming wheel, dies, and baffles, and turns setscrews to adjust guides, spring tension, bead cutter arm, and bead forming wheel cycle according to specifications, using wrenches and screwdriver. Threads specified number of wires from spools through tuber die for rubber coating and into machine for forming into bead layers. Starts machine to feed wire through die and onto forming wheel. Cuts wire to remove bead layer from forming wheel when cycle is complete. Tapes cut end to hold bead together for wrapping or places bead in wrapping machine.
GOE: 06.02.09 STRENGTH: M GED: R3 M2 L2 SVP: 4 DLU: 77

692.682-018 BORING-AND-FILLING-MACHINE OPERATOR (fabrication, nec)

Sets up and operates boring-and-filling machine to fabricate brushes: Installs specified ratchet wheel, cams, stapling head, and drill in machine, using handtools. Mounts roll of wire on spindle and threads wire through stapling mechanism. Fills magazine with material, such as horsehair, nylon, wire, plastic filaments, or vegetable fibers, according to type of brush being made. Positions and clamps wooden or composition brush base in jig under drill, and clamps predrilled base in jig under filling-and-stapling device. Starts machine which simultaneously drills holes in blank base, and inserts and staples brush material in holes of drilled base. Places finished brush on storage rack. May be designated according to type of brush filled as Hair-Brush-Boring-And-Filling-Machine Operator (fabrication, nec); Tooth-Brush-Boring-And-Filling-Machine Operator (fabrication, nec); Wire-Brush-Boring-And-Filling-Machine Operator (fabrication, nec).
GOE: 06.02.09 STRENGTH: M GED: R3 M2 L2 SVP: 5 DLU: 77

692.682-022 BROOM STITCHER (fabrication, nec)

Operates machine to stitch twine through broom fibers to strengthen and shape body of broom: Inserts and tightens jaws in vise that holds broom for stitching. Attaches ratchet and turns lever to set number, rows, and length of stitches. Inserts and clamps brush end of broom in vise. Cuts specified length of twine for each course, using knife. Wraps twine around broom and pulls one end between fibers, using hook, and threads other end through needle. Pushes vise into stitcher and starts machine to stitch fibers. May buckle leather strap around broom to hold it during stitching.
GOE: 06.02.09 STRENGTH: M GED: R3 M2 L2 SVP: 4 DLU: 77

692.682-026 CANDLE-EXTRUSION-MACHINE OPERATOR (fabrication, nec)

Sets up and operates machine to extrude sheets of candle wax or candles: Reviews instructions to determine type product to be produced. Installs speci-

fied die plates in machine, using handtools. Threads wick material through machine guides. Turns valve and dials to transfer wax to machine and to regulate speed, pressure, and temperature of machine. Starts machine that feeds wax and wick through dies to produce candles of specified dimensions or forces wax through dies to produce sheet of candle wax. Adjusts pressure controls to obtain specified dimensions.
GOE: 06.02.18 STRENGTH: L GED: R3 M2 L3 SVP: 4 DLU: 77

692.682-030 COREMAKING-MACHINE OPERATOR (elec. equip.)
Operates machine to mold core and insert carbon rod in core to form cathode of dry cell batteries: Installs extruder bushings and mold on machine, using handtools. Places carbon rods in trough of feeding mechanism. Fills machine hopper with paste (black mix), using shovel. Starts machine that rams paste into mold, drives bar into paste to form hole for carbon rod, inserts rod in paste, tamps paste to compress paste around rod, and ejects finished core onto conveyor belt. Inspects core for defects and off-centered rods. Adjusts rod-centering device and force of impact and length of stroke of ram, using handtools.
GOE: 06.02.20 STRENGTH: L GED: R3 M2 L2 SVP: 4 DLU: 77

692.682-034 ELECTRODE TURNER-AND-FINISHER (elec. equip.)
Sets up and operates machines to perform machining operation, such as boring, threading, and turning on carbon electrodes according to production specifications: Installs specified drilling and threading tools in holders, using handtools. Lifts and centers electrode in chuck of machine, using hoist. Starts machine that automatically drills and threads electrode ends. Positions workpiece in turning lathe. Starts machine, and sets feed and travel controls to machine electrode to specified diameter and surface finish. Verifies conformance of machined workpiece to specifications, using calipers.
GOE: 06.02.09 STRENGTH: M GED: R3 M2 L2 SVP: 4 DLU: 77

692.682-038 FILLING-AND-STAPLING-MACHINE OPERATOR (fabrication, nec)
Operates machine to insert and staple brush-filling material into prebored holes of brush head: Places spool of wire on machine spindle and threads wire into staple machine. Lays material in feeder box. Turns manual-control wheel to test feeding and staple-forming operation. Twists key to clamp brush head in holding block. Turns handwheel and screw adjustment to adjust tilt and height of machine table and positions brush head under filling spout. Depresses pedal to start machine and moves brush head under filling spout to ensure that brush-filling material is inserted and stapled in brush head holes. Readjusts table to accommodate varying angles of holes in brush head.
GOE: 06.02.09 STRENGTH: M GED: R3 M2 L2 SVP: 4 DLU: 77

692.682-042 GAUGE OPERATOR (fabrication, nec)
Operates machine to cut floor covering sheets into tile: Installs specified cutting die, and adjusts feed stroke, air pressure, and suction pick-up on machine, using handtools. Starts machine and feeds floor covering sheets into machine. Removes tiles from machine and transfers tiles to stock area, using handtruck.
GOE: 06.02.09 STRENGTH: L GED: R3 M1 L2 SVP: 4 DLU: 77

692.682-046 PAINT-ROLLER-COVER-MACHINE SETTER (fabrication, nec)
Sets up and operates variety of machines used to fabricate paint roller covers: Changes and adjusts jigs and fixtures, cutters, and chucks on machines, such as sewing, cutting, and reversing machines, using handtools. Fills machine reservoirs with glue and adjusts mechanisms that control flow of glue into machines. Inspects machines to detect malfunctions and adjusts machines. Replaces worn or damaged parts, using handtools.
GOE: 06.02.20 STRENGTH: L GED: R3 M2 L3 SVP: 5 DLU: 77

692.682-050 POWER-DRIVEN-BRUSH MAKER (fabrication, nec)
Sets up and operates filling machine which inserts and fastens brush wire in metal hub to fabricate power-driven circular wire brushes: Inserts specified metal hub in machine holding fixture and tightens bolts using hand wrench. Selects coil of brush wire according to chart, mounts it on feeding reel, and threads end through machine feed rollers. Turns screws to adjust stroke of feeding arms that feed specified amounts of brush wire into machine cutting blade which cuts wire to length. Fills magazine feed with tying wires of specified length. Starts machine which inserts brush wire into hub and ties into place with wire. Notifies supervisor of machine malfunction.
GOE: 06.02.02 STRENGTH: M GED: R3 M2 L2 SVP: 5 DLU: 77

692.682-054 STACKING-MACHINE OPERATOR I (any industry) alternate titles: lamination stacker, machine; plate stacker, machine
Operates machine to stack plates or sheets of material, such as metal or plastic, to assemble laminated products, such as rotor cores and storage battery elements or to form bundles for shipment: Places specified material into one or more feed magazines or holding devices. Moves lever to set automatic feed for number of items specified for stack. Turns screws to adjust opening in feed mechanism to size of item, using measuring instruments or built-in scale and handtools. Starts machine that automatically measures or counts and stacks specified number of pieces in desired arrangement. Clears jams and adjusts machine to correct malfunction, using handtools. Removes finished stack from machine and places stack into basket or into magazine of machine performing subsequent operation. May insert spacers between bundles to form continuous stack.
GOE: 06.02.20 STRENGTH: L GED: R3 M2 L3 SVP: 4 DLU: 77

692.682-058 STRAPPING-MACHINE OPERATOR (wood. container) alternate titles: box strapper; strapper
Operates machine to wind reinforcing metal or plastic bands around ends of boxes or cartons: Places spool of strapping on machine and threads end of strap through jaws of clamp. Adjusts jaws to attain specified tension on strap. Tightens clamp down on box or carton placed in it. Nails end of strap to box. Starts machine that automatically winds strap around box or carton. Nails strap to box, and cuts strap with snips. Releases pressure of clamp on box or carton and removes it from machine.
GOE: 06.04.38 STRENGTH: H GED: R3 M1 L2 SVP: 4 DLU: 77

692.682-062 STRING-WINDING-MACHINE OPERATOR (musical inst.)
Operates lathe-type winding machine to wind wire or other materials over core of wire, nylon, or gut to make musical instrument strings: Places looped end of core over one end of machine and attaches core to other end of machine. Places spool of winding wire or nylon on spool holder and threads end through loop on core. Starts machine and guides covering material along rotating core. Stops machine and cuts covering material with shears or wirecutter. Clips one end of core with wirecutter and removes it from machine. May wind more than one strand of wire or nylon over core. May wind colored silk or rayon on string ends for trim, identification, or protection. May specialize in winding bass strings and be designated Bass-String Winder (musical inst.).
GOE: 06.02.09 STRENGTH: L GED: R3 M2 L2 SVP: 4 DLU: 77

692.682-066 SWEEPER-BRUSH MAKER, MACHINE (fabrication, nec) alternate titles: broom-machine operator
Operates machine to bind fibers on cylindrical core to form brushes used on street sweeping machines: Mounts brush core in machine, turns crank to wind specified amount of cable on holding spool, and staples end of cable to core, using hammer. Sets spool brake to maintain tension between spool and core, using wrench. Aligns carriage wheel guide in spiral groove of core and adjusts material guides and conveyor to feed material onto core according to size of brush, using wrenches. Spreads precut fibers on conveyor. Starts machine that winds cable to bind fibers onto revolving core. Staples or bolts cable to core at completion of winding process. Repairs sweeper brush cores, using handtools.
GOE: 06.02.09 STRENGTH: H GED: R3 M2 L2 SVP: 4 DLU: 77

692.682-070 TWISTING-MACHINE OPERATOR (fabrication, nec)
Sets up and operates twisting machine to twist wire around brush filling-material to make brushes: Fastens specified chuck in machine to accommodate diameter of wire. Turns screws to set stops on machine bed at specified distance from chuck to stop twisting action when wire is twisted to required length, using handtools and rule. Selects specified size of precut looped wire and places on machine bed with looped end over machine hitching post. Inserts straight ends of wire into machine chuck and tightens with hand wrench. Weighs out specified amount of horsehair, nylon, vegetable fibers or other brush material on scale. Distributes material evenly in brush area between ends of wire. Moves lever to start machine that twists wire around brush material. Stacks finished brush in storage bin.
GOE: 06.02.20 STRENGTH: L GED: R3 M2 L2 SVP: 5 DLU: 77

692.685-010 ABRASIVE-BAND WINDER (nonmet. min.)
Tends electrically powered or hand-cranked band-winding machine that joins and shapes precut backing strip with abrasive-coated strip by spirally winding strips on mandrel to produce grinding and polishing tubes or cones: Applies adhesive to backing strip by handbrush or by automatic applicator attached to winding machine. Clips ends of backing strip and abrasive strip to mandrel. Depresses foot switch or turns handcrank to revolve mandrel. Guides strips by hand and depresses pressure roller pedal to feed strips on mandrel. Unclips and slides completed roll from mandrel and places roll in container.
GOE: 06.04.20 STRENGTH: L GED: R2 M1 L1 SVP: 2 DLU: 77

692.685-014 ADHESIVE-BANDAGE-MACHINE OPERATOR (protective dev.)
Tends machine that automatically makes adhesive bandages from cloth and plastic material: Positions specified rolls of materials on machine spindles and locks them in place with plates and setscrews to prevent unrolling. Threads materials through rollers in prescribed sequence. Starts machine that cuts materials to required length, affixes gauze to cloth or plastic tape, fastens crinoline strips to ends, seals completed bandage in paper wrapper, and deposits it on conveyor belt or in bin for subsequent packing. Observes machine during operations to detect jamming, twisted materials, or malfunctions and makes minor adjustments to correct faults.
GOE: 06.04.05 STRENGTH: L GED: R2 M1 L2 SVP: 3 DLU: 77

692.685-018 AIR-HOLE DRILLER (fabrication, nec)
Tends machine that drills airhole in shank of smoking pipe to connect shank hole to bowl chamber: Clamps smoking pipe bowl in jaws of holding device and starts machine. Pulls handle of drill that automatically releases drilling tool into center of shank to bore hole through shank into base of bowl chamber. Removes bowl from clamp after drilling tool automatically stops and holds shank against sanding wheel to face shank for stem fitting.
GOE: 06.04.03 STRENGTH: L GED: R2 M1 L1 SVP: 2 DLU: 77

692.685-022 BEAD PREPARER (rubber goods)
Tends machine that wraps and cements rubberized fabric tape on bead wire used to reinforce airplane deicers: Loads specified reels of bead wire and rub-

berized fabric tape on *letoff racks,* and threads wire and tape through machine. Adjusts feed rollers and tension wheels according to specifications, using handtools. Pours rubber cement and powdered soapstone in dispensers and starts machine. Examines and feels bead wire for loose wrap. Cuts bead wire when windup reel is filled, using pliers.
GOE: 06.04.07 STRENGTH: H GED: R2 M1 L1 SVP: 3 DLU: 77

692.685-026 BRASSIERE-SLIDE-MAKING-MACHINE TENDER, AUTOMATIC (garment)
Tends automatic machine that loops tape through buckles and cuts and fuses tape ends together to fabricate brassiere slides: Fills machine hoppers with plastic buckles. Mounts rolls of tape on brackets and threads machine. Starts machine and observes operation for malfunctions. Reports malfunctions to supervisory personnel. Removes slides from machine following fabrication.
GOE: 06.04.05 STRENGTH: L GED: R1 M1 L1 SVP: 2 DLU: 77

692.685-030 BROOM BUNDLER (fabrication, nec)
Tends machine that binds bundles of brooms for shipment: Stacks specified number of brooms under ram of binding machine. Depresses pedal that lowers ram to compact broom heads and insert twine through heads. Removes brooms from machine and ties twine around heads and handles to form bundle.
GOE: 06.04.38 STRENGTH: M GED: R2 M1 L2 SVP: 2 DLU: 77

692.685-034 BUCKLE-FRAME SHAPER (button & notion) alternate titles: chop-and-frame operator
Tends automatic machine that cuts and shapes wire or fabric-covered wire to form bars, prongs, and buckle frames: Adjusts forming head according to product specified, using handtools. Positions reel of wire on machine spindle and draws end of wire through guides to forming head. Inserts wire against stop and depresses treadle-switch to start machine. Observes automatic feeding of wire into machine or holds switch down with foot and advances wire against stop as specified item is cut, formed, and ejected. May pull levers of hand-bending machine to shape sample items.
GOE: 06.04.09 STRENGTH: L GED: R2 M1 L2 SVP: 3 DLU: 77

692.685-038 CANDLE MOLDER, MACHINE (fabrication, nec)
Tends cast-molding machine that forms candles: Fills machine with liquid wax and turns valve to force steam into jackets to heat molds. Turns valve to transfer wax to molds. Scrapes *flash* from molds, using knife, and depresses pedal to eject candles into trays. Cuts candlewick ends to specified length, using knife. May move lever to force needles, threaded with wicks, through candles or to insert pins into candles, leaving hole for later insertion of wick. May imbed decorative bases in butt ends of candles during cooling. May insert wax cores in molds for application of final wax coating.
GOE: 06.04.19 STRENGTH: M GED: R2 M1 L2 SVP: 4 DLU: 77

692.685-042 CAPPING-MACHINE OPERATOR (elec. equip.) alternate titles: washer-and-capper-machine operator
Tends machine that inserts and tamps washers and affixes cover to dry-cell containers (cans): Inserts washers and dumps caps into feeding mechanisms. Starts machine and observes mirror to inspect units passing on conveyor to ensure washers are at prescribed depth. Inspects capped cells for defects and offcenter carbon rods. Adjusts machine for changes in size of cans or to correct malfunction, using handtools. May tend machine equipped with device that cuts (punches) paper washers from tape, inserts washer, and affixes cap to can.
GOE: 06.04.20 STRENGTH: L GED: R2 M1 L2 SVP: 3 DLU: 77

692.685-046 CELL TUBER, MACHINE (elec. equip.)
Tends machines that wrap dry cells in plasticized material and insert and seal cells in paper tubes or metal sleeves, using any of following methods: (1) Installs roll of plastic film in wrapping machine equipped with sealing unit. Threads plastic film through feeding device to wrapping mechanism. Starts machine and feeds cells to machine. (2) Tends tubing machine, fed by turntables, that inserts metal bottom and dry cell into paper tube and crimps tube over bottom. (3) Tends sleeving machine, fed by turntable, that inserts tubed cell in metal sleeve and positions and crimps metal cap on sleeve. Inspects units for faulty crimping or sealing. Observes machine for malfunctions and makes adjustments, such as retiming machine, using handtools. May be designated according to machine tended as Sleeve-Machine Tender (elec. equip.); Tubing-Machine Tender (elec. equip.); Wrapping-Machine Tender (elec. equip.).
GOE: 06.04.09 STRENGTH: L GED: R2 M1 L1 SVP: 2 DLU: 77

692.685-050 CEMENTER, MACHINE (boot & shoe)
Tends machines that apply margin of rubber or latex cement to rubberized fabric parts used in assembling rubber footwear: Starts machine, picks up uncemented part from book, *board,* tray, frame, or stack and applies cement, using any of following methods: (1) Draws edge of workpiece between preset revolving rollers, exercising care to obtain even coating and prevent part from being misshapen. (2) Depresses pedal to bring rollers together on material passing between rollers. (3) Holds top of *skirtlike upper* along bottom edge between rollers to apply margin of cement all around for subsequent bonding to shoe bottom. Turns setscrews to adjust distances between pickup, wiper, and applicator rollers and blades to regulate amount of cement deposited. Places processed parts on conveyor belt or in books, frames, or stacks. May stack one part in another before cementing [FITTER-PLACER (rubber goods) 753.687-022].
GOE: 06.04.05 STRENGTH: L GED: R1 M1 L1 SVP: 2 DLU: 77

692.685-054 COATING-MACHINE OPERATOR (pen & pencil) alternate titles: painting-machine operator
Tends machines that apply lacquer, paint, or stain to pencils: Pours coating fluid into reservoir of machine. Places pencils on feed conveyor or in hopper

of machine. Starts machine that presses pencils through openings in sides of reservoir to coat them with fluid. Places coated pencils on conveyor that carries them through heated drying unit and drops them into container. Removes coated pencils from container and examines them for evenness of coating. May tend pair of machines that apply successive coats of paint or lacquer to pencils.
GOE: 06.04.21 STRENGTH: M GED: R2 M1 L2 SVP: 2 DLU: 77

692.685-058 CORE SHAPER (toy-sport equip.)
Tends machine that shapes sides or cambers (arches) of wooden or foam core blanks or plastic base strips used in ski manufacturing: Installs specified cutter heads, templates, and guides according to work order, using handtools. Starts machine that shapes core blanks or plastic base strips, following template contours. May be designated according to operation performed as Core Shaper, Sides (toy-sport equip.); Core Shaper, Top (toy-sport equip.).
GOE: 06.04.09 STRENGTH: M GED: R2 M1 L2 SVP: 2 DLU: 77

692.685-062 CROWN-ASSEMBLY-MACHINE OPERATOR (any industry) alternate titles: cap-lining-machine operator; inserting-press operator; lining-machine tender; spot-machine operator
Tends machine that inserts and glues cork, paper, plastic, or aluminum foil in bottlecap shells: Pours glue into pot. Turns valves to adjust gas flame for heating glue and to regulate flow of glue into machine. Mounts roll of lining material on machine spindle and starts machine. Observes discs and shells flowing from hopper into machine and pries jammed discs or shells loose, using poker. Examines glued shells on conveyor and rejects bent shells and offcenter or chipped discs. Pries glued disc from sample shell, using pick, observes quantity and texture of glue on sample, and adjusts valves to maintain specified temperature and rate of flow of glue.
GOE: 06.04.09 STRENGTH: L GED: R2 M1 L1 SVP: 2 DLU: 77

692.685-066 DEICER-ELEMENT WINDER, MACHINE (rubber goods)
Tends machine that winds wire onto drum to form electric heating elements for airplane deicers: Aligns and tapes precut sheet of fabric on drum of machine. Determines location of element parts on fabric and length of element wires, using template. Tapes braided wire connections and solders strips to fabric in specified locations. Brushes rubber cement on fabric, and threads wire into machine. Turns dials to adjust machine that crimps and spaces element wires during winding, and starts machine. Cuts element wires to specified length and tapes ends of wires to fabric. Verifies length and spacing of element wires with rule. Counts number of wires specified for sections of element, and pulls off excess wires. Solders parts, such as *bus bars* and braided connections to element wires, using soldering iron. Cuts fabric, containing formed element, from drum of machine, using scissors, and lays element on stockrack.
GOE: 06.04.20 STRENGTH: L GED: R2 M2 L2 SVP: 4 DLU: 77

692.685-070 DESIGN INSERTER (plastic prod.)
Tends equipment that inlays glass, metal, and plastic figures into pocket knives, money clips, key cases, gearshift balls, and other products: Places product in gas furnace to soften it. Removes product from furnace, using tongs. Places article on machine and depresses pedal to lower ram that indents surface of article. Inserts figure into surface indentation of article by hand or by machine. May tend machine that stamps design on face of article. May be designated according to kind of substance inlaid as INLAYER, SILVER (plastic prod.).
GOE: 06.04.02 STRENGTH: L GED: R2 M1 L2 SVP: 3 DLU: 77

692.685-074 DIELECTRIC-PRESS OPERATOR (auto. mfg.)
Tends dielectric press that bonds together and embosses materials, such as vinyl and fiber panels used for decorating motor vehicle interiors: Places layers of fiber panel, packing, and vinyl in tray on table of press. Pushes tray under ram of press. Pushes button to lower ram and start dielectric action that bonds vinyl and fiber panels. Pulls tray from press at end of cycle, and removes assembled panel. May tend machine that automatically feeds tray to and from press bed.
GOE: 06.04.05 STRENGTH: L GED: R2 M1 L2 SVP: 2 DLU: 90

692.685-078 DYNAMITE-CARTRIDGE CRIMPER (chemical)
Tends crimping presses that crimp and finish ends of filled dynamite cartridges: Installs specified crimping dies and adjusts table as directed, according to diameter and length of cartridges being crimped. Places single cartridges or shuttle (forming block) of cartridges on table under dies, starts machine, and depresses pedal to crimp cartridges. Stacks finished cartridges in case-house buggy (cart).
GOE: 06.02.04 STRENGTH: M GED: R3 M2 L2 SVP: 4 DLU: 77

692.685-082 FILM SPOOLER (photo. appar.)
Tends automatic machine that winds, cuts and prints lines on unexposed film, loads film into cartridges, and seals and packages cartridges for shipment: Loads automatic units with film, labels, backing paper, and cartridges. Observes operations for jams and malfunctions. Adjusts mechanisms, using handtools.
GOE: 06.04.09 STRENGTH: L GED: R2 M1 L1 SVP: 2 DLU: 77

692.685-086 FOILING-MACHINE OPERATOR (ordnance)
Tends automatic machine that punches out disks of waterproof paper and presses them over open end of loaded primer cups to seal out moisture: Positions specially holed plate containing loaded primer cups in holding fixture of feed table and starts machine. Removes plate when machine automatically stops. May examine sealed primer cups and remove defective ones from plate,

using fingers, metal pick, or wax-tipped stick. May load machine with rolls of paper tape.
GOE: 06.04.09 STRENGTH: L GED: R1 M1 L1 SVP: 2 DLU: 77

692.685-090 GARLAND-MACHINE OPERATOR (fabrication, nec)
Tends machine that binds evergreen and conifer twigs with wire to make garlands and wreath stock: Places spool of wire on machine feed spindle and threads wire between crimping gears and through guides to wrapping chamber. Adjusts meter of measuring device that rings bell as specified lengths of garland are formed. Starts machine, inserts ends of twigs into wrapping chamber, and depresses pedal to actuate mechanism that binds twigs into continuous strand of garland. Cuts garland to specified length with wire cutters and places them on table or conveyor. May bend lengths of garland into circle, twist wire ends together, and tie ribbon bow over wire joint to form wreaths. When concerned only with making wreaths, is designated Wreath-Machine Operator (fabrication, nec).
GOE: 06.04.09 STRENGTH: L GED: R2 M1 L1 SVP: 2 DLU: 77

692.685-094 GLUE-MACHINE OPERATOR (pen & pencil) alternate titles: lead-laying-and-gluing-machine operator
Tends machine that places pencil leads in grooves of wooden slats and cements slats together to form pencil blanks: Places pencil leads and wooden slats in feed hoppers of machine. Fills reservoirs of machine with cement. Starts machine that automatically applies cement to grooved surface of slats, places lead in grooves and joins cemented slats to form blank. Stops machine and removes jammed slats or leads.
GOE: 06.04.09 STRENGTH: L GED: R2 M1 L1 SVP: 2 DLU: 77

692.685-098 GLUING-MACHINE OPERATOR (rubber goods)
Tends machine that spreads adhesive onto foam rubber pillow sections: Presses section against revolving disk that applies cement to section. Places coated sections on conveyor passing beneath drying lamps for joining together by other workers. Fills adhesive reservoir as necessary.
GOE: 06.04.21 STRENGTH: L GED: R1 M1 L1 SVP: 2 DLU: 77

692.685-102 KICK-PRESS OPERATOR (protective dev.)
Tends kick press that joins snap fasteners to fabric for use in manufacture of gas mask carriers: Inserts upper half of fastener in plunger of machine and positions lower half on anvil. Places reinforcement patch and fabric over lower half of fastener, guided by pinhole in fabric. Depresses pedal to lower plunger and join fastener parts to fabric.
GOE: 06.04.20 STRENGTH: L GED: R2 M1 L1 SVP: 2 DLU: 77

692.685-106 LAMINATING-MACHINE OPERATOR (furniture)
Tends machine that cements precut plastic covering material to plywood panels to form furniture parts, such as tops for cabinets and tables: Inserts plywood panel between rollers of cement-spreading machine to coat both sides of panel with cement. Positions plastic covering material on sides of panel and places covered panel on bed of press. Starts machine that presses covered panel with heated ram for prescribed time to seal plastic covering material onto plywood panel. May tend automatic machine that presses veneer to panels and trims excess edges.
GOE: 06.04.09 STRENGTH: M GED: R3 M1 L2 SVP: 3 DLU: 77

692.685-110 LAMP-SHADE JOINER (fabrication, nec) alternate titles: paster
Tends machine that bonds edges of precut parchment together to form lampshades: Depresses pedal to raise top presser bar of machine and positions edge of parchment on lower presser bar. Brushes cement on edge of parchment. Bends parchment in circle and positions opposite edge of parchment on top of cemented edge. Releases pedal to lower and lock top presser bar onto parchment to bond edges.
GOE: 06.04.04 STRENGTH: L GED: R1 M1 L1 SVP: 2 DLU: 77

692.685-114 LEVEL-GLASS-VIAL FILLER (cutlery-hrdwr.)
Tends equipment that fills glass vials with alcohol or ether solution and leaves air bubble to form vials used in tools and instruments to determine levelness: Fills rack with vial-filled cups and lowers rack into tank of solution. Lowers weighted glass cover and moves lever to turn on air pressure. Sets timer for designated time cycle. Shuts off air and raises cover when bell rings. Compares bubbles in random sampling of filled vials with master vial for conformance to size. Refills vials or lets vials stand to evaporate excess fluid to regulate size of bubble. Pours solution from jug into tank to replace used fluid.
GOE: 06.04.36 STRENGTH: L GED: R1 M1 L1 SVP: 2 DLU: 77

692.685-118 LIGHT-BULB ASSEMBLER (light. fix.)
Tends variety of machines that assemble electric light bulbs, performing any combination of following tasks: Feeds parts and materials, such as lead and fuse wires, glass tubing, flares, and getter fluid, into machine that automatically shapes and combines them to make mounts (units which furnish light when electricity flows through them). Observes completed mounts for faulty combination of parts and assists mechanic in locating defect in machine. Records number of damaged mounts. Examines machine conveyors for jammed or defective parts when signal indicates stoppage. Removes jammed or defective parts, using tweezers. Feeds glass bulbs and mounts into machine that inserts and seals mount in bulb. Inserts and arranges wire protruding through neck of bulb in cement-filled base as bulb passes on conveyor to basing machine. Observes basing operation as machine carries bulb through series of burners which bake cement, past knives which cut off excess wires, and soldering irons which

solder contact points at bottom and side of base. Inspects completed lamp for identification markings, freedom from dirt and cracks, and to determine condition of filament, using tinted glass. Removes excess solder from base of lamp, using knife. Places defective lamps in salvage bin. Puts lamp in corrugated paper case and packs lamp in carton. Inserts slip identifying contents in carton and places carton on conveyor. Feeds completed stem into annealer to remove glass strains resulting from stem making. Manually places bulb over mount prior to sealing. Removes air impurities from bulb. Secures bases to bulbs in oven where cement is automatically applied and dried. Secures bases to ends of fluorescent light tubes. May be designated according to operation performed as Baser (light. fix.); Sealer (light. fix.). May tend machine that cuts off part of light bulb necks and be designated Neck Cutter (light. fix.).
GOE: 06.04.20 STRENGTH: L GED: R2 M1 L1 SVP: 2 DLU: 77

692.685-122 MAT-MAKING MACHINE TENDER (furniture)
Tends machine that automatically weaves wire and cord or burlap to provide firmness between padding and coil springs of mattresses and upholstered furniture: Mounts roll of burlap on machine rack and threads end between machine rollers. Places cone of wire and spools of twisted paper cord on reels, and inserts wire and cord ends into machine. Starts machine that automatically makes mats. Spreads emerging fabric over table and cuts fabric into mats of specified length, using cutting pliers.
GOE: 06.04.09 STRENGTH: L GED: R2 M2 L2 SVP: 2 DLU: 77

692.685-126 MOUNTER II (light. fix.)
Tends machines that mount glass beads on lead wires, wind filament coils, and clamp coils to lead wires of bead mounts used in incandescent lamps: Fills machine hoppers with glass beads and observes machines for malfunctioning. Inserts completed bead mounts in glass bulbs. Notifies maintenance crew of machine malfunctioning and to replace exhausted wire reels.
GOE: 06.04.09 STRENGTH: L GED: R1 M1 L1 SVP: 3 DLU: 77

692.685-130 PINKING-MACHINE OPERATOR (button & notion)
Tends automatic pinking machine that cuts continuous chain of slide fasteners (zippers) into individual units of preset length with serrated tape ends: Threads end of chain from supply carton through guides and feeding mechanism to cutting die. Starts machine and picks up cut piece from discharge rail. Examines zippers for ragged pinking, short or long tape ends, stops, malformed filament, and sewing defects. Stacks pieces in machine tray and verifies length against previously cut piece. Pulls chain from carton by hand to prevent jamming of machine.
GOE: 06.04.09 STRENGTH: S GED: R2 M1 L2 SVP: 2 DLU: 77

692.685-134 POULTICE-MACHINE OPERATOR (pharmaceut.)
Tends machine that automatically inserts chemical granules between two continuous layers of cloth and cuts and sews edges to make poultices: Places spools of thread and rolls of cloth on spindle of machine. Threads needles, using pliers. Inserts end of cloth into conveyor guide. Dumps or scoops granules into machine hopper and starts machine. Examines poultices for uniformity of stitching, and feels them for specified thickness and firmness and even distribution of granules. Adjusts stroke in insertion rod to correct irregularities in filling to prevent excessive looseness or tautness of product.
GOE: 06.04.09 STRENGTH: L GED: R2 M2 L2 SVP: 4 DLU: 77

692.685-138 PROTECTOR-PLATE ATTACHER (cutlery-hrdwr.) alternate titles: strike-plate attacher
Tends machine that attaches protective metal strike-plates to wooden segments of assembled folding rule: Mounts reels of metal strip on machine spindles and threads strip ends through feed mechanism. Holds unfolded rule against guides and starts machine that cuts off, forms, and fastens pronged protector-plate to each segment of rule. Removes spilled and jammed plates from mechanisms, using screwdriver.
GOE: 06.04.09 STRENGTH: L GED: R1 M1 L1 SVP: 2 DLU: 77

692.685-142 RIBBON INKER (pen & pencil) alternate titles: inking-machine tender
Tends machine that impregnates ribbons with ink to make ribbons for machines, such as typewriters, adding and addressograph machines, and cash registers: Fills ink pan of machine and loads machine roll or spool of silk, cotton, or nylon ribbon. Starts machine to rotate rollers that dip into ink pan and press ink on ribbon. Adjusts speed of machine and amount of ink to be pressed on ribbon according to type of ribbon to be made. Inspects inked ribbons for imperfections. May shape inner curve of divider that separates inks of bicolored ribbons, using file and emery cloth, until curve matches that of inking rollers. May adjust machine guides according to width of ribbon to be inked.
GOE: 06.04.16 STRENGTH: L GED: R2 M1 L2 SVP: 2 DLU: 77

692.685-146 SADDLE-AND-SIDE WIRE STITCHER (print. & pub.) alternate titles: stitcher operator
Tends wire-stitching machine equipped with adjustable table that fastens together pages of pamphlets or magazines: Loads machine with spool of wire and threads wire through machine. Sets table flat for side stitching or tent-shaped for saddle (back) stitching. Positions materials under head of machine and starts machine. Adjusts machine table to accommodate size of materials being stitched.
GOE: 06.04.04 STRENGTH: L GED: R2 M1 L1 SVP: 2 DLU: 77

692.685-150 SANITARY-NAPKIN-MACHINE TENDER (protective dev.)
Tends automatic machine that forms sanitary napkins: Threads nonwoven fabric, plastic inserts, paper, and cotton filling through feed rollers of machine

in prescribed sequence. Fills glue reservoirs. Loads hot-melt pellets in heater unit and sets temperature and flow controls to melt pellets and saturate napkin to impart body to napkin. Starts machine. Examines napkins for defects and segregates damaged items for disposal. Packs finished pads into cartons and places them on conveyor for sealing.
GOE: 06.04.09 STRENGTH: L GED: R2 M1 L2 SVP: 2 DLU: 77

692.685-154   SEAL-EXTRUSION OPERATOR (elec. equip.)
Tends extrusion press that fills grooves of storage battery covers with sealing compound: Attaches cylinder of sealing compound to press or fills drum of press with compound, using bucket. Depresses pedal to extrude sealing compound. Holds and moves inverted cover under vent of press to fill grooves to specified level. Places filled covers on truck. Turns valve to circulate cleaning solution through machine or cleans press, using brush and water.
GOE: 06.04.36 STRENGTH: L GED: R2 M1 L1 SVP: 2 DLU: 77

692.685-158   SEALER, DRY CELL (elec. equip.) alternate titles: sealer operator
Tends preheater, seal dispenser (sealer), and flamer that seals dry cells: Installs sprocket of prescribed size according to diameter of cell. Turns setscrews to adjust sealer and flamer according to height of cells, using handtools.
GOE: 06.04.09 STRENGTH: L GED: R2 M1 L1 SVP: 3 DLU: 77

692.685-162   SEALING-MACHINE OPERATOR (light. fix.)
Tends automatic machine that seals assembly of filament and glass supports (mount) into glass bulb: Fits mount into glass bulb and places assembly in holding sockets of circular disk mounted on vertical shaft. Starts machine that brings assembly past gas flames to weld mount to bulb and cut off excess glass from stem.
GOE: 06.04.19 STRENGTH: L GED: R2 M1 L2 SVP: 3 DLU: 77

692.685-166   SEPARATOR OPERATOR (button & notion)
Tends battery of machines that separate polished buttons from polishing media and sort buttons according to size: Unloads buttons from polishing barrel into container and transports container to separating machine, using handtruck or dolly. Positions container above machine, using electric hoist, and pulls lever to tilt container and dump contents into machine hopper. Moves switches to start machine that removes polishing media and moves buttons through series of screening cylinders that sort buttons according to size.
GOE: 06.04.09 STRENGTH: M GED: R2 M1 L1 SVP: 2 DLU: 77

692.685-170   SKI TOPPER (toy-sport equip.)
Tends machine that bonds plastic strips to tops of skis: Positions ski covered with precut strips on bed of machine. Presses lever or pedal to lower press or activate pressure rollers that bond plastic to ski tops. Examines skis for defects and removes blemishes, using abrasives, blade, and solvent.
GOE: 06.04.20 STRENGTH: L GED: R2 M1 L1 SVP: 2 DLU: 77

692.685-174   SLICING-MACHINE OPERATOR (button & notion)
Tends machine equipped with circular saws that slices pearl button blanks into two or more thinner blanks: Starts machine and positions blanks by hand in jaws of automatic clamps on turret feed mechanism. Observes feeding of blanks toward saw blades and stops machine if blanks appear to require realignment in holders. Removes containers of sliced blanks and places containers on bench or handtruck. May position single blank in holding clamp of manually controlled slicing machine and pull on leverage bar to feed blank into rotating saw blades.
GOE: 06.04.08 STRENGTH: L GED: R2 M1 L1 SVP: 2 DLU: 77

692.685-178   SLINGER, SEQUINS (plastic prod.)
Tends machine that automatically interlaces thread around strings of sequins in such manner as to separate, space, and hold fast sequins. Places spools of thread and string of sequins in machine and inserts ends in feeding mechanism. Observes operation to determine that threads are aligned and have desired tension and that threads and sequins are of same color.
GOE: 06.04.09 STRENGTH: L GED: R2 M1 L2 SVP: 2 DLU: 77

692.685-182   SORTER, MACHINE (button & notion) alternate titles: classifying-machine operator
Tends battery of automatic machines that sort button blanks according to thickness: Loads blanks into machine hopper, using hand scoop. Starts machine that sorts blanks and drops them into separate containers beneath machine. Removes filled containers and carries them to inspection department or storage.
GOE: 06.04.09 STRENGTH: L GED: R2 M1 L1 SVP: 2 DLU: 77

692.685-186   SPIRAL-MACHINE OPERATOR (paper goods)
Tends machine that automatically wraps paper cord or cellophane tape around wire or cord to be used as handles for shopping bags, beverage stirring sticks, and other purposes.
GOE: 06.04.09 STRENGTH: L GED: R1 M1 L1 SVP: 2 DLU: 77

692.685-190   SPUN-PASTE-MACHINE OPERATOR (elec. equip.)
Tends machine and injection equipment that line dry-cell battery cans with liquid paste that serves as separator between anode (can) and cathode (core) and as reservoir for portion of electrolyte: Turns valve to open paste line and admit paste to reservoir of injection device. Starts machine and feeds unlined cans into openings in dial-type holder that positions cans to receive injection of measured amount of paste and spins cans to distribute paste evenly. Pushes unlined cans into opening to eject lined cans, dropping them onto conveyor belt leading to dryer. Removes excess paste from face of dial, using hand scraper.

GOE: 06.04.21 STRENGTH: L GED: R2 M1 L2 SVP: 2 DLU: 77

692.685-194   STAMPING-MACHINE OPERATOR (pen & pencil)
Tends machine that imprints identifying data, such as trademark and type of lead on pencils: Places pencils in machine hopper, and starts machine to lower die-head and stamp data on pencil. Ties pencils into bundles. May install type or dies in machine head and replace colored foil roll in machine.
GOE: 06.04.21 STRENGTH: L GED: R2 M1 L1 SVP: 2 DLU: 77

692.685-198   STAPLER, MACHINE (furniture) alternate titles: wire-stitcher, machine
Tends stapling machine that staples padding to innerspring mattress assemblies: Loads spool of wire into machine. Places spring assembly on table, spreads precut padding on top of spring and positions them under head of machine. Starts machine and holds padding on spring as machine moves around table. May staple padding to spring assembly, using stationary stapling machine or hand stapler.
GOE: 06.04.20 STRENGTH: M GED: R2 M1 L1 SVP: 3 DLU: 77

692.685-202   STAPLING-MACHINE OPERATOR (any industry) alternate titles: wire-stitcher operator
Tends machine that staples together parts of products made from materials, such as plastic, paper, leather, felt, and canvas: Loads machine with wire staples or spool of wire, and positions material under head of machine. Steps on pedal to lower ram that cuts off wire staple and forces it through material to clinch it together. May adjust machine table to accommodate different sizes of materials being stapled.
GOE: 06.04.20 STRENGTH: M GED: R2 M1 L2 SVP: 2 DLU: 77

692.685-206   STOP ATTACHER (button & notion)
Tends semiautomatic press that attaches metal stops to slide fastener stringers: Fills machine hopper with stops. Inserts stringer between press jaws and depresses pedal to drive prongs of stop through tape. Pulls chain through dies to machine stop to position stringer for next stroke. Picks jammed or defective stops from feeder tube, or hopper, using metal pick or tweezers. May tend machine that automatically punches, forms, and attaches stop to stringer. May hold zipper on anvil of *power press* by hand and depress pedal to attach stops to individual zipper. May be designated according to location of stop as Bottom-Stop Attacher (button & notion); Top-Stop Attacher (button & notion). May attach hardware to zipper and be designated according to type of hardware attached as Box Attacher (button & notion); Bridge Attacher (button & notion); Pin Attacher (button & notion).
GOE: 06.04.20 STRENGTH: S GED: R2 M1 L2 SVP: 2 DLU: 77

692.685-210   TAPE COATER (nonmet. min.)
Tends machine that coats cloth tape with abrasive compound for use in polishing roller bearings: Mounts reel of tape of specified size onto machine spindle, and adjusts feed guide to accommodate tape. Fills machine cylinder with abrasive compound, and threads tape through cylinder and onto winding spindle. Scrapes excess compound from coated tape.
GOE: 06.04.21 STRENGTH: L GED: R1 M1 L1 SVP: 2 DLU: 77

692.685-214   TAPER, MACHINE (fabrication, nec)
Tends machine that tapes edges of precut material, such as parchment or fabric, on wire frame to form lampshades: Inserts spool of binding tape on machine spindle and draws tape through machine guides and folding attachment. Depresses pedal to raise holding device and positions edge of material and wire frame in groove of machine bed under pressing head. Releases pedal to lower and lock holding device. Starts machine that presses tape over edges of material and wire frame. Removes lampshade from machine and trims excess tape from shade, using scissors.
GOE: 06.04.09 STRENGTH: L GED: R2 M1 L2 SVP: 2 DLU: 77

692.685-218   THERMOSTAT-ASSEMBLY-MACHINE-TENDER, AUTOMATIC (inst. & app.)
Tends machine that automatically assembles, calibrates, and tests thermostat units: Turns setscrews to regulate speed of machine hoppers. Fills hoppers with workpieces and screws. Adjusts control device that positions workpiece under screw mechanism and sets depth of automatic screwdriver, using handtools. Starts machine that automatically assembles, calibrates, and tests thermostats. Examines thermostat units for defects. May turn dial indicator to set temperature of thermostat. May tend in-line or rotary, self-indexing, multiple-station-and-purpose automatic assembly machine.
GOE: 06.04.20 STRENGTH: L GED: R2 M1 L2 SVP: 3 DLU: 89

692.685-222   TILE-POWER-SHEAR OPERATOR (fabrication, nec)
Operates power shear to cut sheets of floor coverings into tile of specified size: Adjusts stop gauges according to predetermined size. Feeds material under blade and against stop. Depresses pedal that lowers shear and cuts material into tile.
GOE: 06.04.09 STRENGTH: L GED: R2 M1 L1 SVP: 2 DLU: 77

692.685-226   TINSEL-MACHINE OPERATOR (fabrication, nec)
Tends twisting machine that forms tinsel strands: Places spools of tinsel, cotton, and wire on spindles or bobbins and threads material on machine. Starts machine that automatically weaves them into single strand of tinsel. Winds completed strands on cards by hand.
GOE: 06.04.09 STRENGTH: L GED: R2 M1 L1 SVP: 2 DLU: 77

692.685-230   TRIM ATTACHER (cutlery-hrdwr.)
Tends machine that applies metal binding to protect and decorate edges of wooden level bodies: Inserts strips of metal trim in vertical slots of machine.

Stands level body on end under loaded slots and closes gate to lock level in place. Starts ram that forces metal corner strips into grooves in wooden body of level. Examines trimmed levels to detect split or splintered wood, or scratches and dents in metal binding. May install metal end plates on level bodies, using drill press and power screwdriver.
GOE: 06.04.20 STRENGTH: L GED: R2 M1 L2 SVP: 2 DLU: 77

692.685-234 TUBE WINDER, HAND (nonmet. min.) alternate titles: tube maker; winder operator
Tends machine that winds material, such as asbestos or felt paper around mandrel to form insulated pipe-covering: Places mandrel of designated size in winding jig and attaches end of sheet to mandrel. Turns mandrel wheel specified number of times to wind layers of liner, filler, and outer materials, such as adhesive coated asbestos, tar, corrugated and wool felt papers around mandrel. Cuts material from roll sheet, using knife. Lifts and turns mandrel to vertical position. Grasps and shakes tube to drop mandrel from center of tube. Stacks tubes on handtrucks and replaces mandrel in jig. May manually paste and wrap completed tube in canvas outer jacket. May tend machine that winds specified pattern of fiberglass filament around mandrel to produce tubular pipe.
GOE: 06.04.09 STRENGTH: M GED: R2 M1 L2 SVP: 2 DLU: 77

692.685-238 VACUUM-APPLICATOR OPERATOR (fabrication, nec)
Tends machine that applies adhesive luminous coating to aluminum plates for use as signs: Places plate on bed of machine. Positions precut adhesive material on plate, adhesive side down. Positions vacuum head over plate and turns steam valve or starts heat lamps to press and bake plate for specified time. Raises vacuum head and removes plate for further processing. May cut adhesive material from roll, using shears.
GOE: 06.04.21 STRENGTH: M GED: R2 M1 L1 SVP: 2 DLU: 77

692.685-242 WICKER, MOLDED CANDLES (fabrication, nec) alternate titles: wick tender
Tends machine that inserts wicks in openings of molded candles: Threads wick from spool through inserting sleeve and turns hand screws to adjust wick cutter and control motion of ram that compresses wick at bottom of candle. Places candles in holders on turntable and starts machine. Examines finished candles for surface defects and loose wicks and packs them in cartons. May cut and insert wicks by hand.
GOE: 06.04.09 STRENGTH: L GED: R2 M1 L2 SVP: 3 DLU: 77

692.685-246 WINDER (toy-sport equip.) alternate titles: solid center winder; winder, gammeter
Tends machine or series of machines that wind thread, yarn, or rubber strands around spherical molded cores to produce items, such as golf balls, baseballs, and softballs: Positions core in winding machine. Starts machine that winds core to specified size. Removes wound ball, breaks winding material, and ties loose end. Verifies size of ball with preset gauge or tape measure. Weighs baseballs and softballs on scale or verifies compression of golf balls on testing machine to ascertain that winding material in machine is adjusted to specified tension. Turns nut or setscrews of tension springs to adjust tension. Removes empty spools and rethreads machine. May be designated according to article wound as Baseball Winder (toy-sport equip.); Golf-Ball Winder (toy-sport equip.); Softball Winder (toy-sport equip.).
GOE: 06.04.09 STRENGTH: L GED: R2 M1 L2 SVP: 2 DLU: 77

692.685-250 WINDOW-SHADE CUTTER AND MOUNTER (furniture)
Tends machines that cut window shade fabric and rollers to specified size, and install roller end caps and hanging pins, and staple fabric to roller: Installs roll of shade cloth on spindles of window-shade cutter machine. Threads end of cloth through retaining and feed rollers of machine. Turns handle to feed specified amount of cloth into machine. Depresses treadle to cut cloth and fold bottom hem. Clamps shade roller against stop on saw carriage, starts machine, and pushes carriage against saw blade to cut roller to specified length. Removes roller and slips cap over each end. Clamps roller in pin-driving machine, inserts pin in driver, and depresses lever to drive pin through cap into end of roller. Fastens top end of cloth to roller, using hand stapler.
GOE: 06.04.09 STRENGTH: L GED: R2 M1 L1 SVP: 3 DLU: 77

692.685-254 WINDOW-SHADE-RING SEWER (furniture) alternate titles: window-shade-ring coverer
Tends crocheting machine that covers metal rings used as window-shade pulls: Fills magazine with metal rings. Oils machine and threads crocheting needle. Starts machine with hand clutch and observes operation to detect malfunctions. Clips thread and ties ends as rings are covered.
GOE: 06.04.09 STRENGTH: S GED: R2 M1 L1 SVP: 2 DLU: 77

692.685-258 WIRE-TURNING-MACHINE OPERATOR (wood. container) alternate titles: looper
Tends machine that cuts binding wires between successive wirebound *box blanks*, forms loops in wire ends, and drives wire tips into wood. Starts machine and observes boxes to detect uncut wire. Removes boxes from machine.
GOE: 06.04.09 STRENGTH: L GED: R1 M1 L1 SVP: 2 DLU: 77

692.685-262 WOOD-WEB-WEAVING-MACHINE OPERATOR (furniture) alternate titles: loom operator; weaver
Tends wood-web weaving machine that binds together wood slats to form indoor or porch shades: Spreads bundle of wood slats on machine bed. Starts machine and feeds slats into machine jaw which grips and pulls slats over and under warp threads. Stops machine to tie broken warp ends. Positions shade

on stapling machine carriage and depresses pedal to staple molding and splints on top and bottom of shade. May tend machine that binds together plastic slats to form window blinds and be designated Woven-Blind-Loom Tender (furniture).
GOE: 06.04.09 STRENGTH: M GED: R2 M1 L2 SVP: 3 DLU: 77

692.685-266 ZIPPER TRIMMER, MACHINE (button & notion)
Tends power press that cuts excess scoops (links) from slide fastener chains to shorten them to specified length: Measures chain against machine-mounted ruler to determine number of scoops to remove. Positions stringer under die of press and presses pedal to operate cutter. Rubs cut scoops against edge of press to remove them from tape. Examines zippers for broken or missing scoops and discards defective zippers.
GOE: 06.04.34 STRENGTH: S GED: R2 M1 L1 SVP: 2 DLU: 77

692.685-270 ZIPPER-MACHINE OPERATOR (button & notion) alternate titles: chain-machine operator; scoop-machine operator
Tends battery of automatic machines that cut and form metal slide fastener scoops (links) from wire and crimp them onto beaded edge of tape to form side of zipper (stringer): Positions box of beaded tape behind each machine and mounts coil of wire on roller. Threads tape and wire through guides and automatic feeder mechanism and into forming dies. Starts machines, and observes operation to detect malfunctioning, such as jamming. Measures scoops to verify specified dimensions, such as width, spacing, and height of lug, using micrometer. Turns setscrews to adjust jaws for height of lug and depth of cup on scoops, using wrenches. May examine finished product for imperfections, such as malformed or rough-cut scoops, using eye loupe. May tend automatic machine that attaches preformed scoops to tape.
GOE: 06.04.02 STRENGTH: L GED: R2 M1 L2 SVP: 2 DLU: 77

692.685-274 KEYMODULE-ASSEMBLY-MACHINE TENDER (office machines)
Tends machine that automatically assembles components to form modules used in keyboards of electronic computer equipment: Observes machine operations to detect defective parts and to ensure continuous movement of parts, subassemblies, and final assemblies along feed tracks. Removes defective parts from feed tracks and repositions disoriented parts, using pick. Pries jammed parts from track, using pick, or replenishes supply of parts in feeder bowl to remedy machine stoppage. Packs completed assemblies into containers. Notifies mechanic when machine malfunctions repeatedly occur. Periodically cleans feed tracks, machine surface, and work area, using handbrush, broom, airhose, or vacuum cleaner.
GOE: 06.04.09 STRENGTH: L GED: R2 M2 L2 SVP: 2 DLU: 86

692.685-278 DIAPER MACHINE TENDER (protective dev.)
Tends automatic machine that forms disposable diapers: Threads rolls of woodpulp, plastic backing, and nonwoven fabric facing in specified sequence through guides of machine. Fills glue reservoir and fragrance receptacle, and loads diaper tape tabs into dispensing bins. Flips switch to start machine that automatically crushes woodpulp into fiber; sprays fiber to impart fragrance; applies glue to join layers of diapers into continuous strip; affixes tape tabs to strip at designated intervals; applies glue to shape form-fit diapers; cuts strip into individual diapers; and folds diapers in half for packing. Observes operation of machine and examines diapers to detect machine malfunctions. Turns knobs or screws to make minor adjustments to sections of machine, such as rollers, cutting blades, and folding device, using handtools. Notifies maintenance personnel when welding or parts replacement is required.
GOE: 06.04.09 STRENGTH: L GED: R3 M2 L3 SVP: 4 DLU: 86

692.685-282 LAMINATOR, PRINTED CIRCUIT BOARDS (electron. comp.)
Tends laminating machine that automatically bonds assembled layers of laminating materials and printed circuit board (PCB) panels to form multilayer PCB panels: Reads instruction sheet to determine specified materials and laminating procedures. Assembles inner and outer layers of PCB panels and laminating materials over guide pins of holding fixture. Places assembled boards on bay (shelf) of machine. Turns controls to set time, pressure, and temperature of laminating machine according to specifications. Starts machine that applies pressure and heat to bond materials and form multilayer PCB panels. Monitors machine operation and adjusts machine controls to maintain specified temperature and pressure. May compute pressure level for laminating machine. May heat materials in oven to remove moisture or condition materials prior to laminating process.
GOE: 06.04.09 STRENGTH: M GED: R2 M1 L2 SVP: 3 DLU: 86

692.685-286 MOLDER, AUTOMOBILE CARPETS (tex. prod., nec) alternate titles: molder; molder-trimmer
Tends machines that mold nonwoven carpet used in automobiles: Places carpet blank (precut section of nonwoven carpet) into oven that heats carpet to prepare carpet for molding. Sprays insides of stationary mold with silicone fluid, using pump sprayer, to prevent sticking. Places jute backing over steel pins in stationary mold. Removes heated carpet from oven, smooths carpet over mold, and secures carpet over jute on stationary mold. Observes carpet to detect defects, such as wrinkling and drawn edges, that indicate overheating of carpet. Turns dial on oven to adjust heating cycle. Presses button to lower upper mold onto stationary mold to press, cool, shape, and bond carpet and jute backing to fit sections of automobile. Removes carpet from mold and places carpet on trim buck. Presses button to lower holding device that secures carpet in position

for trimming. Trims carpet along trim line, using utility knife. Hammers carpet, using mallet, to remove knockout sections on trim buck. Sprays adhesive onto bottom of exposed carpet to reattach loose jute, using spray can.
GOE: 06.04.09 STRENGTH: L GED: R2 M1 L1 SVP: 3 DLU: 86

692.685-290   TRACK LAMINATING MACHINE TENDER (inst. & app.)
Tends machine that laminates and trims vinyl from aluminum track used in drafting machines: Loads spool of vinyl onto laminating machine wheel, starts machine, and feeds track into machine that automatically laminates vinyl onto track and trims vinyl. Monitors track conveyance and visually examines track to detect lamination and trimming flaws, such as excess vinyl, air bubbles, and oil or adhesive accumulation on edge of track. Smooths air bubbles from lamination and trims excess vinyl, using handtools. Cleans excess oil and adhesive from edge of track, using rag and brush. Rejects defective track. May cut vinyl at joint to separate track sections, using knife or saw.
GOE: 06.04.09 STRENGTH: M GED: R1 M1 L1 SVP: 2 DLU: 90

692.686-010   ASSEMBLY-MACHINE OPERATOR (pen & pencil)
Feeds components, such as barrels, caps, cartridges, and nibs into and removes assembled pens and pencils from automatic assembly machine: Places components in predetermined sequence on revolving spindles or dumps components into hoppers. Lifts assembled pens or pencils from machine spindles and inspects for loose components. Places inspected units on conveyor. May be designated according to component or station as Assembly-Machine Feeder (pen & pencil); Assembly-Machine Offbearer (pen & pencil); Cartridge Feeder (pen & pencil).
GOE: 06.04.20 STRENGTH: L GED: R2 M1 L1 SVP: 2 DLU: 77

692.686-014   BASE REMOVER (light. fix.)
Feeds incandescent lamp bulbs into holders of rotating wheel of machine that carries lamp through series of gas torches to melt cement adhering to base of lamp preparatory to removal of defective bases. Removes lamp from holder as device rotates back to starting position and pulls base and glass bulb apart. Wipes excess cement from bulb and places in rack.
GOE: 06.04.09 STRENGTH: M GED: R1 M1 L1 SVP: 2 DLU: 77

692.686-018   BROOMCORN SEEDER (fabrication, nec) alternate titles: broomcorn scraper
Feeds broomcorn into machine that removes seed or chaff and straightens fibers: Holds stalk and brush end of fibers against teeth of rotating cylinder to remove seed and chaff. May cut stems to size [CUTTER (fabrication, nec) II].
GOE: 06.04.09 STRENGTH: M GED: R1 M1 L1 SVP: 2 DLU: 77

692.686-022   BULB FILLER (light. fix.)
Places bulb in guide of machine that automatically cuts and blows magnesium wire into alloy photoflash bulb to provide material for flashing. Holds open neck of each bulb over air jet to blow loose end of wire into top of bulb. Places bulbs on conveyor leading to sealing machine.
GOE: 06.04.09 STRENGTH: L GED: R1 M1 L1 SVP: 1 DLU: 77

692.686-026   CARBON ROD INSERTER (elec. equip.)
Feeds machines that insert carbon rods, cap, seal, tube, and otherwise assemble dry cells: Removes cells or components from conveyors, containers, or cartons and places them on ramp, conveyor, dial, turntable, or into mechanism that feeds them to core tamping, capping, sealing, tubing, sleeve, or wafer machines. Removes units from discharge conveyor of machine and places them on other conveyor or in trays or boxes. May dump components into hopper of machine.
GOE: 06.04.20 STRENGTH: L GED: R1 M1 L1 SVP: 2 DLU: 77

692.686-030   CUTTER II (fabrication, nec)
Feeds broomcorn stems into lever-type cutter that cuts them for use in making brooms: Shakes stems against table to align ends. Positions stems on table against gauge and depresses pedal or manually lowers blade to cut stems to specified length. May remove seed and straighten fibers [BROOMCORN SEEDER (fabrication, nec)].
GOE: 06.04.09 STRENGTH: M GED: R1 M1 L1 SVP: 2 DLU: 77

692.686-034   DESIGN ASSEMBLER (fabrication, nec)
Positions stacks of floor covering pieces on bed of machine that transfers layer of pieces onto conveyor and fills spaces between pieces with floor covering material to form inlaid floor covering, following pattern guides on machine bed.
GOE: 06.04.19 STRENGTH: L GED: R1 M1 L1 SVP: 2 DLU: 77

692.686-038   DYNAMITE-PACKING-MACHINE FEEDER (chemical) alternate titles: powder shoveler
Feeds dynamite cartridge filling machine with granular or gelatin dynamite: Pushes buggy containing dynamite to packing machine and fills hopper, using wooden shovel. Sweeps spilled dynamite and broken shells from floor and shovels sweepings into boxes. Scrubs empty buggy with sodium carbonate solution, using brush, to neutralize remaining nitroglycerin. May scrub packinghouse floor with sodium carbonate solution.
GOE: 06.04.09 STRENGTH: H GED: R2 M1 L1 SVP: 2 DLU: 77

692.686-042   GROOVER (any industry)
Feeds material, such as plastic or wood, to rotating cutters of grooving machine, or places material in machine hopper, that cuts grooves in material used to make products, such as lead pencils, picture frames, and boxes.
GOE: 06.04.09 STRENGTH: L GED: R1 M1 L1 SVP: 2 DLU: 77

692.686-046   LAMINATED-PLASTIC-TABLETOP-MOLDING WRAPPER (furniture)
Feeds machine that wraps metal molding around edge of laminated plastic tabletops: Clamps tabletop plastic side up in machine bed while coworker

guides molding between edge of tabletop and pressure roller that shapes molding and presses lip into groove along tabletop edge. Transfers wrapped top, automatically released from machine, to conveyor and clamps another top in machine bed.
GOE: 06.04.20 STRENGTH: M GED: R1 M1 L1 SVP: 2 DLU: 77

692.686-050   MOUNTER I (light. fix.) alternate titles: stem-mounting-machine operator
Feeds tungsten filament wire coils into machine that mounts them to stems in electric light bulbs: Inserts coils, using tweezers, into slotted plate of spider mounting machine which automatically drops them into position on lead wires attached to stem and loops these wires over coils to hold them securely. Examines finished mounts emerging from machine for imperfections.
GOE: 06.04.20 STRENGTH: L GED: R1 M1 L1 SVP: 2 DLU: 77

692.686-054   NAIL-POLISH-BRUSH-MACHINE   FEEDER,   AUTOMATIC (fabrication, nec)
Feeds brush bases into machine that automatically fills and staples bristles to fabricate nail and mascara brushes: Fills machine hoppers with bases or inserts base in jig of machine table. Observes machine operation for malfunctions and examines finished brushes for defects. May pack brushes for shipment.
GOE: 06.04.20 STRENGTH: L GED: R2 M1 L1 SVP: 2 DLU: 77

692.686-058   NECKER (jewelry-silver.)
Feeds rolls of cardboard and fabric into machine that automatically wraps materials around each other to form cardboard necks (filler between case and lining of jewelry box). Sets controls to cut strips to prescribed length. Observes machine to detect malfunction. Dumps strips into basket for further processing.
GOE: 06.04.20 STRENGTH: L GED: R1 M1 L1 SVP: 2 DLU: 77

692.686-062   STEM SIZER (fabrication, nec) alternate titles: hurl shaker
Feeds machine that separates broomcorn stems according to thickness: Places stems in screen-bottomed vibrating hopper that separates thin stems. Removes stems from and beneath hopper and stacks stems in storage bins.
GOE: 06.04.09 STRENGTH: M GED: R1 M1 L1 SVP: 2 DLU: 77

692.686-066   THIRD   DRY-CELL-ASSEMBLING-MACHINE   TENDER (elec. equip.)
Removes dry cells from trough of dry-cell-assembling machine and places cells right side up in wooden trays, preparatory to sealing with wax.
GOE: 06.04.20 STRENGTH: L GED: R1 M1 L1 SVP: 1 DLU: 77

692.686-070   PASTER, HAT LINING (hat & cap)
Feeds satin and cardboard squares into gluing machine to assemble hat linings: Presses switch to start gluing machine. Inserts satin and cardboard squares in corresponding feed slot of gluing machine that glues items together. Pours glue into glue trough of machine to maintain required level. Empties hat linings from machine hopper, stacks linings, and places linings in storage for further processing.
GOE: 06.02.27 STRENGTH: L GED: R1 M1 L1 SVP: 3 DLU: 86

692.687-010   SPLICER (fabrication, nec) alternate titles: dry-felt splicer
Splices rolls of felt paper to provide continuous sheets for use in production of hard-surface floor covering, working as member of team: Positions roll ·of felt paper on stand, using power hoist. Cuts ends of material with hooked knife and attaches ends to another roll, using glue or tape. Aligns seam under heated machine iron and lowers iron to seal seam. Examines material for kinks and tears.
GOE: 06.04.34 STRENGTH: M GED: R1 M1 L1 SVP: 2 DLU: 77

693   MODELMAKERS, PATTERNMAKERS, AND RELATED OCCUPATIONS

This group includes occupations concerned with making models or patterns of any combination of metal, clay, plastics, and similar materials. Wood patternmakers are included in Group 661.

693.130-010   SUPERVISOR, MODEL MAKING (clock & watch)
Supervises and coordinates activities of workers engaged in making models, such as mechanical and electric clocks, timers, and controls: Sets up and operates lathe, milling machine, shaper, grinder, and related machines and equipment [MODEL MAKER (clock & watch)]. Trains new workers. Inspects models or fabricated parts for conformance to specifications, using gauges, micrometers, and other precision instruments. Assembles and tests models to verify performance standards. Requisitions materials and parts. Performs other duties as described under SUPERVISOR (any industry) Master Title.
GOE: 05.05.07 STRENGTH: L GED: R4 M3 L4 SVP: 7 DLU: 77

693.131-010   PATTERN-SHOP SUPERVISOR (foundry)
Supervises and coordinates activities of workers engaged in making models, foundry patterns, and prototypes from wood, plastic, plaster, or metal, for use in manufacture of dies, castings, and such products as machinery parts and automobile body parts. Trains workers. Performs duties as described under SUPERVISOR (any industry) Master Title.
GOE: 05.05.07 STRENGTH: L GED: R4 M3 L3 SVP: 8 DLU: 77

693.132-010   PATTERN-GRADER SUPERVISOR (wood prod., nec)
Supervises and coordinates activities of workers engaged in cutting out patterns for shoe lasts: Reads and interprets work orders and lasts specifications.

Trains new workers. Inspects patterns to ensure conformance to specifications [LAST-PATTERN GRADER (wood prod., nec)]. Performs other duties as described under SUPERVISOR (any industry) Master Title.
GOE: 06.02.04 STRENGTH: L GED: R4 M3 L3 SVP: 7 DLU: 77

693.260-018 ENGINEERING MODEL MAKER (inst. & app.; office machines)

Sets up and operates variety of machines to fabricate tooling, patterns, parts, and models for electronic, mechanical or electromechanical instruments, devices, or equipment, such as electromedical and computer equipment; measuring, indicating, and controlling instruments; and surgical and navigational instruments, according to engineering blueprints and specifications: Studies drawings and sketches of proposed product and confers with engineering personnel to plan design details and model operation. Determines machines, tooling, and sequence of operation necessary to produce model parts, tooling, dies, or patterns, utilizing knowledge of machining and fabricating techniques. Lays out reference points and dimensions on assorted materials, such as metals, plastic, and synthetic resins, using measuring instruments and work aids [LAY-OUT WORKER (any industry) I 809.281-010]. Sets up and operates machines, such as milling machines, lathes, grinders, drill press, punch press, and brake, to produce or modify model parts [MACHINIST (machine shop) 600.280-022]. Fits and assembles parts, using handtools or power tools. Wires and solders electrical and electronic connections and components. Inspects and tests model or other product to verify conformance to specifications, using precision measuring instruments, such as calipers, gauges, and micrometers, and test equipment, such as multimeter and oscilloscope. Suggests structural or operational modifications or reworks component parts as required to ensure performance of equipment or parts meets standards. May consult with engineering personnel to evaluate design and performance factors. May specialize in fabricating, testing, and adjusting prototype models of electromedical equipment and be designated Medical-Apparatus Model Maker (inst. & app.).
GOE: 05.05.07 STRENGTH: M GED: R4 M4 L4 SVP: 8 DLU: 90

693.261-010 DEVELOPER PROVER, INTERIOR ASSEMBLIES (aircraft mfg.) alternate titles: developer prover, upholstering; trimmer

Plans, lays out, fabricates, and assembles aircraft upholstery, interior trim, soundproofing, insulating, and related items, to develop prototype parts to verify or modify engineering designs, using precision instruments, handtools, power tools, and shop equipment: Reads and interprets blueprints, sketches, and engineering information to determine design specifications. Plans location and arrangement of parts and assemblies, considering space requirements in aircraft. Lays out dimensions of parts on assorted materials, such as plastic, wood, or cardboard, to develop template for fabricating parts, using measuring and marking instruments. Cuts template to size, using saw, shears, or power cutters. Fabricates and assembles sample parts from assorted fabrics, plastics, and other trim materials, utilizing upholstery craft skills, using templates, handtools, and shop equipment, such as sewing machines, snap fasteners, and power cutters [UPHOLSTERER (aircraft mfg.) 780.384-014]. Installs completed parts and assemblies in aircraft mockup to verify accuracy of fit, using handtools and power tools. Modifies templates as required prior to releasing pattern to production. Collaborates with engineering, tooling, production, and other personnel to resolve developmental, assembly, and installation problems.
GOE: 05.05.15 STRENGTH: M GED: R4 M4 L4 SVP: 6 DLU: 87

693.261-014 DEVELOPMENT MECHANIC (aircraft mfg.) alternate titles: experimental mechanic

Lays out, fabricates, and assembles developmental or experimental structural and mechanical parts and assemblies, and installs parts and assemblies in prototype aircraft or spacecraft, following engineering information, using precision instruments, handtools, power tools, and shop equipment: Reads and interprets blueprints, sketches, loft information, and related engineering data to plan sequence of operations and methods for fabricating, assembling, and installing parts and assemblies. Lays out radii, angle, and dimensions of parts on assorted materials, using precision measuring and marking instruments, such as gauges, calipers, scale, and scriber, applying trigonometric calculations to solve layout problems. Sets up and operates shop equipment, such as bandsaw, lathe, table saw, drill press, shear, and brake, to shape and form parts. Verifies dimensions of parts, using precision measuring instruments. Drills, countersinks, and reams holes in parts and assemblies for bolts, rivets, and other fasteners, using power tools. Aligns and joins structural assemblies, using transit, sight level, handtools, power tools, clamps, and fasteners. Installs experimental parts and assemblies in prototype structure to verify accuracy of layout and assembly. Tests functional performance of installed parts. Confers with engineers to resolve fabrication and installation problems. May fabricate or modify tooling, such as jigs, fixtures, templates, and form blocks. May fabricate and assemble reduced-scale mockups of parts and assemblies. May be designated by type of part or assembly developed as Controls Development Mechanic (aircraft mfg.); Developer-Prover, Mechanical (aircraft mfg.); Fabrication And Structures Development Mechanic (aircraft mfg.); Hydraulic And Plumbing Development Mechanic (aircraft mfg.); Mechanic, Experimental Structural Assembly (aircraft mfg.).
GOE: 06.01.04 STRENGTH: M GED: R4 M4 L4 SVP: 7 DLU: 88

693.261-018 MODEL MAKER (aircraft mfg.)

Lays out, fabricates, and assembles scale models of aeronautical and aerospace products, such as aircraft and missiles, utilizing knowledge of model building, lofting principles, and machining, using precision instruments, tools, machines, and equipment: Reviews engineering information and model design to determine methods and sequence of operations to build model. Lays out design to determine lines and contours for model, according to blueprints, rough sketches, or verbal instructions, using trigonometric calculations and principles of model designing for establishing station lines and index points. Marks radius, contour, angle, and dimensions on materials, such as wood, metal, and plastic, using measuring instruments, crayon, scriber, or other method. Sets up and operates shop equipment, such as saws, planer, jointer, drill press, wood lathe, shear, and brake, to fabricate parts, such as nacelles, wings, and control surfaces. Shapes and hand finishes model to required contours and tolerances, using tools and work aids, such as knives, chisel, file, and sandpaper. Drills, countersinks, and reams holes in parts and assemblies for fasteners, such as bolts, screws, and dowel pins, using power tools. Fits, aligns, and joins model parts, assemblies, and working mechanisms into complete structure, using jigs, fasteners, glue, solder, or other method. Sprays or brushes protective, finish, or decorative coatings, such as enamel, paint, or lacquer, on model surfaces. Develops and constructs holding fixtures, jigs, special tools, fittings, templates, patterns, and molds used to construct models. May construct, operate, and maintain associated test equipment. May install model in wind tunnel and modify model during tests as directed by engineering personnel and be designated Model Builder, Wind Tunnel (aircraft mfg.). May construct models for display, advertising, or sales purposes and be designated Model Builder, Display (aircraft mfg.).
GOE: 06.01.04 STRENGTH: M GED: R4 M4 L4 SVP: 7 DLU: 88

693.261-022 ROCKET-MOTOR MECHANIC (aircraft mfg.)

Fabricates, assembles, and tests experimental solid fuel rocket motor parts and assemblies according to specifications, using handtools, precision instruments, machines, and test equipment: Reads and interprets blueprints, drawings, and engineering information to determine methods and sequence of operations to fabricate experimental units. Sets up and operates machines, such as milling machines, lathes, drill presses, and power saws, to machine parts. Measures parts for conformance to specifications, using calipers and micrometers. Assembles parts into completed units, such as valves and pressure vessels, using handtools. Operates vacuum pressure testing equipment to test assembled units for air leaks. Confers with engineering, supervisory, and manufacturing personnel to exchange technical information. May mix chemicals used in fabrication of composite materials. May operate winding machine to fabricate composite parts for solid fuel rocket motor. May specialize in fabricating, assembling, and testing experimental liquid fuel rocket engines and be designated Rocket-Engine Mechanic, Liquid (aircraft mfg.).
GOE: 05.05.07 STRENGTH: M GED: R4 M4 L4 SVP: 7 DLU: 89

693.280-014 PATTERNMAKER, ALL-AROUND (foundry; plastic prod.)

Fabricates foundry patterns from various materials, such as wood, metal, and plastic, for use in forming molds for castings, according to blueprint specifications and using various machine tools, power tools, and handtools: Studies blueprint of part to be cast, computes dimensions, and plans sequence of operations depending upon material specified for pattern. Measures, marks, and scribes layout on metal casting or woodstock. Sets up and operates various wood and metal machine tools and other power tools to machine, cut, and shape stock or casting to specifications. Pours or spreads materials into mold or over model of pattern or builds laminations of fiberglass cloth and plastic resin to fabricate patterns from assorted materials, such as plaster, plaster, or clay. Assembles pattern sections, using fasteners, such as nails, screws, bolts, glue, or glass cloth and resin. Shapes workpiece to specified finish, using handtools and power tools, such as scrapers, files, sanders, grinders, rasps, and planer. Verifies conformance of finished pattern to blueprint specifications, using templates and measuring instruments, such as scales, calipers, micrometer, and protractor. Applies protective finish or paints pattern sections to indicate method of assembly. Repairs broken or damaged patterns and corrects patterns to compensate for defects in castings. Constructs templates for layout and inspection.
GOE: 05.05.07 STRENGTH: M GED: R4 M4 L3 SVP: 8 DLU: 86

693.281-014 PATTERNMAKER (metal prod., nec)

Constructs prototype springs for use in motor vehicles and lays out and forms spring leaves for use as templates in forming production springs. May construct metal platforms, using handtools and bench tools, and weld pattern on each platform to make lower tow dies of spring-forming machine.
GOE: 05.05.06 STRENGTH: M GED: R4 M3 L3 SVP: 7 DLU: 77

693.281-018 PATTERNMAKER, METAL, BENCH (foundry) alternate titles: filer, metal patterns; patternmaker, bench; patternmaker, hand; scratcher, metal patterns

Fits, assembles, and hand finishes castings and parts in making of metal foundry patterns, using handtools and analyzing specifications according to knowledge of pattern-making methods: Studies blueprint of part to be cast, computes dimensions, and plans sequence of operations. Dresses casting down to specified dimensions, using files, scrapers, powered hand grinders, and drill press. Assembles pattern, using handtools and bolts, screws, and other fasteners. Verifies conformance of pattern dimensions to specifications, using templates and measuring instruments, such as scale, calipers, and micrometer. May make templates for own use in inspecting finished surfaces [TEMPLATE MAKER (any industry)]. May operate welding equipment in assembling pattern [WELDER, COMBINATION (welding)].

GOE: 05.05.06 STRENGTH: M GED: R4 M3 L4 SVP: 8 DLU: 77

693.281-022 PATTERNMAKER, SAMPLE (cutlery-hrdwr.)

Fabricates luggage hardware according to blueprint specifications for use as patterns in quantity production: Lays out design on metal, following specifications, and cuts, forms, and assembles finished parts, using hand and machine metalworking tools. Verifies dimensions of assembled parts against specifications, using calipers and other precision measuring instruments. Fastens assembled hardware to sample luggage, adjusting parts to ensure function of hinges, locks, and closures. Alters hardware according to changes in specifications. May submit finished luggage sample to customer for approval. May design hardware.

GOE: 05.05.06 STRENGTH: L GED: R4 M4 L4 SVP: 7 DLU: 77

693.281-030 TOOL BUILDER (aircraft mfg.)

Lays out, fabricates, assembles, and repairs jigs, fixtures, forms, templates, and related tooling used in manufacturing aircraft parts and assemblies, following blueprints, sketches, and specifications, using handtools, power tools, machines, and equipment: Reviews engineering information, tool design drawings, and other specifications to determine methods and sequence of operations to fabricate tools. Examines blueprint of part for which template, jig, fixture, or other tooling is to be built. Calculates unspecified dimensions, and lays out design on assorted materials to establish and coordinate reference points and tooling holes, using measuring instruments, such as dividers and straightedges. Sets up and operates variety of machines and shop equipment to cut, shape, and finish materials to specified dimensions. Fits, aligns, and assembles tooling components, and measures tooling assembly for conformance to specifications, using precision measuring and checking instruments. Joins assembly components, using bolts, pins, clamps, screws, rivets, or other method. Repairs or reworks tools. May draw sketches and prepare detailed instructions for fabricating or machining to be performed by other workers. May specialize in building specific type tool and be designated Form Block Maker (aircraft mfg.); Jig And Fixture Builder (aircraft mfg.); Machine Tool Fixture Builder (aircraft mfg.); Wood-Tool Maker (aircraft mfg.).

GOE: 06.01.04 STRENGTH: M GED: R4 M4 L4 SVP: 7 DLU: 87

693.361-014 MOCK-UP BUILDER (aircraft mfg.)

Lays out, fabricates, and assembles full-scale master mock-ups and prototypes of experimental and production aircraft and spacecraft structures and components, according to specifications, using machines, handtools, and power tools: Lays out lines and contours of structures and components on metallic and nonmetallic materials, utilizing knowledge of trigonometry to determine radius angles and dimensions, according to engineering drawings, sketches, loft data, or verbal instructions. Sets up and operates shop equipment, such as bandsaw, lathe, planer, and drill press, to fabricate parts, such as ribs, empennage, wings, and landing gear. Drills, countersinks, and reams holes in parts and assemblies for bolts, screws, and other fasteners, using power tools. Forms frames and bases from plaster, using cutting, shaping, and finishing tools. Grinds, files, and sands parts to finished dimensions. Aligns and fits parts and assemblies, using fixtures and precision measuring instruments. Joins parts, using fasteners, such as bolts, screws, and clamps, or glue. Confers with liaison personnel to discuss development problems or to recommend modifications if mock-up cannot be fabricated or assembled as designed.

GOE: 05.05.07 STRENGTH: M GED: R4 M4 L4 SVP: 7 DLU: 88

693.380-010 MODEL MAKER (clock & watch)

Sets up and operates machines, such as modelmaker's lathe, milling and engraving machines, and jig borer to make working models of watch parts and complete watches: Makes bridges, plates, and wheels, cutting teeth on wheels and pinions, and working from blueprints to extremely close tolerances. Makes and threads screws. Assembles complete watches. May design and fabricate own tools.

GOE: 05.05.07 STRENGTH: L GED: R4 M3 L4 SVP: 7 DLU: 77

693.380-014 MODEL MAKER (auto. mfg.) alternate titles: miniature-model maker

Sets up and operates variety of woodworking, metalworking, and plasticworking machines to fabricate component parts, and assembles parts to form miniature models of motor vehicle bodies and accessories, using handtools: Constructs parts, following blueprints, computer generated designs, photographs, and other specifications, using bench lathes, milling machine, drill press, planer, baking oven, grinder, files, chisels, and measuring instruments. Assembles completed parts to form desired unit, using handtools and abrasives. May paint and upholster completed bodies.

GOE: 05.05.07 STRENGTH: L GED: R4 M3 L3 SVP: 8 DLU: 90

693.381-018 MOCK-UP BUILDER (vehicles, nec) alternate titles: mock-up assembler

Constructs full-scale experimental and production trailer mockups according to specifications, using woodworking and metalworking machines and handtools: Lays out lines and contours of trailer structures and components on metal, wood, and plastic materials with crayon and scriber, according to engineering drawings, sketches, lofting data, or verbal instructions, using calipers, scales, gauges, and trigonometry to define radius angles and dimensions. Sets up and operates shop equipment, such as bandsaw, lathe, planer, jointer, and drill press, to shape parts, according to blueprints. Drills, countersinks, and reams holes in parts and assemblies for bolts and screws, using portable power tools. Aligns and fits parts and assemblies, using transit and sight level. Joins

parts together, using bolts, screws, clamps, or glue. Lays out, fits, drills, screws, bolts, and rivets together metal sheeting, upright frames, bottom and top bars, and angle clips, using pneumatic handtools and templates. Marks and cuts openings in sheeting, installs support framing around openings, and installs doors, hinges and catches. Fits, drills, bolts, and rivets metal frame pots, headers, and buck plates to make body section, verifying tolerances with tri-square and rule. Installs insulating material and electrical wiring. Connects water supply and installs fixtures and appliances. Completes model by installing molding, hardware, and accessories.

GOE: 05.05.07 STRENGTH: L GED: R4 M3 L4 SVP: 7 DLU: 77

693.381-022 MOLDER, PATTERN (foundry)

Casts patterns in nonferrous metals for use in high production duplicate castings, applying knowledge of metal characteristics, molding sand, contours of patterns, and pouring procedures: Makes one or more sand molds, using wood pattern to form mold impression of metal pattern to be cast [MOLDER (foundry)]. Pours molten aluminum, bronze, or other nonferrous metal into molds with hand ladle. Machines metal patterns to exact dimensions [PATTERNMAKER, METAL (foundry)]. May make wood patterns used to form sand molds in which metal patterns are cast [PATTERNMAKER, WOOD (foundry)].

GOE: 06.02.24 STRENGTH: M GED: R4 M3 L3 SVP: 7 DLU: 77

693.381-026 ELECTRICAL AND RADIO MOCK-UP MECHANIC (aircraft mfg.)

Lays out, fabricates, and assembles jig boards, wiring templates, and master panels used as production patterns for manufacturing control panels and wiring assemblies for aircraft and space vehicles, using handtools, power tools, precision measuring instruments, and shop equipment: Reads blueprints, assembly drawings, and schematics to determine arrangement and relationship of parts and equipment, reference and location points, dimensional specifications, and circuitry routings. Measures and marks location in mockup for installation of control panels, wiring, junction boxes, switches, and related items. Plans, routes, attaches, and ties wires between designated locations in mockup to form prototype wire harness. Transfers pattern of prototype harness to blank jig board and attaches terminal pins, guide pins, clamps, and holding devices to jig board, using handtools and power tools. Assembles sample wire harness, using jig board, and tests continuity of circuits, using voltmeter, ammeter, and other test equipment. Lays out and fabricates prototype panel boards, using precision measuring instruments, such as square, straightedge, scale, protractor, and scriber, and shop equipment, such as saw and drill press. Fits wire harness assembly and panel board in mockup to verify accuracy of layout and modifies layouts as required. Fabricates wiring template used to locate wire harnesses, terminal connections, and related parts and equipment on control panel assembly, using shop equipment. Installs instruments, terminal outlets, switches, junction boxes, and wire harnesses on sample control panel. Tests continuity and functional performance of control panel assembly, using test equipment, to verify conformance of jig board, master panel, and wiring template layouts to specifications.

GOE: 06.01.04 STRENGTH: L GED: R4 M3 L3 SVP: 7 DLU: 88

693.382-010 LAST-PATTERN GRADER (wood prod., nec)

Operates pattern grading (sizing) machine to cut out paper last patterns for shoe sizes of specified style and cuts out steel patterns for use in manufacturing shoe lasts: Positions customer's last pattern on steel sheet, scribes line around pattern, and cuts along line with metal snips to form steel cutting pattern. Secures pattern on table of grading machine. Adjusts reduction scale of machine to cut specified size paper patterns. Inserts cutting tool and stylus into ends of pantograph arm of machine. Starts machine, turns gear to advance uncut pattern paper from roll into position under cutting tool and lowers stylus to starting point on steel pattern. Guides stylus around pattern, observing action of cutting tool to correct cutting irregularities. Measures paper pattern cut by machine against original pattern to verify reproduction of size and shape. Repeats machine operations to cut out specified number of patterns of given size. Readjusts reduction scale and repeats cutting operation to produce all pattern sizes specified for prescribed shoe style. Staples, tapes, or glues specified sized heel patterns to last patterns when making patterns for LAST-MODEL MAKER (wood prod., nec). May cut insole patterns to customer specifications for use in shoe factories.

GOE: 06.02.04 STRENGTH: M GED: R4 M3 L3 SVP: 7 DLU: 77

694   OCCUPATIONS IN FABRICATION OF ORDNANCE, AMMUNITION, AND RELATED PRODUCTS, N.E.C.

This group includes occupations, not elsewhere classified, concerned with fabricating naval, aircraft, antiaircraft, tank, coast, and field artillery having a bore of over 30mm; specialized components for tanks; ammunition; and related products.

694.131-010 TRACER-BULLET-SECTION SUPERVISOR (ordnance)

Supervises and coordinates activities of workers engaged in charging tracer bullets with powder and shaping them to finished dimensions: Interviews new workers and assigns them to work commensurate with their qualifications. Assigns more experienced workers to train new workers. Makes recommendations for promotion or dismissal of workers. Directs workers engaged in repair of machines and other equipment. Coordinates work of department with that of

related departments. Performs other duties as described under SUPERVISOR (any industry) Master Title.
GOE: 06.01.01 STRENGTH: L GED: R4 M3 L3 SVP: 8 DLU: 77

694.132-010 EXPLOSIVE-OPERATOR SUPERVISOR (ordnance)

Supervises and coordinates activities of workers engaged in fabrication, assembly, and loading of ammunition and ammunition components: Interprets and enforces safety regulations. Devises mechanical methods for production processes. Trains workers in operation of machines and equipment. Directs inspection and gauging of processed or stored materials. May supervise ammunition reclamation and reloading activities and be designated Renovation-Plant Supervisor (ordnance). Performs other duties as described under SUPERVISOR (any industry) Master Title.
GOE: 06.02.01 STRENGTH: L GED: R4 M3 L4 SVP: 8 DLU: 77

694.260-010 LOADING-MACHINE TOOL-SETTER (ordnance)

Sets up battery of automatic machines to assemble primed shell bodies, powder, wads, and shot into complete shotgun shells: Replaces worn or broken machine parts, such as bushings, punches, crimpers, powder and shot chargers, hoppers, springs, and belts, using handtools. Examines samples of assembled shells for defects, such as incomplete crimping, tipped top wads, or blurred printing (identifying data), and verifies shell length and diameter, using fixed gauges. Cuts open sample shells with knife to determine that components are assembled as specified. Diagnoses cause of defect and replaces worn parts or adjusts setscrews, stop nuts, knurled bolts, and wingnuts by trial and error until machine produces acceptable work. Dismantles machine to gain access to defective parts and to clear jams not removable by operator. Submits samples of first-run shells assembled after adjustment or changeover to ballistics for approval before releasing machine to operator. Takes charges of powder and shot from loading mechanisms and weighs them on grain scale to verify accuracy of charges. Turns knob to regulate charge to meet specifications.
GOE: 06.01.02 STRENGTH: L GED: R4 M3 L3 SVP: 6 DLU: 77

694.360-010 PRIMER-CHARGING TOOL SETTER (ordnance)

Sets up charging, varnishing, foiling (tamping), and shaker machines, and assembly presses, used in charging and assembling primers for small arms ammunition: Removes, replaces, and adjusts such tools as punches, punch blocks, pins, dies, and die blocks, using handtools. Peens die mouths in foiling die block and reams die hole with hand reamer to sharpen edges, operates *bench grinder* to grind punches and dies for fitting into blocks, hammers charging and shaker plates on straightening plate to straighten them, and rotates bent punch in drill press to determine high spot and taps with metal block to straighten punch. Examines trays of primers for scratches, dents, and lack of anvil or foiling paper. Measures depth of priming mixture, tamping, and anvil in primer, or primer seating in battery cup, using fixed gauges. Turns setscrews to adjust punch or pin block height. May be limited to primer assembly presses only.
GOE: 06.01.02 STRENGTH: M GED: R4 M3 L3 SVP: 6 DLU: 77

694.362-010 CLIP-LOADING-MACHINE ADJUSTER (ordnance)

Sets up and operates machine to position cartridges into clips preparatory to use in small arms weapons: Adjusts or replaces feeding and clipping units to maintain synchronized operation, using handtools and gauges. Lubricates moving parts of machine. Pushes buttons to start machine and stops it when jams occur. Examines workpieces removed from jams to determine location of malfunctioning unit. Notifies MAINTENANCE MACHINIST (machine shop) for repairs. May give instructions to new machine operators.
GOE: 06.02.20 STRENGTH: L GED: R3 M2 L3 SVP: 4 DLU: 77

694.382-010 SALVAGE-MACHINE OPERATOR (ordnance)

Sets up and operates machines to disassemble rejected cartridges for salvaging metal parts: Replaces punches, fingers, dies, feed plate, and shell holders, using handtools, and turns setscrews and stop nuts to adjust ratchets, springs, gates, and pulldown mechanism to accommodate caliber cartridge being processed. Starts machine and feeds cartridges into slots in dial feed plate by hand. Shakes empty cases in hand tumbler to remove powder. Weighs and records scrap and components. May insert cartridges in jaws of bench device and pull lever to extract bullet.
GOE: 06.02.20 STRENGTH: M GED: R3 M2 L2 SVP: 4 DLU: 77

694.382-014 TRACER-BULLET-CHARGING-MACHINE OPERATOR (ordnance)

Operates multiple-station machine to automatically charge and tamp subigniter, igniter, and tracer powder in bullet jackets to form tracer bullets for military rifle ammunition: Starts machine and watches tracks and stations for malfunctioning and jams. Clears jammed dies, funnels, and bullets, using fingers or wire hook. Observes dies at assembly station and inserts jackets by hand in dies missed at hopper tube, seating them with hammer. Turns setscrews and stopnuts, using handtools, to adjust width of track rails, height of scraper regulating amount of powder scooped, stroke of tamping punch, and timing of die-turning fingers. Replaces worn and damaged punches, dies, knock-out pins, and fingers. Weighs powder samples from each charging station on grain scale and adjusts height of scraper or changes size of scoop to regulate load. Measures depth of charge in bullet with dial indicator for firmness of pack. Empties carrier pouches of powder into reservoir bags at charging stations to replenish supply. Cleans machine, using airhose and steam wand, and washes powder dust from floor with water hose.
GOE: 06.02.09 STRENGTH: H GED: R3 M2 L3 SVP: 4 DLU: 77

694.385-010 SHOTGUN-SHELL-ASSEMBLY-MACHINE OPERATOR (ordnance)

Tends battery of automatic machines that perform any combination of following operations to assemble shotgun shells preparatory to loading with powder and shot: Starts machine that coils paper strip into wad and presses wad into shell body; presses molded base wad into shell body; presses metal head onto body and crimps head to form extractor flange; or presses loaded primer into head. Observes machines for jams in hoppers and feed mechanisms and removes jammed components. Examines assembled shells for defects, such as open seams, wad bulges, damaged mouths, and malformed or tarnished heads. Measures head thickness and diameter, shell length, and primer depth, using fixed gauges and dial micrometer. Weighs coiled paper base wads on grain scale to verify conformance to specifications. May fill hoppers with components and remove filled containers of assembled shells and rejects.
GOE: 06.04.20 STRENGTH: M GED: R2 M1 L2 SVP: 3 DLU: 77

694.585-010 SHELL-SIEVE OPERATOR (ordnance) alternate titles: chip separator

Tends rotary and shaker screens that tumble primed rim-fire cartridge cases to shake out loose particles of priming mixture, sawdust, dirt, and chips and to screen out oversize and malformed cases. Records volume of production.
GOE: 06.04.09 STRENGTH: H GED: R1 M1 L1 SVP: 2 DLU: 77

694.665-010 SHOTGUN-SHELL-LOADING-MACHINE OPERATOR (ordnance) alternate titles: loading-machine operator

Tends battery of automatic machines that assemble shotgun shells and print load information on shell body: Starts machine and observes operation for jams in hoppers, feed tubes and channels, rotary feed plates, and loading and crimping mechanisms. Removes jammed shell components, using fingers or wire hook. Examines samples of completed shells at specified intervals to detect incomplete crimping, bulging wads, and blurred printing. Measures length, head thickness, and diameter, using fixed gauges. Cuts open shell with knife and weighs powder and shot charge on grain scale to ensure charges are within specified limits and wads are correctly placed within shells. Periodically obstructs flow of powder and wads to ensure that automatic warning devices are functioning. Communicates with HOPPER FEEDER (ordnance) and packing workers regarding operational difficulties, quality, quantity, and changeover of shells that corrective action may be taken, using intercom system. Cleans machines of powder, shot, and scrap, using brush and vacuum cleaner. Notifies LOADING-MACHINE TOOL-SETTER (ordnance) of machine malfunctioning.
GOE: 06.04.09 STRENGTH: L GED: R2 M2 L2 SVP: 3 DLU: 77

694.682-010 BULLET-ASSEMBLY-PRESS SETTER-OPERATOR (ordnance)

Sets up and operates automatic machine to cut and size lead wire into bullet cores, fit cores into steel jackets, and shape nose and base of bullets according to specifications: Installs and aligns dies and cutting tools and adjusts pressure and depth of stroke of cutting mechanism according to specifications, using handtools and gauges [STRAIGHT-LINE-PRESS SETTER (ordnance); SWAGING-MACHINE ADJUSTER (ordnance)]. Threads lead wire through machine guides and pulleys [CUT-OFF-MACHINE OPERATOR (ordnance); SWAGING-MACHINE OPERATOR (ordnance)]. Starts machine to obtain sample bullet and to verify machine setup. Examines bullets for defects and conformance to specifications, using gauges.
GOE: 06.02.02 STRENGTH: L GED: R3 M2 L3 SVP: 4 DLU: 77

694.682-014 HYDRAULIC-PRESSURE-AUTO-FRETTAGE-MACHINE OPERATOR (ordnance) alternate titles: cold-work operator

Operates hydraulic-pressure-auto-frettage machine to improve physical characteristics and to detect physical weakness of machined artillery barrels, following specifications: Plugs muzzle end of barrel, sets barrel in vertical container of frettage machine, and tightens clamps to lock barrel in place. Connects water pressure pipes to machine, starts water pumps, and moves controls to apply hydraulic pressure to barrel bore to expand bore to specified diameter. Observes pressure indicators and records pressure and time at specified intervals. Fastens cables around barrel and signals OVERHEAD CRANE OPERATOR (any industry) 921.663-010 to remove barrel from machine.
GOE: 06.02.02 STRENGTH: M GED: R3 M2 L2 SVP: 5 DLU: 77

694.685-010 ANVIL-SEATING-PRESS OPERATOR (ordnance) alternate titles: primer assembler; primer-press operator

Tends *power press* that forces primer anvils into loaded primer cups to form complete primers for small arms cartridges: Aligns specially holed plate containing anvils over matching plate of loaded primer cups. Positions assembled plates in holding fixture, pulls lever to lock plates in place on feed table, and starts machine. Examines assembly for malformations, discolorations, and other defects. May seat anvils, using hand-operated toggle press. May tend shaker machine that fills plates with primer components [SHAKER-PLATE OPERATOR (ordnance)].
GOE: 06.04.20 STRENGTH: L GED: R2 M1 L2 SVP: 3 DLU: 77

694.685-014 BULLET-ASSEMBLY-PRESS OPERATOR (ordnance)

Tends machine that shapes (points) front end of steel-jacketed bullets, inserts and seats lead slugs, shapes (bases) rear of bullets, and sizes external diameter, preparatory to insertion in brass cases to form completed cartridges: Places bullet jackets, containing loose slugs, point downward in *dial* feed stations, or observes operation of automatic machine, clearing clogged feed lines, filling dial feed stations, and pressing jackets firmly into holes.

GOE: 06.04.02 STRENGTH: H GED: R2 M1 L2 SVP: 3 DLU: 77

694.685-018 BULLET-LUBRICATING-MACHINE OPERATOR (ordnance) alternate titles: machine pack-shaker lubricator

Tends shaker machine that inserts small arms cartridges into specially holed plates. Positions filled plates on conveyor that immerses cartridge noses in lubricant to coat bullets, preventing lead deposits within weapon bore when fired.
GOE: 06.04.21 STRENGTH: L GED: R1 M1 L1 SVP: 2 DLU: 77

694.685-022 FUSE-CUP EXPANDER (ordnance)

Tends machine that expands fuse cups into adapters of fragmentation bombs to ensure tightness of fit: Wipes cup threads with cloth and screws cup into bomb cavity, using wrench. Guides bomb from conveyor into machine jig. Pushes lever to force tapered mandrel into fuse cup and expand cup into adapter wall.
GOE: 06.04.02 STRENGTH: L GED: R1 M1 L1 SVP: 2 DLU: 77

694.685-026 LOADING-MACHINE OPERATOR (ordnance) alternate titles: cartridge-loading operator

Tends machine that loads small arms cartridges with powder and inserts bullets: Inserts bullets in holes of dial feed plate and observes cartridge case feed lines for tipped and inverted cases. Notifies LOADING-UNIT TOOL-SETTER (ordnance) of machine malfunction. Measures samples of loaded cartridges for conformance to specifications, using go-not-go gauges. May replenish powder supply.
GOE: 06.04.20 STRENGTH: L GED: R2 M1 L1 SVP: 3 DLU: 77

694.685-030 LOADING-UNIT OPERATOR (ordnance)

Tends machines that load small arms cartridge cases with powder and bullets and crimps cases, working as member of team: Places powder dispensing plate in machine fixture and pushes lever that moves plate under machine hopper to fill holes in plate with powder and return it automatically. Clamps plate of cartridge cases over powder plate and turns over assembly to dump powder into cases. Taps dispensing plate with mallet to dislodge powder residue and removes plate. Measures powder-filled cases, using special gauge, to verify cases are filled. Positions plate of bullets over plate of cartridge cases and pulls bottom slide in bullet plate to drop bullets into cases. Positions cartridge plate on press and pushes lever to lower punches that seat bullets to specified depth in cartridge cases. Places plate of cartridges on press bed and pushes lever to lower crimping block that crimps cartridge cases around bullets. Removes plate from press and examines cartridges for defects, such as dented points, scratches, and loose bullets. Measures samples with fixed gauges to verify conformance to specifications. May be designated according to machine unit tended as Loading-Unit Operator, Crimping (ordnance); Loading-Unit Operator, Powder Charging (ordnance); Loading-Unit Operator, Seating (ordnance).
GOE: 06.04.09 STRENGTH: L GED: R2 M1 L2 SVP: 2 DLU: 77

694.685-034 PELLET-PRESS OPERATOR (ordnance)

Tends press that forms pellets of explosives from mixed powder for use in charging or producing detonators for grenades, bombs, shells, and other ammunition: Rubs graphite on table plate and bottom of feed chute of machine. Aligns dies and punches of machine, and adjusts cogwheels to which punches are attached to regulate punches to produce size pellets specified. Fills machine hopper with powder and moves flywheel to make sample pellet. Weighs pellet on balance scale and determines its size with micrometers. Makes necessary adjustments to machine to produce pellets according to specifications. Operates press by remote control due to fire and explosion hazards.
GOE: 06.04.09 STRENGTH: M GED: R2 M1 L2 SVP: 3 DLU: 77

694.685-038 PRESS TENDER, PYROTECHNICS (chemical) alternate titles: explosives operator

Tends hydraulic press that compresses powder in cardboard cases for use as pyrotechnic (firework) flares and signals: Places cases in mold of press and locks mold. Weighs and pours specified amounts of powder into cases. Pulls lever or pushes button to raise press bed and force ram into mold to compress powder in case. Releases pressure and removes mold. Breaks open molds with mallet and removes containers. May add specified quantities of explosive powder to form igniting charge. May be designated according to type of pyrotechnic loaded as Press Tender, Incendiary Grenade (chemical); Press Tender, Smoke Signal (chemical); Press Tender, Star Signal (chemical).
GOE: 06.04.09 STRENGTH: M GED: R2 M1 L2 SVP: 2 DLU: 77

694.685-042 PRIMER-INSERTING-MACHINE OPERATOR (ordnance) alternate titles: heading-and-priming operator; priming-machine operator

Tends machine that inserts and seats primers in center fire cartridge cases and shotgun shells: Starts machine and feeds cases onto pins of rotating dial plate or fills hopper. Observes flow of primers and cases through feed tracks to detect malfunction or jamming of inserting and seating punches and ejection mechanism. Stops machine to remove jammed primers or cases, using fingers, and notifies PRIMER-INSERTING-MACHINE ADJUSTER (ordnance) of malfunction. Examines primed cases at ejection chute for defects, such as dents or scratches, and measures them for conformance to specifications, using fixed gauges. May tend machine that waterproofs cases [PRIMER-WATERPROOFING-MACHINE OPERATOR (ordnance)].
GOE: 06.04.20 STRENGTH: L GED: R2 M1 L2 SVP: 2 DLU: 77

694.685-046 PRIMER-WATERPROOFING-MACHINE OPERATOR (ordnance) alternate titles: lacquer-machine feeder

Tends semiautomatic machine that daubs and sprays lacquer to base and mouth of cartridge cases to form waterproof seals around primer and bullet:

Pulls lever to start machine and inserts cartridge cases into recesses in *dial* feedplate. Observes mechanisms that *index,* apply and remove excess lacquer, and eject cases. Notifies PRIMER-WATERPROOFING-MACHINE ADJUSTER (ordnance) of machine malfunction. Examines cases to ensure complete coverage of lacquered areas. May tend machine that inserts primer in case [PRIMER-INSERTING-MACHINE OPERATOR (ordnance)].
GOE: 06.04.21 STRENGTH: L GED: R2 M1 L2 SVP: 2 DLU: 77

694.685-050 RIM-FIRE-PRIMING OPERATOR (ordnance) alternate titles: rim-fire charger operator

Tends battery of automatic machines that fill head cavity of rim-fire cartridge cases with priming mixture: Rubs moist priming mixture into holes in charger plate, using rubber handtool. Positions plate in holding fixture of priming machine. Starts machine that punches pellets of primming powder into cases and spins mixture into head cavity. Removes jammed cases from feed channels, using airhose or wire pick. Removes empty charger plate when machine stops.
GOE: 06.04.09 STRENGTH: M GED: R2 M1 L2 SVP: 3 DLU: 77

694.686-010 CLIP-LOADING-MACHINE FEEDER (ordnance)

Feeds clips or loaded cartridges into conveyor slots of feed channels of machine that automatically forces clip over cartridge bases to fasten together specified number of cartridges for use in small arms magazines, working as member of team.
GOE: 06.04.20 STRENGTH: S GED: R1 M1 L1 SVP: 2 DLU: 77

699 MISCELLANEOUS MACHINE TRADES OCCUPATIONS, N.E.C.

This group includes miscellaneous occupations, not elsewhere classified, concerned with feeding, tending, operating, controlling, and setting up machines to work various materials and products.

699.130-010 PRODUCTION SUPERVISOR (any industry)

Supervises and coordinates activities of workers engaged in two or more metal manufacturing processes, such as machining, metal forming, assembling, and welding, applying knowledge of processes involved, production methods, and products. Trains employees in work methods and procedure. Inspects products to verify conformance to specifications and directs setup and adjustments of machines. Performs duties as described under SUPERVISOR (any industry) Master Title.
GOE: 06.02.01 STRENGTH: L GED: R4 M3 L4 SVP: 7 DLU: 77

699.131-010 SUPERVISOR, LUBRICATION (any industry)

Supervises and coordinates activities of workers engaged in lubricating industrial equipment and machinery: Trains workers in lubrication methods, operation of lubrication equipment, and in use of various types and grades of oils and greases. Records lubrication activities to verify equipment is serviced as scheduled. Orders installation of grease cup and other fittings to reduce machine wear. Performs other duties as described under SUPERVISOR (any industry) Master Title.
GOE: 06.04.01 STRENGTH: L GED: R4 M3 L3 SVP: 7 DLU: 77

699.137-010 SUPERVISOR, CLEANING (beverage; can. & preserv.; dairy products; food prep., nec)

Supervises and coordinates activities of workers engaged in cleaning machines, equipment, and work areas in beverage or food industries: Fills container with specified amount of cleaning agent, such as liquid or powdered soap and caustic soda. Directs workers in cleaning machines, such as separators, pasteurizers, evaporators, driers, cookers, fillers, and washers, conveyor lines, and working areas. Starts machines and reports machine, gauge, and other control instrument malfunctions to maintenance department. Performs other duties as described under SUPERVISOR (any industry) Master Title.
GOE: 06.04.01 STRENGTH: L GED: R4 M2 L3 SVP: 7 DLU: 77

699.362-010 AUTOMATED CUTTING MACHINE OPERATOR (aircraft mfg.)

Sets up and operates automated cutting machine to cut assorted materials, such as graphite, bleeder and breather cloth, and fiberglass, used in manufacturing composite (fiber reinforced plastic) aircraft parts and assemblies: Reads cutting requests to determine job specifications, such as part identification number, type and quantity of material required, and cutting instructions. Mounts material onto machine fixture or dispensing device, manually or using overhead crane and handtools. Pulls specified length of material over machine cutting table and cuts material, using knife. Positions material on machine cutting table, following blueprints, sketches, and other specifications, using measuring instruments. Pulls and positions additional plies of material onto cutting table. Positions cutter above material plies in specified location. Loads machine control media or enters commands in computer control console to retrieve preprogrammed cutting instructions. Enters commands to activate vacuum that secures materials to table, identify cutter location coordinates, and start machine. Monitors operation of cutting machine to detect malfunctions and informs supervisor or programmer of problem. Removes cut plies from table, marks part identification on plies, and bags and labels cut material for subsequent production use. Sets up and operates machine to cut test pattern from sample material, and obtains approval of test pattern by quality control, programming, or other authorized personnel prior to cutting production materials. Removes and replaces broken or worn blades, using handtools.

GOE: 06.02.09 STRENGTH: L GED: R3 M2 L3 SVP: 4 DLU: 88

699.380-010 DIE SET-UP OPERATOR, PRINTED CIRCUIT BOARDS (electron. comp.)

Sets up and adjusts punching dies in blanking and piercing machines used to fabricate printed circuit boards (PCB's): Reads job order to determine specified dies to be installed. Removes face block from shaft assembly and installs dies according to specifications, using handtools. Replaces face block and aligns shaft assembly with die. Tightens bolts to secure die base and to prevent movement during machine operation. Turns flywheel by hand to ensure complete compression and expansion cycles. Adjusts shaft height as required and locks shaft assembly in vertical position, using handtools. Starts and stops machine and observes operation to detect machine malfunctions.
GOE: 06.01.02 STRENGTH: H GED: R3 M2 L2 SVP: 3 DLU: 86

699.382-010 FLUID JET CUTTER OPERATOR (aircraft mfg.)

Sets up and operates high-speed water jet cutter to cut and trim parts and materials from assorted materials according to specifications: Reads work order, blueprints, and specifications to determine machine setup, type of material or part, quantity, and finish dimensions. Measures and marks cutting and trimming lines on material or part, using measuring instruments, scriber, or marking pen, or mounts material or part in cutting or trimming fixture. Installs and aligns machine accessories, such as cutting tips, work positioner, plates, fixtures, and shields, using handtools and measuring instruments, or enters coordinate information into computer control panel, using *teach pendant*. Manipulates machine controls, such as buttons, switches, dials, levers, and pedals, to regulate and adjust cutting speed and flow of fluid. Cuts and trims parts by manually moving part or material under stream of fluid along cutting lines, controlling movement of part secured in fixture or on work positioner, or entering commands to retrieve and start preprogrammed cutting or trimming instructions to cut materials mounted on machine bed. Observes displays, cutting or trimming process, and listens to sound of machines to detect malfunctions. Replaces worn or damaged machine parts, such as nozzles, tips, and washers. Measures dimensions of finished part, using measuring instruments, such as micrometers, calipers, and dial indicators, or check fixture. Cleans machines and work area. May scoop or pour abrasive particles into hopper of machine. May trim, sand, and drill parts, using shop equipment. May operate automated cutter and be designated Abrasive Water Jet Cutter Operator (aircraft mfg.); or operate manual cutter and be designated Water Router Operator (aircraft mfg.).
GOE: 06.02.09 STRENGTH: M GED: R3 M2 L3 SVP: 5 DLU: 87

699.384-010 COMPARATOR OPERATOR (any industry) alternate titles: shadowgraph operator

Inspects parts for defects in finish and dimensions, using machine that projects magnified shadows of parts on screen: Reads specifications of part to ascertain form and degree to be magnified. Draws enlarged outline of part to scale on chart (celluloid disk), using scribers, dividers, and straightedge. Places chart over translucent glass disk of comparator (shadowgraph) machine. Inserts specified lens into machine and adjusts mirrors to magnify parts. Positions and secures parts on machine table. Turns light on and moves levers of machine to bring shadows of parts into focus with chart outline. Inspects shadows for imperfections of finish and incorrect dimensions. Prepares reports of findings. May rotate part in holding fixture to examine surfaces and to verify concentricity of parts.
GOE: 06.03.01 STRENGTH: L GED: R3 M3 L3 SVP: 4 DLU: 77

699.482-010 RIVETING-MACHINE OPERATOR I (any industry)

Sets up and operates riveting machine to rivet together parts fabricated from materials, such as sheet metal and plastic, according to work orders and specifications: Positions, aligns, and bolts specified dies over anvil and ram of machine and positions fixtures in machine bed, using micrometer, rule, gauge, shims, and wrenches. Installs cam and spring in anvil to synchronize action or clinching post of lower die with action of ram and with rivet feed agitator or lever when setting up semiautomatic machines which position rivets over anvil. Turns knobs and sets screws to adjust depth and pressure limit of ram stroke. Aligns holes of workpieces and inserts shanks of rivets into holes or onto anvil of machine. Positions rivets or holes in workpieces over anvil or against fixtures. Depresses pedal to lower ram that spreads rivet shank to clinch workpieces. Fills hopper with rivets when operating semiautomatic machines. May set up machines equipped with several rams, or with turret to punch and dimple rivet holes and to reposition workpiece after each operation.
GOE: 06.02.02 STRENGTH: M GED: R3 M2 L3 SVP: 5 DLU: 77

699.587-010 SLITTING-MACHINE-OPERATOR HELPER I (any industry) alternate titles: drum operator; machine-operator helper; rewinder; rewinder-operator helper; slitter-and-rewinder; slitter helper

Assists SLITTING-MACHINE OPERATOR (any industry) I performing any combination of following tasks: Positions roll of material, such as cardboard, felt, metallic foil, paper, plastic, rubberized sheeting, or textile fabrics, at rear of machine, using handtruck or cart. Assembles cores, collars, and shafts on roll and positions roll in machine brackets, using hoist. Places takeup tubes I of specified widths on rewind shaft. Threads material over tension bar, between feed rollers, and under rotary blades and laps end of material around takeup tube. Pushes finished roll to bench and removes shaft. Separates pads (slit sections of roll) by chopping at score-marks and prying pad from roll, using dividing iron. Stacks and weighs pads and records weight and color of load. Moves

load to next process station or to storage, using handtruck. May space cutting blades on machine shaft, according to width specified for strips, and turn setscrew to secure blades in position, using allen wrench. May move mill rolls from stock to machine, using handtruck or cart. Performs other duties as described under HELPER (any industry) Master Title.
GOE: 06.04.09 STRENGTH: H GED: R2 M1 L1 SVP: 2 DLU: 77

699.682-010 BINDING CUTTER, SYNTHETIC CLOTH (tex. prod., nec)

Operates machine, equipped with electrically heated knives, to cut synthetic cloth into binding strips and fuses edges to prevent raveling by melting cloth fibers: Spaces knives on machine shaft, according to specified strip width, and turns setscrews to secure knives in position, using wrench. Mounts cloth roll on machine supports and threads cloth through machine units. Laps end of material around takeup tubes I. Turns dial to regulate temperature of knives and starts machine. Observes operation to detect faulty cutting and winding. Removes narrow rolls of material following process. Replaces defective knives, using handtools and spacing gauges.
GOE: 06.02.05 STRENGTH: M GED: R3 M2 L2 SVP: 4 DLU: 77

699.682-014 CUTTER (glove & mit.; tex. prod., nec)

Operates machine to cut parts for articles, such as gloves or fabric buffing wheels, from multiple layers of material: Presses pedal to activate conveyor on which layers of material have been spread, guides material into position on bed (cutting block) of machine, and releases pedal when specified length of material is under ram. Straightens edges of material layers to prevent partial cuts. Lifts gang die onto rack under ram of machine, using chain hoist, or positions single die on material. Presses pedal or lever to lower ram that forces die through material.
GOE: 06.02.05 STRENGTH: M GED: R3 M2 L2 SVP: 4 DLU: 77

699.682-018 CUTTER OPERATOR (any industry) alternate titles: sheeter operator; slitter sheeter operator

Sets up and operates cutting machine equipped with rotary or reciprocating blades to cut rolls of material, such as cloth, paper, paperboard, cellophane, or plastic into sheets, according to specifications: Reads work order to determine dimensions of sheets to be cut. Inserts shaft into core of one or more rolls and raises and positions roll or rolls on cutter rack, using hoist. Threads ends of material through feed rollers, under or across cutting blades, and aligns material against machine guides. Turns rheostat or handwheel to adjust tension of material and to synchronize timing of cutting blades with rate of material feed to regulate length and width of cut. Starts machine and verifies size of cut material, using rule, or notes accuracy of knife cut on spots of premarked paper. Readjusts machine to ensure specified dimensions of sheet. Starts counting device, conveyor belt, or automatic take off table, or raises platform (bearing pallet) on machines equipped with these devices. Observes operation of machine to detect malfunctions, such as jamming, wrinkling, or tearing of material. Stops machine to make required adjustments. Replaces worn cutting blades, using handtools. May oversee duties of assistant operator. May operate machine equipped with electronic eye to control timing of cutting blades and be designated Spot Cutter (any industry). May be designated according to material cut as Cellophane Sheeter (any industry); Foil Cutter (electron. comp.); Paperboard Sheeter (paper products); Paper Sheeter (any industry); or according to purpose for which material is cut as Envelope Cutter (paper products); Liner Sheeter (any industry); Tag-And-Label Cutter (print. & pub.); Wrapper Sheeter (any industry).
GOE: 06.02.09 STRENGTH: M GED: R3 M2 L2 SVP: 5 DLU: 79

699.682-022 DIE CUTTER (any industry) alternate titles: beam-machine operator; clicker; clicker operator; clicking-machine operator; die-press operator; dinking-machine operator; power-press operator

Operates machine to cut out parts of specified size and shape from materials, such as cardboard, cloth, leather, mica, paper, plastic, or rubber: Places single or multiple layers of material on bed of machine. Turns handwheel to raise or lower head of machine (ram) according to thickness of material or depth of die. Positions one or more cutting dies on material or clamps dies to head of machine and positions material under dies to ensure maximum utilization of material. Depresses pedal or moves lever to activate ram that forces die through material. Removes cut parts from die or bed of machine. Measures parts with rule or compares parts with standard to verify conformance to specifications. Stacks parts in storage area according to size and shape. May sharpen cutting edges of dies, using file or hone. When operating machine to trim hat brims, is designated Rounding-Machine Operator (hat & cap). May be designated according to type of die used as Adjustable-Die Cutter (paper goods); Solid-Die Cutter (paper goods); or according to part cut as Sole-Leather-Cutting-Machine Operator (boot & shoe); Toppiece Cutter (boot & shoe); Trimming Cutter (garment). May be designated: Beam-Press Operator (rubber goods); Box-Toe Cutter (boot & shoe); Brim Cutter (hat & cap); Buckram Cutter (boot & shoe; hat & cap; leather prod.); Cap-Parts Cutter (hat & cap); Double Cutter (boot & shoe); Glove-Parts Cutter (glove & mit.); Handbag-Parts Cutter (leather prod.); Hat-Parts Cutter (leather prod.); Heel-Lift-Beam Cutter (boot & shoe); Helmet-Hat-Brim Cutter (hat & cap); Insole Cutter, Machine (boot & shoe); Label Cutter (garment); Leather-Novelty-Parts Cutter (leather prod.); Lining Cutter, Machine (boot & shoe); Outsole Cutter, Machine (boot & shoe); Shoe-Parts Cutter (boot & shoe); Silk-Lining Cutter, Machine (boot & shoe; hat & cap; leather prod.); Single-Beam Clicker (boot & shoe; hat & cap; leather prod.); Sole-Cutting-Machine Operator (boot & shoe); Top-Lift Cutter (boot & shoe); Trimming Cutter,

Machine (boot & shoe); Twin-Beam Clicker (boot & shoe; hat & cap; leather prod.); Upper Cutter, Machine (boot & shoe).
GOE: 06.02.09 STRENGTH: M GED: R3 M2 L3 SVP: 4 DLU: 77

699.682-026 ROLL-SHEETING CUTTER (tex. prod., nec) alternate titles: trim operator

Operates machine to trim edges and slits rolls of coated fabric or plastic sheeting to specified widths for use as wall and shelf covering: Adjusts knives to cut through pattern (design) on material at exact points so patterns will match in register when butted together. Observes operation to correct deviation of cut from point. May be designated according to material cut as Coated Fabric Cutter (tex. prod., nec); Plastic-Sheeting Cutter (plastic prod.).
GOE: 06.02.09 STRENGTH: M GED: R3 M2 L2 SVP: 4 DLU: 77

699.682-030 SLITTING-MACHINE OPERATOR I (any industry) alternate titles: rip-machine operator; roll-cutting operator; slitter-and-rewinder-machine operator; splitter operator

Operates machine to slit continuous lengths of material, such as cardboard, felt, metallic foil, paper, plastic, rubberized sheeting, or textile fabrics, into strips of specified width: Spaces rotary blades on machine shaft, according to width specified for strips, and turns setscrew to secure blades in position, using allen wrench. Mounts roll or bolt of material on machine supports and threads material over tension bar, between feed rollers, and under rotary blades. Laps ends of slit material around takeup tubes I. Starts machine and observes flow of material through machine to detect irregular cutting and winding. Moves levers to stop, start, and regulate speed of machine and to align material with rotary blades. Disengages winding shaft and removes narrow rolls of material. Stacks material on shelves according to width of material. When slitting aluminum foil into widths, is designated Aluminum-Foil-Spooling-Machine Operator (nonfer. metal). When slitting embroidered cloth into strips for use as decorative trimming, is designated Straight Cutter, Machine (tex. prod., nec). May be designated according to material or product cut as Binding Cutter (hat & cap); Cuff Slitter (glove & mit.); Electric-Tape Slitter (rubber goods); Facing Slitter (garment; knitting); Paper Slitter (elec. equip.; paper & pulp; paper goods); Tape Cutter (garment; knitting).
GOE: 06.02.09 STRENGTH: M GED: R3 M2 L3 SVP: 4 DLU: 77

699.682-034 BEVELER, PRINTED CIRCUIT BOARDS (electron. comp.) alternate titles: finisher

Operates machine to bevel printed circuit board (PCB) connectors: Reads work order to determine specified angle and depth of bevel. Turns knobs to adjust machine cutting tool. Slides PCB along guide over cutting tool to bevel PCB connector. Views beveled edge of sample board connector through magnifying scope to verify angle and depth of cut meet company specifications. Operates machine to bevel all connector edges. Inspects PCB's to detect rough edges, dirty surfaces, and closed holes. Smooths rough edges, using hand file. Cleans dust and deposits from PCB, using airhose, toothbrush, or rag. Scrapes excess plating from holes, using utility knife.
GOE: 06.04.09 STRENGTH: L GED: R2 M1 L2 SVP: 2 DLU: 86

699.685-010 BUTTON-ATTACHING-MACHINE OPERATOR (garment; hat & cap) alternate titles: button bradder; button clamper; button riveter; button tacker; patent-button machine operator, automatic; top-bottom-attaching-machine operator

Tends machine that attaches buttons to articles of apparel, such as work clothing and caps: Places tack in holder on machine bed. Positions premarked article over tack on bed and positions button on garment over tack and under machine ram. Depresses pedal that lowers ram, joining button to article.
GOE: 06.04.05 STRENGTH: L GED: R2 M1 L1 SVP: 2 DLU: 77

699.685-014 CUTTER, MACHINE II (any industry) alternate titles: shearer; straight cutter

Tends machine that cuts materials, such as braid, cardboard, cloth, felt, leather, ribbon, roofing paper, strands of wire, or tape to specified dimensions, by any of following methods: (1) Spaces guide or stop gauge along calibrated scale of cutting table according to length of cut specified and tightens setscrew to secure guide or gauge in position. Stacks single or multiple layers of material on cutting table with edges against stop gauge or pulls material across cutting table to guide. Lowers lever-type blade by hand to cut material. (2) Spaces stop gauge along calibrated scale, according to length of cut specified, and tightens setscrew to secure gauge in position. Places single or multiple layers of material on bed of machine with edges against stop gauge or moves lever to advance material in bed of machine against stop gauge. Depresses pedal to activate lever-type-blade that lowers and cuts material. May tend machine that trims excess material or irregular edges from variety of materials or garment and shoe parts. (3) Mounts roll of material on shaft or positions container of flat folded material at feed end of machine. Threads end of material through guides and automatic feeding device. Turns setscrew to regulate feeding device according to length of cut specified. Starts machine that automatically feeds material under lever-type blade and cuts material into lengths. Stacks lengths of material on table or in handtruck. May change blade, using handtools. When cutting materials for use in making rubber stamp pads, is designated Guillotine Operator (pen & pencil). When trimming feathers for use in making shuttlecocks, is designated Shuttlecock-Feather Trimmer (toy-sport equip.). May be designated according to material or article cut or trimmed as Belt-Loop Cutter (garment); Collar Trimmer (garment); Sample Cutter (garment; textile). May be designated: Band Cutter (garment); Belt Cutter (garment); Braid Cutter (rubber

goods); Elastic Cutter (garment); Foil Cutter (any industry); Hose-Suspender Cutter (garment); Label Cutter (garment; knitting); Piping Blocker (boot & shoe); Ribbon Cutter (garment; Sheet Cutter (tex. prod., nec) I; Strap Cutter (garment); Tape Cutter (garment); Toppiece Chopper (boot & shoe).
GOE: 06.04.09 STRENGTH: L GED: R2 M1 L2 SVP: 2 DLU: 77

699.685-018 EYELET-MACHINE OPERATOR (any industry) alternate titles: button bradder; button clamper; button riveter; eyelet maker; eyelet riveter; eyeletter; grommet-machine operator; grommet maker

Tends machine that crimps eyelets, grommets, snaps, buttons, or similar fasteners to material, such as cloth, canvas, paper, plastic, leather, or rubber to reinforce holes, attach fasteners, or to attach parts, by any of following methods: (1) Pours metal fasteners into hopper of machine. Positions material under machine head according to marking on machine bed or material. Depresses pedal to start machine that feeds fastener from fastener holder, lowers ram to force fastener through material and to crimp fastener edges into material, and material into position for succeeding fasteners. (2) Lays fastener in holder of machine. Positions material over fastener according to marks on material or prepunched holes in material. Depresses pedal to lower machine ram which forces edges of fastener into material. (3) Inserts bottom section of two piece fastener in slot in bed of machine and top section into hole in material. Depresses pedal to lower ram and rivet both sections together. May locate and mark positions of fastener on material. May tend machine that also punches holes for fasteners. May be designated according to type of fastener used as Blind Eyeletter (boot & shoe); Blind Hooker (boot & shoe); according to part attached as Buckle-Attaching-Machine Operator (hat & cap); Hook-and-Eye Attacher, Machine (garment); or according to part made as Chin-Strap Maker (hat & cap); Sweatband Maker (hat & cap). May be designated: Button-Attaching-Machine Operator (any industry); Cap-And-Stud-Machine Operator (rubber goods); Fastener Attacher (any industry); Gripper Attacher (any industry); Snap Attacher (any industry); Snap-Fastener-Machine Operator (any industry).
GOE: 06.04.05 STRENGTH: L GED: R2 M1 L1 SVP: 2 DLU: 77

699.685-022 EYELET-PUNCH OPERATOR (furniture)

Tends machines that automatically fasten fabric, padding, and scrim with eyelets to form felted border panels for mattresses: Loads material on machine reels, inserts ends between rollers, and drops metal eyelets into feed slots of machine. Starts machine and cuts, folds, and bundles boxing as it emerges.
GOE: 06.04.20 STRENGTH: L GED: R2 M1 L1 SVP: 2 DLU: 77

699.685-026 POWER-SCREWDRIVER OPERATOR (any industry) alternate titles: power-nut-runner operator

Tends power screwdriver that tightens bolts, nuts, or drives screws to assemble products fabricated from materials, such as wood, metal, plastic, or other materials: Threads or clamps specified torque chuck onto machine spindle. Inserts shank of specified wrench or screwdriver bit into chuck and tightens it, using chuck wrench. Inserts screw or bolt through holes of workpieces or nut onto stud, and turns screw or bolt to catch thread. Positions bolt or nut under bit, and depresses lever to lower spindle and grip head of screw or nut. Pushes pedal to activate spindle that turns and tightens nut, bolt, or screw to torque limit of chuck. May tend machine that positions screw or bolt into workpiece. May tend machine that is activated by pressing workpiece against chuck. May fill hoppers with screws and tend machine that automatically feeds screw between aligned holes of workpiece.
GOE: 06.04.20 STRENGTH: L GED: R1 M1 L1 SVP: 2 DLU: 77

699.685-030 RIVETING-MACHINE OPERATOR II (any industry)

Tends riveting machine that rivets together parts fabricated from materials, such as plastic, cloth, or leather: Aligns holes of workpieces. Inserts rivet shank through holes or onto anvil of machine. Positions rivet or holes of workpieces over anvil or against fixtures. Presses pedal to lower ram that expands rivet shank and clinches workpieces together. Fills hopper with rivets when tending automatic machine that positions rivets over anvil. May tend machine equipped with rotating die and be designated Rivet Spinner (any industry).
GOE: 06.04.20 STRENGTH: L GED: R1 M1 L1 SVP: 2 DLU: 77

699.685-038 FILLING-MACHINE OPERATOR (nonfer. metal)

Tends machine that fills cavities of aluminum extrusions with cement to form thermal-conduction barriers for use in manufacturing windows and doors: Moves machine controls to regulate extrusion feed rate and speed of cement flow. Adjusts drive wheels, pressure rollers, and cement needle according to extrusion size and cavity to be filled, using wrenches. Starts machine that conveys extrusion on rollers through machine for filling operation. Observes operation to ensure cavity filling meets company standards. Readjusts settings when cavity filling falls below specifications. Stacks filled extrusions discharged from machine into cart with assistance from coworker. Places separator blocks and sticks between extrusion layers to prevent sticking and facilitate cement drying.
GOE: 06.04.36 STRENGTH: L GED: R2 M1 L2 SVP: 3 DLU: 86

699.685-046 PINNER, PRINTED CIRCUIT BOARDS (electron. comp.)

Tends machine that drills pinning holes and inserts metal pins into sets of copper laminated fiberglass boards and backing material preparatory to fabrication of printed circuit boards (PCB's): Fills pinning machine hopper with metal pins. Reads work orders to determine specified PCB's. Positions PCB's on bed of machine. Turns machine levers and handwheels to adjust, align, and hold PCB's for drilling and pinning. Activates machine that drills pinning holes and inserts pins into PCB's to stabilize PCB's during numerical-controlled drill-

ing of component mounting holes. Stacks pinned PCB's for transfer to next work station. May assemble sets of fiberglass PCB's and backing material prior to pinning operation.
GOE: 06.04.09 STRENGTH: M GED: R2 M2 L1 SVP: 2 DLU: 86

699.685-050 PRODUCTION-MACHINE TENDER (auto. mfg.)
 Tends automatic production machines and equipment that machine, stamp, weld, form, move, or apply adhesives to automotive parts, according to specifications and machine operating instructions: Pushes buttons on control panel to start and activate automatic cycles of production machines and equipment. Observes machine operations, material supplies, and position of workpieces to detect malfunctions, needed supplies, or misaligned parts. Adjusts alignment of parts on transfer devices and fixtures, using wrench, screwdriver, or control panel. Pushes buttons and presses keys on *teach pendant* to adjust programmed positions of robots' end-of-arm tools or to reset programs that control robot movements. Inspects welds of arc welding robots and adjusts weld position, amount of electrode wire in weld, or heat setting, using teach pendant. Replenishes workpieces for spot welding robots, adhesive supply for adhesive applying robots, and welding wire for arc welding robots. Lubricates machine parts, using grease gun and oilcan. Removes weld slag from fixtures, using chisel, hammer, or file. Notifies supervisor of machine malfunction or defective auto parts. May be assigned to one type of machine, such as material handling, spot welding, or arc welding robots; automatic spot welder; or punch or drill press. May work as part of team.
GOE: 06.04.02 STRENGTH: M GED: R2 M1 L2 SVP: 3 DLU: 90

699.685-054 TRIMMER, PRINTED CIRCUIT BOARD PANELS (electron. comp.)
 Tends machines that trim and bevel edges of copper laminated fiberglass panels used in fabrication of printed circuit boards (PCB's): Flips switches to activate machines. Positions panel over pegs on bed of trimming (shearing) machine. Presses buttons to lower cutting blade that trims excess edges from fiberglass panel. Removes panel from bed of trimming machine and positions edge of panel against guide on bed of beveling machine. Moves panel along guide and under rotating cutting blade that bevels edges of panel. May clean machines, using airhose, to remove shavings. May count and record number of panels completed.
GOE: 06.04.09 STRENGTH: M GED: R2 M1 L1 SVP: 2 DLU: 86

699.686-010 MACHINE FEEDER (any industry)
 Feeds or removes metal, plastic, or other stock and material from automatic fabricating machines: Places stock into hoppers, onto conveyors of self-centering machine bed, or lifts coils of sheet metal or wire onto feedrack. Removes stock from conveyor and piles it into boxes, truck, or on feed conveyor for next operation. May push dual control buttons to activate machine. May work in pairs to feed or remove pieces from machine. May thread sheet metal or wire through machine. May be designated by machine fed as Shear Operator, Automatic (any industry) II; or by task performed as Punch-Press Feeder (any industry); Punch-Press Offbearer (any industry); Straightening-Machine Feeder (any industry).

GOE: 06.04.09 STRENGTH: M GED: R1 M1 L1 SVP: 2 DLU: 77

699.687-010 HARNESS CLEANER (textile) alternate titles: harness brusher; reed cleaner
 Cleans lint, dust, gum, and size from harness assemblies and loom reeds, using brush or airhose. Scrubs harness assemblies in cleaning solution and hangs them in drying cabinet. May clean and replace worn or damaged *drop wires.*
GOE: 06.04.39 STRENGTH: M GED: R1 M1 L1 SVP: 2 DLU: 77

699.687-014 MACHINE CLEANER (any industry) alternate titles: machine brusher; machine rubber; wiper
 Cleans dust, dirt, grease, and lint from machines and auxiliary equipment, such as tanks and pipelines, in industrial plant or aboard ship, using cleaning solutions, waste, rags, waterhose, pumps, lint vacuum system, airhose, brushes, and scraping tools: Cleans screen on lint vacuum system and replaces worn screen. May clean plant sewage treatment system and water supply wells. May remove machine guards and accessories, using handtools. May paint exposed surfaces of machines to prevent rust. May oil moving parts or wearing surfaces. May clean floors around machine, using broom or vacuum cleaner. May be designated according to machine or part of machine cleaned as Bottle-Packing-Machine Cleaner (any industry); Creel Cleaner (textile); Opening-Machine Cleaner (textile); Pin Cleaner (textile); Rack Cleaner (textile); Shafting Cleaner (any industry). May be designated: Card Cleaner (textile); Guide-Rail Cleaner (textile); Loom Blower (textile).
GOE: 06.04.39 STRENGTH: M GED: R2 M1 L1 SVP: 2 DLU: 86

699.687-018 OILER (any industry) alternate titles: boiler-room helper; greaser and oiler; greaser; hostler; lubricator; machine hostler; oiler and greaser
 Oils and greases moving parts of friction surfaces of mechanical equipment, such as shaft and motor bearings, sprockets, drive chains, gears, and pulleys, according to specified procedures and oral instructions: Fills container, such as oilcan, grease gun, or tank of lubrication truck with specified lubricant. Squirts or pours oil on moving parts and friction surfaces, or into holes, oil cups, or reservoirs. Turns oil cup valves to regulate flow of oil to moving parts. Forces grease into bearings with grease-gun, smears grease on friction surfaces, or packs grease cups by hand. Fills wells and sumps of lubricating systems with oil. Reports machinery defects or malfunctions to supervisor. May clean machines, sweep floors, and transport stock. May be specified according to type of machine or equipment lubricated. May tend machine that automatically oils parts.
GOE: 05.12.08 STRENGTH: M GED: R2 M1 L1 SVP: 3 DLU: 77

699.687-022 ROPE CLEANER (textile)
 Rubs powdered mica onto tension rope of warp beam to prevent rope from slipping and to maintain even tension on warp.
GOE: 06.04.27 STRENGTH: L GED: R1 M1 L1 SVP: 2 DLU: 77

682

7 BENCHWORK OCCUPATIONS

This category includes occupations concerned with the use of body members, handtools, and bench machines to fit, grind, carve, mold, paint, sew, assemble, inspect, repair, and similarly work relatively small objects and materials, such as jewelry, phonographs, light bulbs, musical instruments, tires, footwear, pottery, and garments. The work is usually performed at a set position in a mill, plant, or shop, at a bench, worktable, or conveyor. At the more complex levels, workers frequently read blueprints, follow patterns, use a variety of handtools, and assume responsibility for meeting standards. Workers at the less complex levels are required to follow standardized procedures.

70 OCCUPATIONS IN FABRICATION, ASSEMBLY, AND REPAIR OF METAL PRODUCTS, N.E.C.

This division includes occupations, not elsewhere classified, concerned with fabricating, assembling, and repairing or reconditioning products primarily made of metal, but may include parts of plastic or other materials. Also includes products usually made of metal, such as certain tools, but sometimes made of a substitute metallic-type material, the fabrication of which involves use of tooling and techniques similar to metalworking.

700 OCCUPATIONS IN FABRICATION, ASSEMBLY, AND REPAIR OF JEWELRY, SILVERWARE, AND RELATED PRODUCTS

This group includes occupations concerned with fabricating and repairing solid and plated jewelry, tableware, dresser sets, ornamental articles, trophies, medals, rosaries and ecclesiastical ware, jewelers' findings, and related items made of precious and semiprecious metals, and such alloys as pewter and stainless steel. Includes mounting stones in settings. Lapidary work is included in Group 770; and metal engraving is included in Group 704.

700.130-010 SUPERVISOR (jewelry-silver.)
Supervises and coordinates activities of workers engaged in production of sterling silver or silver-plated hollowware, such as serving pieces, flatware, ecclesiastical items, or trophies: Analyzes characteristics, such as luster, malleability, and attractiveness of workpiece in process to determine whether to stop or continue production of workpiece. Trains new workers. Inspects finished work to ensure adherence to specifications, using micrometer, calipers, height-gauge, and rulers. May operate equipment, such as buffing machine, press, and drophammer to correct defects in product. Performs other duties as described under SUPERVISOR (any industry) Master Title.
GOE: 06.01.01 STRENGTH: L GED: R4 M3 L3 SVP: 7 DLU: 77

700.131-010 SUPERVISOR (jewelry-silver.; plastic prod.)
Supervises and coordinates activities of workers engaged in production of jewelry cases: Trains new employees in all phases of operations. Performs duties as described under SUPERVISOR (any industry) Master Title. May be designated according to workers supervised as Supervisor, Hand Workers (jewelry-silver.; plastic prod.); Supervisor, Machine Workers (jewelry-silver.; plastic prod.).
GOE: 06.02.01 STRENGTH: L GED: R4 M3 L3 SVP: 7 DLU: 77

700.131-014 SUPERVISOR (metal prod., nec)
Supervises and coordinates activities of workers engaged in beating gold strips into leaves of specified dimensions, performing duties as described under SUPERVISOR (any industry) Master Title.
GOE: 06.02.01 STRENGTH: L GED: R4 M3 L3 SVP: 8 DLU: 77

700.131-018 SUPERVISOR, JEWELRY DEPARTMENT (jewelry-silver.)
Supervises and coordinates activities of workers engaged in more than one phase of manufacturing jewelry, such as rings, pins, charms, and medals: Assigns workers to stamping, soldering, enameling, or engraving department. Trains workers in methods of jewelry manufacture, such as model making, casting, polishing and stone cutting. Inspects finished work to ensure adherence to specification, using sight magnifier, micrometer, and loupe. Performs other duties as described under SUPERVISOR (any industry) Master Title.
GOE: 06.02.01 STRENGTH: L GED: R4 M4 L3 SVP: 7 DLU: 77

700.261-010 PEWTERER (jewelry-silver.)
Designs and fabricates pewter products, applying knowledge of metallurgy, mold-making, and pewter casting and finishing: Researches reference materials and consults with interested parties to develop ideas for new products. Designs, drafts, and fabricates models of new casting molds, using drafting tools, lathe, and handtools. Fabricates lathe accessories and modifies handtools to facilitate turning and finishing of cast pieces. Mixes and heats alloy and fills casting molds [PEWTER CASTER (jewelry-silver.) 502.384-010]. Joins cast parts to form product, using solder and blowtorch, and shapes, engraves, and polishes product, using lathe and cutting and polishing tools [PEWTER FINISHER (jewelry-silver.) 700.281-026]. Analyzes production data to determine deviations from standards necessitating replacement of molds or modification of equipment.

GOE: 01.06.02 STRENGTH: M GED: R3 M3 L3 SVP: 8 DLU: 86

700.281-010 JEWELER (jewelry-silver.) alternate titles: bench worker; jewelry jobber; jewelry repairer
Fabricates and repairs jewelry articles, such as rings, brooches, pendants, bracelets, and lockets: Forms model of article from wax or metal, using carving tools. Places wax model in casting ring, and pours plaster into ring to form mold. Inserts plaster mold in furnace to melt wax. Casts metal model from plaster mold. Forms mold of sand or rubber from metal model for casting jewelry. Pours molten metal into mold, or operates centrifugal casting machine to cast article [CENTRIFUGAL-CASTING-MACHINE OPERATOR (jewelry-silver.)]. Cuts, saws, files, and polishes article, using handtools and polishing wheel. Solders pieces of jewelry together, using soldering torch or iron. Enlarges or reduces size of rings by sawing through band, adding or removing metal, and soldering ends together. Repairs broken clasps, pins, rings, and other jewelry by soldering or replacing broken parts. Reshapes and restyles old jewelry, following designs or instructions, using handtools and machines, such as jeweler's lathe and drill. Smooths soldered joints and rough spots, using hand file and emery paper. May be designated according to metals fashioned as Goldsmith (jewelry-silver.); Platinumsmith (jewelry-silver.); Silversmith (jewelry-silver.) I.
GOE: 01.06.02 STRENGTH: S GED: R4 M3 L3 SVP: 7 DLU: 77

700.281-014 JEWELER APPRENTICE (jewelry-silver.) alternate titles: bench-worker apprentice; jewelry-repairer apprentice; craft worker
Performs duties as described under APPRENTICE (any industry) Master Title.
GOE: 01.06.02 STRENGTH: S GED: R4 M3 L3 SVP: 7 DLU: 77

700.281-018 MODEL MAKER I (jewelry-silver.)
Makes models by hand from materials, such as plastic, plaster, wax, and metals, according to prepared design for use as molds in casting silverware articles, using sculpturing, carving, and engraving tools: Cuts, carves, chisels, scrapes, and files plaster, wax, or other plastic materials to make model of article in conformity with design. Makes mold of clay or plaster and casts metal sample of model [MOLD MAKER (jewelry-silver.) I]. Grinds, sharpens, and makes handtools, such as scrapers, cutters, gougers, and shapers. May chase decorative designs on silver blanks to be used as models from which steel-production dies are made [CHASER (jewelry-silver.)]. May make own jigs and fixtures.
GOE: 01.06.02 STRENGTH: L GED: R4 M3 L3 SVP: 7 DLU: 77

700.281-022 SILVERSMITH II (jewelry-silver.)
Assembles and repairs silverware, such as coffee pots, tea sets, and trays: Anneals workpiece in gas oven for prescribed time to soften metal for reworking. Wires parts, such as legs, spouts, and handles, to body to prepare unit for soldering. Solders parts together and fills in holes and cracks with silver solder, using gas torch. Hammers out deformations and levels and sets bottoms, using dollies, hammers, and tracing punches. Shapes and straightens damaged legs, lids, and spouts with pliers. Restores dented embossing on articles, using hammers and punches. Pierces and cuts open design in ornamentation, using hand drill and scroll saw. Glues plastic separators to handles of coffee and teapots. May operate lathe to form articles of silverware out of silver or plated sheet, according to sketches. May hammer metal into shape and solder seams to make handles and spouts. May work with metals other than silver, such as pewter, brass, chromium, and nickel.
GOE: 01.06.02 STRENGTH: L GED: R4 M2 L3 SVP: 7 DLU: 77

700.281-026 PEWTER FINISHER (jewelry-silver.)
Shapes, joins, engraves, and polishes pewter items following casting, using machine and handtools and applying knowledge of finishing processes: Secures cast pewter item onto chuck of lathe, depresses button to activate lathe, and pares inner and outer surfaces of items to remove rough edges and excess material, to shape piece to style specifications, and to impart luster to finish, depending on processing stage, using variety of chipping and cutting tools. Engraves decorative lines on item, using engraving tool. Polishes finished surfaces, using abrasive pad. Determines placement on item of auxiliary parts, such as spouts and handles, using paper facsimile, and marks solder path on item, using grease pencil. Routs out solder path, following marked lines and using routing machine. Places part on jig to stabilize part, aligns auxiliary part with part of jig, and joins parts, using solder and blowtorch. Weighs completed pieces to determine deviation from target weight, and records weight and proc-

essing time required on production records. Carries pieces to next work station. Occasionally fabricates chipping and turning tools, using machine and handtools.
GOE: 01.06.02 STRENGTH: M GED: R3 M2 L2 SVP: 7 DLU: 86

700.381-010 CHAIN MAKER, HAND (jewelry-silver.)
Forms chains of various shapes and designs from gold wire to make jewelry articles according to specifications: Winds wire into coils, using coiling device. Saws coils through one side to form separate links, using handsaw. Assembles links in specified manner to form rope chain or fancy links, using pointed pliers. Solders links to form chain, using gold solder and gas torch. Immerses chain in chemical baths to clean gold. Polishes chain, using jeweler's rouge and felt polishing wheel.
GOE: 06.01.04 STRENGTH: L GED: R4 M2 L3 SVP: 6 DLU: 77

700.381-014 FANCY-WIRE DRAWER (jewelry-silver.)
Draws, shapes, and engraves or embosses precious or base metal wire for use in fabricating precious or costume jewelry, such as chains, box links, and bracelets: Inserts tapered end of metal wire, such as gold, platinum, and silver, through die hole, pulling wire through dies of wire-drawing machine manually to form round, half-round, square, or rectangular jewelry wire. Engraves ornamental designs on surface of wire, using triangular and square-pointed tools, such as gravers and carvers, or embosses wire with decorative patterns, using wire-drawing machine equipped with embossing rollers. Draws, shapes, and embosses ribbon-wire, using rolling mill. Examines dimensions of rolled or drawn wire, using micrometers.
GOE: 01.06.01 STRENGTH: S GED: R4 M3 L3 SVP: 7 DLU: 77

700.381-018 GOLDBEATER (metal prod., nec)
Beats gold strips into gold leaf, using hammers, for use in decorating products, such as books, furniture, and signs: Cuts gold strip into one inch squares and interlaminates squares with leaves of cutch (packet of vellum sheets). Hammers cutch to reduce thickness and expand area of squares to form gold sheets of specified dimensions. Cuts sheets into quarters and interlaminates quartered sheets with leaves of shoder (packet of skins). Hammers shoder to form gold leaf of specified dimensions.
GOE: 06.01.04 STRENGTH: M GED: R3 M2 L2 SVP: 6 DLU: 77

700.381-022 HAMMERSMITH (jewelry-silver.) alternate titles: flat hammerer
Repairs defects in silver hollowware, such as trays, creamers, teapots, and bowls, using hammers, dollies, and tracing punches: Examines article to determine nature of defect, such as dents, uneven bottom, scratches, or holes. Places article on anvil or dolly and pounds out dents or bulges, selecting hammer with head corresponding in curvature with surface of article. Straightens twisted articles by hand. Forms concavity in bottom of article to improve its stability, using tracing punches and hammer. Verifies levelness of bottom edges of article, using straightedge, or by rocking article back and forth on flat surface. Peens edges of scratches or holes to repair defect, using peening hammer.
GOE: 06.01.04 STRENGTH: L GED: R3 M1 L2 SVP: 6 DLU: 77

700.381-026 LAY-OUT WORKER (jewelry-silver.)
Lays out settings and mounts stones in jewelry mounting, following specifications: Compares mounting with design to determine position of settings. Marks and drills holes in mountings to center stones according to design specifications. Decorates raised portions of metal, using engravers' tools. Positions mountings in sandblasting machine to clean and sharpen design preparatory to further processing. May modify existing mountings to reposition jewels [STONE SETTER (jewelry-silver.; optical goods)].
GOE: 01.06.02 STRENGTH: S GED: R4 M2 L3 SVP: 7 DLU: 77

700.381-030 LOCKET MAKER (jewelry-silver.)
Shapes, finishes, and assembles metal parts to fabricate lockets: Stamps design in metal frame with drop press. Cuts edges with chisel or reamer to flatten sides. Solders in lining and places field piece between outer and inner frame to hold picture. Removes rough spots with file and emery paper, and polishes with buffing wire and wire brush. Dips lockets in cleaning solution to remove stains and in solution of gold or other metal to color lockets.
GOE: 06.01.04 STRENGTH: L GED: R3 M2 L2 SVP: 7 DLU: 77

700.381-034 MOLD MAKER I (jewelry-silver.) alternate titles: chaser
Finishes, alters, and repairs metal molds used to cast jewelry articles and trophy figurines, using hand carving and engraving tools: Cuts design in mold and files, grinds, and shapes points, surfaces, and contours. Fits halves of molds together to determine if they close tightly. Drills holes in mold to allow gases to escape during casting. Reshapes pouring funnels of molds to facilitate flow of molten metal. Drills holes in mold and attaches handles, using drill press and screwdriver. Forms sample castings in mold and measures casting to verify dimensions. May grind, sharpen, and make tools.
GOE: 01.06.02 STRENGTH: L GED: R4 M3 L3 SVP: 8 DLU: 77

700.381-038 MOLD-MAKER APPRENTICE (jewelry-silver.) alternate titles: chaser apprentice
Performs duties as described under APPRENTICE (any industry) Master Title.
GOE: 01.06.02 STRENGTH: L GED: R4 M3 L3 SVP: 8 DLU: 77

700.381-042 RING MAKER (jewelry-silver.)
Fabricates rings by any of following methods: (1) Casts rings, using molds of rubber, plaster, wax, sand, and metal. (2) Cuts out ring blanks from flat metal and shapes blanks into ring bands. (3) Ties or twists gold or silver wires together and bends to form rings. Removes gates, solders ends, and files rings to remove excess metal. Cleans and polishes rings by immersing them in metal cleaning or acid solution. May set stones in rings.
GOE: 06.01.04 STRENGTH: L GED: R3 M2 L2 SVP: 7 DLU: 77

700.381-046 SAMPLE MAKER I (jewelry-silver.) alternate titles: crafter
Fabricates sample jewelry articles, according to drawings or instructions: Cuts and shapes metal into findings, using metal cutting and carving tools. Arranges metal findings into specified design, softens findings by heating with gas torch, and shapes findings, using hammer and die. Solders pieces together, and smooths rough surfaces, using wooden mallet, files, or polishing wheel. Attaches decorative trimmings, such as wax flowers, enamel motifs, and stones.
GOE: 01.06.02 STRENGTH: L GED: R3 M2 L2 SVP: 7 DLU: 77

700.381-050 SOLDERER (jewelry-silver.)
Solders together parts of new or broken jewelry, using gas torch and solder: Selects type of solder to be used and lays parts on asbestos board. Lights torch and applies solder and flux to article as needed. Immerses article in water to cool.
GOE: 06.01.04 STRENGTH: S GED: R3 M2 L3 SVP: 5 DLU: 77

700.381-054 STONE SETTER (jewelry-silver.; optical goods) alternate titles: jewelry setter
Sets precious, semiprecious, or ornamental stones in rings, earrings, bracelets, brooches, metal optical frames, and other jeweled items, using handtools: Places item in vise. Cuts and files setting to accommodate stones, using files, chisels, and hand or electric drills. Positions stone in setting and fixes in place by pressing prongs around stone, by raising retaining metal ridge around stone, or by tapping edges of setting with setting tool and hammer, forcing metal against stone. Smooths edges, using emery file and pointed steel tool. Examines union of stone and setting, using magnifying glass. May drill holes in settings preparatory to setting stones in piece. May replace stones in rings. May be designated according to stone set as Diamond Setter (jewelry-silver.) or according to item worked on as Stone Setter, Metal Optical Frames (optical goods).
GOE: 05.05.14 STRENGTH: L GED: R3 M2 L2 SVP: 7 DLU: 77

700.381-058 STONE-SETTER APPRENTICE (jewelry-silver.; optical goods)
Performs duties as described under APPRENTICE (any industry) Master Title.
GOE: 05.05.14 STRENGTH: L GED: R3 M2 L2 SVP: 7 DLU: 77

700.682-010 FLATWARE MAKER (jewelry-silver.)
Operates power press and other machines to stamp out spoons and forks from sterling silver blanks: Positions and secures specified cutting dies in holders of power press, using wrench. Starts press, positions blank, and depresses pedal to cut blank to size. Places cut blank in die holder of drop press. Pulls strap to drop ram onto blank to form bowl or fork end of flatware, regulating force of ram by height from which ram is released. Anneals flatware between initial and final stampings, using torch to heat metal to prescribed temperature. Immerses annealed flatware in specified solution to cool and clean metal. Positions formed fork blanks in holders of tining press and activates cutters that form tines. Shapes handle, bowl, or tines of spoons and forks, using copper model as standard, grinding wheel, emery-belt, wooden mallet, forming blocks, and hand files.
GOE: 06.02.02 STRENGTH: L GED: R3 M2 L2 SVP: 7 DLU: 77

700.682-014 LATHE HAND (jewelry-silver.) alternate titles: sawyer
Operates bench lathe to saw, mill, burr, or bevel metal stock or parts used to make jewelry findings: Secures stock in guide or jig, starts lathe, and moves stock against cutting tool. May manipulate stock against cutting tool without use of guide or jig.
GOE: 06.02.02 STRENGTH: L GED: R3 M1 L2 SVP: 6 DLU: 77

700.682-018 PROFILE-SAW OPERATOR (jewelry-silver.)
Trims excess metal from edges of hollowware, such as trays, platters, bowls, and vegetable dishes after forming on forming press, using circular saw: Selects saw blade according to metal composition of workpiece and mounts it on driving spindle, using wrench. Measures distance from bottom of workpiece to ridge or scallop to contour and adjusts height of saw blade, using dividers, scale, adjustable square, and wrenches. Starts machine and positions hollow side of workpiece over saw blade with top flat against backboard. Guides workpiece against saw following designated ridge or scallop to cut excess metal at same height around edge of workpiece.
GOE: 06.02.02 STRENGTH: L GED: R3 M2 L2 SVP: 3 DLU: 77

700.684-010 ARBORER (jewelry-silver.) alternate titles: bender; ring maker; sizer
Forms ring blank into circular shape, using ring mandrel and rawhide mallet: Files ends of ring blank smooth and square and places blank in ring bending device. Pulls lever to bend blank into semicircle. Places blank on mandrel and hammers blank into circular shape, using rawhide mallet. Slides ring over sizing (measuring) mandrel to verify conformity to specifications.
GOE: 06.04.24 STRENGTH: L GED: R2 M1 L1 SVP: 2 DLU: 77

700.684-014 ASSEMBLER (jewelry-silver.)
Assembles jewelry, such as rings, lockets, bracelets, brooches, and watchcases, using pliers, screwdriver, and jeweler's hammer. May use foot

press. May be designated according to type of product assembled as Bracelet Maker, Novelty (jewelry-silver.); Brooch Maker, Novelty (jewelry-silver.).
GOE: 06.04.23 STRENGTH: S GED: R2 M1 L1 SVP: 3 DLU: 77

700.684-018   BRIGHT CUTTER (jewelry-silver.)
Cuts layer of metal from walls of settings and other surfaces of jewelry articles to reveal bright inner metals: Clamps article in chuck preparatory to cutting. Lubricates cutting tool and pushes tool over surface to remove specified layer of metal.
GOE: 06.02.24 STRENGTH: S GED: R3 M2 L2 SVP: 3 DLU: 77

700.684-022   CHAIN MAKER, MACHINE (jewelry-silver.)
Forms chains for watches and other jewelry articles: Feeds wire into machine. Hooks together ends of chain formed by machine, using pliers, and solders on trimming. May be designated according to type of chain as Novelty-Chain Maker (jewelry-silver.).
GOE: 06.02.23 STRENGTH: L GED: R3 M2 L2 SVP: 3 DLU: 77

700.684-026   DRILLER (jewelry-silver.) alternate titles: drill-press operator
Drills holes and sockets for stones or hinges in pieces of jewelry, such as brooches, rings, and bracelets: Inserts drill bit of specified size in chuck of press and starts drill. Holds piece of jewelry against drill, pressing it until holes or sockets are formed. May use hand drill.
GOE: 06.04.24 STRENGTH: S GED: R2 M1 L2 SVP: 3 DLU: 77

700.684-030   EARRING MAKER (jewelry-silver.)
Assembles pearl earrings according to designs or instructions: Winds wire-threaded pearls, by hand, around metal-looped earring blanks. Cuts end of wire thread with cutter. Fastens pearls on loops by twisting wire with pliers. May paste loops of pearls and single pearls to facing of other loop blank.
GOE: 06.04.23 STRENGTH: S GED: R3 M2 L2 SVP: 3 DLU: 77

700.684-034   FILER (jewelry-silver.) alternate titles: fitter; shaper
Trims and smooths edges, surfaces, and impressed or raised designs of jewelry articles and jewelry findings, using files, chisels, and saws: Places article in holding device or against bench pin. Files or cuts excess metal from surfaces and ornamentations, such as filigree or relief designs. Miters joints and ends of formed ring blanks, using file. May smooth and polish edges and soldered areas of jewelry, using abrasive wheel. May operate motor-driven filing machine.
GOE: 06.04.24 STRENGTH: L GED: R3 M1 L2 SVP: 3 DLU: 77

700.684-038   GOLD CUTTER (metal prod., nec)
Cuts goldleaf sheets to specified sizes and fills interleaved books with cut sheets, using handtools: Removes sheet of goldleaf from mold, using wood pinchers. Places sheets on worktable and smooths sheets preparatory to cutting. Cuts sheets to specified size, using cutting device. Places goldleaf in interleaved book, using wood pinchers. May operate electric cutting machine to cut goldleaf.
GOE: 06.02.24 STRENGTH: L GED: R3 M1 L2 SVP: 4 DLU: 77

700.684-042   HOLLOW-HANDLE-KNIFE ASSEMBLER (jewelry-silver.)
Cements knife blades into hollow handles by performing any combination of following tasks: Weighs, measures, and mixes specified amounts of powder and water together in automatic beater for specified time. Pours cement into drum of centrifugal loading machine, inserts knife handles in perimeter of drum and activates machine to fill handles. Places filled handle in tray. Inserts tang of blade into cement-filled handle and twists blade to align blade with handle. Places assembled knife between spring-loaded holders on vertical endless chain conveyor leading to drying oven or water-curing machine. Removes finished pieces from conveyor and examines them for alignment and excess cement. Twists blade to realign it with handle, and places rejects in tray. Places accepted knives in rack for air drying. Cleans cement from knife, using brush and metal pick. May pour cement into pneumatic cylinder, connect compressed air-hose, place knife handle under cylinder spout, and fill handle by depressing pedal to release cement from cylinder.
GOE: 06.04.23 STRENGTH: L GED: R2 M1 L1 SVP: 2 DLU: 77

700.684-046   JIGSAWYER (jewelry-silver.) alternate titles: jigsaw operator
Cuts out metal jewelry findings according to pattern, using jigsaw: Receives metal sheets with patterns cemented to tops, or prints patterns on printing press and cements onto metal sheets. Assembles several sheets into laminated block with oiled paper between layers to produce multiple findings in one cutting operation. Drills holes for saw blade, using drill press. Mounts blade on jigsaw, starts saw, and guides metal sheet against blade to cut along lines of pattern.
GOE: 06.04.24 STRENGTH: L GED: R2 M1 L1 SVP: 4 DLU: 77

700.684-050   MESH CUTTER (jewelry-silver.)
Cuts metal mesh to specified dimensions to make jewelry articles, such as women's handbags, belts, and watchbands: Detaches small metal squares from mesh by cutting corner rings until desired size and shape of mesh is attained. May complete shaping of mesh with scissors.
GOE: 06.02.24 STRENGTH: S GED: R3 M1 L2 SVP: 3 DLU: 77

700.684-054   OXIDIZER (jewelry-silver.)
Brushes oxide solution on ornamentation (patterned surfaces) of silverware and silver-plated ware to darken crevasses to make design stand out after buffing: Brushes oxide on ornamentation of hollowware, such as bowls, trays, and

coffee pots. Dips ornamented end of knives, forks, and spoons in solution, and wipes excess solution from silverware with cloth to prevent discoloration. Places silverware in mesh basket and immerses it in water to neutralize oxidation. May tend conveyorized machine that automatically oxidizes stainless steel flatware items.
GOE: 06.04.24 STRENGTH: L GED: R2 M1 L2 SVP: 2 DLU: 77

700.684-058   PREPARER, MAKING DEPARTMENT (jewelry-silver.)
Operates equipment and uses handtools to prepare metal jewelry findings for further processing, using handtools and machine tools: Shapes, cuts, and assembles findings, using pliers, shears, arbors, mallets, files, or foot press. Drills holes in findings, using small drill. Cuts off excess metal or makes slots in findings, using bench lathe. Polishes findings on powered abrasive disk or emery wheel. Softens findings by heating them in furnace to prepare them for soft soldering or shaping.
GOE: 06.02.24 STRENGTH: L GED: R3 M2 L2 SVP: 6 DLU: 77

700.684-062   PREPARER, SAMPLES AND REPAIRS (jewelry-silver.)
Duplicates sample jewelry articles by shaping, assembling, and cutting findings for soldering and other operations, using original sample as guide. Repairs jewelry damaged during processing by replacing or reshaping defective parts, using handtools and machine tools.
GOE: 06.02.24 STRENGTH: L GED: R3 M2 L2 SVP: 4 DLU: 77

700.684-066   RING STAMPER (jewelry-silver.) alternate titles: ring striker
Stamps out, shapes, and trims ring and findings blanks for jewelry, such as bracelets, pins, and earrings, performing any of following tasks: Stamps out ring and finding blanks from metal strips, using kick-press or power press. Forms contoured ring body from blank metal, using drop-press. Trims excess metal from edges of contoured ring body. Heats and softens metal blanks preparatory to stamping and shaping operations, using annealing furnace or gas torch. May operate rolling mill to decrease thickness of metal ingots.
GOE: 06.02.24 STRENGTH: L GED: R2 M1 L1 SVP: 5 DLU: 77

700.684-070   SILVERWARE ASSEMBLER (jewelry-silver.)
Assembles silver hollowware, such as lazy susans, teapots, creamers, and chafing dishes: Drills holes in parts, using bench drill. Screws, bolts, or pins base, legs, and lid to body of hollowware, using handtools. Adjusts length of legs, or flattens base with mallet so article stands firm and level. Mixes plastic ingredients, following formula, to form adhesive compound, and glues handle to hollowware. May ream and tap holes, using bench drill and tap. May fasten parts together by swedging. May buff and polish articles after assembly to remove finger marks.
GOE: 06.04.23 STRENGTH: L GED: R2 M1 L1 SVP: 2 DLU: 77

700.684-074   SPINNER (jewelry-silver.)
Stretches and shapes metal into symmetrical forms, using handtools and bench lathe, for use in making jewelry: Mounts work in lathe chuck. Starts lathe and forces handtools against metal to bend and stretch it as specified.
GOE: 06.02.24 STRENGTH: L GED: R3 M2 L2 SVP: 5 DLU: 77

700.684-078   STRETCHER (jewelry-silver.)
Stretches rings to specified size and shape, using stretching device: Slides ring onto hollow arbor (female) having slits running down its length that permit it to contract or expand. Turns wheel to force tapered male arbor into hollow arbor to expand and stretch ring. Repeats operation until ring is stretched and formed as specified.
GOE: 06.04.24 STRENGTH: S GED: R2 M1 L2 SVP: 3 DLU: 77

700.684-082   WATCH-BAND ASSEMBLER (jewelry-silver.)
Assembles ribs of skeleton for expansion metal watch band, using handtools: Inserts coil spring in center eyelet of watch-band rib with pencil-shaped *jigger*. Turns other projecting ends of spring to fasten rib to skeleton.
GOE: 06.04.23 STRENGTH: L GED: R2 M1 L1 SVP: 3 DLU: 77

700.687-010   BENCH WORKER, HOLLOW HANDLE (jewelry-silver.)
Performs any combination of following tasks involved in assembling knife handles and handles for hollowware, such as creamers and sugar bowls: Holds halves of handles against electrodes on spot-welding machine to tack-weld them together. Places handles on rack hooks and dips them in tank of flux. Places knife handle halves in assembly press to fit halves together onto metal holding frame preparatory to soldering. Inserts premeasured amount of solder in hollow handle. Loads handles on screen conveyor that carries them through furnace. Positions soldered handles in fixture of milling machine or belt grinder to face mouth of handles. Positions handle in fixture and depresses pedal that submerges handles into water tank and forces compressed air into fixture. Observes handles to detect air bubbles indicating faulty soldering. Brushes flux on inside of handles and sprinkles them with powdered solder, using reed scoop.
GOE: 06.04.23 STRENGTH: L GED: R2 M1 L1 SVP: 2 DLU: 77

700.687-014   BOILER-OUT (jewelry-silver.)
Coats rings and jewelry fittings with acid solution or wax to protect metal from oxidation during soldering process: Drops fittings into boiling acid solution for specified time, or applies wax to fittings, using brush. Removes acid coated fittings and heats them in oven to harden coating. Dips soldered articles in chemical solutions and water to remove coating.
GOE: 06.04.33 STRENGTH: L GED: R2 M1 L1 SVP: 2 DLU: 77

700.687-018   BRIMER (metal prod., nec)
Applies special powder to both sides of plastic mold sheets to prevent gold strips from sticking to sheet, using powder and plush stick.

GOE: 06.04.33 STRENGTH: S GED: R1 M1 L1 SVP: 2 DLU: 77

700.687-022 CASTER HELPER (jewelry-silver.)
Prepares investment molds for use in casting gold rings: Mixes plaster of paris and water in specified proportion and pours around wax model. Places casting in oven for baking. Cleans finished casting by dipping it in acid and water solution.
GOE: 05.12.10 STRENGTH: L GED: R2 M1 L1 SVP: 3 DLU: 77

700.687-026 CHARGER II (jewelry-silver.) alternate titles: bench hand; set-up and charger
Prepares jewelry findings for subsequent soldering operations: Positions jewelry article on nonflammable work surface, such as asbestos board or pan of crushed emery stone. Selects findings and positions them on jewelry article, using tweezers. Places particle of solder (charge) at junction of jewelry article and finding, using brush or pick.
GOE: 06.04.23 STRENGTH: S GED: R2 M1 L1 SVP: 2 DLU: 77

700.687-030 CUTCH CLEANER (metal prod., nec)
Cleans, dries, and presses cutch sheets (skins) to recondition sheets for reuse, using airhose and hydraulic press: Receives wet sheets that have been washed to remove gold particles, and holds sheets under compressed airhose to remove excess moisture. Places sheets in fanned-out pattern in heated hydraulic press to press and complete drying of sheets. Stacks reconditioned sheets on worktable for reuse.
GOE: 06.04.27 STRENGTH: L GED: R2 M1 L1 SVP: 2 DLU: 77

700.687-034 INSPECTOR (jewelry-silver.)
Examines findings and finished pieces of jewelry for specified size and shape and for defects in enameling, painting, plating, and polishing. Straightens parts or inserts links, using pointed pliers. May measure and weigh completed articles of sterling silver or pieces of jewelry, using balance scale, micrometer, calipers, rulers, and height gauge. May inspect filled books of gold leaf or rolls of metal foil for defects, such as dimensional accuracy, holes or torn corners.
GOE: 06.03.02 STRENGTH: S GED: R3 M2 L2 SVP: 4 DLU: 77

700.687-038 LABORER, GOLD LEAF (metal prod., nec)
Places gold strips between sheets of plastic or skin to form packets (stacks) for beating by GOLDBEATER (metal prod., nec). May be designated Shoder Filler (metal prod., nec) when forming packet for second beating, or Mold Filler (metal prod., nec) when forming packet for third beating.
GOE: 06.04.24 STRENGTH: L GED: R2 M1 L1 SVP: 2 DLU: 77

700.687-042 MELTER (jewelry-silver.)
Melts gold, or gold and silver alloys, using furnace, electric heating unit, or torch, and pours molten metal into ingot molds to prepare metal for use in making jewelry: Places metal in clay crucible. Places crucible in preheated oven or heats crucible with torch to melt metal. Observes color changes in metals to ensure that specified temperature is attained. Pours molten metal into ingot mold. Opens mold, lifts out ingot with tongs, and quenches ingot in water. May operate roller machine to roll ingots into metal strips for use in stamping out jewelry blanks [ROLLER (jewelry-silver.)].
GOE: 06.04.24 STRENGTH: M GED: R2 M1 L2 SVP: 2 DLU: 77

700.687-046 MOLD SHEET CLEANER (metal prod., nec)
Removes gold dust and chips that adhere to plastic sheets, during hammering process: Inserts plastic sheets in opening of glass enclosure and under compressed airhose that blows gold dust and chips from sheets. Stacks cleaned sheets on worktable for reuse.
GOE: 06.04.39 STRENGTH: L GED: R1 M1 L1 SVP: 2 DLU: 77

700.687-050 MOLD-MAKER HELPER (jewelry-silver.) alternate titles: chaser helper
Assists MOLD MAKER (jewelry-silver.) I in making metal molds used to cast jewelry articles: Scrapes, files, and sandpapers surfaces of metal molds so they will close smoothly. Performs duties as described under HELPER (any industry) Master Title.
GOE: 06.04.24 STRENGTH: L GED: R1 M1 L1 SVP: 2 DLU: 77

700.687-054 PLANISHER (jewelry-silver.)
Flattens previously initialed heads of signet rings to remove dents, using press. Positions plunger and arbor holder in press. Slips ring on arbor and inserts arbor in arbor holder. Pushes lever that forces plunger down on head of ring to flatten it and remove dents. Releases lever and removes ring from press.
GOE: 06.04.24 STRENGTH: L GED: R2 M1 L1 SVP: 2 DLU: 77

700.687-058 POLISHER (jewelry-silver.) alternate titles: rubber-off
Smooths and polishes jewelry, such as charms, earrings, pins, rings, and bracelets, using polishing wheel: Selects polishing wheel and dressing compound according to type of metal to be polished and type of finish desired. Applies dressing compound or rouge to rotating wheel and moves article against wheel to remove surface blemishes and produce luster. May apply dressing compound and rub articles with cloth to remove discoloration and produce luster. May immerse jewelry in plating solution for specified time to coat jewelry with gold, silver, or other material. May polish areas of rings that are inaccessible to polishing wheel, using strip of abrasive polishing fabric. May buff jewelry findings with abrasive to produce grain effect (dull, granulated surface) and be designated Grainer (jewelry-silver.). When holding jewelry against lapping disk to smooth soldered joints, rough edges, and file marks, may be designated Lapper (jewelry-silver.). When holding jewelry

against wire-brush wheel to remove stains, oxide coatings, solder flux, and to produce satin-finished surfaces, may be designated Scratch Brusher (jewelry-silver.).
GOE: 06.04.24 STRENGTH: S GED: R2 M1 L2 SVP: 3 DLU: 77

700.687-062 PREPARER (jewelry-silver.) alternate titles: bench hand
Performs any combination of following tasks in preparing cast jewelry findings for further processing: Cuts, saws, or breaks off gates from jewelry castings, using shears, jeweler's saw, pliers, or foot press equipped with cutting tool. Removes burrs and smooths rough edges of casting, using file or grinding wheel. Straightens distorted castings, using foot press equipped with shaping dies. May remove plaster from castings by dipping castings in water and acid solution. May count and separate jewelry casting into containers, according to type, and marks containers with identifying information. May specialize in breaking off gates from jewelry castings and be designated Breaker-Off (jewelry-silver.).
GOE: 06.04.24 STRENGTH: S GED: R2 M1 L1 SVP: 2 DLU: 77

700.687-066 SCRAPER (jewelry-silver.) alternate titles: cutter and edge trimmer
Saws and grinds gates and flash from castings of novelty jewelry and trophy figurines: Starts bandsaw and positions casting against revolving blade to cut off gate. Scrapes off flash and smooths rough surfaces, using belt-sanding machine, rotary file, and hand knife.
GOE: 06.04.24 STRENGTH: L GED: R2 M1 L1 SVP: 2 DLU: 77

701 OCCUPATIONS IN FABRICATION, ASSEMBLY, AND REPAIR OF TOOLS, AND RELATED PRODUCTS

This group includes occupations concerned with hand forging, straightening, tempering, sharpening, assembling, repairing, and reconditioning handtools used in woodworking, metalworking, ceramics, construction, mechanics, agriculture, masonry, sheet metal, jewelry, and watchmaking; setting, filing, welding, or otherwise reconditioning circular or bandsaw blades; and grinding or otherwise reconditioning twist drills, reamers, lathe bits, and other cutting tools used in power and machine tools.

701.137-010 SUPERVISOR, ASSEMBLY-AND-PACKING (cutlery-hrdwr.)
Supervises and coordinates activities of workers engaged in painting and assembling can opener parts, packing completed can opener parts, and packing completed can openers. Performs duties as described under SUPERVISOR (any industry) Master Title.
GOE: 06.04.01 STRENGTH: L GED: R4 M3 L3 SVP: 7 DLU: 77

701.261-010 QUALITY-CONTROL INSPECTOR (cutlery-hrdwr.)
Inspects completed handtools and parts in process, using statistical sampling techniques and following printed procedures, to evaluate quality of products: Selects, according to sampling tables, percentage of production lot of tools, such as planes, bit braces, levels, garden shears, tape, and folding rules. Examines tool or part to judge quality of finish and to detect visible flaws, such as cracks in castings. Measures dimensions and angles for conformance with blueprint or tabular specifications, using measuring instruments. Tests hardness of metal components [HARDNESS INSPECTOR (heat treating)]. Moves working parts of tool by hand to judge smoothness of action. Function tests mitre boxes and saws by making trial cuts to verify accuracy of mitre gauge and absence of saw run-out. Secures drill bit or counter bore in powered chuck and bores holes in wood to evaluate cutting action. Records findings on chart. Rejects or accepts entire production lot according to quality of sample inspected. Notifies supervisor when sampling indicates progressive deterioration in product quality, in order that corrections can be made in machine setup or operating procedure to forestall production of unacceptable work. Verifies accuracy of production gauges against master gauges. Computes percentages, ratios, and proportions of product-quality deviations in order to prepare engineering reports and analyses.
GOE: 06.01.05 STRENGTH: L GED: R4 M3 L3 SVP: 6 DLU: 77

701.381-010 REPAIRER, HANDTOOLS (cutlery-hrdwr.)
Repairs handtools, such as planes, vises, bit braces, levels, tape rules and mitre boxes: Examines defective tools to determine from experience, nature of defect or cause of malfunction, and possibility of repair. Disassembles tool, using screwdrivers, hammers, chisels, punches, and files. Operates power tools, such as drill press, power press, and handmilling machine, to remove screws, pins, rivets, bushings, collars, and jackets. Replaces defective part or repairs part, using files, reaming tools, and vise. Verifies dimensions, straightness, and concentricity of parts, using gauges. Reassembles tool, using hand and power equipment [ASSEMBLER (cutlery-hrdwr.)]. Records nature and extent of repairs performed. Maintains stock of parts.
GOE: 05.10.02 STRENGTH: L GED: R3 M2 L2 SVP: 5 DLU: 77

701.381-014 SAW FILER (any industry) alternate titles: filer
Repairs bandsaw, handsaw, and circular saw blades according to customer's or manufacturer's specifications, using handtools, machine tools, and welding equipment: Examines saw for defects. Cuts broken teeth from saw, using power shear [SHEAR OPERATOR (any industry) I]. Forms teeth on saw blade by beveling joints on grinder and welding or brazing them together. Brazes or welds cracks in saw blades. Straightens twists and kinks in blades, using

straightening press, and hammers out dents in blade on metal table. Adjusts cutting width of teeth, using swage or special pliers. Computes number and angle of teeth to produce specified cut. Clamps blade in saw-filing machine and turns handwheel to adjust distance between teeth, angle of bevel, and depth of cut of file or abrasive wheel. Starts machine that automatically grinds and files saw teeth. May be designated according to type of saw sharpened as Band-Saw Filer (any industry); Circular-Saw Filer (any industry).
GOE: 05.05.07 STRENGTH: M GED: R3 M3 L3 SVP: 6 DLU: 77

701.381-018 TOOL GRINDER I (any industry) alternate titles: cutlery grinder; tool sharpener

Sharpens shears, scissors, hair clippers, surgical instruments, cleavers, and other fine-edged cutting tools, using whetstone and grinding and polishing wheels: Holds cutting edge of tool against rotating wheel or clamps tool in holder or carriage to steady it during sharpening process. Sharpens surgical instruments and razors, using fine-grained grinding wheels, and hones them on whetstone. May sharpen handsaws. May brush heated mixture of glue and grit onto worn grinding wheels to rebuild them. May specialize in sharpening barbers' tools and be designated Barber-Tool Sharpener (any industry). May specialize in sharpening shears and scissors and be designated Scissors Grinder (any industry). May specialize in sharpening tools and implements in homes and business establishments and be designated Grinder (any industry) III.
GOE: 05.05.07 STRENGTH: L GED: R3 M2 L2 SVP: 6 DLU: 77

701.384-010 TOOL-MAINTENANCE WORKER (office machines)

Repairs and adjusts handtools and power tools used in assembling, adjusting, and aligning typewriters: Examines tools for wear and tear. Tests operation of pnuematic tool, such as power socket wrench and power screwdriver, by driving home nuts and screws and by verifying tightness, using handtools, torque wrench, or torque screwdriver. Sharpens and squares ends of screwdrivers, using bench grinder. Brazes or solders loose handles to tools, using gas torch. Repairs or replaces defective jaws of special pliers and wooden tool handles, using mallet and vise. Straightens bent tool shanks in vise or by tapping tool shanks with hammer. Dismantles, cleans, and oils motors for power tools. Discards irreparable tools and requisitions and distributes replacements. May repair worn or defective tool parts, using bench lathes, cut-off machine, drill press, and machinists' tools.
GOE: 06.02.24 STRENGTH: L GED: R2 M1 L1 SVP: 3 DLU: 77

701.684-010 CALIBRATOR (cutlery-hrdwr.)

Calibrates and repairs torque and other wrenches, using test scale and handtools: Sets wrench indicator on end of wrench handle to maximum setting and inserts head of wrench into socket on test scale. Twists wrench until wrench mechanism releases and notes corresponding indication on scale. Adjusts wrench mechanism so that indications on scale coincide with releases of torque wrench, using allen wrench. Disassembles defective wrenches, examines parts, and replaces or repairs parts, using handtools.
GOE: 06.04.24 STRENGTH: L GED: R2 M1 L2 SVP: 4 DLU: 77

701.684-014 INSPECTOR, OPEN DIE (cutlery-hrdwr.)

Inspects cutting dies for conformance with specifications: Examines dies for defects, such as uneven or distorted cutting edge, and for correct identification number. Verifies dimensions of die face, using template. Tags defective dies and routes them to repair shop.
GOE: 06.03.02 STRENGTH: L GED: R3 M2 L2 SVP: 4 DLU: 77

701.684-018 LEVEL-VIAL SETTER (cutlery-hrdwr.) alternate titles: glass setter

Mounts glass vials in level bodies (frames) or vial cases: Inserts vial in body or case, and holds vial in position, using specially designed holder, wood wedges, or paper. Mixes plaster with liquids to desired consistency. Levels frame or case on bench plate, or clamps it in fixture and applies plaster around enclosed vial, using handtools. Adjusts vial to center bubble and smooths plaster, using trowel. Removes excess plaster, using handtools and compressed air-hose.
GOE: 06.04.23 STRENGTH: L GED: R2 M1 L1 SVP: 3 DLU: 77

701.684-022 SAW SETTER (stonework) alternate titles: saw maker

Maintains stonecutting saws in operating condition: Removes broken and bent saw blades from gangsaws. Cuts new blades and cuts holes in ends of blades for mounting in saw frame, using cutting torch. Straightens bent blades, using hammer. Spaces, tightens, and levels blades to set up gangsaws so that stone will be cut, according to specifications. May direct workers engaged in setting blocks of stone on cars to see that they are properly squared and leveled for cutting on gangsaws.
GOE: 05.10.01 STRENGTH: M GED: R3 M1 L2 SVP: 5 DLU: 77

701.684-026 SAW-EDGE FUSER, CIRCULAR (cutlery-hrdwr.)

Fuses diamond and carbon edges to circular steel saw blades, using oven: Weighs carbide, nickel, iron, and diamond ingredients in specified percentages on jeweler's scale. Pours compound in form clamped to saw-blank edges, and places saw blank in oven at preset temperature and under specified atmospheric conditions to fuse compound to saw edge. May operate metalworking tools, such as grinder, lathe, and drill press, to finish edge of saw. May measure edge of saw with micrometer and pressure gauges.
GOE: 06.04.32 STRENGTH: M GED: R2 M2 L2 SVP: 3 DLU: 77

701.684-030 TOOL FILER (pottery & porc.)

Repairs iron and steel tools used by POTTER (pottery & porc.) to form pottery and porcelain ware: Clamps tool to template in vise. Selects files for par-

ticular metal, and files edge of tools to correct contour, following template outline. Inspects reworked tools for adherence to specifications, using templates and angle gauges. May fabricate master tools and templates from rough drawings.
GOE: 05.12.13 STRENGTH: L GED: R3 M1 L2 SVP: 5 DLU: 77

701.687-010 ASSEMBLER (cutlery-hrdwr.) alternate titles: pinner

Joins parts, such as handles, blades, gears, or springs to assemble articles, such as pliers, knives, razors, shears, knife sharpeners, can openers, and ice crushers: Positions parts together, following guides such as holes, edges, and prongs. Rivets, bolts, or screws parts together, using hammer, riveting machine, wrench, or pneumatic screwdriver. May drill, ream, or tap holes in parts of pliers, using drill press. May use clamps, pneumatic or screw presses, and other work aids to hold parts during assembly. May be designated according to article assembled as Assembler, Knife (cutlery-hrdwr.); Electric-Razor Assembler (cutlery-hrdwr.); Shear Assembler (cutlery-hrdwr.).
GOE: 06.04.23 STRENGTH: L GED: R2 M1 L2 SVP: 2 DLU: 77

701.687-014 BLADE BALANCER (agric. equip.)

Weighs lawnmower cutting blades and sorts them into stacks according to weight to ensure that blades of approximately equal weight will be mounted on each mower.
GOE: 06.03.02 STRENGTH: L GED: R1 M1 L1 SVP: 2 DLU: 77

701.687-018 COLD-PRESS LOADER (cutlery-hrdwr.) alternate titles: laborer, cutting tool

Places steel saw blade cores, mixed or segmented diamond materials, and silver solder into molds preparatory to firing core in furnace: Inserts precut silver solder wire into groove in top graphite mold. Places steel blade core in bottom graphite mold. Positions segmented diamonds onto core edge according to size of core, or pours diamond mixture into notches on saw blade edge. Places top mold over bottom mold and lays it on firing platform. May requisition, weigh, and blend diamonds and metal powder alloys. May stamp serial number on saw blade. May be designated according to form of saw blade edge as Notched-Blade Loader (cutlery-hrdwr.).
GOE: 06.04.32 STRENGTH: L GED: R2 M1 L2 SVP: 3 DLU: 77

701.687-022 LEVEL-VIAL CURVATURE GAUGER (cutlery-hrdwr.) alternate titles: glass curvature gauger

Gauges length and degree of curvature of level glasses (vials), using gauge indicator, and sorts or rejects them according to differences in values: Positions vial against indicator button in fixture of machine. Observes point of maximum curve of vial on gauge indicator and rejects vials that do not fall within specified degrees.
GOE: 06.03.02 STRENGTH: L GED: R2 M1 L2 SVP: 3 DLU: 77

701.687-026 LEVEL-VIAL INSPECTOR-AND-TESTER (cutlery-hrdwr.) alternate titles: inspector

Examines and gauges level vials for conformance to specifications and tests for leakage: Loads boxes of sealed vials into evaporating oven, and examines heated vials to detect fluid-loss due to leakage. Gauges length of vials, using go-not-go gauge, and examines vials for clarity of guidelines. Sorts completed vials according to position of bubble in relation to guidelines, to match vials in levels containing more than one vial. May be known according to specific task assigned as Final Inspector (cutlery-hrdwr.); Tester (cutlery-hrdwr.); Vial Gauger (cutlery-hrdwr.).
GOE: 06.03.02 STRENGTH: L GED: R2 M1 L2 SVP: 3 DLU: 77

701.687-030 POWER-CHISEL OPERATOR (cutlery-hrdwr.) alternate titles: featherer

Trims wooden handles of hammers, axes, and hatchets, using portable power chisel, to remove curled shavings (feathers) raised on handle by steel edges of eye when tool head is driven onto handle.
GOE: 06.04.25 STRENGTH: L GED: R2 M1 L1 SVP: 2 DLU: 77

701.687-034 WEDGER, MACHINE (cutlery-hrdwr.)

Mounts steel axe and hatchet heads on wooden handles, using power hammer: Starts slotted end of handle into eye of tool, using hand hammer. Places assembled workpiece headup under power hammer, and moves controls to lower hammer that drives tool head onto handle. Inserts wooden wedge in handle slot, and moves controls to hammer wedge into slot. May operate table saw to trim excess wood from tool eye. May trim end of handle, using abrasive wheel. May mount steel hammer heads on wooden handles manually, using chisel and hammer.
GOE: 06.04.23 STRENGTH: M GED: R2 M1 L1 SVP: 2 DLU: 77

703 OCCUPATIONS IN ASSEMBLY AND REPAIR OF SHEETMETAL PRODUCTS, N.E.C.

This group includes occupations, not elsewhere classified, concerned with laying out, cutting, shaping, and fitting ferrous or nonferrous sheet metal to assemble or repair sheet metal parts and items. Structural sheet metal occupations are included in Division 80.

703.132-010 SUPERVISOR, METAL CANS (tinware)

Supervises and coordinates activities of workers engaged in fabricating tin cans, pails, and other tinware from cut, pressed, or shaped tinplate. Trains new workers. Confers with workers' representatives to resolve grievances. Performs duties as described under SUPERVISOR (any industry) Master Title.

GOE: 06.02.01 STRENGTH: L GED: R4 M3 L3 SVP: 7 DLU: 77

703.381-010 PATTERNMAKER (stonework)
Lays out and cuts sheet metal patterns used to cut stones for building and monuments, working according to blueprints: Calculates dimensions of pattern from blueprints or scale drawings. Lays out and draws pattern on sheet of metal, using square, rule, compass, scribe, and marking pencil. Cuts pattern from sheet, using hand shears. Measures and compares pattern with specification, using rule and caliper. Marks identification figures on pattern and files it in rack according to markings. May draw scale drawings of stone blocks from rough or detailed sketches.
GOE: 05.05.06 STRENGTH: L GED: R4 M3 L3 SVP: 7 DLU: 77

703.684-010 BENCH-SHEAR OPERATOR (furniture)
Cuts sheet metal furniture parts to shape with hand-operated bench shears: Scribes cutting lines on one sheet or receives sample sheet marked by another worker. Places sheet in shears with one line of cut on edge of lower knife. Pulls lever to cut sheet along line. Advances sheet into shears as separate cuts are made on scribed lines until shape is completely cut. Marks other sheets as desired, using first sheet as pattern, and cuts parts from sheets.
GOE: 06.02.25 STRENGTH: M GED: R3 M1 L2 SVP: 5 DLU: 77

703.684-014 CUPBOARD BUILDER (furniture) alternate titles: cabinet finisher
Assembles metal cabinets: Inserts pins in hinges to attach doors to cabinet. Attaches stationary knobs in place with screws. Fits, assembles, and attaches locks to doors. Measures and drills support holes in shelves and shelf brackets and screws shelves in place. Adjusts doors, knobs, and shelves to fit by bending, filing, or hammering them, using handtools.
GOE: 06.02.22 STRENGTH: L GED: R3 M1 L2 SVP: 4 DLU: 77

703.684-018 TEMPLATE CUTTER (cutlery-hrdwr.)
Cuts out metal templates for cutting dies following master pattern, using shears and files: Staples pattern onto sheet metal to form outline for cutting operation, using stapling machine. Cuts template along pattern edge, using shears and file. Removes pattern from template, using hammers and punch. Marks identifying information, such as type, number, and size onto template, using pen or pencil.
GOE: 06.04.24 STRENGTH: L GED: R2 M2 L2 SVP: 2 DLU: 77

703.685-010 PAIL BAILER (tinware) alternate titles: bail attacher; kinker; snapper-on
Tends machine that automatically attaches bails (handles) to pails: Feeds coil of wire into machine, and places plastic handles that are attached automatically to bail by machine into hopper. Turns knobs to time movement of pails on conveyor for attachment of bails. Observes operation of machine to detect jams and malfunctions. Inserts bails in pails missed by machine, using handtool. Inspects bails for quality and reports irregularities to supervisor. May tend machine that fabricates bails for use on metal containers, or welds handles to can covers.
GOE: 06.04.02 STRENGTH: L GED: R3 M1 L2 SVP: 3 DLU: 77

703.685-014 TESTING-MACHINE OPERATOR (tinware) alternate titles: can tester; pail tester
Tends can testing machine that automatically tests cans for leaks: Starts machine and observes operation of machine and conveyor on which cans are carried through machine. Notifies supervisor of defective operation of machine or conveyor. Verifies accuracy of test machine, using standard test can. Places rejected cans on water tester and pulls lever to inject water into cans to indicate leaks. Marks location of leaks for can repairer, using crayon. May apply flux to inside of ear clincher or side seams of can, using flux applicator and reheat soldered seams under gas flame to seal leaks. May reshape bent or dented cans on metal form with mallet. May reheat soldered seams under gas flame to seal leaks. Retests repaired cans. May record number of cans rejected and repaired.
GOE: 06.03.02 STRENGTH: L GED: R2 M1 L1 SVP: 2 DLU: 77

703.687-010 ASSORTER (steel & rel.)
Inspects tinplate for defects and for conformance to specified weight, size, and gauge, and classifies material according to quality: Examines sheets for defects, such as insufficient coating, holes, dirt, bows, or twists. Wipes grease from sheets with cloth and straightens bent corners with handtool. Measures gauge of sheets, using micrometers, and compares measurements with customer specifications. Weighs sheets on scale. Sorts sheets according to defects found and places sheets in piles. Marks identifying information on piles with eraser.
GOE: 06.03.02 STRENGTH: L GED: R3 M2 L2 SVP: 4 DLU: 77

703.687-014 METAL-FINISH INSPECTOR (any industry)
Inspects surfaces of sheet metal articles, such as refrigerator and freezer cabinets, or automobile bodies for burrs, dings, scratches, laminated metal, or other surface defects prior to painting or porcelainizing: Rubs gloved hand over surfaces and examines workpiece. Marks defects for repair, using knowledge of acceptable metal finish standards and specifications. Records recurring defects on inspection report and submits report to quality control department for action. Records and submits daily inspection report.
GOE: 06.03.02 STRENGTH: L GED: R3 M2 L2 SVP: 5 DLU: 77

703.687-018 METAL-FINISH INSPECTOR (furniture)
Examines interior and exterior of assembled lacquered, enameled, or varnished pieces of metal furniture for defects in finish or construction. Rejects

faulty pieces and returns pieces to proper departments for correction. Applies manufacturer's label to accepted pieces.
GOE: 06.03.02 STRENGTH: L GED: R3 M1 L2 SVP: 4 DLU: 77

703.687-022 STEEL-BARREL REAMER (wood. container)
Enlarges and shapes rivet hole in side of steel barrel, using hand reamer.
GOE: 06.04.24 STRENGTH: L GED: R1 M1 L1 SVP: 2 DLU: 77

704 ENGRAVERS, ETCHERS, AND RELATED OCCUPATIONS

This group includes occupations concerned with engraving or etching designs or lettering into surface of flat or curved metal objects, using engravers' handtools and machines or etching acids and inks. Photoengravers and printing plate, die, and roller engravers are included in Division 97.

704.131-010 ENGRAVING SUPERVISOR (engraving)
Supervises and coordinates activities of workers engaged in hand and machine engraving of dies, jewelry, notarial seals, and silverware: Trains new workers. Examines engraved items for conformity to specifications, using mandrel, caliper, and ruler. May lay out patterns for workers [PATTERNMAKER (engraving)]. May be designated according to specification as Die-Engraving Supervisor (engraving); Jewelry-Engraving Supervisor (engraving; jewelry-silver.). Performs other tasks as described under SUPERVISOR (any industry) Master Title.
GOE: 01.06.01 STRENGTH: L GED: R4 M3 L3 SVP: 8 DLU: 77

704.131-014 SUPERVISOR, ENGRAVING (pen & pencil)
Supervises and coordinates activities of workers engaged in fabrication of marking devices, badges, and memorial plates: Interprets customers' orders and assigns and directs workers engaged in selecting size and style of characters used, typesetting master pattern and setup of pantograph for reproduction of pattern, and layout and hand engraving or fabrication of seals, memorial plates, badges, metal tags, and stencils. Inspects in-process and finished work for compliance with customers' orders and quality standards. May operate presses and pantograph, or assist in setting them up. Performs other duties as described under SUPERVISOR (any industry) Master Title.
GOE: 01.06.01 STRENGTH: L GED: R4 M3 L3 SVP: 8 DLU: 77

704.381-010 CHASER (jewelry-silver.)
Reproduces decorative designs on items made of silver, gold, platinum, and other metals, from photographs or drawings: Outlines design on surface of article, using handtools. Positions hollowware over snarling tool (forming head) and raises design area, using foot-powered hammer. Strikes small tools with hammer to indent design area. Pours molten pitch into article to serve as foundation. Melts pitch with blowtorch to remove pitch from completed article. Cuts designs in castings of lamp bases and ornamental statuary.
GOE: 01.06.02 STRENGTH: L GED: R4 M2 L3 SVP: 6 DLU: 77

704.381-014 CHEMICAL-ETCHING PROCESSOR (aircraft mfg.) alternate titles: chemical-milling processor; etcher, aircraft
Etches specified portions of metal parts and materials used in manufacturing aircraft, using immersion equipment, templates, handtools, and precision measuring instruments: Reads work order, blueprints, and process specifications to determine location of etch, finished dimensions, and method and sequence of operations. Cleans surface of parts and materials to ensure uniform adhesion of maskant. Applies maskant to surfaces to be etched, scribes etch lines, using template, and removes maskant from etch areas. Immerses parts and materials in etching solution for specified time, manually or using hoist. Removes objects from etch solution, rinses objects with water, and removes remaining maskant. Measures etched parts and materials for conformance to specifications, using micrometers, scales, and other precision measuring instruments. May immerse parts and materials in successive baths and rinses to perform surface processing in addition to etching, such as pickling, chromodizing, passivating, degreasing, and stripping, and be designated Process Equipment Operator (aircraft mfg.).
GOE: 06.01.04 STRENGTH: M GED: R3 M2 L3 SVP: 6 DLU: 88

704.381-018 ENGINE TURNER (jewelry-silver.)
Cuts designs or lines in jewelry by machine: Marks design or line on jewelry, using ruler and scriber, following sample, sketch, photograph, or standard pattern. Clamps article of jewelry in holding device of machine and cuts design by moving cutting tool along guidelines. Observes progress of work through magnifying glass attached to cutting tool. Sharpens cutting tool.
GOE: 01.06.01 STRENGTH: S GED: R3 M2 L2 SVP: 6 DLU: 77

704.381-022 ENGRAVER APPRENTICE, DECORATIVE (engraving)
Performs duties as described under APPRENTICE (any industry) Master Title.
GOE: 01.06.01 STRENGTH: S GED: R3 M2 L2 SVP: 7 DLU: 77

704.381-026 ENGRAVER, HAND, HARD METALS (engraving)
Lays out and cuts lettering and designs on surfaces of hard metal for hobs, dies, and molds or plates used to imprint designs on paper, metal, plastic, or porcelain products, following sketches and blueprints, and using engraving tools: Computes dimensions of lettering and design, and marks or scribes layout lines on workpiece, using drawing tools, such as straightedge, compass, and scriber. Positions workpiece in vise and cuts designs in surface of workpiece or trims precut designs, using gravers, punches, files, hammer, and shaped

chisels. Sharpens and forms cutting edge of gravers on cutter grinder [TOOL-GRINDER OPERATOR (machine shop)]. May sketch original design for customer. May enlarge or reduce reproduction of pattern according to size of article to be made. May brush surface of metal with acidproof paint to prevent corrosion. May be designated according to type of imprinting device engraved as Stencil Maker (engraving).
GOE: 01.06.01 STRENGTH: M GED: R4 M3 L3 SVP: 8 DLU: 77

704.381-030 ENGRAVER, HAND, SOFT METALS (engraving) alternate titles: carver; decorator

Engraves lettering and ornamental designs on soft metal articles, such as silverware, trophies, aluminum or plastic eyeglass frames, and jewelry articles, according to sketches, diagrams, photographs, or sample workpieces, using engraver's handtools: Lays out design or lettering to be engraved on object by brushing chalklike powder or solution on item and sketching design in powder, locating reference points, and marking outline of design on item, using scribers or gravers, or by imprinting design on surface of item, using inked rubber stamp, and marking outline, using scribers. Mounts piece in chuck and affixes chuck in jeweler's ball (rotating vise) or mounts piece directly in jeweler's ball. Cuts design in workpiece, using chisel-like engraving tools. May sketch original designs. May be designated according to kind of product engraved as Engraver, Flatware (engraving); Engraver, Jewelry (engraving); Engraver, Optical Frames (engraving); or according to specialty as Engraver, Lettering (engraving); Engraver, Ornamental Design (engraving).
GOE: 01.06.01 STRENGTH: S GED: R3 M2 L2 SVP: 7 DLU: 77

704.381-034 ENGRAVER, SEALS (pen & pencil)

Engraves characters and designs in surface of die according to customers' copy or specification, and casts corresponding male die for use in seals, such as corporate or notary seals: Marks vertical centerline on blank or prestamped dies, using compass. Selects style and size of characters and visually spaces characters from centerline to obtain symmetry. Engraves characters in surface of die, using hand stamps and mallet, and restamps closed or distorted characters. Cleans die, using wire brush. Installs finished female die in device (splash) used to impress die in molten seal metal (lead alloy) to form male die (counter). Melts metal in gas-fired crucible and ladles metal onto aluminum foil sheet placed on base of splash. Drops die into metal and allows it to cool. Removes dies from splash, files notch in both to ensure alignment in seal press, and trims excess metal from counter, using knife. Oils faces of dies to prevent sticking. Applies adhesive fabric (sticky-back) to base and ram of press and aligns and mounts dies. Imprints seal on purchase order to verify copy.
GOE: 01.06.01 STRENGTH: S GED: R4 M2 L3 SVP: 6 DLU: 77

704.382-010 ENGRAVER, PANTOGRAPH I (engraving) alternate titles: prototype-machine operator

Sets up and operates pantograph engraving machine to engrave designs or lettering on engraving dies, nameplates, stamps or seals, following two or three-dimensional pattern or blueprint: Positions and secures pattern to workpiece on cutting table, using rule, square, calipers, and fixtures. Sets reduction scale and controls of pantograph to attain specified size of reproduction on workpiece and height, depth, and width of cut. Sharpens cutting tools on cutter grinder [TOOL-GRINDER OPERATOR (machine shop)]. Inserts cutting tool into spindle of machine and secures it with wrench. Starts machine and lowers stylus to beginning point on pattern. Guides stylus over pattern. Observes action of cutting tool and adjusts movement of stylus to ensure accurate reproduction and verifies conformance to specifications, using micrometers and calipers. May observe action of cutting tool through microscope.
GOE: 05.10.05 STRENGTH: M GED: R3 M2 L2 SVP: 6 DLU: 77

704.582-010 ENGRAVER, MACHINE II (engraving)

Operates engraving machine to inscribe letters on flat metal surfaces: Slides master lettering plates onto fixture according to sequence specified on work order. Adjusts gauge on arms of machine according to size of letters. Centers and clamps blank plate on machine. Moves lever that lowers diamond cutting point onto plate. Guides dummy point, that controls cut, over lettering on master plate to inscribe letters on metal.
GOE: 05.10.05 STRENGTH: L GED: R3 M2 L2 SVP: 3 DLU: 77

704.682-010 ENGRAVER, MACHINE I (engraving)

Operates pantograph engraving machine to engrave letters and figures on products, such as badges, fraternal emblems, pendants, and thermometers: Inserts specified letters and figures into pattern frame. Positions and secures workpiece in machine holding fixture and sets stylus at beginning of pattern. Depresses pedal to lower cutting tool onto workpiece. Engraves designs on workpiece by moving stylus around pattern, causing cutting tool to duplicate motion on workpiece. Removes workpiece and places in tray.
GOE: 05.10.05 STRENGTH: S GED: R3 M2 L2 SVP: 3 DLU: 77

704.682-014 ENGRAVER, PANTOGRAPH II (engraving)

Engraves specified characters on metal blanks of articles, such as trophies, trays, badges, and plaques, according to work order: Positions and locks blank metal plate in holding fixture beneath rotary cutting tool. Selects specified lettering template and places template beneath stylus attached to machine cutting tool. Turns knob on machine to set reduction scale to obtain required reproduction ratio on metal plate. Starts machine and guides stylus over template, causing cutting tool to simultaneously duplicate characters on metal plate. Cleans chips from metal plate, using airhose. Examines engraving for quality of cut, burrs, and rough spots. May increase or decrease depth of cut by adjusting

height of worktable. May wipe acid over engraving to darken or highlight inscription. May assemble trophies, using wood base, bolts, and wrench.
GOE: 05.10.05 STRENGTH: L GED: R3 M2 L2 SVP: 3 DLU: 77

704.684-010 ETCHER (engraving)

Etches designs, lettering, and figures on processed plates of brass, steel, copper, zinc, magnesium, or plastic: Mixes acid solution according to formula, and pours mixture into etching tank. Places plate on rack in etching tank, sets tank timing controls, and starts machine that sprays plate with corrosive solution. Removes plate periodically, and measures depth to which metal has been etched, using gauge. Inspects plate to ensure that design is not undercut. Washes plate to remove etching powder and protective ink. May brush etching powder on surface of plate to prevent undercutting of reproduction.
GOE: 01.06.01 STRENGTH: L GED: R3 M2 L2 SVP: 6 DLU: 77

704.684-014 SILK-SCREEN ETCHER (engraving) alternate titles: etcher, hand

Etches lettering, trademarks, or designs through silk screen onto metal objects, such as plates, jewelry, trophies, cutlery, and tools: Positions object to be etched on setup board. Places silk screen of specified design or lettering over object. Brushes specified acid solution through silk screen to etch design on object. Rinses workpiece in neutralizing solution after specified time to remove acid, or places it on conveyor which carries workpiece into bath. May brush acid resistant solution through screen and place workpiece into acid bath to etch pattern on unprotected surface.
GOE: 06.04.24 STRENGTH: L GED: R2 M1 L1 SVP: 3 DLU: 77

704.687-010 CLEANER (engraving) alternate titles: white-work cleaner

Removes excess paint from metal stampings to bring out etched or embossed pattern or lettering, by rubbing surface of pattern with cloth and solvent: Separates stampings that are scratched or marred, or that have been imperfectly finished. May apply paint to unpainted areas of stampings overlooked during painting process, using brush. May remove masking compound from specified areas of metal parts to be chemically etched, using template outline and knife.
GOE: 06.04.39 STRENGTH: L GED: R1 M1 L1 SVP: 2 DLU: 77

704.687-014 ETCHER, HAND (cutlery-hrdwr.)

Etches trademarks on stainless steel knives and forks, using rubber stamp and acid solution: Ties cloth around glass block and pours acid on cloth to form stamp pad. Places cutlery in lime bath. Removes cutlery from bath, presses rubber stamp on acid pad, and stamps cutlery.
GOE: 06.04.24 STRENGTH: L GED: R2 M1 L1 SVP: 3 DLU: 77

705 FILING, GRINDING, BUFFING, CLEANING, AND POLISHING OCCUPATIONS, N.E.C.

This group includes occupations, not elsewhere classified, concerned with filing, grinding, buffing, cleaning, and polishing metal, plastic, or rubber parts or objects other than by use of production machines. Tool sharpening occupations are included in Group 701.

705.381-010 DIE BARBER (machine shop)

Rough-finishes stamping-die-member surfaces, using abrasives and abrading handtools: Lifts and positions die member on bench manually or with hoist. Brushes blue pigment on ridges and grooves left by milling operation. Grinds ridges down until only traces of pigment are visible at bottom of grooves. Uses variety of files, stones, and abrasive cloths and papers to shape and smooth die member. May repair punch and die sets, using bench lathe, portable grinder, and polisher, and abrasive handtools.
GOE: 05.05.06 STRENGTH: M GED: R3 M1 L2 SVP: 7 DLU: 77

705.381-014 EXTRUSION-DIE REPAIRER (nonfer. metal)

Repairs aluminum extrusion dies, according to specifications, using powered handtools: Examines exterior of dies for defects, such as cracks or excessive wear, and observes exterior surface of extrusion samples to determine whether inside of dies need resurfacing or polishing. Secures dies in vise, and determines amount of metal to remove from die opening to restore die to specifications, using diagram and gauges. Selects abrasive bit and secures it in electric tool, and moves tool over die opening surface to remove, polish, or angle surface to specifications, utilizing experience and knowledge of dies. Heats dies with stress cracks in oven to soften metal and taps sides of dies to close cracks, using hammer and bit. Removes rough spots from exterior of repaired dies, using electric deburring tool. Verifies openings of new dies, using calipers and gauges, and monitors sample extrusions to determine whether press dies need repair.
GOE: 05.05.06 STRENGTH: L GED: R3 M3 L3 SVP: 6 DLU: 86

705.384-010 SCRAPER, HAND (machine shop) alternate titles: hand scraper; scraper

Scrapes metal workpieces with handtools to smooth machine ways, surface plates, and bearing surfaces to ensure free action of parts: Positions workpiece on worktable, in vise, or in fixture, and secures it with clamps and wrenches. Files and grinds burrs from workpiece. Applies pigment to surface plate with brush, cloth, or sponge. Positions workpiece and surface plate against each other, rubs one surface against other to determine high spots. Selects hand scraper and scrapes workpiece surface to remove high spots indicated by pigment pattern. Repeats operation until pigment pattern is even over work surface. May inspect workpiece for conformity to specifications, using such instruments

as dial indicator, height gauge, master, surface plate, and gauge blocks. May use powered hand scraper. May polish and buff steel articles, using portable polisher or buffing brush [POLISHER AND BUFFER (any industry) II].
GOE: 06.02.24 STRENGTH: M GED: R3 M1 L2 SVP: 6 DLU: 77

705.481-010 FILER, FINISH (ordnance)

Finishes and fits together metal small arms parts preparatory to assembly, using handtools and machine tools: Removes burrs and rounds sharp edges, using hammer, chisel, files, and scrapers. Sets up and operates drill press and speed lathe [ENGINE-LATHE SET-UP OPERATOR, TOOL (machine shop)], equipped with rotary file or abrasive wheel to remove burrs, smooth interior surfaces of reamed and tapped holes, and to spot face. Polishes movable parts to ensure smoothness of action, using bench polishing jack. Calculates amount of metal to be removed from parts, using micrometer, scales, and gauges, and files excess metal from parts. Trial fits parts to ensure accurate fit. May imprint serial numbers on parts, using hammer and punch dies. May repair and refinish damaged parts returned by customer and be designated Filer Repairer (ordnance).
GOE: 06.01.04 STRENGTH: M GED: R3 M2 L2 SVP: 5 DLU: 77

705.481-014 LAPPER, HAND, TOOL (machine shop) alternate titles: lap hand, tool; precision lap hand

Laps metal objects, such as gauges and machine parts, to specifications within tolerances as fine as 0.00001 inch, applying knowledge of abrasives and *lapping* procedures: Measures workpiece with instrument, such as optical comparator, compares workpiece dimensions with specifications to ascertain amount of stock to be removed, and estimates number of lapping strokes required. Mounts workpiece in fixture, or in power-driven mechanism, using wrenches and keys, and positions work aids, such as parallel bars and rods to guide motion of *lap I* or workpiece. Files grooves in surface of lap to hold *lapping compound.* Applies compound to workpiece and rubs lap across workpiece with rotary or reciprocating motion, feeling friction and applying required pressure based on previous experience, to attain specified tolerance. Measures workpiece to verify comformance to specifications, using special gauges. Straightens or polishes rods by inserting and pressing them between two rollers with lapping compound.
GOE: 05.05.07 STRENGTH: L GED: R3 M3 L2 SVP: 5 DLU: 77

705.484-010 FILER, HAND, TOOL (machine shop) alternate titles: precision filer, hand; tool filer, hand

Files grooved, contoured, and irregular surfaces of metal objects, such as metalworking dies and machine parts, to conform to templates, other parts, layout, or blueprint specifications: Studies blueprint or layout on workpiece, and selects files according to material, size and shape of work, and amount of stock to be removed, applying knowledge of filing procedures. Files workpiece surface to layout lines, and inspects with magnifying glass. Verifies conformity of finished workpiece by positioning workpiece against template or other part, or by measuring dimensions, using instruments, such as vernier calipers, micrometers, and surface gauges. Smooths and polishes workpiece with emery cloth or power buffer, and feels surface with fingers for smoothness. May lay out workpiece [LAY-OUT WORKER (machine shop)] or saw out template or layout [CONTOUR-BAND-SAW OPERATOR, VERTICAL (machine shop)]. May functionally test workpiece by mounting workpiece in press or with other parts and operating press or machine. May specialize according to product as Die Filer (machine tools).
GOE: 05.05.07 STRENGTH: M GED: R3 M2 L2 SVP: 6 DLU: 77

705.484-014 FINAL FINISHER, FORGING DIES (machine shop) alternate titles: die-finisher, forging; forging-die finisher

Grinds and sands contoured metal surfaces to finish forging dies, using handtools: Selects abrasive tools according to operation and dimensions specified. Manipulates powered hand grinder to remove bead, grind curved surfaces to specified radii, remove machining marks, and smooth die surfaces. Sands surfaces of cavity and gutters to facilitate flow of metal during forging. Manipulates handtools, such as files, stones, and emery cloth, to smooth surfaces. Visually and tactually inspects surfaces for flaws and smoothness.
GOE: 05.05.07 STRENGTH: M GED: R3 M2 L2 SVP: 6 DLU: 77

705.582-010 BLADE GROOVER (cutlery-hrdwr.)

Operates machine to grind decorative grooves in steel knife blades: Marks groove length of blade according to bench marks, using chalk. Places tip of blade under rotating abrasive wheel and presses blade against wheel to grind groove in blade. Examines groove in blade for conformance to specified depth and width and dresses abrasive wheel, using handstone. Turns stop nuts to adjust roll and guide according to width of blade and replaces worn abrasive wheel, using wrenches.
GOE: 06.04.24 STRENGTH: L GED: R2 M1 L1 SVP: 2 DLU: 77

705.682-010 GOLD-NIB GRINDER (pen & pencil)

Operates machine to grind pen points to specified size and shape: Inserts pen point blanks into slots on machine holder and clamps blanks into holder. Starts machine that rotates grinding wheel (copper lathe) and advances pen point blanks against wheel to grind fine, medium, or broad points on blanks. Examines ground points for conformance with specifications. Notifies machine repairer of grinding defects. May observe grinding process through magnifying glass.
GOE: 06.04.02 STRENGTH: L GED: R2 M1 L2 SVP: 2 DLU: 77

705.682-014 TRIMMER (jewelry-silver.) alternate titles: facer; straight edger; tipper

Operates bench grinding machine: Holds stainless steel, silver, and silver-plated flatware against emery coated belt or wheel, shaped to match contour of workpiece, which removes burrs, flash, or pressmarks and rounds edges. May remove burrs, using hand file. May change abrasive belts, using handtools.
GOE: 06.02.02 STRENGTH: L GED: R3 M1 L2 SVP: 4 DLU: 77

705.684-010 BENCH GRINDER (any industry)

Moves metal objects, such as castings, billets, machine parts, sheet metal subassemblies, or arrowheads, against abrasive wheel of bench grinder to grind, smooth, or rough-finish objects to specifications: Clamps workpiece in workholder or jig, or holds it in hands, and feeds it against rotating grinding wheel to remove excess metal, scratches, or burs. Examines or measures workpiece for conformance to standards. Guides dressing tool across wheel to true surface. Replaces worn wheels, using wrench. May position workpiece in automatic feed mechanism. May select and mount abrasive wheels of different grit size to grinder to obtain specified finish on workpiece. May start pump and direct coolant flow against wheel.
GOE: 06.04.24 STRENGTH: M GED: R2 M1 L1 SVP: 3 DLU: 77

705.684-014 BUFFER I (any industry) alternate titles: color buffer

Buffs items, such as automobile trim or accessories, hardware, or fabricated plastic parts with cloth buffing wheel: Holds and moves parts against wheel to smooth surfaces, produce specified finish, or cut down plating defects, such as burns or salt deposits, using knowledge of metals and buffing operations. Coats buffing wheel by holding buffing compound stick against revolving wheel. Pushes and manipulates workpiece against buffing wheel to remove scratches and defects and produce specified finish, using knowledge of buffing operations and finishes. Replaces worn buffs, using wrench. Uses care not to cut through plate when buffing plated surfaces. May be designated according to type of material buffed as Buffer, Chrome (any industry); Buffer, Copper (any industry); Buffer, Nickel (any industry). May polish articles [POLISHER (any industry)] and buff articles and be designated Polisher And Buffer (any industry) I. May polish brass eye castings used in fitting wooden shuttles and clean castings in series of chemical solutions and be designated Strapper And Buffer (woodworking).
GOE: 06.04.24 STRENGTH: M GED: R2 M1 L2 SVP: 4 DLU: 77

705.684-018 FILER AND SANDER (woodworking) alternate titles: sander and filer

Shapes metal eye castings to fit in wooden shuttles: Files and sands eye castings to specified shape and smoothness, using vise, hand files, and emery cloth. Removes completed castings from vise and places castings in containers. Cleans brass particles from files by drawing file card (block of wood with even rows of metal pins attached) through file grooves.
GOE: 06.04.24 STRENGTH: L GED: R2 M1 L1 SVP: 3 DLU: 77

705.684-022 GREASE BUFFER (jewelry-silver.)

Holds and turns silverware, such as bowls, tea sets, trays, or flatware, against grease-coated cloth wheel or leather belt to impart specified finish. May remove scratches, spots, or blemishes with pumice stone. May bolt layers of precut cloth onto spindle and form into buff of desired shape by holding rakelike handtool against rotating cloth. May buff silverware to specified final finish, using soft cloth buffing wheel and fine grained rouge or buffing compound and be designated Finisher (jewelry-silver.).
GOE: 06.02.24 STRENGTH: L GED: R2 M1 L2 SVP: 4 DLU: 77

705.684-026 GRINDER I (any industry)

Grinds and smooths surfaces of items, such as automobile or appliance components, prior to finishing operations, using powered portable wheel, disk, or belt grinder: Examines and feels surface of workpiece for defects. Selects grade of abrasive belt, wheel, or disk according to specifications, knowledge of abrasives, and condition of metal, and attaches to grinder. Starts grinder and moves it over surface of workpiece to remove scratches, laminated metal, excess weld material, and burs. Polishes ground areas with finer abrasive to produce smooth, unmarred surface. Replaces worn abrasive disks, wheels, and belts, using wrench. May be designated according to type of grinder operated as Grinder, Belt (any industry); Grinder, Wheel Or Disk (any industry). May grind leaded-in portions of automobile bodies and be designated Grinder, Lead (auto. mfg.).
GOE: 06.04.24 STRENGTH: M GED: R2 M1 L2 SVP: 3 DLU: 77

705.684-030 GRINDER-CHIPPER I (any industry) alternate titles: grinder-dresser; portable grinder operator

Grinds and chips workpiece to groove, bevel, round, or straighten edges or remove excess stock from metal as specified by drawings, job orders, or guidelines or to remove defects, such as shrink cracks and holes, using portable grinders, chipping hammers, pedestal grinders, and hand files: Positions workpiece manually or by using jib of crane. Inserts selected grinding wheel or cutting chisel into portable grinder or power hammer. Positions and manually guides tool along specified guidelines on edge or surface of workpiece. Inspects work, using rule, straightedge, or template. Grinds portable parts on pedestal grinder. Removes sharp edges or burrs, using hand file. Grinds, chips, or brushes off excess weld, splatter, and rust to improve appearance of workpiece. Sharpens chisels and dresses grinding wheels, using grinder and wheel dresser. May cut excess metal from workpiece, using acetylene torch. May climb large assemblies to remove metal from improperly fabricated parts at direction of FITTER (any industry) I or WELDER-FITTER (welding). May be designated according to tool used as Chipper (any industry) I; Grinder (any industry) II.

GOE: 06.02.24 STRENGTH: H GED: R3 M2 L2 SVP: 4 DLU: 77

705.684-034 METAL FINISHER (any industry)
Grinds, files, or sands surfaces of metal items, such as automobile bodies and household appliances, using handtools, power tools, and knowledge of metal finishing techniques: Examines and feels surface of metal to detect defects, such as dents, scratches, or breaks in metal. Removes dents, using hammer and dolly block, and fills uneven surface with molten solder. Smooths surface of item to specified finish, using handtools and powered tools. May polish metal surface, using powered polishing wheel or belt [POLISHER (any industry)].
GOE: 06.04.24 STRENGTH: L GED: R2 M1 L2 SVP: 4 DLU: 77

705.684-038 MOLD FINISHER (machine shop)
Shapes and smooths metal surfaces to finish molds, using handtools: Lifts partially completed mold half with hoist, and positions and secures in holding fixture. Removes burrs and smooths contoured surfaces with powered hand grinder. Positions and hammers specified handtool against mold surface to make sharper impression. Verifies contour of impression with templates. Applies blue pigment to mold surfaces, and presses mold halves together manually to locate high spots. Fits and installs nameplate in mold, using handtools. Inserts preformed metal tabs into slots in mold, verifies height of each insert with preset dial indicator, and hammers mold metal around inserts with pneumatic hammer to secure them. Performs other hand scraping, sanding, and brushing tasks, using handtools, to shape and smooth mold. May make own handtools.
GOE: 06.02.24 STRENGTH: M GED: R3 M2 L2 SVP: 5 DLU: 77

705.684-042 MOTHER REPAIRER (recording)
Repairs metal phonograph record *mother* (matrix): Examines matrix to locate inspection markings that indicate defects, using microscope or magnifying glass. Removes defects, such as bubbles, dirt, and particles of nickel in sound track grooves, using needles and cloths moistened with solvents. Wipes surface of matrix with cleaning solvent to remove inspection markings.
GOE: 06.02.24 STRENGTH: L GED: R3 M2 L2 SVP: 4 DLU: 77

705.684-046 NEEDLE POLISHER (button & notion)
Polishes industrial sewing and knitting needles, using buffing wheels: Picks up rack of needles, using tongs and holds needles against buffing wheels to polish needles to specification. Examines needles by feel and using eye loupe to determine if polished surface meets specifications. Conditions surface of buffing wheels, balances wheels, and aligns tongs to maintain polishing equipment, using handtools. Records quantity of needles polished, date polished, and initials work ticket.
GOE: 06.04.24 STRENGTH: M GED: R2 M1 L1 SVP: 3 DLU: 77

705.684-050 NIB FINISHER (pen & pencil)
Smooths and polishes tips of fountain pen nibs, following specifications and using polishing compounds and abrasive cloths and papers: Applies polishing compound, such as rouge, emery, garnet, or other abrasive cloths or paper. Presses and rotates nib on abrasive cloth or paper to polish it to specified smoothness. Wipes polished nib with cloth and inspects surface for smoothness with magnifying glass and by feeling with fingertips.
GOE: 06.04.24 STRENGTH: L GED: R2 M1 L2 SVP: 4 DLU: 77

705.684-054 PIPE BUFFER (construction)
Cleans and polishes end of pipe, prior to welding in pipeline construction, using portable buffing machine. May operate portable gasoline motor generator to provide electric power for buffer.
GOE: 05.12.18 STRENGTH: M GED: R2 M1 L1 SVP: 2 DLU: 77

705.684-058 POLISHER (any industry)
Removes excess metal and surface defects from such items as hardware, small arms barrels, automobile trim, or accessory parts prior to buffing, bluing, or plating, using revolving abrasive wheel or belt: Selects abrasive belt or wheel according to grain size, type of finish specified, product being polished, or amount of metal to be removed, using knowledge of polishing operations and abrasives. Attaches wheel or belt to drive mechanism. Starts polisher and manipulates workpiece against abrasive wheel or portable wheel against workpiece to remove metal and surface defects. Examines part for acceptability of finish. May be designated according to type of material polished as Polisher, Aluminum (any industry); Polisher, Brass (any industry); Polisher, Bronze (any industry); Polisher, Zinc (any industry).
GOE: 06.04.24 STRENGTH: M GED: R3 M2 L2 SVP: 6 DLU: 77

705.684-062 POLISHER AND BUFFER II (any industry)
Polishes and buffs steel and stainless steel articles, such as ice cream freezer lids, soda fountain dispensers, storage tanks, and display cases, using portable polisher, buffing brush, and emery cloth: Secures workpiece to bench or table and guides abrasive polishing wheel over workpiece to remove scratches and other defects from metal surface. Dips buffing brush into abrasive cake and lubricant. Moves buffing brush over surfaces of workpiece to remove fine scratches and to achieve specified finish. Polishes recessed areas with fine grade emery cloth.
GOE: 06.04.24 STRENGTH: M GED: R2 M1 L2 SVP: 2 DLU: 77

705.684-066 POLISHER APPRENTICE (any industry) alternate titles: metal-polisher-and-buffer apprentice
Performs duties as described under APPRENTICE (any industry) Master Title.
GOE: 06.04.24 STRENGTH: M GED: R3 M2 L2 SVP: 6 DLU: 77

705.684-070 POLISHER, SAND (jewelry-silver.)
Polishes sterling or silver-plated hollowware, such as bowls, dishes, and trays, and flatware, by applying compound of powdered pumice and oil to workpiece while turning it against felt, leather, or brush polishing wheel: Mixes pumice and oil according to established proportions for type of workpiece being polished. Holds workpiece against revolving brush to remove excess solder from joints, using care not to cut through soldered joint.
GOE: 06.02.24 STRENGTH: L GED: R3 M1 L2 SVP: 6 DLU: 77

705.684-074 SNAG GRINDER (foundry) alternate titles: casting finisher; cast-shell grinder; snagger; swing-frame-grinder operator; swing grinder
Cleans and rough finishes surfaces of casting, using powered grinding wheel mounted on counterbalanced frame: Positions casting under grinding wheel manually or using crane or hoist. Grabs grinder handles and pulls wheel down against casting to remove projections, such as gates, fins, and parting lines, from surface. Repositions casting to grind other areas. May change position of belts on motor and pulleys to increase revolutions per minute when grinding wheel wears down. May remove cracks in surfaces of ingots, billets, and forgings, using grinder. May grind castings, using stationary grinder and be designated Stand Grinder (foundry).
GOE: 06.04.24 STRENGTH: M GED: R2 M1 L2 SVP: 3 DLU: 77

705.687-010 JIGGER (jewelry-silver.)
Places pieces of jewelry articles on pins of specially designed jigs to facilitate polishing operations.
GOE: 06.04.34 STRENGTH: L GED: R1 M1 L1 SVP: 2 DLU: 77

705.687-014 LABORER, GRINDING AND POLISHING (any industry) alternate titles: finisher
Cleans, deburrs, polishes, or grinds items of metal, plastic, or rubber, using handtools or powered equipment, performing any combination of following tasks: Scrapes or rubs parts with file, wire brush, or buffing cloth. Holds part against buffing or grinding wheel. Deburrs or polishes parts, using portable grinder, chipping hammer, buffer, deburring tool, or hand pick. Mounts part on revolving spindle or chuck and holds or moves tools, such as file, abrasive stone, or cloth against workpiece to file, grind, polish, or buff surface. Cleans interior surfaces of holes, using reamer. Changes tools on powered equipment. Applies abrasive compound, wax, or other dressing to facilitate cleaning or polishing operation. May be known according to process performed as Buffer (any industry) II; Burrer (machine shop); Burrer-Marker, Axle (machine shop); Top-Edge Beveler (any industry); Wire Brusher (any industry).
GOE: 06.04.34 STRENGTH: M GED: R2 M2 L2 SVP: 2 DLU: 77

705.687-018 METAL SANDER AND FINISHER (furniture)
Removes surface defects, such as burrs and pits, from metal furniture parts and polishes surface: Positions parts in holding device and removes surface defects with hand sanding machine, sandpaper, or file. Polishes surface to smooth finish, using such materials as cleaning powder, pumice, or steel wool. Wipes surface clean with cloth and stacks finished parts.
GOE: 06.04.24 STRENGTH: L GED: R2 M1 L1 SVP: 3 DLU: 77

706 METAL UNIT ASSEMBLERS AND ADJUSTERS, N.E.C.

This group includes occupations, not elsewhere classified, concerned with assembling and adjusting metal units or components, including mechanical assembling or adjusting not requiring overall mechanical knowledge. Occupations concerned with electrical assembling and adjusting are included in Division 72.

706.130-010 SUPERVISOR, COIN-MACHINE (svc. ind. mach.)
Supervises and coordinates activities of workers engaged in production of coin-vending machines: Selects dies or cutting tools, according to design of metal or plastic part to be formed. Sets up automatic equipment, such as forming press, punch press, and power shear. Performs other duties as described under SUPERVISOR (any industry) Master Title.
GOE: 06.01.01 STRENGTH: L GED: R4 M3 L3 SVP: 7 DLU: 77

706.131-010 LABORATORY SUPERVISOR (machine shop)
Supervises and coordinates activities of workers engaged in assembling, final testing, and inspection of miniature ball bearings: Inspects and tests sample bearings on variety of special devices to determine whether bearings conform to specifications. Examines rejected bearings to ascertain whether components are salvageable. Recommends research to update inspection and testing techniques, instrumentation, and correlation of inspection and testing results with manufacturing methods and processes. Performs other duties as described under SUPERVISOR (any industry) Master Title.
GOE: 06.01.01 STRENGTH: M GED: R4 M3 L3 SVP: 8 DLU: 77

706.131-014 SUPERVISOR (office machines)
Supervises and coordinates activities of workers engaged in fabrication of standard and electric typewriters: Examines defective parts to determine whether to stop or continue assembly process, using job knowledge of acceptable quality and manufacturing standards, such as process sheets, blueprints, and sketches. May verify dimensions of parts, using precision measuring instruments. Performs tasks as described under SUPERVISOR (any industry) Master Title. May be designated according to activities of workers supervised as Supervisor, Assembly (office machines) II; Supervisor, Fabrication (office machines);

Supervisor, Inspection (office machines); Supervisor, Soldering (office machines); Supervisor, Type-Bar-And-Segment (office machines).
GOE: 06.02.01 STRENGTH: L GED: R4 M3 L4 SVP: 7 DLU: 77

706.131-018 CHIEF INSPECTOR (office machines)
Supervises and coordinates activities of workers engaged in inspecting office machine parts and assembled mechanical and electromechanical tape-moistening machines, and inspects materials and purchased machine parts, using precision measuring devices: Confers with assembly supervisors to determine staff assignments at assembly inspection stations and to discuss ongoing inspection results. Alerts supervisors when reports indicate major or consistent assembly discrepancies, and meets with punch press supervisor to discuss rejection findings on parts production. Examines raw materials for smoothness and to detect surface defects, such as nicks, burrs, pits, and scratches, following blueprints, sketches, and order specifications. Tests materials for hardness, using hardness tester. Measures materials, using precision measuring instruments such as calipers, micrometers, gauges, and dial indicators. Prepares rejection slips indicating reasons materials or parts failed inspection. Trains new staff and monitors progress. Performs other duties as described under SUPERVISOR (any industry) Master Title.
GOE: 06.03.02 STRENGTH: M GED: R3 M3 L3 SVP: 7 DLU: 86

706.361-010 ASSEMBLER (machinery mfg.)
Assembles machinery, such as crushers and vibrators, according to blueprints and shop orders, for processing materials, such as coal, clay, chemicals, and rock: Positions parts in frame of machine, using hoist, and bolts stationary parts in place, using impact wrench and handtools. Removes burrs and rough spots from parts with hand file and portable pneumatic grinder. Aligns bearings with shafts in machine. Inserts shims and turns setscrews to set clearance between parts, and verifies clearance, using scale and fixed gauges. Fastens lift chain around machine and directs OVERHEAD CRANE OPERATOR (any industry) 921.663-010 in moving machine to storage area. May be designated according to type of machine assembled as Crusher Assembler (machinery mfg.); Vibrator Assembler (machinery mfg.).
GOE: 06.02.22 STRENGTH: M GED: R3 M2 L3 SVP: 5 DLU: 77

706.361-014 ASSEMBLY INSPECTOR (agric. equip.)
Inspects lawn and garden equipment, such as garden tractors, snow blowers, and power lawnmowers for assembly defects, and repairs defects, using handtools: Examines equipment for surface defects, such as paint streaks and scratches and improper decal application. Touches up paint defects, using brush or spray can. Pushes and pulls knobs and levers to test operation of controls, such as engine throttle and clutch lever. Adjusts controls, using pliers, screwdrivers, and wrenches. Observes and listens to equipment during test run to detect defects, such as leaks, malfunctioning controls, and other defects indicated by unusual noises. Examines identification plates and shipping tags to ensure matching of serial numbers.
GOE: 06.01.05 STRENGTH: L GED: R3 M2 L1 SVP: 5 DLU: 77

706.381-010 ALIGNER, TYPEWRITER (office machines)
Adjusts type and type bar of assembled typewriters to obtain even spacing, equalized impression, and alignment of characters, following manual, and using special-purpose handtools: Inserts paper in machine and types row of alternate upper and lower case characters of each key. Examines imprints for defects, such as close spacing and misaligned or unbalanced impressions. Bends or straightens type or type bar to rectify defective impressions, using special-purpose handtools. Turns regulator or impression screw to adjust length of type-bar stroke and to regulate depth of impression, using screwdriver. Spaces and aligns each upper and lower case character, using first aligned key character as guide.
GOE: 06.02.24 STRENGTH: L GED: R3 M2 L2 SVP: 4 DLU: 77

706.381-014 BENCH HAND (furniture)
Cuts and forms metal furniture parts according to blueprints, using handtools and power tools: Lays out furniture parts on metals, using punches, scribers, and templates. Cuts and forms metal parts, using handtools and machines, such as tin snips, drill press, and power hacksaw. Assembles parts to ensure closeness of fit, using handtools, such as screwdriver, wrench, and hammer. Disassembles furniture prior to painting.
GOE: 06.02.24 STRENGTH: M GED: R3 M2 L3 SVP: 6 DLU: 77

706.381-018 FINAL ASSEMBLER (office machines)
Assembles, installs, and adjusts variety of electromechanical units, such as feed drives, control key assemblies, and printing units, on new and rebuilt punched card office machines according to blueprints and written specifications, using handtools, assembly fixtures, and test devices: Reads blueprints to determine position of unit and component parts. Positions components in assembly fixture. Assembles unit and mounts it on office machine frame, using screwdrivers and wrenches. Starts machine and adjusts unit for specified clearances and time cycles, using fixed gauges, test lights, and handtools. Inspects machine to verify that optional equipment changes have been made according to customer order. May operate electric hoist to position unit on office machine frame.
GOE: 06.01.04 STRENGTH: M GED: R3 M2 L3 SVP: 6 DLU: 77

706.381-022 INSPECTOR, TYPEWRITER ASSEMBLY AND PARTS
(office machines) alternate titles: inspector, manufactured parts; inspector, mechanical
Inspects typewriters, subassemblies, and parts for conformance with specifications, using handtools and measuring instruments: Moves parts to determine

binding, looseness, or misalignment. Tests tightness of screws and nuts, using screwdrivers and wrenches. Measures dimensions of parts, distance between them, and shapes of angles and curves to verify conformance to specifications, using comparator, micrometer, dial indicators, and fixed and adjustable gauges. Refers to blueprints and charts for tolerances. Examines parts for surface defects, such as rust, dullness, discoloration, and chipped and scratched finish. Stops production when rejects exceed specified limits. Compiles information to indicate number of, and reasons for, rejects. May train other workers performing inspections. May be designated according to type of assembly monitored as Inspector, Conveyor Line (office machines); Inspector, Final Assembly-Conveyor Line (office machines); Inspector, Floor Sub-Assembly (office machines); Inspector, Station Assembly-Conveyor Line (office machines); or type of parts inspected as Inspector, Purchased Parts (office machines).
GOE: 06.01.05 STRENGTH: M GED: R3 M3 L3 SVP: 6 DLU: 77

706.381-026 OPERATING-TABLE ASSEMBLER (furniture)
Operates metalworking machines to shape prefabricated metal parts and assembles parts to make surgical tables: Mills parts and assembles base of table. Constructs hydraulic-lifting and table-revolving mechanisms, using drilling, reaming, and tapping machines, and installs them in base. Mounts table frame with its various moving or collapsible sections on base, and attaches table plates to frame. Inspects completed table for compliance with specifications. May assemble examining chairs and be designated Examining-Chair Assembler (furniture).
GOE: 06.01.04 STRENGTH: M GED: R4 M3 L3 SVP: 6 DLU: 77

706.381-030 REPAIRER, TYPEWRITER (office machines)
Repairs and adjusts defective typewriters removed from production line, using handtools, power tools, and gauges: Operates typewriter to test functioning of parts and mechanisms to determine repairs required. Disassembles machines to repair or replace defective components, using handtools and holding devices. Bends, taps, turns parts, such as screws, nuts, and type bar, to eliminate binding, looseness, and misalignment, using special handtools. Verifies specified clearance between parts, using spacebars, tension scales, dial indicators, and feeler gauges. Measures rotation of motor drive-wheel to determine speed of wheel, using tachometer. May adjust interrelated typewriter parts to synchronize machine operation and be designated Adjuster (office machines).
GOE: 06.02.24 STRENGTH: M GED: R3 M2 L3 SVP: 6 DLU: 77

706.381-034 SEWING-MACHINE ASSEMBLER (machinery mfg.)
Mounts previously assembled units of power sewing machines onto frames of machines, and fastens units, such as crankshafts, needle arms, and feed rockers to machines, using drill press, handtools, and gauges.
GOE: 06.02.23 STRENGTH: M GED: R3 M2 L2 SVP: 6 DLU: 77

706.381-038 SUBASSEMBLER (machinery mfg.)
Assembles machinery components, such as operating cylinders, electric control cases, transmissions, clutches, and special tools, according to specifications: Transports specified parts from storage to work area manually or by using overhead crane. Removes burrs and rough surfaces from metal parts with hand file or portable pneumatic grinder. Brushes lubricant on moving parts and fits parts together on bench, following blueprints. Inserts shims between parts to realign or level parts and verifies alignment and clearance of parts, using micrometers, scale, and gauges. Bolts, screws, and rivets parts together, using handtools. May operate hydraulic press to force bearings into sleeves and flatten rivets. May set up and operate drill press, bench lathe, and speed lathe. May connect electric wires to terminals of subassembly, using screwdriver. May move subassembly to storage area, using overhead crane.
GOE: 06.02.24 STRENGTH: M GED: R3 M3 L2 SVP: 6 DLU: 77

706.381-042 TURBINE SUBASSEMBLER (engine-turbine)
Assembles steam and gas turbine subassemblies according to drawings, using measuring instruments, handtools, and power tools: Chips, grinds, and files welds and patches on castings and relief areas on cylinder joints to obtain specified clearances or smooth finish, using pneumatic chipping hammer and pedestal grinder. Drills and taps holes in castings to seat nipples and valves, using single-spindle drill press. Fills castings, high pressure cylinders, turbine exhaust ends, gland casings, relay cylinders, compressor cylinders, and compressor heads with water, using high pressure pump to simulate steam pressure in turbine. Measures expansion of unit, using micrometer-scaled rod. Inspects weldments, baffles, valves, valve seats, and piping for leaks. Inserts heating element of electric heater into hollow studs and heats studs to facilitate tightening with wrenches. Bolts or dowels fitted parts together, using wrenches and pneumatic hammer. Measures clearances and spacing, using feeler gauges, calipers, and micrometers. May cut expansion reliefs in cylinders and exhaust end joints, using portable power hacksaw.
GOE: 06.02.22 STRENGTH: M GED: R3 M2 L3 SVP: 6 DLU: 77

706.381-046 WHEELWRIGHT (automotive ser.)
Repairs and aligns defective wheels of automotive vehicles, such as automobiles, buses, and trucks: Examines wheel rims, drums, discs, and wire spokes for damage. Hammers out warps in wheel rim, or places wheel rim in hydraulic press and forces rim into shape with pry bar or hydraulic jacks. Repairs damaged wire spokes, using straightening press, and replaces broken or missing spokes. Examines alignment of wheels on test stand equipped with dial indicator gauge for measuring radial and lateral tolerance. Corrects alignment of wheels, using handtools.
GOE: 05.10.01 STRENGTH: H GED: R3 M1 L2 SVP: 5 DLU: 77

706.381-050 PRECISION ASSEMBLER, BENCH (aircraft mfg.) alternate titles: detail bench assembler

Assembles machined parts into precision aircraft and missile assemblies, such as landing gear struts, brakes, fueling equipment, control linkages, actuators, and gearbox mechanisms, according to specifications, using handtools, power tools, and measuring instruments: Measures parts to determine specified tolerance, using measuring instruments, such as micrometers, calipers, and verniers. Files and buffs parts to fit, using handtools and power tools. Drills, taps, reams, countersinks, and spotfaces bolt holes in parts, using drill press or portable power drill. Positions and aligns parts, using jigs, fixtures, and templates. Bolts, screws, and rivets parts together, using handtools and power tools. Disassembles and replaces parts as required. May lap and hone internal cylindrical surfaces. May test functional performance of assembly. May clean and lubricate parts and assemblies. May mark identifying information on parts.
GOE: 06.02.23 STRENGTH: M GED: R3 M2 L2 SVP: 6 DLU: 87

706.382-010 FUNCTIONAL TESTER, TYPEWRITERS (office machines)

Operates assembled typewriters to test their performances: Types characters in prescribed sequence on sample sheet to evaluate functioning of parts, such as shift, ribbon feed, key levers, tabulator, carriage, and spacebar. Indicates on prepared form condition of machine, such as excessively noisy, binding parts, misaligned type, and jammed backspace. Sends report and defective machines to ALIGNER, TYPEWRITER (office machines) for repair or adjustment. Repeats tests on adjusted or repaired machines to verify corrections.
GOE: 06.03.01 STRENGTH: L GED: R3 M2 L2 SVP: 4 DLU: 77

706.382-014 TESTER, SOUND (machinery mfg.) alternate titles: bearing inspector

Operates sound-testing equipment to detect defects in machinery ball bearing assemblies and diagnoses causes of defects: Turns dials on equipment to specified setting. Slides bearing on adapter arm and starts machine to rotate inner ring of bearing. Listens through headphones to detect sounds that indicate mechanical defect in bearing and to determine probable cause of defect. Separates defective bearings and sorts bearings for scrap or salvage.
GOE: 06.03.01 STRENGTH: L GED: R3 M2 L2 SVP: 4 DLU: 77

706.384-010 INSPECTOR-ADJUSTER, OFFICE-MACHINE COMPONENTS (office machines)

Inspects and adjusts components and subassemblies of high-speed printers used in electronic data systems for conformance with specifications, using testing equipment and handtools: Examines components and subassemblies for defects and faulty workmanship, using schematic drawings and work process specifications. Measures and checks clearances, tensions, alignments, and electric circuitry, using gauges, ohmmeter, and aligning fixtures. Turns adjusting screw to increase or decrease tension and clearance of parts not conforming to specifications. Examines printout of printed characters to determine if height, width, and spacing meet specifications, using plastic template, and adjusts rollers to correct defects, using handtools. Connects frequency meter lead to circuit board of printer and reads meter dial to verify that frequency readings are within prescribed limits. Measures printer motor speed, using motor-speed tester, and routes defective motors to repair shop.
GOE: 06.01.05 STRENGTH: L GED: R3 M2 L3 SVP: 3 DLU: 86

706.387-010 INSPECTOR, AUTOMATIC TYPEWRITER (office machines)

Inspects automatic electric typewriter, used as part of data processing unit, for conformance to specifications: Plugs machine connections into electrical outlets. Tests performance of typewriter by pressing keys, listening for noise variations, and noting malfunction of mechanisms, such as trip margin stop, backspacer, carriage, and shift. Examines typed copy to determine skipping and misalignment of characters. Marks sample sheet with designated symbols to indicate defects. Routes machine, sample sheet, and work ticket to readjusting or repairing departments. May test performance of typewriter, using automatic programmed simulator.
GOE: 06.03.01 STRENGTH: M GED: R3 M2 L2 SVP: 4 DLU: 77

706.387-014 MACHINE TESTER (office machines)

Tests machines, such as calculating or adding machines, manually or automatically to detect malfunctions, using handtools, alignment gauge, and tester: Sets machine on ball swivel mount to facilitate turning in all directions when examining parts. Plugs cord of machine into electrical outlet. Presses keys on keyboard and moves levers in prescribed sequence to test alignment of printing, repeat latch, ribbon and paper feed, correction release, noise, and clearance of type bars, according to checklist. Test-runs battery of machines through fixed computation cycle automatically, using auto typist or tester. Reads arithmetic results recorded on paper tapes of machines and compares them with test chart to verify accuracy. Indicates defects on inspection worksheet and gives worksheet and machine to repairer. May disassemble machine to determine cause of defect. May be designated according to type of inspection done as Clearing Inspector (office machines); Final Inspector (office machines); Sampling Inspector (office machines); Utility Inspector (office machines).
GOE: 06.03.01 STRENGTH: L GED: R3 M2 L2 SVP: 4 DLU: 77

706.481-010 INTERNAL-COMBUSTION-ENGINE SUBASSEMBLER (engine-turbine) alternate titles: bench assembler; group assembler

Fits together mechanical parts at workbench or assembly floor to make subassemblies for internal combustion engines according to drawings or routing

sheets, using handtools and power tools: Places basic part of assembly, such as carburetor, water pump, fuel pump, oil pump, governor, cam housing, gearcase, exhaust housing, remote control, pistons and connecting rods into holding fixture. Bolts, screws, or pins mechanical and electrical parts together, such as push rods, valves, rocker arms, and magnetos, using power wrenches, torque wrench, stud drivers, and hammer. Operates hand or power arbor press to press bushings and seals into housings or onto shafts. Reams tubular worm gear cage to form smooth surface for assembled worm gear, using hand reamer. Tests sealed units, such as relief valves, fittings, and cylinders under air or water pressure [HYDRO-PNEUMATIC TESTER (any industry)]. Applies decals to engine to indicate operating procedure. May be designated according to part assembled as Carburetor Assembler (engine-turbine); Cylinder-Head Assembler (engine-turbine); Gearcase Assembler (engine-turbine); Governor Assembler (engine-turbine); Remote-Control Assembler (engine-turbine); Water-Pump Assembler (engine-turbine).
GOE: 06.02.22 STRENGTH: M GED: R3 M2 L2 SVP: 5 DLU: 77

706.484-010 DRAPERY-ROD ASSEMBLER (retail trade)

Assembles drapery rods to customer's order in retail establishment: Bends rod to customer's specifications to ensure proper fit in window boxes and offsets. Installs drapery pull cords, drapery carriers, master carriers, and end pulleys on drapery rod.
GOE: 05.12.12 STRENGTH: M GED: R2 M1 L2 SVP: 3 DLU: 77

706.587-010 CLEANER-TOUCH-UP WORKER (office machines) alternate titles: touch-up worker

Wipes grease and fingermarks from typewriter parts, such as covers, platen, and keyboard, using cloth and solvent and touches up scratches and nicks in enamel finish, using paint and brush. Notifies supervisor if shade of touchup paint and cover color do not match. Rejects machines with covers too badly marred to touch up. Records serial numbers of machines cleaned. May insert wire to secure typewriter carriage in place for shipping. May attach identifying tags and warranty to typewriter.
GOE: 06.03.02 STRENGTH: L GED: R2 M1 L2 SVP: 3 DLU: 77

706.587-014 SORTER (office machines)

Disassembles and sorts defective typewriter parts and subassemblies into lots to reclaim serviceable parts, using handtools: Lifts containers of rejected mixed parts from assembly lines onto handtruck and transports them to work area. Dismantles subassemblies, using pliers, wrenches, and screwdrivers. Sorts parts into lots for reuse, repair, or salvage according to disposition information on tags and instructions from supervisor. Assigns part number from stock catalog to reusable, repairable, or salvaged parts. Prepares route slips to indicate, according to instructions from supervisor, departments to which parts are to be sent. May bend, straighten, grind, ream or tap defective typewriter parts to remove defects, using handtools and power tools. May extract metal parts from floor sweepings to reclaim salvageable parts, using hand magnet.
GOE: 06.03.02 STRENGTH: L GED: R2 M2 L2 SVP: 3 DLU: 77

706.684-010 AIR-CONDITIONING-COIL ASSEMBLER (svc. ind. mach.) alternate titles: coil fin assembler; plate fin assembler

Assembles prepunched aluminum fin plates and copper tubing to form cooling coils for air-conditioning units, using handtools and other equipment: Places fin plates on worktable and clamps into position. Inserts copper tubing through holes in fin plates. Depresses switch to activate hydraulic rams, forcing them through tubes, to expand tubes and lock fins in position. Joins completed assemblies, using end plates and pneumatic hammer to expand ends of tubes. Heats tube ends and seals joints, using solder. May operate press machine to punch fins and tubes required to fabricate air-conditioning coils.
GOE: 06.02.23 STRENGTH: M GED: R3 M2 L2 SVP: 3 DLU: 77

706.684-014 ASSEMBLER I (office machines) alternate titles: assembler-adjuster

Assembles and adjusts typewriters and office machine assemblies and subassemblies, using blueprints, gauges, handtools, and holding devices: Screws and bolts parts together, using screwdrivers, wrenches, and other handtools. Tests operation of machines and typewriters to detect loose and binding parts and to determine synchronization of related parts. Bends and taps parts into alignment, using pliers and mallets. Turns compensating screws to set parts at specified tensions and clearances. Verifies tensions and clearances of parts, using tension scales and space and feeler gauges. May ream and tap holes and file and fit carriages and covers of equipment, using hand reamer, tap, and file.
GOE: 06.02.23 STRENGTH: M GED: R3 M2 L2 SVP: 4 DLU: 81

706.684-018 ASSEMBLER, PRODUCT (machine shop) alternate titles: assembler; erector

Assembles metal products, such as vacuum cleaners, valves, or hydraulic cylinders, partially or completely, working at bench or on shop floor: Positions parts according to knowledge of unit being assembled or following blueprints. Fastens parts together with bolts, screws, speed clips, rivets, or other fasteners, using handtools and portable powered tools. May remove small quantities of metal with hand files and scrapers to produce close fit between parts. May operate drill presses, punch presses, or riveting machines to assist in assembly operation. May disassemble power brake boosters, air-brake compressors, and valves for salvage of parts and be designated Disassembler, Product (machine shop). May assemble and test patient lifting devices and be designated Assembler, Patient Lifting Device (protective dev.). Usually specializes in assembly of one type of product.

GOE: 06.02.23 STRENGTH: M GED: R3 M2 L2 SVP: 3 DLU: 77

706.684-022 ASSEMBLER, SMALL PRODUCTS I (any industry) alternate titles: bench assembler

Performs any combination of following repetitive tasks on assembly line to mass produce small products, such as ball bearings, automobile door locking units, speedometers, condensers, distributors, ignition coils, drafting table subassemblies, or carburetors: Positions parts in specified relationship to each other, using hands, tweezers, or tongs. Bolts, screws, clips, cements, or otherwise fastens parts together by hand or using handtools or portable powered tools. Frequently works at bench as member of assembly group assembling one or two specific parts and passing unit to another worker. Loads and unloads previously setup machines, such as arbor presses, drill presses, taps, spot-welding machines, riveting machines, milling machines, or broaches, to perform fastening, force fitting, or light metal-cutting operation on assembly line. May be assigned to different work stations as production needs require or shift from one station to another to reduce fatigue factor. May be known according to product assembled.
GOE: 06.04.23 STRENGTH: L GED: R2 M1 L1 SVP: 2 DLU: 79

706.684-026 ASSEMBLER, TYPE-BAR-AND-SEGMENT (office machines)

Assembles typewriter type-bar-and-segment units and bends ends of type bars to specified angles and clearances preparatory to type soldering, using handtools and hand-powered brake: Clamps segment to holding device and inserts type bars into segment slots. Pushes curved wire (fulcrum) through channel in segment and through holes in type bars to hold them in place. Moves bars to determine snugness of fit. Bends type-bars to fit precisely into segment slots, using special pliers. Grinds defective bars to fit, using emery wheel. Positions bar-and-segment assembly to holding plate on braking device. Moves levers to adjust quadrant (scale in degrees) to degree desired, to bend ends of type bars to specified angles and clearances, and to release bent type bars from holding and bending jaws. Removes formed type-bar-and-segment unit from braking device. Positions type-bar-and-segment assembly in guide-installation fixture and installs type guide, using special alignment tools and power screwdriver. Checks outside bars for guide clearance after removal from fixture, using gauge. May be designated according to work performed as Fitter, Type-Bar-And-Segment (office machines); Former, Type-Bar-And-Segment (office machines); Guide-Instsller, Type-Bar-And-Segment (office machines); Spacer, Type-Bar-And-Segment (office machines).
GOE: 06.02.23 STRENGTH: L GED: R3 M2 L2 SVP: 3 DLU: 77

706.684-030 ATOMIZER ASSEMBLER (fabrication, nec)

Assembles component parts of perfume atomizers, such as stems, washers, springs, and plungers, using handtools: Screws completed atomizers onto empty glass containers and places them in boxes.
GOE: 06.04.23 STRENGTH: S GED: R2 M1 L1 SVP: 2 DLU: 77

706.684-034 BAR AND FILLER ASSEMBLER (furniture)

Fits upright filler tubes into crossbars to form sections of metal bed ends: Sets crossbar in place in assembling frame. Sets filler tubes vertically in each hole in bar and presses tubes into bar with lever. Removes section from frame.
GOE: 06.04.22 STRENGTH: L GED: R2 M1 L2 SVP: 2 DLU: 77

706.684-038 BEARING-RING ASSEMBLER (machinery mfg.) alternate titles: unit assembler

Assembles outer rings, inner rings, bearings, and retainer guards to form ball bearing assembly unit used in manufacture of gyros and other commercial equipment: Selects inner ring and places it on pedestal jig. Selects outer ring and places it on pedestal jig. Picks up ball bearings of specified size and number, using magnetic and nonmagnetic needles. Inserts bearings between outer and inner rings, spacing them with nonmagnetic needle. Selects and inserts retaining guard into ball bearing unit assembly. Tests finished assemblies with gauge to determine accurate radial play. May secure ball bearings in position, using rivets and riveting press. May disassemble finished ball bearings rejected, during final inspection.
GOE: 06.04.23 STRENGTH: L GED: R2 M2 L2 SVP: 3 DLU: 77

706.684-042 BENCH ASSEMBLER (agric. equip.) alternate titles: subassembler

Assembles parts to form yard and garden care equipment components, such as reels, steering handles, and gear boxes, following specifications and using handtools and power tools: Fits parts of components together and fastens them with bolts and cotter pins, using handtools and pneumatic impact wrench. Seats inserts, such as bearings and grease seals in hubs and sleeves, using power press. Rivets reel blades to hubs on reel shaft, using pneumatic clinching gun, and sets rivets, using rivet press [RIVETING-MACHINE OPERATOR (any industry) I]. May be designated according to part assembled as Reel Fabricator (agric. equip.).
GOE: 06.04.23 STRENGTH: L GED: R2 M1 L2 SVP: 2 DLU: 77

706.684-046 BENCH HAND (motor-bicycles)

Assembles motorcycle and bicycle subassemblies, using arbor press, drill press, grinder, riveter, or other power bench machines: Positions and clamps metal parts in bed of machines. Starts machines to burr, grind, drill, or polish brake drum, clutch hub, shifter cam, or other subassembly parts, following standard procedures. Removes part from machine and compares part with pattern. Bends tubular sections to specified shape, using handtools. Fits and rivets or spot welds parts together.

GOE: 06.04.22 STRENGTH: M GED: R2 M2 L2 SVP: 3 DLU: 77

706.684-050 DRAWER UPFITTER (furniture) alternate titles: drawer-hardware worker; file-drawer finisher

Assembles drawers for use in metal file cabinets: Inserts slide rod, block, and spring in file drawers to hold file guides. Rivets label holders to drawer fronts. Screws handles to drawers.
GOE: 06.04.23 STRENGTH: M GED: R2 M1 L1 SVP: 4 DLU: 77

706.684-054 FITTER II (any industry)

Fits together components of fabricated metal products, such as boxes, shells, and frames, for window sashes, doors, bicycles, and tubular furniture to prepare them for welding, brazing, or assembly: Positions parts into fixture or frame, examines alignment visually, or verifies alignment, using square, rule, and template. Files and grinds to remove burrs or alter shape. Straightens part by hammering or using straightening press. Secures part to fixture or fastens parts together, using clamps.
GOE: 06.02.22 STRENGTH: H GED: R2 M1 L2 SVP: 5 DLU: 77

706.684-058 HYDRAULIC-CHAIR ASSEMBLER (furniture)

Assembles hydraulic chairs, such as professional, laboratory, and hospital chairs, from prefabricated and finished parts: Assembles hydraulic-lifting and chair-revolving mechanisms and mounts them on base. Assembles chair frame to base and attaches seat, arm, and headrests. Inspects and adjusts completed unit. Rethreads screws, retaps holes, and removes excess paint while assembling, to facilitate work. May be designated according to type of chairs assembled as Dental-Chair Assembler (furniture).
GOE: 06.02.22 STRENGTH: L GED: R3 M2 L2 SVP: 5 DLU: 77

706.684-062 INJECTOR ASSEMBLER (engine-turbine)

Smooths, drills, and tests parts for diesel engine fuel injectors according to specifications, using lapping machine, microscope drill, and testing equipment: Mounts injector check valves on spindle heads. Smooths flat and curved surfaces of valves on rotating disk or semispherically shaped pan containing *lapping compound* for specified time. Examines samples of lapped valves under binocular microscope for nicks and grooves. Clamps injector spray tip in fixture under microscope drill and moves lever to drill holes into tip. Stamps identifying numbers on injector parts, using roll type metal stamper. Clamps body of injector into holding fixture and inserts tip assembly including check valve, barrel and plunger, stem, spring, and retaining nut. Screws injector into testing machine and moves lever to test operation of plunger, spring, and spray tip outlets.
GOE: 06.02.23 STRENGTH: L GED: R3 M2 L2 SVP: 5 DLU: 77

706.684-070 LOCK ASSEMBLER (furniture)

Assembles bases, columns, housings, springs, valves, and tubing to form completed supports for hydraulic chairs, such as dental or barber chairs. May operate any of various metalworking machines to machine rough or inaccurately shaped parts to size.
GOE: 06.02.22 STRENGTH: M GED: R3 M2 L2 SVP: 6 DLU: 77

706.684-074 LOCK ASSEMBLER (cutlery-hrdwr.)

Fastens together parts of locks with screws, bolts, and rivets, using handtools and power tools: Files and fits parts to obtain smooth functioning of lock. Assembles inside lock parts in lock case and rivets side plate in place, using rivet tool. May pack locks in cartons and mark cartons to identify contents.
GOE: 06.04.23 STRENGTH: S GED: R2 M1 L2 SVP: 3 DLU: 77

706.684-078 LOCK INSTALLER (furniture)

Installs slide locks in drawers of metal office furniture, using power drill to cut holes and handtools to screw parts in place.
GOE: 06.04.24 STRENGTH: L GED: R2 M1 L1 SVP: 3 DLU: 77

706.684-082 METAL-BED ASSEMBLER (furniture) alternate titles: panel assembler

Assembles head and foot sections of metal bedstead: Inserts upright fillers in holes in bedpost and in holes in cross filler. Springs legs of frame apart and inserts ends of cross filler into holes in legs. Fits molding to bedpost and drives it into grooves in bedpost with mallet. Forces ends of panel into molding, bottom of panel into cross molding, and ends of cross molding into bedpost, using mallet. May cut panel from stock, using power shear. May bend molding to shape by use of power press. May assemble safety rails and attach motors, pulleys, and cables to bed frame to assemble electric hospital beds. May be designated according to section of bed assembled as Foot-Piece Assembler (furniture); Head-Piece Assembler (furniture).
GOE: 06.02.22 STRENGTH: M GED: R2 M1 L2 SVP: 3 DLU: 77

706.684-086 PLUMBING-HARDWARE ASSEMBLER (plumbing-heat.) alternate titles: assembler; fittings tightener

Assembles plumbing fixtures, such as faucets, stoppers, and shower heads, using handtools and power tools: Screws pipe fittings into grease traps, check valves, and other plumbing fixtures, using pipe wrench or power wrench. Drills holes in fixtures for bolt attachments, using power drill. Fits parts together and secures parts with screws, bolts, or solder, using handtools and flame solderer. May adjust valves and other linkage to ensure free action of moving parts.
GOE: 06.04.23 STRENGTH: L GED: R2 M1 L2 SVP: 2 DLU: 77

706.684-090 SPRING ASSEMBLER (metal prod., nec)

Assembles leaf-type springs, performing any combination of following tasks: Picks up specified spring leaves from conveyor and inserts metal rod through center holes of leaves to align leaves lengthwise and form springs. Removes

rod and attaches leaves together with nut and bolt, using pneumatic wrench. Attaches pads and clips to leaf spring to maintain spring alignment. Places ends of spring under bushing machine and activates machine to insert rubber bushings. May spread grease over surface of spring leaves before assembly, using greasing apparatus or brush. May compress leaves prior to attaching center bolt, using press. May be designated according to specific task performed as Bolt-Up Worker (metal prod., nec); Bushing-And-Broach Operator (metal prod., nec); Catcher (metal prod., nec); Clip Riveter (metal prod., nec); Greaser (metal prod., nec); Pinner (metal prod., nec).
GOE: 06.04.22 STRENGTH: H GED: R2 M1 L1 SVP: 4 DLU: 77

706.684-094 SUBASSEMBLER (office machines)
Fastens together and adjusts variety of subassemblies, such as circuit breakers, brush slides, control panels, and other office machine subassemblies, using assembly fixtures and handtools: Reads blueprints or written instructions to determine position of subassembly components, such as cams, shafts, frames, keys, and brushes. Positions components in assembly fixtures. Fastens subassembly together with bolts, screws, and collars, using wrenches and screwdrivers. May solder parts of subassembly together. Adjusts linkage and clearance of assembled components to specifications, using fixed gauges and handtools. May disassemble and inspect subassemblies of rebuilt machines for conformance to engineering change orders.
GOE: 06.02.23 STRENGTH: L GED: R3 M2 L3 SVP: 4 DLU: 80

706.684-098 VALVE GRINDER (machine shop) alternate titles: valve lapper
Laps valves against valve seats to produce gastight fit, using powered tools: Applies lapping compound to bearing surfaces of valve and seat. Inserts valve stem into valve guide and positions valve against seat. Engages holes or slot in top of valve with projections in powered rotary tool (valve grinder). Presses and rotates valve against seat, using powered tool. May test valve by connecting chamber to hydraulic or pneumatic pressure and observing leaks. May rotate valve against seat, using handtool.
GOE: 06.02.24 STRENGTH: M GED: R3 M2 L2 SVP: 5 DLU: 77

706.684-102 VENDING-MACHINE ASSEMBLER (svc. ind. mach.)
Fastens together components of vending or slot machines and assembles machine, using handtools and power tools, performing any combination of following tasks: Positions, aligns, and fastens specified parts to form subassemblies of coin machines, such as selector button control panels, coin changer chassis, coin chutes, and refrigeration units, using hand press, jigs, and pneumatic screwdriver. Attaches inside components of machine, such as selection drums, evaporator units, ice makers, cup droppers, and motors as machines pass along conveyor line. Positions and attaches door panels, latch assemblies, and instruction panels, using pneumatic screwdriver.
GOE: 06.02.23 STRENGTH: L GED: R2 M1 L2 SVP: 2 DLU: 77

706.684-106 WHEEL LACER AND TRUER (motor-bicycles) alternate titles: wheel assembler; wheel truer
Laces and trues-up (aligns) motorcycle and bicycle wheels according to specifications, using gauges and handtools or power tools: Hooks wire spokes onto perforated hubs and screws nipples of spokes onto rim to lace (assemble) wheel, using special hand wrench. Measures diameter of wheel, using fixed gauge. Grinds protruding end of spokes from inside surface of rim, using portable hand grinder. Mounts tires on wheels [TIRE MOUNTER (fabrication, nec)] and clamps wheel in fixture. Positions dial indicator against tire and rim, turns wheel, and notes points at which wheel needs alignment as indicated by needle deflection on indicator. Turns spoke nipples with wrench to adjust tension of spokes at indicated points to align wheel.
GOE: 06.02.23 STRENGTH: M GED: R2 M1 L2 SVP: 4 DLU: 77

706.684-110 WRAPPER OPERATOR (metal prod., nec)
Wraps extended spring leaf ends around main leaf, using hand-operated wrapping device: Selects and sets eye pin (eye holder) into base of wrapping device. Positions cold main-leaf eye over pin to hold main leaf in place during wrapping. Heats end of second leaf for specified time in furnace and positions leaf behind main-leaf eye, using clamp tongs. Inserts centering pin through center hole in each leaf to align leaves and clamps leaves together with tongs. Pulls lever to move pressure plate against heated end of second leaf forcing it around main-leaf eye.
GOE: 06.04.22 STRENGTH: M GED: R2 M2 L2 SVP: 2 DLU: 77

706.685-010 TYPE-SOLDERING-MACHINE TENDER (office machines)
Tends machine equipped with multiple stations that solders typewriter type to type bars: Clamps type bar and segment-assembly to holding plate of machine. Selects type in designated sequence and positions type between guides, or in matrix plate on machine table. Pulls down first type bar with fingers and seats end of bar in back slot of type. Pushes table or depresses treadle that moves assembly to next station where flux, solder, and coolant air are automatically applied. May apply flux to back slot, using tweezers. May adjust guides for different styles of type, using size blocks and turning setscrews. May remove excess solder to prevent type from binding in type guide, using pencil-flame gas torch and brush or file.
GOE: 06.04.20 STRENGTH: S GED: R2 M1 L2 SVP: 3 DLU: 77

706.685-014 WHEEL-TRUING MACHINE TENDER (motor-bicycles)
Tends truing machine which aligns spoke-wheels: Places loosely laced (spoked) wheel onto rotating bed of machine. Presses buttons to lower ram which clamps wheel into position. Turns knob which rotates turntable to align spoke nipple screws on wheel with advanceable power screwdrivers. Presses button to bring screwdrivers into contact with screw and tighten them. Pushes lever to progressively rotate worktable to align screws with screwdrivers. Removes wheel from machine and mounts on mandrel; places point of dial indicator against rim. Spins wheel and reads dial to ascertain points of diameter and circumference imbalance. Turns spoke nipples with wrench where required to true-up wheel.
GOE: 06.04.24 STRENGTH: M GED: R2 M2 L2 SVP: 2 DLU: 77

706.687-010 ASSEMBLER, PRODUCTION (any industry)
Performs repetitive bench or line assembly operations to mass-produce products, such as automobile or tractor radiators, blower wheels, refrigerators, or gas stoves: Places parts in specified relationship to each other. Bolts, clips, screws, cements, or otherwise fastens parts together by hand, or using handtools or portable power tools. May tend machines, such as arbor presses or riveting machine, to perform force fitting or fastening operations on assembly line. May be assigned to different work stations as production needs require. May work on line where tasks vary as different model of same article moves along line. May be designated according to part or product produced.
GOE: 06.04.22 STRENGTH: L GED: R2 M1 L1 SVP: 2 DLU: 80

706.687-018 FAN-BLADE ALIGNER (elec. equip.) alternate titles: blade aligner; fan-blade truer; line-up-machine operator
Bends metal fan blades by hand to adjust pitch (angle) of blade, and to align blades for vibrationless tracking: Places blade assembly on spindle of gauging fixture, and manually rotates blades between set of pin gauges. Sights across blade surface and tips of gaugepins, and bends and twists blade into contact with pin ends. May use wrench or bending tool to adjust heavy-duty blades and blade carriers. May align and adjust pitch of oil-retaining ring at hub of commercial or industrial fan.
GOE: 06.04.24 STRENGTH: L GED: R2 M1 L2 SVP: 2 DLU: 77

706.687-022 INSPECTOR, ALIGNING (office machines) alternate titles: alining checker
Examines typed characters and exterior features of typewriter, such as serial number and carriage model, for conformance to specifications: Verifies serial number, model carriage, front panel, and type style against specifications. Measures width of type guide, using go-not-go gauge. Compares arrangement of key tops with diagram stick to verify positions of characters. Types line-of-write on sample sheet and examines typing for defects, such as characters above or below line-of-write, heavy or light impressions, cutting into or embossing paper, and uneven spacing or tilted characters. Marks sample sheet with prescribed symbols to indicate defects. Places sheet, ticket, and machine on conveyor for realigning or stamps inspection number on tickets and papers of approved machine and posts serial number to production report. Determines alignment and looseness of specified parts, using screwdriver.
GOE: 06.03.02 STRENGTH: L GED: R3 M2 L2 SVP: 4 DLU: 77

706.687-026 INSPECTOR, TYPE (office machines)
Examines typewriter type under mounted magnifying glass for defects, such as burrs, incomplete or off-center characters, or malformed back blades. Discards defective type. May push type along knifelike blade for ease in examining.
GOE: 06.03.02 STRENGTH: S GED: R2 M1 L2 SVP: 3 DLU: 77

706.687-030 PUSH-CONNECTOR ASSEMBLER (house. appl.) alternate titles: assembler, latches and springs
Installs catches in vacuum cleaner hose couplings, using fingers and metal pry: Positions spring-steel ring in holding groove on inside wall of coupling. Pries ring away from coupling wall, using handtool, and slips latch bar between ring and wall. Positions latch bar so that push button attached to bar protrudes through opening in coupling wall. Inserts second latch bar at opposite point on coupling.
GOE: 06.04.23 STRENGTH: L GED: R2 M1 L1 SVP: 2 DLU: 77

706.687-034 ROLLER-BEARING INSPECTOR (machinery mfg.; motor-bicycles) alternate titles: roller-bearing assembler
Sorts rollers for roller bearings into groups according to diameter or length: Sets gauge slots of machine that automatically ejects off-size rollers, using micrometers and gauges. Feeds rollers into machine hopper. Examines rollers for defects, such as marks, scratches, or other blemishes. Measures bearing retainer for conformance to specification, using height gauge. Fits bearings into retainer rings and packs roller bearings in boxes for shipment. May sort inner and outer rings of ball bearing, according to size, using gauges.
GOE: 06.03.02 STRENGTH: L GED: R2 M1 L2 SVP: 3 DLU: 77

709 MISCELLANEOUS OCCUPATIONS IN FABRICATION, ASSEMBLY, AND REPAIR OF METAL PRODUCTS, N.E.C.

This group includes occupations, not elsewhere classified, concerned with fabricating, assembling, and repairing metal products.

709.134-010 SUPERVISOR, METAL FURNITURE ASSEMBLY (furniture)
Supervises and coordinates activities of workers engaged in assembling and packing metal furniture: Assigns tasks to workers based on workflow. Monitors

work in progress to ensure conformance to set standards and work order specifications. Assists workers in performance of duties to solve work problems or reassigns workers to maintain production at specified levels. Trains new workers. Inspects assembled pieces for conformity to production standards. Reroutes defective furniture for reworking. Enforces worker adherence to safety standards. Examines packaging for furniture to ensure compliance with company standards. Performs other duties as described under SUPERVISOR (any industry) Master Title.
GOE: 06.02.01 STRENGTH: L GED: R4 M3 L3 SVP: 7 DLU: 77

709.137-010 INSPECTION SUPERVISOR (chemical; nonfer. metal)
Supervises and coordinates activities of workers engaged in inspecting materials received, production of uranium fuel elements, and storage of fuel elements in nuclear fuel plant: Assigns workers to inspection stations according to priorities and workers' knowledge of nuclear fuel element processing procedures and techniques. Examines materials and products rejected by subordinates to verify defects and to determine whether defects are within allowable engineering standards. Submits samples of hardware and materials received to quality control personnel to obtain verification of manufacturers' certifications and authorizations to release items for production usage. Compiles and submits reports to quality control engineer. Trains new workers. Performs other duties as described under SUPERVISOR (any industry) Master Title.
GOE: 06.01.01 STRENGTH: M GED: R4 M3 L3 SVP: 8 DLU: 77

709.281-010 LOCKSMITH (any industry) alternate titles: lock expert
Installs, repairs, rebuilds, and services mechanical or electrical locking devices, using handtools and special equipment: Disassembles locks, such as padlocks, safe locks, and door locks, and repairs or replaces worn tumblers, springs, and other parts. Inserts new or repaired tumblers into lock to change combination. Cuts new or duplicate keys, using keycutting machine. Moves lockpick in cylinder to open door locks without keys. Opens safe locks by drilling. May keep records of company locks and keys.
GOE: 05.05.09 STRENGTH: L GED: R4 M3 L3 SVP: 6 DLU: 88

709.281-014 LOCKSMITH APPRENTICE (any industry)
Performs duties as described under APPRENTICE (any industry) Master Title.
GOE: 05.05.09 STRENGTH: L GED: R4 M3 L3 SVP: 6 DLU: 77

709.364-010 INSPECTOR, MAGNETIC PARTICLE AND PENETRANT (any industry)
Inspects chemically treated metallic and nonmetallic parts and assemblies under fluorescent or black lighting for defects, such as fissures, weld breaks, or fractures, using magnetic particle or fluid penetrant inspection processes and equipment, using either of following methods: (1) Immerses or sprays ferrous magnetic metal parts with iron oxide solution. Positions parts between electrodes of magnetic testing equipment and activates switch to induce magnetic field that attracts and accumulates iron oxide particles at defective points. (2) Immerses or sprays nonmagnetic metal or nonmetallic parts with fluid penetrant solution. Rinses excess solution from parts, and dries parts in oven. Examines parts under fluorescent or black lighting to detect defects at or near part surfaces indicated by thick deposits of iron oxide particles or reflection of penetrant solutions. Removes surface defects, using handtools, power tools, or abrasive solutions, or marks part defects for repair or discard depending on nature and extent of defects. Notifies supervisor of defective processing of parts or materials. May be designated by inspection process involved as Inspector, Magnetic Particle (any industry); Inspector, Penetrant (any industry).
GOE: 06.03.01 STRENGTH: M GED: R3 M3 L3 SVP: 5 DLU: 87

709.364-014 TOWEL-CABINET REPAIRER (business ser.)
Services continuous-roll towel cabinets in rest rooms of industrial and commercial establishments: Disassembles cabinet, using handtools, to determine cause of failure reported by towel-service company customer. Repairs or replaces components, such as springs and release mechanism, at scene or returns cabinet to repair shop for more extensive overhaul. May repair or replace related items, such as hot-air hand driers, toilet tissue dispensers, and soap dispensers. May deliver laundered towels to customers on route, according to prescribed schedule.
GOE: 05.10.01 STRENGTH: M GED: R2 M1 L2 SVP: 3 DLU: 77

709.367-010 INSPECTOR, METAL CAN (tinware) alternate titles: can-line examiner; can technician
Inspects and tests metal cans for imperfections, using scaler and measuring devices: Pulls samples of tinplate or aluminum sheeting can bodies and ends from production lines, and inspects them for surface flaws in metal, defective seams, and machining defects, such as scratches, burrs, and dents. Measures sample, using micrometer or gauges, to verify dimensions. Records results of inspection in log for each machine. Stops production line when inspection reveals need for corrective maintenance. Tests cans for bursting strength, using hot oil-pressure tank. Feeds defective test cans through testing machines to verify efficiency of rejection mechanisms. Disassembles and flattens cans or lids, using handpress and cutters. Measures flanges, hooks, seams, curls, countersinks, beads, and inside and outside dimensions of cans, using dial gauges. Immerses coated cans and lids in chemical solutions for specified time to test resistance of coating. Weighs coated and uncoated can samples, and records and compares difference in weight with standard conversion charts to determine amount of coating deposited. Verifies temperature of drying ovens and solder baths to ensure uniformity of heating and melting processes.

GOE: 06.03.01 STRENGTH: L GED: R4 M3 L3 SVP: 5 DLU: 77

709.381-010 ATOMIC-FUEL ASSEMBLER (chemical) alternate titles: fuel assembler; process operator, atomic energy
Prepares fuel elements for use in nuclear reactors or radiographic measuring and detecting devices, performing any combination of following tasks: Strings fuel cells on wire or rod, using tweezers, safety gloves, and radiation shield or box. Enlarges hole in cell as necessary for precise fit, using reamers, files, scrapers, and emery cloth. Inspects completed assembly for flaws, such as burrs or faulty assembly. Stacks prescribed number of assemblies in jig and slips ring or cap over end to form single fuel unit. Cleans inside of metallic tubes, using ultrasonic wand, preparatory to filling with liquid fuel solution. Mixes radioactive solution according to specifications and pours into tube, using remote-controlled slave manipulators. Seals ends of tube by crimping cap or by spot welding cap to tube. Inspects tubes for leakage, using mass spectrometer or disintegration counter. Cleans exterior of tubes, using acetone and cloth or brush. Packs tubes in cartons or lead containers for shipment. Weighs completed assemblies or radioactive materials, using gram scale. Keeps records of materials used, shipping data, and number of units assembled.
GOE: 06.01.04 STRENGTH: L GED: R4 M2 L2 SVP: 4 DLU: 77

709.381-014 MODEL BUILDER (furniture)
Makes parts for and assembles prototypes of metal furniture according to specifications to test practicality of new designs: Lays out and marks parts, following blueprints, sketches, and verbal instructions, using calipers and scribers. Cuts and forms parts from metal, such as steel and aluminum, using lathe, power saw, snips, and handtools. Joins parts, using screwdriver, wrench, and welding torch. May alter design of finished model according to revised specifications.
GOE: 05.05.06 STRENGTH: M GED: R3 M2 L3 SVP: 7 DLU: 77

709.381-018 MODEL MAKER II (jewelry-silver.) alternate titles: jewelry-casting-model maker
Constructs metal models of jewelry articles for use in making molds for casting jewelry parts: Lays out design on metal stock, using gravers. Cuts metal along markings and smooths edges, using handsaw and file. Examines and measures metal parts for conformance to design specifications on scale drawing. Hammers, carves, and scrapes rough model to produce specified relief design, using handtools. Drills holes in model, using drill press. Assembles and solders parts together [SOLDERER (jewelry-silver.) 700.381-050]. Polishes metal surfaces, using abrasive wheel. May make and sharpen tools. May modify design specifications to conform to production requirements. May construct preliminary model of wax or wire.
GOE: 01.06.02 STRENGTH: L GED: R4 M3 L3 SVP: 7 DLU: 77

709.381-022 MODEL-MAKER APPRENTICE (jewelry-silver.) alternate titles: jewelry-casting-model-maker apprentice
Performs duties as described under APPRENTICE (any industry) Master Title.
GOE: 01.06.02 STRENGTH: L GED: R4 M3 L3 SVP: 7 DLU: 77

709.381-026 MOLD STAMPER AND REPAIRER (rubber tire) alternate titles: mold dresser
Repairs and refinishes tire molds and changes lettering plates and bead rings: Repairs nicks, dents, and holes in molds, using ball peen hammer, hand drill, chisels, metal plugs, and acetylene torch. Refinishes repaired area or complete mold with hand-buffing machine and steel wool. Changes bead rings and nameplates showing size and ply to correspond with tires scheduled to be cured, using wrenches. Cleans and maintains inventory of plates, bead rings, and molds. Positions molds in area, using hoist. May add metal to, or remove metal from, plates, rings, and molds, using welding equipment and files. May fill in mold lettering with liquid metal or plugs, buff to smooth finish, and restamp [MOLD STAMPER (machine shop)].
GOE: 05.10.01 STRENGTH: H GED: R3 M2 L2 SVP: 6 DLU: 77

709.381-030 ORGAN-PIPE MAKER, METAL (musical inst.)
Casts metal into sheets and forms metal pipes for pipe organs, using handtools and knowledge of metal properties and pipe making: Melts mixture of lead and tin in melting pot. Pours molten metal onto flat table to form sheets. Brushes sizing onto sheets and cuts sheets, using hook-knife and power shears. Hand-rolls sheets into tubes on mandrel, using handtools. Scrapes edges, using handtool to obtain required angle for soldering and solders seam. Places pipe on mandrel and hammers pipe, using mallet to form and finish mouth. Hand-rolls annealed sheet zinc in similar manner to form larger pipes.
GOE: 05.05.06 STRENGTH: M GED: R3 M2 L2 SVP: 7 DLU: 77

709.381-034 PATTERNMAKER (furniture)
Sketches and constructs patterns from blueprints for use in manufacture of metal furniture parts: Draws outline of part on paper or traces it from blueprint. Transfers outline onto pattern materials, such as metal, plastic, or rubber by tracing over lines. Cuts out pattern with lathe or handtools and power tools, such as tin snips and power hacksaw. Assembles pattern sections, using handtools, such as hammer and screwdriver. Marks identifying number or symbol on pattern.
GOE: 05.05.07 STRENGTH: L GED: R4 M3 L3 SVP: 7 DLU: 77

709.381-038 REED MAKER (machinery mfg.)
Fabricates reed assemblies for textile looms, using machines, handtools, and gauges: Inserts spool of wire in machine that cuts wire into dents (specified

lengths) and consecutively fastens ends of dents to opposing coils of two parallel forming springs. Positions additional forming springs across rows of dents to reinforce assembly and ensure specified spacing of dents. Compresses springs in screw press and wires frame (steel band) around dents to form reed assembly of specified width. Packs lime preparation between dents and dips assembly into solder trough to solder dent ends to frame. Removes lime preparation, wires, and springs, using handtools. Inspects spacing of dents, using micrometer and feeler gauge. Corrects spacing, using straightening tool. Cleans and polishes reed assembly, using portable buffing wheel.
GOE: 06.01.04 STRENGTH: M GED: R3 M2 L2 SVP: 6 DLU: 77

709.381-042 SPRING FORMER, HAND (metal prod., nec) alternate titles: fitter, hand
Shapes semielliptical spring leaves, using hand-forming jack: Reads specifications to determine arch required to shape leaf and computes additional arch required to compensate for unsetting of leaves in subsequent operations. Positions forming die (flexible pattern) over center pin of jack. Bends pattern and secures it to jack with holding pin. Positions center hole of hot leaf over center pin and bends leaf, using clamp tongs. Clamps ends of each leaf to pattern and sprinkles water over leaf to set arch and prevent warping. Immerses leaves in oil and places them in tempering oven [TEMPERER (heat treating)]. Shapes cold leaves on fitting block with sledgehammer.
GOE: 06.02.24 STRENGTH: M GED: R3 M2 L2 SVP: 7 DLU: 77

709.381-046 WIRE-MESH-FILTER FABRICATOR (metal prod., nec)
Fabricates and installs wire-mesh screening in housings of filters used for swimming pools and in motors of jet aircraft, motor boats, and automobiles, following blueprints or sketches, using handtools, power tools, and metalworking tools: Cuts copper or stainless steel wire-mesh screening sections according to dimensional specifications, using hand shears, scissors, or power shears. Joins sections of screening, using spot welding or riveting machines. Solders seams of screen with soldering iron or silver solder and acetylene torch. Applies silver solder and flux to screening crosspieces, and places screening in gas-fired furnace to melt solder, using tongs. Fits screening into housing of filter and solders screening in place. May fabricate and install wire-mesh screening in housing of experimental model fitters and be designated Experimental Fabricator-And-Installer (metal prod., nec).
GOE: 06.02.24 STRENGTH: L GED: R4 M3 L3 SVP: 6 DLU: 77

709.382-010 SEWING-MACHINE TESTER (machinery mfg.)
Sets up and operates new sewing machines to test machine and attachments preparatory to shipment: Feeds piece of cloth into machine to test feeding action. Threads machine and makes prescribed tension adjustments preparatory to test sewing. Starts machine and sews sample piece of cloth, varying stitching pattern and type of stitch to evaluate machine operation. Installs machine attachments, such as hemming, buttonholing, and shirring devices to evaluate operation of attachments. Rejects defective machines and attachments. May verify effectiveness of machine attachments, using detachable gauge. May specialize in attachment testing and be designated Sewing-Machine Attachment Tester (machinery mfg.).
GOE: 06.03.01 STRENGTH: L GED: R3 M2 L2 SVP: 5 DLU: 77

709.384-010 FIRE-EXTINGUISHER REPAIRER (any industry)
Repairs and tests fire extinguishers in repair shops and in establishments, such as factories, homes, garages, and office buildings, using handtools and hydrostatic test equipment: Dismantles extinguisher and examines tubings, horns, head gaskets, cutter discs, and other parts for defects. Replaces worn or damaged parts, using handtools. Cleans extinguishers and recharges them with materials, such as soda water and sulfuric acid, carbon tetrachloride, nitrogen, or patented solutions. Tests extinguishers for conformity with legal specifications, using hydrostatic test equipment. May install cabinets and brackets to hold extinguishers. May sell fire extinguishers.
GOE: 05.10.04 STRENGTH: M GED: R3 M2 L2 SVP: 3 DLU: 77

709.484-010 SILK-SCREEN-FRAME ASSEMBLER (any industry) alternate titles: frame builder, silk-screen; setter-up, silk-screen frame
Builds frames for silk or metal screens used to stencil identifying or operational data on parts or products following blueprints: Bends bar stock to specified shape and dimensions to form frame, using vise and handtools. Solders joints, using soldering iron. Measures and marks location of holes on frame, using rule. Drills and threads holes, using drill press and handtap. Screws guides and stops in holes for use in positioning part in frame.
GOE: 06.04.23 STRENGTH: L GED: R3 M2 L2 SVP: 3 DLU: 77

709.484-014 STRAIGHTENER, HAND (any industry)
Straightens metal workpieces to blueprint specifications, using handtools and knowledge of metal properties: Rolls workpiece on flat surface or mounts and rotates it between centers to ascertain irregularities visually or with dial indicator. Positions workpiece on surface plate or anvil and hammers workpiece at points of irregularity to straighten it. Hammers mandrel through cylindrical objects, such as pipes or tubing to remove dents or kinks. Measures straightened workpiece for conformance with specifications, using straightedge, micrometers, and calipers. May straighten workpiece in straightening press. May heat workpiece in furnace or with heating torch to straighten it. May be designated according to parts straightened as Tool Straightener (any industry); Straightener, Gun Parts (ordnance).
GOE: 06.02.24 STRENGTH: M GED: R3 M2 L2 SVP: 5 DLU: 77

709.587-010 INSPECTOR (cutlery-hrdwr.)
Inspects and examines articles, such as can openers, hacksaw blades, steel rules, and kitchen cutlery for manufacturing defects: Examines parts for defects, such as nicks, defective plating, and incorrect marking. Verifies dimensions of parts, using fixed gauges. Turns handle of can opener to verify meshing of gears. Attaches tag, noting defects, to article and returns it to repair department. May be designated according to article inspected as Hacksaw Inspector (cutlery-hrdwr.); Steel-Rule Inspector (cutlery-hrdwr.).
GOE: 06.03.02 STRENGTH: L GED: R2 M2 L2 SVP: 3 DLU: 77

709.587-014 SPOILAGE WORKER (tinware) alternate titles: can-repairer
Inspects and repairs rejected tin cans and tin-can parts: Inspects parts for defects, such as scratches, dents, nicks, and punctures, and sorts parts according to type of defect. Places can parts over die of straightening fixture and depresses pedal that forces curving plate against die to remove dents or places can body over form and reshapes flanges and side walls, using rubber hammer. Tests cans for leaks, using pressure tester [TESTING-MACHINE OPERATOR (tinware)]. Solders holes in seams, using gas flame and hand-soldering iron. Cleans can parts with damp cloth, water, or solvent. Records source, type, and disposition of reprocessed cans and places cans and can parts in carton. Weighs scrap and routes scrap to salvage department. May observe decorated cans emerging from oven and remove cans with defects, such as faulty printing, malformed seams, or foreign materials.
GOE: 06.03.02 STRENGTH: L GED: R2 M1 L2 SVP: 4 DLU: 77

709.667-010 FABRIC STRETCHER (furniture) alternate titles: bunk assembler; cot assembler; fabric assembler; flat-spring assembler
Clinches wire mesh fabric to metal frames to assemble springs for cots, folding beds, and other furniture: Clamps frame in jig and hooks helical springs to frame bars. Spreads fabric and stretches springs, using hooked handtool, and links spring hooks to loops of fabric. Attaches hooks to secure fabric to frame, using pliers and hammer.
GOE: 06.04.22 STRENGTH: L GED: R2 M1 L1 SVP: 3 DLU: 77

709.682-010 AUTOCLAVE OPERATOR II (chemical)
Operates series of high pressure autoclaves to test fabricated uranium fuel elements for leakage and ruptures in zirconium cladding and weld: Loads fuel elements in metal baskets and places baskets into tank of autoclave, using crane. Closes tank lid, using torque wrench. Turns valve to admit specified amount of water into tank, and closes exhaust outlet of tank. Activates electric heating element, adjust control knobs, and observes gauges to obtain specified temperature and pressure. Monitors guages to prevent rise in temperature and listens for alarm signal that indicates leak or rupture of one or more fuel elements. Presses button to cut off heat elements, opens exhaust water valve to dump hot water, and opens valve to admit cold water to cool elements. Opens autoclave, removes basket, and replaces tested elements. Records serial number of ruptured elements. Periodically tests quality of deionized water in autoclave, using special equipment.
GOE: 06.03.01 STRENGTH: R GED: R3 M2 L3 SVP: 6 DLU: 77

709.684-010 ADJUSTER (furniture)
Bends or shapes doors and drawers so that they fit snugly and work smoothly in assembled metal furniture without binding, using handtools.
GOE: 05.10.01 STRENGTH: M GED: R2 M2 L2 SVP: 3 DLU: 77

709.684-014 ASSEMBLER, METAL FURNITURE (furniture) alternate titles: metal-furniture assembler
Performs any combination of following tasks to assemble metal furniture: Drills holes in parts, such as backrests, covers, and seats, using power drill and template. Fits parts together and fastens them temporarily with clamps and presses. Bolts, staples, or screws parts together, using handtools, such as pliers, wrenches, pneumatic screwdrivers, and staplers. Rivets parts together, using hand or pneumatic hammer. Inserts such parts as casters and scuff plates into holes or slots. Bends fastening devices and fits interlocking parts together with hammer or rubber mallet or by striking parts against floor or workbench. Applies cement to cushions and covers with brush or spray gun, and joins parts by hand. Pulls and fastens drawstrings, wires, or springs to join precut upholstery covers to armrests, seats, and other parts, using handtools. Inserts drawers into slides and adjusts slides to fit drawer surfaces. Packs furniture for shipment. May bend metal parts, using bending machine. May be designated according to parts assembled as Backrest Assembler (furniture); Seat Assembler furniture); or according to type of metal furniture assembled as Art Metal-Chair Assembler (furniture); Office-Chair Assembler (furniture); Table Assembler, Metal (furniture).
GOE: 06.04.22 STRENGTH: M GED: R2 M2 L2 SVP: 2 DLU: 80

709.684-018 ASSEMBLY-LINE INSPECTOR (furniture)
Inspects unfinished metal articles of furniture for defects in metal or poor work: Marks rejected piece with chalk or crayon and returns it to proper department for repairs. Observes and feels welds and bent corners for burrs. Removes burrs, using file or emery paper. May inspect assembled electric hospital beds to certify conformity to production standards.
GOE: 06.03.02 STRENGTH: L GED: R3 M2 L2 SVP: 4 DLU: 77

709.684-022 BABBITTER (machine shop)
Lines bearing surfaces of metal workpieces with babbit (tin alloy) to reduce friction and wear: Melts metal in pot or ladle. Positions workpiece in fixture,

and heats with torch. Pours molten metal from ladle or pot into fixture. Smooths and shapes bearing surfaces to match contours, using hand scraper. May apply acid to workpiece and dip it in molten tin to coat surface preparatory to babbitting.
GOE: 06.02.24 STRENGTH: M GED: R3 M2 L1 SVP: 6 DLU: 77

709.684-026 BIRD-CAGE ASSEMBLER (metal prod., nec)
Fabricates wire birdcages, using handtools and drill press: Cuts wire to specified length, using wirecutter. Positions metal plate in jig, and drills holes around circumference of plate, using drill press. Fits ends of wires into holes in plate, and fastens upper ends of wire together to form cage.
GOE: 06.04.23 STRENGTH: L GED: R2 M1 L1 SVP: 4 DLU: 77

709.684-030 CAGE MAKER (concrete prod.)
Cuts, forms, and welds wire mesh and reinforcing steel to fabricate cages used in reinforcing concrete pipe and other concrete forms, according to blueprint or work order specifications: Obtains roll of wire mesh of specified gauge, and unrolls and stretches out mesh for cutting. Measures mesh with steel rule and cuts strands, using hand or pneumatic cutter. Feeds wire mesh into rollers of bending machine and turns adjusting wheel to shape frame or cage sections. Places formed rods or mesh on floor or in special forming stand preparatory to welding. Tack-welds sections together, using arc-welding equipment. Cuts reinforcing steel, using cutting torch.
GOE: 06.02.24 STRENGTH: M GED: R3 M1 L2 SVP: 5 DLU: 77

709.684-034 CIGARETTE-LIGHTER REPAIRER (any industry)
Repairs and cleans cigarette lighters, using handtools: Disassembles lighter and adjusts or replaces parts, such as spark wheels, injector valves, and clutch gears, using handtools. Removes cotton and defective wick from lighter, inserts new wick, and repacks cotton, using tweezers and picks. Immerses lighters in solution to clean them. Applies polish to lighters and refinishes surfaces, using hand polisher. Inserts flint and fills lighter with fluid or gas. May immerse butane lighters in specified solution to detect leaks. May sell lighters to customers. May compute charges for repairs.
GOE: 05.12.15 STRENGTH: L GED: R2 M1 L2 SVP: 3 DLU: 77

709.684-038 CLIP-BOLTER AND WRAPPER (metal prod., nec) alternate titles: clip wrapper
Clips assembled leaf springs together by any of following methods: (1) Inserts bolt through end holes in U-shaped clip and tightens nut, using impact wrench. (2) Inserts bolt through hole in end of spring and positions spring and clip in holding device. Hammers clip around spring to align hole in clip over bolt. Tightens nut on bolt, using impact wrench. (3) Installs holding die and aligns spring end over clip. Starts press that automatically wraps clip around spring. Reams rough ends from main-leaf eyes, using drill press.
GOE: 06.04.22 STRENGTH: M GED: R2 M2 L1 SVP: 3 DLU: 77

709.684-042 HAND STAMPER (any industry)
Stamps designs or lettering into metal workpieces, using hand stamps (punches) and hammer: Obtains specified stamp from rack and holds and hammers it to imprint workpiece. May use stand or fixture to position stamp or workpiece.
GOE: 06.04.24 STRENGTH: M GED: R2 M1 L2 SVP: 3 DLU: 77

709.684-046 HOT-TOP LINER (steel & rel.)
Lines ingot mold covers (hot-tops) with firebrick and refractory mortar, using handtools: Examines cover to determine necessary repairs. Pries or chips defective lining from inside of cover, using crowbar, hammer, or pneumatic chisel. Cleans covers, using wire brush. Mixes specified amount of refractory mortar powder with water and spreads mixture on inside of cover, using trowel. Positions firebrick and refractory ring in mortar, using trowel, tamping bar, and wire clamps. Mixes specified amounts of molasses and graphite to form base for premixed facing solution and applies base and facing solution to cover, using brush.
GOE: 05.12.09 STRENGTH: H GED: R2 M1 L1 SVP: 3 DLU: 77

709.684-050 KEY CUTTER (any industry) alternate titles: key maker; keysmith; key worker
Cuts notches in key blanks to duplicate notches of original key, using key-duplicating machine: Selects key blank according to size, shape, or code number of original key. Positions original key and blank in vises on carriage of machine and against guides. Turns thumbscrews to secure key and blank in vises. Starts cutting disk of machine. Pushes and pulls horizontally moving carriage of machine to slide notched edge of original key against stationary guide on machine and to move key blank against cutting disk, duplicating notches of original key in bit of blank. Turns thumbscrews and removes keys from vises. Presses and holds duplicated key against revolving wire wheel to remove burrs from key. Positions one key atop other to compare notches of keys. May collect payment from customer and make change. May sell key holders or related novelty items.
GOE: 05.12.13 STRENGTH: L GED: R2 M2 L2 SVP: 2 DLU: 77

709.684-054 MOLD STAMPER (machine shop)
Lays out and stamps lettering and designs manually on tire molds, following blueprints: Positions and clamps mold on worktable manually or using hoist. Reads blueprint to obtain information, such as location and spacing of single letters, words, and designs. Applies blue pigment to mold and measures and marks reference lines with protractor, rulers, and scribers to indicate location of specified stampings. Positions stamps according to layout lines and hammers

stamps to imprint letters and designs in mold in reverse order. Inspects impressions with template to verify uniform depth. May compute spacing of letters. May set up and operate pantograph machine to engrave letters and designs in molds.
GOE: 06.02.31 STRENGTH: M GED: R3 M3 L3 SVP: 6 DLU: 77

709.684-058 REAMER, HAND (machine shop)
Reams drilled holes in metal workpieces, using handtools. Inserts reamer (straight-fluted rotary cutting tool) into hole and twists and pushes it to enlarge, smooth, or improve roundness of hole. Verifies hole specifications, using plug gauge. May place workpieces in vise when reaming out hole.
GOE: 06.02.24 STRENGTH: M GED: R3 M1 L2 SVP: 5 DLU: 77

709.684-062 REPAIRER (furniture) alternate titles: salvage worker
Repairs or replaces damaged metal furniture parts, using handtools and power tools: Welds cracks, using acetylene torch. Files, scrapes, or sands parts to remove dirt, paint, or rust. Melts solder into holes and cracks. Grinds solder until smooth and flush with surrounding metal, using portable grinder. Bends or hammers dented or twisted parts to original shape. Replaces inoperative furniture parts. May reassemble metal furniture.
GOE: 05.10.01 STRENGTH: L GED: R3 M1 L2 SVP: 5 DLU: 77

709.684-066 RIVETER, HAND (any industry)
Rivets together light-gauge metal parts to assemble articles, such as kitchenware, household appliances, and metal furniture, using portable riveting gun or rivet set and hammer: Aligns parts and inserts rivets in rivet holes. Positions parts with rivet head against anvil or die. Places die of rivet gun or rivet set over end of rivet shank. Presses trigger of gun or strikes end of rivet set with hammer to spread rivet over rivet hole. May drill or ream rivet holes, using portable drill. May remove defective rivets, using hand punch.
GOE: 06.04.22 STRENGTH: M GED: R2 M1 L1 SVP: 2 DLU: 77

709.684-070 SALVAGER (petrol. refin.) alternate titles: salvage repairer; valve repairer, reclamation
Repairs defective valves and pipefittings removed from refinery pipelines, following specifications and using handtools and power tools: Clamps valve gauge in vise. Grinds surfaces of valve gauge to specified finish, using portable grinder. Cleans valve parts, using electric buffer and solvents. Verifies dimensions of valve parts, using calipers. Sends parts that require machining to machine shop. Orders new parts by catalog number, size, and type. Assembles and repacks valves, using handtools. Screws valve on testing device and moves handle of hydraulic pump to test valve at specified pressures. Tightens bolts to stop leaks, using wrench. Removes flanges and pipefittings from pipe, using wrenches and acetylene cutting torch. Cleans flanges and fittings, using sandblasting equipment [SANDBLASTER (any industry)]. Paints valves and fittings, using spray gun. Keeps inventory record of valves, flanges, and pipefittings by size and type. May recondition other refinery equipment, such as steam traps, water glasses, tubing, and condenser sections.
GOE: 05.10.02 STRENGTH: H GED: R3 M2 L2 SVP: 5 DLU: 77

709.684-074 SHEARER AND TRIMMER, WIRE SCREEN AND FABRIC (metal prod., nec) alternate titles: screen cutter and trimmer; shearer, screen measurer and trimmer
Cuts and trims edges of wire screening or fabric to specified dimensions, using hand shears and hone: Measures material to locate specified point of cut, using rule, scale, or pattern. Cuts material following line between parallel wires of weave or along edge of pattern. Inspects and hones cut edges to remove burrs and even tips of wires, using magnifying glass and hand hone. May hold workpieces in position for brazing. May clean or polish finished workpiece to remove tarnish, using specified cleaning solution or polishing wheel. May cut and trim wire screening, using scissors, power shears, power slitting machine, and grinding machine. May solder edges of screen of wire cloth to form seam and be designated Seamer (metal prod., nec).
GOE: 06.04.24 STRENGTH: M GED: R2 M1 L2 SVP: 3 DLU: 77

709.684-078 SPRING FITTER (metal prod., nec)
Measures, reshapes, and assembles spring leaves to form set of matched springs: Measures leaves, using ruler and straightedge, and sorts them according to size and shape. Reshapes warped leaves to specifications, using sledge-hammer or shaping press. Selects and positions matched leaves in vise on worktable and presses pedal to compress leaves. Inserts bolts through leaf holes and tightens nut, using wrench. Verifies length and alignment of spring, using straightedge and ruler. May route spring leaves through assembly process after repairing leaves.
GOE: 06.02.24 STRENGTH: M GED: R3 M2 L2 SVP: 5 DLU: 77

709.684-082 STAB SETTER AND DRILLER (cutlery-hrdwr.) alternate titles: blank driller
Fabricates dies used to mark sewing reference points on materials: Positions metal blank on bed of drill press. Aligns drill template over plate. Starts machine and drills holes into blank. Inserts stabs (pointed metal dowels) into holes. Places stab setter (handpunch) over stab and hammers stab into hole.
GOE: 06.02.02 STRENGTH: L GED: R2 M2 L2 SVP: 3 DLU: 77

709.684-086 TORCH-STRAIGHTENER-AND HEATER (any industry) alternate titles: straightener, torch
Straightens metal plates, weldments, and structural shapes or preheats them preparatory to welding or bending, using torch: Selects torch tip from data charts according to thickness, area, and temperature of metal to heat. Screws

tip on torch and connects hoses from torch to tanks of oxygen and fuel gas, such as acetylene. Turns levers to activate flow of gas, lights flame, and adjusts mixture to obtain desired size and color of flame. Holds or guides flame along surface of workpiece to heat and expand metal, to achieve specified straightness, or until color indicates sufficient heating for welding or machine straightening or bending. Measures workpiece with straightedge or template to ensure conformance with specifications. May hammer out bulges and bends. May place workpiece into heating furnace for specified period of time, using jib of crane.
GOE: 05.10.01 STRENGTH: H GED: R3 M2 L2 SVP: 4 DLU: 77

709.684-090 TUBE BENDER, HAND I (any industry) alternate titles: bender, hand
Bends metal and plastic tubing, according to specifications, for use in hydraulic, fuel, and electrical installations: Draws outline of tubing on cardboard or cuts wood forming blocks with band scroll saw, following templates. Screws blocks to forming board, as specified. Bends tubing by hand to conform to outline on cardboard or hammers tubing around forming blocks, using mallet. May heat plastic tubing in hot oil or water to facilitate bending. May operate circular power hacksaw to cut tubing. May bead, burr, and flare tubing. May assemble and test preformed metal tubing for use in hydraulic, fuel, and water systems of aircraft and spacecraft.
GOE: 06.02.24 STRENGTH: L GED: R3 M1 L1 SVP: 4 DLU: 77

709.684-094 UTILITY OPERATOR II (chemical)
Assembles *monotubes*, unloads and stores nuclear reactor fuel elements, and decontaminates work area: Places fuel elements and spacers on rack of monotube loading machine in sequential order. Activates machine that automatically pushes fuel elements and spacers into monotubes. Moves filled monotubes to storage, using recharge machine. Removes tube caps from reactor wall openings and attaches connector to loaded monotube and adapter to reactor tube preparatory to charging-discharging operation, using handtools. Decontaminates work area, using brush, soap, and water. Places radiation exposed safety clothing in laundry bags for cleaning and stacks cleaned clothing on shelves.
GOE: 05.12.12 STRENGTH: M GED: R3 M2 L2 SVP: 3 DLU: 77

709.684-098 WIRE-FRAME-LAMP-SHADE MAKER (fabrication, nec)
Constructs wire lampshade frames, working from blueprints, sketches, and models, using handtools and wireworking machines: Builds jig of heavy gauge wire to fix position of framing members and hold them in position during production assembly and welding operations, using handtools. Inserts forming blocks and wire stops into machines and adjusts stops and rollers, using handtools. Loads automatic wire-cutting machine and feeds lengths of wire cut to size into wire-forming roller and bending machines. Positions top and bottom frame rings over jig and spot welds framing membersto rings.
GOE: 06.02.24 STRENGTH: L GED: R3 M2 L3 SVP: 5 DLU: 77

709.684-102 WIRE-ROPE-SLING MAKER (metal prod., nec)
Fabricates wire rope slings from cut lengths of wire rope: Cuts wire rope to specified length, using hand shears or abrasive cutting wheel. Marks rope at specified points, using chalk, and seizes at marks to facilitate forming sling. Forms loop and makes splice, using either of following methods: (1) on mechanical splice, splits rope by separating three adjacent strands to seizing, leaving other three strands and core intact. Bends sets of strands into desired size loop crossing over with one set. Lays strand sections alternately back into rope grooves until sections are laid into throat. Cuts out core and attaches metal sleeve to base of loop. Presses sleeve onto rope, using mechanical or hydraulic press: (2) on hand splice, forms loop at end of rope to seizing. Places loop in splicing vise or places thimble in loop, when required. Interweaves or tucks loose end of strands into body strands, using marlinespike. Cuts protruding ends and hammers down splice, using block of wood and mallet. Wraps wire over splice, when required. Attaches fittings, such as hooks, shackles, turnbuckles, and sockets, to slings according to customer's order. May apply some fittings by swaging or filling with molten zinc.
GOE: 06.02.24 STRENGTH: M GED: R3 M1 L2 SVP: 5 DLU: 77

709.685-010 GOLD RECLAIMER (metal prod., nec)
Tends equipment that crushes, filters, and separates embedded gold particles from materials, such as broken or scrapped clay, melted crucible, and waste water to reclaim gold for reuse: Fills bin of crusher with material to be processed, using shovel, and starts crusher to grind material into fine powder. Separates gold particles from powder, using special reciprocating table, agitation tank, thickener, and set of troughs. Turns valves and knobs and adds specified amounts of ingredients to waste water in tank. Moves switch to start precipitation process.
GOE: 06.04.02 STRENGTH: M GED: R2 M1 L2 SVP: 3 DLU: 77

709.685-014 HOT BOX OPERATOR (metal prod., nec)
Tends machine that removes wrinkles from rolls of metal foil: Places roll of foil on machine feed roller. Threads foil through tension rollers and heated tunnel, and attaches end of foil to rewind roller. Turns valves and knobs to set required tension of rollers and specified heat of tunnel. Starts and observes operation of machine to detect malfunction. Makes required adjustment or notifies supervisor. Removes wrinkle-free roll of foil from machine for further processing.
GOE: 06.04.02 STRENGTH: L GED: R2 M1 L2 SVP: 2 DLU: 77

709.685-018 ROLLER, GOLD LEAF (metal prod., nec)
Tends machine that forms rolls of gold leaf: Places roll of paper on arbor of machine and feeds paper around tension and rewind rollers. Positions coil

of wax on machine roller and book of gold leaf on machine table. Starts machine and removes gold leaf from book, using pinchers. Places gold leaf on paper passing into machine, and pulls lever to apply wax coating to paper to prevent sticking of gold leaf on rotating roll which is cut to specified length by machine.
GOE: 06.04.34 STRENGTH: L GED: R2 M1 L2 SVP: 3 DLU: 77

709.686-010 LABORER, TIN CAN (tinware)
Performs any combination of following tasks involved in manufacture of tin cans: Opens bales of tinplate, using cutters. Removes rust spots, oil stains, or other surface accumulations, from sheets of tinplate, using steel wool, scouring powder, or cloths soaked in alcohol. Straightens bent or dented tinplate with mallet. Places cans and lids on paint racks, prior to painting process and removes painted items from racks for shipping. Supplies packing-line workers with packing materials. Places units, such as handles and cleats on flux pads and positions nozzles and solder strips on cans on conveyors that pass into ovens used to join items to cans. Packs cans or lids in cardboard containers by hand or using packing machine, or bulk-packs cans in railroad cars or transport trucks with handtools. Lines railroad cars or trucks with paper and installs bulkheads for bulk loading. Sorts cans according to size and type. Feeds flattened can bodies through reforming machine to straighten them. Seals containers with tape, staples, and bands or feeds filled containers through glue machine. Repairs, relabels, and collapses used cartons for subsequent use. Wraps pallet loads of cans with cardboard and paper. Stacks, moves, or loads cans, containers, materials, and supplies around areas of plant by hand, truck, or cart. May inspect units for obvious defects and discard defective items. May be designated according to work assigned as Bag Sealer (tinware); Can-Reforming-Machine Operator (tinware); Can Stacker (tinware); Cleaner (tinware).
GOE: 06.04.24 STRENGTH: H GED: R2 M1 L1 SVP: 2 DLU: 77

709.687-010 CLEANER AND POLISHER (any industry)
Cleans and polishes chromium or nickel plated articles with cloth and liquid cleanser. May remove paint or other foreign matter adhering to surface of article with solvent, knife, or steel wool. May be designated according to type of metal cleaned as Chrome Cleaner (any industry); Nickel Cleaner (any industry).
GOE: 06.04.39 STRENGTH: L GED: R1 M1 L1 SVP: 2 DLU: 77

709.687-014 CLEANER, FURNITURE (furniture) alternate titles: bed washer; furniture cleaner; metal cleaner
Removes dirt, grease, rust, nicks, and scratches from surfaces of metal furniture or parts, using any of following methods: (1) Immerses furniture or parts into series of chemical and water baths, using hoist. (2) Rubs and wipes metal surfaces with cleaning fluid and dry cloth. (3) Rubs surfaces with emery cloth or sandpaper to remove rust and scratches. (4) Moves steam iron covered with damp cloth across laminated tabletops and wipes moisture from cleaned tabletops with cloth. May be designated by type of metal furniture cleaned as Table-And-Desk Finisher (furniture).
GOE: 06.04.39 STRENGTH: M GED: R1 M1 L1 SVP: 2 DLU: 77

709.687-018 HOT-TOP-LINER HELPER (steel & rel.)
Assists HOT-TOP LINER (steel & rel.) in lining covers (hot-tops) for ingot molds: Pries and chips firebrick, mortar, and clay from inside of cover, using tools, such as crowbar or chipping hammer. Attaches crane hooks to lugs of cover. Cleans mold with oxygen lance. Mixes mortar and carries firebrick to repair platform. May signal crane operator to lift and position covers. Performs other duties as described under HELPER (any industry) Master Title.
GOE: 05.12.09 STRENGTH: H GED: R1 M1 L1 SVP: 3 DLU: 77

709.687-022 INSPECTOR (chemical)
Inspects nuclear reactor fuel elements and components for conformance to quality and dimensional specifications: Removes fuel elements and components from conveyors or crates, and inspects them for surface defects, such as pits, cracks, corrosion, and weld beads, using magnifying glass. Examines exposed radiographic films of fuel elements to detect presence of minute voids in elements. Compares defects with standards charts to determine acceptability of each element. Measures interior and exterior dimensions of elements, using ring and plug gauges. Rolls each element through warp gauge to ensure lengthwise alignment. Records number of defective elements and places elements in designated crate.
GOE: 06.03.02 STRENGTH: L GED: R3 M2 L2 SVP: 4 DLU: 77

709.687-026 INSPECTOR, WIRE PRODUCTS (metal prod., nec)
Inspects wire products, such as brassiere frames, oven or refrigerator racks, and wire cloth for conformance with specifications: Places product in fixture, or measures dimensions, using ruler to verify specified size and shape. Examines product for defects, such as broken welds, chipped or unpainted surfaces, holes, or uneven weave. Twists and bends product into alignment, using hands or pliers. Cuts defective sections from wire cloth, using scissors. Staples ends of wire cloth together, using stapling gun. Routes defective products to repair shop.
GOE: 06.03.02 STRENGTH: L GED: R2 M1 L2 SVP: 3 DLU: 77

709.687-030 PROOF-COIN COLLECTOR (government ser.)
Inspects proof (struck from new dies) coins produced by U.S. Mint for imperfections, such as burrs, scratches, and flattened edges. Packs satisfactory units for mailing to coin collectors in specially designed protective envelopes. May inspect medals, lapel buttons, ribbons, and similar items attached to coins for decorative or display purposes.

GOE: 06.03.02 STRENGTH: L GED: R3 M2 L2 SVP: 4 DLU: 77

709.687-034 SALVAGER HELPER (petrol. refin.)
Assists SALVAGER (petrol. refin.) in repairing defective valves and pipefittings removed from refinery pipelines: Dismantles valves, using wrenches. Rethreads pipefittings, using pipe threader. Sorts fittings according to type and size and places them in bins. Performs other duties as described under HELPER (any industry) Master Title.
GOE: 05.12.15 STRENGTH: H GED: R2 M1 L1 SVP: 4 DLU: 77

709.687-038 SPRING INSPECTOR II (metal prod., nec) alternate titles: inspector-and-unloader
Removes springs from conveyor belt and inspects them for defects, such as missing or bent leaves, clips, and bushings, and excessive spacing between leaves: Measures spring dimensions to verify specifications, using rule and micrometer. Marks spring to indicate defects, using crayon. Notifies supervisor when springs indicate specified types and quantity of defects that require rework. Separates and stacks defective and acceptable springs. Straightens defective springs, using hammer.
GOE: 06.03.02 STRENGTH: L GED: R2 M2 L2 SVP: 2 DLU: 77

709.687-042 SPRING TESTER II (metal prod., nec)
Tests resiliency of springs, such as those used in screen doors, using testing device: Attaches weights to spring and notes deflection and recovery of spring. Discards defective springs.
GOE: 06.03.02 STRENGTH: L GED: R2 M1 L2 SVP: 2 DLU: 77

709.687-046 TIN-CONTAINER STRIAGHTENER (tobacco)
Places tobacco tin over form and beats with hammer or mallet, or uses straightening device to remove minor dents from tins.
GOE: 06.04.24 STRENGTH: L GED: R1 M1 L1 SVP: 1 DLU: 77

709.687-050 TUBE BENDER, HAND II (any industry)
Bends metal tubing around forming blocks, or between rollers of bending device to produce components for such products as refrigeration systems or electrical heating units: Marks tubing at point of bend or places end of tubing against stop of bending device. Bends tubing to specified shape around rollers or forming blocks. May slip fittings on tube. May flare tube by forcing end against rotating cone. May be designated according to material formed as Wire Bender, Hand (any industry).
GOE: 06.04.24 STRENGTH: L GED: R2 M1 L1 SVP: 2 DLU: 77

709.687-054 ULTRASONIC TESTER (chemical)
Tests fabricated uranium fuel elements for bonding and element container for thickness in atomic fuel plant, using ultrasonic testing equipment: Pushes buttons and turns dials to activate test equipment. Places fuel element used as standard in test equipment tank, and calibrates ultrasonic sensor chart indicator, comparing chart from test run to standard chart pattern previously obtained. Places untested fuel elements in test tank and observes reading on ultrasonic chart to detect deviations from standard to determine acceptability of elements. Removes fuel elements from tank and places elements in designated cart. Records serial number of rejected fuel elements and type of defects causing rejection. Periodically places standard fuel element in tank and runs test to verify calibration of equipment.
GOE: 06.03.01 STRENGTH: M GED: R3 M2 L2 SVP: 3 DLU: 77

709.687-058 WIRE BENDER (furniture)
Bends wire to form frames for mattress and box-spring assemblies, using wire-bending jig: Positions bending pegs on jig table according to specifications and tightens with wrench. Inserts one or more wires in holding device and depresses pedal to drive bending arms around pegs to bend wire to required angle or bends wire around pegs, using lever. Connects frame edge-wire ends with metal sleeve and rivet sleeve, using hammer and punch.
GOE: 06.04.24 STRENGTH: M GED: R1 M1 L1 SVP: 3 DLU: 77

709.687-062 WIRE-BASKET MAKER (metal prod., nec)
Bends rolled wire-meshing into specified shapes and sizes, using pliers and crimping tool to form such items as fry baskets and waste baskets. May shape wire, using bending jig.
GOE: 06.04.24 STRENGTH: M GED: R2 M1 L1 SVP: 2 DLU: 77

71 OCCUPATIONS IN FABRICATION AND REPAIR OF SCIENTIFIC, MEDICAL, PHOTOGRAPHIC, OPTICAL, HOROLOGICAL, AND RELATED PRODUCTS

This division includes occupations concerned with assembling, fabricating, and repairing scientific, engineering, and medical equipment, photographic and optical goods, clocks and watches, and related products including fabrication of precision optical and ophthalmic lenses, using specialized handtools and bench-type machines.

710 OCCUPATIONS IN FABRICATION AND REPAIR OF INSTRUMENTS FOR MEASURING, CONTROLLING, AND INDICATING PHYSICAL CHARACTERISTICS

This group includes occupations concerned with fabricating and repairing instruments for measuring, controlling, and indicating temperature, pressure and vacuum, fluid flow, liquid level, mechanical motion, rotation, humidity, density, acidity or alkalinity, and combustion, including those used to control home air-conditioning and heating systems and as components in household appliances; dial pressure gauges; scales and balances; and apparatus for testing such physical properties as hardness, tension, torsion, compression, and elasticity. Occupations concerned with instruments for measuring, recording, and controlling electrical characteristics are included in Division 72.

710.131-010 SUPERVISOR, GAS METER REPAIR (utilities)
Supervises and coordinates activities of workers engaged in testing, adjusting, and repairing gas meters: Trains workers in testing and repair of meters. Requisitions and distributes supply of repair parts. Performs other duties as described under SUPERVISOR (any industry) Master Title.
GOE: 05.10.02 STRENGTH: L GED: R4 M3 L3 SVP: 8 DLU: 77

710.131-014 SUPERVISOR, INSTRUMENT MAINTENANCE (any industry) alternate titles: instrument repair supervisor
Supervises and coordinates activities of workers engaged in inspecting, testing, repairing, adjusting, and calibrating instruments, such as altimeters, ammeters, barometers, compasses, position indicators, steam gauges, tachometers, and voltmeters: Prepares work orders indicating malfunctions of instruments. Inspects and tests shop equipment and repaired instruments for conformance to quality control standards, using testing equipment, such as oscilloscope, pressure chamber, ammeter, and voltmeter. May disassemble, adjust, alter, repair, calibrate, and reassemble damaged or defective instruments, using tweezers and handtools. May train workers in inspecting, testing, repairing, and calibrating procedures. Performs other tasks as described under SUPERVISOR (any industry) Master Title.
GOE: 05.05.11 STRENGTH: L GED: R4 M4 L4 SVP: 8 DLU: 88

710.131-018 SUPERVISOR, INSTRUMENT MECHANICS (utilities)
Supervises and coordinates activities of INSTRUMENT TECHNICIANS (utilities) engaged in repairing, adjusting, and calibrating meters, gauges, and remote-control equipment of steam-generating plant: Trains workers in repair of instruments. Develops standard methods and procedures for servicing, repairing, and calibrating instruments and control equipment, applying knowledge of repair procedures, using manufacturers maintenance and repair manuals. Sets up instruments to conduct efficiency and performance tests, performs necessary calculations to determine performance of instruments, and records data for use in future repairs. Submits requisitions for parts and test equipment. May assist workers in repair of instruments. Performs other duties as described under SUPERVISOR (any industry) Master Title.
GOE: 05.05.10 STRENGTH: L GED: R4 M4 L4 SVP: 8 DLU: 77

710.131-022 SUPERVISOR, INSTRUMENT REPAIR (any industry)
Supervises and coordinates activities of workers engaged in installing, inspecting, and renovating meters and other instruments used to measure, regulate, and control chemical and thermal processes and flow of liquids through pipelines: Inspects new and repaired instruments and verifies dimensions of parts, using test stand, gauges and micrometers. Trains new workers to install, inspect, and renovate instruments. Requisitions new parts and instruments. Assists workers in repair of instruments. Performs other duties as described under SUPERVISOR (any industry) Master Title.
GOE: 05.05.10 STRENGTH: L GED: R4 M3 L3 SVP: 7 DLU: 77

710.131-026 SUPERVISOR, METER REPAIR SHOP (utilities)
Supervises and coordinates activities of workers engaged in testing and repairing watt-hour meters, watt-hour demand meters, graphic demand meters, and instrument transformers in meter repair shop of electric power companies: Directs workers engaged in storing and issuing meters and meter repair parts and in making periodic stock inventories. May test electrical metering mechanisms used as standards for accuracy, using meters and instruments mounted on test board. May test protective goods for dielectric strength [RUBBER-GOODS TESTER (elec. equip.; utilities)]. May supervise and coordinate activities of workers engaged in testing and repairing electrical indicating instruments, such as ammeters, voltmeters, frequency meters, phase angle meters, phase rotation indicators, gas detectors, metal detectors, and analysers. May supervise and coordinate activities of workers engaged in testing and repairing clock movements in demand meters and other electric-power-system timing equipment. Performs other duties as described under SUPERVISOR (any industry) Master Title.
GOE: 05.05.10 STRENGTH: L GED: R4 M3 L4 SVP: 8 DLU: 77

710.131-030 SUPERVISOR, METER SHOP (waterworks)
Supervises and coordinates activities of workers engaged in installing, maintaining, removing, and repairing water meters: Instructs workers in methods of repairing and maintaining water meters. Inspects industrial plants, office buildings, and apartments to determine size, number, and type meters required. Requisitions materials and supplies required to clean, maintain, and repair meters. Tests accuracy of meters, using calibrated testing equipment and turns dials and indicators to adjust meters. Performs other duties as described under SUPERVISOR (any industry) Master Title.
GOE: 05.10.02 STRENGTH: M GED: R4 M3 L3 SVP: 7 DLU: 77

710.131-034 SUPERVISOR, SHOP (petrol. & gas) alternate titles: electronics supervisor; supervisor, research shop
Supervises and coordinates activities of INSTRUMENT-MAKER AND REPAIRER (petrol. & gas) in constructing, maintaining, and repairing mechanical

and electronic instruments and equipment used in petroleum prospecting and oil and gas well surveying and servicing: Assists subordinates in constructing, maintaining, and repairing instruments and equipment, using handtools. Inspects work of subordinates, using testing instruments. Performs other duties as described under SUPERVISOR (any industry) Master Title.
GOE: 05.05.10 STRENGTH: L GED: R4 M3 L3 SVP: 8 DLU: 77

710.131-038 SUPERVISOR, INSTRUMENT ASSEMBLY (electron. comp.; inst. & app.)

Supervises and coordinates activities of workers engaged in assembling electronic, electrical, mechanical, and electromechanical instruments, devices, subassemblies, and component parts: Reads work orders, production schedules, product specifications, and parts lists to determine work priorities and material requirements, such as fixtures, tools, supplies, and equipment. Assigns duties to workers. Sets up, or directs other workers to set up, machines and equipment at workstations, such as drill presses, tappers, and riveters. Observes assembly operations and examines product to ensure conformance to specifications, utilizing knowledge of assembly methods and procedures and established quality control standards. Performs other tasks as described under SUPERVISOR (any industry) Master Title.
GOE: 06.01.01 STRENGTH: L GED: R4 M3 L3 SVP: 8 DLU: 90

710.131-042 SUPERVISOR, THERMOSTATIC CONTROLS (inst. & app.)

Supervises and coordinates activities of workers engaged in assembly, repair, inspection, or calibration of thermostatic controls used to regulate household equipment, such as refrigerators, clothes dryers, and air-conditioners: Plans assembly, repair, inspection, or calibration of thermostats according to blueprints, product specifications, and engineering requirements, and assigns work to subordinates. Performs other tasks as described under SUPERVISOR (any industry) Master Title. May prepare requisitions for repair or maintenance of assembly machines, equipment, jigs, and fixtures. May be designated according to activity as Supervisor, Assembly Line (inst. & app.); Supervisor, Calibration (inst. & app.); Supervisor, Inspection (inst. & app.); Supervisor, Rework (inst. & app.).
GOE: 06.01.01 STRENGTH: L GED: R4 M3 L3 SVP: 7 DLU: 89

710.137-010 SUPERVISOR, ASSEMBLY I (office machines)

Supervises and coordinates activities of workers engaged in assembling, testing, adjusting, and calibrating scales, balances, and dynamometers. May dismantle and test scale components to determine cause of defects. Performs other tasks as described under SUPERVISOR (any industry) Master Title.
GOE: 06.02.01 STRENGTH: L GED: R4 M3 L3 SVP: 7 DLU: 77

710.137-014 SUPERVISOR, METER-AND-REGULATOR SHOP (petrol. refin.; utilities)

Supervises and coordinates activities of workers engaged in repairing, adjusting, installing, and testing meters, regulators, gauges, and recording instruments for measuring and regulating flow of gas, water, and petroleum: Inspects completed work to ensure adherance to company specifications. Submits requisitions for supplies and materials needed. Performs other duties as described under SUPERVISOR (any industry) Master Title.
GOE: 05.10.02 STRENGTH: L GED: R4 M3 L4 SVP: 8 DLU: 77

710.261-010 INSTRUMENT REPAIRER (any industry)

Repairs and calibrates speedometers and other automotive gauges and meters, using handtools and test equipment: Confers with customer to determine nature of malfunction. Inspects components, connections, and drive mechanisms to detect defects. Removes instrument from vehicle and disassembles, cleans, and inspects instrument to determine which parts are defective. Replaces worn and defective parts, using handtools. Tests and calibrates instruments, using mechanical and electronic devices, such as voltmeters, pressure generators, and speedometer tester. Installs instruments in vehicle, using handtools. Computes speedometer drive ratio changes for modified vehicles. Maintains stock and parts inventory. May operate jeweler's lathe and other machines to fabricate instrument parts. May repair automotive clocks [WATCH REPAIRER (clock & watch)].
GOE: 05.05.11 STRENGTH: L GED: R4 M3 L4 SVP: 8 DLU: 77

710.281-010 ASSEMBLER AND TESTER, ELECTRONICS (office machines)

Assembles subassemblies into electronic scale, dynamometer, or other force measuring instruments, following specifications, and tests for, diagnoses, and adjusts operating malfunctions: Assembles computer readout printer, scale, and scanner into one unit, using interconnecting cables and handtools. Assembles electronic components, such as frames, chassis boards, resistors, capacitors, circuit breakers, switches, transformers, and condensors into dynamometer or other force measuring instrument, using handtools, soldering iron, bench lathe, and drill press. Measures voltages, using voltmeter, and adjusts voltages to specified value. Varies line voltage, and interprets wave pattern on oscilloscope screen to determine operational accuracy of instrument under varying line voltage conditions. May adjust, repair, or replace parts and code colored wires. May be designated according to type instrument assembled as Dynamometer Assembler And Tester (office machines); Electronic-Scale Assembler And Tester (office machines).
GOE: 06.01.04 STRENGTH: L GED: R4 M3 L3 SVP: 6 DLU: 77

710.281-018 ELECTROMECHANICAL TECHNICIAN (inst. & app.)

Fabricates, tests, analyzes, and adjusts precision electromechanical instruments, such as accelerometers, altimeters, electromedical instruments, gyro-scopes, temperature probes, and x-ray inspection systems, according to blueprints and other specifications, using handtools, metalworking machines, and precision measuring and testing instruments: Operates metalworking machines, such as bench lathe, milling machine, punch press, and drill press to fabricate housings, fittings, jigs, and fixtures, and verifies dimensions, using precision measuring instruments. Assembles wires, insulation, and electrical components, such as resistors and capacitors, following method layouts, using fixtures, binocular microscope, soldering equipment, tweezers, and handtools. Installs electrical assemblies and hardware in housing, using handtools and soldering equipment. Tests assembled instruments for circuit continuity and operational reliability, using test instruments, such as multimeter, oscilloscope, oscillator, electronic voltmeter, and bridge. Analyzes test results and repairs or adjusts instruments according to analysis. Records test results and writes report on fabrication techniques used. May calibrate instruments according to specifications. May specialize in assembly of prototype or production instruments and be designated Development Technician (inst. & app.).
GOE: 05.05.11 STRENGTH: L GED: R4 M4 L4 SVP: 7 DLU: 90

710.281-022 GAS-METER PROVER (utilities) alternate titles: gas-meter adjuster

Tests ability of gas meters to accurately measure specified volume of gas at maximum and average cubic-feet-per-hour capacity and adjusts meters to correct excessive registration error: Connects hoses from prover to meter inlet and outlet and raises prover bell until prover gauge registers zero. Turns valve to allow measured amount of air or gas to pass through meter at specified flowrate. Closes valve and compares registration on meter gauge. Screws fitting into meter outlet to retard flow of gas and repeats test. Turns setscrews to adjust meter and repeats test until meter registration is within specified limits according to prover and meter gas readings. Analyzes test results to determine cause of persistent registration errors. Segregates meters requiring repair. Records test results and date on meter card. May maintain temperature of oil used as gas seal in prover within specified limits to ensure accurate and uniform test readings. May test ability of flowmeters to accurately measure gas and liquid and be designated Flowmeter Test And Certification Technician (inst. & app.).
GOE: 06.01.05 STRENGTH: M GED: R3 M3 L3 SVP: 7 DLU: 77

710.281-026 INSTRUMENT MECHANIC (any industry) alternate titles: instrument repairer

Installs, repairs, maintains, and adjusts indicating, recording, telemetering, and controlling instruments and test equipment, used to control and measure variables, such as pressure, flow, temperature, motion, force, and chemical composition, using precision instruments, and handtools: Disassembles malfunctioning instruments or test equipment, such as bargraphs, electrical ovens, multimeters, environmental cabinets, and weatherometers, and examines and tests mechanisms and circuitry for defects. Replaces or repairs defective parts, using handtools. Reassembles instrument or test equipment, and tests assembly for conformance to specifications, using instruments, such as potentiometer, resistance bridge, manometer, and pressure gauge. Inspects instruments and test equipment periodically and adjusts calibration to ensure functioning within specified standards. May calibrate instruments or test equipment according to established standards. May be designated according to type of instrument repaired as Aircraft Instrument Repairer (air trans.); Panel-Instrument Repairer (any industry); X-Ray-Control-Equipment Repairer (any industry).
GOE: 05.05.10 STRENGTH: M GED: R4 M3 L4 SVP: 7 DLU: 89

710.281-030 INSTRUMENT TECHNICIAN (utilities) alternate titles: oscillograph technician

Inspects, tests, adjusts, and repairs electric, electronic, mechanical, and pneumatic instruments and systems used to indicate, record, and control generating operations in conventional or nuclear power electric generating plant: Inspects meters, indicators, and gauges to detect abnormal fluctuations. Tests accuracy of flowmeters, pressure gauges, temperature indicators, controllers, radiation counters or detectors, and other recording, indicating or controlling instruments to locate defective components in system, using test equipment, such as pressure gauges, mercury manometers, potentiometers, pulse and signal generators, oscilloscopes, transistor curve tracers, and ammeters, voltmeters, and wattmeters. Traces out and tests electronic solid state and vacuum tube circuitry and components to locate defective parts in analog and digital, protection, or radiation monitoring systems, using test equipment, schematics, and maintenance manuals. Removes defective instruments from system, decontaminates, disassembles, and cleans instruments, and replaces defective parts, using handtools. Reassembles instruments and replaces instruments in system, using handtools. Lubricates instruments and replaces defective wiring and tubing. Calibrates readings on instruments according to standards and adjusts phasing and aligns stages to ensure accuracy of recording and indicating function. Records calibrations made, parts and components used, and inventory of parts on hand. Prepares schematic drawings, sketches, and reports to reflect changes or alterations made in instruments, circuits, and sytems. May be designated according to type power plant as Nuclear-Plant-Instrument Technician (utilities); Instrument Repairer, Steam Plant (utilities).
GOE: 05.05.11 STRENGTH: L GED: R4 M3 L3 SVP: 8 DLU: 77

710.281-034 METER REPAIRER (any industry)

Disassembles, cleans, adjusts, repairs, and tests oil, gas, and water meters, using handtools and testing equipment: Connects meter to testing apparatus. Turns valve to permit specified quantity of oil, gas, or water to pass through meter under varying pressure to test meter for leaks and accuracy of recording.

701

Disassembles meter, removing gear train and disk assembly, using handtools. Removes plant growth, rust, and scale from internal housing and parts, using wire brush, electric buffer, and acid. Repairs or replaces warped or broken disks and gears, and grinds and straightens parts to specified tolerance to fit parts to meter, using grinding machine and hydraulic press. Reassembles and tests meter. Tests large capacity meters in industrial plants to determine accuracy of operation. Records materials used and meters repaired. May install meters [WATER-METER INSTALLER (waterworks)]. May read meters [METER READER (utilities; waterworks)].
GOE: 05.10.02 STRENGTH: M GED: R4 M2 L3 SVP: 5 DLU: 77

710.281-038 TAXIMETER REPAIRER (automotive ser.)
Repairs and adjusts taxicab meters: Disassembles meters to determine cause of incorrect or nonregistering of time, mileage, or fare readings. Cleans meters, and repairs or replaces broken or worn parts. Adjusts registering mechanism gears, using handtools. Reassembles meters and makes final adjustments to registering mechanism control gear to meet test specifications.
GOE: 05.05.11 STRENGTH: L GED: R4 M3 L3 SVP: 6 DLU: 77

710.281-042 INSTRUMENT-TECHNICIAN APPRENTICE (utilities)
Performs duties as described under APPRENTICE (any industry) Master Title.
GOE: 05.05.11 STRENGTH: L GED: R4 M3 L3 SVP: 8 DLU: 77

710.360-010 SCALE ASSEMBLY SET-UP WORKER (office machines)
Installs, sets up, and adjusts machines, equipment, tools, jigs and fixtures at scale assembly workbench according to engineering specifications and drawings: Selects parts, components, materials, and tools according to engineering parts list and conveys parts to work station. Reads engineering specifications to determine scale or scale component to be assembled. Installs, sets up, and adjusts machines, tools, equipment, and work aids, such as drill press, kick press, air screwdrivers, engraving machine, soldering equipment, jigs, and fixtures, according to engineering specifications, using handtools. Assembles and tests balance scale or components to determine if equipment is set up according to specifications and readjusts equipment to meet specifications. Explains use of equipment to workers.
GOE: 06.01.02 STRENGTH: L GED: R4 M4 L3 SVP: 7 DLU: 77

710.361-010 MODEL MAKER, SCALE (office machines)
Assembles, tests, and adjusts prototype weight scales according to drawings, using handtools and power tools and metal fabricating machines: Selects prefabricated parts or fabricates parts required to assemble scale, using handtools and metal fabricating machines, such as drill press and bench lathe. Assembles mechanical and electrical parts and subassemblies of scale according to drawing, using handtools and power tools. Tests function and calibration of assembled scale, using test weights. Disassembles scale to determine type error and replaces or adjusts parts to correct error. Adds weight to poise or lever to calibrate scales or drills holes, hones, or twists levers or *pivots* to reduce weight. Informs engineering department of findings and recommends changes in design to correct or improve performance of prototype scale.
GOE: 05.05.11 STRENGTH: L GED: R4 M3 L3 SVP: 7 DLU: 77

710.361-014 TEST EQUIPMENT MECHANIC (aircraft mfg.) alternate titles: engineering test mechanic; structural test mechanic
Plans, lays out, constructs, modifies, tests, and maintains laboratory test equipment and related structural assemblies used to test experimental aircraft and space vehicle parts and assemblies, using precision instruments, handtools, power tools, and shop equipment: Reads and interprets blueprints, engineering drawings, and sketches, or receives verbal instructions, to determine methods and sequence of operations to lay out and construct mechanical, electrical, electronic, pneumatic, or hydraulic test equipment and related structures. Lays out and fabricates parts from assorted materials, such as aluminum, steel, wood, plastic, and graphite composites, using measuring instruments and shop equipment, such as saws, shears, drill presses, lathes, and routers. Fits, aligns, and assembles parts, equipment, specialized test devices, and structural framework to build test units, using precision measuring instruments, such as transit and level, power tools, rivets, bolts, clamps, pins, and other fasteners. Installs, or assists other workers in installing, test specimens in test equipment, using hoist, overhead crane, or related equipment. Assists engineers in operating test equipment to obtain research data on performance of experimental parts and assemblies under varying operational conditions. Diagnoses test equipment malfunctions and services and repairs equipment as required. May repair test specimens damaged during testing to prepare item for retesting. May specialize in constructing mechanical, electrical, electronic, pneumatic, hydraulic, or structural test equipment.
GOE: 06.01.04 STRENGTH: M GED: R4 M4 L4 SVP: 7 DLU: 88

710.381-010 ASSEMBLER II (office machines)
Assembles components and subassemblies of various types of scales: Verifies scale parts requirement list against parts inventory in work area to ensure supply for assembly. Assembles parts and subassemblies, such as base, levers, *stirrups*, pins, charts, indicators, and pendulums, into scale housing, using handtools and powered tools, jigs and fixtures, and plug and go-not-go gauges. Fills cavities with hot lead or lead shot to weight required for specific type scale, as fan type and cylinder type. Drills holes, twists levers, hones pivots, and files parts to ensure clearance, alignment, and accuracy. May assemble complete scale or work at position on assembly line. May test scales for accuracy, using master weights, and adjust parts and calibrate scale, using handtools.

GOE: 06.02.23 STRENGTH: L GED: R3 M2 L2 SVP: 5 DLU: 77

710.381-014 BALANCER, SCALE (office machines) alternate titles: inspector, scales
Inspects, tests, and adjusts scale mechanisms and repairs or replaces defective parts to ensure balance and accuracy of scales, using handtools and test equipment: Rolls test weights to and from position on scale platform and reads dial indications or weight tickets (if scale is so equipped) to verify accuracy of scales. Adjusts parts, such as *loading box,* rack, pendulum weights, and cams, for travel and leverage to determine type of error and coordinate readings with weights. Adjusts and tightens parts, such as locking handle, cam holddowns and ribbons, pendulum lever assembly, and stops for tare-beam lever, using handtools. Reduces friction to minimum in all bearings and parts of scale, using chisels, taps, tin snips, hacksaw, plumb bob, and electric drill. Repairs or replaces defective parts. May install parts in conjunction with balancing operation.
GOE: 06.01.05 STRENGTH: L GED: R4 M2 L2 SVP: 6 DLU: 77

710.381-022 GAS-METER MECHANIC I (utilities) alternate titles: meter tester
Reconditions, tests, and calibrates positive displacement gas meters, using handtools and test equipment: Dismantles gas meter case, diaphragm assembly, and connecting rods, using soldering iron and handtools. Positions and solders diaphragm and diaphragm rings in dismantled meter case. Inserts and solders flow-control valves in place, using soldering iron and guide wires. Moves shaft connected to valve to test freedom of movement. Adjusts shaft, using pliers, or resolders shaft to correct defective operation. Solders index assembly in position and connects assembly to activating mechanism. Moves activating arms to extreme extension to test freedom of movement. Adjusts valve mechanism to calibrate meter registration in accordance with public utilities commission specifications. Repositions and resolders connecting rods to provide sufficient clearance. Resolders case seams to seal meter. Attaches airhose at meter inlet to pressurize meter and test ability to register passage of low air volume. Attaches pressurized meter to fixture which submerges meter under water to test for leaks. May inspect, repair, and maintain gas meters used to measure volume of natural gas flowing from producing wells to processing plant and be designated Field Operator (petrol. & gas).
GOE: 05.10.02 STRENGTH: L GED: R3 M3 L3 SVP: 5 DLU: 77

710.381-026 GAS-REGULATOR REPAIRER (petrol. refin.; pipe lines; utilities)
Tests, repairs, and adjusts regulators (gas governors), relief valves, and related equipment used to control gas pressure in city gas mains and service pipes, pipelines, in-plant gas systems, and petroleum refineries: Dismantles regulator and examines such parts as springs, valves, and diaphragm for wear or deterioration. Cleans corrosion and tar deposits from serviceable parts, using solvents and wire brush. Cuts seat to receive new orifice, taps inspection ports, and performs other repairs to salvage useable materials, using handtools and machine tools. Reassembles regulator with new and reconditioned parts, according to blueprints. Connects regulator to test stand and turns screw adjustment until test-stand gauges indicate regulator inlet and outlet pressures are according to specifications for regulator and type of service. Tests and adjusts pressure setting of relief valves in similar manner. Records work done, pressure adjustment, and related data for each instrument. May install regulators, and such related equipment as gas meters, odorization units, and gas-pressure-telemetering equipment.
GOE: 05.05.09 STRENGTH: M GED: R4 M3 L3 SVP: 7 DLU: 77

710.381-030 HYDROMETER CALIBRATOR (inst. & app.) alternate titles: hydrometer finisher
Calibrates hydrometer tubes, using chemical solutions, marking device, and graduating machine: Mixes solutions of high, medium, and low specific gravity according to formula. Tests solutions, using standard hydrometer, and adjusts specific gravity of solutions. Places specified ballast weight into hydrometer float and seals hydrometer, using sealing compound. Immerses hydrometer into prepared solutions and marks levels of each solution on hydrometer tube. Graduates hydrometer, using engraving machine. Lines paper or metal scale into degrees, using drafter's pen or metal scriber, and secures scale inside hydrometer to ensure lines correspond to graduations on hydrometer.
GOE: 06.01.04 STRENGTH: L GED: R3 M2 L2 SVP: 6 DLU: 77

710.381-034 CALIBRATOR (inst. & app.) alternate titles: calibration technician
Tests and calibrates controlling, indicating, and measuring instruments and devices, such as monochromators, pressure regulators, tachometers, temperature controls, and thermometers, to ensure specified operating performance, using handtools, testing and calibrating instruments and equipment, and precision measuring instruments: Reads quality control manual and testing specifications to obtain data to test or calibrate specific devices. Selects and installs accessories, such as adapters, indicating gauges, or holding devices on test or calibration fixture, and connects instrument or device to fixture, according to specifications, using handtools. Sets controls to regulate factors, such as current flow, timing cycle, pressure, temperature, or vacuum, according to specifications, and activates test or calibration equipment. Observes readings on meters and gauges, and other displays and performance of device or instrument to identify functional defects and determine calibration requirements. Adjusts calibration mechanisms to obtain specified operational performance of device or in-

strument, using handtools and precision measuring and calibrating instruments and equipment. Applies sealing compound on calibration mechanism to prevent readjustment of settings and loss of calibration. Rejects malfunctioning devices and routes devices to specified department for rework or salvaging of parts. May disassemble instrument or device to determine cause of defective operation and notify supervisory personnel of findings.
GOE: 06.01.04 STRENGTH: L GED: R4 M3 L3 SVP: 6 DLU: 90

710.381-042 CALIBRATOR, BAROMETERS (inst. & app.) alternate titles: instrument calibrator
Tests, calibrates, and adjusts aneroid barometers to obtain specified performance, using handtools and test equipment: Places barometer in vacuum chamber and connects barometer to master barometer (mercurial or electronic). Starts vacuum pump to decrease atmospheric pressure in vacuum chamber, and records variances of readings between aneroid and master barometer at different atmospheric pressures, manually or using computer. Calculates adjustments required and calibrates barometer, using handtools, or automatically calibrates barometer to specifications, using computer. Tests calibrated barometer to ensure calibration conforms to master barometer. Prepares and maintains manual or computerized test and calibration records. May test calibration of aneroid barometers, using radio frequency signals recorded on tape. May disassemble, inspect, and replace defective barometer parts.
GOE: 06.01.04 STRENGTH: L GED: R4 M3 L3 SVP: 6 DLU: 90

710.381-046 TESTER, ELECTRONIC SCALE (office machines)
Tests assembled electronic scale components to detect missing parts, loose wires, and defective solder joints, using oscilloscope and voltmeter. Disassembles and repairs or replaces parts.
GOE: 05.10.03 STRENGTH: L GED: R3 M2 L2 SVP: 6 DLU: 77

710.381-050 THERMOSTAT REPAIRER (inst. & app.) alternate titles: field return repairer; production repairer
Repairs defective thermostats used in refrigeration, air-conditioning, and heating equipment, following blueprints and other specifications: Disassembles and examines thermostats to locate and remove defective parts, using handtools. Replaces defective parts, such as bellows, range spring, and toggle switch, and reassembles thermostat according to blueprint specifications, using cam press and handtools. Measures tolerances of assembled parts, using micrometer and calipers. Repairs leaks in valve seats or bellows of automotive heater thermostats, using soft solder, flux, and acetylene torch. Examines thermostat for defects, such as loose screws and dents. Writes repair ticket to identify thermostat and places repaired thermostats in tote boxes. Calibrates thermostat for specified temperature or pressure settings [CALIBRATOR (inst. & app.) 710.381-034].
GOE: 05.10.02 STRENGTH: M GED: R3 M3 L3 SVP: 5 DLU: 77

710.381-054 REPAIRER, GYROSCOPE (inst. & app.) alternate titles: electromechanical instrument mechanic
Tests and repairs gyroscopes according to blueprints and other specifications, using tools and equipment: Tests functional performance of gyroscope, using electronic test equipment. Disassembles mechanical and electrical components of defective gyroscope, following blueprints, using handtools and power tools. Measures parts, using precision measuring instruments, and adjusts fit of parts and balances gimbal (stabilizer), using handtools, power tools, and bench machines. Cleans and replaces parts. Tests and reassembles repaired gyroscope. May repair other precision electromechanical instruments, such as accelerometers and potentiometers.
GOE: 05.05.10 STRENGTH: M GED: R3 M3 L3 SVP: 6 DLU: 89

710.384-010 GAS-REGULATOR-REPAIRER HELPER (petrol. refin.; pipe lines; utilities)
Assists GAS-REGULATOR REPAIRER (petrol. refin.; pipe lines; utilities) in repair and installation of regulators, relief valves, and related equipment: Dismantles and cleans regulators preparatory to repair. Performs regulator pressure-tests as directed. Cuts, threads, and joins pipe sections and fittings to fabricate pipe assemblies to be installed in regulating stations by other workers. Drives truck to haul tools and equipment to regulator station. Performs other duties as described under HELPER (any industry) Master Title.
GOE: 05.10.02 STRENGTH: M GED: R3 M2 L2 SVP: 5 DLU: 77

710.384-014 INSPECTOR (office machines)
Inspects and tests parts, subassemblies, and finished scales and balances for conformance to quality standards, using written specifications, precision measuring instruments, and handtools: Inspects purchased or in-plant-fabricated parts for observable defects and tests specific components for hardness, dimensions and tolerances, using blueprints, hardness testing machine, and precision measuring instruments, such as micrometers, calipers, and thread gauges. Inspects and tests assembled scales and balances for appearance, allowable tolerances, reliability (repeated use), and accuracy (calibration), using master weights. Rejects unacceptable parts, subassemblies, and completed scales and prepares reports indicating defects and suspected cause.
GOE: 06.03.01 STRENGTH: L GED: R4 M3 L3 SVP: 7 DLU: 77

710.384-018 INSTRUMENT-REPAIRER HELPER (any industry)
Assists INSTRUMENT REPAIRER (any industry) I in installing, repairing, and adjusting recording and control instruments: Changes and collects charts on recording instruments. Observes operating condition of instruments and reports abnormal readings to INSTRUMENT MECHANIC (any industry). Drills holes

in masonry or structural steel for installation of instruments, using electric and pneumatic tools. Repairs and finishes parts, using buffers, grinders, and drill press. Paints instrument casings and panels, using brush or spray gun. Carries tools and materials, cleans parts and work areas, and erects hoists and scaffolds. Performs other duties as described under HELPER (any industry) Master Title.
GOE: 05.12.15 STRENGTH: M GED: R3 M2 L2 SVP: 5 DLU: 77

710.384-022 METER INSPECTOR (utilities)
Tests accuracy of gas flowmeters, using testing apparatus: Inserts measuring orifice disk between flanged ends of two metal pipe sections and connects pipe sections with bolts and nuts. Fastens one end of pipe to gas main leaving flowmeter and attaches rubber hose to free (discharge) end of pipe to deflect air currents. Sets frame containing manometer instruments on tripod and connects instruments to nipples on pipe and to flowmeter with rubber tubing. Reads instruments to obtain data, such as specific gravity and temperature of gas, and clocks number of seconds required for specified volume of gas to pass through meter. Computes accuracy of meter, using mathematical formulas based on readings and clocking tests and standard data stamped on orifice disk, and verifies calculations, using tabulated chart. Adjusts meters to correct inaccurate readings. May change recording charts on gas flowmeters [CHART CHANGER (clerical)].
GOE: 06.03.01 STRENGTH: L GED: R3 M3 L3 SVP: 4 DLU: 77

710.384-026 PARKING-METER SERVICER (government ser.)
Inspects, repairs, and maintains parking meters on designated route: Winds meters according to schedule, adjusts mechanisms, and repairs or replaces worn parts, using handtools. Straightens meter standards, using wrenches, and replaces broken glass. Disassembles meter and cleans and oils parts with gasoline and carbon tetrachloride. Keeps records of machine service histories to facilitate preventive maintenance or replacement of meters.
GOE: 05.10.02 STRENGTH: M GED: R3 M2 L2 SVP: 4 DLU: 77

710.384-030 THERMOMETER TESTER (inst. & app.)
Heats and cools thermometers to test flow of mercury, remove excess mercury, and establish calibration reference points: Places thermometer alternately into hot water and crushed ice and rubs thermometer across corrugated pad to force excess mercury and mercury vapor from thermometer into temporary top chamber of thermometer. Spins thermometer in centrifuge to force remaining mercury back into bulb at bottom of thermometer. Observes rise and fall of mercury column and rejects thermometer if particles of mercury or dirt cling to bore, or bore constrictions prevent specified rise and fall of mercury. Heats thermometer at two known temperatures and marks height of mercury column on tube as reference points for calibration.
GOE: 06.03.01 STRENGTH: L GED: R3 M2 L2 SVP: 5 DLU: 77

710.387-010 TESTER, REGULATOR (protective dev.; toy-sport equip.)
Tests and inspects compressed air or oxygen regulators to detect air leaks: Clamps regulator unit into vise on stage above water tank and attaches compressed airhose to intake ports of regulator. Varies pressure of air flowing into regulator, using manual control, and turns regulator handles to determine that valves and pistons are functioning properly. Lowers regulator into tank of water, using power-driven foot pedal. Alters flow of air passing through unit and reads pressure gauges to determine points of high and low air release speeds. Inspects unit for air leaks, using brush to remove normal submersion bubbles. Releases foot pedal to raise regulator from water tank. Unclamps unit and places unit in tray. Marks malfunctioning areas of defective units, utilizing knowledge of components.
GOE: 06.03.01 STRENGTH: L GED: R3 M2 L2 SVP: 4 DLU: 77

710.584-010 SCROLL ASSEMBLER (office machines)
Fastens metal or plastic covers to balance and scale frames to enclose mechanism, using handtools: Fits parts, such as backplates, front and back scrolls, glass lens, and name and patent plates to frame, according to blueprint, using handtools, such as file, drill, and screwdriver.
GOE: 06.04.23 STRENGTH: L GED: R2 M1 L1 SVP: 3 DLU: 77

710.681-018 REGISTER REPAIRER (r.r. trans.) alternate titles: farebox repairer
Cleans and repairs fare registers used in rapid-transit railway stations: Disassembles register, using pliers, screwdrivers, punch, and hammer. Cleans register case with soap and water and working parts with kerosene. Replaces defective parts, makes necessary adjustments, and repaints dial markings, using brush. Reassembles register, oils mechanism, and shellacks or paints outside of case, using brush and spray gun.
GOE: 05.10.02 STRENGTH: L GED: R3 M2 L2 SVP: 6 DLU: 77

710.681-026 THERMOMETER MAKER (inst. & app.)
Fills, shapes, seals, and marks glass tubes to fabricate thermometers, using vacuum tank, micrometer, gas burners, and handtools: Places thermometer tubes in vacuum tank filled with colored liquid and secures tank lid. Turns handle to create vacuum in tank that causes fluid to fill tubes. Holds end of filled tube over gas flame until glass changes color. Inserts air bulb into unheated end of tube and squeezes air into tube to form thermometer bulb. Rotates bulb in preset micrometer to attain specified size. Holds open end of tube over flame to soften glass and seal tube. Immerses tube in temperature controlled hot and cold water tanks to determine reference point for calibrating tubes. Scribes marker at reference points, using file. Heats and cools water in tanks to specified temperatures, using heater, ice, and master thermometer. May blow and

shape glass tubes used to make thermometers [GLASS BLOWER, LAB-ORATORY APPARATUS (glass products; inst. & app.) 772.281-010].
GOE: 06.02.30 STRENGTH: S GED: R3 M2 L2 SVP: 4 DLU: 77

710.684-010 AGATE SETTER (office machines)
Positions, glues, and aligns *agate bearings* in scale housings and bridges, base plates, and spiders: Mixes cement ingredients according to formula. Cleans agate seats, using files. Positions part in holding fixture. Coats agates and part seats with cement, positions agates in seats, and screws clamp into fixture to hold agates in place. Places clamped part and fixture in oven to harden cement. Sights along rods or straightedge to verify alignment of agates. Repositions bearings to correct misalignment, using handtools, or resets agate bearing.
GOE: 06.02.32 STRENGTH: L GED: R3 M1 L2 SVP: 4 DLU: 77

710.684-014 BELLOWS FILLER (inst. & app.)
Fills thermostat bellows with gas or liquid to charge bellows, using vacuum tank or cabinet, crimping equipment, brazing iron, and solder seal equipment, by either of following methods: (1) Inserts capillary tube of bellows into *charging manifold* of cabinet and closes cabinet windows to seal cabinet. Manipulates controls of cabinet to purge capillary tubes of air and fill tubes with gas. Observes gauges to verify that internal temperature of cabinet meets specifications, and turns valve to maintain specified gas pressure in bellows. (2) Positions bellows assemblies into vacuum tank with bulb end down. Closes tank lids, tightens lugs to seal tank, and opens valves to create vacuum in tank. Turns valve on vacuum tank and connection line between vacuum tank and filling tank to draw liquid into tank and force liquid into bellows. Removes bellows from tank or cabinet and crimps bulb end of capillary tube to seal in gas or liquid fill, using crimping equipment. Brazes crimped end of tube, using brazing iron or solder seal equipment. Submerges portion of capillary tube in water, when filling tube with combination of liquid and gas, to partially condense gas. Places filled bellows in tray or storage boxes.
GOE: 06.04.36 STRENGTH: M GED: R3 M2 L2 SVP: 4 DLU: 89

710.684-018 DIAL MAKER (office machines)
Marks balance scale dials by hand or using silk screen equipment: Reads work order to determine type of dial required and selects specified dial blanks from stockroom. Lays out and marks special order dials, using pivoted straightedge, pen, and ink. Marks regular order dials, using silk screen, paint, and squeegee [SCREEN PRINTER (any industry)].
GOE: 06.02.31 STRENGTH: L GED: R3 M2 L2 SVP: 4 DLU: 77

710.684-026 GAS-METER MECHANIC II (utilities) alternate titles: gas-meter repairer
Performs any combination of following tasks to recondition displacement-type gas meters and governors: Cleans meter case, using wire brush or scraper and places meter in grit-blast chamber to remove paint and soil. Removes top, front, and back case panels and valve compartment panels, using soldering iron or gas-fired chamber. Removes internal parts, including valve covers, valve connecting arms, and recording mechanisms, using soldering iron and handtools. Cleans internal compartments and moving parts, using rags and cleaning compound. Repairs internal partition seams, using soldering iron. Replaces stuffing box, using handtools, and lubricates moving parts, using oil gun. Attaches airhose to meter inlet, plugs outlet, and observes gauges for loss of pressure to test internal seams for leaks. Solders top, front, and back case panels in place, using soldering iron. Connects meter to water chamber fixture to submerge meter in water and observes meter to detect leaks. Marks seams to identify leaks, using chalk. Caps inlet and outlet of meter to prevent paint from entering system and places meter on conveyor of electrostatic spray booth. Turns spray booth controls to paint meter. Places painted meter in shipping container.
GOE: 05.10.02 STRENGTH: L GED: R2 M1 L1 SVP: 3 DLU: 77

710.684-030 INSTRUMENT-TECHNICIAN HELPER (utilities)
Assists INSTRUMENT TECHNICIAN (utilities) in repair and maintenance of metering instruments for electric-power generating equipment, such as boilers and turbines: Removes, dismantles, and assembles instruments, using mechanic's and electrician's handtools. Performs other duties as described under HELPER (any industry) Master Title.
GOE: 05.10.02 STRENGTH: L GED: R3 M2 L2 SVP: 4 DLU: 77

710.684-034 METER-REPAIRER HELPER (any industry)
Assists METER REPAIRER (any industry) in installing, adjusting, and repairing volumetrical gas, oil, or water meters: Disconnects meters with wrench and loads meters in truck. Disassembles meters, using handtools. Cleans parts, using solvents and wiping rags. Replaces defective parts and reassembles meters, using handtools. Connects meters to testing apparatus for inspection and adjustment by METER REPAIRER (any industry). Performs other duties as described under HELPER (any industry) Master Title.
GOE: 05.12.15 STRENGTH: L GED: R3 M1 L1 SVP: 4 DLU: 77

710.684-038 SEALER (office machines)
Assembles and seals scale poises and counterweights used in manufacture of balance scales: Weighs poises and counterweights, using microscale, and refers to weight chart to determine amount lead shot to be added to adjust weight. Drills hole in poise, using drill press. Verifies depth of hole, using depth gauge and drill chart. Hammers lead shot into hole to add necessary weight. Inserts shot into cavity of counterweight to and necessary weight, using tweezers. Files or grinds poise or counterweight to reduce weight, using file or power grinder.

Positions plug over cavity of counterweight and seals plug in cavity, using pneumatic press.
GOE: 06.02.24 STRENGTH: M GED: R3 M2 L2 SVP: 5 DLU: 77

710.684-042 BELLOWS ASSEMBLER (inst. & app.)
Performs any combination of following tasks to fabricate bellows assemblies for thermostats: Spins bellows and flanges covers onto bellows, using spinning and flanging machines. Winds copper tubing around circular fixture and cuts tubing to specified length to form capillary tube. Attaches bulb to end of capillary tube, using staking machine, and solders bellows to opposite end of capillary tube, using soft or silver solder, soldering iron or torch, and brazing rod. Cleans bellows assembly to remove foreign material resulting from soldering and brazing operation. Places bellows assemblies on tray and loads tray into drying oven. Clips excess material from bellows assembly, using clipping machine. Examines assemblies for surface defects, such as cracks or pits, and places defective assemblies into boxes for salvage. Maintains production records.
GOE: 06.04.23 STRENGTH: L GED: R2 M1 L2 SVP: 3 DLU: 89

710.684-046 INSTRUMENT ASSEMBLER (inst. & app.)
Assembles instruments and devices, such as barometers, control valves, gyroscopes, hygrometers, speedometers, tachometers, and thermostats, using handtools, power tools, and measuring instruments: Visually examines parts for defects. Fits, aligns, and secures internal and external component parts to assemble finished unit, using handtools, power tools, soldering iron, and measuring instruments. May inspect assembled unit for conformance to specifications, using measuring and testing equipment. May test functional performance of unit, using test equipment. May be designated according to product assembled as Regulator Assembler (inst. & app.); Thermostat Assembler (inst. & app.); Valve Assembler (inst. & app.).
GOE: 06.02.23 STRENGTH: L GED: R3 M2 L2 SVP: 4 DLU: 90

710.684-050 INSTRUMENT INSPECTOR (inst. & app.)
Inspects measuring, indicating, and controlling instruments, such as speedometers, sequence timers, and thermostats, and component parts, for conformance to specifications: Examines components and housings for specified characteristics, such as smoothness and centering of holes, or defects, such as scratches and chips. Measures instrument parts to verify conformance to blueprint specifications, using measuring devices, such as ruler, thread gauge, micrometer, and dial indicator. May use microscope to inspect bearings or other component parts. May test functional performance of instrument, using test equipment. May write inspection reports concerning defective parts and assemblies.
GOE: 06.03.02 STRENGTH: L GED: R3 M2 L2 SVP: 4 DLU: 88

710.685-014 THERMOMETER PRODUCTION WORKER (inst. & app.)
Performs any combination of following tasks to fabricate and test clinical mercury thermometers: Reads work order to determine sequence of tasks and specifications. Tends machines that heat glass capillary tubes to form blister, constrict and adjust blister, fuse bulb to tube, form top chamber, seal end of tube, and fuse tops to form thermometer. Tends vacuum equipment that fills thermometer bores with mercury. Tends centrifuges, shakers, chill tanks, warming tanks, or related machines and equipment that disperse mercury in bore and remove excess mercury or air. Tends automated machines that grade and mark calibration reference points on thermometers. Tends equipment that prints scale on thermometer [SILK-SCREEN PRINTER, MACHINE (any industry) 979.685-010]. Tends heat tank that heats thermometer to standard temperature, and reads thermometer scale to test accuracy. Inspects thermometers to detect defects, such as cracks, cloudiness, and screen printing errors. Records production information, such as number of thermometers processed, number rejected, and reason for rejection.
GOE: 06.04.19 STRENGTH: L GED: R2 M1 L1 SVP: 2 DLU: 89

710.687-014 BELLOWS TESTER (inst. & app.)
Inspects and tests thermostat bellows for conformance to established standards, using test stand and charts: Examines bellows for surface defects, such as dents, cracks, or pits. Inserts bulb end of bellows assembly into dry ice to lower temperature of liquid in bulb to below zero. Connects bellows assembly to fitting on test stand. Turns dial on test stand to indicate zero reading. Removes bellows assembly from dry ice and inserts bulb end into tank of water heated to specified temperature. Reads test stand gauge to ensure expansion height of liquid in bellows conforms to specifications. Rejects bellows if defects exceed established standards or tags bellows for rework. Maintains records of bellows tested and rejected from each lot.
GOE: 06.03.02 STRENGTH: L GED: R3 M2 L2 SVP: 3 DLU: 77

710.687-034 TIE-UP WORKER (office machines)
Ties or bolts moving parts of scales, prior to packing and shipping, to prevent damage: Disconnects and secures mechanisms with screws and bolts at specified points, using handtools. Lifts levers to insert felt pads between pivots and thrusts. Ties installation instruction tags to parts. May package scales.
GOE: 06.04.38 STRENGTH: H GED: R2 M1 L1 SVP: 3 DLU: 77

711 OCCUPATIONS IN FABRICATION AND REPAIR OF OPTICAL INSTRUMENTS

This group includes occupations concerned with fabricating and repairing optical instruments, such as microscopes, field glasses, opera glasses, and telescopes; optical measuring and testing instruments, such as refractometers, spectrometers, spectroscopes, colorimeters, and polariscopes; and optical range finders, bombsights, and fire-control instruments. Occupations concerned with fabricating and repairing optical lenses are included in Group 716.

711.137-010 SUPERVISOR, OPTICAL INSTRUMENTS (inst. & app.)

Supervises and coordinates activities of workers engaged in assembling, repairing, calibrating, and inspecting optical instruments, such as binoculars, telescopes, gunsights, compasses, and other sighting equipment. May inspect work to ensure conformance to product specifications. Performs tasks as described under SUPERVISOR (any industry) Master Title.
GOE: 06.02.01 STRENGTH: L GED: R4 M3 L3 SVP: 7 DLU: 77

711.281-010 INSPECTOR, OPTICAL INSTRUMENT (optical goods)

Inspects, cleans, adjusts and certifies precision optical measuring, sighting, aligning, and leveling instruments to ensure conformance to company, military, and governmental standards, using precision measuring instruments and handtools: Reads written and schematic specifications, handbooks, inspection manuals, and blueprints to determine inspection and certification data, such as required tolerances, adjustment and certification methods, formulas, and measuring instruments required. Inspects instruments to detect surface defects, such as chips, burrs, loose lenses, and mirrors, bent or broken parts, and presence of foreign matter. Removes defects, such as chips and burrs, using hand honing tool. Measures instrument parts, using gauges, and calculates degree of wear and looseness of parts, using established mathematical formulas. Verifies sighting and focal accuracy of instruments, such as transits and alignment scopes, using targets and mirror systems of established heights and distances. Turns setscrews to calibrate instruments to required tolerances. Cleans mirrors and lenses of instrument, using solvent, rags, and brushes, and secures certification tag to instrument. Routes defective instruments to repair or calibration laboratories. Maintains inspection records.
GOE: 06.01.05 STRENGTH: L GED: R4 M4 L4 SVP: 7 DLU: 77

711.281-014 INSTRUMENT MECHANIC, WEAPONS SYSTEM (inst. & app.)

Repairs, tests, and calibrates optomechanical instruments, such as range finders, gun directors, and fire-control instruments, according to specifications, using handtools, bench machines, and precision measuring instruments: Disassembles optomechanical instruments and inspects for defects, such as broken or worn mechanical parts and scratched or defectively coated optical elements. Fabricates replacement parts, using bench lathes, drill presses, and milling machines. Cleans optical element, using cloth, and immerses element in solution to remove defective coating. Files and hones mechanical parts to facilitate meshing of gears. Coats optical element, using coating equipment. Reassembles instruments and adjusts parts to ensure freedom of movement, using handtools. Installs instrument in test fixture or mount, and sights known objective of fixed distance and height to test sighting accuracy of instrument. Adjusts readings on instrument dials to calibrate instrument according to observation. Measures dial graduations and scales to verify accuracy, using precision measuring instruments. Engraves scales and graduations on instrument dials to correct errors, using pantograph engraving machine.
GOE: 05.05.11 STRENGTH: M GED: R4 M3 L3 SVP: 8 DLU: 77

711.381-010 OPTICAL-INSTRUMENT ASSEMBLER (optical goods)

Performs any combination of following duties to assemble optical instruments, such as telescopes, level-transits, and gunsights: Reads work order, blueprints, and sketches to determine assembly procedure. Cleans elements, using tissue, cleaning solution, and compressed air device. Coats optical elements according to specifications [OPTICAL-ELEMENT COATER (optical goods)]. Cements multiple lens assemblies together [CEMENTER (optical goods)]. Picks up element, using vacuum-holding device, and positions element in mounting seat of instrument housing. Inserts and screws locking ring in housing to hold element in place. Applies cement to rings to prevent loosening. Assembles structural and mechanical parts of instrument according to blueprint specifications, using wrenches and screwdrivers. Computes standard trigonometric formulas to determine distance of test target from instrument. Positions target in darkroom tunnel and connects optical instrument to test devices, such as oscilloscope and collimator. Sights instrument on target and reads dials to determine optical center of instrument lens and to verify specified focusing power. Measures elements and instrument parts to verify dimensional specifications, using precision measuring instruments. Records inspection and test data. May set up and operate lathe to modify instrument parts. May paint instrument parts, using brush or spray gun. May fill instrument housing with nitrogen gas to minimize corrosive effects on internal optical surfaces, using vacuum pump.
GOE: 06.01.04 STRENGTH: L GED: R4 M3 L4 SVP: 6 DLU: 77

711.684-010 ASSEMBLY LOADER (inst. & app.)

Selects and arranges specified type and quantity of component parts in trays preparatory to line assembly of surveying instruments: Positions instrument base or support structure (standard) in jig, and spreads bracket of standard to specified width to facilitate attachment of parts, using tongs. Files burrs from bracket holes, using hand file. Selects component parts from stock bins, according to instrument being assembled, and examines parts for defects. Arranges parts in tray and places tray on assembly line conveyor. Tallies number of trays assembled, using counter.
GOE: 06.04.34 STRENGTH: L GED: R2 M1 L1 SVP: 3 DLU: 77

711.684-014 CEMENTER (optical goods)

Cements optical elements together to form units which have specific optical properties: Cleans elements, using solvent, tissue, brush, and compressed air device. Holds elements together to verify fit. Applies cement to element surfaces, using glass rod. Presses and rotates elements together to remove air pockets and distribute cement evenly over joined surfaces. Centers and clamps elements together. Places elements in curing oven for specified period.
GOE: 06.02.30 STRENGTH: S GED: R2 M2 L2 SVP: 5 DLU: 77

712 OCCUPATIONS IN FABRICATION AND REPAIR OF SURGICAL, MEDICAL, AND DENTAL INSTRUMENTS AND SUPPLIES

This group includes occupations concerned with fabricating and repairing dental, medical, surgical, ophthalmic, and veterinary instruments, apparatus, and supplies, other than electrical used by those in the professions, laboratories, and schools; orthopedic, prosthetic, and surgical appliances and supplies, such as arch supports and other foot appliances, fracture appliances, elastic hosiery, abdominal supporters, braces, trusses, bandages, surgical gauze and dressings, adhesive tapes and medicated plasters, and personal safety appliances and equipment; artificial teeth and dental metals, alloys, and amalgams. Occupations concerned with machine sewing trusses, elastic hosiery, and other surgical and orthopedic garments are included in Group 787.

712.131-010 SUPERVISOR, DENTAL LABORATORY (protective dev.)

Supervises and coordinates activities of workers engaged in fabrication, assembly, and repair of full or partial dentures: Reads prescription and consults with DENTIST (medical ser.) 072.101-010 to resolve problems concerning prescription specifications and to establish cost and delivery agreements. Trains new workers in performance of tasks, and fabricates and repairs dentures as needed to expedite work flow. Inspects work in progress and upon completion to ensure conformance to prescription specifications. Requisitions materials and supplies. Performs other duties as described under SUPERVISOR (any industry) Master Title. May be designated according to department supervised as Supervisor, Denture Department (protective dev.); Supervisor, Gold Department (protective dev.); Supervisor, Partial Denture Department (protective dev.); Supervisor, Porcelain Department (protective dev.).
GOE: 05.05.11 STRENGTH: L GED: R4 M3 L4 SVP: 7 DLU: 79

712.132-010 SUPERVISOR, SURGICAL GARMENT ASSEMBLY (protective dev.)

Supervises and coordinates activities of workers engaged in fabricating surgical garments, such as trusses, hosiery, knee and elbow braces, corsets, and belts: Assigns workers to duties, such as laying out, cutting, sewing, and assembling surgical garments. Trains new employees. Inspects garments at various stages of production to verify conformance to specifications. Consults with management and orthopedic specialists and reads trade journals to develop new products. Requisitions materials and supplies. Performs other duties as described under SUPERVISOR (any industry) Master Title.
GOE: 06.02.01 STRENGTH: L GED: R4 M3 L4 SVP: 7 DLU: 77

712.134-010 SUPERVISOR, ARTIFICIAL BREAST FABRICATION (protective dev.)

Supervises, coordinates, and participates in activities of workers engaged in fabricating cosmetic appliances from latex for use as artificial breasts: Explains and demonstrates work techniques and use of equipment to train new employees. Observes workers to ensure that work performance conforms to company standards. Weighs, pours, and mixes prescribed amounts of filtered water and chemicals, using scale and mixing tanks, to prepare latex gel. Places plastic roll on worktable, using hydraulic jack, unrolls plastic, and cuts plastic to specified sizes, according to work order, using portable rotary cutting machine. Molds shells, using vacuum forming machine, and cuts molded sheets into individual shells, using cutting machine. Fills inner shells with latex gel, using weighing and filling device, and imprints outer shell backing with identification data, using printing device. Fuses backing to shells to form cells, using heat sealing machine, inflates cells with airhose, and seals cells, using tacking device. Compiles inventory reports. Performs other duties as described under SUPERVISOR (any industry) Master Title.
GOE: 06.02.01 STRENGTH: M GED: R4 M2 L2 SVP: 6 DLU: 86

712.137-010 SUPERVISOR, FACEPIECE LINE (protective dev.)

Supervises and coordinates activities of workers engaged in fabricating facepieces for military gas masks. Performs duties as described under SUPERVISOR (any industry) Master Title.
GOE: 06.04.01 STRENGTH: L GED: R4 M3 L3 SVP: 7 DLU: 77

712.137-014 SUPERVISOR, FINAL ASSEMBLY AND PACKING (protective dev.) alternate titles: packing-and-final-assembly supervisor

Supervises and coordinates activities of workers engaged in fabrication, assembly, and packing of military gas masks. Performs duties as described under SUPERVISOR (any industry) Master Title.
GOE: 06.02.01 STRENGTH: L GED: R4 M3 L3 SVP: 7 DLU: 77

712.281-014 DESIGNER (protective dev.)

Designs surgical belts and supports, fabricates prototype, and makes production patterns: Draws full-size outline of support on paper according to specifications, body measurements, and anatomical application of support, using mechanical drawing instruments. Cuts drawing into parts to make patterns, marks around patterns on specified cloth, and cuts cloth on marks, using scissors or

electrically powered knife. Sews pieces together, using any combination of single- two-, three- and four-needle, zigzag, square-stitch, and buttonhole sewing machines. Operates eyelet, hook-and-eye, and caps-and-studs machines to attach specified fasteners to supports. Inspects completed sample and makes alterations requested by management. Writes specifications for materials, straps, stays, fasteners, adjustments, and sizes to be produced. Traces patterns on fiberboard or cardboard and cuts out patterns to be used as master patterns. Enlarges and reduces master patterns to make patterns for range of sizes to be produced.
GOE: 05.05.11 STRENGTH: L GED: R4 M2 L3 SVP: 6 DLU: 77

712.381-010 ARCH-SUPPORT TECHNICIAN (protective dev.)
Fabricates steel arch support to fit patient's foot, according to medical prescription: Receives plaster cast of foot from PROSTHETIST (medical ser.) or PODIATRIST (medical ser.). Places protection cloth into cast and fills cast with plaster to mold model of patient's foot. Removes hardened model from cast and traces model outline on paper to use as pattern in cutting support. Selects stainless steel sheet of prescribed thickness and cuts sheet to specified dimensions, using shears, guided by pattern. Hammers steel into prescribed contours to form support and places support against plaster model to determine accuracy of fit. Splits support into front and back pieces when indicated according to prescription, using shears. Polishes support, using abrasive wheel. Glues leather to bottom of arch support to protect shoe, and rivets additional leather across top edge for foot comfort, using riveting tool.
GOE: 05.10.01 STRENGTH: L GED: R3 M2 L2 SVP: 5 DLU: 77

712.381-014 CONTOUR WIRE SPECIALIST, DENTURE (protective dev.)
Makes and repairs contoured wire frames and retainers for teeth used in partial dentures, using power tools and handtools: Examines model of oral impression and reads DENTIST'S (medical ser.) 072.101-010 prescription to determine design of wire frame. Marks pencil tracings on surface of model to indicate position of wire clasps, using *surveyor*. Cuts wire to specified lengths, using wirecutter. Bends and shapes wire around tooth impressions or along base of model, using pliers, knife, and tweezers. Applies investment to wire sections and model to hold sections in alignment, using spatula. Welds or solders wire joints, using special welding and soldering tools. Removes investment. Grinds and polishes wire frame to lustrous finish, using electric grinding and polishing wheel. Reworks or replaces wire sections and missing teeth to repair partial dentures, using acrylic bonding agent. Fabricates wire retainers to straighten teeth, using pliers, tweezers, and similar handtools. Inspects work for adherence to DENTIST'S (medical ser.) specifications.
GOE: 05.05.11 STRENGTH: S GED: R4 M3 L3 SVP: 7 DLU: 77

712.381-018 DENTAL-LABORATORY TECHNICIAN (protective dev.) alternate titles: dental technician
Performs any combination of following tasks to fabricate and repair dental appliances, according to DENTIST'S (medical ser.) 072.101-010 prescription, using handtools, molding equipment, and bench fabricating machines: Reads prescription and examines dental models and impressions to determine type of denture to be made or repaired applying knowledge of dental laboratory techniques. Fabricates full or partial dentures, using wax, plastic, and plaster models, articulators, grinders, and polishers. Casts plastic or plaster models of dentures to be repaired [DENTURE-MODEL MAKER (protective dev.) 712.684-046]. Selects and mounts replacement teeth in model to match color and shape of natural or adjacent teeth, using tooth color scales and tooth illustrations. Molds wax over denture setup to form contours of gums, using knives and spatula [DENTURE WAXER (protective dev.) 712.381-046]. Removes excess plastic and polishes surfaces of cast dentures, using grinding and polishing tools and ultrasonic equipment [FINISHER, DENTURE (protective dev.) 712.381-050]. Rebuilds denture linings to duplicate original thickness, contour, and color according to specifications. Tests repaired dentures for accuracy of occlusion, using articulator. Bends and solders gold and platinum wire to construct wire frames for dentures, using soldering gun and handtools [CONTOUR WIRE SPECIALIST, DENTURE (protective dev.) 712.381-014]. May confer with DENTIST (medical ser.) to resolve problems in design and setup of dentures. May be designated according to type of denture fabricated as Dental Technician, Crown And Bridge (protective dev.); Dental Technician, Metal (protective dev.).
GOE: 05.05.11 STRENGTH: L GED: R4 M3 L4 SVP: 7 DLU: 90

712.381-022 DENTAL-LABORATORY-TECHNICIAN APPRENTICE (protective dev.) alternate titles: dental-technician apprentice
Performs tasks as described under APPRENTICE (any industry) Master Title.
GOE: 05.05.11 STRENGTH: L GED: R4 M3 L4 SVP: 7 DLU: 77

712.381-026 ORTHODONTIC BAND MAKER (protective dev.)
Fabricates metal bands used for dental products, such as braces, inlays, crowns, and bridges: Examines specification sheet to determine dimensions and physical characteristics of band. Cuts and rolls gold ingot to specified size and thickness, using handtools. Melts specified amount of gold, silver, or other metal and pours molten material into molds to cast inlays, crowns, and fixed bridges, using casting equipment. Solders or welds metal pieces together to form band, using soldering iron.
GOE: 05.05.11 STRENGTH: L GED: R4 M3 L4 SVP: 7 DLU: 90

712.381-030 ORTHODONTIC TECHNICIAN (protective dev.)
Constructs and repairs appliances for straightening teeth according to ORTHODONTIST'S (medical ser.) 072.101-022 prescription: Shapes, grinds,

polishes, carves, and assembles metal and plastic appliances, such as retainers, tooth bands, and positioners, using spatula, pliers, soldering torch, and electric grinders and polishers. Tests appliance for conformance to specifications, using articulator.
GOE: 05.05.11 STRENGTH: S GED: R4 M3 L4 SVP: 6 DLU: 78

712.381-034 ORTHOTICS TECHNICIAN (protective dev.)
Fabricates, fits, repairs, and maintains orthotic devices, such as braces and surgical supports, according to specifications and under guidance of ORTHOTIST (medical ser.) 078.261-018 or ORTHOTICS ASSISTANT (medical ser.) 078.361-022: Bends, forms, welds, and saws metal brace structural components to conform to measurements, using hammers, anvils, welding equipment, and saws. Drills and taps holes for rivets, and rivets components together. Shapes plastic and metal around cast of patient's torso or limbs. Covers and pads metal or plastic brace structures, using layers of rubber, felt, plastic, and leather. May also perform functions of PROSTHETICS TECHNICIAN (protective dev.) 712.381-038 and be designated Orthotics-Prosthetics Technician (protective dev.).
GOE: 05.05.11 STRENGTH: M GED: R4 M3 L4 SVP: 6 DLU: 78

712.381-038 PROSTHETICS TECHNICIAN (protective dev.) alternate titles: restoration technician
Fabricates, fits, maintains, and repairs artificial limbs, plastic cosmetic appliances, and other prosthetic devices, according to prescription specifications and under guidance of PROSTHETIST (medical ser.) 078.261-022 or PROSTHETICS ASSISTANT (medical ser.) 078.361-026: Reads specifications to determine type of prosthesis to be fabricated and materials and tools required. Lays out and marks dimensions of parts, using precision measuring instruments and templates. Saws, carves, cuts, and grinds wood, plastic, metal, or fabric to fabricate parts, using rotary sawing and cutting machines and hand cutting tools. Drills and taps holes for rivets and screws, using drill press. Glues, welds, bolts, sews, and rivets parts together to form prostheses, such as artificial limbs. Makes wax or plastic impression of patient's amputated area, prepares mold from impression, and pours molten plastic into mold to form cosmetic appliances, such as artificial ear, nose, or hand. Assembles layers of padding over prosthesis and fits and attaches outer covering, such as leather, sheet plastic, or fiberglass, over device, using sewing machine, rivet gun, and handtools. Mixes pigments according to formula to duplicate skin coloring of patient and applies pigments to outer covering of prosthesis. Polishes finished device, using grinding and buffing wheels. Tests prostheses for freedom of movement, alignment of parts, and biomechanical stability, using plumbline, goniometer, and alignment fixtures. May harness prosthesis to patient's stump, applying knowledge of functional anatomy. May instruct patient in use of prosthesis. May also perform functions of ORTHOTICS TECHNICIAN (protective dev.) 712.381-034.
GOE: 05.05.11 STRENGTH: M GED: R4 M4 L4 SVP: 6 DLU: 77

712.381-042 DENTAL CERAMIST (protective dev.) alternate titles: ceramics technician
Applies layers of porcelain or acrylic paste over metal framework to form dental prostheses, such as crowns, bridges, and tooth facings, according to prescription of DENTIST (medical ser.) 072.101-010: Mixes porcelain or acrylic paste according to prescription to match color of natural teeth. Applies layers of mixture over metal framework, using brushes and spatula. Brushes excess mixture from denture and places denture in furnace to harden. Removes denture from furnace, brushes on additional layer of mixture, and shapes mixture to contour of denture, using spatula. Repeats mixture-application process and baking until denture conforms to specifications. Verifies accuracy of tooth dimensions and occlusion of teeth, using micrometer and articulator. Cleans and polishes dental prostheses, using ultrasonic machine and polishing machine.
GOE: 05.05.11 STRENGTH: S GED: R4 M3 L4 SVP: 7 DLU: 90

712.381-046 DENTURE WAXER (protective dev.) alternate titles: waxer
Molds wax over denture setup to form contour molds of gums, palates, bridges, and other denture surfaces for use in casting plaster models or metal framework of dentures, using molding equipment and handtools: Applies softened wax to base of denture setup and fills spaces between adjacent teeth, using spatula and fingers. Carves and shapes wax, using scraper, knife, and heated spatula to form natural-appearing denture contours. Verifies occlusion of teeth, using articulator. May mix plaster or melt metals and pour plaster or molten metal in contour molds to form model for duplicate casting [DENTURE-MODEL MAKER (protective dev.) 712.684-046]. May construct wax bite blocks and plastic trays [BITE-BLOCK MAKER (protective dev.) 712.684-014].
GOE: 06.02.32 STRENGTH: S GED: R3 M3 L3 SVP: 6 DLU: 90

712.381-050 FINISHER, DENTURE (protective dev.) alternate titles: denture finisher; finisher; finisher-polisher
Polishes, cleans, and adjusts dentures and dental appliances to obtain specified finish, using handtools, polishing wheels, and cleaning equipment: Removes mold from frame, using ejector press, and chips molding material from denture, using hammer and chisel. Smooths and polishes denture and denture frames to remove excess material, using polishing machine. Removes excess plastic from teeth, using sharp pointed tool. Fills chipped or low spots in surfaces of plastic areas with acrylic resins, using brush. Repairs and adjusts metal framework of dentures, using soldering torch and handtools. Verifies occlusion of dentures, using articulator.
GOE: 05.05.11 STRENGTH: L GED: R3 M2 L3 SVP: 5 DLU: 90

712.487-010 INSPECTOR, SURGICAL GARMENT (protective dev.)

Inspects surgical garments, such as belts, hosiery, trusses, braces, and sanitary napkins for conformance to specifications: Examines raw materials to detect dirt particles, discolorations, and other defects and rejects substandard materials. Weighs and measures component parts and completed garment to verify specified weight and dimensional specifications, using scale and gauges. Examines garment at various stages of production for correct positioning of parts and appearance. Inspects packaged garments for appearance and to detect excessive glue. Tags rejected items for rework or disposal. Maintains inspection records and computes level of quality control achieved, using mathematical formulas.
GOE: 06.03.01 STRENGTH: L GED: R3 M3 L2 SVP: 3 DLU: 77

712.664-010 DENTAL CERAMIST ASSISTANT (protective dev.) alternate titles: porcelain finisher; porcelain waxer

Performs any combination of following tasks to assist DENTAL CERAMIST (protective dev.) 712.381-042 in molding dental prostheses, such as crowns, bridges, and tooth facings: Brushes liquid separating solution on tip of tooth die and covers die with wax sheet. Invests wax impressions in plaster molds, and inserts mold in furnace to melt wax. Positions mold in casting machine to cast metal framework. Removes metal framework from mold, using sandblasting equipment or hammer. Smooths rough spots from framework, using abrasive grinding wheel. Mixes porcelain or acrylic resin solution to match color of natural teeth, under direction of DENTAL CERAMIST (protective dev.). Fills wax impression of tooth with graphite solution, plates impression in electroplating machine, removes die (plated impression) from electroplating machine, and applies acrylic resin to base of die, using spatula, to fabricate copper dies for dentures.
GOE: 05.05.11 STRENGTH: S GED: R3 M2 L3 SVP: 6 DLU: 78

712.684-010 ASSEMBLER, SURGICAL GARMENT (protective dev.)

Performs any combination of following tasks to assemble surgical garments and personal safety devices, such as colostomy pouches, trusses, belts, cervical collars, hosiery, and back, knee, wrist, elbow, and ankle braces: Reads work order to determine number and type of parts required to assemble garment. Measures and cuts required pieces, using ruler, templates, knife, and electric or hand shears. Punches holes in material, using punch press or hand punch. Attaches fasteners, such as eyelets or snaps, using rivet, snap-fastening, or eyelet machine. Grinds and polishes parts, using grinding wheel. Bends metal stays (springs) to specified curvature, using bending machine. Applies latex coating to parts or specified areas of parts, using coating machine. Fits and fastens parts together, such as straps, buckles, pads, belts, and stays to assemble garment, using handtools, gluing equipment, and machines, such as punch press, riveting machine, heat-sealing machine, and sewing machine. Weaves elastic thread into outer edges of garments, such as knee, wrist, and elbow braces, to increase elasticity. Places completed garments in boxes or plastic bags for packaging. May be designated according to type garment assembled or material worked with as Elastic Assembler (protective dev.); Latexer (protective dev.) II; Leather Worker (protective dev.); Spring Bender (protective dev.); Truss Assembler (protective dev.).
GOE: 06.02.23 STRENGTH: L GED: R2 M2 L2 SVP: 3 DLU: 78

712.684-014 BITE-BLOCK MAKER (protective dev.)

Forms wax bite blocks and impression trays used by DENTIST (medical ser.) 072.101-010 to take impressions of patients' teeth and adjacent portions of jaw, using molding equipment and handtools: Softens plastic or shellac wafer shaped material, using heated press or gas burner. Spreads and shapes wafer over model of preliminary impression to form tray, using flat-bladed molding tool. Imbeds metal strip in soft material for convenience in handling. Presses soft wax over plaster model of denture to form bite block. Trims excess wax from mold and smooths surface, using knife, spatula, and gas burner. Immerses mold in water to harden wax. Trims and smooths edges and surfaces of trays and bite blocks, using bench lathe equipped with grinding and buffing wheels. Rubs finished piece with cotton to obtain lustrous finish.
GOE: 06.02.23 STRENGTH: S GED: R3 M1 L1 SVP: 4 DLU: 77

712.684-018 FLANGER (inst. & app.) alternate titles: glass-cylinder flanger

Forms flange on open ends of glass tubes used in manufacturing laboratory and medical instruments and apparatus, using gas burner and handtools: Rotates glass tube over gas burner to heat end of tube. Inserts end-opening tool into tube to flare opening and closes jaws of flange-forming tool to shape flange. May rotate flange over gas burner to glaze flange or to add or remove glass to obtain uniformity of finished flare. May trim edge of flange, using cutting tool.
GOE: 06.04.30 STRENGTH: L GED: R2 M1 L1 SVP: 3 DLU: 89

712.684-022 GAS-MASK ASSEMBLER (protective dev.)

Assembles military gas masks, using kick press and handtools: Punches holes in facepiece, using kick press. Attaches valves to facepiece and seals joints, using wire strands, acetone, cement, and tape. Glues hoses to facepiece and canister units. Clinches metal clamps on strips of tape to form head harness and attaches harness to mask. Inserts lenses in eyepieces and crimps rims to seal lenses. May stitch reinforcement patches onto masks and seal stitching with cement.
GOE: 06.04.23 STRENGTH: M GED: R2 M1 L1 SVP: 4 DLU: 77

712.684-026 GLAZIER (inst. & app.)

Glazes tapered ends of glass tubes used in laboratory and medical instruments and apparatus, using gas burner and handtools: Heats tube on gas burner equipped with rolls that revolve tube in flame. Transfers tube between burners, set at graduated degrees of temperature, to expose tube to gradual heating and cooling process. May manually revolve tube on gas burner rolls to heat tube. May periodically glaze glass tubes, using hand torch.
GOE: 06.04.30 STRENGTH: L GED: R2 M1 L1 SVP: 2 DLU: 89

712.684-030 OPAQUER (protective dev.) alternate titles: porcelain-build-up assistant

Applies coating of opaque procelain over cast metal tooth cap, using brush: Mixes porcelain of specified color and water to required consistency. Brushes porcelain mixture over surfaces of metal cap. Places cap in electric oven for specified time to dry and harden porcelain. Removes cap and examines cap to ensure even application and smoothness of coating. Routes workpiece to specified department for application of finish porcelain. May grind and shape dried porcelain to contours of metal cap, using abrasive wheels. May measure dimensions of tooth cap and verify occlusion, using gauges and articulator.
GOE: 06.02.32 STRENGTH: S GED: R3 M2 L2 SVP: 4 DLU: 77

712.684-034 PACKER, DENTURE (protective dev.) alternate titles: molder

Packs plastic material in molds to form base for full or partial dentures: Mixes specified amounts of plastic powder and chemical solution, using spatula. Packs mixture around base of exposed artificial teeth and into cavities of mold sections. Positions sheet of plastic or wax paper or foil over bottom of mold to permit separation of mold from denture. Fits top section of mold over bottom and places assembly in press. Starts press that forces sections together and compresses mixture around teeth to form reproduction of gums. Removes model from press and trims excess plastic from mold, using knife. Submerges mold in hot water for specified time to cure plastic.
GOE: 05.05.11 STRENGTH: L GED: R3 M2 L3 SVP: 5 DLU: 77

712.684-038 REFINER (protective dev.)

Recovers precious metals, such as gold, platinum, and palladium from scrap dentures and extracted teeth, using furnace, retort, and laboratory equipment: Breaks scrap dentures, using hammer, and removes precious metals. Weighs each type metal and records weights. Places metal in retort and positions retort in furnace to melt metal particles. Turns valves to adjust temperature of furnace. Removes retort and pours molten metal solution into beaker, using tongs. Adds specified amounts of chemicals to molten metal solution to separate metal from solution. Pours solution through filter to recover precious dental metals.
GOE: 06.04.24 STRENGTH: L GED: R3 M2 L2 SVP: 4 DLU: 77

712.684-042 FABRICATOR, ARTIFICIAL BREAST (protective dev.)

Fabricates cosmetic appliances from latex for use as artificial breasts, using dies, molded plastic forms, heat-sealing device, and airhose: Places molded form in die, according to size, and positions die on balance scale under spigot of latex gel container. Pushes lever to open spigot to fill molded form, and to close spigot when mold reaches prescribed weight. Imprints mold size and other identification data onto plastic sheet used as backing for form, using printing device. Places imprinted backing in prescribed position over die containing gel-filled mold and fuses backing to molded form, using sealing device, to form inner shell. Inserts inner shell into outer plastic shell and fuses outer shell, using sealing device. Inflates shell to specified shape and firmness, using airhose, and seals opening, using heated rod. Tears excess plastic from edge of form.
GOE: 06.04.02 STRENGTH: L GED: R2 M1 L1 SVP: 2 DLU: 86

712.684-046 DENTURE-MODEL MAKER (protective dev.)

Forms plaster, metal, plastic, or rubber models and molds from dental impressions and wax models of dentures and dental appliances, using casting equipment and handtools: Mixes specified amounts of special plaster and water or other model-making ingredients, by hand or electric mixer-vibrator, to form compound used for models and molds. Pours mixture into impressions to form models for upper and lower dentures. Melts pieces of gold, silver, or other metal, using gas torch, and casts inlays, crowns, and pontics for fixed bridges, using centrifugal casting machine. Packs plasttic mixture or composition rubber strips in molds to cast orthodontic appliances, such as tooth positioners, mouthguards, and retainers. Positions models in articulator and verifies occlusions. Packs plaster or other denture-making ingredient around wax model of denture to form model or matrix for casting denture. Places mold in boiling water to melt wax from cast model. Scrapes remaining wax from model, using knife, and washes model in soapy solution to remove dirt and foreign matter.
GOE: 05.05.11 STRENGTH: L GED: R3 M2 L3 SVP: 5 DLU: 77

712.684-050 INSPECTOR, SURGICAL INSTRUMENTS (inst. & app.)

Inspects surgical instruments, such as needles, needle holders, bandage scissors, forceps, and scalpels, for defects in finish and adherence to standards. Measures instruments for conformance to specifications, using measuring instruments, such as ruler and micrometer. May use microscope or other magnifying device to perform inspection.
GOE: 06.03.02 STRENGTH: L GED: R2 M2 L1 SVP: 2 DLU: 84

712.684-054 SURGICAL-FORCEPS FABRICATOR (inst. & app.)

Performs any combination of following tasks to fabricate radio-frequency cauterizing surgical forceps, according to written instructions: Cuts and strips coaxial wire and solders wire ends to plug terminals and forceps contacts. Applies bonding agent to metal surfaces requiring plastic insulation coating, using brush. Places plug terminals into mold, bolts mold together, and clamps mold

in vise. Injects liquid plastic into mold, using hand-operated pressure gun. Dips forceps into liquid plastic and hangs forceps on stand to drain. Places plug molds and dipped forceps into oven for specified time to cure plastic insulation. Inspects plastic insulation for bubbles and uniformity of thickness. Tests cured plugs and forceps for continuity, using ohmmeter. Trims plastic flash from plugs and forceps, using knife. Plugs forceps into radio-frequency generator and passes forceps along metal grounding plate to test for insulation leaks indicated by sparking. Applies electroplating solution onto contact points of forceps, using battery-powered plating paddle. Fabricates parts, such as plug pins, insulating collars, and fittings for assembly, using handtools, such as wire brush, pliers, drill press, and jeweler's lathe. Weighs and mixes ingredients for plastic compound.
GOE: 06.04.24 STRENGTH: L GED: R3 M2 L2 SVP: 4 DLU: 78

712.687-010 ASSEMBLER, PLASTIC HOSPITAL PRODUCTS (inst. & app.)
Performs any combination of following tasks to assemble and package disposable plastic hospital products, such as hypodermic syringes, catheters, and intravenous apparatus: Reviews work order and selects component parts to assemble specified product. Fits and assembles parts together, using adhesives and handtools, or heats, bonds, and welds parts together, using automatic equipment. Visually inspects products for defects, verifies conformance to specifications, and rejects defective products. Packages assembled product into plastic bag or other container and seals package, using sealing machine. Packs sealed product and instructional information into cartons, and labels cartons with identifying information. May stack cartons in sterilization chamber, seal chamber, and turn valves to admit gas into chamber to sterilize product.
GOE: 06.04.24 STRENGTH: L GED: R2 M1 L1 SVP: 2 DLU: 90

712.687-014 COILER (protective dev.) alternate titles: pinner
Inserts and solders metal coils and pins in base of artificial teeth to form means of attachment to denture: Inserts coil in tooth, using tweezers, and solders pin to coil, using soldering iron. Coats pins with flux.
GOE: 06.04.23 STRENGTH: L GED: R2 M1 L1 SVP: 2 DLU: 77

712.687-018 GAUGER (protective dev.) alternate titles: suture gauger; suture measurer
Sorts and measures strands of surgical sutures according to length and thickness: Places strand on measuring stick to determine length. Inserts each end and center of strand into slot of gauge that automatically registers thickness to 0.001 inch and compares gauge reading with prescribed limits of acceptable suture thicknesses. Rejects strands that fail to meet standards. Sorts acceptable strands by width and length, placing specially cut ends together, to ready them for subsequent clamping onto needles. May wind graded sutures onto spools.
GOE: 06.03.02 STRENGTH: S GED: R2 M1 L2 SVP: 2 DLU: 77

712.687-022 GAS-MASK INSPECTOR (protective dev.)
Inspects assembled gas masks for conformity to specifications: Examines chemical containers, facepieces, straps, and rubber hoses for defects, such as blisters, tears, and faulty stitching. Tests masks for leakage around glass eyepieces, using suction-cup device. Tests chemical containers for content, and for leakage under pressure, using gauge. Tests absorbing quality of chemicals, using smoke meter.
GOE: 06.03.02 STRENGTH: L GED: R3 M2 L2 SVP: 4 DLU: 77

712.687-030 SUTURE POLISHER (protective dev.)
Smooths and polishes sheep gut used in sutures: Fastens sheep gut in adjustable rack. Adjusts rack to hold gut taut. Smooths and polishes gut, using sandpaper.
GOE: 06.04.34 STRENGTH: L GED: R2 M1 L1 SVP: 2 DLU: 77

712.687-034 SUTURE WINDER, HAND (protective dev.) alternate titles: gut winder
Winds single or multiple lengths of surgical catgut onto fiber suture reel: Pulls out holding flaps on reel, inserts end of strand under one flap, and places reel on power-driven wheel. Presses pedal to actuate wheel and guides strand under holding flaps as wheel spins to wind precut lengths or counts wheel revolutions to measure lengths. Turns reels by hand when winding numerous strands. Cuts catgut from spool, using scissors. Inserts completed reels in plastic envelopes for subsequent sterilization, or into glass tubes for future use.
GOE: 06.04.23 STRENGTH: S GED: R2 M1 L1 SVP: 2 DLU: 77

712.687-038 TOOTH INSPECTOR (protective dev.)
Examines, sorts, and packages artificial teeth: Sorts teeth according to type, size, and color shade. Examines teeth to detect surface blemishes and removes blemishes, using brush or scraper. Rejects defective teeth. Packages acceptable teeth in wax-filled casing and stamps identifying information in wax.
GOE: 06.03.02 STRENGTH: L GED: R2 M1 L1 SVP: 2 DLU: 77

713   OCCUPATIONS IN FABRICATION AND REPAIR OF OPHTHALMIC GOODS

This group includes occupations concerned with fabricating and repairing ophthalmic frames and goods, fitting frames on customer, mounting lenses into frames, and molding ophthalmic goods, such as artificial eyes and contact lenses. Occupations concerned with generating, grinding, and polishing ophthalmic lenses are included in Group 716.

713.261-010 ARTIFICIAL-GLASS-EYE MAKER (optical goods) alternate titles: ocularist, glass
Fabricates artificial glass eyes for humans according to physician's prescription or customer specifications, applying knowledge of glass blowing and fabricating techniques: Holds and turns glass tube over gas burner to soften glass to viscous state. Blows into tube to form globe. Superimposes glass of required color on top surface of bulb to form iris. Fuses black glass in center of iris to simulate pupil and fuses clear glass over iris to form cornea. Positions and fuses red glass threads on globe to produce veins of eyeball. Fits artificial glass eyes to patients and makes adjustments for cosmetic correction.
GOE: 05.05.11 STRENGTH: L GED: R4 M2 L4 SVP: 8 DLU: 77

713.261-014 ARTIFICIAL-PLASTIC-EYE MAKER (optical goods) alternate titles: ocularist; plastic-eye technician
Fabricates artificial plastic eyes according to specifications and fits eyes into customer's eye sockets, using precision handtools, measuring instruments, molding devices, and bench fabricating machines: Measures customer's eye socket, using calipers, and measures natural eye to determine size and location of pupil and iris, using scale. Records data on examination card. Selects stock artificial eye approximating size and shape of customer's socket and inserts eye into socket. Fills eye area and questions customer to ascertain that eye fit is comfortable. Applies plastic as required to build up and shape stock eye to conform to customer's eye socket. Examines customer's natural eye to determine iris coloring, eye white shading, and number of eye white veins and records information on examination card. Selects samples of iris, pupil, and white to match eye. Positions artificial eye stock in plaster of paris to prepare mold for casting plastic eye. Pours plastic into mold to form artificial eye. Measures molded eye to determine position for pupil and iris, using rule. Positions and presses pupil and iris into place. Immerses eye in boiling water to set plastic. Paints iris and white of artificial eye to produce color of customer's natural eye according to information recorded on examination card. Draws veins on white of eye, using colored pencil or scratches grooves into eye to represent veins and fills grooves with pigment. Immerses eye in clear plastic solution to produce glassy finish. Examines eye for irregularities in shape and removes irregularities, using dental grinding machine. Polishes eye, using pumice and electric buffing wheel. Fits customer with artificial eye and compares artificial eye with natural eye to ensure centering of iris and pupils and matching of colors. May fit patients with ready-to-wear plastic eyes of standard sizes and colors. May fabricate implants (plastic and mesh devices fitted in eye socket for retention of eye muscles) and conformers (plastic disks placed in eye socket to maintain socket shape prior to fitting of artificial eye), using standard molds and grinding and polishing machines.
GOE: 05.05.11 STRENGTH: L GED: R4 M3 L4 SVP: 8 DLU: 77

713.381-010 LENS-MOLD SETTER (optical goods) alternate titles: mold setter
Assembles molds for casting contact lenses, using handtools, and inspects cast lenses for conformance to specifications, using precision measuring instruments: Selects mold and mold inserts. Positions inserts in mold and shims inserts as indicated by mold insert records. Sets holding pins, using wrench, and routes mold to CONTACT-LENS MOLDER (optical goods). Breaks seal on mold after casting and prys mold apart, using screwdriver and handpress. Peels lens and flashing from mold, using scalpel-like knife. Cuts lenses apart and places lenses in storage box. Inspects lenses, using power determining and optical centering instruments, thickness gauge, shadowgraph, and loupe magnifier, to verify correctness of characteristics, such as inside curve dimension and power, and to detect defects, such as scratches. Alters position of mold inserts to correct lens thickness, using shims. Cleans mold with solvent or routes mold to grinding room for polishing to eliminate defects.
GOE: 06.02.23 STRENGTH: L GED: R3 M3 L2 SVP: 5 DLU: 77

713.384-010 ASSEMBLER, GOLD FRAME (optical goods)
Assembles gold, aluminum, platinum, or other metallic wire eyeglass frames, using handtools: Enlarges predrilled holes and grooves in frame parts, using drills and files. Brushes holes and grooves with acetone to clean openings. Positions frame parts in holding fixture, aligns holes in parts, and inserts and tightens screws to secure parts together. Pushes eye-wires into grooves in frame and taps frame to tighten groove openings and secure wires. Attaches decorative or supportive wire sections to frame or temple pieces according to design specifications, using adhesive compound or soldering equipment.
GOE: 06.01.04 STRENGTH: L GED: R2 M1 L2 SVP: 2 DLU: 77

713.384-014 INSPECTOR, EYEGLASS (optical goods)
Inspects mounted eyeglasses for quality of work and compliance with prescription specifications, using precision optical measuring instrument: Examines frame for proper assembly, and for appearance of engraving and trim. Measures eyesize, temple length, and distance between lenses with ruler. Inspects alignment of lenses, nose pads, and temples with straightedge. Inspects lenses for color, seating in frame, and defects, such as striae, pits, and sharp edges. Examines lenses with power-determining and optical-centering instrument to ensure that optical center, focal center, power of lens, and refractive effect are in accordance with prescription. Returns defective articles for correction.
GOE: 06.01.04 STRENGTH: S GED: R3 M3 L2 SVP: 5 DLU: 77

713.667-010 INSPECTOR, CLIP-ON SUNGLASSES (optical goods)
Inspects assembled clip-on sunglasses for fit, tension of spring clip, and lens defects, using handtools, microscope, and light projector: Trims end of clip

spring, using diagonal cutter, and bends clip with fingers to achieve specified holding tension. Holds sunglasses over light to inspect lenses for matched color shading and scratches. Places sunglasses under microscope or in front of light projector to detect lens distortion, indicated by blurring of instrument crosshairs or of letters on projected chart. Returns rejected sunglasses to assembly workers and explains rework required.
GOE: 06.03.02 STRENGTH: S GED: R2 M1 L2 SVP: 3 DLU: 77

713.681-010 LENS MOUNTER II (optical goods)
Mounts prescription eyeglass lenses in metal, plastic, or combination frames, using handtools: Examines eyeglass prescription to determine style, color, and size of frame. Inspects lenses to detect flaws, such as pits, chips, and scratches. Holds and turns lenses against grinding wheel to remove flaws. Assembles eyeglass frame and attaches ornaments, shields, nose pads, and temple pieces, using pliers and screwdrivers. Drills holes in lenses for mounting on rimless frames, using diamond drill. Immerses plastic frame rims in hot salt solution to soften rims or stretches rims, using hot, metal cone. Inserts and aligns lenses in frame. Verifies frame dimensions and alignment of lenses, using protractor, ruler, and straightedge. Turns lenses in frame to correct alignment, using padded pliers. Immerses plastic frames in cold water to set plastic around lenses. Tightens screws to hold lenses in metal frames. Examines lenses under polarized light to detect stress caused by overtightening screws and adjusts screws as necessary. Heats plastic frame bridge and bends frame according to prescription specifications, using fingers and handtools. Immerses plastic frames in dye for specified period to color frames. Solders broken metal bridges and replaces damaged temples to repair frames, using soldering iron and handtools. Cleans and polishes finished eyeglasses, using cloth and solvent. May be designated according to type frame mounted as Metal-Frame Inserter (optical goods); Plastic-Frame Inserter (optical goods); or according to part assembled as Trim Mounter (optical goods) II.
GOE: 05.05.11 STRENGTH: M GED: R3 M2 L3 SVP: 6 DLU: 77

713.684-010 ASSEMBLER, CLIP-ON SUNGLASSES (optical goods)
Assembles clip-on sunglasses, using handtools and holding fixture: Fits metal frame into slots of plastic frame, presses lenses into metal frame grooves, and places assembly into holding fixture. Fits clip-on attachment into slots of plastic frame top. Inserts and sets screws in holes, using tweezers and jeweler's screwdriver. Examines glasses to ensure that both lenses are of same color and shading.
GOE: 06.04.23 STRENGTH: L GED: R2 M1 L1 SVP: 3 DLU: 77

713.684-014 ASSEMBLER, MOLDED FRAMES (optical goods) alternate titles: frame assembler
Assembles plastic eyeglass frames, using drill press and rivet press: Positions frame parts in jig and drills holes in parts, using drill press. Inserts rivets through holes, positions clips and hinges on rivets, and depresses pedal of pneumatic press to set rivets.
GOE: 06.04.23 STRENGTH: L GED: R2 M1 L1 SVP: 2 DLU: 77

713.684-018 BENCH WORKER (optical goods)
Performs any combination of following activities to prepare plastic eyeglass frames for assembly, using bench-mounted machines and handtools or power tools: Drills or punches holes in frame components, using drill or punch press. Inserts and tightens screws, nuts, and bolts to assemble parts, using handtools. Inserts and expands rivets to assemble parts, using rivet gun. Aligns and miters frame part edges, using mitering machine. Cuts grooves in parts for insertion of lenses, using grooving machine. May be designated according to activity as Groover (optical goods).
GOE: 06.04.24 STRENGTH: L GED: R2 M1 L1 SVP: 3 DLU: 77

713.684-022 EMBOSSER (optical goods)
Imprints identifying information on eyeglass frames according to prescription, using embossing press: Reads prescription to obtain information to be imprinted, such as owner's name, address, and telephone number. Sets type in type bar and slides bar into position in press. Turns knob to lock type bar in place. Positions eyeglass temple in spring clip below type bar. Places metallic foil over temple and pulls handle to lower electrically heated type bar and imprint information on temple. May mount trim on frame and be designated Trim Mounter (optical goods) I. Routes printed and trimmed eyeglasses to inspection section.
GOE: 06.04.37 STRENGTH: L GED: R2 M1 L1 SVP: 3 DLU: 77

713.684-026 EYEGLASS-FRAME TRUER (optical goods)
Bends and adjusts plastic or metal eyeglass frames according to prescription specifications, using jeweler's handtools, such as hammers, screwdrivers, and pliers. Measures frames to determine amount of adjustment required, using gauges and jigs.
GOE: 06.04.02 STRENGTH: L GED: R2 M1 L2 SVP: 3 DLU: 77

713.684-030 FRAME CARVER, SPINDLE (optical goods)
Carves spectacle nose pieces of celluloid, plastics, and other material, using rotary spindle carving tool: Measures designated sample nose piece to determine dimensional specifications, using precision measuring instruments. Mounts specified cutting tool in machine chuck, using handtools. Starts machine and holds and turns nose piece blank against cutting tool to fabricate nose piece according to specifications.
GOE: 06.04.24 STRENGTH: S GED: R2 M2 L2 SVP: 3 DLU: 77

713.684-034 MULTIFOCAL-LENS ASSEMBLER (optical goods) alternate titles: multifocal-button assembler
Fits and secures multifocal lens parts together preparatory to fusing, utilizing adhesive compound or asbestos tape: Dips multifocal button in cleaning solu-

tion and wipes dry. Brushes button and countersink blank to remove dust and lint. Positions button on polished surface of countersink blank. Performs test to detect presence of foreign matter between button and countersink blank, using instrument that indicates foreign matter when pressure is applied to outside edge of button. Recleans surfaces and performs test until instrument indicates lens parts are free of foreign matter. Places spring clamp on blank to hold button in position. Inserts metal peg between button and blank to allow air to escape during fusing, using tweezers. Applies cement to surface contact points around edge of button, using needle applicator, or wraps asbestos tape around button and countersink blank assembly to hold button in place. Removes spring clip and metal peg after cement is set. Places assembled unit in tray for transfer to fusing room.
GOE: 06.04.23 STRENGTH: S GED: R2 M1 L2 SVP: 3 DLU: 77

713.684-038 POLISHER, EYEGLASS FRAMES (optical goods)
Polishes plastic eyeglass frames and temple pieces to remove scratches and pit marks, using polishing wheel: Applies abrasive compound to wheel surface, using brush. Starts machine and holds and turns frame parts against wheel to polish parts and remove defects. Inspects and feels polished parts to verify removal of flaws. Presses sandpaper against polishing wheel to remove abrasive residue in preparation for next sequence.
GOE: 06.04.24 STRENGTH: S GED: R2 M1 L1 SVP: 2 DLU: 77

713.684-042 WASHER (optical goods)
Performs any combination of following duties to clean finished eyeglasses, dye plastic eyeglass lenses, and electroplate metal frames: Washes, rinses, dries, and buffs eyeglasses, using cleaning solution, cloth, and buffing wheel. Mixes trays of dye according to formula and places trays on heating plate to maintain specified temperature. Mounts plastic lenses in holder and immerses lenses in dye for specified period. Compares lens with sample to verify color and immerses lens in dye to correct color as necessary. Immerses metal frames in plating solution for specified period to electroplate frames.
GOE: 06.04.39 STRENGTH: L GED: R2 M1 L1 SVP: 3 DLU: 77

713.687-010 CLIP COATER (optical goods) alternate titles: clip baker; dipper
Coats tips of sunglass clips with protective plastic and cures coated clips in oven: Slides metal clips onto rack and immerses rack in molten plastic to coat tips of metal clips, or applies plastic to tips, using brush. Places racks of clips in oven for specified period to cure plastic. Removes racks, examines coating for proper baking, indicated by color of plastic, and places racks on table for further processing or in oven for further baking.
GOE: 06.04.33 STRENGTH: L GED: R2 M1 L1 SVP: 2 DLU: 77

713.687-014 CONTACT-LENS-FLASHING PUNCHER (optical goods) alternate titles: puncher
Punches flashing from molded plastic contact lenses, using handpress: Places compartmentalized box under openings in press-holding fixture to catch lens after punching. Positions lens in holding fixture and pulls lever to lower hollow punch which cuts flashing from lens. Repeats punching, allowing only lenses of same specifications to fall in same compartment. Labels and routes lenses in envelopes or boxes to stockroom or other work stations.
GOE: 06.04.24 STRENGTH: L GED: R2 M1 L1 SVP: 2 DLU: 77

713.687-018 FINAL ASSEMBLER (optical goods)
Attaches nose pads and temple pieces to optical frames, using handtools: Positions parts in fixture to align screw holes. Inserts and tightens screws, using screwdriver.
GOE: 06.04.23 STRENGTH: S GED: R1 M1 L1 SVP: 2 DLU: 77

713.687-022 INSPECTOR, EYEGLASS FRAMES (optical goods)
Examines eyeglass frames and frame parts, such as temples, rims, nose pads, and bridge pieces, for defects and conformance to dimensional specifications. Feels and visually inspects frames to detect soldering irregularities, rough spots, and scratches. Verifies measurements of frame parts, using ruler and gauges.
GOE: 06.03.02 STRENGTH: S GED: R2 M1 L2 SVP: 3 DLU: 77

713.687-026 LENS INSERTER (optical goods) alternate titles: roll-over loader
Fits lenses into plastic sunglass frames and places frames on conveyor belt that passes under heat lamps which soften frames preparatory to setting of lenses.
GOE: 06.04.23 STRENGTH: S GED: R1 M1 L1 SVP: 2 DLU: 77

713.687-030 LENS MATCHER (optical goods)
Examines and matches colored goggle lenses to obtain pairs and places matched lenses of same shade in box. May inspect lenses for defects.
GOE: 06.03.02 STRENGTH: L GED: R2 M1 L2 SVP: 2 DLU: 77

713.687-034 POLISHER, IMPLANT (optical goods)
Polishes plastic implants used to fill eye socket of person with artificial eye, using polishing cloths and chamois: Cuts emery cloth and chamois cloth into strips, using scissors. Clamps plastic implant in vise, and pulls emery cloth strip back and forth through implant opening to remove rough edges and enlarge opening. Examines implant to verify smoothness and freedom from defects, using eye loupe.
GOE: 06.04.24 STRENGTH: S GED: R2 M1 L1 SVP: 2 DLU: 77

713.687-038 SALVAGER (optical goods)
Examines and dismantles sunglasses to salvage components, such as lenses, clips, and frames, using handtools: Examines sunglasses to determine salvage-

able components. Punches out rivets, using hammer and punch. Removes ornamental jewels, hinges, clips, and other parts and places parts in storage boxes. Cuts, unscrews, springs, or otherwise loosens frames to remove lenses. Stacks lenses by color, grind, shape, and shading. Sorts metal frames by style, and plastic frames by color for reprocessing.
GOE: 06.04.34 STRENGTH: L GED: R2 M1 L1 SVP: 2 DLU: 77

713.687-042 SUNGLASS-CLIP ATTACHER (optical goods) alternate titles: heating-fixture tender; melter
Bonds metal spring clip to plastic clip-on sunglass frames, using electric heating equipment: Pulls lever or slides rod to clamp frames in heating fixture. Removes bonded frames and examines attachment and action of clip for freedom of movement.
GOE: 06.04.23 STRENGTH: L GED: R2 M1 L1 SVP: 2 DLU: 77

714 OCCUPATIONS IN FABRICATION AND REPAIR OF PHOTOGRAPHIC EQUIPMENT AND SUPPLIES

This group includes occupations concerned with fabricating and repairing photographic apparatus, such as still and motion picture cameras and projectors, photocopy and microfilm equipment, blueprinting and diazo-type equipment, and other photographic equipment, parts, and attachments; sensitized film, plates, cloth, and papers; and prepared chemicals packaged for photographic use. Occupations concerned with electronic components are included in Group 726 and bulbs are included in Group 725.

714.131-010 SUPERVISOR, MOTION-PICTURE EQUIPMENT (motion picture; photo. appar.) alternate titles: cinetechnician supervisor
Supervises and coordinates activities of workers engaged in assembling, repairing, remodeling, and maintaining photographing, projecting, sound, and related motion-picture equipment: Inspects malfunctioning equipment to determine extent of work to be performed and directs individuals or groups to make repairs or modifications. Trains new workers in equipment assembly and maintenance. May assign repair crews to motion picture production units. Performs other duties as described under SUPERVISOR (any industry) Master Title.
GOE: 05.05.11 STRENGTH: L GED: R4 M4 L4 SVP: 8 DLU: 77

714.281-010 AIRCRAFT-PHOTOGRAPHIC-EQUIPMENT MECHANIC (photo. appar.) alternate titles: research assembler; research mechanic
Assembles, adjusts, tests, and modifies aircraft cameras according to engineering drawings and sketches, using handtools and bench machines: Reads and interprets engineering drawings and verbal instructions to determine fabrication methods and sequence of fabrication. Lays out reference points and dimensions on parts to be machined, using precision measuring instruments. Fabricates parts to specifications, using bench lathe, milling machine, shaper, and grinder. Measures parts to verify specified dimensions, using micrometer, dial gauges, and vernier caliper. Cuts, bends, drills, and fastens parts to assemble, repair, or modify camera, using handtools. Fabricates and installs electrical assemblies and wiring in camera housing, using handtools and soldering equipment. Tests camera units for operational efficiency, using calibrating instruments, multimeter, and stroboscope and adjusts mechanisms to correct inefficient operation. Installs film in camera and adjusts camera mechanisms to record sharpest image consistent with speed of aircraft, weather conditions, and object or terrain to be photographed. Records test data, prepares reports on fabricating techniques used, and recommends modifications to resolve problems.
GOE: 05.05.09 STRENGTH: L GED: R4 M4 L4 SVP: 8 DLU: 77

714.281-014 CAMERA REPAIRER (photo. appar.)
Repairs and adjusts cameras, using specialized tools and test devices: Disassembles camera, using handtools. Tests and aligns diaphragm, lens mounts, and film transport to minimize optical distortion, using precision gauges. Adjusts range and view finders, using fixed focusing target. Calibrates operation of shutter, diaphragm, and lens carriers with dial settings, using electronic or stroboscopic timing instruments. Fabricates of modifies parts, using bench lathe, grinder, and drill press.
GOE: 05.05.11 STRENGTH: S GED: R4 M4 L4 SVP: 8 DLU: 77

714.281-018 MACHINIST, MOTION-PICTURE EQUIPMENT (motion picture; photo. appar.) alternate titles: cinetechnician; motion-picture-camera repairer
Assembles, repairs, remodels, and services photographing, projecting, editing, sound-recording, and power equipment used in motion picture production, using handtools and bench machines: Reads job order and blueprints to plan work procedures. Disassembles defective equipment, using handtools. Constructs replacement parts (except camera lenses and other optical parts) used to repair or remodel equipment, using machines, such as bench lathes, milling machines, gear cutters, grinders, and drill presses. Finishes, fits, and installs parts, using precision handtools and calibration devices. Measures installed parts for conformance to specifications, using micrometers and calipers. Operates repaired equipment to verify operational efficiency. Cleans and lubricates equipment.
GOE: 05.05.09 STRENGTH: M GED: R4 M4 L4 SVP: 8 DLU: 77

714.281-022 PHOTOGRAPHIC EQUIPMENT TECHNICIAN (photo. appar.)
Assembles, repairs, tests, and maintains still and motion picture cameras and photographic equipment according to customer, blueprint, or work order speci-

fications, using handtools, bench machines, and test equipment: Reads diagrammatic and verbal specifications to determine repairs needed and sequence of operations. Inspects cameras and equipment to locate defects, using jewelers' loupe. Disassembles cameras to gain access to defects. Tests focus of lens system, using optical measuring equipment, and adjusts and repairs lens system to correct defective focusing, using handtools. Measures camera shutter speed, using electronic measuring instrument, and adjusts shutter mechanism to manufacturer's specifications, using handtools. Compares light meter readings with readings of light measuring instrument to verify accuracy of camera light meters. Adjusts light meters to correct defective readings, using handtools. Measures operating speed of movie cameras, using frequency counter and turns camera speed control, using screwdriver, to correct defective operation. Cleans and lubricates cameras and polishes camera lenses, using air gun, ultrasonic cleaning device, cloth, syringe, and tissue paper. May fabricate parts for cameras and related equipment, using machines, such as bench lathe, milling machines, cutters, and grinders.
GOE: 05.05.11 STRENGTH: L GED: R4 M4 L4 SVP: 8 DLU: 77

714.281-026 PHOTOGRAPHIC-EQUIPMENT-MAINTENANCE TECHNICIAN (photo. appar.) alternate titles: technical-maintenance technician
Fabricates, assembles, and repairs photographic equipment except cameras, using handtools and power tools: Examines equipment, such as photograph printers, print washers, driers and straighteners, and mounting presses. Replaces defective wood and metal parts and makes minor repairs, such as cleaning and tightening connections, soldering and welding broken metal parts, and bending and installing piping. Lays out framework dimensions on channel and angle stock, using tape measure, square, and scribe and cuts and grinds stock to dimensional specifications to fabricate equipment parts, using power saws, sanders, grinders, and files. Assembles frames and installs parts according to blueprint specifications, using handtools, such as drills, wrenches, reamers, and hole punches. Installs electrical wiring, following blueprints. Requisitions parts and materials.
GOE: 05.05.09 STRENGTH: L GED: R4 M3 L4 SVP: 7 DLU: 77

714.281-030 SERVICE TECHNICIAN, COMPUTERIZED-PHOTOFINISHING EQUIPMENT (photofinishing)
Analyzes malfunctions in computerized electromechanical photofinishing equipment and replaces or repairs defective components, utilizing knowledge of equipment operation and repair: Examines and tests equipment to determine nature and probable cause of malfunction, using work aids such as voltmeter, ohmmeter, schematic drawings, and equipment specifications. Removes and replaces defective electronic, electrical, mechanical, and plumbing components, such as pipes, valves, printed circuit boards, wiring, switches, thermostats, heaters, motors, pumps, gears, and drive chains, using handtools and following drawings and manufacturer's manuals. Tightens or solders loose connections and fittings, and performs related repairs. Adjusts equipment to manufacturer's specifications, using handtools and measuring instruments. Test operates equipment to ensure that defects have been corrected.
GOE: 05.05.11 STRENGTH: M GED: R4 M3 L4 SVP: 6 DLU: 86

714.381-010 ASSEMBLER, PHOTOGRAPHIC EQUIPMENT (photo. appar.) alternate titles: assembler, precision-mechanical
Assembles and adjusts photographic apparatus, such as motion picture cameras, projectors, film developing equipment, and microfilm equipment, according to blueprint specifications, using handtools and portable power tools: Examines blueprints to determine specifications. Aligns, fits, and bolts components together to assemble mechanisms, subassemblies, and assemblies of photographic apparatus, using handtools, portable power tools, and drill press. Connects electrical wiring according to circuit diagram, using soldering iron. Tests function of assembled units, using precision mechanical, electrical, optical, and sound measuring instruments; and adjusts mechanisms to attain specified functional performance, using handtools. May repair defective products returned to production.
GOE: 06.01.04 STRENGTH: L GED: R4 M3 L3 SVP: 6 DLU: 78

714.381-014 INSPECTOR, PHOTOGRAPHIC EQUIPMENT (photo. appar.) alternate titles: inspector, precision
Inspects parts, subassemblies, and assembled photographic apparatus, such as still and motion picture cameras, magazines, enlargers, flash units, and film developing machines for conformance to verbal and diagrammatic specifications, using precision measuring and testing instruments: Examines blueprints, wiring diagrams, and other specifications to determine parts, dimensions, and tolerances required. Examines equipment for defects, such as missing parts, incorrect serial numbers, flaws in castings, and light leakage. Measures parts to ensure conformance to dimensional specifications, using micrometers, gauges, rules, and other precision measuring instruments. Tests functioning of electronic components, using test instruments, such as voltmeters, oscilloscopes, and signal generators. Trips camera shutters to verify timing, using timing device. Measures focal distance of lenses, using depth micrometer or collimator. Traces electrical wiring and examines connections to detect assembly defects and tests electrical circuits for continuity, using wire diagrams and continuity meter. Examines test film to detect faulty operation of cameras, using projector, viewing screen, and hand lens. Records inspection data and marks or stamps inspection tag to indicate acceptance or rejection of equipment inspected.
GOE: 06.01.05 STRENGTH: L GED: R4 M3 L3 SVP: 6 DLU: 77

714.381-018 PHOTOGRAPHIC-PLATE MAKER (electron. comp.) alternate titles: photographic-process attendant

Prepares photographic plates used to print pattern of aperture masks on sensitized steel: Examines unexposed plate to detect foreign particles or emulsion flaws. Transfers image from master plate to unexposed plate by means of contact exposure and immerses plate in series of chemical and water baths to develop image on plate [DEVELOPER (photofinishing)]. Examines plate over light box in darkroom to detect flaws and verify conformity of pattern with master plate. Measures dot size and center distance, using calibrated microscope, and examines master and production plates for dot damage. Repairs defective plates by filling in missing dots, using photographic touch-up tool and ink. Installs and alignes plates in printing case for DISPLAY-SCREEN FABRICATOR (electron. comp.). Prepares developing solutions, following formula.
GOE: 05.10.05 STRENGTH: L GED: R4 M3 L3 SVP: 6 DLU: 77

714.667-010 SENSITIZED-PAPER TESTER (photo. appar.)

Tests tensile strength and light value of samples of photocopy, blueprint, and other sensitized paper to ensure conformance to specifications, using duplicating machines and testing devices: Inserts paper sample in duplicating machine and starts machine. Removes developed print and compares sample with printed standard to detect variations in color and clarity. Cuts paper sample into strips and clamps ends of strips in tensile strength measuring device. Turns handle of testing device until paper breaks. Records pounds of force required to break paper. Records test data in log.
GOE: 06.03.02 STRENGTH: L GED: R2 M1 L1 SVP: 3 DLU: 77

714.684-010 ASSEMBLER, PRODUCTION LINE (photo. appar.)

Assembles components of cameras, camera magazines, camera shutters, movie projectors, and electronic photographic apparatus, such as exposure meters, using electric riveting press, punch press, soldering iron, and handtools: Screws, rivets, solders, and otherwise fastens and installs parts, following blueprints. Operates assemblies to test for specified functioning and adjusts mechanisms to attain specified functioning, using handtools, gauges, and meters. May be designated according to type of apparatus assembled as Camera Assembler (photo. appar.); Meter Assembler (photo. appar.); Projector Assembler (photo. appar.); or according to part assembled as Synchro Assembler (photo. appar.).
GOE: 06.02.23 STRENGTH: L GED: R3 M2 L2 SVP: 4 DLU: 78

714.684-014 BELLOWS MAKER (photo. appar.) alternate titles: bellows assembler

Builds or repairs camera bellows, using handtools, power tools, and gluing equipment: Selects cardboard cone bellow form according to size of bellows. Cuts paper pattern of cone. Cuts lining and cover materials for bellows, according to pattern, using scissors or electric knife. Stretches lining around cone and glues overlapping edges to cone. Cuts cardboard strips (ribs) and glues strips to lining. Glues cover over ribbed lining and attaches front and rear metal frames, using glue and clamps. Trims excess material from assembly, using scissors and removes dried glue, using solvent and cloth. Compresses assembly over special frame to pleat material and form completed bellows.
GOE: 06.02.32 STRENGTH: L GED: R3 M2 L2 SVP: 4 DLU: 77

714.687-010 CHECKER, FILM TESTS (photo. appar.)

Identifies, wraps, and packages samples of sheet film for in-process testing according to specified procedures: Reads test requests for film in various stages of production and locates, removes, and batches sample sheets of specified film. Wraps, packages, and labels samples according to process stage and characteristics of film selected. Routes samples to testing department. Examines tested film, sorts rejected and approved sheets, and segregates rejected sheets with salvageable areas for cutting. Maintains records of film tested and test results.
GOE: 06.03.02 STRENGTH: L GED: R3 M1 L2 SVP: 4 DLU: 77

715 OCCUPATIONS IN FABRICATION AND REPAIR OF WATCHES, CLOCKS, AND PARTS

This group includes occupations concerned with fabricating and repairing complete mechanical or electric watches and clocks, and mechanical movements used in clockwork-operated devices, such as timers, electric meters, and recorders.

715.131-010 SUPERVISOR (clock & watch)

Supervises and coordinates activities of workers engaged in assembling watches, clocks, and related units, and testing assembled units: Inspects finished work at production stations to ensure conformance to specifications, using loupe and gauges. Trains workers in performance of tasks. Requisitions materials and supplies. Confers with other supervisory personnel to coordinate interdepartmental workflow. Sets up machines and equipment. Performs duties of workers supervised to expedite production. May supervise workers engaged in fabricating watch and clock parts. Performs other duties as described under SUPERVISOR (any industry) Master Title.
GOE: 06.01.01 STRENGTH: L GED: R4 M3 L3 SVP: 7 DLU: 77

715.131-014 SUPERVISOR, DIALS (clock & watch)

Supervises and coordinates activities of workers engaged in blanking, cleaning, brushing, soldering, polishing, plating, printing, and lacquering watch dials: Trains new workers in performance of tasks. Requisitions supplies and materials. Confers with other supervisory personnel to coordinate interdepartmental workflow. Confers with workers' representatives to resolve grievances. Sets up

machines and equipment. Performs other duties as described under SUPERVISOR (any industry) Master Title.
GOE: 06.02.01 STRENGTH: L GED: R4 M3 L3 SVP: 7 DLU: 77

715.131-018 SUPERVISOR, HAIRSPRING FABRICATION (clock & watch)

Supervises and coordinates activities of workers engaged in fabricating watch hairsprings: Trains workers in performance of tasks. Requisitions supplies and materials. Confers with other supervisory personnel to coordinate interdepartmental workflow. Confers with workers' representatives to resolve grievances. Performs other duties as described under SUPERVISOR (any industry) Master Title.
GOE: 06.01.01 STRENGTH: L GED: R4 M3 L3 SVP: 7 DLU: 77

715.131-022 SUPERVISOR, INSPECTION (clock & watch)

Supervises and coordinates activities of workers engaged in inspecting and testing fabricated and assembled parts of watches, clocks, and related units for conformance to company standards: Demonstrates methods of work and use of equipment to train workers. Inspects randomly selected parts and units to ensure conformance to standards, using loupe, gauges, and comparator. Confers with other supervisory and quality control personnel to coordinate interdepartmental workflow and to determine corrective action required. May supervise workers engaged in inspecting and testing tools, dies, gauges, and other precision measuring instruments used in inspection. Performs other duties as described under SUPERVISOR (any industry) Master Title.
GOE: 06.01.01 STRENGTH: L GED: R4 M3 L3 SVP: 7 DLU: 77

715.131-026 SUPERVISOR, MAINSPRING FABRICATION (clock & watch)

Supervises and coordinates activities of workers engaged in fabricating watch mainsprings. Performs duties as described under SUPERVISOR (any industry) Master Title.
GOE: 06.01.01 STRENGTH: L GED: R4 M3 L3 SVP: 7 DLU: 77

715.131-030 SUPERVISOR, TUMBLING AND ROLLING (clock & watch)

Supervises and coordinates activities of workers engaged in deburring, smoothing, and burnishing precision clock and watch parts: Trains workers in performance of tasks. Confers with other supervisory personnel to coordinate interdepartmental workflow. Confers with workers' representatives to resolve grievances. Requisitions supplies and equipment. Performs other duties as described under SUPERVISOR (any industry) Master Title.
GOE: 06.02.01 STRENGTH: L GED: R4 M3 L3 SVP: 7 DLU: 77

715.221-010 INSTRUCTOR, WATCH ASSEMBLY (clock & watch)

Instructs workers in all operations concerned with assembly of watch movements: Conducts lectures on function of various parts and assemblies, and demonstrates assembly activities, such as *overcoiling, putting-in-beat, truing II, poising,* colleting, staking, and *vibrating.* Instructs workers in handling of minute parts with loupe, microscope, and tweezers. May be designated according to assembly operation taught as Instructor, Hairspring (clock & watch).
GOE: 06.02.01 STRENGTH: L GED: R4 M3 L4 SVP: 7 DLU: 77

715.261-010 MECHANICAL TECHNICIAN, LABORATORY (clock & watch)

Performs variety of experiments on watch parts, lubricants, and abrasives used in manufacture of horological instruments to ascertain conformance to production standards: Heats or cools watch parts to specific temperatures in oven or refrigerator. Subjects heated or cooled watch parts to stress tests and records results. Tests lubricants and abrasives used in watch manufacture for conformance to established lubricity and abrasion levels. Analyzes test results to detect deficiencies in watch parts, lubricants or abrasives and suggests modifications in production methods to overcome deficiencies. Recommends new test procedures or testing devices as necessary. May assist in fabrication and installation of new testing devices. May repair ovens or refrigerators.
GOE: 02.04.01 STRENGTH: L GED: R4 M4 L4 SVP: 7 DLU: 77

715.281-010 WATCH REPAIRER (clock & watch) alternate titles: clockmaker; watch adjuster; watchmaker

Repairs, cleans, and adjusts watches, clocks, and related instruments, using watchmaker's tools, measuring instruments, bench machines, and cleaning equipment: Removes mechanism from case and examines mechanism for defective parts or accumulation of foreign matter, using loupe. Disassembles parts, such as hands, mainspring, *escape wheels,* and balance wheel, using pliers, screwdriver, and tweezers. Places parts into watch-cleaning machine and starts machine that cleans, rinses, and dries parts. Tests *truing II* of balance wheel assembly, using truing calipers and trues assembly, using tweezers. Repairs damaged or worn parts, using watchmaker's lathe and drill press. Replaces broken parts, such as mainsprings, hairspring, jewels, stems, escape wheel, and pinions, using handtools. Assembles mechanism and oils moving parts. Places mechanism in demagnetizing machine that automatically removes magnetic properties from mechanism. Replaces mechanism in case and tests assembled instrument for accuracy, using watch-rate recorder. Adjusts balance wheel speed regulator to synchronize reading of instrument with recorder. May repair jewelry [JEWELER (jewelry-silver.) 700.281-010]. May salvage and repair watchcases and be designated Repairer, Watchcases (clock & watch). May repair clocks used in electric power system timing equipment and be designated Time-Clock Repairer (clock & watch). May be designated according to type of

instrument or instrument subassembly repaired as Demand Equipment Repairer (utilities); Repairer, Hairspring (clock & watch).
GOE: 05.05.11 STRENGTH: L GED: R4 M3 L3 SVP: 8 DLU: 90

715.281-014 WATCH REPAIRER APPRENTICE (clock & watch) alternate titles: clockmaker apprentice; watchmaker apprentice

Performs duties as described under APPRENTICE (any industry) Master Title.
GOE: 05.05.11 STRENGTH: L GED: R4 M3 L3 SVP: 8 DLU: 77

715.381-010 ASSEMBLER (clock & watch)

Assembles and installs chime-controlling mechanisms in master clocks according to blueprints and sketches, using watchmaker's tools: Bolts mounting casting which houses clock and chimes mechanisms to inner rear panel of master clockcase. Installs toggle-switch and cut-off secondaries, for opening and closing chime-mechanism circuit, on panel, and makes wire connections. Disassembles, examines, repairs, or adjusts spring-wound clock, and reassembles clock [WATCH REPAIRER (clock & watch)]. adding strike-control parts, such as hour-strike spring to hour mechanism, night-spot cutout to hour hand sleeve-wheel, and minute-mercury ring to minute mechanism. Bolts assembled clock mechanism in position on mounting casting. Assembles parts, such as dial, hour and minute hands, contact springs, motor drum and condenser, and makes wire connections to complete master clock mechanism. Installs completed assembly into master clockcase.
GOE: 06.01.04 STRENGTH: L GED: R4 M2 L3 SVP: 7 DLU: 77

715.381-014 ASSEMBLER, WATCH TRAIN (clock & watch)

Assembles, inspects, and adjusts watch train (center, third, fourth, and *escape wheels* with pinions), using watchmaker's tools, loupe, and holding fixture: Examines parts to ensure freedom from defects, using loupe. Positions *pillar plate* in holding fixture and inserts pivots of wheel staffs into holes drilled in pillar plate jewels, using tweezers. Positions train bridge over wheels, aligns pivots with jewels in bridge, and screws bridge to pillar plate, using tweezers and screwdriver. Inspects assembled watch train for meshing of wheels and pinions and endshake (vertical play) of wheels, using tweezers and loupe [INSPECTOR, WATCH TRAIN (clock & watch)]. Moves jeweled bearings specified distance to correct deficient endshake, using micrometer and hand staking tool.
GOE: 06.01.04 STRENGTH: S GED: R4 M2 L2 SVP: 6 DLU: 77

715.381-018 BANKING PIN ADJUSTER (clock & watch) alternate titles: escapement matcher

Inspects and adjusts position of watch banking pins to limit angle through which pallet swings to point where escape wheel clears pallet stones, using loupe and watchmaker's tools: Turns screw to move eccentrically placed banking pin until impulse face of escape wheel drops off pallet jewel. Moves pallet back and forth to test jewel pin shake (distance between pallet fork and jewel pin), to verify that shake is equal in both pallet positions, using tweezers. Bends pallet to equalize shake, using tweezers. Examines locking motion of escape wheel when guard pin is pressed against safety roller to verify guard pin shake (distance between guard pin and safety roller). Moves guard point out or files point to obtain correct length. Heats pallet to liquefy jewel adhesive, using hot plate, and moves jewels to correct slide, using tweezers. Examines pallet action to verify sufficient clearance between pallet and roller. Increases or decreases clearance between pallet and roller to correct deficiency, using tweezers.
GOE: 06.01.04 STRENGTH: S GED: R3 M2 L2 SVP: 5 DLU: 77

715.381-022 BARREL ASSEMBLER (clock & watch)

Assembles, tests, and adjusts mainspring barrel assembly, using watchmaker's tools, handpress, and loupe: Attaches inner coil of mainspring to arbor of hand-operated mainspring winder, and winds spring within body of winder. Inserts wound spring into mainspring barrel, utilizing plunger inside winder. Presses barrel arbor into position and turns arbor until hook in arbor engages hole in center of coiled spring, using tweezers. Places drop of oil on spring, using hypodermic syringe. Presses barrel cover into place, using handpress. Moves arbor up and down to test endshake (vertical clearance of arbor between cover and bottom of barrel), using tweezers and loupe. Corrects insufficient or excessive endshake [BARREL-ENDSHAKE ADJUSTER (clock & watch)]. May press rounded punch against barrel hub to correct side-shake (clearance between arbor and barrel hole).
GOE: 06.01.04 STRENGTH: S GED: R3 M2 L2 SVP: 6 DLU: 77

715.381-026 BARREL-BRIDGE ASSEMBLER (clock & watch)

Assembles barrel, setting lever, ratchet wheel, and barrel bridge to *pillar plate* to form barrel-bridge assembly, using watchmaker's tools, loupe, and holding fixture: Positions pillar plate on holding fixture and places barrel in plate recess, using tweezers and loupe. Screws barrel bridge with assembled crown wheel and click (pawl) in position over barrel and screws setting lever and ratchet wheel in place, using screwdriver. Holds ratchet wheel in position and tightens ratchet screw, using screwdriver. Positions clutch wheel and winding pinion in place and inserts stem through hole in pillar plate to secure assembly, using tweezers and loupe.
GOE: 06.01.04 STRENGTH: S GED: R3 M2 L2 SVP: 5 DLU: 77

715.381-030 BARREL-ENDSHAKE ADJUSTER (clock & watch)

Tests and adjusts barrel endshake (vertical clearance of arbor between cover and bottom of barrel), using holding fixture and jeweler's tools: Places barrel assembly in holding fixture and moves arbor up and down to test endshake, using tweezers. Estimates from experience whether shake is within acceptable

limits (between 0.015 and 0.02 mm). Actuates arms of holding tool to bend barrel cover sufficiently to correct endshake error.
GOE: 06.01.04 STRENGTH: S GED: R3 M2 L2 SVP: 6 DLU: 77

715.381-034 BLOCKER AND POLISHER, GOLD WHEEL (clock & watch)

Trues, blocks, and polishes gold watch wheels, using handpress, block adhesive, and polishing stones: Flattens (trues) wheel, using handpress. Blocks wheels in recess of disk-shaped block, using adhesive [BLOCKER (clock & watch)]. Rubs wheel on wet stone to rough polish wheel. Applies polishing compound to steel block and rubs wheel on block to polish wheel to required luster. Examines wheel to verify required luster and freedom from defects, using loupe.
GOE: 06.01.04 STRENGTH: S GED: R3 M2 L2 SVP: 5 DLU: 77

715.381-038 CHRONOMETER ASSEMBLER AND ADJUSTER (clock & watch)

Assembles, tests, and adjusts marine chronometers, using watchmaker's tools and loupe: Assembles parts, such as plates, bridges, train wheels, mainspring, and fusee, in specified sequence, using tweezers and watchmaker's tools. Greases and assembles fusee and barrel assembly. Tests assembled parts, such as fusee and barrel and train wheels for specified endshake (vertical movement), using tweezers. Bends parts, such as bridges, to correct insufficient or excessive endshake. Oils and greases bushings and other surfaces requiring lubrication. Cleans parts, such as plates, mainspring barrel, and hands, using buff stick moistened with benzine. Tests operation and fit of parts and subassemblies during assembly and makes adjustments to eliminate any improper fit or malfunctioning. Changes timing weights on balance wheel to correct deficient timing and tightens or replaces loose jewels, using watchmaker's tools.
GOE: 06.01.04 STRENGTH: L GED: R4 M3 L3 SVP: 7 DLU: 77

715.381-042 CHRONOMETER-BALANCE-AND-HAIRSPRING ASSEMBLER (clock & watch)

Assembles and trues balance and hairspring assemblies used in marine chronometers, using *truing II* calipers and watchmaker's tools: Attaches hairspring to collet, using watchmaker's tools. Positions hairspring and collet assembly in truing calipers and bends hairspring to correct deficient truing, using tweezers. Attaches stud to hairspring and screws balance staff into balance wheel. Trues balance wheel, using truing calipers. Fastens balance screws, weights, and timing screws in balance wheel, using screwdriver. Inserts impulse and unlocking rollers in assembly. Poises balance wheel, using truing calipers. Connects hairspring and collet to balance wheel assembly, using watchmaker's tools.
GOE: 06.01.04 STRENGTH: L GED: R3 M2 L2 SVP: 6 DLU: 77

715.381-046 DIAL MAKER (clock & watch) alternate titles: watch-dial maker

Performs any combination of following tasks to fabricate clock and watch dials: Cuts out dial blanks, using handtools. Solders holding feet to dial, using soldering iron. Brushes, buffs, and polishes dial, using variety of abrasive wheels. Plates dials with silver, gold, nickel, or other metals [PLATER (electroplating)]. Stakes numerals and numeral indicators, such as diamonds, to dial [STAKER (clock & watch)]. Prints designs, numerals, and company's name on dials [TRANSFERRER (clock & watch)]. Inspects completed dials for dirt and scratches, completeness of printed designs, and adherence to dimension specifications.
GOE: 06.01.04 STRENGTH: L GED: R3 M2 L2 SVP: 6 DLU: 77

715.381-050 FINAL INSPECTOR (clock & watch) alternate titles: adjuster and inspector; finishing inspector; watch-assembly inspector; watch inspector, final movement

Inspects and tests watch and clock subassemblies and completed watch movements for mechanical and visual defects and makes adjustments to correct defects, using watchmaker's tools and loupe: Inspects banking of pallet, lock, drop, and slide of escapement. Verifies that hairspring is level and centered [INSPECTOR, HAIRSPRING TRUING (clock & watch)], and inspects and adjusts *beat* [PUT-IN-BEAT ADJUSTER (clock & watch)]. Tests endshake (vertical play of wheels), using tweezers, to verify that shake is within acceptable limits. Examines spring to verify centering between regulator pins and centers regulator lever. Examines movement for scratches, and blows out dust or dirt, using airhose. Activates watch and clock movements and compares time indicated with master clock to verify accuracy of movements. Listens to movements in operation to detect excessive noise. Turns time and alarm shafts and pulls alarm buttons to test alarm mechanisms for freedom of movement. Examines external surfaces for defects, such as cracked or scratched cases or crystals, loose or misaligned hands, and faulty printing on dials. Oils or inspects oiling of pallet stones and jeweled bearings. Disassembles movement to point of error and replaces defective parts, using watchmaker's tools. Observes minute parts with aid of loupe. May clean parts with soft leather and polish case with chamois.
GOE: 06.01.05 STRENGTH: L GED: R4 M3 L3 SVP: 7 DLU: 77

715.381-054 HAIRSPRING ASSEMBLER (clock & watch) alternate titles: watch-hairspring assembler

Assembles, inspects, and adjusts watch hairspring and balance assemblies, using watchmaker's tools: Attaches hairspring to collet and stud [COLLETER (clock & watch) 715.684-066; STUDDER, HAIRSPRING (clock & watch) 715.684-186], and assembles parts of hairspring and balance, using punch, stak-

ing tool, tweezers, and other watchmaker's tools. Overcoils spring [OVERCOILER (clock & watch) 715.684-150], and trues spring [HAIRSPRING TRUER (clock & watch) 715.381-058]. Poises balance wheel. Locates vibrating point [HAIRSPRING VIBRATOR (clock & watch) 715.381-062]. Inspects and adjusts hairspring and balance assembly [INSPECTOR HAIRSPRING (clock & watch) I 715.381-066].
GOE: 06.01.04 STRENGTH: L GED: R3 M1 L2 SVP: 5 DLU: 77

715.381-058 HAIRSPRING TRUER (clock & watch)
Examines and adjusts hairspring assemblies to ensure horizontal and circular alignment of hairspring, using *truing II* calipers, loupe, and watchmaker's tools: Mounts hairspring and balance wheel assembly between jaws of truing calipers. Turns wheel of caliper and examines spring to determine if center coils appear as perfect circles, using loupe. Bends inner coil of spring away from or toward collet to locate center of collet in center of spring and to correct errors resulting from faulty colleting of coil, using tweezers. Estimates space between collet and first inner coil to determine if space is within acceptable limits, and bends coil to correct errors, using tweezers. Examines plane of hairspring to determine if coils are parallel to plane of collet and raises or lowers individual coils to correct discrepancies, using tweezers.
GOE: 06.01.04 STRENGTH: S GED: R3 M2 L2 SVP: 6 DLU: 77

715.381-062 HAIRSPRING VIBRATOR (clock & watch)
Locates *vibrating* point (point at which length of spring is such as to cause attached balance wheel to oscillate at specified rate) on clock and watch hairsprings and cuts hairspring at specified point to synchronize oscillation of movements, utilizing one or both of following methods: (1) Fastens free end of spring of hairspring assembly in fixture of electronic vibrating device, and adjusts bed of device until it touches pivot of vertically oscillating balance wheel, as indicated on cathode-ray tube. Observes second cathode-ray tube to determine excess length of spring as vertical swings are translated into corresponding horizontal oscillations. Winds excess length of spring into holding fixture of device and readjusts bed until cathode-ray tube readings are within acceptable limits. Starts shears to cut excess spring at specified distance from vibrating point for attachment to stud. (2) Inserts end of spring into holding tweezers of master balance wheel assembly, and adjusts tweezers until pivots and arms of test and master balances are aligned. Releases lever that gives starting impulse to both balances simultaneously, and observes operation to determine if balances are synchronized. Resets holding point of vibrator tweezers and repeats operation until balances are synchronized. Cuts off spring at specified distance from vibrating point for attachment to stud, using cutting pliers.
GOE: 06.01.04 STRENGTH: L GED: R3 M2 L2 SVP: 6 DLU: 77

715.381-066 INSPECTOR, HAIRSPRING I (clock & watch)
Inspects completed hairspring assemblies, using loupe and watchmaker's tools: Verifies that spring and balance wheel are true in flat and round [INSPECTOR, BALANCE TRUING (clock & watch)], and that mass of balance wheel is equally distributed around axis of rotation [INSPECTOR, POISING (clock & watch)]. Examines positioning of parts to determine that parts are in *beat*, and that *overcoil* is in specified relationship to spring, using loupe. Verifies that parts are securely staked, using tweezers. Separates unsatisfactory assemblies. Observes minute parts and functioning of parts with loupe. May test parts to determine if *vibrating* point has been accurately located, using master balance [HAIRSPRING VIBRATOR (clock & watch)].
GOE: 06.01.05 STRENGTH: S GED: R3 M2 L2 SVP: 6 DLU: 77

715.381-070 INSPECTOR, WATCH ASSEMBLY (clock & watch)
Inspects watch subassemblies and incomplete watch movements for mechanical and visual defects, using watchmaker's tools and loupe: Inspects parts, such as bridges, jewels, and screws, for cracks, scratches, and other surface defects, using loupe. Turns wheels to detect amount of vertical play (endshake) and to ascertain if wheels have sufficient freedom, using tweezers and picks. Winds mainspring to determine wheel characteristics, such as flatness of path and freedom of movement. Examines wheels and pivots for bends and alignment, using loupe. Records defects found.
GOE: 06.01.05 STRENGTH: L GED: R3 M2 L2 SVP: 6 DLU: 77

715.381-074 INSPECTOR, WATCH TRAIN (clock & watch)
Inspects assembled watch train (center, third, fourth, and *escape wheels* with pinions) for vertical play of wheels (endshake), meshing of gears, and cleanliness of movement, using watchmaker's tools and loupe: Moves wheels up and down to test endshake, using tweezers, and determining from experience whether shake is within acceptable limits. Turns center wheel to ascertain that gears mesh and that train turns easily. Examines assembly for cleanliness, oiling of cap jewels, and to determine that wheels are level and in parallel planes, using loupe. Rejects or accepts watch train assemblies and places defective assemblies in trays according to type of defect.
GOE: 06.01.05 STRENGTH: S GED: R4 M2 L3 SVP: 7 DLU: 77

715.381-078 LOCATION-AND-MEASUREMENT TECHNICIAN (clock & watch)
Inspects machined watch parts to ensure that hole locations, contour measurements, and shapes conform, within prescribed tolerances, to blueprint specifications, using coordinate measuring machine (precision optical device) and working to tolerances of up to 0.00001 inch: Places watch part on viewing table of projector, adjusts focus of projector, and installs glass chart on viewing screen preparatory to inspection. Aligns part with specified locations or measurement points on chart and examines projected enlargement to determine if

hole locations, contour, and shape of part fall within tolerance lines etched on chart. Positions part on microscope table of coordinate measuring machine to reexamine part and to obtain precise coordinate measurements. Observes part through microscope and adjusts calibrated controls of measuring machine to center watch part and to determine vertical and horizontal measurements. Compares readings with chart and blueprint specifications and calculates differences between readings and specifications. Records inspection data and interprets findings to supervisory personnel. May operate coordinate measuring machine equipped with spotting and scribing device to locate, spot, and scribe tool, gauge, fixture, and die blanks and be designated Location-And-Measurement Technician, Tool Room (clock & watch).
GOE: 06.01.04 STRENGTH: L GED: R4 M3 L3 SVP: 6 DLU: 77

715.381-082 PALLET-STONE INSERTER (clock & watch)
Sets pallet stones in watch pallets, using tweezers and pallet-stone inserting fixture: Positions pallet over projecting pins in seat of fixture. Manipulates fixture attachments to squeeze sides of stone-holding recesses together to produce friction-tight holding recesses. Inserts stones in recesses, using tweezers.
GOE: 06.02.32 STRENGTH: L GED: R3 M2 L2 SVP: 6 DLU: 77

715.381-086 PALLET-STONE POSITIONER (clock & watch)
Adjusts position of pallet stones to extend each stone specified amount from face of holding recess, using positioning fixture: Fits pallet in fixture beneath binocular microscope. Examines pallet stones through microscope and inserts needle between base of stones and holding recess to force stones upward from recess. Swings fork end of pallet against positioning pins of fixture to force stones specified distance into recess.
GOE: 06.01.04 STRENGTH: S GED: R3 M2 L2 SVP: 6 DLU: 77

715.381-090 SCREWHEAD POLISHER (clock & watch)
Polishes screwheads to produce watch screws of specified dimensions and finish, using blocking equipment and polishing wheels: Fits screws in block, using tweezers and suction device. Applies shellac over screws, heats block to melt shellac, and seats screws in block, using handpress. Grinds block screwheads to remove burrs, using grinding wheel. Polishes screwheads to specified dimensions and finish, using flat-lap polisher [FLAT POLISHER (clock & watch)], or manually oscillates screwheads on polishing stones, using overhead pole or hand stick to apply pressure. Examines and measures screws to verify required finish and dimensional specifications, using loupe and precision gauge. Washes and boils block to remove loose polish and to liquefy shellac. Taps block to remove screws. Rinses, dries, and places screws in beakers for inspection.
GOE: 06.01.04 STRENGTH: S GED: R3 M2 L2 SVP: 5 DLU: 77

715.381-094 WATCH ASSEMBLER (clock & watch)
Assembles, tests, and adjusts complete watch movements according to specifications, using watchmaker's tools and loupe: Attaches hairspring and balance assembly, train, escapement, winding and setting mechanism, mainspring, jeweled bearings, and bridges, using tweezers, hand staker (press), and other watchmaker's tools, and loupe. Inspects movement for accuracy, diagnoses cause of defects, and replaces defective parts. Adjusts subassemblies, such as *truing II* balance and banking escapement.
GOE: 06.01.04 STRENGTH: L GED: R4 M3 L3 SVP: 6 DLU: 77

715.384-010 BALANCE ASSEMBLER (clock & watch)
Screws watch balance and balance bridge assembly to *pillar plate*. Places pillar plate in holding fixture, and positions balance and bridge assembly on plate securing with screws. Tests balance for endshake (vertical play) by gently moving balance, using tweezers, and determining from experience if shake is within acceptable limits. Raises bridge slightly, using tweezers, or disassembles bridge and presses down on reverse side to correct shake. Touches oil-filled hypodermic needle to jewel to oil lower balance jewel prior to assembling. Observes minute parts with aid of loupe and handles parts with tweezers.
GOE: 06.02.23 STRENGTH: S GED: R3 M2 L2 SVP: 3 DLU: 77

715.384-014 INSPECTOR, MECHANISM (clock & watch)
Inspects assembled watch winding and setting mechanisms for mechanical and surface defects, using tweezers and loupe: Moves stem in and out to verify clicking into winding and setting positions and turns stem in each position to test for ease of winding and setting. Moves barrel of mechanism to test for amount of vertical play (endshake), using tweezers, and determining from experience whether shake is within acceptable limits. Examines movement for scratches and presence of dirt, using loupe.
GOE: 06.03.01 STRENGTH: S GED: R3 M2 L2 SVP: 4 DLU: 77

715.384-018 INSPECTOR, POISING (clock & watch)
Inspects *poise* of watch balance wheels to determine if mass of wheel is equally distributed around balance wheel staff, using poising tools and loupe: Mounts wheel in poising tool that supports staff on knife edges as wheel is rotated in channel, using tweezers. Observes rotating wheel to verify evenness of turning, using loupe. Removes screw from uneven or heavy area of wheel and mills screw to decrease weight, using hand milling tool. Rejects and segregates units if balance wheels are out of poise or if general condition of unit does not meet specifications.
GOE: 06.01.05 STRENGTH: S GED: R3 M2 L2 SVP: 4 DLU: 77

715.384-022 INSPECTOR, WATCH PARTS (clock & watch)
Examines and measures watch and clock components, such as pinions, wheels, gears, *pillar plates*, shafts, pallets, wheel and pinion assemblies, and

escapement assemblies to ensure conformance to tolerance specifications and quality standards, using loupe, precision measuring instruments, and electronic timing devices: Reads blueprints and inspection specifications for parts to be inspected to determine types and sequences of inspection and measuring instruments required. Examines components for surface defects, such as scratches, burrs, nicks, and blemishes, using loupe, optical comparator, microscope, and tweezers. Measures components to ensure adherence to dimensional specifications, using precision measuring instruments, such as gauges, calipers, dial indicators, comparascopes, and micrometers. Approves or rejects components according to inspection results and records reasons for rejection. Checks accuracy of measuring instruments, using calibrating equipment. May project watch parts on screen to inspect parts [COMPARATOR OPERATOR (any industry)]. May weigh fine parts, such as timing, balance, and gold screws to ensure conformance to weight specifications, using balances and scales. May test hardness of watch parts [HARDNESS INSPECTOR (heat treating)]. May be designated according to component inspected as Arbor Inspector (clock & watch); Balance-Staff Inspector (clock & watch); Barrel Inspector (clock & watch); Case Inspector (clock & watch); Hands Inspector (clock & watch); Mainspring-Strip Gauger (clock & watch). May be designated: Mainspring-Strip Inspector (clock & watch); Pinion Inspector (clock & watch); Plate Inspector (clock & watch); Screw Inspector (clock & watch).
GOE: 06.01.04 STRENGTH: S GED: R3 M2 L3 SVP: 6 DLU: 77

715.584-010   DIAL REFINISHER (clock & watch)
Refinishes watch dials, according to specifications: Removes original finish and dial markings, such as numerals and calibrations on faceplate, using chemical solution and buffing wheel or wire brush. Applies specified finish to dial, using plating solution. Embosses and retouches markings, using stamping equipment, paint, and brush. Sprays dial with lacquer to preserve finish. May attach numerals to faceplate with rivets. May apply radium to dial markings to form luminous dial.
GOE: 06.04.33 STRENGTH: S GED: R2 M1 L2 SVP: 5 DLU: 77

715.584-014   REPAIRER, AUTO CLOCKS (clock & watch)
Repairs surface defects in battery-operated clocks for motor vehicles, using handtools: Examines rejected clock for defects, such as scratched or broken lens, damaged backplate, and bent or missing hands. Removes and replaces defective parts, using handtools, such as punch, tweezers, staking tool, and screwdriver. Places repaired clock in tray for retiming. Records quantity and type of clocks repaired.
GOE: 06.04.34 STRENGTH: L GED: R2 M1 L1 SVP: 3 DLU: 77

715.584-018   STONER, HAND (clock & watch)
Stones (polishes) watch parts, such as winding wheels and clicks (pawls), to specified thickness, using blocking equipment and polishing stone: Adjusts stops on block corners to specified height indicated by gauge, using screwdriver. Brushes block surface with vaseline to hold wheels or clicks in place. Fits wheels or clicks over protruding pins of block, using tweezers. Places block, face down, on stone. Fits projecting pin of handle in block recess and rubs block against stone with circular motion until touch indicates parts are stoned to size. Verifies thickness of part, using loupe and indicator gauge.
GOE: 06.02.24 STRENGTH: L GED: R2 M1 L1 SVP: 3 DLU: 77

715.660-010   SET-UP WORKER (clock & watch)
Sets up and adjusts staking machines used to assemble clock and watch parts according to blueprints and operation sheets: Confers with department supervisor and reviews operation sheets to determine parts or assemblies to be processed, assembly specifications, and instructions for machine setup. Bolts or screws specified dies into beds of machines according to blueprints, using handtools. Operates machines to press or rivet parts together to form sample assemblies. Examines and measures sample assemblies for adherance to surface and dimensional specifications, using gauges such as micrometers and calipers, and confers with quality control personnel to gain approval of sample for production. Demonstrates operation of machines to production workers and examines work to detect production defects. Oils and cleans machines, using oilcans and cloths.
GOE: 06.01.02 STRENGTH: L GED: R3 M2 L3 SVP: 5 DLU: 77

715.681-010   TIMING ADJUSTER (clock & watch) alternate titles: poiser, balance
Alters weight of watch balance wheels to correct timing of movement, using jeweler's tools and loupe: Receives movement from INSPECTOR, TIMING (clock & watch) with indication of rate of gain or loss in time. Replaces balance wheel screw with one of heavier weight or adds washer of specified weight when movement is fast, using screwdriver. Repeats operation on opposite side of balance wheel to maintain *poise*. Replaces balance wheel or files angle of screw point to reduced weight, using hand file. Repeats operation on opposite side of wheel to maintain poise. Observes minute parts, using loupe.
GOE: 06.02.24 STRENGTH: L GED: R3 M2 L2 SVP: 6 DLU: 77

715.682-010   BARREL FINISHER (clock & watch)
Operates lathe to turn watch gear blanks (barrels) to size preparatory to milling. Positions barrels into chuck of lathe. Starts lathe and holds tool against material. Gauges finished barrels, using measuring device.
GOE: 06.02.02 STRENGTH: S GED: R2 M1 L2 SVP: 3 DLU: 77

715.682-014   COUNTERSINKER (clock & watch)
Operates vertical- or horizontal-drill press to countersink drilled holes in watch parts: Places part in bed or chuck of press. Aligns countersinking bit and

hole, using loupe, and advances bit manually to automatic stop device. Removes part from press and measures depth of countersink, using precision dial gauge. May countersink screw holes around periphery of balance wheels and be designated Countersinker, Balance Screw Hole (clock & watch).
GOE: 06.02.02 STRENGTH: L GED: R2 M2 L1 SVP: 3 DLU: 77

715.682-018   POLISHER (clock & watch)
Operates lathe and rag wheel polisher to smooth and polish edges of watch plates and bridges: Selects basswood *lap I* of specified size to polish recessed or curved surfaces and mounts lap in lathe. Holds bar of abrasive against rotating surface to charge lap. Manipulates bridge or plate against lap to smooth corners and edges. Strings cut parts on wire and pushes parts against revolving edge of rag wheel to polish parts to specified finish. Washes polished parts in benzine to remove cutting and polishing compound. Holds and turns wooden lap against lathe to dress lap.
GOE: 06.02.02 STRENGTH: L GED: R3 M2 L2 SVP: 5 DLU: 77

715.682-022   TAPPER, BALANCE-WHEEL SCREW HOLE (clock & watch)
Operates powered horizontal tapping machine to cut internal threads in screw holes around periphery of watch balance wheel: Places center hole of balance wheel over protruding pin of machine chuck. Turns wheel to align hole with tap and presses handle to starts tap forward into hole. Verifies size of holes, using precision plug gauge. Replaces worn taps.
GOE: 06.02.02 STRENGTH: L GED: R3 M2 L2 SVP: 3 DLU: 77

715.682-026   TOOTH POLISHER (clock & watch)
Operates bench-polishing machine to remove scratches and burrs and to impart polished finish to watch pinion teeth: Positions pinion in machine holder, using tweezers. Depresses pedal to engage lapping wheel and holds abrasive and polishing compound against rotating wheel to dress wheel. Presses machine lever to lower and hold lapping wheel against pinion to remove defects and polish pinion teeth. Releases pedal to stop machine after prescribed period and raises lever to gain access to polished pinion. Depresses pedal of hot air device to melt polishing compound adhered to pinion and to blow pinion into container. Mounts pinion in holding calipers and cleans pinion, using electric brush and cleaning compound. Examines and measures cleaned pinions to verify specified finish and dimensional specifications, using loupe and precision gauges.
GOE: 06.02.02 STRENGTH: L GED: R3 M2 L2 SVP: 5 DLU: 77

715.684-010   ADJUSTER, ALARM MECHANISM (clock & watch)
Adjusts alarm mechanism and lubricates moving parts of electric alarm clock assemblies, using handtools: Clamps lead wires of clock motors to current outlet. Bends alarm striker, turns alarm indicators to specified setting, and pulls and turns set shafts to adjust and set alarm, using tweezers, pliers, and knife. Observes mechanism in operation to verify freedom of moving parts. Lubricates moving parts, using brush and lubricant. Places acceptable assemblies on conveyor for further processing and places defective assemblies in tray for repair. Tallies number of mechanisms adjusted, using counter, and records production.
GOE: 06.04.34 STRENGTH: S GED: R2 M1 L2 SVP: 2 DLU: 77

715.684-014   ASSEMBLER, MOVEMENT (clock & watch)
Assembles watch, clock, and appliance timer movements, using handtools and power tools: Positions front plate assembly in holding fixture. Positions setting and winding mechanisms on front plate and positions escapement, pallet, and train pivot in pivot holes of front plate, using tweezers and loupe. Positions backplate over pillars and aligns pivots of parts with pivot holes in backplate. Fastens backplate to movement, using pneumatic screwdriver. Attaches alarm components to alarm clock movements, installs motors in electric clocks, and assembles motors and appliance timers, using handtools and pneumatic screwdriver. Records quantity of movements assembled.
GOE: 06.04.23 STRENGTH: L GED: R2 M1 L1 SVP: 3 DLU: 77

715.684-018   BALANCE TRUER (clock & watch)
Tests and adjusts watch balance wheels to ensure that rim is concentric with staff axis: Mounts balance wheel and staff on test stand or between jaws of *truing II* calipers, using tweezers, and twirls wheel by hand. Determines that dial gauge readings are within acceptable limits as rim of revolving wheel brushes against gauge arm on test stand, or determines no clearance variation between rim of wheel and caliper index pointer placed above rim, using loupe. Bends rim to eliminate distortions, using tweezers or rim wrench.
GOE: 06.01.04 STRENGTH: L GED: R3 M2 L2 SVP: 4 DLU: 77

715.684-022   BALANCE-BRIDGE ASSEMBLER (clock & watch)
Attaches balance assembly to balance bridge: Positions regulator in nest of holding block and places balance bridge over regulator to fit balance bridge jewel into hole in regulator. Presses bridge into place, using tweezers. Positions balance wheel and hairspring assembly over bridge, and places hairspring stud into hole in bridge. Tightens screw to hold stud securely. Oils balance bridge jewel, using oil-filled hypodermic needle. Observes minute parts, using tweezers and loupe.
GOE: 06.02.23 STRENGTH: L GED: R3 M2 L2 SVP: 3 DLU: 77

715.684-026   BENCH HAND (clock & watch)
Positions screws in rims of balance wheels and secures screws in place, using screwdriver.
GOE: 06.04.23 STRENGTH: S GED: R1 M1 L1 SVP: 2 DLU: 77

715.684-030   BEVELER (clock & watch)
Bevels watch hands to form rounded surface, using ram: Positions watch hand in nest on bed of die, using tweezers, and starts ram. Blows dirt from die after each operation, using compressed-air hose.

GOE: 06.02.24 STRENGTH: S GED: R2 M1 L1 SVP: 3 DLU: 77

715.684-034 BLOCKER (clock & watch) alternate titles: blocker, polishing

Positions flat pieces, such as clutch levers and escape wheels, on circular metal blocks or into recesses in blocks preparatory to grinding operation: Heats block and applies shellac. Places pieces over surface of block, using tweezers. Reheats block, places sheet of paper on top of block, fits press block directly over circular block, and applies pressure in screw press to position pieces firmly in shellac. Removes pieces from press, and inspects parts for proper position prior to grinding process. Blocks parts, such as wheels and screws, using suction device. Heats, shellacs, and presses loaded blocks to secure parts. May spread layer of vaseline over block to hold parts.
GOE: 06.02.24 STRENGTH: L GED: R2 M1 L1 SVP: 4 DLU: 77

715.684-038 BURNISHER, BALANCE WHEEL ARM (clock & watch)

Burnishes chamfer on watch balance wheel arm, using burnishing tool and loupe: Fits balance wheel in work plate of jig and tightens jig to hold wheel in place. Burnishes arm by hand to round and polish edges. Inspects finished wheel, using loupe.
GOE: 06.02.24 STRENGTH: L GED: R2 M1 L1 SVP: 3 DLU: 77

715.684-042 BURRER (clock & watch) alternate titles: burrer, hand; scraper burrer

Removes burrs from rims, edges, and recesses of watch parts, such as pillar plates and barrel bridges, using burring tool. Inspects parts to ensure removal of burrs, using loupe.
GOE: 06.02.24 STRENGTH: L GED: R2 M1 L1 SVP: 3 DLU: 77

715.684-046 CANNON-PINION ADJUSTER (clock & watch)

Attaches and adjusts cannon pinion to arbor of center wheel, using hand punch: Lubricates arbor, using oil-filled hypodermic needle. Positions cannon pinion over center wheel arbor and secures pinion onto arbor, using tweezers or hand punch. Pinches arbor at specified points to loosen or tighten pinion. Observes minute parts, using tweezers and loupe.
GOE: 06.04.23 STRENGTH: L GED: R3 M2 L2 SVP: 3 DLU: 77

715.684-050 CAP-JEWEL PLATE ASSEMBLER (clock & watch)

Attaches cap jewel plate to train and balance bridges: Places bridge in holding fixture and positions cap jewel plate over bridge, aligning cap jewel with hole in bridge. Inserts minute screw into hole with tweezers and screws plate to bridge. Observes minute parts with loupe. May insert screw in hole of balance bridge to facilitate subsequent fastening of hairspring stud.
GOE: 06.02.23 STRENGTH: L GED: R3 M2 L2 SVP: 3 DLU: 77

715.684-054 CASER (clock & watch)

Performs any combination of following duties to insert clock and watch assemblies in cases: Inserts and secures crown and stem into clock and watch movements, using loupe, tweezers, screwdriver, and other jeweler's tools. Cleans case, using airhose, and inserts movement into case. Presses revolving plastic cup against crown or rubs crown against plastic strip to wind movement. Sets watch to specified time prior to testing. Secures watertight cases, using pliers, or places movement in device that tightens case automatically. May remove temporary crown and stem prior to assembly, using handtools. May measure stem, using gauge, and file stem to specified length. May screw crowns onto stems. May test waterproof watches in air pressure and water tanks.
GOE: 06.04.23 STRENGTH: L GED: R2 M1 L2 SVP: 3 DLU: 77

715.684-058 CLOCK ASSEMBLER (clock & watch)

Attaches power cords, cases, dials, and hands to electric clock movements to assemble electric clocks, using handtools: Inserts end of power cord through opening in clock case and splices wires from motor of clock movement to cord, using plastic connectors. Fastens case to clock movement, using pneumatic screwdriver. Positions dial over front plate of movement and attaches hour, minute, and second hands to cannon pinion, using wrench. Aligns clock hands and alarm indicator and pulls alarm button to test mechanism. Snaps plastic crystal into case, affixes label to back of case and places assembled clock on conveyor for further processing.
GOE: 06.04.23 STRENGTH: L GED: R2 M1 L2 SVP: 3 DLU: 77

715.684-062 COLLET DRILLER (clock & watch)

Tends drill press that drills holes in metal collars (collets) prior to assembly with watch escapement movement. Positions collets on bed of drill press, using tweezers. Lowers revolving drill to bore and countersink hole in collets.
GOE: 06.02.02 STRENGTH: L GED: R2 M1 L1 SVP: 2 DLU: 77

715.684-066 COLLETER (clock & watch)

Attaches inner coil of watch hairspring to collet preparatory to assembly to balance wheel: Positions collet over arbor of colleting tool, using tweezers and forces collet into place, using hand punch. Places hairspring over arbor and inserts end of inner coil into hole in collet, using tweezers and loupe. Inserts tapered brass pin into hole in collet and pulls pin through hole to secure hairspring against wall of collet, using tweezers and pliers. Cuts protruding ends of pin with pliers. May examine plane of hairspring and collet to ensure conformance to specifications.
GOE: 06.04.23 STRENGTH: S GED: R2 M1 L2 SVP: 3 DLU: 77

715.684-070 CROWN ATTACHER (clock & watch)

Attaches watch crowns to stem: Inserts stems into chuck of machine and places crown in holding tool. Presses holding tool against revolving stem that automatically screws on crown. May hold stem with pliers and screw crown onto stem by hand.
GOE: 06.04.23 STRENGTH: L GED: R2 M1 L2 SVP: 2 DLU: 77

715.684-074 CROWN-WHEEL ASSEMBLER (clock & watch)

Attaches watch crown wheel and click (pawl on ratchet wheel) to barrel bridge, using tweezers and loupe: Places bridge in holding fixture. Positions and secures crown wheel center (washer) over post in bridge and crown wheel over washer, using screw, tweezers, and loupe. Positions and secures click in bridge. Inserts click spring into position. May lubricate friction points of assembly, using oil-filled hypodermic needle.
GOE: 06.02.23 STRENGTH: S GED: R3 M2 L2 SVP: 3 DLU: 77

715.684-078 CRYSTAL CUTTER (clock & watch)

Grinds improperly fitting watch crystals to specified size and to remove rough or chipped edges, using abrasive wheel. Brushes crystal with lacquer and dries crystal under heat lamp to protect surface of crystal. Examines and measures crystals to ensure conformance to specifications, using loupe, calipers, and micrometer.
GOE: 06.04.30 STRENGTH: L GED: R2 M2 L2 SVP: 3 DLU: 77

715.684-082 DIAL-SCREW ASSEMBLER (clock & watch)

Attaches dial screws to pillar plates preparatory to securing dial to watch, using screwdriver, tweezers, and loupe: Aligns number of pillar plates in holding fixture. Inserts and fastens screws to plates.
GOE: 06.04.23 STRENGTH: S GED: R2 M1 L2 SVP: 2 DLU: 77

715.684-086 DIALER (clock & watch)

Attaches clock or watch dials to movements: Places movement in holding fixture, and positions hour wheel and one or more dial washers over cannon pinion, using punch or hand staking tool. Positions dial over movement, and inserts dial feet into holes in pillar plate or rod. Inserts feeler gauge between dial and plate to facilitate specified fit, tightens screws to secure dial, and removes gauge. Observes minute parts, using loupe and handles parts with tweezers. May snap clock dials in place in faceplate grooves. May attach clock hands, using hand staking tool.
GOE: 06.02.23 STRENGTH: S GED: R3 M2 L2 SVP: 3 DLU: 77

715.684-090 DISASSEMBLER (clock & watch)

Disassembles defective auto clocks for salvage or reuse of parts, using watchmakers' tools: Turns screws and nuts and separates parts, such as case, lens, backplate, hands, and dial, using screwdrivers, pliers, and tweezers. Segregates parts in trays for reuse. Places scrap parts in tray for salvage. Removes date stamp markings from parts, using solvent and cloth. Places dented or bent cases and backplates on metal block and straightens or smooths defective part, using mallet. Records quantity and type of clocks disassembled.
GOE: 06.02.24 STRENGTH: L GED: R2 M1 L1 SVP: 3 DLU: 77

715.684-094 FINAL INSPECTOR, MOVEMENT ASSEMBLY (clock & watch)

Inspects completed watch and clock movements and motors for defects, such as surface blemishes, missing parts, and misalignment of parts, using loupe, watchmaker's tools, and gauges: Winds and activates movements to verify prescribed wheel motion. Examines movements and motors for defects, such as misalignment of parts, missing parts, cracked or broken parts, and deficient oil content on jewels. Replaces or tightens missing screws, using screwdriver; removes scratches on parts, using buffing stick; and oils jewels, using hypodermic syringe. May test performance of motors used in electric clocks and timers, using voltmeter and ammeter and be designated Motor Checker (clock & watch). May be designated according to type of movement inspected as Final Inspector, Balance Wheel (clock & watch).
GOE: 06.01.05 STRENGTH: S GED: R3 M2 L2 SVP: 4 DLU: 77

715.684-098 FINER (clock & watch)

Attaches balance wheel and hairspring assembly to watch or clock movement, using handtools: Positions balance wheel and hairspring assembly between balance stud and balance screw of watch or clock movement assembly, using tweezers. Tightens balance screw to secure balance wheel and hairspring assembly to movement, using wrench. Inserts end of hairspring through eye (slot) of regulator and into hole of hairspring stud, and inserts hairspring wedge into hole of hairspring stud to secure end of spring to stud, using tweezers. Engages *impulse pin* to pallet to activate movement, using tweezers. Oils specified parts of watch or clock assembly, using oil-filled hypodermic needle.
GOE: 06.04.23 STRENGTH: L GED: R2 M2 L2 SVP: 3 DLU: 77

715.684-102 HAIRSPRING ADJUSTER (clock & watch)

Inspects and adjusts watch hairsprings after assembly to *pillar plate* for conformance to mechanical specifications, using loupe, holding device, and tweezers: Mounts assembly in holding device. Examines outer coil to verify that coil is centered between regulator pins, and that positioning of *overcoil* is within acceptable limits, using loupe. Pinches segment of coil to position and level coil, using tweezers. Spins balance wheel to verify that all coils of spring are within same plane and concentric with collet when oscillating. Adjusts coils to correct discrepancies, using tweezers.
GOE: 06.01.04 STRENGTH: L GED: R3 M1 L2 SVP: 4 DLU: 77

715.684-106 HAND FILER, BALANCE WHEEL (clock & watch)

Removes excess metal from inside rim of balance wheel, using radius file: Positions wheel in slot of work jig filing plate. Files excess metal between arm

and inside rim of wheel to obtain specified balance of wheel, using file and loupe. Inspects wheels to ensure conformance to specifications. Shapes files on emery wheel.
GOE: 06.02.24 STRENGTH: S GED: R2 M1 L1 SVP: 3 DLU: 77

715.684-110 HANDS ASSEMBLER (clock & watch)
 Attaches hands to faces of clocks and watches: Places movement in holding fixture of hand staking tool. Positions hour hand on hour wheel and forces hand over arbor to secure friction tight fit, using staking punch. Positions minute hand over cannon pinion of minute wheel and secures fit, using staking punch. Aligns hour hand with specified hour marking, and minute hand with numeral twelve. Bends tips of hands with tweezers to conform to curvature of dial. Presses second hand over fourth wheel arbor and secures fit. Winds watch and observes movement of hands to determine specified clearance between hands, dial, and crystal. Observes and handles minute parts, using loupe and tweezers.
GOE: 06.04.23 STRENGTH: L GED: R2 M2 L2 SVP: 3 DLU: 77

715.684-114 INSPECTOR, BARREL ASSEMBLY (clock & watch)
 Inspects and adjusts mainspring barrel assembly, utilizing either of following methods: (1) Grasps barrel arbor with pliers and locks arbor by means of adjustable ring on plier arms. Holds barrel and turns arbor to wind mainspring. Allows pliers to hang freely to observe spinning motion as result of spring unwinding, indicating faulty assembly. Separates faulty assemblies and places rejected assemblies by type of reject in containers for repair. (2) Winds spring to determine if arbor hook is secured in hole of center coil, using hand winding device. Tests endshake (vertical play) of barrel, using tweezers. Separates faulty barrel assemblies.
GOE: 06.01.05 STRENGTH: S GED: R3 M2 L2 SVP: 6 DLU: 77

715.684-118 INSPECTOR, HAIRSPRING TRUING (clock & watch)
 Examines assembled watch hairsprings to determine if spring is in same plane and concentric with collet, and that space between collet and first inner spring is within acceptable limits, using loupe. Separates faulty assemblies for adjustment by HAIRSPRING TRUER (clock & watch).
GOE: 06.03.02 STRENGTH: S GED: R3 M2 L2 SVP: 4 DLU: 77

715.684-122 INSPECTOR, HAIRSPRING II (clock & watch)
 Examines unassembled hairsprings for flatness and concentricity, using tweezers and loupe: Stretches spring to ensure specified plane and spacing between coils, using tweezers. Examines spring to detect defects, such as blemishes and bent or short tongues, using loupe. Segregates standard and defective springs in boxes for salvage, storage, and shipping. Records inspection data for identification purposes.
GOE: 06.01.05 STRENGTH: S GED: R2 M1 L2 SVP: 3 DLU: 77

715.684-126 INSPECTOR, WHEEL AND PINION (clock & watch)
 Inspects and adjusts assembled watch wheels and pinions for surface and mechanical defects, using tweezers, gauges, and loupe: Examines wheels for levelness, using gauges, and adjusts wheels to correct discrepancies [STRAIGHTENER, HAND (any industry)]. Tests and adjusts endshake (vertical movement) of wheels, using loupe and tweezers. Mounts wheels in gauge and observes gauge readings to verify that wheels and pinions are concentric with staff. Places straightedge on flat surface of wheels and turns wheels, observing wheels to detect passage of light, to test wheels for flatness. Examines wheels to detect scratches and broken teeth, using loupe. Segregates faulty and acceptable assemblies.
GOE: 06.01.05 STRENGTH: S GED: R3 M2 L2 SVP: 4 DLU: 77

715.684-130 JEWEL INSERTER (clock & watch)
 Inserts jewels in jewel settings: Squirts oil over settings on sheet of paper. Moistens tip of wooden peg with oil, picks up individual jewel, and positions jewel in setting, using peg. Presses jewel into setting, using staking tool. Inspects specified number of completed settings to ensure proper seating of jewels, using loupe.
GOE: 06.04.23 STRENGTH: L GED: R2 M2 L2 SVP: 3 DLU: 77

715.684-134 JEWEL STAKER (clock & watch)
 Presses jewels to watch bridges and plates, using staking tool: Positions part in nest of tool, using tweezers and loupe. Presses identifying mark or part on bridge or plate, using hand-operated punch. May press jeweled or metal markers onto dial for use as numerals, using adhesive-tipped stick.
GOE: 06.04.23 STRENGTH: L GED: R2 M2 L2 SVP: 3 DLU: 77

715.684-138 LACQUERER (clock & watch)
 Covers watch dials with lacquer to protect dials preparatory to polishing or plating numerals, or preparatory to final assembling. Dries lacquer in heated cabinets.
GOE: 06.04.33 STRENGTH: S GED: R1 M1 L1 SVP: 2 DLU: 77

715.684-142 MECHANISM ASSEMBLER (clock & watch)
 Assembles parts of watch winding and setting mechanism to *pillar plate*: Positions clutch lever, clutch-lever spring, setting wheel, and minute wheel on plate, using loupe and tweezers. Places yoke over parts, and secures yoke with screws. May oil clutch and winding pinion, using oil-filled hypodermic.
GOE: 06.04.23 STRENGTH: S GED: R2 M1 L2 SVP: 3 DLU: 77

715.684-146 OILER (clock & watch)
 Oils watch parts, such as jeweled bearings, on center, third, fourth, and escape wheels, using oil-filled hypodermic needle or automatic oil dispenser. Observes minute parts, using loupe to determine specified amount of oil applied. May oil industrial motor assemblies.

GOE: 06.04.33 STRENGTH: S GED: R2 M1 L1 SVP: 2 DLU: 77

715.684-150 OVERCOILER (clock & watch)
 Raises and bends outer coil of watch hairsprings to ensure *overcoiling*: Positions balance assembly in holding fixture, using tweezers. Threads stud end of spring through fixture and clamps end securely. Adjusts series of levers to raise outer coil specified distance above plane of spring and straighten raised portion parallel with plane of spring. Pinches and bends outer coil to obtain concentric position with inner coils and to ensure overcoiling, using loupe and tweezers.
GOE: 06.04.23 STRENGTH: S GED: R2 M1 L2 SVP: 3 DLU: 77

715.684-154 PALLET ASSEMBLER (clock & watch)
 Attaches pallet assembly to *pillar plate*: Places pallet arbor into hole in jewel of pillar plate. Places pallet bridge over pallet, aligns hole in jewel with pallet staff, and secures bridge to form assembly, using tweezers, loupe, and screwdriver. Moves pallet up and down, using tweezers, to test and adjust endshake (vertical movement) and estimates movement within acceptable limits. May disassemble pallet and bridge and move pallet bridge jewel to adjust endshake, using hand-operated press.
GOE: 06.04.23 STRENGTH: S GED: R2 M1 L2 SVP: 3 DLU: 77

715.684-158 PALLET RECTIFIER (clock & watch)
 Adjusts passing hollow (crescent-shaped notch) and sizes jewel-hole slots of pallets, using holding fixture and burnishing wheel: Locates pallet over hole in fixture. Pushes pallet into stop against V-shaped lap to adjust passing hollow. Holds pallet against carbide burnisher to size jewel slots according to specified width and depth. Turns fixture during burnishing to round walls of jewel slot.
GOE: 06.02.24 STRENGTH: S GED: R2 M2 L2 SVP: 4 DLU: 77

715.684-162 PEARLER (clock & watch)
 Cuts cone-shaped notch in face of watch dial for use as numerals: Positions dial on bed of press, aligns second and center holes with pins in press. Raises bed of press to bring dial in contact with diamond-cutting tool that automatically cuts cone-shaped notch.
GOE: 06.02.24 STRENGTH: L GED: R2 M1 L1 SVP: 2 DLU: 77

715.684-166 PIN INSERTER, REGULATOR (clock & watch)
 Secures regulator pin in regulator, using jeweler's tools. Positions regulator in holding fixture and places pin in hole of regulator, using tweezers and loupe. Taps pin with hammer and cuts off protruding excess of pin, using pliers. Secures fit of pin, using staking tool.
GOE: 06.04.23 STRENGTH: L GED: R2 M1 L2 SVP: 3 DLU: 77

715.684-170 POLISHER, DIAL (clock & watch)
 Polishes watch dial blanks, using abrasive belt or wheel: Holds blanks against rotating belt or wheel to buff dials, using jeweler's rouge. May rub dial over hone to impart distinctive mat finish to dial and be designated Watch-Dial Stoner (clock & watch). May polish raised numerals on watch dials and be designated Polisher, Numeral (clock & watch).
GOE: 06.02.24 STRENGTH: S GED: R2 M1 L1 SVP: 3 DLU: 77

715.684-174 PUT-IN-BEAT ADJUSTER (clock & watch)
 Aligns hairspring stud with center of roller and roller jewel with line of center on *escape wheel* pallet to ensure *in-beat* of watch movement: Positions balance wheel assembly in fixture of tool, using tweezers, and engages crescent of roller with lever to prevent balance wheel from turning. Engages slot in hairspring collet, using plunger, and turns collet and attached hairspring until stud on outer coil of hairspring is aligned with indicator on balance wheel. Observes minute parts, using loupe.
GOE: 06.02.23 STRENGTH: S GED: R3 M2 L2 SVP: 3 DLU: 77

715.684-178 SET-STAFF FITTER (clock & watch)
 Installs wheel and sleeve assembly in clocks preparatory to inserting hour hand: Places wheel and sleeve assembly over center staff protruding through front frame and meshes assembly with dial wheel pinion. Places time and alarm train onto staff and inserts staff through hole in clock frame. Places clock frame in jig of press that secures assemblies by means of washer and collet.
GOE: 06.04.23 STRENGTH: S GED: R2 M1 L1 SVP: 2 DLU: 77

715.684-182 STAKER (clock & watch) alternate titles: staking-machine
 operator; staking-press operator
 Presses or rivets parts together for use in assembly of watches, clocks, timers, and industrial motors, using staking machine or hand staking tools: Positions parts in specific relationship to each other in recess of die (bed) or fits part in punch of machine, using tweezers and loupe. Activates machine to lower punch that presses or rivets parts together. Places assembled parts on conveyor, in tray, or on table for further processing. May be designated according to parts assembled as Balance-Staff Staker (clock & watch); Hairspring Staker (clock & watch); Pin Inserter (clock & watch); Pinion Staker (clock & watch); Roller Staker (clock & watch).
GOE: 06.04.23 STRENGTH: L GED: R2 M2 L2 SVP: 3 DLU: 77

715.684-186 STUDDER, HAIRSPRING (clock & watch)
 Attaches stud to watch hairspring preparatory to assembly to balance bridge, using studding fixture, loupe, and watchmaker's tools: Positions stud in recess of studding fixture, using tweezers, and broaches hole in stud, using handtool. Inserts end of outer hairspring coil into hole, and forces tapered brass pin through hole to wedge spring in place, using loupe and watchmaker's tools. Cuts off protruding ends of pin, using pliers.
GOE: 06.04.23 STRENGTH: S GED: R2 M1 L1 SVP: 3 DLU: 77

715.684-190 TRANSFERRER (clock & watch) alternate titles: watch-dial printer

Prints numerals, minute and second tracks, and company name onto timepiece dials, using printing equipment: Positions holding fixture and gelatinous head in printer. Places engraved metal plate in holding fixture and spreads ink over plate. Removes excess ink, using spatula. Lowers gelatinous head of transfer printer onto plate to transfer design from plate to head. Moves watch dial into position and lowers gelatinous head to print design on dial. Applies lacquer to specific parts of dial to protect them during brushing operations.
GOE: 06.01.04 STRENGTH: L GED: R3 M1 L1 SVP: 3 DLU: 77

715.684-194 TRUER, PINION AND WHEEL (clock & watch)

Inspects and adjusts electric-clock wheel parts to correct *truing II* of pinion and wheel assemblies, using comparator, loupe, and truing tools: Places part in rotating jig of comparator and projects part onto calibrated screen to determine degree of truing defect [COMPARATOR OPERATOR (any industry) 699.384-010] or examines part to determine defect, using loupe. Bends parts manually to correct truing defect or forces truing tool against rotating part to correct defect.
GOE: 06.01.04 STRENGTH: S GED: R2 M1 L1 SVP: 3 DLU: 77

715.685-010 COLLET GLUER (clock & watch)

Applies glue to hairspring and balance wheel assembly of auto clocks and tends oven that dries glue to secure parts together: Places hairspring and balance wheel assembly in slots of die, using tweezers. Applies glue to inner coil of hairspring to join hairspring to balance staff collet, using glue dispenser. Sets time and temperature controls on bench-mounted oven and places tray of dies containing balance and hairspring assemblies in oven. Pulls trays from oven subsequent to curing of glue and stacks trays on rack for cooling. Pulls hairspring and balance wheel assemblies from dies and places assemblies in tray for further processing.
GOE: 06.04.24 STRENGTH: L GED: R2 M1 L1 SVP: 2 DLU: 77

715.685-014 CUTTER, V-GROOVE (clock & watch) alternate titles: groove turner

Tends lathe that cuts decorative V-shaped circular groove in faces of heattreated watch wheels. Depresses pedal to open chuck, inserts wheel, and releases pedal to secure wheel in chuck. Brushes lubricant on cutter and turns wheel to advance cutter into rotating watch wheel to cut groove.
GOE: 06.04.02 STRENGTH: L GED: R2 M1 L1 SVP: 3 DLU: 77

715.685-018 DEBURRER, MACHINE (clock & watch)

Tends bench lathe that removes burrs and polishes watch parts, such as pinions and wheels: Inserts part in chuck of lathe, using loupe and tweezers. Positions deburring tool on tool rest, starts lathe, and moves tool against part to smooth surface.
GOE: 06.04.02 STRENGTH: L GED: R2 M1 L1 SVP: 3 DLU: 77

715.685-022 DRILLER AND BROACHER (clock & watch)

Tends vertical drill that bores and broaches pinholes in watch regulators: Positions regulator in drilling jig, using tweezers, and closes jig. Places jig on table beneath drill, aligns bushing guide holes of jig with drill, using loupe, and depresses drill to bore holes in regulator. Removes drilled regulator from jig, positions and aligns holes under tapered broach (boring tool), and pulls handle to automatic stop to shape and enlarge holes.
GOE: 06.02.02 STRENGTH: L GED: R3 M2 L2 SVP: 5 DLU: 77

715.685-026 END POLISHER (clock & watch) alternate titles: pivot-end polisher

Tends polishing machine that smooths and imparts specified finish to pivot (staff) ends of pinions and arbors: Pulls spindle handle to insert and position pinion in holder of workpiece. Depresses pedal to start felt-wheel lap rotating across pivot end to polish ends. Charges wheel with lime stick as needed. Inspects ends to detect defects, such as burrs and rough surfaces, using loupe. Performs minor adjustments to machine.
GOE: 06.02.02 STRENGTH: L GED: R2 M2 L2 SVP: 4 DLU: 77

715.685-030 GRINDER II (clock & watch)

Tends jigging machines that grind pivots of watch parts to specified lengths: Pulls spindle handle to open spindle, inserts pinion with tweezers, and releases handle to force pinion into place in chuck. Depresses pedal to start rotating grinding wheel across end of pivot to grind pivot to specified size. Measures pinions to ensure specified lengths, using loupe and precision upright gauge.
GOE: 06.04.02 STRENGTH: L GED: R2 M1 L1 SVP: 3 DLU: 77

715.685-034 INSPECTOR, TIMING (clock & watch) alternate titles: reliability inspector; timer; timing-machine operator

Tends electric timer that verifies timing *beat* of clock, watch, and timer movements and adjusts movements to correct timing defects, using watchmaker's tools and loupe: Sets up timing device for specified type movement. Positions movement in holding fixture and connects movement to timing device. Activates timing device that automatically compares timing beat of test movement with standard and records discrepancies on tape. Adjusts movements to attain accurate beat or routes movement to TIMING ADJUSTER (clock & watch) 715.681-010. Records timing beat defects. Places acceptable movements in tray for assembly.
GOE: 06.01.05 STRENGTH: L GED: R3 M2 L2 SVP: 5 DLU: 77

715.685-038 MAINSPRING WINDER AND OILER (clock & watch) alternate titles: mainspring-winding-machine operator

Tends semiautomatic mainspring-winding machine that winds mainspring into shell (barrel) and lubricates bearing surfaces: Opens chuck, inserts arbor, and fits spring assembly over arbor. Depresses pedal that allows winding and oiling mechanism to wind spring around arbor, and oil spring. Places barrel over spring by hand and removes assembly from chuck. May wind mainspring, using hand-operated spring-winding tool. May reverse mainspring to coil spring in direction used in watch and be designated Mainspring-Reverse Winder (clock & watch).
GOE: 06.04.02 STRENGTH: S GED: R2 M1 L1 SVP: 2 DLU: 77

715.685-042 PINION POLISHER (clock & watch)

Tends lathe that polishes leaves, pivots, or staffs of clock pinions: Clamps part in chuck of lathe. Starts lathe and swings tool rest into position. Forces slip of bell metal against rotating part to smooth surface. Repeats process, polishing part with slip of oilstone and buffing part with rouge to produce smooth, even surface. Examines part for surface defects, using loupe and tweezers. May be designated according to part polished as Pivot Polisher (clock & watch).
GOE: 06.04.02 STRENGTH: L GED: R2 M1 L1 SVP: 3 DLU: 77

715.685-046 POLISHER, BALANCE SCREWHEAD (clock & watch) alternate titles: screwhead polisher

Tends semiautomatic turning lathe that bevels and polishes balance wheel screwheads: Places screw, using tweezers, into threaded chuck and depresses pedal to turn screw firmly into chuck. Turns, bevels, and polishes screwhead by manually feeding diamond tool against rotating head until automatic stop is reached. Depresses pedal to reverse direction of rotating chuck and to remove finished screw. Observes parts, using loupe and tweezers.
GOE: 06.04.02 STRENGTH: S GED: R2 M1 L1 SVP: 3 DLU: 77

715.685-050 PRESS OPERATOR, PIERCE AND SHAVE (clock & watch)

Tends automatic press that pierces holes and shaves corners and holes of watch parts: Cleans work plate of press, using airhose. Positions part in recessed nest or over protruding pins of work plate. Presses button to activate press that automatically pierces and shaves part. Removes finished part from press and measures dimensions of hole, using plug gauge.
GOE: 06.04.02 STRENGTH: S GED: R2 M1 L1 SVP: 2 DLU: 77

715.685-054 PROFILER, HAND (clock & watch)

Tends profiling machine that cuts grooves and recesses in watch parts: Clamps part in chuck. Moves forward and lateral guide handles simultaneously to press model against guide point as cutting progresses. Measures profiled dimensions, using precision indicator gauge and loupe.
GOE: 06.02.02 STRENGTH: L GED: R3 M2 L2 SVP: 4 DLU: 77

715.685-058 SOLDERER (clock & watch)

Tends machine that solders holding feet (used to secure dial to watch movement) to back of watch dials: Places dial on asbestos holding fixture. Positions soldering rings over specified points on dial and positions dial foot in each ring, using tweezers. Lowers weights onto holding feet to secure feet in fixture. Starts machine that automatically moves lighted gas torch into position to solder feet to blank.
GOE: 06.04.02 STRENGTH: L GED: R2 M1 L1 SVP: 2 DLU: 77

715.685-062 TAPPER II (clock & watch)

Tends tapping machine that cuts internal threads in watch-setting levers: Places levers in holding fixture of machine and aligns hole in lever under tap. Starts machine that lowers tap into holes to cut threads. Verifies size of hole, using plug and thread gauges. Removes burrs from tapped hole, using powered burr cutter.
GOE: 06.04.02 STRENGTH: L GED: R2 M1 L1 SVP: 3 DLU: 77

715.685-066 TORQUE TESTER (clock & watch) alternate titles: mainspring-torque tester

Tends torque-testing machine that measures strength of watch mainsprings: Positions barrel in testing holder. Moves controls and reads scale indicating strength of coiled spring. Segregates assemblies into trays according to strength measurements.
GOE: 06.03.02 STRENGTH: L GED: R2 M1 L2 SVP: 3 DLU: 77

715.685-070 TUBING-MACHINE TENDER (clock & watch)

Tends bench-mounted punch press that forms pivot holes in watch hour-hand tubes. Positions hand in nest on bed of press, using tweezers. Activates press that automatically forms hole in hour hand for insertion of pivot.
GOE: 06.04.24 STRENGTH: S GED: R2 M1 L1 SVP: 3 DLU: 77

715.686-010 DESTATICIZER FEEDER (clock & watch)

Feeds auto clock lenses into machine that coats lenses with anti-electrostatic solution: Wipes dust from lenses, using cloth, and examines lenses for imperfections. Discards defective lenses. Presses lenses in clamps of circular conveyor that carries lenses through spray booth for application of solution that dissipates electrostatic charges and prevents further accumulation of charges on lenses. Presses buttons to start and stop conveyor and to activate sprayer. Removes lenses from clamps subsequent to spraying and places lenses in box.
GOE: 06.04.21 STRENGTH: L GED: R2 M1 L1 SVP: 2 DLU: 77

715.686-014 MACHINE FEEDER (clock & watch)

Feeds jeweled settings, right-side-up, into hoppers of automatic machines in clock and watch manufacturing plant, using tweezers.
GOE: 06.04.09 STRENGTH: L GED: R1 M1 L1 SVP: 1 DLU: 77

715.687-010 BAND ATTACHER (clock & watch)

Attaches wrist bands to watches, using handtools: Removes holding pins from case, using handtool, and inserts pins into holes in band. Reattaches pins

in case to secure band. Threads band through hole in women's watchcases, and crimps metal cord ring around band to secure band.
GOE: 06.04.23 STRENGTH: S GED: R1 M1 L1 SVP: 2 DLU: 77

715.687-014 BARREL-CAP SETTER (clock & watch)
Attaches cap (cover) to mainspring barrel assembly, using handtools: Places barrel assemblies in nests of special holder. Positions caps on assemblies, using tweezers, and presses caps firmly in place, using cap press (handtool). Oils assembly, using fountain oiler or oil-filled hypodermic syringe.
GOE: 06.04.23 STRENGTH: S GED: R2 M1 L1 SVP: 3 DLU: 77

715.687-018 CRYSTAL ATTACHER (clock & watch)
Inserts watch crystals into bezels (grooved holding rings) by hand.
GOE: 06.04.23 STRENGTH: S GED: R1 M1 L1 SVP: 2 DLU: 77

715.687-022 DIAL BRUSHER (clock & watch) alternate titles: scratch brusher
Cleans and polishes timepiece dials or dial blanks, using power brushing wheel or handbrush: Applies abrasive powder to dials. Holds dials against rotating brush or manipulates brush over dials to clean and polish dials. Examines surface of dials subsequent to cleaning and polishing to verify specified cleanliness and finish, using loupe. Rinses dials in water or alcohol and dries dials in heated centrifuge.
GOE: 06.04.33 STRENGTH: S GED: R1 M1 L1 SVP: 2 DLU: 77

715.687-026 DIPPER, CLOCK AND WATCH HANDS (clock & watch)
Dips watch and clock hands, mounted on board, into lacquer to cover perforations in hands preparatory to painting with radioactive paint. Skims off film of thickened lacquer from surface of tank before repeating process, using spatula.
GOE: 06.04.33 STRENGTH: S GED: R1 M1 L1 SVP: 2 DLU: 77

715.687-030 FOOT STRAIGHTENER (clock & watch)
Straightens timepiece dial holding feet, using holding device and gauge: Positions dial in holding device, aligning feet with holes in fixture of device. Closes collet of device that squeezes and straightens feet. Places dial in gauge that duplicates watch movement to determine that feet are straight and properly positioned and that center and second holes are correctly placed.
GOE: 06.02.24 STRENGTH: L GED: R2 M1 L1 SVP: 2 DLU: 77

715.687-034 GAUGER (clock & watch)
Measures height of pinions on wheel to ensure conformance to specifications, using gauge: Adjusts pointer of dial gauge to zero mark according to standard pinion on gauge block. Places test wheel and pinion in nest of gauge block, using tweezers, and reads gauge to determine height of pinion. Separates pinions according to acceptable grade.
GOE: 06.01.05 STRENGTH: L GED: R3 M2 L2 SVP: 4 DLU: 77

715.687-038 HAIRSPRING CUTTER I (clock & watch)
Cuts off end of inner coil of watch hairspring to provide sufficient clearance for spring to slip over collet, using tweezers, hand clippers, and loupe. Places spring over gauge to determine if fit is correct.
GOE: 06.02.24 STRENGTH: L GED: R2 M1 L1 SVP: 2 DLU: 77

715.687-042 HAIRSPRING CUTTER II (clock & watch)
Cuts individual hairspring wires to specified length, using hand-operated cutting device: Pulls wire from spool and positions and clamps wire end in cutting stop. Pulls wire taut and cuts wire to specified length, using pivoted cutting blade.
GOE: 06.02.24 STRENGTH: L GED: R2 M1 L2 SVP: 2 DLU: 77

715.687-046 HAMMER ADJUSTER (clock & watch)
Shapes hammers used to strike bells in alarm clocks, using holding fixture: Fits ends of hammers into holding fixture. Bends arms to required shape by hand.
GOE: 06.02.24 STRENGTH: L GED: R1 M1 L1 SVP: 1 DLU: 77

715.687-050 INSPECTOR, BALANCE TRUING (clock & watch)
Inspects watch balance wheels to verify that rim lies in single plane and that plane is perpendicular to staff axis, using *truing II* caliper, tweezers, and loupe. Mounts balance wheel and staff between jaws of truing calipers, using tweezers, and adjusts index pointer above end of balance arm. Turns and examines wheel to verify that space between index and both arms is identical, using loupe. Adjusts index pointer over rim of wheel and verifies that width of light slit between rim and index does not vary as wheel is rotated. Rejects wheels that are not true.
GOE: 06.01.05 STRENGTH: S GED: R3 M2 L2 SVP: 3 DLU: 77

715.687-054 INSPECTOR, BALANCE WHEEL MOTION (clock & watch)
Examines motion of watch balance wheel to verify that wheel swings around an arc of at least 180 degrees, using holding fixture and loupe: Winds and positions watch in holding fixture. Examines swing of wheel utilizing balance arm as point of reference, to verify that swing is at least 180 degrees of arc, using loupe. Disassembles faulty balance wheel movements for repair.
GOE: 06.03.02 STRENGTH: S GED: R2 M2 L2 SVP: 3 DLU: 77

715.687-058 INSPECTOR, BALANCE-BRIDGE (clock & watch)
Examines assembled watch balance bridges to detect scratches and damaged screws and cap jewels, using loupe and tweezers. Centers regulator, using tweezers, and verifies that jewel is properly oiled, using loupe. Segregates faulty balance bridges.

GOE: 06.03.02 STRENGTH: S GED: R2 M1 L2 SVP: 3 DLU: 77

715.687-062 INSPECTOR, CASING (clock & watch)
Inspects assembled watches, clocks, and appliance timers for conformance to company standards: Scans assemblies to detect defects, such as surface blemishes, broken or scratched crystals, faulty plating, tightness of case, and presence of foreign matter. Turns crown and set buttons on assemblies to determine ease of setting and winding. Compares accuracy of watches and clocks with master clock to determine conformance to specified tolerances. Marks type of defects found on assemblies, using pencil or crayon, and places defective assemblies in containers for repair.
GOE: 06.03.02 STRENGTH: L GED: R2 M2 L2 SVP: 3 DLU: 77

715.687-066 INSPECTOR, DIALS (clock & watch) alternate titles: hands-and-dial inspector
Examines clock and watch dials for surface and mechanical defects, using loupe, gauges, and pick: Examines dials for surface defects, such as scratches, finger marks, double lines in printing of numerals, and defective lacquer coating, using loupe. Turns movement, dial side down, to determine if watch hands slip. Inspects hands to determine if they are aligned with numerals, are specified distances apart, and that they do not touch dial or crystal, using gauges. Moves second hand to ascertain if hand slips on arbor, using pick. Inspects dials for centering of center and second holes, using gauges. May bake dials in oven for specified time to harden lacquer coating.
GOE: 06.03.02 STRENGTH: S GED: R3 M2 L3 SVP: 4 DLU: 77

715.687-070 INSPECTOR, SOLDERING (clock & watch)
Inspects soldered dial feet to verify that solder has melted evenly and that feet are held securely. Tests positioning of feet, using go-not-go gauge. May mix flux for use in soldering dial feet.
GOE: 06.03.02 STRENGTH: L GED: R2 M2 L2 SVP: 3 DLU: 77

715.687-074 INSPECTOR, TIMERS (clock & watch)
Examines appliance timers for surface defects and sets timers preparatory to testing: Examines timers for defects, such as scratched dials, dents, and broken or missing parts. Places defective timers in carton for repair. Plugs test light into timer and turns dial of timer to specified setting. Places timer on vertical rack for testing and connects timer cord to electrical outlet. Flips switch of timer to verify that test light burns and that timer functions.
GOE: 06.03.02 STRENGTH: L GED: R2 M2 L2 SVP: 3 DLU: 77

715.687-078 MAINSPRING FORMER, ARBOR END (clock & watch)
Forms arbor end and arbor spiral on watch mainsprings so arbor end will fit snugly around arbor hole, using hand forming tool. Mounts mainspring and arbor blanks in forming tool, using tweezers, and moves levers to form specified end and spiral.
GOE: 06.02.24 STRENGTH: S GED: R2 M2 L2 SVP: 2 DLU: 77

715.687-082 MAINSPRING FORMER, BRACE END (clock & watch)
Bends brace end of watch mainspring to match inside of mainspring barrel, using hand bending tool. Places brace end against pin in center of tool, using tweezers. Turns clamp to secure brace end in tool and manipulates tool handle to bend brace end to specified shape.
GOE: 06.02.24 STRENGTH: S GED: R2 M1 L1 SVP: 2 DLU: 77

715.687-086 MASKER (clock & watch)
Brushes lacquer in second track recess of timepiece dial to prevent removal of finish during polishing and brushes lacquer over trylons (numerical markings) of dial to prevent trylons from being plated during dial-plating operation.
GOE: 06.04.33 STRENGTH: S GED: R1 M1 L1 SVP: 2 DLU: 77

715.687-090 MOTOR POLARIZER (clock & watch)
Polarizes motors used in timers and clocks, using electromagnet: Oils rotor pinion of motor, using oil-soaked cloth. Inserts motor between poles of electromagnet and activates electromagnet to polarize motor. Places polarized motor on conveyor for further processing. Tallies each polarized motor, using counting device, and records daily production.
GOE: 06.04.23 STRENGTH: S GED: R1 M1 L1 SVP: 2 DLU: 77

715.687-094 MOUNTER, CLOCK AND WATCH HANDS (clock & watch)
Mounts clock and watch hands on board preparatory to dipping in lacquer: Presses eyelet end of hand onto adhesive material on board with pointed end extending specified distance over edge of board, using tweezers. Examines mounted hands to ensure that all hands on board are aligned and parallel.
GOE: 06.04.23 STRENGTH: S GED: R1 M1 L1 SVP: 2 DLU: 77

715.687-098 PAINTER, CLOCK AND WATCH HANDS (clock & watch)
Brushes short narrow stripes of radioactive paint on watch and clock hands so that hands will be visible in dark, using artist's brush.
GOE: 06.04.33 STRENGTH: S GED: R1 M1 L1 SVP: 2 DLU: 77

715.687-102 PARTS REMOVER (clock & watch)
Removes watch parts from metal polishing blocks, utilizing one of following methods: (1) Heats block on hot plate to melt shellac, and pushes parts off block, using spatula, or holds block upside down and blows parts off block, using compressed airhose. (2) Heats and places block upside down on bed of handpress. Lowers ram to force parts out. (3) Places blocks in caustic solution to dissolve shellac and loosen parts.
GOE: 06.04.34 STRENGTH: L GED: R1 M1 L1 SVP: 2 DLU: 77

715.687-106 RACKER (clock & watch)
Places electric clocks or electric motors used in clocks and timers on rack and connects lead wires to current outlets preparatory to testing. Records quantity racked, identification number, rack number, and date.
GOE: 06.04.34 STRENGTH: L GED: R1 M1 L1 SVP: 2 DLU: 77

715.687-110 REAMER, CENTER HOLE (clock & watch)
Reams center holes of balance wheels subsequent to recessing operation to clean holes, using hand reamer and loupe.
GOE: 06.02.24 STRENGTH: L GED: R2 M1 L1 SVP: 2 DLU: 77

715.687-114 ROTOR ASSEMBLER (clock & watch)
Assembles rotors used in electric timer motors, using glue dispenser and die: Places rotor disk in die attached to conveyor. Positions rotor shaft, with hub attached, through hole of rotor disk. Presses tip of pencil-shaped glue dispenser against hub of rotor shaft and rotor disk to join parts. Places plastic pinion in die, lifts glued assembly from die, and presses rotor shaft through hole in pinion to complete rotor assembly. Places completed assemblies in tray for further processing.
GOE: 06.04.23 STRENGTH: S GED: R2 M1 L2 SVP: 2 DLU: 77

715.687-118 SET-KEY DRIVER (clock & watch)
Attaches time and alarm setting keys to assembled alarm clock movement, using press: Places keys into holding fixture of press and positions clock movement over keys so that ends of staff protrude through keyholes. Starts press that forces staffs into keys.
GOE: 06.04.23 STRENGTH: L GED: R1 M1 L1 SVP: 2 DLU: 77

715.687-122 SPRING LAYER (clock & watch)
Straightens, shapes, and forms clock springs, using holding fixture and pliers. Winds coiled spring around peg or pin of fixture and bends and shapes spring to specifications, using needle-nosed pliers.
GOE: 06.02.24 STRENGTH: L GED: R2 M1 L1 SVP: 2 DLU: 77

715.687-126 WASHER (clock & watch)
Immerses watch parts in series of cleaning and rinsing solutions to wash parts: Empties parts onto wire screen subsequent to washing and rinsing, and adds sawdust. Shakes screen causing sawdust to absorb moisture from parts and to drop parts through screen. Separates parts according to size, or places parts in box, for transfer to next operation. May dry parts, using electric lamp, centrifugal drier, or tumbling barrel. May weigh parts on balance scale. May mix cleaning solutions. May dip polishing blocks in caustic and soap solutions to remove shellac or vaseline and be designated Block Cleaner (clock & watch). May clean mainspring barrel assemblies, using buff stick dipped in naptha and be designated Mainspring-Barrel-Assembly Cleaner (clock & watch).
GOE: 06.04.39 STRENGTH: L GED: R2 M1 L1 SVP: 2 DLU: 77

715.687-130 WINDER (clock & watch)
Winds assembled watch movements and adjusts watch hands to indicate correct time preparatory to testing: Turns crown of movement against soft plastic sheet or holds crown against revolving plastic cup to wind movement or winds movement by hand. Rewinds movement after specified period and segregates movements that have gained or lost time in excess of specified amount.
GOE: 06.03.02 STRENGTH: S GED: R2 M1 L2 SVP: 3 DLU: 77

716 OCCUPATIONS IN FABRICATION AND REPAIR OF ENGINEERING AND SCIENTIFIC INSTRUMENTS AND EQUIPMENT, N.E.C.

This group includes occupations concerned with grinding, polishing, and coating optical lenses, reflectors, filters, and prisms and ophthalmic eyeglass, sunglass, and contact lenses.

716.130-010 SUPERVISOR (optical goods)
Supervises and coordinates activities of workers engaged in fabricating and inspecting eyeglass, contact, and precision optical lenses: Inspects lenses for defects and adherence to specifications, using devices such as polariscope, magnifying glass, protractor, and power determining instrument. Trains workers in operation of lens processing machinery, theory of optics, and lens handling. Keeps records and prepares reports on machine maintenance, lens breakage and spoilage, inventory and requisition of supplies, and personnel production and assignments. Sets up, adjusts, and repairs lens generators, polishers, edgers, and hardeners, using handtools. Performs other duties as described under SUPERVISOR (any industry) Master Title. May be designated according to type of lens manufactured as Supervisor, Contact Lens (optical goods); Supervisor, Multifocal Lens (optical goods); Supervisor, Precision Optical Elements (optical goods); Supervisor, Sunglasses (optical goods); or according to department as Supervisor, Fusing Room (optical goods); Supervisor, Grinding And Polishing (optical goods). May be designated: Molding-Room Supervisor (optical goods); Supervisor, Inspecting (optical goods); Supervisor, Lens Generating (optical goods).
GOE: 06.01.01 STRENGTH: L GED: R4 M3 L4 SVP: 7 DLU: 86

716.280-010 OPTICIAN APPRENTICE (optical goods; retail trade) alternate titles: ophthalmic-technician apprentice; optical-mechanic apprentice
Performs duties as described under APPRENTICE (any industry) Master Title.

GOE: 05.05.11 STRENGTH: L GED: R4 M4 L4 SVP: 8 DLU: 77

716.280-014 OPTICIAN (optical goods; retail trade) alternate titles: optical mechanic
Sets up and operates machines to grind eyeglass lenses to prescription specifications and assembles lenses in frames: Reads lens and frame specifications from prescription. Selects lens blanks from stock. Sets up and operates machines, such as generator, polisher, edger, and hardener, to fabricate lenses to specifications. Mounts lenses in metal, plastic, or rimless frames. Inspects mounted lenses for conformance to specifications [INSPECTOR, EYEGLASS (optical goods)]. Examines broken lenses to identify original lens prescription, using power determining and optical centering instruments.
GOE: 05.05.11 STRENGTH: L GED: R4 M4 L4 SVP: 8 DLU: 77

716.280-018 OPTICIAN (optical goods) alternate titles: flat optical element maker; optical model maker and tester; precision lens technician
Sets up and operates machine tools to fabricate optical elements and systems, applying knowledge of layout and machining techniques and procedures, shop mathematics, and properties of optical and abrasive materials: Studies work order, blueprints, and sketches to formulate machining plans and sequences. Measures and marks dimensions and reference points to lay out stock for machining. Selects premixed compounds or mixes grinding, polishing, and holding compounds according to formula. Mounts workpiece on holding fixture, using adhesive, friction, or vacuum. Mounts and secures workpiece and tooling in machines. Operates machines, such as saws, lathes, grinders, milling machines, generators, polishers, and edgers to fabricate optics, fixtures, tools, and mountings of specified sizes and shapes. Grinds and polishes optics, using handtools, as required. Measures and tests optics, using precision measuring and testing instruments. May develop specifications and drawings from verbal description. May perform experimental work and research to develop new production methods and procedures applying shop mathematics and knowledge of production techniques. May train and direct other workers.
GOE: 05.05.11 STRENGTH: L GED: R4 M4 L4 SVP: 8 DLU: 77

716.360-010 SIZER, MACHINE (optical goods)
Sets up machines to grind and polish edges or surfaces of lens blanks: Selects specified grinding and polishing tools and secures tools to machine spindles, using handtools. Turns adjustment screws to set radius of grinding and polishing arm stroke according to size of lens holding block. Sets time cycle which automatically stops machines on completion of grinding and polishing process. Tilts and secures generator machine head at required angle with workpiece according to specified curve and thickness of lens. Installs and adjusts lens holders and diamond wheel on edging machines according to diameter of lens. May dress grinding wheel.
GOE: 06.01.02 STRENGTH: L GED: R3 M3 L3 SVP: 7 DLU: 77

716.381-010 INSPECTOR, PRECISION (optical goods) alternate titles: inspector, optical elements; lens inspector
Inspects precision optical and ophthalmic lenses at various stages of production to ensure specified standards have been met, using precision measuring instruments: Reads prescription and work order to ascertain lens specifications. Examines lenses for defects, such as pits, scratches, unpolished areas, bubbles, and chips, using magnifying glass and polarized light. Verifies lens dimensions, such as thickness, size, curve, and position of bifocal element, using mechanical and fixed measuring instruments, such as calibrated microscope, micrometer, and test glass. Compares lens to sample to verify specified color. Mounts lenses on optical centering and power determining instrument, adjusts dials to focus and center test pattern, and compares power, centering, and axis readings with prescription to ensure specified standards have been met. Measures properties, such as coating thickness, angles, curves, and focal length of lens, using electronic, optical, and electromechanical measuring instruments, such as spectrometer, collimator, goniometer, and facimeters. Marks and routes defective lenses for rework or salvage. May clean optics to facilitate inspection. May be designated according to stage in production as Final Inspector (optical goods); In-Process Inspector (optical goods); or according to type lens inspected as Camera-Lens Inspector (optical goods); Contact-Lens Inspector (optical goods); Instrument-Lens Inspector (optical goods); Ophthalmic-Lens Inspector (optical goods); Prism Inspector (optical goods); Reticle Inspector (optical goods).
GOE: 06.01.05 STRENGTH: S GED: R4 M3 L4 SVP: 7 DLU: 78

716.381-014 LAY-OUT TECHNICIAN (optical goods)
Locates and marks centers, axes, and terminal points on ophthalmic lens blanks, draws reference lines, and writes specifications to guide workers who surface or finish lenses: Reads work order to ascertain lens specifications. Examines lens blank to ensure freedom from defects and to verify color and size specifications. Positions lens blank to be surfaced on protractor and marks center, direction of cylinder axis, and position of reading lens segment. Mounts lens blank to be finished in optical centering and power determining instrument and adjusts dials to align and focus target. Compares dial readings with work order to ensure lens blank has been surfaced to meet power and axis specifications. Rejects defective lenses. Depresses marking device on instrument to mark optical center and horizontal axis of lens blank. Writes specifications on lens blank to guide lens fabricating workers. May be designated according to department worked in as Bench-Lay-Out Technician (optical goods); Surface-Lay-Out Technician (optical goods).
GOE: 06.01.04 STRENGTH: S GED: R3 M3 L3 SVP: 6 DLU: 77

716.382-010   LATHE OPERATOR, CONTACT LENS (optical goods) alternate titles: contact-lens cutter

Operates jeweler's lathe to cut inside or outside curvature in contact lens blanks: Reads prescription to determine lens thickness and dioptric power and converts specified dioptric power to radius dimensions, using conversion table. Inserts plastic blank in holding chuck of lathe. Adjusts cutting tool mechanism for specified radius of inside or outside curvature and depth of cut. Starts lathe and turns crank to advance cutting tool. Observes gauge and readjusts lathe to prevent excessive cutting. Pulls control arm to move cutting tool across face of lens. Removes lens from chuck and examines lens for smoothness of cut. Measures lens to verify compliance with specifications, using thickness gauge and calipers. Tapes finished lens to work order and places lens in routing box.
GOE: 06.02.08 STRENGTH: L GED: R3 M3 L3 SVP: 5 DLU: 77

716.382-014   OPTICAL-ELEMENT COATER (optical goods)

Controls vacuum coating equipment to coat optical elements with chemical or metal film to alter reflective properties of elements: Reads work order to ascertain thickness of optical element and type coating material specified. Installs heating filament in coating machine according to type coating applied, using screwdriver. Fills crucible with coating material and positions crucible under heating filament. Secures optical element in jig and centers jig in vacuum chamber of machine to ensure uniform coating of optical surface. Places dome-shaped lid (vacuum bell) over jig or lowers lid equipped with window depending upon machine used. Starts machine that creates vacuum and releases chemicals or metal to form coating on optical element by process of sublimation or atomization. Observes changing colors of element through vacuum bell or through window in lid to determine when element is coated to specifications, or reads exposure meter to determine coating thickness. Applies and removes strip of cellophane to test adherence of coating to optical element. May immerse elements in chemical solution to clean elements. May operate ultrasonic vibrator to clean element. May inspect optical elements prior to coating to detect defects, such as blemishes, abrasions, and rough edges, using microscope. May cement optical elements together to form multiple laminated elements [CEMENTER (optical goods)]. May spray emulsion on lens preparatory to coating.
GOE: 06.02.21 STRENGTH: L GED: R3 M2 L2 SVP: 5 DLU: 77

716.382-018   PRECISION-LENS GRINDER (optical goods) alternate titles: lens grinder; optical technician

Sets up and operates grinding and polishing machines to make lenses, optical flats, and other precision optical elements for optical instruments and ophthalmic goods, such as telescopes, aerial cameras, military optical systems, and eyeglasses: Operates machine to rough-grind blanks of optical glass to approximate size and shape or manually positions and turns blanks against grinding wheel or *lap I*. Blocks optical element in plaster or other compound. Mounts blocked element in machine and operates machine to oscillate and rotate element against abrasive to fine-grind element to final size and shape. Periodically stops machine to inspect and measure elements for accuracy and degree of completion. Polishes surfaces, using lens-polishing machine [PRECISION-LENS POLISHER (optical goods) 716.682-018]. May cement lens elements together to obtain corrected lens assemblies. May mount optical elements in holders or adapters for use in instruments. May be designated according to type of lens ground as Eyeglass-Lens Grinder (optical goods); Instrument-Lens Grinder (optical goods); Multifocal-Button Grinder (optical goods).
GOE: 06.02.08 STRENGTH: L GED: R4 M3 L4 SVP: 7 DLU: 86

716.382-022   PRECISION-LENS-GRINDER APPRENTICE (optical goods) alternate titles: instrument-lens-grinder apprentice; lens-grinder apprentice

Performs duties as described under APPRENTICE (any industry) Master Title.
GOE: 06.02.08 STRENGTH: L GED: R4 M3 L4 SVP: 7 DLU: 77

716.462-010   PRECISION-LENS CENTERER AND EDGER (optical goods)

Operates grinder to edge and bevel precision ophthalmic optical lenses: Reads work order or blueprint to determine edge specifications. Selects lens holding tool of specified size and mounts tool in truing machine. Starts machine and turns handwheel to move cutting tool into lens holding tool to true holding tool. Applies heated pitch or other adhesive to lens holding tool and affixes lens on tool. Passes beam of light through lens and repositions lens on holding tool until beam remains stationary to center lens on tool or centers lens, using collimator. Secures holding tool and lens assembly in fixture of edge grinder. Adjusts grinder for variables, such as speed, rate of feed, and depth and angle of cut. Starts machine and turns handwheel to bring grinding wheel in contact with lens. Observes machine operation; stops machine to measure lens edge, using precision measuring instruments, such as micrometers and calipers; and adjusts machine to grind and bevel edge to specifications. May hold lens against grinding wheel to bevel edges to specified angle. May set up machines for other workers and train workers to operate machines.
GOE: 06.02.08 STRENGTH: L GED: R3 M3 L2 SVP: 6 DLU: 77

716.681-010   BLOCKER AND CUTTER, CONTACT LENS (optical goods)

Blocks contact lens blanks and cuts lenses to specified diameter, using jeweler's lathe and handtools: Immerses *laps I* in molten wax and embeds lens in wax or presses two-faced adhesive tape into depression of lap, using rounded

tool, and affixes lens to tape. Trims excess tape, using knife. Positions lens and lap assembly in blocking device. Presses plunger to center and fasten lens to blocking device. Mounts blocked lens in chuck of jeweler's lathe. Turns crank and observes gauge to set cutting tool for specified diameter. Starts lathe and turns handle to feed cutting tool into lens. Removes cut lens from lathe and smooths burrs, using emery cloth. Places laps in container of solvent to remove tape or wax residue before reuse.
GOE: 06.01.04 STRENGTH: L GED: R3 M2 L3 SVP: 5 DLU: 77

716.681-014   GLASS CUTTER, HAND (optical goods)

Lays out and cuts optical glass to specified dimensions and weight for molding into lens blanks, using templates, balance scale, and glass cutting tool: Examines optical glass stock or molded blanks for defects, such as bubbles, cracks, and scratches, and rejects defective stock. Weighs glass stock to facilitate cutting to specified weight, using balance scale. Traces outline according to dimension specifications, using template. Cuts glass according to pattern, using glass cutter. Grinds rough edges from blank, using rotating grindstone.
GOE: 06.01.04 STRENGTH: L GED: R3 M2 L2 SVP: 4 DLU: 77

716.681-018   LENS POLISHER, HAND (optical goods)

Hand polishes optical elements, such as lenses, prisms, and optical flats, to finish element or remove defects, using jeweler's rouge, polishing cloth or device, precision measuring instruments, and jeweler's lathe: Examines surface of element to detect defects, such as stains and scratches, and measures element to determine amount of finish required, using precision measuring instruments. Rubs rouge onto chamois, using jeweler's rouge stick, or onto polishing device mounted on workbench, using sponge. Rubs chamois over surface of element or oscillates element against polishing device to remove defects from element. Mounts element on spindle of jeweler's lathe, starts lathe, and holds rouge-coated chamois against element to finish element. Verifies dimensions of finished element, using precision measuring instruments, and examines elements to ensure all defects have been corrected, using magnifying glass. Cleans finished elements, using lens cleaning solution, cloth, and paper.
GOE: 06.01.04 STRENGTH: L GED: R3 M2 L2 SVP: 5 DLU: 77

716.681-022   OPTICAL-GLASS ETCHER (optical goods) alternate titles: glass etcher

Etches numerals and graduation lines on prisms and other optical glass surfaces for use in optical instruments, using pantograph engraver: Mounts glass specimens in holder. Dips glass elements in molten wax to obtain uniform protective coating. Positions tracing stylus of pantograph on template and guides stylus around template. Inscribes pattern of lines and numerals on elements in wax coating with needle which is affixed to pantograph arm. Exposes glass to hydrofluoric acid fumes to etch pattern. Cleans glass with water and solvents. Fills etched characters with opaque paste to improve readability. Inspects etched work for uniformity, using calibrated microscope.
GOE: 06.02.30 STRENGTH: S GED: R3 M2 L2 SVP: 4 DLU: 77

716.682-010   EYEGLASS-LENS CUTTER (optical goods) alternate titles: lens cutter

Sets up and operates bench-mounted cutting machine to cut eyeglass lenses to specified size and shape: Selects metal pattern according to prescription specifications and mounts pattern in spring clamp of cutting machine. Sets control dial for specified lens diameter plus allowance for edge grinding. Aligns center and axis marks on lens with markings on pad of cutting machine and lowers cushioned pressure arm of machine which holds lens in position. Lowers cutting arm over lens and turns crank which rotates lens under cutting wheel to determine if machine settings are correct. Presses cutting arm down to hold cutting wheel against lens and turns crank to cut lens. Removes lens from machine and chips excess material from lens edges, using chipping pliers. Routes cut lenses to edging department.
GOE: 06.02.08 STRENGTH: L GED: R3 M2 L2 SVP: 3 DLU: 77

716.682-014   PRECISION-LENS GENERATOR (optical goods)

Sets up and operates lens generating machine to grind ophthalmic and optical element blanks, such as lenses, prisms, and optical flats, to specified curvature and thickness: Reads work orders, sketch, or blueprint to ascertain grinding specifications. Selects specified size holding tool or fabricates tool to fit optic blank. Presses blank into holding tool and mounts tool in generator. Selects specified diamond grinding wheel and secures wheel on generator spindle. Adjusts generator controls to regulate rotation speed of tool and blank, rate of feed, angle of arc, and depth of cut. Positions coolant nozzle over blank and starts generator to grind blank to specified curvature and thickness. Observes generator operation. Stops generator after specified time lapse and measures optic blank to verify curvature and thickness, using precision measuring instruments, such as dial gauge, spherometer, and micrometer. May utilize pitch or vacuum holding device to secure blank on holding tool. May move generator controls manually to grind blank. May operate surface grinder or milling machine to generate optical surfaces. May be designated according to type lens ground as Cataract-Lens Generator (optical goods); Eyeglass-Lens Generator (optical goods); Instrument-Lens Generator (optical goods); Multifocal-Button Generator (optical goods). May operate lens generator to remove scratches and true surface of lens and be designated Truer (optical goods).
GOE: 06.02.08 STRENGTH: L GED: R3 M3 L3 SVP: 6 DLU: 77

716.682-018   PRECISION-LENS POLISHER (optical goods)

Operates polishing machines to polish ophthalmic lenses or optical elements, such as lenses, prisms, and flats for use as contact or eyeglass lenses or in pre-

cision optical instruments: Mounts optical element on holding tool, using tape or cement. Selects *lap I*, according to size of optical element and applies pitch or other adhesive to polishing face of lap. Presses optical element into adhesive to form polishing surface. Mounts holding tool on polishing machine spindle and positions lap and element assembly over tool. Applies abrasive, or positions abrasive flow nozzle over element, and starts machine that polishes element. Observes polishing operation and periodically stops machine to rinse element with water and to test element for conformance to specifications, using test lens, monochromatic light, microscope, and power determining and optical centering instruments. May guide polishing lap manually over element. May mix adhesive according to formula. May be designated according to type of lens polished as Contact-Lens Polisher (optical goods).
GOE: 06.02.08 STRENGTH: L GED: R3 M2 L2 SVP: 7 DLU: 78

716.684-010 BLOCKER, HAND (optical goods)
Affixes precision optical or ophthalmic lens blanks in metal blocks used to hold blanks during grinding and polishing operations: Selects blocks according to size of lens blank and heats blocks or lenses over gas burner to prepare for adherance of pitch or wax. Pours molten pitch into block, using ladle, or melts wax over holding surface of block, using torch. Presses and centers lens blank into wax or pitch. Pushes lens to test for adherance to block and positions blocked lens under fan for cooling. May smooth and remove sharp edges from lens, using grinding wheel. May test centering of lens in block, using lapping machine.
GOE: 06.02.30 STRENGTH: L GED: R3 M1 L1 SVP: 3 DLU: 77

716.685-010 BLOCKING-MACHINE TENDER (optical goods)
Tends *blocking machine* that seals optical or ophthalmic lens blanks in metal blocks preparatory to grinding and polishing of lenses: Applies lacquer to lens blank, using spray gun or brush. Mounts lens and block in blocking machine, aligns marks on lens blank and block, and clamps lens and block in place. Pulls lever to admit molten pitch or metal alloy and water through holes in block and starts machine that bonds lens blank to block. Pours molten pitch or loads solid metal into machine to replenish supply. May tend machine that casts metal block and bonds lens to block in one operation.
GOE: 06.04.08 STRENGTH: L GED: R2 M1 L2 SVP: 3 DLU: 77

716.685-014 DRILLER (optical goods)
Tends bench-mounted, single-spindle drill press that bores holes in optical lenses for attachment of ear and nosepieces: Holds lens against base of drill bit and puts drop of cutting oil over spot to be bored. Starts drill and regulates lever to lower and hold drill bit against lens. Wipes lens with soft cloth to remove cutting oil and glass grindings.
GOE: 06.04.08 STRENGTH: S GED: R2 M1 L1 SVP: 3 DLU: 77

716.685-018 GRINDER, HAND (optical goods) alternate titles: backside grinder
Tends machine that grinds approximate curves on lens blanks preparatory to fine grinding: Selects lens blanks as specified on production order. Places lens blank in holder and positions holder and lens assembly on diamond *lap I* of grinding machine. Lowers spindle of weighted arm onto lens holder to hold lens on lap. Starts machine and moves control arm back and forth to grind lens blanks to specified curvature or holds lens blank against grinding wheel to grind blank. Removes blank from holder and washes blank in water to remove grinding abrasive. Measures blanks to verify specified curvature, using lens gauge.
GOE: 06.04.08 STRENGTH: L GED: R2 M1 L1 SVP: 2 DLU: 77

716.685-022 LENS-FABRICATING-MACHINE TENDER (optical goods)
Tends one or more bench machines that generate, grind, edge, or polish ophthalmic lenses and precision optical elements: Mounts blocked element in machine holding device. Verifies machine settings or adjusts machines for variables, such as speed, machining time, and flow rate of abrasive or coolant. Starts machine that automatically generates, grinds, polishes, or edges optical element. Removes element after specified machining time, rinses element in water, and measures to verify specified dimensions of element, using micrometer, caliper, dial gauge, and shadowgraph. May deblock and clean element in degreasing tank. May be designated according to fabricating process or type lens fabricated as Contact-Lens-Curve Grinder (optical goods); Contact-Lens-Edge Buffer (optical goods); Fusion-Juncture Grinder (optical goods); Lens-Edge Grinder, Machine (optical goods); Lens-Generating-Machine Tender (optical goods); Multifocal-Button Countersink Grinder (optical goods).
GOE: 06.04.08 STRENGTH: L GED: R2 M2 L2 SVP: 4 DLU: 77

716.687-010 DEBLOCKER (optical goods) alternate titles: cleaner
Performs one or more of following duties to deblock and clean precision ophthalmic or optical elements, such as lenses, flats, prisms: Chills blocked element to crystallize pitch or other block adhesive and strikes block with mallet to separate element from block, or heats block to soften adhesive and removes element with fingers. Places lenses and elements in basket and immerses basket in degreasing tank or automatic cleaning machine. Cleans finished surfaces of element with pad and brush and rubs unfinished surfaces on board dusted with abrasive to remove foreign substances. Inspects lens to ensure cleanliness and freedom from defects. Sprays or brushes protective coating on element, allows coating to dry, and places in element tray or wraps in tissue. Replenishes solvents in trays and tanks. Drains molten metal block adhesive from machine or tank for reuse. May clean pitch from surface of block, using hammer, knife, and wire wheel.

GOE: 06.04.39 STRENGTH: L GED: R2 M1 L1 SVP: 3 DLU: 77

716.687-014 GLASS CHECKER (optical goods)
Tests glass stock for color density to determine acceptability of stock for colored lenses, using light transmitting equipment. Inserts colored glass stock in transmission equipment that passes light through stock and registers color density. Reads machine dial and rejects or accepts glass stock according to chart listing density specifications.
GOE: 06.03.02 STRENGTH: L GED: R2 M1 L1 SVP: 2 DLU: 77

716.687-018 INSPECTOR, MULTIFOCAL LENS (optical goods)
Inspects multifocal lenses or lens parts, at various stages of processing, for defects caused by flaws in glass or improper assembly: Examines lenses or lens parts, such as polished multifocal buttons, polished lens blanks, and fused multifocal buttons, for defects, such as scratches or chips on surface or presence of dust or water stains along fused juncture. Measures dimensions of lenses or parts, using lens gauge or millimeter ruler. Places lenses or lens parts in trays for transfer to other departments. Keeps production record. May chill mounted lenses in freezer to contract mounting pitch for ease of lens removal. May remove lenses or lens parts from block by tapping block with hammer. May be designated according to lens or lens part inspected as Fusing-Line Inspector (optical goods); Multifocal-Button Inspector (optical goods); Topside Inspector (optical goods).
GOE: 06.03.02 STRENGTH: L GED: R3 M2 L2 SVP: 3 DLU: 77

716.687-022 LENS EXAMINER (optical goods) alternate titles: inspector-in-process; lens assorter; lens inspector
Performs one or more of following tasks to inspect glass and plastic lens blanks for defects: Removes paint and wax from blank with solvent and razor blade. Rinses blank in water. Examines surface and edges to detect defects, such as pits, scratches, and chips. Inspects blanks with polariscope to detect annealing defects, such as bubbles, striae, fire cracks, or seal checks. Marks defective blanks for rework or salvage, using crayon or pencil. Sorts blanks by grade and type of defect. Weighs lens blanks and records weight for determining shipping costs. May pack blanks in cartons for shipping. May gauge blanks [LENS-BLANK GAUGER (optical goods)]. May assemble nonprecision optical element into mechanical housing.
GOE: 06.03.02 STRENGTH: L GED: R2 M1 L2 SVP: 4 DLU: 77

716.687-026 LENS-BLANK GAUGER (optical goods) alternate titles: clocker; lens assorter; neutralizer; sizer
Measures lens blanks for conformance to specified dimensions, using fixed curvature and thickness gauges, dial indicator, rule, or eye wire. Matches lens blanks with standard lenses to verify focal strength of blanks. Sorts blanks according to size, shape, or focal strength.
GOE: 06.03.02 STRENGTH: L GED: R3 M2 L2 SVP: 3 DLU: 77

716.687-030 LENS-BLOCK GAUGER (optical goods)
Examines blocked lens to determine whether lens blanks are positioned evenly on block, using template. Positions template over blocked lens blank, holds assembly against light, and examines assembly to detect presence of light between blank and template indicating uneven positioning of lens blank on block.
GOE: 06.03.02 STRENGTH: S GED: R2 M1 L2 SVP: 2 DLU: 77

716.687-034 WET INSPECTOR, OPTICAL GLASS (optical goods) alternate titles: optical-glass inspector
Inspects optical glass immersed in chemical bath, to detect striae (internal stresses): Selects premixed chemical solution or mixes liquid chemicals in tank according to refraction index and grade of glass. Immerses glass in bath and focuses Burton lamp, collimating light, or striae scope on glass to detect internal stresses (striae). Marks defective areas with pencil. Writes inspection results and maintains permanent records for each melt. Sorts and grades glass according to type of defect noted. May operate transmission machine [GLASS CHECKER (optical goods)] to examine glass for strain. May saw glass stock [GLASS CUTTER (any industry)].
GOE: 06.03.02 STRENGTH: L GED: R2 M2 L2 SVP: 3 DLU: 77

719 OCCUPATIONS IN FABRICATION AND REPAIR OF SCIENTIFIC AND MEDICAL APPARATUS, PHOTOGRAPHIC AND OPTICAL GOODS, HOROLOGICAL, AND RELATED PRODUCTS, N.E.C.

This group includes occupations, not elsewhere classified, concerned with assembling, fabricating, and repairing scientific and medical apparatus, photographic and optical goods, watches and clocks and related products.

719.261-014 RADIOLOGICAL-EQUIPMENT SPECIALIST (inst. & app.) alternate titles: radiologic electronic specialist
Tests, repairs, calibrates, and assists in installation of radiological and related equipment used in medical diagnosis or therapy, applying technical knowledge of electronic, radiological, and mechanical systems, and user knowledge of computers, and using manuals, test equipment, measuring instruments, handtools, and power tools: Confers with supervisor, manufacturers' representatives, equipment operators, and other workers to discuss and establish work priorities, resolve equipment related problems, and plan installation, pre-

ventive maintenance, and repair procedures. Inspects and tests malfunctioning equipment to determine cause of malfunction, following learned procedures and repair manual instructions, using specialized test and analysis instruments and manufacturers' specifications. Disassembles malfunctioning equipment and removes, replaces, or repairs defective components, and readjusts components to manufacturers' specifications, using handtools, power tools, and measuring instruments. Removes old equipment, prepares space for installation of new equipment, and oversees installation of new equipment by manufacturer. Tests and calibrates equipment at regular or required intervals, using test and measuring instruments and handtools to maintain manufacturers' operational specifications. Selects, devises, designs, and installs mechanical or structural hardware, using tools and utilizing knowledge of mechanics and structures to resolve special equipment operation problems. Maintains records of maintenance and repair work and approved updates of equipment as required by manufacturer. Demonstrates operational procedures for equipment to users. May fabricate hardware, using machine and power tools, handtools, and related equipment. May work for manufacturer and specialize in particular line of equipment.
GOE: 05.05.11 STRENGTH: M GED: R5 M5 L5 SVP: 7 DLU: 89

719.381-014 HEARING-AID REPAIRER (inst. & app.)
Tests and repairs hearing aids, using oscilloscope, electrical test meters, and handtools, following schematic diagram: Tests circuits for shorts, open wires, or defective parts, using electrical test meters. Solders loose connections and replaces defective parts, such as resistors, condensers, batteries, and transistors. Repairs or replaces transformer, microphone, and volume control, using handtools. Cleans and lubricates mechanical parts with solvent and oil.
GOE: 05.10.03 STRENGTH: S GED: R4 M3 L4 SVP: 6 DLU: 78

719.381-018 BLOCK MAKER (protective dev.)
Molds lead blocks to be used as shields in radiation therapy treatments: Lays out x-ray film taken of patient in treatment position and tapes film over grid on lighted table. Sets distances on mold cutting machine, duplicating distances from which x ray was taken. Calculates required thickness of block, based upon equipment to be used in treatment and applying knowledge of geometry. Aligns template and styrofoam piece in blocking tray over x-ray film. Guides hand held stylus along lines drawn on x-ray film or print showing area to be treated, simultaneously cutting styrofoam piece with hot wire to form styrofoam mold used in making block. Sets mold in vise and tightens metal clamps to hold mold securely in position. Pours heated lead alloy into mold to form block. Mounts cooled block on lucite board, using screws. Installs finished block in tray of machine and views superimposed outline of block on x-ray film to verify accuracy of block and adherence to standards. Records patient information on finished block. May transport patients to and from treatment area.
GOE: 05.12.13 STRENGTH: M GED: R3 M3 L3 SVP: 3 DLU: 90

72   OCCUPATIONS IN ASSEMBLY AND REPAIR OF ELECTRICAL EQUIPMENT

This division includes occupations concerned with assembling, fabricating, or repairing equipment, components, and parts for equipment to transmit, control, or convert electrical power; signaling and detection equipment; and home radios, television sets, and phonographs.

720   OCCUPATIONS IN ASSEMBLY AND REPAIR OF RADIO AND TELEVISION RECEIVING SETS AND PHONOGRAPHS

This group includes occupations concerned with assembling and repairing radio and television receivers, recorders, phonographs, and related items. Occupations concerned with sound recording and transcription are included in Group 194.

720.281-010 RADIO REPAIRER (any industry) alternate titles: trouble shooter, radio
Repairs radio receivers, phonographs, recorders, and other electronic-audio equipment, using circuit diagrams and test meters: Tests wiring, tubes, resistors, and other parts, using electronic test equipment, such as voltmeters and oscilloscopes, to locate defects. Replaces defective parts, using handtools, and solders loose connections with soldering iron. May compute charges for labor and materials. May install radios in automobiles [AUTOMOBILE-ACCESSORIES INSTALLER (automotive ser.)]. May be designated according to type of radio repaired as Automobile Radio Repairer (any industry); Radio Repairer, Domestic (any industry).
GOE: 05.10.03 STRENGTH: L GED: R4 M2 L2 SVP: 6 DLU: 77

720.281-014 TAPE-RECORDER REPAIRER (any industry)
Tests, repairs, and adjusts tape-recording machines, following schematic diagrams and manufacturer's specifications, using handtools and electronic testing instruments: Disassembles machine and replaces worn parts, such as sprocket wheels, drive belts, electrical switches, and guide rollers, using handtools. Records voice and listens to playbacks to detect distortion in sound. Tests circuits, using instruments, such as voltmeters, oscilloscopes, audiogenerators, and distortion meters. Replaces defective resistors, condensers, and tubes. Solders loose connections. Tests operation of repaired recorder.
GOE: 05.10.03 STRENGTH: M GED: R4 M3 L2 SVP: 7 DLU: 77

720.281-018 TELEVISION-AND-RADIO REPAIRER (any industry) alternate titles: television repairer
Repairs and adjusts radios and television receivers, using handtools and electronic testing instruments: Tunes receiver on all channels and observes audio and video characteristics to locate source of trouble. Adjusts controls to obtain desired density, linearity, focus, and size of picture. Examines chassis for defects. Tests voltages and resistances of circuits to isolate defect, following schematic diagram and using voltmeter, oscilloscope, signal generator, and other electronic testing instruments. Tests and changes tubes. Solders loose connections and repairs or replaces defective parts, using handtools and soldering iron. Repairs radios and other audio equipment [RADIO REPAIRER (any industry)]. May install television sets [TELEVISION INSTALLER (any industry)].
GOE: 05.10.03 STRENGTH: M GED: R4 M3 L2 SVP: 7 DLU: 77

720.684-010 ASSEMBLY ADJUSTER (comm. equip.) alternate titles: record-changer adjuster
Tests and adjusts assembled phonograph turntable and record-changer unit for specified operation: Adjusts speed of turntable to specified number of revolutions per minute, using screwdriver and stroboscope. Listens for and eliminates noise in bearing. Removes humming noise from coil. Adjusts pickup arm, record magazine, elevator shafts and pads, and transfer lever to positions for accurate automatic record transfer.
GOE: 06.04.34 STRENGTH: L GED: R2 M2 L1 SVP: 3 DLU: 77

720.684-014 PHONOGRAPH-CARTRIDGE ASSEMBLER (comm. equip.) alternate titles: cartridge assembler
Assembles parts into components and components into complete phonograph cartridge assemblies: Positions, fits, and fastens together variety of small parts to make contact block assembly, using tweezers, toothpick, cement stick, and screwdriver. Welds ground piece to contact block, using spot welder. Solders fine wires from coils to contact block, seam in copper shield, and ground piece to shield, using pencil soldering iron. Plugs completed contact block assembly into ohmmeter to test for continuity. Assembles parts of magnet holder and stylus arm, using handpunch, tweezers, cement stick, holding fixture and loupe. Bakes subassembly in small oven to join parts and fix stylus angle. Fits subassemblies into potting assembly, verifies stylus alignement, and screws them together, using screwdriver.
GOE: 06.04.23 STRENGTH: S GED: R2 M2 L2 SVP: 5 DLU: 77

720.687-010 RECORD-CHANGER ASSEMBLER (comm. equip.)
Performs one or more repetitive operations to assemble record changers, such as positioning plates in jig, screwing and bolting parts together, soldering pickup and motor leads, and inserting springs and other small parts, using screwdrivers, wrenches, and soldering iron.
GOE: 06.04.23 STRENGTH: L GED: R2 M1 L1 SVP: 2 DLU: 77

720.687-014 RECORD-CHANGER TESTER (comm. equip.)
Tests automatic record changers for accuracy of record transfer and pickup movement by placing several records on changer and observing performance. Segregates for adjustment record changers not meeting performance standards.
GOE: 06.03.02 STRENGTH: L GED: R2 M1 L1 SVP: 2 DLU: 77

721   OCCUPATIONS IN ASSEMBLY AND REPAIR OF MOTORS, GENERATORS, AND RELATED PRODUCTS

This group includes occupations concerned with assembling and repairing electric motors, power generators, motor-generator sets, railway motors and control equipment; and motors, generators, and control equipment for gasoline-electric and oil-electric buses and trucks. Occupations concerned with winding and assembling coils, magnets, armatures, and related components are included in Group 724.

721.131-010 ELECTRIC MOTOR REPAIRING SUPERVISOR (any industry)
Supervises and coordinates activities of ELECTRIC-MOTOR ANALYST (any industry) and ELECTRIC-MOTOR REPAIRER (any industry) engaged in repairing electric motors, generators, switches, starting devices, and other electrical equipment. Estimates cost of repairs. Performs duties as described under SUPERVISOR (any industry) Master Title.
GOE: 05.05.10 STRENGTH: L GED: R4 M3 L3 SVP: 7 DLU: 77

721.131-014 SUPERVISOR, INSPECTION AND TESTING (elec. equip.)
Supervises and coordinates activities of workers engaged in inspecting and testing parts and subassemblies of electric motors and generators, such as armatures, stators, and field assemblies for conformance to specifications: Assigns workers to inspect parts for defects, such as improperly connected, broken, or cracked leads, surface defects on commutators, and for dimensional specifications of parts and subassemblies. Designates type of test, method and procedure, and equipment to be used in testing parts and subassemblies. Analyzes test data to diagnose cause of malfunctions and schedules repair of products not meeting specifications. Trains workers in use of testing equipment. Performs other duties as described under SUPERVISOR (any industry) Master Title. May be designated according to operation coordinated as Supervisor, Coil And Armature Inspection (elec. equip.); Supervisor, Electric Motor Testing (elec. equip.).
GOE: 06.02.01 STRENGTH: L GED: R4 M3 L3 SVP: 7 DLU: 77

721.261-010 ELECTRIC-MOTOR ANALYST (any industry)
Determines causes of failures in electric motors, following drawings and specifications and using handtools and electrical test meters: Dismantles motor, using handtools. Examines bearings, brackets, and other parts for wear and damage. Tests armature and stator for shorted, grounded, or broken wires, using electrical test meters. Lists causes of motor failures and repairs required and reports adjustment and repair requirements to repairer. May repair mechanical parts and reassemble motor, using handtools and power tools. May rebuild motor.
GOE: 05.07.02 STRENGTH: L GED: R4 M3 L2 SVP: 7 DLU: 77

721.261-014 FINAL TESTER (elec. equip.)
Conducts final test on electrical equipment, such as generators, motors, motor generator sets, switchgear, and control apparatus to determine conformity to specifications, using electrical testing equipment, measuring instruments, and mechanics' and electricians' handtools: Sets up test circuit by connecting unit to power supply, resistors, transformers, meters, and test panels in prescribed sequence. Operates and tests unit under specified conditions by moving levers, handwheels, knobs, and pushbuttons to apply prescribed voltages and current. Observes instruments, such as meters, tachometer, vibrometer, oscilloscope, thermometer, and potentiometer, and makes calculations, using slide rule, to determine resistance, starting torque heat, load, saturation, and other electrical characteristics. Observes and measures mechanical performance, such as ventilation, bearing noise, airgap, and end play, using micrometers, verniers, torsion meters, and other measuring and testing devices. Adjusts controls, such as resistors, relays, and circuit breakers to correct malfunctions. Records findings in test log and forwards findings to engineering department for analysis. May conduct dynamometer test on large motors and generators. May diagnose mechanical or electrical difficulties and suggest changes in design and operating function to engineering department. May mount units to test base.
GOE: 06.01.05 STRENGTH: M GED: R4 M3 L3 SVP: 7 DLU: 77

721.281-010 AUTOMOTIVE-GENERATOR-AND-STARTER REPAIRER (automotive ser.)
Tests, repairs, and rebuilds automotive generators and starters: Tests generator unit to ascertain amperage and voltage output, using voltmeter and ammeter. Disassembles unit and cleans brushes, bearings, shafts, and armatures in solvent and examines parts for wear or defects. Refaces commutator using lathe. Tests starter spring tension, using testing device. Replaces or repairs defective parts, and reinstalls generator in vehicle. Adjusts fan belt tension and voltage output. May charge or replace battery. May be designated according to part repaired as Automotive-Generator Repairer (automotive ser.); Automotive-Starter Repairer (automotive ser.).
GOE: 05.05.05 STRENGTH: M GED: R4 M3 L2 SVP: 6 DLU: 77

721.281-014 ELECTRIC-MOTOR ASSEMBLER AND TESTER (any industry) alternate titles: motor assembler
Assembles and adjusts repaired electric motors to meet specified ratings, using handtools and electrical meters: Cleans motor parts with gasoline. Repairs or replaces damaged parts and assembles motor, using handtools. Measures velocity, horsepower, and current consumption of motor, using electrical meters and mechanical testing devices. Adjusts motor to ratings specified on motor nameplate. May ream and fit motor bearings and grind, turn, and polish parts, using machine tools, such as grinder and lathe.
GOE: 06.02.23 STRENGTH: L GED: R4 M3 L2 SVP: 7 DLU: 77

721.281-018 ELECTRIC-MOTOR REPAIRER (any industry)
Repairs electric motors, generators, and equipment, such as starting devices and switches, following schematic drawings, and using handtools, coil-winding machines, power tools, and test equipment: Disassembles and removes armature, stator, or rotor from housing. Examines coil connections for broken or defective wiring. Tests coils, armatures, stator, rotor, and field coils for continuity, shorts, and grounds and insulation resistance, using test lamp, ammeter, and ohmmeter. Cuts out or removes defective coils and removes insulation from core slots. Cuts and forms insulation and inserts insulation into armature, rotor, or stator slots. Rewinds coils on core while in slots manually or makes replacement coils, using coil-winding machine. Installs and aligns prewound coils in slots, using hammer, drift, or mallet. Replaces defective coil leads and solders connections of coils in specified sequence. Examines bearings, shafts, and other moving parts for excessive wear or defects. Refaces commutators and machines parts to specified tolerances, using machine tools. Assembles and tests motor for specified performance. May be designated according to size of motor repaired as Fractional-Horsepower Motor Repairer (any industry); equipment repaired as Dynamotor Repairer (any industry); or part repaired as Armature Straightener (elec. equip.); Coil-Connector Repairer (elec. equip.); Commutator Repairer (any industry); Field-Coil Repairer (elec. equip.); Stator Repairer (any industry).
GOE: 05.05.10 STRENGTH: M GED: R4 M3 L3 SVP: 7 DLU: 77

721.281-022 MAGNETO REPAIRER (any industry)
Tests and repairs magnetos used in gasoline and diesel engines, using meters, gauges, and handtools: Connects magneto to motor and electrical test panel and starts motor to determine source of malfunction. Disassembles magneto and inspects coils, condenser, and armature for shorts. Repairs or replaces worn or defective parts, using handtools. Verifies polarity of armature. Cleans parts with alcohol or solvent and reassembles unit. Adjusts breaker points, using feeler gauge. Installs magneto in engine.

GOE: 05.05.05 STRENGTH: L GED: R4 M2 L2 SVP: 6 DLU: 77

721.281-026 PROPULSION-MOTOR-AND-GENERATOR REPAIRER (automotive ser.)
Reconditions defective motors and generators of electric buses: Lifts propulsion motors or generators onto worktable, using chain hoist. Disassembles defective units, using handtools. Inspects parts to determine required repairs. Repairs or replaces worn and defective parts, such as carbon brushes, cables, and connecting wires. Reassembles motors and generators. Tests circuitry, using testing lamp.
GOE: 05.05.10 STRENGTH: M GED: R4 M3 L2 SVP: 7 DLU: 77

721.281-030 TESTER, MOTORS AND CONTROLS (elec. equip.)
Tests endurance and performance of electric motors and electrical-control components, such as motor reversers, cam and unit switches, shunt contactors, and magnet valve adapters under simulated operating conditions, in laboratory or production areas, following specified procedures, using testing equipment: Positions motors or parts, such as switches, contacts, and magnetic cores on test rack, and connects leads to power source and test panels. Pulls switch to start equipment and regulates controls for prescribed timing, speeds, and voltages. Turns off lamps and moves rheostat controls of generators to adjust load resistance. Observes and adjusts measuring instruments, such as ammeters and voltmeters, in prescribed sequence, to measure electrical characteristics, such as blow-out, drop-out, pick-up, resistance, electrical stress, and iron content of cores. Examines parts for mechanical defects or failures. Records test data. May replace worn brushes on power supply generator. May be known according to item tested as Transformer Tester (elec. equip.).
GOE: 06.01.05 STRENGTH: M GED: R4 M3 L3 SVP: 6 DLU: 77

721.361-010 INSPECTOR, MOTORS AND GENERATORS (elec. equip.)
Examines electric motors, generators, and parts, such as coils, commutators, armatures, and stators, for compliance with specifications, using measuring devices and test equipment: Examines parts to detect defects, such as faulty insulation, broken wires, burrs, and nicks. Compares windings, soldered connections, and location of parts with schematics and blueprints to ensure compliance with specifications. Verifies dimensional specifications of parts and measures airgap between parts, using micrometers, verniers, calipers, and scale. Tests windings for resistance, shorts, and grounded wires, using testing apparatus. Tags rejected parts and assemblies for repair. Records inspection data.
GOE: 06.01.05 STRENGTH: M GED: R4 M3 L3 SVP: 7 DLU: 77

721.381-010 ELECTRIC-MOTOR FITTER (railroad equip.) alternate titles: car repairer; motor assembler; motor overhauler
Cleans, assembles, and tests motors of locomotives and streetcars: Disassembles motors by removing bolts and nuts from motor case heads, fastening crane hook to case heads and armatures, and directing HOISTING ENGINEER (any industry) to hoist parts from motor cases. Routes armatures to repair shop. Cleans case heads in hot ammonia bath. Scrapes inside of motor cases to remove grease and dirt, and applies insulating paint. Inspects motor lead wires and replaces worn insulation tape. Reassembles motors working with HOISTING ENGINEER (any industry) in handling heavy parts. Connects motor lead wires to power source and tests motor for r.p.m. and overheating, using speed gauges and thermometers.
GOE: 05.05.05 STRENGTH: L GED: R4 M2 L3 SVP: 7 DLU: 77

721.381-014 ELECTRIC-MOTOR-CONTROL ASSEMBLER (elec. equip.) alternate titles: control-panel assembler; panelboard assembler; power-panel assembler
Assembles electric-motor control units, such as transmitters, relays, switches, voltage controls, and starters and mounts units on panel according to drawings and specifications, using handtools and power tools: Cleans parts, using liquid cleaner, airhose, and cloth. Assembles units, using handtools, pneumatic nut runners, power press, and torque wrenches. Lays out and drills mounting holes and mounts units to panel, using scribers, rule, dividers, drill press, portable power drill, reamer, screwdrivers, and wrenches. Adjusts and aligns parts to maintain specified airgap, contact wipe, dimensions, and part movement, using feeler gauges and micrometers. Solders electric wire connections and secures spring guides, setscrews, and spring post to units, using soldering iron and acetylene torch. Tests electrical circuits for resistance, current, and potential difference, using instruments, such as ohmmeter, ammeter, and voltmeter. May be designated according to control assembled as Transmitter Assembler (elec. equip.); Voltage-Regulator Assembler (elec. equip.). May also operate sheet metal forming machines to fabricate housing for synchro-units and be designated Synchro-Unit Assembler (elec. equip.).
GOE: 06.01.04 STRENGTH: M GED: R4 M3 L2 SVP: 6 DLU: 77

721.381-018 GOVERNOR ASSEMBLER, HYDRAULIC (elec. equip.)
Assembles and adjusts mechanical and electrical parts to construct governors for hydraulic turbines, according to specifications, using pneumatic tools, handtools, gauges, and micrometers: Aligns motor mounts and motors on reservoir base and marks location. Removes motors and drills and taps foundation holes. Inserts steel pins in holes to secure motors to base. Positions mechanical parts, such as actuator, kaplan, oil basket, strainers, oil ramp, hydraulic cylinder, valves, and subassemblies to base and inside of reservoir, to form governor unit subassembly. Joins frame, doors, trim, and deck plates to assemble metal cabinet, using handtools. Attaches governor unit subassembly to cabinet frame. Assembles meters, gauges, indicators, switches, and control panels and mounts on unit. Shapes conduit for electrical lines and laces electrical cables,

using soldering iron to secure connections. Assembles pump and fits pipelines, valves, vents, and pressure lines, using plumbers' tools. Tests performance of completed unit for conformance to specifications. Disassembles unit and crates and wraps parts to prepare parts for shipping. Attaches name plates, marks, and other identification on items. May machine and fabricate parts to complete job when drawing changes occur.
GOE: 06.01.04 STRENGTH: M GED: R4 M3 L2 SVP: 7 DLU: 77

721.484-010 ELECTRIC-MOTOR WINDER (elec. equip.) alternate titles: armature-and-rotor winder; coil assembler
Assembles and tests electric motor and generator stators, armatures, or rotors: Inspects cores for defects and aligns laminations, using hammer and drift. Files burrs from core slots, using hand file, portable power file, and scraper. Lines slots with sheet insulation and inserts coils into slots. Cuts, strips, and bends wire leads at ends of coils, using pliers and wire scrapers. Twists leads together to connect coils. Taps coil and end windings to shape, using hammer and fiber block. Tests windings for motor-housing clearance, grounds, and short circuits, using clearance gauge, growler, spring-steel blade, telephone receiver, insulation tester, and resistance bridge. Winds new coils on armatures, stators, or rotors of used motors and generators. May rewind defective coils. May be designated according to motor part wound as Armature Winder (elec. equip.); Rotor Winder (elec. equip.); Stator Winder (elec. equip.).
GOE: 06.02.23 STRENGTH: M GED: R3 M2 L2 SVP: 6 DLU: 77

721.484-014 FIELD-RING ASSEMBLER (elec. equip.) alternate titles: assembler dc field ring; assembler dc field yoke; brush maker; carbon-brush maker; motor-and-generator-brush cutter
Assembles field poles and interpoles to steel housing ring (yoke) to build field rings for dc motors and generators: Slips insulated coils over pole piece and drives fiber spacing wedges between them. Bolts field poles and interpoles to inside face of yoke, adjusting airgap by measuring with micrometer and inserting shims. Lays out, cuts, drills, punches, and forms copper strap to connect coils of large units. Fastens coil connections with bolts.
GOE: 06.02.23 STRENGTH: M GED: R3 M2 L2 SVP: 6 DLU: 77

721.484-018 INSULATION CUTTER AND FORMER (elec. equip.)
Cuts and forms insulation, gaskets, and wedges used in electric motors and generators, performing any combination of following duties: Measures and marks dimensions and holes on insulation material, such as felt, fiber, mica, and fiberglass, using specifications or template. Places sheet of insulation against shearing machine stops, depresses pedal to lower blade to cut strips, or inserts sheet under roller-type holddown and against stops of circular saw to cut strips. Places cut material into bending machine and depresses pedal to rotate movable section around fixed mandrel to shape sides. Holds flat and wedge insulation against pedestal grinder to grind U-shaped bevel in end or inserts mica sheets between drums of drum sander to wear down to specified thickness. Measures thickness of each mica sheet, using micrometer, and stacks sheets according to dimensions. May cut shaped wooden or fiber strips to lengths for wedges, using bandsaw.
GOE: 06.02.32 STRENGTH: L GED: R3 M2 L2 SVP: 3 DLU: 77

721.484-022 SKEIN WINDER (elec. equip.)
Inserts loops of prewound skein of wire into slots of stators for fractional-horsepower motors: Loops skein end and inserts two sides in adjacent coil slots, manipulating wire with fingers. Forms additional loops in skein and inserts in other pairs of slots until entire skein is wound into core.
GOE: 06.02.32 STRENGTH: L GED: R3 M2 L2 SVP: 5 DLU: 77

721.684-010 ARMATURE-WINDER HELPER, REPAIR (any industry)
Assists ARMATURE WINDER, REPAIR (any industry) in repairing electric motors and generators: Burns old insulation from coils, using blowtorch, and strips old coils from armatures and stators, using handsaw and wirecutter. Scrubs mechanical parts of motors, such as shafts, gears, and laminations, using cleaning fluid, wire brush, and scraper. Guides compressed air stream on parts to dry and remove loose dirt. Winds coils, using coil winding machine. Tapes coils by hand or using machine. Dips armatures and stators in enamel or varnish tank to insulate coils and paints motor and generator housings, using brush. Performs other duties as described under HELPER (any industry) Master Title.
GOE: 05.12.16 STRENGTH: M GED: R2 M1 L1 SVP: 3 DLU: 77

721.684-014 ASSEMBLER, CARBON BRUSHES (elec. equip.)
Assembles carbon brushes by performing any of following tasks: Drills hole in precut carbon block, using drill press. Cuts copper wire to specified lengths, using hand shears. Positions and clamps block on workbench. Inserts wire into hole and wedges wire with copper pin, fastens wire with rivet or screw, or solders wire, using soldering iron. Attaches copper eyelet to free end of wire and solders eyelet to wire. Immerses brush in electroplating solution to cover brush with copper coating. Stamps manufacturer's name on brush, using die. May cut carbon to specified size.
GOE: 06.02.23 STRENGTH: L GED: R3 M1 L2 SVP: 4 DLU: 77

721.684-018 COIL CONNECTOR (elec. equip.) alternate titles: connector
Twists ends of coil wires together to connect prewound coils of electric motor and generator parts, such as stators, rotors, and armatures, using soldering equipment and handtools: Lifts or hoists unit with crane to workbench or winding buck. Pounds coils, using hammer, block, and drift to compact and align coils in slots and form leads on strap coils. Cuts protruding insulating material, skins ends of coil wire, and splices lead connections of stator coils, using

pliers. Places leads of armature coils into commutator bar slots and secures leads, using drift and hammer. Brazes or pours molten solder over connections, using brazing torch or soldering pot and ladle. Tapes connections, and laces and ties coil leads to stator end windings or commutator risers, using tape hook [LACER AND TIER (elec. equip.)]. May test unit for short circuit, grounds, and weak insulation. May be known according to motor part connected as Armature Connector (elec. equip.) I; Stator Connector (elec. equip.).
GOE: 06.02.32 STRENGTH: M GED: R3 M2 L2 SVP: 5 DLU: 77

721.684-022 ELECTRIC-MOTOR ASSEMBLER (elec. equip.) alternate titles: assembler; assembly hand
Assembles subassemblies and parts of dynamotors, converters, and electric motors used in instruments, appliances, and power tools, performing any combination of following tasks, using power tools and handtools: Bolts field windings and brush holders into motor housings, using wrenches, screwdrivers, and holding fixtures. Presses bushings and bearings into motor head, using arbor press. Secures fans and gears to armature shaft, using nuts and lock washers, and places armature shaft in bearings. Solders or screws electrical leads to brushes, and switch and cord assembly, using soldering iron. Assembles end brackets and base to housing and fastens assembly with screws. Lubricates gears and other moving parts, using oilcan, paddle, or grease gun. Turns shaft to ensure free movement of parts. May screw covers on motor ends to keep out dirt and moisture during shipment. When replacing defective parts in motors is designated Repairer, Electric Motor (elec. equip.). May be designated according to type motor assembled as Assembbler, Instrument Motors (elec. equip.) or part assembled as Brush-Holder Assembler (elec. equip.).
GOE: 06.04.23 STRENGTH: L GED: R2 M1 L2 SVP: 3 DLU: 77

721.684-026 SPIDER ASSEMBLER (elec. equip.) alternate titles: assembler, caterpillar spider; revolving field assembler; rotating field assembler
Assembles coils, poles, and fastening devices to rotor spider to build rotating field for motors and alternators (generators): Aligns poles on spider and secures with nuts and lockwashers. Slips coil over insulated core (pole) and bolts pole shoe in place over coil and pole piece. Drills and taps holes to fasten clamps with bolts to secure connecting cable between coils. Secures collector rings to shaft, using keys, bolts, and washers or presses rings to shaft, using hydraulic press, or heats rings, using portable gas oven and allows to shrink. May cut, drill, and form copper and steel bar stock for leads and clamps, using electric drill, power saw, and forming fixture.
GOE: 06.02.23 STRENGTH: M GED: R4 M2 L2 SVP: 6 DLU: 77

721.687-010 CLEANER AND PREPARER (elec. equip.)
Cleans and applies paint and masking materials on motor and generator subassemblies to preserve surface for further processing: Brushes solvents onto parts or dips parts into caustic solutions to loosen paint, grease, dirt, and other foreign substances. Rinses parts with hot water. Removes loosened paint, using scraper, wire brush, or portable buffer. Brushes grease and masking compound on subassemblies, inserts cork plugs into holes, and tightens screws to keep insulating material or paint from specified areas. Coats parts with paint or insulating material, using spray gun or dipping tank.
GOE: 06.04.33 STRENGTH: M GED: R1 M1 L1 SVP: 2 DLU: 77

722 OCCUPATIONS IN ASSEMBLY AND REPAIR OF COMMUNICATIONS EQUIPMENT

This group includes occupations concerned with assembling and repairing wire and wireless telephone and telegraph equipment and parts, radio and television broadcasting equipment and parts, electronic field detection apparatus, light and heat emission operating apparatus, object detection apparatus and navigational electronic equipment, aircraft and missile control systems, electronic data processing equipment, and electronic and electric communication and signaling products.

722.131-010 INSTRUMENT-SHOP SUPERVISOR (tel. & tel.)
Supervises and coordinates activities of INSTRUMENT REPAIRERS (tel. & tel.) in repair and maintenance of telephone and telegraphic equipment: Examines and tests equipment, such as telephones, teletypewriters, station and switching apparatus, private-branch-exchange systems, and perforation equipment to determine repairs required, using electrical and electronic testing devices. Assigns workers to repair tasks. Supervises final inspection of equipment to ensure conformance to specifications. May be designated according to type of equipment maintained as Communications-Equipment Supervisor (tel. & tel.); Telegraphic-Instrument Supervisor (tel. & tel.); Telephone-Instrument Supervisor (tel. & tel.). Performs other duties as described under SUPERVISOR (any industry) Master Title.
GOE: 05.05.10 STRENGTH: L GED: R4 M2 L3 SVP: 7 DLU: 77

722.281-010 INSTRUMENT REPAIRER (tel. & tel.) alternate titles: shop repairer
Repairs, tests, and modifies telephone and telegraphic equipment, such as telephones, teletypewriters, tickers, and switchboards, using handtools and power tools: Adjusts component parts of equipment, such as dials, coin tracks, springs, and relays to conform to specifications. Verifies wiring and location of parts, using schematic drawings. Tests and calibrates reassembled equipment, using electrical testing devices, such as ohmmeter and circuit analyzers. Rewires and modifies equipment in accordance with engineering changes and traf-

fic-handling requirements. Cleans instruments and parts, using specified solvents. Maintains daily record of instruments and equipment repaired. May assist in sorting, cataloging, and storing repaired parts and equipment.
GOE: 05.05.10 STRENGTH: M GED: R4 M3 L3 SVP: 7 DLU: 77

722.381-010 ASSEMBLER (tel. & tel.) alternate titles: assembler, equipment; wirer
Wires switchboards, operating tables, and other telegraph apparatus to specifications, using handtools and soldering iron. May test wiring installations, using meters.
GOE: 06.01.04 STRENGTH: L GED: R4 M3 L3 SVP: 7 DLU: 77

722.381-014 INSTRUMENT INSPECTOR (aircraft mfg.; air trans.)
Inspects, tests, and adjusts navigational and control instruments and components for aircraft and aerospace vehicles, according to blueprints, technical orders, manufacturers' data, and other specifications, using precision measuring instruments and testing equipment: Examines instruments and components for defects, such as broken dials and scratched surfaces. Tests functional and operational performance of instruments and components, such as altimeters, airspeed indicators, turn and bank indicators, radar beacon sets, and directional gyroscopes, to determine conformance to specifications, using testing equipment. Inspects, calibrates, and adjusts instruments and components, using precision instruments. Records inspection information. May contact vendors, customers, or others to exchange information or coordinate inspection activities. May interpret inspection information and recommend corrective action for recurring instrumentation problems. May be required to maintain Federal Aviation Administration certification to repair and adjust instruments. May be designated according to type of instruments inspected as Inspector, Radar And Electronics (aircraft mfg.).
GOE: 06.01.05 STRENGTH: M GED: R4 M4 L3 SVP: 7 DLU: 88

722.687-010 SWITCHBOX ASSEMBLER I (comm. equip.)
Inserts metal dovetails of box sides into slots of metal box bottoms, and hammers to clamp parts together to form switchboxes for telephones.
GOE: 06.04.23 STRENGTH: L GED: R1 M1 L1 SVP: 2 DLU: 77

723 OCCUPATIONS IN ASSEMBLY AND REPAIR OF ELECTRICAL APPLIANCES AND FIXTURES

This group includes occupations concerned with assembly and repair of small appliances, such as toasters, grills, mixers, and coffee makers; lighting fixtures; and cord sets, switches, sockets, and related products.

723.131-010 SUPERVISOR, SMALL APPLIANCE ASSEMBLY (house. appl.) alternate titles: supervisor, assembly line
Supervises and coordinates activities of workers engaged in assembly, inspection, testing, repair, and packing of toasters, irons, percolators, and related small electrical appliances: Reviews inspection and test reports to determine causes of appliance defects, such as motors heating up, insufficient revolution per minute, and short and grounded circuits. Performs other duties as described under SUPERVISOR (any industry) Master Title.
GOE: 06.02.01 STRENGTH: L GED: R4 M3 L3 SVP: 7 DLU: 77

723.132-010 SUPERVISOR, FABRICATION DEPARTMENT (light. fix.)
Supervises and coordinates activities of workers engaged in fabricating and assembling wall lamps, floor lamps, and hanging fixtures. Requisitions parts and materials according to design sketches and knowledge of fixture making. Trains workers in operation of equipment. Performs other duties as described under SUPERVISOR (any industry) Master Title.
GOE: 06.02.01 STRENGTH: L GED: R4 M3 L3 SVP: 8 DLU: 77

723.361-010 MODEL MAKER, FLUORESCENT LIGHTING (light. fix.)
Lays out and constructs experimental models of fluorescent lighting fixtures, such as those used in buildings and tunnels, following blueprints, designs, and engineering sketches: Computes dimensions and lays out outline of fixture on sheet metal, using rule, scribe, and drafting tools. Cuts and shapes metal, using hand and power brakes and shears, files, and mallets. Assembles fixture and installs electrical components and wiring, using spot-welding machine and handtools. Fastens glass or plastic lens in place, using clips, bolts, or screws, and tightens fluorescent tube in sockets. Connects fixture to electrical outlet and tests continuity of fixture's circuit, using circuit tester. Records dimensions, bending angles, hole locations, and other specifications, for use in production of fixture. May inspect installed fixtures and make minor repairs.
GOE: 05.05.06 STRENGTH: M GED: R4 M3 L3 SVP: 7 DLU: 77

723.381-010 ELECTRICAL-APPLIANCE REPAIRER (any industry) alternate titles: appliance-service representative; small-appliance repairer
Repairs electrical appliances, such as toasters, cookers, percolators, lamps, and irons, using handtools and electrical testing instruments: Examines appliance for mechanical defects and disassembles appliance. Tests wiring for broken or short circuits, using voltmeters, ohmmeters, and other circuit testers. Replaces defective wiring and parts, such as toaster elements and percolator coils, using handtools, soldering iron, and spot-welding equipment. May compute charges for labor and materials. May assist ELECTRICAL-APPLIANCE SERVICER (any industry) in repairing such appliances as refrigerators and stoves.
GOE: 05.10.03 STRENGTH: L GED: R4 M2 L3 SVP: 6 DLU: 77

723.381-014 VACUUM CLEANER REPAIRER (any industry)
Repairs and adjusts vacuum cleaners, using handtools: Observes ammeter reading and listens to sound of cleaner motor to detect cause of faulty operation. Repairs, adjusts, or replaces defective brushes, belts, fans, control switches, extension cords, electric motors, or other mechanical or electrical parts, using handtools. Lubricates cleaner parts, using grease gun. May sell and demonstrate vacuum cleaners.
GOE: 05.10.03 STRENGTH: M GED: R3 M2 L2 SVP: 6 DLU: 77

723.584-010 APPLIANCE REPAIRER (house. appl.) alternate titles: repairer
Repairs portable, household electrical appliances, such as fans, heaters, vacuum cleaners, toasters, and flatirons, on assembly line: Refers to inspector's checklist, or defect-symbol marked on appliance, to identify defective or malfunctioning part. Disassembles appliance to remove defective part, using power screwdrivers, soldering iron, and handtools. Installs new part, and reassembles appliance. Records nature of repair in log or on mechanical counting device. Maintains stock of replacement parts. May determine repair requirements by connecting appliance to power source or examining parts for defects while disassembling. May file or bend parts to remove burrs or to improve alignment and fit. May hold appliance against buffing or polishing wheel to remove scratches from metal surfaces. May touch up paint defects, using brush or spray gun. May be designated according to part repaired as Heating-Element Repairer (house. appl.); or appliance repaired as Electric-Frying-Pan Repairer (house. appl.); Food-Mixer Repairer (house. appl.); Toaster-Element Repairer (house. appl.); Vacuum-Cleaner Repairer (house. appl.).
GOE: 05.10.03 STRENGTH: M GED: R3 M2 L2 SVP: 3 DLU: 77

723.684-010 ASSEMBLER (house. appl.)
Assembles parts and subassemblies to form portable electrical appliances, power tools, and other products, using fixtures, handtools, and power tools: Inserts screws, bolts, or rivets through holes in parts or subassemblies and tightens fasteners to secure components, such as field windings, fan blades, pulleys, heating elements, thermostats, switches, and timers, using handtools and power tools. Reams bearing holes in housing assembly, using hand reamer, and places armature shaft in bearings of product. Turns setscrew to adjust end play of motor. Hooks lug ends of wires to terminals, tightens bolts, or solders connection to fasten instruments with burner, motor, or outlet cord. May be designated according to product assembled as Deep-Fryer Assembler (house. appl.); Electric-Fan Assembler (house. appl.); Electric-Heater Assembler (house. appl.); Food-Mixer Assembler (house. appl.); Power-Tool Assembler (house. appl.); Steam-Iron Assembler (house. appl.).
GOE: 06.04.23 STRENGTH: L GED: R2 M2 L2 SVP: 3 DLU: 77

723.684-014 ASSEMBLER I (light. fix.) alternate titles: lamp wirer
Assembles component parts to make subassemblies or completed units of lighting fixtures, such as chandeliers, lamps, shades, or reflectors: Threads and pulls wire through lighting fixture body or frame. Strips insulation from ends of wire and attaches ends to terminal or socket lugs, using knife, pliers or stripping tool, and screwdriver. Bolts or screws wired parts together, using screwdriver and other handtools. Inserts incandescent bulb or fluorescent tube into fixture and connects wire to electrical outlet to test unit. May be designated according to type of fixture assembled as Assembler, Fluorescent Lights (light. fix.); Assembler, Incandescent Lights (light. fix.).
GOE: 06.02.23 STRENGTH: L GED: R3 M2 L2 SVP: 3 DLU: 77

723.684-018 ASSEMBLER II (light. fix.)
Assembles metal lighting fixtures, using handtools and drill press: Screws together threaded parts by hand. Bores holes in fixtures, using drill press. Fastens together parts with bolts or screws by hand, or using tools, such as wrenches and screwdrivers. Inserts wire into fixture. May work from blueprints or sketches.
GOE: 06.04.23 STRENGTH: L GED: R2 M1 L2 SVP: 2 DLU: 77

723.684-022 FLASHER ADJUSTER (light. fix.)
Tests and adjusts flasher units used in automobile directional signals, using chuck, meter, and handtools: Inserts flasher into socket of chuck. Observes reading on meter and bends frame of flasher, using pliers, until meter reading is accurate.
GOE: 06.03.02 STRENGTH: L GED: R2 M1 L1 SVP: 2 DLU: 77

723.685-010 HEATING-ELEMENT WINDER (elec. equip.; house. appl.)
Tends machine that winds spiral-spring resistance wire onto mica-plate core to form heating element: Inserts core in slotted shaft of winding motor, and hooks wire end to core. Depresses pedal to start motor that rotates core, and guides wire between thumb and fingers to seat turns of wire in slots at edge of mica plate. Controls core-rotation speed by pressure of hand on brake wheel attached to motor shaft, and stops motor when end of wire is reached. May test heating element, using ohmmeter.
GOE: 06.04.20 STRENGTH: L GED: R2 M1 L1 SVP: 3 DLU: 77

723.687-010 PATCHER (house. appl.)
Covers wired electrical appliance components, such as thermostats used in heating pads, with insulating fabric: Tears piece of adhesive from dispenser roll, and places adhesive on workbench. Positions thermostat on fabric and arranges lead wires to prevent strain on soldered connections. Folds and seals fabric over thermostat, using fingers. May touch lead wires to test terminals and observe signal light to verify wiring continuity.

GOE: 06.04.34 STRENGTH: S GED: R2 M1 L1 SVP: 2 DLU: 77

723.687-014 TESTER AND INSPECTOR, LAMPS (light. fix.)
Inspects and tests lamps after assembly to determine if they are in satisfactory condition: Plugs lamp into electric outlet and turns on switch. Touches metal parts of lamp with exposed ends of live testing wires for indication of short circuit. Inserts metal test rod into lamp socket and touches contact point to ascertain continuity of circuit. Affixes gummed inspection ticket on each lamp found to be satisfactory.
GOE: 06.03.02 STRENGTH: L GED: R2 M1 L2 SVP: 2 DLU: 77

723.687-018 TESTER, WASTE DISPOSAL LEAKAGE (house. appl.)
Tests household waste disposal units for leaks, using air pressure device: Places unit on test stand and pulls lever to secure unit in place. Attaches airhose and fills unit with air. Observes warning light which indicates leakage. Places defective units on bench for rework. Hangs acceptable units on overhead conveyor.
GOE: 06.03.02 STRENGTH: L GED: R2 M2 L2 SVP: 3 DLU: 77

723.687-022 WIPER (light. fix.)
Cleans copper or brass lamp components and assemblies to remove excess paint or smudge, using cloth and solvent: Removes tape around edges or rims of lamps, using wiper and solvent. Dips cloth into solvent and wipes around unpainted areas of lamp component or assembly. Stacks parts or lamps for removal to lacquering section.
GOE: 06.04.39 STRENGTH: L GED: R2 M1 L1 SVP: 2 DLU: 77

724 OCCUPATIONS IN WINDING AND ASSEMBLING COILS, MAGNETS, ARMATURES, AND RELATED PRODUCTS

This group includes occupations concerned with cutting, winding, taping, forming, stripping, connecting, and soldering wire to fabricate, assemble, and repair coils, magnets, armatures, and related products.

724.130-010 SUPERVISOR, ELECTRONIC COILS (elec. equip.; electron. comp.)
Supervises and coordinates activities of workers engaged in winding, assembling, and testing electronic inductor devices, such as coils, filters, and transformers: Analyzes production schedule to plan assignments for section and assigns duties to workers. Examines product for conformance to manufacturing and quality standards. Demonstrates method and sequence for performing duties, and trains workers in operation and control of machines and equipment. Initiates or recommends personnel actions, such as hiring, transferring, promoting, or disciplining. Maintains records and prepares cost, yield and breakage, and maintenance reports. Inventories and requisitions tools, equipment, and supplies for department activities. May be required to set up, adjust, and repair machines and equipment. May be designated according to product assembled or activity involved, as Supervisor, Coil Winding (elec. equip.; electron. comp.); Supervisor, Filter Assembly (elec. equip.; electron. comp); Supervisor, Test and Inspection (elec. equip.; electron. comp.).
GOE: 06.01.01 STRENGTH: L GED: R4 M3 L4 SVP: 8 DLU: 87

724.131-010 SUPERVISOR, COIL WINDING (elec. equip.) alternate titles: armature-and-field-assembly supervisor
Supervises and coordinates activities of workers engaged in winding electric motors and generators: Plans and schedules department activities, utilizing knowledge of motor controls, winding machine operations, insulation characteristics, and types of windings. Plans and inspects machine adjustments. Assigns duties to utilize available machines to complete job order according to specifications, such as number of pieces, number of turns, size of coils or armatures, and type of wire. Schedules dipping and baking of coils and coil assemblies to group products requiring identical insulation and baking time. Adjusts work procedure for inserting prewound coils into rotors and stators, connecting coil groups, and testing wound assembly to utilize abilities of available workers. Performs other duties as described under SUPERVISOR (any industry) Master Title.
GOE: 06.02.01 STRENGTH: L GED: R4 M3 L3 SVP: 7 DLU: 77

724.131-014 TRANSFORMER SHOP SUPERVISOR (any industry)
Supervises and coordinates activities of TRANSFORMER REPAIRERS (any industry) and other workers engaged in testing and repairing distribution, street light, and instrument transformers. Trains new employees. Performs duties as described under SUPERVISOR (any industry) Master Title.
GOE: 05.05.10 STRENGTH: L GED: R4 M3 L3 SVP: 7 DLU: 77

724.281-010 TRANSFORMER TESTER (utilities)
Tests insulation, current resistance, loss of current, and performance of transformers and tests insulating strength of transformer oil, using electrical testing mechanisms: Attaches transformer wires to terminal board mounting various testing meters and to live wire for energizing transformer. Adjusts testing-meter indicators at settings governed by test to be made and volt specifications on transformer tested, employing extensive knowledge of transformers. Successively turns switches which control transmission of current through transformer to testing meters, such as voltmeter, ammeter, and ohmmeter, for testing insulation, resistance, and loss of current. Notes action of circuit breaker which automatically stops flow of current if transformer does not react correctly to test

applied. Tests insulating strength of transformer oil by passing current through oil sample placed in box containing two electrodes. Notes whether current will break down oil, causing arc between electrodes, actuating dielectric meter and indicating oil is of insufficient insulating strength. Tests fuse strength by regulating switch and sending excessive current through transformer. Diagnoses transformer defects and routes rejected transformers for repairs.
GOE: 06.01.05 STRENGTH: M GED: R4 M3 L3 SVP: 7 DLU: 77

724.360-010 SET-UP MECHANIC, COIL-WINDING MACHINES (elec. equip.)
Sets up, adjusts, and maintains machines used to wind, tape, form, strip, or connect wire for electrical coils, using setup charts and handtools: Changes fixtures in automatic coil-winding machines and core-insulating machines, replaces wire supply, and threads wire or insulating paper through tension devices to accommodate different size coils and windings. Turns screws and knobs to adjust settings of electrical switches and counters in automatic armature-and-field-coil-winding machines, using wrenches and screwdriver. Tightens bolts to align pulleys and adjust belt tension. Removes winding jaws from automatic winding machines and holds against powered buffing wheel to smooth surfaces, using *lapping compound*. Changes forming dies and holding devices in coil forming presses and changes cutting blades in wire-stripping machine to accommodate different sizes of wire. Replaces defective parts. Operates power grinder to make specialty tools used in winding department, such as picks, winding hooks, and scrapers.
GOE: 06.01.02 STRENGTH: M GED: R4 M3 L4 SVP: 6 DLU: 87

724.362-010 WIRE COILER (house. appl.)
Sets up and operates wire-coiling machine to coil wire for electrical appliance heating element: Selects wire of specified thickness. Bolts coiling disks to machine to make coils of specified size. Positions electric eye to activate automatic cutting mechanism, allowing for trimming of coil ends, using handtools. Threads wire through guides and between disks and starts machine. Hangs coil of each run to contacts of testing device, pulls switch, and reads watt and voltage input on meters. Resets electric eye, changes disks, or threads different gauge wire into machine to correct discrepancies. May cut wire at end of coil, using wire snips, watching meter for desired length. May use wire-cutting-and-stripping machine [LEAD FORMER (elec. equip.) 691.685-018].
GOE: 06.02.02 STRENGTH: L GED: R3 M2 L3 SVP: 5 DLU: 77

724.364-010 WINDING INSPECTOR AND TESTER (elec. equip.)
Performs any combination of following tasks to inspect and test stators, armatures, or rotors wound with prewound coils, using electrical testing equipment: Tests armatures, rotors, or stators for misconnected leads and insulation breakdown, using oscilloscope or test panel. Determines test hook-up from work ticket and connects coded stator leads to test clips. Turns dials to select specified voltage and current. Closes circuit and observes meter reading or oscillograph pattern. Interprets readings and patterns and records data. Touches one lead from high voltage source to stator or armature core and other lead to each coil lead in stator or armature. Watches for spark which indicates grounded circuit. Places spring steel blade of growler against inside face of stator or drum of armature and rotates over circumference. Observes steel blade for vibration which indicates shorted coils. Inspects lead and end windings for mechanical damage and conformance to specifications, using gauge, rule, or template to measure length and shape. Taps steel die to stamp code on core, using hammer. May inspect alignment of stacked commutators. May bunch and wrap stator leads to protect them until further assembly. May be designated according to item tested and inspected as Armature Tester (elec. equip.) III; Inspector And Shaper, End Windings (elec. equip.); Stator Tester (elec. equip.).
GOE: 06.03.01 STRENGTH: L GED: R3 M2 L2 SVP: 4 DLU: 77

724.381-010 ADJUSTER, ELECTRICAL CONTACTS (elec. equip.)
Adjusts contacts and springs of electrical apparatus, such as relays and switches, to permit opening and closing of circuits and flow of current: Examines apparatus for defects, such as damaged coil cover, bent springs and contacts, misaligned armatures and contacts, and missing parts. Verifies clearance and tension of parts, using feeler and tension gauges and shadowgraph. Turns dials of test equipment to specified settings. Positions apparatus in holding fixture, shadowgraph, or test board and presses control buttons to activate test equipment. Observes meters and lights on test equipment to determine factors, such as amperage required to close contacts, operating sequence and release timing of contacts, and electrical continuity. May verify mechanical operation of apparatus by manipulating apparatus with fingers. Bends parts, such as armature, contacts, and tension springs, to assure apparatus operates as specified, using handtools. Stamps and sorts defective and adjusted apparatus into stock pans for repair or further processing. May be designated according to type of apparatus adjusted as Crossbar-Switch Adjuster (elec. equip.); Relay Adjuster (elec. equip.); Switch Adjuster (elec. equip.); Wire-Spring-Relay Adjuster (elec. equip.). May verify adjustment of relays on sample basis and be designated Relay Checker (elec. equip.). May adjust fluorescent lamp starters and be designated Starter Adjuster (light. fix.).
GOE: 05.10.03 STRENGTH: L GED: R3 M2 L2 SVP: 6 DLU: 77

724.381-014 COIL WINDER, REPAIR (any industry)
Winds coils for repair of electric motor and generator parts, such as rotors, stators, and armatures, using original winding as guide to determine number of turns and size of wire: Winds coil on machine or directly into slots of rotors, stators, and armatures or pounds heavy copper over template to form coils. Op-

erates coil spreading machine to shape rigid coils for placement into slots. Tends coil taping machine or winds tape around coils by hand to insulate coils. Cuts and forms sheet insulation to fit slots, using paper cutter and forming fixture. Inserts coils into slots and pounds, using mallet and block, to compress and shape windings. Twists coil leads together to form groups of coils according to original winding and solders connections, using soldering iron. May paint coils with insulating varnish or enamel. May be designated according to coil wound as Field-Coil Winder (any industry).
GOE: 06.02.32 STRENGTH: L GED: R3 M2 L2 SVP: 5 DLU: 77

724.381-018 TRANSFORMER REPAIRER (any industry) alternate titles: transformer assembler; transformer rebuilder
Cleans and repairs distribution, streetlight, and instrument transformers: Disassembles transformers, using handtools, and opens valve to drain oil. Boils metal transformer case and cover in chemical solution to remove grease, rinses with hose, and dries with cloth to remove dirt and oil. Reassembles transformer, replacing worn or defective parts, using handtools. Solders input and output wires in position and pours compound in transformer-case terminal openings to seal out moisture. Pours oil into transformer until coils are submerged.
GOE: 05.10.03 STRENGTH: M GED: R3 M2 L2 SVP: 7 DLU: 77

724.384-010 ARMATURE TESTER I (elec. equip.) alternate titles: tester, armature or fields; rotor-and-armature bander
Tests armatures and field assemblies for motors to locate short, open, or grounded circuits, using electrical test apparatus that shows defects on panel meters or oscillograph patterns: Places armature in fixture equipped with brush contactors or touches test prods to commutator bars to make bar-to-bar and similar tests. Compares meter readings with fixed calibration on meter to determine shorts, opens, and grounds. Connects master unit, such as armature or field assembly, to terminals of winding tester. Looks into oscilloscope to compare test pattern of each unit tested with master unit. Turns dials to create different test situations and recognizes differences from master pattern. Inspects unit for mechanical defects. Scrapes chips and dirt from commutator slots, using brush and pick. Records quantity and classification of rejects and total number tested. May replace and revarnish string bands, reconnect leads, and resolder connections to repair armatures.
GOE: 05.10.03 STRENGTH: L GED: R3 M2 L2 SVP: 4 DLU: 77

724.384-014 STATIC BALANCER (any industry)
Tests products, such as armatures, fans, and rotors for balance, using static balancer, and adds or removes metal from product to correct imbalance: Rolls parts on two parallel, level, knife edges or rotates part on two pairs of overlapping, narrow, faced rollers and observes point of rest. Removes excess metal from heavy areas, using drill press, bench grinder, chisel and hammer, or files. Adds rivets, washers, or metal wedges to light areas, using handtools to correct balance. May attach parts to mandrel for balancing. May be designated according to part balanced as Armature Balancer (elec. equip.); Fan Balancer (elec. equip.); Rotor Balancer (elec. equip.).
GOE: 06.03.01 STRENGTH: M GED: R3 M2 L2 SVP: 3 DLU: 77

724.684-010 ARMATURE BANDER (any industry)
Winds steel wire around coil slots in armature core to hold coils in position when armature rotates, using banding machine: Lifts or hoists armature to horizontal spindle of banding machine. Shapes exposed parts of coils to specified size, using rawhide hammer. Mounts spool of specified wire and threads wire through guides of machine. Wraps sheet of insulation around core and attaches wire to pin wedged in core or twists first turn around armature, using pliers. Inserts metal clips under wire and turns crank to rotate armature or starts machine that winds wire around armature. Guides wire manually or mechanically to maintain tension. Turns ends of metal clips over wire and solders to hold wires in place. Solders armature leads to commutator and caps riser, using electric soldering iron. May shape coils [COIL SHAPER (any industry)].
GOE: 06.02.24 STRENGTH: M GED: R3 M2 L2 SVP: 5 DLU: 77

724.684-014 ARMATURE CONNECTOR II (elec. equip.)
Inserts lead wires of armature coils into commutator slots to connect armature to commutator. Places armature in holding fixture on workbench and strips insulation from ends of coil wires, using wire scraper or knife. Bends wire leads to conform with curvature of armature and inserts leads into commutator slots, using handtools. Winds and ties cord around coil leads to hold in specified commutator slots. Cuts excess wire from leads, using wirecutter or scissors. May shape end windings, using hammer and fiber block. May test connected armatures by touching contact points to test light. May repair connections by splicing, reconnecting, or reinsulating wires. May dip commutator into solder pot to solder wires into commutator slots. May press commutator on armature shaft, using arbor press. May be designated according to coil leads connected as Primary Connector, Armature (elec. equip.); Secondary Connector, Armature (elec. equip.).
GOE: 06.04.23 STRENGTH: L GED: R2 M2 L2 SVP: 3 DLU: 86

724.684-018 ARMATURE WINDER, REPAIR (any industry) alternate titles: armature repairer
Winds new coils on armatures of used generators and motors: Cuts insulating material to fit slots on armature core. Places insulating material in bottom of core slots. Cuts wire to length and winds in place, or counts turns of wire in coil being replaced and winds on corresponding number. Occasionally inserts and hammers readymade coils in place. May test armatures, solder ends of coils to commutator segments, wind field coils, test motors for defects, and perform

other duties pertaining to motor repairing. May wind new coils on armatures for use in motor vehicles and be designated Armature Winder, Automotive (automotive ser.).
GOE: 06.02.24 STRENGTH: L GED: R3 M2 L2 SVP: 4 DLU: 77

724.684-022 COIL SHAPER (any industry) alternate titles: coil spreader
Spreads and shapes coils to fit armature, rotor, and stator slots, using coil-spreading machine: Moves levers and handwheels to position side clamps, end clamps, spreader bars, or forming blocks which set specified span and angle of knuckle. Places coil in clamp holders and closes clamps, using hand lever. Depresses pedal or pulls levers to spread and shape coils. Aligns and curves coil ends, using rawhide hammer. Releases hand clamps, removes coils, and verifies dimensions of coil, using rule or template.
GOE: 06.02.24 STRENGTH: L GED: R3 M2 L2 SVP: 5 DLU: 77

724.684-026 COIL WINDER (elec. equip.; electron. comp.)
Winds coils used in electrical equipment and instruments, or as electronic components, according to wiring diagrams, sample coil, or work order, using coil-winding machines and handtools: Reviews wiring diagrams and work order or examines sample coil to ascertain type and size of wire specified, and type, size, length, circumference, and primary and secondary windings of coil to be wound. Selects coil-forming device for specified coil and fastens device onto machine arbor, mandrel, or spindle or fastens device between chuck and tail stock. Threads end of wire from reel through tension device, guides, and spreader, bends wire ends to form lead, and attaches lead to coil core. Turns setscrews to adjust tension on wire and sets counter for number of turns specified. Starts machine and manually feeds wire over coil core or spreader to obtain even and uniform winding and shape of coil. Observes counter and stops machine at specified number of coils. Wraps insulation between layers and around wound coil or inserts plastic blocks between turns to form cooling ducts. Cuts wire to form leads, using wire or bolt cutters. Pounds coil with hammer or mallet to shape end windings or remove coil from fixtures. Winds asbestos, cotton, glass mica, paper, or tape around coil, and brushes varnish on coil or dips coil in varnish, epoxy, or wax to reinforce and seal coil. Strips insulation from end of lead wires, threads lead wires through insulating sleeves or slides sleeves over leads, and solders lead wires to terminals. May test coils for winding continuity, using test lamp. May cut and form insulating materials and be known as Insulator Cutter And Former (elec. equip.); or insert insulation in core slots and be known as Insulator (elec. equip.). May wind heavy ribbon, strap, or round wire over fixture to form coil and be designated Coil Former, Template (elec. equip.); Coil Winder, Open Slot (elec. equip.); Coil Winder, Strap (elec. equip.). May be designated according to type of coil wound or work station as Armature Coil Winder (elec. equip.); Audio-Coil Winder (electron. comp.); Bender, Armature Coil (elec. equip.); Bobbin-Coil Winder (electron. comp.); Coil Finisher (elec. equip.; electron. comp.); Coil Taper (elec. equip.). May be designated: Coil Winder, Hand (electron. comp.); Field-Coil Winder (elec. equip.); Filament-Coil Winder (electron. comp.); Helix-Coil Winder (elec. equip.; electron. comp.); Resistor Winder (elec. equip.; electron. comp.); Transformer-Coil Winder (elec. equip.; electron. comp.).
GOE: 06.04.23 STRENGTH: L GED: R2 M2 L2 SVP: 4 DLU: 88

724.684-030 COMMUTATOR ASSEMBLER (elec. equip.) alternate titles: commutator presser; regulator assembler; swedger
Fabricates and undercuts commutators for electric motors and generators, using stacking and holding fixtures, handtools, metalworking machines, and measuring devices: Cuts copper bars of specified thickness into designated lengths and widths, and cuts sheet mica into separators, sleeves, and collars, using power saw. Stacks bars, separated by mica inserts, in stacking sleeve and aligns bars, using dial indicator and mallet. Places bar and mica assembly in fixture and presses assembly together, using hydraulic press. Heats assembly in oven to soften insulation and presses heated assembly to specified circumference, using press. Positions mica collars at ends of bar assembly, and if V-ring is used, presses ring against collar, using arbor press. Secures assembly with bolts and nuts or threaded ring, using wrenches or hammer and drift. Mounts assembly in *indexing* fixture on circular saw or slotting machine, and undercuts mica or slots commutator risers to specified depth. Removes burrs, chips, and foreign matter from commutator, using picks, knives, cloths, solvent, or compressed air. Connects leads to power source for testing commutator. Touches leads from bars onto steel frame to ensure that commutator is not grounded or shorted. May braze or solder resistor or capacitor leads to commutator. May be designated according to operation performed as Commutator Undercutter (elec. equip.); Commutator V-Ring Assembler (elec. equip.).
GOE: 06.02.24 STRENGTH: M GED: R3 M2 L2 SVP: 5 DLU: 77

724.684-034 MAGNET-VALVE ASSEMBLER (elec. equip.)
Fits together bushings, needle valve, springs, washers, and coil into housing to assemble electromagnet valves used to control flow of liquids or gases in diesel equipment: Presses washer-type ring over needle stem to assemble valve stem. Slides collar over stem and turns one-fourth turn to seat ring. Clamps valve stem in fixture and inserts needle valve and spring. Adjusts setscrew to hold needle valve in specified position shown on dial indicator. Inserts assembled valve stem into housing and plugs with bottle cap to hold in position temporarily. Clamps housing in holding fixture, removes bottle cap, and seats brass bushing in opening in valve housing around valve stem, using special tool and hammer. Dips plastic washer and bottom of magnet coil into varnish to form insulation between coil and housing. Wraps coil in paper and bolts and screws coil, springs, and washers, to inside of housing, using ratchet wrench and screwdriver.

GOE: 06.04.23 STRENGTH: L GED: R2 M1 L2 SVP: 3 DLU: 77

724.684-038 MOTOR-AND-GENERATOR-BRUSH MAKER (elec. equip.) alternate titles: wire-brush maker

Cuts, winds, and presses wire gauze to fabricate brushes of specified size for collecting and distributing electric current in generators and motors, using hand shear, mandrel, and hydraulic press: Cuts wire gauze to specified lengths, using hand shears. Winds cut gauze on mandrel to form roll of several thicknesses. Adjusts setscrews on bed of hydraulic press and positions rolled gauze in bed of press which compresses gauze to specified width and thickness. Immerses compressed brush into molten lead, using tongs, and solders end of gauze to fasten exposed flap. Holds gauze against bandsaw to bevel brush end.
GOE: 06.02.24 STRENGTH: L GED: R3 M2 L1 SVP: 4 DLU: 77

724.685-010 ELEMENT WINDING MACHINE TENDER (elec. equip.; inst. & app.)

Tends wire winding machine that automatically winds elements used in electrical and electronic components, equipment, instruments, and devices, following work orders and wiring diagrams, using handtools: Reads work orders and specifications to determine materials required. Loads wire spools onto machine spindles and adjusts machine controls at specified positions, following machine setup instructions and wiring diagrams. Threads specified wire through winding guides or over coil, using handtools, such as tweezers, hook, or spreader. Clamps element or coil onto machine fixture and attaches wire to element or coil, using handtools, such as tweezers, hook, flux, soldering iron, and microscope. Sets winding counter or tension adjustments, and manipulates hand or foot controls to start machine. Observes and monitors machine winding to detect deviations from standards, and to stop or ensure automatic shut-off of machine after specified number of windings. Severs wire manually, using scissors, wire snippers, or cutters, or pushes lever to activate automatic machine wire cutting. May record production information. May mix and apply cement, glue, or varnish to element or coil and heat element or coil in curing oven to reinforce, insulate, and prevent raveling of wire. May test and measure elements and coils for resistance factors and linearity, using ohmmeter, computer, and calipers.
GOE: 06.04.09 STRENGTH: L GED: R3 M2 L2 SVP: 3 DLU: 90

724.685-014 WELD INSPECTOR (elec. equip.)

Tends machine that tests welds of contact disks to spark-breaker arms used in automobile distributors: Positions arm in machine that strikes contact disk with hammer. Discards spark-breaker arms if contact disks break off. Weighs out spark-breaker arms in lots, using scales, and places parts in cartons.
GOE: 06.03.02 STRENGTH: L GED: R2 M1 L1 SVP: 2 DLU: 77

724.687-010 LACER AND TIER (elec. equip.) alternate titles: binder

Laces and ties cotton tape to cover joint formed by soldering coil leads of adjacent coils in one pole phase group: Laces tape through and over wires of joint, loops tape around open leads, and ties tape.
GOE: 06.04.23 STRENGTH: M GED: R1 M1 L1 SVP: 2 DLU: 77

725 OCCUPATIONS IN ASSEMBLY OF LIGHT BULBS AND ELECTRONIC TUBES

This group includes occupations concerned with fabricating and assembling filaments, grids, plates, masks, guns, and other parts and inserting them into bulbs to complete electron tubes and light bulbs.

725.381-010 TUBE REBUILDER (electron. comp.) alternate titles: television-picture-tube rebuilder

Rebuilds cathode ray tubes used in television receivers and display instruments according to specifications, applying knowledge of electronics: Inspects tube for physical defects, such as cracks, scratches, burns, and pits to determine if tube is repairable. Tests display function, such as horizontal fade, color purity, and convergence to locate cause of malfunction, using test equipment. Cuts off glass neck holding electron gun, using hot wire or gas torch. Paints dag (graphite paint) inside bulb to provide conductive surface, using brush. Places bulb and replacement electron gun in lathe equipped with gas torch to weld and anneal parts together. Operates ovens and pumps to seal and evacuate tube. Places rebuilt tube in chamber to age (stabilize) tube. Coats exterior surface of tube with dag, using spray gun. Tests tube function and operation for conformance to specifications. Buffs and polishes display screen surface to remove scratches, using power buffer and abrasive compound.
GOE: 05.05.10 STRENGTH: M GED: R4 M3 L4 SVP: 6 DLU: 88

725.384-010 TUBE ASSEMBLER, ELECTRON (electron. comp.)

Performs any combination of following tasks to fabricate and assemble custom or production electron tubes: Reads work orders, receives verbal instructions, and follows drawings and sample assemblies to fabricate and assemble parts. Winds wire around grid core or mandrel to form filaments, grids, and heaters, using manual or automatic winding machines. Stretches and presses wound grid cores to designated shape, and cuts cores to specified size, using manual or power tools. Forms parts, such as grids, stems, and leads, using special purpose automatic machines. Coats designated parts with specified materials to change conductive properties of parts or provide electrostatic shield for tube elements, using spray equipment, paint brush, pressurized needle, or other coating method. Positions parts, such as grids, spacers, plates, caps, shields, stems, heaters, and radiators, in specified relationship to one another. Mounts

parts in holding fixtures and bonds parts together, using welding and brazing techniques and equipment. Fills bases or top caps of designated tubes with adhesive and attaches bases or caps to glass bulbs and metal shells. Places assembled tube in equipment to remove impurities, create vacuum, and seal tube. Stamps and etches identifying information on tube and tube parts, using printing or etching equipment. Polishes designated parts and assemblies, using buffing wheel. Tends ovens that cure adhesives, inks, and coatings. Assembles parts for cathodes, using microscope. Tests and inspects parts and assemblies for conformance to specifications, using test equipment, precision measuring instruments, and microscope. Tends electronic ageing equipment that stabilize electrical characteristics of tubes. May be designated by duties performed as Electron Gun Assembler (electron. comp.); Stem-Lead Former (electron. comp.); Tube-Component Assembler (electron comp.); Tube Fitter (electron. comp.).
GOE: 06.02.23 STRENGTH: L GED: R2 M2 L2 SVP: 2 DLU: 88

725.684-010 COILED-COIL INSPECTOR (light. fix.)

Examines tungsten filament coils of electric light bulbs for concentricity and burrs by rolling coils under fingers on workbench, using tweezers to separate coils. Measures length of coils, using metric scale. Determines brittleness of coils by stretching occasional coil to breaking point. Places approved coils in labeled glass jars and sets aside rejected coils. Maintains record of material examined.
GOE: 06.03.01 STRENGTH: S GED: R3 M2 L2 SVP: 3 DLU: 77

725.684-014 MOUNTER, HAND (light. fix.)

Mounts tungsten filament coils on bead mounts or stems used in incandescent lamps by either of following methods: (1) Positions hooked ends of pair of stem lead wires on bed of press, slips filament coil ends under hooks with tweezers, and presses pedal to lower die on stem that clamps hooks over ends of coil. May clamp tungsten filament coil to lead wires which have no end hooks. (2) Slips one end of filament coil through lead wire hook of bead mount, using tweezers and magnifying glass, and clamps part in place, using press. Twists filament through loop in bead-mount anchor wire, through tip of other lead wire, and clamps part in place, using press. Pulls tip of anchor wire to tighten loop around filament coil, using tweezers. Inserts two completed mounts in each light bulb.
GOE: 06.04.23 STRENGTH: L GED: R2 M2 L2 SVP: 3 DLU: 77

725.684-018 STEM MOUNTER (light. fix.)

Fastens tungsten wire (filament) to glass stem to form mount for electric light bulb: Loops wire over hooks on glass stem held in revolving table and clinches hooks in place, using pliers. Cements ends to lead wires, using brush and carbon cement.
GOE: 06.04.23 STRENGTH: S GED: R2 M1 L1 SVP: 2 DLU: 77

725.684-022 TUBE ASSEMBLER, CATHODE RAY (electron. comp.)

Performs any combination of following tasks to assemble cathode-ray tubes used in television and display equipment: Removes funnel from rack and places funnel onto conveyorized washing, rinsing, and drying equipment. Positions funnel in rotatable holding chuck to secure funnel for painting. Inserts brush into rotating funnel and paints dag (conductive graphite) coating as indicated by chuck guide to provide electric conductivity. Verifies that aperture mask and display screen fit together according to corresponding numbers. Examines aperture mask and screen in light box to detect misaligned color dots, using microscope. Positions funnel in rotatable chuck equipped with automatic frit dispenser. Moves controls that index frit dispenser around edge of funnel mouth to dispense sealant. Removes frit-coated funnel from chuck and secures funnel in jig for joining display screen assembly onto funnel. Positions display screen assembly on funnel edge and aligns screen with reference points on funnel. Pushes jig onto conveyor leading into oven to fuse funnel and display screen assembly into bulb. Places bulb on holding fixture of sprayer to coat interior surface of bulb with protective layer of lacquer. Places bulb onto holding fixture of evaporation equipment to apply aluminized coating to interior surface of bulb. Places bulb onto conveyor that carries bulb through processing stations to preheat bulb, insert and fuse gun to neck of bulb to form tube, and anneals and cools tube assembly. Places tube onto cart or conveyor for further processing. Inspects tube for imperfections, such as blemishes, coating defects, scratches, bubbles, or stains, using magnifier, ultraviolet light, inspection booth, or unaided vision. May be designated according to duties performed as Aluminizer (electron. comp.); Bulb Assembler (electron. comp.); Dag Coater (electron. comp.); Frit Coater (electron. comp.); Funnel Coater (electron comp.); Gun-Sealing-Machine Operator (electron. comp.); Lacquer Sprayer (electron. comp.).
GOE: 06.02.23 STRENGTH: M GED: R2 M1 L1 SVP: 3 DLU: 89

725.684-026 CATHODE RAY TUBE SALVAGE PROCESSOR (electron. comp.)

Performs any combination of following duties to disassemble salvaged cathode ray tubes for reprocessing: Removes vacuum and electron gun from bulb of salvaged cathode ray tube, using portable air drill. Places bulb on fixture of deband machine and activates machine that cuts metal band that surrounds joint between funnel and viewing screen of bulb. Places debanded bulb on conveyor that carries bulb through series of acid and water baths to loosen and dissolve frit that bonds funnel to viewing screen. Positions bulb on chuck of machine and presses pedal on machine that pneumatically separates funnel from viewing screen. Places funnel and screen in vats of acid and water to remove remaining frit from parts. Examines funnel and screen to ensure all frit was removed during acid processing. Places funnel and screen on cart for further processing.

GOE: 06.02.32 STRENGTH: H GED: R2 M1 L1 SVP: 3 DLU: 88

725.685-010 DISPLAY-SCREEN FABRICATOR (electron. comp.)

Tends equipment that forms and prepares aperture masks and display screens for oscilloscope and television picture tubes: Feeds specified sections of sensitized steel between plates in photographic printing chase to flatten sheet to specification. Sets timer for specified exposure and turns on heliarc lamp to imprint pattern of aperture mask from photographic plate onto steel. Verifies alignment of plates, using microscope. Tends furnace that blackens aperture masks and rings. Feeds mask through series of rollers that flatten mask. Positions mask on bed of forming press and lowers die to form mask. Tends processing equipment to clean, dry, and coat phosphor on inside face of display screen. Positions aperture mask and screen on fixture over time-cycled light source to print color-emitting dots on phosphor coating. Starts cycle to expose coating to light through mask aperture. Marks mating screen and aperture mask with matching numbers for future assembly. Fastens screen in holder on conveyor that carries screen through equipment that develops exposed phosphor, removes unexposed phosphor, and dries screen. May be designated according to process as Aperture-Mask Etcher (electron. comp.); Mask Former (electron. comp.); Screener (electron. comp.).
GOE: 06.04.19 STRENGTH: M GED: R2 M2 L2 SVP: 2 DLU: 89

725.687-010 BEAD INSPECTOR (light. fix.)

Inspects molded glass beads, used in incandescent lamps, for defects: Scoops up beads on prongs of metal forklike device. Examines beads to determine if beads are whole. Moves beads up and down on prongs to gauge diameter; rejects beads that do not slide easily. Breaks or puts aside defective beads, and pours satisfactory beads into containers.
GOE: 06.03.02 STRENGTH: S GED: R2 M2 L2 SVP: 3 DLU: 77

725.687-014 COILER (light. fix.)

Tests incandescent lamps for air leaks, using high-frequency electric ray gun: Spreads completed lamps on table, three sides and top of which are covered by black hood. Depresses switch on high-frequency ray gun which releases electric current through exposed wire protruding from gun. Passes exposed wire over lamps and observes each to ascertain its turning specified shade of blue on contact. Segregates defective lamps from those meeting standards.
GOE: 06.03.02 STRENGTH: L GED: R2 M2 L2 SVP: 3 DLU: 77

725.687-018 FOCUSER (light. fix.)

Observes magnified shadow of lamp filament projected on coordinate lines of dark screen to determine if coil has been properly centered within bulb. Pulls stem to center filament, using tweezers.
GOE: 06.03.02 STRENGTH: S GED: R2 M1 L2 SVP: 3 DLU: 77

725.687-022 GETTERER (light. fix.)

Applies getter (chemical solution) to stems of lead wires used in making incandescent lamps: Picks stem from tray and applies getter on lead wires, using brush. Places stem in tray to dry. Adds thinners to getter and stirs mixture to maintain specified consistency.
GOE: 06.04.33 STRENGTH: S GED: R1 M1 L1 SVP: 2 DLU: 77

725.687-026 QUALITY-CONTROL INSPECTOR (light. fix.)

Examines machine-made light bulbs for defects: Selects sample carton from each lampmaking unit, tests lamps (bulbs) for lighting, and visually examines bulbs for other defects. Records number of defectives and informs department supervisor when percentage of defective lamps exceeds allowable limits, requiring inspection of entire unit output. May open tips of sample bulbs with knife, immerse bulbs in water, measure amounts of water remaining in bulbs, and compare amounts with standard chart to determine whether sufficient gas is injected by machine.
GOE: 06.03.02 STRENGTH: L GED: R3 M2 L2 SVP: 3 DLU: 77

726 OCCUPATIONS IN ASSEMBLY AND REPAIR OF ELECTRONIC COMPONENTS AND ACCESSORIES, N.E.C.

This group includes occupations, not elsewhere classified, concerned with fabricating resistors, inductors, transformers, capacitors, crystals, diodes, semiconductors (solid state), potentiometers and controls, printed circuitry, harness, and similar products for electronic end products, and assembling and repairing accessories, such as speakers, antennas, and related items.

726.130-010 SUPERVISOR, ELECTRONICS PRODUCTION (comm. equip.; electron. comp.; office machines)

Supervises and coordinates activities of workers engaged in fabricating, assembling, testing, inspecting, and repairing electronic products, systems, subassemblies, components, or parts: Analyzes manufacturing requirements, prepares production schedule, and distributes work assignments according to order priorities and worker availability. Reviews work orders, product specifications, and technical instructions to determine facility requirements, and requisitions tools, equipment, and supplies to meet production goals. Demonstrates work methods, such as machine setup, wire routing, assembly, inspection sequence, repair, and test equipment operation. Examines product for defects, utilizing knowledge of manufacturing and quality standards, to ensure conformance to product specifications. Performs other tasks described under SUPERVISOR (any industry) Master Title. May assist subordinates to adjust and repair machines and equipment. May confer with interdepartmental personnel to discuss production procedures and resolve problems. May be designated according to function supervised as Quality Assurance Supervisor (office machines); Supervisor, Electronics Assembly (electron. comp.; office machines); Supervisor, Electronics Inspection (electron. comp.); Supervisor, Electronics Testing (electron. comp.); Supervisor, Television-Chassis Repair (comm. equip.).
GOE: 06.01.01 STRENGTH: L GED: R4 M3 L3 SVP: 7 DLU: 88

726.131-014 SUPERVISOR, HEARING-AID ASSEMBLY (protective dev.)

Supervises and coordinates activities of workers engaged in assembling and repairing hearing aids: Reads assembly orders and repair tickets to determine work priorities, and assigns work to those workers responsible for assembly or repair. Records production, such as type of hearing aids to be assembled, number of units, and date assigned. Monitors work in progress to determine whether production is maintained according to schedule. Confers with workers' representatives to resolve grievances. Demonstrates job tasks to train new workers and assigns experienced workers to assist in training. Compiles weekly and monthly production reports of hearing aids assembled and repaired. Requisitions supplies and equipment as required. Performs other duties as described under SUPERVISOR (any industry) Master Title.
GOE: 06.01.01 STRENGTH: L GED: R3 M3 L3 SVP: 7 DLU: 86

726.131-018 SUPERVISOR, PRINTED CIRCUIT BOARD TESTING (electron. comp.) alternate titles: supervisor, electronic testing; supervisor, functional testing; supervisor, in-circuit testing

Supervises and coordinates activities of workers engaged in repairing and testing performance of printed circuit boards (PCB's) during and after assembly, applying knowledge of electronic theory and circuitry, test procedures, and documentation: Directs training of workers in areas such as test procedures and equipment operation, troubleshooting and repairing, and interpretation of specifications and documentation. Coordinates testing and repair work to ensure completion of work assignment. Monitors repair activities to verify PCB's conform to documentation standards. Performs other duties as described under SUPERVISOR (any industry) Master Title. May supervise activities of workers engaged in assembling PCB's.
GOE: 06.01.01 STRENGTH: L GED: R4 M3 L4 SVP: 8 DLU: 86

726.134-010 SUPERVISOR, PRINTED CIRCUIT BOARD ASSEMBLY (electron. comp.)

Supervises and coordinates activities of workers engaged in assembling, testing, and inspecting printed circuit boards: Directs training of workers in interpreting shop specifications, component recognition, equipment operation, and performance of job duties to ensure conformance to assembly standards. Plans and coordinates work assignments to meet production goals. Examines assembled printed circuit boards, applying knowledge of assembly and quality standards, to ensure specifications are met. Performs other duties as described under SUPERVISOR (any industry) Master Title. May be designated according to stage of assembly as Supervisor, Final (electron. comp.); Supervisor, Post-Wave (electron. comp.); Supervisor, Pre-Wave (electron. comp.). May be designated according to function supervised as Supervisor, Assembly (electron. comp.); Supervisor, Quality Control (electron. comp.); Supervisor, Testing (electron. comp.).
GOE: 06.01.01 STRENGTH: L GED: R4 M3 L4 SVP: 7 DLU: 88

726.261-010 ELECTRONICS ASSEMBLER, DEVELOPMENTAL (any industry) alternate titles: developer-prover, electrical; electrical and electronics development mechanic; prototype assembler, electronics

Assembles, tests, and modifies prototype or custom electronic parts, systems, and apparatus to develop assembly methods and techniques for use by production workers, applying knowledge of electronic theory and assembly techniques: Reads blueprints, wiring diagrams, process sheets, and assembly and schematic drawings, and receives verbal instructions regarding work assignment. Aligns and assembles parts, such as leads, coils, wires, tabs, and terminals into housing, using handtools, power tools, soldering iron, brazing fixture, and welding head. Routes and laces cables [CABLE MAKER (elec. equip.; electron. comp.) 728.684-010]. Installs components and parts, such as switches, coils, transformers, relays, transistors, and semiconductor circuits on chassis, circuit boards, panels, and other units, using handtools, power tools, soldering and welding equipment, and thermocompression bonding, wave soldering, or resistance welding techniques. Routes and attaches wires and connectors to form circuitry and connects assembly to power supply sources, switch panels, or junction boxes. Attaches hardware and seals assembly, using rivets, screws, handtools, power tools, resistance welder or thermocompression bonding. Examines parts for defects, such as pinholes or chips. Test-operates unit to locate defects, measure performance, determine need for adjustment, and verify specified operation, using ohmmeter, oscilloscope, signal generator, and other electronic test instruments. Replaces defective components and wiring, using handtools and soldering iron. Calibrates unit according to specifications. Enters information on production records, logs, and other report forms. May assemble prototype microelectronic units, using binocular microscope. May repair defective units rejected by inspection or test personnel [ELECTRONIC EQUIPMENT REPAIRER (comm. equip.; electron. comp.) 726.381-014].
GOE: 05.05.05 STRENGTH: L GED: R4 M4 L4 SVP: 7 DLU: 89

726.261-014 ELECTRICIAN, RESEARCH (aircraft mfg.)
Develops, lays out, fabricates, tests, and modifies radio, electrical, and electronic systems and assemblies, and test equipment, for aeronautical and aerospace developmental test projects: Plans method and sequence of operations for developmental test project. Lays out, fabricates, and assembles radio, electrical, and electronic systems and assemblies, following engineering data, sketches, and blueprints, utilizing knowledge of electrical and electronic theory, using measuring instruments, handtools, and shop equipment. Sets up and operates test equipment to evaluate performance of developmental parts, assemblies, or systems under simulated operating conditions. Records, analyzes, and interprets test information. Collaborates with engineering and other personnel to solve developmental problems. Modifies parts, assemblies, and systems as required. Constructs, maintains, repairs, calibrates, and modifies test equipment. May develop and fabricate tooling for developmental projects.
GOE: 05.03.05 STRENGTH: M GED: R4 M4 L3 SVP: 7 DLU: 88

726.261-018 ELECTRONICS TESTER (any industry) alternate titles: quality-control-assembly-test technician; technician, test systems; tester, systems; test technician; trouble shooter
Performs variety of electronic, mechanical, and electromechanical tests on electronic systems, subassemblies, and parts to ensure unit functions according to specifications or to determine cause of unit failure, using electronic test instruments: Reads test schedule, work orders, test manuals, performance specifications, wiring diagrams, and schematics to determine testing procedure and equipment to be used. Tests functional performance of systems, subassemblies, and parts under specified environmental conditions, such as temperature change, vibration, pressure, and humidity, using testing devices, such as temperature cabinets, shake-test machines, and centrifuges. Calibrates test instruments according to specifications. Connects unit to be tested to test equipment, such as signal generator, frequency meter, or spectrum analyzer. Reads dials or digital displays that indicate electronic characteristics, such as voltage, frequency, distortion, inductance, and capacitance. Compares results with specifications and records test data or plots test results on graph. Analyzes test results on defective units to determine cause of failure, applying knowledge of electronic theory and using electronic test equipment. Replaces defective wiring and components, using handtools and soldering iron, or records defects on tag attached to unit and returns unit to production department for repair. Confers with engineers, technicians, production personnel, and others regarding testing procedures and results and to resolve problems. May write computer programs to control semiconductor device and electronic component test equipment prior to testing, utilizing knowledge of programming techniques, electronics, test equipment, and testing specifications. May explain and demonstrate testing procedures to other workers. May verify dimensions of pins, shafts, and other mechanical parts, using calipers, vernier gauges, and micrometers. May operate x-ray equipment to verify internal assembly and alignment of parts according to specifications. May devise test equipment setup to evaluate performance and operation of nonstandard or customer returned units. May be designated according to unit tested as Memory-Unit Test Technician (electron. comp.); Television-Receiver Analyzer (electron. comp.); Transmitter Tester (electron. comp.); Tube-Test Technician (electron. comp.).
GOE: 06.01.05 STRENGTH: M GED: R4 M4 L3 SVP: 7 DLU: 90

726.361-014 GROUP LEADER, PRINTED CIRCUIT BOARD ASSEMBLY (electron. comp.)
Assists SUPERVISOR, PRINTED CIRCUIT BOARD ASSEMBLY (electron. comp.) 762.134-010, in coordinating activities of workers engaged in assembling printed circuit boards (PCB's), applying knowledge of PCB assembly techniques, specifications, and production scheduling: Confers with SUPERVISOR, PRINTED CIRCUIT BOARD ASSEMBLY (electron. comp.), and reviews production schedules, specifications, and priorities to plan department work assignments. Requisitions, obtains, and distributes supplies and materials, such as PCB's, electronic components and parts, solder and flux, antistatic bags and wristbands, and schematic drawings and work orders. Assigns duties to assembly workers and oversees department activities. Revises work assignments to meet production schedules and contract priorities. Explains and demonstrates PCB assembly line procedures and techniques to workers. Interprets schematic drawings, specifications, and work orders for workers. Assists workers in resolving technical problems and advises SUPERVISOR, PRINTED CIRCUIT BOARD ASSEMBLY (electron. comp.) of complex production problems. Reads, prepares, collects, and maintains reports, such as individual and department production reports, employee time and attendance records, and component waste reports. Substitutes for absent workers or assists workers to alleviate work overload situations. May assemble sample PCB's, using schematic drawings, handtools, and soldering equipment, to use as work aids. May preform lead wires for electronic components, using forming machines or handtools, and supply preformed parts to assemblers.
GOE: 06.02.23 STRENGTH: L GED: R3 M2 L3 SVP: 5 DLU: 88

726.361-018 GROUP LEADER, PRINTED CIRCUIT BOARD QUALITY CONTROL (electron. comp.)
Assists SUPERVISOR, PRINTED CIRCUIT BOARD ASSEMBLY (electron. comp.) 726.134-010 in coordinating activities of workers engaged in inspecting, testing, and repairing printed circuit boards (PCB's), applying knowledge of electronic theory, test procedures, repair techniques, and quality standards: Confers with SUPERVISOR, PRINTED CIRCUIT BOARD ASSEMBLY (electron. comp.), and reviews production schedules to determine quantity and type of PCB's to be inspected, tested, or repaired. Compiles list of test and inspection personnel and assists in planning department work assignments. Assigns duties to inspection, test, and repair personnel, using knowledge of workers' experience and capabilities. Collects PCB's and components for processing from receiving and assembly departments and distributes PCB's and components to inspection, test, or repair personnel. Oversees department activities and revises work assignments to meet production schedules and contract priorities. Explains inspection, test procedures, and specifications, and demonstrates use of testing equipment and PCB repair techniques to workers. Interprets schematic drawings, procedure changes, and work orders for workers. Assists workers in resolving technical problems, utilizing knowledge of electronic theory, test procedures, and specifications. Confers with technical personnel and department supervisors to report and resolve assembly and testing problems, and reports unresolved problems to SUPERVISOR, PRINTED CIRCUIT BOARD ASSEMBLY (electron. comp.). Requisitions, obtains, and distributes supplies, materials, and equipment, such as electronic components and parts used for repair work, test and inspection specifications and test equipment, fixtures, and handtools. Inspects test equipment to verify equipment functions according to standards. Reports substandard equipment performance to supervisor or maintenance personnel. Reads, prepares, collects, and maintains reports, such as individual and department production reports and test results, employee time and attendance records, and product waste reports. Maintains vendor files. Substitutes for absent workers and assists workers to alleviate work overload situations.
GOE: 06.03.01 STRENGTH: L GED: R3 M3 L3 SVP: 6 DLU: 88

726.361-022 REPAIRER, PROBE TEST CARD, SEMICONDUCTOR WAFERS (electron. comp.)
Replaces and realigns broken, worn, or misaligned probes on probe test cards, using handtools and equipment, to maintain probe cards for wafer probe (electrical test) equipment: Reads specification sheets, manuals, and diagrams to determine probe card wiring and probe positions. Inspects probe cards, using microscope, to detect defects, such as loose wiring and loose, split, or worn probes. Removes, replaces, and re-solders defective wiring and probes, using tweezers and soldering iron. Observes probe card through microscope and aligns probes in specified position over test wafer, using tweezers. Aligns probes on even plane, using tweezers and test equipment. Maintains repair and replacement records. Maintains probe and inventory records, using computer terminal.
GOE: 06.01.04 STRENGTH: L GED: R3 M2 L2 SVP: 4 DLU: 86

726.362-010 GROUP LEADER, SEMICONDUCTOR TESTING (electron. comp.) alternate titles: production aide
Assists SUPERVISOR, ELECTRONICS TESTING (electron. comp.) 726.130-010 in coordinating and monitoring activities of workers engaged in testing electronic devices (components), such as integrated circuits (ICs), transistors, and diodes, on semiconductor wafers, utilizing knowledge of equipment, procedures, and test specifications: Answers questions from workers pertaining to test procedures and test equipment operation. Monitors and expedites flow of materials through testing cycle. Enters test program into test equipment, using computer terminal, and examines test equipment printout to verify test equipment is functioning according to company and manual specifications. Notifies maintenance workers of test equipment malfunctions. Operates or tends equipment to substitute for absentee workers. Maintains production records. Trains workers in equipment operation and test procedures.
GOE: 06.01.05 STRENGTH: S GED: R3 M2 L2 SVP: 7 DLU: 86

726.362-014 WAVE-SOLDERING MACHINE OPERATOR (comm. equip.; electron. comp.; inst. & app.; office machines) alternates titles: flow-solder machine operator
Controls wave-soldering machine or system to solder electronic components onto printed circuit boards (PCB's), according to processing specifications: Reads production schedules and operations manuals and receives verbal instructions regarding sequential start up and operation of wave-soldering machine or system. Moves controls to activate machine or equipment, such as preheater, lead wire cutter, wave-soldering units, and conveyors. Adjusts controls of machines to regulate operating speed and temperature and height of flux, wax, and solder waves. Verifies specific gravity of flux, using hydrometer. Adjusts dimensions of conveyor pallets and rails used to hold and transport PCB's through wave-soldering process, using precision instruments and handtools. Places loaded master pallet and production pallets on conveyor line of wave soldering machine or system and monitors pallets moving through process to verify that timing, temperatures, and dimensions are set according to standards. Observes heat-sensitive color marks or strips placed on PCB's to verify boards have been preheated to specified temperatures. Observes meters, gauges, and indicator lights to ensure that soldering of PCB's conforms to processing standards. Examines samples of soldered boards to detect substandard soldering. Discusses quality of soldering with supervisor and adjusts controls according to instructions. Cleans parts and interiors of machines and replenishes fluids in machines and equipment, using handtools. Performs preventive maintenance on machines and equipment, using handtools. May return substandard boards to workers for repair. May feed or off bear boards or pallets to or from conveyor system.
GOE: 06.02.19 STRENGTH: M GED: R3 M2 L3 SVP: 4 DLU: 88

726.364-010 LEAD HAND, INSPECTING AND TESTING (electron. comp.)
Assists supervisor in coordinating activities of workers engaged in inspecting and testing electronic components for compliance to company standards: Re-

ceives boxes of components and records identifying information on specified forms. Collects random lot samples, according to lot volume and following company guidelines. Distributes components to workers responsible for testing specific components. Instructs new workers in testing equipment operation, component testing sequence, and specification sheet interpretations. Modifies workers' assignments to meet priorities and to adjust work loads according to worker absenteeism. Completes requisition forms to obtain items requested and delivers items to workers. Observes calibration maintenance sheets to verify maintenance of test equipment and notifies designated personnel of unscheduled verification of equipment as warranted by questionable test results. Maintains records that indicate material discrepancies and records information on vendor history forms.
GOE: 06.03.02 STRENGTH: M GED: R3 M2 L3 SVP: 6 DLU: 86

726.364-014 TEST FIXTURE DESIGNER (electron. comp.)

Plots and draws schematics for test fixture heads used in testing printed circuit boards (PCB's) for electrical shorts and breaks, utilizing knowledge of printed circuit design, electronics, and customer specifications: Reviews blueprint to determine customer requirements and beginning and end points of PCB conductor paths. Confers with engineer to resolve questions concerning design of test fixture heads. Refers to blueprint and method sheets and chooses electrical points to be tested, making sure to include critical points along conductor path. Plots electrical points to be tested on layout sheet, using pencil. Chooses drill size to be used in drilling test head, according to test design and engineering specifications. Forwards layout of test points with requested drill size to numerical-control drilling department to be used as guide to drill test head. Reviews blueprints to determine logical and most efficient method to wire test head to frame of test fixture. Draws schematics for TEST FIXTURE ASSEMBLER (electron. comp.) 726.684-098 to follow in wiring test head to test fixture frame. May review schematics with assembler to answer questions regarding correct wiring procedures. May monitor building of test fixture by assembler. May record data regarding completed job.
GOE: 05.03.02 STRENGTH: S GED: R4 M3 L3 SVP: 7 DLU: 86

726.364-018 ELECTRONICS UTILITY WORKER (comm. equip.; electron. comp.) alternate titles: setup worker, electronics

Arranges layout of work stations for workers engaged in fabricating, processing, or assembling electronic equipment and components, such as semiconductor devices, printed circuit boards (PCB's), chassis assemblies, and wire harnesses and cables: Reads specifications, such as process guide, bill of material, wiring diagram, *mechanical print,* and schematic diagram, to determine materials and equipment needed, such as component parts, chemicals and gases, tools, test instruments, and jigs and fixtures, for work stations. Prepares and submits requisitions for equipment, parts, or tools required to initially set up or resupply work stations. Positions materials and equipment in specified arrangement at work stations. May explain or demonstrate work procedures to other workers in fabricating, processing, and assembly functions. May perform fabricating, processing, or assembly work in absence of line worker. May set and adjust controls for processing, fabricating, and assembly line equipment, such as furnaces, process chambers, power supplies, timers, and multimeters. May test assemblies, using testing machines or instruments, such as meters, resistance bridges, and automatic component testers. May repair or rework assembled items by removing, adding, or replacing parts or resoldering or rebonding defective connections, using handtools or power tools.
GOE: 06.04.34 STRENGTH: L GED: R3 M2 L3 SVP: 5 DLU: 88

726.367-010 GREEN INSPECTOR (elec. equip.)

Inspects newly extruded (green) carbon electrodes to detect defects, such as cracks and blisters, and to determine disposition of electrodes: Notifies other personnel to investigate cause of defective electrodes. Weighs and measures dimensions of electrodes to determine if specifications are met, using scale, calipers, and straightedge. Marks disposition of electrodes on parts, using chalk, and records findings and disposition of electrodes. May compute density of electrodes, according to plant formula, using slide rule. May inspect samples of graphitized electrodes or green carbon stock impregnated with pitch or linseed oil and be designated Impregnation Inspector (elec. equip.).
GOE: 06.03.01 STRENGTH: L GED: R3 M2 L2 SVP: 4 DLU: 77

726.380-010 ELECTRONIC EQUIPMENT SET-UP OPERATOR (electron. comp.)

Sets up and operates equipment, such as shearing machine, laminator, and drill, to fabricate single- and multi-layer printed circuit boards (PCB's), following diagrams and specifications: Determines dimensions and tolerances of boards, sequence of operations, and tools and equipment required, according to diagrams and specifications, and measures and marks dimensions and reference points to lay out boards for machining. Sets up and operates shearing machine and drills to cut, form, and drill holes into boards according to specifications. Bevels edge connectors, using slotter, and verifies dimensions and tolerances, using calipers. Sets up and controls laminating and other plating equipment, to apply copper plating and photoresist to boards. Photographs design image and exposes film to produce and develop acid resisting circuitry pattern, using photographic equipment. Etches and retouches circuitry on boards, using etcher. Bonds two or more PCB's together to form multilayer boards, using laminating press.
GOE: 06.01.03 STRENGTH: L GED: R4 M4 L3 SVP: 6 DLU: 88

726.381-010 ELECTRONICS INSPECTOR (comm. equip.; electron. comp.; inst. & app.) alternate titles: quality control inspector; systems inspector

Performs any combination of following tasks to inspect electronic systems, assemblies, subassemblies, components, and parts for conformance to specifications, following blueprints, drawings, and production and assembly manuals: Examines layout and installation of wiring, cables, subassemblies, hardware, and components to detect assembly errors. Compares assembly with parts list to detect missing hardware. Examines joints, using magnifying glass and mirror, and pulls wires and cables to locate soldering defects. Examines alignment of parts and measures parts for conformance to specified dimensions, using precision measuring instruments, such as micrometers, vernier calipers, and gauges. Twists dials, knobs, shafts, and gears to verify freedom of movement. Traces cables and harness assemblies, following cable wiring diagram, to verify routing of wires to specified connections and conformance of cable lacing and insulation to manufacturing standards. Measures plated areas for uniformity and thickness, using micrometers or dial indicators. Verifies location of bolt and rivet holes, using templates, check fixtures, and precision measuring instruments. Examines parts for surface defects, such as chips, scratches, and pinholes. Examines production documents to ensure that all assembly, inspecting, and testing steps were performed according to specifications. Calculates percentage of defective parts, using calculator. Records inspection data, such as serial number, type and percent of defects, and rework required. Resolders broken connections on components and parts. Performs functional and operational tests, using electronic test equipment such as frequency meter, oscilloscope, and signal generator [ELECTRONICS TESTER (any industry) 726.261-018], or performs destructive tests to determine tensile strength of product or part. May inspect and lay out optic axis of raw quartz crystals, using optical inspection equipment, and be designated Inspector, Raw Quartz (electron. comp.). May inspect parts at random and be designated Check Inspector (electron. comp.). May inspect units on assembly line and be designated In-Process Inspector (electron. comp.) or final product and be designated Final Inspector (electron. comp.). May be designated according to type of unit inspected as Inspector, Subassemblies (electron. comp.); Inspector, Tubes (electron. comp.).
GOE: 06.01.05 STRENGTH: L GED: R4 M4 L4 SVP: 6 DLU: 89

726.381-014 ELECTRONIC EQUIPMENT REPAIRER (comm. equip.; electron. comp.) alternate titles: production repairer

Repairs electronic equipment, such as radio and television receivers, radio transmitters, speakers, amplifiers, and related antenna and cable assemblies, according to product specifications, manufacturing instructions and diagrams, using test equipment, handtools, and soldering iron: Reads inspection tag and examines unit to locate defects, such as broken wires, burned-out components, or scratches on cabinet, using model schematics and electronic test equipment. Inspects wiring and removes broken wires from units, using soldering iron and pliers. Cuts new wires to specified lengths, using wire cutters, or obtains precut wires and re-routes and solders wires to specified terminals, following wiring diagram. Repairs defective soldering, using soldering iron. Removes, repairs, or replaces defective components, such as resistors, transformers, and capacitors, using soldering iron and handtools. May brush touch-up paint on cabinet or case, and varnish on exposed wiring.
GOE: 05.10.03 STRENGTH: H GED: R3 M3 L3 SVP: 6 DLU: 88

726.382-010 SEQUENCING-MACHINE OPERATOR (electron. comp.)

Sets up and operates sequencing machine to insert electronic components in programmed sequence onto paper tape for use in machine insertion of components onto printed circuit boards (PCB's): Reads instructions to determine sequence, quantity, and types of components required. Mounts supply reels of components on spindles and threads component supply reel tape through machine. Installs and spaces holding devices on machine according to number of components to be sequenced, using wrench. Mounts paper tape reels onto spindles of machine to receive sequenced components. Keys data into computer terminal to enter program number that controls release of components in prescribed sequence onto paper tape. Presses button to activate machine and observes panelboard light indicators to verify sequencing procedures and to detect machine stoppages. Clears jams in holding devices and splices tapes, using handtools and adhesive tapes. Straightens bent wire leads or cuts damaged component from supply tape, using wire snips. Replaces defective components. Records production information. May operate sequencing machine equipped with verifier that automatically identifies faulty components.
GOE: 06.02.20 STRENGTH: L GED: R3 M2 L3 SVP: 5 DLU: 86

726.384-014 INSPECTOR, CIRCUITRY NEGATIVE (electron. comp.) alternate titles: film inspector

Inspects circuitry film negatives (artwork) for conformance to specifications and touches up defects on negatives to prepare negatives for use in printed circuit board (PCB) fabrication: Compares size and location of hole images on circuitry negative with drilled holes in sample PCB panel to verify conformance of negative to specifications, using light table. Examines circuitry negatives to detect defects, such as under-exposure or over-exposure of negatives, circuitry width, and spacing, using light table and microscope. Fills nicks, scratches, and gaps in circuitry pattern on negatives with pen or plastic tape, removes excess ink from negatives with cotton swab, and cuts flaws and excess film from circuitry negatives to correct and prepare negatives for use in PCB fabrication, using utility knife. Measures circuitry negative for conformance to specified dimensions, using precision-measuring instruments.

GOE: 06.03.01 STRENGTH: L GED: R3 M3 L3 SVP: 5 DLU: 86

726.384-018 INSPECTOR, SEMICONDUCTOR WAFER PROCESSING (electron. comp.)

Inspects semiconductor wafers, using microscope, to identify processing defects: Places wafers on stage of microscope, using tweezers or vacuum wand. Examines surface of wafer and test patterns on wafers, using microscope, and compares wafers to specification diagrams to identify processing defects, such as scratches, contamination, pattern misalignment, photoresist peel, and circuit bridges. Measures specified dimensions of test patterns on wafers, using electronic measuring devices attached to microscope at work station, to verify that wafers meet company specifications. Routes defective wafers to engineering department. Records observations onto processing sheets and log. Cleans inspecting area, using cleaning solution.
GOE: 06.03.01 STRENGTH: S GED: R3 M2 L2 SVP: 4 DLU: 86

726.384-022 PHOTO MASK INSPECTOR (electron. comp.) alternate titles: mask inspector

Inspects master or production photo mask plates used in fabrication of semiconductor devices for defects and to ensure conformance to specifications: Positions photo mask plate on stage of microscope or computer-aided inspection equipment. Focuses and aligns lens with predetermined coordinates on photo mask plate. Inspects photo mask plate for defects, such as misalignment of design, contamination, cracks, pinholes, and streaking, and compares photo mask pattern to original design to verify conformance to specifications. Enters commands to activate computer-aided inspection equipment that automatically scans surface of photo mask plate to locate and record defects. Records inspection information, and sorts photo mask plates according to inspection results. May measure critical dimensions of pattern on photo mask plate and compares dimensions to design requirements, using microscopes with attached calibrated viewing or image shearing apparatus. May photograph surface of defective photo mask plate, using instant-print camera. May operate laser-beam equipment to repair circuitry defects on photo mask plate [LASER-BEAM-TRIM OPERATOR (electron. comp.) 726.682-010]. May tend equipment that removes contaminants and photoresist from surface of photo mask plate [PHOTO MASK CLEANER (electron. comp.) 590.684-034].
GOE: 06.01.05 STRENGTH: L GED: R4 M3 L4 SVP: 6 DLU: 86

726.682-010 LASER-BEAM-TRIM OPERATOR (electron. comp.)

Operates computer-controlled laser machine to trim excess material from electronic components: Reads production sheet to determine specified operation code and enters commands, using control console, to retrieve programmed instructions. Inserts electronic component into holding fixture of laser machine, using tweezers, and presses console buttons to actuate laser beam that automatically trims excess metal and glass from component. Observes light indicator on control panel or monitor to determine if component meets specifications. Removes trimmed component from holding fixture and examines component for defects and completeness of trim, using microscope. May repair holding fixture on laser machine, using handtools, such as allen wrench, wire strippers, hand drill, and soldering iron.
GOE: 06.02.02 STRENGTH: L GED: R3 M3 L3 SVP: 4 DLU: 89

726.682-014 WIRE-WRAPPING-MACHINE OPERATOR (electron. comp.)

Operates computer-controlled semiautomatic machine that wraps wires around electronic-pin connectors: Mounts connector panel on machine pallet that moves panel along programmed path, using wrench and screwdriver. Depresses specified button to start automatic programmed tape for pin sequence and observes panel lights that indicate size of wire prescribed in program. Selects and mounts specified wire on machine spindle. Threads wire through bit of wire-wrap gun, positions gun in support to align gun with pins on connector panel, and depresses trigger of wire-wrap gun to wrap wire on pins. Observes directional lights of machine to determine movement of pallet and gun support. Inspects wire-wrap of completed panels for tightness, neatness of fold, or broken wire.
GOE: 06.02.09 STRENGTH: L GED: R3 M3 L3 SVP: 2 DLU: 86

726.682-018 COORDINATE MEASURING EQUIPMENT OPERATOR (electron. comp.) alternate titles: mechanical inspector

Operates coordinate measuring equipment to measure dimensions of printed circuit boards (PCB's): Reads blueprints to determine dimensions and tolerance specifications for selected PCB's. Positions PCB's on measuring table of equipment, views PCB's on monitor screen, and turns calibrated cranks on equipment to position control bar, with attached camera, over specified sections of PCB's. Flips toggles to lock camera in position, activates digital readout equipment, and records specified measurement of PCB's on inspection sheets. Repeats process to cover all sections of PCB's, including locations of specified drilled holes and samples of routed PCB's. Compares recorded measurements to blueprint dimensions and tolerances and notifies specified persons of discrepancies.
GOE: 06.03.02 STRENGTH: L GED: R3 M3 L2 SVP: 3 DLU: 86

726.682-026 SAW OPERATOR (electron. comp.)

Operates battery of circular saws to cut plastic blocks containing ceramic-coated aluminum rods to length for processing into electronic resistors: Reads job order to determine length of rods required. Secures blocks in clamps of automatic-feed saw, preset to specified length. Closes safety cover and depresses controls to start saw and activate automatic feed. Loads additional saws and monitors sawing operations to detect machine malfunctions. Removes sawed blocks from saws at end of automatic cycle. Holds sawed block against stop of manual-feed saw, starts saw, and feeds block into blade to complete specified cuts. Holds cut blocks under running water to remove debris. Measures cut and washed blocks to verify conformance with job order, using calipers and micrometers. Periodically replaces cog in automatic-feed saw to change length of cut, following identification number on cog and using wrench. Replaces worn or damaged saw blades, using handtools. Cleans work area. Records specified data on production report. May assist maintenance personnel with saw maintenance and repair.
GOE: 06.02.09 STRENGTH: M GED: R3 M2 L1 SVP: 4 DLU: 86

726.684-010 CAPACITOR-PACK-PRESS OPERATOR (elec. equip.) alternate titles: pack-press operator

Presses metal capacitor container over paper-wound packs, using power press: Adjusts fixture according to size of capacitor, using handtools. Folds fiber insulation around pack and bends electrodes by hand to position electrodes for pressing. Places open end of container over pack in holding fixture of machine, engages ram, and depresses pedal to start machine that presses packs into can. Lifts capacitor from machine, straightens electrodes by hand, fills out process tag, and clips tag to capacitor.
GOE: 06.04.34 STRENGTH: M GED: R2 M1 L1 SVP: 4 DLU: 77

726.684-014 ELECTRONIC-SCALE SUBASSEMBLER (office machines)

Assembles parts to make electronic subassemblies for scales: Assembles color-coded wires, tube sockets, resistors, capacitors, terminal strips, and printed circuit boards following diagrams, instruction sheets, or samples, using handtools, such as wire stripper and soldering iron.
GOE: 06.02.23 STRENGTH: L GED: R3 M1 L1 SVP: 3 DLU: 77

726.684-018 ELECTRONICS ASSEMBLER (comm. equip.; electron. comp.; inst. & app.)

Performs any combination of following tasks to assemble electronic components, subassemblies, products, or systems: Reads work orders, follows production drawings and sample assemblies, or receives verbal instructions regarding duties to be performed. Positions and aligns parts in specified relationship to each other in jig, fixture, or other holding device. Crimps, stakes, screws, bolts, rivets, welds, solders, cements, press fits, or performs similar operations to join or secure parts in place, using handtools, power tools, machines, and equipment. Mounts assembled components, such as transformers, resistors, transistors, capacitors, integrated circuits, and sockets, on chassis panel. Connects component lead wires to printed circuit or routes and connects wires between individual component leads and other components, connectors, terminals, and contact points, using soldering, welding, thermocompression, or related bonding procedures and equipment. Installs finished assemblies or subassemblies in cases and cabinets. Assembles and attaches hardware, such as caps, clamps, knobs, and switches, to assemblies. Performs intermediate assembly tasks, such as potting, encapsulating, sanding, cleaning, epoxy bonding, curing, stamping, etching, impregnating, and color coding parts and assemblies. Tends machines that press, shape, or wind component parts. Adjusts or trims materials from components to achieve specified electrical or dimensional characteristics. Performs on-line go-not-go testing and inspection, using magnifying devices, measuring instruments, and electronic test equipment, to ensure parts and assemblies meet production specifications and standards. May perform assembly operations under microscope or other magnifying device. Occupations related to assembly of printed circuit boards and fabrication of integrated circuit chips are defined under separate definitions.
GOE: 06.02.23 STRENGTH: L GED: R2 M1 L2 SVP: 4 DLU: 89

726.684-022 ELECTRONICS INSPECTOR (electron. comp.) alternate titles: checker; inspector, component parts; line inspector

Inspects electronic assemblies, subassemblies, parts, and components for defects, following samples, production illustrations, or using comparator: Examines unit for physical defects, such as broken or missing leads, excess solder, holes in sealing material, unevenly wound coil, coating and plating blemishes, oil leaks, faulty welds, scratches, cracks, and chips. Compares hardware on assemblies, subassemblies, and parts to parts list to verify installation. Examines hardware for specified contact with conductor area. Rejects faulty assembly, part, or component and records type and quantity of defects. May measure parts to verify accuracy of dimensions, using precision measuring instruments. May sort defective components and parts for salvage or scrap. May inspect parts, using microscope or magnifier. May be designated according to item inspected, as Capacitor Inspector (electron. comp.); Electron Gun Inspector (electron. comp.); Filter Inspector (electron. comp.); Resistor Inspector (electron. comp.); Tube Inspector (electron. comp.).
GOE: 06.03.02 STRENGTH: L GED: R3 M2 L2 SVP: 3 DLU: 88

726.684-026 ELECTRONICS TESTER (comm. equip.; electron. comp.; inst. & app.; office machines)

Tests function of electronic assemblies, components, and parts according to established procedures, using computerized or standard test equipment: Connects electronic assembly, component, or part to test instrument, such as ohmmeter, voltmeter, ammeter, resistance bridge, or oscilloscope, or to automatic or computerized test equipment, and turns switch to actuate test equipment. Reads instrument dial or scope, or observes viewing screen, that indicates resistance, capacitance, continuity, and wave pattern or defect, such as short circuit or current leakage. Compares instrument reading or monitor display with

standard and rejects defective units. Records type and quantity of defect. May verify dimensions of parts, using standard gauges. May examine assembly, component, or part for defects, such as short leads, bent plate, or cracked seal. May tend equipment that subjects unit to stress prior to testing. May replace defective components or repair defective wiring after testing. May operate burn-in oven to elevate printed circuit board temperature prior to testing. May adjust circuits in radios and televisions for maximum signal response. May be designated according to unit tested or test equipment used as Auto-Test Equipment Operator (electron. comp.); Solid State Tester (electron. comp.); Tester, Printed Circuit Boards (electron. comp.); Tube Tester (electron. comp.).
GOE: 06.03.02 STRENGTH: L GED: R3 M3 L3 SVP: 3 DLU: 89

726.684-034 ASSEMBLER, SEMICONDUCTOR (electron. comp.) alternate titles: microelectronics processor

Assembles microelectronic semiconductor devices, components, and sub-assemblies according to drawings and specifications, using microscope, bonding machines, and handtools, performing any combination of following duties: Reads work orders and studies assembly drawings to determine operation to be performed. Observes processed semiconductor wafer under scribing machine microscope and aligns scribing tool with markings on wafer. Adjusts scribing machine controls, according to work order specifications, and presses switch to start scribing. Removes scribed wafer and breaks wafer into dice (chips), using probe. Places dice under microscope, visually examines dice for defects, according to procedures, and rejects defective dice. Positions mounting device on holder under bonding machine microscope, and adjusts bonding machine controls according to work order specifications. Positions die (chip) on mounting surface according to diagram. Presses switch on bonding machine to bond die to mounting surface. Places mounted die into holding fixture under microscope of lead bonding machine. Adjusts bonding machine controls according to work order specifications. Views die and moves controls to align and position bonding head for lead bonding according to diagram. Presses switch to bond lead and moves bonding head to points indicated in bonding diagram to attach and route leads as illustrated. Inserts and seals unprotected assembly into designated assembly container device, using welding machine and epoxy syringe, to protect microelectronic assembly and complete device, component, or subassembly package. Examines and tests assembly at various stages of production, using microscope, go-not-go test equipment, measuring instruments, pressure-vacuum tanks, and related devices, according to standard procedures, to detect nonstandard or defective assemblies. Rejects or routes nonstandard components for rework. Cleans parts and assemblies at various stages of production, using cleaning devices and equipment. Maintains records of production and defects. Bonds multiple dice to headers or other mounting devices. Important variations are kinds of equipment used, such as thermal compression, wedge, wire ball, and wobble bonders, items assembled, or procedure performed.
GOE: 06.02.23 STRENGTH: S GED: R3 M2 L2 SVP: 3 DLU: 86

726.684-042 DIE ATTACHER (electron. comp.)

Attaches *dies* to empty integrated circuit (IC) packages to assemble complete semiconductor packages, using welding and gluing equipment: Places empty IC packages on heated chuck of equipment, using tweezers. Deposits bonding material, such as epoxy or gold alloy, on specified location of empty packages, and positions and aligns dies on bonding material in packages, using equipment or handtools. Removes packages with attached dies from chuck and places packages in trays, using tweezers. May place loaded trays in oven to set bonding material. May view positioning of epoxy and die in empty packages through microscope.
GOE: 06.04.23 STRENGTH: L GED: R2 M1 L2 SVP: 2 DLU: 88

726.684-050 FILM TOUCH-UP INSPECTOR (electron. comp.)

Inspects and repairs circuitry image on photoresist film (separate film or film laminated to fiberglass boards) used in manufacture of printed circuit boards (PCB's): Inspects film under magnifying glass for holes, breaks, and bridges (connections) in photoresist circuit image. Removes excess photoresist, using knife. Touches up holes and breaks in photoresist circuitry image, using photoresist ink pen. Removes and stacks finished boards for transfer to next work station. Maintains production reports. May place lint free paper between dry film sheets to avoid scratching circuit images on film.
GOE: 06.03.02 STRENGTH: S GED: R2 M1 L1 SVP: 2 DLU: 86

726.684-054 INSPECTOR, CRYSTAL (electron. comp.) alternate titles: crystal evaluator

Inspects, measures, and tests semiconductor crystal ingots to determine compliance with specifications, using measuring devices and test equipment: Transports ingot to workbench by cart or by hand. Measures ingot *flat*, diameter, and length, using calipers and ruler. Weighs ingots on scales and calculates weight loss due to grinding and sawing. Tests ingot resistivity, using electronic probes. Records weights, measurements, and other test results in logbook and on labels, and attaches labels to ingots. May operate saws to cut off ends of crystal or to cut sample wafers. May tend furnace that heat-treats ingots to alter resistivity to meet specifications. May determine *crystal orientation*, using x-ray machine. May operate grinding machine to bevel ends of crystals. May operate sandblasting machine to remove glaze from ingot surface. May tend equipment that etches ingots to remove surface material. May calculate proportion of impurities, using resistivity readings and specified formula.
GOE: 06.03.02 STRENGTH: H GED: R3 M2 L2 SVP: 4 DLU: 86

726.684-058 INSPECTOR, INTEGRATED CIRCUITS (electron. comp.)

Inspects integrated circuit (IC) assemblies, semiconductor wafers, and IC *dies* for conformance to company standards, using microscope: Reads work order to determine inspection criteria. Places group of items in trays on microscope stage, or positions items individually on stage for inspection, using vacuum pencil or tweezers. Turns knobs on microscope to adjust focus and magnification as required to view items for inspection. Views and inspects items according to company standards to detect defects, such as broken circuit lines, bridged circuits, misalignments, symbol errors, and missing solder. Discards defective items. May remove contaminants from items, using brush or airhose. May use magnifying glass to inspect electronic items.
GOE: 06.03.02 STRENGTH: L GED: R2 M2 L2 SVP: 3 DLU: 86

726.684-062 INSPECTOR, PRINTED CIRCUIT BOARDS (electron. comp.) alternate titles: circuit board inspector; touch-up inspector, printed circuit boards

Performs any combination of following tasks to inspect and repair printed circuit boards (PCB's): Inserts plug gauges into drilled holes of PCB panels to verify conformance to specified dimensions. Measures thickness and dimensions of plating on PCB panels to verify that plating meets specifications, using micrometers, dial indicators, calipers, rulers, eye loupes, and electronic measuring devices. Examines PCB circuitry to detect defects, such as shorts, breaks, excess or missing solder, scratches, cracks, and incorrect layout, using *light table*, eye loupe, magnifier, or microscope. Brushes solder mask ink on PCB's to repair defects in screen printing. Scrapes excess plating, or solder mask ink from PCB's, using utility knife. Repairs broken circuitry, using soldering iron or circuit bonding equipment. Records type and quantity of defective PCB's. Tests adherence of solder mask ink to PCB's, using tape. Tests continuity of PCB circuits, using bare board tester. May inspect inner layers of multilayer PCB's to verify that internal alignment and location of drilled holes meet specifications and be designated X-Ray Technician, Printed Circuit Boards (electron. comp.).
GOE: 06.03.01 STRENGTH: L GED: R3 M2 L2 SVP: 3 DLU: 86

726.684-066 INSPECTOR, SEMICONDUCTOR WAFER (electron. comp.)

Performs any of following duties to inspect, measure, and test semiconductor wafers for conformance to specifications: Inspects wafers under high intensity lamp to detect surface defects, such as scratches, chips, stains, burns, or haze. Measures thickness and resistivity of wafers, using electronic gauges or automated sorting machine. Measures diameter and *flat* of wafers, using calipers. Inspects bow or flatness of wafers, using electronic gauges, or examines surface of wafers under high intensity lamp. Tests for positive or negative conductivity of wafers, using electronic probe and gauge. Determines *crystal orientation* of wafers, using x-ray equipment. Encloses containers of inspected wafers in plastic bags for protection, using heat sealer. Records inspection data on production records or in computer, using computer terminal. May tend equipment that cleans surface of wafers [WAFER CLEANER (electron. comp.) 590.685-102].
GOE: 06.03.02 STRENGTH: L GED: R3 M2 L2 SVP: 3 DLU: 86

726.684-070 PRINTED CIRCUIT BOARD ASSEMBLER, HAND (comm. equip.; electron. comp.; inst. & app.; office machines)

Performs any combination of following duties in assembly of electronic components onto printed circuit boards (PCB's) according to specifications, using handtools: Reads worksheets and wiring diagrams, receives verbal instructions, or follows sample board to determine assembly duties, and selects components, such as transistors, resistors, relays, capacitors, and integrated circuits. Twists, bends, trims, strips, or files wire leads of components or reams holes in boards to insert wire leads, using handtools. Inserts color-coded wires in designated holes and clinches wire ends, using pliers. Press-fits (mounts) component leads onto board. Places plastic insulating sleeves around specified wire leads of components and shrinks sleeves into place, using heat gun. Crimps wire leads on underside of board, using handtools or press. Applies sealer or masking compound to selected parts of board to protect parts from effects of wave solder process. Solders wire leads and joints on underside of board, using soldering iron, to route and connect lead wires to board and between individual components. Installs heat sinks, sockets, faceplates, and accessories on boards, using handtools. May be designated according to unit installed as Socket Assembler (electron. comp.) or stage of production as Post-Wave Assembler (electron. comp.); Pre-Wave Assembler (electron. comp.). May assist other workers in wave-soldering PCB's.
GOE: 06.02.23 STRENGTH: L GED: R3 M1 L2 SVP: 4 DLU: 88

726.684-074 PRINTED CIRCUIT BOARD COMPONENT TESTER, CHEMICAL (electron. comp.)

Tests electronic components for compliance to company standards, using chemicals and soldering equipment: Places droplets of acid on surface of petri dish to prepare for lead (metal) test, using eyedropper. Positions wire lead of component or pin on integrated circuit in acid, places acid-coated wire lead or pin on chemically prepared filter paper, and observes reaction on paper that indicates lead content. Soaks components that do not pass lead test in freon to remove acid from wire leads or pins and repeats test. Refers to vendor list to determine whether components are listed as acceptable. Dips wire leads of components in beaker of liquid flux, solder pot, and beaker of freon to conduct solderability test on wire leads, using metal tongs. Observes solder on wire leads for questionable conditions, such as bending of solder, discoloration, or no solder present, using magnification lamp. Sets aside components of questionable acceptance for approval by engineer. Maintains record of test results.
GOE: 06.03.02 STRENGTH: M GED: R3 M2 L2 SVP: 5 DLU: 86

726.684-078 PRINTED CIRCUIT BOARD COMPONENT TESTER, PRE-ASSEMBLY (electron. comp.)

Tests electronic function of components preparatory to printed circuit board (PCB) assembly for compliance to company standards, using test equipment: Selects and positions test fixture on test equipment panel according to type of component being tested. Keys data into computer keyboard or turns dials and presses buttons to set tolerances on equipment, following company standards guide. Positions components in test fixture or mounts reels containing components on tape onto machine spindle and threads component tape through test machine guides. Activates equipment to start test and observes colored panel lights on equipment to determine whether components meet specifications. Replaces defective components. Verifies dimensions of components, using calipers and specification book. Obtains vendor history file for reference when excessive component defects result during testing. Maintains records of test results. May solder electronic components to test boards prior to testing. May be designated according to unit tested as Capacitor Tester (electron. comp.); Hybrid Tester (electron. comp.); Inductor Tester (electron. comp.); Relay Tester (electron. comp.); Resistor Tester (electron. comp.); Transformer Tester (electron. comp.).
GOE: 06.03.02 STRENGTH: L GED: R3 M2 L2 SVP: 5 DLU: 86

726.684-082 PRINTED CIRCUIT BOARD INSPECTOR, PRE-ASSEMBLY (electron. comp.)

Inspects printed circuit boards (PCB's) preparatory to assembly for compliance to company guidelines, using test equipment: Examines PCB's on light table for breaks in copper foil circuits. Examines PCB's to detect circuit shorts, using magnification lamp. Measures dimensions of PCB's, using ruler. Views inside edges of solder holes to detect irregular surfaces, using eye loupe. Inserts leads to components in solder holes to verify spacing of holes and ease of component insertion. Verifies plating integrity of copper foil circuits and composition of solder through solder holes, using electronic test equipment. May record inspection results to maintain vendor history files.
GOE: 06.03.02 STRENGTH: L GED: R3 M2 L2 SVP: 6 DLU: 86

726.684-086 PRINTED CIRCUIT BOARD ASSEMBLY REPAIRER (electron. comp.)

Performs any combination of following tasks to repair defective printed circuit board (PCB) assemblies, using soldering and desoldering equipment: Examines PCB's under magnifying lamp and reads inspection tags to locate defects, such as insufficient or excess solder and missing or defective components and parts. Solders or resolders missed or defective connections, joints, wiring, and terminals found to be defective or missing after original soldering process. Removes excess solder from connections and clears solder from component holes, using desoldering equipment. Repositions misaligned components, such as resistors, capacitors, and integrated circuits (IC's), and removes and replaces damaged or missing components. Trims long leads, replaces eyelets and rivets, and repairs damaged substrate, using handtools and power tools. Modifies PCB's following shop instructions, using handtools and soldering equipment. Tests soldered connections on PCB's to detect open circuits or shorts, using continuity tester.
GOE: 06.02.23 STRENGTH: L GED: R3 M1 L3 SVP: 4 DLU: 86

726.684-090 REWORKER, PRINTED CIRCUIT BOARD (electron. comp.) alternate titles: reworker

Repairs defective surfaces and circuitry on printed circuit boards (PCB's), using power and handtools, utilizing knowledge of electronic repair techniques: Reads work orders to determine number of PCB's to be repaired, type of repairs required, and method and tools to be used in reworking. Positions PCB's under microscope to examine circuitry. Cuts and removes defective wires, using knife, and positions replacement wire on circuit, using magnetic tweezers. Repairs defective circuitry, using handtools and soldering or welding equipment. Repairs board surface faults, such as excess solder on board or gold plating on connectors, using handtools, and washes solder or liquid gold over specified areas to restore board surfaces. Cleans repaired boards with solvent, using brush and rags. Inspects boards to determine that repairs meet specifications. Removes and stacks repaired boards on racks for movement to next work station. Places PCB's in industrial oven to cure solder mask. May prepare production reports.
GOE: 06.02.23 STRENGTH: L GED: R2 M2 L2 SVP: 3 DLU: 86

726.684-094 SOLDER DEPOSIT OPERATOR (electron. comp.)

Cleans assembled semiconductor packages, coats package leads with flux, and applies solder to package leads, using solder dip machine, to complete semiconductor package assembly: Places packages in holding cases and immerses cases in series of acid baths to clean packages. Places packages in holding fixtures and immerses loaded fixtures in flux bath to coat leads of packages. Pushes button to activate solder pumps of solder-dip machine and places loaded fixtures on conveyor of machine that deposits solder on leads of packages to enhance electrical conductivity of leads. Removes fixtures from conveyor, inspects leads of packages for uniform soldering, and removes solder from top of packages, using needle-nose pliers. Places loaded fixtures in baskets and immerses baskets in series of acid and soap baths to clean packages. Removes packages from fixtures, places packages on trays, and positions loaded trays in oven to dry packages. Removes tray from oven and loads packages into lot box and cleans and maintains solder pot of machine. Maintains production records.
GOE: 06.04.10 STRENGTH: L GED: R2 M2 L2 SVP: 2 DLU: 86

726.684-098 TEST FIXTURE ASSEMBLER (electron. comp.)

Assembles test fixtures used to test electrical circuitry of printed circuit boards (PCB's), according to diagram instructions: Receives test fixture kits, work orders, and diagrams. Positions test fixture boards on worktable and inserts copper sleeves in designated holes of boards as indicated on diagrams. Positions pins flush with fixture board surface, using mallet. Places copper test pins in sleeves previously inserted and positions spacer blocks in prescribed pattern on top and bottom of boards. Inserts screws in spacer blocks and secures blocks to boards, using screwdriver. Positions wires against pins and blocks, following specified pattern, and secures wires around pins or blocks, using wire wrapping gun. Positions fixture cover over spacer blocks on top of test fixture boards and positions metal back on assembled test fixture. Secures cover and back, using screws and screwdriver.
GOE: 06.04.23 STRENGTH: M GED: R3 M2 L2 SVP: 3 DLU: 86

726.684-102 TESTER, SEMICONDUCTOR WAFERS (electron. comp.)

Tests electrical characteristics of circuits on semiconductor wafers, using test equipment: Reads processing documents to determine test specifications. Obtains specified probe cards from inventory and slides probe cards into designated slot on testing equipment. Activates testing equipment and places wafer on chuck of test equipment, using tweezers. Observes wafer through test equipment microscope and aligns wafer under probes of test equipment. Pushes buttons to activate test cycle. Records test readings from printouts or display screen in test log. Compares test readings with specifications manual to identify wafers failing electrical tests. Maintains production records. May clean and maintain test equipment.
GOE: 06.03.02 STRENGTH: S GED: R2 M2 L2 SVP: 3 DLU: 86

726.684-106 TESTER, WAFER SUBSTRATE (electron. comp.)

Tests semiconductor wafer substrate, using testing equipment, such as probe tester, spectophotometer, and curve tracer, to evaluate electrical characteristics of wafer substrate: Places wafer, using tweezers, on test equipment that measures electrical characteristics of wafer substrate, such as resistivity, capacitance, and voltage. Starts equipment and observes equipment readout to determine wafer electrical measurements. Records measurements in production log. Compares measurements with specification sheets to determine if wafer substrate meets company standards. Sorts, boxes, and labels tested wafers. Delivers wafers and process sheets to production line workers. Maintains production records. May inspect wafer substrate surfaces, using ultraviolet lamp, to detect scratches and contamination.
GOE: 06.03.02 STRENGTH: L GED: R3 M2 L3 SVP: 4 DLU: 86

726.684-110 TOUCH-UP SCREENER, PRINTED CIRCUIT BOARD ASSEMBLY (electron. comp.)

Inspects printed circuit board (PCB) assemblies for defects, such as missing or damaged components, loose connections, or defective solder: Examines PCB's under magnification lamp and compares boards to sample board to detect defects. Labels defects requiring extensive repairs, such as missing or misaligned parts, damaged components, and loose connections, and routes boards to repairer. Performs minor repairs, such as cleaning boards with freon to remove solder flux; trimming long leads, using wire cutter; removing excess solder from solder points (connections), using suction bulb or solder wick and soldering iron; or resoldering connections on PCB's where solder is insufficient. Maintains record of defects and repairs to indicate recurring production problems. May reposition and solder misaligned components. May measure clearances between board and connectors, using gauges.
GOE: 06.03.02 STRENGTH: S GED: R2 M1 L2 SVP: 2 DLU: 86

726.685-010 MAGNETIC-TAPE WINDER (recording) alternate titles: cartridge loader

Tends machines that wind magnetic tape into reels or cassette hubs for use in communication and control equipment, instruments, and computers: Positions tape supply reels or cassette hubs on letoff and windup spindles of tape winding machines. Loops tape from supply reels through machine guides and into blank reels or hubs. Turns knob of footage counter devices that automatically cut tape and stop machines when specified length of tape has been wound into blank reels or hubs. Pushes switches to start individual machines and removes wound reels or hubs when machines stop. Scrapes detected surface defects from tape with knife. Splices tape ends together to form continuous loops in cassettes, using bench splicer. Inserts filled and blank hubs into cassettes and attaches covers. Packs reels and cassettes into containers and labels containers for shipment.
GOE: 06.04.02 STRENGTH: L GED: R2 M1 L1 SVP: 2 DLU: 86

726.685-014 INSERTION MACHINE TENDER, ELECTRONIC COMPONENTS (comm. equip.; electron. comp.; office machines) alternate titles: automatic component insertion operator; component insertion operator

Tends computer-controlled machine that automatically inserts electronic components, such as resistors, capacitors, diodes, and integrated circuits, into holes of printed circuit boards (PCB's): Inserts specified program tape into machine or types commands on keyboard to enter program that directs machine to insert components in specified sequence and location on PCB's. Positions paper tape reels or plastic tubes containing components into feeding mechanism to load machine. Positions PCB's on machine bed holding fixtures, starts machine, and monitors machine operation. Removes assembled PCB's from machine bed and inspects PCB's for defects, such as missing components or incomplete insertion. Stops machine and notifies supervisor or maintenance mechanic of machine malfunctions. Records production information such as production levels, machine downtime, and defects. May make minor machine adjustments and

clear machine jams. May manually insert missing components or route defective boards to repair department. May tend semiautomatic or manually controlled machines and position PCB's or components on board by hand.
GOE: 06.04.09 STRENGTH: L GED: R3 M2 L3 SVP: 4 DLU: 88

726.685-018 BREAK-AND-LOAD OPERATOR (electron. comp.)
Tends machine that breaks resistor plates along previously scored lines and loads resistors into magazines for further processing: Attaches guides of specified size to track on machine that feeds resistors into magazine, using allen wrench. Snaps magazine onto machine. Breaks scrap edges from plates. Places plates into feed mechanism of machine and starts machine that automatically breaks plates into columns of resistors which slide down track. Taps column of resistors at bottom of track, using plastic rod, to break column into single resistors that fall into magazine. Clears machine jams, using plastic rod or tweezers. Breaks plates by hand to remove premarked, defective resistors. Fills out job order and production report. Cleans machine and work station, using brush. Carries magazines to storage room and picks up box of plates for next work order.
GOE: 06.04.19 STRENGTH: L GED: R2 M1 L1 SVP: 3 DLU: 86

726.685-022 DEFLASH AND WASH OPERATOR (electron. comp.)
Tends equipment that automatically removes rubber *flash* from resistor ladders (rubber encased resistors) and cleans ladders: Loads resistor ladders into feed chute of machine and starts machine that automatically conveys resistor ladders through abrading chamber that removes flash from ladders. Visually inspects ladders to ensure that flash has been removed. Turns knob to adjust conveyor speed, if necessary, to increase or decrease abrading time. Clears jams on conveyor, using tweezers. Hits chamber of machine with mallet to loosen packed plastic abrading beads. Removes deflashed resistor ladders from conveyor, by hand, and places ladders in wire basket for subsequent cleaning and rinsing. Hangs basket of ladders on travel arm of wash equipment and starts equipment that ultrasonically cleans and rinses deflashed ladders in chemical baths.
GOE: 06.04.19 STRENGTH: M GED: R2 M1 L1 SVP: 3 DLU: 86

726.685-026 DIE ATTACHING MACHINE TENDER (electron. comp.)
Tends *die* attaching machine that bonds dies to semiconductor packages: Loads package carriers, magazines containing dies, and gold pieces, used to attach dies to packages, into designated slots of machine. Starts machine that automatically positions and melts gold on packages and positions dies in packages to form assembled semiconductor packages. Observes operation of machine to ensure that alignment of packages, gold, and dies meets company specifications, using video monitor. Turns knobs on machine to adjust alignment of parts assembled, regulate operation speed, and set temperature of molten gold. Removes magazines of packages for further processing.
GOE: 06.04.09 STRENGTH: L GED: R2 M1 L2 SVP: 2 DLU: 86

726.685-030 DIE TESTER (electron. comp.)
Tests voltage of *dies* containing individual devices, such as diodes and transistors, using computerized testing system, to ensure that dies meet company and manufacturer specifications: Reads production sheets and computer code books to determine test instructions and codes. Keys instructions and codes into computer, using computer terminal. Pours dies into equipment bowl that automatically conveys each die to probe, tests voltage of each die, and sorts dies into specified bottles. Observes equipment operation to detect misfeeds, using built-in microscope. Maintains production records. Records voltage reading on bottle labels. Cleans and maintains testing equipment.
GOE: 06.03.02 STRENGTH: L GED: R2 M2 L2 SVP: 3 DLU: 86

726.685-034 LEAK TESTER, SEMICONDUCTOR PACKAGES (electron. comp.)
Tends testing equipment that detects leaks in semiconductor packages: Loads tubes containing semiconductor packages into canister. Places loaded canister in equipment that replaces air in canister with liquid freon or flushes canister with radioactive isotopes. Pushes buttons and flips switches to activate equipment. Removes loaded canister and places either canister or tube of semiconductor packages in leak testing equipment, such as bubble pot or geiger counter tank, that detects gross and fine leaks in semiconductor packages. Inspects tube of packages in bubble pot, using magnifying glass, to identify packages with bubbles, indicating gross leaks. Observes control panel of geiger counter tank to identify radioactive semiconductor packages, indicating fine leaks. Removes tubes and canisters from leak detection equipment and places defective semiconductor packages in containers, using tweezers. Places accepted semiconductor packages in tubes, using tweezers. Maintains production records.
GOE: 06.03.02 STRENGTH: M GED: R2 M1 L2 SVP: 2 DLU: 86

726.685-038 REFLOW OPERATOR (electron. comp.)
Tends reflow equipment that melts solder on printed circuit boards (PCB's) to redistribute and fuse solder on boards to improve appearance, hardness, and solderability for PCB component assembly: Immerses boards in cleaning solution or places boards in cleaning machine that cleans and removes contaminants from boards before reflow process. Starts reflow equipment and adjusts conveyor speed and temperature of infrared heating units to meet specifications. Feeds PCB's onto conveyor of equipment that applies liquid flux and infrared heat to boards to melt, redistribute, and fuse existing solder on boards and cleans, rinses, and dries boards following reflow process. Observes boards moving on conveyor to monitor flow and operation of reflow process. Removes boards upon completion of process and inspects boards for reflow process de-

fects. May add chemicals to flux solution. May tend soldering equipment. May tend reflow equipment that automatically cleans, rinses, and dries boards before and after reflow process.
GOE: 06.04.19 STRENGTH: M GED: R2 M2 L2 SVP: 2 DLU: 86

726.685-042 ROD TAPE OPERATOR (electron. comp.)
Tends rod taping machine that separates and tapes ceramic coated aluminum rods and winds tape containing rods onto reels for subsequent processing: Places rods onto feed tray of taping machine that aligns rods in parallel configuration, applies tape to secure rods in place, and winds taped rods onto reel. Monitors operation of machine to detect malfunctions. Replaces empty tape rolls and removes full reels of taped rods from machine. May perform duties as described under SCREENER OPERATOR (any industry) 599.685-082 to separate defective slugs (rods cut to specified lengths, approximately one inch or less).
GOE: 06.04.19 STRENGTH: M GED: R2 M1 L1 SVP: 3 DLU: 86

726.685-046 SAW OPERATOR, SEMICONDUCTOR WAFERS (electron. comp.) alternate titles: scriber
Tends sawing machine that automatically scribes semiconductor wafers prior to separating wafers into individual *dies*: Flips switches and presses buttons to activate sawing machine. Places wafer mounted on laminated plastic onto moveable chuck of sawing machine, using tweezers. Presses buttons and turns knobs and dials to adjust saw to specifications and to start sawing cycle. Monitors sawing cycle, using magnified viewer or TV monitor, to verify that wafers are scribed according to specifications and adjusts controls if required. Removes scribed wafer from machine and places wafer in container, using tweezers. May mount wafers on plastic laminate, using mounting device. May visually inspect wafers to identify misalignment of scribe lines. May maintain and clean sawing machine. May separate sawn wafers into dies [WAFER BREAKER, SEMICONDUCTORS (electron. comp.) 726.687-046]. May clean sawn wafers or dies, using cleaning equipment and solutions.
GOE: 06.04.09 STRENGTH: L GED: R2 M1 L2 SVP: 3 DLU: 88

726.685-050 SOLDER-LEVELER, PRINTED CIRCUIT BOARDS (electron. comp.)
Tends processing equipment that prepares and applies solder to copper circuit areas of printed circuit boards (PCB's) or panels: Reads process specifications and activates equipment units, such as conveyors, sprayers, pumps, brushes, air knives (blower mechanism), and solder bath. Adjusts equipment controls to regulate processing factors, such as temperatures, pressures, and speeds, according to specifications. Feeds boards on motorized conveyor leading into series of processing units, such as sprayers, brushes, dryers, and flux rollers, that clean copper circuit areas and apply flux preparatory to solder application. Removes boards from precleaning equipment conveyor and clamps boards to feeding mechanism of solder leveling equipment. Pushes button to activate equipment that automatically lowers board into molten solder bath, lifts boards out of bath, and moves boards past hot-air knives that smooth solder off noncopper areas. Monitors equipment operation and corrects minor malfunctions, such as board misfeeds, conveyor speeds, and temperature settings. Removes board from solder equipment and visually examines boards for completeness of soldering. Notifies supervisor of equipment malfunctions and board defects, such as discolored, missing, or unlevel solder. May reroute defective boards through processing equipment to correct defects. May maintain production records.
GOE: 06.04.21 STRENGTH: L GED: R2 M2 L2 SVP: 3 DLU: 86

726.685-054 TESTER, SEMICONDUCTOR PACKAGES (electron. comp.)
Tends automatic equipment that test functions of semiconductor packages: Reads production documents to determine test specifications. Inserts specified test program (magnetic card) in test equipment to program equipment. Places tubular magazines containing semiconductor packages in feeder mechanism of equipment. Flips switch to activate test cycle. Monitors operation of test equipment to detect misfeeds. Sorts tested semiconductor packages into specified containers. Maintains production records. May tend centrifuge or temperature-cycle machine that places semiconductor packages under stress to cause circuit failure of weak sections during subsequent testing.
GOE: 06.03.02 STRENGTH: L GED: R2 M2 L2 SVP: 3 DLU: 86

726.685-058 WAFER MOUNTER (electron. comp.)
Tends press that mounts semiconductor wafers in templates for polishing: Cleans templates, using cleaning solution and brush or towel, or tends machine that automatically cleans templates. Places cushion in template depressions and places wafers on cushion, or places wafers on waxed template. Positions templates in press and activates press that presses wafers into templates. May tend machine that automatically removes polished wafers from templates. May tend machine that laps templates to restore flatness. May tend press that attaches template to carriers before mounting wafers.
GOE: 06.04.09 STRENGTH: M GED: R2 M1 L2 SVP: 2 DLU: 86

726.685-062 PROGRAMMING EQUIPMENT OPERATOR (electron. comp.) alternate titles: die equipment operator; prom burn-off operator
Tends equipment that automatically transfers programmed information onto integrated circuits (ICs) on *dies* or IC packages, such as PROMs (programmable read only memory): Reads work order that accompanies ICs for processing to determine programming specifications. Secures master PROM or die in equipment. Keys in codes, using computer keyboard and presses buttons to acti-

vate equipment that reproduces master program in programmer. Observes digital displays on equipment to ensure that master program is not defective and to determine when reproduction of program is completed in programmer. Positions blank PROMs and pushes lever to lock PROMs in sockets of programmer; or positions blank dies on platform of die probe equipment, views dies through microscope, and turns knobs on equipment to position specified areas of dies under probes prior to programming. Presses switches to activate programmer that reproduces program on blank PROMs or dies. Observes defect indicator lights to detect defective PROMs or dies and to determine completion of programming. Maintains production records. May load defective PROMs into equipment that exposes PROMs to ultraviolet light for timed intervals to erase programmed information in order to reuse PROMs.
GOE: 06.04.19 STRENGTH: S GED: R3 M2 L3 SVP: 3 DLU: 86

726.685-066   BONDER, SEMICONDUCTOR (electron. comp.)
Tends automatic bonding machine that bonds gold or aluminum wire to integrated circuit dies to connect circuitry to package leads: Reviews schematic diagram or work order to determine bonding specifications. Turns dials to set bonding machine temperature controls and to regulate wire feeding mechanism. Mounts spool of wire onto holder and inserts wire end through guides, using tweezers. Positions semiconductor package into magazine of automatic feed mechanism, and observes package, using microscope or equipment display screen, to ensure connections to be bonded are aligned with bonding wire. Adjusts alignment as necessary. Activates machine that automatically bonds wire to specified connections on semiconductor package leads. Removes packages from bonding machine and places packages in work tray. May test tensile strength of bonded connections, using testing equipment. May locate connections and bond wire to connect circuitry of hybrid circuits, using precision-bonding machine.
GOE: 06.04.09 STRENGTH: S GED: R2 M1 L2 SVP: 2 DLU: 86

726.686-010   WAVE-SOLDER OFFBEARER (electron. comp.)
Removes printed circuit boards (PCB's) from discharge conveyor of automatic wave-soldering machine following completion of soldering process: Places empty carrier on workbench at discharge end of wave-soldering machine conveyor. Removes pallets containing wave-soldered PCB's from conveyor and places pallets in carrier. Examines boards to detect defects, such as missing solder, spots, or warped boards. Submits defective boards to supervisor for approval or correction of defects. Stacks acceptable boards on carrier or in tub for final assembly. May assist others in setting up and operating equipment for wave-soldering process. May assist in cleaning equipment, using scraper and airhose. May complete production report for supervisory use.
GOE: 06.04.40 STRENGTH: M GED: R2 M1 L2 SVP: 2 DLU: 86

726.687-010   ELECTRONICS WORKER (electron. comp.)
Performs any combination of following tasks to clean, trim, or prepare components or parts for assembly by other workers: Receives verbal or written instructions from supervisor regarding work assignment. Cleans and deglosses parts, using cleaning devices, solutions, and abrasives. Trims flash from molded or cast parts, using cutting tool or file. Applies primers, plastics, adhesives, and other coatings to designated surfaces, using applicators, such as spray guns, brushes, or rollers. Fills shells, caps, cases, and other cavities with plastic encapsulating fluid or dips parts in fluid to protect, coat, and seal parts. Prepares wires for assembly by measuring, cutting, stripping, twisting, tinning, and attaching contacts, lugs, and other terminal devices, using handtools, and power tools and equipment. Positions and fastens together parts, such as laminates, electron tube mounts and cages, variable capacitor rotors and stators, paper loudspeaker cones, faceplates, and shells and cases for various electronic components, using handtools and power tools. Prints identifying information on components and parts, using silk screen, transfer press, or electro-etch printing devices, or ink pad and stamp. Moves parts and finished components to designated areas of plant, such as assembly, shipping and receiving, or storage. Loads and unloads parts from ovens, baskets, pallets, and racks. Disassembles and reclaims parts, using heating equipment and handtools.
GOE: 06.04.34 STRENGTH: L GED: R2 M1 L2 SVP: 2 DLU: 88

726.687-014   PLUG WIRER (elec. equip.)
Attaches insulated wire to terminals of electric plugs, using handpress: Positions wire in slot of plug shell and places brass terminal prongs in clamp of press. Moves lever that causes press to force exposed ends of wire into contact with prongs and secures contacts firmly in plug.
GOE: 06.04.23 STRENGTH: L GED: R2 M1 L1 SVP: 3 DLU: 77

726.687-022   ENCAPSULATOR (elec. equip.; electron. comp.)
Performs any combination of following tasks to encapsulate electrical and electronic parts, components, and assemblies with epoxy, plastic, and other protective coating material: Weighs and mixes encapsulating material, following prescribed formula. Positions module or transformer case under outlet of encapsulating fluid tank and moves controls to force preset amount of fluid from tank into module or transformer case. Places components on racks or hooks, dips racks or hooks containing components into encapsulating fluid, and places dipped components on drying frame or into oven to harden coating. Fills capacitor shells or semiconductor caps with encapsulating fluid or applies encapsulating fluid to specified surfaces on component, using manually- or electrically-powered syringe or other applicator. Molds protective casing around component, using compression molding machine. Places component into mold and pours encapsulating fluid into mold to surround component. Heats component

in oven or curing device prior to or after encapsulating to remove moisture or cure encapsulating material. Inspects encapsulation for defects, such as chips and pinholes. Stamps color code or trademark on encapsulated components. Bonds flexible printed circuit boards to rigid boards, using bonding solution and potting equipment. May weigh and mix materials, following formula, and be designated Compound Mixer (elec. equip.; electron. comp.). May be designated Bonder (electron. comp.); Dipper (elec. equip.; electron. comp.); Filler (elec. equip.; electron. comp.); Potter (electron. comp.).
GOE: 06.04.24 STRENGTH: L GED: R2 M1 L2 SVP: 2 DLU: 87

726.687-026   LAMINATION   ASSEMBLER,   PRINTED   CIRCUIT BOARDS (electron. comp.)
Assembles layers of laminating materials and printed circuit board (PCB) panels to prepare for multilayer PCB laminating process: Assembles and aligns inner and outer layers of PCB panels and laminating materials over guide pins in holding fixture to prepare multilayer PCB panels for laminating process, following established procedures. Examines inner layers of panels during assembly for defects, such as chips, dust, or dents. May tend laminating machine that bonds assembled panels to form multilayer PCB panels [LAMINATOR, PRINTED CIRCUIT BOARDS (electron. comp.) 692.685-282]. May heat materials in oven to remove moisture prior to laminating process.
GOE: 06.04.34 STRENGTH: M GED: R2 M2 L2 SVP: 2 DLU: 88

726.687-030   LOADER, SEMICONDUCTOR DIES (electron. comp.)
Loads *dies*, using vacuum wand, into carriers that hold and protect dies during fabrication of semiconductor packages: Pours dies from container onto filter paper. Picks up and places dies circuit-side up in indentations in carrier, using vacuum wand. Secures lid on carrier, using manual pressure. May clean dies prior to loading, using solutions and cleaning equipment. May sort semiconductor devices to remove defective devices marked in inspection department.
GOE: 06.04.40 STRENGTH: S GED: R2 M1 L2 SVP: 2 DLU: 86

726.687-034   MASKER (electron. comp.)
Applies liquefied soldering mask to designated terminal areas of printed circuit boards (PCB's) to prevent molten solder from collecting on circuitry during wave soldering process, using squeeze bottle of soldering mask, and following premasked sample. Removes excess mask from PCB's, using towel. Places masked PCB's in storage racks for movement to next work station.
GOE: 06.04.23 STRENGTH: L GED: R2 M1 L2 SVP: 2 DLU: 88

726.687-038   PREASSEMBLER, PRINTED CIRCUIT BOARD (electron. comp.)
Attaches preassembled components, such as terminal pins, connectors, and labels, to printed circuit boards (PCB's) and stamps identification codes on boards preparatory to further assembly: Examines PCB's for illegible issue numbers and removes and restamps numbers, using eraser and handstamp. Reads work specifications to determine type of labels, components, and locations on PCB's to attach items. Cuts component pins (wires) to specified length, using wire cutters, inserts pins in specified holes on PCB's, and secures pins to PCB's, using holding block and hammer or pneumatically powered stamping device. Affixes labels and tape to boards and stamps identification codes on boards.
GOE: 06.04.34 STRENGTH: L GED: R2 M1 L2 SVP: 2 DLU: 86

726.687-042   SEALER,   SEMICONDUCTOR   PACKAGES   (electron. comp.)
Positions and seals solder-coated lids or tops on semiconductor packages, using heated chuck or automatic furnace: Places lids on semiconductor packages, using tweezers. Places semiconductor packages on heated chuck in nitrogen box or places container of semiconductor packages on furnace conveyor to heat and seal semiconductor packages. Maintains production records.
GOE: 06.04.23 STRENGTH: L GED: R2 M1 L1 SVP: 2 DLU: 86

726.687-046   WAFER BREAKER, SEMICONDUCTORS (electron. comp.)
Breaks semiconductor wafers into individual *dies*, using equipment and handtools: Places semiconductor wafer on pad, using tweezers. Taps wafer, using pencil tip, awl, or tweezers to break wafer into quarters. Places semiconductor wafer quarter on plastic square. Presses semiconductor wafer, using roller or air pressure equipment, to break wafer quarter into individual dies. Places individual dies in containers, using vacuum wand or brush. May break wafers, using chemical solutions and breaking equipment.
GOE: 06.04.34 STRENGTH: S GED: R2 M1 L2 SVP: 2 DLU: 86

727   OCCUPATIONS IN ASSEMBLY OF STORAGE BATTERIES

This group includes occupations concerned with assembling grids, plates, separators, and connectors to form wet- and dry-cell batteries, and filling with electrolyte.

727.130-010   SUPERVISOR, BURNING, FORMING, AND ASSEMBLY (elec. equip.)
Supervises and coordinates activities of workers engaged in assembly and repair of storage batteries: Coordinates activities pertaining to grouping and fusing plates into elements and elements into complete batteries, processing (forming and drying) plates preparatory to final assembly, charging finished batteries, and repairing defective batteries. Adjusts machines or equipment, such as automatic plate stackers and burners, dry-charge processing machine, and sealing

machines. Inspects in-process or finished units, such as elements, batteries, and containers to determine conformance to specifications. Observes meters, thermometers, hydrometers, temperature controls, and operation of machines and equipment to detect malfunction. Performs other duties as described under SUPERVISOR (any industry) Master Title. May be designated according to process supervised as Supervisor, Battery Assembly (elec. equip.); Supervisor, Lead Burning (elec. equip.); Supervisor, Plate Forming (elec. equip.).
GOE: 06.02.01 STRENGTH: L GED: R4 M3 L3 SVP: 7 DLU: 77

727.137-010 SUPERVISOR, DRY-CELL ASSEMBLY (elec. equip.)
Supervises and coordinates activities of workers engaged in producing and assembling components of primary (dry) cells to make batteries: Coordinates activities, such as extruding cores, inserting cores and carbon rods in cans, welding wires (pins) to cans, capping and sealing cells, soldering pins to rods of other cells to make battery, inserting cells in tubes or sleeves, and testing, repairing, and packaging batteries. Inspects subassemblies and finished units for conformance to specifications. May assist machine operators with setup or adjustment of machines for change in size of cans or to correct malfunction. Performs other duties as described under SUPERVISOR (any industry) Master Title.
GOE: 06.02.01 STRENGTH: L GED: R4 M3 L3 SVP: 7 DLU: 77

727.381-010 BATTERY RECHARGER (elec. equip.)
Tests and treats rejected storage batteries and mixes acid solutions: Determines specific gravity of electrolyte in rejected batteries and adjusts solution to specified concentration and height in cells [ACID FILLER (elec. equip.)]. Tests batteries for specific defects [BATTERY TESTER (elec. equip.); FINAL INSPECTOR (elec. equip.)]. Fills batteries with fresh electrolyte, charges battery and tests battery for performance, using voltmeters and ammeters. Segregates batteries that fail performance test. Turns valves to fill vats with specified quantity of acid and water for use in forming and charging processes. Activates agitator to diffuse liquids, and tests solutions for specified concentration, using hydrometer.
GOE: 06.02.32 STRENGTH: M GED: R3 M2 L2 SVP: 5 DLU: 77

727.381-014 BATTERY REPAIRER (any industry) alternate titles: battery tester; storage-battery charger
Repairs and recharges electric-storage batteries: Melts sealing compound on cover, using gas torch. Loosens compound from sides of case, using putty knife. Removes and disassembles cells and inspects parts to detect defects. Replaces defective parts, fuses lead parts, using oxyacetylene torch, reassembles battery, and pours hot seal (tar compound) over cover. Fills cells with acid solution and determines specific gravity of solution, using hydrometer and thermometer. Adds acid or water to obtain specified concentration. Attaches leads from charger to battery posts and starts charger. Reads meters and adjusts rheostat to control flow of current through battery. May repair battery-charging equipment.
GOE: 05.10.03 STRENGTH: M GED: R3 M2 L2 SVP: 6 DLU: 77

727.381-018 DRY-CELL TESTER (elec. equip.)
Tests dry cells and dry-cell batteries to determine length of life, capacity, shelf-life, effects of temperature on battery output, and other characteristics, using direct current voltmeters, ammeters, and programmed test equipment: Mounts cells or batteries on test racks and connects terminals to testing equipment. Discharges cells or batteries through fixed resistances at specified time intervals. Reads meters and records voltages during discharge intervals. Tests cells and batteries for open-circuit voltage and electrical output at specified intervals for prescribed periods to measure shelf-life. May test new compounds as directed.
GOE: 06.03.01 STRENGTH: L GED: R4 M3 L3 SVP: 6 DLU: 77

727.381-022 STORAGE BATTERY INSPECTOR AND TESTER (elec. equip.) alternate titles: battery analyst; quality auditor; test technician
Inspects and tests storage batteries in process of manufacture or before shipment to verify conformity with mechanical, chemical, and electrical specifications, using specified and standardized tests, procedures, and equipment and applying knowledge of battery performance, specifications, manufacture, and construction: Disassembles batteries following specified procedures. Examines battery for defects and measures battery to determine if specifications are met, using such instruments as gauges and scales. Tests specific gravity of battery acid, using hydrometer and thermometer. Places battery in water tank or refrigerator to control temperature and test electrical capacity of battery. Attaches leads to meters and equipment to charge or discharge battery as specified to determine amperage delivered at given rate. Records inspection and test results, compares results with specifications, and writes reports used in correcting manufacturing defects or developing new products. May test and disassemble returned batteries to determine cause of failure.
GOE: 06.01.05 STRENGTH: L GED: R4 M2 L4 SVP: 7 DLU: 77

727.384-010 BATTERY TESTER (elec. equip.) alternate titles: electrical tester, battery
Tests storage batteries, using electric testing instruments: Sets dials on testing instruments according to battery voltage. Places positive and negative wired plugs on posts and intercell-connector terminals of corresponding polarity and observes indicator on instrument that measures resistance capacity in terms of pass or reject. Tests rejected batteries to determine specific defects, using voltmeter. Computes comparative figures and test data to determine deficiencies

and attaches slip to battery indicating type of defect. May test battery assemblies on conveyor line. May test batteries used in field equipment and be designated Battery Tester, Field (elec. equip.).
GOE: 06.03.01 STRENGTH: L GED: R3 M3 L2 SVP: 3 DLU: 77

727.484-010 ACID ADJUSTER (elec. equip.) alternate titles: balancer
Adjusts (balances) specific gravity of electrolyte (acid solution) in battery cells or in plate-forming tanks to concentration specified: Ascertains temperature and specific gravity of solutions, using thermometer and hydrometer. Turns valves or lever to drain acid or water into cells or tanks to adjust specific gravity of solutions. Connects batteries to charging line and charges batteries for specified time.
GOE: 06.04.34 STRENGTH: L GED: R2 M2 L2 SVP: 2 DLU: 77

727.587-010 BATTERY CHARGER (elec. equip.)
Charges storage batteries: Groups batteries on tables according to type and specified rate and length of charge. Attaches positive lead wire (jumper) from current source to positive post and negative lead wire to negative post of group. Starts charge and reads ammeter and adjusts rheostat to obtain specified charging rate. Records data indicating location, type, and number of batteries on circuit and rate and length of charge specified. Marks ends of tables with chalk indicating when batteries are to be disconnected and removed. May ascertain specific gravity of acid in batteries during charge, using hydrometer and thermometer and notify ACID ADJUSTER (elec. equip.) to correct variation. May record instrument readings during charging cycle and regulate current.
GOE: 06.04.34 STRENGTH: L GED: R2 M2 L1 SVP: 3 DLU: 77

727.662-010 LEAD BURNER, MACHINE (elec. equip.) alternate titles: group burner, machine
Sets up and operates rotary lead-burning machine to fuse straps to grouped plates to form storage battery elements: Adjusts machine fixtures and torch, according to size of grouped plates, using handtools. Observes pressure gauge, ignites torch, turns gas and air valves to set flame of specified size and color, and starts machine. Visually inspects fused elements for lead runs, and defective plates and separators. Places specified number of elements in battery box in prescribed position, using shims when necessary. Directs workers engaged in machine stacking of plates (grouping), loading groups into machine, and fitting straps to lugs prior to fusing. Inspects materials prior to grouping for specified size and type. Directs or performs adjustment of feeding mechanisms and electric counter on stacking machine, using handtools. May operate two-station lead-burning machines.
GOE: 06.02.19 STRENGTH: M GED: R3 M2 L2 SVP: 5 DLU: 77

727.664-010 BATTERY ASSEMBLER, DRY CELL (elec. equip.)
Performs any combination of following duties to assemble batteries for commercial use in products, such as photographic equipment, flashlights, and pagers: Fills electrolyte or mercury dispensing devices to specified levels. Pours partial battery assembly parts into respective conveyor line bowl feeders, places spools of metal strips and paper on holding brackets, or positions battery subassemblies in conveyor holding attachments. Observes automatic equipment that cuts blotter and cathode inserts, places inserts in subassembly, joins top and bottom subassembly of batteries, dispenses specified amounts of electrolyte or mercury, and spot welds metal strip to each battery; or tamps pellets into bottom sections of battery subassembly. Positions inserts, such as poly ring and anode ring, in subassembly before or after designated steps of assembly process. Notifies supervisor or setup personnel, or signals coworkers, to stop conveyor when malfunctions occur. Gathers batteries with metal strips attached, and places specified number of batteries in concave work aid that facilitates positioning metal strips over side of batteries in stack prior to spot welding. Positions each battery of stack under spot welder and depresses pedal to spot weld strips to successive stacks of batteries. Spot welds battery top to joined batteries. Inserts battery stacks into battery sleeves with crimped tops, positions battery sleeves in crimping machine, and presses button to crimp bottom of sleeves to secure stacks in sleeves. Positions batteries in test equipment to determine whether batteries meet standard for acceptability. Tends equipment that automatically cuts out blotter and cathode battery inserts and places inserts in partial battery assemblies. Packs batteries meeting company standards for shipment.
GOE: 06.04.23 STRENGTH: M GED: R3 M2 L2 SVP: 4 DLU: 88

727.684-010 BATTERY ASSEMBLER (elec. equip.)
Assembles cells and other components in container (battery case) to make complete storage battery: Inserts cells into container according to prescribed polarity arrangement. Installs covers on cells [CELL COVERER (elec. equip.) 727.687-042] and fits intercell connectors on posts. Burns (fuses) connectors to post. Pours compound over cells to fill cracks and seal battery in case [SEALER (elec. equip.) 727.684-030]. May invert special-type cover onto jig, position cells in cover, ladle molten lead into cover to form posts and connectors and fuse parts to cells, pour plastic seal into grooves, and press container into cover to assemble battery.
GOE: 06.02.23 STRENGTH: L GED: R3 M2 L2 SVP: 4 DLU: 77

727.684-014 BATTERY ASSEMBLER, PLASTIC (elec. equip.)
Performs any combination of following tasks to prepare and assemble components of plastic-cased batteries: Places state-of-charge indicator in case in prescribed channel position and attaches glass mat to rear surface of ball channel, using adhesive. Applies liquid-level lines to case according to drawing, using marking devices. Inserts bushings in post openings in cover to provide

leak-proof junction between post and cover. Places filler-plugs and washers in cover and attaches baffle plate to cell vent to reduce acid spray during charging. Inserts (interleaves) separators of specified size between plates of elements and applies liner to exposed edges and outside plates to insulate surfaces and serve as reservoir for electrolyte. Fits baffle plate onto top of element and between connecting straps to protect tops of separators and reduce acid spray during charging. Inserts cells in single or multicell containers according to specified polarity arrangement. Tests each cell electrically by determining resistance of cell to flow of applied current of specified voltage, using meter. Lubricates inner surface of bushings in cover. Applies cement to top edge of container and positions cover. Places clamps on cover to apply pressure until cement sets. Removes clamps. Fuses wire or cast terminals to posts, using torch. Inspects battery for defects. Applies air pressure to battery submerged in water to detect leaks. Dates, codes, and labels case, using marking and labeling devices. Inspects finished batteries for appearance and packages and seals batteries in cartons.
GOE: 06.04.23 STRENGTH: L GED: R2 M2 L2 SVP: 2 DLU: 77

727.684-018 CELL REPAIRER (elec. equip.) alternate titles: battery tester and repairer
Repairs multiple-cell dry batteries: Inspects batteries for defects, such as dented cans, damaged carbon rods and terminals, and defective sealing. Repairs or replaces defective parts, using handtools. Tests cells and batteries for capacity, using voltmeter. Cuts wires to remove faulty cells, using hand shears. Connects replacement cell to batteries, using soldering iron.
GOE: 06.04.34 STRENGTH: L GED: R2 M2 L2 SVP: 3 DLU: 77

727.684-022 LEAD BURNER (elec. equip.)
Burns (fuses) together lead and lead-alloy connections and builds up storage-battery parts, using oxyacetylene torch and lead bar: Ignites torch, observes color of flame, and turns handwheel or valve to regulate flow of gas and air to obtain flame of specified temperature. Moves flame over contact points of parts to puddle (melt) metal and fuse parts, melting lead bar and adding metal when required. Seals fusion points of parts, such as straps and lugs, posts and links, intercell connecting bar, and sleeves; wires or strips connecting plates and lead forming tanks; and bars connecting dry-charge elements. Guides torch and bar to add metal and build up parts, such as battery posts, to prescribed level, using template to ensure specified height. Fills cavities or corrects malformation in lead parts. May install and remove post builders or burning dams used to position molten lead. May install assembled units and posts in mold, heat mold with torch, and brush liquid soap on mold to prevent sticking.
GOE: 06.04.31 STRENGTH: L GED: R2 M1 L2 SVP: 3 DLU: 77

727.684-026 PLATE ASSEMBLER, SMALL BATTERY (elec. equip.) alternate titles: bench assembler, battery
Assembles plates in series for small batteries: Positions plates vertically between teeth of rack and pushes rack under electrode of welding machine. Places terminal assembly (a short wire welded to screw terminal) on plate edge. Depresses pedal to lower electrode and weld terminal wire to plate, repeating operation until all plates are fitted with terminals. Interleaves positive and negative plates in assembly rack and fuses wire across tops of grouped plates. Cuts wire to separate positive and negative units from series of plates, using knife. Aligns units in jig so grouped plates are parallel.
GOE: 06.02.23 STRENGTH: L GED: R3 M2 L2 SVP: 3 DLU: 77

727.684-030 SEALER (elec. equip.) alternate titles: flamer-sealer
Seals storage battery cells in containers (battery box) to form airtight and watertight battery: Loads thermostatically controlled kettle (preheater) with chunks of compound. Ignites burners and adjusts temperature controls to heat and melt compound. Opens valve to drain compound into pot and empties compound into tank (sealing machine). Holds hose attached to tank and presses lever to control flow of compound over cells. Starts conveyor to move batteries through flamer (fixed and preset gas torches) or manipulates gas torch to melt and level off compound to produce seal. Scrapes excess compound from container, using putty knife and cloth. May clip posts, using handtool. May stamp numbers on battery, using marking dies. May install covers on cells [CELL COVERER (elec. equip.) 727.687-042]. May melt compound in hand-manipulated container and pour compound over cells. May use heated dipper equipped with trigger mechanism to deposit sealing compound over cells.
GOE: 06.04.34 STRENGTH: L GED: R2 M1 L2 SVP: 3 DLU: 77

727.685-010 PLATE SLITTER-AND-INSPECTOR (elec. equip.)
Tends machine that slits panels of storage-battery plates to specified widths, and inspects slit plates for defects in casting or pasting, such as cracked frames (grids), broken lugs, holes, and incomplete or uneven pasting: Adjusts slot in feeding mechanism (plate transfer) to thickness of plate, positions saw according to trim lugs on plate to specified length, and positions cutting rollers according to widths specified for plates. Starts conveyor and slitter. Examines plates and segregates defective plates. Cleans edges of lugs, using handtools and stacks plates on truck. Records date, type of plate, and inspector's name on ticket and attaches ticket to load.
GOE: 06.04.24 STRENGTH: L GED: R2 M2 L2 SVP: 2 DLU: 77

727.687-010 ACID DUMPER (elec. equip.) alternate titles: acid changer; forming acid dumper
Starts conveyors and pushes incoming storage batteries onto conveyor leading to machine which inverts batteries over receiving tank to drain used forming acid or manually unloads batteries from forming trucks, inverts batteries,

and places batteries on rack to drain. Places drained batteries on conveyor leading to refilling station or on truck. May strip connectors and dummy vents from battery before draining, replace them after draining, and refill battery with acid, using vacuum filling machine [ACID FILLER (elec. equip.)]. May ascertain specific gravity of acid in battery, using thermometer and hydrometer and add acid or water to obtain specified concentration.
GOE: 06.04.40 STRENGTH: M GED: R2 M1 L1 SVP: 2 DLU: 77

727.687-014 ACID FILLER (elec. equip.)
Fills storage battery cells with sulfuric acid solutions of specified concentration preparatory to forming and charging: Arranges batteries in groups on tables or trucks according to specified acid concentration. Holds spouts of hoses on gravity flow or siphon-type fillers over battery vents. Adjusts valves manually or pushes pedal to control flow of acid to cells. Fits rubber gaskets on multiple filler head of vacuum filling machine to set level of fill. Positions filler head on battery vents and adjusts controls to start vacuum action and fill cells. May mix acid and water and adjust solution to prescribed specific gravity. May bring acid in insufficiently filled batteries to specified level and be designated Acid Leveler (elec. equip.).
GOE: 06.04.36 STRENGTH: L GED: R2 M1 L1 SVP: 2 DLU: 77

727.687-018 ALUMINUM-CONTAINER TESTER (elec. equip.) alternate titles: battery-container tester, aluminum
Tests efficiency of enamel insulation of finished aluminum battery containers, using electrical testing apparatus and chemical solutions: Places lid on metal fixture wired to instrument panel to test coating on lid. Dips instrument terminal in chemical solution and rubs terminal over surface of lid, observing sparks that indicate insufficient insulation. Outlines areas that emit sparks with crayon to guide workers in applying additional enamel coating. Fills container with chemical solution to test interior insulation. Dips tip of rubber-covered rod, connected to ohmmeter, in solution and observes instrument dial to determine if insulation is effective within specified tolerance. Marks acceptance symbol on satisfactory containers. Moves testing rod around interior of container until panel light indicates defect in container. Pours solution out of container to level of defective area (light goes out when level of solution is below defect). Moves tip of wired bar over surface of container until sparks occur indicating location of defect. Marks and segregates defective containers.
GOE: 06.03.02 STRENGTH: L GED: R2 M2 L2 SVP: 3 DLU: 77

727.687-022 ASSEMBLER, DRY CELL AND BATTERY (elec. equip.)
Performs any combination of following tasks to assemble dry cells and dry batteries: Removes cans (cell containers) from cartons and racks cans in trays. Drops washer into bottom of cans. Pulls lever to drain measured amount of liquid paste into can. Places paper liner (spider) over open end of can. Drops core into can, forcing spider to line can and wrap core. Observes conveyor-fed electrical-test-and-reject mechanism that contacts and tests finished cells and removes defective cells from conveyor. Inserts cells in partitioned containers to make battery. Positions perforated metal plate (cover) on carbon rods of cells in battery to straighten and center rods. Places battery on conveyor leading to next station, where worker removes and returns cover. Bends wires on cells preparatory to soldering of wires to cells in adjacent row. Drains or pours hot asphalt into battery-container, using dispensing device or ladle. Places battery in container and presses it into asphalt. Places finished batteries in cartons. May be designated according to task performed as Core Dropper (elec. equip.); Wire Bender (elec. equip.).
GOE: 06.04.23 STRENGTH: L GED: R1 M1 L1 SVP: 2 DLU: 77

727.687-026 BATTERY CHARGER, CONVEYOR LINE (elec. equip.)
Performs any combination of following tasks to charge storage batteries: Sets acid-filled batteries apart from batteries requiring acid and routes batteries requiring acid to designated areas. Places charging plugs (filler-vent caps) loosely over cells of acid-filled batteries to prevent escape of battery acid during charging process. Clears jams on conveyors leading to and from acid-dumping machine. Reads charging record cards and chalk marks on charging tables to determine batteries ready to be removed. Disconnects charged batteries from electric circuit and slides batteries from table onto conveyor. May carry boxes of plugs to designated areas. May be known as Charging-Plug Placer (elec. equip.).
GOE: 06.04.34 STRENGTH: L GED: R2 M1 L1 SVP: 2 DLU: 77

727.687-030 BATTERY STACKER (elec. equip.) alternate titles: battery loader
Loads batteries from conveyor or handtruck to two-level (double decker) trucks, according to specified polarity arrangement, preparatory to further processing, such as forming or charging. Clamps or pushes connectors or links onto posts. May perform other tasks, such as wiping excess sealing compound from battery, clipping posts, using handtool, inspecting batteries for defective covers or posts, and rejecting defective batteries.
GOE: 06.04.40 STRENGTH: M GED: R1 M1 L1 SVP: 2 DLU: 77

727.687-034 BATTERY-CONTAINER-FINISHING HAND (elec. equip.) alternate titles: container finisher
Sprays, dips, or liquid-treats battery containers and terminal boxes and loads containers and boxes into drying ovens: Rubs surfaces of products, using sandpaper to smooth surfaces preparatory to painting. Arranges items on drying racks after painting and pushes racks into oven, or hooks parts on conveyor which carries parts through drying tunnel. Turns temperature dials as specified according to products being dried. May insert rubber liners through acid vents in containers and glue liners in place. May move materials between processing

stations. May position bolts in slots of jig preparatory to spray painting. May glue labels on containers. May file paint from rims of containers.
GOE: 06.04.33 STRENGTH: L GED: R1 M1 L1 SVP: 2 DLU: 77

727.687-038 BATTERY-PARTS ASSEMBLER (elec. equip.) alternate titles: cell assembly, booker; cell assembly, pinner

Performs any combination of following tasks to complete assembly of storage batteries, according to specification: Threads positive and negative battery plates onto separate connecting bolts, inserts washers between each plate to assemble grouped plates, and attaches nuts to ends of bolts of grouped plates to secure plates, using hydraulic hand wrench. Joins grouped plates and positions joined plates in battery base, or inserts element (cell) in single-cell container or inserts number of cells in multiple-cell containers, according to specified order of polarity. Wraps insulating material around cell or inserts wooden shims in container to secure tight fit. Inserts plastic separating rods (or pins) on plates, following notched guides on each plate. Positions batteries or cell containers in jig and attaches, inserts, or positions battery parts, such as gaskets, washers, battery posts, and battery lids, according to color-coded assembly procedures. Applies glue to edge of lids and positions batteries in vises for specified time to seal batteries. Adds compound to fill cavities to secure tight seal and improve appearance, using hand torch. Tests sealed units for air leaks, using air pressure testing device. Attaches terminal cables, using handtools. Removes excess metal around posts, using handtools. Dips posts in soda solution or brushes paint or molten wax on posts and connectors to prevent acid corrosion. May be designated according to part assembled as Battery-Vent-Plug Inserter (elec. equip.); Element Setter (elec. equip.); Separator Inserter (elec. equip.).
GOE: 06.04.23 STRENGTH: L GED: R2 M1 L2 SVP: 3 DLU: 88

727.687-042 CELL COVERER (elec. equip.)

Fits covers on storage battery cells preparatory to sealing: Burns soda and acid deposits from battery posts, using gas torch. Lubricates bushings. Fits and presses cover of specified size onto cell. May place gasket over threaded posts and screw down locknuts, using wrench. May tap down covers over posts, using mallet. May clip posts, using handtools.
GOE: 06.04.23 STRENGTH: L GED: R2 M1 L1 SVP: 2 DLU: 77

727.687-046 CELL TUBER, HAND (elec. equip.)

Inserts finished dry cells in paper tubes and attaches cover to complete assembly of dry cell batteries: Places cell in tube and positions cover over cell. Positions tubed cell in hand-crimping press and pulls lever to crimp top of tube over cover. Inspects cell to detect faulty crimping and places cell in tray.
GOE: 06.04.23 STRENGTH: L GED: R1 M1 L1 SVP: 2 DLU: 77

727.687-050 ELECTRIC-CONTAINER TESTER (elec. equip.) alternate titles: dielectric-testing-machine operator

Tests aircraft storage battery containers for defects, using dielectric testing device: Places storage battery container on table and connects cables from testing device to battery. Starts device that transmits high voltage electric current through battery. Observes dial on testing device that indicates if container has any defects, such as cracks or holes. Stops device, disconnects cables, and places tested battery aside for further processing. Marks defective battery, using chalk.
GOE: 06.03.02 STRENGTH: L GED: R2 M2 L2 SVP: 3 DLU: 77

727.687-054 FINAL INSPECTOR (elec. equip.) alternate titles: polarity tester

Tests polarity connections on finished storage batteries and inspects final assembly for defects: Positions metal prongs of testing unit over terminals of intercell connecting straps and observes bulb on testing unit that lights when cell arrangement is correct. Examines assembly for defects, such as omission of symbols on battery posts, uneven sealing, and cracked covers.
GOE: 06.03.02 STRENGTH: L GED: R2 M2 L2 SVP: 2 DLU: 77

727.687-058 FORMING-PROCESS-LINE WORKER (elec. equip.)

Performs any combination of following tasks pertaining to forming (treating) storage battery plates: Positions plates or elements in forming tank. Breaks forming lugs from formed plates and pulls lead wires from lugs, using pliers. Collects wires and lugs for salvage. Cleans lugs on positive plates, using brush. Washes formed plates to remove forming acid in running water bath. Stacks washed plates on drying machine. Stacks batteries in specified polarity arrangement on forming trucks. Attaches connectors preparatory to forming. Slides positive and negative plates into slots of partitions that prevent buckling during forming process. Ascertains voltage of batteries, using voltmeter, and adjusts rheostat to regulate current. Reads meter to detect deviations in discharge rate from prescribed range. Removes connectors from posts and plates from forming tanks. Dumps forming acid from batteries. Refills treated batteries with finishing acid. Pumps used forming acid to reclaiming tanks and cleans reclaiming tanks, using brushes, scrapers, and water hose. May be designated according to task performed as Battery Plate Remover (elec. equip.); Lug-Breaker-And-Wire-Puller (elec. equip.); Plate-Put-In Worker (elec. equip.); Plate Washer (elec. equip.); Tank Cleaner (elec. equip.).
GOE: 06.04.24 STRENGTH: M GED: R2 M1 L1 SVP: 2 DLU: 77

727.687-062 INSPECTOR (elec. equip.)

Inspects finished in-process dry cell or storage batteries for defects, such as dents, scratches, short electrodes, or missing parts: Examines batteries to detect defects and places defective batteries in box. May test batteries, using voltmeters and ammeters. May replace damaged parts.

GOE: 06.03.02 STRENGTH: L GED: R2 M1 L1 SVP: 2 DLU: 77

727.687-066 INSPECTOR, CONTAINER FINISHING (elec. equip.) alternate titles: battery-container inspector

Inspects battery containers to determine if finishing and dimensional specifications are met: Examines battery containers for surface defects, such as cracks and damaged terminal posts. Verifies dimensional specifications of battery containers, using templates or other measuring devices. Places covers over cell partitions of battery containers to determine if spacing requirements are met.
GOE: 06.03.02 STRENGTH: L GED: R2 M2 L2 SVP: 2 DLU: 77

727.687-070 LEAD-BURNER HELPER (elec. equip.)

Assists LEAD BURNER (elec. equip.) in preparing storage battery parts for fusing (lead burning): Positions specified number of positive and negative plates in burning rack to ready equipment for fusing lugs to connecting straps. Places intercell connectors on assembled batteries. Places post builders (templates) over posts to aid LEAD BURNER (elec. equip.) I in adding lead to build up posts to specified levels. Removes post builders from posts after burning, using tongs. Places positive and negative post builders in separate containers. Selects burning racks according to size of plates grouped. May stamp polarity symbols on posts, using hand marking dies. May haul plates from storage to burning area, using handtruck. Performs other duties as described under HELPER (any industry) Master Title. May be known according to task performed as Intercell-Connector Placer (elec. equip.); Post-Form Remover (elec. equip.); Rack Loader (elec. equip.).
GOE: 06.04.23 STRENGTH: M GED: R2 M1 L2 SVP: 2 DLU: 77

727.687-074 MOLDED-PARTS INSPECTOR (elec. equip.) alternate titles: molded-grid-and-parts inspector

Inspects molded storage battery parts, such as grids, straps, vent plugs, washers, and gaskets for conformance to specifications: Examines parts for defects, such as cracks, airholes, or other surface defects. Measures parts to determine dimensional accuracy, using gauges, such as micrometers and vernier scales. Rejects faulty parts and prepares inspection reports.
GOE: 06.03.02 STRENGTH: L GED: R3 M2 L2 SVP: 3 DLU: 77

727.687-078 SPARK TESTER (elec. equip.)

Tests encased storage batteries for air-tightness, using electric spark tester: Places frame of tester over battery container and presses plug terminal of testing apparatus to posts of battery. Moves frame of tester over surface of container to detect leaks indicated by bright sparks emitted at contact points. Examines assemblies for defects, such as uneven sealing, misplaced intercell connectors, and covers. Attaches slip to rejected batteries indicating type of defect. May stamp polarity symbols on posts, using hammer and dies.
GOE: 06.03.02 STRENGTH: L GED: R2 M2 L2 SVP: 2 DLU: 77

727.687-082 WAFER-LINE WORKER (elec. equip.) alternate titles: wafer-cell-battery assembler

Performs any combination of following tasks to assemble wafer-type dry cell batteries: Removes stack of cells from machine and inspects and counts cells. Positions stack in handpress and pulls lever to compress stack to form battery. Wraps battery in rubberized wrapping and places wrapped battery on hot iron to seal. Marks positive terminal, using pencil, and places battery in tray. Tests capacity of battery, using voltmeter. Closes and seals ends on hot iron. Touches ends of cell to device to coat ends with hot asphalt. Manually presses carbon end plates on asphalt. Presses copper lead to end plate, using hot iron. Applies strip of tape around battery to hold lead in position. Stamps code on battery, using hand stamp. Rubs cover with emery paper to remove wax from terminal covers and appplies silver wax to terminals, using hot iron. Inserts battery, pads, and bottom in can. Crimps can over bottom, using hand-crimping press.
GOE: 06.04.23 STRENGTH: L GED: R2 M1 L1 SVP: 2 DLU: 77

728 OCCUPATIONS IN FABRICATION OF ELECTRICAL WIRE AND CABLE

This group includes occupations concerned with fabricating insulated, shielded (armored), or waxed electrical conductors made from purchased wire.

728.684-010 WIRE HARNESS ASSEMBLER (elec. equip.; electron. comp.; office machines) alternate titles: cable maker; harness maker; wirer

Routes and ties wires to form wire harness (cable) used in electrical and electronic equipment or systems: Reads instructions, such as work orders, diagrams, and wire lists to determine materials needed and sequence of assembly. Selects wires of specified color, marking, or length, and loops wires between guide pegs on harness board, following color-coded lines or sequential numbers on board or diagram. Wraps and ties wires together at designated points to form harness, manually or using tie-wrap gun. May apply sealing liquid to secure knots in ties, using brush. May attach ends of wires to components, plugs, or terminal strip, using soldering iron or crimping device. May insert cable in plastic tubing or inject plastic sealant around terminals to protect cable from dust and moisture. May test wiring continuity, using continuity tester. May mark identifying data on completed harness.
GOE: 06.02.32 STRENGTH: L GED: R2 M1 L1 SVP: 3 DLU: 88

728.684-014 ELECTRICAL-LINE SPLICER (petrol. & gas) alternate titles: cable splicer

Splices conductor cables used to lower electrical testing or surveying instruments into oil or gas wells or boreholes, using handtools: Unwraps armor

strands (protective covering) from end of cable. Strips insulation from stranded conductor cable, using stripping pliers. Cuts ends of conductor cable, using pliers. Clamps cable ends together in vise to form butt joint. Solders joint, using silver solder and iron. Wraps joint with insulating tape to form smooth insulation of same diameter as original cable. Wraps armor strands over joint. Trims ends of armor strands, using cutters, to form smooth butt joints and solders joints, using silver solder and iron. May test conductor cables, using equipment, such as voltmeters and capacity and resistance bridges.
GOE: 05.10.03 STRENGTH: M GED: R3 M2 L2 SVP: 5 DLU: 77

728.684-018 SPARK TESTER (elec. equip.; nonfer. metal) alternate titles: sparker and patcher

Tests electric wire and cable to locate defects in insulation, using spark tester, and repairs insulation, using portable vulcanizer: Threads wire through spark tester and onto takeup spool. Locates defect indicated by dark spot on insulation. Removes defective insulation with knife and wraps uncured rubber tape around cable to form patch. Clamps electric curing block around patch and turns switch on for specified period. Smooths cured patch, using power grinder. May braze wire lengths together to form continuous cable, using gas torch.
GOE: 06.03.02 STRENGTH: L GED: R2 M2 L2 SVP: 4 DLU: 77

728.684-022 WIREWORKER (elec. equip.; electron. comp.) alternate titles: wire-preparation worker

Performs any combination of following tasks involved in cutting, stripping, taping, forming, and soldering wires or wire leads of components used in electrical and electronic units, such as communication equipment, ignition systems, electrical appliances, test equipment, or other electrical or electronic systems: Cuts wire to specified lengths, using wire cutters and ruler or measuring jig. Strips insulation from wire ends, using stripping tool. Twists wire ends and dips ends into pot of solder to prevent fraying. Solders wires to specified connectors and terminals, using soldering iron, or crimps connectors and terminals to wire ends, using handtools. Wraps numbered or colored identification tape around wires. Rolls wires of identical number or color together and attaches tag to roll. Inserts wires into plastic insulation tubing. Bends, cuts, and crimps component leads to prepare component for mounting onto printed circuit board or other assembly, using handtools. Inserts wires in automatic numbering or color-coding machine to imprint part numbers or color codes. Dips wire or component leads into paraffin solution to insulate wire and leads. Applies protective coatings onto wires, using brush. Tests wire and cable assemblies and repairs defective assemblies. May use automated equipment or bench-mounted devices to cut, strip, bend, or crimp wire. May be designated by type of wire worked as Component Lead Former (electron. comp.).
GOE: 06.04.34 STRENGTH: L GED: R2 M1 L2 SVP: 2 DLU: 86

728.685-010 WIRE PREPARATION MACHINE TENDER (any industry)

Tends machines that automatically cut, strip, and mark identifying stripes or other information on wire used in electrical installations or assemblies: Places reel of specified wire onto play-out spindle of machine and threads wire through feed rolls. Adjusts machine controls to regulate factors, such as wire thickness, pressure, heat, and cutting and stripping length. Starts machine and observes operation to detect machine malfunction. Places boxes under ejection roll or manually removes and bundles or boxes cut, stripped, and marked wire. Examines wire for conformance to specifications and removes defective pieces. Observes automatic counter or counts finished pieces, and records data on tags or boxes. May install drive adjustment and tension or adjustment rolls in machine. May install ram and dies that bend finished pieces of wire to specified angles. May replace dull or broken cutting or stripping blades. May tend machine that automatically bends wire to specified angle. May tend machine that crimps and attaches connectors and terminals to wire ends. May tend numerical control wire preparation machine and be designated Numerical-Control-Wire-Preparation-Machine Tender (aircraft mfg.).
GOE: 06.04.09 STRENGTH: L GED: R2 M1 L2 SVP: 2 DLU: 88

729 OCCUPATIONS IN ASSEMBLY AND REPAIR OF ELECTRICAL EQUIPMENT, N.E.C.

This group includes occupations, not elsewhere classified, concerned with assembling, fabricating, or repairing electrical and electronic equipment.

729.130-010 SUPERVISOR, ELECTRICAL ASSEMBLY (elec. equip.)

Supervises and coordinates activities of workers engaged in assembly, inspecting, and testing of electrical equipment such as motors, generators, voltage regulators, capacitors, and switches, applying knowledge of assembly techniques, machine setup, and testing procedures: Interprets blueprints, specifications, and job orders and assigns work stations to workers. Demonstrates machine setup and operation, and procedures of assembly, wiring, and soldering techniques, using handtools and soldering equipment. Performs other duties as described under SUPERVISOR (any industry) Master Title.
GOE: 06.01.01 STRENGTH: L GED: R4 M3 L3 SVP: 6 DLU: 77

729.131-010 INSPECTOR, CHIEF (elec. equip.)

Supervises and coordinates activities of workers engaged in inspecting and grading quality of graphite electrodes during each step in manufacturing process: Maintains production records, such as grade and quality of electrodes manufactured and types of defects detected in electrodes during inspection. Determines inspection procedures according to plant production schedules and type and size of inspection instruments to be used. Examines defective electrodes

for possible salvage. Performs other duties as described under SUPERVISOR (any industry) Master Title.
GOE: 06.01.01 STRENGTH: L GED: R4 M3 L3 SVP: 6 DLU: 77

729.131-014 RELAY-SHOP SUPERVISOR (utilities) alternate titles: chief, relay tester; lead-relay tester

Supervises and coordinates activities of RELAY TESTERS (utilities) engaged in testing, adjusting, and repairing relays, meters, capacitors, and other parts of electric power-distributing equipment: Schedules periodic tests of all operating equipment. Directs workers in installation of equipment. Prepares diagrams and drawings of new installations. Performs other duties as described under SUPERVISOR (any industry) Master Title.
GOE: 05.05.10 STRENGTH: L GED: R4 M3 L3 SVP: 7 DLU: 77

729.281-010 AUDIO-VIDEO REPAIRER (any industry) alternate titles: audiovisual-aids technician

Installs and repairs audio-video equipment, such as tape recorders, public address systems, slide and motion picture projectors, and record players, using handtools, soldering iron, and special testing equipment. Inspects equipment for defects and repairs or replaces parts. Returns equipment to shop for more complicated repairs.
GOE: 05.05.05 STRENGTH: L GED: R4 M3 L3 SVP: 6 DLU: 77

729.281-014 ELECTRIC-METER REPAIRER (utilities) alternate titles: meter repairer

Inspects, adjusts, and repairs electric meters used for recording electric current consumption: Disassembles defective meters, using handtools. Examines parts of meter for wear and detects warped or bent parts, using straightedge. Soaks electric parts in chemical solutions to clean parts. Removes dirt from other parts, using brushes, sandpaper, and soap and water. Reassembles meter, using new or repaired parts. Turns setscrews or makes other adjustments required to bring meter accuracy within prescribed limits. May test meters for accuracy [ELECTRIC-METER TESTER (utilities)] or for correctness of assembly and dielectric strength, using testing apparatus. May repair demand register mechanism of demand meters. May repair such electric components as instrument transformers and relays. May install meters.
GOE: 05.05.10 STRENGTH: L GED: R4 M2 L3 SVP: 7 DLU: 77

729.281-018 ELECTRIC-METER-REPAIRER APPRENTICE (utilities) alternate titles: meter-repairer apprentice

Performs duties as described under APPRENTICE (any industry) Master Title.
GOE: 05.05.10 STRENGTH: L GED: R4 M2 L3 SVP: 7 DLU: 77

729.281-022 ELECTRIC-TOOL REPAIRER (any industry) alternate titles: power-tool repairer

Repairs electrical handtools and bench tools, such as drills, saws, grinders, and sanders, using lathe, circuit testers, handtools, and power tools: Tests motors, switches, and wiring for grounds, shorts, and loose connections, using electrical circuit testers. Turns motor commutators, using bench lathe. Repairs or replaces defective electrical parts, using handtools, power tools, and soldering and welding equipment. Inspects parts, such as mechanical gears, bearings, and bushings, for wear and damage, and repairs or replaces parts.
GOE: 05.10.03 STRENGTH: L GED: R4 M3 L3 SVP: 6 DLU: 77

729.281-026 ELECTRICAL-INSTRUMENT REPAIRER (any industry) alternate titles: instrument maker; instrument repairer

Repairs, calibrates, and tests instruments, such as voltmeters, ammeters, resistance bridges, galvanometers, temperature bridges, and temperature controlling and recording gauges and instruments, using jewelers' tools, electricians' tools, handtools, and measuring instruments: Tests instruments for resistance, voltage, and other characteristics, using potentiometer, voltage divider, and other testing devices. Disassembles instruments, using handtools, and examines parts for defects. Measures, cuts, and fits glass for meters and instruments, using glass cutter. Repairs or replaces defective parts of instruments, using handtools, soldering equipment, grinders, calipers, micrometers, and dividers. Reassembles instruments, following circuit diagrams and using jewelers' tools. Tests new and repaired instruments, using test board. May operate lathe and drill press to make replacement parts. May plan, construct, and assemble test panels for experimental and production testing. May keep records on repair and calibration of instruments. May rebuild induction cores for electric furnaces. May install, repair, and adjust electronically controlled dynamometers and be known as Dynamometer Repairer (elec. equip.).
GOE: 05.05.10 STRENGTH: L GED: R4 M3 L3 SVP: 6 DLU: 77

729.281-030 ELECTROMEDICAL-EQUIPMENT REPAIRER (any industry) alternate titles: electromedical service engineer

Tests and repairs electromedical equipment, such as electrocardiographs, electroencephalographs, sterilizers, operating room lamps and tables, and diathermy machines, following schematic diagrams and using handtools and test meters: Tests electrical circuits and components to locate shorts, faulty connections, and defective parts, using test meters. Solders loose connections and replaces defective parts, such as tubes, transformers, resistors, condensors, and switches, using handtools and soldering iron. Disassembles equipment and repairs or replaces faulty mechanical parts, such as control lever mechanisms and water impellers. Adjusts and repairs stylus, graph, and other recording mechanisms. May replace x-ray tubes. May be designated according to type of machine or equipment repaired as Diathermy-Equipment Repairer (any industry); Electrocardiograph Repairer (any industry).

GOE: 05.05.11 STRENGTH: M GED: R4 M3 L3 SVP: 6 DLU: 77

729.281-034 INSIDE-METER TESTER (utilities) alternate titles: electric-meter tester, shop; inside tester

Tests electric meters to detect cause of malfunctions and inaccuracy, and repairs meters: Connects meter to test panel mounting standard meter and determines recording accuracy [ELECTRIC-METER TESTER (utilities)]. Changes connections to test panel and observes whether parts, such as coils and magnet, function according to standard. Adjusts test panel controls and observes dials to determine if meter's electrical readings are correct and turns setscrews to correct deviations. Determines if meter gears mesh properly by tactile examination and tightens or loosens screws to make adjustments. Adjusts timing mechanism on demand meters. Makes minor repairs, such as replacing wornout screws, jewels, and registers, and routes meters needing major overhaul to ELECTRIC-METER REPAIRER (utilities). May test accuracy of meters, using stroboscope to compare tested meter disk revolutions to those of standard. May test relays [RELAY TESTER (utilities)]. May install and maintain test boards used to test function and accuracy of meters.

GOE: 05.05.10 STRENGTH: L GED: R4 M3 L3 SVP: 7 DLU: 77

729.281-038 RELAY TESTER (utilities) alternate titles: network-relay tester; relay-shop tester

Tests, cleans, repairs, and adjusts relays used to protect and control functions of equipment, such as circuit breakers, transformers, and automatic switches in generating stations, substations, and distribution facilities: Connects relay to test board and adjusts test board controls to simulate operating conditions. Observes ammeters, voltmeters, and related test board recording and indicating instruments to determine if relay performs all functions correctly, according to specifications of manufacturer and relay history card. Analyzes reactions of relay to tests to identify cause of malfunction. Tightens bolts, springs, and electrical connections, and adjusts screws to correct malfunction. Adjusts electrical, thermal, and timing elements to calibrate relay, according to installation specifications. Dismantles, cleans, or replaces worn or defective relays, using handtools and brush or feather. Records test results, repairs, adjustments, and related data on relay history card. May periodically inspect and test relays at functioning points. May test and repair related equipment, such as telemetering and supervisory-control devices.

GOE: 05.05.05 STRENGTH: L GED: R4 M3 L4 SVP: 7 DLU: 77

729.281-042 WIRER (office machines)

Installs, adjusts, and repairs wiring and cables in punched card office machines and adding machines according to wiring diagrams, blueprints, and engineering specifications, using handtools, soldering iron, and plugging gun: Reads wiring diagrams, blueprints, wire routing and standards sheets, and engineering specifications to determine lengths, types, routing, and colors of wiring and cables to be installed in machines, such as collators, adding machines, reproducing punches, card reader punches, and interpreters. Selects specified wires and cables, routes according to instructions, and fastens connections by bolting, screwing, soldering, or plugging, using wrenches, screwdrivers, soldering iron, and plugging gun (pneumatic gun that forces plug ends of wires into jacks). Inspects previously wired units, such as plugboards, fuse holders, keyboards, and indicator lights, for conformance to specifications, using test devices, such as voltmeters and ohmmeters.

GOE: 06.02.32 STRENGTH: L GED: R3 M3 L2 SVP: 6 DLU: 77

729.281-046 X-RAY-EQUIPMENT TESTER (any industry) alternate titles: x-ray consultant; x-ray equipment servicer; x-ray service engineer

Tests x-ray machines and accessory equipment to locate defects, using voltmeter and laboratory testing instruments: Compares readings on x-ray control meter and timer with measurements taken with standard instruments during machine operation to verify or adjust meter and timer calibration. Tests performance of transformer and measures voltages, using voltmeter, and compares results with standard graphs. May plan layouts of x-ray departments and install equipment.

GOE: 06.01.05 STRENGTH: L GED: R4 M3 L3 SVP: 6 DLU: 77

729.360-010 PROBE TEST EQUIPMENT TECHNICIAN, SEMICONDUCTOR WAFERS (electron. comp.)

Sets up and maintains wafer probe and test equipment that test electrical properties of circuits on semiconductor wafers, following setup manual specifications: Reads process sheet and setup manual to determine test program required and setup specifications. Inserts test probe card in wafer probe equipment. Inserts floppy disk or magnetic tape into slot on test equipment and pushes buttons on test equipment or types commands on keyboard to enter test program. Places sample wafer from specified wafer lot on wafer probe equipment chuck, using vacuum wand or tweezers. Observes wafer through microscope attached to wafer probe equipment and turns knobs on equipment to align and position wafer circuit under probes on probe card, according to setup manual specifications. Activates test equipment to make trial run to ensure correct equipment setup and informs equipment operator that setup is completed. Removes and sharpens worn probes, using handtools and burnishing blade. Replaces defective probes or probe cards and solders joints on replacement probes, using soldering iron. Tests electrical continuity of cable connecting wafer probe and test equipment, using ohmeter. Replaces defective connector cables. Removes, cleans, and refills reservoir of inker on wafer probe equipment that marks defective circuits with ink spot.

GOE: 06.01.02 STRENGTH: L GED: R3 M2 L3 SVP: 5 DLU: 86

729.361-010 INSPECTOR, ELECTROMECHANICAL (inst. & app.)

Inspects and tests components, housings, and finished assemblies of electromechanical instruments and equipment, such as oceanographic instruments, navigational systems, medical diagnostic equipment, and measuring, indicating, and controlling instruments, for conformance to specifications, using magnifying devices, test equipment, and precision measuring instruments: Reviews work orders, blueprints, or other specifications and confers with supervisor, engineer, and other personnel to determine product dimensions and specifications. Examines electrical, structural, and mechanical components and housings for defects in assembly, soldering, bonding, and finish. Measures dimensions and verifies locations of parts, holes, grooves, and other points, using precision measuring instruments, such as calipers, micrometers, gauges, dial indicators, and optical comparators. Tests electrical components and finished devices for electrical functioning, using electrical test equipment, such as oscilloscope, multimeter, voltmeter, and computerized test equipment. Tests functional characteristics, such as freedom of movement, leaks, and torque, and tests performance of device under simulated operating conditions, using specialized test equipment. Maintains records of inspection and test results and presents results to other staff for corrective action. May inspect and calibrate precision measuring instruments used to measure electromechanical instruments and equipment, using calibrating equipment. May inspect and test purchased parts and materials and be designated Receiving Inspector (inst. & app.).

GOE: 06.01.05 STRENGTH: M GED: R4 M3 L4 SVP: 7 DLU: 90

729.381-010 ELECTRICAL-EQUIPMENT TESTER (aircraft mfg.) alternate titles: inspector, precision electrical assembly; tester, electrical accessories

Tests and adjusts electrical equipment and accessories prior to installation in aircraft to ensure conformance to specifications, using precision measuring instruments and testing equipment: Examines electrical equipment and accessories, such as batteries, bells, chimes, solenoids, booster coils, circuit breakers, electric actuators, and starter control valves, for defects. Connects electrical equipment and accessories to testing equipment, such as voltmeter, ammeter, oscilloscope, and torque indicator, and tests for voltages under varying loads, output and input of power at various operating temperatures, amount of current used at different voltages, electrical leakages, short circuits, open circuits, and electric motor torques. Compares test performance results with prescribed values, and adjusts moving parts as indicated by tests, using handtools and measuring instruments. Stamps or attaches tags to approved equipment. Records results of tests. May test effects of vibration on equipment and accessories, using vibration testing equipment. May design, lay out, and construct special testing jigs. May measure parts of electromechanical assemblies for conformance to specifications, using micrometers, calipers, and gauges. May test and adjust electronic equipment.

GOE: 06.01.05 STRENGTH: L GED: R3 M3 L3 SVP: 6 DLU: 88

729.381-014 PIN-GAME-MACHINE INSPECTOR (svc. ind. mach.)

Inspects and repairs pinball and games machines: Plays machine and observes mechanism in operation to detect defects. Disassembles defective machines, using handtools. Adjusts or replaces defective parts, following electrical schematic diagrams. May return machine to department where defect occurred.

GOE: 05.10.03 STRENGTH: L GED: R4 M2 L3 SVP: 5 DLU: 77

729.381-018 STREET-LIGHT REPAIRER (utilities)

Tests, adjusts, and repairs mercury-vapor, fluorescent, electric-arc, or incandescent street lights and traffic signals in shop: Disassembles lamp, using handtools. Tests and examines components to determine need for repair or replacement, using electrical testing devices, such as test lamps, voltmeter, and wattmeter. Repairs or replaces broken connections, defective coils, cracked insulators, and other electrical components. Connects repaired lamp to test circuit and regulates such adjustable components as shunt coils until lamp meets operating specifications, according to electrical gauge readings, using screwdriver. Winds replacement coils on bench lathe and bakes freshly insulated coils in oven. Installs repaired lamp in outside casing or canopy.

GOE: 05.05.05 STRENGTH: L GED: R4 M2 L3 SVP: 7 DLU: 77

729.381-022 WIRER, CABLE (comm. equip.; elec. equip.)

Installs cables and solders wires to connect electrical instruments mounted on control apparatus, such as panelboards and telephone crossbar frames, according to diagrams and blueprints: Pulls assembled crossbar frame or unit to work area, using monorail chain hoist or handtruck. Ties preformed wiring cable to brackets. Positions arms of cable (groups of wires tied off from trunk of cable) and spreads wires to facilitate wiring. May strip insulation from ends of wires with pliers to prepare for connections. Connects color-coded wires to terminals, using soldering iron or pneumatic wire-wrapping tool. Examines and feels wires to detect loose connections. Writes and ties tickets to wires or terminals in apparatus to identify surplus or missing wires. May secure parts, such as diodes and resistors to specified locations on equipment, using soldering iron or screwdriver. Tapes insulating sleeves over auxiliary lead wires of cable. Pulls or carries wired apparatus to storage area. May be designated according to equipment wired as Crossbar-Frame Wirer (elec. equip.); Crossbar-Unit Wirer (elec. equip.); Switchboard Assembler (comm. equip.).

GOE: 05.10.03 STRENGTH: M GED: R3 M2 L2 SVP: 6 DLU: 77

729.384-010 ASSEMBLER, ELECTRICAL ACCESSORIES II (elec. equip.)

Assembles electrical instruments, such as ammeters, galvanometer, and voltmeters, performing any combination of following duties: Winds fine wire

around *coil forms* on winding machine. Joins coils, plates, hairsprings, and other parts, connects and solders wires, using handtools, tweezers, and soldering iron. Inserts and tightens setscrews to secure components to housing. Cleans lens and glass faceplate and cements parts in place. Tests assembled units, using potentiometer and similar equipment to ensure that meters perform according to specifications. May be designated according to type of meter being assembled as Galvanometer Assembler (elec. equip.).
GOE: 06.02.23 STRENGTH: L GED: R3 M2 L2 SVP: 3 DLU: 77

729.384-014 FARE-REGISTER REPAIRER (motor trans.)
Repairs and adjusts electromechanical fare recording boxes used in buses and streetcars: Disassembles unit to locate defects. Tests electrical circuit, using ammeters, ohmmeters, and voltmeters. Inspects mechanical components and repairs or replaces defective or worn parts, using handtools and soldering iron. Cleans, oils, adjusts, and reassembles recording mechanism.
GOE: 05.10.03 STRENGTH: L GED: R3 M2 L2 SVP: 6 DLU: 77

729.384-018 SALVAGE REPAIRER II (utilities)
Reconditions salvaged parts of equipment used in electric-power system and rebuilds equipment, such as air circuit breakers and lightning arrestors: Removes bolts and screws to disassemble salvaged materials, using handtools, and discards parts beyond repair. Dips parts in acid, lye, or soap solution to clean parts, and polishes parts, using buffing wheel. Solders, wraps, and coats lightning rod arrestor wires to connect and insulate wires during repair, using soldering iron, tape, and varnish. Bolts porcelain insulators to wood parts to assemble hot stools (insulated stools on which line workers stand). Replaces broken porcelain insulating parts to rebuild air-circuit breakers and other protective devices, using cement.
GOE: 05.10.03 STRENGTH: M GED: R3 M1 L2 SVP: 5 DLU: 77

729.384-022 WINDING INSPECTOR (house. appl.)
Performs any combination of following tasks to inspect appliance motors and parts, such as armatures and field assemblies: Examines parts, such as commutators, laminations, windings, and shafts for centering of commutator slots, depth of mica undercutting, loose copper and mica chips, positioning and winding of armature coils, and excess varnish or paint. Gauges parts, such as shafts, laminations, commutator bars, for specified length and diameters, using micrometers, fixed and snap gauges, rule, and dial indicator. Places armatures in bearings of bench fixture, rotates armatures manually, and observes dial indicator for eccentricity. Taps offcenter shafts with mallet to straighten shafts. Repairs defects, such as damaged threads and rough commutators, and cleans copper chips from slots, using threading dies, end reamers, knives, picks, brushes, and sandpaper. Routes repairs, such as offcenter commutator slots and shallow undercutting. Stamps date code on acceptable armatures, using rubber stamp. Writes transfer tickets and inspection reports to include quantity and classification of rejected and accepted armatures. May be designated according to part inspected as Brush-Holder Inspector (house. appl.); Commutator Inspector (house. appl.); Shaft Inspector (house. appl.).
GOE: 06.03.01 STRENGTH: L GED: R3 M2 L3 SVP: 4 DLU: 77

729.384-026 ELECTRICAL ASSEMBLER (aircraft mfg.) alternate titles: assembler, radio and electrical; assembler, wire group; bench assembler, electrical
Routes, wires, assembles, and installs electrical and electronic components in aircraft and missile units, such as main junction and terminal boxes, main control switch panels, and instrument and radio panels, according to specifications, using jig boards, handtools, and equipment: Reads work orders, blueprints, and specifications to determine established assembly methods. Cuts wire to specified lengths, using wire cutters. Cuts plastic sleeves and slips sleeves over wire ends to insulate connections. Crimps terminal eyelets and lugs to wire ends, using hand or machine crimping device. Routes, combs, twists, wraps, ties, and attaches wire to terminal points, according to jig board layout, using soldering gun and handtools. Connects wiring to accessories, such as relays, circuit breakers, plugs, condensors, switches, and solenoids, and installs accessory assemblies in electrical or electronic units, using soldering gun and handtools. Conducts functional and continuity tests of electrical assemblies, components, wire harness, and plugs, using ohmmeter, test lights, and other electrical testing instruments. Pots or encapsulates electrical and electronic details [ENCAPSULATOR (elec. equip.; electron. comp.) 726.687-022]. May attach eyelets, terminals, and mounting studs to etched circuit boards.
GOE: 06.02.23 STRENGTH: L GED: R3 M2 L3 SVP: 3 DLU: 87

729.387-010 DEICER INSPECTOR, ELECTRIC (rubber goods) alternate titlès: electric deicer inspector; ice-guard inspector
Inspects electrical airplane deicers for defects and conformance to blueprints: Examines deicers for such defects as cracks, blisters, and separation of rubber plies (layers). Verifes dimensions of deicers and assembly of deicer parts, using rule, snap gauge, and magnifying glass. Weighs deicers to determine conformance to weight tolerance. Examines heat element of deicers under fluoroscope to verify wire spacing and detect broken and loose connections. Marks defective deicers and records inspection results. May clamp deicers to testing device to verify electrical resistance.
GOE: 06.03.01 STRENGTH: L GED: R3 M2 L2 SVP: 4 DLU: 77

729.387-014 DEICER TESTER (rubber goods) alternate titles: final inspector and tester; ice-guard tester
Tests performance of electric airplane deicers: Connects deicer to controlled electric circuit or battery to test for electrical shorts and faulty insulation. Turns

control switch to expose deicer to specified voltage, and observes surface of deicer to detect melting or smoking rubber. May submerge activated deicer in water to detect bubbles or electrical flash that indicate defective area. Dusts deicer with zinc stearate and exposes deicer to specified voltage to test heating performance. Verifies dimensions of deicer, using rule and snap gauge. Marks and sorts defective deicers for scrap or repair. Records test data. May examine rubber plies (layers) of deicer for defects, such as cracks, blisters, and ply separations.
GOE: 06.03.01 STRENGTH: L GED: R3 M2 L2 SVP: 4 DLU: 77

729.387-018 FINISHING INSPECTOR (elec. equip.) alternate titles: final inspector
Inspects brushes, electrodes, nipples, and other graphite products after machining or prior to shipment to verify conformance to specifications: Examines products for defects, such as breaks, burns, cracks, and pits. Measures dimensions of product for conformance to specifications, using calipers, gauges, micrometers, rules, or other inspection tools. Determines cause of defects and whether parts are salvageable or scrap. Records inspection data.
GOE: 06.03.01 STRENGTH: L GED: R3 M2 L3 SVP: 5 DLU: 77

729.387-022 INSPECTOR (house. appl.)
Inspects and tests electrical household appliances, such as ranges, water heaters, and food mixers for appearance and mechanical and electrical characteristics, using testing devices and handtools: Examines metal, glass, and enamel surfaces for scratches, dents, and color matching. Observes alignment of doors, panels, and control dials with adjacent parts. Opens doors and sliding compartments to inspect movement along guides and operation of catches. Taps panels, housing, frame, or frame supports, using fiber hammer, to eliminate binding or align bearings with armature shaft. Connects unit with power source and testing devices, such as wattmeter, voltmeter, and potentiometer. Runs unit through operating cycles, observes meters, and compares readings against standards to determine electrical characteristics. Observes mechanical operation of parts, such as nozzles, blowers, pulleys, and transmission. Records information on inspection ticket. May wrap wire racks, pans, glass, and burner irons in paper and install fiber packing. May specialize in inspection of appearance and mechanical operation and be designated Appliance Inspector (house. appl.). May specialize in electrical testing and be designated Appliance Tester (house. appl.).
GOE: 06.03.01 STRENGTH: L GED: R3 M2 L2 SVP: 4 DLU: 77

729.387-026 INSULATOR TESTER (utilities)
Tests dielectric strength of porcelain insulators, using testing apparatus: Fastens one hooked end of insulator to metal rod of testing set and connects other hook to grounded wire. Turns dial on test set to specified voltage. Presses button to produce voltage and observes meters on test set to verify dielectric strength of insulator. Discards defective insulators.
GOE: 06.03.01 STRENGTH: L GED: R3 M2 L2 SVP: 4 DLU: 77

729.664-010 TEST-DEPARTMENT HELPER (comm. equip.; elec. equip.)
Positions electrical equipment, such as motors, generators, transformers, telephone apparatus, and electrical controls in test area and connects to test equipment preparatory to final testing: Builds up timbers and steel beams on test floor to form base for testing platform. Directs OVERHEAD CRANE OPERATOR (any industry) 921.663-010 or uses jib crane to lift electrical unit to test bench or platform and secures unit, using bolts. Connects equipment to dynamometer or test load, using belt or couplings and adapters. Hooks up electric connections from power supply to unit, using plug, clamp, and screw-type connectors. Observes meters and reports readings to tester.
GOE: 05.12.16 STRENGTH: H GED: R2 M2 L2 SVP: 3 DLU: 77

729.682-010 OPERATOR, CAVITY PUMP (elec. equip.)
Operates pump to inject or extract fluids into or from electrical component cavities to improve component electrical characteristics: Mounts electrical components, such as switches or transformers in holding device. Turns controls or pushes buttons to activate equipment such as welders, cooling systems, heater coils, ammeters, or vacuum and injection pumps. Inserts coupling device into component, reads pressure gauge and turns pump controls to extract or inject fluids such as air, oil, or inert gases at specified pressures and turns off pump. Heats component casing while extracting coupler to seal component, using heating devices such as coil, oven or welder. May connect testing device such as coil or ammeter to component leads and compare reading with specifications, or immerse unit in liquids to determine if unit leaks.
GOE: 06.02.18 STRENGTH: L GED: R3 M2 L3 SVP: 4 DLU: 77

729.684-010 BATTERY-CHARGER TESTER (elec. equip.)
Tests electric battery chargers, using portable testing unit: Clamps battery charger cables to appropriate tester terminals. Pushes control buttons to supply battery charger with specific amount of current that registers on charger meters and compares meter reading with tester meter to determine that meter is registering accurately. Increases current flowing from tester to charger to heat battery charger coil until grease and dirt are burned out. Turns off switches and removes battery charger cables from tester, approving satisfactory battery chargers and returning defective battery chargers for adjustments.
GOE: 06.03.02 STRENGTH: L GED: R3 M2 L2 SVP: 3 DLU: 77

729.684-014 CAPACITOR ASSEMBLER (elec. equip.)
Assembles capacitors for electric transmission equipment, using handtools and soldering equipment: Solders banded porcelain bushing to cover, terminal and tube to top of bushing, and tins areas of bushing holes in top cover, using

stationary or hand gas-heating equipment. Covers bushings with protective cap to prepare covers for sandblasting, buffing, and degreasing. Folds, creases, and pounds insulation to fit over top of wound foil and tissue, using rawhide hammer. Hammers drive screws to fasten nameplate to capacitor. Places cover on capacitor and tightens seal-off screw to hold cover during assembly, using screwdriver. Twists goose-neck filler pipe to capacitor tank and removes pipe after impregnation. Inserts brass plug and seals plug with solder, using gas torch. May bolt capacitors to frames and connect capacitors in banks, using bare copper or insulated conductor. May repair capacitors and be designated Capacitor Repairer (elec. equip.).
GOE: 06.02.23 STRENGTH: M GED: R3 M2 L2 SVP: 4 DLU: 77

729.684-018 DIAL MARKER (elec. equip.)
Draws scale markings by hand on dials of electric meters: Measures and marks specified number of equal distances between calibrations, designated by pinpoints, on dial with dividers or by judging distances. Draws scale according to markings with special pens and black or white ink to contrast with dial. Stamps outline of numbers on scale, using rubber stamp, and fills in outlines with ink. Marks danger points on scale in red ink.
GOE: 01.06.03 STRENGTH: S GED: R2 M2 L2 SVP: 2 DLU: 77

729.684-022 ELECTRIC-SIGN ASSEMBLER (fabrication, nec)
Assembles electric signs, mounts tubing, and connects electrical equipment to sign box: Fastens back of sign to precut metal frame to form sign box, using screws and screwdriver. Fits precut glass, plexiglass, or plastic pane into bottom channel of metal frame. Crimps frame channel to secure pane, using pliers. Attaches tubing support brackets to sign box with self-tapping screws, using screwdriver. Screws or clamps glass elevation posts to brackets. Binds neon sign scroll to posts with wire. Connects wires between tubing electrodes and secondary-winding terminals of transformer. Attaches animation mechanism to back of sign, and connects part to be animated. May assemble fiberboard or cardboard cutout parts for animated window display signs.
GOE: 06.02.22 STRENGTH: M GED: R3 M2 L2 SVP: 3 DLU: 77

729.684-026 ELECTRICAL-CONTROL ASSEMBLER (comm. equip.; elec. equip.)
Assembles protection, communication, and control devices, such as switches, relays, rheostats, transmitters, and switchboards, as laid out in drawings and wiring diagrams: Assembles in predetermined order, contact fingers, shafts, springs, gears, coils, terminals, and push buttons, using handtools, hand arbor press, and assembly fixtures. Fastens units in specified locations in switchbox or case. Cuts, strips, and mounts wires to connect electrical units, using soldering iron, staking machine, and plugging devices. Connects lead wires to buzzer, ohmmeter, or resistance tester to test connections for resistance, shorts, and grounds. May adjust contacts, springs, and shafts to meet specifications. May be designated according to unit assembled as Relay Assembler (elec. equip.); Rheostat Assembler (elec. equip.); Speaking-Unit Assembler (comm. equip.; elec. equip.); Switchbox Assembler (comm. equip.; elec. equip.) II; Telephone-Diaphragm Assembler (comm. equip.; elec. equip.); or according to type of equipment assembled as Assembler, Communications Equipment (comm. equip.; elec. equip.). May assemble strip of switches, of telephone switchboard type, and be designated Jack-Strip Assembler (comm. equip.; elec. equip.).
GOE: 06.02.23 STRENGTH: L GED: R3 M2 L2 SVP: 4 DLU: 77

729.684-030 MOLD OPERATOR (elec. equip.) alternate titles: assembler-insulator
Pours liquid or powdered insulating material into mold to form insulation for electric motor, generator, and switchgear mechanisms: Weighs specified amounts of plaster, cement, metallic, or plastic powders, dumps ingredients into mixing machine, and starts machine. Positions assemblies, such as contact arms, collector rings, rotor shaft coils, and core assemblies, into mold cavity or molding jig, using spacer blocks and pilot pins. Pours mixture into mold and allows mixture to set in hydraulic press or harden in furnace. Removes assembly from mold or jig and scrapes hardened insulation with knife and rasp to trim to specified size. Cuts, bends, shapes, and bolts together pieces of metal to adapt or improvise assembly fixtures to hold parts in mold. May touch leads to meter and observe dial readings to test assembly for electrical continuity. May be designated according to type of material used as Plaster-Of-Paris Molder (elec. equip.) or product insulated as Transformer Molder (elec. equip.).
GOE: 06.02.32 STRENGTH: L GED: R3 M2 L2 SVP: 4 DLU: 77

729.684-034 MOTOR-VEHICLE-LIGHT ASSEMBLER (light. fix.) alternate titles: automobile-light assembler
Assembles bulbs, lenses, socket insulators, springs, and other components to lamp shell to make lights for motor vehicles: Positions and clamps lamp shell in jig on assembly bench or table. Bolts, screws, or crimps specified components to lamp shell, using handtools. Inspects parts for defects, such as cracks or dents, and rejects defective ones. May be designated according to light assembled as Automobile-Headlight Assembler (light. fix.); Automobile-Taillight Assembler (light. fix.); Truck-Head Light Assembler (light. fix.).
GOE: 06.04.23 STRENGTH: L GED: R2 M1 L1 SVP: 3 DLU: 77

729.684-038 REPAIRER, SWITCHGEAR (comm. equip.; elec. equip.)
Repairs defects in electrical apparatus, such as relays and crossbar switches, used in protection, communication, and control devices: Verifies defects, such as burred screws, damaged coils, bent contacts, incorrect stampings, and misassembled parts indicated by inspection ticket. Disassembles apparatus to replace or relocate parts. Bends parts of apparatus, such as contacts and springs,

using handtools to correct alignment, straightness, clearance, and tension defects, and verifies corrections, using gauges. Corrects wrong or illegible stampings, using inked hand stamp. May use equipment to test repaired apparatus for electrical characteristics, such as continuity, resistance, and grounds. May repair wiring defects, such as loose connections and misconnected wires, using soldering iron or wire-wrapping gun. May be designated according to apparatus repaired as Crossbar-Switch Repairer (comm. equip.; elec. equip.); Relay Repairer (elec. equip.); Telephone-Switch Repairer (comm. equip.; elec. equip.).
GOE: 05.10.03 STRENGTH: L GED: R3 M2 L2 SVP: 5 DLU: 77

729.684-042 SAFETY-LAMP KEEPER (mine & quarry) alternate titles: battery charger
Repairs and issues electric lamps and safety lamps used underground by miners: Cleans lamps and batteries, using rags and steel wool. Inspects lamps and replaces defective or worn parts, such as cables, bulbs, wicks, and batteries. Tests batteries to determine strength, using testing device. Inserts batteries into electric charger to restore charge. Fills battery cells with chemicals and distilled water, and fills safety lamp reservoirs with fuel. Keeps record of lamps issued to mine personnel.
GOE: 05.09.01 STRENGTH: L GED: R3 M2 L1 SVP: 4 DLU: 77

729.684-046 SPARK-PLUG ASSEMBLER (elec. equip.)
Assembles components to make spark plugs: Selects base and model according to type of plug to be assembled. Dips end of central electrode in cement and inserts electrode into porcelain insulator. Screws caps over threaded ends of electrodes to form posts for wire connections. Places metal gasket over outer end of porcelain insulator and inserts assembly into metal base (shell). Crimps metal base around insulator, using machine.
GOE: 06.04.23 STRENGTH: L GED: R2 M1 L1 SVP: 2 DLU: 77

729.684-050 STREET-LIGHT-REPAIRER HELPER (utilities)
Performs any combination of following tasks concerned with maintenance and repair of street lighting equipment in repair shop: Dismantles outside case and lamp preparatory to testing and inspection of electrical components by STREET-LIGHT REPAIRER (utilities). Examines components for defects, such as broken connections, cracks, or excessive wear, and replaces defective parts. Cleans lamp cases, reflectors, switches, transformers, and porcelain bases, using brush and solvent. Paints cases, reflectors, and lamp components subject to corrosion, and reassembles lamp and case as directed. Solders or brazes terminals or connectors, using soldering iron or torch. Assists in testing repaired equipment. May stamp metal tags to identify equipment, using embossing machine. May salvage metal from worn out or defective parts.
GOE: 05.12.16 STRENGTH: M GED: R2 M2 L2 SVP: 3 DLU: 77

729.684-054 SUBASSEMBLER (elec. equip.)
Performs any of following tasks to assemble electrical equipment and parts, such as armature cores, coils, electric motors, and switches: Tapes lead wires to coils to facilitate soldering. Solders coil and lead wires, using soldering iron. Trims leads and positions parts in specified relationship to each other, using hands and handtools. Bolts, screws, clips, cements, and fastens parts together, using hands, handtools, or portable powered tools. May remove burrs from parts prior to assembly, using file or electric grinder.
GOE: 06.04.23 STRENGTH: L GED: R2 M1 L2 SVP: 2 DLU: 77

729.684-058 TESTER, ELECTRICAL CONTINUITY (elec. equip.; house. appl.; light. fix.)
Tests electrical units, such as lamps, coils, armatures, and commutators to determine shorts, grounds, or efficiency of unit, using test lamp, meter, or growler: Clamps test wires to electrical unit, screws unit into socket, or inserts lead wires into mercury tube to make contact with testing device. Turns dials to set controls of test equipment and observes meter or test lamp which indicates acceptability of unit. Places armature in growler and manually rotates armature under steel strip. Listens for growling sound and watches for attraction of steel strip to armature surface indicating short circuit. May inspect unit and remove excess solder, mica, or copper chips, using buffing machine, pick, or brush. May demagnetize coils, using demagnetizing equipment. May test carbon pellets with attached shunt wires to determine current flow through pellets, during production of carbon brushes. May be designated according to unit tested as Armature Tester (elec. equip.) II; Carbon Brushes Tester (elec. equip.); Coil Tester (elec. equip.); Commutator Tester (elec. equip.); Electric-Switch Tester (elec. equip.); Light-Bulb Tester (elec. equip.); Resistor Tester (elec. equip.).
GOE: 06.03.02 STRENGTH: L GED: R3 M2 L2 SVP: 3 DLU: 88

729.684-062 WIRER, SUBASSEMBLIES (office machines)
Installs color-coded wires and cables in subassemblies, such as fuse panels, control key assemblies, and relay panels, for punched-card office machines according to wiring diagrams and blueprints by any combination of following tasks: Fastens eyelet or spade types of wire lugs to bolt or screw terminals, using wrenches and screwdrivers. Inserts plug ends of wires and cables into jacks, using pliers or special insertion tools. Attaches wire ends to terminal posts, using pneumatic wire-wrapping gun. May test wiring continuity and connections, using ohmmeter, test lights, or other testing devices.
GOE: 06.02.23 STRENGTH: L GED: R3 M2 L1 SVP: 4 DLU: 77

729.684-066 LAMINATION ASSEMBLER (elec. equip.; electron. comp.) alternate titles: stacking assembler
Stacks, aligns, and secures metal laminations and insulating separators, to assemble laminated cores for electrical parts, such as commutators, coils, arma-

tures, and stators, according to specifications, using either of following methods: (1) Places core laminations and separators into holding device of machine. Starts machine that automatically measures and stacks specified quantity of laminations for each core and inserts separators between laminations. Unloads laminations from machine, and secures laminations using tape or other material. (2) Stacks specified quantity of laminations in holding fixture. Squeezes stack, manually, or presses laminations together in vise or press to reduce kinks or bulges. Measures stack, using rule, and adds or removes laminations and separators to obtain specified dimensions. Aligns edges of laminations, using hammer, and secures laminations, using rubber wrapping material. May place stack of lamination cores into machine that automatically welds laminations into individual cores. May be designated according to method used or type of core assembled as Lamination Stacker, Hand (elec. equip.; electron. comp.); Lamination Stacker, Machine (elec. equip.; electron. comp.); Transformer-Core Assembler (elec. equip.).
GOE: 06.02.23 STRENGTH: L GED: R2 M1 L2 SVP: 3 DLU: 81

729.687-010   ASSEMBLER, ELECTRICAL ACCESSORIES I (elec. equip.; light. fix.) alternate titles: assembler; contact assembler; switchboard contact assembler
Assembles mechanical parts of electrical equipment, such as light sockets, switches, terminal boards, and plugging devices: Fits together parts, such as socket bases, shafts, contact fingers, and springs, in specified sequence, using fixtures, screwdrivers, and air nut runners. Tests actions of moving parts and listens for unusual sounds to detect defective parts or faulty operation. Verifies completed assembly against pictorial drawings. May be designated according to type of equipment assembled as Circuit Breaker Assembler (elec. equip.); Contact-Finger Assembler (elec. equip.); Plug Assembler (elec. equip.); Pull-Socket Assembler (elec. equip.); Push-Button-Switch Assembler (elec. equip.); Terminal-Block Assembler (elec. equip.); Tumbler-Switch Assembler (elec. equip.).
GOE: 06.04.23 STRENGTH: L GED: R2 M1 L2 SVP: 2 DLU: 88

729.687-014   ELECTRODE CLEANER (elec. equip.)
Scrapes surface of graphitized electrodes to loosen particles of coke or encrusted insulating mixture, using scraping tool. Wipes loose material from electrode, using steel wool, and places electrodes into cart for inspection.
GOE: 06.04.39 STRENGTH: L GED: R1 M1 L1 SVP: 1 DLU: 77

729.687-018   LAMINATION SPINNER (elec. equip.) alternate titles: lamination inspector; rotor-lamination inspector; spinner, iron
Spins core laminations on fixture shaft to align slots and wedge grooves: Slides stacks of laminations onto fixture shaft mounted on bench or floor. Spins or rotates laminations manually until key center-hole slots and wedge grooves are aligned. Inserts fixed gauge into peripheral slots to verify alignment and size of slots. Examines circumference of laminations to detect burrs and bent edges. Slides or lifts laminations from fixture shaft. Discards defective laminations and trucks approved laminations to storage. May file burrs from lamination slots.
GOE: 06.04.34 STRENGTH: L GED: R2 M1 L1 SVP: 2 DLU: 77

729.687-022   MICA-WASHER GLUER (mine & quarry)
Builds up (glues) mica washers for use as electrical insulators: Dumps washers into tumbler equipped with series of upright spindles onto which washers fall as tumbler spins. Removes spindles filled with washers, dips spindles into binding solution, and places spindles coated with binding solution into drying oven or ignites coated washers with match to dry washers. Removes spindles from dried washers and splits washers into specified thickness, using knife.
GOE: 06.04.33 STRENGTH: M GED: R2 M2 L2 SVP: 2 DLU: 77

729.687-026   PLATE STACKER, HAND (elec. equip.) alternate titles: grouper; stacker
Groups (interleaves) specified number of positive and negative plates and separators, and places stack on conveyor leading to burning (welding) station. Moves materials about work area, using handtruck.
GOE: 06.04.40 STRENGTH: L GED: R1 M1 L1 SVP: 2 DLU: 77

729.687-030   SALVAGER (utilities)
Dismantles and cleans electric equipment, such as insulators, fuses, wires, wire clamps, and conduit fittings to salvage serviceable materials: Removes rust and deposits of hardened material, using scrapers, wire brush, and abrasive paper. Dips parts in solvents to remove foreign matter. Paints components exposed to weather. Unloads materials from trucks and conveys materials about shop and warehouse, using handtruck. May drive forklift truck.
GOE: 05.12.18 STRENGTH: M GED: R2 M1 L1 SVP: 3 DLU: 77

73   OCCUPATIONS IN FABRICATION AND REPAIR OF PRODUCTS MADE FROM ASSORTED MATERIALS

This division includes occupations concerned with shaping, fitting, trimming, assembling, joining, finishing, and repairing products made from combinations of such materials as metal, wood, plastics, rubber, fabric, and paper.

730   OCCUPATIONS IN FABRICATION AND REPAIR OF MUSICAL INSTRUMENTS AND PARTS

This group includes occupations concerned with fabricating and repairing wind, string, and percussion musical instruments, including pianos and electric or electronic organs. Includes tuning.

730.131-010   SUPERVISOR (musical inst.)
Supervises and coordinates activities of workers engaged in manufacturing musical instruments. Trains new workers. May inspect material at various stages in production to ensure compliance with company standards. May verify accuracy and completeness of records, such as time and production cards. Performs duties as described under SUPERVISOR (any industry) Master Title.
GOE: 06.02.01 STRENGTH: L GED: R4 M3 L3 SVP: 7 DLU: 77

730.281-010   ACCORDION MAKER (musical inst.)
Lays out and constructs accordions, applying knowledge of accordion construction, using handtools and operating variety of wood and metalworking machines: Studies sketch of accordion or customer's specifications to plan work. Measures and marks woodstock to lay out wood parts. Operates woodworking machines, such as saw and sander, and uses carpenter handtools to cut, shape, and finish wood parts of instrument. Measures, cuts, and pleats cardboard to form bellows. Covers bellows with sateen and cloth. Glues leather and places metal guards on corners of bellows. Applies celluloid to accordion parts, such as keys and box ends. Assembles wood and metal parts with screws, nails, or glue, using handtools. Examines fit and finish of instrument and plays notes and chords to inspect completed instrument. May tune accordion reeds and glue reeds in reed blocks [ACCORDION TUNER (any industry)]. May fabricate metal parts, using shop machines and handtools. May repair used instruments [ACCORDION REPAIRER (any industry)]. May be designated according to part made as Bass-Mechanism Maker (musical inst.); Bellows Maker (musical inst.); Box Maker (musical inst.); or by operation performed as Finisher, Accordion (musical inst.).
GOE: 05.05.12 STRENGTH: M GED: R4 M3 L3 SVP: 8 DLU: 77

730.281-014   ACCORDION REPAIRER (any industry)
Repairs and tunes accordions and concertinas, using handtools: Disassembles instrument and parts, such as base and treble mechanisms, bellows, reed blocks, and manuals (keyboards), using handtools. Moves parts, observing their action to detect defects. Files, realigns, and adjusts parts, using handtools. Recovers bellows with sateen and cloth. Glues leather on corners of bellows. Operates woodworking machines and uses handtools to make wood replacement parts. Repairs cracks in celluloid. Solders or removes and replaces defective metal parts. Reassembles instrument and plays notes and chords to determine accuracy of repair. May tune accordion or concertina reeds [ACCORDION TUNER (any industry)]. May repair electronic accordions, using electronic testing equipment, to determine defects and to verify repairs.
GOE: 05.05.12 STRENGTH: M GED: R4 M3 L3 SVP: 7 DLU: 77

730.281-018   ELECTRIC-ORGAN INSPECTOR AND REPAIRER (musical inst.)
Inspects and repairs electric and electronic organs: Plays organ to determine nature of malfunction. Studies circuit diagrams and performs standard tests to locate mechanical, electrical, or electronic difficulties. Replaces defective components and wiring and adjusts mechanical parts, using soldering equipment and handtools. Aligns, adjusts, and calibrates equipment according to specifications, following circuit diagrams and using alignment tools, handtools, and test equipment.
GOE: 05.05.12 STRENGTH: L GED: R4 M3 L4 SVP: 6 DLU: 77

730.281-022   FRETTED-INSTRUMENT MAKER, HAND (musical inst.)
Constructs fretted musical instruments, such as banjos, guitars, and mandolins, by hand, applying knowledge of wood properties and instrument design and construction. May construct bowed instruments [VIOLIN MAKER, HAND (musical inst.)]. May repair bowed instruments [VIOLIN REPAIRER (any industry)]. May repair fretted instruments [FRETTED-INSTRUMENT REPAIRER (any industry)]. May be designated according to instrument made as Guitar Maker, Hand (musical inst.).
GOE: 05.05.12 STRENGTH: L GED: R4 M3 L4 SVP: 8 DLU: 77

730.281-026   FRETTED-INSTRUMENT REPAIRER (any industry)
Repairs fretted musical instruments, such as banjos, guitars, mandolins, and ukuleles, using handtools: Inspects and plays instrument to determine defects. Disassembles instrument, using handtools. Removes, replaces, and dresses (levels) frets, using handtools. Fits wood and metal replacement parts. Reassembles and strings instrument. Adjusts truss rod and bridge to position neck and strings. Plays notes and chords and adjusts string tension to tune instrument. Replaces skin or plastic heads of banjos. Tests and replaces tubes, replaces defective parts, and solders new parts and loose connections on amplifiers, reverberation units, and pickups of electrically amplified instruments. May repair wood bodies or carve wood replacement parts. May be designated according to instrument repaired as Guitar Repairer (any industry).
GOE: 05.05.12 STRENGTH: M GED: R4 M3 L3 SVP: 6 DLU: 77

730.281-030   HARP MAKER (musical inst.)
Shapes and fits harp components to assemble new and repair damaged harps, using handtools and machine tools: Selects wood which will produce desired tonal quality and measures and marks it to lay out design of components. Shapes wood and metal into various parts, using drill press and handtools. Glues wood parts together. Fits metal and wood parts together to form completed harp. Knots each string between soundboard and tuning pin, and turns tuning pin with key to adjust string pitch [HARP REGULATOR (musical inst.)]. Sketches ornamental wood carvings onto graph paper, from customer's description, and orders them made, or carves them himself. May repair damaged harps only and be designated Harp Repairer (any industry).

GOE: 05.05.12 STRENGTH: H GED: R4 M4 L3 SVP: 8 DLU: 77

730.281-034 HARPSICHORD MAKER (musical inst.)

Lays out, machines, fits, assembles, and finishes wood, metal, and plastic parts to build harpsichords, applying knowledge of material properties and harpsichord construction: Measures and marks wood, metal, and plastic to lay out instrument components, applying knowledge of instrument design or following sketch or drawings. Operates woodworking machines and uses handtools to form wooden case parts. Sands and scrapes wood parts and applies varnish, stain, or oil to finish surfaces. Fits and assembles parts, using handtools, to assemble harpsichord case. Files cast metal soundboard to fit soundboard into case, using handtools. Operates drill press to drill holes for tuning pins, following template or drawing that locates holes. Bends metal bridges to specified contour, using vise and handtools, and installs bridges on soundboard. Bends nonmetal bridges to specified contour, using steam and clamps, or saws curve-shaped bridges, using bandsaw, and installs bridges on soundboards. Inserts tuning pins and strings instrument, using various gauge wires. Operates shop machines and uses handtools to cut and shape wood, plastic, and leather to form parts of keyboards and actions. Sets pieces of veneer into surface of wood sides of harpsichord to decorate instrument, using glue. Fits and assembles keyboard and action parts and installs them. Carves, shapes, and tapers plectrum (plucking device), using knive. Tunes instrument to specified pitch, using tuning fork, tuning wrench, and handtools. Visually and tactually examines completed instrument and corrects defects. Repairs used instruments. May apply decorative trim, such as stripes, decals, or gilt to finished instrument [DECORATOR (furniture; toy-sport equip.) 749.684-014]. May design and prepare working drawings to build harpsichords.
GOE: 05.05.12 STRENGTH: H GED: R4 M3 L3 SVP: 6 DLU: 77

730.281-038 PIANO TECHNICIAN (any industry)

Repairs, refinishes, and tunes pianos, using specialized tools and gauges: Tests components, such as keyboard, pedals, and action assembly, using special tools and gauges. Levels keys by inserting paper shims. Detaches action mechanism and replaces faulty, worn, or broken parts, such as hammers, shanks, and joint connections. Aligns hammers and turns screws to adjust striking action of keys [PIANO REGULATOR-INSPECTOR (musical inst.)]. Replaces broken or missing strings [PIANO STRINGER (musical inst.)]. Tunes strings, using tuning hammer and fork [PIANO TUNER (any industry)]. Examines wooden parts for splits, warps, and other defects. Repairs, replaces, resurfaces, and refinishes wooden parts.
GOE: 05.05.12 STRENGTH: M GED: R3 M2 L2 SVP: 7 DLU: 77

730.281-042 PIPE-ORGAN BUILDER (musical inst.)

Lays out, constructs, and assembles electrically controlled pipe organs, using handtools and machines, and following blueprints: Plans layout of organ, following blueprints and sketches of installation site and customer specifications. Operates woodworking machines and uses handtools to cut, shape, fit, and assemble wood components, such as console, wind chest, and wooden pipes. Assembles and installs electrical parts in organ components and solders connecting wires to leads. Examines and tests components prior to transportation to installation site. Fits and assembles component parts of organ in allocated space at installation site [PIPE-ORGAN INSTALLER (musical inst.)]. May voice organ pipes [ORGAN-PIPE VOICER (musical inst.)].
GOE: 05.05.12 STRENGTH: H GED: R4 M3 L3 SVP: 8 DLU: 77

730.281-046 VIOLIN MAKER, HAND (musical inst.)

Constructs bowed musical instruments, such as violins, cellos, and violas, using handtools: Selects wood according to type, grain, and seasoning. Lays out parts to be cut, using templates. Saws, carves, and shapes instrument parts, using handtools. Glues parts together, using jigs, forms, and clamps. Finishes surface with stain and varnish. Strings instrument. Plays instrument to evaluate tonal quality. Relocates bridge and sounding post, or shaves wood from bottom of instrument to improve tone. May repair bowed instruments [VIOLIN REPAIRER (any industry)]. May construct fretted instruments [FRETTED-INSTRUMENT MAKER, HAND (musical inst.)]. May repair fretted instruments [FRETTED-INSTRUMENT REPAIRER (any industry)]. May rebuild and restore bowed instruments and be designated Violin Restorer (musical inst.).
GOE: 05.05.12 STRENGTH: L GED: R4 M3 L3 SVP: 8 DLU: 77

730.281-050 VIOLIN REPAIRER (any industry)

Adjusts and repairs bowed musical instruments, such as cellos, violas, and violins, using handtools: Inspects and plays instrument to determine defects. Disassembles instrument, using handtools. Removes cracked or broken sections, using heated knife and handtools. Glues cracked part, places it in plaster cast, and clamps cast in handpress. Cuts out broken sections, carves replacement parts, and fits replacements to original shape and dimensions of instrument. Reassembles body of instrument, using glue and clamps. Planes and replaces fingerboard, and fits and replaces pegs. Varnishes, rubs, and buffs instruments to protect and decorate them. Strings instrument and fits bridge and soundpost to obtain specified string tension and height. May repair bows. May be designated according to instrument repaired as Bass-Viol Repairer (any industry). When repairing bows, may be known as Bow Repairer (any industry).
GOE: 05.05.12 STRENGTH: L GED: R4 M2 L2 SVP: 7 DLU: 77

730.281-054 WIND-INSTRUMENT REPAIRER (any industry)

Repairs, cleans, and alters brasswind and woodwind musical instruments: Inspects instrument, moves mechanical parts, or plays scale to determine defects. Unscrews and removes rod pins, keys, pistons, and other parts. Removes sol-

dered parts, using gas torch. Reshapes parts, using handtools. Removes dents, using mallet or burnishing tool. Fills cracks in wood instruments, using either of following methods. (1) Inserts pinning wire into crack and covers wire with filler. (2) Operates lathe to cut groove around cracks, applies filler, and clamps retaining band into groove, using hand-operated press. Solders patches over cracks in brass instruments, using silver solder, and files patched area to contour of instrument. Resolders parts, using silver or soft solder. Operates lathe to cut off end of metal tubing, or solders attachments onto tubing to improve instrument's tone or intonation. Washes metal in lacquer-stripping solution and cyanide solution to remove lacquer coating and tarnish. Removes burrs from instrument valves, using scraping tool. Laps valves and pistons so they move freely. Heats key cups to melt shellac and removes pads. Polishes instruments, using rag and polishing compound, buffing wheel, or burnishing tool. Glues new pads and cork pieces on key cups, using hot shellac. Bends and cuts replacement springs and screws them into place. May be designated according to type of instrument repaired as Brasswind-Instrument Repairer (any industry); Woodwind-Instrument Repairer (any industry).
GOE: 05.05.12 STRENGTH: M GED: R4 M2 L2 SVP: 7 DLU: 77

730.281-058 BOW MAKER (musical inst.)

Constructs bows for stringed instruments, using handtools and power tools: Selects specified wood to shape bow, utilizing knowledge of bow styles. Cuts and shapes bow blank from wood, using bandsaw, plane, file, and knife. Positions blank over alcohol flame and bends blank to obtain desired curve of bow. Cuts, glues, and solders ornamental material, such as ebony, ivory, tortoise shell, and silver, to form parts of bow, such as frog and ferrule, using bandsaw, torch, and caliper. Drills or chisels mortise in lead of bow or frog to insert bow hair, using lathe, chisel, and hammer. Ties knot in end of bow hair, combs hair to straighten strands, using brush, and inserts hair into mortise, through ferrule, and into frog of bow. Secures bow hair in place with wooden wedge. Smooths and stains bow to achieve desired appearance, using sandpaper, stain, and rags. Adjusts weight, balance, and stiffness of bow by adding or removing decorative material, using handtools. Replaces bow hair [BOW REHAIRER (any industry) 730.684-022] and repairs bows.
GOE: 05.05.12 STRENGTH: L GED: R3 M2 L3 SVP: 6 DLU: 86

730.361-010 PIANO TUNER (any industry) alternate titles: tonal regulator; tuner

Tunes pianos in private and public establishments, using tuning fork and tuning hammer: Removes board from front of piano to expose strings. Places strips of felt or rubber between strings nearest to string to be tested to mute them. Strikes middle C and compares pitch with that of standard tuning fork. Turns string pin with tuning hammer to adjust tension on string until pitch of string and tuning fork correspond. Tunes remaining notes (strings) by comparing them with middle C and each other. May make initial adjustment of piano strings in factory [CHIP TUNER (musical inst.)].
GOE: 05.05.12 STRENGTH: L GED: R3 M2 L3 SVP: 5 DLU: 77

730.361-014 PIPE-ORGAN TUNER AND REPAIRER (any industry)

Tunes and services pipe organs: Directs helper to depress organ console key and strikes tuning fork to sound A above Middle C. Adjusts pitch of organ A pipes to conform with pitch of tuning fork and adjusts pitch of other pipes with references to pitch of other pipes with reference to pitch of tuned pipes by any combination of following methods: (1) Raises or lowers tuning slides and stoppers of metal and wooden pipes. (2) Rolls or unrolls curled strips of metal across tuning holes of metal pipes. (3) Pinches or spreads metal lips that protrude from mouths of metal pipes. Flares or closes metal pipes, using cone-shaped tool. Cleans pipes, using vacuum cleaner, and repairs or replaces worn parts of pipes, console, bellows, and blower, using handtools and power tools, such as pliers and electric sander. May assemble and install new pipe organs in buildings, such as churches and theatres [PIPE-ORGAN INSTALLER (musical inst.)].
GOE: 05.05.12 STRENGTH: M GED: R4 M3 L3 SVP: 8 DLU: 77

730.367-010 FINAL INSPECTOR (musical inst.)

Inspects finished musical instruments to ascertain conformance to standards for fit, finish, and tone: Fingers moving parts, such as keys and pedals, to inspect operation. Examines fit of parts at joints. Examines finish of instruments for scratches and defective plating or buffing. Corrects defects or notes defects and returns instrument to production department for correction. Plays notes and chords to test tone aurally or uses electronic tuning device. May adjust instrument to obtain specified tone. May be designated by family of instrument or instrument inspected.
GOE: 06.03.01 STRENGTH: L GED: R3 M2 L3 SVP: 5 DLU: 77

730.381-010 ACCORDION TUNER (any industry)

Tunes accordions by aurally comparing pitch of reeds with master reeds and filing reeds to obtain standard pitch: Places set of reeds to be tuned in slots in tuning table. Depresses pedal to operate bellows and presses key to blow or draw air through reed to be tuned and master reed. Files reed being tuned until pitch corresponds to master. Replaces defective leather valves. Measures and mixes glue. Places tuned reeds in reed blocks and secures them with glue. Verifies pitch of master reeds by comparing with pitch of vibrating tuning bar or fork. Files reeds until pitch corresponds to pitch of tuning bar or fork. May disassemble and reassemble used instruments to tune reeds.
GOE: 05.05.12 STRENGTH: L GED: R3 M2 L2 SVP: 6 DLU: 77

730.381-014 BELL MAKER (musical inst.)

Lays out pattern and shapes sheet metal into brass-wind instrument bells and bell necks, using templates, machine tools, handtools, and blueprints: Traces

pattern of bell onto metal, using scribe and template or blueprint. Cuts out bell blank, using hand or power shears. Hammers blank over bell-shaped mandrel, and butts seam, using torch. Brazes seam, using torch. Smooths seam, using notching tool. Operates draw bench or arbor press equipped with expandable lead plug to shape and smooth bell and bell neck over mandrel. Operates spinning lathe to spin bell head and to form bead at tip of bell head [BELL SPINNER (musical inst.)]. Anneals previously shaped bell necks, using hand torch to soften metal for further bending. Removes scratches from bell, using abrasive-coated cloth. May be designated by instrument as Bell Maker, Sousaphones (musical inst.).
GOE: 05.05.12 STRENGTH: M GED: R3 M1 L2 SVP: 7 DLU: 77

730.381-018 BRASS-WIND-INSTRUMENT MAKER (musical inst.) alternate titles: assembler; band-instrument maker

Fabricates or alters brass-wind instrument parts, and assembles parts into completed instruments, ascertaining fabrication and assembly procedures from standard or customer's specifications: Reads specifications and makes calculations to determine procedures for fabricating and assembling instrument. Sets up and operates drawbench, bandsaw, and lathe to draw, cut, and machine instrument tubing. Bends tubing around forming blocks by hand. Measures tubing, using rule, to locate position of holes to be drilled for pistons and valve casings. Operates drill press, honing machine, and lapping machine to drill, hone, and lap metal components. Solders piston and valve components, using silver and soft solder. Hammers bell neck around bell-shaped mandrel, and brazes seams with oxyacetylene torch. Operates spinning lathe to shape bell head around mandrel. Assembles parts, such as braces, slides, valves, pistons, and bell head to form completed instrument, using handtools, measuring devices, and soldering iron. Plates assembled instrument with nickel, copper, or silver [PLATER (electroplating)]. May repair brass-wind instruments. May be designated according to instrument or part made as Saxophone Assembler (musical inst.); Valve Maker (musical inst.) I.
GOE: 05.05.12 STRENGTH: M GED: R4 M4 L4 SVP: 7 DLU: 77

730.381-022 ELECTRIC-ORGAN ASSEMBLER AND CHECKER (musical inst.)

Assembles electronic organ components: Wires, solders, and installs components, such as amplifier switches, keys, and pedals. Performs standard tests to ensure conformance to standards.
GOE: 06.02.23 STRENGTH: L GED: R3 M2 L2 SVP: 6 DLU: 77

730.381-026 HARP REGULATOR (musical inst.)

Completes assembly of harps and tunes them: Screws action to neck, using handtools. Inserts tuning pins in neck. Knots each string between soundboard and tuning pin. Adjusts tuning pins and regulating disks to tune instrument, using handtools and electronic tuning device.
GOE: 06.02.23 STRENGTH: M GED: R3 M2 L1 SVP: 6 DLU: 77

730.381-030 HARP-ACTION ASSEMBLER (musical inst.)

Fits, assembles, and inspects harp actions to obtain specified tolerances and operation: Reams metal parts, using machine tools and handtools. Rivets components to assemble action lines, using riveting machine. Inspects action line with level and micrometer to maintain specified tolerance and moves parts to inspect operation. Assembles action lines between action plates and assembles other metal parts onto plates to complete assembly. Inspects and oils completed action.
GOE: 05.05.12 STRENGTH: M GED: R4 M2 L2 SVP: 6 DLU: 77

730.381-034 METAL-REED TUNER (any industry)

Tunes metal reeds of musical instruments to standard pitch: Dismantles instrument and removes reed blocks, using handtools. Positions reed block over orifice in testing stand and actuates hand-or foot-operated bellows to sound reed. Strikes tuning bar and compares pitch of reed with that of bar to ascertain that reed is sharp or flat. Removes reed block from testing stand, inserts steel plate between reed and block to support reed, and files reed until it matches pitch of tuning bar. Tunes remaining reeds in their chromatic relationship to tuning bar. May lubricate and make repairs and adjustments to other parts of instrument.
GOE: 05.05.12 STRENGTH: L GED: R3 M2 L2 SVP: 7 DLU: 77

730.381-038 ORGAN-PIPE VOICER (musical inst.) alternate titles: voicer

Adjusts metal and wood organ pipes to obtain specified timber and strength of sound: Inserts unvoiced pipes in rack of tuning table and starts electric blower. Depresses key to blow air through unvoiced pipe and voiced master pipe. Listens to difference in tone and determines needed adjustments. Raises or lowers lips of metal flue pipes to regulate airflow over lips, and notches languet (inner tongue), using handtools. Files and raises or lowers reeds in reed pipes. Scrapes and sands lips in wooden pipes and raises or lowers them to regulate airflow. Enlarges or decreases opening in toe hole (hole at base of pipe), using handtools, to regulate loudness of sound. Tunes organ pipes [PIPE-ORGAN TUNER AND REPAIRER (any industry)]. May do final tuning and voicing of pipes in newly installed organs and be designated Organ-Pipe Finisher (musical inst.).
GOE: 05.05.12 STRENGTH: M GED: R4 M2 L2 SVP: 7 DLU: 77

730.381-042 PERCUSSION-INSTRUMENT REPAIRER (any industry)

Repairs percussion instruments, such as drums, cymbals, and xylophones: Removes drum tension rod screws and rods by hand or using drum key. Lifts rim hoop from drum shell and cuts drumhead from hoop. Cuts new drumhead from animal skin, using scissors. Soaks skin in water until it becomes pliable. Stretches skin over rim hoop and tucks it around and under hoop, using hand tucking tool. Reclamps rim hoop onto drum shell to allow drumhead to dry and become taut. Cuts out section around break in drum shells, and cuts new piece to fit, using power saw and handtools. Glues and clamps new piece in place. Removes dents in tympani, using steel-hitting block. Operates drill press or hand power drill to drill hole at inside end of crack in cymbal, gong, or similar instruments to prevent advance of crack, and cuts out section around crack, using shears or grinding wheel. Repairs bass drum and tympani foot mechanisms, and replaces percussion instrument hardware, such as tension rods and rim hoops, and xylophone and marimba bars and wheels as needed, using handtools. Performs other duties, such as sanding, painting, and cleaning drum shells, and regluing simulated pearl onto shells. May solder or weld frames of mallet instruments and metal drum parts. May lay out and shape laminated wood, and apply decorative trim to fabricate drum shells, using handtools, machine tools, blueprints, and shop drawings, and be designated Drum-Shell Maker (musical inst.).
GOE: 05.05.12 STRENGTH: M GED: R3 M2 L2 SVP: 6 DLU: 77

730.381-046 PIPE-ORGAN INSTALLER (musical inst.) alternate titles: organ installer

Assembles and installs components of electrically or mechanically controlled pipe organs, using handtools and following blueprints: Installs and wires components, such as air chests, console, blowers, and airducts, using handtools. Mounts pipes above air chest in predetermined pattern. Secures pipes in wooden racks and fastens racks to chest, using dowels and screws. May tune, maintain, and repair organs [PIPE-ORGAN TUNER AND REPAIRER (any industry)]. May voice pipes [ORGAN-PIPE VOICER (musical inst.)].
GOE: 05.05.12 STRENGTH: M GED: R4 M3 L3 SVP: 7 DLU: 77

730.381-050 PLAYER-PIANO TECHNICIAN (musical inst.)

Installs, tests, and adjusts electronic mechanisms on pianos to convert pianos to self-playing, using handtools and electronic testing equipment and following blueprints: Drills holes in support blocks with portable drill and installs blocks under keyboard at specified angle with whip assembly, consisting of hammers that strike cords to produce musical sounds. Attaches track for mounting music roll and sliding carriage onto key bed of piano, using handtools, and positions electronic control box into carriage. Installs vacuum pump and unit, required to transmit action from music roll through controls to solenoids, using screws and handtools. Places bar containing electrical solenoids on attached support bars, aligning solenoids with whip assembly to ensure engagement of solenoids, whip assembly, and piano hammers. Wires, solders, and installs wiring to piano case and attaches vacuum hose to pump and controls. Places music roll on carrier, starts mechanism, turns controls, and determines if player mechanism functions as required. Makes adjustments or repairs to correct defects, using handtools and electronic testing equipment.
GOE: 05.05.12 STRENGTH: H GED: R3 M3 L3 SVP: 4 DLU: 77

730.381-054 TROMBONE-SLIDE ASSEMBLER (musical inst.)

Assembles, solders, and laps trombone slides: Solders slide components, such as tubing sections, braces, and water valves, using gas torch and soft solder, following pattern to form inner and outer sections. Ascertains whether slides are parallel and straight, using gauges. Inserts plugs into slides, and squeezes or separates them to align them. Pushes outer slide over motor-driven shaft coated with abrasive to smooth inner surface. Brushes lubricant on inner slide surfaces and laps inner and outer slides together by hand. May cut tubes, using rotary power saw. May repair trombone slides.
GOE: 06.01.04 STRENGTH: L GED: R3 M2 L2 SVP: 7 DLU: 77

730.381-058 TUNER, PERCUSSION (musical inst.)

Tunes wood and fiberglass bars used in marimbas and xylophones, metal bars used in bell-lyras and vibraharps, and metal rods used in electronic carillons and tuning forks, using machines and handtools: Strikes bar with mallet and compares tone with tuned block or stroboscope. When tuning wood and fiberglass bars, removes wood and fiberglass with bandsaw and smooths bar with sanding machine or by hand until specified tone is obtained. When tuning metal bars and rods, removes metal with machine grinder and with hand files and scrapers to obtain specified tone. May assemble bars onto instruments. May be designated according to tuning operation performed as Harmonic Tuner (musical inst.); Octave Tuner (musical inst.).
GOE: 05.05.12 STRENGTH: M GED: R3 M2 L2 SVP: 6 DLU: 77

730.384-010 ASSEMBLER, PIANO (musical inst.)

Performs any combination of following tasks to assemble and install components in piano cases or benches: Positions parts in specified relationship to each other preparatory to assembly or installation. Joins parts and bolts, nails, screws, or glues parts to assemble or install parts, using handtools and portable power tools. Planes, sands, and files or adds shims and bushings to obtain specified fit and movement of parts. Machines parts to specifications prior to assembly, using machines, such as circular saw, or single-spindle-drill press. May verify alignment of parts, using ruler and gauge.
GOE: 06.02.22 STRENGTH: L GED: R3 M2 L2 SVP: 4 DLU: 77

730.681-010 PIANO REGULATOR-INSPECTOR (musical inst.) alternate titles: adjuster, piano action

Performs any combination of following tasks to inspect and regulate piano internal actions: Examines piano action components after installation for completeness and operation, and removes, repairs, or replaces defective or broken

parts, using handtools, glue, nails, and power tools, such as saw, sander, and drill. Verifies alignment of parts, using ruler and gauges. Scrapes, files, bends or adds shims and bushings to adjust operation of alignment of parts as specified. Depresses piano keys to verify operation of piano actions and makes adjustments to obtain specified performance. May mix glue. May assemble parts on to complete assembly prior to regulating. May specialize in inspecting and regulating particular type piano actions, such as spinet, upright, or grand.
GOE: 06.01.04 STRENGTH: L GED: R3 M2 L3 SVP: 5 DLU: 77

730.681-014 PISTON MAKER (musical inst.)
Finishes brasswind instrument pistons and assembles piston parts, using handtools: Inserts crooks (curved tubes) through precut holes in piston blank and cuts them to length, using sheet metal snippers or table saw. Places piston blank over mandrel or die and pushes steel balls or works ball-ended handtool through crooks to expand crooks to limits of holes into which they are inserted. Presses in piston bottom and head, using small hand press. Solders bottom plate onto piston, and removes excess solder, using scraping tool. Rough trims crooks, after soldering, using table saw. Operates turning lathe to face and bevel piston ends, and to shape and smooth external surface of piston. Operates drill press to tap threads into piston. Solders crooks to piston blank, using silver solder and gas torch. Grinds piston to final size, using special piston grinder and gauge. Inspects finished pistons for defects, such as holes and dents.
GOE: 06.01.04 STRENGTH: L GED: R3 M2 L2 SVP: 5 DLU: 77

730.681-018 VALVE MAKER II (musical inst.)
Fabricates valves for brass musical instruments, using handtools and machine tools and performing any combination of following tasks: Cuts connecting tubes to specified length, using table saw. Drills connecting tube holes in valve, taps internal and external threads in valve and ballisters, and cuts recess in top of valve or ballisters, using drill press. Fits ballisters onto valve and solders them into place with soft solder. Inserts connecting tubes and braces between valves, and wires (ties) them into place, using pliers. Aligns valves, tubes, and braces, using gauge and hammer. Solders tubes and braces to valves with silver solder. Cuts connecting tubes from interior of piston and bores piston, using honing machine with changeable bits. Hones interior of valve and exterior of piston, using *lapping* machine. Cleans excess solder from joints and deburrs inside of valve, using file, scraping tool, and sandpaper. Depresses piston into valve to ascertain that corresponding valve and piston holes match, and solders piston head to piston when holes are matched. Numbers matched valves and pistons to facilitate final assembly.
GOE: 06.02.24 STRENGTH: L GED: R3 M2 L2 SVP: 6 DLU: 77

730.682-010 SOCKET PULLER (musical inst.) alternate titles: body maker
Operates machine to draw, face (trim), and roll edges of tone holes of musical instruments, such as flutes and saxophones: Bolts mandrel for particular instrument to machine. Brushes compound on drawing buttons and places them in holes in mandrel. Places instrument body on mandrel with tone holes centered over drawing buttons and clamps it in place. Places bushing over revolving shaft head to form drawing die for each sized tone hole and drawing button. Moves controls to lower revolving shaft and screw it into button. Starts drawing machine that raises shaft and drawing button to draw out tone hole. Repeats operation for each tone hole. Changes mandrel and attaches tools to trim and roll back top edge of tone holes.
GOE: 06.02.02 STRENGTH: M GED: R3 M1 L1 SVP: 4 DLU: 77

730.684-010 ASSEMBLER, MUSICAL INSTRUMENTS (musical inst.)
Performs any combination of following tasks to assemble and fasten together parts to form subassemblies or complete musical instruments, such as drums, keyed brass, woodwind, or stringed instruments according to specified instructions or diagrams: Drills, taps, or reams holes to prepare parts for assembly, using drill press or bench-mounted drill. Bends tubing and laps parts by hand to form or join parts. Applies abrasive solvents to sliding joints to cause parts to move freely. Fits or faces parts, using hand file or *bench grinder* to trim parts to fit. Aligns metal brass-wind parts, such as valves, knobs, keys, and bars by sight, by placing them in jigs and clamping them on instrument, or by positioning parts, using rulers or gauges. Screws, clips, solders, and glues parts, such as drum hardware, corks, violin necks, wooden bridges, and metal snares, using handtools, portable powered tools, or hand torches. Removes excess solder, using scraping tool. Winds and bends spring wire around valve keys by hand to install valves on brass-wind instruments. Inserts steel bars and squeezes or separates bars to adjust tube spacing on brass-wind instruments. Cleans inside of tubes of brass-wind instruments with swab and cleaning solvent. Installs electric pick-ups in electrically amplified instruments, using screwdriver and soldering gun. May polish or buff exterior of instruments, using rotating buffing wheel. May cut tubing, using power saw. May inspect instruments for defects and reject instruments not meeting specifications. May be designated according to instrument assembled as Final Assembler, Brass-Wind Instruments (musical inst.); Mounter, Brass-Wind Instruments (musical inst.); Stringed-Instrument Assembler (musical inst.); or by part assembled as Bridge Fitter (musical inst.); Knobber (musical inst.); Neck Fitter (musical inst.). May be designated: Mounter, Clarinets (musical inst.); Mounter, Flutes And Piccolos (musical inst.); Mounter, Keyed Instruments (musical inst.); Mounter, Saxophones (musical inst.); Mounter, Sousaphones (musical inst.); Mounter, Trombones (musical inst.); Mounter, Trumpets And Cornets (musical inst.).
GOE: 06.02.23 STRENGTH: L GED: R3 M2 L2 SVP: 3 DLU: 77

730.684-014 BELL-NECK HAMMERER (musical inst.) alternate titles: folder-and-notcher
Forms and shapes bell necks for brass musical instruments: Bends neck blank down middle by hand. Aligns blank on mandrel, using forming device. Rolls bent blank around mandrel to form seam, using wooden mallet and iron bar. Secures seam for brazing, using notching tool. Smooths brazed seam, using file. Places neck on mandrel and hammers neck to shape it and remove dents, using metal hammer and wooden mallet.
GOE: 06.04.24 STRENGTH: M GED: R2 M1 L1 SVP: 2 DLU: 77

730.684-018 BELLY BUILDER (musical inst.)
Performs any combination of following tasks to fit and assemble wood soundboard, cast metal plate, and wood bridges to wood frame to fabricate back panel of piano: Glues supporting ribs and bridges to soundboard and glues soundboard to frame, using electronic gluing machine, gluing machine, or gluing press. Screws back panel to frame to reinforce gluing, using screws and screwdriver. Notches ribs and back frame to specifications, using chamfering machine. Clamps metal back plate to back panel, using air-clamp table, and measures and marks location for plate, using ruler, calipers, template, or gauge. Shapes bridges to specified height, using template, gauge, plane, and sandpaper. Presses pedal to release air-clamp and removes metal plate. Marks with punch and drills holes in back panel to attach metal plate, using drill press. Locates, marks, and drills bridge pin holes, using template, punch, hammer, and portable drill. Notches treble bridge with shaper machine or handtools. Hammers bridge pins into holes. Repositions metal back plate on back panel and secures plate to panel with bolts and screws. Verifies alignment of plate with back and bridges, using gauges. Inserts shims or removes wood from frame to adjust level of plate to obtain specified alignment. Hammers wood bushings into tuning pin holes in plate. Hammers tuning pins into bushings. May drill holes in bushings, using drill press. May varnish soundboard and ribs. May grind metal plate bearing bar to specified size, using portable grinder.
GOE: 06.02.32 STRENGTH: H GED: R3 M3 L3 SVP: 3 DLU: 77

730.684-022 BOW REHAIRER (any industry)
Replaces bow hair of stringed instrument bows, using handtools: Disassembles bow and removes spent hair, using handtools. Examines and cleans bow parts. Hand-carves replacement wedges and plugs. Selects new hairs of similar color and binds one end with yarn and resin. Secures bound end in one end of bow and secures it with wedges. Combs hair and binds loose ends with yarn and resin. Secures end in bow with wedges.
GOE: 05.05.12 STRENGTH: S GED: R3 M1 L1 SVP: 6 DLU: 77

730.684-026 CHIP TUNER (musical inst.) alternate titles: chipper
Adjusts piano strings to attain specified pitch, in first tuning of partially finished pianos: Rubs strings with wood block to remove irregularities, such as kinks. Plucks specified C or A string with pick and adjusts tuning pin with tuning wrench until pitch of string and tuning fork or bar are in unison. Plucks remaining string and adjusts to specified pitch by aurally comparing with previously tuned strings.
GOE: 06.02.32 STRENGTH: M GED: R3 M2 L3 SVP: 3 DLU: 77

730.684-030 CONSOLE ASSEMBLER (musical inst.)
Assembles and connects organ components, such as speakers, pedal assembly, switch assembly, and amplifiers on mockup. Makes mechanical adjustments to units. Removes units from mockup and installs in organ case.
GOE: 06.02.23 STRENGTH: M GED: R3 M2 L2 SVP: 4 DLU: 77

730.684-034 FRETTED-INSTRUMENT INSPECTOR (musical inst.)
Inspects stringed instruments, such as banjos and guitars, for tone, finish, and mechanical action: Tightens strings of instrument by hand. Plucks and adjusts strings to test tonal quality and intonation. Examines instrument for flaws in construction and finish. Adjusts alignment of parts, using handtools. Files and sands rough areas and applies lacquer over areas with brush. Buffs lacquered areas, using power-buffing wheel.
GOE: 06.01.04 STRENGTH: L GED: R3 M2 L2 SVP: 4 DLU: 77

730.684-038 INSPECTOR, WOODWIND INSTRUMENTS (musical inst.)
Inspects woodwind musical instruments, such as clarinets, saxophones, or flutes, for defective finish and mechanical action, and makes repairs, using handtools and testing devices: Tests soldered joints for strength and keys for spring tension, using testing devices. Solders loose parts and adjusts spring tension, using soldering iron and handtools. Examines instrument for defects in finish, and touches up defects, using buffing wheel. Inserts instrument into device that closes all keys and admits compressed air. Observes manometer to ascertain presence of air leakage. Presses pads with finger to locate leakage and adjusts pad, using handtools. Marks other defects for correction.
GOE: 06.03.02 STRENGTH: L GED: R3 M2 L2 SVP: 4 DLU: 77

730.684-042 KEYBOARD-ACTION ASSEMBLER (musical inst.)
Assembles and adjusts action of electronic organs: Uncrates keyboards and removes keys from keyboard. Sends keyboard to cabinet shop for shaping. Replaces keys in keyboard and locks board in rotor rack. Adjusts travel (up and down action) of keys and spaces with spacing tool. Regulates tension of key springs. Inserts key action screws into slotted ends of keys and levels key ends. Places keyboard end plates in each end of jig and locks plates in place. Removes keyboard from rotor rack and places keyboard in jig between end plates. Drills holes through keyboard and end plates and inserts screws. Removes keyboard from jig and attaches key action mounting brackets to end plates. At-

taches contact plates to underside of keys, using screwdriver. Solders connecting wire across all contact blocks, using soldering iron. Mounts subassembly under keys, using screwdriver. Adjusts level of key ends so key will activate key action.
GOE: 06.02.23 STRENGTH: L GED: R3 M2 L2 SVP: 4 DLU: 77

730.684-046 MANUAL WINDER (musical inst.)
Performs any combination of following tasks to assemble components for electronic organs: Inserts tension rod in manual to ease tension on resistance wires welded to contacts. Inserts contacts through actuators and locks actuators in place. Forms loops on ends of wires, using machine; and attaches loop ends to specified terminals. Winds excess wire into trough for tone control. Removes tension rod and ties assembly into place, using thread. Inserts rows of contacts in manual and wires preset stops for change of organ tone. Inserts contact separators in manual. Cleans bus bars, using chamois and alcohol, and inserts bars in manual to form junctions for electrical circuits. Straightens and replaces contacts, and rewires components to correct defective manuals. Inserts holder and wiring comb. Fastens assembly, using screwdriver.
GOE: 06.02.23 STRENGTH: L GED: R3 M2 L2 SVP: 3 DLU: 77

730.684-050 MUSICAL-STRING MAKER (musical inst.)
Performs any combination of following tasks to fabricate gut strings for musical instruments: Removes sheep intestine from barrel and places it in cleaning solution. Feeds intestines through stripping machine or runs hands or scraper over intestine to remove mucus. Splits intestine into four pieces and splices pieces together to make uniform lengths. Feels strands to select those of uniform size for various strings. Attaches loops to strands and stretches strands over posts. Twists specified number of strands together to form strings. Fumigates, dyes, and bleaches strings. Verifies gauge of string, using micrometer.
GOE: 06.02.32 STRENGTH: L GED: R3 M1 L1 SVP: 4 DLU: 77

730.684-054 PIANO STRINGER (musical inst.)
Threads wires through tuning pins to string pianos, using handtools: Selects specified wire, following chart for particular model, and threads wire through hole in tuning pin, around hitch pin (pin at base of cast plate used to hold string), and through another tuning pin. Cuts wire with cutters and draws it taut, using handtools. Aligns and spaces strings, using handtools. Attaches metal pressure bar, using screws and handtools to stabilize string pressure. May pluck string with pick and adjust tuning pin with tool to bring note to specified range. May insert and hammer tuning pins into previously drilled holes in back panel.
GOE: 06.04.24 STRENGTH: M GED: R2 M1 L2 SVP: 4 DLU: 77

730.684-058 PREASSEMBLER AND INSPECTOR (musical inst.)
Laps pistons and slides of brass musical instruments to ensure that joints slide freely: Screws piston onto shaft attached to handle, and brushes pumice compound onto piston. Inserts piston into matched valve, and laps it until it moves freely. Moves sliding joints to detect binding action. Applies abrasive compounds to slides, and files and laps them until they move freely. Inspects soldered joints for excess solder and rejects unacceptable joints.
GOE: 06.04.23 STRENGTH: L GED: R2 M1 L1 SVP: 4 DLU: 77

730.684-062 RACKER, OCTAVE BOARD (musical inst.)
Assembles octave rack for electronic organ, according to blueprint or diagram: Clamps rack in jig table. Places octave boards in designated rack sections and staples edges to rack, using stapling gun. Solders wires between boards to connect octave board circuits, using electric soldering iron. Positions wire cable on rack and octave boards, according to blueprint or diagram, and solders cable ends to solder buttons on boards. Attaches hinges to rack, using screwdriver.
GOE: 06.02.23 STRENGTH: L GED: R3 M2 L2 SVP: 4 DLU: 77

730.684-066 SANDER-AND-BUFFER (musical inst.)
Sands unlacquered wooden sections of guitars, using sandpaper and portable-power sander. Repairs cracks in wood, using knife and putty. Stains instrument, using brush, pad or spray gun. Rubs stained surface with cloth or felt pad to remove excess stain and evenly distribute stain. Scrapes away shading from binding to top, back, rim, and neck of instruments, using steel scraper tools and sands instrument smooth, using sandpaper. Hand-buffs lacquered sections of guitar, using cheesecloth and buffing compound.
GOE: 06.04.25 STRENGTH: L GED: R2 M1 L2 SVP: 4 DLU: 77

730.684-070 SEAM HAMMERER (musical inst.)
Smooths brazed seam of copper, nickel, silver, or brass musical instruments, using power roller or hammer: Files seam, using metal file. Places instrument on anvil or mandrel with seam uppermost. Starts hammer and moves instrument piece across anvil to expose seam to hammer, or positions workpiece under wheel of rolling machine and activates wheel to compress seam to specified thickness.
GOE: 06.02.24 STRENGTH: L GED: R3 M1 L1 SVP: 3 DLU: 77

730.684-074 SHEET-METAL-PATTERN CUTTER (musical inst.)
Lays out and cuts sheet metal for brass-wind instrument bells and bell necks, using templates and power tools or handtools: Positions templates on sheet metal to obtain minimum of waste. Marks cutting and forming lines on sheet metal with scriber, following outlines of templates. Cuts metal, following guidelines, using hand shears or power shears.
GOE: 06.02.24 STRENGTH: L GED: R2 M2 L1 SVP: 3 DLU: 77

730.684-078 SLIDING-JOINT MAKER (musical inst.)
Cuts tubing, solders tubes together, and fits into brass wind instrument sliding joints: Sets length gauge of table saw, and cuts tubes to length. Secures

tubes in chuck of turning lathe, and works handtools against tube ends to bevel, burr, and ream tubes. Solders tubes, braces, and attachments together and assembles joints, using mallet.
GOE: 06.02.24 STRENGTH: S GED: R3 M2 L2 SVP: 3 DLU: 77

730.684-082 STOPBOARD ASSEMBLER (musical inst.)
Assembles electronic organ stopboards, attaching components, such as stop tabs, brackets, switches, and lights: Drills holes, using electric drill. Attaches holding brackets with screws. Inserts holding screws, stop tabs, and spring clips. Levels stop tabs, using measuring tool. Drills holes and installs stack switch. Attaches bank of indicator lights. Tests lights with battery tester. Installs music rack lighting panel. Attaches face board to exposed ends of stopboard sections, using screwdriver.
GOE: 06.02.23 STRENGTH: L GED: R3 M3 L3 SVP: 4 DLU: 77

730.684-086 TESTER (musical inst.)
Tests pitch of reed and brass instruments by sounding note and observing effect on stroboscope: Sets dial on stroboscope to note to be tested. Plays note on musical instrument into microphone connected to stroboscope. Observes whether revolving lights on stroboscope appear to stand still, indicating correctness of pitch, or move slowly to right or left, indicating sharp or flat. Pushes or pulls tuning slide or pulls out mouthpiece to adjust instrument until exact pitch is obtained. Rejects defective instruments. Tests accuracy of stroboscope by striking standard pitch chime and noting indicator.
GOE: 06.03.02 STRENGTH: L GED: R3 M2 L2 SVP: 6 DLU: 77

730.684-090 TONE CABINET ASSEMBLER (musical inst.) alternate titles: pedal assembler
Assembles pedal board and keyboard-coupler assemblies, and mounts speakers and parts to tone cabinets of electronic organs, following detailed drawings, and using handtools: Cements felt strips to wood frames of chassis. Lays out and drills holes in frame, using ruler, pencil, and hand drill. Mounts metal guide bars in holes and secures them to frame with wood screws. Scribes line for mounting felt to note-mounting channel, using straightedge. Cements felt strips on channel. Fastens pedals to mounting channel, inserts and crimps pedal tension springs on pedal frames, and adjusts tension of springs. Cements felt strips to channel tips. Cuts speaker and speaker adapter portholes in panel of tone cabinet. Installs front and top speakers and solders connecting wires to speakers. Mounts grille cloth over speakers. Cuts hole in rear panel of cabinet for receptacle of connector cable and connects cable wires to speakers. Mounts insulation in speaker enclosures. Assembles keyboard kit and attaches mounts to brackets of keyboard assembly. Cements felt to keynote channels. Clamps keyboard assembly to coupler assembly and attaches assemblies to chassis frame.
GOE: 06.02.23 STRENGTH: M GED: R3 M2 L2 SVP: 3 DLU: 77

730.684-094 TONE REGULATOR (musical inst.)
Compresses or loosens felt on piano hammers to brighten or soften tone of piano strings: Depresses piano key and listens to piano tone. Sands defective hammers with sanding paddle or brushes lacquer on hammer to harden felt and increase tonal brilliance. Jabs felt hammer with needles to soften hammers and increase tonal mellowness. Removes excess felt from hammer, using file. Inspects and adjusts string spacing and striking point of hammers, using wrench and burner. Files burrs from tuning pins.
GOE: 06.04.34 STRENGTH: L GED: R2 M1 L1 SVP: 4 DLU: 77

730.685-010 LOOPER (musical inst.) alternate titles: ball-ender
Tends machine that twists loop around fitting at end of wire musical-instrument strings: Positions cylindrical fitting (brass cylinder with hollow center) onto post on horizontal shaft of looper machine. Inserts wire-string into securing hole in machine table. Draws loose end of wire-string around fitting on shaft and back across machine table. Pulls bar over wire-string on machine table to hold wire-string secure. Depresses treadle, causing wire-looped cylinder to revolve, twisting loop, and fastening fitting to end of wire-string. Stops machine and removes looped fitting from machine. Places wire-string in holder for collection. May test loop strength, using applied tension. May verify gauges of wire with micrometer.
GOE: 06.04.24 STRENGTH: S GED: R2 M1 L2 SVP: 3 DLU: 77

730.685-014 MOUTHPIECE MAKER (musical inst.)
Tends shop machines that form and shape mouthpieces for woodwind instruments: Screws mouthpiece into boring machine that follows template to automatically form base of piece. Positions mouthpiece in chuck of automatic turning lathe and shapes outside of mouthpiece. Feeds mouthpiece in sloping machine to cut slope to specified dimensions. Presses tip of mouthpiece against abrasive wheel to grind to specified curvature. Places mouthpiece in fixture of chambering (shaping) machine to shape inside opening. Cuts and attaches cork around forward part of mouthpiece to ensure fit of mouthpiece into instrument, using knife and glue. Verifies dimensions, using micrometers and gauges. Operates power buffing wheel to buff mouthpiece.
GOE: 06.04.09 STRENGTH: L GED: R3 M2 L2 SVP: 3 DLU: 77

730.686-010 CUTTER, WOODWIND REEDS (musical inst.)
Feeds machines that saw and abrade cane (cultivated bamboo) into woodwind instrument reeds: Places stalk of cane against length guide on table of bandsawing machine that cuts cane to length. Sorts cut pieces by diameter. Splits pieces into strips, using hand-operated splitting device. Places strips into blanking-machine that cuts excess material from strips to form reed blanks.

Places blanks on conveyor belt that feeds against rotating sanding disk. Inserts blank into holding device of cutting machine that tapers one end of reed blank. Removes tapered reeds and sorts, using gauge.
GOE: 06.04.25 STRENGTH: L GED: R2 M1 L1 SVP: 2 DLU: 77

731   OCCUPATIONS IN FABRICATION AND REPAIR OF GAMES AND TOYS

This group includes occupations concerned with fabricating and repairing BB guns, trains, toy musical instruments, models, poker chips, dolls, chess and checker sets, and children's vehicles. Occupations concerned with fabricating such textile products as doll clothing and children's costumes are included in Division 78.

731.131-010   SUPERVISOR, TOY ASSEMBLY (toy-sport equip.)
Supervises and coordinates activities of workers engaged in assembly, cleaning, and painting of metal, plastic, and wooden toys: Assembles toys to aid in meeting schedule or to determine cause of production delays. Directs workers in assembly methods by demonstrating assembly tasks. Trains workers in operation and maintenance of equipment used in assembly and painting of toys on production line. Schedules conveyor line changes according to production requirements. Inspects toys for finish and operation. Maintains production and personnel records. Performs other duties as described under SUPERVISOR (any industry) Master Title. May supervise workers engaged in constructing prototype toys and be designated Supervisor, Model Making (toy-sport equip.).
GOE: 06.02.01 STRENGTH: L GED: R4 M3 L4 SVP: 7 DLU: 77

731.280-010   MODEL MAKER (toy-sport equip.)
Constructs mechanically functioning prototypes of toys from blueprints, using metalworking, woodworking, and plastic-forming machines and handtools: Studies blueprint design and selects stock material, such as aluminum, wood, styrene, and fiberglass, according to design specifications. Lays out design of parts on stock, following blueprints and using measuring and drawing instruments. Designs and casts molds from resin for use in injection-molding and plastic-forming machines. Sets up and operates machines, such as injection-molding machine, vacuum plastic-forming machine, drill press, lathe, jointer, milling machine, and sanding machine, to cut, shape, and sand model parts. Assembles and fastens parts together, using handtools, glue, bolts, nails, and clamps.
GOE: 01.06.02 STRENGTH: L GED: R4 M4 L4 SVP: 7 DLU: 77

731.381-010   DICE MAKER (toy-sport equip.)
Fabricates dice from precut nitric-celloid cubes according to specifications: Places nitric-celloid cubes in electrically heated metal box to remove volatile solvents. Operates milling machine to shape cubes to specified tolerance, according to dimensions specified on work order. Measures cubes with vernier caliper. Operates drill press to drill spots in cubes. Paints spots on cubes, using implement. Finishes dice to tolerance of 0.001 inch, using buffing wheel or draws dice over various grades of sandpaper to achieve dull finish.
GOE: 06.02.24 STRENGTH: L GED: R3 M2 L2 SVP: 6 DLU: 77

731.587-010   FINISHER, HAND (toy-sport equip.)
Dresses and decorates toys or dolls with ready-made clothes, ribbons, and ornaments, such as bells and collars: Glues precut facial features and hats on toy. Directs air from blower over toys to remove dust and lint. Records production. May dress dolls with unfinished garments and sew them onto doll. May glue heads of toys onto bodies.
GOE: 06.04.23 STRENGTH: L GED: R2 M1 L1 SVP: 2 DLU: 77

731.684-010   COIN-MACHINE ASSEMBLER (svc. ind. mach.) alternate titles: switchpanel mounter
Mounts and connects switch panels to control boxes of electric pinball machines. Attaches switch panels to control boxes, using screws and screwdriver, and solders switch panel wires to electric plugs of control boxes, using soldering iron.
GOE: 06.04.23 STRENGTH: L GED: R2 M1 L2 SVP: 3 DLU: 77

731.684-014   DOLL REPAIRER (any industry)
Repairs damaged dolls: Examines doll to determine extent of damage and repairs needed. Disassembles doll to remove damaged parts. Repairs or replaces parts and reassembles doll. Repaints dolls, retouches lips, and cheeks, using paint and brush. Replaces eyelashes and hair, using glue. May package or otherwise prepare repaired doll for shipment or storage.
GOE: 05.10.04 STRENGTH: L GED: R2 M1 L1 SVP: 3 DLU: 77

731.684-018   TOY ASSEMBLER (retail trade)
Assembles knocked-down toys for delivery to customers, using handtools and manufacturer's diagram or instructions.
GOE: 05.12.15 STRENGTH: L GED: R2 M2 L2 SVP: 3 DLU: 77

731.684-022   TOY-ELECTRIC-TRAIN REPAIRER (retail trade)
Repairs toy electric trains in retail toy store, using pliers, screwdrivers, and soldering iron: Removes defective parts and replaces with new ones. Adjusts coils and moving parts. Does touchup painting as required.
GOE: 05.10.03 STRENGTH: L GED: R3 M2 L2 SVP: 3 DLU: 77

731.685-010   ROOTER OPERATOR (fabrication, nec) alternate titles: doll-wig maker, rooted hair; hair-rooting-machine operator
Tends machine that roots (stitches) prescribed quantity of hair onto doll head: Places one or more cones of precurled synthetic hair at rear of machine. Pulls

single strand of hair from cone, threads needle, and positions doll head on machine post. Depresses pedal to activate needle and maneuvers head under needle in prescribed manner until machine stops at end of rooting cycle. Releases pedal to activate device that cuts hair from cone at specified length. Places completed head in containers for removal to finishing department. May tend machine that curls hair as it is being sewn onto doll heads.
GOE: 06.04.09 STRENGTH: S GED: R2 M1 L2 SVP: 3 DLU: 77

731.685-014   STUFFER (toy-sport equip.) alternate titles: blower; toy stuffer
Tends machine that blows filler into stuffed-toy shells: Inserts precut supporting wire into shell. Places shell opening over stuffing machine nozzle. Depresses pedal to blow cotton or chopped foam rubber filler into shell to impart shape to toy. Places stuffed toy in tote box. Records production. May stuff toys by hand.
GOE: 06.04.34 STRENGTH: S GED: R2 M1 L1 SVP: 2 DLU: 77

731.685-018   TIRE SETTER (toy-sport equip.)
Tends machine that attaches rubber tires or semipneumatic tires to wheels of children's vehicles, such as tricycles or bicycles, using either of following methods: (1) Starts machine and positions rubber tire material against machine fence in line with threading hole. Depresses pedal causing machine to thread wire through tire and cut wire to specified length. Inserts protruding ends of wire in slots and holes of machine forming loop with tire. Positions vehicle wheel inside loop formed by tire and depresses pedal to activate machine and draw wire, twist wheel, trim wire, and secure wire on wheel. Slides wheel onto shaft between rollers of machine with wire twist up and depresses pedal causing rollers to push ends of tire over wire-twist to complete tire. (2) Places tire in jaws of machine and starts machine to stretch tire. Positions wheel inside stretched tire on machine, holds wheel, and depresses pedal to release tire onto wheel rim. May install sprocket, dust cap, and secure sprocket with snap ring on bicycle wheel, using metal cone.
GOE: 06.04.34 STRENGTH: L GED: R2 M1 L1 SVP: 2 DLU: 77

731.687-010   ASSEMBLER (svc. ind. mach.)
Assembles ball-propelling units of pinball games, using handtools: Screws cap on rod with pliers and slips spring on rod. Inserts end of rod through hole in housing and attaches pull knob, using screwdriver. Pulls knob to test spring tension of assembly.
GOE: 06.04.23 STRENGTH: L GED: R1 M1 L1 SVP: 2 DLU: 77

731.687-014   FINISHER (fabrication, nec)
Sets doll hair into specified style by combing, brushing, and cutting: Places doll head on holder and combs and brushes hair in prescribed manner to smooth and untangle hair, using wire brush and petroleum jelly. Cuts hair to desired length, using scissors. Sets hair into specified style and secures in place, using rubber bands. Wipes doll face to remove smudges, using damp cloth. Places plastic bag over finished head and tucks edges under base to prevent damage to hair and face.
GOE: 06.04.34 STRENGTH: S GED: R2 M1 L1 SVP: 2 DLU: 77

731.687-018   HACKLER, DOLL WIGS (toy-sport equip.)
Grasps and pulls synthetic hair through teeth or bristles of hackle to remove tangles and soften fibers preparatory to making doll wigs. May arrange and finish doll wigs, using comb, and be designated Wig Comber (toy-sport equip.).
GOE: 06.04.34 STRENGTH: L GED: R2 M1 L1 SVP: 2 DLU: 77

731.687-022   INSPECTOR, TOYS (toy-sport equip.)
Inspects subassembly or finished metal, plastic, and wooden toys for conformance to specifications: Examines toys at end of assembly line for items, such as paint scratches or nicks, inclusion of accessories, operation of moving parts, and decal application. Removes defective toys from line or performs repairs, such as touching up paint, tightening screws, or bending fastening tabs. Cleans toys with damp sponge and transfers them to packing section. Weighs specified quantities to fill orders for toys. May test operation of toys, using testing equipment.
GOE: 06.03.02 STRENGTH: L GED: R3 M2 L2 SVP: 4 DLU: 77

731.687-026   MOLD FILLER, PLASTIC DOLLS (toy-sport equip.)
Fills molds with plastic compound to cast doll heads, arms, and legs: Inspects molds and covers for cleanliness and cleans them as required with solvent and rags. Ignites hand-operated gun and inserts nozzle into fill plug of mold. Presses trigger of gun which automatically discharges premeasured amount of plastic compound into mold. Places cover on mold and bolts it in place, using pneumatic wrench. Pushes mold onto conveyor. May strip mold after curing.
GOE: 06.04.32 STRENGTH: H GED: R2 M1 L1 SVP: 3 DLU: 77

731.687-030   PUZZLE ASSEMBLER (toy-sport equip.)
Fits together pieces of jigsaw puzzles to form completed unit: Removes puzzle forms and paint trays from conveyor and stacks them according to color code. Removes puzzle parts from trays and fits part into form. Places assembled puzzle on conveyor.
GOE: 06.04.23 STRENGTH: L GED: R2 M1 L1 SVP: 2 DLU: 77

731.687-034   TOY ASSEMBLER (toy-sport equip.)
Assembles parts of various materials, such as plastic, wood, metal, or fabric to mass produce toys, performing any combination of following tasks: Selects parts specified and positions parts in designated relationship to each other, using hands, tweezers, or pliers. Assembles and fastens parts of toys together,

using clips, glue, jig, screws, dowels, nails, handtools, and portable powered tools. Inspects toys for specified color and operation of parts. May tend previously set up machines, such as drill press, reamer, welding machine, nailing machine, flanging press, and punch press to drill, cut, weld, trim, fit, or insert toy parts on assembly line. May be designated according to item assembled or material used as Assembler, Toy Voices (toy-sport equip.); Doll-Eye-Setter (toy-sport equip.); Stuffed-Toy Joiner (toy-sport equip.); Toy Assembler, Plastic (toy-sport equip.); Toy Assembler, Wood (toy-sport equip.); Wheel Assembler, Baby Carriage (toy-sport equip.).
GOE: 06.04.23 STRENGTH: L GED: R2 M1 L1 SVP: 2 DLU: 77

731.687-038 WIRE CUTTER (svc. ind. mach.)
Cuts copper wire to specified length, using hand shears, for use in manufacture of pinball machines.
GOE: 06.04.24 STRENGTH: L GED: R1 M1 L1 SVP: 1 DLU: 77

732 OCCUPATIONS IN FABRICATION AND REPAIR OF SPORTING GOODS

This group includes occupations concerned with fabricating and repairing golf and tennis goods, gymnasium and playground equipment, basketballs, fishing gear, decoys, roller skates and ice skates, body-protection equipment, and bowling balls. Occupations concerned with fabricating and repairing athletic and sports apparel are included in Division 78. Occupations concerned with fabricating and repairing small arms are included in Group 736, and occupations concerned with fabricating ammunition are included in Group 737.

732.130-010 SUPERVISOR (toy-sport equip.)
Supervises and coordinates activities of workers engaged in fabricating, assembling, or repairing sporting goods, such as athletic balls, billiard tables, bowling balls, bows and arrows, golf clubs, and under-water equipment: Directs workers in operation of machines and assembly techniques. Tours work area to ascertain progress of scheduled work and observes workers to verify conformity with prescribed work procedures, safety regulations, productivity, and standards of work quality. Occasionally examines assembled products to determine if products meet company specifications. Reports defective machinery and equipment to designated personnel to obtain repairs required. May assemble items to aid in meeting production schedule or determine cause of production delays. Performs other duties described under SUPERVISOR (any industry) Master Title. May be designated according to activity supervised as Assembly Supervisor (toy-sport equip.); Fabrication Supervisor (toy-sport equip.); Repair Supervisor (toy-sport equip.).
GOE: 06.02.01 STRENGTH: L GED: R4 M3 L3 SVP: 6 DLU: 78

732.281-010 CUSTOM SKI MAKER (toy-sport equip.)
Fabricates customized skis, using knowledge of materials and techniques of production: Examines designs and confers with engineering personnel to determine production specifications. Computes deviations from standard specifications required to produce customized skis. Collects parts required and fabricates cams and core form needed to make skis, using planing machine. Turns knobs to adjust temperature of mold press to specified setting. Positions parts, such as heel pad, toe-edge, and shims in female die of mold. Wraps fiberglass around polyurethane foam core, pours epoxy resin over core, and positions core in female die of heated mold press for shaping. Removes ski from die, scrapes edge with putty knife to remove resin flash, and mounts ski in rack to stabilize camber and torsion. Visually inspects finish applied to skis by other production workers to ensure compliance with specifications. Verifies configuration of skis in repose and under stress, using micrometer, rulers, and weight-distribution measurement graph. Records information on materials used and techniques applied to fabricate skis.
GOE: 05.10.01 STRENGTH: L GED: R4 M4 L4 SVP: 7 DLU: 77

732.364-014 SKI-BINDING FITTER-AND-REPAIRER (toy-sport equip.)
Fits and attaches bindings to skis, according to customer needs and ski and boot specifications, and repairs ski bindings and skis, using power tools and handtools: Records customer statistics, such as height, weight, skiing experience, and skiing habits to maintain reference file. Reviews customer data and ski manufacturer specifications to determine method of locating and attaching binding to skis. Measures length of ski-running surface with ruler to locate center of skis. Places skis in clamps, positions drilling-jig on skis, and drills holes, using electric hand drill and utilizing knowledge of composition of skis. Screws bindings to skis, using screwdriver, and secures boots in bindings to ensure required flexibility. Replaces defective bindings, cements separated layers of laminated skis, using epoxy resin and clamps, and sharpens ski edges, using file, to repair skis. Occasionally sells skis when sales staff are busy.
GOE: 06.02.24 STRENGTH: L GED: R4 M3 L3 SVP: 5 DLU: 86

732.381-010 BOW MAKER, CUSTOM (toy-sport equip.)
Selects, laminates, shapes, and finishes woods, plastics, and metals to make archery bows: Selects materials from stock according to customer's specifications, and preshapes parts, using handtools and power tools. Applies specified adhesives between parts. Assembles parts and places assembled bows in glue press to cure. Heats bows in steam box until pliable and clamps bows on form to shape curves and recurves. Trims and smooths bows, using handtools and sandpaper. Stains, paints, and varnishes bows according to specifications. May apply decals to bows. May rework or repair damaged bow and be designated Bow Repairer, Custom (toy-sport equip.). May make arrows, using die cutter to cut feathers used on arrows.

GOE: 01.06.02 STRENGTH: L GED: R4 M2 L2 SVP: 7 DLU: 77

732.381-014 BOWLING-BALL GRADER AND MARKER (toy-sport equip.) alternate titles: grade and center marker
Lays out axis through light and heavy centers of bowling balls and gauges and grades balls according to size, color, and quality: Floats bowling ball in mercury pool and locates and marks center of light side, using plumb bob and grease pencil. Places ball in jig and locates center of heavy side, using center gauge. Examines ball for defects and color quality, measures size with ring gauge, and marks data to be engraved under trademark, using grease pencil. Places rejected balls aside for reworking.
GOE: 06.01.05 STRENGTH: L GED: R3 M2 L2 SVP: 6 DLU: 77

732.381-018 GOLF-CLUB HEAD FORMER (toy-sport equip.) alternate titles: club former
Adjusts loft and lie (angle made by club face to neck) on golf club irons to specified angle, using hammer. Reads work order to determine number and model of club being formed. Reads chart specifying angle of loft and lie for club and measures angles, using bench-size protractor or gauges. Places forging on lead block and hammers neck or head to open or close angles to achieve specified angle dimensions. Inserts shaft and verifies conformance of angles with standards, using gauge.
GOE: 06.02.24 STRENGTH: L GED: R3 M2 L2 SVP: 6 DLU: 77

732.381-022 GOLF-CLUB REPAIRER (toy-sport equip.)
Repairs worn or damaged golf clubs or customized golf clubs according to customer specifications, using handtools: Dismantles golf clubs and replaces worn or damaged parts or parts specified by customer, such as head, shaft, sole plates, and composition inlays in faces of woods, using screws, rivets, epoxies, files, sandpaper, drills, hammers, heating torch, and vise. Wraps shanks of clubs with cord or cements on plastic sleeves to prevent shanks from splitting. Removes old grips. Attaches new grips by applying listing materials to build up handle area and by wrapping leather strip over listing materials, or brushes on adhesive and slips molded rubber grips onto shaft. Reweights clubs by adding or subtracting lead or brass weights to achieve *swing weight* specified. Sands and files faces of woods or hammers heads of irons to change loft or lie of clubs or to open or close faces of clubs. Stains, shellacs, or oils wooden heads and shafts and polishes steel heads on buffing wheel to finish clubs. Cleans and polishes chrome-plated metal golf club heads, using buffing machine and sand-blasting equipment. May make clubs to customer specifications, using ready-made shafts and club heads and be designated Golf-Club Maker (toy-sport equip.); or according to operation performed as Assembler, Golf-Wood Head (toy-sport equip.); or Golf-Club Finisher (toy-sport equip.).
GOE: 05.10.01 STRENGTH: M GED: R3 M2 L2 SVP: 6 DLU: 77

732.384-010 ASSEMBLER, BILLIARD-TABLE (toy-sport equip.)
Assembles new billiard or pool tables, performing any combination of following tasks: Cuts, trims, and installs pool table parts, such as cushions, cloth covering, pockets, and tabletops, using cement, tacks, scissors, hammer, and portable bandsaw. Assembles and installs rails and legs, using handtools. Installs specified pool table accessories, such as coin meter assembly and ball return gullies, using handtools and power tools. May assemble billiard sticks and glue tips on ends, using brush and glue. May repair billiard tables, using handtools and power tools and be designated Billiard-Table Repairer (retail trade; toy-sport equip.); or may be designated according to component assembled as Cushion Former (toy-sport equip.); Cushion Installer (toy-sport equip.); Frame Assembler (toy-sport equip.); Leg Assembler (toy-sport equip.); Pocket Assembler (toy-sport equip.); Rail Assembler (toy-sport equip.); Trim Mounter (toy-sport equip.).
GOE: 05.10.01 STRENGTH: L GED: R3 M2 L2 SVP: 3 DLU: 77

732.384-014 INSPECTOR AND ADJUSTER, GOLF CLUB HEAD (toy-sport equip.) alternate titles: loft and lie inspector and adjuster
Inspects golf club irons to verify conformance with specifications and adjusts angles, using rubber mallet: Measures angle of loft and lie, using gauges. Adjusts neck or head to achieve specified angle dimensions.
GOE: 06.03.02 STRENGTH: L GED: R3 M3 L3 SVP: 4 DLU: 77

732.487-010 BOWLING-BALL WEIGHER AND PACKER (toy-sport equip.)
Weighs bowling balls, computes weight differential between light and heavy sides, records data on box, and packs balls for sales, storage, or shipment: Places ball (heavy side out) on pan of straight-beam-balance scale and reads and records weight. Reverses position of ball on scale pan, reads and records weight, and computes differential between light and heavy sides. Reweighs with heavy side down to ascertain true weight. Records data on packing box, using pen or grease pencil. Packs ball in box and seals box with glue or gummed tape.
GOE: 06.04.38 STRENGTH: L GED: R2 M2 L1 SVP: 4 DLU: 77

732.567-010 INSPECTOR, GOLF BALL (toy-sport equip.)
Inspects and tests golf ball centers and wound cores for conformance to standards and records results: Squeezes liquid centers through wringer to observe cover leaks. Examines wound cores to see that ball is round and that thread condition meets specifications. Passes ball through go-not-go gauges to verify size. Places wound cores on fixture of compression tester, presses pedal to drop ram, and observes gauges to obtain compression reading. Sorts balls

according to compression registered on gauge. Reports compression test results and other quality factors.
GOE: 06.03.02 STRENGTH: L GED: R3 M2 L2 SVP: 3 DLU: 77

732.584-010 BOWLING-BALL ENGRAVER (toy-sport equip.)
Engraves brand name, serial number, and other identification data on plastic bowling balls, using pantograph-routing machine: Inserts cutting bit in router head and secures bit with wrench. Selects and clamps specified pattern (letters or design) under tracing stylus of pantograph-routing machine. Centers bowling ball in jig and clamps ball into position under router head. Starts machine and lowers tracing stylus to beginning point on pattern. Pulls lever, lowering cutting bit onto surface of bowling ball, and guides tracing stylus over pattern, causing router to cut identification data on ball. Examines ball to detect irregular or incomplete engraving and places defective balls aside for rework.
GOE: 06.04.24 STRENGTH: L GED: R2 M1 L2 SVP: 3 DLU: 77

732.584-014 FINISHER (toy-sport equip.)
Shapes and smooths archery bows and tennis racket frames to final contours of prototype designs prior to application of finish coating, using scrapers, files, and emery paper: Clamps bow or frame in padded vise and files off excess wood or fiberglass to give finish shape to item. Scrapes flat surfaces to remove file marks. Shapes tip nocks of bows with circular file. Smooths surfaces to final finish, using vibratory sander and emery paper. Marks item with identification for inspector's reference and records number and type of item finished.
GOE: 06.04.25 STRENGTH: L GED: R2 M1 L2 SVP: 4 DLU: 77

732.587-010 GOLF-BALL TRIMMER (toy-sport equip.)
Shaves *flash* from molded golf balls, using trimming machine: Positions golf ball in locating cup. Depresses pedal to move golf ball against driver cup. Presses degrooving knife against rotating golf ball to shave flash. Releases pedal to drop golf ball in chute. May remove flash from golf balls, using machine that sands flash from surface of ball. Keeps production records.
GOE: 06.04.34 STRENGTH: S GED: R2 M1 L1 SVP: 2 DLU: 77

732.587-014 GOLF-CLUB WEIGHER (toy-sport equip.) alternate titles: golf-club matcher
Weighs golf clubs on scale to obtain *swing weight* for matching irons and sorts clubs according to swing weight: Positions club in holding fixture of scale with grip in holder and head extending over and beyond fulcrum point. Reads pointer on scale indicating swing weight. Wraps heads of weighed clubs in cellophane bag and tapes bag to shaft with colored tape designating swing weight of club. Places weighed and wrapped clubs in tote box with work order.
GOE: 06.03.02 STRENGTH: L GED: R2 M1 L2 SVP: 2 DLU: 77

732.684-010 ARROWSMITH (toy-sport equip.)
Paints decorations and glues nock, head, and feathers on shaft of archery arrows: Applies glue to ends of arrow and places nock on one end and hunting or target head on other end. Positions arrow in rotating cresting (decorating) machine and paints bands of specified color on rotating arrow shaft, using brush. Clamps arrow into fletching (feathering) jig of rotating fletching table leaving edge of quill exposed. Applies glue to exposed edge and positions edge on arrow shaft. Repeats gluing operation until specified number of feathers are glued to arrow. May mix paints according to color chart. May be designated according to duties performed as Crester (toy-sport equip.); Fletcher (toy-sport equip.).
GOE: 06.04.34 STRENGTH: L GED: R2 M2 L2 SVP: 2 DLU: 77

732.684-014 ASSEMBLER (toy-sport equip.)
Assembles water sports equipment, such as diving boards, under-water equipment, and water skis, using handtools and power tools: Positions parts in sequence of assembly following work orders, guides, holes, or edges. Screws precut parts together, using handtools, or glues parts together, using glue and clamps. Reams threads on tanks, using die cutting tool. May bore holes for attachment of accessories, using portable drill. May examine completed items for functioning and conformance to specifications. May be designated according to article assembled as Air-Tank Assembler (toy-sport equip.); Diving-Board Assembler (toy-sport equip.); Water-Ski Assembler (toy-sport equip.).
GOE: 06.04.23 STRENGTH: L GED: R2 M2 L2 SVP: 3 DLU: 77

732.684-018 ASSEMBLER, LIQUID CENTER (toy-sport equip.)
Molds golf ball center covers and encases liquid centers in molded covers: Fills pans with specified amounts of water and chemicals and packs dry ice around pans. Places liquid centers for golf balls in series of pans of chemical solutions to freeze liquid, remove gelatin cover, and clean surface. Centers rubber disks on mold, closes cover, and inserts mold in press. Pulls lever to close press and mold disks into semispheres. Removes mold, places semispheres in upper and lower cavities of molding press, places frozen centers on semispheres, and pulls lever to close mold. Opens mold after prescribed time and removes centers encased in rubber. Pulls *flash* from around centers and places them in dry ice preparatory to vulcanizing.
GOE: 06.04.32 STRENGTH: M GED: R2 M1 L1 SVP: 2 DLU: 77

732.684-022 ASSEMBLER, PING-PONG TABLE (toy-sport equip.)
Assembles parts, such as table-top sections, trim, hinges, and legs, to produce ping-pong tables: Positions table-top sections in jig and applies glue along table edge, using glue and brush. Places wooden trim strips over glue and attaches strips to table edge, using staple gun or power screwdriver. Fastens parts, such as hinges, legs, leg braces, and locks, using power screwdriver.
GOE: 06.04.22 STRENGTH: L GED: R2 M1 L1 SVP: 2 DLU: 77

732.684-026 BALL ASSEMBLER (toy-sport equip.)
Assembles balls from rubber, rubber impregnated fabrics, and leather, on wax-ball lasts (forms), using handtools: Places wax-ball last in holding fixture and brushes on cement. Presses and smooths rubber impregnated fabric panels on last in specified pattern to cover ball last, leaving space for door opening flap for wax removal. Repeats operation, cementing on specified number of plies to form basketball carcass. Inserts bladder into carcass through door opening and inflates to specified pressure. Aligns flaps of door to matching edges of carcass, brushes on cement, and presses flaps down to close door. Brushes cement on molded carcass or receives cemented carcass. Inspects wet adhesive for dried lumps and missed spaces. Aligns precut leather or rubber panels between raised ribs of molded carcass. Presses and smooths panels onto carcass to complete assembly of basketball. Cuts off air valve nipple flush with ball, using scissors or knife. Paints stripes along false seams, using brush and ink. Waxes balls, using paste wax and damp cloth. Buffs ball surface, using power buffer. Affixes decals to balls and labels balls, using stencil and spray gun. May fabricate and repair rubber or plastic ball bladders. May repair returned, worn, or damaged basketballs by putting in new carcasses or repanelling old carcasses. May specialize in one phase of assembly and be designated Carcass Assembler (toy-sport equip.); Door Closer (toy-sport equip.); Leather Coverer (toy-sport equip.); or according to type of ball as Basketball Assembler (toy-sport equip.); Soccer Ball Assembler (toy-sport equip.); Volleyball Assembler (toy-sport equip.).
GOE: 06.04.23 STRENGTH: L GED: R2 M2 L2 SVP: 3 DLU: 77

732.684-030 BASEBALL INSPECTOR AND REPAIRER (toy-sport equip.)
Inspects and grades baseballs or softballs and repairs defects, using handtools: Examines ball for defects, such as crooked, uneven or raised stitches, lumps, and irregular shapes. Straightens crooked stitches by pulling or prying them into place with awl. Places balls with raised stitches into bench press and clamps top of press to flatten stitches. Pushes curved awl through seams to press and smooth lumps under cover of ball. Weighs softballs on scale. Grades baseballs according to model and quality, and grades softballs according to model, quality, and weight. Rejects nonrepairable and misshapened balls.
GOE: 06.03.02 STRENGTH: L GED: R3 M2 L2 SVP: 3 DLU: 77

732.684-034 BASEBALL SEWER, HAND (toy-sport equip.) alternate titles: hand stitcher
Sews leather covers on baseballs and softballs: Places glue-dipped ball in buck frame and stretches both leather covers over ball. Pulls perforated edges of covers together with pliers and tacks covers into place with brads or staples. Sews covers onto ball with harness needle, using waxed linen thread.
GOE: 06.04.27 STRENGTH: L GED: R2 M1 L1 SVP: 3 DLU: 77

732.684-038 BOW MAKER, PRODUCTION (toy-sport equip.)
Fabricates and shapes laminated archery bows: Selects dies according to type bow to be produced and bolts dies to bow press. Applies epoxy resin to precut wood and fiberglass parts for laminating. Aligns parts, following reference marks, and clamps parts to press. Cures bows for specified time to form contour of bow, using bow press. Cuts string nocks in bow tips and bevels bow edge, using abrasive wheels and sanders. Shapes and finishes contour of bow, using belt sanders. Examines bow for twist and adjusts string position to compensate for deficiencies noted. Buffs bow to smooth finish, using power buffer. Measures force required to pull bow string to full draw, using scale and pulley device, to determine if bow meets specifications. May apply decorative or identifying decal to bow. May varnish and stain bow to protect surface. May assemble crossbows and be designated Crossbow Maker (toy-sport equip.). May repair defects in bows damaged in production or returned to factory for repair.
GOE: 06.02.32 STRENGTH: L GED: R3 M3 L2 SVP: 5 DLU: 78

732.684-042 BOW-STRING MAKER (toy-sport equip.)
Makes strings for archery bows: Loops string around posts of jig and ties ends together, waxing ends by hand. Holds end of string and spins hand-winding jig to form loops on both ends. Attaches string to post and winds strands to complete bow string. Winds extra wrapping around string to give protection at point where notch of arrow fits onto string. May wind string, using automatic bow-string making device.
GOE: 06.04.34 STRENGTH: L GED: R2 M1 L1 SVP: 3 DLU: 77

732.684-046 CELLULOID TRIMMER (toy-sport equip.)
Attaches celluloid band to golf club shaft to anchor ends of leather grip: Bevels grip with knife to taper it to shaft. Slides celluloid band onto tapered part of grip and shrinks celluloid to size, using electric heating jig. Applies cement to tapered grip and cements band in place over end of grip. Sands celluloid band, trims it to length with knife, and cleans grip with cleaning fluid.
GOE: 06.04.34 STRENGTH: L GED: R2 M1 L1 SVP: 2 DLU: 77

732.684-050 FEATHER STITCHER (toy-sport equip.) alternate titles: stitcher, hand
Sews feathers of shuttlecocks together by hand: Places shuttlecock in holding device and sews several rows of stitching in feathers above base of shuttlecock, using curved needle. May be designated according to row of stitching worked on as Bottom Stitcher (toy-sport equip.); Middle Stitcher (toy-sport equip.); Top Stitcher (toy-sport equip.).
GOE: 06.04.34 STRENGTH: L GED: R2 M1 L1 SVP: 3 DLU: 77

732.684-054 FISH-STRINGER ASSEMBLER (toy-sport equip.)
Joins parts, such as chain, catches, and swivel, to assemble fish stringer: Positions and holds stringer chain against premeasured marks on worktable to

measure chain. Opens link and separates measured length of chain from stock length, using prying device. Positions swivel over end of link, and presses ends of link together to close link and secure swivel to chain, using bending device. Attaches stringer catches to chain, using clip snaps or pliers. Places completed stringer in box, and seals box, using gummed tape.
GOE: 06.04.23 STRENGTH: L GED: R2 M2 L1 SVP: 2 DLU: 77

732.684-058   FISHING-LURE ASSEMBLER (toy-sport equip.)
Cuts out fishing lure parts from metal strips, and assembles lures, using machines and handtools: Secures specified dies in machine, using wrench. Threads roll of blank metal through machine. Depresses pedal to start machine and cut out parts, such as bodies, spinners, or spoons, from metal strip. Coats surface of lures, such as plugs or popping bugs with paint, using spray gun. Bores holes in cutout parts, using drill press or hand drill. Joins lures and attachments, such as hooks, skirts, or swivel according to model or work ticket specifications, using cement, pliers, or screwdriver.
GOE: 06.02.24 STRENGTH: L GED: R3 M2 L2 SVP: 3 DLU: 77

732.684-062   FISHING-REEL ASSEMBLER (toy-sport equip.) alternate titles: reel assembler
Assembles fishing reels, performing any combination of following tasks: Positions parts, such as washers, levers, springs, line spool, and retaining rings, in slots, holes, or over pins provided on frame of fishing reel. Inserts drive shaft through line spool and frame bearing. Positions side plate assembly containing gears and crankshaft on frame, aligns screw holes, and screws assembly to frame, using powered screwdriver. Places crank on crankshaft and tightens nut with wrench to fasten crank to shaft. Screws parts, such as control knobs and case covers, to frame. Tests and adjusts reel for unrestricted, positive movement of parts by performing such tasks as rotating level crank, pulling fishline off spool, and turning adjustment screws or knobs located on reel. May disassemble reel, realign parts, and remove burrs to rework defective reels, using handtools. May operate arbor and kick presses to perform such tasks as forcing bushings into reel frames, riveting parts to subassemblies, and pressing or staking gears on shafts.
GOE: 06.04.23 STRENGTH: S GED: R2 M1 L1 SVP: 2 DLU: 77

732.684-066   FISHING-ROD ASSEMBLER (toy-sport equip.) alternate titles: fishing-rod trimmer
Assembles fishing rods from rod blanks, line guides, ferrules, handles, and reel seats: Heats rod cement over alcohol lamp and drip-melts it into ferrules, rod tip, and reel seat and handle socket. Presses ferrules, rod tip, and other parts onto rod blank while cement is hot and fluid. Aligns and spaces line guides on rod, and secures, using rod-winding-thread. Winds additional bands of rod-winding-thread at ends of rod tip and ferrules to strengthen and decorate rod. May apply varnish, lacquer, or shellac to rod and windings. May repair rods and replace tips, line guides, ferrules, and windings. May assemble kits of fishing rod parts.
GOE: 06.04.23 STRENGTH: L GED: R2 M1 L2 SVP: 2 DLU: 77

732.684-070   FISHING-ROD MARKER (toy-sport equip.)
Marks layout on fishing rods, according to specified marking pattern, to indicate where guides are to be attached or decorative striping or winding applied: Reads work order to ascertain specified pattern board and fastens pattern board to workbench. Lays rod against pattern and marks layout on rod corresponding to markings on pattern. May suspend rods on two parallel bars, allowing rods to roll to their natural center of gravity, and mark this position to indicate area for attachment of side guides.
GOE: 06.02.31 STRENGTH: L GED: R2 M1 L2 SVP: 3 DLU: 77

732.684-074   FLY TIER (toy-sport equip.) alternate titles: artificial-fly tier; bait tier; fly winder
Makes artificial fish flies and lures, using feathers, fur, thread, and fishhooks, according to prototype design: Clamps fishhook in vise and wraps thread around shank or hook. Pulls feathers or fur of specified color or type from quill or pelt, positions on hook, and wraps in place with thread. Repeats operation to simulate wings, legs, and tail of insect. Wraps thread or colored wire around shank of hook in continuous spirals to form body of insect. Ties and cuts off thread. May brush dope on windings to waterproof and hold them in place.
GOE: 06.04.23 STRENGTH: S GED: R2 M1 L2 SVP: 4 DLU: 77

732.684-078   GOLF-CLUB ASSEMBLER (toy-sport equip.)
Assembles golf clubs, using one of following methods: (1) Verifies wood golf club parts against job order specifications. Cuts shaft of club to specified length, using bench mounted circular abrasive saw. Slides trim ring over tip of shaft to embellish shaft-head joint. Squeezes glue into hole of golf club head neck and inserts club shaft into hole. Positions club assembly in holding fixture of drill press and drills hole through neck of wood head and shaft with drill. Inserts steel pin into hole to strengthen connection of head to shaft. Removes club from holding fixture and stacks aside for further processing. (2) Reads job order to determine specifications, such as shaft-head alignment and swingweight of iron golf clubs. Slides ferrule (plastic collar) over tip of club shaft to embellish shaft-head joint. Inserts club shaft into socket in head of club. Positions club assembly on swingweight scale and reads scale to determine swingweight of club. Removes club head from shaft and pours lead powder into socket of club head to adjust swingweight to specification. Squeezes glue onto tip of club shaft, inserts shaft into iron club head, and aligns shaft with head in specified manner. Stacks club aside for further processing.
GOE: 06.04.23 STRENGTH: L GED: R2 M1 L1 SVP: 3 DLU: 77

732.684-082   GRIP WRAPPER (toy-sport equip.) alternate titles: gripper
Wraps leather strips around or slips rubber tubes on articles, such as golf clubs, tennis rackets, and archery bows to form grips or handles, using one of following methods: (1) Positions workpiece in machine that rotates article. Brushes or smears adhesive on area to be wrapped. Staples, tacks, or otherwise fastens end of leather strip to starting position of grip. Starts machine and feeds leather strip onto rotating workpiece to wrap handle area, taking care to align edges of strip against one another without overlap or open spaces. Trims excess leather at end of grip with knife and fastens with tape or sleeve. (2) Places workpiece in vise. Wraps two-way tape around area to be gripped. Aligns and slides rubber tube onto workpiece to fully cover grip area. May wind nylon cord around neck of wood golf club head, using turning machine, and be designated Wood-Club-Neck Whipper (toy-sport equip.).
GOE: 06.04.27 STRENGTH: L GED: R2 M1 L1 SVP: 3 DLU: 77

732.684-086   GUIDE WINDER (toy-sport equip.)
Attaches line guides or applies decorative trim to fishing rods according to oral or written specifications: Obtains specified thread and guides and feeds thread through dispenser or places spool on thread holder. Clamps rod in holding fixture or rotating device. Depresses pedal to rotate rod or to rotate thread dispenser around rod, or turns rod manually. Winds thread around rod in continuous wraps for specified distance, controlling wrap spacing by moving rod or thread as each wrap is completed. Positions guide on rod, holds or tapes leg to secure guide, and continues wrapping until guide leg is wound to rod as specified. Trims loose ends with razor or knife. May apply cement to hold loose ends.
GOE: 06.04.34 STRENGTH: S GED: R2 M2 L2 SVP: 3 DLU: 77

732.684-090   PELOTA MAKER (toy-sport equip.)
Sews together layers of cotton, rubber, and goat skin to make pelotas (ball used in jai alai) of specified size and weight. Removes scratched or damaged layers and sews on new ones.
GOE: 06.04.34 STRENGTH: L GED: R2 M1 L1 SVP: 4 DLU: 77

732.684-094   RACKET STRINGER (toy-sport equip.)
Strings tennis and badminton rackets with synthetic fiber or animal gut strings: Clamps racket in stand and threads warp (main strings) through holes in bow. Clamps ends of strings in jaws of tensioner arms, depresses pedal to tighten strings to prescribed tension, and locks strings in place by wedging awl in hole with string until next set of holes are strung, or string is tied. Threads weave (cross strings) through holes in bow, weaves them through main strings, applies tension, and secures them similarly to main strings. May wrap bow at intervals with bands of colored thread to strengthen and decorate it. May varnish wooden parts of racket. May replace leather or plastic grips on racket handle.
GOE: 06.02.32 STRENGTH: L GED: R3 M2 L2 SVP: 5 DLU: 77

732.684-098   ROLLER-SKATE ASSEMBLER (toy-sport equip.)
Assembles parts of roller skates: Fits rubber cushions into brackets, and rivets brackets to frame, using air rivet gun. Inserts axle through hole in frame, and mounts wheels on axle. Places nut and washer on threaded end of axle, and tightens nut, with wrench. Rivets leather strap to frame, using air rivet gun. May insert ball bearings into retaining cups of wheels.
GOE: 06.04.23 STRENGTH: L GED: R2 M1 L1 SVP: 2 DLU: 77

732.684-102   ROLLER-SKATE REPAIRER (any industry)·
Repairs roller skates by disassembling skates, and cleaning and replacing bearings, wheels, and other worn parts, using handtools and power tools. May repair attached shoes and leather straps.
GOE: 05.12.15 STRENGTH: L GED: R2 M2 L1 SVP: 4 DLU: 77

732.684-106   SHAPER, BASEBALL GLOVE (toy-sport equip.) alternate titles: steamer and shaper
Forms pocket, opens fingers, and smooths seams to shape baseball gloves, using heated forms, mallets, and hammers: Pulls glove over heated hand-shaped form to open and stretch finger linings. Pounds fingers and palm of glove with rubber mallet and ball-shaped hammer to smooth seams and bulges, and form glove pocket. Removes glove from form, inserts hand into glove, and strikes glove pocket with fist while examining glove visually and tactually to ensure comfortable fit.
GOE: 06.04.27 STRENGTH: M GED: R2 M1 L1 SVP: 2 DLU: 77

732.684-110   SKI BASE TRIMMER (toy-sport equip.)
Joins polyethylene-plastic base-strips and steel edges to fabricate ski base-layer, using handtools and work aids: Selects specified base-strips and steel edges for joining. Tapes logo (manufacturer's symbol) in position on toe area of base-strip and inserts strip into roller that presses logo into position on base-strip. Applies adhesive onto steel edge and base-strip, using glue bottle and adhesive dispenser. Positions steel edge in jig and inserts base strip into steel edge. Trims base-strip to conform to bend of steel edge and cuts strip to conform to heel-plate of steel edge, using hand plane, knife, and template. Inserts heel-patch between base-strip and heel-plate, and presses assembly into specified position to fabricate base-layer, using special handtool designed to apply rubbing pressure on plastic strip. Examines assembly to determine if assembly falls within specified fabrication tolerances and discards base-layers failing to meet tolerances. Carries accepted base-layers to designated press molds for further processing.
GOE: 06.04.34 STRENGTH: M GED: R2 M1 L1 SVP: 2 DLU: 77

732.684-114 SKI MOLDER (toy-sport equip.)
Fabricates sock (inner-construction, ski-component) and aligns sock with other ski parts in die press that molds components into partially fabricated ski: Places fiberglass lay-up (mat of specified size) on worktable, pours epoxy resin over lay-up, and spreads resin with paddle to facilitate saturation. Positions ski core on lay-up, places foot-pad on top of core, and pours resin over core and foot-pad. Folds lay-up around core and foot-pad to form sock, cuts sock to contour of ski toe (front) with scissors and template, and aligns sock assembly in specified manner within mold press. Places ski base layer in press with sock assembly in specified alignment and activates press to shape and mold layers.
GOE: 06.04.32 STRENGTH: L GED: R3 M1 L2 SVP: 3 DLU: 77

732.684-118 SKI REPAIRER, PRODUCTION (toy-sport equip.)
Repairs defects in skis damaged in production or defective in material, using handtools and power tools: Examines designated defects and markings on ski to determine type repair required. Selects specified fiberglass mat patch and positions patch over defect. Pours epoxy resin on patch to cause patch to adhere to ski. Places patched area into heated mold press to shape and dry patch. Removes ski from mold press and trims patched area with knife. Drills holes and trims damaged area to provide access to defect for skis having defects in plastic base layer, using portable drill and knife. Aligns polyethylene-plastic sliver with defect in base layer and rubs soldering iron over sliver to melt plastic into defect. Smooths repaired ski to remove excess patching, using belt sander. May repair and refinish user-damaged skis in ski manufacturer's service shop.
GOE: 06.02.24 STRENGTH: L GED: R2 M1 L1 SVP: 5 DLU: 77

732.684-122 SPORTS-EQUIPMENT REPAIRER (any industry)
Repairs and replaces sporting and athletic equipment, such as fishing tackle, tennis rackets, or archery equipment: Restrings tennis rackets with animal gut or synthetic string. Replaces defective parts of fishing tackle, such as reels and rods. Replaces metal points on arrow shafts. Refinishes surfaces of sporting and athletic equipment with lacquer or paint. May carve wooden parts for sporting and athletic equipment, using handtools and powered woodworking tools. May make new gun stocks and pistol grips. May reglue and rewind bamboo sections of fly rods. May rewind shafts of bows and arrows. May be designated according to type of sporting or athletic equipment repaired as Archery-Equipment Repairer (any industry); Fishing-Tackle Repairer (any industry); Football-Pad Repairer (any industry); Tennis-Racket Repairer (any industry).
GOE: 05.10.04 STRENGTH: L GED: R3 M2 L2 SVP: 4 DLU: 77

732.684-126 SURFBOARD MAKER (toy-sport equip.)
Shapes and finishes planks of plastic foam, reinforced with wood, to form surfboards, using hand plane, electric hand plane, and electric sander: Verifies shape and dimensions with fiberboard template. Coats with resin and covers with fiberglass. Applies coat of resin and finishes with sandpaper and polishing compounds to achieve desired luster. May attach skeg to rear of board, using fiberglass to obtain required conformity. May repair damaged surfboards by inserting polyurethane foam in damaged area and laminating over the repaired area with fiberglass.
GOE: 06.04.24 STRENGTH: M GED: R2 M2 L2 SVP: 3 DLU: 77

732.684-130 INSPECTOR (toy-sport equip.) alternate titles: process inspector
Examines finished items, such as golf clubs, golf balls, bowling balls, baseball gloves, baseballs, skis, bows, fishing rods, or lures, for conformance to specified standards: Visually and tactually examines workpiece for plating or coating defects or mars, scratches, pits, or tears in surface. Inspects markings for location, readability, and form. Inspects product for completeness and accuracy of assembly, warp, and holes, and makes repairs, using handtools, filler, and wax. Inspects overall product to determine if structural formation meets specifications. Marks defects and routes workpiece to station for repair, salvage, or scrap. Prepares report or otherwise keeps record of defects. May confer with workers regarding quality of work. May weigh product, such as bowling balls, to determine conformity to weight specifications. May package product.
GOE: 06.03.01 STRENGTH: L GED: R3 M2 L3 SVP: 3 DLU: 78

732.685-010 BASE-FILLER OPERATOR (toy-sport equip.)
Tends machine that stuffs baseball base covers with materials to form baseball bases: Dumps filler material in machine hopper or positions material between jaws of machine. Positions cover to receive filler and activates machine to force material into cover. Removes stuffed base from machine and examines base to ensure base meets company specifications. May operate sewing machine to close open end of base.
GOE: 06.04.36 STRENGTH: L GED: R2 M1 L1 SVP: 2 DLU: 77

732.685-014 FEATHER SAWYER (toy-sport equip.) alternate titles: cutter
Tends machine that cuts and trims feathers for archery arrows: Starts cutting machine. Positions feathers on wheel of machine so that cutting blade cuts through center of quill and trims edges. Sorts and grades feathers. Dumps residue in discard box.
GOE: 06.04.09 STRENGTH: L GED: R2 M1 L1 SVP: 2 DLU: 77

732.685-018 FIXING-MACHINE OPERATOR (toy-sport equip.) alternate titles: shuttlecock assembler
Tends machine that inserts (presses) feathers in cork bases of badminton shuttlecocks: Positions cork base of shuttlecock in chuck of machine. Places feathers in punching tool of machine. Depresses pedal to press feathers into predrilled holes of cork base. Repeats operation until all holes in cork are filled with feathers. Packs assembled shuttlecocks in cardboard tubes.
GOE: 06.04.20 STRENGTH: M GED: R2 M1 L1 SVP: 3 DLU: 77

732.685-022 GUIDE-BASE WINDER, MACHINE (toy-sport equip.) alternate titles: guide winder
Tends bench machine that winds thread around specified areas of fishing rod blanks to form base for line guides: Clamps rod end in chuck and adjusts rod supporting fixtures by loosening setscrews and moving fixtures until rod is level. Feeds thread through playout device and needle eye. Turns setscrew to adjust tension on playout device to specified pressure. Slides playout devices along track until needles are adjacent to markings on rod, indicating where base winds start, and tightens setscrew. Pulls length of thread through needle and clamps or tapes end to rod. Depresses lever causing rod to rotate and playout devices to traverse along track as thread is wound around rod. Stops machine and cuts thread as each area is wound to specified length. Cements thread end to rod. Inspects rods to verify that they are wound to specification. Adjusts setup of machine to correct faulty winding.
GOE: 06.04.09 STRENGTH: L GED: R2 M1 L1 SVP: 2 DLU: 77

732.685-026 MACHINE SNELLER (toy-sport equip.)
Tends machine that attaches snells (leaders) to fishhooks: Threads snell from spool through guides to machine chuck. Starts machine and inserts hook between chuck jaws. Depresses pedal to actuate chuck that spins and wraps snell around hook shank, and cuts snell to predetermined length. Removes snelled hook from machine, threads snell through eye of hook, and ties overhand loop knot in end to facilitate attaching to fishing line. May attach snelled hooks to display cards. May tie second hook above first to make special baiting hookup.
GOE: 06.04.34 STRENGTH: L GED: R2 M1 L1 SVP: 2 DLU: 77

732.685-030 SINKER WINDER (toy-sport equip.)
Tends machine that automatically twists sinker pin and clinches pin to lead slug to fabricate sinkers for fish lines: Places lead slug and sinker pin in position on machine and inserts sinker pin into predrilled hole in lead slug to form assembly unit. Presses switch to engage winding element of machine and start die rotating. Places assembly unit with pin shank down into machine die that automatically twists and clinches assembly to produce sinkers for fish lines.
GOE: 06.04.20 STRENGTH: L GED: R2 M1 L1 SVP: 2 DLU: 77

732.685-034 STUFFING-MACHINE OPERATOR (toy-sport equip.)
Tends machine that injects stuffing into protective athletic equipment, such as baseball chest protectors, catcher's mask linings, and boxing gloves: Pushes length of workpiece over pipe of stuffing machine. Depresses pedal to start machine that forces stuffing material into workpiece. Pulls workpiece off pipe as article is stuffed. Fills hopper of stuffing machine when empty.
GOE: 06.04.05 STRENGTH: L GED: R2 M1 L1 SVP: 2 DLU: 77

732.685-038 TRIMMING-MACHINE OPERATOR (toy-sport equip.) alternate titles: trimmer, machine
Tends machine that trims ragged leather edges from shuttlecock bases: Positions base in trimming machine. Depresses pedal to actuate cutting tool that trims and smooths edge of leather-covered cork base.
GOE: 06.04.05 STRENGTH: L GED: R1 M1 L1 SVP: 2 DLU: 77

732.686-010 HAY SORTER (toy-sport equip.)
Removes foreign matter from hay, packs it in trough, and pushes it toward machine that bundles and ties it into disk form for use as archery target. Removes target from machine.
GOE: 06.04.34 STRENGTH: M GED: R1 M1 L1 SVP: 1 DLU: 77

732.687-010 ADHESIVE PRIMER (toy-sport equip.)
Applies adhesive to edge strips of partially fabricated ski to prepare ski for attachment of top layer, using roller and adhesive: Examines ski for defects, such as holes and bumps. Rubs bumps with abrasive cloth to smooth surface. Marks holes on skis with chalk and stacks marked skis aside for rework. Applies adhesive to edge strips, using roller and places skis in wheeled rack for movement to next processing station.
GOE: 06.04.33 STRENGTH: M GED: R1 M1 L1 SVP: 2 DLU: 77

732.687-014 ASSEMBLER, FISHING FLOATS (toy-sport equip.)
Assembles and packs transparent plastic-bubble fishing floats by inserting filling tube through end holes of molded float halves and snapping halves together. Places assembled units into plastic bags and closes bags, using stapler.
GOE: 06.04.23 STRENGTH: L GED: R1 M1 L1 SVP: 2 DLU: 77

732.687-018 BASE FILLER (toy-sport equip.)
Stuffs canvas bags with excelsior or felt pads to form baseball base: Turns bag to place sewn edges inside and smooth seams outside. Stuffs bags with excelsior or felt pads by hand. Places bag on pressing machine and pulls lever to lower head that compresses stuffing to prescribed thickness. Inserts anchor straps through loops sewn on bag. May fill football dummies, medicine balls, and punching bags with materials, such as cotton, felt, cattle hair, and rubberized hair. May mold and assemble plastic base covers, using plastic, mold, and curing oven. May assemble and seal vinyl covered bases, using electric sealing iron.
GOE: 06.04.23 STRENGTH: L GED: R1 M1 L1 SVP: 1 DLU: 77

732.687-022 CASTING-PLUG ASSEMBLER (toy-sport equip.)
Attaches gang hooks to wooden casting plugs used for fishing, using screwdriver: Inserts screw through eye of gang hook and into previously drilled hole in body of plug. Tightens screw with screwdriver.

GOE: 06.04.23 STRENGTH: L GED: R1 M1 L1 SVP: 2 DLU: 77

732.687-026   GOLF-CLUB WEIGHTER (toy-sport equip.) alternate titles: weighter

Weights wooden golf club heads to achieve specified *swing weight:* Screws stop on portable drill or inserts drill bit of specified length and width. Clamps club head into vise and drills hole in head. Pours molten lead from ladle into hole or places threaded cylindrical metal weights in drilled hole, and inserts wood screw to hold metal weights. May reweight finished clubs, by adding or subtracting weight as specified.
GOE: 06.04.34 STRENGTH: L GED: R2 M1 L1 SVP: 2 DLU: 77

732.687-030   LABORER (toy-sport equip.)

Performs any combination of following tasks in manufacture of sports equipment: Glues layers of feathers together and cuts layers to size to form feathered arrowrests for bows. Holds feathers against brushing wheel or hot wire to brush or trim arrow feathers. Rubs and smooths sports equipment to improve appearance or utility, using filler, solvent, wax, or abrasive, and rags. Positions items of sports equipment in racks for painting. Melts lead in pan and pours lead into mold to form such items as fish baits and lead sinkers. Assembles golf ball covers and cores preparatory to molding. Cuts golf club shaft to specified length, using power saw. Cleans material, work aids, and equipment to expedite fabrication of sports equipment, using solvent, rags, and handtools. Cuts, trims, and glues parts into specified position on sports equipment, using glue, knife, and scissors. Transports and positions material at molds, machines, or worktables, using cart. Dips item of sports equipment or rubs glue or starch on item to facilitate further processing. Sprays sand with airhose onto diving boards to provide safety tread. May examine molded items, such as clay trapshooting targets, for chips and cracks and discard defective targets.
GOE: 06.04.34 STRENGTH: M GED: R1 M1 L1 SVP: 2 DLU: 77

732.687-034   LACER (toy-sport equip.) alternate titles: hand lacer

Laces footballs, punching bags, or baseball gloves and mitts, using lacing needle and awl: Pushes end of fabric, plastic, or leather lace through eyelets of article with awl or lacing needle. Pulls lace through eyelet. Repeats operation and ties and cuts lace after article is laced as specified.
GOE: 06.04.34 STRENGTH: L GED: R2 M1 L1 SVP: 3 DLU: 77

732.687-038   LEADER TIER (toy-sport equip.) alternate titles: leader assembler

Fabricates fishing leaders from cable wire and synthetic fiber line: Attaches snaps, swivels, and other accessories to precut lengths of plastic- or nylon-coated cable wire, and secures ends of cable with plastic or nylon sleeves and adhesives. Forms loop in ends of precut lengths of stainless steel wire and wraps ends back around wire to secure them. Ties loop knots in centers and ends of precut lengths of line to facilitate attachment of weights or hooks. May coil completed leaders and attach them to display cards or insert them in plastic envelopes. May test tensile strength of leader material, using tensiometer. May attach precut length of line to fishhook in manner to facilitate attachment of line or lure and be designated Sneller, Hand (toy-sport equip.).
GOE: 06.04.34 STRENGTH: L GED: R2 M1 L1 SVP: 2 DLU: 77

732.687-042   LINING INSERTER (toy-sport equip.) alternate titles: baseball-glove stuffer; inserter; lining stuffer

Inserts padded leather lining into baseball gloves: Places lining on form and pulls glove over lining. Pushes thumb lining into glove, using bench post.
GOE: 06.04.23 STRENGTH: M GED: R2 M1 L1 SVP: 2 DLU: 77

732.687-046   MOLD CLEANER (toy-sport equip.)

Heats metallic bowling ball mold parts on electric plate and scrapes and buffs ball to remove residue, using scraper and power-driven rotary wire brush. May spray mold components with parting material to prevent corrosion and to prepare them for assembly.
GOE: 06.04.39 STRENGTH: L GED: R1 M1 L1 SVP: 2 DLU: 77

732.687-050   MOLD STRIPPER (toy-sport equip.) alternate titles: breaker

Separates and removes molds from cured plastic bowling balls and grinds off sprues and ridges preparatory to truing and finishing balls: Removes thumbscrews or clamps from molds and pries molds from balls. Screws core support bolts out of balls with wrench. Grinds sprues and seam ridges from balls, using powered grind wheel. May fill core supporting bolt holes with plastic to mark heavy side of ball.
GOE: 06.04.24 STRENGTH: L GED: R1 M1 L1 SVP: 2 DLU: 77

732.687-054   MOLDER, INFLATED BALL (toy-sport equip.) alternate titles: press operator, carcass

Shapes completed footballs, volleyballs, and soccer balls, or vulcanizes plied ball carcasses, such as basketball carcasses, using internal pressure molding presses: Places ball or carcass in bottom half of heated molding press and inserts inflating stem in valve plug of workpiece. Closes and locks mold. Inflates workpiece to specified air pressure, removes inflating stem, and turns dial on timeclock to control heating cycle. Inserts deflating stem through hole in mold and into valve of ball or carcass after specified time and deflates workpiece to regulation playing pressure. Opens press, pulls out stem, and removes ball or carcass. May repair rejected balls for remolding. May mold plastic material to form bladderless inflatable balls, using heated curing ovens and molds.
GOE: 06.04.32 STRENGTH: M GED: R2 M1 L1 SVP: 2 DLU: 77

732.687-058   MOLDER, WAX BALL (toy-sport equip.) alternate titles: press operator, wax ball

Casts wax-ball lasts (forms) used in assembly of basketball carcasses: Places heated half mold on scale of mold and inserts mold into water-cooled centrifuge

that rotates mold and solidifies wax into hollow ball. Removes mold after specified time, unscrews top, and pulls out wax ball. Breaks off flash with fingers.
GOE: 06.04.32 STRENGTH: M GED: R2 M1 L1 SVP: 2 DLU: 77

732.687-062   PAINTER AND GRADER, CORK (toy-sport equip.)

Paints tops of leather-covered corks used as base for badminton shuttlecocks, using handbrush. Examines corks and grades them according to quality.
GOE: 06.04.33 STRENGTH: L GED: R2 M1 L1 SVP: 2 DLU: 77

732.687-066   REVERSER (toy-sport equip.) alternate titles: turner

Reverses partially assembled footballs, volleyballs, soccer balls, punching bags, or ball gloves that are inside-out to bring edges of sewn seams inside and leather or plastic cover outside: Places specified areas of inside-out article on turning post and pulls part of article over post. Repositions article on post and repeats operation until article is completely reversed.
GOE: 06.04.34 STRENGTH: M GED: R2 M1 L1 SVP: 2 DLU: 77

732.687-070   SOFTBALL CORE MOLDER (toy-sport equip.) alternate titles: molder

Forms softball cores, using heated presses: Weighs loose wad of kapoc, rags, or paper on scale and stuffs specified amount into heated press. Turns wheel to close press and mold softball core. Removes molded core from press after specified period and wraps with cord to hold core together until wound. May shape and cure vinyl dipped softballs, using rolling machine and heated molding press.
GOE: 06.04.32 STRENGTH: M GED: R2 M1 L1 SVP: 2 DLU: 77

732.687-074   SPIN-TABLE OPERATOR (toy-sport equip.)

Polishes surface of bowling balls, using abrasives and ball-spinning device: Places preground ball in holder of spin table and depresses pedal to spin ball. Presses abrasives against spinning ball to abrade surface. Splashes water on ball to reduce friction. Applies polishing compound to ball with rag. Lifts and turns ball in holder of spin table to effect polishing of surface. Wipes moisture from ball and places it in rack.
GOE: 06.04.24 STRENGTH: M GED: R2 M1 L1 SVP: 3 DLU: 77

732.687-078   TARGET TRIMMER (toy-sport equip.)

Trims excess straw from surface of wrapped and tied archery targets with powered trimmer: Places target on flat surface, lowers powered trimmer into position, and guides it over target to remove loose and excess straw. Turns target over and trims other side. Trims edges with hand shears. Reinforces target center with hemp rope and sews rope handle to target with needle and thread.
GOE: 06.04.34 STRENGTH: M GED: R2 M1 L1 SVP: 2 DLU: 77

732.687-082   WAX-BALL KNOCK-OUT WORKER (toy-sport equip.)

Crushes and removes wax-ball lasts (forms) from basketball carcasses, using club, scraping tool, and airhose: Strikes carcass with bat to break wax ball. Shakes pieces out through opening in carcass. Scrapes wax particles from carcass and removes particles and dust with airhose.
GOE: 06.04.39 STRENGTH: M GED: R1 M1 L1 SVP: 2 DLU: 77

732.687-086   WEIGHER (toy-sport equip.) alternate titles: balancer; weight tester

Weighs and adjusts weight of shuttlecocks: Places shuttlecock (purposely made underweight) on balance scale and reads weight on meter. Positions lead disks on center of cork base of shuttlecock with tweezers until specified weight is indicated by meter (weight must be standard to ensure uniform speed of shuttlecock in flight). Presses lead disks into drilled cork with hand punch.
GOE: 06.04.34 STRENGTH: L GED: R2 M2 L1 SVP: 2 DLU: 77

733   OCCUPATIONS IN FABRICATION AND REPAIR OF PENS, PENCILS, AND OFFICE AND ARTISTS' MATERIALS, N.E.C.

This group includes occupations, not elsewhere classified, concerned with fabricating and repairing such products as pen points, mechanical pencils, refill cartridges, and related products and such office and artists' materials as lead pencils, carbon and stencil paper, inked ribbons, airbrushes, palettes, artists' colors and waxes, and rubber and metal hand stamps, dies, and seals.

733.130-010   SUPERVISOR, PLATING AND POINT ASSEMBLY (pen & pencil)

Supervises and coordinates activities of workers engaged in plating and assembling components of ballpoint pens: Reviews production schedule to ascertain number and type of ballpoint pen parts to be plated. Sets up machines and equipment to prepare for plating operations. Performs other duties as described under SUPERVISOR (any industry) Master Title.
GOE: 06.01.01 STRENGTH: L GED: R4 M3 L3 SVP: 7 DLU: 77

733.131-010   SUPERVISOR, RUBBER STAMPS AND DIES (pen & pencil)

Supervises and coordinates activities of workers engaged in fabrication of rubber box die and rubber-faced hand stamps: Interprets customers order and supervises workers engaged in typesetting, heating and pressing plastic used to form matrix, pressing and vulcanizing rubber in matrix to form dies, and trimming and cementing dies for hand stamps to wooden mount. Inspects finished dies for conformity with orders. Adjusts temperature and pressure of vulcanizing press which produces box dies of specified height. May engrave signature

in rubber for use as hand stamps [ENGRAVER, RUBBER (pen & pencil)]. Performs other duties as described under SUPERVISOR (any industry) Master Title.
GOE: 06.02.01 STRENGTH: L GED: R4 M4 L3 SVP: 7 DLU: 77

733.137-010 SUPERVISOR, ASSEMBLY (pen & pencil)
Supervises and coordinates activities of workers engaged in assembling and printing information on ballpoint pens, fiber tip pens or mechanical pencil parts. Maintains time and production records. May train new workers. Performs other duties as described under SUPERVISOR (any industry) Master Title.
GOE: 06.02.01 STRENGTH: L GED: R4 M3 L4 SVP: 7 DLU: 77

733.137-014 SUPERVISOR, FINISHING DEPARTMENT (pen & pencil)
Supervises and coordinates activities of workers engaged in tipping, end-trimming, and stamping and packing wooden pencils and assembly of wood-cased ballpoint pens: Notifies setup worker of needed adjustments on tipping, trimming, stamping and packaging machines, according to size, shape and type of pencil to be processed. Inspects samples of processed pencils for defects, such as loose metal tips, broken eraser plugs, and splintered ends. Examines pencils to verify stamped information and type of tip on pencil against production specifications. Examines pen refills to verify conformance to specifications. Requisitions supplies, such as sandpaper, cardboard containers, and stamping foil. May adjust assembly machines, using handtools. May train new workers. Performs other duties as described under SUPERVISOR (any industry) Master Title.
GOE: 06.02.01 STRENGTH: L GED: R4 M3 L3 SVP: 7 DLU: 77

733.137-018 SUPERVISOR, INSPECTION (pen & pencil)
Supervises and coordinates activities of workers engaged in inspecting, packing and shipping of ballpoint pens or mechanical pencils. Performs other duties as described under SUPERVISOR (any industry) Master Title. May supervise workers engaged in inspecting material used in manufacture of pens and pencils.
GOE: 06.02.01 STRENGTH: L GED: R4 M3 L4 SVP: 7 DLU: 77

733.281-010 BALLPOINT PEN CARTRIDGE TESTER (pen & pencil)
Tests ballpoint pen cartridges to determine conformity to company specifications: Selects and weighs cartridges to determine conformance to weight specifications. Inserts cartridges into holding devices on testing machine, starts machine that moves paper, and counts circular marks made by cartridges. Examines defective cartridges under microscope to determine cause of malfunction and photographs ballpoint to obtain visible evidence of malfunction, using camera.
GOE: 06.03.01 STRENGTH: L GED: R3 M2 L2 SVP: 5 DLU: 77

733.364-010 QUALITY-CONTROL TECHNICIAN, INKED RIBBONS (pen & pencil)
Inspects and tests office machine ribbons to ensure adherence to order specifications and company quality standards, using testing equipment: Inspects production line operations, such as aligning ribbon on spool, joining ribbon ends, placing ribbon in cartridge, and packing ribbon for shipment to ensure quality standards are met. Inserts sample of inked ribbon and paper in typewriter, types several symbols on paper, and places paper on reflectance testing machine to obtain ink impregnation reading. Weighs ribbon sample to verify ink impregnation level, using scale. Tests and measures tensile strength and thickness of ribbon sample, using tension testing machine and measuring instrument. Records test results to maintain inspection log and notifies workers when ribbon fails to meet specifications. Completes final inspection form to release product for shipment.
GOE: 06.03.02 STRENGTH: L GED: R3 M3 L3 SVP: 5 DLU: 86

733.381-010 ENGRAVER, RUBBER (pen & pencil) alternate titles: engraver, signature
Engraves outline of signature impressed on rubber and cuts away excess rubber: Applies varnish to surface of rubber blank to clean and fill surface. Removes excess varnish with cloth wiper. Presses facsimile of signature onto rubber to transfer signature from paper. Removes paper and coats rubber with powder. Cuts outline of impression in rubber and cuts excess rubber away from impression, using knife and graver. Applies cement to back of stamp and to wood mount and presses stamp on mount manually.
GOE: 05.10.05 STRENGTH: L GED: R4 M3 L2 SVP: 7 DLU: 77

733.381-014 RUBBER-STAMP MAKER (pen & pencil) alternate titles: stamp maker
Molds stamp dies, assembles parts to fabricate rubber handstamps and composes type: Places type in chase. Proofreads copy or type in chase. Places chase and molding compound in press to form mold for rubber die, positions uncured rubber on top of mold, and places mold and rubber in vulcanizer to form rubber die. Joins parts, such as mounts, dies, and handles, to assemble handstamps [STAMP MOUNTER (pen & pencil)].
GOE: 06.01.04 STRENGTH: L GED: R4 M3 L3 SVP: 6 DLU: 77

733.384-010 REPAIRER, PENS AND PENCILS (pen & pencil) alternate titles: salvage clerk
Repairs and adjusts defective ballpoint pens and mechanical pencils in pen and pencil manufacturing plant: Examines pens or pencils to determine needed repairs or adjustments, or follows specifications on repair tags. Disassembles pens and pencils, using handtools, such as pliers and screwdrivers. Replaces defective parts, such as ink cartridges and screw mechanisms, and assembles parts of pens or pencils by hand or using machines that press and clinch interlocking parts together.
GOE: 06.02.32 STRENGTH: L GED: R3 M2 L3 SVP: 3 DLU: 77

733.684-010 PAINT-BRUSH MAKER (fabrication, nec) alternate titles: brush maker; rubber-stamp assembler
Fills metal ferrules with hog bristle, horsehair, vegetable fiber, or nylon, using either of following methods: (1) Twists material into tuft and dips base of tuft into cement. Ties string around base of tuft, redips tuft in cement, and inserts tuft in hole of brush head. (2) Weighs out specified amount of bristles, using balance scale and inserts base end of bristles into ferrule. Separates bristles with metal blade, and inserts wooden or aluminum plug (wedge) into bristles to press them against sides of ferrule to form brush head. Immerses flag end of brush head in flaxseed gum to hold filling material in brush shape during vulcanizing process. Measures length of bristles, using gauge. May cut bristles to varying lengths to taper tip of brush head, using metal form and scissors. May make wire drawn brushes [BRUSH FILLER, HAND (fabrication, nec) 739.687-046].
GOE: 06.04.34 STRENGTH: L GED: R2 M2 L2 SVP: 4 DLU: 77

733.684-014 PEN-AND-PENCIL REPAIRER (any industry)
Repairs and replaces parts of fountain pens and mechanical pencils, using electric buffer, handtools, and magnifying lens: Repairs or replaces ink sacs, plungers, barrels, and other parts, using handtools. Places pen points on straightening block and rubs them with mandrel to straighten points. Twists and turns points with pliers under magnifying lens to align points. Washes pens and pencils in cleaning solution. Removes engraving and polishes pens and pencils, using electric buffer. May operate pantograph engraving machine or stamping machine to inscribe names on pens and pencils. May operate bench lathes to cut out parts for pens and pencils. May sell pens and pencils. May requisition replacement parts for pens and pencils.
GOE: 05.12.15 STRENGTH: L GED: R3 M1 L2 SVP: 4 DLU: 77

733.684-018 STAMP MOUNTER (pen & pencil)
Joins parts, such as mounts, dies, and handles, to assemble rubber handstamps: Measures and marks wood mount and cuts woodstock for stamp mounts, using circular table saw. Positions and holds wooden mount on table, under bit of boring machine and pulls lever or depresses pedal to lower bit into mount, drilling hole for stamp handle. Hammers stamp handle into hole in mount. Cuts out and trims rubber die (type) from multistamp molded sheet, using scissors. Brushes cement onto back of rubber die and bottom of mount and positions and presses die onto mount. Applies ink to stamp die and stamps die onto paper, forming identification label. Inserts label between plastic facing and top or side of stamp mount.
GOE: 06.04.34 STRENGTH: L GED: R2 M2 L1 SVP: 2 DLU: 77

733.685-010 ASSEMBLER (pen & pencil)
Tends automatic pen and pencil assembly machines: Aligns workpiece in specified position against fixtures or under ram of machine. Depresses lever or pedal or turns handwheel to activate ram that bends or presses components together. Screws threaded barrels and caps together by hand to form completed pens or pencils. Places clips in holding devices of machine that prints trademark or clips. Inspects finished workpiece with magnifying glass. May be designated according to component assembled as Cartridge Assembler (pen & pencil); Nib Assembler (pen & pencil).
GOE: 06.04.20 STRENGTH: L GED: R2 M2 L2 SVP: 2 DLU: 77

733.685-014 FILLING-MACHINE OPERATOR (pen & pencil)
Tends machine that pumps ink into tubes (reservoirs) to permeate marking pen fillers or fills ballpoint refills, using any of following methods: (1) Places fillers in tubes and inserts nozzle of filler machine into tube and pushes button to start machine that pumps specified amount of ink into tubes. (2) Inserts cotton filler into cartridge tube by hand. Places tube into holding device of inking machine. Depresses pedal to start filling mechanism. (3) Fills hopper of machine with refill components for ballpoint pen. Starts machine that automatically fills tube with ink, joins ballpoint to inked tube, and crimps tube to seal ink in tube.
GOE: 06.04.36 STRENGTH: M GED: R2 M2 L2 SVP: 2 DLU: 77

733.685-018 GROOVING-MACHINE OPERATOR (pen & pencil) alternate titles: bench-boring-machine operator
Tends machine that cuts internal threads in pen or mechanical pencil barrels: Positions and aligns pen or pencil barrel in holding device of machine. Inserts threading tap into spindle of machine and turns lever to secure tap. Presses switch to start machine. Moves lever or depresses pedal that advances pen or pencil barrel onto rotating tap that cuts internal threads in barrel.
GOE: 06.04.09 STRENGTH: L GED: R2 M1 L1 SVP: 2 DLU: 77

733.685-022 RIBBON WINDER (pen & pencil) alternate titles: spooler; typewriter-ribbon winder
Tends machine that winds typewriter ribbons onto spools: Sets yardage indicator on machine according to ribbon length specified on work order to control number of revolutions. Places ribbon supply reel on mandrel and draws ribbon around rollers and through ribbon guide to prepare ribbon for winding. Adjusts ribbon guide, according to width of ribbon. Places empty spool on spindle and attaches end of ribbon from supply reel to spool. Turns knob to zero dial of footage counter and depresses pedal to wind ribbon onto spool or turns reel that winds ribbon onto spool. Observes dial of footage counter and stops ma-

chine at specified point. Examines ribbon during winding to detect defects in fabric, inking, and winding. Removes completed spool from spindle and attaches hooks or eyelets onto ends of ribbons to facilitate attaching to empty spool on typewriter. Attaches fasteners over end of ribbon to prevent unwinding.
GOE: 06.04.09 STRENGTH: L GED: R2 M2 L2 SVP: 3 DLU: 77

733.685-026 SMOOTHER (pen & pencil) alternate titles: pen-point smoother

Tends machine that smooths rough edges from pen point tips: Places pen points into molds on hinged holding device and closes device to hold pen points stationary during smoothing process. Sprinkles polishing rouge on felt wheel and starts machine. Inserts tongue of holding device into groove on machine bed and moves holding device back and forth in groove as pen point tips work against rotating felt wheel or guides holding device against rotating wheel by hand to smooth surface of pen point tips. Feels tips of pen points with fingers to detect rough areas.
GOE: 06.04.24 STRENGTH: S GED: R2 M1 L1 SVP: 2 DLU: 77

733.685-030 TIP BANDER (pen & pencil) alternate titles: tip-banding-machine operator

Tends machine that applies decorative or identifying band of paint to metal tips of pencils: Dumps tips into machine hopper and pours paint into reservoir of machine. Starts machine that feeds tips against paint roller. Turns valve to regulate stream of air that blows tip from conveyor into tray. Places tray in storage rack.
GOE: 06.04.21 STRENGTH: L GED: R2 M1 L1 SVP: 2 DLU: 77

733.685-034 TIPPING-MACHINE OPERATOR (pen & pencil) alternate titles: tipper

Tends machine that fastens metal caps and erasers to ends of wooden pencils or rounds pencil ends: Places pencils, ferrules (metal ring or caps), and erasers in separate hoppers and starts machine that installs and fastens ferrule to pencil, inserts eraser in ferrule, and imprints specified data on pencil. Removes tipped pencils from machine and examines pencils for defects, such as broken erasers or loose ferrules. Ties accepted pencils into designated size bundles.
GOE: 06.04.20 STRENGTH: L GED: R2 M2 L2 SVP: 2 DLU: 77

733.687-010 ASSEMBLER, MARKING DEVICES (pen & pencil) alternate titles: marker assembler

Performs any combination of following duties to assemble stencil marking and ink applying devices: Selects parts according to specifications. Aligns parts following guides, such as contours, edges, slots, or fastening devices. Joins parts manually or using handtools, such as wrenches and power screwdrivers, or positions parts on holding device of machine bed under ram, and moves lever to lower ram, joining parts. Performs other tasks, such as cleaning parts, using air gun; fitting ink chambers; and positioning marker in holder of air pressure device that tests marker for leaks in ink valve and chamber. May be designated according to part assembled as Fountain-Brush Assembler (pen & pencil); Fountain-Roller Assembler (pen & pencil); Pen Assembler (pen & pencil).
GOE: 06.04.23 STRENGTH: L GED: R2 M2 L2 SVP: 2 DLU: 77

733.687-014 ASSEMBLER, MECHANICAL PENCILS AND BALL-POINT PENS (pen & pencil) alternate titles: air-hammer operator; bench-assembler operator; small kick-press operator; small press operator; tip tightener

Assembles parts of ballpoint pens and mechanical pencils: Selects pen or pencil parts according to color or work-ticket specifications. Places parts together, guided by edges, holes, and slots, and fastens devices, such as clips or prongs on parts. Joins parts, using any of following methods: (1) Positions parts in holding device under ram of press and depresses pedal that lowers ram, forcing interlocking parts together. (2) Positions parts in holding device of machine that clinches prongs or clips, joining parts. (3) Fits interlocking parts together, or screws threaded parts together by hand. Fills mechanical pencils with specified quantity of lead. May use pneumatic or screw clamps and other work aids that hold parts during assembly. May glue plastic miniature display tops to plunger mechanism on mechanical pencils, using plastic solvent and brush. May assemble parts of desk-pen sets [DESK-PEN-SET ASSEMBLER (pen & pencil) 733.687-034].
GOE: 06.04.23 STRENGTH: L GED: R2 M2 L2 SVP: 2 DLU: 77

733.687-018 BANDER (pen & pencil)

Fastens metal bands onto pen barrels: Slips band into groove on barrel. May insert and squeeze part in hand squeezer or crimping tool to tighten band in place.
GOE: 06.04.23 STRENGTH: L GED: R2 M1 L1 SVP: 2 DLU: 77

733.687-022 CHALK CUTTER (pen & pencil)

Loads lengths of extruded chalk into die, locks die in place, and runs hand cutter through holes in die to cut chalk to specified lengths. Opens die, places cut chalk in trays for drying, and disposes of excess chalk.
GOE: 06.04.34 STRENGTH: M GED: R1 M1 L1 SVP: 2 DLU: 77

733.687-026 CLAMPER (pen & pencil) alternate titles: hydraulic-press operator

Clamps stacks of cemented wooden pencil slats to hold them while cement dries: Places clamp between jaws of press and positions cemented slats in clamp. Depresses pedal to close jaws of press and press slats together. Turns

bolts to tighten clamp, using wrench. Depresses pedal to open press and places clamped slats on washer conveyor to remove excess cement from slats. May clamp stacks of cemented pencil slats, using hand clamps.
GOE: 06.04.25 STRENGTH: M GED: R1 M1 L1 SVP: 2 DLU: 77

733.687-030 DATER ASSEMBLER (pen & pencil)

Assembles parts of dater or number handstamps performing any combination of following tasks: Selects parts according to specifications. Applies cement and joins ends of rubber letter or number bands. Positions bands around metal bar and fits bar onto end of stamp frame. Positions band and turner wheels and washers inside circular bands and inserts rivet pin through stamp frame and band wheels, securing parts of stamp. Nails wood handle to frame. May use jig to hold and stretch rubberbands while assembling stamp parts. May be designated according to task performed as Cementer (pen & pencil).
GOE: 06.04.23 STRENGTH: L GED: R2 M1 L2 SVP: 2 DLU: 77

733.687-034 DESK-PEN-SET ASSEMBLER (pen & pencil) alternate titles: bench-assembler operator

Joins parts, such as swivel, penholder, and base to assemble desk-pen sets. Selects parts, according to work ticket specifications. Screws threaded parts together, using portable power screwdriver, or positions parts on bed and under ram of machine and presses switch to lower ram, joining interlocking parts. Glues felt onto bottom of base.
GOE: 06.04.23 STRENGTH: L GED: R2 M1 L1 SVP: 2 DLU: 77

733.687-038 DIPPER (pen & pencil)

Immerses bundles of wooden pencil slats into vat to coat them with wax solution. Loads slats in cage of hoist and pulls handle to lower cage into solution. Raises cage, removes slats, and stacks them on handtruck. May apply paint to coat or decorate wooden pencils by dipping or using screw-type ram dipper.
GOE: 06.04.33 STRENGTH: M GED: R1 M1 L1 SVP: 2 DLU: 77

733.687-042 INSPECTOR (pen & pencil) alternate titles: nib adjuster

Inspects fountain pens for defects: Examines nib under magnifying glass and inserts feeler gauge between fountain pen points to determine whether spacing between points conforms to specifications. Opens and closes pen points to adjust spacing between points, using handtools. Writes with fountain pen to determine legibility and ease of writing. Places rejected pens aside for rework. Places inspected pens in carton.
GOE: 06.03.02 STRENGTH: L GED: R2 M1 L2 SVP: 3 DLU: 77

733.687-046 INSPECTOR, BALL POINTS (nonfer. metal)

Inspects metal alloy pen ball points for defects: Picks up ball point with tweezer and places it under microscopic lens to examine for holes or other flaws. Measures approximately every 40th point with micrometer to determine if specifications are met and removes rejects. May test ballpoint pens and refills for conformity to specifications, using centrifuge, magnifying glass, and microscope.
GOE: 06.03.02 STRENGTH: L GED: R2 M2 L2 SVP: 3 DLU: 77

733.687-050 INSPECTOR, FINAL ASSEMBLY (pen & pencil)

Inspects ballpoint pens or mechanical pencils for defects, such as scratched or cracked barrels and faulty mechanisms: Compares color, style, and printed information on pen or pencil with written specifications. Depresses plunger of ballpoint pens to test retracting action of cartridge (refill). Discards defective items and returns repairable items for rework. May write with ballpoint pens to test inking mechanism. May remove substandard printing, using rag and solvent.
GOE: 06.03.02 STRENGTH: L GED: R2 M2 L2 SVP: 3 DLU: 77

733.687-054 INSPECTOR, RUBBER-STAMP DIE (pen & pencil)

Examines rubber handstamp dies (type) for defects: Examines stamp dies under magnifying glass for defects in molded rubber, such as loose or incomplete letters or designs. Compares stamp die to customer specifications to verify characters or designs.
GOE: 06.03.02 STRENGTH: L GED: R3 M1 L1 SVP: 4 DLU: 77

733.687-058 NIB INSPECTOR (pen & pencil)

Inspects fountain pen nibs to ensure that smoothness, contour, and dimensions conform to specifications, using magnifying glass and dial and fixed gauges: Examines nibs with magnifying glass and by feeling with fingertips to detect surface defects, such as scratches, pits, and cracks. Verifies dimensions of nibs, using preset measuring instruments, such as dial indicators, calipers, and micrometers. Tags rejected nibs to indicate types of defects.
GOE: 06.03.02 STRENGTH: L GED: R3 M2 L2 SVP: 3 DLU: 77

733.687-062 PENCIL INSPECTOR (pen & pencil) alternate titles: pencil sorter

Examines wooden pencil slats, wood-cased ball point pens, or painted wooden pencils for defects, such as dents, misplaced lead, scratches, or split ends. Trims slivers from around ferrules of wooden pencils, using knife. Sorts and marks defective pencils. May maintain production records.
GOE: 06.03.02 STRENGTH: L GED: R2 M1 L1 SVP: 2 DLU: 77

733.687-066 STAMP-PAD FINISHER (pen & pencil)

Places inking pads for stenciling rollers or handstamps in metal cases. May apply cement to pad or case to secure parts.
GOE: 06.04.23 STRENGTH: L GED: R1 M1 L1 SVP: 1 DLU: 77

733.687-070 STAMP-PAD MAKER (pen & pencil)

Fabricates rubber stamp pads: Places precut pieces of muslin, felt, and rubberized backing in sequence in fixture on assembly table. Applies glue to ex-

tended edges of muslin and folds edges around backing. Places pad in inking device and pulls lever to lower pad into reservoir which impregnates it with ink under pressure. May place inked pad into metal case and cover case with lid.
GOE: 06.04.23 STRENGTH: L GED: R2 M1 L1 SVP: 2 DLU: 77

733.687-074 STENCIL INSPECTOR (pen & pencil)
Inspects duplicating stencils for defects prior to mounting on backing sheets: Holds stencil over fluoroscope to determine presence of defects, such as holes, tears, and imperfect surface. Discards defective stencil. Places layer of paper between stencils to protect them. May measure stencil for conformance to size.
GOE: 06.03.02 STRENGTH: L GED: R2 M1 L1 SVP: 2 DLU: 77

733.687-078 WASHER (pen & pencil)
Washes excess glue from clamped wooden pencil slats, using water and sponge. Turns valve to start flow of water onto slats and rubs all sides of clamped slats with sponge. Places washed slats in handcart and pushes loaded cart to kiln for further processing.
GOE: 06.04.39 STRENGTH: H GED: R1 M1 L1 SVP: 1 DLU: 77

734 OCCUPATIONS IN FABRICATION AND REPAIR OF NOTIONS

This group includes occupations concerned with fabricating such items as pins, needles, plumes, brushes, artificial flowers, buttons, and zippers. Includes curling and dyeing feathers. Occupations concerned with fabricating ornamental buttons from precious metals are included in Group 700.

734.131-010 SUPERVISOR II (button & notion)
Supervises and coordinates activities of workers engaged in making plastic artificial articles, such as flowers, foliage, and butterflies: Reads work orders to ascertain articles scheduled, material requirements, and to plan work sequences. Assigns specific duties to workers and gives work direction for performing duties. Inspects articles at various stages of production to ensure conformance with customer and company specifications. Records daily production. Performs other duties as described under SUPERVISOR (any industry) Master Title.
GOE: 06.04.01 STRENGTH: L GED: R4 M2 L3 SVP: 5 DLU: 77

734.384-010 BUTTON-CUTTING-MACHINE OPERATOR (button & notion) alternate titles: button cutter; shaper
Cuts button blanks from shells: Holds shell against machine fixture by hand or using tongs. Moves lever or depresses pedal to advance tubular saw into shell and cut out button blank. Determines location for cuts according to size, shape, and condition of individual shell in order to obtain maximum number of blanks. Replaces dulled saws, using wrenches. May reset and sharpen saws, using hand files.
GOE: 06.02.30 STRENGTH: L GED: R2 M1 L1 SVP: 3 DLU: 77

734.481-010 WIRE-FRAME MAKER (button & notion)
Bends wires into frames used for forming plastic flowers, leaves, and butterflies, using jig and soldering iron: Bends wire around jig following specified instructions, using fingers and pick. Cuts wire after frame is formed, using wire cutters. Solders together wires that overlap to strengthen frame, using flux and soldering iron. Builds up button of solder in center of petals when framing flowers. Presses lever that removes frame from jig. Examines frame to ensure shape meets specifications. Cuts excess wire from frame, using wire cutters. Records daily production figures.
GOE: 06.04.24 STRENGTH: L GED: R2 M2 L2 SVP: 3 DLU: 77

734.584-010 NEEDLE GRINDER (button & notion)
Grinds industrial knitting and sewing needles to sharpen points, using grinding wheels: Activates stone and wire-brush wheels and alternately presses needle against each rotating wheel to sharpen point. Applies emery to wire-brush wheel as needed to facilitate grinding process. Visually and tactually examines needle to ensure conformance to specifications. Records production.
GOE: 06.04.24 STRENGTH: L GED: R2 M1 L2 SVP: 2 DLU: 77

734.684-010 FEATHER SHAPER (button & notion)
Trims, cuts, bones, straightens, and curls feathers for use in decorations for displays and garments, using handtools, such as knives and scissors: Draws feather between knife and thumb to curl feather or cuts portion from quill, using knife, to make feather soft and wavy or applies steam to make feather smooth and straight. Trims feather to specified shape, using scissors. May wire, glue, paste, or sew feathers to form specified design. May be designated according to work performed as Brancher (button & notion); Curler (button & notion); Cutter (button & notion); Feather Boner (button & notion); Feather Trimmer (button & notion).
GOE: 06.04.34 STRENGTH: S GED: R2 M1 L2 SVP: 2 DLU: 77

734.684-014 FEATHER-DUSTER WINDER (tex. prod., nec)
Fabricates feather dusters, using scissors, shears, and winding machine: Clamps wooden handle in chuck of winding machine. Pulls wire from reel and attaches wire to grooved end of handle. Starts machine to rotate handle and inserts quills under wire as it winds around handle. Stops machine and cuts wire, using shears. Tacks paper cuff around wire and wraps end of wire around tack. Trims feathers to specified length, using scissors.
GOE: 06.04.23 STRENGTH: L GED: R2 M1 L1 SVP: 3 DLU: 77

734.684-018 INSPECTOR-REPAIRER (button & notion)
Examines frames or plastic articles during various stages of manufacture and reworks article to meet specifications: Inspects frames for unsoldered wires and solders contact points, using soldering iron. Examines formed articles for holes in plastic or deformations and brushes liquid epoxy or plastic to repair defect. Inspects decorated articles for missed paint areas or defective decoration and paints areas needing rework, using artist's brush. Discards articles that cannot be reworked. Occasionally bends finished article into specified shape and seals article in plastic bag, using heated iron.
GOE: 06.03.02 STRENGTH: L GED: R3 M2 L2 SVP: 4 DLU: 77

734.684-022 SLIDE-FASTENER REPAIRER (button & notion) alternate titles: zipper repairer
Repairs and adjusts defective slide fasteners (zipper chains): Examines rejected fasteners for type of defect and extent of repair required. Pries excess or broken scoops (teeth) and damaged slides from chain, using metal pin. Separates prongs of replacement scoops with pin, and secures scoops to tape, using hand pliers. Cuts chain to specified length, using hand cutting tool. Inserts and secures bottom stop to tape ends of chain, using pinchers, to hold tapes together and provide stop for slide. Positions slide on chain and crimps sides of slides over scoops to mesh links and to provide even sliding action, using crimping tool. Tests zipper by drawing slide over scoops.
GOE: 06.04.24 STRENGTH: L GED: R2 M2 L2 SVP: 2 DLU: 77

734.684-026 WIRE-FRAME DIPPER (button & notion)
Immerses preshaped wire frames in liquid plastic to form articles, such as flowers and foliage, prior to decorating, using either of following methods: (1) Slides metal tube over wire stem of frame to prevent coating of stem. Immerses frame in plastic solution, slides tube down to base of petals, and observes frame to ensure that plastic has covered area within frame. Secures stem on holder above container to allow excess plastic to drip into container. Removes article from holder, removes tube, and places article on drying rack. (2) Dips wire frame in plastic solution and removes article after area within frame is filled. Bends holding wire and hangs filled in frame on hook of conveyor to dry. Mixes plastic solutions according to formula. Records daily production.
GOE: 06.04.33 STRENGTH: L GED: R2 M1 L1 SVP: 2 DLU: 77

734.685-010 STAMPER (button & notion)
Tends handpress that imprints design on wooden buttons: Positions and fastens die in handpress. Places button in holder under die and pulls lever to lower die that imprints design on button.
GOE: 06.04.25 STRENGTH: M GED: R2 M1 L1 SVP: 2 DLU: 77

734.685-014 BUTTON MAKER AND INSTALLER (tex. prod., nec)
Tends button machine that assembles buttons and inserts buttons into pillow and cushion shells prior to stuffing: Positions specified metal button dies in machine, according to work order, and flips switch to activate machine. Turns knob to set counter that tallies number of buttons assembled. Places button covers and metal button parts in specified sequence in dies and depresses pedal to activate automatic assembly cycle of machine. Picks up buttons from machine discharge bin and cuts away excess covering material, using scissors. Inserts one end of button ties into openings on back of buttons, places opposite end of ties into inserting tool, and pushes tool through precut holes in pillow or cushion shells. Removes ties from tool and inserts ties into openings of other buttons on opposite side of shells. Places assembled items in storage area. Periodically cuts additional button covers from specified fabrics, using handpress.
GOE: 06.04.09 STRENGTH: M GED: R2 M1 L1 SVP: 2 DLU: 86

734.687-010 ACETONE-BUTTON PASTER (button & notion)
Brushes or drops acetone cement on backs of buttons to attach metal shanks of buttons and presses shank into softened plastic.
GOE: 06.04.23 STRENGTH: S GED: R1 M1 L1 SVP: 2 DLU: 77

734.687-014 ASSEMBLER (tex. prod., nec) alternate titles: table worker
Assembles fabric badges from such materials as metal bars, ribbon, and metal buttons, using any of following methods: (1) Slides hanger on back of metal bar through hemmed edge of ribbon. (2) Brushes cement onto back of metal or plastic bar and presses edge of ribbon onto bar. (3) Positions ribbon over back of metal button and presses circular wire pin against ribbon and under back edge of button. (4) Brushes cement onto buckram backing of rosette and presses edge of ribbon onto rosette. (5) Pushes pin on back of metal button through center of rosette and bends prongs of pin back to hold rosette in place. May trim and clean fabric badge, using scissors and cleaning cloth. May cement labels onto back of badges, using brush and cement.
GOE: 06.04.23 STRENGTH: L GED: R2 M1 L1 SVP: 2 DLU: 77

734.687-018 ASSEMBLER (button & notion)
Inserts paper label in back of celluloid or metal advertising buttons and forces shaped stickpin under rim.
GOE: 06.04.23 STRENGTH: S GED: R1 M1 L1 SVP: 2 DLU: 77

734.687-022 BOBBIN DISKER (glass mfg.) alternate titles: disk setter
Inserts specified disk into recess at head of bobbin, using fingers, or positions disk on top of stationary metal rod and slides bobbin over rod and disk to identify type or size of fiberglass yarn to be wound on bobbin.
GOE: 06.04.23 STRENGTH: L GED: R2 M1 L1 SVP: 2 DLU: 77

734.687-026 BUCKLE INSPECTOR (button & notion)
Examines finished metal buckles and clasps for defects, such as bent or broken parts, dents, scratches, and plating or lacquering imperfections. Sets aside

defective buckles for rework. Places protective plastic tip over buckle prong. Wraps specified number of buckles in tissue paper preparatory to packaging. May count and weigh sample lot, using scale, to ascertain weight per gross, in order that items may be packaged by weight rather than by actual count.
GOE: 06.03.02 STRENGTH: L GED: R2 M1 L1 SVP: 2 DLU: 77

734.687-030 BUCKLE SORTER (button & notion)
Sorts metal buckles and parts according to size and kind, and removes bent or broken ones. Dumps container of buckles on bench and separates them into piles or containers. Removes pieces of tumbling-barrel shot jammed in buckles, using metal pick.
GOE: 06.03.02 STRENGTH: L GED: R2 M1 L2 SVP: 3 DLU: 77

734.687-034 BUCKLE-WIRE INSERTER (button & notion)
Pushes reinforcing wire through tubular material for use in making buckle frames. Cuts off material to match length of reinforcing wire, using scissors.
GOE: 06.04.23 STRENGTH: S GED: R1 M1 L1 SVP: 1 DLU: 77

734.687-038 BUTTON GRADER (button & notion)
Examines completed pearl buttons and sorts them according to grade: Observes buttons on conveyor belt or worktable, and sorts into containers according to shade and purity of color, and degree of iridescence. Discards buttons with defects, such as spots, chips, cracks, or toolmarks. May examine completed plastic buttons for defects.
GOE: 06.03.02 STRENGTH: S GED: R2 M1 L2 SVP: 4 DLU: 77

734.687-042 BUTTON RECLAIMER (knitting)
Examines buttons for defects, such as chips and cracks, and separates defective buttons from acceptable ones.
GOE: 06.03.02 STRENGTH: S GED: R1 M1 L1 SVP: 2 DLU: 77

734.687-046 BUTTON-AND-BUCKLE MAKER (any industry) alternate titles: buckle-and-button maker; covered button maker
Covers buttons and buckles with fabric, leather, or other material, using pedal-operated press: Cuts covering from layers of material, using die-cutting machine. Places button or buckle in press with covering over it. Depresses pedal to lower plunger and clamp covering and metal parts together. Releases pedal and removes covered article.
GOE: 06.04.27 STRENGTH: L GED: R2 M1 L1 SVP: 3 DLU: 80

734.687-050 COVERED-BUCKLE ASSEMBLER (button & notion) alternate titles: buckle assembler; buckle coverer; buckle gluer
Brushes glue over surface of metal buckle frames and presses precut leather or fabric over frame. Trims excess material with shears.
GOE: 06.04.27 STRENGTH: L GED: R1 M1 L1 SVP: 3 DLU: 77

734.687-054 GRINDER, HAND (button & notion)
Inserts button blanks in slot of grinding machine and pulls grinder against button to grind flat surfaces.
GOE: 06.04.34 STRENGTH: L GED: R1 M1 L1 SVP: 2 DLU: 77

734.687-058 HOT-STONE SETTER (button & notion)
Sets rhinestones in plastic buttons by heating rhinestones on hot metal plate and inserting them in indentations in buttons. Presses stones into buttons with tweezers or metal guard fitted over finger.
GOE: 06.04.23 STRENGTH: S GED: R1 M1 L1 SVP: 2 DLU: 77

734.687-062 INSPECTOR, SLIDE FASTENERS (button & notion)
Inspects samples of slide-fastener (zipper) chains and scoops (links) for defects and conformance to chart specifications for height, width, and spacing of scoops, using micrometers: Measures dimensions of chain and spacing of scoops, using micrometers and ruler, and counts number of scoops per length of chain. Examines chain and scoops for such defects as smashed, cracked, burred, or missing scoops, or for uneven spacing, using optical glasses or eye loupe. Opens and closes zipper to determine ease of sliding and smooth action of slider. Tallies defects found according to type, and prepares report. May examine finish of lacquered chains.
GOE: 06.03.02 STRENGTH: L GED: R3 M2 L2 SVP: 4 DLU: 77

734.687-066 QUILL-BUNCHER-AND-SORTER (tex. prod., nec)
Separates quills into specified groupings, such as skirts (short), wing, pointer, tail, and white quills, preparatory to processing into feather dusters. Bunches specified number of each kind of quill and secures them with clamps. Discards broken quills.
GOE: 06.03.02 STRENGTH: S GED: R2 M1 L2 SVP: 3 DLU: 77

734.687-070 SHELL-GRADER (button & notion) alternate titles: shell sorter
Grades pearl shells used in making pearl buttons: Examines shells and grades them according to size, thickness, curvature, color, and imperfections. Sorts shells into grading bins. Places graded shells in containers of water to soften them for cutting operations. May transport cases of shells from storage, using handtruck.
GOE: 06.03.02 STRENGTH: L GED: R3 M1 L2 SVP: 4 DLU: 77

734.687-074 SLIDE-FASTENER-CHAIN ASSEMBLER (button & notion) alternate titles: assembler, slide fastener stringers; puller; zipper joiner
Joins together stringers (sides) of slide fasteners, using slider jig: Aligns links of stringer with links of other stringer and inserts ends of stringers in slider jig. Pulls ends of stringers through jig to interlock links. Examines fastener for

defects, such as crooked, broken, flattened, or misaligned links. Cuts out defective section, using scissors, and splices sections, using adhesive tape or hand stapler. May sew sections together to prevent raveling, using serging sewing machine. May tend machine rollers that pull stringers through jig.
GOE: 06.04.23 STRENGTH: S GED: R2 M1 L1 SVP: 2 DLU: 77

734.687-078 SLIDER ASSEMBLER (button & notion; garment) alternate titles: slider attacher; zipper-slide attacher
Attaches slides onto garment zipper: Clamps slide in holding device on worktable and threads bottom links of zipper chains through slide. Grasps bottom of zipper and pulls chains through slide, meshing links to close zipper. Removes slide from holding device and positions garment on machine bed with zipper bottom against guide. Depresses pedal that lowers machine head to fasten metal clamp or staple around bottom of chains. May depress pedal that closes rollers on chains and pulls them through slide automatically.
GOE: 06.04.23 STRENGTH: L GED: R2 M1 L2 SVP: 2 DLU: 77

734.687-082 SORTER (button & notion)
Examines pearl or plastic button blanks on moving conveyor and discards those with defects, such as wormholes, loose spots, uneven backs, cracks, or chips. May examine unpolished plastic buttons for tool marks, off-center thread holes, and unfinished shape.
GOE: 06.03.02 STRENGTH: S GED: R2 M1 L2 SVP: 3 DLU: 77

734.687-086 SPLITTER, HAND (button & notion)
Splits pearl button blanks into two or more blanks, using hand knife and mallet. Holds blank edge-up on bench or block. Positions knife blade along top edge of blank, steadies blade and blank with thumb and fingers of one hand, and taps blade with mallet to split blank.
GOE: 06.04.34 STRENGTH: S GED: R1 M1 L1 SVP: 2 DLU: 77

734.687-090 STICKER (button & notion) alternate titles: leaf sticker
Glues paper-covered wire to artificial flowers to stiffen and strengthen them. May emboss simulated veins on leaves.
GOE: 06.04.23 STRENGTH: S GED: R1 M1 L1 SVP: 1 DLU: 77

734.687-094 ZIPPER TRIMMER, HAND (button & notion) alternate titles: zipper measurer
Measures slide fastener chains and cuts excess scoops (links) from chains to shorten chains to specified length: Measures chain against bench mounted ruler to determine number of scoops to remove. Cuts each scoop from tape, using pincers. Rubs scoops against edge of bench to remove them from tape. Cuts tape between chains to form individual zipper, using scissors. Examines zippers for broken or missing scoops and discards defective zippers. May count and record number of zippers produced.
GOE: 06.04.24 STRENGTH: S GED: R2 M2 L2 SVP: 2 DLU: 77

735 OCCUPATIONS IN FABRICATION AND REPAIR OF JEWELRY, N.E.C.

This group includes occupations, not elsewhere classified, concerned with fabricating and repairing jewelry.

735.381-010 BENCH HAND (jewelry-silver.) alternate titles: bench worker
Cuts out, files, and solders parts for jewelry articles, such as bracelets, brooches, emblems, and rings, performing any combination of following tasks: Cuts out, using power saw or handsaw. Shapes, trims, and smooths parts, using files. Joins parts together, using solder and torch. May bend ring settings and brooch clasps, using pliers. May assemble finished parts of jewelry articles.
GOE: 06.01.04 STRENGTH: L GED: R3 M2 L1 SVP: 6 DLU: 77

735.381-014 PEARL RESTORER (jewelry-silver.) alternate titles: pearl peeler
Peels, shapes, smooths, and polishes genuine pearls to remove surface defects and attain uniform color, using knife, grinding stone, and abrasives: Peels outer layers to remove damaged areas and obtain natural, uniform color, using knife. Selects abrasive and grinding stone to produce smooth finish, utilizing knowledge of natural pearl structure, abrasives, and grinding operations. Shapes, smooths, and polishes pearls, using abrasives and grinding stone. Cleans surface of pearls, applying rag and oil mixtures.
GOE: 05.05.14 STRENGTH: L GED: R3 M2 L2 SVP: 6 DLU: 77

735.381-018 SAMPLE MAKER II (jewelry-silver.)
Reproduces original designs of jewelry articles in wax, prepares design specifications, and computes production costs: Molds original designs in wax, using modeling tools. Writes design specifications, such as metal content and weight and type of alloy. Computes cost of labor and material to determine production costs of jewelry articles. May form metal samples from wax molds [MODEL MAKER (jewelry-silver.) II].
GOE: 05.03.02 STRENGTH: S GED: R4 M2 L2 SVP: 6 DLU: 77

735.587-010 COLORING CHECKER (jewelry-silver.)
Records plating instructions for jewelry articles and inspects plated articles for quantity and quality: Receives jewelry articles with order card and transcribes plating instructions onto order sheet. Routes order and plating instructions to STRINGER (jewelry-silver.). Verifies quantity of articles and inspects plated articles for uniformity of surface and unplated areas. May keep records, such as rate cards, pricelists, or daily production reports.

GOE: 06.03.02 STRENGTH: L GED: R3 M1 L1 SVP: 4 DLU: 77

735.681-010 BRACELET AND BROOCH MAKER (jewelry-silver.) alternate titles: brooch-and-bracelet maker

Assembles jewelry parts to form decorative articles, such as bracelets and brooches: Joins parts and attaches decorations, using gas torch, soldering iron, pick, and tweezers. Sets stones and forms settings, using pliers, gas torch, or soldering iron.

GOE: 06.02.23 STRENGTH: L GED: R3 M2 L1 SVP: 7 DLU: 77

735.684-010 BEAD STRINGER (jewelry-silver.)

Strings bead necklaces on wire or thread: Counts number of beads in necklace. Cleans beads in soap and water or other cleaning solution. Sorts beads according to size, color, or original pattern. Guides needle through hole in beads and strings them into necklace of graduated or uniform sized beads. Ties knot in thread or bends wire and attaches fastener. May be designated according to type of beads strung as Pearl Stringer (jewelry-silver.). May restring bead necklaces on wire or thread.

GOE: 06.04.34 STRENGTH: S GED: R2 M1 L2 SVP: 3 DLU: 77

735.684-014 STONER (jewelry-silver.)

Smooths enameled surface of jewelry articles, using abrasive stone: Fastens jewelry article in wooden chuck (jeweler's block). Rubs moist abrasive stone across article to remove excess enamel and produce smooth surface. Brushes or washes article to remove loose particles. May remove excess enamel, using buffing machine.

GOE: 06.04.24 STRENGTH: S GED: R2 M1 L2 SVP: 4 DLU: 77

735.684-018 TROPHY ASSEMBLER (jewelry-silver.)

Assembles trophies to customer's specifications, using drill press and handtools: Selects parts, such as base, tubing, metal plates, figures, and hardware from stock. Drills holes in base or plaque, using electric drill or drill press. Glues felt to bottom of base, or screws in metal feet. Staples or tapes metal plate to base. Bolts parts together, using screwdriver and socket wrench. Touches up scratch marks with scratch remover and polishes assembled trophy. May attach marble or onyx decoration to formed column with adhesive tape. May wrap trophy in tissue paper preparatory to shipping.

GOE: 06.02.24 STRENGTH: L GED: R3 M2 L2 SVP: 5 DLU: 77

735.687-010 DIPPER (jewelry-silver.) alternate titles: etcher, enameling; washer-off

Immerses enameled jewelry, jewelry findings, and other articles in acid and water baths to clean them. Dries cleaned articles by placing them in sieve and exposing them to steam or hot air, placing them in oven, by rolling them in heated sawdust, or by placing them in centrifugal drier.

GOE: 06.04.39 STRENGTH: L GED: R2 M1 L1 SVP: 2 DLU: 77

735.687-014 LINKER (jewelry-silver.) alternate titles: linker-up; plier worker

Attaches links, trimmings, and findings to bracelets, necklaces, and pendant chains, using pointed pliers: Grips link with pliers, or positions link in slot of linking ring (screwhead soldered on ring). Twists link joint open with pliers. Slides finding, link, or trimming into open link and clinches link joint to close it. May refer to sketch to verify order of assembly. May cut chains or ribbons into specified lengths, using cutter. May attach glass beads to findings by threading end pin (piece of wire with head) through bead and opening in finding, and twisting or looping pin to hold bead in place. May hook metal links together and be designated Link Assembler (jewelry-silver.); or repair broken jewelry chains previously soldered, using handtools and gas torch, and be designated Chain Mender (jewelry-silver.).

GOE: 06.04.23 STRENGTH: S GED: R2 M1 L2 SVP: 3 DLU: 77

735.687-018 PAINTER (jewelry-silver.)

Brushes protective covering onto specified sections of jewelry articles to protect sections during electroplating, sandblasting, and polishing operations: Brushes or dabs lacquer or molten wax onto jewelry to prevent damage to coated areas during electroplating or sandblasting. Brushes shellac on sandblasted areas to protect areas during polishing. May correct plating defects, using paint and brush.

GOE: 06.04.33 STRENGTH: S GED: R2 M2 L2 SVP: 2 DLU: 77

735.687-022 PIN-OR-CLIP FASTENER (jewelry-silver.) alternate titles: finding fastener

Fastens pins and clips to jewelry items, such as brooches and earrings: Positions jewelry item between jaws of machine. Selects pin or clip and fits end of pin or clip into holes of jewelry item. Depresses pedal to close jaws and squeeze joints together. Inspects jewelry for defects and rejects defective pieces. May mount jewelry on cards [CARDER (any industry)].

GOE: 06.04.23 STRENGTH: S GED: R2 M1 L1 SVP: 2 DLU: 77

735.687-026 RACKER (jewelry-silver.)

Arranges pieces of jewelry in rows on wire screens, or fastens pieces to racks with clamps or fabricated hooks, preparatory to plating, degreasing, and enameling. May brush particles of foreign matter from pieces of jewelry preparatory to painting. May place painted jewelry in trays for inspection.

GOE: 06.04.34 STRENGTH: L GED: R1 M1 L1 SVP: 2 DLU: 77

735.687-030 SORTER (jewelry-silver.)

Sorts jewelry articles, such as pins, emblems, rings, and casting patterns for control and inventory purposes: Separates items by type, size, and style. Counts

and records total items in each separate grouping. Requests additional articles from production department when such items are needed to complete specified inventory levels. May maintain inprocess record controls of patterns during casting and processing of gold jewelry.

GOE: 06.03.02 STRENGTH: S GED: R2 M2 L2 SVP: 3 DLU: 77

735.687-034 STONE SETTER (jewelry-silver.)

Sets ornamental stones, such as pearls, rhinestones, and colored glass in metal or plastic jewelry articles by one of following methods: (1) Brushes paste or applies cement across settings or depressions in article or deposits glue in settings with pick. Places stone in each setting, using tweezers or other pickup tool. (2) Places stone in setting and presses prongs around stone with handtool. (3) Bores hole in setting, using hand drill. Inserts rivet in hole and hammers rivet ends flat. Positions stone in setting and presses rivet around stone with handtools. May paint decorations on article. May be designated according to method of setting stones as Pronger (jewelry-silver.); Stone Gluer (jewelry-silver.); or according to type of stone set as Pearl Hand (jewelry-silver.); Rhinestone Setter (jewelry-silver.).

GOE: 06.04.30 STRENGTH: S GED: R1 M1 L1 SVP: 2 DLU: 77

735.687-038 SWEDGER (jewelry-silver.)

Assembles costume jewelry, using foot press: Inserts prongs (rivets) of one finding into corresponding holes of another, and shapes findings with pliers to obtain fit. Positions findings under swedging (riveting) tool in press. Depresses pedal or moves lever to lower swedging tool that spreads and flattens prongs to combine findings.

GOE: 06.04.23 STRENGTH: L GED: R2 M1 L1 SVP: 2 DLU: 77

735.687-042 WIRE DRAWER (jewelry-silver.) alternate titles: roller

Forms wire of specified shape and diameter, preparatory to further processing in fabrication of jewelry articles, using either of following methods: (1) Draws bar of metal through successively smaller holes in hardened steel plate. (2) Feeds bar of metal into mill and turns crank to actuate rollers that compress metal in groove to produce round or square wire.

GOE: 06.04.24 STRENGTH: L GED: R2 M1 L1 SVP: 2 DLU: 77

736 OCCUPATIONS IN FABRICATION AND REPAIR OF ORDNANCE AND ACCESSORIES

This group includes occupations concerned with inspecting, fitting, assembling, and repairing small arms, repeating weapons, and related ordnance.

736.131-010 AUTOMOTIVE-TIRE-TESTING SUPERVISOR (ordnance)

Supervises and coordinates activities of workers engaged in testing durability of standard and bulletproof tires and inner tubes, caterpillar tracks, and bulletproof gas tanks for military vehicles, performing duties as described under SUPERVISOR (any industry) Master Title.

GOE: 06.01.01 STRENGTH: L GED: R4 M3 L3 SVP: 8 DLU: 77

736.131-014 FIREARMS-ASSEMBLY SUPERVISOR (ordnance)

Supervises and coordinates activities of workers engaged in assembling and packing firearms. May set up machines for tool tryout or prototype job to solve setup problem. Performs duties as described under SUPERVISOR (any industry) Master Title.

GOE: 06.04.01 STRENGTH: L GED: R4 M3 L3 SVP: 7 DLU: 77

736.131-018 INSPECTION SUPERVISOR I (ordnance)

Supervises and coordinates activities of workers engaged in inspecting firearms. Trains new workers. Performs duties as described under SUPERVISOR (any industry) Master Title.

GOE: 06.01.01 STRENGTH: L GED: R4 M3 L3 SVP: 7 DLU: 77

736.281-010 GUN EXAMINER (ordnance)

Examines small arms returned by customers for repair to determine causes of malfunctioning: Reads correspondence to ascertain request or complaint. Disassembles gun, using handtools. Examines components, and measures dimensions and clearances, using gauges, to detect malfunction. Test-fires guns to evaluate performance of loading, firing, ejection mechanisms, and accuracy of bore and sights. Prepares list of parts and repair operations required to restore function of weapon. Determines whether customer or company is responsible for malfunction and records information for subsequent billing. May replace worn or broken parts and be designated Gun Examiner And Repairer (ordnance).

GOE: 06.01.05 STRENGTH: M GED: R4 M3 L3 SVP: 6 DLU: 77

736.367-010 AUTOMOTIVE-TIRE TESTER (ordnance)

Tests pneumatic tires and tubes, bulletproof gasoline tanks, caterpillar tracks, and similar equipment to determine that they meet minimum specifications for use on military vehicles: Mounts ordinary pneumatic or bulletproof tires and tubes on tire-testing machines or on appropriate vehicles. Inflates tires to prescribed pressure and manipulates controls to operate machines and simulate driving conditions, or drives vehicles, observing indicators and noting tire conditions. Directs other workers in firing specified number of bullets into tires at specified places and in taking photographs of test results. Fills and weighs bulletproof gasoline tanks and directs other workers in firing bullets through tanks. Weighs pierced tanks to determine extent of gasoline loss. Mounts military tank tracks on special testing machines and manipulates controls to test tracks under induced conditions. Observes results and notes instrument read-

ings. Prepares reports indicating results of wear or bullet holes on material tested. Interprets test results, using charts and tables.
GOE: 06.03.01 STRENGTH: M GED: R4 M3 L4 SVP: 7 DLU: 77

736.381-010 ASSEMBLER I (ordnance) alternate titles: final assembler
Assembles and adjusts small arms parts to specifications and tests moving parts to detect malfunctions: Verifies dimensions of parts, using gauges. Screws, pins, and bolts parts together to assemble weapon, using handtools and power tools. Tests action of weapon to detect malfunctions. Disassembles weapon and files, scrapes, and reams parts to fit, using emery cloth, hand files, reamers, and bench grinder. May test-fire weapon, using dummy ammunition.
GOE: 06.02.23 STRENGTH: L GED: R3 M3 L2 SVP: 5 DLU: 77

736.381-014 FITTER, VENTILATED RIB (ordnance) alternate titles: rib matcher and fitter
Mounts and aligns ventilated (elevated) ribs to shotgun barrels to facilitate aiming: Selects and positions ribs to dovetailed posts on top of gun barrel. Mounts rib to barrel by dovetailing each rib slot and barrel post along barrel. Locks barrel in vise and measures height of rib at breech end, using pin gauge, to determine amount rear end post must be reduced to lower rib to specified height. Hammers and files post and squeezes rib slot, using handtools and fixtures, to fit rib post at specified height. Files and fits each rib slot to each post along barrel to align and level rib. Stamps identifying data on rib and barrel, using punches and hammer. Operates bench drill press to drill holes in barrel for retaining pins and sighting beads.
GOE: 06.02.24 STRENGTH: M GED: R3 M2 L2 SVP: 5 DLU: 77

736.381-018 PROCESS INSPECTOR (ordnance)
Inspects rocket motors, cases, and fuel mixtures for conformance with specifications and verifies standard work procedures and process conditions involved in loading rocket-motor cases with fuel: Weighs and records weights of fuel mixtures and ingredients on inspection reports. Observes fuel mixing, case preparation, and lining activities for conformity to specified procedures and records variations on inspection report. Observes and records weight of lined cases. Examines linings for voids, pockmarks, and other defects. Observes charts, meters, and gauges on casting-control console to verify conformity of process conditions to specifications and records readings. Correlates gauge readings to estimate flow of fuel pumped (cast) into motor case. Observes meters and charts on curing-control panel to verify specified process conditions in curing oven. Examines cured rocket motors for defects, such as voids in propellant, presence of foreign bodies, and paint defects on motor case.
GOE: 06.01.05 STRENGTH: L GED: R3 M2 L3 SVP: 6 DLU: 77

736.384-010 PROOF INSPECTOR (ordnance) alternate titles: proof tester; shooter
Fires small arms weapons to test loading, firing, and ejection mechanisms: Places gun in fixture of proof-shoot box, and loads it with ammunition. Fires gun specified number of times manually and by remote control to test its shock resistance and function of loading, firing, and extraction mechanisms. Examines gun and spent cartridges for indications of mechanical defects. Measures chamber and bore for conformance to specifications, using gauge. Records firing malfunctioning on tag, and routes gun to repair shop. May keep daily inspection records.
GOE: 06.03.01 STRENGTH: L GED: R3 M2 L2 SVP: 3 DLU: 77

736.387-010 INSPECTOR, ASSEMBLY (ordnance)
Inspects and tests small arm units during subassembly and assembly stages to ensure that mechanical action, finish, and assembly conform to specifications: Tests firearms for specified cocking and trigger action, using gauges. Examines wood and metal parts of weapons to detect flaws in finish. Pushes gauge through bore of gun to verify straightness of barrel. Measures dimensions and clearances of components to verify conformance with specifications, using gauges. Tests tightness of screws, bolts, and pins, using handtools. Records on tags firearms rejected and reasons. May be designated according to processing stage as Final Inspector (ordnance).
GOE: 06.03.01 STRENGTH: L GED: R3 M2 L2 SVP: 4 DLU: 77

736.387-014 PROOF-TECHNICIAN HELPER (ordnance) alternate titles: laboratory-mechanic helper
Tests and inspects small arms, artillery weapons, ammunition, and bombs for safety and quality control: Obtains sample ammunition from production lot for ballistic testing. Sets up targets on ranges. Fires weapons to determine mechanical function, accuracy, and velocity under variable conditions. Records number of defective pieces and sends them to laboratory for analysis. Cleans and maintains weapons used in testing.
GOE: 06.03.01 STRENGTH: H GED: R3 M2 L3 SVP: 4 DLU: 77

736.481-010 SIGHT MOUNTER (ordnance)
Attaches and adjusts telescopic and other special sights to shotguns and rifles: Locates and marks position for mounting holes, using scales and dividers. Operates drill press to drill and tap mounting holes and screws sights on barrel. Positions gun in holding fixture. Sights through bore and moves fixture to align gun with target. Turns setscrews on sight mount to align telescopic sight with fixed target. Routes gun for test firing.
GOE: 06.02.24 STRENGTH: L GED: R3 M3 L2 SVP: 5 DLU: 77

736.587-010 BARREL LOADER AND CLEANER (ordnance)
Loads automatic pistols and revolvers with cartridges for test firing and cleans and oils tested guns: Fills magazine or cylinder of weapon with specified type of ammunition. Unscrews retaining pin to remove cylinder or pulls magazine from test-fired guns and removes empty shells and live ammunition. Cleans cylinders and barrel with wire brush and swabs gun with oil. Stamps test mark on frame, using hammer and punch. Records number of firearms tested.
GOE: 06.04.34 STRENGTH: M GED: R2 M1 L1 SVP: 2 DLU: 77

736.684-010 ALIGNER, BARREL AND RECEIVER (ordnance)
Assembles and aligns rifle barrels and receivers, using handtools and power tools, using either of following methods: Mounts barrel in vise and screws receiver onto barrel, using wrench. (1) Positions assembled barrel and receiver in concentricity gauge and marks areas on barrel where metal must be removed or raised to bring barrel and receiver into alignment. Remounts barrel in vise, removes receiver, and scrapes metal from barrel shoulder, or peens receiver chamber, using hammer and peening tool to raise metal to form shim. Mounts sighting bars at each end of barrel, sights between bars, and twists receiver to align bars. (2) Positions assembled barrel and receiver in alignment gauge. Tightens receiver and barrel to adjust alignment according to dial gauge reading, using pneumatic gauge. May screw barrel into receiver to specified pressure, using torque wrench.
GOE: 06.02.23 STRENGTH: M GED: R3 M2 L1 SVP: 3 DLU: 77

736.684-014 ASSEMBLER II (ordnance) alternate titles: subassembler
Assembles small arms subassemblies, such as cartridge clips, triggers, ejectors, and bolts, using handtools and power tools: Drills, reams, countersinks, and polishes parts, using power tools. Screws, pins, bolts, and rivets parts to form subassembly. Straightens warped parts, using bench and handtools. Examines subassemblies for nicks, burrs, and machine marks, and verifies accuracy of assembly, using gauges. Smooths parts to remove defects and improve fit, using emery cloth and hand file.
GOE: 06.04.23 STRENGTH: L GED: R2 M1 L1 SVP: 3 DLU: 77

736.684-018 BARREL FINISHER (ordnance)
Smooths and polishes outside surfaces of shotgun barrels preparatory to bluing, using files, striker tools, and emery cloth: Positions and secures barrel in vise. Files off excess metal and surface blemishes, such as toolmarks, ripples, pits, and flat spots. Examines and feels surface of barrel to determine smoothness. Rubs barrel to obtain satin finish, using various grades of emery cloth. May secure barrel in filing jig and file with striker tool to taper breech end, using surface as guide. May remove excess solder from joints.
GOE: 06.04.24 STRENGTH: M GED: R2 M1 L2 SVP: 4 DLU: 77

736.684-022 BARREL REPAIRER (ordnance)
Repairs scratched or dented steel shotgun barrels, using handtools: Examines damaged barrel to determine salvageability. Positions and secures barrel in bench vise. Draws (stretches) metal from adjoining barrel surface to fill nicks, dents, and scratches by tapping edges with peening hammers. Smooths repaired area and removes blemishes, using handtools and emery cloth. Removes worn inscriptions, such as serial numbers and trademarks, using peening hammers, files, and scrapers. Replaces inscriptions, using punch dies and mallet [MARKER (ordnance)].
GOE: 05.10.01 STRENGTH: M GED: R2 M1 L1 SVP: 5 DLU: 77

736.684-026 BARREL STRAIGHTENER I (ordnance)
Straightens small arms barrels to remove bends and crooks, using either line or ring method: (1) Positions barrel in straightening press, sighting it toward frosted glass plate across which is drawn black horizontal line. Sights through barrel, noting two line-shadows cast longitudinally along interior by reflected light from frosted glass. Tightens jaws of press to bend barrel at points where shadows are not straight to straighten barrel (line method). (2) Positions barrel on special fixture. Sights through barrel toward light, noting position of three ring-shadows cast inside bore by light passing through ring scribed on smoked glass at far end of barrel (eccentric rings denote bend in barrel). Removes crooked barrel from fixture and strikes it with soft metal mallet against babbitt block to remove bend indicated by position of rings (ring method).
GOE: 06.02.24 STRENGTH: L GED: R3 M1 L2 SVP: 4 DLU: 77

736.684-030 FRONT-SIGHT ATTACHER (ordnance)
Attaches front sights to shotgun and rifle barrels: Secures barrel in vise and screws threaded shank of sight into hole near muzzle. Shears off excess shank extending into bore, using hammer and chisel. Files sheared end of shank with file until edge is smooth with inside of gun barrel. Feels sheared joint and sights through bore or inserts plug gauge into bore to verify smoothness. May drill and tap hole in barrel to accommodate front sight, using drill press and tap.
GOE: 06.04.23 STRENGTH: L GED: R2 M1 L1 SVP: 2 DLU: 77

736.684-034 GAS-CHECK-PAD MAKER (ordnance)
Makes gas-check pads of plastic and wire screening to be used in breechblocks of bag-loading cannons: Mixes specified quantity of ingredients, such as vaseline, powdered asbestos, and graphite in agitator to form puttylike substance. Presses specified amount of mixture between dies in hydrostatic press to form disk. Shapes brass wire screening into similar shape, using snips and soldering iron. Embeds wire in disk, using hydrostatic press. Coats pad with graphite paint and stencils identifying data on pad. Wraps pad in wax paper.
GOE: 06.02.32 STRENGTH: L GED: R3 M2 L2 SVP: 4 DLU: 77

736.684-038 SOLDERER, BARREL RIBS (ordnance)
Mounts and solders ribs to shotgun barrels to form double barrels and for use as aiming sight: Brushes flux onto shotgun barrels to prepare surface for

soldering. Files and fits dovetail butts of barrels together and hammers pin through holes in barrels to lock them together. Inserts spacers between barrels and mounts barrels in fixture. Aligns rib between barrels and drives wedges between rib and barrels to secure rib. Heats assembly in gas-fired oven to specified temperature for soldering. Melts and flows solder along adjoining edges of rib and barrels, using gas torch. Positions and secures barrels and sighting ribs in aligning fixture and solders ribs to barrels. Drills vent and bead holes in barrels, using bench drill. Places soldered barrels in wire basket and moves barrels through acid bath tanks and rinse water, using overhead hoist, to remove excess solder and flux.
GOE: 06.04.31 STRENGTH: L GED: R2 M1 L1 SVP: 3 DLU: 77

736.684-042 TARGETEER (ordnance) alternate titles: aligner; sighter
Fires small arms weapons at fixed targets to test accuracy of sights and mechanical functions of weapons: Positions target at specified distance. Mounts weapon on tripod, or mechanical rest. Aims weapon and fires series of shots at target. Examines target to determine shot pattern and accuracy of sight. Adjusts sights to attain specified accuracy, using handtools. Examines indentations on cartridge face to detect defective striking of firing pin. Records firing deficiencies on target or tag, and routes gun to repair shop.
GOE: 06.03.02 STRENGTH: L GED: R3 M1 L1 SVP: 3 DLU: 77

736.687-010 GREASER (ordnance) alternate titles: cleaner-greaser; oiler and packer, gun parts
Greases small arms and artillery pieces to prevent corrosion during shipment or storage: Coats parts with grease, using swabs and brushes, or dips parts into grease pot. May dismantle units, such as breech or firing mechanism to facilitate application of grease.
GOE: 05.12.08 STRENGTH: M GED: R1 M1 L1 SVP: 2 DLU: 77

736.687-014 INSPECTOR, BARREL (ordnance)
Tests shotgun and rifle barrel forging for straightness prior to machining: Places barrel on roller supports of test device. Positions stem of dial indicator against barrel. Rotates barrel and notes deflection of indicator needle. Rejects barrels which deflect needle beyond specified limits.
GOE: 06.03.02 STRENGTH: L GED: R2 M1 L2 SVP: 3 DLU: 77

736.687-018 INSPECTOR, LIVE AMMUNITION (ordnance)
Examines magazines and chambers of guns after final test firing to ensure removal of live ammunition. Records number and disposition of guns passing through department.
GOE: 06.03.02 STRENGTH: L GED: R1 M1 L1 SVP: 2 DLU: 77

737 OCCUPATIONS IN FABRICATION OF AMMUNITION, FIREWORKS, EXPLOSIVES, AND RELATED PRODUCTS

This group includes occupations concerned with assembling, loading, and inspecting small arms and artillery ammunition, bombs, mines, grenades, chemical warfare projectiles, flares, explosive charges, and related products. Occupations concerned with processing explosive chemicals are included in Division 55.

737.131-010 SUPERVISOR, FIREWORKS ASSEMBLY (chemical)
Supervises and coordinates activities of workers engaged in mixing powders and assembling parts to produce fireworks: Ignites fireworks and observes resultant sound and color to verify use of specified proportions and mixtures of powders. Prepares reports and discusses test results with production manager. May train new workers and set up machines and equipment to meet production requirements. Performs other duties as described under SUPERVISOR (any industry) Master Title. May be designated according to type of product manufactured or function supervised as Floatlight-Loading Supervisor (chemical); Incendiaries Supervisor (chemical); Pyrotechnic-Loading Supervisor (chemical).
GOE: 06.02.01 STRENGTH: M GED: R4 M2 L3 SVP: 7 DLU: 77

737.132-010 PRIMER SUPERVISOR (ordnance)
Supervises and coordinates activities of workers engaged in shaping, charging, foiling, and assembly of cartridge primers. Performs other duties as described under SUPERVISOR (any industry) Master Title.
GOE: 06.02.01 STRENGTH: L GED: R4 M2 L3 SVP: 7 DLU: 77

737.134-010 INSPECTION SUPERVISOR II (ordnance)
Supervises and coordinates activities of workers engaged in making final inspections of small-arms ammunition and artillery shells and cases: Determines from blueprints type and size of gauges or inspection instruments to be used. Examines rejected parts to ascertain whether they may be salvaged or scrapped. Consults with various department heads concerning the correction of defects attributed to malfunction of machines and equipment during manufacturing processes. Recommends improvements to companies supplying raw materials when tests indicate that their products have been the cause of defects. May train newly assigned workers. Performs other duties as described under SUPERVISOR (any industry) Master Title.
GOE: 06.01.01 STRENGTH: L GED: R4 M2 L3 SVP: 8 DLU: 77

737.137-010 INSPECTOR, CHIEF (ordnance)
Supervises and coordinates activities of personnel engaged in inspecting ammunition and ammunition components: Keeps records of storage and processing. Assigns subordinates to routine inspection of stores or processes. Studies

inspection reports and directs action to remedy unsafe conditions and to dispose of unserviceable materials. Performs other duties as described under SUPERVISOR (any industry) Master Title.
GOE: 06.01.01 STRENGTH: L GED: R4 M3 L3 SVP: 7 DLU: 77

737.137-014 POWDER-AND-PRIMER-CANNING LEADER (ordnance) alternate titles: primer-and-powder-canning leader
Supervises and coordinates activities of workers engaged in drying, canning, and storing cartridge primers and propellant powder for small-arms ammunition. Performs other duties as described under SUPERVISOR (any industry) Master Title.
GOE: 06.01.01 STRENGTH: L GED: R4 M3 L3 SVP: 8 DLU: 77

737.137-018 SUPERVISOR (ordnance)
Supervises and coordinates activities of workers engaged in manufacture, loading, assembly, drying, or storage of ammunition. Performs other duties as described under SUPERVISOR (any industry) Master Title. May inspect material or products to ensure compliance with manufacturing standards. May be designated according to activity supervised as Supervisor, Ammunition-Loading (ordnance); Supervisor, Powder-And-Primer-Canning (ordnance); Supervisor, Propellant-Charge-Loading (ordnance); Supervisor, Pyrotechnic-Loading (ordnance).
GOE: 06.02.01 STRENGTH: L GED: R4 M4 L3 SVP: 8 DLU: 77

737.137-022 SUPERVISOR, BELT-AND-LINK ASSEMBLY (ordnance) alternate titles: belt-and-link-shop supervisor
Supervises and coordinates activities of workers engaged in loading belts, chains, and clips with small-arms ammunition for automatic and semiautomatic weapons. Performs other duties as described under SUPERVISOR (any industry) Master Title.
GOE: 06.02.01 STRENGTH: L GED: R4 M3 L3 SVP: 8 DLU: 77

737.364-010 PROCESS CHECKER (ordnance) alternate titles: inspector, materials and processes
Inspects and tests small arms ammunition to verify conformance with variety of qualitative specifications: Collects quantity of cartridges or shotgun shells as they emerge from loading and assembling machines. Tests crimping of case around bullet, using bench device that registers force required to withdraw bullet from case. Cuts open shotgun shells to verify correct placement of wads, shot, and powder. Weighs powder from several individual shells on balance scale and computes average weight. Weighs shot pellet load from individual shell on shadowgraph scale and counts number of pellets in load, using pellet-counting device, and computes number of pellets per ounce; estimates average pellet size, using graduated device. Reports patterns in ammunition defects that indicate loading or assembly machine malfunctions or maladjustments to machine adjuster or supervisor. Records test results in tabular, graphic, or narrative form for quality control purposes.
GOE: 06.03.01 STRENGTH: L GED: R3 M3 L2 SVP: 3 DLU: 77

737.367-010 INSPECTOR III (ordnance)
Inspects ammunition, ammunition components, loading plants, and magazine areas to detect unsafe or unserviceable items and to enforce safety regulations: Inspects cartridges and other metallic items for corrosion or physical defects. Visually examines explosive components for deterioration, freedom of movement of parts, clearances between parts, and dimensions of specified parts, using measuring devices. Inspects physical condition of plant buildings and magazines for adequate safety equipment. Observes methods of storing and handling ammunition and actions of plant personnel for compliance with safety regulations. Inspects incoming and outgoing shipments for proper loading, bracing, and marking. Prepares reports on findings. May observe loading process for quality of production and observance of safety regulations. May supervise personnel engaged in salvage or destruction of unserviceable ammunition and explosives.
GOE: 06.03.01 STRENGTH: L GED: R4 M3 L3 SVP: 6 DLU: 77

737.381-010 ASSEMBLER, IGNITER (ordnance)
Assembles, tests, and packages rocket engine ignition charges, following written instructions and wiring diagrams: Sifts and weighs out specified quantities of propellant powder and pours it into container. Seals container with solder or adhesive to form igniter. Assembles main charge and igniter to form ignition cap. Stamps or marks identification on cap, using crayon. Attaches wires to terminal pins of ignition cap according to wiring diagram, using pliers, soldering iron, and screwdriver. Tests wiring for continuity, using continuity checker. Tests ignition cap for air leaks, using vacuum pump. Places tested caps on shipping tray, or seals them in moistureproof bag.
GOE: 06.02.23 STRENGTH: L GED: R3 M3 L3 SVP: 6 DLU: 77

737.387-010 DROP TESTER (ordnance)
Tests cartridge primers for sensitivity to impact by dropping weight onto sample primers from measured heights: Secures primer or primed cartridge case in test fixture and positions firing pin over primer. Raises steel ball in electromagnetic holder to specified height on calibrated column. Presses switch to cut power from electromagnet which drops ball onto firing pin in test fixture to detonate primer. Tests groups of primers from same production sample at several specified drop-heights, and records percentage of fires and misfires at each height. May plot test results on graph to develop primer sensitivity curve, or apply standardized statistical formulas to estimate sensitivity characteristics of entire production lot of primers.

GOE: 06.03.01 STRENGTH: L GED: R3 M3 L2 SVP: 3 DLU: 77

737.387-014 INSPECTOR I (ordnance)
Inspects interior and exterior of bomb and artillery shell components for defects: Visually examines components to detect defective material and work quality, such as cracks or incorrect size. Verifies accuracy of critical dimensions, using direct-reading electric limit gauge. Pressure-tests welded joints to ensure airtightness, using compressed air and soap solution. Tests strength of fitted and welded joints, using special hydraulic equipment.
GOE: 06.03.01 STRENGTH: M GED: R3 M2 L2 SVP: 5 DLU: 77

737.387-018 PRESSURE-TEST OPERATOR (ordnance)
Measures propellant force of powder charge by firing small arms cartridges and shotshells in pressure-testing device: Selects test barrel according to type and caliber of cartridge to be fired. Secures breech end of barrel in fixture containing breech-block, hammer, and firing pin, using handtools and gauges. Inserts *gas check* and steel piston into vent in barrel wall. Positions lead or copper slug of standard length on piston and tightens yoke-mounted setscrew which acts as anvil to secure it. Fires cartridge and measures compressed slug for reduction in length, using micrometer. Converts reduction in slug length to pressure expressed in pounds-per-square inch, using conversion chart. Computes average pressure for specified number of cartridges. May perform velocity tests on projectiles.
GOE: 06.03.01 STRENGTH: L GED: R3 M3 L2 SVP: 4 DLU: 77

737.487-010 PROPELLANT-CHARGE LOADER (ordnance)
Measures quantities of explosives and loads them into propellant charge bags: Measures approximate quantity of powder, using volumetric weighing machine. Weighs charge on scale. Verifies weight on second scale. Empties charge into charge bag. Sews opening together at top of bag, using sewing machine.
GOE: 06.04.34 STRENGTH: M GED: R2 M2 L2 SVP: 2 DLU: 77

737.587-010 BANDOLEER STRAIGHTENER-STAMPER (ordnance)
Prepares fabric bandoleer belts for packing with clips of small arms cartridges: Cuts open bundles of bandoleer belts, unfolds, straightens, examines stitching for imperfections, and counts them into lots of specified quantity. Stamps each belt with order and caliber data. Records number of belts counted and issued to BANDOLEER PACKERS (ordnance).
GOE: 06.04.37 STRENGTH: S GED: R1 M1 L1 SVP: 2 DLU: 77

737.587-014 FIREWORKS ASSEMBLER (chemical) alternate titles: pyrotechnic assembler
Performs any combination of following duties in assembling pyrotechnics (fireworks) and signal flares: Weighs specified quantities of powder or scoops powder into premeasured scooping device, and loads them into cans, cones, tubes, or other casings, or fills containers to predetermined level. Applies sealing compound to container from bulb syringe to seal in powder, or places cap or lid on container and secures them by crimping with machine or handtool. Drills or punches holes in caps or lids for insertion or attachment of fuse or wick. Attaches igniter ring atop open end of signal flares. Attaches and secures components of assemblies, using handtools. Inspects items at various stages of completion for inaccuracies in assembly and for obvious flaws. Packs specified number of flares or finished fireworks in cartons for storage or shipment. Stencils identifying information, such as type of firework, date of manufacture, and lot number, on assembled item or carton. May assemble cartons from flattened state, seal packed cartons, and attach shipping label onto carton.
GOE: 06.04.23 STRENGTH: L GED: R2 M1 L1 SVP: 2 DLU: 77

737.587-018 PRIMER BOXER (ordnance)
Fills linen boxes with charged primers for inspection or storage: Pours water into catch pan. Places sieve tray of primers over catch pan so excess primer mixture will fall through sieve into water as primers are moved about. Scoops primers from sieve, and pours them into box to specified height. Marks lot ticket and places it in box. Empties and scrubs catch pan.
GOE: 06.04.38 STRENGTH: L GED: R2 M1 L2 SVP: 2 DLU: 77

737.684-010 ASSEMBLER, MECHANICAL ORDNANCE (ordnance)
Assembles solid, liquid, or gas-powered mechanical and electromechanical torpedo engines according to drawings and specifications, using torque wrench and handtools: Reads instructions or drawings to plan assembly sequence. Positions basic workpiece on workbench or clamps workpiece in floor fixture. Lays out parts and subassembly elements required to assemble engine. Fits parts together and bolts or screws parts to basic workpiece in specified locations, using torque wrench and handtools. Colors each fitting after torque is applied, using felt tip pen. Verifies dimensions and clearances of parts to ensure conformance to written specifications, using preset gauges. Confirms operation of assembled unit, using air and water pressure test equipment. Requests inspector approval of assembled unit before proceeding to next assembly stage. Fits together subassemblies, such as fuel pumps and gear trains, according to drawings or instructions, using handtools, and bolts subassemblies to specified positions on unit.
GOE: 06.02.22 STRENGTH: M GED: R3 M3 L3 SVP: 3 DLU: 77

737.684-014 BOMB LOADER (ordnance)
Performs any combination of following tasks to load, assemble, and pack aerial bombs: Tends machine that loads and compresses thermite and explosive charges into steel noses of bombs. Assembles bombs by joining together component parts and sections, using handtools, cement, riveting machines, and jigs.

Spray-paints and tapes nose of bombs to seal perforations. Stamps identification numbers on bombs, using stamping machines. Binds cluster of bombs together with steel bands preparatory to packing to prevent accidental discharge. Packs clusters of bombs into moistureproof steel boxes, using chain hoist. Seals container lids with putty and packs loaded containers into wooden shipping crates, closing crates with hammer and nails. May be designated according to type of bomb loaded as Thermite-Bomb Loader (ordnance).
GOE: 06.02.22 STRENGTH: M GED: R3 M2 L2 SVP: 3 DLU: 77

737.684-018 FIREWORKS MAKER (chemical)
Makes bombs, fountains, colored lights, and set pieces for use as fireworks, following blueprints or pictures: Weighs, mixes, and sifts powder ingredients, according to formula, to produce various color and noise effects. Ignites portion of mixed ingredients to determine whether color meets specifications. Rams and pounds powder into casings or tubes, using wooden rods and mallet. Inspects fireworks for faulty wrapping or other defects and tests for sound by firing samples. Assembles and fastens together fireworks to form figures and scenes, using wire, cardboard, and handtools. May use previously prepared chemicals [MIXER (chemical) II].
GOE: 06.02.32 STRENGTH: M GED: R3 M1 L2 SVP: 6 DLU: 77

737.684-022 FUSE ASSEMBLER (ordnance)
Loads and assembles component parts of time and nose fuses, performing any combination of following tasks: Assembles essential portions of fuses, bolting and crimping parts together with press. Drills charge holes, using drill press. Loads parts with explosive charges, forcing them in place with semiautomatic hydraulic and pneumatic presses. Joins together various subassemblies with housing structure and screws or crimps them in place. Sets delay-action screw in place in time fuses and glues small disks of onionskin around screw to hold it firmly in place. Shellacks unprotected surfaces with brush.
GOE: 06.02.23 STRENGTH: L GED: R3 M2 L2 SVP: 3 DLU: 77

737.684-026 INSPECTOR, SALVAGE (ordnance) alternate titles: cartridge gauger; salvage-machine operator
Salvages rejected loaded cartridges, performing any combination of following tasks: Measures and weighs cartridges, using fixed and adjustable gauges and direct-reading shadowgraph scale, or feeds cartridges into gauge-and-weigh machine [GAUGE-AND-WEIGH-MACHINE OPERATOR (ordnance)] to verify rejection. Feeds cartridges into dial plate on automatic power press that straightens sides and deepens shoulders of cases or punches out defective primers. Positions cartridge in lathe chuck and moves lever to feed cutting tool to cut head diameter and cannelure to specified size. Inserts cartridge into fixture of machine that draws bullet from cartridge case. Dumps powder from cartridge and drops emptied case into chute.
GOE: 06.04.34 STRENGTH: L GED: R2 M2 L1 SVP: 2 DLU: 77

737.684-030 POWDER WORKER, TNT (ordnance)
Screens, melts, and pours TNT into projectile cases: Pours TNT powder into hopper of screening machine which reduces lumps by agitation. Pours powder into revolving steam-heated kettle and adjusts controls to permit steam to flow in pipes around kettle, heating and melting TNT. Empties melted explosive into buckets through valves. Tests temperature of TNT with thermometer and cools it to prescribed temperature, using power-operated paddle. Pours molten TNT into shell and bomb cases. Breaks off crystallized TNT scrap and returns it to melting pot. Drills threaded holes in charge into which boosters are loaded. Loads shells and bombs with TNT powder, pouring explosive into cases by hand and pressing powder down with hydraulic press.
GOE: 06.02.32 STRENGTH: M GED: R3 M2 L2 SVP: 4 DLU: 77

737.684-034 PRODUCTION ASSEMBLER (ordnance)
Performs any combination of following duties to assemble ordnance and related devices, such as fuses, detonators, flares, ammunition, primers, and projectile boosters: Weighs powder and chemicals, according to formula and places ingredients in mixer. Starts mixer and mixes powder with chemicals, and pours specified amount of mixture into cavity of ordnance device. Places ordnance unit under microscope, positions components to be connected according to diagram, and solders or welds parts together. Positions parts of device to be assembled in prescribed order and fastens parts together, using screws, bolts, and handtools.
GOE: 06.04.23 STRENGTH: L GED: R2 M2 L2 SVP: 3 DLU: 77

737.684-038 SHELL ASSEMBLER (ordnance)
Assembles component parts of artillery shells for shipment to loading arsenal: Lifts shells onto bench. Screws fuse plugs into base of shells, and adapters (reducing brushings pierced and threaded in center to receive fuses) into nose, using hand and pneumatic wrenches. Smears petroleum jelly onto unlacquered shell surfaces. Screws plugs into nosefuse holes. Cleans and reams threads. May lacquer shells and metal parts by brushing, spraying, or dipping.
GOE: 06.04.23 STRENGTH: M GED: R2 M1 L2 SVP: 5 DLU: 77

737.685-010 GAUGE-AND-WEIGH-MACHINE OPERATOR (ordnance)
Tends machine that gauges and weighs cartridges and examines cartridges for defects: Scoops handful of cartridges from bin and arranges them with heads in one direction. Rolls cartridges from hand to hand and examines them for such defects as dents, scratches, and missing or inverted primers. Places acceptable cartridges on inclined chute for gravity feeding into gauging and weighing mechanisms. Starts machine and observes operation to detect jamming. Removes misaligned cartridges from gravity chute, using special hook tool. Moves

lever to eject jammed cartridges. Notifies GAUGE-AND-WEIGH-MACHINE ADJUSTER (ordnance) of machine malfunction. May examine cartridges carried past work station in nests of rotating conveyor table and press button to drop out defective cartridges. May tend machine that gauges but does not weigh cartridges and be designated Gauging-Machine Operator (ordnance).
GOE: 06.03.02 STRENGTH: L GED: R2 M1 L2 SVP: 3 DLU: 77

737.685-014 SHAKER-PLATE OPERATOR (ordnance) alternate titles: loading-unit plate filler; plate filler
Tends machine that positions small arms cartridges or components in specially holed plates and inspects parts for conformance to standards: Places plate on shaker bed and scoops parts from hopper onto plate. Starts machine and spreads parts over oscillating plate by hand or with stick to fill depressions. Stops machine and shakes plate to invert parts not upended. Examines cartridges and components for defects, such as dents, burrs, scratches, and reversed or missing parts, using magnifying glass for minute parts. Removes defective parts, using tweezers, pick, or wax-tipped stick. Inverts parts, using transfer plate, to examine both ends. May record quantity of rejections according to type of defect. May shake parts through gauging screens to verify conformance to specified dimensions.
GOE: 06.03.02 STRENGTH: L GED: R2 M1 L2 SVP: 2 DLU: 77

737.685-018 WAX POURER (chemical)
Tends equipment that melts and pours paraffin into cardboard tubes in manufacture of signal flares: Scans invoice to determine number of flares required. Climbs ladder and dumps paraffin blocks into vat and activates heating element to melt paraffin. Observes temperature gauge to determine when melting point is reached and looks into vat to verify liquid condition of paraffin. Turns valve to allow gravity-fed liquid paraffin to flow into pressure vat. Adjusts pressure vat controls to prescribed setting and flips switch to activate heating element. Places flare tube in rack with open end up and examines closed end for openings. Squeezes sealant into tubes to seal defective closed ends. Positions racked tubes under spout and depresses treadle to fill tubes with specified amount of paraffin. Advances each row of tubes under spout until all tubes are filled with paraffin. Carries racked tubes to next work station. Scrapes paraffin residue from worktable, using scraper. Maintains production records.
GOE: 06.04.19 STRENGTH: M GED: R2 M1 L1 SVP: 2 DLU: 77

737.687-010 ASSEMBLER (ordnance)
Performs any combination of following duties to assemble fittings on fragmentation bombs: Wipes nose-adapter threads with cloth and solvent. Dries adapter, using airhose. Coats interior threads of adapters with thin layer of grease. Brushes nose-plug threads with fast-drying paint, and screws plug into adapter. Screws adapter into nose section of bomb. Attaches components of fin-stabilizer unit to bomb, using pliers and wire.
GOE: 06.04.23 STRENGTH: L GED: R2 M1 L1 SVP: 2 DLU: 77

737.687-014 BAG LOADER (ordnance)
Loads ammunition charge bags with previously weighed quantities of powder: Receives cup containing powder from CHECK WEIGHER (ordnance). Inserts funnel into bag opening. Pours charge into bag through funnel, shaking bag to settle powder.
GOE: 06.04.36 STRENGTH: M GED: R1 M1 L1 SVP: 1 DLU: 77

737.687-018 BLASTING-CAP ASSEMBLER (ordnance) alternate titles: electric-blasting-cap assembler
Performs any combination of following duties to assemble blasting caps: Dips lengths of wire into insulating compound and wraps them with cloth tape. Cuts wires in cutting machine. Inserts wires, having short piece of platinum wire soldered to one end, into fiber plug. Seals plug with fiber disk.
GOE: 06.04.23 STRENGTH: L GED: R2 M1 L1 SVP: 2 DLU: 77

737.687-022 BOOSTER ASSEMBLER (ordnance)
Assembles elements of explosive shell boosters, performing any combination of following duties: Places cushion disks in bottoms of booster cups. Stamps cooper washers with identifying data and glues onionskin disks over holes. Puts together parts of releasing mechanism (rotors) and assembles them with stamped washers and housings (body pieces) to complete boosters. Gauges overall length of completed units, using snap gauges.
GOE: 06.04.23 STRENGTH: L GED: R2 M2 L1 SVP: 2 DLU: 77

737.687-026 CHECK WEIGHER (ordnance)
Weighs each cup containing powder charge again after weighing by SHADOWGRAPH-SCALE OPERATOR (ordnance) to ascertain its adherence to specifications. Returns cups of inexact weight to original SHADOWGRAPH-SCALE OPERATOR (ordnance) to be check-weighed for third time. Passes satisfactory charges on to BAG LOADER (ordnance).
GOE: 06.03.02 STRENGTH: S GED: R1 M1 L1 SVP: 2 DLU: 77

737.687-030 CORE LOADER (ordnance)
Loads dumbbell-shaped ammunition charge bags (cores) with black powder: Fills hopper of air-powered filling machine with black powder. Blows powder into one end of bag by inserting machine feedpipe through hole in handle of bag and moving controls to blow powder into end. Removes bag from pipe and reinserts pipe into bag so that pipe faces unfilled end of bag. Moves controls to fill empty end of bag with powder. Stops up hole in handle with clamp.
GOE: 06.04.36 STRENGTH: L GED: R1 M1 L1 SVP: 1 DLU: 77

737.687-034 DEMOLITION SPECIALIST (ordnance)
Disposes of explosive wastes and rejected powder-charged products in accordance with established safety regulations: Collects explosive wastes, rejected

ordnance devices, and products saturated with explosive materials from production areas in containers. Sorts material by type and places material in rubber containers. Pours water or other counteracting agents into containers to neutralize material and places material in open area until disposal. Stores rejected products in bunkers. Loads truck with waste, transports, and positions waste in specified manner for disposal. Sets fire to waste products and materials and ensures complete destruction of all items.
GOE: 05.12.03 STRENGTH: H GED: R2 M1 L1 SVP: 4 DLU: 77

737.687-038 DETONATOR ASSEMBLER (ordnance)
Loads and assembles component parts of shell detonators, performing any combination of following duties: Loads detonator cup with explosives, such as black powder and tetryl, using power press. Inserts loaded cup in detonator holder and screws holder into detonator head. Assembles head with activating mechanisms that start explosion of shell when it strikes. Gauges completed detonator for length.
GOE: 06.04.23 STRENGTH: L GED: R2 M1 L1 SVP: 2 DLU: 77

737.687-042 EXPLOSIVE OPERATOR I (ordnance)
Unloads, cleans, and reloads defective assemblies and component parts of high-explosive shells and bombs: Removes fuses with wrench, working behind protective barriers. Washes out explosive charges with water, destroying or salvaging explosive. Removes paint and grease from shells and bombs, using chemicals and shot-blast machine. Disassembles shells and bombs for inspection. Makes minor alterations in shape and size, using engine lathe. Assembles and paints components. Reloads bombs and shells with high explosives [EXPLOSIVE OPERATOR (ordnance) II].
GOE: 06.04.34 STRENGTH: L GED: R2 M2 L2 SVP: 3 DLU: 77

737.687-046 EXPLOSIVE OPERATOR II (ordnance)
Performs any combination of following tasks, which require a working knowledge of open explosives, concerned with manufacturing, assembling, and loading of fuses, detonators, primers, boosters, shells, and bags: Weighs, blends, and pours explosives into containers, compressing powder into pellets, screwing together threaded parts of shells, and checking dimensions of ammunition. May be designated according to type of explosive manufactured as Explosive Operator, Bomb (ordnance); Explosive Operator, Fuse (ordnance); Explosive Operator, Grenade (ordnance).
GOE: 06.04.34 STRENGTH: L GED: R2 M2 L2 SVP: 2 DLU: 77

737.687-050 IGNITER CAPPER (ordnance)
Ties protective cotton cap over igniter end of propellant charge. Ties tag containing identifying data to charge.
GOE: 06.04.34 STRENGTH: L GED: R1 M1 L1 SVP: 1 DLU: 77

737.687-054 INSPECTOR II (ordnance)
Examines shell and bomb explosive assemblies, such as time fuses, nose fuses, delay-action detonators, and relays, to determine their conformity to specifications: Inspects time fuses and nose fuses, observing packing of charge for firmness, tests action of plunger and restraining spring for freedom of movement, examines wiring for defective soldered connections, and examines shaping of metal. Tests interrupter action in revolving chuck. Gauges boosters for body length and lockpin length. Inspects detonators, relays, and primers, using magnifying glass to examine loading. Observes wet primers for evenness of charge. Reads data stamped on assemblies or on tag attached to assemblies to ensure that data is legible and complete.
GOE: 06.03.02 STRENGTH: L GED: R3 M2 L2 SVP: 4 DLU: 77

737.687-058 INSPECTOR, BULLET SLUGS (ordnance)
Examines bullet slugs or cores for defects to ensure conformance to specifications: Rolls slugs or cores by hand across bench, scoops slugs or cores onto moving belt for inspection as they pass by, or aligns them on grooved inspection plate by pushing plate into pile of slugs or cores and shaking plate to remove excess. Examines slugs or cores for defects, such as pits, burrs, and fins. Picks out defective slugs or cores with fingers or wax-tipped stick and drops them into scrapbox.
GOE: 06.03.02 STRENGTH: L GED: R2 M1 L2 SVP: 3 DLU: 77

737.687-062 INSPECTOR, FIREWORKS (chemical)
Inspects and tests assembled and partially assembled pyrotechnics (fireworks): Examines parts for defects, such as nicks, cracks, or holes. Screws standard test piece on threaded parts to determine acceptable fit and alignment. Verifies component dimensions for conformance to specifications, using fixed gauge. Segregates defective assemblies for reconstruction, salvage, or further analysis. May be designated according to part inspected as Firing-Pin Gauger (chemical); Pellet-Post Inspector (chemical).
GOE: 06.03.02 STRENGTH: L GED: R2 M1 L2 SVP: 3 DLU: 77

737.687-066 INSPECTOR, SHELLS (ordnance)
Inspects cartridge cases and bullet jackets for defects, such as burrs, dents, discolorations, and scratches, as they pass along conveyor or are held in frames. Removes defective cases and jackets by hand. May measure samples to verify specified dimensions, using fixed gauges. May inspect bullet jackets and cores at various stages of manufacture to ensure compliance with production specifications.
GOE: 06.03.02 STRENGTH: L GED: R2 M2 L1 SVP: 2 DLU: 77

737.687-070 LABORER, AMMUNITION ASSEMBLY I (ordnance)
Assembles component parts of tracer shells, signals, flares, and other pyrotechnics, performing any combination of following tasks: Loads relays (devices

for transferring ignition sequence to various charges in shell) with black powder pellets. Tends press that pushes powder charge tightly into relay. Assembles and loads mine fuses with red phosphorous and black powder. Installs relays in shells and screws them in place. Loads shells with tracer powder, tamps pellets with automatic press, and seals chamber with celluloid disk. May cut and sew silk to assist in making of signal flare parachutes.
GOE: 06.04.23 STRENGTH: M GED: R2 M1 L1 SVP: 3 DLU: 77

737.687-074 LABORER, AMMUNITION ASSEMBLY II (ordnance)
Assembles and packs complete rounds of ammunition (projectile and cartridge), performing any combination of following tasks: Greases threads on fuses and starts them into threaded fuse sockets. Screws fuses into place, using screw press. Places primers in cartridge cases and stamps them in place, using press. Weighs and inserts propellants into cartridge cases. Brushes band of adhesive compound around base of projectile to seal cartridge. Gauges completed shells, using simple acceptance jigs. Stamps shell data on cartridge, using rubber stamp or stamping machine. Packs completed rounds in cardboard tubes. Stamps shell data on tubes, dips tubes in molten paraffin, and packs tubes in crates. Screws pierced and threaded plugs into bases of aerial bombs. Screws rod-supporting fin assembly into threaded hole in plug. Slips metal sleeves about bombs and packs them in metal containers, attaching tags with identification data to containers.
GOE: 06.04.34 STRENGTH: M GED: R2 M1 L1 SVP: 2 DLU: 77

737.687-078 LACQUER-PIN-PRESS OPERATOR (ordnance)
Deposits drop of lacquer inside cartridge primer cup to seal in anvil and foil paper and to waterproof primer charge, using hand powered bench device (lacquer-pin press): Pulls lever to lower pin plate of press to dip tips of pins into tray of lacquer. Positions plate containing assembled primer cups in fixture beneath lacquer-tipped pins. Pulls lever to lower pin plate and deposit lacquer in primers. Places primer-filled plate in hot air oven to dry lacquer. Empties lacquer from tray into waste can at prescribed intervals and refills tray from supply can.
GOE: 06.04.33 STRENGTH: L GED: R1 M1 L1 SVP: 1 DLU: 77

737.687-082 MANUAL-PLATE FILLER (ordnance)
Positions parts for small arms ammunition in specially holed plates or frames for inspection, assembly, or further processing: Scoops parts onto plate or frame, spreads them over surface, and shakes frame manually to arrange parts in holes or indentations, open ends up. Positions with fingers parts that are not seated during shaking.
GOE: 06.04.24 STRENGTH: L GED: R1 M1 L1 SVP: 2 DLU: 77

737.687-086 MERCURY-CRACKING TESTER (ordnance)
Examines completed cartridge case for cracks: Cleans cases by dipping them in solution of nitric acid and rinsing them in water. Dips cases into mercurous nitrate solution. Heats chemically treated cases over flame and examines cases for discolorations, indicative of cracks. Discards defective cases.
GOE: 06.03.02 STRENGTH: L GED: R1 M1 L1 SVP: 2 DLU: 77

737.687-090 MIXER II (chemical)
Weighs and mixes chemicals according to formula for use as explosive ingredients in pyrotechnics (fireworks): Examines chemicals to ensure that color and texture conform to specifications. Weighs prescribed quantities of chemicals. Rubs powdered chemicals through screens to obtain specified fineness. Mixes screened powders to obtain uniform blend. May dump powdered chemicals onto stone table, blend them with linseed oil, using roller, and mix blended material with additional chemicals by machine. May tend tumbling machine to obtain finer powders. May cure and dry mixture. May be designated according to type of powder mixed as Floatlight-Powder Mixer (chemical); Incendiary-Powder Mixer (chemical); Photoflash-Powder Mixer (chemical); Pyrotechnic Mixer (chemical); Starter-Cup-Powder Mixer (chemical).
GOE: 06.04.34 STRENGTH: H GED: R2 M2 L2 SVP: 2 DLU: 77

737.687-094 PACKER-FUSER (chemical)
Assembles and packs pyrotechnic devices: Packs designated number of sparklers of specified color in carton, discarding defective sparklers. Perforates other pyrotechnic devices, such as firecrackers and display cones, with awl or knife to permit insertion of wick. Dips wick in glue and inserts wick in hole. Wraps device in paper and packs device for storage or shipment.
GOE: 06.04.38 STRENGTH: L GED: R1 M1 L1 SVP: 1 DLU: 77

737.687-098 PRIMER ASSEMBLER (ordnance)
Loads and assembles component parts of wet and dry bomb and shell primers, performing any combination of following tasks: Loads primer cups with explosives, using power presses to seat explosive. Loads other primer parts with explosives. Assembles primer cups with rings and washers and rolls assembly on cloth soaked with gluelike explosive compound. Inserts primer in holder and presses it in place so that compound sticks. Crimps primer in place with press.
GOE: 06.04.23 STRENGTH: M GED: R2 M1 L1 SVP: 3 DLU: 77

737.687-102 PRIMER CHARGER (ordnance) alternate titles: cup filler
Fills small arms ammunition primer cups with dry or wet priming mixture, using one of following methods: (1) Positions specially holed plate filled with primer cups in fixture beneath charging plate. Dumps dry powder on charging plate and rubs it into holes, using rubber spreading tool. Pushes levers to retract retaining plate between charging plate and cup plate, to start pneumatic vibrator that shakes powder into primer cups. (2) Dumps wet mixture onto charging plate, kneads it into holes and scrape off excess with rubber blade. Super-

imposes powder-filled plate over cup-filled plate and punches mixture into primer cups, using knock out fixture. May operate varnish pin-press [LACQUER-PIN-PRESS OPERATOR (ordnance)] and foiling-tamping press [FOILING-MACHINE OPERATOR (ordnance)].
GOE: 06.04.34 STRENGTH: M GED: R2 M1 L1 SVP: 3 DLU: 77

737.687-106 PRIMER INSPECTOR (ordnance)
Examines cartridge primers for defects, such as lack of powder or improperly inserted anvil. Removes faulty primers with tweezers or wax-tipped stick. May fill specially holed boards with primers, using shaker machine [SHAKER-PLATE OPERATOR (ordnance)], or pour primers into boxes for transfer to subsequent operations. May use magnifying glass to examine primers.
GOE: 06.03.02 STRENGTH: L GED: R2 M1 L2 SVP: 3 DLU: 77

737.687-110 PROPELLANT-CHARGE-ZONE ASSEMBLER (ordnance)
Assembles and ties together charge bags loaded with explosives: Lifts bags from barrels and positions them on bench. Joins and secures four tying straps over top of assembly. Slips circumference gauge over completed charge zone to determine that size of charge is within prescribed limits.
GOE: 06.04.23 STRENGTH: M GED: R2 M1 L1 SVP: 3 DLU: 77

737.687-114 SALVAGER I (ordnance)
Inspects machinegun ammunition links for machining defects: Visually inspects links for burrs, dents, and other obvious defects. Checks links with fixed gauges and dial indicator gauges for accuracy of dimensions. Places acceptable links in container and defective links in another for salvage.
GOE: 06.03.02 STRENGTH: L GED: R3 M1 L2 SVP: 4 DLU: 77

737.687-118 SALVAGER II (ordnance)
Inspects, tests, and reclaims discarded parts of explosive shells, such as fuses, boosters, and detonators in manufacturing plant, using micrometers, measuring instruments, and knowledge of blueprints to determine salvage value of materials.
GOE: 06.03.02 STRENGTH: L GED: R3 M2 L2 SVP: 3 DLU: 77

737.687-122 SCREW-EYE ASSEMBLER (ordnance)
Screws metal eyes into threaded holes inside bottom of artillery cartridge cases to form anchor, to which ammunition bags are tied and held within case.
GOE: 06.04.23 STRENGTH: L GED: R1 M1 L1 SVP: 1 DLU: 77

737.687-126 SHADOWGRAPH-SCALE OPERATOR (ordnance)
Weighs powder charges on scale, which uses shadow of a needle as indicator: Receives container, holding powder charge and weighs container. Adds or removes quantities of powder to secure exact quantity of charge.
GOE: 06.03.02 STRENGTH: S GED: R2 M1 L2 SVP: 2 DLU: 77

737.687-130 SHELLACKER (ordnance)
Brushes shellac over foil that will be stamped into small disks and used to seal powder in cartridge primer cups. Prepares solution by dissolving shellac in solvent and straining mixture. Hangs coated strips on rack to dry. May cut foil into strips.
GOE: 06.04.33 STRENGTH: L GED: R2 M1 L1 SVP: 3 DLU: 77

737.687-134 TAPPER, HAND (ordnance)
Places empty artillery cartridge cases on table and cuts threads in two previously drilled holes on inside surface for insertion of screw eyes by SCREW-EYE ASSEMBLER (ordnance), using handtap.
GOE: 06.04.24 STRENGTH: M GED: R1 M1 L1 SVP: 1 DLU: 77

737.687-138 VARNISHING-UNIT OPERATOR (ordnance)
Varnishes or lacquers heads and mouths of cartridge cases to make waterproof seal between heads and primers and between cartridge mouths and bullets: Positions varnishing plate over plate of cartridge cases and inverts to transfer cases to varnishing plate. Positions plate of cases in fixture of manually powdered varnishing device. Moves levers to dip upper and lower blocks of pins to reservoirs of varnish and then onto primers and into mouths of cases. Wipes excess varnish from cases with cloth and examines them for completeness of coverage. Sets plate of cases on air blower screen to dry.
GOE: 06.04.33 STRENGTH: L GED: R2 M1 L1 SVP: 2 DLU: 77

739 OCCUPATIONS IN FABRICATION AND REPAIR OF PRODUCTS MADE FROM ASSORTED MATERIALS, N.E.C.

This group includes occupations, not elsewhere classified, concerned with fabricating and repairing products from assorted materials.

739.130-010 SUPERVISOR, BIT AND SHANK DEPARTMENT (fabrication, nec)
Supervises and coordinates activities of workers engaged in sawing, shaping, and fitting bits and shanks of smoking pipes: Informs workers engaged in sawing operations of changes in style and number of stummels to saw for each style. Determines from production schedule quantity and style of bits to be bent, and number of each style bit needed. Inspects stummels and bits at each work station to ensure conformance to company standards. Sets up machines. Performs other duties as described under SUPERVISOR (any industry) Master Title.
GOE: 06.02.01 STRENGTH: L GED: R4 M3 L3 SVP: 7 DLU: 77

739.131-010 SUPERVISOR I (fabrication, nec)
Supervises and coordinates activities of workers engaged in cutting, sewing, tacking, and tipping umbrellas: Observes machine operations to detect mal-

functioning equipment. Repairs or adjusts equipment, using handtools. May train new employees. May cut patterns from cardboard, according to sketches or customer's specifications. Performs other duties as described under SUPERVISOR (any industry) Master Title.
GOE: 06.02.01 STRENGTH: L GED: R4 M2 L3 SVP: 7 DLU: 77

739.131-014 SUPERVISOR II (fabrication, nec)
Supervises and coordinates activities of workers engaged in fabricating, finishing, sanding, painting, and decorating plastic and papier mache mannequins and display structures. Inspects work at various stages of production to ensure conformance to plant standards. Performs duties as described under SUPERVISOR (any industry) Master Title.
GOE: 01.06.02 STRENGTH: L GED: R4 M2 L3 SVP: 7 DLU: 77

739.132-010 SUPERVISOR, CORNCOB PIPE MANUFACTURING (fabrication, nec)
Supervises and coordinates activities of workers engaged in making corncob pipes: Trains workers in operation of machines used to cut, shape, bore, and smooth corncob pipe bowls. Directs maintenance workers in repair of machinery. Records personnel and production data. May supervise workers packing and shipping pipes. Performs other duties as described under SUPERVISOR (any industry) Master Title.
GOE: 06.02.01 STRENGTH: L GED: R3 M2 L3 SVP: 6 DLU: 78

739.134-010 SUPERVISOR, ASSEMBLY ROOM (fabrication, nec)
Supervises and coordinates activities of workers engaged in assembling caskets: Inspects caskets for fit of assembled parts and overall appearance to determine conformance to company standards. Trains workers in assembly of caskets. May mix glue with water or steam. Performs duties as described under SUPERVISOR (any industry) Master Title.
GOE: 06.04.01 STRENGTH: L GED: R4 M3 L3 SVP: 7 DLU: 77

739.134-014 SUPERVISOR, DISPLAY FABRICATION (fabrication, nec)
Supervises and coordinates activities of workers engaged in fabricating smoking pipe displays: Studies sketches to determine patterns necessary for fabrication or to devise procedure to be used in absence of patterns. Verifies setup of woodworking machines, using tape ruler and information from sketch or pattern. Supervises work of DISPLAY FABRICATOR (fabrication, nec) 860.684-022. Constructs model displays, using handtools, sketch, and woodworking machines, such as bandsaw and variety saw. Performs other duties as described under SUPERVISOR (any industry) Master Title.
GOE: 06.04.01 STRENGTH: M GED: R4 M3 L3 SVP: 7 DLU: 86

739.137-010 ASSEMBLY SUPERVISOR (any industry)
Supervises and coordinates activities of workers engaged in assembling parts or assemblies into units, such as carburetors, refrigerators, vacuum cleaners, electric motors, or vending machines, applying knowledge of assembly process, tools, equipment, products, and production methods. Reports machine and equipment malfunctions to maintenance personnel. Performs duties as described under SUPERVISOR (any industry) Master Title.
GOE: 06.02.01 STRENGTH: L GED: R4 M2 L3 SVP: 7 DLU: 77

739.137-014 SUPERVISOR, LAMP SHADES (fabrication, nec)
Supervises and coordinates activities of workers engaged in cutting silk, parchment, and fiberglass from lampshade patterns, attaching shades to metal frames, applying trimmings to shades, and wrapping and packing completed lampshades. Performs other duties as described under SUPERVISOR (any industry) Master Title.
GOE: 06.02.01 STRENGTH: L GED: R4 M2 L2 SVP: 7 DLU: 77

739.137-018 SUPERVISOR, PIPE MANUFACTURE (fabrication, nec)
Supervises and coordinates activities of workers engaged in patching, sanding, staining, or polishing smoking pipes: Interprets job requirements and schedules processing to meet requirements. Routes defective pipes to designated workers for repair. Specifies formulas to be mixed and used to patch, stain, varnish, and lacquer pipes. Observes pipes at various stages of patching, sanding, or finishing to ensure conformance to standards. Performs other duties as described under SUPERVISOR (any industry) Master Title. May be designated according to activity supervised as Supervisor, Dyeing And Finishing Department (fabrication, nec); Supervisor, Patching Department (fabrication, nec); Supervisor, Sanding Department (fabrication, nec).
GOE: 06.04.01 STRENGTH: L GED: R4 M3 L3 SVP: 7 DLU: 78

739.137-022 SUPERVISOR, WALL MIRROR DEPARTMENT (glass products)
Supervises and coordinates activities of workers engaged in assembly, inspection, and packing wall and furniture mirrors: Orders specified size, type, and quantity of mirror, frames, backs, hardware, and packing cartons required to meet production schedules. Patrols work area and examines items on production line to ensure conformity to specifications. Trains new workers in job duties. Performs other duties as described under SUPERVISOR (any industry) Master Title.
GOE: 06.02.01 STRENGTH: L GED: R3 M3 L3 SVP: 5 DLU: 77

739.261-010 EXHIBIT BUILDER (museums) alternate titles: exhibition specialist; exhibit technician; museum craft worker; experimental-display builder; model maker
Constructs and installs museum exhibit structures, electric wiring, and fixtures of materials, such as wood, plywood, and fiberglass, using handtools and power tools: Studies sketches or scale drawings for temporary or permanent display or exhibit structures, such as framework, fixtures, booths, or cabinets to determine type, amount, and cost of material needed. Confers with exhibit planning and art personnel to discuss structural feasibility of plans and to suggest alternate methods of displaying objects in exhibit. Cuts, assembles, and fastens parts to construct framework, panels, shelves, and other exhibit components of specified materials, using handtools and power tools. Sprays or brushes paint, enamel, varnish, or other finish on structures, or creates special effects by applying finish with cloth, sponge, or fingers to prepare structure for addition of fittings. Mounts fittings and fixtures, such as shelves, panelboards, and shadowboxes to framework, using handtools or adhesives. Installs electrical wiring, fixtures, apparatus, audiovisual components, or control equipment in framework, according to design specifications. Installs or affixes murals, photographs, mounted legend materials, and graphics in framework or on fixtures. Assembles, installs, or arranges structures in exhibit galleries working with maintenance and installation personnel. Tests electrical, electronic, and mechanical components of exhibit structure to verify operation. May maintain inventory of building materials, tools, and equipment, and order supplies as needed for construction of exhibit fixtures. May assign duties to and supervise work of carpentry, electrical, and other craftworkers engaged in constructing and installing exhibit components. May assist in placement of display accessories and collection objects or specimens. May be designated according to speciality as Exhibit Carpenter (museums); Exhibit Electrician (museums); or job location as Planetarium Sky Show Technician (museums); Science Center Display Builder (museums).
GOE: 01.06.02 STRENGTH: M GED: R4 M4 L4 SVP: 7 DLU: 86

739.281-010 PACKAGING TECHNICIAN (paper goods)
Lays out, fabricates, assembles, and tests samples of corrugated paperboard and plastic containers: Sketches design details or makes scale drawings of containers used for shipping, protecting, or displaying items, indicating construction dimensions, using drawing instruments and shipping requirements. Lays out dimensions of container on paperboard, cuts along specified lines with knife or saw and assembles sample container, using adhesive or staples. Lays out dimensions of production templates for cartons and cuts out templates, using power tools. Cuts out specified plastic parts, using handtools and power tools. Tests ability of container to withstand shipping requirements, using strain, strength, and stress test equipment. Records results of tests.
GOE: 06.01.04 STRENGTH: M GED: R4 M3 L3 SVP: 6 DLU: 77

739.281-014 ULTRASONIC TESTER (any industry)
Conducts ultrasonic tests on fabricated metallic and nonmetallic parts and products to identify discontinuities: Reviews work orders, test procedure sheets, and product acceptance criteria to determine test specifications. Attaches specified crystal probe transducer to ultrasound test device and moves switch to actuate device. Calibrates and adjusts ultrasonic test equipment to required standards and settings, applying knowledge of ultrasonic testing procedures. Sprays couplant (light oil which acts as medium) or other liquid over part to be tested, moves transducer over part to be tested, and observes CRT (cathode ray tube) screen to detect patterns of discontinuity, such as cracks, inclusions, bonding defects, or porosity. Marks defective areas of part or product and prepares report of test findings. May set up and operate computerized inspection equipment.
GOE: 05.07.01 STRENGTH: M GED: R4 M3 L3 SVP: 6 DLU: 90

739.361-010 DISPLAY MAKER (fabrication, nec)
Designs, fabricates, assembles, or installs displays, exhibits, and models of point-of-sale displays: Designs displays or exhibits from pictures or sketches or according to verbal instructions from customer. Lays out, cuts, shapes, and finishes wood, plastic, plexiglass, sheet metal, and hardboard parts of displays, using woodworking machines, metal machines, and handtools, according to drawings or blueprints. Cuts glass to specified shape with glasscutter. Assembles parts with nails, screws, bolts, and glue, using handtools. Confers with designer, customer, or salesperson regarding refinements, additions, and adjustments. May disassemble display to make working drawings for production run and to produce estimates for accounting and sales departments. Reassembles display and sends it to prospective customer. May wire display for illumination, audio, or video. May travel and set up display on designated site. May specialize in making diorama models and be designated Diorama Model-Maker (fabrication, nec).
GOE: 01.06.02 STRENGTH: M GED: R4 M4 L3 SVP: 7 DLU: 77

739.381-010 CANVAS WORKER (ship-boat mfg.; tex. prod., nec)
Lays out canvas, plastic, rubber, and other materials and fabricates and assembles material into sails, awnings, tents, and tarpaulins: Lays out full scale drawings on sail loft floor, according to blueprints or sketches, using chalk. Cuts pattern from paper according to full scale drawing. Marks outline on material with crayon. Cuts material with shears or power cutter. Sews sections of material together on power sewing machine. Installs grommets, metal fittings, and fasteners by machine. When hand-sewing grommets, measures and marks off grommet holes on material, punches holes, using mallet, punch, and hardwood block, and sews galvanized iron ring to edge of hole, using sailmaker's palm and sail twine. Splices, inserts, and hems manila or wire rope in edges to relieve strain or sews rope at points where sail is attached to boom or mast. Secures rope or cable to finished article. Wraps and sews parts of rope or wire that are subject to chafing. Installs and adjusts completed product on shipboard. Examines completed sails for conformance to specifications. May make awning

frames [AWNING-FRAME MAKER (tex. prod., nec)]. May be designated according to type of product made as Awning Maker (tex. prod., nec); Sailmaker (ship-boat mfg.; tex. prod., nec); Tentmaker (tex. prod., nec).
GOE: 06.01.04 STRENGTH: M GED: R4 M3 L2 SVP: 7 DLU: 77

739.381-014 CANVAS-WORKER APPRENTICE (ship-boat mfg.; tex. prod., nec) alternate titles: sail, tent, and awning-maker apprentice
Performs duties as described under APPRENTICE (any industry) Master Title.
GOE: 06.01.04 STRENGTH: M GED: R4 M3 L2 SVP: 7 DLU: 77

739.381-018 DIE MAKER (paper goods) alternate titles: steel-rule die maker
Constructs dies from plywood and steel rule, for use in paper cutting and scoring machines, using blueprints, handtools, and machine tools: Lays out and draws die design on plywood sheet, according to blueprint specifications, using such drafting tools as compasses, scribes, calipers, pencils, and rulers. Saws pieces (blocks) from sheet, using table, band, and jigsaws. Sands and polishes blocks to specified dimensions and smoothness, using belt sander. Measures and cuts steel rule to specified length, using tape measure, power hacksaw, and shears. Bends pieces of steel rule to form tab cutting knives and grinds edge to specified sharpness on grinding wheel. Places chase on assembly table, positions wooden blocks in chase, and inserts knives and scoring rules between blocks according to blueprints. Turns bolts on chase to fasten blocks and knives in place, using wrench. May fasten blocks and knives in chase with quoins and mallet.
GOE: 05.05.06 STRENGTH: M GED: R4 M3 L3 SVP: 8 DLU: 77

739.381-022 DIE-MAKER APPRENTICE (paper goods) alternate titles: steel-rule-die-maker apprentice
Performs duties as described under APPRENTICE (any industry) Master Title.
GOE: 05.05.06 STRENGTH: M GED: R4 M3 L3 SVP: 8 DLU: 77

739.381-026 EXPERIMENTAL ASSEMBLER (any industry)
Assembles, inspects, tests, and adjusts variety of optical, electrical, and mechanical devices on pilot run basis to improve assembly methods and to discover and correct deficiencies in materials, specifications, and equipment prior to production runs: Reads and interprets blueprints, diagrams, schematics, and narrative instructions to determine required parts and tools and lays out workbench to provide assembly arrangement. Assembles up to 100 units or components of optical, electrical, or mechanical devices, such as slide projectors, plastic tape dispensers, duplicating machines, and ribbon-bow-making machines, using power tools and handtools. Inspects, tests, and adjusts assembled devices for specified functioning, using light meter, ammeter, voltmeter, stopwatch, rulers, feeler gauges, spring tension tester, torque tester, and depth micrometer.
GOE: 05.05.11 STRENGTH: M GED: R4 M4 L4 SVP: 6 DLU: 77

739.381-030 FABRICATOR, SHOWER DOORS AND PANELS (struct. metal)
Fabricates hinged shower doors, sliding doors, and stationary panels, using power tools and handtools: Cuts aluminum channel rail stock to specifications, using rail saw. Drills and punches assembly holes. Rivets piano hinge to rail. Polishes rails, using buffing machine. Measures and cuts glass panels. Fits rubber molding around edge of glass panels and assembles rails on panels. Inserts metal screws to secure rails to panels. Positions, drills, and attaches fixtures, such as towel rod, door catch, and handles.
GOE: 06.02.22 STRENGTH: M GED: R3 M3 L2 SVP: 5 DLU: 77

739.381-034 FIGURE REFINISHER AND REPAIRER (retail trade)
Repairs and refinishes mannequins used to display wearing apparel on sales floor or in store window: Fills cracks and chips with putty and sandpapers surface. Mixes paint to match flesh color on mannequin and applies paint with brush or spray gun. Retouches features with paint, using airbrush. Glues on wigs and eyelashes. Keeps inventory records of mannequin arms, wigs, and display fixtures.
GOE: 01.06.02 STRENGTH: L GED: R3 M2 L2 SVP: 5 DLU: 77

739.381-038 INSET CUTTER (fabrication, nec)
Lays out and cuts decorative insets for hard-surface floor covering: Lays out design and makes pattern from blueprint, using drafting tools. Selects material according to type and color specified on pattern. Lays out materials according to pattern colors, exercising care to obtain maximum utilization of material. Transfers design section to material by tracing over pattern and carbon paper. Aligns two or more layers of material, to be cut simultaneously, using straightedge and T-square. Cuts or gouges out design section, using gouging tools or guides electrical cutting machine over pattern lines. Places specified tile material on heated warming table and directs rays of portable heater onto area being cut to soften material and prevent cracking. Cuts specified design sections from brass or aluminum for insertion in inset. Assembles sections to form complete design and fastens parts together with masking tape. Fills in gouged lines of hand-carved designs with oil, aluminum, or bronze paint to enhance appearance of finished product.
GOE: 01.06.02 STRENGTH: L GED: R4 M3 L3 SVP: 6 DLU: 77

739.381-042 MANNEQUIN WIG MAKER (fabrication, nec)
Makes wigs for mannequin out of synthetic hair according to style specifications: Places layer of cellophane over head model. Molds sheet of wet buckram over cellophane to form wig foundation. Selects strands of hair and combs, cuts, and blends them according to specified length and color. Folds ends of strands and glues short side of fold to foundation. Pins tape over glued section, to secure hair in position, on foundation. Combs, curls, and fastens hair in place to style wig according to specifications, using tape, pins, comb, and curling rods. Dries hair under electric drier and sprays wig with lacquer to set hair style.
GOE: 06.01.04 STRENGTH: S GED: R3 M2 L2 SVP: 6 DLU: 77

739.381-046 MANNEQUIN-MOLD MAKER (fabrication, nec) alternate titles: mold maker
Builds plaster or plastic molds of display models: Lays model on bench, packs clay around model to centerline of figure, and greases exposed part of model. Prepares plaster of paris and smears it on upper part of figure, shaping it to form base of mold. Applies reinforcing strips of hemp fiber over mold body and covers hemp with layer of plaster. Applies successive layers of liquid plastic, glass fiber mesh cloth, and liquid resin around model. Removes supporting clay from figure, turns mold over, and applies plaster of paris and hemp fiber or plastic, cloth, and resin to remainder of figure to complete mold.
GOE: 06.01.04 STRENGTH: M GED: R4 M2 L2 SVP: 7 DLU: 77

739.381-050 SOUVENIR AND NOVELTY MAKER (metal prod., nec) alternate titles: souvenir assembler
Fabricates souvenirs and novelty items from materials, such as sea shells, pine needles, driftwood, wooden stock, cloth scraps, skins, and parts of animals: Studies samples, patterns, or drawings to become familiar with items to be made and materials needed to fabricate souvenir or novelty items; or employs artistic ability and creative talent to design items. Constructs items by one of following methods: (1) Molds or builds forms of plaster of paris or wood, using handtools. Examines animal skins and cuts skin ɔ fit form, using knife and scissors. Attaches skin to form with tacks and glue. Attaches items, such as lighters, ash trays, and light fixtures, using adhesives and handtools. Combs and brushes fur to improve appearance. (2) Assembles cleaned, sanded, and waxed driftwood in artistic display and attaches driftwood to wooden base with glue or screws. (3) Arranges pine needles into specified patterns to fabricate baskets, coasters, and utility mats and stitches needles in place with raffia. (4) Constructs rag dolls following pattern, sewing parts together, stuffing doll with filler material, embroidering features on doll face, and placing designated clothing on doll. (5) Builds items, such as sailboats, fish, and animals from woodstock, using handtools and power tools. Cuts out shape of item with coping, hand, or jigsaw and completes item by carving and sanding wood. Buffs, polishes, paints, or varnishes item to produce desired finish. (6) Cleans, cuts, or grinds sea shells and coral with handtools and power tools to prepare coral and shells for use as souvenir or novelty items. Arranges items on display board, in glass jars, or into novelty items, such as figurines, lamps, or paperweights, using jewelry findings, pipe cleaners, glue, wire, plaster of paris, and handtools. May keep records pertaining to cost of supplies and income from sales.
GOE: 01.06.02 STRENGTH: L GED: R3 M3 L3 SVP: 5 DLU: 77

739.381-054 SURVIVAL-EQUIPMENT REPAIRER (government ser.)
Inspects, maintains, and repairs aircraft and marine survival equipment, or flight safety equipment, such as life rafts, inflatable jackets, marker buoys, flare cases, helmets, and pressure suits, using handtools.
GOE: 05.10.01 STRENGTH: M GED: R3 M2 L2 SVP: 6 DLU: 77

739.381-058 WIG MAKER (fabrication, nec)
Lays out, sews, and fastens together materials and hair strands to make wigs and transformations: Draws or pins wig pattern on model of customer's head. Places sections of gauze, lace, net, ribbon, and springs over pattern and sews sections together to form wig foundation [FOUNDATION MAKER (fabrication, nec)]. Hooks strands of hair into foundation holes, using ventilating needle (similar to crochet needle), blends shades of hair to give natural appearance, and ties ends of strands to foundation [VENTILATOR (fabrication, nec)]. Weaves hair to form speciality hairpieces, such as braids, switches, and chignons. Arranges woven hair in specified position and sews hair together to form hairpiece. May repair wigs. May supervise or train other workers.
GOE: 05.05.15 STRENGTH: S GED: R3 M2 L3 SVP: 7 DLU: 77

739.384-010 DIAMOND MOUNTER (machine tools)
Positions and mounts industrial diamonds in tools used for dressing and *truing I* grinding wheels and for machining metal, according to type and size of tool by one of following methods: (1) Places tools shank in press and moves controls to force diamond into shank. Applies solder and flux around diamond and places tool into electric induction furnace for specified time to bond diamond to shank. (2) Inserts wire through hole in diamond and twists wire around pin on tool shank. Positions mold around diamond and shank and pours molten metal into mold to cast tool containing diamond. (3) Presses powdered metal into mold around diamond on tool shank and places in sintering furnace for specified time to fabricate tool containing diamond. (4) Aligns and clamps diamond in tool shank. Cleans joints of diamond and shank, using wire brush and cleaning solution. Bonds shank and diamond together, using brazing alloy and acetylene hand torch.
GOE: 06.02.32 STRENGTH: L GED: R3 M3 L3 SVP: 4 DLU: 77

739.384-014 FOUNDATION MAKER (fabrication, nec) alternate titles: blocker and sewer
Lays out and sews together materials, such as ribbon, net, and gauze, to make foundations for wigs and transformations: Draws and cuts pattern of hair-

piece according to customer's head measurements. Shapes and pins pattern to head model. Draws lines on pattern to indicate position of foundation. Stretches and pins wet gauze over foundation area. Cuts ribbon and pins it to model to form skeleton structure of foundation. Fits and sews elastic and springs to foundation to ensure snug fit. Fits and sews net and lace to gauze and springs to form front and back portions of foundations.
GOE: 06.02.27 STRENGTH: L GED: R3 M2 L1 SVP: 5 DLU: 77

739.384-018   HAIR PREPARER (fabrication, nec) alternate titles: hair blender

Bleaches, dyes, and blends human hair used in making hair pieces: Soaks hair in soap and water to remove foreign matter and separates hair into strands. Mixes and blends ingredients to make bleaches and dyes according to formula. Dips strands into bleaching and dyeing solutions to obtain desired color. Hangs bleached and dyed strands on lines to air dry. Arranges and combs strands to blend them to specified hue and grade. May wash and soak hair in acid and soda solutions to thin hair and burn roots, preparatory to making theatrical hair pieces.
GOE: 06.02.32 STRENGTH: L GED: R3 M1 L1 SVP: 7 DLU: 77

739.384-022   VENTILATOR (fabrication, nec)

Fastens human hair to foundation material to make wigs: Arranges specified strands of hair between cards equipped with rows of wire teeth. Pulls several strands through teeth of card, cuts ends even, and forms loops in ends. Hooks strands in holes of foundation (on head model) with ventilating needle (similar to fine crochet needle) and knots them to fasten hair securely. Cuts off uneven ends protruding beyond knots and repeats operations until wig is completed according to sample or instructions. Combs out hair when wig is finished. May be designated according to area of wig worked on as First Front Ventilator (fabrication, nec); Part Maker (fabrication, nec).
GOE: 06.02.32 STRENGTH: S GED: R3 M1 L1 SVP: 5 DLU: 77

739.387-010   CASKET INSPECTOR (fabrication, nec)

Examines assembled caskets visually and tactually to determine their conformance to specifications: Inspects casket lining for irregularities, such as faulty design, discoloration of material, unconcealed tacks, and bulges in padding. Opens and closes top panel to determine presence of obstructions. Blows out inside and outside of casket to remove dust, using compressed air gun. Inspects casket exterior for defects, such as torn covering, nicks, spots, incompleteness, misalignment, and imperfect finish. Keeps rejection records, noting such factors as number of units inspected, number of units rejected, and reason for rejection. Removes spots from lining and cover with solvent. Identifies types of defects and returns caskets to workers for correction. May touch up scratches, using felt tip pen, and steam wrinkles from casket lining, using portable steamer.
GOE: 06.03.01 STRENGTH: L GED: R3 M1 L1 SVP: 5 DLU: 77

739.387-014   HAIR-SAMPLE MATCHER (fabrication, nec) alternate titles: hair blender; hair mixer

Selects strands of human hair and blends them to match customer's hair preparatory to making hair piece: Selects strands from stock according to texture, shape, type, color, and composition of customer's natural hair. Arranges and combs strands to match variations in natural hair caused by graying, bleaching, or dyeing. Weighs and ties hair with string.
GOE: 05.05.15 STRENGTH: S GED: R3 M2 L1 SVP: 5 DLU: 77

739.484-010   CHRONOGRAPH OPERATOR (ordnance) alternate titles: ballistics tester

Measures velocity of projectiles fired from various types and sizes of weapons to determine performance of weapon or ammunition, using chronograph: Loads and aims weapon and fires projectile through electron-beam screens that activate chronograph. Converts chronograph reading of elapsed time to velocity in feet-per-second, using reference charts. Records data on inspection forms and calculates average velocity of projectiles tested.
GOE: 06.03.01 STRENGTH: L GED: R3 M3 L3 SVP: 3 DLU: 77

739.484-014   FIRE-EQUIPMENT INSPECTOR (any industry)

Inspects, tests, and repairs conduits and fire-fighting equipment to secure property against fires: Turns valves to force water through lines to test them for leaks, breaks, and stoppage. Replaces and repairs defective sections of hoses and pipelines, using handtools. Inserts wire rod in hose of fire extinguishers to remove stoppages. Tests and cleans fire extinguishers and recharges them with solvents, sulfuric acid, carbon tetrachloride and chemicals [FIRE-EXTINGUISHER REPAIRER (any industry)]. Maintains inventory of equipment and fills out inspection tags and reports. Reports unsatisfactory conditions to FIRE MARSHAL (any industry). May repair gas masks. May service and drive firetruck. May test for presence of gases, using gas scope or explosive meter.
GOE: 05.07.01 STRENGTH: L GED: R3 M2 L3 SVP: 4 DLU: 77

739.484-018   SMOKING-PIPE REPAIRER (any industry)

Repairs pipes and cigar and cigarette holders according to customer's specifications, using lathe: Fits rubber or plastic mouthpiece blank in lathe chuck. Guides tools against revolving blank to drill and ream airhole and to turn end of blank to fit pipe or holder. Carves blank with scraper or presses blank against grinding and buffing wheel to shape mouthpiece according to customer's specifications. Heats pipe stem over flame to bend stem to specified angle. Cuts threads on stem and pipe shank, using tap and die. Repairs broken or cracked shanks with cement, metal bands, or screws.

GOE: 05.10.01 STRENGTH: L GED: R3 M2 L2 SVP: 5 DLU: 77

739.587-010   INSPECTION CLERK (fabrication, nec) alternate titles: roll-up helper

Records pattern and color defects and quality of hard-surface floor covering as directed by INSPECTOR (fabrication, nec) II and labels finished goods: Records yardage and defects on inspection record sheet. Cuts out defective sections of floor covering, using knife. Records shade and yardage on ticket for each piece of material cut from roll. Adjusts controls that actuate and position grade indicator to mark section of material specified by INSPECTOR (fabrication, nec) II. Affixes label to remnant roll of floor covering to indicate such information as number of pieces in roll and yardage of each piece. Attaches labels to packaged floor covering.
GOE: 06.04.37 STRENGTH: H GED: R3 M3 L2 SVP: 4 DLU: 77

739.664-010   CANDLEMAKER (fabrication, nec)

Forms candles according to one of following methods: (1) Strings wicks through notches or rings of dipping frame, according to length of candle to be formed. Dips wicks manually or with aid of motorized mechanism into vat of molten wax mixture to build up candles to specified circumference. Cuts or trims candles to specified sizes, using knife or hand die. Grades candles according to type, color, and size. (2) Inserts wick through center of molds and attaches ends to racks. Pours molten wax mixture into molds, using container or opens valves to admit wax into molds. Adjusts steam and coolant valves to maintain prescribed thermometer reading in mold. Turns handcrank of ejection mechanism to release candles from molds into rack after specified time. Scrapes remaining wax from molds, using handtools. May record production data, such as name, color, and quantity of candles. May add color ingredients to molten wax, according to specifications.
GOE: 06.04.32 STRENGTH: M GED: R2 M1 L1 SVP: 4 DLU: 77

739.667-010   SPOT PICKER, MOLDED GOODS (fabrication, nec) alternate titles: spot picker

Inspects and patches designs on linoleum and related floor coverings: Examines floor covering to detect pattern defects as floor covering passes over repair table. Removes spots of misplaced color, using tweezers. Builds up low spots, covers empty spaces, and corrects lines in designs on floor covering, by patting and rubbing in matching color mix, using fingers or spatula. Removes excessive color, using scraper. Usually works as member of team.
GOE: 06.03.02 STRENGTH: L GED: R2 M1 L1 SVP: 3 DLU: 77

739.684-010   ARTIFICIAL-CANDY MAKER (fabrication, nec) alternate titles: novelty-candy maker

Carves, molds, or assembles imitation candy made from wood, plaster of paris, or styrofoam for use as display items: Shapes material to resemble candy by sculpturing in wood or by casting plaster in molds prepared by other workers. Paints pieces to resemble candy coloring, using spray gun. Applies decorations with glue, according to design.
GOE: 06.02.32 STRENGTH: L GED: R3 M2 L2 SVP: 5 DLU: 77

739.684-014   ARTIFICIAL-FLOWER MAKER (button & notion) alternate titles: flower arranger; foliage arranger

Cuts out and assembles materials, such as fabric, wood, and paper, performing any combination of following tasks to make artificial foliage, such as flowers, wreaths, and trees: Cuts out flower parts, such as leaves and petals from paper, fabric, or plastic, using handtools, such as scissors, knives, hammers, and dies. Stamps out flower parts with hand-operated or power-driven machine. Places roll of material on spindle of machine that automatically forms artificial-flower stems. Prints veining on artificial leaves, using stamps and handpress. Dips flowers into specified dye and squeezes out excess dye, using hands. Fastens twigs and buds to steel wire to form branches by hand or using twisting machine. Wires or glues flower parts to stem or branch. Fastens artificial flowers and foliage to wreath stand and inserts cones and grass decorations to form artificial wreath. May wrap stems with green and brown paper to effect natural appearance. May be designated according to product produced as Wreath And Garland Maker, Hand (button & notion); or shape artificial flower petals from fabric, using tweezers, heated metal ball, and wooden form, and be designated Petal Shaper, Hand (button & notion).
GOE: 06.04.34 STRENGTH: L GED: R2 M1 L1 SVP: 3 DLU: 77

739.684-018   BROOMMAKER (fabrication, nec) alternate titles: winder

Fabricates brooms from broomcorn fibers, using one of following methods: (1) Inserts and clamps broom handle in winder (rotating vise). Threads end of wire from reel through hole in handle and nails, ties, or staples wire to handle. Places layers of fiber onto handle and depresses pedal to rotate handle to wrap wire around fiber. Spreads fibers around under wire as winder turns. Trims excess fiber around each layer, using knife. Hooks leather strap around body of broom to secure it while winding subsequent layers. Pounds fibers to pack and shape broom shoulders, using mallet. Wraps and fastens wire around neck of broom handle with stapler. Weighs brooms on scales to verify conformance to standard. (2) Gathers cut and graded broomcorn into bundle according to size required for broom. Inserts broom handle into plastic cone and staples cone to broom handle, using stapling machine. Dips base of broomcorn bundle in pot of hot tar, inserts base into cone, flattens cone and broomcorn into fan-flare shape, using vise. Staples cone to broomcorn, using stapling machine, and stacks brooms for further processing. May pull broom through stemmer (comb-like device) to remove coarse or short fibers.
GOE: 06.04.34 STRENGTH: L GED: R2 M1 L1 SVP: 4 DLU: 77

739.684-022 BRUSH MATERIAL PREPARER (fabrication, nec)
Prepares hog bristles and other brush-filling materials, such as horsehair, nylon, and vegetable fibers for use in brushes: Aligns bristles, to ensure that flagged ends are together, and discards defective bristles. Ties bundle of bristles to prevent bending and places it in rack. Uses hoist to lower rack of bundles into vat of boiling water to remove natural curl of bristle. Removes rack after specified time and places it on dolly or in oven to dry. Places bundle of bristles in carton and labels carton according to length, origin, grade, and color of contents or spreads bristles in rows on tray for mixing and blending operations. Prepares other brush-filling materials by straightening, combing, cutting, and tying them according to type of material and intended use. Holds bundle of material against grinding wheel to flag ends, to trim butt ends, and to polish material. Selects filling material according to formula and lays it on workbench in prescribed manner prior to processing by mixing machine. May pack material in carton. May place bristles in sterilizer to kill germs. May dye bristles specified color, using dyeing vat. May shape, soften, and clean bristles, using machines that cut, split, and grind bristles.
GOE: 06.02.32 STRENGTH: M GED: R2 M1 L1 SVP: 5 DLU: 77

739.684-026 BUFFER (fabrication, nec) alternate titles: polisher; tripoler
Polishes parts of assembled smoking pipes: Secures buffing wheel on machine arbor, using wrench. Dips part into polishing compound or applies compound with fingers. Starts machine and guides part against rotating wheel, varying pressure to impart luster and seal pores of briar. May be designated according to part of pipe polished as Bit Tripoler (fabrication, nec); or according to compound used as Lacquer Polisher (fabrication, nec); Shellac Polisher (fabrication, nec).
GOE: 06.04.34 STRENGTH: L GED: R2 M1 L1 SVP: 3 DLU: 78

739.684-030 BUFFING-AND-POLISHING-WHEEL REPAIRER (any industry) alternate titles: buff-wheel fabricator; disk recoater; polishing-wheel repairer
Repairs cloth buffing and polishing wheels, using handtools, standard charts, tracing lathe, and arbor press: Clamps worn wheel in steam cleaning machine to remove abrasives and bonding materials. Dismantles cleaned wheels, using handtools, and salvages cloth inserts depending upon size and condition. Assembles buffing and polishing wheels according to standard charts, by pressing inserts and spacers on wheel shaft, using arbor press. Mounts assembled wheel on tracing lathe to turn wheel surface to specified shape. Sprays or brushes abrasive bonding material on surface of polishing wheel and places it in oven to dry. Repairs polishing wheels by recoating with specified abrasive bonding material. May mount completed polishing and buffing wheels on machine.
GOE: 06.04.34 STRENGTH: M GED: R2 M1 L1 SVP: 3 DLU: 77

739.684-034 CASE FINISHER (leather prod.) alternate titles: case assembler; instrument-case finisher; leather-case finisher
Assembles and finishes suitcases and radio, jewelry, and instrument cases, and lines or covers them with material, such as leather, velvet, or satin, performing any combination of following tasks: Inserts hinge wings into slots in top and bottom sections of case and secures them in grooves, using pinch pliers, or rivets, nails, or screws hinges in position. Opens case and verifies lid angle, using table gauge. Cuts specified material to size, using pattern and shears, or obtains precut fabric. Brushes glue on area to be covered. Positions material on inner or outer surfaces of case and smooths out wrinkles, using fingers. Trims excess fabric from joints, seams, and edges, using knife. Glues or nails bracing blocks to case and covers blocks with material. Presses cushion or pad into upper and lower sections of case. Examines case for misalignment of edges, and opens and closes lid to test action of hinges and spring. Holds case over air nozzle and presses pedal to remove dust and lint. Packs cases in shipping cartons. May crimp lids to case or crimp bottoms to case frame, using pneumatic-powered crimper. May repair or replace hinges, linings, and springs and be designated Case Repairer (leather prod.).
GOE: 06.04.27 STRENGTH: L GED: R3 M2 L2 SVP: 2 DLU: 80

739.684-038 CLIP-AND-HANGER ATTACHER (glass products)
Attaches clamps, clips, and hangers to precut fiberboard backing for mirrors, using handtools, power-driven tools, and riveting machine: Places backing on table. Marks location of clamps, clips, or hangers, using tape measure, template, and pencil. Drills holes at marked locations with electric hand drill. Attaches clamps, clips, or hangers to backing, using pneumatic screwdriver. Attaches support brackets to backing when mirrors are to be attached to furniture, using riveting machine and handtools. Places gummed felt pads over exposed screwheads and rivets to protect mirror finish. Glues hanging instruction labels to back. Stacks completed mirror backs on pallet.
GOE: 06.04.34 STRENGTH: L GED: R2 M2 L2 SVP: 4 DLU: 77

739.684-042 CURTAIN-ROLLER ASSEMBLER (furniture)
Assembles curtain rollers for use in window curtains: Slips and attaches coiled spring over shaft. Slides assembly into tube and plugs end with fiber insert. Rivets small lever to ratchet plate to hold wound curtains in place. Drills holes and slots in retaining rods, using drill press.
GOE: 06.04.23 STRENGTH: L GED: R2 M1 L1 SVP: 3 DLU: 77

739.684-046 DECORATOR (leather prod.) alternate titles: hardware assembler
Attaches metal findings onto leather to decorate articles, such as belts, gloves, and handbags, using either of following methods: (1) Positions template on precut leather article. Punches holes in leather, following markings on template, using hammer and punch. Inserts findings, such as buttons, locks, and ornaments, into holes and clinches findings, using hammer and prying tool. (2) Brushes cement onto fittings, positions fittings on premarked leather article, and presses fittings to leather.
GOE: 06.04.27 STRENGTH: L GED: R2 M2 L1 SVP: 2 DLU: 77

739.684-050 DEICER ASSEMBLER, ELECTRIC (rubber goods)
Assembles precut rubberized fabric, gum-rubber ply stocks, and wiring elements to make electric deicers for airplanes: Determines location for rubber ply (layers) stock and wiring elements on building form, following guidelines on form or using template and blueprints. Positions rubber ply stocks and element in specified sequence on building form, and secures them in place with rubber cement. Solders wire element connections at specified locations. Compresses assembled ply stocks with roller to remove wrinkles and promote adherence. Cuts and cements strips of gum rubber around wires for insulation and reinforcement. Trims excess ply stock from assembled deicer with knife. May verify electrical resistance of deicer by clamping deicer lead wires to testing device. May cover deicer with nylon blanket and tape it to building form (preparatory to curing). May assemble pneumatic deicers and be designated Deicer Assembler, Pneumatic (rubber goods).
GOE: 06.02.22 STRENGTH: M GED: R3 M2 L2 SVP: 5 DLU: 77

739.684-054 DEICER FINISHER (rubber goods)
Solders thermostats and terminal connections on airplane deicers to complete assembly: Solders thermostats and terminal connections to lead wires of deicer, using electric soldering iron. Measures and cuts gum rubber strips to reinforce lead wires. Buffs rubber ply (layer) around lead wires of deicer, using portable electric buffer. Slips lead boss (molded rubber cover) onto lead wires, and secures lead boss to deicer with gum rubber strips. Presses gum rubber strip together with fingers to induce adherance. Cures gum rubber strips on deicer, using spotcuring press.
GOE: 06.04.34 STRENGTH: L GED: R2 M2 L2 SVP: 4 DLU: 77

739.684-058 DEICER-ELEMENT WINDER, HAND (rubber goods) alternate titles: heating-element builder
Constructs electric heating elements for airplane deicers: Measures and cuts base stock for element from rubberized fabric to fit specified jig. Positions base stock on jig and secures stock with jig bar. Lifts reel of specified wire to letoff rack and clamps end of wire to jig by turning setscrew. Threads wire between poles of jig following specified pattern. Pushes wires down to base of poles, and tightens expansion screw on jig to remove slack from wires, using handtools. Brushes flux on wires to clean them preparatory to soldering. Solders parts, such as *bus bars,* jumper and lead wires, to element to make specified electrical circuit. Examines element to ensure that solder joints are secured. Cements precut sections of rubberized fabric cover stock over wires with rubber cement, and presses them together, using roller. Trims excess base and cover stock from edges of element with knife. May clamp formed element to testing device to verify electrical resistance.
GOE: 06.02.32 STRENGTH: L GED: R2 M1 L1 SVP: 4 DLU: 77

739.684-046 DECORATOR (leather prod.) alternate titles: hardware assembler
Attaches metal findings onto leather to decorate articles, such as belts, gloves, and handbags, using either of following methods: (1) Positions template on precut leather article. Punches holes in leather, following markings on template, using hammer and punch. Inserts findings, such as buttons, locks, and ornaments, into holes and clinches findings, using hammer and prying tool. (2) Brushes cement onto fittings, positions fittings on premarked leather article, and presses fittings to leather.
GOE: 06.04.27 STRENGTH: L GED: R2 M2 L1 SVP: 2 DLU: 77

739.684-050 DEICER ASSEMBLER, ELECTRIC (rubber goods)
Assembles precut rubberized fabric, gum-rubber ply stocks, and wiring elements to make electric deicers for airplanes: Determines location for rubber ply (layers) stock and wiring elements on building form, following guidelines on form or using template and blueprints. Positions rubber ply stocks and element in specified sequence on building form, and secures them in place with rubber cement. Solders wire element connections at specified locations. Compresses assembled ply stocks with roller to remove wrinkles and promote adherence. Cuts and cements strips of gum rubber around wires for insulation and reinforcement. Trims excess ply stock from assembled deicer with knife. May verify electrical resistance of deicer by clamping deicer lead wires to testing device. May cover deicer with nylon blanket and tape it to building form (preparatory to curing). May assemble pneumatic deicers and be designated Deicer Assembler, Pneumatic (rubber goods).
GOE: 06.02.22 STRENGTH: M GED: R3 M2 L2 SVP: 5 DLU: 77

739.684-054 DEICER FINISHER (rubber goods)
Solders thermostats and terminal connections on airplane deicers to complete assembly: Solders thermostats and terminal connections to lead wires of deicer, using electric soldering iron. Measures and cuts gum rubber strips to reinforce lead wires. Buffs rubber ply (layer) around lead wires of deicer, using portable electric buffer. Slips lead boss (molded rubber cover) onto lead wires, and secures lead boss to deicer with gum rubber strips. Presses gum rubber strip together with fingers to induce adherance. Cures gum rubber strips on deicer, using spotcuring press.
GOE: 06.04.34 STRENGTH: L GED: R2 M2 L2 SVP: 4 DLU: 77

739.684-058   DEICER-ELEMENT WINDER, HAND (rubber goods) alternate titles: heating-element builder

Constructs electric heating elements for airplane deicers: Measures and cuts base stock for element from rubberized fabric to fit specified jig. Positions base stock on jig and secures stock with jig bar. Lifts reel of specified wire to letoff rack and clamps end of wire to jig by turning setscrew. Threads wire between poles of jig following specified pattern. Pushes wires down to base of poles, and tightens expansion screw on jig to remove slack from wires, using handtools. Brushes flux on wires to clean them preparatory to soldering. Solders parts, such as *bus bars,* jumper and lead wires, to element to make specified electrical circuit. Examines element to ensure that solder joints are secure. Cements precut sections of rubberized fabric cover stock over wires with rubber cement, and presses them together, using roller. Trims excess base and cover stock from edges of element with knife. May clamp formed element to testing device to verify electrical resistance.
GOE: 06.02.32 STRENGTH: L GED: R2 M1 L1 SVP: 4 DLU: 77

739.684-062   FINISHER, BRUSH (fabrication, nec)

Finishes brushes, performing any combination of following tasks: Holds wooden brush surface against sanding wheel and buffer to sand and polish brush heads and handles. Trims, tapers, and shapes brush-filling material according to prescribed standards by pushing brush over rotary trimmer, feeding it into trimming machine, or holding brush over blades of clipping machine. Removes dust and loose filling material by placing brush in centrifugal cleaning machine, holding it against cleaning brush, or feeding it into combing machine. Dips brush handle in varnish or lacquer or sprays handle with varnish or lacquer and hangs it on rack to dry. Paints identifying stripes on brush handle. Examines brush for conformity to job specifications and defects and makes corrections, such as retouching varnished or lacquered surface and hand-trimming filling material. Repairs cracked handles and bent ferrules. Separates and reroutes brushes that cannot be repaired to corrective work station. May flatten ferrule, using press machine, and nail band or ferrule to brush. May attach handle to brush.
GOE: 06.04.34 STRENGTH: L GED: R2 M1 L2 SVP: 3 DLU: 77

739.684-066   FOOT-MITER OPERATOR (wood prod., nec) alternate titles: hand-miter operator

Miters and cuts molding stock for picture frames to specified length and angle, using miter knife: Turns screws to adjust feed guides to width of molding and to adjust stop that measures molding for cutting. Turns handwheel to raise or lower miter bars that protect edges from splintering. Inserts molding between guides and depresses foot treadle or pulls hand lever to lower knife that cuts one end of stock at 45 degree angle. Places molding against stop and under second blade that cuts other end to specified length and 45 degree angle. May make several cuts with knife to complete full cut of thick stock.
GOE: 06.04.25 STRENGTH: L GED: R2 M2 L1 SVP: 2 DLU: 77

739.684-070   FORM COVERER (fabrication, nec)

Fits and fastens cloth covering on papier mache bust or mannequin forms: Selects cover according to size of bust of mannequin. Pulls cover over form, smoothing and fitting it manually. Tacks and pastes end of cover to inside of torso openings. Slits cover at arm and neck openings, and pastes cover to edges of openings.
GOE: 06.04.27 STRENGTH: L GED: R2 M1 L1 SVP: 3 DLU: 77

739.684-074   FRAME REPAIRER (glass products)

Repairs surface defects in plastic mirror frames and mirrors: Examines frame or mirror to detect defects, such as rough edges, cracks, and blisters on frame and scratches on mirror. Unscrews brackets holding mirror within frame, using pneumatic screwdriver, and removes mirror from frame. Clamps frame in vise to hold frame in position for repair. Fills cracks in frame with putty. Sands and touches up defective area, using sandpaper and paint. Trims rough edges from frames with wire cutters. Hand buffs scratched area on mirrors, to remove scratches, using felt block and polishing compound. Reassembles repaired mirrors and stacks nonrepairable items aside.
GOE: 06.04.34 STRENGTH: L GED: R2 M2 L2 SVP: 3 DLU: 77

739.684-078   FRAMER (glass products; wood prod., nec)

Installs mirrors or pictures in wooden, plastic, or metal frames, performing any combination of following tasks: Assembles frames from precut material and glues, nails, screws, or staples material together, using clamps, handtools, and power tools. Places glass, picture, or mirror into frame. Inserts wooden strips between mirror and frame or covers mirror edge with stripping to secure mirror in position. Positions backing, such as corrugated paper or cardboard, over back of picture or mirror. Staples backing to frame or locates and marks points on backing where hangers are to be placed, using ruler and pencil. Drills holes with portable electric drill and bolts or screws hangers to mirror backing. Places mirror backing in frame and attaches backing to mirror frame, using clips, screws, staples, and handtools. Bolts wings to frame to form border of shadow-box mirrors. May mount picture on mat before framing. May perform all operations of cutting, shaving, and drilling to prepare frame parts from stock molding according to customer or company specifications. May pack mirrors or pictures for shipment.
GOE: 06.04.34 STRENGTH: M GED: R2 M2 L2 SVP: 3 DLU: 77

739.684-082   FURNITURE   ASSEMBLER-AND-INSTALLER   (retail trade)

Uncrates, assembles, installs, and repairs furniture and office equipment in customers' homes or offices: Uncrates and assembles items, using handtools. Repairs and paints dents and scratches in metal or wood. Cleans, repairs, and replaces safe and file drawers, locks, catches, and slides. May repair or replace damaged vinyl or fabric upholstery material, using handtools, patching, needle, and thread.
GOE: 05.10.01 STRENGTH: H GED: R3 M2 L1 SVP: 4 DLU: 77

739.684-086   HAIR WORKER (fabrication, nec) alternate titles: hackler

Combs, sorts, and prepares human or synthetic hair for making wigs, switches, and hair pieces: Pulls loose strands of hair across teeth of stationary comb to remove tangles. Separates hair strands according to length and ties them in groups. Washes human hair with soap and water and dries it in oven. Throws ends of hair against hackle (steel-bristled brush) and pulls hair through teeth to disentangle and straighten strands; places hair between cardboard sheets with ends protruding. Removes hair roots by brushing ends with brush containing row of needles. May mix various shades of hair to obtain routine blends.
GOE: 06.04.34 STRENGTH: L GED: R2 M1 L1 SVP: 5 DLU: 77

739.684-090   HANDBAG FRAMER (leather prod.) alternate titles: framer

Attaches hinged metal frames to leather or fabric handbags: Spreads grooves in frame, using automatic opening device or pliers. Brushes cement into grooves. Trims edges and corners of bag fabric, using scissors. Clamps frame in frame-tightening device, and pushes edges and corners of bag into grooves with fingers and punch. Depresses pedal of tightening device to pinch sides of grooves around edges and corners of bag fabric. May record production. May be designated according to type of handbag framed as Coin-Purse Framer (leather prod.); Pocketbook Framer (leather prod.); Purse Framer (leather prod.).
GOE: 06.04.23 STRENGTH: L GED: R2 M1 L1 SVP: 2 DLU: 77

739.684-094   LAMP-SHADE ASSEMBLER (fabrication, nec)

Performs any combination of tasks involved in assembly of lampshades and lampshade collars: Applies glue to edges of shade fabric and backs of shade attachments, such as collars, ornaments, and trimmings. Folds glued edges of fabric around wire frame, and presses attachments onto fabric. Secures shade to frame by stringing cord through shade perforations and lacing cord around frame rings. Tapes edges of parchment shades to prevent tearing of parchment. Places pattern over shade skirt, marks points of attachment on skirt, and staples skirt to shade. Rubs various colored paints on inner and outer surfaces of paper and parchment shades to produce antique finish, using rubber sponge. May heat seams in press to set glue.
GOE: 06.04.23 STRENGTH: S GED: R2 M1 L1 SVP: 2 DLU: 77

739.684-098   LAST IRONER (wood prod., nec) alternate titles: ironer

Fits and nails steel plates to bottoms of wooden or plastic shoe lasts: Straps last to ironing jack (holding device) and positions steel sole and heel plates of specified size on bottom of lasts. Nails steel plates to last bottoms and shapes plates to contour of last, using hammer. Files edges of last bottoms and steel plates to form smooth, flush edges.
GOE: 06.04.27 STRENGTH: M GED: R2 M1 L1 SVP: 3 DLU: 77

739.684-102   LAST MARKER (wood prod., nec)

Positions paper shoe last pattern of specified size and style on bottom of wood last turning and draws outline around pattern for LAST TRIMMER (wood prod., nec).
GOE: 06.04.34 STRENGTH: L GED: R2 M1 L1 SVP: 2 DLU: 77

739.684-106   LAST REMODELER-REPAIRER (boot & shoe; wood prod., nec) alternate titles: remodeler

Remodels and repairs out-of-style, worn, or damaged shoe lasts, performing any combination of following tasks: Saws kerfs into specified areas of last toe, applies glue, and hammers wedges of last material into kerfs to build up toe area. Saws, files, and sands toe of last to specified shape, using handtools and portable sanders. Drills holes in splintered areas of lasts, using electric drill. Brushes glue on wood or fiber pegs and hammers pegs into holes in last. Cuts pegs off at surface of last, using handsaw or powered saw. Verifies shape, using templates and sole patterns. Replaces worn or damaged hardware and trim on last, such as hinge pins, hinges, thimble sleeves, fiber and leather heel trim, or rubber tack holders, using handtools and powered bench tools. Sands varnish from last and dips or sprays last with varnish to refinish. Polishes last, using power buffer. Paints identifying stripes on last according to specified code. May stamp style, size, and width numbers on last.
GOE: 05.10.01 STRENGTH: M GED: R3 M2 L2 SVP: 4 DLU: 77

739.684-110   LAST REPAIRER (boot & shoe; wood prod., nec)

Repairs shoe lasts: Drills holes in splintered areas of wooden last, using electric drill. Brushes glue on wood or fiber pegs, and hammers pegs into holes in last. Cuts pegs off at surface of last, using handsaw or powered saw. Files repaired area of last with hand file to smooth surface. Patches holes and cracks in defective plastic lasts, and smooths patched or rough areas, using sanding wheel or file and sandpaper. May stamp style, size, and width numbers on last.
GOE: 06.04.25 STRENGTH: M GED: R2 M1 L1 SVP: 3 DLU: 77

739.684-114   LAST-REPAIRER HELPER (boot & shoe)

Removes and replaces worn cords that join blocks and lasts. Glues on thin patches of leather at designated points to build up lasts. Nails heel plates to lasts that clinch tacks driven through upper and insole during shoe construction. Fills tack holes and grooves around bottom of last with plastic wood, using putty knife.
GOE: 06.04.34 STRENGTH: L GED: R2 M1 L1 SVP: 2 DLU: 77

739.684-118   MANNEQUIN MOUNTER (fabrication, nec) alternate titles: balancer

Attaches arms, legs, and pedestals to display form bodies: Trims openings with knife to fit socket blocks. Tacks block in opening. Sets arm or leg in place in socket block. Inserts pedestal into cavity of bust form and tacks form to pedestal. Sets form on workbench between aligning bars. Aligns bust form with bars to balance it and nails form to pedestal.
GOE: 06.02.22 STRENGTH: L GED: R3 M2 L2 SVP: 5 DLU: 77

739.684-122   MANNEQUIN SANDER AND FINISHER (fabrication, nec) alternate titles: paper finisher

Smooths, patches, paints, and corrects contour defects in papier mache and plastic mannequins: Removes waves with metal rasp and smooths surfaces with sandpaper or power sander. Fills holes with plaster. Builds up surface of mannequin, using plaster, paper, burlap, and cement. Brushes plaster over mannequin surface, sandpapers it to smooth finish, and sprays it with flesh-colored lacquer.
GOE: 06.02.32 STRENGTH: L GED: R3 M1 L1 SVP: 3 DLU: 77

739.684-126   MAT CUTTER (wood prod., nec)

Cuts materials to form bordering frames (mats) for pictures: Measures and marks materials, such as matboards, fabrics, or paper according to size and width of picture. Inserts material in holding device and cuts with knife or razor blade to form bordering frame. May cut backing board to size, using knife or saw.
GOE: 06.04.34 STRENGTH: L GED: R2 M1 L1 SVP: 2 DLU: 77

739.684-130   MOUNTER, SMOKING PIPE (fabrication, nec)

Assembles bits and stummels of smoking pipes by one of following methods: (1) Reams hole in shank, using reamer. Inserts tenon end of bit into hole and aligns mouthpiece with pipe bowl, using hands. May insert filter. (2) Places filter in shank, secures bit in chuck, and starts machine to screw bit into shank. Removes pipe from machine. Tightens bit and aligns mouthpiece with pipe bowl, using wrench.
GOE: 06.04.23 STRENGTH: L GED: R2 M1 L1 SVP: 2 DLU: 77

739.684-134   NEEDLE-BOARD REPAIRER (tex. prod., nec) alternate titles: needle setter

Repairs needle board by replacing defective needles: Positions needle board on repair rack or bench. Pulls out dull, broken, or bent needles with pliers. Reverses board and inserts new barbed needles into drilled holes and hammers them tight. May prepare new needle boards by inserting needles according to specified pattern.
GOE: 06.04.34 STRENGTH: L GED: R2 M1 L2 SVP: 3 DLU: 77

739.684-138   OIL-SEAL ASSEMBLER (leather prod.)

Assembles oil seals by placing and positioning specified number of metal, leather, and rubber parts in specified sequence in metal case, using fingers and handtools: Arranges and stacks parts on workbench. Inspects and discards parts having defects, such as scratches and burs. Inserts and aligns parts in metal case, following specified sequence. Records number of oil seals assembled and stacks them in pan. May position springs around periphery of parts, using handtool. May examine oil seal after crimping and closing in press for exterior defects as cuts and nicks.
GOE: 06.04.23 STRENGTH: S GED: R2 M2 L2 SVP: 3 DLU: 77

739.684-142   PAINT-ROLLER COVERMAKER (fabrication, nec)

Performs any combination of following tasks in fabricating paint roller covers: Cuts material to shape for use in making roller covers, following pattern and using handtools. Flattens stitching in lambskin material with hand flattener to produce smooth surface. Combs nap of material, bevels ends, and shaves nap, using beveler or shear machine, to provide uniform size and form to cover. Feeds material into machine that cuts material to specified length. Feeds material into machine that reverses fabric and inserts and glues tube into fabric or glues and inserts core (tube) into lambskin material to fabricate paint roller cover.
GOE: 06.02.32 STRENGTH: L GED: R2 M1 L1 SVP: 2 DLU: 77

739.684-146   PICTURE FRAMER (retail trade; wood prod., nec) alternate titles: fitter

Frames pictures in custom-made or stock frames: Mounts picture on backing, using glue. Cuts mounted picture to fit frame, using papercutter or power saw. Cuts glass to fit frame, using glass-cutting tool. Cleans glass and places it in upturned frame. Places picture on top of glass. Cuts piece of cardboard to fit frame, and places it on back of picture. Pushes or taps brads into frame or uses stapler to staple picture in place. Glues paper cover to back of frame. Attaches screw eyes and wire to frame, using handtools or staple gun. May frame oil paintings that do not require glass fronts or paper covers. May repair and redecorate old or broken frames.
GOE: 01.06.02 STRENGTH: L GED: R3 M1 L1 SVP: 5 DLU: 77

739.684-150   SCREEN MAKER (paper goods)

Builds printing screens used to reproduce designs on wallpaper: Cuts and assembles wood or metal frames of specified dimensions for printing screens, using saw, miter box, and other handtools, or fits together screen frame from precut and pregrooved parts. Clamps frame to screen stretcher and lifts bolt of specified screening material to letoff rack. Pulls screening material over frame and secures edges of screening on anchor pins of screen stretcher. Turns adjustment wheels on screen stretcher to stretch and straighten screening. Examines

and feels screen to determine straightness and tension. Staples or glues screening materials to frame.
GOE: 06.04.34 STRENGTH: L GED: R2 M1 L1 SVP: 3 DLU: 77

739.684-154   TICKET-CHOPPER ASSEMBLER (furniture)

Assembles prefabricated components of ticket choppers: Fits and aligns parts, such as legs, sides, doors, and chopper, by riveting, screwing, or otherwise fastening parts together. Marks holes to be drilled and bores them, using power drill. Secures parts with rivets, and flattens rivet ends with hammer. Screws chopper and handwheel to partially assembled box. Places glass panes in grooves in front and on top of box. Attaches locks, hinges, and other hardware to completed box, using rivets and hammer.
GOE: 06.04.22 STRENGTH: M GED: R2 M1 L2 SVP: 5 DLU: 77

739.684-158   TIRE MOUNTER (fabrication, nec) alternate titles: tire assembler

Assembles hard rubber tires and wheel rims for articles, such as lawn mowers and baby carriages: Places rubber tire into jaws of spreading device and depresses pedal to close jaws and stretch tire. Positions wheel rim on spindle mandrel at center of tire. Pushes button to open jaws that release tire onto rim and removes wheel from spreading device.
GOE: 06.04.23 STRENGTH: L GED: R2 M1 L1 SVP: 2 DLU: 77

739.684-162   UMBRELLA TIPPER, HAND (fabrication, nec) alternate titles: framer; tacker

Handsews umbrella covers to frames: Tacks cover to ribs along seams and sews corners to tip of rib. Sews ties to outside of cover to hold umbrella when folded.
GOE: 06.04.27 STRENGTH: S GED: R2 M1 L1 SVP: 2 DLU: 77

739.684-166   VENETIAN-BLIND ASSEMBLER (furniture; retail trade)

Assembles aluminum, plastic, and nylon parts to form venetian blinds, using handtools and power tools: Installs cord lock, cord drum cradle, worm gear, and braces in position within head (top) portion of venetian blind, using pedal-operated riveter or press and handtools. Attaches tapes and cords. Places required number of slats through loops in tape and threads cord through holes in slats. Trims and fastens end of tape to bottom rail. Places caps on bottom rail to close ends and secure tape in position. Pulls lowering, raising, and turning cords to detect and adjust functioning defects. Wraps and packs blinds for shipment. May tend power press to form and cut slats, head, and hardware attached within head. May assemble shades with vertical louvers and be designated Vertical-Shade Assembler (furniture).
GOE: 06.04.22 STRENGTH: M GED: R2 M2 L2 SVP: 3 DLU: 77

739.684-170   WEAVER (fabrication, nec) alternate titles: mounter; weft maker

Interlaces hair strands in prescribed sequence, using weaving fixture, and sews weft (woven piece) to mounting cord to make hair pieces, such as switches and braids: Attaches threads of designated color and texture to rods and pegs of weaving fixture. Turns pegs to tighten threads. Cuts strands from tuft of matched hair, using scissors and interweaves root ends around and between threads in prescribed sequence. Pulls strands straight and weaves successive strands to complete weft. Cuts and knots thread ends. Fastens mounting cord of specified color to hub of mounting reel and turns reel handle to wind cord. Hand sews free end of cord to end of weft with matching thread. Turns mounting reel to twist weft seam around cord. Loops end of cord and sews remaining seam to loop, folding seam at intervals to smock (gather) hair.
GOE: 06.02.32 STRENGTH: S GED: R2 M1 L1 SVP: 4 DLU: 77

739.684-174   WOODEN-SHADE HARDWARE INSTALLER (furniture)

Installs draw cord and pulley hardware to complete assembly of wood indoor or porch shades: Places shade on table and measures length and width of shade to verify dimensions. Lays out and drills holes for lock pulley and screw eyes on wooden shade mounting strip, using pencil, ruler, and hand or power drill. Screws lock pulley and screw eye into place and threads draw cord through pulley to screw eye to complete assembly. Packs shade in box for shipment.
GOE: 06.02.22 STRENGTH: M GED: R3 M2 L2 SVP: 3 DLU: 77

739.684-178   WOVEN-WOOD SHADE ASSEMBLER (furniture)

Assembles woven-wood shades, performing any combination of following tasks: Cuts woven-wood material to specified length and width, using scissors or razor blade. Verifies length of shade material with tape measurer, applies glue to bottom slats of shade material, rolls slat over, and clamps slats with hand clamp to allow glue to dry and form hem or valance. Attaches headrail to top of shade material, using handtools, pneumatic stapler, and portable electric drill. Cuts specified design along bottom of shade material or valance and attaches fringe to cut portion, using shears and glue. Installs pulley in headrail, using handtools, cuts cord with knife, and threads cord through shade and pulleys to complete assembly of shade. Pulls cord to cause movement of shade to detect and adjust functioning defects. Examines damaged shades to determine extent of damage and repairs damage, using handtools, tape, glue, and needle.
GOE: 06.02.27 STRENGTH: M GED: R2 M2 L2 SVP: 3 DLU: 77

739.684-182   WREATH AND GARLAND MAKER (fabrication, nec)

Assembles wreaths and garlands, using conifer boughs and artificial decorations: Cuts conifer boughs to length, using pruning shears, and sorts them according to shade of color. Ties boughs to garland cord or circled wreath form with wire, spacing boughs to attain uniform appearance. Attaches specified decorations, such as holly, artificial berries, glass balls, and ribbon.

GOE: 06.04.23 STRENGTH: L GED: R2 M1 L2 SVP: 2 DLU: 77

739.684-186 PIPE STEM REPAIRER (fabrication, nec)

Repairs or replaces defective pipe stems, using stem mounter, press, grinding wheel, and handtools: Inspects pipes to determine defects. Removes and replaces defective screw-stem assemblies, using screwdriver, glue, press, and stem mounter. Smooths ends of unlevel pipe bowl shank to eliminate cracks between shank and stem, using grinding wheel. Heats defective adjustomatic stems, inserts stems in pipe bowl shank, and twists stems, using pipe stem wrench, to adjust alignment of stem and bowl. Replaces broken push-bit stems, using press machine.

GOE: 06.04.34 STRENGTH: S GED: R2 M1 L1 SVP: 6 DLU: 86

739.684-190 CASKET ASSEMBLER (fabrication, nec) alternate titles: fitter

Assembles wooden caskets from preformed panels and moldings and attaches supplemental hardware: Nails and glues side, end, and bottom sections together to form casket body. Assembles preformed sections of top frame, using hammer, glue, clamping nails, and bar clamps. Locates and marks midpoint of top frame, using ruler and pencil. Glues and nails panelboard and brace block between sides at midpoint for reinforcement. Positions template over top edge of body or measures body with ruler to locate position of hinges and catches, and recesses positions, using hammer and chisel or portable router. Drills holes at specified locations, using portable power drill. Installs hardware, such as corners, handles, hinges, and catches, using hand or power screwdriver. Sands and planes edges between body, top frame, and top panel to form tight joint, using planer or portable sander. Attaches top panel to top frame, using hand or powered screwdriver. Measures, cuts, and attaches ornamental molding or beading to casket body, using saw, hammer, miter box, and ruler. Sets nailheads, using hammer and nail set. Fills cracks and nail holes with wood filler or plaster of paris by hand or with putty knife. Smooths joints and edges, using sandpaper and handtools. May cut or trim wood to specified size for use in assembly of casket, using cutoff saw. May be designated according to part of casket assembled as Body Maker (fabrication, nec); Cap Maker (fabrication, nec); Molding Fitter (fabrication, nec); Panel Fitter (fabrication, nec); Top-Frame Fitter (fabrication, nec); Top-Frame Maker (fabrication, nec).

GOE: 06.02.22 STRENGTH: M GED: R3 M2 L2 SVP: 3 DLU: 78

739.685-010 ASSEMBLER, FINGER BUFFS (tex. prod., nec)

Tends machine that forms finger buffs to lacings to produce fabric buffing wheels: Positions lacings over center guide of circular tray (form) and secures lacing with weight. Inserts *finger buffs* under points of lacing, using marks on tray as guides. Positions tray under ram of pressing machine and depresses pedal to lower ram that forces points of lacing into material. Removes assembled buffing wheel from tray. May tend pressing machine to press parts assembled by other workers, and be designated Lacing Presser (tex. prod., nec). May tend press to insert cardboard, wood, or metal cores in cloth buffing wheels, and be designated Core Inserter (tex. prod., nec).

GOE: 06.04.20 STRENGTH: L GED: R2 M1 L1 SVP: 2 DLU: 77

739.685-014 BRUSH MAKER, MACHINE (fabrication, nec)

Tends machine that inserts and secures bristles into ferrule to form paint brush heads: Places bristles on feed belt and stacks ferrules in vertical feeding magazine. Starts machine, observes movement of bristles on belt, and taps bristles on belt with fingers to control level of bristles. Turns wheel to position specified amount of bristles for brush head and to facilitate placement of ferrule around bristles. Notifies supervisor when machine malfunction occurs. Verifies length of bristles in brush head, using gauge. Combs bristles with electric brush to straighten bristles and packs completed brush head in box.

GOE: 06.04.20 STRENGTH: L GED: R2 M1 L1 SVP: 2 DLU: 77

739.685-018 BRUSH-HEAD MAKER (fabrication, nec)

Tends machine that glues brush bristles within ferrule to form brush head, using either of following methods: (1) Places specified weights of epoxy glue and acid in tank of pouring machine for mixing. Holds brush under machine spout that dispenses glue into ferrule to cover bristles to designated height and secure bristles in place. Places glued brush head into tray for drying. (2) Inserts brush base, of ferrule and bristles, into holes of machine table that rotates under glue head that dispenses glue into bristles in ferrule. Removes brush head and inserts plastic core into ferrule. Positions brush head in air-operated press that forces core into position within ferrule. Places brush head in drying rack and inserts rack into oven for curing and drying.

GOE: 06.04.20 STRENGTH: L GED: R2 M1 L1 SVP: 2 DLU: 77

739.685-022 CLIPPER (fabrication, nec)

Tends rotary or lever-type machine that cuts brooms to specified length and removes rough fiber ends: Sets indicator gauge according to broom length specified, positions broom on turntable, and pushes table to feed edge of broom into rotating circular knife; or moves stop along scale on table to set machine according to length of broom specified, places broom on table against stop, and lowers blade by hand. May examine brooms and remove defective fibers or twine. May attach metal cap to handle tip, using hammer and nails. May sew brooms together at brush end with needle and thread, tie handles with twine, and wrap brooms in paper for shipping.

GOE: 06.04.09 STRENGTH: M GED: R2 M1 L1 SVP: 2 DLU: 77

739.685-026 MOP MAKER (tex. prod., nec) alternate titles: mop-machine operator

Tends broom-winding machine that attaches mopheads to handles: Places spool of wire or twine on wire holder and threads wire or twine through machine guides. Inserts mop handle into chuck of winding machine and turns handwheel to tighten chuck, securing handle in chuck. Threads wire or twine through hole in handle and ties wire or twine around handle by hand. Positions mop yarn around handle and depresses pedal to start machine that rotates handle and winds wire or twine around yarn strands, securing yarn to handle. Drives nail into handle and twists end of wire around nail, or ties twine with looping device to secure wound twine to handle. Removes mop from machine. May trim ends of yarn to even mophead. May tend machine that cuts yarn into lengths for use as mopheads [CUTTER (tex. prod., nec) 686.685-022]. May tend machine to bore holes in handles.

GOE: 06.04.20 STRENGTH: L GED: R2 M1 L1 SVP: 2 DLU: 78

739.685-030 PAINT-ROLLER WINDER (fabrication, nec) alternate titles: spiral winder

Tends machine that winds and glues fabric on tubing to make paint rollers: Fills glue spreader reservoir. Turns thermostat control knobs to maintain glue at specified temperature or dips paint roller into glue to apply glue evenly to roller. Mounts tubing on power-driven machine spindles and starts machine to rotate tube. Turns valve to regulate flow of glue and to distribute it evenly over surface or rotating tube. Positions, holds, and feeds precut fabric against glued surface of rotating tube as fabric is spirally wound and glued on tube. Removes wound tube from machine spindles. May glue and trim fabric, using handtools to repair paint roller covers. May glue loose ends to paint roller covers, using gluing machine. May bevel ends of roller cover, using spindle beveling machine.

GOE: 06.04.05 STRENGTH: L GED: R2 M1 L1 SVP: 3 DLU: 77

739.685-034 SHANK THREADER (fabrication, nec)

Tends machine that cuts threads inside shank of smoking pipes: Places pipe bowl in holding fixture and starts machine threading device. Pushes shank against revolving tool of threading device that cuts threads inside predrilled shank hole. Removes pipe from holding device and examines threaded shank for conformance to standards.

GOE: 06.04.03 STRENGTH: L GED: R2 M1 L1 SVP: 2 DLU: 77

739.685-038 STACKING-MACHINE OPERATOR II (any industry)

Tends stacking machine that stacks metal or plastic plates or sheets to assemble laminated products, such as rotor cores or storage battery elements, or to form bundles for shipment: Places specified material into one or more feed magazines or holding devices of machine. Starts machine that counts and stacks specified number of pieces for each assembly or bundle. Places stack in basket or in magazine of machine for further processing. May insert spacers between bundles to form continuous stack.

GOE: 06.04.02 STRENGTH: M GED: R2 M1 L1 SVP: 2 DLU: 77

739.685-042 STEM-PROCESSING-MACHINE OPERATOR (fabrication, nec)

Tends bench machine that automatically fabricates pipestems for corncob pipes: Examines wooden dowels for cracks and chips, and discards defective dowels. Positions dowel in holding device of stem processing machine. Presses button to start machine that automatically shapes dowel to form pipestem, bores airhole in stem, and taps ferrule onto stem. May dip end of pipestem in glue, tap stem into pipe bowl, and apply decal to pipe bowl [ASSEMBLER, CORNCOB PIPES (fabrication, nec)].

GOE: 06.04.03 STRENGTH: L GED: R2 M1 L1 SVP: 2 DLU: 77

739.685-046 TAPPER, BIT (fabrication, nec)

Tends press that inserts bushing into end of smoking pipe bits which connects bit to shank: Places rubber bit in hot water to expand hole. Places bit and bushing in opening of press and activates automatic mechanism that forces bushing into end of bit. Allows bit to cool and contract around bushing.

GOE: 06.04.34 STRENGTH: S GED: R2 M1 L1 SVP: 2 DLU: 77

739.685-050 TAPPER, SHANK (fabrication, nec)

Tends machine that screws bushing into shank of smoking pipe for use in connecting stem to shank: Places previously glued bushing on threaded projection of tapping machine and holds threaded end of shank against bushing until they are screwed together. Reverses machine to remove threaded projection from bushing.

GOE: 06.04.20 STRENGTH: S GED: R2 M1 L1 SVP: 2 DLU: 77

739.685-054 UMBRELLA TIPPER, MACHINE (fabrication, nec)

Tends machine that attaches metal or plastic tips to corners of prestitched umbrella covers: Positions tips in machine fixture and holds corner of cover in position to receive tips. Presses pedal of machine to release tips and secure tips to corners of cover. May sew tips in place with needle and thread [UMBRELLA TIPPER, HAND (fabrication, nec) 739.684-162].

GOE: 06.04.20 STRENGTH: S GED: R1 M1 L1 SVP: 2 DLU: 77

739.685-058 WREATH MACHINE TENDER (button & notion)

Tends machines that form straw into rope, wraps yarn around straw rope to form floral wreath bases, and winds vinyl around floral wreath bases to cover straw and complete floral wreaths: Mounts spools of yarn on spindles of roping machine and draws yarn through guide. Starts roping machine that moves straw through forming and tying mechanism to form straw rope. Winds straw rope around ring guide specified number of times and starts machine that automatically winds yarn around ring of straw rope to form wreath base. Positions straw wreath base and starts machine that automatically rotates wreath base and winds vinyl around base to cover straw. Examines wreath form to ensure straw is cov-

ered and places completed form on worktable. May be designated according to machine tended as Roping Machine Tender (button & notion); Wreath Wrapper, Machine (button & notion).
GOE: 06.04.09 STRENGTH: M GED: R2 M1 L1 SVP: 2 DLU: 77

739.687-010 ASSEMBLER-ARRANGER (fabrication, nec) alternate titles: arranger-assembler
Assembles decorative wall plaques by hand: Arranges flowers or other ornamental material, according to prepared design, and glues parts on pasteboard, plastic, or wooden background. Places sheet of glass over design and applies gummed tape around edges to hold glass in place. May assemble decorative arrangement, using twisting machine to fasten arrangement together.
GOE: 06.04.23 STRENGTH: L GED: R2 M1 L1 SVP: 2 DLU: 77

739.687-014 ASSEMBLER, CORNCOB PIPES (fabrication, nec) alternate titles: bit setter; borer, stem; ferruler; reamer; stem assembler; stem setter
Joins parts, such as bowls and stems, to assemble corncob pipes, performing any combination of following tasks: Dips end of pipestem in glue and taps stem into pipe bowl, using mallet. Hammers metal ferrule onto end of pipestem and holds end of stem over rotating reamer to enlarge hole in stem for insertion of mouthpiece. Positions pipe bowl over flexible airhose and bends hose to release air that blows sawdust from reamed bowl. Inserts paper filter or metal cleaner into mouthpiece of pipe and taps mouthpiece into pipestem, using mallet. May apply decals to pipes. May hold pipe bowl over rotating reamer to cut end of stem that protrudes into bowl or bevel end of pipe stem for insertion into pipe bowl, using cutting blade. May rotate pipe on heated die or against flame to char and color pipe bowl.
GOE: 06.04.23 STRENGTH: L GED: R1 M1 L1 SVP: 2 DLU: 78

739.687-018 ASSEMBLER, FILTERS (glass products)
Assembles fiberglass filters for use in industrial and domestic heating and cooling units: Places layer of precut treated fiberglass between perforated metal sides for reinforcement. Inserts assembly in cardboard frame and folds sides of frame over edges of reinforcements. Secures sides in place, using glue and staples. Seals edges of frame, using gummed tape.
GOE: 06.04.23 STRENGTH: L GED: R2 M1 L1 SVP: 3 DLU: 77

739.687-022 ASSEMBLER, GARMENT FORM (fabrication, nec)
Joins together prefabricated, linen-covered papier mache garment form sections to hold, fit, or shape garments being manufactured or altered. Inserts pedestal into cavity of assembled form and fastens form to pedestal, using handtools.
GOE: 06.04.23 STRENGTH: L GED: R2 M2 L1 SVP: 2 DLU: 77

739.687-026 ASSEMBLER, FILTERS (auto. mfg.)
Assembles air, fuel, and oil filters for use on internal combustion engines used to power equipment, such as motor vehicles, aircraft, locomotives, and agricultural, construction, industrial, and marine equipment, performing any combination of following tasks: (1) Folds, convolutes, and cures filter paper. Places roll of paper on holder and threads paper through machine. Observes machine for jamming or overcuring. (2) Assembles pack (filter paper), metal tube, and jacket (perforated filter paper) into unit. (3) Dips ends of unit in liquid plastic solution. (4) Places metal, plastic, or cardboard disks on ends of unit. (5) Places unit in machine that automatically fastens sealers on ends.
GOE: 06.04.23 STRENGTH: L GED: R2 M2 L2 SVP: 2 DLU: 78

739.687-030 ASSEMBLER, SMALL PRODUCTS II (any industry)
Performs any combination of following duties to assemble parts of various materials, such as plastic, wood, metal, rubber, or paperboard, to produce small products, such as roller skates, toys, shoe lasts, musical instrument parts, or loudspeakers: Positions parts in specified relationship to each other, using hand, tweezers, or tongs. Bolts, screws, clips, cements, or otherwise fastens parts together by hand, using handtools, portable powered tools, or bench machines. Performs fastening, force fitting, or light cutting operations, using machines such as arbor presses, punch presses, taps, spot-welding or riveters.
GOE: 06.04.23 STRENGTH: L GED: R2 M1 L1 SVP: 2 DLU: 81

739.687-034 BEADER (furniture)
Installs plastic molding strips into slotted edges of metal tabletops, using mallet and bandsaw: Positions center of molding strip over leading edge of tabletop as it moves along conveyor, and pushes tongue of molding into slot along entire edge of tabletop. Pounds molding with mallet to seat molding firmly in slot. Lifts tabletop from conveyor onto worktable, and cuts off overlapping ends of molding, using bandsaw. Pounds trimmed ends of molding into slot to form tight joint. Heats molding strips in hot water tank prior to installation when specified on job order.
GOE: 06.04.24 STRENGTH: M GED: R1 M1 L1 SVP: 2 DLU: 77

739.687-038 BLOCK INSPECTOR (fabrication, nec)
Observes wooden match blocks passing on conveyor and removes those containing pitch pockets, faulty grain, and knots.
GOE: 06.03.02 STRENGTH: L GED: R1 M1 L1 SVP: 2 DLU: 77

739.687-042 BROOMCORN GRADER (fabrication, nec) alternate titles: broomcorn sorter
Sorts broomcorn fibers according to specified length and quality to determine fibers to be used as cores, or outer layer: Opens bales of broomcorn stems with wire cutter. Examines and removes stems which are short, off-color, broken,

or do not otherwise meet standards. Measures lengths of standard stems or panicles, using grading table scale. Determines grade of stems according to length, color, and fineness of fiber. Bundles and labels graded broomcorn. May remove seeds and straighten fibers [BROOMCORN SEEDER (fabrication, nec)] or cut stalks to length.
GOE: 06.03.02 STRENGTH: L GED: R2 M1 L2 SVP: 3 DLU: 77

739.687-046 BRUSH FILLER, HAND (fabrication, nec) alternate titles: draw hand
Fills prebored brush heads with hog bristles, horsehair, nylon, vegetable fiber, or other brush-filling materials: Secures brush base in bench fixture. Threads wire through hole in brush head. Loops end of wire around filling material, pulls material through hole in brush head, and ties wire to secure material. Repeats process until holes are filled.
GOE: 06.04.23 STRENGTH: S GED: R2 M2 L2 SVP: 3 DLU: 77

739.687-050 CANDLE CUTTER (fabrication, nec) alternate titles: wick cutter
Cuts wicks, using scissors and knife, to separate candles after wax-dipping process: Places candles, assembled on metal frame, on revolving stand. Rotates stand by hand and cuts wicks at butt end. Removes candles from frame and examines for defects in shape and finish. May grade candles according to size and type. May trim ends, using hand dies.
GOE: 06.04.34 STRENGTH: M GED: R1 M1 L1 SVP: 2 DLU: 77

739.687-054 CANDLE MOLDER, HAND (fabrication, nec)
Molds candles by hand: Places wick over center of one section of mold, presses mold halves together and fastens with rubberband. Pours wax through opening and places mold in water to harden wax. Separates mold and removes candle. Scrapes excess wax from candle surface, using knife, and examines for surface defects and uniformity of color.
GOE: 06.04.32 STRENGTH: L GED: R2 M1 L1 SVP: 3 DLU: 77

739.687-058 CLEANER (fabrication, nec) alternate titles: wiper
Wipes smoking pipes with cloth to remove dust, putty, and other foreign matter: Places pipes in box or bin according to style. May clean inside of bit, using pipe cleaner.
GOE: 06.04.39 STRENGTH: L GED: R2 M1 L1 SVP: 2 DLU: 77

739.687-062 CLEANER, SIGNS (fabrication, nec)
Cleans and polishes electrical and outdoor signs and letters: Washes glass, plastic, and painted signs and letters with cleaning agent and water, cleaning compound, or acid solution and cloth or brush to remove dirt, stains, and other foreign matter. Dries surfaces, using cloth, chamois, or squeegee. Rubs metal signs and letters with cleaning agent to remove dirt and corrosion, and polishes with clean cloth.
GOE: 05.12.18 STRENGTH: M GED: R2 M1 L1 SVP: 2 DLU: 77

739.687-066 COMPACT ASSEMBLER (jewelry-silver.)
Joins upper and lower halves of vanity compacts: Inserts pins in hinges to join halves, using fingers or tweezers. Attaches spring catch lock by pressing it into place with pinching tool. Fits mirror on inside of cover.
GOE: 06.04.23 STRENGTH: S GED: R2 M1 L1 SVP: 2 DLU: 77

739.687-070 DIGGER (fabrication, nec)
Digs into bowl and shank of smoking pipe blank with pointed tool to remove rough spots and smooth surface: Examines bowl and shank for imperfections. Digs out rotten briar, or stones and smooths rough spots with a pointed tool, exercising care not to dig too deep into wood. Fills holes with putty to give smooth surface to bowl and shank.
GOE: 06.04.25 STRENGTH: S GED: R2 M1 L2 SVP: 3 DLU: 77

739.687-074 DUST-BRUSH ASSEMBLER (house. appl.)
Installs hollow-centered dust brush in vinyl plastic housing to form vacuum cleaner attachment: Loads plastic housings into tank of warm water to soften plastic material and increase elasticity. Removes warmed housing from water, and places housing in bench fixture. Inserts back of brush in housing, and presses down on brush with fingers to expand heat-softened wall of housing, and force brush into retaining groove. May remove plastic housing from mold while housing is still warm and elastic, and place housing in bench fixture, rather than place housing in warm water to soften.
GOE: 06.04.23 STRENGTH: L GED: R1 M1 L1 SVP: 2 DLU: 77

739.687-078 DUST-MOP MAKER (tex. prod., nec) alternate titles: dry-mop maker
Inserts triangular shaped metal rod through binding material sewn to yarn strands to form dust mopheads. Ties ends of binding material to secure mophead to rod.
GOE: 06.04.23 STRENGTH: L GED: R1 M1 L1 SVP: 2 DLU: 77

739.687-082 EXAMINER (fabrication, nec)
Inspects and packs umbrellas preparatory to shipping: Examines covers for pattern matching, tears, and stitching defects. Clips loose threads from umbrella, using scissors. Inspects frames for defects, such as bent ribs and missing tips. Stacks rejected umbrellas for correction. Inserts accepted umbrellas in wrappers and packs them in cartons according to types, sizes, and pattern designs. Records types and quantities of packed umbrellas. May hold opened umbrella over steam nozzle to smooth covering.
GOE: 06.03.02 STRENGTH: L GED: R2 M1 L1 SVP: 2 DLU: 77

739.687-086 EYE-DROPPER ASSEMBLER (glass products)
Slips rubber bulbs over ends of glass tubes to form eye droppers.

GOE: 06.04.23 STRENGTH: S GED: R2 M1 L1 SVP: 2 DLU: 77

739.687-090 FILLER (fabrication, nec)
Fills cavities in exterior surface of corncob pipe bowls with plaster of paris: Mixes plaster paste and water. Places cob bowl on revolving spindle. Applies plaster to sides and ends of bowl by hand, filling cavities and smoothing exterior surfaces of bowl. May apply sealer to interior of hickory pipe bowls to seal bowls.
GOE: 06.04.34 STRENGTH: L GED: R1 M1 L1 SVP: 2 DLU: 77

739.687-094 FIRE-EQUIPMENT-INSPECTOR HELPER (any industry) alternate titles: fire-and-safety helper
Assists FIRE-EQUIPMENT INSPECTOR (any industry) in testing, inspecting, and repairing fire-fighting equipment. Performs other duties as described under HELPER (any industry) Master Title.
GOE: 05.07.01 STRENGTH: M GED: R2 M2 L2 SVP: 3 DLU: 77

739.687-098 FLOOR WORKER (wood prod., nec)
Removes centers from cork or plastic washers, using screening box: Dumps washers into screening box. Presses washers against wire-mesh bottom or shakes box to remove centers from washers. Dumps washers into cartons for shipping.
GOE: 06.04.34 STRENGTH: L GED: R1 M1 L1 SVP: 1 DLU: 77

739.687-102 GASKET INSPECTOR (nonmet. min.) alternate titles: picker
Separates precut gaskets from strips of cork, rubber, or composition material and examines gaskets for defects, such as cuts or flaws in material. Sorts gaskets according to type and places gaskets on table for packing.
GOE: 06.03.02 STRENGTH: L GED: R2 M1 L1 SVP: 2 DLU: 77

739.687-106 INSPECTOR I (fabrication, nec)
Inspects boxed matches to ensure that they meet product specifications: Opens sample cases of matches from each pallet load and inspects boxes for labeling and packing. Examines matches for quality of coating. Ignites several matches to ascertain that they strike and burn efficiently and safely. Routes rejected loads for further inspection, salvage, or disposal. May inspect match strip sections for defects, such as tears, uneveness, incomplete slitting, and compressed heads.
GOE: 06.03.02 STRENGTH: L GED: R2 M1 L2 SVP: 3 DLU: 77

739.687-110 INSPECTOR III (furniture) alternate titles: checker
Inspects metal furniture and parts for defects: Verifies color of furniture against work ticket specifications. Feels and visually inspects furniture and parts for defective quality and damage, such as unwelded joints, wrinkled or torn upholstery, and dents. Marks defective areas with chalk or crayon, and segregates furniture and parts requiring repair.
GOE: 06.03.02 STRENGTH: L GED: R2 M1 L1 SVP: 3 DLU: 77

739.687-118 INSPECTOR, WREATH (fabrication, nec)
Inspects holiday decorations made from twigs and boughs, such as wreaths and door charms, for completeness and quality: Examines pieces received from individual workers or on conveyor belt to ascertain that specified greens and decorative items have been combined in required proportions, that each assembly is full and symmetrical, and that binding wires are tight and secure. Trims protruding twigs, boughs, and wire ends with pruning shears or nippers.
GOE: 06.03.02 STRENGTH: L GED: R2 M1 L1 SVP: 3 DLU: 77

739.687-122 MOP-HANDLE ASSEMBLER (tex. prod., nec) alternate titles: handle maker
Assembles handles for detachable mopheads, performing any of following tasks: Inserts butt end of handle into spring, positions lever between spring and handle, and fastens spring and lever to handle, using automatic stapler. Positions metal head over end of handle and fastens head to handle, using automatic stapler. Pulls wire bail over metal head and inserts end of bail through holes in levers.
GOE: 06.04.23 STRENGTH: L GED: R2 M1 L1 SVP: 2 DLU: 77

739.687-126 NAILER (tinware)
Fastens wooden bottoms in metal jackets used as protective covering for containers, such as gasoline and oilcans: Fits jackets over cans and inserts circular wooden block into jackets, flush with edge of jackets and against bottoms of cans. Drives nails through lower rim of jackets into wooden bottoms.
GOE: 06.04.23 STRENGTH: L GED: R1 M1 L1 SVP: 2 DLU: 77

739.687-130 ORNAMENT MAKER, HAND (fabrication, nec)
Cuts, folds, glues, and assembles holiday ornaments and wrappings, such as tinsel balls, artificial holly wreaths and trees, Christmas tree lights, and ribbon, using handtools, such as scissors, pliers, wirecutters, and staplers.
GOE: 06.04.23 STRENGTH: L GED: R2 M1 L1 SVP: 3 DLU: 77

739.687-134 PAINT-ROLLER ASSEMBLER (fabrication, nec)
Performs any combination of following tasks to assemble paint rollers: Places shaped metal rod in fixture of ram press machine and aligns paint roller handle with end of rod and machine ram. Depresses pedal activating ram that forces handle onto rod. Assembles roller cage (body) to extended metal rod of handle and secures cage to rod with locknut or screw. Places plastic end cap over locknut or screw to cover end of roller, using capping machine or by hand. Examines roller for ease of movement and correct alignment and places roller in container.

GOE: 06.04.23 STRENGTH: L GED: R2 M1 L1 SVP: 2 DLU: 77

739.687-138 PART MAKER (jewelry-silver.)
Forms and lines parts for use in jewelry and instrument cases, performing any combination of following duties: Glues specified fabric on cardboard blanks to make lining base. Inserts cotton pad in lining to form cushion. Places glue-coated fabric on precut metal strip in jig and pulls handle of heating device to fold and seal fabric around strip to form bracelet-type watch holder. Places covered bracelet band on metal cylinder and shapes by hand or in groove of forming device and turns handle to shape band around form. Inserts wire spring in lining pad and positions pad and bracelet on holders in fixture. Pulls feeder that picks up and fits spring into groove on bracelet. Pulls lever of fastening device to press spring in place and fasten bracelet to pad or inserts bracelet into groove by hand. Records number and type of parts made. May be designated according to specific part made as Bracelet-Form Coverer (jewelry-silver.); Bracelet Former (jewelry-silver.); Cushion Maker, Hand (jewelry-silver.); Lining Maker, Hand (jewelry-silver.); Pad Assembler (jewelry-silver.).
GOE: 06.04.27 STRENGTH: L GED: R2 M1 L2 SVP: 3 DLU: 77

739.687-142 PATCH DRILLER (fabrication, nec)
Examines briar pipe stummels and removes defects, using drill: Examines and feels pipes to detect cracks, splits, and decayed wood. Guides pipe against rotating drill, varying angle of cut and pressure on pipe, according to type and size of defect. Deposits pipes in boxes according to size of drillings.
GOE: 06.04.25 STRENGTH: L GED: R2 M1 L1 SVP: 3 DLU: 77

739.687-146 PATCHER (fabrication, nec) alternate titles: inspector; repairer
Examines smoking pipes for cracks, splits, and holes: Fills imperfections with putty, using knife and fingers. May mix putty according to formula. May insert paper filter into pipe stem upon completion of examination and repair of pipe. May be designated according to size of defects patched as Fine Patcher (fabrication, nec); Rough Patcher (fabrication, nec).
GOE: 06.04.34 STRENGTH: L GED: R2 M1 L1 SVP: 3 DLU: 78

739.687-150 PIPE-SMOKER-MACHINE OPERATOR (fabrication, nec)
Tends machine that breaks in (chars) new pipe bowls: Inserts pipes into suction tubes on machine, fills bowls with tobacco, and lights tobacco, using torch. Turns valve on and off to pull air through pipes in simulated series of puffs. Removes pipes from machine, empties ashes, and wipes bowl with cloth. Inspects interior of charred bowls to verify conformance to company standards. Places processed pipes in box.
GOE: 06.04.18 STRENGTH: L GED: R2 M1 L1 SVP: 2 DLU: 77

739.687-154 POLISHING-PAD MOUNTER (optical goods) alternate titles: pad maker
Applies pitch and mounts cloth pads on surface of metal *laps I* used for polishing lens surfaces: Heats metal laps over gas flame. Rubs bar of pitch or pours molten pitch on heated lap surface and positions cloth pad on lap. Places cup-shaped holder of same curve as lap over cloth pad and clamps assembly in bench press until pitch sets. May apply pad or remove old pad, using knife.
GOE: 06.04.34 STRENGTH: L GED: R2 M1 L1 SVP: 2 DLU: 77

739.687-158 POURER (fabrication, nec) alternate titles: candle pourer
Pours molten wax to form candles by either of following methods: (1) Positions metal pins in center of molten wax to form holes for candle wicks and pours specified quantity of wax into molds to form candles. (2) Positions preassembled wicks and metal bases in containers. Pours measured amount of wax into each container to anchor wick assembly. Positions series of funnels (pouring assembly) above glasses and moves lever to fill glasses with wax. Trims wicks to uniform length with scissors. Packs finished candles in cartons.
GOE: 06.04.32 STRENGTH: L GED: R1 M1 L1 SVP: 2 DLU: 77

739.687-162 PULL-OUT OPERATOR (fabrication, nec)
Pulls out sheets of dried felt-base floor covering from racks in drying oven: Removes one sheet and splices end to next sheet, continuing drawing-out operation until all sheets have been removed.
GOE: 06.04.40 STRENGTH: L GED: R2 M1 L1 SVP: 3 DLU: 77

739.687-166 SELECTOR (fabrication, nec) alternate titles: stummel selector
Classifies smoking pipe stummels according to quality of briar and length of shank: Examines stummels for defects, such as cracks, splits, and decayed wood. Measures length of shank, using gauge. Classifies stummels according to specifications for each grade and places them in designated boxes. Dips high grade stummels in alcohol to bring out grain of briar and sorts them according to distinctiveness of grain. Discards defective briars. May inspect damaged pipes to determine method of salvage.
GOE: 06.03.02 STRENGTH: L GED: R3 M1 L2 SVP: 3 DLU: 78

739.687-170 SMOKING-PIPE LINER (fabrication, nec)
Coats chambers of pipe bowls with syrup or honey mixture to improve taste of pipes during breaking-in process: Cleans dust and other foreign particles from bowl and shank, using airhose. Dips brush or swab in specified syrup or honey mixture and applies mixture to chamber of pipe bowl to coat and sweeten bowl. Sets bowl aside to dry.
GOE: 06.04.33 STRENGTH: L GED: R1 M1 L1 SVP: 2 DLU: 77

739.687-174 STAINER (fabrication, nec)
Dips smoking pipe stummels into staining solution and places them on conveyors or in sawdust to dry. Places dry pipes in containers according to style.

GOE: 06.04.33 STRENGTH: L GED: R2 M1 L1 SVP: 2 DLU: 77

739.687-178 STARCHER (button & notion) alternate titles: sizer
Brushes on or immerses fabric in gelatin to stiffen fabric for use in making artificial flowers. Drapes fabric over poles to dry.
GOE: 06.04.34 STRENGTH: L GED: R1 M1 L1 SVP: 2 DLU: 77

739.687-182 TABLE WORKER (fabrication, nec) alternate titles: spotter
Examines squares (tiles) of felt-based linoleum material passing along on conveyor and replaces missing and substandard tiles.
GOE: 06.03.02 STRENGTH: S GED: R1 M1 L1 SVP: 2 DLU: 77

739.687-186 TRAVERSE-ROD ASSEMBLER (furniture)
Assembles traverse curtain rods for shipment: Secures rod in bench fixture and inserts and attaches pull cord, master slides, nylon sliders, and pulleys into rod slot. Slips retaining brackets over ends of rod to complete assembly. Stacks rods in boxes. May cut cord to specified length before insertion into rod slot. May adjust functioning of traverse rod to meet specifications, using handtools. May dismantle defective or damaged traverse rods to salvage parts, using handtools.
GOE: 06.04.23 STRENGTH: M GED: R1 M1 L1 SVP: 2 DLU: 77

739.687-190 UMBRELLA FINISHER (fabrication, nec)
Mounts puffs, enlarges handle hole, and glues handles on umbrellas: Places leather or cloth puffs over umbrella rod to cover top. Hammers ferrule over end of rod to secure puff in position. Reams socket of handle to enlarge hole, using floor-mounted electric drill. Spreads glue inside hole with brush and inserts handle into rod of umbrella frame. Opens umbrella cover and steams it over nozzle of steamer to remove wrinkles. Examines umbrellas and sets aside defective umbrellas for corrective processing. Inserts completed umbrellas into paper of plastic tubes preparatory to packing.
GOE: 06.04.34 STRENGTH: L GED: R1 M1 L1 SVP: 2 DLU: 77

739.687-194 VACUUM-BOTTLE ASSEMBLER (glass products)
Assembles vacuum bottles by placing plastic saddle in container bottom, inserting glass bottle in saddle, slipping metal locking ring over bottle, placing plastic stopper in mouth of bottle, and screwing plastic drinking cup onto threaded mouth of bottle.
GOE: 06.04.23 STRENGTH: L GED: R2 M1 L1 SVP: 1 DLU: 77

739.687-198 VENETIAN-BLIND CLEANER AND REPAIRER (any industry)
Cleans and repairs venetian blinds, using handtools: Dusts and washes blinds, using cloth, vacuum, brush, water and detergent. Hangs blinds on rack to dry. Examines blinds to detect defective or worn parts, such as cord, tape, or slats, and replaces parts, using handtools. May install blinds. May assemble blinds.
GOE: 05.12.18 STRENGTH: M GED: R2 M1 L1 SVP: 2 DLU: 77

739.687-202 WICK-AND-BASE ASSEMBLER (fabrication, nec) alternate titles: base-and-wick assembler
Fastens candlewicks to metal bases to make candles: Inserts wick through hole in base. Strikes flange of wick hole with metal die to crimp base onto wick. Ties specified number of assemblies together by twisting wicks to hold assemblies together. Places group of assemblies in containers. May tend wick-cutting machine that cuts wicks prior to assembly.
GOE: 06.04.23 STRENGTH: M GED: R2 M1 L1 SVP: 2 DLU: 77

739.687-206 BRUSH LOADER AND HANDLE ATTACHER (fabrication, nec)
Attaches plastic handles to wire ends of brush heads to assemble household brushes: Positions brush heads in fixtures attached to machine conveyor, following specified procedures. Aligns ends of plastic brush handles with heated wire ends of brush heads on conveyor, pushes hollow end of handles against heated wires, and twists handles to secure brush heads to handles. Occasionally adjusts temperature control of induction welder that heats brush head wire ends to maintain specified setting.
GOE: 06.04.34 STRENGTH: L GED: R2 M1 L1 SVP: 2 DLU: 86

739.687-210 PIPE STEM ALIGNER (fabrication, nec)
Inspects and aligns smoking pipe stems with pipe bowls, using pipe stem wrench, according to specifications.
GOE: 06.04.34 STRENGTH: M GED: R2 M1 L1 SVP: 1 DLU: 86

74 PAINTING, DECORATING, AND RELATED OCCUPATIONS

This division includes occupations concerned with applying decorative or protective materials, such as paint, enamel, varnish, shellac, stain, or oil to articles by brushing, spraying, wiping, or hand-dipping, includes preparing surface of the article, mixing coating ingredients, handrubbing filled or coated surfaces, and related activities.

740 PAINTERS, BRUSH

This group includes occupations concerned with covering or decorating surfaces, using brushes.

740.221-010 INSTRUCTOR, DECORATING (pottery & porc.)
Instructs workers in painting decorations on plates, bowls, saucers, and other bisque dinnerware: Demonstrates decorating techniques, such as brush stroking, color mixing and blending, and design highlighting to trainees. Explains procedures for adding water or glycerine to obtain prescribed consistency of paint. Evaluates and prepares reports of trainees' progress during various stages of training program. Recommends advancement, transfer, or termination of trainees to management. Consults with management and engineering personnel and recommends new techniques for improving quality of decorating process. May maintain production reports and attendance records.
GOE: 01.06.03 STRENGTH: L GED: R4 M2 L3 SVP: 7 DLU: 77

740.381-010 DECORATOR (glass mfg.; glass products) alternate titles: glass artist; pyroglazer
Paints pictures or designs onto surfaces of glassware, such as tumblers, vases, or bowls, using brush and following pattern or design: Mixes ceramic paints to obtain color specified on pattern. Places glassware onto table or workbench. Sketches outline of picture or design onto glassware. Paints design or picture onto glassware. Compares finished product with pattern. Places painted glassware onto moving conveyor. May rub in dry color on sandblasted areas of glass articles to tint them.
GOE: 01.06.03 STRENGTH: L GED: R4 M2 L3 SVP: 6 DLU: 77

740.381-014 LUSTER APPLICATOR (glass mfg.; glass products) alternate titles: hand decorator
Applies paint to exterior or interior of glassware, such as tumblers, vases, or bowls to tint glass and to apply luster to glassware: Mixes color with oil and water to obtain desired consistency. Centers glassware on balanced wheel and balances glassware on wheel with weights. Turns pivot pole with one hand to rotate wheel and glassware, and holds paint brush to glassware while resting arm on support to steady hand to apply thin layer of paint. Examines glassware for brush strokes. Places painted glassware onto moving conveyor.
GOE: 01.06.03 STRENGTH: L GED: R3 M2 L2 SVP: 6 DLU: 77

740.381-018 PAINTER (button & notion)
Applies paint to wire-framed, clear-plastic articles, such as flowers, leaves, and butterflies used in artificial artistic arrangements, to impart natural coloring, using brush: Selects specified colors of stain paint and adds paint thinner to each color to attain desired consistency. Applies successive coats of paint to plastic articles, using brush, to attain desired shades and hues necessary to achieve natural lifelike appearance. Removes excess paint, using brush or cotton swab. Hangs articles on rack to dry after each coat of paint. Maintains daily production record.
GOE: 01.06.03 STRENGTH: S GED: R3 M2 L2 SVP: 5 DLU: 77

740.484-010 STRIPER, HAND (any industry)
Paints stripes, letters, or decorative edges on bicycle frames, motorcycle fenders and tanks, utensils, or other stamped products, using handbrushes and enamel or lacquer. Marks area to be stamped, lettered, or decorated, using rule or template. Mixes paint and matches colors according to specifications, or uses prepared paints.
GOE: 01.06.03 STRENGTH: L GED: R3 M2 L2 SVP: 6 DLU: 77

740.681-010 LINER (pottery & porc.) alternate titles: bander; decorator, hand; gilder; line decorator
Draws line of color or gold around edge or rim of bisque or glost ware, such as cups and plates, with brush: Sets ware on wheel and centers it. Starts wheel revolving. Holds brush against spinning ware, resting arm or hand on support to steady it and make line straight. Draws lines on handles and oval or irregular-shaped ware freehand. May use hand roller to apply decorative color to ware edges. May mix color glazes by hand to obtain specified color shade. May paint bands or lines on exterior and interior of glassware, such as tumblers, vases, and bowls, and be designated Bander, Hand (glass mfg.; glass prod.).
GOE: 01.06.03 STRENGTH: S GED: R3 M1 L1 SVP: 5 DLU: 77

740.684-010 CHARGER I (jewelry-silver.)
Applies decorative colored enamel pastes to jewelry articles by hand, following specifications or sample articles: Places article in holding device and applies paste, using spatula, tweezers, or pick. Removes excess paste, using blotter or special brush to push back surplus enamel that spreads over design.
GOE: 01.06.03 STRENGTH: S GED: R3 M1 L1 SVP: 3 DLU: 77

740.684-014 DECORATOR (pottery & porc.)
Paints decorations on plates, bowls, saucers, and other flat and hollow bisque dinnerware prior to glazing, using brush and following sample or design: Adds water to specified color of paint to obtain desired consistency. Turns ware by hand or using turntable and applies underglaze paint to smooth and raised surfaces, following ware sample or designs stamped or embossed on ware. Rubs ware with sponge, pumice stone, or abrasive cloth to remove excess paint and to achieve desired shaded effect in design. Stamps identification mark on bottom of ware, using rubber stamp. May carve holes in greenware, according to specified pattern to produce features such as bank slots and eyes. May paint glazed ware. May apply decals to glazed ware.
GOE: 01.06.03 STRENGTH: S GED: R3 M1 L1 SVP: 5 DLU: 81

740.684-018 ENAMELER (jewelry-silver.)
Applies decorative enamel to jewelry articles, such as pins, earrings, insignia, and award medals, using handtools and electric oven: Cleans jewelry in baths of acid and water, and scrubs surfaces with brush. Mixes ground colored enamel and distilled water, according to specifications. Applies enamel of various colors to designated areas of jewelry to form specified design, using spatula or pick. Places metal tray containing jewelry in electric oven to melt and fuse

enamel to jewelry. Immerses jewelry in baths of acid and water to remove oxide scale. Rubs enameled surfaces with abrasive stone to smooth and remove excess enamel. Reheats enamel in oven to produce luster.
GOE: 01.06.03 STRENGTH: S GED: R3 M2 L2 SVP: 4 DLU: 77

740.684-022 PAINTER, BRUSH (any industry) alternate titles: painter, hand

Brushes paint, lacquer, rustproofing agent, or other coating onto metal, woodstock, or fabricated items, using brush: Places workpiece on bench, stanchion, or floor. Cleans surfaces, using hand scraper, wire brush, sandpaper, or turpentine. Pours desired amount of thinner into paint. Paints articles, using brush. Cleans brushes and floor, using solvent or soap and water. May transfer items to and from work area, using hoist or handtruck. May be designated according to article painted as Last-Code Striper (wood prod., nec); Painter, Drum (any industry); Painter, Mannequin (fabrication, nec); Pipe Coater (steel & rel.); or according to coating applied as Japanner (any industry); Lacquerer (machine shop); Car Varnisher (railroad equip.).
GOE: 06.04.33 STRENGTH: M GED: R2 M1 L1 SVP: 2 DLU: 77

740.684-026 TOUCH-UP PAINTER, HAND (any industry) alternate titles: hand painter; retoucher; salvage painter

Paints articles, such as clock or instrument hands and dials, engraved surfaces, glass tubes, and ceramics, to cover or touch up articles, using brush: Inspects workpiece for inspector's markings or defects. Wipes, scrapes, sands, or applies cleaning solution to surface to prepare for retouching. Dips brush into specified paint or protective coating solution and applies it to surface of article specified. Brushes paint over surface and wipes it from unengraved area to paint engraved etchings. May apply coating of material, such as plastic wax or removable paint to mask surfaces for plating, painting, or metalizing. May straighten parts, such as clock dials or hands, using jig or bench press preparatory to painting. May paint original items, such as dials for custom-built instruments, freehand or using stencil or tracing device.
GOE: 06.04.33 STRENGTH: L GED: R2 M1 L1 SVP: 2 DLU: 88

740.687-010 BUTTON SPINDLER (button & notion) alternate titles: spindler

Paints rims or other parts of buttons, using artist's paintbrush and spinning device: Positions button on continuous spinning device and holds brush against part of button to be painted. Presses knee lever to activate knock-out device that automatically removes button from spinning device.
GOE: 06.04.33 STRENGTH: S GED: R1 M1 L1 SVP: 2 DLU: 77

740.687-018 PAINTER, EMBOSSED OR IMPRESSED LETTERING (any industry)

Colors identification or model numbers, brand names, or designs embossed or impressed in articles, using brush or roller: Positions workpiece on bench. Cleans area to be painted, using solvent-soaked cloth. Brushes or rolls paint, lacquer, or ink of specified color over embossed or impressed lettering or design. Wipes excess material from surrounding surfaces, leaving embossed or impressed areas coated with coloring material. May be designated according to article decorated as Dice Spotter (toy-sport equip.); Painter, Battery Brand And Vent Plug (elec. equip.).
GOE: 06.04.33 STRENGTH: L GED: R2 M1 L1 SVP: 2 DLU: 77

740.687-022 PAINTER, PANEL EDGE (furniture) alternate titles: paint and table edger

Applies paint to unfinished edges of plastic panels, using hand roller, prior to assembly of panels into tabletops. Wipes excess paint from top of edges, using rag. Stacks panels on pallet for transporting to assembly line.
GOE: 06.04.33 STRENGTH: L GED: R1 M1 L1 SVP: 2 DLU: 77

741 PAINTERS, SPRAY

This group includes occupations concerned with covering or decorating surfaces, using spray guns and stencils.

741.684-010 ARTIST, MANNEQUIN COLORING (fabrication, nec) alternate titles: decorator

Applies paint or lacquer to papier mache mannequin to simulate parts of body and articles of clothing: Sets mannequin on revolving table in spraybooth. Masks parts preparatory to spraying, using gummed paper. Selects color according to part to be colored, such as red for lips, blue for eyes, and black for shoes, and sprays figure, using airbrush. May attach eyelashes to eyes of finished display forms. May specialize in one phase of coloring, such as tinting of body or painting of eyes.
GOE: 01.06.03 STRENGTH: L GED: R3 M1 L2 SVP: 4 DLU: 77

741.684-014 FOAM-GUN OPERATOR (plastic prod.)

Sprays mixture of resins and activators (foam) on reinforced plastic products, such as shower stalls, bathtubs, and automobile body parts, using foam gun: Turns valves to obtain specified mixture, quantity, and force of resin and activator to gun nozzle. Directs spray onto workpiece to insulate, reinforce, or build up thickness of product, according to specifications. Moves sprayed items to curing area, using dolly. Cleans nozzle and spray equipment, using menthol chloride.
GOE: 06.02.24 STRENGTH: M GED: R3 M2 L2 SVP: 3 DLU: 77

741.684-018 PAINTER, AIRBRUSH (any industry)

Coats, decorates, glazes, retouches, or tints articles, such as fishing lures, toys, dolls, pottery, artificial flowers, greeting cards, and household appliances,

using airbrush: Stirs or shakes coating liquid and thinner to mix solution to specified consistency. Pours solution into airbrush container, couples airbrush to airhose, and starts compressor or opens valve on compressed-air line. Turns adjusting sleeve on nozzle of airbrush to regulate spray pattern to size of workpiece or area to be sprayed. Presses button on airbrush to spray coating over workpiece, or to spray specified designs and decorations on workpiece, spraying freehand or using stencils, masks, screens, and tape. Cleans airbrush nozzle and hose with solvent. May be designated according to article sprayed as Bait Painter (toy-sport equip.).
GOE: 01.06.03 STRENGTH: L GED: R3 M1 L1 SVP: 5 DLU: 77

741.684-022 PAINTER, MIRROR (glass products) alternate titles: paint sprayer

Sprays heated paint onto silvered surface of glass to protect silver coating: Starts conveyor that moves silvered glass through painting and drying areas. Starts pump that circulates hot water through hose to heat paint and starts heating units of drying ovens. Turns valve to start paint flowing to spray gun and directs spray over surface of glass. Observes heat pump indicator and air pressure gauge to determine that specified temperature and air pressure are maintained. Turns thermostat to regulate temperature of ovens.
GOE: 06.04.33 STRENGTH: M GED: R3 M2 L2 SVP: 4 DLU: 77

741.684-026 PAINTER, SPRAY I (any industry) alternate titles: spray-gun operator

Sprays surfaces of machines, manufactured products, or working area with protective or decorative material, such as paint, enamel, glaze, *gel-coat*, or lacquer, using spray gun: Cleans grease and dirt from product, using materials, such as lacquer thinner, turpentine, soap, and water. Applies masking tape over parts and areas that are not to be coated [MASKER (any industry) 749.687-018]. Fills cavities and dents with putty to attain smooth surface. Selects and mixes coating liquid to produce desired color, according to specifications, using paddle or mechanical mixer. Pours coating liquid into spray container and connects gun to airhose, using wrenches. Turns sprayer valves and nozzle to regulate width and pressure of spray according to knowledge of painting technique. Pulls trigger and directs spray onto work surface to apply prime or finish coat. Coats areas inaccessible to hand sprayer, using brush. Cleans spraying equipment and brushes with solvent. May heat and spray wax onto products after they are tested. May use acid, wire brush, or steel wool to remove rust from metal. May paint designs on rug surfaces for decorative purposes or for use as guidelines in carving rugs, using spray gun and stencil, and be designated Stenciler (carpet & rug). May be designated according to article sprayed as Hat Sprayer (hat & cap); Painter, Ordnance (ordnance); Sprayer, Railroad Car (r.r. trans.); or according to material used as Gel-Coat Sprayer (ship-boat mfg.; toy-sport equip.); Porcelain-Enamel Sprayer (any industry). May be designated: Ceramic Sprayer (brick & tile; pottery & porc.); Enameler (pottery & porc.); Enamel Sprayer (any industry) I; Glaze Sprayer (auto. mfg.); Lacquer Sprayer (any industry) I; Painter, Insignia (aircraft mfg.; auto. mfg.); Panel Finisher (paint & varnish); Primer Sprayer (aircraft mfg.; auto. mfg.); Sprayer, Auto Parts (auto. mfg.); Thinner Sprayer (auto. mfg.). May act as lead person in group.
GOE: 05.10.07 STRENGTH: M GED: R3 M2 L2 SVP: 4 DLU: 89

741.684-030 PORCELAIN-ENAMEL REPAIRER (any industry) alternate titles: appliance painter-and-refinisher; slusher

Repairs porcelain enamel finish on commercial and household appliances or fixtures: Inspects marked defects, such as chipped or cracked surfaces to ascertain extent of damage and determine repair procedures. Removes old porcelain or smooths rough spots, using sandpaper, emery stone, and power grinder. Turns spray gun nozzle and valves to set spray pattern and to adjust air pressure. Coats defective area with enamel, using spray gun, to fill holes or other flaws. Cleans spray gun, paintbooths, hoses, and pressure tanks, using solvent, putty knife, and brush. May brush on porcelain. May replace damaged appliance panels or trim, using screwdriver, wrench, or pliers.
GOE: 06.04.33 STRENGTH: H GED: R3 M1 L1 SVP: 2 DLU: 77

741.685-010 SPRAY-PAINTING-MACHINE OPERATOR (any industry) alternate titles: automatic-spray-machine operator

Tends spray-painting machine that automatically applies lettering, diagrams, or designs on products, such as speedometer faces, automobile steering-wheel hubs, and radio or television control knobs: Places workpiece in masking jig and depresses pedal to clamp workpiece against stencil mask. Depresses pedal to spray exposed area of workpiece through mask. Removes product from jig and examines coating for smears, runs, incomplete painting, and similar flaws. Removes and places paint saturated masks in mask-washing machine for cleaning. May record production.
GOE: 06.04.09 STRENGTH: M GED: R2 M1 L1 SVP: 2 DLU: 77

741.687-010 PAINT-SPRAY INSPECTOR (any industry) alternate titles: finish inspector

Inspects finishes, such as paint, lacquer, or porcelain enamel on items, such as household appliances, automobiles, toys, or bicycles while items move along production line or in inspection bays to ascertain conformance to standards: Examines workpiece for scale, cracks, shade variances, or unpainted areas. Marks workpiece with symbol to indicate defective area and type of repair needed. Records number and type of units rejected and reasons for rejection. May mark other defects, such as loose welds and loose or missing parts. May inspect decals, identification markings or stenciling on workpiece to ensure specified lo-

cation, clarity, and alignment. May record number and types of metal and paint defects, using hand held, programmed data collector.
GOE: 06.03.02 STRENGTH: L GED: R2 M1 L2 SVP: 2 DLU: 86

741.687-014 PAINTER HELPER, SPRAY (any industry) alternate titles: paint-spraying-machine-operator helper; sprayer helper

Assists PAINTER, SPRAY (any industry) I 741.684-026 to spray-paint surfaces of materials or products, performing any combination of following tasks: Loads and moves materials to work area, using handtruck or dolly. Fills containers with prescribed quantities of paint and thinner. Applies masking to articles [MASKER (any industry) 749.687-018]. Installs specified nozzles in spray guns. Replaces screens and filters. Cleans and prepares surface of articles to be painted, using solvent, sandpaper, wire brush, and scraper. Pushes painted articles to and from drying oven, using handtruck. Cleans spray and drying chamber, conveyor, tanks, hoses, and nozzles, using solvent, brushes, and cloths. Racks workpieces on conveyor; and inspects, marks, and transfers finished pieces to stockroom or shipping areas. Positions articles in jigs or erects ladders and scaffolds. Performs other duties as described under HELPER (any industry) Master Title.
GOE: 05.12.03 STRENGTH: M GED: R2 M1 L1 SVP: 3 DLU: 81

741.687-018 PAINTER, SPRAY II (any industry) alternate titles: painter, rough

Performs duties as described under PAINTER, SPRAY (any industry) I 741.684-026 where coating of surface or product is required without need for finished appearance. Sprays manufactured articles on assembly line, or travels to work site to spray materials, such as waterproofing, adhesive, foam, or paint, onto surfaces of articles. May be designated according to article sprayed as Coil Sprayer (electron. comp.); Mica-Parts Sprayer (electron. comp.); Painter, Barrel (petrol. refin.); or according to coating applied as Enamel Sprayer (any industry) II; Lacquer Sprayer (any industry) II; Sizing Sprayer (furniture). May be designated: Dag Sprayer (electron. comp.); Doper Operator (tinware); Lipcoat Sprayer (any industry); Painter, Blackwall Tire (rubber tire); Painter, Chassis (auto. mfg.); Painter, Electric Motor (any industry); Silicator (chemical); Special-Lining Applier (any industry); Spray Cementer (leather prod.); Sprayer (boot & shoe); Tile Sprayer (brick & tile); Timber Sprinkler (mine & quarry); Undercoat Sprayer (aircraft mfg.; auto. mfg.); Waterproofer (boot & shoe).
GOE: 06.04.33 STRENGTH: M GED: R2 M1 L1 SVP: 2 DLU: 90

741.687-022 STRIPER, SPRAY GUN (any industry) alternate titles: gun striper; mechanical striper; pencil striper

Paints decorative stripes on manufactured articles, using spray gun and templates: Fills reservoir of spray gun with paint or enamel. Positions straightedge, template, or other guide on article to be striped, and pulls trigger of gun to apply paint or enamel as gun is moved along surface. Touches up stripe, using brush, and wipes excess paint from surface, using cloth and turpentine. May stripe articles against molding or in groove of article without use of guide. May paint decorative stripes or spiral designs on articles such as bisque ware or wheels as they revolve on turntable or mandrel, using spray gun equipped with specified striping nozzle. May be designated according to product or article striped as Pottery Striper (pottery & porc.); Washing-Machine Striper (house. appl.).
GOE: 06.04.33 STRENGTH: L GED: R2 M1 L1 SVP: 2 DLU: 77

742 STAINING, WAXING, AND RELATED OCCUPATIONS

This group includes occupations concerned with applying liquid or paste materials to produce natural finishes on wood and similar materials.

742.134-010 SUPERVISOR, FINISHING (furniture)

Supervises and coordinates activities of workers engaged in applying finishing coats of liquid mixture of paint, varnish, solvent, and stain to wood furniture surfaces and rubbing and polishing surfaces to desired luster: Reviews work tickets to plan production schedules. Confers with supervisors of other departments to coordinate flow of materials and products. Determines finishing materials required for operations and requisitions materials from supply area. Inspects finish of furniture at various stages to verify conformance to company standards. Trains new workers. May monitor pressure gauges and turn valves to adjust flow of finish material, such as stain, paint, or lacquer, to spray guns. Performs other duties as described under SUPERVISOR (any industry) Master Title.
GOE: 06.02.01 STRENGTH: M GED: R4 M3 L3 SVP: 7 DLU: 79

742.684-010 RUBBER (furniture; wood prod., nec) alternate titles: burnisher; finisher

Rubs previously applied finish coat on furniture or other articles to produce lustrous or dull finish: Applies oil or wax to surface of article. Sprinkles powdered pumice stone on surface. Rubs surface with cloth or steel wool, or guides rubbing tool equipped with felt pad over surface to produce desired finish. Wipes residue from surface of article with cloth. May be designated according to type of finish obtained as Duller (furniture); Satin Finisher (furniture; wood prod., nec). May stain light spots and rub dark spots with sandpaper or steel wool to produce uniform coloring and be designated Brush Shade-Hand (furniture). May rub freshly stained furniture to produce highlights (thin spots in stain) and be designated High-Lighter (furniture).
GOE: 06.04.25 STRENGTH: M GED: R2 M1 L1 SVP: 3 DLU: 79

742.684-014 STAINER (furniture; wood prod., nec)

Stains parts of furniture or mirror and picture frames and other furniture items, using brush, pad, sponge, or spray gun, or by dipping parts or frames into vat of stain by hand. Rubs stained surface with cloth or felt pad to wipe off excess stain and distribute it evenly over surface. May be designated according to method of applying stain as Brush Stainer (furniture).
GOE: 06.04.33 STRENGTH: M GED: R2 M1 L1 SVP: 3 DLU: 78

742.687-010 WIPER (furniture) alternate titles: rubber; wiper-blender

Rubs surfaces of furniture, to which filler, stain, glaze, or washcoat has been applied, to remove surplus filler or finish: Rubs filler into pores of open-grained wood and spreads stain, glaze, or washcoat evenly over wood surfaces, using brush, cloth, or power rubbing tool. Wipes surfaces with cloth to remove excess filler or finish. May apply filler or finish to surfaces. May smooth rough spots on surfaces of furniture prior to application of glaze, using steel wool. May be designated according to coat wiped as Filler Wiper (furniture); Glaze Wiper (furniture); Stain Wiper (furniture); Washcoat Wiper (furniture).
GOE: 06.04.25 STRENGTH: M GED: R2 M1 L1 SVP: 2 DLU: 79

749 PAINTING, DECORATING, AND RELATED OCCUPATIONS, N.E.C.

This group includes occupations, not elsewhere classified, concerned with hand-dipping, cleaning, masking, and other activities involved in painting and decorating.

749.131-010 SUPERVISOR, DECORATING (pottery & porc.)

Supervises and coordinates activities of workers engaged in decorating ceramic dinnerware: Examines production schedule to determine type of dinnerware to decorate and type of decoration specified. Assigns tasks to workers, such as stamping or painting designs or lines on dinnerware and applying decals or colored underglaze to dinnerware. Confers with other supervisors to coordinate workflow. Requisitions required supplies and equipment. Demonstrates decorating techniques to workers and inspects decorated items to ensure compliance with company specifications and standards. Establishes and maintains worker training programs. Performs other duties as described under SUPERVISOR (any industry) Master Title. May be designated according to specific method of decorating as Supervisor, Decaling (pottery & porc.).
GOE: 01.06.03 STRENGTH: L GED: R4 M3 L3 SVP: 7 DLU: 77

749.131-014 SUPERVISOR, PAINT DEPARTMENT (any industry)

Supervises and coordinates activities of workers engaged in mixing paint, preparing surface of object to be painted, painting object, and drying or baking paint on object: May compute paint mixture formulas. May plan and program sequence of tasks for robots in spray paint booth. May move controls to adjust furnace temperatures, paint supply, hydraulic pressure, or conveyor speeds. May inspect painted surfaces for paint coverage, flow of paint, and color quality. May measure thickness and viscosity of paint applied to objects, using measuring devices. May be required to have experience with particular materials or products painted and application methods. Performs duties as described under SUPERVISOR (any industry) Master Title.
GOE: 06.02.01 STRENGTH: L GED: R4 M4 L3 SVP: 7 DLU: 86

749.134-010 SUPERVISOR, FINISHING (fabrication, nec)

Supervises and coordinates activities of workers engaged in spray painting, sanding, rubbing, and polishing wooden and metal caskets: Inspects casket finish in process and upon completion for smoothness of sanding, uniformity of staining, finish applications, and rubbing and polishing effects, to determine conformance to company standards. Demonstrates techniques to train new employees in finishing caskets. Performs duties as described under SUPERVISOR (any industry) Master Title.
GOE: 06.02.01 STRENGTH: L GED: R4 M2 L3 SVP: 8 DLU: 77

749.137-010 CHEST-PAINTING AND SEALING SUPERVISOR (ordnance) alternate titles: chest-painting leader

Supervises and coordinates activities of workers engaged in painting, striping, and lettering wooden chests for packing small-arms cartridges, and in cutting, forming, soldering, and painting metal liners for chests. Performs other duties as described under SUPERVISOR (any industry) Master Title.
GOE: 06.02.01 STRENGTH: L GED: R4 M3 L3 SVP: 8 DLU: 77

749.381-010 GILDER (any industry) alternate titles: gold charmer; gold-leaf gilder; metal-leaf gilder; metal-leaf layer

Covers surfaces of items, such as books, furniture, harps, and signs, with metal leaf, such as aluminum, gold, or silver, to decorate them, using brushes, T-shaped handtool, and hands: Brushes sizing (thin glue) on sections of items which are to be covered with leaf (gilded), according to design. Transfers leaf from supply book onto pallet. Rubs camel-hair brush in hair to electrify brush and picks up leaf with brush, or picks up leaf with T-shaped, felt-edged tool, and lays leaf over sizing; or presses sheets or ribbons of leaf onto sizing by hand. Smooths leaf over surface and removes excess, using brush. Rubs leaf with polished burnishing agate, cotton pad, or gloved hand to polish leaf or simulate worn metal finish. May brush or spray protective lacquer coat over gilded surface.
GOE: 01.06.03 STRENGTH: L GED: R3 M1 L1 SVP: 6 DLU: 77

749.587-010 RACKER (toy-sport equip.)

Clamps arrows in rack preparatory to dipping: Aligns arrows in row and slides one end of row into rack slot. Builds successive layers of arrows by sep-

arating rows with dividers until rack is filled. Clamps ends of arrows in rack to hold them securely. Removes dividers and transfers loaded rack to painting department. Keeps records of arrows racked.
GOE: 06.04.34 STRENGTH: L GED: R2 M1 L2 SVP: 2 DLU: 77

749.684-010 DECAL APPLIER (any industry) alternate titles: decal transferrer; design transferrer; print applier
Applies decal designs to surfaces by moisture process: Cleans surface to be covered, using moist cloth. Submerges decal in water to moisten adhesive and backing paper. Positions decal on surface visually or using template and smooths out air bubbles with roller or edge board. Slides backing paper from decal and wipes off excess adhesive with damp cloth. May cut out decals from sheet with scissors. May varnish over design. When applying decals to chinaware, may be designated Print Decorator (pottery & porc.).
GOE: 06.04.34 STRENGTH: L GED: R2 M1 L1 SVP: 2 DLU: 77

749.684-014 DECORATOR (furniture; toy-sport equip.)
Applies decorative designs to furniture or inflatable athletic balls by hand, performing any combination of following duties: Positions specified stencil on item and sprays or brushes paint into stencil opening to apply decorative designs or lettering, using spray gun or brush. Applies decal designs to surfaces by moisture process [DECAL APPLIER (any industry) 749.684-010]. Brushes shellac, paint, or gilt onto surface of furniture to form decorative designs, stripes, or letters. May be designated according to duties performed as Stenciler (furniture) or Striper (furniture).
GOE: 01.06.03 STRENGTH: L GED: R2 M1 L1 SVP: 4 DLU: 87

749.684-018 DECORATOR, LIGHTING FIXTURES (light. fix.) alternate titles: lamp decorator
Decorates lighting fixtures, such as lamp bases and chandeliers with designated designs by squeezing decorating material from plastic tube onto fixture: Mixes decorative material with water to obtain specified consistency. Pours material into plastic tube. Squeezes tube to eject decorating material onto workpiece while moving tube with free arm motion to form specified designs, such as flower petals.
GOE: 01.06.03 STRENGTH: L GED: R3 M1 L2 SVP: 3 DLU: 77

749.684-022 EDGE STAINER II (leather prod.)
Stains edges of leather articles, such as wallets and key cases, using either of following methods: Fills reservoir of spray gun or roller device with color of stain specified on work ticket. (1) Presses button to activate blower that removes spray mist and fumes from spray booth. Positions bundle of leather articles on turntable and pulls lever to lower ram that holds and compresses bundle for staining. Manually rotates turntable and sprays stain on edges of bundled articles, using spray gun. (2) Presses button and turns set screws to activate stain-saturated roller and to regulate amount of stain on roller. Holds and turns edges of leather articles against roller to stain edges. Places stained articles on worktable or revolving turntable to dry. May mix tinting liquids and stains to match color of leather articles. May be designated according to method of staining as Roller Stainer (leather prod.); Spray Stainer (leather prod.).
GOE: 06.04.33 STRENGTH: L GED: R2 M1 L1 SVP: 3 DLU: 77

749.684-026 FINISHER (wood. container)
Paints assembled wooden containers with primary coat of paint, using brush. Applies finish coat of paint over primary coat when it has dried, using spray equipment.
GOE: 06.04.33 STRENGTH: M GED: R2 M1 L1 SVP: 4 DLU: 77

749.684-030 FRAME TRIMMER I (wood prod., nec) alternate titles: shader and toner
Paints contrasting color of paint on mirror-or picture-frame molding: Compares color of mixed paint with sample and adds paint to mixture to match sample. Lays strip of molding face up on table. Dips cloth pad, steel wool, or sponge in paint and rubs pad over surface, or applies paint to portions of molding with brush or roller.
GOE: 06.04.33 STRENGTH: L GED: R2 M1 L1 SVP: 2 DLU: 77

749.684-034 LACQUERER (jewelry-silver.)
Coats surfaces of ornamental figurines and trophies with lacquer to preserve surface gloss: Adds thinner to lacquer to obtain desired viscosity. Verifies viscosity of lacquer in vat, using viscometer. Places metal objects in wire basket and immerses basket in lacquer, using hand-operated hoist, or sprays objects with lacquer, using spray gun.
GOE: 06.02.24 STRENGTH: L GED: R3 M2 L1 SVP: 3 DLU: 77

749.684-038 PAINTER, TOUCH-UP (any industry) alternate titles: final-touch-up painter; finish repairer; spot sprayer
Brushes or sprays paint to cover scratches, chips, or repairs in painted finish of items, such as refrigerator cabinets, washing machines, or automobile bodies: Cleans and prepares surface for painting, using water, solvent, and scraper. Applies thin, even coat of finish material, such as paint or lacquer, to sanded area, using spray gun. Sprays lacquer or thinner material over finish coats to blend in spots and eliminate halo around repair. Paints chipped spots with brush. Compares color of paint supply with color chart and workpiece and remixes it to match standard colors. Maintains spray painting equipment. May mark identifying code on workpiece to indicate destination for further processing.
GOE: 05.10.07 STRENGTH: M GED: R3 M1 L1 SVP: 4 DLU: 77

749.684-042 PUTTY GLAZER (any industry)
Applies coating of putty, mastic, or similar material to imperfections in manufactured articles, preparatory to application of paint or other final coating: In-

spects surface of article for defects, such as holes, cracks, and indentations. Spreads material over flaws, using dauber or knife, and brushes or spreads thinned putty or sealer over surface to conceal blemish. May spray article with prescribed coating, using spray gun. May prepare surface for finishing coat, using wire brushes, sandpaper, power grinder, or sandblasting equipment. May tend oven to bake article before or after application of final coating. May be designated according to article coated as Wheel Filler (auto. mfg.).
GOE: 06.04.33 STRENGTH: M GED: R2 M1 L1 SVP: 3 DLU: 77

749.684-046 STOVE REFINISHER (any industry)
Cleans, removes rust, polishes, and enamels used stoves and ranges: Dips stove or range shell and fittings into caustic solution which removes dirt and grease, using block and tackle. Transfers dipped article to drying oven. Removes rust from parts, using power-driven rotary wire buffer, and polishes brightwork surfaces on polishing wheel. Dips parts or article in enamel vat, using hoist, and transfers article to drying oven for prescribed time. May similarly refinish other articles, such as refrigerator cabinets, washing machines, and clothes driers.
GOE: 05.12.14 STRENGTH: H GED: R2 M1 L1 SVP: 3 DLU: 77

749.684-050 PAINT TRIMMER, PIPE BOWLS (fabrication, nec)
Trims excess paint from metal bands on shanks of smoking pipes, using paint trimmer and file: Examines pipe stummels to detect metal bands with excess paint. Places stummel bowl over paint trimmer stud, lowers trim blade, and rotates pipe stummel to trim off excess paint. Files excess paint from metal band around pipe bowl shank on designated pipe styles, using file. May operate tumbler barrel to smooth pipe stems and perform duties as described under TUMBLER OPERATOR (any industry) 599.685-110.
GOE: 06.04.34 STRENGTH: M GED: R2 M1 L1 SVP: 2 DLU: 86

749.684-054 WALLCOVERING TEXTURER (paper goods)
Applies paint to decorate textured wallcoverings in prescribed pattern: Reads production card and paint sample book to determine information, such as colors specified, patterns, and methods of paint application. Positions roll of wall covering stock on worktable, and tapes end of stock to takeup reel of drier used to dry painted stock. Drips specified paint onto stock, using stick or sponge depending on paint application method specified for pattern, dips paint roller into paint solvent, and spreads paint onto stock, according to pattern. Places blotting paper on wet paint, and rubs paper to remove excess paint and achieve pattern design. Pushes button to activate drier takeup reel to move painted wall covering into drier and unpainted stock onto worktable. Removes dried rolls of wallcovering and repeats process, using additional paints to achieve final pattern. Observes wallcovering in drier for breaks and tapes wallcovering together to repair breaks. Sprays water repellent on specified wallcovering, using spray gun.
GOE: 06.04.33 STRENGTH: M GED: R2 M1 L2 SVP: 3 DLU: 86

749.686-010 STRIPER, MACHINE (motor-bicycles)
Feeds motorcycle and bicycle fenders in machine that paints decorative trim on fenders: Inserts and guides fenders between paint wheels of machine that paints decorative stripes on fenders. Removes fenders from discharge end of machine and positions them on rack to dry. Examines stripes for consistency and thickness of paint. Wipes excess paint from fenders, using rag. Pours paint in machine reservoir to replenish supply. Removes drive mechanism and paint wheels from machine, using hex-key wrench, and cleans parts with brush and solvent.
GOE: 06.04.33 STRENGTH: L GED: R2 M1 L1 SVP: 2 DLU: 77

749.687-010 DIPPER AND DRIER (woodworking)
Immerses wooden articles, such as curtain-pole ends and doorstops in bath of paint or dye to form protective or decorative coating on articles: Hammers articles onto nails protruding from sides of reels (wooden disks with holes at centers), using rubber mallet. Dips article in bath, holding reel in horizontal position. Mounts reels on shafts of drying machines which rotate reels to hasten drying process. Pulls dried articles from nails by hand.
GOE: 06.04.33 STRENGTH: H GED: R1 M1 L1 SVP: 2 DLU: 87

749.687-014 KEG VARNISHER (wood. container)
Mixes varnish and dryer in tank. Dips and rolls keg in mixture to varnish surface.
GOE: 06.04.33 STRENGTH: M GED: R1 M1 L1 SVP: 2 DLU: 77

749.687-018 MASKER (any industry) alternate titles: body masker; taper
Covers specified areas of metal or wooden parts to be spray-painted, using masking tape, cardboard, or paper: Marks area to be masked on parts or articles, such as aircraft and automobile assemblies, lamp bases, or motorcycle fenders, using rule or template. Cuts or tears paper or cardboard to specified size. Secures masking in place with gummed tape to protect parts while surrounding areas are spray-painted. May smooth unmasked surface, using sandpaper. May dip or coat article with liquid wax instead of applying masking. May tape precut masks or stencils to article.
GOE: 06.04.34 STRENGTH: L GED: R2 M1 L1 SVP: 3 DLU: 77

749.687-022 PAINTER, SKI EDGE (toy-sport equip.)
Applies stain to ski edges, using felt-tip dauber: Pours specified amounts of enamel and mineral spirits in bowl and stirs mixture with plastic stick to prepare stain. Positions and clamps ski in vise to secure ski for daubing. Scrapes and washes ski edge, using razor blade, putty knife, cotton cloth, and solvent. Slides and dabs stain-saturated dauber along ski edge to apply stain. Wipes off

excess stain, using cotton pad. Occasionally conceals blemishes, such as rough spots and pits, using filler, blade, knife, steel wool, and abrasive cloth.
GOE: 06.04.33 STRENGTH: L GED: R2 M1 L1 SVP: 2 DLU: 77

749.687-026 PLASTERER (furniture) alternate titles: plasterer, spot
Fills in nicks, welding and die marks, and imperfections in metal furniture with plaster (special quick-drying metal filler) after priming coat is dry and preparatory to application of finishing coats, using putty knife to smooth filled spots. May smooth metal surfaces with sandpaper.
GOE: 06.04.33 STRENGTH: L GED: R2 M1 L1 SVP: 2 DLU: 77

749.687-030 STRIPPER (furniture) alternate titles: finish remover
Removes paint, lacquer, stain, or other finish from furniture and furniture parts by rubbing surface with cloth, brush, steel wool, and solvent to prepare them for refinishing. Immerses small articles in vat filled with solvent before rubbing. Blows excess solvent from surface with airhose or wipes surface dry with cloth.
GOE: 06.04.39 STRENGTH: M GED: R2 M1 L1 SVP: 2 DLU: 77

749.687-034 PIPE RACKER (fabrication, nec)
Inserts paper into pipe bowls and inserts dummy stems into bowl shanks to protect openings in stummels during painting process: Places pipes over pegs on bowl tray in specified sequence. Twists and removes stems, places stems in corresponding position on pipe stem tray, places dummy stem in pipe bowl shank, inserts paper into pipe bowl to plug bowl during painting. Replaces plugged bowl on peg. Examines painted pipe bowls, following painting process, to verify conformance to company standards. Removes paper from bowl, using pick. Twists and removes dummy stems and places tray of painted bowls in heated storage area to cure paint.
GOE: 06.04.34 STRENGTH: L GED: R3 M2 L2 SVP: 3 DLU: 86

75   OCCUPATIONS IN FABRICATION AND REPAIR OF PLASTICS, SYNTHETICS, RUBBER, AND RELATED PRODUCTS

This division includes occupations, not elsewhere classified, concerned with laying out, marking, cutting, carving, shaping, scraping, pressing, fitting, modeling, cementing, bench molding, and bench casting of products from plastics, synthetics, rubber, and related materials.

750   OCCUPATIONS IN FABRICATION AND REPAIR OF TIRES, TUBES, TIRE TREADS, AND RELATED PRODUCTS

This group includes occupations concerned with fabricating or repairing solid and pneumatic tires, pneumatic casings, inner tubes tire treads, and related products for such conveyances as vehicles, airplanes, farm equipment, and children's vehicles. Includes recapping and retreading automobile tires. Such minor repairs as patching inner tubes and sealing punctures in tubeless tires are included in Group 915.

750.130-010 SUPERVISOR (rubber tire)
Supervises and coordinates activities of workers engaged in manufacturing rubber tires and tubes. Inspects products in process to ensure adherence to specifications. Performs other duties as described under SUPERVISOR (any industry) Master Title. May be designated according to process involved as Bead Supervisor (rubber tire); Curing Supervisor (rubber tire); Millroom Supervisor (rubber tire); Rubber-Compounder Supervisor (rubber tire); Stock-Preparation Supervisor (rubber tire); Tire-Building Supervisor (rubber tire); Tire-Finishing Supervisor (rubber tire); Tire-Room Supervisor (rubber tire); Tube-Room Supervisor (rubber tire).
GOE: 06.02.01 STRENGTH: L GED: R4 M2 L4 SVP: 7 DLU: 77

750.132-010 RETREAD SUPERVISOR (rubber tire)
Supervises workers engaged in vulcanizing, retreading, and recapping automobile tires. Performs duties as described under SUPERVISOR (any industry) Master Title.
GOE: 06.02.01 STRENGTH: M GED: R4 M2 L3 SVP: 5 DLU: 77

750.367-010 QUALITY-CONTROL INSPECTOR (rubber tire)
Inspects completed rubber products or products in process for conformance to specifications: Inspects products for such items as width, weight, length and markings, using ruler, thickness and hardness gauge, protractor, and book of specifications. Verifies temperatures and pressures on machine recording instruments. Tags substandard products and discusses defects with department supervisors to correct them. Writes report on all substandard products. May inspect storage area to ensure specified racking of rubber goods. May inspect mixing machine to ensure that it is functioning according to specifications.
GOE: 06.03.01 STRENGTH: L GED: R3 M3 L2 SVP: 4 DLU: 77

750.382-010 TIRE TECHNICIAN (rubber tire)
Tests experimental and sample production tires to determine strength, wearability, and cause of failure: Inflates tire on test machine, and adjusts controls to simulate road conditions, such as speed, weight-mileage check, and roadbed. Operates test equipment, such as autographic load-deflection recording mechanism, deflection machine, dead-load pressure gauge checking machine,

and deflection-variation measurement machine, to evaluate tire uniformity, quality, and durability. Maintains periodic follow up on test until tire fails or has run for specified time. Cuts cross section from test tires, new experimental tires, or actual road tested tires with power saw. Counts bead wires and plies in cross section, verifies angle of plies with protractor, and measures specified areas on tire to ascertain effects of testing. Records test results and prepares graphs to compare test results.
GOE: 06.03.01 STRENGTH: M GED: R3 M3 L3 SVP: 5 DLU: 77

750.384-010 TIRE BUILDER, AUTOMOBILE (rubber tire)
Builds pneumatic tires on collapsible drum device from rubber components, such as beads, ply stock, tread, and sidewalls: Positions ply stitcher rollers and drum according to width of stock, using handtools and gauges. Rubs cement stick on drum edge to provide adhesive surface for plies. Pulls ply from supply rack and aligns with edge of drum. Depresses pedal to rotate drum, winds specified number of plies around drum to form tire body. Cuts ply at splice point and presses ends together to form continuous band. Brushes solvent onto ply to ensure adhesion and repeats process as specified, alternating direction of each ply to strengthen tire. Pushes switch to move bead setters that press prefabricated beads onto plies and to position rollers that turn edges of plies under and over beads. Winds chafers and breaker onto plies. Aligns tread with guide, Starts drum to wind tread onto plies, and splices ends. Starts rollers that bond tread and plies as drum revolves. Depresses pedal to collapse drum and lifts tire onto conveyor. May turn ends of plies under and over beads with steel rod. May build heavy-service or limited production tires for aircraft, trucks, or equipment and be designated Tire Builder, Heavy Service (rubber tire).
GOE: 06.02.29 STRENGTH: M GED: R3 M2 L2 SVP: 3 DLU: 77

750.384-014 TUBE BUILDER, AIRPLANE (rubber tire)
Cuts and cements rubber stock to build airplane tire tubes: Places templates on calendered gum stock, traces patterns, and cuts stock with scissors, holding edges at angle to obtain beveled cut. Washes edges with solvent and brushes on cement. Joins stock together to form tube by lapping and bonding edges with hand roller. Marks valve location with template and inserts valve in tube.
GOE: 06.02.29 STRENGTH: L GED: R2 M1 L1 SVP: 4 DLU: 77

750.387-010 TIRE CLASSIFIER (rubber tire)
Examines defective tires rejected by TIRE INSPECTOR (rubber tire) to determine extent of repair and disposition of tires: Segregates tires according to defects, such as spread cords, ply separations, buckles, and blisters, and sends them to TIRE REPAIRER (rubber tire). Probes defects with handtools to determine extent of damage. Prepares daily report of defects. Recommends disposal of nonrepairable tires. May repair minor defects, such as puncturing blisters or applying patches, to prepare tires for storage.
GOE: 06.03.01 STRENGTH: L GED: R3 M1 L2 SVP: 3 DLU: 77

750.681-010 TIRE REPAIRER (rubber tire)
Repairs defects in cured tires as identified by TIRE INSPECTOR (rubber tire), using handtools and rubber patch: Examines and probes tire with awl to determine extent of defect. Buffs blemishes from tire, using portable buffer. Cuts out rubber around cracks and buffs area to prepare it for patching. Cements gum rubber patch into cutout to build up defective area. Rolls down patch with hand stitcher and punctures air pockets in patch to remove trapped air. Buffs and trims excess patch rubber from tire. Replaces treads by cutting defective tread from plies, buffing ply surface, and cementing new tread onto plies. May tend vulcanizing machine to cure patch on tire for specified time. May replace imprinting plates on electronic replating machine to change or clarify markings on tire.
GOE: 06.02.29 STRENGTH: M GED: R3 M1 L2 SVP: 3 DLU: 77

750.684-010 BAND BUILDER (rubber tire) alternate titles: pocket builder
Builds *bands* for use in manufacturing truck tires: Positions ply stock on drum and aligns stock with sides of drum. Depresses pedal to rotate drum while guiding ply onto drum to form band. Swabs wrinkles with benzol and smooths by hand. Splices ends of plies by pressing with fingers. Repeats operation, reversing angle of splice until specified number of plies are formed into band. Depresses pedal or pulls lever to move rollers against band and rotate drum to bond plies. Pushes pedal to collapse drum and pulls band from drum.
GOE: 06.04.29 STRENGTH: L GED: R2 M2 L2 SVP: 2 DLU: 77

750.684-014 BEAD BUILDER (rubber tire)
Wraps rubberized tape around coiled and rubber coated wire to reinforce tire bead: Positions bead on machine guide wheels and sets roller clamps to hold bead. Applies end of stock(bead-wrap fabric, gum-filler strip, or bead-flipper fabric) to bead. Starts machine and guides stock from roll onto bead as it rotates. Cuts stock with scissors and presses loose ends onto bead with fingers. Releases clamps and lifts bead to rack. Tags and ties specified quantity and type of bead into bundles. May be designated according to stock applied as Bead Filler (rubber tire); Bead Flipper (rubber tire); Bead Wrapper (rubber tire).
GOE: 06.04.07 STRENGTH: L GED: R2 M1 L2 SVP: 3 DLU: 77

750.684-018 GREEN-TIRE INSPECTOR (rubber tire)
Inspects uncured tires: Measures tread width and sidewall dimensions with ruler and gauge. Weighs tires for conformance to specified tolerance, and keeps weight records on all tires. Verifies thickness of liner and ply stock to be used in tire fabrication, using dial thickness gauge. Stamps approved tires, and marks rejected tires.

GOE: 06.03.02 STRENGTH: L GED: R3 M2 L2 SVP: 4 DLU: 77

750.684-022 TIRE BUILDER (automotive ser.) alternate titles: retreader; tire rebuilder

Builds (molds) semi-raw rubber tread onto buffed tire casing to prepare tire for vulcanization in recapping or retreading process: Applies rubber cement to casing, using brush or spray gun preparatory to application of camelback (new rubber treads). Selects camelback according to whether tire is to be retreaded or recapped, tire width, and tread thickness specified. Rolls camelback onto casing by hand, and cuts it with knife. Rolls hand roller over rebuilt casing, exerting pressure, to ensure adhesion between camelback and casing. May place rebuilt casing in mold for vulcanization process.
GOE: 05.12.12 STRENGTH: H GED: R2 M1 L1 SVP: 3 DLU: 77

750.684-026 TIRE GROOVER (automotive ser.)

Cuts grooves in treads of worn, vulcanized, or retreaded tires, using hand cutting tool: Fastens tire on holder. Pulls electrically heated grooving knife around circumference of tread to form grooves, following old design or laying out new design. Cuts crosswise grooves in tread in similar manner.
GOE: 05.12.13 STRENGTH: M GED: R2 M1 L2 SVP: 3 DLU: 77

750.684-030 TIRE INSPECTOR (rubber tire) alternate titles: final inspector

Inspects cured tires to ensure conformance to standards: Lifts tire manually or with hoist onto turntable. Revolves table to inspect for sidewall cracks, foreign material, and blisters. Feels beads to detect kinks and feels inner surface of tire to detect spread cords, ply separations, or buckles. May trim toe of bead and mold overflow with knife [TIRE TRIMMER, HAND (rubber tire) 750.684-034]. Marks defects and sorts tires for removal to balance and label, repair, or classification sections. May use fluoroscope or camera to detect flaws in tires. May inspect inner tubes. May be designated according to type of tire inspected as Passenger-Tire Inspector (rubber tire); Truck-Tire Inspector (rubber tire).
GOE: 06.03.02 STRENGTH: L GED: R3 M2 L2 SVP: 4 DLU: 77

750.684-034 TIRE TRIMMER, HAND (rubber tire)

Trims excess rubber formed on solid or pneumatic tires during curing process, using knives: Lifts tire onto turntable or machine-driven rollers, or works on overhead or roller conveyors. Trims excess rubber from tread, sidewall, and inside diameter of tires as tire is rotated manually or mechanically. Lifts tire from table or pulls lever to remove it from rollers. May buff tires to remove defects and foreign matter and impart smooth finish, using power buffing wheel. May remove burrs and marks from rim band of solid tires, using power hand grinder or wire brush. May paint rim bands of solid tires with rust inhibiting coating. May be designated Solid-Tire Finisher (rubber tire).
GOE: 06.04.29 STRENGTH: H GED: R2 M1 L2 SVP: 2 DLU: 77

750.684-038 TIRE VULCANIZER (automotive ser.) alternate titles: cementer; patcher

Vulcanizes breaks and holes in casings and treads of motor vehicle tires: Cuts and trims broken sections of tire with knife. Scrapes and cleans area, using electrically or air-rotated wire brush. Coats break on inside of tire with rubber cement. Cuts raw and corded rubber patches and rolls them into rupture, using hand roller, to ensure adhesion. Covers rupture on outside of tire with tread rubber and works rubber into hole with hand roller. Trims patch, using knife. Places tire in tire mold of vulcanizing machine which has been heated to specified temperature. Adjusts air or steam bag inside tire, inflating it to exert pressure on tire in mold. Clamps tire in mold and allows it to remain until rubber is vulcanized and patch fused with surrounding rubber. May inspect and rebuff tire.
GOE: 05.12.12 STRENGTH: H GED: R2 M1 L1 SVP: 3 DLU: 77

750.684-042 TIRE-BLADDER MAKER (rubber tire)

Fabricates *bladders* used in tire curing presses, performing any of following duties: Brushes rubber cement on ends of skived rubber stock and splices stock into ring shape, using press to fuse ends. Removes spliced stock and weighs it on preset scale to ascertain conformance to specifications. Places ring in press that forms and cures bladder. May place spliced ring in stock preheater to soften it prior to molding. Dips cured bladder in water tank to cool it after molding. Trims and smooths bladder, using knife, hot knife, and hand buffer. Bolts steel fittings, used to attach bladder to curing press, to finished bladder, using handtools.
GOE: 06.04.29 STRENGTH: M GED: R2 M2 L2 SVP: 2 DLU: 77

750.684-046 TUBE BALANCER (rubber tire)

Tests tubes for airplane tires to ensure conformance to balance specifications and glues patch to tube to equalize weight: Inflates tube with airhose, and fits it over hub of gravity balance wheel to locate heavy area. Determines overweight and selects balance patch to equalize weight. Hand buffs and brushes cement on area to which patch is applied. Bonds patch to area, using hand roller.
GOE: 06.04.29 STRENGTH: M GED: R2 M1 L1 SVP: 3 DLU: 77

750.684-050 TUBE REPAIRER (rubber tire)

Repairs defects in cured tubes: Cuts out defective areas, such as buckles, cracks, and thin spots, with scissors. Buffs cut edge, washes with solvent, and brushes cement on area to be repaired. Applies uncured gum patch and bonds with hand roller. Removes defective valves, washes area, and applies new valve. Spot-cures repairs on automatic or manually operated air-ram press (hot plate). Buffs repaired areas to smooth finish with hand buffing machine.

GOE: 06.04.29 STRENGTH: M GED: R2 M1 L1 SVP: 3 DLU: 77

750.685-010 SQUEEGEE TENDER (rubber tire)

Tends unit of *band* building machine that rolls *squeegee* and gum strip onto ply stock: Lifts rolls of gum strip and squeegee onto letoff rods of machine and threads stock through series of guide rollers. Lifts bias-cut ply stock from conveyor to apron of machine. Turns setscrews to adjust apron guide and provide even application of squeegee and gum on ply stock. Starts machine to run squeegee and gum onto ply stock and to accumulate ply stock in *festoon* for BAND BUILDER (rubber tire). Splices each succeeding section of ply stock to previous one by hand to form continuous strip.
GOE: 06.04.07 STRENGTH: H GED: R2 M1 L1 SVP: 3 DLU: 77

750.685-014 TIRE RECAPPER (automotive ser.)

Tends machines that recap and retread tires for reuse: Inspects tire to determine whether it is suitable for recapping and rejects tire if damaged beyond repair. Pushes tire against power buffing wheels, using tire holder, to prepare tire for recapping or retreading. Builds new tread onto buffed casing, using brush or spray gun to apply rubber cement, and hand roller to cause tread to adhere to casing. Tends mold that vulcanizes tread onto tire and molds tread design, and adjusts controls to inflate air bag within tire to specified pressure and heat mold to required temperature. May tend machine that automatically ingests, extrudes, and applies rubber to buffed tire.
GOE: 05.12.12 STRENGTH: M GED: R2 M1 L1 SVP: 4 DLU: 77

750.687-010 INNER-TUBE INSERTER (rubber tire) alternate titles: tuber

Installs inner tubes and flaps in tires preparatory to shipping: Positions tire under hydraulic spreader clamps. Pushes switch to activate clamps that spread sidewall of tire. Inserts inner tube in tire with valve located at point marked by TIRE BALANCER (rubber tire). Inflates inner tube, using airhose. Inserts flap over inner tube to prevent damage.
GOE: 06.04.29 STRENGTH: H GED: R1 M1 L1 SVP: 2 DLU: 77

750.687-014 TIRE BALANCER (rubber tire) alternate titles: tire spotter

Inspects cured tires for conformance to balance specifications: Lifts tire onto balance table manually or with hoist. Pulls lever to spread holding fixture that secures tire in position. Releases lock that permits balance table to float freely on mounting and bubble gauge to function. Observes bubble gauge to determine if tire balance is within specified limits. Marks tire where gauge indicates lightest area, for location of inner-tube valve. Lays aside unacceptable tires and lifts acceptable tires onto conveyor. May affix identification labels on acceptable tires.
GOE: 06.04.29 STRENGTH: M GED: R2 M1 L1 SVP: 2 DLU: 77

750.687-018 TIRE INSPECTOR (automotive ser.)

Inspects used tires to be retreaded for automobiles, buses, trucks, and other automotive vehicles: Examines breaks in cord, bead and sidewall. Places tire on tirespreading machine and examines inner surface of tire for breaks. Marks breaks with chalk to indicate repairs required prior to retreading. Rejects tires that cannot be broken.
GOE: 06.03.02 STRENGTH: L GED: R3 M2 L2 SVP: 4 DLU: 77

750.687-022 TIRE SORTER (rubber tire)

Sorts cured and uncured tires according to size and type as indicated by identification number on tire: Compares number on tire and numbers on pallets, conveyors, hand or rock trucks leading to further processing, such as curing, finishing, buffing, or testing, and places tire on conveyance. Sorts uncured tires and places them on saddles (storage racks) prior to automatic curing.
GOE: 06.03.02 STRENGTH: L GED: R2 M1 L2 SVP: 3 DLU: 77

751 LAYING OUT AND CUTTING OCCUPATIONS, N.E.C.

This group includes occupations, not elsewhere classified, concerned with laying out, marking, and cutting of plastics, fiberglass, synthetics, rubber, and related materials.

751.381-010 PATTERNMAKER (engraving)

Lays out and cuts plastic patterns used for pantograph engraving according to sketches or blueprints, using drafting instruments and engraving tools: Establishes reference points on plastic sheet and computes layout dimensions, following blueprints. Marks or scribes lines on plastic sheet, using drawing tools, such as straightedge, compass, and scriber. Cuts out pattern, using jeweler's handsaw or jigsaw. May tend injection molding machine to form plastic patterns.
GOE: 01.06.01 STRENGTH: L GED: R4 M3 L3 SVP: 7 DLU: 77

751.387-010 STOCK PREPARER (plastic prod.)

Cuts milled plastic materials or rubber molding compounds to size for compression or transfer molding processes, using die press or papercutter. Weighs preforms to verify required weights. Discards off-standard pieces. Stacks preforms on trays for delivery to mold room. Records number of preforms prepared.
GOE: 06.04.34 STRENGTH: L GED: R2 M1 L1 SVP: 3 DLU: 77

751.584-010 COLD-ROLL INSPECTOR (plastic-synth.)

Examines continuous sheet of plastics material passing over artificially lighted glass inspection table and cuts out defective areas: Stops progress of plastics

sheet and removes spots, color streaks, wrinkles, and other defects, using knife or scissors. Applies solvent to ends of defective material, laps ends, and pounds lapped material with hands to reform continuous sheet. Threads material through equipment. Turns wheels to synchronize speed of cold rolls with flow of sheeting. Records weight of defective material.
GOE: 06.03.02 STRENGTH: L GED: R2 M1 L2 SVP: 4 DLU: 77

751.684-010 CUTTER-INSPECTOR (nonmet. min.)
Inspects for defects mesh tubular knit plastic mesh used to fabricate scouring pads: Mounts roll of mesh onto turntable spindle. Pulls end of mesh across table to align cutting guide thread with mark on table. Pulls handle of hinged knife blade to cut mesh to specified length. Inspects mesh as it is unwound to detect defects, such as skipped or uneven stitches.
GOE: 06.03.02 STRENGTH: L GED: R2 M1 L2 SVP: 2 DLU: 77

751.684-014 CUTTER, HAND (rubber goods) alternate titles: knife cutter; stock cutter; trimmer, hand
Performs any combination of following tasks to cut gaskets, diaphragms, or parts for hydraulic valves, radios, airplane deicers, and footwear from rubber sheeting, uncured rubber slabs, plastic, or cork: Mounts sheeting roll in letoff rack by hand or with hoist and pulls sheeting from roll or positions material on table. Cements sheets together to build up required thickness or piles together layers for cutting multiple parts. Places template on material, traces outline with pencil, and cuts out parts with scissors or cuts around template with knife. Places cut parts on truck for removal to next process station. Trims top of footwear following outline of binding or flash from molded heels or soles. Cuts slot on side or V in front of footwear to permit insertion of foot. Pares excess rubber or fabric from lasted toe to reduce thickness and prevent outsole from bulging at toe. Stamps sizes on shoe soles, using stamp and pad, and places finished outsoles in *book*. Embosses trademark on arch, using pedal-controlled press. May be designated according to part cut as Outsole Cutter, Hand (rubber goods).
GOE: 06.04.34 STRENGTH: L GED: R2 M1 L1 SVP: 2 DLU: 77

751.684-018 CUTTER, HOT KNIFE (boot & shoe; rubber goods)
Cuts parts for rubber footwear from uncured sheet rubber, using electrically heated knife: Presses knife onto rubber and guides it around outline on fabric lining. Strips and cuts away web (scrap) stock and throws into container. Cleans rubber deposit from knife edge, using file.
GOE: 06.04.29 STRENGTH: L GED: R2 M1 L2 SVP: 3 DLU: 77

751.684-022 FOXING CUTTER, HOT KNIFE (boot & shoe; rubber goods)
Cuts uncured rubber strips to specified lengths for use as foxing with electrically heated knife (hot knife): Places tray-filled parallel strips on worktable. Cuts rows of strips into equal lengths with diagonal ends for firmer bonding, using sample or judging length from experience. Swabs strips with benzine to restore adhesiveness for assembling to footwear. Sets tray of cut foxing on assembly line or stacks them on table.
GOE: 06.04.29 STRENGTH: L GED: R2 M1 L1 SVP: 2 DLU: 77

751.684-026 PREFORM PLATE MAKER (ship-boat mfg.)
Constructs wooden or paper templates for laying-out cutting lines on fiberglass materials used in manufacturing plastic boats: Positions sheets of paper on sections of molds for hulls, decks, or other parts of boat. Fits paper over contours and into corners of molds and marks outline with chalk. Removes paper from molds and cuts pattern, using scissors. Marks pattern with identifying data. Positions paper pattern on strips of wood and scribes outline of pattern on strips. Cuts wood strip according to markings, using power handsaw. Assembles strips to form template, using screws, nails, and braces. Positions template or pattern on fiberglass material and outlines pattern with chalk or crayon. Cuts material, following outline and using power cutter. Inspects rolls of materials received and stores them on shelves.
GOE: 06.02.31 STRENGTH: M GED: R3 M2 L2 SVP: 5 DLU: 77

751.686-010 HOSE CUTTER, MACHINE (rubber goods) alternate titles: cutting-table operator
Feeds cured rubber hose into machine that automatically cuts hose to specified lengths, or cuts hose, using miter box and knife. Coils cut hose as it emerges from machine and lifts it onto skid or conveyor for removal to packing area. May attach coupling hardware to hose.
GOE: 06.04.07 STRENGTH: H GED: R2 M1 L1 SVP: 2 DLU: 77

751.687-010 HOSE CUTTER, HAND (rubber goods)
Measures, rerolls, and cuts rubber hose to specified lengths: Positions reels of hose in letoff rack and empty reels in powered windup rack. Verifies diameter on hose, using gauges. Threads end of hose through measure meter and onto empty reel. Depresses pedal and guides hose onto windup rack. Examines hose for defects, such as snags, cuts, and bulges. Observes measuring meter and cuts hose to specified lengths, using knife. Weighs hose and records information on identification tag. May attach metal couplings or fittings to each end of hose.
GOE: 06.04.29 STRENGTH: H GED: R2 M1 L1 SVP: 3 DLU: 77

752 FITTING, SHAPING, CEMENTING, FINISHING, AND RELATED OCCUPATIONS, N.E.C.

This group includes occupations, not elsewhere classified, concerned with fitting, shaping, cementing, finishing, and similarly working plastic, fiberglass synthetics, rubber, and related materials.

752.684-010 BALLOON MAKER (rubber goods)
Cuts out inflatable rubber figures, such as animals and comic characters, for use in parades and carnivals. Punches hole and inserts air valve in each component member of figure, cements valve in place, and cements members together and to body of figure, forming inflatable balloon. Inflates figure and inspects for leaks.
GOE: 06.02.29 STRENGTH: L GED: R3 M2 L2 SVP: 3 DLU: 77

752.684-014 BELT BUILDER (rubber goods)
Builds up plies (layers) of rubberized fabric and gum to fabricate transmission and conveyor belts: Pulls fabric and gum plies of specified width onto table from rolls on letoff rack and aligns edge with previously laid ply. Cuts ply to length with scissors and bonds plies together, using rollers and stitchers. Builds up specified number of plies and trims irregular edges with scissors or knife. Splices belting to obtain specified belt. Inserts end of finished belt between pressure rollers that bond plies and roll belt onto windup rack. Signals OVERHEAD CRANE OPERATOR (any industry) 921.663-010 to lift and position rolls of stock and belting in work area. Measures finished belts with ruler and gauges for conformance to blueprints. May operate calender machine that coats and feeds plies direct to building table [CALENDER OPERATOR, FOUR-ROLL (plastic prod.; rubber goods; rubber tire)].
GOE: 06.04.29 STRENGTH: H GED: R2 M2 L2 SVP: 2 DLU: 77

752.684-018 BIT BENDER (fabrication, nec)
Softens and bends rubber or plastic smoking pipe bits, using either of following methods: (1) Places bits into machine drums that distribute bits onto conveyor that moves under ultraviolet lamps to soften bits. Bends softened bit, according to pipe style, using pliers. (2) Places bit in tube of hot water to soften bit. Positions bit in shaping bed of die and depresses lever to force platen against bit to shape bit.
GOE: 06.04.02 STRENGTH: L GED: R2 M1 L1 SVP: 3 DLU: 78

752.684-022 BUFFER (plastic prod.)
Removes ridges and rough edges from fiberglass or plastic castings. Holds casting against rotating buffing wheel to grind off ridges. Lifts casting from machine and places it in container.
GOE: 06.04.24 STRENGTH: M GED: R2 M1 L1 SVP: 2 DLU: 77

752.684-026 CATHETER BUILDER (rubber goods)
Cuts and shapes rubber surgical tubing for medical use: Seals one end of tubing with rubber plug and cuts sealed end to specified shape with knife. Fills tubing with water to aid curing process and ties off end. Lubricates shaped end when tubing dries, and pushes it into glass curing form. Holds vacuum hose over hole in end of form to draw tubing into curing form. Folds extending tied end of tubing down against outside of form, wraps it with tape, and covers hole in tube with cement to make tube airtight. Places form in rack for curing. Removes cement from hole after curing to allow air to enter and pulls tubing from form.
GOE: 06.04.29 STRENGTH: L GED: R2 M1 L1 SVP: 4 DLU: 77

752.684-030 HOSE MAKER (rubber goods) alternate titles: hose builder
Assembles rubberized fabric, rubber tubing, and gum rubber ply (layer) stocks to fabricate industrial hose: Lifts mandrel, using hoist, and locks end of mandrel in motorized chuck, using wrench. Swabs rubber tubing and ply stocks with solvent and rubber cement to clean them and provide adhesive surfaces. Aligns strips and sheets of ply stock with rubber tubing as specified. Depresses pedal to rotate mandrel and guides ply stock onto rubber tubing to form hose. Rolls assembled hose to ensure adherence of plies, using mechanical or hand roller and stitcher. Smooths wrinkles and presses loose plies together, using fingers and roller. Cements brand on assembled hose prior to curing. Measures dimensions of hose with rule, calipers, and gauges, and cuts off excess rubber with knife. Wraps fabric around hose to prepare hose for curing. Clamps or cements metal fittings to ends of hose, using rubber cement and handtools. May load and unload hose in autoclave heater, using hoist. May move cured hose to storage area, using hoist.
GOE: 06.02.27 STRENGTH: M GED: R3 M2 L2 SVP: 3 DLU: 77

752.684-034 PADDED-PRODUCTS FINISHER (rubber goods)
Repairs defects and finishes padded automotive products, such as dashboards and door panels: Pours or injects with hypodermic needle padding solution (liquid rubber foam) into defects, such as wrinkles and faulty adhesion between padding and plastic covering. Clamps molding form to repaired area and sets it aside to dry. Cuts out wrinkled plastic and selects piece of matching plastic and cements it to defective part. Repairs defects, such as abrasions, faulty embossing, and discoloration, using knives, scissors, hand buffing wheel, and spray gun. Removes wrinkles by softening plastic, using heat lamps, and pressing out wrinkles by hand. Applies solvents, cement, putties or paints to finish product.
GOE: 06.04.27 STRENGTH: M GED: R2 M1 L2 SVP: 3 DLU: 77

752.684-038 RUBBER-GOODS ASSEMBLER (rubber goods)
Assembles rubber goods, such as water bottles, ice bags, swim fins, water goggles, rubber gloves, and ring cushions: Cements and stretches molded opening in goods to insert styrene eyepieces, closures, and ferrules. Clamps buckles and straps to fins and goggles, using air vise and handtools. Wraps fabric tape around inserted closures and ferrules to hold them in place and stretches band of rubber around tape. Brushes cement on valves and closures. May be designated according to product assembled as Bottle Assembler (rubber goods);

Goggles Assembler (rubber goods); Graphite-Disk Assembler (rubber goods); Ice-Bag Assembler (rubber goods).
GOE: 06.04.23 STRENGTH: L GED: R2 M1 L1 SVP: 2 DLU: 77

752.684-042 RUBBER-TUBING SPLICER (rubber goods) alternate titles: splicer

Splices rubber tubing into continuous strips for use as automobile window and door seals: Measures and cuts extruded rubber to specified length, using gauge and knife. Brushes rubber cement on ends of tubing and positions tubing in splicing fixture. Clamps fixture in heated press to complete splice. Removes spliced tubing from press and fixture after specified time. May examine splice for breaks or irregularities.
GOE: 06.04.29 STRENGTH: L GED: R2 M1 L2 SVP: 2 DLU: 77

752.684-046 SELF-SEALING-FUEL-TANK BUILDER (rubber goods) alternate titles: fuel-cell assembler

Builds up layers of synthetic and rubber sheeting on plaster form to make self-sealing fuel tanks for airplanes: Brushes solution on specified plaster form to provide smooth surface. Fits specified layers of synthetic and rubber sheeting on form and smooths out wrinkles with hands and hand roller. Brushes cement between layers of rubber to provide adhesive surface. Locates areas for fittings on fuel tank, using templates and ruler, and makes cutouts with knife. Cements fittings on fuel tank, rubber reinforcement strips over base of fittings, and reinforcement strips of gum rubber over seams of fuel tank.
GOE: 06.02.29 STRENGTH: H GED: R3 M2 L2 SVP: 4 DLU: 77

752.684-050 SKIN FORMER (rubber goods)

Places skin (plastic sheeting) over jigs to form padded automotive products, such as dashboards and door panels: Lifts precut skin from oven conveyor and stretches it over jig. Depresses pedal to create vacuum in jig to draw skin over jig contours, and smooths wrinkles with hands. Sponges skin with water to cool skin and set shape. Trims excess skin with knife. Releases vacuum and lifts formed skin to rack. Sets oven controls for specified temperature. Presses conveyor cycle buttons to move skins to and from oven.
GOE: 06.04.32 STRENGTH: L GED: R2 M1 L1 SVP: 3 DLU: 77

752.685-010 SECTIONAL-BELT-MOLD ASSEMBLER (rubber goods) alternate titles: v-belt mold assembler and curer

Tends machine that presses belts to attain V-shape: Stretches belts around molds and fastens several molds together with metal rod and nut. Positions assembled molds between twin parallel power rollers, using hoist. Threads water-soaked cloth liner through tension guides and around molds. Pulls pressure roll down to molds and starts rollers that press belts to attain V-shape and wrap molds with liner. Ties cord around liner to secure it.
GOE: 06.04.07 STRENGTH: H GED: R2 M1 L1 SVP: 3 DLU: 77

753 OCCUPATIONS IN FABRICATION AND REPAIR OF RUBBER AND PLASTIC FOOTWEAR

This group includes occupations concerned with fabricating and repairing molded rubber and plastic footwear, and vulcanized rubber-solid fabric-top footwear, including rubbers, rubber boots, and galoshes. Occupations concerned with footwear made from leather and other materials are included in Group 690 and Group 788.

753.381-010 BOOTMAKER, HAND (rubber goods)

Builds odd lot, odd size, and specially designed rubber footwear, such as boots, arctics, and gaiters, using handtools: Pushes last onto bench jack. Selects parts in prescribed sequence from *books* and frames and assembles them on last, positioning and aligning them in designated relationship to other parts, using form gauges to locate exact position of such parts as grommet, strap, or buckle. Swabs some parts with benzine or naphtha to restore tackiness and brushes others with rubber cement for better adhesion. Presses parts onto previously assembled parts with fingers and rolls them with handtools for tighter bond. Pares (skives) and trims off excess rubber, using knife and scissors. Pulls last bearing completed article from jack and sets aside for transfer to vulcanizer.
GOE: 06.02.29 STRENGTH: L GED: R3 M2 L2 SVP: 4 DLU: 77

753.467-010 CLASSIFIER (rubber goods)

Examines rubber or plastic footwear rejected by inspectors and determines whether it can be salvaged as seconds or thirds or must be cut up as scrap: Inspects and segregates pairs by throwing them into separate containers. Keeps running tally of classifications according to grade. Computes percentage in each classification to total pairs in bracket (lot), according to work ticket, and notifies supervisor of recurring defects (pattern). Sets aside rejected pair from pattern for examination by fabricating department. May compute percentages, using calculator or slide rule.
GOE: 06.03.01 STRENGTH: L GED: R3 M2 L2 SVP: 3 DLU: 77

753.584-010 MACHINE-MADE-SHOE UNIT WORKER (boot & shoe)

Performs any combination of following tasks, as member of crew of rotating machine (merry-go-round) on which plastic soles are molded onto presewn fabric uppers to form low top sport shoes: Holds nozzle of hose to sprue hole of mold and squeezes release on hose handle to fill space between mold and lasted shoe with liquid plastic. Releases lever to stop flow when plastic oozes from toe end of mold into catch pan. Passes insole between rollers to coat underside with latex cement and places it on tray of machine station to partially dry as it is carried one rotation around machine. Brushes sole inside molded shoe with latex cement for bonding with insole and sets on machine tray to dry. Pulls excess plastic from around molded sole, using pliers. Digs and removes plastic plug from sprue hole and excess deposit from toe pan, using pliers. Removes previously cemented insole and molded shoe from machine trays, inserts insole in shoe, and places shoe on adjacent table for pressing insole. Selects pair of right and left lasts according to size and style shoe being processed and sets on pins in machine table. Places shoes on lasts and pushes knobs to lower padded rams that press insoles into shoes. Removes shoes as rams automatically retract after preset time and pushes them along table. Examines shoes for such defects as loose stitching and off center or incomplete molding, and throws them into tote boxes, according to size and acceptance or rejection. Verifies color of shoe with color specified on box label. Removes smudges, using cloth moistened with naphtha or benzine.
GOE: 06.04.32 STRENGTH: L GED: R2 M1 L2 SVP: 2 DLU: 77

753.587-010 SORTER (boot & shoe)

Sorts rubber footwear according to style, size, and width: Picks footwear from container, identifies style, and locates size and width numbers for sorting. Mates (pairs), counts, tags, and places pairs of footwear on conveyor or in racks or packing boxes. Records quantities of sorted pairs by style and size on form.
GOE: 06.03.02 STRENGTH: L GED: R2 M1 L1 SVP: 2 DLU: 77

753.684-010 BUFFING-AND-SUEDING-MACHINE OPERATOR (boot & shoe) alternate titles: sueding-and-buffing-machine operator

Holds rubber soles against power-driven abrasive-covered wheel to obtain soft or suede finish. Changes abrasive collar on wheel for different degrees of finish, using wrench.
GOE: 06.04.05 STRENGTH: L GED: R2 M1 L1 SVP: 2 DLU: 77

753.684-014 CUT-AND-COVER LINE WORKER (boot & shoe)

Fits, places, and joins together on conveyor belt, precut parts and subassemblies of uncured and fabric lined rubber to form uppers or legs for rubber footwear: Adds and joins parts, such as toe piece counters, vamp, binder strip, in designated sequence. Swabs designated parts with benzine-moistened swab to restore tackiness for adherence to other parts. Stamps identifying data on designated part, using hand stamp. Dusts pocket (gusset) with powder to prevent parts sticking together.
GOE: 06.04.27 STRENGTH: L GED: R2 M1 L1 SVP: 2 DLU: 77

753.684-018 HOOKER-LASTER (boot & shoe)

Mounts fabric shoe uppers on rotating lasts of machine (merry-go-round) to produce fabric top shoes with plastic soles: Pulls and stretches fabric upper and hooks hemmed edge over pins protruding from instep and heel of last, using claw-tipped lasting tool, to secure fabric. Taps puckered fabric at toe and heel with lasting tool to flatten it and permit free flow of plastic during molding of sole. Cuts ends from draw string, using ring knife or hook blade of lasting tool. Pulls lever that releases catch and automatically turns and lowers last and closes top of sole mold.
GOE: 06.04.27 STRENGTH: L GED: R2 M1 L2 SVP: 3 DLU: 77

753.684-022 LASTER (boot & shoe)

Attaches uppers of fabric top footwear to insoles: Holds last on which upper and insole are premounted to rollers of machine. Inserts projecting margin of upper fabric between folding rollers and presses workpiece upward against flattening roller. Turns workpiece until fabric of upper is folded and pressed against insole all around. Places lasted footwear on conveyor for attaching outsole.
GOE: 06.04.27 STRENGTH: L GED: R2 M1 L2 SVP: 3 DLU: 77

753.684-026 REPAIRER (boot & shoe)

Repairs and salvages defective rubber footwear, such as boots, gaiters, overshoes, and fabric-upper footwear: Examines articles to determine location and extent of defect and method of repair. Swabs loose edges of seams with benzine or naphtha to restore tackiness and rolls or stitches seam to make tighter bond for stress and waterproofing. Presses edges with heated knife to smooth them. Moistens misaligned, creased, or wrong part, such as binding, toecap, heel, outsole, or foxing, with solvent. Pulls defective section from underpart and repositions or replaces part. Trims (skives) excess rubber from insoles to remove bulge of outsole or heel, using knife. Cleans soiled spots with solvent-moistened swab or cloth, soap or detergent, and water.
GOE: 06.04.29 STRENGTH: L GED: R2 M1 L1 SVP: 4 DLU: 77

753.684-030 ROLLER-STITCHER (boot & shoe)

Presses together layers of uncured rubber parts or sections of rubber footwear, as they pass by on lasts on conveyor line, using hand rolling or stitching tools: Presses tool against designated area or part of workpiece, such as shank, midsole, toecap, outsole, or foxing, and rolls it back and forth or follows designated path around edge or seam until layers are pressed together. Removes footwear from end of conveyor line and rolls and stitches (rolls indentations along narrow strip) seams around edge of outsole as final assembly operation.
GOE: 06.04.29 STRENGTH: L GED: R2 M1 L1 SVP: 2 DLU: 77

753.687-010 CLIPPER (boot & shoe)

Cuts threads connecting rubber footwear parts, using scissors. Snips off thread ends. Examines parts for loose or missing stitches and for prescribed margins. Arranges parts in boxes or places them on conveyor for next operation. May be designated according to parts separated as Clipper, Counters

(rubber goods); Clipper, Outside Back Stay (rubber goods); Clipper, Tongues (rubber goods).
GOE: 06.04.29 STRENGTH: L GED: R2 M1 L1 SVP: 2 DLU: 77

753.687-014 DEBRANDER (boot & shoe) alternate titles: brander; rebrander
Melts brand name from articles of plastic footwear, such as rubbers or overshoes, for sale under another vendor's name, using electrically heated tool resembling soldering iron. Cleans adhering plastic from tool tip by rubbing on wire brush.
GOE: 05.12.10 STRENGTH: L GED: R1 M1 L1 SVP: 2 DLU: 77

753.687-018 FINAL INSPECTOR (boot & shoe) alternate titles: packing inspector; reinspector
Inspects articles of vulcanized rubber or cured slush cast plastic footwear, such as boots, gaiters, overshoes, or fabric-upper sportswear, for misplaced, misaligned, or missing parts, overcuring, undercuring, discolorations, and mismating of size, width, color, or style preparatory to packing: Determines acceptability of article, based on adherence to specifications and on acquired job knowledge of acceptable standards. Measures thickness of uppers, using dial micrometer. Marks defects with chalk and sets rejects aside for disposal by CLASSIFIER (rubber goods).
GOE: 06.03.02 STRENGTH: L GED: R3 M2 L2 SVP: 3 DLU: 77

753.687-022 FITTER-PLACER (rubber goods)
Fits and places precut or prepared parts upon others, as they pass by on conveyor belt, to form subassembly of parts for rubber footwear: Removes parts from *book,* board, frame, bundle, or container and places them on sheet rubber or other parts. Aligns and places parts to allow adequate margins for subsequent joining, where specified. Presses parts together with fingers, and repositions parts to remove wrinkles. Strips off and discards parts that are misplaced, wrinkled beyond correction, or are not tacky. May remove subassembled parts from belt and arrange on board, in frame, or in book for subsequent use.
GOE: 06.04.23 STRENGTH: L GED: R1 M1 L1 SVP: 2 DLU: 77

753.687-026 MAKING-LINE WORKER (boot & shoe) alternate titles: assembler, rubber footwear
Places parts and joins seams to assemble rubber footwear articles as they pass by on conveyor jacks, performing any combination of following tasks: Places last on conveyor jack. Removes upper from conveyor, wraps around last, and presses back seam at heel to hold upper onto last. Turns or pulls last upright in position for next operation. Joins seams, such as back, toe, pocket, and top, allowing specified margin and pressing seams with fingers to ensure complete union. Removes part from book, frame, board, or stack and adds part to workpiece by fitting and placing in designated location, each worker performing one operation, at successive stations, until article is completed. Aligns parts, using other parts as guides or according to markings stamped on parts or metal form gauges. Swabs dry parts with benzine or naphtha to restore tackiness.
GOE: 06.04.27 STRENGTH: L GED: R2 M1 L2 SVP: 3 DLU: 77

753.687-030 MOLD FILLER AND DRAINER (boot & shoe)
Casts plastic footwear, performing any combination of following tasks, and working as member of crew: Fills mold under spigot, or mold fills automatically as it moves on conveyor. Empties mold into vat and places it top down on rotary conveyor rack to drain off excess. Removes mold after one rotation and places on conveyor that carries it through oven to gel (set) and dry. Repeats entire process to increase wearability by adding second thickness. Holds mold under spigot and adds liquid, tipping mold back and forth to build up even thickness of sole. Adds additional plastic to heel area to increase thickness of heel.
GOE: 06.04.32 STRENGTH: L GED: R2 M1 L1 SVP: 2 DLU: 77

753.687-034 MOLD-INSERT CHANGER (boot & shoe)
Changes metal inserts in molds for rubber soles according to size and pattern indicated on worksheet: Selects designated insert, places insert in cavity of mold, and taps it with plastic hammer to wedge it securely in mold. Taps insert through holes in bottom of mold to remove it, using punch and hammer. Replaces inserts in designated bins.
GOE: 06.04.32 STRENGTH: M GED: R2 M1 L1 SVP: 3 DLU: 77

753.687-038 PACKING-LINE WORKER (rubber goods)
Performs any combination of following tasks as member of conveyor line crew, to finish and pack plastic or rubber footwear: Sorts and mates pairs and places them on conveyor. Opens or closes buckles, snaps fasteners together, inserts laces in eyelets, and ties loops (frogs) around buttons. Counts and tallies production or records on counter. Wraps pair in tissue, places them in shoe box, and packs boxes in cartons. Places rejects in boxes or racks for repair or mating.
GOE: 06.04.38 STRENGTH: L GED: R2 M2 L1 SVP: 2 DLU: 77

753.687-042 STOCKLAYER (boot & shoe)
Piles plies (layers) of cloth, rubber, or rubberized fabric for cutting rubber footwear parts, using winding drum: Selects beam (roll) of material according to job order. Positions beam in cradle, using hoist. Clamps end of material in slot in winding drum, notes yardage indicator reading, and moves lever to engage clutch and start material winding. Stops machine when specified number of turns have been recorded on indicator. Cuts through plies, using knife. Tapes or ties ends of unused material, marks amount left on roll, and returns it to storage.

GOE: 06.04.34 STRENGTH: M GED: R2 M1 L1 SVP: 2 DLU: 77

754 OCCUPATIONS IN FABRICATION AND REPAIR OF MISCELLANEOUS PLASTICS PRODUCTS

This group includes occupations concerned with bench molding, fitting, and finishing plastics and fiberglass products. Structural work occupations are included in Division 80.

754.130-010 DECORATING-AND-ASSEMBLY SUPERVISOR (plastic prod.)
Supervises and coordinates activities of workers engaged in welding and assembling components into plastic products and printing logos on products: Inspects processed plastic components and products to verify conformance to customer specifications and company standards. Demonstrates machine operations to new employees and assigns trainees to work with experienced workers for continued on-the-job training. Diagnoses machine malfunctions and assists workers in determining corrective actions required. Performs other duties as described under SUPERVISOR (any industry) Master Title.
GOE: 06.04.01 STRENGTH: L GED: R4 M2 L3 SVP: 5 DLU: 86

754.137-010 SUPERVISOR, SAMPLE (plastic-synth.)
Supervises and coordinates activities of workers engaged in cutting plastic sheets to specified size for samples, waxing and polishing samples, stamping identifying data on samples, and preparing sample orders for shipment. Trains new employees. Examines samples to detect defects in color, mottle pattern, and surface finish. Performs duties as described under SUPERVISOR (any industry) Master Title.
GOE: 06.04.01 STRENGTH: L GED: R4 M3 L3 SVP: 7 DLU: 77

754.381-010 INTERNAL CARVER (plastic prod.)
Carves designs on paperweights, calender backs and stands, letter openers and handles, and other clear plastics products, using electric hand drill.
GOE: 06.01.04 STRENGTH: L GED: R4 M3 L3 SVP: 7 DLU: 77

754.381-014 PATTERNMAKER, PLASTICS (plastic prod.) alternate titles: jig and form maker; plug maker
Fabricates patterns, fixtures, jigs, and templates, used in producing plastic articles, from wood or metal stock, following blueprints and using handtools, power tools, and measuring instruments: Lays out cutting lines on stock, using scribe, compass, rule, triangles, and French curves. Cuts stock, using power saw, power shear, and handtools. Assembles pieces, using rivets, bolts, nails, or glue. Smooths surface of assembly, using plane and power sander. Verifies dimensions of assembly, using calipers, rule, and compass. Sprays coat of parting agent, such as sealing lacquer or wax on surface of assembly. May cover pattern with plastic-impregnated fabric to make preforms. May remove preform from pattern when plastic has cured, using airhose.
GOE: 05.05.07 STRENGTH: L GED: R4 M3 L3 SVP: 6 DLU: 77

754.381-018 PLASTICS FABRICATOR (aircraft mfg.; plastic prod.) alternate titles: plastics bench mechanic; plastics fabricator and assembler
Fabricates, assembles, reworks, and repairs plastic products, applying knowledge of working characteristics of plastics and bonding techniques, using precision instruments, handtools, power tools, machines, and equipment: Reads and interprets blueprints, work orders, and related documentation to determine methods and sequence of operations and dimensional and finish specifications. Lays out cutting lines on plastic materials, such as sheet stock and fiberglass or graphite cloth, following template pattern, blueprints, sketches, or sample part, using measuring and marking instruments. Cuts material to size, using shears, knives, cutters, scissors, router, or saw. Mixes ingredients, such as resins, catalysts, fillers, accelerators, and colors, according to formulas, manually or using mixer. Sets up and operates forming machines and presses, or laminates plastic cloth and resins or preimpregnated cloth onto layup mold or bonding fixture, to shape parts. Wraps bonding fixture or mold in vacuum bagging materials, attaches fittings to mold or fixture, such as vacuum connections, thermocouples, and probes, and exhausts air from vacuum bag to prepare lamination for curing or bonding. Operates oven to cure parts. Trims, drills, reams, countersinks, grinds, and finishes parts to specifications, using templates, handtools, and power tools. Verifies dimensions of parts, using precision instruments, such as dial indicators, micrometers, and calipers. Fits and assembles parts and attaches hardware and fittings, such as brackets and hinges, using clamps, jigs, fixtures, power tools, and fasteners. Applies tape, foam, or other type of adhesives to assembly for subsequent bonding in autoclave. Repairs and reworks damaged or defective parts and assemblies by lay up, foaming, cementing, molding, potting, casting, or similar methods. May heat parts or materials to facilitate shaping, using oven or heat gun. May fabricate and assemble parts from fiber reinforced plastics (composites) and assorted materials, such as metal and honeycomb, and be designated Bonding And Composite Fabricator (aircraft mfg.); Composites Fabricator And Assembler (aircraft mfg.). May press, smooth, trim, measure, and adjust composite tape during automatic application of tape onto mold or fixture by numerical-control tape laying machine, using scale, knife, and scraper. May wind fiberglass, graphite, nylon, or other natural or synthetic fiber or filament around parts, using filament winding machine, manually applying layers of resinous materials to part at specified intervals during winding process. May be designated by type of part or activity involved as Experimental Plastics Fabricator (aircraft mfg.); Filament-Wound Parts Fab-

ricator (aircraft mfg.); Plastic Parts Fabricator (aircraft mfg.); Plastic-Sign Fabricator (plastic prod.); Plastics Rework And Repair Mechanic (aircraft mfg.).
GOE: 06.01.04 STRENGTH: M GED: R4 M4 L4 SVP: 7 DLU: 88

754.684-010 ASSEMBLER (plastic prod.) alternate titles: fabricator
Performs any combination of tasks involved in assembly of plastic articles, such as bags, baby pants, coolers, fiberglass chairs, containers, trays and inflatable toys: Marks cutting lines on plastic sheet of sections to be assembled, following template. Cuts sections from sheet, using knife, scissors, or power cutting machine. Positions sections on jig and aligns seams and air valves. Brushes glue along edges of section, seals edges with hot iron or electric-sealing machine, and trims edges with scissors. Examines articles for defects, such as smeared paint, cuts, and wrinkled seams. Fills inflatable article with air and submerges it in water to detect leaks. Positions plastic patch over leak and fuses it to article, using electric sealing machine. Cleans markings and dirt from article with solvent, folds article, and places it in bag for shipment. Heats cooler brackets, using hot plate, and secures cooler, using bench fixture. Presses bracket into depressed section of cooler to attach bracket. May record number of articles packed. May sort plastic sheets in bins. May seal decorative pieces of adhesive-backed cloth on garment parts, using automatic heat sealer and be designated Thermoelectric-Heat-Sealing-Machine Operator (tex., nec).
GOE: 06.04.24 STRENGTH: M GED: R2 M2 L1 SVP: 4 DLU: 77

754.684-014 ASSEMBLER-AND-GLUER, LAMINATED PLASTICS (plastic prod.)
Assembles plastics laminates, using handtools and electrically heated press: Mixes urea resin glue with water and applies glue to surfaces of wooden boards, using hand spreader. Lays laminates between wooden boards and places unit into press. Removes unit after specified heating time and routes off excess material. Joins self edge, backsplash, or molding edge to laminates, using hacksaw, miter, snips, mallet, and nails. Solders open joints of metal edges, using electric soldering iron. Buffs assembled unit with steel wool, and places it into cabinet.
GOE: 06.04.24 STRENGTH: M GED: R2 M1 L2 SVP: 3 DLU: 77

754.684-018 BIT SHAVER (fabrication, nec) alternate titles: head facer
Shaves and smooths mouthpieces of smoking pipe bits: Pushes bit against sander to smooth rubber bits, and against revolving blade to shave excess material from plastic bits. May use holding device to hold bit during smoothing or shaving process.
GOE: 06.04.34 STRENGTH: S GED: R2 M1 L1 SVP: 2 DLU: 77

754.684-022 CASTER (plastic prod.) alternate titles: pourer
Casts thermosetting plastic resins in mold to form plastic products: Coats mold sections with parting agents, such as soap, wax, or lacquer, using brush or spray gun. Assembles sections of mold, using C-clamps, nuts, bolts, and wrench. Weighs specified amounts of resin, catalyst, pigment, and hardening agent, using balance scale, and mixes them in container, using mixing machine or paddle. Pours mixture into mold and places mold in oven or water-bath cooker to cure. Removes product from mold, using airhose and handtools. May be designated according to product cast as Foam Caster (nonmet. min.); Foam Molder (clock & watch).
GOE: 06.02.24 STRENGTH: M GED: R2 M1 L2 SVP: 4 DLU: 77

754.684-026 DRILLER, HAND (button & notion)
Drills holes in plastic buttons for setting rhinestones, using powered bench drill: Inserts specified bit in drill chuck. Places button against guide and presses button against rotating bit to form hole. Determines position and spacing of holes by looking at sample button, exercising care to drill hole evenly and neatly and to depth required to hold stone.
GOE: 06.04.24 STRENGTH: L GED: R2 M1 L1 SVP: 2 DLU: 77

754.684-030 FINISHER, HAND (plastic prod.)
Trims and smooths molded, laminated, or machined plastics products, using handtools and sandpaper: Examines products for scratches, cracks, and other blemishes, and patches them with plastic fabrics. Scrapes, cuts, files, and sands products to remove gates, burrs, flashing, runners, and other forms of excessive material, using files, knives, and sandpaper. Washes products in soap, naphtha, or other cleaning solution to remove dirt, grease, and stains.
GOE: 06.04.24 STRENGTH: M GED: R2 M1 L1 SVP: 3 DLU: 77

754.684-034 KNOCK-OUT HAND (plastic prod.)
Removes plaster-forming mandrels from cured plastic products: Places product in tank of water to loosen product from mandrel. Pounds product with mallet to break plaster, utilizing knowledge of plastics to avoid damaging product. Immerses product in water to wash out remaining plaster. Cuts bands of reinforcing tape from product, using knife.
GOE: 06.04.32 STRENGTH: M GED: R2 M1 L1 SVP: 3 DLU: 77

754.684-038 PLASTIC DUPLICATOR (machine tools)
Casts plastic reproductions of models, patterns, and prototype parts: Examines part to determine sections that can be cast and assembled to obtain reproduction. Constructs boxlike enclosure around section of part to be duplicated. Brushes or sprays surface of section with parting agent to prevent plastic from sticking to surface. Casts part, using either of following methods: (1) Brushes plastic facing coat on section of part to be cast. Mixes plastic resin and brushes thin, uniform coat over facing coat. fiberglass glass cloth to approximate size of cast and places it over resin. Brushes cloth to smooth it, applies additional coat of resin, and repeats procedure until alternate layers of fiberglass and resin

are built up to specified thickness. (2) Brushes plastic facing coat on section of part to be cast, mixes plastic resin, and pours it into enclosure until cast is of specified thickness. Removes hardened cast from section. Files, grinds, and sands cast to remove jagged edges and to cut cast down to specified dimensions. Forms base and bracing structure to support cast, using handtools and liquid adhesive. May assemble casts to produce completed model, pattern, or prototype. May bolt or otherwise fasten metal inserts to casts at specified points.
GOE: 06.02.24 STRENGTH: M GED: R3 M2 L2 SVP: 5 DLU: 77

754.684-042 PLASTICS WORKER (aircraft mfg.) alternate titles: composite worker
Performs any combination of following tasks to fabricate plastic aircraft and missile parts, accessories, and trim according to specifications: Cuts fiberglass or graphite (composite) cloth to size, following template or blueprints, using cutting machine, scissors, or knife. Marks identifying information on material and assembles materials in kits for subsequent laminating. Applies parting agent to mold or bonding fixture. Impregnates cloth with resins by dipping cloth in solutions, feeding cloth between rollers of impregnating machine, or brushing resin onto cloth. Applies layers of impregnated cloth or prepreg onto mold or fixture in predetermined ply sequence, and presses cloth to fit contours of mold, smooth surface, and remove air pockets and excess resin, using squeegee, scraper, or spatula. Fits and laps ends of cloth, using scissors or knife. Encases molded laminate in bagging material and bleeder cloth, attaches vacuum bagging apparatus, such as thermocouples, probes, and vacuum connections, to mold or bonding fixture, and exhausts air from vacuum bag to seal laminate for curing. Tests seal on vacuum bagging apparatus, using leak detector. Trims, drills, burrs, grinds, sands, and finishes cured parts to specifications, using templates, fixtures, handtools, and power tools. Prefits and assembles cured parts into assemblies or subassemblies, using jigs, fixtures, power tools, and fasteners, such as rivets and bolts. Applies adhesives to surface of assembled parts for bonding in autoclave. May assist PLASTICS FABRICATOR (aircraft mfg.; plastic prod.) 754.381-018 in fabricating plastic or composite first article parts and assemblies or parts and assemblies involving compound or complex contours, working to close tolerances. May tend oven to cure parts. May assist AUTOCLAVE OPERATOR (aircraft mfg.) 553.362-014 in loading and unloading parts from autoclave. May form and cure rubber parts, using heat lamps or vacuum molding machine. May be designated by type of plastic or specific activity involved as Bagger (aircraft mfg.); Composite Assembler (aircraft mfg.); Composite Bond Worker (aircraft mfg.); Composite Laminator (aircraft mfg.); Composite Layup Worker (aircraft mfg.); Composite Trim And Drill Worker (aircraft mfg.); Kitter (aircraft mfg.); Plastic Parts Fabricator-Trimmer (aircraft mfg.); Smooth And Burr Worker, Composites (aircraft mfg.).
GOE: 06.02.24 STRENGTH: M GED: R3 M2 L2 SVP: 5 DLU: 88

754.684-046 PLASTICS REPAIRER (plastic prod.)
Repairs plastic products, such as dresser sets, luggage, decorative panels, desk tops, and stands: Examines product for defects, such as blisters, cracks, and broken joints. Grinds defects, using power grinder, to smooth surface and form base for bonding compound. Fills cracks and cements broken joints with compound. Allows compound to set, and removes excess compound with rag dipped in acetone.
GOE: 06.04.24 STRENGTH: L GED: R2 M1 L2 SVP: 3 DLU: 77

754.684-050 LAMINATOR, PREFORMS (plastic prod.) alternate titles: preformer, impregnated fabrics; squeegeer and former
Lays up fiberglass and resin-coated fabrics on plaster, steel, or wooden forms to mold plastic parts for products, such as boats, sporting equipment, automobile bodies, and airplane seats: Cleans form with solvent and sprays it with parting agent, such as wax or soap. Cuts fabric to specified size, following pattern or template and using knife or scissors. Measures and mixes plastic resins, coloring agents, and catalyst as specified, using scales and portable mixer. Spreads compound on form, positions fabric on compound, and rubs fabric with squeegee to remove air bubbles. Applies additional layers of compound and fabric to build up specified number of laminations. Trims edges of laminated fabric, using scissors or knife. Allows part to cure and removes it from mold. May paint part, using spray gun. May drill and cut part, following template and using power drill and power saw. Sprays mixture of chopped fiberglass, resin, and catalyst on mold to form laminations, using spray gun. May tend machine that wraps resin impregnated fabric strips around mandrel to form plastic rods.
GOE: 06.04.24 STRENGTH: M GED: R2 M1 L2 SVP: 4 DLU: 81

754.685-010 TAB-MACHINE OPERATOR (nonmet. min.)
Tends tab machine that secures threads of plastic mesh scouring ball with plastic label: Slips slotted label over base of threads and positions ball into slot of machine so that threads run length of machine. Presses switch to activate machine that folds and heat seals plastic tape over label and threads to secure threads and hold shape of ball. Turns dial to regulate heat of sealing dies. Turns thumbscrew to loosen and tighten spindle when replacing roll of plastic tape.
GOE: 06.04.02 STRENGTH: L GED: R2 M1 L1 SVP: 2 DLU: 77

754.685-014 ASSEMBLY-MACHINE TENDER (plastic prod.)
Tends variety of machines that weld and assemble components into plastic products and stamp or silk-screen logos on products: Positions plastic products or components on fixtures of hot-stamp, silk-screening, and ultrasonic welding machines, and presses buttons or treadles to actuate machines that apply logos to product or weld components together. Dumps plastic components into vibrat-

ing hoppers of assembly machine that automatically assembles components to form plastic products. Observes machine operations to detect malfunctions and clears jams and blockages, using screwdriver. Positions plastic bottles or components on conveyor or turntable of hot-stamp, flame cleaner, or stamping machines that automatically apply logos or remove molding residue from bottles or fit components into single part. Inspects decorated and assembled finished products for defects, such as discolored logos or misaligned bottle caps. Packs finished products into cartons.
GOE: 06.04.20 STRENGTH: L GED: R2 M1 L1 SVP: 2 DLU: 86

754.687-010 LABORER, GENERAL (plastic prod.)
Performs any combination of following duties in fabrication of plastic products: Removes molds from ovens, and places them on table. Removes foliage, flower, fruit, and other castings from molds. Cleans molds and returns them to CASTER (plastic prod.). Strips stamped, sealed, or cut plastic bodies from plastic panel. Dips castings or products in solvent to cleanse them. Smooths surfaces of objects with soft cloth. Dapples vinyl inks of various colors onto surfaces of fruit and other castings or products to approximate natural colors and conditions. Fastens or cements leaves or foliage to pineapples, peaches, and other vinyl products. Attaches safety pins to convention badges. Assembles pieces of tablet holders in wooden tray to prepare products for subsequent sealing of seams by machine. Inserts tabs and pencils into slots of tablet holders.
GOE: 06.04.39 STRENGTH: M GED: R2 M1 L1 SVP: 2 DLU: 77

754.687-014 SEQUINS STRINGER (plastic prod.)
Strings plastic sequins on thread for use as decoration on wearing apparel: Doubles length of thread and hooks it onto cut near end of needle loaded with sequins. Slides sequins from needle onto doubled thread. Cuts off excess thread. Pulls one strand of thread from sequins and ties ends to form loop. Ties specified number of loops in bunch.
GOE: 06.04.24 STRENGTH: L GED: R1 M1 L1 SVP: 2 DLU: 77

759 OCCUPATIONS IN FABRICATION AND REPAIR OF PLASTICS, SYNTHETICS, RUBBER, AND RELATED PRODUCTS, N.E.C.

This group includes occupations, not elsewhere classified, concerned with fabricating and repairing plastics, synthetics, rubber, and related products.

759.135-010 SUPERVISOR, SCOURING PADS (nonmet. min.)
Supervises and coordinates activities of workers engaged in tending machines to manufacture knit plastic mesh scouring pads: Examines product at various production stages to detect defects, such as skipped stitches in knitting and incorrect folding. Trains workers in use of machines and in techniques used in folding and tying units of knit plastic mesh tubing to form scouring pads. Performs other duties as described under SUPERVISOR (any industry) Master Title.
GOE: 06.02.01 STRENGTH: M GED: R4 M3 L3 SVP: 7 DLU: 77

759.137-010 SUPERVISOR I (rubber goods)
Supervises and coordinates activities of workers engaged in testing, printing, and assembling dipped latex products, such as balloons, gloves, and prophylactics: Trains new workers in production methods. Inspects quality of work. Performs other duties as described under SUPERVISOR (any industry) Master Title. May be designated according to area supervised as Supervisor, Assembling (rubber goods); Supervisor, Printing (rubber goods); Supervisor, Testing (rubber goods).
GOE: 06.02.01 STRENGTH: L GED: R4 M3 L3 SVP: 7 DLU: 77

759.261-010 PROTOTYPE-DEICER ASSEMBLER (rubber goods)
Assembles and tests experimental electric or pneumatic airplane deicers according to specifications: Assembles experimental deicers. Tests deicers under simulated flying conditions for pressure leaks, electrical resistance, and shorts, using electric or air pressure testing equipment. Examines deicers to locate ruptures, cracks, or weak spots. Records test results. May instruct customers in installation, repair, or maintenance of deicers.
GOE: 06.01.05 STRENGTH: M GED: R4 M3 L3 SVP: 6 DLU: 77

759.364-010 HOSE INSPECTOR AND PATCHER (rubber goods)
Inspects and repairs rubber hose, using handtools, vulcanizing equipment, and hydrostatic test equipment: Examines hose and couplings for defects, such as cracks, checks, and faulty seal around couplings. Tests hose, using hydrostatic (water or air) test equipment, to detect leaks and weaknesses in hose walls [HOSE TESTER (rubber goods)]. Cuts out defective area, using knife or saw, or strips rubber coating from fabric backing. Applies cement and cuts and cements patch to fabric backing or cements ends together after removal of defective section. Inserts repaired section in bench-molding machine and turns steam valve to vulcanize patch at specified temperature. Replaces couplings, steel bands, and gaskets, using pliers or crimping machine. Records vulcanizing time, nature of defects discovered, and repairs completed on quality control report. May repair hose returned by customers, according to nature of complaint specified on work ticket.
GOE: 06.03.01 STRENGTH: L GED: R3 M2 L2 SVP: 4 DLU: 77

759.381-010 RUBBER-GOODS TESTER (elec. equip.; utilities) alternate titles: safety-equipment tester
Tests rubber protective goods, such as gloves, sleeves, blankets or mats, and heavy hoods, used by workers working on high-voltage power lines and equip-

ment: Examines rubber goods to detect defects, such as blisters, breaks, or deterioration. Clips rubber goods to metal rod of dielectric-strength-testing machine and partially submerges articles in water tank of machine. Manipulates controls to discharge excessive voltage through metal rod and rubber goods to water. Observes apparatus for flash or opening of circuit breaker, indicating defective goods. Reads milliammeter on panel to determine if amount of current passed through article to water is within prescribed tolerance. Discards defective equipment. May inflate gloves on special apparatus to detect defects. May make mechanical tests on goods for conformance to purchase specifications, using testing apparatus, such as micrometers, rulers, and tensile-testing machine.
GOE: 06.01.05 STRENGTH: L GED: R3 M2 L3 SVP: 6 DLU: 77

759.384-010 SELF-SEALING-FUEL-TANK REPAIRER (rubber goods) alternate titles: fuel-cell repairer
Repairs defects in self-sealing rubber fuel tanks for use on airplanes: Examines fuel tanks to detect location and extent of defects, such as blisters, ply separations, cracks, and loose seams. Cuts away rubber in defective area with knife and smooths edges with portable buffer. Positions and cements specified patch material in defective area, using hand roller. Cuts out and replaces defective tank fittings and rubber reinforcement strips with handtools, following blueprints. Clamps electric platen on repaired area to vulcanize it. Cleans foreign material from inside of fuel tank, using wire brush, buffer, and vacuum hose. May position fuel tank on jig to verify location of fittings and screw holes.
GOE: 06.04.29 STRENGTH: M GED: R2 M1 L1 SVP: 4 DLU: 77

759.484-010 ROLL BUILDER (rubber goods)
Builds up plies (layers) of natural and synthetic rubber on metal cores for use on commercial and industrial machines: Positions metal core in building machine by hand or by use of hoist, and applies rubber cement with brush. Pulls ply of rubber from roll in rack onto worktable. Washes rubber plies with solvent and starts machine to revolve core. Wraps specified number of plies around core and splices ends. Starts automatic machine rollers or uses hand roller to compress rubber plies and remove wrinkles and trapped air. Measures thickness of roll, using calipers. Cuts roll to length with knife. Cements and applies finish rubber strips to each end. Wraps finished roll with strips of cloth preparatory to curing.
GOE: 06.04.29 STRENGTH: M GED: R2 M1 L2 SVP: 3 DLU: 77

759.664-010 BRAIDER SETTER (rubber goods)
Repairs broken or knotted yarn in braided jacket of firehose: Reverses braiding machine to unbraid yarn to defective area. Untangles knots, ties broken strands, and turns spools of yarn to take up slack. Starts machine and signals BRAIDING-MACHINE TENDER (rubber goods) when defect is corrected. Changes pitch gear on braiding machine as specified, using wrench, and verifies pitch of braid with rule. Moves supplies to BRAIDING-MACHINE TENDER (rubber goods) using handtrucks. May inflate hose to specified diameter to prepare it for covering.
GOE: 06.04.06 STRENGTH: M GED: R2 M1 L1 SVP: 2 DLU: 77

759.664-014 EXPANSION-JOINT BUILDER (rubber goods) alternate titles: expansion-joint finisher
Fabricates expansion joints for ends of rubber hose to permit coupling of hose to pipes or ducts according to blueprints and customer specifications: Examines blueprints and work ticket to determine dimensions and type of joint to be fabricated. Applies solution of soapstone and water to end of hose and builds up specified number of layers of rubber and fabric around end of hose or on mandrel to form expansion joint. Wraps joint with tape and steel curing plates preparatory to vulcanizing, using rule and calipers to ensure conformance to specifications. Removes tape and curing plates or rubber reinforcing material after vulcanizing and trims or grinds joint to specified diameter and contour, using knife and portable grinder. Applies precured rubber patches to cover defects, such as low spots or surface cracks. Marks and punches bolt holes in joint, using templates, scriber, and hand punch. Paints joint, using brush, and hangs completed joint to dry.
GOE: 06.02.29 STRENGTH: M GED: R3 M2 L2 SVP: 4 DLU: 77

759.664-018 ROLLER MAKER (print. & pub.)
Recovers and reconditions used printing-press rollers, using handtools and such equipment as melting pot and chopping machine: Strips cover from roller manually or with knife, separating meltable from nonmeltable materials. Feeds meltable scrap into chopping machine and dumps chopped material into heated melting pot. Weighs out, mixes, and melts ingredients to form molding compound in mixing kettle, according to formula. Paints roller cores, using brush. Winds twine around roller ends and other areas needing packing. Fits stars (centering devices) in position on cores and molding cylinder. Oils cylinder, using oilcan, and inserts cores in cylinder. Attaches bottom plate, water, and drain lines to molding cylinder, using wrenches. Couples lines from compressor to kettle containing molding compound and to pressure gun used to force molding compound into cylinder. Controls flow of compound according to signals from another worker observing operation from raised platform. Pours cold water over surface of cylinder to congeal molding compound. Inspects finished rollers for imperfections, trims excess molding compound from edges, and directs steam over surface of roller covers to remove wrinkles, using steam hose.
GOE: 06.02.32 STRENGTH: M GED: R3 M1 L1 SVP: 4 DLU: 77

759.684-010 AIRPLANE-GAS-TANK-LINER ASSEMBLER (rubber goods)
Cuts and cements sheets of rubber to make shock absorbers for airplane gas tanks: Cuts rubber sheets to specified size, using scissors or roller-cutter. Brush-

es rubber cement on sheets and presses them together. Hangs completed sheets on revolving drums that pass through curing oven.
GOE: 06.04.29 STRENGTH: L GED: R2 M1 L1 SVP: 2 DLU: 77

759.684-014 BASE-PLY HAND (rubber goods)
Cements rubber ply (layer) to metal forming plate and lays out parts locations on pneumatic deicers: Places rolls of gum rubber and rubberized fabric ply stocks in letoff racks, using hoist. Pulls rubber ply stocks from roll, aligns rubber plies with edge of forming plate, and cuts plies to size with scissors and knife. Rolls rubber plies with hand roller to remove wrinkles and promote adherence to forming plate. Stencils location of deicer parts on rubber plies, using template and inked brush. Locates centerline on plies by aligning chalk-line with guide marks on forming plate. Carries plied-up forming plate to storage rack.
GOE: 06.02.29 STRENGTH: H GED: R2 M1 L1 SVP: 3 DLU: 77

759.684-018 BELT-BUILDER HELPER (rubber goods)
Performs following duties to build up plies (layers) of rubberized fabric and gum to produce transmission and conveyor belting: Moves rolls of stock to belt-building area, using lift truck or handtruck. Positions stock rolls in letoff rack, using hoist. Pulls fabric and gum plies of specified width onto belt-building table from roll in letoff rack or calender, and aligns edge with previously laid ply. Compresses plies together, using rollers and stitchers. Builds up specified number of plies and trims irregular edges with scissors or knife. Inserts end of finished belt between pressure rollers that bond plies, and rolls finished belt onto windup rack.
GOE: 06.04.29 STRENGTH: H GED: R2 M1 L1 SVP: 3 DLU: 77

759.684-022 BUFFER (rubber goods; rubber tire)
Buffs rubber articles to clean, smooth, repair, trim, or roughen for cementing, using hand or power buffer: Starts buffer and holds article against it, or holds buffing wheel against article. Changes buffing wheel according to operation performed or type of finish required, using wrench. May weigh, sort, and pack articles for further processing or shipping. May be designated according to article buffed as Tire Buffer (rubber tire); White-Sidewall-Tire Buffer (rubber tire).
GOE: 06.04.29 STRENGTH: M GED: R2 M1 L1 SVP: 2 DLU: 77

759.684-026 DEICER REPAIRER (rubber goods) alternate titles: ice-guard repairer
Repairs defective parts of airplane deicers: Cuts out premarked defects, such as cracks and blisters, from rubber plies of deicer with knife. Buffs defective area to prepare it for patching, using portable electric buffer. Mends wiring defects in electric deicers, using soldering iron. Cuts out and patches defective spots in rubberized-fabric air tubes and manifolds of pneumatic deicers. Swabs defective area of rubber plies with rubber cement to provide adhesive surface. Positions uncured rubber patch on defective area and rolls down with hand roller to promote adherence. Trims excess rubber from patch with knife. Cures and vulcanizes patch, using portable vulcanizing equipment. Lifts repaired deicer to handtruck for removal to inspection department. May be designated according to type of deicer repaired as Deicer Repairer, Electric (rubber goods); Deicer Repairer, Pneumatic (rubber goods).
GOE: 06.04.34 STRENGTH: L GED: R2 M1 L2 SVP: 4 DLU: 77

759.684-030 DEICER-KIT ASSEMBLER (rubber goods)
Assembles rubber ply stock, molded rubber parts, blueprints, and tools for use in airplane deicer kit box: Selects precut rubber plies (layers) and molded rubber parts from bins for specified deicers. Verifies thickness of rubber ply parts with snap gauge, and lays parts in kit box. Selects specified items, such as punches, dies, blueprints, and templates, and places them in kit box with rubber parts. Weighs loaded kit box to determine conformance to weight specifications. Attaches identification tag to box and places kit box in storage rack.
GOE: 06.04.34 STRENGTH: M GED: R2 M1 L1 SVP: 3 DLU: 77

759.684-034 FOLDER-TIER (nonmet. min.)
Reverses lengths of tubular knit plastic mesh to form scouring ball: Stretches tubing over post and pulls tubing down length of post. Pulls bottom of tubing up to form double-walled tube. Slides tubing off post and pulls out guide thread. Pushes tubing across bed of device that ties string around middle of tube. Flexes interior walls of tubing with fingers to enlarge cavity and pushes mass of tubing into itself to form scouring ball.
GOE: 06.04.24 STRENGTH: L GED: R2 M1 L1 SVP: 2 DLU: 77

759.684-038 HOSE WRAPPER (rubber goods)
Wraps strips of fabric around rubber hose to maintain shape of hose during curing: Inserts end of hose-covered mandrel into powered chuck. Pulls end of fabric strip from hand reel and starts strip around end of hose. Starts machine and guides fabric strip onto hose. May mark curing time on hose, using crayon. May load hose onto storage rack, using hoist, or into steam-heated oven for curing. May unwrap fabric strips from cured hose.
GOE: 06.04.34 STRENGTH: H GED: R2 M1 L2 SVP: 2 DLU: 77

759.684-042 MAT REPAIRER (rubber goods)
Repairs molded rubber automobile floor mats: Cuts out defects, such as holes, snags, and tears, in mat with knife. Smooths defective area of mat with emery cloth to prepare surface for rubber patch. Cuts uncured rubber patch to size with knife. Cements rubber patch to defective area and trims off excess rubber. Positions mat in vulcanizer to cure patch for specified time. Cuts felt padding to size with shears and cements it to back of mat on repaired area.
GOE: 06.04.29 STRENGTH: L GED: R2 M1 L1 SVP: 2 DLU: 77

759.684-046 PATCHER, BOWLING BALL (toy-sport equip.)
Reams out and fills surface holes and scratches, and vulcanizes filling material to patch bowling balls: Reams out surface flaws in bowling balls to uniform depth, using electrically powered router. Pours liquid resin into holes on ball surface to fill flaw. Positions patched balls in heated bench presses and clamps tops of presses down on patched areas of balls to compress and vulcanize patch. Turns timer dial of presses to control heating cycle. May remove excess resin, using drill. May smooth surface, using powered sander and fine sandpaper.
GOE: 06.04.02 STRENGTH: M GED: R2 M1 L1 SVP: 3 DLU: 77

759.684-050 RUBBER LINER (machinery mfg.) alternate titles: liner; rubber insulator
Lines interior of tanks, valves, pipes, and similar articles with rubber sheeting to prevent corrosion of vessel, and to minimize contamination, shock, ignition, or explosion hazards to contents. May inject compressed air into vessel to bond lining to vessel walls, and introduce live steam or place article in autoclave to vulcanize rubber lining. May prepare vessel for application of lining by sandblasting, scraping, or painting interior surfaces. May test lining for holes and faulty seams, using device that creates spark on contact with metal vessel through apertures in rubber. May visit equipment sites to install linings. May be designated according to article lined as Tank Insulator, Rubber (machinery mfg.); Valve Liner, Rubber (machinery mfg.).
GOE: 06.02.29 STRENGTH: M GED: R3 M1 L2 SVP: 4 DLU: 77

759.684-054 RUBBER-GOODS REPAIRER (any industry)
Repairs rubber products, such as life rafts and vests, gas-tank linings, inner tubes, and rubber vent systems, using oven or autoclave and steam curing iron: Cements rubber patch to torn or damaged areas and vulcanizes patch, using steam curing iron. Cuts rubber into pieces, covers metal and other surfaces with pieces, and places rubber article in oven or autoclave to bond surfaces. May make gaskets, washers, and hose, using molds and dies.
GOE: 06.02.29 STRENGTH: L GED: R3 M1 L1 SVP: 4 DLU: 77

759.684-058 SPLICER (rubber tire) alternate titles: cord splicer; ply splicer; stock roller;
Splices bias-cut rubberized-fabric stock into plies for use in tire building: Inspects plies and tears off sections having such defects as uncalendered spots or torn fabric. Aligns and splices sections of ply stock by overlapping ends and pressing together with fingers. Presses pedal to wind spliced plies on spool. Determines when spool is loaded by counting plies or observing stop-mark on liner. Guides ply onto spools by hand to prevent wrinkling. May splice stock cut from and tend automatic bias cutting machine. Winds assembled plies onto spool; or cuts it to lengths, using bar cutter, and slides assembly onto conveyor. Notifies maintenance department of machine malfunction.
GOE: 06.04.29 STRENGTH: L GED: R2 M1 L2 SVP: 2 DLU: 77

759.684-062 TUBE-AND-MANIFOLD BUILDER (rubber goods)
Builds tubes and manifolds of rubberized fabric for use in pneumatic airplane deicers: Lifts roll of rubberized fabric sheeting to letoff racks and unwinds it onto table. Lays out and draws outline of specified size tubes and manifolds on rubberized fabric, using rule, template, and chalkline. Cuts outlined section from rubberized fabric, using scissors and knife. Positions and wraps cut fabric section around metal forming bar, and aligns and splices edges by pressing gum tape over edges of fabric on bar, using roller. Pulls out forming bar and blows soapstone into rubberized tubing with airhose to prevent inner surfaces from sticking together. Winds number of tubing sections required for one deicer onto reel. Attaches identification tag to loaded reel and carries it to storage rack.
GOE: 06.02.29 STRENGTH: M GED: R2 M1 L2 SVP: 3 DLU: 77

759.684-066 V-BELT BUILDER (rubber goods)
Builds up plies (layers) of rubber and filler to form V-belts: Hoists rolls of calendered rubber for belt base and filler from storage to worktable, using hoist. Sets drum to specified circumference by turning wheel and verifies size with rule. Pulls rubber from rolls and measures and cuts it with scissors. Brushes rubber cement on sides of rubber, lays one or more plies of rubber around drum, and splices ends. Threads end of cemented belt cord from spool through lathe guide and spots ends at edge of base rubber on drum. Sets gauge to wind specified cords per inch around length of base rubber and starts drum revolving. Lays one or more plies of filler rubber on top of cord. Starts pressure rollers that compress material on drum. Positions notched cutting bar across front of drum and cuts belting to specified width by holding knife in notches and pressing knife against revolving drum. Collapses drum and places cut belts on rack.
GOE: 06.02.29 STRENGTH: M GED: R3 M1 L2 SVP: 4 DLU: 77

759.684-070 SPLICER (protective dev.)
Splices ends of safety ropes to prevent raveling: Cuts polypropylene rope to specifications, using electric knife. Inserts end of rope through protective plastic washer in eye of ring or hook. Unravels and interweaves strands to retain ring or hook at end of rope. Holds spliced section of rope over heated coil to fuse strands.
GOE: 06.04.34 STRENGTH: L GED: R2 M1 L1 SVP: 2 DLU: 86

759.684-074 RUBBER-GOODS INSPECTOR-TESTER (rubber goods)
Inspects and tests rubber materials, parts, or products for conformance to specifications: Visually and tactually examines items for defects, such as soils, cracks, and breaks. Verifies dimensions and weights of articles, using scales, calipers, templates, and other measuring instruments, following specifications

and blueprints. Verifies strength, durability, and permeability of materials and products, using tensile strength, compression, inflation, and water tests. Sorts, counts, or marks articles according to size, grade, or color. Records inspection and testing data. May trim excess materials from articles, using knife, scissors, cutting machines, or buffing wheels. May cut out and replace defective areas to salvage parts or products. May bundle or pack goods for shipment. May be designated according to product inspected as Balloon Tester (rubber goods); Hose Tester (rubber goods); Inner-Tube Tester (rubber tire); Rubber-Gasket Inspector-Trimmer (rubber goods); V-Belt Inspector (rubber goods). May be designated: Adhesion Tester (rubber goods); Boot Tester (rubber goods); Calender Inspector (rubber goods); Catheter Finisher-And-Inspector (rubber goods); Dielectric Tester (rubber goods); Hose Inspector (rubber goods); Inflation Tester (rubber goods); Inspector (rubber goods); Inspector And Tester (rubber goods); Inspector, Fuel Hose (rubber goods); Matting Inspector (rubber goods); Mattress Inspector (rubber goods); Molded-Goods Inspector-Trimmer (rubber goods); Padded-Products Inspector-Trimmer (rubber goods); Piston-Cup Inspector (rubber goods); Rubber-Goods Finisher (rubber goods); Rubber-Goods Inspector-Trimmer (rubber goods; rubber reclaim.; rubber tire); Rubber-Goods Tester, Water (rubber goods; rubber tire); Slab Inspector (rubber reclaim.).
GOE: 06.03.02 STRENGTH: L GED: R3 M2 L3 SVP: 4 DLU: 78

759.687-010 DEICER INSPECTOR, PNEUMATIC (rubber goods)
Inspects pneumatic airplane deicers for defects: Inflates deicers with specified amount of air pressure, using hose. Observes air pressure gauge and examines rubberized fabric tubes and manifold of deicers to detect leaks. Sorts and marks defective deicers for repair or scrap. May pull rip strip (rubberized fabric) from deicer to form vent channel, and punch ventholes in specified locations, using die and mallet.
GOE: 06.03.02 STRENGTH: L GED: R3 M2 L2 SVP: 4 DLU: 77

759.687-014 HOSE-COUPLING JOINER (rubber goods) alternate titles: assembler-crimper; coupler
Joins metal couplings to cured rubber hose: Attaches expansion shaft to air-powered expander device, using handtools. Positions specified expansion ring on shaft and coupling on end of hose. Slips hose over expansion shaft and starts expander device that spreads expansion ring and locks coupling to hose. Cuts hose to specified length before attaching couplings, using miter box and knife. May bolt coupling hardware to hose, using wrench.
GOE: 06.04.34 STRENGTH: H GED: R2 M1 L2 SVP: 2 DLU: 77

76 OCCUPATIONS IN FABRICATION AND REPAIR OF WOOD PRODUCTS

This division includes occupations concerned with fabricating and repairing complete wooden articles, or subassemblies of wooden structures, involving the use of woodworking handtools and power tools.

760 BENCH CARPENTERS AND RELATED OCCUPATIONS

This group includes occupations concerned with laying out stock and shaping, assembling, and smoothing wood articles, using saws, planers, and other carpentry tools.

760.684-010 BENCH CARPENTER (woodworking)
Assembles precut and prefabricated wooden parts to form complete units, using woodworking hand and power tools: Reads blueprints, shop drawings, or written instructions to determine method and sequence of assembling parts. Measures, shapes, adjusts, trims, and sands parts and joints to make parts fit snugly, using rulers, handtools, and sandpaper. Applies glue and inserts dowels or screws to fasten subassemblies together and form complete unit, using handtools and clamps. May install hardware in subassemblies or into completed unit. May work on an assembly line and be responsible for only one phase of assembly process.
GOE: 06.04.25 STRENGTH: H GED: R2 M2 L2 SVP: 3 DLU: 77

760.684-014 BOX MAKER, WOOD (wood. container) alternate titles: carpenter, box; case maker; rate builder
Cuts lumber and assembles cut lumber into boxes and crates, using handtools or power tools: Measures, marks, and saws boards to specified size, using ruler, pencil, and power saws. Assembles and nails boards together, using hammer, power stapler, or nailing machine. Repairs damaged containers by replacing damaged parts, using handtools. Salvages used crating by removing nails from board with hammer, nail puller, or crowbar and by sawing ends with portable electric handsaw. May sharpen saw, using file. May insert cardboard fillers, felt pads, and wooden separators in containers. May build crate around material, using ruler, handtools, and pneumatic nailer. When repairing wooden boxes, may be known as Box Repairer (wood. container) I.
GOE: 06.02.25 STRENGTH: M GED: R3 M2 L2 SVP: 3 DLU: 77

761 OCCUPATIONS IN LAYING OUT, CUTTING, CARVING, SHAPING, AND SANDING WOOD PRODUCTS, N.E.C.

This group includes occupations concerned with marking, cutting lines on stock, and bending, shaving, carving, sawing, and sanding wood products, using abrasives, handtools, templates, and other devices and materials.

761.130-010 SUPERVISOR, BRIAR SHOP (fabrication, nec)
Supervises and coordinates activities of workers engaged in fabricating smoking pipe stummels from briar blocks: Studies production schedules to determine style and number of stummels to be sawed from blocks. Surveys stummels in stockroom and prepares work order indicating style and quality of stummels needed. Informs workers when to prepare for change-over to new style. Inspects graded stummels to verify conformance to standards. Records quality and quantity of pipes produced from specific suppliers' briar blocks. Trains workers in setup of machines. Performs other duties as described under SUPERVISOR (any industry) Master Title.
GOE: 06.02.01 STRENGTH: L GED: R4 M3 L3 SVP: 7 DLU: 77

761.131-010 SUPERVISOR, LAST-MODEL DEPARTMENT (wood prod., nec)
Supervises and coordinates activities of workers engaged in shaping wooden and plastic heel and shoe last models: Compares specifications with last patterns to verify style and measurements, using measuring instruments. Designates pattern to be used and informs workers of style and measurement specifications required. Completes forms to requisition work material and supplies, such as sandpaper, wood, and plastic stock. Examines completed lists to verify conformance with customer and company specifications. Performs other duties as described under SUPERVISOR (any industry) Master Title.
GOE: 06.01.01 STRENGTH: L GED: R4 M3 L3 SVP: 8 DLU: 77

761.281-010 CARVER, HAND (woodworking) alternate titles: wood carver, hand
Carves ornamental designs into wooden furniture parts, using handtools and woodworking machines: Studies sketches and dimensions of ornamental designs submitted by architect, customer, or design department, visualizes finished product, and draws design to scale, using drawing instruments. Transfers design to wooden furniture part by tracing over drawing and carbon paper with stylus. Clamps furniture part in vise and roughs out design freehand or by cutting along lines marked on wood, using chisel and mallet, jigsaw, and router. Selects chisels, gouges, files, and rasps and determines sequence of their use according to intricacy of design. Cuts, trims, or touches up roughed out design, using handtools to finish design. Verifies dimensions of carving, using rule and dividers. Taps *stippling tool* with mallet to stipple design. May saw precut wooden blocks into rough shaped decorative items, using chain saw and portable power saw. May finish carvings roughed out on router, spindle carver, or wood-carving machine and be designated Skin Carver (furniture).
GOE: 01.06.02 STRENGTH: L GED: R4 M4 L3 SVP: 8 DLU: 87

761.281-014 EXPERIMENTAL-BOX TESTER (wood. container)
Designs and constructs boxes for experimental and test purposes. Measures and tests strength of boxes made by competitors, disassembles boxes, and records findings.
GOE: 05.05.02 STRENGTH: L GED: R4 M3 L4 SVP: 7 DLU: 77

761.281-018 MARQUETRY WORKER (furniture)
Designs, fabricates, and inlays marquetry in custom furniture: Designs and draws marquetry patterns to scale, using drafting tools. Computes quantities of wood needed for shaping marquetry design blocks, and selects woods, such as ebony, teak, and walnut, for marquetry designs according to color, strength, and grain. Shapes pieces of wood to form pattern, using power saws, handsaws, planers, and jigs. Measures wood pieces to verify dimensions, using calipers, scales, and pattern. Applies glue to wood pieces, assembles pieces according to pattern, and clamps pieces between boards to prevent damage and to form marquetry block. Selects wood in which pattern will be mounted and cuts openings in surface of wood and specified piece of furniture to form inlay openings for sections of marquetry block, using routers, chisels, and planers. Saws marquetry block to obtain cross-sections of specified thickness for inlay. Glues and places sections into inlay openings of wood surface and positions wood with marquetry design into opening on furniture. Trims design to fit opening, and sands surface of furniture to attain desired finish, using handtools and power sander. Cleans furniture and applies stain, lacquer, or shellac in prescribed order to finish custom furniture.
GOE: 05.05.08 STRENGTH: L GED: R4 M4 L3 SVP: 7 DLU: 86

761.381-010 BOAT-OAR MAKER (woodworking)
Performs carpentry necessary to cut and shape oars, using special planes, drawknives, and other handtools: Clamps oar in vise. Shapes blade, loom (shaft from handle to blade), and handle, trimming edges and rounding corners according to specified dimensions. Smooths and sands surface preparatory to varnishing or painting. Usually identifies work with personal markings on blade.
GOE: 06.02.25 STRENGTH: M GED: R3 M2 L2 SVP: 6 DLU: 77

761.381-014 JIG BUILDER (wood. container) alternate titles: setter
Builds jigs used as guides for assembling oversized or special type box shooks, following blueprints: Measures and marks position of stops on worktable, according to blueprint, using tape measure and chalk. Nails stops to worktable as indicated by layout. May build first shook on layout as demonstration.
GOE: 05.10.01 STRENGTH: M GED: R3 M2 L2 SVP: 6 DLU: 77

761.381-018 LAST-MODEL MAKER (wood prod., nec) alternate titles: model maker
Shapes wood blocks into shoe last models according to specifications and diagrams, using copy lathe and handtools: Lays out and cuts specified size and

shape templates for use in constructing last models and to verify dimensions and contour of finished last models, using scribe, measuring instruments, and razor cutter. Procures last model with backpart (heel of last to ball of last) having same size and shapes as that specified on order. Mounts last model and wood block in copy lathe that automatically turns down end of block to match backpart of last model. Removes model and partially turned wood block from lathe and measures model at prescribed points to verify duplication. Clamps partially turned block in vise. Shapes toe area to specified size and contour, using files, drawknives, spokeshaves, sandpaper, and glass. Verifies contour and size with templates and sole patterns. Sands last model to specified size and finish. Hammers tacks along edges to protect model from wear on copy lathes. Files tack heads flush with last. May shape new last models from wood blocks, plastic, or leather, using handtools only, when last models of identical backpart specifications are not available. May specialize in fashioning and fabricating last models for shoe heels or shoe soles.
GOE: 06.01.04 STRENGTH: M GED: R4 M4 L4 SVP: 6 DLU: 77

761.381-022 PATTERN MARKER I (woodworking)
Lays out outlines of frames and furniture parts on woodstock to guide machine operators, working from blueprints, job orders, or models: Studies architectural drawing or blueprint of part or full assembly to be made. Selects stock lumber of necessary size and measures and marks with rule, square, and pencil or crayon, outlines of cuts to be made by various machine operators. May calibrate and record machining dimensions on stock or pattern for use in production as guide for machining parts. May trace outlines from blueprints for decorative or irregular cutting on bandsaw. May trace around patterns to indicate cutting lines.
GOE: 06.02.31 STRENGTH: L GED: R4 M4 L3 SVP: 7 DLU: 77

761.381-026 SKI MAKER, WOOD (toy-sport equip.)
Fabricates skis from wood, using handtools and powered machines: Cuts rough forms for skis, using electrically powered cutting machine. Soaks ski forms in hot water until pliable and places them in bending frame for shaping. Operates shaper to form ridges on top of ski. Pairs skis according to size, weight, and grain of wood. Sands skis and scrapes them with handtool to correct variations in thickness. Operates shaper to form grooves on underside of ski according to type of ski, such as plain, racing, or jumping skis. Finishes surface, using sandpaper. May apply varnish or paint to finished ski.
GOE: 06.02.25 STRENGTH: M GED: R3 M3 L2 SVP: 5 DLU: 77

761.381-030 SMOKING-PIPE MAKER (fabrication, nec)
Performs all hand and machine operations to make smoking-pipe bowls and stems from briar blocks: Sets up preselected block in fixture of wood-turning lathe. Sets up cutters in lathe chuck, and moves block forward to cause cutters to partially turn and face bowl of pipe. Replaces cutting tools to bore inside of bowl. Clamps block in *frazing machine* and forces it against cutters that duplicate lower part of bowl and shank to preselected pipe shape. Places shank in holder of drill press and drills and reams shank hole. Selects appropriate bit and drills airhole from mortice hole through shank into bowl chamber. Removes bowl from drill press and digs into bowl and shank to remove rotten briar and rough spots, using sharp handtool. Threads shank and stem, using threading machine. Inserts metal bushing in shank with handtool. Inspects pipe for flaws, cracks, or irregularities. Dips pipe in stain solution to highlight grain and color of briar and wipes pipe dry with soft cloth. Coats inside bowl chamber with specified mixture to sweeten bowl, using brush. Screws or presses stem into shank to assemble pipe, using handtools. Holds assembled pipe against sanding and buffing wheels to finish and polish surface.
GOE: 06.02.03 STRENGTH: L GED: R4 M2 L2 SVP: 7 DLU: 77

761.381-034 STOCK CHECKERER I (ordnance) alternate titles: checkerer, hand
Carves checkered designs and borders in wooden gunstocks, forearms, and slide handles to provide decorative gripping surfaces: Positions paper or plastic pattern on workpiece and dusts with powdered chalk to transfer outline to surface of wood. Secures workpiece in holding device to facilitate tooling over pattern area. Engraves grooves and decorative borders within chalked outline, using hand checkering and rabbeting tools. May rout recesses in workpiece, using carving tools, and insert wood or metal inlays. May sketch and engrave special designs, such as scrolls, oak leaves, birds, or animals, and be designated Carver And Checkerer, Specials (ordnance). May carve borders only and be designated Borderer (ordnance); or repair defective checkering on worn or damaged stocks and be designated Repairer And Checker (ordnance).
GOE: 01.06.02 STRENGTH: L GED: R3 M2 L3 SVP: 5 DLU: 77

761.381-038 STOCK MAKER, CUSTOM (ordnance) alternate titles: gunstock repairer; outside repairer, special; shaper
Lays out, fabricates, and finishes standard or wooden gunstocks: Selects wooden blanks according to customer's specifications. Draws outline on blanks following pattern or template. Cuts along outline with bandsaw to form rough stock; and shapes recesses in stock, using chisels, gauges, and rabbeting tools. Bores holes to specified depth in butt of gun, using drill press or brace and bit; and inserts weights to attain specified balance. Attaches frame and trigger assembly to stock and screws barrel into frame. Mounts gun in holding device of layout table and locates and draws finish outline, centerline, pitch, pull, and drop, using pencil, scribe, straightedge, square, and butt drop gauge. Shapes contours, using drawknives, chisels, gauges, rasps, and files. Finishes stock, using sandpaper, emery cloth, steel wool, oil, stain, and varnish.

GOE: 01.06.02 STRENGTH: L GED: R4 M3 L3 SVP: 7 DLU: 77

761.682-010 LATHE SANDER (woodworking)
Operates lathe or vacuum spindle machine to remove toolmarks and smooth round wooden parts: Positions part to be sanded between headstock and tailstock of lathe, and closes tailstock against part to hold it in place, or places part on rubber cup of vacuum spindle. Starts machine and presses sandpaper of specified grade over and around rotating part. Inspects or feels part to ascertain whether surface is smooth. Removes sanded part from machine. May apply wax or other finishes while part is rotating on machine. May be designated according to machine as Vacuum-Spindle Sander (furniture).
GOE: 06.04.25 STRENGTH: M GED: R2 M1 L1 SVP: 2 DLU: 77

761.682-014 SANDER, MACHINE (woodworking)
Operates one or more sanding machines equipped with sanding belts or sanding heads, such as disks, drums, spools, or brushes mounted on vertical or horizontal spindles to smooth surfaces and edges of hand held wooden parts, boards, or furniture parts: Turns handwheels to adjust tension of sanding belt or to adjust height or angle of table or spindle. Presses button or switch to start machine. Holds and turns stock by hand against sanding head or belt or places stock on table or in jig and pushes stock back and forth against sanding head or belt, until rough surfaces and edges of stock are smooth. Examines and feels stock to verify smoothness. Replaces worn sandpaper belts, or sandpaper on sanding heads, using handtools. May cut sandpaper to designated size and shape prior to replacement on machine, using scissors. May select and mount sanding head on spindle according to shape of article to be sanded, using screwdriver or wrench. May be designated according to type of machine operated as Belt Sander (woodworking); Spindle Sander (woodworking); according to type sanding head used as Brush Sander (woodworking); Disk Sander (woodworking); Pneumatic-Drum Sander (woodworking); Spool Sander (woodworking); or according to area of article sanded as Edge Sander (woodworking).
GOE: 06.02.03 STRENGTH: M GED: R2 M1 L1 SVP: 3 DLU: 79

761.682-018 SPINDLE CARVER (woodworking) alternate titles: carver, machine; carving-machine operator
Sets up and operates bench-mounted, single-spindle carving machine to carve decorative designs on wooden furniture stock, following drawing or sample: Studies drawing of design or stock sample of item to be carved and selects cutter according to size and shape of design and type of wood. Attaches cutter to machine spindle, using wrenches and pliers. Starts machine and holds and guides stock against rotating cutter to carve design identical to drawing or sample. May install grinding wheel on spindle and sharpen cutter by holding it against rotating grinding wheel. May attach carving guide and rest stock against guide to cut design in stock.
GOE: 06.02.03 STRENGTH: L GED: R3 M2 L2 SVP: 5 DLU: 78

761.684-010 GOLF-CLUB FACER (toy-sport equip.) alternate titles: facer
Shapes faces of golf club woods to achieve specified contours, using one of following methods: (1) Clamps head of golf club wood in vise and selects file of tooth size, according to amount of material to be removed. Files contours on face. (2) Moves wood head against belt sander to shape face to specified contours. Places serrated cutters and spacers on arbor of motor in specified pattern to set up scoring apparatus. Starts motor and presses face of club into cutters to score face. Measures loft of club with protractor and visually compares faced club with prototype to verify contours.
GOE: 06.02.25 STRENGTH: L GED: R3 M2 L1 SVP: 4 DLU: 77

761.684-014 JIG BUILDER (metal prod., nec)
Builds wood jigs, used as guides in welding wire display racks, following sketch or sample: Lays out and marks jig dimensions on plywood stock according to written instructions or measurements taken from sample. Adjusts saw guides and cuts grooves in plywood to hold wires in place for welding, using table saw. Positions and attaches wood stops to plywood at wire crossing points and drills holes in plywood at crossing points to facilitate welding, using drill press and handtools.
GOE: 06.04.25 STRENGTH: M GED: R2 M2 L1 SVP: 3 DLU: 77

761.684-018 PANEL-LAY-UP WORKER (woodworking)
Matches and gathers boards of specified grain, color, and width to form panels: Inspects boards in stockpile and selects sides with matching grain and color for panel surface. Assembles pieces on table or conveyor, in sequence, and marks them with crayon for reassembly in gluing machine. Measures width of panel to verify work order requirements, using ruler. May place rejected boards on conveyor for reprocessing. May be designated according to type of panel assembled as Piano-Sounding-Board Matcher (musical inst.).
GOE: 06.03.02 STRENGTH: L GED: R3 M2 L2 SVP: 4 DLU: 77

761.684-022 PATTERN MARKER II (woodworking) alternate titles: band-saw marker; marker
Marks outlines of irregularly shaped parts on woodstock to provide cutting guides for machine operators: Arranges specified patterns on stock to obtain maximum number of pieces with most effective utilization of wood grain. Traces patterns with pencil or other marking device. May nail pieces of thin stock together for identical parts to be cut simultaneously. May be designated according to woodstock being marked as Veneer Marker (woodworking).
GOE: 06.04.25 STRENGTH: L GED: R2 M2 L2 SVP: 2 DLU: 77

761.684-026 POLISHER (woodworking)
Holds and moves articles, such as baseball bats, wooden tool handles, handbag frames, and shoe lasts against revolving canvas belt or rotating cloth-cov-

ered wheel or disk to smooth and polish their surfaces: Activates polishing apparatus and holds polishing compound stick against belt, wheel, or disk to coat it. Presses and turns articles against belt, wheel or disk, to remove scratches and defects, and to polish surface of article to specified finish. Replaces worn buffs, using wrenches. May be designated according to article polished as Last Polisher (wood prod., nec); Wood Buffer (musical inst.).
GOE: 06.04.25 STRENGTH: M GED: R2 M1 L1 SVP: 2 DLU: 77

761.684-030 SANDER (fabrication, nec) alternate titles: hand sander; topper
Cleans, shapes, and smooths parts of smoking pipes: Positions specified grade of sandpaper on sanding machine spindle and turns nut to secure sandpaper. Starts machine and holds part, such as bowl or stem, against rotating disk, using varying pressure, or positions pipe bowl on spindle and holds sandpaper against revolving bowl to clean, shape, or smooth pipe. May be designated according to degree of sanding as Fine Sander (fabrication, nec); Rough Sander (fabrication, nec); or according to part or area sanded as Bit Sander (fabrication, nec); Bottom Sander (fabrication, nec); Bowl Topper (fabrication, nec); Shank Sander (fabrication, nec); or according to sanding objective as Putty Remover (fabrication, nec). May sand shank to fit flush with stem and be designated Flusher (fabrication, nec). May position pipe bowl on spindle and hold sandpaper against revolving bowl to smooth and shape bowl.
GOE: 06.04.34 STRENGTH: L GED: R2 M1 L1 SVP: 2 DLU: 78

761.684-034 SANDER, PORTABLE MACHINE (woodworking)
Smooths wood surfaces to facilitate finishing, using portable belt, disk, orbital, or vibrator sanding machine: Attaches sheet, disk or belt of abrasive material to machine rollers or platen, and secures it with thumbscrews or clamps. Starts machine and guides it over surfaces by hand. Inspects and feels stock for smoothness. May remove excess glue from joints, using knife, scraper, or wood chisel. May sand wood surface by hand, using sandpaper.
GOE: 06.04.25 STRENGTH: L GED: R2 M1 L1 SVP: 2 DLU: 80

761.684-038 SHAPER, HAND (furniture) alternate titles: scraper, hand
Dresses and smooths curved wooden furniture parts by clamping roughly sawed or shaped part in vise and shaping it to specified contours and finish, using tools, such as spokeshave, plane, rasps, and power sander.
GOE: 06.02.25 STRENGTH: L GED: R3 M1 L1 SVP: 4 DLU: 77

761.684-042 STOCK PATCHER (ordnance) alternate titles: patcher-wood welder; stock repairer
Repairs defective or damaged wooden gunstocks and forearms (grips): Trims outline of holes, cracks, chips, and splintered sections to form seat for patch, using punches, chisels, and hammers. Selects wood of matching grain and color and shapes wedges or dowels to form patch, using knives, files, benchsaw, and sanding wheel. Brushes patch with adhesive and positions it in seat. Places patched section between pole plates of heating machine to set adhesive. Trims patch flush with stock surface. Melts stick shellac into scratches, patched section, dents, and blemishes to fill damaged areas, using soldering iron or heated file. Removes excess shellac from repaired area, using sandpaper. May attach specified bakelite cap or ebony tip on stock.
GOE: 06.02.25 STRENGTH: L GED: R3 M1 L1 SVP: 3 DLU: 77

761.684-046 STOCK SHAPER (ordnance)
Scrapes, files, and sands machine-shaped gunstocks to remove excess wood and impart finished appearance to surfaces: Positions and secures stock in vise. Inserts filing jigs into routed recesses and secures them with screws. Scrapes and files wood to fit surfaces flush with jigs and butt-plate and to finish curves and contours of flutes. Smooths areas of stock, using sandpaper and emery cloth. Presses stock against sanding drum to impart smooth finish to stock.
GOE: 06.04.25 STRENGTH: M GED: R2 M1 L1 SVP: 3 DLU: 77

761.684-050 PANEL CUTTER (furniture)
Cuts plywood or particleboard to form end panels for display fixtures, using portable router: Reads work order to determine style of panel and type of woodstock to be used. Selects pattern and places pattern on woodstock, such as plywood or particleboard. Clamps pattern and woodstock to workbench. Guides portable router around edge of pattern to cut panel from woodstock. Cuts grooves in specified panels, using shaper.
GOE: 06.04.25 STRENGTH: M GED: R2 M2 L2 SVP: 2 DLU: 86

761.684-054 TOUCH-UP CARVER (fabrication, nec)
Carves decorative designs on wood smoking pipes to correct defects, using carving machine or pneumatically powered portable drill: Places designated carving bit in carving machine or drill chuck and tightens bit in chuck, using chuck wrench or pliers. Pushes button to start rotation of carving bit. Holds smoking pipe bowl and shank against bit to recarve designated pattern to specified depth on patched pipe or to correct carving defects.
GOE: 06.04.25 STRENGTH: M GED: R3 M1 L1 SVP: 3 DLU: 86

761.684-058 WIRE BRUSH OPERATOR (fabrication, nec)
Cuts pattern on smoking pipe bowl, using rotating wire brush: Places wire brush attachments over wire brush machine shaft and secures brush on shaft, using wrench. Pushes lever to start wire brush rotating. Holds and turns pipe bowl against rotating wire brush, using varying pressure, to cut pattern on specified surfaces of bowl.
GOE: 06.04.25 STRENGTH: M GED: R2 M1 L1 SVP: 2 DLU: 86

761.687-010 SANDER, HAND (woodworking)
Smooths surface of wooden articles, such as furniture parts, mirror frames, caskets, and cabinet panels preparatory to finishing, or between finish coats, using sandpaper and steel wool. Feels surface of sanded article for smoothness. May scrape article with chisel or scraper to remove burrs, splinters, and excess glue. May mark defects, such as knotholes, cracks, and splits to facilitate repair of article. May be designated Finish Sander (woodworking); First-Coat Sander (woodworking).
GOE: 06.04.25 STRENGTH: L GED: R2 M1 L1 SVP: 2 DLU: 79

762 OCCUPATIONS IN ASSEMBLING WOOD PRODUCTS, N.E.C.

This group includes occupations, not elsewhere classified, concerned with fitting, joining, or interlacing wood products by using bolts, nails, rivets, screws, and adhesives.

762.134-010 SUPERVISOR, COMPONENT ASSEMBLER (mfd. bldgs.)
Supervises and coordinates activities of workers engaged in assembling components for manufactured buildings: Examines completed components to determine whether components, such as cabinets, sink tops, door casings, and closets, conform to specifications. Trains new workers in component assembly techniques. Performs other duties as described under SUPERVISOR (any industry) Master Title.
GOE: 06.02.01 STRENGTH: M GED: R4 M3 L3 SVP: 8 DLU: 77

762.384-010 GLUED WOOD TESTER (woodworking) alternate titles: tester
Conducts laboratory tests to determine quality and strength of glued wood products, utilizing knowledge of wood species and strength of glued wood products: Soaks plywood in water for specified time and removes plywood from water to air dry, repeating procedure until glued plywood separates to determine soaking effect upon glue. Glues samples of wood together, places samples in oven, and increases temperature at specified intervals until glued samples break apart to determine heat effect upon glue. Tests tensile strength of glue, using pneumatic testing device to pull glued blocks apart. Determines moisture content of wood by weighing sample before and after baking in electric oven. Compiles test data and records results. Examines and measures stock in various stages of production to detect variations from standards. Prepares graphs and charts to show trends in waste of material and substandard lumber.
GOE: 06.03.01 STRENGTH: L GED: R4 M3 L4 SVP: 7 DLU: 77

762.484-010 REEL ASSEMBLER (woodworking)
Assembles precut wooden pieces to form reels for winding cables or strands: Measures parts, using measuring tape and rule, and assembles them, using hammer. Weighs, marks, and attaches tags to full reels. Rolls reels to stock house. May grease reels to waterproof them.
GOE: 06.04.22 STRENGTH: H GED: R2 M2 L2 SVP: 3 DLU: 77

762.684-010 ASSEMBLER (wood. container)
Assembles precut parts of wooden cases for use in carrying industrial tools and equipment: Fastens wooden parts of case together with rivets or nuts and bolts. Drills holes in precut metal strips and screws strips to edges of case. Rivets hardware, such as hinges, fasteners, and metal corners to case to complete assembly.
GOE: 06.04.22 STRENGTH: M GED: R2 M2 L1 SVP: 3 DLU: 77

762.684-014 ASSEMBLER, COMPONENT (mfd. bldgs.; vehicles, nec)
Assembles manufactured building and travel trailer components, such as sinks, cabinets, closets, counters, doors, and partitions, using hand and power tools: Obtains precut parts and subassemblies specified on parts list. Positions precut parts and subassemblies on worktable according to blueprint specifications or assembly instructions and examines joints to ensure snug fit. Applies glue to parts, using brush or spray gun, and fastens parts together to form component, using staple gun, hammer, or power screwdriver. Positions component or measures to locate position for hardware, such as door knobs, rollers, or faucets, and bores holes or cuts grooves for hardware, such as door hinges, pulls, door knobs, or rollers, using power saw and drill. Fastens hardware in place and hangs doors in frames, using screwdriver and drill. Positions and secures sink or lavatory fixtures in specified position, using pipe wrench. May cut precut lumber to alter dimensions to meet specifications, using power saw and tape measure. May bend portion of wooden counter top to form backsplash, using bending machine. May be designated according to component assembled as Cabinet Assembler (mfd. bldgs.; vehicles, nec); Counter Top Assembler (mfd. bldgs.; vehicles, nec); Partition Assembler (mfd. bldgs.; vehicles, nec).
GOE: 06.02.22 STRENGTH: M GED: R3 M2 L2 SVP: 3 DLU: 77

762.684-018 ASSEMBLY OPERATOR (woodworking)
Fits parts, such as shuttle eyes, tension devices, plates, and spindles, into wooden shuttles: Smooths interior surfaces of openings in shuttles or spindles, using chisel or cutting machine with rotating knives. Bores holes for final assembly, using boring machine. Positions parts in specified opening and screws or bolts them in place, using handtools. Tests tension devices for resistance.
GOE: 06.04.25 STRENGTH: L GED: R2 M2 L2 SVP: 3 DLU: 77

762.684-022 BASKET MENDER (wood. container)
Trims and repairs rattan baskets prior to application of protective coating: Trims ends of rattan rods and reeds, using knives and shears. Removes thin hairlike strands of reed by singeing with gas torch. Reweaves defective sections of baskets to repair baskets. Removes and replaces defective reeds and rods. Rejects baskets unsuited for repair.

GOE: 06.04.34 STRENGTH: L GED: R2 M1 L1 SVP: 3 DLU: 77

762.684-026 BOX MAKER (fabrication, nec)

Assembles wooden boxes from prepared sections or precut boards for use as shipping or burial cases, using either of following methods, using hand or power tools: (1) Places ends of box in form on workbench, and nails side sections and bottom panels to ends, using hammer or pneumatic nailer. Turns unit over, positions top panels on box, nails batten to panels to reinforce top, and tacks top to box. (2) Clamps and fastens precut boards together to form end, side, and bottom sections and nails sections together, using hand clamps, braces, corrugated fasteners, hammer, and pneumatic nailer. Turns unit over, clamps and nails braces to boards to form top, and tacks top to box. Trims and smooths edges and corners of assembled box, using hand plane, drawknife, and sandpaper. Conveys assembled boxes to storage area, using handtruck. May mark box size on ends of boxes. May paint surfaces of boxes, using spray gun.
GOE: 06.04.25 STRENGTH: M GED: R2 M1 L1 SVP: 2 DLU: 77

762.684-030 CURTAIN-STRETCHER ASSEMBLER (woodworking)

Assembles component parts of adjustable curtain stretchers: Drills holes and slots according to markings on wooden parts. Fits parts together to form frame, bolting slotted parts together to permit size adjustment. Connects frame to prop by inserting removable brace into drilled holes of frame and prop.
GOE: 06.04.22 STRENGTH: L GED: R2 M2 L1 SVP: 2 DLU: 77

762.684-034 DOOR ASSEMBLER I (woodworking)

Assembles prepared machined parts (stiles, rails, panels, and bars) into doors, according to prescribed patterns, using glue, maul, and jig: Spaces glue-discharge pipes to correspond with dowel holes in stiles, using wrench and sample stile. Places stile on edge of glue tank and depresses pedal to fill dowel holes with glue. Drops glued stile horizontally with dowel holes up into jig on floor. Grasps rails and panels, in sequence, from stacks behind glue tank and aligns protruding dowels from each piece into glued holes of stile on floor. Taps pieces with maul to start dowels into holes. Glues and places second stile over protruding dowel pins of rails and panels and drives assembly partially together with maul. Tips door on bottom edge and stacks door vertically against rack for removal to CLAMPER (woodworking).
GOE: 06.04.22 STRENGTH: M GED: R2 M1 L1 SVP: 3 DLU: 77

762.684-038 EDGE BANDER, HAND (furniture) alternate titles: veneer-edge bander

Glues veneer bands to edges of case tops and tabletops by hand: Applies glue to veneer strips or edges of top with roller or brush and positions strips on edges. Places top in clamp and closes clamp to hold veneer strips against edges of top until glue is dry. Removes top and trims and smooths joints and edges of veneer with portable laminate trimmer and sandpaper. May cut veneer strips to specified length with handsaw. May use electrically heated or steam-heated clamp to facilitate drying of glue.
GOE: 06.04.22 STRENGTH: M GED: R2 M1 L1 SVP: 2 DLU: 77

762.684-042 GRIP ASSEMBLER (woodworking)

Assembles gripping units that hold bobbins in wooden shuttles and inserts assembled units in shuttles: Removes burrs from edges of slots inside shuttles, using small knife. Fastens T-shaped shim to bobbin holder (grip) with leather straps and fits grip assembly into slots in shuttle chamber. Inserts tapered rod through length of shuttle and grip assembly to align parts, and screws assembled unit to shuttle. Measures position of unit in shuttle, using gauges, and adjusts unit to specified position, using handtools. Inserts specified bobbin in grip assembly and makes adjustments to obtain specified position and tension of bobbin. Repairs damaged grip units by tapping bent parts with hammer.
GOE: 06.02.23 STRENGTH: L GED: R3 M2 L2 SVP: 4 DLU: 77

762.684-046 HARDWARE ASSEMBLER (woodworking)

Attaches hinges to wooden bifold doors with power screwdriver, working as member of three-member crew: Pushes cart of matched doors to feed end of conveyor. Removes and places matched pair of doors face to face on their side edges onto conveyor that conveys doors to stop guide under jigs. Places offset hinges in jigs; and flips switch to activate bars that grasp, lift, and hold doors in position under jigs. Screws hinges to doors, using power screwdriver, to join doors. Depresses foot bar to release joined doors onto conveyor for subsequent packing.
GOE: 06.04.23 STRENGTH: M GED: R2 M1 L1 SVP: 2 DLU: 77

762.684-050 NAILER, HAND (any industry)

Assembles wooden products, such as boxes, packing cases, kegs, pallets, furniture frames, door and window units, and hogshead subassemblies, using handtools: Positions workpiece on table, floor, easel, or jig, according to verbal instructions, and nails or staples materials together at designated points, using hammer, pneumatic gun, or staple gun. Drives nails in carvings, molding, and scroll work, using hammer, before attaching to furniture. Attaches metal cleats to bottoms of nail kegs to reinforce containers, using hammer and nails. Clinches exposed nail ends and places assembled unit aside for further processing or shipment. May insert bolts in predrilled holes and tighten bolts with wrench. May glue joints before nailing. May record production. May repair containers and be designated Box Repairer (any industry). May be designated according to product assembled as Box Maker, Wood (any industry); Panel Maker (woodworking).
GOE: 06.04.22 STRENGTH: M GED: R2 M1 L1 SVP: 3 DLU: 80

762.684-054 SCARF GLUER (millwork-plywood)

Glues scarfed plywood panels together to form panels of specified length: Spreads glue on scarfed edge of panels, using roller, brush or putty knife.

Places panels on worktable, fits glued-scarfed edges together to form joint, and staples corners of panel to hold them together while being pressed. Removes staples from cured panels and sands excess glue from surface of joint, using portable sander. Stacks finished panels on pallets and brands grade and trademark on edge, using electric branding iron. May verify strength of bonded joint, using pneumatic test equipment. May push panels into hot-plate press and close press to cure joint.
GOE: 06.04.25 STRENGTH: H GED: R2 M1 L1 SVP: 4 DLU: 77

762.684-058 SIDING STAPLER (millwork-plywood)

Glues and staples wood strips and wedges on edges of plywood panels to make siding panels: Places plywood panels and wood strips near workbench. Examines each panel and rejects those with defects. Positions acceptable panel on workbench with finish surface down. Feeds wood strip through rollers that apply glue to bottom side and glues strip along one surface edge of panel. Positions wood wedge on end of panel and staples strip and wedge to panel, using staple gun. Stacks and ties completed panels in bundles to protect finish surfaces from damage during storage or shipment. Paints edges of bundled panels with weather proofing compound, using spray gun. Cuts rejected panels into strips, using table saw. Fills glue container, adding catalyst to obtain prescribed color. Records production.
GOE: 06.04.25 STRENGTH: H GED: R2 M2 L2 SVP: 2 DLU: 77

762.684-062 TRUSS ASSEMBLER (millwork-plywood)

Assembles precut wooden parts to build trusses and similar supports or wall sections used in building construction: Moves specified precut parts to work area and positions parts in jig by hand or using overhead crane, following supervisor's instructions and blueprint specifications. Places metal reinforcement plates over connecting joints and connects parts at joints, using hammer, screwdriver, or pneumatic staple gun. Verifies dimensions of precut parts and accuracy of assembly, using ruler and gauges.
GOE: 05.10.01 STRENGTH: M GED: R3 M2 L2 SVP: 3 DLU: 77

762.684-066 WOODEN-FRAME BUILDER (furniture)

Assembles wood frames for box springs and studio couches, using handtools: Positions precut frame parts, such as sides, ends, and braces in fixture, and glues, staples, and screws them together to fabricate box spring frame, using handtools, hand stapler, and glue applicator. Trims and smooths edges of frame, using saw and planer. Nails, screws, bolts, and glues precut couch framing and attaches legs, arms, and back pieces, using handtools. Nails, screws, or bolts plywood or other material to frame to form bedding box. May cut wood parts, according to specifications, using power tools. May attach hardware, such as caster, hand-pulls, and spring hinges. May staple spring assembly to wooden frame to form box spring unit, using pneumatic staple gun. May be designated according to type of frame assembled as Box-Spring-Frame Builder (furniture); Studio-Couch-Frame Builder (furniture).
GOE: 06.04.25 STRENGTH: M GED: R2 M1 L1 SVP: 2 DLU: 77

762.685-010 EDGE BANDER, MACHINE (furniture; millwork-plywood)

Tends machine that glues veneer bands to edges of case tops, tabletops, and plywood panels, using either of following methods: (1) Pours glue in reservoir of banding machine. Places stack of veneer strips in feed chutes. Adjusts conveyor and trimming saws to width and thickness of panels or tops to be banded. Starts machine and feeds stock into machine that applies glue to edges of stock, pulls veneer strips from feed chute onto edges, dries glue on heated plates, and trims strips flush with edges. Regulates speed of belts that convey stock through machine. Sets temperature control to regulate heat of drying plates. (2) Brushes glue on edges of panels or tops. Adjusts stop on bander machine to width of stock. Sets dial on temperature gauge to heat ram and stop according to thickness of stock. Aligns stock and veneer strips between ram and stop. Depresses pedal to activate ram that presses stock against stop and bonds veneer strips to edges of stock. Places stock on worktable for edge trimming and sanding. May mix glue.
GOE: 06.04.03 STRENGTH: M GED: R2 M2 L2 SVP: 3 DLU: 78

762.686-010 EDGE-BANDING-MACHINE OFFBEARER (furniture; millwork-plywood)

Off bears machine that glues veneer bands to edges of case tops, tabletops, and plywood panels. Stacks banded stock on pallet for movement to storage or further processing.
GOE: 06.04.03 STRENGTH: M GED: R1 M1 L1 SVP: 2 DLU: 77

762.687-010 BANDER (wood. container)

Attaches reinforcing metal bands to ends of wood boxes, using *strapping tool*: Threads strapping tool with metal band. Positions band around ends of box. Pumps handle of tool to tighten band. Pulls lever on machine to crimp and fasten band with metal clip.
GOE: 06.04.25 STRENGTH: M GED: R1 M1 L1 SVP: 2 DLU: 77

762.687-014 BOX INSPECTOR (wood. container) alternate titles: assembling inspector

Inspects and repairs wood boxes: Examines partially or completely assembled boxes and crates for defects, such as cracks, nicks, holes, and diagonally driven and protruding nails. Removes diagonally driven nails and drives in protruding nails, using hammer. Smooths rough spots and edges, using sanding block or wire brush. Rejects substandard boxes. May sort assembled boxes according to specified groups.
GOE: 06.03.02 STRENGTH: L GED: R2 M1 L2 SVP: 2 DLU: 77

762.687-018 BOX REPAIRER II (wood. container) alternate titles: box-shook patcher
Examines box shooks and blanks for cracks, knots, holes, and loose binding wire. Fills defects with cement and wood and staples loose binding wires to sides of boxes.
GOE: 06.03.02 STRENGTH: L GED: R2 M1 L1 SVP: 3 DLU: 86

762.687-022 CLAMP-JIG ASSEMBLER (woodworking)
Assembles and clamps together wooden parts for such products as door frames and furniture parts, using jig equipped with power clamping device: Places precut wooden parts in jig in specified sequence and position, and activates mechanism that clamps parts together. Releases clamp and stacks completed items on skid. May turn crank to adjust width of jig. May brush glue on wooden parts or squirt glue in dowel or tenon holes before assembling parts. May be designated according to product as Hollow-Core Door-Frame Assembler (wood prod., nec); Louver-Door Assembler (wood prod., nec).
GOE: 06.04.22 STRENGTH: M GED: R2 M2 L2 SVP: 2 DLU: 78

762.687-026 CROSSBAND LAYER (millwork-plywood) alternate titles: core layer, plywood; glue spreader helper
Stacks glued *crossbands* alternately with *core stock* to assemble plywood panels for bonding, working as member of team: Grasps glue-coated crossbands as they emerge from glue spreader and places them cross-grained between *back sheet*, core stock, and *face sheet* placed by VENEER-STOCK LAYER (millwork-plywood) 762.687-066 until specified ply is obtained. Discards broken crossbands. Pushes assembled panels down conveyor to hot-plate press for bonding into plywood. May assist GLUE SPREADER, VENEER (millwork-plywood; wood prod., nec) 569.685-042 to clean rollers of glue spreader. May brush glue on irregularly shaped veneer sheets that will not fit in glue spreader. May assemble 3-ply panels alone, laying back sheet, glued core or inner sheet, and face sheet in sequence, and be designated Plywood Builder (millwork-plywood).
GOE: 06.04.25 STRENGTH: M GED: R2 M1 L1 SVP: 2 DLU: 78

762.687-030 DOOR CORE ASSEMBLER (woodworking)
Assembles hollow-core or solid-core doors in teamwork, using either of following methods: (1) Inserts preassembled hollow or solid door cores between glue rollers that coat both sides with glue, and alternately stacks cores on press dolly between pairs of veneer panels to assemble doors. Positions lock blocks, cross sticks, and corrugated cardboard spacers within frames of hollow cores. Pushes loaded dolly into press. (2) Inserts braces, stiles, rails, and filler boards between glue rollers, and alternately stacks them in position between pairs of veneer panels on elevator platform that automatically descends as each hollow-core door is assembled. Pushes stack of assembled doors from platform rollers onto conveyor rollers for transfer to press.
GOE: 06.04.22 STRENGTH: M GED: R2 M1 L1 SVP: 2 DLU: 77

762.687-034 GLUER (woodworking)
Applies glue to surfaces of wooden pieces and clamps them together to form larger pieces or complete units, such as panels, tub bottoms, and tennis rackets: Spreads glue on surfaces to be joined, using brush or hand roller, or by drawing wood across roller partially submerged in glue. Assembles and aligns pieces, and fastens them together until glue dries, using bar clamps, hand clamps, vise, or radial-arm clamp carrier. Presses pedal when using clamp carrier to move racks containing clamped units around frame of device and back to working position. May reinforce joints with nails, screws, or brads, using handtools. May mix glue. May be designated according to type of clamping device used as Clamp-Carrier Operator (woodworking). May be designated according to product as Box Gluer (wood. container); Panel Maker (fabrication, nec).
GOE: 06.04.22 STRENGTH: M GED: R2 M2 L2 SVP: 3 DLU: 78

762.687-038 GLUER-AND-WEDGER (woodworking) alternate titles: wedger-and-gluer
Glues and shapes fibrous veneer strips to sides and ends of wooden shuttle blanks: Brushes glue on veneer strips and aligns them on sides of shuttle blanks to form even surface. Clamps several veneered shuttle blanks together in rack and hangs racks in drying room. Removes racks and brushes glue on underside of veneer strips at tapered shuttle ends, and hammers wooden wedges around tapered ends of shuttles in rack to shape strips to shuttle form. Returns racks to drying rooms.
GOE: 06.04.25 STRENGTH: L GED: R2 M1 L1 SVP: 2 DLU: 77

762.687-042 HANDLE ASSEMBLER (woodworking)
Attaches metal parts, such as webs and ferrules, to wooden tool and implement handles: Positions metal parts on handle, and drills holes for bolts or rivets, using portable power drill. Inserts bolts or rivets in holes, and tightens or fastens them, using handtools or riveting press. May stamp handles with name or size. May pack handles for shipment. May dip or spray handles to color or preserve them. May be designated according to handle assembled as Saw-Handle Assembler (woodworking); Shovel-Handle Assembler (woodworking); Snath-Handle Assembler (woodworking).
GOE: 06.04.22 STRENGTH: M GED: R2 M1 L1 SVP: 2 DLU: 77

762.687-046 HARDWARE ASSEMBLER (wood. container) alternate titles: box-hinge and lock attacher
Attaches hardware, such as hinges, latches, or lockplates, to wooden boxes, using either of following methods: (1) Inserts hardware in magnetized holder of ram or die of press. Positions box in jig beneath ram and depresses pedal

to press and attach hardware to box. (2) Fits and attaches hardware to grooves on wooden box, using hammer and nails. May be desiignated according to method used as Box Nailer (wood. container); Hardware Press Operator (wood. container).
GOE: 06.04.23 STRENGTH: L GED: R2 M1 L1 SVP: 2 DLU: 77

762.687-050 KNOCK-UP ASSEMBLER (woodworking)
Glues and drives tenons of precut wood parts into mortises of other parts to assemble wood products, such as window sashes, door frames, boxes, or furniture or cabinet parts: Brushes glue on tenons or into mortises. Places wood parts on worktable according to specified pattern and sequence and drives tenons of parts into mortises of adjacent parts, using mallet. Inserts mullions between stiles and rails of multipane windows and fastens them with glue. Stacks completed items on skid. May insert wedges into mortises to fasten parts together. May operate *clamp machine* to squeeze tenons into mortises. May be designated according to product assembled as Door Assembler (woodworking) II; Sash Assembler (woodworking).
GOE: 06.04.22 STRENGTH: M GED: R2 M1 L1 SVP: 2 DLU: 77

762.687-054 PARTITION ASSEMBLER (wood. container)
Hammers wood partitions into grooves of other partitions to form sections in bottle boxes. Presses partition clips against top edges of partitions and into box ends to fasten partitions.
GOE: 06.04.23 STRENGTH: L GED: R1 M1 L1 SVP: 1 DLU: 77

762.687-058 SCREEN TACKER (woodworking)
Installs screening in door or window screen frames: Positions roll of screening material on rack and places door or window frame on worktable. Pulls screening material over frame opening, and cuts screen to fit opening, using roller cutter. Forces edge of screen into frame groove, using roller or chisel-like setting tool. Nails molding strip over frame groove or rolls brading cord or spline into groove to secure edge of screen. When rolling in screens, may be designated Screen Roller (woodworking).
GOE: 06.04.34 STRENGTH: L GED: R2 M1 L1 SVP: 2 DLU: 77

762.687-062 SHEET TURNER (millwork-plywood)
Stacks veneer sheets on table to supply VENEER-STOCK LAYER (millwork-plywood) engaged in assembling plywood panels: Removes *back sheets*, *face sheets*, and *core stock* from pallets and places sheets in separate stacks on table supplying VENEER-STOCK LAYER (millwork-plywood). Turns exterior side of back sheet down and places back sheet on top of face sheet to ensure that exterior of sheets are on outside of finished panels. Slides back and face sheets toward VENEER-STOCK LAYER (millwork-plywood) to facilitate handling of sheets by VENEER-STOCK LAYER (millwork-plywood).
GOE: 06.04.40 STRENGTH: M GED: R1 M1 L1 SVP: 2 DLU: 77

762.687-066 VENEER-STOCK LAYER (millwork-plywood) alternate titles: face layer
Stacks veneer sheets alternately with glued *crossbands* to assemble plywood panels for bonding, working as member of team: Positions layup board on conveyor against backstop and inserts poles in socket at end to form jig. Places *back sheets* on layup board to start assembly of individual panels. Places *core stock* between crossbands placed by CROSSBAND LAYER (millwork-plywood) until specified ply is obtained. Places *face sheets* on tops of individual panels to complete panels. Pushes assembled panels down conveyor to hotplate press for bonding into plywood. May turn back and face sheets during assembly of panels to ensure that exterior sides of sheets are on outside of finished panels. May stack chemically treated paper on veneer sheet to make plywood with smooth face sheet suitable for painting or application of wallpaper or cloth.
GOE: 06.04.25 STRENGTH: M GED: R2 M1 L1 SVP: 2 DLU: 77

762.687-070 WOODENWARE ASSEMBLER (woodworking)
Assembles wooden articles, such as ladders, stools, benches, and folding chairs from prefabricated parts; and fastens them together with bolts, nails, or screws, using hand or power tools. May place parts in jig and force parts together for assembly, using pneumatic press. May fasten sections together and attach brackets, using riveting machine. May inspect ladders for conformance to plant and government standards. May be designated according to product assembled as Towel-Rack Assembler (woodworking). May read work orders to determine materials required, number of assemblers needed, and time required to complete work order. May adjust pneumatic bench press according to blueprint of wooden article to be manufactured.
GOE: 06.04.22 STRENGTH: M GED: R2 M1 L2 SVP: 3 DLU: 78

763 OCCUPATIONS IN FABRICATION AND REPAIR OF FURNITURE, N.E.C.

This group includes occupations, not elsewhere classified, concerned with inlaying, installing, molding, weaving, polishing, and related activities concerned with fabricating and repairing furniture.

763.134-010 SUPERVISOR, QUALITY CONTROL (furniture)
Supervises and coordinates activities of workers engaged in inspecting and repairing finished and unfinished wooden furniture to ensure conformance of furniture to company and customer specifications: Confers with supervisory personnel concerned with assembly of furniture to determine type and quantity of furniture to be processed. Measures wooden parts and assembled furniture articles, using tape measure, ruler, and calipers, to ensure conformance with

blueprint specifications. Scans and feels surface of furniture for construction and finishing defects to determine if quality standards are met. Compares color on finished furniture with master color sample to determine if colors match. Records type and quantity of furniture articles processed daily and reports production to office personnel. Performs other duties as described under SUPERVISOR (any industry) Master Title.
GOE: 06.02.01 STRENGTH: M GED: R4 M4 L3 SVP: 6 DLU: 77

763.134-014 SUPERVISOR, FURNITURE ASSEMBLY (furniture)
Supervises and coordinates activities of workers engaged in assembling wood furniture: Determines amount, type, and availability of furniture subassemblies and supplies required for furniture assembly. Examines samples of furniture assembled to ensure conformance to specifications, and instructs workers in methods of correcting defects. Performs other duties as described under SUPERVISOR (any industry) Master Title.
GOE: 06.02.01 STRENGTH: L GED: R3 M3 L3 SVP: 7 DLU: 86

763.380-010 FURNITURE RESTORER (museums) alternate titles: furnishings conservator; coater
Restores and preserves historical furniture in collection of museum or similar institution, using variety of handtools and power tools and applying knowledge of antique fabrics and wood furniture: Examines furnishings to determine type of material, extent of deterioration or damage, or date of construction to verify authenticity and plan restoration. Sets up and operates variety of woodworking machines to fabricate, repair, reinforce, and replace parts of furniture. Cuts, shapes, and attaches parts according to blueprints or drawings, using handtools. Matches materials for color, grain, and texture. Strips old finish from furnishings, using solvents and abrasives. Fills cracks, depressions, and other blemishes, using plastic wood or lacquer stick. Treats warped or stained surfaces to restore original contour and color. Glues or replaces veneer sections. Smooths surfaces, using power sander or abrasive material. Washes or bleaches furniture surfaces to prepare surface for application of finish. Selects coatings, such as stain, lacquer, or varnish according to type wood, and brushes or sprays material onto surface to protect surface and produce desired appearance. Polishes, sprays, or waxes finished pieces. Removes damaged or deteriorated coverings from upholstered furniture. Repairs, reinforces, or replaces components, such as springs, webbing, and padding. Selects fabric for new covering, using knowledge of period and style of furniture or following instructions of CURATOR (museums) 102.017-010. Tacks, sews, glues, or staples covering to furniture frame to attach upholstery. Refurbishes leather coverings of furnishings, using softeners, solvents, adhesives, stains, or polishes. Replaces damaged coverings with leather pieces of appropriate color, grain, and weight. Stencils, gilds, embosses, or paints designs or borders on restored pieces to reproduce original appearance. May advise curatorial staff on environmental conditions necessary for preservation of furnishings in exhibit and storage areas. May fabricate replicas of period furniture for use in exhibits. May be designated according to specialty as Finish Specialist (museums); Upholstery Restorer (museums).
GOE: 05.05.08 STRENGTH: L GED: R4 M3 L4 SVP: 6 DLU: 86

763.381-010 FURNITURE FINISHER (woodworking) alternate titles: furniture refinisher; recoater; refinisher; wood finisher
Finishes or refinishes damaged, worn, or used furniture or new high-grade furniture to specified color or finish, utilizing knowledge of wood properties, finishes, and furniture styling: Disassembles article, masks areas adjacent to areas being finished, or removes accessories such as knobs and hinges, using handtools, to prepare article for finishing. Removes old finish from surfaces, using steel wool, sandpaper, or solvent and putty knife. Removes excess solvent with cloth immersed in paint thinner or sal soda. Applies plastic-putty, wood putty, or lacquer-stick to surface, using spatula or knife, to fill nicks, depressions, holes, and cracks. Smooths surface for finishing, using sandpaper or power sander. Selects finish ingredients and mixes them by hand or machine to obtain specified color or shade or to match existing finish. Brushes or sprays successive coats of stain, varnish, shellac, lacquer, or paint on workpiece. Grains wood or paints wood trim, using graining roller, comb, sponge, or brush. Polishes and waxes finished surfaces. May restore wood to natural color, using bleaching acid and neutralizer. May spread graining ink over metal portions of surfaces with cheesecloth to simulate wood-grainlike finish. May finish piano and organ cases and be designated Piano-And-Organ Refinisher (woodworking). May finish mirror and picture frames and be designated according to type of finish applied as Powder Gilder (wood prod., nec); Whitener (wood prod., nec). May finish television receiver cabinets and be designated Television-Cabinet Finisher (woodworking). May finish wooden parts of custom-made firearms and be designated Finisher, Special Stocks (ordnance). May stain and finish surfaces of new furniture pieces to simulate antiques, bringing out highlights and shadings by rubbing surfaces with abrasives or cloth, and be designated Antiquer (furniture).
GOE: 05.05.08 STRENGTH: L GED: R4 M2 L2 SVP: 7 DLU: 77

763.381-014 FURNITURE-FINISHER APPRENTICE (woodworking) alternate titles: wood-finisher apprentice
Performs duties as described under APPRENTICE (any industry) Master Title.
GOE: 05.05.08 STRENGTH: L GED: R4 M2 L2 SVP: 7 DLU: 77

763.681-010 FRAME REPAIRER (furniture)
Repairs frames of sofas and chairs damaged during upholstering in furniture plant: Removes upholstery, burlap, or webbing to expose splits or breaks in

frames. Glues and secures splits with screws, dowels, or nails, using handtools. Cuts out or chisels away broken parts of frames, using handsaw, portable power saw, or hammer and wood chisel. Cuts replacement parts to fit adjacent parts of frames and glues and dowels replacement parts to frames.
GOE: 05.10.01 STRENGTH: H GED: R3 M3 L2 SVP: 6 DLU: 86

763.684-010 ASSEMBLY INSPECTOR (furniture) alternate titles: inspector
Inspects unfinished furniture for surface defects and conformance to company standards: Cleans dust from drawers and external surfaces of furniture, using airhose. Examines surface for defects, such as loose or blistered veneer, cracks, knots, exposed nails, warping, loose joints, splits, dents, or scratches. Feels surface to detect rough spots. Marks defective areas with chalk for resanding or repair. Inspects fit of doors and drawers and tightness of joints. May make minor repairs to furniture, such as nailing drawer slides and drawer stops to case, sanding rough areas, and scraping off excess glue. May record number of units inspected.
GOE: 06.03.02 STRENGTH: M GED: R3 M1 L2 SVP: 5 DLU: 79

763.684-014 CABINET ASSEMBLER (furniture)
Assembles radio, television, and phonograph cabinets, using handtools: Fits prefabricated wooden parts together. Trims and smooths parts to fit, using handtools and sandpaper. Inserts screws or dowels in predrilled holes, and fastens parts together with screwdriver, glue, and clamps. Installs hardware, such as hinges, catches, and knobs, on assembled cabinet. May cut baffle cloths and plastic screens to specified size and install them in cabinets, using hand or machine cutters, screwdriver, and stapling gun.
GOE: 06.02.22 STRENGTH: L GED: R3 M2 L3 SVP: 3 DLU: 77

763.684-018 CANER I (furniture) alternate titles: weaver
Weaves twine and strips of cane or other flexible material onto furniture frames to form woven seats, backs, or other panels: Cuts strips or twine to length, using knife. Inserts strips or twine through frame holes and interlaces strips within frame openings in horizontal, vertical, and diagonal directions to form woven panels of specified patterns. Pulls strips taut and loops ends of strips in and out of holes to form decorative edges. Staples or tacks twine to frames. May water-soak cane or other material fibers to increase pliability for weaving. May clamp frames in fixtures to hold frames for weaving. May weave strips or twine on tables and wire racks to form decorative edges.
GOE: 06.02.32 STRENGTH: L GED: R3 M1 L1 SVP: 3 DLU: 77

763.684-022 CANER II (furniture)
Installs or replaces prewoven panels of cane, willow, or rattan in furniture frames: Cuts damaged panel from furniture frame, using knife. Pries wooden splines from grooves in frame, using chisel. Places frame in water to soften dried glue and adhering panel of cane or willow, and scrapes surfaces clean. Brushes glue into grooves around frame opening and stretches water-soaked panel over opening. Forces edges of panel into grooves, using wedge and mallet or pneumatic press. Brushes glue over panel edges in grooves, and forces splines into grooves flush with surface. Trims excess material, using knife. May cut prewoven panels to size, using pattern and scissors or cutting machine.
GOE: 06.04.25 STRENGTH: L GED: R2 M1 L1 SVP: 3 DLU: 78

763.684-026 CASE FITTER (furniture) alternate titles: prefitter
Fits doors, trays, and drawers into unfinished wooden furniture: Trims and shapes edges of uneven or misshapened parts, using chisel, file, sandpaper, and hand plane, or by drawing edges over jointer blade. Pushes thumbtacks into drawer slides to level drawers and to facilitate sliding. Fits prehinged doors to cases and marks and drills holes for insertion of screws, using portable power drill. Attaches doors to cases or sets them aside for painting. Slides drawers in and out to test fit of drawers, and tests doors for ease of opening and closing. May repair, replace, or lubricate defective hardware, using handtools and portable power tools. May be designated according to part fitted as Door Fitter (furniture); Drawer Fitter (furniture).
GOE: 05.10.01 STRENGTH: M GED: R3 M1 L1 SVP: 3 DLU: 78

763.684-030 DRAWER LINER (furniture)
Glues velveteen, felt, or other lining material to bottom or over entire inside of drawers which are used for storage of silver, coins, or other tarnishable articles: Brushes glue evenly on parts to be covered. Positions and smooths precut lining on glue by hand and cuts or trims it as necessary to fit part.
GOE: 06.04.27 STRENGTH: L GED: R2 M1 L1 SVP: 2 DLU: 77

763.684-034 FINISH PATCHER (furniture) alternate titles: finish cleaner; finish repairer; refinisher; retoucher
Repairs defects, such as holes, cracks, and scratches, in finish of furniture or furniture stock: Examines each defective article to determine method of repair. Fills holes and cracks with shellac or wax, using heated blade to melt and spread wax and shellac. Removes varnish and smooths cracks and scratches with sandpaper. Applies stain to match furniture surface and varnish to protect surface, using brush or spray gun. Smooths and shapes repaired surface with sandpaper, pumice stone, steel wool, or chisel. Nails, screws, or glues broken or split parts together. Rubs glossy spots with pumice stone and oil, and polishes dull spots with wax to match surrounding finish. Dabs moistened cloth to and presses heated blade against dents and scratches to draw indentations to surface. May chisel out defective sections and replace them with patch matching color and grain.
GOE: 05.10.01 STRENGTH: M GED: R3 M1 L2 SVP: 4 DLU: 79

763.684-038 FURNITURE ASSEMBLER (furniture) alternate titles: parts assembler

Assembles wooden parts or assemblies to form sections, frames, or complete articles of furniture: Trims joints to fit, using handtools. Blows dust from mortises and areas to be glued, using airhose. Spreads glue on surfaces to be joined by drawing wood across roller partially submerged in glue, by using brush dipped in glue, or by using glue-filled squeeze bottle. Knocks connecting parts together with mallet or compresses assembled parts in clamp until glue has dried. Wipes excess glue from joints with rag. Drills holes and drives screws into parts to join parts or to reinforce glued joints, using power drill and screwdriver. Attaches glue blocks, metal braces, corner blocks, drawer guides, tops, molding, shelves, dust bottoms, back panels, or skids with nails, screws, glue, or staples, using handtools and power tools. Inspects and verifies accuracy of assembled article for conformance to specified standards, using square and tape measure. Smooths irregular joints with rasp and sandpaper, and levels chair legs, using circular leveling saw. May drill holes and attach hardware, such as drawer guides, drawer locks, catches, and latches, using power drill and handtools. May slide drawers in and out to test ease of movement, and adjust ill-fitting drawers, using handtools. May be known in establishment according to part or article assembled. May work as member of team along conveyor line.
GOE: 06.02.22 STRENGTH: M GED: R3 M2 L2 SVP: 4 DLU: 80

763.684-042 HARDWARE ASSEMBLER (furniture) alternate titles: mounter; upfitter

Attaches hardware, such as drawer pulls, locks, latches, or metal ornaments, to finished furniture, using handtools and power screwdriver: Examines drawings or work ticket to ascertain location and type of hardware to be mounted to furniture. Attaches wooden molding, decorative carvings, trim, and hardware to furniture, using nails, screws, adhesive spray gun, handtools, and power screwdriver. Staples plastic tabs on top edges of drawers or brushes liquid paraffin on drawer edges to facilitate ease of opening and closing drawers. Wraps keys, trays, and drawer dividers in paper and places them inside cabinet. Inserts felt-backed metal clips between drawers and furniture case to hold drawers during shipment. May hang doors by screwing hinges to predrilled holes. May press electric iron against inside panel of furniture case drawers to burn brand name on drawer.
GOE: 06.04.22 STRENGTH: L GED: R2 M1 L1 SVP: 3 DLU: 80

763.684-046 LAG SCREWER (furniture) alternate titles: pin-machine operator

Inserts lag bolts in table legs, using pin machine: Inserts lag screw in hole of table leg or in drill of machine. Pushes leg against rotating drill or pulls lever to lower drill onto leg. Verifies depth of screw in leg, using gauge. Stacks legs on handtruck and conveys them to storage or assembly area.
GOE: 06.04.23 STRENGTH: L GED: R2 M2 L2 SVP: 2 DLU: 77

763.684-050 LAMINATOR, HAND (furniture)

Cements precut laminated plastic covering materials to plywood panels to form furniture parts, such as cabinet tops, countertops, tabletops, and desktops: Applies cement to surface of plywood panels, using brush. Glues plastic laminated covering material to plywood panel to form furniture part and smooths surface with rollers. Wipes acetone on edges of covering and panel with rag and solvent to remove excess cement. Examines edges of laminated part to detect ridges, and removes excess material with file or electric hand trimmer. May attach metal molding trim to edges, using glue and handtools. May cut plastic laminated material and plywood to specified size and shape, using handtools and power tools. May clamp laminated plastic in place until glue sets, using clamps or vise. May install laminated plastic tops on furniture and be designated Plastic-Top Installer (furniture). May cover tops of kitchen and bathroom fixtures and be designated Cabinet Assembler (mfd. bldgs.).
GOE: 06.04.22 STRENGTH: M GED: R2 M1 L1 SVP: 3 DLU: 77

763.684-054 LEATHER TOOLER (furniture)

Covers wooden table or desk tops with leather: Cuts cardboard pattern to contour of tabletop or desk top and cuts outline of pattern on leather, using knife or shears. Applies adhesive to table or desk top and to leather, and presses leather onto top, shaping and stretching it to remove wrinkles and prevent buckling as adhesive dries. Trims excess leather, using knife. Applies goldleaf or other decorative design to leather, using heated die or printing roller and stencil. May spray lacquer over leather to protect surface of leather.
GOE: 06.02.27 STRENGTH: L GED: R3 M2 L2 SVP: 5 DLU: 77

763.684-058 PIANO CASE AND BENCH ASSEMBLER (musical inst.)

Performs any combination of following tasks to assemble piano frames, cases, and benches, using carpenter's handtools, templates, jigs, and woodworking machines: Fits keybeds, shelves, music racks, and other case parts for assembly by sawing, drilling holes, and sanding material to fit, using handtools, bandsaw, jig, drill press, and sandpaper. Applies glue to side pieces and back frame parts with brush and positions material in clamp for drying, or gives material to GLUING-MACHINE OPERATOR, ELECTRONIC (woodworking) for gluing and clamping. Installs additional pieces, such as pedalboard, toe rails, music racks, keycover rod, hardware, and decorative items, using handtools, work aids, and portable power tools. May be designated according to item assembled as Bottom Board And Truss Leg Installer (musical inst.); Key-Bed Installer (musical inst.); Piano Bench Assembler (musical inst.); Side Gluer (musical inst.); Top Case Assembler (musical inst.).
GOE: 06.04.25 STRENGTH: L GED: R2 M2 L2 SVP: 2 DLU: 77

763.684-062 PLASTIC-TOP ASSEMBLER (furniture)

Stacks sheets of glue-coated plywood, fiberboard, and plastic, in specified sequence for pressing into laminated tops for furniture, such as dressers, tables, and desks. Builds tops by matching sets, by matching color, type of finish, and grain pattern of face sheets. May tend cold press to compress stack [HYDRAULIC-PRESS OPERATOR (millwork-plywood)].
GOE: 06.04.22 STRENGTH: H GED: R2 M1 L1 SVP: 2 DLU: 77

763.684-066 SLOT ROUTER (furniture)

Cuts (routes) slots for attaching molding on tabletops, using portable power router: Pushes tabletop from pallet onto worktable. Reads work order to ascertain dimensions and position of slot. Selects and inserts router tool in chuck of router, using wrench. Adjusts guide stop and base plate for depth and position of slot, using rule, and secures item in place, using wing nuts. Positions router on tabletop with guide against edge and starts router. Moves router around periphery of tabletop to cut slot. Pushes slotted tabletop onto rollers of conveyor. Cleans work area.
GOE: 06.04.25 STRENGTH: H GED: R2 M2 L2 SVP: 2 DLU: 77

763.684-070 STOCK-PARTS INSPECTOR (furniture) alternate titles: inspector and patch worker; parts inspector; putty-and-patch worker

Inspects furniture parts for defects and repairs defective parts: Examines furniture parts, such as table and cabinet tops, end panels, and furniture legs for knot holes, cracks, splits, scratches, raised veneer, and defective sanding. Selects filler to match color, type, and species of stock piece, and fills cracks, holes, and dents with filler, using putty knife. Places electric iron on repaired wood defect to dry filler. Smooths rough places with sandpaper and hand plane. Verifies pieces inspected against cutting orders. Orders replacement parts, indicating number of pieces needed, pattern number, and dimensions. May cut out defects, using portable electric saw or knife, and glue patch for patch strips in cutout area. May fill splits with glue and clamp stock for specified time to allow glue to dry.
GOE: 06.03.02 STRENGTH: L GED: R3 M2 L2 SVP: 4 DLU: 78

763.684-074 TABLE-TOP TILE SETTER (brick & tile)

Covers tabletops with mosaic tile squares to form decorative design: Glues cardboard pattern to top of table. Places template over pattern and marks off design, using pencil. Cuts out marked-off portion, using handknife. Applies glue to surface of mosaic tile and tabletop. Sets multicolored squares in position to form prescribed design and color pattern.
GOE: 06.04.30 STRENGTH: L GED: R2 M2 L2 SVP: 4 DLU: 77

763.684-078 WICKER WORKER (furniture)

Fabricates wicker furniture from peeled and softened rattan, reed, or willow sticks: Clamps or secures frame pieces in fixtures. Heats frame pieces and other sticks with blowtorch, and bends them to desired shape. Fastens sticks together with bolts, nails, and screws. Weaves wickers in, through, and around frame, cutting off and concealing or weaving together loose ends to finish edges. Winds wickers around joints to strengthen and conceal them. May be designated according to material used as Rattan Worker (furniture); Reed Worker (furniture); Willow Worker (furniture).
GOE: 06.04.25 STRENGTH: M GED: R3 M1 L2 SVP: 5 DLU: 77

763.687-010 BLOW-OFF WORKER (furniture)

Cleans outside surfaces and inside drawers of furniture, using airhose and cloth, to remove dust, dirt, and chips preparatory to spray finishing.
GOE: 06.04.39 STRENGTH: L GED: R1 M1 L1 SVP: 2 DLU: 77

763.687-014 CHAIR INSPECTOR AND LEVELER (furniture)

Inspects wooden chairs or stools for defects in construction or finish to ensure conformance with manufacturing standards: Places chair, stool, or frame on bench to determine if item stands level. Slides uneven items over circular saw flush with top of bench to cut excess length from legs. Inspects wooden surfaces for defects in finish, such as cracks, splits, and protruding splinters, and marks defects with chalk or crayon. Stacks defective chairs or stools in designated area. May repair defects in finish, using stain stick. May assemble wooden furniture parts.
GOE: 06.03.02 STRENGTH: L GED: R2 M1 L2 SVP: 3 DLU: 79

763.687-018 DISTRESSER (furniture)

Marks surface of furniture with crayon or strikes surface with rough edged object, such as chain, broken bottle, or rock, to distress (simulate antique) furniture finish: Reads work ticket to ascertain items to be distressed or receives oral instructions from supervisor. Swings chain against surface of furniture to cause dents in surface. Taps surface with wooden hammer containing protruding nails to produce pattern of holes in surface. Scrapes pointed end of metal rod across surface to produce random scratches. Marks surface with crayon to produce desired antique finish. May apply stain to wood furniture to produce antique effect.
GOE: 06.04.25 STRENGTH: L GED: R2 M1 L1 SVP: 3 DLU: 79

763.687-022 DRAWER WAXER (furniture)

Applies wax to drawer slides and unexposed sprayed surfaces of drawer, using brush or cloth. May sand inside of drawer with portable sanding machine or sandpaper-covered wood block.
GOE: 06.04.33 STRENGTH: L GED: R1 M1 L1 SVP: 1 DLU: 77

763.687-026 FINISHED-STOCK INSPECTOR (furniture) alternate titles: final inspector

Inspects completed furniture for defects in finish, construction, or upholstery, to ensure conformance with manufacturing standards: Verifies color, pattern,

and grade of upholstery, using ticket specifications and shop orders. Inspects upholstery cover for rips in fabric or seams. Feels upholstery padding to determine if padding conforms to specified degree of firmness. Examines wooden surfaces for defects in assembly, wood, or finish. Marks defects with tape. Removes wrinkles, using hand steamer and soil marks, using cleaning fluid. May stamp or mark furniture to indicate acception or rejection. May repair minor defects in finish, using heated blade, wax, lacquer, and stain stick. May be designated according to inspection performed as Finish Inspector (furniture); or product inspected as Chair Inspector (furniture); Radio-And-Television-Cabinet Inspector (furniture); Sofa Inspector (furniture).
GOE: 06.03.02 STRENGTH: L GED: R3 M2 L2 SVP: 4 DLU: 80

763.687-030 CANE CUTTER (furniture)
Cuts cane and rattan for use in furniture manufacture: Places rolls of cane on holding device, and pulls cane to mark on work surface according to length specified; or positions rattan on work surface to cut ends for mitering. Pulls lever to lower blade and cut cane or rattan, according to instructions. Stacks cane and rattan for further processing.
GOE: 06.04.25 STRENGTH: M GED: R2 M1 L1 SVP: 1 DLU: 86

764 COOPERAGE OCCUPATIONS

This group includes occupations concerned with laying out stock and shaping, assembling, and smoothing barrels, casks, and similar containers.

764.134-010 SUPERVISOR, COOPERAGE SHOP (wood. container)
Supervises and coordinates activities of workers engaged in fabricating or repairing kegs, barrels, or hogsheads: Assigns duties to workers and coordinates activities with other supervisors to maintain production schedule. Patrols work area to observe functioning of machines and directs workers in adjusting machines that fail to meet production standards. Examines finished product to determine whether product meets company specifications. Trains new workers. May purchase wood from supplier for use in producing staves and maintain records of transactions. Performs other duties as described under SUPERVISOR (any industry) Master Title. May be designated according to process supervised as Supervisor, Barrel Assembly (wood. container); Supervisor, Heading (wood. container); Supervisor, Stave Finishing (wood. container).
GOE: 06.02.01 STRENGTH: L GED: R4 M2 L3 SVP: 7 DLU: 77

764.387-010 HEAD INSPECTOR (wood. container) alternate titles: quality-control-inspector, heading
Examines finished heading and barrelheads for defects to verify conformance to specifications: Measures finished heading and barrelheads, using tape measure and circular gauge, and inspects them for defects, such as knots, wormholes, and defective jointing, to determine and grade quality of work. Applies chemical to jointed edges of heading to determine sap line in heading, using cloth applicator. Sets aside defective heads for repair. Records results of examination and amount of wood used in heading, and submits quality control report to supervisor. May inspect and mark centers of heading blanks prior to sawing and be designated Head-Inspector-And-Center Marker (wood. container).
GOE: 06.03.01 STRENGTH: L GED: R3 M2 L3 SVP: 4 DLU: 77

764.387-014 MATERIAL INSPECTOR (wood. container) alternate titles: stave grader; stave inspector
Examines sample of staves in shipment to determine price to be paid for shipment: Takes sampling of staves from freight car. Examines staves for defects, such as cracks, warpage, knots, and excessive sap content. Separates and grades staves according to number and type of defects found. Marks grade on staves, using pencil. Inspects bilge, if staves have been jointed, and measures length and width of staves, using tape measure. Computes total usable width of staves in car and prices entire carload based on grading and calculations. May record price paid for staves and quantity purchased. May supervise workers engaged in operation of dry kiln.
GOE: 05.07.06 STRENGTH: L GED: R4 M3 L3 SVP: 5 DLU: 77

764.684-010 BARREL BRANDER (wood. container)
Burns initials or trademark of manufacturer on staves or heads of barrel (or keg): Lays barrel horizontally on carriage of brander and turns handwheel, raising carriage and forcing barrel against hot iron. Turns handwheel to rotate barrel in carriage and bring another stave in contact with iron. Lowers carriage and removes barrels when specified number of staves have been branded. May use hand-operated, gasoline-fired branding iron. May heat irons bearing single letter or mark and apply irons to barrels. May stamp consecutive numbers on barrel staves to facilitate reassembly by customers.
GOE: 06.04.37 STRENGTH: M GED: R2 M1 L1 SVP: 2 DLU: 77

764.684-014 BARREL CHARRER (wood. container) alternate titles: barrel burner; charrer; charring-room worker, barrel
Burns interior of headless barrel (or keg) to prepare it for aging whiskey: Fits charring rings in each end of barrel to protect surface in which croze is to be cut. Fires gas burner or fire pot containing wood scraps and shavings, and places barrel over flame. Covers top end of barrel with metal plate and allows burning to continue for specified period, according to depth of char desired. Removes plate and quenches burning interior with wet mop or spray from hose. May use device equipped with lever to lower metal hood or exhaust chimney onto top end of barrel to create draft during charring and timer that automatically raises hood or chimney when specified charring time has elapsed.

May burn one side of whiskey barrelhead in oven or over fire pot and be designated Head Charrer (wood. container).
GOE: 06.04.18 STRENGTH: M GED: R2 M1 L1 SVP: 4 DLU: 77

764.684-018 BARREL RAISER (wood. container) alternate titles: barrel maker; keg raiser; raiser; setter-up; setting-up-and-windlass-machine operator
Assembles wooden barrel shells in raising stand. Places staves inside truss hoop and forming rings to form barrel shell. Loops cable of windlass around top of barrel and moves leg control to draw staves together. Slips truss ring on top of barrel shell and presses pedal to release cable. Removes shell from raising stand. May insert truss and forming rings in raising stand. May place barrels on heat tunnel conveyor.
GOE: 06.04.22 STRENGTH: M GED: R2 M1 L1 SVP: 4 DLU: 77

764.684-022 COOPER (wood. container) alternate titles: barrel repairer; shop cooper
Replaces staves, heads, and hoops, using windlass and handtools to repair barrels: Loops cable of windlass around top of barrel and turns handle to compress staves and loosen hoops. Removes defective stave and inserts and aligns new stave, using wooden mallet. Shapes top edge of stave to conform with others, using saw to trim and spokeshave to bevel inside and outside edges. Cuts croze, using hand crozer. Replaces and tightens hoops. Removes head hoop, using cooper's hammer, and pries out head, using prybar. Inserts edge of new head in croze of staves and forces head into place by hand or using mallet. Replaces head hoop. May rebuild entire barrel. May loosen hoops and force caulking between staves to repair leaking stave joints. May plug knotholes and wormholes with wooden plugs. May tend machine that compresses barrel shell to facilitate removal of forming rings and placement of temporary truss hoops. May build new barrels, buckets, casks, kegs, and tubs, using handtools, and be designated according to type built as Slack Cooper (wood. container); Tight Cooper (wood. container).
GOE: 05.10.01 STRENGTH: M GED: R3 M1 L1 SVP: 5 DLU: 78

764.684-026 HOGSHEAD COOPER I (wood. container) alternate titles: cask maker
Repairs collapsible mats (staves wired or banded together) for reuse as tobacco containers: Examines hogshead mat to extent of damage. Removes damaged or broken staves, hinges, wire hoops, or metal bands from hogshead mat, using hammer, crowbar, pliers, or portable circular saw. Positions and nails precut staves or stave patches into hogshead mats, using staple gun or hammer. Straightens or replaces precut wire hoops or metal bands. Threads wire hoop through wire hinge or metal band into metal hinge and secures hinge to hoop or band, using hammer. Nails hoops or bands to staves, using staple gun or hammer. May replace defective cleats (blocks made of wood or metal), using handtools.
GOE: 06.04.22 STRENGTH: H GED: R2 M1 L1 SVP: 2 DLU: 77

764.684-030 TANK ASSEMBLER (wood. container) alternate titles: tank cooper;
Assembles boards, staves, and rods to form tanks: Arranges boards in shape of bottom and marks identification on each board to facilitate assembling. Marks location of dowel holes in boards or staves and drills holes. Drives croze of staves on bottoms with hammer until tank is completed. Places and tightens washers, rods, and nuts on rectangular tanks to make boards secure. Inspects tank for quality, smoothing uneven joints with drawknife. Marks identification on staves and disassembles tanks to prepare them for shipment. May place metal hoops around staves to withstand pressure. May be designated according to shape or section of tank assembled as Circular-Tank Cooper (wood. container); Rectangular-Tank Cooper (wood. container); Tank-Bottom Assembler (wood. container); Tank-Stave Assembler (wood. container).
GOE: 06.02.25 STRENGTH: M GED: R3 M2 L2 SVP: 4 DLU: 77

764.687-010 AIR-AND-WATER FILLER (wood. container) alternate titles: air-and-water-tester
Injects compressed air and water into barrels preparatory to inspection by BARREL INSPECTOR, TIGHT (wood. container): Drives rubber valve into bunghole, using hammer. Inserts nozzle into valve and pulls lever to inject air and water into barrel until specified pressure is attained within barrel as determined by automatic cutoff. Removes nozzle from barrel and sets barrel aside for inspection. May taper bunghole prior to insertion of valve and nozzle, using reaming machine. May inject air or water only and be designated Air Filler (wood. container); Barrel Waterer (wood. container).
GOE: 06.04.36 STRENGTH: H GED: R2 M1 L1 SVP: 2 DLU: 77

764.687-014 ASSEMBLER, FAUCETS (wood. container)
Assembles wooden parts to make faucets for wine and beer kegs and barrels. Brushes glue on faucet parts and fits parts together. Hammers spigot in faucet, using mallet.
GOE: 06.04.23 STRENGTH: L GED: R2 M1 L1 SVP: 2 DLU: 77

764.687-018 BARREL DRAINER (wood. container) alternate titles: barrel-bung-remover and dumper
Empties water from barrel that has been inspected by BARREL INSPECTOR, TIGHT (wood. container) or weighed, by rolling barrel onto stand and pulling bung from hole by hand, or using bung puller.
GOE: 06.04.40 STRENGTH: H GED: R1 M1 L1 SVP: 1 DLU: 77

764.687-022 BARREL INSPECTOR, TIGHT (wood. container) alternate titles: air tester; barrel tester and drainer; final inspector; final tester; keg inspector

Examines heads and staves of tight barrels or kegs, containing water and compressed air, to determine if they are liquid tight: Rolls and tumbles barrel to spread water over interior of barrel. Examines barrel for faulty stave joints, leaks, loose or defective hoops, and material defects, such as streaks, cross grains, wormholes, and knotholes, in stave and heading material. Marks defects with chalk and rolls barrel to COOPER (wood. container). May make minor repairs to barrel, such as plugging wormholes, knotholes, and small leaks.
GOE: 06.03.02 STRENGTH: L GED: R2 M1 L2 SVP: 4 DLU: 77

764.687-026 BARREL LINER (wood. container) alternate titles: barrel coater

Coats interior of tight barrels and kegs with sealing material, such as hot paraffin and pitch, to prevent leakage and contact of stored liquid with wood: Melts sealer in heating tank. Places bunghole of barrel over vertical spout of tank and pulls lever to open compressed-air valve that forces melted sealer into barrel, or pours dipperful of melted sealer into bunghole and tumbles, rolls, and shakes barrel to coat and seal inner surface of barrel. Drains excess sealer from barrel into drain trough. Scrapes sealer from bunghole with piece of steel and replaces bung. Scrapes hardened sealer from drain trough.
GOE: 06.04.33 STRENGTH: M GED: R2 M1 L1 SVP: 2 DLU: 77

764.687-030 BARREL MARKER (wood. container) alternate titles: barrel roller

Lays out and marks position of center hoops on barrel for BARREL ASSEMBLER (wood. container): Pushes marker (bung attached to center of metal strap, length of which is desired distance between center hoops) into bunghole of barrel with strap parallel to stave into which bunghole is cut. Marks barrel with chalk at each end of strap to locate position of center hoops. Removes marker from bunghole and rolls barrel to position near hooping machine.
GOE: 06.04.25 STRENGTH: L GED: R2 M1 L1 SVP: 2 DLU: 77

764.687-034 BARREL-CHARRER HELPER (wood. container) alternate titles: charrer helper; charring-room-worker helper, barrel

Assists BARREL CHARRER (wood. container) in burning interior of headless barrels (or kegs) to prepare them for aging whiskey. Performs duties as described under HELPER (any industry) Master Title.
GOE: 06.04.18 STRENGTH: M GED: R2 M1 L1 SVP: 2 DLU: 77

764.687-038 BARREL-RAISER HELPER (wood. container) alternate titles: raiser helper; setting-up-and-windlass-machine-operator helper

Assists BARREL RAISER (wood. container) in assembling wooden barrel shells. Performs other duties as described under HELPER (any industry) Master Title.
GOE: 06.04.22 STRENGTH: M GED: R2 M1 L1 SVP: 2 DLU: 77

764.687-042 BUNG DRIVER (wood. container)

Covers bunghole of barrel with burlap cloth and hammers bung and cloth into hole to prevent dirt from entering barrel before it is filled.
GOE: 06.04.22 STRENGTH: L GED: R1 M1 L1 SVP: 1 DLU: 77

764.687-046 CHANNEL INSTALLER (wood. container)

Fits metal channel around heading of hogshead. Taps channel with mallet to force channel over edges of heading.
GOE: 06.04.22 STRENGTH: M GED: R2 M1 L1 SVP: 2 DLU: 77

764.687-050 COOPER HELPER (wood. container) alternate titles: barrel-repairer helper; hand-cooper helper

Assists COOPER (wood. container) in repairing barrels. Performs duties as described under HELPER (any industry) Master Title.
GOE: 05.12.12 STRENGTH: M GED: R2 M2 L2 SVP: 2 DLU: 77

764.687-054 CULLER (wood. container) alternate titles: barrel-stave inspector; stave inspector and culler; stave matcher

Examines barrel staves after jointing: Examines *bilge of stave* and rejects those not conforming to specification. Examines and rejects staves containing defects, such as knots, wormholes, and checks. Ties accepted staves into bundles, or arranges and fits staves by width between stops of matching rack until total number of staves equals desired barrel circumference. May grade staves for quality of work, and record production and results of examination.
GOE: 06.03.02 STRENGTH: L GED: R2 M1 L2 SVP: 3 DLU: 77

764.687-058 HEADER (wood. container) alternate titles: header-up; head setter

Installs circular head in croze (groove) of slack or tight barrel: Loosens temporary head loop on barrel by striking hoop, using hammer. Picks up head with spiked tool and fits head into croze of barrel. Draws staves around head, using windlass machine or other equipment. Replaces temporary head hoop with regular head hoop. Taps hoop lightly with hammer to tighten it around barrel and sets barrel aside.
GOE: 06.04.22 STRENGTH: M GED: R2 M1 L1 SVP: 2 DLU: 77

764.687-062 HEADING MATCHER AND ASSEMBLER (wood. container) alternate titles: doweler; heading pinner

Inserts dowels in pieces of barrel-heading material and assembles pieces to form blank from which barrelhead is cut: Selects, inspects, and arranges specified number of heading material according to size, using gauge, to produce tight fit of barrel when assembled. Hammers dowels into one edge of each piece, using hammer, and lays strip of *flagging* along doweled edges. Fits dowels into dowel holes and hammers pieces together to assemble head blank. Stacks assembled heading blanks on floor or on conveyor for movement to next work station.
GOE: 06.04.22 STRENGTH: L GED: R2 M2 L2 SVP: 3 DLU: 77

764.687-066 HEADING REPAIRER (wood. container)

Repairs tight barrelhead, using either of following methods: (1) Separates sections of barrelhead with chisel, inserts strips of *flagging* between sections, and hammers them together to enlarge barrelhead to fit croze of barrel. (2) Removes section of head, replaces it with wider board, and sends head to TURNING-MACHINE OPERATOR (wood. container) 667.685-066 for processing.
GOE: 06.04.25 STRENGTH: L GED: R2 M1 L1 SVP: 3 DLU: 77

764.687-070 HOGSHEAD COOPER II (wood. container) alternate titles: patented-hogshead assembler

Assembles patented hogsheads from prefabricated mats (staves wired together), hoops, and headings, performing any combination of following duties: Stands mat on ends to form cylinder or positions mat around circular form. Inserts tie wire between loops of mats and twists tie wire to fasten ends together, using wire twisters; or fastens mat together by aligning hinges attached to hoops and inserting metal pin through hinge. Positions heading in hogshead shell. Encircles bottom edge of hogshead with metal band and inserts ends of band through *pinch cleat* into jaws of *strapping tool*. Pumps handle of tool to tighten band around hogshead and crimp pinch cleat over end of band. Breaks or cuts surplus ends of metal band, using hatchet, and hammers nails through holes in band to secure bands to staves.
GOE: 06.04.22 STRENGTH: H GED: R2 M1 L1 SVP: 2 DLU: 77

764.687-074 HOGSHEAD COOPER III (wood. container) alternate titles: hogshead builder

Assembles precut staves and metal bands to form hogshead shells: Places staves in cradle of circular frame until lower portion of hogshead is formed. Inserts liner ring to support staves and places staves over ring to complete hogshead shell. Pulls lever to tighten frame bands around staves and hammers stave ends even. Braces open ends of hogshead shell with wooden boards and positions metal hoops around both ends of shell. Tightens hoop, using hoop puller, and nails hoops to staves. Releases levers, removes braces, and rolls shell to succeeding station. Works as member of team to assemble hogshead shells. May assemble and nail together precut boards or nail shaped parts to shell to form bottom of hogshead [NAILER, HAND (any industry)]. May fasten wire hoops around hogshead to secure staves [HOGSHEAD HOOPER (wood. container)].
GOE: 06.04.22 STRENGTH: H GED: R2 M1 L1 SVP: 2 DLU: 77

764.687-078 HOGSHEAD HOOPER (wood. container) alternate titles: hooper

Fastens precut lengths of wire (hoops) around hogshead to secure staves: Places wooden board in open end of hogshead to brace staves at opening. Encircles hogshead with wire lengths and inserts wire ends into wire tightener or wire twister. Pumps lever of tightener or turns twister to tighten wire around hogshead and to fasten wire ends together. Bends wire ends under wire hoop and hammers wire flat or cuts wire ends, using wire cutter. Removes brace from open end of hogshead and rolls hogshead to succeeding work station. May staple hoop to staves, using pneumatic staple gun.
GOE: 06.04.22 STRENGTH: M GED: R1 M1 L1 SVP: 2 DLU: 77

764.687-082 HOGSHEAD MAT ASSEMBLER (wood. container)

Assembles precut staves, cleats (wooden blocks), and metal bands to form hogshead mats: Places cleats in jig on worktable and spaces staves on cleats, using metal disks as spacing guides. Positions metal band across staves and inserts pins in preriveted hinges on ends of band to secure staves to jig. Hammers nails through holes in band to secure staves to band. Drills hole in stave through hole in hinge leaf, using portable electric drill, to facilitate bolting mats together to form hogshead shell. Pulls pins from band hinges to release mat from jig. Stacks mats on floor.
GOE: 06.04.22 STRENGTH: M GED: R2 M1 L1 SVP: 2 DLU: 77

764.687-086 HOGSHEAD MAT INSPECTOR (wood. container)

Inspects hogshead mats (prefabricated staves banded together) for nailing defects: Positions mat on worktable and inspects mat for nailing defects. Removes misdriven nails and hammers nails through band into stave. Bolts hinges to mats to complete mat assembly, using socket wrench.
GOE: 06.03.02 STRENGTH: L GED: R2 M1 L2 SVP: 3 DLU: 77

764.687-090 LEAK HUNTER (beverage) alternate titles: couper; patcher; repairer

Inspects barrels filled with beer or whiskey to detect and repair leaking barrels: Walks between rows of stacked barrels and examines each barrel for leaks. Caulks holes or seams, using wicking (twisted cotton), wooden plugs, or strips of adhesive canvas. Records serial number of barrel repaired and date. May examine barrels of beer in shipping area to detect leakage and push leaking barrels aside for removal to dumping area.
GOE: 05.12.12 STRENGTH: M GED: R2 M1 L1 SVP: 2 DLU: 77

764.687-094 LEVELER I (wood. container) alternate titles: barrel leveler

Taps ends of barrel staves against metal truss, using hammer, or lifts barrel (or keg) and drops it end down on floor to align ends of staves and to smooth and round barrel shell. May hammer truss hoops on barrel.

GOE: 06.04.22 STRENGTH: M GED: R1 M1 L1 SVP: 2 DLU: 77

764.687-098 PLUGGER (wood. container)
Hammers wooden plugs in small holes in barrel and places iron hoops over barrel for BARREL ASSEMBLER (wood. container).
GOE: 06.04.22 STRENGTH: L GED: R1 M1 L1 SVP: 1 DLU: 77

769 OCCUPATIONS IN FABRICATION AND REPAIR OF WOOD PRODUCTS, N.E.C.

This group includes occupations, not elsewhere classified, concerned with fabricating and repairing wood products.

769.130-010 SUPERVISOR, FABRICATION (wood prod., nec)
Supervises and coordinates activities of workers engaged in cutting, fitting, and joining preshaped molding to form picture frames: Demonstrates machine functions, work methods, and techniques to train workers, such as machine cutters, drillers, bevelers, spray or automatic spraying machine painters, and hand or machine assemblers in duties. Examines parts or finished articles for defects to maintain qualitative standards. Performs other duties as described under SUPERVISOR (any industry) Master Title.
GOE: 06.02.01 STRENGTH: L GED: R4 M2 L3 SVP: 7 DLU: 77

769.134-010 SUPERVISOR, DIMENSION WAREHOUSE (furniture)
Supervises and coordinates activities of workers engaged in receiving, storing, and issuing dimensional woodstock; sanding stock; and assembling stock parts to form furniture components: Computes stock requirements, based on inventory and production schedules, and requisitions material needed. Inspects stock in process for dimensional accuracy and quality of construction to ensure adherence to company standards. Demonstrates new or more efficient work methods to workers. Observes sanding and assembling operations and reassigns personnel to alleviate detected bottlenecks. Trains new workers. Performs other duties as described under SUPERVISOR (any industry) Master Title.
GOE: 06.02.01 STRENGTH: M GED: R4 M3 L3 SVP: 7 DLU: 77

769.137-010 STOCKING-AND-BOX-SHOP SUPERVISOR (ordnance)
Supervises and coordinates activities of workers engaged in manufacture of stocks, guards, and other wooden parts of rifles and machine guns and in construction of wooden shipping boxes. Performs other duties as described under SUPERVISOR (any industry) Master Title.
GOE: 06.02.01 STRENGTH: L GED: R4 M3 L3 SVP: 7 DLU: 77

769.137-014 SUPERVISOR, ASSEMBLY (woodworking)
Supervises and coordinates activities of workers engaged in assembling wooden parts or assemblies to form sections, frames, or completed articles, using knowledge of wood products and assembly processes: Analyzes work orders to determine production schedules. Determines amounts of woodstock and other materials required for assembly, based on production schedules, and requisitions materials from storage area. Prepares work tickets and gives oral instructions to workers pertaining to type of assemblies to be processed. Inspects parts, assemblies, or completed articles to verify conformance to company standards. Trains new workers in methods of assembly. Confers with supervisors in other departments to coordinate flow of materials and products into and out of department. Performs other duties as described under SUPERVISOR (any industry) Master Title. May be designated according to method of assembly as Supervisor, Gluing (woodworking).
GOE: 06.02.01 STRENGTH: L GED: R4 M3 L3 SVP: 7 DLU: 78

769.381-010 COMPO CASTER (wood prod., nec) alternate titles: ornamenter, hand
Compounds and casts ornamenting putty (compo) into designs and glues designs to picture moldings: Measures glue, resin, linseed oil, and water into separate gluepots and weighs them. Melts glue and resin and combines ingredients into one pot. Inspects mixture to ascertain viscosity and pours it into tube that contains whiting (powdered chalk). Stirs, kneads, and shapes putty into loaf. Presses loaf into mold with hand and thumbs. Clamps board over filled mold and places it in press. Pushes button or turns handwheel to activate and release press. Removes casting, trims design, and places it on table to harden. Brushes glue on back of hardened ornament and lays it in place on blank picture molding.
GOE: 06.02.32 STRENGTH: L GED: R3 M2 L2 SVP: 6 DLU: 77

769.387-010 WOODWORK-SALVAGE INSPECTOR (ordnance) alternate titles: salvage inspector, wood parts
Examines rejected wooden parts of small arms weapons to determine salvageability: Inspects parts to determine whether cause of damage resulted from defective wooden stock, machine malfunction, or faulty assembly. Routes salvageable parts to repair department. Records findings in salvage report.
GOE: 06.03.01 STRENGTH: L GED: R3 M2 L2 SVP: 4 DLU: 77

769.664-010 SHAKER REPAIRER (grain-feed mills)
Repairs shaker tables and reel frames used in processing corn products: Places frame on worktable, assisted by another worker. Examines screen surface to detect weak spots and holes. Removes old bolting cloth, using tack pullers and pincers. Cuts new cloth piece, stretches it over panel, and tacks it in place. May tack strip of bias tape over edges to hold cloth securely. Repairs damaged wood frames and builds new ones, using handtools. Remounts reel frames on reels, using wrench and screwdriver. Replaces shaker tables on supporting springs.

GOE: 06.04.25 STRENGTH: H GED: R2 M1 L1 SVP: 2 DLU: 77

769.684-010 BASKET ASSEMBLER II (wood. container)
Performs any combination of following tasks in fabrication of reed and wicker baskets: Cuts out premarked basket bottoms from flakeboard sheet, using bandsaw. Drills specified number of rod holes around edge of each bottom, using gauge and drillpress. Dips end of presized birch dowels into glue pot and inserts rods into holes of bottoms to form basket frames for WEAVER (wood. container). Bevels ends of soaked reed handle, using knife, and attaches handle to woven basket by inserting ends through woven sides, at specified points, to base of basket. Immerses basket into glue drum to bind woven reed and leaf material to rods and give luster to finished basket.
GOE: 06.04.34 STRENGTH: L GED: R2 M1 L1 SVP: 2 DLU: 77

769.684-014 BASKET PATCHER (wood. container)
Inspects and repairs defective baskets and basket covers, using handtools: Examines basket or covers for defects, such as knotholes, split or misaligned staves, and unstapled parts. Places basket or cover over form or on table to facilitate repair. Loosens, tightens, bends, or replaces basket or cover parts, using hammer and nails. Stacks repaired baskets and covers on floor to conserve space.
GOE: 06.04.34 STRENGTH: L GED: R2 M1 L1 SVP: 2 DLU: 77

769.684-018 BENDER, HAND (woodworking)
Bends pliable wooden parts by hand after steaming: Places stock in vat of boiling water. Removes stock from vat when pliable and places part in form. Presses stock around form and clamps free end of stock to form. Places form containing stock on handtruck and transfers them to kiln to dry and set in permanent shape.
GOE: 06.04.25 STRENGTH: L GED: R2 M1 L1 SVP: 2 DLU: 77

769.684-022 FINAL INSPECTOR, SHUTTLE (woodworking)
Inspects completely assembled wooden shuttles for imperfections: Examines wood and fiber (veneered) surfaces and measures dimensions of shuttles [SHUTTLE INSPECTOR (woodworking)]. Ascertains that metal tips are securely attached to tapered shuttle ends, that eyeholes are aligned, and that bobbin-grips and other parts of shuttle are positioned as specified. Tightens loose screws, using handtools. May imprint trade name on shuttles, using stamping machine.
GOE: 06.03.01 STRENGTH: L GED: R3 M2 L2 SVP: 4 DLU: 77

769.684-026 OIL DIPPER (woodworking)
Oils and polishes wooden shuttles and saws openings for insertion of shuttle eyes: Places shuttles in wire basket and lowers basket into tank, using hoist. Turns valves to fill tank with heated oil, drain tank, and dry oil-coated shuttles. Inspects shuttles to ensure specified oiling and buffs surfaces of oiled shuttle, using leather-covered wheel. Cuts eye openings in shuttle shoulders, using jigsaw.
GOE: 06.04.25 STRENGTH: M GED: R2 M1 L1 SVP: 3 DLU: 77

769.684-030 PATCHER (woodworking) alternate titles: patch setter
Repairs defects in surfaces of finished lumber, wood doors, veneer sheets, and plywood panels to improve appearance and increase market value, performing any combination of following tasks: Examines material to be repaired to determine type of repair needed. Mixes specified amounts of colored putties or patching compound with paint thinner to obtain workable consistency and fills defects, such as cracks, splits, and crevices with mixture, using putty knife. Cuts defective sections from material, using portable router or saw. Glues and sets shims, or trims and inserts wood patches in locations where defects have been cut out, using glue and hammer. Brushes water on dents and raises grain in dent with hot iron. Smooths patched areas, using hand sander. Stacks patched material on conveyor for movement to next processing station. May press patch into position and cure glue, using electronic-heat press. May be designated according to product repaired as Door Patcher (woodworking); Plywood Patcher (millwork-plywood).
GOE: 06.04.25 STRENGTH: M GED: R2 M2 L1 SVP: 3 DLU: 78

769.684-034 REELER (woodworking)
Fabricates and repairs wooden reels for winding wire: Cuts lumber according to templates, using portable saw. Bolts or screws pieces together to assemble reel and reel heads and installs steel axle core in reel, using handtools and power tools. Paints reels with spray gun and stencils specifications on sides of reel. Repairs reels or dismantles reels for scrap or salvage.
GOE: 06.04.25 STRENGTH: H GED: R2 M1 L1 SVP: 2 DLU: 77

769.684-038 REPAIRER, ASSEMBLED WOOD PRODUCTS (woodworking)
Repairs surface defects of wood products, such as sashes, doors, furniture, cabinet work, mirror frames, and picture frames to prepare them for finishing, gilding, painting, or packaging: Visually inspects workpiece for rough edges, surface nicks, dents, nail holes, cracks, open seams, veneer blisters, glue, dirt, or inspector's marks. Trims and smooths rough edges and surfaces, and removes scratches, dirt, and glue, using knife, scraper, sandpaper, and portable electric sander. Applies moisture and heat to remove dents, using wet sponge and electric iron. Fills cracks, seams, depressions, and nail holes with filler, such as putty. Touches up defects and filler, using stain, paint, or touchup crayons. Lifts and glues loose veneer to surface. May cut out damaged or blistered veneer or molding and trim, fit, and glue matching piece in place. May reglue defective joints [GLUER (woodworking) 762.687-034]. May be designated by

product repaired as Repairer, Mirror And Picture Frame (wood prod., nec); Repairer, Sash And Door (wood prod., nec); Repairer, Wood Furniture (furniture).
GOE: 05.10.01 STRENGTH: M GED: R3 M1 L2 SVP: 5 DLU: 79

769.684-042   SAMPLE MAKER, VENEER (millwork-plywood)
Cuts and glues veneer samples on display boards for use by sales personnel and furniture manufacture customers: Selects samples of veneer strips from various wood species. Cuts samples to specified uniform size, using handsaw and tape measure. Pastes label containing identifying information, such as species, grade, and marketing data, on each sample. Positions and glues samples on wooden display board to provide rigidity and facilitate handling and storage of display boards.
GOE: 06.04.25 STRENGTH: L GED: R2 M1 L1 SVP: 3 DLU: 77

769.684-046   SHUTTLE INSPECTOR (woodworking)
Inspects wooden shuttles before attachment of parts for defects in material and work quality: Measures exterior and interior dimensions of shuttles, using calipers, gauges, squares, and rulers, to ensure conformance to specifications. Examines surfaces of shuttles for defects, such as knots, splits, and scratches, and returns defective shuttles for repairs. May attach metal shuttle tips to wooden shuttles.
GOE: 06.03.01 STRENGTH: L GED: R3 M2 L2 SVP: 4 DLU: 77

769.684-050   STOCK-PARTS FABRICATOR (ship-boat mfg.)
Lays out, cuts, and laminates woodstock for boat components such as bulkheads and doors: Traces outline of component part on plywood stock, using pattern and marking devices. Cuts part from stock along lines scribed from pattern, using portable jigsaw. Cuts grooves in part to accommodate interpanel wiring, using portable router, and positions precut electrical wiring in grooves. Applies contact cement to plastic laminate sheet and component part, using glue roller. Positions and glues sheet on part and presses out air bubbles, using roller. Trims edges of laminate sheet to shape of component part, using portable router.
GOE: 06.02.25 STRENGTH: M GED: R3 M1 L1 SVP: 3 DLU: 77

769.684-054   WEAVER (wood. container) alternate titles: basket maker; wicker worker
Weaves baskets of specified size and shape by interlacing paper strips, willow, rattan, or other materials: Removes precut rattan stakes (rods) from soaking tank and glues or staples rods into solid or woven bottom of basket. Places completed bottom in form that conforms to shape of basket to be woven. Weaves reeds through rods to form sides of basket. Interlaces ends of rods or weaves reed strips through upper portion of rods to form braid around top of basket, using handtools. May make solid bottom boards, using bandsaw, drill press, and carpenter's handtools. Cuts off excess ends of rods, using cutting shears. May interlace reeds through stakes, secured in screw blocks, to form parts of basket, such as woven bottom. May design baskets. May be designated according to type of basket woven as Hamper Maker (wood. container); Market-Basket Maker (wood. container) II; or according to material used as Rattan Worker (wood. container); Willow Worker (wood. container).
GOE: 06.04.34 STRENGTH: S GED: R2 M1 L2 SVP: 4 DLU: 77

769.684-058   REPAIRER, VENEER SHEET (furniture)
Repairs defects in decorative veneer sheets and tapes veneer border to sheets: Holds veneer sheets against light and examines sheets for defects, such as splits, holes, thin spots, and untaped veneer strips. Moistens tape, using sponge, and presses tape to veneer splits to pull splits together, using flat pressing tool. Cuts and inserts splinters or sections of veneer in holes of sheet, using knife, sponge, and tape; or applies wood putty to opening in sheets, using putty knife. Sands wood particles that overlap veneer joints, using sandpaper and wood block. Positions and tapes shaped veneer borders around perimeter of veneer sheets to add decorative appearance.
GOE: 06.03.02 STRENGTH: M GED: R2 M1 L1 SVP: 2 DLU: 86

769.685-010   PANEL EDGE SEALER (millwork-plywood) alternate titles: edge plugger
Tends machine that automatically applies putty to side edges of plywood panels to seal crevices; and seals crevices in end edges of panels, using putty gun: Injects putty into crevices in end edges of panels stacked on handtruck, using putty gun, and pushes handtruck into position over feeder mechanism of edge-sealing machine. Adjusts automatic feeding and discharge elements of machine according to panel thickness, using wrench. Starts machine that feeds panels between injection heads, that apply putty to edges of panels to seal crevices, and mechanism that stacks processed panels at discharge end of machine. Monitors operation of machine and adjusts control mechanism, using wrench, to ensure specified application of putty and stacking of panels. Brushes excess putty from edges of panel with handbrush. Transfers pump from empty to full barrel of putty to replenish supply for machine. Removes and cleans putty heads, using wrench and cleaning solution.
GOE: 06.04.21 STRENGTH: M GED: R2 M1 L1 SVP: 2 DLU: 77

769.687-010   BASKET GRADER (wood. container)
Inspects finished baskets for defects, such as splits in wood, discoloration, warping, and rot. Discards imperfect baskets and stacks accepted ones in tiers to conserve space and to ensure that baskets conform to size standards. Ties each tier with twine and transfers baskets to storage area.
GOE: 06.03.02 STRENGTH: L GED: R2 M1 L1 SVP: 2 DLU: 77

769.687-014   BOBBIN INSPECTOR (woodworking)
Examines and rejects finished wooden bobbins with imperfections, such as splinters, cracks, rough finish, and defective spindle holes.

GOE: 06.03.02 STRENGTH: L GED: R2 M1 L1 SVP: 2 DLU: 77

769.687-018   CANOE INSPECTOR, FINAL (ship-boat mfg.)
Inspects canoes and rowboats prior to painting for flaws in work and blemishes in aluminum or wood. Vacuums interior of boat. May partially submerge canoes under pressure in water to test for water tightness.
GOE: 06.03.02 STRENGTH: L GED: R2 M1 L1 SVP: 4 DLU: 77

769.687-022   FRAME TRIMMER II (wood prod., nec) alternate titles: filler and sander
Sands wooden mirror or picture frames with sandpaper preparatory to finishing and staining to remove nicks or rough edges. Spreads putty over nail holes, using spatula or knife. May touch up marred or discolored spots with matching color paint.
GOE: 06.04.25 STRENGTH: L GED: R2 M1 L1 SVP: 2 DLU: 77

769.687-026   INSPECTOR (woodworking)
Inspects dimensional woodstock, wooden furniture, or wood products, such as doors, panels, window sashes, and window screen frames for defects and conformance to machining specifications: Visually examines and feels surface of woodstock or products to detect defects, such as mismatched veneer, dents, splits, blemishes, loose and uneven joints, holes, and faulty sanding. Verifies conformance of woodstock or products to dimensional specifications, using ruler, caliper, gauges, and square. Records quantity of material approved and rejected on inspection report. May sand uneven areas, using sandpaper, and fill dents and cracks, using filler and putty knife.
GOE: 06.03.02 STRENGTH: L GED: R2 M2 L2 SVP: 3 DLU: 78

769.687-030   INSPECTOR, PICTURE FRAMES (wood prod., nec)
Inspects wood picture frames for conformance to specifications: Examines frames for defects, such as defective shading, splinters, and uneven corners. Knocks uneven corners of frame together, using stick. Removes sides of frame containing defects, and passes side to designated worker for reprocessing. Records production.
GOE: 06.03.02 STRENGTH: L GED: R2 M1 L2 SVP: 3 DLU: 77

769.687-034   PLUG SORTER (woodworking)
Picks out split, broken, or knotty cedar plugs, used to fill holes resulting from removal of spikes in railroad ties or telephone poles, as they pass on conveyor.
GOE: 06.03.02 STRENGTH: L GED: R1 M1 L1 SVP: 2 DLU: 77

769.687-038   PUTTY MIXER AND APPLIER (wood. container)
Mixes oil, drier, and water with whiting (powdered chalk) to make putty. Fills holes in wood with putty, using putty knife.
GOE: 06.04.34 STRENGTH: L GED: R1 M1 L1 SVP: 1 DLU: 77

769.687-042   SORTER II (wood prod., nec) alternate titles: cork sorter
Examines, grades, and sorts corks according to degree of porosity and number and size of cracks.
GOE: 06.03.02 STRENGTH: L GED: R1 M1 L1 SVP: 2 DLU: 77

769.687-046   VENEER MATCHER (millwork-plywood) alternate titles: splicer matcher
Matches precut veneer strips according to grain, pattern, and shade to form face sheet of specified size: Lays strips of veneer on table and inspects them for defects. Stacks rejected strips aside for removal. Arranges suitable pieces in order of similar grain, pattern, and shade to form face sheet of specified minimum width. Numbers strips in sequence for assembly and stacks them on pallet. May trim end pieces to size, using knife. May assemble strips into flitches in matched pattern sequence for assembly. May match and tape together veneer sheets for use in furniture manufacture and be designated Veneer Matcher (furniture).
GOE: 06.03.02 STRENGTH: L GED: R3 M1 L1 SVP: 4 DLU: 77

769.687-050   VENEER-STOCK GRADER (wood. container)
Inspects veneer stock, used in making slat baskets and wirebound boxes, and removes defective stock containing splits, knots, or other surface flaws. Sorts and stacks material on table or in bins according to size and intended use. May distribute stock to assembly workers.
GOE: 06.03.02 STRENGTH: L GED: R2 M1 L1 SVP: 2 DLU: 77

769.687-054   WOODWORKING-SHOP HAND (woodworking) alternate titles: mill laborer; woodworking-shop laborer
Performs any combination of following duties to facilitate cutting, finishing, storing, cleaning, and shipping wood products, and inspects products prior to shipment: Stacks lumber or wood products on floor or in bins to supply machine operators or assemblers, or in kiln cars, yard, or shed for storage or seasoning. Places sticks between lumber to permit air circulation, and binds stacks together during seasoning. Hammers shaped steel bands into timbers and railroad ties to prevent splitting during seasoning and inserts bolts or metal dowels through split timbers to hold parts together. Dismantles crates and removes nails and other metal from wooden parts to salvage material, using handtools. Applies filler, putty, or other material, using brush, putty knife, and fingers to fill wood pores, holes, cracks, or other indentations. Removes paint, lacquer, and other finishes from wood products, using solvent, steel wool, brush, and cloths, and sands rough spots, using sandpaper or sanding machine, to prepare surfaces for finishing. Traces patterns on lumber stock as guide for machine operator. Attaches articles to wires, cord, or hooks preparatory to dipping. Dips article into vats to coat them with paint, asphalt, or other ingredients. Marks

furniture surfaces with crayon or rough-edged object to simulate antique finish. Brushes surfaces with glue preparatory to covering surfaces with leather, paper, or other materials. Nails together lumber for cutting, and places lumber on machine table. Examines materials and products for defects, finish, and grade, and accuracy of dimension and matching panels, using measuring instruments. Stamps grade on product and weighs and records units processed and inspected. Changes cutterheads and blades, adjusts belts, and performs other duties as instructed to facilitate setting up woodworking machines. Loads and unloads materials from railroad cars, trucks and barges by hand, using handtruck or industrial truck to move material to designated areas. Cleans cars and trucks and lines them with paper preparatory to loading.
GOE: 06.04.25 STRENGTH: V GED: R2 M1 L1 SVP: 2 DLU: 81

769.687-058 BRIAR-WOOD SORTER (fabrication, nec)
Sorts briar-wood blocks used in making pipe stummels, using metal gauge: Removes briar-wood block from bin and compares block with metal gauge to determine size classification of block. Tosses block into specified burlap bag, according to shape and dimensions of block. Discards scrap briar-wood.
GOE: 06.03.02 STRENGTH: M GED: R2 M1 L1 SVP: 2 DLU: 86

77 OCCUPATIONS IN FABRICATION AND REPAIR OF SAND, STONE, CLAY, AND GLASS PRODUCTS

This division includes occupations concerned with handcraft and related activities involving specialized handtools and power tools used in grading, cutting, and polishing precious or semiprecious stones, including natural or synthetic gems, jewel bearings, and diamond wiredrawing dies; cutting and polishing ornamental and structural stone; forming, decorating, and finishing porcelain, pottery, tiles, and other ceramic products; molding, shaping, and decorating artistic and laboratory glassware, pressed lenses, and other handmade glass products; and producing commercial or industrial abrasives.

770 OCCUPATIONS IN FABRICATION AND REPAIR OF JEWELRY, ORNAMENTS, AND RELATED PRODUCTS

This group includes occupations concerned with precious and semiprecious, natural and synthetic, ornamental and industrial stones, gems, jewel bearings, and diamond dies.

770.131-010 JEWEL SUPERVISOR (clock & watch)
Supervises and coordinates activities of workers engaged in fabricating watch jewels from raw stock. Performs duties as described under SUPERVISOR (any industry) Master Title.
GOE: 06.04.01 STRENGTH: L GED: R4 M3 L4 SVP: 7 DLU: 77

770.131-014 SUPERVISOR, DIAMOND FINISHING (jewelry-silver.)
Supervises and coordinates activities of workers engaged in girdling, brilliandeering, and lopping diamonds, and marks defects on diamonds to be removed by cutter: Examines rough diamonds with magnifying glass to detect defects in color, quality, and physical structure. Outlines defects to be removed by diamond cutter, using ink pen. Distributes cut diamonds to workers for finishing process. Trains new workers in job duties. May cleave (split) diamonds to remove imperfections. Performs other duties as described under SUPERVISOR (any industry) Master Title.
GOE: 05.05.14 STRENGTH: L GED: R4 M3 L3 SVP: 8 DLU: 77

770.261-010 BRILLIANDEER-LOPPER (jewelry-silver.)
Cuts and polishes facets, table, and culet on diamonds, using table-mounted polishing plate: Mixes bort (diamond dust and oil), starts motor that spins plate, applies bort to plate with fingers, and presses leather strap against plate to work bort into surface. Positions diamond in cup of dop and aligns dop in holding device to set angle of diamond for cutting. Lowers diamond onto spinning plate, exercising core to prevent damaging diamond. Positions holding device between guide pins on table or holds device in hands and regulates pressure of diamond against spinning plate with hand or metal weight. Examines diamond frequently to ensure that angle and position of cuts are within specified limits. Measures cuts, using loupe and gauges, and feels diamond to determine that cuts are with grain. Removes and replaces polishing plate as necessary, using wrench. May saw diamonds, using bench lathe. May cut and polish facets, tables, and culets on girdled diamonds and be designated Blocker (jewelry-silver.). May be designated according to section of diamond cut as Bezel Cutter (jewelry-silver.); Pavilion Cutter (jewelry-silver.).
GOE: 05.05.14 STRENGTH: S GED: R3 M2 L2 SVP: 6 DLU: 77

770.261-014 GIRDLER (jewelry-silver.)
Laps girdle on rough diamonds, using diamond girdling lathe, and utilizing knowledge of diamond finishing techniques: Examines diamond to determine site, width, and shape of stone to be girdled and selects flat or hollow tipped dop, depending on surface of diamond. Screws dop onto end of heating rod, heats dop over gas flame, places cement on tip of dop, and presses diamond onto cement in position to facilitate girdling. Selects two dop-mounted diamonds and screws one onto lathe and one onto *girdling stick.* Starts lathe and works irregular shaped sides of stick diamond against lathe diamond to remove

points and lap girdles on diamonds. Examines diamonds during girdling, using loupe or magnifying glass, to determine that girdles are shaped to specifications. Heats dop to soften cement and removes diamond from dop. Lubricates, dismantles, and cleans lathe and motor, and replaces motor belt as required.
GOE: 05.05.14 STRENGTH: S GED: R3 M2 L2 SVP: 6 DLU: 77

770.267-010 DIAMOND EXPERT (jewelry-silver.)
Examines rough diamonds with magnifying glass to detect defects in color, quality, and physical structure. Marks sections of stone with india ink to outline defects to be removed by diamond sawyers. May appraise diamonds for customers.
GOE: 05.05.14 STRENGTH: S GED: R4 M3 L3 SVP: 8 DLU: 77

770.281-010 DIAMOND SELECTOR (jewelry-silver.) alternate titles: diamond assorter; diamond grader
Selects diamonds according to type and size, for use in cutting tools and ring mountings: Studies grade, quality, color (skin), and physical structure of rough or finished diamonds. Sorts stones according to quality and type, using magnifying glass or loupe. Determines size of stone, using measuring gauge or sizing plate, and sorts diamonds of same size into containers. May weigh stones, using diamond weighing scale, to verify weight.
GOE: 05.05.14 STRENGTH: S GED: R4 M2 L3 SVP: 8 DLU: 77

770.281-014 GEM CUTTER (jewelry-silver.) alternate titles: cutter; lapidary; stonecutter
Cuts, shapes, and polishes precious and synthetic gems: Positions rough stone in holder and holds stone against edge of revolving saw or lapidary slitter impregnated with diamond dust to cut and slit stone. Removes cut stone and places it in lapidary stick. Selects shaping wheel and applies abrasive compound. Holds lapidary stick against revolving shaping wheel and lapidary disk to further shape stone and grind facets. Examines stone for accuracy of cut, using magnifying glass. Polishes stone, using felt or canvas-covered polishing wheel, and polishing compounds, such as tripoli or rouge. May use mechanical facet-cutting device. May cut and polish diamonds for industrial purposes and be designated Industrial-Diamond Polisher (jewelry-silver.).
GOE: 05.05.14 STRENGTH: S GED: R4 M3 L3 SVP: 6 DLU: 77

770.381-010 BEAD MAKER (jewelry-silver.) alternate titles: glass-bead maker; glass blower
Makes glass beads and decorative jewelry findings, such as petals and leaves: Melts end of solid glass rod, using gas burner. Picks up small globule of molten glass on end of metal wire and twirls wire until sphere is formed to make solid bead, or rolls globule of glass in groove of block of hard wood to form bead of correct diameter and contour. To make solid decorative findings, flattens globule into disk with spatula, and shapes disk by twisting and elongating it with pliers, or shapes disk in specially setup embossing dies in handpress. To make hollow glass articles, picks up globule of molten glass with blowpipe and inflates it to size of sample article by blowing into pipe or inflates globule to half-size of finished article and places it in metal mold, inflating it fully so that glass will assume shape of mold cavity. Cools and solidifies glass article by holding it over jet of compressed air, or dips article into water to cool and solidify glass. May shape heated rods into novelty items, such as fish, boats, and pins and be designated Glass-Novelty Maker (glass prod.).
GOE: 01.06.02 STRENGTH: L GED: R3 M2 L2 SVP: 7 DLU: 77

770.381-014 DIAMOND CLEAVER (jewelry-silver.) alternate titles: cleaver; splitter
Splits rough diamonds along premarked lines to remove imperfections, such as internal spots and flaws, and to obtain optimum value from stones: Positions diamond in holder and presses diamond-studded tool along premarked lines to make incision for splitting. Places steel blade in incision and taps blade with jeweler's hammer to split stone.
GOE: 05.05.14 STRENGTH: S GED: R3 M2 L2 SVP: 6 DLU: 77

770.381-018 DIAMOND DRILLER (machine tools) alternate titles: driller, fine-diamond dies
Drills minute channels in industrial diamonds for use in wire-drawing dies, using drill, lathe, and handtools: Positions diamond in chuck of lathe equipped with diamond-charged wire (drilling point) or forms wax cup around diamond by hand, fills cup with diamond dust mixture, and inserts steel needle into lathe to act as drilling tool. Regulates speed of revolutions and reciprocating action of drilling mechanism. Advances cutting point of drill according to specifications covering depth and contour of channel, working to tolerance of 0.0001 inch. Examines depth and shape of channel with microscope and regrinds point of drill. Drills backout (hole drilled from opposite side of stone to meet channel) to prevent chipping surface of stone. Laps inner wall of channel by means of machine that revolves stone as rotating wire or needle rocks back and forth in channel, working to hole diameter tolerance of 0.0000018 inch. Tests accuracy of die hole by pulling specified length of wire through die and measuring its resistance in Wheatstone bridge having readings translated into wire diameter or by taking a series of readings along length of wire with electronic micrometer. Secures stone in metal mounting, using molten solder. May drill cavity (spot) in face of stone to hold diamond dust mixture, by pressing pointed end of diamond chip against revolving stone, using pliers. May be designated according to operation performed as Finisher, Fine-Diamond Dies (machine tools).
GOE: 06.01.04 STRENGTH: L GED: R3 M2 L2 SVP: 5 DLU: 77

770.381-022 DIAMOND-DIE POLISHER (machine tools) alternate titles: die cutter, diamond; die polisher

Laps and polishes bores of diamond wire drawing dies to specified dimensions: Positions die in holding device of machine. Inserts steel needle in machine spindle, positions needle inside bore of die and starts machine which rotates needle in bore. Dabs progressively finer diamond-dust paste or solution on needle during lapping operation. Pulls specified gauge wire through bore and measures wire with micrometer to verify bore dimension. Inspects bore of die for cracks and other defects, using magnifying glass or microscope. Replaces worn needles and sharpens points on grinder. May insert and press hand lapping tool in bore of rotating die. May drill initial bore, using diamond drills.
GOE: 06.01.04 STRENGTH: L GED: R3 M2 L2 SVP: 5 DLU: 77

770.381-026 JEWEL BLOCKER AND SAWYER (clock & watch) alternate titles: jewel sawyer

Cuts boules (raw stock from which jewels are fashioned) into small squares by successive blocking and sawing operations: Secures boule on block with melted sealing wax preparatory to sawing. Cuts boules into half moons (boule cross sections), using saw equipped with diamond-impregnated circular copper blade. Turns indexing handle to move saw blade for successive cuts. Blocks half moons and saws them into strips. Blocks and saws strips into squares. Trues blades after diamond dust has been pressed into cutting rim in hydraulic press, by peening on flat metal surface until metal is so distributed throughout blade that blade does not snake (shimmy) when turning.
GOE: 06.01.04 STRENGTH: L GED: R3 M2 L2 SVP: 6 DLU: 77

770.381-030 JEWEL-MAKER (clock & watch)

Grinds, drills, and finishes sapphire jewel bearings for use in precision instruments, such as compasses, meters, and chronometers: Grinds and faces sapphire blanks to flatten surfaces, and turns edges, to form bearings of specified size and thickness. Drills and finishes holes in centers of bearings.
GOE: 06.01.04 STRENGTH: L GED: R4 M3 L3 SVP: 7 DLU: 77

770.381-034 OLIVING-MACHINE OPERATOR (clock & watch) alternate titles: jewel-oliving-machine operator

Grinds olive-shaped contour on bearing surface of olive-jewel hole: Fits wire strung with jewels, and on which wire diamond dust is spread, in holding bow. Holds bow so that jewel is rotated between shaped rotating wheels of machine while rocking bow back and forth so that action of wire on rotating jewel will wear away sides of hole to olive shape. Repeats bowing operation on rest of jewels on string. Inspects jewels for shape of olive and measures hole size with graduated, tapered needle.
GOE: 06.01.04 STRENGTH: S GED: R3 M2 L2 SVP: 5 DLU: 77

770.381-038 SAPPHIRE-STYLUS GRINDER (comm. equip.)

Grinds sapphire stylus to specified shape for use in machine that records sound on wax or plastic master plate, using abrasive cutting wheel.
GOE: 06.01.04 STRENGTH: S GED: R3 M2 L2 SVP: 5 DLU: 77

770.381-042 SPOTTER (machine tools)

Locates and marks specified drilling position on surfaces of diamonds used as dies: Places diamond under microscope and moves it at various angles until clear channel through gem can be seen. Forms indentation in diamond surface to mark spot for drilling, using diamond chips held in pliers. Drills starting hole of minute dimensions, using electrically powered hand drill.
GOE: 05.05.14 STRENGTH: L GED: R4 M3 L3 SVP: 6 DLU: 77

770.382-010 LATHE OPERATOR (jewelry-silver.) alternate titles: sawyer

Operates lathe type saw to saw rough diamonds along premarked lines preparatory to shaping operation, using bench lathes: Attaches sawing wheel (bronze plate) to lathe and applies abrasive compound. Positions stone in cement holder of lathe, starts lathe, and presses diamond against revolving wheel to groove stone along premarked lines. Adjusts arm of lathe to apply pressure required to saw diamond. Periodically examines sawing operation to ensure standard production.
GOE: 06.02.08 STRENGTH: L GED: R3 M2 L3 SVP: 6 DLU: 77

770.382-014 PHONOGRAPH-NEEDLE-TIP MAKER (comm. equip.) alternate titles: grinder, needle tip; needle grinder; single-pointed operator

Sets up and operates grinding machines to grind and polishes precious-stone tips of phonograph needles to specified point and finish: Mounts tip in holding shank, using tweezers, chemical dropper, and soldering iron. Sets up grinding wheel, dresses wheel with dressing tool, mounts shank containing tip in spindle or chuck, and grinds tip to form specified point, observing grinding under microscope or through loupe or viewing lens. Polishes tip on buffing wheel. May hold mounted tip against preset grinding wheel to do preliminary grinding. May examine finished tip for accuracy, using shadowgraph.
GOE: 06.02.08 STRENGTH: L GED: R3 M2 L2 SVP: 5 DLU: 77

770.582-010 FACER (clock & watch)

Operates lathe to polish faces of jewel bearings: Affixes boxwood lap (polishing disk) impregnated with diamond dust to faceplate of lathe. Starts lathe and moves bearing against revolving lap, using pointed stick to facilitate handling jewel bearing. Inspects polished bearings to ensure conformance with standard, using magnifying glass.
GOE: 06.02.30 STRENGTH: L GED: R3 M2 L2 SVP: 4 DLU: 77

770.682-010 JEWEL-BEARING BROACHER (clock & watch) alternate titles: broacher; pinner, jewel bearing

Operates lathe to finish holes drilled in partially processed jewel bearings: Inserts bearings in lathe chuck. Dips brass wire (broach) in diamond dust, in-serts it into bearing hole, and rubs away high spots, working within tolerances of 0.0001 inch. Inspects holes with magnifying glass and measures them with gauges and micrometers. Bevels edges of holes.
GOE: 06.02.30 STRENGTH: L GED: R3 M2 L2 SVP: 5 DLU: 77

770.682-014 JEWEL-BEARING DRILLER (clock & watch)

Operates bench lathes to drill holes of specified size in jewel bearings: Sharpens diamond drill, using diamond cutter and other tools. Mounts chuck in lathe and inserts shaped and ground sapphire bearing between jaws of chuck, using tweezers. Starts lathe and holds drill against center of bearing, cutting halfway through. Reverses bearing in chuck and drills through center of bearing from other side until holes meet.
GOE: 06.01.04 STRENGTH: L GED: R3 M2 L2 SVP: 4 DLU: 77

770.682-018 JEWEL-BEARING FACER (clock & watch) alternate titles: flat-grinder operator

Operates lathe to grind jewel bearings to specified thickness: Mounts fixture in chuck of lathe and inserts jewel bearing into recess of fixture, using tweezers. Mounts grinding disk impregnated with diamond dust on opposite faceplate of lathe. Manipulates controls to bring bearing into contact with grinding disk and to govern grinding process, working to tolerances of 0.0005 inch. Examines bearings, using measuring instruments, such as gauges and micrometers, to ensure conformance with specifications.
GOE: 06.02.08 STRENGTH: L GED: R3 M2 L2 SVP: 4 DLU: 77

770.682-022 JEWEL-BEARING TURNER (clock & watch)

Operates lathe to turn edges of partially processed jewel bearings: Chips edges of ground sapphires to approach disk shape, using chisel and hammer. Mounts bearing in chuck of lathe. Starts lathe and presses diamond cutter against circumference of bearing. Examines shaped bearing, using magnifying glass and dial micrometers, to ensure conformance with specifications.
GOE: 06.02.30 STRENGTH: L GED: R3 M2 L2 SVP: 4 DLU: 77

770.682-026 JEWEL-HOLE DRILLER (clock & watch)

Operates battery of horizontal, multispindle, drilling machines to drill center holes in round jewel bearing blanks: Puts molten shellac on end of work spindle and centers jewel on spindles, using small, hand centering tool. Fits drill bits in soft shellac in drill head. Trues up (aligns) bit by holding bit lightly with tweezers to detect any play indicative of poor alignment; straightens bit by moving its tip slightly to eliminate play. Inserts work spindle, applies diamond dust with wire to drilling point, and removes jewel when spindle spring opens and thus indicates hole is drilled. Inspects holes for size by manually turning them on standard bit used as gauge.
GOE: 06.02.02 STRENGTH: L GED: R3 M2 L2 SVP: 5 DLU: 77

770.684-010 JEWEL GRINDER II (clock & watch) alternate titles: grinder, outside diameter

Grinds outside diameter (periphery) of watch jewels to size, using diamond-bonded wheel under water jet: Fits wire filled with jewels in small holding tool (shaped similar to small bucksaw) and turns adjusting screw to pull wire taut. Positions rubber holding wheel so distance between grinding wheels is identical to specified outside diameter of jewels. Holds jewels against grinder, moving holder back and forth until jewels are ground sufficiently to pass between wheels. Measures jewel diameter with precision jaw gauge and regrinds if necessary.
GOE: 06.04.30 STRENGTH: L GED: R2 M1 L2 SVP: 3 DLU: 77

770.684-014 JEWEL-HOLE CORNERER (clock & watch)

Smooths hole corners on flat side of bar jewels: Dips tapered point of cornering tool in mixture of diamond dust and oil. Secures jewel by putting tool point into jewel hole, and holding jewel on revolving rubber disc until action of cornering tool and dust shape corner in revolving jewel.
GOE: 06.04.30 STRENGTH: L GED: R2 M1 L1 SVP: 3 DLU: 77

770.684-018 ROUGH OPENER, JEWEL HOLE (clock & watch) alternate titles: jewel-hole rough opener

Opens (enlarges) holes in jewels by drawing tapered wire through holes by hand: Strings inch-long row of jewels on wire. Inserts row in space between holders in center of holding tool and pulls wire back and forth through center openings to wear away inside diameter. Applies diamond dust to wire to act as abrasive and speed enlarging. Unwinds tapered wire gradually from spool and feeds larger portion of wire through jewels as opening operation proceeds.
GOE: 06.02.30 STRENGTH: L GED: R2 M1 L1 SVP: 2 DLU: 77

770.685-010 FLAT SURFACER, JEWEL (clock & watch) alternate titles: jewel polisher

Tends *lapping* machine that polishes flat surfaces (ends) of round jewel bearings: Blocks in molten shellac in circular row near outside edge of flat, circular steel block. Sets blocks, usually four or five at once, in holding chuck and turns screw press to force blocked jewels against diamond dusted revolving lap. Observes polishing to detect signs of overheating and removes hot block for cooling before shellac melts and jewels are damaged by being turned on edge. Examines finish of jewels for appearance with loupe and verifies thickness with upright dial gauge.
GOE: 06.04.08 STRENGTH: L GED: R2 M1 L2 SVP: 3 DLU: 77

770.685-014 JEWEL GRINDER I (clock & watch)

Tends centerless grinding machine that fashions round jewels from square blanks: Positions and aligns row of square jewels on edge in trough. Brushes

bead of honey on row of jewels, places row on rest of grinder, and secures row in place with spring device that applies pressure against each end of row. Starts grinder that rotates and grinds jewels, which are held in place in triangular area formed by grinding wheel, driving wheel, and rest. Measures outside diameter of round jewels for size on jaw gauge.
GOE: 06.04.08 STRENGTH: L GED: R2 M1 L2 SVP: 3 DLU: 77

770.685-018 JEWEL-BEARING GRINDER (clock & watch)
Tends lathe that grinds sapphire jewel-bearing blanks flat on both sides: Applies diamond dust to surface of grinding disk (lap). Mounts lap in revolving chuck. Inserts single bearings into cavity at base of holder (rod) and holds bearings against revolving lap to grind them on one side. Mounts several bearings on metal disk coated with adhesive material, and holds disk against lap to grind other side of bearing.
GOE: 06.04.08 STRENGTH: L GED: R3 M2 L2 SVP: 4 DLU: 77

770.685-022 JEWEL-BEARING POLISHER (clock & watch)
Tends lathe that polishes internal surfaces of holes in jewel bearings: Inserts jewel bearing into chuck of lathe. Starts lathe and polishes surfaces by inserting splint coated with ground diamond dust into hole of bearing. Cleans hole with splint dipped in benzene. Inspects hole under magnifying glass to ensure that polished surfaces conform to standard.
GOE: 06.04.08 STRENGTH: L GED: R3 M2 L2 SVP: 4 DLU: 77

770.685-026 JEWEL-CORNER-BRUSHING-MACHINE OPERATOR (clock & watch)
Tends machine that shapes and smooths outside (lead-in) corner of bar jewels: Blocks jewels with melted shellac on circular metal block. Places block in spindle of machine and positions work against brush. Turns on power and allows machine to run until, from experience and by touching block to estimate its temperature (heated by friction), worker knows jewels are shaped and smoothed. Inspects jewels under loupe to determine if corner is properly finished.
GOE: 06.04.08 STRENGTH: L GED: R2 M1 L1 SVP: 3 DLU: 77

770.685-030 JEWEL-CUPPING-MACHINE OPERATOR (clock & watch)
Tends cupping machine that cuts and polishes oilcups in jewel bearings: Depresses pedal to open chuck, inserts jewel with tweezers, and releases pedal to clamp jewel in place. Lowers head holding diamond and borax broaching tool to working position, starts machine, and loads other machines. Removes finished jewel when machine automatically stops. Examines cupped jewels for correctness of cut. Verifies dimensions of recess on upright gauge.
GOE: 06.04.08 STRENGTH: L GED: R2 M1 L2 SVP: 3 DLU: 77

770.685-034 TURNER, MACHINE (clock & watch)
Tends grinding machine that grinds sapphire squares to disk shape, for use as jewel bearings: Glues specified number of sapphire squares together to form stack. Positions stack between abrasive and rubber rolls of grinding machine and starts machine that grinds sapphires to disk shape. May operate similar machine equipped with diamond-dust-coated wheel to smooth edges of sapphire disk.
GOE: 06.04.08 STRENGTH: L GED: R3 M1 L2 SVP: 4 DLU: 77

770.687-010 ARTIFICIAL-PEARL MAKER (jewelry-silver.) alternate titles: pearl dipper; pearl maker
Dips glass beads in solution of pearl lacquer to make pearls: Sticks beads on pins or toothpicks and mounts them on wooden blocks. Sets blocks in device that dips beads in solution. Cuts pearls off pins with knife. May finish pearls by applying glue, stringing on thread, and linking together.
GOE: 06.04.33 STRENGTH: L GED: R1 M1 L1 SVP: 2 DLU: 77

770.687-014 DIAMOND SIZER AND SORTER (clock & watch; jewelry-silver.)
Sorts diamonds according to size for use in watches and jewelry, using sieve, loupe, and precision measuring instruments: Reads work orders to determine sizes required to fit mountings. Measures diamonds, using gauge and loupe, or sorts diamonds, using sieve of specified diameter, to segregate sizes required. Places diamonds of specified size in containers. May size and sort jewels other than diamonds and be designated Jewel Sorter (clock & watch).
GOE: 06.03.02 STRENGTH: S GED: R3 M2 L2 SVP: 4 DLU: 77

770.687-018 JEWEL GAUGER (clock & watch)
Measures inside and outside diameters of watch jewels and segregates jewels according to size: Gauges inside diameter of jewel hole by slipping jewel on graduated, tapered needle. Places jewel in precision jaw gauge and measures its outside diameter. Segregates jewels according to size and rejects those jewels failing to meet tolerances as fine as 0.0001 inch. May measure hole size of jewel bearings, using go-not-go gauge. May be designated according to measurements made as Jewel-Diameter Gauger (clock & watch); Jewel-Hole Gauger (clock & watch).
GOE: 06.03.02 STRENGTH: S GED: R3 M2 L2 SVP: 4 DLU: 77

770.687-022 JEWEL INSPECTOR (clock & watch) alternate titles: inspector, jewels
Examines watch jewels for defects, such as cracks, rough cuts and cups, misshapen holes, and chips, using microscope: Places quantity of jewels on glass table, which is lighted from beneath, and positions each jewel individually beneath microscope with tweezers. Turns jewel to view all surfaces. Segregates rejects according to type of defect.

GOE: 06.03.02 STRENGTH: S GED: R3 M3 L2 SVP: 4 DLU: 77

770.687-026 JEWEL STRINGER (clock & watch)
Strings watch jewels on wire for further processing, using tweezers and loupe. Strings jewel settings, right side up, on wire for transfer to feeding tubes of automatic shaving press.
GOE: 06.04.30 STRENGTH: S GED: R2 M1 L1 SVP: 2 DLU: 77

770.687-030 PULVERIZER (jewelry-silver.) alternate titles: cracker; enamel cracker; enamel pulverizer
Pulverizes pieces of enamel to be used in decorating jewelry settings, using mortar and pestle: Places lumps of enamel crystals in mortar and crushes them by striking pestle with hammer. Pours pulverized material through sieve. Recrushes those pieces that do not pass through sieve.
GOE: 06.04.34 STRENGTH: L GED: R2 M1 L1 SVP: 2 DLU: 77

770.687-034 ROCK BREAKER (retail trade; stonework)
Breaks rocks into small pieces for use in fabricating novelties, such as mineral specimen cards, ash trays, book ends, and paperweights, using hammer.
GOE: 05.12.07 STRENGTH: L GED: R2 M1 L1 SVP: 2 DLU: 77

771 STONE CUTTERS AND CARVERS

This group includes occupations concerned with cutting, shaping, and finishing granite, slate, marble, and other types of stone.

771.137-010 SUPERVISOR, SLATE SPLITTING (stonework)
Supervises and coordinates activities of workers engaged in splitting slate for use as flagstone, caping, window sills, and flooring: Examines quarried slabs and indicates thickness for workers to split stone for maximum utilization. Measures thickness of split stone to verify conformance to standards. Performs other duties as described under SUPERVISOR (any industry) Master Title.
GOE: 06.04.01 STRENGTH: L GED: R3 M2 L2 SVP: 5 DLU: 77

771.281-010 STENCIL CUTTER (stonework) alternate titles: blaster; rubber cutter; shape carver
Lays out inscriptions and decorative designs on stenciling material applied to stone and cuts out stencil preparatory to sandblasting: Applies stenciling material to stone surface by spreading cement over surface of stone and positioning material on stone, stripping cloth from adhesive surface of material and positioning adhesive surface on stone. Aligns pattern on stencil, using rule and square, and marks over pattern with straightedge to transfer carbon lettering and design to stenciling material. Cuts out lettering and designs along marks to expose stone surface for sandblasting, using stencil knife. Trims and smooths edges of stencil to ensure detailed reproduction of intricate designs.
GOE: 01.06.01 STRENGTH: M GED: R4 M2 L2 SVP: 6 DLU: 77

771.281-014 STONE CARVER (stonework) alternate titles: hand carver; sculptor
Carves designs and figures in full and bas-relief on stone, employing knowledge of stone-carving techniques and sense of artistry to produce carving consistent with designer's plans: Analyzes artistic objects or graphic materials, such as models, sketches, or blueprints; visualizes finished product; and plans carving technique. Lays out figures or designs on stone surface by freehand sketching, marking over tracing paper, and transferring dimensions from sketches or blueprints, using rule, straightedge, square, compass, calipers, and chalk, or scriber. Selects chisels and pneumatic tools and determines sequence of their use according to intricacy of design or figure. Roughs out design freehand or by chipping along marks on stone, using mallet and chisel or pneumatic tool. Shapes, trims, or touches up roughed out design with appropriate tool to finish carving. Periodically compares carving with sketches, blueprints, or model and verifies dimensions of carving, using calipers, rule, straightedge, and square. Moves fingers over surface of carving to verify smoothness of finish. May smooth surface of carving with rubbing stone. May be designated according to type of work as Monument Carver (stonework); or according to kind of stone carved as Granite Carver (stonework); Marble Carver (stonework).
GOE: 01.06.02 STRENGTH: M GED: R4 M4 L4 SVP: 8 DLU: 77

771.381-010 STONECUTTER APPRENTICE, HAND (stonework) alternate titles: granite cutter apprentice
Performs duties as described under APPRENTICE (any industry) Master Title.
GOE: 05.05.01 STRENGTH: M GED: R4 M3 L3 SVP: 7 DLU: 77

771.381-014 STONECUTTER, HAND (stonework) alternate titles: chisel worker; stone dresser; stoneworker
Cuts, shapes, and finishes rough blocks of building or monumental stone according to diagrams or patterns: Traces around pattern or transfers dimensions from diagrams to stone, using rule, straightedge, compass, square, and chalk or scriber. Selects surfacing tools according to finish specified or step in finishing process. Chips fragments of stone away from marks on stone, working surface of stone down to specified finish. Verifies progress of finishing to ensure adherence to specifications, using straightedge, level, plumb, and square. May dress surface of stone with bushhammer. May cut decorative designs in stone surface. May cut moldings or grooves in stone that cannot be reached by machine. May drill holes in stone. May be designated according to product as Building Stonecutter (stonework); Curbing Stonecutter (stonework); Monument Stonecutter (stonework).

GOE: 05.05.01 STRENGTH: M GED: R4 M3 L3 SVP: 7 DLU: 77

771.384-010 COPER, HAND (stonework) alternate titles: cutter; marble coper

Cuts rough-sawed slabs of stone, using pneumatic hammer, into blocks used for capping (coping) of brick or stone walls: Measures and marks slab according to specifications, using square, rule, straightedge, chalk, or crayon. Selects cutting chisel and inserts it into pneumatic hammer. Chips slab along markings with pneumatic hammer to form breaking groove. Inserts coping tool in groove and taps it to break stone, using hammer or mallet. May turn slab and cut groove in opposite side to facilitate breaking. May smooth edges of broken stones, using chisels and mallet. May smooth edges of broken stones, using grinder.

GOE: 06.02.30 STRENGTH: H GED: R3 M1 L2 SVP: 3 DLU: 77

771.484-010 BEVELER (stonework)

Bevels and smooths edges of marble or slate slabs, using handtools: Positions slabs on workbench. Marks width of bevel on slab edges, using rule, square, straightedge, and scribe. Removes excess slab material along edge markings to produce bevel of specified angle, using rasp. Smooths beveled edges with fine file. May finish smoothed edges, using sandpaper.

GOE: 06.02.30 STRENGTH: H GED: R3 M2 L2 SVP: 5 DLU: 77

771.684-010 ROCK SPLITTER (stonework) alternate titles: block maker; driller

Splits rough dimension stone into smaller units, such as paving blocks, ashlar, or rubble, using airhammer, wedges, and shims: Scans stone to determine rift and grain lines of splitting, usually at right angles to each other. Chips rough edges from stone, using chipping hammer. May be designated according to product made as Paving-Block Cutter (stonework) II. May split rough slabs of slat into sheets for use as coping, flooring, and roofing and be designated Slate Slitter (stonework).

GOE: 05.12.07 STRENGTH: H GED: R3 M1 L1 SVP: 6 DLU: 77

772   GLASS BLOWING, PRESSING, SHAPING, AND RELATED OCCUPATIONS, N.E.C.

This group includes occupations, not elsewhere classified, concerned with such handmade products as art glassware, laboratory apparatus, and tableware. Occupations concerned with such machine mass-produced products as bottles and light-bulb blanks are included in Group 575.

772.281-010 GLASS BLOWER, LABORATORY APPARATUS (glass products; inst. & app.) alternate titles: glass technologist

Develops specifications for glass component parts and apparatus, such as test tubes, retorts, and flasks, used in medical and laboratory products, and blows and shapes glass to required dimensions, applying knowledge of glass technology and glass blowing techniques: Develops sketch into blueprint specifications, correlates product design, and determines type of glass to use to fabricate product, utilizing knowledge of factors, such as effects of heat, vacuum, and corrosive chemicals. Heats glass tubing to pliable stage, using gas flame. Blows tubing into specified form, using compressed air or own breath. Shapes, bends, or joins sections of blown glass tubing, using flaring, pressing, and flattening handtools, and stop cork. Inspects and measures product to verify conformance to specifications, using instruments, such as micrometers, calipers, magnifier, and ruler. May anneal product, using annealing oven. May cut glass tubing to specified size and polish tube edges, using hand cutting and polishing wheels. May operate lathe grinder [GLASS GRINDER, LABORATORY APPARATUS (glass products; inst. & app.) 775.382-010] to grind stopcocks and joints to modify glass products. May operate glass blowing lathe [GLASS BLOWING LATHE OPERATOR (glass products) 772.482-010] to join and shape glass tubing.

GOE: 05.05.11 STRENGTH: M GED: R4 M2 L3 SVP: 8 DLU: 90

772.381-010 GLASS BENDER (fabrication, nec) alternate titles: glass blower; glass-tube bender

Heats and bends glass tubes to form scroll of electric neon signs according to pattern: Tacks asbestos pattern onto workbench. Cuts length of tubing required to form letters, using file. Holds tube over gas burner at point to be bent, rotating tube to heat it uniformly. Places rubber hose over end of tubing. Blows into hose to prevent glass from collapsing and bends tube by hand. Superimposes bent tubing on asbestos pattern to ensure accuracy. When letter or scroll has been formed, places electrode in each end of tube and heats with gas burner to fuse in place. Paints or tapes portions of tubing to separate letters. Repairs broken scroll by replacing with new sections of tubing. May charge tubing with gas [NEON-TUBE PUMPER (fabrication, nec)].

GOE: 01.06.02 STRENGTH: L GED: R4 M3 L3 SVP: 8 DLU: 77

772.381-014 PATTERNMAKER (fabrication, nec)

Lays out pattern of neon sign lettering for use in fabricating scroll, using sketch: Fastens sheet of paper to worktable and blocks in letters, using drafting instruments and pencils. Transcribes letters from sketch to pattern, and outlines sign borders. Superimposes full scale drawing of sign on pattern and perforates pattern along pencil lines, using stylus or perforating tool. Places perforated pattern on asbestos sheet, and dusts pattern with powdered charcoal to form outline on asbestos sheet. Darkens outline with pencil.

GOE: 01.06.03 STRENGTH: L GED: R4 M3 L4 SVP: 8 DLU: 77

772.381-018 WARE FINISHER (glass mfg.) alternate titles: glassware finisher

Finishes hand pressed or blown glassware by forming and attaching lips, handles, and pedestals: Cuts required gob (lump) from molten glass, using shears. Forms gob into handle, using wooden paddles to shape handle. Drops gob into hand-press mold to form pedestal. Presses handle and pedestal to glassware to attach them. Shapes handle and forms lips by rubbing and pressing with carbon stick. Smooths pedestal, using wooden buffer. May be known by article attached as Foot Caster (glass mfg.).

GOE: 06.01.04 STRENGTH: L GED: R3 M2 L2 SVP: 6 DLU: 77

772.381-022 GLASS BLOWER (glass mfg.) alternate titles: blower; gaffer

Shapes gather (gob of molten glass) into glassware by blowing through blowpipe: Receives blowpipe from GATHERER (glass mfg.) 575.684-026 and examines gather on blowpipe for imperfections, utilizing knowledge of molten glass characteristics. Blows through pipe to inflate gather while rotating pipe to prevent sagging and to obtain desired shape, or blows and rotates gather in mold or on board to obtain final shape. May dip end of blowpipe into molten glass to collect gather on head of pipe. May strike neck of finished article to separate article from blow pipe. May pull gather with tongs to aid in shaping. May use compressed air to inflate gather. May be designated according to article blown as Bottle Blower (glass mfg.).

GOE: 06.01.04 STRENGTH: L GED: R3 M2 L2 SVP: 7 DLU: 79

772.482-010 GLASS-BLOWING-LATHE OPERATOR (glass products)

Operates glassblowing lathe to join and shape glass or plastic tubing, according to blueprints and work orders: Selects, inserts, and clamps specified mandrels in head and tailstock of lathe, using wrenches. Turns knobs to adjust rotation speed. Inserts and clamps tube and other glass parts of various lengths, shapes, and diameters to be joined in chucks, using mallet and wrenches. Lights fixed jets and hand torches and turns gas valves to adjust height and color of flames and obtain specified temperature. Turns handwheels to move head and tailstock and bring workpieces in contact with flames. Blows through hose connected to center of chuck to shape glass or maintain air pressure within tube. Selects and manipulates spatula, hand torches and tips, and glass rods to shape, seal, splice, imbed, and weld rotating parts according to specifications. Uses hand torch and fixed jets to anneal joined or shaped areas. Turns handwheels to move head and tailstock and stretch or separate heated stock to specifications. May manually move glass tube over flame and blow it into specified shape.

GOE: 06.02.08 STRENGTH: L GED: R3 M2 L3 SVP: 6 DLU: 77

772.684-010 DEFECT REPAIRER, GLASSWARE (glass mfg.)

Repairs forming defects in glassware, using acetylene torch and molds: Ignites torch and moves flame over defective area to soften glass for reworking. Inserts softened glassware in mold for reshaping and removes glassware from mold after reshaping. Examines finished glassware to ensure defect is repaired.

GOE: 05.09.03 STRENGTH: L GED: R2 M1 L2 SVP: 3 DLU: 77

772.684-014 HOT-WIRE GLASS-TUBE CUTTER (glass products)

Holds and rotates glass tubing against hot wire to cut tubing to specified length: Sets guide at specified distance, using rule and wrench. Turns on electric current to heat wire. Places glass tube against guide and hot wire. Turns tubing to heat glass. Places hot glass under stream of cold water, causing it to break along heated line.

GOE: 06.04.30 STRENGTH: L GED: R2 M1 L1 SVP: 2 DLU: 77

772.684-018 WARM-IN WORKER (glass mfg.)

Reheats blown or pressed glassware in furnace to fire-polish glassware and make it malleable for further processing: Clamps snap (long-handled pincers) on hot glassware, grasps snap, and inserts glassware into furnace opening (glory hole). Rotates ware to heat it evenly to ensure retention of its molded shape. Withdraws ware from furnace when it is heated to an orange-red color. May remove or add clay to furnace opening to enlarge or reduce its size to accommodate glassware being processed. May adjust fans to control ventilation that blows fire blast back into furnace and cools snap handle.

GOE: 06.04.30 STRENGTH: L GED: R2 M1 L1 SVP: 3 DLU: 77

772.684-022 WATCH-CRYSTAL MOLDER (glass products)

Molds glass and plastic watch crystals: Places glass or plastic blank on mold of specified shape and size. Heats glass with hand torch or softens plastic in oven until it conforms to contour of mold. Holds crystal against revolving wheel to polish surface. May cut glass or plastic blanks. May grind edges of crystal.

GOE: 06.02.32 STRENGTH: S GED: R3 M1 L1 SVP: 4 DLU: 77

772.687-010 GLASS-WORKER, PRESSED OR BLOWN (glass mfg.) alternate titles: glass technologist

Performs any combination of following tasks to produce pressed or blown glassware from molten glass: Balances gather (gob of molten glass) on blowpipe, and blows through and simultaneously rotates blowpipe to maintain gather in globular form for blocking, redipping, or final shaping. Moves controls that open hinged molds to receive gather for shaping by press or attaches blower head to opening of blank-filled mold and turns valve to admit compressed air that shapes blank to mold contour. Removes glassware from mold, using pincers or fork, or catches ware from inverted molds on paddle (tray) and carries ware to reheating furnace, glazing machine, or lehr. Strikes glassware with metal bar to break (crack off) ware from blowpipe. Removes excess glass from

ware, using bar, hand cutter, flame, or saw. Inspects glassware for defects, such as cracks, chips, and malformations.
GOE: 06.02.30 STRENGTH: L GED: R2 M1 L2 SVP: 2 DLU: 77

772.687-014 SPOTTER (glass mfg.)
Locates and marks apex of curvature of formed glassware to provide index point for cutting operations: Holds flat edge of glassware on illuminated bullseyed board. Locates shadow of mold indentation and positions marking pencil on glassware until pencil shadow falls in center of indentation shadow. Marks center of indentation on glassware to indicate apex of curvature. Inspects glassware for visable defects.
GOE: 06.03.02 STRENGTH: L GED: R2 M1 L2 SVP: 2 DLU: 77

773 OCCUPATIONS IN COLORING AND DECORATING BRICK, TILE, AND RELATED PRODUCTS

This group includes occupations concerned with such coloring and decorating tasks as printing designs on brick, tile, and related products, and arranging tiles into designs for use as table tops, flooring, and similar purposes.

773.131-010 PASTER SUPERVISOR (brick & tile)
Supervises and coordinates activities of workers engaged in arranging mosaic tile on pattern boards and pasting backing on arrangements, setting up and operating automatic tile-gluing machine, inspecting sheets of tile for defects, and packing tile in cartons. Trains new workers. Performs duties as described under SUPERVISOR (any industry) Master Title.
GOE: 06.02.01 STRENGTH: M GED: R4 M2 L3 SVP: 7 DLU: 77

773.381-010 TILE DECORATOR (brick & tile) alternate titles: decorator
Prints lettering or designs on unglazed tile, using silk-screen process: Reads job order and examines drawing of design to determine method of making stencil. Cuts stencil by hand or photographs design on film. Selects colored glaze and thins it, using glaze thinner and stirring sticks. Prints design on tile, using silk-screen process. Catalogs and stores screens for future orders. May trace, transfer, stamp, or stipple designs on tile, using brushes, stamps, sponges, stencils, or decalcomanias. May load tile in kiln and sort and grade fired tile.
GOE: 01.06.03 STRENGTH: L GED: R3 M2 L3 SVP: 4 DLU: 77

773.487-010 CLAY-STAIN MIXER (brick & tile)
Mixes powdered stains for coloring clay used to make mosaic tiles, following charts and formulas: Reads formula to determine materials required, and scans chart to determine ratio of stain to tonnage of clay. Calculates quantity of materials needed, and weighs dry ingredients. Pours ingredients into container and writes identifying information on container. Adds stain to clay during blending process.
GOE: 06.04.34 STRENGTH: M GED: R3 M2 L2 SVP: 3 DLU: 77

773.684-010 COLORER (brick & tile) alternate titles: hand decorator; top-tile decorator
Applies colored glazes to tile following stamped or outlined design: Reads job order for work procedure and examines color sketches to determine colors to be applied. Fills bulb of applicator with specified glaze color. Applies glaze to design following color scheme on sketches. Cleans used applicator bulbs. May spray glaze onto tile, using spray gun. May apply liquid gold to tile, using china painting brush.
GOE: 01.06.03 STRENGTH: M GED: R3 M2 L3 SVP: 4 DLU: 77

773.687-014 PASTER (brick & tile) alternate titles: tile paster
Arranges tiles into designs for such use as flooring or sink tops and pastes paper on tile to preserve arrangement of design: Inserts individual colored tiles in slots in form-board following sample design. Pastes sheet of paper on top of tile arrangement. Places sheets of tiles in cartons.
GOE: 06.04.30 STRENGTH: M GED: R2 M1 L1 SVP: 3 DLU: 77

773.687-010 PASTING INSPECTOR (brick & tile)
Inspects mosaic tiles pasted on backing sheets for defects: Inspects tiles pasted on sheets for defects, such as coloring shades and chipped or cracked tile. Examines layout to determine that specified tile arrangement and color scheme have been carried out. Examines backing to determine that specified backing was used, tiles are firmly pasted onto backing, and spacing and position of tiles is uniform. Maintains department production records.
GOE: 06.03.02 STRENGTH: L GED: R2 M1 L1 SVP: 4 DLU: 77

774 OCCUPATIONS IN FABRICATION AND REPAIR OF POTTERY AND PORCELAIN WARE

This group includes occupations concerned with forming, decorating, and finishing pottery and porcelain ware.

774.130-010 SUPERVISOR, CLAY SHOP (pottery & porc.)
Supervises and coordinates activities of workers engaged in forming, inspecting, and finishing pottery and porcelain ware: Directs workers in casting, jiggering, and finishing ware. Sets up machine units, installs dies and shaping tools, and adjusts and sets controls of forming machines and equipment. Adjusts controls on drying ovens to regulate temperature and drying time for ceramic ware. Demonstrates to workers techniques in handling ware to avoid

breakage; recognizing and evaluating extent of defects, such as cracks, chips, and pinholes, refinishing defective ware; use of grading and color charts in sorting ware; and rubbing ware surfaces with abrasives to remove rough spots. Performs other duties as described under SUPERVISOR (any industry) Master Title.
GOE: 06.01.01 STRENGTH: L GED: R4 M3 L3 SVP: 7 DLU: 77

774.381-010 THROWER (pottery & porc.) alternate titles: clay thrower; pot maker
Molds plastic clay into such ware as vases, urns, saggers, and pitchers, as clay revolves on potter's wheel: Positions ball of clay in center of potter's wheel and starts motor, or pumps treadle with foot to revolve wheel. Presses thumbs down into center of revolving clay to form hollow. Presses on inside and outside of emerging clay cylinder with hands and fingers, gradually raising and shaping clay to desired form and size. Constantly adjusts speed of wheel to conform with changing tenacity (firmness) of clay as piece enlarges and walls become thinner, judging degrees of change by feel. Smooths surfaces of finished piece, using rubber scrapers and wet sponge. Verifies size and form, using calipers and templates. Pulls wire held taut between both hands through base of article and wheel to separate finished piece, or removes piece from wheel to dry. May form saggers only and be known as Sagger Former (pottery & porc.).
GOE: 06.02.30 STRENGTH: M GED: R3 M2 L3 SVP: 7 DLU: 77

774.382-010 POTTERY-MACHINE OPERATOR (pottery & porc.) alternate titles: jigger operator; pot maker
Operates pug mill, jigger machine, and drying chamber, that form, dry, and finish ceramic ware, such as bowls, cups, plates, and saucers: Adjusts and sets controls of pug mill that mixes, extrudes, cuts, and deposits clay charges in or over molds as specified. Installs shaping tool in head of jiggering unit, using handtools. Sets controls to regulate temperature of drying chamber. Installs trimming tools and abrasives on arms of ware-finishing unit, using handtools. Starts machine unit and conveyors and observes lights and gauges on panelboard to verify operational efficiency. Examines finished ware for defects and measures dimensions, using rule and thickness gauge. Adjusts pressures, temperatures, and trimming tool settings as required. May operate jigger machine only and be designated Potter (pottery & porc.). May form urns and planters, using jolly, and be designated Jollier (pottery & porc.).
GOE: 06.02.08 STRENGTH: M GED: R3 M2 L2 SVP: 5 DLU: 77

774.384-010 INSPECTOR II (pottery & porc.)
Examines ceramic and porcelain products at various stages of manufacture for defects and adherence to standards: Examines ware surfaces for defects, such as pin marks, glaze runs, chips, cracks, mold marks, and deformities. Marks correctable defects with pencil, or finishes ware, using trimming tools, abrasives, and sponges. Feels edges (rims) and surfaces of ware with finger tips to detect rough spots. Smooths rough spots, using pumice stone or wet sponge and abrasive powder. Mixes ceramic and porcelain ingredients and examines mixture for foreign matter. May verify measurements of metal dies for machine forming presses, using calipers, gauges, and micrometers. Maintains records of test results, and prepares analysis of defect causes based on test results. May measure viscosity and specific gravity of mixed ceramic, porcelain, and glaze batches, using viscometer and volume device. May test durability of ware at prescribed temperatures, using electric oven. May conduct chipping test, using impact tester.
GOE: 06.03.01 STRENGTH: L GED: R2 M1 L1 SVP: 5 DLU: 82

774.684-010 BISQUE CLEANER (pottery & porc.) alternate titles: bisque finisher; bisque grader; grinder; scourer; scraper
Cleans and finishes bisque ware by hand preparatory to glazing: Examines ware for visible defects. Fills cracks, pinholes, and scratches with liquid clay, using brush. Grinds down rough spots with abrasive stones, smooths ware surfaces with sandpaper, and cleans ware with airhose. Holds surface of earthenware against sanding wheel to remove warps, grog (clay fragments), and scratches. Verifies dimensional accuracy of ware to ensure correct fit of lids on such items as compotes and teapots, using templates. Discards substandard pieces.
GOE: 06.04.30 STRENGTH: L GED: R2 M1 L1 SVP: 4 DLU: 77

774.684-014 DIPPER (pottery & porc.)
Dips bisque ware, ceramic tile, or greenware in solution to cover article with protective glaze: Grasps article with tongs or fingers and dips it in tub of glaze solution. Twists and turns article to spread glaze over surface and shakes off excess. Sets article on rack to dry. Rubs glaze over missed areas, using fingers. May pour glaze on ceramic tile or hold tile against roller to apply glaze. May clean edges of ceramic tile, using wire brush.
GOE: 06.02.30 STRENGTH: L GED: R3 M1 L1 SVP: 5 DLU: 77

774.684-018 FINISHER (pottery & porc.) alternate titles: fettler; shaper; sponger
Trims and smooths edges and surfaces of greenware preparatory to bisque firing: Trims excess clay from ware. Positions circular pieces, such as plates and cups, in center of whirler. Starts whirler revolving and moves variousshaped knives over ware surface, following contours of piece, to remove rough spots and mold marks. Smooths ware surfaces, using abrasive cloth, felt, and moist sponge. May be designated according to type of ware finished as Flatwork Finisher (pottery & porc.). May finish handles preparatory to joining them to such ware as cups and be designated Handle Finisher (pottery & porc.).

GOE: 06.04.30 STRENGTH: L GED: R2 M1 L1 SVP: 4 DLU: 81

774.684-022 HANDLER (pottery & porc.) alternate titles: handle sticker; sticker

Attaches handles and knobs to cups and other greenware preparatory to bisque firing: Trims ends of handle to fit ware. Dips ends of handle in slip (semiliquid clay) and presses handle onto clay piece in position specified. Trims and smooths joint, using handtools and wet sponge. May finish ware before attaching handles [FINISHER (pottery & porc.)].
GOE: 06.02.30 STRENGTH: L GED: R3 M1 L1 SVP: 5 DLU: 77

774.684-026 PLASTER-DIE MAKER (pottery & porc.) alternate titles: ram-die maker

Casts plaster dies for hydraulic ram press that forms pottery ware: Places wire mesh over die face of master model and presses or taps mesh with wooden mallet to contour of model. Wires nonmetallic conduit to wire mesh. Removes wire mesh assembly and sponges soap solution on model surface to separate die halves after casting. Lowers steel die rings over outside rim of each half of model and places wire mesh assembly over model face. Wires assembly to die rings. Mixes hydrostone (powdered plaster) with water and pours mixture into each half of model to top of die ring. Separates die from model and attaches airhose to die to remove water from dies. Sponges remaining moisture from dies. Places finished dies in storage rack.
GOE: 06.02.30 STRENGTH: H GED: R3 M1 L1 SVP: 5 DLU: 77

774.684-030 SAGGER MAKER (pottery & porc.)

Pounds clay over mold or frame to shape sagger sides and bottom, using maul: Lays pliable clay in circular or rectangular frame and pounds to shape to form of frame, using maul. Hammers slabs of clay over iron frame and cuts into strips to form sides, using knife. Folds strips around drum or wooden mold placed on prepared bottom to form sagger sides. Wets ends of strip and applies hand pressure to join. Plucks spare clay off bottom to fasten to sides, using wooden plucking tool. Smooths surface, using knife and wooden paddle and removes mold. Places sagger in drying room.
GOE: 06.04.30 STRENGTH: M GED: R2 M1 L1 SVP: 3 DLU: 77

774.684-034 STICKER-ON (nonmet. min.)

Attaches clay arms to clay figurines by wetting shoulders of figurine with sponge, and dipping tops of arms into wet clay and pressing them onto shoulders. Washes off excess clay to smooth joints, using syringe. Removes clay from between fingers of figurine, using hooked tool.
GOE: 06.04.30 STRENGTH: L GED: R2 M1 L1 SVP: 2 DLU: 77

774.684-038 TURNER (pottery & porc.)

Shapes green (unfired) clayware, using lathe: Positions clayware on lathe, starts machine, and guides edge of handtool against revolving ware until ware object is trimmed to specified shape and size. May verify accuracy of shape and dimensions of object, using calipers and templates.
GOE: 06.02.30 STRENGTH: M GED: R3 M2 L2 SVP: 6 DLU: 77

774.684-042 WARE DRESSER (pottery & porc.) alternate titles: back grinder; back polisher

Dresses and polishes glazed and decorated ware and segregates ware into standard grades: Chips pin marks from bottom of ware with dressing iron. Grinds down dressed spots and other defects, such as glaze droplets, kiln dirt, and color spots, using grinding wheel. Polishes dressed ware, using power buffer. Verifies shape and dimensional accuracy of ware, using templates. Segregates pieces into standard grades according to number and type of defects in form, color, and uniformity of glaze coverage.
GOE: 06.04.30 STRENGTH: L GED: R3 M1 L1 SVP: 4 DLU: 77

774.684-046 PATCHER (pottery & porc.)

Fills holes and attaches parts to greenware ceramic figures prior to firing: Breaks off pieces of clay of matching color used to patch greenware, and fills holes formed during casting. Applies water to clay, and shapes clay to contour of greenware, using handtools. Forms holes in greenware at designated locations to vent steam created during firing. Applies wet clay to designated locations on greenware, and attaches clay parts, such as heads, arms, legs, or musical instruments, to complete greenware figures. Smooths clay used to attach parts to figure. Inserts wire in specified greenware to form legs and feet, and adjusts wires to level greenware. Counts greenware and records total on forms for production records. Places greenware on trays, covers greenware with towels or sponge pads, and places trays on racks to await further processing.
GOE: 06.04.30 STRENGTH: L GED: R2 M1 L1 SVP: 3 DLU: 86

774.687-010 BISQUE GRADER (pottery & porc.)

Sorts, selects, inspects, and stamps bisque ware; and fills orders: Sorts ware according to size. Taps pieces with trimming iron to detect cracks and selects sound pieces for underglaze decoration. Rejects cracked and malformed pieces. May sort ware into first and second grades. Stamps trademark or other inscription on bottom of ware with rubber stamp.
GOE: 06.03.02 STRENGTH: L GED: R3 M2 L3 SVP: 3 DLU: 77

774.687-014 LACER (nonmet. min.)

Attaches lace decorations to clay figurines prior to baking: Cuts specified length of lace with scissors, dips it in clay, and presses it lightly onto figure, arranging it with pointed stick.
GOE: 06.04.30 STRENGTH: S GED: R2 M1 L1 SVP: 2 DLU: 77

774.687-018 PRINT INSPECTOR (pottery & porc.) alternate titles: decorator inspector

Inspects printed decoration on pottery and porcelain ware: Compares printed decoration and quality of workmanship of ware with sample and discards mis-

printed ware. Returns salvageable pieces for rework. Rubs ware with abrasive stone or wet sponge to remove paint spots.
GOE: 06.03.02 STRENGTH: L GED: R3 M1 L1 SVP: 4 DLU: 77

774.687-022 WARE CLEANER (pottery & porc.) alternate titles: finisher

Smooths surface of pressed, cast, or glaze-dipped clay products to remove flash, cracks, and loose material, using fingers, pick knife, sponge, or sandpaper: Trims soft flash or picks loose clay from indentations of cast or pressed clay products, using pick knife and wet sponge. Smooths hardened surface, using sandpaper. Wipes fingers over glazed surfaces to distribute glaze evenly over checks and cracks prior to firing. Wipes excess glaze solution from dipped article, using rags, wet sponge, or suction device.
GOE: 06.04.30 STRENGTH: L GED: R2 M1 L1 SVP: 2 DLU: 77

774.687-026 TESTER (pottery & porc.)

Tests toilet bowls for compliance with company standards, using any of following methods: (1) Positions water tank suspended from overhead rail over water inlet of toilets, and pulls lever to lower water tank gasket onto water inlet of bowls preparatory to flushing. Places rags in bowls and pulls handle of water tank to force water into bowls and flush rags through flush channels. Removes rags caught on obstructions or rough surfaces, using plunger. Marks bowls requiring smoothing of flush channels, using grease pencil. (2) Tips bowls, inserts tip of squeeze bottle containing dye into specified hole in base of bowls, and squirts dye into opening to detect leaks in bowls. Marks bowls to indicate leaks. (3) Places level in several directions across rim of bowls and observes bubble of level to determine levelness of bowls. Marks bowls to indicate need for further grinding of bowl base. Removes defective bowls from conveyor line for further processing. When using dye to test bowls, may be designated Dye Tester (pottery & porc.); or when flush testing, may be designated Flush Tester (pottery & porc.).
GOE: 06.03.02 STRENGTH: H GED: R2 M1 L1 SVP: 2 DLU: 86

775 GRINDING, FILING, POLISHING, FROSTING, ETCHING, CLEANING, AND RELATED OCCUPATIONS, N.E.C.

This group includes occupations concerned with grinding, filing, polishing, frosting, etching, cleaning, and similar working of sand, stone, clay, and glass products.

775.130-010 SUPERVISOR, FINISHING (glass mfg.)

Supervises and coordinates activities of workers engaged in grinding and polishing pressed or blown glassware: Inspects products for defects and adherence to specifications. Directs or assists workers in machine setup and operating techniques. Requisitions materials and supplies. Performs other duties as described under SUPERVISOR (any industry) Master Title. May be designated according to department supervised as Supervisor, Crack-Off (glass mfg.); Supervisor, Grinding (glass mfg.); Supervisor, Polishing (glass mfg.).
GOE: 06.02.01 STRENGTH: L GED: R4 M3 L3 SVP: 8 DLU: 77

775.131-010 SUPERVISOR, CONCRETE-STONE FINISHING (concrete prod.)

Supervises and coordinates activities of workers engaged in repairing, etching, and polishing ornamental stone-faced or plain surfaced concrete products. Demonstrates methods of troweling, dry brushing, and acid etching. Inspects work for quality, quantity, and size. Performs duties as described under SUPERVISOR (any industry) Master Title.
GOE: 05.05.01 STRENGTH: L GED: R4 M3 L3 SVP: 7 DLU: 77

775.134-010 CUTTING SUPERVISOR (glass products)

Supervises and coordinates activities of workers engaged in cutting flat glass or mirrors to customer specifications. Cuts and finishes plywood patterns according to blueprints for use by GLASS CUTTER (any industry). Trains new workers in glass cutting techniques. Performs other duties as described under SUPERVISOR (any industry) Master Title.
GOE: 06.02.01 STRENGTH: M GED: R4 M4 L3 SVP: 6 DLU: 77

775.281-010 SURFACE-PLATE FINISHER (stonework)

Inspects surface of stone plates to determine areas requiring lapping, and levels stone surface to specified tolerance for use as surface plates: Builds bed of timbers on floor beneath head of lapping machine. Positions stone on timbers, using hoist. Aligns stone with arm of lapping machine and levels stone on timbers, using wedges, blocks, and spirit level. Moves straightedge over stone to detect uneven areas on stone surface. Wets stone surface, using hose, and applies abrasive to stone, using brush. Selects lapping block (metal or stone) according to uniformity of stone surface or step in finishing process. Lifts block onto stone, using hoist. Secures block to arm of lapping machine, using wrench. Starts machine and presses buttons to guide spinning block over uneven areas of stone surface. Moves tolerance dial indicator through specified patterns on stone and observes dial to detect tolerance deviations. Changes lapping blocks according to readings from tolerance dial indicator and laps surface down to level finish. Laps stone by hand to level surface to specified tolerance. Sights through convex lens of collimator at specified positions on stone surface to determine whether surface plate has been finished within prescribed limitations of accuracy and determine tolerance deviation of plate's surface. Prepares graph of collimator readings, indicating tolerance deviation at any point on surface of plate. Drills adapter holes in surface plate to facilitate attachment of measuring instruments, using diamond drill.

775.684-050 MARK-UP DESIGNER (glass mfg.)
Lays out and cuts stencils and traces designs on glassware for etching or grinding: Sketches design on cardboard with drafting instruments, following blueprints. Cuts out designs along lines, using razor blade or knife. Positions stencil on glass and brushes stenciling ink over stencil to transfer design onto glass or positions glass over stencil and traces design on glass with china-marking pencil or brush pen. Draws freehand design on glass when limited number of one design is to be etched or ground. May immerse glassware in acid bath before tracing design.
GOE: 06.02.31 STRENGTH: M GED: R3 M2 L3 SVP: 3 DLU: 77

775.684-054 PATCH SANDER (stonework)
Sands repaired areas of sandstone table and counter tops, using portable sander and sandpaper: Moves portable sander equipped with abrasive disc across patched area of stone top down to level of stone. Feels and examines sanded area to detect rough areas and sands patched sections, using sandpaper. Replaces abrasive disc on portable sander, using wrench.
GOE: 06.04.30 STRENGTH: M GED: R1 M1 L1 SVP: 2 DLU: 77

775.684-058 POLISHER (glass mfg.; glass products)
Polishes edges or surfaces of flat glass, using polishing wheels: Pours polishing compound into hopper of automatic feeder or applies compound to polishing wheel with brush. Holds and turns glass edge or engraved or beveled surface against white (cork) polishing wheel for rough polishing. Presses glass edge, or scratched, engraved, or beveled surface against felt polishing wheel for final polishing or to remove scratches. Wipes polished area and examines glass for smoothness. May be designated according to area polished as Edge Polisher (glass products); Engravings Polisher (glass products); Scratch Polisher (glass products).
GOE: 06.04.30 STRENGTH: H GED: R2 M1 L1 SVP: 4 DLU: 77

775.684-062 WATCH-CRYSTAL EDGE GRINDER (glass products) alternate titles: edge grinder, machine
Grinds edges of watch-crystal blanks, using abrasive wheel: Places blank on die of specified size and clamps die and blank in chuck. Starts grinding wheel and adjusts flow of water on wheel. Holds blank against wheel and grinds it until die is stopped by guide. Rotates blank and die until all edges are ground.
GOE: 06.04.30 STRENGTH: S GED: R2 M1 L2 SVP: 4 DLU: 77

775.685-010 CUTTING-MACHINE TENDER, DECORATIVE (glass mfg.)
Tends automatic cutting machine that cuts designs in glassware. Depresses pedal to raise holding fixture and places glassware in fixture. Pushes button to index fixture to cutting stations which cut designs in glassware. Removes finished glassware and places it in tray.
GOE: 06.04.08 STRENGTH: L GED: R2 M1 L1 SVP: 2 DLU: 77

775.687-010 FINISHER (nonmet. min.)
Finishes surfaces of plaster castings, such as lamp bases, statues, figurines, and architectural ornaments, by patching holes in chipped places, using spatula. Removes excess plaster, using scraping tool, and smooths surface of casting with damp sponge, steelwool, or sandpaper. Attaches member parts, such as horns, to figurines, using fresh plaster to moisten surface and pressing parts onto figurine. May deepen defect or mar surface of article to impart antiqued appearance.
GOE: 06.04.30 STRENGTH: M GED: R2 M1 L1 SVP: 2 DLU: 77

775.687-014 GLASS DRILLER (glass mfg.)
Drills premarked holes in glass lampshades for attachment of frames or fixtures, using electric hand drill.
GOE: 06.04.30 STRENGTH: L GED: R2 M1 L2 SVP: 2 DLU: 77

775.687-018 GLASS-CUTTER HELPER (any industry)
Assists GLASS CUTTER (any industry) in cutting and handling glass or mirrors: Carries glass or mirrors to worktable and places cutting tools on table. Removes excess glass from working area. Measures layout dimensions, using tape measure, and counts cut glass or mirrors to verify measurements and quantity cut. Performs other duties as described under HELPER (any industry) Master Title.
GOE: 06.04.30 STRENGTH: H GED: R2 M1 L2 SVP: 3 DLU: 77

775.687-022 GOLD BURNISHER (pottery & porc.)
Rubs hollowware with burnishing brush or polishing cloth to polish gold band or trim. Mounts flatware on rotating spindle and applies pressure to ware surface with burnishing brush to polish it. Examines and discards defective pieces. May rub surface of ware with rag or steelwool to remove excess paint and produce antiqued appearance.
GOE: 06.04.24 STRENGTH: S GED: R2 M1 L1 SVP: 2 DLU: 77

776 OCCUPATIONS IN FABRICATION AND REPAIR OF ASBESTOS AND POLISHING PRODUCTS, ABRASIVES, AND RELATED MATERIALS

This group includes occupations concerned with such activities as blending, coating, cutting, gluing, and forming asbestos and polishing products, abrasives, and related materials.

776.487-010 GRINDING-WHEEL INSPECTOR (nonmet. min.)
Inspects and tests finished grinding wheels for adherence to specifications: Inserts spindle in wheel, and mounts spindle on tripod. Spins wheel and examines it for defects, such as heavy spots, uneven faces, and cracks. Measures diameter and width of wheel, using calipers and tape measure. Mounts wheel on machine that spins it at specified number of revolutions per minute to test it for cracks and soft spots. Weighs wheels on balance scale and stacks them in pile according to grade and weight. Marks defective wheels to be refinished or discarded. May record number, size, and type of wheels inspected.
GOE: 06.03.01 STRENGTH: M GED: R3 M2 L2 SVP: 4 DLU: 77

776.667-010 INSPECTOR (nonmet. min.) alternate titles: inspector, brake lining
Inspects asbestos brake linings for defects: Examines linings for cracks, blisters, and other imperfections to ensure adherence to specifications. Measures width and thickness of linings to ensure attainment of specified tolerances, using calipers or other measuring devices. Discusses discrepancies with machine operators or supervisory personnel and keeps record of rejects. May determine resistance of lining stock to surface abrasion, using hardness testing device.
GOE: 06.03.02 STRENGTH: L GED: R3 M2 L3 SVP: 4 DLU: 77

776.684-010 BELT MAKER (nonmet. min.) alternate titles: sleeve maker; sleeve wheel maker
Cuts and glues sandpaper to form cylindrical sleeves or endless belts for sanding drums or machines: Inserts paper of specified width and grit in bench fixture and cuts it to length, using knife and guide bar. Presses ends of paper against grinding wheel to remove grit and form smooth margin for lapping and gluing. Spreads glue on ends and overlaps them to form cylindrical sleeves or endless belts. Presses glued ends in lever press to set glue.
GOE: 06.04.34 STRENGTH: M GED: R2 M1 L2 SVP: 2 DLU: 77

776.684-014 POLISHING-WHEEL SETTER (any industry) alternate titles: wheel setter
Replaces worn abrasive surface on leather or felt polishing wheels, canvas belts, and metal or fiber disks, and balances wheels: Immerses wheel or disk in solution to soften glue. Mounts wheel on electrically driven, pedestal-mounted spindle, using wrench, and holds pumice stone against rotating wheel to remove compacted abrasive. Rubs fingers over wheel surface to detect abrasive fragments. Brushes binding agent on wheel or disk. Rolls wheel in tray of abrasive powder or sprinkles powder over disk to cover surface with abrasive. Pounds wheel or disk with wooden block to force abrasive into binding agent. Centers wheel on static balancer to locate placement for lead weight to balance wheel. Removes lead weight from heavy side of wheel or nails counterweight to opposite side to balance wheel.
GOE: 05.10.04 STRENGTH: M GED: R2 M1 L2 SVP: 3 DLU: 77 .

776.687-010 BELT-MAKER HELPER (nonmet. min.)
Assists in forming and packaging abrasive belts, performing any combination of following tasks: Brushes adhesive onto splice lap area of end of abrasive-coated strip and holds end of strip in position on press bed. Helps to wind abrasive belts into compact coil, by hand, and wraps coil in moistureproof plastic film, places plastic-wrapped coils in boxes, and seals boxes with tape. Inserts metal spindle through core of roll of abrasive-coated material, hooks overhead hoist chains to ends and moves roll along rail from storage to work area. Presses hoist control button to lower roll, positioning spindle on rack.
GOE: 06.04.38 STRENGTH: L GED: R1 M1 L1 SVP: 1 DLU: 77

777 MODELMAKERS, PATTERNMAKERS, MOLDMAKERS, AND RELATED OCCUPATIONS

This group includes occupations concerned with building clay or plaster models and patterns of one-of-a-kind or mass-produced products made of metallic or plaster materials; and making molds used in casting or forming such items as three-dimensional maps, trophies, or jewelry.

777.081-010 MODELER (brick & tile)
Molds from plaster of paris original models for special designs in decorative tile, such as fountains and waterspouts, sculpturing model by cutting, scraping, and finishing. May construct wooden molds for use in casting original clay models, using carpenter's handtools, or may supervise CARPENTER, MOLD (brick & tile; concrete prod.) in preparing wooden molds from original models.
GOE: 01.06.02 GED: R4 M4 L4 SVP: 5 DLU: 77

777.131-010 SUPERVISOR, MOLD SHOP (pottery & porc.)
Supervises and coordinates activities of workers engaged in casting plaster dies and block, case, and production molds used to form ceramic pottery ware: Examines design sketches and production schedules to determine type of plaster models to be formed and quantities of production dies and molds to be cast. Inspects completed products for accuracy of dimensions, fitting, and alignment, and presence of surface defects, using dial indicators, gauges, calipers, and rules. Trains new workers in preparing plaster batches to specified consistency, handling and storing dies and molds to avoid surface damages, and verifying dimensions with aid of precision instruments. Assists workers in solving problems in casting and finishing products with aid of blocks, trimming knives, hand scrapers, and wet sponges. Performs other duties as described under SUPERVISOR (any industry) Master Title.
GOE: 06.01.01 STRENGTH: M GED: R4 M3 L3 SVP: 8 DLU: 77

777.261-010 MODEL MAKER I (any industry)
Constructs scale model of objects: Builds and molds models, using clay, metal, wood, fiberglass, other substance, depending on industry for which

model is constructed, such as ship and boat building or automobile manufacturing.
GOE: 01.06.02 STRENGTH: L GED: R5 M3 L3 SVP: 7 DLU: 77

777.281-010 CONCRETE SCULPTOR (concrete prod.)
Constructs models and molds for use in casting concrete garden furniture and statuary: Constructs metal armature for use as framework to support figure while modeling. Shapes model, following drawings or pictures, by modeling clay with hands and handtools. Brushes successive coats of rubber paint on clay model to form cast. Covers cast with layers of fiberglass to form shield. Cuts hardened fiberglass shield in sections with hand or power tools and removes shield from model. Removes rubber cast from clay model by peeling or cutting into sections. Reassembles sections of fiberglass shield around rubber cast and fills cast with concrete.
GOE: 01.06.02 STRENGTH: H GED: R4 M2 L2 SVP: 7 DLU: 77

777.281-014 MODEL MAKER (pottery & porc.) alternate titles: modeler; patternmaker
Constructs model of particular piece of ware to be used in casting molds: Forms model by carving it from plaster or from clay or both, or by shaping material with hands as it revolves on spinning table [THROWER (pottery & porc.)], or by shaving it with steel cutting tools as it revolves [TURNER (pottery & porc.)].
GOE: 01.06.02 STRENGTH: M GED: R4 M3 L2 SVP: 7 DLU: 77

777.281-018 PATTERNMAKER, PLASTER (aircraft mfg.) alternate titles: loft patternmaker; model maker, plaster and plastic; patternmaker, plaster and plastic
Plans, lays out, and constructs master full-scale models, forms, mockups, check jigs, and plaster patterns for casting master tooling used in manufacturing aeronautical and aerospace products, utilizing knowledge of plaster patternmaking, metal forming, and foundry practices and procedures, using precision instruments, tools, and equipment: Studies engineering tool design data, loft information, and blueprints to determine sequence of operations and to develop layout for constructing master model. Lays out, locates, and aligns steel skeletons and master contour templates on surface table or other base structure to form model frame, using precision measuring instruments and devices, such as micrometers, calipers, and transit. Forms plaster over template frame and hand finishes plaster to peripheral dimensions of contour templates, using scrapers, fairing tools, and other handtools. Verifies finished dimensions of master model, using precision instruments. Scribes butt, water, and station lines on master model to establish location points, reference lines, and contours for subsequent pattern casting. Casts plaster pattern (splash) from sections of master model, and recasts pattern to produce working patterns of contour templates, check templates, and related tooling. May fabricate master patterns, jigs, templates, or mockups from materials other than plaster, such as wax, plastic, and fiberglass. May cut out and fabricate flat contour templates from engineering or loft information.
GOE: 06.01.04 STRENGTH: M GED: R4 M4 L4 SVP: 7 DLU: 88

777.361-010 EAR-MOLD LABORATORY TECHNICIAN (plastic prod.)
Makes wax pattern of ear and molds plastic impression of ear for use in hearing aids, using handtools, grinder, and polishing wheels: Forms red designing wax into shape of ear, using spatulas, brushes, and gas burner. Mixes ingredients to make plaster and pours it over wax pattern to form plaster mold of ear. Removes plaster mold from wax pattern. Mixes ingredients to make plastic compound and pours it into plaster mold to form impression of ear. Applies hot and cold water and air to mold to harden plastic liquid in cavity of mold. Removes rough casting of ear from mold. Grinds and polishes casting to obtain plastic ear impression, using electric grinder and polishing wheels. Examines impression for blemishes, and places it in box for shipment.
GOE: 05.05.11 STRENGTH: M GED: R4 M3 L2 SVP: 7 DLU: 77

777.381-010 MODEL MAKER, FIBERGLASS (concrete prod.)
Makes fiberglass model or molds for casting concrete products: Brushes wax on model to prevent adhesion of fiberglass. Lays up fiberglass on top of model to form mold, building layers of resin and fiberglass around model for smooth, hard finish. Constructs and repairs wooden molds, using carpenter tools.
GOE: 01.06.02 STRENGTH: M GED: R4 M3 L3 SVP: 8 DLU: 77

777.381-014 MODEL-AND-MOLD MAKER (brick & tile)
Forms plaster models from drawings or blueprints, and constructs molds from model to cast brick or tile products: Mixes water and powder or catalytic compound, and clay, according to specifications, to form plaster. Places plaster on worktable. Cuts, shapes, and finishes plaster according to model specifications, using knife, strips of wood, and fingers. Pours measured amount of plaster into wooden mold form. Coats dry model with soap solution to facilitate removal. Places model into wet plaster to form hand of mold. Removes model from hardened half mold and repeats process to form completed mold.
GOE: 01.06.02 STRENGTH: L GED: R4 M2 L2 SVP: 6 DLU: 77

777.381-018 MODEL-AND-MOLD MAKER, PLASTER (concrete prod.)
Makes plaster models or molds for casting concrete products, such as cornices, panels, and grave markers: Lays out profile of product on sheet metal, following working drawings or blueprints. Cuts out template of profile, using hand shears, and nails template to wood guide, to make modeling frame. Mixes water and plaster to required consistency in tub, using paddle. Brushes liquid soap on modeling frame to prevent adhesion of plaster. Scoops up mixed plas-

ter and places it on modeling frame. Builds up layers of plaster and reinforcing hemp, allowing time for hardening between layers, and pushes template across built up material to remove excess plaster and form model or mold to required dimensions. Cuts off sections of hardened model or mold, using saw. Lays out sections to form mold pattern and cements sections together with burnt shellac. Fills joints or defects with plaster and smooths plaster with hands and molding tools. May make sectional mold impressions of existing models. May make molds or models of clay. May be designated according to specialty as Model Maker, Plaster (concrete prod.); Mold Maker, Plaster (concrete prod.).
GOE: 01.06.02 STRENGTH: L GED: R4 M3 L3 SVP: 7 DLU: 77

777.381-022 MOLD MAKER II (jewelry-silver.)
Fabricates plaster molds from models of jewelry articles and trophy figurines preparatory to casting metal molds: Presses one side of model into clay. Builds up clay around exposed half of model to retain plaster. Mixes plaster powder with water and pours it around exposed half of model to form mold. Allows plaster to set and removes clay and model from plaster mold. Brushes loose particles from mold and applies shellac to preserve mold and to prevent absorption of moisture. Covers surfaces of mold with dry bone powder to prevent shellacked surface from sticking in sand mold.
GOE: 06.01.04 STRENGTH: L GED: R3 M1 L2 SVP: 7 DLU: 77

777.381-034 PLASTER MOLDER I (foundry) alternate titles: patternmaker, pressure cast
Lays out parting line on patterns and casts plaster molds according to blueprints, sketches, and oral instructions, applying knowledge of metal characteristics, pattern contours, and pouring procedures: Locates and scribes parting line on wood, metal, or plastic patterns, using measuring instruments, such as calipers, square, depth gauge, and straightedge. Mixes plaster powder and water according to standard formula. Places cope and drag (upper and lower half of flask) on molding table. Pours liquid plaster into drag and positions pattern in plaster up to parting line. Removes excess plaster, using straightedge, and allows mold to harden. Places cope on completed drag, and makes depressions in plaster around drag pattern to ensure accurate joining of mold halves for casting. Brushes parting agent on surfaces of mold, pattern, and flask and pours liquid plaster into cope. Separates cope and drag after specified time and removes pattern. Repairs cracks and broken edges of molds, using molder's handtools, such as spoon, trowel, and slick. Removes excess plaster from molds, using knife or bandsaw. Joins cope and drag sections of mold together by aligning them in flask and pouring liquid plaster over them. May cut gates and risers into baked mold. May position cores in drag and assemble mold. May pour molten metal into molds, using hand ladle.
GOE: 06.02.30 STRENGTH: M GED: R4 M3 L3 SVP: 7 DLU: 77

777.381-038 PLASTER-PATTERN CASTER (machine tools) alternate titles: loft patternmaker
Casts and finishes plaster patterns used in making precision sand molds for dies, tools, and machine parts, according to specifications: Constructs boxlike enclosure around part to be cast, filling in cracks and openings with clay. Lubricates surface with parting agent that prevents plaster from sticking to part. Mixes plaster and pours it into enclosure. Reinforces plaster with hemp fiber and small steel rods or heavy wire. Removes hardened plaster cast from enclosure. Patches broken edges and fractures, using clay or plaster. Trims plaster pattern to tolerance by scraping and shaping plaster surfaces by hand following blueprint, using flat metal scrapers. Verifies dimensions, using measuring instruments, such as calipers, vernier gauge, and protractor. Makes identifying marks on pattern with crayon, inked rubber stamps, or pointed tool. Shellacs finished surfaces to harden and smooth them.
GOE: 01.06.02 STRENGTH: M GED: R4 M3 L3 SVP: 7 DLU: 77

777.381-042 RELIEF-MAP MODELER (any industry) alternate titles: three-dimensional-map modeler
Makes plaster relief-map models from which molds are prepared to produce duplicate scale models of land forms: Mixes plaster, water, and retarder in container. Punches holes in map's surface, using stippler or scorer so that plaster will adhere. Pours plaster over sea-level contour map, and spreads it evenly over surface with brush or spatula. Covers drainage, river, and city lines with transparent media or leaves border without plaster to preserve lines. Builds mound or elevation of plaster around spot elevation pins, leaving pinhead exposed. Observes printed lines indicating contour planes, and consults reference map to ascertain number, elevations, and shapes of contours to be built up with plaster. Pours and spreads plaster on contour planes of successively higher elevations. Fills with plaster angles formed by contour planes at two successive elevations to achieve natural and realistic surface appearance. Removes excess plaster and smooths surface of model with file and sandpaper.
GOE: 01.06.02 STRENGTH: L GED: R4 M3 L3 SVP: 6 DLU: 77

777.381-046 SAND TESTER (foundry) alternate titles: sand technologist
Tests sand to determine its usability for making sand molds or cores: Collects samples of sand mixes and compresses sand into sample piece, using specimen sand rammer. Determines properties of sand samples, such as moisture content, permeability, compression and shear strength, clay content, and sand-grain size and distribution, using sand-test equipment, such as moisture teller, permeability meter, sand-strength tester, and sieve set. May perform similar tests on ladle lining refractories. May test quality of incoming materials, such as cereal or core oils to be used in sand mixes by mixing and testing sand samples.

GOE: 06.01.05 STRENGTH: L GED: R3 M2 L2 SVP: 6 DLU: 77

777.684-010 FORM MAKER, PLASTER (plastic prod.) alternate titles: molder; slusher

Casts plaster patterns used in shaping plastic or plastic-impregnated materials: Brushes inside of mold sections with lubricant, and bolts sections together. Mixes specified amounts of plaster and water in mixing machine. Pours plaster into mold and positions mold in machine that rolls mold to distribute mixture evenly and facilitate drying. Repeats operation, after each layer of plaster has set, to build casting to specified thickness. Removes bolts from mold and pries sections apart, using bar. Removes fins and flanges from pattern, using scraper. Fills bubble holes and smooths uneven surfaces with wet plaster. Places pattern in drying room to cure. May coat pattern with sealing lacquer.
GOE: 06.02.30 STRENGTH: H GED: R3 M2 L2 SVP: 4 DLU: 77

777.684-014 MOLD MAKER (nonmet. min.)

Constructs molds used for casting plaster objects, such as ashtrays, plaques, figurines, and statuary, using wet plaster, treated fiberglass, or liquid rubber: Covers model of object from which mold is to be made with lubricant to prevent mold from sticking to model. Immerses portion of model in container of wet plaster to make half of mold and allows plaster to harden. Immerses other half of model to complete mold. Makes section of fiberglass mold by covering portion of model with layers of fiberglass treated to harden when allowed to set. Allows fiberglass to harden and repeats process, covering other portions of model until mold is complete. Sprays liquid rubber over model to make rubber mold, using spray gun. Allows rubber to harden and pulls model from rubber mold. Removes mold sections of plaster or fiberglass mold form. Bores holes in edges of sections of mold for insertion of bolts to hold sections together, using power drill, or binds sections together with cord. Smooths surfaces of mold, using scraping tool and sandpaper.
GOE: 06.02.30 STRENGTH: L GED: R3 M1 L2 SVP: 5 DLU: 77

777.684-018 MOLD MAKER (pottery & porc.) alternate titles: block and case maker; blocker; caser

Casts plaster block molds, case molds, and working molds used in forming pottery ware, using models, clay, and plaster: Places model in clay with upper half of model exposed. Brushes soap solution on exposed half of model. Places wooden form around model or builds up wooden box sides. Mixes plaster and pours it over exposed half of model to form one half of block mold. Allows plaster to harden, removes wooden box sides, and turns mold over, leaving model in plaster mold. Removes clay, smooths surface of mold, using knife and scrapers and applies soap solution. Replaces box sides around mold and pours in plaster to form other half of block mold. Casts case mold in similar manner, using block mold as pattern.
GOE: 06.02.30 STRENGTH: H GED: R3 M1 L2 SVP: 6 DLU: 78

779 OCCUPATIONS IN FABRICATION AND REPAIR OF SAND, STONE, CLAY, AND GLASS PRODUCTS, N.E.C.

This group includes occupations, not elsewhere classified, concerned with fabricating and repairing sand, stone, clay, and glass products.

779.131-010 SUPERVISOR I (nonmet. min.)

Supervises and coordinates activities of workers engaged in molding, casting, and finishing plaster statuary, plaques, and other art objects. Performs duties as described under SUPERVISOR (any industry) Master Title.
GOE: 01.06.02 STRENGTH: L GED: R4 M3 L3 SVP: 8 DLU: 77

779.281-010 CLAY MODELER (any industry)

Molds full-sized or scale models of products, such as automobiles, automobile parts, television sets, radios, washers, refrigerators, caskets, or boats from clay following artist's sketches or from verbal instructions: Builds rough lumber form to fit around model or centers preformed lath-covered wood frame on grid platform. Kneads clay into slots between laths so clay will adhere to frame. Molds clay by hand to approximate shape. Pulls sheet aluminum forming tool over surface of clay to shape areas that have constant cross sections. Shapes sculptured surfaces, using various types of sculptor's tools and scrapers. Verifies uniformity and smoothness of curved surfaces with splines and sweeps. Scrapes clay from high areas and builds up and smooths low areas to attain desired shape. Cuts cardboard templates for use as guides to shape symmetrical sections. Takes measurements from completed half of model and duplicates them on unfinished half to make both sides symmetrical. Covers bumpers, lights, door handles, and other parts with aluminum foil to simulate chrome or colored glass.
GOE: 01.06.02 STRENGTH: L GED: R4 M3 L4 SVP: 7 DLU: 77

779.381-010 GLAZIER, STAINED GLASS (glass products) alternate titles: glazier artist

Selects and cuts colored glass for use in stained-glass windows in churches, memorials, and residences, following original pattern: Selects bits of glass of color, thickness, and texture that will yield color shade shown in original design. Selects and places one piece of glass over another (double-plating) if exact color cannot be found. Cuts glass according to various shapes of pattern pieces, using glasscutter. Assembles glass, according to design, and solders joints of lead stripping between glass pieces. May reinforce with steel rods. Repairs stained glass windows by replacing broken glass and straightening buck-

led sections. Repairs stained glass lamp shades by replacing broken glass and soldering joints of lead stripping. When assembling glass between lead strippings only, may be designated JOINER (glass prod.).
GOE: 01.06.02 STRENGTH: M GED: R4 M3 L3 SVP: 7 DLU: 77

779.381-014 MOSAIC WORKER (glass products; nonmet. min.)

Cuts, shapes, and sets blocks of colored glass, enamel, marble, or ceramic tile for installation on walls, ceilings, or panels or for use as table tops or decorative screens, according to specifications: Brushes glue over surface of manila paper on which sections of design have been drawn in reverse, according to full-size drawings and tile charts. Selects color and type of tile specified for section according to tile charts. Cuts or breaks tile to shape and size, using hand-cutters and hammer. Positions tile, finished-side down, on glue-covered paper, using fingers or tweezers. Applies completed tile sections to surface previously covered with mastic cement and removes manila paper. Applies colored cement grout to seal joints of tile after section has been installed and washes surface with damp cloth. May apply tile to wall, ceiling, or panels on which design has been drawn.
GOE: 01.06.02 STRENGTH: L GED: R3 M2 L2 SVP: 5 DLU: 77

779.381-018 REPAIRER, ART OBJECTS (any industry)

Repairs and restores objects of art, such as figurines and vases made of antique or fine porcelain, glass, or semiprecious stone: Fits together broken or otherwise marred pieces with wires and glue or other adhesive. Refinishes surfaces with lacquer or paint. Restores decorative patterns by repainting blemished lines or creating new designs.
GOE: 01.06.02 STRENGTH: S GED: R4 M3 L3 SVP: 7 DLU: 77

779.381-022 TRACER (construction; stonework) alternate titles: decorator

Lays out or traces lettering and designs on surface of marble and granite to prepare stone for cutting, using any of following methods: Positions stone on bench, stool, or floor with aid of other workers, hoist, or crane. (1) Lays paper bearing lettering and design on stone, centers paper and traces outline with stylus. (2) Lays out lettering with drafting instruments and sketches designs freehand, working to specifications. (3) Centers and pastes paper bearing lettering and design on face of stone.
GOE: 01.06.02 STRENGTH: H GED: R4 M3 L3 SVP: 7 DLU: 77

779.387-010 FINAL INSPECTOR (glass products)

Inspects defective glass or mirrors to determine salvageability: Examines glass or mirrors to determine extent of defect and routes product for repair, cutting to smaller size, or stripping of silver and paint. Writes replacement tickets for glass or mirror to be cut down or stripped. Marks area of mirror to be salvaged, using crayon or wax pencil. Measures mirror or glass to determine footage loss, using ruler. Records number of glass or mirror pieces replaced, type of glass and defect, size, and footage loss. May examine damaged mirrors returned by customers. May buff mirrors to remove scratches and surface defects, using portable buffing wheel and polishing compound.
GOE: 06.03.01 STRENGTH: M GED: R3 M2 L2 SVP: 5 DLU: 77

779.387-014 INSPECTOR I (concrete prod.)

Inspects finished plaster wallboard for conformance to specifications: Inspects sides, edges, and ends of wallbaord for surface defects. Measures length, width, and thickness, using rule and micrometer. Weighs sample on scale. Tests sample for hardness by penetrating board edge with knife. Cuts across board surface and observes peel-back of surface paper. Measures unabsorbed moisture in board, using moisture sensitive meter. Records quantity of board produced and number and types of rejects. May test hardness of wallboard, using hardness meter.
GOE: 06.03.01 STRENGTH: L GED: R3 M2 L2 SVP: 6 DLU: 77

779.584-010 PATTERNMAKER (glass products)

Lays out and cuts pattern pieces for stained-glass windows: Places cartoon (full-size working drawing) over pattern paper and traces *cutlines*, using stylus, to transfer cartoon to paper. Cuts out pattern pieces, using double-bladed pattern shears. Marks pattern part to indicate relative location in design, using pencil.
GOE: 06.02.31 STRENGTH: L GED: R3 M2 L2 SVP: 6 DLU: 77

779.681-010 MICA SPLITTER (mine & quarry) alternate titles: splitter

Splits mica to sheets of specified dimensions and trims defects from mica sheets, using knife: Measures thickness of mica sheets, using dial or caliper-type micrometer, to determine amount of mica to remove. Locates cleavage plane in mica and inserts point of knife between layers. Peels layers of mica from sheets to reduce thickness of sheets. Gauges mica sheets with micrometer to determine amount of mica to remove and to verify thickness of split sheets. Examines mica for defects, such as stains, cracks, or scale and trims defects, using knife. Deposits mica sheets into containers according to size and rejects sheets that fail to meet thickness specifications. Compares mica to templates of parts being produced and deposits mica in container according to part. May measure length of sheets with rule and trim excess mica from sheets, using scissors or knife. May rub edges of mica sheets over sandpaper-covered portion of worktable to locate cleavages in sheets.
GOE: 06.02.30 STRENGTH: S GED: R3 M2 L3 SVP: 4 DLU: 77

779.684-010 CEMENT FITTINGS MAKER (concrete prod.)

Casts concrete pipe sections to mold fittings, performing combination of following duties: Tamps concrete into steel molds and smooths edges, using trowel, to cast elbows, lids, or traps. Places fittings on pallets or shelves to harden

and adheres hardened sections to complete assembly. Dips hardened sections into grout (liquid cement) to facilitate waterproofing. Divides pipe sections, using saw, trowel, or hammer to form Y-shapes or T-shapes and seals joints with grout. Transports finished fittings to yard, using handtruck. Mixes grout and concrete. Cleans and lubricates molds. May prepare production records.
GOE: 06.04.32 STRENGTH: H GED: R2 M1 L2 SVP: 4 DLU: 77

779.684-014   CONCRETE-PIPE MAKER (concrete prod.) alternate titles: poured-pipe maker

Casts concrete pipes and manhole covers, performing any combination of following duties: Moves overhead crane to position steel mold sections reinforcing cage on pallet, and to insert mold core and pouring plate. Fastens mold sections together, using wrenches to tighten screw clamps and bolts and nuts. Positions manhole form into side of reinforcing cage and fastens manhole form with tie wire to provide side hole in manhole casting. Inserts pins through apertures in mold to form holes in casting for insertion of hoisting bar. Brushes or sprays mold and core with oil to prevent concrete from adhering. Positions concrete-filled pouring bucket over pouring plate on top of mold, using hoist. Strikes trip bar of bucket to release concrete onto pouring plate and into mold. Bolts pneumatic vibrator to mold, using wrench, and starts vibrator to settle concrete in mold; or presses switch to start vibrator and holds internal vibrator with worm drive tube submerged in concrete to compress concrete poured in mold. Places steam hoses inside filled mold, lowers curing box over mold with hoist or covers mold with canvas and allows steam to cure concrete. Dismantles mold and core after concrete has cured. Inserts and cements metal ladder rungs into precast holes inside manholes.
GOE: 06.04.32 STRENGTH: H GED: R2 M1 L2 SVP: 2 DLU: 78

779.684-018   FETTLER (brick & tile) alternate titles: tile edger

Grinds and sands ceramic products, such as clay slabs, refractory tiles, ceramic tiles, and bisque tiles to remove defects, press marks, or rough spots: Grinds, brushes, or scrapes surface of ceramic product to remove rough spots, press marks, and defects, using power grinder and wire or stiff brush. Smooths (fettles) edges and surface of product, using sandpaper or handstone. Discards broken or poorly pressed tile. Stacks ceramic tile or clay slates in specified pattern on boards, plates, trays, or in saggers. May measure dimensions of tile for conformance to specifications, using gauge. May tend machine that automatically fettles tile.
GOE: 06.04.30 STRENGTH: L GED: R2 M1 L1 SVP: 3 DLU: 78

779.684-022   GLASS CUTTER, OVAL OR CIRCULAR (glass mfg.)

Cuts sheet glass into oval or circular shapes, using cutting table equipped with manually guided cutting tool suspended above surface of glass: Adjusts cutter to produce specified shape and guides cutting tool, mounted on steel rod, over glass to score and cut surface.
GOE: 06.04.30 STRENGTH: M GED: R2 M1 L2 SVP: 3 DLU: 77

779.684-026   GLASS-LINED TANK REPAIRER (beverage) alternate titles: tank refinisher

Patches fractured glass linings of steel tanks used for storing beer: Crawls inside tank and locates fractured lining areas. Melts fractured area, using propane torch. Removes melted material with burning knife. Heats and dries cleaned area. Heats patching material in bucket to specified temperature and consistency, using torch. Applies hot liquid patching material with paint brush. Smooths material after it has set, using torch.
GOE: 05.10.01 STRENGTH: L GED: R3 M1 L2 SVP: 3 DLU: 77

779.684-030   INSPECTOR-REPAIRER, SANDSTONE (stonework)

Examines and repairs sandstone table and counter tops, using handtools: Examines and feels sandstone for defects, such as flaking or bubbles in paint, pits, cracks, and chipped areas, and for variations in surface texture. Sands top and edges of stone, using fine grit abrasive paper. Fills cracks and holes with stone cement to level of stone surface or to match corner or edge of stone, using spatula. Applies flame of propane torch to defective painted area to ensure adhesion of stone cement to painted surface. Reads blueprint specifications and verifies dimensions and location of holes in table and counter tops, using tape and micrometer.
GOE: 05.10.01 STRENGTH: V GED: R3 M2 L2 SVP: 3 DLU: 77

779.684-034   LEVEL-VIAL SEALER (cutlery-hrdwr.) alternate titles: capper

Rotates tips of alcohol-filled glass vials to be used in levels against pinpoint gas flame to melt glass and seal hole in tip. Taps sealed vials on wooden block to see if they will break.
GOE: 06.04.30 STRENGTH: S GED: R2 M1 L1 SVP: 2 DLU: 77

779.684-038   MIRROR SPECIALIST (glass products; wood prod., nec)

Performs any combination of following tasks involved in mirror production: Loads and unloads conveyors and feeds and off bears machines, such as washers, polishers, bevelers, edgers, and seamers. Cleans mirrors by hand with powdered pumice. Cuts fiberboard or plywood to size for mirror backs, using table saw. Rivets clips and hangers on fiberboard backs, using riveting machine. Drills holes in glass and unframed mirrors to accommodate bolts, screws, and cords, using single-spindle drilling machine. Folds prescored cartons and pads over form, inserts mirror, and closes and staples carton. Cuts lumber and assembles pieces to form boxes or crates, using handtools and power tools. Packs mirrors in excelsior-filled crates and labels and addresses them, using stencil. May install and fasten mirrors into prepared frames by nailing and gluing wood

blocks to frames around back of mirror and tacking wood or cardboard backs to blocks.
GOE: 06.04.08 STRENGTH: H GED: R2 M1 L1 SVP: 3 DLU: 77

779.684-042   PIPE FINISHER (brick & tile) alternate titles: corrugator; finisher

Finishes socket or spigot ends of green sewer pipe, using handtools: Aligns pipe on roller conveyor, bench, or stand. Trims socket, using hand or machine trimmers. Smooths inside and outside of barrel and overlap of spigot, using handtools, sponges, and water. Shines light inside of barrel and examines interior to detect defects or blisters. Bursts blisters with knife and patches defective area with clay. Coats outside of socket with grease, oil, or water to retard drying process, using hand applicator or swab.
GOE: 06.04.30 STRENGTH: M GED: R2 M1 L1 SVP: 3 DLU: 77

779.684-046   PLASTER MAKER (nonmet. min.) alternate titles: caster

Casts plaster art objects, such as statuary and plaques, using flexible molds: Assembles mold that consists of inner shell and outer casing. Mixes specified proportions of water and plaster, by hand or using mechanical mixer, and pours mixture into rubber mold. Shakes and squeezes mold to eliminate air bubbles, and smooths plaster mixture at mouth of mold, with spatula. Flexes mold to remove casting, when plaster has set. Places casting in oven to dry. May be designated according to object cast as Plaque Maker (nonmet. min.).
GOE: 06.02.30 STRENGTH: M GED: R3 M1 L2 SVP: 5 DLU: 77

779.684-050   PLASTIC MOLDER (fabrication, nec)

Constructs plastic segments of mannequins and display forms, using molds, liquid plastic, and glass fiber cloth: Brushes paste wax onto inside surfaces of mold halves to facilitate removal of molded form. Inserts aluminum fitting block corresponding to segment of form being constructed into recess of mold. Brushes coat of liquid plastic onto inside surfaces of mold halves. Lays strips of glass fiber mesh on surface of mold cavity and fastens ends of strips to inside projections of fitting blocks. Brushes liquid resin adhesive over glass fiber strips. Builds up form to specified thickness with alternate layers of glass fiber strips and adhesive. Sprinkles chopped glass fiber particles on built-up area and applies final coat of liquid adhesive. Clamps halves of mold together and places it on rack to dry. Removes dried form from mold and places it on rack for finishing.
GOE: 06.02.32 STRENGTH: L GED: R3 M1 L2 SVP: 3 DLU: 77

779.684-054   SECOND CUTTER (glass mfg.) alternate titles: glass breaker; glass cutter, hand

Cuts glass sheets by hand to reduce sheets to specified dimensions or eliminate blemishes: Examines sheet of glass for defects, such as breaks, chips, scratches, and blisters. Scores kerf on glass surface, using T-square and cutting tool. Breaks scored sheet into specified sizes by use of pincers or by snapping kerf over crossbar. Places defective glass in cullet (waste glass) bin. Measures and scores glass sheet into standard size plates, using ruler and glass-cutting wheel or splitter (diamond cutting tool). Breaks off plates and places them on racks. Works as member of two-person team when cutting at discharge end of lehr. May be designated according to work area as Lehr Cutter (glass mfg.); Warehouse Cutter (glass mfg.).
GOE: 06.04.30 STRENGTH: M GED: R2 M2 L2 SVP: 3 DLU: 77

779.684-058   STONE REPAIRER (stonework) alternate titles: sticker

Mends broken marble slabs to restore them to usable condition, using either of following methods: (1) Cleans broken surfaces with wire brush. Heats surfaces with gas torch. Smears shellac evenly over heated surfaces from stick while playing torch flame on stick to thoroughly melt shellac. Presses broken surfaces of slabs tightly together and wipes surplus shellac from joint. Clamps sections together and allows shellac to dry. May drill holes into opposing surfaces of broken slab sections with drill press or portable electric drill and join broken slab sections with dowel pins in addition to shellac. (2) Lays broken grooved sections of slab wrong side up on bench and fits them together. Heats marble along groove with blowtorch. Inserts sulfur-coated steel rod to completely fill groove (sulfur expands during cooling to lock rod in groove). Scrapes off excess sulfur and allows joint to set.
GOE: 05.10.01 STRENGTH: L GED: R3 M2 L3 SVP: 5 DLU: 77

779.687-010   BREAKER (glass products) alternate titles: glass breaker

Breaks excess glass from glass stock along lines cut by GLASS CUTTER (any industry), using notched tool, glass pinchers, or pliers, to form products, such as watch crystals, meter dials, goggle lenses, or mirrors.
GOE: 06.04.30 STRENGTH: H GED: R2 M1 L1 SVP: 2 DLU: 77

779.687-014   CARTRIDGE LOADER (elec. equip.)

Fills cartridge cores of heating units with cement and holds them against motor-operated vibrating shaft to pack cement. Places cores in containers preparatory to further processing.
GOE: 06.04.34 STRENGTH: L GED: R1 M1 L1 SVP: 1 DLU: 77

779.687-018   GLASS-BULB SILVERER (glass products)

Coats interiors of ornamental glass balls with silvering solution: Pours solution into balls through small openings. Holds stopper over openings and shakes balls until interior surfaces are covered. Pours surplus silvering solution out of balls.
GOE: 06.04.33 STRENGTH: S GED: R1 M1 L1 SVP: 2 DLU: 77

779.687-022   INSPECTOR, GLASS OR MIRROR (glass products) alternate titles: face cleaner; glass inspector; mirror inspector

Inspects glass or mirrors to detect imperfections, such as scratches, seeds (sandholes), chips, or cracks: Examines glass or mirror at discharge end of glass

washing and drying machine or silvering range, or places glass or mirror on padded table under light. Turns glass or mirror in circular motion to inspect both sides. Wipes gloved hand over glass or mirror to remove dust. Marks defects with crayon or wax pencil. May move glass or mirror onto skids or conveyors. May keep record of rejections, type of defects, and footage loss. May glue labels onto mirrors.
GOE: 06.03.02 STRENGTH: M GED: R3 M2 L2 SVP: 4 DLU: 78

779.687-026   MICA INSPECTOR (mine & quarry) alternate titles: inspector
Inspects articles formed from mica for defects, such as spots, streaks, scratches, and cracks: Spreads articles over illuminated table and scans them for defects, or places articles on bed of microscope, using tweezers or pneumatic lifting device, and examines articles through microscope to detect defects not visible to naked eye. Rejects defective articles. Packs high quality or optical grade mica in protective paper or envelopes and packs parts in plastic boxes.
GOE: 06.03.02 STRENGTH: S GED: R3 M2 L2 SVP: 4 DLU: 77

779.687-030   MICA SIZER (mine & quarry)
Splits built-up mica washer rods into washers of specified thickness, using rod splitter: Positions built-up mica washer rod on work surface and pulls lever to press rod against sharp edged cutting blade to cut off washers of specified thickness.
GOE: 06.04.30 STRENGTH: S GED: R2 M2 L1 SVP: 3 DLU: 77

779.687-034   STOCK SHEETS CLEANER-INSPECTOR (glass products)
Cleans, inspects, and polishes stock sheets (large mirrors): Places stock sheets on vertical tabletop and depresses pedal to move tabletop to flat position. Cleans and inspects mirror and removes surface scratches, using portable scratch polishing wheel. Measures mirror with ruler and records size. Cuts defective edges from mirror with glasscutter. Glues label on mirror. Packs mirror in shipping crate.
GOE: 06.03.02 STRENGTH: M GED: R3 M2 L2 SVP: 4 DLU: 77

779.687-038   WAXER (glass products) alternate titles: glass-etcher helper
Brushes coat of wax on glass speedometer and radio dials, leaving stenciled numbers and figures free for etching.
GOE: 06.04.33 STRENGTH: S GED: R1 M1 L1 SVP: 2 DLU: 77

78   OCCUPATIONS IN FABRICATION AND REPAIR OF TEXTILE, LEATHER, AND RELATED PRODUCTS

This division includes occupations concerned with laying out, marking, and cutting materials; hand-sewing or machine-sewing parts of mass-produced products, such as drapes, slip covers, sheets, pillowcases, and ready-to-wear apparel; fitting and stitching made-to-measure garments and accessories; hand knitting complete garments, garment parts, or accessories; hand weaving and embroidering to embellish or repair garments and accessories; fabricating footwear, except molded rubber and plastics; and other activities concerned with fabricating or repairing garments, canvas goods, house furnishings, and related products.

780   OCCUPATIONS IN UPHOLSTERING AND IN FABRICATION AND REPAIR OF STUFFED FURNITURE, MATTRESSES, AND RELATED PRODUCTS

This group includes occupations concerned with upholstering such products as furniture, automobile seats, and caskets, and forming, stuffing, and assembling padding, mattresses, and bedsprings.

780.131-010   SUPERVISOR, CUTTING-AND-SEWING DEPARTMENT (furniture)
Supervises and coordinates activities of workers engaged in spreading, marking, cutting, and sewing fabric used in upholstered furniture: Inspects processed parts to verify dimensions, color, quantity, and style against work order or sample. Trains employees in operations. Performs other duties as described under SUPERVISOR (any industry) Master Title. May be designated according to specialty as Supervisor, Cutting Department (furniture); Supervisor, Sewing Department (furniture).
GOE: 06.02.01 STRENGTH: L GED: R4 M3 L3 SVP: 8 DLU: 79

780.131-014   SUPERVISOR, UPHOLSTERY DEPARTMENT (any industry)
Supervises and coordinates activities of workers engaged in padding, covering, trimming, or renovating upholstered articles, such as furniture, mattresses, or vehicle seats: Reviews production schedules and computes amounts of padding, fabric, and supplies necessary to achieve production. Assigns workers to stations according to workers' abilities and qualifications. Observes workers performing duties and interprets drawings, sketches, and work orders for workers based on knowledge of upholstery methods, style, and design of articles. Analyzes inventories of fabrics and materials to determine production costs and estimates. Inspects upholstered articles to verify conformance to customer's order or company standards. Performs other duties as described under SUPERVISOR (any industry) Master Title.

GOE: 06.01.01 STRENGTH: L GED: R4 M3 L3 SVP: 7 DLU: 79

780.134-010   SUPERVISOR, COVERING AND LINING (fabrication, nec)
Supervises and coordinates activities of workers engaged in covering and lining caskets: Inspects caskets for exposed edges of material, faulty lining installation, fit of casket top after covering, and overall appearance, to determine conformance to company standards. Demonstrates procedures to train new employees in lining and covering caskets. Performs duties as described under SUPERVISOR (any industry) Master Title. May cut cloth, using hand shears.
GOE: 06.02.01 STRENGTH: M GED: R4 M2 L2 SVP: 8 DLU: 77

780.134-014   SUPERVISOR, SPRING-UP (furniture)
Supervises and coordinates activities of workers engaged in cutting and installing webbing and springs in chair and sofa frames and cushions prior to upholstering. Examines frames and cushions at work stations to ensure specified materials are being used and work meets manufacturing standards. Performs other duties as described under SUPERVISOR (any industry) Master Title.
GOE: 06.02.01 STRENGTH: M GED: R4 M3 L3 SVP: 7 DLU: 78

780.137-010   SUPERVISOR, MATTRESS AND BOXSPRINGS (furniture)
Supervises and coordinates activities of workers engaged in padding and covering assembled spring units to make finished mattresses and box springs: Schedules flow of cotton and sisal through *garnett machines* for cleaning and felting. Directs workers in covering of spring unit with sisal pad and in boxfilling and closing, tape- and roll-edging, and tufting. Performs other duties as described under SUPERVISOR (any industry) Master Title. May set up machines. May be designated according to department as Supervisor, Border Department (furniture); Supervisor, Cutting-And-Sewing Room (furniture); Supervisor, Finishing Department (furniture).
GOE: 06.02.01 STRENGTH: L GED: R4 M2 L2 SVP: 7 DLU: 77

780.381-010   AUTOMOBILE UPHOLSTERER (automotive ser.)
Repairs or replaces upholstery in automobiles, buses, and trucks: Removes old upholstery from seats and door panels of vehicle. Measures new padding and covering materials, and cuts them to required dimensions, using knife or shears. Adjusts or replaces seat springs and ties them in place. Sews covering material together, using sewing machine. Fits covering to seat frame and secures it with glue and tacks. Repairs or replaces convertible tops. Refurbishes interiors of streetcars and buses by replacing cushions, drapes, and floor coverings. May be designated according to specialty as Body Trimmer (automotive ser.); Bus Upholsterer (automotive ser.); Top Installer (automotive ser.).
GOE: 05.05.15 STRENGTH: M GED: R3 M2 L3 SVP: 6 DLU: 77

780.381-014   AUTOMOBILE-UPHOLSTERER APPRENTICE (automotive ser.) alternate titles: passenger-car-upholsterer apprentice; upholsterer apprentice
Performs duties as described under APPRENTICE (any industry) Master Title.
GOE: 05.05.15 STRENGTH: M GED: R3 M2 L3 SVP: 6 DLU: 77

780.381-018   FURNITURE UPHOLSTERER (any industry) alternate titles: upholsterer
Repairs and rebuilds upholstered furniture, using handtools and knowledge of fabrics and upholstery methods: Removes covering, webbing, and padding from seat, arms, back, and sides of workpiece, using tack puller, chisel, and mallet. Removes defective springs by cutting cords or wires that hold them in place. Replaces webbing and springs or reties springs [SPRINGER (furniture) 780.684-106]. Measures and cuts new covering material [CUTTER, MACHINE (any industry) I 781.684-014]. Installs material on inside of arms, back, and seat, and over outside back and arms of wooden frame. Tacks or sews ornamental trim, such as braid and buttons, to cover or frame [UPHOLSTERY TRIMMER (furniture) 780.684-126]. May operate sewing machine to seam cushions and join various sections of covering material. May repair wooden frame of workpiece. May refinish wooden surfaces [FURNITURE FINISHER (woodworking) 763.381-010]. May upholster cornices and be designated Cornice Upholsterer (any industry). May repair seats, carpets, curtains, mattresses, and window shades of railroad coaches and sleeping cars and be designated Upholsterer (r.r. trans.).
GOE: 05.05.15 STRENGTH: M GED: R4 M3 L3 SVP: 7 DLU: 81

780.381-022   FURNITURE-UPHOLSTERER APPRENTICE (any industry) alternate titles: upholsterer apprentice
Performs duties as described under APPRENTICE (any industry) Master Title.
GOE: 05.05.15 STRENGTH: M GED: R4 M3 L3 SVP: 7 DLU: 77

780.381-026   UPHOLSTERER, LIMOUSINE AND HEARSE (auto. mfg.)
Upholsters interior of limousine and hearse bodies, performing any combination of following duties: Selects and cuts material to specifications, using shears and pattern. Sews material together, using sewing machine. Installs padding, and fastens and sews covering material in place in body of vehicle. May fasten interior and exterior trim to vehicle body. May design new patterns.
GOE: 06.02.27 STRENGTH: M GED: R3 M2 L3 SVP: 5 DLU: 90

780.381-030   PAD HAND (leather prod.) alternate titles: pad cutter and assembler
Cuts, assembles, and joins fabrics, leather, or other materials to form cushioned seat of saddle: Positions pattern on material and cuts material, using knife or scissors. Positions padding, such as cotton batting, foam rubber, or mohair

between covers. Sews edges of covers to form pad, using needle and thread. Inserts pad between leather covers of saddle seat and sews edges of covers to form cushioned seat.
GOE: 06.02.32 STRENGTH: L GED: R3 M2 L3 SVP: 5 DLU: 77

780.381-034 SLIPCOVER CUTTER (retail trade; tex. prod., nec)
Cuts material for slipcovers according to size and shape of furniture to match patterns and ensure economical use of material: Reads order to determine type and amount of material required, and obtains materials from stockroom. Determines from experience and knowledge of materials approximate yardage necessary to cover furniture, allowing for shrinkage and stitching. Measures, drapes, and smooths material, wrong-side-out, over sections of furniture to ensure most economical use and to serve as guide in matching shades, colors, and designs in cloth. Determines cutting lines by pinning or marking fabric, using shape of furniture as outline. Cuts fabric along marked lines. Pins cut pieces together and fits assembled unit over furniture, making adjustments with pins to attain required fitting. Wraps fitted pieces together and delivers to shop for sewing. Records amount of time required for each assignment. May visit customer's home to cut material for slipcovers. May cut material for draperies. May cut out slipcover parts from patterns, using rotary knife.
GOE: 05.05.15 STRENGTH: L GED: R3 M2 L3 SVP: 6 DLU: 77

780.381-038 UPHOLSTERER, INSIDE (furniture)
Upholsters inside sections of chairs and sofas, utilizing knowledge of upholstery materials and methods: Lifts frame of article and places it on workbench. Tacks material along front rail, outside and inside arms, and onto top outside back. Places padding and material over seat springs and tacks material onto frame to complete seat upholstery. Repeats operation to upholster arms. Places and shapes layers of padding over inside back and tacks material to complete inside upholstery of article. May use grooved foam rubber padding and work excess material into grooves to produce channeled effect and secure material with buttons, using needle, thread, and cotton. May cover burlap with horsehair and cover it with muslin to prepare article for tufting. May cut openings in muslin and push horsehair away from opening and secure it with buttons to create tufting effect.
GOE: 06.02.27 STRENGTH: M GED: R3 M3 L3 SVP: 6 DLU: 79

780.384-010 AUTOMOBILE-SEAT-COVER-AND-CONVERTIBLE-TOP INSTALLER (automotive ser.) alternate titles: automobile-upholstery-trim installer; top-and-seat-cover fitter
Fits and installs automobile seat covers and convertible-top: Examines standard pattern or removes automobile seat or top and measures it to determine amount of cover material required. Cuts material, using shears, and places it on pattern or pins it to seat or top frame. Marks material with chalk to indicate where it is to be sewed, reinforced, and decorated. Secures completed covers, using tacks, staples, and pliers. May operate sewing machine.
GOE: 05.05.15 STRENGTH: M GED: R3 M3 L3 SVP: 6 DLU: 77

780.384-014 UPHOLSTERER (aircraft mfg.)
Lays out, fabricates, and assembles aircraft upholstery, insulation, soundproofing, and interior trim items from assorted materials, according to specifications, using handtools, power tools, machines, and shop equipment: Stacks, aligns, and smooths materials on cutting table. Draws cutting lines on materials, such as leather, fabric, rubber, cork, fiberglass, and plastic, following patterns, templates, sketches, or blueprints, using chalk, pencil, paint, or other method. Cuts along marked lines, using power cutters, scissors, knives, or shears. Drills or punches holes in material. Sews, staples, glues, and cements materials to assemble upholstery or trim items, using handtools, power tools, machines, and equipment. Attaches snap fasteners, grommets, buckles, cords, and other accessories to upholstery or trim items, using handtools or equipment. Attaches binding or applies solutions to edges of cut material to prevent raveling. Hand sews buttons, hooks, or other fasteners onto fabric. Covers aircraft parts, such as tubing and duct work, with specified materials.
GOE: 06.02.32 STRENGTH: M GED: R3 M2 L3 SVP: 6 DLU: 87

780.587-010 SORTER, UPHOLSTERY PARTS (furniture) alternate titles: bundler; upholstery bundler; upholstery handler
Collects, sorts, counts, and bundles upholstery parts in furniture sewing department: Collects parts and carries parts to worktable. Sorts, counts, and stacks parts according to color, quantity, material, and part-number specifications on work ticket. Marks identifying number on top part in stack, using chalk. Copies color, quantity, material, and part number from work ticket onto production report form, using pen or pencil. Ties stacked parts into bundle, using string [PACKAGER, HAND (any industry) 920.587-018]. Carries bundled parts to storage area and places bundles in bins or on shelves according to part number.
GOE: 06.03.02 STRENGTH: M GED: R2 M1 L2 SVP: 3 DLU: 79

780.682-010 SEWING-MACHINE OPERATOR (furniture) alternate titles: tick sewer
Operates sewing machine to join mattress parts, such as covers. May be designated according to part joined as Cover Assembler (furniture). Performs duties as described under SEWING-MACHINE OPERATOR, REGULAR EQUIPMENT (any industry) Master Title.
GOE: 06.02.05 STRENGTH: L GED: R3 M1 L1 SVP: 4 DLU: 77

780.682-014 SLIP-COVER SEWER (tex. prod., nec)
Operates sewing machine to join parts, stitch piping or welt to seams, and stitch pleats to form slip covers: Guides parts under machine needle to join them. Positions piping or welt on seam and guides under machine needle to strengthen and decorate covers. Folds pleats in covers, using ruler to measure width and distance between pleats, and guides them under machine needle to stitch pleats. Performs duties as described under SEWING-MACHINE OPERATOR, REGULAR EQUIPMENT (any industry) Master Title.
GOE: 06.02.05 STRENGTH: L GED: R3 M1 L1 SVP: 4 DLU: 77

780.682-018 UPHOLSTERY SEWER (any industry)
Operates sewing machine to join cut fabric parts to fabricate upholstery coverings for aircraft, automobile, boat, household, and railroad furnishings: May sew pull bands into seams of upholstery parts. May sew welts or false pleats into upholstered furniture covers and be designated Welt Sewer (furniture). May sew cord into fabric to make boxpleats and be designated Boxing-Machine Operator (furniture). May be designated according to section or part seamed as Cover Maker (furniture); Cushion Closer (furniture; tex. prod., nec); Cushion Maker (furniture) II. Performs duties as described under SEWING-MACHINE OPERATOR, REGULAR EQUIPMENT (any industry) Master Title.
GOE: 06.02.05 STRENGTH: L GED: R3 M2 L2 SVP: 4 DLU: 79

780.684-010 BACK PADDER (furniture) alternate titles: upholsterer helper
Assembles padded wooden backs for metal chairs, performing any combination of following duties: Joins padding material, such as wood fiber or cotton, to wooden backplate, using hand stapler or staple gun. Inserts end of padded backplate in stretched cover and depresses pedal to lower ram that forces entire padded plate into cover. Inserts and aligns cardboard strips between cover edges and bottom edge of backplate. Staples cover edges and cardboard strips to backplate. Trims excess material from cover edges with scissors. Burns holes through cover to coincide with predrilled holes in backplate, using heated handtool. Inserts tubular metal frame supports into holes and joins to backplate, using hammer or pneumatic screwdriver.
GOE: 06.04.27 STRENGTH: L GED: R2 M1 L1 SVP: 2 DLU: 77

780.684-014 BAND-TOP MAKER (furniture) alternate titles: band-top assembler
Assembles and rivets metal strips into rectangular latticework used in construction of bedsprings: Lays specified number of long bands on worktable, evenly spaced and parallel. Inserts rivets and rivet collars through holes in bands. Lays cross bands over long bands, lining up holes with protruding rivet shanks. Strikes shanks with hammer to flatten rivets and secure bands together, forming lattice.
GOE: 06.04.22 STRENGTH: L GED: R2 M1 L1 SVP: 3 DLU: 77

780.684-018 BOX-SPRING MAKER I (furniture)
Assembles, upholsters, or repairs box springs, using handtools: Fastens coil springs to slats of wood frame, using hammer and nails or stapler. Clips edgewire to border coils with metal clips and pliers and interlaces coils with twine to secure springs in position. Measures and cuts padding and upholstering fabric, using tape measure and scissors or knife. Spreads materials over coils and staples them to frame to upholster box spring.
GOE: 06.04.34 STRENGTH: M GED: R2 M1 L1 SVP: 3 DLU: 77

780.684-022 BOX-SPRING MAKER II (furniture)
Staples padding and fabric on coil spring units to upholster box springs: Spreads padding over springs and tucks it in corners of assembly. Places fabric over padding, pulls it to obtain smooth surface, and staples fabric to wood frame, using stapling hammer. Nails fabric handles to frame and tacks dust cloth to bottom of frame, using hammer. May compress spring assembly to facilitate stapling of fabric to frame, using hydraulic or air press.
GOE: 06.04.22 STRENGTH: H GED: R2 M1 L1 SVP: 3 DLU: 77

780.684-026 CASKET COVERER (fabrication, nec) alternate titles: casket trimmer
Fits and glues fabric covering to outside of casket body, top frame, and top panel: Brushes glue over sides and ends of casket body, top frame, and top panel. Spreads fabric over glued surface, pulling, pressing, and smoothing cover over casket surfaces. Trims excess fabric at corners. Folds edge of cover under bottom and glues, tacks, or staples it to bottom. Tacks or glues trimming material over seams and exposed edges. Cuts and glues paper cover to bottom of casket. May attach hinges to fasten top frame to body. May attach top panel to top frame with screws. May be designated according to part of casket covered as Body Coverer (fabrication, nec); Cap Coverer (fabrication, nec); Panel Coverer (fabrication, nec); Top Coverer (fabrication, nec); Top-Frame Coverer (fabrication, nec).
GOE: 06.04.27 STRENGTH: M GED: R2 M1 L1 SVP: 3 DLU: 77

780.684-030 CASKET LINER (fabrication, nec) alternate titles: casket upholsterer
Pads and lines inside of bodies and tops of caskets: Spreads layer of excelsior evenly over bottom of casket and spreads layer of cotton over excelsior. Cuts cloth from supply roll, using hand shears, and tacks or staples cloth over bottom padding. Pads and covers sides and ends of casket with cotton and crepe. Staples or tacks lining over padding. Tacks or staples prepared lining into top panel or cuts or drapes lining material into top, depending on casket style. May attach handles and supporting hardware. May fit and glue fabric to inside of casket cover body to fashion designs onto head panels.
GOE: 06.02.22 STRENGTH: H GED: R3 M1 L1 SVP: 3 DLU: 79

780.684-034 CHAIR UPHOLSTERER (furniture) alternate titles: chair trimmer
Upholsters chairs having no springs: Cuts out and molds padding material in place on arms, seats, or backs, and covers padding with cotton wadding.

Stretches and tacks or staples canvas, burlap, or denim over wadding, leaving opening for further filling. Molds and packs wadding under cover, using hands or rod to eliminate lumps. Closes opening with tacks when packing is completed. Stretches precut upholstery covering over covered padding and tacks it in place. Sews or glues trimming over tacks and raw edges of upholstery. May glue foam cushions to particle board backing to form seat cushions for chairs. May glue upholstery material onto shaped foam to make cushions for upholstered furniture.
GOE: 06.02.27 STRENGTH: M GED: R3 M2 L2 SVP: 5 DLU: 77

780.684-038 COTTON DISPATCHER (furniture)
Tears or cuts cotton wadding or cushioning material to specified size or shape for use in padding upholstered furniture or slip seats: Measures specified length on cotton roll of width and thickness indicated on work ticket and tears cotton apart or places form over wadding and cuts around form. Cuts edging to required length.
GOE: 06.04.27 STRENGTH: M GED: R2 M1 L1 SVP: 2 DLU: 77

780.684-042 CRUSHER (fabrication, nec) alternate titles: smocker
Crushes (puffs) cloth to form three-dimensional geometric patterns for fancy linings in caskets: Lays material on female crushing die and fits male crushing die or crushing rod over material and into depression of female die. Steams material on crushing board to set shape, using steam hose. Removes male dies or crushing rods. Brushes or sprays glue onto screen and presses backing material against screen. Lays backing material on raised portion of facing material on crushing board. Wipes cloth over backing material to stick fabrics together. Removes and hangs finished article to dry. May sew linings and pillows.
GOE: 06.04.27 STRENGTH: M GED: R2 M1 L1 SVP: 2 DLU: 77

780.684-046 CUSHION BUILDER (furniture) alternate titles: upholsterer
Secures padding over cushion springs, previously tied into metal frames to form furniture cushions: Places padding on springs and frame. Fastens padding in place, using needle and cord. Sews inner covering of cotton material and outer covering over padded frame. Routes padded cushion to other workers for final sewing.
GOE: 06.04.22 STRENGTH: L GED: R2 M1 L1 SVP: 3 DLU: 77

780.684-054 CUSHION MAKER I (furniture) alternate titles: cushion assembler; cushion filler; cushion-mat maker; cushion stuffer; machine stuffer, automatic
Fills cushion covers with moss, hair, kapok, down, foam cushions, or spring units, using any of following methods: (1) Stuffs loose fibers, layers of material, or foam cushions into cover with hands. Beats cushions with hands to smooth out lumps. (2) Places layers of cotton wadding or foam cushions in forming box of stuffing machine, or tears and cuts wadding, covers cushion-spring assembly and places wrapped spring assembly in box. Lowers top of forming box and pushes lever or turns handwheel to close side panels and compress cushioning material. Slips cover over open end of forming box and depresses pedal to eject cushioning material into cover. (3) Dumps down, kapok, or other fibers into hopper of blower. Holds end of cushion cover over spout of blower and starts blower to fill cover. Weighs cushion and adds or removes material to obtain cushion of specified weight. May sew ends of cushion covers after filling, using needle and thread or power sewing machine.
GOE: 06.04.23 STRENGTH: M GED: R2 M1 L1 SVP: 4 DLU: 79

780.684-058 EDGE ROLLER (furniture)
Installs and pads first covering on upholstered pieces, such as armrests and chair seats not equipped with springs, to prepare piece for final covering. Spreads cotton, kapok, or moss padding evenly over part. Draws and tacks covering of canvas, burlap, or denim tightly over padding, using upholstery tacks and hammer.
GOE: 06.04.22 STRENGTH: L GED: R2 M1 L1 SVP: 3 DLU: 77

780.684-062 FABRICATOR, FOAM RUBBER (any industry) alternate titles: assembler; cementer; foam fabricator
Cuts and assembles padded articles, such as mattresses or cushions, from molded foam rubber sheets, pads, or scrap: Positions and measures or marks pattern outline on foam rubber piece, using tape measure and crayon or pencil. Cuts around measurement or pattern outline, using electric knife or bandsaw. May place two identical pieces together, brush cement along edge, and press edges of pieces together to form cushion or mattress. May cement strips around edges of assembled pieces and over seams to provide smooth finish and reinforce seams. May staple spring material to wood frame and leno or sisal cloth to top of springs to form box-spring unit.
GOE: 06.04.29 STRENGTH: L GED: R2 M1 L1 SVP: 2 DLU: 77

780.684-066 FILLER (tex. prod., nec) alternate titles: stuffer
Fills pillows, cushions, and comforters with down, kapok, wool, or other filler, using filling machine: Ties or holds opening of cover around discharge tube of filling machine and presses button to start blower that sucks filling into cover. Estimates amount of filler blown into cover by either timing blower or weighing articles. Stuffs filling into open end of cover, using metal rod. May stuff covers by hand. May be designated according to article filled as Cushion Filler (tex. prod., nec); Pillow Filler (tex. prod., nec); Sleeping-Bag Filler (tex. prod., nec); or according to kind of filler used as Down Filler (tex. prod., nec).
GOE: 06.04.23 STRENGTH: L GED: R2 M1 L1 SVP: 2 DLU: 77

780.684-070 MATTRESS FINISHER (furniture) alternate titles: finisher, hand; stitcher, hand
Tufts and stitches mattresses to finish them: Measures and marks off tufting points on both sides of mattress with rule and crayon. Threads cotton tufts or

tufting buttons and sews through mattress to tie them to tufts or buttons on under side. Stitches mattress border (boxing) to side padding to stiffen mattress edge and prevent sagging through displacement of padding. Gathers corners of padding to shape and to stitch rolled edge and preserve box-like shape of mattress. May tend equipment, such as tape-edge, roll-edge, or tufting machines. May be designated by specific function or specialty as Roll-Edge Stitcher, Hand (furniture); Side-Stitcher (furniture).
GOE: 06.02.27 STRENGTH: M GED: R3 M2 L2 SVP: 3 DLU: 77

780.684-074 MATTRESS MAKER (furniture)
Pads and covers innerspring assemblies to form mattresses: Cuts cover material, using electric cutting knife and scissors, and spreads and staples burlap, leno, or sisal cloth to both sides of innerspring assemblies. Spreads padding over sides of innerspring and tends tape-edge machine that sews cover over padding. Tufts mattresses by hand or by tending machine to hold padding in place. Sews roll edges on mattress by hand or by machine.
GOE: 06.02.27 STRENGTH: M GED: R3 M1 L2 SVP: 4 DLU: 77

780.684-078 PADDER, CUSHION (furniture) alternate titles: seat padder
Assembles seat pads, backrest pads, and arm covers for metal chairs, using pneumatic press and handtools: Positions specified material, such as cotton, foam-rubber padding, or precut leather, on base of pneumatic press. Depresses pedal or pushes handle to lower press onto materials. Draws wire through passage around edge of material and twists ends of wire together to tighten covering, using pliers. Hammers upholstery clips through covering to fasten edge to bottom of frame. Removes excess covering with scissors. Releases pedal or pulls handle to raise press. May assemble backrest pads or arm covers, using pliers, scissors, glue, and wire.
GOE: 06.04.22 STRENGTH: L GED: R2 M1 L1 SVP: 3 DLU: 77

780.684-082 PANEL COVERER, METAL FURNITURE (furniture) alternate titles: side-piece coverer
Covers sheet metal sections of furniture with precut cotton padding and upholstery materials, such as fabric, leather, or plastic: Selects sheet metal panel, padding, and upholstery material according to work ticket. Coats surface of panel with glue, using brush or spray gun. Positions and presses padding on panel and trims excess cotton from edge, using scissors. Positions upholstery material over padding and pulls material taut to remove wrinkles. Presses edges of upholstery material onto prongs protruding from back of panel and bends prongs to secure material, using hammer. Trims excess material from edges with scissors. May be designated according to type of panel padded as Back-Panel Padder (furniture); Inside-Panel Padder (furniture); Side-Panel Padder (furniture).
GOE: 06.04.22 STRENGTH: L GED: R2 M1 L1 SVP: 2 DLU: 77

780.684-086 PANEL MAKER (furniture) alternate titles: panel coverer
Pads and covers panels for use in upholstered furniture: Places precut felt or cotton batting over cardboard or wood panel and stretches covering material over padding. Staples edges of material to back of panel so that material is tight, smooth, and even. May sew edging on panels, using sewing machine.
GOE: 06.04.27 STRENGTH: L GED: R2 M1 L1 SVP: 3 DLU: 77

780.684-090 POCKETED-SPRING ASSEMBLER (furniture) alternate titles: racker
Sews together sections of pocketed coil springs to assemble innersprings for mattresses: Cuts sections of uniform length from chain of pocketed coils with shears, and spreads specified number in layer across pegs of vertical rack. Sews fabric of pocket sections together (length and width of assembly), using needle and thread. Turns assembly over and repeats process.
GOE: 06.04.22 STRENGTH: L GED: R2 M1 L1 SVP: 3 DLU: 77

780.684-094 SLIP-SEAT COVERER (furniture)
Pads and covers slip-seats (removable chair seats), using one of following methods: (1) Places padding on wooden panel, stretches cover over padding, and tacks or staples edges of cover to panel. (2) Inserts foam rubber cushion in cover and tacks or staples cushion to wooden backing panel. (3) Places cover, right side down, on form under air press. Lays padding, fiber filling, and backing panel over cover. Opens valve to lower press against backing panel to compress assembly. Cuts excess padding and filler from panel, using shears. Draws edges of cover over panel and tacks or staples edge to panel. May staple, tack, or paste material content tag to backing panel.
GOE: 06.04.27 STRENGTH: M GED: R2 M1 L1 SVP: 3 DLU: 77

780.684-098 SPRING ASSEMBLER (furniture) alternate titles: coil placer; coil-spring assembler
Assembles and fastens coil springs in wire frames to form box spring units for beds or chairs: Lays bed of crossed wiring in jig and clinches or wires coil springs to wiring. Fastens tops of coils together with tie wires or metal clips. Clips edge wire to tops of outside coil springs, using clipping tool. Cuts protruding ends of wires, using pliers. May staple springs to wooden frame individually or as assembled unit, using stapler. May attach channel-shaped rim to top coils of bedsprings by crimping edges of channel together over wire, using handtools. May be designated according to type of spring as Bedspring Assembler (furniture); Chair-Spring Assembler (furniture); Cushion-Spring Assembler (furniture).
GOE: 06.04.22 STRENGTH: M GED: R2 M1 L1 SVP: 2 DLU: 77

780.684-102 SPRING CLIPPER (furniture)
Cuts and clips spring to form assembly units of specified size and shape: Cuts spring assembly units, using wire cutters. Fits units together, according to

specifications, using *clinching tool*. Clinches border wire to spring assembly to reinforce unit.

GOE: 06.04.24 STRENGTH: L GED: R2 M1 L2 SVP: 3 DLU: 77

780.684-106 SPRINGER (furniture) alternate titles: hand-tier; spring set-ter; spring tacker; spring tier; spring upholsterer

Installs webbing and springs in furniture frames preparatory to upholstering: Tacks or staples ends of webbing strips to side of frame, using tack hammer or staple gun. Stretches webbing across frame with *webbing stretcher* and tacks ends to opposite side of frame. Tacks strips to back of frame and weaves them through crosspieces to cover opening. Cuts webbing overlap with hand shears. Positions coil springs on webbing and fastens spring to webbing with needle and twine or with metal clips, using *clinching tool*. Tacks twine to edges of frame opening and laces and ties twine to springs to stabilize and secure them in place. Cuts burlap or canvas to cover springs, places cover on springs, and tacks to edges of frame. May install zigzag or no-sag springs in backs of sofa and chair frames, using metal clips and hammer. May tack metal support strap on frame, using hammer. May fasten border wire to springs, using metal clips or by twisting crimp wire around border wire and top of spring. May cover frame opening by attaching web-fabric panels to frame with small springs. May sew heavy paper over border wire, using needle and stitching twine to soften edge.

GOE: 06.02.32 STRENGTH: H GED: R3 M1 L2 SVP: 4 DLU: 79

780.684-110 TESTER, CONVERTIBLE SOFA BEDSPRING (furniture)

Repairs assembly and operational defects in convertible-sofa bedsprings preparatory to framing and upholstering: Examines unit for missing parts, and tightens loose rivets with pneumatic riveting gun. Places mattress in unit, pulls unit open and pushes it closed to test ease of operation. Adjusts pivot bolts and straightens connecting rods and brackets, using handtools. Rubs rough surfaces and joints with thinner and solvent to remove excess paint and grease and minimize friction.

GOE: 06.02.24 STRENGTH: M GED: R3 M1 L2 SVP: 4 DLU: 77

780.684-114 TRIMMING ASSEMBLER (furniture) alternate titles: cover assembler

Selects upholstery trimmings, such as gimp, braid, or fringe, to match material used for covering furniture. Cuts off amount required to complete upholstering of each furniture unit.

GOE: 06.02.23 STRENGTH: L GED: R3 M2 L2 SVP: 3 DLU: 77

780.684-118 UPHOLSTERER, OUTSIDE (furniture)

Upholsters outside sections of furniture such as chairs and sofas, utilizing knowledge of upholstery procedures: Tacks cardboard, padding, and upholstery material to top, side, and bottom rails of outside arms, fitting and shaping materials to obtain specified contour. Tacks covering material to top, bottom, and side rails of back frame and sews upholstery covering edges onto inside back and outside arm coverings with needle and thread to complete upholstery of furniture piece. Tacks cover to bottom rails to enclose bottom area. Attaches trimming material, such as gimp, braid, binding, skirts, and panels to upholstered frames, using glue, staples, nails, or tacks. May screw leg units to frame.

GOE: 06.04.27 STRENGTH: M GED: R3 M1 L2 SVP: 5 DLU: 79

780.684-122 UPHOLSTERY REPAIRER (furniture)

Repairs or replaces damaged or defective upholstery on chairs or sofas: Examines upholstery to locate defects. Sews tears or rips with needle and thread. Pulls tacks or staples from defective upholstery, using hammer or pliers, and removes upholstery from frame. Tacks, sews, or staples replacement upholstery to frame. May cut covering from bolt of cloth, using part removed as pattern, or may carry defective parts to cutters to have replacement parts cut to specifications.

GOE: 05.05.15 STRENGTH: M GED: R3 M1 L1 SVP: 6 DLU: 77

780.684-126 UPHOLSTERY TRIMMER (furniture) alternate titles: gimp tacker

Attaches gimp, braid, binding, skirts, or other trimming material to upholstered frames, following instruction on work ticket, using glue, staples, nails, or tacks.

GOE: 06.04.27 STRENGTH: M GED: R2 M1 L2 SVP: 3 DLU: 79

780.684-130 WEBBING TACKER (furniture)

Stretches and tacks or staples webbing to underside of couch or chair frames to provide foundation for springs: Stretches and tacks or staples specified number of webbing pieces to sides of frame. Secures ends of other pieces to end of frame. Weaves pieces lengthwise through crosspieces and stretches and secures them to other end of frame until opening is covered with interlaced webbing.

GOE: 06.04.27 STRENGTH: H GED: R2 M1 L1 SVP: 3 DLU: 77

780.684-134 UPHOLSTERER, ASSEMBLY LINE (furniture)

Upholsters one section of sofa, chair, or furniture frames, using one of following methods: (1) Attaches spring assembly section to seat and back of frame with clips or ties springs with twine and tacks ends of twine to frame. (2) Places padding and covering over seat springs and tacks or staples covering to frame to complete seat upholstering, using tack hammer or powered staple gun. (3) Places padding and covering over inside of arms and tacks or staples covering to frame to complete inside arms. (4) Places layers of padding over inside back, shaping padding to specifications, and tacks or staples covering over padding to make inside back. (5) Tacks or staples cardboard, padding, and uphol-

stery material to top, side, and bottom rails of outside arms, fitting and shaping materials to obtain smooth contour.(6) Tacks or staples covering material to top, bottom, and side rails of back frame, and sews upholstery covering edges to adjoining inside back and outside arm coverings with needle and thread to complete upholstery of furniture piece. (7) Tacks or staples cover to bottom rails to enclose bottom area. May attach trimming material, such as gimp, braid, binding, skirts, and panels to upholstered frames, using glue, staples, nails, or tacks. May screw leg units to frame. May be designated according to part or pieces upholstered as Arm Maker (furniture); Back Maker (furniture); Seat Maker (furniture).

GOE: 06.04.27 STRENGTH: L GED: R2 M1 L1 SVP: 3 DLU: 86

780.685-010 MATTRESS-FILLING-MACHINE TENDER (furniture)

Tends machine that compresses padded spring assemblies and inserts them into prefabricated covers to form mattresses: Spreads precut and weighed cotton bats into compression box of filling machine. Places sisal-covered innerspring assembly on top of batting and spreads cotton batting on top of spring, stuffing excess at ends into springs. Pushes cover over discharge spout and depresses pedal to compress and insert padded spring into cover. May operate sewing machine to close open end of mattress cover. May build up layers of batting in compression box without innerspring to make crib pads and be designated Crib-Pad Maker (furniture).

GOE: 06.04.20 STRENGTH: M GED: R2 M1 L1 SVP: 2 DLU: 77

780.685-014 STUFFING-MACHINE OPERATOR (furniture) alternate titles: pad maker

Tends machine that cleans and fluffs filling and blows it into prefabricated covers to form mattress or other upholstered pads: Weighs filling material, such as cotton or sisal, to obtain specified weight and dumps into hopper of machine. Places cover over discharge tube and starts machine that cleans, fluffs, and blows filling material into cover. Removes filled cover and closes end, using sewing machine. Places pad on table and strikes it with wood pole to beat and level filling. Turns pad over and repeats process. May fill pad by piling required amount of filling on table and slipping cover over pile. May pad by hand [TUFTER, HAND (furniture) 780.687-050] or by machine [TUFTING-MACHINE OPERATOR (furniture) 687.685-014].

GOE: 06.04.36 STRENGTH: M GED: R2 M1 L2 SVP: 3 DLU: 78

780.685-018 WIRE-BORDER ASSEMBLER (furniture) alternate titles: topper

Tends machine that attaches edge-wire frame to coil spring assemblies with *helical springs:* Places spring assembly on table and positions edge wire on top of springs. Inserts helical spring in spinner and depresses pedal to start and control speed of spinner. Guides emerging helical spring so that it joins edge wire and tops of coil springs on ends and sides of assembly. Removes surplus helical spring, using nipper, and crimps end with pliers. Turns and positions assembly to attach edge wire to remaining ends or sides. Turns spring assembly over and repeats process.

GOE: 06.04.20 STRENGTH: H GED: R2 M1 L1 SVP: 3 DLU: 77

780.687-010 BORDER MEASURER AND CUTTER (furniture) alternate titles: border measurer

Winds border fabric around pegs to obtain specified lengths for mattresses and cuts fabric into lengths, using scissors. May sew together ends of border with sewing machine.

GOE: 06.04.27 STRENGTH: L GED: R1 M1 L1 SVP: 1 DLU: 77

780.687-014 CLIPPER AND TURNER (furniture)

Clips ends of innersprings, using wirecutter and pliers, and turns wires under spring to prevent them from piercing mattress. Cuts excess material from *helical springs* and crimps ends around coil spring loops, using pincers.

GOE: 06.04.24 STRENGTH: M GED: R1 M1 L1 SVP: 2 DLU: 77

780.687-018 HASSOCK MAKER (tex. prod., nec)

Fills sewed hassock covers with precut polyfoam filler: Places filler inside tack (cover) and centers evenly between ends of cover. Places hassock in pleater and draws strings together to pleat and close ends. Attaches buttons to ends of hassock with cord and hook. May stuff filling material, such as cotton, excelsior, or kapok, into hassock cover and compress it under hydraulic press to shape and firm hassock.

GOE: 06.04.34 STRENGTH: M GED: R2 M1 L1 SVP: 2 DLU: 77

780.687-022 INSPECTOR II (furniture)

Examines mattresses and box springs for defects prior to packaging: Inspects surfaces for puckers, gathers, and irregular corners. Measures length and width of mattress and box spring to ensure conformity with specifications, using tape measure. Cuts loose threads and fabric ends from mattresses meeting standards and removes defective ones from conveyor. May use water on surfaces to shrink puckers, using spray gun.

GOE: 06.03.02 STRENGTH: L GED: R2 M1 L2 SVP: 4 DLU: 77

780.687-026 MATTRESS STRIPPER (furniture)

Strips and removes padding from used mattresses preparatory to reconditioning them: Places mattress on table. Cuts tufts or buttons and stitching, using knife or scissors, or rips cover off to open mattress, and removes padding.

GOE: 06.04.27 STRENGTH: M GED: R1 M1 L1 SVP: 4 DLU: 77

780.687-030 MATTRESS-SPRING ENCASER (furniture) alternate titles: spring encaser

Covers innerspring assemblies with cotton or sisal fabric to prevent upholstery material from shifting: Spreads precut fabric on table, lays innerspring on

fabric, and spreads fabric on top of spring. Draws edges together and sews edges with needle and twine or staples edges together, using hand stapler. Positions sisal on innerspring unit and staples perimeter, using pneumatic staple gun.
GOE: 06.04.22 STRENGTH: L GED: R2 M1 L1 SVP: 2 DLU: 77

780.687-034 PADDING GLUER (furniture)
Fastens padded edging to sofa and chair frames prior to upholstering, using glue and *clinching tool:* Cuts strips of foam rubber and burlap edging to fit seat edges and armrests of sprung-up chair and sofa frames, using knife. Applies glue to seat edge, armrests and foam rubber strips, using spray gun, and presses surfaces together. Aligns and attaches burlap edging to edges of seats, using clinching tool. Slides sprung-up frames to conveyor and loads frames onto conveyor. Cleans spray gun with solvent and refills glue tank.
GOE: 06.04.27 STRENGTH: H GED: R2 M1 L1 SVP: 2 DLU: 77

780.687-038 SPRING COVERER (furniture)
Staples or tacks burlap, canvas, denim, or synthetic material over springs in furniture frames prior to upholstering where fabric is not installed by SPRING-ER (furniture). Cuts covering material to specified size, using scissors. Sews twine through covering material and around coil springs to stabilize them.
GOE: 06.04.27 STRENGTH: H GED: R2 M1 L1 SVP: 2 DLU: 77

780.687-042 STAPLER, HAND (furniture) alternate titles: sisal operator; wire stitcher, hand
Staples padding to both sides of innerspring or top of boxspring assemblies: Places spring assembly on table, spreads leno or sisal cloth over top of springs, and staples it to edge wire and tops of spring coils. Spreads padding over cloth, folding edges over edge wire and into coils, and staples it to edge wire. Turns innerspring assembly over and spreads cloth and padding and staples them to assembly. May fasten padding to edge wire, using hog rings and pliers. May hand sew padding to springs. May staple covering to boxsprings, using hydraulic press. May staple coil spring assembly to wood frame and be designated Stapler, Coil Unit (furniture).
GOE: 06.04.22 STRENGTH: M GED: R2 M1 L1 SVP: 2 DLU: 77

780.687-046 STUFFER (tex. prod., nec)
Stuffs pads and cushions with filling material, such as excelsior, foam rubber, kapok, or cotton, by hand.
GOE: 06.04.23 STRENGTH: L GED: R1 M1 L1 SVP: 1 DLU: 78

780.687-050 TUFTER, HAND (furniture) alternate titles: button tufter; pad tufter
Sews and tufts mattresses and pad to hold filling in place: Places mattress or pad in press and moves button to lower press head. Tilts press to upright position. Pushes needle carrying tufting cords through mattress or pad at openings in press head. Ties buttons or knots tufts to cord ends on both sides. Moves button to raise press head and removes mattress or pad.
GOE: 06.04.27 STRENGTH: H GED: R2 M1 L1 SVP: 2 DLU: 77

780.687-054 UPHOLSTERER HELPER (any industry)
Assists AUTOMOBILE UPHOLSTERER (automotive ser.) or FURNITURE UPHOLSTERER (any industry) to repair and rebuild upholstered furniture or automobile seats: Rips or cuts away worn covering material and padding from frame and pulls tacks from frame, using tack puller. Lifts furniture onto worktable. May remove spots from upholstery, using cleaning fluids. May assist in rebuilding of fabric automobile tops. Performs other duties as described under HELPER (any industry) Master Title.
GOE: 06.04.27 STRENGTH: H GED: R2 M1 L1 SVP: 3 DLU: 77

780.687-058 UPHOLSTERY CLEANER (furniture)
Cleans upholstery on new furniture preparatory to storage or shipping: Inspects spots to ascertain composition, selects solvent, and applies it to spot with cloth or brush. Cleans dust, lint, and cloth scraps from fabric, using airhose or vacuum cleaner. Applies steam to upholstery from steam hose to raise nap, brighten color, and tighten fabric. May smooth upholstery into folds or push padding to corners of cushions and backs with pick. May rub exposed wooden parts with furniture polish. When applying steam to cleaned upholstery, may be designated Steam Cleaner (furniture).
GOE: 06.04.39 STRENGTH: M GED: R2 M1 L1 SVP: 2 DLU: 78

780.687-062 BACK TUFTER (furniture)
Attaches tufting buttons to foam cushions for use in backs of upholstered furniture: Positions cushion on worktable and spreads and smooths upholstery fabric over cushion. Selects matching (color) button, punches button by hand through precut hole in cloth and cushion, and secures button to cushion with spring washer. Forces cloth around button into pleats, using wedge and fingers.
GOE: 06.04.27 STRENGTH: M GED: R1 M1 L1 SVP: 2 DLU: 86

780.687-066 INSPECTOR I (furniture)
Inspects wood frames and metal springs of upholstered furniture to ensure assembled parts meet company specifications: Examines wood furniture frames to detect defects, such as loose joints, splits, and warped areas. Marks defects with chalk for repair. Inspects metal springs installed in frames for defects, such as misalignment and faulty attachment to frame. Measures position of springs in frame, using ruler, to ensure assembly is mounted according to specification. Examines fabric covering spring assembly to ensure that fabric is taut and secured to springs.
GOE: 06.03.02 STRENGTH: M GED: R3 M2 L2 SVP: 6 DLU: 86

780.687-070 SKIRT PANEL ASSEMBLER (furniture) alternate titles: skirt clipper
Fastens rigid plastic-coated fabric between upholstery skirt panel and liner, and presses panel for smoothness and shape, using steam iron and presser: Cuts threads joining sewn panels, using scissors. Presses panels right-side out, using hand steam iron. Cuts coated fabric from roll and inserts fabric between panel and liner and staples fabric to parts to impart body to panel prior to final assembly. Presses assembled panel to flatten seams and shape panel, using steam presser. Examines panel to ensure specifications are attained. Places pressed panels in designated area.
GOE: 06.04.27 STRENGTH: L GED: R2 M2 L2 SVP: 3 DLU: 86

781 LAYING OUT, MARKING, CUTTING, AND PUNCHING OCCUPATIONS, N.E.C.

This group includes occupations, not elsewhere classified, concerned with laying out, marking, cutting, and punching garment, canvas goods, and house furnishing parts from single or multiple layers of material preparatory to piecing up, fitting, and stitching or machine-sewing.

781.131-010 SUPERVISOR, PATTERN MARKING (garment)
Supervises and coordinates activities of workers engaged in marking, reproducing, and assembling paper garment patterns for use by manufacturers: Observes operations to verify that pattern parts are marked for fabric weave lines, coded to specifications, reproduced clearly, and assembled in specified order. Modifies new patterns, using knowledge of mathematics and pattern-making principles. Determines layout for various pattern sizes to prevent waste and estimates material yardage required. Trains new workers to mark, reproduce, and assemble patterns. Performs other duties as described under SUPERVISOR (any industry) Master Title.
GOE: 05.03.02 STRENGTH: L GED: R4 M3 L3 SVP: 7 DLU: 77

781.134-010 SUPERVISOR, CUTTING DEPARTMENT (any industry)
Supervises and coordinates activities of workers engaged in spreading, marking, and cutting fabrics: Determines quantity and type of material to be cut and cutting patterns or dies to be used, according to cutting orders and design specifications. Directs MARKERS (any industry) I 781.384-014 in positioning patterns or paper markers on lays of cloth to ensure that pattern and weave of parts match when assembled and to minimize waste. Examines cut parts for conformance to outline, notches, and other markings on pattern. Trains workers by demonstrating work methods and techniques and use of spreaders and cutting equipment. Performs other duties as described under SUPERVISOR (any industry) Master Title.
GOE: 06.02.01 STRENGTH: L GED: R4 M3 L3 SVP: 6 DLU: 78

781.287-010 CLOTHING-PATTERN PREPARER (garment) alternate titles: dopster
Determines style and size of standard patterns and any variations to be used in cutting out made-to-measure clothing: Prepares work order ticket, using previously recorded notations indicating customer's measurements and style and fabric preferences. Designates standard patterns to be used in cutting each article of clothing. Makes notations on ticket to indicate to MARKER (any industry) I any variations from standard patterns necessary to fit individual customer, utilizing knowledge of pattern-modification techniques.
GOE: 06.02.31 STRENGTH: S GED: R4 M4 L3 SVP: 6 DLU: 77

781.361-010 ASSISTANT DESIGNER (garment)
Lays out, marks, and cuts muslin pattern and garment parts for manufacturer of women's sportswear, using design sketch, master pattern, and scissors: Traces outline of specified paperboard pattern onto muslin fabric, and cuts muslin pattern, using scissors. Positions and pins muslin pattern sections onto dressmaker model form for marking of style lines by designer. Removes marked sections from model and traces style lines on pattern, using tracing wheel and carbon paper. Positions and pins garment and muslin patterns onto form for designer to approve that patterns conform in proportion, harmony, and balance to design-sketch concept. Traces and cuts garment fabric parts, following muslin pattern. Advises workers who sew garment parts together on procedures, such as type of stitching, positioning of collars and sleeves on garments, and correcting defects.
GOE: 05.05.15 STRENGTH: L GED: R3 M2 L3 SVP: 7 DLU: 86

781.361-014 PATTERNMAKER (furniture; garment; tex. prod., nec)
Draws and cuts out sets of master patterns for articles, such as garments, parachutes, and upholstery, following sketches, sample articles and design specifications: Examines sketches or sample articles and design specifications to ascertain number, shape, and size of pattern parts and quantity of cloth required to make finished article, using knowledge of manufacturing processes and characteristics of fabrics. Discusses design specifications with designer, when necessary. Draws outlines of parts on paper, using drafting instruments, such as calipers, squares, straight and curved rules, and pencils. Draws details on outlined parts to indicate position of pleats, pockets, buttonholes, and other items. Marks outlined garment parts with lines and notches that serve as guides in joining parts of garment. Cuts out master patterns, using scissors and knife, and marks size and style information on patterns. May draw and cut out sets of patterns of different sizes, following master patterns [PATTERN GRADER-CUTTER (garment) 781.381-022]. May fabricate template from plywood, trace around template with chalk to outline pattern on material, and cut off parts,

using power shears [DEVELOPER PROVER, INTERIOR ASSEMBLIES (aircraft mfg.) 693.261-010].
GOE: 05.03.02 STRENGTH: L GED: R4 M3 L3 SVP: 6 DLU: 78

781.381-010 CARTOON DESIGNER (tex. prod., nec)
Lays out and draws embroidery cartoon on pattern paper to form embroidery pattern for emblems, according to specifications: Lays out and draws sketch of cartoon, using drafting instruments, such as triangle, pencils, and crayons. Places customer-approved cartoon in enlarging apparatus. Positions pattern paper on drawing board beneath enlarger and pushes button to illuminate enlarger. Looks through eyepiece of enlarger and traces image of cartoon onto pattern paper to form embroidery pattern. Writes specifications on border of pattern and marks identifying information on outside of pattern, using pencil.
GOE: 01.02.03 STRENGTH: S GED: R4 M3 L3 SVP: 7 DLU: 77

781.381-018 LEATHER STAMPER (leather prod.) alternate titles: decorator; leather tooler; tooler
Cuts, stamps, stains, or paints lettering and decorative designs on leather products, such as belts, handbags, luggage, saddles, and novelty items: Draws design and lettering on wet leather with stylus or transfers design by placing pattern or template on leather and pounding with mallet. Cuts outline of design and lettering with knife. Bevels and flares edges of cuts and fills in design and background, using various stamping tools and mallet. May trim and punch leather pieces and sew them together by hand or machine. May apply various colors and shades of stain to design and background and be designated Spanisher (leather prod.).
GOE: 01.06.02 STRENGTH: L GED: R3 M1 L1 SVP: 5 DLU: 77

781.381-022 PATTERN GRADER-CUTTER (garment)
Draws and cuts out sets of patterns for specified ranges of garment sizes, grading (increasing or decreasing dimensions) master pattern for each size within set, using either of following methods: (1) Obtains data from charts that specify modifications of master pattern dimensions necessary to produce patterns of various sizes. Positions master pattern on paperboard and drafts reference points on paperboard to modify dimensions of master pattern, according to specification charts, using drafting instruments. Draws lines between reference points, producing outline of graded pattern. (2) Positions master pattern in clamp of grading device and places paperboard under pattern. Turns knobs to set dial indicator at specified size and moves master pattern through series of reference points on paperboard. Marks reference points on paperboard. Draws lines between reference points, producing outline of graded pattern. Marks location of notches in graded patterns that serve as guides for joining garment parts. Cuts out graded patterns, using scissors, and marks garment size, sections, and style number on each pattern piece.
GOE: 05.03.02 STRENGTH: L GED: R3 M3 L3 SVP: 6 DLU: 77

781.381-030 SAIL-LAY-OUT WORKER (tex. prod., nec)
Lays out and draws pattern of sail on floor, following design specifications and dimensions: Calculates dimensions and specifications from sales order and enters data on worksheet. Computes dimensional allowances for draft of sail and stretching of sail cloth, and corrects dimensional specifications of pattern. Draws actual size and shape of sail on floor with chalk, chalkline, and measuring tape. May supervise other workers in shop engaged in cutting, sewing, and finishing cloth to produce complete sail. May lay out and cut sail cloth [SAIL CUTTER (tex. prod., nec)].
GOE: 05.05.15 STRENGTH: M GED: R4 M3 L2 SVP: 8 DLU: 77

781.381-034 GRADER MARKER (garment)
Draws and cuts sets of garment patterns, grading (increasing or decreasing pattern dimensions) master pattern for each set, and draws marker pattern for use in cutting garment material: Receives set of master garment patterns from PATTERNMAKER (furniture; garment; tex. prod., nec) 781.361-014 for grading. Positions paperboard, grading device, and master pattern in specified sequence on worktable to mark reference points that serve as guides for joining garment part and pattern outline. Turns knobs on grading device to set dial indicators at specified settings, utilizing reference chart and reference points on master pattern. Marks reference points on paperboard and draws lines between points to outline pattern. Cuts paperboard along pattern outline, using scissors, and marks each pattern section with information, such as garment style, size, and number. Positions carbon paper, marking paper with printed measurements, and complete paperboard pattern sets on worktable, and arranges patterns on marking paper to minimize waste and to determine material needed to position complete pattern set. Draws outline of patterns on marking paper for use in cutting garment material.
GOE: 05.03.02 STRENGTH: L GED: R3 M2 L3 SVP: 6 DLU: 86

781.384-014 MARKER I (any industry) alternate titles: pattern marker
Arranges patterns and marks identifying numbers, assembly guidelines, and outline of patterns on lay of cloth, leather, paper, or other materials to facilitate cutting and sewing operations, employing knowledge of marking, cutting, and manufacturing processes to minimize waste: Selects lay of material and patterns according to specifications. Compares pattern with cutting order to verify style of garment, size scale, type and yardage of cloth, and number of garments to be cut. Positions pattern on lay according to type, print, or weave of material, so that parts match when assembled and waste is minimized, using rules and squares as work aids. Outlines patterns on top of materials, using chalk stick, dust bag, crayon, soap, or wax. May mark part size and model number within outlines. May pin marked paper or outlined patterns onto material. May notch,

drill, and mark holes in lay to serve as guides for attachment of other parts, using notcher, electric drill, or electric drill equipped with cartridge containing fluorescent marking solution. May be designated according to type of material marked as Canvas Marker (tex. prod., nec), or according to article marked as Dress Marker (garment); Hat Marker (hat & cap); Shirt Marker (garment).
GOE: 06.02.31 STRENGTH: L GED: R3 M2 L2 SVP: 4 DLU: 78

781.384-018 SAIL CUTTER (tex. prod., nec)
Spreads sail cloth over floor pattern and cuts cloth into specified lengths and shapes for subsequent sewing into complete sail: Lays first width of sail cloth over pattern and fastens it into position, using weights or awls. Marks outline of sail on cloth, following pattern and allowing margin of material to overlap for seams. Cuts cloth along outline, using hand shears. Draws seam guidelines on edge of cloth with pencil to mark seam overlap. Spreads succeeding widths of cloth over pattern in specified manner and cuts with hand shears until sail is complete. Draws lines across joints of cloths with pencil as guides to match cloths for assembly. Picks up, marks, and stacks cloths in order of sewing. Lays out and cuts reinforcing patches for sails. Trims sails after machine seaming and creases edges by hand to prepare for machine finishing. May prepare sails for repair by opening seams and cutting out defective cloth or rope with hand shears. May shrink cotton cloths before cutting by soaking in water. May lay out and draw sail patterns on floor [SAIL-LAY-OUT WORKER (tex. prod., nec)].
GOE: 06.02.27 STRENGTH: L GED: R3 M2 L2 SVP: 4 DLU: 77

781.484-010 PLEAT PATTERNMAKER (garment; tex. prod., nec)
Lays out cardboard patterns as specified for use in making pleats in fabrics: Computes dimensions of pleats according to length of material, and size and style of garment specified on work ticket. Measures and marks top and bottom of pattern into designated widths for pleats, using ruler and protractor. Punches hole in cardboard to mark positions, using pin. May score pleat crease lines and fold pattern.
GOE: 06.02.31 STRENGTH: L GED: R3 M3 L2 SVP: 5 DLU: 77

781.667-010 ASSEMBLER (glove & mit.)
Sorts glove parts after cutting according to size, style, type of material, and color. Stacks specified number of parts for each style in box or tray. Stores extra parts in bins. May carry dies from storage to cutting machine and assist DIE CUTTER (any industry) in mounting gang dies onto rack of machine.
GOE: 06.03.02 STRENGTH: L GED: R2 M1 L2 SVP: 2 DLU: 77

781.682-010 TRIMMER, MACHINE (garment; knitting)
Operates sewing machine equipped with cutting blade attachment to trim excess fabric from material or article. Depresses pedal to start machine, moves hand and foot controls, and guides material or articles under blade to trim excess fabric and facilitate subsequent operation. May be designated by type of article or material trimmed as Collar Trimmer (garment; knitting); Brassiere-Cup-Mold Cutter (garment).
GOE: 06.02.05 STRENGTH: L GED: R2 M1 L1 SVP: 2 DLU: 77

781.684-010 CARPET CUTTER I (carpet & rug) alternate titles: cut order hand; rug cutter
Measures and cuts carpet from stock rolls to specified dimensions or according to diagrammed instructions, using tape measure, triangle, chalkline, and hand cutting tool: Unrolls carpeting on floor, measures cutting dimensions, using triangle and tape measure, and marks cutting guide lines, using chalkline. Inserts and aligns hand cutting tool under carpet, and pushes and guides cutting tool across carpet to cut required size and shape carpet from stock roll. Rerolls carpeting to be returned to storage and rolls up cut carpet to facilitate further operations.
GOE: 06.02.27 STRENGTH: M GED: R2 M2 L2 SVP: 4 DLU: 77

781.684-014 CUTTER, MACHINE I (any industry) alternate titles: cloth-cutting-machine operator
Cuts multiple layers of fabric into parts for articles, such as canvas goods, house furnishings, garments, hats, stuffed toys, and upholstered furniture, using portable electric cutter: Inserts base of cutter under layers of fabric, starts cutter, and guides cutter around edges of pattern or template or along markings on fabric to cut out parts. Drills holes through layers of fabric, using electric drill, or cuts notches in edges of parts with scissors or electric cutter to mark parts for assembly. Sharpens blade with abrasive stone or belt attached to cutter as quality of cut indicates dull blade. Changes cutter blades, using screwdriver or wrench. May guide layers of fabric around blade of stationary cutter (bandsaw), according to pattern markings. May spread fabric on table preparatory to cutting [SPREADER, MACHINE (any industry) 781.685-010]. May arrange patterns on top ply of fabric and mark outline of pattern on fabric with chalk or crayon [MARKER (any industry) I 781.384-014]. May separate cutting waste according to color of material. May be designated according to type of cutting machine used as Circular-Knife Cutter, Machine (any industry); Straight-Knife Cutter, Machine (any industry); or according to type of material, article, or part cut as Canvas Cutter, Machine (tex. prod., nec); Cover Cutter, Machine (furniture; tex. prod., nec); Drapery Cutter, Machine (tex. prod., nec); Garment-Parts Cutter, Machine (garment); Hat-Parts Cutter, Machine (hat & cap). May be designated: House-Furnishings Cutter, Machine (tex. prod., nec); Terry-Cloth Cutter, Machine (tex. prod., nec); Upholstery Cutter, Machine (furniture).
GOE: 06.02.27 STRENGTH: M GED: R3 M2 L2 SVP: 5 DLU: 79

781.684-018 CUTTER, ROTARY SHEAR (tex. prod., nec)
Cuts toweling into individual towel lengths, using rotary shear: Pushes boxes of material into feeding position and threads toweling under guides on cutting

table. Pulls material across table and guides rotary shear along cut marks woven into material to cut toweling into individual lengths. Presses button on side of rotary shear to tally production. Stacks towels on table. May feed cloth from finishing ranges onto cutting table.
GOE: 06.04.27 STRENGTH: L GED: R2 M1 L2 SVP: 3 DLU: 77

781.684-022   CUTTING INSPECTOR (tex. prod., nec)
Examines parts of articles, such as bedspreads, curtains, or draperies, prior to assembly to detect cutting defects: Compares parts with pattern to determine accuracy of cutting. Trims parts to fit pattern, using scissors. Marks parts at specified places to indicate assembly point, using chalk or pencil.
GOE: 06.03.02 STRENGTH: L GED: R3 M1 L1 SVP: 3 DLU: 77

781.684-026   DRAPER (garment; knitting)
Examines fit and hang of garments, and marks location of trimmings and fasteners to be added and defects to be corrected: Positions garment on sized model form and examines fit and hang of garment for conformity to model. Indicates defects, such as wrinkles, bulges, or puckers, and positioning of fasteners and trimming, such as belts, buttons, sashes and snaps, by pinning garment or marking with chalk. May be designated according to garment draped as Coat Draper (garment); Dress Draper (garment).
GOE: 06.02.31 STRENGTH: L GED: R3 M2 L3 SVP: 4 DLU: 77

781.684-030   DRAPERY-HEAD FORMER (retail trade)
Forms heading in drapes, using shears, steam iron, and sizing device: Lays drapes on table to straighten fabric. Measures fabric to specification and fastens material to table, using sizing device and clamps. Cuts uneven edges of material with shears. Folds material over crinoline and presses material with steam iron to form heading.
GOE: 06.04.27 STRENGTH: L GED: R2 M1 L1 SVP: 2 DLU: 77

781.684-034   LAY-OUT-MACHINE OPERATOR (tex. prod., nec) alternate titles: prehemmer; tabler
Measures curtains, draperies, and bedspreads to determine if lengths meet specifications and pins or marks hems in them, using layout table: Slides adjustable straightedge of layout table to specified position, using graduated marks of table as guide. Clamps edge of material to straightedge and spreads material over table. Verifies length of material against scale and removes surplus with shears. Folds edges of material and pins them in place to form hems.
GOE: 06.04.27 STRENGTH: L GED: R3 M1 L1 SVP: 4 DLU: 77

781.684-038   NYLON-HOT-WIRE CUTTER (tex. prod., nec)
Marks and cuts nylon webbing and cord for parachute harness and lines, using heated wire cutter: Positions article on board under marking guide and marks assembly and sewing guides, using pencil. Depresses pedal to lower heated wire that cuts and seals edges of nylon to prevent raveling.
GOE: 06.04.27 STRENGTH: L GED: R2 M2 L1 SVP: 3 DLU: 77

781.684-042   PERFORATOR (tex. prod., nec) alternate titles: pattern-perforating-machine operator
Punches designs on paper to form embroidery patterns (stencils), using either of following methods: (1) Inserts needle in holder of electric perforating tool and turns dial to regulate perforating speed. Positions paper on felt pad beneath tool and presses button to start tool. Guides needle over paper following predrawn design, to perforate paper and form embroidery pattern (stencil). (2) Inserts pins into foam rubber pad, following drawings or paper patterns. Positions paper over pins and presses paper against pins to perforate paper and form pattern.
GOE: 06.04.26 STRENGTH: L GED: R2 M1 L1 SVP: 3 DLU: 77

781.684-046   RUG CLIPPER (carpet & rug) alternate titles: carver; clipper; rug cutter
Guides cutting head of powered clipper over surface of hooked and tufted rugs to cut nap to uniform length or to cut design into rug, following guidelines. Measures depth of cut, using ruler. May vacuum rug to remove cut yarn. May comb pile to raise uncut loops, using steel-toothed comb, and cut loops, using scissors.
GOE: 06.04.27 STRENGTH: M GED: R2 M2 L2 SVP: 3 DLU: 77

781.684-050   RUG-SAMPLE BEVELER (carpet & rug) alternate titles: sample finisher
Trims edges of sample rug swatches, using beveling machine, and glues beveled edges to prevent raveling: Holds rug sample edge against guide on feed bed of beveling machine, and moves edge under blade that cuts edges on slant for appearance. Inserts beveled edge into slit of glue bottle, turns bottle upside down, and slides edges of rug sample through slit to glue edge and prevent raveling.
GOE: 06.04.27 STRENGTH: L GED: R1 M1 L1 SVP: 2 DLU: 77

781.684-054   SLITTER (knitting)
Slits welt of hose for use in making panty hose or leotards, using one of following methods: (1) Positions welt of hose on edge of board equipped with electrically heated protruding wire, aligns mark on welt with slot, and pulls welt down to specified point on board passing through heated wire and slitting welt. (2) Pulls hose over upright board, aligns mark on welt with slot, and pulls welt down to specified point on board. Slits welt using solder iron equipped with heated wire. (3) Pulls hose over board, aligns welt over slot, and pulls welt down to specified point on board. Slits welt by pushing small flat iron equipped with electrically heated wire along slotted area under welt. May control tem-

perature of wire by adjusting heat gauge. May scrape residue from wire, using knife or metal object.
GOE: 06.04.27 STRENGTH: L GED: R2 M1 L1 SVP: 2 DLU: 77

781.684-058   TRIM-STENCIL MAKER (any industry) alternate titles: pattern-punching-machine operator
Lays out and traces patterns on paper to make stencils used for cutting cloth upholstery: Arranges master patterns on paper in such manner as to minimize waste when cloth is cut. Traces patterns on paper, using pencil. Perforates paper, using hand punch or by guiding automatic punch around traced lines so that pattern will be transferred to material when chalk powder is dusted over stencil.
GOE: 06.04.26 STRENGTH: L GED: R2 M2 L2 SVP: 3 DLU: 77

781.684-062   WASTE SALVAGER (garment) alternate titles: small-piece cutter
Sorts usable pieces of cloth from cloth discarded after cutting, and cuts garment parts from salvaged pieces: Cuts out defects, using hand shears, following instructions on cutting ticket. Positions pattern on material and cuts around pattern, using hand shears or electric knife. Stacks garment parts according to size, style, and color. May separate defective cloth according to color and type.
GOE: 06.02.27 STRENGTH: L GED: R3 M1 L2 SVP: 3 DLU: 77

781.684-066   MATERIAL ASSEMBLER (furniture)
Gathers and assembles specified upholstery materials and accessories for use in manufacture of upholstered furniture: Reads work ticket to determine type and quantity of materials needed by upholsterers to upholster unit according to specifications. Gathers materials and accessories, such as *edge rolls*, polyfoam or dacron padding, plywood panels, and metal fasteners, from storage areas and places materials with designated furniture frame to facilitate subsequent processing. Cuts edge rolls and polyfoam to specified length and pattern, using electric cutter. Sprays edges of back and seat cushions with glue.
GOE: 06.04.27 STRENGTH: M GED: R2 M2 L2 SVP: 4 DLU: 86

781.684-070   SAMPLE CUTTER (furniture)
Cuts upholstery fabric into squares for use as sample swatches, using electric knife, scissors, and pinking machine: Reads sample list to determine specified fabric and pattern and quantity of swatches to be fabricated. Spreads fabric on table in single or multiple layers. Positions pattern over fabric to ensure fabric design is on swatch area and traces outline of pattern, using chalk. Removes pattern and cuts along outline, using scissors, electric knife, and pinking machine, to form swatch. Punches holes in swatches, using drill press.
GOE: 06.02.27 STRENGTH: V GED: R2 M1 L1 SVP: 3 DLU: 86

781.684-074   CUTTER, HAND I (any industry)
Cuts out, shapes, or trims material or articles, such as canvas goods, garment parts, hats and caps, house furnishings, or knit goods, to facilitate subsequent operations, using scissors or knife: Unrolls and lays out material along calibrated scale on cutting table or measures material with ruler and cuts material into lengths, using scissors or knife. Positions pattern or template on material or marks around pattern or template, using chalk or pencil, and cuts out parts, using scissors or knife. Cuts notches in edges of parts to mark them for assembly. Shapes or trims excess material from parts. May match materials for color or shade. May cut or trim knit goods, using hot-wire device. May mark identification numbers on parts. May spread cloth on table in single or multiple lays prior to cutting. May assemble and fold articles after cutting. May be designated according to type of material or article cut as Applique Cutter, Hand (tex. prod., nec); Bedspread Cutter, Hand (tex. prod., nec); Blanket Cutter, Hand (tex. prod., nec); Canvas Cutter, Hand (tex. prod., nec); Curtain Cutter, Hand (tex. prod., nec); Drapery Cutter, Hand (tex. prod., nec); Garment-Parts Cutter, Hand (garment). May be designated: Hat-And-Cap-Parts Cutter, Hand (hat & cap); Knit-Goods Cutter, Hand (knitting); Terry-Cloth Cutter, Hand (tex. prod., nec).
GOE: 06.02.27 STRENGTH: L GED: R3 M1 L2 SVP: 4 DLU: 80

781.684-078   CUTTER APPRENTICE, HAND (any industry)
Performs duties as described under APPRENTICE (any industry) Master Title.
GOE: 06.02.27 STRENGTH: L GED: R3 M1 L2 SVP: 4 DLU: 77

781.685-010   SPREADER, MACHINE (any industry) alternate titles: layer up
Tends machine that spreads cloth in successive layers on table to prepare cloth for cutting: Positions bolt of cloth on carriage of machine, turns handle to align edge of cloth with marks on table, threads cloth end through feed rollers, and clamps cloth to end of table. Starts machine that automatically spreads cloth in even layers as it moves back and forth over table, or pushes machine along track over cutting table. Inspects cloth as it is spread to detect defects, such as dye shadings and holes. Cuts out defects with hand shears. Laps ends of cloth at points marked on table. Straightens edges and smooths layers of cloth with hands. Turns handwheel to adjust feeding mechanism of machine according to weight of cloth. Cuts cloth from roll, using hand shears. May mark pattern outlines on top ply of cloth [MARKER (any industry) I 781.384-014]. May cut spread cloth [CUTTER, MACHINE (any industry) I 781.684-014].
GOE: 06.04.05 STRENGTH: H GED: R3 M2 L2 SVP: 3 DLU: 78

781.687-010   ASSEMBLER (garment; glove & mit.) alternate titles: assorter; bundler; bundle tier; feeder; fitter, factory; folder; matcher; piecer-up; tier
Assembles specified number of selected garment, glove, or mitten parts into bundles for distribution to production workers: Selects parts required to make

complete article according to size, style, and color, following style guides or applying knowledge of styles. Counts specified number of garment parts of same size, style, and color and ties parts into bundles by hand. Ties production ticket to bundles of parts. Stacks bundles onto handtruck according to style, size, and color. May mark parts to indicate points of assembly or openings to be cut, using chalk or pencil, or by cutting notches with scissors. May replace defective parts found while assembling bundles. May assemble completed suit ensembles, such as coat, vest, and pants. May notify cutting department of need for additional parts to replace stock shortage.
GOE: 06.03.02 STRENGTH: L GED: R2 M1 L2 SVP: 3 DLU: 78

781.687-014 CLOTH EXAMINER, HAND (textile) alternate titles: fabric inspector; finished-cloth checker; shader and folder; stretcher

Examines finished cloth for defects, such as grease spots, tears, and variations in color, finish, and dimensions: Measures width of cloth with ruler to detect variations from customer and plant standards. Turns through cloth folds or pulls cloth over inspection frame and feels and scans cloth to detect defects and variations in color and finish. Cuts defects from cloth, using scissors, or marks defects with chalk, thread, or label to indicate yardage allowance for defects. Records yardage for each cut of cloth examined. Routes cloth that does not conform to customer and plant specifications to CLOTH GRADER (textile). May tear sample strip from each cut of cloth. May count folds to determine yardage in each cut of cloth. May be designated according to specialization as Cloth-Colors Examiner (textile); Cloth-Cutting Inspector (textile).
GOE: 06.03.02 STRENGTH: L GED: R2 M1 L1 SVP: 3 DLU: 77

781.687-018 CLOTH TEARER (garment) alternate titles: tearer

Tears pieces from hemmed bolts of cloth prior to their fabrication into articles, such as handkerchiefs. Tears cloth, beginning at nick in cloth and stopping at opposite hem. Cuts through hem with scissors. May nick edge of cloth by folding and impaling it on equally spaced spikes on table and snipping edge with scissors. May tear cloth woven in special pattern so that pattern is centered in each article.
GOE: 06.04.27 STRENGTH: M GED: R2 M1 L1 SVP: 2 DLU: 77

781.687-022 CUTTER HELPER (any industry)

Assists in cutting materials for articles, such as bedspreads, curtains, draperies, garment parts, and glove parts: Spreads material on cutting table. Removes cut material from table and lays it over rack or in handtruck. Performs other duties as described under HELPER (any industry) Master Title.
GOE: 06.04.27 STRENGTH: L GED: R2 M1 L1 SVP: 2 DLU: 77

781.687-026 CUTTER, HAND II (any industry)

Cuts narrow material, such as buckram, elastic, labels, lace, or ribbon to specified length with scissors or knife, using either of following methods: (1) Unrolls material from spool or bolt along calibrated scale on cutting table or measures material with ruler and cuts material into lengths, using scissors. (2) Winds strand of material around reel or pegs on cutting table and cuts material at specified points, using scissors or knife. May tie lengths of material into bundles. May be designated according to type of material or article cut as Band Cutter (knitting); Elastic Cutter, Hand (any industry); Lacing Cutter (plastic synth.); Venetian-Blind-Tape Cutter (furniture).
GOE: 06.04.27 STRENGTH: L GED: R2 M1 L1 SVP: 2 DLU: 78

781.687-030 CUTTER, HAND III (any industry) alternate titles: dinker; mallet-and-die cutter

Cuts out parts of articles from materials, such as cloth, felt, leather, or plastic, using dies and mallet: Spreads one or more layers of material on table, positions specified die on material, and strikes die with mallet to force die through material. May be designated according to product cut as Felt-Pad Cutter (button & notion); Glove Cutter (glove & mit.; leather prod.); Petal Cutter (button & notion).
GOE: 06.04.34 STRENGTH: M GED: R1 M1 L1 SVP: 2 DLU: 77

781.687-034 GLOVE-PARTS INSPECTOR (glove & mit.) alternate titles: leather-piece inspector

Inspects and sorts parts of leather gloves or mittens after cutting: Examines parts to detect defects, such as holes, scars, and cutting nicks. Trims part to remove defects, using hand shears. Feels leather part to determine weight and thickness. Sorts parts according to color, weight, and quality standards for specified styles and leather parts of comparable quality required to make complete glove or mitten [ASSEMBLER (garment; glove & mit.)].
GOE: 06.03.02 STRENGTH: L GED: R3 M1 L2 SVP: 4 DLU: 77

781.687-038 GOODS LAYER (textile) alternate titles: cloth layer-out

Lays out cloth in preparation for sewing into continuous strips: Cuts bands from bale with wire snips and removes burlap wrapping. Stacks folded cloth on floor or handtruck with ends exposed to facilitate sewing. Records lot numbers and total yardage of cloth laid out on work ticket.
GOE: 05.09.02 STRENGTH: M GED: R2 M1 L1 SVP: 2 DLU: 77

781.687-042 MARKER (garment; retail trade; tex. prod., nec)

Marks sewing guides on garments or material, using chalk, crayon, or pencil, to facilitate further sewing operations, by any of following methods: (1) Measures specified distance from edge or reference point on article, using ruler or tape measure, and marks sewing guides for position of buttons, buttonholes, snap or gripper fasteners, hems, cuffs, buckram, crinoline, or other trimmings. (2) Turns screws to set chalk holders in position along horizontal bar of lever-type marking device, according to size of garment. Positions garment on table beneath bar and depresses pedal or moves lever to lower bar that marks position of buttonhole or buttons. (3) Aligns weave and print of adjacent edges of garment parts, following markings (notches), and marks sewing guidelines. (4) Positions pattern on garment and marks around pattern, or lays transfer paper on stack of garments beneath lever-type marker and lowers marker to transfer sewing guides to material. May trim excess material from hemlines, using scissors. May place buttons in garment pocket. May be designated according to marking objective as Button-Buttonhole Marker (garment); Hem Marker (garment; retail trade; tex. prod., nec); Matcher (garment); Pocket Marker (garment).
GOE: 06.04.27 STRENGTH: L GED: R2 M1 L1 SVP: 2 DLU: 77

781.687-046 MARKING STITCHER (garment)

Draws thread through several layers of garment parts to mark points for attachment of other parts, using handpowered machine: Places spool of thread on spindle and draws thread through guide and eye of needle. Positions several layers of garment parts on machine bed under needle. Depresses lever that forces needle downward to draw thread through parts, following markings on fabric. Cuts thread between layers of fabric, using scissors, leaving thread through each part to serve as guide for attachment of other parts, such as flaps and pockets.
GOE: 06.04.27 STRENGTH: L GED: R2 M1 L1 SVP: 2 DLU: 77

781.687-050 RIBBON CUTTER (narrow fabrics)

Cuts woven narrow fabrics, such as labels, ribbon, or webbing from loom, using scissors. May thread fabric through portable measuring device as it is wound onto roll. May transport boxes of fabric to storage.
GOE: 06.04.27 STRENGTH: H GED: R2 M1 L1 SVP: 2 DLU: 77

781.687-054 RUG-BACKING STENCILER (carpet & rug)

Stencils designs on rug backing material, using mop, lampblack solution, and perforated paper patterns to prepare backing for hooking operations: Measures and cuts material, using ruler and scissors. Assembles spiked frame on floor, using screwdriver, and pulls material taut over spikes. Positions and pins pattern to material and mops lampblack solution onto pattern to transfer design. Dry mops pattern to remove solution and removes material from frame. May stretch material onto hooking frame and remove hooked rug from frame.
GOE: 06.04.27 STRENGTH: M GED: R2 M1 L1 SVP: 3 DLU: 77

781.687-058 SPREADER I (any industry) alternate titles: cloth layer; cloth spreader

Spreads layers of cloth on table preparatory to marking and cutting parts for such articles as garments, mattress or upholstery covers, and bedspreads: Mounts roll of cloth in rack at end of table. Unreels successive lengths of cloth onto table, spreading each length evenly on length beneath. Places weights on cloth, fastens edges of fabric lay, using stapler, or clamps edges of cloth to hold material in position for cutting. May measure specified length of material to be cut according to work order or verbal instructions. May cut out parts, using scissors. May assemble cut garment parts. May work as member of two-person team and position, secure with metal rules, and cut cloth, using shears, rather than folding successive layers, to allow front surface of each layer to face upwards.
GOE: 06.04.27 STRENGTH: M GED: R2 M1 L1 SVP: 2 DLU: 77

781.687-062 STAMPER I (tex. prod., nec)

Transfers decorative designs from paper embroidery stencils (patterns) onto fabric articles, such as armbands, banners, and shirts to serve as guides for embroidery or other sewing operations, using either of following methods: (1) Positions stencil on fabric and brushes stamping solution through perforations to form outline of design on fabric. (2) Rubs powdered marking chalk over perforated pattern with blackboard eraser to force powder through perforations onto fabric.
GOE: 06.04.27 STRENGTH: L GED: R2 M1 L1 SVP: 2 DLU: 77

781.687-066 STENCILER (garment; tex. prod., nec)

Applies chalk, fluorescent powder, or fluorescent solution to perforated stencil to mark garment part for cutting or for subsequent sewing operations, such as making darts, attaching pockets, or embroidering.
GOE: 06.04.27 STRENGTH: L GED: R2 M1 L1 SVP: 2 DLU: 77

781.687-070 TRIMMER, HAND (any industry) alternate titles: finisher; hand clipper

Trims ravelings, loose threads, or excess material from articles, such as garments, hosiery, textile products, embroidered articles, or bolts or rolls of cloth, using scissors. May scan trimmed articles for soiled spots and stitching and dyeing defects. May clean spots or stains from articles, using cleaning fluids, rags, brushes, or sponges. May be designated according to material trimmed as Cloth Trimmer, Hand (textile); Facing-End Trimmer (knitting).
GOE: 06.04.27 STRENGTH: L GED: R2 M1 L1 SVP: 2 DLU: 77

782 HAND SEWERS, MENDERS, EMBROIDERERS, KNITTERS, AND RELATED OCCUPATIONS, N.E.C.

This group includes occupations, not elsewhere classified, concerned with basting, trimming, stitching, and related handwork to join, shape, decorate, finish, or repair garments and accessories or related products. Price being the controlling factor, this work is most extensively performed on fine-quality garments and tailored apparel.

782.361-010 CORSET FITTER (retail trade)

Fits and alters foundation garments, such as girdles and corsets, to customer's measurements: Measures customer, using tape measure, and records measurements on alteration tag. Pins garment at various points or marks with chalk to indicate alterations required. Sews garment by hand or machine, performing alterations, such as adjusting length of garment, garters, or straps, or taking in darts.
GOE: 05.05.15 STRENGTH: L GED: R3 M2 L3 SVP: 7 DLU: 77

782.361-014 EMBROIDERY PATTERNMAKER (retail trade; wholesale tr.)

Draws designs on tracing paper and transfers them onto cloth to provide guide for embroidery: Sketches patterns with pencil, selecting or creating designs approved by customer. Guides pattern under needle of machine that perforates pattern lines. Rubs wax, powder, or charcoal over perforated lines with wet brush or pouncer to transfer pattern outline to cloth, providing guide for embroidery.
GOE: 01.06.03 STRENGTH: L GED: R4 M3 L3 SVP: 6 DLU: 77

782.381-010 HAT TRIMMER (laundry & rel.)

Replaces and sews hat trimmings, such as linings, hatbands, ribbons, and ornaments on cleaned hats, by hand or using sewing machine: Cuts ribbons and leathers to length, using scissors. Folds ribbon to form bows and other ornaments, and stitches them to hat. Bastes linings and ribbons to hat, using needle and thread. Blind stitches (whips) leather to hat to form sweatband, by hand or sewing machine. Folds ribbon to form binding, by hand or uses sewing machine equipped with binding attachment. May cut and rip out stitches to remove trimmings before hat is cleaned. May scrub lining ribbons and bows of women's hats and press them with hand iron. May reshape artificial flower ornaments by hand to freshen them.
GOE: 06.02.27 STRENGTH: L GED: R3 M1 L2 SVP: 5 DLU: 77

782.381-014 ORIENTAL-RUG REPAIRER (any industry)

Reweaves damaged areas of oriental or other expensive rugs, following color, pattern, and weave of rug: Tacks damaged area of rug onto wooden frame. Trims and removes tuft yarns and backing twine of damaged area, using scissors or knife. Inserts needle and twine into edge of damaged area, draws twine across area and into opposite edge, and interlaces twine to form rug backing. Selects tuft yarn, according to kind of yarn in rug, color, and pattern of rug. Weaves yarn into backing twine, using needle, and following pattern and weave of rug, to form rug pile. Trims loose thread ends. May stretch oriental rugs to restore shape of rug and remove wrinkles or misshapen areas [ORIENTAL-RUG STRETCHER (any industry)].
GOE: 05.05.15 STRENGTH: M GED: R4 M3 L3 SVP: 6 DLU: 77

782.381-018 RUG REPAIRER (laundry & rel.)

Repairs and remodels rugs and carpets: Cuts patch from corner or edge of defective rug, or from carpet material or another rug of similar color and pattern for use in repair of damaged rug. Darns holes in rug-backing by hand, using cross-stitch to sew fibers together. Selects matching rug fibers and stitches them to rug-backing with needle and thread to reburl (reweave) damaged area and restore nap (pile). Patches rug by stitching edges of rug and patch together with carpet stitch. Remodels rugs by cutting to required size and shape, using hand shears. Binds edges of rugs by operating serging machine, or sews edges of rug or carpet, using needle and thread.
GOE: 05.05.15 STRENGTH: M GED: R3 M2 L3 SVP: 6 DLU: 77

782.381-022 WEAVER, HAND (personal ser.) alternate titles: french weaver; inweaver; overweaver; repair weaver; reweaver; section weaver; thread weaver

Weaves threads or patches into fabric articles to repair holes, tears, or worn places, using weavers' hand needles: Cuts patch from seam or hem allowance of article, using scissors. Pins article to padded block. Reweaves defective area by either of following methods: (1) Pulls lengthwise and crosswise threads from patch. Inserts ballpoint or latch needle some distance from edge of hole and interlaces it over and under threads of article running perpendicular to needle, across hole or worn area, and into fabric on opposite side, following original pattern. Inserts raveled thread in needle and pulls needle and thread through fabric, leaving thread ends projecting from fabric. Repeats interlacing of raveled threads (reweaving) until hole or worn area is filled. Pulls strands back and forth with fingers until woven part forms color or pattern design of article. (2) Ravels threads from edge of hole and patch, leaving frayed appearance, and pins or bastes patch under hole so that pattern matches. Interlaces needle over and under threads of article perpendicular to needle. Inserts end of raveled patch thread and pulls needle and thread through fabric. Repeats process until loose (raveled) ends around hole are rewoven into patch. Turns article over and repeats process to reweave thread ends of patch into fabric of article. Cuts off projecting thread ends and marks repaired area with thread to facilitate inspection. May press article, using steam iron or damp cloth and dry iron.
GOE: 05.05.15 STRENGTH: S GED: R3 M2 L2 SVP: 5 DLU: 77

782.487-010 NETTING INSPECTOR (tex. prod., nec) alternate titles: inspector and mender; mender

Inspects and mends netting: Stretches netting over frame and examines rows of mesh for defects, such as broken twine and irregular knots. Measures mesh

with rule to ensure that net meets size specifications. Ties loose mesh with net-mending needle and cuts loose ends of twine with knife or scissors. Folds net preparatory to stretching or packing. May tie strips of netting together.
GOE: 06.03.02 STRENGTH: L GED: R2 M2 L2 SVP: 3 DLU: 77

782.684-010 CANVAS REPAIRER (any industry)

Repairs damaged or worn tent, awning, or other canvas articles: Spreads canvas on worktable and examines it for holes, tears, and worn areas. Trims edges of damaged area, using scissors or knife. Patches holes, sews tears, or darns defective area, using needle and thread or sewing machine. Stamps grommets into edges of canvas, using mallet and punch or eyelet machine. May repair leatherette fabrics. May measure structures for canvas coverings, using tape measure.
GOE: 06.04.27 STRENGTH: H GED: R2 M1 L1 SVP: 4 DLU: 77

782.684-014 CROCHETER, HAND (knitting)

Crochets edges, seams, and decorative pieces for garments, using crochet needles and yarn. May crochet coverings for buckle frames, buttons, and other similar trimmings.
GOE: 06.02.27 STRENGTH: L GED: R3 M1 L2 SVP: 5 DLU: 77

782.684-018 EMBROIDERER, HAND (tex. prod., nec) alternate titles: decorator, hand

Embroiders ornamental designs by hand over stamped or stenciled designs on fabric material: Fastens embroidery hoop over fabric to keep fabric taut. Threads needle with kind and color of thread specified on work ticket. Sews along cut lines of stamped design, utilizing knowledge of various stitches that may be required. May place fabric in frame instead of embroidery hoop to keep fabric taut. May use strings of beads instead of colored thread for ornamental work. May pin design on fabric preparatory to embroidering. May be designated according to specialty performed or item worked on as Initial Maker (garment); Quilt Sewer, Hand (tex. prod., nec).
GOE: 06.02.27 STRENGTH: S GED: R3 M1 L2 SVP: 5 DLU: 77

782.684-026 FISH-NET STRINGER (tex. prod., nec) alternate titles: net hanger; slugger

Strings fish netting to meter lines or ropes to form gill or pound nets, using needles and thread or twine, using either of following methods: Ties seaming twine or thread to end of meter line or rope. (1) Runs twine through outside meshes of netting, and over and under meter line to string gill net, using needles. (2) Draws shuttle-type wooden needle through successive meshes of netting, brings needle over and under rope at specified distance, and makes half hitch to fasten twine to rope. May be designated according to type of net strung as Gill-Net Stringer (tex. prod., nec); Webbing Seamer, Pound Net (tex. prod., nec).
GOE: 06.04.27 STRENGTH: L GED: R2 M1 L1 SVP: 3 DLU: 77

782.684-030 HOSIERY MENDER (knitting) alternate titles: darner; mender, hand; mender, machine

Mends defects in hosiery, panty hose, or leotards (tights), such as holes, runs, and pulled threads, using one or combination of following methods: (1) Sews holes with needle and thread. (2) Stretches portion of hose containing hole or run over mending cup and secures one end of broken thread, using needle and thread. Reknits dropped stitch or run, using latch needle. Bastes across other end of broken thread. Clips loose threads from hose with scissors. (3) Stretches hose over mending cup and moves powered-mending device across hose to return picked or pulled thread to position. Pulls hose on inspection form or over mending cup to locate defects. May smooth and fix mend, using electric iron. May be designated Greige Mender (knitting) when repairing undyed hose or Finish Mender (knitting) if repairing dyed hose.
GOE: 06.02.27 STRENGTH: L GED: R3 M1 L1 SVP: 3 DLU: 81

782.684-034 KNITTER (tex. prod., nec)

Knits garments, such as sweaters, dresses, and suits, and accessories, using yarn and needles determined by type of garment and stitch specified and individual measurements for garment. May sew linings, buttons, and fasteners onto garments. May shape, block, and steam garments.
GOE: 06.02.27 STRENGTH: L GED: R3 M3 L2 SVP: 5 DLU: 77

782.684-038 MATCH-UP WORKER (garment) alternate titles: damage cutter; thread cutter

Removes damaged parts of completed garments, following information on repair tags or markings on parts: Cuts and pulls threads to remove damaged parts, using scissors or knife. Obtains replacement parts from cutting department and routes garments and replacement parts to sewing department. May be designated according to type of garment repaired as Corset Repairer (garment).
GOE: 06.04.27 STRENGTH: L GED: R2 M1 L1 SVP: 4 DLU: 77

782.684-042 MENDER (carpet & rug; textile)

Mends torn or defective portions of unfinished or finished cloth or carpets and rugs by handweaving: Examines cloth or rug for tears or defects, or marking that indicate imperfections. Reweaves thread or yarn to close holes or repair defects, using needle and thread or *burling iron,* and blends repair thread or yarn with existing pattern. Draws missing warp or filling threads through cloth and pulls out coarse and surplus threads, using burling iron, tweezers, and needle and thread. Pulls loosely woven threads through back of cloth to reduce slack, using tweezers. May trim yarn from defect, using scissors. May weave patch into hole, pounding repaired area smooth, and be designated Rug Mender (carpet & rug).

GOE: 06.02.27 STRENGTH: L GED: R3 M1 L2 SVP: 4 DLU: 77

782.684-046 MENDER, KNIT GOODS (garment; knitting)

Repairs defects, such as holes, runs, dropped or pulled threads, and needles lines, in knitted cloth and garments, using needle and thread or latch needle: Examines cloth or garment to detect defects or markings indicating defects. Sews up holes, using needle and thread. Reknits runs and replaces broken threads, using latch needle. Pulls knots to wrong side of garment, using hook. May operate sewing machine to resew defective seams or sew up holes in fabric. May clean soil spots from fabric or garment, using spray gun and cleaning fluid.

GOE: 06.02.27 STRENGTH: L GED: R3 M1 L1 SVP: 3 DLU: 77

782.684-050 PASSEMENTERIE WORKER (tex. prod., nec) alternate titles: fringer; hand; sewer, hand

Fashions and hand sews cloth, braid, silk, and other materials to make ornaments for dresses, coats, and housefurnishings. Attaches fasteners and trimmings (passementerie), such as tassels, braids, cords, loops, and beads to ornaments. May tie colored ribbons into bows and do hand embroidery and fagoting. May weave or knot yarn to make braid or fringe and hand sew knots to prevent raveling.

GOE: 06.04.27 STRENGTH: L GED: R2 M1 L1 SVP: 4 DLU: 77

782.684-054 PINNER (tex. prod., nec)

Decorates fabrics or garments with embroidery or applique, performing any combination of following tasks: Positions and pins designs or pattern on fabric, following stamped pattern. Hangs embroidered fabrics in heating cabinet or irons fabric to char buckram. Rubs and kneads cloth with hand or scrapes it with blunt instrument to loosen charred buckram. Examines finished fabric for imperfections and loose threads. Cuts off loose threads, using scissors. Removes stains from fabric, using cloth and cleaning fluid. Counts pieces and verifies number with work ticket.

GOE: 06.04.27 STRENGTH: L GED: R2 M1 L1 SVP: 3 DLU: 77

782.684-058 SEWER, HAND (any industry) alternate titles: assembler; bander; band sewer; garment finisher; garment sewer, hand; hand stitcher; hand tacker; needleworker; table worker, sewing; trimmer

Joins and reinforces parts of articles, such as garments, curtains, parachutes, stuffed toys, or sews buttonholes and attaches fasteners to articles, or sews decorative trimmings to articles, using needle and thread: Selects thread, according to specifications or color of parts. Aligns parts, fasteners, or trimmings, following seams, edges, or markings on parts. Sews parts with various types of stitches, such as felling tacking, stitch and basting. Trims excess thread, using scissors or knife. May trim edges of parts, using scissors or knife. When sewing fasteners or trimmings to articles, may be designated Finisher, Hand (garment). May be designated according to stitch sewn as Baster, Hand (garment); Feller, Hand (garment). May be designated according to article or part sewn as Armhole Baster, Hand (garment); Bow Attacher (garment); Bow Tacker (hat & cap) I; Buttonhole Maker, Hand (garment); Buttonhole Tacker (garment); Button Sewer, Hand (garment); Collar Feller (garment). May be designated: Collar Tacker (garment); Drapery Sewer, Hand (tex. prod., nec); Dressmaker (garment); Edge Maker (garment); Hook-And-Eye Attacher (garment); Label Sewer, Hand (any industry); Lapel Baster (garment); Lapel Padder (garment); Lining Finisher (garment); Neck Feller (garment); Sleeve Baster (garment); Sleeve-Bottom Feller (garment); Tacker (garment); Top-Collar Baster (garment); Trimming Finisher (garment).

GOE: 06.04.27 STRENGTH: L GED: R2 M1 L1 SVP: 3 DLU: 78

782.684-062 WEAVER, HAND (narrow fabrics; textile) alternate titles: endless-belt finisher; splicer

Weaves sections of loom-woven belting to finish them or join them to form endless belts: Ties selvages together to secure belts. Inspects belting and removes loose filling threads. Draws warp threads over and under filling threads, using hook. Cuts warp threads to specified length, using tape measure and shears, and ties or laps warp threads together to join belts. Counts number of filling and warp threads per square inch and draws new filling and warp threads through belting to maintain specified weave pattern and to finish belting. May use hurdle fork to move filling threads close together when weaving narrow belting.

GOE: 06.02.27 STRENGTH: L GED: R2 M1 L2 SVP: 3 DLU: 77

782.687-010 BASTING PULLER (garment)

Breaks, cuts, or pulls basting stitches or loose threads from completed garments or garment parts, using fingers, scissors, or bodkin. Brushes chalk marks and lint from garments.

GOE: 06.04.27 STRENGTH: L GED: R1 M1 L1 SVP: 2 DLU: 77

782.687-014 BUTTONER (garment; knitting)

Buttons or snaps garments to prepare them for pressing or packing. Cuts off excess threads between buttons or around buttonholes, using hand shears. May turn garment right side out before buttoning.

GOE: 06.04.27 STRENGTH: L GED: R1 M1 L1 SVP: 1 DLU: 77

782.687-018 CLOTH-BALE HEADER (textile) alternate titles: bale coverer; burlapper

Sews lapped edges of burlap that protects bales or rolls of cloth during shipment, using needle and thread.

GOE: 06.04.27 STRENGTH: M GED: R1 M1 L1 SVP: 2 DLU: 77

782.687-022 ELASTIC-TAPE INSERTER (garment)

Inserts and draws elastic tape through hem channel of stretch garments, using leader: Selects strip of elastic of same length and width as hem channel, by aligning strip over hem. Pins tape to leader, using safety pin, inserts leader into hem channel, and draws tape through it. Unpins leader and hand staples channel at ends of hem to secure tape for sewing operation. May pin two leg bands together to make pair.

GOE: 06.04.27 STRENGTH: L GED: R2 M1 L1 SVP: 2 DLU: 77

782.687-026 PINNER (garment; tex. prod., nec) alternate titles: table draper

Positions and pins trimming and other ornamentation onto garments or garment parts, preparatory to sewing, according to paper patterns or markings. May be designated according to type of trimming or ornamentation as Lace Pinner (garment; tex. prod., nec).

GOE: 06.04.27 STRENGTH: L GED: R1 M1 L1 SVP: 2 DLU: 77

782.687-030 PULLER-THROUGH (glove & mit.)

Pulls loose ends of stitching threads from outside through to inside of gloves and mittens with hook, knots threads, and cuts off loose ends with scissors.

GOE: 06.04.27 STRENGTH: S GED: R1 M1 L1 SVP: 1 DLU: 77

782.687-034 RAVELER (knitting)

Unravels rows of excess fabric along looped seams of knitted garments by cutting several stitches with scissors and pulling out yarn by hand.

GOE: 06.04.27 STRENGTH: L GED: R1 M1 L1 SVP: 1 DLU: 77

782.687-038 RIPPER (garment; retail trade; tex. prod., nec)

Cuts or rips stitches from sections of articles or garments to prepare them for resewing, using ragor blade, scissors, or seam ripper. Pulls out loose threads. May be designated Garment Ripper, Alterations (garment).

GOE: 06.04.27 STRENGTH: L GED: R2 M1 L1 SVP: 2 DLU: 77

782.687-042 RUG BRAIDER, HAND (carpet & rug) alternate titles: braided-rug maker

Makes braided rugs by hand from strips of wool, cotton, or synthetic materials: Selects strips in matching, contrasting, or blending colors and interweaves three or more at time to form continuous braid. Lays braid on flat surface. Coils or bends it into shape, stitching edges together by hand. May cut material into strips and sew ends together by hand or machine. May dye materials.

GOE: 06.04.27 STRENGTH: L GED: R2 M1 L1 SVP: 2 DLU: 77

782.687-046 SACK REPAIRER (any industry) alternate titles: bag patcher; sack mender

Repairs worn or torn burlap and cloth sacks, using needle and thread or sewing machine. Cuts burlap or cloth to form patches for sacks, using shears. May close open end of sack to prepare sack for filling through valve.

GOE: 06.04.27 STRENGTH: S GED: R2 M1 L1 SVP: 2 DLU: 77

782.687-050 SECONDS HANDLER (knitting)

Sorts repaired knitted garments according to size, style, and color. Folds garments and places them in stockroom.

GOE: 06.03.02 STRENGTH: L GED: R2 M1 L1 SVP: 2 DLU: 77

782.687-054 TAPE STRINGER (garment; knitting)

Threads tape, ribbon, or yarn through tubing, lace, or garment parts, using bodkin. May tie ends into bow.

GOE: 06.04.27 STRENGTH: L GED: R1 M1 L1 SVP: 1 DLU: 77

782.687-058 THREAD MARKER (garment) alternate titles: basting marker

Sews temporary basting stitches along markings on garment parts to mark position of vees, pleats, and other garment parts to serve as guides for subsequent sewing operations, using needle and thread.

GOE: 06.04.27 STRENGTH: L GED: R2 M1 L2 SVP: 2 DLU: 77

783 FUR AND LEATHER WORKING OCCUPATIONS

This group includes occupations concerned with cutting, piecing, shaping, and sewing prepared skins of fur-bearing animals and leather to fit, alter, finish, or repair fur or fur-lined garments and accessories; and the fabrication of leather articles, such as harnesses, luggages, pocketbooks, purses, saddles, and other leather products. Fabrication and repair of hats, caps, gloves, and related products are included in Group 784. Fabrication and repair of footwear is included in Group 788.

783.131-010 SUPERVISOR, FURRIER SHOP (fur goods)

Supervises and coordinates activities of workers engaged in manufacture, alteration, and repair of fur garments: Inspects pelts for conformity with dressing and dyeing specifications. Directs workers in matching furs, and in cutting, shaping, and sewing operations. Inspects finished garments for conformance to standards of workmanship and pattern. Performs other duties as described under SUPERVISOR (any industry) Master Title. May sort, match, and cut pelts [FUR CUTTER (fur goods); FUR SORTER (fur goods)]. May discuss alterations or repairs with customer. May supervise one group of workers, such as FUR FINISHERS (fur goods), and be designated Fur Finisher, Head (fur goods).

GOE: 05.05.15 STRENGTH: L GED: R4 M3 L4 SVP: 7 DLU: 77

783.132-010 SUPERVISOR (leather prod.)

Supervises and coordinates activities of workers engaged in cutting, assembling, and joining parts to form articles, such as belts, briefcases, gun cases and

holsters, handbags, wallets, and other leather products: Trains workers in operation of machine cutters and sewing machines. Examines parts or finished articles for defects. Prepares requisition forms to order supplies. Performs other duties as described under SUPERVISOR (any industry) Master Title. May be designated according to department supervised as Assembly-Department Supervisor (leather prod.); Cloth-And-Leather-Department Supervisor (leather prod.); Cutting-Department Supervisor (leather prod.); Sewing-Department Supervisor (leather prod.).
GOE: 06.02.01 STRENGTH: L GED: R4 M3 L4 SVP: 5 DLU: 80

783.261-010   FURRIER (fur goods) alternate titles: fur repairer; fur tailor
Designs, makes, alters, restyles, and repairs fur garments, applying principles of fur garment construction and styling. May purchase pelts required to make garment. May estimate cost of making, repairing, or restyling garment. May sell furs [SALESPERSON, FURS (retail trade)].
GOE: 05.05.15 STRENGTH: L GED: R4 M3 L3 SVP: 8 DLU: 77

783.361-010   CUSTOM-LEATHER-PRODUCTS MAKER (leather prod.)
Lays out, cuts, and assembles custom leather products, such as belts, purses, sandals, and garments, from original designs or existing patterns: Examines customer's sketch or sample of leather product to be fabricated and confers with customer regarding specifications of product. Draws outline of leather parts on paper or cardboard to form pattern, and cuts out pattern pieces, using square, compass, ruler, pencil, and scissors. Selects leather, positions pattern on leather, and cuts leather parts, using knife and shears. Assembles leather products according to sketch, utilizing knowledge and experience and work devices, such as sewing machine, needle and thread or leather lacing, glue and clamps, or rivets and riveting tool. Applies liquid dyes, soaks leather in water, or engraves designs on leather to obtain special effects or shapes. Attaches buckles, metal rings, decorative brads, or grommets according to design, using handtools. Stitches or glues fabric or leather linings according to product design. Occasionally displays items and sells them to customers.
GOE: 05.05.15 STRENGTH: L GED: R3 M2 L3 SVP: 7 DLU: 86

783.381-010   FUR CUTTER (fur goods)
Selects and cuts pelts to make, alter, or repair garments or other fur articles: Selects required number of fur pelts and matches them for size, color, texture, and quality. Arranges pelts on pattern according to design and color, placing finest pelts where they will show to best advantage and give garment symmetrical appearance. Numbers pelts to indicate their pattern location. Cuts off inferior or unusable parts, such as heads, necks, sides, rumps, and tails. Slits skin of furs into diagonal strips, leaving uncut margin at edge, to obtain specified length and shape of pelt, using furrier's knife. Cuts pelts to shape them to garment pattern.
GOE: 06.02.27 STRENGTH: L GED: R3 M3 L2 SVP: 7 DLU: 77

783.381-014   FUR FINISHER (fur goods) alternate titles: fur sewer; fur tailor
Completes, alters, and repairs fur garments, sewing by hand or using sewing machine: Sews interlining to inside of fur skin by hand or using blindstitch sewing machine. Selects lining pattern or measures garment shell or old lining, cuts out lining parts, and sews parts together, using sewing machine. Sews lining into shell, using sewing machine or needle and thread. Sews on hooks, rings, hem tape, buttons, monograms, and padding for collars and cuffs, using needle and thread. May baste lining parts together by hand to facilitate machine sewing. May sew preassembled lining into shell. May sew linings only and be designated Fur Liner (fur goods). May replace linings and repair damaged skins and be designated Lining Finisher (laundry & rel.).
GOE: 06.02.27 STRENGTH: L GED: R3 M2 L2 SVP: 6 DLU: 77

783.381-018   HARNESS MAKER (leather prod.; retail trade)
Cuts, assembles, and joins leather and other parts of harnesses, following customer specifications concerning color and thickness of leather and size or type of harness, to fabricate new or repair damaged or worn harness: Traces outline of part on material. Cuts parts along outline from leather or canvas [CUTTER, HAND (any industry) I]. Assembles and joins edges of parts, using needle and thread or stitching machine. Inserts harness strap ends through buckles, rings, or other hardware, and loops and joins end to body of strap, using stitching machine or hand riveting tool. Punches buckle holes in harness, using awl or punch. Carves specified design on material, using handtools. Laces leather thong around article to form decorative edge. Applies paint and liquid dressing to harness to produce glossy finish, using brush or sponge. Cuts lining from fleece, following pattern and glues it to inside of saddle or holster. May clean harness. May specialize in replacing damaged harness parts, such as bridle, breast, or body harness and be designated Harness Repairer (leather prod.).
GOE: 05.05.15 STRENGTH: M GED: R3 M3 L3 SVP: 7 DLU: 77

783.381-022   LUGGAGE MAKER (leather prod.)
Covers and lines luggage frames with fabric, leather, imitation leather, or vinyl plastics and attaches hardware to complete luggage according to sketches or customer's order: Measures luggage frame with rule to determine size of cover material. Cuts material to size with guillotine knife, drapes material over frame, and trims it to fit, using scissors or knife. Spreads glue over back of material with brush and glues material to frame. Sews edges of material to frame, using foot-controlled stitching machine, to provide additional bond. Drills holes for rivets and attaches handles and hardware, using foot-controlled rivet punch machine. Cuts lining to fit inside of frame and glues it in place. Sews welting, piping, or chafing strips to decorate or protect luggage, using

stitching machine. May build wooden luggage frames. May operate stamping machine to stamp initials on luggage [STAMPING-PRESS OPERATOR (any industry)]. May repair or renovate worn or damaged luggage [LUGGAGE REPAIRER (any industry)].
GOE: 06.02.27 STRENGTH: M GED: R3 M2 L3 SVP: 7 DLU: 77

783.381-026   SADDLE MAKER (leather prod.)
Cuts, assembles, and joins leather parts and other materials to form saddle, following specifications, such as size of saddle, color and grain of leather, or type of saddle: Cuts out parts, according to specifications. Joins edges of parts to form saddle tree cover, using needle and thread or stitching machine. Positions covering and cushioning materials, such as cotton batting, foam rubber, or mohair over saddle tree. Joins covering to saddle tree, using cement, nails, needle and thread, or stitching machine. Attaches accessories or ornamentation to saddle with rivets or needle and thread. Applies paint and liquid dressing to produce glossy finish, using brush or sponge. May cut and stamp lettering and decorative designs into surface of leather, [LEATHER STAMPER (leather prod.)]. May be designated according to type of saddle made as Western-Saddle Maker (leather prod.). May specialize in replacement of damaged saddle parts, such as cushioned seats, canvas girths, cinches, and saddle bags and be designated Saddler (leather prod.; retail trade).
GOE: 05.05.15 STRENGTH: H GED: R3 M3 L3 SVP: 8 DLU: 77

783.384-010   FUR SORTER (fur goods) alternate titles: fur grader; fur matcher
Assorts fur skins into single-garment bundles according to shading, size, pattern, and density of fur: Compares pelts with sample pelt of each grade, stroking fur to feel its density, to see undercolor, and to judge height of hair. Selects those pelts that match or blend and have same thickness and length of fur. Judges number required for particular garment to be manufactured, and assembles them into bundles.
GOE: 06.03.01 STRENGTH: L GED: R3 M1 L2 SVP: 7 DLU: 77

783.387-010   FUR-REPAIR INSPECTOR (retail trade)
Inspects fur garments or pieces, following customer instructions, to determine cost of remodeling or repair: Examines article for frayed linings, worn spots and tears, and determines alterations needed to remodel article. Marks pattern and work ticket to indicate alterations or repairs to be made. Examines remodeled or repaired articles to verify repairs. May remodel or repair fur articles. May be designated according to type of article inspected as Coat-Repair Inspector (retail trade).
GOE: 05.05.15 STRENGTH: L GED: R3 M2 L2 SVP: 8 DLU: 77

783.681-010   FUR BLENDER (leather mfg.) alternate titles: fur dyer; fur tinter
Tints, bleaches or dyes furs according to specifications by applying liquid dye or bleaching compound to tips of guard hair or to all surface hair, using feather or brush to produce lustrous finish and to accentuate colors and shades of furs.
GOE: 01.06.02 STRENGTH: L GED: R3 M1 L2 SVP: 6 DLU: 77

783.682-010   FUR-MACHINE OPERATOR (fur goods) alternate titles: fur joiner; fur operator; fur sewer
Operates *fur machine* to join fur strips and pelts into garment parts or garments, such as collars, cuffs, linings, coats, and capes: Selects thread according to color, places spool on spindle, and draws thread through machine guides, tensions and needle eye. Inserts bobbin into shuttle and draws thread through guide and looper eye. Depresses pedal to open horizontal *feed cups*, aligns pelt edges and positions them between cups, and releases pedal to close cups against pelts. Guides fur strips or pelts between feed cups and across horizontal needle to join fur strips or pelts to form garment parts or garment, following markings on pelts and designer's pattern. May cut slits in fur pelt to separate it from strips, using knife, to let out pelts. May alter finished garment, such as removing excess fur to reduce highlighted color in fur texture, following designer's instructions. May join edges of lambskin strips to form paint roller covers.
GOE: 06.02.05 STRENGTH: L GED: R3 M2 L2 SVP: 6 DLU: 77

783.682-014   SEWING MACHINE OPERATOR (leather prod.)
Operates sewing machine to join parts of leather products, such as suitcases, handbags, and wallets. May operate machine equipped with shirring attachment. May operate machine equipped with wrapping and folding attachment to join parts of handbag handles and be designated Handle Sewer (leather prod.). May cut thread, using blade attached to machine or scissors. May oil machine and change needles. When joining or decorating handbag parts with decorative stitches, is designated Fancy Sewer (leather prod.). May be designated according to parts joined as Applique Sewer (leather prod.); Lining-Parts Sewer (leather prod.); or according to article assembled and sewed as Briefcase Sewer (leather prod.); Handbag Finisher (leather prod.). Performs duties as described under SEWING MACHINE OPERATOR, REGULAR EQUIPMENT (any industry) Master Title.
GOE: 06.02.05 STRENGTH: L GED: R3 M1 L1 SVP: 3 DLU: 80

783.684-010   ASSEMBLER, LEATHER GOODS I (leather prod.)
Assembles leather products, such as coin purses, handbags, keycases, pocket secretaries, or wallets, performing any combination of following duties: Turns handbag inside out and presses inner folds against flat-edged rod to sharpen creases. Punches holes in leather to facilitate attaching straps, snaps, or trim, using awl or perforating machine. Attaches buttons, clasps, straps, or trim to

leather parts, using eyelet machine. Folds and creases or pleats edges, using scissors, creasing iron, hammer, or *folding bone*. Applies cement to edges or parts, and presses parts together to secure parts. May sew edges or parts, using sewing machine. May select and match materials to assemble. May be designated according to article assembled as Assembler, Handbags (leather prod.); Coin-Purse Assembler (leather prod.); Keycase Assembler (leather prod.); Pocket-Secretary Assembler (leather prod.); Wallet Assembler (leather prod.).
GOE: 06.02.27 STRENGTH: L GED: R3 M2 L2 SVP: 3 DLU: 78

783.684-014 FUR NAILER (fur goods)
Lays out pelts and secures them to board to stretch and block pelts into desired shape: Brushes skin side of fur with water, to dampen it. Positions, stretches, and shapes pelt, skin side up, and nails or staples to board. Positions paper pattern over pelt and marks outline, using crayon, to indicate sections of pelt to be trimmed and to mark sewing guidelines for assembly operations. Removes dried furs from board. May trim fur along pattern outline, using knife, to obtain smooth edge. May moisten, press, and comb fur, using brush, steam and dry irons, and comb, to restore nap and luster to fur.
GOE: 06.02.31 STRENGTH: L GED: R3 M2 L2 SVP: 6 DLU: 77

783.684-018 INSPECTOR-REPAIRER (leather prod.)
Examines coin purses, handbags, wallets, and other leather articles for defects, such as missing seam stitches, faulty frame alignment, and blemishes, and repairs minor defects, using handtools: Trims excess material and thread from articles, using clippers. Wipes spots and stains from articles, using cleaning solution and cloth. Brushes stain on cuts, cements loose edges, presses out wrinkles, and aligns frame, using brushes, heated iron, pliers, and screwdriver. May place inserts, such as coin purses, combs, and tissue paper into articles. Attaches inspection tag to articles and records articles inspected. May place article in plastic bag prior to packing.
GOE: 06.03.02 STRENGTH: L GED: R3 M2 L2 SVP: 3 DLU: 80

783.684-022 LEATHER CUTTER (leather prod.)
Lays out, marks, and cuts leather or skins into parts for articles, such as holsters, belts, gun cases, garments and garment trim, surgical appliances, and paint roller covers, using leather knife or shears: Lays leather or skins on cutting table and positions pattern pieces on leather or skins to determine number of cuts. Marks outline of pattern on leather or skins, using pencil. Cuts around outline, using leather knife or shears. Turns screws on strap knife to adjust width of cut when cutting leather for rifle slings and gun case handles. Lays leather side on table, positions dies on leather to obtain maximum number of cuts from side, and strikes die with mallet to cut out part. May stack and tie cut pieces together. May cut parts with guillotine cutter. May punch holes in parts, using kick press.
GOE: 06.02.27 STRENGTH: L GED: R3 M2 L2 SVP: 4 DLU: 77

783.684-026 LEATHER WORKER (leather prod.)
Punches holes, installs rivets, and finishes edges of leather products, such as holsters, rifle cases, and belts, using handtools: Marks holes in article, using template and marking pencil. Punches holes for rivets, snaps, or buttons, using hand punch. Fastens parts together, using rivets, stitching machine, needle and thread, or adhesive. Attaches eyelets and metal decorations to article, using hammer and punch. Cuts around edge of article to smooth edge, using knife. Brushes stain on cut edge to match color of article. Rubs finished article with damp cloth to clean leather and rubs paste wax on surface, using cloth, to produce shine. May emboss designs on leather surface. May be designated according to article fabricated or repaired as Holster Maker (leather prod.); Rifle-Case Repairer (leather prod.).
GOE: 06.02.27 STRENGTH: M GED: R3 M2 L2 SVP: 5 DLU: 77

783.684-030 UTILITY BAG ASSEMBLER (leather prod.)
Assembles leather utility bags, using handtools and power tools: Brushes cement on underside of utility bag frame, positions frame unit in zipper template and zipper on cemented surface of unit to align and join zipper to unit prior to stitching operation. Brushes cement on bottom of bag frame flaps, positions metal frame bar on cemented surface, and folds leather flaps over bars. Places frame unit on bar cutter bed, depresses pedal to lower ram that holds unit in position, and pulls bar cutter knife handle to trim ends of zipper and frame. Brushes stain on cut ends. Positions frame on bending machine template, depresses pedal to lower ram that holds unit in position, and presses ends of unit down to shape frame into utility bag opening. Positions frame unit and carrying strap on anvil of stapling machine and depresses pedal to staple frame and strap. May hold seam between jaws of hammering device that straightens stitched seam and pushes seam out to form bead.
GOE: 06.04.23 STRENGTH: L GED: R2 M1 L2 SVP: 2 DLU: 77

783.685-010 COVERING-MACHINE TENDER (leather prod.)
Tends pneumatic-powered machine that stretches and presses precemented leather part over metal keycase half to form decorative covering on keycase: Turns knobs and handles to actuate heating element in machine and open air valves. Places metal keycase half in machine ram-head depression, and positions precemented leather part in bottom die jaws of machine. Presses buttons to open air valves that force ram head down into die jaws to cover keycase half with leather. Removes part from machine and inspects leather for defective covering. Presses loose edges of leather into snap slot, using *folding bone*.
GOE: 06.04.20 STRENGTH: L GED: R2 M1 L1 SVP: 2 DLU: 77

783.685-014 CREASER (leather prod.)
Tends heated press to fold and crease edges of leather for products, such as coin purses, wallets, and cigarette cases: Positions die in ram and turns

setscrews to secure die. Positions and bolts template guide on machine guide, using screwdriver and wrench. Turns rheostat to adjust heating element in ram to specified temperature. Folds leather part along fold line, using fingers. Positions folded part in guide template, and depresses pedal to lower heated creasing ram onto leather part to crease fold in edge of leather. Releases pedal to raise ram and removes part from machine.
GOE: 06.02.05 STRENGTH: L GED: R3 M1 L2 SVP: 4 DLU: 77

783.685-018 DISK-AND-TAPE-MACHINE TENDER (leather prod.)
Tends machine that affixes reinforced tape and plastic disks to closing snaps of flaps on leather articles, such as coin purses and wallets: Threads roll of linen tape on machine spools and pulls tape over and through rollers and guide. Places disk on tape on bed of machine and positions snap of coin purse flap over disk. Depresses pedal to activate mechanism that affixes tape and disk to snap and cuts tape.
GOE: 06.04.05 STRENGTH: L GED: R2 M1 L1 SVP: 2 DLU: 77

783.685-022 LAMINATOR II (leather prod.)
Tends machine that laminates (bonds) leather and plastic parts of leather articles, such as wallets, purses, and eyeglass cases: Presses buttons to activate heat element and conveyor, and turns knobs to adjust pressure of rollers. Positions precemented parts together and places them on conveyor belt that moves parts under heating element and through rollers to laminate parts.
GOE: 06.04.20 STRENGTH: L GED: R2 M1 L1 SVP: 2 DLU: 77

783.685-026 MARKING-MACHINE TENDER (boot & shoe; leather prod.)
Tends machine that prints stitch markings on leather parts to guide worker during stitching operations: Selects type of printing die, template guide, and ink cloth to use in machine according to specifications. Positions roll of ink cloth in machine holding arms and threads cloth through rollers. Positions printing die in machine and turns setscrews to secure die. Positions and bolts template in bed of machine, using screwdriver and wrench. Positions leather part in template and pulls lever to move ink cloth and die onto leather part to mark stitching guidelines. Releases lever and removes leather part.
GOE: 06.04.05 STRENGTH: L GED: R2 M1 L1 SVP: 2 DLU: 77

783.687-010 ASSEMBLER, LEATHER GOODS II (leather prod.)
Assembles leather products, performing any combination of following duties: Cuts loose threads from product, using scissors. Affixes cardboard backing to lining, using double-sided-gum tape. Cements cardboard to metal handle and staples preassembled leather parts to cardboard, prior to sewing operation, to assemble handles for handbags or luggage. Attaches handles to frame, using rings and pliers. Brushes cement on parts, such as tabs, slots, marks, and edges, and presses parts together to join them. Cements decorative leather or fabric strips onto metal frames to assemble handbags. Inverts presewn plastic or vinyl linings and inserts them in bags. Inserts plastic windows, card and photo holders, memo pads, ballpoint pens, identification cards, and price tags into specified sections of article. May stuff article with wadded paper to give shape to article. May place finished article in display box. May be designated according to job duties as Filler And Trimmer (leather prod.); Frame Coverer (leather prod.); Handle Attacher (leather prod.); Handle Maker (leather prod.).
GOE: 06.04.23 STRENGTH: L GED: R3 M1 L2 SVP: 2 DLU: 80

783.687-014 FUR TRIMMER (fur goods)
Trims blocked fur garments to remove excess fur around chalk-marked pattern on inside of garment, using hand knife.
GOE: 06.04.27 STRENGTH: L GED: R2 M1 L2 SVP: 3 DLU: 77

783.687-018 HIDE INSPECTOR (leather mfg.) alternate titles: hide examiner
Examines shipments of hides or skins for compliance with specifications, such as grade, type, and weight, and for defects, such as cuts or scars. Records data on work ticket.
GOE: 06.03.02 STRENGTH: L GED: R3 M2 L2 SVP: 4 DLU: 77

783.687-022 MATCHER, LEATHER PARTS (leather prod.)
Matches pieces of leather to be used in manufacture of leather products. Examines leather for defects, such as cuts and blemishes. Matches and sorts specified number of pieces of same color, texture, and size. May count number of pieces inspected and matched.
GOE: 06.03.02 STRENGTH: L GED: R2 M1 L2 SVP: 3 DLU: 77

783.687-026 PASTER, HAND OR MACHINE (leather prod.)
Presses belt tops and linings together, using hands and machine filled with paste: Loads hopper of machine and feeds belt top and lining through machine to apply coat of paste. Aligns belt top and lining by hand and runs parts through mangle to press them together. May apply paste to belt top and lining, using brush or spray gun. When top and lining are partially dry, aligns and presses them together by hand.
GOE: 06.04.23 STRENGTH: L GED: R2 M1 L1 SVP: 2 DLU: 77

783.687-030 TABLE WORKER (leather prod.)
Inserts sheets of waxed paper between precemented parts of small leather articles to prevent parts from sticking together. Places stacks of parts in boxes and carries boxes to next work station for further processing.

GOE: 06.04.27 STRENGTH: L GED: R1 M1 L1 SVP: 1 DLU: 77

784 OCCUPATIONS IN FABRICATION AND REPAIR OF HATS, CAPS, GLOVES, AND RELATED PRODUCTS

This group includes occupations concerned with working textile and leather materials into hats, caps, and gloves.

784.130-010 SUPERVISOR, CAP-AND-HAT PRODUCTION (hat & cap)

Supervises and coordinates activities of workers engaged in cutting, assembling, sewing, trimming, and blocking, men's and boy's caps and hats: Reviews work orders to determine staffing requirements and to plan and schedule production operations. Requisitions materials. Trains workers in operation of equipment, such as sewing machines, kick presses, cutting machines, and knives. Inspects samples of products for adherence to specifications for cutting, sewing, sizing, and blocking. May select and distribute materials to be assembled to workers. Performs other duties as described under SUPERVISOR (any industry) Master Title. May be designated according to department as Supervisor, Body Department (hat & cap); Supervisor, Braid Department (hat & cap); Supervisor, Finishing Department (hat & cap); Supervisor, Harvest-Hat Department (hat & cap); Supervisor, Sewing Deparment (hat & cap). May supervise and coordinate activities of workers engaged in blending fur cuttings and be designated Supervisor, Back Shop (hat & cap).
GOE: 06.02.01 STRENGTH: L GED: R4 M3 L3 SVP: 7 DLU: 78

784.132-010 SUPERVISOR (glove & mit.)

Supervises and coordinates activities of workers engaged in glove and mitten manufacturing activities, such as cutting, sewing, inspecting, and shipping: Examines gloves or mittens for defects, such as irregular stitches and misaligned parts. Instructs workers in operation and minor maintenance of sewing machines, and in methods to detect and correct defective work. Instructs workers in turning and pressing gloves or mittens made of materials, such as flannel, cotton, canvas, and leather. Performs other duties as described under SUPERVISOR (any industry) Master Title.
GOE: 06.02.01 STRENGTH: L GED: R4 M3 L3 SVP: 7 DLU: 78

784.261-010 MILLINER (retail trade)

Fabricates hats for individual customer or for store's stock: Cuts pattern from material to desired size and shape, using original design or adapting or copying existing model. Lays pattern on material and cuts material, following pattern. Molds, drapes, and blocks material, using hat forms and steam iron. Sews lining and other sections of hat together and trims with materials, such as ribbon, veil, feathers, and flowers, using needle and thread or sewing machine. Reproduces hats in various colors and materials. Alters stock hats to customer's wishes by changing ornaments and veiling.
GOE: 01.06.02 STRENGTH: L GED: R4 M2 L2 SVP: 6 DLU: 77

784.361-010 PATTERNMAKER (hat & cap) alternate titles: caster; mold maker; plaster whittler; whittling-room operator

Casts plaster hat-making patterns from sample hat and shapes patterns to specified form and dimensions, using hand knife: Melts and pours thin, even layer of wax over hat to stiffen it. Presses hat into loose sand to create impression that duplicates dimensions and shape of hat. Mixes plaster powder with water and pours it into sand impression to form pattern. Lifts pattern from sand after it hardens. Whittles, cuts, and scrapes plaster from pattern with hand knife to achieve specified form and dimensions, measuring and comparing pattern with hat, using rule and tape.
GOE: 01.06.02 STRENGTH: L GED: R4 M3 L3 SVP: 7 DLU: 77

784.387-010 INSPECTOR (hat & cap) alternate titles: brusher; hat measurer; passer; racker; repairer; selector; trimmer

Inspects finished or partially finished hats, caps, hat parts, and millinery for defects and damage, and repairs less extensive flaws: Examines articles for irregularities, such as faulty coloring, shaping, sizing, and stitching. Rejects or returns extensively damaged articles to originating department for repair. Informs supervisor regarding types of article defects or damage. Repairs less extensive damage, performing any combination of following tasks: Trims excess material and loose or protruding threads, using clippers or scissors. Removes spots or stains from article, using sponge and water, and brushes surface of hat to remove dust or foreign matter. Applies sizing solution to cover holes or thin spots, using dauber or brush. Resews loose stitches and size tags, using needle and thread. Hangs or stacks hats and caps on rack or on table for packing. May be designated according to specific inspection function as Hat-Body Inspector (hat & cap); Hat-Cone Inspector (hat & cap); Trimming Inspector (hat & cap).
GOE: 06.03.01 STRENGTH: L GED: R2 M1 L1 SVP: 3 DLU: 78

784.387-014 LEATHER GRADER (glove & mit.) alternate titles: leather sorter

Examines and grades pieces of leather used to make gloves and mittens: Examines leather to detect defects, such as scars and holes and feels leather to detect thin and thick areas. Grades and stacks leather according to number of defects, thickness, and color.
GOE: 06.03.01 STRENGTH: M GED: R3 M2 L2 SVP: 5 DLU: 77

784.587-010 HAT-BODY SORTER (hat & cap)

Sorts and stacks hats, according to color, size, and style, for further processing: Pulls hat over marked *plug* to measure hat size. Marks size in hat crown, using pencil or crayon. Stacks hats on shelf, according to color, size, and style specified. May compare and sort hats for height of crown and width of brim. May place adhesive-backed size and brand label in hat. May place inverted hat body over steam tank to remove excess gloss.
GOE: 06.03.02 STRENGTH: L GED: R2 M1 L2 SVP: 2 DLU: 77

784.682-010 GLOVE SEWER (glove & mit.)

Operates sewing machine to join or decorate glove and mitten parts or finished article: Guides parts under machine needle to join thumb pieces to back and palm; to assemble finger pieces and join pieces to glove; to join sides of cuffs or cuff to glove; to stitch around fingers, thumb, and sides of glove to close glove openings; to sew on knuckle strap or finger tips; to join parts of mittens; or to stitch knit linings to elastic wristbands to complete cuffs. May repair gloves with defective stitching and be designated Mender (glove & mit.). May be designated according to part sewn or operation performed as Closer (glove & mit.); Fingerer (glove & mit.); Fourchette Sewer (glove & mit.); Knuckle-Strap Sewer (glove & mit); Mitten Stitcher (glove & mit); Palm-And-Back Forger (glove & mit). May be designated: Strapper (glove & mit); Thumb Sewer (glove & mit.); Tipper (glove & mit.); Wrist Closer (glove & mit.); Wrister (glove & mit.); Wrist Liner (glove & mit.). Performs duties as described under SEWING-MACHINE OPERATOR, REGULAR EQUIPMENT (any industry) Master Title.
GOE: 06.02.05 STRENGTH: L GED: R3 M1 L2 SVP: 4 DLU: 79

784.682-014 HAT-AND-CAP SEWER (hat & cap)

Operates sewing machine to join, decorate, or reinforce hat or cap parts or finished article: Guides parts under machine needle to form crown, sides, brim, sweatband, or visor, or to join parts together to fabricate article. May join *reeding* onto hat parts to reinforce them and be designated Brim-Welt-Sewing-Machine Operator (hat & cap); Cap Sizer (hat & cap); Leather Fitter (hat & cap); Reeding-Machine Operator (hat & cap); Wire-Machine Operator (hat & cap). May be designated according to part sewn as Chin-Strap Sewer (hat & cap). May be designated: Brim Stitcher (hat & cap) II; Label Sewer (hat & cap); Lining Maker (hat & cap); Ribbon-Sweatband Operator (hat & cap); Straw-Hat-Machine Operator (hat & cap); Tip Maker (hat & cap); Top Stitcher (hat & cap). Performs duties as described under SEWING-MACHINE OPERATOR, REGULAR EQUIPMENT (any industry) Master Title.
GOE: 06.02.05 STRENGTH: L GED: R3 M1 L1 SVP: 3 DLU: 77

784.684-010 BOW MAKER (garment; hat & cap)

Folds and shapes ribbon sections to form decorative bows: Clips ends of folded ribbons to form tips of bow, using scissors, and folds tips of sewn ribbon sections according to specified style of bow. Glues sticker to back of shaped tip to secure tip in place. Folds and positions crosspiece in center of bow and secures in place, using wet glue sticker. Irons ribbon section to curve and shape ribbon to crown of hat. Ties western-style bows and lingerie bows by hand.
GOE: 06.04.27 STRENGTH: L GED: R2 M1 L1 SVP: 3 DLU: 78

784.684-014 BRIM IRONER, HAND (hat & cap) alternate titles: brim setter; hat-brim curler

Presses felt-hat brims to smooth, curl, and shape brim, using hand iron (shackle): Sets hand iron on heated plate to heat iron. Places cardboard protector ring over crown to protect sides from hot iron. Moistens brim, using damp sponge. Lifts iron from heated plate, inserts hat brim edge into forming slot of iron, and places hat on worktable. Presses iron around brim to smooth, curl, and shape hat brim. May place hat brim over steam hose to improve finish and remove iron marks. May shape and form depressions and creases in hat crown by hand according to style of hat.
GOE: 06.04.27 STRENGTH: L GED: R2 M1 L1 SVP: 3 DLU: 78

784.684-018 CAP MAKER (hat & cap) alternate titles: cap-machine operator; cap operator

Aligns cap parts and joins them to form finished cap, using needle and thread or sewing machine: Assembles parts, such as visors, covers, sweatbands, and ornaments, and joins them, using needle and thread; or operates sewing machine [HAT-AND-CAP SEWER (hat & cap)] to join parts. May join parts with basting stitches. May be designated according to type of cap joined as Dress-Cap Maker (hat & cap); Uniform-Cap Operator (hat & cap).
GOE: 06.04.27 STRENGTH: L GED: R2 M1 L2 SVP: 4 DLU: 77

784.684-022 DECORATOR (hat & cap) alternate titles: hat trimmer

Sews or glues decorative trimmings to articles, such as hats, caps, or millinery: Pulls article over block to secure article for trimming. Pins trimmings, such as artificial flowers, bows, and ribbons, on article, following sample or specifications. Cements or sews trimmings to article, according to size and type of trimming, using brush, cement gun, or needle and thread. Cements label inside article, using brush. May cut, sew, cement, or tie ribbons or cloth parts to make trimmings and be designated Braided-Band Assembler (hat & cap). May lace decorative material through precut slots and holes and be designated Hat Lacer (hat & cap). May be designated by article trimmed as Ladies'-Hat Trimmer (hat & cap).
GOE: 06.04.27 STRENGTH: L GED: R2 M1 L2 SVP: 3 DLU: 78

784.684-026 FLANGER (hat & cap) alternate titles: brim flanger; brim shaper; flanging operator; hat-brim curler

Presses hat brims to set shape and impart specified finish, using hand iron and heated sandbag: Inserts hat in specified size flange (metal or wood collar)

with brim resting on flange. Spreads pressing cloth over hat brim and ties cloth to base of form, using cord. Dampens cloth with sponge and irons brim, using dry or steam iron. Lowers preheated sandbag, suspended by rope and pulley, onto brim to set and shape brim against flange. Raises sandbag after specified time and unties cord. Examines hat for flaws in shape and appearance. May be designated according to type of hat flanged as Felt-Hat-Flanging Operator (hat & cap); Panama-Hat Flanger (hat & cap); Wool-Hat Flanger (hat & cap).
GOE: 06.04.27 STRENGTH: L GED: R2 M1 L2 SVP: 3 DLU: 78

784.684-030 FOUNDATION MAKER (hat & cap)
Makes foundations to provide shape and form for hats and caps: Positions wire, cardboard, or plastic foundation between layers of knitted or woven fabric. Staples or hand-sews fabric together after insertion of foundation. May insert cardboard between layers of fabric to provide stiffening for hat or cap brims. May brush paste on cap-visor lining and apply fabric or plastic covering to lining. May be designated according to material used as Wire-Shape Maker (hat & cap).
GOE: 06.04.34 STRENGTH: S GED: R2 M1 L2 SVP: 2 DLU: 77

784.684-034 HARDENER (hat & cap) alternate titles: hand hardener; manual hardener
Kneads fur felt hat cones to mat together interlocking fibers and harden cones for shaping into hats: Wraps wet cones in burlap, squeezes wrapped cones to extract water, and removes cones from burlap. Rolls cones in blanket and kneads to interlock fibers and harden cones. Unrolls blanket, refolds and repositions cones in blanket, and repeats kneading until cones are sufficiently hardened to withstand subsequent handling and shaping into hats. Stacks hardened cones on bench or tray.
GOE: 06.04.27 STRENGTH: L GED: R2 M1 L2 SVP: 4 DLU: 77

784.684-038 HAT BRAIDER (hat & cap)
Cuts, braids, and shapes felt-covered wire to form head clips (women's hats): Pulls several feet of tubing from spool and cuts to specified length, using cutting pliers. Wraps tubing over nail driven into worktable and braids tubing to form decorative head clip. Crimps together exposed wire at ends of tubing to form continuous loop, cutting sharp ends to prevent injury to wearer's head. Spreads tubing with fingers and forces it over knee to form head shape. Packs completed head clips in cartons for shipment.
GOE: 06.04.34 STRENGTH: L GED: R2 M1 L1 SVP: 3 DLU: 77

784.684-042 HAT MAKER (hat & cap)
Assembles ladies' hats by folding, draping, pinning, and sewing fabric, trimmings, and presewn hat parts to unfinished hat bodies, following color and design specifications or sample hat: Slips hat body onto block to secure hat for assembly. Folds, twists, and drapes material, such as satin or silk, around crown and brim to shape and decorate hat. Pins material in place. Sews parts, such as brim and trimmings to hat body, using needle and thread. May cut, glue, cement, or sew ribbon or cloth, to form trimmings, such as artificial flowers or bows. May cement trimmings to hat, using brush. When working under instructions of FASHION DESIGNER (profess. & kin.) to assemble sample hats, may be designated Hat-Designer Helper (hat & cap).
GOE: 06.02.27 STRENGTH: L GED: R3 M1 L2 SVP: 5 DLU: 77

784.684-046 MENDER (hat & cap)
Repairs damaged straw, woven-paper, or knitted hats or caps, using needle and thread: Repairs holes by weaving thread over them, selected to match original fabric. Stitches together cut or torn fabric. May be designated according to type of hat repaired as Woven-Paper-Hat Mender (hat & cap).
GOE: 06.04.34 STRENGTH: S GED: R2 M1 L1 SVP: 3 DLU: 77

784.684-050 ROUNDER, HAND (hat & cap) alternate titles: brim rounder; hand trimmer; welt-edge rounder
Cuts hat brims or cones to trim excess material from irregular edges, according to one of following methods: (1) Places hat on worktable and cuts excess material from raw or sewn welt edge, using adjustable razor cutting tool. (2) Pulls hat cone over block, places cutting edge against material, and turns mounted hat cone under cutting blade to remove excess material. May affix label inside hat crown to identify hat size.
GOE: 06.04.27 STRENGTH: L GED: R2 M1 L1 SVP: 2 DLU: 78

784.684-054 SIZER, HAND (hat & cap) alternate titles: sizer
Dips felt hat cones in hot water to shrink cones and wrings them to remove excess water. Kneads cone to mat together and strengthen interlocking fibers. Rolls cone, using rolling pin, to remove wrinkles and smooth surface. Inserts and spreads hands inside cone to enlarge and shape it. Measures cone, using ruler, and repeats dipping and kneading process until cone has shrunk to specifications.
GOE: 06.04.27 STRENGTH: L GED: R2 M1 L1 SVP: 3 DLU: 77

784.684-058 SIZER, MACHINE (hat & cap) alternate titles: starter; stumper
Moistens, folds, wraps, and places unfinished felt hat bodies in machine that agitates bodies to harden and shrink fur fibers to specified size: Sprinkles hat bodies with hot water or immerses bodies to shrink them. Wrings bodies to remove excess water, using hands. Folds hat bodies in prescribed manner and wraps burlap around folded bodies to protect fur fibers. Places bundle of bodies between machine rollers that agitate bodies, causing further shrinking and matting together of interlocking fibers. Measures bodies, using ruler. Continues refolding and passing hat bodies between rollers until bodies have become firm and have shrunk to specified size.

GOE: 06.04.16 STRENGTH: L GED: R2 M1 L1 SVP: 2 DLU: 78

784.684-062 SLICKER (hat & cap) alternate titles: lurer
Brushes felt hats to clean hats and applies polish and wax to surface to impart smooth, finished appearance: Brushes hat to remove dust, lint, and loose fibers and rotates hat over steampipe to remove excess gloss and condition fibers. Pulls hat onto block of revolving spindle and depresses pedal to start block rotating. Brushes silk polish (banana oil solution) onto hat to produce gloss. Applies wax to lure (cloth pad), rubs pad against heated iron to melt wax, and holds heated pad against rotating hat to smooth and finish appearance of felt. May place hi-roll hat in metal jig to shape and sharpen style lines.
GOE: 06.04.33 STRENGTH: L GED: R2 M1 L1 SVP: 3 DLU: 78

784.684-066 SMOOTHER (hat & cap)
Shapes felt-hat cones after dyeing to smooth, shape, and remove wrinkles. Pulls hat cone over metal block, presses and rubs hat to smooth and shape cone, and folds and stacks shaped cones flat on worktable for further processing.
GOE: 06.04.27 STRENGTH: L GED: R1 M1 L1 SVP: 2 DLU: 77

784.684-070 STEAMER-BLOCKER (hat & cap; knitting)
Positions hats or caps on shaped blocks to steam headwear and impart specified size and shape: Pulls hat linings, hats, or caps onto hat blocks. Holds block over steam jet, using hands to smooth and shape fabric. Places knit headwear on perforated aluminum head forms. Depresses pedal to force steam through form to soften headwear while shaping it by hand, using padded asbestos gloves. Sews hat brims to crowns, using needle and thread.
GOE: 06.04.27 STRENGTH: L GED: R2 M1 L1 SVP: 2 DLU: 77

784.684-074 TOP-HAT-BODY MAKER (hat & cap) alternate titles: silk-top-hat-body maker
Builds top-hat bodies from shellacked muslin, shellacks assembled body, and irons top, crown, and brim: Wraps several layers of shellacked muslin around shaped hat block to form crown of hat. Cuts several layers of muslin to shape of brim, using knife, slides them over crown, and fastens them to crown with tape to form brim. Cuts out top for hat, using scissors or knife, and fastens it to crown with tape. Applies several coats of shellac to hat body, using brush. Cuts brim to specified width when shellac is dry, using *rounding jack* [ROUNDER, HAND (hat & cap)]. Slips felt cover over hat body and presses top, crown, and brim, using iron. May press brim over flange to press and curl brim [FLANGER (hat & cap)]. May assemble collapsible opera hat body.
GOE: 06.04.27 STRENGTH: L GED: R2 M1 L1 SVP: 3 DLU: 77.

784.684-078 TRIMMER (hat & cap) alternate titles: hat-band attacher; specialty trimmer
Attaches buttons, studs, snaps, chin straps, braid, and ornamental bands to caps, using needle and thread, stapler, or handpress. Attaches ornamental hat bands, using hot-glue gun or adhesive tape. May operate sewing machine to attach bands, chin straps, or bows.
GOE: 06.04.27 STRENGTH: L GED: R2 M1 L1 SVP: 2 DLU: 78

784.685-010 BAND-AND-CUFF CUTTER (glove & mit.)
Tends machine that cuts wristbands or knuckle straps for gloves or mittens: Positions rolls of banding material on holders and draws ends through guides. Starts material under revolving wheel set with dies that cut material to shape and size, or starts material under fingers that pull material under blade that cuts it to length. Stacks specified number of cut bands in box. May tend machine with sewing attachment to sew over edge of material before cutting.
GOE: 06.04.05 STRENGTH: L GED: R2 M1 L1 SVP: 2 DLU: 77

784.685-014 BRIM STITCHER I (hat & cap)
Tends one or more sewing machines that automatically sew circular row of stitches on hat brims to reinforce and decorate brims: Turns screw to position guide on bed of machine. Inserts hat brim into guide, under presser foot and needle. Performs duties as described under SEWING-MACHINE OPERATOR, AUTOMATIC (any industry) Master Title.
GOE: 06.04.05 STRENGTH: L GED: R2 M1 L1 SVP: 2 DLU: 77

784.687-010 BRIM RAISER (hat & cap) alternate titles: steam finisher; straw-hat-brim-raiser operator; straw-hat finishing operator
Dampens strawhats, using sponge, and holds hats over steam jet to cause straw to swell and resume shape after hat has been pressed.
GOE: 06.04.27 STRENGTH: L GED: R2 M1 L1 SVP: 2 DLU: 77

784.687-014 CARROTER (hat & cap) alternate titles: brusher, hand
Applies chemical solution onto fur pelts, using brush, to condition fur fibers for manufacture of felt hats.
GOE: 06.04.33 STRENGTH: L GED: R2 M1 L1 SVP: 2 DLU: 77

784.687-018 CROWN POUNCER, HAND (hat & cap) alternate titles: felt-hat-pouncing operator, hand; hand pouncer; pouncer
Slips unfinished hat over specified size hat block and rubs crown in one direction to remove excess fibers and impart smooth finish. Feels surface of crown to ascertain when specified texture has been attained. Removes hat from block and places it on wheeled rack.
GOE: 06.04.27 STRENGTH: L GED: R2 M1 L1 SVP: 3 DLU: 77

784.687-022 EAR-MUFF ASSEMBLER (hat & cap)
Assembles ear muffs by inserting wire loops of adjustable metal headband into presewn fur or fabric ear covers, selected according to color and material specifications.

GOE: 06.04.23 STRENGTH: L GED: R2 M1 L1 SVP: 2 DLU: 77

784.687-026 ENDBAND CUTTER, HAND (hat & cap) alternate titles: endbander; endband sizer; sizing end-bander
Measures and cuts end bands (ear flaps) to size for caps: Positions band against size gauge to measure band, and cuts band, according to size specified on work ticket, using scissors. Bundles cut parts, using ribbon or string.
GOE: 06.04.27 STRENGTH: S GED: R2 M1 L1 SVP: 2 DLU: 77

784.687-030 FLOORWORKER-DISTRIBUTOR (hat & cap)
Selects and distributes materials, such as unfinished hat bodies and trimmings, to workers engaged in assembling and trimming hats. May inspect finished work. May oversee activities and maintain production records of assembly workers.
GOE: 06.04.40 STRENGTH: L GED: R2 M1 L1 SVP: 2 DLU: 77

784.687-034 GLOVE PAIRER (glove & mit.) alternate titles: gauntlet pairer
Matches right- and left-hand gloves according to size, style, and color, and stacks them in lots of specified number of pairs. May tie gloves in lots onto cardboard, by hand or with tying machine, to prepare them for packing. May insert pair of gloves into plastic bag and pack specified number of pairs into shipping carton.
GOE: 06.03.02 STRENGTH: L GED: R2 M1 L1 SVP: 2 DLU: 77

784.687-038 GLOVE TURNER (glove & mit.)
Turns gloves and mittens right-side-out: Pulls thumb and each finger of glove over *turner tube*, depresses pedal to lower rod that pushes tips of fingers into tube, and pulls partially turned glove from tube. Pulls thumb and each finger over shaped form (punch-out stick) to complete turning and to push out finger tips. May pull turned glove over heated form to press glove [GLOVE FORMER (glove & mit.; laundry & rel.) 363.687-010] and be designated Glove Turner-And-Former (glove & mit.).
GOE: 06.04.27 STRENGTH: L GED: R2 M1 L1 SVP: 3 DLU: 78

784.687-042 INSPECTOR-PACKER (hat & cap)
Inspects, repairs, and packs repaired finished hats or caps: Inspects hats or caps for flaws, such as poor stitching and improperly placed visors, bands, or ornaments. Makes minor repairs to hats or caps, such as sewing in missed stitches, using needle and thread, clipping loose threads, using scissors, and fastening loose ornaments. Sorts hats or caps into piles according to size. Lines boxes or cartons with tissue paper and packs hats or caps in containers. Marks contents on outside of containers. May spray hats, using airhose, to remove lint prior to packing. May perform final finishing operations, such as buckling chin straps. May be designated according to hat as Felt-Hat Inspector And Packer (hat & cap); Strawhat Inspector And Packer (hat & cap).
GOE: 06.03.02 STRENGTH: L GED: R2 M1 L2 SVP: 2 DLU: 78

784.687-046 LINER (glove & mit.)
Inserts cloth linings in leather mittens: Places lining on specified size metal form and pulls mitten over lining. Folds wristlets back over lining preparatory to stiching to leather. Removes lined mitten from form.
GOE: 06.04.27 STRENGTH: L GED: R2 M1 L1 SVP: 2 DLU: 77

784.687-050 MATERIAL ASSEMBLER (hat & cap) alternate titles: trim preparer
Sorts and assembles cap, hat, or millinery parts and trimming material according to color, quantity, size, or style, to facilitate attachment to article: Measures and cuts ribbon or other material, following specifications, using ruler and scissors. Gathers and bundles parts and trimmings specified for each hat, such as flowers, feathers, ribbons, and sweatbands, using pins or twine. May maintain records of materials issued to HAT MAKER (hat & cap) 784.684-014 and of ribbon inventory. May be designated according to material cut as Ribbon Cutter (hat & cap).
GOE: 06.03.02 STRENGTH: L GED: R3 M1 L2 SVP: 3 DLU: 78

784.687-054 OPENER I (hat & cap)
Slits rabbit pelts along abdomen and opens them out, using knife. Cuts off ears, tail, and feet and places parts in bags to be processed as inferior fur. Piles opened skins, fur sides together, to facilitate processing of fur into felt hats. May cover skins with burlap and tie into bundles, using string.
GOE: 06.04.27 STRENGTH: L GED: R2 M1 L1 SVP: 2 DLU: 77

784.687-058 POWDERER (hat & cap)
Rubs or sprays powder of specified color onto unfinished felt hat bodies, using powder-filled cloth bag or compressed-air gun, to stiffen, finish, or prepare bodies for further processing.
GOE: 06.04.33 STRENGTH: L GED: R2 M1 L1 SVP: 2 DLU: 78

784.687-062 SINGER (hat & cap)
Holds felt hats over flame to burn away protruding hairs prior to finishing operations: Depresses pedal to release steam from jet and holds and turns hat, mounted on block, in current of steam to moisten felt. Activates gas jet and turns hat in flame to burn away protruding hairs without scorching felt. May place hat body on revolving block to burn off excess fuzz or lint.
GOE: 06.04.27 STRENGTH: L GED: R2 M1 L1 SVP: 2 DLU: 77

784.687-066 SMOKE-ROOM OPERATOR (hat & cap)
Tends burning room to bleach strawhats with burning sulfur: Loads racks with hats and wheels them into room. Pours powdered sulfur into pan provided

with electric heating unit, closes door of room, and turns electric switch to burn sulfur in pan. Turns on ventilator fan and removes hats after specified time.
GOE: 06.04.34 STRENGTH: M GED: R1 M1 L1 SVP: 2 DLU: 77

784.687-070 STICKER (hat & cap) alternate titles: sticker-on
Glues pieces of hides, such as rabbit, beaver, muskrat, or nutria to paper sheets to facilitate machine cutting of fur from skin: Brushes glue onto paper sheets. Presses fur, skin side down, onto glued surface to create fur area large enough to be accommodated by clipping machine that cuts fur from skins.
GOE: 06.04.27 STRENGTH: L GED: R1 M1 L1 SVP: 2 DLU: 77

784.687-074 STRAW-HAT BRUSHER (hat & cap)
Cleans and polishes strawhats: Slips hat on wooden block, wipes powdered sulfur onto hat with cloth, and brushes hat by hand.
GOE: 06.04.39 STRENGTH: L GED: R2 M1 L1 SVP: 2 DLU: 77

784.687-078 STRAW-HAT-WASHER OPERATOR (hat & cap) alternate titles: stiff-straw-hat washer
Rubs strawhats with damp sponge to remove excess sizing: Slips hat over shaped hat block, rubs surface with damp sponge, and hangs hat on rack to dry. May hold hat over steam jet to soften sizing, preparatory to rubbing with sponge, or place hats in tub equipped with steam jets and cover top of tub with burlap cloth to allow steam to soften sizing and condition straw and be designated Steamer (hat & cap).
GOE: 06.04.27 STRENGTH: L GED: R1 M1 L1 SVP: 1 DLU: 77

784.687-082 WIRE INSERTER (hat & cap)
Cuts and inserts wire into crown of caps to shape and support crown: Measures wire, using ruler. Positions wire on bed of cutter beneath blade and presses lever to cut wire to specified length. Bends wire to form circle and fastens ends of wire together with metal clip. Inserts circular wire into crown of cap, using fingers.
GOE: 06.04.34 STRENGTH: L GED: R2 M1 L1 SVP: 2 DLU: 77

784.687-086 HAT CONDITIONER (hat & cap) alternate titles: muller
Sprays felt hats with water and refrigerates hats to condition hat fibers in fancy finish department of hat manufacturer: Sprays hats with fine mist, using water spray nozzle, and positions burlap around hats to confine moisture. Places hats in refrigerated room for chilling to condition hat fibers. Removes hat after specified time and places hats on racks for further processing.
GOE: 06.04.27 STRENGTH: L GED: R1 M1 L1 SVP: 2 DLU: 86

784.687-090 SWEATBAND SHAPER (hat & cap)
Shapes sweatbands to conform to hat crowns, using heated metal blocks: Places hats on heated metal blocks, according to hat size. Removes hats after specified time. Places hats on racks and pushes racks to designated location for further processing.
GOE: 06.04.27 STRENGTH: M GED: R1 M1 L1 SVP: 2 DLU: 86

785 TAILORS AND DRESSMAKERS

This group includes occupations concerned with performing all tasks required to design and produce finished made-to-measure garments or to perform specialized stitching and machine-sewing requiring tailoring skill in the manufacture or alteration of ready-made or tailored apparel.

785.131-010 SUPERVISOR, ALTERATION WORKROOM (retail trade)
Supervises and coordinates activities of workers engaged in altering ready-to-wear garments: Assigns duties to workers according to type of garment and alteration to be performed. Examines work of subordinates periodically to detect faulty work. Performs duties of absent workers and assists workers to maintain production when necessary. Trains new employees. Requisitions supplies. Confers with workers, customers, and other supervisors regarding garment alterations. Performs other duties as described under SUPERVISOR (any industry) Master Title.
GOE: 05.05.15 STRENGTH: L GED: R3 M3 L3 SVP: 6 DLU: 77

785.261-010 ALTERATION TAILOR (garment; personal ser.; retail trade) alternate titles: alterer; busheler
Alters clothing to fit individual customers or repairs defective garments, following alteration or repair tags or marks on garments: Examines tag or garment to ascertain necessary alterations. Removes stitches from garment, using ripper or razor blade. Shortens or lengthens sleeves and legs, expands or narrows waist and chest, raises or lowers collar, and inserts or eliminates padding in shoulders while maintaining drape and proportions of garment. Trims excess material, using scissors. Resews garment, using needle and thread or sewing machine. Repairs or replaces defective garment parts, such as pockets, pocket flaps, and coat linings. May fit garments on customer to determine required alterations [GARMENT FITTER (retail trade) 785.361-014]. May press garment, using hand iron [PRESSER, HAND (any industry) 363.684-018] or pressing machine [PRESSER, MACHINE (any industry) 363.682-018]. May be designated according to type of garment altered or repaired as Tailor, Men's Ready-To-Wear (retail trade); Tailor, Women's-Garment Alteration (retail trade); or according to garment part altered or repaired as Pants Busheler (Retail trade); Vest Busheler (retail trade).
GOE: 05.05.15 STRENGTH: L GED: R4 M3 L3 SVP: 7 DLU: 81

785.261-014 CUSTOM TAILOR (garment; personal ser.; retail trade) alternate titles: made-to-measure tailor; tailor
Develops designs and makes tailored garments, such as suits, topcoats, overcoats, and other dress clothing, applying principles of garment design, construc-

tion, and styling: Confers with customer to determine type of material and garment style desired. Measures customer for size and records measurements for use in preparing patterns and making garment. Develops designs for garments or copies existing designs. Draws individual pattern for garment or alters standard pattern to fit customer's measurements. Outlines patterns of garment parts on fabric and cuts fabric along outlines, using scissors. Assembles garments, sewing padding to coat fronts, lapels, and collars to give them shape and joining garment parts with basting stitches, using needle and thread or sewing machine. Fits basted garment on customer and marks areas requiring alterations. Alters garment and joins parts, using needle and thread or sewing machine. Sews buttons and buttonholes to finish garment. May press garment [PRESSER, HAND (any industry); PRESSER, MACHINE (any industry)]. May supervise activities of other workers in tailoring shop. May specialize in making garments and be designated Coat Tailor (garment). May perform specific tasks in tailor shop and be designated Coat Fitter (garment); Try-On Baster (garment).
GOE: 05.05.15 STRENGTH: L GED: R4 M3 L3 SVP: 8 DLU: 77

785.261-018 TAILOR APPRENTICE, ALTERATION (garment; personal ser.; retail trade) alternate titles: alterer apprentice
Performs duties as described under APPRENTICE (any industry) Master Title.
GOE: 05.05.15 STRENGTH: L GED: R4 M3 L3 SVP: 7 DLU: 77

785.261-022 TAILOR APPRENTICE, CUSTOM (garment; personal ser.; retail trade) alternate titles: made-to-measure-tailor apprentice; master-tailor apprentice
Performs duties as described under APPRENTICE (any industry) Master Title.
GOE: 05.05.15 STRENGTH: L GED: R4 M3 L3 SVP: 8 DLU: 77

785.361-010 DRESSMAKER (any industry)
Makes women's garments, such as dresses, coats, and suits, according to customer specifications and measurements: Discusses with customer type of material, pattern, or style to be used in making garment. Measures customer to determine modification from pattern, using tape measure. Positions and pins pattern sections, such as collar, sleeve, or waist, on fabric, and cuts fabric with scissors following pattern edge. Pins or bastes together fabric parts in preparation for final sewing. Sews fabric parts by hand or operates single-needle sewing machine that joins fabric parts to form garment. Sews *felling stitch* in hem of garment by hand to conceal thread. Presses garment, using hand iron, to smooth seams and remove wrinkles [PRESSER, HAND (any industry)]. May draft standard pattern according to measurements of customer and adapt pattern to obtain specified style. May make garment according to picture furnished by customer.
GOE: 05.05.15 STRENGTH: L GED: R3 M3 L3 SVP: 7 DLU: 77

785.361-014 GARMENT FITTER (retail trade)
Fits ready-to-wear garments on customer to designate alterations required for desired fit of garment: Studies garment on customer and measures pieces, such as sleeves, pants, and hems. Pins altering folds or marks on cloth with chalk at seams, darts, or necklines to indicate alterations to be made. Measures and marks hem to specified length. Records required alterations and instructions concerning alterations on tag and attaches tag to garment, or calls out instructions to salesperson for recording on alteration tag. May alter garment, using sewing machine, as required by work load. May be designated according to garment fitted as Men's Garment Fitter (retail trade); Women's Garment Fitter (retail trade).
GOE: 05.05.15 STRENGTH: L GED: R3 M2 L2 SVP: 6 DLU: 77

785.361-018 SAMPLE STITCHER (garment) alternate titles: sample maker; sample maker, original; sample sewer; sample tailor
Marks and cuts out material and sews parts of new style garments, following patterns, sketches, and design specifications, to prepare sample garments: Selects garment parts and threads, according to design specifications. Positions and aligns parts of sample garment together, following markings on parts, sketches, and patterns. Sews parts and attaches accessories and ornamentations, using needle and thread or sewing machine. Drapes garment on model form, examines fit and hang of garment, and marks garment to indicate position of fasteners and trimmings, such as sashes, belts, and emblems. May sew fasteners and trimmings to garments, using needle and thread or sewing machine. May mark and cut materials to obtain garment parts, following patterns or designer's sketches. May press garments by hand or machine. May join dress parts to prove correctness of pattern as to fit and hang of garment and be designated Duplicate Maker (garment).
GOE: 05.05.15 STRENGTH: L GED: R4 M3 L3 SVP: 6 DLU: 77

785.361-022 SHOP TAILOR (garment; retail trade)
Performs specialized hand and machine sewing operations in manufacture of made-to-measure or ready-to-wear clothing, applying knowledge of garment construction and fabrics: Trims and shapes edges of garment parts preparatory to sewing and cuts excess material from seam edges, using shears or knife. Fits collar facing to underfacing, trims edge of undercollar with shears, and sews undercollar to collar. Bastes collar or sleeves to coat body and sews collar or sleeves to coat with permanent stitches. Stitches shoulder padding, coat facing, and lining together at armhole. Bastes and sews canvas material in various coat parts, such as undercollar, shoulder, and front edge. Joins shoulder padding to coat with basting stitches. May sew on buttons and make buttonholes to finish suits. May be designated according to tasks performed or garments sewn as

Coat Baster (garment; retail trade); Coat Padder (garment; retail trade); Collar Setter (garment; retail trade); Lapel Padder (garment; retail trade); Sleeve Tailor (garment; retail trade); Suit Finisher (garment; retail trade). May be designated: Top-Collar Maker (garment; retail trade); Undercollar Baster (garment; retail trade); Undercollar Maker (garment; retail trade); Vest Tailor (garment; retail trade).
GOE: 05.05.15 STRENGTH: L GED: R4 M3 L3 SVP: 7 DLU: 77

785.361-026 SHOP TAILOR APPRENTICE (garment; retail trade) alternate titles: finisher-tailor apprentice
Performs duties as described under APPRENTICE (any industry) Master Title.
GOE: 05.05.15 STRENGTH: L GED: R4 M3 L3 SVP: 7 DLU: 77

786 SEWING MACHINE OPERATORS, GARMENT

This group includes occupations concerned with operating regular sewing machines, tending semiautomatic machines to sew garments (as defined in GARMENT INDUSTRY), or to ultrasonically seam garments in imitation of sewing.

786.132-010 SUPERVISOR, GARMENT MANUFACTURING (garment)
Supervises and coordinates activities of workers engaged in sewing, pressing, and inspecting garments in one department of manufacturing establishment: Inspects work for adherence to specifications. Notifies mechanic when machines malfunction. Trains workers in assembly of new style garments. Performs other duties as described under SUPERVISOR (any industry) Master Title. May be designated according to department supervised as Supervisor, Finishing Department (garment); Supervisor, Inspection Department (garment); Supervisor, Sewing Room (garment).
GOE: 06.02.01 STRENGTH: L GED: R4 M2 L3 SVP: 6 DLU: 78

786.682-010 APPLIQUER, ZIGZAG (garment)
Operates *zigzag sewing machine* to sew appliques, monograms, embroidery, or lace on designated places of garment to decorate or reinforce garment. Performs duties as described under SEWING-MACHINE OPERATOR, REGULAR EQUIPMENT (any industry) Master Title.
GOE: 06.02.05 STRENGTH: L GED: R2 M1 L1 SVP: 3 DLU: 77

786.682-014 ARMHOLE BASTER, JUMPBASTING (garment)
Operates *jumpbasting sewing machine* to temporarily secure fabric layers in position at armhole seam of coat or jacket: Positions armhole on machine bed and bastes to secure outer fabric, shoulder pad, and canvas interlining at armhole seam. Repositions armhole and bastes on inside of coat to secure lining. Performs duties as described under SEWING-MACHINE OPERATOR, REGULAR EQUIPMENT (any industry) Master Title.
GOE: 06.02.05 STRENGTH: L GED: R2 M1 L1 SVP: 3 DLU: 77

786.682-018 ARMHOLE FELLER, HANDSTITCHING MACHINE (garment)
Operates sewing machine that simulates handstitching to sew sleeve lining to coat lining: Turns knob to adjust machine for depth of needle penetration, depending on type of fabric. Positions armhole of coat lining with partially sewn sleeve lining on bed of machine, folds raw edge of sleeve lining at top of armhole, aligns lining edges, and depresses pedal to sew parts together. Folds edge with fingers and presses knee lever to gather sleeve lining to fit armhole of coat lining. Performs duties as described under SEWING-MACHINE OPERATOR, REGULAR EQUIPMENT (any industry) Master Title.
GOE: 06.02.05 STRENGTH: L GED: R2 M1 L1 SVP: 2 DLU: 77

786.682-022 ARMHOLE-SEW-AND-TRIM OPERATOR, LOCKSTITCH (garment)
Operates lockstitch sewing machine equipped with edgecutter to sew prebasted layers at armhole seam of coat or jacket and cut away excess fabric. Positions armhole on machine bed and sews through sleevehead, sleeve, canvas, shoulder pad, and outer coat fabric while edgecutter trims excess fabric. Performs other duties as described under SEWING-MACHINE OPERATOR, REGULAR EQUIPMENT (any industry) Master Title.
GOE: 06.02.05 STRENGTH: L GED: R2 M1 L1 SVP: 3 DLU: 77

786.682-026 BACK MAKER, LOCKSTITCH (garment)
Operates lockstitch sewing machine to make complete back of coat or jacket: Aligns center back edges from shoulder to vent, matching fabric pattern, if any, and guides edges under needle to join. Hems vent edge or attaches rectangular piece of lining fabric or tape, to conceal raw edge of vent. May attach tape to back neckline. May raise (topstitch) center back seam by sewing specified distance from seam line to reinforce, flatten, and decorate back seam and vent. Performs other duties as described under SEWING-MACHINE OPERATOR, REGULAR EQUIPMENT (any industry) Master Title.
GOE: 06.02.05 STRENGTH: L GED: R2 M1 L1 SVP: 3 DLU: 77

786.682-030 BASTING-MACHINE OPERATOR (garment)
Operates basting machine to temporarily maintain position of garment edges or layers in preparation for pressing or final sewing operation. May attach bridle (length of tape stretched taut) to canvas interlining along bend of coat lapel to maintain roll line. May baste edges on front of coat to maintain sharp edge and be designated Edge Baster (garment). Performs other duties as described under SEWING-MACHINE OPERATOR, REGUALR EQUIPMENT (any industry) Master Title.

GOE: 06.02.05 STRENGTH: L GED: R2 M1 L1 SVP: 3 DLU: 77

786.682-034 BINDER, CHAINSTITCH (garment)
Operates chainstitch sewing machine equipped with folder to fold and attach binding material over raw edge of garment to give finished appearance. Performs other duties as described under SEWING-MACHINE OPERATOR, REGULAR EQUIPMENT (any industry) Master Title.
GOE: 06.02.05 STRENGTH: L GED: R2 M1 L1 SVP: 3 DLU: 77

786.682-038 BINDER, COVERSTITCH (garment)
Operates *coverstitch sewing machine* equipped with folder to fold and attach binding material over raw edge of knit garment to give finished appearance. Performs duties as described under SEWING-MACHINE OPERATOR, REGULAR EQUIPMENT (any industry) Master Title.
GOE: 06.02.05 STRENGTH: L GED: R2 M1 L1 SVP: 3 DLU: 77

786.682-042 BINDER, LOCKSTITCH (garment)
Operates lockstitch sewing machine equipped with folder to fold and attach binding material over raw edge of garment to give finished appearance. Performs other duties as described under SEWING-MACHINE OPERATOR, REGULAR EQUIPMENT (any industry) Master Title.
GOE: 06.02.05 STRENGTH: L GED: R2 M1 L1 SVP: 3 DLU: 77

786.682-046 BLINDSTITCH-MACHINE OPERATOR (garment)
Operates *blindstitch sewing machine* to join fabric layers, or attach tape or parts to garment, with stitching that does not penetrate to outer surface of garment. Adjusts machine for depth of needle penetration, depending on fabric. Performs duties as described under SEWING-MACHINE OPERATOR, REGULAR EQUIPMENT (any industry) Master Title. May attach one edge of curtain (waistband lining) to pants and be designated Curtain Feller, Blindstitch (garment).
GOE: 06.02.05 STRENGTH: L GED: R2 M1 L1 SVP: 2 DLU: 77

786.682-050 CANVAS BASTER, JUMPBASTING (garment)
Operates *jumpbasting sewing machine* to temporarily attach canvas interlining to front of coat. Positions front of coat on canvas interlining and bastes outer surface, allowing fullness as required by style of coat. Performs duties as described under SEWING-MACHINE OPERATOR, REGULAR EQUIPMENT (any industry) Master Title.
GOE: 06.02.05 STRENGTH: L GED: R2 M1 L1 SVP: 3 DLU: 77

786.682-054 CHAINSTITCH SEWING MACHINE OPERATOR (garment)
Operates chainstitch sewing machine to join garment parts, or attach trim to garment. Performs duties as described under SEWING-MACHINE OPERATOR, REGULAR EQUIPMENT (any industry) Master Title. May attach tape or trim, ruffle and attach ruffled trim, or fold and sew stripping, using machine attachments, such as ruffler or folder.
GOE: 06.02.05 STRENGTH: L GED: R3 M1 L2 SVP: 3 DLU: 78

786.682-058 COAT JOINER, LOCKSTITCH (garment)
Operates lockstitch sewing machine to join side panels to back of coat or jacket: Positions edges, joining matching fabric pattern as necessary and guides fabric under needle, manipulating fabric to provide fullness over chest area. May fold edge of coat panel according to marks to form vent. May attach tape around back of armhole, flattening seams, pulling tape taut, and manipulating coat fabric to ease-in fullness. Performs other duties as described under SEWING-MACHINE OPERATOR, REGULAR EQUIPMENT (any industry) Master Title.
GOE: 06.02.05 STRENGTH: L GED: R2 M1 L1 SVP: 3 DLU: 77

786.682-062 COLLAR BASTER, JUMPBASTING (garment)
Operates *jumpbasting sewing machine* to baste collar to neckline of coat, manipulating fabric to follow curve of neckline and provide fullness at shoulder area. Performs duties as described under SEWING-MACHINE OPERATOR, REGULAR EQUIPMENT (any industry) Master Title. May baste front section of top collar to lapel facing. May baste cuff.
GOE: 06.02.05 STRENGTH: L GED: R2 M1 L1 SVP: 3 DLU: 77

786.682-066 COLLAR FELLER, HANDSTITCHING MACHINE (garment)
Operates sewing machine that simulates handstitching to join undercollar to neckline of garment. Adjusts machine for depth of needle penetration, depending on fabric. Performs duties as described under SEWING-MACHINE OPERATOR, REGULAR EQUIPMENT (any industry) Master Title. May operate machine to join top collar to neckline of garment.
GOE: 06.02.05 STRENGTH: L GED: R2 M1 L1 SVP: 2 DLU: 77

786.682-070 COLLAR SETTER, LOCKSTITCH (garment)
Operates lockstitch sewing machine to attach collar to neckline of garment: Positions edges of one or more layers of collar on neckline and joins collar to neckline of garment, manipulating fabric to align edges according to markings. Performs duties as described under SEWING-MACHINE OPERATOR, REGULAR EQUIPMENT (any industry) Master Title. On styles requiring separate joining of collar layers, may join unattached edge to neckline and be designated Collar Closer, Lockstitch (garment). May set cuffs instead of collars and be designated Cuff Setter, Lockstitch (garment).
GOE: 06.02.05 STRENGTH: L GED: R2 M1 L1 SVP: 3 DLU: 77

786.682-074 COLLAR SETTER, OVERLOCK (garment)
Operates *overlock sewing machine* to attach collar to neckline of garment: Positions collar on neckline and joins parts, manipulating fabric to align edges according to markings. Performs duties as described under SEWING-MACHINE OPERATOR, REGULAR EQUIPMENT (any industry) Master Title. May set cuffs instead of collars, with or without intermittent shirring, and be designated Cuff Setter, Overlock (garment).
GOE: 06.02.05 STRENGTH: L GED: R2 M1 L1 SVP: 3 DLU: 77

786.682-078 COVERSTITCH-MACHINE OPERATOR (garment)
Operates *coverstitch sewing machine* to join parts of knit garments, or to attach narrow fabric, such as tape, lace, or borders, to edges, or to flatten presewn seams. Performs duties as described under SEWING-MACHINE OPERATOR, REGULAR EQUIPMENT (any industry) Master Title.
GOE: 06.02.05 STRENGTH: L GED: R2 M1 L1 SVP: 2 DLU: 77

786.682-082 CUP SETTER, LOCKSTITCH (garment)
Operates lockstitch sewing machine to set brassiere cups to foundation garment or swim suit. Aligns cup with lining or body of garment, following markings, and joins parts, manipulating fabric to conform to shape of cup. Performs other duties as described under SEWING-MACHINE OPERATOR, REGULAR EQUIPMENT (any industry) Master Title.
GOE: 06.02.05 STRENGTH: L GED: R2 M1 L1 SVP: 3 DLU: 77

786.682-086 ELASTIC ATTACHER, CHAINSTITCH (garment)
Operates multiple needle chainstitch sewing machine equipped with tension regulator and folder to sew elastic band or stripping to garment parts: Adjusts tension regulator to stretch elastic for specified dimension. Guides garment edge into folder, aligns elastic with folded edge, and sews along edge to attach. Performs other duties as described under SEWING-MACHINE OPERATOR, REGULAR EQUIPMENT (any industry) Master Title.
GOE: 06.02.05 STRENGTH: L GED: R2 M1 L1 SVP: 3 DLU: 77

786.682-090 ELASTIC ATTACHER, COVERSTITCH (garment)
Operates *coverstitch sewing machine,* equipped with tension regulator, to sew elastic stripping to waistline or other opening of knit garments, such as underwear. Adjusts tension regulator to stretch elastic for specified dimension. Aligns elastic on edge of opening and guides under needles to attach. Performs duties as described under SEWING-MACHINE OPERATOR, REGULAR EQUIPMENT (any industry) Master Title.
GOE: 06.02.05 STRENGTH: L GED: R2 M1 L1 SVP: 3 DLU: 77

786.682-094 ELASTIC ATTACHER, OVERLOCK (garment)
Operates *overlock sewing machine,* equipped with tension regulator, to sew elastic stripping to waistline or other opening of garment: Adjusts tension regulator to stretch elastic for specified dimension. Aligns elastic on garment edge and guides parts under needle to overedge and join them. Performs duties as described under SEWING-MACHINE OPERATOR, REGULAR EQUIPMENT (any industry) Master Title.
GOE: 06.02.05 STRENGTH: L GED: R2 M1 L1 SVP: 3 DLU: 77

786.682-098 ELASTIC ATTACHER, ZIGZAG (garment)
Operates *zigzag sewing machine* to sew elastic strip to edge of garment: Positions elastic strip on garment edge. Stretches elastic with fingers to maintain tension while sewing or operates zigzag machine equipped with tension regulator. Performs duties as described under SEWING-MACHINE OPERATOR, REGULAR EQUIPMENT (any industry) Master Title.
GOE: 06.02.05 STRENGTH: L GED: R2 M1 L1 SVP: 3 DLU: 77

786.682-102 FACING BASTER, JUMPBASTING (garment)
Operates *jumpbasting sewing machine* to baste facing to front of coat, manipulating fabric to provide fullness. Performs duties as described under SEWING-MACHINE OPERATOR, REGULAR EQUIPMENT (any industry) Master Title. May be designated by first or second step in basting of facing as Second Facing Baster (garment); Underbaster (garment).
GOE: 06.02.05 STRENGTH: L GED: R2 M1 L1 SVP: 3 DLU: 77

786.682-106 FELLED-SEAM OPERATOR, CHAINSTITCH (garment)
alternate titles: felling-machine operator
Operates multiple-needle, chainstitch sewing machine to join edges of garments or garment parts with *felled seam:* Guides edge of garment through folding attachment or folds edge according to style specifications to form seam. Presses knee control to lower machine arm. Positions folded garment edge under needle and releases knee control to raise machine arm. Guides garment edge under needle and against gauge. Performs duties as described under SEWING-MACHINE OPERATOR, REGULAR EQUIPMENT (any industry) Master Title.
GOE: 06.02.05 STRENGTH: L GED: R2 M1 L1 SVP: 3 DLU: 77

786.682-110 FLATLOCK-SEWING-MACHINE OPERATOR (garment)
Operates *flatlock sewing machine* equipped with cutting attachment to join parts of knitwear with flat, nonraveling seams. Places garment part around arm of machine with fabric edges together and operates machine to seam parts and cut excess fabric from seam. Performs duties as described under SEWING-MACHINE OPERATOR (any industry) Master Title.
GOE: 06.02.05 STRENGTH: L GED: R2 M1 L1 SVP: 3 DLU: 77

786.682-114 FRONT MAKER, LOCKSTITCH (garment)
Operates lockstitch sewing machine equipped with attachments, such as folding attachment or topstitching guide, to make front of bodice for women's and children's garments. Sets, joins, and attaches parts as specified to complete front or other parts of bodice, according to style. Performs other duties as described under SEWING-MACHINE OPERATOR, REGULAR EQUIPMENT (any industry) Master Title.

GOE: 06.02.05 STRENGTH: L GED: R2 M1 L1 SVP: 4 DLU: 77

786.682-118 FRONT-EDGE-TAPE SEWER, LOCKSTITCH (garment)

Operates lockstitch sewing machine equipped with edgecutter to sew prebasted front edge of coat or jacket: Sews across top edge of lapel. Lowers edgecutter to side of needle, positions tape along front edge of coat, and guides parts under needle to sew tape and cut away excess fabric from coat layers (outer fabric, canvas, and facing). Raises edgecutter and sews tape to bottom front corner of coat, easing in tape at corner. Performs other duties as described under SEWING-MACHINE OPERATOR, REGULAR EQUIPMENT (any industry) Master Title.

GOE: 06.02.05 STRENGTH: L GED: R2 M1 L1 SVP: 4 DLU: 77

786.682-122 FUR-MACHINE OPERATOR (garment) alternate titles: feed-cup-sewing-machine operator

Operates *fur machine* to join bulky or heavy material, such as sheepskin pelts, fake fur, or leather, into garments or garment parts: Depresses pedal to open horizontal *feed cups,* positions edges of material between cups, and releases pedal to close cups. Guides edges of material between feed cups and across path of horizontal needle to join them. Performs duties as described under SEWING-MACHINE OPERATOR, REGULAR EQUIPMENT (any industry) Master Title.

GOE: 06.02.05 STRENGTH: L GED: R3 M1 L1 SVP: 7 DLU: 77

786.682-126 HEMMER, BLINDSTITCH (garment) alternate titles: feller

Operates *blindstitch sewing machine* equipped with folder to hem bottom or edges of garment. Adjusts machine for depth of needle penetration depending on fabric. Guides garment edge into folder and under needle to sew folded edge with stitches not visible on outer surface of garment. May book (hem) margins of seams and be designated Bookseamer, Blindstitch (garment). Performs other duties as described under SEWING-MACHINE OPERATOR, REGULAR EQUIPMENT (any industry) Master Title.

GOE: 06.02.05 STRENGTH: L GED: R2 M1 L1 SVP: 2 DLU: 77

786.682-130 HEMMER, CHAINSTITCH (garment)

Operates chainstitch sewing machine equipped with folder and guides edges of garment, such as shirt, into folder to hem garment. Performs other duties as described under SEWING-MACHINE OPERATOR, REGULAR EQUIPMENT (any industry) Master Title.

GOE: 06.02.05 STRENGTH: L GED: R2 M1 L1 SVP: 2 DLU: 77

786.682-134 HEMMER, LOCKSTITCH (garment)

Operates lockstitch sewing machine equipped with folder to hem edges of garment, such as shirt. Performs other duties as described under SEWING-MACHINE OPERATOR, REGULAR EQUIPMENT (any industry) Master Title.

GOE: 06.02.05 STRENGTH: L GED: R2 M1 L1 SVP: 2 DLU: 77

786.682-138 HEMMER, OVERLOCK (garment)

Operates *overlock sewing machine* equipped with S-shaped folder to hem garment edge. Guides garment edge into folder and simultaneously sews over raw edge and over folded-back top of hem to secure hem and cover raw edge with stitching. Performs duties as described under SEWING-MACHINE OPERATOR, REGULAR EQUIPMENT (any industry) Master Title.

GOE: 06.02.05 STRENGTH: L GED: R2 M1 L1 SVP: 2 DLU: 77

786.682-142 HEMSTITCHING-MACHINE OPERATOR (garment)

Operates hemstitching sewing machine, equipped with folder, to sew decorative line of stitched perforations. Performs duties as described under SEWING-MACHINE OPERATOR, REGULAR EQUIPMENT (any industry) Master Title.

GOE: 06.02.05 STRENGTH: L GED: R2 M1 L1 SVP: 2 DLU: 77

786.682-146 JUMPBASTING-MACHINE OPERATOR (garment)

Operates *jumpbasting sewing machine* to secure parts of coat in position, either permanently or in preparation for permanent sewing. Performs duties as described under SEWING-MACHINE OPERATOR, REGULAR EQUIPMENT (any industry) Master Title.

GOE: 06.02.05 STRENGTH: L GED: R2 M1 L1 SVP: 2 DLU: 77

786.682-150 LAPEL PADDER, BLINDSTITCH (garment)

Operates *blindstitch sewing machine* to attach canvas interlining to lapel of coat, manipulating fabric to ease-in fullness so lapel rolls outward. Adjusts machine for depth of needle penetration, depending on fabric, and sews lines of stitching, following contour of lapel. May sew lines of stitching on coat collar instead of lapel and be designated Collar Padder, Blindstitch (garment). Performs other duties as described under SEWING-MACHINE OPERATOR, REGULAR EQUIPMENT (any industry) Master Title.

GOE: 06.02.05 STRENGTH: L GED: R2 M1 L1 SVP: 3 DLU: 77

786.682-154 LINING BASTER, JUMPBASTING (garment)

Operates *jumpbasting sewing machine* to baste lining to coat, manipulating fabric to distribute lining fullness, in preparation for permanent attachment. Folds and sews pleats in lining. When basting coat with vent, folds and bastes lining to vent edges. Performs duties as described under SEWING-MACHINE OPERATOR, REGULAR EQUIPMENT (any industry) Master Title.

GOE: 06.02.05 STRENGTH: L GED: R2 M1 L1 SVP: 4 DLU: 77

786.682-158 LINING FELLER, BLINDSTITCH (garment)

Operates *blindstitch sewing machine* equipped with vertical guide to join bottom of lining to garment with stitches that are invisible on outer surface of gar-

ment: Adjusts stitch-penetration depth, depending on fabric. Folds under edge of lining and positions on outer fabric. Guides edge of lining against vertical guide to maintain fabric position and join undersurfaces. May join lining at cuff. Performs other duties as described under SEWING-MACHINE OPERATOR, REGULAR EQUIPMENT (any industry) Master Title.

GOE: 06.02.05 STRENGTH: L GED: R2 M1 L1 SVP: 3 DLU: 77

786.682-162 LINING MAKER, LOCKSTITCH (garment)

Operates lockstitch sewing machine to make garment lining: Seams sides, shoulders, and sleeves of lining and sews darts, if any. Folds and sews pleat in back of lining for extra fullness. Sets sleeve lining to body lining. Performs other duties as described under SEWING-MACHINE OPERATOR, REGULAR EQUIPMENT (any industry) Master Title.

GOE: 06.02.05 STRENGTH: L GED: R2 M1 L1 SVP: 2 DLU: 77

786.682-166 LINING SETTER, LOCKSTITCH (garment) alternate titles: outsewer; sew-out operator

Operates lockstitch sewing machine to set edge of lining to garment edges, either directly or by first joining lining to facing and then setting facing to garment edge. May operate machine equipped with edgecutter to set lining and trim excess fabric. Performs other duties as described under SEWING-MACHINE OPERATOR, REGULAR EQUIPMENT (any industry) Master Title.

GOE: 06.02.05 STRENGTH: L GED: R2 M1 L1 SVP: 3 DLU: 77

786.682-170 LOCKSTITCH-MACHINE OPERATOR (garment) alternate titles: single-needle operator

Operates lockstitch sewing machine equipped with guides to perform sewing operations, such as seaming garment parts along similarly shaped edges, attaching narrow fabrics (tape, lace or other trim), or sewing reinforcing fabric: Matches edges or positions tape, trim, or piece of fabric on mark and operates machine to attach to garment. Performs other duties as described under SEWING-MACHINE OPERATOR, REGULAR EQUIPMENT (any industry) Master Title. May operate machine equipped with ruffling attachment to ruffle material and attach ruffled trim to garment, or operate machine equipped with shirring attachment to shirr while attaching trim. May operate two-needle variation of lockstitch machine to attach tape or trim and be designated Double-Needle Operator, Lockstitch (garment).

GOE: 06.02.05 STRENGTH: L GED: R3 M1 L2 SVP: 3 DLU: 81

786.682-174 LOCKSTITCH-SEWING-MACHINE OPERATOR, COMPLETE GARMENT (garment)

Operates lockstitch sewing machine equipped with various attachments to sew complete garment, exclusive of finishing operations. May make shell of garment (complete garment exclusive of lining) and be designated Shell Maker, Lockstitch (garment). Performs other duties as described under SEWING-MACHINE OPERATOR, REGULAR EQUIPMENT (any industry) Master Title.

GOE: 06.02.05 STRENGTH: L GED: R3 M1 L2 SVP: 4 DLU: 77

786.682-178 MULTINEEDLE-CHAINSTITCH-MACHINE OPERATOR (garment) alternate titles: multineedle shirrer

Operates multineedle chainstitch sewing machine to shirr garment parts by any of following methods: (1) Guides garment part under shirring presser foot that evenly spaces gathers under needle; (2) guides part under needles of machine threaded with elastic thread; (3) guides parts and elastic cord under needles to shirr fabric. Secures specified number of needles into machine head. Performs duties as defined under SEWING-MACHINE OPERATOR, REGULAR EQUIPMENT (any industry) Master Title. May sew multiple rows of flat trim to garment part. May sew decorative threads between rows of shirring, or shirr fabric with decorative stitch and be designated SMOCKING-MACHINE OPERATOR (garment).

GOE: 06.02.05 STRENGTH: L GED: R2 M1 L1 SVP: 3 DLU: 77

786.682-182 NECKTIE OPERATOR, POCKETS AND PIECES (garment)

Operates chainstitch sewing machine to join parts of necktie. Aligns edges of tie pieces and joins parts to make face (outer surface) of tie. Seams tie pocket (lining) to tips of tie. Performs other duties as described under SEWING-MACHINE OPERATOR, REGULAR EQUIPMENT (any industry) Master Title.

GOE: 06.02.05 STRENGTH: L GED: R2 M1 L1 SVP: 3 DLU: 77

786.682-186 NECKTIE-CENTRALIZING-MACHINE OPERATOR I (garment) alternate titles: necktie stitcher

Operates *necktie-centralizing sewing machine* equipped with hook in front of needle to seam length of necktie and attach reinforcing strip with stretchable one-thread stitch. Folds tie fabric lengthwise, superimposes and aligns reinforcing strip along edge, and stitches through layers to join. Performs duties as described under SEWING-MACHINE OPERATOR, REGULAR EQUIPMENT (any industry) Master Title.

GOE: 06.02.05 STRENGTH: L GED: R2 M1 L1 SVP: 3 DLU: 77

786.682-190 NECKTIE-CENTRALIZING-MACHINE OPERATOR II (garment) alternate titles: slipstitch-machine operator

Operates *necktie-centralizing machine* equipped with feed track and stationary needle to seam length of necktie and simultaneously attach reinforcing strip with stitch simulating handstitiching: Positions reinforcing strip on feed track. Folds tie fabric lengthwise and positions above strip. Operates machine and manipulates edges continuously to align and guide tie fabric into track.

GOE: 06.02.05 STRENGTH: I GED: R2 M1 L1 SVP: 3 DLU: 77

786.682-194　OVERLOCK SEWING MACHINE OPERATOR (garment)

Operates *overlock sewing machine,* equipped with edgecutter, to serge, seam, or attach tape or trim to garment and cut away excess material: Overedges one ply of fabric to prevent fraying, or overedges two or more plies to join garment parts. Performs duties as described under SEWING-MACHINE OPERATOR, REGULAR EQUIPMENT (any industry) Master Title. May operate overlock machine equipped with shirring mechanism to shirr and attach trim to garment. May operate overlock machine that sews reinforcing row of stitches while overedging and be designated Safety-Stitch-Machine Operator (garment).
GOE: 06.02.05 STRENGTH: L GED: R2 M1 L1 SVP: 3 DLU: 80

786.682-198　OVERLOCK-MACHINE OPERATOR, COMPLETE GARMENT (garment)

Operates *overlock sewing machine* equipped with edgecutter to sew complete garment, exclusive of finishing operations. Performs duties as described under SEWING-MACHINE OPERATOR, REGULAR EQUIPMENT (any industry) Master Title. May operate machine equipped with intermittent shirring mechanism to shorten edge of one garment part in order to join edges of dissimilar length.
GOE: 06.02.05 STRENGTH: L GED: R3 M1 L2 SVP: 4 DLU: 77

786.682-202　PANTS OUTSEAMER, CHAINSTITCH (garment) alternate titles: pants closer

Operates chainstitch sewing machine to sew outside seam of pants, pushing front pants pocket out of way, matching notches, and aligning fabric pattern, if any. Performs other duties as described under SEWING-MACHINE OPERATOR, REGULAR EQUIPMENT (any industry) Master Title.
GOE: 06.02.05 STRENGTH: L GED: R2 M1 L1 SVP: 3 DLU: 77

786.682-206　PICKED-EDGE SEWING-MACHINE OPERATOR (garment)

Operates picked-edge sewing machine to sew stitchline specified distance from edge on outer surface of garment part, duplicating hand top stitching in appearance: Threads needle with precut lengths of thread, using threading hook attached to frame. Depresses pedal to start machine equipped with double-ended needle that moves between top and bottom chucks to insert thread at preset distances, simulating saddle stitch or short-length stitch. Pulls loop of thread from needle, using pick.
GOE: 06.02.05 STRENGTH: L GED: R2 M1 L1 SVP: 2 DLU: 77

786.682-210　POCKET SETTER, LOCKSTITCH (garment) alternate titles: pocket maker

Operates lockstitch sewing machine to join cut parts to form pockets and to set pockets into or onto garment, according to style and markings. May topstitch pocket edges or attach welting, piping, or trim to pockets. May cut material for welting, using scissors. May cut pocket openings, match corners, or cut excess fabric from seam, using scissors. Performs other duties as described under SEWING-MACHINE OPERATOR, REGULAR EQUIPMENT (any industry) Master Title.
GOE: 06.02.05 STRENGTH: L GED: R3 M1 L1 SVP: 4 DLU: 77

786.682-214　REPAIR OPERATOR (garment)

Operates lockstitch sewing machine to repair or replace damaged or defective parts of garments: Examines repair tags and markings on garment to locate defects or damage, such as irregular stitches or torn or snagged parts. Removes stitches, using scissors or ripper (pointed handtool). Joins replacement parts to garment and sews missing or improperly sewn stitches on garment parts. Performs duties as described under SEWING-MACHINE OPERATOR, REGULAR EQUIPMENT (any industry) Master Title.
GOE: 06.02.05 STRENGTH: L GED: R3 M1 L2 SVP: 3 DLU: 77

786.682-218　SEAT JOINER, CHAINSTITCH (garment)

Operates chainstitch sewing machine to join seat seam of pants with curved stitchline from bottom of zipper to waistline at center back, matching inseams and varying seam allowance according to size. Performs other duties as described under SEWING-MACHINE OPERATOR, REGULAR EQUIPMENT (any industry) Master Title.
GOE: 06.02.05 STRENGTH: L GED: R2 M1 L1 SVP: 3 DLU: 77

786.682-222　SHOULDER JOINER, LOCKSTITCH (garment)

Operates lockstitch sewing machine to sew shoulder seam of coat or jacket. Aligns seam edges, moving canvas and shoulder pad aside, and guides edges under needle to sew shoulder seam, working in fullness of fabric with fingers. Performs other duties as described under SEWING-MACHINE OPERATOR, REGULAR EQUIPMENT (any industry) Master Title.
GOE: 06.02.05 STRENGTH: L GED: R2 M1 L1 SVP: 3 DLU: 77

786.682-226　SLEEVE MAKER, LOCKSTITCH (garment)

Operates lockstitch sewing machine to make coat sleeve. Seams edges of sleeve parts, following markings and manipulating fabric to provide fullness over elbow area. May attach separate cuffs or fold raw bottom edge of sleeve and sew to make cuff with or without vent. Performs other duties as described under SEWING-MACHINE OPERATOR, REGULAR EQUIPMENT (any industry) Master Title.
GOE: 06.02.05 STRENGTH: L GED: R2 M1 L1 SVP: 2 DLU: 77

786.682-230　SLEEVE SETTER, LOCKSTITCH (garment)

Operates lockstitch sewing machine to set sleeve to garment: Aligns edge of sleeve on edge of armhole and manipulates sleeve material under needle to con-

form to dissimilar shape of opening and to distribute fullness at shoulder. May set either seamed or unseamed sleeve sleeve. May operate machine with edgecutting attachment, seam guide, or folding attachment. Performs other duties as described under SEWING-MACHINE OPERATOR, REGULAR EQUIPMENT (any industry) Master Title.
GOE: 06.02.05 STRENGTH: L GED: R2 M1 L1 SVP: 4 DLU: 77

786.682-234　SLEEVE SETTER, OVERLOCK (garment)

Operates *overlock sewing machine* equipped with edge cutter and intermittent shirring mechanism to set sleeve to garment: Aligns edge of sleeve on edge of armhole and manipulates sleeve material under needle to conform to dissimilar shape of opening. Presses knee lever to engage intermittent shirring mechanism and distributes sleeve fullness at shoulder. Performs duties as described under SEWING-MACHINE OPERATOR, REGULAR EQUIPMENT (any industry) Master Title. May set either seamed or unseamed sleeve. May operate variation of overlock machine that sews separate reinforcing row of stitches while overedging and be designated Sleeve Setter, Safety-Stitch (garment).
GOE: 06.02.05 STRENGTH: L GED: R2 M1 L1 SVP: 3 DLU: 77

786.682-238　TOPSTITCHER, LOCKSTITCH (garment)

Operates lockstitch sewing machine to sew one or two rows of stitching specified distance from edge or seam of garment part to reinforce seam, prevent edge rolling, or emphasize design. May be designated according to part of garment outlined as Armhole Raiser, Lockstitch (garment); Fly Raiser, Lockstitch (garment). May sew along edges of coat and be designated Edge Stitcher, Lockstitch (garment). Performs other duties as described under SEWING-MACHINE OPERATOR, REGULAR EQUIPMENT (any industry) Master Title.
GOE: 06.02.05 STRENGTH: L GED: R2 M1 L1 SVP: 3 DLU: 77

786.682-242　TOPSTITCHER, ZIGZAG (garment)

Operates *zigzag sewing machine* to sew row of stitching specified distance from either edge or seam of garment for decorative effect. Performs duties as described under SEWING-MACHINE OPERATOR, REGULAR EQUIPMENT (any industry) Master Title.
GOE: 06.02.05 STRENGTH: L GED: R2 M1 L1 SVP: 3 DLU: 77

786.682-246　TUNNEL-ELASTIC OPERATOR, CHAINSTITCH (garment)

Operates two-needle chainstitch sewing machine equipped with folder to enclose elastic strip inside fold of fabric at garment opening: Inserts end of elastic strip and edge of garment into folder. Guides edge of garment under needles to enclose elastic in hem between two rows of stitching. May operate machine equipped with different type of folder to either enclose elastic in binding or folded tape at garment edge. Performs other duties as described under SEWING-MACHINE OPERATOR, REGULAR EQUIPMENT (any industry) Master Title.
GOE: 06.02.05 STRENGTH: L GED: R2 M1 L1 SVP: 3 DLU: 77

786.682-250　TUNNEL-ELASTIC OPERATOR, LOCKSTITCH (garment)

Operates lockstitch sewing machine equipped with folder to enclose elastic strip inside fold of fabric at garment opening: Inserts end of elastic strip and edge of garment into folder. Guides edge of garment under needle to hem garment and enclose elastic strip in hem. May operate machine equipped with different type of folder to either enclose elastic in binding or in folded tape at garment edge. Performs other duties as described under SEWING-MACHINE OPERATOR, REGULAR EQUIPMENT (any industry) Master Title.
GOE: 06.02.05 STRENGTH: L GED: R2 M1 L1 SVP: 3 DLU: 77

786.682-254　TUNNEL-ELASTIC OPERATOR, ZIGZAG (garment)

Operates *zigzag sewing machine* equipped with folder to enclose elastic strip inside fold of fabric at garment opening: Inserts end of elastic strip and edge of garment into folder. Guides edge of garment under needle to hem garment and enclose elastic strip in hem. Performs duties as described under SEWING-MACHINE OPERATOR, REGULAR EQUIPMENT (any industry) Master Title. May operate machine equipped with different type of folder to either enclose elastic in binding or in folded tape at garment edge.
GOE: 06.02.05 STRENGTH: L GED: R2 M1 L1 SVP: 3 DLU: 77

786.682-258　ULTRASONIC-SEAMING-MACHINE OPERATOR (garment)

Operates *ultrasonic seaming machine* to hem, attach garment parts, or join layers by fusing thermoplastic material in simulated stitch pattern: Presses knee lever to raise *horn* and positions garment parts on machine bed. Depresses pedal to start machine and guides material under horn to fuse material. May replace *stitching wheel* under bed of machine to change stitching pattern.
GOE: 06.02.05 STRENGTH: L GED: R2 M1 L2 SVP: 2 DLU: 77

786.682-262　UTILITY OPERATOR (garment) alternate titles: reserve operator

Operates sewing machines to join garment parts: Guides garment parts under needle or needles to join parts, following markings, aligning edges, and distributing fullness. Performs duties as described under SEWING-MACHINE OPERATOR, REGULAR EQUIPMENT (any industry) Master Title. May substitute for absent workers or assist workers temporarily behind in production.
GOE: 06.02.05 STRENGTH: L GED: R3 M1 L2 SVP: 4 DLU: 77

786.682-266　WAISTBAND SETTER, LOCKSTITCH (garment)

Operates lockstitch sewing machine to sew waistband to upper edge of pants or skirt. Positions waistband on upper edge of garment, aligning markings, and

guides parts under needle to attach waistband to garment. Performs other duties as described under SEWING-MACHINE OPERATOR, REGULAR EQUIPMENT (any industry) Master Title.
GOE: 06.02.05 STRENGTH: L GED: R2 M1 L1 SVP: 2 DLU: 77

786.682-270 WAISTLINE JOINER, LOCKSTITCH (garment)
Operates lockstitch sewing machine to join bodice and skirt of garment: Aligns edges of bodice and skirt, matching seams, notches, or pleats, and guides parts under needle to sew seam. Performs other duties as described under SEWING-MACHINE OPERATOR, REGULAR EQUIPMENT (any industry) Master Title.
GOE: 06.02.05 STRENGTH: L GED: R2 M1 L1 SVP: 3 DLU: 77

786.682-274 WAISTLINE JOINER, OVERLOCK (garment)
Operates *overlock sewing machine* equipped with edgecutter and shirring mechanism to join bodice and skirt of garment and shirr fabric at wasitline: Positions bodice and skirt on machine bed, operates machine to join parts and cut away excess fabric, and presses knee lever to shirr edge of skirt or bodice as needed to match markings and seams. Performs duties as described under SEWING-MACHINE OPERATOR, REGULAR EQUIPMENT (any industry) Master Title.
GOE: 06.02.05 STRENGTH: L GED: R2 M1 L1 SVP: 4 DLU: 77

786.682-278 ZIGZAG-MACHINE OPERATOR (garment)
Operates *zigzag sewing machine* to join layers of material, seam garment parts, or attach trim to garment. Performs duties as described under SEWING-MACHINE OPERATOR, REGULAR EQUIPMENT (any industry) Master Title. May operate machine equipped with different cams to sew decorative stitches, such as scallops. May operate variation of zigzag machine to join adjacent edges or flatten seams with decorative crisscross stitch and be designated Fagoting-Machine Operator (garment).
GOE: 06.02.05 STRENGTH: L GED: R2 M1 L1 SVP: 2 DLU: 77

786.682-282 ZIPPER SETTER, CHAINSTITCH (garment)
Operates chainstitch sewing machine equipped with zipper presser foot to set slide fastener in garment opening: Positions one side of zipper tape along one edge of seam opening matching marks or notches on seam edge and tape. Guides edges under needle and zipper presser foot to sew zipper tape along one side, across bottom, and up other side to set zipper in opening. Performs other duties as described under SEWING-MACHINE OPERATOR, REGULAR EQUIPMENT (any industry) Master Title.
GOE: 06.02.05 STRENGTH: L GED: R2 M1 L1 SVP: 3 DLU: 77

786.682-286 ZIPPER SETTER, LOCKSTITCH (garment)
Operates lockstitch sewing machine equipped with zipper presser foot to set slide fastener in garment opening: Positions one side of zipper tape along one edge of seam opening, matching marks or notches on seam edge and tape. Guides edges under needle and zipper presser foot to sew zipper tape along one side, across bottom, and up other side to set zipper in opening. May assemble fly in pants and set zipper in fly and be designated Fly Setter (garment). Performs other duties as described under SEWING-MACHINE OPERATOR, REGULAR EQUIPMENT (any industry) Master Title.
GOE: 06.02.05 STRENGTH: L GED: R2 M1 L1 SVP: 3 DLU: 77

786.685-010 BUTTON-SEWING-MACHINE OPERATOR (garment) alternate titles: fastener-sewing-machine operator
Tends semiautomatic, *short-cycle sewing machine* that sews buttons or other fasteners onto garments: Positions garment or garment part under needle. Pours buttons into hopper for automatic feeding into holding clamp or places button or fastener in clamp and starts machine. Variations are in type of attachment (spot-tack or thread-shank) and in type of button or fastener (flat or shank button; snap or hook-and-eye fastener). May tend same machine to spot-tack when not attaching buttons or fasteners.
GOE: 06.04.05 STRENGTH: L GED: R2 M1 L1 SVP: 2 DLU: 77

786.685-014 BUTTONHOLE-MACHINE OPERATOR (garment)
Tends semiautomatic, *short-cycle sewing machine* that cuts and stitches buttonholes in garments: Positions garment or garment part under needle, starts machine that automatically stitches and cuts buttonhole, and cuts thread. May adjust stitching and cutting mechanisms of machine to alter size of buttonholes. May tend machine that cuts and stitches gimp-reinforced (eyelet-ended or teardrop) buttonholes in garments, such as coats or jackets, and be designated Gimp-Buttonhole-Machine Operator (garment).
GOE: 06.04.05 STRENGTH: L GED: R2 M1 L1 SVP: 2 DLU: 77

786.685-018 EMBROIDERY-MACHINE OPERATOR (garment)
Tends semiautomatic sewing machine with multiple-sewing heads controlled by pattern chain that embroiders designs on garments or garment parts: Positions garment or part over embroidery hoops arranged in hoop frame, following edges or markings on fabric. Places hoop frame on machine bed and turns thumbscrews to secure frame to machine. Presses button to start machine that sews design onto garment or part and stops, or sews one color of multiple-color design and stops. When sewing multiple-color designs, rethreads machine with subsequent colors of thread and starts machine to complete design. Removes hoop frame from machine on completion of design and removes garment or part from hoops.
GOE: 06.04.05 STRENGTH: L GED: R2 M1 L1 SVP: 2 DLU: 77

786.685-022 PIPED-POCKET-MACHINE OPERATOR (garment) alternate titles: welt-pocket-machine operator
Tends semiautomatic sewing machine that folds, sews, and cuts fabric to make piped or welt pocket openings: Positions garment section, strips of fabric,

and reinforcing material in clamp and depresses pedal to lower and close clamp. Presses knee lever to activate machine cycle that automatically folds and attaches strips with two rows of stitching, cuts opening and corner slits, and pushes piping through opening. May adjust stitching and cutting mechanisms and change knives to regulate size of opening. May change needles, thread machine, and adjust thread tension. May operate piped-buttonhole machine and be designated Piped-Buttonhole-Machine Operator (garment).
GOE: 06.04.05 STRENGTH: L GED: R2 M1 L1 SVP: 2 DLU: 77

786.685-026 PROFILE-STITCHING-MACHINE OPERATOR (garment) alternate titles: contour stitcher; longseam-machine operator; runstitching-machine operator
Tends semiautomatic machine that sews stitching along contour to join, attach, serge, topstitch, or hem garment parts: Positions fabric layers or garment part under needle, against guide, or in clamp or template, and starts machine that performs preset sewing cycle to make garment part (such as collar), attach garment part (such as patch pocket), or automatically sew along fabric edge to serge, seam, hem, or topstitch. When tending machine equipped with template, removes garment part from template at end of sewing cycle.
GOE: 06.04.05 STRENGTH: L GED: R2 M1 L1 SVP: 2 DLU: 77

786.685-030 SEWING-MACHINE OPERATOR, SEMIAUTOMATIC (garment)
Tends one or more semiautomatic sewing machines that attach, join, reinforce, or decorate garments or garment parts, or perform other preset cycle operations, such as buttonhole making: Threads machine and adjusts thread tensions. Positions fabric layers, garment, or garment part in holding device on machine bed or according to guides, edges, or markings, and starts machine. Notifies SUPERVISOR, GARMENT MANUFACTURING (garment) 786.132-010 if machine malfunctions. May select supplies, such as fasteners and thread, according to specifications or color of fabric. May change needles and oil machine.
GOE: 06.04.05 STRENGTH: L GED: R2 M1 L2 SVP: 2 DLU: 81

786.685-034 TACKING-MACHINE OPERATOR (garment)
Tends semiautomatic, *short-cycle sewing machine* that sews concentration of stitches, such as bar, spot, or triangle, to attach or secure part, such as strap, garter, label, belt loop, or cuff, or reinforce stress point, such as pocket corner or bottom of fly.
GOE: 06.04.05 STRENGTH: L GED: R2 M1 L1 SVP: 2 DLU: 77

786.685-038 ULTRASONIC-SEAMING-MACHINE OPERATOR, SEMI-AUTOMATIC (garment)
Tends semiautomatic, *ultrasonic seaming machine* to seal dart edges, cut and seal edges of buttonholes, or cut tubing (or belt lengths) and seal ends by heat fusion. Positions garment or garment part under horn of machine, following markings. Depresses pedal to activate machine that heat-fuses garment parts with or without stitch pattern and with or without cutting.
GOE: 06.04.05 STRENGTH: L GED: R2 M1 L1 SVP: 1 DLU: 77

786.685-042 BUTTONHOLE-AND-BUTTON-SEWING-MACHINE OPERATOR (garment)
Tends semiautomatic sewing machines that cut and stitch buttonholes and sew buttons and other fasteners to garments: Pours buttons into hopper for automatic feeding into holding clamp of sewing machine or places buttons and fasteners in clamp. Turns knobs to adjust stitching and cutting mechanisms of machine to set size of buttonholes according to garment styles. Positions garment, garment parts, buttons, or fasteners under needle, and starts short-cycle sewing machine that cuts and stitches buttonholes in garment or parts or sews buttons and fasteners to garment. Cuts threads, using scissors.
GOE: 06.04.05 STRENGTH: L GED: R2 M1 L2 SVP: 2 DLU: 86

787 SEWING MACHINE OPERATORS, NONGARMENT

This group includes occupations concerned with machine-sewing textile, leather, fur, and related products, except garments as defined in GARMENT INDUSTRY.

787.132-010 SEWING SUPERVISOR (any industry)
Supervises and coordinates activities of workers engaged in operating sewing machines to assemble articles, such as curtains and drapes, fabric camping equipment, and stuffed toy shells: Examines articles to ensure adherence to quality standards. Trains workers by demonstrating work methods and machine operation. Performs other duties as described under SUPERVISOR (any industry) Master Title. May be designated according to activity supervised as Curtain Supervisor (tex. prod., nec); Drapery Supervisor (tex. prod., nec); Embroidery Supervisor (tex. prod., nec); Supervisor, Camp Department (tex. prod., nec); Supervisor, Sleeping-Bag Department (tex. prod., nec); Supervisor, Stuffed-Toy Shells (toy-sport equip.).
GOE: 06.02.01 STRENGTH: L GED: R4 M3 L3 SVP: 6 DLU: 77

787.132-014 SUPERVISOR, SEWING ROOM (fabrication, nec)
Supervises and coordinates activities of workers engaged in preparing casket linings, and pillows: Measures and cuts cloth according to size, color, and style of lining, using hand shears. Inspects seams, shirring, embroidering, and crushing for conformance to company standards. Demonstrates sewing and crushing techniques to train new employees. May operate shirring machine to gather ma-

terial. Performs other duties as described under SUPERVISOR (any industry) Master Title.
GOE: 06.02.01 STRENGTH: L GED: R4 M2 L3 SVP: 5 DLU: 77

787.132-018 SUPERVISOR, STITCHING DEPARTMENT (tex. prod., nec)
Supervises and coordinates activities of workers engaged in operating sewing machines to produce decorative trimming or stitching, such as tucking, shirring, and embroidering: Directs workers in techniques or procedures in sewing new designs. Assigns new designs and materials to workers to ensure continuous workflow. Records number of pieces processed by worker for production cost records. Performs other duties as described under SUPERVISOR (any industry) Master Title.
GOE: 06.02.01 STRENGTH: L GED: R4 M2 L2 SVP: 7 DLU: 77

787.381-010 LAMP-SHADE SEWER (fabrication, nec)
Fabricates lampshades from material, such as silk, following patterns and using scissors, needle and thread, and sewing machine: Places specified material on table and marks cutting lines on materials, following pattern. Cuts shade sections from material, using scissors. Sews sections together to form shade covering, using single needle sewing machine. Winds tape around upper and lower rings of frame. Draws shade covering over frame and bastes covering to tape on rings. Sews material to frame and trims material with scissors. Sews trimming around top and bottom of shade. Sews wire to edge of shade to reinforce edge and retain shape.
GOE: 06.02.27 STRENGTH: L GED: R3 M2 L2 SVP: 6 DLU: 77

787.682-010 BINDER (any industry) alternate titles: binding-end stitcher; binding-machine operator; taper
Operates sewing machine equipped with folding attachment to sew binding material over edges or seams of articles, such as camping equipment, linens, parachutes, gloves and mittens, or hats and caps, to reinforce, prevent raveling, and give finished appearance: Places roll of binding on holder and draws end through folding attachment. Positions edge of article between folds of binding material and guides article and material under needle. Performs duties as described under SEWING-MACHINE OPERATOR, REGULAR EQUIPMENT (any industry) Master Title. When binding blankets, folds binding material at end of seam to form corners and sews over folded corner. When binding fitted sheets, matches curved edges of sheet and guides edges under needle to form sheet corners. May operate sewing machine equipped with shirring mechanism to gather binding as binding is attached to article. May be designated according to article or part bound as Band-Lining Bander (hat & cap); Blanket Binder (tex. prod., nec); Ear-Flap Binder (hat & cap); Fitted Sheet Binder (tex. prod., nec); Flap-Lining Binder (hat & cap); Helmet Binder (hat & cap). May be designated: Parachute Taper (tex. prod., nec); Pot-Holder Binder (tex. prod., nec); Screen-Vent Binder (hat & cap); Soft-Hat Binder (hat & cap). May bind rug samples and be designated Sample Processor (carpet & rug).
GOE: 06.02.05 STRENGTH: L GED: R3 M1 L1 SVP: 4 DLU: 78

787.682-014 CARPET SEWER (carpet & rug; retail trade) alternate titles: fringe-binder operator; leno sewer; sewing-machine operator, carpet and rugs
Operates sewing machine to join carpet sections or braided yarn strips to form rug and finish edges, performing any combination of following duties: Joins sections of carpeting to form rug of desired size or continuous length (runner). Sews decorative trimmings on rugs, borders on runners, or binding to prevent edges from raveling. Operates sewing machine that loops yarn into fringe and stitches fringe to edge of rug. Joins braided strips of yarn to form round or oval rug of desired size. Joins widths of leno cloth used on backing of rugs. May join sections of carpet together, using seaming tape and liquid cement. Performs other duties as described under SEWING-MACHINE OPERATOR, REGULAR EQUIPMENT (any industry) Master Title.
GOE: 06.02.05 STRENGTH: M GED: R3 M2 L2 SVP: 3 DLU: 77

787.682-018 DRAPERY OPERATOR (retail trade) alternate titles: drapery worker
Operates sewing machine to join precut pieces of material to form finished draperies: Folds edges of material by hand and guides them under machine needle to form hems. Determines number of pleats required, according to width of finished drapery. Gathers pleats by hand and guides material under machine needle to tack pleats [TACKING-MACHINE OPERATOR (any industry)]. May measure and cut material according to specifications, using rule and scissors. Performs duties as described under SEWING-MACHINE OPERATOR, REGULAR EQUIPMENT (any industry) Master Title.
GOE: 06.02.05 STRENGTH: L GED: R3 M1 L2 SVP: 4 DLU: 77

787.682-022 EMBROIDERY-MACHINE OPERATOR (any industry) alternate titles: monogram-machine operator
Operates sewing machine to embroider name, initial, or decorative designs on garments, household articles, material, or uniforms and to stitch cording, braid, or emblems on material or garments, following stamped design or working freehand without guide or markings: Reads work order to determine type and location of embroidery. Selects size and color thread and draws it through machine guides and bobbin. Turns setscrews to regulate machine settings. Positions article under presser foot and presses pedal or knee control to start machine and control speed of sewing. Guides fabric under needle with left hand or turns handcrank under feed bed to guide material, following stamped pattern or by freehand. Observes sewing operation to detect defects in stitching that

indicate machine malfunction and notifies supervisor of malfunction. May draw guide freehand on fabric. May pin tissue paper pattern on fabric to be used as guide. May use embroidery hoops to hold fabric taut. May smooth embroidered area, using hand iron. May repair defective embroidery or fill in blanks left by embroidery machine. May operate automatic embroidery machines with multiple sewing heads controlled by perforated pattern tape. May be designated according to type of work done as Cloth Numberer (tex. prod., nec); Letterer (garment). When operating embroidery machine to sew tape or braiding to garment to form embroidery design, may be designated Corder (garment; tex. prod., nec).
GOE: 06.02.05 STRENGTH: L GED: R3 M2 L2 SVP: 4 DLU: 77

787.682-026 HEMMER (any industry) alternate titles: plain-goods hemmer
Operates sewing machine equipped with folding attachment to hem articles, such as curtains and draperies, gloves and mittens, sheets, towels, and pillowcases: Guides edge of material through folding attachment and under machine needle. Inserts and sews labels into hem. May reinforce hem by backstitching at ends of seam. May fold hem manually. When operating machine to hem curtains and draperies to form rod inserts, is designated HEADER (tex. prod., nec). May be designated according to article or part hemmed as Pillowcase Sewer (tex. prod., nec); Sheet Sewer (tex. prod., nec); Towel Sewer (tex. prod., nec); Window-Shade-Cloth Sewer (furniture); Wrist Hemmer (glove & mit.). Performs duties as described under SEWING-MACHINE OPERATOR, REGULAR EQUIPMENT (any industry) Master Title.
GOE: 06.02.05 STRENGTH: L GED: R3 M1 L1 SVP: 4 DLU: 77

787.682-030 MENDER (any industry)
Operates sewing machine to repair defects, such as tears and holes in garments, linens, curtains, draperies, and blankets: Patches, darns, or reweaves holes or tears in garments, curtains, or linens, and resews ripped seams. Sews fringe, tassels, and ruffles onto drapes and curtains. Sews buttons and trimming on garments after they have been cleaned. Operates sewing machine to restitch or replace binding ribbon on edge of blankets. May cut curtains to specified measurements and hem edges. May shorten or lengthen hems to alter size of garments. May replace pockets in coats or trousers. May sew identifying labels and emblems on uniforms, linens, or diapers for linen supply or diaper service. May repair defective stitching on articles. May be designated according to type of article sewn as Sewer, Linen Room (hotel & rest.) or machine used as Darning-Machine Operator (any industry). May examine lace webbing for defects and be designated Examiner-Mender (tex. prod., nec). Performs duties as described under SEWING-MACHINE OPERATOR, REGULAR EQUIPMENT (any industry) Master Title.
GOE: 06.02.05 STRENGTH: L GED: R3 M1 L2 SVP: 4 DLU: 78

787.682-034 OVEREDGE SEWER (any industry)
Operates sewing machine equipped with rotary cutter to trim raw edges from articles and sew edges with overedge stitch to decorate and reinforce them and prevent raveling. Guides edges under needle and through trimming attachment. Performs duties as described under SEWING-MACHINE OPERATOR, REGULAR EQUIPMENT (any industry) Master Title.
GOE: 06.02.05 STRENGTH: L GED: R3 M1 L2 SVP: 4 DLU: 77

787.682-038 ROLL-OR-TAPE-EDGE-MACHINE OPERATOR (furniture)
Operates sewing machine to stitch rolled edges of filled and tufted mattresses to reinforce their boxlike shape, or to stitch padding and fabric covering around innersprings used in mattress: Positions mattress on table and adjusts machine according to thickness of mattress. Rolls and inserts mattress edge under machine needle, starts machine, and guides edge under needle as machine travels slowly around table. Places innersprings on table and spreads felt or foam rubber padding and covering over springs. Inserts edges of covering and border panel under needle and tape feed of machine and guides tape and edges under needle to join them as machine travels slowly around table. Performs duties as described under SEWING-MACHINE OPERATOR, REGULAR EQUIPMENT (any industry) Master Title.
GOE: 06.02.05 STRENGTH: M GED: R2 M1 L1 SVP: 3 DLU: 77

787.682-046 SEWING-MACHINE OPERATOR (any industry)
Operates sewing machine to join, gather, hem, reinforce, or decorate articles. Performs duties as described under SEWING-MACHINE OPERATOR, REGULAR EQUIPMENT (any industry) Master Title.
GOE: 06.02.05 STRENGTH: L GED: R3 M2 L2 SVP: 5 DLU: 77

787.682-050 SEWING-MACHINE OPERATOR (knitting; protective dev.)
Operates sewing machine to join parts of surgical appliances and garments and orthopedic supports. May position filling material and springs in truss pads and braces. May guide leather parts, such as covers under machine needle to join them. Performs duties as described under SEWING-MACHINE OPERATOR, REGULAR EQUIPMENT (any industry) Master Title.
GOE: 06.02.05 STRENGTH: L GED: R2 M1 L1 SVP: 3 DLU: 81

787.682-054 SEWING-MACHINE OPERATOR (toy-sport equip.)
Operates sewing machine to join parts of stuffed toys: Fits together parts, such as ear, head, or body assembly, prior to sewing. Stitches assembly inside out and combines individual assemblies into completed toys. Adjusts thread tension guides. May stitch opening closed after filling and be designated Closer (toy-sport equip.). Performs duties as described under SEWING-MACHINE OPERATOR, REGULAR EQUIPMENT (any industry) Master Title.

GOE: 06.02.05 STRENGTH: L GED: R2 M1 L1 SVP: 3 DLU: 77

787.682-058 SEWING-MACHINE OPERATOR II (tex. prod., nec)
Operates sewing machine to join parts of fabricated textile products, canvas products, and trimmed and stamped art goods: May insert wire or draw-string cord under edge of material to fabricate articles, such as clothes pin bags, laundry bags, or ironing board covers. May be designated according to function performed as Core-Covering Sewer (tex. prod., nec); Filter-Cloth Maker (tex. prod., nec); Finger-Buff Sewer (tex. prod., nec); Parachute-Accessories Attacher (tex. prod., nec); Parachute-Crown Sewer (tex. prod., nec); Parachute-Cushion Installer (tex. prod., nec); Parachute-Panel Joiner (tex. prod., nec). May stitch binding tape or zippers to exposed edges of canvas products. May stamp grommets into edges of canvas products, using mallet and punch or eyelet machine. May be designated according to type of article joined or type of stitch sewn as Awning Assembler (tex. prod., nec); Cloth Joiner, Tents (tex. prod., nec); Sail Finisher, Machine (tex. prod., nec); Tent Assembler (tex. prod., nec). May operate double-needle machine to trim or reinforce fabric used for stamped art goods (decorative cloth) or products, such as coat, dress, and millinery trimming and be designated according to operation performed as Hemstitching-Machine Operator (tex. prod., nec); Mender (tex. prod., nec). May fold bag material so that edges meet prior to sewing, sew mailing tags into seams, or close seams missed during assembly of textile bags. May be designated according to type of bag or material sewn as Burlap-Bag Sewer (tex. prod., nec); Canvas-Bag Maker (tex. prod., nec); Charge-Bag Sewer (tex. prod., nec); Cotton-Bag Sewer (tex. prod., nec); Jute-Bag Sewer (tex. prod., nec); Waterproof-Bag Sewer (tex. prod., nec). Performs other duties as described under SEWING-MACHINE OPERATOR, REGULAR EQUIPMENT (any industry) Master Title.
GOE: 06.02.05 STRENGTH: L GED: R3 M2 L2 SVP: 4 DLU: 78

787.682-066 SEWING MACHINE OPERATOR I (tex. prod., nec) alternate titles: joiner; seamer
Operates sewing machine to join, reinforce, or decorate parts of household articles, such as bedspreads, curtains, drapes, bed linens, mopheads and quilts: Guides parts under machine needle to sew stiffening material to tops of drapery panels, or elastic to fitted articles, or to stitch ruffles to curtains and chair pads, or to sew tape, fringe, or welt to seams or edges of articles to decorate or reinforce them. May oil machine, change needles, and secure modifying attachments to machine. May be designated according to article or parts of articles assembled as Bedspread Seamer (tex. prod., nec); Buckram Sewer (tex. prod., nec); Cover Assembler (tex. prod., nec); Elastic Sewer (tex. prod., nec); Fringer (tex. prod., nec); Lining Sewer (tex. prod., nec). May be designated: Mophead Sewer (tex. prod., nec); Panel Sewer (tex. prod., nec); Quilt Sewer (tex. prod., nec); Taping Machine Operator (tex. prod., nec). May mark patterns on articles with chalk and sew along markings to decorate articles. Performs duties as described under SEWING-MACHINE OPERATOR, REGULAR EQUIPMENT (any industry) Master Title.
GOE: 06.02.05 STRENGTH: L GED: R3 M2 L2 SVP: 3 DLU: 78

787.682-074 SEWING-MACHINE OPERATOR (knitting)
Operates sewing machine to join parts of socks or stockings: Guides parts under machine needle or between feed cups to stitch open edges of foot, leg, and welt of full-fashioned hose; or to join ends of elastic bands and attach bands to tops of seamless hose and tights; or to close toes in seamless hose or socks; or aligns edge or slit of leg, panty, and crotch part to sew pantyhose. May record number of hose sewn. May be designated according to part sewn or operation performed as Seamer (knitting); Seamer, Elastic Band (knitting); Seamer, Pantyhose (knitting); Tacker, Elastic Band (knitting); Toe Sewer (knitting). When operating machine that slits and sews crotch portions of hose together to form pantyhose, may be designated Pantyhose-Crotch-Closing-Machine Operator (knitting). Performs duties as described under SEWING-MACHINE OPERATOR, REGULAR EQUIPMENT (any industry) Master Title.
GOE: 06.02.05 STRENGTH: L GED: R2 M1 L1 SVP: 3 DLU: 81

787.682-078 SHIRRING-MACHINE OPERATOR (any industry) alternate titles: gatherer; ruffler
Operates sewing machine equipped with shirring attachment to shorten or decorate edges of material with gathers or puckers for use in fabricating articles, such as buffing wheels, curtains and tie-backs, casket interiors, hats and caps, and decorative folds in fabrics for garment trimmings: Turns screws to adjust tension of thread, length of stitch, and spacing and width of shirred runnings. Presses knee control to raise gathering device, positions edge of material beneath needle, and lowers gathering device onto material. Trims excess thread and material from shirred material, using scissors or knife-blade attachment. Performs duties as described under SEWING-MACHINE OPERATOR, REGULAR EQUIPMENT (any industry) Master Title.
GOE: 06.02.05 STRENGTH: L GED: R2 M1 L1 SVP: 4 DLU: 78

787.682-082 TUCKING-MACHINE OPERATOR (any industry) alternate titles: corder; cording-machine operator; graduate tucker; pleater; ruching-machine operator
Operates sewing machine equipped with tucking attachment to fold and sew uniform or graduated decorative tucks in products, such as decorative cloth fabrics and hats and caps: Turns screws to adjust tension of thread, length of stitch, and spacing and width of tucks. Places material over adjustable guide blade and swings blade into position against needle or moves lever to lower presser foot with attached tucking device and folds material over tucking device

and against guide beneath needle. Moves lever to lock presser foot and tucking device onto material. Trims excess material and thread from tucked article, using blade attached to machine or scissors. When sewing graduated tucks, attaches specified cam to machine to control progressive size change in tucks. May sew lace or braid into seam of tuck. When operating machine with attachment that feeds gimp under fabric to form round, puffed tucks, is designated Air Tucker (tex. prod., nec). Performs duties as described under SEWING-MACHINE OPERATOR, REGULAR EQUIPMENT (any industry) Master Title.
GOE: 06.02.05 STRENGTH: L GED: R3 M1 L1 SVP: 4 DLU: 77

787.682-086 ZIPPER SETTER (any industry)
Operates sewing machine equipped with guides that prevent needle from contacting metal to sew slide fasteners in openings or on parts of articles, such as mattresses, blankets, cushions, upholsteries, sleeping bags and other camping equipment, and quilt covers: Places roll of zippers on holder, or selects zipper of specified length, and draws end of zipper through guides. Cuts zippers from roll after sewing, using scissors. Attaches zipper slide to zipper and opens zipper before sewing stops on each end of zipper opening. When sewing zippers on plastic material, operates machine equipped with folding attachment to sew binding material over seam. Performs duties as described under SEWING-MACHINE OPERATOR, REGULAR EQUIPMENT (any industry) Master Title.
GOE: 06.02.05 STRENGTH: L GED: R3 M1 L1 SVP: 4 DLU: 77

787.685-010 FASTENER-SEWING-MACHINE OPERATOR (any industry) alternate titles: hook-and-eye-sewing-machine operator
Tends one or more machines that automatically sew fasteners, such as hooks and eyes, to continuous strips of binding tape. Fills hopper of machine with fasteners. May measure hook and eye spacing, using ruler, and examine tape for defects, such as misplaced stitching or discoloration. May tend machine equipped with button sewing adaptor to stitch metal tips to corners of umbrella covers and be designated Tipping-Machine Operator (fabrication, nec). Performs duties as described under SEWING-MACHINE OPERATOR, AUTOMATIC (any industry) Master Title.
GOE: 06.04.05 STRENGTH: L GED: R2 M1 L2 SVP: 2 DLU: 77

787.685-014 FOLDER-SEAMER, AUTOMATIC (any industry)
Tends machine that folds, stitches, and cuts cloth into lengths to form articles, such as bags, finger-buffs, pillowcases, straps, or tie-backs. May turn handwheel or thumbscrew to adjust tension on roll of cloth. May tend machine that sews string into hem of draw-string bag and be designated Sheet Cutter (tex. prod., nec) II. May be designated according to article fabricated as Bag-Making-Machine Tender (tex. prod., nec); Belt-Loop Maker (garment); Pillowcase Sewer, Automatic (tex. prod., nec); Sewer-And-Cutter, Finger-Buff Material (tex. prod., nec); Strap-Machine Operator, Automatic (garment); Tie-Back-Sewer, Automatic (tex. prod., nec). Performs duties as described under SEWING-MACHINE OPERATOR, AUTOMATIC (any industry) Master Title.
GOE: 06.04.05 STRENGTH: L GED: R2 M1 L2 SVP: 3 DLU: 77

787.685-018 HEMMER, AUTOMATIC (tex. prod., nec) alternate titles: side hemmer
Tends one or more automatic sewing machines that hem continuous lengths of material: Threads material through feed rollers, machine guides, and hem-folding attachment. Starts machine that sews continuous hem and stops as material runs out or thread breaks. When tending machine that sews hemstitch, may be designated Gang-Hemstitching-Machine Operator (tex. prod., nec). May be designated according to product hemmed as Curtain Hemmer, Automatic (tex. prod., nec); Drapery Hemmer, Automatic (tex. prod., nec); Ruffling Hemmer, Automatic (tex. prod., nec). Performs duties as described under SEWING-MACHINE OPERATOR, AUTOMATIC (any industry) Master Title.
GOE: 06.04.05 STRENGTH: L GED: R3 M1 L1 SVP: 3 DLU: 77

787.685-022 HEMMING-AND-TACKING-MACHINE OPERATOR (furniture) alternate titles: border-machine operator; padded-box sewer
Tends automatic sewing machine that tacks padding to prequilted fabric and hems fabric to form quilted border panels for mattresses and box springs: Inserts rolls of fabric and padding into machine brackets and threads them through guides. May tend automatic machine that only sews hem on fabric to form border panel. May sew cloth handles to border panels, using sewing machine. May insert ventilating eyelets and attach handles to border panels, using punching and crimping machine. Performs duties as described under SEWING-MACHINE OPERATOR, AUTOMATIC (any industry) Master Title.
GOE: 06.04.05 STRENGTH: L GED: R2 M1 L1 SVP: 2 DLU: 77

787.685-026 PLEATER (tex. prod., nec) alternate titles: l-tacker
Tends machine that sews pleats in drapery panels: Folds top of panel at designated places to form pleat. Positions folded pleat under presser foot and starts machine that stitches L-pattern to secure pleat. May tend machine equipped with jig that forms pleat prior to sewing. May tend machine that stitches pleat and sews ring to drapery panel at pleat and be designated Ring Attacher (tex. prod., nec). Performs duties as described under SEWING-MACHINE OPERATOR, AUTOMATIC (any industry) Master Title.
GOE: 06.04.05 STRENGTH: L GED: R3 M1 L1 SVP: 3 DLU: 77

787.685-030 SERGING-MACHINE OPERATOR, AUTOMATIC (any industry)
Tends machine that automatically binds edges of articles with serging stitch to reinforce edges, prevent raveling, or give finished appearance. May tend ma-

chine with blade attachment to trim raw edges. Performs duties as described under SEWING-MACHINE OPERATOR, AUTOMATIC (any industry) Master Title.
GOE: 06.04.05 STRENGTH: L GED: R3 M1 L2 SVP: 3 DLU: 77

787.685-034 SEWING-MACHINE OPERATOR, ZIPPER (button & notion)

Tends one or more automatic sewing machines that stitch cord to edge of continuous length of tape to reinforce it for attachment to zipper chain: Mounts cheeses, cones, or bobbins of cord on holders of machines. Threads cord and tape through guides and tension bars. Starts machine that automatically stitches cords to tape. Observes machine for automatic stopping which indicates defective feed or broken thread. Tapes together broken ends of cord or thread. Examines sewn tape for loose cords or dropped stitching. Adjusts cord tensions and guide positions, using screwdriver and pliers. May tend machines that sew spiral or ladder-shaped filament between layers of tape to form side of zipper and be designated Sewing-Machine Operator, Plastic Zipper (button & notion). Performs duties as described under SEWING-MACHINE OPERATOR, AUTOMATIC (any industry) Master Title.
GOE: 06.04.05 STRENGTH: L GED: R2 M1 L1 SVP: 2 DLU: 77

787.685-038 SHIRRING-MACHINE OPERATOR, AUTOMATIC (tex. prod., nec) alternate titles: ruffler

Tends one or more automatic sewing machines that gather continuous lengths of material used for ruffles or valances. Turns thumbscrew or lever to change number of gathers per inch according to specifications. May be designated according to article shirred as Valance Shirrer (tex. prod., nec). Performs duties as described under SEWING-MACHINE OPERATOR, AUTOMATIC (any industry) Master Title.
GOE: 06.04.05 STRENGTH: L GED: R2 M1 L1 SVP: 3 DLU: 77

787.685-042 TACKING-MACHINE OPERATOR (any industry)

Tends machine that sews pattern of stitches, such as circles or rectangles, to attach parts, such as labels or straps, reinforce seam ends, or decorate articles. May be designated according to parts tacked as Band Tacker (any industry); Bow Tacker (hat & cap) II; Label Tacker (tex. prod., nec); or according to stitches sewn as Bar Tacker (any industry). May attach reinforcing pieces to finger tips of gloves and be designated Tip Sewer (glove & mit.). May tend machine that tacks lead wire, thermostats, and line cord onto fabric body and be designated Tacker (elec. equip.). Performs duties as described under SEWING-MACHINE OPERATOR, AUTOMATIC (any industry) Master Title.
GOE: 06.04.05 STRENGTH: L GED: R2 M1 L1 SVP: 3 DLU: 78

787.685-046 TOE-CLOSING-MACHINE TENDER (knitting)

Tends machine that automatically closes toe of sock: Presses pedal to start machine and guides edges of open toe of sock onto feed guide that automatically feeds edges onto revolving dial of machine and through sewing mechanism to close toe. Performs duties as described under SEWING-MACHINE OPERATOR, AUTOMATIC (any industry) Master Title.
GOE: 06.04.05 STRENGTH: L GED: R2 M1 L1 SVP: 2 DLU: 77

787.685-050 TRIMMING SEWER, AUTOMATIC (garment; tex. prod., nec)

Tends battery of automatic sewing machines to assemble several widths of trimming material, such as lace, ribbon, or braid. Changes cloth guides on machine according to width of material. Threads ends of material through guides according to sequence of assembly. May tend machine to join trimming material to articles, such as garments, lingerie, or valances. Performs duties as described under SEWING-MACHINE OPERATOR, AUTOMATIC (any industry) Master Title.
GOE: 06.04.05 STRENGTH: L GED: R2 M1 L1 SVP: 3 DLU: 77

787.685-054 SEWING-MACHINE OPERATOR, PAPER BAGS (paper goods)

Tends automatic sewing machines that stitch folded and glued bottoms of multiwall paper bags to provide additional bag strength: Presses buttons to start machines and observes automatic operation of machines to detect malfunctions. Performs duties as described under SEWING-MACHINE OPERATOR, AUTOMATIC (any industry) Master Title.
GOE: 06.04.04 STRENGTH: L GED: R2 M1 L1 SVP: 4 DLU: 86

787.686-010 BAG SEWER (paper goods) alternate titles: bag-end sewer

Feeds paper tubes into machine that stitches ends or sews glued tape to one or both ends to seal bags or to form overlap for self-sealing paper bags: Depresses pedal to start machine conveyor. Lifts tubes from load table and positions tubes individually on conveyor leading to machine mechanism that stitches ends and cuts strings and tape. May be designated according to number of ends sewed as Double-End Sewer (paper goods); Single-End Sewer (paper goods).
GOE: 06.04.04 STRENGTH: L GED: R2 M1 L1 SVP: 2 DLU: 77

788 OCCUPATIONS IN FABRICATION AND REPAIR OF FOOTWEAR

This group includes occupations concerned with fabricating leather, fabric, and plastic footwear, including house slippers and indoor or outdoor athletic shoes. Occupations concerned with fabricating and repairing molded rubber and plastic footwear are included in Group 753.

788.131-010 SUPERVISOR (boot & shoe)

Supervises and coordinates activities of workers in cutting, *lasting*, fitting, bottoming, and heeling departments of shoe manufacturing plant: Instructs workers in determining hide areas from which to cut shoe parts and in selecting cutting dies. Examines shoe parts to verify efficient utilization of hides. Requisitions supplies, such as cement, nails, heels, and dowel lifts. Instructs workers in operation of machinery and techniques used in application of dressings and colorings. Repairs malfunctioning equipment, such as cutting machine, stitcher, buffer, and bed laster by adjusting or replacing defective parts. Performs other duties as described under SUPERVISOR (any industry) Master Title. May be designated according to department supervised as Bottoming-Room Supervisor (boot & shoe); Cutting-Room Supervisor (boot & shoe); Fitting-Room Supervisor (boot & shoe); Heel-Room Supervisor (boot & shoe); Lasting-Room Supervisor (boot & shoe).
GOE: 06.02.01 STRENGTH: L GED: R4 M4 L3 SVP: 7 DLU: 78

788.137-010 SUPERVISOR, PACKING (boot & shoe)

Supervises and coordinates activites of workers engaged in finishing and packing shoes: Examines shoes for specified coloring, dressing, and polishing, for defects, such as cuts, nicks, and scratches, and for pairing of shoes according to style and size. May train workers in operation of machinery and techniques used in application of dressings and colorings. Performs other duties as described under SUPERVISOR (any industry) Master Title.
GOE: 06.02.01 STRENGTH: L GED: R4 M3 L3 SVP: 7 DLU: 77

788.222-010 INSTRUCTOR (boot & shoe)

Instructs workers to tend or operate machines used to manufacture boots and shoes, utilizing knowledge of machine function and process: Teaches workers to tend or operate machines used to stitch, fold, skive, stamp, crease, perforate, or staple shoe parts. Identifies and describes functions of machine parts, and explains adjustment and maintenance requirements. Demonstrates steps required to prepare machines for operation. Examines work of trainees and instructs workers to detect and correct defective work. Assists experienced workers to improve work techniques.
GOE: 06.02.01 STRENGTH: L GED: R4 M3 L4 SVP: 6 DLU: 78

788.261-010 ORTHOPEDIC-BOOT-AND-SHOE DESIGNER AND MAKER (boot & shoe; protective dev.)

Fabricates boots and shoes for deformed feet according to prescription and patient's measurements: Studies prescription to determine degree of deformity and type of correction to be built into shoe. Measures foot, using calipers, tape measure, rule, and other measuring devices and instruments, and applying knowledge of foot anatomy and orthopedic shoe-making techniques. Discusses boot and shoe styles available with customer to determine customer's desires. Makes plaster cast of foot when exact measurements are required. Designs paper patterns for shoe parts and cuts out leather from pattern, using knives. Marks and punches out eyelets, and inserts and clinches metal rings in holes, using eyelet riveter. Tacks insole on last and draws upper over last with pliers, tacking upper in place. Inserts foam cushioning or arch support material, such as steel, leather, or cork, under insole to support or cushion foot. Sews sole and upper together, using sewing machine. Glues cork, leather, wood, or rubber material to build up extension of outer sole to specified height. Buffs surface of sole and curves sole upward to provide stable walking surface. May fabricate arch supports which can be inserted in regular shoes.
GOE: 05.05.15 STRENGTH: L GED: R4 M3 L4 SVP: 7 DLU: 77

788.281-010 DESIGNER AND PATTERNMAKER (boot & shoe) alternate titles: master-pattern maker; model maker

Prepares master pattern of shoe upper design and cuts pattern into individual parts preparatory to making template: Pencils markings, such as cone, back seam, or shank edge onto sized wooden last. Positions kraft paper on last and trims paper along markings, using knife or scissors. Traces outline onto manila paper, cardboard, or pressboard, using cut form or last mold as pattern. Draws details, such as stitching or ornamentation according to design specifications, using drafting instruments. Cuts traced design into individual patterns of shoe parts, such as quarters, saddles, and vamps, using scissors or knife. May compile manufacturing data from design specifications. May prepare pattern template.
GOE: 05.05.15 STRENGTH: L GED: R4 M4 L3 SVP: 7 DLU: 77

788.381-010 COBBLER (boot & shoe) alternate titles: shoe repairer; shoe stitcher, odd

Repairs shoes damaged in manufacturing process: Inspects shoe or reads ticket to determine defects. Removes damaged parts, using handtools, such as knife, hammer, *lasting tool,* prying tool, and tack puller. Operates stitching machine or stitches by hand to repair broken or missed stitches and to replace parts. Relasts shoe to remove defects, such as wrinkles from outer parts, bunching of inner parts, and crooked seams. Aligns and cements parts, such as edges, bindings, heels, soles, and uppers of shoe by hand. May fill holes and cracks in shoes, using colored wax filler. May be designated according to part of shoe repaired as Cobbler, Sole (boot & shoe); Cobbler, Upper (boot & shoe); Lining Repairer (boot & shoe); or according to method of shoe construction as Cobbler, McKay (boot & shoe).
GOE: 06.02.27 STRENGTH: M GED: R3 M1 L2 SVP: 5 DLU: 77

788.381-014 SHOEMAKER, CUSTOM (boot & shoe)

Makes boots and shoes, using hand and machine tools: Makes patterns, using form of foot and pattern paper, and outlines patterns on leather. Cuts out parts

with shears and knife, and sews them together on machine to form uppers. Marks eyelets, punches them out, and inserts metal rings and clinches them on machine. Assembles last and attaches it to stand. Tacks insole on last and draws upper over last, tacking it in place. Trims upper with knife and sews on welt. Attaches outer sole to lasted upper by sewing it on or by roughening surface of sole with rasp and wire brush, coating it with cement and hammering it. Tacks on rand, leather lifts to build heel base, and heel. Trims and buffs edges of sole and heel, using knife and buffing wheel. Brushes dressing dye on shoe and polishes it by holding it against rotating brush. May roughen outsole and cement rubber or fiber sole to it. May design and make women's fashion or custom shoes of materials, such as leather, fabric, and straw and be designated Custom-Shoe Designer And Maker (boot & shoe).
GOE: 05.05.15 STRENGTH: L GED: R4 M3 L3 SVP: 6 DLU: 77

788.384-010   INSPECTOR (boot & shoe)
   Inspects finished and partially finished shoes and shoe parts for imperfections and repairs less extensive damages: Examines parts or shoes for defects, such as uneven or broken stitching, lining wrinkles, or excess cement. Marks extensively damaged parts or shoes with chalk or attaches repair tag and routes them to departments for repair. Cuts out defective stitching, using scissors or knife, and tends stitching machine to repair defect, or brushes on adhesive to replace defective stitching or part. Removes wrinkles from material, using moistening mixture and brush, and portable electric hot air blower. May be designated according to part or kind of shoe inspected or to department as Bottoming-Room Inspector (boot & shoe); Casual-Shoe Inspector (boot & shoe); Dress-Shoe Inspector (boot & shoe); Fitting-Room Inspector (boot & shoe); Lining Inspector (boot & shoe); Packing-Room Inspector (boot & shoe). May be designated: Quarter Inspector (boot & shoe); Sock-Lining Examiner (boot & shoe); Upper Inspector (boot & shoe); White-Shoe Examiner (boot & shoe).
GOE: 06.03.01 STRENGTH: M GED: R3 M2 L2 SVP: 5 DLU: 78

788.387-010   UPPER-LEATHER SORTER (boot & shoe) alternate titles: leather grader
   Receives, stores, sorts, and issues upper shoe leather for cutting operations: Verifies contents of bundles of leather against delivery form. Stores bundles in bins or on shelves according to code, color, or supplier's designation. Sorts leather according to quality, thickness, and color. Compares pieces of leather to match color and grain. Inspects leather for defects, such as open grains, scars, and undercuts. Fills orders for upper leather from stock. Bundles leather and attaches work order for issuance to workers. May carry or handtruck bundles to workers. May sort and store other shoe upper material, such as synthetics and cloth.
GOE: 06.03.01 STRENGTH: M GED: R3 M2 L2 SVP: 4 DLU: 77

788.584-010   HEEL SORTER (boot & shoe)
   Sorts and grades leather heels: Sorts right and left heels into groups. Examines groups for defects, such as nicks, scars, brittleness, and texture, to grade heels. Records information on grading sheet. Places heels in containers for discard, reprocessing, shipment, or storage.
GOE: 06.03.02 STRENGTH: S GED: R3 M2 L2 SVP: 4 DLU: 77

788.584-014   MARKER, HAND (boot & shoe) alternate titles: cut-out marker; upper marker
   Marks lines or numbers that serve as guides for subsequent operations on shoe parts: Selects pattern, following specifications. Places and aligns pattern on part. Marks lines with crayon, pencil, or pen, following slots in pattern. When marking location of heel seat, positions heel and scratches line on sole in front of heel, using knife point. Pencils in identifying numbers according to job ticket. May attach identifying tags. May be designated according to part marked as Heel Marker (boot & shoe); Lining Marker (boot & shoe); or according to guidelines marked as Eyelet-Row Marker (boot & shoe); Fancy-Stitch Marker (boot & shoe).
GOE: 06.04.27 STRENGTH: L GED: R2 M1 L1 SVP: 2 DLU: 77

788.587-010   JOB PUTTER-UP AND TICKET PREPARER (boot & shoe)
   Gathers and prepares hides and schedules leather cutting operations for shoe production, according to standard procedures: Gathers bundled hides from storage bins according to work ticket. Records quantity and length of hides from tag on bundle. Scrapes paper labels from hides with knife to prepare hides for cutting. Sorts work tickets according to number of shoes, stock number, type of hide, and shoe widths required to arrange daily work for CLICKING-MACHINE OPERATOR (boot & shoe; glove & mit.; leather prod.) Bundles sorted tickets for distribution by another worker.
GOE: 05.09.02 STRENGTH: M GED: R3 M2 L2 SVP: 3 DLU: 77

788.667-010   ODD-SHOE EXAMINER (boot & shoe) alternate titles: back-shoe operator
   Examines shoe uppers for defective leather parts and distributes replacement parts to processing area: Cuts stitching in shoe upper with knife or scissors and rips out defective parts. Writes specifications for replacement parts on work order and delivers it to initial processing area. Carries replacement parts to and from various departments to accomplish specified processing, such as cutting, marking, and stitching. Delivers replacement parts to fitting department for assembly to upper of shoe. Converses with department supervisors to correct irregular flow of replacement parts.
GOE: 06.03.02 STRENGTH: L GED: R3 M1 L1 SVP: 3 DLU: 77

788.684-010   ASSEMBLER FOR PULLER-OVER, HAND (boot & shoe) alternate titles: back tacker; hand assembler; laster, hand
   Inserts cement covered counter between lining and shoe upper to prepare upper for further lasting operations: Places counter on wire screen, dips screen

in liquid cement, and drains excess cement from counter. Positions last on *pin jack*. Inserts counter between lining and upper. Pulls shoe upper onto last and aligns back seam of upper with guide marks on last. Tacks upper to last, using *lasting tool*.
GOE: 06.04.27 STRENGTH: L GED: R3 M1 L1 SVP: 3 DLU: 77

788.684-014   ASSEMBLER, SANDAL PARTS (boot & shoe)
   Joins precemented sandal parts: Places pattern on outsole as guide for positioning vamp and quarter straps. Places vamp and quarter strap ends in pattern slots on outsole. Loops vamp straps to form weave pattern. Removes pattern from outsole. Hammers strap ends to join onto outsole. Presses insole onto inner side of outsole. Positions joined parts on machine under heated presser head and depresses pedal to apply heat and pressure to parts.
GOE: 06.04.27 STRENGTH: L GED: R2 M1 L2 SVP: 2 DLU: 77

788.684-018   BINDING FOLDER, MACHINE (boot & shoe) alternate titles: braid folder
   Folds presewn binding over edge of shoe uppers to smooth and finish edge, using folding machine: Guides upper under heating element to soften cement on unfolded binding. Positions upper on machine and depresses pedal to fold binding over raw edge of upper and cement it to side of upper. Bends or folds corners of bindings to lie smoothly and pounds them with handtool. May be designated according to type of binding used as French-Binding Folder (boot & shoe).
GOE: 06.04.27 STRENGTH: L GED: R3 M1 L2 SVP: 4 DLU: 77

788.684-022   BLEMISH REMOVER (boot & shoe) alternate titles: color repairer; dull shoe repairer; filler; leather repairer; shoe repairer
   Removes color blemishes and fills in cracks or scratches on shoes: Applies prepared color with cloth, hand spray, or crayon to obtain or restore specified color. Applies prepared filler, using cloth or hand spray, to fill cracks and scratches. May blend prepared pigments to match shoe color, using spatula. May cement or rub cut or nicked areas of shoe. May be designated according to type or color of shoe as Russet Repairer (boot & shoe).
GOE: 06.04.33 STRENGTH: L GED: R2 M1 L1 SVP: 4 DLU: 77

788.684-026   BOTTOM FILLER (boot & shoe) alternate titles: cushion cementer; insole-bottom filler; insole filler
   Fills insole depression with compound to provide cushion for ball of foot and even surface for attachment of outsole: Spreads heated compound on insole, using spatula. Positions shoe on machine and depresses pedal to lower heated plate that presses and smooths compound. May press and smooth compound by hand, using spatula. May fill heated reservoir with compound.
GOE: 06.04.32 STRENGTH: M GED: R2 M1 L1 SVP: 2 DLU: 77

788.684-030   BOTTOM WHEELER (boot & shoe)
   Imprints designs, lines, or notches on bottom of outsole to decorate, finish, or mark shoe sole: Presses and guides heated scoring (seat wheeling) tool, notching tool (branding iron), or inked rod (striping rod) on sole to imprint design. Loads processed shoes on wheeled rack and pushes rack to storage area.
GOE: 06.04.27 STRENGTH: L GED: R2 M1 L1 SVP: 3 DLU: 77

788.684-034   BOW MAKER (boot & shoe)
   Assembles bows to be used as ornamental shoe parts: Selects precut strips of material, such as leather, plastic, or fabric, following ticket specifications. Ties strips into bows by hand. Joins bow parts, using hand stapler. May sew bow parts together by hand. May brush cement onto parts and press parts together.
GOE: 06.04.27 STRENGTH: L GED: R2 M1 L1 SVP: 2 DLU: 77

788.684-038   BUTTONHOLE MAKER (boot & shoe)
   Makes buttonholes for shoes: Sets button fly of quarter against gauge of machine. Depresses lever which brings down knife to cut buttonhole and stitcher to automatically stitch all around buttonhole.
GOE: 06.04.27 STRENGTH: L GED: R2 M1 L1 SVP: 3 DLU: 77

788.684-042   CRIPPLE WORKER (boot & shoe)
   Cuts or pulls defective leather or fabric parts from shoe uppers and cements replacement parts: Cuts stitching with knife or scissors and pulls defective part, such as vamp, box-toe, or lining from upper. Tags and routes defective parts to cutting department to obtain replacement parts. Cements replacement parts to upper. May cut and pull defective stitching from upper to permit restitching.
GOE: 06.02.27 STRENGTH: L GED: R3 M1 L1 SVP: 3 DLU: 77

788.684-046   FINGER COBBLER (boot & shoe)
   Repairs damaged outer surface of leather shoes: Examines shoe for defects, such as scuffs, cracks, and blemishes. Spreads glue on defects and presses leather with heated iron rod to seal. Buffs defective area with sandpaper or by holding shoe against buffing wheel. Wipes defective area with rag to remove foreign material. Mixes waxes to obtain matching color or selects matching crayon stick. Spreads wax on defective surface. Rubs repaired area with rag to polish and blend surfaces.
GOE: 06.02.27 STRENGTH: L GED: R3 M1 L2 SVP: 4 DLU: 77

788.684-050   FLAMER (boot & shoe) alternate titles: shoe singer; singeing-torch operator; singer and unloader
   Singes surplus threads from shoe uppers, using gas flame or torch, or cuts excess threads, using knife or scissors.
GOE: 06.04.27 STRENGTH: M GED: R2 M1 L1 SVP: 2 DLU: 77

788.684-054 HAND SEWER, SHOES (boot & shoe) alternate titles: hand lacer; hand trimmer; moccasin sewer

Sews shoe parts, such as heel ends, plugs, and quarters, to vamp or raises decorative stitches (kicker) in backstay of casual shoes: Soaks skived or nonskived parts in water to soften them. Positions lasted shoe on pin jack and pulls and tacks parts to last with lasting tool. Punches stitch openings in parts with awl. Inserts waxed thread through punched openings to join skived shoe parts to vamp or raise decorative stitching in backstay. Removes tacks and shapes seam, using lasting tool. May hold unskived shoe parts in hand and insert metal tipped lace through perforations to join parts to vamp. Smooths and polishes seams, using rubbing stick. May join parts of unlasted shoes, pulling needle and waxed thread through perforated stitch openings.
GOE: 06.04.27 STRENGTH: L GED: R2 M1 L1 SVP: 2 DLU: 77

788.684-058 HEEL ATTACHER, WOOD (boot & shoe) alternate titles: wood-heel cementer

Glues wood heels to lasted shoes: Brushes liquid cement on heel seat. Positions heel on heel seat of shoe and pushes pedal to lock shoe in holding fixture. Inserts drill bit through guide hole in last and drills hole in top of heel for temporary holding screw, using hand drill or portable electric drill. Turns screw through heel seat into heel with pneumatic screwdriver to hold heel against outsole of shoe until glue dries.
GOE: 06.04.34 STRENGTH: L GED: R2 M1 L1 SVP: 4 DLU: 77

788.684-062 HEEL-SEAT FITTER, HAND (boot & shoe)

Trims, tacks, and pounds heel seat to prepare shoes for heel attachment: Selects heels according to specified size and style. Positions lasted shoe on stationary pin jack. Positions heel on heel seat and scratches line to indicate area to be trimmed. Trims heel seat to fit heel, using knife. Tacks heel seat to insole and pounds seat to conform leather to contour of heel, using hammer. Repositions heel on heel seat to verify fit.
GOE: 06.04.34 STRENGTH: L GED: R2 M1 L1 SVP: 4 DLU: 77

788.684-066 INKER (boot & shoe)

Applies ink, stain, color, glaze, or dope to edges, along seams, or to shoe parts to color, clean, or protect parts, using brush, cloth, or spray gun. May clean shoes or shoe parts, using dry sponge or cloth and cleaning fluids. May be designated according to part treated as Edge Inker (boot & shoe); Edge Inker, Heels (boot & shoe); Edge Inker, Uppers (boot & shoe); or according to coating substance as Dope Edger (boot & shoe); or according to type of finish as Antiquer (boot & shoe).
GOE: 06.04.33 STRENGTH: M GED: R2 M1 L1 SVP: 2 DLU: 77

788.684-070 INTERLACER (boot & shoe) alternate titles: weaver

Weaves decorative designs in shoe uppers. Draws strips of material, such as fabric or leather, between slits in shoe upper to weave decorative design.
GOE: 06.04.27 STRENGTH: S GED: R2 M1 L2 SVP: 3 DLU: 77

788.684-074 LASTER, HAND (boot & shoe)

Pulls and secures linings and uppers over last to form leather shoes of designated size: Pulls cloth or leather lining tightly and smoothly over wooden last and secures to insole with cement. Trims away excess material with knife. Pulls assembled upper onto last and draws upper over last and insole. Drives temporary tacks into insole to secure upper until welt stitching or cementing is completed, or drives permanent lasting tacks through upper, lining, insole, and against steel bottom of last to clinch tacks into insole and permanently secure upper to insole. May tack sole to upper in preparation for final soling operations.
GOE: 06.04.27 STRENGTH: M GED: R2 M1 L1 SVP: 2 DLU: 77

788.684-078 LASTING-MACHINE OPERATOR, HAND METHOD (boot & shoe) alternate titles: counter tacker

Tacks counters and lining to shoe insole: Removes last from rack and positions it on spindle of machine. Tightens and smooths lining, counter, and upper on left side of shoe, using hand pincers. Removes last from spindle and positions it under tacking hammer of machine. Presses pedal to start machine and guides left side of shoe through tacking mechanism. Repeats operation on right side.
GOE: 06.04.27 STRENGTH: L GED: R2 M1 L1 SVP: 4 DLU: 77

788.684-082 OUTSIDE CUTTER, HAND (boot & shoe) alternate titles: carver; hand shoe cutter; modeler; sample cutter; shoe cutter; upper cutter-out; upper-leather cutter; vamp-and-whole-shoe cutter, hand

Cuts upper shoe parts from leather or other material, using hand knife: Selects material and cutting pattern according to specifications. Marks defects, such as brands, cuts, and scars, using chalk, and cuts leather against grain to minimize stretch. Positions pattern over material on cutting board. Draws knife along edge of pattern to cut parts. Bundles cut parts. Marks size on top part, using pencil.
GOE: 06.02.24 STRENGTH: L GED: R3 M2 L2 SVP: 4 DLU: 77

788.684-086 PULLER AND LASTER, MACHINE (boot & shoe)

Pulls shoe upper over last and shapes toe and forepart sections of shoe, using lasting machine: Places upper in steamer to soften upper. Presses last against jack lever that closes pincers on upper edges and lifts heel of last to stretch upper. Positions toe of last on machine toe plate and depresses pedal to raise toe plate and cause pincers to grip upper edges. Depresses pedal to move heated wipers across toe and forepart sections of upper and press precemented edges onto insole. Turns knobs to adjust wiper position or pressure.

GOE: 06.04.27 STRENGTH: L GED: R2 M1 L2 SVP: 3 DLU: 77

788.684-090 PULLER OVER, MACHINE (boot & shoe)

Stretches toe, vamp, and quarters of shoe upper over sides of last and tacks upper onto insole and bottom of last, using pull-over machine: Positions lasted upper on machine. Pulls lever to stretch upper over last. Pushes second lever to clamp upper in position and depresses pedal to start tacking operation.
GOE: 06.04.27 STRENGTH: L GED: R2 M1 L1 SVP: 4 DLU: 77

788.684-094 RASPER (boot & shoe)

Files insoles and nails that protrude through insoles, using rasping machine: Cuts protruding nail ends, using wire cutters. Presses and holds shoe against revolving shaft of rasping machine to file nails and smooth insole. May hold shoe under air nozzle and depress pedal to blow filings from inside of shoe. May pound nails and tacks that protrude through insoles, using hammer, to smooth insoles. May pull nails with tack remover. May be designated according to part rasped as Forepart Rasper (boot & shoe); Heel-Nail Rasper (boot & shoe); Insole Rasper (boot & shoe).
GOE: 06.04.27 STRENGTH: L GED: R2 M1 L1 SVP: 2 DLU: 77

788.684-098 SAMPLE SHOE INSPECTOR AND REWORKER (boot & shoe)

Inspects sample and nonsample uppers and shoes and removes imperfections: Examines sample uppers for blemishes, such as wrinkles, rough seams, and bulges. Removes blemishes with handtools, such as electric irons, hammers, and knives. Disassembles blemished nonsample shoes received from packing inspectors and sample uppers having defects, such as broken stitches, torn parts, and discolored materials, for reassembly by other workers.
GOE: 06.03.02 STRENGTH: L GED: R3 M1 L2 SVP: 5 DLU: 77

788.684-102 SCREW REMOVER (boot & shoe)

Pushes hook-eye of screw, used temporarily to hold heel to shoe, into chuck of screw-remover machine to loosen and remove screw from heel, heel-seat, and last. Pushes pedal to start machine.
GOE: 06.04.27 STRENGTH: L GED: R2 M1 L1 SVP: 2 DLU: 77

788.684-106 SLIP LASTER (boot & shoe) alternate titles: last inserter; relaster

Replaces last in shoe upper prior to bottoming, using one of following methods: (1) Places broken last (open at hinge) on stationary *pin jack*. Positions shoe upper on last and pulls heel section of last down to stretch upper. (2) Places toe of upper onto last. Inserts shoe horn device in heel section of upper and depresses pedal to pull upper onto last. May align sock lining between last and insole. May tack upper parts, such as vamp strap or wrapper onto last, using *lasting tool*. May immerse uppers in softening solution to prevent seams from splitting. May remove upper from last.
GOE: 06.04.27 STRENGTH: L GED: R2 M1 L1 SVP: 2 DLU: 77

788.684-110 SOLE SEWER, HAND (boot & shoe) alternate titles: sole stitcher, hand

Sews outsoles to custom-made shoe by hand: Attaches pig bristle to end of cord to make point that will enter awl holes easily. Waxes cord by drawing it through ball of wax. Marks guideline around welt of shoe. Softens sole with water-soaked sponge. Cuts groove, using grooving tool, along line of marking on sole to make channel stitch. Cuts groove in welt along marked line to make invisible stitch. Makes hole through welt and sole with awl. Inserts one end of cord through hole and draws it about halfway through. Punches another hole and inserts both ends of cord through hole from opposite sides to form lock stitch. Continues punching and stitching operations in straight line, locking threads each time. Pounds down sole, using shoemaker's hammer, and levels off sole by rolling round piece of wood forward and backward over sole until surface is smooth and even. Smooths stitching (straight stitch) with piece of flat bone if stitching shows on welt.
GOE: 06.02.27 STRENGTH: L GED: R3 M1 L3 SVP: 6 DLU: 77

788.684-114 THREAD LASTER (boot & shoe) alternate titles: stitchdown-thread laster; stitchdown-thread-lasting-machine operator

Attaches shoe upper to insole, using stitchdown-thread-lasting machine: Sets last, with insole attached, on table and pulls upper over last by setting toe and end of upper in jaws of machine. Holds upper against insole on shoe rest. Depresses lever which lowers feeder onto upper edge. Pushes lever to start machine and guides shoe into feeding mechanism that sews upper to insole.
GOE: 06.04.05 STRENGTH: R3 M1 L2 SVP: 3 DLU: 77

788.684-118 TREE DRILLER (boot & shoe)

Presses last (tree) against power drill bit at specified point to drill hole through last into heel seat of women's shoes to receive retaining screw which secures wooden heel to shoes.
GOE: 06.04.27 STRENGTH: L GED: R2 M1 L1 SVP: 3 DLU: 77

788.684-122 UPPER-AND-BOTTOM LACER, HAND (boot & shoe)

Assembles parts of novelty shoes by lacing parts together with braided cloth or leather strips: Fashions upper portion of shoe by lacing quarters to vamp. Aligns perforated upper and sole, inserts tipped lacer, and draws parts together by lacing backward around shoe on either side. Ties lacer at top of heel. Smooths outside of shoe sole and heel stitches by pounding with hammer.
GOE: 06.04.27 STRENGTH: L GED: R2 M1 L2 SVP: 3 DLU: 77

788.684-126 WOOD-HEEL FINISHER (boot & shoe) alternate titles: breast finisher; heel finisher

Trims and smooths leather that covers breast and shank of wood heels, performing any of following duties: Trims and splits projecting edges of breast

flap with knife or scissors. Brushes cement onto shank and lodge. Inserts heel flap against heel breast and under top lift. Bevels and smooths edges of breast flap with beveling stick. Smooths wrinkles from heel covering with heated iron or hot air. May be designated according to task performed as Wood-Heel Cementer (boot & shoe); Wood-Heel-Flap Inserter (boot & shoe); Wood-Heel-Flap Rubber (boot & shoe); Wood-Heel-Flap Trimmer (boot & shoe).
GOE: 06.04.27 STRENGTH: S GED: R2 M1 L1 SVP: 3 DLU: 77

788.684-130 WRINKLE CHASER (boot & shoe) alternate titles: flamer, after lasting; ironer; presser
Irons wrinkles from shoes or shoe parts: Inspects shoes or parts for inside or outside wrinkles. Removes wrinkles, using heated hand or stationary iron, or hot air blower and awl-shaped handtool. May be designated according to part of shoe smoothed or ironed as Lining Ironer (boot & shoe); Wood-Heel-Cover Ironer (boot & shoe).
GOE: 06.04.27 STRENGTH: L GED: R2 M1 L1 SVP: 2 DLU: 77

788.685-010 FLARE BREAKER (boot & shoe) alternate titles: cookie breaker
Tends machine that bends flare to conform to shape of arch: Wets flare to make it pliable. Holds lasted insole against hexagon-shaped roller that beats flare against arch contour of last.
GOE: 06.04.05 STRENGTH: L GED: R1 M1 L1 SVP: 2 DLU: 77

788.685-014 FOLDING-MACHINE TENDER (boot & shoe) alternate titles: fold skiver; tip cementer; topline-beading-machine tender
Tends bench-mounted machine to fold and press precemented edges of shoe parts together: Positions parts on bed of machine and depresses pedal to lower presser foot to fold part and press edges together.
GOE: 06.04.05 STRENGTH: L GED: R2 M1 L1 SVP: 2 DLU: 77

788.685-018 STOCK FITTER (boot & shoe) alternate titles: fitting room operator; insole-and-outsole preparer; sole cutter
Cuts and shapes leather insoles and outsoles for further processing, performing any combination of following duties: Tends machine to stamp out insole or outsole blanks. Trims blanks to pattern size by feeding through sole-rounding machine. Sorts blanks according to designated quality standards. Feeds blanks into splitting machine to cut to desired thickness. Shaves edges of soles at shank to improve appearance and to increase flexibility. Roughens band around edge of outsole. Applies bank of cement around edge of outsole. May cement cord platforms, staple wedgies to platforms, and cut and turn channels for welt shoes. May cement filler to ball of insole to prevent squeaking of finished shoe.
GOE: 06.02.27 STRENGTH: L GED: R3 M1 L1 SVP: 6 DLU: 77

788.685-022 TONGUE PRESSER (boot & shoe)
Tends machine that shapes and removes wrinkles from tongue of leather shoes. Presses foot switch to close upper and lower halves of heated forming die that shapes and removes wrinkles from tongue.
GOE: 06.04.05 STRENGTH: L GED: R2 M1 L1 SVP: 2 DLU: 77

788.685-026 TOP FORMER (boot & shoe) alternate titles: top ironer; upper shaper
Tends machine that shapes shoe uppers on heated forming die: Positions shoe upper on heated forming die and pulls lever to bring padded pressing arm against shoe to shape back part of upper. Releases lever after specified time and removes shoe upper from die.
GOE: 06.04.05 STRENGTH: L GED: R2 M1 L1 SVP: 2 DLU: 77

788.685-030 WRAP TURNER (boot & shoe)
Tends machine that turns wrap on platformed shoe to prepare for cementing: Brushes liquid leather softener on wrap to prevent tearing. Holds toe of shoe upside down so that wrap fits over stationary U-shaped horn of machine. Depresses pedal that lowers flat, toe-shaped piece against bottom of shoe at toe, pressing shoe downward below walls of horn, to reverse wrap. Performs same operation at heel of shoe. Turns wrap on sides by hand.
GOE: 06.04.05 STRENGTH: L GED: R2 M1 L1 SVP: 2 DLU: 77

788.687-010 ANTISQUEAK FILLER (boot & shoe) alternate titles: antisqueak applier; antisqueak chalker; chalker, soles; flare chalker; outsole paraffiner
Applies liquid coating to shoe parts, or cements cushioning material between parts, to prevent squeaking due to friction or wear. Brushes coating of liquid chalk, paraffin, or wax on parts, such as heel bases, flares, and outsoles.
GOE: 06.04.33 STRENGTH: L GED: R1 M1 L1 SVP: 2 DLU: 77

788.687-014 BOTTOM BLEACHER (boot & shoe) alternate titles: bleacher; bottom scrubber
Applies bleaching liquid to bottom of leather outsoles of lasted shoes, using brush or cloth, to lighten color of outsoles. May apply stain, using cloth or sponge. May apply cleaning fluid to remove foreign matter.
GOE: 06.04.33 STRENGTH: L GED: R1 M1 L1 SVP: 2 DLU: 77

788.687-018 BRUSHER (boot & shoe)
Holds and turns shoes against revolving brushes to clean and polish them: Coats revolving wheel with wax, using wax black. Holds shoe against wheel to apply wax, then against revolving bristle and cloth wheels to polish shoe. May clean, wax, and polish shoe heels and soles and be designated Edge Polisher (boot & shoe). May be designated according to part of shoe worked on as Bottom Brusher (boot & shoe); Heel Brusher (boot & shoe).

GOE: 06.04.33 STRENGTH: L GED: R1 M1 L1 SVP: 2 DLU: 77

788.687-022 BUCKLER AND LACER (boot & shoe)
Threads laces through eyelets and buckles straps on finished shoes in preparation for shipping.
GOE: 06.04.27 STRENGTH: S GED: R1 M1 L1 SVP: 2 DLU: 77

788.687-026 CASER, SHOE PARTS (boot & shoe) alternate titles: caser; counter caser
Gathers and sorts shoe parts for delivery to other departments or workers: Collects parts, such as heels, quarters, linings, and outsoles from baskets, bins, or racks, following quality, quantity, size, and style specifications. Sorts parts according to identifying numbers and bundles or places them in containers for delivery. Receives and stores parts. May examine parts for defects, such as cracks or rough finishes. May copy identifying numbers from order ticket onto shoe parts or containers, using crayon or pencil. May stamp container number onto order ticket, using ink stamp.
GOE: 06.03.02 STRENGTH: M GED: R3 M2 L2 SVP: 3 DLU: 78

788.687-030 CEMENTER, HAND (boot & shoe) alternate titles: gluer; gummer; material combiner; paster
Joins precemented shoe parts, or applies cement to join parts, using any of following methods: (1) Brushes cement onto parts. (2) Sprays cement onto parts, using spray gun. (3) Rubs parts over cement-covered roller. (4) Feeds and pulls parts between cement-covered rollers. May align precemented parts, following seams or edges, markings on parts, or template guides, and press parts together by hand or using handtools. May trim excess material from cemented parts. May mark location of heel seat, using pencil. May roughen shoe parts in preparation for cementing. May brush solvent on parts to activate cemented surface. May hammer holding nail through stacked lifts and place heels in press to dry and be designated Heel Builder, Hand (boot & shoe). May be designated according to parts cemented as Arch-Pad Cementer (boot & shoe); Bottom Cementer (boot & shoe) II; Box-Toe Cementer (boot & shoe); Heel Cementer (boot & shoe); Heel Coverer (boot & shoe). May be designated: Heel Padder (boot & shoe); Shank Cementer, Hand (boot & shoe); Sock Liner (boot & shoe); Sole Layer, Hand (boot & shoe); Upper Doubler (boot & shoe).
GOE: 06.04.27 STRENGTH: L GED: R1 M1 L1 SVP: 2 DLU: 78

788.687-034 COLOR MATCHER (boot & shoe) alternate titles: heel sprayer, first; uniformer
Inspects shoes for color uniformity and rectifies defects: Examines outer surface of finished shoes for spots of light or irregular coloring. Mixes coloring solutions until matching color is obtained. Sprays solution on defective area of shoe with spray gun or applies solution by hand, using rag or finger. Polishes repaired area with rag to blend with other shoe surface.
GOE: 06.03.02 STRENGTH: S GED: R2 M2 L1 SVP: 4 DLU: 77

788.687-038 DRESSER (boot & shoe) alternate titles: luster repairer; quarter doper; shoe dresser
Applies liquid dressing or dye on shoes to produce glossy finish, using brush, sponge, or spray gun: Applies dressing by method specified for particular style of shoe. May apply hot water and alcohol to back of shoe to soften leather and prevent splitting of back seam when last is removed. May apply filler to prepare leather for dressing operation.
GOE: 06.04.33 STRENGTH: L GED: R2 M1 L1 SVP: 2 DLU: 77

788.687-042 FINISHING TRIMMER (boot & shoe) alternate titles: cover cutter; cover remover; goring cutter; gusset ripper
Cuts and removes temporary protective plastic covers, *gore* reinforcing tape, or stitches from closed gussets from shoes prior to dressing and packing operations: Presses shoe against friction-heated trimming wheel or inserts knife or other handtool between upper of shoe and cover, cutting cover at welt. Removes material by hand and places shoe on rack.
GOE: 06.04.27 STRENGTH: L GED: R2 M1 L1 SVP: 2 DLU: 77

788.687-046 FLOORWORKER, LASTING (boot & shoe)
Marks shoe parts rejected in lasting inspection, distributes rejected parts for repair, and locates repaired parts: Marks or tags damaged uppers. Pulls last from damaged upper and returns upper to department of origin or to worker for repair. Locates and gathers repaired parts. Procures replacements for damaged lasts.
GOE: 05.09.03 STRENGTH: L GED: R2 M1 L2 SVP: 2 DLU: 77

788.687-050 FOLDER, HAND (boot & shoe) alternate titles: flat folder
Folds precemented edges of shoe parts that cannot be folded by machine to form finished edges, and tamps edges with hammer to crease and cleave material. May apply cement with brush or finger under nonadhesive edges. May hammer prefolded edge of insole cover over arch pad to flatten cover edge and be designated Hammerer, Tab (boot & shoe).
GOE: 06.04.27 STRENGTH: L GED: R2 M1 L1 SVP: 2 DLU: 77

788.687-054 GOLF-SHOE-SPIKE ASSEMBLER (boot & shoe) alternate titles: golf-stud riveter
Attaches studs or spikes to golf shoe soles and heels by one of following methods: (1) Sets leather sole right side up on anvil. Depresses pedal causing magnetized driver to push rivet end of stud through sole and clinch it into bottom of sole or heel. (2) Threads spikes into metal inserts that have been molded into plastic soles and heels of completed shoes. Holds shoe against bench-mounted air wrench, inserts spike head into socket, and presses shoe against

revolving wrench until spike is threaded securely. Repeats operation until each spike in sole and heel is assembled to shoe.
GOE: 06.04.27 STRENGTH: M GED: R2 M1 L1 SVP: 2 DLU: 77

788.687-058   HEEL DIPPER (boot & shoe)
Dips heels in cement prior to heel covering operation: Places heels in wire basket. Immerses basket in cement solution to coat heels. Raises basket, allowing excess cement to drain. Places heels on drying rack. May attach heels to bar used to hold heels for dipping in cement.
GOE: 06.04.33 STRENGTH: L GED: R1 M1 L1 SVP: 2 DLU: 78

788.687-062   INSOLE-AND-HEEL-STIFFENER (boot & shoe) alternate titles: channel-lip stiffener, insoles; rib-stiffener and heel-dipper
Applies stiffening solution to insoles in preparation for *lasting* by dipping toe and heel of insole in tank, and guiding channel of insole under roller of machine onto which stiffening solution is automatically fed. May dip heel sections into solution and place them on drying rack and be designated Heel Dipper, Insole (boot & shoe).
GOE: 06.04.27 STRENGTH: L GED: R1 M1 L1 SVP: 2 DLU: 77

788.687-066   LABORER, BOOT AND SHOE (boot & shoe)
Performs any combination of following tasks in shoe factory: Removes lasts from assembled shoes by hand. Sorts lasts according to size and stores them in bins. Gathers leather scraps for salvage. Stacks and stores leather parts according to size and shape. Transfers shoes in various stages of completion to workers for further processing. Sweeps floors and cleans work benches. May off bear products of leather cutting and shaping machines. May sand heels on sanding machine, and burnish work boots.
GOE: 06.04.40 STRENGTH: M GED: R2 M1 L1 SVP: 2 DLU: 77

788.687-070   LACER I (boot & shoe)
Inserts permanent laces through two lower eyelets of shoes and ties them to prevent loss. May attach descriptive tag to shoe.
GOE: 06.04.27 STRENGTH: L GED: R1 M1 L1 SVP: 2 DLU: 77

788.687-074   LACING-STRING CUTTER (boot & shoe) alternate titles: string cutter
Cuts and removes temporary lacing strings that hold shoe uppers together during *lasting* operations, using knife.
GOE: 06.04.27 STRENGTH: L GED: R1 M1 L1 SVP: 1 DLU: 77

788.687-078   LAST CHALKER (boot & shoe) alternate titles: last dipper; last greaser; last waxer
Treats lasts (shoe molds) to prevent lining from sticking at box toe and counter when shoe is lasted. Paints toe and heel of last with paste or chalky preparation.
GOE: 06.04.33 STRENGTH: L GED: R1 M1 L1 SVP: 2 DLU: 77

788.687-082   LAST CLEANER (boot & shoe)
Cleans wooden shoe lasts by pressing them against rotating abrasive wheel to remove dried cement. Stacks cleaned lasts according to size on rack.
GOE: 06.04.39 STRENGTH: L GED: R1 M1 L1 SVP: 1 DLU: 77

788.687-086   LAST PULLER (boot & shoe)
Removes lasts from shoes by either of following methods: (1) Places shoe on *pin jack* and pulls sharply on heel seam, causing hinge of last to open and release shoe. (2) Places shoe on pin jack and depresses pedal to force shoe against vertically moving rubber belt that lifts heel section from last. Removes shoe from last by hand.
GOE: 06.04.27 STRENGTH: L GED: R2 M1 L1 SVP: 2 DLU: 77

788.687-090   LEATHER SOFTENER (boot & shoe)
Softens leather shoe parts by one of following methods: (1) Places shoe parts, by case lots, on rack and pushes rack into humidifier. Turns valves to control heat and moisture in humidifier. Records rack number and time or date of placement in humidifier. Pushes rack of softened parts to other workers. (2) Dips bundles of welt strips into water and places bundles in humidifying room to maintain moisture in strips. (3) Places outsoles on rack, places rack on dipping frame, and lowers frame into trough of softener solution, using power hoist. Pushes rack of softened outsoles into humidifying room. (4) Sprays softening solution on shoe parts, using spray gun. (5) Pulls shoe part along roller that applies softening solution to part. (6) Wipes flesh side of leather with dampened rag or sponge to maintain pliability. May place sheets of fiberboard or leatherboard in softening solution, place softened board on skid, and cover stack of boards with plastic sheet to retain moisture. May be designated according to part treated as Heel-Cover Softener (boot & shoe); Sole Wetter (boot & shoe); Upper Muller (boot & shoe); Vamp Wetter (boot & shoe); Welt Treater (boot & shoe).
GOE: 06.04.27 STRENGTH: M GED: R2 M1 L1 SVP: 2 DLU: 77

788.687-094   MOLDER, SHOE PARTS (boot & shoe) alternate titles: conformal pad former; plastic insert molder
Molds preshaped piece of plastic to form shoe parts, such as arch supports and counters: Softens plastic piece in oven and positions it in mold. Pulls lever that lowers die to press and shape part. Removes shaped part from mold. May mark part to indicate size, using marking pencil.
GOE: 06.04.32 STRENGTH: L GED: R2 M1 L1 SVP: 2 DLU: 77

788.687-098   PAINTER, BOTTOM (boot & shoe) alternate titles: bottom stainer; sole stainer
Applies ink or stain onto bottoms of leather outsoles and heels, using brush, sponge, or spray gun, to color bottoms and prepare surface for polishing. May

press shoe bottom against machine bristle rollers that remove excess stain and impart preliminary finish.
GOE: 06.04.33 STRENGTH: L GED: R1 M1 L1 SVP: 2 DLU: 77

788.687-102   PEGGER (boot & shoe)
Hammers wooden pegs into heel and arch of boots to strengthen shank and keep boot waterproof: Places boot on *pin jack* and shapes edge of sole, using hammer. Marks row for pegs around heel and arch, using marking tool. Punches holes for pegs, using awl and hammer. Selects length of peg according to thickness of boot, places peg in hole, and hammers peg into boot. Repeats operation for each side of shank.
GOE: 06.04.27 STRENGTH: L GED: R2 M1 L1 SVP: 2 DLU: 77

788.687-106   SCRAP SORTER (boot & shoe)
Sorts and bags scrap leather to salvage usable pieces for further processing: Gathers scrap leather from cutting operations. Sorts trimmed material according to kind and use. Places sorted scrap in bags.
GOE: 06.03.02 STRENGTH: L GED: R1 M1 L1 SVP: 2 DLU: 77

788.687-110   SHANK INSPECTOR (boot & shoe) alternate titles: shank picker; shank sorter
Examines steel arch shanks for imperfections, such as burrs or excess metal, and packs them in container. Discards defective shanks.
GOE: 06.03.02 STRENGTH: L GED: R2 M1 L1 SVP: 2 DLU: 77

788.687-114   SHANK TAPER (boot & shoe) alternate titles: shank paperer
Presses strips of gummed paper tape on shoe upper to protect it during sanding of outsole.
GOE: 06.04.27 STRENGTH: S GED: R1 M1 L1 SVP: 2 DLU: 77

788.687-118   SHANK-PIECE TACKER (boot & shoe) alternate titles: shanker; shank tacker
Positions and affixes metal shank piece to shank of shoes to support arch, using hammer and tacks or stapler.
GOE: 06.04.27 STRENGTH: L GED: R1 M1 L1 SVP: 2 DLU: 77

788.687-122   SHOE CLEANER (boot & shoe) alternate titles: treer
Removes foreign matter, such as grease and cement from finished shoes, using art gum, knife, and cleaning fluids. Applies dressing to cleaned area to restore color and finish, using brush or spray gun and dressing or colored paint. May wrap shoe ornaments with paper for protection during packing and shipping. May spray disinfectant on inside of shoes to sanitize them and be designated Sanitizer (boot & shoe).
GOE: 06.04.39 STRENGTH: M GED: R2 M1 L1 SVP: 2 DLU: 77

788.687-126   SHOE COVERER (boot & shoe)
Places canvas, paper, or plastic covers over partially assembled shoes to protect uppers during processing. Inserts toe of shoe into end of cover, pulls cover over heel, and secures cover with rubberband or tacks edges of cover to insole.
GOE: 06.04.27 STRENGTH: L GED: R1 M1 L1 SVP: 2 DLU: 77

788.687-130   SHOE TURNER (boot & shoe)
Turns inverted shoe-vamp strap right side out: Pulls tubular strap down over vertical rod. Depresses pedal to lower second rod onto folded end of strap. Pulls up on bottom part of vamp strap to turn strap right side out. Releases pedal and removes strap. Bundles parts for delivery to other workers. May press adhesive cloth tape to inside of perforated leather uppers to prepare them for stitching. May pull boot upper onto turning rod frame, clamp top of upper to turning bar, and pull bar forward to turn boot upper right side out and be designated Boot Turner (boot & shoe).
GOE: 06.04.27 STRENGTH: L GED: R2 M1 L1 SVP: 2 DLU: 77

788.687-134   SOLE SCRAPER (boot & shoe)
Scrapes excess ink dressing from edge of shoe soles with metal scraper or knife to minimize clogging of sandpaper when sanding edges of sole.
GOE: 06.04.27 STRENGTH: M GED: R1 M1 L1 SVP: 2 DLU: 77

788.687-138   STEEL-BOX-TOE INSERTER (boot & shoe)
Inserts steel box toe into forepart of safety shoe: Places toe of lasted shoe in steam box to soften leather and positions steamed shoe on *pin jack*. Pulls tacks and upper-holding wire from toe area of shoe, using *lasting tool*. Draws upper leather back from toe area by hand and inserts steel box toe over lining. Brushes cement onto vamp edge of box toe and covers edge with felt strip to prevent friction between metal and upper leather. Pulls upper leather back over toe area, using lasting tool. Tacks edges of shoe upper to last, using hammer.
GOE: 06.04.27 STRENGTH: M GED: R2 M1 L1 SVP: 2 DLU: 77

788.687-142   TABLE WORKER (boot & shoe)
Performs any combination of following tasks in stitching room, using handtools: Cements doubles (cloth backing) together. Brushes cement on shoe parts. Counts number of parts and verifies total against work ticket. Sorts parts. Cuts and ties threads.
GOE: 06.04.27 STRENGTH: L GED: R2 M1 L1 SVP: 2 DLU: 77

788.687-146   TACK PULLER (boot & shoe) alternate titles: anchor-tack puller; insole-tack-puller, hand
Pulls temporary holding tacks from insole and upper of lasted shoe, using tack-pulling tool or pincers. May remove toe-wire and tacks from lasted shoes, using tack puller and pincers.
GOE: 06.04.27 STRENGTH: L GED: R1 M1 L1 SVP: 2 DLU: 77

788.687-150 TRIMMER, HAND (boot & shoe)
Trims excess material from edges or decorative openings of shoe parts, using handtools, such as knife and shears, and following specifications, markings, or template outline.
GOE: 06.04.27 STRENGTH: L GED: R2 M1 L1 SVP: 2 DLU: 77

788.687-154 VAMP CREASER (boot & shoe) alternate titles: crimper
Tends crimping machine that creases shoe vamps (part of shoe over instep) by one of following methods: (1) Positions leather model of vamp on vamp to be creased and places them under heated machine head. Depresses pedal to lower head and crimp vamp and model against parallel walls. (2) Places assembled shoe over die in machine head and stamps crease into vamp where foot bends. May place vamp over steamer to soften leather prior to crimping.
GOE: 06.04.05 STRENGTH: L GED: R2 M1 L1 SVP: 2 DLU: 77

788.687-158 VAMP-STRAP IRONER (boot & shoe) alternate titles: shoe ironer
Creases turn-stitched seams of lined vamp strap: Pushes steel insert into open end of strap to hold seams flat. Moistens strap with sponge and places strap on ironing bed. Depresses pedal to lower hot-iron plate and iron strap. Releases pedal, removes strap from ironing bed, and withdraws insert.
GOE: 06.04.27 STRENGTH: S GED: R1 M1 L1 SVP: 2 DLU: 77

788.687-162 WELT-BUTTER, HAND (boot & shoe)
Cuts off excess welt at heel seat of lasted shoe, using knife.
GOE: 06.04.27 STRENGTH: L GED: R2 M1 L1 SVP: 2 DLU: 77

788.687-166 WHITE-SHOE RAGGER (boot & shoe)
Brushes liquid polish on white leather shoes and rubs shoes with rag to give glossy and finished appearance. May apply polish to white leather of multicolored shoes, using artist's brush.
GOE: 06.04.33 STRENGTH: S GED: R1 M1 L1 SVP: 2 DLU: 77

789 OCCUPATIONS IN FABRICATION AND REPAIR OF TEXTILE, LEATHER, AND RELATED PRODUCTS, N.E.C.

This group includes occupations, not elsewhere classified, concerned with fabricating and repairing textile, leather, fur, and related products.

789.132-010 SUPERVISOR IV (tex. prod., nec)
Supervises and coordinates activities of workers engaged in laying out, cutting, and sewing material for household articles, such as bed linens, curtains, drapes, or slipcovers: Examines finished articles for defects, such as uneven seams and missed stitches, to maintain qualitative standards. Trains workers in laying out and cutting material and in sewing machine operation. Performs other duties as described under SUPERVISOR (any industry) Master Title. May be designated according to article fabricated or department as Cutting-And-Sewing Supervisor (tex. prod., nec); Drapery Room Supervisor (retail trade; tex. prod., nec); Pillow-And-Cushion-Department Supervisor (tex. prod., nec).
GOE: 06.02.01 STRENGTH: L GED: R3 M3 L2 SVP: 6 DLU: 78

789.132-014 SUPERVISOR I (tex. prod., nec)
Supervises and coordinates activities of workers engaged in cutting, sewing, inspecting, and turning textile bags: Measures and examines bags at various stages of processing to verify conformance to specifications. Informs workers when variations in size and defects in sewing, stringing, and turning are detected. Orders machine adjustments or changes in work procedure to restore production to specifications or to introduce changes in bag styles. Performs other duties as described under SUPERVISOR (any industry) Master Title. May be designated according to department as Cutting-Department Supervisor (tex. prod., nec).
GOE: 06.02.01 STRENGTH: L GED: R4 M3 L3 SVP: 6 DLU: 77

789.132-018 SUPERVISOR III (tex. prod., nec)
Supervises and coordinates activities of workers engaged in fabricating and repairing awnings, boat covers, drop and ground cloths, sails, tarpaulins, and tents made from canvas, synthetic, and vinyl material: Directs workers in cutting, assembling, and sewing material. Examines parts and finished or repaired articles for defects, such as holes and missed stitches, to maintain qualitative standards. Estimates cost of repairing damaged or worn articles. Trains employees in work procedures and machine operation. May interpret blueprints and draw layouts or patterns for workers. Performs other duties as described under SUPERVISOR (any industry) Master Title. May supervise workers engaged in fabricating and repairing canvas products and be designated Supervisor, Canvas Products (tex. prod., nec).
GOE: 06.02.01 STRENGTH: L GED: R4 M3 L3 SVP: 7 DLU: 78

789.132-022 SUPERVISOR, NET MAKING (toy-sport equip.)
Supervises and coordinates activities of workers engaged in making nets from purchased netting for games, such as badminton, basketball, tennis, or volleyball: Directs workers in measuring, cutting, and sewing netting and tape and in crimping grommets into tape for support ropes and cables. Inspects nets for conformance to specifications. Trains workers in job duties and machine operation. Performs other duties as described under SUPERVISOR (any industry) Master Title.
GOE: 06.02.01 STRENGTH: L GED: R4 M3 L3 SVP: 7 DLU: 77

789.132-026 SUPERVISOR, PARACHUTE MANUFACTURING (tex. prod., nec)
Supervises and coordinates activities of workers engaged in marking, cutting, sewing, inspecting, and folding parachutes. Trains workers in sewing machine operation and in method of inserting suspension lines. Inspects parachutes during fabrication to detect defects, such as missing stitches, underlap or overlap in seams, pleats or puckers in cloth, and unsewn suspension lines. Performs other duties as described under SUPERVISOR (any industry) Master Title.
GOE: 06.02.01 STRENGTH: L GED: R4 M2 L3 SVP: 7 DLU: 77

789.134-010 SUPERVISOR II (tex. prod., nec)
Supervises and coordinates activities of workers engaged in fabricating and decorating products, such as armbands, banners, and emblems. Requisitions supplies, such as bobbins, fabric, needles, and thread. Performs other duties as described under SUPERVISOR (any industry) Master Title.
GOE: 06.02.01 STRENGTH: L GED: R4 M2 L3 SVP: 7 DLU: 77

789.134-014 SUPERVISOR II (protective dev.)
Supervises and coordinates activities of workers engaged in assembling locking devices and splicing safety ropes and nets: Requisitions materials needed to process customer orders. Trains and directs workers in assembly techniques. Performs other duties as described under SUPERVISOR (any industry) Master Title.
GOE: 06.02.01 STRENGTH: M GED: R4 M3 L4 SVP: 7 DLU: 86

789.137-010 BOXING-AND-PRESSING SUPERVISOR (knitting)
Supervises and coordinates activities of workers engaged in inspecting and sorting bundles of knitted garments according to style preparatory to shipment. Performs duties as described under SUPERVISOR (any industry) Master Title.
GOE: 06.02.01 STRENGTH: L GED: R4 M3 L3 SVP: 6 DLU: 77

789.137-014 SUPERVISOR, WEBBING (tex. prod., nec)
Supervises and coordinates activities of workers engaged in fabricating and repairing fish nets. Performs duties as described under SUPERVISOR (any industry) Master Title.
GOE: 06.02.01 STRENGTH: L GED: R4 M3 L3 SVP: 7 DLU: 77

789.222-010 INSTRUCTOR, APPAREL MANUFACTURE (textile) alternate titles: instructor; overseer
Instructs workers to tend or operate knitting, looping, and sewing machines, using knowledge of machine function and process: Plans training schedule to ensure workers achieve standard production in specified time. Demonstrates methods of cleaning, threading, replacing needles, changing guides, lubricating, tension adjusting, and operating machines. Examines work of trainees to detect defects and instructs worker in methods to detect and correct defective work. Records production of worker to determine progress according to training schedule. Recommends transfer of worker from one operation to another based on progress made. May sew or loop sample articles to determine steps in assembly for new styles. May teach hand knitting, looping, and sewing to workers.
GOE: 06.02.01 STRENGTH: L GED: R4 M3 L3 SVP: 6 DLU: 77

789.261-010 BOAT-CANVAS MAKER-INSTALLER (tex. prod., nec)
Lays out, assembles, and installs custom and production model convertible tops, cockpit covers, and side curtains for boats according to customer specifications: Sketches design according to customer's description of item desired. Measures boat for part to be made, using tape. Makes pattern from measurements, and lays out and cuts material, using hand shears. Sews material according to markings, using power sewing machine [SEWING-MACHINE OPERATOR (tex. prod., nec) II]. Cuts and bends aluminum tubing to form framework, using metal-cutting saw and pipe-bending jig. Assembles framework, attaches material, and installs finished product on boat, using handtools, electric drill, and nuts and bolts.
GOE: 05.05.15 STRENGTH: M GED: R3 M3 L3 SVP: 6 DLU: 77

789.381-010 BEADWORKER (fabrication, nec)
Sews beads and other ornaments to leather articles, such as belts, purses, and moccasins, to form decorative designs: Draws original design on paper or executes design by threading beads together on hand loom. Stitches beads individually or in clumps onto leather article to transfer from drawing or loom. May prepare deerskin or other hide for beading by rubbing with stones to soften leather. May stitch materials, such as bird claws, feathers, and animal teeth, to leather to form contrasting design. May prepare dyes for coloring materials from berries or other natural substances, according to shade desired and knowledge of dye properties of available materials. May prepare thread from leather sinews for attaching ornaments.
GOE: 01.06.03 STRENGTH: L GED: R3 M1 L2 SVP: 6 DLU: 77

789.381-014 PATTERN CHART-WRITER (paper goods)
Makes scale drawings of dresses and their parts for use in reproducing commercial patterns and to illustrate style of garment and manner in which parts should be assembled, working from sample dresses or designer's sketches: Draws completed pattern and its separate parts, identifying counterparts of completed pattern with letters or numbers. Writes instructions for arranging pattern parts on material preliminary to cutting, and for assembling parts into garment.
GOE: 05.03.02 STRENGTH: L GED: R3 M2 L2 SVP: 5 DLU: 77

789.381-018 TRAWL NET MAKER (tex. prod., nec)
Lays out and cuts pattern, and fabricates trawl nets, using handtools and prefabricated net materials: Draws diagram to lay out parts for net, computing di-

mensions in number of meshes required along each seam. Lays out patterns for net parts on paper, using rule and pencil or marking crayon. Cuts patterns with scissors. Stretches netting materials on table or floor and cuts net parts with scissors, following patterns. Hangs net parts on pins along wall, over frames, or holds seams together with hands and toes to align seams. Threads twine, wound on shuttles (needles), through adjacent meshes of parts and ties half-hitch knots around knots of mesh to secure seam. Hangs net to metering lines. Similarly attaches prefabricated bag (used as trap to release fish onto deck from suspended net) to truncated end of net.
GOE: 06.01.04 STRENGTH: M GED: R3 M2 L3 SVP: 6 DLU: 77

789.382-010 CLICKING-MACHINE OPERATOR (boot & shoe; glove & mit.; leather prod.)

Operates clicking machine (die cutter) to cut out parts from leather or similar materials for articles, such as gloves, shoes, and small leather products, according to finish, grain, and pattern of material: Selects material and cutting dies according to specifications on work ticket. Turns handwheel to adjust depth of cut of clicking machine ram according to thickness of material and die. Lays material on cutting block and positions dies on material to match grain and weave of adjacent parts and to obtain desired cuts. Pulls horizontally swinging ram over dies to cut out parts. Counts parts to verify quantity against work ticket. May bundle parts and mark identification data on top part, using pencil. May smooth wooden cutting block, using hand plane or rasp. May cut out parts, using knife. May cut out shoe parts to repair shoes damaged in processing and be designated Cripple Cutter (boot & shoe). May be designated according to material or article as Leather Cutter (glove & mit.; leather prod.).
GOE: 06.02.05 STRENGTH: M GED: R3 M2 L2 SVP: 5 DLU: 80

789.387-010 QUALITY-CONTROL CHECKER (garment)

Inspects garments, such as men's shirts, during manufacturing operations to determine number of defects per worker and reasons for rejects by examiners: Cuts swatches from bolts of fabric to determine variations in dye lot shades. Counts number of pattern parts and lays of cloth prior to cutting to ensure accuracy of cutting operation with minimum waste. Counts number of stitches per inch during sewing operation to detect inconsistencies in sewing machine settings. Tests strength of collar-stay fusion, using tensiometer. Folds collars in half to detect unevenness of attachment. Examines garment and parts for defects, such as unfinished raw edges, broken buttons or hooks, uneven stripes or plaids, puckers in seams, loose threads or stitches, or incorrect packaging assortment. Records number and type of defects for each worker. Returns rejected part or garment to department to be reworked.
GOE: 06.03.01 STRENGTH: L GED: R3 M2 L3 SVP: 5 DLU: 77

789.387-014 SAMPLE SELECTOR (tex. prod., nec)

Selects materials, such as buckram, metal bars, and ribbon, and joins parts to form sample fabric badge or selects sample fabric badges from files, according to customer order. May wrap badges in tissue paper and pack them in boxes for shipment.
GOE: 06.02.27 STRENGTH: S GED: R2 M1 L1 SVP: 4 DLU: 77

789.484-010 DIAGRAMMER AND SEAMER (carpet & rug)

Cuts sections from rugs and joins sections together to form special size or shape rug, following diagrammed instructions: Reads instructions to determine rugs to be cut and obtains rugs from storage. Compares diagram with rugs spread on floor to estimate shape of required rug, lines along which to cut sections from rugs, and to visualize order in which sections can be joined to obtain required pattern. Computes area surface of sections needed to determine cutting lines. Measures and marks cutting guidelines, using tape measure, chalk, and yardstick. Guides portable electric cutter along chalkline to cut sections from rugs. Places cut sections upside down, matching edges, and nails sections to floor. Positions webbing tape over chutting edges, and spreads glue, using putty knife, onto tape so that glue seeps through webbing, adhering tape to backing material to seam sections together. Removes nails when glue dries, turns rug over, and clips uneven pile yarn along seams, using electric clippers, to make seams invisible.
GOE: 06.02.31 STRENGTH: M GED: R4 M4 L3 SVP: 5 DLU: 77

789.484-014 FINISHER, HAND (tex. prod., nec)

Fastens grommets, and hand sews reinforcing patches, ropes, rings, and snaps to such canvas products as awnings, sails, and tents: Sews reinforcing patches, ropes, snaps, eyelets, and rings to specified areas of canvas, using thread, palm, and needle. Measures and draws grommet holes on canvas with ruler and pencil. Cuts holes and fastens grommet to canvas using hammer, punch, and wooden block, or operates grommet machine to fasten grommets to canvas [EYELET-MACHINE OPERATOR (any industry)]. Splices rope and wire to metal fittings, seizes (binds) ends and sews to canvas. Threads ropes through grommets or ties to canvas. May taper rope by shaving it with knife, and sew rope to canvas. May repair defective canvas by patching or replacing ropes or grommets. May be designated according to type of article finished as Awning Finisher (tex. prod., nec); Sail Finisher, Hand (tex. prod., nec); Tent Finisher (tex. prod., nec).
GOE: 06.02.27 STRENGTH: M GED: R3 M1 L2 SVP: 5 DLU: 77

789.487-010 PLEAT TAPER (tex. prod., nec)

Measures unhemmed edge of pleated material for conformance to size specifications, using ruler. Tapes pleats in place, using masking tape. Folds material and stacks it on table according to size and color.
GOE: 06.03.01 STRENGTH: L GED: R1 M1 L1 SVP: 2 DLU: 77

789.587-010 BOXING INSPECTOR (garment)

Examines garments after folding or boxing to detect imperfections, such as shaded parts, holes, twisted straps, loose buttons, or open seams and to determine if garments are folded and boxed according to specifications. Refolds disarranged garments. Records type and number of imperfections detected.
GOE: 06.03.02 STRENGTH: L GED: R2 M1 L2 SVP: 3 DLU: 77

789.587-014 INSPECTOR, FABRIC (any industry) alternate titles: folder inspector; inspector and clipper

Examines articles made from fabric, such as bags, bed linens, canvas products, or house furnishings, to detect soil and assembly defects: Measures length or width of article to detect variation from customer or plant specifications, using tape or rule. Spreads article over table or rack and scans article to detect defective stitching, loose threads, color variations between thread and fabric, and uneven seams, corners, pleats, or hems. Cuts excess threads with scissors. Marks defects with gummed label or chalk. Stacks articles that fail to meet specifications on handtruck or table. Records number and type of defects. Folds articles according to customer or plant specifications. May examine paired articles, comparing designs to detect irregular alignment. May inspect tufted articles, scanning article to detect uneven or ragged tufts. May work as member of team to examine large articles, such as blankets, bedspreads, and draperies. May be designated according to article inspected as Bag Inspector (tex. prod., nec); Bedspread Inspector (tex. prod., nec); Blanket Inspector (tex. prod., nec); Curtain Inspector (tex. prod., nec); Dish-Cloth Inspector (tex. prod., nec); Drapery Inspector (tex. prod., nec). May be designated: Inspector, Canvas Products (tex. prod., nec); Returned-Goods Inspector (tex. prod., nec); Sheet Inspector (tex. prod., nec); Towel Inspector (tex. prod., nec).
GOE: 06.03.02 STRENGTH: L GED: R3 M1 L2 SVP: 3 DLU: 77

789.587-018 PARACHUTE MARKER (tex. prod., nec)

Folds rectangular signal-flare parachutes in four and marks corner representing center of parachute with pencil prior to further processing. Records number of parachutes folded on production sheet.
GOE: 06.04.27 STRENGTH: M GED: R2 M1 L1 SVP: 2 DLU: 77

789.587-022 RUG INSPECTOR II (carpet & rug)

Inspects carpets and rugs to detect defects in weaving, tufting, or hooking, soil spots, uncut pile, and loose threads: Spreads rug on table or examines rug spread on floor to detect soil spots, missing stitches, holes, loose threads, uncut pile, defectively bound edges, and faulty shearing, and to determine that color, design, and fabrication meet specifications. Measures pile height and rug dimensions, using ruler and tapeline. Marks defect on rug. Cuts uncut pile, loose yarn ends, and long fringe yarn, using scissors. Selects yarn of color to match rug, threads hooked needle, and hooks yarn to backing in blank areas of rug to fill in missing pile or yarn. May rub soil spots with cloth and cleaning solution to remove soil and restore natural color to rug pile. May glue backing strip around back edge of rug. May attach tassels to edge of rug, using plunger needle and yarn. May affix gummed label to rug, using heated iron. May work as member of two-worker team when inspecting large rugs.
GOE: 06.03.02 STRENGTH: L GED: R3 M2 L2 SVP: 4 DLU: 77

789.587-026 SAMPLE CLERK (textile)

Cuts cloth into swatches and attaches them to cards for production records or distribution to salesmen and customers: Compares cloth for color and style with standard sample which meets design specifications. Examines cloth for defects in weave, shade, finish, and dimensions, and rejects imperfect cloth. Stacks cloth according to style and cuts to specified size, using pinking machine. Spaces samples on card and attaches them to card, using paste and brush or hand stapling machine. Prints style number and color on sample card, using rubber stamps [TICKETER (textile)]. Records and files description of orders filled.
GOE: 06.04.27 STRENGTH: L GED: R2 M1 L1 SVP: 3 DLU: 77

789.684-010 BOW MAKER (any industry)

Forms ornamental bows for hair or dress wear, by hand: Winds length of ribbon on rack to form bows. Cuts ribbon into sections with scissors and ties folds together at middle with twine to form bow. Inserts bobby pin or safety pin through twine, and removes bows from rack. Arranges artificial flower or lace medallion on bow as specified, and ties them together with twine or ribbon. May sew comb attachment to middle section of underside of bow, using needle and thread.
GOE: 06.04.27 STRENGTH: L GED: R2 M1 L2 SVP: 3 DLU: 77

789.684-014 BUFFING-WHEEL FORMER, HAND (tex. prod., nec)

Folds and gathers cloth within metal ring to form buffing wheels, using hand-actuated forming and pressing device: Lifts roll of cloth onto holder or draws end from box and threads end through guides and over steam pipes. Positions front section of forming drum on rod at specified distance from rear section. Pulls material over drum and centers it over space between drum sections. Secures cloth edges over pins across drum. Turns valve or depresses pedal to admit steam to pipes to soften material. Turns crank to wind specified amount of material around drum. Pushes lever to close jaws of pressing device that forces cloth between drum sections, folding and gathering cloth in center. Removes front section of drum. Pulls half of gathered cloth forward from pressing jaws, slides ring over cloth to secure gathers in center, and turns cloth over ring to cover it. Raises lever to open jaws of pressing device and removes buffing wheel.
GOE: 06.04.27 STRENGTH: L GED: R2 M1 L1 SVP: 3 DLU: 77

789.684-018 CANOPY STRINGER (tex. prod., nec)
Threads shroud lines through perpendicular seams of parachute canopy for connecting canopy to parachute harness: Spreads canopy on table and places vent over holders. Secures end of line in barbs of insertion needle and working from interior dome of canopy outward, inserts shroud lines through holes in opposite panel seams so that center of line lays in semicircle around top hem. Threads and pulls line down through panel seam, drawing it out just above reinforcements attached to bottom hem of canopy. Pins shroud lines at hem and vent, according to markings on line, to facilitate stitching of lines to canopy. Braids lines to prevent tangling, cooperating with co-worker so that each advances one panel seam in same circular direction as stringing progresses. May thread shroud lines through horizontal seams of aerial recovery parachutes. May insert line into itself, using insertion needle, to form endless vent line.
GOE: 06.02.27 STRENGTH: L GED: R3 M2 L2 SVP: 4 DLU: 77

789.684-022 HAIR CLIPPER, POWER (leather mfg.)
Clips hair from cattle or horse tails, using electric clippers, so that hair falls into container or onto conveyor. Throws sheared tail into separate container.
GOE: 06.04.34 STRENGTH: L GED: R2 M1 L1 SVP: 2 DLU: 77

789.684-026 MOLDER, SHOULDER PAD (garment)
Shapes fabric shoulder pads over steam-heated metal molds: Positions and shapes precut fabric over heated mold. Allows fabric to remain on mold until sufficiently heated to retain shape of mold. Removes shaped pad from mold and places pad in basket for further processing.
GOE: 06.04.27 STRENGTH: L GED: R2 M1 L1 SVP: 2 DLU: 77

789.684-030 NET MAKER (tex. prod., nec) alternate titles: knotter, hand; knotter
Interlaces and knots twine to form nets: Selects gauge and twine according to size specified on work ticket. Wraps twine around needle (twine holder) that facilitates interlacing and knotting of twine. Extends and ties ends of foundation line to poles. Ties twine to end of line with clove hitch and positions gauge against line. Loops twine around gauge and knots twine onto foundation line, forming half mesh. Removes gauge and repeats operation to form row of half meshes. Holds gauge against half-mesh, pulls twine around gauge, and ties sheep bend knot onto half-mesh, forming mesh. Repeats operation with succeeding half meshes to form net. Unties foundation line and pulls line from net. May be designated according to type of net made as Safety-Net Maker (tex. prod., nec); Tennis-Net Maker (tex. prod., nec).
GOE: 06.04.27 STRENGTH: L GED: R2 M1 L1 SVP: 3 DLU: 77

789.684-034 PARACHUTE FOLDER (tex. prod., nec)
Folds circular or rectangular parachutes preparatory to further processing, using any of following methods: (1) Hangs circular parachute canopy on wall hook, prior to attachment of shroud lines, and folds canopy lengthwise along seams, one panel over another. Removes canopy from hook and rolls canopy from top to bottom. (2) Spreads circular canopy on table, after shroud lines are attached, and straightens canopy and lines to eliminate wrinkles, tangles, or coils. Clamps shroud lines to table edge with vise, loops lines through hook in wall, and pulls lines taut. Splices loops in ends of shroud lines, using cotton twine. Folds canopy lengthwise along seams, one panel over another. Rolls canopy from top to bottom, removes shroud lines from hook, wraps lines around rolled canopy, and secures bundle with rubber bands. (3) Folds rectangular canopy in half lengthwise and spreads canopy on table with shroud lines hanging over table edge. Folds canopy fanwise so that shroud lines are grouped together. Straightens lines to eliminate coils and tangles, and ties lines and flare suspension cords together. Cuts off excess line and cord ends, using scissors. Rolls canopy from top to bottom and wraps lines and cords around canopy.
GOE: 06.04.27 STRENGTH: H GED: R2 M1 L1 SVP: 3 DLU: 77

789.684-038 PARACHUTE MENDER (tex. prod., nec) alternate titles: mender
Patches damaged parachute canopies, using needle and thread and sewing machine. Replaces defective shrouds and splices connections between shrouds and harness, using handtools.
GOE: 05.10.04 STRENGTH: L GED: R3 M1 L1 SVP: 3 DLU: 77

789.684-042 RAWHIDE-BONE ROLLER (leather prod.)
Cuts, rolls, and ties strips of rawhide to form toy bones for dogs. Cuts strips of specified size from sheets of wet, processed rawhide, using knife. Rolls strips and ties knots in ends to form bone shaped toy.
GOE: 06.04.27 STRENGTH: L GED: R2 M1 L1 SVP: 2 DLU: 77

789.684-046 RIGGER (tex. prod., nec)
Fits finished canvas to metal frame to prepare awning for installation: Inserts metal frame and roller into pockets at lower end and sides of awning cloth. Drills holes in aluminum roller, using portable electric drill, and screws in spring roller, using screwdriver. Threads rope through grommets, blocks, and pockets and ties rope to awning cloth and frame. May bundle awnings into lots and attach work ticket.
GOE: 06.04.34 STRENGTH: M GED: R2 M1 L1 SVP: 2 DLU: 77

789.684-050 THREAD CUTTER (any industry) alternate titles: trimming-machine operator
Trims loose threads from edges or seams of articles, such as garments, hats, linens, and surgical appliances, using either of following methods: (1) Moves edges or seams of article over stationary cutting head equipped with vacuum attachment that draws threads between reciprocal blades to cut threads. (2)

Spreads article on table or pulls article over form and guides electric hand clippers equipped with vacuum hose along edges or seams of article to cut threads. When trimming knitted garments, pulls loose threads through several stitches with latch needle or ties threads from converging seams to secure stitching. May cut short or thick threads unsuitable for machine cutting, using scissors.
GOE: 06.04.27 STRENGTH: L GED: R2 M1 L1 SVP: 2 DLU: 77

789.684-054 ELECTRIC BLANKET WIRER (tex. prod., nec) alternate titles: shuttler
Installs wire and safety thermostats in electric blankets, using shuttle devices, worktable, and wire shears, working as member of two-person team: Places electric blanket shell on worktable that contains illuminated surface panels. Observes prewoven channels in blanket shell, made visible by light passing through blanket shell, to identify channel openings. Threads heater element wire through channels of blanket shell, using shuttle device and working with team member at opposite side of table. Inserts thermostats with attached connecting wires into thermostat channels of blanket shell, using shuttle device. Cuts installed heater element wire at specified points, using wire shears, and fastens cut ends to connecting wires of thermostats to align and secure assembly for subsequent processing, using clamps. May inspect blankets to detect defects, such as closed channels or excessive blanket length. May cut out faulty wires and rewire blanket.
GOE: 06.02.27 STRENGTH: M GED: R2 M1 L1 SVP: 3 DLU: 86

789.685-010 ORNAMENT SETTER (garment; tex. prod., nec) alternate titles: nailhead puncher; stud setter
Tends kick press that attaches ornaments, such as nailheads, rhinestones, and pearls, to cloth, leather, or plastic materials or to finished garments: Selects dies, according to specification, and positions dies in ram and bed of machine. Turns setscrews to secure dies. Selects ornaments according to specifications. Places self-fastening ornament in die of ram, or places ornament and metal fastener in upper and lower dies of machine. Positions material or garment on bed and under ram of machine, following markings on material or garment. Depresses pedal to lower ram that clinches metal fasteners, attaching ornament. May operate machine equipped with vacuum mechanism that holds ornament in die on ram of machine in preparation for attachment. May be designated according to type of ornamentation fastened to garments as Nailhead Setter (garment; tex. prod., nec); Rhinestone Setter (garment; tex. prod., nec).
GOE: 06.04.34 STRENGTH: S GED: R2 M1 L2 SVP: 3 DLU: 77

789.687-010 BAG CUTTER (tex. prod., nec) alternate titles: textile-scrap salvager
Reclaims usable material from used or defective textile bags: Cuts or pulls stitches from seam to open bag. Inspects material to locate defects and cuts usable material into largest possible bag dimension, using electric rotary cutter. Sorts and stacks reclaimed material according to specified bag sizes.
GOE: 06.04.27 STRENGTH: L GED: R2 M1 L1 SVP: 2 DLU: 77

789.687-014 BAG LINER (tex. prod., nec)
Places cotton bag on form and pulls burlap bag down over it to line burlap bag.
GOE: 06.04.27 STRENGTH: L GED: R1 M1 L1 SVP: 2 DLU: 77

789.687-018 BONER (garment; protective dev.) alternate titles: stayer; stripper
Inserts stays (bones or steels) into prepared pockets of women's foundation garments, such as corsets or brassiers, or into casings of surgical appliances: Selects number and size stays to be inserted and pushes stays into pockets or casings by hand or using metal punch. May mark dot on support appliance, using pencil and template. May cut excess leather, cloth, and threads from appliance, using scissors, and inspect appliance for sewing defects.
GOE: 06.04.34 STRENGTH: L GED: R2 M1 L1 SVP: 2 DLU: 77

789.687-022 BUFFING TURNER-AND-COUNTER (tex. prod., nec)
Assembles cloth disks to be used to make fabric buffing wheels: Inserts rod in center hole of stack of disks. Turns disks so woven threads in cloth layers are at angle to those in adjoining layers to reduce fraying of edges in finished product. Counts specified number of disks to make one wheel while turning them. Removes turned and counted disks from rod and stacks them in tray. Lays paper strip on stack to separate each group of disks required to make one wheel.
GOE: 06.04.23 STRENGTH: S GED: R1 M1 L1 SVP: 2 DLU: 77

789.687-026 BUFFING-WHEEL INSPECTOR (tex. prod., nec)
Inspects fabric buffing wheels to detect defective stitching, frayed edges, loose strings, or other defects. Trims edges or strings, using hand shears, and stacks wheels with defective stitching for resewing. Counts inspected buffing wheels of same quality and style to fill orders or replace stock.
GOE: 06.03.02 STRENGTH: L GED: R2 M1 L1 SVP: 2 DLU: 77

789.687-030 CLIPPER (any industry)
Separates chain-sewn or knitted articles, such as garment parts, textile bags, or curtains, prior to assembly into completed article: Clips connecting threads or material between articles, using scissors or knife, or guides connecting thread or material under rotary cutter to separate articles. Pulls ends of thread from knitted part and twists threads around revolving wheel to separate individual parts from chain-knitted strip. May sort, count, and store separated articles in bins according to style, color, and size. May be designated according to article separated as Collarette Separator (knitting); Collar Separator (knitting); Cotton-

Bag Clipper (tex. prod., nec); Cuff Separator (knitting); Jute-Bag Clipper (tex. prod., nec); Rib-Trim Separator (knitting). May be designated: Sleeve Separator (knitting).
GOE: 06.03.02 STRENGTH: L GED: R1 M1 L1 SVP: 2 DLU: 77

789.687-034 CLOTH-STOCK SORTER (tex. prod., nec; textile)
Sorts finished articles or cloth by style and color for subsequent processing, according to ticket attached to cloth. Stores article or cloth or conveys it on handtruck to various departments. Records data on article or cloth stored and distributed.
GOE: 06.03.02 STRENGTH: L GED: R2 M1 L2 SVP: 2 DLU: 77

789.687-038 COVER INSPECTOR (furniture)
Inspects sewed parts of cushion and upholstery covers for stitching defects and conformity to specifications: Marks defects with chalk and rips out faulty seams. Measures skirts with yardstick. Records number of defects found. May carry defective covers to sewing department and identify defects to be repaired. May be designated according to type of cover inspected as Cushion-Cover Inspector (furniture; tex. prod., nec); Sofa-Cover Inspector (furniture).
GOE: 06.03.02 STRENGTH: L GED: R3 M2 L2 SVP: 3 DLU: 78

789.687-042 EXAMINER (glove & mit.) alternate titles: inspector trimmer
Inspects gloves and mittens for material flaws and variations in colors, and pulls seams to detect defective stitching. Grades gloves and mittens according to specifications. Separates gloves with stitching defects for resewing. May pair gloves of same grade, size, style, and color, and stack gloves in lots. May pull threads from outside to inside with hook, knot threads, and cut them, using scissors [PULLER-THROUGH (glove & mit.)]. May pack gloves in boxes.
GOE: 06.03.02 STRENGTH: L GED: R2 M1 L1 SVP: 3 DLU: 77

789.687-046 FINAL ASSEMBLER (garment)
Assembles garments, such as skirts, blouses, and jackets, for final inspection: Ties bows, draws belts through belt loops, closes slide fasteners, and buttons, snaps, or buckles garment openings. Trims long ends of thread or loose threads from garments, using scissors. Attaches specified tag denoting size of completed ensemble.
GOE: 06.04.27 STRENGTH: L GED: R2 M1 L1 SVP: 2 DLU: 77

789.687-050 FINISHER (tex. prod., nec) alternate titles: examiner; trimmer
Inspects, finishes, and counts embroidered or trimmed fabrics preparatory to shipping: Examines fabric for broken threads, skipped stitches, cuts in material, stains, or other imperfections. Trims loose or hanging threads, using scissors. Brushes or sponges out soiled spots with cleaning fluid. Counts pieces of fabric to verify work ticket. Bundles damaged and imperfect materials for repairing.
GOE: 06.03.02 STRENGTH: L GED: R2 M1 L1 SVP: 2 DLU: 77

789.687-054 FLOCKER (tex. prod., nec)
Cements flock onto fabric articles, such as banners and flags to give them velvety or woolly appearance: Brushes sizing onto article to stiffen article and to hold flock. Spreads flock over sized material and places article on tray. Presses button to start vibrating rollers on machine. Positions and holds tray on vibrating rollers that fluffs flock to give article velvety or woolly appearance.
GOE: 06.04.33 STRENGTH: L GED: R2 M1 L1 SVP: 2 DLU: 77

789.687-058 FOLDER (tex. prod., nec) alternate titles: waterproof-material folder
Folds pieces of waterproofed or padded bag material preparatory to sewing so that ends match evenly and burlap is to outside. Creases fold with hand and places pieces on handtruck.
GOE: 06.04.27 STRENGTH: L GED: R1 M1 L1 SVP: 2 DLU: 77

789.687-062 FRINGER (carpet & rug; tex. prod., nec)
Pulls out specified number of warp and filling threads or selvage yarns to form fringe on woven tablecloths or rugs. Trims excess threads from fringe, using scissors.
GOE: 06.04.27 STRENGTH: L GED: R1 M1 L1 SVP: 2 DLU: 77

789.687-066 GARMENT FOLDER (garment; knitting)
Folds garments for bagging or boxing, following guide marks on table or using folding board (cardboard or metal form). Secures folds with metal clips. May insert tissue paper between folds. May make final inspection of garment. May pack garments in bags and boxes [PACKAGER, HAND (any industry)]. May be designated according to garment folded as Shirt Folder (garment; knitting).
GOE: 06.04.38 STRENGTH: L GED: R1 M1 L1 SVP: 2 DLU: 77

789.687-070 GARMENT INSPECTOR (any industry) alternate titles: trimmer
Inspects garments for defects in sewing, knitting, or finishing: Spreads garment on table or draws garment over inspection form. Scans garment to detect defects, such as faulty seaming, incorrect sleeve or collar setting, misaligned fasteners or trim, and variations in color of fabric. Examines fabric for mispicks, slubs, runs, dropped stitches, holes, or stains. Marks defects, using chalk, thread, tags, tape, or pins. Measures garment at designated places, using tape measure or following markings on table, to determine that garments conform to standard size. Trims excess material and thread ends from garment, using scissors, or tends trimming machine to remove excess material and loose

threads [THREAD CUTTER (any industry) 789.684-050]. Folds garment or hangs it on hanger or rack. May remove spots and stains from garments [SPOT CLEANER (garment; knitting) 582.684-014]. May inspect surgical garments and appliances, such as belts, hosiery, or knee and ankle braces, and be designated Inspector (protective dev.).May examine cut garment parts to detect inaccuracies in cutting and be designated Cutting Inspector (garment). May be designated according to production stage as Finished-Garment Inspector (garment; knitting); Greige-Goods Inspector (knitting); Seconds Inspector (garment; knitting).
GOE: 06.03.02 STRENGTH: L GED: R2 M1 L2 SVP: 3 DLU: 78

789.687-074 GARMENT TURNER (garment; knitting)
Turns garments right side out preparatory to folding: Turns garments by hand or pulls garment over shaped form to reverse garment. Turns closed portion of garment, such as foot of child's sleeper, by pulling garment over suction tube, pressing closed portion in mouth of tube, and turning garment from tube onto form. Pulls garment over form and depresses pedal to activate air suction that turns garment right side out. May button garment. May be designated according to type of garment or garment part turned as Shirt Turner (garment; knitting); Sleeve Turner (garment; knitting).
GOE: 06.04.27 STRENGTH: L GED: R1 M1 L1 SVP: 2 DLU: 77

789.687-078 GARMENT-ALTERATION EXAMINER (retail trade) alternate titles: alteration inspector; outgoing inspector
Examines altered garments to ensure compliance with standards: Removes lint and loose threads from garment. Examines garment to ascertain that it is pressed, that buttons are sewed on, and that alterations have been completed. Matches suit jacket, pants, or other parts to see that customer receives complete garment. May verify cost of alterations with sales check. May place garment in protective bag.
GOE: 05.05.15 STRENGTH: L GED: R3 M1 L1 SVP: 4 DLU: 77

789.687-082 HARNESS RIGGER (tex. prod., nec) alternate titles: parachute-harness rigger
Threads breast shields, buckles, snaps, and other hardware devices on straps of parachute harness to position them for stiching into place: Clamps harness onto table with wire clamps. Slides canvas breast shield fitted with snap onto one harness strap and slides shield fitted with buckle ring onto other strap. Attaches pair of backstraps to harness and slides snap onto one strap and buckle ring onto other strap. Crosses backstraps and pulls them through buckles mounted on opposite harness straps. Places assembled harness in bin.
GOE: 06.04.27 STRENGTH: L GED: R2 M2 L1 SVP: 2 DLU: 77

789.687-086 HARNESS-AND-BAG INSPECTOR (tex. prod., nec)
Inspects parachute deployment bags and harnesses to detect defects in assembly, stitching, or webbing, using checklist: Unfolds back pad, seat pack, or accessory, such as protector flap, cone panel, ripcord pocket, or riser pocket, and examines them for flaws, such as defective material and stitching or loose eyelets. Determines if accessories are at specified location, using straightedge, and pulls accessories to ensure that they are securely attached to seat pack. Lays harness on table and checks measurements of straps and assembly points, using ruler or measurements marked on table. Inspects harness for defects, such as damaged webbing, poor stitching, smears in silk-screen printing, and attachment of component parts. Marks defects with pins. Lifts stitches with point of scissors to determine whether correct tension was used, and trims loose threads with scissors. May be designated according to part or parts inspected as Back-Pad Inspector (tex. prod., nec); Harness Inspector (tex. prod., nec); Seat-Pack Inspector (tex. prod., nec).
GOE: 06.03.02 STRENGTH: L GED: R2 M1 L2 SVP: 2 DLU: 77

789.687-090 LABORER, CANVAS SHOP (tex. prod., nec)
Performs any of following tasks in laying out, cutting, sewing, fabricating, and assembling canvas products, such as awnings, tents, and tarpaulins: Carries or handtrucks supplies to work stations. Unrolls cloth from bolt, cuts cloth to specified length with hand shears, and spreads cloth on table for pattern layout and cutting. Stacks and marks cut cloth according to work order. Rolls cloths into bundles. Ties and tags bundles. Inspects finished products for defects, such as tears, missing rope, or hardware, defective sewing, dirt, or stains. Folds, ties, and packs finished products. Trims threads from machine-sewed items with shears to prepare them for finishing. Sews rings, snaps, or ropes to canvas by hand, using palm and needle. May tend grommet machine to attach grommets to canvas. May assist in installing awnings. May be designated according to work performed as Awning Spreader (tex. prod., nec); Ring Sewer (tex. prod., nec).
GOE: 06.04.27 STRENGTH: M GED: R2 M1 L1 SVP: 2 DLU: 77

789.687-094 LACER (protective dev.)
Threads laces through eyelets and adjustment buckles of surgical supports to provide adjustments for fitting support to wearer: Selects laces according to type of support. Threads laces through eyelets of support and buckles eyelets in specified sequence. Adjusts laces and places straps in buckles. May tack ends of laces to reinforce them, using tacking machine. May place support on frame to hold support in position.
GOE: 06.04.27 STRENGTH: L GED: R2 M1 L1 SVP: 2 DLU: 77

789.687-098 MIXER II (tex. prod., nec)
Mixes, by hand, various grades and quantities of cotton and wool waste, or waste thread, according to specifications, for use as wiping, rubbing, and polishing or packing material.

GOE: 06.04.27 STRENGTH: L GED: R1 M1 L1 SVP: 2 DLU: 77

789.687-102   MONOGRAM-AND-LETTER PASTER (tex. prod., nec) alternate titles: paster

Cements cardboard letters or monograms onto fabric articles, such as armbands, banners, and shirts to prepare article for embroidering: Marks position of letter or monogram on article, according to specifications, using chalk and ruler. Brushes cement onto letter or monogram and positions it on marked area of article. Presses letter or monogram onto article.
GOE: 06.04.27 STRENGTH: L GED: R2 M1 L1 SVP: 2 DLU: 77

789.687-106   MOPHEAD TRIMMER-AND-WRAPPER (tex. prod., nec)

Trims uneven strands of yarn from mopheads, using shears, wraps mopheads with paper or inserts mopheads into bags, and packs mopheads into carton: May separate chain-sewn mopheads [CLIPPER (any industry)]. May glue labels or stamp identifying data on bundles. May compress mopheads preparatory to wrapping, using handpress.
GOE: 06.04.38 STRENGTH: L GED: R1 M1 L1 SVP: 2 DLU: 77

789.687-110   PAIRER (tex. prod., nec)

Places hemmed drapery lining over hemmed drapery panel and hangs resulting assembly over rack preparatory to seaming. Works as member of team to prepare assemblies for multiple-paneled draperies.
GOE: 06.04.27 STRENGTH: L GED: R1 M1 L1 SVP: 1 DLU: 77

789.687-114   PARACHUTE INSPECTOR (tex. prod., nec)

Inspects parachutes and lines to detect flaws in materials and fabrication: Spreads parachute or part, such as canopy and shroud webbing, on glass-topped table or over fluorescent light, and examines them for flaws, such as defective material and stitching, crooked hems, and tears. Pulls on shroud lines and suspension cords to ensure tightness of knots. Rips out defective stitching, hems, seams, and taped edges, and trims excess fabric at edges, using scissors. Pins pieces of colored cloth over defective areas. May be designated according to part inspected as Canopy Inspector (tex. prod., nec); Hem Inspector (tex. prod., nec); Shroud-Web Inspector (tex. prod., nec).
GOE: 06.03.02 STRENGTH: L GED: R2 M1 L1 SVP: 2 DLU: 77

789.687-118   PARACHUTE-LINE TIER (tex. prod., nec)

Ties shroud lines and suspension cords to signal-flare parachutes: Threads ends of shroud lines through eyelets in edge of parachute and ends of suspension cords through eyes of swivels to which flares are attached. Ties knots in lines and cords to secure them. May cut holes in parachute edge for insertion of shroud lines, using scissors. May verify length of attached suspension cords or shroud lines, using flexible steel tape. May tend machine that attaches eyelets to parachutes. May be designated according to line or cord attached as Shroud-Line Tier (tex. prod., nec); Suspension-Cord Tier (tex. prod., nec).
GOE: 06.04.27 STRENGTH: M GED: R2 M2 L1 SVP: 2 DLU: 77

789.687-122   PILLOW CLEANER (tex. prod., nec) alternate titles: cushion sweeper

Holds pillow against revolving brushes of machine equipped with suction fan to remove dust, lint, and feathers from ticking (cover) of pillow.
GOE: 06.04.39 STRENGTH: L GED: R1 M1 L1 SVP: 1 DLU: 77

789.687-126   POMPOM MAKER (knitting)

Fabricates pompoms for knitted headwear: Gathers spools of yarn according to type and color specified on work order. Positions and secures winding wheel on workbench. Threads yarn through tension devices and guides of winding wheel. Manually rotates wheel to form skein of yarn. Ties string around yarn, pulls yarn from wheel, and cuts yarn between strings to form pompom, using handsaw or scissors. Fluffs yarn by hand into shape of pompom.
GOE: 06.04.27 STRENGTH: L GED: R1 M1 L1 SVP: 1 DLU: 77

789.687-130   QUILT STUFFER (tex. prod., nec) alternate titles: filler; wool-batting worker

Fills quilt or comforter covers with precut sheets of cotton or wool batting, or synthetic materials, preparatory to sewing and quilting, using one of following methods: (1) Selects filler and places it smoothly between unsewn cover pieces, securing cover together with snap clamps. (2) Spreads filler on inverted cover, sewn on three sides, and turns cover right side out over fillers. (3) Places cover, sewn on three sides, over frame that holds it open, and places filler on movable table to slide filler into cover. May fill sleeping bags and cushions. May tend automatic quilting machines.
GOE: 06.04.23 STRENGTH: L GED: R2 M1 L1 SVP: 2 DLU: 77

789.687-134   RAG SORTER AND CUTTER (tex. prod., nec) alternate titles: cutter

Scans rags for hardware, such as buttons and snaps, and holds rags against rotating blade that cuts hardware from rags and cuts rags into specified sizes. Sorts rags into bins according to color and fabric.
GOE: 06.03.02 STRENGTH: L GED: R1 M1 L1 SVP: 2 DLU: 77

789.687-138   RAKER (carpet & rug) alternate titles: rug scratcher

Combs rugs to pull out short yarns, uncut loops, and pull up yarn ends, using *scratching tool.* Pushes tool back and forth across surface of rug and clips uncut loops and long yarn ends, using scissors.
GOE: 06.04.27 STRENGTH: L GED: R1 M1 L1 SVP: 2 DLU: 77

789.687-142   REDYE HAND (knitting)

Sorts and bags hose, panty hose, and tights that are to be redyed, according to style, size, and length: Examines article to locate markings knitted in foot

and welt that designate style and size. Measures overall length of article with scale to determine length classification. Records on production sheet quantity, type, size, and style of articles processed and prepares ticket for bag, indicating style number, quantity, and size. Bags hose of identical style, size, and length, attaches ticket to bag, and stores bags in bins.
GOE: 06.03.02 STRENGTH: L GED: R3 M1 L1 SVP: 3 DLU: 77

789.687-146   REMNANT SORTER (textile)

Sorts cloth remnants or seconds according to length and folds and ties them into bundles. May cut defects from cloth or cut cloth into smaller articles, such as pillowcases or washcloths, using scissors. May record identifying information on tag and tie tag to bundle. May sort seconds and be designated Cloth-Seconds Sorter (textile). May measure fabric pieces for use as drop cloths and sort pieces according to size, weight (thickness), fabric type, and color and be designated Sorter (tex. prod., nec).
GOE: 06.03.02 STRENGTH: L GED: R2 M1 L1 SVP: 2 DLU: 77

789.687-150   REMNANTS CUTTER (textile)

Cuts defective cloth along markings made by INSPECTOR, FABRIC (any industry), using hand shears. When cutting labels from sheets to be sold as seconds, is known as Label Cutter (textile). May sort remnants according to style and type.
GOE: 06.04.27 STRENGTH: L GED: R1 M1 L1 SVP: 1 DLU: 77

789.687-154   RIVETER, HAND (garment)

Secures rivets in prepunched holes of garment parts, such as overall pockets, to reinforce them: Pushes soft metal rivet through hole in material and rests base of rivet on anvil. Slides rivet burr over upper end of rivet, holds rivet set over upper end of rivet, and strikes top of rivet set with hammer to secure rivet.
GOE: 06.04.27 STRENGTH: L GED: R2 M1 L1 SVP: 2 DLU: 77

789.687-158   RUG-INSPECTOR HELPER (carpet & rug)

Lifts and carries rugs to inspection rack: Pulls rug onto rack. Tags flaws on repairable rugs and returns rugs to mending department. Staples labels to corner of rugs requiring no further processing. Clips or sews in loose ends, using scissors or needle. Pushes loaded racks to packaging department or to coating department.
GOE: 06.04.40 STRENGTH: M GED: R2 M1 L1 SVP: 3 DLU: 77

789.687-166   SEAM STEAMER (garment) alternate titles: pipe steamer

Slips knitted woolen garments over aluminum steam pipes adjusted to size of garment being steamed and releases steam which smooths and flattens seams.
GOE: 06.04.27 STRENGTH: L GED: R1 M1 L1 SVP: 1 DLU: 77

789.687-170   STEAMER (tex. prod., nec)

Steams rolled pleat patterns in which fabrics are pleated, so that fabric will retain pleats: Places rolled patterns in upright position in steam cabinet for specified period. Removes steamed patterns and places them on racks to cool.
GOE: 06.04.16 STRENGTH: M GED: R1 M1 L1 SVP: 2 DLU: 77

789.687-174   THREAD SEPARATOR (tex. prod., nec) alternate titles: thread drawer

Separates webs of lace into smaller pieces preparatory to winding onto cards: Cuts ends of web even with scissors. Counts out prescribed number of sections (bands), pulls thread to separate lace between sections, and folds sections.
GOE: 06.04.27 STRENGTH: S GED: R1 M1 L1 SVP: 2 DLU: 77

789.687-178   TIE PRESSER (knitting)

Removes wrinkles from knitted ties, using cardboard form and steamtable: Opens valve to allow steam to escape through holes in steamtable. Inserts cardboard form in opening of tie to extend it to full width. Passes tie across holes of steamtable to press it. Folds pressed tie.
GOE: 06.04.27 STRENGTH: L GED: R2 M1 L1 SVP: 2 DLU: 77

789.687-182   TURNER (any industry) alternate titles: clipper and turner

Turns articles, such as clothing, clothing parts, coin purse linings, stuffed toy shells, or textile bags, right side out, according to one of following methods: (1) Pulls article or part downward over lower vertical rod of holding device and folds end of article or part over end of rod. Depresses pedal that closes jaws of holding device and pulls article upward, over upper rod, to reverse it. Releases pedal and removes article from upper rod. (2) Places end or edge of article over rod or form and draws rest of article downward over rod or form to reverse it. (3) Slides article over pipe and pushes end of article through pipe, using rod. (4) Reverses article by hand. May clip loose threads and thread between chain-sewn articles, using scissors. May turn bags over form equipped with blade to cut thread between chain-sewn bags. May insert gathering string into hem of bags, using needle. May turn garments having closed portions, using air-activated suction tube. May be designated according to article or part turned as Belt Turner (garment); Collar Turner (garment); Cuff Turner (knitting); Hose Turner (knitting); Inverter-And-Clipper (leather prod.); Necktie Turner (garment); Reverser (tex. prod., nec).

GOE: 06.04.27 STRENGTH: L GED: R1 M1 L1 SVP: 2 DLU: 78

79 BENCHWORK OCCUPATIONS, N.E.C.

This division includes benchwork occupations, not elsewhere classified.

790 OCCUPATIONS IN PREPARATION OF FOOD, TOBACCO, AND RELATED PRODUCTS, N.E.C.

This group includes occupations, not elsewhere classified, concerned with preparing food, tobacco, and related products.

790.134-010 SUPERVISOR, CIGAR MAKING, HAND (tobacco)
Supervises and coordinates activities of workers engaged in inspecting wrappers, rolling bunches, and wrapping bunches with wrapper leaves to produce handmade cigars. Confers with other department supervisors to coordinate flow of filler, binder, and wrapper tobacco into department. Reads production schedule to determine style, length, diameter, and color wrapper required for daily cigar production. Measures length, diameter, and weight of cigars, using gauge and scales, and examines wrapper leaves and bundles to ensure company standards are met. Trains new workers and maintains production records. Performs other duties as described under SUPERVISOR (any industry) Master Title.
GOE: 06.04.01 STRENGTH: L GED: R3 M2 L3 SVP: 6 DLU: 77

790.381-010 TOBACCO BLENDER (retail trade)
Blends various kinds of tobacco to customers' orders or for sale in retail establishment, using formulas: Pours tobaccos on table or into mixing box. Removes sticks and off-colored grains. Kneads tobaccos or shakes tobaccos in mixing box to effect blend. Squeezes handful of tobacco into wad and observes it unraveling or through magnifying lens to determine moisture content. Sprays tobacco with oils, cloves, and other spices and kneads tobacco to blend in flavoring. Pours blend into can and seals it. Records method of packing and contents of can on tag and attaches to can. Weighs and packs tobacco in canister or pocket-sized cans, boxes, and bags.
GOE: 05.10.08 STRENGTH: M GED: R3 M2 L2 SVP: 6 DLU: 77

790.684-010 BUNCH MAKER, HAND (tobacco) alternate titles: binder roller; binder; bunch breaker; buncher, hand
Rolls cigar filler and binder leaves into bunches preparatory to wrapping: Tears or cuts section of binder leaf to specified size. Rolls filler between palms and binder around filler to form bunch. Applies glue or twists end of binder to secure binder. Places bunches in molds and secures top on molds to compress bunches to specific size and shape.
GOE: 06.04.28 STRENGTH: L GED: R2 M2 L1 SVP: 4 DLU: 77

790.684-014 CIGAR MAKER (tobacco) alternate titles: finished-cigar maker; out-and-out cigar maker, hand; stogie maker, hand
Rolls cigars by hand: Rolls filler, wraps filler with binder [BUNCH MAKER, HAND (tobacco)], and wraps bunch with wrapper leaf [ROLLER, HAND (tobacco)]. Presses cigars in molds to obtain finished shape [MOLD PRESSER (tobacco)].
GOE: 06.04.28 STRENGTH: L GED: R2 M2 L2 SVP: 5 DLU: 77

790.684-018 PATCH WORKER (tobacco) alternate titles: cigar patcher; patcher; reroller, hand
Repairs defective or damaged cigars: Examines rejected cigars for defects, such as holes, loose seams, color spots, and loose tucks. Cuts out color spots. Pastes piece of wrapper leaf of matching color on cigar to patch holes. Pastes loose seams together. Discards unrepairable cigars. May open rejected cigars to salvage tobacco [REJECT OPENER (tobacco)].
GOE: 06.04.28 STRENGTH: L GED: R2 M1 L1 SVP: 3 DLU: 77

790.684-022 ROLLER, HAND (tobacco) alternate titles: cigar roller; suction-plate roller, hand; suction roller; wrapper, hand
Rolls wrapper tobacco leaves around bunches to make cigars: Smooths wrapper leaf on table and cuts leaf to specified shapes, using template and knife. Lays bunches on wrapper and rolls them together. Secures end of wrapper with glue and trims cigar to specified length, using knife or cigar cutter. Places cigars in rack.
GOE: 06.04.28 STRENGTH: L GED: R2 M2 L2 SVP: 5 DLU: 77

790.687-010 CANDY CUTTER, HAND (sugar & conf.)
Cuts candy into squares, using knife consisting of series of disk blades evenly spaced on shaft with handle at each end. Dips knife in water periodically to prevent candy from adhering to knife. May separate pieces of candy and arrange them on trays. May be designated according to candy cut as Caramel Cutter, Hand (sugar & conf.).
GOE: 06.04.28 STRENGTH: L GED: R2 M1 L1 SVP: 2 DLU: 77

790.687-014 CIGAR PACKER (tobacco) alternate titles: cigar packer and grader; cigar packer and picker; cigar packer and shader; cigar packer and sorter; cigar sorter
Sorts cigars according to color and loads cigars in handpress prior to wrapping in cellophane and banding: Examines cigars to detect variations in color and lays them in separate piles. Places cigars of same color in press box, placing paper strip and board or cardboard between successive layers. Places board over top row of cigars and sets box in press. Turns handwheel of press to apply pressure to box. May inspect cigars for imperfections. May keep record of ci-

gars received. May be designated by type of cigar packed as Stogie Packer (tobacco).
GOE: 06.04.28 STRENGTH: L GED: R2 M1 L2 SVP: 3 DLU: 77

790.687-018 LUMP INSPECTOR (tobacco) alternate titles: lump receiver
Inspects lumps of tobacco for defects in wrapper leaf, such as holes and rough spots. Repairs tears or holes in wrapper leaf, using glue and piece of wrapper leaf. May stack lumps on handtruck.
GOE: 06.03.02 STRENGTH: L GED: R2 M1 L1 SVP: 2 DLU: 77

790.687-022 MOLD PRESSER (tobacco) alternate titles: mold carrier
Distributes scrap tobacco to BUNCH MAKER, HAND (tobacco) or BUNCH MAKER, MACHINE (tobacco) and presses bunches in molds, using handpress: Pushes cases of tobacco to machine and scoops tobacco into machine hopper. Carries press molds to worker and removes molds filled with bunches. Positions filled molds in handpress and turns handle of press to compress bunches into uniform cigar shape. Loads compressed bunches onto handtruck for BUNCH TRIMMER, MOLD (tobacco).
GOE: 06.04.28 STRENGTH: M GED: R2 M1 L1 SVP: 2 DLU: 77

790.687-026 REJECT OPENER (tobacco) alternate titles: reject opener and filler
Opens rejected cigars to reclaim tobacco: Opens wrapper and examines bunch to determine whether bunch can be rewrapped. Places bunches that can be rewrapped in box. Opens defective bunches and places filler and binder tobacco in separate boxes for reuse.
GOE: 06.04.28 STRENGTH: L GED: R2 M1 L1 SVP: 3 DLU: 77

790.687-030 TWISTER, HAND (tobacco) alternate titles: hand roller; tobacco roller; twist maker
Rolls leaves of tobacco together to form twists of chewing tobacco: Overlaps leaves of tobacco on table and rolls leaves together or places filler tobacco on leaves and rolls leaves over filler to form roll, using fingers and palms of hands. Folds roll in middle and rolls again to form twist. Periodically weighs twists to determine whether weight is within prescribed limits.
GOE: 06.04.28 STRENGTH: L GED: R1 M1 L1 SVP: 2 DLU: 77

794 OCCUPATIONS IN FABRICATION OF PAPER PRODUCTS, N.E.C.

This group includes occupations, not elsewhere classified, concerned with such activities as assembling boxes and envelopes from precut blanks and assembling party favors.

794.684-010 BAG REPAIRER (paper goods)
Repairs defective paper bags and tubes by sewing, gluing, valving, and sleeving: Inspects and sorts bags according to type of repair needed to remedy defect. Removes and replaces defective sleeves, repastes seams with handbrush, or resews seams with sewing machine. Sets aside repaired articles and discards bags and tubes that cannot be repaired.
GOE: 06.04.26 STRENGTH: L GED: R2 M1 L1 SVP: 2 DLU: 77

794.684-014 BOX MAKER, PAPERBOARD (any industry)
Fabricates cartons, boxes, and other paper products from laminated, corrugated, or plain paperboard materials: Measures and marks or traces outline of carton on paperboard sheet, using template, pattern, ruler, and marking pencil. Cuts sheets along markings to form carton blanks, using bandsaw or papercutter. Feeds blanks or paperboard sheets into machines that slit, score, slot, form, or glue them, or folds blanks along scored lines and tapes or stitches (staples) edges together to form cartons. Assembles and fits slotted pieces together to form partitions for cartons. Glues strips of cellophane on carton to form windows in container. Counts specified number of cartons and ties them into bundles for shipment, using twine or wire. May glue linen strips to tops and backs of boxes to form hinges. May paste or glue paper edgings or linings to boxes to form trimmings.
GOE: 06.04.26 STRENGTH: M GED: R2 M1 L1 SVP: 2 DLU: 77

794.684-018 EXPANSION ENVELOPE MAKER, HAND (paper goods)
Scores, folds, glues, and assembles precut cardboard blanks and cloth tape to make expanding envelopes, performing any combination of following tasks: Glues cloth tape to edges of strips of cardboard to reinforce expanding side pieces (gussets) of envelopes. Scores cardboard strips, using hand operated scoring machine or handtool, and bends gussets along scored lines to make accordion fold and attachment flaps. Scores and folds cardboard lining blanks along edges to make surface for attachment of gussets. Feeds lining blanks into machine that gums edges or spreads glue on edges with brush. Positions gummed lining edges and gusset flaps together on forming block and places them in screw press or feeds them under roller press to seal them together. Feeds envelope front and back sections into glue spreading machine to coat edges with glue and assembles sections with gussets and linings on wood form to complete expanding envelope. May be designated according to part produced as Gusset Maker (paper goods); or according to type of envelope as Five-Piece-Expansion Maker, Hand (paper goods); One-Piece-Expansion Maker, Hand (paper goods).
GOE: 06.04.26 STRENGTH: L GED: R2 M1 L1 SVP: 2 DLU: 77

794.684-022 PAPER-NOVELTY MAKER (paper goods) alternate titles: copyist; novelty maker
Makes paper candy and nut cups and miscellaneous paper novelties, such as hats, placecards, and party favors: Cuts out paper with scissors, using samples

or patterns as guides. Folds and pleats paper by hand. Pastes parts together. May use sewing machine to pleat and stitch parts together to form completed item. May originate new designs.
GOE: 06.02.26 STRENGTH: L GED: R2 M1 L1 SVP: 2 DLU: 77

794.684-026 PAPIER MACHE MOLDER (fabrication, nec) alternate titles: paper layer
Builds up display forms of papier mache sheets: Greases inside of form-mold halves with brush. Coats one side of papier mache sheets with paste and tears sheets into pieces to fit mold. Lays unpasted side of sheet against inside of mold and presses it in place by hand, leaving lap projections at side of mold. Builds up form to desired thickness, fitting and smoothing each sheet to mold. Places halves of mold together, pastes and presses lap projections of each half of form together, and removes completed form from molds. Pastes and papers neck and skirt openings of form to smooth edges.
GOE: 06.02.26 STRENGTH: L GED: R3 M2 L2 SVP: 4 DLU: 77

794.684-030 SAMPLE MAKER, HAND (paper goods)
Fabricates sample paper or polyethylene bags by hand for use by sales department: Cuts, folds, and fastens bags, adds eyelets, and attaches handles, according to specifications, using rules, scissors, and paste brushes.
GOE: 06.04.26 STRENGTH: S GED: R2 M1 L2 SVP: 3 DLU: 77

794.687-010 ASSEMBLER, PRINTED PRODUCTS (print. & pub.)
Assembles printed products, such as cards, programs, menus, wedding and business invitations, and calendars, performing any combination of following tasks: Assembles and folds printed sheets or cards into various shapes or designs. Attaches seals, lace, sachet bags, ribbon, or other paper or metallic inserts on specified products, using glue, plastic tape, or staples. Applies glue to folded edges of product with brush. Glues and inserts sheets on specified products by machine. Examines finished products for defects. May trim products to specified size, using trimming machine. May insert envelope into fold of card. May box and wrap cards and other products. May be classified according to products assembled and be classified Assembler, Cards and Announcements (print. & pub.). May be classified according to method of assembly and be designated Hand Worker (print. & pub.).
GOE: 06.04.26 STRENGTH: L GED: R2 M1 L1 SVP: 2 DLU: 86

794.687-014 COLOR-CARD MAKER (paint & varnish)
Cuts cards from colored sheets, using paper cutter, and mounts cards on color-advertising folders: Cuts sheets into cards of specified dimensions, using paper cutter. Sorts cards into stacks according to color. Positions cards in handpress according to color section-number on card folder. Brushes glue on back of cards. Positions card folder over cards and pulls lever to close press and glue cards to folder. Removes folder from press and stacks it on table.
GOE: 06.04.26 STRENGTH: L GED: R2 M1 L1 SVP: 2 DLU: 77

794.687-018 COUNTER, HAND (paper goods)
Counts sheets of paper, using fingers to separate fanned edges into groups of threes, fours, or fives, to facilitate counting. Separates sheets into units of specified quantity and stacks units on pallets or conveyors. May collate covers with filler sheets to facilitate fabrication of tablets.
GOE: 06.03.02 STRENGTH: L GED: R2 M1 L2 SVP: 3 DLU: 77

794.687-022 FOLDER, HAND (paper goods) alternate titles: envelope folder; hand folder; table worker
Folds, gums, and finishes by hand die-cut blanks to make envelopes: Scores blank, using spatula or scoring tool. Folds envelope blanks according to pattern and creases folds by hand or with spatula. Applies gum to edges of flaps with brush or stick and seals flaps before gum dries. Applies gum to open flap with stick and allows it to dry. Folds down open flaps and packs completed envelopes in specified boxes. May attach cellophane strips or other decorations to envelopes by hand.
GOE: 06.04.26 STRENGTH: L GED: R2 M1 L1 SVP: 3 DLU: 77

794.687-026 FORWARDER (print. & pub.)
Trims and rounds sewed signatures and pastes covers on signatures to form books: Trims edges of sewed signatures. Rounds back of sewed signatures by working outer signatures forward toward fore-edge with fingers and pounding back into required curvature with hammer. Pastes end papers on book covers and pastes covers on sewed signatures to form finished books. May be designated according to type of book completed as Blankbook Forwarder (print. & pub.).
GOE: 06.04.26 STRENGTH: L GED: R2 M1 L1 SVP: 3 DLU: 77

794.687-030 GLUER AND SLICER, HAND (paper goods)
Glues one end of stack of paper and slices stack into sections for making such products as legal tablets, notebooks, and scratch pads: Brushes coat of glue on end of stack, covers end with cheesecloth and brushes glue over cheesecloth. Pushes stack along conveyor into drying chamber. Slices sections from stack, using slicing knife and stacks them on skids. May not cover end of stack with cheesecloth when gluing such items as scratch pads.
GOE: 06.04.26 STRENGTH: H GED: R2 M1 L1 SVP: 2 DLU: 77

794.687-034 PAPER-PATTERN FOLDER (paper goods)
Folds pattern pieces for complete garment and inserts them into envelope for shipment.
GOE: 06.04.26 STRENGTH: L GED: R1 M1 L1 SVP: 1 DLU: 77

794.687-038 PATTERN RULER (tex. prod., nec)
Scores and folds crease lines on pleat patterns: Positions straightedge along punched holes in pattern and scores pattern with scriber. Folds pattern at crease lines to form pleats.

GOE: 06.04.27 STRENGTH: L GED: R1 M1 L1 SVP: 2 DLU: 77

794.687-042 PUNCHBOARD ASSEMBLER I (paper goods) alternate titles: punchboard inserter; punchboard stuffer
Inserts numbered pieces of creased paper into holes of cardboard punchboards, and tokens or coins in holes at top of boards and covers tokens or coins with transparent material. Staples wooden punch to base of card.
GOE: 06.04.23 STRENGTH: L GED: R2 M1 L1 SVP: 2 DLU: 77

794.687-046 PUNCHBOARD ASSEMBLER II (paper goods)
Combines perforated cardboard sheets to make punchboards by inserting sheets, to which glue has been applied, over pins of metal plate to align them and pressing sheets together, using piece of metal.
GOE: 06.04.23 STRENGTH: L GED: R1 M1 L1 SVP: 1 DLU: 77

794.687-050 SCRAPPER (paper goods) alternate titles: air-hammer stripper; breaker; knocker-off; peeler
Removes excess material from prescored cardboard carton blanks, performing any combination of following duties: Strips waste from blanks stacked on pallet, using airhammer and chisel. Places edge of chisel on cutting mark at top of stack and pushes hammer down through stack to remove excess material. Places stack of precut blanks on worktable and strikes edge with hammer to knock out scored corners or edges. Places stack of trimmed blanks on worktable and brushes edges of stack with steel brush or sandpaper. Removes damaged or defective blanks. Strikes flap edges with hammer to bend flaps. Piles smoothed blanks on pallet and removes to storage area, using handtruck.
GOE: 06.04.39 STRENGTH: H GED: R2 M1 L1 SVP: 2 DLU: 77

794.687-054 STRINGER (paper goods) alternate titles: hand worker
Adds wire tie or binding string to paper tags by tying or twisting precut lengths of string or wire through holes in ends of tag. May count tags and tie them into bundles of prescribed number. May be designated according to type of tag as Garment-Tag Stringer (paper goods).
GOE: 06.04.23 STRENGTH: L GED: R1 M1 L1 SVP: 1 DLU: 77

794.687-058 TABBER (paper goods) alternate titles: inserter; tagger
Inserts paper identification tabs into slots of guide devices attached to index filecards.
GOE: 06.04.23 STRENGTH: L GED: R1 M1 L1 SVP: 1 DLU: 77

794.687-062 TRIMMER, HAND (paper goods)
Pulls or cuts with scissors excess paper from edges of paper doilies as they are ejected from fabricating machine. Counts and bundles trimmed doilies.
GOE: 06.04.26 STRENGTH: L GED: R1 M1 L1 SVP: 1 DLU: 77

795 GLUING OCCUPATIONS, N.E.C.

This group includes occupations concerned with fastening together assorted materials by the application of viscid (sticky) substances such as glue, paste, or gum and the positioning of these materials together. Occupations concerned with assembling complete products, such as furniture, plywood, and fiberglass are not included here but are listed under their respective groups.

795.684-014 EDGE STRIPPER (paper goods; wood. container) alternate titles: edger
Glues strips of printed paper trim onto box edges: Lays paper edging strips on table, printed side down, and brushes on paste or glue. Aligns strip on edge of box so that edge bisects strip, smooths strip down on either side of edge, folds strip at corners, and continues applying strip until all edges of box and lid are trimmed.
GOE: 06.04.26 STRENGTH: S GED: R2 M1 L2 SVP: 4 DLU: 77

795.684-018 GLOBE MOUNTER (print. & pub.)
Pastes segments of world map over spherical forms to make globes delineating surface of earth: Mixes prescribed amounts of flour and water to make paste. Spreads paste on glass plate with handbrush, and places gores (segments) of printed map on glass plate to soak and absorb paste. Mounts gores on marked globe and smooths gores with burnishing iron. Sponges excess paste from finished globe with water and sets it aside to dry.
GOE: 06.04.26 STRENGTH: L GED: R2 M1 L1 SVP: 3 DLU: 77

795.684-022 TIPPER (print. & pub.) alternate titles: gluer; hand gluer
Glues together edges of printed business forms, using glueboard and gluepot applicator: Adjusts slots in glueboard to accommodate width of sheets to be glued. Positions applicator pins in gluepot to apply glue to edges of forms at specified points. Inserts paper sheets singly into slot at top of gluepot and moves lever, causing spreading pins to apply glue to edge of sheet. Positions sheet in slot of glueboard and presses it against preceding sheet until specified number of forms are assembled in numerical sequence. Removes completed forms and places on rack. Counts out assembled forms into round lots for shipment. Records number and kind of forms assembled during shift.
GOE: 06.04.26 STRENGTH: L GED: R2 M2 L1 SVP: 3 DLU: 77

795.684-026 WADER-BOOT-TOP ASSEMBLER (rubber goods) alternate titles: boot-liner maker; suit maker
Cements precut rubber and rubberized fabric parts to fabricate wader boot tops and boot liners for rubber boots: Selects parts according to worksheet and lays them on workbench for cementing. Brushes rubber cement on edges to be joined or brushes benzine over previously applied adhesive to restore tackiness,

and assembles cemented parts in specified sequence to form complete article. Pulls boot liner over last and cements on sole piece. Trims excess material, using scissors. Places strip of gum rubber over joined seam and rolls it to make firm bond, using handroller. Attaches eyelets and snap buttons at designated points, using grommeting machine. Hangs completed article on rack for cement to dry. Marks around template on spare stock and cuts out needed parts, such as straps or reinforcement tabs, using scissors.
GOE: 06.04.29 STRENGTH: L GED: R2 M1 L2 SVP: 2 DLU: 77

795.687-010 COVERER, LOOSELEAF BINDER (print. & pub.)
Glues simulated leather, plastic, or other material over cardboard fillers to make covers for looseleaf binders, using automatic gluing machine and handtools: Fills glue reservoir, starts machine, and feeds precut sheets of material through rollers to spread glue over surface. Removes glued sheets and arranges them on worktable. Places center angle iron at specified position on glued cover sheet and presses it down on glue. Positions cardboard filler over cover sheet and folds protruding margins back over edges of filler. Presses ends of cover with flat handtool and taps corner folds with hammer to flatten and smooth them. Presses glued cover down over inside ends of angle iron. May apply paper or fabric lining over inside of covers.
GOE: 06.04.27 STRENGTH: L GED: R2 M2 L1 SVP: 4 DLU: 77

795.687-014 GLUER (any industry) alternate titles: cementer
Glues material such as paper, cloth, leather, wood, metal, glass, rubber, or plastic together, following specified procedures: Applies adhesive to surface of material by brushing, spraying, dipping, rolling, holding material against rotating saturated brush, or feeding part between saturated rollers. Presses glued materials together manually, presses material with hand roller, or clamps materials in fixture to bond material together and set glue. May perform limited assembly of preglued material. May trim excess material from cemented parts. May wipe surplus adhesive from seams, using cloth or sponge. May visually inspect completed work. May be designated according to article glued as Arrow-Point Attacher (toy-sport equip.); Gasket Attacher (machinery mfg.); Nock Applier (toy-sport equip.); Pad Attacher (any industry); Sample Mounter (any industry); or according to gluing method used as Adhesive Sprayer (any industry). May be designated: Box Coverer, Hand (paper goods); Glue Spreader (furniture); Paper-Cone Maker (electron. comp.); Rubber Attacher (toy-sport equip.).

GOE: 06.04.34 STRENGTH: L GED: R1 M1 L1 SVP: 2 DLU: 89

795.687-018 GLUER, WET SUIT (plastic prod.)
Glues together precut pieces of rubberized plastic to assemble skindiving outfits, such as wet suits, hoods, and jackets, forming watertight, bonded seams after subsequent curing.
GOE: 06.04.29 STRENGTH: L GED: R2 M1 L1 SVP: 2 DLU: 77

795.687-022 LINING CEMENTER (hat & cap)
Cements lining to caps and hats, performing any combination of following tasks: Brushes cement onto base of crown or underside of sweatband, positions lining in crown of hat, and presses with fingers to smooth and join lining to crown. Applies paste to linings of cap visors, using brush, and applies lacquered cloth covering to linings to complete visor assembly. Pours glue onto glass plate, presses dowel pins of spotting jig onto plate, presses jig against cardboard, and positions lining tip on cardboard to affix lining to cardboard. Applies paste to cardboard squares and manually presses silk hat lining to squares.
GOE: 06.04.27 STRENGTH: L GED: R1 M1 L1 SVP: 1 DLU: 78

795.687-026 TENNIS-BALL COVERER, HAND (toy-sport equip.) alternate titles: felt coverer; felter, tennis balls
Cements felt covers to molded rubber balls to produce tennis balls: Aligns and smooths pieces of previously glued and cut felt over molded ball to cover ball. Rolls ball between palm and workbench or strokes cover with dull implement to secure felt to ball.
GOE: 06.04.27 STRENGTH: L GED: R2 M1 L1 SVP: 2 DLU: 77

795.687-030 TENNIS-BALL-COVER CEMENTER (toy-sport equip.) alternate titles: felt cementer
Spreads cement on rolls of felt used to cover tennis balls: Unrolls roll of felt on steamtable, securing edges to table with hooks to keep it straight and uniform. Applies cement to felt with leather strap, spreading cement over surface with handbrush. Allows first coat to set, applies second, and rerolls felt. May thin cement with gasoline or benzol. Wears gas mask when fumes become too objectionable.
GOE: 06.04.34 STRENGTH: L GED: R1 M1 L1 SVP: 2 DLU: 77

8 STRUCTURAL WORK OCCUPATIONS

This category includes occupations concerned with fabricating, erecting, installing, paving, painting, repairing, and similarly working structures or structural parts, such as bridges, buildings, roads, transportation equipment frames and structures, cables, girders, plates, and frames. The work generally occurs outside a factory or shop environment, except for factory production line occupations concerned with fabricating, installing, erecting, or repairing structures. Tools used are handtools or portable power tools, and such materials as wood, metal, concrete, glass, and clay are involved. Stationary machines are frequently used in structural work occupations, but the worker's relationship to machines is usually secondary in importance as compared to use of handtools and portable power tools. Workers are frequently required to have a knowledge of the materials with which they work, e.g., stresses, strains, durability, and resistance to weather.

80   OCCUPATIONS IN METAL FABRICATING, N.E.C.

This division includes occupations concerned with fabricating, erecting, and repairing building frames and ornamental metalwork, bridges, trestles, marine craft and structures, boilers, storage tanks, drilling rigs, towers, and other structures generally assembled from heavy structural plates, beams, and castings; fitting and assembling vehicle bodies, airframes, prefabricated door casings and window frames, air ducts, and other structural units assembled from stock or preformed sheet metal and structural shapes; and assembling or repairing boats, automobile bodies, and other structural units partially or entirely constructed of rigid plastics or fiberglass.

800   RIVETERS, N.E.C.

This group includes occupations, not elsewhere classified, concerned with joining structural shapes and members with rivets.

800.662-010 RIVETER, HYDRAULIC (any industry) alternate titles: bull riveter; hydraulic-bull-riveter operator; multiple-pressure-riveter operator

Operates hydraulic riveting machine to rivet steel plate sections together: Selects dies according to size of rivet and type of head to be formed and installs dies in machine, using wrench. Signals RIVETER HELPER (any industry) to hoist plates into position, line up rivet holes with rivet die, insert hot rivets in holes, and hold metal bar or die against rivet head. Starts machine and adjusts valve to regulate pressure according to size of rivet. Moves lever to force piston and die against rivet shank to form head. May operate portable machine and be designated Riveter, Portable Machine (any industry).
GOE: 06.02.02 STRENGTH: M GED: R3 M1 L1 SVP: 5 DLU: 77

800.682-010 RIVETER, PORTABLE PINCH (any industry)

Operates pinch riveting machine to rivet together plates, castings, and structures, such as bars, beams, and rounds: Pulls and clamps pulley rope to position pinch riveter, suspended from monorail, at work level. Installs specified dies in bed and ram of rivet press, and turns bolt to set specified gap between dies, using wrench. Slides press along monorail to position dies over rivets. Starts press to lower ram that spreads and shapes rivet shank.
GOE: 06.02.02 STRENGTH: M GED: R3 M1 L1 SVP: 4 DLU: 77

800.684-010 RIVETER (railroad equip.)

Rivets structural members, assemblies, and parts of railroad cars, using portable riveting, dimpling, and drilling machines and handtools: Reads work orders, blueprints, and operation sheets to determine sequence of operations and type size and hole pattern of rivets. Removes temporary bolts or fasteners and inserts rivets in predrilled holes. Places drive head of rivet gun against rivet shank and pulls trigger to actuate hammer that spreds rivet, or spreads rivet, using rivet set and hammer. Rivets together adjoining edges of parts and assemblies, using portable rivet squeezer. Places two dies of rivet squeezer over head and shank of rivet, and presses trigger to activate dies that flatten shank of rivet. Drills and reams rivet holes and drills out defective rivets. Forms dimples around rivet holes, using portable dimpling gun or stationary dimpling machine. May align and assemble parts to be riveted, using jigs, holding fixtures, pins, clamps, and fasteners. May buck rivets.
GOE: 05.10.01 STRENGTH: M GED: R3 M1 L1 SVP: 4 DLU: 77

800.684-014 RIVETER, PNEUMATIC (any industry)

Rivets together parts, such as structures, plates, and castings, using pneumatic hammer: Inserts die, corresponding to size of rivet head, in head of hammer. Places die against shank of rivet held in hole by RIVETER HELPER (any industry) or by clamping fixture, and presses trigger to pound and shape head on rivet shank. May place rivet set (steel bar with cup-shaped end) over shank and strike set with sledge to shape rivet. May clean or align rivet holes, using metal dowel in pneumatic hammer. May bolt parts together, using wrench and nut runner. May remove and replace defective rivets, using cutting torch, power tools, and riveting equipment.
GOE: 05.10.01 STRENGTH: H GED: R3 M1 L1 SVP: 4 DLU: 77

800.687-010 RIVETER HELPER (any industry) alternate titles: rivet bucker; rivet catcher; rivet sticker

Performs any combination of following tasks to assist in riveting structural parts or assemblies together: Lifts structural parts into position for riveting, using hoist. Aligns rivet holes, using clamps, duft pins, and hammer. Bolts parts together to temporarily secure structure for riveting, using impact wrench. Pushes riveting machine along monorail to position machine over rivet. Reams misaligned rivet holes, using portable drill and hand reamer. Positions rivets in rivet holes or catches hot rivets thrown by RIVET HEATER (heat treating), using bucket, and inserts rivets into holes, using tongs. Presses metal bucking bar or die against rivet head to maintain position of rivet in hole. Heats bucking bar, using gas torch, and shapes bar according to specifications, using handtools. Removes temporary fitting bolts and unsatisfactory rivets, using cutting torch and handtools. Performs other duties as described under HELPER (any industry) Master Title.
GOE: 05.12.12 STRENGTH: H GED: R2 M1 L1 SVP: 3 DLU: 77

801   FITTING, BOLTING, SCREWING, AND RELATED OCCUPATIONS

This group includes occupations concerned with joining structural parts and components with bolts, screws, and related fasteners, or by fitting (placing) reinforcing steel or iron in forms to strengthen concrete. Fitting, bolting, screwing, and related occupations concerned with the assembly of transportation equipment only are included in Group 806.

801.131-010 SUPERVISOR, CHIMNEY CONSTRUCTION (construction)

Supervises and coordinates activities of workers engaged in constructing reinforced concrete chimneys and similar structures: Reads blueprints and measures distances to lay out chimney. Directs workers in setting forms, erecting and wiring reinforcing steel, pouring and puddling concrete, and advancing scaffolding as erection of chimney progresses. Observes progress of work to ensure safety of installations and conformance of work to specifications. Verifies dimensions, using rule and spirit level. Performs other duties as described under SUPERVISOR (any industry) Master Title.
GOE: 05.05.01 STRENGTH: L GED: R4 M3 L2 SVP: 8 DLU: 77

801.131-014 SUPERVISOR, FITTING (any industry)

Supervises and coordinates activities of workers engaged in aligning and fitting component parts to assemble fabricated metal products, applying knowledge of product design, layout, strength of materials, and properties of metal: Reads blueprint specifications to determine assembly sequence. Requisitions equipment, such as jigs, base blocks, and rigging, and assigns equipment to workers according to work performed. Trains workers in performance of tasks, such as laying out, fitting, and aligning fabricated metal parts. Performs other duties as described under SUPERVISOR (any industry) Master Title.
GOE: 06.02.01 STRENGTH: L GED: R4 M4 L3 SVP: 8 DLU: 77

801.131-018 SUPERVISOR, RIDE ASSEMBLY (amuse. & rec.)

Supervises and coordinates activities of circus or carnival workers engaged in assembling and disassembling mechanical rides, such as ferris wheel and merry-go-round: Hooks up electrical connections to power source, lubricates moving parts, and inspects equipment for safety. May operate ride. Performs other duties as described under SUPERVISOR (any industry) Master Title.
GOE: 05.12.15 STRENGTH: M GED: R4 M2 L2 SVP: 7 DLU: 77

801.134-010 SUPERVISOR, REINFORCED-STEEL-PLACING (construction) alternate titles: supervisor, ironworking; supervisor, metal placing; supervisor, rod placing

Supervises and coordinates activities of workers engaged in placing reinforcing steel in forms to strengthen concrete. Reads blueprints and measures forms to ensure that steel rods or wire mesh are positioned according to specifications. Performs other duties as described under SUPERVISOR (any industry) Master Title.
GOE: 05.05.06 STRENGTH: L GED: R4 M3 L3 SVP: 8 DLU: 77

801.137-010 SUPERVISOR, ASSEMBLY (agric. equip.)

Supervises and coordinates activities of workers engaged in assembling balers, combines, motors, tractors, lawn mowers, rotary tillers, and other agri-

cultural and lawn/garden machines and equipment: Coordinates work of production and stock control departments to maintain flow of material to assembly line. Inspects defective parts and directs routing of rejects to salvage or rework department. Investigates and determines causes of assembly defects and orders corrective action. Studies present layout of equipment to effect changeover of assembly line for processing new models. Performs other duties as described under SUPERVISOR (any industry) Master Title. May be designated according to component assembled as Motor-Assembly Supervisor (agric. equip.).
GOE: 06.02.01 STRENGTH: L GED: R4 M3 L2 SVP: 7 DLU: 77

801.137-014 SUPERVISOR, INSPECTION (agric. equip.)

Supervises and coordinates activities of workers engaged in inspecting agricultural equipment for defects. Evaluates defective inspected parts to determine disposition, and directs routing of rejects to salvage or rework department. Performs duties as described under SUPERVISOR (any industry) Master Title.
GOE: 06.01.01 STRENGTH: L GED: R4 M3 L3 SVP: 7 DLU: 77

801.261-010 ASSEMBLER, MINING MACHINERY (machinery mfg.) alternate titles: assembler, hydraulic backhoe; assembler, portable oil-well drilling rig; hydraulic and mechanical assembler

Assembles mining machinery, such as continuous miners, loading machines, cutting machines, locomotives, hydraulic backhoes, and portable oil well drilling rigs according to blueprints and written specifications, using handtools, power handtools, and other powered equipment: Reads blueprints and written specifications to plan assembly sequence. Operates crane or directs OVERHEAD CRANE OPERATOR (any industry) 921.663-010 to move structural framework and machine parts to assembly area. Studies blueprints to plan logical assembly sequence. Positions specified gears, drive shafts, bearings, clutches, and other component parts in housings on frame of machine, using electric hoist. Aligns and levels parts with spacers and shims, and sets clearance between parts, using micrometers, feeler gauges, calipers, and scale. Bolts cover plates, electric motors, and hydraulic pumps to machine frame in specified locations, using torque wrench. Lays out hydraulic hose on machine, away from moving parts, to facilitate servicing machine and connects hydraulic hose to pumps and specified fittings, using wrench. May measure and cut hydraulic hose for installation in machine. May clean parts preparatory to assembly, using solvent, cleaning cloths, and air gun. May assemble and test subassemblies, such as drive shaft, clutch, and transmission, using acetylene welding, heating, and cutting equipment and test stands. May install electrical wiring in assembled units according to schematic drawings. May drive mobile machinery to test performance.
GOE: 05.05.09 STRENGTH: M GED: R4 M4 L3 SVP: 7 DLU: 77

801.261-014 FITTER I (any industry) alternate titles: jig fitter; bridge worker; housesmith; iron erector; ironworker; steel erector; structural-iron erector; structural-iron worker; structural-steel erector

Lays out, positions, aligns, and fits together fabricated parts of structural metal products in shop, according to blueprint and layout specifications, preparatory to welding or riveting: Plans sequence of operation, applying knowledge of geometry, effects of heat, and allowances for weld shrinkage, machining, and thickness of metal. Sets up face block, jigs and fixtures. Locates and marks centerlines and reference points onto floor or face block and transposes them to workpiece, using tape, chains, plumb bob, and squares. Moves parts into position, manually or by hoist or crane. Aligns parts, using jack, turnbuckles, wedges, drift pins, pry bars, and hammer. Removes high spots and cuts bevels, using hand files, portable grinders, and cutting torch. Gives directions to WELDER, ARC (welding) to build up low spots or short pieces with weld. Straightens warped or bent parts, using sledge, hand torch, straightening press, or bulldozer. Positions or tightens braces, jacks, clamps, ropes, or bolt straps, or bolts parts in positions for welding or riveting. May use transit to locate reference points and erect ladders and scaffolding to fit together large assemblies. May tack weld and be designated Fitter-Tacker (any industry).
GOE: 05.05.06 STRENGTH: H GED: R4 M4 L2 SVP: 7 DLU: 77

801.261-018 ROTARY-ENGINE ASSEMBLER (engine-turbine)

Assembles and tests industrial rotary engines, following blueprints and using handtools and power tools: Inspects parts and housing to verify conformity to parts list and blueprint specifications, using micrometer, feeler gauges, and dial indicators. Inspects wiring harnesses for defects, rewires defective harnesses, and connects terminals of harness wires as indicated, following schematics. Tests and adjusts magnetos, using timing light. Dips parts into cleaning tank of ultrasonic cleaning equipment to clean part surfaces, and hones cleaned parts to smooth finish, using hand files and emery paper. Aligns housing on fixture, using jib crane and measuring tools, to position housing for insertion of parts, working as member of team. Sizes and finishes holes in housing and parts to specified tolerances, using power drills and reamers. Inserts or attaches and secures holding pins, seals, pipes, and tubing, using measuring instruments and handtools or power tools. Positions engine on test block, aligns engine with brake, and bolts engine to bed of block. Connects piping and attachments, using handtools, to supply engine with water, oil, fuel, and exhaust lines and systems during test operation. Connects test panel lines, starts engine, and observes gauges to verify that parts function according to specifications. May disassemble and repair engines. May fabricate engine parts.
GOE: 06.02.22 STRENGTH: H GED: R4 M3 L4 SVP: 6 DLU: 86

801.361-010 BLOWER AND COMPRESSOR ASSEMBLER (machinery mfg.)

Fits and aligns machined parts, such as bearings, diaphragms, impeller wheels, blower casings, shafts, and *gear cages* to assemble compressors, blowers, and vacuum pumps, according to drawings and specifications, using handtools, power drills, and portable gas heating equipment: Scrapes bearings to fit shafts, using hand scraper, blue chalk, and abrasive paper. Screws and bolts together mechanical parts, such as gears, vanes, needle bearings, and ring gear, to assemble gear cage assembly, using wrenches and screwdrivers. Shrinks impeller wheel, sleeves, spacers, and balance piston onto shaft to form spindle, using portable gas heating equipment. Caulks metal sealing strips into seams of impeller wheels, sleeves, and balance piston to form seal between impeller wheel and diaphragm, using hammer and caulking chisel. Lifts and positions spindle into casing (cylinder) to align diaphragm to spindle and upper and lower blower casing, using *lead wires*, micrometers, and calipers. Levels beams supporting bedplates over test pit, using transit, *master straightedge*, and levels. Aligns and levels blower, induction gear, oil tank, and drive unit on bedplate to mark mounting holes, using gauges, rules, punch, and scribes. Drills, taps, and reams holes for mounting bolts, coupling guards, and dowel pins, using portable drill press. Installs inlet and discharge piping to blower, using handtools, and attaches instruments, such as barometers, thermometers, pressure gauges, thermocouples, and speed indicator to blower. Dismantles unit from test pit and cleans and oils parts prior to shipment. Makes specified tests to determine blower performance, using electrical test equipment, and records instrument readings. May be designated according to equipment assembled as Compressor Assembler (machinery mfg.); Pump Assembler (machinery mfg.).
GOE: 06.02.22 STRENGTH: H GED: R4 M3 L3 SVP: 6 DLU: 77

801.361-014 STRUCTURAL-STEEL WORKER (construction)

Performs any combination of following duties to raise, place, and unite girders, columns, and other structural-steel members to form completed structures or structure frameworks, working as member of crew: Sets up hoisting equipment for raising and placing structural-steel members. Fastens steel members to cable of hoist, using chain, cable, or rope. Signals worker operating hoisting equipment to lift and place steel member. Guides member, using tab line (rope) or rides on member in order to guide it into position. Pulls, pushes, or pries steel members into approximate position while member is supported by hoisting device. Forces members into final position, using turnbuckles, crowbars, jacks, and handtools. Aligns rivet holes in member with corresponding holes in previously placed member by driving drift pins or handle of wrench through holes. Verifies vertical and horizontal alignment of members, using plumb bob and level. Bolts aligned members to keep them in position until they can be permanently riveted, bolted, or welded in place. Catches hot rivets tosssd by RIVET HEATER (heat treating) in bucket and inserts rivets in holes, using tongs. Bucks (holds) rivets while RIVETER, PNEUMATIC (any industry) uses airhammer to form heads on rivets. Cuts and welds steel members to make alterations, using oxyacetylene welding equipment. May specialize in erecting or repairing specific types of structures and be designated Bridge-Maintenance Worker (construction); Chimney Builder, Reinforced Concrete (construction); Scaffold Builder, Metal (construction); Structural-Steel-Equipment Erector (construction).
GOE: 05.05.06 STRENGTH: H GED: R3 M2 L3 SVP: 7 DLU: 77

801.361-018 STRUCTURAL-STEEL-WORKER APPRENTICE (construction) alternate titles: bridge worker apprentice; ironworker apprentice; steel-erector apprentice

Performs duties as described under APPRENTICE (any industry) Master Title.
GOE: 05.05.06 STRENGTH: H GED: R3 M2 L3 SVP: 7 DLU: 77

801.361-022 TANK SETTER (petrol. & gas) alternate titles: tank builder

Erects metal tanks used to store crude oil at oil fields, utilizing knowledge of overall construction techniques and using handtools: Directs helpers in grading area for tank base. Verifies grade, using spirit level. Bolts tank sections together and inserts felt or asbestos sealing strips between joints to assemble and erect tank bottoms, sides, and covers, using wrenches. Bolts attachments, such as ladders, pipe flanges, gauges, and valves, to tank, using wrenches. Directs helpers in erection of scaffolds and assembly of tank sections. May erect wooden tanks [TANK ERECTOR (construction)].
GOE: 05.05.06 STRENGTH: M GED: R4 M2 L2 SVP: 7 DLU: 77

801.381-010 ASSEMBLER, METAL BUILDING (construction)

Assembles prefabricated metal buildings according to blueprint specifications, using handtools, power tools, and hoisting equipment: Erects frame of building, using hoist. Bolts steel frame members together. Attaches wire and insulating materials to framework. Bolts sheet metal panels to framework. Reads blueprint to determine location of items, such as doors, windows, ventilators, and skylights and installs items, using cutting torch, wrenches, and power drill. Trims excess sheet metal, using cutting torch, power saw, and tin snips.
GOE: 05.05.06 STRENGTH: M GED: R3 M2 L2 SVP: 6 DLU: 77

801.381-014 FITTER (machine shop)

Fits and assembles structural frameworks and housings from materials, such as angle iron, I-beams, and plate steel, using handtools and welding equipment and following blueprint specifications: Examines blueprints and materials list to obtain parts specifications. Lays out parts dimensions on worktable, using square, chalk line, and soapstone. Tack-welds scrap metal to outline to provide

jig for assembly. Positions parts in jig and files, chisels, and grinds parts, as indicated, to fit them together. May heat parts with acetylene torch and bend them in vise, on anvil, or around stakes mounted in table. Tack-welds fitted parts together or directs FITTER HELPER (any industry) to tack-weld parts. May heat parts with acetylene torch and dip parts in cyanide bath to harden. Periodically compares dimensions of assembly to blueprint specifications, using square, rule, and calipers. Works to tolerances of .0625 inch. May anneal parts with acetylene torch to remove stresses of welding. May fasten parts together with acetylene torch and brazing rod.
GOE: 05.05.06 STRENGTH: M GED: R3 M3 L2 SVP: 7 DLU: 77

801.381-018   MAJOR-ASSEMBLY INSPECTOR (agric. equip.) alternate titles: assembly inspector; finished-goods inspector
Inspects parts and component assemblies of agricultural equipment, such as tractors and combines, for compliance with blueprint specifications, using precision measuring instruments: Inspects parts, such as housings, shafts, and gears, before assembly, for location and diameter of threaded holes, shaft diameter, and gear tooth angle and spacing, using micrometers, scales, and templates. Measures completed assemblies for fit and clearance of parts, using micrometers, calipers, height gauges, and rules. Examines parts for rough spots, casting flaws, and scratches. Records number of items rejected and reason for rejection.
GOE: 06.01.05 STRENGTH: M GED: R3 M2 L2 SVP: 6 DLU: 77

801.384-010   ASSEMBLER, WIRE-MESH GATE (metal prod., nec)
Fabricates frames from pipe stock and special fittings and installs wire mesh fencing to assemble gates, using handtools and power tools: Cuts pipe stock to specified size, using hacksaw, power saw, or pipe-cutting machine. Inserts pipe ends into corner fittings and verifies length of frame, using template. Drills holes through pipe and fittings and bolts them together, using power wrenches. Untwists wire, using pliers, and removes link to cut wire mesh to size, using hand shears. Inserts metal straps into terminal links of wire mesh. Fits clamps around metal straps and pipe. Stretches wire and bends clamp around pipe, using special handtool. Drills holes in frame and bolts scrolls and ornamental castings to gate. Finishes welded pipe joints, using file or hammer and chisel, and paints joints to retard rusting.
GOE: 06.02.22 STRENGTH: M GED: R3 M1 L1 SVP: 4 DLU: 77

801.663-010   ASSEMBLY-INSPECTOR HELPER (agric. equip.)
Assists ASSEMBLY INSPECTOR (agric. equip.) in testing power lawnmowers: Selects lawnmower for test run, according to instructions, and moves mower from assembly line to test area, using hoist. Pours fuel in tank and starts engine. Pushes or drives mower around test area and moves controls, such as gearshift and steering mechanisms on signal from ASSEMBLY INSPECTOR (agric. equip.). Places mower on shipping base, using hoist. Performs other duties as described under HELPER (any industry) Master Title.
GOE: 06.03.02 STRENGTH: L GED: R2 M1 L1 SVP: 3 DLU: 77

801.664-010   LINER REPLACER (mine & quarry; smelt. & refin.)
Replaces metal liners in ore processing equipment, such as mills, crushers, chutes, and hoppers, using handtools: Loosens worn liners, using wrenches. Signals OVERHEAD CRANE OPERATOR (any industry) 921.663-010 to remove old liner and position replacement. Adjusts new liner, using sledge, pry bar, and hydraulic jacks. Bolts liner in place, using wrenches. May tend furnace to melt zinc. May pour molten zinc onto inner surfaces of equipment to prepare equipment for new lining.
GOE: 05.12.12 STRENGTH: M GED: R2 M1 L1 SVP: 3 DLU: 77

801.664-014   UTILITY WORKER, MERCHANT MILL (steel & rel.)
Performs any combination of tasks involved in preparing rolling mill for rolling rods, bars, rounds, and flats: Assembles roll stands, rolls, guides, and rest bars of rolling mill, using hammers and wrenches. Installs repeaters or tables on rolling line, using handtools. Grinds surface of repeater guides to ensure smooth passage of steel through mill, using portable grinder. Sorts and stores guides, tools, and other mill equipment. Cuts scrap to charging box size, using scrap shear or torch, and places scrap in charging box. Hooks crane slings to rolls, mill equipment, scrap, or charging boxes, and signals OVERHEAD CRANE OPERATOR (any industry) 921.663-010 to position load in specified areas. Removes steel piled up in furnace, using rake or tongs and chain.
GOE: 05.12.15 STRENGTH: M GED: R2 M1 L2 SVP: 5 DLU: 77

801.664-018   ROLL BUILDER (steel & rel.)
Assembles roll stands used on rolling mills according to orders, using handtools: Reads orders to ascertain shape and size of structural product to be rolled and to determine procedures for assembling stands. Attaches slings of crane to rolls in racks and signals OVERHEAD CRANE OPERATOR (any industry) 921.663-010 to position rolls in stands. Inserts rolls in housing, installs roll bearings, and bolts rolls in place, using handtools. Installs specified guides on stands, using handtools. Grinds guides, using portable grinder, to ensure smooth passage of steel through mill. Disassembles roll stands removed from line and examines parts to determine need for replacement. Sorts and stores rolling equipment. Records size, quantity, and condition of rolls.
GOE: 05.05.06 STRENGTH: M GED: R3 M2 L3 SVP: 5 DLU: 78

801.667-010   INSPECTOR, SHIPPING (agric. equip.) alternate titles: inspector, finished machines and bundles
Examines agricultural equipment, such as tractors, combines, and balers, for surface defects, prior to shipment: Examines painted surfaces for scratches, surfaces of parts, such as hydraulic shafts and chains for specified protective coat-

ing, and grills, ports, and vents for required sealing against entrance of dust, dirt, and foreign material. Reads labels, tags, identification plates, and stenciled markings to ensure that items, such as serial and part numbers, correspond. Compares unit with shipping order to determine if correct accessories, such as boxes of spare parts and tools, are present. Examines unit to ensure that accessories and parts are securely mounted and that parts, such as radiator and transmission, do not leak. Notifies supervisor of defects.
GOE: 06.03.02 STRENGTH: L GED: R3 M1 L1 SVP: 4 DLU: 77

801.684-010   JIG FITTER (machinery mfg.)
Assembles frames, bases, and other component parts of industrial machines and equipment in jigs preparatory to welding, using electric crane and handtools: Verifies shape of metal parts according to blueprint specifications, using templates. Examines metal parts to detect defects, such as rough spots and burrs, and removes defects, using hand file and portable powered grinder. Lifts and fits parts in jig according to blueprint, using electric crane and handtools. Clamps parts in position in jig, using wrench. Tack-welds parts together [WELDER, TACK (welding) 810.684-010] in preparation for final welding. Lifts and moves assembly from jig to welding area using electric crane.
GOE: 06.02.24 STRENGTH: M GED: R3 M2 L1 SVP: 5 DLU: 77

801.684-014   PATTERN GATER (foundry)
Fastens two or more metal patterns to metal match plate, using screws: Cuts metal strips from stock, using hacksaw, for use as gates and risers, and fastens strips to match plate, using screws. Applies solder or other compound to joints to achieve smooth finish. May fabricate pattern parts, using tools, such as disc sander, joiner, planer, and router. May shellac finished pattern, using brush.
GOE: 06.04.24 STRENGTH: M GED: R2 M1 L1 SVP: 4 DLU: 77

801.684-018   PLAYGROUND-EQUIPMENT ERECTOR (retail trade)
Erects prefabricated playground equipment for schools, recreational centers, and institutions: Assembles parts, such as swings, horizontal ladders, basketball standards, slides, and other equipment, using wrenches, stocks and dies, and other tools to join parts with flanges, and sleeve and elbow joints. Mixes and places cement around bases of standards. Performs necessary carpentry work.
GOE: 05.12.12 STRENGTH: H GED: R3 M1 L1 SVP: 3 DLU: 77

801.684-022   PROGRESSIVE ASSEMBLER AND FITTER (agric. equip.) alternate titles: assembler, lawn-and-garden machinery; assembler, tractor; case assembler; main-line assembler
Assembles farm or lawn-and-garden machinery, such as tractors, harvesters, plow disks, rakes, roto-tillers, and snow throwers at one station of progressive assembly line, using handtools and power tools: Files edges and reams holes to align parts, such as chains, gears, housings, transmissions, radiators, fuel lines, and wheels with main assembly. Bolts or clips parts to assembly, using tools, such as prys, hammers, and pneumatic wrenches and drills. Sets clearance between parts to prescribed tolerances, using fixed gauges and tools, such as torque wrenches and screwdriver. Positions parts, such as control mechanisms, and connecting rods in housing and secures parts with bolts, rivets, cotter pins, and keys, using hamme, wrench, and pliers. Pours lubricating oil into housing and fastens housing cover plates, using wrench. Mounts assembled units in test fixture, connects unit to electric motor, and starts motor to test performance of unit. May work from blueprints or sketches.
GOE: 06.04.22 STRENGTH: M GED: R2 M1 L1 SVP: 3 DLU: 77

801.684-026   REINFORCING-METAL WORKER (construction) alternate titles: reinforcing-bar setter; reinforcing-iron worker; reinforcing-steel erector; reinforcing-steel placer; reinforcing-steel setter; reinforcing-steel worker
Positions and secures steel bars in concrete forms to reinforce concrete: Determines number, sizes, shapes, and locations of reinforcing rods from blueprints, sketches, or oral instructions. Selects and places rods in forms, spacing and fastening them together, using wire and pliers. Cuts bars to required lengths, using hacksaw, bar cutters, or acetylene torch. May bend steel rods with handtools or rodbending machine. May reinforce concrete with wire mesh. May weld reinforcing bars together, using arc-welding equipment.
GOE: 05.05.06 STRENGTH: H GED: R3 M1 L1 SVP: 6 DLU: 77

801.687-010   ASSEMBLER HELPER, INTERNAL COMBUSTION ENGINE (engine-turbine)
Prepares internal combustion engines for final assembly and testing, performing any of following duties: Pushes or pulls motor aside, using hook, or pushes engine on casters between assembly stations. Pulls masking tape from engine to permit further assembly and adjustment. Removes temporary holding screws to permit attachment of permanent assemblies, using handtools. Lubricates engine, using grease guns, grease fittings, brushes, and oilcans. Wipes oil and dirt from outside surface of engine, using rags. Clamps engine to carrying frame and raises it to overhead conveyor line, using power hoist.
GOE: 06.04.40 STRENGTH: H GED: R2 M1 L1 SVP: 2 DLU: 77

801.687-014   FITTER HELPER (any industry) alternate titles: plate-worker helper; welder-fitter helper
Assists FITTER (any industry) I or WELDER-FITTER (welding) to position, align, and fit together fabricated plates, structural shapes, and weldments preparatory to assembly into structural fabricated products, performing following tasks: Holds, positions, and reads tape or rods to assist in layout. Places and moves blocking, braces, and jigs to hold parts. Hammers wedges and drift pins, and turns turnbuckles, using lever. Pulls pry bars to align parts. Grinds or chips

rough edges, surplus weld, or scale, using portable grinder or airhammer. Positions and turns clamps, and bolts together butt straps or parts, using hand or power wrench. Performs any combination of incidental tasks, such as transporting tools, fixtures, and parts, assisting welders, bucking rivets, reaming holes, and sweeping area. May be known according to task performed as Lay-Out Helper (any industry). Performs other duties as described under HELPER (any industry) Master Title.
GOE: 05.12.12 STRENGTH: H GED: R2 M1 L1 SVP: 3 DLU: 77

801.687-018   TANK-SETTER HELPER (petrol. & gas) alternate titles: tank-builder helper
Assists TANK SETTER (petrol. & gas) in erecting metal tanks used to store crude oil, performing following tasks: Shovels and spreads dirt over designated area and pulls straightedge (plank) over surface to tank base. Brushes sealing compound on felt or asbestos strips used to seal tank joints. Bolts tank sections together to assemble tanks and inserts sealing strips in joints. Erects scaffolds. Carries tools and materials. Performs other duties as described under HELPER (any industry) Master Title.
GOE: 05.12.12 STRENGTH: M GED: R2 M1 L1 SVP: 2 DLU: 77

804   TINSMITHS, COPPERSMITHS, AND SHEET METAL WORKERS

This group includes occupations concerned with laying out, cutting to size, bending or shaping, and soldering, brazing, riveting, or crimping sheet metal, such as copper, steel, aluminum, galvanized iron, and tinplate, to fabricate or repair sheet metal items, such as gutters, hot and cold air vents, cabinets, and light tanks.

804.281-010   SHEET-METAL WORKER (any industry) alternate titles: sheet-metal mechanic
Plans, lays out, fabricates, assembles, installs, and repairs sheet metal parts, equipment, and products, utilizing knowledge of working characteristics of metallic and nonmetallic materials, machining, and layout techniques, using handtools, power tools, machines, and equipment: Reads and interprets blueprints, sketches, or product specifications to determine sequence and methods of fabricating, assembling, and installing sheet metal products. Selects gauge and type of sheet metal, such as galvanized iron, copper, steel, or aluminum, or nonmetallic material, such as plastics or fiberglass, according to product specifications. Lays out and marks dimensions and reference lines on material, using scribers, dividers, squares, and rulers, applying knowledge of shop mathematics and layout techniques to develop and trace patterns of product or parts [SHEET-METAL LAY-OUT WORKER (any industry) 809.281-010] or using templates. Sets up and operates fabricating machines, such as shears, brakes, presses, forming rolls, and routers, to cut, bend, block and form, or straighten materials. Shapes metal material over anvil, block, or other form, using handtools. Trims, files, grinds, deburrs, buffs, and smooths surfaces, using handtools and portable power tools. Welds, solders, bolts, rivets, screws, clips, caulks, or bonds component parts to assemble products, using handtools, power tools, and equipment. Installs assemblies in supportive framework according to blueprints, using handtools, power tools, and lifting and handling devices. Inspects assemblies and installation for conformance to specifications, using measuring instruments, such as calipers, scales, dial indicators, gauges, and micrometers. Repairs and maintains sheet metal products. May operate computer-aided-drafting (CAD) equipment to develop scale drawings of product or system. May operate laser-beam cutter [LASER-BEAM-MACHINE OPERATOR (welding) 815.682-010] or plasma arc cutter [ARC CUTTER, PLASMA ARC (welding) 816.364-010] to cut patterns from sheet metal. May be designated by type of metal as Coppersmith (any industry); Tinsmith (any industry); or according to type of activity as Fabricator, Special Items (any industry); Model Maker, Sheet-Metal (any industry); Product-Development Worker (any industry); Roofer, Metal (construction); Sheet-Metal Installer (any industry); Sheet-Metal Worker, Maintenance (any industry); Shop Mechanic (any industry).
GOE: 05.05.06 STRENGTH: M GED: R4 M4 L3 SVP: 7 DLU: 88

804.281-014   SHEET-METAL-WORKER APPRENTICE (any industry)
Performs duties as described under APPRENTICE (any industry) Master Title. Frequently specializes, after completing apprenticeship program, in such areas as ventilation and air-conditioning, restaurant equipment, architectural sheet metal work, warm-air heating systems, sheet metal roofing, and electric-sign construction.
GOE: 05.05.06 STRENGTH: M GED: R4 M4 L3 SVP: 7 DLU: 77

804.481-010   HOOD MAKER (tex. prod., nec)
Fabricates and assembles sheet metal hoods used to protect awnings, using handtools and portable power tools: Selects specified steel sheet from stock. Lays out and marks hood parts on steel sheet, indicating lines for bending, cutting, and drilling according to drawings, sketches, or verbal instructions, using scale, rule, scribe, and punch. Cuts metal pieces to size, using hand or bench shears. Bends metal into specified shapes, using manually operated brake machine or hammers metal to shape, using wooden mallet. Drills holes into metal, using electric hand drill, or punches holes, using hammer and punch. Hammers edges of metal parts to form seams, using mallet. Screws, bolts, or rivets hood together and attaches supports, using handtools. May install hood on building. May fabricate awning frames [AWNING-FRAME MAKER (tex. prod., nec)].
GOE: 05.05.06 STRENGTH: M GED: R4 M3 L3 SVP: 5 DLU: 77

804.684-010   CUTTER, ALUMINUM SHEET (ship-boat mfg.)
Cuts sheet aluminum to specified shape for use as boat hulls and decks, using portable saw: Stacks sheets of aluminum on cutting table and positions pattern on top sheet. Outlines pattern on sheet, using scribe. Guides saw around outline to cut out hull or deck parts. Drills holes along edges of cutout parts at specified points to mark locations for attachment of parts, using portable electric drill.
GOE: 06.04.24 STRENGTH: M GED: R2 M1 L1 SVP: 2 DLU: 77

804.684-014   EXTRUSION BENDER (ship-boat mfg.)
Cuts and bends aluminum extrusions into specified shapes for use as trim, fasteners, and bumper guards on fiberglass boats, using handtools and portable power tools: Obtains precut extrusions from stock, or cuts extrusions to specified length, using hacksaw. Places blocks in jig and bends extrusions to shape around blocks. Clamps extrusions in position in jig and drills holes through extrusions, using power drill. Bolts extrusions together, using wrench. Releases clamps and removes extrusions from jigs. Tapes inner surface of extrusions to form watertight seal. Bends aluminum trim in jigs, and attaches trim to exposed edges of parts, such as plastic panels and seats. Forces trim into position, using rubber mallet. Crimps edges of trim to fasten trim in position, using crimping tool.
GOE: 06.02.24 STRENGTH: L GED: R3 M2 L2 SVP: 4 DLU: 77

805   BOILERMAKERS

This group includes occupations concerned with assembling, erecting, and repairing boilers and related equipment, attachments, and accessories. Includes laying out, cutting, fitting and bolting, welding, or riveting heavy metal plates, boiler tubes, and castings.

805.131-010   SUPERVISOR, BOILERMAKING (struct. metal)
Supervises and coordinates activities of workers engaged in assembly, erection, and repair of boilers, tanks, vats, and pressure vessels: Lays out reference points of columns or plates on foundation, following blueprints. Directs workers in selection of type and location of rigging and equipment to lift parts into position. Directs welders to assemble unit. Lays out location and position of drums and *headers* on frame to ensure specified alignment of tubes. Verifies dimensions of accessories, such as chutes, fan stands, uptakes, stacks, and ladders needed to adapt boiler or tank to location. Directs workers in repair of boilers, tanks, vats, and pressure vessels. May construct templates of wood, paper, or sheet metal to facilitate layout tasks. Performs other duties as described under SUPERVISOR (any industry) Master Title. May be designated according to work activities or workers supervised as Supervisor, Boilermaking Shop (struct. metal); Supervisor, Field Assembly-And-Erection (struct. metal); Supervisor Mechanic, Boilermaking (struct. metal).
GOE: 05.05.06 STRENGTH: M GED: R4 M4 L3 SVP: 8 DLU: 77

805.137-010   SUPERVISOR, BOILER REPAIR (any industry)
Supervises and coordinates activities of workers engaged in maintenance and repair of stationary steam boilers and boiler house auxiliaries, performing duties as described under SUPERVISOR (any industry) Master Title.
GOE: 05.05.06 STRENGTH: M GED: R4 M3 L3 SVP: 8 DLU: 77

805.261-010   BOILERMAKER APPRENTICE (struct. metal)
Performs duties as described under APPRENTICE (any industry) Master Title.
GOE: 05.05.06 STRENGTH: H GED: R4 M4 L3 SVP: 7 DLU: 77

805.261-014   BOILERMAKER I (struct. metal) alternate titles: boiler-maker, assembly and erection
Assembles, analyzes defects in, and repairs boilers, pressure vessels, tanks, and vats in field, following blueprints and using handtools and portable power tools and equipment: Locates and marks reference points for columns or plates on foundation, using *master straightedge*, squares, transit, and measuring tape, and applying knowledge of geometry. Attaches rigging or signals crane operator to lift parts to specified position. Aligns structures or plate sections to assemble boiler frame, tanks, or vats, using plumb bobs, levels, wedges, dogs, or turnbuckles. Hammers, flame-cuts, files, or grinds irregular edges of sections or structural parts to facilitate fitting edges together. Bolts or arc-welds structures and sections together. Positions drums and *headers* into supports and bolts or welds supports to frame. Aligns water tubes and connects and expands ends to drums and headers, using tube expander. Bells, beads with power hammer, or welds tube ends to ensure leakproof joints. Bolts or welds casing sections, uptakes, stacks, baffles, and such fabricated parts as chutes, air heaters, fan stands, feeding tube, catwalks, ladders, coal hoppers, and safety hatch to frame, using wrench. Installs manholes, handholes, valves, gauges, and feedwater connection in drums to complete assembly of water tube boilers. Assists in testing assembled vessels by pumping water or gas under specified pressure into vessel and observing instruments for evidence of leakage. Repairs boilers or tanks in field by unbolting or flame cutting defective sections or tubes, straightening plates, using torch or jacks, installing new tubes, fitting and welding new sections and replacing worn lugs on bolts. May rivet and caulk sections of vessels, using pneumatic riveting and caulking hammers. May line firebox with refractory brick and asbestos rope and blocks [BRICKLAYER, FIREBRICK AND REFRACTORY TILE (construction)]. May fabricate such parts as stacks, uptakes, and chutes to adapt boiler to premises in which it is installed [BOILERMAKER (struct. metal) II].

GOE: 05.05.06 STRENGTH: H GED: R4 M4 L3 SVP: 7 DLU: 77

805.361-010 BOILER HOUSE MECHANIC (any industry) alternate titles: boiler mechanic; heating-equipment repairer; station mechanic

Maintains and repairs stationary steam boilers and boiler house auxiliaries, using handtools and portable power tools: Cleans or directs other workers to clean boilers and auxiliary equipment, using scrapers, wire brush and cleaning solvent. Inspects and repairs boiler fittings, such as safety valves, regulators, automatic-control mechanisms, and water columns, and auxiliary machines, such as pumps, draft fans, stokers, and burners. Replaces damaged boiler tubes and plates [BOILERMAKER (struct. metal) I]. Repairs or replaces high-pressure piping, using power saw, gas torch, threading die, and welding equipment. May patch boiler insulation with cement. May paint surface of equipment, using brush. May perform water pressure test by pumping water into system to determine location of leaks. May remove and replace defective firebrick, using hammer and chisel. May operate lathe and milling machine to repair or make parts, such as valve stems and pump shafts.
GOE: 05.05.06 STRENGTH: M GED: R4 M3 L3 SVP: 7 DLU: 77

805.361-014 BOILERMAKER FITTER (struct. metal)

Positions, aligns, and secures structural parts and related assemblies of pressure vessels, such as boilers, tanks, and vats in specified relationship for subsequent permanent assembly by BOILERMAKER (struct. metal) I or WELDER, BOILERMAKER (struct. metal). Locates and marks position of parts, using measuring tape, transit, square, and plumb bob. Signals RIGGER (any industry) to lift parts into position. Aligns parts to specified fit, using dogs, wedges, turnbuckles, jacks, hammers, and *drift pins*. Cuts, files, and grinds seams and joints to attain specified fit, using cutting torch, file, and power grinder. Straightens or reshapes bent plates or structure, using hammer, jacks, and torch. Clamps, bolts, or tack-welds parts in place for final welding or bolting. Climbs framework or ladders to position, fit, or secure parts. May fit plates, structures, or pipes to repair ships.
GOE: 05.05.06 STRENGTH: H GED: R4 M3 L2 SVP: 7 DLU: 77

805.381-010 BOILERMAKER II (struct. metal) alternate titles: boilermaker mechanic

Assembles boilers, tanks, vats, and pressure vessels according to blueprint specifications, using power tools and handtools: Reads blueprint to determine location and relationship of parts. Connects firetubes to heads or watertubes to drums and *headers* of boilers, by expanding and belling ends, using tube expander and beading ends, using power hammer. Drills and taps holes for installation of studs, using portable drill. Tightens bolts to assemble frames, using hand or power wrenches. Mounts casings of watertube boilers, or attaches davit heads, burners, or furnace casing to firetube boilers, using wrenches. Bolts or screws accessories, such as manholes, handholes, fans, gauges, and valves to vessel, using handtools or power wrenches. Replaces defective parts, using power wrenches, prying bars, or handtools. May install and repair refractory brick [BRICKLAYER, FIREBRICK AND REFRACTORY TILE (construction)]. May thread and install stay bolts, using pipe wrench and dies. May remove and replace rivets and caulk seams to repair riveted shells and structures, using pneumatic chisel, riveter, and caulking hammer. May cut out defective parts, using acetylene torch. Distinguish from BOILERMAKER (struct. metal) I who assembles and repairs boilers and related pressure vessels. May be designated according to work setting or location as Boilermaker, Central Steam Plant (struct. metal); Boilermaker, Industrial Boilers (struct. metal); Boilermaker, Ship (struct. metal).
GOE: 05.05.06 STRENGTH: M GED: R3 M2 L2 SVP: 7 DLU: 77

805.664-010 BOILERMAKER HELPER II (struct. metal)

Assists boilermaking personnel in assembling, installing, repairing, and testing steam boilers, pressure vessels, and other removable structures in ships, central steam plants, and in industrial plants. Loads structural parts of boilers, pressure vessels, or tanks on pallets, using hoist. Attaches slings to pallets or onto parts for moving by crane. Assists in positioning parts in jigs and attaches clamps or other holding devices to fit parts together. Grinds welds or seams to fit, using portable grinder. Removes boiler casings, grades, handrails, manhole, and handhole covers to facilitate access to boilers or other vessels for repair, using handtools. Assists in positioning boiler tubes as specified in boiler drums and *headers*. Cleans scale from boiler tubes, using rotary pneumatic brush equipment. Mixes mortar used for laying firebrick in firebox. Replaces and reassembles gratings, ladders, handrails, and other disassembled structures after repairs are completed. Performs other duties as described under HELPER (any industry) Master Title.
GOE: 05.12.12 STRENGTH: H GED: R2 M2 L2 SVP: 5 DLU: 77

805.667-010 BOILER HOUSE INSPECTOR (any industry) alternate titles: boiler cleaner, chief

Visually inspects boilers and water and steam connection pipes to locate leaks and defective parts. Notifies work crew of repairs to be made. Visually inspects repaired boilers to ensure completion of repair job and notifies BOILER OPERATOR (any industry) to resume operation of boiler. Inspects cleaning equipment, such as hand and powered wire brushes and chipping tools, and orders replacements.
GOE: 05.07.01 STRENGTH: L GED: R3 M1 L1 SVP: 6 DLU: 77

805.687-010 BOILERMAKER HELPER I (struct. metal)

Performs following tasks to assist BOILERMAKER (struct. metal) I in assembly, erection, and repair of boilers, tanks, vats, and pressure vessels, in field: Conveys tools, equipment, and parts to work area by hand or using handtrucks. Cleans boilers and tanks, using scrapers and steam or water hoses. Cleans work area and places salvageable material in bins. Attaches slings, ropes, or cables to objects, such as plates, tubes, and drums, following signals of RIGGER (any industry). Positions and holds parts for BOILERMAKER (struct. metal) I to fit, clamp, or weld parts in specified alignment. Bolts or unbolts assemblies, using handtools, such as wrenches, screwdrivers, and prying bars. Performs other duties as described under HELPER (any industry) Master Title.
GOE: 05.12.12 STRENGTH: H GED: R2 M1 L1 SVP: 2 DLU: 77

806 TRANSPORTATION EQUIPMENT ASSEMBLERS AND RELATED OCCUPATIONS

This group includes occupations concerned with assembling transportation and related equipment, such as motor vehicles, aircraft, rail equipment, motorcycles and bicycles, boats, and components, parts, and accessories. Body work is included in Group 807, and painting is included in Group 845.

806.130-010 SUPERVISOR, ENGINE ASSEMBLY (engine-turbine)

Supervises and coordinates activities of workers engaged in assembly of internal combustion engines: Reviews routing sheets to determine type of engine to assemble. Examines engine parts at assembly bench or line for agreement with routing sheet. Confers with supervisor to arrange assembly line, supplies, and parts to facilitate assembly of engines. Corrects stoppages on line by reassigning workers, reporting breakdown of machines to maintenance department, or supervising repair of machines. Sets up arbor presses, special jigs, and holding fixtures for assembly of engines. Performs other duties as described under SUPERVISOR (any industry) Master Title.
GOE: 06.01.01 STRENGTH: L GED: R4 M3 L2 SVP: 8 DLU: 77

806.131-010 SUPERVISOR, ALUMINUM BOAT ASSEMBLY (ship-boat mfg.)

Supervises and coordinates activities of workers engaged in assembly of aluminum boats: Trains and assists workers in performance of tasks, such as cleaning, drilling, riveting, painting, and inspecting aluminum boats and component parts. Performs other duties as described under SUPERVISOR (any industry) Master Title.
GOE: 06.01.01 STRENGTH: M GED: R4 M3 L3 SVP: 8 DLU: 77

806.131-014 SUPERVISOR, ASSEMBLY (motor-bicycles)

Supervises and coordinates activities of workers engaged in assembling and repairing forks, frames, transmissions, or other motorcycle components: Trains workers in assembly and repair procedures. Performs duties as described under SUPERVISOR (any industry) Master Title. May be designated according to department as Supervisor, Frame Assembly (motor-bicycles); Supervisor, Motorcycle And Wheel Assembly (motor-bicycles); Supervisor, Transmission And Fork Assembly (motor-bicycles). May supervise and coordinate activities of workers engaged in assembly and repair of bicycles, wheels, and parts.
GOE: 06.02.01 STRENGTH: L GED: R4 M3 L3 SVP: 8 DLU: 77

806.131-018 SUPERVISOR, BOAT OUTFITTING (ship-boat mfg.)

Supervises and coordinates activities of workers engaged in outfitting and installing engines in fiberglass boats: Trains and assists workers in performance of tasks, such as installing engines and outfitting boats with such fixtures as metal trim, seats, and windshields. Inspects engine placement for conformance to specifications, using rulers and levels. Rubs fingers over boat surfaces to detect rough edges. Confers with other supervisory personnel to coordinate interdepartmental workflow. Coordinates loading and shipping schedules. Performs other duties as described under SUPERVISOR (any industry) Master Title.
GOE: 06.02.01 STRENGTH: L GED: R4 M3 L2 SVP: 8 DLU: 77

806.131-022 SUPERVISOR, ERECTION SHOP (railroad equip.)

Supervises and coordinates activities of workers engaged in fitting, welding, and riveting railroad car components, such as beams, center sills, crossbearers, sides, ends, and roofing, to make car framework. Performs duties as described under SUPERVISOR (any industry) Master Title.
GOE: 06.02.01 STRENGTH: M GED: R4 M3 L3 SVP: 8 DLU: 77

806.131-026 SUPERVISOR, INSPECTION AND TESTING (motor-bicycles)

Supervises and coordinates activities of workers engaged in inspecting and testing motorcycle parts and assemblies: Examines and measures rejected parts and assemblies to determine type of defect. Notifies engineering personnel of malfunctioning inspecting and testing equipment. Trains workers in inspecting and testing procedures. Performs duties as described under SUPERVISOR (any industry) Master Title.
GOE: 06.01.01 STRENGTH: L GED: R4 M3 L3 SVP: 8 DLU: 77

806.131-030 SUPERVISOR, RIGGER (ship-boat mfg.)

Supervises and coordinates activities of workers engaged in installation and repair of rigging, and in hoisting and positioning machinery, equipment, and structural parts aboard ships. Performs duties as described under SUPERVISOR (any industry) Master Title.
GOE: 05.05.06 STRENGTH: L GED: R4 M3 L2 SVP: 8 DLU: 77

806.131-034 SUPERVISOR, SHIPFITTERS (ship-boat mfg.)

Supervises and coordinates activities of workers engaged in fabricating and installing metal structural parts, such as bulkheads, plates, and frames in ships.

Inspects installations, such as decks and engine foundations, for conformance with specifications. May supervise workers engaged in repairing structural parts of ships. May direct moving and launching of ships. Performs other duties as described under SUPERVISOR (any industry) Master Title.
GOE: 05.05.06 STRENGTH: M GED: R4 M3 L3 SVP: 8 DLU: 80

806.131-038 SUPERVISOR, INSPECTION (aircraft mfg.)
Supervises and coordinates activities of workers engaged in inspecting and testing raw materials and manufactured products in accordance with customer and company quality standards. Performs other duties as described under SUPERVISOR (any industry) Master Title.
GOE: 06.01.01 STRENGTH: L GED: R4 M4 L4 SVP: 7 DLU: 87

806.131-042 SUPERVISOR, PRODUCTION DEPARTMENT (aircraft mfg.)
Supervises and coordinates activities of workers engaged in fabricating, assembling, modifying, or repairing parts, assemblies, tooling, and related items used in manufacturing aircraft and space vehicles: Analyzes work orders, schematics, and other specifications to determine parts and assemblies requiring fabrication, modification, or repair. Trains employees in work methods and procedures. Inspects work to ensure adherence to standards and specifications. Requisitions replacement materials, tools, and equipment. Performs other duties as described under SUPERVISOR (any industry) Master Title.
GOE: 06.01.01 STRENGTH: M GED: R4 M4 L4 SVP: 8 DLU: 87

806.134-010 SUPERVISOR, MOTOR VEHICLE ASSEMBLY (auto. mfg.)
Supervises and coordinates activities of workers engaged in assembling motor vehicles, such as automobiles, trucks, buses, or limousines: Directs workers in welding, assembly, inspection, and repair techniques, utilizing knowledge of assembly procedures and specifications. Confers with other supervisory personnel to coordinate activities of individual departments within plant. Assigns training of new employees to qualified workers or performs training duties. Performs other duties as described under SUPERVISOR (any industry) Master Title. May be designated according to component assembled or installed as Supervisor, Engine Assembly (auto. mfg.); Supervisor, Seat Assembly (auto. mfg.); or stage of assembly as Supervisor, Body Assembly (auto. mfg.); Supervisor, Chassis Assembly (auto. mfg.); Supervisor, Final Assembly (auto. mfg.); Supervisor, Trim Assembly (auto. mfg.); Supervisor, Truck-Trailer Assembly (auto. mfg.).
GOE: 06.02.01 STRENGTH: L GED: R4 M4 L4 SVP: 7 DLU: 90

806.134-014 SUPERVISOR, FIBERGLASS BOAT ASSEMBLY (ship-boat mfg.)
Supervises and coordinates activities of workers engaged in laminating fiberglass casts on boat molds and assembling fiberglass boats and component parts: Reads work orders and blueprints to determine materials needed and requisitions materials. Trains and assists workers in performance of tasks, such as laminating, assembling, painting, and inspecting boats and component parts. Visually and tactually inspects component parts of boats to detect air pockets, defects in thickness, or other failures to conform to blueprint specifications. Performs other duties as described under SUPERVISOR (any industry) Master Title. May supervise workers engaged in laminating and assembling ship components made of fiberglass and be designated Supervisor, Fiberglass-Ship-Component Assembly (ship-boat mfg.).
GOE: 06.02.01 STRENGTH: M GED: R4 M3 L3 SVP: 8 DLU: 80

806.137-010 SUPERVISOR, CAR INSTALLATIONS (railroad equip.)
Supervises and coordinates activities of workers engaged in installing doors, walls, flooring, insulation, heaters, ventilators, generators, and other equipment and materials in exteriors and interiors of railroad cars. Performs duties as described under SUPERVISOR (any industry) Master Title.
GOE: 06.02.01 STRENGTH: L GED: R4 M3 L2 SVP: 7 DLU: 77

806.137-014 SUPERVISOR, ORDNANCE TRUCK INSTALLATION (ordnance)
Supervises and coordinates activities of workers engaged in assembly and installation of tools, equipment, and materials in ordnance mobile shop trucks: Directs assembly and installation in truck bodies, of benches, tools, and machinery according to diagrams and blueprints. Performs other duties as described under SUPERVISOR (any industry) Master Title.
GOE: 05.10.01 STRENGTH: L GED: R4 M3 L3 SVP: 7 DLU: 77

806.137-018 SUPERVISOR, SHIPPING TRACK (railroad equip.)
Supervises and coordinates activities of workers engaged in final assembly and preparation of railroad cars for shipment to customers: Trains new workers in performance of tasks, such as installing exterior fixtures, touching up stenciled letters and designs, sandblasting to clean exterior surfaces, caulking to waterproof, and testing and adjusting air brake systems of railroad cars. Monitors performance of tasks, machinery and equipment, and condition of work areas to ensure adherence to company standards. Reports machinery and equipment malfunctions to maintenance personnel. Performs other duties as described under SUPERVISOR (any industry) Master Title.
GOE: 06.02.01 STRENGTH: L GED: R4 M3 L3 SVP: 7 DLU: 77

806.137-022 QUALITY ASSURANCE SUPERVISOR (auto. mfg.)
Supervises and coordinates activities of workers engaged in inspecting and testing assembled motor vehicles, components, and parts, as vehicles and subassemblies proceed through stages of assembly process, applying knowledge of quality assurance standards and procedures: Reviews quality assurance instructions, assembly specifications, and production schedules to determine method of conducting inspections and tests, sequence of operations, and work assignments. Directs workers in quality assurance inspection and testing, to assure that establishment and regulatory standards are met. Assigns training of new workers to qualified workers. Reviews reports and confers with quality assurance, production, management, and engineering personnel to solve work-related problems. Performs other duties as described under SUPERVISOR (any industry) Master Title. May be designated according to stage of assembly as Quality Assurance Supervisor, Body (auto. mfg.); Quality Assurance Supervisor, Trim (auto. mfg.); Quality Assurance Supervisor, Chassis (auto. mfg.); Quality Assurance Supervisor, Final (auto. mfg.).
GOE: 06.01.01 STRENGTH: L GED: R4 M3 L4 SVP: 7 DLU: 88

806.261-010 INTERNAL-COMBUSTION-ENGINE INSPECTOR (engine-turbine) alternate titles: inspector and tester; inspector; erector
Inspects internal combustion engines after test for conformance to blueprints and specifications, using measuring instruments and handtools: Reviews performance test report and compares log data, such as temperature, lubrication compression, horsepower, fuel consumption, and manifold pressure with specifications. Signs inspection tag to release engines from test floor or analyzes data to locate assemblies and parts not functioning according to specifications. Measures dimensions of disassembled parts and assemblies, such as pistons, cylinder liners, valves, bearings, shafts, governors, injectors, or carburetors, and clearances between moving and stationary parts, using scale, micrometers, special tools, and gauging setups. Compares measurements with specifications to locate faulty parts. Records findings and notifies supervisor of results of inspection. May inspect incoming materials for conformance with specifications. May disassemble engines during inspection process. May supervise crating and shipping of engines to consignees. May be designated according to type of engine inspected as Diesel-Engine Inspector (engine-turbine); Gasoline-Engine Inspector (engine-turbine).
GOE: 06.01.05 STRENGTH: M GED: R4 M3 L4 SVP: 7 DLU: 77

806.261-014 RIGGER (ship-boat mfg.) alternate titles: loft rigger; outside rigger
Fabricates, installs, and repairs rigging and weight-handling gear on ships and attaches hoists and pulling gear to rigging to lift, move, and position machinery, equipment, structural parts, and other heavy loads aboard ship: Forms slings and towing bridles by looping and splicing cable or by crimping metal sleeve around cable end and body of cable, using crimping tool. Splices and ties rope to form nets, ladders, and other rigging. Installs hooks, swivels, and turnbuckles in rigging. Reeves lines through blocks and pulleys. Sews canvas or leather covers on rigging at friction points, using sail twine and sailmaker's palm and needle. Selects and attaches gear, braces, and cushions, according to weight and distribution of load, availability of hoisting machinery, and presence of obstacles, such as ship's structural members and jutting buildings, which might interfere with maneuverability of incorrectly rigged hoisting gear. Signals workers operating cranes or other equipment to move load. Installs beam clamps, pad eyes, gallows frames, and other supporting structures for rigging gear. Controls movement of heavy equipment through narrow openings or in confined spaces, using jacks, pulley blocks, chainfalls, and rollers. Lays out and handles lines, snubs lines on cleats or bollards, or hauls in lines with capstans to assist SHIPWRIGHT (ship-boat mfg.) in ship drydocking operations. Installs or repairs ship's rigging, such as mast or antenna rigs, small boat handling gear, and winch or windlass rigging. Installs masts, booms, yardarms, and gaffs, working aloft as required. Rigs and hangs scaffolds and stages that require blocks and pulleys.
GOE: 05.05.06 STRENGTH: H GED: R4 M2 L2 SVP: 7 DLU: 77

806.261-018 RIGGER APPRENTICE (ship-boat mfg.) alternate titles: erector appentice
Performs duties as described under APPRENTICE (any industry) Master Title.
GOE: 05.05.06 STRENGTH: H GED: R4 M2 L2 SVP: 7 DLU: 77

806.261-022 TESTER, ROCKET MOTOR (aircraft mfg.) alternate titles: tester, rocket engine
Test fires rocket motor or rocket engine to determine performance characteristics, using testing, measuring, and recording instruments and equipment, and mathematical formulas: Positions, or directs other workers to position, motor or engine on test stand, using hoist or overhead crane. Attaches measuring and testing instruments, controls, and computerized data acquisition equipment, using handtools. Test operates motor or engine for specified test periods under varying operational conditions to determine performance characteristics, such as motor thrust, chamber pressure, and burn rate. Calculates performance data using computer, calculator, and standard formulas. Records and interprets test results for analysis by engineers or others.
GOE: 06.01.05 STRENGTH: M GED: R4 M4 L4 SVP: 8 DLU: 88

806.261-026 MARINE-SERVICES TECHNICIAN (ship-boat mfg.)
Repairs and maintains boats and similar vessels in marine service facility: Examines repair or installation orders, drawings, and vessel, utilizing knowledge based on past experience to determine extent of repairs required or modifications necessary for installation of equipment, accessories, and hardware. Consults with supervisor regarding installation or repair problems, sequence of

operations, and time required to complete repair or installation. Removes vessels from water, using movable lift crane or marine railway. Positions and secures blocking at bottom and sides of vessels according to size, weight, and weight distribution of vessels, using fasteners, handtools, and power tools. Removes flaked paint, barnacles, and encrusted debris from hulls of vessel, using scrapers, scrubbers, power washers, and sandblast equipment. Removes damaged or rotted sections from wooden or fiberglass vessels, using drill, saw, and handtools. Fabricates and installs wooden replacement parts, using drawings, measuring instruments, work aids, handtools, power tools, and woodworking machines and equipment, such as saws, drill press, shaper, planer, and steam cabinet. Caulks wooden hulls with cotton to prevent leaks. Grinds and sands edges around removed fiberglass sections. Mixes fiberglass bonding resin and catalyst, cuts fiberglass cloth to size, and impregnates cloth with mixture. Positions layers of impregnated cloth over damaged area, and smooths area to match contour of hull, using rollers, squeegee, and power sander. Mixes and applies paint or gel coat to boats with hand and spray equipment, utilizing knowledge of color mixing, matching techniques, and application procedures. Tests engine, transmission, rigging, propeller, navigational, and related systems to diagnose malfunctions, using various measuring instruments. Replaces or repairs defective components, or fabricates new components. Installs and tests steering gear, sanitation and refrigeration systems, cabinetry, electrical systems and accessories, hardware, trim, and related components, following manufacturer's instructions and drawings.
GOE: 05.05.02 STRENGTH: H GED: R4 M3 L3 SVP: 7 DLU: 86

806.261-030 INSPECTOR, ASSEMBLIES AND INSTALLATIONS (aircraft mfg.) alternate titles: inspector, assembly
Inspects assemblies, such as fuselage, tail, and wings, joining of assemblies into major structure, installation of parts, equipment, and accessories, or complete aircraft for conformance to specifications and quality standards: Reads and interprets blueprints, engineering documents, and inspection manuals and procedures to determine methods and sequence of inspection. Examines parts and assemblies for physical characteristics, such as surface finish, color, and texture, and for defects, such as cracks, scratches, and loose connections. Measures parts and assemblies for dimensional accuracy and adherence to blueprint specifications. Inspects assembly, mating, and installation of parts, assemblies, and equipment for alignment, fit, clearance, tension, throw limits, torque, and related factors, using fixtures, jigs, and precision measuring and checking instruments, such as scales, protractor, tensiometer, and gauges. Conducts or witnesses functional or operational tests of partial or completed units, such as landing gear, auto pilot, engine controls, and rudders, to verify conformance to specifications, using test equipment. Accepts or rejects assemblies or installations, and recommends repair, rework, or replacement of component parts. Confers with engineering, production, and inspection personnel to exchange inspection information. May be designated according to assembly or installation inspected as Inspector, Subassembly (aircraft mfg.); Inspector, Final Assembly (aircraft mfg.); Inspector, Final Assembly, Electrical (aircraft mfg.); Inspector, Final Assembly, Mechanical (aircraft mfg.); Inspector, Structures (aircraft mfg.); Inspector, Engines And Components Assembly (aircraft mfg.); Inspector, Experimental Assembly (aircraft mfg.); Inspector, Electrical And Electronic Installations (aircraft mfg.).
GOE: 06.01.05 STRENGTH: M GED: R4 M4 L4 SVP: 7 DLU: 89

806.261-034 INSPECTOR, MATERIAL DISPOSITION (aircraft mfg.)
Inspects rejected or obsolete aircraft parts, assemblies, or materials to determine disposition, utilizing knowledge of production processes, repair methods, and cost, using precision measuring instruments: Reviews rejection slips to determine method of inspection required. Inspects and measures parts to determine nature and extent of defect, using surface plate or table and precision measuring instruments, such as calipers, gauges, and micrometers. Compares inspection results with specifications and consults with manufacturing, engineering, and other personnel to determine possibility and practicability of salvaging rejected parts, assemblies, or materials. Evaluates inspection data, considering value, costs involved, production delays, quality, appearance, and related factors, and recommends final disposition, such as scrap, return to vendor, salvage, or rework. Records inspection results and recommendations for disposition of parts, assemblies, or materials. May investigate rejections of parts and assemblies to determine corrective action to prevent recurrence and be designated Material Review Board Representative, Quality Control (aircraft mfg.).
GOE: 06.01.05 STRENGTH: M GED: R4 M4 L4 SVP: 7 DLU: 88

806.261-038 INSPECTOR, MISSILE (aircraft mfg.)
Inspects and tests missile components and ground support equipment, according to blueprints and specifications, using precision measuring instruments and test equipment: Examines components of missile systems, such as electrical, electronic, instrumentation, mechanical, propulsion, hydraulic, and pneumatic, for conformance to quality standards. Tests functional performance of system components, using test equipment. Inspects and measures parts and assemblies for alignment, location, dimension, fit, location of bolt and rivet holes, and fastening to ensure conformance to blueprints and specifications, using jigs, fixtures, sight levels, and precision measuring instruments. Inspects ground equipment, such as missile boosters, launch pads, and shelters, for conformance to standards and specifications. Visually and tactilely examines ablative coating on exterior surfaces of missile to ensure uniform application. Conducts or witnesses operational testing to verify that missile systems adhere to specifications. Analyzes inspection and test results and prepares inspection reports indicating

acceptance, rejection, or rework required. Confers with customers, engineering, production, and inspection personnel to exchange information, such as test results or proposed modifications to missile system. May inspect and test missile systems prior to flight or delivery to customer and be designated Inspector, Missile Final Assembly (aircraft mfg.); Missile Inspector, Preflight (aircraft mfg.). May inspect space vehicle components during final assembly and be designated Space Vehicle Inspector, Preflight (aircraft mfg.).
GOE: 06.01.05 STRENGTH: L GED: R4 M4 L4 SVP: 7 DLU: 89

806.261-042 INSPECTOR, OUTSIDE PRODUCTION (aircraft mfg.)
Inspects and tests aircraft, space capsule, and missile parts, assemblies, and materials at subcontractor's plant or airline maintenance base for conformance to engineering requirements and specifications, using blueprints, test equipment, and precision measuring instruments: Sets up and adjusts hardness testers to test metal parts for specified hardness. Inspects dimensions, alignment, and assembly of machined parts and tools, such as landing gears, brakes, gear boxes, jigs, and fixtures, using measuring instruments and devices, such as surface plate, height gauges, calipers, and micrometers. Approves or rejects parts, assemblies, and materials, and prepares inspection reports. Consults with vendors and subcontractors regarding interpretation of specifications, rejection, rework, salvage or other disposition of parts, and related issues. May inspect surfaces of metal parts and assemblies subsequent to or following chemical milling, heat treating, and micro-particle cleaning for defects or surface contaminants, using inspection devices. May examine and test ordnance devices and pyrotechnic apparatus, such as ejection seats, under simulated operating conditions to ensure specified operational characteristics. May specialize according to parts inspected, such as machined parts, plastics, sheet metal, and precision assemblies, or according to process involved, such as welding or electroplating.
GOE: 06.01.05 STRENGTH: L GED: R4 M4 L4 SVP: 7 DLU: 88

806.261-046 INSPECTOR, PLASTICS AND COMPOSITES (aircraft mfg.)
Inspects and tests plastic and composite aircraft and aerospace parts, assemblies, and structures for work quality, dimensional accuracy, and conformance to engineering drawings and specifications, using precision measuring and testing instruments and equipment: Reads inspection logs and operation sheets to determine nature and sequence of inspection. Reviews blueprints and production diagrams to visualize layout and assembly procedures, locate critical references, determine parts and materials requirements, dimensions, and finish specifications. Inspects laminated and molded structures during all phases of fabrication and assembly to ensure adherence to specifications. Visually inspects parts and assemblies for fissures, porosity, delaminations, contour, and other physical characteristics. Measures parts and assemblies for dimensional accuracy, using precision measuring instruments, templates, jigs, and fixtures. Verifies location of installed fasteners and hardware. Reads pyrometers, timers, and pressure instruments to verify that operation of curing ovens and other equipment conforms to specifications. Examines assembly surfaces subsequent to curing to ensure specified smoothness and evenness of finish. Sets up and operates test equipment to perform pressure and functional testing of parts and assemblies, and to measure physical properties, such as thickness and hardness. Calculates and records test results. Accepts or rejects parts and assemblies, and prepares documentation to record inspection results, rework required, and disposition of unacceptable products. Confers with production, liaison, inspection, and other personnel to coordinate inspection process and to discuss inspection results. May inspect and test bonding of parts from metal and nonmetallic materials, such as graphite and fiberglass, and be designated Metal Bond Inspector (aircraft mfg.). May be designated by material or process as Inspector, Advanced Composite (aircraft mfg.); Inspector, Plastics Fabrication-Developmental (aircraft mfg.); Inspector, Production Plastic Parts (aircraft mfg.); Inspector, Structural Bonding (airccraft mfg.).
GOE: 06.01.05 STRENGTH: L GED: R4 M4 L4 SVP: 7 DLU: 87

806.261-050 OPERATIONAL TEST MECHANIC (aircraft mfg.) alternate titles: systems checkout mechanic
Conducts final operational testing and troubleshooting of entire electrical, hydraulic, oxygen, pneumatic, fuel, surface control and rigging systems, and component parts installed in aircraft, under simulated flight conditions, according to blueprints, diagrams, engineering documents, and specifications, using precision instruments and test equipment: Locates and disassembles structural, mechanical, electrical, or other parts and assemblies to facilitate testing, using blueprints, diagrams, handtools, and power tools. Attaches fittings, clamps, lines, and hoses to test equipment, such as hydraulic test bench, pressure or vacuum test cart, and fuel quantity calibration equipment, and connects test equipment to system components to be tested. Operates test consoles, test equipment, and aircraft controls, or observes operation of system components, such as control surfaces and landing gear, being operated by other workers to determine system performance under simulated flight conditions. Communicates with other workers during system checkout, using radio headset or other communication device. Operates steering cart or aircraft controls to move aircraft. Interprets and analyzes test results to diagnose malfunctions. Adjusts, replaces, or repairs defective components, or documents rework to be completed by others. Records operational test and rework information. Fabricates test aids as required. May perform operational testing of specific electrical, mechanical, or other aircraft system and be designated Checkout Mechanic, Hydraulic And Rigging (aircraft mfg.); Electrical Checkout Mechanic (aircraft mfg.); Mechanic, Electrical Operational Test (aircraft mfg.); Mechanic, General Operational Test (aircraft mfg.).

GOE: 06.01.05 STRENGTH: M GED: R4 M3 L3 SVP: 8 DLU: 88

806.264-010 HULL INSPECTOR (ship-boat mfg.)
Inspects construction of hulls, compartments, tanks, and decks of ships for conformance to plans and specifications: Examines hulls, hull fittings, and riveting for defects, and alignment of plating and framing. Inspects painted surfaces and caulked edges and seams. Observes testing of tanks, decks, and compartments for strength of material and watertightness. Opens and closes doors, manhole covers, hatches, and hull valves, by hand or remote controls, to verify fit and ease of operation. Inspects heating and ventilation systems to verify size of vent ducts, and to ensure that installation meets specifications. Starts blowers, and measures volume and velocity of air in system, using measuring devices, such as meters and gauges. Inspects piping and valves of ship's service system during pressure test for leakage and strength of material. Records inspection data. May inspect commissioned vessels, afloat or in drydock, for corrosion or deterioration in outer hull, double bottoms, sea chests, and other structural parts.
GOE: 05.07.01 STRENGTH: L GED: R4 M2 L2 SVP: 8 DLU: 77

806.264-014 INSPECTOR, AIRCRAFT LAUNCHING AND ARREST-ING SYSTEMS (government ser.)
Inspects mechanical and structural construction and installation, and monitors operational testing of aircraft catapults and arresting gear systems used on aircraft carriers, according to contract specifications: Examines system components, such as pumps, valves, cables, and air and steam lines for defects and faulty installation. Compares operational functioning with contract specifications to ensure serviceability and safety. Tests questionable components, using standard instruments and gauges. Monitors operational testing of equipment and assists in determining causes of malfunctioning equipment. Prepares reports of findings to facilitate modifications.
GOE: 05.07.01 STRENGTH: M GED: R4 M4 L4 SVP: 6 DLU: 77

806.281-010 DYNAMOMETER TESTER, ENGINE (auto. mfg.) alternate titles: engine tester
Tests completed motor vehicle engines prior to mounting in chassis, using conventional or computerized dynamometer, and adjusts and repairs engines to ensure performance conforms to specifications: Lifts engine onto stand, using hoist, and aligns and bolts engine in place. Bolts coupling to dynamometer and engine shaft and attaches fuel and coolant lines, using handtools. Starts engine to drive dynamometer. Reads gauges on instrument panel to determine that power developed at specified speeds, timing, and other engine specifications meet standards. Screws gauge into spark plug opening of successive cylinders while engine is running to verify compression ratios. Reverses drive by cutting off engine and moving switches, causing dynamometer to drive engine. Reads gauges to determine power necessary to turn engine. Adjusts carburetor, sets clearances between tappets and valves, and regulates timing, using feeler gauge, timing light, and handtools. Listens for internal noise, such as piston slap, knocks, taps, and gear noises that indicate irregularities in engine operation, using stethoscope-like instrument, and determines location and cause of malfunctions. Repairs or replaces carburetor, spark plugs, and fuel pump, or fills out report for repairs involving disassembly of engine. May test engine mounted on chassis and be designated Dynamometer Tester, Chassis (auto. mfg.).
GOE: 06.01.05 STRENGTH: M GED: R4 M3 L3 SVP: 6 DLU: 89

806.281-014 EXPERIMENTAL MECHANIC, ELECTRICAL (motor-bicycles)
Builds, modifies, and tests electrical parts to improve motorcycle performance, using handtools, metal fabricating machines, and testing equipment: Positions and clamps parts in fixtures on test bench. Attaches oscilloscope, pyrometer, voltmeter, spark tester, or other test equipment to armature coil, generator, spark plugs, voltage regulator, or other electrical parts. Reads dials and meters to determine amperage, voltage, electrical output and input at specified operating temperature, and to detect open circuits, short circuits, or other electrical malfunctions. Analyzes performance of parts tested to determine deviation from specifications. Disassembles and examines parts to determine cause of malfunction, using handtools. Operates drill press, grinders, engine lathe, or other machines to modify parts tested or to fabricate experimental parts for testing. Compiles and submits reports of test results to engineering department and recommends design or material changes.
GOE: 05.05.10 STRENGTH: L GED: R4 M4 L3 SVP: 7 DLU: 77

806.281-018 FINAL INSPECTOR, MOTORCYCLES (motor-bicycles)
Inspects and tests new motorcycles prior to shipment to ensure conformance with specified standards, using mechanic's handtools and specification sheets: Turns screws and bolts to adjust brake, carburetor, clutch, or timing of motor to attain specified performance, using handtools. Activates motor and runs stationary motorcycle at various speeds, and records unusual sounds or vibration in motor, rear end, or transmission. Drives motorcycle over test area to detect malfunctions in engine and defects in body assembly. Observes instrument dials and gauges on dashboard and records deviations from standards, such as performance vibration, low oil pressure, discharging battery, or stiff action. Compiles written report approving unit for shipment or specifies reason for disapproval. When test riding only, may be designated Test Rider (motor-bicycles).
GOE: 06.01.05 STRENGTH: L GED: R4 M2 L2 SVP: 7 DLU: 77

806.281-026 INSPECTOR, PRECISION ASSEMBLY (aircraft mfg.)
Inspects and tests precision parts and assemblies, such as landing gear, control columns, boosters, and impellers, used in manufacturing aircraft and aircraft

engines, for conformance to blueprints, drawings, and other specifications, using precision measuring instruments and testing equipment: Visually examines parts for completeness, relationship of component parts, quality, and obvious defects. Measures clearances, dimensions, alignment, mesh, and fit of component parts, using precision measuring instruments, such as boroscope, micrometers, calipers, and gauges. Compares measurements to blueprints, drawings, and specifications to determine if parts conform to acceptable tolerances. Connects assemblies to bench test equipment, and conducts functional and continuity tests to determine if working mechanisms adhere to established standards. Records inspection results to document acceptance, rejection, or rework required of inspected parts and assemblies. May plan method and sequence of inspection and testing when written information is not provided.
GOE: 06.01.05 STRENGTH: L GED: R4 M4 L3 SVP: 7 DLU: 88

806.281-058 CARPENTER, PROTOTYPE (ship-boat mfg.)
Fits and installs bulkheads, sole, and cabinets in prototype fiberglass boats, and cuts pattern for production sailboats: Reads preliminary blueprints to determine bulkhead dimensions and position. Transfers dimensions to marine plywood, using tape measure, square, and marking devices. Cuts wood to specified dimensions, using portable electric saw. Lifts and carries wood and climbs scaffolds to position plywood in hull. Pushes and pulls to position bulkhead in accordance with specifications. Marks and trims bulkhead to remove excess material and ensure bulkhead matches hull contour. Attaches bulkhead to pawl with clamps to immobilize bulkhead. Applies liquid adhesive to back of trim fabric and surface to be covered, using brush. Lays fabric on adhesive-coated area and smooths material with hands to remove wrinkles. Slides and shoves prebuilt cabinets into specified position. Transfers measurements of fitted parts to plywood, using tape measure, square, and marking devices. Cuts wood, using portable electric saw, to make pattern for production sailboat.
GOE: 05.05.02 STRENGTH: H GED: R4 M3 L3 SVP: 7 DLU: 86

806.283-010 TEST DRIVER II (auto. mfg.)
Drives prototype or experimental vehicles, such as automobiles, trucks, motor homes, or buses, under test conditions to obtain performance data: Drives vehicle over test tracks, city streets, or highways to perform specified tests. Gathers data on vehicle performance, such as braking action, stability, and maneuverability. Listens for unusual noises from engine, transmission, differential, and body parts, indicating possible defects. Copies readings from special test equipment. Records information, such as miles traveled and gas, oil, or water consumed, brake operation, noises detected, and general performance on standard form. May install special testing equipment specified for tests. May perform maintenance duties, such as gassing car, changing oil, or lubricating car.
GOE: 05.07.02 STRENGTH: L GED: R4 M3 L3 SVP: 7 DLU: 90

806.283-014 TEST DRIVER I (auto. mfg.) alternate titles: car tester; chassis driver; overland driver; road tester
Drives completed motor vehicle, as vehicle comes from assembly line, on proving ground under simulated road conditions, and observes performance to detect mechanical and structural defects: Examines vehicle before road testing to ensure that equipment, such as electrical wiring, hydraulic lines, and fan belts are installed as specified, and verifies that vehicle has been serviced with oil, gas, and water. Drives vehicle to simulate actual driving conditions. Listens for rattles and excessive mechanical noise, and moves controls to test functioning of equipment, such as horn, heater, wipers, and power windows. Writes inspection report on standardized form indicating defects or malfunctions.
GOE: 06.03.01 STRENGTH: L GED: R3 M2 L3 SVP: 6 DLU: 90

806.361-014 ASSEMBLER-INSTALLER, GENERAL (aircraft mfg.) alternate titles: line assembler, aircraft
Builds up and joins structural assemblies, such as wing, tail, and fuselage, and installs functional units, parts, or equipment, such as landing gear, control surfaces, doors, stowage units, fuel and oil tanks, wire harnesses, and floorboards, according to specifications, using handtools and power tools: Locates and marks reference points and holes for installation operations, using jigs and templates, or measures from previously established or marked station lines or index points, using measuring instruments, such as scales, micrometer, and square. Cuts, trims, files, drills, reams, cements, or solders assembled units prior to installation, using handtools and power tools. Bolts, screws, or rivets accessories, such as brackets, pulleys, and clips to fasten, support, or hang components and installations. Aligns and fits structural assemblies manually or signals OVERHEAD CRANE OPERATOR (any industry) 921.663-010 to position assemblies for joining. Bolts, clamps, and rivets assemblies to fuselage. Installs functional units, parts, or equipment in structural assembly according to blueprints and specifications, using handtools and power tools. Inspects and tests installed units, parts, and equipment to ensure that fit, clearance, alignment, and functional performance comply with standards, using measuring instruments and test equipment.
GOE: 06.02.22 STRENGTH: M GED: R4 M3 L3 SVP: 6 DLU: 87

806.361-018 FINAL INSPECTOR, TRUCK TRAILER (auto. mfg.)
Examines assembled truck trailers for conformance to manufacturing specifications: Measures parts and compares dimensions with work orders and blueprints, using steel tape, fixed gauges, and micrometers. Inspects electrical wiring, following wiring diagrams and color codes. Compares part numbers with assembled units to determine that undercarriage, braking system, wheels, tires, and latching support meet specifications. Examines welded and painted surfaces for flaws. Records type of items examined and defects found. Stamps items that meet specifications.

GOE: 06.01.05 STRENGTH: L GED: R4 M3 L4 SVP: 8 DLU: 89

806.361-022 INSPECTOR, FABRICATION (aircraft mfg.)
Inspects metallic and nonmetallic aircraft parts, such as extrusions, tubing, skins, access doors, fuel and oil tank sections, and air ducts, for conformance to standards and specifications: Reads and interprets inspection manuals, blueprints, engineering drawings, and specifications to determine inspection method and procedures and allowable tolerances. Examines parts for defects, such as cracks, corrosion, pits, and stress and fatigue marks. Measures dimensions, contours, trim lines, angles, radii, and coordination of parts for conformance to blueprints and specifications, using precision measuring instruments and devices, such as surface plate, surface table, micrometers, calipers, protractor, and contour templates. Calculates allowable dimensional deviations, utilizing knowledge of shop math. Verifies configuration of component parts and location of fastener holes, using check fixtures and measuring instruments. Inspects welding, heat treating, bonding, brazing, and machining of parts for conformance to specifications. Observes or conducts testing of parts to ensure that functional performance and physical characteristics conform to fabrication standards and specifications, using testing and measuring equipment. Accepts or rejects parts and records inspection results. Discusses test results with quality assurance, production, and engineering personnel. May review inspection results prepared by other inspectors. May be designated according to fabrication process involved as Inspector, Machined Parts (aircraft mfg.); Inspector, Sheet Metal Parts (aircraft mfg.); Inspector, Welded Parts (aircraft mfg.).
GOE: 06.01.05 STRENGTH: M GED: R4 M4 L3 SVP: 6 DLU: 88

806.361-026 NEW-CAR GET-READY MECHANIC (automotive ser.; retail trade) alternate titles: car checker; make-ready mechanic
Inspects and services new automobiles on delivery to dealer or customer, and makes minor repairs or adjustments to place vehicle in salable condition, using handtools, portable power tools, and specification sheets: Inspects vehicle for obvious damage and missing major components. Records discrepancies and signs acceptance slip for each vehicle delivered. Inspects vehicle for loose or misaligned items, such as trim, doors, and hardware, and positions defective items according to specifications, using handtools. Starts engine and drives automobile to test steering, brakes, transmission, and engine operation. Activates power equipment, such as electric windows, seats, radio, horn, lights, and directional signals to ensure specified operating standards. Washes car and vacuums interior. Inspects surfaces to detect minor chips and scratches in paint and touches up imperfections, using brush applicator and factory-supplied matching paint. Installs optional equipment specified by customer or dealer, such as outside mirrors, rugs, and seat covers, using handtools. Installs standard components, such as hubcaps and wiper blades, using handtools. Pours antifreeze into radiator according to seasonal requirements. Polishes car to remove preservative coating and road film accumulated during transit. May spray undercoating material on vehicle, using spray gun. May tune engine, using mechanic's tools and test equipment. May install or repair major mechanical, hydraulic, or electromechanical equipment, such as radios, air-conditioners, power steering units, and power brakes, using mechanic's handtools.
GOE: 05.10.02 STRENGTH: M GED: R3 M2 L2 SVP: 6 DLU: 87

806.361-030 AIRCRAFT MECHANIC, ARMAMENT (aircraft mfg.) alternate titles: armament assembler; armament installer
Assembles, installs, and adjusts aircraft armament parts, assemblies, and accessories, according to specifications, using handtools, power tools, and measuring instruments: Cleans and oils armament parts, units, and accessories. Attaches armament mounts to aircraft, using handtools and power tools. Assembles armament system components, such as guns, gun cameras, bomb racks, missile pods, and firing devices, using measuring instruments, handtools, and power tools. Installs parts, assemblies, and accessories in specified location on aircraft, using handtools, power tools, and lifting devices. Installs and connects control cables to electronically controlled units, using handtools, ring locks, cotter keys, threaded connectors, turnbuckles, and related devices, and adjusts cables to specified tolerances. Aligns, adjusts, and synchronizes aircraft armament, using sighting devices and handtools. Tests functional performance of installed units and adjusts, repairs, or replaces malfunctioning units. Prepares and loads live ammunition, missiles, and bombs onto aircraft, according to established procedure. May assist in operational checkout of entire armament system, including test firing, on ground or during test flight.
GOE: 06.01.04 STRENGTH: M GED: R4 M3 L3 SVP: 7 DLU: 89

806.364-010 INSPECTOR, EXHAUST EMISSIONS (auto. mfg.)
Inspects and tests motor vehicle emission control systems, using handtools and computerized testing equipment: Attaches test circuit leads to vehicle ignition system and inserts exhaust probe in tail pipe. Starts and accelerates engine to specified speed. Observes dials and meters of testing equipment to determine exhaust emission content and records readings on chart. Compares computer printout to exhaust emissions chart to detect variations. Examines emission control systems to determine cause of faulty operation. Adjusts and replaces defective parts, using handtools. Records incidence of recurring defects and consults with department heads or plant engineers to initiate corrective measures.
GOE: 06.03.01 STRENGTH: L GED: R3 M3 L3 SVP: 5 DLU: 90

806.367-010 UTILITY WORKER, LINE ASSEMBLY (auto. mfg.) alternate titles: group leader; team coordinator
Determines conditions impeding flow of work on motor vehicle assembly line and notifies responsible personnel that corrective action is necessary: Informs workers of supervisor's instructions. Notifies supervisor of substandard assembly work and defective parts, tools, equipment, and material, or other conditions which hinder assembly process. Notifies supervisor of excessive number of damaged or defective parts, and requests replacement supply of standard parts to expedite work flow. Discusses methods of resolving recurring production problems with workers and supervisors, utilizing knowledge of assembly process. Observes material stock along assembly line and notifies materials-handling personnel or supervisor of impending shortages. Serves temporarily as ASSEMBLER, MOTOR VEHICLE (auto. mfg.) 806.684-010 in work-congested areas. Instructs new workers and demonstrates new or changed operations. May substitute for workers at moving-line assembly operation. May work as member of assembly group (team) and be assigned to different stages of production process. May participate in group meetings to exchange job related information.
GOE: 06.04.01 STRENGTH: M GED: R3 M2 L3 SVP: 4 DLU: 90

806.367-014 QUALITY ASSURANCE GROUP LEADER (auto. mfg.) alternate titles: team coordinator; team leader
Assists QUALITY ASSURANCE SUPERVISOR (auto. mfg.) 806.137-022 in coordinating and monitoring activities of workers engaged in inspecting and testing assembled motor vehicles, components, and parts, as vehicles and subassemblies proceed through stages of assembly process, applying knowledge of quality assurance standards and procedures: Confers with supervisor and reviews assembly specifications and production schedules. Assigns workers to work stations and monitors department activities. Interprets standards and procedures, and assists workers in resolving technical problems. Reports unresolved problems to supervisor. Demonstrates tools, equipment, and work aids used in performing quality assurance tasks. May attend management meetings to represent work group and record minutes of meeting. May conduct work group (team) meetings to relay management information to workers, and solicit response to work-related problems. May perform duties of absent workers to maintain work schedules.
GOE: 06.03.02 STRENGTH: L GED: R3 M2 L3 SVP: 5 DLU: 87

806.367-018 QUALITY ASSURANCE MONITOR (auto. mfg.)
Inspects and tests assembled motor vehicle, components, and parts as vehicle and subassemblies proceed through stages of assembly process, performing any combination of following tasks, to assure that assembly work and materials meet establishment and regulatory standards, using conventional and electronic test equipment and machines: Pries welded surfaces of vehicle body apart to observe welded seams and compare characteristics of spot welds with standards. Conducts nondestructive ultrasonic tests on unpainted vehicle body to assure that production welding standards have been met. Inspects vehicle subassemblies and parts received from suppliers to detect substandard materials prior to distribution to assembly line. Inspects painted vehicle to detect defects in painted surfaces. Measures gaps between vehicle doors, deck lid, hood, and body, and flushness of parts to vehicle body. Measures force required to close vehicle doors and deck lids, operate door-opening buttons, and turn key in doors and deck lid locks. Verifies predetermined torque settings on bolts and nuts used to assemble parts, subassemblies and vehicle body. Verifies and calibrates setting of pneumatic powered and hand torque wrenches. Inspects trim parts and components of vehicle body, such as molding, instrument control panel, wire harnesses, and seat belts. Inspects and tests chassis parts and components, such as engine and transmission, and suspension, brake, and exhaust systems. Functionally tests electrical and mechanical systems of completed motor vehicle. Drives completed vehicle on test track to determine origin of wind noise, squeaks, and rattles. Records results of individual observations and tests, using printed graphic and written forms, electronic data collecting equipment, or keyboard of central computer system. Reviews overall quality of vehicle leaving one stage of production prior to entering next or final stage. Observes assembly and quality assurance process to trace cause of production defects, and confers with production and quality assurance workers and supervisors, and engineering personnel to resolve problems. Attends meetings to obtain and discuss report of production defects observed and recorded by quality audit personnel (centralized auditing unit), for later discussion with department workers and supervisor. Corrects substandard work or replaces defective parts, using handtools and power tools. May work as member of quality assurance group (team) and be assigned different work stations as monitoring needs require. May be designated according to stage of assembly process as Quality Assurance Monitor, Body (auto. mfg.); Quality Assurance Monitor, Chassis (auto. mfg.); Quality Assurance Monitor, Final (auto. mfg.); Quality Assurance Monitor, Trim (auto. mfg.).
GOE: 06.03.02 STRENGTH: L GED: R3 M2 L3 SVP: 5 DLU: 87

806.380-010 RIVETING MACHINE OPERATOR, AUTOMATIC (aircraft mfg.)
Sets up and operates riveting machines that automatically drill, countersink, and rivet aircraft assemblies, such as wing panels and fuselage sections: Reads and interprets blueprints, engineering drawings, and specifications to determine setup and operating procedures. Positions, aligns, and levels parts to be assembled in machine locating tools, or loads part in automatic work positioner installed on machine, using hoist or overhead crane. Selects and installs tools, such as drills, countersinks, rams, rivet injector, and chamfer tools in machine spindles, using handtools. Loads control media, such as tape or disk, in machine. Adjusts controls to synchronize control media, parts, and machine, and to regulate depth of countersink, air pressure, and ram stroke. Fills hopper with

rivets or other fasteners. Starts machine, observes operation, monitors displays, and readjusts machine to ensure riveted assemblies conform to specifications. Operates machine manually or from automatic settings. Replaces defective cutting tools. May assemble parts prior to loading parts on machine, using rivet gun and bucking bar. May be designated by type of media controlling machine as Riveting Machine Operator, Programmed Control (aircraft mfg.); Riveting Machine Operator, Tape Control (aircraft mfg.).
GOE: 06.01.03 STRENGTH: M GED: R4 M3 L3 SVP: 6 DLU: 88

806.381-014 AIRCRAFT MECHANIC, ENVIRONMENTAL CONTROL SYSTEM (aircraft mfg.)
Lays out, assembles, installs, tests, and adjusts aircraft environmental control systems according to specifications, using handtools, power tools, machines, and test equipment: Lays out location of assemblies and parts, such as turbines, heat exchanges, valves, cylinders, struts, pumps, instruments, lines, and fittings on aircraft, using layout tools, such as scribers, rules, steel tape, and center punches. Measures, cuts, and bends tubing and other materials, using machines, such as saws, brakes, and tube bending equipment. Assembles, installs, and hooks up system components, using handtools, power tools, and fasteners, such as bolts, screws, rivets, and clamps. Tests functional performance of installed systems and portions of systems for malfunctions or leaks, using test equipment.
GOE: 06.01.04 STRENGTH: M GED: R4 M3 L3 SVP: 7 DLU: 88

806.381-018 AIRCRAFT MECHANIC, RIGGING AND CONTROLS (aircraft mfg.) alternate titles: aircraft mechanic, rigger; assembler-installer, cable controlled systems
Assembles and installs rigging and control assemblies and systems that actuate aircraft structures, such as rudder, elevator, canopy, and wing surfaces, according to specifications, using handtools, power tools, and equipment: Reads and interprets blueprints, production illustrations, and other specifications to determine location, identity, and relationship of parts. Assembles, hangs, connects, and installs rigging and control assemblies and systems, including cables, cylinders, components of ailerons and flaps, pulleys, mountings, and brackets, working from established station lines and index points, using templates, jigs, fixtures, handtools, and power tools. Sets, adjusts, and synchronizes rigging and control system components to established tolerances and requirements. Verifies specified tension of cables, using tensionmeter. Operates rigging and control systems to determine functional performance, and reworks or adjusts system components accordingly. May install mechanical linkages and actuators.
GOE: 06.01.04 STRENGTH: M GED: R4 M4 L3 SVP: 6 DLU: 88

806.381-022 ASSEMBLER, AIRCRAFT POWER PLANT (aircraft mfg.) alternate titles: engine buildup mechanic
Builds up aircraft power plant according to blueprints and specifications, using handtools, power tools, and equipment: Positions and secures engine on assembly fixture, using hoist. Connects auxiliary component parts, wiring, cables, lines, and accessory units to engine according to blueprints and assembly procedures, using handtools and power tools. Fits, trims, aligns, and adjusts parts and components, using handtools, power tools, and measuring instruments. Solders, lugs, routes, and ties electrical components. Tests installed parts and accessories for leakage, continuity, and functionality, using test equipment. Reworks, repairs, or replaces faulty components. May install engine in nacelle or other structural assembly. May assemble and install propeller components. May remove engine from crate or packing container.
GOE: 06.02.22 STRENGTH: M GED: R3 M2 L3 SVP: 6 DLU: 88

806.381-026 ASSEMBLER, AIRCRAFT, STRUCTURES AND SURFACES (aircraft mfg.) alternate titles: aircraft mechanic, structures; assembler-installer, sturctures; structures assembler
Assembles tail, wing, fuselage, or other structural section of aircraft, space vehicles, and missiles from parts, subassemblies, and components, such as frames, bulkheads, doors, stabilizers, and landing gear, following blueprints and specifications, using handtools, power tools, and measuring instruments: Positions and aligns subassemblies in jigs or fixtures, using measuring instruments, such as protractors and dividers, following blueprint station lines and index points. Trims and files parts to fit, and verifies fitting tolerances, using measuring instruments, such as gauges and calipers. Drills, reams, and countersinks holes in subassemblies, and bolts, rivets, or otherwise fastens subassemblies into structural assembly, using handtools and power tools. Locates holes to be drilled in structural assembly for installation of parts and components, using jigs, templates, and measuring instruments. Drills holes in structure and attaches brackets, hinges, braces, and clips to secure installations. Installs parts and components, such as incidental plumbing, electrical, rigging, or other functional items, in main structure, using handtools and power tools. May specialize in assembling and installing parts, structural components, and subassemblies to build wing assemblies and be designated Assembler-Installer, Wing Structures (aircraft mfg.).
GOE: 06.01.04 STRENGTH: M GED: R4 M3 L3 SVP: 6 DLU: 88

806.381-034 ASSEMBLER, TUBING (aircraft mfg.) alternate titles: tube bender-assembler
Fabricates and assembles tubing components for air, fuel, oil, hydraulic, and related systems of aircraft and spacecraft, according to specifications, using handtools, power tools, machines, equipment, and measuring instruments: Reads work order, blueprints, sketches, and bend data charts, or works from master

tubing templates to determine tubing dimensions, configuration, and finish specifications. Establishes location of cutouts, holes, and trim lines of parts and relationship of parts to each other, using measuring instruments, such as rule, scales, and dividers. Sets up and operates variety of manual and power machines to cut, bend, form, swage, flare, bead, and burr tubing according to specifications. Attaches fittings, such as nuts, sleeves, collars, and caps, to tubing components, using handtools. Aligns, fits, and assembles tubing components in jigs and fixtures for subsequent welding. Modifies holding fixtures and jigs to conform to configuration of tubing samples by placing and fastening guides, stops, cradles, clamps, and rotation holders, using handtools. Measures and inspects tubing components for conformance to master tube data, using master template or measuring instruments. Tests tubing assemblies for leaks and other defects, using pressure testing equipment. Marks identifying information on tubing, using electro-chemical etching device, label, rubber stamp, or other method. Cleans and lubricates tubing and assemblies. May weld tubing and fittings, using tack-welder, induction brazing chamber, or other equipment. May operate tube-straightening machine. May operate oven to form nylon, plastic, and shrink tubing. May set up and operate computer-controlled tube bending systems to bend and check tubing.
GOE: 06.01.04 STRENGTH: M GED: R3 M3 L3 SVP: 6 DLU: 88

806.381-042 CABLE ASSEMBLER AND SWAGER (aircraft mfg.) alternate titles: cable assembler; cable cutter and swager
Fabricates and tests aircraft cable assemblies, such as control cables, tow-target cables, and engine slings, following blueprints and specifications, using measuring instruments, handtools, and machines: Reads and interprets blueprints, work orders, and specifications to determine sequence of operations, type and size of cable and fittings required, quantity, and finished dimensions. Measures and cuts cable to required length, considering cable stretch and metal flow resulting from swaging operations, using cable cutter or saw. Selects and installs dies, jigs, shims, or other accessories in swaging machine, using handtools. Assembles fittings onto cable in specified location. Positions fitting and cable between dies of swaging machine, and depresses pedal to activate machine that swages fittings onto cable, turning cable assembly by hand as fitting is swaged onto cable. Verifies dimensions of cable assembly and position of fittings, using measuring instruments. Tests holding capacity of cable assembly, using proofloading machines. Repairs and reworks cable assemblies as required. May form loops or splices in cables, using clamps and fittings, or by reweaving cable strands. May solder cable ends. May apply lubricants and protective coatings to cable assemblies. May operate crimping machine. May mark identifying information on cable assemblies. May fabricate cable templates.
GOE: 06.02.22 STRENGTH: M GED: R3 M3 L3 SVP: 6 DLU: 88

806.381-046 SHIPFITTER (ship-boat mfg.) alternate titles: fitter
Lays out and fabricates metal structural parts, such as plates, bulkheads, and frames, and braces them in position within hull of ship for riveting or welding: Lays out position of parts on metal, working from blueprints or templates and using scribe and handtools. Locates and marks reference lines, such as center, buttock, and frame lines. Positions parts in hull of ship, assisted by RIGGER (ship-boat mfg.). Aligns parts in relation to each other, using jacks, turnbuckles, clips, wedges, and mauls. Marks location of holes to be drilled and installs temporary fasteners to hold part in place for welding or riveting. Installs packing, gaskets, liners, and structural accessories and members, such as doors, hatches, brackets, and clips. May prepare molds and templates for fabrication of nonstandard parts. May tack weld clips and brackets in place prior to permanent welding. May roll, bend, flange, cut, and shape plates, beams, and other heavy metal parts, using shop machinery, such as plate rolls, presses, bending brakes, and joggle machines.
GOE: 05.05.06 STRENGTH: H GED: R4 M3 L2 SVP: 8 DLU: 77

806.381-050 SHIPFITTER APPRENTICE (ship-boat mfg.)
Performs duties as described under APPRENTICE (any industry) Master Title.
GOE: 05.05.06 STRENGTH: H GED: R4 M3 L2 SVP: 8 DLU: 77

806.381-058 TRAILER ASSEMBLER I (auto. mfg.) alternate titles: assembler, truck-trailer
Assembles prefabricated parts to build metal and wood truck trailers, following blueprints, performing any combination of following tasks: Lays out, fits, drills, screws, bolts, and rivets together metal sheeting, upright frames, bottom and top bars, and angle clips, using pneumatic and hydraulic handtools and machines, and templates. Assembles and fastens together preassembled trailer side and top sections to trailer frame. Marks and cuts openings in sheeting, installs support framing around openings, and installs preassembled doors, handles, hinges, and catches. Fits, drills, bolts, and rivets metal frame posts, headers, and buckplates together to make rear trailer body section, verifying tolerances with square and rule. Assembles and bolts undercarriage in position and mounts tires on wheels. Drills, bolts, and rivets frames, metal and plywood sheeting, lock assemblies, hinges, and bracket angles to assemble doors for trailer bodies. Installs insulating material between framing and outer plates of doors. Screws holding brackets in place and strings wiring for lighting system. Applies sealant to assembled sections. Welds parts. May be designated according to part assembled as Custom-Frame Assembler (auto. mfg.); Trailer-Body Assembler (auto. mfg.).
GOE: 06.02.22 STRENGTH: M GED: R3 M2 L2 SVP: 3 DLU: 89

806.381-062 INSTALLER, ELECTRICAL, PLUMBING, MECHANICAL (ship-boat mfg.)

Installs electrical circuitry and fixtures, plumbing and plumbing fixtures, and engines in sailboats, using power and handtools: Reads blueprints and work diagrams to determine length and size of wire needed. Measures and cuts wire to specified length, using tape measure and electrician's pliers. Strips insulation from ends of wire, using electrician's knife, and connects wire to terminals, using screwdriver. Strings wire harness beneath hull flange to secure harness with nylon strap. Pulls length of wire from harness at specified points to complete branch circuits. Drills holes in bulkhead and cabin and mounts panels and fixtures, using electric drill and screwdriver. Places toilet in prescribed location on toilet pedestal and secures toilet with bolts, using hand-held wrench. Places sink in countertop cutout, applies sealant around edge of sink, using caulking gun, and secures sink with fasteners, using wrench. Forces ends of prescribed, precut hoses over intake and discharge fittings to provide water for plumbing system and engine cooling. Installs and tightens hose clamps to form watertight seal, using wrench and screwdriver. Operates saw to cut holes for valves, outlets, and propellor drive shaft. Inserts valve and outlet fittings through hole to provide watertight fit. Operates overhead hoist controls to position engine in boat. Pushes and pulls engine to position engine over mount rails. Inserts stub shaft in engine drive coupling to aid in aligning engine on mount rails and to locate position for shaft gland on stern post. Drills holes in engine mount rails, using portable electric drill, inserts bolts, and tightens bolts, using wrench, to secure engine to boat. May lead and give directions to other workers performing same duties.
GOE: 05.05.05 STRENGTH: M GED: R3 M3 L3 SVP: 7 DLU: 86

806.381-066 AIRCRAFT MECHANIC, PLUMBING AND HYDRAULICS (aircraft mfg.) alternate titles: assembler, aircraft, plumbing and hydraulics; hydraulic and plumbing installer

Lays out, assembles, installs, and tests plumbing and hydraulic systems and components in aircraft, following blueprints and production illustrations, using handtools, power tools, and test equipment: Lays out location of parts and assemblies, such as surface control boosters, landing gears, vacuum units, and fuel, oil, oxygen, and water systems, according to specifications, using measuring and marking instruments. Assembles and installs parts and assemblies, using handtools and power tools. Adjusts working mechanisms of installed parts and assemblies to blueprint specifications. Conducts pressure, leak, and functional tests of installed systems, using test equipment. Repairs or replaces malfunctioning system components. May fabricate parts incidental to assembly and installation, using shop equipment.
GOE: 06.02.22 STRENGTH: M GED: R3 M3 L3 SVP: 7 DLU: 88

806.381-070 CUSTOM VAN CONVERTER (auto. mfg.; automotive ser.)

Performs any combination of following duties to customize vans according to specifications and work orders, using handtools, power tools and welding equipment: Measures interior of van to determine area to be modified. Fabricates and installs walls, cabinets, and supports. Cuts wall and floor sections of vehicle body for installation of customized interior components and specialized equipment, according to specifications. Installs new top on vehicle body to increase headroom. Installs electrical systems, such as wire harnesses, electrical outlets, and electrical/electronic controls for specialized equipment. Tests electrical systems, using ohmmeter and voltmeter. Positions and installs appliances in vehicle according to specifications. Installs customized interior components, such as carpet, linoleum, wall covering and preassembled windows, according to customer orders. Prepares and paints vehicle surfaces and parts, using spray paint equipment. Installs specialized equipment, such as wheelchair lift, steering and braking systems, for use by handicapped persons.
GOE: 05.05.02 STRENGTH: M GED: R4 M3 L3 SVP: 5 DLU: 88

806.381-074 INSPECTOR, PROCESSING (aircraft mfg.)

Inspects aircraft and space vehicle parts, assemblies, and materials for results or effects of manufacturing processes or operations, such as anodizing, painting, etching, passivating, sandblasting, and chemical milling, for conformance to specifications, using precision measuring instruments and equipment: Examines surfaces of processed parts, assemblies, and materials for uniformity of finish, color, and area covered, and to detect defects, such as corrosion, blistering, pinholes, and dents. Measures dimensions of parts, assemblies, and materials before, during, and after processing cycles for conformance to blueprints, engineering data, shop orders, and other specifications, using precision measuring instruments, such as micrometers and gauges, and equipment. Verifies that temperature ranges and density of processing mixtures and solutions adhere to specifications. Approves or rejects parts, assemblies, and materials, and prepares documentation indicating reason for rejection, rework required, and disposition of parts. May inspect parts and materials for soundness, hardness [HARDNESS INSPECTOR (heat treating) 504.387-010], and for effects of heat-treating [HEAT-TREAT INSPECTOR (heat treating) 504.281-010], using testing equipment.
GOE: 06.01.05 STRENGTH: L GED: R3 M3 L3 SVP: 5 DLU: 88

806.381-078 INSTALLER, INTERIOR ASSEMBLIES (aircraft mfg.) alternate titles: cabin furnishings installer

Installs aircraft interior furnishings, trim, and accessories, such as carpeting, sidewalls, doors, windows, seats, partitions, galleys, and passenger service units, according to specifications, using handtools and power tools: Reads and interprets blueprints, drawings, and production procedures to determine measurements and installation procedures. Measures and marks installation areas in aircraft interior, using measuring and marking instruments and templates. Drills, reams, countersinks, rivets, trims, and files parts and assemblies, using handtools and power tools. Fits and installs items in aircraft, using handtools, power tools, and fasteners, such as screws, rivets, bolts, and speednuts. Fabricates and installs supporting structural devices, such as clips, brackets, angles, gussets, and doublers, using shop equipment. Tests functional performance of installed items. Reworks installations as required.
GOE: 06.01.04 STRENGTH: M GED: R4 M3 L3 SVP: 6 DLU: 87

806.381-082 PRECISION ASSEMBLER (aircraft mfg.)

Assembles, tests, and repairs aircraft and space vehicle precision hydraulic and structural subassemblies, assemblies, and incidental mechanical units, such as landing gear, elevator, and control stands, according to blueprints and specifications, using handtools, power tools, precision instruments, and test equipment: Reads and interprets blueprints, specifications, and related documents to determine methods and sequence of operations. Examines component parts for defects. Measures parts to ensure conformance to specified dimensions and lays out reference points for holes, trim lines, and part locations, using precision measuring instruments. Drills, reams, trims, shims, files, and smooths parts, using handtools and power tools, to ensure fit and clearance of component parts. Aligns, fits, and assembles hydraulic, structural, and mechanical components into completed assembly, using jigs, fixtures, measuring instruments, handtools, and power tools. Tests functional performance of completed assemblies, such as booster units and aircraft heaters, using test equipment. Reworks, replaces, and realigns parts, adjusts valves, retorques fittings, and retests units to ensure conformance to specifications.
GOE: 06.01.04 STRENGTH: M GED: R4 M4 L4 SVP: 7 DLU: 89

806.383-010 ROADABILITY-MACHINE OPERATOR (auto. mfg.)

Drives completed motor vehicle onto roller drums of computerized roadability machine that tests mechanical and electrical systems of vehicle: Drives vehicle onto roller drums of test machine, and connects computer cables of machine to terminals of vehicle instrument control panel. Moves shift lever through range of gears, to run rear wheels of rear-wheel drive vehicles and front wheels of front-wheel drive vehicles at specified speeds for computer testing of vehicle components, such as transmission, cruise control, and brake system. Observes computer video display screen of test machine to verify that vehicle performance conforms to specifications. Attaches computer printout of test results to inspection document in vehicle. Disconnects test cables, and drives vehicle to repair or shipping area.
GOE: 06.01.05 STRENGTH: L GED: R3 M2 L3 SVP: 4 DLU: 90

806.384-014 INSPECTOR, RETURNED MATERIALS (auto. mfg.) alternate titles: salvage inspector; service-claims inspector; service dismantler

Tests, dismantles, and inspects motor vehicle parts returned as defective to determine cause of defects: Examines unit for cracked or missing components. Tests unit under simulated operating conditions to determine nature of defect, using computerized testing equipment. Dismantles unit and inspects components for conformance to specifications, using instruments, such as micrometers, indicator gauges, hardness testers, calipers, and sine bars. Determines cause of defect and prepares report of findings. Routes unit to department for replacement, repair, or salvage. May judge validity of customer's claim of defective parts or work. May specialize according to type of product inspected.
GOE: 06.03.01 STRENGTH: M GED: R3 M2 L3 SVP: 5 DLU: 90

806.384-022 ROCKET-TEST-FIRE WORKER (ordnance)

Prepares rocket-motor cases for test firing and cleans cases subsequent to firing: Conveys rocket-motor case to test area, using forklift truck. Positions case in heat-conditioning chamber, using lift truck, and turns dial on control panel to heat case to specified temperature. Positions case on test stand, using hoist, and attaches thermocouples from test stand to case preparatory to test-firing. Removes case from stand subsequent to firing and immerses case in chemical bath to remove liner and propellant residue, using hoist.
GOE: 05.11.04 STRENGTH: M GED: R3 M1 L1 SVP: 5 DLU: 77

806.384-030 ASSEMBLER, METAL BONDING (aircraft mfg.) alternate titles: assembler, bonding

Bonds aircraft and space vehicle parts and assemblies, such as sheet metal skins to honeycomb core, according to blueprints and specifications, using handtools, power tools, and equipment: Reads process charts, work orders, and specifications to determine sequence of bonding operations, amount of bonding agent to be applied, and areas to be bonded. Examines parts to verify that prior processes have been completed and that identifying information corresponds with specifications. Measures, trims, fits, forms, and shapes mating surfaces of parts to ensure required contact can be accomplished, using measuring instruments, handtools, and power tools. Cleans dust, dirt, oil, and other foreign matter from contact surfaces, using cleaning solutions and rags. Positions, aligns, fits, and assembles parts, materials, and incidental functional items on jigs, fixtures, platen or project plates, using handtools, power tools, and fasteners. Applies primer and metal bonding film, foam, or other adhesives to bonding surfaces. Dries and cures parts and assemblies, using vacuum fixtures or presses with heated platens. Adjusts curing oven controls to regulate pressure, time, and heating temperature. Loads and unloads assemblies from oven, manually or using equipment. May mix adhesives.
GOE: 06.02.24 STRENGTH: M GED: R3 M2 L3 SVP: 5 DLU: 88

806.384-034 ASSEMBLER, SUBASSEMBLY (aircraft mfg.) alternate titles: detail assembler

Assembles parts, such as spars, ribs, and braces, to form structural subassemblies of aircraft, such as airfoils, control surfaces, fuselage tops and bulkheads, doors, and windows, according to specifications, using handtools and power tools: Reads and interprets blueprints and specifications to determine assembly sequence, tooling requirements, measurements, and allowable tolerances. Marks reference lines and points on parts, using templates, or by measuring from blueprint index points and station lines, using rule, protractor, and divider. Cuts, trims, files, and deburrs parts, using handtools or power tools. Measures parts to verify dimensions, using precision instruments, such as micrometers and calipers. Fits and assembles parts and fittings, such as braces, hinges, brackets, keyways, and nut plates, in jigs and fixtures, using clamps. Drills, reams, and countersinks holes, using power tools. Deburrs keyways, holes, and cable grooves, using burring tool. Marks reference symbols on parts for subsequent riveting. Installs bolts, screws, rivets, and other fasteners to join parts, using power tools. Cements, tapes, and glues parts as required. May install electric and hydraulic components. May bend tubing. May make temporary assembly fixtures. May buck rivets.
GOE: 06.02.22 STRENGTH: M GED: R3 M2 L3 SVP: 5 DLU: 87

806.384-038 PRESSURE SEALER-AND-TESTER (aircraft mfg.) alternate titles: sealer, aircraft

Cleans, seals, and tests aircraft pressurized sections and cavities, according to blueprints and specifications, using handtools, power tools, and pressure testing equipment: Reads and interprets blueprints and process specifications to determine area to be sealed, volume of pressure to be applied, and allowable tolerances. Applies cleaning solvent or other solution to interior and exterior surfaces of section to be sealed, such as fuel and water tanks, integral wings, and fuselage, using brushes, rags, spray guns, liquid vacuum cleaners, and air hoses. Applies sealing compounds to surfaces, using fillet guns, brushes, and similar equipment. Dries sealant, using heat lamps and compressed hot air. Bolts access doors and hatches, disconnects plumbing lines, electrical cable and rigging, and caps connections with plugs and threaded fixtures to make section airtight. Sets up and operates pressure-testing equipment to detect leakage. Visually and audibly checks for leakage of areas under pressure, and applies sealing tape, cement, liquid rubber, grommets, and other aids to eliminate leakage. Reinstalls accessories disconnected prior to test. May repair structural defects, using tools and equipment. May seal and test integral wing sections serving as fuel cells, working within closed or difficult areas to access, and be designated Fuel Tank Sealer And Tester (aircraft mfg.) or Integral Tank Sealer (aircraft mfg.). May seal and pressurize aircraft fuselage sections and be designated Pressurization Mechanic (aircraft mfg.) or Pressurizer (aircraft mfg.). May set up and operate air pressure cabinet located outside section being tested by others to maintain constant internal pressure and be designated Pressurization Mechanic, Air Control (aircraft mfg.).
GOE: 06.02.24 STRENGTH: L GED: R3 M2 L3 SVP: 4 DLU: 88

806.387-014 WHEEL INSPECTOR (r.r. trans.)

Inspects railroad wheels for defects and measures wheel flange for wear, using gauges, micrometer, and similar measuring instruments: Examines and feels surface of wheels for cracks and wear. Marks defective area with chalk or paint. Strikes wheel with hammer and listens to sound to detect flaws in metal. Measures wheel flange for wear and gauge (distance) between wheels, using micrometer and similar measuring instruments. Prepares reports describing defects in wheels and amount of wear in wheel flange, with recommendations for repair, replacement, or scrapping.
GOE: 05.07.01 STRENGTH: L GED: R3 M2 L2 SVP: 8 DLU: 77

806.464-010 BOAT RIGGER (retail trade; ship-boat mfg.) alternate titles: boat accessories installer; outboard-motorboat rigger

Installs accessories in outboard or inboard motorboats: Drills holes, attaches brackets, and installs accessories, such as lights, batteries, ignition switches, fuel tanks, and guide pulleys, using handtools and power tools. May change propellors and adjust motors to obtain maximum performance. May install outboard and inboard motors and controls, using handtools. May load boats on trailers and make deliveries to customers.
GOE: 05.10.01 STRENGTH: M GED: R3 M2 L1 SVP: 4 DLU: 77

806.481-010 ASSEMBLER, ALUMINUM BOATS (ship-boat mfg.)

Assembles aluminum boats, performing any combination of following tasks: Bends edges of precut hull bottom, using roller-bending device and hammer. Positions hull sides along bottom and clamps them in place. Drills holes through hull sides, using portable electric drill. Rivets hull bottom and sides together, using pneumatic rivet gun. Bolts wooden gunnel strips and transom in place to stiffen hull. Positions parts, such as ribs, stringers, seats, and flotation tanks in hull, using rule and template and following blueprints. Clamps parts in place, drills holes, and bolts or rivets parts to hull. Drills holes in hull, following layout marks and installs accessories, such as cleats, lights, and windshields. Seals seams with aluminum caulking compound to prevent hull leakage. Files rough edges with hand file.
GOE: 06.02.22 STRENGTH: M GED: R3 M2 L2 SVP: 5 DLU: 77

806.481-014 ASSEMBLER, INTERNAL COMBUSTION ENGINE (engine-turbine) alternate titles: engine assembler

Assembles internal combustion engines according to standard procedures, using handtools, power wrenches, and gauges, performing any of following op-

erations on assembly line: Positions and bolts crankcase, block, and trunion support together to form basic unit of engine, using wrenches, hammer, and power hoist. Mounts crankshaft and camshaft to bearings and tightens bearing caps, using power wrench. Presses gears, sheave, flywheel, or sprocket to shafts, using hand or hydraulic press, and locks them with keys and pins. Inserts cylinder sleeves into engine block or casing and fits piston and connecting rod assembly into cylinder and bolts it to crankshaft. Aligns engine parts, such as camshaft and crankshaft gears, and sets timing and clearances between fixed or moving parts, using aligning gauges, dial indicator, feeler gauges, and timing light. Examines parts or observes movement of completed assemblies to detect malfunction, and discards or replaces defective parts or assemblies. Flares and connects copper or brass tubing for lubricating and cooling systems, using flaring tools and wrenches. May cut and bend tubing to conform to curvature of engine, using bending fixtures and tubing cutters. May lap cylinder counterbore and valve seats to seat cylinder sleeves and valves, using hand lapping tool and compound. May disassemble, polish, buff, and reassemble motors for demonstration purposes and be designated Assembler, Show Motor (engine-turbine). May be designated according to type of engine assembled as Diesel-Engine Assembler (engine-turbine); Gasoline-Engine Assembler (engine-turbine); Motorcycle-Engine Assembler (engine-turbine); Outboard-Motor Assembler (engine-turbine).
GOE: 06.02.22 STRENGTH: M GED: R4 M3 L3 SVP: 6 DLU: 77

806.667-010 HELPER, METAL HANGING (mfd. bldgs.)

Assists METAL HANGER (mfd. bldgs.; vehicles, nec) in installation of sheet metal panels, molding, and exterior parts, using handtools and portable power tools: Secures bottom edge of siding to frame, and attaches accessories, such as reflectors and light covers, using screwdriver. Performs other duties as described under HELPER (any industry) Master Title.
GOE: 06.04.22 STRENGTH: L GED: R1 M1 L1 SVP: 2 DLU: 77

806.684-010 ASSEMBLER, MOTOR VEHICLE (auto. mfg.) alternate titles: quality worker; team member

Assembles motor vehicles, such as automobiles, trucks, buses, or limousines, at assigned work stations on moving assembly line, performing any combination of following repetitive tasks according to specifications and using handtools, power tools, welding equipment, and production fixtures: Loads stamped metal body components into automated welding equipment that welds together components to form body subassemblies. Positions and fastens together body subassemblies, such as side frames, underbodies, doors, hoods, and trunk lids, to assemble vehicle bodies and truck cabs preparatory to body welding process. Bolts, screws, clips, or otherwise fastens together parts to form subassemblies, such as doors, seats, instrument control panels, steering columns, and axle units. Installs mechanical and electrical components and systems, such as engine, transmission, and axle units; pumps; wire harnesses; instrument control panels; and exhaust, brake, and air-conditioning systems. Fits and adjusts doors, hoods, and trunk lids. Seals joints and seams, using caulking gun. Fastens seats, door paneling, headliners, carpeting, molding, and other trim into position. Fills vehicle systems with brake and transmission fluids, engine coolant, and oil. May apply precut and adhesive coated vinyl tops and pads to vehicle roofs. May verify quality of own work and write description of defects observed on documents attached to vehicle bodies. May enter and retrieve production data, using computer terminals. May work as member of assembly group (team) and be assigned different work stations as production needs require or shift from one station to another to reduce fatigue factor. May participate in group meetings to exchange job related information. May be designated according to component assembled or installed as Assembler, Engine (auto. mfg.); Assembler, Seat (auto. mfg.); or stage of assembly as Assembler, Body (auto. mfg.); Assembler, Chassis (auto. mfg.); Assembler, Final (auto. mfg.); Assembler, Trim (auto. mfg.).
GOE: 06.04.22 STRENGTH: M GED: R2 M1 L2 SVP: 2 DLU: 90

806.684-014 ASSEMBLER, BICYCLE I (motor-bicycles)

Assembles bicycles, using handtools and portable power tools: Positions *head* of frame in drill press and pulls lever to drill holes for name plate. Fastens name plate to frame, using brads and hammer. Positions frame in hydraulic press and pulls lever to press bushings in head and *hanger* of frame. Positions frame on post and attaches kickstand to frame, using retaining pin and pliers. Slides sprocket and cone onto crank and inserts crank assembly in frame. Turns locknut to secure crank assembly in frame, using wrench. Positions and secures drive chain, using snap-on tool. Installs front fork assembly, using air wrench and lock pliers. Positions fender and brace in riveting machine and depresses pedal to rivet brace to fender. Bolts fender assembly to frame, using air wrench. Positions wheels in front and rear fork assemblies and secures wheels to frame, using air wrench. Fingers spokes to verify tension and tightens or loosens spokes, using nipple wrench. Bolts seat post to frame, using air wrench. May examine finished bicycle for defects in paint finish and assembly [INSPECTOR, BICYCLE (motor-bicycles)].
GOE: 06.04.22 STRENGTH: L GED: R2 M1 L1 SVP: 4 DLU: 77

806.684-018 ASSEMBLER, CAMPER (vehicles, nec)

Assembles camper bodies and installs interior units according to diagrams and written specifications, performing any combination of following tasks: Assembles and secures floor to camper frame, using power screwdriver. Fastens side and end sections to frame, using hammer and screwdriver. Spreads mastic

on floor and lays linoleum tile, using trowel and tile roller. Installs interior paneling and prefabricated cabinets, using staple gun. Uncrates refrigerator, stove, and water container, and inspects exterior surfaces to detect dents and scratches. Connects water supply and drainage lines to sink, using wrenches. Slides appliances into specified cabinets and glues molding around edges of cabinets to secure appliances, using glue gun. Attaches hinges to cabinet doors and installs doors on cabinets, using screwdriver. May be designated according to part assembled or unit installed as Appliance Installer (vehicles, nec); Cabinet-And-Trim Installer (vehicles, nec); Floor Finisher (vehicles, nec); Floor Framer (vehicles, nec); Side Framer (vehicles, nec).
GOE: 06.04.22 STRENGTH: M GED: R3 M2 L2 SVP: 3 DLU: 77

806.684-022   ASSEMBLER, DECK AND HULL (ship-boat mfg.) alternate titles: deck and hull assembler
Joins deck and hull sections of fiberglass boats, using handtools and portable power tools: Positions deck on hull and seals seam with caulking compound, using caulking gun. Lays aluminum gunwale strip along deck and hull seam and hammers it into place with mallet. Places drilling template along gunwale strip and drills rivet holes through strip with portable electric drill. Rivets or bolts deck and hull together, using rivet gun or impact wrench. Forces rubber bumper rail into gunwale strip with special roller and cuts off surplus strip with hacksaw. Hammers protective and decorative aluminum channel trim around deck and cabin edges with mallet. May trim edges of transom opening with saw prior to installing protective trim. May sand edges and interior of decks and hull, using power sander. May install miscellaneous hardware, such as mooring cleats, toerails, bulkhead panels, and pulpits, using handtools [BOAT OUTFITTER (ship-boat mfg.)].
GOE: 06.02.22 STRENGTH: H GED: R3 M1 L1 SVP: 3 DLU: 77

806.684-026   ASSEMBLER, INSULATION AND FLOORING (ship-boat mfg.)
Sprays fiberglass foam insulation in boat bottoms and installs boat flooring, using pneumatic spray gun, handtools, and portable power tools: Turns valve to open air line of spray gun, secures spray gun hose to foam barrel, and attaches nozzle to spray gun. Reads gauges to ensure specified air pressure, temperature, and chemical mixture of foam. Squeezes spray gun trigger to start flow of foam to boat bottom. Selects precut stringers, used to reinforce motor-mount areas, according to model number of boat. Positions and secures stringers to specified area of boat bottom, using fiberglass mats, resin, and squeegee. Selects prefabricated flooring according to type and size of boat and positions flooring over solidified foam insulation. Drills holes in flooring and insulation, using portable power drill, and fastens flooring to boat bottom, using screwdriver. Spreads wood putty over screwheads and caulks edges of flooring to make boat waterproof, using caulking gun and putty knife. Pushes boat to next station in assembly line.
GOE: 06.04.34 STRENGTH: M GED: R2 M1 L1 SVP: 3 DLU: 77

806.684-038   AUTOMOBILE-ACCESSORIES INSTALLER (automotive ser.)
Installs automobile accessories, such as heaters, radios, antennas, safety seat belts, seat covers, or special clamps, and mirrors: Drills and taps holes, assembles and fits accessories to automobile, and tightens bolts and clamps. May be designated according to specialty as Radio Installer, Automobile (automotive ser.).
GOE: 05.10.02 STRENGTH: M GED: R2 M1 L2 SVP: 4 DLU: 77

806.684-046   CAR TRIMMER (railroad equip.)
Installs interior fixtures in railroad cars, using handtools and portable power tools: Positions and bolts seats in place, using wrench. Bolts door tracks and posts to side of car, using impact wrench. Guides door into tracks, using hoist. Positions and fastens windows in casings, using screwdrivers. Rubs paraffin over window guides to ensure smooth operation. Installs and aligns steps and ladders, using wrenches, jacks, hoist, and sledge. Measures to determine location of other fixtures, such as curtains, handles, signal cords, and door hardware, using gauges, and secures fixtures in place, using screwdrivers and portable power tools.
GOE: 06.04.22 STRENGTH: H GED: R3 M2 L1 SVP: 3 DLU: 77

806.684-050   DOOR ASSEMBLER (mfd. bldgs.; vehicles, nec)
Fabricates parts and assembles precut wood and metal doors for use in mobile homes, trailers, or prefabricated buildings: Positions specified wood frame members in jig and nails or staples members together to form doorframe. Packs insulation between frame members. Marks and cuts sheet metal to conform to dimensions of doorframe, using ruler and powered shear. Bends sheet metal to fit over doorframe, using handbrake. Attaches metal panels to doorframe, using handtools or rivet gun. Marks locations of window and lock on door, using templates, and cuts openings in door, using electric router or power shears. Installs lock assembly and prefabricated window assembly in door, using handtools. Marks positions of hinges on door, using template, and screws hinges to doors, using screwdriver. May attach metal and rubber weather stripping for exterior doors.
GOE: 06.02.22 STRENGTH: M GED: R3 M2 L1 SVP: 3 DLU: 77

806.684-054   FIBERGLASS LAMINATOR (ship-boat mfg.; vehicles, nec) alternate titles: laminator
Laminates layers of fiberglass on molds to form boat decks and hulls, or fiberglass bodies of golf carts: Selects precut fiberglass mat, cloth, and woodbracing materials, according to model number of boat or golf cart. Places

layers of mat and cloth in mold and smooths out wrinkles by hand. Trims excess material from mold, using hand shears. Mixes catalyst into resin and saturates cloth and mat with mixture, using brush. Works saturated mat and cloth into shape of mold with hands and squeegee, to remove air bubbles and smooth surfaces. Bonds wood reinforcing strips to deck and cabin structures, using resin-saturated fiberglass. Cuts hardened fiberglass from mold with trimming knife. May specialize in molding part of boat and be designated Deck Molder (ship-boat mfg.); Hull Molder (ship-boat mfg.). May install stringers and flooring in hull [OVERLAY PLASTICIAN 806.684-106]. May spray chopped fiberglass, resin, and catalyst on mold, using pneumatic spray gun with chopper attachment. May remove hulls and decks from mold [HULL AND DECK REMOVER (ship-boat mfg.) 809.667-010]. May inspect, clean, and assemble molds prior to start of work. May apply wax to surface of mold to facilitate assembly and removal of laminated parts. May apply resin to surfaces of mold prior to placement of fiberglass mats.
GOE: 06.02.32 STRENGTH: M GED: R3 M2 L1 SVP: 4 DLU: 80

806.684-066   INSTALLER-INSPECTOR, FINAL (vehicles, nec)
Installs attachment in fold-out-top campers and inspects campers preparatory to shipment, using handtools and portable power tools: Fits mattress and pad in specified location in camper. Spreads canvas fold-out top over camper body and attaches top to body, using staple gun and pop-rivet tool. Zips prefabricated door into fold-out top. Opens and closes top to test ease of movement and folds top into camper body. Hooks up water system hose to outlet and reads gauges to detect leaks in system. Turns faucet to test operation of camper water system. Connects electrical cord to camper outlet and tests lights, outlets, and refrigerator to ensure conformance to standards. Examines interior paneling, cabinets, linoleum flooring, and fixtures to determine that components meet company specifications and have been installed according to work orders. Attaches inspection tag to camper, listing any defects in unit. Routes defective unit to repair department and pushes completed unit to shipping area.
GOE: 06.03.02 STRENGTH: L GED: R3 M2 L2 SVP: 4 DLU: 77

806.684-070   INSTALLER, METAL FLOORING (railroad equip.)
Installs prefabricated metal flooring in railroad cars preparatory to welding, using handtools and portable power tools: Measures transverse centerline of car to determine location of flooring, using location fixtures. Positions flooring sections in specified relationship to side sill or longitudinal centerline, using rule, gauge, and pry bars. Secures flooring to underframe of car in preparation for welding, using wedges and jacks.
GOE: 05.12.12 STRENGTH: H GED: R2 M1 L1 SVP: 4 DLU: 77

806.684-074   INSTALLER, MOVABLE BULKHEAD (railroad equip.)
Installs movable bulkheads and bulkhead trolley in railroad cars, using handtools and portable power tools: Measures and marks centerline on roof and floor of car, using chalkline and gauges. Positions and secures overhead rail assembly in car according to marked centerlines, using cotter pins, wedges, and clamps. Positions and secures trolley-beam assembly to rail assembly, using wire. Guides bulkhead onto trolley, using hoist, and bolts bulkhead to trolley, using impact wrench. Pushes bulkhead along overhead trolley-and-rail assembly to end of car and depresses lever to lock bulkhead in place. Installs and bolts bottom bulkhead track to underframe of car, using power drill and impact wrench. Grinds track surfaces to remove burrs and rough edges, using portable grinder.
GOE: 05.10.01 STRENGTH: H GED: R3 M1 L1 SVP: 4 DLU: 77

806.684-082   TRAILER ASSEMBLER II (auto. mfg.) alternate titles: trailer assembler, paneling; trailer-sections assembler
Assembles sections of trailer bodies, following diagrams, using jigs and fixtures, handtools, and power tools: Positions and aligns metal rails, frames, and sheeting in jigs and fixtures, using measuring tape and square to verify alignment of parts. Drills holes in parts at designated points, using power hand drill and drill template. Rivets parts together to form fabricated sides, top, front, and rear sections, using power rivet gun. Installs plywood panels, insulation, and flooring in interiors of trailer bodies. May cut structural truck body parts or trim excess metal from parts, using power saws. May weld steel door frames. May seal riveted seams, using caulking compound. May paint truck body parts. May work as member of assembly team.
GOE: 06.02.22 STRENGTH: H GED: R3 M2 L2 SVP: 3 DLU: 89

806.684-086   MOLD LAMINATOR (concrete prod.; ship-boat mfg.) alternate titles: plug-and-mold finisher
Builds up layers of fiberglass and resin over plug (wooden or plaster pattern) to form molds for plastic product sections or to be used in casting concrete products, using handtools and portable power tools: Fills cracks, depressions, and holes on plug surface with plastic filler material and sandpapers plug to smooth surface. Applies and buffs wax on plug to obtain glossy surface. Brushes surface of plug with water-soluble parting agent to facilitate removal of mold. Covers plug with fiberglass cloth and trims off excess cloth with shears. Mixes specified proportions of resin and catalyst and brushes mixture on cloth. Works mixture into cloth with hands and squeegee to remove air bubbles and to smooth surface. Examines layer of fiberglass and resin after hardening for rough spots and air bubbles and sandpapers defective areas. Laminates additional layers of fiberglass to initial layer to obtain mold of specified thickness. Removes plug from mold, using wooden tool and airhose. Trims excess fiberglass from edge of mold with knife. Inspects completed mold for surface defects. May bond mold to tubular holding device with resin-saturated fiberglass strips. May repair and modify fiberglass molds, using handtools.

GOE: 06.02.32 STRENGTH: M GED: R3 M1 L1 SVP: 4 DLU: 77

806.684-090 MOTORCYCLE ASSEMBLER (motor-bicycles)

Assembles complete motorcycles, performing any combination of following tasks: Positions and clamps frame in fixture on conveyor line. Bolts fork, motor, transmission, rear and front wheels, chain drives, handlebars, lights, seats, and other parts to frame, using handtools or power tools. Turns gas or spark handle controls, and adjustment screws on distributor and carburetor to set spark and gas feed. Turns screws to adjust chain drive and clutch to specified tension. Focuses headlight on testing board and turns adjustment screws to align beam of light. Lubricates motorcycle with grease gun. Records motor and sales numbers. May relieve assemblers and be known as Utility Assembler (motor-bicycles).

GOE: 06.02.22 STRENGTH: H GED: R3 M1 L1 SVP: 5 DLU: 77

806.684-094 MOTORCYCLE SUBASSEMBLER (motor-bicycles)

Assembles forks, frames, transmissions, or other subassemblies of motorcycles, using handtools or power tools: Positions parts or components in holding fixture on bench. Drills, taps, and reams holes in parts, using handtools, power tools, or single-spindle drill press. Bolts, screws, fits, or presses parts together, using screwdriver, wrench, arbor press, or flexible power press. Aligns and adjusts movement of parts or sets clearance between parts, using dial indicators, feeler gauges, or snap gauges. Examines parts or observes their operation in subassembly to detect defective parts. Replaces defective parts, using handtools. May test assembled units, such as transmissions, under simulated operating conditions. May be designated according to component assembled as Brake Assembler (motor-bicycles); Clutch Assembler (motor-bicycles); Fork Assembler (motor-bicycles); Frame Assembler (motor-bicycles); Handle-Bar Assembler (motor-bicycles); Transmission Assembler (motor-bicycles).

GOE: 06.04.22 STRENGTH: H GED: R3 M2 L1 SVP: 5 DLU: 77

806.684-098 ORDNANCE TRUCK INSTALLATION MECHANIC (ordnance)

Assembles and installs ordnance equipment in mobile repair vehicles according to standard procedures, performing one or combination of following duties: Assembles sheet metal workbenches for installation into trucks, using handtools. Mounts and secures workbenches in trucks, using handtools. Measures to determine locations for installations in truck and installs bench grinders, lathes, milling machines, and other mechanical equipment, using power hoist, handtools, and measuring instruments. Stocks truck with handtools, spare parts, and auxiliary equipment, such as oilcans, hand grinders, and flashlights. Compares contents of truck against equipment checklist to ensure completeness of installations.

GOE: 06.02.22 STRENGTH: M GED: R3 M2 L1 SVP: 3 DLU: 77

806.684-102 OUTFITTER, CABIN (ship-boat mfg.)

Installs fixtures and appliances in cabin of fiberglass or metal boat, using handtools and portable power tools: Measures and marks location of fixtures, such as windows, doors, and trim, using carpenter's square and rule. Cuts and drills fastening holes, using portable power saw and drill. Inserts fasteners and secures fixtures and appliances to superstructure, using power screwdriver. Installs prefabricated bulkheads to separate cabin compartments, using carpenter's tools. Applies adhesive wall covering to specified sections, using handbrush. Installs wall paneling in specified locations, using carpenter's tools. May perform duties as described under GROUP LEADER (any industry) Term Title.

GOE: 06.04.22 STRENGTH: M GED: R3 M2 L2 SVP: 5 DLU: 77

806.684-106 OVERLAY PLASTICIAN (ship-boat mfg.) alternate titles: boat bottomer

Installs wooden stringers and precut plywood sheets in molded fiberglass boat hulls to strengthen boat bottoms, using fiberglass bonding agent and handtools: Obtains precut stringers and plywood sheets according to model number of boat. Mixes catalyst into resin to control setting rate of bonding agent and saturates strips of fiberglass mat with mixture, using brush. Lays strips between stringer and hull and clamps stringers in place with special holding device. Lays strips of material along seams of stringers to reinforce bond and smooths out air bubbles by hand. Covers hull bottom interior and tops of stringers with saturated strips. Positions plywood flooring on bottom of boat and places clamps or weights on flooring to press it against hull and stringers. May install precut wood flotation tanks, seat supports, and bulkheads. May install plastic blocks of flotation material, fiberglass gasoline tanks, and other fiberglass fixtures.

GOE: 06.02.24 STRENGTH: M GED: R2 M1 L1 SVP: 4 DLU: 77

806.684-114 RAILROAD-CAR-TRUCK BUILDER (railroad equip.)

Assembles frames, beams, brakes, and springs to form railroad car truck and wheel units, using handtools: Positions bolster on erection block and lowers side frames and brake beams into bolster slots, grooves, and recesses, using hoist. Slips brakeshoes into receptacles and secures brakeshoes with pin, using hammer. Assembles brake parts, such as bottom rods, traverse plates, fulcrum, and levers and secures unit to brake beams and shoes, using bolts and cotter pins. Sets springs on studs in spring housing and places adapters in grooves on axle wheel bearings. Lifts complete truck unit over truck wheel assemblies, using hoist, and lowers it onto adapters. Pushes truck and wheel assembly along track for next operation.

GOE: 06.04.22 STRENGTH: H GED: R3 M1 L1 SVP: 3 DLU: 77

806.684-118 REPAIRER, GENERAL (auto. mfg.)

Installs, replaces, or repairs parts on motor vehicle bodies, using handtools and power tools and following specifications and inspection reports: Reads specifications and inspection reports to determine incorrectly installed, missing, or defective parts. Installs, replaces, or repairs parts, such as wheels, doors, interior and exterior trim, and vinyl tops. Installs or tightens missing or loose screws, bolts, and fasteners, using power tool. Applies sealant to window seams, using caulking gun, and removes excess sealant, using handtool. Indicates items repaired on repair sheet. May drive vehicle from assembly line or holding area to work station. May work as member of team and be assigned to different work stations as production needs require.

GOE: 06.04.22 STRENGTH: M GED: R3 M2 L2 SVP: 4 DLU: 90

806.684-122 RIGGER HELPER (ship-boat mfg.)

Assists RIGGER (ship-boat mfg.) in moving, lifting, and positioning machinery and structural members of ships under repair or construction: Positions chain falls or hoists, air pullers, and block and tackle as directed by RIGGER (ship-boat mfg.). Pulls or slacks off on rigging, following hand signals, to maneuver equipment in close quarters, lay keel and bilge blocks in drydock, and position ship in drydock. May issue and maintain rigging gear in rigging loft and be designated Rigging-Loft Repairer (ship-boat mfg.). Performs other duties as described under HELPER (any industry) Master Title.

GOE: 05.05.06 STRENGTH: H GED: R3 M1 L1 SVP: 5 DLU: 77

806.684-126 ROOF FITTER (railroad equip.)

Aligns, fits, and secures roof onto railroad cars, using handtools and portable power tools: Positions spreading device and chain jack inside car, using hoist. Manipulates controls on spreading device or chain jack to push out or pull in sides of car to specified width. Attaches holding device between sides of car to retain specified width. Erects scaffolding in car to facilitate climbing to roof area, using carpenter's tools. Climbs scaffolding and brushes sealing compound on top plates of car. Signals crane operator to lower prefabricated roof onto top plates of car. Aligns and fastens roof onto car, using impact wrench. Bends roof flanges over sides of car, using hammer or mallet. Reams holes in roof and top plate of car and inserts drift pins preparatory to riveting. Disassembles and removes spreading device, jack, and scaffolding, using handtools.

GOE: 06.02.22 STRENGTH: H GED: R3 M2 L1 SVP: 4 DLU: 77

806.684-130 SKIN-LAP BONDER (aircraft mfg.)

Seals aircraft fuselage skin-laps preparatory to riveting, using handtools and sealing compound: Reads blueprints, work orders, and specifications to determine skin-lap to be sealed and type of sealant to be used. Cleans skin-lap area, using solvent, cloth, and brush. Applies specified sealing compound to skin-lap area, using fairing tools, roller, and sealing gun. Cleans bonded area to remove excess sealant subsequent to riveting, using solvent and cloth. May mix adhesives, cements, and similar sealing compounds.

GOE: 06.04.24 STRENGTH: M GED: R3 M2 L3 SVP: 3 DLU: 87

806.684-134 TRANSMISSION TESTER (auto. mfg.) alternate titles: gear tester

Tests assembled motor vehicle transmissions under simulated operating conditions to detect malfunctioning: Lifts transmission onto testing fixture, using hoist. Flushes gears with oil. Attaches transmission shaft to engine. Starts engine and depresses pedal to engage gears in transmission. Varies engine speeds and shifts gears to test each gear combination. Listens to sounds of gears meshing at different speeds and feels smoothness of gears shifting to detect malfunction. Prepares reports of test results.

GOE: 06.03.02 STRENGTH: L GED: R3 M2 L3 SVP: 4 DLU: 77

806.684-142 RUNNING RIGGER (ship-boat mfg.)

Splices wire and nylon rope to fabricate items, such as halyards, outhaul assemblies, reef lines, lazy jacks, and lifelines: Selects size and type of rope specified on work order and pulls rope through length meter to measure rope. Wraps masking tape around rope to mark points where rope is to be spliced and cuts rope, using soldering iron with rope cutting attachment. Wraps nylon thread around ends of rope or burns end of rope, using soldering iron, to seize ends and prevent fraying. Pushes marlinspike through rope to separate strands and passes fid through casing of rope to interweave strands and splice ropes to join unlike ropes into one continuous length or to form eyes for attaching hardware. Coils rope and ties end of rope around center of coil to secure rope for storage or transport. Threads lifeline rope through stanchions on boat decks and splices shackle to end of rope to install lifelines.

GOE: 06.02.32 STRENGTH: M GED: R3 M3 L2 SVP: 4 DLU: 86

806.684-146 BOAT OUTFITTER (ship-boat mfg.) alternate titles: assembler, plastic boat; boat garnisher; final assembler, boat

Installs parts, such as hatches, marine hardware, metal trim, seats, cabinets, and windshields on fiberglass, aluminum, or wooden boats, using handtools and portable power tools: Locates and marks position of hardware, seats, and other parts according to specifications, using rule, template, and marking device. Cuts or grinds mounting bases or brackets, using portable electric saws and grinders, and bolts or screws them in place. Drills holes and bolts hardware, hatches, and other parts in place, using handtools. Applies caulking compound under spray rails, windshields, and around windows, using caulking gun. Saws aluminum trim to specified lengths and cements, crimps, screws, or pounds trim into place, using hacksaw, crimping device, adhesives, screwdriver, and mallet. Inspects completed boat for defects and writes report of appraisal. May grind interior and exterior contours of hull to remove burrs and rough edges, using portable grinder. May paint pinstriping and lettering on boat, using stencil and brush. May measure, cut and install insulation in designated sections of boats, using handtools. May be designated according to part installed as Plastic Out-

fitter (ship-boat mfg.); Trim Installer (ship-boat mfg.) Windshield Installer (ship-boat mfg.); Window Installer (ship-boat mfg.); Wood And Hardware Outfitter (ship-boat mfg.).
GOE: 05.10.01 STRENGTH: M GED: R3 M2 L2 SVP: 4 DLU: 80

806.684-150 ROUTER OPERATOR, HAND (aircraft mfg.; railroad equip.)
Routs and trims metallic and nonmetallic parts and materials to provide cutouts for windows, air vents, and tubing runs, used in manufacturing transportation equipment, such as aircraft and railroad cars, using portable router and handtools: Selects and installs specified type and size bit and collar combinations in hand router, guided by template, jig, or fixture markings or information obtained from blueprints and specifications. Positions and secures parts or materials to be routed, template, and router guide on router board, jig, or fixture, using bolts, screws, clamps, handtools, and power tools. Moves router along guide to cut openings in parts and materials or to trim excess material. Grinds, smooths, or deburrs parts, using handtools or power tools. May drill coordinating holes in parts or materials, using drill motor.
GOE: 06.02.24 STRENGTH: M GED: R3 M1 L2 SVP: 4 DLU: 88

806.687-010 ASSEMBLER, BICYCLE II (motor-bicycles)
Assembles bicycles on assembly line, performing one or a combination of tasks as described under ASSEMBLER, BICYCLE (motor-bicycles) I, using handtools and portable power tools. May assemble and package bicycle subassemblies, such as shift levers, axles, and reflectors and be designated Bicycle Subassembler (motor-bicycles).
GOE: 06.04.22 STRENGTH: L GED: R1 M1 L1 SVP: 2 DLU: 77

806.687-018 FINAL INSPECTOR (auto. mfg.) alternate titles: checker
Inspects completed motor vehicle for conformance to specifications: Examines vehicle for installation of specified accessories, such as radio, heater, and defroster. Tests operation of windows, doors, lights, and controls on instrument panel. Examines seats, headlining, and door paneling for spots or tears in upholstery, and car exterior for chips and scratches on painted surfaces. Records defects on checklist. May inspect components of vehicle and be designated Chassis Inspector (auto. mfg.); Trim Inspector (auto. mfg.).
GOE: 06.03.02 STRENGTH: L GED: R3 M2 L3 SVP: 4 DLU: 90

806.687-022 HELPER, METAL BONDING (aircraft mfg.) alternate titles: metal-bonding worker
Performs variety of tasks to assist ASSEMBLER, METAL BONDING (aircraft mfg.) 806.384-030 and METAL-BONDING PRESS OPERATOR (aircraft mfg.) 553.382-026 in fabricating bonded aircraft and space vehicle parts and assemblies. Performs duties as described under HELPER (any industry) Master Title.
GOE: 06.04.24 STRENGTH: M GED: R2 M2 L2 SVP: 3 DLU: 88

806.687-026 INSPECTOR, ALUMINUM BOAT (ship-boat mfg.)
Inspects aluminum boats and canoes to detect leaks, using water-test tank: Lifts and places boat in test tank with aid of other workers. Positions bow and stern of boat under hydraulic ram. Presses lever to activate ram that pushes and holds boat down in water of tank. Inspects rivets to detect leaks and marks leaking areas, using crayon. Tightens or replaces leaking rivets, using rivet gun. Records number of boats inspected and repairs required on worksheet.
GOE: 06.03.02 STRENGTH: M GED: R2 M1 L2 SVP: 3 DLU: 77

806.687-030 INSPECTOR, BICYCLE (motor-bicycles)
Inspects bicycles for defects in assembly and finish: Examines bicycle to detect missing equipment, flaws in paint, and alignment of frame, sprockets, and wheels. Turns pedals, spins wheels, and moves parts to verify specified adjustment. Informs bicycle repairer of defects. May perform assembly line duties [ASSEMBLER, BICYCLE (motor-bicycles) II].
GOE: 06.03.02 STRENGTH: L GED: R2 M1 L1 SVP: 2 DLU: 77

806.687-034 INSTALLER, DOOR FURRING (railroad equip.)
Installs prefabricated furring strips and insulation material into metal railroad car doors, using handtools: Positions and aligns door frame on assembly rails, using hoist. Removes paint from studs in door frame, using paint remover and brush. Applies sealing compound to designated points in frame, using caulking gun. Positions furring strips over sealing compound and bolts furring to frame, using impact wrench. Fits prescribed amounts of insulation material between furring strips.
GOE: 06.04.22 STRENGTH: H GED: R2 M1 L1 SVP: 2 DLU: 77

806.687-042 OUTBOARD-MOTOR INSPECTOR (engine-turbine)
Inspects outboard motors at end of assembly line for conformance to factory standards, preparatory to shipment: Examines motor for missing parts, dents, scratches, and paint imperfections, such as runs and spots. Moves shifting lever into drive positions, pulls starter rope, opens cover latches and doors, moves tilt lever, release lever, starter lock, and reverse lock, to verify operation of parts. Records defects on inspection tag.
GOE: 06.03.02 STRENGTH: L GED: R3 M2 L2 SVP: 4 DLU: 77

806.687-046 ROLLER (ship-boat mfg.)
Positions, smooths, and compresses layers of fiberglass on boat hulls to strengthen weak spots and eliminate air pockets, using metal or fiber rollers: Positions fiberglass cloth on stress points of boat hull according to specifications. Sprays resin compound over fiberglass, using portable spray gun. Smooths and compresses fiberglass to eliminate air pockets and strengthen hull,

using rollers. Cuts excess fiberglass material from hull, using scissors. Cleans rollers, using acetone solution. Pushes boat hull to next work station in assembly line.
GOE: 06.04.27 STRENGTH: M GED: R2 M1 L1 SVP: 3 DLU: 77

806.687-050 SHIPFITTER HELPER (ship-boat mfg.)
Assists SHIPFITTER (ship-boat mfg.) in fabricating, assembling, and installing bulkheads, plates, frames, stanchions, and other heavy steel structural parts within hull of ship by performing following tasks: Obtains tools and materials from storage and carries them or arranges for their transportation to work site. Assists SHIPFITTER (ship-boat mfg.) in establishing reference points on structural member or steel parts to indicate bending, cutting, drilling, and other machining necessary to fabricate steel into ship members. Holds workpieces during welding operations. Cleans slag from welds, using slag hammer and wire brush. Grinds welds smooth, using portable grinder. Measures and cuts metal pieces to specifications, using gas cutting equipment. Tightens bolts, using hand and power wrenches. Assembles and fits gaskets, packing, and liners in place. Tightens turnbuckles of guy wires to hold bulkheads and stanchions in position for welding. Performs other duties as described under HELPER (any industry) Master Title.
GOE: 05.12.12 STRENGTH: H GED: R2 M1 L1 SVP: 2 DLU: 77

807 STRUCTURAL REPAIRERS, TRANSPORTATION EQUIPMENT

This group includes occupations concerned with repairing vehicle bodies, parts, components, and attachments for such transportation equipment as automobiles, aircraft, rail equipment, motorcycles, boats, travel trailers, motor homes, and military vehicles.

807.137-010 SUPERVISOR, AUTOMOBILE BODY REPAIR (automotive ser.) alternate titles: automobile-body repair chief
Supervises and coordinates activities of workers engaged in repairing and painting damaged bodies and body parts of automotive vehicles: May examine damaged vehicle and estimate cost of repairs [SHOP ESTIMATOR (automotive ser.)]. Performs other duties as described under SUPERVISOR (any industry) Master Title.
GOE: 05.05.06 STRENGTH: L GED: R4 M3 L3 SVP: 7 DLU: 77

807.261-010 AIRCRAFT BODY REPAIRER (air trans.)
Repairs sheet and extruded metal structural parts of aircraft and missiles according to design specifications, using handtools and power tools and metalworking machinery: Reads design specifications or examines sample parts to determine fabrication procedures and machines and tools required. Removes rivets and other fasteners to facilitate removal of defective part, using power drill and punch, or cuts out defective part, using power shears, hacksaw, and file. Locates and marks dimension and reference lines on defective or replacement part, using templates, scribes, compass, and steel rule. Sets up and operates metal fabricating machines, such as saws, brakes, shears, drill press, and grinders, to repair defective part or fabricate new part. Reinstalls repaired or replacement parts for subsequent riveting or welding, using clamps and wrenches. Confers with other workers to expedite heat treating, anodizing, or other specified processing of repair parts. May signal crane operator to fit and align heavy parts. May stretch skin and panel sheets to remove surface tension, using sheet metal hand forming tools.
GOE: 05.05.06 STRENGTH: M GED: R4 M3 L3 SVP: 7 DLU: 77

807.267-010 SHOP ESTIMATOR (automotive ser.)
Estimates cost of repairing damaged automobile and truck bodies, on basis of visual inspection of vehicle and familiarity with standard parts, costs, and labor rates: Examines damaged vehicle for dents, scratches, broken glass, and other areas requiring repair, replacement, or repainting. Sights along fenders to detect frame damage, or positions vehicle in frame-aligning rig that indicates location and extent of misalignment. Examines interior for evidence of fire or water damage to upholstery and appointments. Determines feasibility of repair or replacement of parts, such as bumpers, fenders, and doors, according to familiarity with relative costs and extent of damage. Computes cost of replacement parts and labor to restore vehicle to condition specified by customer, using standard labor and parts cost manuals. Enters itemized estimate on job order card or estimate form and explains estimate to customer. May estimate cost of mechanical, electrical, or other repairs where shop performs both body work and mechanical servicing of vehicles [AUTOMOBILE-REPAIR-SERVICE ESTIMATOR (automotive ser.) 620.261-018]. May estimate cost of repainting, converting vehicles to special purposes, or customizing undamaged vehicles, depending on specialty of shop.
GOE: 05.07.01 STRENGTH: L GED: R4 M3 L3 SVP: 6 DLU: 78

807.281-010 TRUCK-BODY BUILDER (auto. mfg.; automotive ser.) alternate titles: body builder
Constructs and repairs metal truck bodies and trailers according to specifications, using handtools and power tools: Lays out dimensions on metal stock, such as sheet metal and angle iron, using square, rule, and punch. Fits and assembles components, using handtools and portable power tools, such as drill, riveter, and welding apparatus [SHEET-METAL WORKER (any industry) 804.281-010]. Welds together body parts and braces [WELDER, COMBINATION (welding) 819.384-010]. Measures and cuts woodstock and installs wood floors, interiors, insulations, and fixtures, using handtools, such as ham-

mer, file, and screwdriver, and power tools, such as bandsaw, sander, and hand drill. Installs electrical wiring for dome lights, taillights, brake lights, and other equipment according to specified procedures. May spray or brush paint, primer, or protective coating on wood and metal surfaces.
GOE: 05.05.06 STRENGTH: M GED: R3 M3 L2 SVP: 5 DLU: 90

807.361-010 AUTOMOBILE-BODY CUSTOMIZER (automotive ser.)
Installs custom equipment to alter appearance of automotive vehicle according to customer specifications, using handtools and power tools: Reads specifications or confers with customer to determine modifications desired. Cuts opening in vehicle body for installation of customized windows, using templates, and power shears or chisel. Measures and marks vinyl material and cuts material to size for roof installation, using rule, straightedge, and hand shears. Cuts and bends metal trim to specified size and configuration, using power shears and chrome-bending die. Fits and secures windows, vinyl roof, and metal trim, using caulking gun, adhesive brush, and mallet.
GOE: 05.05.06 STRENGTH: M GED: R3 M2 L2 SVP: 6 DLU: 77

807.361-014 BOAT REPAIRER (ship-boat mfg.)
Repairs wooden and fiberglass boats according to blueprints and customer specifications, using handtools and power tools: Confers with customer or supervisory personnel and reads blueprints to determine repairs needed and plan sequence of operations. Examines boat to determine location and extent of defect. Cuts out defective area, using power saw, drills, and handtools. Measures and records dimensions of defective area and lays out dimension lines and reference points on materials, using rules, straightedge, squares, and scribing instruments. Sets up and operates saws, joiners, planers, and shapers to fabricate repair parts. Positions and fits repair part in boat and secures part to boat, using caulking gun, adhesive, or carpenter's handtools. Cuts fiberglass material to specified size and patches defective surfaces [BOAT PATCHER, PLASTIC (ship-boat mfg.)]. Smooths repaired surfaces, using power sander. Installs fittings and equipment according to customer specifications, using handtools and portable power tools. Hand brushes or sprays paint or other finishing solution on repaired areas and waxes and buffs area to specified finish.
GOE: 05.05.02 STRENGTH: M GED: R4 M3 L3 SVP: 7 DLU: 77

807.381-010 AUTOMOBILE-BODY REPAIRER (automotive ser.) alternate titles: automobile-body worker; body-line finisher; body repairer, bus; dent remover; door repairer, bus; metal bumper; metal shrinker; metal worker; touch-up finisher, metal
Repairs damaged bodies and body parts of automotive vehicles, such as automobiles, buses, and light trucks according to repair manuals, using handtools and power tools: Examines damaged vehicles and estimates cost of repairs [SHOP ESTIMATOR (automotive ser.) 807.267-010]. Removes upholstery, accessories, electrical and hydraulic window-and-seat-operating equipment, and trim to gain access to vehicle body and fenders. Positions dolly block against surface of dented area and beats opposite surface to remove dents, using hammer. Fills depressions with body filler, using putty knife. Removes damaged fenders, panels, and grills, using wrenches and cutting torch, and bolts or welds replacement parts in position, using wrenches or welding equipment. Straightens bent automobile frames, using pneumatic frame straightening machine. Files, grinds, and sands repaired surfaces, using power tools and handtools. Refinishes repaired surface, using paint spray gun and sander. Aims headlights, aligns wheels, and bleeds hydraulic brake system. May paint surfaces after performing body repairs and be designated Automobile-Body Repairer, Combination (automotive ser.). May repair or replace defective mechanical parts [AUTOMOBILE MECHANIC (automotive ser.) 620.261-010].
GOE: 05.05.06 STRENGTH: M GED: R3 M3 L3 SVP: 7 DLU: 81

807.381-014 BONDED STRUCTURES REPAIRER (aircraft mfg.) alternate titles: bonder, rework and repair
Repairs aircraft and space vehicle bonded structures according to blueprints and specifications, using handtools, power tools, and equipment: Reads inspection reports, rework instructions, and blueprints to determine type of repair, tools required, and to plan sequence of operations. Positions and secures bonded structure in fixture or bonding form, or attaches fixture to structure, using clamps and handtools. Examines structure to determine location, nature, and extent of defect or damage. Spreads plastic film over area to be repaired to prevent damage to surrounding area. Drills holes in structure to gain access to internal defect or damage. Scribes around repair area and cuts out defective or damaged section, using power tools and equipment. Laminates variety of metallic and nonmetallic materials, such as aluminum, fiberglass, plastic, and honeycomb, to fabricate replacement section. Trims and shapes replacement section to specified size, using handtools and power tools. Injects adhesive into cutout areas, using injection gun. Fits replacement section into cutout area and secures section in place, using adhesive tape and tack iron. Cures bonded structure, using portable or stationary curing equipment. Cleans, strips, primes, and sands structural surfaces and materials prior to bonding.
GOE: 06.02.32 STRENGTH: M GED: R3 M2 L3 SVP: 6 DLU: 88

807.381-018 FRAME REPAIRER (motor-bicycles)
Repairs motorcycle frames according to written instructions or visual examination, using bandsaw and welding and aligning equipment: Reads work tickets or examines frame to determine extent and type of damage. Cuts bent, broken, or cracked tubular parts from frame, using bandsaw. Measures defective area of frame and selects tubular sections to replace cutout part. Positions and

clamps replacement part and frame in welding fixture. Welds replacement part to frame, using arc or acetylene welding equipment [WELDER COMBINATION (welding)] or brazes part to frame, using brazing torch [BRAZER, ASSEMBLER (welding)]. Aligns frames after repairing [FRAME STRAIGHTENER (motor-bicycles)].
GOE: 05.10.01 STRENGTH: H GED: R3 M2 L1 SVP: 7 DLU: 77

807.381-022 SERVICE MECHANIC (auto. mfg.)
Services, repairs, and installs accessories and metal sections on new and used metal trailers: Examines workmanship and tests, adjusts, and repairs wheel alignments, bearings, lights, and brake assemblies of new trailers. Adjusts, and services motor-cooling systems in refrigerated trailers. Replaces and repairs worn and defective parts. Overhauls used and wrecked trailer bodies, following shop orders or specifications. Lays out, fits, drills, screws, rivets, and welds new assemblies to other trailer sections, using pneumatic tools, welding and burning equipment, and handtools. May install metal or wood flooring.
GOE: 05.10.01 STRENGTH: M GED: R3 M2 L3 SVP: 6 DLU: 77

807.381-026 STREETCAR REPAIRER (railroad equip.) alternate titles: car-body inspector
Performs any combination of following tasks to inspect and repair streetcar bodies, following blueprints and wiring diagrams and using handtools, power tools, and electrical test equipment: Examines car roof for wear and damage and repairs defective sections, using specified roofing material, cement, nails, and waterproof paint. Cuts sheet metal strips and bolts strips to sign frame joints, installs glass panes, and trims frayed or torn sign material to repair streetcar route signs, using handtools. Tests current continuity of car wiring, using ammeter. Engages controls to drive streetcar specified distance and pushes light and signal switches to test electrical system of car. Replaces defective wiring and insulation and tightens electrical connections, using handtools. Glues ends of window sash frames together, screws weather stripping and brass channels to frame, and installs glass panes to repair window sashes, using handtools. Unbolts defective slats from frame and front gate of lifeguard, drills boltholes in new slats and bolts slats in place, using power wrench and drill. Removes defective sandbox from beneath platform of car, fills new box with sand, and installs box on car, using handtools. Records condition of car, repairs made, and work to be performed by repair shop. May be designated according to specific activity performed as Car-Roof Repairer (railroad equip.); Destination-Sign Repairer (railroad equip.); Electrical Inspector (railroad equip.); Sash Repairer (railroad equip.); Streetcar Sandbox And Lifeguard-Unit Repairer (railroad equip.).
GOE: 05.10.04 STRENGTH: H GED: R4 M2 L2 SVP: 6 DLU: 77

807.381-030 AUTO-BODY REPAIRER, FIBERGLASS (automotive ser.)
Repairs damaged fiberglass automobile bodies, using pneumatic tools and knowledge of fiberglass repair techniques: Cuts away damaged fiberglass, using air grinder. Smooths edges of painted surface, using sandpaper or air-powered sander. Masks surrounding undamaged surface, using masking tape. Cuts plastic separating film, using shears, and tapes film to outside repair area. Mixes polyester resin and hardener according to specifications and applies mixture to repair area, using brush. Soaks matting in resin mixture and layers matting over repair area to specified thickness. Peels separating film from repair area and washes repair surface with water. Occasionally secures new panel to repair area, using C-clamp. Applies and spreads body filler manually to re-establish surface. Manually files away excess filler to match original contour. Smooths filler, using air sander. Cleans repair area with air gun.
GOE: 05.10.01 STRENGTH: M GED: R3 M2 L2 SVP: 7 DLU: 86

807.484-010 FRAME STRAIGHTENER (motor-bicycles) alternate titles: frame aligner; straightener-and-aligner
Straightens and aligns motorcycle frames according to specifications, using aligning table, jigs, gauges, jack, and handtools: Turns screws to adjust and set gauges and stops on jigs. Positions and clamps frame in fixtures on aligning table. Examines frame to ascertain degree of aligning required, using height and level gauges. Realigns frame, using hammer, pry bar, or jack, and measures frame to verify alignment.
GOE: 05.10.01 STRENGTH: H GED: R3 M2 L2 SVP: 5 DLU: 77

807.664-010 MUFFLER INSTALLER (automotive ser.)
Replaces defective mufflers and pipes on automobiles, buses, trucks, and other automotive vehicles according to factory or customer specifications, using handtools and power tools: Removes defective muffler, using hacksaw, wrenches, air-powered tools, or acetylene torch. Selects replacement muffler according to automotive vehicle model and customer's preference. Bolts or tack welds new muffler in place. Bends and shapes tailpipe sections according to customer specifications, using pipe-bending machine. Welds tailpipe sections to muffler or exhaust pipe, using arc welding equipment. Aligns muffler and tailpipe within frame and bolts hangers to frame to secure muffler.
GOE: 05.10.01 STRENGTH: M GED: R3 M2 L2 SVP: 4 DLU: 77

807.667-010 FLATCAR WHACKER (saw. & plan.)
Inspects and repairs rail-type logging equipment: Examines rail flatcar attachments, such as stakes, cables, straps, and cross timbers to detect defects. Repairs or replaces attachments, using handtools, such as wrenches, pry bars, and hammers. Inspects frame and wheel assembly of flatcar and notifies maintenance personnel when repairs are needed.
GOE: 05.12.12 STRENGTH: H GED: R2 M1 L1 SVP: 3 DLU: 77

807.684-010 AUTOMOBILE-BUMPER STRAIGHTENER (automotive ser.) alternate titles: bumper straightener

Repairs damaged automobile bumpers preparatory to replating: Selects specified make and model bumper from storage yard. Positions bumper in hydraulic press and starts press to restore original shape to bumper, using templates to verify contours. Removes smaller dents, using sledgehammer. Positions bumper in bench vise and grinds out hammer marks, dimples, scratches, and rust areas, using portable grinding wheel. May cut and weld sections from several bumpers to form single salvageable unit, using flame cutting and welding equipment.
GOE: 05.12.12 STRENGTH: H GED: R2 M1 L1 SVP: 3 DLU: 77

807.684-014 BOAT PATCHER, PLASTIC (ship-boat mfg.) alternate titles: assembly detailer; patcher, plastic boat

Repairs and repaints defects in fiberglass boat hulls, decks, and cabins, using handtools and power tools: Examines parts for defects, such as cracks and holes. Drills out defective areas or smooths rough edges, using portable electric drill and grinder. Cuts out patch of fiberglass material, using shears. Mixes resin and catalyst, dips patch in solution, and places patch over defect. Shapes and smooths edges to match contour of patched area. Fills holes with plastic filler material. Smooths repaired surfaces, using sandpaper or power disk sander. Mixes plastic paint with catalyst and sprays repaired surfaces, using spray gun. Cuts out damaged wood bracing strips, using portable electric saw. Replaces and bonds strips in place with saturated fiberglass mat. Touches up flaws, using paintbrush. May polish repainted sections.
GOE: 06.02.24 STRENGTH: M GED: R3 M1 L1 SVP: 4 DLU: 77

807.684-018 AIRCRAFT SKIN BURNISHER (aircraft mfg.)

Burnishes and hand finishes sheet metal stock or fabricated aircraft skins to remove surface defects, such as scratches, mars, and blemishes, and to restore surface to uniform grain, color, and luster, using burnishing tools: Reads work order and burnishing specifications. Lubricates area to be burnished, and rubs burnishing tool over lubricated metal surfaces to remove surface imperfections. Polishes surfaces to restore area to original luster or finish, by hand or using power tools. Brushes solutions onto skin surfaces to remove stains. Examines burnished area and surrounding skin to determine uniformity of grain, color, and finish.
GOE: 06.04.24 STRENGTH: L GED: R3 M1 L2 SVP: 3 DLU: 88

807.684-022 FLOOR SERVICE WORKER, SPRING (automotive ser.)

Removes leaf springs from automotive vehicles to facilitate repair or replacement and replaces springs, using handtools: Raises vehicle, using hydraulic jack or hoist. Places mounting stands under vehicle to decrease leaf spring pressure. Removes shock absorbers, U-bolts, and shackle pins to gain access to springs, using impact wrench and handtools. Removes leaf springs and conveys springs to repair shop. Reinstalls repaired or replacement springs, using handtools.
GOE: 05.12.12 STRENGTH: H GED: R2 M1 L1 SVP: 4 DLU: 77

807.684-026 INSTALLER, SOFT TOP (automotive ser.) alternate titles: assembler, convertible top

Installs convertible top assemblies on automobile bodies: Bolts rubber molding to specified points on bottom of convertible assembly frame. Positions assembly on automobile body and bolts metal frame and rear edge of fabric to body. Trims off excess fabric from rear edge, using shears. Connects hydraulic lift to assembly and raises top. Adjusts bolts and top bows of metal frame to tighten fabric. Turns setscrews to adjust height and movement of side windows. Screws metal caps to frame to protect fabric at points of greatest wear. May install fabric on top assemblies.
GOE: 06.04.22 STRENGTH: M GED: R2 M1 L2 SVP: 2 DLU: 77

807.684-034 WATER LEAK REPAIRER (auto. mfg.)

Detects and seals areas of water leaks on motor vehicle bodies, using ultraviolet light, caulking gun, and handtools: Illuminates areas of inner compartments of vehicle bodies, using ultraviolet light (black light) to detect water inside compartments. Seals areas suspected of water leaks, using caulking gun. Aligns parts, such as hoods, doors, and deck lids (trunks) to fit body contours to correct cause of water leaks, using handtools. May work as part of team.
GOE: 06.03.02 STRENGTH: L GED: R2 M1 L2 SVP: 3 DLU: 90

807.687-010 AUTOMOBILE-BODY-REPAIRER HELPER (automotive ser.)

Performs duties as described under HELPER (any industry) Master Title.
GOE: 05.12.12 STRENGTH: M GED: R2 M1 L1 SVP: 2 DLU: 77

807.687-014 STREETCAR-REPAIRER HELPER (railroad equip.) alternate titles: car-body-inspector helper

Performs any combination of following tasks to assist STREETCAR REPAIRER (railroad equip.) in repairing streetcar bodies, using handtools: Tightens loose bolts and screws and replaces worn or broken *stirrups*, using handtools. Replaces or tightens worn or loose weather stripping on windows, using handtools. Repairs torn upholstery, using needle and thread. Lubricates car, using oil gun. Performs other duties as described under HELPER (any industry) Master Title.
GOE: 05.12.12 STRENGTH: H GED: R2 M1 L1 SVP: 3 DLU: 77

809 MISCELLANEOUS OCCUPATIONS IN METAL FABRICATING, N.E.C.

This group includes occupations, not elsewhere classified, concerned with fabricating structures from metal and related materials.

809.130-010 SUPERVISOR, ASSEMBLY DEPARTMENT (struct. metal)

Supervises and coordinates activities of workers engaged in assembling metal sash, screen doors, and storm doors and windows. Sets up or supervises setup of machinery, according to work order specifications and instructions from management. May design and fabricate full-sized or miniature screens or storm windows and doors to be used as samples, using handtools and power equipment. Performs other duties as described under SUPERVISOR (any industry) Master Title.
GOE: 06.02.01 STRENGTH: L GED: R4 M3 L3 SVP: 7 DLU: 77

809.130-014 SUPERVISOR, METAL FABRICATING (any industry) alternate titles: shop supervisor; steel fabricating supervisor

Supervises and coordinates activities of workers engaged in fabrication and assembly of structural, ornamental, or sheet metal products, applying knowledge of layout, product design, machine function, capacities and output, properties of metal, and strength of materials: Analyzes work orders and blueprints to determine information, such as material to be used, type of operations, and sequence of operations required. Requisitions dies, fixtures, and material. Examines defective machinery to determine cause of malfunction and reports need for machine repairs. Trains workers in operation of equipment. Sets up and operates machines to make test runs and experimental products. Inspects work in progress and finished products. Performs other duties as described under SUPERVISOR (any industry) Master Title. May be designated by product fabricated as Boiler-Shop Supervisor (any industry); Sheet-Metal-Shop Supervisor (any industry); Structural Steel-Shop Supervisor (any industry); Tank-Shop Supervisor (any industry).
GOE: 05.10.01 STRENGTH: M GED: R4 M3 L3 SVP: 8 DLU: 78

809.131-010 SUPERVISOR, FABRICATION AND ASSEMBLY (toy-sport equip.)

Supervises and coordinates activities of workers engaged in fabricating and assembling playground equipment, such as swings, slides, park tables, and benches: Explains and demonstrates duties to new workers. Inspects work in progress and finished product to verify conformance to standards and quality of work. Performs other duties as described under SUPERVISOR (any industry) Master Title.
GOE: 06.02.01 STRENGTH: L GED: R4 M3 L3 SVP: 7 DLU: 77

809.131-014 SUPERVISOR, ORNAMENTAL IRONWORKING (construction)

Supervises and coordinates activities of workers engaged in installing prefabricated ornamental ironwork, such as window and door frames, elevator fronts, and fences: Examines blueprints and confers with employer to determine location and type ironwork to be installed, plan installation procedures, and resolve problems in securing specified units. Demonstrates and explains work procedures and safety practices to workers. Inspects preparation and installation of ironwork to ensure adherence to building specifications. Performs other duties as described under SUPERVISOR (any industry) Master Title.
GOE: 05.05.06 STRENGTH: M GED: R4 M3 L3 SVP: 7 DLU: 77

809.131-018 SUPERVISOR, STRUCTURAL-STEEL ERECTION (construction) alternate titles: iron-and-steel-work supervisor; steel-erecting pusher

Supervises and coordinates activities of work crews engaged in erecting structural steel: Marks locations for new rivet holes to rectify errors. Directs workers to drill and ream new holes. Assists workers in performance of tasks, such as riveting, welding, bolting, and chipping, using protable power tools. Performs other duties as described under SUPERVISOR (any industry) Master Title. May supervise workers engaged in erecting steel power transmission towers and poles and be designated Tower Supervisor (construction). May be designated according to activity of workers supervised as Supervisor, Riveting (construction).
GOE: 05.05.06 STRENGTH: M GED: R4 M3 L3 SVP: 8 DLU: 77

809.134-010 SUPERVISOR, GRINDING AND SPRAYING (struct. metal)

Supervises and coordinates activities of workers engaged in rough surface grinding and spray painting structural and ornamental metalwork articles: Reads work order specifications to determine supply requirements and coordinates interdepartmental work flow. Trains new workers and demonstrates work procedures and assists workers in performance of tasks. Inspects completed pieces to verify conformance of finish to company standards. Performs other duties as described under SUPERVISOR (any industry) Master Title.
GOE: 06.02.01 STRENGTH: H GED: R4 M3 L3 SVP: 5 DLU: 77

809.134-014 SUPERVISOR, METAL HANGING (mfd. bldgs.)

Supervises and coordinates activities of workers engaged in installing exterior aluminum siding on manufactured buildings: Reads blueprints and written specifications to determine materials needed and requisitions materials from warehouse. Distributes materials to workers. Assists workers in performance of tasks as described under METAL HANGER (mfd. bldgs.; vehicles, nec). Performs other duties as described under SUPERVISOR (any industry) Master Title.
GOE: 06.02.01 STRENGTH: H GED: R4 M3 L3 SVP: 7 DLU: 77

809.261-010 ASSEMBLER, GROUND SUPPORT EQUIPMENT (aircraft mfg.) alternate titles: ground equipment mechanic

Lays out, fabricates, and assembles missile ground support equipment and related structures according to blueprints and engineering specifications, using handtools and power tools: Reads and interprets blueprints and engineering

specifications to determine methods and procedures for assembling equipment and structures, such as missile loading systems, storage shelters, and launching equipment. Lays out reference lines on parts, assemblies, and accessories, using measuring and marking instruments. Drills, rivets, reams, taps, countersinks, trims, files, grinds, and forms parts and assemblies, using handtools and power tools. Assembles, aligns, and fits component parts, assemblies, and accessories preparatory to final assembly and welding at missile launch site, using handtools and power tools. Reworks assemblies according to engineering specifications. Verifies symmetry of completed assemblies, using surveying instruments. Discusses assembly sequence, tooling requirements, modifications, and related issues with engineers, liaison personnel and others. May test assembled mechanisms and assemblies following specified testing procedures, using test equipment.
GOE: 05.05.06 STRENGTH: M GED: R4 M3 L3 SVP: 7 DLU: 89

809.281-010 LAY-OUT WORKER I (any industry)
Lays out reference points and dimensions on sheets, plates, tubes, and structural shapes for fabricating, welding, and assembling into structural metal products: Plans and develops layout as outlined on blueprints and templates, applying knowledge of trigonometry, product design, effects of heat, and allowances for curvature and thickness of metal. Details location and sequence of cutting, drilling, bending, rolling, punching, and welding operations, using instruments, such as compass, protractor, dividers, and rule. Marks curves, lines, holes, dimensions, and welding symbols onto workpiece, using scribes, soapstone, and punches. May design and make templates of wood, paper, or metal [TEMPLATE MAKER (any industry)]. May fit and align fabricated parts for welding or assembly operations [FITTER (any industry) II]. May be designated according to type material laid out as Sheet-Metal Lay-Out Worker (any industry); Structural-Steel Lay-Out Worker (any industry).
GOE: 05.05.06 STRENGTH: M GED: R4 M4 L3 SVP: 8 DLU: 77

809.381-010 FABRICATOR-ASSEMBLER, METAL PRODUCTS (any industry)
Fabricates and assembles metal products, such as window sashes, casements, doors, awning frames, shells, cases, and tubular products, such as golf carts or furniture, as specified by work orders, diagrams, and templates, using handtools, power tools, and metalworking machinery: Lays out and marks reference points onto components, using template, rule, square, compass, and scale [LAY-OUT WORKER (any industry) II 809.381-014]. Operates machines, such as shears, cutoff saws, brakes, punch press, form roll and drill press, to cut and shape components to specified dimensions [MACHINE OPERATOR (any industry) II 619.685-062]. Fits [FITTER (any industry) II 706.684-054] and assembles components, using fixtures, handtools, and portable power tools, such as grinders, drills, power wrenches, and riveters. Operates machines, such as arbor presses, riveting press, brazing machine, and resistance-welding machines, to complete assembly. May weld components together. May be designated by specialty as Awning-Frame Maker (fabrication, nec); Metal Screen, Storm Door, And Window Builder (struct. metal); Tubular-Products Fabricator (any industry).
GOE: 06.02.24 STRENGTH: M GED: R3 M2 L2 SVP: 5 DLU: 78

809.381-014 LAY-OUT WORKER II (any industry) alternate titles: duplicator; lay-out maker
Traces patterns and marks specifications for fabricating operations onto sheet metal, metal plates, and structural shapes, using templates, measuring instruments, and handtools: Measures stock, using rule to locate center line for positioning template. Tapes, clamps, bolts, or holds template on workpiece. Marks bending and cutting lines, using scribe, and punches or spot drills location of holes, using center punch or hand drill. May lay out straight lines and location of holes detailed on blueprints.
GOE: 06.02.31 STRENGTH: M GED: R3 M3 L2 SVP: 5 DLU: 77

809.381-018 MILKING-SYSTEM INSTALLER (agric. equip.; retail trade)
Installs and services automatic milking systems in barns and milkhouses, using handtools and power tools: Confers with customer to ascertain needs, sketches layout, and estimates costs for optimum equipment layout. Drills holes and bolts milking equipment, such as control panels, pumps, wash sinks, feed stalls, and gates, in specified locations. Cuts metal pipe to specified length, using hacksaw and vise. Installs and levels piping system, using pipe cutters, wrenches, and spirit level. Starts vacuum pump, calibrates vacuum gauges, and connects test instruments, such as *pulsation recorder and stability gauge*, to monitor system performance. Dismantles and cleans system. Replaces defective or malfunctioning system parts, using wrenches and washing equipment.
GOE: 05.05.09 STRENGTH: H GED: R4 M3 L3 SVP: 6 DLU: 77

809.381-022 ORNAMENTAL-IRON WORKER (construction) alternate titles: housesmith; metal-trim erector; ornamental-iron erector
Installs prefabricated ornamental ironwork, other than structural ironwork, such as metal window and door frames, motor-driven and automatic power doors, metal trim and paneling, and aluminum curtain-wall frames: Measures and marks layout for installation, according to blueprints, using rule, template, square, and compass. Welds brackets to lintels, sills, columns, and other structural framework. Drills holes in metal, concrete, and masonry structure, using portable power drills, airhammer, and handtools. Cuts, miters, and bevels metal trim and cover plates to size, using handsaws or portable power saws. Bolts,

clips, welds, or solders ironwork together and to brackets or anchors. Verifies level and plumbness, using level or plumb bob. Bolts newell posts, balusters, and other parts of stairways and stair rails to supports or embeds them in sockets. Fastens cover plates and molding in place with metal screws to finish and trim work. Installs equipment, such as motor-driven or automatic doors, following procedures provided by manufacturer. May locate and mark reference points, dig postholes, mix concrete, and erect ornamental fences, using transit, posthole digger, and handtools. When working with bronze, is designated ORNAMENTAL-BRONZE WORKER (construction). May fabricate frames for mounting glass in ornamental cast stonework. May be designated according to equipment installed as Metal-Sash Setter (construction); Ornamental-Rail Installer (construction); Steel-Door Setter (construction); Steel-Sash Erector (construction).
GOE: 05.05.06 STRENGTH: H GED: R4 M3 L3 SVP: 7 DLU: 77

809.381-026 ORNAMENTAL-IRON-WORKER APPRENTICE (construction) alternate titles: ornamental-metal-erector apprentice
Performs duties as described under APPRENTICE (any industry) Master Title.
GOE: 05.05.06 STRENGTH: H GED: R4 M3 L3 SVP: 7 DLU: 77

809.381-030 PNEUMATIC-TOOL OPERATOR (ship-boat mfg.)
Performs any of following duties involved in chipping, caulking, drilling, and riveting steelplates, beams, and other structural parts of ships under construction or repair, using pneumatic tools: Caulks overlapping seams between steelplates to make seams watertight, using caulking tool. Chips, cuts, trims, and bevels metal to various shapes and sizes, using handtools and pneumatic hammer. Drills, reams, and countersinks rivet and bolt holes, pipe openings, or other holes in steelplate, steel beams, and angle iron, using portable drilling machines. Heats rivets in forge to specified temperature. Presses steel bar (dolly) against head of hot rivet while RIVETER, HAND (any industry) hydrostatically tests rivet from opposite side. Tests compartments, tanks, and other watertight parts for leaks, using water and air pressure.
GOE: 05.05.06 STRENGTH: M GED: R3 M2 L2 SVP: 7 DLU: 77

809.381-034 SOLAR-FABRICATION TECHNICIAN (machine shop)
Fabricates and assembles metal solar collectors according to job order specifications, using machine shop tools and equipment: Lays out and marks reference points on metal tubing and sheets according to job order specifications, using rule and scriber. Aligns, cuts, and drills copper tubing to form pipe sections, using jig, bandsaw, and drill press. Smooths edges of pipe sections, using file and T-bar. Inserts other precut pipes into drilled holes of pipe sections according to job order specifications, and brazes joints to form manifold unit. Aligns and bends copper sheeting to form absorber plate, using power brake. Aligns manifold unit with grooves of absorber plate, squirts liquid solder into grooves, and bakes assembly to permanently bond joints, using oven. Sprays black paint on assembly to facilitate solar heat absorption, using paint sprayer. Aligns and bends galvanized sheeting to form enclosure frame parts of solar collector, using power brake. Drills holes into frame parts and screws or rivets parts together, using pneumatic drill and rivet gun. Inserts absorber plate and manifold assembly into enclosure frame, and rivets sections together. Caulks assembly corners to prevent water leaks, using caulk gun. Cuts and inserts insulation into enclosure frame to provide heat retention. Aligns and rivets frame end to assembly. Rivets covering to unit to complete solar collector assembly. Packs solar collectors into cardboard boxes for shipment, using tape, strapping, and crimper. Records product identification information on packed boxes.
GOE: 06.02.24 STRENGTH: H GED: R3 M3 L2 SVP: 4 DLU: 86

809.382-010 BALANCING-MACHINE SET-UP WORKER (any industry) alternate titles: dynamic-balancer set-up worker
Sets up and operates dynamic balancing machine to locate points of imbalance on engine or electric motor parts, such as spindles, impeller wheels, armatures, rotors, and flywheels: Positions bearing pedestals according to size of workpiece, installs bearings and keys on pedestal, and aligns drive motor with belt pulleys or drive adapter of balancing machine, using handtools. Adjusts stroboscope light to specified intensity and focus. Signals crane operator to position workpiece on pedestals and fastens test weight to specified point on workpiece, using hammer, pliers, and welding equipment. Starts machine to rotate workpiece. Moves controls of machine and observes dials, meters, or trace patterns on screen to determine points of imbalance on workpiece.
GOE: 06.03.01 STRENGTH: M GED: R4 M3 L3 SVP: 7 DLU: 77

809.484-010 AWNING-FRAME MAKER (tex. prod., nec) alternate titles: frame bender
Fabricates and assembles metal frames for awnings and dock shelters according to sketches, drawings, or verbal instructions, using handtools and portable power tools: Selects specified size and type of pipe or other raw or finished frame material from stock to use in forming frame parts, such as front bars, extension arms, uprights, armlifts, slide rods, and rafters. Measures and marks metal, using tape measure and crayon. Fastens metal in vise and cuts to size, using hand or power hacksaw. Threads pipe ends, using thread cutters. Drills holes in metal, using electric powered drill. Screws and bolts sections together to assemble frame, using tees, unions, screwdriver, and wrenches. May bend metal to specified angle, using hand bending tool. May disassemble frame and pack for transporting to installation site. May assemble canvas to metal frames [RIGGER (tex. prod., nec)]. May hang awnings [AWNING HANGER (construction; retail trade; tex. prod., nec)]. May measure installation site for awning to obtain dimensions.

GOE: 05.10.01 STRENGTH: M GED: R3 M2 L1 SVP: 5 DLU: 77

809.484-014 TEMPLATE MAKER, TRACK (any industry)
Fabricates and assembles track templates for flame-cutting machines from aluminum bar stock and precut plywood board, using handtools and measuring instruments: Positions and tacks or staples template layout onto specified template board, using hammer or staple gun, or draws specified radial shapes onto board, using compass. Measures and cuts aluminum bars to specified length, using hand shears or saw. Bends bar to contour of template design, using hand roll and handtools. Tacks bent bars to template board along layout lines or pattern, using hammer. Changes track sections of template on flame-cutting machine when used for more than one job. Dismantles track templates and straightens bar for reuse, using straightening roll [STRAIGHTENING-ROLL OPERATOR (any industry)].
GOE: 05.10.01 STRENGTH: L GED: R3 M2 L1 SVP: 3 DLU: 77

809.664-010 ALUMINUM-POOL INSTALLER (construction)
Assembles aluminum swimming pool at work site, using handtools and portable power tools: Directs other workers to excavate pool site according to customer specifications. Assembles and installs structural parts, such as underground piping and bottom and side panels of pool, using power drill, rivet gun, spot-welding equipment, and handtools. Erects aluminum fencing around pool, using handtools. Lays precut carpet on deck around pool, using handtools.
GOE: 05.10.01 STRENGTH: M GED: R3 M2 L1 SVP: 4 DLU: 77

809.667-010 HULL AND DECK REMOVER (ship-boat mfg.) alternate titles: boat puller
Removes fiberglass boat decks and hulls from molds, using handtools: Pries edge of hull or deck from mold, using wooden tool, and taps mold, using mallet to loosen cast. Inserts airhose between mold and cast, or in hole in mold, and opens valve to blow cast loose. Grasps and works cast loose from mold. Places cast on dolly with help of other workers or clamps special lifting tool to tabs on hull and pushes hoist lever to fit loosened hull from mold. May assemble and temporarily join structural members, such as hull, deck, and headlines, using hoist, weights, and clamps. May grind edges of decks and hulls preparatory to removing from mold, using disk sander.
GOE: 06.04.34 STRENGTH: H GED: R2 M1 L1 SVP: 3 DLU: 78

809.681-010 ASSEMBLER, UNIT (struct. metal)
Fabricates and assembles custom-built products, such as doors, windows, window screens, and metal awnings according to work orders, diagrams, or layout, using handtools, power tools, and metalworking machinery: Aligns component parts in jig or straightens and squares parts, using measuring instrument and straightener. Smooths edges to obtain specified fit, using file or grinder. Straightens components, using hammer or straightening press. Traces reference lines to lay out points for screw and rivet holes, using rule and scribe or template. Drills or punches screw and rivet holes, using punch or drillpress or portable power drill. Assembles component parts to form completed unit, using handtools and portable power tools [ASSEMBLER, PRODUCTION LINE (struct. metal)]. Measures panels and lifts and turns latches to inspect and test them for conformance to specifications. May operate riveter, power press, or airhammer to assemble units. May polish surfaces, using portable buffing and polishing tools. May be designated by product assembled as Fireproof-Door Assembler (struct. metal); Metal-Door Assembler (struct. metal); Metal-Window-Screen Assembler (struct. metal).
GOE: 06.02.22 STRENGTH: M GED: R3 M2 L2 SVP: 4 DLU: 77

809.684-010 ASSEMBLER, PRODUCTION LINE (struct. metal) alternate titles: assembler-fitter; crimper-assembler
Performs any combination of following assembly line tasks to assemble structural parts, such as metal sashes, doors, windows, and window screens, using handtools and portable power tools: Assembles frame components, such as tops, bottoms, sides, panels, and molding in jigs or fixtures. Smooths edges of components to obtain specified fit, using grinder or file. Punches or drills holes for fastening, using hole punch or power drill. Aligns holes and screws or bolts frame components together, using screwdriver or wrench. Positions hardware, such as locks, hinges, catches, and swivels on frame and fastens hardware to frame, using screwdriver, nut runner, and hand riveter. Cuts screens to specified size, using measuring jig and hand shears. Positions screen over frame and secures screen in groove, using disk roller. Spreads glue, putty, or plastic compound on frame and positions precut glass panes into frame. Rolls plastic or metal spline into groove and trims excess spline, using knife, or crimps edges of groove to hold screen or glass in place, using crimping tool. Assembles components of lock, such as bolts, washers, and spring. Inspects workpiece to detect scratches or burs. Positions workpiece in measuring jig to verify dimensions. May lay out reference points for drilling holes in frame members, using template, rule, and square. May cut channels and molding to specified length, using pinch cutter, shears, or cutoff saw. May cut glass to specified size, using glass cutter. May be designated according to part assembled as Channel Installer (struct. metal); Door-Lock Installer (struct. metal); Frame Assembler (struct. metal); Hardware Installer (struct. metal); Kick-Plate Installer (struct. metal); Screen Installer (struct. metal); Spliner (struct. metal). May perform duties as described under GROUP LEADER (any industry) Term Title.
GOE: 06.04.22 STRENGTH: M GED: R2 M1 L1 SVP: 3 DLU: 77

809.684-014 CASKET ASSEMBLER, METAL (fabrication, nec)
Assembles metal caskets, performing any combination of following tasks, using handtools and welding equipment: Places precut sheet metal sections into

jig to form casket body or lid. Solders joints and hand files or machine grinds rough surfaces [SOLDERER-ASSEMBLER (welding)]. Saws and bevels wooden slats to specified dimension, using handsaw and jointer. Inserts slats under flange of casket body or lid and nails slats into place. Fits lid onto casket body and bends flange of casket body by hand to facilitate tight fit. Drills holes in lid, using power drill and bolts hinge to lid, using wrench. Welds hinge to casket body, using spot-welding machine. May weld joints, using arc-welding machine [WELDER, ARC (welding)].
GOE: 06.04.22 STRENGTH: M GED: R3 M1 L1 SVP: 4 DLU: 77

809.684-018 DRILLER, HAND (any industry) alternate titles: driller, portable
Drills rivet or bolt holes in material, such as metal, wood, or plastic, following layout marks and using portable power drill: Punches indentations along layout marks to guide drill bit, using center punch and hammer. Fastens specified drill bit in chuck of drill. Drills holes, replaces drill bit with specified reamer, tap, or countersink, and enlarges, threads, or countersinks holes. Sharpens cutting tools, using power grinder. May align offcenter holes in structural members, using *drift pins*, and bolt members together, using wrench.
GOE: 06.04.34 STRENGTH: M GED: R2 M1 L1 SVP: 2 DLU: 77

809.684-022 FINISHER, FIBERGLASS BOAT PARTS (ship-boat mfg.) alternate titles: ballaster; grinder
Grinds, repairs, and cleans molded fiberglass parts preparatory to assembly into boats, using handtools and portable power tools: Attaches abrasive disk to grinder and grinds molded parts to remove excess fiberglass and smooth edges. Checks flange of molded parts with thickness gauge to determine if more grinding is necessary. Trims excess fiberglass extending from edge of boat hull, using chisel and mallet. Inspects parts to detect defective areas and cuts out defective areas, using chisel and mallet or portable drill. Applies putty to ground-out areas to repair surfaces, using trowel. Waxes and polishes molded parts, using buffer, paste wax and cloth. May paint repaired areas, using spray gun. May install ballast forms in boat hull, using power hoist and handtools.
GOE: 06.04.34 STRENGTH: M GED: R2 M2 L2 SVP: 3 DLU: 78

809.684-026 GRINDER-CHIPPER II (any industry) alternate titles: grinder, rough
Grinds and chips weld splatter, high spots, burrs, slag, and rust from surface of fabricated metal structures and parts to improve appearance or prepare for painting, using portable or pedestal grinders, chipping hammers, and wire brushes: Positions workpiece on worktable manually or using jib or crane. Inserts specified grinding wheel, wire brush, or cutting chisel into portable grinder or power hammer. Pulls trigger to activate power tool and positions and guides tool along high or defective spots on surface of workpiece. May chip or grind out pits or cracks. Grinds portable pieces, using pedestal grinder. May sharpen chisels and dress grinding wheel, using pedestal grinder or wheel dresser. May paint fabricated parts, using spray gun [PAINTER, SPRAY (any industry) I]. May be designated according to tool used as Chipper (any industry) II; Grinder (any industry) IV.
GOE: 06.04.24 STRENGTH: H GED: R2 M1 L1 SVP: 3 DLU: 77

809.684-030 METAL HANGER (mfd. bldgs.; vehicles, nec)
Installs sheet metal panels, molding, and exterior parts and accessories on manufactured building and travel trailer frames and bodies, using handtools and power tools: Positions panels on body frame, by hand or using chain hoist. Fastens panels to frame, using hammer, drill, rivet gun, stapler, and screwdriver. Trims panels to shape of coach, using tin snips. Lays out window, door, and vent areas on panels according to blueprints, using pencil, ruler, and template. Cuts opening, using electric router and tin snips. Nails and screws insulation to roof frame. Measures, cuts, and installs molding strips to corners, using rule, hammer, hacksaw, and screwdriver. Applies sealer compound around window edges, vent openings, and roof seams, using putty knife. Sets prefabricated window units, screens, and louvers in openings and fastens them in place with screws or rivets. Installs accessories, such as visors, lights, brackets, and railings, using screwdriver. Fastens metal threshold and door casing on body frame, hangs door, and attaches weather stripping, doorstops, striker plate, and molding, using handtools. May assemble window unit. May tend machines that cut or shape metal panels preparatory to hanging [MACHINE OPERATOR (any industry) I 616.380-018]. May be designated according to part installed as Door Installer (mfd. bldgs.; vehicles, nec) I; Roof-Panel Hanger (mfd. bldgs.; vehicles, nec); Side-Panel Hanger (mfd. bldgs.; vehicles, nec); Window Installer (mfd. bldgs.; vehicles, nec).
GOE: 06.02.22 STRENGTH: M GED: R3 M2 L2 SVP: 4 DLU: 77

809.684-034 REPAIRER, FINISHED METAL (any industry)
Repairs surface defects, such as dings, dents, and buckles, in finished metal items, such as automobile bodies, refrigerators, or other appliances, using dolly blocks, ding and pick hammers, and other handtools: Visually examines and feels surface of workpiece to determine extent of defect. Holds dolly block against defect and hammers opposite side to smooth surface, being careful not to stretch surface or mar finish. Cleans and polishes repaired area, using buffer and cloth. May file dings to remove burrs and rough spots. Polishes working surfaces of dolly blocks and hammers, using naphtha-soaked emery cloth to prevent scratching or gouging of workpiece.
GOE: 06.02.24 STRENGTH: H GED: R3 M1 L1 SVP: 5 DLU: 77

809.684-038 WHEEL ASSEMBLER (mfd. bldgs.; vehicles, nec)
Mounts wheels and tires on chassis of mobile home: Positions wheel and spring assembly on chassis brackets, using chain hoist. Bolts wheel assembly

to brackets, using hand or power wrench. Mounts tires on wheel assembly, fastening nuts with tire wrench. May bolt front wheel jack to chassis. May attach brake wires to brake housing and thread wires through holes in cross-members to front of chassis. May spray chassis with rust-resistant paint or undercoat material.
GOE: 06.04.22 STRENGTH: M GED: R2 M1 L1 SVP: 2 DLU: 77

809.684-042 PANEL LAMINATOR (struct. metal)
Laminates precut materials to form doors and portable wall sections used in prefabricated metal buildings: Reads work order to determine materials to be laminated, such as steel, aluminum, urethane, vinyl hardboard, and gypsum, and to determine size and color. Measures materials to verify size. Applies adhesive to materials, using spray gun. Positions and presses materials together on conveyor in prescribed order and aligns materials, using mallet. Pushes button to start conveyor and activate pinch roller that presses sections together and removes air pockets. Removes completed panel from conveyor and places panel on pallet.
GOE: 06.04.22 STRENGTH: H GED: R2 M1 L1 SVP: 3 DLU: 86

809.687-010 DUCT MAKER (construction; mfd. bldgs.)
Cuts and shapes fiberglass sheet to form heating and air-conditioning ducts, using handtools: Places sheet on worktable for cutting. Measures and marks sheet according to specifications, using tape measure and marker. Cuts wedge shaped grooves according to marking to facilitate folding, using straightedge and knife. Folds sheet to form rectangular duct and fastens open edge of duct, using pneumatic stapler. Cuts aluminum tape according to length of duct and tapes edge of duct to make air tight seal. Writes model number on completed sections of duct with felt pen. Moves ducts to designated storage area.
GOE: 06.04.24 STRENGTH: L GED: R2 M1 L2 SVP: 2 DLU: 77

809.687-014 HELPER, MANUFACTURING (aircraft mfg.) alternate titles: general helper
Assists workers engaged in fabricating, assembling, installing, and processing materials, parts, and assemblies for aircraft and aerospace products, performing any combination of following tasks: Sorts and counts parts and materials. Examines parts and materials for defects. Feeds, loads, or removes parts from machines. Loads and unloads racks, baskets, skids, dollies, and conveyors. Moves or carries parts, materials, and equipment. Files, trims, saws, buffs, drills, and deburrs parts, using handtools and power tools. Wraps and unwraps parts, tools, and equipment. Marks identifying information on parts and materials. Places, positions, clamps, or holds parts and materials during assembly, installation, or machining. Lubricates and cleans parts, assemblies, and equipment. Cleans and sweeps work area. Performs other duties as described under HELPER (any industry) Master Title.
GOE: 06.04.34 STRENGTH: M GED: R2 M1 L1 SVP: 2 DLU: 88

809.687-018 INSPECTOR AND TESTER (struct. metal)
Inspects metal sashes, window screens, windows, and doors for appearance and accuracy of fabrication and assembly: Feels sides of workpiece for burrs, ravelled screening, or defective packing of screening, glass, or splines. Slides panels up and down to ensure specified alignment. Verifies dimensions, using fixed gauge, rule, or square. Returns defective workpiece for repair or performs such minor repairs as tightening screws, adjusting balance, and rolling or hammering out small dents, using handtools. May apply gummed tape around frame, screen, or glass, pack pieces according to size, and insert screens and glass panels into frames to prepare pieces for shipping.
GOE: 06.03.02 STRENGTH: L GED: R2 M1 L2 SVP: 3 DLU: 77

809.687-022 LABORER, SHIPYARD (ship-boat mfg.)
Performs following tasks in shipyards: Loads vehicles, using handtruck or dolly. Washes trucks and other vehicles. Cleans ships, piers, drydocks, and other working areas, using broom and water hose. Opens shipping crates, using hammer and pinchbar. Sorts lumber, metals, and other scrap materials. Collects and burns trash. Mixes and pours cement on inner bottoms of ships and around joints on decks to prepare surfaces for tile or to make joints watertight. Removes paint and scale from ships' metal surfaces, using hand or powered wire brushes. Conveys materials and tools to work site.
GOE: 05.12.03 STRENGTH: H GED: R2 M1 L1 SVP: 2 DLU: 77

809.687-026 MOLD PREPARER (ship-boat mfg.) alternate titles: mold finisher
Cleans and waxes fiberglass boat molds preparatory to molding: Washes molds, using sponge. Waxes and polishes interior of mold, using cloth, or electric buffer. Brushes parting agent on mold to facilitate removal of cast after molding.
GOE: 06.04.39 STRENGTH: L GED: R2 M1 L1 SVP: 2 DLU: 77

81 WELDERS, CUTTERS, AND RELATED OCCUPATIONS

This division includes occupations primarily concerned with joining, surfacing, or otherwise fabricating or repairing structures or parts of metal or other weldable material, such as plastic or glass, applying the following welding or cutting processes: arc; gas; resistance; solid state (friction, ultrasonic, cold, explosion, diffusion); and other processes, such as electroslag, electron beam, induction, thermit, and laser beam. Welders in this division are distinguished from workers using welding equipment in other divisions by their knowledge of and experience in welding technology and in being primarily concerned with the equipment and technology of welding. Workers classified in other divisions may use welding equipment, but their knowledge and experience are primarily in assembly or repair techniques. For example, welders who work on storage batteries can be found in Group 727.

810 ARC WELDERS AND CUTTERS

This group includes occupations concerned with welding processes in which joining is produced by heating with an arc or arcs, with or without the application of pressure and with or without the use of filler metal.

810.382-010 WELDING-MACHINE OPERATOR, ARC (welding)
Sets up and operates arc welding machine that welds together parts of fabricated metal products, as specified by blueprints, layouts, welding procedures, and operating charts: Welds flat, cylindrical, or irregular parts that may be clamped, tack-welded, or otherwise positioned. May position weld line parallel to carriage. Turns cranks or pushes buttons to align electrode on welding head over weld joint to weld linear joints, or adjust length of radial arm to position electrode over weld joint when welding radial joints. Clamps cylindrical workpieces onto turning rolls under stationary head to weld circular joints. Threads specified electrode wire from reel through feed rolls and welding head. Turns welding head to set specified angle of electrode. May fill hopper with specified flux and direct nozzle or gravity feed over weld line, or adjust shielding gas or gas mixture flow rate. Turns knobs to set current, voltage, and slope, and synchronize feed of wire and flux with speed of welding action. May set limit switch which automatically stops machine at end of weld. Starts machine and observes meters and gauges, or observes welding action for compliance with procedures. Visually examines welds for adherence to specifications. May grind welded surfaces for penetrant test. Adjusts machine setup to vary size, location, and penetration of bead. May install track template to weld irregularly shaped seams. May make trial run before welding and record setup and operating data. May layout, fit, and tack workpieces together. May preheat workpiece, using hand torch or heating furnace. May reweld defective joints, using hand-welding equipment. May remove surplus slag, flux, and spatter, using brush, portable grinder, and hand scraper. May operate machine equipped with two or more heads. May be designated according to type of welding machine operated as Welding-Machine Operator, Electro-Gas (welding); Welding-Machine Operator, Gas-Metal Arc (welding); Welding-Machine Operator, Gas-Tungsten Arc (welding); Welding-Machine Operator, Plasma Arc (welding); Welding-Machine Operator, Submerged Arc (welding).
GOE: 06.02.19 STRENGTH: M GED: R4 M4 L3 SVP: 6 DLU: 77

810.384-010 WELDER APPRENTICE, ARC (welding)
Performs duties as described under APPRENTICE (any industry) Master Title.
GOE: 05.05.06 STRENGTH: H GED: R4 M4 L3 SVP: 5 DLU: 77

810.384-014 WELDER, ARC (welding)
Welds together metal components of products, such as pipelines, automobiles, boilers, ships, aircraft, and mobile homes, as specified by layout, blueprints, diagram, work order, welding procedures, or oral instructions, using arc-welding equipment: Obtains specified electrode and inserts electrode into portable holder or threads consumable electrode wire through portable welding gun. Connects cables from welding unit to obtain amperage, voltage, slope, and pulse, as specified by WELDING ENGINEER (profess. & kin.) 011.061-026 or WELDING TECHNICIAN (profess. & kin.) 011.261-014. Starts power supply to produce electric current. Strikes (forms) arc which generates heat to melt and deposit metal from electrode to workpiece and join edges of workpiece. Manually guides electrode or gun along weld line, maintaining length of arc and speed of movement to form specified depth of fusion and bead, as judged from color of metal, sound of weld, and size of molten puddle. Welds in flat, horizontal, vertical, or overhead positions. Examines weld for bead size and other specifications. May manually apply filler rod to supply weld metal. May clean or degrease weld joint or workpiece, using wire brush, portable grinder, or chemical bath. May repair broken or cracked parts and fill holes. May prepare broken parts for welding by grooving or scarfing surfaces. May chip off excess weld, slag, and spatter, using hand scraper or power chipper. May preheat workpiece, using hand torch or heating furnace. May position and clamp workpieces together or assemble them in jig or fixture. May tack assemblies together. May cut metal plates or structural shapes [ARC CUTTER (welding) 816.364-010]. May be designated according to type of equipment used as Welder, Carbon Arc (welding); Welder, Flux-Cored Arc (welding); Welder, Gas-Metal Arc (welding); Welder, Gas-Tungsten Arc (welding); Welder, Hand, Submerged Arc (welding); Welder, Plasma Arc (welding); Welder, Shielded-Metal Arc (welding). May operate other machine shop equipment to prepare components for welding. May be designated according to product welded as Welder, Boilermaker (struct. metal). Important variations include types of metals welded, subprocesses used, trade name of equipment used, work site (in-plant, job shop, construction site, shipyard), method of application (manual, semiautomatic), high-production or custom, level of ambidexterity required, type of joints welded (seam, spot, butt). May be required to pass employer performance tests or standard tests to meet certification standards of governmental agencies or professional and technical associations.
GOE: 05.05.06 STRENGTH: H GED: R4 M4 L3 SVP: 5 DLU: 89

810.664-010 WELDER, GUN (welding) alternate titles: spot welder, line; spot welder, body assembly

Welds or tack-welds overlapping edges of positioned components to fabricate sheet metal assemblies, such as panels, refrigerator shells, and automobile bodies, using portable spot-welding gun: Positions and clamps electrode under overlapping edges of workpiece. Presses electrode against workpiece at specified weld points to complete circuit between electrodes and heat metal to joining temperature. Removes electrode after specified period of time. May adjust equipment for automatic timing of current. May periodically attend group meetings to learn new or modified tasks. May position and clamp workpieces together. May examine welded components to detect defects.

GOE: 06.04.31 STRENGTH: M GED: R2 M2 L2 SVP: 2 DLU: 89

810.684-010 WELDER, TACK (welding) alternate titles: tacker

Welds short beads at points specified by layout, welding diagram, or by FITTER (any industry) I 801.261-014, along overlapping edges of metal parts to hold parts in place for final welding. Performs tasks of FITTER HELPER (any industry) 801.687-014. May tack-weld, using hand, submerged, or gas-shielded arc welding equipment. May tack-weld, using portable spotwelding gun [WELDER, GUN (welding) 810.664-010].

GOE: 05.10.01 STRENGTH: H GED: R3 M2 L2 SVP: 5 DLU: 80

811 GAS WELDERS

This group includes occupations concerned with welding in which joining is produced by heating with a gas flame or flames, with or without the application of pressure, and with or without the use of filler metal.

811.482-010 WELDING-MACHINE OPERATOR, GAS (welding) alternate titles: welder, gas, automatic

Sets up and operates oxy-fuel-gas-welding machine to weld metal parts, according to work order, blueprints, layout, and operating charts: Clamps workpieces into holding fixture on machine bed, movable carriage, or turntable. Positions and clamps or bolts welding torch onto overhead carriage, radial arm, or into stationary fixture at specified angle and distance from workpiece. Turns cranks to align torch with weld line. Selects torch tip, filler wire, and flux, according to charts or thickness and type of metal. Fills hoppers with flux and positions spout over weld line. Places reel of filler wire onto spindle and threads end through feed rolls to welding seam. Connects hoses from torch to regulator valves and cylinders of oxygen and fuel gas. Turns regulator valves to start flow of gases, lights torch, and adjusts gas mixture and pressure to obtain flame of desired size and color. Turns knobs to synchronize movement of torch or workpiece, feed of flux and filler with welding action, and sets switch to stop machine at end of weld. Starts machine, observes welding action, and examines weld for defects. Adjusts machine setup to vary bead size and other weld characteristics. May record setup and operating data. May reweld defective joints, using handtorch. May preheat workpiece in furnace. May lay out, fit, and tack-weld workpieces together. May operate machine equipped with two or more welding torches. May remove surplus flux, slag, and splatter, using wirebrush, portable grinder, and hand scraper.

GOE: 06.02.19 STRENGTH: M GED: R3 M3 L2 SVP: 6 DLU: 77

811.684-010 WELDER APPRENTICE, GAS (welding)

Performs duties as described under APPRENTICE (any industry) Master Title.

GOE: 05.05.06 STRENGTH: M GED: R3 M3 L3 SVP: 5 DLU: 77

811.684-014 WELDER, GAS (welding)

Welds metal parts, using gas welding equipment as specified by layout, welding diagram, or work order: Positions parts in jigs or fixtures on bench or floor, or clamps parts together along layout marks. Selects torch, torch tip, filler rod and flux, according to welding chart specifications or type and thickness of metal. Connects regulator valves and hoses to oxygen and fuel gas cylinders, and welding torch. Turns regulator valves to activate flow of gases, lights torch and adjusts gas mixture and pressure, to obtain desired flame, based on knowledge of gas-welding techniques. Holds torch at proper angle to metal and guides along weld joint, applying filler rod to molten area to form weld. Examines weld for bead size and other specifications. Repairs broken or cracked metal objects, fills holes, and builds up metal parts. May apply flux to workpiece instead of filler rod. May preheat workpiece in furnace or with torch. May layout, position and tack weld workpieces. May weld along vertical or overhead weld lines. May scarf or groove weld prior to applying filler metal, using gas welding equipment. May chip or grind off excess weld, slag, or spatter [GRINDER-CHIPPER (any industry) II]. May clean or degrease parts, using wire brush, portable grinder, or chemical bath. May cut metal plates or structural shapes using gas torch. May be designated according to type of gases used such as Welder, Acetylene (welding); Welder, Oxyacetylene (welding); Welder, Oxyhydrogen (welding). Important variations include type of metal welded, products, subprocesses, trade name of equipment, worksite (inplant), job shop, construction site, shipyard), high-production or custom, level of ambidexterity required or type of joints welded (seam, spot, butt). May be required to pass employer performance tests or standard tests to meet certification standards of governmental agencies or professional and technical associations.

GOE: 05.05.06 STRENGTH: M GED: R3 M3 L3 SVP: 5 DLU: 77

812 RESISTANCE WELDERS

This group includes occupations concerned with welding processes in which joining is produced by heat obtained from resistance of the base metal to electric current in a circuit of which the workpiece is a part, and by the application of pressure. Machine tenders in this group are included in Group 819 as WELDING-MACHINE TENDER (welding).

812.360-010 WELDER SETTER, RESISTANCE MACHINE (welding)

Sets up resistance welding and brazing machines that join or bond metal components, such as panels, frames, yokes, tubes, and containers, according to specifications and blueprints: Lays out and marks weld points and position of components on workpiece, using rule, square, templates, and scribe. Selects, positions, aligns, and bolts electrodes, jigs, holding fixtures, guides, and stops onto machine, using measuring instruments and handtools. Turns knobs to set and sychronize electric current, pressure, timing cycle, and automatic feed and transfer equipment specified by welding machine chart or record of previous work. Computes and records setting for new work, applying knowledge of metal properties, principles of welding, and shop mathematics. Makes trial weld. Adjusts electrode gap and feed rollers to thickness of metal. Dresses electrodes, using tip dresser, file, emery cloth, or dressing wheel. Devises and builds fixtures. Gives directions to WELDING-MACHINE OPERATOR, RESISTANCE (welding) in operation of machine. May inspect electrical circuits of machine and perform maintenance tasks, such as replacing defective tubes and relays. May set up welding stations on automatic production lines. Important variations include material types, finish required, and types of joints welded (spot, butt, seam).

GOE: 06.01.02 STRENGTH: M GED: R4 M4 L3 SVP: 7 DLU: 77

812.682-010 WELDING-MACHINE OPERATOR, RESISTANCE (welding)

Sets up and operates resistance welding machine to join metal parts, according to blueprints, work orders, or oral instructions: Turns machine dials to set air and hydraulic pressure, amperage, and joining time, according to specified type of metal, weld, and assembly. May select, install, and adjust electrodes. Aligns workpieces, using square and rule. May hold pieces together manually, fasten into jigs, or secure with clamps to align in specified assembly position. Holds part between electrodes or positions on machine worktable. Depresses pedal or pulls trigger to close electrodes and form weld at point of contact. Releases pedal or trigger after specified welding time. Cleans electrodes, using file, tip dresser, emery cloth. May operate machine which automatically releases electrodes from metal after welding cycle. May devise and build fixtures to hold pieces. May inspect finished work. May operate machine equipped with two or more electrodes which weld at several points simultaneously. Important variations include types of joints welded (seam, spot, butt) and types of materials welded (aluminum, steel). May be designated according to type of resistance-welding machine operated as Flash-Welding-Machine Operator (welding); Percussion-Welding-Machine Operator (welding); Projection-Welding-Machine Operator (welding); Upset-Welding-Machine Operator (welding).

GOE: 06.02.19 STRENGTH: M GED: R4 M4 L3 SVP: 6 DLU: 77

813 BRAZING, BRAZE-WELDING, AND SOLDERING OCCUPATIONS

This group includes occupations concerned with processes in which joining is produced by heating the base metals (metals to be joined) to a suitable temperature and supplying a filler metal to complete the joint. Brazing and braze-welding requires heating the base metals above 800 degrees F. (427 degrees C.) but below their melting point. Soldering requires heating the base metals below 800 degrees F. (427 degrees C.) and below their melting point. Machine tenders in this group are included in Group 819 as WELDING-MACHINE TENDER (welding). SOLDERER (jewelry-silver.) can be found in Group 700.

813.360-010 BRAZING-MACHINE SETTER (welding)

Sets up variety of brazing machines which braze (bond) or solder metal components, according to blueprint, work order, data chart, and layout specifications: Selects, positions, aligns, and bolts holding fixtures, guides, and stops onto machine to position and hold workpieces, using measuring instuments and handtools. Selects or bends tubing and wire to form heating coils, installs coils to electrodes, and turns knobs to set electrical current when setting up induction-brazing machines [BRAZER, INDUCTION (welding)]. Connects hoses from cylinders of oxygen and fuel gas, such as acetylene or natural gas, to regulator valves and one or more welding torches. Selects and installs nozzles to torches. Turns valves and installs gears and cams to set timing devices which shut off electrical current or gas pressure, move workpieces, or fill coils with water to cool workpiece after brazing, and synchronize movement of conveyor or rotary table with brazing action. May install positioning or ejecting fixtures. Makes trial runs, readjusts machine, and records setup data. May set up thermal brazing machines [BRAZING-MACHINE OPERATOR (welding)]. May set up resistance-brazing machines [BRAZER, RESISTANCE (welding)], brazing furnaces [BRAZER, FURNACE (welding)], and gas welding machines [WELDING-MACHINE OPERATOR, GAS (welding)].

GOE: 06.01.02 STRENGTH: M GED: R4 M4 L3 SVP: 7 DLU: 77

813.360-014 SETTER, INDUCTION-HEATING EQUIPMENT (welding)
Sets up induction heating equipment used to braze, heat-treat, and spot-weld metal parts: Selects induction coil according to heating chart, or bends copper tubing by hand, to form coil, following electrical formulas. Attaches power and coolant lines to ends of coil, using flaring tool, nuts and washers, and wrenches. Sets dial controls to regulate current, heating-cycle time, and coolant-flow pressure. Turns wheel and reads meter to tune power-supply oscillators for maximum output. Shims coil-holder and work-holding fixture to center parts within coil for heating. Trains workers to braze and solder metals and examines their work for completeness of bonding. Cleans, lubricates, and adjusts equipment to maintain efficient operation using airhose, cleaning fluid, and handtools.
GOE: 06.01.02 STRENGTH: L GED: R3 M3 L3 SVP: 5 DLU: 77

813.382-010 BRAZER, INDUCTION (welding) alternate titles: brazer, electronic; solderer, electronic
Sets up and operates induction heating equipment to braze (bond) together metal components, according to blueprint, work order, or layout specifications: Positions and clamps fixtures and stops into machine, using square, rule, and template. Selects heating coil, or bends copper or alloy tubing or wire into coils, which outline joint to be brazed. Bolts or screws coil to electrode. Turns knobs to adjust electrical current for type and thickness of metal, as computed from data charts. Places wire, strip, or preformed piece of brazing alloy over edges of components and brushes flux along seams to be joined. Assembles and positions workpieces into holding fixture. Starts electric current in coils to heat workpiece and melt alloy. Turns off current and allows workpiece to cool, or directs stream of water or air onto workpiece, or turns handle to fill coil with water to cool workpiece. Removes workpiece, using tongs or tweezer, when brazed metal has solidified, as indicated by color. May connect holding fixture to electrode instead of using heating coil. May set timing control to shut off current automatically after specified period of time. May anneal finished workpiece to relieve internal stress [ANNEALER (heat treating)]. May dip workpiece into chemical bath to remove impurities or flux. May bond workpieces together with soft solder and be known as Solderer, Induction (welding).
GOE: 06.02.10 STRENGTH: M GED: R3 M3 L2 SVP: 5 DLU: 77

813.382-014 BRAZING-MACHINE OPERATOR (welding) alternate titles: brazing-machine operator, automatic; flame-brazing-machine operator; soldering-machine operator, automatic
Sets up and operates thermal brazing machine which bonds components of fabricated metal products as specified by work orders, blueprints, and data charts: Selects torch tips, braze alloy, and flux, according to type and thickness of metal, data charts, or previous brazing record. Screws tips to torches. Positions and clamps torches at specified distance and angle to workpiece. Aligns and clamps holding fixtures to machine bed, table, or conveyor, using rule, square, and handtools. Aligns and clamps workpieces into fixtures. Fills hoppers with flux and positions spout to direct flow, or manually brushes flux onto seams of workpieces. Loads reel of brazing wire onto machine holder and threads end through automatic feed rolls. Positions preformed pieces of braze alloy along seams of workpiece, or manually applies alloy to seams during brazing. Connects hoses from oxygen and fuel gas cylinders to regulator valves and torches. Turns valves to start flow of gases, lights torch, and adjusts mixture to obtain flame of desired size and color. Turns knobs to synchronize movement of conveyor, rotary table, or oscillating carriage with feed of wire, flux, and brazing action. Starts machine which moves workpiece to flame or moves torch to workpiece to melt alloy into seam. Moves workpiece away from machine to cool. Removes and examines finished pieces for defective seams. May dip pieces into water or acid bath to cool and clean them. May operate machine which automatically moves pieces before air jet or into cooling chamber. May manipulate levers or crank to control movement of machine. May bond workpieces with soft solder and be designated Soldering-Machine Operator (welding).
GOE: 06.02.19 STRENGTH: M GED: R3 M3 L2 SVP: 5 DLU: 77

813.482-010 BRAZER, FURNACE (welding) alternate titles: solderer, furnace
Operates electric, gas, or oil-fired furnace to braze (bond) or solder metal components, as specified by work orders, sketches, and charts: Turns knobs and observes recording instruments, gauges, and pyrometer te maintain furnace and cooling chamber temperature specified for type of metal and brazing or soldering alloy used. Aligns and clamps together components or positions components in holding fixtures under specified pressure. Brushes on flux and places wire or preformed pieces of brazing or soldering alloy over joints. Places workpieces into furnace or onto conveyor, or into containers, such as baskets, trays, or retorts. Loads containers into furnace or onto furnace conveyor, manually or by hoist. Transfers workpieces from furnace to cooling chamber, using pole, hook, or by turning cranks. May install fixtures into furnace or onto conveyor, using rule, square , template, and handtools. May operate furnace which drops brazed products into quenching tank. May solder metals, such as tin, zinc, brass, and nickel, to strips of gold or silver preparatory to making jewelry articles and be designated Rolled-Gold Plater (jewelry-silver.).
GOE: 06.02.10 STRENGTH: M GED: R3 M2 L3 SVP: 4 DLU: 77

813.682-010 BRAZER, RESISTANCE (welding)
Operates spot welding machine to braze (bond) metal parts together: Places flux and wire or strip of brazing alloy between workpieces. Adjusts electric current and timing cycle of machine to heat metal to bonding temperature. Re-moves workpiece, using tongs, and cools workpiece, using air or water. May cut carbon electrodes to specified size and shape, using cutoff saw.
GOE: 06.02.19 STRENGTH: H GED: R3 M2 L2 SVP: 4 DLU: 77

813.684-010 BRAZER, ASSEMBLER (welding) alternate titles: brazer; torch brazer
Brazes (bonds) together components to assemble metal parts as specified by layout, work order, or blueprints, using hand torch: Aligns and clamps workpieces together, using rule, square, or template or sets up and places them in fixtures, jigs, or vise. Cleans joints of workpieces, using wire brush or by dipping them into cleaning solution. Selects torch tip, flux, and brazing alloy from data charts or work order. Connects hoses from torch to regulator valves and cylinders of oxygen and specified fuel gas, acetylene or natural. Turns valves to start flow of gases, lights flame, and adjusts pressure and mixture of gases to obtain desired color and size of flame. Brushes flux onto joint of workpiece or dips braze rod into flux to prevent oxidation of metal. Guides torch and rod along joint or seam of workpiece to heat to brazing temperature and melt braze alloy to bond workpieces together. Examines seam and rebrazes defective joints. May braze together broken parts and cover holes to repair leaks. May specialize in bonding parts with soft solder and be designated Solderer, Torch (welding) II. May melt and separate brazed joints, using hand torch or furnace, remove and straighten components, and rebraze joints to repair misaligned or damaged assemblies and be designated Brazer, Repair And Salvage (welding). May braze together seams of metal sheets, strips, screening, or wire cloth, using torch mounted on manually guided crawler, and be designated Brazer, Crawler Torch (welding).
GOE: 06.02.22 STRENGTH: M GED: R4 M3 L3 SVP: 5 DLU: 77

813.684-014 SOLDERER-ASSEMBLER (welding) alternate titles: production solderer; returned-goods repairer
Solders together components to assemble fabricated metal items, as specified by work orders, diagrams, or layout, using soldering iron: Aligns and clamps parts together, using rule, square, or handtools, or positions items in fixtures, jigs, or vise. Dips parts in cleaning solution, or brushes or sprinkles flux along seams. Heats soldering iron in gas flame or electric induction coil, or plugs iron in electrical outlet. Plunges tip of iron into cleaning compound and rubs tip onto specified tin alloy to clean and tin tip. Guides tip along seam to heat workpiece to bonding temperature and dips bar or wire of specified soft solder in seam to solder joint. May dip workpieces into molten solder or place solder strip between seams and heat seam with iron to sweat items together. May clean workpiece, using file, handbrush, or grinder. May grind, cut, or bend edges to fit fabricated parts together, using power grinder and handtools. May use hand torch to solder joints inaccessible to hand iron. May solder broken parts or cover holes to repair leaks. May melt and separate soldered joints, using hand torch, iron, or furnace, and remove and straighten components and resolder joints to repair misaligned or damaged assemblies and be designated Solderer, Assembly Repair (welding).
GOE: 06.02.22 STRENGTH: M GED: R3 M2 L3 SVP: 4 DLU: 77

813.684-018 SOLDERER-DIPPER (welding)
Dips metal parts into molten solder to bond them together, using any combination of following methods: (1) Twists, crimps, clamps, or holds parts together and dips them into solder for specified time. Removes and holds parts together until color indicates solder has set. (2) Dips parts separately and solders them together with hand iron, heating one part and pressing it against another, or placing clamped parts into furnace. (3) Clamps workpiece into fixture over solder pot and depresses lever to raise level of solder or move workpiece into solder. May dip units, such as radiator cores, using jib or crane. May place solder bars into container and turn knobs to specified position to melt solder and regulate its temperature.
GOE: 06.04.31 STRENGTH: L GED: R2 M2 L2 SVP: 2 DLU: 77

813.684-022 SOLDERER, PRODUCTION LINE (welding)
Solders together components of metal products on production line, using hand soldering iron and soft solder: Dips workpieces into chemical solution or brushes or powders flux along joints to remove impurities. Places workpieces into fixtures or manually holds them together at designated point. Plunges soldering iron into chemical to clean tip. Positions tip of heated soldering iron and wire or bar of solder to joint until solder melts and seeps into joint. Guides iron and solder along seams. Removes workpiece when color indicates that solder has cooled and bonded workpieces together. May sweat together workpieces coated with solder. May solder with self-fluxing solder. May adjust controls of gas flame or electric induction coils to specified point on dial to heat soldering iron.
GOE: 06.04.31 STRENGTH: L GED: R2 M2 L2 SVP: 2 DLU: 77

813.684-026 SOLDERER, TORCH I (welding)
Fills holes, indentations, and seams of fabricated metal products, using solder and gas torch: Prepares area to be soldered, using hand and powered tools, such as hacksaw, chisel, hammer, grinder, and wire brush. Brushes acid solution onto area to clean area. Moves oxyacetelene torch over area to heat acid and wipes surface, using cloth, to remove dirt and excess acid. Rubs stick of solder on heated area and melts solder, using torch. Smooths soldered area with alternate strokes of paddle and torch, leaving soldered section slightly higher than surrounding area for later filing.
GOE: 06.04.31 STRENGTH: L GED: R2 M2 L2 SVP: 2 DLU: 77

813.684-030 SOLDERER, ULTRASONIC, HAND (welding)
Solders metal components, using electric-ultrasonic soldering equipment: Positions component in fixture. Preheats joint area to temperature above solder

melting point, using oxy-fuel torch. Turns dials to set intensity and duration of ultrasonic impulse, according to work order specifications. Pushes button to turn on electric-ultrasonic equipment. Fills joint with solder and positions *ultrasonic horn* on outside of joint to transfer energy impulse from equipment to workpiece, to bond solder and base metal.
GOE: 06.04.31 STRENGTH: L GED: R2 M2 L2 SVP: 3 DLU: 77

813.685-010 BRAZER, CONTROLLED ATMOSPHERIC FURNACE (welding) alternate titles: hydrogen braze-furnace operator
Tends brazing furnace equipped to introduce mixture of gases, which removes oxides from, and prevents oxidation of metal and braze alloy during brazing. Turns handle and knobs and observes gauges to start pump or gas generator and to maintain specified flow of gas into combustion and cooling chamber. Visually inspects brazed metal components periodically and discards defective parts.
GOE: 06.02.19 STRENGTH: L GED: R3 M2 L3 SVP: 4 DLU: 77

814   SOLID STATE WELDERS

This group includes occupations concerned with a group of welding processes in which joining is produced essentially at temperatures below the melting point of the base metals being joined without the addition of a filler metal. Pressure may or may not be used. Processes included are cold welding, explosion welding, diffusion welding, ultrasonic welding, and friction welding. Machine tenders in this group are included in Group 819 as WELDING-MACHINE TENDER (welding). Forge welding occupations are included in Division 61.

814.382-010 WELDING-MACHINE OPERATOR, FRICTION (welding)
Operates friction-welding machine to join metal components, according to work orders, specification tables, and diagrams: Installs, aligns, and adjusts fixtures and stops, using handtools and precision measuring devices, such as micrometers, calipers, verniers, and gauges. Positions parts to be welded into rotating and stationary cylinders of machine holding devices and aligns cylinders in parallel position, using wrench. Turns knobs to regulate speed and timing of rotating cycle and pressure force of stationary cylinder. Presses button to activate machine motor and depresses pedal to start friction-welding cycle to perform trial run. Removes welded parts from machine, using wrench. Periodically inspects workpieces, using precision measuring devices. May perform maintenance operations before and after machine functioning, such as greasing machine, adjusting tension of drive belts, and maintaining specified level of hydraulic fluids and coolants.
GOE: 06.02.19 STRENGTH: L GED: R3 M3 L2 SVP: 5 DLU: 77

814.682-010 WELDING-MACHINE OPERATOR, ULTRASONIC (welding)
Operates welding machine and related equipment to convert ultrasonic vibrations into heat energy to fuse metal components: Observes activity meter for specific amount of power drawn from generator or power supply, according to charts. Turns controls to set clamping pressure, force-amplitude ratio, and velocity, according to work order specifications. Presses buttons to adjust controls for automatic timing of weld and hold cycles. Places workpiece in holding fixture on conveyor and pushes button or depresses pedal to start automatic weld cycle. Observes machine in operation and reports malfunctions to supervisor. Removes welded workpiece from fixture. Removes and replaces worn or damaged *ultrasonic horn*. Important variations include fabrication requirements and type of ultrasonic welding (spot, ring, line, continuous-seam/scan).
GOE: 06.02.19 STRENGTH: M GED: R3 M3 L3 SVP: 4 DLU: 77

814.684-010 WELDER, EXPLOSION (welding)
Welds fabricated metal products within firing chamber of explosion welding equipment, applying knowledge of metal characteristics and explosives: Spreads buffer material in base part of holding device and spreads explosive powder material in upper part of holding device. Positions workpieces in holding device and adjusts to form acute angle. Positions device with contents in firing chamber, closes door of chamber, and turns handle to lock door. Presses detonator button on firing chamber to trigger explosion that forces holding device to close, locking and joining metal workpieces. Unlocks and opens chamber door and removes holding device. Opens holding device, removes welded metal workpiece, and places workpiece in receptacle for further processing.
GOE: 06.02.24 STRENGTH: M GED: R3 M3 L2 SVP: 5 DLU: 77

815   ELECTRON-BEAM; ELECTROSLAG; THERMIT; INDUCTION; AND LASER-BEAM WELDERS

This group includes occupations concerned with the following processes: Electron-beam welding; thermit welding; electroslag welding; induction welding; and laser-beam welding. Machine tenders in this group are included in Group 819 as WELDING-MACHINE TENDER (welding).

815.380-010 WELDER SETTER, ELECTRON-BEAM MACHINE (welding)
Sets up electron-beam welding machine to join together metal components through emission of electrons in vacuum chamber onto workpiece, according to welding charts and specifications: Turns knobs to set voltage and welding

speed according to specifications. Turns knobs to set focus of electron beam, beam current, vacuum level and deflection, according to welding charts of parameter settings and equipment setup experience. Turns controls to start air-pumping and water-cooling systems. Positions metal components into present fixture. Pushes cycle button to automatically start power supply and to weld component. Inspects welded component for defects according to knowledge of metal characteristics and electron-beam welding equipment. Cleans gun cartridge, using cleaning solution, and replaces damaged filament, using handtools. Replaces worn seal in vacuum chamber, using wrench.
GOE: 06.01.02 STRENGTH: L GED: R4 M3 L3 SVP: 6 DLU: 77

815.382-010 WELDING-MACHINE OPERATOR, ELECTRON BEAM (welding)
Sets up and operates electron beam welding machine to join metal workpieces according to specifications, applying knowledge of electron-beam welding: Cleans and assembles part, using solvents, degreasing equipment, and press or oven. Checks part for magnetic field, using Gauss meter, and places part on automatic demagnetizer. Selects holding fixture according to size and type of workpiece and installs fixture into welding position. Selects *target block* and fastens block to fixture to make beam adjustments and prevent damage to equipment. Turns on power supply and water cooling and air pumping systems. Closes chamber door and activates pumping stages to create vacuum. Reviews specifications or examines sample parts to determine equipment settings, applying knowledge of electron-beam welding and metal characteristics. Adjusts current setting to heat filament or cathode and adjusts high voltage setting on anode. Aligns target block in horizontal and lateral directions, using hand and foot controls. Rotates polarized filter to darken image in optical viewing system. Activates beam and adjusts anode voltage and beam current to regulate depth of weld. Adjusts current to magnetic lens to focus beam in specific positions. Moves workpiece under electron beam during welding, using handtools. Turns off beam, opens chamber, and removes target block. Inspects section of workpiece for depth of weld penetration, width of joining cracks, holes, and inclusions, using microscope. Performs mechanical strength tests and records results. Cleans weld chamber and replaces filament, using handtools.
GOE: 06.02.19 STRENGTH: M GED: R4 M3 L3 SVP: 6 DLU: 77

815.382-014 WELDING-MACHINE OPERATOR, ELECTROSLAG (welding)
Operates electroslag welding machine, which uses heat produced by resistance of molten flux to electrical current, to fuse metal components: Places metal components in fixture and tightens holding braces, using wrench. Turns dials to start cooling water supply and to activate power sources and control cabinet. Turns knobs to set voltage, wire feed speed, and welding current, according to welding charts and work orders. Presses automatic cycle button to strike arc and start welding process. Adds premeasured flux to joint to create molten flux pool of specified depth. Turns control to start oscillation. Listens for change in sound of welding process or measures flux pool depth, using steel rod, to determine if additional flux is required. Adds flux throughout welding cycle to maintain stable operation. Observes electrode wire feed to ensure that wire enters and melts in flux. Presses button to stop welding current, power supply, and wire feed. Removes copper weld retaining shoes, using hammer. May remove tabs containing accumulated weld, using oxy fuel or arc cutting equipment. May inspect welded joints for defects, and fills holes, using arc welding equipment. May remove slag, using oxy fuel torch. Important variations are fabrication requirements, weldment design, quality, construction site facilities, and type of electroslag equipment (single-wire nonoscillating, double-wire oscillating, and multiwire oscillating).
GOE: 06.02.19 STRENGTH: H GED: R3 M3 L3 SVP: 4 DLU: 77

815.682-010 LASER-BEAM-MACHINE OPERATOR (welding)
Operates laser-beam machine, which produces heat from concentrated light beam, to weld metal components: Pushes button to open safety enclosure at rear of laser cavity. Positions metal components in fixture and places components on fixture-holding table inside cavity. Pushes button to close safety enclosure. Aligns rear mirror of laser cavity, using micrometer screws, according to chart specifications. Types instructions, using teletype machine, to computer that automatically places fixture-holding table in operative position. Sights reference mark through microscope and turns controls to move fixture to welding position. Teletypes instructions to initiate weld cycle and to return fixture-holding table to unload position. Pushes button to open safety enclosure and removes fixtures containing welded components. Cleans optics, using brush, and replaces used flash tubes. May cut metal components, using laser-beam machine, and be designated Laser-Beam Cutter (welding).
GOE: 06.02.19 STRENGTH: L GED: R3 M3 L3 SVP: 4 DLU: 77

815.682-014 WELDING-MACHINE OPERATOR, THERMIT (welding)
Operates thermit welding machine to join metal components, such as crankshafts, ship stern frames, machine parts, and railroad and craneway rails. Aligns and secures parts in holding fixture. Cuts gap in parts parallel to joint, using gas torch. Places wax pattern and mold box around gap. Places gate and riser patterns into specific positions. Pulls plug to automatically pour specified amount of thermit material into mold box. Ignites kerosene preheater to melt wax and dry mold, using gas torch. Places powder on thermit material and ignites compound, using gas torch, to start thermit welding reaction. Breaks mold, using handtools. Cuts off gates and risers, using gas torch.

GOE: 05.10.01 STRENGTH: M GED: R3 M3 L3 SVP: 3 DLU: 77

816   THERMAL CUTTERS AND ARC CUTTERS

This group includes occupations concerned with severing or trimming materials, using thermal or electric-arc cutting equipment.

816.364-010   ARC CUTTER (welding) alternate titles: arc-air operator; burn-out-scarfing operator

Cuts, trims, or scarfs metal objects to dimensions, contour, or bevel specified by blueprints, work order, or layout, using arc-cutting equipment: Positions workpiece onto table or into fixture or with jib or crane. Selects carbon or metal-coated carbon electrode, gas nozzle, electric current, and gas pressure, according to thickness and type of metal, data on charts, or record of previous runs. Inserts electrode and gas nozzle into holder and connects hose from holder to compressed gas supply. Connects cables from power source to electrode and workpiece or fixture, to obtain desired polarity. Turns knobs to select amperage. Turns lever to adjust jet of gas to blow away molten metal. Strikes arc and guides electrode along lines to cut (melt) through metal. May cut off chips or sprues and burn out cracks and holes. May use holder having two electrodes. May cut without using gas jet. May use nonconsumable tungsten electrode and gases, such as helium or carbon dioxide, and be designated Arc Cutter, Gas-Tungsten Arc (welding). May use plasma-arc cutting torch and gases, such as nitrogen and carbon dioxide, and be designated Arc Cutter, Plasma Arc (welding).
GOE: 05.05.06 STRENGTH: M GED: R3 M3 L3 SVP: 5 DLU: 77

816.464-010   THERMAL CUTTER, HAND I (welding) alternate titles: burner, hand; cutter, gas; flame gouger; torch cutter

Cuts, trims, or scarfs metal objects to dimensions, contour, or bevel specified by blueprints, layout, work order, or oral instructions, using thermal-cutting equipment: Lifts and positions workpiece onto table, manually or using jib or crane. Connects hoses from torch to oxygen tank and fuel gas tank, such as acetylene or propane. Selects torch tip, gas pressures, speed of cut, and allows for width of cut, according to thickness and type of metal as computed from charts. Installs torch tip and turns handle to start and adjust pressure of fuel gas. Lights torch and adjusts flow of oxygen to obtain desired mixture, as indicated by color and size of flame. Directs flame on workpiece to heat it to oxidizing temperature, as indicated by color of metal. Squeezes lever or trigger to release additional jet of oxygen which burns path through metal. Guides flame along cutting line, observing cutting to judge angle, distance of torch, and speed of movement. Removes and inspects finished workpiece. Chips or grinds burrs from edges, using power chisel or portable grinder. May lay out cutting lines, using rule, square, compass, or by tracing from template. May cut damaged or worn pieces from metal structure, such as bridge or building frames, ship plates, or pipelines. May install special tip to cut grooves into metal joints preparatory to welding and be designated Flame Scarfer (welding).
GOE: 05.10.01 STRENGTH: H GED: R3 M3 L3 SVP: 5 DLU: 77

816.482-010   THERMAL-CUTTING-MACHINE OPERATOR (welding) alternate titles: burning-machine operator; flame-cutting-machine operator; flame planer; gas-cutting-machine operator; radiagraph operator

Sets up and operates thermal cutting machines which cut metal plates and structural shapes to dimensions, contour, and bevel specified by blueprints, layout, work orders, and templates: Lifts, positions, and clamps metal stock onto bed of machine. Connects hoses from torch to regulator valves and cylinders of oxygen and fuel gas, such as acetylene, hydrogen, or propane. Selects torch tip and computes gas pressure and mixture, and speed of cut, according to type and thickness of metal, data charts, or record of previous cuts. Installs tip to torch. Pushes button to adjust sliding arm from side or overhead carriage to position torch over cutting line, and to adjust height of head over workpiece to make longitudinal cuts. Adjusts length of radial arm to cut out arcs or circles. Tilts angle of torch to cut bevels. Pushes buttons and reads gauges to obtain selected gas pressure and mixture and set speed of cutting action. Pushes button to automatically light torch, preheat metal to oxidizing temperature, and open valve to release additional oxygen to cut through metal. Pushes button to automatically position torch at cutting line and to start machine moving along line. May maintain records of operating data. May lay out cutting lines, using rule, tape, and square. May preheat metal to remove surface impurities, using hand torch. May clamp two or more plates together for simultaneous cutting. May be designated according to equipment used as Electronic-Eye-Thermal-Cutting-Machine Operator (welding); Magnetic-Thermal-Cutting-Machine Operator (welding); Thermal-Cutting-Tracer-Machine Operator (welding); Track-Template-Thermal-Cutting-Machine Operator (welding); Plasma-Cutting-Machine Operator (welding).
GOE: 06.02.19 STRENGTH: M GED: R3 M3 L3 SVP: 5 DLU: 77

816.682-010   SCARFING MACHINE OPERATOR (steel & rel.)

Sets up and operates, from control booth, scarfing machine to cut surface defects from rolled steel slabs: Reads rolling orders to ascertain scarfing instructions and determine machine setup. Selects specified number of torches and installs tips in torches, using handtools. Clamps torches in machine at specified angle and connects hoses from gas and air manifolds onto torches. Opens manifold valves, observes pressure gauges, and turns valve wheels to regulate gas and oxygen pressure. Moves console controls to ignite torches and adjust gas

and oxygen mixture to obtain specified color of flame. Moves controls to position machine on rolling line, to activate rolling conveyor, and to ignite torches. Observes operation to ensure defects have been removed from slab and rescarfs slab as needed. Opens water spray valve to flush scale and metal from scarfed slab. Moves controls to move machine away from rolling line. Cleans and changes tips as needed. Prepares production reports and cleans work area. Assists other workers to repair scarfing machine.
GOE: 06.02.02 STRENGTH: L GED: R3 M2 L2 SVP: 5 DLU: 86

816.684-010   THERMAL CUTTER, HAND II (welding) alternate titles: salvage cutter; scrap burner; scrap cutter

Dismantles metal assemblies, such as automobiles, machines, building girders, and pipelines, or cuts scrap metal to size for shipping, using thermal-cutting equipment, such as flame-cutting torch or plasma-arc equipment: Connects hoses from hand torch to cylinders of oxygen and fuel gas, or turns knobs to adjust settings of arc-cutting equipment. Turns handle to open gas valve to specified pressure. Lights torch and adjusts flow of oxygen to obtain desired mixture, as indicated by color and size of flame. Directs flame on workpiece to heat it to oxidizing temperature, as indicated by color of metal. Squeezes lever or trigger to release additional jet of oxygen which cuts path through metal. Guides flame or arc across workpiece and observes cutting action to judge speed of movement. May change cutting tips or adjust gas pressure or arc-welding equipment to cut metal of different types and thickness. May climb ladders or work on scaffolds to disassemble structures.
GOE: 05.12.11 STRENGTH: H GED: R2 M1 L1 SVP: 2 DLU: 77

819   WELDERS, CUTTERS, AND RELATED OCCUPATIONS, N.E.C.

This group includes occupations, not elsewhere classified, concerned with welding, brazing, soldering, cutting, and related processes. LEAD BURNER, MACHINE (elec. equip.) and LEAD BURNER (elec. equip.) I are included in Group 727.

819.131-010   LEAD-BURNER SUPERVISOR (welding)

Supervises and coordinates activities of workers engaged in burning (welding) lead and lead alloy parts according to blueprints, specifications, or orders, applying knowledge of melting characteristics of lead: Directs workers and participates in fabricating, installing, and repairing equipment, such as lead pipes, floors, valves and tank linings. Interprets drawings and specifications and orders materials. Performs other duties as described under SUPERVISOR (any industry) Master Title.
GOE: 05.05.06 STRENGTH: M GED: R4 M3 L3 SVP: 7 DLU: 77

819.131-014   WELDING SUPERVISOR (welding)

Supervises and coordinates activities of workers engaged in welding and cutting of products and structures, such as auto, aircraft, and ship components, pipes, boilers, and mobile homes, applying knowledge of welding and cutting techniques, materials, and equipment, and fabrication requirements: Analyzes work orders and blueprints to determine need for supplies and sequence of operations required. Requisitions supplies, such as weld rods, gas, flux, and fixtures. Inspects work or confers with WELD INSPECTOR (welding) I 819.281-018 and WELD INSPECTOR (welding) II 819.687-010 to maintain specified standards and quality. Trains workers in operation of equipment. May set up machines or make trial welds to make test runs and experimental products. May supervise brazing and soldering operations. May supervise fitting and assembly of structural frames. May supervise workers engaged in making tubing from flat steel strips by electric-weld process and be designated Welding Supervisor, Electric-Weld Pipe Mill (welding). Important variations include location of workers supervised, such as in-plant, job-shop, construction site, or shipyard. Performs other duties as described under SUPERVISOR (any industry) Master Title.
GOE: 06.02.01 STRENGTH: L GED: R4 M4 L3 SVP: 8 DLU: 88

819.132-010   SUPERVISOR, FLAME CUTTING (steel & rel.)

Supervises and coordinates activities of workers engaged in removing defects from and cutting heavy gauge steel plates into specified sizes and shapes, using flame cutting, welding, chipping, and grinding machines and equipment: Reviews orders to ascertain size, shape, and gauge of steel plate ordered and examines plate marked by inspection personnel to plan unit work and sequence of operations. Observes flame cutting and plate conditioning activities to ensure expedient, quality, and maximum production. Trains workers in operation of equipment and performance of assigned duties. Inspects equipment for need of repair and arranges for maintenance. Performs other duties as described under SUPERVISOR (any industry) Master Title.
GOE: 06.02.01 STRENGTH: L GED: R4 M3 L3 SVP: 7 DLU: 86

819.281-010   LEAD BURNER (welding) alternate titles: lead welder

Welds lead or lead alloy, using gas torch or arc welding equipment, to install and repair lead items according to oral instructions or dimensional data from blueprints: Installs or repairs equipment, such as lead pipes, valves, floors, and tank linings. Cuts lead sheets or pipe, using powered saws, hand shears, or chipping knife. Levels and scrapes edges or surfaces, using hand scraper, and positions parts for burning. Ignites torch and adjusts valves to obtain flame of specified size and color or adjusts arc welding equipment to obtain specified arc. Welds in flat, vertical, horizontal, or overhead positions. Melts lead bar or wire to add lead to joint. Bonds lead to steel or copper to produce homo-

geneous lead lining or cover, using flux. Places hand molding irons on heavy joints or corners to hold them in position. Heats forms and dresses lead pipes, elbows, and parts, using handtools, torch, or arc welding equipment. Places asbestos strip under joints to prevent heating of supporting surface. May pour molten lead into permanent or sand molds to cast parts. May melt scrap in kettle and cast or extrude melted scrap into bars or wire for reuse. Important variations include type of joint welded (butt, spot, seam).
GOE: 05.05.06 STRENGTH: M GED: R4 M3 L3 SVP: 7 DLU: 77

819.281-014 LEAD-BURNER APPRENTICE (welding)
Performs duties as described under APPRENTICE (any industry) Master Title.
GOE: 05.05.06 STRENGTH: M GED: R4 M3 L3 SVP: 7 DLU: 77

819.281-018 WELD INSPECTOR I (welding) alternate titles: welding tester
Inspects and tests welded joints of work in progress and of completed units for visible defects, correct dimensions, joint strength, bead formation, weld penetration, and conformance with layout, blueprint, and work order specificatons, applying knowledge of welding principles and metallurgical properties: Examines joint to detect flaws, such as cracks, cold weld, spatter, and undercuts, using flashlight and magnifying glass. Inspects joints for hidden cracks and pits, using magnaflux machine and ultrasonic testing equipment. Performs stress tests on joint, using stress testing equipment, or prepares sample for stress testing, and reviews results. Verifies alignment and dimensions of product and setup of machines and fixtures used for work in progress. Observes techniques and performance of welders in shop or at construction site. Marks defective pieces and recommends scrapping or methods for reworking. Records inspection data. Analyzes x-ray photographs of welded joints. May weld, test, and inspect metal samples to determine most effective welding process and technique and be designated Performance-Test Inspector (welding).
GOE: 06.01.05 STRENGTH: M GED: R4 M4 L3 SVP: 7 DLU: 77

819.281-022 WELDER, EXPERIMENTAL (welding)
Analyzes engineering data and welds experimental parts and assemblies to determine most effective welding processes, using various welding techniques and equipment: Analyzes engineering drawings and specifications to plan welding operations where procedural information is unavailable. Lays out parts and assemblies according to specifications. Develops templates and other work aids to hold and align parts. Determines type of welding to be used, such as metallic arc, inert gas, electrode, and oven treatment, applying knowledge of metals to be joined, contours and angles to be formed, and specified stress tolerances. Welds components in flat, vertical, or overhead positions, and adjusts amperage, voltage, and speed during joining to assure required weld deposit. Inspects grooves, angles, gap allowances, and related aspects of assembly to ensure conformance to specifications, using micrometer, caliper, and related precision measuring instruments. Observes hydrostatic, x ray, dimension tolerance, and other tests on welded surfaces to evaluate quality of weld and conformance to production requirements.
GOE: 05.05.06 STRENGTH: L GED: R4 M4 L3 SVP: 8 DLU: 77

819.361-010 WELDER-FITTER (welding)
Lays out, fits, and welds fabricated, cast, and forged components to assemble structural forms, such as machinery frames, tanks, pressure vessels, furnace shells, and building and bridge parts, according to blueprints and knowledge of welding and metallurgy: Selects equipment and plans layout, assembly, and welding, applying knowledge of geometry, physical properties of metal machining and welding techniques. Lays out, positions, aligns, and fits components together. Bolts, clamps, and tack-welds parts to secure in position for welding [WELDER, TACK (welding)]. Sets up equipment and welds parts, using arc, gas-shielded arc, submerged arc, or gas welding equipment [WELDER, COMBINATION (welding)]. May assemble parts by bolting and riveting. May repair products by dismantling, straightening, reshaping, and reassembling parts, using cutting torch, straightening press, and handtools, and be designated Welder, Structural Repair (welding). May specialize in using one welding process and be designated Welder-Fitter, Arc (welding); Welder-Fitter, Gas (welding). May specialize in fitting and welding components of metal tools, dies, and fixtures and be designated Welder, Tool And Die (welding).
GOE: 05.05.06 STRENGTH: M GED: R4 M3 L3 SVP: 7 DLU: 77

819.361-014 WELDER-FITTER APPRENTICE (welding)
Performs duties as described under APPRENTICE (any industry) Master Title.
GOE: 05.05.06 STRENGTH: M GED: R4 M3 L3 SVP: 7 DLU: 77

819.381-010 WELDER-ASSEMBLER (machinery mfg.)
Assembles and tack-welds steel frames and other component parts of machinery and equipment in preparation for final welding: Measures and marks locations for metal components on assembly table, following blueprints. Lifts and positions components on assembly table, using electric crane, jacks, and shims. Verifies position of metal components in assembly, using straightedge, combination square, calipers, and rule. Clamps metal components to assembly table for welding. Removes rough spots from castings, using portable powered grinder and hand file, to fit and assemble parts. Tack-welds parts in preparation for final welding. Moves assembly to storage area, using electric crane.
GOE: 05.05.06 STRENGTH: M GED: R3 M3 L2 SVP: 6 DLU: 77

819.384-010 WELDER, COMBINATION (welding)
Welds metal components together to fabricate or repair products, such as machine parts, plant equipment, mobile homes, motors, and generators, according

to layouts, blueprints, or work orders, using brazing and variety of arc and gas welding equipment: Welds metal parts together, using both gas welding [WELDER, GAS (welding)] or brazing [BRAZER, ASSEMBLER (welding)] and any combination of arc welding processes [WELDER, ARC (welding)]. Performs related tasks, such as thermal cutting and grinding. Repairs broken or cracked parts, fills holes, and increases size of metal parts. Positions and clamps together components of fabricated metal products preparatory to welding. May locate and repair cracks in industrial engine cylinder heads, using inspection equipment and gas torch, and be designated Repairer, Cylinder Heads (welding). May perform repairs only and be designated Welder, Repair (welding). May be required to pass employer performance tests or standard tests to meet certification standards of governmental agencies or professional and technical associations.
GOE: 05.05.06 STRENGTH: M GED: R4 M3 L3 SVP: 6 DLU: 77

819.384-014 WELDER APPRENTICE, COMBINATION (welding)
Performs duties as described under APPRENTICE (any industry) Master Title.
GOE: 05.05.06 STRENGTH: M GED: R4 M3 L3 SVP: 6 DLU: 77

819.664-010 PLATE CONDITIONER (steel & rel.)
Removes and repairs surface defects in steel plates, using hammer and chisel, portable power grinder, and arc welding machine: Determines method required for reconditioning plate based upon examination of plate or following instructions of supervisory personnel. Chips out rolled-in scale from plate, using hammer and chisel, or grinds overfills to plate level, using portable electric grinder. Fills in depressions or chipped out areas of plate, using arc welding machine. Brushes welded area to remove flux, using wire brush, and grinds filled in area to remove excess metal and to smooth plate, using portable electric grinder. Reworks plate to meet standards as directed by inspection personnel. Stamps or marks identification on plate, using steel dies, hammer, or chalk. Attaches sling to plate and crane hook and signals worker operating crane to lift and position plate on or remove plate from workbench.
GOE: 06.04.24 STRENGTH: L GED: R2 M2 L2 SVP: 4 DLU: 86

819.666-010 MACHINE HELPER (welding)
Performs any combination of following tasks involved in use of welding, flame cutting, and brazing machines and furnaces: Transfers workpieces, tools, and supplies. Inserts welding rods into holders, screws tips to torches, or places reels of wire onto rack and threads ends through feed rolls to help set up machine. Positions workpieces and fixtures, and clamps or bolts parts into bed of machine or onto conveyor. Removes corrosion, slag, grease, and excess flux from workpieces, using wire brush, scraper, vacuum hose, portable grinder, or chemical solution. Fills hoppers with flux or brushes flux and inserts braze or solder alloy along seams of workpiece. Turns handles or cranks to move workpieces through machine. Bolts portable machines to workpieces, using wrench. Removes finished work from machine with tongs, or hoist. Tags or marks identifying data on work pieces. Oils and cleans machines. May cut scrap to size, using hand torch. May be designated by machine as Brazer Helper, Furnace (welding); Brazer Helper Induction (welding); Brazing-Machine-Operator Helper (welding); Flame-Cutting-Machine-Operator Helper (welding); Soldering-Machine-Operator Helper (welding); Welding-Machine-Operator Helper, Arc (welding); Welding-Machine-Operator, Gas (welding).
GOE: 05.12.11 STRENGTH: H GED: R2 M1 L2 SVP: 2 DLU: 77

819.684-010 WELDER, PRODUCTION LINE (welding)
Welds metal parts on production line, using previously set up gas- or arc-welding equipment: Turns valves to release fuel gas and oxygen and ignites mixture, or inserts specified weld rod into portable holder, clamps cable onto workpiece or jig, and strikes arc. Guides electrodes, or torch and filler rod, along horizontal weld line at specified speed and angle to melt and deposit metal from filler rod or electrode onto workpiece. May skip (tack) weld designated spots to secure workpieces for other welders. May use different equipment and be designated Brazer, Production Line (welding); Welder, Production Line, Arc (welding); Welder, Production Line, Combination (welding); Welder, Production Line, Gas (welding).
GOE: 06.04.31 STRENGTH: M GED: R2 M2 L2 SVP: 2 DLU: 77

819.685-010 WELDING-MACHINE TENDER (welding)
Tends welding, brazing, or soldering equipment that joins metal components of products, such as auto, aircraft, and jewelry parts, brackets, panels, housings, and electric circuit boards: Lifts metal parts and loads in welding, brazing, or soldering machine. Moves lever to lock parts in position. Presses foot controls or pushes buttons to start machine which automatically welds, brazes, or solders, and unloads parts onto conveyor. Observes operation of machine to detect malfunctioning, and reports malfunctions to MACHINE SETTER (any industry) 616.360-022 or supervisor. Inspects joined components for defects. May unload parts from machine and place on conveyor. May clean metal parts, using wire brush. May tend machine that solders tin can bodies and be designated Side-Seam Tender (welding). May tend machine that welds ends of wire together to form continuous coil and be designated Wire-Drawing-Machine Tender (welding). May be designated Spot Welder (welding). Variations are based on type of machine tended, such as resistance-welding machine, cold-welding machine, soldering/brazing machine, diffusion-welding machine, or laser-beam machine.
GOE: 06.04.02 STRENGTH: M GED: R2 M1 L1 SVP: 2 DLU: 88

819.686-010 MACHINE FEEDER (welding) alternate titles: machine helper

Feeds metal components and removes finished assemblies from brazing, soldering, or welding machines or furnaces: Places or clamps workpieces into holding fixtures, or onto heating fixtures, trays, or conveyor in specified order. Positions preformed piece of brazing alloy between edges of parts and brushes flux along seams of workpiece. Removes finished assemblies after they have passed through heated induction coil and furnace, between electrodes, or over gas flame, and through cooling chamber or water. May feed bonding wire and powdered or liquid flux into machine which brushes flux and feeds wire to seams of workpiece. May load components into hopper of machine which automatically positions them into fixtures. May examine finished parts and separate defective pieces. May be designated by machine fed as Brazing-Furnace Feeder (welding); Brazing-Machine Feeder (welding); Soldering-Machine Feeder (welding); Welding-Machine Feeder (welding).
GOE: 06.04.31 STRENGTH: L GED: R2 M1 L1 SVP: 2 DLU: 77

819.687-010 WELD INSPECTOR II (welding)

Inspects welded or soldered joints and seams for defects, such as cracks, cold weld, spatter, and undercuts: Tests joints or seams, using either of following methods: (1) Connects test-fittings to pipe, turns valve to admit compressed air, and immerses pipe in water, or brushes soapy water onto pipe to locate leaks. (2) Probes soldered joints, using pointed tool, to locate defects. Marks location of defects, using crayon, and routes defective parts to repair area. May use dye penetrants or magna-flux equipment during inspection.
GOE: 06.03.02 STRENGTH: L GED: R3 M2 L2 SVP: 4 DLU: 77

819.687-014 WELDER HELPER (welding)

Performs any combination of following duties to assist workers in welding, brazing, and thermal and arc cutting activities: Moves workpieces, tools, and supplies, manually or by handtruck. Lifts, moves and holds, or clamps workpieces to table, into jigs, or into position as directed, manually or by using hoist, pry bars, wrenches, hammer, and wedges. Cleans workpieces to remove impurities, such as slag, rust, and grease, using wire brush, portable grinder, hand scraper, or chemical solutions. Connects hoses from hand torch to oxygen and fuel gas cylinders or connects cables from power source to electrode holder and workpiece or fixture. Starts gasoline engine to activate electric generators. Places workpieces into furnace to preheat for specified time. Removes, tags or marks, and moves finished work. May attach grappling equipment to objects preparatory to movement by crane. May be designated according to type of activity as Thermal-Cutter Helper (welding).
GOE: 05.12.11 STRENGTH: H GED: R2 M1 L1 SVP: 2 DLU: 77

82 ELECTRICAL ASSEMBLING, INSTALLING, AND REPAIRING OCCUPATIONS

This division includes occupations concerned with assembling, installing, erecting, and repairing electrical equipment and related structures designed for electric power generation, transmission, and distribution; communication, signaling, and object detection; process control, fire control, and data processing; transportation and materials-handling; heating, air-conditioning, refrigeration, and illumination; and other industrial, commercial, and domestic electrical applications.

820 OCCUPATIONS IN ASSEMBLY, INSTALLATION, AND REPAIR OF GENERATORS, MOTORS, ACCESSORIES, AND RELATED POWERPLANT EQUIPMENT

This group includes occupations concerned with assembling components and premachined parts; connecting electrical circuits; testing circuitry and operation of generators, motors, accessories, controls, and related equipment; and making on-site repairs to operating equipment.

820.131-010 ELECTRICIAN SUPERVISOR, SUBSTATION (utilities) alternate titles: electric-repair supervisor; special inspecting-and-testing supervisor

Supervises and coordinates activites of ELECTRICIAN, SUBSTATION (utilities) engaged in installing and repairing circuit breakers, transformers, and other electrical equipment in substation of power system: Examines workers' tools and equipment and installed safety devices, such as hoses and blankets. Directs workers to de-energize lines and equipment and to post warning signs. Inspects completed work and directs workers to restore electrical service. Trains workers in installation and repair of electrical equipment. May supervise and coordinate activities of workers engaged in erecting transmission towers and structural framework of substation [LINE SUPERVISOR (utilities)]. Performs other duties as described under SUPERVISOR (any industry) Master Title.
GOE: 05.05.05 STRENGTH: L GED: R4 M4 L4 SVP: 8 DLU: 77

820.137-010 TRANSFORMER ASSEMBLY SUPERVISOR (elec. equip.)

Supervises workers engaged in assembling electric transformers: Assigns and coordinates either hand or machine operations, such as stacking, brazing, assembly, electrical wiring, and testing. Interprets winding designs to locate malfunctions as indicated by negative test reports. Directs workers or participates in adjusting machines or equipment. Inspects finished or in process parts, vis-

ually or using electrical test equipment, such as ohmmeters and wattmeters, to determine conformance to specifications. Records data, such as time and production figures. Performs other duties as described under SUPERVISOR (any industry) Master Title.
GOE: 06.02.01 STRENGTH: L GED: R4 M4 L4 SVP: 7 DLU: 77

820.261-010 ELECTRICIAN APPRENTICE, POWERHOUSE (utilities)

Performs duties as described under APPRENTICE (any industry) Master Title.
GOE: 05.05.05 STRENGTH: M GED: R4 M4 L3 SVP: 8 DLU: 81

820.261-014 ELECTRICIAN, POWERHOUSE (utilities)

Repairs and maintains electrical equipment in generating station or powerhouse: Tests defective equipment to determine cause of malfunction or failure, using voltmeters, ammeters, and related electrical testing apparatus. Notifies plant personnel of necessary equipment downtime requiring changes from normal generating and transmission equipment operation to maintain uninterrupted service. Repairs and replaces equipment, such as relays, switches, supervisory controls, and indicating and recording instruments. Tests and repairs switchboard and equipment circuitry, interpreting wiring diagrams to trace and connect numerous wires carrying current for independent functions. Cleans and repairs brushes, commutators, windings, and bearings of generators, motors, and converters. May test and maintain transmission equipment, performing such duties as oiling circuit breakers and transformers [ELECTRICIAN, SUBSTATION (utilities)].
GOE: 05.05.05 STRENGTH: M GED: R4 M4 L3 SVP: 8 DLU: 77

820.261-018 ELECTRICIAN, SUBSTATION (utilities)

Inspects, tests, and maintains substation electrical equipment, such as oil circuit breakers and transformers: Inspects and tests equipment to detect malfunctioning and determine resistance and load, using voltmeter and ammeter. Tests insulators and bushings of equipment for power leakage by imposing specified voltage on insulation through testing apparatus and calculating insulation loss. Tests oil in circuit breakers and transformers for dielectric strength [TRANSFORMER TESTER (utilities)]. Repairs or rebuilds oil circuit breakers, transformers, and lightning arrestors by replacing worn parts. Disconnects voltage regulators for removal by other workers by loosening bolts and screws and connects replacement regulator to high-voltage line. Periodically replenishes oil in circuit breakers and transformers not needing repair. Inspects switches before repairing or replacing equipment to ensure power cutoffs. Does not repair electrical machinery, such as generators and converters [ELECTRICIAN, POWERHOUSE (utilities)]. May set forms and pour concrete footings for heavy equipment installation. May paint, repair, and maintain substation buildings.
GOE: 05.05.05 STRENGTH: M GED: R4 M4 L3 SVP: 8 DLU: 77

820.361-010 CORROSION-CONTROL FITTER (pipe lines; utilities)

Installs and inspects rectifier stations and anodes used to minimize corrosive effects of static-electricity discharge between gas pipeline and ground: Measures electric current present in ground, using voltmeter, ammeter, and resistivity meter. Compares electrical quantities with written standard to identify ground areas in which electric current exceeds permissible maximum. Buries rectifier or anode near pipe. Welds connector to pipe, using thermite welding device, and connects wire between connector and anode to complete circuit. Installs insulating flanges at pipe joints to isolate sections of pipe protected by rectifier stations. Periodically tests rectifiers to verify efficiency and replaces defective units.
GOE: 05.05.05 STRENGTH: M GED: R4 M3 L3 SVP: 7 DLU: 77

820.361-014 ELECTRIC-MOTOR-AND-GENERATOR ASSEMBLER (elec. equip.) alternate titles: assembler-erector; motor-and-generator assembler

Fits together parts and subassemblies to build electric motors, generators, and gasoline engine-generator sets, using machinist's tools, precision instruments, and following blueprints and specifications: Files and scrapes burrs from parts and cleans parts with solvent and compressed air. Fits bearings to armature or rotor shafts, using Prussian blue and hand scraper to locate and reduce high spots. Shrinks bushings, couplings, and pinions on shafts, in electric oven. Positions rotors and armatures into stator or field ring and slides heads over shaft and against housing ends manually or with hoist. Secures assembly, using bolts and wrenches. Aligns heads to allow rotor or armature to turn freely and inserts shims under rotor support to adjust airgap between rotor and stator, measuring clearance with precision instruments. Fits carbon brushes to curvature of commutator or collector rings by sand brushing or rotating in seating fixture. Cuts and strips wire leads and crimps or solders connecting lugs to them. Screws leads to brush holders. Packs chamber with grease to lubricate bearings. Assembles external parts, such as fans, covers, exciters, control panels, space heaters, and piping, to build special units. May level and align unit on customer's bedplate or on test base in testing department and couple unit to drive motor or test instruments. May dismantle equipment after testing and examine parts for evidence of wear. May be designated according to power source of unit as Engine-Generator Assembler (engine-turbine).
GOE: 06.01.04 STRENGTH: M GED: R4 M4 L4 SVP: 6 DLU: 77

820.361-018 REGULATOR INSPECTOR (utilities)

Inspects, tests, and maintains voltage regulators and auxiliary equipment that control line voltage within specified range: Tightens connections and replaces defective regulator parts, such as motor controls, fuses, or capacitors. Observes readings and calculates line-drop compensator settings which allow for resist-

ance and reactance voltage drops in primary feeder and main circuits. Adjusts line-drop compensators and reads meters to sustain voltage within specified range. Computes electrical characteristics, such as impedence, power factor, and phase angle. Oils moving parts of regulator and changes oil in motor-bearing housings. Files contact points to remove carbon and provide smooth surface for electrical contact. Clips voltmeter to regulator and records voltage on inspection report. Sends defective motors and parts to repair department. May make voltmeter and ammeter tests on transmission lines and auxiliary equipment. Compiles service report indicating parts replaced and corrections made in voltage range and transformer ratios. May order replacement parts to replenish inventories. May set regulator to deliver specified constant voltage before removing motor for repair to avoid interruption to service.
GOE: 05.05.05 STRENGTH: M GED: R4 M4 L3 SVP: 7 DLU: 77

820.381-010 BATTERY MAINTAINER, LARGE EMERGENCY STORAGE (utilities)

Services and repairs storage batteries maintained in generating plants and substations as electric power source for lighting purposes and operation of motors, switchgear, and electric appliances during interruptions of normal power supply: Tests condition of electrolyte in each cell, using hydrometer and thermometer, and adds water or acid, according to specifications. Measures electrical energy level of batteries to ensure that potential energy meets minimum requirements. Connects batteries to portable charger and adjusts rheostat to raise energy level of undercharged cells. Replaces deteriorated plates in cells and cleans out sediment that accumulates in bottom of battery case. Compiles operating and maintenance records.
GOE: 05.10.03 STRENGTH: L GED: R3 M3 L3 SVP: 6 DLU: 77

820.381-014 TRANSFORMER ASSEMBLER I (elec. equip.)

Connects coils to terminals and builds up supporting structure of power transformers, according to wiring and structural diagrams: Wraps insulation around coil and secures with adhesive tape. Drives fiber wedges between coil and core, using mallet to hold coil around leg of transformer core. Crimps leads to magnet (coil) wire, using hand or hydraulic crimper and tapes connections. Crimps tags to lead wires to conform with wiring diagram. Assembles support structure, clamping angles, terminals, tanks, or cabinet panels, using gas or electric welding equipment, welding jigs, tie bolts, nut runner, drill press, and power drill. Brazes coil leads to specified tanks of terminal strip. May fabricate coils and assemble component parts to build electric power, distribution, or specialty transformers according to blueprints and wiring or structural diagrams. Winds copper wire around jig, fixture, or spindle to form primary coil. Fabricates secondary coil on copper plate of specified thickness, using drill, calipers, and bandsaw. May be designated according to type of transformer assembled as Distribution-Transformer Assembler (elec. equip.); Power-Transformer Assembler (elec. equip.); Specialty-Transformer Assembler (elec. equip.); or by type of core used as Hypercil-Core-Transformer Assembler (elec. equip.).
GOE: 06.01.04 STRENGTH: M GED: R4 M4 L3 SVP: 6 DLU: 78

820.662-010 MOTOR-ROOM CONTROLLER (utilities)

Controls generation and distribution of electrical power from in-plant power station to plant facilities, such as rolling mills or machine shops, and maintains equipment in efficient and safe operating condition: Operates switchboard controls and monitors indicating and recording instruments to maintain adequate flow of electric power to current-consuming machinery and processes, and to prevent overloading of electrical generating and distribution equipment. Repairs or replaces defective motor-generator sets, transformers, switchgear, circuitry, and driving motors. Compiles power consumption and equipment performance and repair records.
GOE: 05.06.01 STRENGTH: M GED: R4 M4 L3 SVP: 8 DLU: 77

820.684-010 TRANSFORMER ASSEMBLER II (elec. equip.)

Assembles transformers according to specifications, performing any combination of following tasks: Reads work order to determine assembly procedure specified by customer. Cleans coils to remove materials accumulated during production processing. Removes accessories from coils, using screwdriver, and wraps coils with paper and tape, leaving ends of wire leads exposed. Inserts ends of wire leads of cores and coils into wire stripping machine to remove coating from wires. Inspects and twists stripped wires together by hand to join designated colored wires. Disassembles cores to facilitate attachment of coils and attaches cores to coils, using cloth tape and glue. Secures core/coils, using metal strapping, metal cutters, and band clippers. Positions wooden wedges that facilitate further processing of units in designated openings of core/coils, using rubber hammer. Turns knobs to set controls of test machine to verify that core/coils operate within specified range, attaches clips to wire leads of core/coils, and observes machine dials to determine test results. Routes defective core/coils for rework. Places component parts of terminals in press, activates press to join parts; or positions parts in fixture and joins parts, using solder and soldering iron, to fabricate terminals. Attaches terminals to core/coils, according to work order, using handtools, spacers, and soldering iron. Applies adhesive to inside of transformer case side sections. Positions and aligns wires and terminals of core/coils with openings in sections. Positions core/coil and side sections in welding machine, aligns seams of sections for welding, and presses buttons to activate welding machine to weld seams. Attaches clip probes to transformer terminals, and activates test equipment to determine whether units meet specifications. Positions, inserts, and attaches transformer parts, such as insulation panels, front and back metal covers, and base plates to complete assembly of transformers, using handtools. Stamps identification numbers on base of transformer, using metal dies and hammer. Repairs transformers with minor defects.

GOE: 06.02.22 STRENGTH: H GED: R3 M1 L2 SVP: 3 DLU: 87

821 OCCUPATIONS IN ASSEMBLY, INSTALLATION, AND REPAIR OF TRANSMISSION AND DISTRIBUTION LINES AND CIRCUITS

This group includes occupations concerned with erecting and repairing power lines and circuits for transmission and distribution of electricity, and assembling and erecting related equipment and structures.

821.131-010 ELECTRICAL-INSTALLATION SUPERVISOR (utilities) alternate titles: service inspector

Supervises and coordinates activities of ELECTRIC-METER INSTALLER (utilities) I and ELECTRIC-METER REPAIRER (utilities) engaged in installing, testing, adjusting, and repairing meters for recording electric current consumption: Reviews work orders to verify specifications of wire sizes and metering equipment according to National Electric Code and company requirements. Visits installation sites and inspects installed meters and other electrical appliances for conformance to specifications and safety standards. Consults with customers, electric-wiring contractors, and commercial department representatives to determine space requirements, availability of customer-service outlets, and types of metering equipment for special installations. Issues meter test or repair orders to workers. Examines meters, instruments, and phase transformers to verify accuracy of tests and completion of repairs or adjustments. Performs other duties as described under SUPERVISOR (any industry) Master Title.
GOE: 05.05.05 STRENGTH: L GED: R4 M4 L4 SVP: 8 DLU: 77

821.131-014 LINE SUPERVISOR (utilities)

Supervises and coordinates activities of workers engaged in construction and repair of overhead and underground power lines: Determines and locates cause of current interrruptions. Trains workers in repair of power lines. Performs other duties as described under SUPERVISOR (any industry) Master Title. May specialize in supervising workers engaged in erecting poles and power lines and be designated Line-Construction Supervisor (utilities). May specialize in supervising workers engaged in making emergency repairs and be designated Emergency-Crew Supervisor (utilities). May specialize in supervising workers engaged in erecting steel transmission towers and be designated Line Supervisor, Tower (utilities).
GOE: 05.05.05 STRENGTH: L GED: R4 M4 L4 SVP: 8 DLU: 77

821.131-018 SERVICE SUPERVISOR II (utilities)

Supervises and coordinates activities of TROUBLE SHOOTER (utilities) II and VOLTAGE TESTER (utilities) engaged in testing electric power distribution lines for overloads and voltage and current fluctuations, in installing service drops from poles to customers' premises, and in repairing regulators, switchgears, and line installations. Trains workers in job duties. Prepares reports of abnormal line conditions, such as overload, low voltage, and transformer outage conditions. Performs other duties as described under SUPERVISOR (any industry) Master Title.
GOE: 05.05.05 STRENGTH: L GED: R4 M4 L4 SVP: 8 DLU: 77

821.131-022 STEEL-POST-INSTALLER SUPERVISOR (utilities)

Supervises and coordinates activities of STEEL-POST INSTALLER (utilities) and WIRER, STREET LIGHT (utilities) engaged in installing, removing, and wiring steel-post street lights. Examines poles to verify accuracy of installation and alignment. Trains workers in work procedures. Performs other duties as described under SUPERVISOR (any industry) Master Title.
GOE: 05.05.05 STRENGTH: L GED: R4 M4 L4 SVP: 7 DLU: 77

821.131-026 WIREWORKER SUPERVISOR (utilities) alternate titles: electrician-constructor supervisor

Supervises and coordinates activities of workers engaged in installing, repairing, and maintaining electrical equipment and wiring in and around generating and distribution stations of power and light company. Performs duties as described under SUPERVISOR (any industry) Master Title.
GOE: 05.05.05 STRENGTH: L GED: R4 M4 L4 SVP: 8 DLU: 77

821.261-010 CABLE TELEVISION LINE TECHNICIAN (radio-tv broad.)

Maintains and repairs cable television cables and equipment: Measures signal strength at amplifiers or at customer's terminal boxes, using field strength meter. Repairs or replaces worn components to ensure acceptable signal strength. Climbs utility pole and connects test television sets to amplifiers. Observes set to evaluate reception and determine cause of faulty reception. Repairs defective cable systems. Answers customers' inquiries or complaints and explains cost and operation of cable service. May communicate with COMMUNICATIONS ELECTRICIAN SUPERVISOR (any industry) 823.131-010, using two-way radio or telephone, to receive instructions or technical advice. May report unauthorized use of cable system to COMMUNICATIONS ELECTRICIAN SUPERVISOR (any industry). May clean and maintain tools, test equipment, and motor vehicle.
GOE: 05.05.05 STRENGTH: H GED: R3 M3 L3 SVP: 6 DLU: 88

821.261-014 LINE MAINTAINER (any industry)

Installs, maintains, and repairs telephone and telegraph and electrical power lines between installations of industrial plant: Directs workers in setting poles.

Climbs poles and installs hardware, lightning arresters, telephone repeaters, telephone and telegraph wires, and other equipment [LINE INSTALLER-REPAIRER (tel. & tel.)]. Installs electrical power cables and auxiliary equipment [LINE ERECTOR (construction; utilities)]. Makes repairs and replacements to maintain lines. May be designated according to area of operations as Line Maintainer, District (any industry).
GOE: 05.05.05 STRENGTH: M GED: R4 M4 L3 SVP: 7 DLU: 77

821.261-018 RELAY TECHNICIAN (utilities)
Performs electrical tests and repairs concerned with maintenance and performance evaluation of in-service relays to prevent and remedy abnormal behavior or failure of transmission and distribution lines and equipment: Connects test apparatus to troubled circuit. Analyzes test results and interprets electrical diagrams to locate defective relay. Opens and closes switches to isolate defective relay and makes adjustments or removes relay for repair. Tests circuit and equipment to evaluate such factors as insulation quality, which affect function of relays. Analyzes test data to determine performance characteristics of relays and effect of system modifications on relay performance. Prepares reports of work performed.
GOE: 05.05.05 STRENGTH: L GED: R4 M4 L3 SVP: 8 DLU: 77

821.261-022 SERVICE RESTORER, EMERGENCY (r.r. trans.)
Restores street railway service after power failures, accidents, and equipment breakdowns, working as member of crew: Drives truck equipped with tools and materials to job site. Diagnoses cause of difficulty to facilitate restoration of service. Repairs or replaces parts or materials, such as trolley wire, insulators, conductor-bar assemblies, and lighting fixtures [LINE INSTALLER, STREET RAILWAY (r.r. trans.)]. Repositions derailed cars on tracks with aid of other workers and mechanical hoisting equipment. Erects portable structures at scene of fire to facilitate laying fire hose across street, and to permit streetcars and buses to pass underneath. Raises or disconnects trolley wires to facilitate house-moving operations. May repair malfunctioning streetcar units at scene when towing to repair barn is not feasible. May repair or replace track, switches, and accessories to facilitate temporary service.
GOE: 05.05.05 STRENGTH: H GED: R4 M2 L3 SVP: 7 DLU: 77

821.261-026 TROUBLE SHOOTER II (utilities)
Locates source of electric power line disturbance or failure and replaces or repairs defective equipment and accessories: Proceeds to troubled sector as directed by DISPATCHER, SERVICE OR WORK (utilities) or joins line crew under supervision of LINE SUPERVISOR (utilities). Tests powerlines and auxiliary equipment to identify defective voltage regulators, transformers, switches, and related accessories causing line disturbances, such as voltage fluctuations, using direct reading and recording electrical testing instruments. Climbs poles and towers to repair or replace overhead conductors, switches, transformers, fuses, and related equipment, using precautionary work methods and insulated tools, ladders, and platforms when working on or near energized circuits. Opens switches to deenergize disturbed or fallen lines to facilitate repairs or to remove electrical hazards. May repair street-light circuitry. May locate and correct electrical trouble in building circuits. May install watt-hour meters and connect service drops between power line and consumer. May patrol power lines and periodically telephone dispatcher's office for trouble assignments. May respond to fire alarms to disconnect power from buildings and extinguish fires on power poles or other utility property.
GOE: 05.05.05 STRENGTH: M GED: R4 M4 L3 SVP: 8 DLU: 77

821.281-010 CABLE TELEVISION INSTALLER (radio-tv broad.)
Installs cable television cables and equipment on customer's premise, using electrician's tools and test equipment: Measures television signal strength at utility pole, using electronic test equipment. Computes impedance of wire from pole to house to determine additional resistance needed for reducing signal to desired level. Installs terminal boxes and strings lead-in wires, using electrician's tools. Connects television set to cable system and evaluates incoming signal. Adjusts and repairs cable system to ensure optimum reception. May collect installation fees and explain cable service operation to subscriber. May communicate with COMMUNICATIONS ELECTRICIAN SUPERVISOR (any industry) 823.131-010, using two-way radio or telephone, to receive instructions or technical advice and to report problems to be repaired by CABLE TELEVISION LINE TECHNICIAN (radio-tv broad.) 821.261-010. May report unauthorized use of cable system to COMMUNICATIONS ELECTRICIAN SUPERVISOR (any industry). May clean and maintain tools, test equipment, and motor vehicle.
GOE: 05.10.03 STRENGTH: H GED: R4 M4 L3 SVP: 5 DLU: 88

821.361-010 CABLE INSTALLER-REPAIRER (utilities) alternate titles: electrician, underground
Installs and repairs underground conduit and cable systems used to conduct electrical energy between substations and consumers: Installs and repairs conduits following blueprints. Pulls cables through ducts [CABLE PULLER (construction; utilities)]. Splices cables together or to overhead transmission line, customer service line, or street light line [CABLE SPLICER (construction; utilities); tel. & tel.; utilities)]. Installs and repairs transformers, fuse boxes, bus bars, relays, and other electrical equipment in manhole and underground substations [UNDERGROUND REPAIRER (utilities)] according to wiring diagrams and specifications. Reinsulates or replaces worn cables and wires. Tests electric cables and equipment wiring to detect broken circuits or incorrect connections, using test lamp, voltmeter, ammeter, and thermocouple indicator.

GOE: 05.05.05 STRENGTH: M GED: R4 M4 L3 SVP: 8 DLU: 77

821.361-014 ELECTRIC-METER INSTALLER I (utilities)
Installs, disconnects, removes, and reconnects electric power meters used to record current consumption of residential, commercial, and industrial customers: Splices and connects covered insulated cable to bus bar in pull box or on switchboard. Mounts meter, and other electric equipment for high load installations, such as time clocks, transformers, and circuit breakers, on racks or wall, using electrician handtools. Installs and connects cable from pull box to meter socket or transformer. Attaches color-coded wires from current transformer to test blocks and from test blocks to meter terminals for testing purposes. Tests meter for current flow and recording of current consumption. Disconnects and seals meter on cut-off order or removes seal and reconnects meter on cut-in orders. Removes, replaces, and reconnects meters when current consumption is too high for existing installation. Installs temporary service meter for recording current consumption during construction. Splices and connects jumper cables from current transformer onto bus bar on switchboard to provide temporary power for customer during change of meter and cables or when customer's service equipment is defective. Records meter and installation data on meter cards, work orders, and field service orders. Locates, diagnoses, and clears electrical trouble on customers' premises. Performs minor repairs and changes faulty or incorrect wiring on customers' premises. May be designated according to specialty as Meter Installer-And-Remover (utilities).
GOE: 05.05.05 STRENGTH: L GED: R4 M4 L3 SVP: 7 DLU: 77

821.361-018 LINE ERECTOR (construction; utilities)
Erects, maintains, and repairs wood poles and prefabricated light-duty metal towers, cable, and related equipment to construct transmission and distribution power lines used to conduct electrical energy between generating stations, substations, and consumers: Directs and assists GROUND HELPERS (tel. & tel.; utilities) in attaching crossarms, insulators, lightning arresters, switches, wire conductors, and auxiliary equipment to poles preparatory to erection, as instructed by LINE SUPERVISOR (utilities), and assists in erection of poles or towers and adjustment of guy wires. Climbs erected poles or towers and installs equipment, such as transformers, which are ordinarily installed after poles are erected. Strings wire conductors between erected poles with assistance of GROUND HELPERS (tel. & tel.; utilities) and adjusts slack in conductors to compensate for contraction and elongation of conductors due to temperature variations, using winch. Splices, solders, and insulates conductors and related wiring to join sections of power line, and to connect transformers and electrical accessories. May trim trees and brush prior to new construction, during repair of damaged lines, or as part of routine maintenance [TREE TRIMMER (tel. & tel.; utilities)].
GOE: 05.05.05 STRENGTH: H GED: R4 M3 L3 SVP: 7 DLU: 77

821.361-022 LINE INSTALLER, STREET RAILWAY (r.r. trans.) alternate titles: line installer, trolley
Installs, inspects, and maintains street-railway electrical and related equipment, such as poles, feeder cables, trolley wires and supports, and high-tension lines, following blueprints, manuals, and work orders: Replaces worn or broken poles and straightens leaning poles, securing pole in position in ground with guy wires, using block and tackle. Cuts faulty sections from overhead wires and splices in new wire, anchoring severed ends with block and tackle while new wire and splicing fixtures are being installed. Installs clinch ears (clamps) that connect trolley wire to supporting cross cables, and switches that throw trolley pole from one trolley wire to another, using hammer and clinching iron. Installs running boards that carry trolley wires under overhead crossings by clamping boards to beams or girders. Strings cable from pole to pole with assistance of ground crew. Tests electrical installations, using various testing devices.
GOE: 05.05.05 STRENGTH: M GED: R4 M4 L3 SVP: 7 DLU: 77

821.361-026 LINE REPAIRER (utilities) alternate titles: hiker; line servicer
Repairs and replaces transmission and distribution power lines between generating stations, substations, and consumers, requiring use of precautionary work methods and safety equipment due to electrical hazards present when working on or near energized conductors and electrical accessories: Opens switches or clamps grounding device to energized equipment to deenergize lines or accessories as directed by LINE SUPERVISOR (utilities). Climbs poles or rides in bucket attached to truck-mounted boom to remove broken or defective wires. Secures new wires to crossarm insulators and splices wire to adjoining sections of line to complete circuit. Transfers wires from defective poles to poles erected by GROUND HELPERS (tel. & tel.; utilities). Installs pole hardware and such auxiliary equipment as transformers, lightning arresters, switches, fuses, and insulators, using handtools. Suspends insulated ladders and platforms from pole crossarms and covers energized lines with rubber mats to facilitate safe handling of high-voltage lines without interrupting service by power shutoff, and uses insulated poles (hot sticks) fitted with mechanically or hydraulically operated grasping and crimping tools. May service streetlight systems [STREET-LIGHT SERVICER (utilities)]. May patrol power lines [ELECTRIC POWER LINE EXAMINER (utilities)]. Qualifications of workers in this classification include work experience in terms of maximum voltage of power lines repaired, such as 120-240 volt secondary circuits, 2,300-4,000 volt distribution lines, or 138 kilovolt transmission lines. Power line repairers experienced in repair of energized or deenergized conductors suspended from electrically conductive metal towers, commonly one-hundred feet or more above ground, may be designated Line Repairer, Tower (utilities).

GOE: 05.05.05 STRENGTH: H GED: R4 M4 L4 SVP: 7 DLU: 77

821.361-030 LINE-ERECTOR APPRENTICE (construction; utilities)

Performs duties as described under APPRENTICE (any industry) Master Title.

GOE: 05.05.05 STRENGTH: H GED: R4 M3 L3 SVP: 7 DLU: 77

821.361-034 POWER-TRANSFORMER REPAIRER (utilities) alternate titles: transformer assembler

Repairs power transformers used in electric generating stations and substations to step-up voltage of current being fed out over high-voltage power lines or to step-down voltage of incoming current prior to being fed to lower voltage distribution lines or electric equipment: Drains and filters transformer oil. Loosens bolts to free transformer cover, laminations, coils, and other internal and external parts. Signals OVERHEAD CRANE OPERATOR (any industry) 921.663-010 to raise heavy transformer components and subassemblies. Dismantles lamination assembly preparatory to cleaning and inspection. Conveys defective coils to coworker for rewinding. Climbs into transformer case, cleans inner surfaces with scrapers and solvent, and examines case for defects, such as cracked weldments. Reassembles transformer, using new and reconditioned parts as specified. Operates pump to fill reassembled transformer with oil. May work at site of transformer installation. May wind replacement coil.

GOE: 05.05.05 STRENGTH: M GED: R4 M3 L2 SVP: 7 DLU: 77

821.361-038 TOWER ERECTOR (construction; utilities)

Erects structural steel, wood, or aluminum transmission towers and installs electric cables and auxiliary equipment to construct transmission and high-voltage distribution power lines between generating stations and substations: Repairs and performs scheduled maintenance on towers, cables, and auxiliary equipment. Frequently works more than one hundred feet above ground when erecting upper portion of towers, and when installing insulators, cables, and electrical accessories on completed towers. May trim trees and remove brush along right-of-way [TREE TRIMMER (tel. & tel.; utilities)].

GOE: 05.05.05 STRENGTH: H GED: R4 M3 L2 SVP: 7 DLU: 77

821.364-010 UTILITIES SERVICE INVESTIGATOR (utilities) alternate titles: electric-meter inspector

Investigates reports of METER READERS (utilities; waterworks) concerning evidence of tampering with watt-hour meters and related wiring which interferes with correct metering of electric current consumed: Requests permission of customer to examine meter. Examines meter for evidence of tampering. Examines wiring connecting meter to outside power lines and building circuits. Removes unauthorized wires or devices illegally installed to bypass current past meter, or to obstruct normal meter function. Turns on bulb of known wattage and observes movement of meter disk, determining accuracy of disk rotation in relation to current consumed by bulb. Replaces blown fuses and repairs minor defects, such as loose wiring connections or insulators. Removes meters showing evidence of tampering and informs customer of discontinuance of service, pending settlement with company. Compiles inspection report, confirming or denying suspected tampering, and reports needed major repairs. May serve court summons and testify in court as company witness during criminal prosecution.

GOE: 05.10.02 STRENGTH: L GED: R4 M3 L3 SVP: 6 DLU: 77

821.367-010 CONSTRUCTION CHECKER (utilities) alternate titles: inspector and clerk; power-line inspector

Inspects and prepares reports concerned with construction and maintenance of overhead or underground electric-power line projects or extensions: Inspects pole installations to ensure compliance with work order specifications, and records items requiring correction, such as loose guy wires, hanging wires, defective conduits or vaults, and incorrect location of equipment on pole. Records identification data on installed equipment, such as transformers, wires or cables, poles or vaults, and guys. Checks line and transformer capacities and phase hook-ups to provide data required for adjustment of power load and phase balance. Draws sketches of installation and location of equipment, such as transformers, switches, fuse boxes, lines, and guys so that map records can be corrected. May prepare list of hardware and materials used on specified construction project.

GOE: 05.05.05 STRENGTH: M GED: R4 M4 L3 SVP: 6 DLU: 77

821.367-014 SAFETY INSPECTOR (utilities)

Inspects equipment, tools, and working conditions to ensure safety of workers engaged in construction and maintenance of overhead and underground power lines: Inspects safety belts, ladders, ropes, rubber goods, and tools and replaces those not meeting safety requirements. Observes crews at work and reports laxity in safety precautions, such as failure to use goggles, rubber gloves, and other safety devices. Examines conditions of ditches and tunnels and recommends use of braces to prevent cave-ins endangering workers. Investigates accidents to determine causes and devises preventive measures. May instruct workers in use of safety equipment and safe work methods.

GOE: 05.03.06 STRENGTH: L GED: R4 M3 L3 SVP: 8 DLU: 77

821.381-010 ELECTRIC-METER TESTER (utilities) alternate titles: meter tester

Tests accuracy of meters used for recording electric current consumption and makes necessary adjustments, using following methods: (1) Connects meter to standard (specially calibrated electric meter mechanism) and adjusts standard's dials to meter being tested. Pushes switch and allows needle on standard to revolve specified number of turns or for clocked period. Compares meter and standard calibrated dials to ascertain accuracy of meter. (2) Connects testing instruments, such as wattmeter, voltmeter, and ammeter, across coils of meter and allows load to pass through meter for clocked period. Computes watt-hours of current consumed, using instrument readings and time factor. Compares watt-hour computations with dial on tested meter to determine meter accuracy. Adjusts meters by loosening or tightening screws, using screwdriver. Inspects wiring of installed meters for improper connections or diversions of current. May make minor repairs and recommend meter removal for major repair. May clean mechanism with solution and small brush. May calculate inaccurate meter variations from standard. May set up auxiliary equipment to route current around installed meter during testing to avoid interruption to service. Does not perform tests on inaccurate meters to diagnose malfunctioning if inaccuracy cannot be corrected by screw adjustment [INSIDE-METER TESTER (utilities) 729.281-034].May be designated according to types of meters tested as Tester, Demand Meters (utilities); Meter Tester, Polyphase (utilities); Meter Tester, Primary (utilities); Meter Tester, Single Phase (utilities).

GOE: 05.05.10 STRENGTH: L GED: R4 M4 L3 SVP: 7 DLU: 77

821.381-014 VOLTAGE TESTER (utilities) alternate titles: service tester

Tests electric power lines and auxiliary equipment to compile data concerning circuit conditions affecting efficiency of electric service and accuracy of current-consumption meters, using test instruments: Climbs poles or descends into underground vaults to gain access to power line equipment. Connects voltmeters, ammeters, and recording-demand meters to energized circuitry, transformers, and electrical accessories, using insulated pole fitted with grasping device. Records registration of direct-reading instruments. Periodically returns to change charts of recording meters. Tests building circuitry and such current-consuming apparatus as x-ray machines and motors to collect data regarding actual voltage requirements and fluctuations. Submits meter readings and charts to supervisory personnel. Inspects wiring, switchgear, and current-control apparatus for mechanical defects. May adjust voltage regulators.

GOE: 05.05.05 STRENGTH: M GED: R4 M4 L3 SVP: 7 DLU: 77

821.381-018 WIND-GENERATING-ELECTRIC-POWER INSTALLER (construction; utilities)

Assembles, installs, and maintains electrical and mechanical parts, such as alternators, generators, and rotors of electric power generating windmills, according to production specifications, using tools and equipment: Assembles and adjusts alternator components according to production specifications, using handtools, drill presses, grinders, and micrometers. Welds steel supports to alternator for mounting on windmill tower, using welding equipment. Crates alternator for shipment to installation site. Attaches cables to alternator and pulls lever to activate truck-mounted hoist to position alternator on windmill tower. Secures alternator to tower structure, using bolts and wrenches. Attaches electric cables, windmill motor, and rotor to alternator, according to schematic, using handtools. Replaces bent or defective parts of windmill and lubricates machinery to service equipment, using handtools, oilcan, and grease gun.

GOE: 05.05.05 STRENGTH: H GED: R4 M3 L3 SVP: 8 DLU: 86

821.564-010 LABORATORY HELPER (utilities)

Assists workers engaged in testing, adjusting, and repairing electrical transmission and distribution equipment in laboratory repair shop, performing any combination of following tasks: Cuts lead wires to length and attaches connectors according to requirements of equipment to be tested. Connects lead wires to equipment and test-apparatus as directed. Observes and records, or calls out readings of test-apparatus meters, and turns test-apparatus switches and dials as directed to assist in making tests requiring numerous connection changes, or when testing equipment is in locations not accessible to test-apparatus. Cleans, paints, and removes minor defects from items, such as meter boxes, protective covers, and mounting brackets. Performs other duties as described under HELPER (any industry) Master Title. May be designated according to worker assisted as Electric-Meter-Repairer Helper (utilities); Electric-Meter-Tester Helper (utilities); Relay-Tester Helper (utilities).

GOE: 05.12.16 STRENGTH: M GED: R2 M2 L2 SVP: 3 DLU: 77

821.667-010 HELPER, ELECTRICAL (utilities) alternate titles: electrician helper

Assists electrical workers in installation, maintenance, and repair of electric-power generation and distribution equipment, underground cables, and related facilities, performing any combination of following tasks: Places barricades around open manholes and excavations, and below crewmembers working overhead to protect workers and public from injury. Digs trenches, places shoring, and lowers tools and materials to workers in excavations and vaults. Positions reels of electric cable along side trench or manhole, and guides cable as it is pulled into ducts to prevent damage to lead sheath. Breaks up concrete to facilitate installation or repair of equipment, using airhammer. Rigs scaffolds and hoists, and helps move heavy machine parts to assist in assembly and repair of generators, converters, switchgear, and related equipment at generating station or substation, as directed. May drive truck. May trim trees and clear undergrowth along right-of-way. Performs other duties as described under HELPER (any industry) Master Title. May be designated according to worker assisted as Cable Installer-Repairer Helper (utilities); Duct-Layer Helper (construction; utilities); Electrician Helper, Powerhouse (utilities); Electric-Meter-Installer Helper (utilities); Wirer Helper (utilities).

GOE: 05.12.16 STRENGTH: H GED: R2 M2 L2 SVP: 3 DLU: 77

821.684-010 ELECTRIC-METER INSTALLER II (utilities)
Installs electric watthour meters in preinstalled meter-connection boxes to connect service: Breaks seal on box previously connected to building wiring, using pliers, and tests box for current flow with test lamp. Fits meter onto prongs extending from top of box and turns setscrews to secure prongs to meter, using screwdriver. Fastens meter to wall with screws and seals with sealing device. Connects electric service and tests for specified voltage, phase, and polarity, using handtools and test instruments. Disconnects customer service on request or default in payment of account. Records meter reading before connecting or after disconnecting service, and submits work report to supervisor.
GOE: 05.10.03 STRENGTH: L GED: R3 M3 L2 SVP: 4 DLU: 77

821.684-014 TOWER ERECTOR HELPER (construction; utilities)
Assists TOWER ERECTOR (construction; utilities) in erection of transmission towers, installation of tower hardware, and stringing of transmission lines or cables, working as member of crew: Unloads structural members of tower and electrical hardware from trucks. Bolts members together to form tower assemblies, using handtools. Positions assemblies in place for installation on tower, using block and tackle. Raises or lowers hardware, tools, and other materials to workers on tower, using handline. Assists in stringing transmission cables. Performs other duties as described under HELPER (any industry) Master Title. May be designated according to specialty as Ground Helper (tel. & tel.; utilities); Ground Helper, Street Railway (r.r. trans.).
GOE: 05.10.01 STRENGTH: V GED: R3 M2 L2 SVP: 5 DLU: 77

821.684-018 WIRER, STREET LIGHT (utilities)
Connects electric street lights to power circuit: Pulls wires leading from underground conduit, and wires leading from lamppost light socket, outside opening in lamppost base. Bares ends of wires and connects them together and to proper terminals. Wraps tape around wire connections for insulation. Fastens lamppost lid in place.
GOE: 05.12.16 STRENGTH: L GED: R3 M3 L2 SVP: 3 DLU: 77

821.684-022 TROLLEY-WIRE INSTALLER (mine & quarry)
Installs and maintains electric wire in underground mine to provide power source for mine locomotives: Drives dinkey engine equipped with tools and materials to underground job site. Operates pneumatic drill to bore hanger holes in top of tunnel. Inserts and secures trolley wire hanger in roof holes. Strings transmission cable (trolley wire) from hanger to hanger, using wrench. Repairs damaged wire and hangers. Relocates transmission cables which are no longer used to other areas of mine.
GOE: 05.10.04 STRENGTH: H GED: R3 M2 L2 SVP: 3 DLU: 86

821.687-010 STEEL-POST INSTALLER (utilities) alternate titles: laborer, pole crew; pole setter
Installs steel posts used to support street lights, traffic signals, and power lines: Guides post into position on previously installed base as it is lowered by truck-mounted hoist. Sights post against previously installed post, or uses carpenter's level, and inserts shims under post until post is vertical. Tightens bolts to secure post to base, using wrench.
GOE: 05.12.12 STRENGTH: M GED: R2 M2 L2 SVP: 3 DLU: 77

822 OCCUPATIONS IN ASSEMBLY, INSTALLATION, AND REPAIR OF WIRE COMMUNICATION, DETECTION AND SIGNALING EQUIPMENT

This group includes occupations concerned with erecting, installing, or repairing overhead and underground telephone and telegraph lines and equipment; and installing or repairing wiring and equipment within buildings to provide communication, detection, and signaling services.

822.131-010 CENTRAL-OFFICE-REPAIRER SUPERVISOR (tel. & tel.) alternate titles: installation supervisor; maintenance chief; operations chief; wire chief
Supervises and coordinates activities of workers engaged in construction, installation, testing, maintenance, and repair of electric power equipment, such as powerplants, cables, wiring, and teleprinters in central offices and at outside facilities: Directs placing and removal of cross-connections on wire-distributing frames. Directs installation of traffic trunklines through switchboard and switchroom. Schedules periodic inspections and tests of equipment to prevent service interruptions. Keeps records of trouble reports and repairs made. Performs other duties as described under SUPERVISOR (any industry) Master Title. May be designated according to area supervised as Central-Office Supervisor (tel. & tel.); City-Plant Supervisor (tel. & tel.); District-Plant Supervisor (tel. & tel.); Inside-Plant Supervisor (tel. & tel.); Outside-Plant Supervisor (tel. & tel.).
GOE: 05.05.05 STRENGTH: L GED: R4 M4 L4 SVP: 7 DLU: 77

822.131-014 CUSTOMER-FACILITIES SUPERVISOR (tel. & tel.) alternate titles: maintenance supervisor; manager, service; service-center supervisor
Supervises and coordinates activities of workers engaged in installation, repair, and maintenance of telephone facilities, such as private and public telephones, switchboards, teletypewriters, and related electromechanical equipment: Inspects customer's premises to determine location of telephone and installation

procedures. Directs installation of telephones and auxiliary equipment, such as brackets, wires, and clamps. Connects wiring to outside cable terminals, tests installed instruments and circuits continuity or to locate malfunctions, using tone and flicker sets. Directs workers in repair or replacement of faulty equipment. Performs other duties as described under SUPERVISOR (any industry) Master Title. May be designated according to particular activity supervised as Installation Supervisor (tel. & tel.); Transmission-Maintenance Supervisor (tel. & tel.); or Manager, Prorate (tel. & tel.) when supervising EQUIPMENT INSPECTOR (tel. & tel.) 822.261-014 in rural areas.
GOE: 05.05.05 STRENGTH: L GED: R4 M4 L4 SVP: 7 DLU: 77

822.131-018 LINE SUPERVISOR (tel. & tel.)
Supervises and coordinates activities of telephone or telegraph workers engaged in construction, removal, and rearrangement of open-wire and carrier cable communication equipment: Examines work order and wiring diagrams to determine installation or repair procedures. Inspects connections, fittings, and installed wire and cable sections for conformance to specifications. Performs duties as described under SUPERVISOR (any industry) Master Title.
GOE: 05.05.05 STRENGTH: L GED: R4 M4 L4 SVP: 7 DLU: 77

822.131-022 PROTECTIVE-SIGNAL SUPERINTENDENT (business ser.) alternate titles: burglar-alarm superintendent
Supervises and coordinates activities of workers engaged in construction, installation, inspection, and maintenance of electrical protective signaling systems installed on subscribers' premises and central station of protective service organization: Reviews work order and surveys subscriber's premises to plan protective system layout. Estimates labor, material, and construction costs. Consults with architects, builders, and electrical and sprinkler contractors concerning installation of protection devices. Plans circuit layouts and arranges facility rental agreements with wire lessors. Devises work schedules and procedures. Requisitions material and facilities. Verifies progress of work against schedules. Inspects completed installations for conformance to specifications and safety standards, and explains system operating procedures to customer. May contact prospective subscribers to explain services and solicit new business.
GOE: 05.02.02 STRENGTH: L GED: R4 M4 L4 SVP: 7 DLU: 80

822.131-026 SIGNAL SUPERVISOR (r.r. trans.)
Supervises and coordinates activities of workers engaged in installing and repairing railroad signals and signal equipment: Reads work orders stating location and extent of damage to or malfunction of signal equipment to determine number of workers and type of equipment and materials needed for repairs. Inspects signal equipment to determine sequence of repair. Directs and assists workers in installing or repairing signal equipment, such as interlocks, automatic signals, and crossing protections. Inspects completed work for conformance to company specifications. Compiles reports at end of day indicating work completed, location, materials used, and number of worker-hours required for each job. Performs other duties as described under SUPERVISOR (any industry) Master Title.
GOE: 05.05.05 STRENGTH: L GED: R4 M4 L3 SVP: 7 DLU: 77

822.131-030 TEST-DESK SUPERVISOR (tel. & tel.)
Supervises and coordinates activities of TROUBLE LOCATORS, TEST DESK (tel. & tel.) engaged in locating and clearing trouble on telephone line circuits. Performs duties as described under SUPERVISOR (any industry) Master Title.
GOE: 05.05.05 STRENGTH: S GED: R4 M3 L3 SVP: 7 DLU: 77

822.261-010 ELECTRICIAN, OFFICE (tel. & tel.) alternate titles: electrician, station, assistant
Makes operating adjustments in submarine cable repeater and terminal circuits and apparatus, and rearranges connections in cables to maintain continuity of service. Communicates with other cable stations, using manual telegraph.
GOE: 05.05.05 STRENGTH: L GED: R4 M3 L3 SVP: 7 DLU: 77

822.261-014 EQUIPMENT INSPECTOR (tel. & tel.)
Inspects layout and equipment in telegraph central office to determine extent of construction, replacement, or modification required to maintain or improve efficiency of installation: Inspects plant to determine accuracy of layout specifications for modification or installation of equipment, estimates costs, prepares and submits report. Inspects work being performed during construction or modification to determine compliance with specifications. Examines reports of voltage and load tests on equipment to ensure adequacy of power and circuits.
GOE: 05.07.01 STRENGTH: L GED: R4 M4 L3 SVP: 8 DLU: 77

822.261-018 MAINTENANCE INSPECTOR (tel. & tel.)
Inspects and tests plant and office telegraph equipment: Examines plant equipment and reviews maintenance records to ensure that equipment has been installed and maintained according to prescribed practices. Conducts load and voltage tests for specific line capacities, and operating tests on circuits, relays, repeaters, and terminal equipment, to determine maintenance required. Compares test results with predetermined standards to ensure that equipment is operating at required service level. Prepares report on inspections, indicating repair or replacement needs.
GOE: 05.07.03 STRENGTH: M GED: R4 M3 L3 SVP: 8 DLU: 77

822.261-022 STATION INSTALLER-AND-REPAIRER (tel. & tel.)
Installs, maintains, and repairs telephone station equipment, such as telephones, coin collectors, telephone booths, and switching-key equipment: Inspects subscriber premises to determine method of installation. Climbs pole to

attach outside (drop) wires. Assembles telephone equipment, mounts brackets, and connects wire leads, using handtools and following installation diagrams or work order. Tests newly installed equipment and repairs or replaces faulty equipment, using test telephone and other testing devices. May be designated according to specific task performed as Station Installer (tel. & tel.); Station Repairer (tel. & tel.). May maintain telephones, lines, and equipment in primarily small rural areas and be designated Section Maintainer (tel. & tel.).
GOE: 05.05.05 STRENGTH: L GED: R4 M4 L3 SVP: 7 DLU: 77

822.261-026 TESTING-AND-REGULATING TECHNICIAN (tel. & tel.) alternate titles: automatic maintainer; repeater attendant; technician, terminal and repeater; tester, equipment; wire-and-repeater technician

Tests and adjusts telegraph repeaters and terminal apparatus to maintain continuity of service: Operates test board (switchboard composed of testing equipment) and other testing devices to trace and diagnose wiring and circuit deficiencies between stations [TROUBLE LOCATOR, TEST DESK (tel. & tel.)]. Replaces or regulates repeaters, relays, switches, and other equipment, using handtools. Communicates with other telegraph offices by teletypewriter equipment concerning operational problems. May be designated according to equipment tested and adjusted as Telegraph-Repeater Technician (tel. & tel.).
GOE: 05.05.05 STRENGTH: L GED: R4 M3 L3 SVP: 7 DLU: 77

822.267-010 LINE INSPECTOR (tel. & tel.) alternate titles: inspector, line

Inspects telegraph lines, cables, and underground plant to determine extent of construction, replacement, or maintenance work necessary to maintain or improve efficiency of communication system: Estimates costs of improvements and prepares report on findings and recommendations. Consults with field engineering personnel and operations personnel concerning advisability of improvements. May investigate right-of-way for new installations [RIGHT-OF-WAY AGENT (any industry)].
GOE: 05.07.03 STRENGTH: L GED: R4 M3 L3 SVP: 7 DLU: 77

822.281-010 AUTOMATIC-EQUIPMENT TECHNICIAN (tel. & tel.) alternate titles: technician, automatic; telegraph-equipment maintainer

Analyzes problems and repairs manual and automatic telegraphic transmitting and receiving apparatus, such as teletypewriters, facsimile-recording devices, and switching equipment: Tests and adjusts equipment, using testing devices, such as signal generators and ohmmeters, following blueprints and wiring diagrams, and using handtools. Tests and regulates telegraph repeaters [TESTING-AND-REGULATING TECHNICIAN (tel. & tel.)]. When repairing and maintaining equipment in branch offices, may be designated Operations Technician (tel. & tel.). May be designated according to type of equipment maintained or repaired as Printer Maintainer (tel. & tel.); Telegraphic-Typewriter Repairer (tel. & tel.).
GOE: 05.05.05 STRENGTH: M GED: R4 M4 L3 SVP: 7 DLU: 77

822.281-014 CENTRAL-OFFICE REPAIRER (tel. & tel.) alternate titles: central-office maintainer

Tests, analyzes defects, and repairs telephone circuits and equipment in central office of telephone company, using test meters and handtools: Locates electrical, electronic, and mechanical failures in telephone switching equipment, using milliammeter boxes, schematic drawings, computer printouts, or trouble tickets. Installs, repairs, and adjusts equipment, such as switches, relays, and amplifiers, using handtools. Removes connections on wire distributing frames and solders or splices wires to terminal lugs, following diagrams [FRAME WIRER (tel. & tel.)]. May maintain telephone switching equipment at private establishments, such as hotels and office buildings [PRIVATE-BRANCH-EXCHANGE REPAIRER (tel. & tel.)]. May diagnose, isolate, and clear electrical faults in circuit [TROUBLE LOCATOR, TEST DESK (tel. & tel.)]. When servicing equipment for intercommunity telephone lines, may be designated Toll Repairer, Central Office (tel. & tel.).
GOE: 05.05.05 STRENGTH: L GED: R4 M3 L3 SVP: 7 DLU: 77

822.281-018 MAINTENANCE MECHANIC, TELEPHONE (any industry) alternate titles: electrician, telephone

Installs, tests, and repairs communication equipment, such as public address and intercommunication systems, wired burglar alarms, switchboards, telegraphs, telephones, and related apparatus, including coin collectors, telephone booths, and switching keys, using schematic diagrams, testing devices, and handtools: Installs equipment according to layout plans and connects units with inside and outside service wires. Maintains equipment and analyzes operational malfunctioning with testing devices, such as oscilloscopes, generators, meters, and electric bridges, to locate and diagnose nature of defect and ascertain repairs to be made. Examines mechanism and disassembles components to replace, clean, adjust or repair parts, wires, switches, relays, circuits, or signaling units, using handtools. Operates and tests equipment to ensure elimination of malfunction. May climb poles to install or repair outside service lines. May repair cables, lay out plans for new equipment, and estimate material required.
GOE: 05.05.05 STRENGTH: L GED: R4 M4 L3 SVP: 7 DLU: 77

822.281-022 PRIVATE-BRANCH-EXCHANGE REPAIRER (tel. & tel.) alternate titles: pbx repairer; telephone repairer

Analyzes and repairs defects in communication equipment, such as telephone switchboards, teletypewriters, and mobile radiophones on customers' premises: Tests equipment to locate malfunctions, using circuit diagrams, polar probes,

meters, and telephone test set. Isolates and analyzes malfunction to determine method of repair, according to knowledge of equipment and test readings. Repairs or replaces defective equipment, using handtools, soldering iron, or wire wrap gun. Retests equipment to verify completeness of repair. May install equipment [PRIVATE-BRANCH-EXCHANGE INSTALLER (tel. & tel.)].
GOE: 05.05.05 STRENGTH: M GED: R4 M2 L3 SVP: 7 DLU: 77

822.281-026 SIGNAL MAINTAINER (r.r. trans.) alternate titles: signal inspector; signal repairer

Inspects, tests, and repairs electric gate crossings, signals, and signal equipment within division of railroad system: Drives truck along track route and stops truck to inspect and test gate crossings, signals, and signal equipment, such as interlocks and hotbox detectors. Inspects batteries to ensure that batteries are filled with battery water or to determine need for replacement. Tests signal circuit connections, using standard electrical testing equipment. Replaces defective wiring, broken lenses, or burned-out light bulbs. Cleans lenses of lamps with cloths and solvent. Lubricates moving parts on gate crossing mechanisms and swinging signals. Inspects electrical units of railroad grade crossing gates to detect loose bolts, defective electrical connections and parts. Tightens loose bolts, using wrench, and tests circuits and connections by opening and closing gate. Compiles reports indicating mileage or track inspected, repairs made, and equipment requiring replacement. May inspect mechanical gate crossings and repair defective cables on hand-operated gates and test air lines and air cylinders on pneumatically operated gates.
GOE: 05.05.05 STRENGTH: M GED: R4 M3 L3 SVP: 7 DLU: 77

822.281-030 TECHNICIAN, PLANT AND MAINTENANCE (radio-tv broad.)

Repairs and maintains coaxial cables and related equipment for cable-television system: Climbs into underground tunnels and passageways to reach television transmission cables. Determines cause of signal breakdown, using blueprints and schematic diagrams, electrical measuring instruments, and knowledge of communication equipment. Repairs equipment, such as coaxial cables and current amplifiers, and performs regular maintenance on cable system, using measuring instruments and handtools.
GOE: 05.05.05 STRENGTH: M GED: R4 M3 L3 SVP: 7 DLU: 77

822.281-034 TECHNICIAN, SUBMARINE CABLE EQUIPMENT (tel. & tel.)

Repairs, adjusts, and maintains machines and equipment used in submarine-cable office or station to control cable traffic, using electrical meters and handtools: Examines malfunctioning machines and equipment, such as automatic transmitters, direct writers, perforating machines, printers and relays, and siphon recorders, to determine defects, using meters, such as voltmeter, ohmmeter, and capacity meter. Makes adjustments, or dismantles machines for repairs or replacement of parts, using handtools. May make temporary or emergency repairs with improvised parts or sections. Duties may be performed by CENTRAL-OFFICE REPAIRER (tel. & tel.).
GOE: 05.05.05 STRENGTH: M GED: R4 M4 L3 SVP: 7 DLU: 77

822.361-010 CABLE TESTER (tel. & tel.)

Tests insulated wires in aerial, underground, or submarine multiple-conductor cables to determine continuity, insulation, and correctness of cable loading, using standard testing procedures and impedance, resistance, and frequency oscillating meters. Listens for sound of escaping insulating gas from hole in cable sheathing to locate defects in cable. Determines continuity, insulation, capacity imbalance, and cable loading, using meters, such as capacity and resistance bridges. Prepares report identifying location and cause of malfunctions. May drive motor vehicle along route of cable, climb poles, and ride in cable car from pole to pole on cable strand to perform tests. May direct CABLE SPLICER (construction; tel. & tel.; utilities) in correction of malfunction.
GOE: 05.05.05 STRENGTH: M GED: R4 M3 L3 SVP: 7 DLU: 77

822.361-014 CENTRAL-OFFICE INSTALLER (tel. & tel.) alternate titles: equipment installer

Installs equipment used to select, connect, and disconnect telephone lines in telephone company central office, following diagrams and using handtools and power tools: Positions switching and power apparatus according to floor plans, using chain hoist when necessary. Connects outgoing and incoming telephone trunk lines to central office equipment, using handtools and following diagrams. Connects and solders wires, using soldering iron. Tests operation of equipment after installation, using electrical testing equipment, such as electrical pulse repeaters and ohmmeters.
GOE: 05.05.05 STRENGTH: M GED: R4 M3 L3 SVP: 7 DLU: 77

822.361-018 PROTECTIVE-SIGNAL INSTALLER (business ser.) alternate titles: burglar-alarm installer; installer

Installs electrical protective signaling systems used to notify central office of fire, burglary, or other irregularities on subscribers' premises: Installs wires, conduits, and signaling units, following blueprints of electrical layouts and building plans and using handtools, power tools and soldering iron. May repair signaling systems [PROTECTIVE-SIGNAL REPAIRER (business ser.)]. Usually is required to possess identification card issued by local authorities.
GOE: 05.05.05 STRENGTH: M GED: R4 M3 L2 SVP: 7 DLU: 77

822.361-022 PROTECTIVE-SIGNAL REPAIRER (business ser.) alternate titles: burglar-alarm installer and servicer

Inspects, repairs, and replaces electrical protective-signaling systems, such as burglar alarms: Examines signaling installation to ensure sound connections and

unbroken insulation. Tests circuits, following wiring specifications, using electrical testing devices, such as ohmmeter or voltmeter. Tightens loose connections and disconnects and replaces defective parts and wiring, using electrician's handtools. Adjusts controls to test operation of signaling units on subscriber premises and transmission of signals to central station and police and fire departments. Recommends new installation or modification of existing equipment to meet subscriber needs. May install equipment [PROTECTIVE-SIGNAL INSTALLER (business ser.) 822.361-018]. Usually is required to possess identification card issued by local authorities.
GOE: 05.05.05 STRENGTH: M GED: R4 M3 L3 SVP: 7 DLU: 80

822.361-026 TRANSMISSION TESTER (tel. & tel.)
Tests and operates telephone equipment in telephone office that services lines extending between communities (toll-office): Tests equipment, using voltmeters, ammeters, transmission measuring sets, impedance bridges, vacuum-tube testing sets, and other electrical measuring devices. Records types and results of tests performed on worksheet. Connects broadcasting equipment into telephone circuits in preparation for radio and television transmission service.
GOE: 05.07.03 STRENGTH: L GED: R4 M3 L3 SVP: 7 DLU: 77

822.361-030 TROUBLE LOCATOR, TEST DESK (tel. & tel.) alternate titles: dispatcher
Locates malfunctions in telephone or telegraph lines, using switchboard composed of electrical testing instruments, and coordinates maintenance crew's work to remove malfunction: Tests lines to find cause and location of malfunction, using switchboard equipped with audible and visual alarms and electrical testing devices, such as voltmeter and resistance meter. Reports nature of trouble to inside and outside maintenance crews and directs and coordinates trouble-clearing activities. May dispatch maintenance crews to malfunctioning area. May contact subscribers to investigate reported trouble.
GOE: 05.06.01 STRENGTH: S GED: R4 M2 L3 SVP: 6 DLU: 77

822.381-010 EQUIPMENT INSTALLER (tel. & tel.)
Installs telegraphic transmitting and receiving equipment in telegraph company offices and on customers' premises, following floor-plan sketches and wiring diagrams: Installs and connects equipment, such as teletypewriters, tickers, facsimile-recording devices, and reperforators, using handtools and soldering iron. Tests equipment for circuit continuity, using testing instruments, such as voltmeter and ohmmeter. May wire and assemble equipment prior to installation [ASSEMBLER (tel. & tel.)]. May be designated according to equipment installed as Call-Box Wirer (tel. & tel.); Telegraphic-Typewriter Installer (tel. & tel.); Telegraph-Repeater Installer (tel. & tel.); Teletype Installer (tel. & tel.); Ticker Installer (tel. & tel.); Time-Signal Wirer (tel. & tel.).
GOE: 05.05.05 STRENGTH: M GED: R4 M3 L3 SVP: 7 DLU: 77

822.381-014 LINE INSTALLER-REPAIRER (tel. & tel.)
Installs and repairs telephone and telegraph lines, poles, and related equipment, according to diagrams, and using electrician's handtools: Digs holes, using power auger or shovel, hoists poles upright in holes, using truck-mounted winch, and fills and tamps holes, using cement, earth, and tamping device. Ascends poles or enters tunnels and sewers to cut in feeder lines, attach appliances, such as terminal boxes and repeaters, and repair or replace defective lines and auxiliary equipment. Unreels and strings lines from pole to pole and from pole to building, installs hardware, such as conduits and insulators, and attaches appliances on lines. Pulls lines through ducts by hand or with use of winch. When assisting in installation and removal of plant equipment, such as callboxes and clocks, in city locations, may be designated Line Installer-Repairer, City (tel. & tel.). When patrolling telephone lines between communities, may be designated Toll-Line Repairer (tel. & tel.). When patrolling telephone or telegraph lines between two established points or in designated areas, may be designated Line Maintainer, Section (tel. & tel.).
GOE: 05.05.05 STRENGTH: H GED: R4 M3 L3 SVP: 7 DLU: 77

822.381-018 PRIVATE-BRANCH-EXCHANGE INSTALLER (tel. & tel.) alternate titles: pbx installer
Installs telephone switchboards and specialized communication equipment, such as intercommunications systems, telephoto circuits, mobile radio-telephones, and teletypewriters, on customers' premises: Connects telephone or telegraph cable terminals to inside wires and switchboard, following diagrams and using handtools, soldering iron, and wire wrap gun. Tests and adjusts installation, using voltmeter, ammeter, and test telephone set [PRIVATE-BRANCH-EXCHANGE REPAIRER (tel. & tel.)]. May be designated according to type of equipment installed and maintained as Private-Branch-Exchange Installer, Mobile Radio (tel. & tel.); Private-Branch-Exchange Installer, Teletypewriter (tel. & tel.); Radio Installer (tel. & tel.); Telephoto Installer (tel. & tel.); Teleprinter Installer (tel. & tel.); Video Installer (tel. & tel.).
GOE: 05.05.05 STRENGTH: H GED: R4 M3 L3 SVP: 7 DLU: 77

822.381-022 TELEGRAPH-PLANT MAINTAINER (tel. & tel.) alternate titles: equipment installer; maintainer, central office; maintainer, equipment; maintainer, plant
Installs, maintains, and repairs electrical and mechanical equipment (other than automatic or manual transmitting and receiving equipment) in central office of telegraph company, according to written and graphic specifications: Installs and wires equipment, such as clocks, switching apparatus, repeaters, relays, conveyor belts, and pneumatic tubes, using handtools, power tools, soldering equipment, metal fasteners, and brackets. Tests installed equipment for circuit continuity and operational performance, using testing devices, such as ohmmeter and voltmeter.

GOE: 05.05.05 STRENGTH: M GED: R4 M3 L3 SVP: 7 DLU: 77

822.664-010 PROTECTIVE-SIGNAL-INSTALLER HELPER (business ser.)
Assists PROTECTIVE-SIGNAL INSTALLER (business ser.) to install protective signaling systems by erecting conduits, pulling wires, fastening pipe straps, and making soldered connections. Makes small installations independently. Performs other duties as described under HELPER (any industry) Master Title. Usually is required to possess identification card issued by local authorities.
GOE: 05.10.03 STRENGTH: M GED: R3 M2 L2 SVP: 5 DLU: 77

822.684-010 FRAME WIRER (tel. & tel.)
Connects wires from telephone lines and cables to distributing frames in telephone company central office, using soldering iron and handtools: Solders connections, following diagram or oral instructions. Strings distributing frames with connecting wires. Tests circuit connections, using voltmeter or ammeter. Removes and remakes connections to change circuit layouts. Cleans switches and replaces contact points, using vacuum hose, solvents, and handtools. Lubricates moving switch parts. Assists TROUBLE LOCATOR, TEST DESK (tel. & tel.) in locating and correcting malfunction in wiring on distributing frame.
GOE: 05.10.03 STRENGTH: M GED: R3 M3 L3 SVP: 4 DLU: 77

822.684-014 PROTECTIVE-SIGNAL-REPAIRER HELPER (business ser.) alternate titles: burglar-alarm-repairer helper
Assists PROTECTIVE-SIGNAL REPAIRER (business ser.) to repair electrical protective signaling systems: Examines electrical units for loose connections and broken insulation. Tightens connections, using wrench. Disassembles defective parts of system, using handtools. Removes and replaces defective wiring and solders connections, using soldering iron. Performs other duties as described under HELPER (any industry) Master Title. Usually required to possess identification card issued by local authorities.
GOE: 05.10.03 STRENGTH: M GED: R3 M2 L2 SVP: 6 DLU: 77

822.684-018 SIGNAL MAINTAINER HELPER (r.r. trans.) alternate titles: assistant signal maintainer
Assists SIGNAL MAINTAINER (r.r. trans.) to install and repair railroad signals and signal equipment, working as member of crew: Loads and unloads equipment and supplies from trucks or flatcars. Digs holes, using post-hole digger, lines holes with wooden forms, and mixes and pours concrete to build concrete foundations. Assists SIGNAL MAINTAINER (r.r. trans.) in installing signals, making electrical connections to units, and performing routine maintenance and repair on equipment. Performs other duties as described under HELPER (any industry) Master Title. May install precast concrete foundations. May climb poles or dig trenches to install wiring, conduit, and related hardware.
GOE: 05.12.16 STRENGTH: H GED: R2 M2 L2 SVP: 3 DLU: 77

823 OCCUPATIONS IN ASSEMBLY, INSTALLATION, AND REPAIR OF ELECTRONIC COMMUNICATION, DETECTION, AND SIGNALING EQUIPMENT

This group includes occupations concerned with assembling equipment components; connecting and testing circuitry; installing equipment to provide electronic communication, detection, signaling, recording, analyzing, and computing services; and making on-site repairs in buildings, ships, trains, and aircraft.

823.131-010 COMMUNICATIONS ELECTRICIAN SUPERVISOR (any industry) alternate titles: chief technician
Supervises and coordinates activities of workers engaged in assembly, installation, maintenance, and repair of electronic communications equipment: Examines premises, plans, and specifications to determine work procedures, estimate costs, and requisition needed materials and equipment. Contacts load dispatching personnel to obtain work clearances on lines and equipment. Assigns duties to workers and requisitions materials, tools, and supplies. Inspects assembled, installed, or repaired equipment, such as transmitters and receivers, power and telephone line carriers, microwave devices, or cable television lines to verify conformance to company standards and government regulations. Tests electronic installations, using testing apparatus. Reviews work orders, trouble reports, and time and equipment records for completeness and accuracy. Prepares daily operating reports summarizing labor, materials, and equipment charges for work performed. Performs other duties as described under SUPERVISOR (any industry) Master Title.
GOE: 05.05.05 STRENGTH: H GED: R4 M4 L4 SVP: 7 DLU: 88

823.131-014 RIGGER SUPERVISOR (radio-tv broad.; tel. & tel.) alternate titles: rigger, chief
Supervises and coordinates activities of workers engaged in wiring and repairing antenna systems for radio communications and radio and television broadcasting. Performs duties as described under SUPERVISOR (any industry) Master Title. May supervise workers engaged in operation and repair of radio transmitters.
GOE: 05.05.06 STRENGTH: L GED: R4 M3 L3 SVP: 7 DLU: 77

823.131-018 SUPERVISOR, AVIONICS SHOP (air trans.)
Supervises and coordinates activities of workers engaged in scheduled inspection, servicing, and maintenance of avionics equipment for commercial air-

line: Reviews service schedules to determine work sequence, methods, and crew and equipment requirements. Assigns duties to workers according to abilities and service priorities. Trains new workers and interprets work procedures, company rules, and safety regulations. Inspects avionic equipment and assemblies to verify conformance to specifications. Signs off completed work and initiates certification as airworthy. Develops revisions in service manuals, test panels, and instruments to increase efficiency and up-date service techniques. Keeps production and inventory records. Performs other duties as described under SUPERVISOR (any industry) Master Title.
GOE: 05.05.10 STRENGTH: L GED: R4 M4 L4 SVP: 8 DLU: 77

823.131-022 SUPERVISOR, RADIO INTERFERENCE (electron. comp.)

Supervises and coordinates activities of RADIO INTERFERENCE INVESTIGATORS (electron. comp.) engaged in locating origin of radio and television interference: Determines, from complaint, location and type of interference caused by electrical power lines or equipment. Assigns workers to investigate complaints and assists in solving more difficult interference problems. Consults with electrical contractors, appliance dealers, and departmental staff to eliminate interference problems. Reviews inspection reports and prepares summary of investigative actions. Performs other duties as described under SUPERVISOR (any industry) Master Title.
GOE: 05.05.05 STRENGTH: L GED: R4 M4 L4 SVP: 8 DLU: 77

823.131-026 SUPERVISOR, SOUND TECHNICIAN (business ser.)

Supervises and coordinates activities of workers engaged in installing, servicing, and repairing commercial sound systems in businesses, offices, and industrial work places: Reads sales orders to ascertain specifications of units to be installed; to determine components, coaxial cable, fittings, and connectors required; and to prepare installation orders for crew. Scans installation site to determine degree of difficulty of installation and to ascertain equipment needs. Assigns installation tasks to individual workers, according to their skills and experience. Explains and demonstrates tasks to workers to impart knowledge and upgrade skill level. Oversees work in progress to ensure quality of work and professional appearance of installation. Turns volume and tone controls to adjust sound levels to harmonize with room size and ambient noises and to test installation. Prepares checklist to indicate inspection of each step and completion of installation. Writes listing to indicate work performed; components installed; distances wired; coaxial cable, fittings, and connectors used; and hours of work expended. Reads reports of malfunctions to diagnose probable cause and to ascertain make, model, and size of installation. Prepares work order and dispatches SOUND TECHNICIAN (any industry) 829.281-022 to repair and service system components. Performs other duties as described under SUPERVISOR (any industry) Master Title.
GOE: 05.05.05 STRENGTH: L GED: R4 M3 L3 SVP: 7 DLU: 86

823.261-010 PUBLIC-ADDRESS SERVICER (any industry) alternate titles: electronic-sound technician; public-address-system operator

Installs and repairs sound-amplifying systems used at public and private assemblages, using handtools and electronic test meters: Positions loudspeakers on posts or other supports. Strings cable from loudspeakers to amplifiers. Places microphones in position near speaker, orchestra, or other attraction, and plugs microphone wires into amplifiers. Switches on installation. Listens to sound output and adjusts volume controls or repositions microphones. Tests and repairs equipment in shop, using handtools, soldering iron, and electronic test meters. May test and repair sound recorders, radio and television receivers, and other electronic equipment. May drive sound truck. May install and repair mobile sound-amplifying system in truck and be designated Sound-Truck Operator (any industry).
GOE: 05.05.10 STRENGTH: M GED: R4 M3 L2 SVP: 7 DLU: 77

823.261-014 RADIO INTERFERENCE INVESTIGATOR (electron. comp.) alternate titles: radio-interference trouble shooter

Drives vehicle and operates radio equipped with directional antenna to locate origin of radio and television interference caused by electric power lines and electrical equipment: Drives to area of complaint of interference or power leakage and turns on radio. Directs car toward source of interference, guided by increase in volume of noises on radio as car nears defective line or apparatus. Examines lines and equipment to determine cause of interference or leakage. Initiates order to have defects corrected or recommends to owner of equipment correction of condition causing interference. May make minor repairs or replacement of power lines and equipment, using handtools. May locate interference by entering complainant's home and turning on lights and appliances and noting effect on radio or television reception. May attach special analyzing device to radio which measures and analyzes interference noises. May investigate voltage complaints and make voltage tests [VOLTAGE TESTER (utilities)].
GOE: 05.05.05 STRENGTH: L GED: R4 M4 L3 SVP: 7 DLU: 77

823.261-018 RADIO MECHANIC (any industry)

Tests and repairs radio transmitting and receiving equipment in accordance with diagrams and manufacturer's specifications, using electrical measuring instruments, wiring diagrams, and handtools: Examines equipment for damaged components and loose or broken connections and wires. Attaches test leads or plugs in test equipment to unit being tested, turns knobs on equipment to specified settings, and observes dial readings to test radio circuitry for defects. Tests equipment for factors such as power output, frequency power, noise level, audio

quality, and dial calibration, using oscilloscopes, radio frequency and wattmeter, ammeters, and voltmeters. Replaces defective components and parts, such as transistors, coils, and integrated circuits, using soldering iron, wire cutters, and handtools. Removes and replaces defective units that are not repairable. Inserts plugs into receptacles and bolts or screws leads to terminals to connect radios and equipment to power source, using handtools. Turns setscrews to adjust receivers for sensitivity and transmitters for maximum output. Tests batteries with hydrometer and ammeter and charges batteries. Required to have Federal Communications Commission Radiotelephone Operator's license. May install, test, adjust, modify, and repair intercommunication systems. May specialize in testing and repairing radio transmitting and receiving equipment in motor vehicles and commercial and government establishments.
GOE: 05.05.10 STRENGTH: M GED: R4 M3 L3 SVP: 6 DLU: 80

823.261-022 ANTENNA INSTALLER, SATELLITE COMMUNICATIONS (any industry)

Installs, tests, and repairs antennas and related equipment that receive communication satellite signals, following specifications and using handtools and test instruments: Reviews installation specifications, building permit, manufacturer's instructions, and government ordinances to determine installation site for antenna. Measures distance from landmarks to identify exact site location. Visually inspects installation site to identify obstructions, such as trees or buildings, that could distort or block microwave signals from satellite. Discusses site location and construction requirements with customer. Digs hole for footing to support antenna base, using gasoline-powered auger, posthole digger, or shovel. Assembles and installs prefabricated form in hole to cast concrete base, using handtools, plumb rule, and level, following specifications. Mixes, pours, and finishes concrete, using concrete mixer, trowel, and float. Inserts pedestal mounting bolts in wet concrete. Digs trench and lays underground cable to connect antenna base to source of power in customer's building. Attaches antenna base to footing after concrete dries, using handtools. Assembles and attaches electronic and structural components of antenna, with co-worker, applying knowledge of electronics and electricity, following installation guidelines, and using handtools. Attaches antenna to base, using nuts, bolts, and handtools. Climbs ladder to install antenna when area is inaccessible from ground. Orients antenna to direction and altitude of communication satellite, using surveying instruments and following charts of satellite position. Solders connections to electronic controls, using soldering gun and wire cutters. Connects antenna and television set to signal converter control box, using handtools. Tests installed system for conformance to specifications, using test equipment, such as multimeters and oscilloscope. Observes picture on television screen to evaluate reception. Instructs customer in use of equipment. Replaces or repairs defective parts, using handtools and test equipment. May construct pole or roof mounts for antenna base, using carpenter's tools. May reinforce roof of building to provide secure installation site, using carpenter's tools. May install antennas and related equipment to receive satellite signals for such purposes as telephone, telex, facsimile, data, or radio communication.
GOE: 05.05.05 STRENGTH: M GED: R3 M3 L3 SVP: 6 DLU: 86

823.261-026 AVIONICS TECHNICIAN (aircraft mfg.; air trans.) alternate titles: avionics and radar technician; avionics mechanic; radio and radar technician

Inspects, tests, adjusts, and repairs avionics equipment, such as radar, radio, pulse, navigation, auto pilot, and compass systems, installed in aircraft and space vehicles, using handtools and test equipment: Inspects components of avionics equipment for defects, such as loose connections and frayed wire, and for accuracy of assembly and installation. Tests avionics equipment under simulated or actual operating conditions to determine performance and airworthiness, using test equipment, such as oscilloscopes, digital meters and counters, and circuit analyzers. Adjusts, repairs, or replaces defective components based on analysis of test results, following blueprints, schematics, handbooks, and other technical documents, using handtools. Calibrates installed or repaired equipment to prescribed specifications. Adjusts frequencies of radio sets by signaling ground station and turning setscrews. Must possess Radiotelephone License issued by Federal Communications Commission. May accompany flight crew to perform in-flight adjustments and to determine and record required post-flight repair work. May sign overhaul documents for equipment replaced or repaired. May operate ground station for air-to-station check of radar or other equipment.
GOE: 05.05.10 STRENGTH: L GED: R4 M4 L4 SVP: 6 DLU: 88

823.261-030 DATA COMMUNICATIONS TECHNICIAN (any industry)

Installs and repairs data communications lines and equipment for computer system, using handtools and test instruments: Reviews work orders to move, change, install, repair, or remove data communications equipment, such as modems, cables, and wires. Reads technical manuals to learn correct settings for equipment. Measures, cuts, and installs wires and cables. Splices wires or cables, using handtools or soldering iron. Connects microcomputer or terminal to data communications lines, using handtools and following diagrams and manuals. Disassembles equipment and inspects and tests wiring to locate and repair problem. Modifies equipment in accordance with user request. Tests communication lines to ensure that specifications are met, using testing instruments such as voltmeter and data scope. Enters commands into computer to test equipment. Reads messages on computer screen to verify that data is being transmitted between locations according to specifications. May plan layout and installation of data communications equipment. May demonstrate use of equipment.

GOE: 05.05.05 STRENGTH: M GED: R4 M3 L4 SVP: 7 DLU: 90

823.281-014 ELECTRICIAN, RADIO (any industry) alternate titles: radio-communications mechanician; radio mechanic; station mechanic

Adjusts, installs, tests, and repairs high-powered stationary and mobile radio transmitting equipment, using handtools and testing instruments and following wiring diagrams: Adjusts controls and tests frequencies of transmitters, using frequency meter. Listens to radio range station at frequent intervals during broadcasts to detect flaws in transmission and adjusts controls to eliminate flaws. Operates emergency truck transmitter to ensure its readiness for immediate use. Examines equipment and replaces defective condensers, switches, tubes, and transistors. Tests equipment with instruments, such as circuit analyzers, audiometers, and voltmeters. Repairs components of radio transmitting equipment and intercommunication telephone system, using handtools. May be designated according to equipment serviced as Marine-Radio Installer-And-Servicer (any industry); Radiotelegraph Operator-Servicer (any industry).
GOE: 05.05.05 STRENGTH: L GED: R4 M4 L3 SVP: 7 DLU: 77

823.281-018 METEOROLOGICAL-EQUIPMENT REPAIRER (any industry) alternate titles: electronics technician

Installs, maintains, and repairs electronic, mercurial, aneroid, and other types of weather-station equipment, using handtools and electronic testing instruments: Tests meteorological instruments for compliance with printed specifications and schematic diagrams, using voltmeters, oscilloscopes, tube testers, and other test instruments. Replaces defective parts, using handtools and soldering iron. Inspects barometers, thermographs, and hydrographs, including recording mechanisms, and repairs, adjusts, or replaces defective parts. Calibrates graphs and other recording devices. Installs radar and two-way radio systems to detect and communicate weather signals. Adjusts and repairs masts, supporting structures, clearance lights, control panels, control cabling and wiring, and other electrical and mechanical devices and equipment, using handtools.
GOE: 05.05.10 STRENGTH: M GED: R4 M3 L3 SVP: 7 DLU: 77

823.281-022 RIGGER (radio-tv broad.)

Wires radio-broadcasting and radio-communications antenna systems, wood or steel antenna towers, and supporting catenaries. Repairs antennas by replacing broken or defective wires, insulators, and lamps. Paints antenna towers and otherwise keeps antenna systems in state of good repair.
GOE: 05.05.06 STRENGTH: M GED: R4 M3 L3 SVP: 7 DLU: 77

823.361-010 TELEVISION INSTALLER (any industry)

Installs and adjusts television receivers and antennas, using handtools: Selects antenna according to type of set and location of transmitting station. Bolts crossarms and dipole elements in position to assemble antenna. Secures antenna in place with bracket and guy wires, observing insurance codes and local ordinances to protect installation from lightning and other hazards. Drills and waterproofs holes in building to make passages for transmission line. Connects line between receiver and antenna and fastens line in place. Tunes receiver on all channels and adjusts screws to obtain desired density, linearity, focus, and size of picture. Orients antenna and installs reflector to obtain optimum signal reception.
GOE: 05.10.03 STRENGTH: M GED: R3 M3 L3 SVP: 6 DLU: 77

823.684-010 ANTENNA INSTALLER (any industry)

Installs antennas for radio or television receiving sets: Sets up wooden or metal mast and secures in place with guy wires and base plate, using handtools. Attaches single dipole antenna to mast for FM radio reception or antenna composed of several directors plus dipole antenna and reflector for television reception. Positions antenna with directors toward station transmitters or toward reflection point to obtain optimum signal. Attaches lead-in wire to dipole antenna and other end to set. May install lightning arrester on lead-in wire.
GOE: 05.12.16 STRENGTH: M GED: R3 M2 L2 SVP: 4 DLU: 77

824 OCCUPATIONS IN ASSEMBLY, INSTALLATION, AND REPAIR OF LIGHTING EQUIPMENT AND BUILDING WIRING, N.E.C.

This group includes occupations, not elsewhere classified, concerned with wiring buildings and adjacent yards to provide electricity for power and lighting; assembling and installing lighting equipment, conduit switches, junction and fuse boxes, and related accessories and controls; and repairing wiring and components.

824.137-010 ELECTRICIAN, CHIEF (motion picture)

Supervises and coordinates installation, maintenance, and operation of all electrical lighting equipment in motion picture studios and outside locations: Confers with DIRECTOR, MOTION PICTURE (motion picture); ART DIRECTOR (motion picture; radio-tv broad.), and other key personnel regarding lighting specifications for specific sets. Prepares requisitions or issues work orders for purchase or construction of special electrical equipment. Arranges with local utility company for use of power lines or transformers when filming scenes on outside locations. Inspects sets after equipment is installed to ensure conformance with lighting equipment requirements.
GOE: 05.05.05 STRENGTH: L GED: R4 M3 L3 SVP: 7 DLU: 77

824.137-014 STREET-LIGHT-SERVICER SUPERVISOR (utilities)

Supervises and coordinates activities of STREET-LIGHT SERVICER (utilities) engaged in inspecting, servicing, and repairing street lamps and equipment:

Determines material requirements and prepares requisitions. Performs other duties as described under SUPERVISOR (any industry) Master Title.
GOE: 05.05.05 STRENGTH: L GED: R4 M3 L3 SVP: 7 DLU: 77

824.261-010 ELECTRICIAN (construction) alternate titles: wirer

Plans layout, installs, and repairs wiring, electrical fixtures, apparatus, and control equipment: Plans new or modified installations to minimize waste of materials, provide access for future maintenance, and avoid unsightly, hazardous, and unreliable wiring, consistent with specifications and local electrical codes. Prepares sketches showing location of wiring and equipment, or follows diagrams or blueprints, ensuring that concealed wiring is installed before completion of future walls, ceilings, and flooring. Measures, cuts, bends, threads, assembles, and installs electrical conduit, using tools, such as hacksaw, pipe threader, and conduit bender. Pulls wiring through conduit, assisted by ELECTRICIAN HELPER (any industry) 829.684-022. Splices wires by stripping insulation from terminal leads, using knife or pliers, twisting or soldering wires together, and applying tape or terminal caps. Connects wiring to lighting fixtures and power equipment, using handtools. Installs control and distribution apparatus, such as switches, relays, and circuit-breaker panels, fastening in place with screws or bolts, using handtools and power tools. Connects power cables to equipment, such as electric range or motor, and installs grounding leads. Tests continuity of circuit to ensure electrical compatibility and safety of components, using testing instruments, such as ohmmeter, battery and buzzer, and oscilloscope. Observes functioning of installed equipment or system to detect hazards and need for adjustments, relocation, or replacement. May repair faulty equipment or systems [ELECTRICIAN, MAINTENANCE (any industry) 829.261-018]. May be required to hold license. May cut and weld steel structural members, using flame-cutting and welding equipment. May be designated according to work location as Mine Electrician (mine & quarry).
GOE: 05.05.05 STRENGTH: M GED: R4 M4 L3 SVP: 7 DLU: 88

824.261-014 ELECTRICIAN APPRENTICE (construction)

Performs duties as described under APPRENTICE (any industry) Master Title.
GOE: 05.05.05 STRENGTH: M GED: R4 M4 L3 SVP: 7 DLU: 77

824.281-010 AIRPORT ELECTRICIAN (air trans.)

Plans layout, installs, inspects, and maintains lighting systems, lights, and beacons at airport or flying field: Inspects lighting systems and advises MANAGER, AIRPORT (air trans.) of need to repair or upgrade airport lighting systems. Installs lighting systems in compliance with Federal Aviation Administration recommendations. Inspects beacon and lights, such as boundary, runway, obstacle, and airport-control lights, replacing defective lenses or bulbs and cleaning or repairing equipment. May drive and operate floodlight truck at crashes or other emergencies. May place warning flares about airfield during power failure or emergency. May be on constant call to make emergency repairs.
GOE: 05.05.05 STRENGTH: M GED: R4 M4 L3 SVP: 7 DLU: 77

824.281-014 ELECTRIC-DISTRIBUTION CHECKER (construction; utilities)

Inspects and tests electric distribution equipment and wiring outside and within buildings to verify conformance of installation with construction and building code specifications, or to determine feasibility of increasing electrical load: Examines wires and auxiliary equipment, such as fuses, insulators, and switches to ascertain conformance to specifications on work orders, utilizing thorough knowledge of types, sizes, and styles of equipment. Compares layout and methods of installation to blueprints and sketches and marks differentiations on drawings. Climbs poles to compare printed data on transformers with work orders and to examine wires and auxiliary equipment on poles. Approves installations or records inaccuracies on work orders. Tests lines, transformers, and other distribution equipment, using such devices as ohmmeters, voltmeters, and thermocouple indicators to measure voltage drop between points in circuitry, locate cause of electrical disturbances, and determine actual electrical load on system. Tests for temperature and presence of explosive gases in vicinity of electrified equipment.
GOE: 05.05.05 STRENGTH: L GED: R4 M3 L3 SVP: 8 DLU: 77

824.281-018 NEON-SIGN SERVICER (fabrication, nec)

Services and repairs plastic, neon and illuminated signs in response to trouble calls: Ascends ladder or operates hydraulic or electric hoist to examine sign and determine cause of malfunction. Performs operations, such as rewiring, removing defective parts, and installing new parts, using electricians' tools. Removes sign or part of sign for shop repairs, such as structural fabrication, scroll repair, or transformer repair.
GOE: 05.05.10 STRENGTH: M GED: R4 M2 L2 SVP: 7 DLU: 77

824.381-010 STREET-LIGHT SERVICER (utilities) alternate titles: street-light repairer

Maintains and repairs mercury-vapor, fluorescent, electric-arc, or incandescent street lights and traffic signals: Climbs ladder or stands in tower-truck bucket to reach lamp. Tests circuits and electric components to locate grounded wires, broken connections, or defective current-control mechanisms, using electrical testing instruments. Replaces blown fuses and bulbs, faulty transformers, photoelectric timers, electrodes, and wires, using electricians' handtools. See LINE REPAIRER (utilities) and TROUBLE SHOOTER (utilities) II for classification of workers also qualified to work on high-voltage power lines. May install and repair traffic signals only and be designated Traffic-Signal Repairer (utilities).

GOE: 05.05.05 STRENGTH: M GED: R4 M3 L3 SVP: 7 DLU: 77

824.664-010 STREET-LIGHT-SERVICER HELPER (utilities)
Assists STREET-LIGHT SERVICER (utilities) in making emergency or permanent repairs to street lights, working as member of crew: Places warning signs, flags, or barriers at repair site. Opens manholes or vaults to gain access to underground circuits or erects ladders for repairing overhead equipment. Unloads tools, parts, and supplies from truck as directed. Flips switches to energize or de-energize circuits preparatory to repair of equipment. Disassembles, cleans, and reassembles lighting fixtures and equipment, using handtools. Tests transformers and transformer gaskets, using ammeter and air pump. Replenishes service truck supply of replacement parts, tools, and equipment.
GOE: 05.12.16 STRENGTH: M GED: R3 M3 L2 SVP: 4 DLU: 77

824.681-010 ELECTRICIAN (mfd. bldgs.)
Installs and repairs wiring, electrical fixtures, and fuse boxes in prefabricated and modular homes, using handtools: Reads blueprints to determine locations of equipment and conformance to building and safety codes. Measures, cuts, and installs conduit in specified panels, using handtools. Measures for location of receptacles with tape measure and installs receptacles. Cuts and connects wires according to diagrams to install fixtures, such as switches, light fixtures, and fuse boxes. Tests continuity of circuits to ensure safety, using ohmmeter. Repairs faulty systems. May direct workers in boring holes in studs and running wiring. May train new workers in electrical system installation procedures.
GOE: 05.05.05 STRENGTH: L GED: R3 M2 L3 SVP: 4 DLU: 77

824.683-010 NIGHT-PATROL INSPECTOR (fabrication, nec)
Patrols scheduled route to inspect operation of illuminated and animated signs: Drives company car along scheduled route at night. Inspects signs covered by company maintenance contract for specified appearance and operation. Reports faulty operation to service department. May perform minor repairs, such as replacing light bulbs.
GOE: 05.08.03 STRENGTH: L GED: R2 M1 L2 SVP: 2 DLU: 77

824.684-010 NEON-TUBE PUMPER (fabrication, nec)
Charges illuminated sign tubing with rare (inert) gases: Attaches formed sign tubing to pumping unit through fused tubulations (glass nipples). Removes air from tubing by means of vacuum pump. Bombards tubing with high-voltage electric current to eliminate gaseous impurities. Reduces vacuum in tubing to specified point, using vacuum pump and vacuum gauge. Connects and opens rare gas bottle to admit rare gas, such as neon, argon, helium, krypton, xenon, distilled mercury, or blue gas (depending on color desired) to specified pressure as indicated by pressure gauge. Tests sign by connecting electrodes to secondary winding of transformer and observing color of light. Seals tubing by heating and closing tubulations. Connects tubing to transformer and operates several hours to age tubing (consume gaseous impurities). May paint or tape tubing to separate symbols.
GOE: 05.05.10 STRENGTH: L GED: R3 M2 L2 SVP: 5 DLU: 77

825 OCCUPATIONS IN ASSEMBLY, INSTALLATION, AND REPAIR OF TRANSPORTATION AND MATERIAL-HANDLING EQUIPMENT, N.E.C.

This group includes occupations, not elsewhere classified, concerned with wiring and repairing electrical power units and controls for transportation and material-handling equipment, and adjusting or repairing electrical components and circuits.

825.131-010 ELECTRICIAN SUPERVISOR (ship-boat mfg.)
Supervises and coordinates activities of workers engaged in installation and repair of wiring and electrical equipment aboard ship and in shipyard facilities, performing duties as described under SUPERVISOR (any industry) Master Title.
GOE: 05.05.05 STRENGTH: M GED: R4 M3 L3 SVP: 8 DLU: 77

825.131-014 ELEVATOR-CONSTRUCTOR SUPERVISOR (construction)
Supervises and coordinates activities of workers engaged in installation of electric and hydraulic freight and passenger elevators, escalators, and dumbwaiters. Performs duties as described under SUPERVISOR (any industry) Master Title.
GOE: 05.05.09 STRENGTH: M GED: R4 M3 L3 SVP: 8 DLU: 77

825.137-010 SUPERVISOR, LINE DEPARTMENT (r.r. trans.)
Supervises and coordinates activities of line crew engaged in installing and maintaining street railway electrical equipment, such as trolley wires, switches, and signals: Assigns crews to jobs and inspects trucks to see that materials are loaded. Inspects work at various sites to ascertain that work is accomplished according to specifications. Plans for future projects, drawing rough sketches in field, and arranges for supplemental services to facilitate departmental activities. Maintains time records for salary purposes. Participates in grievance procedures. Performs other duties as described under SUPERVISOR (any industry) Master Title.
GOE: 05.05.05 STRENGTH: L GED: R4 M3 L3 SVP: 7 DLU: 77

825.261-010 ELECTRIC-TRACK-SWITCH MAINTAINER (r.r. trans.)
Installs, inspects, and repairs electric-railway track switches, section lines, and intercommunication systems, following blueprints and work orders: Installs

switch-controlling mechanism on trolley wire, using handtools. Connects wiring to switch in track bed, and inspects electrical switch system to ascertain that system functions according to standards. Maintains high tension lines, deenergizing lines for power company as repairs are requested. Installs and maintains section lines and intercommunication systems. May install and maintain mechanical parts of track switch.
GOE: 05.05.05 STRENGTH: M GED: R4 M4 L3 SVP: 7 DLU: 77

825.261-014 ELEVATOR EXAMINER-AND-ADJUSTER (any industry)
alternate titles: elevator inspector
Inspects and adjusts installed freight and passenger elevators and escalators to meet factory specifications and safety codes, using handtools and measuring instruments: Inspects door installations for plumbness, lap, and working action. Adjusts mechanism of doors, using handtools. Inspects car hoistway and mechanical installations for alignment and clearance. Tests power consumption and line voltage changes of motors and motor-generator sets under no-load and full-load conditions to detect overload factors, using tachometer, voltmeter, and ammeter. Adjusts counterweights and regulates controls to compensate for power overload. Inspects wiring connections and control panel hookups, and adjusts switches to meet specifications for gap and timing. Tests and adjusts safety controls, such as brakes and governors. Turns valve or pushes switches to adjust pump pressures, fluid levels, and power supply on hydraulic units of elevators. Operates elevator to determine power demands at various car speeds. May compile service reports to verify conformance of each unit to prescribed standards.
GOE: 05.07.03 STRENGTH: L GED: R4 M3 L3 SVP: 8 DLU: 77

825.261-018 ELECTRICIAN, AIRCRAFT (aircraft mfg.; air trans.) alternate titles: aircraft and engine electrician, field and hangar; aircraft mechanic, electrical
Installs, adjusts, tests, modifies, repairs, and maintains electrical and electronic parts, assemblies, systems, and equipment in prototype, developmental, or production aircraft, engines, and components: Installs electrical and electronic parts, assemblies, systems, and equipment in aircraft, according to blueprints, wiring diagrams, and other specifications, using handtools and power tools. Sets up and operates ground support and test equipment, such as test carts, panels, ground power unit, and ground servicing cart, to perform functional and continuity test of electrical and electronic systems. Interprets test results to diagnose malfunctions, and adjusts, repairs, or replaces defective parts. Modifies components according to blueprint specifications and engineering drawings. Fabricates parts and test aids as required. May accompany aircraft on test flight to perform functional tests or to make in-flight adjustments.
GOE: 05.05.05 STRENGTH: M GED: R4 M3 L3 SVP: 7 DLU: 88

825.281-014 ELECTRICIAN (water trans.)
Repairs and maintains electrical equipment, such as generators, alternators, motors, and intercommunication systems aboard ship: Moves controls at distribution board (switchboard) to maintain electrical load within capacity of generators. Starts standby generator when load nears capacity of operating generator. Performs routine tests to ensure that electric motors are driving pumps, blowers, and refrigerating machinery. Tests wiring for short circuits, using voltmeter and ammeter. Replaces and cleans commutator brushes. Removes and replaces fuses and defective lights. May be classified according to degree of authority held as Electrician, Chief (water trans.); Electrician, Second (water trans.); Electrician, Third (water trans.); or equipment worked on as Electrician, Sound (water trans.); or area of operations as Electrician, Deck (water trans.). Must hold certificate as Electrician issued by U.S. Coast Guard.
GOE: 05.05.05 STRENGTH: L GED: R4 M3 L3 SVP: 7 DLU: 77

825.281-022 ELECTRICIAN, AUTOMOTIVE (automotive ser.)
Repairs and overhauls electrical systems in automotive vehicles, such as automobiles, buses, and trucks: Confers with customer to determine nature of electrical malfunction. Determines malfunction of electrical system by visual inspection and by use of testing devices, such as oscilloscope, voltmeter, and ammeter. Adjusts ignition timing and measures and adjusts distributor breaker-point gaps, using *dwell meter* or thickness gauge. Tests and repairs starters, generators, and distributors. Repairs or replaces defective wiring in ignition, lighting, air-conditioning, and safety control systems, using electrician's handtools. Rebuilds electrical units, such as starters, generators, and door controls. May estimate cost of repairs based on parts and labor charges. May be designated according to specialty as Electrical Repairer, Internal Combustion Engines (automotive ser.; engine-turbine); Electrical-Unit Rebuilder (automotive ser.); Electrician, Bus (automotive ser.); Ignition-And-Carburetor Mechanic (automotive ser.); Windshield-Wiper Repairer (automotive ser.).
GOE: 05.05.10 STRENGTH: L GED: R4 M3 L3 SVP: 7 DLU: 77

825.281-026 ELECTRICIAN, LOCOMOTIVE (railroad equip.)
Installs and maintains electrical wiring and equipment, such as motors, generators, air-conditioning units, electrical outlets, and lighting fixtures of railroad locomotives and cars, streetcars, and subway coaches: Measures, cuts, threads, bends, assembles, and installs conduits that connect to control panels and junction boxes, using hacksaw, pipe benders, pipe-threading tools, and other handtools. Splices wires with knife or cutting pliers and solders connections to fixtures, outlets, and equipment. Tests circuit connections, using electrical test equipment. Installs and tests electrical equipment, such as air-conditioning, heating, and ignition systems, generator brushes, and commutators. Installs and repairs headlights in locomotives and streetcars. Repairs electrical equipment,

such as panel lighting, circuit breakers, junction boxes, voltage regulators, and reverse current relays. May recharge storage batteries. May rewind armatures. May be designated according to specialty as Accessories Repairer (railroad equip.); Electrician, Control Equipment (railroad equip.); Wirer, Passenger Car (railroad equip.).
GOE: 05.05.05 STRENGTH: M GED: R4 M3 L3 SVP: 7 DLU: 77

825.281-030 ELEVATOR REPAIRER (any industry) alternate titles: electrician, elevator-maintenance; elevator mechanic; elevator-repair mechanic; maintenance mechanic, elevators
Repairs and maintains elevators, escalators, and dumb-waiters to meet safety regulations and building codes, using handtools, power tools, test lamps, ammeters, voltmeters, and other testing devices: Locates and determines causes of trouble in brakes, motors, switches, and signal and control systems, using test lamps, ammeters, and voltmeters. Disassembles defective units and repairs or replaces parts, such as locks, gears, cables, electric wiring, and faulty safety devices, using handtools. Installs push-button controls and other devices to modernize elevators. Lubricates bearings and other parts to minimize friction.
GOE: 05.05.05 STRENGTH: M GED: R4 M3 L3 SVP: 7 DLU: 77

825.281-034 ELEVATOR-REPAIRER APPRENTICE (any industry) alternate titles: electrician apprentice, elevator maintenance
Performs duties as described under APPRENTICE (any industry) Master Title.
GOE: 05.05.05 STRENGTH: M GED: R4 M3 L3 SVP: 7 DLU: 77

825.281-038 EXPERIMENTAL-ROCKET-SLED MECHANIC (aircraft mfg.)
Installs, adjusts, and repairs recording and control instruments and structural components in experimental rocket sleds according to blueprints, using handtools, power tools, and test equipment: Mounts instruments, such as telemetering transmitter, strain gauges, and cameras on sled, using portable power drill, handtools, and soldering iron. Inspects firing control circuits, instruments, and recording systems, using test equipment, such as ammeter, voltmeter, and oscilloscope. Adjusts test settings for hydraulic or other braking mechanism. Positions and secures ballast in sled to obtain specified weight distribution and balance. Repairs firing control mechanisms, recording systems, and other structural and mechanical parts and devices after test completion, using handtools, power tools, and welding equipment. May modify rocket motors or related hardware, using metal or composite reforming tools or welding equipment.
GOE: 05.05.05 STRENGTH: M GED: R4 M3 L3 SVP: 7 DLU: 87

825.361-010 ELEVATOR CONSTRUCTOR (construction) alternate titles: elevator builder; elevator erector; elevator installer; elevator mechanic
Assembles and installs electric and hydraulic freight and passenger elevators, escalators, and dumbwaiters, determining layout and electrical connections from blueprints: Studies blueprints and lays out location of framework, counterbalance rails, motor pump, cylinder, and plunger foundations. Drills holes in concrete or structural steel members with portable electric drill. Secures anchor bolts or welds brackets to support rails and framework, and verifies alignment with plumb bob and level. Cuts prefabricated sections of framework, rails, and other elevator components to specified dimensions, using acetylene torch, power saw, and disc grinder. Installs cables, counterweights, pumps, motor foundations, escalator drives, guide rails, elevator cars, and control panels, using handtools. Connects electrical wiring to control panels and electric motors. Installs safety and control devices. Positions electric motor and equipment on top of elevator shaft, using hoists and cable slings. May be designated according to type of equipment installed as Elevator Constructor, Electric (construction); Elevator Constructor, Hydraulic (construction); Escalator Constructor (construction).
GOE: 05.05.06 STRENGTH: H GED: R4 M3 L3 SVP: 7 DLU: 77

825.361-014 VIBRATOR-EQUIPMENT TESTER (machinery mfg.) alternate titles: tester, vibrator equipment; top-lift and automatic-window repairer
Tests electrical and mechanical vibrator feeders and conveyors for conformance to specifications. Clips cable of test board to electric vibrator equipment. Turns dials and observes meters to operate electric vibrator equipment at specified cycle, voltage, and amperage levels. Holds end of scale against vibrator equipment to pick up vibration. Reads scale mark that shows distinct double image and determines vibrating frequency on conversion chart. Starts motor of mechanical vibrator equipment and verifies vibrating frequency. Advises ASSEMBLER (machinery mfg.) to add or remove vibrator bars from electrical vibrator equipment or weights from drive shaft of mechanical vibrator equipment, to correct vibrating deficiencies. May inspect vibrator equipment for loose bearings and bolts, using stethoscope. Records test data.
GOE: 06.01.05 STRENGTH: L GED: R3 M3 L3 SVP: 6 DLU: 77

825.381-010 AIRCRAFT MECHANIC, ELECTRICAL AND RADIO (aircraft mfg.)
Lays out, assembles, installs, and tests radio and electrical systems in aircraft and missiles, according to specifications, using handtools and precision testing equipment: Assembles units, such as switches, electrical controls, and junction boxes, and connects units to major units, such as radio systems, instruments, magnetos, and inverters, using handtools and soldering iron. Lays out installation of major units in aircraft, using scribe, scale, and protractor. Installs and

connects units, according to wiring diagrams, using handtools and soldering iron. Tests units, using equipment, such as circuit continuity tester, oscilloscope, and voltmeter, and adjusts or repairs malfunctioning units.
GOE: 06.02.23 STRENGTH: M GED: R4 M3 L3 SVP: 7 DLU: 89

825.381-014 AUTOMATIC-WINDOW-SEAT-AND-TOP-LIFT REPAIRER (automotive ser.)
Disassembles, repairs, installs, adjusts, and services hydraulic and electromagnetic automatic lift mechanisms used to raise and lower automobile windows, seats, and tops.
GOE: 05.10.03 STRENGTH: L GED: R3 M3 L3 SVP: 4 DLU: 77

825.381-018 CONTROLLER REPAIRER-AND-TESTER (railroad equip.) alternate titles: control inspector
Adjusts, cleans, repairs, and tests electric control equipment of commuter and rapid transit cars or streetcars, following wiring diagrams and using specialized test equipment and handtools: Blows dirt from relays and switches, using airhose. Examines parts, such as control points, relays, and wiring, and adjusts or replaces defective parts. Observes operation of relays to verify conformance to specifications. Disassembles electric controller cylinders and replaces defective parts, such as copper contact segments, insulation disks, and spacing washers. Examines systems for short circuits or broken wires preparatory to high potential test, using megameter, and tests for defective circuits. Assembles and paints controller cylinders and tests cylinders to verify specified operation.
GOE: 05.05.05 STRENGTH: M GED: R4 M3 L3 SVP: 7 DLU: 77

825.381-026 ELECTRICAL INSPECTOR (aircraft mfg.; air trans.) alternate titles: inspector, electrical bench; inspector, precision electrical assembly
Inspects and tests electrical parts, assemblies, and accessories prior to installation in aircraft for conformance to specifications and quality standards, using precision measuring instruments and test equipment: Examines parts and assemblies, such as wire harnesses, control panels, coaxial cables, and electrical jig boards, for completeness of assembly, quality, and conformance to blueprints, production illustrations, engineering drawings, and specifications. Inspects wiring of assemblies for accuracy of stripping, soldering, and crimping, and for defects, such as frayed wires, loose connections, and cracks. Verifies wire and cable length, dimensions, and clearance of parts, using precision instruments. Tests continuity and performance of parts, assemblies, and accessories, using test equipment. Records acceptance or rejection of parts on inspection report, and indicates reason for rejection.
GOE: 06.01.05 STRENGTH: L GED: R4 M3 L3 SVP: 7 DLU: 77

825.381-030 ELECTRICIAN (ship-boat mfg.) alternate titles: electrician, marine; electrician, outside
Installs and repairs wiring, fixtures, and equipment for all electrical services aboard ship and in shipyard facilities, following blueprints and wiring diagrams: Installs conduit to bulkheads with brackets and screws, using handtools, and threads wires through conduit to terminals, such as connection boxes, circuit breakers, voltage regulators, and switch panels. Strips insulation from wire ends and solders ends to terminals, using stripping pliers and soldering iron. Connects power-supply circuits to radio, radar, sonar, fire control, and other electronic equipment. Tests electrical characteristics, such as voltage, resistance, and phase angle, in circuits, using voltmeters, ohmmeters, and phase rotation indicators. May construct instrument panels, using handtools, rulers, dividers, and power drills, following specifications. May be designated according to work location as Electrician, Ship (ship-boat mfg.); Electrician, Shop (ship-boat mfg.); Electrician, Yard (ship-boat mfg.).
GOE: 05.05.05 STRENGTH: M GED: R4 M3 L3 SVP: 8 DLU: 77

825.381-034 ELECTRICIAN APPRENTICE (ship-boat mfg.) alternate titles: marine-electrician apprentice
Performs duties as described under APPRENTICE (any industry) Master Title.
GOE: 05.05.05 STRENGTH: M GED: R4 M3 L3 SVP: 8 DLU: 77

825.381-038 THIRD-RAIL INSTALLER (r.r. trans.)
Installs third (power-supply) rails on electric elevated or subway railway tracks: Treats wooden insulator blocks by soaking for specified time in hot paraffin. Assembles trolley chairs by forcing top and bottom castings onto wooden insulator blocks with compressed-air press, drilling bolt holes through castings and blocks with power drill, and driving rivets into holes, using rivet gun. Paints anchor blocks with preservative to protect against rot. Installs trolley chairs beneath third rail at ends of rail sections by boring holes through tie and bottom castings and screwing trolley chairs to tie. Installs anchor blocks at center of third-rail sections, bolting block to rail and tie. Arc welds copper bands at junction of rails to provide unbroken electrical connections between rail sections [WELDER, ARC (welding)]. Fastens and positions annunciator rails to third-rail at specified points so contact will be made with third-rail shoe of passing trains. May specialize in installation and maintenance of conduit systems for electric street railways and be designated Conduit Installer (r.r. trans.).
GOE: 05.10.01 STRENGTH: M GED: R3 M2 L2 SVP: 5 DLU: 77

825.664-010 ELEVATOR-CONSTRUCTOR HELPER (construction) alternate titles: elevator-erector helper
Assists ELEVATOR CONSTRUCTOR (construction) to install freight and passenger elevators: Raises and moves heavy machinery and equipment, using hoists, dollies, rollers, wire rope, and cable slings. Holds material in position

to assist in installing rails and supporting framework. Drills holes in concrete or steel, using portable electric drill. Assembles and bolts rails, elevator motor, car, and control panels preparatory to installation. Performs other duties as described under HELPER (any industry) Master Title.
GOE: 05.12.12 STRENGTH: H GED: R3 M2 L2 SVP: 3 DLU: 77

825.684-010 ELECTRICIAN HELPER, AUTOMOTIVE (automotive ser.)
Assists ELECTRICIAN, AUTOMOTIVE (automotive ser.) to repair automotive vehicle electrical equipment: Disassembles electrical units, such as starters and generators, using handtools. Removes and replaces defective parts, such as armatures, brushes, and wires. Washes parts. May lift motors and generators, using mechanical hoist, and move parts about repair shop, using handtruck. Performs other duties as described under HELPER (any industry) Master Title.
GOE: 05.12.16 STRENGTH: M GED: R2 M2 L2 SVP: 2 DLU: 77

825.684-014 ELEVATOR-REPAIRER HELPER (any industry)
Assists ELEVATOR REPAIRER (any industry) to service and repair freight or passenger elevators, performing any combination of following duties: Assists in moving and raising elevator components, using hoists, dollies, and rollers. Assists in disassembly and assembly of elevator components, using mechanic's handtools. Cleans equipment, using scrapers and cleaning compound, and lubricates equipment with grease guns. Performs other duties as described under HELPER (any industry) Master Title.
GOE: 05.12.15 STRENGTH: H GED: R3 M2 L2 SVP: 3 DLU: 77

825.684-018 BATTERY CHARGER (any industry)
Inspects, recharges, and replaces batteries of electric industrial trucks: Disconnects electrical leads and removes battery from industrial truck, using handtools and hoist. Checks fluid levels and specific gravity of cells and adds water and acid, using hydrometer, thermometer, and siphons, to ensure fluid concentration meets specifications. Cleans electrical leads and battery poles to provide contact surface, using wire brush. Attaches battery to battery charger and manipulates controls of battery charger to start flow of electricity into battery. Installs recharged battery in industrial truck. May remove and replace other defective electrical components, such as motor, switches, wires, and rheostats. May lubricate truck's moving parts, using grease gun.
GOE: 05.12.16 STRENGTH: M GED: R2 M2 L1 SVP: 3 DLU: 86

826 OCCUPATIONS IN ASSEMBLY, INSTALLATION, AND REPAIR OF INDUSTRIAL APPARATUS, N.E.C.

This group includes occupations, not elsewhere classified, concerned with assembling, installing, and repairing industrial apparatus involving electrical circuitry.

826.131-010 ELECTRICAL SUPERVISOR (petrol. & gas)
Supervises and coordinates activities of workers installing, repairing, and inspecting oil field electrical equipment, such as primary and secondary power lines, transformers, submarine cables to offshore well sites, and electric motors. Inspects work for compliance with government electrical codes and company standards. Performs other duties as described under SUPERVISOR (any industry) Master Title.
GOE: 05.05.05 STRENGTH: L GED: R4 M4 L4 SVP: 7 DLU: 77

826.131-014 SUPERVISOR, ELECTRICAL ASSEMBLIES (elec. equip.; machinery mfg.)
Supervises and coordinates activities of workers engaged in fabrication of subassemblies and assembly of electrical equipment, such as electric welding machines, conveyors, and other electrically powered machine tools: Confers with engineering and management staff to establish assembly procedures and production schedules. Interprets and modifies blueprints and wiring diagrams in accordance with assembly specifications. Inspects and tests assembled components and equipment, using oscilloscopes, voltmeters, ammeters, and other test instruments. Suggests design modifications to increase product efficiency and production output. Trains new workers and resolves personnel problems. Performs other duties as described under SUPERVISOR (any industry) Master Title.
GOE: 06.02.01 STRENGTH: L GED: R4 M4 L4 SVP: 7 DLU: 77

826.261-010 FIELD-SERVICE ENGINEER (photo. appar.)
Installs and repairs microfilming, film-developing, and auxiliary photographic equipment at customers' premises: Assembles equipment and connects water and electrical lines, using handtools and following wiring diagrams and blueprints. Tests equipment performance and demonstrates operation and servicing of equipment to customer. Examines faulty equipment and processed film, interprets laboratory reports, and analyzes customer complaints to diagnose equipment malfunction. Repairs defective units, using handtools and repair manuals. Schedules service calls according to customer location and urgency of need. Recommends equipment design changes or upgrading as needed. Interviews prospective buyers and reports leads to sales personnel.
GOE: 05.05.13 STRENGTH: L GED: R4 M4 L3 SVP: 8 DLU: 77

826.361-010 ASSEMBLER AND WIRER, INDUSTRIAL EQUIPMENT (elec. equip.; machinery mfg.) alternate titles: panel assembler and wirer
Installs electrical wiring and assembles components in control cabinets, electrical and industrial equipment, and related industrial apparatus, according to

blueprints and wiring diagrams: Squares, aligns, and assembles bases, sills, cabinet frames, or equipment structural components, on floor or floor plate, using jacks, clamps, squares, plumb line and dial indicator. Lays out diagram for electrical installations according to wiring specifications. Drills and taps holes in specified locations for mounting control units, using handtools and drill press. Attaches breakers, relays, contactors, bus bars, transformers, insulators, regulator cabinets, condenser units, motor and generator sets, meters, plugging devices, and fuse blocks to mounting holes with bolts and screws, using wrenches, screwdrivers, and nut runners. Cuts, strips, bends, and forms wire cable, conduit, pipe, and tubing used to connect circuits and subassemblies, using hacksaw, bandsaw, pipe cutters, and mechanical or hydraulic pipe or cable benders. Connects color-coded wires, using mirrors in compact areas. Solders connections and crimps connectors to wire ends, using soldering iron and pliers. Tests and adjusts electrical assemblies, using electrician's handtools and test equipment. Discusses errors in diagrams or production order with supervisor or engineer to clarify assembly problems. May be designated according to unit assembled as Assembler Dielectric Heater (elec. equip.); Control-Cabinet Assembler (elec. equip.); Welding-Machine Assembler (elec. equip.).
GOE: 06.01.04 STRENGTH: M GED: R4 M3 L3 SVP: 6 DLU: 82

826.381-010 FABRICATOR, INDUSTRIAL FURNACE (machinery mfg.)
Assembles and installs structural and electrical components to fabricate high-temperature industrial furnaces: Lays refractory brick to insulate furnace interior, using masonry trowel and mortar. Drills holes in brick to provide openings for heater elements, wiring, and instruments, according to shop drawings and schematics. Attaches manual or power door opening mechanisms and chain and heater guards, using power tools. Installs and wires heater elements, instruments, gauges, motors, and controls, following electrical schematics and blueprints. Tests assembled unit for operational defects and makes necessary adjustments. Operates paint sprayer to paint furnace as specified. Places completed unit in crate for shipment.
GOE: 05.10.01 STRENGTH: H GED: R3 M3 L3 SVP: 6 DLU: 77

826.384-010 CELL REPAIRER (chemical)
Assembles, installs, maintains, and repairs electrolytic cells, performing any combination of following duties: Starts concrete mixer and pours concrete slurry into assembled molds to cast sections of electrolytic cells, such as tops, bottoms, rings, and partitions [CELL MAKER (chemical)]. Positions copper bars, graphite blades, or carbon electrodes in cylindrical form (jig), and secures them by pouring molten lead into jig to fabricate anode units [ANODE BUILDER (chemical)]. Wraps asbestos diaphragm paper and perforated steel screen around jig assembly to fabricate cathode pots [POT BUILDER (chemical)]. Disconnects, dismantles, and replaces spent or defective electrolytic cell units, such as anodes and cathodes [CELL CHANGER (chemical)]. Cleans electrolytic cells, cell assemblies and glassware, and washes cathode screens to remove asbestos [CELL CLEANER (chemical)]. Coats cathode screens by dipping screens in asbestos slurry [CATHODE MAKER (chemical)]. Records data, such as condition of cell units, parts used, and date of change. May inspect defective cells and measure voltage drop, using voltmeter. May bolt current jumper to adjacent cells to shunt current around defective cell.
GOE: 06.02.32 STRENGTH: H GED: R3 M2 L2 SVP: 5 DLU: 77

826.684-010 ANODE BUILDER (chemical)
Fabricates anode units for use in electrolytic cells, using handtools and power tools: Paints cell bottoms, using brush. Assembles cylindrical form jig with handtools and hoist, and positions copper bars, graphite blades, or carbon electrodes in jig. Opens valve to admit melted lead to jig, or pours in lead to specified level, using container to secure copper bars, graphite blades, or carbon electrodes in place. Lifts anode assembly from jig, using hoist, and positions anode in cell bottom. Fills tar pot with mastic or tar mixture and turns valve on pot to heat mastic tar to pouring temperature. Opens spigot to fill container with mastic or tar, and pours it into anode assembly to prevent corrosion of lead and cell bottom and leakage around joints and copper bars. May operate jackhammer to dismantle spent anode units. May position graphite blades in cell bottom, using power wrench. May join electrode to electrical conductor with holding rings or lead bands.
GOE: 06.02.32 STRENGTH: H GED: R3 M2 L2 SVP: 4 DLU: 77

826.684-014 CELL CHANGER (chemical)
Replaces spent anodes or cathodes used in electrolytic cells, according to replacement schedule, using handtools and power tools: Disconnects electrical and pipe connections and removes retaining bolts to free cells, using wrenches. Removes cell top and cathode assembly, using tension handles, prybars, and hoist. Measures thickness of cathode blade and length of anode to determine remaining usable life, using ruler, and inspects anode for deterioration. Adjusts anode and cathode spacing, using handtools. Records cell and cathode number and condition of anode and cathode. Scrapes and washes putty and dirt from cell assembly, using hand scraper and steam or water hose, or cleans cathode bars and cell bottom with power grinder and acid. Cleans and smooths electrical connections, using emery cloth. Transfers defective units to cell repair room and obtains replacement parts, using cart or crane. Positions cell bottom, anode, cathode, and cell top in place, using hoist. Bolts assemblies together, replaces sight glasses, funnels, and percolator pipes, and secures electrical connections to *bus bar*, using handtools. Seals joints with putty, mortar, and asbestos, using putty extruder and knife. Turns valves to start brine flow. Records new parts used and date of change. May repair cells [CELL REPAIRER (chemical)]. When draining and cleaning mercury electrolytic cells, replacing mer-

cury, and timing rate of flow of mercury to ensure efficient operation, may be designated Mercury-Cell Cleaner (chemical).
GOE: 05.10.03 STRENGTH: H GED: R3 M2 L2 SVP: 5 DLU: 77

826.684-018 CELL INSTALLER (chemical)
Removes defective mercury electrolytic cells from rocker mechanism and installs new cells, using handtools: Removes bolts and rocker assembly that hold cell bottom in place on rocker mechanism, using wrenches. Signals OVER-HEAD CRANE OPERATOR (any industry) 921.663-010 to remove defective cell and position replacement cell on rocker mechanism. Visually levels cell on mechanism and bolts it into place. Cements glass sight tubes in sides of concrete bottom and bolts copper hanger beneath cell bottom. May raise or lower cell bottom, using leveling jacks, and time rate of flow of mercury, using stopwatch, to ensure that cell is mounted in accordance with efficient operating requirements.
GOE: 05.12.12 STRENGTH: M GED: R3 M2 L2 SVP: 6 DLU: 77

826.684-022 POT BUILDER (chemical) alternate titles: cathode builder; diaphragm builder
Assembles cathode pots for use in electrolytic cells, using handtools and hoist: Assembles cathode rings on ends of cylindrical form jig, using handtools and hoist. Wraps asbestos diaphragm paper around inner and outer jig assembly and applies glue to secure asbestos in place. Wraps perforated steel diaphragm screens around assembly and clasps ends together or secures screen in place with metal hoops, using handtools. Wraps asbestos tape around cathode rim or hammers iron band around top to attain airtight connection. Applies putty, asbestos compound, and paint, using putty knife, putty extruder, and brush, to seal cathode connections and joints. Removes cathode assembly from jig, using hoist. May cut asbestos paper to required size. May insert rubber gaskets or solder overlapping metal at joints to attain airtight connections. May perform duties of CELL REPAIRER (chemical).
GOE: 05.10.03 STRENGTH: H GED: R3 M2 L2 SVP: 4 DLU: 77

827 OCCUPATIONS IN ASSEMBLY, INSTALLATION, AND REPAIR OF LARGE HOUSEHOLD APPLIANCES AND SIMILAR COMMERCIAL AND INDUSTRIAL EQUIPMENT

This group includes occupations concerned with installing service lines, connecting leads, and assembling components and accessories to install or repair large household electrical appliances and equivalent commercial and industrial installations, such as refrigerators, freezers, air-conditioners, heaters, washers, driers, and their related controls.

827.131-010 ELECTRICAL-APPLIANCE-SERVICER SUPERVISOR (any industry)
Supervises and coordinates activities of ELECTRICAL-APPLIANCE SERVICER (any industry) engaged in servicing, repairing, and installing electrical household appliances. Requisitions tools, supplies, and replacement parts. Performs other duties as described under SUPERVISOR (any industry) Master Title.
GOE: 05.10.03 STRENGTH: L GED: R4 M4 L4 SVP: 7 DLU: 77

827.131-014 SUPERVISOR, MAJOR APPLIANCE ASSEMBLY (house. appl.)
Supervises and coordinates activities of workers engaged in assembly, inspection, testing, repair, and packing of major household appliances: Assigns duties to workers according to production schedules. Reads inspection and test reports to determine nature and cause of appliance defects. Recommends designs, tooling, and assembly modifications to increase efficiency or improve product quality. Trains workers and resolves employee grievances. Performs other duties as described under SUPERVISOR (any industry) Master Title.
GOE: 06.02.01 STRENGTH: L GED: R4 M4 L4 SVP: 7 DLU: 77

827.131-018 SUPERVISOR, AIR-CONDITIONING INSTALLER (any industry)
Supervises activities of workers engaged in fabricating, installing, and repairing air-conditioning systems in residential and commercial buildings: Inspects and measures building to determine airflow requirements. Plans and draws layout and dimensions of ductwork, applying knowledge of sheet metal fabrication and air-conditioning system design, using pencil and ruler, and following specifications from air-conditioning equipment manufacturers and customer. Obtains price quotations on materials and purchases materials, such as sheet metal, compressors, and fans, from suppliers and tests equipment to verify that equipment is functioning. Schedules air-conditioning installation assignments. Examines installed air-conditioning systems to verify that system is functioning, using test instruments. Compiles labor and material cost figures and supporting media for billing purposes. Attends classes and seminars on air-conditioning components and system design to update skills. May instruct workers in sheet metal fabrication in shop. May supervise sheet metal fabrication in shop and resolve problems to maintain production schedule. Performs other duties as described under SUPERVISOR (any industry) Master Title.
GOE: 05.10.04 STRENGTH: L GED: R4 M4 L4 SVP: 7 DLU: 86

827.261-010 ELECTRICAL-APPLIANCE SERVICER (any industry) alternate titles: appliance-service representative
Installs, services, and repairs stoves, refrigerators, dishwashing machines, and other electrical household or commercial appliances, using handtools, test

equipment, and following wiring diagrams and manufacturer's specifications: Connects appliance to power source and test meters, such as wattmeter, ammeter, or voltmeter. Observes readings on meters and graphic recorders. Examines appliance during operating cycle to detect excess vibration, overheating, fluid leaks, and loose parts. Disassembles appliance and examines mechanical and electrical parts. Traces electrical circuits, following diagram, and locates shorts and grounds, using ohmmeter. Calibrates timers, thermostats, and adjusts contact points. Cleans and washes parts, using wire brush, buffer, and solvent, to remove carbon, grease, and dust. Replaces worn or defective parts, such as switches, pumps, bearings, transmissions, belts, gears, blowers, and defective wiring. Repairs and adjusts appliance motors. Reassembles appliance, adjusts pulleys, and lubricates moving parts, using handtools and lubricating equipment. May be known according to appliance repaired as Clothes-Drier Repairer (any industry); Coffee-Maker Servicer (any industry); Dishwashing-Machine Repairer (any industry); Electric-Range Servicer (any industry); Electric-Refrigerator Servicer (any industry); Washing-Machine Servicer (any industry).
GOE: 05.05.10 STRENGTH: M GED: R4 M3 L3 SVP: 7 DLU: 77

827.261-014 ELECTRICAL-APPLIANCE-SERVICER APPRENTICE (any industry) alternate titles: major-appliance-servicer apprentice, electrical
Performs duties as described under APPRENTICE (any industry) Master Title.
GOE: 05.05.10 STRENGTH: M GED: R4 M3 L3 SVP: 7 DLU: 77

827.361-010 AIR-CONDITIONING-UNIT TESTER (svc. ind. mach.)
Tests efficiency of heating and air-conditioning equipment under simulated operating conditions: Connects heating and air-conditioning equipment to facilities, such as heating units, waterlines, and spray devices to set up controlled temperature and moisture conditions. Constructs cardboard air ducts and other accessories for use in testing equipment. Couples gauges and instruments to system and starts equipment. Observes and records readings of instruments, such as thermometers, psychrometers, thermocouples, air flowmeters, voltmeters, ammeters, and pressure and draft gauges. Informs supervisor of unusual noise and instrument readings during operation of equipment. May plot instrument reading data.
GOE: 06.01.05 STRENGTH: L GED: R3 M2 L2 SVP: 6 DLU: 77

827.361-014 REFRIGERATION MECHANIC (svc. ind. mach.)
Fabricates and assembles components of refrigeration systems for environmental test equipment according to blueprints or schematic drawings and knowledge of refrigeration systems, using handtools, powered tools and welding equipment: Reads blueprints or schematic drawings to determine location, size, capacity, and type of components, such as compressor, condenser, expansion tank, valves, and tubing or piping needed to build refrigeration system. Mounts compressor, condenser, and other components in specified locations on frame, using handtools and arc or acetylene welding equipment. Cuts, bends, and brazes specified tubing to inlets and outlets of components to form liquid and suction lines of refrigeration system, using knowledge of metal properties. Installs expansion and control valves, using acetylene torch and wrenches. Adjusts valves according to specifications. Removes air from system and charges system with specified amount and type of refrigerant [GAS CHARGER (svc. ind. mach.)]. Tests lines, components, and connections for leaks with leak detector which indicates presence of refrigerant [GAS-LEAK TESTER (svc. ind. mach.)]. Attaches thermocouples to various points of refrigeration system and test-operates equipment to evaluate functioning and cooling capacity of system. Records pressure and temperature readings from gauges and *temperature potentiometer* during test run. Compares reading with specifications to evaluate performance of system, and adjusts or replaces parts as indicated. May fabricate and assemble structural portions of test equipment. May assemble and mount electrical wiring circuits, controls, and recording devices. May fabricate and assemble cascade and multiple stage refrigeration systems.
GOE: 05.05.09 STRENGTH: H GED: R4 M3 L3 SVP: 7 DLU: 77

827.381-010 CONTROL-PANEL TESTER (elec. equip.)
Inspects and tests electrical panels used to control machinery, equipment, and systems for conformance with specifications, following blueprints and wiring schematics, and using electrical testing equipment and instruments: Compares wiring and location of control devices on panel with blueprints and wiring diagrams to verify assembly. Examines wiring for loose or faulty connections. Connects leads from panel onto power source leads to prepare for testing activities. Turns rheostat to impose and regulate current loads onto panel controls and observes action of relays, cut-outs, and other devices for conformance with specifications. Tests wiring circuits and controls to isolate and locate causes of malfunctions, using electrical instruments, such as voltmeter, ammeter, and ohmmeter. Records causes of malfunctions on test sheet and routes defective panels for rework. May change defective control devices on panel, using handtools, and solder loose or faulty wiring.
GOE: 06.01.05 STRENGTH: L GED: R4 M4 L3 SVP: 7 DLU: 77

827.384-010 REFRIGERATOR TESTER (svc. ind. mach.)
Inspects and tests refrigeration units to evaluate functional operation of system, using knowledge of refrigeration systems and operating specifications: Connects unit to electrical outlet and starts compressor. Observes units to detect malfunction and ensure that cooling is taking place. Tests compressors on nonfunctioning units for specified wattage, using watt-meter. Times operating cycle of unit, using watch and replaces relay switches, or orders compressor

replacement to regulate length of operating cycle. Feels lines and other components at various points in system to determine if unit is functioning. Examines coolant lines for damage and accumulations of frost indicating constriction or obstruction in lines. Records and attaches inspection tag to malfunctioning units, indicating type and location of defects. May attach gauges to verify conformance of unit to temperature, pressure, B.T.U., and other operational specifications. May work in controlled temperature room.
GOE: 06.03.01 STRENGTH: L GED: R3 M2 L3 SVP: 5 DLU: 77

827.485-010 GAS CHARGER (svc. ind. mach.) alternate titles: charging-board operator
Tends charging board that charges cooling units of refrigerators, freezers, or air-conditioners with gas refrigerant, using one of following methods: (1) Sets indicator on charging board to control volume and type of refrigerant for unit being charged, following work order specifications. Determines pressure in refrigeration unit, using mercury gauge. Attaches filler hose from refrigeration tank to unit. Presses button to fill charging tank and pump refrigerant into compressor. (2) Turns indicator to specified setting and attaches filler hose to fill charging bomb. Mounts filled bombs on refrigeration unit. Attaches vacuum hose to unit to draw refrigerant into compressor. Weighs bombs before and after filling to ascertain weight of charge. Adjusts timers to maintain specified weight.
GOE: 06.04.36 STRENGTH: M GED: R2 M2 L2 SVP: 2 DLU: 77

827.584-010 ELECTRICAL-APPLIANCE PREPARER (any industry) alternate titles: uncrater
Assembles and tests electrical appliances, such as ranges, refrigerators, and washing machines, to prepare appliance for delivery and installation, using handtools and test lamp: Uncrates appliances, using pry bar, wire cutters, and nail puller. Assembles appliance parts, using screws and handtools. Connects appliance to electric current to test performance. Locates faulty circuits with test lamp. Solders and wraps wires with friction tape to repair insulation. Washes and polishes appliances. Examines exterior of appliance for chips, scratches, and dents. Keeps records of appliances received, assembled, and delivered. May be designated according to type of appliance assembled and tested as Dishwasher Preparer (any industry); Electric-Range Preparer (any industry); Electric-Refrigerator Preparer (any industry); Washer-Drier Preparer (any industry).
GOE: 05.12.16 STRENGTH: H GED: R2 M2 L2 SVP: 3 DLU: 77

827.584-014 GAS-LEAK TESTER (svc. ind. mach.)
Performs one or more of following tasks to test assembled and charged refrigeration units for refrigerant leaks: Adjusts controls to set balance and range of electronic leak tester. Moves nozzle of tester along refrigerant lines, condenser, and compressor and listens for buzzer indicating presence of gas. Narrows range of tester and probes area to pinpoint exact location of leak. Turns valve of gas tester to adjust flow of gas to copper flame-ring and ignites gas. Moves suction hose, joined to flame-ring, along surfaces of refrigeration unit and observes flame for change in color denoting presence of leaking refrigerant gas. Wraps wet litmus paper around joints of refrigeration unit and observes paper for color change indicating refrigerant leak. Marks number of defective part or joint on inspection tag, according to blueprint numbering chart, and attaches tag to unit. Records number and location of leaks on inspection chart.
GOE: 06.03.02 STRENGTH: L GED: R2 M1 L1 SVP: 2 DLU: 77

827.585-010 FOAM CHARGER (svc. ind. mach.)
Tends equipment that blows foam insulation into cooler and refrigerator doors and cabinet walls, using portable foam gun: Connects foam pump and nitrogen pressure tank to resin and catalyst barrels. Turns valve to regulate nitrogen pressure at specified level. Connects hose from freon tank to gun and adjusts freon pressure. Opens gun valve and conducts foam test to ensure proper mixture of ingredients. Inserts nozzle of gun into compartment openings and blows specified amounts of foam insulation into doors and cabinet walls. Inserts plugs into openings to seal filled compartment. Regulates overhead electric heaters to maintain constant room temperature. Records number and type of units filled on daily production record. Cleans equipment and work area. May prepare units to receive insulation.
GOE: 06.04.36 STRENGTH: M GED: R2 M2 L2 SVP: 3 DLU: 77

827.661-010 HOUSEHOLD-APPLIANCE INSTALLER (any industry)
Installs household appliances, such as refrigerators, washing machines, stoves, and related appliances, in mobile homes or customers' homes, using handtools: Levels refrigerators and adjusts doors. Connects water pipes to washing machines, using plumbing tools. Observes complete cycle of automatic washers and dryers and makes adjustments. Lights and adjusts pilot lights on gas stoves and examines valves and burners for gas leakage and specified flame. May assemble and install prefabricated kitchen cabinets in conjunction with appliances. May stain or finish cabinets.
GOE: 05.10.04 STRENGTH: H GED: R3 M3 L3 SVP: 6 DLU: 77

827.684-010 APPLIANCE ASSEMBLER, LINE (house. appl.; svc. ind. mach.)
Assembles major household or commercial appliances, such as ranges, ovens, washing machines, dryers, refrigeration units, water heaters, and dishwashers, using handtools: Obtains specified parts or subassemblies. Aligns holes, inserts screws or bolts, and tightens them, using nut runner or power screwdriver, to assemble preformed panels and support brackets to base. Bolts subassemblies, such as motors, pumps, transmissions, control panels, blowers, heating units, and doors, using wrenches and power nut runners. Aligns doors, brackets,

racks, and moving parts before tightening to achieve appearance, fit, and movement specified. Packs or folds insulation between panels. Connects electrical wires on control panel to motors, heating units, or blowers, according to color and length of wire, by forcing plug connectors together and sliding plastic insulators over connection. Lubricates moving parts, using grease paddle or oil-can. May place panels in fixture to align for bolting. May clamp test wires to machine and observe meter and light to test for shorts, grounds, and wattage. May be designated according to appliance assembled as Air-Conditioning-Unit Assembler (svc. ind. mach.); Assembler, Coolers (svc. ind. mach.); Automobile Air-Conditioner Assembler (svc. ind. mach.); Clothes-Drier Assembler (house. appl.); Electric-Range Assembler (house. appl.); Washing-Machine Assembler (house. appl.).
GOE: 06.02.22 STRENGTH: M GED: R3 M2 L2 SVP: 3 DLU: 77

828 OCCUPATIONS IN FABRICATION, INSTALLATION, AND REPAIR OF ELECTRICAL AND ELECTRONICS PRODUCTS, N.E.C.

This group includes occupations, not elsewhere classified, concerned with assembling, installing, erecting, and repairing electrical and electronic products.

828.131-010 SUPERVISOR, ELECTRONIC CONTROLS REPAIRER (engine-turbine)
Supervises and coordinates activities of workers engaged in repair of electronic controls of diesel engines and generators: Trains workers in diagnosis and repair of electronic controls of diesel engines and generators in heavy equipment, such as tractors, cranes, and compressors, using test equipment and following repair manuals, blueprints, diagrams, and schematics. Reviews service calls to determine type of equipment needing repair, equipment location, and nature of problem and schedules workers for service assignments. Orders supplies and materials and maintains service records. Assists workers in repair of electronic controls at job site or in maintenance shop. Performs other duties as described under SUPERVISOR (any industry) Master Title.
GOE: 05.05.10 STRENGTH: M GED: R4 M4 L3 SVP: 8 DLU: 86

828.161-010 SUPERVISOR, ELECTRONICS SYSTEMS MAINTENANCE (any industry)
Supervises and coordinates activities of workers engaged in repair and maintenance of electronic equipment used in air navigational aids or in communications, monitoring, industrial control, or instrumentation systems. Participates in testing, modification, repair, and maintenance of radar, microwave links, indicator plotter, radar beacon, omnirange receivers and transmitters [ELECTRONICS MECHANIC (any industry)]. Maintains log of repair and maintenance activities occurring during shift.
GOE: 05.05.05 STRENGTH: L GED: R5 M5 L4 SVP: 8 DLU: 77

828.251-010 ELECTRONIC-SALES-AND-SERVICE TECHNICIAN (profess. & kin.)
Analyzes technical requirements of customer desiring to utilize electronic equipment, and performs installation and maintenance duties. Determines feasibility of using standardized equipment, and develops specifications for equipment required to perform additional functions. Installs, maintains, and repairs equipment.
GOE: 05.05.05 STRENGTH: M GED: R4 M3 L3 SVP: 7 DLU: 77

828.261-010 ELECTRONIC-ORGAN TECHNICIAN (any industry) alternate titles: electric-organ technicianc;
Installs, tests, adjusts, and repairs electronic organs, pianos, or related musical instruments, using circuit diagrams, service manuals, and standard test equipment: Places speakers along wall or in sound chambers, or mounts speakers on wall. Wires speakers to console. Tunes or adjusts instruments and amplification systems, using electronic test equipment and handtools. May be designated according to specialized function as Electronic-Organ Installer (any industry); Electronic-Piano Installer (any industry); Organ Tuner, Electronic (any industry).
GOE: 05.05.12 STRENGTH: L GED: R4 M3 L3 SVP: 6 DLU: 77

828.261-014 FIELD SERVICE ENGINEER (profess. & kin.) alternate titles: field service representative; field technical assistant
Installs and repairs electronic equipment, such as computer, radar, missile-control, avionics, and communication systems, in field installations: Consults with customer or supervisor to plan layout of equipment. Studies blueprints, schematics, manuals, and other specifications to determine installation procedures. Installs or oversees installation of equipment according to manufacturer's specifications. Operates system to demonstrate equipment and to analyze malfunctions. Interprets maintenance manuals, schematics, and wiring diagrams, and repairs equipment, utilizing knowledge of electronics and using standard test instruments and handtools. Instructs and directs workers in servicing and repairing equipment. Consults with engineering personnel to resolve unusual problems in system operation and maintenance. May instruct workers in electronic theory. May supervise workers in testing, tuning, and adjusting equipment to obtain optimum operating performance. May advise management regarding customer satisfaction, product performance, and suggestions for product improvements.
GOE: 05.05.05 STRENGTH: L GED: R4 M4 L4 SVP: 7 DLU: 88

828.261-018 SENIOR TECHNICIAN, CONTROLS (pipe lines)
Develops design modifications and provides technical assistance to workers engaged in installation, modification, and repair of gas compressor station controls and instruments: Tours compressor station and inspects or tests station control apparatus, using standard test equipment and handtools. Confers with superintendent to determine operational problems and efficiency of automatic control systems. Analyzes operational problems and develops modifications in design to improve efficiency. Trains workers and provides technical assistance in installation, maintenance, and repair techniques. Confers with manufacturers' representatives and submits proposed design modifications to improve efficiency of compressor station controls and instrumentation.
GOE: 05.01.08 STRENGTH: L GED: R4 M4 L4 SVP: 7 DLU: 77

828.261-022 ELECTRONICS MECHANIC (any industry) alternate titles: communication technician; electronics-equipment mechanic; electronics specialist; electronics-system mechanic; electronics technician; maintenance engineer
Repairs electronic equipment, such as computers, industrial controls, audio and video systems, radar systems, telemetering and missile control systems, transmitters, antennas, and servomechanisms, following blueprints and manufacturers' specifications, and using handtools and test instruments: Converses with equipment operators to ascertain problems with equipment before breakdown, and to determine if breakdown is due to human error or mechanical problems. Tests faulty equipment and applies knowledge of functional operation of electronic units and systems to diagnose cause of malfunction. Tests electronic components and circuits to locate defects, using oscilloscopes, signal generators, ammeters, and voltmeters. Replaces defective components and wiring and adjusts mechanical parts, using handtools and soldering iron. Aligns, adjusts, and calibrates equipment according to specifications. Calibrates testing instruments. Maintains records of repairs, calibrations, and tests. May enter information into computer to copy program from one electronic component to another, or to draw, modify or to store schematics, applying knowledge of software package used. May install equipment in industrial or military establishments and in aircraft and missiles. May operate equipment, such as communication equipment or missile control systems in ground and flight test, and be required to hold license from governmental agency. May be designated according to type of equipment repaired as Customer-Engineering Specialist (office machines); Electronics Mechanic, Computer (any industry); Radar Mechanic (any industry); Voting-Machine Repairer (government ser.).
GOE: 05.05.10 STRENGTH: M GED: R4 M4 L4 SVP: 7 DLU: 89

828.261-026 ELECTRONICS-MECHANIC APPRENTICE (any industry) alternate titles: electronics-technician apprentice
Performs duties as described under APPRENTICE (any industry) Master Title.
GOE: 05.05.10 STRENGTH: M GED: R4 M4 L4 SVP: 7 DLU: 77

828.281-018 MISSILE FACILITIES REPAIRER (military ser.)
Repairs missile weapons system support facilities and equipment: Inspects, services, and replaces electrical, hydraulic, and mechanical components of missile weapons systems real-property-installed equipment, facilities, and ground support equipment, such as missile pedestals, crib suspensions, pendulum links, shock mounts, maintenance work platforms, erection booms, umbilical brackets, and suspension devices. Services support equipment with fuel, lubricants, hydraulic fluid, and air. Operates auxiliary motor generators, battery systems, and portable self-powered handling equipment. Aligns missile to launcher, using equipment such as collimator systems.
GOE: 05.10.01 STRENGTH: V GED: R3 M3 L3 SVP: 4 DLU: 77

828.281-022 RADIOACTIVITY-INSTRUMENT MAINTENANCE TECHNICIAN (petrol. & gas) alternate titles: radioactivity technician
Repairs and services electrical radioactivity-detecting instruments used to locate radioactive formations in oil- or gas-well boreholes, using special testing apparatus. Tests electronic, electrostatic, and electromagnetic elements and circuits of instruments with special laboratory testing apparatus to locate defective parts and to verify precise adjustments. Services special subsurface instruments containing radium or radioactive compounds.
GOE: 05.05.11 STRENGTH: L GED: R4 M4 L4 SVP: 7 DLU: 77

828.281-026 COMPUTERIZED ENVIRONMENTAL CONTROL INSTALLER (electron. comp.)
Installs and repairs programmable, computer-based control systems for regulating residential and commercial environmental energy equipment, such as heating, ventilating and air-conditioning (HVAC) systems, heat pumps, boilers, and chillers, applying knowledge of computer control systems and environmental energy equipment: Reads specifications, diagrams, and schematics detailing computer control installation requirements and existing environmental energy equipment design and layout. Installs, mounts, and connects specified computer hardware, such as central processing unit, keyboard, CRT display, temperature sensor, analog to digital converter, and interconnect wiring to interface with environmental energy equipment control circuits, using handtools and power tools. Types commands on input keyboard or inserts disk into disk drive to start and run computerized environmental control system through operating sequence. Tests control circuits to verify system operation or diagnose malfunctions, using voltmeter and oscilloscope. Isolates faults to computer controls or environmental energy units based on test results, specification data, and

symptoms. Tests circuitry of faulty computer controls, using voltmeter, oscilloscope, and logic analyzer to isolate malfunctions to circuit board. Replaces faulty circuit boards, using handtools. Maintains records of installation, test results, and repairs.
GOE: 05.05.05 STRENGTH: L GED: R4 M4 L4 SVP: 7 DLU: 86

828.381-010 EQUIPMENT INSTALLER (any industry)
Installs electronic control panels and related mechanical or electrical equipment, such as motor generator units, battery chargers, utility reels, and darkroom equipment, in panel trucks following blueprint specifications: Measures distances with rule to lay out work in body of truck. Drills holes and bolts metal framework and supports in place, using electric drill and wrenches. Cuts, drills, and fits brackets, supports, covers, and fixtures from metal sheet, strap or bar stock, using metal cutting saws, drill press, grinders, and files. Bolts and screws control panels and assembled operating units to framework. Connects electrical wiring and cables, using electricians' handtools. Installs lighting fixtures, outlets, switches, wall boxes, and terminal boards.
GOE: 05.10.04 STRENGTH: M GED: R4 M3 L3 SVP: 7 DLU: 77

828.381-018 ASSEMBLER, ELECTROMECHANICAL (aircraft mfg.; electron. comp.; inst. & app.)
Assembles, tests, and repairs precision electromechanical parts, assemblies, and equipment, such as gyros, servomechanisms, electronic instruments, radar, and missile controls, according to blueprints, diagrams, and specifications, using handtools, power tools, precision instruments, and test equipment: Reads blueprints, schematics, and technical orders to determine methods and sequence of assembly operations. Examines parts for surface defects. Aligns, fits, and assembles component parts into completed units, using handtools, power tools, fixtures, and templates. Verifies dimensions and clearances of parts to ensure conformance to blueprint specifications, using instruments, such as micrometers, calipers, and height gauges. Solders and bolts electrical and electronic components in specified location on assembly [ELECTRONICS ASSEMBLER (comm. equip.; electron. comp.; inst. & app.) 726.684-018]. Tests functional performance of completed electromechanical assemblies, using test equipment. Repairs, reworks, and calibrates assemblies to meet operational tolerances. May fabricate parts, using shop equipment.
GOE: 06.01.04 STRENGTH: M GED: R4 M3 L3 SVP: 7 DLU: 89

829 OCCUPATIONS IN INSTALLATION AND REPAIR OF ELECTRICAL PRODUCTS, N.E.C.

This group includes occupations, not elsewhere classified, concerned with assembling, installing, erecting, and repairing electrical equipment and related structures.

829.131-010 CABLE SUPERVISOR (construction; tel. & tel.; utilities) alternate titles: cable-splicing supervisor
Supervises and coordinates activities of workers engaged in installation, maintenance, and repair of underground, aerial, and buried cables and electrical equipment for power-utility, communication, or street-railway systems: Directs installation of main and feeder cables through conduit, splicing and lead-coating cable sections, connecting wires to terminals, and installing terminal and junction boxes, transformers, and other equipment in underground vaults or overhead platforms. Performs other duties as described under SUPERVISOR (any industry) Master Title. May be designated according to specialty as Underground Supervisor (utilities).
GOE: 05.05.05 STRENGTH: L GED: R4 M3 L3 SVP: 8 DLU: 77

829.131-014 ELECTRICIAN SUPERVISOR (any industry)
Supervises and coordinates activities of ELECTRICIAN, MAINTENANCE (any industry) 829.261-018 and ELECTRICIAN (construction) 824.261-010 engaged in construction, maintenance and repair of electric power, lighting, and communication systems of buildings, factories, and transportation equipment: Plans wiring and installation of equipment and fixtures, such as motors, generators, switches, circuit breakers, and fuse boxes, according to blueprints, schematic drawings, and sketches. Inspects wiring and fixtures for conformance to company specifications or local electrical codes, using test equipment, such as voltmeter and ohmmeter. Performs other duties as described under SUPERVISOR (any industry) Master Title. May supervise workers in maintenance of electrical systems and be designated Building-Maintenance Supervisor, Electrical (any industry); Electrician Supervisor, Maintenance (any industry). May supervise workers specializing in electrical systems of transportation equipment and be designated Electrician Supervisor, Airplane (air trans.); Electrician Supervisor, Automotive (automotive ser.); Electrician Supervisor Locomotive (railroad equip.). May be designated according to workers supervised as Circuit-Breaker Supervisor (utilities); Power-Transformer-Repair Supervisor (utilities); Service-Transformer-Repair Supervisor (utilities).
GOE: 05.05.05 STRENGTH: L GED: R4 M3 L3 SVP: 8 DLU: 81

829.131-018 INSTALLATION SUPERINTENDENT, PIN-SETTING MACHINE (construction)
Supervises and coordinates activities of workers engaged in installing automatic pin-setting machines in bowling alleys. Performs duties as described under SUPERVISOR (any industry) Master Title.
GOE: 05.05.09 STRENGTH: L GED: R4 M3 L3 SVP: 8 DLU: 77

tions of utility district: Trains workers in maintenance of equipment. Inspects work for conformance to specifications. Patrols telephone lines to look for broken insulators, storm damage, and leaning poles. Performs other duties as described under SUPERVISOR (any industry) Master Title.
GOE: 05.05.05 STRENGTH: L GED: R4 M3 L3 SVP: 8 DLU: 77

829.261-010 COMPLAINT INSPECTOR (utilities)
Inspects and locates cause of defective electric service on customer's premises and repairs wiring and connections: Examines interior wiring, switches, fuses, circuit breakers, light sockets, and connections to appliances to detect irregularities or defects. Repairs or replaces defective or worn parts. Tests voltage on wire to meter to determine overload or underload [VOLTAGE TESTER (utilities)] and recommends new wiring arrangement to correct inadequacies. Examines and repairs broken lines from distribution pole to building or requests LINE REPAIRER (utilities) or TROUBLE SHOOTER (utilities) II to examine and repair connections and outside wiring if trouble cannot be located within building. May make minor repairs to appliances and report major defects to ELECTRICAL-APPLIANCE SERVICER (any industry).
GOE: 05.05.05 STRENGTH: L GED: R4 M3 L3 SVP: 7 DLU: 77

829.261-014 DENTAL-EQUIPMENT INSTALLER AND SERVICER (wholesale tr.)
Installs and services dental office equipment, such as hydraulic chairs and electric or pneumatic drill units, according to manufacturer's service manuals: Installs equipment and assembles specified hydraulic, pneumatic, and electrical connections, using handtools and power tools. Replaces obsolete or faulty equipment as ordered. Repairs or replaces defective or worn parts, such as motors, clutches, and switches. Performs routine servicing of equipment, such as lubricating gears and repacking bearings. May install and repair dental plumbing. May install, service, test, and calibrate dental x-ray equipment.
GOE: 05.10.02 STRENGTH: M GED: R4 M4 L3 SVP: 6 DLU: 77

829.261-018 ELECTRICIAN, MAINTENANCE (any industry) alternate titles: electrical repairer
Installs and repairs electrical systems, apparatus, and electrical and electronic components of industrial machinery and equipment, following electrical code, manuals, schematic diagrams, blueprints, and other specifications, using handtools, power tools, and electrical and electronic test equipment: Installs power supply wiring and conduit for newly installed machines and equipment, such as robots, conveyors, and *programmable controllers*, following electrical code and blueprints, using handtools and voltage tester. Connects power supply wires to machines and equipment, and connects cables and wires between machines and equipment, following manuals, schematic diagrams, and blueprints, using handtools and test equipment. Diagnoses malfunctioning apparatus, such as transformers, motors, and lighting fixtures, using test equipment, and replaces damaged or broken wires and cables, using handtools. Tests malfunctioning machinery, using test equipment, and discusses malfunction with other maintenance workers, such as MACHINE REPAIRER, MAINTENANCE (any industry) 638.261-030 and TOOL MAKER, MAINTENANCE (machine shop) 601.280-042, to diagnose malfunction. Replaces faulty electrical components of machine, such as relays, switches, and motors, and positions sensing devices, using handtools. Diagnoses and repairs or replaces faulty electronic components, such as printed circuit boards [ELECTRONICS TESTER (any industry) 726.261-018], using electronic test equipment and handtools. Replaces electric motor bearings and rewires motors. May push buttons and press keys on robot controller, *teach pendant*, and programmable controller to program automated machinery, such as robots, to operate automated machinery, to test for malfunctions, and to verify repairs. May plan layout of wiring and install wiring, conduit, and electrical apparatus in buildings [ELECTRICIAN (construction) 824.261-010]. May diagnose and replace faulty mechanical, hydraulic, and pneumatic components of machines and equipment. May be required to hold electrician's license. May be designated according to equipment repaired as Circuit-Breaker Mechanic (utilities); Electrician, Crane Maintenance (any industry); Electrician, Rectifier Maintenance (utilities); Salvage Repairer (utilities) I; Time Clock Repairer (elec. equip.); Transformer-Coil Winder (utilities); or according to work location as Electrician, Machine Shop (machine shop); Electrician Refinery (petrol. refin.); Underground Repairer (utilities). May be designated: Watch Electrician (tel. & tel.); Wirer, Maintenance (utilities).
GOE: 05.05.05 STRENGTH: M GED: R4 M4 L4 SVP: 8 DLU: 88

829.281-010 AUTOMATIC-DOOR MECHANIC (construction)
Installs, services, and repairs opening and closing mechanisms of automatic doors used in self-service grocery stores and similar establishments: Bores and cuts holes in flooring, using handtools and power tools. Sets in and secures floor treadle for activating mechanism and connects hydraulic powerpack and electrical panelboard to treadle. Covers treadle with carpeting and screws or nails down chrome strips around edges. Tests system by stepping on treadle. Repairs nonoperating systems, using handtools, blueprints, and schematic diagrams. May install frames and door units, using cutting tools and handtools. May install systems actuated by electronic-eye mechanism.
GOE: 05.10.03 STRENGTH: M GED: R3 M2 L2 SVP: 6 DLU: 77

829.281-018 IN-FLIGHT REFUELING SYSTEM REPAIRER (military ser.)
Inspects, tests, modifies, and repairs aircraft in-flight refueling systems and associated equipment, using electrical test instruments and special handtools,

applying knowledge of system wiring diagrams, technical publications, and design characteristics: Repairs in-flight refueling electrical devices, such as elevation, telescope, and azimuth control assemblies and limit switches. Conducts detailed tests of in-flight refueling electrical systems, using ohmmeter, voltmeter, and electrical and hydraulic systems to ensure maximum operation efficiency, using wiring diagrams and technical publications. Adjusts end play, spacing, clearance, and specified torque on in-flight refueling components. Inspects seals, gaskets, hoses, tubing, hydraulic motors, fuel pumps, valves, filters, accumulators, and plumbing installations for leakage and functional operation. Fabricates wiring assemblies for replacing damaged cables and wiring in electrical systems.
GOE: 05.10.02 STRENGTH: L GED: R3 M3 L3 SVP: 7 DLU: 77

829.281-022 SOUND TECHNICIAN (any industry) alternate titles: inter-com installer; inter-com servicer
Installs, maintains, and services sound and intercommunication systems, multiple antenna systems, closed circuit TV systems, and associated apparatus: Installs coaxial cable and interconnecting cable and wiring. Tests installation to verify proper functioning. Tests, trouble-shoots, and services equipment. May install high-fidelity or stereophonic components or systems for playing musical recordings in homes or business establishments.
GOE: 05.05.05 STRENGTH: H GED: R4 M3 L3 SVP: 6 DLU: 77

829.361-010 CABLE SPLICER (construction; tel. & tel.; utilities) alternate titles: electrician, cable-splicing; splicer
Splices overhead, underground, or submarine multiple-conductor cables used in telephone and telegraph communication and electric-power transmission systems: Climbs utility poles or towers, utilizes truck-mounted lift bucket, or descends into sewers and underground vaults where cables are located. Cuts lead sheath from installed cable to gain access to defective cable connections, using hacksaw. Cuts and peels lead sheath and insulation from newly installed cables and conductors preparatory to splicing. Tests (traces or phases-out) each conductor to identify corresponding conductors in adjoining cable sections, according to electrical diagrams and specifications, to prevent incorrect connections between individual communication circuits or electric power circuits, using test lamp or bell system. Cleans, tins, and splices corresponding conductors by twisting ends together or by joining ends with metal clips and soldering each connection. Covers conductors with insulating or fireproofing materials. Fits lead sleeve around cable joint and wipes molten lead into joints between sleeve and cable sheath to produce moistureproof joint. Fills completed sleeve with insulating oil. May work on energized circuits to avoid interruption of service. May locate and repair leaks in pressurized cable. May work on board marine craft when splicing underwater cable and be designated Jointer, Submarine Cable (tel. & tel.; utilities).
GOE: 05.05.05 STRENGTH: L GED: R4 M3 L3 SVP: 7 DLU: 77

829.361-014 CABLE-SPLICER APPRENTICE (construction; tel. & tel.; utilities) alternate titles: splicer apprentice
Performs duties as described under APPRENTICE (any industry) Master Title.
GOE: 05.05.05 STRENGTH: L GED: R4 M3 L3 SVP: 7 DLU: 77

829.361-018 CIRCULATING PROCESS INSPECTOR (elec. equip.) alternate titles: inspector, process
Inspects machined parts and mechanical or electrical assembly of electrical equipment to detect defective assemblies and ensure quality of production: Verifies dimensions and location or alignment of layouts of mechanical assemblies and electrical contacts, using micrometers, calipers, squares, rules, protractors, dial indicators, scales, and gauges. Compares machined surfaces with finished blocks. Examines parts to detect cracks, flaws, damaged surfaces, and burrs to ensure completeness. Stops defective assembly or machining operations and notifies supervisor. Examines colored wires connected to terminals of apparatus to verify wiring locations, and examines connections for excessive or loose solder. Tests electrical characterisitics, such as resistance, short circuits, continuity, and grounds, using test equipment. Prepares inspection reports and records specified information on inspection tickets. May operate bench lathe to machine salvageable parts. May connect loose wires to terminals, using soldering iron or wire-wrapping gun. May be designated according to product inspected as Transformer Inspector (elec. equip.); Wiring Inspector (elec. equip.).
GOE: 06.01.05 STRENGTH: L GED: R3 M3 L3 SVP: 6 DLU: 77

829.381-010 PINSETTER ADJUSTER, AUTOMATIC (toy-sport equip.)
Inspects and adjusts automatic pinsetters, following blueprints, using handtools and gauges: Inspects pinsetter for defects and missing components following blueprint parts list. Mounts components or returns machine to assembly department for reworking. Rolls pinsetter to test bay and connects drive mechanism and power source. Adjusts microswitches, spring tension, traverse or circuit stops, cams, and other control mechanisms to specified settings, using handtools. Operates pinsetters to detect malfunctioning. Measures and regulates height and sweep of rake, using fixed gauge and handtools. Runs machine through complete cycle and inspects for pinsetting accuracy. Tests automatic shutoffs by running undersized pins through mechanism. Examines and adjusts each pin and pickup scissor to correct malfunctions.
GOE: 05.05.10 STRENGTH: M GED: R4 M3 L3 SVP: 6 DLU: 77

829.667-010 CABLE-SPLICER HELPER (construction; tel. & tel.; utilities)
Assists CABLE SPLICER (construction; tel. & tel.; utilities) to join ends of multiple-conductor cables used in telephone and telegraph communication sys-

tems and electric-power transmitting equipment by performing routine duties: Positions splicer's cart, opens manholes, hangs splicer's platform in position, and supplies splicer with tools and equipment. Tends small gasoline engine to pump water from underground conduit tunnels or to supply fresh air to worker in tunnel. Cuts lead tubing with hacksaw to form covering over spliced cables. Tends gasoline heater to melt lead and paraffin. Assists CABLE SPLICER (construction; tel. & tel.; utilities) in boiling out wet cables and affixing cables in tunnel racks or to poles. May pull cables through ducts and conduits [CABLE PULLER (construction; utilities)]. Performs other duties as described under HELPER (any industry) Master Title.
GOE: 05.12.16 STRENGTH: M GED: R2 M2 L2 SVP: 3 DLU: 77

829.667-014 PINSETTER-MECHANIC HELPER (any industry)
Assists PINSETTER MECHANIC, AUTOMATIC (any industry) in repair and maintenance of automatic pinsetting bowling equipment: Carries tools and test apparatus to and from job site. Loosens bolts to assist in dismantling pinsetting equipment. Cleans equipment and parts, using solvent and rags. May perform routine oiling and greasing of moving parts. Performs other duties as described under HELPER (any industry) Master Title.
GOE: 05.12.15 STRENGTH: H GED: R2 M2 L2 SVP: 2 DLU: 77

829.684-010 BATTERY INSPECTOR (railroad equip.; r.r. trans.)
Services and repairs railway car electrical equipment, using handtools, test equipment, and wiring diagram: Inspects electrical connections, wiring, charging relays, charging resistance box, and storage batteries, following wiring diagram and using voltmeter and hydrometer. Fills batteries with water and replaces defective wiring, fuses, brushes, coils, armatures, sockets, and light bulbs. Examines fan motor brushes and fills fan grease cups. Records defective equipment and batteries serviced.
GOE: 05.10.03 STRENGTH: L GED: R3 M3 L3 SVP: 4 DLU: 77

829.684-014 BODY WIRER (vehicles, nec) alternate titles: coach wirer; electrician, wiring; wirer
Installs circuit wiring in travel trailers and similar vehicles for lights, ignition, starting motors, and other electrical apparatus, following diagrams and color code: Locates and marks positions for outlet boxes on walls and ceiling, using templates or jigs. Cuts openings and drills holes for wire, light fixtures, outlet boxes, and fuse holders, using electric drill and router. Threads wires or preassembled cables through holes in floor or sides of vehicles and secures them to frame, using clips or staples. Installs fixtures and boxes in openings, using screwdriver. Connects terminals to power source to test operation of fixtures.
GOE: 05.05.05 STRENGTH: L GED: R3 M2 L3 SVP: 4 DLU: 90

829.684-018 CABLE PULLER (construction; utilities) alternate titles: cable placer; cable rigger
Pulls lead-sheathed electrical cables for electric power systems through ducts: Pushes long, flexible, steel ribbon (fish tape) or rods through duct. Attaches wire to rod or fish tape and pulls wire through duct. Attaches wire to cable and pulls cable through duct by hand or using winch. May pull ball or mandrel through duct to ensure clear passage for cable.
GOE: 05.12.16 STRENGTH: H GED: R2 M1 L1 SVP: 4 DLU: 77

829.684-022 ELECTRICIAN HELPER (any industry) alternate titles: wirer helper
Assists ELECTRICIAN (construction) 824.261-010 or ELECTRICIAN, MAINTENANCE (any industry) 829.261-018 to install and repair electrical wiring, fixtures, and equipment, performing any combination of following tasks: Gathers tools and supplies to be used at work site, according to instructions. Measures, cuts, and bends wire and conduit, using ruler and handtools. Drills holes for wiring, using power drill, and pulls or pushes wiring through opening. Traces out short circuits in wiring, using knowledge of wiring and test meter. Assists in lifting, positioning, and fastening objects, such as wiring, conduit, and motors. Performs minor repairs, such as replacing fuses, light sockets, bulbs, and switches, using handtools. Maintains tools and equipment and keeps supplies and parts in order. Disassembles defective electrical equipment, replaces defective or worn parts, and reassembles equipment, using handtools. Performs other duties as described under HELPER (any industry) Master Title.
GOE: 05.12.16 STRENGTH: M GED: R3 M2 L2 SVP: 3 DLU: 82

829.684-026 ELECTRICIAN HELPER (ship-boat mfg.)
Assists ELECTRICIAN (ship-boat mfg.) in installing and repairing wiring, fixtures, and equipment aboard ship and in shipyard facilities: Supplies ELECTRICIANS (ship-boat mfg.) with materials and tools, using handtools, or by carrying material. Measures and cuts pipe conduit to specified length, using steel tape and hacksaw. Threads conduit ends, using pipe threader, and connects couplings and conduit fittings, using wrench. Fabricates conduit support brackets from strap iron strips, using hacksaw, shaping dies, hammer, and punch. Secures brackets to bulkheads with screws and bolts and pulls wires through conduit leading to connection boxes, switch panels, and other terminals. Strips insulation from wire ends, using wire stripping pliers. Ties or screws wires to terminals for subsequent soldering. Performs other duties described under HELPER (any industry) Master Title.
GOE: 05.12.16 STRENGTH: M GED: R2 M1 L1 SVP: 3 DLU: 77

84   PAINTING, PLASTERING, WATERPROOFING, CEMENTING, AND RELATED OCCUPATIONS
This division includes occupations concerned with preparing surfaces to be covered; mixing coating ingredients; erecting scaffolding; and applying protec-

tive or decorative materials, such as cement, concrete, lacquer, paint, plaster, and wallpaper, to structural surfaces by spraying, brushing, troweling, or hand-pressing.

840   CONSTRUCTION AND MAINTENANCE PAINTERS AND RELATED OCCUPATIONS
This group includes occupations concerned with applying paint and related materials to machinery, equipment, buildings, bridges, tanks, and marine hulls and superstructures, using brushes and spray guns.

840.131-010 SUPERVISOR, PAINTING (construction)
Supervises and coordinates activities of workers engaged in applying decorative and protective coats of paint, varnish, stain, enamel, or lacquer to exterior or interior surfaces, trimming, and fixtures of buildings or other structures: Assists workers in mixing and blending paint, removing old paint from surfaces, repairing and cleaning surfaces, and applying coatings to surfaces. May supervise workers covering room interiors with wallpaper or fabric and assist workers in removing old wallpaper, repairing cracks and holes in structural surfaces, measuring and cutting coverings, and applying wallpaper or fabric to interiors. Performs other duties as described under SUPERVISOR (any industry) Master Title.
GOE: 05.10.07 STRENGTH: L GED: R4 M3 L3 SVP: 8 DLU: 86

840.131-014 SUPERVISOR, PAINTING, SHIPYARD (ship-boat mfg.)
Supervises and coordinates activities of workers engaged in painting parts, equipment, ships, and buildings in ship and boat building establishment: Trains new workers in operation of painting equipment. Inspects surface of area to be painted to determine worker assignments, such as sandblasting, wire brushing, scraping, and painting. Examines surfaces subsequent to painting to verify adherence to specified standards. Performs other duties as described under SUPERVISOR (any industry) Master Title.
GOE: 05.10.07 STRENGTH: L GED: R4 M3 L3 SVP: 8 DLU: 77

840.381-010 PAINTER (construction)
Applies coats of paint, varnish, stain, enamel, or lacquer to decorate and protect interior or exterior surfaces, trimmings, and fixtures of buildings and other structures: Reads work order or receives instructions from supervisor or homeowner regarding painting. Smooths surfaces, using sandpaper, brushes, or steel wool, and removes old paint from surfaces, using paint remover, scraper, wire brush, or blowtorch to prepare surfaces for painting. Fills nail holes, cracks, and joints with caulk, putty, plaster, or other filler, using caulking gun and putty knife. Selects premixed paints, or mixes required portions of pigment, oil, and thinning and drying substances to prepare paint that matches specified colors. Removes fixtures, such as pictures and electric switchcovers from walls prior to painting, using screwdriver. Spreads dropcloths over floors and room furnishings, and covers surfaces, such as baseboards, door frames, and windows with masking tape and paper to protect surfaces during painting. Paints surfaces, using brushes, spray gun, or paint rollers. Simulates wood grain, marble, brick, or tile effects. Applies paint with cloth, brush, sponge, or fingers to create special effects. Erects scaffolding or sets up ladders to perform tasks above ground level. May be designated according to type of work performed as Painter, Interior Finish (construction); Painter, Maintenance (any industry); or according to type of material used as Calciminer (construction); Varnisher (construction). May also hang wallpaper and fabrics [PAPERHANGER (construction) 841.381-010]. May wash surfaces prior to painting with mildew remover, using brush.
GOE: 05.10.07 STRENGTH: M GED: R3 M2 L2 SVP: 7 DLU: 88

840.381-014 PAINTER APPRENTICE, SHIPYARD (ship-boat mfg.)
Performs duties as described under APPRENTICE (any industry) Master Title.
GOE: 05.10.07 STRENGTH: M GED: R3 M2 L2 SVP: 7 DLU: 77

840.381-018 PAINTER, SHIPYARD (ship-boat mfg.)
Prepares wood, fiberglass, and metal surfaces for painting, and paints parts, equipment, interiors, and exteriors of ships, boats, and shipyard and marina buildings, using brushes, spray guns, and rollers: Mixes solvents according to formula, and immerses parts in solution or washes surfaces to remove grease, rust, scale, and dirt. Burns off old paint, using blowtorch. Smooths wooden and plaster surfaces, using sandpaper, scrapers, and sanding machines. Fills cracks and holes with patching plaster, putty, or plastic wood. Washes and treats surfaces with oil, turpentine, and other preparations. Brushes and rubs filler material into grained wood to prepare surfaces for painting. Mixes and matches colors of paint, varnish, stain, shellac, and calcimine. Operates spray painting equipment or brushes or rolls paint on surfaces. Sands surfaces between coats and polishes final coat to specified finish. May spray or brush hot plastics or pitch on surfaces. May bake finishes on painted and enameled articles in baking oven. May cut glass and install window and door panes. May hang wallpaper. May cut stencils, and brush or spray lettering and decorations on surfaces.
GOE: 05.10.07 STRENGTH: M GED: R3 M2 L2 SVP: 7 DLU: 77

840.681-010 PAINTER, STAGE SETTINGS (motion picture) alternate titles: painter, set
Paints walls, exteriors and interiors of buildings, furniture, and other portions of motion picture sets, using brush, roller, or spray gun: Blends paints, matches colors, or uses premixed paint or stain. Paints surfaces or objects on set to rep-

resent stonework, surface marble effects, and wood grain. May paint or burn wood and other surfaces of articles used in motion picture sets to create appearance of age, deterioration, or usage and be designated Ager (motion picture).
GOE: 01.06.03 STRENGTH: L GED: R3 M2 L1 SVP: 7 DLU: 77

840.684-010 GLASS TINTER (glass products) alternate titles: colored-liquid-plastic applier
Applies colored liquid plastic to glass surface of installed windows and doors to reduce interior heat and glare from sunlight, using spray gun: Fills spray reservoir with solution. Applies plastic coating to glass surfaces from top of window or door and working downward to apply smooth, uniform coat. Positions collection trough at bottom of coated surface to reclaim excess liquid.
GOE: 06.04.33 STRENGTH: M GED: R2 M1 L2 SVP: 5 DLU: 77

840.687-010 PAINTER HELPER, SHIPYARD (ship-boat mfg.)
Assists PAINTER, SHIPYARD (ship-boat mfg.) performing any combination of following duties: Pours specified amounts of chemical solutions into stripping tanks. Places articles, such as cabinets, metal furniture, and paint containers into stripping tanks and removes articles after prescribed period of time. Fills cracks in plaster surfaces with putty or epoxy compounds, using putty knife. Smooths surfaces to be painted, using wire brush, sandpaper, or portable sanding and buffing equipment. Strips masking tape over surfaces not to be painted. Performs other duties as described under HELPER (any industry) Master Title.
GOE: 05.12.12 STRENGTH: M GED: R2 M2 L1 SVP: 3 DLU: 77

841 PAPERHANGERS

This group includes occupations concerned with applying wallpaper, advertising material, and fabrics to walls, ceilings, and signs.

841.137-010 SUPERVISOR, BILLPOSTING (business ser.)
Supervises and coordinates activities of BILLPOSTERS (business ser.): Examines poster panels to verify specified size and sequential arrangement. Performs other duties as described under SUPERVISOR (any industry) Master Title.
GOE: 05.12.01 STRENGTH: L GED: R4 M2 L3 SVP: 6 DLU: 77

841.381-010 PAPERHANGER (construction)
Covers interior walls and ceilings of rooms with decorative wallpaper or fabric, using handtools: Measures walls and ceiling to compute number and length of strips required to cover surface. Sets up pasteboard and erects scaffolding. Marks vertical guideline on wall to align first strip, using plumb bob and chalkline. Smooths rough spots on walls and ceilings, using sandpaper. Fills holes and cracks with plaster, using trowel. Removes paint, varnish, and grease from surfaces, using paint remover and water soda solution. Applies acetic acid to damp plaster to prevent lime from bleeding through paper. Applies sizing (thin glue) to waterproof porous surfaces, using brush, roller, or pasting machine. Measures and cuts strips from roll of wallpaper or fabric, using shears or razor. Mixes paste to desired consistency and brushes paste on back of wallpaper or fabric, using paste brush. Trims selvage (rough edge) from strips, using straightedge and trimming knife. Places paste-coated strips on wall or ceiling to match adjacent edges of figured strips, and smooths strips with dry brush or felt-covered roller to remove wrinkles and bubbles. Smooths joints with seam roller and trims excess material at ceiling and baseboard, using knife. Removes old paper, using water, steam machine, or chemical remover and scraper. May apply paint to interior or exterior surface of buildings [PAINTER (construction)].
GOE: 05.05.04 STRENGTH: M GED: R4 M2 L2 SVP: 7 DLU: 77

841.684-010 BILLPOSTER (business ser.)
Attaches advertising posters on surfaces, such as walls and billboards, using handtools: Removes old poster, using scraping tool. Mixes paste-powder with water to form paste. Smears paste on wall or billboard surface, using brush. Aligns poster sections on billboard and smooths sections, using long-handled brush. Staples or tacks posters on fences, walls, or poles. Climbs ladder to work from deck at bottom of elevated billboard. May work from scaffolding.
GOE: 05.12.14 STRENGTH: L GED: R2 M1 L1 SVP: 2 DLU: 77

842 PLASTERERS AND RELATED OCCUPATIONS

This group includes occupations concerned with applying plaster, stucco, and related materials to structural surfaces.

842.131-010 SUPERVISOR, DRY-WALL APPLICATION (construction)
Supervises and coordinates activities of workers engaged in erecting metal studs and suspension ceiling grids and applying plasterboard or other wallboard to ceilings and walls of buildings: Studies blueprints and estimates worker-hours and materials required to complete job, applying mathematical formulas. Measures and marks location of metal framing on walls and ceilings. Inspects work to ensure adherence to company standards and building codes. Trains and assists workers in performance of duties. Performs other duties as described under SUPERVISOR (any industry) Master Title.
GOE: 05.05.04 STRENGTH: V GED: R4 M3 L3 SVP: 7 DLU: 77

842.131-014 SUPERVISOR, LATHING (construction)
Supervises and coordinates activities of workers engaged in fastening wooden, metal, or rockboard lathing to walls, ceilings, and partitions of buildings

to provide supporting base for plaster, fireproofing, or acoustical material: Measures and marks partition locations and center lines, plumbs and levels vertical and horizontal alignment of walls and ceilings, and draws guidelines to correct irregularities. Inspects work in progress to verify adherence to specifications. Trains and assists workers as described under SUPERVISOR (any industry) Master Title. Performs duties as described under SUPERVISOR (any industry) Master Title.
GOE: 05.10.01 STRENGTH: M GED: R4 M3 L3 SVP: 8 DLU: 77

842.131-018 SUPERVISOR, PLASTERING (construction)
Supervises and coordinates activities of workers engaged in applying coats of plaster, stucco, cement, and fireproofing materials to surface of structures to produce protective or decorative finish: Analyzes blueprints to determine surface area to be covered and estimates worker-hours and materials requirements applying mathematical formulas. Demonstrates mixing, plastering, cementing and other techniques to workers. Inspects material application for uniform thickness, surface flaws, and consistency of mix. Inspects finished surface to verify quality of work and adherence to specifications. Performs other duties as described under SUPERVISOR (any industry) Master Title.
GOE: 05.05.04 STRENGTH: L GED: R4 M3 L3 SVP: 7 DLU: 77

842.134-010 SUPERVISOR, TAPING (construction)
Supervises and coordinates activities of workers engaged in sealing joints between plasterboard and other wallboard to prepare wall for painting or papering: Estimates material and worker-hour requirements to complete job, applying mathematical formulas. Monitors operation of electric mixing machines and makes minor machine adjustments. Inspects work in progress to ensure quality meets company standards and adheres to building codes. Trains and assists workers in performance of tasks. Performs other duties as described under SUPERVISOR (any industry) Master Title.
GOE: 05.10.01 STRENGTH: M GED: R4 M3 L3 SVP: 6 DLU: 77

842.361-010 LATHER (construction)
Fastens wooden, metal, or rockboard lath to walls, ceilings, and partitions of buildings to provide supporting base for plaster, fireproofing, or acoustical material, using handtools and portable power tools: Erects horizontal metal framework to which laths are fastened, using nails, bolts, and studgun. Drills holes in floor and ceiling, using portable electric tool, and drives ends of wooden or metal studs into holes to provide anchor for furring or rockboard lath. Wires horizontal strips to furring to stiffen framework. Cuts lath to fit openings and projections, using handtools or portable power tools. Wires, nails, clips, or staples lath to framework, ceiling joists, and flat concrete surfaces. Bends metal lath to fit corners, or attaches preformed corner reinforcements. Wires plasterer's channels to overhead structural framework to provide support for plaster or acoustical ceiling tile. May install metal casings around openings, metal window stools, and metal trim and plaster grounds (wood or metal strips) nailed to studding to provide guide for PLASTERER (construction). May weld metal frame supports to steel structural members. May be designated according to type of lath applied as Metal Lather (construction); Rockboard Lather (construction); Wood Lather (construction); or according to task performed as Metal Furrer (construction).
GOE: 05.10.01 STRENGTH: M GED: R3 M2 L2 SVP: 6 DLU: 77

842.361-014 LATHER APPRENTICE (construction)
Performs duties as described under APPRENTICE (any industry) Master Title.
GOE: 05.10.01 STRENGTH: M GED: R3 M2 L2 SVP: 6 DLU: 77

842.361-018 PLASTERER (construction)
Applies coats of plaster to interior walls, ceilings, and partitions of buildings, to produce finished surface, according to blueprints, architect's drawings, or oral instructions, using handtools and portable power tools: Directs workers to mix plaster to desired consistency and to erect scaffolds. Spreads plaster over lath or masonry base, using trowel, and smooths plaster with darby and float to attain uniform thickness. Applies scratch, brown, or finish coats of plaster to wood, metal, or board lath successively. Roughens undercoat with scratcher (wire or metal scraper) to provide bond for succeeding coats of plaster. Creates decorative textures in finish coat by marking surface of coat with brush and trowel or by spattering surface with pebbles [STUCCO MASON (construction) 842.381-014]. May install lathing [LATHER (construction) 842.361-010]. May mix mortar. May install guide wires on exterior surface of buildings to indicate thickness of plaster to be applied. May install precast ornamental plaster pieces by applying mortar to back of pieces and pressing pieces into place on wall or ceiling and be designated Ornamental-Plaster Sticker (construction). May specialize in applying finish or rough coats of plaster and be desigated Plasterer, Finish (construction); Plasterer, Rough (construction). May apply plaster with spray gun and be designated Plasterer, Spray Gun (construction). May perform maintenance work only and be designated Plasterer, Maintenance (construction).
GOE: 05.05.04 STRENGTH: M GED: R3 M2 L2 SVP: 7 DLU: 81

842.361-022 PLASTERER APPRENTICE (construction)
Performs duties as described under APPRENTICE (any industry) Master Title.
GOE: 05.05.04 STRENGTH: M GED: R3 M2 L3 SVP: 7 DLU: 77

842.361-026 PLASTERER, MOLDING (concrete prod.; construction) alternate titles: plasterer, ornamental
Molds and installs ornamental plaster panels and trim, and runs (casts) ornamental plaster cornices and moldings by either of following methods: (1)

Spreads freshly mixed plaster on table or in forms with trowel when molding and installing ornamental trim. Shapes plaster by hand, using template and cuts trim to size after plaster has hardened. Applies coat of plaster to wall and presses trim into position. (2) Nails wooden strips to wall and ceiling to serve as guide for template when casting (running) cornices or moldings. Applies plaster to wall or ceiling, using trowel. Pushes template over plaster, striking off excess plaster until desired shape and smoothness of molding is obtained.
GOE: 05.05.04 STRENGTH: M GED: R4 M2 L3 SVP: 7 DLU: 77

842.361-030 DRY-WALL APPLICATOR (construction) alternate titles: dry-wall installations mechanic; dry-wall installer; gypsum dry-wall systems installer
Plans gypsum drywall installations, erects metal framing and furring channels for fastening drywalls, and installs drywall to cover walls, ceilings, soffits, shafts, and movable partitions in residential, commercial, and industrial buildings: Reads blueprints and other specifications to determine method of installation, work procedures, and material, tool, and work aid requirements. Lays out reference lines and points for use in computing location and position of metal framing and furring channels and marks position for erecting metalwork, using chalkline. Measures, marks, and cuts metal runners, studs, and furring channels to specified size, using tape measure, straightedge and hand-and portable power-cutting tools. Secures metal framing to walls and furring channels to ceilings, using hand and portable power tools. Measures and marks cutting lines on drywall, using square, tape measure, and marking devices. Scribes cutting lines on drywall, using straightedge and utility knife and breaks board along cut lines. Fits and fastens board into specified position on wall, using screws, hand or portable power tools, or adhesive. Cuts openings into board for electrical outlets, vents or fixtures, using keyhole saw or other cutting tools. Measures, cuts, assembles and installs metal framing and decorative trim for windows, doorways, and vents. Fits, aligns, and hangs doors and installs hardware, such as locks and kickplates [CARPENTER (construction) 860.381-022]. Worker is usually assisted by other workers.
GOE: 05.05.04 STRENGTH: V GED: R3 M3 L3 SVP: 7 DLU: 81

842.381-014 STUCCO MASON (construction) alternate titles: plasterer, stucco; stucco worker
Applies weatherproof, decorative covering of Portland cement or gypsum plaster to outside building surfaces, using handtools: Erects scaffolds. Applies various coats of material, using same technique as PLASTERER (construction). Decorates final or finish coat by marking coat with sand, or with brush or trowel, or by spattering with small stones. May nail wire mesh, lath, or similar material to outside surfaces to serve as binding device to hold stucco in place. May apply stucco, using spray gun. May install guide wires on surface of buildings to indicate thickness of stucco to be applied.
GOE: 05.05.04 STRENGTH: M GED: R4 M3 L3 SVP: 7 DLU: 77

842.664-010 TAPER (construction; mfd. bldgs.) alternate titles: dry-wall finisher; finisher; wallboard and plasterboard; sheetrock taper; taper and bedder; taper and floater
Seals joints between plasterboard or other wallboards to prepare wall surface for painting or papering: Mixes sealing compound by hand or with portable electric mixer, and spreads compound over joints between boards, using trowel, broadknife, or spatula. Presses paper tape over joint to embed tape into compound and seal joint, or tapes joint, using mechanical applicator that spreads compound and embeds tape in one operation. Spreads and smooths cementing material over tape, using trowel or floating machine to blend joint with wall surface. Sands rough spots after cement has dried. Fills cracks and holes in walls and ceiling with sealing compound. Installs metal molding at corners in lieu of sealant and tape. Usually works as member of crew. May apply texturing compound and primer to walls and ceiling preparatory to final finishing, using brushes, roller, or spray gun. May countersink nails or screws below surface of wall prior to applying sealing compound, using hammer or screwdriver.
GOE: 05.10.01 STRENGTH: M GED: R3 M2 L2 SVP: 5 DLU: 81

842.665-010 PLASTER-MACHINE TENDER (construction)
Tends machine that pumps plaster or stucco through spray-gun for application to ceilings, walls, and partitions of buildings: Starts and stops machine on signals from PLASTERER (construction). Fills hopper of machine with plaster. Turns valves to regulate pump and compressor. Assists in erecting scaffolds.
GOE: 05.12.06 STRENGTH: L GED: R2 M1 L1 SVP: 4 DLU: 77

842.684-010 DRY-WALL SPRAYER (mfd. bldgs.)
Sprays vinyl base compound on interior sheetrock walls of factory-built modular homes to produce plaster effect: Measures and pours compound ingredients into mixing vat according to mixing chart and blends ingredients, using electric blender. Pours compound into spray gun reservoir. Connects airlines to spray gun and adjusts nozzle to required spray density. Pulls trigger, and directs spray onto wall surfaces to produce plaster appearance. Adjusts spraying distance, spray density, and air pressure as required to enhance plaster effect. Inspects sprayed surfaces to detect missed areas and corrects defects, using knife and spray gun.
GOE: 06.04.33 STRENGTH: M GED: R3 M2 L1 SVP: 4 DLU: 77

842.684-014 DRY-WALL APPLICATOR (construction; mfd. bldgs.) alternate titles: dry-wall nailer; sheetrock installer
Installs plasterboard or other wallboard to ceiling and interior walls of building, using handtools and portable power tools: Installs horizontal and vertical

metal or wooden studs for attachment of wallboard on interior walls, using handtools. Cuts angle iron and channel iron to specified size, using hacksaw, and suspends angle iron grid and channel iron from ceiling, using wire. Scribes measurements on wallboard, using straightedge and tape measure, and cuts wallboard to size, using knife or saw. Cuts out openings for electrical and other outlets, using knife or saw. Attaches wallboard to wall and ceiling supports, using glue, nails, screws, hammer, or powered screwdriver. Trims rough edges from wallboard to maintain even joints, using knife. Nails prefabricated metal pieces around windows and doors and between dissimilar materials to protect drywall edges. Work is usually performed with other workers. May remove plaster, drywall, or paneling during renovation project, using crowbar and hammer.
GOE: 05.10.01 STRENGTH: M GED: R2 M2 L2 SVP: 6 DLU: 81

843 WATERPROOFING AND RELATED OCCUPATIONS

This group includes occupations concerned with applying waterproofing and caulking materials to structures.

843.134-010 SUPERVISOR, DOPING (construction) alternate titles: joint supervisor
Supervises and coordinates activities of workers engaged in coating pipeline with protective covering: Directs workers engaged in removing rust and scale from pipeline, covering pipeline with adhesive asphalt compound, and wrapping pipe with materials, such as glass cloth and felt paper, to protect pipe from electrolytic decomposition. Locates insufficient covered areas, using electronic detector, and directs workers to apply additional dope (adhesive compound) and wrapping. Performs other duties as described under SUPERVISOR (any industry) Master Title.
GOE: 05.10.07 STRENGTH: L GED: R4 M2 L3 SVP: 7 DLU: 77

843.137-010 SUPERVISOR, WATERPROOFING (construction)
Supervises and coordinates activities of workers engaged in preparing and applying waterproofing and dampproofing materials to structural surfaces, such as masonry and concrete. Performs duties as described under SUPERVISOR (any industry) Master Title.
GOE: 05.10.07 STRENGTH: L GED: R4 M3 L3 SVP: 7 DLU: 77

843.384-010 WOOD CAULKER (ship-boat mfg.)
Caulks seams between planking in hull or deck of wooden ships or boats to make them watertight by either of following methods: (1) Guides caulking tool that automatically forces caulking material into seam. Hammers material into seam, using tamping tool. Heats marine glue in melting pot. Fills glue runner (funnel) with glue and guides runner along seam to fill seam with glue. Removes excess glue, using scraper. (2) Pushes cotton line and hemp rope into seam and hammers them in place, using caulking iron and mallet. Smears hot pitch over seam, using mop, or spreads putty in seam. May hammer old caulking from seams, using reaming iron and mallet.
GOE: 05.12.14 STRENGTH: M GED: R2 M1 L1 SVP: 3 DLU: 77

843.482-010 METAL SPRAYER, CORROSION PREVENTION (any industry) alternate titles: metalizer, field operation; metal sprayer, protective coating
Controls portable flame spray equipment to spray corrosion-resistant coatings, such as zinc or aluminum, on objects, such as plates, tanks, and structural shapes according to specifications: Cleans and roughens surface of object to be coated, using sandblasting equipment [SANDBLASTER (any industry)]. Selects nozzle to accommodate size of wire to be melted and sprayed and screws nozzle into place on metalizing gun. Inserts wire into rear of gun and through feed rollers and nozzle. Connects hoses from gun to air compressor and tanks of oxygen and fuel gas, such as acetylene. Turns knobs to synchronize speed of wire feed, air pressure, and flow of oxygen and fuel indicated on dials to specifications computed from data charts. Ignites gases to melt wire and presses button or trigger to release compressed air which atomizes and sprays molten metal onto workpiece. Directs spray over surface of workpiece in specified pattern to obtain coating of required thickness as indicated by electromagnetic gauge or amount of wire used. May spray or brush paint or apply sealing material on coated surface for decoration or further protection [PAINTER, SPRAY (any industry) I]. May flame-spray nonmetallic objects, such as glass or plastics.
GOE: 05.12.14 STRENGTH: M GED: R3 M2 L2 SVP: 5 DLU: 77

843.684-010 STEEL-PLATE CAULKER (any industry) alternate titles: caulker
Caulks seams between plates of boilers, tanks, pressure vessels, or ships to make them watertight: Connects airhose to caulking hammer and inserts caulking chisel in hammer socket. Positions chisel on edge of seam and presses trigger of hammer to pound edge of overlapping plate into surface of adjoining plate to seal seam. May use hand caulking tool to close seams.
GOE: 05.12.14 STRENGTH: M GED: R2 M1 L1 SVP: 4 DLU: 77

843.684-014 UNDERCOATER (automotive ser.) alternate titles: rust proofer
Sprays protective compound onto chassis and underbody of automobiles and trucks to minimize rust and corrosion and to eliminate noise: Drives vehicle onto overhead rack. Removes headlights and other accessories, using handtools.

Steam cleans or pressure washes underside of vehicle preparatory to application of protective compound. Drills holes for interior spraying as required, using electric drill. Sprays specified areas of vehicle, using spray gun. Inserts plastic plugs to reseal holes subsequent to spraying. Replaces accessories and removes overspray and excess seepage from body seams and joints, using cloth and solvents. May mask painted or chromed surfaces to prevent exposure to undercoating spray, using tape. May spray firewall, underside of hood, and interior of trunk compartment.
GOE: 05.12.14 STRENGTH: L GED: R2 M1 L1 SVP: 3 DLU: 77

844 CEMENT AND CONCRETE FINISHING AND RELATED OCCUPATIONS

This group includes occupations concerned with covering, leveling, and smoothing cement and concrete surfaces.

844.364-010 CEMENT MASON (construction) alternate titles: cement finisher; cement paver; concrete finisher; concrete floater
Smooths and finishes surfaces of poured concrete floors, walls, sidewalks, or curbs to specified textures, using handtools or power tools, including floats, trowels, and screeds: Signals concrete deliverer to position truck to facilitate pouring concrete. Moves discharge chute of truck to direct concrete into forms. Spreads concrete into inaccessible sections of forms, using rake or shovel. Levels concrete to specified depth and workable consistency, using hand held screed and floats to bring water to surface and produce soft topping. Smooths, and shapes surfaces of freshly poured concrete, using straightedge and float or power screed. Finishes concrete surfaces, using power trowel, or wets and rubs concrete with abrasive stone to impart finish. Removes rough or defective spots from concrete surfaces, using power grinder or chisel and hammer, and patches holes with fresh concrete or epoxy compound. Molds expansion joints and edges, using edging tools, jointers, and straightedge. May sprinkle colored stone chips, powdered steel, or coloring powder on concrete to produce prescribed finish. May produce rough concrete surface, using broom. May mix cement, using hoe or concrete-mixing machine. May direct subgrade work, mixing of concrete, and setting of forms. May specialize in finishing steps and stairways and be designated Step Finisher (construction). May break up and repair old concrete surfaces, using pneumatic tools, and be designated Cement Mason, Maintenance (any industry). May spread premixed cement over deck, inner surfaces, joints, and crevices of ships and be designated Cementer (ship-boat mfg.).
GOE: 05.05.01 STRENGTH: H GED: R3 M3 L2 SVP: 7 DLU: 81

844.364-014 CEMENT-MASON APPRENTICE (construction) alternate titles: cement-finisher apprentice; concrete-finisher apprentice
Performs duties as described under APPRENTICE (any industry) Master Title.
GOE: 05.05.01 STRENGTH: H GED: R3 M3 L2 SVP: 7 DLU: 77

844.461-010 CONCRETE-STONE FINISHER (concrete prod.)
Finishes ornamental stone facings and surfaces of concrete structural products: Fills holes with grout or mix to repair imperfections in structural panels, floor and roof slabs, highway dividers, grave markers, and ornamental flowerpots, using sponge, trowel, chisel, and hammer. Cuts out damaged areas and drills holes for reinforcing rods, using power saw and drill. Positions reinforcing rods and builds wooden mold around area to be repaired, using handtools. Mixes cement, aggregate, and coloring by hand and fills mold to match specifications of product being finished, using trowel, tamper, and scraper. Polishes stone facings to lustrous finish, using polishing machine [STONE POLISHER, MACHINE (stonework)], or applies acid solution to stone facing to remove excess facing mix around stones, using brush. Smooths rough spots on stone facing, using hand chisel and abrasive stone. Washes facing with water to remove excess acid and abrasive, using hose.
GOE: 05.05.01 STRENGTH: M GED: R4 M3 L3 SVP: 7 DLU: 77

844.681-010 CELL MAKER (chemical)
Casts concrete sections of electrolytic cells, such as tops, bottoms, collars, brine traps, and partitions, using handtools and power tools, hoist, and concrete mixer: Assembles iron molds, using hoist, and bolts sections together, using handtools. Washes and scrapes molds to remove dirt, using water hose and hand scraper, and brushes surface of molds with grease, oil, or tallow, to facilitate removal of molds from concrete. Shovels specified amounts of cement, rock, sand, insulating material, and water into concrete mixer, and starts machine to mix concrete to specified consistency. Shovels or dumps concrete into mold and tamps concrete, using power vibrator. Inserts reinforcing steel members in concrete. Tests hardness of concrete by touch, and removes molds, using wrenches and hoist. Finishes surface of section, using trowel or portable grinder, and transfers section to curing tank for water or tar immersion, using hoist. May install electrical connections, and weld or solder connections in place. May inventory and requisition supplies. May cast concrete rings for mercury cells, impregnating them in bath of molten tar, and tending steam chamber to dry coated rings and be designated Ring Maker (chemical). May cast concrete cell covers and fabricate cover parts, such as anode pins, using power tools and handpress, and be designated Cover Maker (chemical).
GOE: 06.02.30 STRENGTH: M GED: R3 M2 L2 SVP: 5 DLU: 77

844.684-010 CONCRETE RUBBER (concrete prod.) alternate titles: cement patcher; cement rubber; concrete pointer; concrete polisher
Finishes surface of concrete products or structural elements after forms have been removed: Mixes sand, cement, and water in specified proportions to make cement grout or slurry. Wets surface of concrete to bond surface. Fills holes and cracks with grout or slurry and smooths surface, using trowel. Clamps wooden forms to corners and pours grout or slurry into forms to patch broken corners. Chips, scrapes, rubs, and grinds high spots, ridges, and rough projections from surface to remove defective concrete, using pneumatic chisel or handtools. Cleans chipped area, using wire brush. Feels and observes surface to detect irregularities and rough or uneven surfaces. Selects abrasive stone according to finish specified or step in finishing process. Wets concrete surface and rubs surface with stone to obtain specified finish. May apply muriatic acid to concrete to clean surface.
GOE: 05.10.01 STRENGTH: M GED: R3 M1 L1 SVP: 5 DLU: 77

844.687-010 CEMENT SPRAYER HELPER, NOZZLE (concrete prod.; construction)
Assists CEMENT SPRAYER, NOZZLE (concrete prod.; construction) to apply stucco, cement mortar, or concrete to exposed earth, masonry, or steel surfaces: Moves and holds supply hose as spraying progresses, using rope sling. Drags screed over finished surface to cut and clean spots from surface. Cuts and squares corners, using trowel. Assists workers engaged in erecting and moving scaffolds and in coupling and uncoupling pipe. Performs other duties as described under HELPER (any industry) Master Title.
GOE: 05.12.09 STRENGTH: H GED: R1 M1 L1 SVP: 2 DLU: 77

845 TRANSPORTATION EQUIPMENT PAINTERS AND RELATED OCCUPATIONS

This group includes occupations concerned with applying paint and related materials to transportation equipment, including automobiles, trucks, trailers, aircraft, and railway cars.

845.381-010 PAINTER APPRENTICE, TRANSPORTATION EQUIPMENT (aircraft mfg.; air trans.; automotive ser.)
Performs duties as described under APPRENTICE (any industry) Master Title.
GOE: 05.10.07 STRENGTH: M GED: R3 M2 L3 SVP: 6 DLU: 77

845.381-014 PAINTER, TRANSPORTATION EQUIPMENT (aircraft mfg.; air trans.; automotive ser.)
Paints surfaces of transportation equipment, such as automobiles, buses, trucks, and aircraft, applying knowledge of surface preparation and painting techniques, using spray painting equipment, power tools, and work aids: Cleans, sands, and applies chemical solutions to prepare and condition surfaces prior to painting. Mixes and thins paint or other coating to specified color and consistency according to standard formulas or color charts, using spatula or mixing equipment and viscometer. Masks and covers surfaces not to be painted. Sprays specified amount or thickness of primer, protective, decorative, or finish coatings, such as paint, lacquer, sealer, or enamel, onto prepared surfaces, using spray equipment. Strips, sands, masks, and repaints surfaces, and blends and polishes finish to match surrounding areas, manually or using portable power tools. May apply or retouch paint, using brush. May lay out and paint insignias, symbols, designs, or other markings on painted surfaces, according to blueprints or specifications, using stencils, patterns, measuring instruments, brushes, or spray equipment. May regulate controls on equipment to cure and dry paint or other coatings. May set up portable ventilators, exhaust units, ladders, and scaffolding prior to painting. May operate lifting and moving devices to move materials and equipment and access areas to be painted. May remove accessories from motor vehicles, such as chrome, mirrors, and windshield wipers, prior to repainting. May be designated according to vehicle painted as Auto-Body Painter (automotive ser.); Painter, Aircraft (aircraft mfg.; air trans.); Painter, Aircraft-Production (aircraft mfg.); Painter, Automotive (automotive ser.); Painter, Decorative-Commercial Aircraft (aircraft mfg.).
GOE: 05.10.07 STRENGTH: M GED: R3 M2 L3 SVP: 6 DLU: 89

845.381-018 PAINT SPRAYER, SANDBLASTER (concrete prod.)
Spray paints and sandblasts heavy equipment, such as concrete mixer trucks, boom trucks, and payloaders, using spray gun and sandblasting equipment: Cleans grease, dirt, dried concrete, old paint, and rust from equipment, using solvent, water, rags, brushes, pneumatic wire brush, and chipping hammer. Cleans and prepares surface for painting, using air-powered sandblasting equipment. Applies paper and masking tape to protect unpainted surfaces, such as windows and trim. Stencils lettering and other identifying information on vehicles according to specifications. Selects paint according to company color scheme and specifications. Stirs paint, pours paint into spray container, and applies primer or finish coat of paint, using spray gun. Paints areas inaccessible to spray gun, using paint brush. Disassembles paint and sandblasting equipment and cleans equipment, using solvent, wire brushes, and dry cloth.
GOE: 05.10.07 STRENGTH: M GED: R3 M2 L1 SVP: 4 DLU: 86

845.681-010 RAILROAD-CAR LETTERER (r.r. trans.) alternate titles: painter, railroad car
Paints railroad freight cars and applies decalcomania lettering: Removes old paint, using blowtorch or paint remover and hand scraper. Mixes and matches

paints, following color charts. Paints cars, using brushes or spray gun. Cuts stencils, tacks stencils on car, and paints over stencils with brush or spray gun. Applies decalcomania lettering to interior and exterior surfaces of car. Paints black line around letters and numbers for emphasis, using brush.
GOE: 01.06.03 STRENGTH: L GED: R3 M2 L2 SVP: 7 DLU: 77

845.684-010 CAR SCRUBBER (railroad equip.) alternate titles: car cleaner; passenger-car scrubber
Cleans surfaces of railroad cars preparatory to painting: Strips car of articles, such as sign frames, signal cords, curtains, seat cushions, and window frames, using handtools. Sweeps or blows dirt from car, using broom or airhose. Scrubs surfaces of car, using brush, sponge, and cleaning solution. Rubs varnished surfaces of car, after painting, with powdered pumice stone and cloth to attain smooth even finish. Scrapes excess paint from window glass, using sharp edged instrument. May sand surface areas to remove paint, using emery cloth, and sandpaper. May mask areas not to be painted, using tape and masking liquid.
GOE: 05.12.18 STRENGTH: M GED: R2 M1 L1 SVP: 3 DLU: 77

845.684-014 PAINTER HELPER, AUTOMOTIVE (automotive ser.) alternate titles: sander
Assists PAINTER, TRANSPORTATION EQUIPMENT (aircraft mfg.; air trans.; automotive ser.) 845.381-014 by preparing surfaces of automotive vehicles, such as automobiles, buses, and trucks, for repainting and polishes repainted vehicles: Sands rough spots on automotive vehicle. Sprays scratched areas with filler solution, using spray gun. Applies paper and masking tape to protect unpainted surfaces, such as bumpers, windows, and chrome trim. Removes gloss from intermediate coats of paint, using wet sandpaper, to ensure adherence of next coat. Polishes final coat of paint, using polishing compound and cloth. Paints surfaces not readily accessible, such as wheels and underside of fenders, using brush and spray gun. May remove and replace chrome moldings and trim. May brush or spray undercoating material on replaced parts. Performs other duties as described under HELPER (any industry) Master Title.
GOE: 05.12.12 STRENGTH: M GED: R2 M1 L1 SVP: 4 DLU: 77

849 PAINTING, PLASTERING, WATERPROOFING, CEMENTING, AND RELATED OCCUPATIONS, N.E.C.

This group includes occupations, not elsewhere classified, concerned with painting, plastering, waterproofing, cementing, and related activities.

849.137-010 DISPATCHER (construction)
Supervises and coordinates activities of workers engaged in weighing, mixing, and shipping concrete and concrete aggregates. Performs duties as described under SUPERVISOR (any industry) Master Title.
GOE: 05.09.01 STRENGTH: L GED: R4 M3 L3 SVP: 6 DLU: 77

849.381-010 AIRPLANE COVERER (aircraft mfg.; air trans.) alternate titles: dope-and-fabric worker; doper
Fabricates, installs, and sprays cloth airplane surface coverings, using handtools and portable power tools: Marks dimensions of surface on cloth parts, using chalk and templates. Cuts cloth to size, using scissors or cutting machine. Operates sewing machine to stitch cloth to form envelope that fits structure to be covered and reinforces envelope with cloth tape. Fastens fabric parts to structure, using cement, needle and thread, or metal strips and screws. Sprays covering with water to produce smooth surface. Applies diluted dope to prime and tighten fabric, using handbrush. Brushes on clear and silver dope to strengthen and preserve fabric. Applies pigmented dope, using brush or spray gun to color and finish fabric. May fabricate patterns and templates.
GOE: 06.01.04 STRENGTH: M GED: R3 M2 L2 SVP: 7 DLU: 77

849.484-010 BOILER RELINER, PLASTIC BLOCK (foundry) alternate titles: plastic installer
Relines furnace with plastic block refractory material, using handtools: Removes worn or damaged lining, using handtools. Measures furnace wall and cuts required number of sheets from plastic block, using saw. Drills holes in wall and bolts overlapping layers of plastic to walls. Hammers surface to compress layers into solid sheet.
GOE: 05.10.01 STRENGTH: M GED: R2 M2 L1 SVP: 4 DLU: 77

849.665-010 PUMP TENDER, CEMENT BASED MATERIALS (concrete prod.; construction)
Tends one or more machines that pump concrete, grout, or dry mixtures of sand and cement through hoses to fill forms and crevices or to coat surfaces: Positions hose or temporary pipeline and snaps couplings together. Shovels materials into hopper, moves lever to discharge materials from skip into hopper, or signals CONCRETE-MIXING-TRUCK DRIVER (construction) to fill hopper with concrete. Moves controls to start and operate mixer. Starts pump or compressor and turns valves to regulate air pressure and flow of materials through hose. May aim hose nozzle into space to be filled or at surface to be coated. May lubricate and repair machinery. May be designated according to type of machine tended as Cement-Gun Operator (concrete prod.; construction); Concrete-Gun Operator (construction); Concrete-Pump Operator (construction); Grout-Pump Operator (construction).
GOE: 05.12.06 STRENGTH: L GED: R2 M1 L1 SVP: 4 DLU: 77

849.684-010 BOAT BUFFER, PLASTIC (ship-boat mfg.)
Applies buffing compound with brush and buffs hulls, decks, and cabins of fiberglass boats to impart glossy finish, using portable electric buffer. May sand rough areas, using sandpaper.

GOE: 06.04.24 STRENGTH: M GED: R1 M1 L1 SVP: 3 DLU: 77

85 EXCAVATING, GRADING, PAVING, AND RELATED OCCUPATIONS

This division includes occupations concerned with operating heavy earth-moving equipment in removal and placement of earth materials and grading earth surfaces; laying concrete and other hard-surface paving materials in highway, airport, and related construction; building surface or subsurface drainage systems and pipelines; and related activities including blasting, haulage, and pick-and-shovel work.

850 EXCAVATING, GRADING, AND RELATED OCCUPATIONS

This group includes occupations concerned with removing earth materials to and from open or underground excavations, including mines; dredging irrigation ditches, canals, and inland or offshore marine channels; and related activities, such as tending air locks and operating underground haulage equipment. Occupations in extraction of minerals are included in Division 93.

850.133-010 SUPERVISOR, RECLAMATION (mine & quarry)
Supervises and coordinates activities of workers engaged in restoration of land areas following surface mining operations: Studies engineering survey data and confers with mining officials to establish reclamation program in conformance with regulations. Directs grading crews to fill, grade, and contour land or to prepare certain areas for impoundment of water in artificial lakes. Inspects equipment for compliance with safety regulations. Maintains records of land areas restored.
GOE: 05.11.02 STRENGTH: L GED: R4 M3 L4 SVP: 7 DLU: 77

850.137-010 SUPERVISOR, CORE DRILLING (construction) alternate titles: test-boring crew chief
Supervises and coordinates activities of field crew engaged in obtaining substrata core samples for analysis of geological character of ground, nature of ore, or type and strength of foundation materials: Directs workers engaged in transporting bulldozers, trucks, core drills, and other machinery and equipment to work area. Directs workers engaged in boring operations and determines sequence of drilling, bit pressure, rate of feed, and location of drillings to comply with specifications. Removes cores and samples of formations from borings, and conducts preliminary geological classification based on color and density of sample, and type of material, such as clay, gravel, or silt. Marks location and hole number on sample or container for laboratory analysis. Records location, depth, and soil content of borings for use as reference by design and layout personnel, and for inclusion in subsequent construction contracts. Cooperates with property owners and municipal officials to avoid damage to property and equipment. Performs other duties as described under SUPERVISOR (any industry) Master Title.
GOE: 05.11.01 STRENGTH: L GED: R4 M3 L3 SVP: 7 DLU: 77

850.137-014 SUPERVISOR, LABOR GANG (construction)
Supervises and coordinates activities of work crews engaged in digging and backfilling excavations for laying of pipelines or structure footings. Performs duties as described under SUPERVISOR (any industry) Master Title. May be designated according to specific activities of workers supervised as Supervisor, Backfilling (construction); Supervisor, Ditching (construction).
GOE: 05.12.01 STRENGTH: M GED: R4 M2 L3 SVP: 6 DLU: 77

850.137-018 SUPERVISOR, RIPRAP PLACING (construction)
Supervises and coordinates activities of workers engaged in placing stone on earthen slopes of structures, such as dikes and dams, to prevent soil erosion. Performs duties as described under SUPERVISOR (any industry) Master Title.
GOE: 05.12.01 STRENGTH: L GED: R4 M3 L2 SVP: 6 DLU: 77

850.381-010 MINER (construction)
Drills and blasts earth and rock excavations to construct underground shafts and tunnels for projects, such as roads, railways, and waterways: Sets up pneumatic drilling machinery and moves lever controlling drilling action to drill blastholes in *tunnel heading* according to spacing, angle, and depth of hole specified by SUPERVISOR, TUNNEL HEADING (construction). Loads blastholes and fires powder charges to loosen earth and rock [BLASTER (any industry)]. Wedges, nails, or bolts timber or steel retaining structures to prevent cave-ins. May work in caissons. When concerned with erection of breast boards (timber bracing) to shore tunnel heading, may be designated Breast Worker (construction).
GOE: 05.11.01 STRENGTH: H GED: R4 M3 L2 SVP: 7 DLU: 77

850.387-010 INSPECTOR OF DREDGING (water trans.)
Estimates quantity of material dredged from bed of waterway, according to depth of residue deposited in scow, to ensure that dredging depth conforms to engineering specifications. Keeps records of findings. May drop measured lengths of weighted cable from scow to verify dredging depth.
GOE: 05.07.01 STRENGTH: L GED: R4 M3 L3 SVP: 6 DLU: 77

850.467-010 GRADE CHECKER (construction)
Sets grade stakes to guide earth moving equipment operators in sloping highways and fill embankments, using measuring instruments and handtools: Reads

survey stakes along highway right-of-way to determine grade specification for embankment. Measures horizontally and vertically, in specified ratio, from survey stake to juncture of embankment and initial excavation, using survey rod and eye level. Sets grade stakes, using hatchet, and chalk-marks excavation reference points on stake. Repeats measuring and staking at specified intervals to form horizontal stakeline along embankment. Observes excavating activities to verify conformance to stake references and notifies equipment operators or supervisor of deviations.
GOE: 05.03.01 STRENGTH: L GED: R3 M2 L2 SVP: 4 DLU: 77

850.662-010   HORIZONTAL-EARTH-BORING-MACHINE OPERATOR (construction) alternate titles: boring-machine operator; tunneling-machine operator

Sets up and operates boring machine to drill horizontal holes through earth banks for installation of pipelines under highways, railroads, canals, and other obstructions: Assembles and positions machine, augers, and casing pipes. Signals operator of crane to lower boring equipment into previously dug starter hole. Verifies depth and level of boring position, using surveyor's level and spirit level. Starts engine and moves levers to rotate and feed auger into earth, and simultaneously activates hydraulic ram that forces casing into hole. Retracts auger and forces earth cuttings back through casing to permit coupling additional sections of casing and auger. May operate machine which flushes and pumps earth cuttings from hole. May operate boring machine that drives pilot hole through earth bank and pulls auger bit back through bank to cut hole of required diameter.
GOE: 05.11.01 STRENGTH: M GED: R3 M2 L2 SVP: 5 DLU: 77

850.662-014   ROCK-DRILL OPERATOR II (construction) alternate titles: drifter

Operates drill supported by upright column, to drill through rock in construction work, such as tunnels, highways, or dams: Fits bit in chuck of drifter (drill). Regulates valve to release compressed air that activates drill. Turns screw to feed drill into rock. Regulates flow of water to remove dust and debris from hole, or blows dust out of hole with compressed air.
GOE: 05.11.01 STRENGTH: H GED: R3 M1 L1 SVP: 5 DLU: 77

850.663-010   DREDGE OPERATOR (construction; mine & quarry) alternate titles: dredge pumper

Operates power-driven dredge to excavate and maintain navigable channels in waterways and to mine sand and gravel at bottom of lakes, rivers, and streams: Directs workers engaged in placing shore anchors and cables, laying additional lengths of pipes from dredge to shore, and in pumping water from pontoons. Starts and stops engines to operate equipment. Moves levers to place dredge in position for excavation, engage hydraulic pump, raise and lower suction boom, and control rotation of cutterhead. Lowers anchor pole to verify depth of excavation, using winch, or scans depth gauge to determine depth of excavation. Starts power winch that draws in or lets out cable to change position of dredge, or pulls in and lets out cable manually.
GOE: 05.11.01 STRENGTH: M GED: R3 M2 L2 SVP: 5 DLU: 77

850.663-014   ELEVATING-GRADER OPERATOR (construction) alternate titles: plow holder; plow shaker

Operates self-powered or tractor-drawn elevating grader to plow and scrape up dirt and deposit dirt in trucks, stockpiles, or earth fills: Starts engine to drive machine or signals TRACTOR OPERATOR (any industry) to guide movement of tractor-drawn machine. Moves levers to raise and lower plowing disk and conveyor.
GOE: 05.11.01 STRENGTH: M GED: R3 M1 L1 SVP: 6 DLU: 77

850.663-018   LOCK TENDER II (construction)

Operates electrically powered locomotive or electrically driven winch to move narrow-gauge railroad car into or out of material lock (pressurized air chamber) during sewer or tunnel construction: Observes signals of LOCK TENDER (construction) I, to determine when specified air pressure has been reached. Couples cars or fastens winch hook to cars, and moves hand or foot controls to engage winch or start locomotive.
GOE: 05.11.01 STRENGTH: L GED: R3 M1 L1 SVP: 4 DLU: 77

850.663-022   MOTOR-GRADER OPERATOR (construction) alternate titles: blade-grader operator; motor-patrol operator; power-grader operator; road grader; road-hogger operator

Operates self-propelled grader to spread and level dirt, gravel, and stone, to grade specifications in construction and maintenance of earthwork structures, such as highways, streets, airports, dikes, and temporary roads: Drives grader and moves levers to regulate height and angle of grader blade, lower scarifier that loosens packed soil to permit grading, and to tilt front wheels of grader when making sharp turns. Drives grader in successive passes over working area, observing reference stakes or hand signals of assisting worker, to level surface to specified grade. Feels lever and listens to sound of engine to determine depth of cut. May perform fine or rough grading and be designated Motor Grader, Fine Grade (construction); Motor Grader, Rough Grade (construction). May operate tractor drawn grader to cut and smooth subgrade on street and highway paving projects and be designated Subgrader Operator (construction).
GOE: 05.11.01 STRENGTH: M GED: R3 M1 L1 SVP: 5 DLU: 77

850.663-026   STRIPPING-SHOVEL OPERATOR (mine & quarry)

Operates stripping shovel to remove overburden at strip mine or open pit preparatory to extracting operations: Moves levers and depresses pedals to scoop

up blast-loosened dirt and rock from top of coal, ore, or rock seam and to deposit overburden in void left by preceding strip. Piles heavy rock at base and lighter materials on top to build permanent *spoil pile*. Signals BULLDOZER OPERATOR (any industry) I, to scrape scattered rock and dirt into pile within reach of shovel. May repair and replace shovel parts, such as gears, bearings, and bucket teeth, using handtools.
GOE: 05.11.02 STRENGTH: M GED: R3 M1 L1 SVP: 5 DLU: 77

850.682-010   SHIELD RUNNER (construction) alternate titles: erector operator; hydraulic operator; shield operator

Sets up and operates equipment to advance steel framework (shield) within tunnel during construction: Turns handcrank to regulate hydraulic valves that advance jacks used to push forward tunnel shield that supports overlying ground during tunnel construction. Moves levers to regulate movement of steel arm attached to shield to lift metal segments of *tunnel heading* into position.
GOE: 05.11.01 STRENGTH: L GED: R3 M1 L1 SVP: 5 DLU: 77

850.683-010   BULLDOZER OPERATOR I (any industry) alternate titles: grader operator

Operates tractor equipped with concave blade attached across front to gouge out, level, and distribute earth and to push trees and rocks from land preparatory to constructing roads and buildings or planting crops, or in mining, quarrying, and lumbering operations: Fastens attachments to tractor with clevis or wedge-pin hitches. Connects hydraulic hoses, belts, mechanical linkage, or power takeoff shaft to tractor to provide power to raise, lower, or tilt attachment. Moves levers to control tool bars, carriers, and disks. Moves levers and depresses pedals to maneuver tractor and raise, lower, and tilt attachment to clear right-of-way. Feels lever and listens for stalling action of engine to estimate depth of cut. Drives bulldozer in successive passes over terrain to raise or lower terrain to specified grade following markings on grade stakes or hand signals. Greases, oils, and performs minor repairs on tractor, using grease gun, oilcans, and handtools. When required to work to close tolerances, may be designated Fine-Grade-Bulldozer Operator (any industry). When operating bulldozer to loosen soil, may be designated Scarifier Operator (any industry). May be designated according to type of tractor operated as Crawler-Tractor Operator (any industry); Forest Fire Equipment Operator (government ser.); or attachment added as Angledozer Operator (any industry). May operate bulldozer to scrape surface clay to determine existence and types of clay deposits or to gather clay into piles preparatory to removal to brick-and-tile manufacturing plant and be designated Scraper Operator (mine & quarry).
GOE: 05.11.01 STRENGTH: H GED: R3 M2 L2 SVP: 5 DLU: 81

850.683-014   DITCHER OPERATOR (r.r. trans.)

Operates railcar-mounted toothed bucket to scoop fallen rock from ditches beside railroad track for removal to landfill area. Moves levers to guide bucket to scooping and dumping areas and dumps load in designated areas. Stops or resumes operation in response to railroad traffic signals.
GOE: 05.11.01 STRENGTH: L GED: R3 M1 L1 SVP: 4 DLU: 77

850.683-018   DRAGLINE OPERATOR (any industry)

Operates power-driven crane equipped with dragline bucket, suspended from boom by cable to excavate or move sand, gravel, clay, mud, coal, or other materials: Drives machine to work site. Moves hand levers and depresses pedals to rotate crane on chassis and position boom above excavation point, to raise and lower boom, to lower bucket to material, to drag bucket toward crane to excavate or move material, to place bucket over unloading point, and to tilt bucket to release material. May direct workers engaged in placing blocks and outriggers to prevent capsizing of machine when lifting heavy loads. May be designated according to type of chassis or power unit as Crawler-Dragline Operator (any industry); Diesel-Dragline Operator (any industry); Electric-Dragline Operator (any industry); Gasoline-Dragline Operator (any industry); or material excavated as Clay Hoister (cement); Walking-Dragline Operator (any industry).
GOE: 05.11.04 STRENGTH: M GED: R3 M2 L2 SVP: 5 DLU: 77

850.683-022   FORM-GRADER OPERATOR (construction) alternate titles: concrete-paving-form grader

Operates machine equipped with adjustable, revolving cutterhead to cut trench for concrete road to specified grade: Aligns grader with stakes and guidelines on ground. Lowers cutterhead and aligns depth gauge marker with guideline to control depth of trench. Moves throttle to regulate speed of machine and cutterhead. Raises and lowers cutterhead to reduce base material by making several shallow passes. Observes spiral conveyor that automatically moves loose dirt to side of trench.
GOE: 05.11.01 STRENGTH: L GED: R3 M2 L1 SVP: 4 DLU: 77

850.683-026   MUCKING-MACHINE OPERATOR (construction) alternate titles: mucker operator

Operates powered shovel or scraper loader (mucking machine) to hoist earth and rock, excavated from *tunnel headings*, onto cars or trucks: Moves levers to control movement of machine on narrow gauge track and to activate buckets or scrapers that scoop up or dig into materials and deposit them into dinkey cars or sweep materials from sides and bottom of tunnel heading and deposit materials on machine mounted conveyor.
GOE: 05.11.01 STRENGTH: L GED: R3 M1 L1 SVP: 3 DLU: 77

850.683-030   POWER-SHOVEL OPERATOR (any industry)

Operates power-driven machine, equipped with movable shovel, to excavate or move coal, dirt, rock, sand, and other materials: Receives written or oral in-

structions from supervisor regarding material to move or excavate. Pushes levers and depresses pedals to move machine, to lower and push shovel into stockpiled material, to lower and dig shovel into surface of ground, and to lift, swing, and dump contents of shovel into truck, car, or onto conveyor, hopper, or stockpile. Observes markings on ground, hand signals, or grade stakes to remove material, when operating machine at excavation site. May tend mining machinery, such as pulverizer. May be designated according to type of power unit as Diesel-Power-Shovel Operator (any industry); Electric-Power-Shovel Operator (any industry); Gasoline-Power-Shovel Operator (any industry). May operate power shovel equipped with duck-bill scoop and be designated Duck-Bill Operator (mine & quarry). May operate power shovel which digs by pulling dipper toward machine and be designated Back-Hoe Operator (any industry). May operate power shovel on which excavating bucket runs outward along horizontal boom to dig into materials and be designated Skimmer-Scoop Operator (any industry). May operate power shovel designed to be converted to crane, skimmer scoop, backhoe, or dragline and be designated Convertible-Power-Shovel Operator (any industry).
GOE: 05.11.01 STRENGTH: M GED: R3 M1 L1 SVP: 5 DLU: 80

850.683-034 ROCK-DRILL OPERATOR I (construction)
Drives and operates tractor-mounted rock drilling machine to drill explosive-charge holes through hard materials to facilitate blasting operations: Moves lever to set out-rigger jacks to level machine. Verifies level of machine, using spirit level. Inserts steel drill or rock bit into chuck. Moves levers to start, stop, and control drilling speed of machine. Drills holes and observes depth gauge on drill stem to verify depth of hole specified by BLASTER (any industry). May be designated according to type of machine operated as Reciprocating-Drill Operator (any industry); Rotary-Rock-Drilling-Machine Operator (any industry).
GOE: 05.11.01 STRENGTH: L GED: R3 M2 L2 SVP: 5 DLU: 77

850.683-038 SCRAPER OPERATOR (construction)
Operates tractor-drawn or self-propelled scraper to move, haul, and grade earth on construction sites, such as roadbeds, ditch banks, and water reservoirs: Moves switches, levers, and pedals to control loading gate on bucket (scraper), to adjust depth of cut, to raise and close filled bucket for hauling, and to spread or dump earth.
GOE: 05.11.01 STRENGTH: M GED: R3 M1 L2 SVP: 5 DLU: 77

850.683-042 TOWER-EXCAVATOR OPERATOR (construction) alternate titles: cable-tower operator; guyline operator; slackline operator; tower-dragline operator
Operates power machinery to activate dragline bucket slung between portable towers or to excavate and load sand, gravel, earth, or similar material into trucks or onto conveyors: Moves hand and foot levers to raise and lower bucket, load and dump bucket, and move bucket along slack line slung between towers to unloading point. May direct workers engaged in changing position of towers.
GOE: 05.11.04 STRENGTH: L GED: R3 M1 L1 SVP: 5 DLU: 77

850.683-046 UTILITY-TRACTOR OPERATOR (construction)
Drives pneumatic-tired tractor and controls grading or digging attachments to move and level materials, such as dirt and gravel, for construction of driveways, parking lots, and streets: Moves levers to engage gears to raise and lower attachment. Adjusts and controls bulldozer attachment to level earth to specified depth. Pulls grader attachment over cutout to trim edges, level surface, and spread rock. Controls back-hoe, trench-digging attachment, or lift-scoop attachment to dig and backfill trenches.
GOE: 05.11.01 STRENGTH: L GED: R3 M1 L1 SVP: 4 DLU: 77

850.684-010 EXCAVATOR (any industry)
Digs at archeological excavation sites to unearth pottery, bones, implements, and other archeological specimens, using shovel, pickax, scraper, and dusting broom.
GOE: 05.12.03 STRENGTH: H GED: R3 M1 L1 SVP: 3 DLU: 77

850.684-014 HORIZONTAL-EARTH-BORING-MACHINE-OPERATOR HELPER (construction) alternate titles: boring-machine-operator helper
Performs any combination of following duties to aid in drilling of horizontal holes for installation of pipelines under highways, railroads, canals, and other obstructions: Lays foundation timbers for boring machine and places timber braces to hold machine in place. Couples auger sections together and bolts sections to drive shaft. Removes dirt from hole, using shovel. Removes seepage water from boring machine pit, using portable sump. May place props between hydraulic rams and end of casing pipe. May hammer steel wedges into shaft collar to lock auger drive to ram yoke. May weld sections of casing pipe together, using arc-welding equipment.
GOE: 05.12.02 STRENGTH: H GED: R2 M1 L1 SVP: 2 DLU: 77

850.684-018 STRIPPING-SHOVEL OILER (mine & quarry) alternate titles: oiler
Lubricates stripping shovel used to remove overburden at strip mine or open pit: Observes panel to determine efficiency of automatic lubrication system. Heats dope (heavy duty lubricant) in dope box and sprays lubricant onto gears and other moving parts. Oils and greases shovel while in operation, using hand grease gun and oilcan. Inspects parts, such as swing pinions, boom pins, hoist gears, brakes, boom cable, and supports to detect wear. Records production, re-

pairs, and downtime. May start driving mechanism of shovel and guide shovel into working position. May operate stripping shovel [STRIPPING-SHOVEL OPERATOR (mine & quarry)]. May lubricate other mining and quarrying equipment and be designated Dragline Oiler (mine & quarry); Walking-Dragline Oiler (mine & quarry).
GOE: 05.12.08 STRENGTH: H GED: R3 M1 L1 SVP: 6 DLU: 77

851   DRAINAGE AND RELATED OCCUPATIONS

This group includes occupations concerned with placing, joining, aligning, and sealing pipes in excavations, using caulking tools, sealing compounds, ropes, pipe-supporting equipment, and other devices and materials.

851.137-010 BANK BOSS (construction) alternate titles: levee superintendent
Supervises and coordinates activities of workers engaged in placing shore sections of discharge pipe from suction dredge and in grading material discharged from dredge onto shore. Determines location of discharge pipes, applying knowledge of material flow rate, capacity of fill leveling equipment, irregularities of terrain, and ultimate use of landfill. Performs duties as described under SUPERVISOR (any industry) Master Title.
GOE: 05.12.01 STRENGTH: L GED: R4 M3 L3 SVP: 7 DLU: 77

851.137-014 SUPERVISOR, SEWER MAINTENANCE (government ser.)
Supervises and coordinates activities of workers engaged in repair and maintenance of sewers: Directs workers in connecting sewer lines to mains. Inspects construction of new sewers and manholes to ensure conformance with specifications, according to blueprints. Directs workers in cleaning storm, water, and sewer catch basins, repairing broken sewer lines, and replacing worn and damaged parts. May assist workers in repairing breaks in sewers. May operate and repair equipment, such as jackhammers, pumps, air compressors, and other equipment, used in repair and maintenance of sewers. May direct workers in operation of mobile closed-circuit television monitoring system to inspect internal areas of sewer lines.
GOE: 05.12.01 STRENGTH: L GED: R4 M3 L3 SVP: 6 DLU: 77

851.262-010 SEWER-LINE REPAIRER, TELE-GROUT (sanitary ser.)
Operates mobile television and chemical sealing units to conduct internal inspection of sewer lines and to seal defects for prevention of water infiltration: Locates line sections to be inspected, using map, and determines setup procedures. Turns knobs to activate television equipment for video viewing. Adjusts TV camera and monitors controls for optimal clarity and contrast. Locates and identifies infiltration points and sewer defects to determine extent of sewer line damage. Prepares description of each sewer defect, and records pertinent data, including exact location of defect. Photographs screen picture of serious or unusual irregularities, using camera. Determines chemical composition of sealing compound based on type of sealing activity necessary to seal defects, and oversees preparation of compound. Turns control knobs of sealing unit to inflate packer to desired pressure, to air test infiltration point, to determine volume of needed sealing compound, and to pump correct amount of sealing chemicals. Turns air release valve to deflate packer after allowing specified time for sealing compound to set. Communicates with workers, using intercom system, and confers with supervisors to discuss condition of sewer lines, based on television inspection. Services, adjusts, and makes minor repairs to equipment and attachments. Gives directions to workers in efficient and safe use of television and grout, in work methods, and safety precautions. Drives television and grout unit truck.
GOE: 05.10.01 STRENGTH: L GED: R4 M3 L2 SVP: 7 DLU: 86

851.362-010 SEWER-LINE PHOTO-INSPECTOR (sanitary ser.)
Operates camera to photograph inside of sewer lines to conduct inspection and determine need for repairs: Locates line sections to be photographed, using map. Determines setup procedures. Floats rope used to pull camera to adjacent manhole to thread sewer lines. Directs workers in setting up cable stands over manholes. Loads camera with film and inspects battery of camera. Depresses button on camera to photograph small blackboard giving location of manhole, manhole number, data, and weather conditions for future reference. Attaches pulling cable to camera and instructs workers to position camera in sewer line and to turn cable stand handles that enable camera to move inside pipe. Snaps pictures at designated intervals until camera reaches downstream manhole. Detaches camera from cable, rewinds cable into reel, and disassembles equipment. Removes film and batteries from camera and sends film to be developed. Confers with supervisor to discuss condition of sewer lines as indicated in developed photographs. Drives pickup truck to haul crew and equipment. Services, adjusts, and makes minor repairs to camera, equipment, and attachments. Communicates with supervisor, using radio telephone. Gives directions to workers in efficient and safe use of camera and equipment, work methods, and safety precautions. Prepares daily report listing lines photographed.
GOE: 05.07.01 STRENGTH: M GED: R3 M2 L2 SVP: 5 DLU: 86

851.383-010 IRRIGATION SYSTEM INSTALLER (construction)
Installs underground pipe for farm irrigation systems performing any combination of following tasks: Drives straight-bed truck with attached pole trailer [POLE-TRUCK DRIVER (construction; tel. & tel.; utilities)] to deliver pipe, risers, and pump stands to installation site. Operates crawler-type trench digger to dig trench along prestaked route. Measures plastic pipe to specified length and cuts pipe, using handsaw. Applies plastic cement to pipe and coupler, using

brush, and fits pipe and coupler together. Attaches risers to pipe at specified intervals, using plastic cement and fittings. Digs hole for pump stand, using shovel, and lowers stand and assembled pipe into excavation by hand. Welds mating collar to pump stand [WELDER, ARC (welding)]. Operates crawler-type tractor to cover pipe [BULLDOZER OPERATOR (any industry) I].
GOE: 05.11.01 STRENGTH: M GED: R3 M2 L2 SVP: 5 DLU: 77

851.663-010 SEPTIC-TANK INSTALLER (construction)
Operates back-hoe (trench-excavating machine) to dig trenches for installation of septic tanks and drain lines for sewage disposal system: Reads blueprints to determine location of septic tank and drainpipes. Operates back-hoe to dig and refill trenches for septic tank and tile drainpipes and to transfer crushed rock or gravel to provide drainage base for pipes. Lowers septic tank into excavation, using back-hoe as hoist. Directs workers engaged in spreading crushed rock and gravel, in laying tile drainpipe, and in connecting drainpipes to branch sewers. May verify levels of rock or gravel, base, and tile drainpipe, using surveyor's or carpenter's level.
GOE: 05.11.01 STRENGTH: M GED: R3 M2 L2 SVP: 4 DLU: 77

853   PAVING OCCUPATIONS, ASPHALT AND CONCRETE

This group includes occupations concerned with combining asphaltic or concrete ingredients at mobile batching plants; applying asphalt or concrete to roadbeds and other substructures; and shaping and finishing asphalt or concrete; involves operating or tending machines for mixing, spreading, compacting, and leveling paving materials, and using trowels, screeds, rakes, shovels, and other devices.

853.133-010 SUPERVISOR, ASPHALT PAVING (construction)
Supervises and coordinates activities of workers engaged in spreading, rolling, and tamping asphalt or similar material to form surfaces of highways, streets, parking lots, and aircraft landing strips: Calculates number of trucks required to haul asphalt from mix plant according to capacity of vehicles, traffic conditions, distance from work site, and productivity of drivers. Tours work site to ascertain progress in meeting time schedules and to detect insufficient utilization of workers and equipment.Measures slope and thickness of paving to verify compliance with contract. Performs other duties as described under SUPERVISOR (any industry) Master Title. May supervise workers engaged in patching asphalt paving and be designated Supervisor, Patching (construction).
GOE: 05.11.01 STRENGTH: L GED: R4 M3 L3 SVP: 8 DLU: 77

853.137-010 SUPERVISOR, MIXING PLACE (construction)
Supervises and coordinates activities of workers engaged in mixing ingredients into concrete and in pouring and finishing concrete in highway and airport runway construction. Performs duties as described under SUPERVISOR (any industry) Master Title.
GOE: 05.10.01 STRENGTH: L GED: R4 M3 L2 SVP: 7 DLU: 77

853.663-010 ASPHALT-PAVING-MACHINE OPERATOR (construction) alternate titles: asphalt-spreader operator; bituminous-paving-machine operator; blacktop-paver operator; blacktop spreader; mechanical-spreader operator; paving-machine operator, asphalt or bituminous
Operates machine that spreads and levels hot-mix bituminous paving material on subgrade of highways and streets: Bolts extensions to screed to adjust width, using wrenches. Lights burners to heat screed. Starts engine and controls paving machine to push dump truck and maintain constant flow of asphalt into hopper. Observes distribution of paving material along screed and controls direction of screed to eliminate voids at curbs and joints. Turns valves to regulate temperature of asphalt flowing from hopper when asphalt begins to harden on screed.
GOE: 05.11.01 STRENGTH: M GED: R3 M1 L1 SVP: 5 DLU: 77

853.663-014 CONCRETE-PAVING-MACHINE OPERATOR (construction)
Operates concrete paving machine to spread and smooth freshly poured concrete surfaces for concrete roads and landing field: Starts machine, engages clutch, and shifts gears to control machine's movement along rails on concrete forms. Moves levers and turns handwheels to lower attachment that spreads wet concrete within forms. Observes surface of concrete to point out low spots for workers to add concrete. Operates machine with attachments to successively vibrate, screed, strike-off (remove excess from), and float surface of concrete, to spray on curing compound, and cut expansion joints. When cutting expansion joints, places strips of material, such as cork, asphalt, or steel, in joints, or places roll of expansion-joint material on machine that automatically inserts material into joints. When operating machine to screed and float surface, may be designated Concrete-Finishing-Machine Operator (construction). May be designated according to specific function of machine attachment as Center-Line-Cutter Operator (construction); Curing-Machine Operator (construction); Gang-Vibrator Operator (construction); Joint-Machine Operator (construction); Longitudinal-Float Operator (construction). May be designated: Screed Operator (construction); Spreader Operator (construction); Strike-Off-Machine Operator (construction); Vibrating-Screed Operator (construction).
GOE: 05.11.01 STRENGTH: M GED: R3 M1 L1 SVP: 3 DLU: 77

853.663-018 ROAD-OILING-TRUCK DRIVER (construction) alternate titles: bituminous-distributor operator; oil sprayer; oil-spreader operator; oil-spreader-truck operator; road-oil distributor
Drives and operates truck equipped with tank to spray oil or bituminous emulsions on road surfaces: Connects hose from storage tank to truck tank and moves lever to fill pressure tank with bituminous liquid. Regulates burner to heat liquid. Starts auxiliary pump. Drives truck at constant speed to obtain uniform distribution of oil. May signal worker to open discharge valve.
GOE: 05.11.01 STRENGTH: L GED: R3 M1 L1 SVP: 5 DLU: 77

853.663-022 STONE-SPREADER OPERATOR (construction) alternate titles: spreader box operator
Operates stone-spreading machine to lay gravel, stone, and cold-mix asphalt on road surfaces: Hooks spreader to rear of dump truck and trips truck tailgate latch. Signals DUMP-TRUCK DRIVER (any industry) to hoist dump body and dump material into spreader hopper. Adjusts hopper opening to ensure required amount of material is deposited on road surface. Drags material from truck bed, using shovel, to distribute material along length of hopper.
GOE: 05.11.01 STRENGTH: L GED: R3 M1 L1 SVP: 5 DLU: 77

853.665-010 ASPHALT-DISTRIBUTOR TENDER (construction) alternate titles: oil-distributor tender
Tends bituminous distributor on rear of road-oiling truck that sprays tar, asphalt, road oils, and emulsions over highways, streets, and parking areas: Snaps or screws on spray bars to attain required width of spray. Turns valve to regulate flow of material at specified rate. Moves levers to adjust height of spray bar from road surfaces. Signals ROAD-OILING-TRUCK DRIVER (construction) or ASPHALT-PAVING-MACHINE OPERATOR (construction) to start and stop truck or paving machine. Observes distribution of material over road surface to ensure uniform distribution. Turns handwheels to set angle and depth of screed. Verifies depth specifications of compacted asphalt, using depth gauge. Monitors flow gauges, tachometer, and temperature gauge. Oils and lubricates equipment.
GOE: 05.12.14 STRENGTH: L GED: R2 M2 L1 SVP: 2 DLU: 77

853.683-010 CURB-MACHINE OPERATOR (construction)
Drives and operates machine to extrude concrete and asphalt curbing on parking lots: Reads specifications to determine location, width of base, and shape of curbing to be installed. Lays string between reference points and sprays paint along string to form curb-machine guide marks. Brushes cement and water mix onto pavement to provide bond between curbing and pavement. Selects and installs specified curb-forming die into machine, using handtools. Fills hopper of machine with asphalt or concrete mix, using shovel. Starts machine motor, engages clutch, and guides machine that extrudes curbing along guidelines. Smooths edges of curbing, using trowel, and cuts expansion joints in curbing at specified intervals, using edger. Maintains and repairs machine, using mechanics' handtools. Drives curbing machine onto truck trailer and drives truck to transport machine to job site.
GOE: 05.11.01 STRENGTH: H GED: R3 M2 L1 SVP: 4 DLU: 77

853.683-014 HEATER-PLANER OPERATOR (construction) alternate titles: asphalt-surface-heater operator; heater operator
Drives and controls machine that heats and scrapes road surface to smooth surface: Starts burner (heating unit) of machine. Presses lever to lower heating unit over pavement to soften pavement. Turns handwheels to lower and position scraper blade. Drives machine over road to smooth surface.
GOE: 05.11.01 STRENGTH: M GED: R3 M1 L1 SVP: 3 DLU: 77

853.683-018 JOINT-CLEANING-AND-GROOVING-MACHINE OPERATOR (construction) alternate titles: joint-cleaning-machine operator; pavement-joint-cleaning-machine operator ; safety-grooving-machine operator
Operates machine to clean expansion joint grooves or to cut new grooves in concrete or asphalt pavement, and to rout out cracks in concrete and asphalt pavement: Installs cutters in cutterhead and mounts cutterhead on cone of main drum shaft, using handtools. Guides machine along joint or crack, sighting through mirror fastened to front of machine. Lowers and raises cutter according to sounds of blades in contact with paved surface to cut safety grooves in specified paved sections. Measures to verify depth of grooves, using depth gauge and adjusts cutting blades according to depth specifications. Cleans and replaces cutters when dirty or worn.
GOE: 05.11.01 STRENGTH: M GED: R3 M1 L1 SVP: 4 DLU: 77

853.685-010 ASPHALT-HEATER TENDER (construction)
Tends portable or stationary heating unit to heat asphalt for application on road surfaces: Lights fire and opens fuel valves to regulate fuel supply. Screws hose connections to heater unit to connect circulating system between tank and unit. Starts pump to circulate asphalt through heating unit. Observes temperature gauge and adjusts blower and damper controls to regulate heat and maintain required temperature.
GOE: 05.12.10 STRENGTH: L GED: R2 M1 L1 SVP: 3 DLU: 77

859   EXCAVATING, GRADING, PAVING, AND RELATED OCCUPATIONS, N.E.C.

This group includes occupations, not elsewhere classified, concerned with excavating, grading, paving, and related activities.

859.133-010 SUPERVISOR, RIGHT-OF-WAY MAINTENANCE (utilities)

Supervises and coordinates activities of workers engaged in maintaining roads and flood-control facilities along electric power transmission line right-of-way: Reviews work orders to determine types of equipment required for job. Examines maps and blueprints to determine location of transmission line and directs crews to job site. Directs crews in constructing, maintaining, and rerouting sections of roadways and in repairing culverts, retaining walls, bridges, and dikes. Directs paving of areas in and around power plants. Instructs workers in operation of equipment, such as tractors and road graders. Performs other duties as described under SUPERVISOR (any industry) Master Title.
GOE: 05.12.01 STRENGTH: L GED: R4 M3 L3 SVP: 7 DLU: 77

859.137-010 SUPERVISOR, GRADING (construction) alternate titles: supervisor, excavating

Supervises and coordinates activities of workers engaged in excavating and grading right-of-way for construction of projects, such as highways, streets, drainage ditches, and dams: Measures distances from reference points to locate boundaries of construction site. Directs work crews engaged in operating vehicles and machines to dump, scrape, and spread dirt. Verifies curvature of graded surface, using hand level. Performs other duties as described under SUPERVISOR (any industry) Master Title. May supervise bituminous paving crew [SUPERVISOR, ASPHALT PAVING (construction)]. May supervise work crew engaged in operating machines to tamp, roll, and smooth surface for subgrade of highway and be designated Supervisor, Fine Grading (construction). May supervise workers engaged in laying drainage tile and concrete and metal culverts and be designated Supervisor, Culvert Laying (construction). May be designated according to activity of workers supervised as Supervisor, Dumping (construction); Supervisor, Rough Grading (construction).
GOE: 05.11.01 STRENGTH: L GED: R4 M3 L3 SVP: 7 DLU: 77

859.137-014 SUPERVISOR, PILE DRIVING (construction)

Supervises and coordinates activities of workers engaged in driving pilings into ground to provide foundations for structures, such as buildings and bridges, and retaining walls for earth embankments, such as cofferdams: Directs workers engaged in operating machines to drive metal, concrete, and wood piling and metal and wood sheets (sheet piling). May direct workers engaged in setting charges of explosives to remove defective piling. Performs other duties as described under SUPERVISOR (any industry) Master Title.
GOE: 05.11.01 STRENGTH: L GED: R4 M3 L3 SVP: 8 DLU: 77

859.137-018 SUPERVISOR, TUNNEL HEADING (construction) alternate titles: header boss; shifter

Supervises and coordinates activities of tunnel construction crew engaged in sinking shafts, boring tunnels, placing tunnel segments, moving shield forward, and excavating in front of sheild: Determines spacing, alignment, and depth of blast holes. Verifies that shoring, bracing, and movement of tunnel shield conform to safety regulations. Performs other duties as described under SUPERVISOR (any industry) Master Title.
GOE: 05.12.01 STRENGTH: L GED: R4 M3 L3 SVP: 7 DLU: 77

859.261-010 BLASTER (any industry) alternate titles: firer; shooter

Assembles, plants, and detonates charges of industrial explosives to loosen earth, rock, stumps, or to demolish structures to facilitate removal: Examines mass, composition, structure, and location of object to be blasted, estimates amount and determines kind of explosive to be used, and marks location of charge holes for drilling. Assembles primer (blasting cap and fuse or electric squib and booster charge) and places primer with main charge in hole or near object to be blasted. Covers charge with mud, sand, clay, or other material and tamps firm to improve detonation and confine force of blast. Signals to clear area of personnel and equipment. Lights fuse or connects wires from charge to battery or detonator to detonate charge. May operate jackhammer, hand drill, or electric drill to bore holes for charges. May climb cliffs or banks to plant explosive charge, using ropes and safety harness, and be designated High Scaler (construction). May set and detonate explosive charges to improve flow of water into wells and be designated Shooter, Water Well (construction).
GOE: 05.10.06 STRENGTH: H GED: R4 M4 L4 SVP: 7 DLU: 77

859.267-010 STREET-OPENINGS INSPECTOR (utilities) alternate titles: public improvement inspector

Inspects construction and excavation of gas or electric sites to ensure precautions are taken to prevent damage to company facilities: Interprets blueprints and work order specifications and marks location of underground facilities and dimensions of trenches to be dug, using stakes and chalkline. Observes progress of work and reports extent of damages, such as broken or exposed pipes and cables or caved-in vaults, and urgency of repairs required. May coordinate gas or power construction and maintenance projects with underground work of municipal departments and other utilities.
GOE: 05.07.01 STRENGTH: L GED: R4 M3 L3 SVP: 8 DLU: 77

859.281-010 GRAVEL INSPECTOR (construction)

Tests samples of gravel to determine suitability for use in highway construction: Weighs sample before and after heating to determine moisture content. Screens gravel through numbered screens to determine coarseness of sample. May perform other duties in material testing laboratory, such as hardness tests, breakage tests, density tests for flexible base, compression and tensile strength tests, and tests for stress and strain [LABORATORY TESTER (any industry)].
GOE: 05.07.01 STRENGTH: L GED: R4 M3 L3 SVP: 5 DLU: 77

859.362-010 WELL-DRILL OPERATOR (construction) alternate titles: rotary-drill-rig operator; water-well driller

Sets up and operates portable drilling rig (machine and related equipment) to drill wells: Extends stabilizing jackscrews to support and level drill rig. Moves levers to control power-driven winch that raises and extends telescoping derrick. Bolts trusses to derrick and machine frame. Assembles drilling tools, using handtools or power tools. Moves levers and pedals to raise and lower drill tools and well casing into well bore. Moves levers and pedals and turns handwheels to control action of machine that drills or punches well bore and lowers casing into well. Pours water into well or pumps water or slush into well to cool drill bit and remove drillings. Listens to sounds of drilling machine and feels cable or brake to determine changes in rock formations being penetrated or variations in drilling process. Moves levers to adjust stroke and impact of cable tool drilling machine or changes drill bits of rotary drilling machine according to nature of strata encountered. Replaces drill bit with tool to collect samples of earth or rock being penetrated. Inspects core samples to determine nature of strata encountered or takes samples to laboratory for analysis. Records drilling progress and geological data. Splices worn or broken cable. Fabricates well casings and builds up worn drill bits, using oxyacetylene cutting and welding equipment. Retrieves lost equipment from bore holes, using fishing (specialized retrieval) tools and equipment. May repair drill bits, using forging furnace, hammer, and anvil. May be designated according to type drilling rig operated as Well-Drill Operator, Cable Tool (construction); Well-Drill Operator, Rotary Drill (construction). May operate well-drilling rig to restore irrigation, industrial, and domestic water wells to active production and be designated Well-Reactivator Operator (construction).
GOE: 05.11.03 STRENGTH: H GED: R4 M3 L3 SVP: 7 DLU: 77

859.682-010 EARTH-BORING-MACHINE OPERATOR (construction; utilities) alternate titles: earth-auger operator; hole-digger operator; post-hole digger

Operates earth-boring machine, mounted on truck or tractor, to dig holes for poles or posts: Sets auger of specified size into drill spindle, using bolts or pins. Starts drilling engine and moves levers to regulate rate of speed and depth of penetration of auger. May drive truck or tractor to work site. May operate hoist to lift power line poles into position in drilled holes.
GOE: 05.11.01 STRENGTH: M GED: R3 M1 L1 SVP: 4 DLU: 77

859.682-014 FOUNDATION-DRILL OPERATOR (construction)

Operates drilling unit, mounted on truck or crawler track, to drill holes for concrete pier and footing foundations: Raises and lowers boom to specified angle for drilling. Swings boom, controls hoist drums, raises and lowers drill, hoists drill bit, bell reamer, casing, and reinforcement steel into position, and controls rotary table that drives drill into earth. Observes drill stem during drilling operation and increases or decreases brake pressure on drill stem hoist drum to prevent swaying motion. Raises drill stem and swings boom to discharge dirt from drill bit or *bell reamer*. Observes type of earth formation penetrated to determine need for lowering casing into hole to seal off water and prevent cave-in of soft formations.
GOE: 05.11.01 STRENGTH: L GED: R3 M2 L2 SVP: 5 DLU: 77

859.682-018 PILE-DRIVER OPERATOR (construction) alternate titles: hoisting engineer, pile driving

Operates pile driver mounted on skids, barge, crawler treads, or locomotive crane to drive piling as foundations for structures, such as buildings, bridges, and piers: Moves hand and foot levers to control diesel-, electric-, gasoline-, or steam-powered hoisting equipment to position piling leads, hoist piling into leads, and position hammer over top of pile. Moves levers and turns valves to activate power-driven hammer, or raise and lower drophammer which drives piles to required depth. May be designated according to type of power used to activate pile driver as Compressed-Air-Pile-Driver Operator (construction); Diesel-Pile-Driver Operator (construction); or type of piles driven as Concrete-Pile-Driver Operator (construction); Sheet-Pile-Driver Operator (construction); Wood-Pile-Driver Operator (construction); or type of mounting used as Pile-Driver Operator, Barge Mounted (construction). May be designated: Drop-Hammer-Pile-Driver Operator (construction); Electric-Pile-Driver Operator (construction); Steam-Pile-Driver Operator (construction).
GOE: 05.11.01 STRENGTH: M GED: R3 M2 L2 SVP: 5 DLU: 77

859.683-010 OPERATING ENGINEER (construction; mine & quarry) alternate titles: heavy-equipment operator

Operates several types of power construction equipment, such as compressors, pumps, hoists, derricks, cranes, shovels, tractors, scrapers, or motor graders, to excavate, move, and grade earth, erect structural and reinforcing steel, and pour concrete or other hard surface paving materials: Turns valves to control air and water output of compressors and pumps. Adjusts handwheels and depresses pedals to drive machines and control attachments, such as blades, buckets, scrapers, and swing booms. Repairs and maintains equipment. May operate machinery on sales lot or customer's property to demonstrate saleable features of construction equipment and be designated Demonstrator, Construction Equipment (wholesale tr.).
GOE: 05.11.01 STRENGTH: M GED: R3 M1 L2 SVP: 6 DLU: 82

859.683-014 OPERATING-ENGINEER APPRENTICE (construction; mine & quarry) alternate titles: heavy-equipment-operator apprentice

Performs duties as described under APPRENTICE (any industry) Master Title.

GOE: 05.11.01 STRENGTH: M GED: R3 M1 L2 SVP: 6 DLU: 77

859.683-018 RAILWAY-EQUIPMENT OPERATOR (r.r. trans.)

Operates several types of heavy equipment, such as rail-mounted tamping machines, brooms, graders, and ballast cleaning machines to tamp ballast beneath and between ties, to clean tracks, to clean and redistribute ballast, and to grade and level ballast on railroad tracks: Pulls levers and depresses pedals to drive machines and control attachments, such as blades, hydraulic turntables, jacks, brooms, and tampers. Tightens loose bolts and adjusts blades, using wrenches. Lubricates machines, changes oil, and fills hydraulic reservoirs to specified levels. May be designated according to type equipment operated as Ballast-Cleaning-Machine Operator (r.r. trans.); Ballast-Regulator Operator (r.r. trans.); Tamping-Machine Operator (r.r. trans.); Track-Broom Operator (r.r. trans.).

GOE: 05.11.01 STRENGTH: M GED: R3 M2 L2 SVP: 4 DLU: 77

859.683-022 REINFORCING-STEEL-MACHINE OPERATOR (construction)

Drives and operates machine that lays, spaces, and automatically ties steel rods used to reinforce concrete highway paving: Starts machine, engages clutch, and shifts gears to control machine's movement along concrete forms. Observes function of machine to detect irregular spacing of rods and missed ties. Notifies supervisor of equipment malfunction. Maintains equipment according to specifications.

GOE: 05.11.01 STRENGTH: L GED: R3 M1 L1 SVP: 4 DLU: 77

859.683-026 ROAD-MIXER OPERATOR (construction) alternate titles: rotary-soil-stabilizer operator; roto-mixer operator; stabilizer operator; stabilizing-machine operator; traveling-plant operator

Drives and operates machine that mixes waterproofing and binding material with soil to stabilize soil for road surfaces and airport runways: Pushes levers and turns wheels to set depth of scoop and rotary blades that pick up and pulverize soil. Starts engine to propel machine and power-rotary digging and mixing blades. Starts pump and adjusts valve to feed waterproofing compounds and binding materials, such as cement, chemicals, and bituminous binders into mixing mechanism. Steers machine in prescribed path. Inspects earth falling from machine and adjusts valves to regulate flow of liquid, judging content of mixture by appearance of poured soil. May be designated according to type of equipment operated as Pulvi-Mixer Operator (construction); Single-Pass-Soil-Stabilizer Operator (construction).

GOE: 05.11.01 STRENGTH: L GED: R3 M1 L1 SVP: 5 DLU: 77

859.683-030 ROAD-ROLLER OPERATOR (construction) alternate titles: roller operator; roller, pneumatic; roll operator

Drives heavy rolling machine (road roller) to compact earth fills, subgrades, flexible base, and bituminous surface to grade specifications preparatory to construction of highways, streets, and runways: Moves levers, depresses pedals, turns handwheels, and pushes throttle to control and guide machine. Drives machine in successive overlapping passes over surface to be compacted. Determines speed and direction of machine, based on knowledge of compressibility of material under changing temperatures, so that ridges are not formed by excessive pressure. Pushes hand roller and pounds surfaces, using hand tamp, or guides portable power roller over areas not accessible to road roller. May be designated according to surface rolled as Road-Roller Operator, Hot Mix (construction); Subgrade-Roller Operator (construction); or according to source of power used as Diesel-Roller Operator (construction); Gas-Roller Operator (construction).

GOE: 05.11.01 STRENGTH: L GED: R2 M1 L1 SVP: 3 DLU: 77

859.684-010 LANE-MARKER INSTALLER (construction)

Installs button-type lane markers along paved highways and streets, using handtools: Sets signs and cones adjacent to work site to divert flow of traffic. Measures and marks installation locations between survey control points, using tape, string, and chalk. Blends epoxy compounds to form specified mix, using spoon. Applies epoxy to marked locations along roadway, using putty knife, and twists plastic markers to position into epoxy. Sights along button line to verify alignment.

GOE: 05.12.14 STRENGTH: M GED: R2 M2 L1 SVP: 3 DLU: 77

859.687-010 BLASTER HELPER (any industry) alternate titles: powder carrier; shooter's helper

Assists BLASTER (any industry) in placing and detonating explosives used to loosen earth and rock, performing any combination of following tasks: Carries explosive bags, cartridges, or powder to blasting area and deposits explosive device in previously drilled holes as directed. Shovels earth or drill cuttings into holes after placement of charge and tamps earth to confine and increase force of detonation, using shovel or pole. Connects explosive cord to blasting cap and lead wire to firing device, or attaches fuse to charge. Fires charge on signal from BLASTER (any industry). Performs other duties as described under HELPER (any industry) Master Title.

GOE: 05.12.02 STRENGTH: H GED: R2 M1 L1 SVP: 3 DLU: 77

86 CONSTRUCTION OCCUPATIONS, N.E.C.

This division includes craft and noncraft occupations, not elsewhere classified, concerned with building and repairing structures.

860 CARPENTERS AND RELATED OCCUPATIONS

This group includes occupations concerned with fabricating, installing, and repairing structures and structural members made of wood and materials that can be worked like wood, such as plastic and fiberglass, using bandsaws, ripsaws, planers, braces, hammers, and other carpentry tools and woodworking machines.

860.131-010 SUPERVISOR, ACOUSTICAL TILE CARPENTERS (construction)

Supervises and coordinates activities of workers engaged in installing acoustical tile to walls and ceilings of buildings: Measures and marks centerlines, guidelines, and location of hooks that hold ceiling suspension grid, according to blueprints and written specifications, to lay out work, using level, plumbline, chalkline, and tape measure. Directs workers in various installation tasks, such as suspending metal grids from ceilings, aligning and butting tile with joints of previously laid tile, and securing tiles with nails, screws, staples, or glue. Inspects smoothness of surfaces, alignment and butting of tiles, and fastening of tile for adherence to specifications. Performs other duties as described under SUPERVISOR (any industry) Master Title.

GOE: 05.10.01 STRENGTH: H GED: R4 M4 L3 SVP: 8 DLU: 77

860.131-014 SUPERVISOR, BOATBUILDERS, WOOD (ship-boat mfg.) alternate titles: carpenter supervisor, wooden ship

Supervises and coordinates activities of workers engaged in building, repairing, or modifying wooden boats, life rafts, floats, or pontoons: Assigns workers to specific duties, such as building pilot houses, cockpits, or cabins, installing masts or booms, laying keels and installing ribs, and fabricating and installing rudders and rudder controls. Directs workers in such procedures as installing skylights, desks, chairs, cabins, and other structural units and furnishings. Inspects specific assemblies, such as door panels, ceiling panels, and wall coverings, for conformance to dimensional specifications and quality standards, using level, square, and measuring instruments and applying knowledge of carpentry. Trains new workers in use of equipment and tools. Performs other tasks as described under SUPERVISOR (any industry) Master Title.

GOE: 05.05.02 STRENGTH: L GED: R4 M3 L3 SVP: 7 DLU: 80

860.131-018 SUPERVISOR, CARPENTERS (construction)

Supervises and coordinates activities of workers engaged in construction, installation, and repair of wooden structures and fixtures: Examines blueprints to determine dimensions of structure. Lays out floorplan and cabinetwork, using rule, framing square, and calipers. Selects materials and structural units, such as lumber, prefabricated doors and cabinets of wood or plastic, and paneling, and inspects them to ensure conformance with provisions of building code and local ordinance. Determines sequence of activities concerned with fabrication, assembly, and erection of structure. Assigns workers to such tasks as cutting material to size, building concrete forms, erecting wooden framework, and laying flooring. Inspects work performed by subcontractors, including ductwork, wiring, and pipe installations, to ensure conformance with specifications. Installs doors, builds stairs, and lays hardwood floors. May supervise workers engaged in building timber structures, such as cofferdams, trestles, and supports for concrete forms. May make cost estimates for contracts. Performs other duties as described under SUPERVISOR (any industry) Master Title. May be designated according to area of specialization as Bowling-Alley-Installation Supervisor (construction); Cofferdam-Construction Supervisor (construction); Form-Building Supervisor (construction); Timbering Supervisor (construction).

GOE: 05.05.02 STRENGTH: M GED: R4 M4 L3 SVP: 8 DLU: 77

860.131-022 SUPERVISOR, JOINERS (ship-boat mfg.)

Supervises and coordinates activities of workers engaged in fabricating, installing, and repairing wooden furnishings in ships or boats: Assigns specific tasks to workers, such as installing interior wood paneling in cabins, laying tile or linoleum on decks, installing soundproofing materials to equipment spaces, and installing laminated plastic or fiberboard surfaces on tables or workbenches. Confers with supervisory personnel of other crafts to coordinate worker assignments and to achieve maximum production. Performs other duties as described under SUPERVISOR (any industry) Master Title.

GOE: 05.05.02 STRENGTH: L GED: R4 M4 L3 SVP: 8 DLU: 77

860.131-026 SUPERVISOR, MOLD CONSTRUCTION (concrete prod.)

Supervises and coordinates activities of workers engaged in fabrication and repair of wooden forms and molds used for casting concrete products: Requisitions materials, tools, and parts for machinery required to fabricate or repair wooden molds and forms. Inspects products at various stages of construction to ensure conformance to standards. Measures, cuts, shapes, and assembles materials to repair or construct molds and forms according to blueprint specifications, using ruler, handtools, and power tools. Performs other duties as described under SUPERVISOR (any industry) Master Title.

GOE: 06.01.01 STRENGTH: M GED: R4 M3 L3 SVP: 7 DLU: 77

860.137-010 CARPENTER-LABOR SUPERVISOR (construction)

Supervises and coordinates activities of workers engaged in supplying materials to workers who construct, erect, install, and repair wooden structures and

fixtures. Directs work crew to strip forms and dismantle temporary wooden structures. May supervise workers engaged in pouring concrete into wooden forms. Performs other duties as described under SUPERVISOR (any industry) Master Title.
GOE: 05.12.01 STRENGTH: L GED: R4 M3 L3 SVP: 7 DLU: 77

860.261-010 CARPENTER INSPECTOR (any industry)
Inspects buildings, desks, cabinets, tables, and other wooden structures and equipment in establishments to ensure specified standards of maintenance. Reports nature and extent of repairs needed or directs CARPENTERS, MAINTENANCE (any industry) to make repairs. Keeps records of conditions before and after repairs. May make repairs within limits of preventive maintenance.
GOE: 05.07.01 STRENGTH: M GED: R4 M2 L3 SVP: 7 DLU: 77

860.281-010 CARPENTER, MAINTENANCE (any industry) alternate titles: carpenter, repair
Constructs and repairs structural woodwork and equipment in establishment, working from blueprints, drawings, or oral instructions: Builds, repairs, and installs counters, cabinets, benches, partitions, floors, doors, building framework, and trim, using carpenter's handtools and power tools. Installs glass in windows, doors, and partitions. Replaces damaged ceiling tile, floor tile, and wall coverings. May build cabinets and other wooden equipment in carpenter shop, using woodworking machines, such as saws, shaper, and jointer [CABINET-MAKER (woodworking) 660.280-010]. May install items, such as window shades, venetian blinds, and curtain rods, wall fans, and door locks for tenants. May be designated according to place at which work is performed as Carpenter, Mine (mine & quarry); or according to specific items made or maintained as Flume Maker (mine & quarry); Frame Maker (leather mfg.); Meat-Cutting-Block Repairer (any industry).
GOE: 05.05.02 STRENGTH: M GED: R4 M4 L3 SVP: 7 DLU: 86

860.281-014 CARPENTER, SHIP (ship-boat mfg.)
Fabricates and repairs ship's structural woodwork and wooden gear according to blueprints, drawings, and diagrams: Builds floors, doors, and partitions, using woodworking machines, saws, hammers, braces, and other carpenters' tools. Moves controls of winch and windlass to raise or lower anchor. Greases running gear and anchor windlass. Replaces defective chains or stanchions on lifelines or guardrails. Sounds water tanks with tape and plumb bob. Computes and logs sounding findings.
GOE: 05.05.02 STRENGTH: M GED: R4 M3 L3 SVP: 7 DLU: 77

860.361-010 BOATBUILDER, WOOD (ship-boat mfg.)
Fabricates, repairs, or modifies wooden boats, life rafts, and pontoons, according to blueprints, using handtools, power tools, and measuring instruments: Lays out full-scale outline of boat on mold-loft floor, using crayon, scales, and protractor, following blueprints and table of offsets. Establishes dimensional reference points on layout and makes templates of parts. Scribes dimensional lines on lumber, following templates. Cuts and forms parts, such as keel, ribs, and sidings, using carpenter's handtools and power tools [MACHINIST, WOOD (woodworking) 669.380-014]. Attaches overhead hoist to precut sections of boat hull and signals coworker to position timbers according to layout of boat, using hoist. Secures timbers together following specified procedure, using adhesive, hardware, and handtools or power tools. Assembles shell of boat by forming steam-softened sidings on mold, removing mold, and securing sidings to keel, or by securing ribs to keel and covering ribs with planking. Builds and installs structures, such as pilot house, cabin, rudder, and foundations for machinery, shafting, and propeller's supports, and installs preformed decking, masts, booms, and ladders, according to blueprints, using handtools, power tools, scale, calipers, and gauges. Work is usually performed with other workers. May caulk seams [WOOD CAULKER (ship-boat mfg.) 843.384-010]. May specialize in fabricating particular part of boat and be designated Bulkhead Carpenter (ship-boat mfg.); Bulwark Carpenter (ship-boat mfg.); Hull Builder (ship-boat mfg.); Keel Assembler (ship-boat mfg.).
GOE: 05.05.02 STRENGTH: M GED: R3 M3 L2 SVP: 6 DLU: 80

860.361-014 BOATBUILDER APPRENTICE, WOOD (ship-boat mfg.)
Performs duties as described under APPRENTICE (any industry) Master Title.
GOE: 05.05.02 STRENGTH: M GED: R3 M3 L2 SVP: 6 DLU: 77

860.381-010 ACOUSTICAL CARPENTER (construction) alternate titles: acoustical-material worker; metal-tile lather
Mounts acoustical tile to walls and ceilings of buildings to reduce reflection of sound and to decorate rooms: Measures and marks surface to lay out work, according to blueprints and drawings. Inspects furrings, mechanical mountings, and masonry surface for plumbness and level, using spirit or water level. Nails or screws molding to wall to support and seal joint between ceiling tile and wall. Scribes and cuts edges of tile to fit wall where wall molding is not specified. Mounts tiles, using any of following methods: (1) Applies cement to back of tile and presses tile into place, aligning with layout marks and joints of previously laid tile. (2) Nails channels or wood furring stips to surfaces to provide mounting for tile. Places building paper between tile and furring strip preparatory to application of butt-edge tile. Nails, screws, or staples tile to wooden furring strips. (3) Hangs dry lines (stretched string) to wall molding to guide positioning of main runners. Drives hanger inserts into reinforced concrete ceiling, using power fastening tool, and suspends and bends hanger wires at points touching dry lines. Threads wires through holes in main runners, and cuts and attaches cross supports to suspended runners and wall molding, using snips,

clips, and rivet gun. Cuts tiles for fixtures and borders, using keyhole saw, and inserts tiles into supporting framework. May wash concrete surfaces with washing soda and zinc sulfate solution before mounting tile to increase adhesive qualities of surfaces.
GOE: 05.05.02 STRENGTH: M GED: R4 M3 L2 SVP: 7 DLU: 77

860.381-022 CARPENTER (construction)
Constructs, erects, installs, and repairs structures and fixtures of wood, plywood, and wallboard, using carpenter's handtools and power tools, and conforming to local building codes: Studies blueprints, sketches, or building plans for information pertaining to type of material required, such as lumber or fiberboard, and dimensions of structure or fixture to be fabricated. Selects specified type of lumber or other materials. Prepares layout, using rule, framing square, and calipers. Marks cutting and assembly lines on materials, using pencil, chalk, and marking gauge. Shapes materials to prescribed measurements, using saws, chisels, and planes. Assembles cut and shaped materials and fastens them together with nails, dowel pins, or glue. Verifies trueness of structure with plumb bob and carpenter's level. Erects framework for structures and lays subflooring. Builds stairs and lays out and installs partitions and cabinet work. Covers subfloor with building paper to keep out moisture and lays hardwood, parquet, and wood-strip-block floors by nailing floors to subfloor or cementing them to mastic or asphalt base. Applies shock-absorbing, sound-deadening, and decorative paneling to ceilings and walls. Fits and installs prefabricated window frames, doors, doorframes, weather stripping, interior and exterior trim, and finish hardware, such as locks, letterdrops, and kick plates. Constructs forms and chutes for pouring concrete. Erects scaffolding and ladders for assembling structures above ground level. May weld metal parts to steel structural members. When specializing in particular phase of carpentry, is designated according to specialty as Combination-Window Installer (construction); Lay-Out Carpenter (construction). When specializing in finish carpentry, such as installing interior and exterior trim, building stairs, and laying hardwood floors, is designated Finish Carpenter (construction). When erecting frame buildings and performing general carpentry work in residential construction, is designated House Carpenter (construction). May remove and replace sections of structures prior to and after installation of insulating materials and be designated Building-Insulating Carpenter (construction; retail trade). May perform carpentry work in construction of walk-in freezers and environmental test chambers and be designated Carpenter, Refrigerator (svc. ind. mach.). May be designated: Door Hanger (construction); Finished-Hardware Erector (construction); Garage-Door Hanger (construction); Hardwood-Floor Installer (construction); Jalousie Installer (construction); Stair Builder (construction); Trim Setter (construction); Weather Stripper (construction); Wood-Sash-And-Frame Carpenter (construction); Wood-Strip-Block Floor Installer (construction).
GOE: 05.05.02 STRENGTH: M GED: R4 M3 L3 SVP: 7 DLU: 88

860.381-026 CARPENTER APPRENTICE (construction)
Performs duties as described under APPRENTICE (any industry) Master Title.
GOE: 05.05.02 STRENGTH: M GED: R4 M3 L3 SVP: 7 DLU: 77

860.381-030 CARPENTER, BRIDGE (r.r. trans.) alternate titles: bridge repairer
Repairs wooden railroad bridges, trestles, and tunnel supports, and replaces decayed, split, or crooked timbers, working as member of crew: Strikes timbers with hammer and listens to sound to detect decay. Installs temporary support to hold structure in place while decayed timber is removed. Loosens nuts and bolts that hold timber in place, using hand wrench or air-powered wrench. Removes timber, using crowbar, or hammers on timber to slide it out of place. Measures and cuts replacement timber to required size, using handsaw or electric saw. Bores bolt holes in timber, using electric drill. Slides new timber into place and secures it with nuts and bolts. May replace defective railroad ties supporting track on bridge.
GOE: 05.05.02 STRENGTH: H GED: R4 M2 L2 SVP: 7 DLU: 77

860.381-034 CARPENTER, MOLD (brick & tile; concrete prod.) alternate titles: mold-forms builder; patternmaker
Constructs and repairs wooden brick-and-tile molds and patterns or constructs wooden forms for molding concrete mixtures in manufacture of concrete products, and performs general maintenance carpentry duties: Lays out and marks measurements on material from blueprints, drawings, or samples, shapes material to size with handtools or power saw, fits mold sections with hand plane, chisel, or jointer, and joins sections with wood screws to construct new molds or patterns. Removes damaged or worn parts and fashions and screws new parts in place to repair molds. Performs general maintenance carpentry, such as repairing wooden doors, sills, floors, and stairways [CARPENTER, MAINTENANCE (any industry)]. May cut sheet metal mold linings and edge coverings to size, using chisel, hacksaw, and shears, and screw them in place. May make rubber molds when irregular surfaces (undercuts) of product require flexible molds. May make plastic molds by applying successive layers of liquid plastic and fiberglass cloth around model.
GOE: 05.05.02 STRENGTH: M GED: R4 M3 L3 SVP: 7 DLU: 77

860.381-038 CARPENTER, RAILCAR (railroad equip.)
Installs and repairs woodwork, such as flooring, wall linings, sidings, posts, sills, and window sashes, in railcars, including freight cars and cabooses: Inspects interior of railcar to detect broken, damaged, or cracked woodwork. Estimates amount and kind of lumber required for repairs or installation. Measures

and cuts required lumber and plywood materials to specified size, using ruler and handsaw or power saw. Repairs or replaces defective woodwork, using handtools. Installs tongued-and-grooved or plywood flooring and wall linings, using pneumatic squeezing, nailing, and stapling devices. Replaces broken door and window glass. May install aisle runners, rafters, and roof canvas to flooring and roofs of streetcars or cable cars and be designated Carpenter, Streetcar (railroad equip.).
GOE: 05.05.02 STRENGTH: M GED: R4 M3 L3 SVP: 7 DLU: 77

860.381-042 CARPENTER, ROUGH (construction) alternate titles: bracer

Builds rough wooden structures, such as concrete forms, scaffolds, tunnel and sewer supports, and temporary frame shelters, according to sketches, blueprints, or oral instructions: Examines specifications to determine dimensions of structure. Measures boards, timbers, or plywood, using square, measuring tape, and ruler, and marks cutting lines on materials, using pencil and scriber. Saws boards and plywood panels to required sizes. Nails cleats (braces) across boards to construct concrete-supporting forms. Braces forms in place with timbers, tie rods, and anchor bolts, for use in building concrete piers, footings, and walls. Erects chutes for pouring concrete. Cuts and assembles timbers to build trestles and cofferdams. Builds falsework to temporarily strengthen, protect, or disguise buildings undergoing construction. Erects scaffolding for buildings and ship structures and installs ladders, handrails, walkways, platforms, and gangways. Installs door and window bucks (rough frames in which finished frames are inserted) in designated positions in building framework, and braces them with boards nailed to framework. Installs subflooring in buildings. Nails plaster grounds (wood or metal strips) to studding to provide guide for PLASTERER (construction). Fits and nails sheathing (first covering of boards) on outer walls and roofs of buildings. Builds sleds from logs and timbers for use in hauling camp buildings and machinery through wooded areas. When specializing in particular phase of rough carpentry, is designated according to specialty as Carpenter, Cradle And Dolly (ship-boat mfg.); Dock Builder (construction); Falsework Builder (construction); Scaffold Builder (construction; ship-boat mfg.); Sheather (construction); Timber Setter (construction). When building and repairing timber structures which support sawmill machinery, is designated Construction Millwright (saw. & plan.). When performing rough carpentry work above ground on sewer or tunnel projects, is designated Surface Carpenter (construction).
GOE: 05.05.02 STRENGTH: H GED: R4 M4 L2 SVP: 7 DLU: 77

860.381-046 FORM BUILDER (construction) alternate titles: carpenter, form; wood-form builder

Constructs built-in-place or prefabricated wooden forms, according to specifications, for molding concrete structures: Studies blueprints and diagrams to determine type and dimension of forms to be constructed. Saws lumber to blueprint dimensions, using handsaw or power saw, and nails lumber together to make form panels. Erects built-in-place forms or assembles and installs prefabricated forms on construction site according to blueprint specifications, using handtools, plumb rule, and level. Inserts spreaders and tie rods between opposite faces of form to maintain specified dimensions. Anchors and braces forms to fixed objects, using nails, bolts, anchor rods, steel cables, planks, and timbers.
GOE: 05.05.02 STRENGTH: H GED: R4 M3 L2 SVP: 7 DLU: 77

860.381-050 JOINER (ship-boat mfg.) alternate titles: boat joiner

Fabricates, assembles, installs, or repairs wooden furnishings in ships or boats according to blueprints, using handtools, power tools, and measuring instruments: Lays out, cuts, assembles, and installs wooden parts, such as deckhouses, doors, sashes, paneling, battery cribs, and refrigerator doors, using woodworking handtools and power tools, scales, square, and calipers. Installs hardware and gaskets, using handtools. Lays linoleum on deck or ladder treads, using mastic, spreaders, and linoleum-cutting tools. Installs fiberglass or cork insulation on sides of ship below waterline to prevent water condensation. Cuts, fits, and installs glass in skylights, cabins, and other parts of ship or boat. Molds, bends, and laminates wood to form parts of ship, using steam chambers, clamps, glue, and jigs. Fabricates, assembles, and installs desks, chairs, and cabinets, using woodworking machinery, such as jigsaws, planers, jointers, mortisers, and tenoners. Shapes irregular parts to fit and joins matched grain wood, such as oak, mahogany, and teak.
GOE: 05.05.02 STRENGTH: M GED: R4 M3 L3 SVP: 6 DLU: 80

860.381-054 JOINER APPRENTICE (ship-boat mfg.)

Performs duties as described under APPRENTICE (any industry) Master Title.
GOE: 05.05.02 STRENGTH: M GED: R4 M3 L3 SVP: 6 DLU: 77

860.381-058 SHIPWRIGHT (ship-boat mfg.) alternate titles: carpenter, ship; woodworker

Constructs or repairs ships, following blueprints or ship's plans: Sights, plots, and marks reference points and lines on building dock or shipway to maintain alignment of vessel during construction or repair, using transit, plumb bob, tapes, and levels. Builds keel and bilge blocks, cradles, and shoring for supporting ships in drydock, marine railways, shipways, or building docks, using woodworking handtools and power tools. Positions and secures blocking and other structures on dock platform, according to ship's blueprints. Aligns vessel over blocks [DOCK HAND (ship-boat mfg.)]. Establishes reference points and lines on ship's hull for locating machinery and other equipment, in accordance

with ship's alignment and shape. Fabricates and installs furring pieces, aprons, uprights, and other wood framing in ship. Shapes, finishes, and installs wooden spars, masts, and cargo and boat booms. Trims wooden frames and other timbers, using broadax and adz. Spikes or bolts metal fittings, plates, and bulkheads to wooden parts of ship, using brace and bits, augers, mauls, and wrenches.
GOE: 05.05.02 STRENGTH: M GED: R4 M4 L3 SVP: 8 DLU: 77

860.381-062 SHIPWRIGHT APPRENTICE (ship-boat mfg.) alternate titles: carpenter apprentice, ship

Performs duties as described under APPRENTICE (any industry) Master Title.
GOE: 05.05.02 STRENGTH: M GED: R4 M4 L3 SVP: 8 DLU: 77

860.381-066 TANK BUILDER AND ERECTOR (construction) alternate titles: tank maker, wood

Constructs and erects wooden tanks for storing liquids according to blueprint specifications: Cuts and shapes tank parts from redwood, fir, and cypress lumber, using power-driven saws and carpenter's handtools. Fits parts together and tests holding properties of tanks and adjusts tank sections to make them watertight and airtight. Directs hoisting of tank parts onto buildings and assembles them, using handtools.
GOE: 05.05.02 STRENGTH: M GED: R4 M3 L3 SVP: 7 DLU: 77

860.381-070 TANK ERECTOR (construction) alternate titles: carpenter, wooden-tank erecting

Assembles and erects precut parts at work site to construct wooden storage or processing tanks and vats: Computes reference points from blueprints, diagrams, and other specifications, using measuring instruments. Measures and marks position of dunnage (subjoints) on foundation and lifts dunnage into place, manually or using powered hoist. Wedges leveling shims under dunnage, using carpenter's level and handtools. Forms tank bottoms, headings (ends) for horizontally mounted circular tanks, and ends and sides for rectangular tanks, by inserting wooden dowels into corresponding holes in sides of boards and hammering boards together. Hammers croze of staves over edge of tank bottoms or heads to form sides of circular tanks, and hammers endboards into crozed bottoms and sides to assemble rectangular tanks. Inspects and shapes parts for fit during assembly, using hand plane or saw and carpenter's rule. Positions metal hoops or rods around tank, affixes washers, lugs, and nuts, and tightens nuts, using wrenches. Positions tank or vat on foundation, using powered hoist and secures them on foundation, using handtools. May assemble scaffolding, using handtools. May cut openings for drain outlets, fill pipes, and manholes, using drills and saws. May install metal outlet covers and force sealant between metal flanges and wooden parts of tank, using wrenches and caulking tools. May install mechanical agitators or other machinery in tank [MILLWRIGHT (any industry)].
GOE: 05.05.02 STRENGTH: V GED: R4 M3 L3 SVP: 7 DLU: 77

860.664-010 CARPENTER I (mfd. bldgs.)

Erects prefabricated buildings at building sites, using carpenter's handtools: Directs TRUCK-CRANE OPERATOR (any industry) in positioning floor, wall, ceiling, and roof panels on house foundation. Aligns and fastens panels, using chalkline, hammer, and nails. Cuts openings in floor panels for wiring, using power saw. Measures, cuts, and fastens siding, exterior trim, and sheetrock to frame members, using tape measure, power saw, nails, and hammer. May direct workers engaged in assembling prefabricated buildings.
GOE: 05.10.01 STRENGTH: M GED: R3 M2 L2 SVP: 4 DLU: 77

860.664-014 JOINER HELPER (ship-boat mfg.)

Performs any combination of following tasks to assist JOINER (ship-boat mfg.) in constructing and repairing wooden and plastic parts of vessels, such as cabin paneling, cabinets, and deck structures: Cuts wooden battens to specified size, using portable power saw. Attaches battens to bulkheads, using glue, screws, and powered screwdriver. Cuts mahogany, oak, or birch paneling to specified size, and holds paneling in place while JOINER (ship-boat mfg.) secures paneling to battens. Cuts insulating or sound-absorbing material, such as fiberglass, cork, or felt, into specified shape, following templates or oral directions and using shears, rules, knives, and straightedge. Hammers retaining holders into studs to hold insulation in place, and tapes seams of insulation to obtain smooth joint. Spreads rubber or plastic cement on decks to be covered with tile or linoleum. Cuts tile or linoleum to fit in corners and around equipment, using cutting tools. Applies glue to joints or edges of cabinet or furniture parts, using brush, assembles parts together, and places assembled parts in clamps until glue has dried. Covers tables and desks with laminated plastic covering material. Smooths boat surfaces to remove defects, such as ridges, tool marks, glue, and excess caulking material, using hand sander.
GOE: 05.10.01 STRENGTH: M GED: R3 M2 L1 SVP: 4 DLU: 77

860.664-018 SHIPWRIGHT HELPER (ship-boat mfg.) alternate titles: carpenter helper; woodworker helper

Performs following tasks to assist SHIPWRIGHT (ship-boat mfg.) in constructing and repairing ships: Holds plumb bobs, sighting rods, and other equipment to aid SHIPWRIGHT (ship-boat mfg.) in establishing reference points and lines of ship, to position ship in drydock or to load machines and equipment. Positions and secures keel and bilge blocks, cradles, shoring, and other structures in drydock or shipway to support ship, using handtools and power tools. Drives wedges or packing between ship's hull and blocks to adjust height of blocking, using sledge. Obtains tools, equipment, and materials from storage

and carries them to work site. Assembles plates, bolts, and other metal fittings. Drills bolt holes in timbers or decking and tightens bolts, using portable power drill and handtools and power wrenches.
GOE: 05.12.12 STRENGTH: H GED: R2 M1 L1 SVP: 4 DLU: 77

860.681-010   CARPENTER II (mfd. bldgs.)
Assembles prefabricated building wall panels, using handtools and power tools: Reads blueprints to determine type of wall panel required. Selects precut studs, measures top and bottom leaders, and marks studs and leader locations, using tape measure. Lays materials on worktable according to markings to fabricate wall frame. Aligns sheetrock on frame. Locates, marks, and cuts receptacle openings in sheetrock, using tape measure, template, and handsaw. Reads specification sheet to determine types of windows and siding required on outside of wall panel. Selects and installs prefabricated windows in prepared openings, using hammer and nails. Measures, marks, cuts, and fastens siding and molding to form outside wall of panel, using tape measure and handtools. Moves completed panel to shipping area, using electric hoist. May direct workers in fastening studs and sheetrock. May operate nailing and routing machines to assemble wall panels and components.
GOE: 06.02.22 STRENGTH: M GED: R3 M2 L2 SVP: 5 DLU: 77

860.684-010   BUILDER, BEAM (mfd. bldgs.)
Cuts and assembles lumber to build false ceiling beams for prefabricated homes: Measures and marks lumber according to specification sheet for beam dimensions, using tape measure and marker. Positions and cuts lumber on workbench, using table saw. Aligns and interlaces different sizes of lumber to obtain specified dimension of beams. Measures beam to determine conformance to specifications, using tape measure. Stores beams on storage rack.
GOE: 06.04.25 STRENGTH: M GED: R3 M2 L2 SVP: 3 DLU: 77

860.684-014   SIDER (mfd. bldgs.)
Applies siding and installs prefabricated doors and windows to exterior wall panels of prefabricated and modular homes, following work orders and using handtools: Lays out siding on sheathing, and cuts siding to fit, using square and hand or portable power saw. Fastens siding to sheathing using hammer, nails, and power tacker. Drills vent holes in wall panels, using power drill, and inserts vents. Fastens tarpaper weather stripping around perimeter of door and window openings, using power tacker. Positions and aligns windows and doors in openings, using tape measure. Fastens doors and windows to wall panel studs, using hammer and nails. Moves completed panels to storage area, using electric hoist. May install precut insulation between wall studs.
GOE: 05.10.01 STRENGTH: H GED: R3 M1 L2 SVP: 3 DLU: 77

860.684-018   CAR BLOCKER (any industry)
Fabricates and installs braces to prevent shifting or damage to products shipped in railroad cars: Determines size of bracing needed, using tape measure. Selects lumber and cuts boards, using power saw. Assembles boards and fits or wedges braces into position to prevent load from shifting during transit. Nails braces to car floor or walls, using hand- or air-powered hammer. May secure load with banding machine and clincher. May place and inflate dunnage bags with compressed air between sections of load or between ends and sides of car and load. May cover load with tarpaulin.
GOE: 05.12.12 STRENGTH: M GED: R2 M2 L2 SVP: 3 DLU: 86

860.684-022   DISPLAY FABRICATOR (fabrication, nec)
Fabricates and assembles parts to manufacture smoking pipe sales displays: Traces pattern or sketch onto construction material or marks dimensions of parts on material, using ruler and pencil. Cuts out display parts along marked lines, using machines such as bandsaw and variety saw. Wipes stain on parts, using rag, or applies paint or varnish, using portable spray gun. Places parts in specified sequence and assembles parts to form displays, using pneumatic stapler. Assembles packing carton, inserts display into carton, and seals carton, using pneumatic stapler. Attaches shipping information to carton, using pneumatic stapler, or writes address on carton, using crayon.
GOE: 06.04.22 STRENGTH: H GED: R3 M2 L2 SVP: 2 DLU: 86

861   BRICK AND STONE MASONS AND TILE SETTERS

This group includes occupations concerned with preparing and laying brick, concrete block, tile, marble, and related materials, using chisels, hammers, trowels, and other handtools and implements.

861.131-010   BRICKLAYER SUPERVISOR (construction)
Supervises and coordinates activities of workers engaged in laying brick, tile, cinderblock, and other materials to construct or repair structures, such as walls, arches, sewers, and partitions: Assigns workers to specific duties. Inspects work in progress to determine conformance to specifications. Trains new workers in use of handtools. May supervise workers engaged in laying only tile and be designated Tile Setter Supervisor (construction). Performs duties as described under SUPERVISOR (any industry) Master Title.
GOE: 05.05.01 STRENGTH: M GED: R4 M3 L3 SVP: 8 DLU: 77

861.131-014   CHIMNEY SUPERVISOR, BRICK (construction)
Supervises and coordinates activities of CHIMNEY BUILDERS, BRICK (construction) engaged in erecting brick chimneys or smokestacks for industrial plants: Measures distances and lays first tier of bricks to lay out specified circumference and curvature of chimney. Directs workers engaged in raising scaffolds and inspects scaffolding for conformance to safety regulations. Inspects work to ensure conformity to specifications, using spirit level. Lays out openings in chimney and supervises installation of templates. May keep time and progress records. Performs other duties as described under SUPERVISOR (any industry) Master Title.
GOE: 05.05.01 STRENGTH: M GED: R4 M3 L3 SVP: 8 DLU: 77

861.131-018   STONEMASON SUPERVISOR (construction)
Supervises and coordinates activities of workers engaged in erecting stone structures, such as piers, walls, and abutments and laying walks, curbstones, and other types of masonry. Performs duties as described under SUPERVISOR (any industry) Master Title.
GOE: 05.05.01 STRENGTH: L GED: R4 M3 L3 SVP: 8 DLU: 77

861.131-022   SUPERVISOR, MARBLE (construction)
Supervises and coordinates activities of workers engaged in cutting, tooling, and setting marble and granite slabs in construction and repair of floors and walls of buildings: Estimates amount and type of materials needed. Trains new workers in use of handtools and methods of cutting, tooling, and setting of marble or granite slabs. Maintains time reports. Inspects work in progress to determine adherence to specifications. Performs duties as described under SUPERVISOR (any industry) Master Title.
GOE: 05.05.01 STRENGTH: H GED: R4 M3 L3 SVP: 8 DLU: 77

861.131-026   SUPERVISOR, TERRAZZO (construction)
Supervises and coordinates activities of workers engaged in mixing, applying, and finishing cement, sand, pigment and marble chips to floors, stairways and cabinet fixtures: Estimates materials needed. Trains new workers in use of handtools and equipment for mixing, applying, and finishing terrazzo surfaces. Prepares production reports. Inspects work in progress to determine adherence to specifications. Performs duties as described under SUPERVISOR (any industry) Master Title.
GOE: 05.05.01 STRENGTH: M GED: R4 M3 L3 SVP: 8 DLU: 77

861.134-010   SUPERVISOR, SMOKE CONTROL (steel & rel.)
Supervises and coordinates activities of workers engaged in patching and repairing coke oven components to ensure oven smoke emissions comply with company and government air pollution regulations: Observes oven operations to detect smoke emissions and inspects ovens to ascertain cause of smoke. Determines oven repairs required, utilizing knowledge of oven structure, and confers with designated personnel to coordinate scheduling of repairs. Reviews technical literature on recent developments in controlling smoke emissions and consults with engineering and management personnel to evaluate feasibility of implementing new methods. Develops smoke emissions programs, conducts tests to determine effectiveness of programs, and prepares reports of test results for management. Performs other duties as described under SUPERVISOR (any industry) Master Title.
GOE: 06.04.01 STRENGTH: L GED: R4 M3 L3 SVP: 7 DLU: 86

861.361-010   COMPOSITION-STONE APPLICATOR (construction)
Casts composition stone and applies it over surfaces of structures to provide decorative coating: Nails tar paper and lath over wall to be covered. Mixes and spreads mortar over lath with trowel, to form base for precast stone. Measures wall surface and marks lines with straightedge to lay out prescribed pattern. Lines interiors of molds with treated paper to prevent sticking and sprinkles pulverized coloring over paper. Fills molds with composition-stone mixture to produce stones of various sizes and shapes and allows mixture to set and absorb coloring. Positions molds along guidelines on wall, according to prescribed sequence for color and size. Presses molds in place to force out surplus water and to set stone. Removes molds and peels paper from surface when precast stone and mortar have hardened. Trims precast stone with caulking trowel, to fit corners, edges, and other structural shapes. Directs workers who mix mortar for plaster and composition stone, and prepares molds, following factory specifications. May smooth surfaces with waterproofing tool and buffer.
GOE: 05.05.01 STRENGTH: L GED: R3 M2 L2 SVP: 7 DLU: 77

861.361-014   MONUMENT SETTER (construction) alternate titles: setter; tombstone setter
Sets stone at cemetery gravesites to erect monuments, following diagrams and written specifications: Lays out foundation for monument, using rule and staked lines. Digs trench for foundation, using pick and shovel. Mixes mortar [MORTAR MIXER (concrete prod.; construction)] and pours mortar into trench to prepare foundation for setting base stone. Removes sections of monument from truck bed and guides stone onto foundation, using skids, hoist, or truck crane. Aligns and levels stone, using rule, square, plumbline, wedges, and crowbar. Spreads mortar on stone with trowel and sets subsequent sections of stone in position according to numbers or letters marked on stone. Fills joints between stone with mortar and finishes joints, using trowel. Removes excess mortar from monument, using water and brush. Works as member of team to erect monuments.
GOE: 05.05.01 STRENGTH: H GED: R4 M2 L3 SVP: 7 DLU: 77

861.381-010   ACID-TANK LINER (construction)
Assembles and installs acid-proof brick lining in metal tanks used for processing and storing of acid: Cleans inside of tank to remove foreign matter, such as rust, scale, and grease, using sandblasting equipment. Removes dust from tank lining, using gasoline dampened cloth. Applies specified coats of primer cement to lining of tank, using spray gun. Heats plastic sheet, using torch, to

fuse plastic coating onto primer cement. Rolls sheet to ensure that inner surface of sheet is attached to primer cement, using hand roller. Tests plastic lining with electrostatic tester to ensure against defects, such as pin holes and cracks. Cuts bricks to specified shape to ensure against crystallizing of cement and seepage of acid into lining. Lays bricks over lining and applies specified coats of plastic cement. Fuses bricks to plastic lining, using torch and applies acid-proof cement to brick joints, using trowel.
GOE: 05.05.01 STRENGTH: M GED: R4 M3 L3 SVP: 7 DLU: 77

861.381-014 BRICKLAYER (brick & tile) alternate titles: kiln repairer
Repairs and rebuilds tunnel, periodic, and shuttle kilns used to burn tile, brick, and sewer pipe: Examines kilns after burning cycles to determine need for repair. Lays firebrick to construct casing walls, flues, feather walls, and burner wickets, using mortar, trowels, plumbobs, hammers, and brick. Spreads plastic refractories over exposed brickwork to protect against deterioration by heat. Lays brick flooring in periodic kilns. May be designated according to type of kiln repaired as Tunnel-Kiln Repairer (brick & tile; pottery & porc.).
GOE: 05.05.01 STRENGTH: M GED: R3 M2 L2 SVP: 8 DLU: 77

861.381-018 BRICKLAYER (construction)
Lays building materials, such as brick, structural tile, and concrete cinder, glass, gypsum, and terra cotta block (except stone) to construct or repair walls, partitions, arches, sewers, and other structures: Measures distance from reference points and marks guidelines on working surface to lay out work. Spreads soft bed (layer) of mortar that serves as base and binder for block, using trowel. Applies mortar to end of block and positions block in mortar bed. Taps block with trowel to level, align, and embed in mortar, allowing specified thickness of joint. Removes excess mortar from face of block, using trowel. Finishes mortar between brick with pointing tool or trowel. Breaks bricks to fit spaces too small for whole brick, using edge of trowel or brick hammer. Determines vertical and horizontal alignment of courses, using plumb bob, gaugeline (tightly stretched cord), and level. Fastens brick or terra cotta veneer to face of structures, with tie wires embedded in mortar between bricks, or in anchor holes in veneer brick. May weld metal parts to steel structural members. May apply plaster to walls and ceiling, using trowel, to complete repair work [PLASTERER (construction)]. May be designated according to material used as Cinder-Block Mason (construction); Concrete-Block Mason (construction); Terra-Cotta Mason (construction); or work performed as Bricklayer, Maintenance (any industry). When specializing in construction of specified structures, is designated according to specialty as Bricklayer, Sewer (construction); Chimney Builder, Brick (construction). May be designated: Block Setter, Gypsum (construction); Hollow-Tile-Partition Erector (construction); Plaster-Block Layer (construction); Silo Erector (construction).
GOE: 05.05.01 STRENGTH: H GED: R4 M3 L3 SVP: 8 DLU: 77

861.381-022 BRICKLAYER APPRENTICE (construction)
Performs duties as described under APPRENTICE (any industry) Master Title.
GOE: 05.05.01 STRENGTH: H GED: R4 M3 L3 SVP: 8 DLU: 77

861.381-026 BRICKLAYER, FIREBRICK AND REFRACTORY TILE (construction) alternate titles: brickmason
Lays firebrick and refractory tile to build, rebuild, reline, or patch high-temperature or heating equipment, such as boilers, ovens, furnaces, converters, cupolas, ladles, and soaking pits, according to job orders and blueprints: Lays out work, using chalklines, plumb bobs, tapes, squares, and levels. Calculates angles and courses for building walls, arches, columns, corners, and bottoms. Removes burned or damaged brick and cleans surface of setting, using sledgehammer, pry bar, pneumatic chipping gun, scraper, and wire brush. Cuts brick to size, using brick hammer or powered abrasive saw. Spreads fire-clay mortar over brick with trowel and lays brick in place. Spreads or sprays refractories over exposed bricks to protect bricks against deterioration by heat, using trowel or spray gun. Positions or bends special frame or hanger over casings to lay arches. Cuts, notches, or drills openings to provide outlets, pyrometer mountings, brackets, and heating elements, using handtools. Patches or replaces firebrick linings of ladles and furnace tap holes. Constructs refractory forms for controlling quantity and flow of molten materials from furnace to rolling machines. May replace bolts, brackets, and heating elements, repair coke oven doors, weld cracks or holes in shell, or perform other repairs. May pack insulation into shells and frames to insulate heating equipment, such as furnaces, boilers, and ovens. May be designated according to structure worked on as Bessemer-Bottom Maker (steel & rel.); Coke-Oven Mason (steel & rel.); Door Repairer (steel & rel.); Furnace Mason (construction); Lip-And-Gate Builder (glass mfg.); Open-Hearth Door-Liner (steel & rel.); Vessel Liner (steel & rel.). When specializing in repair and replacement of firebrick and refractory tile in casings or linings of equipment, is designated Firebrick-And-Refractory Tile Repairer (construction).
GOE: 05.05.01 STRENGTH: M GED: R3 M3 L2 SVP: 6 DLU: 82

861.381-030 MARBLE SETTER (construction)
Cuts, tools, and sets marble slabs in floors and walls of buildings and repairs and polishes slab previously set in buildings: Trims, faces, and cuts marble to specified size, using power sawing, cutting, and facing equipment and handtools. Drills holes in slab and attaches bracket. Spreads mortar on bottom of slab and on sides of adjacent slabs. Sets block in position, tamps it into place, and anchors bracket attachment with wire. Fills joints with grout. Removes excess grout from marble with sponge. Cleans and bevels cracks or

chips on slabs, using handtools and power tools. Heats cracked or chipped area with blowtorch and fills defect with composition mastic that matches grain of marble. Polishes marble and other ornamental stone to high luster, using power tools or by hand.
GOE: 05.05.01 STRENGTH: H GED: R4 M2 L3 SVP: 7 DLU: 77

861.381-034 SOFT-TILE SETTER (construction; retail trade) alternate titles: tile setter
Applies decorative steel, aluminum, and plastic tile (known as soft tile to distinguish from ceramic tile) to walls and cabinets of bathrooms and kitchens: Measures surface to locate center points and draws horizontal and vertical guidelines through them. Brushes waterproof compound over plaster surfaces to seal pores. Spreads adhesive cement over wall, using trowel or broad knife. Positions tile on cement, following specified pattern. Presses tile into cement. Removes excess cement from joints between tile to clean finished surface, using damp cloth or cleaning compound. Rolls sheet wall covering with hand roller to press into cement. May wipe grout into joints of tile to seal them. May be designated according to type of tile applied as Metal-Tile Setter (construction; retail trade); Plastic-Tile Layer (construction; retail trade).
GOE: 05.05.01 STRENGTH: L GED: R4 M2 L3 SVP: 7 DLU: 77

861.381-038 STONEMASON (construction)
Sets stone to build stone structures, such as piers, walls, and abutments, or lays walks, curbstones, or special types of masonry, such as alberene (acid-resistant soapstone for vats, tanks, and floors), using mason's tools: Shapes stone preparatory to setting, using chisel, hammer, and other shaping tools. Spreads mortar over stone and foundation with trowel and sets stone in place by hand or with aid of crane. Aligns stone with plumbline and finishes joints between stone with pointing trowel. May spread mortar along *mortar guides* to ensure joints of uniform thickness. May clean surface of finished wall to remove mortar, using muriatic acid and brush. May be designated according to masonry work performed as Alberene-Stone Setter (construction); Artificial-Stone Setter (construction); Curb Setter (construction); Flagsetter (construction); Granite Setter (construction); Gutter-Mouth Cutter (construction). May set cut and dressed ornamental and structural stone in buildings and be designated Stone Setter (construction).
GOE: 05.05.01 STRENGTH: M GED: R4 M3 L3 SVP: 7 DLU: 77

861.381-042 STONEMASON APPRENTICE (construction) alternate titles: stone rigger; stone-setter apprentice
Performs duties as described under APPRENTICE (any industry) Master Title.
GOE: 05.05.01 STRENGTH: M GED: R4 M3 L3 SVP: 7 DLU: 77

861.381-046 TERRAZZO WORKER (construction) alternate titles: artificial-marble worker; floor grinder
Applies cement, sand, pigment, and marble chips to floors, stairways, and cabinet fixtures to attain durable and decorative surfacing according to specifications and drawings: Spreads roofing paper on surface of foundation. Spreads mixture of sand, cement, and water over surface with trowel to form terrazzo base. Cuts metal division strips and presses them into terrazzo base so that top edges form desired design or pattern and define level of finished floor surface. Spreads mixture of marble chips, cement, pigment, and water over terrazzo base to form finished surface, using float and trowel. Scatters marble chips over finished surface. Pushes roller over surface to imbed chips. Allows surface to dry, and pushes electric-powered surfacing machine over floor to grind and polish terrazzo surface. Grinds curved surfaces and areas inaccessible to surfacing machine, such as stairways and cabinet tops, with portable hand grinder. May precast terrazzo blocks in wooden forms. May perform finishing operations only and be designated Terrazzo Polisher (construction).
GOE: 05.05.01 STRENGTH: M GED: R4 M2 L3 SVP: 7 DLU: 77

861.381-050 TERRAZZO-WORKER APPRENTICE (construction)
Performs duties as described under APPRENTICE (any industry) Master Title.
GOE: 05.05.01 STRENGTH: M GED: R4 M2 L3 SVP: 7 DLU: 77

861.381-054 TILE SETTER (construction) alternate titles: tile fitter; tile layer; tile mason
Applies tile to walls, floors, ceilings, and promenade roof decks, following design specifications: Examines blueprints, measures and marks surfaces to be covered, and lays out work. Measures and cuts metal lath to size for walls and ceilings with tin snips. Tacks lath to wall and ceiling surfaces with staple gun or hammer. Spreads plaster base over lath with trowel and levels plaster to specified thickness, using screed. Spreads concrete on subfloor with trowel and levels it with screed. Spreads mastic or other adhesive base on roof deck, using serrated spreader to form base for promenade tile. Cuts and shapes tile with tile cutters and biters. Positions tile and taps it with trowel handle to affix tile to plaster or adhesive base. May be designated according to type of work done as Roof-Promenade-Tile Setter (construction).
GOE: 05.05.01 STRENGTH: M GED: R4 M3 L3 SVP: 7 DLU: 77

861.381-058 TILE SETTER APPRENTICE (construction)
Performs duties as described under APPRENTICE (any industry) Master Title.
GOE: 05.05.01 STRENGTH: M GED: R4 M3 L3 SVP: 7 DLU: 77

861.381-062 TILE-CONDUIT LAYER (construction)
Lays tile conduit that insulates and protects water or steampipes: Lays runners in previously excavated trench and checks slope with carpenter's level,

digging out or filling in with loose earth. Splits drain tile longitudinally and places halved tiles on runners, fitting spigot end of each half tile into bell end of adjacent tile. Mixes mortar of cement, oakum, and water, and applies it to edges of top half of tiles after PIPE FITTER (construction) has laid water or steampipes in bottom tiles already in position. Places top half sections on corresponding bottom half tiles and seals joints between sections by forcing mortar into bell end of tiles [PIPE LAYER (construction)].
GOE: 05.10.01 STRENGTH: M GED: R3 M2 L2 SVP: 6 DLU: 77

861.664-010 MARBLE FINISHER (construction) alternate titles: marble helper; marble mason helper; marble mechanic helper; marble setter helper

Supplies and mixes construction materials for MARBLE SETTER (construction) 861.381-030, applies grout, and cleans installed marble: Moves marble installation materials, tools, machines, and work devices to work areas. Mixes mortar, plaster, and grout, as required, following standard formulas and using manual or machine mixing methods. Moves mixed mortar or plaster to installation area, manually or using wheelbarrow. Selects marble slab for installation, following numbered sequence or drawings. Drills holes and chisels channels in edges of marble slabs to install metal wall anchors, using power drill and chisel. Bends wires to form metal anchors, using pliers, inserts anchors into drilled holes of marble slab, and secures anchors in place with wooden stake and plaster. Moves marble slabs to installation site, using dolly, hoist, or portable crane. Fills marble joints and surface imperfections with grout, using grouting trowel or spatula, and removes excess grout, using wet sponge. Grinds and polishes marble, using abrasives, chemicals, and manual or machine grinding and polishing techniques. Cleans installed marble surfaces, work and storage areas, installation tools, machinery, and work aids, using water and cleaning agents. Stores marble, installation materials, tools, machinery, and related items. May modify mixing, material moving, grouting, polishing, and cleaning methods and procedures, according to type of installation or materials. May repair and fill chipped, cracked, or broken marble pieces, using torch, spatula, and heat sensitive adhesive and filler. May secure marble anchors to studding, using pliers, and cover ends of anchors with plaster to secure anchors in place. May assist MARBLE SETTER (construction) to saw and position marble. May erect scaffolding and related installation structures.
GOE: 05.05.01 STRENGTH: V GED: R2 M1 L1 SVP: 5 DLU: 86

861.664-014 TERRAZZO FINISHER (construction) alternate titles: terrazzo helper; terrazzo mechanic helper; terrazzo worker helper

Supplies and mixes construction materials for TERRAZZO WORKER (construction) 861.381-046, applies grout, and finishes surface of installed terrazzo: Moves terrazzo installation materials, tools, machines, and work devices to work areas, manually or using wheelbarrow. Measures designated amounts of ingredients for terrazzo or grout, using graduated containers and scale, following standard formulas and specifications, and loads portable mixer, using shovel. Mixes materials according to experience and requests from TERRAZZO WORKER (construction) 861.381-046, and dumps mixed materials that form base or top surface of terrazzo into prepared installation site, using wheelbarrow. Applies curing agent to installed terrazzo to promote even curing, using brush or sprayer. Grinds surface of cured terrazzo, using power grinders, to smooth terrazzo and prepare for grouting. Spreads grout across terrazzo to fill surface imperfections, using trowel. Fine grinds and polishes surface of terrazzo, when grout has set, using power grinders. Washes surface of polished terrazzo, using cleaner and water, and applies sealer, according to manufacturer's specifications, using brush. Installs grinding stones in power grinders, using handtools. Cleans installation site, mixing and storage areas, tools, machines, and equipment, using water and various cleaning devices. Stores terrazzo installation materials, machines, tools, and equipment. May modify mixing, grouting, grinding, and cleaning procedures according to type of installation or material used. May assist TERRAZZO WORKER (construction) 861.381-046 to position and secure moisture membrane and wire mesh prior to pouring base materials for terrazzo installation. May spread marble chips or other material over fresh terrazzo surface and press into terrazzo, using roller. May cut divider and joint strips to size as directed. May assist TERRAZZO WORKER (construction) 861.381-046 to lay terrazzo. May cut grooves in terrazzo stairs, using power grinder, and fill grooves with nonskid material.
GOE: 05.05.01 STRENGTH: V GED: R2 M1 L2 SVP: 5 DLU: 86

861.664-018 TILE FINISHER (construction) alternate titles: tile mechanic helper; tile setter helper

Supplies and mixes construction materials for TILE SETTER (construction) 861.381-054, applies grout, and cleans installed tile: Moves tiles, tilesetting tools, and work devices from storage area to installation site manually or using wheelbarrow. Mixes mortar and grout according to standard formulas and request from TILE SETTER (construction), using bucket, water hose, spatula, and portable mixer. Supplies TILE SETTER (construction) with mortar, using wheelbarrow and shovel. Applies grout between joints of installed tile, using grouting trowel. Removes excess grout from tile joints with wet sponge and scrapes corners and crevices with trowel. Wipes surface of tile after grout has set to remove grout residue and polish tile, using nonabrasive materials. Cleans installation site, mixing and storage areas, and installation machines, tools, and equipment, using water and various cleaning tools. Stores tile setting materials, machines, tools, and equipment. May apply caulk, sealers, acid, steam, or related agents to caulk, seal, or clean installed tile, using various application devices

and equipment. May modify mixing, grouting, grinding, and cleaning procedures according to type of installation or material used. May assist TILE SETTER (construction) to position and secure metal lath, wire mesh, or felt paper prior to installation of tile. May cut marked tiles to size, using power saw or tile cutter.
GOE: 05.05.01 STRENGTH: V GED: R2 M1 L2 SVP: 5 DLU: 86

861.684-010 CUPOLA PATCHER (foundry) alternate titles: cupola liner

Repairs and rebuilds lining of cupola: Mixes sand, clay, and other refractory materials and applies mixture, using trowels and other handtools, to burned areas in brick lining of cupola. Tears out badly burned brick linings and relines cupola with new firebrick, using bricklayer's tools. Closes and props drop-doors of cupola and lines furnace bottom with sand. Builds and repairs clay troughs through which metal runs from taphole to ladle. May use air chisel to remove burned brick.
GOE: 05.05.01 STRENGTH: M GED: R3 M1 L1 SVP: 4 DLU: 77

861.684-014 PATCHER (steel & rel.)

Repairs parts of coke ovens, such as oven jambs, floors, walls, and roofs, regenerator walls, and standpipe joints and linings with refractory materials, using handtools, spray gun, and sandblast machine: Mixes slurry according to specifications, and shapes bricks. Lays brick to patch defective areas or resets jamb or charging hole castings, and smooths work by sandblasting.
GOE: 05.10.01 STRENGTH: H GED: R2 M1 L1 SVP: 4 DLU: 77

861.684-018 TILE SETTER (mfd. bldgs.)

Lays tile and installs cabinets in bathrooms of manufactured buildings: Selects color of tile according to specification sheet. Lays out sheets of floor tile and cuts backing to fit, using shears. Applies adhesive to subfloor and wall with brush and trowel. Cuts wall tiles to fit around tub fixtures, using hand cutter, and presses tiles into place. Wipes grout between tiles and removes excess with wet sponge. Selects bathroom accessories from stock. Installs and anchors fixtures in designated positions, using handtools.
GOE: 05.12.09 STRENGTH: M GED: R2 M1 L2 SVP: 2 DLU: 77

861.684-022 REPAIRER, KILN CAR (brick & tile)

Repairs kiln cars: Sweeps dust and chipped brick from beds of empty kiln cars, using broom. Scrapes loose or chipped mortar from sides of kiln cars, using trowel. Pours water and mortar mix into wheelbarrow, stirs mixture, and spreads and smooths mortar onto sides of kiln cars to repair heat-resistant cover, using trowel. Replaces broken refractory blocks on beds of kiln cars and straightens uneven blocks, using rubber mallet. Lubricates kiln car wheels, using grease gun. May position wooden frame over frame of kiln car, pour mortar into wooden frame, lay insulation mat over mortar, and place refractory slabs and bricks in prescribed order over mat to build new kiln cars.
GOE: 05.12.08 STRENGTH: M GED: R2 M1 L2 SVP: 3 DLU: 86

861.687-010 BRICKLAYER HELPER, FIREBRICK AND REFRACTORY TILE (construction) alternate titles: brickmason helper

Performs any combination of following duties to assist BRICKLAYER, FIREBRICK AND REFRACTORY TILE (construction) in repairing and rebuilding furnaces, ovens, ladles, and similar structures: Removes burned and damaged brick and cleans surfaces of settings, using bar, hammers, chisels, and wire brush. Sweeps and removes refuse from casings. Conveys tools and materials to work site. May mix mortar, using powered mixer. Performs other duties as described under HELPER (any industry) Master Title.
GOE: 05.12.09 STRENGTH: H GED: R2 M1 L1 SVP: 3 DLU: 77

861.687-014 PATCHER HELPER (steel & rel.) alternate titles: helper, patcher

Assists PATCHER (steel & rel.) in mixing slurries and in making repairs to coke ovens and auxiliary equipment. Screens refractory materials, stacks bricks for preheating, and performs other duties as described under HELPER (any industry) Master Title.
GOE: 05.12.09 STRENGTH: H GED: R1 M1 L1 SVP: 2 DLU: 77

862 PLUMBERS, GAS FITTERS, STEAM FITTERS, AND RELATED OCCUPATIONS

This group includes occupations concerned with assembling and installing gas, steam, plumbing, and related fixtures, pipes, and fittings in structures, using pipe-cutting and pipe-threading tools, welding equipment, and other pipe-fitting tools and equipment.

862.131-010 PIPE-FITTER SUPERVISOR (construction)

Supervises and coordinates activities of workers engaged in fabricating, assembling, installing, and maintaining piping, fixtures, and equipment for gas, steam, hot water, fire sprinkler system, or oil heating, cooling, lubricating, and industrial processing systems: Assigns workers to specific duties. Inspects completed processing systems to determine conformance to specifications. Trains new workers in use of equipment and tools. Performs duties as described under SUPERVISOR (any industry) Master Title. May supervise workers engaged in working on high-pressure systems and be designated Steam-Fitter Supervisor (construction). May supervise workers engaged in maintenance and repair work and be designated Pipe-Fitter Supervisor, Maintenance (any industry); Steam-Fitter Supervisor, Maintenance (any industry).
GOE: 05.05.03 STRENGTH: M GED: R4 M3 L3 SVP: 8 DLU: 77

862.131-014 PIPE-FITTER SUPERVISOR (ship-boat mfg.)
Supervises and coordinates activities of workers engaged in installing and maintaining piping systems of ships: Inspects installation of equipment, such as lockers, heating and air-conditioning units, and lavatory facilities to ensure standard requirement. Verifies dimensions of pipes, fittings, and valves, using micrometers, rulers, and levels. Performs duties as described under SUPERVISOR (any industry) Master Title.
GOE: 05.05.03 STRENGTH: M GED: R4 M3 L3 SVP: 8 DLU: 77

862.131-018 PLUMBER SUPERVISOR (construction)
Supervises and coordinates activities of workers engaged in assembly, installation, and repair of pipes, fittings, and fixtures of heating, water supply, and waste disposal systems for buildings: Trains new workers. Inspects work in progress and completed work to determine conformance to specifications. Performs duties as described under SUPERVISOR (any industry) Master Title. When supervising workers who specialize in maintenance and repair of heating, water, and drainage systems in industrial or commercial establishments, is designated Plumber Supervisor, Maintenance (construction).
GOE: 05.05.03 STRENGTH: M GED: R4 M3 L3 SVP: 8 DLU: 77

862.131-022 SUPERVISOR, PIPELINES (petrol. & gas) alternate titles: gang supervisor, pipe lines; roustabout, head
Supervises and coordinates activities of workers engaged in operating digging and pipelaying machines and in installation of pipe, pumps, valves, and meters to construct and maintain pipelines. Performs duties described under SUPERVISOR (any industry) Master Title. May be designated according to work location as Oil-Field Pipeline Supervisor (petrol. & gas).
GOE: 05.11.01 STRENGTH: L GED: R4 M3 L3 SVP: 7 DLU: 77

862.132-010 WELL-POINT PUMPING SUPERVISOR (construction)
Supervises and coordinates activities of workers engaged in erecting pumping systems, pumping subsurface water, and operating and maintaining pumps to provide underground and drinking water at construction sites. Performs duties as described under SUPERVISOR (any industry) Master Title.
GOE: 05.12.01 STRENGTH: L GED: R4 M3 L3 SVP: 7 DLU: 77

862.134-010 SUCTION-DREDGE-PIPELINE-PLACING SUPERVISOR (construction) alternate titles: shore-working supervisor; suction-dredge-dumping supervisor
Supervises and coordinates activities of workers engaged in transporting and joining pipe to provide outlet for excavated material discharged from dredge. Directs workers engaged in connecting pipe, tightening joints, and guiding pipe sections into place. Performs other duties as described under SUPERVISOR (any industry) Master Title.
GOE: 05.05.03 STRENGTH: H GED: R4 M3 L3 SVP: 7 DLU: 77

862.134-014 SUPERVISOR, WATER SOFTENER SERVICE (business ser.)
Supervises and coordinates activities of workers engaged in installation and maintenance of water conditioning equipment: Coordinates operation of plant regeneration equipment to keep customer exchange tanks regenerated and ready for delivery. Trains workers in installation and maintenance of equipment. Supervises workers engaged in shipping and receiving of water conditioning materials and equipment. Assigns service routes to WATER-SOFTENER SERVICER-AND-INSTALLER (business ser.) according to customer location. Compiles cost of installation and service of water conditioning units to determine customer cost. Inspects installed units to determine malfunctioning of system, using gauges and analyzers, and notifies repair worker of repair required. Adjusts customers complaints. Performs other duties as described under SUPERVISOR (any industry) Master Title.
GOE: 05.10.01 STRENGTH: L GED: R4 M3 L4 SVP: 8 DLU: 77

862.137-010 MAINS-AND-SERVICE SUPERVISOR (utilities) alternate titles: gas-distribution supervisor
Supervises and coordinates activities of workers engaged in constructing, maintaining, and repairing gas mains and in servicing pipes from mains to customer's premises: Marks work order diagram to indicate location of installations. Measures distances with tape and marks pavement or earth to indicate location of pipes requiring repairs, referring to work order diagram or map of mains and services. Inspects work in progress and directs workers to test pipes for leaks. May direct workers engaged in installation of meters and regulators to establish initial service for customer. May direct workers engaged in installing bonding, insulation, and counter-current generators to protect pipes against electrolytic corrosion. Performs other duties as described under SUPERVISOR (any industry) Master Title. May be designated according to activity as Leak-Gang Supervisor (utilities); Service-Crew Supervisor (utilities).
GOE: 05.05.03 STRENGTH: L GED: R4 M3 L3 SVP: 7 DLU: 77

862.137-014 STEAM-DISTRIBUTION SUPERVISOR (utilities) alternate titles: chief-maintenance supervisor
Supervises and coordinates activities of workers engaged in installing, maintaining, and repairing steam-distribution lines and equipment: Maintains blueprints or maps of entire steam-distribution system. Authorizes all installation locations and maintenance work to avoid contact and interruption with other electric, gas, and water underground installation. Inspects all pipe connections and equipment installations before turning on steam. Performs other duties as described under SUPERVISOR (any industry) Master Title.
GOE: 05.05.03 STRENGTH: L GED: R4 M3 L3 SVP: 7 DLU: 77

862.137-018 WATER-AND-SEWER-SYSTEMS SUPERVISOR (waterworks) alternate titles: water-maintenance supervisor; water-service supervisor; water supervisor
Supervises and coordinates activities of workers engaged in installing, maintaining, repairing, and servicing water distribution and sewage facilities: Assigns work activities to crewmembers concerned with excavating and backfilling trenches and culverts, installing, repairing, and replacing water and sewer mains, joining and caulking pipeline, repairing valves and hydrants, drilling and installing taps in mains, and performing related street repairs, working from land plats, maps, and other diagrams. Requisitions materials and equipment, such as pipes, special fittings and unions, cranes, draglines, air compressors, and welders. Inspects work to determine conformance to specifications. May prepare reports concerned with such items as human resource utilization, time records, work progress, and disposition of materials. Performs other duties as described under SUPERVISOR (any industry) Master Title.
GOE: 05.05.03 STRENGTH: M GED: R4 M3 L3 SVP: 7 DLU: 77

862.261-010 PIPE FITTER (ship-boat mfg.) alternate titles: pipe fitter, marine
Lays out, installs, and maintains ships' piping systems, such as steam heat and power, hot water, hydraulic, air pressure, and oil lines, following blueprints, and using handtools and shop machines: Plans layout of pipe sections, allowing for conformance to specifications, holes, and obstructions. Cuts and bores holes in bulkheads and decks for installation of pipes. Operates shop machines to cut and thread pipe and pipe fittings, such as valves, traps, and thermostats. Packs pipe with sand to avoid contortion of pipe and bends pipe to specified shape on pipe-bending fixture. Bolts or welds pipe brackets to support pipe systems. Connects pipes to fixtures, such as radiators, laundry, and galley equipment, pumps, and tanks, using wrench, and solders joints to seal connections, using hand torch. Repairs, packs, and adjusts valves. Tests installed systems for leaks and to ensure that system meets specifications, using hydrostatic and other pressure test equipment.
GOE: 05.05.03 STRENGTH: H GED: R4 M4 L3 SVP: 7 DLU: 77

862.281-010 COPPERSMITH (ship-boat mfg.)
Lays out, cuts, bends, and assembles pipe sections, pipefittings, and other parts from copper, brass, and other nonferrous metals: Lays out full-scale floor drawings or makes templates, following blueprints of pipe assemblies. Builds framework on bending slab to use as guide for bending, shaping, and joining assemblies. Cuts pipe, using handtools or shop machinery, and packs it with sand, rosin, or other material to prevent flattening during bending. Heats bend area with gas torch to soften metal and bends pipe, allowing for stretch at outside radius and compression at inside radius, using pipe-bending machines. Reheats and hammers pipe to eliminate wrinkles resulting from bending. Solders or brazes flanges on end of pipe. Flares or bells pipe mouths, using belling and flaring tools and mallet. Bends tubing to form coils for parts, such as feed water or oil heater. Lays out patterns and templates on sheet stock, using knowledge of geometry. Bends, hammers, bumps, razes, and planishes sheet stock to fabricate such parts as expansion joints, tanks, heads, cowls, and air chambers, using handtools, gas torches, and shop machinery. Sweats, rivets, solders, or brazes seams to obtain finished part. Coats parts by dipping them in mixture of molten tin and lead to prevent erosion, galvanic, and electrolytic action. Conducts hydrostatic tests to detect leaks in fabricated pipe. May install piping aboard ship.
GOE: 05.05.03 STRENGTH: M GED: R4 M2 L3 SVP: 8 DLU: 77

862.281-014 COPPERSMITH APPRENTICE (ship-boat mfg.)
Performs duties as described under APPRENTICE (any industry) Master Title.
GOE: 05.05.03 STRENGTH: M GED: R4 M2 L3 SVP: 8 DLU: 77

862.281-018 OIL-BURNER-SERVICER-AND-INSTALLER (any industry)
Installs and services automatic oil burners in furnaces in homes and commercial establishments, using handtools and pipe-threading tools: Assembles and positions oil-storage tank between furnace and wall of building. Drills holes in wall and affixes oil inlet and outlet pipes from storage tank through holes to outside of building. Removes ashpit and grate bars from furnace and installs burner in opening. Seals space around burner with plaster. Connects pipe to storage tank and burner to convey oil. Installs thermostatic control and damper in chimney. Observes color and height of flame and volume of smoke emitted to determine causes of faulty operation. Examines flue draft, using draftstat, and changes balance weight to adjust damper. May install and service automatic coal stokers.
GOE: 05.05.03 STRENGTH: M GED: R3 M1 L2 SVP: 7 DLU: 77

862.281-022 PIPE FITTER (construction) alternate titles: plumber, pipe fitting
Lays out, assembles, installs, and maintains pipe systems, pipe supports, and related hydraulic and pneumatic equipment for steam, hot water, heating, cooling, lubricating, sprinkling, and industrial production and processing systems, applying knowledge of system operation, and following blueprints: Selects type and size of pipe, and related materials and equipment, such as supports, hangers, and hydraulic cylinders, according to specifications. Inspects work site to determine presence of obstructions and to ascertain that holes cut for pipe will not cause structural weakness. Plans installation or repair to avoid obstructions and to avoid interfering with activities of other workers. Cuts pipe, using saws,

pipe cutter, hammer and chisel, cutting torch, and pipe cutting machine. Threads pipe, using pipe threading machine. Bends pipe, using pipe bending tools and pipe bending machine. Assembles and installs variety of metal and nonmetal pipes, tubes, and fittings, including iron, steel, copper, and plastic. Connects pipes, using threaded, caulked, soldered, brazed, fused, or cemented joints, and handtools. Secures pipes to structure with brackets, clamps, and hangers, using handtools and power tools. Installs and maintains hydraulic and pneumatic components of machines and equipment, such as pumps and cylinders, using handtools. Installs and maintains refrigeration and air-conditioning systems, including compressors, pumps, meters, pneumatic and hydraulic controls, and piping, using handtools and power tools, and following specifications and blueprints. Increases pressure in pipe system and observes connected pressure gauge to test system for leaks. May weld pipe supports to structural steel members. May observe production machines in assigned area of manufacturing facility to detect machinery malfunctions. May operate machinery to verify repair. May modify programs of automated machinery, such as robots and conveyors, to change motion and speed of machine, using *teach pendant*, control panel, or keyboard and display screen of *robot controller* and *programmable controller*. May be designated Steam Fitter (construction) when installing piping systems that must withstand high pressure. May be designated according to type of system installed as Pipe Fitter, Ammonia (construction); Pipe Fitter, Fire-Sprinkler Systems (construction); Pipe Fitter, Gas Pipe (construction); or type of piping used as Pipe Fitter, Plastic Pipe (construction); Pipe Fitter, Soft Copper (construction). May be designated: Airdox Fitter (mine & quarry); Freight-Air-Brake Fitter (railroad equip.); Instrument Fitter (construction); Maintainer, Sewer-And-Waterworks (construction); Pipe Fitter, Maintenance (any industry); Pipe Fitter, Welding (construction); Pneumatic-Tube Fitter (construction); Sprinkler-And-Irrigation-System Installer (construction); Tuyere Fitter (steel & rel.).
GOE: 05.05.03 STRENGTH: H GED: R4 M3 L3 SVP: 7 DLU: 88

862.281-026 PIPE-FITTER APPRENTICE (construction)
Performs duties as described under APPRENTICE (any industry) Master Title. Frequently specializes, after completing apprenticeship program, in such areas as refrigeration [REFRIGERATION MECHANIC (any industry)]; air-conditioning [HEATING-AND-AIR-CONDITIONING INSTALLER-SERVICER (construction)]; general pipefitting [PIPE FITTER (construction); PIPE FITTER (ship-boat mfg.)]; or gas, oil, hot water, and steam heating systems [OIL-BURNER-SERVICER-AND-INSTALLER (any industry); GAS-APPLIANCE SERVICER (any industry)].
GOE: 05.05.03 STRENGTH: H GED: R4 M3 L3 SVP: 7 DLU: 77

862.361-010 FURNACE INSTALLER (utilities)
Installs and regulates gas-burner units in building-heating furnaces to convert furnaces from wood, coal, or oil to gas: Directs helper to prepare furnace for installation of gas burner unit. Lays brick foundation [BRICKLAYER (construction)] in furnace ashpit and positions heating unit on foundation. Draws sketch of pipes and fittings required to connect gas burner to gas supply. Measures, cuts, threads, bends, and installs pipe between burner and gas supply with assistance of helper, using pipefitters' tools. Installs thermostat in heated area and makes wiring connections between building terminal box, switchbox, burner motor, and thermostat [ELECTRICIAN (construction)]. Ignites gas burner and adjusts gas-flow and air-supply control valves until observation of gas flame indicates correct combustion.
GOE: 05.05.05 STRENGTH: M GED: R4 M2 L3 SVP: 7 DLU: 77

862.361-014 GAS-MAIN FITTER (utilities) alternate titles: pipe fitter
Lays pipe to repair and extend nonwelded gas mains and to install or repair service pipes between mains and residences: Drills hole in section of main to which new pipe will be fitted and inserts inflated rubber bag to seal off flow of gas. Removes faulty pipe by unscrewing bolts at joint with hand wrench. Lays gas mains by fitting spigot end of one pipe section into bell end of another. Bolts joints together. Places wooden blocks under pipe to adjust pipe to line and grade, testing gradient with carpenter's level. Fastens steel cap over free end of gas-main extensions. Drills hole or installs reducing fitting in main where service pipes begin. Bolts saddle clamp around main, preparatory to welding. Drills hole through welded saddle clamp into main, using power drill. Cuts, threads, and screws together sections of pipe forming service line, and lays service line in trench. Bolts end of service line to saddle clamp, using special compression coupling to produce gas-tight connection. Removes rubber expanding bag to resume flow of gas and caps holes with screw plugs. Installs various gas-main attachments, such as *drips,* ells, and tees. Tests pipe for weak joints by forcing air into pipe with air compressor and coating joints with soap and water, and notes formation of bubbles, indicating leak. Tightens bolts or repairs leaky joints. May install gas meters. May install pipes beneath roads, lawns, or locations where not feasible to dig trenches, by forcing pipe through earth with special pipe jack. May direct crew in excavating trench and positioning pipe. May fuse bonds to pipe joints, using holder and flash chemicals (cadweld), to concentrate high temperatures at point of fusion. May install and repair service lines only and be designated Pipe Fitter, Street Service (utilities).
GOE: 05.05.03 STRENGTH: M GED: R4 M2 L3 SVP: 7 DLU: 77

862.361-018 PIPE FITTER, DIESEL ENGINE I (engine-turbine) alternate titles: piper
Installs oil, air, fuel, and water lines on diesel engines, using blueprints and process documents to determine pipe size, location of connection, and angles of bends: Cuts pipe and bends to specified angle, using tube bending machine [BENDING-MACHINE OPERATOR (any industry) I]. Brazes connections to

pipe, using holding fixtures and gas furnace. Bolts pipe to pipe supports on engine, using wrenches. Brazes or welds pipe to engine, using acetylene and arc welding equipment. May visually estimate angles and bend small pipe and tubing to conform to curvature of engine, using bending fixtures and handtools. May fabricate piping for stock. May replace worn or broken pipes on diesel engines.
GOE: 05.05.03 STRENGTH: M GED: R4 M3 L3 SVP: 7 DLU: 77

862.361-022 STEAM SERVICE INSPECTOR (utilities) alternate titles: inspector, outside steam-distribution; manhole-and-underground-steam-line inspector
Installs, inspects, and repairs underground steam mains and auxiliary equipment: Turns valve to shut off steam and to blow steam from pipe section to be worked on, using valve key, wrench, or special bar. Places pipe in previously dug ditch and bolts or welds pipe sections together, using handtools or welding equipment. Cuts threads and fits pipe [PIPE FITTER (construction)], and fastens expansion joint over connection by turning couplings with wrench. Installs or replaces auxiliary equipment, such as pressure regulating valves, gaskets, and steam traps, using pipefitting tools. Enters manholes periodically and examines steam lines and equipment for vapor leakage or loose connections and feels street surface above mains for heat indicative of steam leakage. Repacks expansion joints and repairs steam traps and other defective equipment. Operates motorized pump to remove water from flooded manholes. May repair steam meters.
GOE: 05.05.03 STRENGTH: H GED: R4 M3 L3 SVP: 7 DLU: 77

862.381-014 INDUSTRIAL-GAS FITTER (utilities) alternate titles: industrial servicer
Installs gas-heating units in industrial boilers, and rebuilds firebox of coal-burning boilers to utilize gas, following blueprints and written specifications: Dismantles old firebox and removes obstructing boiler parts. Positions shoring to support boiler when portions of masonry supporting boiler must be removed. Installs or modifies metal structures inside firebox that support refractory lining, according to blueprints. Lays firebox [BRICKLAYER, FIREBRICK AND REFRACTORY TILE (construction)] and installs boiler parts previously removed. Installs required number of gas burners in firebox. Measures, cuts, threads, bends, and installs gas supply and feeder pipes between gas burners and previously installed gas meter [PIPE FITTER (construction)]. Installs air supply pipes between motor-blower and gas burners. Removes shoring, replaces masonry, and inspects all pipe joints and gas burners for leakage or incorrect installation.
GOE: 05.10.01 STRENGTH: H GED: R3 M2 L2 SVP: 7 DLU: 77

862.381-022 PIPE FITTER, DIESEL ENGINE II (engine-turbine)
Installs high and low pressure piping and tubing for lubrication, cooling, and steam systems of turbines, compressors, condensers, pumps, and generators according to graphic and oral instructions: Lays out full size sketch of assembly on table, using layout tools. Bends, assembles, and positions pipe on sketch, using coupling joints and hydraulic bending machine. Brazes or tack welds piping and fittings into position [WELDER, TACK (welding)]. Climbs in and out of erection pit and onto erection platform to bolt piping to products. Tags or stamps items to identify parts during reassembly. May heat pipe to facilitate bending, using portable gas heating equipment. May install air, fuel, and water lines on diesel engines [PIPE FITTER, DIESEL ENGINE (engine-turbine) I].
GOE: 05.05.03 STRENGTH: H GED: R4 M2 L3 SVP: 7 DLU: 77

862.381-030 PLUMBER (construction)
Assembles, installs, and repairs pipes, fittings, and fixtures of heating, water, and drainage systems, according to specifications and plumbing codes: Studies building plans and working drawings to determine work aids required and sequence of installations. Inspects structure to ascertain obstructions to be avoided to prevent weakening of structure resulting from installation of pipe. Locates and marks position of pipe and pipe connections and passage holes for pipes in walls and floors, using ruler, spirit level, and plumb bob. Cuts openings in walls and floors to accommodate pipe and pipe fittings, using handtools and power tools. Cuts and threads pipe, using pipe cutters, cutting torch, and pipe-threading machine. Bends pipe to required angle by use of pipe-bending machine or by placing pipe over block and bending it by hand. Assembles and installs valves, pipe fittings, and pipes composed of metals, such as iron, steel, brass, and lead, and nonmetals, such as glass, vitrified clay, and plastic, using handtools and power tools. Joins pipes by use of screws, bolts, fittings, solder, plastic solvent, and caulks joints. Fills pipe system with water or air and reads pressure gauges to determine whether system is leaking. Installs and repairs plumbing fixtures, such as sinks, commodes, bathtubs, water heaters, hot water tanks, garbage disposal units, dishwashers, and water softeners. Repairs and maintains plumbing by replacing washers in leaky faucets, mending burst pipes, and opening clogged drains. May weld holding fixtures to steel structural members. When specializing in maintenance and repair of heating, water, and drainage systems in industrial or commercial establishments, is designated Plumber, Maintenance (any industry).
GOE: 05.05.03 STRENGTH: H GED: R4 M3 L3 SVP: 7 DLU: 77

862.381-034 PLUMBER APPRENTICE (construction)
Performs duties as described under APPRENTICE (any industry) Master Title.
GOE: 05.05.03 STRENGTH: H GED: R4 M3 L3 SVP: 7 DLU: 77

862.381-038 THREAD INSPECTOR (petrol. & gas) alternate titles: pipe-thread inspector

Inspects threads on joints of steel casings, tubings, drillpipes, and other tubular oil well equipment to detect defects and to determine conformance to specified tolerances in taper, lead, and threads per inch, using precision gauges and instruments: Measures machined threads and outside diameter of pipes to determine thread size, taper, threads per inch, and size of pipe to ensure clearance for lowering pipe into well, using thread gauge and micrometer. Determines whether combinations of thread elements will form joints capable of withstanding weight of entire string of piping in well and of preventing entrance of outside fluids or gases, applying knowledge of standard and obsolete thread forms.
GOE: 05.07.01 STRENGTH: L GED: R4 M3 L3 SVP: 6 DLU: 77

862.662-010 PIPE-CLEANING-AND-PRIMING-MACHINE OPERATOR (construction)

Operates pipe cleaning and priming machine to clean rust, scale, and dirt from pipelines, and to apply prime coating of hot asphalt: Selects cleaning and priming head to fit pipe and bolts them to machine-driven pulley. Bolts scraping knives and steel wire brushes to inside of cleaning head and bristle brushes inside priming head. Adjusts spring tension on knives and brushes with handtools. Signals TRACTOR OPERATOR (any industry) to lift and slide pipe cleaning and priming machine over end of pipe. Starts engine and moves levers to rotate cleaning and priming heads around pipe, and to propel machine along pipeline. Opens valve to start flow of hot asphalt coating onto pipe surfaces. May operate machine to remove heavy deposits of scale, rust, or other foreign matter from pipes preparatory to cleaning and coating and be designated Pipe-Cleaning-Machine Operator (construction).
GOE: 05.11.01 STRENGTH: L GED: R3 M2 L2 SVP: 6 DLU: 77

862.681-010 PLUMBER (mfd. bldgs.)

Installs bath plumbing systems in manufactured buildings, according to blueprints: Reads blueprints to determine type of plumbing system required. Writes cutting list that specifies sizes and quantity of copper pipe to be cut by PLUMBING ASSEMBLER-INSTALLER (mfd. bldgs.). Marks locations and bores holes in floor joists for pipes, using tape measure, template, and power auger. Selects and inserts precut pieces of copper tubing and fittings in holes. Connects tubing and fittings, using solder paste or solder and torch, to form sewer, drain, and water lines. Selects plumbing fixtures, such as toilets, sinks, and tubs, from storage. Squares tubing projecting through floor to ensure snug fit of fixtures, using square, wedges, and hammer, and solders fixtures to tubing. Squares fixtures with level. May direct workers engaged in preassembly and installation of wall systems, such as risers, air chambers, and shower assemblies.
GOE: 05.05.03 STRENGTH: M GED: R3 M2 L2 SVP: 6 DLU: 77

862.682-010 PIPE CUTTER (mfd. bldgs.)

Operates machine to cut, thread, and ream pipes, and assembles pipes, according to blueprints, to form mobile home water system, using handtools: Measures and marks pipes to be cut and threaded, using tape measure and pencil. Positions and secures pipe in chuck of machine. Starts machine and turns handwheel to engage pipe with dies that cut threads. Pulls lever to lubricate pipes and dies, and turns handwheel to activate reaming tool to burr inside of pipe. Moves lever to open dies, and turns handwheel to disengage dies from pipe. Repositions pipe in chuck and aligns cutting wheels with mark on pipe. Starts machine and turns handle to apply pressure on cutting wheels. Applies sealing compound to threads and fittings with brush and joins pipes in sequence specified, according to blueprints, to form water system, using wrench and vise.
GOE: 06.02.02 STRENGTH: M GED: R4 M2 L3 SVP: 4 DLU: 77

862.682-014 PIPE-WRAPPING-MACHINE OPERATOR (construction; pipe lines)

Operates pipe-wrapping machine to coat pipelines with asphalt or other corrosion-resisting compounds and wrap them spirally with fabrics, such as glass cloth and felt paper, to form protective coating that prevents electrolytic decomposition of oil and gas pipelines: Inspects paper holders and observes flow of hot compounds into reservoir to maintain adequate supply of materials. Starts engine and moves levers to activate mechanism that rotates paper head around pipe and propels machine along pipeline. Turns valves to regulate flow of dope to coat pipe. Adjusts brake tension on paper reels with handtools to ensure tight wrapping.
GOE: 05.11.01 STRENGTH: L GED: R3 M1 L2 SVP: 5 DLU: 77

862.684-010 JUNCTION MAKER (brick & tile) alternate titles: branch maker; fitting maker

Joins sections of unbaked sewer pipe at specified angles to form junctions, using jigs and handtools: Positions green pipe in cutting jig or places pattern or diagram on end of pipe section and cuts pipe to specified angle and length or cuts holes in pipe, using knife or wire cutter. Roughens cut edge and side of second pipe section to facilitate coupling, using comb-like tool. Dampens roughened surfaces of pipes to ensure that clay bonds together. Joins pipe sections and molds clay around joint. Cuts and smooths hole in second pipe at inner junction, using handtools. May insert bracing inside pipe to ensure shape of pipe during drying and firing.
GOE: 06.02.30 STRENGTH: M GED: R2 M1 L2 SVP: 5 DLU: 77

862.684-014 LABORER, CONSTRUCTION OR LEAK GANG (utilities)

Performs any combination of following tasks in laying, repairing, and extending underground gas and steam mains and distribution pipes: Erects barricades and places lanterns around work site to protect workers from street traffic. Breaks up pavement, using airhammer, and digs ditches preparatory to laying or removing pipe. Maneuvers pipe sections, valves, and fittings into position, and holds pieces steady while worker tightens threaded connections. Cuts, threads, and joins pipe sections as directed. Assists PIPE CAULKER (construction) in caulking pipe joints. Mixes and lays concrete to raise top of manhole to level of new street construction. Patches cracks in underground vault walls with concrete and brushes or sprays walls with waterproof compound. May drive truck and tend mobile ventilating equipment to supply fresh air to workers in underground vaults.
GOE: 05.12.12 STRENGTH: H GED: R2 M1 L1 SVP: 4 DLU: 77

862.684-018 PIPE-FITTER HELPER (ship-boat mfg.)

Assists PIPE FITTER (ship-boat mfg.) in assembling and installing aboard ships and boats pipe assemblies for systems, such as propulsion, fresh water, and heat: Requisitions tools and equipment for workers. Fills pipe with sand or melted resin to prevent pipe distortion during bending operations. Holds pipes during bending and installation. Fits assemblies into place aboard ship by screwing and bolting them together and connecting them to tanks, pumps, and other systems, using wrenches and other handtools. Immerses pipe in chemical solution to remove dirt, oil, and scale. Cleans shop machine with solvent and rags and sweeps working areas. Performs other duties as described under HELPER (any industry) Master Title.
GOE: 05.12.12 STRENGTH: H GED: R3 M1 L2 SVP: 5 DLU: 77

862.684-022 PIPE-FITTER HELPER (construction) alternate titles: fitter helper

Assists PIPE FITTER (construction) to assemble and install piping for air, ammonia, gas, and water systems: Cuts or drills holes in walls to permit passage of pipes, using pneumatic drill. Selects specified type and size of pipe. Mounts pipe hangers and brackets on walls and ceiling to hold pipe. Assists PIPE FITTER (construction) to install valves, couplings, and other fittings. May disassemble and remove damaged or worn pipe. Performs other duties as described under HELPER (any industry) Master Title. May assist in installation of high-pressure piping and be designated Steam-Fitter Helper (construction). May assist in installation of gas burner to convert furnaces from wood, coal, or oil and be designated Furnace Installer Helper (utilities).
GOE: 05.12.12 STRENGTH: H GED: R2 M1 L2 SVP: 3 DLU: 77

862.684-026 PLUMBING ASSEMBLER-INSTALLER (mfd. bldgs.)

Assembles and installs manufactured building bathroom hardware, fixtures, and plumbing, under direction of PLUMBER (mfd. bldgs.): Cuts copper tubing according to written instructions, using power saw. Connects, solders, and squares pipes, using solder paste or solder and torch, vice, and level. Selects preassembled wall plumbing units, such as risers, air chamber, and valves, according to diagram. Fastens units to studs with metal braces, using hammer and nails. Selects, assembles, and installs fixtures, such as tub, sink, toilet, and shower fixtures, using handtools. Applies glue to vanity and sets vanity in place.
GOE: 06.02.22 STRENGTH: M GED: R3 M1 L2 SVP: 4 DLU: 77

862.684-030 WATER REGULATOR AND VALVE REPAIRER (waterworks)

Inspects, maintains, repairs, and replaces control devices, such as water pressure regulators, gate valves, and hydrants on water mains in water treatment and distribution systems: Inspects, disassembles, and repairs damaged or malfunctioning control devices of water distribution systems, using handtools. Cleans parts of rust and scale, using scraper and emery cloth. Lubricates wearing surfaces of movable parts. Replaces defective parts or installs new control devices, using handtools. Turns pentagonal nut, using wrench or handwheel to adjust control devices regulators to control water pressure and flow for operating conditions, such as water main leaks, shut-offs, and for trial and emergency purposes. May grind valve seat to remove surface flaws to avoid leakage, using special grinding tool. Prepares requisitions and reports concerning materials needed to effect repairs, cause, and extent of damage to equipment.
GOE: 05.10.02 STRENGTH: M GED: R3 M2 L2 SVP: 5 DLU: 77

862.684-034 WATER-SOFTENER SERVICER-AND-INSTALLER (business ser.)

Installs and services water-softener tanks: Tests water quality for acidity, iron content, and hardness, using test kit. Examines plumbing system to determine connections, pipes, and pipe fittings required. Cuts, threads, and installs pipes, control valves, and couplings, using wrenches, pipe cutters, pipe threaders, and gas soldering equipment. Installs tank and attaches pipes and hoses to tank, fills tank with water, and inspects tank and pipes for leaks or other defects. Connects hoses of portable regenerating equipment to water-softener tank, and operates equipment to regenerate tank with chemicals to restore water-softener qualities at specified time intervals. Replaces sodium chloride in brine holding tank of automatic soft water conditioning system on specified schedule.
GOE: 05.10.01 STRENGTH: H GED: R3 M2 L2 SVP: 4 DLU: 86

862.687-010 COOLING-PIPE INSPECTOR (construction) alternate titles: pipe inspector

Inspects cooling pipes used in concrete structures, such as dams, retaining walls, and other structures, to locate defective pipes, leaking couplings, or defective fittings, prior to covering of pipe with poured concrete. Tightens joints or couplings with hand wrench to eliminate leaks.
GOE: 05.07.01 STRENGTH: L GED: R3 M1 L2 SVP: 5 DLU: 77

862.687-014 HOLIDAY-DETECTOR OPERATOR (construction) alternate titles: electric-detector operator; jeeper operator; pipe jeeper

Tests coating and wrapping of pipelines for holidays (inadequately coated areas), using electric detecting machine: Places jeeper (encircling coiled spring) around pipe. Closes switch to complete electric circuit between battery or generator and jeeper. Pushes jeeper along pipeline and listens for signal which indicates defect in pipe coating and cover. Moves jeeper back and forth over area where signal occurs until electric arcing is observed. Marks holiday with crayon.
GOE: 05.07.01 STRENGTH: L GED: R2 M1 L2 SVP: 2 DLU: 77

862.687-018 HYDRO-PNEUMATIC TESTER (any industry)

Tests boilers, tanks, fittings, pipes, and similar objects to detect and locate leaks, using compressed air or water pressure: Installs fittings on object to seal outlets and connects object to high-pressure air or water line, using handtools. Activates air compressor or water pump until gauge registers specified internal pressure. Observes gauge for loss of pressure indicative of leaks, and examines object for escaping air or water to detect leaks. Marks object at source of leaks for subsequent repair. May apply soap solution to surface of object or immerse object to facilitate location of air leaks. May test object under high pressure to ensure compliance with product safety ratings. May be designated according to type of test used as Hydrostatic Tester (any industry); Pneumatic Tester (any industry).
GOE: 06.03.02 STRENGTH: L GED: R3 M2 L2 SVP: 4 DLU: 77

862.687-022 OIL-BURNER-SERVICER-AND-INSTALLER   HELPER (any industry)

Assists OIL-BURNER-SERVICER-AND-INSTALLER (any industry) in installing and servicing automatic oil burners in homes and commercial establishments: Carries tools and equipment, such as burners, pipes, pipefittings, handtools, portable power tools, plaster, and insulating materials from truck to work site. Loosens bolts and screws of ashpit and grate bars. Lifts disassembled parts from work area. Hands tools and parts to worker drilling holes in walls, installing oil storage tanks, pipes, and insulating materials. Loosens bolts of oil burners, using wrenches, and removes and cleans oil strainer and sediment bowl with rag. Performs other duties as described under HELPER (any industry) Master Title.
GOE: 05.12.12 STRENGTH: H GED: R1 M1 L1 SVP: 2 DLU: 77

863   ASBESTOS AND INSULATION WORKERS

This group includes occupations concerned with covering and lining structures with asbestos, cork, canvas, tar paper, magnesia, and related materials, using saws, knives, rasps, trowels, and other tools and implements.

863.134-010 BUILDING-INSULATION SUPERVISOR (construction) alternate titles: insulation supervisor

Supervises and coordinates activities of work crew engaged in inserting insulating material in walls, floors, ceilings, and roofs of buildings. Assigns workers to specific duties. Demonstrates to new workers techniques of cutting and installing insulation. Inspects installed insulation to determine conformance to specifications. Performs duties as described under SUPERVISOR (any industry) Master Title. May be designated according to type of insulating material used as Mineral-Wool-Insulation Supervisor (construction).
GOE: 05.10.01 STRENGTH: L GED: R4 M3 L3 SVP: 7 DLU: 77

863.134-014 SUPERVISOR, INSULATION (construction)

Supervises and coordinates activities of workers engaged in applying insulating material to exposed surfaces of equipment, such as boilers, tanks, air ducts or pipes: Estimates and requisitions necessary materials and supplies. Assigns workers to specific duties. Demonstrates to new workers techniques of cutting and applying insulation. Inspects applied insulation for conformance to specifications. Compiles production and worker performance reports. Resolves employee grievances. Performs duties as described under SUPERVISOR (any industry) Master Title.
GOE: 05.10.01 STRENGTH: M GED: R4 M3 L3 SVP: 8 DLU: 77

863.364-010 INSULATION-WORKER APPRENTICE (construction) alternate titles: insulator apprentice

Performs duties as described under APPRENTICE (any industry) Master Title.
GOE: 05.10.01 STRENGTH: M GED: R3 M2 L3 SVP: 6 DLU: 77

863.364-014 INSULATION WORKER (construction)

Applies insulating material to exposed surfaces of structures, such as air ducts, hot and cold pipes, storage tanks, and cold storage rooms: Reads blueprints and selects required insulation material (in sheet, tubular, or roll form), such as fiberglass, foam rubber, styrofoam, cork, or urethane, based on material's heat retaining or excluding characteristics. Brushes adhesives on or attaches metal adhesive-backed pins to flat surfaces as necessary to facilitate application of insulation material. Measures and cuts insulation material to specified size and shape for covering flat or round surfaces, using tape measure, knife, or scissors. Fits, wraps, or attaches required insulation material around or to structure, following blueprint specifications. Covers or seals insulation with preformed plastic covers, canvas strips, sealant, or tape to secure insulation to structure, according to type of insulation used and structure covered, using staple gun, trowel, paintbrush, or caulking gun.

GOE: 05.10.01 STRENGTH: M GED: R3 M2 L3 SVP: 6 DLU: 86

863.381-010 CORK INSULATOR, REFRIGERATION PLANT (construction) alternate titles: insulation worker, interior surface

Applies insulating slabs of cork or fiberglass to walls, floor, and ceiling: Embeds parallel rows of slabs in hot asphalt spread on surfaces or spreads cement mortar on slab with trowel and sticks it to surface. Nails slabs to walls and ceiling construction for additional security. May leave narrow space between wall and slab, if wall structure is rough and uneven, and fill space with cement mortar. May construct false ceiling by nailing slabs to wooden framework or by wiring slabs to T-irons. May construct cork partition walls by cementing rows of cork slabs one upon another. May finish cork surface of walls and ceiling with cement plaster or asphalt mastic compound. May spread concrete over floor slabs to form wearing floor [CEMENT MASON (construction); PLASTERER (construction)].
GOE: 05.10.01 STRENGTH: L GED: R3 M2 L2 SVP: 7 DLU: 77

863.381-014 PIPE COVERER AND INSULATOR (ship-boat mfg.)

Covers boilers, pipes, tanks, and refrigeration units, with insulating materials, such as asbestos, cork, plastic, and magnesia to reduce loss or absorption of heat, prevent moisture condensation, and to deaden sound: Wires prefabricated asbestos covering around steam and hot water piping, using handtools. Trowels mastic or brushes cement on asbestos cloth to obtain smooth finish and covers piping with cloth. Fits thermoblock and magnesia-block insulation around insulating boilers, evaporators, and turbines. Wires insulation on machinery and staples wire netting over insulation. Trowels cement on wire netting to protect insulating material. Wires cork on salt water, refrigeration, and air-conditioning piping and cements cloth over insulating material to obtain smooth finish. Cuts sheets of insulation into sections, using handsaw and miter box. Fits and cements sections around fittings. Covers gas piping of refrigeration or air-conditioning systems with molded plastic. Fabricates detachable insulation for valves or similar fitting by measuring connections, preparing patterns, cutting asbestos cloth, stuffing cloth with amosite (plastic pipe covering), and sewing cover together on power sewing machine. Wires detachable covers on valves or fittings, using handtools. Installs fiberglass or spun glass on ventilating systems to deaden sound and prevent vibration.
GOE: 05.10.01 STRENGTH: M GED: R4 M2 L3 SVP: 8 DLU: 77

863.664-010 BLOWER INSULATOR (railroad equip.; retail trade; wholesale tr.) alternate titles: hose handler

Blows insulating material into spaces within walls, floors, and ceilings, using hose attached to blower, to insulate buildings or railway cars: Inserts nozzle of hose through opening into spaces to be filled. Signals INSULATION-POWER-UNIT TENDER (construction; retail trade; wholesale tr.) to start blower. Turns valve to regulate insulation flow from hose nozzle, and moves hose to distribute insulating material evenly. Climbs ladder or erects scaffold to reach working position. Seals insulation access holes of railway car with wooden bungs or metal caps, using hammer and punch. May insulate walls by covering them with sheets of insulating material, using nails or lacing wire.
GOE: 05.12.14 STRENGTH: M GED: R2 M1 L1 SVP: 5 DLU: 77

863.684-010 COMPOSITION-WEATHERBOARD APPLIER (construction) alternate titles: composition-siding worker

Applies composition weatherboard to exterior of buildings, using carpenter's handtools: Cuts, fits, and nails sections of composition weatherboard to building. Trims sections around windows, doors, and other apertures with molding. Fastens reinforced copper corners to building.
GOE: 05.12.12 STRENGTH: M GED: R2 M1 L1 SVP: 4 DLU: 77

863.684-014 SIDER (construction; mfd. bldgs.; retail trade) alternate titles: siding applicator

Applies asbestos, aluminum, pulpwood fiber, plastic panels, brick veneer, or porcelainized metal siding to building exteriors to provide decorative or insulating surfaces: Attaches tar paper, building paper, or other material to building surface, using nails or adhesive cement to provide insulating base. Fastens wood or metal laths to surface, using screws or nails. Fits and fastens siding material to laths, using rule, measuring tape, handtools, power tools, nails, screws, or bolts. Cuts and trims material to shape when fitting siding around windows or corners, using knife, shears, or portable power saw. Waterproofs surface by filling joints or cracks with caulking compound, using putty knife, trowel, or caulking gun. May apply precut siding or may cut material to size and shape at work site. May attach siding to surface of building, using adhesive cement. May attach siding by interlocking pieces through tabs provided at edges, following sequence indicated by numbers printed on reverse of each piece. May specialize in type of siding applied and be designated Aluminum-Siding Installer (construction; retail trade); Asbestos-Siding Installer (construction; retail trade); Concrete-Panel Installer (construction; retail trade); Ornamental-Brick Installer (construction; retail trade); Plastic-Panel Installer (construction; retail trade); Porcelain-Enamel Installer (construction; retail trade).
GOE: 05.10.01 STRENGTH: M GED: R3 M2 L2 SVP: 4 DLU: 77

863.685-010 INSULATION-POWER-UNIT TENDER (construction; retail trade; wholesale tr.) alternate titles: feeder worker power-unit operator

Tends gasoline engine-driven compressor unit used to blow insulating materials into ceiling and wall spaces of buildings: Pushes button or turns handcrank to start engine. Moves lever to start air compressor. Empties bags of rock wool into hopper of feeding unit where wool is blown by compressed air through

hose to sections within ceiling and walls of buildings to obtain insulation against heat or cold. Services engine and compressor unit.
GOE: 05.11.01 STRENGTH: L GED: R2 M1 L1 SVP: 4 DLU: 77

864   FLOOR LAYING AND FINISHING OCCUPATIONS

This group includes occupations concerned with finishing inlaid, hardwood, or composition floors, and laying asphalt, carpet, cork, linoleum, and rubber blocks or sheet materials, using rollers, knives, trowels, sanding machines, and other devices.

864.381-010   CARPET LAYER (retail trade)

Lays carpet and rugs: Measures and cuts carpeting to size according to floor sketches, using carpet knife. Sews sections of carpeting together by hand. Cuts and trims carpet to fit along wall edges, openings, and projections. May lay linoleum.
GOE: 05.10.01 STRENGTH: H GED: R3 M2 L2 SVP: 7 DLU: 77

864.481-010   FLOOR LAYER (construction; retail trade) alternate titles: floor coverer; floor-covering-tile layer

Applies blocks, strips, or sheets of shock-absorbing, sound-deadening, or decorative covering to floors, walls, and cabinets: Disconnects and removes obstacles, such as appliances and light fixtures. Sweeps, scrapes, sands, or chips dirt and irregularities from base surfaces, and fills cracks with putty, plaster, or cement grout to form smooth, clean foundation. Measures and cuts covering materials, such as rubber, linoleum or cork tile, and foundation material, such as felt, according to blueprints and sketches, using rule, straightedge, linoleum knife, and snips. Spreads adhesive cement over floor to cement foundation material to floor for sound-deadening, and to prevent covering from wearing at board joints. Lays out centerlines, guidelines, and borderlines on foundation with chalkline and dividers. Spreads cement on foundation material with serrated trowel. Lays covering on cement, following guidelines, to keep tile courses straight and butts edges of blocks to match patterns and execute designs. Joins sections of sheet covering by overlapping adjoining edges and cutting through both layers with knife to form tight joint. Rolls finished floor to smooth it and press cement into base and covering. May soften area of floor covering with butane torch to fit materials around irregular surfaces. May lay carpet [CARPET LAYER (retail trade)]. May be designated according to type of floor laid as Asphalt-Tile-Floor Layer (construction; retail trade); Cork-Tile-Floor Layer (construction; retail trade); Linoleum-Floor Layer (construction; retail trade); Linoleum Layer (construction; retail trade); Linoleum-Tile-Floor Layer (construction; retail trade); Rubber-Tile-Floor Layer (construction; retail trade).
GOE: 05.10.01 STRENGTH: M GED: R3 M2 L2 SVP: 6 DLU: 77

864.481-014   FLOOR-LAYER APPRENTICE (construction; retail trade) alternate titles: floor-coverer apprentice

Performs duties as described under APPRENTICE (any industry) Master Title.
GOE: 05.10.01 STRENGTH: M GED: R3 M2 L2 SVP: 6 DLU: 77

864.684-010   FLOOR AND WALL APPLIER, LIQUID (construction)

Applies liquid glaze and colored chips to floors and walls to form seamless covering: Applies primer coat of liquid vinyl to floor with squeege and allows surface to dry. Mixes specified amounts of liquid glaze and catalyst, which hardens glaze, and spreads glaze to floor with notched steel trowel. Sprinkles colored chips over surfaces after allowing surface to dry for specified time. Applies second coat of liquid glaze with finishing trowel. Sands surface with floor sander, and applies additional coats of liquid glaze. Repeats procedure when applying seamless covering to walls except primer and liquid glaze are applied with roller and wall surface is sanded by hand.
GOE: 05.10.07 STRENGTH: M GED: R3 M1 L2 SVP: 4 DLU: 77

864.687-010   CARPET-LAYER HELPER (retail trade)

Assists CARPET LAYER (retail trade) to lay carpeting on floors and stairs by performing any combination of following duties: Stretches and tacks carpeting to floors. Cuts rug padding to specified size and tacks it in place on floor, using hammer. Trims carpeting to fit around openings, using knife. Nails metal treads across door openings to hold carpet in place. Performs other duties as described under HELPER (any industry) Master Title.
GOE: 05.10.01 STRENGTH: H GED: R2 M1 L2 SVP: 3 DLU: 77

865   GLAZIERS AND RELATED OCCUPATIONS

This group includes occupations concerned with preparing and setting glass in structures, using bolts, screws, putty, grinding and buffing wheels, glass-cutting tools, and other materials and devices.

865.131-010   GLAZIER SUPERVISOR (construction)

Supervises and coordinates activities of GLAZIERS (construction) engaged in cutting and installing glass in windows, skylights, store fronts, and showcases, or on surfaces, such as building fronts, interior walls, ceilings, and tabletops. Trains new workers. Inspects installed glass to ensure work meets specifications. Performs duties as described under SUPERVISOR (any industry) Master Title.
GOE: 05.10.01 STRENGTH: L GED: R4 M3 L3 SVP: 7 DLU: 77

865.361-010   MIRROR INSTALLER (construction)

Installs custom mirrors on walls, ceilings, and doors in homes and commercial establishments, according to work orders and diagrams, with assistance of helper, using handtools: Loads and arranges mirrors on truck, according to sequence of customer orders. Covers each mirror section with burlap to prevent nicks, scratches, and breakage. Drives to customer location and unloads mirrors, equipment, and tools. Moves furniture to clear work site area and covers floor and furniture with drop cloths. Measures mirrors and dimensions of area to be covered by mirrors, using ruler, chalked cord, work order, and diagram. Determines plumb of walls or ceilings, using plumb line and level. Installs furring strips and shims to level wall surface and provide solid backing for mirrors, using ruler, saw, hammer, and nails. Cuts metal mounting strips and moldings to required lengths, using hacksaw or metal cutters. Attaches strips and moldings to wood, plaster, or concrete walls, using nails, screws, and stud gun. Applies mastic cement, putty, or screws in mirrors with predrilled holes to position and secure mirrors. Accepts payment for completed work.
GOE: 05.10.01 STRENGTH: H GED: R3 M2 L2 SVP: 6 DLU: 86

865.381-010   GLAZIER (construction) alternate titles: glass setter; glass-worker; glazier, plate glass

Installs glass in windows, skylights, store fronts, and display cases, or on surfaces, such as building fronts, interior walls, ceilings, and tabletops: Marks outline or pattern on glass, and cuts glass, using glasscutter. Breaks off excess glass by hand or with notched tool. Fastens glass panes into wood sash with glazier's points, and spreads and smooths putty around edge of panes with knife to seal joints. Installs mirrors or structural glass on building fronts, walls, ceilings, or tables, using mastic, screws, or decorative molding. Bolts metal hinges, handles, locks, and other hardware to prefabricated glass doors. Sets glass doors into frame and fits hinges. May install metal window and door frames into which glass panels are to be fitted. May press plastic adhesive film to glass or spray glass with tinting solution to prevent light glare. May install stained glass windows. May assemble and install metal-framed glass enclosures for showers and be designated Shower-Enclosure Installer (construction). May be designated according to type of glass installed as Glazier, Structural Glass (construction); Plate-Glass Installer (construction).
GOE: 05.10.01 STRENGTH: M GED: R3 M2 L2 SVP: 7 DLU: 77

865.381-014   GLAZIER APPRENTICE (construction)

Performs duties as described under APPRENTICE (any industry) Master Title.
GOE: 05.10.01 STRENGTH: M GED: R3 M2 L2 SVP: 7 DLU: 77

865.684-010   GLASS INSTALLER (automotive ser.) alternate titles: auto-glass worker; glazier; windshield installer

Replaces broken or pitted windshields and window glass in motor vehicles: Removes broken glass by unscrewing frame, using handtools. Cuts flat safety glass according to specified pattern, using glasscutter. Smooths cut edge of glass by holding against abrasive belt. Applies moistureproofing compound along cut edges and installs glass in vehicle. Weatherproofs window or windshield and prevents it from rattling by installing rubber channeling strips around sides of glass. Installs precut replacement glass to replace curved windows. May replace or adjust parts in window-raising mechanism.
GOE: 05.10.01 STRENGTH: M GED: R3 M1 L2 SVP: 4 DLU: 77

865.684-014   GLASS INSTALLER (woodworking) alternate titles: glass inserter; glass setter; glazier

Installs glass in millwork products, such as doors, window sashes, china closets, and office partitions: Places door or sash on worktable and inserts precut glass in opening, or inserts glass as products pass on conveyor, using either of following methods: (1) Inserts precut molding into window opening around edges of glass and taps molding against glass edges, using hammer and wood block. Tacks molding to frame, using hammer or staple gun. (2) Fastens glass into window opening, driving glazier's points into frame over glass, using point-driving tool. Presses and smooths putty into angle formed by glass and wood to make joint watertight, using putty knife. May spread sealing compound around edges of opening before inserting glass, using air gun or knife. May fit framed glass into openings in doors and screw frame to door, using screwdriver. May cut glass [GLASS CUTTER (any industry) 775.684-022]. May be designated according to glass installed as Door-Glass Installer (saw. & plan.); Window Assembler (saw. & plan.).
GOE: 06.04.30 STRENGTH: M GED: R2 M1 L2 SVP: 3 DLU: 87

865.684-018   GLAZIER, METAL FURNITURE (furniture)

Installs glass in doors or other openings in metal furniture, using handtools and power tools: Lays doorframe on glazing block. Inserts and forces rubber cushions in cleats (grooves) of doorframe. Sets glass in place on cushion. Taps upper and lower glazing strips in place in cleats over glass. Lays side strips in place and bores holes in strips at door corners. Screws strips onto doorframe.
GOE: 06.02.22 STRENGTH: M GED: R3 M1 L2 SVP: 5 DLU: 77

865.684-022   REFRIGERATOR GLAZIER (svc. ind. mach.)

Installs airtight plate glass windows in refrigerator display cases and walk-in coolers, using handtools and portable powered drill: Measures and cuts adhesive tape, rubber, or plastic gasket material to fit around outside edge of pane to form airtight seal. Fits gasket material around glass and secures window assembly in cabinet.

GOE: 06.02.22 STRENGTH: L GED: R3 M1 L2 SVP: 4 DLU: 77

866   ROOFERS AND RELATED OCCUPATIONS

This group includes occupations concerned with covering roofs and exterior walls of structures with slate, asphalt, aluminum, wood, and related materials, using brushes, knives, punches, hammers, and other tools.

866.131-010   ROOFING SUPERVISOR (construction)

Supervises and coordinates activities of workers engaged in covering roofs with roofing materials: Schedules work and assigns duties to workers. Demonstrates to new workers techniques of applying various types of roofing material. Inspects work in progress and when completed to determine conformance to specifications. Performs other duties as described under SUPERVISOR (any industry) Master Title.
GOE: 05.10.01 STRENGTH: M GED: R4 M2 L3 SVP: 7 DLU: 77

866.381-010   ROOFER (construction)

Covers roofs with roofing materials other than sheet metal, such as composition shingles or sheets, wood shingles, or asphalt and gravel, to waterproof roofs: Cuts roofing paper to size, using knife, and nails or staples it to roof in overlapping strips to form base for roofing materials. Aligns roofing material with edge of roof, and overlaps successive layers, gauging distance of overlap with chalkline, gauge on shingling hatchet, or by lines on shingles. Fastens composition shingles or sheets to roof with asphalt, cement, or nails. Punches holes in slate, tile, terra cotta, or wooden shingles, using punch and hammer. Cuts strips of flashing and fits them into angles formed by walls, vents, and intersecting roof surfaces. When applying asphalt or tar and gravel to roof, mops or pours hot asphalt or tar onto roof base. Applies alternate layers of hot asphalt or tar and roofing paper until roof covering is as specified. Applies gravel or pebbles over top layer, using rake or stiff-bristled broom. May construct and attach prefabricated roof sections to rafters [CARPENTER (construction)]. May attach shingles to exterior walls and apply roofing paper and tar to shower pans, decks, and promenades to waterproof surfaces. When specializing in one type of roofing materials, is designated according to specialty as Aluminum-Shingle Roofer (construction); Asbestos-Shingle Roofer (construction); Asphalt, Tar, And Gravel Roofer (construction); Composition Roofer (construction); Roofer, Gypsum (construction); Slate Roofer (construction); Tile-And-Terra-Cotta Roofer (construction); Wood-Shingle Roofer (construction).
GOE: 05.10.01 STRENGTH: M GED: R3 M2 L2 SVP: 7 DLU: 77

866.381-014   ROOFER APPRENTICE (construction)

Performs duties as described under APPRENTICE (any industry) Master Title.
GOE: 05.10.01 STRENGTH: M GED: R3 M2 L2 SVP: 7 DLU: 77

866.684-010   ROOFER APPLICATOR (construction)

Sprays roofs, sidings, and walls with urethane or polyurethane foam to bind, seal, insulate, or soundproof sections of structures: Flips switches to start generator, air compressor, and heaters. Turns nozzle on spray gun to obtain specified consistency of mixture. Directs foam onto surfaces, and determines thickness of foam, using probe. Connects hose of nitrogen tank to spray compound supply tank when spraying is completed, and turns valves to inject nitrogen into supply tank to prevent crystallization of compounds in tank.
GOE: 05.12.14 STRENGTH: L GED: R3 M1 L2 SVP: 6 DLU: 77

869   MISCELLANEOUS CONSTRUCTION OCCUPATIONS, N.E.C.

This group includes occupations, not elsewhere classified, concerned with building and repairing structures.

869.131-010   CABIN-EQUIPMENT SUPERVISOR (air trans.)

Supervises and coordinates activities of workers engaged in repairing and overhauling aircraft cabin fixtures: Reads schedules to plan work sequences and assigns workers to duties, such as disassembling and repairing passenger seats, flight attendant buffets, cargo containers, cutting carpeting, upholstery material, and leather and plastic paneling, reconditioning seat belts and other safety equipment; and sewing drapes and slip covers. Performs other duties as described under SUPERVISOR (any industry) Master Title.
GOE: 05.10.01 STRENGTH: L GED: R4 M3 L3 SVP: 7 DLU: 77

869.131-014   CONCRETING SUPERVISOR (construction)

Supervises and coordinates activities of work crews engaged in preparing and applying concrete for fabricating, covering, and reinforcing structures, including buildings, bridges, highways, and dams: Oversees workers who place forms for molding concrete, install reinforcing steel, and convey, pour, finish, and cure concrete. Reads specification sheets for information, such as sizes of aggregates and proportions of cement and water required, to ensure that concrete is mixed according to specifications. Inspects bracing and shoring of concrete forms to ensure their stability before and during pouring. Indicates positions for pouring chutes and runways, cranes, or paving machines to facilitate conveying concrete from mixer to forms. Trains new workers. Directs workers who pour, vibrate, screed, and float concrete, to ensure that concrete is compacted to desired consistency and surface is finished to specified uniformity and smoothness. Examines concrete, after forms are stripped, and gives instruction to workers to repair defects, such as roughness and honeycombed appearance. Prescribes methods for curing concrete, such as covering surface of green (fresh) concrete with burlap, plastic, earth, straw, or chemical compound, to prevent green concrete from drying out rapidly or freezing. Supervises workers engaged in spraying cement mortar or concrete to cover exposed earth, masonry, and steel surfaces and forcing grout (thin mixture of sand, cement, and water) into drilled holes, spaces between foundations and surrounding earth, and fissures in rock foundations, to reinforce structures. Records data, such as time spent on various phases of job and yardage and distribution of concrete poured. May collect samples of each concrete mix for laboratory analysis. May be designated according to workers supervised as Cement-Finishing Supervisor (construction); Concrete-Paving Supervisor (construction); Concrete-Pouring Supervisor (construction); Curb Supervisor (construction); Grout Supervisor (construction). When supervising workers engaged in preparing, setting, and removing tunnel forms for molding concrete in sewer and tunnel construction, may be designated Form-Setter Supervisor (construction); Tunnel-Form-Placing Supervisor (construction). When supervising workers who mold and install reinforced concrete wall slabs, may be designated Tilt-Wall Supervisor (construction). Performs other duties as described under SUPERVISOR (any industry) Master Title.
GOE: 05.05.01 STRENGTH: L GED: R4 M3 L3 SVP: 7 DLU: 77

869.131-018   FIELD-ASSEMBLY SUPERVISOR (mfd. bldgs.)

Supervises and coordinates activities of workers engaged in erecting prefabricated homes at construction site: Verifies alignment of floor, walls, ceilings, and roof panels positioned on house foundation visually and with level for compliance with specifications. Trains new workers in construction procedures and techniques. Installs prefabricated exterior doors, using handtools. Maintains production and time records and requisitions supplies. Performs other duties as described under SUPERVISOR (any industry) Master Title. May supervise workers installing trim and components in prefabricated homes and be designated Trim-Crew Supervisor (mfd. bldgs.).
GOE: 05.10.01 STRENGTH: M GED: R4 M3 L3 SVP: 7 DLU: 77

869.131-022   HOUSE-MOVER SUPERVISOR (construction)

Supervises and coordinates activities of workers engaged in moving houses and buildings: Inspects buildings for structural weaknesses, such as warped joist, dry rot and termite erosion, and inadequate framing. Supervises workers in positioning of beams, cribbing, hydraulic jacks, dollies, chaining of dollies to house beams, and positioning of structure at new site. Directs workers to raise or lower hydraulic jacks at various locations to align house and verify alignment of house, using transit. Performs other duties as described under SUPERVISOR (any industry) Master Title. May supervise workers engaged in demolishing structures, salvaging materials, and removing debris.
GOE: 05.10.01 STRENGTH: H GED: R4 M3 L3 SVP: 7 DLU: 77

869.131-026   STEEL-PAN-FORM-PLACING SUPERVISOR (construction) alternate titles: steel-floor-pan-placing supervisor

Supervises and coordinates activities of workers engaged in placing and erecting metal pan forms for prestressed concrete structures and removing, cleaning, and storing forms: Lays out stringers and marks guidelines to locate positions for pans (concrete forms). Directs workers engaged in erecting stringers and shoring to support metal pan forms while concrete is being poured and cured. Trains new workers. May supervise worker engaged in installation of reinforcing steel, and pouring and finishing of concrete and be designated Concreting Supervisor (construction). Performs other duties as described under SUPERVISOR (any industry) Master Title.
GOE: 05.10.01 STRENGTH: M GED: R4 M3 L3 SVP: 7 DLU: 77

869.131-030   SUPERVISOR, MANUFACTURED BUILDINGS (mfd. bldgs.; vehicles, nec)

Supervises and coordinates activities of workers engaged in one or more phases of fabrication, assembly, and furnishing of manufactured buildings and travel trailers: Inspects manufactured buildings and travel trailers to ensure assembly and furnishings meet specifications and floor plans. Informs workers of defects and suggests repair methods. May lay out and build assembly jigs. May be designated according to type of work supervised as Assembly Supervisor (mfd. bldgs.; vehicles, nec); Subassembly Supervisor (mfd. bldgs.; vehicles, nec); Final-Finish Supervisor (mfd. bldgs.; vehicles, nec); Millroom Supervisor (mfd. bldgs.; vehicles, nec); Supervisor, Travel Trailer (vehicles, nec). Performs other duties as described under SUPERVISOR (any industry) Master Title.
GOE: 06.02.01 STRENGTH: M GED: R4 M3 L3 SVP: 7 DLU: 77

869.131-034   TANKAGE SUPERVISOR (construction) alternate titles: tank-builder supervisor

Supervises and coordinates activities of workers engaged in erecting and maintaining metal tanks used to store liquid materials, such as crude oil, gasoline, and heating oil: Installs and maintains tank components, such as automatic gauges, valves, and vents. May supervise workers engaged in cleaning and painting tanks. Performs other duties as described under SUPERVISOR (any industry) Master Title.
GOE: 05.05.06 STRENGTH: M GED: R4 M3 L3 SVP: 7 DLU: 77

869.131-038   SUPERVISOR, SWIMMING-POOL MAINTENANCE (construction)

Supervises and coordinates activities of workers engaged in construction, repair, and maintenance of swimming pools: Measures and marks pool excavation site, using transit and stakes. Directs workers in mixing, pouring, and leveling cement to form pool floor and in assembling prefabricated pool walls and lin-

ing. Cuts openings for plumbing into sides of pool and directs workers in installation of fixtures, such as pipes, spigots, valves, and pumps. Oversees installation of pool solar-heating system components. Inspects work in progress and completed pool installation to verify adherence to specifications. Trains new workers in work methods and assists workers in pool construction, maintenance, and repair. May secure contracts for pool installation and write customer orders. Performs other duties as decribed under SUPERVISOR (any industry) Master Title.
GOE: 05.02.02 STRENGTH: M GED: R4 M3 L3 SVP: 7 DLU: 86

869.133-010 CLEARING SUPERVISOR (construction) alternate titles: clean-up supervisor; right-of-way supervisor

Supervises and coordinates activities of workers engaged in clearing way for structures, such as buildings, bridges, highways, and pipelines: Directs workers engaged in cutting timber, burning brush, blasting stumps, and grading and leveling land. Directs workers engaged in constructing temporary bridges and roads to provide access to construction site. Directs workers engaged in restoring property, such as land, roadways, drainage ditches, and fences, damaged by construction activity. Confers with CLAIM AGENT (petrol. & gas; pipe lines) to ensure that restorations comply with agreements. May load and fire charges of explosives to blast stumps [BLASTER (any industry)]. Performs other duties as described under SUPERVISOR (any industry) Master Title.
GOE: 05.11.01 STRENGTH: L GED: R4 M3 L3 SVP: 7 DLU: 77

869.134-010 FENCE-ERECTOR SUPERVISOR (construction)

Supervises and coordinates activities of FENCE ERECTORS (construction) engaged in setting and stretching wire mesh fences, and building wooden or concrete fences. Performs duties as described under SUPERVISOR (any industry) Master Title.
GOE: 05.10.01 STRENGTH: L GED: R4 M3 L3 SVP: 7 DLU: 77

869.134-014 SUPERVISOR, ADJUSTABLE-STEEL-JOIST-SETTING (construction)

Supervises and coordinates activities of workers engaged in erecting adjustable steel joists to support concrete floor-slab forms in building construction. Performs duties as described under SUPERVISOR (any industry) Master Title.
GOE: 05.05.06 STRENGTH: L GED: R4 M3 L3 SVP: 7 DLU: 77

869.134-018 SUPERVISOR, PIPELINE MAINTENANCE (pipe lines) alternate titles: crew supervisor; maintenance-crew supervisor; pipe-line maintenance supervisor

Supervises and coordinates activities of workers engaged in maintenance of oil and gas pipelines and pipeline facilities, such as pumping units, compressor stations, tank farms, and right-of-ways: Directs workers engaged in patrolling, inspecting, repairing, and installing pipelines and communication systems, painting pipes and tanks, and in clearing right-of-way. Orders digging and backfilling of culverts and drainage ditches, involving use of trucks, bulldozers, and backhoes. Instructs new workers in work methods, operation of equipment, and safety regulations. Inspects work in progress and completed work to ensure adherence to specifications. Supervises construction or removal of pipelines and pipeline facilities. Performs other duties as described under SUPERVISOR (any industry) Master Title.
GOE: 05.12.01 STRENGTH: L GED: R4 M3 L3 SVP: 8 DLU: 77

869.134-022 TRACK-LAYING SUPERVISOR (construction) alternate titles: extra-gang supervisor; rail gang supervisor; track layer, head; track leader

Supervises and coordinates activities of workers engaged in laying and repairing railroad tracks: Measures distances from reference stakes to locate positions for installation of trackage, switches, and crossovers. Verifies alignment of rails by measuring distances from rails to predetermine center line. Supervises TRACK-SURFACING-MACHINE OPERATOR (construction) and TRACK LAYER (construction) in repair of railroad tracks. Performs other duties as described under SUPERVISOR (any industry) Master Title.
GOE: 05.11.01 STRENGTH: L GED: R4 M3 L4 SVP: 7 DLU: 77

869.134-026 SUPERVISOR, ASBESTOS REMOVAL (construction)

Supervises and coordinates activities of workers engaged in removing asbestos from ceilings, walls, floors, and other structures: Reviews job specifications, inspects work site, and confers with contracting agent to evaluate removal project. Estimates length of time, number of workers, and equipment and supplies required to accomplish project. Hires new workers and instructs workers in safety and removal procedures. Assigns and supervises workers in specific tasks, such as setup of equipment and removal and clean-up of asbestos. Monitors and inspects quality of work during project. Examines workers' equipment, such as respirator systems, air evacuation and filtration systems, and air quality testing devices, to ensure that they meet company and government safety standards. May maintain project records and order supplies. May assist workers in removal activities. Performs other duties as described under SUPERVISOR (any industry) Master Title.
GOE: 05.10.01 STRENGTH: M GED: R3 M3 L3 SVP: 6 DLU: 86

869.137-010 TRAFFIC-MAINTENANCE SUPERVISOR (government ser.)

Supervises and coordinates activities of workers engaged in installing and repairing traffic signals, erecting signs or devices, such as traffic islands and barriers, and in painting traffic-control lines on pavement. When traffic control maintenance is a police responsibility, may be designated Traffic-Maintenance Officer (government ser.). May be designated according to responsibility as Paint-Crew Supervisor (government ser.); Traffic-Signal Supervisor, Maintenance (government ser.); Traffic-Sign Erection Supervisor (government ser.).
GOE: 05.10.01 STRENGTH: M GED: R4 M3 L3 SVP: 7 DLU: 77

869.137-014 WRECKING SUPERVISOR (construction)

Supervises and coordinates activities of TRACTOR-CRANE OPERATOR (any industry) and other workers engaged in razing structures, salvaging materials, and removing debris. Performs duties as described under SUPERVISOR (any industry) Master Title.
GOE: 05.11.01 STRENGTH: L GED: R4 M3 L3 SVP: 7 DLU: 77

869.261-010 HOUSE MOVER (construction)

Prepares buildings for moving from one site to another on trailer truck or rollers, determining most suitable technique based on knowledge of structures and moving-permit regulations: Observes size, shape, and position of building to determine placement of beams and route of travel. Cuts large buildings into sections, using carpentry tools, to facilitate moving building, and to comply with permit regulations. Breaks holes in foundation or removes underpinning, using steel cutters and carpentry tools. Directs workers in positioning timbers or steel beams under house. Positions jacks under beams and raises house. Rolls pneumatic-tired dollies under beams, lowers house onto dollies, and fastens dollies to beams, using chains. Bolts crossbeam to supporting beams to provide tow-bar to move house. Attaches winch-cable to crossbeams. Directs TRACTOR-TRAILER-TRUCK DRIVER (any industry) in moving building to new location and positioning it on new site. May turn guilding arm of rear dollies, using block and tackle to assist truck driver to negotiate sharp turns. May erect foundation. May lower and level house on foundation at new location, using hydraulic jacks. May confer with city and highway officials to obtain permit to move house over streets and roads. May direct CARPENTER HELPERS, HARDWOOD FLOORING (construction).
GOE: 05.10.01 STRENGTH: H GED: R4 M3 L3 SVP: 6 DLU: 77

869.261-014 MECHANICAL-TEST TECHNICIAN (inst. & app.)

Fabricates test structures and installs electronic recording instruments according to schematics, blueprints, and engineering specifications, to provide test facilities for research on aircraft arresting gear: Constructs monorail anchoring stands and footings, using arc welder, drill press, press brake, and handtools. Lays out reference points at test site for installation of monorail, using transit and level. Installs monorail, using handtools. Loads and positions moving and still cameras to record test results. Installs device for triggering test stages. Installs electronic equipment, such as galvanometer and oscillograph, following schematics, to record temperature, pressure, velocity, and force. Tests, adjusts, and repairs recording instruments to replace defective electrical components and to solder loose connections, using voltmeter, ohmmeter, and handtools. Prepares report of test observations.
GOE: 05.05.06 STRENGTH: M GED: R4 M3 L3 SVP: 7 DLU: 77

869.261-018 POURED-CONCRETE-WALL TECHNICIAN (construction)

Surveys and marks construction site, and constructs concrete buildings, using surveying instruments, blueprints, handtools, and power tools, working as member of crew: Reads structural specifications, such as blueprints, building plans, sketches, and plot maps of site location to ascertain dimensions of structure and types of materials to be used. Measures and bolts together wooden or metal sections to form walls, windows, and door frames, using handtools and power tools. Surveys excavation site to ensure specified angles and dimensions of structure footings, using surveying instruments, such as transit and theodolite. Measures distances to points, using steel tape, and records station numbers, distances, and elevations in logbook. Stakes corners of building site and signals BULLDOZER OPERATOR (any industry) I 850.683-010 to excavate area to specified depth. Lays building and wall footings and trues corners, using plumb bob and string, chalk, stakes, footing and wall forms, and hammer. Signals CONCRETE-MIXING-TRUCK DRIVER (construction) 900.683-010 and guides pouring chute that dumps cement into wall and footing cavities. Smooths tops of poured cement, using trowel. Removes wooden forms after cement has dried to free walls and footings, using hammer. Sprays asphalt on outer wall surfaces and footings to waterproof structures. Installs subgrade drainage tile and connects tile to specified points at sewer drain.
GOE: 05.10.01 STRENGTH: H GED: R4 M3 L3 SVP: 7 DLU: 86

869.261-022 REPAIRER, RECREATIONAL VEHICLE (vehicles, nec)

Repairs recreational vehicles, such as campers, travel trailers, and motor homes according to customer service request or work order: Confers with customer or reads work order to determine nature and extent of damage to vehicle. Inspects, examines, or tests parts or item to be repaired or replaced. Lists parts needed, estimates costs, and plans work procedure, using parts list, technical manuals, diagrams, and personal knowledge. Removes damaged exterior panels of vehicle, using handtools. Repairs and replaces structural frame members, seals leaks, and replaces or repairs malfunctioning items, such as heaters, stoves, refrigerators, or water pumps, using equipment and tools, such as drill press, wrenches, and saws. Repairs electrical wiring, plumbing, and gaslines (propane), using items such as caulking compounds, electrical wiring and tape, and plastic or copper pipe. Refinishes wood surfaces on cabinets, doors, moldings, and walls, using woodworking tools, spray equipment, paints, and varnishes. Inspects, examines, and tests functional parts of vehicle, using pressure gauges, ohmmeter, and other test equipment, according to work order, to verify completeness of work performed on new or repaired units before delivery to customer.

GOE: 05.10.01 STRENGTH: M GED: R4 M3 L3 SVP: 6 DLU: 86

869.261-026   WIND TUNNEL MECHANIC (aircraft mfg.)
Constructs, modifies, maintains, and services wind and propulsion tunnel research facilities used to test models of aircraft components, utilizing knowledge of engineering test methods and procedures, using handtools, power tools, machines, and equipment: Installs and aligns mechanical, hydraulic, and pneumatic test equipment and models on support structures, using handtools, power tools, and precision instruments. Installs instrumentation, such as thermocouples and pressure taps, on model and test equipment. Inspects test setup and operates equipment to detect and correct malfunctions. Maintains instrumentation equipment and accessories, such as pressure valves, icing indicators, drive units, spray units, and pumps. Confers with engineering and other personnel during testing and modifies model, test support structure, or test equipment as directed.
GOE: 05.10.04 STRENGTH: M GED: R4 M4 L4 SVP: 7 DLU: 87

869.281-010   FURNACE INSTALLER-AND-REPAIRER, HOT AIR (any industry) alternate titles: furnace worker; heating worker
Installs and repairs hot-air furnaces, stoves, and similar equipment in accordance with diagrams and other specifications, using handtools and pipe-threading tools: Constructs foundation of concrete or other noncombustible material. Assembles and positions heating units in accordance with diagrams, using handtools. Cuts holes in floors and walls to form air duct outlets. Installs air ducts, smoke pipes, blowers, and stokers, following blueprints of building and using handtools. Installs fuel pipes, using dies, pipe cutters, and pipe wrenches. Wraps insulating asbestos around air ducts. Connects and adjusts timers and thermostats. Inspects inoperative heating units to locate causes of trouble. Disassembles heating unit and replaces or repairs defective parts, using handtools. Cuts, bends, and crimps sheet metal to repair furnace and stove casing and pipes, using crimpers, files, snips, handbrakes, and sheet metal hammers. Reassembles and starts heating unit to test operation.
GOE: 05.05.09 STRENGTH: M GED: R4 M3 L3 SVP: 7 DLU: 77

869.281-014   HOUSE BUILDER (construction)
Builds and repairs houses, barns, commercial buildings, garages, and similar structures according to rough sketches or verbal orders, typically performing duties of several building trades crafts workers, especially those of BRICKLAYER (construction); CARPENTER (construction); PAINTER (construction); PAPERHANGER (construction); PLASTERER (construction). Worker is not expert in any one trade and work usually does not possess finish of more specialized workers. May prepare own building plans. May sublet portions of work to specialists. This job is generally found in rural areas where specialists in individual building trades are not available.
GOE: 05.05.02 STRENGTH: M GED: R3 M3 L3 SVP: 7 DLU: 77

869.281-018   YARD INSPECTOR (ship-boat mfg.)
Examines various units of vessels during construction for faulty work quality and compliance with blueprint specifications and Navy standards, using measuring tools: Inspects welded joints for specified fusion. Examines structural units to determine that frames, plates, and foundations are assembled, according to blueprint specifications. Examines installation of machinery and gear, checking on alignment and operation. Checks installation and operation of electrical wiring and equipment. Examines piping and sheet metalwork. Supervises tests on tanks, pipes, and bulkheads.
GOE: 05.07.01 STRENGTH: L GED: R4 M3 L3 SVP: 7 DLU: 77

869.287-010   BRIDGE INSPECTOR (r.r. trans.)
Inspects railroad bridges, trestles, culverts, and waterways to detect damage or wear and to ensure structures conform to safety regulations, building codes, and railroad engineering specifications: Inspects waterways to determine need for cleaning, straightening, or enlargement. Inspects masonry in tunnels, culverts, and waterways to detect cracks in concrete or signs of settlement. Verifies alignment of bridge with road track, using levels and similar gauging instruments. Observes installation of guardrails on bridges to ensure construction according to specifications. Inspects fire protection equipment, such as fire alarms, sprinkler systems, and water barrels, on bridges and in tunnels. Determines need for repainting structures to prevent rust or excessive weathering. Measures clearance between bridges and roads to ensure sufficient clearance for passage of vehicles, in accordance with local building codes and specifications. Inspects piles, posts, and timbers to determine if decayed, split, or crooked. Strikes wooden supports with hammer and listens for sounds indicating decay. Inspects bolts and rivets at joints of floor beams, stringers, and panel points to ensure they are securely fastened. Inspects steel girders to detect buckling. Inspects drainage systems to detect obstructions. Inspects inside of tunnels to detect excessive vegetation growth. Prepares reports of findings, noting location and type of structure, defect, and extent of damage.
GOE: 05.07.01 STRENGTH: M GED: R4 M4 L3 SVP: 7 DLU: 77

869.361-010   CONDUIT MECHANIC (construction; utilities) alternate titles: duct layer
Builds and repairs concrete underground vaults and manholes, and installs ducts to provide installation and maintenance facilities for underground power cables: Installs sheeting, shoring, and bracing for excavation. Builds wooden forms and erects steel reinforcing for concrete vaults and manholes. Directs workers engaged in pouring concrete into forms, and removes forms after concrete has set. Installs brackets and braces, and cuts apertures required for installation of electric equipment and ducts. Lays drainpipe and connects it to sewer system. Forces air through ducts to test for obstructions, using air compressor.

Demolishes or trims vaults and manholes, using pneumatic tools, working in proximity to high-voltage electric cables and equipment. Cuts and lays tile or fiber ducts, using portable power saw and grinder and brickmason's handtools. Cuts, threads, bends, and installs metal conduit. May lay precast concrete ducts.
GOE: 05.05.06 STRENGTH: H GED: R3 M3 L3 SVP: 7 DLU: 77

869.361-014   HYDRAULIC-JACK ADJUSTER (construction)
Sets up hydraulic jacks used to raise precast concrete floors and roof slabs: Guides threaded lift rods, raised by STRUCTURAL-STEEL WORKERS (construction), through holes in jack frames. Slips lift nut (nut cap) over end of rod and inserts hinged nut to fasten lift rod onto jack. Mounts hydraulic motor to jack, using handtools. Fits drive chain around gears on motor and lift nuts. Pulls idler gear arm to adjust tension of drive chain and bolts it in position. Snaps hose fittings and electric wiring in place to connect jacks to control panel and pump. Observes performance of jacks during lifting operations and signals LIFT-SLAB OPERATOR (construction) when malfunction occurs.
GOE: 05.05.06 STRENGTH: M GED: R3 M2 L2 SVP: 6 DLU: 77

869.361-018   SIGN ERECTOR-AND-REPAIRER (fabrication, nec)
Erects wood or metal framework for use as billboards for outdoor advertisements: Examines blueprints and measures distances with rule and tape to lay out work. Cuts wooden structural parts to shape and size, using power-driven woodworking machines. Directs HOLE-DIGGER-TRUCK DRIVER (construction; tel. & tel.; utilities) in digging holes and setting poles to support structure. Drills holes in masonry or concrete walls with portable power drill, and installs anchor bolts, working from swinging scaffold to install supports on side of buildings. Bolts or nails billboard framework to supports, and directs WELDER, ARC (welding) in welding metal joints. Bolts, nails, or screws wood or metal panels to framework to form base for billboards. Bolts, screws, or clips metal trim in place to form decorative seal for joints between panel and framework. Erects scaffolds and hoists. Repairs billboards by replacing defective parts. May fabricate sign parts, using woodworking and·metalworking machines. May paint completed billboard. May install floodlight fixtures. May dig post holes by hand and secure posts in holes.
GOE: 05.05.06 STRENGTH: M GED: R3 M2 L2 SVP: 6 DLU: 77

869.367-010   ASSISTANT CONSTRUCTION SUPERINTENDENT (construction)
Assists superiors in directing activities of workers concerned with construction of buildings, dams, highways, pipelines, or other construction projects: Assists superiors in planning construction procedures, specifications, work schedules, and material needs. Inspects work in progress to ensure that work conforms to specifications and adherence to work schedules.
GOE: 05.02.02 STRENGTH: L GED: R3 M3 L3 SVP: 7 DLU: 77

869.367-014   MEASURER (retail trade)
Measures windows and doors of customer's home to facilitate custom installation of metal doors, windows, and screens, using folding rule and tape measure. Prepares work order containing window and door dimensions and other customer specifications. May estimate cost of installation.
GOE: 05.09.02 STRENGTH: M GED: R3 M2 L2 SVP: 3 DLU: 77

869.367-018   PIPELINE CONSTRUCTION INSPECTOR (construction)
Inspects materials and quality of work of pipeline construction for conformance to specifications: Observes preparation of right-of-way for conformance to contract agreement. Verifies depth and alignment of trenches, using tape measure. Examines bottom of trench for rocks or other hard objects that might damage pipe coatings. Examines surface and x-ray films of welded joints to detect external and internal welding defects. Observes coating and wrapping of pipe or pipe joints for conformance to specifications and verifies accuracy of coating by observing or conducting electrical tests for holidays (inadequately coated areas on pipe). Advises supervisor regarding corrections to be made.
GOE: 05.07.01 STRENGTH: L GED: R4 M3 L3 SVP: 8 DLU: 77

869.381-010   HOUSE REPAIRER (construction)
Repairs and remodels houses and small buildings, according to blueprints or oral instructions: Measures distances and marks reference points on existing structure to lay out work. Removes defective members, existing siding, sheathing, and trim, using pinch bar, portable power saw, hammer, and other carpenter's handtools. Cuts lumber to size and shape, using hand or portable power saw. Nails and screws new framework, sheathing, and trim in place. Fills cracks and other defects in plaster or plasterboard with patching plaster, using trowel. Sands plaster patch after drying to match existing surface. Paints interior and exterior surfaces to specified color and texture. Replaces or installs new electrical fixtures, plumbing hardware, and brickwork, using pliers, screwdrivers, wrenches, and trowel.
GOE: 05.10.04 STRENGTH: M GED: R4 M3 L3 SVP: 7 DLU: 77

869.381-014   LABORATORY-EQUIPMENT INSTALLER (construction)
Installs laboratory and hospital equipment, such as chemical-resistant tables, laboratory benches, hoods for fumes, and operating-room sinks, according to blueprints, using carpentry and plumbing tools: Measures distances on wall or floor with rule or tape to lay out installation. Drills holes in masonry or steel framework with portable electric drill. Assembles equipment and anchors it to framework, using tap-in socket or expansion bolts.
GOE: 05.10.01 STRENGTH: V GED: R3 M3 L3 SVP: 7 DLU: 77

869.381-018   PIPE INSTALLER (construction; utilities)
Installs conduit pipe used to protect electrical wiring in buildings and transportation equipment: Reads blueprints to determine size, position, and amount

of conduit pipe required. Cuts threads, and bends pipe, using handtools and power tools. Installs pipe in walls, ceilings, and floors.
GOE: 05.10.01 STRENGTH: H GED: R3 M2 L3 SVP: 7 DLU: 77

869.381-022 SAFE-AND-VAULT SERVICE MECHANIC (business ser.; wholesale tr.) alternate titles: safe repairer; vault mechanic

Installs and repairs safes and vault doors in banks and other establishments: Installs vault doors and deposit boxes in banks, according to blueprints, using equipment, such as powered drills, taps and dies, and truck crane and dolly. Removes, repairs, adjusts, and reinstalls safes, vault doors, vault compartments, hinges, and other vault and safe equipment, using handtools and other machines and equipment, such as lathes, drill presses, and welding and acetylene cutting apparatus. Tests and repairs locks and locking devices [LOCKSMITH (any industry)]. Removes interior and exterior finishes and sprays on new finishes.
GOE: 05.05.06 STRENGTH: H GED: R3 M3 L3 SVP: 7 DLU: 77

869.381-026 SIGN ERECTOR I (fabrication, nec) alternate titles: sign hanger

Erects preassembled illuminated signs on buildings or other structures, according to sketches, drawings, or blueprints: Measures location for sign and marks points where holes for expansion shields are to be drilled, using measuring tape and chalk. Drills holes, using star drill. Drives expansion shield into hole with hammer, and secures lag bolts in shield, using wrench. Attaches hanging pole for sign to building front with lag bolts, and secures pole with guy wires attached from pole to lag bolts. Secures cornice hook on roof, rigs block and tackle, and hoists sign into position, or operates hydraulic boom to position sign. Secures sign to hanging pole with hooks. Makes electrical connections to power source and tests sign for correct operation. May prewire sign before installing. May use welding equipment when installing sign. May mount plastic signs with adhesives. May fabricate signs according to specifications and be designated Sign Maker (fabrication, nec).
GOE: 05.05.06 STRENGTH: M GED: R4 M2 L3 SVP: 7 DLU: 77

869.381-030 STEEPLE JACK (construction)

Constructs, maintains, and demolishes elevated structures, such as smokestacks, water tanks, and steeples, according to specifications: Climbs ladder attached to structure; assembles and climbs interlocking ladder; constructs and climbs scaffolding tower around structure; attaches block and tackle to cable, fastened on structure or on boom of adjoining erection tower; or uses crane to hoist self in boatswain chair. Positions and welds fabricated steel sections to structure; lays bricks and lines concrete brick and stone chimneys; fills mortar joints of fractures; installs lightning protection devices; applies paint and waterproofing solutions; sandblasts to clean and polish; positions and nails ladders, rails, and scaffolding to structure; or constructs and repairs roofs, using such roofing materials as asphalt and shingles. Demolishes structure by any of following methods: Dismantles sections and chutes section to ground; cuts out section of base, shores up with timbers and dynamites or burns timbers to collapse structure; or cuts structure at base, using cable attached to block and tackle fastened to boom of adjoining erection tower, to lower structure to ground. May fasten brackets onto structure, lay planks on brackets and attach guard rail on brackets to construct scaffold. May repair brick chimneys and smokestacks and be designated Chimney Repairer (construction).
GOE: 05.05.06 STRENGTH: M GED: R3 M3 L3 SVP: 7 DLU: 77

869.381-034 TIMBER FRAMER (mine & quarry) alternate titles: timber repairer

Cuts, fits, installs, and repairs supporting timbers and other framework in underground mine, using carpentry tools: Measures and cuts timbers for roof supports and framing, such as ladders, chutes, walls, and ventilation doors, using handsaw or power saw, square, and rule. Sets roof timbers and inserts wedges to hold them in place. Erects cribbing to increase support or control ventilation [STOPPING BUILDER (mine & quarry)]. Mortises joints with saw, chisel, or adz, and bores boltholes with brace and bit or power drill. Installs braces to repair or shore up loose timbering, using hammer and spikes. May set and wedge props (posts) in place as temporary support for roof or working face. May cut timbers to size and load them onto cars for haulage to mine. May build wooden forms, and mix and pour concrete supports. May set and bolt together steel roof supports and insert wedges to hold supports in place.
GOE: 05.05.02 STRENGTH: H GED: R3 M2 L2 SVP: 6 DLU: 77

869.384-010 REPAIRER, MANUFACTURED BUILDINGS (mfd. bldgs.; vehicles, nec)

Repairs defective units and systems in mobile, modular, and prefabricated homes and travel trailers, using handtools and power tools: Connects water hose to inlet pipe of plumbing system and tests operation of water closets and sinks. Examines and pressure-tests pipes and connections to detect leaks. Repairs leaks with caulking compound or replaces pipes, using pipe wrench. Connects electrical system to outside power source and activates switches to test operation of appliances and light fixtures. Locates and repairs frayed wiring, broken connections, or incorrect wiring, using ohmmeter, soldering iron, tape, and handtools. Opens and closes doors, windows, and drawers to test their operation and trims edges to fit, using jack-plane or drawknife. Resets hardware, using chisel, mallet, and screwdriver. Refinishes wood surfaces on cabinets, doors, moldings, floors, and walls, using power sander, putty, wood finish or paint and brush. May install furniture in mobile home [INSTALLER (mfd. bldgs.; vehicles, nec)]. May seal open side of modular units or double-wide mobile homes to prepare them for shipment, using polyethylene sheets, nails, and hammer.

May drive truck to transport mobile and modular homes or travel trailers. May position mobile home for permanent occupancy on customer's lot, using building blocks, bubble levels, hydraulic jacks, lumber, shingles, and handtools. May be designated Servicer, Travel Trailers (vehicles, nec).
GOE: 05.10.01 STRENGTH: H GED: R3 M2 L2 SVP: 4 DLU: 77

869.387-010 POLE INSPECTOR (utilities) alternate titles: field inspector; pole tester

Inspects power line poles for rot or other deterioration: Examines poles supporting power line. Taps pole with hammer and listens for vibrations indicating internal decay. Tests defective poles with probing bar or bores into poles with brace and bit or auger to determine extent of rot. Drives wooden pegs into bored holes to seal against moisture, using hammer. Prepares reports indicating condition and draws diagrams showing location of poles, with recommendations for pole replacement or type of treatment required to arrest rotting or restore poles. Collects sample of unusual type of rot for laboratory analysis. May estimate labor and materials costs of repairing or replacing poles. May examine attachments to poles and report conditions hazardous to power line facilities.
GOE: 05.07.01 STRENGTH: M GED: R3 M2 L2 SVP: 5 DLU: 77

869.463-010 SWIMMING POOL INSTALLER-AND-SERVICER (construction)

Performs any combination of following tasks in constructing, installing, and servicing swimming pools at commercial and residential sites: Plots length and width of pool site, according to specifications, and marks corners of site, using stakes and sledgehammer. Confers with customer to ensure that pool location and dimensions meet customer's demands. Operates backhoe to dig, shape, and grade walls of in-ground pool. Assembles and aligns wall panel sections, using nuts, bolts, electric air gun, and transit. Pours premixed concrete mixture between dirt wall and wall panels to establish footing (foundation base) to anchor bottoms of wall panels and cross braces. Dumps and spreads gravel into hollow foundation to form drain field, using wheelbarrow, shovel, and rake. Digs trenches, spreads gravel, and lays drain tiles uphill of pool site to divert ground water. Lays out and connects pipelines for water inlets, return valves, and filters, using handtools. Snaps coping section to inside upper edge of wall panels around pool circumference to secure liner edge and protect pool users. Mixes prescribed amounts of cement, sand, and water, and pours mixture into foundation. Spreads and smooths mixture evenly throughout foundation, using trowel, and allows mixture to set. Assembles heater parts, connects gas, oil, or electric lines, and starts heater to verify working order of unit. Installs liner into pool, starts pump to fill pool with water, and installs return valves. Builds concrete deck around pool. Lays out and assembles prefabricated parts of above-ground pool, installs liner, connects plumbing lines, starts pump, and checks pool for leaks. Maintains and repairs pool and equipment, advises customers, and sells chemicals to prevent pool water problems.
GOE: 05.10.01 STRENGTH: V GED: R4 M4 L4 SVP: 8 DLU: 86

869.481-010 AWNING MAKER-AND-INSTALLER (furniture; retail trade)

Fabricates and installs fiberglass and metal awnings for homes and commercial and industrial establishments: Measures windows, doors, and other openings for size of awning and cuts and assembles frame [AWNING-FRAME MAKER (tex. prod., nec)]. Lays out and cuts fiberglass sheets to size with circular saw or cuts metal slats to proper length with handtools or power tools and bolts to frame. Drills holes in window and door frames, masonry, or brick, and mounts brackets. Hangs awnings in brackets. Installs and fastens control rod to louvers or awnings, and tests for ease of operation. May solder frame parts. May paint awnings desired color, using spray gun. May assemble venetian blinds [VENETIAN-BLIND ASSEMBLER (furniture; retail trade)].
GOE: 05.10.01 STRENGTH: M GED: R3 M3 L2 SVP: 5 DLU: 77

869.484-010 AWNING HANGER (construction; retail trade; tex. prod., nec) alternate titles: awning erector; awning installer

Attaches rigid or roll-up canvas, metal, or plastic awnings onto buildings, using handtools and power tools: Measures installation site of awning, such as door, window, and store front, and marks location for frame brackets and hinges. Drills holes into brick, stone, or wood. Screws or nails frame fittings into place. Mounts awning frame to fittings and fastens into position with handtools. Attaches crank roller to frame and building as required. Rolls or lifts awning and makes adjustments to canvas, metal, plastic, ropes, and frame to correct operating defects. May measure buildings to develop specifications for fabrication of awnings. May install awning hoods. May fabricate awning frame [AWNING-FRAME MAKER (tex. prod., nec)]. May assemble awning to frame [RIGGER (tex. prod., nec)]. May repair canvas coverings [CANVAS REPAIRER (any industry)].
GOE: 05.10.01 STRENGTH: H GED: R3 M2 L2 SVP: 4 DLU: 77

869.484-014 DRAPERY HANGER (retail trade) alternate titles: installation worker, draperies; installer

Installs draperies in customers' homes: Measures area to be covered, and delivers finished draperies to customers' homes. Screws and bolts brackets and hangers onto wall, using handtools. Hangs and arranges draperies to enhance appearance of room. May install window shades and venetian blinds.
GOE: 05.10.01 STRENGTH: M GED: R3 M2 L2 SVP: 5 DLU: 77

869.484-018 VENETIAN-BLIND INSTALLER (furniture; retail trade)

Installs venetian blinds in customer's home or business establishment: Measures and marks location for hanging brackets, using rule and pencil. Drills

bracket holes in cement, plaster, or wood and installs brackets, using hand or electric drill and screwdriver. Secures blinds in brackets and pulls lowering, raising and tilting cords to detect and adjust functioning defects. Measures installation site to obtain specifications for fabrication of blinds. May sell venetian blinds and assist customer in color selection of blinds. May clean and repair venetian blinds [VENETIAN-BLIND CLEANER AND REPAIRER (any industry)]. May assemble new venetian blinds [VENETIAN-BLIND ASSEMBLER (furniture; retail trade)].
GOE: 05.10.01 STRENGTH: M GED: R3 M2 L2 SVP: 4 DLU: 77

869.487-010 MEASURER (struct. metal)
Measures door and window openings in buildings for metal-framed doors and windows: Measures opening for size of door or window required. Records measurements for fabricators and assemblers. May adjust and repair faulty doors or windows, using manual and portable power tools.
GOE: 05.09.02 STRENGTH: M GED: R3 M2 L2 SVP: 4 DLU: 77

869.564-010 LINE WALKER (petrol. & gas; petrol. refin.; pipe lines) alternate titles: line rider
Patrols oil and gas pipelines and communication systems on foot, horseback, or in automobile to locate and repair leaks, breaks, washouts, and damaged utility wires and poles: Inspects pipelines to detect evidence of leaks, such as oil stains, odors, and dead vegetation. Repairs small leaks, using caulking tools, hammers, clamps, and wrenches. Reports large leaks and washouts to district office. Inspects telephone and telegraph wires to locate broken insulators, wires and fallen poles, and reports findings. Inspects operation of automatic drip bleeder on gaslines to detect malfunctions, such as clogged valves, and adjusts or repairs valves, using handtools. Installs and replaces warning signs along road and water crossings. Prepares inspection reports.
GOE: 05.07.01 STRENGTH: L GED: R3 M2 L3 SVP: 4 DLU: 77

869.567-010 SURVEYOR HELPER (any industry)
Performs any of following duties to assist in surveying land: Holds level or stadia rod at designated points to assist in determining elevations and laying out stakes for mapmaking, construction, mining, land, and other surveys. Calls out reading or writes station number and reading in notebook. Marks points of measurement with elevation, station number, or other identifying mark. Measures distance between survey points, using steel or cloth tape or surveyor's chain. Marks measuring points with keel (marking crayon), paint sticks, scratches, tacks, or stakes. Places stakes at designated points and drives them into ground at specified elevation, using hammer or hatchet. Cuts and clears brush and trees from line of survey, using brush hook, knife, ax, or other cutting tools. May perform duties as directed by LAND SURVEYOR (profess. & kin.) or SURVEYOR ASSISTANT, INSTRUMENTS (profess. & kin.). May perform one operation and be designated Brush Clearer, Surveying (any industry); Staker, Surveying (any industry); Surveyor Helper, Chain (any industry); Surveyor Helper, Rod (any industry).
GOE: 05.12.02 STRENGTH: M GED: R3 M1 L2 SVP: 4 DLU: 77

869.662-010 LIFT-SLAB OPERATOR (construction) alternate titles: slab lifting engineer; slab lifting supervisor
Operates hydraulic jacks to raise precast concrete floors and roof slabs into position: Directs HYDRAULIC-JACK ADJUSTERS (construction) engaged in erecting scaffolds, hoisting and installing hydraulic jacks on top of support columns, erecting lift rods, and fastening them to jack and support plates set in concrete slab. Measures and marks grade lines on support columns. Connects pump and jacks to control panel, and positions panel on slab so that jacks and grade marks may be observed during lifting. Starts pump and moves levers and valves on control panel to regulate action of jacks. Signals worker to verify grade with rule. Adjusts control valves when slab has reached predetermined position. Directs welding crew to weld supporting collars or brackets to column. May drive truck, equipped with winch, to raise jacks to position on support columns, and to lift and remove equipment from slab.
GOE: 05.12.04 STRENGTH: M GED: R4 M2 L3 SVP: 7 DLU: 77

869.664-010 CONCRETE-BUILDING ASSEMBLER (mfd. bldgs.)
Performs any combination of following duties concerned with assembling concrete buildings at construction site, working as member of crew: Positions column location templates at specified locations on prepared concrete foundations for installing wall panel support columns. Nails template to floor, using cement nails and hammer. Enlarges recessed area around reinforcement rod projecting from floor at column installation site to ensure proper height of column when installed, using hammer and chisel. Wets area with water to ensure bonding of mortar, and applies mortar with trowel. Installs column in wet mortar with protruding pipe end of column down over rod. Aligns and braces column vertically, using bubble lever, board, nails, and hammer. Nails upper column support templates to top of columns, using hammer and measures distance between columns, using tape. Installs outside and inside wall panels that have tongue-and-groove edges, using pneumatic hoist. Inserts pin through hoist hooks and holes in concrete wall panels to lift and position panels between columns. Signals worker to operate hoist to maneuver panel past rough spots in grooves of columns. Removes obstructions in grooves with hammer and chisel. Patches holes, cracks, and joints in assembled sections of building, using mortar and trowel.
GOE: 05.12.12 STRENGTH: H GED: R2 M2 L2 SVP: 4 DLU: 77

869.664-014 CONSTRUCTION WORKER I (construction)
Performs any combination of following duties on construction projects, usually working in utility capacity, by transferring from one task to another where

demands require worker with varied experience and ability to work without close supervision: Measures distances from grade stakes, drives stakes, and stretches tight line. Bolts, nails, aligns, and blocks up under forms. Signals operators of construction equipment to facilitate alignment, movement, and adjustment of machinery to conform to grade specifications. Levels earth to fine grade specifications, using pick and shovel. Mixes concrete, using portable mixer. Smooths and finishes freshly poured cement or concrete, using float, trowel, or screed. Positions, joins, aligns, and seals pipe sections. Erects scaffolding, shoring, and braces. Mops, brushes, or spreads paints or bituminous compounds over surfaces for protection. Sprays materials such as water, sand, steam, vinyl, paint, or stucco through hose to clean, coat, or seal surfaces. Applies caulking compounds by hand or with caulking gun to seal crevices. Grinds, sands, or polishes surfaces, such as concrete, marble, terrazzo, or wood flooring, using abrasive tools or machines. Performs variety of tasks involving dextrous use of hands and tools, such as demolishing buildings, sawing lumber, dismantling forms, removing projections from concrete, mounting pipe hangers, and cutting and attaching insulating material. Work is usually performed with other workers. May be designated according to duties performed as Batterboard Setter (construction); Billboard-Erector Helper (construction); Bricklayer, Paving Brick (construction); Caulker (construction). May be designated: Carpenter Helper, Maintenance (construction); Cement Mason, Highways And Streets (construction); Cement Sprayer, Nozzle (concrete prod.; construction); Concrete-Wall-Grinder Operator (construction); Corrugated-Sheet-Material Sheeter (construction); Cradle Placer (construction); Dampproofer (construction); Drain Layer (construction); Duct Installer (construction; mfd. bldgs.); Fine Grader (construction); Fitter (construction; pipe lines); Floor Finisher (construction); Floor-Sanding-Machine Operator (construction); Form-Builder Helper (construction); Form Setter, Metal-Road Forms (construction); Form Setter, Steel Forms (construction); Form Setter, Steel-Pan Forms (construction); Foundation-Drill-Operator Helper (construction); Glazier Helper (construction); Ground Wirer (construction); Holder, Pile Driving (construction); Hydrant-And-Valve Setter (construction); Insulation Installer (construction); Joist Setter, Adjustable Steel (construction); Laborer, Adjustable Steel Joist (construction); Laborer, Carpentry, Dock (construction); Layer-Out, Plate Glass (construction); Lightning-Rod Erector (construction); Ornamental-Iron-Worker Helper (construction); Painter, Rough (construction); Painter, Structural Steel (construction); Paint-Stripping-Machine Operator (construction); Permastone Dresser (construction); Pile-Driving Setter (construction); Pipe Caulker (construction); Pipe Layer (construction); Pipeline Worker (construction); Plumber Helper (construction); Pointer, Caulker, And Cleaner (construction); Pump-Erector Helper (construction); Receiver Setter (construction); Roofer, Vinyl Coating (construction); Seat Installer (construction); Septic-Tank Servicer (construction); Sewer Tapper (construction); Shorer (construction); Stone Polisher (construction); Tapping-Machine Operator (construction); Tuck Pointer (construction); Waterproofer (construction); Well-Drill-Operator Helper, Cable Tool (construction); Well-Drill-Operator Helper, Rotary Drill (construction); Wrecker (construction).
GOE: 05.10.01 STRENGTH: H GED: R3 M3 L3 SVP: 4 DLU: 88

869.664-018 SEWER-LINE REPAIRER (sanitary ser.)
Repairs and maintains municipal storm and sanitary sewer lines, performing any combination of following tasks: Inspects manholes to locate stoppage. Runs cleaning rods through rod guide, fits front end of rod with auger, using wrench, and lowers guide into position. Thrusts rods into invert and advances them until auger reaches obstruction. Rotates rods manually with turning pin, or attaches end of rod to portable power rodder to rotate rods. Pulls lever and depresses pedal of machine to advance cleaning tool to encounter obstruction and to rotate cable or rods until obstacle is broken. Retracts rods to drag out obstructions, such as roots, grease, and other deposits. Cleans and repairs catch basins, manholes, culverts, and storm drains, using handtools. Lays brick to raise manhole walls to prescribed street level, using masonry tools. Measures distance of excavation site, using tape measure, and marks outline of area to be trenched according to direction of supervisor. Breaks asphalt and other pavement, using airhammer, pick, and shovel. Cuts damaged section of pipe with cutters and removes broken section from ditch. Replaces broken pipes and reconnects pipe sections, using pipe sleeve. Inspects joints to ensure tightness and seal before backfilling. Packs backfilled excavation, using air and gasoline tamper. Taps mainline sewers to install sewer saddles. Replaces manhole covers. Updates sewer maps and manhole charting. Drives pickup trucks to haul crew, materials, and equipment. Services, adjusts, and makes minor repairs to equipment, machines, and attachments. Communicates with supervisor and other workers, using radio telephone. Prepares records showing actions taken, human resource and equipment utilization, and disposition of material. Requisitions tools and equipment. Operates sewer cleaning equipment including power rodder, high velocity water jet, sewer flusher, bucket machine, wayne ball, and vac-all. Cleans and disinfects domestic basements and other areas flooded as a result of sewer stoppages. May lead workers in large repair and construction crew and direct other workers in efficient and safe use of machines, work methods, and safety procedures.
GOE: 05.12.12 STRENGTH: H GED: R3 M2 L2 SVP: 6 DLU: 86

869.665-010 AUXILIARY-EQUIPMENT TENDER (construction)
Tends one or more portable power-driven pumps, compressors, or generators to provide power for tools, machinery, and equipment, to remove water, or to maintain air supply at construction site: Connects hoses, pipelines, or power cables, using wrench, and fills fuel tank. Starts power unit, pump, or compressor, and sets controls to regulate air pressure or electricity. Observes temperature,

pressure, or amperage gauges and adjusts controls to maintain specified level. Lubricates, maintains, and repairs equipment, using handtools. May be designated according to equipment tended as Compressor Operator (construction); Generator Tender, Portable (construction); Lock Tender (construction) I; Pump Tender (construction).
GOE: 05.11.01 STRENGTH: M GED: R3 M2 L2 SVP: 6 DLU: 77

869.667-010 COLUMN PRECASTER (mfd. bldgs.)
Performs any combination of following duties concerned with making concrete columns to be used as wall panel and ceiling supports in concrete buildings: Cleans forms of concrete residue, using putty knife, hammer, chisel, wire brush, and broom. Sprays oil on forms to prevent concrete from sticking to form, using pressure sprayer. Assembles forms, using bolts and wrench. Places opened sided aluminum column forms on form bed in specified alignment. Positions pipe inside columns and tapes end of pipe to prevent entry of concrete, using masking tape. Attaches end pieces of forms that hold pipe and concrete when concrete is poured. Inserts metal spacers into open side of column to stabilize column sides during pouring of concrete. Signals CONCRETE-MIXING-TRUCK DRIVER (construction) to position mixer to fill columns. Moves discharge chute of mixer to distribute concrete. Operates electric vibrator to evacuate air bubbles and allow even distribution of concrete in column form. Disassembles and removes column form, using wrench, hammer, and chisel. Inserts and secures sleeve fittings on end of pipe, using screwdriver. Places cast columns in storage area.
GOE: 06.04.32 STRENGTH: H GED: R2 M1 L1 SVP: 2 DLU: 77

869.667-014 SIGNALER (construction) alternate titles: highballer
Signals or relays signals to operators of hoisting equipment engaged in raising or lowering loads and pumping or conveying materials, such as concrete and gunite, by telephoning, blowing whistle, motioning by hand or flag, or by pulling bell cord. May remove dogs, chains, or slings from hoisted material.
GOE: 05.12.04 STRENGTH: L GED: R2 M1 L2 SVP: 2 DLU: 77

869.681-010 CONCRETE-FENCE BUILDER (construction)
Constructs concrete block and mortar post and installs precast concrete panels to build fences: Lays out fence, according to blueprint specifications, using level and tape measure. Operates earth moving equipment to clear and level land [OPERATING ENGINEER (construction; mine & quarry)]. Operates power-auger to dig post holes [EARTH-BORING-MACHINE OPERATOR (construction; utilities)]. Positions reinforcing iron in holes, and places preshaped wood forms around hole. Mixes and pours concrete into forms or lays concrete blocks to form fence post, using mixer, wheelbarrow, or trowel. Positions precast concrete panels between block or concrete post, using crane.
GOE: 05.05.01 STRENGTH: H GED: R3 M2 L2 SVP: 6 DLU: 77

869.682-010 CIRCULAR SAW OPERATOR (construction)
Operates circular saw to cut concrete or asphalt along marked line to facilitate installation and repair of utility systems and equipment: Installs specified diamond edged circular blade, using handtools. Positions and lowers guide arm of saw over marked cutting line. Connects water hose to supply coolant between cutting blade and surface. Starts motor and pushes lever to lower blade into concrete surface until specified depth has been attained. Pulls lever to activate self-propelled saw along marked line. Guides saw along line, using handle bars attached to saw. Changes worn cutting blades and makes minor repairs, using handtools.
GOE: 05.10.01 STRENGTH: M GED: R3 M1 L2 SVP: 5 DLU: 77

869.682-014 CORE-DRILL OPERATOR (construction)
Operates core drilling equipment to drill holes of specified size in walls or slabs of concrete to facilitate installation and repair of utility systems and equipment: Locates and marks position for drill base, using rule and chalk. Secures drill base to floor, using bolts and wrench. Bolts drill stand to base, mounts drill motor on stand, and levels drill by turning screws at base of drill, using wrench. Connects equipment to electrical outlet, and attaches water hose which supplies coolant for drill. Attaches diamond tipped core drill to drill rod, and fastens rod in machine, using wrench and other handtools. Starts motor and turns crank to move drill into specified drilling position. Observes pressure gauge to maintain specified pressure on drill bit with crank. Tapes plastic bags to finished walls to prevent water damage. Lubricates equipment and makes minor repair, using grease gun and handtools.
GOE: 05.11.03 STRENGTH: M GED: R3 M1 L2 SVP: 5 DLU: 77

869.683-010 FORM-TAMPER OPERATOR (construction) alternate titles: form tamper; form-tamping-machine operator; tamping-machine operator, road forms
Operates gasoline powered machine to tamp earth solidly around foundation form: Lifts and positions machine on single rail of form. Pushes lever to engage crankshaft and activate tamping arms. Pushes or pulls machine manually, using Y-shaped handle to balance and guide machine along rail. Removes or places earth at sides of form, using shovel.
GOE: 05.11.01 STRENGTH: H GED: R2 M1 L2 SVP: 3 DLU: 77

869.683-014 RIGGER (construction)
Operates power winch, equipped with cathead, to haul and slack ropes and cables to move barge or skid-mounted piledriver into position and hold piledriver leads in position for driving piling at angles: Attaches lines to piling or snubbing post to pull or anchor piledriver. Winds and releases ropes or cables on winch drum to move barge, piledriver, or piledriver leads. Fastens lines to piledriver platform or barge to hold it in place while driving piles.

GOE: 05.11.01 STRENGTH: H GED: R3 M1 L2 SVP: 4 DLU: 77

869.683-018 TAMPING-MACHINE OPERATOR (construction) alternate titles: asphalt-tamping-machine operator; hydraulic-hammer operator; tamper operator
Operates crawler-tire or pneumatic-tire mounted tamping machine to compact earthen fills and finished road materials: Drives machine to work area. Moves levers to control tamping action of machine. May operate machine with interchangeable hammers to cut or break up pavement and drive guardrail posts into earth.
GOE: 05.11.01 STRENGTH: L GED: R3 M1 L2 SVP: 5 DLU: 77

869.684-010 ASSEMBLER (mfd. bldgs.; vehicles, nec) alternate titles: framer
Performs any combination of following duties to assemble mobile and modular homes or travel trailer coaches, following blueprints and verbal instructions, using handtools and power tools: Positions precut frame members in jigs and nails, rivets, or bolts members together to assemble wall, floor, and roof frames, using carpenter tools. Positions wheel and spring assembly on brackets of chassis, using chain hoist, and bolts assembly to chassis, using power wrench. Installs tires on wheels, using power tire changer and tire tools. Positions and fastens precut metal beams on front of chassis to form tongue and attaches jack-and-hitch assembly to tongue, using arc-welding equipment. Sprays undercoating compound on floor frame and chassis with spray gun. Installs furring strips, insulation, and plywood flooring over floor frame, using carpenter's tools, staple gun, insulation tape, and gang-nail press. Positions and bolts chassis-and-wheel assembly to floor frame, using hoist and impact wrench. Erects side, end, and roof sections, using hoist or crane, and fastens sections to floor frame, using rivet gun or welding equipment and carpenter's tools. Assembles and installs preformed sections of sheet metal to form heating and air-conditioning ducts, using power screwdriver and aluminum tape. Stuffs insulation batting between wall frame members, and attaches wood or metal paneling to form interior walls, using brush, glue gun, rivet gun, and hammer. Lays out and cuts openings in wall and floor panels, according to blueprint specifications, to facilitate installation of windows, vents, electrical outlets, and heat registers, using rule, power saw, and tin snips. Fastens registers in openings, using screwdriver. May install electrical wiring and copper tubing and perform other duties as described under INSTALLER (mfd. bldgs.; vehicles, nec) 869.684-026. May lead and give directions to other workers. May be designated according to section assembled as Floor Finisher (mfd. bldgs.); Floor Framer (mfd. bldgs.); Roof Framer (mfd. bldgs.); Sheller (mfd. bldgs.); Side Framer (mfd. bldgs.); Wheel Installer (mfd. bldgs.). May assemble utility buildings and be designated Assembler, Utility Buildings (mfd. bldgs.).
GOE: 06.02.22 STRENGTH: M GED: R3 M2 L2 SVP: 4 DLU: 79

869.684-014 ASSEMBLER, SKYLIGHTS (plastic prod.)
Assembles and polishes plexiglass dome skylights, using handtools and electric buffer: Places aluminum frame on assembly table. Masks frame with adhesive-backed cork tape. Attaches dome to frame, using electric drill, electric screwdriver, or electric riveting gun. Polishes dome to remove blemishes, using electric buffer. Stacks domes on pallet. May move pallet to shipping department, using dolly.
GOE: 06.04.24 STRENGTH: M GED: R2 M1 L2 SVP: 3 DLU: 77

869.684-018 ASSEMBLER, SUBASSEMBLY (mfd. bldgs.; vehicles, nec)
Joins precut wood, metal, and plastic board pieces to assemble roof, sidewall, and floor subassemblies of manufactured buildings or travel trailer coaches, using assembly jig, handtools, and power handtools: Positions and aligns roof trusses, girders, studs, and other frame members in assembly jig, according to blueprint specifications. Fastens frame members together, using hammer and nails, gang-nail-press, or welding equipment. Attaches insulation and furring strips to framework, using pneumatic stapler. Attaches plywood, plasterboard, or metal sheathing to framework to form interior wall, ceiling, and subfloor of home, using power screwdriver and stapler, glue gun, hammer and nails, or pneumatic nailer. Trims sheathing overlap, using portable router. Measures, marks, bores, or cuts out sections of sheathing to facilitate installation of utility outlets and wiring, according to blueprints, using templates, power drill, and router. Moves completed subassembly to storage or assembly area. May be designated according to specific work performed as Roof Assembler (mfd. bldgs.) II; Interior Wall Assembler (mfd. bldgs.); Floor Assembler (mfd. bldgs.); Frame Assembler (mfd. bldgs.).
GOE: 06.04.22 STRENGTH: M GED: R3 M2 L2 SVP: 3 DLU: 77

869.684-022 FENCE ERECTOR (construction) alternate titles: iron-worker; wire-fence erector; wire-fence builder
Erects and repairs metal and wooden fences and fence gates around industrial establishments, residences, or farms, using power tools and handtools: Lays out fence line, using tape measure, and marks positions for postholes. Digs postholes with spade, posthole digger, or power-driven auger. Blasts rock formations with dynamite to facilitate digging of postholes. Sets metal or wooden post in upright position in posthole. Mixes concrete by hand or by use of cement mixer. Pours concrete around base of post or tamps soil into posthole to embed post. Aligns posts, using line or by sighting along edges of posts. Verifies vertical alignment of posts with plumb bob or spirit level. Attaches fence-rail support to post, using hammer and pliers. Cuts metal tubing, using pipe cutter and inserts tubing through rail supports. Completes top fence rail of metal fence by connecting tube sections by use of metal sleeves. Attaches rails

or tension wire along bottoms of posts to form fencing frame. Stretches wire, wire mesh, or chain link fencing between posts and attaches fencing to frame. Assembles gate and fastens it in position, using handtools. Saws required lengths of lumber to make rails for wooden fence. Nails top and bottom rails to fence posts, or inserts them in slots on posts. Nails pointed slats to rails to construct picket fence. Erects alternate panel, basket weave, and louvered fences. May weld metal parts together, using portable gas welding equipment. May be designated according to material used as Metal-Fence Erector (construction); Wire-Fence Erector (construction); Wooden-Fence Erector (construction); or according to specific duty performed as Fence-Gate Assembler (construction); Fence Setter (construction); Fence Stretcher (construction).
GOE: 05.10.01 STRENGTH: H GED: R3 M2 L2 SVP: 5 DLU: 77

869.684-026   INSTALLER (mfd. bldgs.; vehicles, nec) alternate titles: final finisher

Performs any combination of following duties to install fixtures and appliances and lay floor covering in mobile and modular homes and travel trailer coaches, using handtools and power tools: Locates, measures, and outlines installation areas for fixtures, such as partitions, doors, window facing, cabinets, and trim; and appliances, such as stoves, refrigerators, and heaters; using blueprint, tape measure, and chalk. Drills holes, attaches brackets and other holding devices, and installs fixtures and appliances, using power drills and screwdrivers. Measures, cuts, and flares copper tubing used as gas supply line and connects tubing to range, furnace, and heater, using cutter, flaring tools, and pliers. Connects water supply and drainage pipelines to sinks, bathtubs, shower, and toilet, using wrenches. Connects wiring to electrical appliances, using screwdriver and pliers. Measures, cuts out, and lays floor covering, such as linoleum tile and carpet, using tape measure, knife, cement trowel, and staple gun. Measures, cuts out, and attaches metal and wood molding around sink tops, cabinets, counter edges, and carpeting. Installs hardware, such as doorknobs, rods, racks, and holders. May drill holes through floor and bolt floor to metal chassis of mobile home, using drill, bolts, and impact wrench. May uncrate appliances and inspect for defects, such as dents or scratches. May direct activities of other workers. May be designated according to article installed as Appliance Installer (mfd. bldgs.; vehicles, nec); Cabinet-And-Trim Installer (mfd. bldgs.; vehicles, nec); Door Installer (mfd. bldgs.; vehicles, nec) II; Hardware Installer (mfd. bldgs.; vehicles, nec); Tile Installer (mfd. bldgs.; vehicles, nec).
GOE: 06.02.22 STRENGTH: M GED: R3 M2 L2 SVP: 4 DLU: 77

869.684-030   LAWN-SPRINKLER INSTALLER (construction)

Installs underground lawn sprinkler systems: Lays out plastic or copper tubing, according to sketch or blueprint. Digs trenches with shovel or by use of ditching machine. Cuts tubing to desired length, using handtools. Connects lengths of tubing, using paintbrush and solvent to fuse ends of plastic tubing, and handtorch and solder to join metal piping and connections. Makes connection to water main, using handtools. Turns valve to start water flow and observes operation to detect leaks. Installs electrical and mechanical control mechanisms for automatic operation. Fills trench with dirt after installation, using shovel.
GOE: 05.10.01 STRENGTH: M GED: R3 M2 L2 SVP: 5 DLU: 77

869.684-034   LAY-OUT WORKER (mfd. bldgs.)

Lays out wall, ceiling, and floor panels to facilitate fabrication of modular homes: Reads production schedule and observes drawings to determine style of panels to be assembled and to determine materials required. Lays out materials, such as studs, joists, and headers of designated dimensions on worktable, using tape measure. Assist in assembly of panels, using nailing gun.
GOE: 06.02.31 STRENGTH: M GED: R3 M2 L2 SVP: 6 DLU: 77

869.684-038   PANEL INSTALLER (mfd. bldgs.) alternate titles: ceiling installer; closet builder; interior paneler, partition setter

Installs prefabricated wooden or plastic board panels to form closets, walls, and ceilings in mobile or modular homes, using handtools and power tools: Conveys or assists other workers to convey panels to floor of home. Positions panels in sequence specified by blueprints and verifies alignment, using measuring tape and template. Fastens panels to specified sidewall and floor areas and to adjacent panels to form closets and dividing walls, using power screwdriver and staple gun. Lifts and positions ceiling panels in place, using hoist and nails or screws panels to roof truss, using hammer, staple gun or power screwdriver. Punches holes in ceiling and wall panels to facilitate installation of heating, plumbing and appliance vents, using hammer. May cut panel sections to required dimensions, using table saw.
GOE: 06.04.22 STRENGTH: M GED: R2 M1 L1 SVP: 2 DLU: 77

869.684-042   ROOF ASSEMBLER I (mfd. bldgs.)

Assembles roof sections of modular homes, performing any combination of following tasks: Positions and attaches precut plywood sheets onto wood or metal roof frames, using jig, adjustable vise clamps, and powered screwdriver or nail gun. Applies rubber cement or asphalt to plywood surface, using adhesive gun or roller, and lays plastic covering or asphalt felt paper in overlapping pattern to cover roof surface. Cuts roof covering to required length, using knife. Brushes plastic covering to smooth and remove air pockets, using broom. Attaches felt covering to roof, using staple gun. Positions and attaches plasterboard sheets to ceiling side of roof frame to form ceiling, using powered screwdriver. Operates electric hoist to move roof section between work stations. May install insulation between rafters to insulate roof, using stapler. May position and attach shingles to roof, using space gauge and pneumatic staple gun.

GOE: 06.04.22 STRENGTH: M GED: R3 M1 L2 SVP: 3 DLU: 77

869.684-046   ROUSTABOUT (petrol. & gas) alternate titles: connection worker; gang worker; roughneck

Assembles and repairs oil field machinery and equipment, using handtools and power tools: Digs holes, sets forms, and mixes and pours concrete into forms, to make foundations for wood or steel derricks, using posthole digger, handtools, and wheelbarrow. Bolts or nails together wood or steel framework to erect derrick. Dismantles and assembles boilers and steam engine parts, using handtools and power tools. Bolts together pump and engine parts. Connects tanks and flow lines, using wrenches. Unscrews or tightens pipe, casing, tubing, and pump rods, using hand and power wrenches and tongs.
GOE: 05.10.01 STRENGTH: H GED: R3 M1 L2 SVP: 5 DLU: 77

869.684-050   SHEETROCK APPLICATOR (mfd. bldgs.)

Fastens sheetrock to interior surface of manufactured building wall panels, using handtools: Installs blanket insulation between studs of exterior walls. Covers insulation with plastic moisture barrier and tacks plastic to studs. Selects required length of sheetrock and lays sheetrock on frame. Measures and marks position of electrical outlets, using tape measure and template. Cuts openings with handsaw. Squares frame, positions, and fastens sheetrock, using tape measure, nails, hammer, screws, and powered screwdriver. Cuts openings for windows and excess sheetrock, using router. Moves completed panel to next work station, using electric hoist.
GOE: 06.04.34 STRENGTH: M GED: R2 M1 L1 SVP: 3 DLU: 77

869.684-054   SIGN ERECTOR II (fabrication, nec)

Erects, assembles, and maintains roadside signs and billboards at designated locations, using handtools and power tools: Digs hole with post hole digger or shovel. Places wood or metal post in hole. Fills hole with cement and tamps cement to hold post in vertical position. Operates airhammer to drive channel-metal post into ground. Bolts, screws, or nails plywood or metal sign panels to sign post or frame, using handtools. Replaces worn and damaged signs. Repaints rusted signs. May erect metal sign support structure over highways. May operate banding machine to band signs on utility poles. May dismantle and number signs sections for transfer and reassembly at new locations and be designated Advertising-Display Rotator (business ser.).
GOE: 05.10.01 STRENGTH: H GED: R3 M2 L2 SVP: 3 DLU: 77

869.684-058   STOPPING BUILDER (mine & quarry) alternate titles: braddisher; ventilation worker

Builds doorways and brattices (ventilation walls or partitions in underground passageways) of materials, such as canvas, wood, concrete, brick, or concrete block as specified to construct partition to control circulation of air through passageways and working areas. Erects partitions to support roof in areas unsuited to timbering or bolting. May install rigid and flexible air ducts to transport air into work areas. May drill and blast obstructing bolders to reopen ventilation shafts.
GOE: 05.10.01 STRENGTH: H GED: R3 M1 L2 SVP: 5 DLU: 77

869.684-062   STULL INSTALLER (concrete prod.)

Installs stulls (wooden cross-bracing) inside partially cured concrete pipes to maintain round contour of pipes during curing process: Saws boards to specified length, using table saw. Nails crosspiece to end of each board. Inserts first stull at one end of pipe to span diameter and wedges stull ends tightly in place, using hammer and wedges. Wedges two more stulls crosswise to first stull and nails stulls together at intersection. Installs additional stulls in same manner at center and opposite end of pipe.
GOE: 05.12.12 STRENGTH: M GED: R2 M1 L1 SVP: 2 DLU: 77

869.684-066   TRIMMER (mfd. bldgs.) alternate titles: installer, molding and trim

Fabricates and installs molding and trim in manufactured buildings, using handtools and power tools: Measures and cuts wooden and plastic molding and trim to specified size, using hand shears, miter box, and radial saw. Reads blueprint to determine location for installation and fastens molding and trim to interior surfaces of manufactured buildings, using pneumatic stapler and hammer.
GOE: 06.04.25 STRENGTH: M GED: R2 M1 L1 SVP: 2 DLU: 77

869.684-074   UTILITY WORKER (mfd. bldgs.; vehicles, nec)

Performs any combination of following tasks in manufacture of mobile homes and travel trailers: Tends woodworking and metalworking machines to cut and shape wood and metal parts. Cuts, shapes, and assembles parts, using handtools and power tools. Installs parts, household appliances, furnishings, and fixtures, using handtools and power tools. Trains inexperienced workers. Assists, relieves, or substitutes for INSTALLER (mfd. bldgs.; vehicles, nec); ASSEMBLER (mfd. bldgs.; vehicles, nec); and PLUMBER (mfd. bldgs.).
GOE: 06.02.22 STRENGTH: M GED: R3 M2 L2 SVP: 5 DLU: 77

869.684-078   VENEER STAPLER (ship-boat mfg.) alternate titles: boat wrapper

Staples successive layers of veneer lamina strips over boat frames preparatory to bonding to build up small hulls: Positions mucilage-faced strips over frames, laying each strip at an angle to lower one and securing strips with hand-stapling machine. Cuts off excess lengths of wood. Inspects hull visually and tactually for gaps on surface. Cuts and fits veneer wedges into gaps and secures them with staples. Repeats strip laying and stapling until desired thickness is attained.
GOE: 06.04.25 STRENGTH: M GED: R3 M1 L2 SVP: 4 DLU: 77

869.684-082   ASBESTOS REMOVAL WORKER (construction)

Removes asbestos from ceilings, walls, beams, boilers, and other structures, following hazardous waste handling guidelines: Assembles scaffolding and seals

off work area, using plastic sheeting and duct tape. Positions mobile decontamination unit or portable showers at entrance of work area. Builds connecting walkway between mobile unit or portable showers and work area, using handtools, limber, nails, plastic sheeting, and duct tape. Positions portable air evacuation and filtration system inside work area. Sprays chemical solution over asbestos covered surfaces, using tank with attached hose and nozzle, to soften asbestos. Cuts and scrapes asbestos from surfaces, using knife and scraper. Shovels asbestos into plastic disposal bags and seals bags, using duct tape. Cleans work area of loose asbestos, using vacuum, broom, and dust pan. Places asbestos in disposal bags and seals bags, using duct tape. Dismantles scaffolding and temporary walkway, using handtools, and places plastic sheeting and disposal bags into transport bags. Seals bags, using duct tape, and loads bags into truck.
GOE: 05.10.01 STRENGTH: H GED: R3 M2 L2 SVP: 2 DLU: 86

869.685-010 KETTLE TENDER (construction) alternate titles: burner; dope firer; dope heater; furnace tender; heater worker
Tends portable kettle that heats tar, asphalt, lead, or sealing compound for use as protective coating for pipelines, roofs, and pavement: Cuts asphalt, tar, or other corrosion-resistant compound into pieces with ax and places pieces in kettle. Maintains fire under kettle to bring materials to required temperature, judging heat from appearance of materials and gauges on kettle. May remove adhering asphalt from rakes or tamping irons by heating them or by use of fuel oil. May be designated according to material heated as Leadite Heater (construction); Tar Heater (construction).
GOE: 05.12.10 STRENGTH: M GED: R1 M1 L1 SVP: 2 DLU: 77

869.687-010 AWNING-HANGER HELPER (construction; retail trade; tex. prod., nec) alternate titles: installation helper
Assists AWNING HANGER (construction; retail trade; tex. prod., nec) to install canvas, wood, metal, and plastic awnings and to assemble and erect carports, patio covers, and metal panel fences. Digs post holes, using post hole digger or powered drill. Mixes concrete in mortar box or wheelbarrow, using hoe or shovel. Drills holes. Bolts and screws brackets to building to hold frame. Holds awnings during installation and lowers or raises awnings to observe their operation. Performs other duties as described under HELPER (any industry) Master Title.
GOE: 05.12.12 STRENGTH: H GED: R2 M1 L1 SVP: 3 DLU: 77

869.687-014 CAMOUFLAGE ASSEMBLER (ordnance)
Inserts steel wool by hand into openings of frames made of wood and chicken wire to make fireproof camouflage barriers.
GOE: 06.04.34 STRENGTH: L GED: R1 M1 L1 SVP: 2 DLU: 77

869.687-018 CLEANER (mfd. bldgs.)
Cleans interiors of manufactured buildings and makes minor repairs to correct defects, following oral instructions: Cleans interior of manufactured buildings, using broom, mop, dust cloth, and vacuum cleaner. Fills nail holes in woodwork, using putty and knife. Repairs minor defects, such as loose wall panels, missing trim, and defective door catches, using pneumatic stapler and screwdriver. Paints woodwork and soiled sections of ceiling, using paint and brush. Loads manufactured buildings components for shipment to construction site [LOADER (mfd. bldgs.)]. May hang curtains, using tape measure, curtain rods, screws and power screwdriver.
GOE: 05.12.18 STRENGTH: M GED: R2 M1 L1 SVP: 2 DLU: 77

869.687-022 CONCRETE-FLOAT MAKER (concrete prod.)
Performs any combination of following tasks concerned with fabricating and casting concrete moorage floats: Flattens, cuts, and bends rolled wire mesh to fabricate reinforcing cages, using flattening table, power cutters, bending table, and metal fastening clinchers. Assembles and seals cardboard cartons for use as cores for buoyancy chambers, using masking tape and shellac. Cuts reinforcing rods to specified length, using hydraulic cutters. Erects and fastens steel form sections with connecting pins. Settles concrete poured on bottom of form, using pneumatic vibrator. Places pair of wire cages in steel form and positions with metal spacers. Inserts cartons in cages. Places pouring plate on mold over cages, shovels poured concrete from plate into sides around cages, and settles it with vibrator. Lifts pouring plate aside and shoves rods into concrete to reinforce sides. Fills space on top of cages with concrete and levels concrete with trowel. Drives drainage tubes through top of tank into cartons, using hammer, and shoves fitting bolts into tank through holes in sides of mold. Strips forms, using hammer and pry bar. Sprays tank with sealer, using hand sprayer, and stamps trade name, using hand die.
GOE: 05.12.12 STRENGTH: M GED: R2 M1 L1 SVP: 2 DLU: 77

869.687-026 CONSTRUCTION WORKER II (construction)
Performs any combination of following tasks, such as erecting, repairing, and wrecking buildings and bridges; installing waterworks, locks, and dams; grading and maintaining railroad right-of-ways and laying ties and rails; and widening, deepening, and improving rivers, canals, and harbors, requiring little or no independent judgment: Digs, spreads, and levels dirt and gravel, using pick and shovel. Lifts, carries, and holds building materials, tools, and supplies. Cleans tools, equipment, materials, and work areas. Mixes, pours, and spreads concrete, asphalt, gravel, and other materials, using handtools. Joins, wraps, and seals sections of pipe. Performs variety of routine, nonmachine tasks, such as removing forms from set concrete, filling expansion joints with asphalt, placing culvert sections in trench, assembling sections of dredge pipeline, removing wallpaper, and laying railroad track. Many of these jobs are not full time; project

size and organization of work determine whether workers spend their time on one job or transfer from task to task as project progresses to completion. Some workers habitually work in one branch of industry, whereas others transfer according to availability of work or on seasonal basis. Work is usually performed with other workers. May be designated according to specific work performed as Air-Hammer Operator (construction); Asphalt-Plant Worker (construction); Asphalt Raker (construction); Backer-Up (construction); Bell-Hole Digger (construction); Brick Cleaner (construction). May be designated: Bricklayer Helper (construction); Brick-Paving Checker (construction); Cage Tender (construction); Carpenter Helper, Hardwood Flooring (construction); Cement-Mason Helper (construction); Clamper (construction); Cold Patcher (construction); Concrete-Pump-Operator Helper (construction); Concrete-Vibrator Operator (construction); Connector Hand (construction); Crank Hand (construction); Crushed-Stone Grader (construction); Curb-Setter Helper (construction); Dope Pourer (construction); Dredge Pipe Installer (construction); Dump Grader (construction); Filter-Bed Placer (construction); Floor-Finisher Helper (construction); Floor-Layer Helper (construction; retail trade); Form-Setter Helper (construction); Form Stripper (concrete prod.; construction); Form Tamper (construction); Grader (construction); Grader Tamper (construction); Grouter Helper (construction); Hod Carrier (construction); Hoosier Pole Hand (construction); Inserter (construction); Joint Filler (construction); Laborer, Batching Plant (construction); Laborer, Bituminous Paving (construction); Laborer, Cement-Gun Placing (construction); Laborer, Concrete Paving (construction); Laborer, Corrugated-Iron-Culvert Placing (construction); Laborer, Electric Power And Transmission Line (construction; utilities); Laborer, Heading (construction); Laborer, Pile Driving, Ground Work (construction); Laborer, Pipeline (construction); Laborer, Plumbing (construction); Laborer, Road (construction); Laborer, Shaft Sinking (construction); Laborer, Shore Dredging (construction); Laborer, Steel Handling (construction); Laborer, Stone Block Ramming (construction); Laborer, Wrecking And Salvaging (construction); Loft Worker, Pile Driving (construction); Material Hauler (construction); Miner Helper (construction); Mixer, Hand, Cement Gun (construction); Mold Maker (construction); Mortar Mixer (concrete prod.; construction); Mucker (construction); Mucker, Cofferdam (construction); Mud-Jack Nozzle Worker (construction); Oil Sprayer (construction); Painter Helper (construction); Paperhanger, Pipe (construction); Paper Latcher (construction); Paper Spooler (construction); Paving-Bed Maker (construction); Paving Rammer (construction); Pipe-Layer Helper (construction); Pipe-Machine Operator (construction); Plasterer Helper (construction); Portable Grout-Mixer Operator (concrete prod.; construction); Puddler, Pile Driving (construction); Reinforcing-Iron-Worker Helper (construction); Reinforcing-Steel Worker, Wire Mesh (construction); Riprap Placer (construction); Roofer Helper (construction); Roofer Helper, Vinyl Coating (construction); Sheeting Puller (construction); Sheet-Pile-Hammer Operator (construction); Skip Tender, Concrete Mixing Or Batch Plant (construction); Slicer (construction); Squeegee Finisher (construction); Stain Remover (construction); Stone-And-Concrete Washer (construction); Stonemason Helper (construction); Stone Unloader (construction); Structural-Steel-Worker Helper (construction); Subgrade Tester (construction); Track Layer (construction); Track-Repairer Helper (construction); Trench Trimmer, Fine (construction); Wallpaper Remover, Steam (construction); Wall Washer (construction); Waterproofer Helper (construction); Well Digger (construction); White Washer (construction).
GOE: 05.12.03 STRENGTH: V GED: R2 M1 L1 SVP: 2 DLU: 79

869.687-030 FURNACE-INSTALLER-AND-REPAIRER HELPER, HOT AIR (any industry) alternate titles: furnace repairer helper
Assists FURNACE-INSTALLER-AND-REPAIRER, HOT AIR (any industry) in installing and repairing hot-air furnaces: Carries tools and components, such as furnace, casing, duct sections, and materials to work area. Cleans fire pots, smoke, and hot-air ducts [FURNACE CLEANER (any industry)]. Holds furnace parts in place for assembling. Loosens or tightens nuts, screws, and bolts in assembling or dismantling furnace, using handtools. Performs other tasks as described under HELPER (any industry) Master Title.
GOE: 05.12.12 STRENGTH: H GED: R2 M1 L1 SVP: 2 DLU: 77

869.687-034 HOUSE-MOVER HELPER (construction)
Assists HOUSE MOVER (construction) to move buildings from one site to another on trailer trucks or rollers, performing any combination of following duties: Disconnects water and sewer lines, using wrenches, sledgehammer, chisel, or block and tackle. Raises building uniformly to prevent cracking of walls, using screw jacks and shoring blocks. Positions timbers or steel beams under buildings as directed. Lowers buildings onto trailer or roller, and attaches towing cables, chains, or rope at specified locations. Assists in lowering building onto new location.
GOE: 05.12.04 STRENGTH: H GED: R1 M1 L1 SVP: 2 DLU: 77

869.687-038 INSPECTOR (mfd. bldgs.)
Inspects manufactured buildings for conformance to specifications during specified intervals of assembly line construction: Measures dimensions and spacing of structural members in building components, such as walls, floors, ceilings, closets and windows for conformance to specifications, using square, plumb, and tape measure. Compares room dimensions, wall alignments, plumbing, and electrical elements with blueprints. Fills plumbing system with air to check for leaks, using air pump and pressure gauge. Tests electrical system for completeness of circuits, using ohmmeter. Inspects surfaces of walls, floors, and ceilings for defects, such as color irregularities, warped sections, and cracks. Compares furnishings of manufactured buildings with customer's order to en-

sure compliance. Prepares inspection report on findings for SUPERVISOR, MANUFACTURED BUILDINGS (mfd. bldgs.; vehicles, nec).
GOE: 06.03.02 STRENGTH: L GED: R3 M2 L3 SVP: 6 DLU: 77

869.687-042 TIMBER-FRAMER HELPER (mine & quarry)
Assists TIMBER FRAMER (mine & quarry) to cut and erect supports in mine: Places and holds timbers, such as posts, headers, and cap-pieces in position for sawing and notching. Saws, hews, and nails timbers as directed, performing duties as described under HELPER (any industry) Master Title.
GOE: 05.12.12 STRENGTH: H GED: R2 M1 L1 SVP: 3 DLU: 77

89   STRUCTURAL WORK OCCUPATIONS, N.E.C.

This division includes occupations, not elsewhere classified, concerned with structural work.

891   OCCUPATIONS IN STRUCTURAL MAINTENANCE, N.E.C.

This group includes occupations, not elsewhere classified, concerned with structural assembly and maintenance.

891.131-010 DOCK SUPERVISOR (ship-boat mfg.) alternate titles: supervisor, ship maintenance services
Supervises and coordinates activities of workers engaged in drydocking, painting, cleaning, and repairing vessels: Analyzes vessel's blueprints and specifications to determine size, shape, and number of keel and bilge blocks required to support vessel. Directs DOCK HAND (ship-boat mfg.) in assembling, positioning, and securing blocks to floating drydock platform, marine railway, or floor of graving dock. Sights reference points for positioning vessel over blocks, using transit, and directs DOCK HAND (ship-boat mfg.) in aligning of vessel over blocks. Directs workers in pumping operations to raise vessel and in positioning, flooding, and pumping caisson (gate) in graving dock. Directs workers engaged in cleaning and maintenance of vessel. Oversees flooding operations and removal of vessels from drydock. Performs other duties as described under SUPERVISOR (any industry) Master Title. May supervise SHIPWRIGHT (ship-boat mfg.) and be designated Shipwright Supervisor (ship-boat mfg.).
GOE: 05.12.18 STRENGTH: L GED: R4 M3 L3 SVP: 7 DLU: 77

891.137-010 MAINTENANCE SUPERVISOR (any industry) alternate titles: building-and-grounds supervisor; building-maintenance supervisor, mechanical; building supervisor
Supervises and coordinates activities of workers engaged in maintaining and repairing physical structures and utility systems of buildings and maintaining grounds: Directs workers engaged in painting and performing structural repairs to masonry, woodwork, and furnishings of buildings, and maintaining and repairing building utility systems, such as electrical wiring and controls, heating and ventilating systems [UTILITIES-AND-MAINTENANCE SUPERVISOR (any industry) 899.131-018]; and water distributing and plumbing systems [PLUMBING SUPERVISOR, MAINTENANCE (construction) 862.131-018]. Directs workers engaged in ground maintenance activities, such as mowing lawns, trimming hedges, removing weeds, and raking and disposing of leaves and refuse. Requisitions tools, equipment, and supplies. Inspects completed work for conformance to blueprints, specifications, and standards. Performs other duties as described under SUPERVISOR (any industry) Master Title. May supervise workers engaged in installing, servicing, and repairing mechanical equipment.
GOE: 05.02.02 STRENGTH: L GED: R4 M3 L3 SVP: 7 DLU: 87

891.137-014 SUPERVISOR, AIRCRAFT CLEANING (air trans.)
Supervises and coordinates activities of workers engaged in cleaning interiors and exteriors of airplane: Trains new workers. Observes work procedures and inspects completed work to ensure adherence to efficiency and safety standards, quality of work, and cleaning requirements. Inventories and orders replacement cleaning and sanitary supplies. Records inspection results and sanitary supplies used on cleaning report. Performs duties as prescribed under SUPERVISOR (any industry) Master Title.
GOE: 05.12.01 STRENGTH: L GED: R4 M3 L3 SVP: 7 DLU: 77

891.137-018 SUPERVISOR, TANK CLEANING (water trans.)
Supervises and coordinates activities of TANK CLEANER (any industry) engaged in cleaning ship's tanks for storing volatile liquids: Determines work sequence and equipment required from job order. Instructs worker in connecting steam, air, and water hoses to equipment located on shore. Inspects completed work for conformance to standards. Maintains record of work accomplished. Performs other duties as described under SUPERVISOR (any industry) Master Title.
GOE: 05.12.01 STRENGTH: M GED: R4 M3 L3 SVP: 7 DLU: 77

891.564-010 PIPE CHANGER (mine & quarry)
Changes, rotates, and cleans pipes that carry materials, such as concentrate slurry and tailings throughout iron ore processing plant: Removes bolted couplings or flanges and changes precut pipe sections or replaces hoses on cyclone feed and discharge lines, concentrate lines, and tailings lines, using wrenches, chain hoist, and impact wrench. Loosens bolted couplings and rotates pipe, using chain wrench so that inner pipe surfaces are worn evenly by abrasive

slurry. Stencils direction and date of rotation on pipe. Inserts pipe cleaner (cylindrical go-devil with scraper and leather fins) into pipe through trap and notifies pumping section to start material flow to force cleaner through pipe to clean out deposits. Removes cleaner at end of pipe. Disassembles, transports, and reassembles pipe sections in new mining areas, using handtools.
GOE: 05.12.12 STRENGTH: H GED: R2 M1 L2 SVP: 3 DLU: 77

891.684-010 DOCK HAND (ship-boat mfg.)
Performs following duties concerned with drydocking and cleaning exteriors of ships and maintenance of drydock and piers: Positions keel blocks on dock platform and builds bilge blocks as directed by DOCK SUPERVISOR (ship-boat mfg.), using handtools and clamps. Opens flood valves in floating drydock sections to submerge platform. Winds up docking lines, using winch, or snubs lines over dock cleats to position ship over drydock. Starts pumps to remove water from drydock sections and turns pump controls to keep dock platform on even keel. Washes or steam cleans exterior of ship's hull to remove marine growth and loose paint, using high-pressure water hose, or steam-cleaning equipment. Scrapes barnacles or other marine growth from hull with long-handled scraper and chips rust or paint from hull with pneumatic tool. Erects stages and scaffolds to reach sections of hull. Opens and closes flood valves on drydock when removing ship from dock, to keep dock platform on even keel as it submerges. Floods or drains caisson (gate) of graving drydock and assists in floating caisson in or out of position across drydock entrance.
GOE: 05.12.18 STRENGTH: H GED: R2 M1 L2 SVP: 3 DLU: 77

891.684-014 RUBBER AND PLASTICS WORKER (military ser.)
Inspects, repairs, replaces, and modifies soundproofing and sweat proofing equipment aboard drydocked or moored submarines: Inspects submarines to detect hazards or malfunctions. Replaces worn or defective rubber and plastic items, such as grommets. Sprays soundproofing material on internal submarine walls, using compressor. Affixes neoprene sheets to submarine walls. Shapes and finishes plastic and rubber items, using handsaws, sanders, grinders, or drill presses.
GOE: 05.10.01 STRENGTH: H GED: R3 M3 L3 SVP: 4 DLU: 77

891.684-018 SWIMMING-POOL SERVICER (any industry) alternate titles: maintenance worker, swimming pool; pool servicer
Cleans, adjusts, and performs minor repairs to swimming pools and auxiliary equipment: Removes leaves and other debris from surface of water, using net. Cleans bottom and sides of pool, using such aids as underwater vacuum cleaner, hose, brush, detergent, acid solution, and sander. Inspects and replaces loose or damaged tile. Cleans and repairs filter system. Adjusts and performs minor repairs to heating and pumping equipment, using mechanic's handtools. Dumps chemicals, in prescribed amounts, to purify water in pool. Prepares service report of materials used and work performed.
GOE: 05.10.04 STRENGTH: M GED: R3 M1 L2 SVP: 4 DLU: 77

891.684-022 BUILDING CLEANER (any industry)
Cleans brick, stone, or metal exterior of structures, using cleaning agents, such as sand, acid solution, and steam: Cleans limited section of surface to determine strength of cleaning agents needed to prepare desired surface finish. Erects swinging scaffold, positions ladders, or assembles metal scaffolding to facilitate cleaning of structures. Pours specified portions and type of cleaning agents into hoppers or tanks of truck-mounted pumping equipment, and turns valves of equipment to produce steam and pump cleaning agents through hoses. Presses levers of spray nozzles to regulate flow of cleaning agent over structure surface. Cleans excessively stained surface areas, using brushes and cleaning compound. Sprays concrete floor to etch surface for cleaning and applies filler compound to seal floor surface. Cleans exterior surfaces of vehicles, using high pressure hoses and cleaning solutions. Cleans rugs on premise of customer, using chemicals, handbrushes, or portable scrubbing machine. Replaces worn parts of cleaning equipment and maintains equipment, using handtools.
GOE: 05.10.01 STRENGTH: H GED: R3 M2 L2 SVP: 4 DLU: 86

891.685-010 STEAM-CLEANING-MACHINE OPERATOR (construction)
Tends one or more portable generators used to generate steam for steam-cleaning exposed surfaces of masonry structures: Connects hose line and electric leads to source of water supply and electric power. Starts pump to force water through generator coils. Fills tanks with cleaning compounds. Starts fire under generator when water coils are full. Turns valves to regulate flow of water and cleaning compound through hose line. Observes pressure gauge to ensure that required steam pressure is maintained. Flushes generator coils with scale remover to clean them.
GOE: 05.11.01 STRENGTH: L GED: R2 M1 L1 SVP: 4 DLU: 77

891.687-010 CHIMNEY SWEEP (any industry) alternate titles: chimney cleaner; cleaning operator
Cleans soot from chimneys: Removes pipe connecting furnace to flue, using handtools. Cleans soot from chimney pit, using vacuum cleaner that automatically discharges into receptacle mounted on truck. Cleans connecting pipes with brush, replaces pipe, and seals joints with cement. Closes fireplace openings and other outlets to clean chimney from above. Lowers weighted bag down flue, withdraws bag which expands and scrapes soot from lining of chimney. Empties bag and inspects interior of chimney to ensure completion of cleaning process, using reflecting light of mirror. May make oral or written reports to request services of CHIMNEY REPAIRER (business ser.). May brush interior of chimney, boilers, and furnaces.
GOE: 05.12.18 STRENGTH: M GED: R2 M1 L1 SVP: 3 DLU: 77

891.687-014 FURNACE CLEANER (any industry)
Cleans fire pots, ducts, vents, registers, air chambers, and filter screens of domestic furnaces: Scrapes soot and ash from fire pot and smoke chambers, using scraper and wire brush. Cleans filter screens, using solvent. Removes dust-clogged air filters and places clean filters into brackets. Brushes and washes dust from air chamber and ducts, using wire or fiber brush. Removes loose soot, ash, and dust, using hand scoop and portable vacuum cleaner. Examines seams of furnace section for defects, such as cracks, and reports defects to customer or furnace repairer. May extract dust from ducts and jackets, using vacuum equipment. May tighten nuts, bolts, and screws on furnace, using handtools.
GOE: 05.12.18 STRENGTH: M GED: R2 M1 L1 SVP: 2 DLU: 77

891.687-018 PROJECT-CREW WORKER (any industry)
Cleans walls, floors, ceilings, and structural members of buildings, using steam-cleaning equipment, brooms, and scrapers, and removes spillage and overflow of materials being processed or manufactured, with shovel and rake. Applies sealer to tile and concrete floors to protect them against subsequent spillage, using mop or brush. Sprays insecticides and fumigants over cleaned areas to prevent insect and rodent infestation.
GOE: 05.11.01 STRENGTH: M GED: R2 M1 L1 SVP: 3 DLU: 77

891.687-022 TANK CLEANER (any industry)
Cleans interiors of boilers, storage tanks, industrial processing tanks, kilns, and tank and refrigerator railroad cars to remove emulsion and incrustations, using shovels, squeegees, brooms, scrapers, hoses, water, and solvents: Drains tank, connects hose to water or steam lines, and sprays walls, roof, and bottom of tank to flush residue, such as oil, acid, grease, and sludge through tank openings. Scrapes and scrubs walls, using detergents, solvents, scrapers, and brushes to remove incrustations, scale, or deposits of coke or catalyst. Sweeps up debris and shovels sludge into buckets or wheelbarrows or down chutes. Removes chemical residues and other liquids from tank bottoms with squeegees or pump and suction hoses. May dry tanks with wood shavings or portable air-drying equipment. May test gas content of tanks. May add specified chemicals to industrial tanks to maintain and replenish tank processing solutions. May be designated according to type of tank cleaned as Acid-Tank Cleaner (petrol. refin.); Boiler Cleaner (any industry); Plating-Tank Cleaner (electron. comp.); Tank-Car Cleaner (petrol. refin.).
GOE: 05.12.18 STRENGTH: H GED: R2 M1 L1 SVP: 3 DLU: 86

891.687-030 TUBE CLEANER (any industry)
Cleans scale from inside of tubes that are used in boilers, kilns, and stills to circulate hot air or water: Removes plugs or assemblies from tube ends, using handtools. Pushes compressed-air rotary scraper or wire brush through tubes to scrape scales from interior surfaces. Flushes or blows out loosened deposits, using water or airhose. May inspect tubes by drawing electric light through them. May be designated according to type of tube cleaned as Boiler-Tube Reamer (any industry); Evaporator Repairer (chemical); Flue Cleaner (any industry); Still Cleaner, Tube (petrol. refin.); Tar Heat-Exchanger Cleaner (petrol. refin.). May steam clean outside of boiler tubes and be designated Boiler-Tube Blower (any industry).
GOE: 05.12.18 STRENGTH: M GED: R2 M1 L1 SVP: 2 DLU: 77

899 MISCELLANEOUS STRUCTURAL WORK OCCUPATIONS, N.E.C.

This group includes miscellaneous occupations, not elsewhere classified, concerned with structural work.

899.130-010 SUPERVISOR, CANAL-EQUIPMENT MAINTENANCE (waterworks) alternate titles: maintenance supervisor
Supervises and coordinates activities of workers engaged in repair and maintenance of irrigation canal gates, waterways, recorder wells (concrete lined sumps housing instruments to measure canal water level), and other canal structures. Orders erection of prefabricated concrete forms and scaffolding and directs workers in operation of sandblasting gear, air compressors, welding equipment, cement mixers, and truck-cranes. Inspects completed work for compliance to specifications. Performs duties as described under SUPERVISOR (any industry) Master Title.
GOE: 05.06.03 STRENGTH: M GED: R4 M3 L3 SVP: 8 DLU: 77

899.131-010 LABOR-CREW SUPERVISOR (construction; utilities)
Supervises and coordinates activities of workers engaged in constructing manholes, transformer vaults, and substation foundations, in installing street light poles, and in laying pipe and ductwork for telephone, electric, water and sewage systems, and gas and oil lines: Reads blueprints and interprets data, including angles required in bending pipe, mixture of concrete most suitable for soil conditions, locations for placement of pipe sections, and type and amount of insulating wrapping and adhesive compound required to protect pipe. Directs activities of workers engaged in inspecting pipe for deficiencies by use of x-ray equipment or by means of high-pressure air tests, of workers engaged in removing rust and applying protective coating to pipe, of workers engaged in laying pipe on land or underwater, of workers engaged in performing dredging, underwater blasting and backfilling activities, and of workers engaged in digging up and removing pipelines. Performs other duties as described under SUPERVISOR (any industry) Master Title. May be designated according to area of specialization as Duct-Layer Supervisor (construction; utilities); Fab-

rication Supervisor (construction); Lower-In Supervisor (construction); Pipe-And-Test Supervisor (construction); Pipe-Laying Supervisor (construction); River-Crossing Supervisor (construction); Take-Up Supervisor (construction).
GOE: 05.12.01 STRENGTH: L GED: R4 M3 L3 SVP: 8 DLU: 77

899.131-014 LOCK MAINTENANCE SUPERVISOR (construction)
Supervises and coordinates activities of workers engaged in installation, alteration, repair, and maintenance of structures, machines, equipment, and utility systems used to operate canal locks: Confers with project engineer on planning of work project relative to maintenance, repair, or alteration of items, such as buildings, utility systems, spillway gates, lock and dam walls; and walks and streets at lock site. Schedules work project to minimize interference with canal operation. Requisitions and verifies materials and equipment delivered to work site. Inspects work in progress and completed projects to ensure conformance to specifications. Trains workers in work methods and procedures. Performs other duties as described under SUPERVISOR (any industry) Master Title.
GOE: 05.10.04 STRENGTH: H GED: R4 M4 L3 SVP: 8 DLU: 77

899.131-018 UTILITIES-AND-MAINTENANCE SUPERVISOR (any industry) alternate titles: maintenance-and-utilities supervisor
Supervises and coordinates activities of workers engaged in maintaining building utility systems, such as electrical wiring and control systems, heating, ventilating, water supply, steam generating, and related pipe systems. Performs other duties as described under SUPERVISOR (any industry) Master Title. May compile reports of cost of completed work. May inspect systems to determine preventative maintenance needs. May supervise workers engaged in maintaining and repairing processing equipment and machinery [MAINTENANCE-MECHANIC SUPERVISOR (any industry) 638.131-022]. May supervise workers engaged in maintaining buildings and grounds.
GOE: 05.06.02 STRENGTH: L GED: R4 M3 L3 SVP: 8 DLU: 86

899.131-022 UTILITY SUPERVISOR, BOAT AND PLANT (ship-boat mfg.)
Supervises and coordinates activities of workers engaged in preparing boats for shipment: Supervises workers engaged in cleaning interior and exterior surfaces of boats. Examines equipment on boat to determine compliance with specifications. Reports deficiencies and reinspects boats after repairs. Constructs staging and dollies for shipment of boats, according to specifications, using rules, dividers, squares, and marking instruments. Cuts and drills materials at points marked to form joints, holes for fasteners, casters, or reinforcements, using hand and portable power tools. Fits and fastens pieces together, using handtools. Loads boat onto transport trailer, using electric hoist. Positions hoist hooks on slings attached to boat cradle to lift and lower boat onto trailer. Tightens chain fasteners, using clamp lever, to secure boat to trailer. Installs and maintains plant electrical, water, and compressed air systems, using power tools and handtools. Performs other duties as described under SUPERVISOR (any industry) Master Title.
GOE: 06.01.01 STRENGTH: M GED: R4 M3 L3 SVP: 7 DLU: 77

899.133-010 SUPERVISOR, LABOR GANG (any industry) alternate titles: boss; bull-gang supervisor; field supervisor; floating-labor-gang supervisor; general-labor supervisor; group supervisor, yard; overseer; yard-labor supervisor
Supervises and coordinates activities of workers engaged in cleaning and maintenance of industrial buildings and grounds: Inspects work areas to determine type of work required and materials and equipment to be used. Directs workers in projects, such as construction of ditches and roadways and grading drainage areas. Operates equipment, such as bulldozers and graders and trains workers in equipment operation. Performs other duties as described under SUPERVISOR (any industry) Master Title.
GOE: 05.12.01 STRENGTH: M GED: R4 M3 L3 SVP: 7 DLU: 77

899.134-010 HIGHWAY-MAINTENANCE SUPERVISOR (government ser.)
Supervises and coordinates activities of workers engaged in maintaining highways, municipal and rural roads, and rights-of-way in safe condition: Routinely inspects all primary and secondary roads in maintenance district. Plans and coordinates all maintenance to roads. Performs other duties as described under SUPERVISOR (any industry) Master Title.
GOE: 05.11.01 STRENGTH: M GED: R4 M3 L3 SVP: 8 DLU: 77

899.137-010 AIRPORT-MAINTENANCE CHIEF (air trans.) alternate titles: superintendent, maintenance, airports; gang boss; gang pusher
Supervises and coordinates activities of workers engaged in repairing and maintaining airport facilities: Reviews maintenance records and inspects facilities to determine repair needs. Prepares work specifications in accordance with regulations governing airport facilities. Requisitions materials and supplies. Assigns crews to repair of asphalt and concrete runways, taxiways, approaches, ramp and concourse lighting systems, patching and cleaning of loading aprons, roads and sidewalks, cleaning of drains, painting of buildings, and cultivating of lawns, shrubs, and other planted areas. Inspects work for compliance with specifications. Prepares maintenance reports. Estimates annual maintenance expenditures for use in preparation of budget. Performs other duties as described under SUPERVISOR (any industry) Master Title.
GOE: 05.10.04 STRENGTH: L GED: R4 M3 L3 SVP: 7 DLU: 77

899.137-014 SUPERINTENDENT, TRACK (construction)
Supervises and coordinates activities of workers engaged in maintenance and construction of racetrack buildings, grounds, and parking facilities: Inspects

premises to determine extent of repairs. Studies soil test reports to plan maintenance of racetrack surface, such as watering, discing, and grading. Compiles cost estimates of repairs and new construction and submits estimates to management for approval. Supervises workers engaged in repairing and maintaining buildings, removing and replacing top soil, watering, discing, and grading track surface, planting and plowing vegetation on track oval to renovate track, planting and trimming flowers, shrubs, and grass to maintain landscape; and repairing and rebuilding parking facilities. Compiles reports of human resources utilized, work progress, and disposition of materials. Performs other duties as described under SUPERVISOR (any industry) Master Title.
GOE: 05.12.01 STRENGTH: L GED: R4 M3 L3 SVP: 6 DLU: 77

899.137-018 SUPERVISOR, MAINTENANCE (petrol. refin.)
Supervises and coordinates activities of workers engaged in construction, maintenance, and cleaning activities at petroleum refinery. Performs duties as described under SUPERVISOR (any industry) Master Title. May supervise workers engaged in cleaning stills, storage tanks, and distillation towers only and be designated Supervisor, Tank Cleaning (petrol. refin.).
GOE: 05.12.01 STRENGTH: L GED: R4 M3 L3 SVP: 7 DLU: 77

899.261-010 DIVER (any industry) alternate titles: submarine worker
Works below surface of water, using scuba gear (self-contained underwater breathing apparatus) or in diving suit with air line extending to surface to inspect, repair, remove, and install equipment and structures: Descends into water with aid of DIVER HELPER (any industry), and communicates with surface by signal line or telephone. Inspects docks and bottoms and propellers of ships. Repairs vessels below water line, replacing missing or leaking rivets with bolts. Caulks leaks in ships or caissons. Guides placement of pilings for structures, such as docks, bridges, cofferdams, and oil drilling platforms. Lays, inspects, and repairs underwater pipelines, cables, and sewers, using handtools. Cuts and welds steel, using oxyycetylene cutting torch and arc-welding equipment, utilizing air balloon device for working underwater. Cleans debris from intake and discharge strainers. Removes obstructions from marine railway or launching ways with pneumatic and power handtools. Levels rails by driving wedges beneath track with maul or sledgehammer. Removes launching cradles and sliding ways from keels of newly launched vessels, using power and handtools. Places rigging around sunken objects and hooks rigging to crane lines. Rigs explosives for underwater demolitions. Searches for lost, missing, or sunken objects, such as bodies, torpedoes, sunken vessels, and equipment. Places recording instruments below surface of water preparatory to underwater tests or experiments. May set sheet pilings for cofferdams. May drill holes in rock for blasting purposes at bottom of lake or harbor and be designated Marine Driller (construction). May work in flooded mines. May use armored diving equipment for dangerous missions. May photograph underwater structures or marine life. May place sandbags around pipelines or base of cofferdam to provide structural support.
GOE: 05.10.01 STRENGTH: H GED: R4 M3 L3 SVP: 7 DLU: 77

899.261-014 MAINTENANCE REPAIRER, INDUSTRIAL (any industry) alternate titles: maintenance associate; plant-maintenance worker; utility repairer
Installs, maintains, and repairs machinery, equipment, physical structures, and pipe and electrical systems in commercial or industrial establishments, following specifications, blueprints, manuals, and schematic drawings, using handtools, power tools, hoist, crane, and measuring and testing instruments: Visually inspects and tests machinery and equipment, using electrical and electronic test equipment. Listens for unusual sounds from machines or equipment to detect malfunction and discusses machine operation variations with supervisors or other maintenance workers to diagnose problem or repair machine. Dismantles defective machines and equipment and installs new or repaired parts, following specifications and blueprints, using precision measuring instruments and handtools [MACHINE REPAIRER, MAINTENANCE (any industry) 638.261-030]. Cleans and lubricates shafts, bearings, gears, and other parts of machinery, using rags, brushes, and grease gun. Installs and repairs electrical apparatus, such as transformers and wiring, and electrical and electronic components of machinery and equipment [ELECTRICIAN, MAINTENANCE (any industry) 829.261-018]. Lays out, assembles, installs, and maintains pipe systems and related hydraulic and pneumatic equipment, and repairs and replaces gauges, valves, pressure regulators, and related equipment [PIPE FITTER (construction) 862.281-022]. Repairs and maintains physical structure of establishment [MAINTENANCE REPAIRER, BUILDING (any industry) 899.381-010]. May install machinery and equipment according to blueprints and other specifications [MILLWRIGHT (any industry) 638.281-018]. May install, program, or repair automated machinery and equipment, such as robots or *programmable controllers*. May set up and operate machine tools, such as lathe, grinder, drill, and milling machine to repair or fabricate machine parts, jigs and fixtures, and tools. May operate cutting torch or welding equipment to cut or join metal parts. May fabricate and repair counters, benches, partitions, and other wooden structures.
GOE: 05.05.09 STRENGTH: H GED: R4 M4 L3 SVP: 8 DLU: 88

899.281-010 CANAL-EQUIPMENT MECHANIC (waterworks)
Repairs and maintains gates and other structures of irrigation canals, using handtools, power tools, and welding equipment: Disassembles gate-moving gear at dam sites to remove worn or damaged gate cable, using mechanics' handtools. Slides fitting over new cable and pours molten zinc over fitting to secure fitting to cable. Threads cable around drum of gate lifting apparatus and

bolts fitting to gate. Welds broken parts of gates and other dam structures. Builds scaffolding and working platforms, using handtools. Sandblasts old paint and corrosion from gates. Paints gates, using spray gun. Lubricates gear trains, gear boxes, cables, and other fittings, using hand grease gun. Mixes concrete and repairs or constructs wells and pumps, using jackhammer, air drill, and water pump. Constructs and repairs structural and mechanical parts of checks, turnouts, and wasteways along canals. May repair and maintain inland waterway structures and equipment and be designated Lock-And-Dam Equipment Repairer (water trans.).
GOE: 05.10.01 STRENGTH: H GED: R3 M3 L3 SVP: 6 DLU: 77

899.364-010 CHIMNEY REPAIRER (business ser.)
Cleans, repairs, relines, remortars, and modifies chimneys of private residences, according to home owners' desires, using wire brush, hammer, chisel, trowel and mortar, brick, tile, metal pipe, and other handtools: Temporarily seals all openings into chimney to prevent soot leakage, using newspaper or plastic sheet and masking tape. Climbs ladders to roof of building and lowers weighted wire brush or scraper on rope down chimney to remove soot adhering to inside of chimney or removes soot from trap at chimney base by hand or by use of vacuum cleaner. Replaces loose or missing bricks or loose mortar. Relines chimney with double-walled metal pipe, inserting pipe in sections from top, when converting to gas heat. Cements outside of chimney in attic. Makes any other masonry repairs to chimney, such as relining chimney with tile or refacing chimney with decorative stone. May install dampers in fireplaces. May widen fireplace opening and install fans at top of chimney to correct draft.
GOE: 05.10.01 STRENGTH: M GED: R3 M2 L2 SVP: 5 DLU: 77

899.364-014 ARTIFICIAL-FOLIAGE ARRANGER (retail trade)
Cuts out, assembles, and installs artificial foliage, such as trees, shrubs, and flowers, to achieve aesthetic effects in commercial and industrial locations, using handtools and working as member of team: Receives instructions from supervisor, and reviews work orders to determine materials needed, such as soil, stones, styrofoam, planters, and artificial floral items, to complete customer's request. Selects, cuts, and assembles materials to form artificial flowers, trees, and shrubs, utilizing experience and knowledge of floral design and using clips, wire, glue, colored tape, scissors, and wire cutters. Loads materials into van, and drives van to deliver artificial floral displays to customer's premise. Arranges displays at customer's premise to create natural effect, utilizing ground covers, such as gravel, pinebark, and soil, according to effect desired by customer. Services arrangements to replace or repair damaged items and to rearrange displays as specified by customer. Prepares daily reports of materials used in each arrangement to maintain inventory records.
GOE: 05.12.12 STRENGTH: M GED: R3 M2 L2 SVP: 5 DLU: 86

899.381-010 MAINTENANCE REPAIRER, BUILDING (any industry) alternate titles: building repairer
Repairs and maintains physical structures of commercial and industrial establishments, such as factories, office buildings, apartment houses, and logging and mining constructions, using handtools and power tools: Replaces defective electrical switches and other fixtures. Paints structures, and repairs woodwork with carpenter's tools. Repairs plumbing fixtures. Repairs plaster and lays brick. Builds sheds and other outbuildings.
GOE: 05.10.01 STRENGTH: M GED: R4 M3 L3 SVP: 7 DLU: 81

899.384-010 TRANSPORTATION-EQUIPMENT-MAINTENANCE WORKER (museums) alternate titles: maintenance worker; renovator; transportation-museum helper
Assists in restoration or maintenance of transportation equipment, such as automobiles, ships, aircraft, streetcars, or locomotives, displayed by museums or similar institutions through performance of any combination of following tasks: Repairs or replaces interior components of equipment, such as wooden panels, seat cushions, window molding, or dashboards, using handtools and power tools, and utilizing carpentry, metalworking, and upholstering techniques. Cuts lumber or sheet metal to designated size, installs components, such as brake assemblies, rudders, or propellers, or welds metal sections, to assist other workers in reconstruction or renovation of exterior structural sections and accessories. Cleans surfaces with wire brush and solvent, applies rustproofing agent to surfaces, vacuums and dry cleans upholstered components, brushes or sprays paint, lacquer, or other coating on cleaned surfaces, or stencils and paints letters or designs on equipment or vehicles to restore or simulate original appearance. Builds, repairs, and installs wooden steps, scaffolds, and walkways to gain access to or permit improved view of exhibited equipment. May be designated according to specialty of institution as Antique-Auto-Museum-Maintenance Worker (museums); according to principal activity as Maintenance Carpenter (museums); or according to job location as Exhibit Cleaner (museums).
GOE: 05.05.06 STRENGTH: M GED: R3 M2 L3 SVP: 5 DLU: 86

899.484-010 MOBILE-HOME-LOT UTILITY WORKER (retail trade) alternate titles: maintenance worker, house trailer
Performs variety of duties at sales lot, to prepare new and used units, such as campers, travel trailers, mobile homes, and motor homes for display and sale: Unpacks crated furnishings and places them in proper location within trailer. Assembles and adjusts lines and hoses for utility fittings, using handtools. Cleans and polishes interior and exterior of units for sale. Repairs or replaces items, such as furniture, plumbing fixtures, electrical system, and bottled gas fittings to refurbish units. Repairs plumbing, electrical system, and bottled gas fittings. Installs linoleum and wall and floor tile. Paints furniture and parts of

interior, using spray gun or brush. May drive truck to pick up and deliver mobile houses over long and short distances.
GOE: 05.10.04 STRENGTH: H GED: R3 M1 L2 SVP: 6 DLU: 77

899.487-010   TESTER (rubber goods)
Tests rubber bladders, used with sections of inflatable buildings, for air leaks, using compressed airhose and mercury manometer: Attaches valve to bladder, using screwdriver. Inflates bladder to specified pressure with compressed airhose. Checks pressure using manometer. Records air temperature. Rechecks pressure and records air temperature periodically. Computes change in pressure due to temperature change, using formula. Removes valves and deflates bladder.
GOE: 06.03.01 STRENGTH: L GED: R2 M1 L2 SVP: 3 DLU: 77

899.664-010   DIVER HELPER (any industry) alternate titles: diver assistant; diver tender; life-line attendant
Helps DIVER (any industry) into diving suit, inspects diving equipment, and maintains communications with submerged DIVER (any industry) by lifeline or telephone: Helps DIVER (any industry) into suit equipped with hardshell headpiece (helment), breathing hose, belt and breast weights, and leaded feet. Examines equipment to ensure no obstructions in airhose and communication line exist and that air pressure is in accordance with DIVER'S (any industry) specifications. Hands equipment to DIVER (any industry) and helps diver into water. Attends lifeline and telephone to receive signals from DIVER (any industry), such as tugs on lifeline and instructions on telephone, to pull in or let out lifeline and airhose. Maintains check on time diver is submerged, weather conditions, and air compressor to ensure safety of DIVER (any industry). May be assigned only to letting out and taking in airhose and be designated Hose Tender (any industry).
GOE: 05.12.12 STRENGTH: M GED: R3 M1 L2 SVP: 3 DLU: 77

899.664-014   SEWER-PIPE CLEANER (business ser.) alternate titles: electric-sewer-cleaning-machine operator
Removes roots, debris, and other refuse from clogged sewer lines and drains, using portable electric sewer cleaning machine, and repairs breaks in underground piping: Positions or disassembles sewer trap machine at sewer or drain outlet. Removes drain cover, using wrench. Installs rotary knives on flexible cable, mounted on reel of machine, according to diameter of pipe to be cleaned. Starts machine to feed revolving cable into opening, stopping machine and changing knives as necessary to conform to diameter or contour of pipe. Withdraws cable to deposit accumulated residue removed from pipe in containers for disposal. Observes residue for evidence of mud, indicating broken sewer line. Measures distance from sewer opening to suspected break, using plumbers' snake, tapeline, or by estimating position of cutting head within sewer. Notifies coworkers to dig out ruptured line or digs out shallow sewers, using shovel. Removes and replaces broken tile section or pipe, using caulking compound and cement to form watertight joint. Replaces or directs replacement of earth. Replaces dull knives and performs repairs on machine, using handtools. May estimate cost of service to customer. May clean sewage collection points and sanitary lines in streets and sewage plants.
GOE: 05.12.12 STRENGTH: M GED: R3 M1 L2 SVP: 3 DLU: 77

899.682-010   DIVER PUMPER (construction; fishing & hunt.)
Operates portable hand pump or motor-driven air compressor to provide fresh air to DIVER (any industry): Places air pump or air compressor where DIVER (any industry) enters water. Turns hand crank or starts compressor motor to pump air. Observes pressure gauge to ensure required pressure is maintained. Oils cylinders and bearings of pump and replaces air filters.
GOE: 05.12.06 STRENGTH: M GED: R3 M1 L1 SVP: 4 DLU: 77

899.684-010   BONDACTOR-MACHINE OPERATOR (foundry)
Sprays interior surfaces of cupolas with refractory mixture to reline interiors, using spray equipment: Loads specified amount of material, such as clay, sand, and water into mixing tank of machine and starts machine to mix ingredients. Installs preformed metal scaffolding in interior of cupola, using handtools. Opens compressed-air valves on machine to force mixture into hose, climbs scaffolding with hose, and sprays surfaces. May chip clay from interior of cupola, lay bed of cupola, or repair ladle linings.
GOE: 05.12.14 STRENGTH: M GED: R3 M1 L1 SVP: 3 DLU: 77

899.684-014   HIGHWAY-MAINTENANCE WORKER (government ser.) alternate titles: highway worker
Maintains highways, municipal and rural roads, and rights-of-way in safe condition, performing combination of following duties: Erects and repairs guardrails, highway markers, and snow fences, using handtools and nails, and power tools. Dumps, spreads, and tamps asphalt, using pneumatic tamper to patch broken or eroded pavement. Drives truck [TRUCK DRIVER, HEAVY (any industry)] to transport crew and equipment to work site. May drive snow-removal equipment, consisting of truck or tractor equipped with adjustable snowplow and blower unit, and be designated Snow-Plow Operator, Truck (government ser.); Snow-Plow Tractor Operator (government ser.). May drive tractor with mower attachment to cut grass around airfield runways.
GOE: 05.12.12 STRENGTH: M GED: R3 M1 L2 SVP: 3 DLU: 77

899.684-018   LAMINATOR (rubber goods)
Glues rubberized fabric and foam to form sections of inflatable buildings: Measures and cuts strips of fabric to specified length, using tape measure and knife. Cleans edges of fabric with solvent and glues strips of fabric together, overlapping edges for specified size. Cleans strip of joined fabric with solvent, and applies glue to strip of foam and fabric, working as member of crew. Fits glued sections together, and repeats process until fabric is covered with foam. Applies glue to other side of foam and to other strip of fabric. Attaches fabric to foam by hand or uses hand roller while crewmember holds and guides fabric. Trims rubberized fabric to specified size, and cuts openings for doors and windows, using template and knife. Inserts metal framed doors and windows in openings. Cleans and attaches edges of frame and fabric, using solvent and tape.
GOE: 06.02.22 STRENGTH: M GED: R2 M1 L2 SVP: 3 DLU: 77

899.684-022   MAINTENANCE-REPAIRER HELPER, INDUSTRIAL (any industry) alternate titles: general-maintenance helper; maintenance mechanic helper
Assists MAINTENANCE REPAIRER, INDUSTRIAL (any industry) 899.261-014 in repairing and maintaining machinery, equipment, physical structures, and plumbing and electrical systems of industrial establishment, using handtools and power tools: Dismantles machines or equipment, replaces defective parts and motors, and adjusts feed mechanisms. Cleans and lubricates machine parts, such as shafts, pulleys, gears, and bearings, using rags, brushes, grease gun, and oilcan. Replaces or repairs machine belts. Removes dust, dirt, grease, and waste material from machines. Paints machines or equipment to prevent corrosion. Bends and cuts conduit and wire, and drills holes in walls, floors, and ceilings for electrical connections. Connects wire to motors, fixtures, and other electrical equipment, replaces switches and fuses, and splices wire and insulates wire with friction tape. Bends, cuts, and threads pipe, cuts openings in walls, ceilings, and floors for pipes, and seals pipe joints with sealing compound. Cuts out and joins parts for worktables, benches, shelves and other furnishings, using power tools and handtools. Patches or replaces plaster or plaster board and paints walls, ceilings, and trim of building. Clears clogged drains, and replaces plumbing fixtures. Performs other duties as described under HELPER (any industry) Master Title. May operate welding machine to repair or join metal parts.
GOE: 05.10.04 STRENGTH: H GED: R3 M1 L2 SVP: 5 DLU: 89

899.684-026   PIPELINER (pipe lines)
Maintains and repairs pipelines, pumping stations, and tank farms by performing any combination of following duties as member of crew: Removes rust and foreign substances from meters and valves, using sand blasting equipment. Pours corrosion resistant material over pipe or applies material with brush or spray gun. Wraps pipe with strips of paper or fabric to prevent corrosion and leakage. Drives and operates such equipment as backhoes, bulldozers, and side booms to dig ditches, lay pipe, and backfill ditches. Positions materials, pipes, fittings, and pumping equipment for carpenters, mechanics, and welders. Installs screw-pipe and manifold connections, using wrenches and pipe tongs. Cleans storage tanks, using squeegees and rakes. Dismantles and restores items, such as fences, gates, and water lines, that inhibit pipeline work, using earth moving equipment, pick, and shovel. Cuts brushes, trees, and weeds with axes and hoes; digs drainage ditches, using shovel; and gathers trash, pipe parts, and equipment to clear grounds along pipelines right-of-way. Spreads chemical pellets along right-of-way for control of tree growth. Loads and unloads trucks. May walk along line to detect leaks [LINE WALKER (petrol. & gas; petrol. refin.; pipe lines)]. May operate pumping equipment [PUMPER (any industry)]. May operate pipe-cleaning-and-wrapping machines to apply dope and wrap pipe.
GOE: 05.10.04 STRENGTH: H GED: R3 M1 L2 SVP: 5 DLU: 77

899.684-030   PORTABLE SAWYER (railroad equip.)
Saws holes in wood panels, using portable saber saw in railroad car manufacturing establishment: Lifts panel onto worktable, places template on panel, and scribes around template with pencil to mark cutting outline. Bores starter hole in specified position on panel, using portable electric drill. Inserts saw blade into hole, starts saw, pushes blade against wood, and guides saw along scribed cutting line to make cut specified. Removes cut panel from worktables to stockpile.
GOE: 06.02.25 STRENGTH: M GED: R3 M2 L1 SVP: 3 DLU: 77

899.684-034   SHAFT MECHANIC (mine & quarry) alternate titles: shaft repairer; shaft tender
Inspects, repairs, and replaces mine shaft parts, such as timbers, cage guides, guardrails, and cable, using handtools. Tightens joints of compressed air, steam, and water pipes in shaft, using pipe wrenches. May build doors and brattices of canvas or wood. May erect partitions of concrete, concrete block, or brick.
GOE: 05.10.01 STRENGTH: H GED: R3 M1 L2 SVP: 5 DLU: 77

899.684-038   STRIPPER AND TAPER (rubber goods)
Applies bias tape over seams of rubberized fabric to protect and reinforce sections of inflatable buildings: Lifts and attaches sections of buildings to circular frame, working as member of crew. Turns handcrank to roll first section of building to top of frame. Cleans seams with solvent, and applies glue to seam and bias tape. Attaches and centers tape on seams, using hand roller and hand pressure. Turns handcrank to position other sections of building and repeats bonding process. Removes, straightens, and cuts tape to correct flaws, using solvent to loosen glue. Reglues corrected sections. Removes completed building, using handcrank.
GOE: 06.04.29 STRENGTH: M GED: R2 M1 L1 SVP: 3 DLU: 77

899.684-042   WINDOW REPAIRER (any industry)
Repairs and adjusts metal and wooden casement windows, storm windows and doors, and jalousies, using handtools and portable power tools: Repairs or

replaces locks, hinges, and cranks. Realigns windows and screens to fit casements. Oils moving parts of sections. May cut and install glass. May paint windows, using brush or spray equipment.
GOE: 05.12.12 STRENGTH: M GED: R2 M1 L1 SVP: 4 DLU: 77

899.684-046 MAINTENANCE WORKER, MUNICIPAL (government ser.)
Performs any combination of following duties to maintain and repair property of municipality, using variety of machines, tools, and equipment: Receives written work orders or verbal instructions from municipal administrator. Cuts grass and trims weeds on town property and parks, using lawn mower and weed trimmer. Digs flower beds and plants flowers, using gardening tools. Constructs decorative flower garden borders from wood, using handtools. Cleans buildings, washes windows, and empties trash cans, using brooms, cleaning supplies, and floor buffer. Paints interior and exterior walls and trim, using paint and painting tools. Operates backhoe to dig trenches for water and sewer pipe. Drives truck and loads fallen tree limbs and roadside trash onto truck, and delivers refuse to landfill. Repairs streets and sidewalks with asphalt, cold patching materials, and concrete, using shovel, hand roller, trowel, level, and long-handled tamp. Removes and replaces damaged parking meters and traffic signs. Operates snow removal equipment to maintain streets, sidewalks, and driveways. Reads water meters and records reading in logbook. Maintains and repairs municipal buildings' plumbing and electrical systems, including replacing worn or defective parts, such as switches and fuses. Repairs or replaces building brick, stone, and concrete. Maintains and repairs wood parts of buildings, using carpenter tools. Replaces worn or damaged parts, such as hoses, wiring, and belts, in machines

and equipment, such as truck, street sweeper, and riding mower. Hand washes vehicles.
GOE: 05.12.12 STRENGTH: H GED: R3 M2 L3 SVP: 5 DLU: 86

899.687-010 DECORATOR, STREET AND BUILDING (any industry)
Installs decorations, such as flags, lights, and bunting, on streets, on or in buildings, halls, and booths for events, such as parades, conventions, and festivals: Strings and connects electric wiring and lights. Hangs decorations in streets and in or on buildings and structures, using wire, rope, and handtools, working from ladders or elevated truck platforms. Constructs framework to support displays, using woodworking machines and handtools. May build and decorate parade floats and be designated Float Builder (any industry).
GOE: 05.12.12 STRENGTH: V GED: R2 M1 L1 SVP: 4 DLU: 77

899.687-014 LABORER, AIRPORT MAINTENANCE (air trans.)
Maintains and repairs airport facilities and grounds by performing any combination of following tasks: Operates sweeping machine to clean streets of dust and trash [STREET-SWEEPER OPERATOR (government ser.)]. Operates power mower to mow lawns and fields of airport. Plants, waters, fertilizes, and prunes shrubs and plants to beautify airport grounds. Drives light truck to haul dirt and trash and to move equipment. Cleans runway drain ditches, catch basins, and drains, and fills holes in fields and grounds, using shovels, hoe, and rake. Repairs damaged fences, replaces defective or damaged parking meters and weathered traffic signs, using handtools. May assist maintenance workers in performing repairs to electrical, plumbing, or heating systems.
GOE: 05.12.12 STRENGTH: M GED: R2 M1 L1 SVP: 2 DLU: 77

9 MISCELLANEOUS OCCUPATIONS

This category includes occupations concerned with transportation services; packaging and warehousing; utilities; amusement, recreation, and motion picture services; mining; graphic arts; and various miscellaneous activities. Occupations concerned with activities listed above and involving extensive record keeping are found in Category 2. Occupations concerned with hoisting and conveying of logs are included in this category. Other logging occupations are found in Category 4.

90   MOTOR FREIGHT OCCUPATIONS

This division includes occupations concerned with transporting cargo over highways, city streets, or within compounds of industrial, construction, or mining areas, by driving vehicles powered by gasoline, diesel, propane, or related fuels, or electricity.

900   CONCRETE-MIXING-TRUCK DRIVERS

This group includes occupations concerned with driving a truck and controlling a mounted concrete mixer to mix concrete and transport it to construction sites and dumping mixed concrete into chutes leading to forms.

900.683-010   CONCRETE-MIXING-TRUCK DRIVER (construction) alternate titles: batch-mixing-truck driver; moto-mix operator; ready-mix-truck driver; transit-mix operator
Drives truck equipped with auxiliary concrete mixer to deliver concrete mix to job sites: Drives truck under loading hopper to receive sand, gravel, cement, and water and starts mixer. Drives truck to location for unloading. Moves levers on truck to release concrete down truck chute into wheelbarrow or other conveying container or directly into area to be poured with concrete. Cleans truck after delivery to prevent concrete from hardening in mixer and on truck, using water hose and hoe. May spray surfaces of truck with protective compound to prevent adhering of concrete. May assemble cement chute.
GOE: 05.08.03 STRENGTH: M GED: R3 M1 L1 SVP: 3 DLU: 86

902   DUMP-TRUCK DRIVERS

This group includes occupations concerned with driving a dump truck to transport sand, gravel, coal, and similar cargo.

902.683-010   DUMP-TRUCK DRIVER (any industry)
Drives truck equipped with dump body to transport and dump loose materials, such as sand, gravel, crushed rock, coal, or bituminous paving materials: Pulls levers or turns crank to tilt body and dump contents. Moves hand and foot controls to jerk truck forward and backward to loosen and dump material adhering to body. May load truck by hand or by operating mechanical loader. May be designated according to type of material hauled as Coal Hauler (any industry); Dust-Truck Driver (any industry); Mud Trucker (steel & rel.). May be designated according to type of equipment driven for off-highway projects as Dump-Truck Driver, Off-Highway (any industry).
GOE: 05.08.01 STRENGTH: M GED: R3 M1 L1 SVP: 2 DLU: 80

903   TRUCK DRIVERS, INFLAMMABLES

This group includes occupations concerned with driving trucks to transport liquid, dry, or gaseous cargoes of inflammable, explosive, volatile, radioactive, or otherwise dangerous material.

903.683-010   EXPLOSIVES-TRUCK DRIVER (ordnance)
Drives specially modified truck to transport explosive material. Loads and unloads containers according to prescribed safety methods and observes safety regulations in transit. Keeps record of materials moved.
GOE: 05.08.01 STRENGTH: M GED: R3 M1 L2 SVP: 3 DLU: 77

903.683-014   POWDER-TRUCK DRIVER (ordnance)
Drives specially modified truck to transport gunpowder from freight cars and motor trucks to and from storage magazines and blending houses. Stores kegs, drums, and boxes of various type powders according to prescribed safety methods and follows safety regulations in transit.
GOE: 05.08.01 STRENGTH: M GED: R3 M1 L2 SVP: 3 DLU: 77

903.683-018   TANK-TRUCK DRIVER (petrol. refin.; retail trade; wholesale tr.)
Drives tank truck to deliver gasoline, fuel oil, lubricating oil, or liquefied petroleum gas to customers: Drives truck into position to load at filling rack. Opens valves or starts pumps to fill tank. Reads gauges or meters and records quantity loaded. Drives truck to customer's premises. Connects hose to tank and opens valves. Records amount delivered and issues ticket to customer. May attach ground wire to truck. May be designated according to type of fuel delivered as Fuel-Oil-Delivery Driver (petrol. refin.; retail trade; wholesale tr.); Gas-Delivery Driver (petrol. refin.; retail trade; wholesale tr.). May drive trailer truck and be designated Trailer-Tank-Truck Driver (petrol. refin.; retail trade; wholesale tr.).

GOE: 05.08.01 STRENGTH: M GED: R3 M1 L2 SVP: 3 DLU: 81

904   TRAILER-TRUCK DRIVERS

This group includes occupations concerned with driving semitrailer or full-trailer trucks to transport cargo.

904.383-010   TRACTOR-TRAILER-TRUCK DRIVER (any industry) alternate titles: semi-truck driver; trailer-truck driver
Drives gasoline or diesel-powered tractor-trailer combination, usually long distances, to transport and deliver products, livestock, or materials in liquid, loose, or packaged form: Drives truck to destination, applying knowledge of commercial driving regulations and skill in maneuvering vehicle in difficult situations, such as narrow passageways. Inspects truck for defects before and after trips and submits report indicating truck condition. Maintains driver log according to I.C.C. regulations. May assist workers in loading and unloading truck. May transport new automobiles or trucks from manufacturers or rail terminals to dealers and be designated Transport Driver (motor trans.). May drive tractor with two trailers hitched in tandem and be designated Double-Bottom Driver (any industry). May drive tractor-trailer combination to deliver poles for utility and construction companies and be designated Pole-Truck Driver (construction; tel. & tel.; utilities). May work as member of two-person team driving tractor with sleeper bunk behind cab and be designated Long-Haul-Sleeper Driver (any industry). May drive tractor-trailer combination to deliver or spray water and be designated Water-Truck Driver (construction; petrol. & gas) I.
GOE: 05.08.01 STRENGTH: M GED: R3 M2 L3 SVP: 4 DLU: 81

904.683-010   LOG-TRUCK DRIVER (logging) alternate titles: log hauler
Drives truck, equipped with long-tongued trailer, to haul logs from forest to mill or storage yard: Maneuvers truck into loading position according to signals from loading crew. Fastens chain or cable binders around logs to secure load on trailer during transit. May release binders and start power hoist to dump logs. May assist in loading and unloading logs, using crane hook or cant hook. May raise empty trailer to carrying position on truck bed, using hoist, for deadhead (empty) trip to forest. May steer trailer from cab attached to rear end of log trailer and be designated Trailer Steerer (logging).
GOE: 05.08.01 STRENGTH: M GED: R3 M1 L2 SVP: 4 DLU: 79

905   TRUCK DRIVERS, HEAVY

This group includes occupations concerned with driving trucks of 3 tons or greater capacity.

905.483-010   MILK DRIVER (dairy products) alternate titles: milk hauler
Drives insulated tank truck to transport bulk milk between farms, dairies, and commercial establishments: Examines milk to detect sediment or stale odor, and takes sample for laboratory analysis. Observes level gauge of storage tank and computes and records weight of milk in tank. Connects hose and turns valves to pump milk into truck. Washes truck. May clean and sterilize tank. May load and drive refrigerated van to haul cans of milk.
GOE: 05.08.01 STRENGTH: M GED: R3 M2 L2 SVP: 3 DLU: 77

905.663-010   GARBAGE COLLECTOR DRIVER (motor trans.)
Drives packer-type truck, dump truck, or truck equipped with hydraulic lifting device to collect garbage and trash, and transports load to disposal area. Records mileage and fuel consumption.
GOE: 05.08.03 STRENGTH: M GED: R3 M1 L1 SVP: 3 DLU: 77

905.663-014   TRUCK DRIVER, HEAVY (any industry)
Drives truck with capacity of more than 3 tons, to transport materials to and from specified destinations: Drives truck to destination, applying knowledge of commercial driving regulations and area roads. Prepares receipts for load picked up. Collects payment for goods delivered and for delivery charges. May maintain truck log, according to state and federal regulations. May maintain telephone or radio contact with supervisor to receive delivery instructions. May load and unload truck. May inspect truck equipment and supplies, such as tires, lights, brakes, gas, oil, and water. May perform emergency roadside repairs, such as changing tires, installing light bulbs, tire chains, and spark plugs. May position blocks and tie rope around items to secure cargo during transit. When driving truck equipped for specific purposes, such as fighting fires, digging holes, and installing and repairing utility company lines, may be designated Fire-Truck Driver (petrol. & gas); Hole-Digger-Truck Driver (construction; tel. & tel.; utilities). When specializing in making deliveries, may be designated Delivery-Truck Driver, Heavy (any industry). May be designated according to

type of truck driven as Truck Driver, Flatbed (logging). May be designated according to kind of cargo transported as Water Hauler (logging).
GOE: 05.08.01 STRENGTH: M GED: R3 M2 L2 SVP: 4 DLU: 81

905.663-018 VAN DRIVER (motor trans.) alternate titles: furniture-mover driver

Loads furniture into van, drives truck to specified destination, and unloads furniture: Drives van to loading point and consults householder on furniture to be moved. Gives directions to VAN-DRIVER HELPER (motor trans.) in moving articles to van. Wraps furniture with blankets to prevent damage. Wraps dishes and fragile items in packing paper and packs them into containers. Loads truck, using dollies and handtruck, distributing weight evenly, forming compact load, and utilizing space. Drives van to destination and unloads cargo. Obtains customers signature or collects payment for services. May service van [GAS-AND-OIL SERVICER (motor trans.)]. May remove window frames and erect block and tackle on house to remove bulky items. May move delicate equipment or instruments for industrial firms. May deliver items such as furniture and large appliances to department store customers and be designated Bulk Driver (motor trans.).
GOE: 05.08.03 STRENGTH: V GED: R3 M2 L3 SVP: 4 DLU: 77

905.683-010 WATER-TRUCK DRIVER II (construction; petrol. & gas)

Drives tank truck to transport water for construction projects or to provide water for use in drilling shallow bore-holes on petroleum-prospecting sites. May insert pipe in refilled trenches and other excavations, and operate auxiliary pump on truck to pump water into fill to settle and compact dirt. May drive truck equipped with sprinkling attachment to settle dust on roadways and streets and to saturate flexible base for compaction. May drive truck equipped with trailer [TRACTOR-TRAILER-TRUCK DRIVER (any industry)].
GOE: 05.08.01 STRENGTH: M GED: R3 M1 L2 SVP: 3 DLU: 77

905.687-010 TRUCK-DRIVER HELPER (any industry) alternate titles: driver helper; trucker helper

Assists TRUCK DRIVER, HEAVY (any industry) by performing any combination of following tasks: Loads and unloads vehicles by hand or by use of handtruck or dolly. Pads, stacks, and secures items in position on truck to prevent damage during shipment. Delivers and stacks merchandise on customer's premises and collects payment or obtains receipt for goods. Performs other duties as described under HELPER (any industry) Master Title.
GOE: 05.12.03 STRENGTH: H GED: R2 M1 L1 SVP: 2 DLU: 77

905.687-014 VAN-DRIVER HELPER (motor trans.) alternate titles: furniture mover; van helper

Assists VAN DRIVER (motor trans.) in loading and unloading moving van: Wraps dishes and fragile items in paper or corrugated cardboard and packs them in barrels. Rolls up rugs, removes pictures from walls, and loads furniture into van. Arranges articles in truck to form compact load, using ropes and padding to secure goods and prevent breakage. Performs other duties as described under HELPER (any industry) Master Title.
GOE: 05.12.03 STRENGTH: V GED: R2 M1 L1 SVP: 3 DLU: 77

906 TRUCK DRIVERS, LIGHT

This group includes occupations concerned with driving trucks of less than 3 tons capacity.

906.683-010 FOOD-SERVICE DRIVER (hotel & rest.) alternate titles: food-service agent

Drives truck to deliver refrigerated and electric-warming cabinets containing previously prepared meals to airports, and unloads cabinets into airplanes: Loads cabinets into truck and moves truck to flight field. Maneuvers truck beneath airplane to be loaded and moves truck levers to elevate truck bed to level of airplane door. Unloads cabinets into airplane and connects electrical cords of cabinets to electrical outlets of airplane. Presents billing form to designated airline representative and collects receipt. Loads empty cabinets onto truck and returns them to commissary kitchen.
GOE: 05.08.03 STRENGTH: M GED: R2 M1 L1 SVP: 3 DLU: 77

906.683-014 LIQUID-FERTILIZER SERVICER (agriculture)

Drives truck to deliver liquid fertilizer to field location and pumps fertilizer into tractor-drawn applicator tank: Drives truck, containing supply tank filled with fertilizer, to area to be fertilized. Couples hose from supply tank to feeder tank mounted on tractor. Opens valves on feed pipes to synchronize flow of fertilizer onto soil with speed of tractor, using pipe wrench. Inspects tanks, hose, piping and couplings for leaks and replaces defective parts, using handtools. Records quantity of fertilizer applied.
GOE: 05.08.03 STRENGTH: M GED: R3 M1 L1 SVP: 3 DLU: 77

906.683-018 TELEPHONE-DIRECTORY-DISTRIBUTOR DRIVER (business ser.)

Drives automobile or truck to transport telphone directories from central storage facilities to distribution area: Loads vehicle with assigned number of books and drives to distribution district, parking vehicle in convenient or centralized location. Distributes books to TELEPHONE-DIRECTORY DELIVERERS (business ser.) for delivery to residences and business establishments indicated on address lists. May transport TELEPHONE-DIRECTORY DELIVERERS (business ser.) to distribution area. May deliver telephone directories, on foot, after parking vehicle.

GOE: 05.08.03 STRENGTH: L GED: R2 M1 L2 SVP: 3 DLU: 77

906.683-022 TRUCK DRIVER, LIGHT (any industry)

Drives truck with capacity under 3 tons to transport materials in liquid or packaged form and personnel to and from specified destinations, such as railroad stations, plants, residences, offices, or within industrial yards: Verifies load against shipping papers. Drives truck to destination, applying knowledge of commercial driving regulations and roads in area. Prepares receipts for load picked up. Collects payment for goods delivered and for delivery charges. May maintain truck log according to state and federal regulations. May maintain telephone or radio contact with supervisor to receive delivery instructions. May drive truck equipped with public address system through city streets to broadcast announcements over system for advertising or publicity purposes. May load and unload truck. May inspect truck equipment and supplies, such as tires, lights, brakes, gas, oil, and water. May perform emergency roadside repairs, such as changing tires, installing light bulbs, fuses, tire chains, and spark plugs. May be known in establishment according to type of activity as Crew-Truck Driver (any industry); Insect Sprayer, Mobile Unit (government ser.); Mail-Truck Driver (any industry); Motor-Vehicle-Escort Driver (business ser.); Pick-Up Driver (motor trans.); Service-Parts Driver (automotive ser.); Sprinkler-Truck Driver (any industry).
GOE: 05.08.01 STRENGTH: M GED: R3 M2 L2 SVP: 3 DLU: 87

909 MOTOR FREIGHT OCCUPATIONS, N.E.C.

This group includes occupations, not elsewhere classified, concerned with motor freight transportation.

909.127-010 SAFETY COORDINATOR (motor trans.) alternate titles: supervisor

Coordinates safety traffic program and instructs truck and trailer drivers in matters pertaining to traffic and safety regulations, and care of equipment: Instructs drivers regarding company regulations, penalties for infraction of rules, or safety and conservation measures. Rides with drivers to detect errors in handling cargo or driving vehicle. Patrols highway to detect violation of company regulations by drivers and to observe condition of vehicles and road. Reroutes truck as result of unsatisfactory road conditions. Investigates accidents involving company trucks, questions witnesses and drivers to determine causes of accidents and makes adjustments in accordance with governmental regulatory agencies' and company procedures. Directs transfer of cargo from damaged truck to substitute vehicle to ensure scheduled delivery. Analyzes accident reports obtained from governmental agencies to determine driver's need for additional training. Trains supervisors in such matters as safety and conservation of equipment and driving hazards. Confers with department heads concerning such problems as accident rates and abuse of equipment, and recommends measures to improve safety records and to conserve equipment.
GOE: 11.10.05 STRENGTH: L GED: R4 M3 L3 SVP: 7 DLU: 77

909.137-010 DRIVER SUPERVISOR (motor trans.)

Supervises and coordinates activities of TRACTOR-TRAILER-TRUCK DRIVER (any industry) 904.383-010 and TRUCK DRIVERS, HEAVY (any industry) 905.663-014 engaged in operating motor vehicles to haul materials for motor freight company or in off-highway haulage activities at industrial site. Performs duties as described under SUPERVISOR (any industry) Master Title.
GOE: 05.08.01 STRENGTH: L GED: R4 M3 L4 SVP: 7 DLU: 78

909.137-014 GARBAGE-COLLECTION SUPERVISOR (motor trans.) alternate titles: rubbish-collection supervisor; trash-collection supervisor

Supervises and coordinates activities of workers engaged in collecting garbage and other refuse and transporting refuse to disposal plants or areas. Assigns routes and trucks to workers. Performs other duties as described under SUPERVISOR (any industry) Master Title.
GOE: 05.08.03 STRENGTH: L GED: R4 M3 L3 SVP: 6 DLU: 77

909.137-018 TRUCK SUPERVISOR (motor trans.)

Supervises and coordinates workers engaged in loading and transporting machinery and industrial equipment, such as construction machinery, or field drilling and pumping equipment, tanks, vessels, compressors and pumps for chemical plants, refineries and pipeline pump stations: Observes installation of old machinery and equipment or studies sizes and weights of new equipment from bills of lading and other specifications, and plans procedures for dismantling and loading equipment. Trains workers in rigging hoists, and dismantling and loading equipment. May plan transportation route by consulting road and city maps to ensure clearance and load limits of roads, bridges and overhead obstructions, such as power lines and underpasses, utilizing knowledge of state regulations regarding size and weight of loads, traffic speeds, and use of clearance lights. May supervise maintenance and repair of trucks. Performs other duties as described under SUPERVISOR (any industry) Master Title.
GOE: 05.12.01 STRENGTH: L GED: R4 M3 L4 SVP: 8 DLU: 77

909.663-010 HOSTLER (motor trans.) alternate titles: hook-up driver; yard spotter

Drives trucks or tractors at vehicle parking or docking area to move, position, or park trucks or trailers: Drives trucks to and from service department and around dock area for motor freight transportation company. Spots (positions) loaded and unloaded trailers at assigned dock space for unloading or loading,

using tractor. Connects loaded semitrailers to tractors for TRACTOR-TRAIL-ER-TRUCK DRIVER (any industry). May service trucks and tractors [GAS-AND-OIL SERVICER (motor trans.)]. May drive buses along municipal streets to deliver replacement vehicle to operator with disabled vehicle and be designated Bus Driver, Garage (motor trans.).
GOE: 05.08.03 STRENGTH: M GED: R3 M2 L2 SVP: 4 DLU: 77

909.687-014 LABORER, GENERAL (motor trans.)
Performs variety of manual tasks around dock area of motor freight transportation company as directed: Sweeps dock area and cleans truck yard, using broom, shovel, and wheelbarrow. May clean interior and exterior of trucks [CLEANER (any industry) II].
GOE: 05.12.18 STRENGTH: H GED: R1 M1 L1 SVP: 2 DLU: 77

91 TRANSPORTATION OCCUPATIONS, N.E.C.

This division includes occupations, not elsewhere classified, concerned with moving people or materials by means of automotive and railway vehicles, aircraft, freshwater or seagoing vessels, pipes, and pumps. Includes loading bulk materials into conveyances; directing course of carrier; routing materials; minor repair and maintenance of carriers; and related activities.

910 RAILROAD TRANSPORTATION OCCUPATIONS

This group includes occupations concerned with transporting passengers and freight by controlling movement of trains, trolleys, and other railway vehicles; collecting fares from passengers and giving information incidental to driving vehicles; supplying fuel; adjusting alignment of tracks; signaling operational information; physically shifting railway cars in classification yards; cleaning and lubricating equipment; and related activities.

910.137-010 BAGGAGE-AND-MAIL AGENT (r.r. trans.)
Supervises and coordinates activities of workers engaged in loading and unloading mail and baggage: Coordinates work schedules in accordance with train schedules to ensure that transfer of mail and luggage is completed in allotted time. Assigns duties to workers. Observes workers serving passengers to ensure workers are courteous and helpful. Supervises workers sorting, loading, and unloading sacks of mail. Notifies STATION AGENT (r.r. trans.) I when transfer of mail and baggage has been completed following prescribed rules and regulations. Recommends new methods of transferring mail and luggage onto and from trains. Reviews workflow and production charts to determine need for additional workers.
GOE: 05.12.01 STRENGTH: L GED: R4 M3 L3 SVP: 6 DLU: 77

910.137-014 CAR-CLEANING SUPERVISOR (r.r. trans.) alternate titles: railroad-car-cleaning supervisor
Supervises and coordinates activities of workers engaged in cleaning railroad freight and passenger cars: Assigns daily work schedules to workers. Requisitions supplies, such as hoses, sponges, brushes, shovels, and cleaning solvents from supply room. Inspects cleaned cars to ensure that interior and exterior are washed, protruding nails removed from floor and sides, holes in floor and sides are covered with boards, doors are securely closed, and for worn out parts of defects on railway cars. Prepares report each day indicating number and type of cars cleaned and ready for use, following ICC regulations, and reports areas needing repairs. When supervising workers engaged in cleaning only passenger cars, may be designated Passenger-Car-Cleaning Supervisor (r.r. trans.). Performs other duties as described under SUPERVISOR (any industry) Master Title.
GOE: 05.12.01 STRENGTH: L GED: R3 M3 L3 SVP: 6 DLU: 77

910.137-018 CIRCUS-TRAIN SUPERVISOR (amuse. & rec.)
Supervises and coordinates activities of workers engaged in loading and unloading circus animals and equipment on and off train: Verifies train schedules with train officials to determine when train will be ready to load or unload. Arranges for water supply for animals and disposal of rubbish. Performs other duties as described under SUPERVISOR (any industry) Master Title.
GOE: 05.12.01 STRENGTH: L GED: R4 M3 L3 SVP: 6 DLU: 77

910.137-022 CONDUCTOR, YARD (r.r. trans.) alternate titles: engine supervisor; head switcher; yard supervisor
Supervises and coordinates activities of switch-engine crew engaged in switching railroad cars within yard of railroad, industrial plant, or similar location to facilitate loading and unloading of cars or making up or breaking up of trains: Notifies YARD ENGINEER (r.r. trans.) of switching orders and, whereby, which cars are to be moved to specified locations of yard, using radio, telephone, verbal, or hand signals. Gives instructions to SWITCH TENDER (r.r. trans.) to throw track switches and to YARD COUPLER (r.r. trans.) to couple and uncouple cars. May keep records, number, origin, destination, and cargo of cars switched. May coordinate activities of switching crew from locomotive cab, caboose, or control tower. May assist workers to couple and uncouple cars, throw track switches, or other activities involved in switching railroad cars, as necessary. May supervise workers engaged in maintenance and repair of diesel locomotives and be designated Locomotive-Engine Supervisor (any industry).
GOE: 05.08.02 STRENGTH: L GED: R4 M3 L3 SVP: 6 DLU: 77

910.137-026 FREIGHT-LOADING SUPERVISOR (r.r. trans.)
Supervises and coordinates activities of workers engaged in loading and unloading incoming and outgoing freight at railroad stations: Determines number

of workers and equipment required to load or unload freight, using information obtained from waybills, other shipping records, and personal experience. Examines each item of freight for size and weight to determine sequence of loading so that maximum amount of freight can be loaded into each car. Gives instructions to MATERIAL HANDLER (any industry) to load freight into cars. Records description of each item of freight and number of car in which it is loaded. Compares items of freight loaded or unloaded with listing on waybill or other shipping records to ensure that all freight is routed to specified destination. Informs adjustment department of damaged freight. May notify railway clerical employee to affix door seal when freight car has been loaded. Performs other duties as described under SUPERVISOR (any industry) Master Title.
GOE: 05.12.01 STRENGTH: L GED: R4 M3 L3 SVP: 6 DLU: 77

910.137-034 ROAD SUPERVISOR OF ENGINES (r.r. trans.) alternate titles: railroad supervisor of engines
Supervises and coordinates activities of train and engine crews on train carrying freight: Measures height and width of special loads to ensure that load limits are in accordance with rules and regulations, and that load will pass through tunnels and over bridges and trestles on scheduled route. Ensures that sufficient number of engines are available to haul load. Notifies LOCOMOTIVE ENGINEER (r.r. trans.) of specified speed and route and special stops. Prepares reports at end of run to explain delays or accidents. Explains mechanical and electrical function of engine to workers, using charts and diagrams. Demonstrates operation of locomotive to workers. Observes workers to evaluate their performance in use of locomotive and in their understanding of operating rules and signals. May recommend hiring, firing, and other personnel actions of train and engine crew workers.
GOE: 05.08.02 STRENGTH: L GED: R4 M3 L4 SVP: 7 DLU: 77

910.137-038 STATION AGENT I (r.r. trans.) alternate titles: agent-telegrapher; freight and passenger agent
Supervises and coordinates activities of workers engaged in selling tickets and checking baggage at railroad station not served by STATION MANAGER (r.r. trans.): Assigns shift schedules to workers to ensure adequate service to patrons. Keeps daily records of attendance. Sells tickets to patrons [TICKET AGENT (any industry)]. Answers inquiries from patrons concerning schedules and departures and arrivals of trains. Requisitions supplies. Relays train orders and messages [TELEGRAPHER (r.r. trans.)]. Inspects buildings to detect maintenance needs. Verifies records of daily ticket sales and cash receipts. May train new employees. May supervise and coordinate activities of workers engaged in maintaining buildings and grounds of railroad station. May perform duties of EXPRESS CLERK (motor trans.; r.r. trans.).
GOE: 07.01.02 STRENGTH: L GED: R4 M3 L4 SVP: 6 DLU: 77

910.137-046 YARD MANAGER (any industry)
Supervises and coordinates activities of workers engaged in loading, transferring, and operating trains and locomotives in industrial yard. May direct workers engaged in handling and storing objects in yard. May direct workers engaged in inspecting and maintaining rolling stock. Performs duties as described under SUPERVISOR (any industry) Master Title.
GOE: 05.12.01 STRENGTH: L GED: R4 M3 L3 SVP: 6 DLU: 77

910.167-010 CAR CHASER (beverage) alternate titles: car spotter
Directs movement of grain-freight cars in plant yard, and selects cars for grain loading: Signals railroad crew and plant workers to move cars in specified sequence to meet grain loading and unloading schedules. Marks or points out cars for use. Walks along tracks on railroad siding to examine empty grain cars to ascertain size, type, and cleanliness. Selects cars for future loading and prepares list of car numbers.
GOE: 05.09.03 STRENGTH: L GED: R3 M2 L3 SVP: 6 DLU: 77

910.167-014 TRAIN DISPATCHER, ASSISTANT CHIEF (r.r. trans.)
Assigns locomotives, cabooses, and crews to trains to obtain most efficient use of equipment and personnel within assigned railroad territory: Determines number of locomotives to be allocated to trains based on type of freight and number and destinations of freight cars to be moved. Assigns locomotives and cabooses to trains and schedules departure and movement of trains on specific tracks and sidings according to ultimate destination of individual freight cars. Schedules and assigns initial, replacement, or emergency crews to trains depending upon available work time of individual crews and purpose of trip. Routes locomotives scheduled for preventive maintenance to destinations in proximity to designated maintenance facility to minimize cost of transfer to service site.
GOE: 05.09.02 STRENGTH: S GED: R4 M2 L3 SVP: 7 DLU: 86

910.263-010 RAIL-FLAW-DETECTOR OPERATOR (r.r. trans.)
Operates rail-flaw-detection machine aboard rail-flaw-detector-railroad car to detect defects in railroad tracks and analyzes graphic recording to determine any and type of defect: Synchronizes electronic recording equipment, meters, and other apparatus of rail-detector car or machine, using handtools. Fills container located at base of rail-detector car with paint so that machine will automatically mark section of defective rail. Starts machine and signals worker to operate rail-detector car along tracks. Analyzes graphic recordings to determine type of defects detected and prepares reports on findings. Replaces rolls of sensitized paper and tubes of ink as necessary. Tests electronic components of rail-flaw-detection machine, using tube and circuit tester.
GOE: 05.07.01 STRENGTH: L GED: R4 M3 L3 SVP: 6 DLU: 77

910.362-010 TOWER OPERATOR (r.r. trans.) alternate titles: signal-tower operator

Operates switching equipment in control tower to route train traffic in railroad yard or at switching point, following switching orders, train schedules, and safety regulations: Reads switching orders and schedules of inbound and outbound traffic to ascertain time trains will enter or leave yard, sequence of movement, and tracks on which trains are to be routed. Observes approaching trains and moves switches on control panel to set traffic signals and to activate track switches that regulate traffic. Receives and transmits switching orders by telephone or telegraph. May control track switches and train signals at junction point on rapid-transit or street-railway line and be designated Interlocking Tower Operator (r.r. trans.).
GOE: 05.03.03 STRENGTH: L GED: R3 M2 L3 SVP: 5 DLU: 77

910.363-010 FIRER, LOCOMOTIVE (r.r. trans.) alternate titles: assistant engineer

Monitors locomotive instruments and watches for dragging equipment, obstacles on right-of-way, and train signals during run: Inventories supplies, such as fuel, water, and sand, to ensure safe, efficient operation during run. Inspects locomotive to detect damaged or worn parts. Observes oil, temperature, and pressure gauges on dashboard to ascertain if engine is operating safely and efficiently. Observes track from left side of locomotive to detect obstructions on tracks. Observes train signals along route and verifies their meaning for LOCOMOTIVE ENGINEER (r.r. trans.). Observes train as it goes around curves to detect dragging equipment and smoking journal boxes. Observes signals from workers in rear of train and relays information to LOCOMOTIVE ENGINEER (r.r. trans.). Signals YARD COUPLER (r.r. trans.) to set handbrakes on cars and to throw track switches when switching cars from train at way stations. Operates locomotive during emergency. May start diesel engine to warm engine before run. May be designated according to kind of locomotive as Firer, Diesel Locomotive (r.r. trans.); Firer, Electric Locomotive (r.r. trans.); or according to type of traffic as Road-Freight Firer (r.r. trans.); Road-Passenger Firer (r.r. trans.).
GOE: 05.08.02 STRENGTH: L GED: R4 M2 L3 SVP: 6 DLU: 77

910.363-014 LOCOMOTIVE ENGINEER (r.r. trans.)

Drives electric, diesel-electric, or gas-turbine-electric locomotive, interpreting train orders, train signals, and railroad rules and regulations, to transport passengers or freight: Inspects locomotive before run to verify specified fuel, sand, water, and other supplies. Synchronizes watch with that of CONDUCTOR, PASSENGER CAR (r.r. trans.) or CONDUCTOR, ROAD FREIGHT (r.r. trans.) to ensure departure time from station or terminal is in accordance with time schedule. Receives starting signal from CONDUCTOR, PASSENGER CAR (r.r. trans.) or CONDUCTOR, ROAD FREIGHT (r.r. trans.) and moves controls, such as throttle and airbrakes to drive locomotive. Interprets train orders, train signals, and railroad rules and regulations to drive locomotive, following safety regulations and time schedule. Calls out train signals to FIRER, LOCOMOTIVE (r.r. trans.) for verification of meaning to avoid errors in interpretation. Confers with CONDUCTOR, ROAD FREIGHT (r.r. trans.) or traffic control center personnel via radiophone to issue or receive information or instructions concerning stops, delays, or oncoming trains. Observes track to detect obstructions. Inspects locomotive after run to detect damaged or defective equipment. Prepares reports to explain accidents, unscheduled stops, or delays. May lubricate moving parts of locomotive. May drive diesel-electric rail-detector car to transport rail-flaw-detecting machine over railroad and be designated Rail-Flaw-Detector-Car Operator (r.r. trans.). May be designated according to type of locomotive driven as Locomotive Engineer, Diesel (r.r. trans.); Locomotive Engineer, Electric (r.r. trans.); or according to type of traffic assigned as Road Engineer, Freight (r.r. trans.); Road Engineer, Passenger (r.r. trans.).
GOE: 05.08.02 STRENGTH: L GED: R4 M2 L3 SVP: 7 DLU: 77

910.363-018 YARD ENGINEER (r.r. trans.) alternate titles: locomotive engineer

Drives switching locomotive within yard of railroad, industrial plant, quarry, construction project, or similar location to switch railroad cars for loading, unloading, and makeup or breakup of trains: Reads switching orders received from CONDUCTOR, YARD (r.r. trans.). Observes traffic signals in yard or in cab and operates locomotive in accordance with railroad rules and regulations. Observes arm or lantern signals from YARD COUPLER (r.r. trans.) or SWITCH TENDER (r.r. trans.) and moves controls to drive locomotive backwards or forwards to switch and couple cars. May assist in cleaning and lubricating engine. May talk to CONDUCTOR, YARD (r.r. trans.) or other yard workers via radio-telephone to give or receive switching information. May be designated according to type of locomotive driven as Locomotive Engineer, Gasoline (any industry). May operate switching diesel engine and be designated Engineer, Remote Control, Diesel (r.r. trans.). When employed by establishment other than railroad to operate switching locomotive at industrial plant, quarry, construction project, or similar location, may be designated Industrial-Locomotive Operator (any industry).
GOE: 05.08.02 STRENGTH: L GED: R3 M2 L3 SVP: 5 DLU: 77

910.364-010 BRAKER, PASSENGER TRAIN (r.r. trans.)

Performs any combination of following duties on passenger train: Inspects equipment, such as couplings, airhose, journal boxes, and handbrakes, to ensure that they function properly. Assists passengers to board and leave train. Places passengers' baggage in rack above seats on train. Answers questions from passengers concerning train rules, station, and timetable information. Turns knobs and pushes switches on control panel to regulate air-conditioning, heating, and lighting on train for comfort of passengers. Sets warning signals, such as flares, flags, lanterns, or torpedoes, in front of and at rear of train during emergency stops to warn oncoming trains. Makes minor repairs to couplings, airhoses, and journal boxes, using handtools. Reports to CONDUCTOR, PASSENGER CAR (r.r. trans.) any equipment requiring major repair. Collects tickets, fares, and passes from passengers.
GOE: 09.01.04 STRENGTH: L GED: R3 M2 L3 SVP: 4 DLU: 77

910.367-010 BRAKE COUPLER, ROAD FREIGHT (r.r. trans.)

Performs any combination of following duties, working as member of train crew: Inspects couplings and airhoses to ensure that they are securely fastened. Inspects journal boxes to ensure that they are lubricated. Inspects handbrakes on cars to ensure that they are released before run begins. Walks on top of cars and peers down between them to inspect couplings, airhoses, and journal boxes. Sets warning signals, such as flares, flags, lanterns, or torpedoes, in front of and at rear of train during emergency stops to warn oncoming trains. Climbs ladder to top of car and turns brakewheel to set car brakes or rides atop car to control its speed when it is shunted. Pulls or pushes track switch to reroute cars during breakup at way stations. Signals LOCOMOTIVE ENGINEER (r.r. trans.) to start or stop train when coupling or uncoupling cars. Rides in cab of engine or cupola of caboose to observe signals from other crewmembers. Makes minor repairs to couplings, airhoses, and journal boxes. Reports to CONDUCTOR, ROAD FREIGHT (r.r. trans.) any equipment requiring major repairs.
GOE: 05.12.05 STRENGTH: M GED: R3 M2 L3 SVP: 4 DLU: 77

910.367-014 CAR DISTRIBUTOR (r.r. trans.) alternate titles: car supplier; chief clerk, yard office

Selects railroad freight cars according to type and amount of cargo to be transported, and directs railroad train and switching crews by radio, telephone, telegraph, and switch-list to segregate specific empty freight cars from trains, and route them to other railroad divisions or designated shippers, according to information received from TRAIN DISPATCHER (r.r. trans.). Keeps record of all transactions.
GOE: 07.04.05 STRENGTH: S GED: R4 M2 L3 SVP: 5 DLU: 77

910.367-018 ENGINE DISPATCHER (r.r. trans.)

Assigns engines to LOCOMOTIVE ENGINEERS (r.r. trans.) for train runs or for switching operations at railroad yard, industrial plant, quarry, construction project, or similar location: Reads train orders or switching orders to ascertain length of run scheduled, type and tonnage of cargo to be transported, or number of switch engines required to complete switching assignments for day. Assigns engine according to size and horsepower and records number and type of engine assigned. Keeps records of number of engines and types of engines available, in use, and in repair or service shops. Notifies HOSTLER (r.r. trans.) when engine can be delivered to switching crew or train crew. When employed by establishment other than railroad, may be designated Dispatcher, Industrial Locomotive (any industry).
GOE: 05.09.02 STRENGTH: S GED: R3 M2 L3 SVP: 4 DLU: 77

910.367-022 LOCOMOTIVE OPERATOR HELPER (r.r. trans.)

Watches for and relays traffic signals from yard workers to YARD ENGINEER (r.r. trans.) in railroad yard, industrial plant, quarry, or other location: Reads switching orders received from CONDUCTOR, YARD (r.r. trans.) or YARD ENGINEER (r.r. trans.) and confirms them with YARD ENGINEER (r.r. trans.). Observes signals and traffic in yard from left side of cab in switch engine and relays information to engineer. Signals YARD COUPLER (r.r. trans.) to set handbrakes on cars or to throw track switches, using arm or lantern signals.
GOE: 05.12.20 STRENGTH: L GED: R2 M2 L2 SVP: 3 DLU: 77

910.367-026 PASSENGER REPRESENTATIVE (r.r. trans.)

Accompanies CONDUCTOR, PASSENGER CAR (r.r. trans.) through train, verifies tickets and seat reservations, and records information, such as number of passengers scheduled to leave train at each stop. Answers passengers' questions and suggests activities and accommodations available at passengers' destination. May assist or relieve CONDUCTOR, PASSENGER CAR (r.r. trans.) by taking tickets in designated coaches or entire train. May inspect kitchen and dining area to ensure sanitation requirements are maintained. May investigate passenger complaints.
GOE: 09.01.04 STRENGTH: L GED: R3 M2 L3 SVP: 4 DLU: 77

910.367-030 WAY INSPECTOR (r.r. trans.) alternate titles: maintenance inspector; track inspector; track supervisor

Inspects railroad roadbed and equipment to detect damage, wear, or defective equipment requiring repair: Observes condition of roadbed from railcar. Stops car and examines switches, fishplates, and rails to detect damaged, worn, or defective equipment, loose bolts, and rotted ties. Manually operates switches to determine that they are in operating condition. Inspects signals and track wiring to determine continuity of electrical connections. Walks along track to observe condition of roadbed, noting looseness of ballast to determine if it requires repacking. Directs section crews to repair or replace defective equipment or to reballast roadbed. Inspects completed work to verify that repairs conform to governmental regulations. Prepares reports, indicating equipment or roadbed in need of repair, location, nature of damage, and repairs made by section crew.
GOE: 05.07.01 STRENGTH: L GED: R3 M2 L3 SVP: 5 DLU: 77

910.382-010 CAR-RETARDER OPERATOR (r.r. trans.) alternate titles: railroad-car retarder operator; retarder operator

Controls track switches and car-retarder system from elevated tower to route and regulate speed of freight cars entering railroad classification yard and couple them to make up trains: Reads switching orders to ascertain routing of cars. Ascertains from YARD ENGINEER (r.r. trans.) number of car to be shunted over hump (rise in yard) into classification yard and compares number with switching orders to determine track to which car should be routed. Observes lights on panelboard that indicate if track switches are open or closed. Notifies YARD ENGINEER (r.r. trans.) when to shunt car and presses button on panelboard that throws track switch to route car onto designated track. Observes car as it coasts down decline of hump and presses button on panelboard that activates retarder (braking device) to reduce speed of car as it reaches end of track or car to which it is to be coupled.
GOE: 05.12.05 STRENGTH: S GED: R3 M2 L3 SVP: 5 DLU: 77

910.384-010 TANK-CAR INSPECTOR (petrol. refin.)

Inspects and repairs refinery tank cars: Examines wheels, bearings, brakes, and safety appliances for defects. Replaces defective brakerod pins, tightens safety appliances, and packs bearings with grease. Examines valves, plugs, and tank seams, and seals leaks, using caulking compound.
GOE: 05.10.02 STRENGTH: M GED: R3 M2 L3 SVP: 4 DLU: 77

910.387-010 PERISHABLE-FRUIT INSPECTOR (wholesale tr.)

Adjusts temperature, humidity, and ventilation in railroad cars to control maturing process and minimize spoilage of fruit in transit: Travels with shipment from point of origin to destination, examines fruit, and records dates, time, and conditions of produce at designated points en route. Monitors temperature and humidity gauges, opens or closes car vents, and orders car iced or heaters installed to maintain optimum conditions. Prepares and submits report to consignor at end of trip.
GOE: 05.10.08 STRENGTH: L GED: R3 M2 L3 SVP: 5 DLU: 77

910.387-014 RAILROAD-CAR INSPECTOR (r.r. trans.) alternate titles: brake inspector; car checker; classification inspector; equipment inspector; journal-box inspector

Inspects railroad cars for structural defects and tests mechanical equipment, such as brakes, airhoses, and couplings to ensure that they are in operating condition: Observes cars from elevated platform or from ground as cars roll by, or climbs aboard train to test equipment and to locate defects. Examines car roofs, ice hatches, brake beams, doors, and floors for structural defects and obstructions. Turns handwheel to test brakes and ascertain that they are in operating condition. Inspects and tests airhoses for leakage. Inspects wheel trucks for dragging equipment. Opens journal boxes to determine that they are filled with grease. Prepares reports on findings, indicating number of car and type of repair required. May inspect electrical circuitry and recommend improvements or repairs to electrical operations. May tag cars in need of immediate repairs. May place lanterns or flags in front and rear of train to warn other workers that inspection is being performed. May inspect locomotives. May be designated according to type of car inspected as Passenger-Car Inspector (r.r. trans.).
GOE: 05.07.01 STRENGTH: L GED: R3 M2 L3 SVP: 5 DLU: 77

910.583-010 LABORER, CAR BARN (r.r. trans.)

Drives streetcars to designated stations in car barn for servicing and storage, according to odometer reading, maintenance charts, and schedule of anticipated car needs: Compares odometer of streetcar with maintenance charts to ascertain if car requires greasing, cleaning, or replacement of equipment, such as motors or compressors. Reads daily car schedule to ascertain number of cars required for next day's run. Drives streetcars to their designated tracks. Records number of cars sent to repair station, servicing needed, and number of units available for use.
GOE: 05.08.02 STRENGTH: L GED: R3 M2 L2 SVP: 4 DLU: 77

910.663-010 TRACK-MOVING-MACHINE OPERATOR (construction; mine & quarry) alternate titles: hydraulic-jack operator; track-laying-machine operator

Operates vehicle that automatically moves and lays track or rails to construct, repair, or maintain railroad tracks or mining car tracks: Drives vehicle over section of track or rail to be moved. Pushes control to close grasping device on track or rail section, raise and move section to specified location. Engages mechanism that lays track or rail to specified gauge.
GOE: 05.11.01 STRENGTH: V GED: R2 M2 L2 SVP: 4 DLU: 77

910.664-010 YARD COUPLER (r.r. trans.)

Switches railroad cars within yard of railroad, industrial plant, quarry, construction project, or similar location to load and unload cars or to make up and break up trains: Receives oral or written instructions from CONDUCTOR, YARD (r.r. trans.) indicating which cars are to be switched and track assignment. Raises coupling lever to uncouple cars. Signals SWITCH TENDER (r.r. trans.) to throw track switches and YARD ENGINEER (r.r. trans.) to move cars, using lantern or arm signals. Climbs ladder to top of car and turns handwheel to set brakes or to control speed of car when it has been shunted. Connects airhose to cars when making up trains, using wrench. Throws track switches where no SWITCH TENDER (r.r. trans.) is stationed to shunt cars to different sections of yard. May talk to CONDUCTOR, YARD (r.r. trans.) or YARD ENGINEER (r.r. trans.) via radiophone to give or receive switching information. May climb onto moving cars to set handbrakes and be designated Car Rider (r.r. trans.). When employed by establishment other than railroad,

may be designated Industrial-Yard Brake Coupler (any industry); or according to locomotive involved as Brake Coupler, Dinkey (any industry).
GOE: 05.12.05 STRENGTH: M GED: R3 M2 L2 SVP: 4 DLU: 77

910.667-010 CAR INSPECTOR (railroad equip.) alternate titles: railroad-car inspector

Inspects railroad cars or streetcars at terminals for damage, such as broken windows, jammed doors, defective locks, worn or damaged seats, and malfunctioning rest room facilities. Notifies train dispatcher if damage requires car to be moved to shop for repair. May make minor repairs.
GOE: 05.07.01 STRENGTH: L GED: R3 M2 L3 SVP: 4 DLU: 77

910.667-014 CONDUCTOR (r.r. trans.)

Performs variety of duties on streetcar, subway, suburban or elevated train, or motorbus: Collects fares or tickets from passengers. Issues transfers. Opens and closes doors. Signals operator to stop or proceed. Announces stops. Answers questions of passengers concerning schedules, routings, and fares. Preserves order among passengers.
GOE: 09.05.08 STRENGTH: M GED: R3 M2 L3 SVP: 4 DLU: 77

910.667-018 LOADING INSPECTOR (r.r. trans.) alternate titles: industrial clerk

Inspects loaded freight cars to ascertain that materials and goods, such as automobiles, lumber, or containers of explosives are securely braced and blocked according to loading specifications. Measures height and width of loads to ensure that they will pass over bridges and through tunnels on scheduled route. Ensures that warning signs are posted on cars containing explosives and radioactive or inflammatory materials. Records discrepancies detected and notifies loading crews to reload cars or insert additional bracing or packing.
GOE: 05.07.01 STRENGTH: L GED: R3 M2 L3 SVP: 4 DLU: 77

910.667-022 PERISHABLE-FREIGHT INSPECTOR (r.r. trans.)

Observes loading of perishable goods, such as drug products, fruits, or fish into railroad cars to ensure that loading crews comply with prescribed handling procedures for each type of shipment. Notifies worker or plant manager of special treatment required for unusual shipments. Records description of freight condition and handling activities.
GOE: 05.12.01 STRENGTH: L GED: R3 M2 L3 SVP: 3 DLU: 77

910.667-026 SWITCH TENDER (r.r. trans.)

Throws track switches within yard of railroad, industrial plant, quarry, construction project, or similar location to switch cars for loading, unloading, making up, and breaking up of trains: Receives oral or written instructions from CONDUCTOR, YARD (r.r. trans.), YARD COUPLER (r.r. trans.) or YARD MANAGER (r.r. trans.). Observes arm or lantern signal from YARD COUPLER (r.r. trans.) and relays information to HOSTLER (r.r. trans.) or throws track switch to facilitate shunting of cars to different locations in yard. May couple and uncouple cars for makeup and breakup of trains. May ride atop cars that have been shunted and turn handwheel to control speed of car or stop it at specified position. May wave arm or lantern to signal YARD ENGINEER (r.r. trans.) to start or stop engine.
GOE: 05.12.05 STRENGTH: M GED: R2 M1 L2 SVP: 2 DLU: 77

910.667-030 TRANSFER-TABLE OPERATOR HELPER (railroad equip.; r.r. trans.)

Assists TRANSFER-TABLE OPERATOR (r.r. trans.; railroad equip.) in moving railroad cars within railroad yard or railroad car manufacturing establishment: Uncouples car, connects towing cable to car, and removes wheel blocks from behind wheels. Determines that tracks are clear and signals TRANSFER-TABLE OPERATOR (r.r. trans.; railroad equip.) to pull car onto transfer table. Signals TRANSFER-TABLE OPERATOR (r.r. trans.; railroad equip.) to stop motion of car at designated point, or engages handbrake to stop motion of car, releases cable from car and places wheel blocks behind wheels to prevent motion. May tend switches to start and stop oven that dries freshly painted cars. May signal TRANSFER-TABLE OPERATOR (r.r. trans.; railroad equip.) to move cars into and out of drying oven.
GOE: 05.12.04 STRENGTH: H GED: R2 M1 L1 SVP: 3 DLU: 77

910.677-010 PASSENGER SERVICE REPRESENTATIVE II (r.r. trans.)

Stands at gate in railroad or rapid-transit station to admit passengers holding tickets or tokens, or at an exit to prevent unauthorized entrance of passengers. Tears or punches tickets to prevent their reuse. May count tickets to tally number of passengers boarding train. May give passengers and guests boarding passes.
GOE: 09.05.08 STRENGTH: L GED: R2 M1 L2 SVP: 2 DLU: 77

910.683-010 HOSTLER (r.r. trans.)

Drives electric, diesel-electric, steam, or gas-turbine-electric locomotive to designated stations in railroad roundhouse to be cleaned, serviced, or repaired: Receives locomotive from LOCOMOTIVE ENGINEER (r.r. trans.) at termination of run. Observes oil, air, and steam pressure gauges and water level to ensure that locomotive is operating efficiently. Pushes or pulls levers to control movement of locomotive. Drives locomotive to various stations in roundhouse to be repaired, cleaned, or supplied with coal, fuel oil, water, lubricating oil, and sand, following instructions from ENGINE DISPATCHER (r.r. trans.). Drives locomotive from roundhouse to switching area and delivers serviced locomotive to engine crew.
GOE: 05.08.02 STRENGTH: L GED: R3 M2 L2 SVP: 4 DLU: 77

910.683-014 MOTOR OPERATOR (r.r. trans.)

Drives elevated suburban, or subway train, observing signal system of railroad. Starts, slows, or stops train on signal. May open and close doors.

GOE: 05.08.02 STRENGTH: L GED: R3 M2 L2 SVP: 5 DLU: 77

910.683-018 TRACK-SURFACING-MACHINE OPERATOR (construction)

Operates one or more machines mounted on flat-bed railroad trucks to spread, shape, and tamp ballast; raise, level, and align track; and prepare track foundation of crushed stone according to specifications: Moves levers and brake pedal to guide machine into position. Adjusts controls to activate jacks, tampers, and scraper blades. Strings wire guidelines through leveling or aligning fixture. Attaches line to rails or trailer extensions (buggies) coupled to machine to set up equipment. Turns wheels to adjust guidelines for track alignments and grades, following specifications. Observes indicator arms to verify level and alignment of track. When concerned with jack-tamping machine, may be designated Jack-Tamp Operator (construction). May control track-lining machine and be designated Track-Liner Operator (construction). May operate machines that lay ties and lay rails to construct, repair, or maintain track [TRACK-MOVING-MACHINE OPERATOR (construction; mine & quarry)].
GOE: 05.11.01 STRENGTH: V GED: R3 M2 L2 SVP: 3 DLU: 77

910.683-022 TRANSFER-TABLE OPERATOR (railroad equip.; r.r. trans.)

Drives transfer table, containing power winch, to move rolling stock within railroad yard: Drives table to area where equipment, such as crane, car, or locomotive is located. Starts table revolving to align track of table with track on which equipment is located. Pulls equipment onto transfer table, using winch. Drives table with rolling stock to transport equipment to specified area. May position table to bridge gap between ends of tracks.
GOE: 05.11.04 STRENGTH: M GED: R3 M1 L2 SVP: 3 DLU: 77

910.684-010 GRINDING-MACHINE OPERATOR, PORTABLE (r.r. trans.) alternate titles: track-grinder operator

Dresses and reshapes worn or damaged railroad switch points and frogs, using portable power grinder: Starts gasoline engine that activates grinding wheel. Holds face or rim of wheel against steel rail parts to remove imperfections and impart appropriate shape, restoring rail for safe, smooth operation. Performs running repairs to grinding machine, lubricates unit, and changes worn or chipped grinding wheels. May repair and adjust track switches, using wrenches and specified replacement parts. May grind ends of newly laid rails to attain smooth joint.
GOE: 05.10.01 STRENGTH: M GED: R2 M2 L2 SVP: 3 DLU: 77

910.684-014 TRACK REPAIRER (r.r. trans.) alternate titles: section-gang worker; track laborer

Installs and repairs railroad track on specified territory of railroad, using portable grinder, spike puller, spike driver, and tie adz, to grind ends of rails, remove old spikes, drive new spikes, cut ties to fit fishplates, and perform related maintenance, working as member of crew: Operates single- or multiple-head spike puller to pull old spikes from tie. Raises rail, using hydraulic jack, to facilitate removal of old tie and installation of new tie. Operates tie-adzing machine to cut portion of tie so that tie plate can be inserted to hold rail. Drills holes through rails, tie plates, and fishplates for insertion of bolts and spike, using power drill. Operates single- or multiple-head spike driving machine to drive spike into tie and secure rail. Operates track-wrench machine to tighten or loosen bolts at joints that hold ends of rails together. Operates rail saw to cut rails to specified lengths. Operates portable grinder to grind worn ends of rails. Sprays ties, fishplates, and joints with oil to protect them from weather. May paint railroad signs, such as speed limits and gate-crossing warnings. May oversee workers and act as section leader.
GOE: 05.12.12 STRENGTH: H GED: R3 M2 L2 SVP: 4 DLU: 81

910.687-010 BAGGAGE HANDLER (r.r. trans.)

Loads and stores baggage on passenger train: Inspects tags on baggage to ensure that baggage is routed to designated train. Loads baggage in car according to destination recorded on tags, placing baggage to be unloaded last in rear of car. Unloads baggage from train onto trailers at destination.
GOE: 05.12.03 STRENGTH: H GED: R2 M1 L1 SVP: 2 DLU: 77

910.687-014 CAR COOPER (any industry) alternate titles: car whacker

Prepares railroad freight cars for loading with grain, ores, packaged goods, and other items: Opens side drop or hopper-bottom doors of cars. Sweeps, scrapes, and shovels rubbish from floors. Hammers down or removes protruding nails from floors and sides. Closes car doors and hammers wooden wedges through latches to secure them. May line interior of cars and doors with paper or cardboard. May repair holes in floors and sides by nailing boards over them. May mix caulking compound and caulk cracks in cars, using handtools. May patch holes in roofs with asphalt coating. May wash interior and exterior of cars, using water hose, disinfectants, brushes, and brooms [CLEANER (any industry) III]. May seal doors of loaded cars. May move cars on track, using capstan winch or car bar. May spray cars with insecticides to destroy insects and rodents. May record data, such as car number, condition of car for shipment, and date fumigated.
GOE: 05.12.18 STRENGTH: M GED: R2 M1 L1 SVP: 2 DLU: 77

910.687-018 CAR ICER (food prep., nec; meat products) alternate titles: car ice-bunker filler; icer, air conditioning; refrigerator-car icer

Fills bunkers of railroad refrigerator cars with ice and rock salt to preserve foodstuffs, such as citrus fruits, bananas, and meat, during shipment. Breaks up

blocks of ice, using bar and pick. May blow crushed ice over perishable products, using ice crushing machine equipped with blower device.
GOE: 05.12.03 STRENGTH: H GED: R2 M1 L1 SVP: 2 DLU: 77

910.687-022 FREIGHT-CAR CLEANER, DELTA SYSTEM (r.r. trans.)

Performs any combination of following duties to clean freight cars at Delta system (central cleaning station): Pushes buttons on control panel to activate track switches, conveyors, vacuum cleaner, warning siren, and winch. Hooks cable to string of cars and starts winch to move cars. Removes grain doors and places them on conveyor to storage area. Removes nails, cleats, crate bracings, and shipping paper from walls and floor, using clawhammer and crowbar. Tosses debris onto incinerator conveyor. Sweeps debris out car door into conveyor pit below track, using broom. Pushes and pulls vacuum cleaner nozzle over floor to remove debris, such as wood chips, sawdust, grain, flour, and powdered chemicals. Washes down ceiling and walls with water, using hose, to remove dust. Pushes button to route cleaned cars to side tracks.
GOE: 05.12.18 STRENGTH: H GED: R2 M1 L1 SVP: 2 DLU: 77

910.687-026 TRACK OILER (r.r. trans.)

Cleans out switches and greases rails around curves on streetcar tracks: Drives three-wheeled motorcycle, equipped with cleaning apparatus and lubricants, along track. Pumps water from electric track-switch box with manually operated suction pump. Sweeps dirt from track switch with broom. Greases curves in rails with grease stick so that flanges on car wheels will be able to adjust to curves without breaking. Throws rock salt over switches during cold weather to counteract freezing.
GOE: 05.12.18 STRENGTH: L GED: R2 M1 L1 SVP: 2 DLU: 77

911   WATER TRANSPORTATION OCCUPATIONS

. This group includes occupations concerned with conveying passengers and cargo by controlling movement of ships, boats, and other vessels; securing vessels in dock; opening and closing canal locks; and related activities.

911.131-010 BOATSWAIN (water trans.)

Supervises ABLE SEAMAN (water trans.) 911.364-010 and DECKHAND (water trans.) 911.687-022 engaged in cleaning decks and lifeboats, and chipping, scraping, wirebrushing, and painting decks, sides, and superstructure: Examines cargo-handling gear and lifesaving equipment and supervises crew engaged in repairing or replacing defective gear and equipment. May be required to be certified by U.S. Coast Guard as ABLE SEAMAN (water trans.) 911.364-010.
GOE: 05.12.18 STRENGTH: H GED: R4 M2 L3 SVP: 7 DLU: 86

911.131-014 LOCK TENDER, CHIEF OPERATOR (water trans.) alternate titles: canal-lock tender, chief operator; chief lock-operator

Supervises and coordinates activities of LOCK OPERATOR (water trans.) to open locks and dams on canal for vessels requiring passage: Assigns to LOCK OPERATOR (water trans.) tasks of mooring boats awaiting passage through canal, raising or lowering water level, opening and closing gates and valves of locks and dams, operating navigation lights and traffic signals, and compiling records of vessels using canal, and of weather and water conditions. Determines which of two locks to use according to needs of traffic. Controls and operates gas, steam, and hydroelectric generating units. Installs mechanical and electrical equipment. Repairs lock machinery motors, generators, power lines, and other electrical equipment [ELECTRICIAN, MAINTENANCE (any industry)]. Operates machinery to open and close locks. Reports needed repairs to lock maintenance department. May observe craft approaching locks to determine size and speed of vessel and issues instructions to vessel operator violating canal regulations.
GOE: 05.05.09 STRENGTH: M GED: R4 M3 L3 SVP: 7 DLU: 77

911.133-010 CADET, DECK (water trans.)

Learns and performs all deck and navigational duties aboard ship under supervision of deck officer to become eligible for U.S. Coast Guard license and position as MATE, SHIP (water trans.): Observes loading and unloading of cargo holds to learn methods of handling and stowing of cargo. Inspects lifesaving and visual-signaling equipment for defects. Directs crew engaged in repair of defective equipment. Stands watch during specified periods while ship is underway. On graduation from maritime academy and successful completion of license examination, is eligible for position as MATE, SHIP (water trans.).
GOE: 05.04.02 STRENGTH: L GED: R4 M4 L3 SVP: 6 DLU: 77

911.137-010 BARGE CAPTAIN (water trans.) alternate titles: scow captain

Supervises and coordinates activities of workers on towed barge that transports cargo on lakes, bays, sounds, and rivers: Directs workers engaged in loading and unloading barge to ensure that cargo is loaded according to balancing specifications. Inspects barge to ensure that craft is seaworthy. Signals TUGBOAT CAPTAIN (water trans.) to tow barge to destination. Logs barge's movements and ports-of-call. Steers barge when it has steering equipment.
GOE: 05.12.01 STRENGTH: M GED: R4 M3 L3 SVP: 6 DLU: 77

911.137-014 DERRICK-BOAT CAPTAIN (water trans.) alternate titles: derrick-boat runner

Supervises and coordinates activities of crew operating derrick mounted on barge: Directs placing and mooring of boat. Supervises crew in placing rigging

and operating derrick to lift and move objects and materials. Prepares progress and personnel reports. Must possess license issued by U.S. Coast Guard to operate self-propelled derrick boat or to operate derrick boat outside continental limits of the United States.
GOE: 05.12.01 STRENGTH: L GED: R4 M3 L3 SVP: 7 DLU: 77

911.137-018 HEADER (water trans.) alternate titles: dock boss; gang boss; hatch supervisor; ship boss; stevedoring supervisor
Supervises and coordinates activities of STEVEDORE (water trans.) II engaged in loading and unloading ships' cargoes: Assigns duties to workers, and explains methods of handling, stowing, securing cargo, and setting up hoisting equipment. Determines what cargo requires special handling and how it is to be stowed in ship's hold. Signals WINCH DRIVER (water trans.) to raise or lower cargo. May estimate dunnage (paper and timber) required to brace and arrange cargo in ship's hold to prevent cargo damage. May maintain inventory of dunnage. May be designated according to work area as Header, Dock (water trans.); Header, Ship (water trans.); or kind of cargo stowed as Cotton Header (water trans.).
GOE: 05.12.01 STRENGTH: L GED: R3 M3 L3 SVP: 6 DLU: 77

911.137-022 SUPERINTENDENT, STEVEDORING (water trans.)
Supervises and coordinates activities of workers engaged in loading and unloading of ship's cargoes: Studies bills of lading to determine sequence of loading operations, taking into consideration cargo space available, shipping instructions, and knowledge of cargo stowage. Calculates number of hours and personnel required for loading or unloading ship and places order for personnel. Inspects load-test certificates of ship's booms and cargo handling gear to ensure they meet safety regulations, and that cargo will not exceed specified load capacity. Directs activities of workers engaged in loading or unloading materials requiring special handling, such as explosives, locomotives, and other machinery. Supervises workers engaged in checking and loading cargo to ensure that cargo is loaded in specified sequence and in accordance with shipping instructions. Prepares report of stevedoring activities, such as time, hours, personnel, cargo handling gear used, and submits report to accounting department. Inspects dock areas to ensure safety regulations are being observed. May supervise and coordinate activities of workers engaged in loading and unloading barges. May supervise container-handling activities and be designated Stevedoring Superintendent, Container Handling (water trans.).
GOE: 05.11.04 STRENGTH: L GED: R4 M3 L3 SVP: 7 DLU: 81

911.137-026 SUPERVISOR, FERRY TERMINAL (water trans.) alternate titles: ferry-terminal agent
Supervises and coordinates activities of workers engaged in selling tickets and directing pedestrian and vehicular traffic to and from ferry boats at ferry terminal: Schedules and assigns work to subordinates. Interprets tariff regulations and changes in operating procedures to subordinates. Prepares daily revenue reports and receipts for bank deposit. Oversees loading of vehicles aboard ferries to prevent accidents, overloading, and imbalanced loading. Observes vehicles on dock and prohibits loading of excessively large vehicles. Directs receipt and loading of cargo aboard ferry. Notifies contractors of supply shortages, such as ferry fuel and janitorial and office supplies.
GOE: 11.11.03 STRENGTH: L GED: R4 M3 L4 SVP: 5 DLU: 77

911.167-010 DISPATCHER, TUGBOAT (water trans.)
Dispatches tugboats to guide ships entering or leaving port and to tow barges and log rafts: Receives written or oral customer request for services. Determines equipment required, such as tugs, barges, or derricks according to size, location and work performed. Selects tugboat captain from roster and notifies captain of order requirements, using radiotelephone. Obtains ship berthing and bunkering permits from port authorities. Reviews weather data and navigation charts and estimates time required to perform requested services. Maintains records and prepares bills for services. May notify captain of tugboat by radiotelephone of order changes. May dispatch work crews to tugboats in response to emergency requests from captain.
GOE: 07.04.05 STRENGTH: S GED: R4 M3 L4 SVP: 6 DLU: 77

911.263-010 DEEP SUBMERGENCE VEHICLE OPERATOR (military ser.)
Commands and pilots deep submergence vehicle (small noncombatant submarine) to obtain oceanographic research information, recover other sunken vessels or objects from ocean floor, and to transport passengers, such as scientists, researchers, and technicians to ocean bottom: Conducts predive and postdive inspection of vehicle to ensure vehicle is seaworthy and life support systems are functioning in specified manner. Reads gauges to verify hydraulic fluid, air pressure, and oxygen are at designated levels. Navigates vehicle based on such knowledge as ocean, currents, and vehicle characteristics. Pushes and pulls control levers on console to steer vehicle. Pushes switches to supply power to various units, such as mainpower supply and mechanical arms which are located outside of vehicle and are used to pick up, collect, or move objects on ocean floor. Monitors sonar and navigational aids. Directs subordinates in their activities. Occasionally instructs students in operation of vehicle.
GOE: 05.04.02 STRENGTH: L GED: R3 M2 L2 SVP: 7 DLU: 77

911.362-010 LOCK OPERATOR (water trans.) alternate titles: canal-structure operator
Controls machinery to open and close locks and dams on canal: Observes gauges and turns valves to increase or decrease water level in lock. Observes positions of vessels and tie-up of mooring lines in lock to ensure optimum utili-

zation of lock space and prevent vessel damage. Logs data, such as water levels, weather conditions, and type, number, and destination of vessels. Starts motors to open gates and sections of dams for passage of vessels. Turns on navigation lights and traffic signals along canal. Cleans, oils, and makes minor repairs to equipment. Collects lock slips (vessel identifications slips) from vessel operators and submits slips to supervisor. Ties or slips line-eyes over bitts on lock deck to secure vessels. May direct activities of workers engaged in mooring vessels in lock.
GOE: 05.11.04 STRENGTH: L GED: R3 M2 L2 SVP: 5 DLU: 77

911.363-010 FERRYBOAT OPERATOR (water trans.) alternate titles: ferry operator
Operates power ferryboat to transport passengers, motor vehicles, and freight across river: Signals passengers to board ferryboat and directs loading of motor vehicles and freight. Signals DECKHAND (water trans.) to raise loading ramp and to pull guard chain across entry. Starts engine to move ferryboat to opposite side of body of water. Collects fares from customers or signals FERRYBOAT-OPERATOR HELPER (water trans.) to collect fares. Determines course and speed of ferryboat, utilizing knowledge of weather conditions and water currents. Reverses engines and steers boat into landing pier. Inspects, lubricates, and performs emergency repairs to railings, pontoons, and winches to ensure safe operation of ferry. May maintain operations log.
GOE: 05.04.02 STRENGTH: L GED: R3 M2 L2 SVP: 6 DLU: 77

911.363-014 QUARTERMASTER (water trans.)
Steers ship and maintains visual communications with other ships: Steers ship under direction of ship's commander or navigating officer, or directs helmsman to steer, following designated course. Stands by wheel when ship is on automatic pilot and verifies accuracy of course by comparing with magnetic compass. Relays specified signals to ships in vicinity, using visual signaling devices, such as blinker light and semaphore. Gives directions to crew engaged in cleaning wheelhouse and quarter deck (afterpart of upper deck reserved as promenade for officers and sometimes cabin passengers). Maintains ship's log while in port, and stands gangway watch to prevent unauthorized persons from boarding ship. May be required to be certificated by U.S. Coast Guard as ABLE SEAMAN (water trans.).
GOE: 05.04.02 STRENGTH: L GED: R3 M3 L3 SVP: 6 DLU: 77

911.364-010 ABLE SEAMAN (water trans.) alternate titles: able-bodied seaman
Performs following tasks on board ship to watch for obstructions in vessel's path and to maintain equipment and structures: Stands watch at bow or on wing of bridge to look for obstructions in path of vessel. Measures depth of water in shallow or unfamiliar waters, using leadline, and telephones or shouts information to bridge. Turns wheel on bridge or uses emergency steering apparatus to steer vessel as directed by MATE, SHIP (water trans.). Breaks out, rigs, overhauls, and stows cargo-handling gear, stationary rigging, and running gear. Overhauls lifeboats and lifeboat gear and lowers or raises lifeboats with winch or falls. Paints and chips rust on deck or superstructure of ship. Must hold certificate issued by U.S. Government. When working aboard vessels carrying liquid cargoes, must hold tanker operator's certificate. May stow or remove cargo from ship's hold [STEVEDORE (water trans.) II]. May be concerned with only one phase of duties, as maintenance of ship's gear and decks or watch duties, and be known as Deckhand, Maintenance (water trans.); Watchstander (water trans.).
GOE: 05.12.03 STRENGTH: H GED: R3 M2 L2 SVP: 5 DLU: 77

911.364-014 BOAT LOADER I (water trans.) alternate titles: dock hand; pier hand; wharf hand; wharf operator; wharf tender
Connects hose couplings to enable liquid cargo, such as petroleum, gasoline, heating oil, sulfuric acid, and alum liquor, to be pumped from and into barges and tankers: Reads timetable to determine name of ship, location of pier, and number and types of hoses to be connected. Climbs aboard ship and lowers measuring tape and thermometer into each tank to measure depth and temperature of liquid cargo to be unloaded. Positions coupling of pier hose next to valve of ship, using winch and boom, and connects coupling to valve, using wrench. Attaches ground wire to hose to prevent explosion caused by static electricity generated when liquid cargo flows through hose. Opens valve to allow flow of cargo through hose and signals worker aboard ship to start pumps to unload cargo. Signals worker aboard ship to pump ballast from cargo tanks in order to prepare transfer of cargo onto ship. Signals worker on shore to pump liquid cargo onto ship. May be designated according to water vessel loaded as Barge Loader (water trans.).
GOE: 05.12.06 STRENGTH: M GED: R2 M2 L2 SVP: 3 DLU: 77

911.584-010 MARINE OILER (water trans.) alternate titles: oiler; striker
Oils and greases moving parts, such as gears, shafts, and bearings, of engines and auxiliary equipment used to propel maritime vessels: Examines machinery for specified pressure and flow of lubricants. Fills oilcups on machinery with grease and lubricating oil, according to machinery lubrication instructions. Reads pressure and temperature gauges and records data in engineering log. Assists ENGINEER (water trans.) in overhauling and adjusting machinery. May lubricate deck machinery when vessel is unloading cargo.
GOE: 05.12.08 STRENGTH: M GED: R3 M2 L2 SVP: 4 DLU: 77

911.663-010 MOTORBOAT OPERATOR (any industry)
Operates motor-driven boat to carry passengers and freight, take depth soundings in turning basin, serve as liaison between ships, ship to shore, harbor and

beach area patrol, or tow, push, or guide other boats, barges, logs, or rafts: Casts off securing lines and starts motor. Starts boat and steers boat with helm or tiller. Maintains equipment, such as range markers, fire extinguishers, boat fenders, lines, pumps, and fittings. Services motor by changing oil and lubricating parts. Cleans boat and repairs hull and superstructure, using handtools, paint, and brushes. May tune up, overhaul, or replace engine. May give directions for loading and seating in boat. May be designated according to type of boat operated as Boat Tender (logging); Boomboat Operator (logging); Charter-Boat Operator (amuse. & rec.); Sightseeing-Boat Operator (water trans.); Water-Taxi Driver (water trans.); or operate motor-driven boat to haul fish or other marine life from offshore fishing vessel to buyer and be designated Run-Boat Operator (water trans.).
GOE: 05.08.04 STRENGTH: M GED: R3 M2 L3 SVP: 5 DLU: 77

911.663-014   STEVEDORE I (water trans.)
Operates material-handling equipment, such as power winch, grain trimmer, crane, and lift truck, to transfer cargo into or from hold of ship and about dock area: Operates crane or winch to load or unload cargo, such as automobiles, crates, scrap, and steel beams, using hook, magnet, or sling attached in accordance with signals from other workers. Moves controls to start flow of grain from spouts of grain trimmer, stopping flow and repositioning spout over each hatch when previous hatch is filled. Drives lift truck along dock or aboard ship to transfer bulk items, such as lumber, pallet-mounted machinery, and crated products within range of winch. Drives tractor to transfer loaded trailers from warehouse to dockside. May position and fasten hose lines to ships' cargo tanks when loading or unloading liquid cargo, such as animal fats, vegetable oils, molasses, or chemicals. May perform variety of manual duties, such as lashing and shoring cargo aboard ship, attaching slings, hooks, or other lifting devices to winch for loading or unloading, and signaling other workers to move, raise, or lower cargo. May direct activities of cargo gang consisting of STEVEDORE (water trans.) II. May be designated according to equipment operated as Lift-Truck Operator (water trans.); Tractor Operator (water trans.); Winch Operator (water trans.).
GOE: 05.11.04 STRENGTH: M GED: R3 M2 L2 SVP: 5 DLU: 77

911.664-010   FERRYBOAT OPERATOR, CABLE (water trans.) alternate titles: ferry operator
Pulls ferryboat guided by overhead cable to transport passengers and freight across river: Signals passengers to board ferryboat and directs workers engaged in loading of freight [FERRYBOAT-OPERATOR HELPER (water trans.)]. Pays out rope on one side of ferryboat and pulls in rope on other side to propel ferryboat across river. Inspects equipment, such as cables, ropes, pontoons, and railings and repairs or replaces defective equipment.
GOE: 05.12.03 STRENGTH: M GED: R2 M2 L2 SVP: 3 DLU: 77

911.664-014   SAILOR, PLEASURE CRAFT (water trans.)
Performs any of following duties to assist skipper to operate and maintain privately owned or charter sailing yacht: Dusts and waxes furniture and polishes wood trim, sweeps floors and decks, and polishes brass and other metal parts. Inspects, repairs, and maintains sails and rigging. Paints or varnishes surfaces. Makes emergency repairs to auxiliary engine. Adjusts sails and rigging and steers boat when underway. May stow supplies and equipment and record data in log, such as weather conditions and distance traveled.
GOE: 05.12.18 STRENGTH: H GED: R3 M2 L2 SVP: 5 DLU: 77

911.667-010   FERRYBOAT-OPERATOR HELPER (water trans.) alternate titles: ferryboat helper
Assists FERRYBOAT OPERATOR, CABLE (water trans.) in operation of cable-guided ferryboat to transport passengers, motor vehicles, and freight across river, by performing following duties: Signals vehicle operators to drive vehicles onto ferryboat, or drives vehicles onto ferryboat. Places blocks under wheels of vehicles. Transfers freight onto ferryboat, using handtruck or power truck. Raises ferryboat gates by hand or by turning windlass. Unties stay ropes from dock. Collects fares from customers. Refuels engines and lubricates mechanical equipment. Performs other duties as described under HELPER (any industry) Master Title.
GOE: 05.12.03 STRENGTH: H GED: R2 M2 L2 SVP: 2 DLU: 77

911.667-014   HATCH TENDER (water trans.)
Signals WINCH DRIVER (water trans.) to transfer cargo from dock to ship's hold, or from ship's hold to dock: Observes workers attaching or detaching slings to or from loads to determine moment for signaling. Waves arms to indicate ready signal for transfer of cargo. May alternate jobs with WINCH DRIVER (water trans.).
GOE: 05.12.04 STRENGTH: L GED: R2 M1 L1 SVP: 2 DLU: 77

911.667-018   SOUNDER (any industry) alternate titles: group leader, river-and-harbor soundings
Measures depth of water at designated points along navigable waterway, using lead-weighted line marked to indicate depth, to facilitate charting of waterways and determine need for dredging or other marine construction activity.
GOE: 05.12.05 STRENGTH: M GED: R3 M2 L2 SVP: 2 DLU: 77

911.677-010   TICKET TAKER, FERRYBOAT (water trans.)
Raises and lowers deck of landing bridge to make bridge level with deck of ferryboat, and collects or punches tickets of passengers at ferryboat terminal: Starts windlass to adjust level of landing bridge for vehicles and pedestrians to board ferryboat, or tosses gangplank pull-ropes to workers who secure gang-

plank to deck of ferryboat. Inspects security of gangplank fastenings to dock. Opens doors or gates to admit passengers aboard ferryboat, and collects tickets or punches commuter tickets as pedestrians and vehicles go aboard. Closes doors and gates upon whistled signal from ferryboat, pulls gangplank back onto dock, and starts windlass to unhook ferryboat from landing bridge. Provides passengers information about ferryboat schedules. May move stalled or driverless vehicles and freight-loaded wagons on and off ferries, using industrial truck.
GOE: 05.12.04 STRENGTH: M GED: R2 M2 L2 SVP: 2 DLU: 77

911.687-010   BOAT-LOADER HELPER (water trans.) alternate titles: dock helper; pier hand helper; wharf helper; wharf-tender helper
Assists BOAT LOADER (water trans.) I to pump liquid cargo, such as petroleum, gasoline, heating oil, sulfuric acid, and alum liquor, from and into barges and tankers: Catches mooring hawsers and ties them around dock posts to secure vessels. Couples hoses to valves on ship's tanks and turns handwheels to open or close valves. Removes lines from vessels and casts off hawsers. Drains loading hoses and places them on dollies. Cleans oil and waste materials from dock, using squeegees, broom, and rags. May be designated according to vessels loaded as Barge-Loader Helper (water trans.).
GOE: 05.12.06 STRENGTH: V GED: R2 M1 L1 SVP: 2 DLU: 77

911.687-014   CLEANER III (any industry)
Cleans coal or coke from holds of ships, docks, or areas around chutes, conveyors, crushers, coke ovens, and screens, using airhose, brooms, scrapers, shovels, and wheelbarrow. May feed coal, using shovel and wheelbarrow, through crusher to obtain sample for laboratory analysis. May extinguish minor oven door fires, using water hose. May be designated according to work area as Belt Cleaner (steel & rel.); Boat Cleaner (steel & rel.); Dock Cleaner (steel & rel.).
GOE: 05.12.18 STRENGTH: M GED: R2 M1 L1 SVP: 2 DLU: 77

911.687-018   COAL TRIMMER (water trans.) alternate titles: boat puller
Positions barges to be loaded with coal under coal tipple, using electric winch or hand ropes. May spread coal evenly with shovel in holds of ships.
GOE: 05.12.04 STRENGTH: H GED: R2 M1 L1 SVP: 3 DLU: 77

911.687-022   DECKHAND (water trans.)
Performs any combination of following duties aboard watercraft, such as dredges, ferryboats, scows, and river boats: Handles lines to moor vessel to wharves, tie up vessel to another vessel, or rig towing lines. Sweeps and washes decks, using broom, brushes, mops, and firehose. Lowers and mans lifeboat in case of emergencies. Stands steering watches or lookout watches while underway. Moves controls or turns handwheels to raise or lower passenger or vehicle landing ramps or kelp-cutter mechanism. Inserts blocks under wheels of vehicles to prevent them from moving on ferryboats. Loads or unloads material from barges, scows, and dredges. Paints lifeboats, decks, and superstructure of vessel, using brush. Lubricates machinery and equipment. Splices and repairs cables and ropes, using handtools. Examines cables that holds vessels in tow and tightens cables to ensure vessels are snug. May tour decks during watch to caution passengers engaged in unsafe practices, and ensures departure of passengers at end of voyage. Deckhands are designated according to type of craft as Barge Hand (water trans.); Dredge Deckhand (water trans.); Ferryboat Deckhand (water trans.); Pilot-Boat Deckhand (water trans.); Scow Deckhand (water trans.); Tugboat Deckhand (water trans.).
GOE: 05.08.04 STRENGTH: H GED: R2 M1 L1 SVP: 4 DLU: 77

911.687-026   LINES TENDER (water trans.) alternate titles: laborer, marine terminal
Secures and removes ship's docking lines to and from dock: Catches lines heaved from ship attempting to dock. Drags lines to bitts on dock and slips eye of docking lines over bitts. Removes lines from bitts when ships depart. May drive vehicle to pull in docking lines.
GOE: 05.12.03 STRENGTH: H GED: R2 M1 L1 SVP: 2 DLU: 77

911.687-030   ORDINARY SEAMAN (water trans.)
Stands deck department watches and performs variety of duties to preserve painted surfaces of ship and to maintain lines, running gear, and cargo-handling gear in safe operating conditon: Watches from bow of ship or wing of bridge for obstructions in path of ship. Turns wheel while observing compass to steer and maintain ship on course. Mops or washes down deck, using hose to remove oil, dirt, and debris. Chips and cleans rust spots from deck, superstructure, and sides of ship, using hand or air chipping hammer and wire brush. Paints chipped area. Splices wire rope, using marlinespike, wirecutters, and twine.
GOE: 05.12.18 STRENGTH: M GED: R3 M1 L1 SVP: 4 DLU: 77

912   AIR TRANSPORTATION OCCUPATIONS

This group includes occupations concerned with fueling, cooling, heating, and ventilating aircraft; repacking parachutes; and related minor repair and maintenance activities.

912.167-010   DISPATCHER (air trans.) alternate titles: airplane dispatcher; helicopter dispatcher
Authorizes, regulates, and controls commercial airline flights according to government and company regulations to expedite and ensure safety of flight: Analyzes and evaluates meteorological information, such as speed and direction

of winds, visibility, and presence of storms, to determine potential safety of flight and desirable route. Computes amount of fuel needed according to type of aircraft, distance of flight, weather conditions, and fuel regulations prescribed by Federal Aviation Agency. Prepares flight plan containing information, such as maximum allowable gross takeoff and landing weights, weather, and landing field conditions. Signs authorization to release flight for takeoff. Delays or cancels flight if unsafe conditions prevail. Studies weather and pilot's position reports and terrain maps to evaluate progress of flight. Recommends flight plan alterations, such as changing course or altitude, canceling stops, or taking extra fuel. Prepares log of flights, delays, and cancellations, and lists reasons for changes in schedules or flight plans. Must be licensed by Federal Aviation Administration.
GOE: 05.03.03 STRENGTH: S GED: R5 M4 L4 SVP: 8 DLU: 77

912.364-010 AIRPORT ATTENDANT (air trans.)
Performs any combination of following duties in maintenance of small airports and in servicing aircraft: Periodically inspects buildings and hangars to detect fire hazards and violations of airport regulations. Examines firefighting equipment to detect malfunctions and fills depleted fire extinguishers. Performs necessary minor repairs to fire trucks and tractors. Fills light bombs with kerosene and positions bombs on landing field to illuminate danger areas. Cleans, fills, and lights smokepots used to indicate wind direction, and repairs or replaces windsock and other wind indicating devices. Replaces defective bulbs or burnt-out fuses in lighting equipment, such as landing lights and boundary lights. Fills holes and levels low places and bumps in runways and taxiing areas. Cuts grass on airport grounds [LABORER, AIRPORT MAINTENANCE (air trans.)]. Patrols airfield to ensure security of aircraft and facilities. Verifies and reports specified amount of gasoline and oil supplies. Blocks and stakes down airplanes. Records airport data, such as number of planes stored in hangars, plane landings and departures, and number of passengers carried on planes. May wash and clean cabins and exterior surfaces of airplanes. May fill airplane tanks with gasoline and oil [LINE-SERVICE ATTENDANT (air trans.)]. May be required to possess Red Cross first-aid certificate to render emergency treatment to victims.
GOE: 05.10.04 STRENGTH: M GED: R3 M2 L3 SVP: 5 DLU: 77

912.367-010 FLIGHT-INFORMATION EXPEDITER (air trans.)
Determines flight times of airplanes and transmits information to flight operations and Air Traffic Command centers: Evaluates data, such as weather conditions, flight plans, ramp delays, and enroute stopovers, to determine arrival and departure times for each flight, using aids, such as weather charts, slide rule, and computer. Transmits identity and type of airplane, flight locations, time of arrival and departure, and names of crewmembers to Air Traffic Command to obtain clearance for flight over restricted areas. Notifies departments of airline of pending arrival of inbound flight to ensure that personnel are available to load or unload fuel, baggage, and cargo.
GOE: 07.04.05 STRENGTH: L GED: R4 M4 L4 SVP: 5 DLU: 77

912.367-014 TRANSPORTATION AGENT (air trans.) alternate titles: departure clerk; operations agent; service coordinator
Expedites movement of freight, mail, baggage, and passengers through airline terminal by performing following tasks: Prepares airway bill of lading on freight from consignors and routes freight on first available flight. Telephones consignees to report arrival of air freight. Obtains flight number, airplane number, and names of crewmembers from teletyped message of DISPATCHER (air trans.), and records data on airplane's flight papers. Records baggage, mail, and freight weights, and number of passengers on airplane's papers and teletypes data to flight's destination. Positions ramp for loading of airplane. Verifies passengers' tickets as they board plane. Oversees or participates in loading cargo to ensure completeness of load and even distribution of weight. Removes ramp, and signals pilot that personnel and equipment are clear of plane. May load and unload freight and baggage by operating forklift truck.
GOE: 07.05.01 STRENGTH: L GED: R3 M3 L3 SVP: 5 DLU: 77

912.662-010 IN-FLIGHT REFUELING OPERATOR (military ser.)
Operates air refueling systems aboard aircraft tanker to refuel airborne aircraft: Confers with receiver aircraft pilot to direct aircraft into air refueling position, using radio. Presses buttons and switches on control panel to extend inflight boom and connect tanker and receiver aircraft. Presses button to start refueling process. Monitors control panel light to detect equipment malfunctions. Contacts receiver aircraft pilot, using radio to inform pilot of progress being made during refueling, to advise pilot of action necessary to maintain safe refueling position, and inform pilot of steps to be taken during equipment malfunction or emergencies. Calculates in-flight weight and balance status of aircraft and notifies tanker pilot of necessary flight correction.
GOE: 05.06.03 STRENGTH: S GED: R4 M3 L3 SVP: 6 DLU: 77

912.663-010 AIRPORT UTILITY WORKER (air trans.)
Services aircraft, working as member of crew, performing any combination of following tasks: Directs incoming and outgoing aircraft near terminal area to assist pilot's maneuvering of aircraft, using visual hand or light signals. Operates service vehicles to replenish fuel, water, and waste system chemicals and to remove liquid waste. Cleans exterior or interior of aircraft, using portable platform, ladders, brushes, rags, waterhose, and vacuum. Positions and removes boarding platform to unload or load aircraft passengers. Unloads and loads luggage and cargo from aircraft, using tow truck with luggage carts. Traces lost baggage for customers and prepares lost baggage claims.

GOE: 05.12.06 STRENGTH: H GED: R3 M2 L3 SVP: 4 DLU: 86

912.682-010 AIRCRAFT LAUNCH AND RECOVERY TECHNICIAN (military ser.)
Operates aircraft launching and recovery equipment, such as hydraulic or steam catapults, barricades, arresting gear, and visual landing aids to launch or recover aircraft on aircraft carriers and land based airfields: Operates arresting gear or catapult consoles and controls to fire catapults, raise and lower arresting gear, and blast deflectors and control other launch and recovery equipment. Calibrates, adjusts, and tests launch and recovery equipment, using electrical and mechanical test equipment and handtools. Disassembles catapults, arresting gear, and other equipment and replaces defective parts, using handtools. Splices broken arresting gear cables, using cable splicing tools. Records in log aircraft launches, recoveries, and maintenance performed on equipment. Occasionally directs aircraft launch or recovery operations, using visual hand or light signals.
GOE: 05.10.02 STRENGTH: H GED: R4 M3 L3 SVP: 5 DLU: 77

912.684-010 PARACHUTE RIGGER (air trans.) alternate titles: parachute packer
Folds parachutes according to specifications and packs chutes in bag: Draws canopy of parachute from pack cover to its full length on surface of long bench. Straightens shrouds to eliminate coils or tangles. Folds canopy lengthwise on its seams, one segment over another. Loops each shroud and forces it into retaining clip of pack cover. Folds canopy in fanfold arrangement and places in pack cover. Places pilot chute over parachute canopy, forces spring flat with hands, and secures it in place with release devices, such as ripcord, barometric pressure release, electromechanical release, or explosive charge. Inspects canopy, shroud, buckles and harness straps for damage or wear. Must be licensed by Federal Aviation Administration. May be designated Master Rigger (air trans.) when additionally qualified through experience to meet Federal Aviation Administration requirements.
GOE: 06.04.38 STRENGTH: M GED: R3 M2 L2 SVP: 5 DLU: 77

912.687-010 LINE-SERVICE ATTENDANT (air trans.)
Services aircraft prior to flight according to specifications: Fills fuel and oil tanks and examines tires for specified air pressure. Adds water and other cooling agents as required to batteries and liquid-cooled engine radiators. Fills landing gear struts with hydraulic fluid. May clean exterior and interior of aircraft. May load and unload containers of food, beverages, and dishes for in-flight meal services. May deice aircraft wings and assemblies, using glycol mixture. May assist mechanics in repair of aircraft.
GOE: 05.12.06 STRENGTH: M GED: R3 M2 L2 SVP: 2 DLU: 77

913 PASSENGER TRANSPORTATION OCCUPATIONS, N.E.C.

This group includes occupations, not elsewhere classified, concerned with conveying passengers by driving automobiles and buses; assigning vehicles and drivers to routes; and directing arrivals and departures of vehicles.

913.133-010 ROAD SUPERVISOR (motor trans.) alternate titles: superintendent, drivers
Supervises BUS DRIVERS (motor trans.) and coordinates bus schedules to maintain service: Gives instructions to BUS DRIVERS (motor trans.) in operation of various types of buses. Observes and records number of passengers on buses. Studies reports and devises new schedules according to passenger traffic patterns. May adjust complaints of passengers regarding service.
GOE: 09.03.03 STRENGTH: L GED: R4 M3 L4 SVP: 6 DLU: 77

913.133-014 SUPERVISOR, CAB (motor trans.)
Supervises and coordinates activities of workers engaged in operation department of taxicab company: Hires workers, such as TAXI DRIVERS (motor trans.); TAXICAB STARTER (motor trans.); and TAXICAB COORDINATOR (motor trans.) and supervises their activities. Drives automobile around city to investigate honesty and operating efficiency of TAXI DRIVERS (motor trans.). May investigate accidents and robberies and settle claims, following company policy. May aid drivers in locating difficult addresses, utilizing maps and knowledge of city.
GOE: 09.03.03 STRENGTH: L GED: R4 M3 L4 SVP: 7 DLU: 77

913.167-010 BUS DISPATCHER, INTERSTATE (motor trans.) alternate titles: dispatcher
Dispatches interstate or long-distance buses according to schedule and oversees BUS DRIVERS (motor trans.) and BUS ATTENDANTS (motor trans.) while they are at terminal: Issues orders for station departure of buses at specified hours, according to schedule. Arranges for extra buses and drivers in case of accidents or heavy traffic. Announces incoming and outgoing buses over public address system in bus terminal. May supervise loading, unloading, and checking of baggage or express shipped by bus. May inspect drivers' appearance and physical condition prior to dispatch.
GOE: 07.04.05 STRENGTH: L GED: R4 M3 L3 SVP: 5 DLU: 77

913.167-014 DISPATCHER, BUS AND TROLLEY (motor trans.) alternate titles: transit-operations supervisor
Supervises and coordinates activities of operators of buses, transit coaches, and trolleys in city or urban transportation system to convey passengers according to schedule: Records movement and location of vehicles and road crews to inform other departments or public regarding current schedules and routes.

Receives telephone or radio reports of accidents, delays, fires, equipment break-downs, and other operating or maintenance difficulties. Reports difficulties and dispatches orders to other divisions to maintain or restore service and schedules. Dispatches extra vehicles and emergency crews to scene of accident or break-down, advising them of location of trouble and proximity of feeder lines and power circuits. Maintains log of scheduled runs, numbers of vehicles, and names of drivers. Records calls and emergencies. Makes report of all accidents. May suspend or call in operators for infractions of operating regulations.
GOE: 07.04.05 STRENGTH: L GED: R4 M3 L4 SVP: 7 DLU: 77

913.167-018 SCHEDULE MAKER (motor trans.)
Prepares schedules for local or long-distance transportation systems, such as bus or streetcar lines: Studies changing traffic situations and schedules of com-peting lines. Determines number of vehicles and trips to be run. Assigns vehicle operators to runs. Prepares schedules indicating times of arrival and departure of vehicles or cars at crosslines or junction points where transfer passengers can be picked up. Studies passenger riding patterns and traffic conditions. Es-tablishes emergency and regular routes according to land topography and exist-ing hazards. Arranges number of stops, length of route, and runs per shift for route, according to union-management contract and cost per mile. Prepares drafts of new schedules. Estimates costs of revised schedules.
GOE: 07.05.01 STRENGTH: L GED: R4 M3 L4 SVP: 5 DLU: 77

913.363-010 BUS DRIVER, DAY-HAUL OR FARM CHARTER (agri-culture)
Drives bus to transport workers between recruiting point and agricultural work area: Ascertains from employer work to be performed, number of workers required, and area or field where workers are required. Parks bus at loading area for workers to board according to referral information furnished by recruit-ing agency, or selects workers from group applying for work. Admonishes indi-viduals to be seated and orderly while en route to job. May assign duties to youthful day workers and supervise their activities in field and be designated Day-Haul Youth Supervisor (agriculture).
GOE: 09.03.01 STRENGTH: M GED: R3 M2 L2 SVP: 3 DLU: 77

913.367-010 TAXICAB STARTER (motor trans.) alternate titles: cab starter; dispatcher
Dispatches taxicabs in response to telephone requests for service: Maintains operational map showing location of each cab. Contacts drivers of assigned sec-tor by radio or telephone to relay request for service. Logs calls relayed to each driver and address of patron. Arranges for relief cab or driver.
GOE: 07.04.05 STRENGTH: S GED: R3 M2 L2 SVP: 3 DLU: 77

913.463-010 BUS DRIVER (motor trans.) alternate titles: chauffeur, motorbus; coach operator
Drives bus to transport passengers over specified routes to local or distant points according to time schedule: Assists passengers with baggage and collects tickets or cash fares. Regulates heating, lighting, and ventilating systems for passenger comfort. Complies with local traffic regulations. Reports delays or accidents. Records cash receipts and ticket fares. May make repairs and change tires. May inspect bus and check gas, oil, and water before departure. May load or unload baggage or express checked by passengers in baggage compartment. May transport pupils between pickup points and school and be designated Bus Driver, School (motor trans.). May drive diesel or electric powered transit bus to transport passengers over established city route and be designated Motor-Coach Driver (motor trans.); Trolley-Coach Driver (motor trans.).
GOE: 09.03.01 STRENGTH: M GED: R3 M2 L2 SVP: 4 DLU: 81

913.463-014 STREETCAR OPERATOR (r.r. trans.) alternate titles: trol-ley-car operator
Drives electric-powered streetcar to transport passengers, collects fares, and gives information to passengers: Drives streetcar in accordance with traffic reg-ulations and observes traffic lights and other vehicles on street to avoid acci-dents. Opens and closes doors and starts and stops streetcar to allow passengers to enter or leave vehicle. Collects fares from passengers and issues change and transfers. Answers questions from passengers concerning fare, schedules, and routings. Records readings of coin receptor at beginning and end of shift to ver-ify amount of money received during shift.
GOE: 09.03.01 STRENGTH: L GED: R3 M2 L2 SVP: 3 DLU: 77

913.463-018 TAXI DRIVER (motor trans.) alternate titles: cab driver
Drives taxicab to transport passengers for fee: Picks up passengers in re-sponse to radio or telephone relayed request for service. Collects fee recorded on taximeter based on mileage or time factor and records transaction on log. Reports by radio or telephone to TAXICAB STARTER (motor trans.) 913.367-010 on completion of trip. May drive limousine or custom-built sedan to pick up and discharge airport passengers arriving or leaving on scheduled flights and be designated Chauffeur, Airport Limousine (motor trans.).
GOE: 09.03.02 STRENGTH: M GED: R3 M2 L2 SVP: 3 DLU: 81

913.663-010 CHAUFFEUR (any industry)
Drives automobile to transport office personnel and visitors of commercial or industrial establishment. Performs miscellaneous errands, such as carrying mail to and from post office. May make overnight drives and extended trips requiring irregular hours. May be required to have chauffeurs license. May clean vehicle and make minor repairs or adjustments.
GOE: 09.03.02 STRENGTH: L GED: R3 M2 L2 SVP: 3 DLU: 77

913.663-014 MOBILE-LOUNGE DRIVER (motor trans.)
Drives mobile lounge to transport aircraft passengers between airport termi-nal building and aircraft on runway.

GOE: 09.03.01 STRENGTH: L GED: R3 M2 L2 SVP: 3 DLU: 77

913.663-018 DRIVER (motor trans.) alternate titles: shuttle-bus driver; van driver
Drives minibus, van, or lightweight truck to transport clients, trainees, or company personnel: Drives vehicle from individual or central loading area to social services or rehabilitation center, training location, job site, or other des-tination according to assigned schedule. May assist disabled passengers into and out of vehicle. May secure passengers' wheelchairs to restraining devices to sta-bilize wheelchairs during trip. May operate radio or similar device to commu-nicate with base station or other vehicles to report disruption of service. May clean and service vehicle with fuel, lubricants, and accessories. May keep records of trips and behavior of passengers. May perform other duties when not driving, such as custodial and building maintenance tasks.
GOE: 09.03.01 STRENGTH: M GED: R2 M2 L2 SVP: 3 DLU: 86

913.683-010 AMBULANCE DRIVER (medical ser.)
Drives ambulance to transport sick, injured, or convalescent persons: Places patients on stretcher and loads stretcher into ambulance, usually with help of AMBULANCE ATTENDANT (medical ser.). Takes sick or injured persons to hospital, or convalescents to destination, using knowledge and skill in driving to avoid sudden motions deterimental to patients. Changes soiled linen on stretcher. Administers first aid as needed. May shackle violent patients. May report facts concerning accident or emergency to hospital personnel or law en-forcement officials.
GOE: 05.08.03 STRENGTH: V GED: R3 M2 L2 SVP: 4 DLU: 77

914 PUMPING AND PIPELINE TRANSPORTATION OCCUPATIONS

This group includes occupations concerned with conveying materials, such as oil, gas, water, coal, slurry, and pulp, by operating or tending pipeline pumps, and opening and closing valves. Pipeline construction and repair is included in Group 869. Occupations concerned with pumping activities in the treatment, purification, and distribution of water for irrigation and water supply are found in Group 954.

914.131-010 SUPERVISOR, PUMPING (smelt. & refin.)
Supervises and coordinates activities of workers engaged in maintaining pipe-lines and in pumping slurry, tailings, water, and other liquids in ore-processing plant. Tours pumping stations and pipelines to ensure removal of slurry, tailings, and water. Performs other duties as described under SUPERVISOR (any industry) Master Title.
GOE: 06.01.01 STRENGTH: L GED: R4 M3 L4 SVP: 7 DLU: 77

914.132-010 COMPRESSOR-STATION ENGINEER, CHIEF (pipe lines) alternate titles: plant superintendent
Supervises and coordinates activities of workers engaged in operation and maintenance of compressor-station equipment, such as gas compressors, station-ary engines, and pipelines to transmit natural gas: Directs workers to start or stop compressors to increase or decrease gas pressure. May operate equipment during emergencies. May supervise workers engaged in operation and mainte-nance of automobiles, trucks, and related equipment. Performs duties as de-scribed under SUPERVISOR (any industry) Master Title.
GOE: 05.02.01 STRENGTH: L GED: R4 M3 L4 SVP: 8 DLU: 77

914.132-014 STATION ENGINEER, CHIEF (pipe lines) alternate titles: oil-pump-station operator, chief; station chief
Supervises and coordinates activities of workers engaged in operating and maintaining main-line pump station: Directs STATION ENGINEER, MAIN LINE (pipe lines) to start or stop pumping equipment and increase or decrease pumping rates, line pressures, and rate of oil flow. Directs GAUGERS (petrol. & gas; petrol. refin.; pipe lines) in sampling, gauging, and testing oil, and in controlling flow of oil. Reports on oil movements and pipeline operations to DISPATCHER, OIL (petrol. & gas; petrol. refin.; pipe lines), using teletype or telephone. Schedules maintenance and repair of pumps, engines, generators, and corrosion-mitigation and pneumatic-control equipment. Performs other duties as described under SUPERVISOR (any industry) Master Title. May operate pump-ing equipment and supervise workers and be designated Station Engineer, Oper-ating Chief (pipe lines).
GOE: 05.06.03 STRENGTH: L GED: R4 M3 L4 SVP: 8 DLU: 77

914.132-018 SUPERVISOR, CELLARS (beverage)
Supervises and coordinates activities of workers engaged in storing finished beer and pumping beer to filling machines: Turns valves that regulate flow of refrigerant in cooling equipment to maintain specified temperatures in cellars. Directs PUMPER, BREWERY (beverage) in transferring beer into storage tanks and from tanks to filling machines, following production schedule specifica-tions. Reads meters and records quantity of beer pumped. Verifies type and des-tination of beer pumped to filling machines against order specifications. Exam-ines tanks, pumps, and lines for cleanliness. Performs other duties as described under SUPERVISOR (any industry) Master Title.
GOE: 05.12.01 STRENGTH: L GED: R4 M2 L2 SVP: 7 DLU: 77

914.132-022 SUPERVISOR, FIELD PIPELINES (pipe lines) alternate ti-tles: district supervisor; gauger, chief delivery; terminal-gauger supervisor
Supervises and coordinates activities of workers constructing, operating, and maintaining oil field pipeline gathering system: Directs gauging, sampling, test-

ing, and pumping of products from individual wells to central point for dispatch by main pipeline to refineries and terminals. Reviews bids for pipeline repair work from construction firms, and recommends acceptance or rejection of bids. Inspects installation of new pipelines and repair of equipment, such as pumps, engines, tanks, and reservoirs. Performs other duties as described under SUPERVISOR (any industry) Master Title.
GOE: 05.02.01 STRENGTH: L GED: R4 M3 L4 SVP: 7 DLU: 77

914.134-010 GAUGER, CHIEF (petrol. & gas; petrol. refin.; pipe lines) alternate titles: chief gauger; district gauger
   Supervises and coordinates activities of GAUGERS (petrol. & gas; petrol. refin.; pipe lines) controlling flow of oil into pipelines and gauging amount of oil stored in tanks or railroad cars. May oversee loading and shipment of oil and preparation of loading reports and bills of lading. Performs duties as described under SUPERVISOR (any industry) Master Title.
GOE: 05.06.03 STRENGTH: L GED: R4 M3 L4 SVP: 7 DLU: 77

914.137-010 DISTRIBUTION SUPERVISOR (pipe lines; wholesale tr.)
   Supervises and coordinates activities of workers engaged in loading petroleum products, such as oils, kerosene, and gasoline into tank trucks, and schedules delivery of products to retail service stations or distributors: Reviews written or telephone shipping orders specifying type and volume of product to be loaded, shipping priorities, and delivery dates to prepare delivery schedules for truckdrivers, employing knowledge of routes, time required for loading, and average customer demands. Compiles and submits reports to regional office. Develops and implements preventive maintenance program for tank trucks. Performs other duties as described under SUPERVISOR (any industry) Master Title.
GOE: 05.09.01 STRENGTH: S GED: R4 M3 L4 SVP: 6 DLU: 77

914.137-014 LOADING-RACK SUPERVISOR (petrol. refin.)
   Supervises and coordinates activities of workers engaged in loading and unloading petroleum products, such as oils, gasoline, and kerosene into and from tank cars and trucks: Receives shipping orders and instructions as to type, specification, and volume of material to be loaded, loading priorities, dates of incoming and outgoing shipments, shipping destinations, and availability of storage tanks, tank cars, and trucks. Prepares schedules indicating car numbers and specifications and volume of material to be loaded. Directs workers in spotting and moving tank cars and trucks in yard, in inspecting and cleaning tank cars and trucks, and in loading and sampling petroleum products. Inspects condition of cars or trucks rejected for loading and arranges for their repair or cleaning. Reviews loading and laboratory sample records to verify conformity of load to specifications. Performs other duties as described under SUPERVISOR (any industry) Master Title.
GOE: 05.12.01 STRENGTH: L GED: R4 M3 L4 SVP: 7 DLU: 77

914.137-018 SUPERVISOR, DOCK (petrol. refin.; pipe lines) alternate titles: terminal supervisor; wharf tender, head
   Supervises and coordinates activities of workers involved in loading and unloading crude oil and liquid and packaged petroleum products, such as gasoline, kerosene, fuel oil, motor oil, and grease into and from barges, ships, or tankers at marine terminal: Receives instructions pertaining to vessel movements, types and quantities of crude oil and petroleum products to be received or delivered, facilities to be used, and loading schedules. Directs BOAT LOADERS (water trans.) I and STEVEDORES, DOCK (water trans.) in spotting and mooring vessels, in inspecting oil tanks, and in connecting oil pipelines. Orders GAUGERS (petrol. & gas; petrol. refin.; pipe lines) to open or close pipelines and tank valves to control and divert oil flow and to gauge and sample oil. Reads gauging and pumping reports and bills of lading to verify receipt or delivery of specified products. May supervise workers engaged in loading and unloading tank cars and trucks, and receiving, storing, and issuing petroleum products [LOADING-RACK SUPERVISOR (petrol. refin.)]. Performs other duties as described under SUPERVISOR (any industry) Master Title.
GOE: 05.12.01 STRENGTH: L GED: R4 M3 L4 SVP: 7 DLU: 77

914.167-010 DISPATCHER, CHIEF II (petrol. & gas; petrol. refin.; pipe lines) alternate titles: district superintendent, gas and gasoline; general-office dispatcher; superintendent, pressure
   Coordinates activities of GAS DISPATCHER (pipe lines; utilities) to deliver natural gas from oil fields through pipelines to delivery points: Reviews customer purchase requests to gather information for scheduling gas movements from various fields. Prepares schedules and notifies GAS DISPATCHER (pipe lines; utilities) by radio, teletype, or telephone to release specific amount of gas from well. Reviews periodic reports of gas pressures and volume of gas delivered to ensure safe operation of pipelines. Keeps records of deliveries of gas, pressures maintained, and shutdowns of lines. May coordinate transfer of liquid petroleum products by pipeline.
GOE: 05.02.01 STRENGTH: S GED: R4 M3 L4 SVP: 7 DLU: 77

914.167-014 DISPATCHER, OIL (petrol. & gas; petrol. refin.; pipe lines) alternate titles: oil dispatcher
   Directs and coordinates field activities of workers who route and control flow of oil and petroleum products through pipelines from point of origin, such as wells and storage tanks to delivery points, such as terminals, carriers, refineries, and tank farms, according to delivery schedules: Reviews oil movement schedules and notifies field personnel, such as DISPATCHER, RELAY (pipe lines); STATION ENGINEER, MAIN LINE (pipe lines); and GAUGERS (petrol. & gas; petrol. refin.; pipe lines), by teletype, telephone, and field radio as to type

and quantities of oil to be moved, facilities and storage stock to be used, destinations, operating procedures, and pumping and delivery schedules. Studies data on oil and oil movement, such as temperatures, pressures, specific gravities, sediment and contamination content, and pumping rates, and ensures compliance with schedules and contract specifications by dispatching instructions to field personnel to increase or decrease pumping rates and pressures, to switch and inject feeder streams of crude and blend oil, and to gauge and test oil. Compares pumping reports with delivery reports to ascertain quantity of oil delivered. Computes data for production reports and for instruction changes relative to pumping rates and pressures, using calculator and slide rule. When scheduling and directing movement of petroleum products through processing, storage, and shipping departments of refineries, may be designated Dispatcher, Refinery (pipe lines).
GOE: 05.02.01 STRENGTH: S GED: R4 M4 L4 SVP: 7 DLU: 77

914.362-010 COAL PIPELINE OPERATOR (pipe lines)
   Controls, from master panel, semiautomatic processing plant that pulverizes and mixes coal with water and introduces resulting slurry into pipeline for transportation. Moves controls to start and regulate conveyors, pumps, grinding mills, tank agitators, and auxiliary equipment that convert coal to slurry of specified density and acidity, following standard procedures. Reviews laboratory reports and observes panel lights, flowmeters, and recording instruments to maintain standard conditions in plant and pipeline. Gives directions to assistant to open valves that regulate admission of slurry into pipeline and to make manual adjustments to processing and distribution equipment. Maintains operating log from instrument readings. May control booster pumping stations from panel or direct station operations by telephone.
GOE: 06.02.18 STRENGTH: L GED: R3 M3 L3 SVP: 4 DLU: 77

914.362-014 CONSTRUCTION-AND-MAINTENANCE   INSPECTOR (petrol. refin.)
   Inspects petroleum-dispensing equipment and machinery at wholesale distributing plants of refinery for defects: Operates air-elimination and pumping equipment to detect malfunctions. Pumps petroleum from storage tanks into calibrated cans or tests tank trucks to verify accuracy of recording meters. Compiles reports of inspection data.
GOE: 05.07.01 STRENGTH: L GED: R3 M3 L3 SVP: 5 DLU: 77

914.362-018 STATION ENGINEER, MAIN LINE (pipe lines) alternate titles: pump-station operator; station operator
   Operates electric, diesel, gas, or automated pumping equipment to pump and route petroleum products through pipelines at main-line or terminal stations according to instructions and destination: Turns valves and starts engines to pump oil through station. Reads flow and pressure meters, and turns valves to vary pumping rate and line pressure, according to specifications. Turns handwheel or directs GAUGER (petrol. & gas; petrol. refin.; pipe lines) to open or close pipeline valves to direct flow of oil to storage tanks according to grade; to direct flow of oil through station and along pipeline, according to destination; or to switch oil to alternative pipelines to prevent contamination between grades. Inspects pumping equipment to detect malfunctioning and leaks. Lubricates machinery, and repairs and adjusts pumps and equipment, using handtools. Records pressures, temperature, and flow rates, and maintains records of oil stock and oil receipts. May pump natural gas or natural gas liquid products. May gauge and test oil or direct work of GAUGERS (petrol. & gas; petrol. refin.; pipe lines). May use radiotelephone equipment.
GOE: 05.06.03 STRENGTH: L GED: R3 M2 L3 SVP: 7 DLU: 77

914.382-010 OIL PUMPER (petrol. & gas) alternate titles: oil-well pumper; pumper
   Operates steam, gas, gasoline, electric, or diesel pumps and auxiliary equipment to restore and control flow of oil from wells: Opens valves to regulate flow of oil from wells to storage tanks or into pipelines. Turns valves to adjust pressure of separator which separates natural gas from oil. Reads flowmeters, gauges oil in tanks with calibrated steel tape, and prepares reports of amount and quality of oil pumped and in storage. Collects and bottles samples of oil for laboratory analysis. Lubricates and repairs pumps, using grease gun, oilcan, and handtools. Examines pipelines for leaks. Reports major breakdowns and well difficulties. May test and treat oil to reduce water and sediment content according to specifications for pipeline transportation of oil.
GOE: 05.06.03 STRENGTH: L GED: R3 M3 L3 SVP: 6 DLU: 77

914.382-014 PUMPER-GAUGER (chemical; petrol. refin.; pipe lines)
   Operates pumps and manifold systems to load petro-chemical products, such as caustic soda, methanol, and styrene into trucks, barges, and tank cars: Reads loading order or receives instructions from supervisor. Determines movement of products through lines from storage tanks to tank trucks, barges, and tank cars utilizing knowledge of interconnections, pipeline capacities, manifolds, and pumps. Inspects and weighs vessels to prevent contamination and to satisfy loading procedures. Coordinates product movement activities with other workers to ensure continuous flow of product. Starts pumps, observes pressure and flowmeters, and turns valves to regulate flow of product to loading vessel according to loading procedures. Signals other pumper-gaugers to open and close hatch valves and to gauge, sample, and determine temperature of tank contents. Records operating data, such as products and quantities pumped, storage tank used, gauge readings, and operating time. Inspects valves, flanges, manifolds throughout system and tightens connections, using handtools. Delivers product samples to laboratory and affixes product warning placards onto vessel. Oper-

ates blenders and heaters to mix, blend, and heat products. May perform variety of tests to determine viscosity, specific gravity, and flash point of sample contents.
GOE: 05.06.04 STRENGTH: M GED: R4 M3 L3 SVP: 7 DLU: 77

914.382-018 PUMPER-GAUGER APPRENTICE (chemical; petrol. refin.; pipe lines)
Performs duties as described under APPRENTICE (any industry) Master Title.
GOE: 05.06.04 STRENGTH: M GED: R4 M3 L3 SVP: 7 DLU: 77

914.382-022 PUMPER, HEAD (petrol. & gas) alternate titles: field operator
Operates pumps and auxiliary equipment to produce artificial flow of oil or gas from wells in oil field: Starts pumps and opens valves to pump oil from wells into storage tanks. Starts compressor engines and diverts oil from storage tanks into compressor units and auxiliary equipment to recover natural gas from oil. Opens valves to return compressed gas to bottoms of specified wells to repressurize them and force oil to surface. Operates engines and pumping units from central powerplant to shut off wells according to production schedule and to switch flow of oil into unfilled storage tanks. Reads tank gauges and pump meters, and keeps production records. May supervise OIL PUMPERS (petrol. & gas) and other workers engaged in producing oil from wells. May repair gas and oil meters and gauges [INSTRUMENT MECHANIC (any industry)].
GOE: 05.06.03 STRENGTH: L GED: R3 M3 L3 SVP: 7 DLU: 77

914.384-010 GAUGER (petrol. & gas; petrol. refin.; pipe lines) alternate titles: field gauger; pipe-line gauger; tank-farm gauger; terminal gauger
Gauges and tests amount of oil in storage tanks, and regulates flow of oil and, other petroleum products into pipelines at wells, tank farms, refineries, and marine and rail terminals, following prescribed standards and regulations: Gauges quantity of oil in storage tanks before and after delivery, using calibrated steel tape and conversion tables. Lowers thermometer into tanks to obtain temperature reading. Turns bleeder valves, or lowers sample container into tank to obtain oil sample. Tests oil to determine amount of bottom sediment, water, and foreign materials, using centrifugal tester. Calculates test results, using standard formulas. Records readings and test results. Starts pumps, and opens valves on pipelines and tanks to regulate and direct flow of oil from and into tanks, according to delivery schedules. Reads automatic gauges at specified time intervals to determine flow rate of oil into or out of tanks and amount of oil in tanks. Inspects pipelines, valves, and flanges to detect malfunctions, such as loose connections and leaks. Tightens connections with wrenches, greases and oils valves, using grease gun and oilcan. Reports leaks or defective valves to maintenance personnel. Clamps seal around valves to secure tanks. May gauge tanks containing petroleum and natural gas byproducts, such as condensate or natural gasoline. May operate pumps, teletype, and mobile radio. May clean pumps, machinery, and equipment. May issue delivery or receiving tickets. May record meter and pressure readings at gas wells. May regulate flow of products into pipelines, using automated pumping equipment. When gauging oil received from and delivered to terminals, tank farms, and refineries, may be designated Gauger, Delivery (pipe lines).
GOE: 05.06.03 STRENGTH: M GED: R3 M3 L3 SVP: 6 DLU: 77

914.485-010 BARREL FILLER II (beverage)
Tends pumps to transfer wine from storage tanks to barrels: Inserts nozzle of automatic filler stem into vent of barrel, turns switch and observes readings of meter to verify filling of barrel with specified amounts of wine. Weighs wine-filled barrels and deducts tare (weight of empty barrel) to determine weight of wine, using platform scale. Marks or stencils information on barrels, such as weight and type of wine. May load filled barrels on trucks or railroad cars [INDUSTRIAL-TRUCK OPERATOR (any industry)].
GOE: 06.04.37 STRENGTH: H GED: R2 M2 L1 SVP: 3 DLU: 77

914.585-010 GAS-TRANSFER OPERATOR (chemical)
Tends equipment to transfer liquid gases from processing equipment to tank trucks and storage tanks: Connects hose and starts pumps until specified quantity of gas has been transferred, as indicated by gauge. Ensures that specified type of gas is pumped, using portable gas analyzer. Records type and quantity of gas pumped, truck number, and departure time. Positions truck in loading area. May refuel and fill oil well of tank trucks. May fill railway tank cars. May evacuate air space between inner and outer tanks of trucks or railway tank cars, using vacuum pump.
GOE: 06.04.12 STRENGTH: L GED: R2 M2 L2 SVP: 2 DLU: 77

914.665-010 PIGMENT PUMPER (rubber reclaim.) alternate titles: checker; drum filler; pigment supplier; solvent-station attendant
Tends equipment that pumps solvents, pigments, and caustics into storage tanks for use in processing reclaim rubber: Dips pigment samples from tank car or container for laboratory analysis. Connects hose couplings between tank cars and pipelines. Starts pumps and opens valves to direct flow of liquid pigments into specified storage or supply tanks. Reads flowmeter to ascertain quantity of stock entering tank. Directs transfer of drums and bags of material from freight cars to specified storage areas and notifies supervisor when supplies drop to specified levels. May schedule delivery of pigments. May convey dry pigments to production areas, using electric truck.
GOE: 05.12.06 STRENGTH: M GED: R2 M1 L1 SVP: 4 DLU: 77

914.665-014 PUMPER, BREWERY (beverage) alternate titles: cellar worker
Tends power-driven pumps that transfer wort, beer, or liquified yeast mixture to various sections of brewery: Receives signal from point of destination indicating time of fluid transfer. Connects flexible hose and stationary lines to pumps and vessels containing specified fluid and notifies worker at destination point of line prior to transfer of fluid. Turns valves and starts pump to admit and control flow of liquid through lines. Collects random samples of fluid from vessels for laboratory testing, using beaker. May tend automated equipment to transfer liquids through various processes. May observe thermometers and turn valves to regulate flow of beer through refrigeration unit to maintain specified temperature of product [COOLING-MACHINE OPERATOR (beverage)]. May pump two or more varieties of beer into one tank to blend mixture. May record types and amounts of beer pumped. May clean pumps and lines by flushing with cleansing solutions and water. May be designated according to plant location or product transferred as Bottle-House Pumper (beverage); Cellar Pumper (beverage); Wort Pumper (beverage); Yeast Pumper (beverage).
GOE: 06.04.40 STRENGTH: M GED: R3 M2 L2 SVP: 3 DLU: 77

914.667-010 LOADER I (any industry) alternate titles: car filler; liquid loader; tank-car loader; truck loader
Pumps liquid chemicals, liquid petroleum products, and other liquids into or from tank cars, trucks, or barges: Verifies tank car numbers with loading instructions to ensure accurate placement of cars by crew. Connects ground cable to carry off static electricity. Removes and replaces or gives directions to another worker to remove and replace dome caps, using wrenches. Inspects interior for cleanliness and exterior for leaks or damage. Swings loading spout over dome and turns valve to admit liquids to tank. Lowers gauge rod into tank or reads meter to verify specified volume of liquids loaded. Lowers sample bottle into tank for laboratory testing. Copies load specification on placard and tacks placard to tank. Seals outlet valves on car. When unloading cars, connects hose to outlet plugs on cars and attaches special dome, using wrenches. Starts pumps or turns valves to admit compressed air into tank car and force liquids into storage tanks. May test sample for specific gravity, using hydrometer, and record reading on loading slip. May clean interior of tank cars or tank trucks, using mechanical spray nozzle. May inspect rupture disc, vacuum relief valve, rubber gaskets on valves and cover plates, and replace defective parts, using wrenches. May pump nitrogen or compressed air into car to test for leaks. May be designated according to material loaded and unloaded as Acid Loader (chemical); Caustic Loader (chemical); Fats And Oils Loader (soap & rel.).
GOE: 06.04.40 STRENGTH: M GED: R3 M2 L2 SVP: 5 DLU: 77

914.682-010 PUMPER (any industry) alternate titles: circulator; pump-machine operator; pump operator; pump runner; pump tender; siphoner
Operates power-driven pumps that transfer liquids, semiliquids, gases, or powdered materials, performing any combination of following duties: Observes pressure gauges and flowmeters, and adjusts valves to regulate speed of pumps and control pressure and rate of flow of materials. Transfers materials to and from storage tanks, processing tanks, trucks, railroad cars, ships, canals, and mines. Pumps crude oil from wells. Maintains pumps and lines by replacing filters and gaskets, tightening connections, and adjusting pumps, using handtools. May transfer liquids by siphoning. May connect pipelines between pumps and containers or storage tanks being filled or emptied. May collect samples of materials for laboratory analysis. May determine density of liquids, using hydrometer. May record quantity of item pumped. May inventory contents of storage tank, using calibrated rod, or by reading mercury gauge and tank charts. Usually receives verbal or written orders from superior as to amount to be pumped and is not responsible for mixing or processing. May be designated according to material pumped or area of work as Acid Pumper (chemical); Glycol-Service Operator (plastic-synth.); Irrigating-Pump Operator (agriculture); Tailings-Dam Pumper (smelt. & refin.); Yard Pumper (any industry).
GOE: 05.06.03 STRENGTH: M GED: R3 M2 L3 SVP: 5 DLU: 77

914.685-010 FISH BAILER (fishing & hunt.)
Tends pumps to unload fish from hold of ship into screening tank on dock: Swings end of suction hose over hold of ship, and clamps hose in position. Forces fish from various parts of hold to point under suction pipe, using water hose. Climbs into hold of ship to guide suction hose into hard-to-reach areas.
GOE: 03.04.03 STRENGTH: M GED: R1 M1 L1 SVP: 2 DLU: 77

914.687-010 LABORER, PIPELINES (pipe lines)
Maintains area around pump stations and pipelines, and services equipment, performing any combination of following tasks: Loads and unloads materials, tools, and equipment onto and from trucks by hand. Digs drainage ditches, cuts brush, and clears ground around pipe, using pick, shovel, wheelbarrow, and ax. Cleans feeder pipes with scrapers and steel brushes. Paints pipe, using brush and spray gun. Assists in carrying and laying of feeder pipes.
GOE: 05.12.03 STRENGTH: H GED: R2 M1 L1 SVP: 2 DLU: 77

914.687-014 LOADER HELPER (any industry)
Assists LOADER (any industry) I in pumping liquid chemicals, petroleum products, and other liquids into or from tank cars, trucks, or barges, performing any combination of following duties: Cleans tanks, using brooms, hose, and cleaning compound. Removes and replaces dome caps, using wrenches. Attaches ground cable to truck to prevent sparks due to static electricity when

flammable or volatile material is to be loaded or unloaded. Connects hose to outlet plugs at bottom of tank to prepare car for unloading. Disconnects hose and replaces plugs after unloading, using wrenches. Performs other duties as described under HELPER (any industry) Master Title.
GOE: 05.12.06 STRENGTH: M GED: R2 M1 L1 SVP: 3 DLU: 77

914.687-018 PUMPER HELPER (any industry)
Assists PUMPER (any industry) in pumping liquids from one vessel to another, from storage tanks to processing equipment, or from one process to another: Moves levers to adjust pumping pressure. Cleans pumps, using solvent and rags, lubricates pumps, using oilcan and grease gun. Dismantles pumps to be repaired and reassembles parts, using handtools. Tightens pipe connections between pumps and vessels, using wrenches. May collect random samples of liquid for laboratory analysis. Performs other duties as described under HELPER (any industry) Master Title.
GOE: 05.12.06 STRENGTH: M GED: R2 M1 L1 SVP: 2 DLU: 77

915 ATTENDANTS AND SERVICERS, PARKING LOTS AND AUTOMOTIVE SERVICE FACILITIES

This group includes occupations concerned with parking, cleaning, polishing, lubricating, and refueling trucks, buses, and automobiles, and related servicing activities.

915.133-010 SUPERVISOR, PARKING LOT (automotive ser.)
Supervises and coordinates activities of workers engaged in parking automobiles in parking lot or storage garage: Prepares daily collection report and bank deposit. Performs other duties as described under SUPERVISOR (any industry) Master Title. May actuate parking meters in parking lot, using key. May verify daily reports against meter readings.
GOE: 09.04.02 STRENGTH: L GED: R3 M2 L2 SVP: 4 DLU: 78

915.134-010 TIRE-SERVICE SUPERVISOR (automotive ser.) alternate titles: manager, tire service
Supervises and coordinates activities of workers engaged in servicing and repairing automobile and truck tires and tubes: Examines damaged, defective, or flat tires to determine feasibility of repair and assigns workers to tasks, such as removing nails, changing tubes, installing boots, and changing tires on vehicles. May direct activities of workers engaged in repairing, relining, and adjusting vehicle brakes. Performs other duties as described under SUPERVISOR (any industry) Master Title.
GOE: 05.12.01 STRENGTH: L GED: R4 M3 L3 SVP: 6 DLU: 77

915.137-010 CAR-WASH SUPERVISOR (automotive ser.)
Supervises and coordinates activities of workers engaged in washing and polishing automobiles and performing related services in automatic car wash: Inventories supplies, such as detergents, brushes, and tire-blacking compound. Quotes prices to customers desiring such services as automobile waxing and polishing. Accepts payment and makes change. Supervises personnel engaged in polishing and washing automobiles or parts of vehicles not washed by automatic mechanism. Inspects equipment for wear and arranges for repair or replacement as necessary. Resolves customer complaints. Keeps records of daily receipts, employee time and wage data, and supplies used. May participate in washing, polishing, and performance of other services during peak periods.
GOE: 05.12.01 STRENGTH: L GED: R3 M2 L2 SVP: 5 DLU: 77

915.467-010 AUTOMOBILE-SERVICE-STATION ATTENDANT (automotive ser.) alternate titles: filling-station attendant; gas-station attendant; gas tender; service-station attendant
Services automobiles, buses, trucks, and other automotive vehicles with fuel, lubricants, and accessories: Fills fuel tank of vehicles with gasoline or diesel fuel to level specified by customer. Observes level of oil in crankcase and amount of water in radiator, and adds required amounts of oil and water. Adds necessary amount of water to battery, and washes windshield of vehicle. Lubricates vehicle and changes motor oil [LUBRICATION SERVICER (automotive ser.) 915.687-018]. Replaces accessories, such as oil filter, air filter, windshield wiper blades, and fan belt. Installs antifreeze and changes spark plugs. Repairs or replaces tires [TIRE REPAIRER (automotive ser.) 915.684-010]. Replaces lights, and washes and waxes vehicle. Collects cash from customer for purchases and makes change or charges purchases, using customer's credit card. May adjust brakes [BRAKE ADJUSTER (automotive ser.) 620.684-018]. May sell batteries and automobile accessories usually found in service stations. May assist in arranging displays, taking inventories, and making daily reports.
GOE: 05.10.02 STRENGTH: M GED: R3 M2 L2 SVP: 3 DLU: 81

915.473-010 PARKING-LOT ATTENDANT (automotive ser.) alternate titles: automobile parker; parking attendant; parking-lot chauffeur; parking-station attendant; spotter
Parks automobiles for customers in parking lot or storage garage: Places numbered tag on windshield of automobile to be parked and hands customer similar tag to be used later in locating parked automobile. Records time and drives automobile to parking space, or points out parking space for customer's use. Patrols area to prevent thefts from parked automobiles. Collects parking fee from customer, based on charges for time automobile is parked. Takes numbered tag from customer, locates automobile, and surrenders it to customer, or directs customer to parked automobile. May service automobiles with gasoline,

oil, and water. When parking automobiles in storage garage, may be designated Storage-Garage Attendant (automotive ser.). May direct customers to parking spaces.
GOE: 09.04.02 STRENGTH: L GED: R2 M1 L1 SVP: 2 DLU: 81

915.477-010 AUTOMOBILE-SELF-SERVE-SERVICE-STATION ATTENDANT (automotive ser.) alternate titles: cashier, automobile services; gasateria attendant; station attendant
Sells fuel, lubricants, and accessories, at self-service station to operators of automobiles, buses, trucks, and other automotive vehicles: Allows customer to fill fuel tank of automotive vehicle with fuel, such as gasoline or diesel fuel, to desired level. Checks level of oil in crankcase and amount of water in radiator, and adds oil and water as requested by customer. Collects cash from customer for purchases and makes change or charges purchases, using customer's credit card. Prepares daily report of fuel, oil, and accessories sold. May lubricate vehicle, change motor oil, and replace accessories, such as oil filter, air filter, windshield wiper blades, and fan belt. May install antifreeze, change spark plugs, make minor brake adjustments, and repair or replace tires. May fill fuel tanks for customers. May service fishing boats and pleasure craft or drive tow boat vehicle to haul boats to and from dock and parking area and be designated Marine-Service-Station Attendant (water trans.)
GOE: 09.04.02 STRENGTH: L GED: R3 M2 L2 SVP: 3 DLU: 81

915.583-010 LOT ATTENDANT (retail trade)
Verifies receipt of new cars delivered to dealer and parks cars in new car lot in orderly manner: Compares serial numbers of incoming cars against invoice. Inspects cars to detect damage and to verify presence of accessories listed on invoice, such as spare tires and radio and stereo equipment. Records description of damages and lists missing items on delivery receipt. Parks new cars in assigned area according to model. Assigns stock control numbers to cars, and catalogs and stores keys. Reparks cars, following sales, to maximize use of space and maintain lot in order. Delivers sold cars to new car preparation department. Services cars in storage to protect tires, battery, and finish against deterioration.
GOE: 05.08.03 STRENGTH: L GED: R3 M2 L3 SVP: 3 DLU: 86

915.587-010 GAS-AND-OIL SERVICER (motor trans.) alternate titles: gas-and-oil checker
Refuels and oils motor vehicles, such as trucks and buses, in company garage: Refills vehicle radiator and washes windows of vehicle. Transports materials, such as filled and empty oil drums, using forklift. Compiles mileage records, fuel consumption log, and storage tank inventory.
GOE: 05.12.06 STRENGTH: M GED: R2 M1 L1 SVP: 2 DLU: 86

915.667-010 CAR-WASH ATTENDANT, AUTOMATIC (automotive ser.)
Performs any combination of following duties in automatic car wash: Directs patron to entrance of wash station or guides automobile onto wheel track of automatic mechanism. Cleans front and rear of vehicle, using brush and detergent. Activates wash mechanism and observes operation to detect equipment malfunctions. Notifies supervisor when malfunctions occur. Receives payment from customer or issues change for coin-operated equipment. Fills detergent and wax tanks, lubricates equipment, and replaces spray jets and hoses as needed. May vacuum interior of automobile.
GOE: 09.04.02 STRENGTH: L GED: R2 M2 L1 SVP: 2 DLU: 81

915.667-014 PARKING LOT SIGNALER (automotive ser.) alternate titles: general lot attendant
Directs vehicle drivers to specific parking spot, using hand signals: Lifts, positions, and removes barricades to open or close parking areas at direction of SUPERVISOR, PARKING LOT (automotive ser.) 915.133-010. Signals vehicle drivers with hands or flashlight to parking area or to spot within parking area at activities, such as sporting events, concerts, and expositions.
GOE: 09.04.02 STRENGTH: L GED: R2 M1 L1 SVP: 2 DLU: 86

915.684-010 TIRE REPAIRER (automotive ser.) alternate titles: tire-and-tube repairer; tire-and-tube servicer; tire fixer; tire servicer
Repairs damaged tires of automobiles, buses, trucks, and other automotive vehicles: Raises vehicle, using hydraulic jack, and unbolts wheel, using lug wrench. Removes wheel from vehicle by hand or, when repairing giant tires of heavy equipment, by use of power hoist. Locates puncture in tubeless tire by visual inspection or by immersing inflated tire in water bath and observing air bubbles emerging from puncture. Seals puncture in tubeless tire by inserting adhesive material and expanding rubber plug into puncture, using handtools. Separates tubed tire from wheel, using rubber mallet and metal bar or mechanical tire changer. Removes inner tube from tire and inspects tire casing for defects, such as holes and tears. Glues boot (tire patch) over rupture in tire casing, using rubber cement. Inflates inner tube and immerses it in water to locate leak. Buffs defective area of inner tube, using scraper, and patches tube with adhesive rubber patch or seals rubber patch to tube, using hot vulcanizing plate. Reassembles tire onto wheel, and places wheel on balancing machine to determine counterweights required to balance wheel. Hammers required counterweights onto rim of wheel. Cleans sides of white wall tires and remounts wheel onto vehicle. Responds to emergency calls to make repairs or replacements of damaged tires at customer's home or on road. May be designated according to specialty as Giant-Tire Repairer (automotive ser.); Tire Changer (automotive ser.); Tire Changer, Aircraft (air trans.); Tire Changer, Road Service (automotive ser.). May rotate tires to different positions on vehicle, using tire changing machine, handtools, and tire balancing machine.

GOE: 05.12.15 STRENGTH: H GED: R2 M1 L1 SVP: 3 DLU: 81

915.687-010 AUTOMOBILE-SEAT-COVER INSTALLER (automotive ser.)

Installs prefabricated seat covers in automobiles: Places covers over seats and backs, smoothing them by hand to remove wrinkles. Fastens covers by closing zippers, joining snap fasteners, or securing them to cushion frame or springs.
GOE: 05.12.12 STRENGTH: M GED: R2 M1 L1 SVP: 2 DLU: 77

915.687-014 GARAGE SERVICER, INDUSTRIAL (any industry)

Services trucks, buses, automobiles, and other automotive equipment used in industrial or commerical establishments: Inspects equipment to ascertain gasoline, oil, and water requirements. Tests batteries and tires. Changes oil and lubricates automotive equipment [LUBRICATION SERVICER (automotive ser.) 915.687-018]. May keep record of gas and oil supplied to each vehicle and gasoline and oil supplies in storage tanks.
GOE: 05.12.08 STRENGTH: M GED: R2 M1 L1 SVP: 3 DLU: 86

915.687-018 LUBRICATION SERVICER (automotive ser.) alternate titles: greaser; lubrication technician; oiler

Lubricates moving parts of automotive vehicles, such as automobiles, buses, and trucks: Injects grease into units, such as springs, universal joints, and steering knuckles, using hand or compressed-air powered grease gun. Inspects fluid level of steering gear, power steering reservoir, transmission, differential, rear axle housings, and shackles. Checks air pressure of tires. Lubricates moving parts with specified lubricants. Drains oil from crankcase and refills crankcase with required amount of oil. Sprays leaf springs with lubricant, using spray gun. Adds water to radiator and battery. Replaces oil and air filters. May sell lubrication and safety inspection services and maintain related records on regular customers, following up periodically with telephone, mail, or personal reminders.
GOE: 05.12.08 STRENGTH: M GED: R2 M1 L1 SVP: 4 DLU: 77

915.687-022 PORTER, USED-CAR LOT (retail trade; wholesale tr.) alternate titles: car cleaner; car porter; used-car-lot attendant

Cleans and services used cars at used-car lot: Cleans interior and exterior of cars being offered for sale. Repairs and changes tires. Keeps used-car lot neat and orderly. May clean and change spark plugs or replace windshield wiper blades and arms. May pick up and deliver cars to customers. May clean new cars. May replenish fluids for battery, radiator, crankcase, transmission, and brakes. May replace battery.
GOE: 05.12.18 STRENGTH: M GED: R2 M1 L1 SVP: 2 DLU: 82

915.687-026 STEAM CLEANER (automotive ser.) alternate titles: automobile washer, steam

Cleans engines, bodies, and chassis of automotive vehicles, using high pressure steam hose and detergent solution: Starts boiler to generate steam. Sprays steam and detergent solution over vehicle chassis, engine, or parts, to remove dirt and grease. Lowers engine or chassis parts into tank of detergent solution, by hand or by use of hoist, to clean inaccessible surfaces. Scrapes off adherent grime and grease, using wire brush or putty knife. May spray vehicle body with steam and caustic compound to remove paint. May clean forging dies and be designated Steam-Clean-Machine Operator (forging).
GOE: 05.12.18 STRENGTH: M GED: R2 M1 L1 SVP: 2 DLU: 77

915.687-030 TAXI SERVICER (motor trans.)

Services taxicab fleet and maintains terminal yard and office in orderly condition: Refuels and lubricates taxicabs [GAS-AND-OIL SERVICER (motor trans.)]. Changes and repairs tires [TIRE REPAIRER (automotive ser.)]. Cleans parking area and removes rubbish. Cleans offices and equipment [CLEANER, COMMERCIAL OR INSTITUTIONAL (any industry)].
GOE: 05.12.18 STRENGTH: M GED: R2 M1 L1 SVP: 2 DLU: 77

915.687-034 AUTOMOBILE DETAILER (automotive ser.)

Cleans and refurbishes new and used automobiles, performing any combination of following duties: Washes vehicle exterior to clean cars, using cleaning solution, water, cloths, and brushes. Applies wax to auto body, and wipes or buffs surfaces to protect surfaces and preserve shine, using cloth or buffing machine. Vacuums interiors of vehicles to remove loose dirt and debris, using vacuum cleaner. Cleans upholstery, rugs, and other surfaces, using cleaning agents, applicators, and cleaning devices. Applies revitalizers and preservatives to vinyl or leather surfaces, and treats fabrics with spot and stain resistant chemicals to preserve and protect interior components. Cleans engine and engine compartment with steam cleaning equipment and various cleaning agents to remove grease and grime. Applies special purpose cleaners to remove foreign materials which do not respond to normal cleaning procedures, utilizing experience and following recommendations of product manufacturer. Paints engine components and related parts, using spray gun or aerosol can and masking material. Applies paint to chipped body surfaces of vehicle, using container of touchup paint. Applies dyes and reconditioning chemical to vinyl tops of vehicle to restore color and condition.
GOE: 05.12.18 STRENGTH: M GED: R2 M1 L1 SVP: 2 DLU: 86

919 MISCELLANEOUS TRANSPORTATION OCCUPATIONS, N.E.C.

This group includes occupations, not elsewhere classified, concerned with transportation. Occupations, not elsewhere classified, concerned with transportation and involving extensive record keeping activities are found in Group 248.

919.162-010 DISPATCHER, TRAFFIC OR SYSTEM (motor trans.; r.r. trans.)

Dispatches workers and equipment to prevent or rectify service disruptions of local transit system, using radiophone equipment: Receives reports of actual or anticipated disruptions and determines action required to rectify condition. Issues instructions to workers for maintenance and repair of roadway and structures. Coordinates movement of workers and equipment throughout system, using telephone communications system. Listens to radio traffic reports to alert TRAFFIC INSPECTOR (motor trans.; r.r. trans.) of conditions affecting schedules. Records service disruptions, time, and action taken. May supervise activities of maintenance crews.
GOE: 07.04.05 STRENGTH: S GED: R4 M3 L3 SVP: 7 DLU: 77

919.223-010 INSTRUCTOR, BUS, TROLLEY, AND TAXI (motor trans.; r.r. trans.)

Instructs students in driving buses, trolleys, or taxicabs, and evaluates their progress: Explains mechanical and electrical functions of various vehicles, using diagrams, charts, and jacked-up chassis. Demonstrates operation of vehicles to students. Observes students while driving to evaluate their performance and progress. Instructs students in methods of keeping records of cash receipts and accident reports. May instruct students in operating monorail trains.
GOE: 09.03.03 STRENGTH: L GED: R4 M3 L3 SVP: 6 DLU: 77

919.363-010 NEW-CAR INSPECTOR (motor trans.)

Inspects new cars prior to loading onto carriers: Examines car for scratches, dents, and broken glass. Drives car to detect motor noises, transmission malfunctions, and brake failure. Records findings. Drives cars onto trailer truck. Keeps record of cars until delivery.
GOE: 06.03.01 STRENGTH: L GED: R3 M2 L2 SVP: 4 DLU: 77

919.663-010 DELIVERER, CAR RENTAL (automotive ser.; retail trade) alternate titles: washer driver

Delivers rental cars to customers, and services them prior to delivery: Sweeps out and vacuum cleans interior of rental automobile. Washes windows and exterior of automobile, using water and other cleansing compounds and cloth. Regulates tire pressure and adds gasoline and oil. Adds water to battery and radiator. Delivers automobile to customer at specified pickup point. Collects rental payment and deposit from customer; and observes that customer reads and signs rental contract. May deliver new or used automobiles to customer from automobile dealership.
GOE: 05.08.03 STRENGTH: L GED: R2 M2 L2 SVP: 3 DLU: 77

919.663-014 DINKEY OPERATOR (any industry) alternate titles: larry-car operator; trammer

Controls dinkey engine powered by electric, gasoline, steam, compressed air, or diesel engine to transport and shunt cars at industrial establishment or mine: Controls movement of dinkey that transports coal, rock, timber, slag, or supplies by moving power controls and brake levers. Signals BRAKE HOLDER (any industry) by hand or whistle to couple cars. Positions cars for loading or unloading according to signals of DUMPER (any industry). Inspects engine at beginning and end of shift. May move levers to open or tilt cars to dump materials. May throw switches and couple cars. May fuel and lubricate engine. May inspect track for defects and assist in repairing track and installing additional rails and ties. May be designated according to kind of power used as Dinkey Operator, Compressed Air (any industry); according to work area as Dinkey Operator, Mine (mine & quarry); or material hauled as Dinkey Operator, Slag (smelt. & refin.); Dinkey Operator, Slate (mine & quarry). May operate flatcar equipped with derrick and be designated Derrick-Car Operator (r.r. trans.). May operate railcar to transport personnel and equipment in area of logging camp and be designated Rail-Car Operator (logging).
GOE: 05.11.04 STRENGTH: L GED: R3 M2 L2 SVP: 4 DLU: 77

919.663-018 DRIVER-UTILITY WORKER (auto. mfg.; automotive ser.)

Demonstrates, and delivers to purchasers, new and reconditioned buses, trucks, tractors, fire engines, and other heavy vehicles. Picks up and delivers parts, using light truck.
GOE: 05.08.03 STRENGTH: M GED: R3 M1 L1 SVP: 4 DLU: 77

919.663-022 ESCORT-VEHICLE DRIVER (motor trans.)

Drives vehicle equipped with warning lights and signs to escort trucks hauling mobile homes on public thoroughfares: Precedes escort and maintains specified distance between pilot vehicle and escort to provide warning to other motorists and to clear traffic at locations. Communicates by two-way radio with truck and other pilot vehicle drivers to coordinate changes in speed and route, emergencies, or traffic congestion.
GOE: 05.08.03 STRENGTH: S GED: R2 M1 L2 SVP: 2 DLU: 77

919.663-026 TOW-TRUCK OPERATOR (automotive ser.) alternate titles: tow-car driver; wrecker operator

Drives tow-truck to move motor vehicles damaged by accident, stalled, or ticketed by police for traffic violation: Receives call or is dispatched to location by repair garage, automobile association, or police department by radio or telephone. Attaches antisway bar to vehicle by means of cable, chains, or other grappling devices, and hoists one end of vehicle, using hand or powered winch, to tow vehicle to repair garage or to police department's impounding area. May make minor repairs to vehicles along highway, such as replacing spark plugs, batteries, and light bulbs, and connecting loose wires. May perform other duties when not engaged in towing, such as AUTOMOBILE-SERVICE-STATION

ATTENDANT (automotive ser.); TIRE REPAIRER (automotive ser.). May dismantle vehicles to salvage parts, using such handtools as wrenches, pry bar, and hacksaws [AUTOMOBILE WRECKER (wholesale tr.)]. May remove, bend, or cut parts of damaged vehicles preparatory to towing.
GOE: 05.08.03 STRENGTH: M GED: R2 M1 L2 SVP: 3 DLU: 77

919.664-010 TEAMSTER (any industry) alternate titles: freighter; hauler; skinner; team driver; toter
Drives one or more draft animals to pull materials, vehicles, or implements, such as logs, wagons, grading scrapers, fertilizer spreaders, plows, or scoops: Jiggles, pulls, and slackens reins, and gives oral commands to control movement of team. May harness and hitch team to material, vehicle, or implement. May load and unload vehicle or manipulate levers, pedals, or holding devices to release material. May groom, feed, and water team and clean stable [STABLE ATTENDANT (any industry)]. May repair harness. May drive one or team of horses to skid logs from forest and be designated Snaker (logging). May be designated according to type of vehicle driven as Cart Driver (any industry); Dray Driver (any industry); Wagon Driver (any industry); or according to kind of animals driven as Horse-And-Wagon Driver (any industry); Mule Driver (any industry); or according to number of animals driven as Four-Horse Hitch Driver (any industry); Six-Horse Hitch Driver (any industry); Long-Line Teamster (any industry).
GOE: 03.04.05 STRENGTH: M GED: R2 M1 L1 SVP: 3 DLU: 77

919.682-010 BRIDGE OPERATOR, SLIP (r.r. trans.) alternate titles: bridge tender; slip tender
Controls horizontally and vertically adjustable bridge, between wharf and scow lashed to wharf, to allow railroad cars to be driven from land to scow: Moves bridge controls to extend and align bridge tracks with tracks on barge. Controls vertical movement of bridge in accordance with sinking of scow during loading. May lash scow to wharf with steel cable drawn taut by winch or windlass when tugboat brings scow into position.
GOE: 05.11.04 STRENGTH: L GED: R3 M2 L2 SVP: 4 DLU: 77

919.683-010 DOCK HAND (air trans.)
Operates motorboat to transport passengers or cargo to and from anchored amphibious airplanes and operates tractor to remove planes from water: Loads cargo or directs passengers aboard motorboat. Pilots boat to plane or dock and discharges cargo or passengers. Positions wheeled beaching gear at end of ramp in water and, standing in water, pushes and pulls plane over ramping gear. Drives tractor to draw plane and gear up ramp onto shore for removal to hangar. Cleans plane interiors and exteriors.
GOE: 05.08.04 STRENGTH: H GED: R2 M2 L2 SVP: 4 DLU: 77

919.683-014 DRIVER (auto. mfg.; automotive ser.) alternate titles: car driver
Drives completed motor vehicle off assembly line to specified repair, shipping, or storage area. May test performance of parts, such as lights, horn, and windshield wipers. May drive completed vehicle onto railroad freight car and secure vehicle for shipping. May drive customer's vehicle to and from service area of repair shop and be designated Car Jockey (automotive ser.).
GOE: 05.08.03 STRENGTH: L GED: R2 M1 L1 SVP: 2 DLU: 90

919.683-018 RAIL-TRACTOR OPERATOR (steel & rel.) alternate titles: ingot buggy operator
Drives electric car mounted on rails, to transport ingots and slabs from soaking pits to mill-approach-conveyor table: Drives car to position car for receiving material from soaking pit. Drives car to mill-approach-conveyor table. Pulls lever to raise tilting cradle of car and deposit material on table. May operate car by remote control from pulpit and be designated Table Operator (steel & rel.).
GOE: 05.11.04 STRENGTH: L GED: R3 M2 L2 SVP: 4 DLU: 77

919.683-022 STREET-SWEEPER OPERATOR (government ser.) alternate titles: tractor-sweeper driver
Drives sweeping machine that cleans streets of trash and other accumulations: Fills water tank of machine from hydrant. Drives sweeper along street near curb. Moves controls to activate rotary brushes and water spray so that machine automatically picks up dust and trash from paved street and deposits it in dirt trap at rear of machine. Pulls lever to dump refuse in piles at curb for removal. May be employed by industrial plant, shopping center, or other establishment to drive modified sweeper through parking lots, factory aisles, or along private roads and be designated Power-Sweeper Operator (any industry). May drive machine that sucks leaves into vacuum chamber and be designated Leaf-Sucker Operator (government ser.). May drive vehicle equipped with rotating brushes to remove sand and litter from newly constructed highways and be designated Sweeper Operator, Highways (construction).
GOE: 05.11.01 STRENGTH: L GED: R2 M1 L1 SVP: 3 DLU: 77

919.683-026 TRACKMOBILE OPERATOR (any industry)
Operates trackmobile to transport railcars or trailers to designated station areas: Drives trackmobile onto track and aligns steel wheels with rails. Moves lever that activates hydraulic device to raise rubber tires allowing steel wheels of vehicle to rest onto rails. Moves levers to couple trailers or railcars. Drives trackmobile to move railcars or trailers to specified areas, such as weighing, loading, and cleaning.
GOE: 05.08.02 STRENGTH: M GED: R2 M1 L2 SVP: 3 DLU: 77

919.683-030 DRIVER, STARTING GATE (amuse. & rec.)
Steers vehicle equipped with rear folding barrier (gate) that allows alignment and positioning of horses abreast of gate prior to official start of sulky (harness) race. Accepts control of vehicle acceleration from HORSE-RACE STARTER (amuse. & rec.) 153.267-010 who simultaneously actuates folding of gate at starting point of race. Drives vehicle off track to clear path for race.
GOE: 05.08.03 STRENGTH: L GED: R2 M1 L1 SVP: 2 DLU: 86

919.687-010 CHECKER (motor trans.)
Counts and herds cattle, hogs, or sheep as they are unloaded from shipping trucks in stockyard and verifies information on ticket, such as number of head, identifying markings on livestock, and designated commission agency: Marks time of arrival on ticket and gives it to shipper as receipt. Herds livestock into separate pens according to markings which identify commission agency to which stock is assigned. May mark identification on stock, using shears or chalk.
GOE: 05.09.01 STRENGTH: L GED: R1 M1 L1 SVP: 2 DLU: 77

919.687-014 CLEANER II (any industry)
Cleans interiors and exteriors of transportation vehicles, such as airplanes, automobiles, buses, railroad cars, and streetcars: Cleans interior of vehicle, using broom, cloth, mop, vacuum cleaner, and whisk broom. Cleans windows with water, cleansing compounds, and cloth or chamois. Replenishes sanitary supplies in vehicle compartments. Removes dust, grease, and oil from exterior surfaces of vehicles, using steam-cleaning equipment, or by spraying or washing vehicles, using spraying equipment, brush or sponge. May polish exterior of vehicle. May fumigate interior of vehicle, using fumigating gases or sprays. May be designated according to type of vehicle cleaned as Airplane Cleaner (air trans.); Automobile Washer (automotive ser.); Bus Cleaner (automotive ser.); Car Cleaner (r.r. trans.); Coach Cleaner (r.r. trans.); Truck Washer (dairy products). When cleaning aircraft interiors may be designated Cabin-Service Agent (air trans.).
GOE: 05.12.18 STRENGTH: M GED: R2 M1 L1 SVP: 1 DLU: 77

919.687-018 SAFETY INSPECTOR, TRUCK (automotive ser.; motor trans.)
Inspects diesel and gasoline motortrucks to ensure that trucks are equipped with accessories prescribed by law: Inspects truck for accessories, such as tools, chains, flares, and first aid kit. Inspects air lines and electric circuits, and reports needed repairs. May drive truck inside terminal yard and garage and position trailer for repair, loading, or unloading. May service vehicle with fuel and water.
GOE: 05.07.01 STRENGTH: L GED: R3 M2 L2 SVP: 4 DLU: 77

919.687-022 SUPPLIES PACKER (any industry) alternate titles: pack-train driver
Transports supplies and equipment by pack animals to places inaccessible by other means of transportation. Assembles equipment, loads and straps it on animals to prevent dislodgment during transit. Leads animals to destination.
GOE: 03.04.05 STRENGTH: H GED: R3 M2 L2 SVP: 5 DLU: 77

92 PACKAGING AND MATERIALS HANDLING OCCUPATIONS

This division includes occupations concerned with preparing and arranging materials and products in bulk and nonbulk forms for distribution or storage; moving and loading or unloading equipment, materials, and products; operating or tending filling, packing, and wrapping machines or conveyors; driving forklifts, lumber carriers, and related material-handling machinery and equipment; and using scoops, handtrucks, and wheelbarrows to load and move materials.

920 PACKAGING OCCUPATIONS

This group includes occupations concerned with assembling containers; pouring and placing materials and products into containers; covering articles or goods with cellophane, paper, and other wrapping materials; cleaning, closing, labeling, stenciling, and stacking articles and containers; and operating or tending filling, packing, or wrapping machines.

920.130-010 SUPERVISOR, PACKING (sugar & conf.)
Supervises and coordinates activities of workers engaged in packing sugar: Reads job order schedules to ascertain grist, type of containers, and packing priority. Directs changing of screens and machine setup according to work order specifications. Observes process stations to verify conformance of packaging, sugar sampling, and package weighing to quality control standards. Performs other duties as described under SUPERVISOR (any industry) Master Title.
GOE: 06.04.01 STRENGTH: L GED: R4 M3 L3 SVP: 6 DLU: 77

920.132-010 PACKAGING SUPERVISOR (any industry)
Supervises and coordinates activities of workers engaged in packaging products and materials for storage or shipment: Studies production order to ascertain type and quantity of product, containers to be used, and other packaging requirements. Inspects products prior to packaging and returns rejected products to production departments. Observes packaging operations and inspects containers to verify conformance to specifications. Starts, adjusts, and repairs packaging machinery, or notifies maintenance department. Trains workers in operation of equipment. Requisitions containers and other supplies for delivery to work stations. Performs other duties as described under SUPERVISOR (any industry) Master Title. May be designated according to type of container filled as Barrel

Filler, Head (any industry); Bottling Supervisor (any industry); Can Supervisor (any industry).
GOE: 06.04.01 STRENGTH: L GED: R4 M2 L3 SVP: 6 DLU: 86

920.132-014 SUPERVISOR, CARTON AND CAN SUPPLY (beverage)
Supervises and coordinates activities of workers engaged in forming cartons and stamping date on beer cans: Adjusts conveyors and can dating and carton forming machines. Verifies cans, can dates, and cartons against order specifications. Performs other duties as described under SUPERVISOR (any industry) Master Title.
GOE: 06.02.01 STRENGTH: L GED: R4 M3 L3 SVP: 7 DLU: 77

920.137-010 PACKING-HOUSE SUPERVISOR (agriculture; wholesale tr.) alternate titles: house supervisor; packing-shed supervisor
Supervises and coordinates activities of workers engaged in receiving, grading, storing, and shipping fruits and vegetables: Trains workers in grading and packing procedures in accordance with customers' specifications. Inspects storage area to determine freshness of produce and indicates produce to be packed and removed. Inspects packaged produce for conformance to customers' specifications. Directs workers engaged in icing loaded railroad cars or trucks. Performs other duties as described under SUPERVISOR (any industry) Master Title. May repair packing equipment and machinery. May supervise workers engaged in constructing packing crates and boxes. May specialize in packing specific produce, such as apples, citrus fruit, or potatoes, or be designated according to produce packed as Banana-Ripening-Room Supervisor (wholesale tr.).
GOE: 06.02.01 STRENGTH: L GED: R4 M3 L3 SVP: 6 DLU: 79

920.137-014 SORTING SUPERVISOR (brick & tile)
Supervises and coordinates activities of workers engaged in sorting tile and brick according to color and grade and in packing materials in cartons. Performs duties as described under SUPERVISOR (any industry) Master Title.
GOE: 06.02.01 STRENGTH: M GED: R4 M2 L3 SVP: 6 DLU: 77

920.137-018 SUPERVISOR (sugar & conf.)
Supervises and coordinates activities of workers engaged in inspecting boxes of packaged chewing gum, wrapping boxes in cellophane, packing boxes in cartons, or unwrapping packages of defective gum. Trains new employees and evaluates work performance. Performs duties as described under SUPERVISOR (any industry) Master Title. May be designated according to process as Supervisor, Inspection Room (sugar & conf.); Supervisor, Unwrapping Room (sugar & conf.); Supervisor, Wrapping Room (sugar & conf.).
GOE: 06.02.01 STRENGTH: L GED: R4 M3 L3 SVP: 5 DLU: 77

920.137-022 SUPERVISOR, FILLING-AND-PACKING (paint & varnish)
Supervises and coordinates activities of workers engaged in filling, coding, labeling, and packaging containers of paints and related products. Plans filling and labeling methods, according to knowledge of operations and type and quantity of product. Performs duties as described under SUPERVISOR (any industry) Master Title.
GOE: 06.04.01 STRENGTH: L GED: R3 M2 L3 SVP: 5 DLU: 77

920.137-026 SUPERVISOR, PACKING AND WRAPPING (any industry)
Supervises and coordinates activities of workers engaged in packing or wrapping products and materials to protect them from damage during storage or shipment: Studies production orders and confers with other department supervisors to ascertain type and quantity of product to be shipped and packing requirements, such as containers or wrapping material to be used, and to coordinate department's activities with other departments. Inspects products prior to packing and wrapping and places rejected products aside or returns them to production departments. Observes packing and wrapping operations to verify conformance to specifications. Trains workers in packing and wrapping procedures. Performs other duties as described under SUPERVISOR (any industry) Master Title. May supervise workers engaged in cleaning upholstered furniture of foreign material prior to packing and be designated Supervisor, Inspect, Clean-Up, And Wrap (furniture). May supervise workers engaged in final assembly of mirrors before packing and be designated Supervisor, Packing (glass products).
GOE: 06.04.01 STRENGTH: M GED: R4 M2 L3 SVP: 7 DLU: 86

920.380-010 SETTER, JUICE PACKAGING MACHINES (can. & preserv.)
Sets up and adjusts can filling and sealing machines and caser machines to package juice in juice processing establishment: Selects filler tubes according to size of cans to be filled and installs and adjusts tubes in filling and sealing machines, following production specifications and using wrench. Adjusts tension controls on filling and sealing machines to regulate pressure of filling, capping, and sealing mechanisms, following operation manual and using screwdriver. Sets and adjusts caser machine controls that position feed hopper, folding and pressure rollers, and conveyor guides to encase products in conformity with size and shape specifications, using mechanic's handtools. Starts machines, monitors filling, sealing, and casing operations, and adjusts machines to conform with operations specifications and production requirements. Replaces worn or damaged machine parts. Dismantles, cleans, and reassembles machines. Cleans machines and lubricates moving parts [MACHINE CLEANER (any industry) 699.687-014]. Occasionally installs cables to connect machines to power source, using electrician's handtools.
GOE: 06.01.02 STRENGTH: M GED: R4 M3 L3 SVP: 6 DLU: 86

920.387-010 INSPECTOR, PACKAGING MATERIALS (pharmaceut.) alternate titles: packaging inspector
Examines, measures, and tests containers and materials used to package drug and cosmetic products for conformity to specifications: Examines and rejects tubes, bottles, cartons, caps, stoppers, and related materials containing such flaws as chips, cracks, torn labels, or discoloration. Measures containers and cap samples to verify specified dimensions, using micrometer, gauge, or caliper. Fills containers with liquid and pours into graduate to verify container capacity. Records inspection or test results. May test components, such as stoppers and seals, using hardness tester. May count, pour, or weigh out contents of sample containers to verify data on label. May determine viscosity of fluids, using viscometer. May convert liquid measure to avoirdupois weight, using calculating machine or slide rule.
GOE: 06.03.01 STRENGTH: L GED: R3 M3 L2 SVP: 4 DLU: 78

920.482-010 ICICLE-MACHINE OPERATOR (dairy products)
Operates machine to form, fill, and seal tubelike cellophane container with flavored sweet water to make icicle: Adds flavor extract to sweet water in tank according to formula. Connects hose lines from tank to icicle machine. Mounts roll of cellophane on spindle of machine and threads end of cellophane through guide rollers into feed mechanism. Adjusts spindle counterweights to regulate tension on cellophane. Starts machine and turns valves to admit sweet water into spout of machine. Turns on heating element that fuses seams of cellophane. Moves levers to control flow of icicle fluid into machine. Removes packaged icicles from discharge end of machine. Places icicles into containers and places containers on conveyor.
GOE: 06.02.15 STRENGTH: L GED: R3 M2 L2 SVP: 4 DLU: 77

920.586-010 MASKING-MACHINE FEEDER (plastic-synth.)
Feeds machine that covers plastic sheets with paper to protect sheets during final processing and shipping: Feeds sheets between rollers of masking machine. Lifts masked sheets from discharge end of machine and places sheets on trucks. Segregates masked sheets according to quality as indicated on tickets. Places masked sheet over lighted table or rack to make previously marked defective areas visible, and traces outlines onto masked surface, using crayon.
GOE: 06.04.02 STRENGTH: M GED: R2 M1 L1 SVP: 2 DLU: 77

920.587-010 CLOTH-BOLT BANDER (textile) alternate titles: backer and bander, cloth; folded-cloth taper; taper
Fastens paper bands around bolts of cloth preparatory to wrapping or shipping: Places bolt of cloth on table over paper bands stacked in slots. Folds edge of cloth under and fastens band near each end of bolt, using tape or glue. Marks yardage on end of center board and records yardage according to lot number. May wrap cloth. May paste labels on center board.
GOE: 06.04.38 STRENGTH: M GED: R2 M1 L1 SVP: 2 DLU: 77

920.587-014 LABEL CODER (any industry) alternate titles: label marker
Cuts notches in container or bottle labels to indicate data, such as type, batch, date, and destination of product, following predetermined code: Turns setscrews to space and lock blades of notching device according to coding guide, using ruler. Clamps stack of labels on bed of notching device and pushes bed forward to force labels against blades. Prepares label-coding report. May insert or remove symbols, using tweezers to set up carton-coding wheels. May wash defective labels from bottles.
GOE: 06.04.26 STRENGTH: L GED: R2 M1 L1 SVP: 2 DLU: 77

920.587-018 PACKAGER, HAND (any industry) alternate titles: hand packager
Packages materials and products manually, performing any combination of following duties: Cleans packaging containers. Lines and pads crates and assembles cartons. Obtains and sorts product. Wraps protective material around product. Starts, stops, and regulates speed of conveyor. Inserts or pours product into containers or fills containers from spout or chute. Weighs containers and adjusts quantity. Nails, glues, or closes and seals containers. Labels containers, container tags, or products. Sorts bundles or filled containers. Packs special arrangements or selections of product. Inspects materials, products, and containers at each step of packaging process. Records information, such as weight, time, and date packaged. May stack, separate, count, pack, wrap, and weigh bakery products and be designated Bakery Worker (bakery products). May apply preservative to aircraft and spaceship parts, package parts for shipment, and be designated Wrapper and Preserver (aircraft mfg.). May be designated according to whether high-production or small-lot packaging as Fancy Packer (retail trade; wholesale tr.); specific packaging duty performed as filling, wrapping, packing, labeling, and container cleaning as Sack Sewer, Hand (any industry); kinds of equipment used or product packaged as Candle Wrapper (fabrication, nec); Carton Stapler (any industry); or whether packager performs associated duties as final assembly before packaging product as Novelty-Balloon Assembler And Packer (rubber goods). May weigh and package meat in retail store and be designated Meat Wrapper (retail trade). May be designated: Bagger (any industry); Bow Maker, Gift Wrapping (any industry); Box Maker, Cardboard (any industry); Box Wrapper (any industry); Bundler (any industry); Candy Packer (sugar & conf.); Caser, Rolled Glass (glass mfg.); Coil Strapper (steel & rel.); Container Filler (any industry); Filler (any industry); Furniture Packer (retail trade); Grader, Sausage And Wiener (meat products); Guncotton Packer (chemical); Inserter, Promotional Item (any industry); Inspector-Packager (any industry); Lidder (any industry); Mattress Packer (furniture); Packager, Meat (meat products); Packer, Dried Beef (meat products); Packer, Foamed-In-Place (any industry); Packer, Sausage And Wiener (meat products); Piece-Goods Packer (textile); Scaler, Sliced Bacon (meat products); Sponge Packer (wholesale tr.); Stamper (any industry); Table Worker (any industry); Tube Packer (rubber tire); Wrapper (any industry); Wrapper,

Hand (can. & preserv.); Wrapping Remover (any industry). Workers who tend packaging machines are classified under PACKAGER, MACHINE (any industry) 920.685-078.
GOE: 06.04.38 STRENGTH: M GED: R2 M1 L1 SVP: 2 DLU: 88

920.587-022 SAMPLE CLERK, HANDKERCHIEF (garment)
Packs sample kits containing specified handkerchief styles for sales personnel. Records samples assigned to each salesperson. Sends soiled samples to be cleaned and returns samples to sales personnel.
GOE: 06.04.38 STRENGTH: L GED: R2 M1 L2 SVP: 2 DLU: 77

920.587-026 MARKER, SEMICONDUCTOR WAFERS (electron. comp.)
Scribes identifying information onto semiconductor wafer, using metal stylus (scribe): Obtains container loaded with semiconductor wafers and removes wafers from container, using tweezers. Marks lot number and description number in designated area of wafers, following specifications and using metal stylus. Records production data. Cleans containers, using soap and water.
GOE: 06.04.37 STRENGTH: L GED: R2 M1 L2 SVP: 2 DLU: 86

920.665-010 CARTON-PACKAGING-MACHINE OPERATOR (tobacco) alternate titles: packing-machine inspector
Tends machine that packs and seals packaged tobacco products into cartons: Examines packaged products on conveyor to detect defects, such as defective folds or seams in wrappers or tear tape, offcentered stamps, or dents in cans. Removes defective packages and notifies CIGARETTE-PACKING-MACHINE OPERATOR (tobacco) or TOBACCO-PACKING-MACHINE OPERATOR (tobacco). Observes flow of cartons into machine and removes defective cartons. Notifies MACHINE ADJUSTER (tobacco) of machine malfunction. May form and place cartons on machine. May turn setscrews to set carton-holding guides to accommodate cartons of various sizes. May be known according to product packaged as Cigarette-Boxing-Machine Operator (tobacco). Workers who package product by hand are classified under PACKER (tobacco).
GOE: 06.04.38 STRENGTH: L GED: R2 M1 L2 SVP: 2 DLU: 77

920.665-014 RACK-ROOM WORKER (beverage) alternate titles: corker; filler; racker; stacker; stamper
Tends machines that fill metal kegs with beer in keg-filling (racking) room of brewery: Pushes metal keg or barrel onto conveyor leading to racking machine. Lifts barrel from conveyor and positions barrel on machine. Lowers filling arm of counter-pressure filling machine (racker), and fits nozzle into bung. Turns valves that pressurize barrel and start flow of beer. Turns valve that releases filling arm when sight glass indicates barrel is full and raises arm. Pounds wooden plug into bung, using mallet. Presses pedal to roll barrel onto conveyor. Affixes revenue stamp over taphole, using staples or glue. Rolls barrel from conveyor to loading chute or storage area. Washes machine and floor, using hose.
GOE: 06.04.38 STRENGTH: M GED: R2 M1 L1 SVP: 2 DLU: 77

920.667-010 CIGARETTE-PACKAGE EXAMINER (tobacco) alternate titles: cellophane-wrapping examiner; package reinspector; packing-machine inspector
Examines packages of cigarettes to detect packing or wrapping defects: Gathers sample package from each packing and wrapping machine and weighs package to determine whether weight of cigarettes and package conforms to standards. Pulls tear tape, removes cellophane wrapper, and examines glue line to detect defective gluing. Opens packages with defective folding, printing, or stamp alignment and returns cigarettes for rewrapping. Records weight and number of defective packages from each machine. Notifies CELLOPHANE WRAPPER, MACHINE (any industry) or CIGARETTE-PACKING-MACHINE OPERATOR (tobacco) of defects.
GOE: 06.03.02 STRENGTH: L GED: R2 M1 L2 SVP: 4 DLU: 77

920.667-014 SNUFF-CONTAINER INSPECTOR (tobacco)
Examines filled snuff containers, such as cans, tumblers, and casings to determine if weight of container and wrapping conform to company standards: Weighs random containers on scales to detect variations from weight tolerances. Examines containers for defects, such as loosely sealed or misplaced labels and stamps. Discards defective containers for salvage, and notifies packing workers of defects. May replace missing labels on containers.
GOE: 06.03.02 STRENGTH: L GED: R2 M1 L2 SVP: 3 DLU: 77

920.680-010 FILLING-MACHINE SET-UP MECHANIC (food prep., nec)
Sets up filling and sealing machines to pack potato chips in bags: Selects spouts according to size of bags being filled and attaches spouts to circular conveyor of filling machine, using handtools. Adjusts height of conveyor that moves filled bags from spouts of circular conveyor. Sets filling-machine scales according to weight specified for filled bags. Starts heating unit of sealing machine and sets date on stamping unit of sealing machine. Fills inkwell of stamping unit and regulates flow of ink onto stamp pad. Places container under conveyor to catch chips from overflow of filling machine and dumps chips into filling-machine hopper. Distributes supplies, such as bags and boxes, to workers engaged in tending machines. Transports boxes of potato chips to storage area, using handtruck.
GOE: 06.01.02 STRENGTH: M GED: R3 M1 L2 SVP: 3 DLU: 77

920.684-010 CRATER (any industry) alternate titles: boxer; carpenter, packing; case maker
Fabricates wooden crates or boxes, using woodworking handtools and powered tools, and packs such items as machinery, vehicles, or other large or odd-

shaped products: Reads blueprints, shipping notices, and other specifications, and inspects product to determine size and shape of container, materials to be used, and types of supports and braces to be used. Lays out dimensions on materials with ruler, measuring tape, and pencil. Saws materials to size, using handsaws and powered saws. Assembles materials, using nailing or stapling machine, screws, bolts, glue, and handtools. Places product in container, manually or using hoist. Bolts heavy pieces to bottom of container or skid. Wraps and pads product with excelsior, paper or other packing material. Builds crate around large or odd-shaped articles. Nails cover on crate. Wraps and tightens metal bands around crate, using banding equipment. Attaches identification labels or stencils containing such information as shipping destination, weight, and type of product contained on crate. Repairs broken crates. May cover military tanks and other equipment with neoprene or other protective covering to protect them during shipment. May count items to be packed to ensure compliance with shipping orders. May weigh loaded crate. May move container to shipping area, and move lumber, paper, and other wrapping supplies to crating area, using hand or industrial truck. May sharpen saw blades, using file. May be designated according to item crated as Machinery Crater (machinery mfg.); Refrigerator Crater (svc. ind. mach.), or specific duty performed as Crate Repairer (any industry).
GOE: 06.04.38 STRENGTH: M GED: R3 M2 L2 SVP: 3 DLU: 87

920.685-010 BALING-MACHINE TENDER (any industry) alternate titles: baler operator; baling-press operator; press operator; tie puller; waste baler
Tends machine that compresses and binds paper, cloth, or other loose materials to facilitate handling: Trucks or carries materials to baling machine. Places materials in compression chamber of baling machine. Moves lever or electric switch, causing ram to compress material. Threads tie bands around bale and twists or clamps ends of bands to tighten bands. Opens compression chamber doors and removes bale from machine. May truck bales to storage place, weigh bales, and record weight. May line compression chamber of baling machine with paper, burlap, or other covering before baling. May sew or tie wrapping in place after baling, and stencil bales. May be designated according to material baled as Cloth Baler (textile); Feather Baler (text. prod., nec); Metal Baler (any industry); Paper Baler (paper goods); Rag Baler (laundry & rel.); Tobacco Baler (tobacco); Corn-Husk Baler (grain-feed mills); Hair Baler (leather mfg.); Leather Baler (leather mfg.); Offal Baler (leather mfg.); Scrap Baler (nonfer. metal; steel & rel.).
GOE: 06.04.38 STRENGTH: H GED: R2 M1 L1 SVP: 2 DLU: 81

920.685-014 BANDER-AND-CELLOPHANER, MACHINE (tobacco)
Tends machine that wraps trademark band and cellophane wrapper around cigars: Loads hopper with cigars and magazine with trademark bands. Places roll of cellophane on spindle and threads cellophane through guides and tension rollers into machine. Starts heating unit that seals cellophane wrapper. Starts machine and turns thumbscrews to set guides and regulate tension of cellophane fed into machine. Inspects cigars for defective banding or wrapping. Packs wrapped cigars in boxes.
GOE: 06.04.38 STRENGTH: L GED: R2 M1 L1 SVP: 2 DLU: 77

920.685-018 BB SHOT PACKER (ordnance) alternate titles: shot-tube-machine tender
Tends machine that automatically fills paper tubes with BB shot for air rifles and crimps tube ends: Starts machine and observes action to detect malfunctioning. Fills stations on dial plate manually with tubes from hopper when automatic feed skips. Removes damaged tubes from feeder plate. Examines BB shot tubes for grease smears, tears, and malformed ends. Stamps cardboard box flats with identifying data. Folds flats into boxes and fills with shot-filled tubes. Places filled boxes on rollers for sealing.
GOE: 06.04.38 STRENGTH: L GED: R2 M1 L1 SVP: 2 DLU: 77

920.685-022 BLOCKER (tex. prod., nec)
Tends machine that automatically fastens cardboard disks to sides of core or tube to form reel: Places bottom half of disk on machine bed. Places filled roll of ribbon on disk, and top half of disk on roll. Trips pedal to bring hammer down and press disk on core to complete reel. Stamps and packs reels in boxes. May adjust machine.
GOE: 06.04.38 STRENGTH: M GED: R2 M1 L1 SVP: 2 DLU: 77

920.685-026 BOTTLE PACKER (beverage) alternate titles: caser
Tends machine that inserts filled beer bottles into cardboard cartons: Positions empty carton on platform below automatic packer. Presses pedal to raise platform to packer level and to deposit bottles in carton. Releases pedal and pushes full carton onto conveyor. Straightens or resets partitions in carton.
GOE: 06.04.38 STRENGTH: L GED: R2 M1 L1 SVP: 2 DLU: 77

920.685-030 CANDLE WRAPPING-MACHINE OPERATOR (fabrication, nec)
Tends machine that wraps candles in plastic material, decorative paper or foil: Installs roll of wrapping material in machine, and threads end of roll through machine guides. Moves controls to set suction pickup mechanism for specified vacuum to produce uniformly wrapped product without damage to wrapper. Places candles in cups of rotating machine table, replenishing supply as candles are automatically wrapped. May pack candles in box.
GOE: 06.04.38 STRENGTH: L GED: R2 M1 L1 SVP: 2 DLU: 77

920.685-034 CARDER (any industry) alternate titles: card assembler; carding-machine operator
Tends machine that stitches articles, such as hairpins, hooks and eyes, knitting needles, and snap fasteners, onto cards for sales presentation: Mounts cones

of threads onto spindles and threads ends through guides. Stacks cards in gravity fed hopper. Starts machine and observes machine for jams as articles drop down feeder tubes and are stitched onto moving card. Cuts stitching between cards to separate cards, using scissors, and stacks filled cards. May attach articles on cards, using staples, elastic, or metal fasteners. May be designated according to type of article mounted as Metal-Hairpin Carder (any industry); Pin Inserter (any industry).
GOE: 06.04.38 STRENGTH: L GED: R2 M1 L1 SVP: 2 DLU: 77

920.685-038 CASE PACKER AND SEALER (tobacco) alternate titles: container-packer operator
Tends machine that packs and seals cartons of cigarettes in shipping cases: Starts machine and conveyor belt and observes flow of cartons on conveyor to determine whether cartons are filled and sealed according to specifications and that date stamp is legible. Removes defective cartons. Shapes collapsible cases and places open end of case over mouthpiece of packing unit, or loads blank shipping cases onto feed magazine. May adjust counting and weighing mechanism on packing machine.
GOE: 06.04.38 STRENGTH: L GED: R2 M1 L2 SVP: 3 DLU: 77

920.685-042 CASE-LOADER OPERATOR (beverage) alternate titles: can-bander operator; six-pack-loader operator; six-pack packer
Tends machines and equipment that pack cartons with beer containers for shipment, using any of following methods: (1) Stacks flattened six-pack cartons in rack of machine. Starts machine that automatically opens carton, loads carton with cans of beer, and closes and moves carton onto conveyor. Clears jams when machine automatically stops and presses button to restart machine. (2) Opens and places cartons on conveyor of machine that automatically loads and seals cartons with four six-packs. (3) Folds back flaps of carton bottom and holds carton against chute of loading machine. Moves lever of machine to load carton with four six-packs and drops filled carton onto conveyor for transfer to sealing machine. (4) Starts machine that automatically receives, assembles, loads, and seals cartons. May turn setscrews to adjust such devices as carton opener and gluer.
GOE: 06.04.38 STRENGTH: M GED: R2 M1 L1 SVP: 2 DLU: 77

920.685-046 CIGAR BRANDER (tobacco)
Tends machine that stamps trademark on cigar wrapper: Fills ink well on machine. Positions cellophane-wrapped cigars on conveyor leading into machine and starts machine. Places trays at delivery end of machine to catch branded cigars and removes filled trays. Observes machine operation to determine that stamping conforms to specifications. Cleans ink roller and type, using ink solvent and rags. May tend similar machine that brands directly on cigar.
GOE: 06.04.37 STRENGTH: L GED: R2 M1 L1 SVP: 2 DLU: 77

920.685-050 CIGARETTE-PACKING-MACHINE OPERATOR (tobacco) alternate titles: packaging operator
Tends machine that forms cigarette package, fills packages with cigarettes, wraps packages with cellophane, and attaches stamps: Pulls lever to lock tray of cigarettes over hopper and removes bottom of tray to allow cigarettes to fall into hopper. Fills label hopper and stamp hopper, and pours paste into receptacle. Places spool of paperbacked foil on spindle and threads foil through rollers and guides. Starts machine and inspects packages for defects in folding, centering of labels, or gluing of stamp and wrapper. Cleans machine, using brush, and turns thumbscrews to adjust guides and rollers. May tend machine with cellophane-wrapping attachment [CELLOPHANE WRAPPER, MACHINE (any industry)].
GOE: 06.04.38 STRENGTH: L GED: R2 M1 L2 SVP: 3 DLU: 77

920.685-054 COTTON-ROLL PACKER (protective dev.)
Tends machine that rolls absorbent surgical cotton into rolls and packs rolls in cardboard cartons for shipment: Places empty shipping cartons on conveyor rollers. Pushes button to start automatic cotton-layer machine that rolls absorbent cotton between paper. Inserts rolled cotton in cardboard containers. Fills shipping cartons with containers and places glued paper tape on tops to seal cartons.
GOE: 06.04.38 STRENGTH: L GED: R2 M1 L1 SVP: 2 DLU: 77

920.685-058 FEED WEIGHER (grain-feed mills) alternate titles: feed elevator worker
Tends machine that fills and sews tops of sacks of stockfeed: Shakes bag open, places bag under chute, and presses pedal that releases preweighed batch of feed into sack. Lifts filled sack on bag-closing machine conveyor, folds end of sack, and clamps sewing unit in place. Starts sewing device which automatically sews tops of bag. May hand sew tops of filled sacks. May weigh filled sacks, using platform scales.
GOE: 06.04.38 STRENGTH: H GED: R2 M1 L1 SVP: 2 DLU: 77

920.685-062 HYDRAULIC-PRESS OPERATOR (tobacco) alternate titles: hogshead-press operator; prize jacker
Tends hydraulic press that packs tobacco into hogsheads (containers) for storage or shipment: Reads scales to determine whether specified amount of tobacco has been packed in hogshead and *charger*. Pulls hogshead and charger from chute or packing line, using metal hook, and positions hogshead under ram of press. Pushes lever to lower ram or to raise hogshead against ram to press tobacco into hogshead. Removes hogshead from press and pulls charger from hogshead onto rack, using hook, or raises charger from hogshead, using

electric hoist. May place metal reinforcement corset around hogshead to prevent staves from bursting under pressure. [Workers who tend machines that fill and ram-pack hogsheads are classified as PACKER OPERATOR, AUTOMATIC (tobacco)].
GOE: 06.04.38 STRENGTH: H GED: R2 M1 L2 SVP: 2 DLU: 77

920.685-066 LABELING-MACHINE OPERATOR (recording)
Tends machine that attaches gummed identification labels to phonograph records: Places labels on machine spindle and turns on heating element in ram of machine. Positions record on machine bed and presses pedal to start labeling mechanism. Removes labeled record while simultaneously positioning unlabeled record on machine. Repeats operations to label reverse side of record. May tend machine that attaches labels and punches hole in center of records in same operation.
GOE: 06.04.37 STRENGTH: L GED: R2 M1 L1 SVP: 2 DLU: 77

920.685-070 LACE-ROLLER OPERATOR (leather prod.) alternate titles: belt roller
Tends machine that winds leather belting or shoelaces onto cardboard or wooden spool for shipment: Mounts and clamps roll of leather stripping on spindle of winding machine. Slides empty spool onto winding axle, and threads leather between pressure rollers, under machine counter, and onto spool. Starts machine that winds leather onto spool. Observes machine counter and stops machine after specified amount of leather has been wound onto spool. Cuts leather from roll, using knife. Removes spool from winding axle and packs spool in shipping container or wraps spool in paper.
GOE: 06.04.05 STRENGTH: M GED: R2 M1 L1 SVP: 2 DLU: 77

920.685-074 PACKAGE SEALER, MACHINE (any industry)
Tends machines that seal filled cardboard boxes, cartons, paper, cellophane, or plastic bags: Fills glue and water reservoir. Inserts rolls of paper tape into holders. Starts sealing machine and observes operation to detect faulty sealing and prevent conveyor jamming. Feeds cartons into machine and removes cartons from discharge conveyor. Feeds filled cellophane or glassine bags into machine that heats and seals top of bag. May adjust holding guides and conveyor line tripping mechanism that regulates movement of carton through gluing and flap-turning mechanism. May pack containers. May stamp identifying data on carton. May inspect contents of package to verify size, color, or brand of article. May be designated according to product packaged as Cigarette-Carton Sealer (tobacco); type of machine operated as Box-Sealing-Machine Catcher (any industry); Hot-Sealing-Machine Operator (any industry); or task performed as Box-Sealing-Machine Feeder (any industry).
GOE: 06.04.38 STRENGTH: M GED: R2 M1 L1 SVP: 2 DLU: 81

920.685-078 PACKAGER, MACHINE (any industry) alternate titles: machine operator, packaging
Tends machine that performs one or more packaging functions, such as filling, marking, labeling, banding, tying, packing, or wrapping containers: Starts machine and observes operation to detect malfunctions of machine. Stops machine and reports malfunction to supervisor. Makes minor adjustments or repairs, such as opening valves, changing forming and cutting dies, setting guides, or clearing away damaged product containers. Inspects filled container to ensure that product is packaged according to specifications. May feed product to conveyors, hoppers, or other feeding devices, and unload packaged product. May replenish packaging supplies, such as wrapping paper, plastic sheet, boxes, cartons, glue, ink, or labels. May mount supplies on spindles or place supplies in hopper or other feeding device. May position and hold container in machine and depress pedal, press button, or move lever to clean, glue, label, sew, or staple container. May cut stencils and stencil information on container, such as lot number or shipping destination. May tally number of units of product packaged or record information, such as size, weight, and type of products packaged. May be designated according to specific function or functions performed by machine tended as Bottle Washer, Machine (any industry) II; Capping-Machine Operator (any industry); Container-Maker-Filler-Packer Operator (any industry); Filling-Machine Operator (any industry); Labeler, Machine (any industry); Wrapping-Machine Operator (any industry). May be designated: Aerosol-Line Operator (any industry); Bag Printer (chemical); Blister-Packing-Machine Tender (any industry); Bread-Wrapping-Machine Feeder (bakery products); Candy-Wrapping-Machine Operator (sugar & conf.); Carton-Gluing-Machine Operator (any industry); Cellophane Wrapper, Machine (any industry); Cover Marker (paint & varnish); Glassine-Machine Tender (any industry); Packing-Machine Tender (any industry); Palletizer Operator (any industry) II; Sack Sewer, Machine (any industry); Silk Screener (optical goods); Spring Crater (furniture); Stencil Cutter, Machine (any industry); Tea-Bag-Machine Tender (food prep., nec); Tire Wrapper (automotive ser.; rubber tire); Tube-Filling-Machine Operator (can. & preserv.; chemical); Tying-Machine Operator (any industry); Wrapping-And-Packing-Machine Operator (any industry). Workers who package products by hand are classified under PACKAGER, HAND (any industry) 920.587-018. May act as lead worker.
GOE: 06.04.38 STRENGTH: M GED: R2 M1 L1 SVP: 2 DLU: 86

920.685-082 PACKER OPERATOR, AUTOMATIC (tobacco) alternate titles: press operator, automatic
Tends packing machine and press that fill containers with tobacco: Positions empty container under *charger* and pushes button to lower charger onto container. Starts flow of tobacco into container and observes signal lights to determine stage of filling-packing. Reads scales to determine when specified weight

is attained. Pushes buttons to lower hydraulic ram into container to press tobacco and to divert flow of tobacco to another container. Raises ram and charger and removes container. May record grade and district (locality where grown) on ticket and staple ticket onto container. [Workers who tend machines that only ram-pack hogsheads (containers) are classified as HYDRAULIC-PRESS OPERATOR (tobacco)].
GOE: 06.04.15 STRENGTH: L GED: R2 M1 L1 SVP: 2 DLU: 77

920.685-086 PACKING-MACHINE-PILOT CAN ROUTER (tobacco) alternate titles: pilot-can router
Tends machine that fills chute of snuff-filling or pipe-tobacco-filling machine with cans. Shifts lever to direct flow of cans into chutes.
GOE: 06.04.38 STRENGTH: L GED: R2 M1 L1 SVP: 2 DLU: 77

920.685-090 ROLL FINISHER (paper & pulp) alternate titles: roll wrapper
Tends machines to wrap and seal rolls of paper for shipment: Places paper roll and wrapping roll on steel rollers opposite each other, using hoist. Glues end of wrapping roll on paper roll, moves lever to wind wrapping paper around paper roll, and cuts and glues wrapping paper at end of wrap, using knife and brush. Crimps wrapping paper over ends of paper roll and glues paper heads and caps over ends to seal. Pushes wrapped-paper roll between electrically heated pressure plates of capping machine and pulls lever to move plates against ends to seal heads. May insert wooden plug in ends to maintain contour of wrapped roll. May stencil shipping information on wrapped roll and attach labels. May roll or truck wrapped roll to weighing scale. May wrap and seal pony (small) rolls of paper and be designated Pony-Roll Finisher (paper & pulp).
GOE: 06.04.38 STRENGTH: H GED: R2 M1 SVP: 2 DLU: 77

920.685-094 SNUFF-PACKING-MACHINE OPERATOR (tobacco)
Tends machine that fills cans with snuff and seals lids on cans: Presses buttons to start or stop machine. Observes operation of machine for malfunctions and to determine if cans are filled and sealed according to specifications. May fill hopper of machine with lids. May weigh random sample of filled can to determine if weight specifications are met. May turn handwheel to increase or decrease rate of feed when filled cans deviate from weight specifications.
GOE: 06.04.38 STRENGTH: L GED: R2 M1 L1 SVP: 2 DLU: 77

920.685-098 TOBACCO-PACKING-MACHINE OPERATOR (tobacco) alternate titles: packing-and-stamping machine operator
Tends machines that fill packages with tobacco: Fills wrapper magazine with wrappers or mounts roll of paper on machine spindle and pulls end of paper through rollers to folding mechanism. Turns screw or wheel to set automatic weighing mechanism to feed specified amount of tobacco into each package. Notifies FEEDER-CATCHER, TOBACCO (tobacco) and PACKING-MACHINE CAN FEEDER (tobacco) to start feeding tobacco and tins to machine. Observes filling of packages to ensure each pack is filled with tobacco. Inspects packages for defects, such as torn paper, dents in tins, loose tops on tins, and defective sealing. Weighs packages periodically to verify accuracy of weighing mechanism. May be designated according to tobacco or container packed as Bag-Filler-Machine Operator (tobacco); Can-Filling-Machine Operator (tobacco); Pouch-Making-Machine Operator (tobacco); Smoking-Tobacco-Packing-Machine Hand (tobacco).
GOE: 06.04.38 STRENGTH: L GED: R2 M1 L2 SVP: 3 DLU: 77

920.685-102 WRAPPER (metal prod., nec) alternate titles: rewinder
Tends rewinding machine that winds wire-screen cloth from loose rolls into tight rolls for shipment: Attaches end of roll of wire to winding mechanism. Starts machine and examines screens for defects during operation. Stops machine and removes roll when meter indicates specified footage has been wound.
GOE: 06.04.38 STRENGTH: L GED: R2 M1 L2 SVP: 3 DLU: 77

920.685-106 CUBING-MACHINE TENDER (concrete prod.)
Tends machine that stacks and binds cured concrete blocks into packages of specified dimensions for shipping: Places strapping tape on machine feed spindles and threads tape through guides and rollers of machine. Presses buttons to activate conveyor that positions blocks under binding mechanism of machine, and flips switch to start machine that automatically wraps strapping tape around specified number of blocks to form cube-shaped packages. Presses buttons to set machine pressure gauges that regulate tension of strapping tape. Observes blocks on conveyor to detect imperfections, such as chips, cracks, or discolorations, and replaces defective blocks. Manually rearranges blocks on conveyor, when required, to maintain prescribed order. Stops conveyor and machine when jams occur and clears jams, using metal bar. Adjusts machine guides to package blocks of different styles and sizes, using wrench. May attach identification tags to packages. May tend machine that stacks and binds brick into packages and be designated Strapping-Machine Tender (brick & tile).
GOE: 06.04.38 STRENGTH: H GED: R2 M1 L1 SVP: 2 DLU: 86

920.685-110 BUNDLE TIER AND LABELER (saw. & plan.)
Tends bundling machine that ties and labels stacks of lumber: Fills machine hoppers with labels and staples. Depresses pedal to activate conveyor that brings stacks of lumber to machine. Slides stack of lumber onto machine conveyor. Pushes stack into machine that automatically clamps boards together and staples label on end of boards. Ties cord around stack while stack is clamped in machine to form bundle. Pushes bundle along conveyor after bundle is automatically released from machine. May tally number of bundles on production sheet.

GOE: 06.04.38 STRENGTH: M GED: R2 M1 L1 SVP: 2 DLU: 81

920.685-114 COTTON BALER (agriculture) alternate titles: presser, cotton ginning
Tends hydraulic press that bales ginned cotton: Spreads piece of burlap or jute bale covering on bed of chamber in press. Starts equipment that dumps and tamps bulk cotton in chamber. Observes level of cotton in chamber and stops loading equipment when chamber contains required amounts of cotton. Positions loaded chamber under ram of press. Starts press to compress cotton. Fastens bands around bale and loads bale on handtruck. Moves handtruck onto platform of scale and records weight of bale. May determine number of compressed bales to be obtained from bulk cotton, according to total weight of cotton.
GOE: 03.04.01 STRENGTH: M GED: R2 M2 L2 SVP: 3 DLU: 80

920.686-010 BANDER-AND-CELLOPHANER HELPER, MACHINE (tobacco) alternate titles: banding-and-cellophane-wrapping-machine-operator helper
Assists BANDER-AND-CELLOPHANER, MACHINE (tobacco) in wrapping trademark band and cellophane wrapper around cigars. Performs other duties as described under HELPER (any industry) Master Title.
GOE: 06.04.38 STRENGTH: L GED: R2 M1 L1 SVP: 2 DLU: 77

920.686-014 COTTON-BALL BAGGER (protective dev.)
Removes absorbent cotton surgical sponges from automatic balling machine, observes sponges for size and shape, and fills bags with specified number of sponges. Places filled bags in cartons for shipment. May fold and seal plastic bag tops, using electric iron.
GOE: 06.04.38 STRENGTH: L GED: R2 M1 L1 SVP: 2 DLU: 77

920.686-018 FOLDING-MACHINE FEEDER (tex. prod., nec)
Feeds pillowcases, towels, or other articles into machine that folds articles for wrapping. May start, stop, and adjust machine.
GOE: 06.04.05 STRENGTH: L GED: R1 M1 L1 SVP: 2 DLU: 77

920.686-022 ORDER FILLER, LINSEED OIL (oils & grease)
Fills cans, drums, and other containers with linseed oil for shipment: Connects hose from oil storage tank to scale hopper. Places empty container beneath hopper outlet. Adjusts scales and opens oil storage tank valve to permit flow of oil into scale hopper (flow of oil automatically stops at specified weight). Opens hopper valve to fill container with oil. Screws bung in place or seals cover on container manually. May fill empty containers with oil directly from storage tank and weigh filled containers, using platform scales. May stencil shipping information, such as oil blend, weight, and consignee's name and address on containers. May move filled containers to storage area.
GOE: 06.04.36 STRENGTH: M GED: R2 M1 L1 SVP: 2 DLU: 77

920.686-026 PACKING-FLOOR WORKER (tobacco)
Unloads boxes of cigars from handpresses and keeps packed cigar containers in order: Turns handscrews to relieve pressure on press and lifts packing box to rack. Prepares identifying labels and attaches labels to boxes in rack. Transfers rack to stockroom, using lift truck. Attaches labels to press to prevent mixing different types of cigars during packing. Turns handwheel to move pressing head against stacked boxes. Supplies CIGAR PACKER (tobacco) with empty boxes and moves material to and from bench.
GOE: 06.04.40 STRENGTH: M GED: R2 M1 L1 SVP: 2 DLU: 77

920.686-030 PACKING-MACHINE CAN FEEDER (tobacco) alternate titles: can feeder; tin-can feeder
Places cans, paper packs, or glass tumblers on conveyor belt of machine that automatically fills containers with tobacco products. May inspect containers for defects.
GOE: 06.04.38 STRENGTH: L GED: R2 M1 L1 SVP: 2 DLU: 77

920.686-034 PAD-MACHINE FEEDER (saw. & plan.)
Feeds machine that compresses and wraps excelsior to make pads used in packing furniture and other products: Spreads excelsior on feed conveyor and observes operation to detect jamming of material and packaging defects. May fill glue reservoir, mount roll of paper on machine, and adjust conveyor guides and speed controls.
GOE: 06.04.09 STRENGTH: L GED: R1 M1 L1 SVP: 2 DLU: 77

920.686-038 POLY-PACKER AND HEAT-SEALER (protective dev.)
Feeds machine that seals sterilized dressings into plastic bags and packs bags in cardboard cartons: Inserts sterilized dressing into plastic bag and folds open end to prepare for sealing. Feeds folded end into machine that seals bag. Presses and examines bag for airtight seal. Packs specified number of bags in cardboard cartons.
GOE: 06.04.38 STRENGTH: L GED: R2 M1 L1 SVP: 2 DLU: 77

920.686-042 PRESS BUCKER (any industry)
Removes pressed bales of material, such as cotton, hay, wastepaper, waste metals, and rags from baling machine, using hook. May push bales to storage area, using handtruck. When removing pressed bales of materials by shoving steel band through press platen, is designated Band Shover, Press (agriculture).
GOE: 05.12.03 STRENGTH: H GED: R1 M1 L1 SVP: 1 DLU: 77

920.686-046 SPOOLER, SEQUINS (plastic prod.) alternate titles: sequins winder
Winds strings of plastic sequins on spools preparatory to shipment: Pulls string of sequins through yardage indicator and cuts off specified length. Exam-

ines string for broken threads, knots, and irregular lay of sequins. Feeds string into winding machine that winds string on spool.
GOE: 06.04.38 STRENGTH: L GED: R2 M1 L1 SVP: 2 DLU: 77

920.686-050 TRAY FILLER (tobacco) alternate titles: packing presser; tray packer
Fills trays with cigars and loads press that compresses cigars into square shape for packing: Places cigars previously sorted for color onto packing trays, and carries trays to press. Stacks trays on bed of press and places paper between trays. Turns handwheel to lower head of press that compresses cigars.
GOE: 06.04.15 STRENGTH: L GED: R2 M1 L1 SVP: 2 DLU: 77

920.687-010 APPLE-PACKING HEADER (agriculture)
Affixes lids on apple-filled barrels, using foot-operated or power-driven press, or hand mallet and cooper's iron. May rearrange top layer of fruit to make lid fit properly. May fasten lids on other containers.
GOE: 03.04.01 STRENGTH: L GED: R2 M1 L1 SVP: 2 DLU: 77

920.687-014 BAGGER (retail trade) alternate titles: grocery packer
Bags groceries at grocery store: Packs grocery items in sacks or cartons, arranging heavy and bulky items at bottom of sack or carton. Verifies price of grocery item in question against price of items on stock shelf, upon request. Carries packed sacks, or places sacks in grocery cart, and pushes cart to customer's vehicle, upon request. Places groceries into customer's vehicle. Collects shopping carts from parking lot and surrounding areas and returns carts to store. Replaces cleaning and packing supplies used at grocery checkout counter. Returns grocery items left at checkout counter to specified stock shelves. Cleans work area and carries empty bottles and trash to storeroom. May price and place grocery articles on shelves. May assist in unloading delivery trucks.
GOE: 09.05.10 STRENGTH: M GED: R2 M1 L1 SVP: 2 DLU: 82

920.687-018 BAGGER (garment; laundry & rel.)
Covers garments or household articles with plastic or paper bags by any of following methods: (1) Hangs garment or article on stand and covers with plastic bag. (2) Pulls plastic from rolls, sliding plastic material over article and tearing plastic at perforations to form bag of desired size. (3) Hangs garment on holder in machine and pulls plastic from roll to envelop garment. Pushes button or moves lever to close heating irons that cut and seal plastic to form bag of desired dimensions. Hangs bagged article on slide rail or rack. (4) Drops shirts or folded articles into machine that automatically envelops articles in plastic bags and drops articles into box. Removes boxes from beneath machine when filled and replaces boxes.
GOE: 06.04.35 STRENGTH: L GED: R1 M1 L1 SVP: 1 DLU: 77

920.687-022 BALE SEWER (agriculture)
Sews burlap covering on baled agricultural produce, such as cotton or hops: Pulls edges of covering material together, folds in end flaps and secures end flaps temporarily with awl. Threads spring-eye sack needle with twine and sews seams. May weigh, stencil, and tag bales. May wrap double compressed bales with metal bands for export shipment. May be designated Sewer, Head (agriculture) when working in bed of press. May sew burlap covering on baled produce, using portable sewing machine.
GOE: 06.04.38 STRENGTH: M GED: R1 M1 L1 SVP: 2 DLU: 77

920.687-026 BANDER, HAND (paper goods)
Wraps printed paper bands (labels), plain unprinted bands, or ribbons, around specified number of prestacked paper items, such as napkins, envelopes, towels, or notebook paper. Brushes glue on one end of band and presses ends together. Stacks banded packages on table or places packages in containers. May be designated according to type of paper item banded as Napkin-Band Wrapper (paper goods); Papeterie-Table Assembler (paper goods); Towel Bander (paper goods).
GOE: 06.04.38 STRENGTH: L GED: R1 M1 L1 SVP: 1 DLU: 77

920.687-030 BANDER, HAND (tobacco) alternate titles: cigar bander, hand
Wraps trademark band around cigars: Moistens or applies paste to tip end of band and presses ends of band together around cigars. Places banded cigars aside for further processing.
GOE: 06.04.38 STRENGTH: S GED: R2 M1 L1 SVP: 2 DLU: 77

920.687-034 BANDOLEER PACKER (ordnance)
Packs small arms ammunition in bandoleer belt pockets: Compares ammunition identification data stenciled on belt with work order to ensure packing of specified caliber cartridges. Places cardboard separator between two filled ammunition clips and slides clips into cardboard packet. Holds bandoleer pocket open with spoonlike tool and inserts packet into pocket. Closes pocket flaps and piles belt on handtruck.
GOE: 06.04.38 STRENGTH: L GED: R1 M1 L1 SVP: 1 DLU: 77

920.687-038 BLUEPRINT TRIMMER (any industry) alternate titles: blueprint assembler; cutter; trimmer
Cuts blueprints, measures print margins, punches holes in prints, and folds, staples, and labels blueprints for shipment: Cuts individual print from continuous strip of processed prints, using shears. Verifies dimensions of blueprint margins, using ruler, and cuts off excess, using shears. Punches holes in blueprint, using paper punch, and folds prints. Staples specified number of prints to folded edges of wrapping paper to form bound set. Writes name and address of customer on wrapping. May sort prints according to numerical code. May examine blueprints for defects, such as clarity and double image.

GOE: 06.04.26 STRENGTH: L GED: R2 M1 L1 SVP: 2 DLU: 77

920.687-042 BOTTLING-LINE ATTENDANT (beverage) alternate titles: line operator
Prepares filled whiskey bottles for packing and shipping, performing any combination of following duties: Pastes labels and tax stamps on filled whiskey bottles as bottles pass on conveyor. Examines bottles to ascertain that labels and stamps have been correctly applied. Straightens labels and stamps on bottles. Presses stamps on necks of bottles. Wipes excess glue and moisture from bottles. Packs whiskey bottles into cartons. Pastes identification labels on cartons. May be known according to task performed as Bottle-Label Inspector (beverage); Stamp Presser (beverage); Strip-Stamp Straightener (beverage).
GOE: 06.04.38 STRENGTH: L GED: R1 M1 L1 SVP: 1 DLU: 77

920.687-046 BUNDLER, SEASONAL GREENERY (forestry)
Bundles decorative greens (forest greenery) and Christmas trees for shipments, performing combination of following tasks: Examines greens and discards branches with discolored or sparse leaves. Arranges greens into bundles as specified, weighs greens, ties greens into bundles, and records number and type of bundles. Sorts Christmas trees on conveyor belts according to size and quality of trees. Ties specified number, size, and quality of trees into bundles and affixes tags to bundles. May trim greens or trees, using hatchet. May be designated according to task performed as Baler (forestry); Buncher (forestry); Tagger (forestry); Trimmer (forestry).
GOE: 03.04.04 STRENGTH: M GED: R2 M1 L1 SVP: 2 DLU: 77

920.687-050 CAN INSPECTOR (beverage; can. & preserv.) alternate titles: seam checker
Inspects lid seams of closed food or beverage cans to ascertain if lids conform to sealing specifications: Collects random samples of filled cans discharged by closing machine. Cuts out center of lid, using can opener, and empties contents. Measures thickness of lid seam, using micrometer. Removes crimped edge of lid (lid hook), using pliers, and measures thickness of crimped edge of can wall (can hook), using micrometer. Records measurements of seam and can hook. May measure thickness of bottom seam prior to filling operations. May empty contents of defective cans into new cans and place on closing-machine conveyor.
GOE: 06.03.02 STRENGTH: L GED: R2 M1 L2 SVP: 3 DLU: 77

920.687-054 CAN PATCHER (can. & preserv.)
Places rejected can on scale to ascertain amount of off-weight, and adjusts contents to bring weight to standard. Places repacked cans on lidding machine conveyor. May repack contents of cans improperly packed by machine.
GOE: 06.04.28 STRENGTH: L GED: R2 M2 L2 SVP: 2 DLU: 77

920.687-058 CAN RECONDITIONER (can. & preserv.)
Examines and reconditions rusted and soiled cans containing food: Taps cans with mallet to determine if cans meet vacuum specification and sets rejects aside [VACUUM TESTER, CANS (can. & preserv.)]. Removes rust from cans, using revolving wire brush and buffer. Immerses cans in washing solution to remove dirt. Stacks or packs reconditioned cans. May relabel cans.
GOE: 06.03.02 STRENGTH: L GED: R2 M1 L2 SVP: 3 DLU: 77

920.687-062 CARDBOARD INSERTER (knitting)
Inserts cardboard in stretchable socks to shape socks for display: Places cardboard insert through opening in sock form and pulls sock over form. Removes sock containing insert from form. May be designated Tissue Inserter (knitting).
GOE: 06.04.27 STRENGTH: L GED: R1 M1 L1 SVP: 1 DLU: 77

920.687-066 CARRIER PACKER (protective dev.)
Packs military gas masks in canvas carriers: Inserts gas-mask canisters into carriers, using manually operated table jig. Ties facepieces around cardboard forms, using string, and inserts facepieces and hose tubes of masks into carriers. Tightens straps in buckles of carriers to obtain compact units for military use. Places gas masks on conveyor for transfer to shipping rooms.
GOE: 06.04.38 STRENGTH: M GED: R2 M1 L1 SVP: 2 DLU: 77

920.687-070 CARTON INSPECTOR (tobacco) alternate titles: carton searcher
Inspects cartons filled with packaged tobacco products to determine whether flaps or wrappers are sealed and cartons are printed or marked as specified. May observe cartons passing on conveyor and remove lightweight carton at signal from electronic checking device. May maintain inspection records.
GOE: 06.03.02 STRENGTH: L GED: R2 M2 L2 SVP: 3 DLU: 77

920.687-074 COTTON TIER (agriculture) alternate titles: tie-out worker
Fastens metal bands around bales of cotton that are compressed in press: Inserts metal band through channel in upper ram of press to worker on opposite side of compressed bale who returns band through channels in lower ram to encircle bale. Bends end of band and fastens band to hook of buckle on opposite end of band. When working on opposite side of compressed bale to return metal bands through channels, may be designated Returner (agriculture).
GOE: 03.04.01 STRENGTH: L GED: R1 M1 L1 SVP: 2 DLU: 77

920.687-078 CRATE LINER (furniture)
Lines crates and boxes used to pack furniture with protective lining to protect furniture during shipment: Spreads wrapping paper in crate box. Cuts corrugated paperboard and fits paperboard in crate. Lays excelsior pads in crate for packing specified units. Glues cardboard pads in corner of crate to make cushions for furniture. Assists PACKAGER, HAND (any industry) to place fur-

niture in box or crate. Transfers packed crates and boxes to loading platform, using handtruck.
GOE: 06.04.38 STRENGTH: M GED: R2 M1 L1 SVP: 2 DLU: 77

920.687-082 DENTAL FLOSS PACKER (protective dev.)
Assembles dental floss packages: Mounts dental floss cutter in container top, using jig, and locks cutter in place, using cap. Cuts away excess floss from roll, using scissors. Positions roll in bottom half of container and mounts cutter top. Threads end of dental floss through cutting mechanism. Places completed unit in shipping container.
GOE: 06.04.34 STRENGTH: L GED: R2 M1 L1 SVP: 2 DLU: 77

920.687-086 FISH PACKER (can. & preserv.) alternate titles: fish-house worker
Packs dressed fish in ice and records weight: Reads orders to determine quantity, size, and variety of fish to be packed. Selects and weighs fish and records weights. Shovels layer of ice in box and fills body cavity of each fish with ice. Places fish in box and fills remainder of box with ice. May assemble boxes, stencil addresses on boxes, and band packed boxes with metal straps.
GOE: 06.04.28 STRENGTH: H GED: R2 M1 L1 SVP: 2 DLU: 77

920.687-090 FLOOR WORKER (sugar & conf.)
Performs any combination of following tasks to facilitate wrapping and packing of chewing gum: Copies from registers (counters) on machines number of cartons of chewing gum filled by each packing machine. Empties containers of scrap gum into barrel for reprocessing. Distributes packaging materials to workers. Replaces packages of gum that were previously removed from carton for inspection. Scans stacks of cellophane-wrapped cartons passing on conveyor belt to detect defective wrapping. Removes cellophane from defectively wrapped cartons and returns cartons for rewrapping.
GOE: 06.04.38 STRENGTH: L GED: R2 M1 L1 SVP: 2 DLU: 77

920.687-094 GREENS TIER (wholesale tr.)
Ties bunches of forest greenery together for eventual sale to consumer by placing greenery in pressure clamp and presses pedal to hold bunches together while tying. Releases pedal and removes bunch from clamp.
GOE: 06.04.38 STRENGTH: M GED: R1 M1 L1 SVP: 1 DLU: 77

920.687-098 HANDKERCHIEF FOLDER (garment)
Folds handkerchiefs prior to packaging. May fold fancy handkerchiefs, such as men's dress handkerchiefs, into specified shapes and place handkerchiefs in cellophane envelopes.
GOE: 06.04.27 STRENGTH: L GED: R2 M1 L1 SVP: 2 DLU: 77

920.687-102 HOGSHEAD OPENER (tobacco) alternate titles: hogshead hand; hogshead stripper; hogshead unpacker; hogshead wrecker
Opens sealed hogsheads of tobacco, using hammer, hatchet, and wire clippers: Removes nails from headbands and cuts metal band and wooden liner. Raises hogshead to upright position, using hoist. Cuts wire bands and remaining headband, removes head, and allows staves to fall on floor or cuts wire bands and lifts hogshead from packed tobacco. On patented hogsheads, cuts tie wire and headbands or removes pins from eyelets, catches sections of staves as staves fall from hogshead, and removes head.
GOE: 06.04.28 STRENGTH: H GED: R2 M1 L2 SVP: 2 DLU: 77

920.687-106 LABEL REMOVER (beverage)
Removes damaged or improperly applied labels from filled whiskey bottles: Places bottles into container of warm water to loosen labels. Rubs or scrapes labels from bottles, using fingers or blade. Wipes bottles with cloth to remove excess moisture and glue. Places bottles on conveyor for relabeling.
GOE: 06.04.39 STRENGTH: L GED: R2 M1 L1 SVP: 2 DLU: 77

920.687-110 LINE-OUT WORKER I (tobacco) alternate titles: head-out worker; hogshead liner
Nails heads onto hogsheads of tobacco prior to shipment or storage: Fits precut boards into hogshead to form head and nails wooden crossbar to assembled pieces to secure pieces. Inserts metal rim in hogshead, places prefabricated head within rim, and lowers hydraulic ram to force head into hogshead. Inserts and nails liner (thin wooden strip) to inside top edge of hogshead to hold head in place. Nails head through side of hogshead to secure head. May weigh hogshead prior to shipment.
GOE: 06.04.38 STRENGTH: M GED: R2 M1 L2 SVP: 2 DLU: 77

920.687-114 LINE-OUT WORKER II (tobacco)
Seals hogsheads of tobacco prior to shipment or storage: Places prefabricated head in hogshead and climbs onto hogshead to press head down. Forces head into hogshead, using metal bar, body weight, and foot pressure. Positions metal band around top edge of hogshead, inserts ends of band into ratchet tool, and moves lever to tighten band. Secures band to hogshead, using clamps and crimping tool, or by inserting fasteners through perforations in band into hogshead. Bends end of band to break off excess band. Removes metal reinforcement from hogshead and rolls or pushes hogshead from work area.
GOE: 06.04.38 STRENGTH: H GED: R2 M1 L1 SVP: 2 DLU: 77

920.687-118 LINEN-SUPPLY LOAD-BUILDER (laundry & rel.)
Assembles laundered uniforms and linen for DRIVER, SALES ROUTE (retail trade; wholesale tr.) of linen supply establishment, according to load sheet showing quantity, description, size, or color of articles requisitioned. May attach labels, emblems, and monograms to articles, such as industrial uniforms, using sewing machines.

GOE: 05.09.01 STRENGTH: L GED: R2 M1 L2 SVP: 2 DLU: 77

920.687-122 MACHINE-PACK ASSEMBLER (ordnance)
Places small arms cartridges nose-to-head for packaging: Positions cartridge-filled shaker plate over double transfer plate and releases catch to drop cartridges nose-down into alternate holes in transfer plate. Turns transfer plate over and repeats to fill remaining holes. Pulls slides in transfer plate that release cartridges in nose-to-head arrangement into packaging-bench fixture.
GOE: 06.04.38 STRENGTH: L GED: R1 M1 L1 SVP: 2 DLU: 77

920.687-126 MARKER II (any industry) alternate titles: labeler; stamper
Marks or affixes trademarks or other identifying information, such as size, color, grade, or process code, on merchandise, material, or product, using one or more methods, such as metal punch and hammer, crayon, rubber stamp and ink, electric pencil, branding iron, acid and stencil, sand-grit and stencil, or tags. May inspect items before marking. May attach gummed labels to merchandise, material, or product, using tag dispensing machine. May clean items. May use printing mechanism or labeling press. When marking is performed as task of packaging duties, worker should be classified according to type of packaging performed as PACKAGER, HAND (any industry) 920.587-018; PACKAGER, MACHINE (any industry) 920.685-078; or BALING-MACHINE TENDER (any industry) 920.685-010.
GOE: 06.04.37 STRENGTH: L GED: R2 M1 L1 SVP: 2 DLU: 84

920.687-130 PACKER (tobacco) alternate titles: carton filler; case packer; case sealer
Packs wrapped or packaged tobacco products into cartons or packs filled cartons in shipping containers: Examines tobacco products for defects, such as excess moisture in chewing tobacco plugs, loosely sealed wrappers, coupons, or labels, or misplaced stamps. Seals and loads container onto handtruck or skid or onto conveyor leading to case-sealing machine or shipping room. May form shipping container or attach label onto container. May weigh product to verify accuracy of packing machine scales. May hand stamp or stencil identifying information on cartons or shipping containers. May be designated according to product packed as Cut-Plug Packer (tobacco); Smoking-Tobacco Packer, Hand (tobacco); Twist Packer (tobacco). Workers who tend machines to package products are classified under CARTON-PACKAGING-MACHINE OPERATOR (tobacco).
GOE: 06.04.38 STRENGTH: M GED: R2 M1 L1 SVP: 2 DLU: 77

920.687-134 PACKER, AGRICULTURAL PRODUCE (agriculture) alternate titles: packer
Packs agricultural produce, such as bulbs, fruits, nuts, eggs, and vegetables, for storage or shipment, performing any combination of following duties: Lines box, barrel, basket, carton, or crate with treated paper, cardboard, excelsior, or prepared padding, or inserts paper trays or separators in container. Places rows of produce in layers in containers, and inserts excelsior, shredded cellophane, or paper trays after each layer and over top layer of produce, or scoops produce into container. Wraps produce in treated paper, foil, or plastic film wrap before placing produce in container. Packs exposed top layer of produce, arranging produce in successive rows in container. Positions basket liner upside down over ring of produce on pallet and fills basket liner with specified amount of produce. Places basket upside down over filled liner on pallet. Pushes basket and pallet over conveyor rollers onto table of turning frame, clamps basket and pallet in place, and moves lever to turn basket upright. Fits lid on container and nails, wires, or tapes in place. Stamps grade, brand, and date of packing on container. Washes and trims produce, such as lettuce and carrots, preparatory to packing, working in warehouse or on harvesting machine in field. Sorts produce according to size, color, and grade before packing. May weigh packed produce and add or remove produce from container to obtain specified weight. May be designated Apple Packer (agriculture; wholesale tr.); Basket Turner (agriculture); Face-And-Fill Packer (agriculture); Lettuce Trimmer (agriculture); Ring Packer (agriculture; wholesale tr.); Topper Packer (agriculture); Apricot Packer (agriculture; wholesale tr.); Avocado Packer (agriculture; wholesale tr.); Boxer (agriculture); Capper (agriculture); Cherry Packer (agriculture; wholesale tr.); Citrus-Fruit Packer (agriculture; wholesale tr.); Crater (agriculture); Crate Tier (agriculture; wholesale tr.); Culled-Fruit Packer (agriculture); Egg Packer (agriculture; wholesale tr.); Fruit Packer, Face-And-Fill (agriculture; wholesale tr.); Fruit Packer, Wrap-And-Place (agriculture; wholesale tr.); Header (agriculture; wholesale tr.); Lider (agriculture; wholesale tr.); Make-Up Market Worker, Truck Garden (agriculture); Melon Packer (agriculture); Mushroom Packer (agriculture); Pear Packer (agriculture; wholesale tr.); Plant Packer (agriculture); Plant Wrapper (agriculture); Plum Packer (agriculture; wholesale tr.); Ring Facer (agriculture); Seed Packer (agriculture); Tobacco Packer (agriculture); Tree Wrapper (agriculture).
GOE: 03.04.01 STRENGTH: M GED: R2 M1 L1 SVP: 2 DLU: 81

920.687-138 PAPER INSERTER (glass mfg.)
Pulls *lites*, stacked on end, slightly forward while simultaneously inserting paper between lites to protect glass from surface damage. Pastes labels on lites, preparatory to packing.
GOE: 06.04.38 STRENGTH: L GED: R1 M1 L1 SVP: 2 DLU: 77

920.687-142 PRIZER (tobacco) alternate titles: hogshead filler; hogshead packer; loose-hand packer; packer
Packs tobacco into hogsheads for storage or shipment, performing any combination of following tasks: Climbs into hogshead and pulls hands of tobacco from stick held by FEEDER-CATCHER, TOBACCO (tobacco) or receives

hands of tobacco and packs tobacco into hogshead. Tramples tobacco hands, strips, or stems fed into hogshead by chute. Pulls charger from movable rack onto top of hogshead so tobacco can be packed above top of hogshead. Opens chute to feed tobacco into hogshead until specified weight is indicated by scale. Stands on platform above hogshead and packs tobacco, using T-shaped stick, as tobacco is fed into hogshead by chute. May be designated according to stage at which packed as Green-Prize Packer (tobacco).
GOE: 06.04.38 STRENGTH: M GED: R2 M1 L1 SVP: 2 DLU: 77

920.687-146 REPACK-ROOM WORKER (beverage)
Repacks cartons of beer or distilled liquor damaged in packaging: Removes containers, such as bottles or cans, from damaged or unclean cartons and places containers in another carton. Replaces damaged containers with containers of identical size, label, and crown. Seals top flaps of carton, using glued tape. Duplicates identification, code, and date number found on damaged cartons, using hand stamps. Positions letters and numbers in hand stamps, using picks and tweezers. Sets repacked carton on conveyor or stacks in storage area. May move carton to storage area, using handtruck. Maintains supply of various-sized bottles and cans, using different types of labels, crowns, and lids. May keep records of material used. May pack orders for shipping.
GOE: 06.04.38 STRENGTH: L GED: R2 M1 L2 SVP: 2 DLU: 77

920.687-150 ROSIN-BARREL FILLER (chemical)
Fills barrels with rosin: Places pipe through opening in barrel head to direct flow of rosin. Hammers hoops down on barrel to tighten staves. Seals leaks in barrels, using clay.
GOE: 06.04.36 STRENGTH: L GED: R1 M1 L1 SVP: 1 DLU: 77

920.687-154 SAMPLE WORKER (any industry)
Prepares articles, such as curtains, draperies, rugs, or towels, for use as display samples, performing any combination of following duties: Assembles garments or articles into sets, and folds articles. Pins or glues identification tickets or labels to articles. Wraps paper bands around article, securing ends of band with glue, or inserts articles into plastic or cellophane bags. Arranges articles in boxes in attractive display and stores samples according to style, size, and color. Fills customer or sales orders, following order ticket. Records number of articles received, sample sets prepared, and samples shipped. Inventories samples in stock and requisitions replacement articles. May tend machine to print identification tickets or labels.
GOE: 06.04.38 STRENGTH: L GED: R3 M1 L2 SVP: 3 DLU: 77

920.687-158 SHINGLE PACKER (saw. & plan.) alternate titles: shingle weaver
Packs shingles or shakes into bundles for shipment: Lays shingles or shakes in jig with small ends interwoven to form bundle. Counts shingles or shakes to ensure specified quantities. Binds bundles with shingle bands or steel band, using stapler or crimping tool. When packing shakes, may be designated Shake Packer (saw. & plan.).
GOE: 06.04.38 STRENGTH: H GED: R2 M1 L1 SVP: 2 DLU: 78

920.687-166 SHOE PACKER (boot & shoe) alternate titles: shoe handler
Packs paired shoes, according to case number, in cartons for shipment. May inspect shoes for defects prior to packing.
GOE: 06.04.38 STRENGTH: L GED: R2 M1 L1 SVP: 2 DLU: 77

920.687-170 SHOT BAGGER (ordnance) alternate titles: shot packer; volumetric weigher
Fills canvas bags with lead shot for shipment, using dispenser with volumetric measuring chamber: Pushes wheeled packing stand beneath bin containing size shot ordered. Hooks feed pipe from dispenser to bin spout. Pulls levers to permit shot to flow from storage bin through pipe into volumetric measuring chamber and from chamber into bag. Closes mouth of bag with wire, using wire-twisting tool. Weighs sample bags at prescribed intervals and turns knob to adjust measuring chamber capacity to produce specified weight.
GOE: 06.04.36 STRENGTH: L GED: R2 M1 L1 SVP: 2 DLU: 77

920.687-174 SNUFF-BOX FINISHER (tobacco)
Glues covers and labels on paper boxes of snuff: Places cardboard disk in opening of round box and applies glue to inner edge of box extending beyond disk. Folds edges over and presses edges onto disk. Glues labels onto top and sides of box.
GOE: 06.04.38 STRENGTH: L GED: R2 M1 L1 SVP: 2 DLU: 77

920.687-178 STENCILER (any industry) alternate titles: marker, shipments
Marks size, lot number, contents, or other identifying information or symbols on containers or directly on article by placing stencil on container or article and rubbing ink or paint brush across open lettering, or by spraying paint on stencil. May mix paints or lacquers. May be designated according to type of container stenciled as Carton Stenciler (any industry); Drum Stenciler (beverage); Sack Stenciler (any industry).
GOE: 06.04.37 STRENGTH: L GED: R1 M1 L1 SVP: 2 DLU: 77

920.687-182 STERILIZER (beverage) alternate titles: sterilizer operator
Sterilizes wine containers, such as barrels or metal tanks: Hammers and pulls bungs from barrels or unscrews cap from tank, using handtools, such as mallet and wrench. Inserts nozzle of steam pipe through vent and flushes steamed container with water, to clean container. Ignites and inserts sulfur stick (candle) into container to kill bacteria. Repaints barrelheads, using brush, lacquer, or paint. Removes sulfur fumes from container, using compressed air.

GOE: 06.04.39 STRENGTH: H GED: R2 M1 L1 SVP: 2 DLU: 77

920.687-186 TABLE-COVER FOLDER (tex. prod., nec)
Folds tablecloths preparatory to packaging, using table equipped with rollers: Places cover on table with one edge on rollers. Lays cardboard tube on cover at rollers and winds cover around tube. Pulls tube from cover, smooths cover flat, and folds cover to specified size to fit into bag. Stacks folded table covers. May fold tablecloths without using rollers.
GOE: 06.04.27 STRENGTH: L GED: R2 M1 L1 SVP: 2 DLU: 77

920.687-190 TIE BINDER (garment) alternate titles: bander; bundler
Binds neckties together prior to packing: Places cardboard forms beneath and on top of stack of folded neckties. Binds stack of ties, using rubberbands, paper strips, or tape. May stamp information, such as number of ties and tie style on cardboard forms. May slide paper or plastic identification bands onto ties or insert labels into pretied knot.
GOE: 06.04.38 STRENGTH: L GED: R2 M1 L1 SVP: 2 DLU: 77

920.687-194 VACUUM TESTER, CANS (can. & preserv.) alternate titles: cap inspector
Taps lids of cans or jars with stick as they pass on conveyor to determine if container is vacuum sealed. Removes defective containers for reprocessing. May feed containers into vacuum chamber to determine if cans are sealed.
GOE: 06.03.02 STRENGTH: L GED: R1 M1 L1 SVP: 2 DLU: 77

920.687-198 WOOL SACKER (agriculture) alternate titles: tromper; wool tamper
Packs wool fleeces in burlap bags preparatory to shipping: Fastens bag around device that holds bag open. Tosses tied fleeces into sack and tramps on bundles to compact. Removes sack from holder and sews open end with needle and twine. Ties ears (hand grips) on each bag.
GOE: 03.04.01 STRENGTH: M GED: R2 M1 L1 SVP: 2 DLU: 77

920.687-202 WORM PACKER (agriculture) alternate titles: worm sorter
Packs earthworms into containers according to size: Scoops growth media and specified number of worms of designated sizes into containers, and date stamps containers for delivery to sales outlet. May dry worms under heat lamps, and grind and package worms for sale as tropical fish food.
GOE: 03.04.01 STRENGTH: L GED: R1 M1 L1 SVP: 1 DLU: 77

921 HOISTING AND CONVEYING OCCUPATIONS

This group includes occupations concerned with lifting and moving materials, machines, and products, and stacking and dumping materials and products, using power-operated equipment, such as cranes, hoists, winches, conveyors (including pneumatic conveyor systems), stackers, rotary dumpers, and industrial trucks; attaching ropes, chains, slings, and other devices to objects being moved; signaling machine operators and guiding moving loads; and related activities.

921.130-010 RIGGING SUPERVISOR (construction)
Supervises and coordinates activities of workers engaged in erecting and operating machines to hoist and convey machinery and equipment, such as structural beams, metal tanks, and wall and floor slabs, at construction site: Specifies locations for movement and erection of derricks, hoists, and cranes, using knowledge of various methods of sliding and lifting equipment. Directs workers engaged in splicing ropes and metal cables to form hoisting slings. Performs other duties as described under SUPERVISOR (any industry) Master Title.
GOE: 05.11.01 STRENGTH: M GED: R4 M3 L3 SVP: 8 DLU: 77

921.131-010 HOOK TENDER (logging) alternate titles: hooker
Supervises and coordinates activities of workers engaged in yarding and loading logs in *high lead,* slack line, or similar cable yarding system: Determines location of blocks, guy lines, spar, and yarding and loading equipment, according to location and size of landing and type of terrain. Inspects rigging for defects and unsafe conditions, and oversees repair or replacement. Directs rigging crew in setting side and tail blocks, rigging spars, notching anchor stumps, raising guy lines, and installing running tackle. Observes yarding system in operation, and directs relocation of rigging to relieve equipment strain or to extend range of system. Informs RIGGING SLINGER (logging) of log removal sequence, capacity of yarding system and equipment, and related factors. Coordinates dismantling and moving of equipment to new site. Trains workers in safety regulations and activities, such as splicing cable, maintaining equipment, and rigging and operating yarding systems. May supervise crew of tractor yarding workers. Performs duties as described under SUPERVISOR (any industry) Master Title.
GOE: 05.12.04 STRENGTH: L GED: R3 M2 L2 SVP: 7 DLU: 77

921.132-010 TRACK SUPERVISOR (grain-feed mills)
Supervises and coordinates activities of workers engaged in loading and unloading railroad cars at grain elevator and operates equipment that unloads railroad cars: Confers with SUPERINTENDENT, GRAIN ELEVATOR (beverage; grain-feed mills) to obtain daily work schedule and resolve operating problems. Confers with GRAIN MIXER (grain-feed mills) to coordinate loading and unloading activities with blending and weighing activities. Assigns workers to duties and issues instructions regarding sequence of activities and railroad cars to be loaded and unloaded. Directs workers to connect car puller cables to railroad cars and pulls lever to start winding mechanism that pulls cars into position

for loading or unloading. Signals weigher when cars are in position and observes lights to detect signal to commence loading or unloading, using signallight system. Pushes and pulls levers and pushes buttons to control rotary dumping equipment that clamps cars in place and tilts and jogs car to dump grain into receiving chute [CAR-DUMPER OPERATOR (beverage)]. Directs DUMPER (any industry) to open hopper doors on railroad cars and presses button to start conveyor that elevates grain to weigh station. Directs workers to position spout into railroad cars for loading of grain, signals weigher to commence loading, and observes signal lights to detect when specified amount of grain has been loaded. May drive tractor to pull railroad cars onto side tracks. Performs other duties as described under SUPERVISOR (any industry) Master Title.
GOE: 05.12.01 STRENGTH: L GED: R3 M2 L2 SVP: 4 DLU: 77

921.133-010 CRANE-CREW SUPERVISOR (any industry)
Supervises and coordinates activities of OVERHEAD CRANE OPERATOR (any industry) 921.663-010 engaged in unloading steel, machinery, timbers, and other heavy cargo from trucks or railway cars at construction site or yard of industrial establishment. Performs duties as described under SUPERVISOR (any industry) Master Title.
GOE: 05.11.04 STRENGTH: L GED: R4 M2 L3 SVP: 7 DLU: 77

921.133-014 LOAD-OUT SUPERVISOR (mine & quarry)
Supervises and coordinates activities of workers engaged in operating machines and equipment to separate sand and gravel according to size, and in testing, stockpiling, and loading sand and gravel into railroad cars and trucks: Reviews car loading orders and issues directions to workers to expedite railroad car and truck loading. Notifies CAR CLEANER (mine & quarry) and YARD ENGINEER (r.r. trans.) to clean and position specified railcars for loading. Determines causes of malfunctioning equipment and notifies MAINTENANCE-MECHANIC SUPERVISOR (any industry). Orders changes in ratio of material, according to test results, to conform to plant or customer specifications. Coordinates changes in plant setup to maintain production specifications. Collects railroad car loading records at specified intervals and submits records to office. Maintains record of vibrating screen setup in plant. Trains new workers. May make minor repairs to machinery and equipment, using handtools. Performs other duties as described under SUPERVISOR (any industry) Master Title.
GOE: 05.12.01 STRENGTH: M GED: R3 M2 L3 SVP: 4 DLU: 77

921.133-018 MATERIAL-HANDLING SUPERVISOR (any industry) alternate titles: stock supervisor; traffic supervisor; warehouse supervisor
Supervises and coordinates activities of workers engaged in lifting, transporting, storing, and loading materials and products by use of conveyors, cranes, hoists, or industrial trucks, applying knowledge of plant layout and material-handling equipment and procedures: Studies receiving or shipping notices, requests for movement of raw materials and finished products, and reports of warehousing space available to develop schedule for material handling activities. May confer with supervisors of other departments to coordinate flow of materials or products. May verify or prepare records, such as routing slips, material requisitions, and job orders. May supervise activities of shipping and receiving personnel. May train new workers. Performs duties as described under SUPERVISOR (any industry) Master Title.
GOE: 05.12.01 STRENGTH: L GED: R4 M2 L3 SVP: 7 DLU: 77

921.137-010 COAL-YARD SUPERVISOR (any industry) alternate titles: coal-and-ash supervisor; millroom supervisor; supervisor, coal handling
Supervises and coordinates activities of workers engaged in receiving, weighing, and unloading coal in yard of industrial plant, in unloading coal from barges into coal hoppers, and in blending, pulverizing, and conveying coal to various processing units or storage areas. May supervise loading of ashes. May supervise unloading of coal from boats and be designated Supervisor, Dock (steel & rel.). Performs duties as described under SUPERVISOR (any industry) Master Title.
GOE: 05.12.01 STRENGTH: L GED: R4 M3 L3 SVP: 8 DLU: 77

921.137-014 MATERIAL-CREW SUPERVISOR (construction; mfd. bldgs.) alternate titles: supervisor, loading
Supervises and coordinates activities of workers engaged in loading materials or prefabricated house components for use on construction projects: Selects materials to be loaded according to size and type specified in orders, and specifies sequence of loading. Directs workers in loading and unloading materials on trucks, dinkey cars, or barges, attaching slings and other lifting devices to facilitate handling with cranes. Performs other duties as described under SUPERVISOR (any industry) Master Title.
GOE: 05.11.04 STRENGTH: M GED: R4 M2 L3 SVP: 7 DLU: 77

921.260-010 RIGGER (any industry) alternate titles: crane rigger; hook tender; slinger; yard rigger
Assembles rigging to lift and move equipment or material in manufacturing plant, shipyard, or on construction project: Selects cables, ropes, pulleys, winches, blocks, and sheaves, according to weight and size of load to be moved. Attaches pulley and blocks to fixed overhead structures, such as beams, ceilings, and gin pole booms, with bolts and clamps. Attaches load with grappling devices, such as loops, wires, ropes, and chains, to crane hook. Gives directions to OVERHEAD CRANE OPERATOR (any industry) 921.663-010 or HOISTING ENGINEER (any industry) engaged in hoisting and moving loads to en-

sure safety of workers and material handled, using hand signals, loudspeaker, or telephone. Sets up, braces, and rigs hoisting equipment, using handtools and power wrenches. Splices rope and wire cables to make or repair slings and tackle. May direct workers engaged in hoisting of machinery and equipment into ships and be designated Machinery Erector (ship-boat mfg.). When hoisting and moving construction machinery onto truck beds, may be designated Machine Mover (construction).
GOE: 05.11.04 STRENGTH: H GED: R4 M2 L2 SVP: 6 DLU: 77

921.364-010 RIGGING SLINGER (logging)
Directs CHOKE SETTERS (logging) in *high lead,* slack line, or similar log yarding system: Determines sequence of logs to be yarded, according to guidelines established by HOOK TENDER (logging). Issues directions to crew regarding logs to be yarded, positioning and securing of *chokers,* and position of crew during movement of logs. Signals YARDING ENGINEER (logging) to control positioning of choker cables for setting and yarding of logs over cutting area, using portable radio transmitter. Signals to inform others of fire, injuries, need for repairs or revisions to rigging, and other conditions. Trains new workers in choker setting techniques, safety practices, and whistle signals. May perform choker setting duties. May lead workers in installing, moving, and dismantling yarder rigging.
GOE: 05.12.04 STRENGTH: M GED: R3 M1 L2 SVP: 5 DLU: 77

921.365-010 GRAIN RECEIVER (grain-feed mills) alternate titles: elevator tender
Tends conveyors and weighs carload shipments of grain, such as corn or milo, and routes grain to steep tanks: Weighs car spotted on scales to record and verify weight against consignment sheet. Notifies MATERIAL HANDLER (any industry) that car is ready for unloading. Weighs empty car. Starts conveyor to move grain from unloading pit to elevator. Sets batching scale at specified weight and starts conveyor that transfers grain to scale bin until balance is achieved. When notified, pulls lever to empty bin and starts conveyor to transfer grain to steep tanks. Maintains batch records.
GOE: 06.03.01 STRENGTH: L GED: R2 M2 L1 SVP: 2 DLU: 77

921.382-010 CONVEYOR OPERATOR, PNEUMATIC SYSTEM (food prep., nec) alternate titles: bulk-system operator; flour distributor; pneumatic-systems operator
Operates panelboard to control pneumatic conveyor system that transfers flour from railroad cars, through blending, sifting, and weighing units to storage bins for subsequent processing into macaroni products: Opens hatch of railroad hopper car to admit air, and connects pneumatic hose to car outlet and to intake pipe of specified bin. Sets timing devices, turns switches, and pushes buttons on panelboard to start and control movement of material through specified processing units to storage bins. Observes lights on board to follow progress of material, or to detect need for changing or bypassing operations. Diverts material flow by pressing button governing specific bin or processing unit. Records car number, weight, and type of material in car, name of sender, and location of material in storage bin or unit. Operates pneumatic air compressor [AIR-COMPRESSOR OPERATOR (any industry)] in conjunction with panelboard, to transfer and distribute flour. May dump bags of special flour into hopper for distribution through processing units.
GOE: 05.06.04 STRENGTH: L GED: R3 M2 L2 SVP: 4 DLU: 77

921.563-010 COKE LOADER (steel & rel.)
Operates equipment, such as conveyor or winch to transfer coke to railroad cars and trucks: Notifies switching department to deliver specified type of car. Estimates and records amount of coke in bins. Starts conveyor and operates winch to position car under boom-conveyor for loading. Inspects boarding and locking of open-top box cars and wedging of side drop and hopper cars to prevent loss of coke in transit. Observes and records car number, carrier, customer, tonnage, and grade and condition of coke. Signals INDUSTRIAL-LOCOMOTIVE OPERATOR (any industry) to move loaded cars. Oils, lubricates, and adjusts conveyors, crushers, and other equipment, using handtools and lubricating equipment. Cleans spillage from tracks, walks, driveways, and conveyor decking, using airhose, broom, and shovel. Cleans hoppers, using bar.
GOE: 05.11.04 STRENGTH: M GED: R3 M2 L2 SVP: 5 DLU: 77

921.565-010 CEMENT LOADER (cement) alternate titles: bulk cement loader; bulk loader
Tends pneumatic conveyor, or belt, auger, or bucket conveyor to load and unload bulk cement onto tank trucks or railroad tank and hopper cars: Inserts loading nozzle in opening on tank trucks. Starts pump and turns lever to open slide on storage bins. Observes weight indicator on scale and regulates speed of feed to fill tank in truck. Records weight on sales slip. Tends winch to position railroad tank cars under loading nozzles. Inserts nozzles in loading ports of car and turns on pump to feed in cement. Records weight loaded on manifest. May tend equipment that inserts flexible pipe into railroad tank and hopper cars and tank trucks. May bag cement [PACKAGER, MACHINE (any industry)]. May be designated according to vehicle loaded as Cement-Railroad-Car Loader (cement); Cement-Truck Loader (cement).
GOE: 06.04.40 STRENGTH: H GED: R2 M1 L1 SVP: 2 DLU: 77

921.583-010 TRANSFER-CAR OPERATOR, DRIER (nonmet. min.) alternate titles: drier unloader
Operates transfer car to move carloads of pipe and boiler covering moldings from driers to work and storage areas: Presses button to raise door of drier. Pulls and pushes carloads of moldings along track out of drier to loading plat-

form. Weighs moldings for moisture content and compares weight to wall chart. Places wet moldings onto car to be returned to drier. Pushes car of dry moldings onto transfer car. Operates transfer car to move moldings to production departments or storage. Records identification number of each car removed from each drier on production sheet. May tend machine that automatically cuts boiler moldings to specified size and packages moldings.
GOE: 05.11.04 STRENGTH: H GED: R2 M1 L1 SVP: 2 DLU: 77

921.662-010 CAR-DUMPER OPERATOR (beverage) alternate titles: car unloader; dumper
Controls equipment that tilts railroad cars to dump grain into receiving hopper for transfer to storage elevator: Pulls lever to activate clamp that fastens car into position on dumping platform. Breaks car seal and pushes open sliding door. Starts conveyor leading from receiving hopper into elevator, and energizes electromagnet which removes metal from grain. Receives signals, and pushes and pulls levers of dumping machinery in sequence to tilt and jog car until car is empty. Returns car to upright position and releases holding mechanism. May remove wood and paper falling from tipped car, using grappling hooks. May guide grain from car, using wood or metal plank. May pull box cars onto and off of dumping platform, using winch and cable.
GOE: 05.11.04 STRENGTH: L GED: R3 M1 L1 SVP: 4 DLU: 77

921.662-014 CHARGE-MACHINE OPERATOR (chemical)
Operates machine to recharge nuclear reactor in nuclear plant: Reads work orders and confers with supervisor to determine reactor tube loading sequence. Reads thermometer to ensure that water temperature is at level specified for charging operation. Pushes button to raise charge-discharge machine to specified height for removal of loaded *monotubes* from wall-storage racks. Turns levers to position machine in horizontal alignment with specified wall rack, and moves transfer-arm controls to remove tubes from rack. Pushes buttons to move charging machine and align serially-numbered monotube with specifically-numbered reactor-wall opening. Activates charging machine pump to force water into monotube and push piston forward to fill reactor tube with fuel elements and to clear irradiated elements out of reactor.
GOE: 06.02.11 STRENGTH: L GED: R3 M2 L3 SVP: 5 DLU: 77

921.662-018 CONVEYOR-SYSTEM OPERATOR (any industry) alternate titles: conveyor console operator
Operates console to control automated conveyor system that receives, sorts, distributes, and conveys bulk or packaged materials or products to and from loading dock and storage area, and between departments or processes: Reads production and delivery schedules and confers with supervisor to determine sorting and routing procedures. Presses buttons and turns dials to start conveyor system and regulate speed of conveyors. Observes materials or products moving on conveyors, or observes lights on control panel to monitor flow and operation of system. Moves switches or pushes buttons to route order to designated areas and to raise, lower, and align conveyor with specific adjoining conveyors. Contacts work stations by telephone or intercom to request movement of order or to notify work stations of shipment enroute and approximate delivery time. Stops equipment and clears jams, using handtools. Observes operation to detect equipment malfunction and informs supervisor when malfunction occurs. May operate elevator system in conjunction with conveyor system. May weigh trucks and railroad cars before and after loading, or read scale that continually weighs product on conveyor to ascertain when specified tonnage has been loaded and record weight on loading ticket. May join sections of conveyor frames at temporary working areas and connect power units. May collect samples of materials for analysis. May lubricate moving parts of conveyors. May operate scoop to load materials onto conveyor. May record data, such as weight and type of material moved and condition of equipment. May be designated according to product moved as Bulk-Loader Operator (water trans.); Coal-Conveyor Operator (any industry); Grain Distributor (grain-feed mills); or according to type of equipment as Grain-Elevator Operator (grain-feed mills); Screen Operator (cement); Suction Operator (agriculture).
GOE: 05.12.04 STRENGTH: M GED: R3 M2 L2 SVP: 3 DLU: 82

921.662-022 MARINE RAILWAY OPERATOR (ship-boat mfg.) alternate titles: ways operator
Operates power-driven winches to pull boats, yachts, and barges from water to repair or reconditioning areas: Attaches cables to dolly on marine railway and pulls lever on winch to lower dolly into water. Signals boat operator to align boat to dolly. Positions block under boat for support and pulls winch lever to haul boat from water to specified area. May repair winch and hauling equipment.
GOE: 05.11.04 STRENGTH: H GED: R3 M2 L2 SVP: 4 DLU: 77

921.662-026 TIPPLE OPERATOR (saw. & plan.)
Operates tipple chain conveyor to move presorted lumber from holding racks to stacking platform: Moves control buttons to align tipple with holding racks which hold lumber requested. Pulls levers to release stops at ends of holding racks, allowing lumber to move down to tipple conveyor chain which transfers lumber to stacking platform. Straightens lumber as it moves on conveyor to prevent jams.
GOE: 05.12.04 STRENGTH: M GED: R2 M1 L1 SVP: 3 DLU: 77

921.663-010 OVERHEAD CRANE OPERATOR (any industry) alternate titles: crane operator, cab; crane operator, ground control; traveling-crane operator
Operates traveling or stationary overhead crane (cab- or ground controlled) to lift, move, and position loads, such as machinery, equipment, products, and

solid or bulk materials, using hoisting attachments, such as hook, sling, electromagnet, or bucket: Observes load hookup and determines safety of load. Manipulates or depresses crane controls, such as pedals, levers, and buttons, to regulate speed and direction of crane and hoist movement according to written, verbal, or signal instructions. Cleans and maintains crane and hoisting mechanism. Inspects crane for defective parts and notifies supervisor of defects or malfunctions. May attach load to hook or other crane accessory prior to operating crane and be designated Crane Operator-Hooker (steel & rel.) or Crane Operator-Hooktender (aircraft mfg.). May be designated by type of crane operated or material handled as Bridge Crane Operator (any industry); Charging Crane Operator (foundry; steel & rel.); Cinder Crane Operator (foundry; steel & rel.) I; Gantry Crane Operator (any industry); Hot-Metal Crane Operator (foundry; nonfer. metal; steel & rel.) I; Ingot Stripper (steel & rel.) I; Scrap Crane Operator (steel & rel.) I; Tower Whirler Operator (any industry); Wall Crane Operator (foundry).
GOE: 05.11.04 STRENGTH: L GED: R3 M2 L2 SVP: 5 DLU: 87

921.663-014 CHERRY-PICKER OPERATOR (construction) alternate titles: car changer
Operates cherry picker (pneumatic hoist attached to structural framework) which moves on rails along tunnel side to hoist loaded dinkey cars from mucking machine to front of train: Hooks hoist line into lift-hooks on dinkey car. Moves lever to activate pneumatic hoist that lifts car. Pushes hoist block and signals DINKEY OPERATOR (any industry) to move train to position empty car at mucking machine. Pushes hoisting frame along rails to front of train and operates hoist to place car in position on rails.
GOE: 05.11.01 STRENGTH: M GED: R2 M1 L1 SVP: 3 DLU: 77

921.663-018 CHIP UNLOADER (paper & pulp)
Unloads wood chips from railroad cars or trucks, using materials-handling equipment: Drives rail-mounted trackmobile to spot railroad cars on scale and on ramp above chip storage bins for unloading. Records gross and net weight of car. Releases bottom doors of car, allowing chips to fall into bin. Starts conveyor that carries chips to stockpile or to inside storage bins [CHIP-BIN CONVEYOR TENDER (chemical; paper & pulp)]. Gathers sample of chips from each car for analysis. Shunts empty cars to spur tracks. Signals driver to position truck for unloading. Attaches hoist cable and hook and starts hoist to lift loaded trailer from tractor bed. Opens tailgate of trailer, allowing wood chips to fall into bin. Lowers trailer onto tractor bed and secures tailgate. May attach electric vibrator to side of railroad cars to dislodge chips that have become tightly packed in transit. May unload barges.
GOE: 05.11.04 STRENGTH: M GED: R2 M1 L1 SVP: 3 DLU: 77

921.663-022 DERRICK OPERATOR (any industry) alternate titles: crane operator
Operates electric-, diesel-, gasoline-, or steam-powered guy-derrick or stiff-leg derrick (mast supported by fixed legs or tripod), to move products, equipment, or materials to and from quarries, storage areas, and processes, or to load and unload trucks or railroad cars: Pushes and pulls levers and depresses pedals to raise, lower, and rotate boom and to raise and lower load line in response to signals. May inspect and lubricate cables, pulleys, guides, and drums. May be known according to material moved as Log-Yard Derrick Operator (saw. & plan.); or equipment controlled as Stiff-Leg Derrick Operator (wood prod., nec).
GOE: 05.11.04 STRENGTH: M GED: R3 M1 L1 SVP: 4 DLU: 77

921.663-026 HOIST OPERATOR (mine & quarry)
Controls hoisting machinery to raise and lower cages (elevators), skips (boxlike containers), and mine cars at mines or quarries: Moves levers and pedals to operate hoist in response to arm, bell, or buzzer signals. Observes dial indicator and marks on cable or drum to ascertain that desired position has been reached. Applies hand or foot brake and moves lever to lock hoist. Inspects, lubricates, and adjusts brakes and equipment. May be designated according to type of machinery controlled as Chain-Hoist Operator (mine & quarry); Electric-Hoist Operator (mine & quarry); Steam-Hoist Operator (mine & quarry); Tugger Operator (mine & quarry); or according to location of machinery as Slope-Hoist Operator (mine & quarry); Tower-Hoist Operator (mine & quarry).
GOE: 05.11.02 STRENGTH: M GED: R3 M1 L2 SVP: 4 DLU: 77

921.663-030 HOISTING ENGINEER (any industry) alternate titles: hoisting-machine operator
Operates compressed air, diesel, electric, gasoline, or steam drum hoists to control movement of cableways, cages, derricks, draglines, loaders, railcars, or skips to move workers and materials for construction, logging, mining, sawmill, and other industrial operations: Starts hoist engine and moves hand and foot levers to wind or unwind cable on drum. Moves brake lever and throttle to stop, start, and regulate speed of drum in response to hand, bell, telephone, loud-speaker, or whistle signals or by observing dial indicator or marks on cable. May fire boiler on steam hoist. May operate hoist with more than one drum. May repair, maintain, and adjust equipment. May be designated according to equipment controlled as Cableway Operator (any industry); Cage Operator (any industry); Gin-Pole Operator (construction); Inclined-Railway Operator (any industry); Skip-Hoist Operator (any industry). May transfer logs from trucks to railroad cars and be designated Transfer Engineer (logging).
GOE: 05.11.04 STRENGTH: M GED: R3 M1 L1 SVP: 4 DLU: 77

921.663-034 IRRADIATED-FUEL HANDLER (chemical)
Operates machines and equipment to package, store, and convey irradiated fuel elements in underwater storage basin of nuclear reactor plant: Operates

crane to pull tram cars along underwater track and position cars under discharge outlets of nuclear reactor to be loaded with irradiated fuel elements. Pulls loaded tram cars from discharge outlets to mechanism that automatically tilts cars to unload irradiated elements onto underwater table. Manipulates handgrips of mechanical arms to place fuel elements into baskets and operates crane to transfer baskets to prepackaging storage area. Moves specified baskets from prepackaging storage area to packaging area and unloads baskets of irradiated elements onto packaging machine that automatically inserts fuel elements into canisters and secures lids on canisters. Operates crane to transfer loaded canisters to two-year, underwater, storage cubicles. Records number of canisters in each cubicle. Operates crane to remove specified canisters from storage, transfer canisters to lead cask, raise lead shipping cask to surface, and load cask onto railroad car for shipment.
GOE: 05.11.04 STRENGTH: M GED: R3 M1 L1 SVP: 5 DLU: 77

921.663-038 LOCOMOTIVE-CRANE OPERATOR (any industry) alternate titles: railroad-crane operator
Operates crane that travels on railroad tracks to lift and move objects: Starts gasoline or diesel engine. Pushes pedals and pulls levers to move, control speed, and stop crane, turn crane boom, and raise or lower cables attached to load. Inspects and compares weight of load with lifting capacity of crane to ensure against overloading crane. Moves controls to move and position load by sight or at direction of LABORER, HOISTING (any industry). Inspects cables and grappling devices for wear. May install or replace cables. May perform maintenance tasks, such as oiling machine. May direct helpers engaged in placing blocking and outrigging under crane when lifting loads. May operate crane in which hoisting mechanism is pneumatically powered. May be designated by type of power unit as Diesel-Locomotive-Crane Operator (any industry); Electric-Locomotive-Crane Operator (any industry); Gasoline-Locomotive-Crane Operator (any industry).
GOE: 05.11.04 STRENGTH: M GED: R3 M1 L2 SVP: 5 DLU: 77

921.663-042 MONORAIL CRANE OPERATOR (any industry)
Operates electrically powered monorail crane to lift, move, and load machinery, equipment, and materials: Moves foot and hand controls to guide crane along overhead rail and to raise and lower load cable. Raises, moves, and lowers load following signals of worker on floor. May switch crane between rails by signaling other workers to throw switches. May operate crane from hand held control box. May inspect, clean, and lubricate crane. May be designated by material moved as Acid-Crane Operator (steel & rel.); Cinder-Crane Operator (foundry; steel & rel.) II; Scrap-Crane Operator (steel & rel.) II; Stock-Crane Operator (steel & rel.); or operation performed as Charging-Crane Operator (foundry; steel & rel.) II; Cold-Roll Packer, Sheet Iron (steel & rel.); Hot-Metal-Crane Operator (foundry; smelt. & refin.; steel & rel.) II; Ingot Stripper (steel & rel.) II.
GOE: 06.04.40 STRENGTH: L GED: R2 M1 L1 SVP: 3 DLU: 77

921.663-046 PNEUMATIC-HOIST OPERATOR (construction; mfd. bldgs.)
Operates pneumatic hoist to lift concrete panel walls of modular buildings: Hauls concrete wall panels to installation site, using handtruck. Lifts panel with aid of coworker to position panel for hoist hookup. Positions hoisting bracket on panel to align holes in panel and bracket, and inserts locking pin to secure linkage for hoisting. Pulls chain to activate hoist to raise panel for lateral movement. Operates hoist to raise and lower panel between grooved columns as signaled by coworkers. Removes any rough spots from panel or grooves, using hammer and chisel. Disconnects hoisting bracket from panel.
GOE: 05.11.01 STRENGTH: V GED: R2 M1 L1 SVP: 3 DLU: 77

921.663-050 SCRAPER-LOADER OPERATOR (mine & quarry) alternate titles: dragger; slusher operator
Operates hoisting engine and cable-drawn scraper or scoop, to load coal, ore, or rock into mine cars or onto conveyor in underground mine: Moves hoist into working place on car and sets up on timber foundation. Sets up snatch blocks (pulleys) and eyebolt, and anchors firmly to post or wall. Connects electric power lines and starts hoist. Moves levers to activate cable which drags scraper into face of ore, then drags full scraper to mine car for dumping. Moves hoist from place to place, using mine car. Lubricates, adjusts, and repairs engine and auxiliary equipment.
GOE: 05.11.02 STRENGTH: H GED: R3 M1 L2 SVP: 4 DLU: 77

921.663-054 TOWER-CRANE OPERATOR (construction)
Operates tower crane to lift and move building materials from ground storage areas and trucks to top of building under construction: Climbs ladder inside vertically mounted tower to gain access to control pad suspended under crane boom. Pushes or pulls levers on control console to rotate counter-balanced horizontally mounted boom to extend or retract trolley along boom, and to raise and lower hook to which loads are attached. Controls crane movement in response to hand signals or radio commands by supervisor or signaler. May operate crane from remote console on top of building. May operate radio-controlled crane.
GOE: 05.11.01 STRENGTH: L GED: R3 M1 L2 SVP: 5 DLU: 77

921.663-058 TRACTOR-CRANE OPERATOR (any industry) alternate titles: crawler-crane operator; tractor-crane engineer
Operates diesel-, gasoline-, or electric-powered crane mounted on crawler treads to lift and move material and objects: Starts engine and drives crane to work site, steering crane by moving levers and pressing pedals that control motion of crawler treads. Pushes and pulls levers and presses pedals in response to hand signals to rotate crane on chassis and raise and lower crane boom and loadline. May lubricate motor and moving parts of crane. May be designated according to attachment as Clamshell Operator (any industry) I; Demolition-Crane Operator (any industry) I; Electromagnet-Crane Operator (any industry) I; Orange-Peel Operator (any industry) I.
GOE: 05.11.04 STRENGTH: M GED: R3 M1 L1 SVP: 4 DLU: 77

921.663-062 TRUCK-CRANE OPERATOR (any industry) alternate titles: mobile-crane operator
Operates gasoline- or diesel-powered crane mounted on specially constructed truck chassis to lift and move materials and objects: Drives truck to work site and directs activities of LABORER, HOISTING (any industry) in placing blocks and outriggers to prevent capsizing when lifting heavy loads. Starts crane engine. Moves levers and pedals to rotate crane on chassis, to raise and lower crane boom, and to raise and lower loadline. May operate crane according to signals from helper. May bolt boom sections together to extend or modify boom for pile driving or high lifting. May be designated according to type of power used as Diesel-Truck-Crane Operator (any industry); Gasoline-Truck-Crane Operator (any industry); or according to attachment as Clamshell Operator (any industry) II; Demolition-Crane Operator (any industry) II; Electromagnet-Crane Operator (any industry) II; Orange-Peel Operator (any industry) II.
GOE: 05.11.04 STRENGTH: M GED: R3 M1 L1 SVP: 5 DLU: 77

921.663-066 YARDING ENGINEER (logging) alternate titles: yarder operator
Operates yarding machine to pull logs from cutting area to landing: Controls direction, speed, and braking of cable drums to position *chokers* or grapples over logs, pull logs across cutting area, lift logs over tree trunks and other obstructions, and position logs for loading onto trucks, using pedals and hand levers in response to whistle or horn code signals. May drag blocks, cable, and other equipment to rigging crew. May raise steel tower, or prerigged spar, and tension guy lines. May drive self-propelled yarder between yarding sites. May be designated according to type of yarding system used as High-Lead Yarder (logging); Sky-Line Yarder (logging); Slack-Line Yarder (logging); or according to type of equipment operated as Grapple-Yarder Operator (logging); Steel-Spar Operator (logging); Triple-Drum Operator (logging). May control machinery on deck of pullboat in cypress forest and be designated Pullboat Engineer (logging).
GOE: 05.11.04 STRENGTH: L GED: R3 M1 L2 SVP: 6 DLU: 77

921.663-070 TRUCK LOADER, OVERHEAD CRANE (nonfer. metal)
Operates overhead crane with hand held control box to load trucks with bundles of aluminum extrusions: Reviews daily truck-delivery schedules to determine information, such as description of orders, sequence of deliveries, and special loading instructions. Weighs bundles, using floor scale, and records weight for company records. Attaches hook or sling of crane to bundles, and presses buttons on control box to hoist and move bundles to loading area or onto trucks, according to unloading sequence. Inspects bundle packaging for conformance to customer requirements. Removes and batches packing tickets. Occasionally loads, restacks, or unloads bundles from trucks by hand or using industrial truck. Directs truck drivers backing vehicles into loading bays and uncovers, covers, and secures loads for delivery.
GOE: 05.11.04 STRENGTH: M GED: R2 M1 L2 SVP: 4 DLU: 86

921.664-010 LINE MOVER (railroad equip.)
Spots railroad cars and railroad-car-truck assemblies on production lines for further processing in locomotive and car building establishment using one of following methods: (1) Attaches one end of push-pole against tractor and other end against assemblies on rails. Signals TRACTOR OPERATOR (any industry) vocally or by hand to push car or car-trucks on rails to specified location. (2) Attaches chain and clevises to assemblies and tractor and signals operator to pull assemblies to specified location.
GOE: 05.12.04 STRENGTH: M GED: R3 M1 L1 SVP: 3 DLU: 77

921.664-014 RIGGER (logging) alternate titles: second rigger
Installs blocks and guy lines for *high lead*, slack line, or similar log yarding system: Cuts notch around anchor stumps specified by HOOK TENDER (logging), using chain saw and ax. Wraps cable around stump and secures it in position with spikes and U-bolts. Installs block, pulls winch cable through block, and secures cable to yarding blocks and guy lines. Signals winch operator to haul yarding blocks and guy lines to anchor stumps, and secures them to anchor stumps. Splices cable to make rigging parts or repair broken or worn cable, using marlin spikes, vise, hammer, and wire cutters. Dismantles yarding system and loads rigging onto trucks for removal to new yarding site. May install yarding cables, *choker* cables, cable swivels, carriages, and related rigging. May rig and erect wooden spars. May climb wooden spars, using climbing spurs and safety rope, to install or repair rigging. May lead activities of crew and be designated Head Rigger (logging).
GOE: 05.12.04 STRENGTH: V GED: R3 M2 L2 SVP: 5 DLU: 77

921.665-010 CEMENT-BOAT-AND-BARGE LOADER (cement)
Tends pipeline system that conveys dry cement from storage silos to ships and barges at cement plant loading dock: Screws flexible hose to dock pipeline and inserts and secures hose to loading port of ship or barge. Ties lines to hose to support hose during loading operation. Turns handwheels to open or close valves and route cement from designated silos through pumps and to vessel,

according to loading orders. Signals SILO TENDER (cement) to start and stop pumps. Monitors movement of cement through pipelines and tightens couplings or repairs loose connections, using handtools. Observes movement of tide, vessel, and hose hookup in relation to pier, and adjusts ship mooring and hose support lines to ensure continuous and safe operation. Observes cargo hold of vessel to determine completion of loading. Disassembles ship-to-shore hookup, and cleans pipes, hoses, and fittings.
GOE: 05.12.06 STRENGTH: V GED: R2 M1 L1 SVP: 2 DLU: 77

921.667-010 BOAT-HOIST-OPERATOR HELPER (retail trade)
Assists BOAT-HOIST OPERATOR (retail trade) to move, lift, and lower yachts and cruisers into and out of water and performs related job tasks: Guides hoist operator by hand and voice signals to maneuver wheeled hoist around obstructions and into loading position above boat. Positions and connects hoist slings for lifting boats. Signals hoist operator to lift or lower boat and guides hoist operator to safely maneuver suspended boat to launching slip, display area, or repair shop. Manually steadies boat as vessel is raised from or lowered into water to prevent bumping into pilings. Positions keel and hull support blocks to support boat being lowered to ground or onto skid. Disconnects and stows slings. Directs stream of water under high pressure from hose against exterior of boat to clean hull of silt, mud, and marine growth. Sands boat surfaces by hand in preparation for painting. Paints boat bottoms, using brush. Assists in mechanical servicing and repairing of boats. Assists other workers in boat repair facility.
GOE: 05.12.04 STRENGTH: H GED: R1 M1 L1 SVP: 2 DLU: 77

921.667-014 CHASER (logging)
Directs placement of logs brought to landing by *high lead* rig or tractor and unhooks *chokers* from logs: Hand signals YARDING ENGINEER (logging) or LOGGING-TRACTOR OPERATOR (forestry; logging; saw. & plan.) where to drop logs on landing for reloading onto logging trucks. Pulls end of choker from bell (sliding fastener) on choker cable to open noose. Signals operator to pull choker free of logs. Cuts knots and limbs from logs, using ax and chain saw. Attaches equipment, such as chokers, lines, blocks, and fire equipment, to outbound rigging as indicated by whistle signals from RIGGING SLINGER (logging). May mark logs [LOG MARKER (logging)]. May be designated Cat Chaser (logging) in tractor logging operations or Water Chaser (logging) when working on floating logs.
GOE: 05.12.04 STRENGTH: H GED: R2 M1 L1 SVP: 3 DLU: 77

921.667-018 DUMPER (any industry) alternate titles: bulk loader
Dumps materials, such as coal, chemicals, flue dust, grain, ore, sugar, and salt, into and from railway cars, trucks, or other vehicles, according to specific instructions: Positions and blocks vehicles by signaling LOCOMOTIVE ENGINEER (r.r. trans.) 910.363-014 or TRUCK DRIVER, HEAVY (any industry) 905.663-014, or by using winch and car jack or powered tractor to spot cars and set brakes. Positions spout, chute, and conveyor over or into car, truck, bin, or storage pile and opens slide in spout or chute to start flow of material into or from vehicles. Positions vehicle over storage bin and opens air valve, side door, or car hopper door, starts conveyors, pneumatic conveyors, or elevators, and adjusts dampers to feed materials to specified bin. May use power scoop to pull grain from car into receiving chute. May collect grain sample, using probe. May drive truck onto ramp, secure it with blocks, and attach hook from electric hoist to front end of trailer or truck and push button to activate hoist or move lever of hydraulic lift to elevate front end of truck as tailgate is opened to dump material. May vibrate hopper to facilitate flow into slurry pit, using airhammer. May open solvent tank valve and start pump to wash and transfer residue of materials to saturator and other tanks. May observe pressure gauges and adjust valves to maintain specified pumping pressure. May record car identifying information, such as weight and volume of material loaded and number of cars dumped or filled. May be designated according to kind of vehicle unloaded as Car Dumper (any industry); according to kind of material unloaded as Grain Unloader (grain-feed mills); or according to type of equipment used as Spout Positioner (any industry); Wincher (any industry).
GOE: 05.12.03 STRENGTH: H GED: R2 M1 L1 SVP: 2 DLU: 82

921.667-022 LABORER, HOISTING (any industry) alternate titles: crane follower; crane hooker; hitcher; hooker; oiler; signaler
Assists workers engaged in operating derricks, cranes, power shovels, or other hoisting machines used to lift and move machinery, equipment, or materials, such as concrete, castings, structural steel, stone slabs, mill rolls, scrap metal, pipe, dirt, and logs, performing any combination of following duties: Couples and uncouples railroad cars and throws railroad track switches. Affixes hook, bucket, electromagnet, or demolition ball to crane; or affixes rope, cable, chain, sling, or other grappling equipment or attachments to object being lifted or to lifting mechanism. Places blocking, out-riggers, or screw-jacks in position to hold crane or shovel upright when lifting heavy loads. Places supports in position to receive load. Signals operator, vocally or with hand signals, to guide operator in lifting and moving loads when view from crane or shovel cab is obstructed. Pushes or pulls load as it is lowered, until it is deposited in desired place. Secures load to trucks or railcars, using ropes, chains, or bands. Lubricates moving parts of crane or shovel with grease gun or oilcan. May install extension sections to boom, using pins and cotter keys, or nuts and bolts. May lay track or timber runways on which tread-wheeled machines move. May drive truck-mounted crane from one work location to another. May be designated according to equipment used, attachments made, or area worked in as Concrete-Bucket Hooker (construction); Floor Worker, Transfer Bay (nonfer. metal); Lo-

comotive-Crane-Operator Helper (any industry); Log Hooker (millwork-plywood; saw. & plan.); Magnet Placer (steel & rel.); Pit-Worker, Power Shovel (any industry); Power-Shovel-Operator Helper (any industry); Truck-Crane-Operator Helper (any industry) Master Title. Performs other duties as described under HELPER (any industry) Master Title.
GOE: 05.12.04 STRENGTH: M GED: R2 M1 L1 SVP: 3 DLU: 78

921.667-026 WHARF WORKER (water trans.)
Moves grain spouts to load grain into holds of ships: Unlashes grain spout, and lowers, raises, and changes direction of spout to test operation of guide ropes and hand winches. Lowers spout into hold of ship and directs spout toward specified compartment. Signals CONVEYOR-SYSTEM OPERATOR (any industry) to start flow of grain. Moves spout in various directions to load grain evenly into compartment.
GOE: 05.12.03 STRENGTH: M GED: R1 M1 L1 SVP: 2 DLU: 77

921.682-010 LOADER, MALT HOUSE (beverage) alternate titles: kiln loader; malt loader
Controls equipment to transfer steeped or malted barley to or from germinating compartments or drying kilns in malt house: Presses switch to position overhead spout under chute, and pulls handle to open chute and dump barley onto compartment or kiln floor. Lifts and removes compartment door to permit entrance of power shovel, using winch. Moves levers and presses pedals of power shovel to transfer malted barley from compartment onto conveyor. Climbs ladder into compartment to clean interior, using scraper, shovel, and high-pressure water hose.
GOE: 05.12.04 STRENGTH: M GED: R2 M1 L1 SVP: 3 DLU: 77

921.682-014 PALLETIZER OPERATOR I (any industry)
Operates console that controls automatic palletizing equipment to sort, transfer, and stack on pallets containers of finished products, such as sugar, canned vegetables, citrus juice, and cigarettes: Reads production and delivery schedules and stacking pattern to determine sorting and transfer procedures, arrangement of packages on pallet, and destination of loaded pallet. Observes packages moving along conveyor to identify packages and to detect defective packaging, and presses console buttons to deflect packages to predetermined accumulator or reject lines. Turns selector switch on palletizer to control stacking arrangement of packages on pallet and to transfer loaded pallet to storage or delivery platform. Supplies loading equipment with empty pallets. Stops equipment to clear jams. Informs supervisor of equipment malfunction. May keep record of production and equipment performance. May operate depalletizing equipment and be designated Depalletizer Operator (any industry).
GOE: 06.04.40 STRENGTH: L GED: R3 M1 L1 SVP: 4 DLU: 77

921.682-018 STACKER-AND-SORTER OPERATOR (saw. & plan.)
Operates machines to sort and stack lumber: Activates conveyor chain that positions lumber stack over hoist. Moves controls to lift hoist and slide single layers of lumber onto chains of sorting machine where boards drop into storage pockets according to length. Starts chain conveyor in bottom of pocket to transfer lumber onto powered rollers for machine stacking preparatory to kiln drying or shipping. Records number of pieces removed from storage, using mechanical hand counter.
GOE: 05.12.04 STRENGTH: M GED: R2 M1 L1 SVP: 3 DLU: 77

921.682-022 TRANSFER CONTROLLER (saw. & plan.) alternate titles: jump-roll operator; separator
Operates conveyor system in sawmill to route lumber, cants, and timber to processing operations according to size, grade, and specie, or type of processing required: Raises and lowers cross chains by moving levers and pedals to shift boards, timbers, or cants from one set of conveyor rolls to another or from rolls to platform. Raises stop blocks to stop lumber at specified points along rolls. Stops and reverses conveyors to re-route cants for further processing. May operate electric hoist to move cants to stockpile. May operate cut-off saw to cut cants to specified lengths.
GOE: 05.12.04 STRENGTH: M GED: R2 M1 L1 SVP: 3 DLU: 77

921.683-010 BOAT-HOIST OPERATOR (retail trade)
Operates mobile boat hoist to lift and lower yachts and cruisers in and out of water, and to move boats to designated storage areas: Starts hoist engine and pushes and pulls levers to move and maneuver four-wheeled boat hoist to straddle boats for moving. Passes sling ends under straddled boat hull, shackles sling ends to winch span, and moves levers to operate power-winch to raise boat clear of support blocks or skids. Drives hoist to move suspended boat to designated location or to hoisting dock to lower boat into water. Operates winch to lower boat to point just above ground surface. Places keel blocks under keel and lowers boat onto keel blocks. Slides and positions hull support blocks and frames against boat bottom for vertical support. Loosens and pulls slings from underneath boat. Drives hoist to dock and lowers boat until slings are slack and signals boat operator to back boat out to clear slings and dock. Operates winch to raise slings out of water or leaves slings in water to pick up another boat. Operates truck to tow empty skids around display or shop areas. Jacks up skids and cradled boats and places dollies under skids to facilitate moving boats in display area. Mounts propellers on shafts to prepare new boats for launching. Operates boats to maneuver boats in and out of slips. Performs related boat handling duties.
GOE: 05.11.04 STRENGTH: H GED: R3 M1 L1 SVP: 3 DLU: 77

921.683-014 BOOM-CONVEYOR OPERATOR (any industry) alternate titles: loader-head operator; stacker attendant
Controls boom conveyors to move materials, such as coal, ore, and gravel, to and from railroad cars or processing station, and storage piles: Starts speci-

fied boom conveyor and conveyor belts, and adjusts height, swing, and extension of boom according to size of storage pile or position of car. Opens side gates of railroad cars or gates of processing station to dump material onto conveyor that carries it to storage pile. Positions boom conveyor over railroad car and starts flow of materials from plant or storage pile to load car. Regulates conveyor speed to prevent spilling or weight variations among cars. Observes gauges and lights on control panel to detect malfunctions of conveyor system. Diverts materials to storage bins or notifies plant or tipple operator to stop supply of materials during emergency. Lubricates machine, using grease gun and oilcan. May drive mobile boom conveyor to designated work area. May be known as Stacker Operator (any industry).
GOE: 05.12.04 STRENGTH: L GED: R2 M1 L1 SVP: 3 DLU: 79

921.683-018 CANTILEVER-CRANE OPERATOR (water trans.) alternate titles: container crane operator
Operates electrically powered crane equipped with cantilevers (structural-steel framework which can be lowered to horizontal position and extended over deck or hold of vessel) on which hoisting gear is supported to load or unload container cargo from vessels: Moves controls or levers and presses pedals to activate electrical power, move tower in position alongside vessel, and lower cantilever over deck or hold of vessel. Moves controls to lower hoisting gear for attachment of sling to container, lift and move container along cantilever, and lower and position container on dock, or on vessel deck or hold. Raises cantilever to vertical position when positioning crane to avoid hitting superstructure of vessel. May follow hand signals of other worker. May operate cantilever crane equipped with clamshell to load or unload bulk materials.
GOE: 05.11.04 STRENGTH: L GED: R3 M2 L2 SVP: 5 DLU: 77

921.683-022 COAL-EQUIPMENT OPERATOR (utilities)
Operates locomotives and bulldozers and controls conveyor systems to transport and pile coal for use in boilers of generating plant: Operates locomotive to haul coal car over unloading bins. Pushes lever of car shaker or car turner to empty coal from car into bins. Starts and controls conveyor that transfers coal to and from bins, bunkers, and storage pile. Operates bulldozers and front-end loaders to shape and compact coal storage pile to minimize possibility of spontaneous combustion. Lubricates and adjusts conveyor systems, bulldozers, and other coal-moving equipment. May loosen frozen coal in gondolas, using steam hose or blowtorch. May collect coal samples for laboratory tests. May tend crusher that reduces size of coal. May operate tugboat to move and position barges for unloading. May read meters and record weight of coal in logbook.
GOE: 05.11.02 STRENGTH: M GED: R3 M2 L3 SVP: 4 DLU: 78

921.683-030 CUPOLA HOIST OPERATOR (foundry)
Operates skip hoist, using levers and foot brakes, to lift pig iron, coke, and limestone to top of cupola furnace for CUPOLA CHARGER (foundry). Maintains and lubricates hoisting machinery.
GOE: 06.04.40 STRENGTH: L GED: R3 M1 L2 SVP: 4 DLU: 77

921.683-034 DERRICK-BOAT OPERATOR (water trans.) alternate titles: barge-crane operator; deck-engine operator; derrick-barge operator; floating-derrick operator; scow-derrick operator
Operates derrick mounted on boat or barge to lift and move heavy objects: Moves control levers and pedals of hoist to rotate, raise, or lower derrick boom and to raise or lower loadline and load attached to it. May move controls of small engines or hoists to push against bottom of body of water with spuds (heavy poles) to move barge from place to place. When derrick boat is self-propelled, operator may be required to possess Master's license issued by U.S. Government.
GOE: 05.11.04 STRENGTH: L GED: R3 M1 L2 SVP: 5 DLU: 77

921.683-038 ELEVATOR OPERATOR, FREIGHT (any industry) alternate titles: elevator operator, service
Operates elevator to transport materials and equipment between floors of industrial or commercial establishment: Moves control levers, or pushes buttons to control movement of elevator. Opens and closes safety gate and door of elevator at each floor where stop is made. May load and unload elevator. May transport freight from elevator to designated area, using handtruck. May transport passengers.
GOE: 05.12.04 STRENGTH: H GED: R2 M1 L1 SVP: 2 DLU: 77

921.683-042 FRONT-END LOADER OPERATOR (any industry) alternate titles: loader operator; wheel loader operator
Operates straight or articulated rubber-tired tractor-type vehicle equipped with front-mounted hydraulically powered bucket or scoop to lift and transport bulk materials to and from storage or processing areas, to feed conveyors, hoppers, or chutes, and to load trucks or railcars: Starts engine, shifts gears, presses pedals, and turns steering wheel to operate loader. Moves levers to lower and tilt bucket and drives front-end loader forward to force bucket into bulk material. Moves levers to raise and tilt bucket when filled, drives vehicle to work site, and moves levers to dump material. Performs routine maintenance on loader, such as lubricating, fueling, and cleaning.
GOE: 05.11.04 STRENGTH: M GED: R2 M1 L1 SVP: 3 DLU: 81

921.683-046 HYDRAULIC-BOOM OPERATOR (smelt. & refin.)
Operates hydraulic boom to lift copper anodes from casting mold and place anodes in cooling tank: Moves levers to position hydraulic boom and cable line over cast anode, lift copper anode from mold, and place anode into slot of rack in cooling tank. Lifts filled rack from tank and places rack on railroad flatcar. Records number of anodes cast. Cleans mold, changes pouring ladles, and sweeps work area, as part of work crew.
GOE: 06.04.40 STRENGTH: M GED: R2 M1 L1 SVP: 3 DLU: 77

921.683-050 INDUSTRIAL-TRUCK OPERATOR (any industry)
Drives gasoline-, liquefied gas-, or electric-powered industrial truck equipped with lifting devices, such as forklift, boom, scoop, lift beam and swivel-hook, fork-grapple, clamps, elevating platform, or trailer hitch, to push, pull, lift, stack, tier, or move products, equipment, or materials in warehouse, storage yard, or factory: Moves levers and presses pedals to drive truck and control movement of lifting apparatus. Positions forks, lifting platform, or other lifting device under, over, or around loaded pallets, skids, boxes, products, or materials or hooks tow trucks to trailer hitch, and transports load to designated area. Unloads and stacks material by raising and lowering lifting device. May inventory materials on work floor, and supply workers with materials as needed. May weigh materials or products and record weight on tags, labels, or production schedules. May load or unload materials onto or off of pallets, skids, or lifting device. May lubricate truck, recharge batteries, fill fuel tank, or replace liquefied-gas tank. May be designated according to article moved as Lead Loader (smelt. & refin.); process in which involved as Stripper Truck Operator (smelt. & refin.); or type of truck operated as Electric-Truck-Crane Operator (any industry); Fork-Lift-Truck Operator (any industry); Tier-Lift-Truck Operator (any industry). May be designated: Burnt-Lime Drawer (concrete prod.); Casting Trucker (foundry); Electric-Freight-Car Operator (r.r. trans.); Electric-Truck Operator (any industry); Gasoline-Truck Operator (any industry); Metal-Storage Worker (nonfer. metal); Package-Lift Operator (any industry).
GOE: 06.04.40 STRENGTH: M GED: R2 M1 L1 SVP: 3 DLU: 82

921.683-054 JAMMER OPERATOR (logging) alternate titles: stiff-neck loader
Operates gasoline- or diesel-powered jammer (A-frame hoist mounted on truck chassis) to load logs on truck and to lift trailer from logging truck to ground.
GOE: 05.11.04 STRENGTH: L GED: R2 M1 L1 SVP: 3 DLU: 77

921.683-058 LOG LOADER (logging) alternate titles: grapple operator; heel-boom operator
Operates heel-boom log loader equipped with cable, hydraulic, or pneumatically controlled grapples to load logs onto log trucks. Selects logs to be loaded according to specie and size required to attain balanced and compact load. May be designated according to type of machine operated as Shovel-Loader Operator (logging).
GOE: 05.11.04 STRENGTH: L GED: R3 M1 L2 SVP: 4 DLU: 78

921.683-062 SKIP OPERATOR (steel & rel.) alternate titles: scale-and-skip-car operator
Controls scale car (larry car) and skip hoist to transfer raw materials from storage bins to blast furnace: Moves controls of scale car to position car under chute of storage bin. Pulls lever to open bin filling car with raw materials, such as iron ore, coke, limestone, or sinter. Drives car onto scale to weigh materials in car. Positions car on skip pit and pulls lever to dump contents into skip car. Moves control of skip hoist to transport skip car up inclined ramp and dump contents into charging bell of furnace. Records data, such as number of charges, weight of materials, and stock levels in furnace.
GOE: 06.04.40 STRENGTH: L GED: R2 M2 L2 SVP: 4 DLU: 77

921.683-066 SORTING-GRAPPLE OPERATOR (logging)
Operates mobile crane equipped with heel-boom and hydraulic grapples to sort and stack logs in sorting yard according to species, grade, size, and designated use markings on log: Starts crane engine and moves levers and pedals to move and position machine boom and grapple to pick up individual logs. Moves levers to grasp log with grapples, force log against heel of boom, raise log to horizontal position, and rotate boom to position log on specified pile.
GOE: 05.11.04 STRENGTH: L GED: R3 M1 L2 SVP: 6 DLU: 77

921.683-070 STRADDLE-TRUCK OPERATOR (any industry) alternate titles: straddle buggy operator
Drives four-wheeled vehicle that carries loads of materials beneath its elevated frame for short hauls within or near plant: Starts vehicle and drives astride load of materials, such as lumber, bundled sheet metal, cased citrus juice, or empty skids. Pushes and pulls levers to raise and lower lifting mechanism equipped with hook, or to control hydraulic systems equipped with clamps (attached to underside of frame) that grasp, lift, and hold material or products for transport to designated area. Drives machine to specified delivery point, and moves levers to lower load to ground. Makes minor adjustments to vehicle. When conveying lumber, may be designated Lumber-Carrier Driver (saw. & plan.).
GOE: 06.04.40 STRENGTH: L GED: R2 M1 L1 SVP: 3 DLU: 77

921.683-074 TOWER-LOADER OPERATOR (water trans.) alternate titles: coal-tower operator
Operates mechanical loading tower to load ships and barges with bulk raw materials, such as coal, iron ore, or iron pellets: Moves controls, levers, and depresses pedals to position tower for loading operations, to lower conveyor directly over vessel hatch, and to position chute to guide materials into hold of ship. Starts conveyor belt to convey materials from stockpile or gondola cars

into hold of vessel. Moves chute controls to spread materials evenly throughout hold of vessel. Adjusts and makes minor repairs to tower and accessory equipment.

GOE: 05.11.04 STRENGTH: L GED: R3 M2 L3 SVP: 5 DLU: 77

921.683-078 TRANSFER-CAR OPERATOR (brick & tile)

Drives electrically powered transfer car on railroad tracks to transport carloads of brick or tile to and from loading station, drying tunnel, kiln, sorting area, or other designated area: Flips switches, moves levers, and depresses pedals to move transfer car to loading station and aligns rails on transfer car with rails on loading platform. Hooks winch cable to carload of brick or tile and operates winch to pull loaded drier car or kiln car onto transfer car. Drives transfer car to specified drier or kiln and aligns transfer car rails with rails into kiln or drier. Hooks cable to loaded car and operates winch to pull car into drier or kiln. Pulls car of dried or fired brick or tile from drying tunnel or kiln and transfers car to sorting area, processing department, or storage area. May manually push or pull loaded or empty cars onto or off transfer car. May open and close drying tunnel or kiln doors, using hook or by pressing button or moving lever. May move dried brick from drier cars to kiln cars, using hoist. May operate automated system that loads brick onto drier cars and moves cars through drying tunnel.

GOE: 05.11.04 STRENGTH: M GED: R2 M1 L1 SVP: 2 DLU: 78

921.683-082 WINCH DRIVER (water trans.)

Operates steam or electric winch to hoist or lower cargo in or out of ship's hold: Inspects booms, lashings, and wire rope to assure safe operation. Moves levers to raise, lower, and turn load. Follows hand signals of HATCH TENDER (water trans.) to control movement of load when it is obscured. May alternate work with HATCH TENDER (water trans.).

GOE: 05.11.04 STRENGTH: L GED: R3 M1 L2 SVP: 4 DLU: 77

921.683-086 YARD WORKER (ship-boat mfg.)

Operates winch to move towboats or other vessels from shop to yard, and launches vessels, using winch: Pushes buttons or levers of automatic or hand jacks to raise vessel off ground. Positions dolly on tracks under ship. Releases jacks to lower vessel onto dolly. Pushes button or turns crank to actuate winch that pulls dolly and vessel into yard. Transfers vessel from dolly to cradle on launching rails, using jacks and other supports. Lowers cradle and vessel into water, using winch.

GOE: 05.12.04 STRENGTH: M GED: R2 M1 L1 SVP: 4 DLU: 77

921.685-010 BOAT LOADER II (water trans.)

Tends winch and loading chute to load boats and barges with iron ore at dock: Selects pocket of ore from list submitted by dock supervisor. Starts power winch that moves boat, by means of cables looped over dock pilings at bow, along rail and stern of boat until hatch is opposite ore pocket. Pulls overhead cables to lower ore chute, allowing ore to flow into hatch. Trims or evens distribution of ore in hold by raising and lowering chute to prevent listing of boat.

GOE: 05.12.04 STRENGTH: M GED: R2 M1 L1 SVP: 3 DLU: 77

921.685-014 BULL-CHAIN OPERATOR (saw. & plan.) alternate titles: deck worker; log-deck tender

Tends chain conveyor that hauls logs up chute from pond to saw or barker deck. May activate kicker arms that push log conveyor to deck.

GOE: 05.12.04 STRENGTH: L GED: R2 M1 L1 SVP: 2 DLU: 77

921.685-018 CAGER OPERATOR (can. & preserv.)

Tends stacking machine that loads sealed cans or jars of baby food into metal baskets for processing in retorts: Pushes basket, mounted on dolly, onto hydraulic lift mounted at floor level and located at discharge platform of filling machine. Presses button and moves lever to activate lift that raises adjustable bottom of basket up to level of platform. Presses button to activate device that slides jars of baby food from platform into basket. Places divider over each layer of jars in basket. Activates lift that lowers adjustable bottom of basket for subsequent layers of jars until basket is filled. Attaches tag to basket to identify type of baby food packed.

GOE: 06.04.40 STRENGTH: H GED: R2 M1 L1 SVP: 2 DLU: 77

921.685-022 CHIP-BIN CONVEYOR TENDER (chemical; paper & pulp) alternate titles: chip deliverer; chip-silo tender

Tends equipment that conveys wood chips from chippers, cleaning machines, or yard storage to storage tanks and digester bins: Starts conveyor belts and elevators to convey specified wood chips to designated bins and tanks. Adjusts feed mechanism by valve or lever control to regulate flow of wood chips to prevent overloading of belt. Cleans belts, using shovel, broom, and airhose, and lubricates machinery. May set trippers or slides to divert chips from belt into specified bins. May measure tanks to determine amount of chips in storage. May unload chips from railroad cars or trucks, using pneumatic tube.

GOE: 06.04.40 STRENGTH: M GED: R1 M1 L1 SVP: 2 DLU: 77

921.685-026 CONVEYOR TENDER (any industry) alternate titles: belt tender; conveyor monitor; receiver, bulk system

Tends conveyor or conveyor system that moves materials or products by belt, auger, or bucket conveyors to and from stockpiles, bins, silos, processing operations, or departments, or to load and unload railroad cars and trucks: Moves levers or pushes buttons to start conveyor. Loads conveyor by hand, lift, or hoist, or by opening gates, chutes, or hoppers. Observes movement of materials or products on conveyor and dislodges jams, using pole, bar, handtools, or by

hand. Notifies supervisor of equipment malfunction. Lubricates moving parts, using grease gun and oilcan. May position deflector bars, gates, chutes, or spouts to divert flow of materials from one conveyor onto another conveyor. May move and assemble portable conveyor sections and plug in electric cords to start conveyors. May clean work area, using shovel and broom. May tend conveyor motors in grain elevator and be designated Grain-Elevator-Motor Starter (grain-feed mills).

GOE: 06.04.40 STRENGTH: M GED: R2 M1 L1 SVP: 2 DLU: 81

921.685-030 COOKER LOADER (oils & grease) alternate titles: charge loader; tank charger

Tends conveyor that feeds offal, bone, or meat into cookers: Opens cooker lid and conveyor chute above cooker. Starts conveyor and observes ammeter or marker in cooker to determine when to stop conveyor, or sets timer to stop conveyor automatically. Cleans working area, using broom and water hose. May tend related equipment that breaks and chops material prior to cooking. May tend conveyor that feeds horizontal, steam-heated melters (cooking vessels) and be designated Melter Loader (meat products).

GOE: 06.04.40 STRENGTH: L GED: R1 M1 L1 SVP: 2 DLU: 77

921.685-034 DRIER-TAKE-OFF TENDER (elec. equip.)

Tends conveyor that regulates movement of storage-battery plates through drying machine. Removes dried plates emerging from drier on conveyor and stacks plates on dollies or skids. Moves loaded dollies or skids to stockroom and empty ones to takeoff station, using electric lift truck.

GOE: 06.04.40 STRENGTH: L GED: R2 M1 L1 SVP: 2 DLU: 77

921.685-038 DUMP OPERATOR (any industry) alternate titles: car-dumper operator; tipple worker

Tends mechanical or electrical dumping equipment to dump materials, such as grain, raw materials, coal, or ore, from mine cars, railroad cars, or trucks into bins or onto conveyor for storage, reloading, or further processing, using either of following methods: (1) Observes that car or truck is spotted accurately on bed of rotary dump. Moves controls to secure clamps over couplings that hold car while being tipped. Starts motor or pulls lever that tips car and dumps contents. Releases clamps to remove car. (2) Opens bottom or side doors of car or truck spotted over gravity dump. Moves controls to lower car shakeout device into car and to start vibration that loosens remaining coal or ore. May hook winch cables to cars to draw them onto dumping bed. May couple and uncouple cars. May be required to maintain records of unloading operations. May be designated according to type of equipment tended as Car-Shakeout Operator (cement; mine & quarry); Rotary-Dump Operator (mine & quarry; steel & rel.); or according to material unloaded as Grain Unloader, Machine (grain-feed mills).

GOE: 05.11.04 STRENGTH: L GED: R2 M1 L1 SVP: 3 DLU: 80

921.685-042 ELECTRIC-FORK OPERATOR (agriculture)

Tends powered hoist to load vine crops, such as green peas or lima bean vines onto conveyor of viner (pea or bean-shelling machine): Pushes hoisting fork into pile of vine crops, and starts hoist that lifts vine crops and drops vines into viner. Rakes up scattered vines and pitches vines into viner, using pitchfork.

GOE: 03.04.01 STRENGTH: H GED: R1 M1 L1 SVP: 2 DLU: 77

921.685-046 FRUIT DISTRIBUTOR (agriculture)

Tends conveyor to distribute citrus fruit to packers' work stations: Tends conveyor, patrols catwalks beside conveyors and monitors flow of fruit passing to each packing station. Reroutes flow of fruit to maintain adequate supply to each packer. Turns wing nut on rail of conveyor to loosen deflector bar. Pushes or pulls on rod to move longitudinal deflector bar regulating flow of fruit to approximate packing speed of each worker. Turns wing nut to clamp rod attached to deflector bar in place. Repeats task to adjust all deflector bars necessary to obtain desired flow of fruit to packers.

GOE: 05.12.04 STRENGTH: L GED: R2 M1 L1 SVP: 2 DLU: 77

921.685-050 PRODUCTION-SUPPLY-EQUIPMENT TENDER (food prep., nec) alternate titles: production helper

Tends equipment that conveys shelled corn and vegetable oil between processes in plant producing foods, such as corn chips and cheese puffs: Starts bucket-type conveyor or pneumatic conveyor that transfers shelled corn from freight cars and trucks to corn storage elevator. Moves levers to control flow of corn from elevator to hoppers of cleaning and grinding machines. Connects pipe, tightens coupling with wrenches, and starts pumps to transfer vegetable oils from tank cars to storage tanks. Opens valves to transfer oils from storage tanks to cooking vats in production areas of plant. Collects oil and corn grain samples for laboratory analysis. Sprays corn storage elevators and conveyor belts with insecticide and seals elevator for specified period to eliminate insects. May weigh trucks before and after unloading [GRAIN RECEIVER (grain-feed mills)].

GOE: 06.04.15 STRENGTH: M GED: R3 M1 L2 SVP: 4 DLU: 77

921.685-054 SORTER OPERATOR (saw. & plan.) alternate titles: lumber sorter, machine

Tends sorting mechanism and grades green lumber as lumber passes on conveyor to designated racks: Determines length and thickness of board by comparing board with gauged marks on machine table. Lifts end of board and feels wood to estimate moisture content. Routes board to appropriate holding rack by pressing specified button on control panel. May grade and route veneer to designated bin and be designated Veneer Sorter (millwork-plywood).

GOE: 05.07.06 STRENGTH: L GED: R2 M1 L1 SVP: 4 DLU: 77

921.685-058 SPOUT TENDER II (chemical)
Tends railcar loading devices to load bulk material, such as phosphatic fertilizer, into hopper cars and boxcars: Presses buttons on hand held control box to position loading spout and feed conveyor over compartment of hopper car. Presses buttons to start spout feed conveyor and to start flow of material from overhead bin onto feed conveyor. Observes flow of material into hopper car and presses buttons on control box to change position of spout to assure equal weight distribution in hopper car. Collects sample of material from spout as each compartment is filled to make up composite sample for laboratory analysis. Closes hinged hatch covers on top of hopper car. Attaches grain doors (wooden inner doors) to contain material in boxcar, using hammer and nails. Moves lever to position hydraulically powered loading chute into boxcar. Presses buttons to start flow of material from overhead bin and to start slinger unit (high speed conveyor in curved end of chute) which throws material to ends of boxcar. Moves levers to swivel slinger to distribute load evenly. Cleans boxcars and hopper cars to eliminate product contamination, using broom and shovel.
GOE: 05.12.04 STRENGTH: L GED: R2 M1 L1 SVP: 3 DLU: 77

921.685-062 STACKER TENDER (millwork-plywood)
Tends control panel that controls raising and lowering of stacking tables in veneer bins, and conveyor that conveys stacks of veneer sheets from filled bins for further processing: Observes control panel lights to determine status of each bin being loaded and pulls lever to lower veneer stacking table of respective bin to unloading position when panel light indicates bin is full. Paints identifying information on end of veneer stack, using paint spray can. Pushes buttons to open bin gate and to activate conveyor to convey veneer stack from bin for further processing. Pushes lever to raise veneer stacking table to loading position. Observes control panel lights to detect faulty operation of stacking machine and stops conveyor and machine when malfunction occurs. Pulls lever on control panel or releases valve manually at bin to lower stacking table and pulls jammed veneer sheet into bin. Pushes button to start timer whenever machine breakdowns occur and records downtime according to type of machine breakdown.
GOE: 06.04.40 STRENGTH: L GED: R2 M1 L1 SVP: 3 DLU: 77

921.685-066 TRANSFER OPERATOR (paper & pulp)
Tends equipment that distributes logs and wood-blocks to saws, barkers, washers, splitters, chippers, and grinders according to size and species of wood: Observes logs and blocks to determine wood species and to estimate diameter and length of logs and condition of wood and bark. Pushes button kickers, or moves lever or pedal controls to start transfer chains and conveyors to distribute and convey logs and blocks to appropriate machines. Breaks up jams on conveyors, using pike pole, or *picaroon*. May remove oversized blocks or those having knots or decayed portions. May saw or split oversized blocks.
GOE: 06.04.40 STRENGTH: M GED: R2 M1 L1 SVP: 3 DLU: 77

921.685-070 UNSCRAMBLER (can. & preserv.)
Tends machine that automatically unscrambles cans or jars of cooked food products from retort baskets into straight line to facilitate further processing: Lowers retort basket to top of hydraulic lift, using hoist, and clamps basket onto lift. Adjusts conveyor sides to permit passage of cans or jars, and pushes button to activate conveyor. Moves levers to activate lift that raises tiers of cans or jars to conveyor height and to activate arm which moves containers from retort basket to conveyor. Observes flow on conveyor and removes warped or bent cans and repositions cans causing bottlenecks. Repeats operation for each layer of cans or jars in basket. Moves empty basket to designated area, using overhead hoist.
GOE: 06.04.40 STRENGTH: M GED: R1 M1 L1 SVP: 2 DLU: 77

921.686-010 CARTON-COUNTER FEEDER (tobacco)
Sorts and feeds cartons of damaged or stale cigarettes according to brands into tracks of conveyor that carries cartons through automatic counting device and down chute for reprocessing.
GOE: 06.03.02 STRENGTH: L GED: R1 M1 L1 SVP: 2 DLU: 77

921.686-014 CONVEYOR FEEDER-OFFBEARER (any industry) alternate titles: carton catcher; dumper-bulk system
Feeds and off bears conveyor or conveyor system performing any of following tasks: Picks up materials or products from pallet, handtruck, or dolly, and places materials or products onto conveyor, or opens bins or chutes to dump bulk material onto conveyor, or hangs products on chain or overhead conveyor, or transfers materials or products from one conveyor to another conveyor, and aligns materials or products on conveyor to prevent jams. Dislodges jams by hand or pole. Removes materials or products from discharge end of conveyor and stacks materials or products on trays, pallets, or handtrucks. May feed and off bear conveyor that conveys material or products through machines or equipment operated or tended by another worker. May inspect materials or products for damage or for conformity to specifications. May push material or products between machines or departments on roller conveyor. May move materials or products to or from conveyor, using handtruck, dolly, or electric handtruck. May start or stop conveyor. May open cartons or shipping containers and place contents on conveyor. May use hoist to load or unload conveyor. May stencil, tag, stamp, or write identifying information on packaged products. May record production. May keep work area clean and orderly.
GOE: 06.04.40 STRENGTH: M GED: R1 M1 L1 SVP: 2 DLU: 86

921.686-018 LOG-HAUL CHAIN FEEDER (paper & pulp; saw. & plan.)
Rolls logs from railroad cars onto moving log-haul chain: Cuts wires and stakes that bind load to car. Breaks jam of logs on car and rolls them one by one on log-haul chain. Cleans log haul and car.
GOE: 05.12.04 STRENGTH: H GED: R2 M1 L1 SVP: 2 DLU: 77

921.686-022 POND WORKER (millwork-plywood; paper & pulp; saw. & plan.) alternate titles: chute feeder; jacker feeder; log-chain feeder; poler; sinker puller; slip feeder
Feeds logs onto conveyor that moves logs from pond to saw or barker deck: Stands on catwalk, flatboat, raft, or floating logs and guides logs onto conveyor, using pike pole. Raises sunken logs, using hoist. May operate powered winch to raise sunken logs. May be designated according to work station as Boat Worker (saw. & plan.); Log Rider (saw. & plan.).
GOE: 05.12.04 STRENGTH: H GED: R1 M1 L1 SVP: 2 DLU: 77

921.687-010 CAR-DUMPER-OPERATOR HELPER (beverage) alternate titles: car-unloader helper
Performs following tasks in dumping grain from railroad cars: Slides open and secures car doors. Removes wood and paper from grain flowing from tipped cars, using grappling hooks. Positions metal plank in car to guide grain dumped into hopper. Sweeps empty car and closes door. May lower road crossing gates at rail and road intersection.
GOE: 05.12.04 STRENGTH: M GED: R2 M1 L1 SVP: 2 DLU: 77

921.687-014 CHOKE SETTER (logging)
Fastens *choker* cables around logs for yarding from cutting area to landing: Pulls choker cables from tractor winch or main-line of yarding machine, passes ball (one end) under and around log, and secures end to bell (sliding fastener) to form noose. May clear brush and earth from under log, using ax and shovel. May assist RIGGING SLINGER (logging) in installing and dismantling rigging of high lead or similar yarding system. May be designated Cat Hooker (logging) in tractor yarding.
GOE: 05.12.04 STRENGTH: V GED: R1 M1 L1 SVP: 2 DLU: 77

921.687-018 LOADER (mfd. bldgs.)
Loads prefabricated home components and modular home units on trucks for shipment to construction site: Loads components in reverse order of house construction sequence and according to size, using electric hoist. Straps completed shipment stacks, using banding tool and clamps. Lifts modular home units from assembly line trailer and lowers unit onto truck bed for shipment, using hydraulic jacks.
GOE: 05.12.04 STRENGTH: M GED: R2 M1 L2 SVP: 3 DLU: 77

921.687-022 LOG LOADER HELPER (logging) alternate titles: second loader
Loads logs onto trucks or railroad cars, performing any combination of following tasks: Hand signals directions for hoisting of trailer from truck chassis and positioning of truck for loading. Connects brake and electrical lines and trailer to truck. Positions railcars for loading, using power winch, pinchbar, and car hand brakes. Secures tongs, slings, or other attachment to log, guides loading of logs by hand and using hand signals, and releases attachments. Trims protruding limbs and knots, using ax and chain saw. Marks log with specified symbols, using paint spray can or branding hammer. Secures load with chains, cables, or steel straps. May roll logs up ramp and position logs on truck, using peavey or cant hook. May be designated according to type of loading equipment involved as Jammer Operator Helper (logging); Grapple Operator Helper (logging); or work location as Loader Helper, Sorting Yard (logging).
GOE: 05.12.04 STRENGTH: M GED: R1 M1 L1 SVP: 2 DLU: 77

921.687-026 RIGGER HELPER (any industry)
Assists RIGGER (any industry) in setting up, bracing, and rigging hoisting equipment, performing duties as described under HELPER (any industry) Master Title.
GOE: 05.12.04 STRENGTH: H GED: R2 M1 L1 SVP: 3 DLU: 77

921.687-030 RIGGER, THIRD (logging)
Carries blocks (pulleys) and cable to RIGGER (logging), threads cables through blocks, and performs similar tasks while working as member of crew engaged in installing blocks, cables, and other rigging used in skidding logs.
GOE: 05.12.04 STRENGTH: V GED: R1 M1 L1 SVP: 2 DLU: 77

921.687-034 WOOD HANDLER (paper & pulp)
Monitors flow of wood in chute and conveyors, and breaks up jams to maintain uninterrupted supply of wood to grinders: Stands beside conveyor and pushes and pulls crossed or interlocked blocks into alignment on belt, using pike pole. Picks up fallen blocks of wood and tosses wood back onto conveyor.
GOE: 05.12.04 STRENGTH: M GED: R1 M1 L1 SVP: 2 DLU: 77

922 OCCUPATIONS IN MOVING AND STORING MATERIALS AND PRODUCTS, N.E.C.

This group includes occupations, not elsewhere classified, concerned with loading and moving materials and products, using work aids, other than machines, such as handtrucks, electric handtrucks or dollies, and wheelbarrows; shoveling, carrying, sorting, and stacking materials and products; and stock checking or records keeping not included in Division 22. Loading and moving materials and products by means of pumping equipment is included in Group 914.

922.137-010 SENIOR-COMMISSARY AGENT (air trans.)
Supervises and coordinates activities of workers engaged in receiving, storing, preparing, assembling, and loading supplies aboard aircraft, such as linens, glasses, emergency kits, and beverages for airline commissary: Reads shipping documents and inspects storage areas to determine space available for storage. Plans commissary supply schedule according to number and type of flights scheduled for departure. Directs workers as to amount and type of supplies to be assembled and loaded on each flight. Conducts inventories to determine supply requirements and orders replacements from main warehouse. Compiles receipt and disbursement data and computes balance. Contacts catering service, supply vendors, and other flight stations to coordinate equipment and supply balance. Trains new workers. Performs duties as described under SUPERVISOR (any industry) Master Title.
GOE: 05.09.01 STRENGTH: M GED: R4 M3 L3 SVP: 7 DLU: 77

922.137-014 SUPERVISOR, HIDE HOUSE (leather mfg.)
Supervises and coordinates activities of workers engaged in inspecting, storing and unloading incoming hides or skins. Performs duties as described under SUPERVISOR (any industry) Master Title.
GOE: 06.02.01 STRENGTH: M GED: R3 M2 L2 SVP: 7 DLU: 77

922.137-018 SUPERVISOR, LOADING AND UNLOADING (any industry)
Supervises and coordinates activities of workers engaged in loading and unloading cargo from conveyances, such as railroad cars, trucks, and ships, and in moving and storing materials or products: Assigns job tasks to worker according to loading and unloading schedules, and observes loading of conveyance to determine conformance to loading patterns and to prevent shifting or damage to materials or products during transit. Verifies materials loaded or unloaded against work order or bill of lading. Directs workers to move materials or products to storage areas or production departments. Trains new employees in job duties. Performs duties as described under SUPERVISOR (any industry) Master Title. May schedule sequence of transportation usage, routes of transportation vehicle operators, or movement of materials into and out of storage area. May be designated according to materials handled, work location, or specialization as Bull-Gang Supervisor (tobacco); Munitions-Handler Supervisor (ordnance); Platform Supervisor (any industry); Supervisor, Case Loading (beverage); Supervisor, Loading (any industry); Supervisor, Shipping (bakery products); Supervisor, Shipping Room (beverage); Supervisor, Unloading (any industry).
GOE: 05.12.01 STRENGTH: M GED: R4 M2 L2 SVP: 6 DLU: 82

922.137-022 SUPERVISOR, OPEN-HEARTH STOCKYARD (steel & rel.)
Supervises and coordinates activities of workers engaged in stocking raw materials and scrap used for open-hearth furnace charging operations. Directs workers in filling charging boxes with scrap, loading boxes on charging buggies (low flatbed railroad car), weighing scrap, and positioning buggies on charging floor. Performs duties as described under SUPERVISOR (any industry) Master Title.
GOE: 05.12.01 STRENGTH: M GED: R4 M2 L2 SVP: 8 DLU: 77

922.137-026 WAREHOUSE TRAFFIC SUPERVISOR (wholesale tr.)
Supervises and coordinates activities of workers engaged in unloading and placing tobacco on auction warehouse floor and directs traffic to and from warehouse: Directs drivers of loaded vehicles to unloading site, and empty vehicles to exits, to expedite unloading of vehicles and avoid traffic congestion. Directs workers to place loads of tobacco in designated areas on warehouse floor. May estimate amount of floor space available to prevent overcrowding of warehouse floor. Performs other duties as described under SUPERVISOR (any industry) Master Title.
GOE: 05.12.01 STRENGTH: L GED: R3 M2 L2 SVP: 5 DLU: 77

922.137-030 YARD SUPERVISOR (forestry)
Supervises and coordinates activities of workers engaged in receiving and shipping Christmas trees: Inspects operations of yard to ensure that orders for trees are filled and company standards regarding processing of trees are adhered to. Inspects trees received from SUPERVISOR, CHRISTMAS-TREE FARM (forestry) and private individuals, and writes invoices to indicate number and sizes of trees accepted. Confers with MANAGER, CHRISTMAS-TREE FARM (forestry) regarding shipping schedules, tree production, and size of work force required. Performs other duties as described under SUPERVISOR (any industry) Master Title.
GOE: 05.09.01 STRENGTH: L GED: R3 M2 L2 SVP: 6 DLU: 77

922.587-010 PRIMING-MIXTURE CARRIER (ordnance)
Moves explosive priming mixture from isolated storage houses to primer and rimfire charging departments: Supplies outside window boxes, near charging stations, with containers of various type mixtures according to work order. Records type and quantity of mixtures received and distributed. Turns valves to replenish water in humidifying trays in wet mixture houses and reports abnormal temperature in dry mixture houses. May flush storage houses, using hose, to prevent accumulation of explosive dust. May wash residue from empty containers with neutralizing solution.
GOE: 05.12.03 STRENGTH: L GED: R2 M1 L2 SVP: 2 DLU: 77

922.665-010 FLUMER I (sugar & conf.) alternate titles: beet flumer
Tends equipment that conveys water and sugar beets from storage bins through flume to washroom: Pushes button to start equipment and turns steam and water valves to admit heated water into flume. Turns crank to raise storage bin gate to start flow of sugar beets into flume. Turns valves to increase or decrease flow of water and beets through flume into washroom according to bell, telephone, or light signals. Observes flow of beets in flume to detect jamming and loosens jams, using bar. Notifies supervisor of equipment malfunction. May maintain equipment, using handtools.
GOE: 06.04.40 STRENGTH: L GED: R2 M1 L1 SVP: 3 DLU: 77

922.665-014 BIN TRIPPER OPERATOR (steel & rel.)
Tends discharge end of conveyor system that moves raw materials in blast furnace to storage bins: Inspects bins and notifies CONVEYOR-SYSTEM OPERATOR (any industry) 921.662-018 of required material, such as iron and manganese ore, limestone, clay, or sinter. Moves control to position tipper over bin. Opens valve to turn on water spray to settle dust. Notifies CONVEYOR-SYSTEM OPERATOR (any industry) when bin is full. Presses switch to stop conveyor for malfunctions. Scrapes and cleans bins and bin areas, using bar, scraper, shovel, and broom.
GOE: 06.04.40 STRENGTH: L GED: R2 M1 L1 SVP: 3 DLU: 86

922.667-010 YARD WORKER, USED BUILDING MATERIALS (retail trade)
Salvages and stores used building materials: Stacks cleaned lumber according to size and condition. Sorts and stores used millwork, plumbing fixtures, heating equipment, and structural steel. Cuts lumber to customer's specifications, using power saw. Fills customer's order and loads materials on car or truck.
GOE: 05.09.01 STRENGTH: M GED: R2 M2 L2 SVP: 3 DLU: 77

922.684-010 LOCKER-PLANT ATTENDANT (retail trade; wholesale tr.)
Performs any combination of following duties in frozen-food locker plant: Wraps food in protective paper or plastic film and ties package by hand or machine. Stamps identifying label and weight on package. Packs wrapped packages in baskets and places them in freezing room until frozen, then transfers them to designated storage lockers. Records items packed, weight, and locker numbers, and sends data to business office. Fills orders from customers' lockers on written request and retail orders from stock. Slices, grinds, and cubes meat by machine. Cleans work area in processing room. May cut beef, pork, or other meat into roasts, chops, steaks, or other forms as requested by customer [MEAT CUTTER (retail trade; wholesale tr.)]. May sell containers for freezing fruits and vegetables. May issue receipts for foods left for freezing. May collect service fees from customers.
GOE: 05.09.01 STRENGTH: M GED: R3 M1 L2 SVP: 4 DLU: 77

922.686-010 DUMPER (chemical)
Dumps nitrocellulose into trough for transfer to explosives-manufacturing equipment: Rolls barrels of nitrocellulose from railroad car to dumping room over wooden rails. Removes lock rims and lids of barrels, using handtools. Upturns barrels over water jet in trough and strikes bottom with rubber mallet to loosen contents. May pump slurry to agitating and blending tubs.
GOE: 06.04.40 STRENGTH: H GED: R1 M1 L1 SVP: 1 DLU: 77

922.686-014 LOWERATOR OPERATOR (fabrication, nec)
Removes wrapped felt-base rugs and felt-base floor coverings from machine that automatically conveys them to lower floor for final processing. Weighs rugs and coverings, using floor scale, and sorts them according to grade. Moves products to storage rooms, using handtruck. Records weights and grades of products.
GOE: 06.03.02 STRENGTH: M GED: R1 M1 L1 SVP: 2 DLU: 77

922.687-010 BIN FILLER (tobacco) alternate titles: bin packer; leaf binner; leaf tinner
Packs tobacco filler leaves in storage bin, positioning leaves in rows to prevent breakage. Covers leaves with rubber sheet and closes bin.
GOE: 06.04.38 STRENGTH: L GED: R1 M1 L1 SVP: 2 DLU: 77

922.687-014 BINDER-AND-WRAPPER PACKER (tobacco)
Packs binder and wrapper tobacco leaves in cases preparatory to storage: Picks up leaves by stems and places them in case. Places burlap covering over leaves, climbs into case, and walks on covering to compact tobacco, removing burlap for use in repeating process for subsequent layers. Nails boards over top of case and conveys case to storage room, using handtruck.
GOE: 06.04.38 STRENGTH: M GED: R2 M1 L1 SVP: 2 DLU: 77

922.687-018 BOBBIN SORTER (glass mfg.; plastic-synth.; textile) alternate titles: bobbin salvager; spool salvager
Sorts bobbins or spools according to type or number and places bobbins in specified bin or box. Inspects bobbins or spools for defects. Removes waste yarn from bobbins or spools [BOBBIN CLEANER, HAND (any industry)]. May remove identification stickers or disks from cleaned bobbins or spools. May convey sorted bobbins or spools to specified work station, using handtruck.
GOE: 06.03.02 STRENGTH: L GED: R2 M1 L1 SVP: 2 DLU: 77

922.687-022 BOLT LOADER (saw. & plan.) alternate titles: car loader
Loads and stacks halved or quartered stave-logs in cars that are rolled into steam tunnel [STEAM-TUNNEL FEEDER (saw. & plan.)].
GOE: 06.04.40 STRENGTH: H GED: R1 M1 L1 SVP: 2 DLU: 77

922.687-026 BULL-GANG WORKER (tobacco) alternate titles: hogshead roller; load-out worker; roller
Moves hogsheads of tobacco, between departments, onto scales, and onto truck or boxcars by rolling or using handtruck. Stacks hogsheads in tiers or re-

moves hogsheads from stack, using skids and stick or iron bar. Works as member of team when stacking and loading hogsheads. May call hogshead number and grade stenciled on hogshead to BOOKING PRIZER (tobacco) as hogsheads are rolled onto scale.
GOE: 06.04.40 STRENGTH: V GED: R1 M1 L1 SVP: 2 DLU: 77

922.687-030 CAN FILLER (tobacco)
Fills carrying cans with tobacco leaves from storage bins: Removes tobacco leaves from storage bins and spreads tobacco on table to separate leaves stuck together. Places tobacco in can in manner that prevents leaves from being compressed. Places cover on can and carries can to scales to be weighed.
GOE: 06.04.36 STRENGTH: M GED: R1 M1 L1 SVP: 1 DLU: 77

922.687-034 CAR PINCHER (steel & rel.) alternate titles: car shifter
Moves railroad cars or tank cars in yard or at loading dock, using pinchbar inserted under car wheel to position domes of railcars under loading spouts. May place planks between coke ovens and top of railroad car to provide path for wheelbarrows. May daub coke oven doors with clay to regulate air intake.
GOE: 05.12.03 STRENGTH: H GED: R1 M1 L1 SVP: 1 DLU: 77

922.687-038 COAL SAMPLER (utilities)
Collects coal samples from hopper cars or coal bunkers preparatory to testing: Inserts specified size of pipe in car or bunker, using sledgehammer, to facilitate gathering coal sample. Dumps coal from pipe into container and records sample source. Carries sample to testing laboratory.
GOE: 05.12.03 STRENGTH: L GED: R2 M1 L1 SVP: 2 DLU: 77

922.687-042 COTTON SAMPLER (agriculture; textile) alternate titles: sampler
Removes samples of cotton from bales for classification purposes: Cuts bale band and burlap covering, using shears and knife. Opens outside layers of cotton, and pulls or cuts samples from interior of each side of bale. Tears stub from bale identification tag, places stub in sample, and wraps samples in paper. May transfer bales of cotton to platform scales, using handtruck.
GOE: 06.04.27 STRENGTH: L GED: R2 M1 L1 SVP: 2 DLU: 77

922.687-046 ICER (wholesale tr.) alternate titles: top icer
Deposits layer of crushed ice on fresh food products packed in barrels, boxes, or crates, to refrigerate them during shipment: Scrapes off surplus ice and passes crate along conveyor system, slides crate to LIDDER (any industry), or places lid on container and moves container to storage or shipping area, using handtruck. May shovel ice into ice compartment of food distribution trucks. May be designated according to container in which product is packed as Box Icer (can. & preserv.); Crate Icer (can. & preserv.); or according to product iced as Fish Icer (can. & preserv.; wholesale tr.).
GOE: 05.12.03 STRENGTH: H GED: R1 M1 L1 SVP: 1 DLU: 77

922.687-050 INSTALLER (museums)
Moves, installs, and stores paintings, statuary, and other art objects in art museum: Places protective pads on handtruck platform and lifts paintings, statuary, or other art objects onto handtruck and places protective pads between and around objects to ensure against damage. Pushes handtruck from shipping-receiving area to storage or display gallery as directed by supervisor. Places objects to be stored in designated sections of storage area. Removes objects to be displayed from handtruck, hangs paintings, and positions statuary and other objects in cabinets or on stands as directed. Dismantles exhibit components, as directed, and moves art objects, cabinets, and other display items to storage area. Moves designated objects from storage area to shipping room.
GOE: 05.12.03 STRENGTH: H GED: R2 M1 L1 SVP: 2 DLU: 77

922.687-054 LABORATORY-SAMPLE CARRIER (any industry) alternate titles: sample gatherer; sampler
Collects samples of products or raw materials for laboratory analysis, performing any combination of following tasks: Turns valves or dips sample container to transfer liquid samples from pipeline, processing equipment, tanks, or other vessels to test tubes, bottles, or buckets. Transfers dry samples, such as ore, grain, crystals, powder, or granular material to containers, using shovel, hand scoop, sample stick, or handtool. Labels sample containers with identifying data, location of sample, and time collected. Delivers samples to laboratory for analysis. Cleans sample containers, using specified cleaning agents and brushes or scrapers. Gathers samples at specified locations, stages of processing, and time interval. May collect samples of radioactive waste, following prescribed safety procedures, and be designated Sampler, Radioactive Waste (chemical).
GOE: 05.09.03 STRENGTH: L GED: R2 M1 L1 SVP: 2 DLU: 78

922.687-058 LABORER, STORES (any industry) alternate titles: order picker; parts picker; stock selector; warehouse worker
Performs any combination of following tasks to receive, store, and distribute material, tools, equipment, and products within establishments: Reads production schedule, customer order, work order, shipping order, or requisition to determine items to be moved, gathered, or distributed. Conveys materials and items from receiving or production areas to storage or to other designated areas by hand, handtruck, or electric handtruck. Sorts and places materials or items on racks, shelves, or in bins according to predetermined sequence, such as size, type, style, color, or product code. Sorts and stores perishable goods in refrigerated rooms. Fills requisitions, work orders, or requests for materials, tools, or other stock items and distributes items to production workers or assembly line. Assembles customer orders from stock and places orders on pallets or

shelves, or conveys orders to packing station or shipping department. Marks materials with identifying information, using stencil, crayon, or other marking device. Opens bales, crates, and other containers, using handtools. Records amounts of materials or items received or distributed. Weighs or counts items for distribution within plant to ensure conformance to company standards. Arranges stock parts in specified sequence for assembly by other workers. May use computer to enter records. May compile worksheets or tickets from customer specifications [ORDER DETAILER (clerical) 221.387-046]. May drive vehicle to transport stored items from warehouse to plant or to pick up items from several locations for shipment. May complete requisition forms to order supplies from other plant departments. May prepare parcels for mailing. May maintain inventory records. May restock aircraft commissary supplies, such as linens, glasses, emergency kits, and beverages, and be designated Commissary Agent (air trans.). May be known according to specific duty performed as Cloth-Bin Packer (textile); Cooler Worker (dairy products); Order Filler (any industry); Produce Clerk (retail trade) II; Tool Chaser (any industry).
GOE: 05.09.01 STRENGTH: M GED: R2 M1 L1 SVP: 2 DLU: 88

922.687-062 LABORER, WHARF (can. & preserv.) alternate titles: dock worker; fish pitcher; lumper; wharf hand
Unloads catch from fishing vessels and conveys fish from wharf to fish-dressing or storage area, performing any combination of following tasks: Loads cargo net, crane bucket, or conveyor with catch from hold of boat, by hand or with shovel or pew (hooked prong). Dumps catch from cargo net or crane bucket onto dock platform and sorts catch according to species, size, or grade. Pushes cart of fish to fish-cleaning tables and dumps fish on table, or piles fish on floor and covers them with chipped ice for temporary storage. Shovels fish scrap into cart and pushes cart to disposal area. May assist boat crew in mooring boat at dock. May clean fish [FISH CLEANER (can. & preserv.; fishing & hunt.)].
GOE: 06.04.40 STRENGTH: H GED: R1 M1 L1 SVP: 2 DLU: 77

922.687-066 LAST PUTTER-AWAY (boot & shoe; rubber goods) alternate titles: dead header; returner, lasts
Sorts and stores lasts (shoe molds) in numbered bins, in racks, or on skids, according to size and style. Picks up lasts in assembly area and transports them to storage room for sorting and placing in bins, using handtruck.
GOE: 05.09.01 STRENGTH: M GED: R1 M1 L1 SVP: 2 DLU: 77

922.687-070 LUMBER HANDLER (woodworking) alternate titles: lumber piler; lumber racker; lumber stacker; lumber sticker
Stacks lumber on kiln cars, in yard, or in shed to dry or store, performing any combination of following tasks: Places lumber piece by piece in layers, leaving space between edges of adjacent pieces. Places sticks between layers as stack rises to permit circulation of air and bind stack together. Stands on ground and hands lumber to another worker on top of stack. Positions timbers on kiln car, ground, or shed floor to build foundation for lumber stacks. Places blocks against wheels of loaded kiln car in dry kiln to prevent movement of car. Unloads lumber from stacks or kiln cars. Places lumber, veneer, or plywood on conveyor for further processing. Loads and unloads stacking machine, working in teamwork with other workers [STACKER, MACHINE (woodworking) 569.685-066]. May stack bundles of laths or barrel staves. May attach identity card to stacks of lumber and record number of stacks by species for supervisor. May carry materials, such as lumber, mortar mix, and nails to sales counter or load materials onto delivery trucks. May be designated according to purpose of stacking as Kiln Stacker (woodworking).
GOE: 05.12.03 STRENGTH: H GED: R2 M1 L1 SVP: 2 DLU: 81

922.687-074 LUMBER SORTER (woodworking) alternate titles: lumber puller; racker; separator
Sorts lumber or veneer according to grade markings and size: Removes boards from sorting table, handtruck, or conveyor and stacks in piles or places boards in rack or on conveyor, according to grade marking, length, or use of boards. Gauges length of boards by sight, by marks on sorting table, or by measuring with rule. May remove defective lumber from conveyor and stack lumber according to grade, length, species, and color. May hand stamp grade markings on boards or stack of lumber. May be designated according to sorting equipment used as Racker (saw. & plan.).
GOE: 06.03.02 STRENGTH: M GED: R1 M1 L1 SVP: 2 DLU: 77

922.687-078 PAPER STRIPPER (paper goods; print. & pub.)
Reads work order to determine amount and type of paper required for printing. Strips outside wrapper from rolls of printing paper or wallpaper stock and cuts away torn, soiled, or creased sections, using knife, to prepare stock for printing. Conveys stock to printing machines, using handtruck. May move raw materials, such as pigment and chemicals to other departments, using handtruck.
GOE: 05.12.19 STRENGTH: H GED: R1 M1 L1 SVP: 2 DLU: 77

922.687-082 PULP PILER (logging) alternate titles: pulp roller
Stacks pulpwood logs in piles at skidway or landing near logging road or stream. Places logs on pile by hand, or guides logs into position with cant hook as log is lifted by mechanical means.
GOE: 05.12.03 STRENGTH: H GED: R1 M1 L1 SVP: 2 DLU: 77

922.687-086 RETURNED-GOODS SORTER (textile)
Sorts defective cloth returned to textile mill or processing establishment. Opens shipping cases, using claw hammer, knife, and wirecutters. Lifts cloth from cases and deposits it in specified bins preparatory to cutting, inspection, or other processes.

GOE: 06.03.02 STRENGTH: L GED: R2 M1 L2 SVP: 2 DLU: 77

922.687-090 STEVEDORE II (water trans.)
Loads and unloads ships' cargoes: Carries or moves cargo by handtruck to wharf and stacks cargo on pallets or cargo boards to facilitate transfer to and from ship. Stacks cargo in transit shed or in hold of ship as directed by HEADER (water trans.). Attaches and moves slings used to lift cargo. Guides load being lifted to prevent swinging. Shores cargo in ship's hold to prevent shifting during voyage. May be designated according to area in which work is performed as Stevedore, Dock (water trans.); Stevedore, Front (water trans.); Stevedore, Hold (water trans.).
GOE: 05.12.03 STRENGTH: V GED: R2 M1 L1 SVP: 2 DLU: 77

922.687-094 TIMBER PACKER (saw. & plan.)
Loads logs or sawed lumber onto flatcars, trucks, and boats, packing tightly and securing load with stakes, chains, and cables so that load will not shift in transit.
GOE: 05.12.03 STRENGTH: H GED: R1 M1 L1 SVP: 2 DLU: 77

922.687-098 TIN STACKER (tinware)
Carries punched blanks from scroll shear to punch press, by hand or on handtrucks. Picks up scrap from scroll shear and punch press, using shovel, scrap fork, or by hand, and deposits it in bins or in scrap chute. May weigh scrap tin and record weight in logbook.
GOE: 06.04.40 STRENGTH: H GED: R1 M1 L1 SVP: 1 DLU: 77

922.687-102 YARD LABORER (paper & pulp)
Moves and stores material and maintains yard and grounds of paper and pulp plant by performing any combination of following tasks: Shovels wood chips, pulpwood, sulfur, and limerock into trucks or onto conveyors. Cleans chips or bark from conveyors; bark, leaves, and twigs from water canal, and burns refuse. Removes driftwood from canal, using hoist. May load waste paper from paper machines into carts. May stack bundles of woodpulp and dump pulp and waste paper into beaters. May dig ditches and install pipelines from railroad tank cars to facilitate unloading of chemicals used in paper manufacture.
GOE: 05.12.03 STRENGTH: H GED: R1 M1 L1 SVP: 1 DLU: 77

929   PACKAGING AND MATERIALS HANDLING OCCUPATIONS, N.E.C.

This group includes occupations, not elsewhere classified, concerned with packaging and materials handling.

929.131-010 SUPERVISOR, SALVAGE (petrol. refin.) alternate titles: reclamation supervisor
Supervises and coordinates activities of workers engaged in salvaging valves, flanges, pipefittings, tubes, and traps, and in sorting, storing, and issuing reclaimed articles. Determines salvageability of defective parts, based on knowledge of availability and cost of replacements. Performs duties as described under SUPERVISOR (any industry) Master Title.
GOE: 05.10.01 STRENGTH: L GED: R4 M3 L3 SVP: 7 DLU: 77

929.132-010 SUPERVISOR, REACTOR FUELING (chemical)
Supervises and coordinates activities of workers engaged in receiving and storing reactor fuel elements, recharging reactor, loading *monotubes,* packaging, storing, and shipping irradiated fuel elements in a nuclear reactor plant: Reads production schedules to determine time and sequence of reactor recharging, monotube loading, packaging, and storing activities. Reads exposure-availability (amount of exposure to radiation permitted individual workers) and personnel rosters to compile work schedules. Explains and demonstrates work tasks to new workers and assigns them to experienced workers for further training. Performs other duties as described under SUPERVISOR (any industry) Master Title.
GOE: 05.12.01 STRENGTH: L GED: R4 M3 L3 SVP: 6 DLU: 77

929.133-010 YARD SUPERVISOR (woodworking)
Supervises and coordinates activities of workers engaged in unloading, storing, and distributing materials, such as coal, logs, lumber, wastepaper, and sulfur in yard of industrial plant: Confers with plant personnel and plans and allocates use of materials handling equipment, such as conveyors, cranes, tractors, and trucks, according to material to be moved and production requirements. Directs workers engaged in keeping records of materials received and used. Trains new workers. May inspect incoming materials and verify invoices. May inspect machines and equipment and direct workers engaged in maintenance and repair work. May supervise workers engaged in drying lumber in kiln [KILN OPERATOR (woodworking) 563.382-010]. May supervise workers engaged in booming (gathering) and sorting logs in log pond. Performs other duties as described under SUPERVISOR (any industry) Master Title.
GOE: 05.12.01 STRENGTH: L GED: R4 M3 L3 SVP: 7 DLU: 78

929.137-010 GENERAL-HANDLING SUPERVISOR (smelt. & refin.)
Supervises and coordinates activities of workers engaged in sorting, stacking, and weighing metal pigs and metal scrap, and in receiving, checking, storing, and distributing raw materials, such as coke, chlorine, and gasoline. Performs duties as described under SUPERVISOR (any industry) Master Title.
GOE: 05.12.01 STRENGTH: L GED: R4 M2 L2 SVP: 6 DLU: 77

929.137-014 POLEYARD SUPERVISOR (utilities)
Supervises and coordinates activities of workers engaged in receiving, grading, sorting, framing, and storing wooden poles used to support electric power

transmission lines: Directs workers engaged in peeling, bucking, boring, and painting poles. Examines poles for conformance to specifications. May direct workers to recondition poles. May prepare requisitions and collect money from sale of poles from yard. Performs duties as described under SUPERVISOR (any industry) Master Title.
GOE: 05.12.01 STRENGTH: L GED: R4 M2 L3 SVP: 7 DLU: 77

929.137-018 WAREHOUSE SUPERVISOR (motor trans.) alternate titles: labor-gang supervisor
Supervises and coordinates activities of workers engaged in loading, unloading, recording, arranging, routing, and delivery of incoming and outgoing freight in a freight storage warehouse of a motor transportation firm. Performs duties as described under SUPERVISOR (any industry) Master Title. May be designated according to activity as Supervisor, Car-Loading-And-Unloading (motor trans.).
GOE: 05.12.01 STRENGTH: L GED: R4 M3 L3 SVP: 7 DLU: 77

929.137-022 WAREHOUSE SUPERVISOR (any industry)
Supervises and coordinates activities of workers engaged in receiving, transporting, stacking, order filling, shipping, and maintaining stock records in warehouse. Supervises labeling and casing or packing of materials or products. Trains new workers. May be known by specific area worked as Cooler Supervisor (dairy products). Performs duties as described under SUPERVISOR (any industry) Master Title.
GOE: 05.09.01 STRENGTH: L GED: R4 M3 L3 SVP: 7 DLU: 81

929.137-026 YARD SUPERVISOR (smelt. & refin.)
Supervises and coordinates activities of workers engaged in receiving, storing, issuing, and shipping equipment, materials, and supplies, such as machinery, lumber, chemicals, fuel oils, scrap iron, and ore concentrate: Weighs railroad cars and trucks containing shipments, and verifies shipments against delivery records. Inspects incoming shipments, notifies freight agent of damages, and compiles claim reports. Informs railroad crews of spotting site for incoming cars. Performs other duties as described under SUPERVISOR (any industry) Master Title.
GOE: 05.12.01 STRENGTH: L GED: R4 M2 L3 SVP: 7 DLU: 77

929.137-030 YARD SUPERVISOR, BUILDING MATERIALS OR LUMBER (retail trade; wholesale tr.)
Supervises and coordinates activities of workers engaged in loading and unloading materials and in using and maintaining machines and equipment in lumber yard or building materials yard: Coordinates shipments in and out of yard and inspects for specified quantity and quality. Directs workers in loading and unloading materials and in use and care of machines and equipment, such as stackers, carriers, planes, saws, and concrete mixers. Performs other duties as described under SUPERVISOR (any industry) Master Title.
GOE: 05.12.01 STRENGTH: M GED: R4 M4 L3 SVP: 7 DLU: 77

929.137-034 YARD SUPERVISOR, COTTON GIN (agriculture)
Supervises and coordinates activities of workers engaged in receiving bulk cotton in cotton ginning establishment: Directs workers engaged in unloading bulk cotton and routing it to storage bins or to ginning stands through vacuum conveyor pipes. Maintains records of quantity and location of stored cotton. May assist in repairing equipment, such as conveyor systems, trailers, and storage bins. May sample cotton [COTTON SAMPLER (agriculture; textile)]. Performs other duties as described under SUPERVISOR (any industry) Master Title.
GOE: 05.12.01 STRENGTH: L GED: R4 M3 L3 SVP: 6 DLU: 77

929.367-010 PRESERVATION INSPECTOR, MARINE EQUIPMENT (government ser.) alternate titles: equipment processor, storage
Directs or participates in preparation of equipment, such as naval guns and other ordnance materiel for mothballing (storage): Inspects materiel for condition to determine feasibility of storage, type of preservative application required, and degree of dismantling necessary. Identifies materiel and parts according to knowledge of equipment function and comparison with catalog specifications to select preservative treatment best suited to each piece of equipment. Ascertains condition to determine need for scraping, washing, brushing, or other treatment preparatory to storage. Directs or assists in moistureproofing of materiel, using preservative agents applied by brushing, spraying, or dipping.
GOE: 05.03.09 STRENGTH: M GED: R4 M2 L2 SVP: 6 DLU: 77

929.381-010 CARPET CUTTER (retail trade)
Measures, marks, and cuts carpeting and linoleum, using measuring and marking devices and knife, or cutting machine, to get maximum number of usable pieces from standard sized rolls, following floor dimensions or diagrams. May be designated according to type of floor covering cut as Linoleum Cutter (retail trade).
GOE: 05.10.01 STRENGTH: H GED: R3 M2 L2 SVP: 5 DLU: 77

929.382-010 LOAD-TEST MECHANIC (aircraft mfg.) alternate titles: proof-load mechanic
Sets up and operates equipment to load-test tooling and material handling apparatus, such as jigs, fixtures, cables, metal and fabric slings, chains, binders, and tie rods: Reads specifications to determine load-test procedures. Positions and secures tooling or apparatus to be tested in holding devices, manually or using crane or forklift. Attaches load-test equipment to test specimen, according to specifications. Adjusts test equipment controls to apply specified weight or

pressure to test specimen to determine holding or handling capacity or to determine maximum load at which item fatigues or breaks. Examines tooling and handling apparatus for structural failure or misuse. Records test information. Attaches inspection tags to tooling or apparatus.
GOE: 06.03.01 STRENGTH: H GED: R3 M2 L3 SVP: 6 DLU: 89

929.583-010 YARD WORKER (agriculture)
Drives tractor to move spots (trailers of cotton) to suction shed, storage building, or other designated areas of cotton gin yard: Loads bales of cotton into trailer and unloads and stores bales. Keeps record of supplies issued from warehouse and delivers supplies to gin workers. May clean gin yard as directed.
GOE: 05.11.04 STRENGTH: M GED: R3 M2 L1 SVP: 3 DLU: 77

929.587-010 NUT-AND-BOLT ASSEMBLER (nut & bolt) alternate titles: nutter-up
Couples and packages nuts and bolts: Screws nut on bolt by hand and holds nut in chuck of nut-turning machine that spins and tightens nut on bolt. Weighs or counts specified amounts of nuts and bolts, and records number of units on production form. Pushes box or carton along bench or onto conveyor. May tie long bolts into bundles, using wire. May feed nuts and bolts into hopper of machine that automatically couples and packages nuts and bolts.
GOE: 06.04.38 STRENGTH: L GED: R1 M1 L1 SVP: 2 DLU: 77

929.663-010 LOGGING-TRACTOR OPERATOR (forestry; logging; saw. & plan.)
Drives straight or articulated tractor equipped with one or more accessories, such as bulldozer blade, grapple, logging arch, cable winches, hoisting rack, and crane boom, to skid, load, unload, or stack logs, pull stumps, or clear brush. Gives or receives signals from coworkers regarding moving logs. May build or repair logging and skid roads. May drive logging tractor equipped with crawler treads. May saw felled trees into lengths [BUCKER (logging) 454.684-010]. May be designated according to accessory equipment operated as Logging-Arch Operator (logging); Logging-Tractor Operator, Swamp (logging); Log-Stacker Operator (logging; saw. & plan.); Skid-Grapple Operator (logging); Skidder Operator (forestry; logging).
GOE: 03.04.02 STRENGTH: M GED: R3 M1 L1 SVP: 4 DLU: 79

929.683-014 TRACTOR OPERATOR (any industry)
Drives gasoline or diesel powered tractor to move materials, draw farm implements, tow trailers, pull out objects imbedded in ground, or pull cable of winch to raise, lower, or load heavy material or equipment: Fastens attachments, such as graders, plows, and rollers, to tractor with hitchpins. Releases brake, shifts gears, and depresses accelerator or moves throttle to control forward and backward movement of tractor. Steers tractor by turning steering wheel and depressing brake pedals. May lubricate and repair tractor and attachments. May be designated according to type of power utilized as Diesel-Tractor Operator (any industry); Gasoline-Tractor Operator (any industry); Tractor Operator, Battery (mine & quarry). May operate tractor mounted with wide spread pneumatic or metallic treads to transport materials over marshes or swamps and be designated Marsh-Buggy Operator (construction). May operate tractor equipped with laser leveling equipment to level large fields for farming or industrial purposes and be designated Tractor Operator, Laser Leveling (any industry).
GOE: 05.11.04 STRENGTH: M GED: R3 M2 L2 SVP: 3 DLU: 80

929.684-010 PACKER (ordnance)
Packs rocket-motor cases in special containers for shipment: Paints shipping containers, using spray gun. Transports motor cases from curing oven on overhead conveyor and lowers cases into shipping container, using hoist. Removes handling rings or slings from case, using hand or power wrenches. Clamps or bolts cover plates over ends of motor case. Clamps cover on shipping container, using wrenches.
GOE: 06.04.38 STRENGTH: M GED: R2 M1 L2 SVP: 3 DLU: 77

929.685-010 CRATE OPENER (furniture)
Tends machine that restrains compressed bedsprings to permit uncrating in mattress manufacturing establishment: Moves crates of compressed bedsprings to bed of uncrating machine, using handtruck. Presses button to lower hydraulic press onto compressed bedsprings and cuts shipping wires and bands, using wire cutters. Presses button to raise press, expanding bedsprings from compressed state. Removes shipping wires and bands from bedsprings and moves bedsprings to processing area, using handtruck.
GOE: 06.04.24 STRENGTH: H GED: R2 M1 L1 SVP: 2 DLU: 77

929.685-014 TYING-MACHINE OPERATOR (paper goods; tex. prod., nec)
Tends tying machine that automatically wraps and ties string around bundles of products, such as cardboard boxes and finished canvas goods: Threads string through machine wrapping arm. Positions specified number of items to be tied on machine table. Depresses pedal that passes wrapping arm around items, ties knot, and cuts off string. May visually inspect products for defects. May keep production records.
GOE: 06.04.38 STRENGTH: L GED: R1 M1 L1 SVP: 2 DLU: 77

929.685-018 TYING-MACHINE OPERATOR, LUMBER (woodworking) alternate titles: binder; bundler
Tends machine that wraps and ties bundles of lumber with wire or twine: Places roll of wire or twine on machine spindle and threads through guides to knotter and cutter. Stacks specified number of boards or furniture parts on ma-

chine table and clamps pile in place. Starts machine and depresses pedal that actuates machine to wrap and tie wire or twine around pile and cut wire or twine free from roll. Stacks bundled stock on dolly or sets bundles on conveyor belt. May wrap ends of bundle with paper or fabric before tying.
GOE: 06.04.38 STRENGTH: H GED: R2 M1 L1 SVP: 2 DLU: 77

929.686-014 BAND SALVAGER (agriculture) alternate titles: band straightener
Salvages tie bands from uncompressed cotton bales for reuse on compressed cotton bales: Straightens bands, using rubber mallet, or feeds bands through powered rollers that flatten and straighten them. Cuts bands to required length for tying compressed bales, using tablemounted cutting device with preset cutting blades. Deposits excess pieces of banding into container for splicing by BAND MAKER (agriculture). May bend end of each band and attach fastening buckle onto bent end.
GOE: 06.04.24 STRENGTH: L GED: R1 M1 L1 SVP: 1 DLU: 77

929.686-018 CRAYON-SORTING-MACHINE FEEDER (pen & pencil)
Loads crayons and pencils of various colors into hopper of machine, starts machine, and observes operation as machine sorts them into specified quantities for packing. Clears jams in machine. Keeps record of boxes completed.
GOE: 06.04.09 STRENGTH: L GED: R2 M1 L1 SVP: 2 DLU: 77

929.686-022 FEED-IN WORKER (grain-feed mills)
Opens damaged sacks of flour and meal and dumps contents into chutes that carry it to feed department for resacking. Cleans sacks, using suction-pipe cleaner. Turns sack inside out and repeats operation. Places cleaned sacks on handtruck and conveys them to supply room.
GOE: 05.12.03 STRENGTH: H GED: R1 M1 L1 SVP: 2 DLU: 77

929.687-010 CUTTER, BANANA ROOM (wholesale tr.)
Cuts hands of bananas from stalks for packing preparatory to shipment. Counts bananas. Determines, according to ripeness, room in which bananas will be stored.
GOE: 06.04.28 STRENGTH: M GED: R2 M1 L1 SVP: 2 DLU: 77

929.687-014 KILN DRAWER (brick & tile) alternate titles: drawer
Removes burned clay products, such as sewer pipe, brick, refractories, and roofing tile, from tunnel kiln cars or periodic kilns, by hand or using hoist: Places pallet on drawing dock and lifts and stacks product on pallet. Examines products for defects, such as cracks, chips, and distortions. Grades and sorts products. Removes and places kiln furniture, such as tie brick, clamp, and holders, in box for reuse. Discards setting rings in waste bin. Cleans used kiln and door brick. May load clay products onto kiln cars prior to firing process. May stock clay products on pallets or place products in carton for shipment.
GOE: 05.12.03 STRENGTH: H GED: R2 M1 L1 SVP: 2 DLU: 78

929.687-018 LABORER, HIGH-DENSITY PRESS (agriculture) alternate titles: hoist worker
Loads compressed bales of cotton onto handtrucks or tractor-drawn trailers: Secures hooks to bale and lifts bale onto trailer or handtruck, using hoist. May stencil identifying information on bale, using brush and stencil.
GOE: 06.04.40 STRENGTH: L GED: R1 M1 L1 SVP: 2 DLU: 77

929.687-022 LABORER, SALVAGE (any industry) alternate titles: reclaimer; salvager; trash collector; waste collector
Salvages materials in industrial or commercial establishment, performing any combination of duties: Collects reusable items or waste materials, such as lumber, paper, rags, fiber, yarn, rubber, beer and soft drink bottles, chemicals, and scrap metal, in scrap gondolas, barrels, or other containers, using handtruck, industrial truck, or wheelbarrow. Inspects materials and sorts items or materials into piles or places in bins or barrels according to type, size, condition, coloring, marking, or other characteristics. Salvages reusable materials and disposes of waste by pouring into sewer or waste containers, loading onto vehicle, or by burning or baling waste. Moves reusable materials to production department or storage. Separates metal particles from waste, using wire screen or magnet. Attaches labels to waste and salvage containers to identify contents. Weighs materials and containers and keeps records of total amount of waste collected. Dumps waste material, such as broke (waste paper and pulp), into machine tank for reprocessing. Makes minor repairs to scrap containers, such as bumping out dents, using handtools. May be designated according to kind of material salvaged as Broke Handler (paper & pulp); Lumber Salvager (any industry); Metal Salvager (any industry); Rag Sorter (any industry); Sack Sorter (any industry); Scrap Sorter (any industry); or specialized assignment as Scrap Burner (any industry).
GOE: 06.04.40 STRENGTH: M GED: R2 M1 L1 SVP: 2 DLU: 77

929.687-026 LINER INSERTER (tobacco)
Pulls plastic liner over carton-shaped or hogshead-shaped form. Lowers form, suspended from ceiling into open containers, using rope and pulley, working as member of two-person team. Overlaps edges of plastic liner over top edge of container and removes form. May insert paper liner into containers.
GOE: 06.04.38 STRENGTH: L GED: R1 M1 L1 SVP: 2 DLU: 77

929.687-030 MATERIAL HANDLER (any industry) alternate titles: distributor; floor worker; line supply; loader and unloader; servicer; stacker; utility worker
Loads, unloads, and moves materials within or near plant, yard, or work site, performing any combination of following duties: Reads work order or follows

oral instructions to ascertain materials or containers to be moved. Opens containers, using steel cutters, crowbar, clawhammer, or other handtools. Loads and unloads materials onto or from pallets, trays, racks, and shelves by hand. Loads materials into vehicles and installs strapping, bracing, or padding to prevent shifting or damage in transit, using handtools. Conveys materials from storage or work sites to designated area, using handtruck, electric dolly, wheelbarrow, or other device. Secures lifting attachments to materials and conveys load to destination, using hand-operated crane or hoist, or signals crane or hoisting operators to move load to destination [LABORER, HOISTING (any industry) 921.667-022]. Counts, weighs, and records number of units of materials moved or handled on daily production sheet. Attaches identifying tags or labels to materials or marks information on cases, bales, or other containers. Loads truck for INDUSTRIAL-TRUCK OPERATOR (any industry) 921.683-050. Stacks or assembles materials into bundles and bands bundles together, using banding machine and clincher. Clamps sections of portable conveyor together or places conveyor sections on blocks or boxes to facilitate movement of materials or products. Removes samples of materials, labels with identifying information, and takes samples to laboratory for analysis [LABORATORY-SAMPLE CARRIER (any industry) 922.687-054]. Lifts heavy objects by hand or using power hoist, and cleans work area, machines, and equipment, using broom, rags, and cleaning compounds, to assist machine operators. Makes simple adjustments or repairs, such as realigning belts or replacing rollers, using handtools. Assembles crates to contain products, such as machines or vehicles, using handtools and precut lumber. Shovels loose materials, such as sand, gravel, metals, plastics, or chemicals, into machine hoppers or into vehicles and containers, such as wheelbarrows, scrap truck, or barrels. May occasionally operate industrial truck or electric hoist to assist in loading or moving materials and products. May be designated according to material handled as Filling Hauler, Weaving (textile); according to method of conveying materials as Lugger (agriculture); according to machine or equipment loaded or unloaded as Blunger Loader (pottery & porc.); Vehicle Unloader (any industry); or according to work station as Outside Trucker (any industry); Platform Loader (any industry). May be designated: Bale Piler (textile); Batch Trucker (rubber tire); Bobbin Handler (textile); Car Loader (any industry); Cloth Hauler (textile); Coal Passer (any industry); Compress Trucker (agriculture); Hogshead Dumper (tobacco); Kiln Car Unloader (brick & tile); Laborer, Yard (any industry); Loader (any industry) II; Lumber-Yard Worker (woodworking); Merchandise Carrier (any industry); Mold Mover (toy-sport equip.); Oven Stripper (any industry); Oven Unloader (any industry); Packaging-Machine-Supplies Distributor (tobacco); Slab Picker (saw. & plan.); Powder Trucker (chemical; ordnance); Rack Carrier (paper goods); Racker (any industry); Retort Loader (chemical); Roper (agriculture); Roving Stock Handler (textile); Scrap Wheeler (machine shop); Segregator (agriculture; wholesale tr.); Sugar Trucker (grain-feed mills); Tire Trucker (rubber tire); Trucker, Hand (any industry).
GOE: 05.12.03 STRENGTH: H GED: R2 M1 L1 SVP: 3 DLU: 89

929.687-034 MUNITIONS HANDLER (ordnance)
Loads, unloads, and stores ammunition and ammunition components in magazines (storage areas): Moves materials between magazines and carries materials by hand, handtrucks, and roller conveyors. Secures cargoes in carriers, using blocks and stays. Cleans magazines and adjacent area. Crates and cases materials for specific orders. Inspects packaging and materials.
GOE: 06.04.40 STRENGTH: H GED: R2 M1 L1 SVP: 2 DLU: 77

929.687-038 RETURNED-CASE INSPECTOR (beverage)
Reconditions and cleans used beer cartons, performing any combination of following tasks: Removes carton from conveyor. Lifts out partitions and discards damaged ones. Dumps out dirt or foreign matter. Places dirty or damaged carton on conveyor or into chute for disposal or repair. Inserts bottom pad and partitions in usable cartons and places carton on conveyor for transfer to box or packaging room. May wash cartons, using sponge and cleaning solution.
GOE: 06.04.39 STRENGTH: L GED: R1 M1 L1 SVP: 2 DLU: 77

929.687-042 ROLL COVERER, BURLAP (textile) alternate titles: burlapper; wrapper-and-bagger, sheeting
Wraps or ties pieces of burlap around rolls of cloth or inserts rolls into burlap bag to protect cloth during shipment. Trims excess twine and burlap, using scirrors. May sew burlap [CLOTH-BALE HEADER (textile)].
GOE: 06.04.38 STRENGTH: M GED: R1 M1 L1 SVP: 2 DLU: 77

929.687-046 SCALER-PACKER (meat products)
Weighs and packs meat cuts and meat byproducts: Weighs hams, butts, ribs, loins, skins, and inedible meat products on scales by truckload, cartons, boxes, or individual cuts. Wraps or packs cuts or carcass parts according to weight, grade, or customer order. May trim cuts. May form boxes, close flaps, or tend strapping (carton closing) machine. May inspect products for quality. May record quantity, type product, and weight for quality control. May stencil shipping information on cartons.
GOE: 06.03.02 STRENGTH: M GED: R2 M1 L2 SVP: 3 DLU: 77

929.687-050 WRAPPER COUNTER (tobacco)
Counts specified number of tobacco wrapper leaves and ties leaves in bundle. Attaches ticket to bundle showing number of leaves in bundle. Wraps bundle in cellophane to preserve moisture content until tobacco is used in making cigars.
GOE: 06.04.38 STRENGTH: L GED: R2 M1 L1 SVP: 2 DLU: 77

929.687-054 PALLETIZER (nonfer. metal)
Secures battens (grooved strips of wood) around bundles of packaged metal extrusions to form protective shipping pallets, using *strapping tool*: Presses

conveyor controls to position packaged extrusions under strapping tool. Measures dimensions of bundles, using ruler, and cuts battens to required size, using power saw. Positions battens, cardboard strips, and metal or plastic strapping around bundles in specified fashion, according to written instructions. Threads strapping through strapping tool and secures battens with strapping, using strapping tool, to form protective pallet around extrusions. Removes palletized bundles from conveyor for further processing, using pneumatic hoist.
GOE: 06.04.38 STRENGTH: L GED: R2 M2 L2 SVP: 2 DLU: 86

929.687-058 BANDER, HAND (any industry) alternate titles: baler; load clerk; packager and strapper
Fastens plastic or metal bands around stacks, bundles, or palletized articles prior to storage or shipment, using *strapping tool* and clamps: Counts number of articles to be banded to verify number specified on work order. Unwinds plastic or metal banding material from reel, wraps band around stack or bundle, inserts loose end of banding material into strapping tool, and cinches and crimps banding material and clamp with strapping tool to secure articles during storage or shipment. Counts and records number of banded bundles. May operate hydraulic jack lift or truck to move articles before or after bundling. May cut lumber or other reinforcing material, using handsaw or power saw, and include reinforcing material in bundle or nail lumber together to protect articles during storage or shipment. May stack bundled articles on pallet by hand. May band articles to pallet to secure articles for moving. May mark or stencil size of article, customer's name, order number, address, or other identifying data on visible portion of bundle or shipping ticket with markers, brushes, or paint.
GOE: 06.04.38 STRENGTH: H GED: R2 M2 L2 SVP: 2 DLU: 86

929.687-062 WEIGHER, PRODUCTION (any industry)
Weighs quantities of materials for use in production processes, using balance, platform, or floor scales: Places loose or packaged material on scales and adds or removes portions of material to obtain specified weight. Reads work order or formula to determine types and quantities of materials to weigh. Records weight of materials used for production records, or maintains perpetual inventory of materials used and on hand. May dump materials in prescribed sequence into chute or hopper or onto conveyor belt. May transfer weighed materials to production or storage areas, using handtruck or power truck. May sort weighed materials into designated bins or containers, according to weight or type. May be designated according to type of scale used or material weighed as Batch Weigher (chemical); Compounder (rubber reclaim.); Feather Grader (tex. prod., nec); Operator, Scales (plastic-synth.); Rubber Compounder (nonfer. metal; plastic-synth.; rubber goods; rubber tire); Shadow-Graph-Weight Operator (toy-sport equip.); Stock Mixer (textile; tex. prod., nec); Weigher-And-Charger (fabrication, nec). May weigh plant products as part of packing process and be designated Weigher, Packing (any industry).
GOE: 06.03.02 STRENGTH: M GED: R2 M1 L2 SVP: 3 DLU: 81

93 OCCUPATIONS IN EXTRACTION OF MINERALS

This division includes occupations concerned with quarrying and with the extraction of minerals, such as coal, ores, crude petroleum, and natural gas. Includes crushing, screening, washing, flotation, and other processes of extracting materials at or near the mining site.

930 EARTH BORING, DRILLING, CUTTING, AND RELATED OCCUPATIONS

This group includes occupations concerned with drilling wells, undercutting coal seams, sawing and splitting virgin rock, and related activities involved with tapping water- or mineral-bearing formations, obtaining samples of substrata, and loosening or removing materials, using handtools, and hydraulic, electric, or pneumatic power tools, cutting and drilling machines, and other devices. Occupations concerned with construction excavating are found in Groups 850 and 859.

930.130-010 TOOL PUSHER (petrol. & gas) alternate titles: superintendent, drilling
Supervises and coordinates activities of workers engaged in drilling oil and gas wells in area consisting of one or more wellsites: Directs workers to erect, dismantle, and move drilling rigs, and drilling crews in setting up and operating power units, draw works and other drilling equipment. Plans delivery of drilling tools, fuel, water, and other supplies for use at drill site. Orders type of drilling bits to be used, according to type of strata encountered. Directs workers in mixing drilling mud and circulating mud in borehole, and in use of special drilling mud to prevent blowouts from gas pressure. Orders installation of control head (valve device) to control flow when well begins to produce gas or oil. May supervise operations at producing wells to maintain and regulate flow of gas or oil [SUPERVISOR, PRODUCTION (petrol. & gas)]. Performs other duties as described under SUPERVISOR (any industry) Master Title. May supervise PROSPECTING DRILLERS (petrol. & gas) drilling shallow boreholes for use in seismic prospecting or to obtain core samples and be designated Tool Pusher, Shallow-Exploratory Drilling (petrol. & gas).
GOE: 05.02.05 STRENGTH: L GED: R4 M2 L3 SVP: 8 DLU: 77

930.131-010 FIELD SUPERVISOR, OIL-WELL SERVICES (petrol. & gas)

Supervises and coordinates activities of workers engaged in setting up, testing, and servicing equipment at oil or gas wells, or boreholes, running instruments in and out of wells, electrical well logging, gun perforating, and temperature surveying. Orders maintenance and repair of equipment, such as cables, vehicles, and test instruments. Performs duties as described under SUPERVISOR (any industry) Master Title.
GOE: 05.02.05 STRENGTH: L GED: R4 M3 L3 SVP: 7 DLU: 77

930.134-010 QUARRY SUPERVISOR, DIMENSION STONE (mine & quarry)

Supervises and coordinates activities of workers engaged in quarrying dimension stone: Schedules production or maintenance assignments of workers. Marks area or dimensions of blocks to be removed from stone mass, using chalkline. Fills blast holes with blasting agents and detonator, and notifies workers to evacuate area. Detonates explosive, using blasting machine, to separate block from stone mass [BLASTER (mine & quarry)]. Signals HOISTING ENGINEER (any industry) to lift blocks from pit to stockpile area. Inspects blocks for defects such as cracks or discolorations. Computes dimensions of and marks identifying data on blocks. Fastens dogs into drilled holes in stone to facilitate loading on truck. Compiles production and shipping records. Performs other duties as described under SUPERVISOR (any industry) Master Title.
GOE: 05.11.02 STRENGTH: H GED: R4 M3 L3 SVP: 6 DLU: 77

930.167-010 TECHNICAL OPERATOR (petrol. & gas) alternate titles: drilling inspector

Charts pressure, temperature, and other characteristics of oil and gas well boreholes or producing wells, using special subsurface instruments, and interprets findings for use in determining further drilling or producing procedures: Directs workers in assembling wire line hoisting gear and attaching line to instruments. Gives directions to HOIST OPERATOR (petrol. & gas) to lower clinograph into well to determine variation of well from vertical (instrument records variation on chart). Informs ROTARY DRILLER (petrol. & gas) of variation from vertical. Lowers weighted wire into well and reads depth of well from recording wheel. Lowers depth bomb into well that records pressure at various depths to determine rate of natural flow of oil from well. Lowers thermometers and other instruments with accompanying recording devices through tubing, casing, drill pipe, or open borehole. Raises instruments from well and removes chart recordings. Measures, converts, records, and interprets data for use by engineering personnel and management in determining drilling or production procedures. May calibrate recording devices. May repair and maintain instruments. May be designated according to specialty as Bottom-Hole-Pressure-Recording Operator (petrol. & gas).
GOE: 05.03.04 STRENGTH: L GED: R4 M3 L3 SVP: 6 DLU: 77

930.261-010 FISHING-TOOL TECHNICIAN, OIL WELL (petrol. & gas) alternate titles: oil-well-fishing-tool operator

Analyzes conditions of unserviceable oil or gas wells and directs use of special well-fishing tools and techniques to recover lost equipment and other obstacles from boreholes of wells: Confers with SUPERINTENDENT, DRILLING AND PRODUCTION (petrol. & gas) to gather information regarding size of pipes and tools and borehole conditions in wells. Plans fishing methods and selects tools for removing obstacles, such as liners, broken casing, screens, and drill pipe from wells. Directs drilling crew in applying weights to drill pipes, in using special tools, in applying pressure to circulating fluid (mud), and in drilling around lodged obstacles or specified earth formations, using whipstocks and other special tools. Observes load variations on strain gauge, mudpump, and motor pressure indicators, and listens to sounds of engines and rotary chains to detect signs of faulty operations or unusual conditions in wells. Quotes prices to customer and prepares reports of services rendered, tools used, and time required, to serve as basis for billing customer. May direct drilling crew in installation of well-bottom equipment.
GOE: 05.03.04 STRENGTH: L GED: R4 M3 L3 SVP: 7 DLU: 77

930.261-014 FORMATION-TESTING OPERATOR (petrol. & gas) alternate titles: oil-well formation tester; testing-tool operator

Analyzes samples of fluids from specified formations in oil well to determine productivity of strata, using special testing equipment: Assembles valve device and automatic pressure recorder on drilling floor, using handtools. Directs ROTARY DRILLER (petrol. & gas) to lower section of drill pipe containing instruments into well to specified depth. Opens valve by surface control to obtain sample of fluids in valve device and to chart pressure of fluid-giving formation. Closes valve and directs ROTARY DRILLER (petrol. & gas) to raise pipe and equipment. Analyzes chemical content of sample and interprets pressure readings to determine presence and quantity of oil, gas, water, or other materials in formation. May send sample of fluids from formation to laboratory for analysis. May perforate boreholes [PERFORATOR OPERATOR, OIL WELL (petrol. & gas)].
GOE: 05.07.05 STRENGTH: L GED: R4 M3 L3 SVP: 6 DLU: 77

930.267-010 OIL-PIPE INSPECTOR (petrol. & gas) alternate titles: pipe inspector

Inspects steel tubing, casing, drill pipe, and other tubular oil well equipment for defects, using magnetic and optical inspection equipment: Positions scanner (ring-shaped object containing induction coils) around pipe and connects wire to automatic graph recorder. Presses switch to start self-propelled scanner along pipe length and observes lines on graph that indicate location, type, and extent of metal blemishes, cracks, and molecular weakness. Inspects interior of pipe for surface imperfections, using optical instrument. Reports findings to engineering personnel.
GOE: 05.07.01 STRENGTH: L GED: R4 M3 L4 SVP: 6 DLU: 77

930.361-010 SERVICE-UNIT OPERATOR, OIL WELL (petrol. & gas) alternate titles: oil-well-sounding-device operator

Operates equipment to increase oil flow from producing wells, or to remove stuck pipe, casing, tools, or other obstructions from drilling wells, using specialized subsurface tools and instruments: Directs SAMPLE-TAKER OPERATOR (petrol. & gas) to assemble and connect pipe and hydraulic lines of flushing equipment to wellhead. Starts pumps which circulate water, oil, or other fluid through well, removing sand and other materials obstructing free flow of oil. Perforates well casing or sidewall of borehole with explosive charge [PERFORATOR OPERATOR, OIL WELL (petrol. & gas)]. Assembles and lowers detection instruments into wells having drill pipe, drilling tools, or other obstructions wedged in well. Interprets instrument readings to ascertain depth of obstruction. Directs lowering of specialized equipment to point of obstruction and pushes switches or pulls levers to back-off pipe by chemical or explosive action, or to sever pipe at point of obstruction, permitting recovery of pipestring and resumption of drilling operations. Assembles and operates sound wave generating and detecting mechanisms for determining fluid level in wells. May operate hoist to lower and raise tools [HOIST OPERATOR (petrol. & gas)].
GOE: 05.11.03 STRENGTH: L GED: R3 M2 L2 SVP: 7 DLU: 77

930.363-010 CLEAN-OUT DRILLER (petrol. & gas) alternate titles: well cleaner

Operates truck-mounted hoist equipped with derrick to clean out and restore old and damaged oil or gas wells: Moves lever to raise derrick over wellhead. Directs CLEAN-OUT-DRILLER HELPER (petrol. & gas) to jack up truck body and to center hoisting cable over borehole. Assembles and attaches cleanout tools to cable, using handtools. Moves winch lever to lower tools into well. Cleans sand, paraffin, or pipe scale from well, using special scaling and bailing tools. Removes debris from well, using bailer. Lowers blocks composed of soft lead or covered with wax, tar, or soap to take impression of broken equipment in well. Lowers grappling tools into well to probe for and remove obstruction, using hoist. Lowers and raises swabbing tool that creates vacuum and draws well fluids through pipe screens and well perforations, using hoist. May be designated according to specific activity as Bailer (petrol. & gas); Swabber (petrol. & gas).
GOE: 05.11.03 STRENGTH: M GED: R3 M2 L2 SVP: 5 DLU: 77

930.364-010 OIL-PIPE-INSPECTOR HELPER (petrol. & gas)

Inspects tubular metal equipment as assistant to OIL-PIPE INSPECTOR (petrol. & gas) by performing any combination of following tasks: Inspects interior and exterior of tubing, casing, drill pipe, and other tubular metal equipment used in drilling and producing oil or gas wells to detect incrustations, cracks, or other defects, using mechanical and electronic instruments. Interconnects electric conductor cables to instruments, control panels, and generator sets, using wrenches and screwdrivers. Rolls and segregates pipe on rack for inspection. Inserts magnetic poles (shooting prods) into ends of pipe and sprinkles magnetic powder on magnetized pipe to reveal exterior defects. Observes surface of pipe and paints colored bands on pipe to indicate nature and location of defect. Inserts tubular instrument through interior of pipe. Clamps self-propelled electronic instrument to pipe, observes instrument moving lengthwise on pipe, and marks location and nature of defect on pipe. Cleans and repairs equipment. Performs other duties as described under HELPER (any industry) Master Title.
GOE: 05.07.01 STRENGTH: H GED: R3 M2 L1 SVP: 5 DLU: 77

930.382-010 DRILLER, MACHINE (construction; mine & quarry) alternate titles: driller operator

Sets up and operates self-propelled or truck-mounted drilling machine to bore blasting holes in overburden at strip mine, open pit, or construction site: Positions and stabilizes machine, using jacks, and lowers drill shaft into position. Moves levers to start and advance drill into overburden, ore, or rock formation. Stops drill to install additional drill stems. Observes operation to detect binding or stoppage of drill. Removes drill when specified depth has been reached. Replaces broken or worn parts, using handtools, and lubricates equipment. May charge and set off explosives in blasting holes. May be assisted by DRILLER HELPER (construction; mine & quarry). May be designated according to type of drill operated as Tractor-Drill Operator (construction; mine & quarry); Rotary-Drill Operator (construction; mine & quarry); Wagon-Drill Operator (construction; mine & quarry).
GOE: 05.11.02 STRENGTH: H GED: R3 M2 L2 SVP: 5 DLU: 77

930.382-014 PIPE TESTER (petrol. & gas)

Operates hydraulic pump and auxiliary equipment to test oil well tubing or casing for high-pressure leaks: Attaches wire line pulley to crown block of rig, and hydraulic hose to testing tool, pump, and source of water, using wrenches. Lowers testing tool and high-pressure packing device into pipe to seal it and retain water in specified section, using winch. Moves lever on hydraulic pump to fill section with water under specified pressure and observes gauge to detect leaks [HYDRO-PNEUMATIC TESTER (any industry)].
GOE: 05.07.01 STRENGTH: M GED: R3 M3 L2 SVP: 5 DLU: 77

930.382-018 PROSPECTING DRILLER (petrol. & gas) alternate titles: core driller; driller; rotary driller, prospecting; shot-hole driller

Operates portable rotary drilling rig to drill shallow boreholes to obtain samples of earth formations, for placement of explosives in seismic prospecting, or for other tests to discover petroleum: Positions truck-mounted derrick at drilling area specified on field map. Starts rig and moves throttles and clutches to raise and lower drilling pipes. Counts sections of drill rod to determine depth of borehole. Selects coring bit and barrel. Withdraws core barrel from hole and extracts core from barrel. Records depths at which samples were taken. Repairs equipment, using handtools.
GOE: 05.11.03 STRENGTH: M GED: R3 M3 L2 SVP: 6 DLU: 77

930.382-022 ROTARY DERRICK OPERATOR (petrol. & gas)

Rigs derrick equipment and operates pumps to circulate mud through drill hole: Sets and bolts crown block to posts at top of derrick. Strings cables through pulleys and blocks. Clamps holding fixture on end of hoisting cable. Weighs clay, and mixes drilling mud, using portable power mixer. Starts pumps that circulate mud through drill pipe and borehole to cool drill bit and flush out drill-cuttings. Cleans and oils pulleys, blocks, and cables. May repair pumps [PUMP SERVICER (any industry)].
GOE: 05.11.03 STRENGTH: M GED: R3 M2 L2 SVP: 5 DLU: 77

930.382-026 ROTARY DRILLER (petrol. & gas) alternate titles: core driller; driller; well driller

Operates gasoline, diesel, electric, or steam draw works to drill oil or gas wells: Observes pressure gauge and moves throttles and levers to control speed of rotary table which rotates string of tools in borehole, and to regulate pressure of tools at bottom of borehole. Connects sections of drill pipe, using handtools and powered wrenches and tongs. Selects and changes drill bits according to nature of strata, using handtools. Pushes levers and brake pedals to control draw works which lowers and raises drill pipe and casing into and out of well. Examines operation of slush pumps to ensure circulation and consistency of mud (drilling fluid) in well. Examines drillings or core samples from bottom of well to determine nature of strata. Fishes for and recovers lost or broken bits, casing and drill pipes from well, using special tools attached to end of drill pipe or cable. Keeps record of footage drilled, location and nature of strata penetrated, and materials used. Caps well or turns valves to regulate outflow of oil from well. Repairs or replaces defective parts of machinery, using handtools. May lower and explode charge in borehole to start flow of oil from well. May specialize in drilling underwater wells from barge-mounted derricks or drilling platforms and be designated Rotary Driller, Marine Operations (petrol. & gas).
GOE: 05.11.03 STRENGTH: M GED: R3 M2 L2 SVP: 6 DLU: 77

930.382-030 WELL PULLER (petrol. & gas) alternate titles: casing puller; pipe puller; pulling-machine operator; rig operator; tube puller; work-over rig operator

Controls power hoisting equipment to pull casing, tubing, and pumping rods from oil and gas wells for repair and to lower repaired equipment, testing devices, and servicing tools into well: Attaches cable clamp to top of pump rod or casing and starts winch or hydraulic jack that raises rod or casing. Disconnects sections of rod or casing, using hand and power wrenches and tongs. Runs packer (plug device) into well to control flow of oil, water, or gas during well-pulling operations. Lowers swabber into well to clear mud from screens at bottom of well and to establish flow of oil. Lowers pressure-recording device into well and interprets charts. Lowers special tools into well to fish for broken rods and tubing and to scrape paraffin and incrustations from casing or tubing. Plugs well with cement [CEMENTER, OIL WELL (petrol. & gas)]. Tests pipe for leaks, using hydraulic-testing equipment. May drive truck equipped with portable hoisting equipment. May be designated according to type of equipment used as Hydraulic Oil-Tool Operator (petrol. & gas).
GOE: 05.11.03 STRENGTH: H GED: R3 M2 L2 SVP: 5 DLU: 77

930.383-010 CHANNELING-MACHINE RUNNER (mine & quarry) alternate titles: channeling-machine operator

Operates track-mounted steam or electrically powered machine to cut channels in quarry stone to facilitate separating stone blocks from mass: Lays track for machine along line at which stone is to be split. Moves levers to start machine moving across face of stone, and to control vertical reciprocating drills which cut shallow channel by shattering action applied to surface of stone. Lubricates machine and replaces dulled bits and worn or damaged parts. May operate portable channeling machine.
GOE: 05.11.02 STRENGTH: M GED: R3 M2 L1 SVP: 4 DLU: 77

930.482-010 DRILLING-MACHINE OPERATOR (mine & quarry) alternate titles: horizontal-drill operator

Operates mobile drilling machine to drill blastholes horizontally in underground mine or in face of strip mine: Drives machine into room where coal, salt, or ore has been undercut. Measures undercuttings with steel rod to determine depth of undercut and location of holes to be drilled. Marks hole locations and boundaries of cut on ribs and face, using chalk. Moves controls to position drill. Starts drill and advances it into rib or face to specified depth. Repositions machine to drill additional holes in specified pattern. Observes electric power cable when moving machine to avoid damage to cable. May drill blastholes in roof to prepare for blasting.
GOE: 05.11.02 STRENGTH: M GED: R3 M2 L1 SVP: 6 DLU: 77

930.662-010 LONG-WALL SHEAR OPERATOR (mine & quarry)

Operates equipment to shear coal from long-wall face in mine: Moves levers to control movement of equipment and to adjust speed and height of cut into coal face during initial pass and during subsequent clean-up passes. Signals other crew members to communicate need to adjust speed of equipment to rate of installation of roof supports and to adjust speed of conveyor to volume of coal needing removal. Listens for unusual sounds that indicate equipment malfunctions. Assists in routine lubrication and maintenance of equipment.
GOE: 05.11.02 STRENGTH: H GED: R3 M2 L2 SVP: 5 DLU: 86

930.663-010 SHALE PLANER OPERATOR (mine & quarry)

Operates track-mounted machine to cut shale from wall face of pit and tends continuous conveyor system used for loading shale in dinkey car or dump truck: Guides and assists crew in resetting planer rails, supports, and blocking from back to front of planer, using jacks, shovel, sledgehammer and pinch bar. Drives machine over rails to pit face. Moves planer levers to control depth of cut and to rotate swivel cutting boom as shale is depleted from area. Presses button to activate conveyor belt and pushes or pulls chain handles to regulate conveyor movement. Lubricates and maintains machine, using handtools, replacement parts, and grease gun.
GOE: 05.11.02 STRENGTH: M GED: R3 M2 L3 SVP: 4 DLU: 77

930.664-010 CASER (petrol. & gas)

Performs any combination of following tasks as member of casing crew: Removes thread protectors from casing sections, using pipe wrenches. Attaches pull-in cable to section of casing and signals crew member to hoist casing onto derrick platform. Attaches cable clamp on casing. Signals rig operator to hoist casing. Pushes or pulls suspended casing to position and align casing section for coupling. Tightens threaded casing sections, using spin rope or spin chain and casing tongs. Removes handslips (curved metal wedges) from casing section to enable rig operator to lower string of coupled casing into borehole. Places handslips around casing at wellhead (after rig operator lowers casing string into borehole to position casing for further coupling) to prevent string of casing from falling into borehole during change or addition of casing sections. Pushes or pulls suspended casing sections while on casing board on derrick tower to assist crew members on derrick floor in stabbing (aligning) casing sections.
GOE: 05.12.12 STRENGTH: V GED: R1 M1 L1 SVP: 3 DLU: 77

930.664-014 CLEAN-OUT-DRILLER HELPER (petrol. & gas)

Cleans out and restores old or damaged gas or oil wells, using handtools, as assistant to CLEAN-OUT DRILLER (petrol. & gas): Unloads cleanout tools and equipment at well site. Levels truck bed at wellhead and aligns hoist cable over borehole, using hand-operated jacks. Assembles and attaches specified cleanout tools, such as bailers and swabs, to cable, using wrenches. Guides tools into borehole. Pushes filled bailer to dumping position and unscrews bailer gate to dump mud, water, and debris removed from well. Guides cable lifting tools from well onto hoist drum, using pinchbar. Dismantles and cleans tools and equipment, using wrenches. Oils and greases machinery. Performs other duties as described under HELPER (any industry) Master Title.
GOE: 05.12.02 STRENGTH: H GED: R2 M1 L1 SVP: 3 DLU: 77

930.665-010 LONG-WALL-MINING-MACHINE TENDER (mine & quarry)

Tends equipment that plows across face of coal strata in underground or strip mine: Monitors electronic control panel which activates machine. Observes indicator lights and gauges on control panel to detect machine malfunction. Advances plow blade through coal strata by remote control on electronic or radio signal from TAILER (mine & quarry). Listens for unusual sounds that would indicate equipment malfunctions. May assist in routine maintenance or repair of machinery.
GOE: 05.11.02 STRENGTH: L GED: R3 M2 L2 SVP: 5 DLU: 77

930.666-010 DRILLER HELPER (construction; mine & quarry)

Bores or burn blasts holes in overburden at strip mine, open pit, quarry, or construction site, as assistant to DRILLER, MACHINE (construction; mine & quarry): Signals DRILLER, MACHINE (construction; mine & quarry) to position machine. Adds, positions, and replaces drill stems, burners, casings, cables, and hoses to assist in drilling operation. Pulls electric cables and water hoses clear of machine treads. Observes ground surface and machine operation for indications of unsafe conditions. Collects ore samples for laboratory analysis. Lubricates and cleans equipment. Performs other duties as described under HELPER (any industry) Master Title.
GOE: 05.12.02 STRENGTH: H GED: R2 M2 L2 SVP: 2 DLU: 77

930.666-014 TAILER (mine & quarry) alternate titles: long-wall-mining-machine helper

Works at opposite end of coal strata assisting LONG-WALL-MINING-MACHINE TENDER (mine & quarry) to advance plow blade through face of coal in underground or surface mine: Pulls levers to adjust depth of penetration of blade. Signals LONG-WALL-MINING-MACHINE TENDER (mine & quarry) by electronic buzzer or two-way radio when machine plow blade is properly positioned. Adjusts and makes minor repairs to equipment, using handtools. May assist in positioning jacks, timbers, or roof supports to prevent cave-ins when working underground.
GOE: 05.12.02 STRENGTH: L GED: R2 M1 L1 SVP: 3 DLU: 77

930.667-010 SHALE PLANER OPERATOR HELPER (mine & quarry)

Cuts and moves shale from open pit, performing any combination of following laboring tasks to assist SHALE PLANER OPERATOR (mine & quarry): Shovels loose shale from travel area of planer. Signals truck driver to posi-

tion vehicle for receiving shale from planer hopper. Monitors movement of shale along conveyor leading from hopper to truck or railcar. Frees jams in planer hopper, using metal pinch bar. Assists in laying tracks and bed supports for planer, using pick, shovel, sledgehammer, and other handtools.
GOE: 05.12.02 STRENGTH: H GED: R2 M1 L1 SVP: 2 DLU: 77

930.682-010 CORE-DRILL OPERATOR (any industry) alternate titles: shot-core-drill operator; test borer; test-hole driller; wash driller

Sets up and operates drilling equipment to obtain solid core samples of strata for analyzing geological characteristics of ground, nature of ore, or strength of foundation material: Drives or guides truck-mounted drilling equipment onto metal or wood foundation, or assembles equipment in position. Connects power lines to equipment. Attaches diamond churn, alloy, or percussion bit to drill rod, and fastens rod in machine, using wrench or other handtools. Starts power unit. Moves clutch and throttle to control rotation and feed of drill bit into ground. Couples additional lengths of drill rod as bit advances. Withdraws drill rod from hole after specified depth has been reached and extracts core from hollow barrel located behind drilling bit. Records depths from which core samples are taken. Lubricates machine, using grease gun, and replaces parts, such as worn winch cables. May replace diamonds in bit as they become worn, chipped, or lost, where diamond drill is used [DIAMOND MOUNTER (machine tools)]. May operate water pump to pump water down borehole to cool drill bit. May be designated according to type of drill used as Diamond Driller (any industry).
GOE: 05.11.02 STRENGTH: M GED: R3 M2 L2 SVP: 6 DLU: 77

930.683-010 CONTINUOUS-MINING-MACHINE OPERATOR (mine & quarry)

Operates self-propelled continuous mining machine to mine coal in underground mine: Drives machine into position at working face. Moves levers to sump (advance) ripper bar or boring head into face of coal seam. Starts machine to gather coal and convey it to floor or shuttle car. May repair, oil, and adjust machine and change cutting teeth, using wrench. May move lever to raise and lower hydraulic safety bar that supports roof above machine until ROOF BOLTERS (mine & quarry) or TIMBER FRAMER (mine & quarry) complete their work.
GOE: 05.11.02 STRENGTH: M GED: R3 M2 L2 SVP: 5 DLU: 77

930.683-014 CUTTER OPERATOR (mine & quarry) alternate titles: coal-cutting-machine operator; cutting-machine operator; undercutter

Operates self-propelled machine to saw channel along working face of coal, salt, or other nonmetal mine to facilitate blasting: Drives unit into working area on tracks or crawler treads. Starts endless chain equipped with teeth that travel around edge of cutter bar and cut into working face. Moves levers to advance cutter bar into face and across bottom or down side of face to complete horizontal or vertical cut. May adjust and repair machine and replace dull teeth, using wrench and pry bar. May shovel debris from channel to facilitate blasting. May cut entries between rooms and haulageways and be designated Entry-Driver Operator (mine & quarry). May cut slots along working face of salt mine deposits and be designated Side-Shearing-Machine Operator (chemical).
GOE: 05.11.02 STRENGTH: M GED: R3 M2 L2 SVP: 6 DLU: 77

930.683-018 DERRICK WORKER, WELL SERVICE (petrol. & gas)

Operates power hoist in truck-mounted, pulling-machine derrick to transfer rod sections to and from derrick racks to rod lifting clamps as sections are removed or returned to oil well: Climbs ladder attached to side of derrick to rod platform. Presses rod hoist control pedal on rod platform to lower *rod transfer device* (rod bottle) to proximity of rod sections suspended in derrick. Attaches transfer device to rod sections and releases pedal to raise rod sections for disconnection of rod lifting clamp (rod elevator). Unlatches lifting clamp and presses pedal to lower rod sections while manually guiding sections into rod holding slots attached to derrick. Descends derrick ladder to tubing platform and fastens safety belt to prepare to transfer tubing sections. Disconnects lifting clamp (tubing elevators) from tubing sections that have been raised into derrick, disconnected from subsequent sections in wellhole, and lowered onto *ground racking board*. Guides tubing sections into slots of tubing rack to stand sections in derrick. Guides tubing sections from tubing rack slots to tubing platform and attaches lifting clamp to sections after defective tubing is replaced, casing repaired, or other oil well service performed. Aligns tubing sections perpendicularly over wellhole to assist in connection of tubing sections and prevent damage to threads of sections. Unfastens safety belt and climbs ladder to rod platform to prepare to transfer rod sections. Presses rod control pedal to lower rod transfer device to rod sections in holding slots. Attaches device to rod sections and releases pedal to lift rod sections from holding slots. Guides sections over wellhole and presses pedal to lower sections to wellhole for connection to rods in wellhole. Connects lifting clamp to rod sections and disconnects transfer device. Periodically turns adjustment screw on rod hoist control stand to regulate power of hoist. Occasionally operates pump to circulate fluid or mud into wellhole. Occasionally connects oil well head attachments, loads tools, and performs similar duties.
GOE: 05.11.03 STRENGTH: H GED: R2 M1 L1 SVP: 3 DLU: 77

930.683-022 HARVESTER OPERATOR (chemical)

Drives and controls specially equipped tractor to harvest salt from granulator beds: Drives machine to designated bed. Positions discharge spout over gondola

car, and depresses clutch to engage harvester. Moves handles to lower scraper equipped with revolving fingers that break up salt and load it onto conveyor for transfer to discharge spout. Moves levers and throttle to control speed of tractor to harvest maximum quantity of salt according to thickness of salt in bed.
GOE: 05.11.04 STRENGTH: L GED: R3 M1 L1 SVP: 4 DLU: 77

930.683-026 ROOF BOLTER (mine & quarry) alternate titles: bolting-machine operator; raise driller

Operates self-propelled machine to install roof-support bolts in underground mine: Positions safety jack to support roof until bolts can be installed. Drives machine into position, inserts bit in drill chuck, and starts drill. Moves lever to advance bit into roof at specified distance from rib or adjacent bolt. Removes bit from chuck and replaces with bolt. Starts hydraulic action which forces bolt into hole. Starts rotation of chuck to turn bolt and open expansion head to exert pressure upon rock formation. Tests bolt for specified tension, using torque wrench. May install truss bolts traversing entire ceiling span and tighten ends of anchored truss bolts, using turnbuckle.
GOE: 05.11.02 STRENGTH: M GED: R3 M1 L1 SVP: 4 DLU: 77

930.684-010 FLAME CHANNELER (construction; mine & quarry) alternate titles: jet channeler; jet-piercer operator

Cuts holes or channels in rock masses to separate block from quarry mass, using jet-piercing torch: Ignites oxygen-kerosene burner and connects water hoses. Positions boom and lowers jet burner to burn or cut hole or channel in rock formation. Adjusts valves and controls to regulate descent or progress of burner as specified. Repairs and replaces parts, using handtools. Keeps production records. May install casing to prevent cave-ins. May use acetylene torch to ignite burner. May lay out pattern for hole or channels to be cut.
GOE: 05.11.02 STRENGTH: M GED: R2 M1 L1 SVP: 4 DLU: 77

930.684-014 FLOOR WORKER, WELL SERVICE (petrol. & gas)

Rigs well service pulling machine on oil well and assembles and disassembles rod and tubing sections, using hand wrenches or power tongs: Pulls lever or turns handle to extend hydraulic or screw-type jacks to support and level pulling machine and derrick. Fastens derrick guy lines to ground-anchors to stabilize derrick. Unloads handtools and power tools from truck and attaches power tools to cables hanging from derrick. Connects pulling machine hydraulic hoses to rod and tubing tongs and other power tools. Unscrews connections on wellhead, using handtools and removes pumping unit head. Attaches lifting clamp (rod elevator) to rod sections in wellhole and places lifting clamp on hook of hoist line. Disconnects rod sections as they are removed from wellhole, using hand wrenches or power tongs. Disconnects and removes hook from hoist line after rod sections have been removed from wellhole and attaches tubing lifting clamp (tubing elevator). Attaches lifting clamps to tubing in wellhole. Disconnects tubing sections as they are removed from wellhole, using hand wrenches or power tongs. Guides uncoupled tubing sections from wellhole to racking board to stand pipe in derrick or guides end of tubing section to ground rack and pushes section to slide it down rack and lay it on ground. Guides tubing and rod sections from derrick or ground rack to wellhole and connects to sections in wellhole, using hand wrenches or power tongs, after repairing oil well pump, replacing defective tubing, or performing similar oil well service. Detaches lifting clamps from sections lowered into wellhole. Assembles and tightens wellhead connections, using hand wrenches and replaces pumping unit head. Disconnects hydraulic hoses and cables from power tools and loads on truck. Unfastens derrick guy lines from ground-anchors and pushes lever or turns handle to contract hydraulic or screw-type jacks. Performs minor maintenance on tools and equipment, such as changing dies in tongs and hand wrenches and changing worn hydraulic hoses on power equipment. Washes tools, equipment, and pulling machine with diesel fuel or other cleaning solution. Shovels dirt around well location to cover spilled oil and cleans oil from wellhead connections.
GOE: 05.12.02 STRENGTH: H GED: R2 M1 L1 SVP: 3 DLU: 77

930.684-018 JACKHAMMER OPERATOR (mine & quarry) alternate titles: air-drill operator; air-hammer operator; plug-drill operator

Drills holes in ore or rock in mine or quarry to facilitate blasting and quarrying, using jackhammer: Connects steam or compressed-air and water lines to hammer. Inserts drill in chuck, trips trigger to start hammer, and leans on hammer to force drill into solid mass. Changes drill or adds lengths as depth of hole increases. Replaces or sharpens bits. Lubricates hammer. May lay steam, compressed-air, or water pipelines. May be designated according to type of drill operated as Tripod-Drill Operator (mine & quarry).
GOE: 05.12.02 STRENGTH: H GED: R2 M2 L1 SVP: 2 DLU: 77

930.684-022 QUARRY PLUG-AND-FEATHER DRILLER (mine & quarry) alternate titles: rock splitter

Separates blocks of rough dimension stone from quarry mass, using jackhammer, wedges, and feathers (shims): Marks desired dimensions on stone, using rule and chalkline, and cuts groove along outline, using chisel. Drills holes along outline with jackhammer [JACKHAMMER OPERATOR (mine & quarry)]. Inserts wedges and feathers into holes and drives wedges with sledgehammer to split stone from mass. May set charge of explosives to split rock [BLASTER (mine & quarry)]. May drill holes into side of stone broken from mass, insert dogs or attach sling, and direct movement of stone from area. May be designated according to type of stone separated as Sandstone Splitter (mine & quarry).

GOE: 05.12.02 STRENGTH: H GED: R2 M1 L1 SVP: 4 DLU: 77

930.684-026 ROTARY-DRILLER HELPER (petrol. & gas) alternate titles: driller helper; rotary helper; roughneck

Assists ROTARY DRILLER (petrol. & gas) in operating machinery to drill oil or gas wells, using handtools and power tongs and wrenches. Assembles and disassembles casings and pipe sections, using hand and power wrenches and tongs. Sets curved metal wedges around pipe string at wellhead to prevent string from falling into well during change or addition of pipe sections. Tightens or loosens threaded joints between sections, using tongs or chain wrenches. Guides lower end of pipe sections to or from well opening. Loosens or tightens joints, using cathead (winch). Mixes drilling mud (clay and sand slush), using power agitators. Reads gauge to ascertain pressure on drilling tools at bottom of well and reports irregularities to ROTARY DRILLER (petrol. & gas). Repairs drilling machinery, slush pumps, and derricks. Digs drainage ditches, racks tools, and cleans drilling floor around rig. May assist in erecting and dismantling rigs. Performs other duties as described under HELPER (any industry) Master Title. May be known according to specific duty performed as Back-Up Worker (petrol. & gas); Cathead Worker (petrol. & gas); Lead-Tong Worker (petrol. & gas); Pipe Racker (petrol. & gas).

GOE: 05.12.02 STRENGTH: H GED: R2 M1 L1 SVP: 4 DLU: 77

930.685-010 MUD-PLANT OPERATOR (petrol. & gas)

Tends machine that mixes mud for use in drilling oil and gas wells: Weighs sand, clay, and other dry materials on scale and dumps materials into hopper of mixing machine. Turns water valve and opens hopper gate to admit specified quantity of water and dry mix into mixing chamber of machine. Tests mud sample for viscosity, using viscometer. Starts pumps that force mud to drilling wells. Lubricates, adjusts, and repairs machinery, using handtools and grease gun. Replaces defective parts of mud pumps and hoisting equipment, using handtools and following repair orders.

GOE: 05.11.03 STRENGTH: H GED: R3 M2 L2 SVP: 4 DLU: 77

930.687-010 BOTTOM-HOLE-PRESSURE-RECORDING-OPERATOR HELPER (petrol. & gas)

Unloads recording equipment at well site for use in determining pressure in oil or gas wells: Attaches conductor cable to instrument and tightens clamps, fittings, and electrical connections, using wrenches and screwdrivers. Observes coiling of conductor cable on hoist drum to prevent damage to cable. Dismantles equipment after use. May drive truck to and from well site when working as member of crew.

GOE: 05.12.03 STRENGTH: M GED: R2 M2 L1 SVP: 3 DLU: 77

930.687-014 CORE-DRILL-OPERATOR HELPER (any industry) alternate titles: drill-runner helper; shot-core-drill-operator helper; test-bore helper; wash-driller helper

Assists CORE-DRILL OPERATOR (any industry) in setting up and operating drilling equipment to obtain core samples used in determining geological character of ground, nature of ore, or strength of foundation material: Labels samples of strata indicating area and depth from which sample was obtained. Lubricates machines and assists in making repairs to machine and equipment, such as replacing worn winch cables, or adjusting drill stems, engines, and pumps. May be designated according to type of drill used as Diamond-Driller Helper (any industry).

GOE: 05.12.02 STRENGTH: H GED: R2 M2 L2 SVP: 2 DLU: 77

930.687-018 CUTTER-OPERATOR HELPER (mine & quarry)

Undercuts coal, salt, or nonmetallic ore in underground mine to assist CUTTER OPERATOR (mine & quarry): Shovels loose material to clear working area for machine. Observes movement of machine to prevent damage to electric power cable. Braces machine from rear, using pole or bar as lever, to prevent sideways sliding of machine due to pressure on cutter bar. Lubricates cutter bar and performs other duties as described under HELPER (any industry) Master Title.

GOE: 05.12.02 STRENGTH: H GED: R2 M1 L1 SVP: 2 DLU: 77

931 BLASTING OCCUPATIONS

This group includes occupations concerned with preparation, placement, and detonation of explosives to shatter, dislodge, or move earth, coal, ore-bearing material, and stone in open pit or underground mines and quarries. Occupations concerned with blasting for construction purposes are found in Group 859.

931.261-010 BLASTER (mine & quarry) alternate titles: dynamiter; firer; shooter; shot firer; shot lighter

Determines strength and pattern of blast required and charges and detonates explosives in surface or underground mine, pit, or quarry to fracture or separate stone or minerals from solid formations: Studies formation to determine amount, type, and location of explosive charge required. Marks pattern of drill holes or issues drilling instructions for depth and placement of blast holes. Inserts, packs, or pours explosives, such as dynamite, ammonium nitrate, black powder, or slurries into blast holes and compacts charge, using tamping rod. Positions assembled primer and blasting cap in hole at depth that will cause most effective explosion. Connects electric wire to primer and covers charge or fills blast hole with clay, drill chips, sand, or other material. Tamps material to secure charge and prevent force of blast from escaping through blast hole. Inspects blasting area to ensure that safety laws are observed and signals work-

ers to clear area. Connects wires to electrical firing device and pushes plunger, turns dial, or presses buttons to set off single or multiple blasts. May compile record of blasts. May keep inventory of blasting agents on hand. May transport blasting agents to blasting area, using light truck [EXPLOSIVES-TRUCK DRIVER (ordnance)].

GOE: 05.10.06 STRENGTH: M GED: R4 M3 L2 SVP: 7 DLU: 77

931.361-010 SAMPLE-TAKER OPERATOR (petrol. & gas) alternate titles: oil-well-electrical-wall-sampling-device operator

Obtains sample of earth formations in sidewalls of oil well boreholes, using electrically exploding device: Loads explosives into gun chambers of tubular firing device. Connects gun chambers to electric detonating cable, using handtools. Signals HOIST OPERATOR (petrol. & gas) to lower sample-taking gun into well. Observes wire line measuring device, weight indicator, and instrument panel of control equipment in truck to position sample-taking gun at specified point in well. Moves controls to set off electrical igniters that fire cylinders into sidewall of rock formation to obtain sample of earth. Signals HOIST OPERATOR (petrol. & gas) to raise equipment and sample from well. May be required to have license for handling explosives. May operate hoist to lower and raise tools and equipment from well.

GOE: 05.12.02 STRENGTH: M GED: R3 M2 L1 SVP: 5 DLU: 77

931.361-014 SHOOTER (petrol. & gas) alternate titles: oil-well shooter; torpedo shooter; well shooter

Detonates torpedoes in bored oil wells to start or renew flow of oil in wells: Connects torpedo and electric cable terminals, using wrench. Signals HOIST OPERATOR (petrol. & gas) to lower torpedo into well. Presses switch or drops go-devil (detonating device) down well to detonate charge. May load torpedoes with explosives. May be required to have license for handling explosives.

GOE: 05.10.06 STRENGTH: L GED: R3 M2 L2 SVP: 6 DLU: 77

931.361-018 SHOOTER, SEISMOGRAPH (petrol. & gas) alternate titles: shot-hole shooter

Detonates dynamite or other explosive charges in shallow boreholes to set up seismic waves that are recorded by seismic instruments and interpreted to reveal subsurface rock formations likely to contain petroleum deposits: Lowers explosives into borehole and pushes switch to detonate charge [SHOOTER (petrol. & gas)]. Moves, stores, and maintains inventories of high explosives. Repairs and services electric wiring and other shooting equipment and automotive equipment. Sets up shortwave radio or field telephone equipment to transmit and receive shooting information. May drive truck to transport explosives and shooting equipment. May admit water into borehole to serve as tamping for explosive charge. May be required to be licensed by federal government to handle explosives.

GOE: 05.10.06 STRENGTH: M GED: R3 M2 L2 SVP: 6 DLU: 77

931.382-010 PERFORATOR OPERATOR, OIL WELL (petrol. & gas) alternate titles: gun perforator; oil-well gun-perforator operator

Operates truck-mounted hoisting equipment and electrical control panel to position and explode charges in oil or gas wells to pierce drill pipes, casings, tubings, and fracture earth formations: Assembles tools and equipment at well site, using handtools. Lowers perforating gun into well, using hoist. Observes odometer, weight indicator, and instrument panel in truck, and positions gun at predetermined point in well. Moves controls at panelboard to detonate charge in gun which propels bullets through wall of bore to pierce or fracture oil- or gas-bearing formations, or to ignite chemical charge which burns fissures in rock formations for passage of oil or processing fluid, such as mud or cement. Observes instrument on control panel to verify detonation of charge in gun. Repairs electrical instruments, using electrician's handtools. Loads perforating guns at well site for special shots.

GOE: 05.11.03 STRENGTH: H GED: R3 M2 L2 SVP: 6 DLU: 77

931.384-010 GUN-PERFORATOR LOADER (petrol. & gas)

Loads explosive powder or chemicals into gun perforators and carriers used in shooting or burning holes through tubing, casings, and earth formations: Assembles perforators, using special handtools. Cleans, gauges, and lubricates gun ports distributed along barrel. Removes gun port, using special wrench. Inserts waterproof sealer and bullet into gun port. Places specified powder charge in powder chamber and screws gun port in place. Screws igniting charge (booster) in place on gun barrel and connects lead wire to cable connection with screwdriver. Inserts special fuse (prima-cord) into carrier of jet perforators. Threads jet-shaped charge on fuse and inserts it into carrier and through port, using special tongs. Inserts specified powder charge in chamber of sidewall sample-taking cylinder and assembles cylinders, using special wrenches. Packs cylinders into boxes for field loading into core barrels. Stores loaded guns, explosives, and related materials in storeroom according to established safety procedures. Maintains inventory records and orders new supplies. May keep gun and explosive records in compliance with local and federal laws.

GOE: 05.10.06 STRENGTH: V GED: R3 M2 L2 SVP: 5 DLU: 77

931.664-010 TIER-AND-DETONATOR (mine & quarry)

Wires and detonates explosives in specified sequence to blast overburden in open pit copper mine: Lays main line of *primacord* between rows of charged blastholes and ties cord into main line to form blast pattern. Ties specified lengths of delaying fuses into pattern to time sequence of explosions. Connects blasting cap and flips switch on electronic blasting device to detonate charge upon signal from SUPERVISOR, BLASTING (mine & quarry).

GOE: 05.12.02 STRENGTH: M GED: R2 M2 L2 SVP: 2 DLU: 77

931.667-010 POWDER LOADER (mine & quarry)
Loads explosives into blastholes to prepare for blasting overburden in open pit copper mine, working as member of crew: Measures depth of blasthole, using weighted tape measure, and consults SUPERVISOR, BLASTING (mine & quarry) to determine amount of explosives needed. Cuts specified lengths of *primacord* and attaches primer to end of cord. Lowers cord into hole and ties upper end to stake. Signals EXPLOSIVES-TRUCK DRIVER (ordnance) to drive truck into position near blasthole. Positions hopper funnel over hole and admits specified amount of explosives. Shovels drill cuttings to fill and tamp hole. Places safety cones around blast area to alert other workers.
GOE: 05.12.02 STRENGTH: M GED: R2 M2 L2 SVP: 2 DLU: 77

931.684-010 DUMPER-BAILER OPERATOR (petrol. & gas)
Dumps sand and cement over shot of nitroglycerine in oil or gas wells to provide tamp and bridge (protective shielding) over area to be shot, using special bailer and hoist: Determines amount and consistency of tamping materials and cement according to size, depth, and similar characteristics of borehole. Selects tools, such as packers for use in borehole. Assembles and attaches tools and bailer to hoist line. Loads sand or other tamping materials into bailer and lowers bailer and tamping tools into borehole, using hoist. Mixes cement to specified consistency, using portable mixer. Loads cement in bailer, using bucket. Lowers and dumps cement in borehole, using hoist. Cleans and repairs equipment.
GOE: 05.11.03 STRENGTH: H GED: R3 M2 L1 SVP: 5 DLU: 77

932 LOADING AND CONVEYING OPERATIONS

This group includes occupations concerned with moving workers, equipment, and extracted materials, using motor cars, chutes, hoists, elevators, conveyors, shovels, picks, and other devices.

932.132-010 BANK BOSS (mine & quarry)
Supervises and coordinates activities of workers operating machinery, such as front-end loaders, bulldozers, and conveyors used in loading bank coal into trucks and railroad cars. Assists workers with faulty equipment. Performs duties as described under SUPERVISOR (any industry) Master Title.
GOE: 05.11.04 STRENGTH: L GED: R4 M3 L3 SVP: 7 DLU: 77

932.132-014 SURFACE SUPERVISOR (mine & quarry)
Supervises and coordinates activities of workers engaged in operating equipment to move personnel, machinery, and supplies to various levels of underground mine: Consults with supervisory personnel to establish daily work schedule. Coordinates use of hoisting devices to raise or lower equipment that transports personnel, machinery, and supplies to and from various mine levels. Directs workers who load and unload materials from trucks or railroad cars. Inspects equipment to detect malfunctions and schedules repairs as needed. Conducts safety meetings and resolves grievances.
GOE: 05.11.02 STRENGTH: L GED: R4 M3 L4 SVP: 8 DLU: 77

932.167-010 DISPATCHER (mine & quarry) alternate titles: car distributor; haulage boss; motor boss; passing boss; turn keeper
Coordinates movements of haulage trips (trains) in underground mine to or from working force or dump area: Schedules movements of trains hauling coal, ore, refuse, personnel, or supplies in accordance with capacity of system, interval between trains, and length and direction of trains. Directs movements of special vehicles, such as emergency and repair railcars, to minimize interference with scheduled operations, using telephone, radio, or track signals. Reroutes trains in event of emergency, such as power failure, explosion, fire, or accident. Investigates cause of train delays, using telephone, and reschedules subsequent operations. Transmits reports of accidents or system malfunctions to repair crew and SAFETY ENGINEER (profess. & kin.). Keeps records of train movements, or monitors movements on lighted panelboard showing location of each train in system. May move controls to throw track switches and regulate movement of trains.
GOE: 07.04.05 STRENGTH: L GED: R4 M3 L3 SVP: 6 DLU: 77

932.363-010 HOIST OPERATOR (petrol. & gas) alternate titles: winch operator
Operates truck-mounted hoist to lower and raise instruments and tools into and out of oil or gas wells on electric conductor cable, used to perform well services and surveys, such as directional drilling, electric well logging, perforating, sidewall sample taking, and free-point shooting: Signals and assists other workers in loading and unloading truck; assembling and connecting instruments and tools to conductor cable, using wrenches and special handtools; and in attaching cable pulley to hoist block of drilling rig or to special pulley-mount placed in position over borehole (rigging up). Operates hoist to lower and raise instruments and tools in well [HOISTING ENGINEER (any industry)], observing signals of engineering personnel. Loads log recorder with film to prepare for logging of oil or gas well boreholes. Observes indicator to verify depth of instruments in borehole. Drives truck to and from well site when working as member of crew. Repairs and maintains truck and other mobile equipment. May repair cables and hoisting equipment. May load explosive charges in such tools as gun or jet perforators.
GOE: 05.11.02 STRENGTH: M GED: R3 M2 L2 SVP: 5 DLU: 77

932.664-010 BRAKE HOLDER (any industry) alternate titles: car rider; coupler; dukey rider; gang rider; nipper; patcher; rope rider; set rider; swamper; tail-end rider; trailer; train conductor; trip rider; tub rider
Throws switches and couples, or attaches to cable, cars being hauled by locomotive or hoisted by cable or chain in mines, quarries, or industrial plants: Uncouples loaded cars at their destination or uncouples and distributes empty cars to sidings or to loading areas. Moves switches to route cars and signals DINKEY OPERATOR (any industry) to start or stop cars. May open and close ventilation doors in mines. May open or close chute gates to load or unload cars. May crush oversize rock or ore on grizzly to prevent clogging, using sledgehammer. May remove and tag ore samples for laboratory analysis. May be designated according to type of hauling machine as Dinkey-Operator Helper (any industry).
GOE: 05.12.03 STRENGTH: M GED: R2 M1 L1 SVP: 3 DLU: 77

932.664-014 SPOUT TENDER I (chemical)
Pulls cable to regulate flow of salt from harvesting machine into gondola cars: Observes position of gondola passing loading spout and pulls cable to position deflector plate for loading salt into car. Pulls cable to reverse plate position and change salt flow to next spout to complete loading of car. Signals HARVESTER OPERATOR (chemical) to stop conveyor when cars are filled.
GOE: 05.12.03 STRENGTH: M GED: R2 M1 L2 SVP: 2 DLU: 77

932.667-010 BOTTOMER I (mine & quarry) alternate titles: foot tender
Works at foot of haulage slope or plane leading to surface of mine: Engages clips or grips by means of which mine cars are attached to hoisting cable for haulage to surface, working at foot of haulage slope or plane leading to surface of mine. Disengages clips or grips as cars are lowered to landing and moves cars onto track sidings for distribution in mine. Signals HOIST OPERATOR (mine & quarry) with bell or buzzer to raise cars.
GOE: 05.12.04 STRENGTH: H GED: R2 M1 L1 SVP: 3 DLU: 77

932.667-014 LOADING-SHOVEL OILER (mine & quarry)
Lubricates diesel or electric loading shovel at strip mine or quarry: Oils and greases bearings, cables, gears, and other friction areas, using grease gun and oilcan. Assists in routine maintenance and repair of machine. May shovel dirt and coal to keep bench (top of exposed coal or ore seam) clear. May keep power cable clear of treads as shovel moves into position. May guide trucks into loading position, using hand or voice signals.
GOE: 05.12.08 STRENGTH: M GED: R2 M1 L1 SVP: 3 DLU: 77

932.683-010 CAR DROPPER (mine & quarry) alternate titles: car pincher; car runner; spragger
Controls movement of railroad or mine cars to position cars for loading or unloading at sidings, loading chutes, tipples, or scales, performing any combination of following tasks: Pushes or rides cars down slope. Guides and stops cars by switching, applying brakes, or placing scotches (wooden wedges) between wheel and rail. Uncouples and positions railroad car under loading chutes by inserting pinch bar under car wheels, using bar as fulcrum and lever to move car. Hooks cable to car and controls cable drum brake to ease car down incline. Opens and closes bottom doors of cars to dump contents. May assist in cleaning and preparing cars for loading.
GOE: 05.12.03 STRENGTH: M GED: R2 M1 L1 SVP: 3 DLU: 77

932.683-014 LOADING-MACHINE OPERATOR (mine & quarry) alternate titles: loader; machine
Drives self-propelled electric loading machine equipped with gathering arms and conveyor to load shattered coal, rock, or ore into shuttle or mine cars in underground mine: Drives machine into pile of material blasted from working face. Moves levers to raise and swivel multisectioned conveyor boom and to start conveyor boom and gathering-arm motors. Advances machine to gather material and convey it into car at rear. Stops gathering arms when car is full. Pries off loose material from roof and moves it into path of machine with crowbar. Moves trailing electrical cable clear of obstructions, using rubber safety gloves. May replace hydraulic hoses, headlight bulbs, and gathering-arm teeth.
GOE: 05.11.02 STRENGTH: M GED: R3 M2 L2 SVP: 5 DLU: 77

932.683-018 MECHANICAL-SHOVEL OPERATOR (mine & quarry) alternate titles: loader operator; mucking-machine operator; shovel operator
Operates power shovel that loads coal or rock into mine cars or onto conveyors in underground mines: Drives rubber-tired, crawled-tread, or rail-mounted machine into working place. Makes power connections and starts machine. Moves levers to force shovel into pile, lift and revolve shovel, and dump contents into mine car or onto conveyor. Advances machine into pile as digging progresses. Lubricates, adjusts, and repairs machine.
GOE: 05.11.02 STRENGTH: M GED: R3 M2 L2 SVP: 5 DLU: 77

932.683-022 SHUTTLE-CAR OPERATOR (mine & quarry)
Drives diesel or electrically powered shuttle car in underground mine to transport materials from working face to mine cars or to conveyor: Positions shuttle car under discharge conveyor of loading machine and observes that materials are loaded according to specifications. Maneuvers shuttle car to keep its nose under discharge conveyor. Controls conveyor which runs entire length of shuttle car to apportion load as loading progresses. Drives loaded shuttle car to ramp and moves controls to discharge load into mine car or onto conveyor. May move mine cars into position to be loaded from shuttle car. May charge batteries when operating battery-powered vehicle.

GOE: 05.11.02 STRENGTH: M GED: R3 M2 L2 SVP: 4 DLU: 80

932.685-010 AERIAL-TRAM OPERATOR (mine & quarry)

Tends aerial tramway (buckets attached to overhead cables and pulleys supported by towers) to convey refuse, coal, ore, and other materials from plant or mine to spoil pile, conveyor, railroad car, boat, or plant: Pushes buttons to start reel and winding cable, causing tram buckets to move between loading and dumping areas. Pulls levers to position buckets for loading and pushes button to dump load, or observes signal panel and listens for malfunction of automatic dumping equipment. Lubricates and repairs machinery. May remove or replace buckets.

GOE: 05.11.04 STRENGTH: L GED: R2 M1 L1 SVP: 3 DLU: 77

932.687-010 CHUTE LOADER (mine & quarry) alternate titles: loader; railroad-car loader

Loads trucks, railroad cars, or conveyors with sand, gravel, coal, crushed stone, or other minerals: Pulls levers or presses buttons to open and close chute of storage bin to regulate flow of materials. Loosens clogged material, using metal bar or compressed air. May position cars under chute [CAR DROPPER (mine & quarry)]. May spray water on materials to settle dust. May keep record of materials loaded. May pry and blast loose mined coal impounded behind battery (stop gate) of storage chute in steeply pitching seams, to load mine cars, and be designated Battery Starter (mine & quarry).

GOE: 05.12.03 STRENGTH: M GED: R1 M1 L1 SVP: 1 DLU: 77

933 CRUSHING OCCUPATIONS

This group includes occupations concerned with reducing bulky materials to convenient sizes, using sledgehammers and crushing machines.

933.664-010 CRUSHER SETTER (mine & quarry)

Adjusts gaps of cone crushers used to reduce taconite ore to specified size: Lowers lead cone into operating crusher that compresses cone to size of crusher gap. Measures compressed cone with rule to determine amount of adjustment of crusher opening. Signals OVERHEAD CRANE OPERATOR (any industry) 921.663-010 to turn threaded crusher bowl to set gap at specified opening. Drives wedges and bolts locking links to secure bowl, using sledges, pliers, and pry bars.

GOE: 06.01.02 STRENGTH: M GED: R2 M1 L1 SVP: 3 DLU: 77

933.687-010 GRIZZLY WORKER (mine & quarry; smelt. & refin.) alternate titles: chute blaster; chute tapper; sorter

Prods and breaks ore or rock in underground mine or quarry to keep it moving through grizzly and chute leading to storage, crusher, or loading station: Loosens clogged ore, using bar or pick. Pushes ore dumped from mine cars or trucks through grizzly with bar, and breaks boulders with hydraulic ram or sledgehammer. May discard oversized lumps. May move levers to dump ore from cars. May remove samples of ore for laboratory analysis.

GOE: 05.12.07 STRENGTH: H GED: R1 M1 L1 SVP: 2 DLU: 77

934 SCREENING AND RELATED OCCUPATIONS

This group includes occupations concerned with cleaning, separating, and sizing coal, ore, stone, and related materials, using gravity and centrifugal separators, vibrating screens, and related equipment.

934.685-010 CONE OPERATOR (mine & quarry)

Tends cone (gravity device) to separate slate and rock from coal: Presses buttons to start conveyor and regulate flow of material into top of cone. Turns valve to regulate flow of water into bottom of cone and maintain specified pressure to carry coal off with overflow while rock and slate fall to bottom. Pulls lever to open slate gate at bottom and draw off impurities.

GOE: 05.12.07 STRENGTH: L GED: R2 M1 L1 SVP: 3 DLU: 77

934.685-014 SAND PLANT ATTENDANT (concrete prod.; mine & quarry)

Tends equipment that separates sand according to texture and grade: Presses buttons or flips switches on control panel to start conveyors, washing, and separating (classifying) units. Adjusts controls of classifying tanks to obtain specified grade of sand. Observes color of sand to determine clay content and notifies supervisor when excess clay or equipment malfunction is detected. Lubricates conveyor idlers, using grease gun, and assists in routine equipment maintenance. Shovels sand spillage clear of moving equipment parts and work area.

GOE: 05.12.07 STRENGTH: M GED: R2 M2 L1 SVP: 2 DLU: 77

934.685-018 SHAKER TENDER (concrete prod.; mine & quarry)

Tends shaker (vibrating or reciprocating screen) that sizes crushed coal, ore, or rock for industrial use or for further processing: Opens and closes chute gates to regulate flow of materials onto shaker table. Picks out refuse and impurities. Unclogs conveyors and screens, and shovels spillage onto conveyors or screens. May change screens. May collect and label batch samples for quality control inspection.

GOE: 05.12.07 STRENGTH: M GED: R2 M2 L1 SVP: 3 DLU: 77

934.685-022 SPIRAL RUNNER (mine & quarry)

Tends battery of spirals (mechanical devices that separate minerals from other materials by centrifugal force): Starts equipment and opens feedlines admitting material into spirals. Examines samples and regulates spirals so that excessive amount of minerals is not lost.

GOE: 05.12.07 STRENGTH: M GED: R2 M1 L1 SVP: 4 DLU: 77

934.687-010 FOOT WORKER (chemical)

Moves levers to adjust chute gate and regulate flow of salt from crusher to vibrating screens that separate salt into various sizes preparatory to shipment or refining. Cleans clogged screens with rod. May tip mine cars to dump rock salt into bins, leading to crusher [CRUSHER TENDER (any industry)].

GOE: 05.12.07 STRENGTH: M GED: R2 M1 L1 SVP: 2 DLU: 77

939 OCCUPATIONS IN EXTRACTION OF MINERALS, N.E.C.

This group includes occupations, not elsewhere classified, concerned with extraction of minerals.

939.130-010 SUPERVISOR, POND (chemical)

Supervises and coordinates activities of workers engaged in pumping salt water to ponds and testing brine concentrate in production of salt by solar evaporation: Orders pumping sequence for each pond to move salt water through prescribed series of concentrating ponds and into crystallizing ponds according to specified density of water. Specifies density to maintain in each pond and sequence of ponds to use as salt concentration increases. Inspects ponds, floodgates, valves, and pumps, and reports needed repair or maintenance. May compile report on pond operations. May direct workers in draining granulator beds and laying gondola tracks on beds. Performs other duties as described under SUPERVISOR (any industry) Master Title.

GOE: 05.12.01 STRENGTH: L GED: R4 M3 L3 SVP: 7 DLU: 77

939.131-010 QUARRY SUPERVISOR, OPEN PIT (mine & quarry)

Supervises and coordinates activities of workers engaged in blasting, removing, and crushing mineral ores in open-pit mines (quarries): Plans location and drilling of blast holes to ensure maximum extraction of ore and provide access roads for trucking ores out of mine. Trains workers in drilling blast holes and in loading and shooting explosive charges. Directs POWER-SHOVEL OPERATORS (any industry) and TRUCK DRIVERS (any industry) in stripping new diggings and in loading and removing ores from mine. Directs CRUSHER TENDER (any industry) in breaking ore into pieces preparatory to extraction of valuable minerals. Performs other duties as described under SUPERVISOR (any industry) Master Title.

GOE: 05.02.05 STRENGTH: L GED: R4 M3 L3 SVP: 7 DLU: 77

939.131-014 SUPERVISOR, PRODUCTION (petrol. & gas) alternate titles: lease supervisor

Supervises and coordinates activities of workers engaged in pumping, gauging, and treating oil from wells within specified oil field area: Directs workers in operation and adjustment of pump engines, pumps, gauges, oil treating units, and control heads (valve devices controlling flow of oil). Inspects work of crews replacing pump rods and casing in wells, treating wells to increase flow or improve quality of oil and constructing or repairing oil field equipment and buildings. Designates allowable flow of oil from wells in accordance with proration regulations and agreements. May direct drilling of wells. Performs other duties as described under SUPERVISOR (any industry) Master Title.

GOE: 05.02.02 STRENGTH: L GED: R4 M3 L3 SVP: 8 DLU: 77

939.131-018 WELL PULLER, HEAD (petrol. & gas) alternate titles: head well-puller

Supervises and coordinates activities of WELL PULLER (petrol. & gas) in cleaning and servicing producing oil and gas wells, and in pulling pumping rods, casing, and tubing from wells, for repair or replacement. May oversee installation of tubing in new wells. May swab wells to induce flow of oil [CLEAN-OUT DRILLER (petrol. & gas)]. Performs duties as described under SUPERVISOR (any industry) Master Title.

GOE: 05.12.02 STRENGTH: H GED: R4 M3 L3 SVP: 7 DLU: 77

939.132-010 DREDGE OPERATOR SUPERVISOR (mine & quarry)

Operates dredge used to mine metal-bearing sands or gravels from bottom of lakes and streams, and supervises other dredge workers: Operates winch to position dredge. Moves controls to lower endless bucket-conveyor to bottom of lake or stream. Starts conveyor to scoop up ore-bearing sand or gravel from bottom and deposit it upon dredge. Directs disassembly, loading, unloading, and reassembly of dredge and related equipment. Supervises and coordinates activities of other workers engaged in primary preparation of ore by screening and amalgamation.

GOE: 05.11.01 STRENGTH: M GED: R4 M3 L3 SVP: 7 DLU: 77

939.132-014 OIL-WELL-SERVICES SUPERVISOR (petrol. & gas)

Supervises and coordinates activities of workers engaged in operating pumping and blending equipment to cement, acidize, and fracture oil and gas wells: Confers with SUPERINTENDENT, DRILLING AND PRODUCTION (petrol. & gas) to determine well conditions, pipe sizes, and characteristics of oil-or-gas-bearing rock formations to be treated. Computes amount of cement, acid, or fracturing material to be used and devises procedures to be followed according to conditions of individual wells. Directs workers in mixing and blending of cement, acid, and other chemicals and in assembling and connecting pipe and pipe fittings between pumping equipment and well head. Observes dials and pressure gauges to ensure that specified pump pressure is being maintained and that equipment is functioning properly. Informs workers when adjustments are needed and directs maintenance and repair of equipment. Assigns new em-

ployees to experienced worker for on-the-job training and assists in training. Evaluates job performance of workers and recommends personnel actions, such as promotions, pay raises, or discharges. May operate blending and pumping equipment and connect pipe and pipe fittings between pumping equipment and well head during peak work periods or for training purposes. May contact established customers to solicit work and maintain good will.
GOE: 05.11.03 STRENGTH: L GED: R4 M3 L3 SVP: 8 DLU: 77

939.137-010 CHIEF DISPATCHER (petrol. & gas)
Supervises and coordinates activities of dispatching and clerical personnel in field offices, and advises on types of oil well services for specific drilling or production problems: Advises customers regarding services best suited for specific drilling or production problems, utilizing knowledge of local conditions gained through field experience, to select type of service required. Computes material quantities and quotes prices for service. Dispatches oil well servicing crews, using telephone or radio, to perform services, and oversees clerical activities in field office. Performs other duties as described under SUPERVISOR (clerical) Master Title.
GOE: 07.04.05 STRENGTH: S GED: R4 M4 L4 SVP: 7 DLU: 77

939.137-014 PIT SUPERVISOR (mine & quarry) alternate titles: dimension-quarry supervisor; strip-mine supervisor
Supervises and coordinates activities of workers engaged in strip or pit mining or in quarrying: Studies contour maps and aerial photographs to determine locations for roads and cuts. Supervises road construction crew and lays out blast pattern. Supervises drilling and shooting crews in drilling blast holes and detonation of charges. Plans location of spoil pile (dump area) to allow maximum room for stripping. Coordinates stripping, drilling, blasting, quarrying, and loading activities, and assists workers with faulty equipment. Determines property lines and legal limits of operations in order to comply with rights of adjoining property owners and mining laws. Schedules running and major repair work on drilling machine and stripping and loading shovels. Requisitions supplies, such as explosives, lubricants, bits, and machine parts. Observes mining operation to detect violation of safety regulations and compiles safety and production records. May supervise crushing operations. May train new workers. May be designated according to specific work performed as Supervisor, Drilling And Shooting (mine & quarry); Supervisor, Blasting (mine & quarry). Performs other duties as described under SUPERVISOR (any industry) Master Title.
GOE: 05.02.05 STRENGTH: L GED: R4 M3 L3 SVP: 7 DLU: 77

939.137-018 SECTION SUPERVISOR (mine & quarry) alternate titles: machine boss; mine captain; muck boss; room boss; shift boss
Supervises and coordinates activities of workers engaged in underground, surface, or pit mining in specified section of mine: Coordinates activities, such as timbering, roof bolting, track-laying, undercutting, drilling, blasting, loading, and conveying of coal, ore, or rock. Examines malfunctioning equipment and orders transfer of faulty unit to surface shop or orders repair at work site. Inspects section for hazards, such as gas, falling rock, squeezes, and poor ventilation, using devices, such as safety lamps, anemometer, and crowbar. Maintains records of production, area mined, and location of personnel and equipment. Orders and distributes supplies, such as bits, wire, machine parts, bulbs, and chalk. May evaluate ore in precious-metal mine and be designated Specimen Boss (mine & quarry). May be designated according to specific equipment used as Auger Supervisor (mine & quarry). Performs other duties as described under SUPERVISOR (any industry) Master Title.
GOE: 05.02.05 STRENGTH: M GED: R4 M3 L3 SVP: 7 DLU: 80

939.137-022 SUPERVISOR, HARVESTING (chemical)
Supervises and coordinates activities of workers engaged in harvesting, transporting, washing, and stockpiling raw salt from crystallization pond beds: Plans shift activities and directs workers to pond beds designated for harvesting. Directs workers in laying of gondola tracks on salt bed. Coordinates harvesting with transporting, washing, and stockpiling activities to ensure continuity in production. Requests field repairs and maintenance of equipment. Directs relocation of conveyor to obtain stockpiles of specified size. Enforces safety regulations. Maintains records of production, pond status, and reasons for production delays.
GOE: 05.12.01 STRENGTH: L GED: R3 M3 L3 SVP: 5 DLU: 77

939.167-010 CONTROLLER, COAL OR ORE (mine & quarry) alternate titles: ore grader
Coordinates loading, dumping, and blending of coal or ore at shipping dock, mill, tipple, or preparation plant: Studies schedules to ascertain required blends, grades, and sizes of material to be processed. Studies analysis sheets and selects materials which will meet specifications. Notifies workers to deliver specified cars for loading, designates loading sequence, and indicates whether cars are to be caulked or plugged to retain powdered coal, oiled to reduce dust, or salted to prevent freezing. Notifies workers to load or dump materials. Prepares control sheet to record loading and dumping activities and variances in production.
GOE: 05.12.01 STRENGTH: S GED: R3 M3 L3 SVP: 6 DLU: 77

939.281-010 MINER I (mine & quarry)
Mines ore, coal, or rock in underground mine, performing any combination of following tasks in areas where high production equipment is limited by economic factors or natural formations: Cuts channel under working face to facilitate blasting, using pick, or by operating cutting machine. Operates mounted or unmounted power drill to bore blasting holes in working face. Charges and

shoots (sets off) explosives or air charges to blast down materials. Shovels shattered materials into mine cars or onto conveyor. Installs timbering, roof bolts, or cribs, to support walls and roof. Lays track to accommodate mine cars or track-mounted equipment. May mine rock in coal mine at contract price per ton or footage of advance and be designated Rock Contractor (mine & quarry). May mine ore, coal, or rock, using pick and shovel, and be designated Miner, Pick (mine & quarry). When digging passageways between rooms, may be designated Entry Miner (mine & quarry). May do development work, such as opening up new passageways, air vents, auxiliary tunnels, rooms, and shafts to facilitate mining, and be designated Drift Miner (mine & quarry); Raise Miner (mine & quarry); Shaft Sinker (mine & quarry); Stope Miner (mine & quarry); Tunnel Miner (mine & quarry).
GOE: 05.11.02 STRENGTH: V GED: R4 M3 L2 SVP: 6 DLU: 77

939.362-010 DISPATCHER, OIL WELL SERVICES (petrol. & gas)
Dispatches oil well servicing crews to service assignments and relays communications to crews and other field personnel, using telephone and radio communication equipment: Receives telephone requests for services from customers and relays information to crews and field personnel, using telephone and radio. Dispatches crews to oil well servicing assignments. Prepares time reports and other records. Confers with customer regarding drilling or production problems and outlines types of services available. May compute quantities of materials required and quote prices for services. May refer customer inquiries regarding production problems or available services to sales personnel.
GOE: 07.04.05 STRENGTH: S GED: R3 M3 L3 SVP: 5 DLU: 77

939.362-014 PANELBOARD OPERATOR (mine & quarry; smelt. & refin.) alternate titles: additive-plant operator; conveyor attendant; crusher operator; grinding-mill operator; mill attendant; switch-house operator; wash-box operator
Operates panelboard to control conveying, blending, washing, crushing, and sizing of coal, rock, sand, gravel, or ore to prepare it for commercial or industrial use or for further processing: Pushes levers and buttons to start plant machinery. Studies customer orders or work schedules and adjusts controls to draw specified amounts and proportions of different grades of materials from storage bins onto conveyors. Observes dials and gauges to route materials through series of screens, wash boxes, crushers, and driers. Reads ammeters to determine load on conveyors and regulates loads to adjust blends. Observes panel lights and meters for indication of overloads, malfunctions, or plugged chutes, and shuts down plant, reroutes materials, or adjusts controls to regulate feed. Notifies maintenance and loading personnel of delays or malfunctions. Observes operation to determine that refuse and tailings are removed as specified. May operate equipment to dump material from cars.
GOE: 06.02.18 STRENGTH: L GED: R4 M3 L3 SVP: 5 DLU: 77

939.364-010 OBSERVER HELPER, SEISMIC PROSPECTING (petrol. & gas) alternate titles: observer helper; recorder helper, seismograph; seismograph-operator helper
Performs any combination of following tasks in seismic prospecting for petroleum-bearing rock strata: Drives equipment truck to work sites. Unloads and carries explosives and seismometers to designated locations on terrain. Unreels and connects electrical cables between seismometers and recording equipment in truck. Guides drill pipe and casing into shotholes. Loads shotholes with explosives. Runs water or pours sand into shotholes to tamp charge. Washes printed seismograph records with solutions. Repairs automotive and prospecting equipment. May be designated according to specific duty performed as Prospecting-Driller Helper (petrol. & gas); Shooter Helper, Seismograph (petrol. & gas).
GOE: 05.12.03 STRENGTH: M GED: R2 M2 L1 SVP: 4 DLU: 77

939.382-010 DRY-PLACER-MACHINE OPERATOR (mine & quarry)
Operates trailer-mounted machine to recover gold from sand: Positions conveyor from front-end loader to machine. Connects terminals from portable generator to control panel, using wrench. Starts machine and adjusts speed of feed conveyor to avoid overloading. Observes flow of fine sand from conveyor to screens and inclined riffle tables. Adjusts speed of bellows to force air through sand and float it over riffles, allowing gold-bearing particles to collect. Dries wet sand, using heat lamps.
GOE: 05.11.02 STRENGTH: M GED: R3 M2 L1 SVP: 4 DLU: 77

939.462-010 OIL-WELL-SERVICE OPERATOR (petrol. & gas)
Controls pumping and blending equipment to acidize, cement, or fracture gas or oil wells and permeable rock formations: Consults with SUPERINTENDENT, DRILLING AND PRODUCTION (petrol. & gas) to determine well conditions, pipe sizes, and amounts of acid, cement, or fracturing chemicals to be used. Gives directions to OIL-WELL-SERVICE-OPERATOR HELPER (petrol. & gas) to unload pipes, fittings, and chemicals, and to correct pipes between pumps and well, using handtools. Mixes acids, chemicals or dry cement according to service specified by customer. Observes meters and pressure gauges to regulate quantity and consistency of materials and to control pump pressure. May perform routine maintenance on vehicles and equipment. May be designated according to specialty as Acidizer (petrol. & gas); Acidizer, Water Well (construction); Cementer, Oil Well (petrol. & gas); Formation-Fracturing Operator (petrol. & gas).
GOE: 05.11.03 STRENGTH: H GED: R4 M3 L3 SVP: 6 DLU: 77

939.485-010 SANDFILL OPERATOR (mine & quarry)
Tends equipment that mixes cement, ore residues, and water into slurry and pumps slurry to fill worked out excavations in underground mine: Opens valves

to transfer ore residues (sand) from mill and admit water to mixing tank. Starts mixer that blends slurry to specified consistency. Opens valves to transfer slurry to excavations (stopes) and to flush distribution lines. Adds measured amounts of cement to slurry when hard-surface fill is specified. Washes residue from tanks and records amount of slurry produced and deposited in mine. May be designated according to area worked as Sandfill Operator, Surface (mine & quarry); Sandfill Operator, Underground (mine & quarry).
GOE: 05.12.07 STRENGTH: M GED: R2 M2 L1 SVP: 3 DLU: 77

939.585-010 DUST SAMPLER (mine & quarry)
Tends equipment that measures amount of coal dust suspended in air in underground coal mine: Places sampling devices in predetermined locations in mine at beginning of work shift. Monitors apparatus periodically to ensure that dust suspension remains within safe limits. Removes collected samples at end of shift, records suspension level, and mails sample to central laboratory for analysis. Cleans and maintains equipment daily.
GOE: 05.07.04 STRENGTH: L GED: R2 M2 L2 SVP: 3 DLU: 77

939.663-010 OBSERVER HELPER, GRAVITY PROSPECTING (petrol. & gas) alternate titles: gravity-prospecting-operator helper; recorder helper, gravity prospecting
Drives truck to transport gravity prospecting personnel and equipment to petroleum-exploration areas. Sets up gravity meter, torsion balance, and other gravity-measuring instruments under direction of OBSERVER, GRAVITY PROSPECTING (petrol. & gas). May read thermometer and barometer and record readings.
GOE: 05.08.03 STRENGTH: M GED: R2 M2 L1 SVP: 3 DLU: 77

939.667-010 CAGER (mine & quarry) alternate titles: lander; skip tender
Pushes mine cars onto and off mine shaft cage and informs workers when cage is used to carry mine personnel: Pushes or pulls loaded cars off cage at surface and replaces with cars that are empty or loaded with supplies. Pulls empty cars from cage at bottom or intermediate levels of mine and moves onto sidings for distribution and loading. Gives directions to workers in loading of cage to ensure conformance to safety regulations. Signals HOIST OPERATOR (mine & quarry) with bell or buzzer when cage is to be moved. May load cage with materials and equipment to be lowered into mine. May record number of containers and estimate production weights. May tend automatic elevator. May be designated according to level in mine shaft at which work is performed as Bottomer (mine & quarry) II; Foot Cager (mine & quarry); Head Cager (mine & quarry); Top Cager (mine & quarry).
GOE: 05.12.04 STRENGTH: H GED: R2 M1 L2 SVP: 3 DLU: 77

939.667-014 QUARRY WORKER (mine & quarry)
Performs any combination of following tasks in rock quarry: Removes mud and muck from surface of stone, using pick, shovel, and steam hose. Chips irregularities from stone slabs to produce uniform, rectangular shapes and reduce shipping weights, using pick. Loosens blasted stone, using pick and crowbar. Cuts notches (dog-holes) in blocks of stone with pick and hammer, and attaches hoisting cables, hooks, or slings to stone. Breaks stone into pieces, using sledgehammer. Loads broken rock into boxes to be hoisted from quarry, using shovel, stone fork, or hands. Loosens blasted stone with bar or pick and skids rock into position for breaking.
GOE: 05.12.03 STRENGTH: H GED: R2 M1 L1 SVP: 2 DLU: 77

939.667-018 SHORE HAND, DREDGE OR BARGE (construction; mine & quarry)
Attaches cable to tree, log, or other anchor on shore to permit use of winch to position barge or dredge: Receives signals from barge or dredge. Disengages cable and moves it to new position. Attaches cable to tree, or attaches cable to log and digs hole to bury log. May use explosives to form anchorages. May assist in loading barge. May ferry fuel and supplies to barge or dredge. May perform routine maintenance duties on dredge.
GOE: 05.12.04 STRENGTH: H GED: R2 M1 L1 SVP: 4 DLU: 77

939.682-010 MONITOR CAR OPERATOR (mine & quarry)
Operates monitor car to mix water and phosphate ore into slurry of specified density for further processing: Starts water pump and adjusts rate of water flow from nozzle. Moves levers to aim nozzle that sprays high pressure jet of water at ore pile to increase density of slurry or into sump to dilute slurry to specified consistency. Observes gauges and presses buttons to regulate volume and rate of slurry flow through pipeline to mill for further processing.
GOE: 06.02.18 STRENGTH: L GED: R3 M2 L1 SVP: 6 DLU: 77

939.682-014 PNEUMATIC-JACK OPERATOR (petrol. & gas)
Operates pneumatic jack on offshore oil drilling barge that raises or lowers barge to facilitate drilling: Moves levers to start jack which is lowered to caisson on ocean floor for purpose of lifting barge to facilitate drilling. Coordinates movement of jack with movement of other jacks on barge. Raises jack to lower barge back into water so that barge may be moved to another drilling location.
GOE: 05.11.03 STRENGTH: H GED: R3 M2 L2 SVP: 5 DLU: 77

939.684-010 JACK SETTER (mine & quarry)
Places hydraulic jacks, timbers, and posts in specified locations to form roof support system in underground mine: Examines hydraulic lines and tightens connections, using wrenches. Helps place temporary posts or timbers under roof support beams when hydraulic jack failure occurs, or to supplement jacks in supporting roof. Advances coal conveyors and jack units forward to facilitate making new series of cuts in coal strata, using built-in or portable horizontal jacks.

GOE: 05.12.02 STRENGTH: M GED: R3 M2 L1 SVP: 5 DLU: 77

939.684-014 MINER, PLACER (mine & quarry) alternate titles: sluice tender
Mines precious metals from sand and gravel by placer method: Constructs inclined trough (sluice box) with riffles or cleats at bottom. Shovels ore-bearing sand or gravel into stream of water running through sluice box and observes operation to ensure that loose metals are being caught behind riffles. Removes obstructions and repairs leaks. Diverts flow of water and scoops out accumulated metals. May use high-pressure water system to wash sand and gravel into sluices and be designated Nozzle Worker (mine & quarry); Placer Miner, Hydraulic (mine & quarry).
GOE: 05.12.02 STRENGTH: H GED: R3 M1 L1 SVP: 4 DLU: 77

939.684-018 OIL-WELL-SERVICE-OPERATOR HELPER (petrol. & gas)
Assists OIL-WELL-SERVICE OPERATOR (petrol. & gas) in controlling blending and pumping equipment to treat oil or gas wells and permeable rock formations with cement, acid, or chemicals: Drives truck equipped with acid pumps, mixers, and related equipment to well site. Unloads and assembles pipes and pumping equipment, using handtools. Dumps acids, cement, or other treating materials in mixer to blend solution. Opens valve as directed to admit specified amounts of solution into well. Dismantles and loads equipment on truck after treatment. May be designated according to duty performed as Acidizer Helper (petrol. & gas); Cementer Helper (petrol. & gas); Formation-Fracturing-Operator Helper (petrol. & gas).
GOE: 05.12.07 STRENGTH: H GED: R3 M2 L2 SVP: 5 DLU: 77

939.685-010 POND TENDER (chemical)
Tends equipment that pumps brine (sea water) through series of concentrating and crystallizing ponds to produce salt by solar evaporation: Turns valves to open floodgates and fill primary concentration ponds. Starts pumps that fill concentrating ponds in specified sequence to facilitate crystallizing process and to empty primary concentrating pond. Tests samples of brine solution for density, using hydrometer. Dilutes brine by pumping it through ponds and into granulator beds, according to specified time sequence. Records hydrometer readings and pumping operations. Pumps water into granulator beds after salt has been harvested.
GOE: 05.12.06 STRENGTH: M GED: R2 M2 L1 SVP: 4 DLU: 77

939.685-014 WASHER-AND-CRUSHER TENDER (mine & quarry)
Tends battery of machines that convey, wash, crush, and separate quarried stone to produce sand and gravel: Presses button to start belt conveyor that conveys material to blade mill. Pulls lever to start blade mill that washes and separates rock, sand, and gravel from clay and other foreign matter. Starts vibrating screens that separate materials according to size. Presses button to start cone crusher that crushes oversized rocks. Observes flow of materials to detect jams or equipment malfunction. Stops machine and notifies supervisor of malfunction or breakdown.
GOE: 05.12.07 STRENGTH: L GED: R2 M2 L2 SVP: 3 DLU: 77

939.686-010 LOADING-MACHINE-OPERATOR HELPER (mine & quarry)
Loads shattered coal, rock, or ore into shuttle or mine cars in underground mine, to assist LOADING-MACHINE OPERATOR (mine & quarry): Positions machine in proximity of receiving conveyance, such as shuttle car or conveyor. Maintains flow of materials through loading material into conveyance. Frees jams and performs routine maintenance on conveyor. Assists in repair and maintenance of loading machine. May relieve LOADING-MACHINE OPERATOR (mine & quarry) in operation of loading machine.
GOE: 05.12.02 STRENGTH: M GED: R2 M1 L1 SVP: 3 DLU: 77

939.687-010 BELT PICKER (mine & quarry)
Removes lumps of slate, wood, wire, clay, or other impurities from extracted minerals passing on conveyor belt, picking table, or shaker screen: Throws lumps of usable material into bins for further processing. Routes impurities to disposal area. May assist in changing conveyor belts or screens and repairing plant equipment.
GOE: 05.12.07 STRENGTH: L GED: R1 M1 L1 SVP: 1 DLU: 77

939.687-014 COMPANY LABORER (mine & quarry) alternate titles: cleaner; digger; laborer, mine; scraper
Works in underground or surface mine, pit, or quarry, or at tipple, mill, or preparation plant, performing any combination of following tasks: Cleans working areas and haulage tracks; digs and maintains drainage ditches; or shovels muck, ore, coal, or rock aside, into cars, or onto conveyors. Pushes loaded mine cars from working face to haulage road and couples cars together for transportation to surface. Positions and adjusts bits on drill shaft and places cables, jacks, roof bolts, and related equipment in specified locations. Trims protrusions from walls and roofs of underground passageways and rooms. Strips (cleans) residue of rock and dirt from exposed coal, ore, or rock formations. Loads, separates, or sorts materials at working face, using shovel or wheelbarrow. Throws calcium or salt around interiors of railroad cars to prevent coal or ore from freezing to cars during winter. May be known according to specific work performed as Car Cleaner (mine & quarry); Car Salter (mine & quarry); Loader (mine & quarry); Mucker (mine & quarry); Shoveler (mine & quarry); Stripper (mine & quarry); Trimmer (mine & quarry).
GOE: 05.12.03 STRENGTH: H GED: R2 M1 L1 SVP: 2 DLU: 80

939.687-018   LABORER (petrol. & gas) alternate titles: roustabout
Performs any combination of following tasks in and about oil fields and pipelines, using handtools: Digs trenches for building foundations or for drainage around oil wells, storage tanks, and other installations. Fills excavations with dirt, using shovels. Loads and unloads trucks by hand or using handtrucks. Mixes concrete, using hoe and shovel. Carries concrete and tamps it into building forms. Bails spilled oil into buckets and barrels. Cleans and performs routine adjustments to machinery, using handtools, solvent, and rags. Cuts down trees and brush around oil field installations to reduce fire hazard or clear way for roads. Rolls and segregates pipe sections on racks in material yard to position pipes for testing. Connects pipe ends and hydraulic hose, using wrenches. Paints oil storage tanks, pumping units, and auxiliary equipment, using brush or spray painting equipment. May clean and service motor vehicles and auxiliary equipment.
GOE: 05.12.03 STRENGTH: V GED: R1 M1 L1 SVP: 1 DLU: 77

939.687-022   LATRINE CLEANER (mine & quarry)
Pushes mine toilet cars or drives self-propelled tank cars onto hoist to be raised to surface. Rolls cars off hoist to disposal area and flushes contents into sewer with water. Refills containers with chemical solution and returns cars to mine.
GOE: 05.12.18 STRENGTH: M GED: R1 M1 L1 SVP: 2 DLU: 77

939.687-026   ROCK-DUST SPRAYER (mine & quarry)
Sprays water or rock dust onto walls, roof, and floor of underground mine workings to mix with coal dust deposits and prevent explosions, using portable compressed-air pump and hose. Mixes rock dust with water and sprays slurry during working hours, to reduce amount of suspended coal dust in air while miners are present.
GOE: 05.12.14 STRENGTH: M GED: R2 M1 L1 SVP: 2 DLU: 77

939.687-030   SAMPLE WASHER (petrol. & gas)
Pulverizes cuttings and cores removed from oil or gas well boreholes, using hammer or small power crusher. Washes cuttings through various-sized mesh screens to separate samples and fossils from soil and other foreign matter. Places samples in bags and attaches identification tags.
GOE: 05.12.07 STRENGTH: L GED: R1 M1 L1 SVP: 2 DLU: 77

939.687-034   SAND FILLER (mine & quarry)
Fills stopes (underground openings from which ore has been mined) with sand to prevent cave-ins of ground surrounding worked out areas: Opens pipe valves to pump sand, waste minerals, and water resulting from treatment of ore, until stopes are filled sufficiently to support walls and roofs. Switches flow from one stope to another to allow time for water to drain off. Plugs holes and cracks in stope with burlap bags and scrap timber to prevent sand from leaking out when dry. May install temporary pipelines from slurry main to distribute slurry in several stopes consecutively.
GOE: 05.12.03 STRENGTH: M GED: R2 M1 L1 SVP: 2 DLU: 77

95   OCCUPATIONS IN PRODUCTION AND DISTRIBUTION OF UTILITIES

This division includes occupations concerned with generation, transmission, and distribution of electricity; generation and distribution of steam for heat and power, including marine propulsion; generation of utility gas, and storage and distribution of natural and manufactured gas for power, illumination, or heating purposes; filtration, purification, and distribution of water for domestic, commercial, or industrial consumption; and collection, treatment, and disposal of sewage and refuse.

950   STATIONARY ENGINEERS

This group includes occupations concerned with operation and maintenance of engines, turbines, air compressors, generators, motors, boilers, and auxiliaries to supply light, heat, refrigeration, ventilation, air-conditioning, and mechanical or electrical power for buildings, industrial plants, and mining or oil field operations.

950.131-010   REFRIGERATING ENGINEER, HEAD (any industry) alternate titles: refrigeration operator, head; refrigeration supervisor
Supervises and coordinates activities of REFRIGERATING ENGINEERS (any industry) engaged in operating refrigerating equipment to provide ice or to cool refrigerating rooms in establishments, such as ice cream plants, frozen food warehouses, and meat packing plants: Directs REFRIGERATION MECHANICS (any industry) in repair of equipment. May participate in repair work, using handtools. Performs duties as described under SUPERVISOR (any industry) Master Title.
GOE: 05.06.02 STRENGTH: L GED: R4 M3 L4 SVP: 7 DLU: 77

950.131-014   STATIONARY-ENGINEER SUPERVISOR (any industry) alternate titles: boiler house supervisor; station supervisor; steam-station supervisor; watch engineer
Supervises and coordinates activities of STATIONARY ENGINEER (any industry) and other workers operating and maintaining stationary engines and mechanical equipment, such as steam engines, air compressors, vacuum and centrifugal pumps, filters, turbines, boilers, and ventilating and refrigerating equip-

ment. May supervise MAINTENANCE REPAIRER, INDUSTRIAL (any industry). Performs duties as described under SUPERVISOR (any industry) Master Title.
GOE: 05.06.02 STRENGTH: L GED: R4 M3 L3 SVP: 7 DLU: 77

950.362-010   ENGINEER, EXHAUSTER (steel & rel.) alternate titles: engineer, byproduct
Operates turbo-blower or steam-driven exhausters and pumps to draw gas resulting from baking of coal through coolers, and into byproducts and benzol-refining plants: Reads pressure and vacuum gauges, thermometers, and flowmeters, and turns hand valves or regulates speed of exhausters and pumps to maintain specified temperatures and pressures. Inspects and repairs equipment, using handtools. Lubricates equipment. Pumps surplus gas to outside consumers [GAS-PUMPING-STATION OPERATOR (utilities)]. Cleans equipment. Records temperatures and pressures at various process stations. May remove ammonium sulfate from gas [SATURATOR OPERATOR (chemical; steel & rel.)].
GOE: 05.06.04 STRENGTH: L GED: R3 M3 L3 SVP: 7 DLU: 77

950.362-014   REFRIGERATING ENGINEER (any industry) alternate titles: cooling-system operator; operating engineer; stationary engineer, refrigeration
Operates freon, carbon-dioxide, or ammonia gas-cooling systems to refrigerate rooms in establishments, such as slaughtering and meat packing plants and dairies, in air-condition buildings, or to provide refrigeration for industrial processes: Opens valves on equipment, such as compressors, pumps, and condensers to prepare system for operation and starts equipment and auxiliary machinery. Observes temperature, pressure and ampere readings for system and equipment and adjusts controls or overrides automatic controls to obtain specified operation of equipment. Records temperature, pressure, and other readings on logsheet at specified intervals. Measures density of brine, using hydrometer, and adds calcium chloride to lower temperature to specified degree. Connects hose from supply tank to compressor to replace coolant. Makes periodic inspection of equipment and system to observe operating condition and need for repair or adjustment. Adjusts controls to isolate and clear broken lines for repair or shuts down equipment. May repack pumps and compressors, clean condensers, and replace worn or defective parts using hand and power tools. When operating refrigeration or air-conditioning equipment aboard ship, may be known as Reefer Engineer (water trans.) and must have endorsement on Merchant Mariner's document as Refrigerating Engineer.
GOE: 05.06.02 STRENGTH: M GED: R4 M3 L3 SVP: 7 DLU: 77

950.382-010   BOILER OPERATOR (any industry) alternate titles: boiler house operator; control-room operator; firer, boiler; steam-power-plant operator
Operates automatically fired boilers to generate steam that supplies heat or power for buildings or industrial processes: Lights gas- or oil-fed burners, using torch. Starts pulverizer and stoker to grind and feed coal into furnace of boiler. Observes pressure, temperature, and draft meters on panel to verify specified operation of automatic combustion control systems, feed water regulators, stoker, pulverizer, and burners. Turns valves and adjusts controls to set specified fuel feed, draft openings, water level, and steam pressure of boiler. Observes boiler and auxiliary units to detect malfunctions and makes repairs, such as changing burners and tightening pipes and fittings. May test and treat boiler feed water, using specified chemicals. May maintain log of meter and gauge readings and record data, such as water test results and quantity of fuel consumed. May be designated according to fuel burned, type of boilers, or class of license required.
GOE: 05.06.02 STRENGTH: M GED: R4 M3 L3 SVP: 7 DLU: 81

950.382-014   GAS-COMPRESSOR OPERATOR (any industry) alternate titles: gas-lift engineer
Operates steam or internal combustion engines to transmit, compress, or recover gases, such as butane, nitrogen, hydrogen, and natural gas in various production processes: Moves controls and turns valves to start compressor engines, pumps, and auxiliary equipment. Monitors meters, gauges, and recording instrument charts to ensure specified temperature, pressure, and flow of gas through system. Observes operation of equipment to detect malfunctions. Records instrument readings and operational changes in operating log. May operate purification tanks (scrubbers) to purify air or byproduct gases. May tend pumps to mix specified amounts of acids and caustics with water for use in purifying gases. May perform minor repairs on equipment, using handtools. May conduct chemical tests to determine sulfur or moisture content in gas. May be designated according to type of gas compressed or recovered as Butadiene-Compressor Operator (chemical); Butane-Compressor Operator (petrol. refin.); Ethylene-Compressor Operator (chemical). May operate equipment to control transmission of natural gas through pipelines and be designated Compressor-Station Engineer (pipe lines).
GOE: 05.06.02 STRENGTH: M GED: R4 M3 L3 SVP: 7 DLU: 77

950.382-018   GAS-ENGINE OPERATOR (any industry)
Operates stationary internal-combustion engines, using natural gas for fuel, to supply power for equipment, such as electrical generators and air or gas compressors: Starts auxiliary air compressor and turns compressed air and fuel valves to start engine. Observes gauges and meters and adjusts controls to regulate ignition, governor, lubrication and cooling systems, and load distribution between engines. Observes operation of equipment, such as generators or com-

pressors to detect malfunctions. May specialize in engines designed for specific processes and be designated Gas-Engine Operator, Compressors (any industry); Gas-Engine Operator, Generators (any industry).
GOE: 05.06.01 STRENGTH: M GED: R3 M2 L2 SVP: 6 DLU: 77

950.382-022   ROTARY-RIG ENGINE OPERATOR (petrol. & gas) alternate titles: diesel-engine engineer; gas-engine engineer

Operates gasoline, natural gas, or diesel engines to supply power for rotary oil well drilling machinery: Starts engines and observes drilling operations to provide power under operating conditions. Assembles and dismantles pumps and other drilling equipment, using handtools. Loosens and tightens threaded sections of drill pipe and well casing. Lubricates and repairs equipment.
GOE: 05.06.02 STRENGTH: M GED: R4 M3 L3 SVP: 7 DLU: 77

950.382-026   STATIONARY ENGINEER (any industry) alternate titles: maintenance engineer; operating engineer; power-plant operator; watch engineer

Operates and maintains stationary engines and mechanical equipment, such as steam engines, air compressors, generators, motors, turbines, and steam boilers to provide utilities, such as light, heat, or power for buildings and industrial processes: Reads meters and gauges or automatic recording devices at specified intervals to verify operating conditions. Records data, such as temperature of equipment, hours of operation, fuel consumed, temperature or pressure, water levels, analysis of flue gases, voltage load and generator balance. Adjusts manual controls or overrides automatic controls to bring equipment into recommended or prescribed operating ranges, switch to backup equipment or systems, or to shut down equipment. Visually inspects equipment at periodic intervals to detect malfunctions or need for repair, adjustment or lubrication. Maintains equipment by tightening fittings, repacking bearings, replacing packing glands, gaskets, valves, recorders, and gauges, and cleaning or replacing burners or other components, using handtools and power tools. May be required to hold license issued by state or municipality, restricting equipment operated to specified types and sizes. May oil and lubricate equipment [OILER (any industry) 950.685-014]. May perform water titration tests and pour chemical additives, such as water softener, into treatment tank to prevent scale buildup and to clean boiler lines. May record operation and maintenance actions taken during shift in operators logbook. May specialize in equipment designed for industrial processes and be designated Acid-Concentration-Plant-Equipment Engineer (any industry); Air-Compressor-Station Engineer (any industry); Diesel-Engine Operator, Stationary (any industry); Water-Pumping-Station Engineer (any industry).
GOE: 05.06.02 STRENGTH: M GED: R4 M4 L3 SVP: 7 DLU: 88

950.382-030   STATIONARY-ENGINEER APPRENTICE (any industry) alternate titles: operating-engineer apprentice, stationary; power-plant-operator apprentice

Performs duties as described under APPRENTICE (any industry) Master Title.
GOE: 05.06.02 STRENGTH: M GED: R4 M4 L3 SVP: 7 DLU: 77

950.485-010   HUMIDIFIER ATTENDANT (textile; tobacco) alternate titles: humidifier-maintenance worker; humid-system operator

Tends humidifying system that keeps moisture content of air in rooms or departments at specified level: Computes moisture content of air, using hygrometer or chart recorder (pneumatic controller). Sets thermostat controls and adjusts valves controlling waterflow to increase or decrease moisture. Replaces worn or broken parts, such as fans, sprinkler heads, and pipe sections, using handtools. Cleans equipment, using airhose, brushes, and rags. May drain water from pipes and air reservoir. May test electrical system to determine specified voltage, using voltage meter.
GOE: 05.06.02 STRENGTH: L GED: R3 M2 L2 SVP: 6 DLU: 77

950.562-010   PANELBOARD OPERATOR (chemical) alternate titles: vessel ventilation system operator

Operates panelboard to control ventilation system of nuclear waste processing plant: Adjusts panelboard controls to maintain specified pressure, temperature, and airflow through ventilation pipes and holding vessels, and to regulate level of nuclear radiation in work area. Observes gauges and meters to monitor operation of fans and pumps, and to detect equipment malfunctions. Informs and directs maintenance personnel to area of malfunctioning equipment. Records data to maintain record of operation of ventilation system as related to safety standards established by Atomic Energy Commission.
GOE: 05.06.04 STRENGTH: L GED: R4 M4 L4 SVP: 7 DLU: 77

950.585-010   VENTILATION EQUIPMENT TENDER (any industry) alternate titles: air-control tender; blower-room attendant; exhaust tender; heating-and-ventilating tender; scrubber-system attendant; ventilation mechanic

Tends ventilating and heating equipment, such as fans, vacuum pumps, air compressors, vents and ducts, and lubrication-oil coolers used in buildings or industrial processes: Adjusts valves to regulate temperature of lubrication oil and flow of water through system. Moves controls to regulate speed of fans and to adjust vents and ducts. Records gauge readings, repairs completed, and time lost because of inoperative equipment. Writes repair work order tickets and out-of-order tags preparatory to equipment repair. Inspects equipment to detect excessive noise and heat. Replaces gauges and tightens and caulks leaky fittings, using wrenches, hammers, and caulking tool. Cleans carbon deposits, pitch, and grease from fans, vents, and ducts, using scrapers, hammer, and compressed air or steam.

GOE: 05.06.02 STRENGTH: L GED: R3 M2 L3 SVP: 4 DLU: 77

950.585-014   BOILER-OPERATOR HELPER (sugar & conf.)

Assists BOILER OPERATOR (any industry) 950.382-010 in operation and maintenance of coal-fired boilers: Turns valves that regulate water flow into full ash hoppers to form slurry and flush slurry into ash grinder. Turns switches that activate vacuum pumps to remove fly ash from full fly ash hoppers. Turns valves and flips switches that activate pumps to replace contaminated water in boiler system. Obtains water samples from designated locations of boiler system and carries samples to testing laboratory. Performs chemical and physical water quality laboratory tests according to prescribed standards. Records and gives results of tests to other workers for use in adjustment of equipment operation.
GOE: 05.06.02 STRENGTH: L GED: R3 M2 L3 SVP: 4 DLU: 86

950.685-010   AIR-COMPRESSOR OPERATOR (any industry) alternate titles: compressor engineer; compressor operator

Tends air compressors driven by steam, electric, or gasoline powered units, to generate and supply compressed air for operation of pneumatic tools, hoists, and air lances: Starts power unit to build up specified pressure in compressor. Adjusts controls or sets automatic controls to maintain continuous air supply to pneumatic tools or equipment. Observes temperature and pressure gauges and adjusts controls accordingly. Lubricates and cleans equipment. May connect pipelines from compressor to pneumatic tools or equipment. May repair low pressure steam boilers that furnish power for air compressor units by disassembling unit of boiler and replacing damaged parts, using handtools. May be designated according to type of equipment operated as Air-Compressor Operator, Stationary (any industry); Compressor Operator, Portable (any industry).
GOE: 05.06.02 STRENGTH: M GED: R3 M2 L2 SVP: 5 DLU: 77

950.685-014   BOILER-ROOM HELPER (any industry) alternate titles: boiler-operator helper; oiler; powerhouse oiler

Assists STATIONARY ENGINEER (any industry) in operation and maintenance of stationary steam boilers and auxiliary steam equipment, such as pumps, compressors, and air-conditioning system, performing any combination of following tasks: Starts auxiliary equipment. Opens valves and adjusts regulators to control flow of steam or water through pipelines, or to blow sludge and scale from pressure system. Cleans and lubricates pumps. Dusts tubes, and removes slag from furnace tubes and brickwork of coal-fired boiler, using steam or compressed air. Opens drains and washes boilers. Performs maintenance tasks, such as packing valves, repairing pipelines, and replacing gauge glasses. May regulate volume of water in boilers and in auxiliary equipment. Performs other duties as described under HELPER (any industry) Master Title.
GOE: 05.06.02 STRENGTH: L GED: R2 M2 L2 SVP: 4 DLU: 77

951   FIRERS AND RELATED OCCUPATIONS

This group includes occupations concerned with firing coal-, gas-, or oil-fueled boilers and furnaces, and tending auxiliary equipment to supply steam or hot air. Includes marine firers. Process firers are included in Category 5; locomotive firers in Group 910; and fire fighters in Group 373.

951.685-010   FIRER, HIGH PRESSURE (any industry) alternate titles: boiler tender; firer, boiler; stoker

Tends portable or stationary high pressure boilers that supply heat or power for engines, turbines, and steam-powered equipment, such as steam shovels, pile drivers, or cranes, or industrial processes: Shovels fuel, such as coal or coke, into firebox or conveyor hopper, or turns valves and moves controls to regulate flow of fuel, such as gas, oil, or pulverized coal, into firebox. Reads gauges and moves controls to maintain specified steam pressure and water level in boiler. Removes ashes from firebox, using shovel and bucket. May clean and repair boilers. May treat boiler feed water, using specified chemicals. May be required to hold license issued by state or municipality. May be designated according to type of boiler tended as Firer, Automatic Stoker (any industry); Firer, Portable Boiler (any industry); Firer, Stationary Boiler (any industry); or type of equipment supplied with power as Firer, Locomotive Crane (any industry); Firer, Pile Driver (any industry); Firer, Steam Shovel (any industry); or type of installation as Firer, Powerhouse (any industry).
GOE: 05.06.02 STRENGTH: M GED: R3 M2 L3 SVP: 5 DLU: 77

951.685-014   FIRER, LOW PRESSURE (any industry) alternate titles: boiler operator

Tends low pressure boilers that supply steam heat for office buildings, apartment houses, or industrial establishments: Shovels coal or coke into firebox to feed fuel into boiler; turns valves to regulate flow of gas, oil, or pulverized coal into firebox; or moves controls to regulate fuel feeding speed of automatic stoker. Reads gauges and moves controls to maintain specified steam pressure, temperature, and water level in boiler. Cleans burner, using tools, such as shovel, wire brush, and scraper. May perform maintenance duties, such as cleaning boiler room and removing waste from building. May be required to hold license issued by state or municipality.
GOE: 05.06.02 STRENGTH: M GED: R2 M2 L2 SVP: 5 DLU: 78

951.685-018   FIRER, MARINE (water trans.)

Tends boilers aboard vessel to maintain steam at specified pressure: Installs atomizing tips on end of burner barrels with wrench. Inserts barrels in burners. Connects fuel-oil lines to burners. Ignites fuel with torch. Adjusts burners to maintain steam pressure at specified level. Cleans drip pans, atomizing tips,

burner barrels, and work area, using steam connections, solvent, or rags. Must have certificate issued by U.S. Coast Guard. May operate soot-blowers to clean combustion residue on generating tubes. May regulate amount of water in boiler and be known as Firer-Watertender (water trans.).
GOE: 05.06.02 STRENGTH: M GED: R3 M3 L3 SVP: 5 DLU: 77

951.686-010 FUEL-HOUSE ATTENDANT (saw. & plan.)
Opens fuel conveyor chute by moving levers and rakes sawmill waste, such as chips, sawdust, and shavings, into hopper of furnace. May lubricate conveyor system, using grease gun and oilcan. May move panelboard controls to regulate proportions of bark, chips, sawdust, and shavings that are fed to boilers.
GOE: 05.12.04 STRENGTH: M GED: R2 M1 L1 SVP: 2 DLU: 77

952 OCCUPATIONS IN GENERATION, TRANSMISSION, AND DISTRIBUTION OF ELECTRIC LIGHT AND POWER

This group includes occupations concerned with controlling equipment in powerplants utilizing fossil fuels, hydraulic power, and atomic energy; monitoring and controlling equipment in manned or remote-controlled substations and standby generating plants; and related activities concerned with generation, transmission, and distribution of electricity for utilization by domestic, commercial, and industrial consumers.

952.131-010 SUBSTATION OPERATOR, CHIEF (utilities)
Supervises and coordinates activities of workers engaged in operating and maintaining electrical and mechanical equipment at electrical substation used to control flow of current through transmission lines: Directs switching operations to drop station voltage load under low frequency conditions in order to determine loss of generator sources, and to resynchronize transmission lines after power separation during emergencies. Inspects equipment, such as control and meter boards, relays, circuit breakers, and transformer lines to ensure operating efficiency. Records instrument readings at designated intervals and completes daily and monthly reports to indicate data, such as current loads, voltage loads, outages, and inspections. Performs other duties as described under SUPERVISOR (any industry) Master Title.
GOE: 05.06.01 STRENGTH: L GED: R4 M3 L3 SVP: 8 DLU: 77

952.132-010 OPERATIONS SUPERVISOR, NUCLEAR POWER PLANT (utilities)
Supervises and coordinates activities of workers engaged in operation and control of thermonuclear reactor, turbine generator, and auxiliary equipment at electric generating station: Devises and writes operating procedures for reactor, turbine generator, and auxiliary equipment, based on review and interpretation of government regulations, technical manuals, and conferences with manufacturer's representatives. Oversees activities of workers, reviews status reports of station operations, and monitors and analyzes readings of instrumentation systems to ensure that reactor and auxiliary equipment are operated safely and in accordance with Nuclear Regulatory Commission regulations. Confers with supervisory personnel to coordinate activities of operations and maintenance workers engaged in performance of routine and emergency shutdowns and maintenance of equipment and machinery. Prepares training outlines and instructs workers in such subjects as mathematics, reactor physics, and electrical theory, according to federal regulatory requirements. Performs other duties as described under SUPERVISOR (any industry) Master Title.
GOE: 05.06.01 STRENGTH: L GED: R5 M5 L5 SVP: 8 DLU: 86

952.137-010 CHIEF LOAD DISPATCHER (utilities) alternate titles: chief dispatcher; system operator, chief
Supervises and coordinates activities of LOAD DISPATCHERS (utilities) engaged in controlling operations of generating stations, substations, and distribution lines of electric power system. May inspect substations [SUBSTATION INSPECTOR (utilities)] to verify accuracy of instrument readings with load dispatching office. Performs duties as described under SUPERVISOR (any industry) Master Title.
GOE: 05.06.01 STRENGTH: L GED: R4 M3 L4 SVP: 7 DLU: 77

952.137-014 HYDROELECTRIC-STATION OPERATOR, CHIEF (utilities) alternate titles: production superintendent, hydro
Supervises and coordinates activities of workers engaged in operating and controlling hydroelectric generating equipment: Analyzes defective operation and directs HYDROELECTRIC-STATION OPERATORS (utilities) to adjust equipment to minimize interruptions of power demands. Inspects equipment and initiates maintenance repair orders. Notifies WATERSHED TENDER (waterworks) when subnormal speed of generating units requires adjustment of reservoir floodgates to increase pressure of water which rotates water wheels. Performs duties as described under SUPERVISOR (any industry) Master Title.
GOE: 05.06.01 STRENGTH: L GED: R4 M3 L3 SVP: 7 DLU: 77

952.137-018 SUPERINTENDENT, LOCAL (utilities) alternate titles: distribution district supervisor
Supervises and coordinates activities of workers located in small communities or rural areas, and engaged in installing, removing, or repairing electric meters and service lines, repairing overhead distribution system, reading meters, and making service collections. Performs other duties as described under SUPERVISOR (any industry) Master Title.
GOE: 05.05.05 STRENGTH: L GED: R4 M3 L3 SVP: 7 DLU: 77

952.137-022 TURBINE OPERATOR, HEAD (utilities)
Supervises and coordinates activities of workers engaged in operating turbine-driven generators in steam-electric generating plant: Reviews work orders from STATIONARY-ENGINEER SUPERVISOR (any industry) or SWITCHBOARD OPERATOR (utilities) to determine specified power necessary for allocating load capacity to turbines. Notifies TURBINE OPERATOR (utilities) to increase or decrease power loads to turbines and to transfer loads when equipment malfunctions. Evaluates reports from TURBINE ATTENDANT (utilities) and observes recording instrument readings to determine operating status of equipment.
GOE: 05.06.01 STRENGTH: L GED: R4 M3 L3 SVP: 7 DLU: 77

952.137-026 SUPERVISOR, OPERATIONS (utilities)
Supervises and coordinates activities of POWER-PLANT OPERATORS (utilities) 952.382-018, AUXILIARY-EQUIPMENT OPERATORS (utilities) 952.362-010, and other workers engaged in operating and controlling coal-fired electric generating equipment to produce electricity: Confers with SUPERINTENDENT, GENERATING PLANT (utilities) 184.167-166 to resolve electric generating problems and to report work activities and personnel matters. Coordinates repair of malfunctioning equipment with maintenance department, and inspects repaired equipment prior to return to service. Assigns new workers to experienced personnel for training, according to established training procedure. Studies equipment modification and operating procedure materials to improve supervisory skills and techniques and to increase worker productivity. Performs other duties as described under SUPERVISOR (any industry) Master Title.
GOE: 05.06.01 STRENGTH: L GED: R4 M3 L4 SVP: 7 DLU: 86

952.167-010 DISPATCHER, SERVICE OR WORK (utilities) alternate titles: trouble dispatcher
Dispatches workers, such as TROUBLE SHOOTERS (utilities) II; LINE REPAIRERS (utilities); and STREET-LIGHT REPAIRERS (utilities) for normal maintenance or emergency repairs to electric-power transmission and distribution lines and related equipment: Receives trouble calls from police, fire departments, and company offices. Records time, location, and nature of trouble and relays information to workers assigned to area in which work occurs, using telephone or radio. Receives work reports and makes reassignments. Informs work crews of changes in weather conditions and system status affecting safety, and answers questions requiring knowledge of system layout and electric equipment operation and repair. Relays and records all messages between line crews and LOAD DISPATCHER (utilities) concerning switching operations. May requisition supplies. May dispatch workers to answer customer service calls [DISPATCHER, SERVICE (utilities)].
GOE: 07.04.05 STRENGTH: S GED: R4 M3 L3 SVP: 7 DLU: 77

952.167-014 LOAD DISPATCHER (utilities) alternate titles: dispatcher, electric power; power dispatcher; system dispatcher; system operator
Coordinates activities of personnel engaged in operating generating stations, substations, and lines of electric power system or electrified railway system to ensure adequate production and distribution of electricity to meet power demands: In smaller system, calculates load estimates according to corrected weather and consumer-demand records and notifies SWITCHBOARD OPERATOR (utilities) at generating stations of electric power required to meet fluctuating demands; or in larger systems receives load schedule for various generating stations from POWER-PLANT OPERATOR (utilities). Monitors control board showing operating condition of lines and equipment throughout system and makes adjustments or directs workers to make adjustments as conditions warrant. Directs SUBSTATION OPERATOR (utilities) and other workers to deenergize malfunctioning circuits or adjusts switches to ensure safety of maintenance crew and avoid interruptions of service during repairs. Notifies maintenance crew of location and deenergization of troubled sector, and verifies that workers are clear of repaired equipment before directing energization of circuit. Contacts other utilities by telephone to arrange exchange of power according to existing contracts or in emergency and coordinates tie-in with other systems. Compiles operational records. May operate console of computer which is programmed to automatically perform load-control functions. May calculate discharge rate of water in reservoirs utilizing reports of rain, river flow, and water level in reservoirs, and directs setting of watergates at hydroelectric plant to coordinate water flow and power generation with irrigation and flood control requirements. May compute bills for power delivered to interconnected utilities. May be responsible for section of system and be designated Load Dispatcher, Local (utilities).
GOE: 05.06.01 STRENGTH: L GED: R4 M3 L3 SVP: 8 DLU: 77

952.261-010 SUBSTATION INSPECTOR (utilities)
Inspects and tests electric current-converting and distribution equipment in attended or unattended substations to verify operating efficiency and accuracy of equipment: Examines transformers, oil switches, fuses, lighting arresters, voltage regulators, and related equipment, and tests circuitry, using standard electrical testing apparatus, to verify that new equipment is correctly installed and wired. Inspects automatic supervisory-controls in unattended stations to verify their performance of supervisory functions, according to specifications and cumulative station-operation records. Performs acceptance and performance tests under direction of engineering personnel to evaluate performance of new and operating equipment. Calculates average and peak load conditions of station from electric recording instrument data and compiles report of load conditions

and test results for equipment performance evaluation and system planning purposes. Repairs or replaces blown fuses and defective switches or wires. Opens switches to deenergize station circuitry and distribution lines preparatory to repairs by maintenance workers or linecrews. May control operation of attended station in absence of regular operator. May patrol power lines [ELECTRIC POWER LINE EXAMINER (utilities)]. When inspecting unattended substations, may be designated Substation Inspector, Automatic (utilities).
GOE: 05.06.01 STRENGTH: L GED: R4 M3 L3 SVP: 7 DLU: 77

952.362-010 AUXILIARY-EQUIPMENT OPERATOR (utilities) alternate titles: pump-room operator

Controls and maintains auxiliary equipment, such as pumps, fans, compressors, filters, feedwater heaters, chlorinators, and condensers that supply water, fuel, lubricants, air, and auxiliary power for turbines, generators, boilers, and other power-generating plant facilities: Opens and closes valves and switches in prescribed sequence upon receipt of signal from TURBINE OPERATOR (utilities) 952.362-042 or POWER-PLANT OPERATOR (utilities) 952.382-018 to start or shut down auxiliary units. Reads temperature, pressure, and r.p.m. gauges to verify that units are operating at specified capacity, and listens for sounds from machinery that warn of mechanical malfunction. Replenishes electrolyte in batteries and oil in voltage transformers and resets tripped electric relays. Assists ELECTRICIAN, POWERHOUSE (utilities) 820.261-014 in making electrical repairs. Cleans and lubricates equipment and collects oil, water, and electrolyte samples for laboratory analysis to prevent equipment failure or deterioration. Tightens leaking glands and pipe joints and reports need for major equipment repairs to POWER-PLANT OPERATOR (utilities). When working in nuclear-powered generating station, may help transfer fissionable material between vehicles and storage area. May fire up and shut down automatically regulated boilers [FIRER, HIGH PRESSURE (any industry) 951.685-010].
GOE: 05.06.01 STRENGTH: M GED: R3 M2 L3 SVP: 5 DLU: 80

952.362-014 FEEDER-SWITCHBOARD OPERATOR (utilities)

Operates switchboard to control distribution of electric power over feeder circuits between generating station and substations of electric power system: Selects and moves control switches as directed by LOAD DISPATCHER (utilities) to cut in and cut out feeder circuits. Observes control-board indicators to detect circuits automatically cut off due to line disturbances and turns controls to cut in spare feeder to carry load of cutoff circuit. Tags switches of feeders automatically cut off to warn next operator of defective lines. Records readings of meters indicating temperature of transformers and voltage and frequency of electricity in feeders.
GOE: 05.06.01 STRENGTH: L GED: R3 M2 L2 SVP: 6 DLU: 77

952.362-018 HYDROELECTRIC-STATION OPERATOR (utilities)

Controls electrical generating units and related mechanical and hydraulic equipment at hydroelectric-generating station: Operates switchboard and manually operated controls to control water wheels, generators, and auxiliary hydroelectric-generating station equipment and distribute power output among generating units, according to power demands [SWITCHBOARD OPERATOR (utilities)]. Operates feeder switchboard to control distribution of electric power over feeder circuits between generating station and substations [FEEDER-SWITCHBOARD OPERATOR (utilities)]. Records control-board meter and gauge readings, inspects operating equipment, and notifies HYDROELECTRIC-STATION OPERATOR, CHIEF (utilities) of conditions indicating abnormal equipment operation. May perform minor maintenance on equipment, such as replacing generator brushes, cleaning insulators, and lubricating machines.
GOE: 05.06.01 STRENGTH: L GED: R4 M3 L3 SVP: 7 DLU: 77

952.362-022 POWER-REACTOR OPERATOR (utilities) alternate titles: nuclear plant control operator; reactor operator

Controls nuclear reactor that produces steam for generation of electric power and coordinates operation of auxiliary equipment: Adjusts controls, under supervision, to start and shut down reactor and to regulate flux level, reactor period, coolant temperature, and rate of flow, control rod positions, and other control elements that affect power level within reactor, following standard instructions and prescribed practices. Dispatches orders and instructions to plant personnel through radiotelephone or intercommunication system to coordinate operation of such auxiliary equipment as pumps, compressors, switchgears, and water-treatment systems. May assist in preparing, transferring, loading, and unloading nuclear fuel elements. May be required to hold Nuclear Reactor Operator's license. May be required to hold Radiotelephone Operator's license. May control dual purpose reactors that produce plutonium and steam. May control operation of auxiliary equipment, such as turbines and generators [SWITCHBOARD OPERATOR (utilities); TURBINE OPERATOR (utilities)].
GOE: 05.06.01 STRENGTH: M GED: R4 M3 L3 SVP: 7 DLU: 77

952.362-026 SUBSTATION OPERATOR (utilities) alternate titles: power-switchboard operator; receiving-distribution-station operator

Controls equipment, such as current converters, voltage transformers, and circuit breakers, that regulate flow of electricity through substation of electric power system and over distribution lines to consumers: Records readings of switchboard instruments to compile data concerning quantities of electric power used for substation operation and amounts distributed from station. Communicates with LOAD DISPATCHER (utilities) to report amount of electricity received into substation, and to receive switching instructions. Observes switchboard instruments to detect indications of line disturbances, such as grounded,

shorted, or open circuits. Pulls circuit breaker switch or pushes buttons to interrupt flow of current in disturbed line preparatory to repair, and to connect alternate circuit to carry load of deenergized lines. Records temperature of transformers at specified intervals. May inspect equipment, such as transformers, pumps, fans, batteries, and circuit breakers to detect defects. May calculate average and peak load conditions from electric recording instrument data and compile periodic report of load variations for system planning purposes. May locate and replace defective fuses and switches, using test lamp and handtools. May be designated according to primary function of substation as Substation Operator, Conversion (utilities); Substation Operator, Distribution (r.r. trans.; utilities); Substation Operator, Transforming (utilities). May operate auxiliary generators and be designated Substation Operator, Generation (utilities). May control several remote-controlled substations from central station switchboard and be designated Substation Operator, Automatic (utilities).
GOE: 05.06.01 STRENGTH: L GED: R4 M3 L3 SVP: 7 DLU: 77

952.362-030 SUBSTATION OPERATOR APPRENTICE (utilities)

Performs duties as described under APPRENTICE (any industry) Master Title.
GOE: 05.06.01 STRENGTH: L GED: R4 M3 L3 SVP: 7 DLU: 77

952.362-034 SWITCHBOARD OPERATOR (utilities) alternate titles: generator-switchboard operator

Controls central switchboard in electric generating plant to distribute power output among generators according to generator capacity and power demands, and to regulate flow and distribution of power from generators to transmission power lines: Determines number of generators required to meet power demands according to load estimates received from LOAD DISPATCHER (utilities). Notifies TURBINE OPERATOR (utilities) to start additional generators when switchboard gauges indicate power demands are approaching capacity of operating generators. Observes synchroscope, voltmeters, and frequency indicators, and operates switchboard controls to synchronize speed of incoming generator with operating units, and to adjust generator output voltage and frequency to match output of operating generators. Closes switch to connect incoming generator to *bus bar* at instant when synchroscope indicates generator is in phase with outgoing power lines. Operates switchboard controls to disconnect generators from bus bar as power demand decreases or when equipment malfunctions. Constantly observes switchboard meters and gauges to verify operating status of equipment. Compiles records of switching and generating operations. May operate switches to control distribution of power over feeder circuits between generating station and substations [FEEDER-SWITCHBOARD OPERATOR (utilities)]. May control automatic steam-generating boiler from switchboard during normal operations and direct other workers who shut down and repair equipment [BOILER OPERATOR (any industry)]. May start, shut down, and monitor operation of turbogenerators by remote control from central switchboard [TURBINE OPERATOR (utilities)]. May control feeder circuits that supply power to production or process equipment in industrial establishment which produces its own electric power.
GOE: 05.06.01 STRENGTH: L GED: R4 M3 L3 SVP: 7 DLU: 77

952.362-038 SWITCHBOARD OPERATOR (chemical) alternate titles: powerhouse attendant

Controls powerhouse equipment, such as converters, rectifiers, transformers, and generators, to direct, distribute, and maintain power to chemical processing equipment, according to demand: Moves switches on central control panel to regulate converters and rectifiers to convert alternating current or direct current and transmit it to electrolytic cell department, according to production demand. Observes demand meters, gauges, and recording instruments and moves controls to ensure efficient power utilization, equipment operation, and maintain power distribution, according to departmental demands. Monitors gauges, alarms, and oscilloscopes to detect and prevent damage to equipment and disruption of power. Records operational data, such as chart and meter readings, power demand and usage, malfunctions and repairs, and operating time. Cleans, lubricates, repairs, and adjusts equipment, using handtools. May turn valves to regulate pressure on lines drawing chlorine to electrolytic cells. When controlling specific equipment only, may be designated by unit as Motor-Generator-Set Operator (chemical); Rectifier Operator (chemical).
GOE: 05.06.01 STRENGTH: L GED: R4 M3 L3 SVP: 7 DLU: 77

952.362-042 TURBINE OPERATOR (utilities) alternate titles: turbogenerator operator

Controls steam-driven turbogenerators in electric or nuclear power generating station: Starts or signals AUXILIARY-EQUIPMENT OPERATOR (utilities) to start turbines and boiler auxiliary units. Adjusts throttle and vacuum-breaker valve to engage governor that regulates speed of turbines and notifies SWITCHBOARD OPERATOR (utilities) that turbine-driven generators can be synchronized with auxiliary units. Monitors panelboard to control operations of turbines to detect equipment malfunctions. Stops turbines when malfunctions occur, following operating instructions. Records instrument readings at specified intervals. May perform minor maintenance or equipment, using handtools. When controlling operation by remote control, may be designated Central-Control-Room Operator (utilities).
GOE: 05.06.01 STRENGTH: L GED: R4 M3 L3 SVP: 7 DLU: 77

952.364-010 TROUBLE SHOOTER I (utilities)

Performs variety of duties as assigned by DISPATCHER, SERVICE (utilities) in answer to trouble or service calls of electricity customers: Switches on

or shuts off electricity to installed meters on order for resumption or discontinuance of service. Tests meters to determine absence or presence of current, using portable test lamp. Attaches and removes out-of-service tags for information of METER READER (utilities; waterworks). Attempts to locate source of lesser interruptions to service and makes minor repairs, such as replacing floor plugs, wall switches, or appliance cords. Reports major interruptions to service for repair by other workers. Notifies customer of malfunctioning appliances and advises customer to call electrician.
GOE: 05.10.03 STRENGTH: L GED: R3 M2 L2 SVP: 5 DLU: 77

952.367-010 LOAD CHECKER (utilities) alternate titles: demand inspector

Surveys electrical equipment and appliances used in industrial plants, commercial establishments, and private homes to compile data for purposes such as forecasting power demands, establishing rates, and improving service: Examines fixtures, appliances, and equipment, and records wattage required for their operation. Attaches meters to appliances and equipment and measures power consumption for specified period. May suggest changes in consumer's equipment to reduce electrical hazards, minimize power loss, and increase efficiency of electric power utilization. May perform minor repairs to meters, wiring, and appliances, using handtools.
GOE: 05.09.01 STRENGTH: L GED: R3 M3 L3 SVP: 6 DLU: 77

952.367-014 SWITCHBOARD OPERATOR ASSISTANT (utilities) alternate titles: generating-substation-operator assistant; power-plant assistant; switchboard-operator helper

Compiles gauge readings and performs other tasks as directed by SWITCHBOARD OPERATOR (utilities) in electric-generating plant: Records gauge and meter readings on switchboard and panelboards at specified intervals. Opens and closes switches to regulate generation and flow of electric power. Cleans and oils mechanical and electrical equipment and reports malfunctions, such as meter fluctuations, abnormal sounds, and overheating. May assist in performing tests to diagnose and locate cause of equipment malfunction. May work in substation that distributes and generates electric power and be designated Substation Operator Helper, Generation (utilities).
GOE: 05.06.01 STRENGTH: L GED: R3 M3 L3 SVP: 7 DLU: 77

952.381-010 SWITCH INSPECTOR (utilities)

Inspects and maintains automatic switches that turn street lights on and off: Climbs pole, using ladder or climbing spurs, and opens switchbox. Examines switch to detect such defects as burned contacts or faulty mercury tubes. Tests switch and circuit to locate short circuits or grounded wires, using test lamp. Repairs or replaces broken or defective parts, using handtools.
GOE: 05.10.03 STRENGTH: M GED: R3 M2 L3 SVP: 5 DLU: 77

952.382-010 DIESEL-PLANT OPERATOR (utilities)

Controls and maintains diesel-electric generating units to produce electric power for distribution or to supply electric power for plant equipment: Starts diesel engines and synchronizes generators with other power sources. Inspects equipment to detect malfunctions. Performs minor repairs and adjustments on equipment, using handtools. Records instrument readings in log. Issues switching orders to open, close, and tag electric circuits [SWITCHBOARD OPERATOR (utilities)].
GOE: 05.06.01 STRENGTH: L GED: R4 M3 L3 SVP: 6 DLU: 77

952.382-014 POWER OPERATOR (tel. & tel.) alternate titles: telephone-plant power operator

Operates and maintains central-office equipment such as motors, generators, storage batteries, and motor-driven apparatus, used to furnish or transmit power for telephone or telegraph operation.
GOE: 05.06.01 STRENGTH: M GED: R3 M3 L2 SVP: 7 DLU: 77

952.382-018 POWER-PLANT OPERATOR (utilities) alternate titles: power engineer; powerhouse engineer; power-plant engineer

Operates boilers, turbines, generators, and auxiliary equipment at generating plant to produce electricity: Monitors control board and regulates equipment, according to procedures and information obtained from recording and indicating instruments. Adjusts controls of water and cold feed systems, blowers, and igniters to start up or shut down boilers. Controls operation of boiler auxiliary equipment, such as water and vacuum pumps, coal driers and pulverizers, steam condensers, and soot blowers to ensure efficient operation of boilers. Adjusts boiler controls to provide steam at specified temperature and pressure for turbine loads according to power demands. Adjusts controls to regulate speed, voltage, and phase of incoming turbines to coincide with voltage and phase of power being generated. Synchronizes incoming generating units with units in operation and closes circuit breaker at exact instant of coincidence. Monitors gauges to determine effect of generator load on related equipment, such as *bus bars* and voltage regulators. Adjusts transformer controls to regulate flow of power between generating stations and substations. Operates switchgear to regulate and transfer power loads to protect maintenance workers engaged in repairing or cleaning equipment. Records malfunctions of equipment, instruments, or controls on logsheet.
GOE: 05.06.01 STRENGTH: M GED: R4 M4 L4 SVP: 8 DLU: 77

952.464-010 CABLE MAINTAINER (utilities)

Maintains pressure in oil-filled and gas-filled cables used to transmit high-voltage electricity: Computes amount of oil or gas required for given section of cable, using standard specifications. Pumps oil or gas into cable until specified pressure is attained. Installs relay (regulating devices) used to control pressure inside cables. Attaches temporary reservoirs to ends of cable to maintain pressure during installation of cable. Tests cables with manual pressure gauges. Reports cable sheath defects and joint failure for repair.
GOE: 05.06.01 STRENGTH: L GED: R3 M3 L3 SVP: 5 DLU: 77

952.567-010 TURBINE ATTENDANT (utilities)

Records meter and instrument readings, such as oil and steam temperature and pressure of hydro-electric turbines and related generators that produce electricity. Notifies STATIONARY-ENGINEER SUPERVISOR (any industry) when recording instruments indicate machine malfunctions. Cleans and lubricates equipment.
GOE: 05.09.03 STRENGTH: L GED: R3 M2 L3 SVP: 4 DLU: 77

952.665-010 LABORER, POWERHOUSE (utilities)

Performs any combination of following duties in power plants, such as electrical power companies, industrial plants, and central heating plants: Assists in control and maintenance of coal conveying equipment, using handtools and lubricating equipment. Shovels coal spillage onto conveyors. Takes samples of coal and carries samples to laboratory for analysis. Loads trucks or railcars with fly ash from dust collectors, using suction hose. Starts and stops pumps, opens and closes floodgates, and adjusts valves of ash sluice system. Sweeps, washes, cleans, and paints buildings, floors, and equipment. Assists in inspection, maintenance, and repair of rail tracks, ties, and roadbeds, using shovels, picks, sledgehammers, jacks, and cutting torches. Maintains roads, lawns, shrubs, and flowers, using power mowers and gardener's handtools. Drives, loads, and unloads trucks to transport personnel and equipment. Keeps logs on equipment and materials and submits production reports to supervisor.
GOE: 05.12.04 STRENGTH: H GED: R2 M1 L1 SVP: 3 DLU: 80

952.667-010 STREET-LIGHT CLEANER (utilities) alternate titles: arc trimmer; boulevard-glassware cleaner; boulevard-glassware replacer; carbon-lamp cleaner; lamp cleaner, street-light; street-light changer-and-renewer; street-light inspector

Patrols route to clean and replace street light globes and illuminators: Turns crank to lower street lights suspended from utility poles or stands in hydraulically operated tower-truck bucket to reach lamps installed on top of street light posts. Removes and cleans globe or diffuse (lens). Replaces defective illuminating elements, such as incandescent bulbs, fluorescent tubes, or carbon electrodes. Performs repairs, such as replacing corroded reflectors and connecting loose wires. Reports defects for repair by STREET-LIGHT SERVICER (utilities). May drive truck.
GOE: 05.12.18 STRENGTH: L GED: R2 M1 L1 SVP: 2 DLU: 77

952.687-010 HYDROELECTRIC-PLANT MAINTAINER (utilities) alternate titles: general utility worker

Performs grounds-keeping and plant maintenance tasks in hydroelectric generating station: Turns handwheel to open alternate water intake and to close clogged intake preparatory to cleaning water intake screens. Removes accumulated logs, weeds, fish, silt, and driftwood from screen or rack, using crab-hoist, rake, shovel, and water hose. Mows lawn, trims hedges, rakes and burns leaves and refuse, and shovels snow from driveways and sidewalks. Cleans and lubricates equipment. Assists in erecting scaffolds, and disassembling and moving heavy equipment.
GOE: 05.12.18 STRENGTH: M GED: R2 M1 L1 SVP: 3 DLU: 77

952.687-014 SUBSTATION-OPERATOR HELPER (utilities)

Assists SUBSTATION OPERATOR (utilities) in controlling flow of electricity through transmission lines, and in operation of equipment for converting direct current into alternating current: Performs other duties as described under HELPER (any industry) Master Title. May record gauge and meter readings. May clean and lubricate auxiliary equipment, such as rotary converters, transformers, blowers, and circuit breakers.
GOE: 05.06.01 STRENGTH: L GED: R2 M1 L1 SVP: 5 DLU: 77

953   OCCUPATIONS IN PRODUCTION AND DISTRIBUTION OF GAS

This group includes occupations concerned with monitoring and controlling equipment to regulate volume and pressure of gas in city mains and distribution lines; purify, liquefy, store, and regasify natural gas.

953.132-010 SUPERVISOR, LIQUEFACTION-AND-REGASIFICATION (utilities)

Supervises and coordinates activities of workers engaged in operation and maintenance of compressors, scrubbers, evaporators, and refrigeration equipment that liquefy and regasify natural gas: Directs LIQUEFACTION-AND-REGASIFICATION-PLANT OPERATOR (utilities) to initate liquefaction and regasification of gas for storage and distribution. Directs GAS DISPATCHER (pipe lines; utilities) to release stored gas into distribution system according to supply and demand. Requisitions supplies and materials. Trains new personnel. Performs other duties as described under SUPERVISOR (any industry) Master Title.
GOE: 05.06.04 STRENGTH: L GED: R4 M3 L4 SVP: 8 DLU: 77

953.137-010 GAS-PUMPING-STATION SUPERVISOR (utilities)

Supervises and coordinates activities of workers engaged in providing adequate pressure on gas dispensed from gasholders. Performs duties as described under SUPERVISOR (any industry) Master Title.

GOE: 05.06.03 STRENGTH: L GED: R4 M3 L3 SVP: 7 DLU: 77

953.137-014 PRESSURE SUPERVISOR (utilities) alternate titles: pressure-control supervisor; regulation supervisor

Supervises and coordinates activities of workers engaged in controlling gas pressure and moisture condensate in mains of city gas-distribution system to meet consumer demands and state regulations: Analyzes hourly estimates of pressure required to meet consumer demands for gas, based on weather conditions, time of day, and customer contracts. Compares estimates with pressure chart readings and teletype reports of actual amount of gas consumed to determine pressure adjustments required. Notifies PRESSURE CONTROLLER (utilities) by telephone or teletype to adjust gas regulators at city gate and customer stations to control pressure. Directs DRIP PUMPER (pipe lines; utilities) in keeping mains free from condensate and in thawing frozen condensate from pipes and meters. Performs other duties as described under SUPERVISOR (any industry) Master Title.
GOE: 05.06.03 STRENGTH: L GED: R4 M3 L3 SVP: 7 DLU: 77

953.137-018 SERVICE SUPERVISOR I (utilities) alternate titles: complaint supervisor; superintendent, service

Supervises and coordinates activities of workers engaged in installing, adjusting, testing, and removing gas meters, regulators, and appliances on customers' premises, and in resolving customers' complaints. Performs duties as described under SUPERVISOR (any industry) Master Title. May be designated according to type of installation or service as Industrial-Gas-Servicer Supervisor (utilities).
GOE: 05.10.02 STRENGTH: L GED: R4 M3 L3 SVP: 7 DLU: 77

953.167-010 GAS DISPATCHER (pipe lines; utilities)

Coordinates flow of natural gas throughout distribution system of public utility or pipeline to ensure volume and pressure of gas required for consumers demands: Monitors telemetering panelboard to determine gas pressure and volume, and records instrument readings in log. Reviews correlating data, such as gas quality, pressure and temperature with variables affecting consumer demand, such as weather conditions and time of day to forecast load adjustments. Adjusts controls to regulate gas flow and pressure through system or telephones GAS-COMPRESSOR OPERATOR (any industry) to increase or decrease pressure in pipelines according to forecast. Directs GAS-PUMPING-STATION OPERATOR (utilities) to pump gas from holding station into distribution system and return according to supply and demand. Informs station personnel to regulate flow of gas from wells into system to maintain specified pressure and volume in pipelines. Records data, such as gas pressure and volume from outlying stations. Observes colorimeter to detect deviations in mixture of natural gas with manufactured gas according to specified Btu rating. Notifies mixing station personnel when deviations occur. May discontinue gas service to specified areas when emergencies or gas shortages exist.
GOE: 05.06.03 STRENGTH: S GED: R4 M3 L3 SVP: 8 DLU: 77

953.281-010 FIELD-MECHANICAL-METER TESTER (petrol. refin.; pipe lines; utilities) alternate titles: mechanical-meter tester; meter inspector

Installs, tests, and maintains mechanical metering, regulating, indicating, and testing instruments and equipment used in *production and distribution of gas: Tests, installs, and maintains gas, steam, and water instruments and apparatus, such as meters, governors, calorimeters, flowmeters, and pyrometers used in gas generating plants, holders, and distribution lines [GAS-REGULATOR REPAIRER (petrol. refin.; pipe lines; utilities); INSTRUMENT MECHANIC (any industry)]. Installs, tests, and maintains mechanical testing equipment, such as gas *provers*. Conducts physical tests on gas, steam, and water. Correlates test data, performs technical calculations, and writes reports.
GOE: 05.05.09 STRENGTH: M GED: R4 M4 L4 SVP: 8 DLU: 77

953.362-010 FUEL ATTENDANT (any industry)

Controls equipment to regulate flow and pressure of gas from mains to fuel feedlines of gas-fired boilers, furnaces, kilns, soaking pits, smelters, and related steam-generating or heating equipment in such establishments as power plants, steel mills, pottery works, chemical plants, and petroleum refining facilities: Opens valve on feedlines to supply adequate gas for fuel when boilers are to be put in operation and to maintain standard pressure on gaslines. Closes valve to reduce gas pressure when increase in gas consumption by boilers causes pressure to rise. Observes, records, and reports flow and pressure gauge readings on gas mains and fuel feedlines.
GOE: 05.06.02 STRENGTH: L GED: R3 M2 L2 SVP: 5 DLU: 77

953.362-014 LIQUEFACTION-AND-REGASIFICATION-PLANT OPERATOR (utilities)

Controls operation of compressors, scrubbers, evaporators, and refrigeration equipment to liquefy and regasify natural gas: Turns valves to admit flow of natural gas through scrubbers that remove harmful gases and water and starts compressors and refrigeration units that liquefy and transfer gas to storage tanks. Starts pumps and adjusts controls of auxiliary equipment to transfer liquid gas from storage tanks and to regulate temperature and pressure of units that regasify liquid gas into distribution lines. Signals workers engaged in tending auxiliary equipment, such as pumps and cooling towers. Repairs equipment, using handtools. May post meter and gauge readings in logbook.
GOE: 05.06.04 STRENGTH: M GED: R4 M3 L3 SVP: 7 DLU: 77

953.362-018 PRESSURE CONTROLLER (utilities)

Controls volume of gas in city distribution mains to ensure adequate gas supply according to consumer demand: Determines required governor adjustments to maintain specified gas pressure and volume according to consumer-demand estimates, based on weather conditions and time of day or night, or receives governor adjustment instructions from PRESSURE SUPERVISOR (utilities). Changes position or number of weights on balance lever or turns valves to adjust governors located at various regulating stations within city. Operates switchboard to adjust governors which are remotely controlled by electric telemetering equipment. May overhaul gas governors [GAS-REGULATOR REPAIRER (petrol. refin.; pipe lines; utilities)]. May change charts in recording meters [CHART CHANGER (clerical)]. May clean pits housing governors, using suction pump and shovel. May determine causes of abnormal pressure variances and make corrective recommendations, such as installation of pipe to relieve overloading.
GOE: 05.06.03 STRENGTH: M GED: R3 M3 L3 SVP: 7 DLU: 77

953.364-010 GAS-METER INSTALLER (utilities) alternate titles: gas fitter; meter installer

Installs residential-type gas meters and regulators in buildings, using handtools: Turns valve to adjust gas burners on appliances, using screwdriver. Inspects appliances to detect gas leaks, using portable testing device, and notifies customer of needed repair. Shuts off gas supply to installed meters, following instructions [CUSTOMER-SERVICE REPRESENTATIVE (tel. & tel.; utilities; waterworks)]. Removes meters from vacated or abandoned buildings. Prepares work orders indicating data, such as meter number, date, and location of installation.
GOE: 05.10.02 STRENGTH: M GED: R3 M2 L3 SVP: 6 DLU: 77

953.367-010 GAS-LEAK INSPECTOR (pipe lines; utilities) alternate titles: leak locator; maintenance inspector

Inspects underground and exposed gas pipelines and enclosed areas to detect and locate leaks, using testing instruments: Walks or rides along pipelines and observes terrain for evidence of leaks, such as decayed vegetation, gas odor, and water bubbles. Drives bar into ground at intervals near pipe, using sledgehammer, preparatory to testing subsurface for traces of gas. Inserts combustible-gas indicator-probe into hole and reads indicator to determine location of leak. Inspects exposed pipes in buildings, manholes, vaults, and valve boxes for leaks, using combustible indicator. Notifies maintenance department of location and condition of facilities inspected and tested. May make temporary repairs, using repair dope or gastight clamps. May drive vehicle equipped with detection devices to aid in locating leaks.
GOE: 05.07.01 STRENGTH: L GED: R3 M2 L2 SVP: 5 DLU: 77

953.367-014 GAS-METER CHECKER (utilities) alternate titles: meter-and-service-line inspector

Inspects gas service lines and meters on customers' premises to detect tampering or improper use of gas: Examines meter case and meter connections for signs of tampering or improper use. Pulls meter with both hands to determine if meter can be tilted, causing it to register slowly. Examines visible gas lines and pipe joints for irregular connections. Submits inspection reports to supervisory personnel.
GOE: 05.07.01 STRENGTH: L GED: R3 M2 L2 SVP: 5 DLU: 77

953.367-018 HOUSE-PIPING INSPECTOR (utilities)

Inspects and tests new gas-pipe installations in buildings to determine conformance to company and city requirements: Screws coupling into gasline to facilitate attachment of hardpump testing set. Pumps air and reads gauge to determine specified amount of air pumped into gasline. Patches gauge to detect fall in pressure indicating leaks in gasline. Observes pressure gauge while joints are being tightened by coworkers to determine when leak has been detected and repaired. Tests joints with soap and water and observes bubble formation to detect leaks. Examines flue openings of gas-heating appliances to determine conformance to specifications. Notifies customer of needed repairs. Prepares inspection report. May inspect installations, such as gas mains, services (pipes from mains to residences), meters, and regulators and be designated Utility Inspector (utilities). May test for presence of subsurface gas to detect leaks in underground gaspipes [GAS-LEAK INSPECTOR (pipe lines; utilities)].
GOE: 05.07.01 STRENGTH: L GED: R3 M2 L3 SVP: 5 DLU: 77

953.382-010 GAS-PUMPING-STATION OPERATOR (utilities) alternate titles: compressor-house operator; engineer, booster and exhauster; engineer, gas-pumping station; gas-substation operator

Controls operation of steam, gas, or electric-motor-driven compressor to maintain specified pressures on high and low pressure mains dispensing gas from gasholders: Observes pressure gauges to determine consumption rate variations and turns knobs or switches to regulate pressures. Opens valves to allow gas to flow into and out of compressors. Reads gas meters and records amount of gas received and dispensed from holders. May clean, lubricate, and adjust compressors, using handtools. May regulate gas governors to maintain specified pressure [PRESSURE CONTROLLER (utilities)].
GOE: 05.06.03 STRENGTH: L GED: R3 M2 L3 SVP: 5 DLU: 77

953.387-010 CYLINDER INSPECTOR-AND-TESTER (chemical) alternate titles: cylinder tester; gas-cylinder inspector; hydrostatic tester

Inspects gas cylinders to detect surface defects and tests elasticity of cylinder walls: Removes valve from cylinder, using wrench or valve-removal machine Inspects exterior and interior of cylinder to detect dirt, rust scale, dents, and arc burns. Fills cylinder with water, seals cylinder and immerses cylinder in

water-filled jacket, using chain hoist. Screws fittings and turns valve or starts pump to create pressure that expands cylinder wall. Compares pressure gauge or burette reading with specifications and segregates cylinders that exceed prescribed expansion limits. Stamps test data and company symbol on cylinder. Records test results, cylinder serial number, and test date. May weigh cylinder. May be designated according to size of cylinder inspected as Ton-Cylinder Inspector (chemical).
GOE: 06.03.01 STRENGTH: M GED: R3 M3 L3 SVP: 4 DLU: 77

953.583-010 DRIP PUMPER (pipe lines; utilities)
Drives tank truck equipped with suction pump to drain condensate from gas pipeline drips: Drives truck to drip location and connects hose from truck tank to drip valve. Measures condensate in tank with calibrated pole or reads tank meter. Opens pressure valve to force condensate into truck tank, or starts suction pump to draw out condensate when gas pressure is low. Records amount of condensate drawn at each drip location. May use hand-operated suction pump to drain condensate when truck is not equipped with automatic pump.
GOE: 05.11.03 STRENGTH: L GED: R3 M2 L2 SVP: 3 DLU: 77

953.584-010 HELPER, LIQUEFACTION-AND-REGASIFICATION (utilities)
Assists LIQUEFACTION-AND-REGASIFICATION-PLANT OPERATOR (utilities) in maintenance of equipment in natural gas plant: Observes operation of equipment to detect malfunctions and reports findings to maintenance personnel. Performs minor repairs, using handtools. Records instrument readings at specified intervals. Performs other duties as described under HELPER (any industry) Master Title.
GOE: 05.10.02 STRENGTH: L GED: R3 M2 L3 SVP: 5 DLU: 77

953.667-010 GAS-LEAK INSPECTOR HELPER (pipe lines; utilities)
Assists GAS-LEAK INSPECTOR (pipe lines; utilities) in locating and detecting leaks in underground and exposed pipelines: Carries testing equipment and handtools to and from vehicle to test site. Places barricades and safety signs at test area and directs traffic to protect workers and public. Measures distances of leak from reference point, using rule or tape, and records data, such as instrument readings in survey report. Assists in performing temporary repairs, using handtools. May drive vehicle equipped with detection devices along inspection route. Performs other duties as described under HELPER (any industry) Master Title.
GOE: 05.07.01 STRENGTH: M GED: R3 M3 L3 SVP: 4 DLU: 77

953.684-010 GAS-PUMPING-STATION HELPER (utilities)
Assists GAS-PUMPING-STATION OPERATOR (utilities) in maintenance of equipment in gasholder station: Carries handtools to and from work area. Inspects equipment to detect malfunctions, such as overheating and noisy compressor. Assists in repairing equipment, using handtools. May paint equipment to prevent corrosion. Performs other duties as described under HELPER (any industry) Master Title.
GOE: 05.12.06 STRENGTH: M GED: R2 M1 L2 SVP: 4 DLU: 77

953.687-010 GAS-METER-INSTALLER HELPER (utilities)
Assists GAS-METER INSTALLER (utilities) to install residential-type gas meters and regulators in buildings: Carries handtools and meters to and from vehicle and work site. Disconnects meters or regulators, using handtools. Ignites gas appliances after meter installation. Performs other duties as described under HELPER (any industry) Master Title.
GOE: 05.12.15 STRENGTH: M GED: R2 M1 L2 SVP: 2 DLU: 77

954 OCCUPATIONS IN FILTRATION, PURIFICATION, AND DISTRIBUTION OF WATER

This group includes occupations concerned with controlling treatment plant equipment to purify and clarify water, and to transfer, distribute, and regulate pressure and flow of water; controlling equipment to convey water in irrigation systems; and controlling gates and valves in aqueducts and dams to supply waterpower.

954.130-010 SUPERVISOR, PUMPING STATION (waterworks) alternate titles: water-plant-pump-operator supervisor
Supervises and coordinates activities of workers engaged in operating equipment, such as pumps, valves, turbines, and electric motors to transfer, distribute, and regulate pressure and flow of raw and processed water: Trains workers in operation and maintenance of equipment. Records data, such as reservoir water elevation, power consumption, and equipment and human resource utilization. Inspects equipment and requisitions supplies. Performs other duties as described under SUPERVISOR (any industry) Master Title.
GOE: 05.06.03 STRENGTH: L GED: R4 M4 L3 SVP: 7 DLU: 77

954.132-010 SUPERVISOR, WATER TREATMENT PLANT (waterworks)
Supervises and coordinates activities of workers engaged in operating and maintaining equipment in water treatment plant: Directs activities of workers engaged in filtering, chemically treating, pumping, and testing fresh and processed water in preparation for human or industrial use. Plans daily work schedule and assigns tasks to workers based upon priority of work and expertise of individual workers. Inspects equipment, such as filters, chlorine indicators, ba-

sins, filtered water basins, and pumps, to detect malfunctions. Directs workers in repair of equipment or reports need for repairs to designated authority. Maintains records on chemical usage and storage, equipment operation, and personnel attendance. Performs other duties as described under SUPERVISOR (any industry) Master Title. May be required to meet licensing or certification standards established by regulatory agency concerned.
GOE: 05.02.01 STRENGTH: L GED: R4 M3 L3 SVP: 6 DLU: 86

954.362-010 DITCH RIDER (waterworks) alternate titles: canal tender; ditch tender; water tender; zanjero
Controls irrigation system to convey water to farms in assigned area, according to rights, or as instructed by WATER CONTROL SUPERVISOR (waterworks) or other officials, for irrigating fields and crops: Contacts water users to determine quantity of water needed, and time and duration of delivery. Computes and requisitions quantity of water required. Operates gates, checks, turnouts, and wasteways to regulate waterflow into canals and laterals (individual supply ditches). Measures or estimates diversions of water from canals and to water users, and calculates and records quantities delivered for use in computing charges to farmers. Patrols assigned area by foot, horseback, or motor vehicle to detect leaks, breaks, weak areas, or obstructions and damage to irrigation system. Removes debris and makes emergency repairs to banks, structures, gates, and canal roads. Fills holes and exterminates rodents. Writes reports and records daily deliveries, number of users, amount of water used, and other data required by law or company. May prepare reports on condition of system and equipment, and replacements or repairs needed. May supervise crew workers cleaning ditches, raising ditch banks, repairing concrete and wooden structures, erecting fences and gates, and other maintenance work after irrigating season has passed. May take annual crop census and make weed and other surveys. May patrol canal at night to determine that water is flowing in prescribed volume into users' ditches.
GOE: 05.06.03 STRENGTH: M GED: R4 M3 L3 SVP: 4 DLU: 77

954.367-010 WATER-SERVICE DISPATCHER (waterworks)
Dispatches service crews to repair water mains: Receives calls from consumers regarding pressure complaints, service requests, and leaks in mains. Dispatches service crew, using telephone or radio. Increases pumpage rate, conduit flow, and reservoir elevation. May keep log on dispatching activities.
GOE: 07.04.05 STRENGTH: L GED: R3 M2 L3 SVP: 4 DLU: 77

954.382-010 PUMP-STATION OPERATOR, WATERWORKS (waterworks) alternate titles: pumping-plant operator; water-plant-pump operator
Operates pumping equipment to transfer raw water to treatment plant, or distribute processed water to residential, commercial, and industrial establishments: Turns valves, pulls levers, and flips switches to operate and control turbine- or motor-driven pumps that transfer water from reservoir to treatment plant, or to transfer processed water to consumer establishments. Reads flowmeters and gauges to regulate equipment according to water consumption and demand. Inspects equipment to detect malfunctions, such as pump leaks or worn bearings. Repairs and lubricates equipment, using handtools. Records data, such as utilization of equipment, power consumption, and water output in log. May operate equipment to treat and process raw water [WATER-TREATMENT-PLANT OPERATOR (waterworks)]. May test water for chlorine content, alkalinity, acidity, or turbidity to determine potability of water, following color analysis standards. May operate hydroelectric equipment to generate power.
GOE: 05.06.03 STRENGTH: L GED: R3 M2 L3 SVP: 5 DLU: 77

954.382-014 WATER-TREATMENT-PLANT OPERATOR (waterworks) alternate titles: filter operator; purifying-plant operator; water-control-station engineer; water filterer; water purifier
Controls treatment plant machines and equipment to purify and clarify water for human consumption and for industrial use: Operates and controls electric motors, pumps, and valves to regulate flow of raw water into treating plant. Dumps specified amounts of chemicals, such as chlorine, ammonia, and lime into water or adjusts automatic devices that admit specified amounts of chemicals into tanks to disinfect, deodorize, and clarify water. Starts agitators to mix chemicals and allows impurities to settle to bottom of tank. Turns valves to regulate water through filter beds to remove impurities. Pumps purified water into water mains. Monitors panelboard and adjusts controls to regulate flow rates, loss of head pressure and water elevation, and distribution of water. Cleans tanks and filter beds, using backwashing (reverse flow of water). Repairs and lubricates machines and equipment, using handtools and power tools. Tests water samples to determine acidity, color, and impurities, using colorimeter, turbidimeter, and conductivity meter. Adds chemicals such, as alum into tanks to coagulate impurities and to reduce acidity. Records data, such as residual content of chemicals, water turbidity, and water pressure. May operate portable water-purification plant to supply drinking water.
GOE: 05.06.04 STRENGTH: M GED: R3 M3 L3 SVP: 5 DLU: 88

954.382-018 WATERSHED TENDER (waterworks) alternate titles: aqueduct-and-reservoir keeper; dam tender; needle-valve operator; reservoir caretaker
Controls equipment to regulate waterflow and water level in reservoirs: Turns valves and pulls levers to regulate waterflow through aqueduct and floodgates. Reads gauges and meters to control specified waterflow, water levels, and water pressure in reservoir. Records data, such as water level, turbidity, temperature, and flow rate. Lubricates and performs minor repairs to equipment, using

handtools. Patrols area to detect property damage and to prevent trespassing. May tend heating apparatus to prevent freezing of valves and gates. May add chemicals to water to retard organic growth such as algae.
GOE: 05.06.03 STRENGTH: L GED: R3 M2 L2 SVP: 5 DLU: 77

954.385-010 BASIN OPERATOR (waterworks)
Tends and maintains desilting basin that removes silt from river water entering irrigation system: Reads dials and gauges to determine if equipment is operating according to specifications. Inspects sluice hoppers of clarifiers to detect clogged valves. Flushes valves to clear them. Inspects and repairs ventilating blowers, pumps, and corrosion protection system. Removes trash from slots of influent channels, using steel rake. Sluices sand and silt from ends of channels, using high-pressure hose. Lubricates machinery and gear boxes or clarifiers. Records equipment malfunctions and corrective actions taken. Cleans basin area, pilot houses, and equipment. Patrols dam area and compound to guard against fire, trespassing, or property damage.
GOE: 05.12.07 STRENGTH: M GED: R3 M2 L2 SVP: 4 DLU: 77

954.564-010 WATER-METER INSTALLER (waterworks)
Installs watermeters in consumer establishments, using handtools: Turns mainline valve to close waterflow through line. Disconnects water pipe and connects watermeter to outlet and inlet pipe unions, using wrench. Examines pipes to detect leaks and informs consumer to close faucets. Opens mainline valve to admit waterflow into building. Records meter readings [METER READER (utilities; waterworks)]. May install and repair water system pipes and accessories, using equipment such as pneumatic jackhammer and plumber's handtools.
GOE: 05.10.01 STRENGTH: M GED: R3 M2 L2 SVP: 4 DLU: 77

954.587-010 WATER-FILTER CLEANER (waterworks) alternate titles: laborer, filter plant; sand-cleaning-machine operator; water-filterer helper
Cleans water filter beds: Holds suction pipe to transfer sand and gravel from filter bed onto regrading screens. Washes and simultaneously screens sand and gravel to remove foreign particles and grade material according to size, using water hose. Turns handle to backwash (reverse waterflow) filter to remove chemical precipitates and impurities. Scrapes and removes dirt from side of filter bed, using metal scraper. Reverses action of suction pipe to return gravel and sand to filter bed. Records daily production. May clean and redistribute sand in filter bed, using sand cleaning machine. May lubricate and repair defective filtering equipment.
GOE: 05.12.18 STRENGTH: M GED: R2 M1 L1 SVP: 2 DLU: 77

955 OCCUPATIONS IN DISPOSAL OF REFUSE AND SEWAGE

This group includes occupations concerned with equipment to regulate flow of radioactive or sewage waste and sludge through pumps, conveyors, blowers, chlorinators, vacuum filters, and other decontaminating equipment; controlling equipment to burn garbage, refuse, and sludge cake; collecting garbage and refuse from homes and business establishments; and related activities such as street cleaning and snow removal. Includes occupations concerned with landfill operations. Occupations concerned with the transportation of garbage and trash to disposaal areas are found in Group 909.

955.130-010 SUPERVISORY WASTEWATER-TREATMENT-PLANT OPERATOR (sanitary ser.) alternate titles: sewage plant supervisor; solid waste facility supervisor
Supervises and coordinates activities of workers engaged in operating and maintaining equipment in wastewater (sewage) treatment and disposal facility: Directs activities of workers in power generating, grit removal, pump and blower, and sludge filtration departments. Tests sewage and water supply to prevent contamination, using chemicals and testing equipment. Inspects equipment, such as pumps, sediment tanks, filters, and chlorinators to detect malfunctions. Confers with engineering personnel and directs workers in repair and maintenance of machinery and equipment. May direct workers in maintenance of buildings and grounds. Performs duties as described under SUPERVISOR (any industry) Master Title.
GOE: 05.02.01 STRENGTH: L GED: R4 M4 L4 SVP: 7 DLU: 77

955.131-010 SUPERVISOR, INCINERATOR PLANT (sanitary ser.)
Supervises and coordinates activities of incinerator plant workers engaged in operation, maintenance, and repair of incinerator furnaces and auxiliary equipment, such as grates, fans, compressors, temperature controls, overhead electric cranes, and ventilating and hydraulic equipment: Directs activities of workers engaged in tasks such as weighing and unloading refuse trucks, moving rubbish to furnace hoppers, operating incinerator furnaces, repairing furnace refractory linings, and removing ashes. Assists workers in repairing facilities and equipment, applying knowledge of principles of combustion and safety procedures, and using handtools. Maintains personnel records. Trains workers in performance of duties and safety procedures. Inspects incinerator furnace and other equipment to detect need for maintenance and repair. Performs other duties as described under SUPERVISOR (any industry) Master Title.
GOE: 05.06.04 STRENGTH: L GED: R4 M2 L2 SVP: 5 DLU: 86

955.133-010 SANITARY-LANDFILL SUPERVISOR (sanitary ser.)
Supervises and coordinates activities of workers engaged in landfill operations, utilizing knowledge of local, state, and federal laws regulating waste dis-

posal: Directs operations, such as spreading and compacting solid waste and spraying insecticides to control insects and pests. May assist in selecting new sites according to community population. Performs other duties as described under SUPERVISOR (any industry) Master Title.
GOE: 05.11.01 STRENGTH: L GED: R4 M3 L3 SVP: 7 DLU: 77

955.137-010 SNOW-REMOVING SUPERVISOR (government ser.)
Supervises removal of snow from thoroughfares and public places, such as airports, government buildings, and streets. Performs duties as described under SUPERVISOR (any industry) Master Title.
GOE: 05.11.01 STRENGTH: M GED: R4 M3 L3 SVP: 6 DLU: 77

955.167-010 DISPATCHER, RADIOACTIVE-WASTE-DISPOSAL (chemical)
Coordinates activities of workers engaged in mixing and controlling flow of chemicals and radioactive waste through pipelines, storage tanks, and sampling areas: Reviews processing schedule to determine receiving and transferring priorities, and notifies workers of type and quantities for processing, destinations, pumping schedule, and operating procedures. Monitors panelboard to ensure temperatures, pressures, pH readings, and contamination content of waste chemicals conform with schedule and processing specifications. Recommends change of pumping rates and pressures that will ensure rate of flow of chemicals or radioactive waste follows specifications. Reviews reports to verify accuracy of amounts received, processed, transferred, or stored.
GOE: 06.01.01 STRENGTH: L GED: R4 M4 L4 SVP: 7 DLU: 77

955.222-010 INSTRUCTOR, WASTEWATER-TREATMENT PLANT (sanitary ser.)
Instructs wastewater treatment plant personnel in operation and maintenance of treatment plant facilities to improve efficiency and meet regulatory certification requirements: Trains personnel in operation and maintenance of treatment plant machines and equipment and demonstrates operation of machines and equipment. Instructs personnel in other procedures, such as selection of sampling sites, laboratory techniques, record keeping, safety measures, and care of lift stations. Administers tests and maintains records of students' progress. Assembles materials, schedules courses, and designs contents of courses to meet specific needs of plant personnel. Provides technical assistance to plant staff and serves as troubleshooter in solving problems in operations. Maintains examination records and coordinates training program with state certification program.
GOE: 05.06.04 STRENGTH: L GED: R4 M3 L3 SVP: 6 DLU: 86

955.362-010 WASTEWATER-TREATMENT-PLANT OPERATOR (sanitary ser.) alternate titles: disposal-plant operator; sewage-plant operator; utilities operator
Operates sewage treatment, sludge processing, and disposal equipment in wastewater (sewage) treatment plant to control flow and processing of sewage: Monitors control panels and adjusts valves and gates manually or by remote control to regulate flow of sewage. Observes variations in operating conditions and interprets meter and gauge readings and tests results to determine load requirements. Starts and stops pumps, engines, and generators to control flow of raw sewage through filtering, settling, aeration, and sludge digestion processes. Maintains log of operations and records meter and gauge readings. Gives directions to WASTEWATER-TREATMENT-PLANT ATTENDANTS (sanitary ser.) and SEWAGE-DISPOSAL WORKERS (sanitary ser.) in performing routine operations and maintenance. May collect sewage sample, using dipper or bottle and conduct laboratory tests, using testing equipment, such as colorimeter. May operate and maintain power generating equipment to provide steam and electricity for plant. May be designated according to specialized activity or stage in processing as Activated-Sludge Operator (sanitary ser.); Grit-Removal Operator (sanitary ser.); Pump-And-Blower Operator (sanitary ser.); Sludge-Control Operator (sanitary ser.); Sludge-Filtration Operator (sanitary ser.).
GOE: 05.06.04 STRENGTH: L GED: R4 M4 L3 SVP: 6 DLU: 77

955.362-014 INCINERATOR OPERATOR II (sanitary ser.)
Controls operation of multiple-hearth incinerator furnaces and related equipment to burn sludge in wastewater treatment plant: Pushes buttons and turns valves to ignite burners, release combustion air, add fuel, control hearth dampers, set hearth temperatures, and set length of burning cycles. Observes meters and gauges on central control room panel to verify that flows, pressures, and temperatures are within specifications. Turns controls to make routine adjustments, following standard procedures. Notifies worker controlling sludge filter press to adjust feed rate of waste material into incinerator hopper to maintain incinerator efficiency. Opens hearth doors and observes operation of waste raking mechanism to verify that burned residue is swept to succeeding hearth. Periodically records specified meter and gauge readings on incinerator log. Calculates and records values for number of tons of waste material fed per hour and quantity of auxiliary fuel burned per ton of waste material, to document efficiency of incinerator operation. Monitors and adjusts controls of auxiliary equipment, such as exhaust emissions, scrubbers, and incinerator heat recovery unit, following prescribed procedures. Removes and cleans equipment parts, such as valves, burners, and oxygen analyzers, following manuals and using handtools.
GOE: 05.06.04 STRENGTH: M GED: R3 M2 L3 SVP: 4 DLU: 86

955.382-010 CLARIFYING-PLANT OPERATOR (textile)
Controls equipment to clean and neutralize waste bleach water preparatory to discharge into natural waterways: Starts pumps or opens valves to transfer

waste bleach water from bleaching tanks to settling and mixing tanks. Tests water to determine acidity, using titration equipment, and calculates quantity of chemicals required to neutralize water. Opens valves to admit specified amount of chemicals into mixing tank and starts motor to mix chemicals with water. Starts pumps or opens valves to discharge water and accumulated sludge into waterway.
GOE: 06.02.16 STRENGTH: L GED: R3 M2 L2 SVP: 4 DLU: 77

955.382-014 WASTE-TREATMENT OPERATOR (chemical)
Controls heat exchange unit, pumps, compressors, and related equipment to decontaminate, neutralize, and dispose of radioactive waste liquids collected from chemical processing operations: Removes sample of liquid from collection tank, using pipette. Pours sample into dish and bakes dish under heat lamp to evaporate water, leaving radioactive residue. Tests residue with Geiger counter and compares reading with chart to determine whether radioactivity level is within prescribed safety limits. Determines degree of acidity or alkalinity in liquid, using pH meter, and adds acid or alkali to neutralize liquid. Starts pump and admits waste liquid into sewer for disposal or into storage tanks for evaporation, according to degree of radioactivity. Transfers radioactive waste liquid from storage tanks to heat exchange unit. Operates heat evaporation system to reduce volume of liquid, and observes gauges and adjusts controls during process to maintain steam pressure, temperature, and liquid at specified levels. Starts compressed-air pump to blow slurry on bottom of evaporator into lead container for permanent storage. Records data, such as number of gallons of waste pumped into sewer system or storage tanks, or reduced by heat exchange unit, and radioactivity levels. May monitor panelboard to control operation of recovery systems that store or dispose of radioactive waste and be designated Nuclear-Waste-Process Operator (any industry).
GOE: 06.02.11 STRENGTH: L GED: R4 M4 L4 SVP: 6 DLU: 77

955.383-010 WASTE-DISPOSAL ATTENDANT (any industry)
Disposes of radioactive equipment and wastes, performing any combination of following duties: Loads contaminated equipment and lead pigs of waste material onto truck, using forklift. Drives truck to storage area and removes load. Shovels specified quantities of ingredients into and tends concrete mixer. Pours or shovels concrete into forms to make disposal coffins (containers). Lifts contaminated equipment or wastes from lead pigs and places them in coffin, using stainless steel rods. Pours concrete into coffin to encase waste. Loads coffins onto truck, using forklift, and transports them to burial ground or arranges for burial at sea. Records amount and type of equipment and waste disposed. May accompany coffins for burial at sea. May clean contaminated equipment for reuse by operating sand blasters, filtering pumps, and steam cleaners or by scrubbing with detergents or solvents. Workers must follow prescribed safety procedures and federal laws regulating waste disposal.
GOE: 05.12.03 STRENGTH: H GED: R3 M2 L2 SVP: 5 DLU: 77

955.463-010 SANITARY LANDFILL OPERATOR (sanitary ser.) alternate titles: solid waste facility operator
Performs any combination of following duties to dispose of solid waste materials at landfill site: Operates heavy equipment, such as bulldozer, front-end loader, and compactor, to excavate landfill site, transport solid waste materials, and to spread and compact layers of waste and earth cover. Directs incoming vehicles to dumping area. Examines cargo to prohibit disposal of caustic waste, according to government regulations. Sprays poisons and other specified chemicals over waste material to control disease carrying pests. Drives truck to distribute oil or water over landfill to control dust. Weighs vehicles entering and leaving site and collects dumping fees.
GOE: 05.11.01 STRENGTH: M GED: R2 M1 L1 SVP: 5 DLU: 86

955.585-010 WASTEWATER-TREATMENT-PLANT ATTENDANT (sanitary ser.) alternate titles: sewage-plant attendant
Tends pumps, conveyors, blowers, chlorinators, vacuum filters, and other equipment used to decontaminate wastewater (sewage) by settling, aeration, and sludge digestion: Removes obstructions, such as coarse materials from barscreens, to accelerate influent through initial screening process. Adjusts pipe valves to regulate flow velocity through settling tanks to separate sludge by sedimentation. Turns air and steam valves to aerate effluent, and to control temperature in sludge digestion tanks. Observes temperature gauges to determine lubrication of equipment. Reads charts, flow meters, and gauges to detect equipment malfunctions. Collects samples, makes process reports, and performs minor repairs on equipment as directed by WASTEWATER-TREATMENT-PLANT OPERATOR (sanitary ser.). May be designated according to station assignments as Activated-Sludge Attendant (sanitary ser.); Grit Station Attendant (sanitary ser.); Pump-And-Blower Attendant (sanitary ser.); Sludge-Control Attendant (sanitary ser.); Sludge-Filtration Attendant (sanitary ser.).
GOE: 05.12.07 STRENGTH: M GED: R3 M2 L2 SVP: 4 DLU: 77

955.667-010 INCINERATOR PLANT LABORER (sanitary ser.)
Signals GARBAGE COLLECTOR DRIVER (motor trans.) 905.663-010 to dump refuse in specific area of collection pit to maintain even distribution of refuse, using hand. Cleans spills from floor of receiving area, using rake, broom, and hose. Loads noncombustible material into containers and carries containers to pickup area for removal.
GOE: 05.12.20 STRENGTH: M GED: R2 M1 L1 SVP: 1 DLU: 86

955.685-010 INCINERATOR OPERATOR I (sanitary ser.)
Tends one or more incinerator furnaces that burn refuse, such as sludge, trash, and garbage: Pulls mechanism to release refuse from hopper into inciner-

ator. Moves levers to ignite burners, to adjust blowers and dampers that regulate airflow and temperature, and to control charging, discharging, and quenching mechanisms of furnace. Opens furnace door and agitates burning refuse to facilitate combustion, using stoking hoe. Moves levers to open grate and drop ashes and noncombustible material from furnace at end of burning cycle. Replaces refractory linings of furnace, using firebrick and mortar. Cleans debris from furnace room floor, using rake and broom. May assist SUPERVISOR, INCINERATOR PLANT (sanitary ser.) 955.131-010 in maintenance and repair of cranes, conveyor equipment, and exhaust system, using handtools.
GOE: 05.06.02 STRENGTH: M GED: R2 M1 L1 SVP: 2 DLU: 86

955.687-010 SEWAGE-DISPOSAL WORKER (sanitary ser.)
Cleans and maintains equipment in sewage disposal plant to facilitate flow and treatment of sewage: Cleans filter screens, processing tanks, and walkways, using hose, brushes, and chemical solutions. Cleans precipitates, such as grit, sludge, trash, and muck from sump, catch basin and grit chamber, using shovel, rake, and hand pump. Lubricates equipment, such as pumps and valves. Opens and closes gates and valves according to gauge readings or warning lights on equipment. Collects samples of decontaminated refuse for testing. May conduct test on sewage sample, using colorimeter. May maintain grounds and outbuildings [GROUNDSKEEPER, INDUSTRIAL-COMMERCIAL (any industry)]. May be designated according to equipment cleaned as Catch-Basin Cleaner (sanitary ser.).
GOE: 05.12.18 STRENGTH: H GED: R2 M1 L1 SVP: 2 DLU: 77

955.687-014 SNOW SHOVELER (government ser.) alternate titles: snow remover
Shovels snow into truck or open sewer from streets and other public thoroughfares. Chops ice and packed snow, using pick or ice-chopper, to clear area around catch basins, fire hydrants, and street corners. May spread salt or thawing chemicals onto roadway from rear of moving truck, using shovel.
GOE: 05.12.18 STRENGTH: H GED: R1 M1 L1 SVP: 1 DLU: 77

955.687-018 STREET CLEANER (government ser.) alternate titles: street sweeper
Sweeps refuse from municipal streets, gutters, and sidewalks into pile and shovels refuse into movable container that is pushed from place to place. May pick up paper and similar rubbish from lawns, flower beds, or highway median strips, using spike-tipped stick.
GOE: 05.12.18 STRENGTH: L GED: R1 M1 L1 SVP: 1 DLU: 77

955.687-022 GARBAGE COLLECTOR (motor trans.)
Collects refuse on designated route within municipality and dumps refuse from containers onto truck. May be designated according to refuse collected as Trash Collector (motor trans.). May drive truck [GARBAGE COLLECTOR DRIVER (motor trans.)]. May start hoisting device that raises refuse bin attached to rear of truck and dumps contents into opening in enclosed truck body.
GOE: 05.12.03 STRENGTH: V GED: R1 M1 L1 SVP: 1 DLU: 77

956 OCCUPATIONS IN DISTRIBUTION OF STEAM

This group includes occupations concerned with maintenance and servicing of steam distribution systems.

956.267-010 INSPECTOR, CHIEF (utilities)
Inspects steam-heat systems in buildings served by steam utility company to determine effect of system modifications reported by BUILDING-EQUIPMENT INSPECTOR (utilities) on steam-metering equipment and billing rates and to determine cause of abnormal steam consumption or other evidence of system malfunction: Investigates changes made in equipment layout by customers and determines if changes affect metering equipment and rates. Determines causes for abnormal meter readings by inspecting customers' steam-utilization equipment and steam lines to detect malfunctioning, and makes minor repairs and adjustments or recommends major overhaul by other workers. Submits reports on special investigations.
GOE: 05.07.01 STRENGTH: M GED: R4 M4 L3 SVP: 7 DLU: 77

956.387-010 BUILDING-EQUIPMENT INSPECTOR (utilities)
Examines steam-heat systems and records steam-meter readings at regular intervals to verify accuracy of meter registration and to ensure economical service to customers of steam utility company: Examines steam-distribution equipment, such as meters, steam traps, safety valves, and pipes, for loose connections or other defects and makes minor repairs and adjustments. Notifies INSPECTOR, CHIEF (utilities) of necessary major repairs and of changes, such as installation of additional steam-utilization equipment or repositioning of pipes which might affect metering equipment or steam rates. Reads meters and compares readings with previous recordings to detect fluctuations indicative of meter or equipment defects. Submits meter readings for billing purposes and reports equipment status. May notify customer of equipment requiring repair.
GOE: 05.07.01 STRENGTH: L GED: R3 M3 L2 SVP: 6 DLU: 77

959 OCCUPATIONS IN PRODUCTION AND DISTRIBUTION OF UTILITIES, N.E.C.

This group includes occupations, not elsewhere classified, concerned with power generation, utilities, and sanitation.

959.131-010 HEATING-PLANT SUPERINTENDENT (any industry) alternate titles: chief engineer
Supervises and coordinates activities of workers engaged in producing and distributing steam heat and hot water in commercial or industrial establishments, and in maintaining mechanical equipment, such as boilers, pipe systems, pump, hot water generators, hot air furnaces, and air-cooling units. Performs duties as described under SUPERVISOR (any industry) Master Title.
GOE: 05.06.02 STRENGTH: L GED: R4 M3 L3 SVP: 8 DLU: 77

959.137-010 DISPATCHER, CHIEF, SERVICE OR WORK (utilities)
Supervises and coordinates activities of DISPATCHERS, SERVICE OR WORK (utilities) and power line workers to increase efficiency of work crews and equipment in routine maintenance and emergencies, such as floods or fire: Assigns duties to workers according to priority of trouble calls received. Relays information and technical instructions between linecrews and appropriate department heads concerning power line troubles requiring action not covered by standard operating procedures. Verifies that all switching operations are accurately recorded and reported to ensure safety of linecrews. May supervise DISPATCHERS, SERVICE (utilities).
GOE: 07.04.05 STRENGTH: L GED: R4 M3 L3 SVP: 7 DLU: 77

959.137-014 DISPATCHER, SERVICE, CHIEF (utilities) alternate titles: service-order dispatcher
Supervises and coordinates activities of DISPATCHERS, SERVICE (utilities) engaged in receiving and reviewing service calls, performing duties as described under SUPERVISOR (clerical) Master Title. May make investigations and tabulations concerning trends, causes, and effects of factors necessitating service calls.
GOE: 07.04.05 STRENGTH: S GED: R4 M3 L3 SVP: 7 DLU: 77

959.137-018 ORDER DISPATCHER, CHIEF (utilities)
Coordinates and supervises activities of WORK-ORDER-SORTING CLERKS (utilities) engaged in routing and scheduling orders for installation and removal of gas meters and installation of main extensions and service connections. May direct service connection construction crews to areas or zones to equalize work loads. May assign trucks to transport crews to job sites. May order materials from storeroom. May maintain records and assist in preparation of reports.
GOE: 07.05.01 STRENGTH: S GED: R4 M2 L3 SVP: 6 DLU: 77

959.137-022 SUPERVISOR, HOME-ENERGY CONSULTANT (utilities) alternate titles: supervisor, energy conservation representative
Supervises and coordinates activities of workers engaged in performing domestic-energy-consumption audits for customers of public utilities: Confers with customers and utility representatives to determine customer needs, appointment times, availability of representatives, and scheduling conflicts. Reschedules energy audits accordingly. Reads federal program guidelines, journals, and related reports to ascertain federal program requirements and recent developments concerning energy conservation techniques. Attends energy seminars, staff meetings, and training sessions to assess effectiveness of energy audit program. Suggests to management changes in brochures, community workshops, or audit procedures to improve community acceptance. Prepares written reports that reflect assessment of program and submits them to management and department officials. Performs other duties as described under SUPERVISOR (any industry) Master Title.
GOE: 05.02.01 STRENGTH: S GED: R4 M3 L4 SVP: 6 DLU: 86

959.167-010 DISPATCHER, SERVICE (utilities) alternate titles: schedule clerk; trouble dispatcher
Dispatches customer service workers to install, service, and repair electric, gas, or steam powered service systems or appliances, or cable television systems: Reviews work orders from departments or complaints from customers and records type and scope of service to be performed. Determines and schedules orders according to urgency. Contacts supply storekeeper to verify availability of parts and equipment to ensure scheduled work performance. Receives check in calls from service workers by radio, telephone, or in person. Informs workers of type and location of work to be performed and dispatches workers to job. Keeps records of repairs, installation, removal of equipment or appliances, and hours required on each job. May maintain records, using computer terminal. May be designated according to utility as Telegraphic-Service Dispatcher (tel. & tel.).
GOE: 07.04.05 STRENGTH: S GED: R4 M3 L3 SVP: 4 DLU: 88

959.361-010 CUSTOMER SERVICE REPRESENTATIVE (utilities) alternate titles: field inspector; special-gas-and-electric service investigator
Investigates customer complaints concerning gas leakage or low pressure, and abnormal consumption of gas or electricity by gas and electric appliances: Ascertains number and type of appliances used on premises to determine rate of utility consumption. Turns off appliances and observes gas or electric meter to detect power leakage. Examines meter and appliance connections for defects, such as shorts, grounds, and loose pipe joints to determine power loss or gas leakage. Covers gas pipe joints with soapsuds and watches for bubble formation to determine position of leak. Performs repairs and adjustments, such as cleaning and regulating gas burner jets, and replacing defective meters and gas regulators, using handtools. Shuts off service and notifies repair crew of major repairs required, such as replacement of underground pipes or electric wiring. May perform emergency repairs to gas service pipes between gas main and

building. May collect delinquent accounts. May recommend and write specifications for distribution changes, such as house wiring, and relocation of poles or service lines, utilizing necessary right-of-way grants. May investigate illegal use of gas or electricity [GAS-METER CHECKER (utilities); UTILITIES SERVICE INVESTIGATOR (utilities)].
GOE: 05.10.04 STRENGTH: L GED: R3 M2 L3 SVP: 6 DLU: 77

959.367-010 ELECTRIC POWER LINE EXAMINER (utilities)
Patrols overhead electric power lines and reports damaged or defective power line equipment and facilities: Patrols on foot, by automobile, boat, or other means of transportation to detect unsafe or defective power lines. Taps poles with hammer to detect rot or splits caused by weather conditions. Pulls guy wires and anchors to detect slack or looseness. Observes crossarms, insulators, transformers, switches, pole hardware, and overhead conductors, using binoculars, to detect evidence of deterioration, storm damage, and vandalism. Writes periodic report of observations. Climbs poles to examine equipment not observable from ground and makes minor repairs, such as tightening loose guy wires. Notifies trouble dispatching personnel by telephone or radio of necessary major repairs. May open and close switches as directed by supervisory personnel.
GOE: 05.07.01 STRENGTH: L GED: R3 M2 L3 SVP: 6 DLU: 77

959.367-014 FACILITY EXAMINER (tel. & tel.)
Examines telephone transmission facilities to determine equipment requirements for providing subscribers with new or additional telephone services: Climbs telephone poles or stands on truck-mounted boom to examine terminal boxes for available connections. Designates cables available for use. Visits subscribers' premises to arrange for new installations, such as telephone booths and telephone poles.
GOE: 05.05.05 STRENGTH: L GED: R3 M2 L3 SVP: 6 DLU: 77

959.367-018 ENERGY-CONSERVATION REPRESENTATIVE (utilities)
Inspects homes of utility company customers to identify conditions that cause energy waste and suggests actions to reduce waste: Interviews customer to obtain data relating to household energy use, such as type of heating system, number of persons home during day, furnace temperature setting, and prior heating costs. Draws sketch of house, measures house perimeter, windows, and doors, using tape measure, and records dimensions on sketch for use in heat-loss calculations. Inspects areas of house, such as attics, crawl spaces, and basements, and notes conditions that contribute to energy waste, such as loose-fitting windows, uninsulated pipes, and deficient insulation. Reads hot water tank label to ascertain tank heat-loss rating and determine need for tank insulation blanket. Examines furnace air filters and heat exchanger to detect dirt in filters and soot buildup in exchanger that retard efficient furnace operation. Confers with customer and recommends action to be taken to reduce energy waste, such as weatherstripping, reducing hot water temperature setting, and adding insulation. Informs customer of types and prices of energy efficiency items sold by utility. Gives customer pamphlets describing energy conservation improvements and sources of loans. Occasionally wraps insulating blanket around hot water tank, using adhesive strips. Calculates area of windows and house volume, using calculator, and records results on computer input form to provide data for computer calculation of heat-loss estimates that are mailed to customer.
GOE: 05.07.01 STRENGTH: M GED: R3 M3 L3 SVP: 3 DLU: 86

959.574-010 SERVICE REPRESENTATIVE (utilities; waterworks)
Discontinues or connects service to consumer's establishment, following written or oral instructions: Locates curb cock (valve) at customer's establishment and turns valve to shut off or to permit flow of gas or water, using handtools. Records meter readings [METER READER (utilities; waterworks)]. Investigates consumer complaints of high service cost. Inspects meters, valves, and pipes to detect defects, such as leaks or malfunctioning meters, using testing equipment. Tightens pipe connections to prevent leaks, using wrench. Recommends necessary repairs to consumer. May collect delinquent accounts. May install meters [WATER-METER INSTALLER (waterworks); GAS-METER INSTALLER (utilities)].
GOE: 05.10.01 STRENGTH: M GED: R3 M2 L2 SVP: 3 DLU: 77

959.684-010 POLE FRAMER (utilities; wood prod., nec) alternate titles: line-and-frame poler
Cuts notches for crossarms and installs step sockets in telephone, telegraph, and electric-power transmission poles: Sights down pole to determine straightest side so that poles will line up evenly when erected. Saws tip of pole to point with chain saw. Saws two parallel cuts at specified place on pole and cuts out wood between cuts with adz to make crossarm notch. Drills bolthole through pole at center of crossarm notch, using electric drill. Measures intervals for step sockets on opposite sides of pole. Drills holes and drives step sockets in place with small ax. Loads and unloads poles from railroad cars or truck, using rope, skids, and cant hook.
GOE: 05.12.12 STRENGTH: M GED: R2 M1 L2 SVP: 3 DLU: 77

96 AMUSEMENT, RECREATION, MOTION PICTURE, RADIO AND TELEVISION OCCUPATIONS, N.E.C.

This division includes occupations, not elsewhere classified, concerned with projecting images on screens; posing for painters and photographers, and standing-in for actors and actresses; erecting, raising, and lowering scenery and positioning microphones and other equipment on sets and stages; creating and editing sound effects; monitoring and controlling equipment in radio and television broadcasting studios to regulate sound and picture quality; adjusting lights; supplying properties; and preparing ice for skating rinks.

960   MOTION PICTURE PROJECTIONISTS

This group includes occupations concerned with operating motion-picture projectors and related equipment to provide motion-picture entertainment or for other viewing purposes.

960.132-010 CHIEF PROJECTIONIST (motion picture)
Supervises and coordinates activities of workers engaged in projecting motion picture film in motion picture studio: Trains workers in methods and techniques of operating projectors. Observes workers and projection operations to verify conformance with established operating procedures. Requisitions supplies and materials. Performs other duties as described under SUPERVISOR (any industry) Master Title.
GOE: 05.10.05 STRENGTH: S GED: R4 M2 L3 SVP: 8 DLU: 77

960.362-010 MOTION-PICTURE PROJECTIONIST (amuse. & rec.; motion picture) alternate titles: audiovisual equipment operator; process projectionist; projectionist; theater projectionist
Sets up and operates motion picture projection and sound-reproducing equipment to produce coordinated effects on screen: Inserts film into top magazine reel of projector. Threads film through picture aperture of projector, around pressure rollers, sprocket wheels, and sound drum or magnetic sound pickup on film, and onto spool that automatically takes up film slack. Regulates projection light and adjusts sound-reproducing equipment. Monitors operation of machines and transfers operation from one machine to another without interrupting flow of action on screen. Rewinds broken end of film onto reels by hand to minimize loss of time. Inspects and rewinds projected films for another showing. Repairs faulty sections of film. Operates stereopticon (magic lantern) or other special-effects equipment to project picture slides on screen. Cleans lenses, oils equipment, and makes minor repairs and adjustments.
GOE: 05.10.05 STRENGTH: L GED: R4 M2 L2 SVP: 6 DLU: 80

960.382-010 AUDIOVISUAL TECHNICIAN (any industry) alternate titles: audiovisual-equipment operator; projectionist
Operates audiovisual or sound-reproducing equipment to provide or complement educational or public service programs offered by institutions, such as museums, zoos, or libraries: Operates motion picture projecting equipment to show films in auditorium or lecture hall for entertainment or enlightenment of visitors to institution. Operates film, slide, video, audio tape, or turntable equipment to project or produce still or moving pictures, background music, oral commentary, or sound effects to illustrate, clarify, or enhance impact of presentation by TEACHER (museums) 099.227-038. Coordinates equipment operation with material presented, according to notations in script or instructions of speaker. Maintains equipment in working condition. Makes minor adjustments and repairs to equipment, and notifies maintenance personnel when correction of major malfunction is required. Positions, installs, and connects equipment, such as microphones, amplifiers, and lights.
GOE: 05.10.05 STRENGTH: M GED: R4 M3 L3 SVP: 3 DLU: 86

961   MODELS, STAND-INS, AND EXTRAS, N.E.C.

This group includes occupations, not elsewhere classified, concerned with posing for painters and photographers; and standing-in for actors and actresses and appearing as extras in motion picture and television productions. Fashion models in garment industry, and in retail and wholesale trade are included in Group 297.

961.364-010 DOUBLE (motion picture; radio-tv broad.)
Portrays image of star performer, facing away from camera or at long range, for motion-picture or television films: Imitates gestures and mannerisms of star performer, such as in standing, walking, climbing stairs, and mounting or riding horse. Dresses in same costume as person portrayed. May be designated according to type of work performed as Photographic Double (amuse. & rec.); Riding Double (amuse. & rec.).
GOE: 01.08.01 STRENGTH: L GED: R3 M1 L2 SVP: 3 DLU: 77

961.367-010 MODEL, PHOTOGRAPHERS' (any industry)
Poses for pictures taken by PHOTOGRAPHER, STILL (profess. & kin.) to be used for advertising purposes: Applies special makeup to face and styles hair to enhance appearance, considering factors, such as color, camera techniques, and facial features. Poses as directed or strikes suitable interpretive poses for promoting and selling merchandise or fashions. May specialize in one category of modeling, such as high fashion, illustration, or art. May specialize in modeling one part of body, such as hands, legs, or face.
GOE: 01.08.01 STRENGTH: L GED: R3 M1 L1 SVP: 4 DLU: 77

961.667-010 MODEL, ARTISTS' (any industry)
Poses as subject for paintings, sculptures, and other types of art for translation into plastic or pictorial values by PAINTER (profess. & kin.) or SCULPTOR (profess. & kin.).
GOE: 01.08.01 STRENGTH: L GED: R3 M1 L1 SVP: 3 DLU: 77

961.667-014 STAND-IN (motion picture; radio-tv broad.)
Substitutes for star performer to achieve desired angle, lighting effects, and background for motion picture or television scene preliminary to taking picture. Must have same general proportions, complexion, and other physical characteristics as person for whom worker is stand-in.
GOE: 01.08.01 STRENGTH: L GED: R2 M1 L1 SVP: 2 DLU: 77

962   OCCUPATIONS IN MOTION PICTURE, TELEVISION, AND THEATRICAL PRODUCTIONS, N.E.C.

This group includes occupations, not elsewhere classified, concerned with erecting, raising, and lowering scenery and positioning microphones and other equipment on sets, television studios, and outdoor locations; adjusting and controlling lighting to achieve desired camera effects; creating and editing sound and visual effects; installing rigging for acrobats and related entertainers; supplying properties, such as costumes and props; and controlling equipment to regulate sound and picture quality in motion pictures, radio, television, theatrical, and related productions. Occupations concerned with cutting and splicing of film and videotape are included in Group 976.

962.132-010 SUPERVISING FILM-OR-VIDEOTAPE EDITOR (motion picture; radio-tv broad.)
Supervises and coordinates activities of workers engaged in editing and assembling filmed scenes photographed by others: Reviews edited and assembled film on screen or edited videotape on monitor, to detect errors. Studies script and confers with producers and directors concerning layout or editing techniques to increase dramatic or entertainment value of production. Trims film segments to specified lengths and assembles segments in sequence that presents story with maximum effect, or edits videotape to correct errors, using editing equipment. Performs other duties as described under SUPERVISOR (any industry) Master Title. May operate studio or portable, shoulder-mounted camera [CAMERA OPERATOR (motion picture; radio-tv broad.) 143.062-022]. May be designated according to specialty as Supervising Editor, Feature (motion picture; radio-tv broad.); Supervising Editor, News Reel (radio-tv broad.); Supervising Editor, Trailer (motion picture; radio-tv broad.).
GOE: 01.01.01 STRENGTH: M GED: R5 M3 L5 SVP: 8 DLU: 89

962.134-010 RECORDIST, CHIEF (motion picture) alternate titles: operative supervisor
Supervises and coordinates activities of workers engaged in servicing and operating recording machines, power supply units, and allied equipment: Assigns workers to test and repair defective equipment. Reads production schedule to ascertain recording machines to be used and informs workers. Places sound film sections under microscope of densitometer and records densitometer readings on test forms to determine density of film. Examines film under microscope to determine width of noise reduction line on film, and records readings. Reads instructions to determine amount of current to be used on exposure lamp of each film recording machine, and what adjustments are necessary. Performs other duties as described under SUPERVISOR (any industry) Master Title.
GOE: 05.10.05 STRENGTH: L GED: R4 M3 L4 SVP: 7 DLU: 77

962.137-010 GRIP BOSS (motion picture) alternate titles: supervisor, grips
Supervises and coordinates activities of workers engaged in rigging and dismantling equipment, maintaining buildings and grounds, sewing material to make tents, backing, and scrim, and operating cranes, booms, or dollies to move cameras in motion picture studio or on location: Reads script and confers with DIRECTOR, MOTION PICTURE (motion picture) and DIRECTOR OF PHOTOGRAPHY (motion picture; radio-tv broad.) to determine type equipment needed. Requisitions supplies and equipment. Plans schedule to coordinate activities of construction, sewing room, and production workers. Performs other duties as described under SUPERVISOR (any industry) Master Title.
GOE: 05.12.01 STRENGTH: L GED: R4 M3 L4 SVP: 8 DLU: 77

962.137-018 SUPERVISOR, COSTUMING (motion picture; radio-tv broad.)
Supervises and coordinates activities of workers engaged in storing, altering, making, renting, and buying costumes and other wardrobe accessories for cast: Confers with DIRECTOR, MOTION PICTURE (motion picture) or PRODUCER (radio-tv broad.), and studies script and research material to determine style of dress according to period and characters to be represented. May sketch and design costumes. Performs other duties as described under SUPERVISOR (any industry) Master Title.
GOE: 01.02.03 STRENGTH: S GED: R4 M3 L4 SVP: 7 DLU: 77

962.137-022 SUPERVISOR, PROP-MAKING (motion picture)
Supervises and coordinates activities of workers engaged in fabricating, installing, and operating props and special effects equipment in studio or on location, according to script specifications or oral instructions. May be designated according to workers supervised as Supervisor, Drapery Hanging (motion picture); Supervisor, Special Effects (motion picture); Supervisor, Stage Carpentry (motion picture); Supervisor, Upholstering (motion picture). Performs other duties as described under SUPERVISOR (any industry) Master Title.
GOE: 01.06.02 STRENGTH: L GED: R4 M4 L3 SVP: 8 DLU: 77

962.137-026 SUPERVISOR, PROPERTIES (motion picture)
Supervises and coordinates activities of personnel engaged in obtaining, moving, and fabricating props used in motion pictures: Reads script and confers

with DIRECTOR, MOTION PICTURE (motion picture) to determine prop requirements for designated scenes. Assigns personnel to fabricate props, to obtain prefabricated props from inventory, or to buy or rent props from outside sources. Assumes responsibility for safekeeping and placement of props on sets during shooting of scenes. Instructs GRIP (motion picture; radio-tv broad.) to remove and store props at completion of shooting. May decorate sets.
GOE: 05.12.01 STRENGTH: L GED: R4 M3 L4 SVP: 8 DLU: 77

962.162-010   DIRECTOR, TECHNICAL (radio-tv broad.) alternate titles: switching operator

Coordinates activities of radio or television studio and control-room personnel to ensure technical quality of picture and sound for programs originating in studio or from remote pickup points: Plans and arranges for special effects requested by supervisory personnel. Assigns work to technical personnel engaged in controlling and maintaining lights, audio and video control equipment, microphones, and cameras. Observes picture through monitor and gives instruction to VIDEO OPERATOR (radio-tv broad.) 194.282-010 concerning shading or CAMERA OPERATOR, TELEVISION (radio-tv broad.) 143.062-022 concerning composition desired. Controls switcher-mixer unit to switch cameras, fade from one picture to another, or superimpose one image upon another as indicated by script or as cued by DIRECTOR, PROGRAM (radio-tv broad.) 184.167-030.
GOE: 05.02.04 STRENGTH: L GED: R5 M2 L4 SVP: 8 DLU: 88

962.167-010   MANAGER, SOUND EFFECTS (radio-tv broad.) alternate titles: sound-effects supervisor

Coordinates activities of workers engaged in preparing and producing sound effects for radio, film, and video tape productions: Assigns duties to SOUND-EFFECTS TECHNICIAN (radio-tv broad.) and other studio personnel engaged in producing sound effects for various productions. Consults with production management personnel, DIRECTOR, RADIO (radio-tv broad.) or SOUND CUTTER (motion picture), and SCREEN WRITERS (motion picture; radio-tv broad.), to determine special sound effects required for production presentation.
GOE: 01.06.02 STRENGTH: S GED: R5 M4 L5 SVP: 7 DLU: 77

962.167-014   PROGRAM ASSISTANT (radio-tv broad.) alternate titles: associate director; production assistant; production coordinator; stage manager

Performs any combination of following or similar duties as directed by DIRECTOR, PROGRAM (radio-tv broad.) 184.167-030 or PRODUCER (radio-tv broad.) 159.117-010 in rehearsal and broadcast of television programs: Distributes copies of script and arranges for rehearsal quarters. Prepares and distributes rehearsal call sheets. Lays out acting areas on stage floor, using tape and following floor plan. Times scenes during rehearsal and calculates overall program timing. Contacts guest and members of cast to verify that makeup has been applied. Verifies that specified films, slides, titles cards, and similar items are ready for broadcast. Directs personnel in rehearsal and broadcast of sign-ons and sign-offs, station breaks, film feature programs, and other programs composed of non-live video elements. Notifies various departments of changes in daily operation schedules. Oversees distribution of studio equipment, such as scenery, cameras, and microphones. Transmits instructions received over telephone headset to performers and others on set orally, or using body gestures. Prepares report of daily on-air activities. May direct production of sound effects. May prepare rehearsal call sheets, reports, daily on-air activity report, memos, or scripts, using computer.
GOE: 01.03.01 STRENGTH: L GED: R4 M2 L3 SVP: 5 DLU: 89

962.167-018   PROPERTY COORDINATOR (amuse. & rec.; radio-tv broad.)

Provides stage properties for theatrical production: Purchases or rents properties from merchants and museums or obtains properties from theater or warehouse. Arranges with PROP MAKER (amuse. & rec.; motion picture) for construction of period furniture and properties. Arranges properties on stage for each scene. Clears or directs clearing of properties from stage at conclusion of each scene. Performs minor repairs on props, using handtools. Cleans props or sends to property shop for maintenance. Keeps record of purchases and submits bill and purchase order to designated authority. When accompanying show on tour, packs and unpacks properties. May arrange for transportation of properties.
GOE: 05.02.06 STRENGTH: V GED: R4 M1 L3 SVP: 7 DLU: 77

962.261-010   PLANETARIUM TECHNICIAN (museums) alternate titles: astro-technician; technical specialist

Installs, modifies, operates, and maintains sound and projection equipment used in presentation of planetarium classes and shows: Consults with personnel who plan classes and shows to determine feasibility of achieving specified effects, modifications in equipment necessary to create desired effects, and additional equipment or properties to be incorporated into technical equipment layout. Modifies projectors, electro-optic equipment, console controls, and auxiliary instruments, following script or lecture outline, to adjust equipment for producing desired visual effects, basing modifications on knowledge of equipment capabilities, and using handtools, precision instruments, and circuitry diagrams. Selects tapes of musical compositions from planetarium files and records portions of each, as designated in script, to produce tape recording with musical background. Modifies sound system to permit synchronization of recorded commentary and background music with visual presentation. Installs special effect properties, such as models of space ships or slides of ancient interpretations of

constellations, in designated positions in dome of theater, and secures properties to control wires or machinery to facilitate manipulation of properties according to script or lecture outline, using handtools. Operates electro-optic, audio, and auxiliary equipment to present show or to complement presentation of class lectures. Repairs and maintains equipment, using handtools and precision calibrating and testing instruments, applying knowledge of electronic circuitry and electro-optics, and following manufacturer's maintenance instructions and diagrams. Constructs and installs permanent or temporary displays, incorporating electromechanical or electronic components, in planetarium's exhibit area.
GOE: 05.10.05 STRENGTH: M GED: R4 M4 L4 SVP: 7 DLU: 86

962.261-014   STAGE TECHNICIAN (amuse. & rec.)

Installs rigging, lighting, sound equipment, and scenery, and erects stages for theatrical, musical, and other entertainment events in arenas, stadiums, theaters, studios, and other amusement places: Reads stage layout specifications and blueprints and confers with MANAGER, STAGE (amuse. & rec.) 159.167-018 to determine type and location of sets, props, scenery, lighting, and sound equipment required for specific event. Assembles props provided by production company, constructs additional props, scenery, or stages, and attaches braces that support scenery frames in upright position, using carpenter's handtools and power tools. Climbs ladder or scaffolding to ceiling grid, crawls and balances on beams, inserts ends of cables or ropes through ceiling grid, and attaches cables to scenery, curtains, equipment, support pipes, and counterbalance weights [GRIP (amuse. & rec.; radio-tv broad.) 962.684-014]. Positions lighting fixtures on and around stage area, clamps light fixtures to supports, connects electrical wiring from fixtures to power source and control panel [LIGHTING-EQUIPMENT OPERATOR (amuse. & rec.) 962.381-014], positions sound equipment, such as microphones, speakers, and amplifiers, on and around stage area, and connects electrical lines to power source and mixing console [PUBLIC-ADDRESS SERVICER (any industry) 823.261-010], utilizing knowledge of electrical codes and use of electrician's handtools and power tools. Pulls cables that raise and lower scenery, curtains, and equipment [FLYER (amuse. & rec.; radio-tv broad.) 962.687-018] and operates lighting and sound equipment during rehearsals and performances, following audio or visual cues.
GOE: 05.10.04 STRENGTH: H GED: R4 M3 L4 SVP: 7 DLU: 86

962.262-010   FILM OR VIDEOTAPE EDITOR (motion picture; radio-tv broad.) alternate titles: cutter

Edits motion picture film, television or cable television video tape, and sound tracks: Evaluates and selects scenes in terms of dramatic and entertainment value and story continuity. Trims film segments to specified lengths and reassembles segments in sequence that presents story with maximum effect, or edits video tape, using editing equipment. Reviews assembled film or edited video tape on screen or monitor and makes corrections. Confers with supervisory personnel and others concerning filming of scenes. May specialize in particular field of film or video editing, such as feature, news, sound, sound effects, or music.
GOE: 01.01.01 STRENGTH: L GED: R5 M2 L4 SVP: 8 DLU: 88

962.267-010   SIGHT-EFFECTS SPECIALIST (amuse. & rec.) alternate titles: electrician, master

Provides special stage lighting and sight effects for theatrical performances and directs electrical crew engaged in installing and arranging lighting and wiring equipment: Studies work drawings of stage sets showing light details. Confers with producing personnel and studies continuity script to determine lighting of sets and special sight effects desired. Suggests changes and orders special mechanical stage contrivances to obtain mobile or stationary sight effects, such as forests burning, oceans rolling, or other scenic effects. Attaches stereopticon lens on lamp and operates lamp from rear of stage to project pictures of desired effects on scrim (transparent curtain), following cue sheet. Directs crew in setting up and arranging electrical equipment and lights for use on stage and in theater. May originate designs for artistic lighting of sets.
GOE: 05.10.03 STRENGTH: L GED: R4 M3 L3 SVP: 8 DLU: 77

962.281-010   PROP MAKER (amuse. & rec.; motion picture)

Fabricates and assembles props, miniatures, and sets for motion pictures and theatrical productions from a variety of materials, using handtools and woodworking and metalworking machines and equipment: Analyzes sketches, blueprints, and verbal instructions to determine type props and other materials needed and equipment required. Measures and marks cutting lines on material, using work aids, such as jigs and fixtures, micrometers, calipers, and templates. Fabricates parts, using machinery, such as drill press, metal and wood lathes, power saws, router, and milling machine. Assembles parts into props, miniatures, and sets, using handtools and equipment, such as screwdrivers, wrenches, hammers, and welding apparatus. Rigs and controls moving or functioning elements of sets that depict action.
GOE: 01.06.02 STRENGTH: M GED: R4 M4 L4 SVP: 7 DLU: 77

962.281-014   SOUND-EFFECTS TECHNICIAN (radio-tv broad.)

Produces artificial sounds that are transmitted and synchronized with production being presented to simulate aural impression of action being broadcasted to listener or viewer. Reproduces recorded sounds from previously prepared phonograph records or tape.
GOE: 01.06.02 STRENGTH: L GED: R4 M3 L4 SVP: 6 DLU: 77

962.281-018   SPECIAL EFFECTS SPECIALIST (amuse. & rec.; motion picture; radio-tv broad.)

Fabricates, installs, and activates equipment to produce special effects, such as rain, snow, explosions, and other mechanical and electrical effects as re-

quired by script for television, motion picture, and theatrical productions: Reads script to determine type of special effects required. Mixes chemicals to produce special effects, following standard formulas. Constructs towers and similar objects used in making effects, using handtools and machine tools. Fabricates parts for special effects from materials, such as wood, metal, plaster, and clay, using handtools and power tools. Installs special effects, using handtools.
GOE: 01.06.02 STRENGTH: M GED: R4 M3 L3 SVP: 6 DLU: 77

962.361-010 OPTICAL-EFFECTS LAYOUT PERSON (motion picture) alternate titles: assistant camera operator; optical-effects-line-up person; plotter

Locates and marks frames of motion picture film to identify film segments for optical effects processing: Reads work order or optical effects specifications sheets to ascertain optical effects specifications and location of subject material on original photography film. Mounts single or multiple rolls of film on spindles of winding device, locates marked start frame of film, and aligns start frame in start position of synchronizer-counter device to locate and identify film frames specified for optical effects. Turns crank on winding device to advance film and observes film passing over viewing light box to detect damage or unclean condition. Cleans film using cleaning solutions and velvet cloth. Repairs minor damage, such as torn sprocket holes, using tape. Periodically stops film when viewing more than one roll simultaneously and compares numbers printed on film edges to ensure synchronization of films. Stops film when counter reading matches number indicated on work order for start of first optical effect. Reviews subject matter within film frame and compares to description on work order to ensure match when work order does not include reference numbers. Marks reference frame of film, using film notcher, tape, or other marking device to indicate optical effect starting point. Marks symbols and numbers on film edge or leader to indicate type of effect and length. Advances film to additional reference frames indicated, and marks designated frames to show reference points within individual optical effects. Prepares count sheet indicating position, length, and type of optical effects required for films which do not have prepared specification sheets. Splices strips of leader material to film, and assembles designated segments of film in specified relationship, using splicing device. May confer with clients regarding optical effects requirements and production problems. May determine artwork requirements and requisition artwork. May review and approve finished optical effects. May load and unload film from camera magazine, and mount and remove magazines from camera. May change subtitle cards when filming subtitles.
GOE: 01.06.02 STRENGTH: L GED: R3 M3 L3 SVP: 6 DLU: 86

962.362-010 COMMUNICATIONS TECHNICIAN (education)

Performs a variety of duties involved in producing motion picture film in audio-visual department of educational institution: Selects areas and locations for filming motion pictures according to specifications. Sets up lighting equipment. Selects picture and sound takes to conform film to script. Assists in designing and building sets for film production. Requisitions props. Edits and splices motion picture film. Operates projectors, video tape recorders, and sound recording equipment to inspect and preview film for clients. Packages and ships film.
GOE: 01.03.01 STRENGTH: L GED: R4 M2 L3 SVP: 7 DLU: 77

962.362-014 LIGHT TECHNICIAN (motion picture; radio-tv broad.) alternate titles: operator, lights; set electrician, assistant chief

Sets up and controls lighting equipment for television broadcast or motion picture production: Confers with directors and studies script to determine lighting effects required. Sets up spot, flood, incandescent, and mercury vapor lights, reflectors, and other equipment. Switches lights on during broadcast, following script or instructions from directors. Makes minor repairs, such as replacing broken cables on equipment. May lead and give directions to workers while performing same duties.
GOE: 05.10.03 STRENGTH: L GED: R4 M2 L3 SVP: 7 DLU: 87

962.381-010 DRAPER (motion picture; radio-tv broad.)

Lays out patterns and cuts fabrics to make drapes, curtains, and items, such as banners, flags, bunting, pennants, and tapestries, for motion-picture or television sets, and hangs items on set: Measures windows or wall areas to be covered and lays out dimensions on fabrics, following specifications. Cuts fabrics and routes cut articles to sewing shop to be sewn. Installs brackets, rods, and similar mountings on sets, using screws, handtools, and power drills, and hangs draperies or other items on mountings.
GOE: 05.05.15 STRENGTH: M GED: R3 M2 L2 SVP: 7 DLU: 77

962.381-014 LIGHTING-EQUIPMENT OPERATOR (amuse. & rec.) alternate titles: electrician, front

Controls lighting equipment, such as floodlamps, strip lights, and spotlights from projection room and front or backstage areas of theater to cast spotlight on stage performers: Places spotlights in specified locations in theater and connects wiring for lighting. Moves spotlight to follow movements of performers with beam of light, according to instructions on prepared cue sheet. Turns color wheel, causing light to be diffused through varicolored gelatin disks to change color of light. Cleans and adjusts light, replacing carbons or bulbs as needed. May insert varicolored gelatin sheets in frame to assemble color wheel.
GOE: 05.12.16 STRENGTH: L GED: R4 M2 L3 SVP: 6 DLU: 77

962.381-018 MINIATURE-SET CONSTRUCTOR (motion picture) alternate titles: miniature-set builder; model-set artist; set-model builder

Constructs miniature models of motion picture sets used in filming backgrounds, titles, and special effects according to scale. Cuts materials, such as

wood, cardboard, or plastic to specified dimensions, using handtools. Fits and glues or tacks cutouts to form three-dimensional set pieces. Builds landscapes, using plaster of paris or modeling clay to represent trees and bushes. Trims and paints completed miniature set.
GOE: 01.06.02 STRENGTH: L GED: R4 M4 L3 SVP: 7 DLU: 77

962.382-010 RECORDIST (motion picture)

Controls equipment to record sound originating on motion-picture set, using magnetic film, optical film, and acetate disk recording equipment: Tests and sets up recording mechanism according to specifications. Starts recorder and synchronizes sound with film. Observes operation to ensure that sound is properly recorded. May be designated according to equipment used as Disk Recordist (motion picture); Film Recordist (motion picture).
GOE: 05.10.05 STRENGTH: L GED: R3 M2 L2 SVP: 6 DLU: 77

962.382-014 SOUND CUTTER (motion picture) alternate titles: editing-machine operator; editor, sound

Edits and synchronizes music, dialogue, and sound effects of motion picture film and video tape into single sound-print for film or video-tape production: Loads combination sound-and-picture reproducing machine with picture and sound-track films and video tape. Starts machine, views action through aperture, and listens to sound being reproduced, using earphones. Notes dupe sheet for sound effects to accompany or punctuate action. Determines that sound matches picture or dupe sheet indicates sound-effect insertion. Stops machine at such points and marks symbol on film with grease pencil or notches symbol on video tape, using electronic device. Rewinds prints onto reels by reversing action of machine. Sets reels on rewinder, turns handle until both sound and picture are unwound to points marked by symbol, and splices sound effect into sound print.
GOE: 01.06.02 STRENGTH: S GED: R4 M3 L4 SVP: 6 DLU: 77

962.384-010 MICROPHONE-BOOM OPERATOR (motion picture; radio-tv broad.) alternate titles: boom operator

Moves levers on adjustable boom to position microphone in proximity of performers during filming of motion picture or television broadcasts: Attaches microphone to rubber supports at end of boom and places preamplifier in container attached to boom as directed by SOUND MIXER (motion picture; recording; radio-tv broad.) 194.262-018. Connects microphone wires to preamplifier and preamplifier wires to sound mixing apparatus. Positions microphone so as not to cast shadows or come in view of camera. Moves boom according to script and position of performers.
GOE: 05.10.05 STRENGTH: L GED: R3 M1 L2 SVP: 5 DLU: 87

962.664-010 HIGH RIGGER (amuse. & rec.; radio-tv broad.)

Installs rigging to raise, lower, or support equipment, such as scenery, lighting equipment, ladders, and nets for theatrical performances on stage or television studio: Climbs ladders, poles, or scaffolding to determine position for rigging and connects, hangs, or attaches cables, ropes, and blocks (pulley) across loft area of stage. Tests rigging to ensure that it is workable. Erects high ladders for acrobatic performances by connecting successive short lengths of ladder to top of erected portion, using clamps, wrenches, and hammers. Installs motors used to move curtains and track on which scenery and curtains move, using handtools and power tools.
GOE: 05.10.01 STRENGTH: V GED: R3 M2 L2 SVP: 6 DLU: 77

962.664-014 RECORDING STUDIO SET-UP WORKER (recording)

Arranges sound recording equipment in studio preparatory to recording session following work order specifications: Reads work order to determine position of equipment and arranges equipment, such as consoles, isolation booths, microphones, tape machines, amplifiers, music stands, and musical instruments, by hand or using handtrucks and dollies. Connects equipment electrical lines to outlets according to oral or written instructions. Dismantles equipment subsequent to recording session and returns items to storage. Maintains storage area and assists in maintaining tape library.
GOE: 05.12.03 STRENGTH: M GED: R3 M1 L1 SVP: 4 DLU: 77

962.665-010 DUBBING-MACHINE OPERATOR (motion picture; radio-tv broad.)

Tends film or magnetic tape dubbing machines that play back recordings of music, dialogue, or sound effects to facilitate synchronization of sound motion-picture film action by RERECORDING MIXER (motion picture; radio-tv broad.): Loads reels of film or tape onto machine and passes lead-end over and around sprockets, wheels, tension rollers, and magnetic tape head or over photo-electric cell apertures. Starts machines, unwinds film or tape, and stops machine when mark on tape or film indicates beginning of sound. Switches machine to automatic for control by RERECORDING MIXER (motion picture; radio-tv broad.). Informs RERECORDING MIXER (motion picture; radio-tv broad.) that machines are loaded and ready for playback. Removes reels when recordings are finished and rewinds tape or film onto original reel.
GOE: 05.10.05 STRENGTH: M GED: R3 M1 L1 SVP: 3 DLU: 77

962.684-010 ACROBATIC RIGGER (amuse. & rec.) alternate titles: rigger

Erects equipment for aerial and acrobatic acts in shows, such as circus, variety show, and carnivals, working as member of crew: Drills holes in floor of stage or platform, using electric drill, and fastens metal floor plates to hold vertical steel rods. Screws steel rods to holding plates and stretches wire or rope between rods, using handtools. Climbs ladder to attach ropes, swinging trapeze,

and other rigging to ceiling area. Fastens rigging and pulleys to hooks or poles in ceiling. Erects net under aerial and highwire acts for safety of performers. Lowers and raises trapezes and nets during performance.
GOE: 05.10.01 STRENGTH: H GED: R3 M1 L1 SVP: 6 DLU: 77

962.684-014 GRIP (amuse. & rec.; radio-tv broad.)
Erects sets and moves scenery on stage for theatrical productions on stage and television studio, using handtools and power tools and equipment: Ties sets upright with lash lines. Hooks stage brace onto set and adjusts brace to straighten and support set. Connects lines to overhead steel work to support hanging units, using handtools and power tools. Fits and hangs painted backdrops and curtains. Inserts weights as specified to counter balance hanging units. Changes scenery between acts or scenes according to script.
GOE: 05.10.01 STRENGTH: V GED: R3 M2 L2 SVP: 5 DLU: 87

962.684-018 MOTOR-POWER CONNECTOR (motion picture)
Connects sound, camera, and lighting motors of motion-picture apparatus to common power source by means of portable junction box and cables: Selects types and lengths of cable according to type equipment to be connected and accessibility to power source. Maintains connections while camera and sound equipment are in use. May manipulate microphone boom [MICROPHONE-BOOM OPERATOR (motion picture; radio-tv broad.)].
GOE: 05.10.03 STRENGTH: L GED: R3 M1 L1 SVP: 5 DLU: 77

962.684-022 PROP ATTENDANT (amuse. & rec.)
Readies stage, equipment, and seating area of theater prior to performances, and produces special lighting and sound effects during performances, using various equipment and devices: Lifts, places, and repositions special effect props, such as breakaway walls, dry ice in smoke/fog generator, and stage elevators, for use by performers during show. Starts, connects, and tests light and sound equipment, such as microphones, magnetic tape players, amplifiers, and stage lighting system, prior to show. Cleans and prepares stage, seating, and dressing areas prior to show [CLEANER, COMMERCIAL OR INSTITUTIONAL (any industry) 381.687-014]. Pushes buttons, presses and flips switches, and turns valves to achieve special sound and lighting effects and to raise and lower scenery and stage curtain during performance, following sight or sound cues. Hands props to performers and assists performers with costume changes during show. May order makeup supplies and props to replace those used or damaged during shows. Prior to show may test equipment and during show may tend equipment that activates and controls animated characters.
GOE: 05.12.16 STRENGTH: M GED: R3 M2 L3 SVP: 2 DLU: 86

962.687-010 DOLLY PUSHER (radio-tv broad.) alternate titles: assistant camera operator
Pushes television camera dolly around studio, as directed by CAMERA OPERATOR, TELEVISION (radio-tv broad.), to follow action of scene being broadcast.
GOE: 05.12.03 STRENGTH: V GED: R2 M1 L1 SVP: 2 DLU: 77

962.687-014 FILM LOADER (motion picture)
Loads and unloads film magazines, as directed, prior to and following photographing of motion-picture scenes. May perform other duties on set location, such as marking stage floor with chalk to designate actors' and actresses' positions, clapping hinged boards together to designate start of scene, and recording scene number and related information on slate to identify scene.
GOE: 05.12.03 STRENGTH: M GED: R2 M1 L1 SVP: 2 DLU: 77

962.687-018 FLYER (amuse. & rec.; radio-tv broad.)
Lowers or raises scenery and curtains by pulling ropes from position above or to one side of stage. Follows prepared cue sheet, bell, or light signals to make required changes during performance.
GOE: 05.12.04 STRENGTH: V GED: R2 M1 L1 SVP: 3 DLU: 77

962.687-022 GRIP (motion picture; radio-tv broad.) alternate titles: property handler
Performs any combination of following tasks in motion picture or television studio or set location: Moves control levers and wheels to guide cranes, booms, and dollies that move cameras and other equipment. Sews canvas and other materials to make and repair tents, tarps, scrims, and backings, using sewing machine. Erects canvas covers to protect camera from rain on location. Cuts gelatin and fiberglass light diffusers to fit metal frame of camera and inserts diffusers into frame. Rigs and dismantles frames, scaffolding, backdrops, prefabricated dressing rooms, camera platforms, and tents for set in studio or on location, using carpenter's handtools. May be designated according to department assigned as Construction Grip (motion picture); Production Grip (motion picture); Sewing Room Grip (motion picture).
GOE: 05.12.04 STRENGTH: H GED: R2 M1 L2 SVP: 5 DLU: 77

969 MISCELLANEOUS AMUSEMENT AND RECREATION OCCUPATIONS, N.E.C.

This group includes occupations, not elsewhere classified, concerned with miscellaneous amusement and recreation occupations.

969.137-010 SUPERVISOR, CIRCUS (amuse. & rec.)
Supervises and coordinates activities of workers engaged in cleaning various areas, moving equipment, and erecting tents and rigging in circus, carnival, or other exhibition, performing duties as described under SUPERVISOR (any industry) Master Title.

GOE: 05.12.01 STRENGTH: L GED: R4 M2 L2 SVP: 6 DLU: 77

969.137-014 SUPERVISOR, SHOW OPERATIONS (amuse. & rec.)
Supervises and coordinates activities of performers and technicians in amusement or theme park: Reviews and adjusts performance schedule to ensure number of performances meets anticipated attendance. Arranges shift assignments of performers and technicians. Talks to guests in person or by telephone to answer questions and resolve complaints. Performs other duties as described under SUPERVISOR (any industry) Master Title.
GOE: 01.03.01 STRENGTH: L GED: R4 M4 L4 SVP: 6 DLU: 86

969.367-010 CUSTODIAN, ATHLETIC EQUIPMENT (amuse. & rec.) alternate titles: manager, equipment
Keeps stock of new and used athletic supplies, such as balls, gloves, bats, shoes, and uniforms, and issues supplies to players: Keeps record of supplies in stock and supplies issued to players. Informs officials when additional supplies are needed. Inspects supplies in stock to detect those requiring repair or cleaning. Repairs torn or damaged supplies or sends supplies out for repair. Issues new or clean supplies to players in exchange for supplies that are worn or dirty. Packs and unpacks supplies for road trips and ensures that arrangements are made for transportation. Accompanies players on trips. Modifies protective supplies, such as adding additional arch supports to shoes, padding uniforms and helmets, or preparing slings for injured players, under specific directions from INSTRUCTOR, SPORTS (amuse. & rec.; education) or ATHLETIC TRAINER (amuse. & rec.; education). May prepare budget estimate for supplies. May purchase supplies. May wash soiled uniforms and other supplies in automatic washing machine or may arrange to have supplies laundered.
GOE: 05.09.01 STRENGTH: M GED: R3 M2 L2 SVP: 5 DLU: 77

969.381-010 WARDROBE-SPECIALTY WORKER (motion picture; radio-tv broad.)
Makes, repairs, alters, and revamps special wardrobe items and accessories, such as military hats and caps, badges, shoes, belts, and leather pouches, or other leather, suede, and canvas items, working from patterns and diagrams, and using handtools and power sewing machines.
GOE: 05.05.15 STRENGTH: L GED: R3 M3 L2 SVP: 7 DLU: 77

969.664-010 FIREWORKS DISPLAY SPECIALIST (chemical) alternate titles: setter-off; setter-up
Assembles and sets off fireworks displays at fairs, expositions, or celebrations, according to picture programs or diagrams: Advises committee as to distance audience should be from setoff site of display, according to wind direction and velocity, considering fallout of sparks and acid, and types of fireworks used. Lays out setoff arrangement. Directs workers to set mortars (pipes used to fire aerial shells) apart from ground display, and places barrier of sandbags, railroad ties, or boxes of gravel between mortars to avoid detonating shells from sparks. Assembles framework and affixes display to framework, using hammer, saw, nails, scissors, and twine. Ties fuses of components to lead fuse to create simultaneous fireworks display. Determines appropriate time for setting off of display, according to environmental conditions.
GOE: 05.10.06 STRENGTH: M GED: R4 M2 L2 SVP: 5 DLU: 77

969.685-010 SNOWMAKER (amuse. & rec.)
Tends artificial snow making equipment of ski resort to produce artificial snow along ski trails: Rides chair lift or drives snow-terrain vehicle along ski trails to reach snow equipment. Attaches hoses from snow equipment to nozzles of above-ground outlets for underground compressed air and water pipelines, using wrenches. Turns outlet valves to adjust compressed air and water mixture to obtain desired snow spray. Returns defective or frozen snow equipment to ski lodge for repair, using snow vehicle. Repositions equipment periodically to direct snowfall to other sections of trail, or closes valves to shut off equipment when snow coverage is completed. Cleans dirt and frozen snow from equipment, using handtools.
GOE: 05.12.18 STRENGTH: H GED: R2 M1 L1 SVP: 2 DLU: 86

969.687-010 CIRCUS LABORER (amuse. & rec.)
Performs variety of tasks in cleaning floors and moving equipment for amusement show, such as fair, circus, or carnival, as directed: Cleans and sweeps show area after each performance. Cleans floor after elephants and horses perform. Moves wild animal cages, acrobatic equipment, and carries other properties to show area. Leads horses, elephants, and other animals into show area. Loads and unloads animals and equipment on and off train. May work as member of team to erect and dismantle canvas tents and place seats.
GOE: 05.12.18 STRENGTH: M GED: R2 M1 L1 SVP: 2 DLU: 77

969.687-014 ICE MAKER, SKATING RINK (amuse. & rec.)
Prepares floor for use as ice-skating rink and removes ice after use: Sprays floor of rink (which has been chilled by ammonia pipes), using water hose, to obtain ice layer of specified thickness. Skates behind tractor to guide scraper blades that smooth surface of rink. Turns valves to force steam through piping in floor to melt ice. Breaks ice, using chisel, and shovels ice into drain or sump. Mops water. May maintain order among patrons and protect property during skating sessions.
GOE: 05.12.18 STRENGTH: M GED: R2 M1 L2 SVP: 2 DLU: 77

97 OCCUPATIONS IN GRAPHIC ART WORK

This division includes occupations concerned with handsetting text or display type; making and mounting plates of line or continuous tone illustrations; assembling hand- or machine-set type, plates, and spacing material to make up pages and forms; reproducing type, illustrations, pages, and forms by photoengraving, lithographic process, electrotyping, or stereotyping to make plates for printing presses; copying lettering, lines, or designs, and retouching artwork; etching or engraving printing rollers; developing and printing film and prints; bookbinding; and related graphic arts activities. Occupations concerned with cold type typesetting and word processing are found in Division 20.

970 ART WORK OCCUPATIONS, BRUSH, SPRAY, OR PEN

This group includes occupations concerned with copying or altering designs or lettering following layout or other directions; retouching original artwork, including photographic negatives or positives, using brush, spray, airbrush, or pen; drawing lines, such as column rules, on page layouts; and related artwork. Creating layouts and producing original art are included in Division 14.

970.131-014 SUPERVISOR, ARTIST, SUSPECT (government ser.)
Supervises and coordinates activities of workers engaged in forming composite images of persons suspected of criminal activities: Assigns duties to and trains new workers. Participates in activities of ARTIST, SUSPECT (government ser.) 970.361-018 to arrange and enhance set of facial features to form composite images of persons suspected of criminal activities. Performs other duties as described under SUPERVISOR (any industry) Master Title.
GOE: 01.06.01 STRENGTH: L GED: R4 M3 L3 SVP: 7 DLU: 86

970.137-010 SUPERVISOR, SIGN SHOP (fabrication, nec)
Supervises and coordinates activities of workers engaged in constructing and painting signs: Reviews work orders and visits future site of sign to determine size of sign, materials needed to construct sign, and media needed to convey requested message. Orders material not already on inventory. Assigns work to PAINTER, SIGN (any industry) 970.381-026; SIGN ERECTOR (fabrication, nec) I 869.381-026; SIGN WRITER, HAND (any industry) 970.281-022; or other workers based upon current work load, priority of work to be completed, and expertise of available workers. Performs other duties as described under SUPERVISOR (any industry) Master Title. May prepare periodic department budget based upon knowledge of historic and projected costs of personnel, materials, and replacements and additions to tool and equipment inventory.
GOE: 05.10.04 STRENGTH: L GED: R4 M3 L4 SVP: 8 DLU: 86

970.281-010 AIRBRUSH ARTIST (profess. & kin.) alternate titles: photograph restorer
Restores damaged and faded photographs or colors and shades drawings to simulate photographs, using airbrush: Examines drawing or photographic print to determine coloring, shading, and changes required. Cuts out masking template, using shears, and positions templates on control areas to be sprayed. Mixes ink or paint solutions according to color specifications and spraying consistency desired. Sprays solution over control area to fill in and blend missing parts of photograph or to give depth, perspective, and tone to drawing, using airbrush. Builds up or changes photograph backgrounds to block out undesirable or distracting details, using airbrush. Inks borders and lettering on illustrations and paints in details missing from photographs, using pen, brush, and drafting instruments. Rubs eraser over specified areas and applies white ink to highlight illustrations, using brush or pen. May specialize in mechanical and industrial designs and be designated Airbrush Artist, Technical (profess. & kin.); or in photograph restoring and be designated Airbrush Artist, Photography (profess. & kin.).
GOE: 01.06.03 STRENGTH: S GED: R4 M2 L3 SVP: 7 DLU: 77

970.281-014 DELINEATOR (profess. & kin.) alternate titles: renderer
Renders perspective drawings of buildings and manufactured products for display or advertising purposes working from sketches and blueprints and using pencil, pen, charcoal, watercolors, or airbrush. May be designated according to specialization as Architectural Renderer (profess. & kin.); Industrial Renderer (profess. & kin.).
GOE: 01.02.03 STRENGTH: S GED: R4 M3 L3 SVP: 7 DLU: 77

970.281-018 PHOTOGRAPH RETOUCHER (photofinishing) alternate titles: retoucher
Retouches photographic negatives and prints to accentuate desirable features of subject, using pencils or watercolors and brushes: Examines negative to determine which features should be accented or minimized. Paints negative with retouching medium so that retouching pencil will mark surface of negative. Shades negative with pencil to smooth facial contours, conceal stray hairs, wrinkles, or blemishes, and soften harsh highlights. Brushes watercolors on print to accentuate lights and shadows and produce clear and attractive features.
GOE: 01.06.03 STRENGTH: S GED: R4 M2 L3 SVP: 6 DLU: 77

970.281-022 SIGN WRITER, HAND (any industry) alternate titles: card writer, hand; show-card writer
Writes, paints, or prints signs or showcards used for display or other purposes, using brushes. May cut out letters and signs for display purposes from wallboard or cardboard, by hand or machines, such as electrically powered jigsaw or bandsaw.
GOE: 01.06.03 STRENGTH: S GED: R4 M3 L3 SVP: 5 DLU: 77

970.281-026 SKETCH MAKER, PHOTOENGRAVING (print. & pub.) alternate titles: artist, color separation
Sketches cloth designs onto transparent paper for subsequent transfer to printing rollers by photographic process, using drafting tools and artists' work aids:

Studies customer's design to locate one complete repeat of pattern. Lays out reference points on design according to location of pattern repeat and motifs within repeat, using ruler, dividers, and pencil. Places design on lighted drafting table, covers design with sheet of transparent paper, and transfers reference points from design to paper. Holds paper against design with stylus and sketches each color (segments of design) in pattern repeat on separate sheet of paper, using pen, brush, sponge, opaque, india ink, and watercolors. Varies intensity of sketch according to design so that printing rollers will be etched in manner that will produce shades and tones of color. Corrects flaws left in design by artist or designer and alters design to make it practical for printing, employing knowledge of fabrics, colors, and etching and printing techniques. Assembles sketches into composite sketch and compares composite with design to determine if parts of design join together to reproduce complete design. Routes sketches to PHOTOGRAPHER, PHOTOENGRAVING (electron. comp.; print. & pub.) for transfer to film.
GOE: 01.02.03 STRENGTH: S GED: R4 M3 L3 SVP: 7 DLU: 77

970.361-010 FORM DESIGNER (print. & pub.) alternate titles: form drafter
Develops office forms, such as invoices and production sheets, according to clients' specifications, using drafting instruments. Draws and submits initial draft to client. Makes changes according to client's specifications. Prepares final form of approved design for printing.
GOE: 01.06.01 STRENGTH: L GED: R3 M3 L3 SVP: 6 DLU: 77

970.361-014 REPEAT CHIEF (print. & pub.) alternate titles: inspector
Examines and corrects defects in films used to transfer designs onto printing rollers: Examines films to detect pinholes, defective screens, loss of contour, and exposure errors. Paints out pinholes, fills in defective screens, and alters contour of images on film, using brushes and opaque. Returns overexposed or underexposed films to PHOTOGRAPHER, PHOTOENGRAVING (electron. comp.; print. & pub.) for correction. Measures image on film to verify conformance to specifications, using steel tape. Routes acceptable prints to REPEAT-PHOTOCOMPOSING-MACHINE OPERATOR (print. & pub.) for use in composing master film for transferring image to sensitized copper printing rollers. Compares master film with original design and examines repeat joinings (lines along which repeats of design are joined) through magnifying lens to detect repeats that are out of register. Returns unsatisfactory films to REPEAT-PHOTOCOMPOSING MACHINE OPERATOR (print. & pub.) for correction of defects.
GOE: 05.10.05 STRENGTH: S GED: R4 M3 L3 SVP: 7 DLU: 77

970.361-018 ARTIST, SUSPECT (government ser.)
Selects set of facial features from inventory, and arranges features to form composite image of persons suspected of criminal activities based on descriptions obtained from victims and witnesses to crimes: Assembles and arranges outlines of features, such as head contours, noses, eyes, lips, chins, and hair lines and styles, to form composite image, according to information provided by witness or victim. Operates photocopy or similar machine to reproduce composite image. Draws moles, scars, and other identifying marks, using pens, pencils, and other artist's work aids, to retouch copy. Alters copy of composite image until witness or victim is satisfied that composite is best possible representation of suspect. Classifies and codes components of image, using established system, to help identify suspect. Searches, or helps witness or victim to search, police photograph records, using classification and coding system, to determine if existing photograph of suspect is available.
GOE: 01.06.01 STRENGTH: L GED: R4 M3 L3 SVP: 6 DLU: 86

970.381-010 COLORIST, PHOTOGRAPHY (photofinishing) alternate titles: tinter, photograph
Applies oil colors to portrait photographs to produce natural, lifelike appearance, according to specifications, using cotton swabs and brushes: Dips cotton swab in photographic colors, and applies color onto face of portrait freehand. Wipes excess color from portrait to produce specified shade, using cotton swab. Applies color to shaded spots of face, cheeks, and lips, using cotton-tipped wooden stick, and rubs color to blend with color previously applied. Applies color to eyes, using camel's hair spotting brush. May color scenic or other photographs.
GOE: 01.06.03 STRENGTH: S GED: R3 M1 L2 SVP: 6 DLU: 77

970.381-014 DECORATOR, MANNEQUIN (fabrication, nec)
Paints facial expressions on mannequins according to established standards, using artists' brushes and airbrush: Inspects mannequin heads to detect imperfections, such as scratches, chips, and cracks and discards defective heads. Mixes paint for eyes, brows, lips, and cheeks according to established formulas. Brushes paint on specified areas of mannequin to create lifelike appearance, using sample mannequin as guide. Applies paint to cheeks of mannequin, using airbrush. Measures and cuts eyelash strips, using rule and scissors. Attaches eyelash to mannequin, using pins. Sprays preservative coating on mannequin, using airbrush.
GOE: 01.06.03 STRENGTH: L GED: R3 M2 L2 SVP: 6 DLU: 77

970.381-018 LAY-OUT FORMER (business ser.)
Prepares advertising layout for reproduction according to customer specifications, utilizing knowledge of display techniques: Cuts out and trims photograph, drawing, or color sketch in order to create balanced layout and focus consumer attention on advertisement, using cutting tools and stencils. Mounts layout units on backing material and draws lines to indicate position of units, using pen.

Draws functional and decorative borders around layout, using marking and measuring instruments. Positions hand-lettered copy on layout. Writes reproduction instructions outside layout border.
GOE: 01.06.03 STRENGTH: S GED: R4 M2 L3 SVP: 7 DLU: 77

970.381-022 PAINTER, HAND (any industry) alternate titles: artist; decorator; filler-in tinter
Paints decorative freehand designs on objects, such as pottery, cigarette cases, and lampshades, using handbrushes: Sketches design, using pencil or permanent ink. Grinds colors on pottery tile, using palette knife, to mix colors and oils to desired consistency. Paints freehand or within sketched design, using mixed colors, or applies pure colors, one over another, to produce desired shade, allowing time for drying between applications. May stipple (create designs by dabbing dots on ware). May trace design prior to painting or sketch guidelines for decals and be designated Sketch Liner (pottery & porc.).
GOE: 01.06.03 STRENGTH: S GED: R4 M2 L3 SVP: 7 DLU: 77

970.381-026 PAINTER, SIGN (any industry) alternate titles: letterer
Designs, lays out, and paints letters and designs to create signs, using measuring and drawing instruments, brushes, and handtools: Reads work orders to determine type of sign specified, work procedures, and materials required. Sketches design on paper, using drawing instruments, such as angles, rulers, and shading pencils. Lays out design on plastic, silk, or tin to prepare stencil, or on paper to draw pounce pattern, using measuring and drawing instruments. Sketches or follows pattern to draw design or lettering onto objects, such as billboards and trucks, using stencils and measuring and drawing instruments. Brushes paint, lacquer, enamel, or japan over stencil, or paints details, background, and shading to fill in outline or sketch of sign, using paintbrush or airbrush. When painting window signs, draws outline of sign on outside window, using chalk, or dusts pounce pattern to mark outline and paints inside of window following drawing or outline, using brush. When making gold or silver leaf signs, forms sign by either of following methods: (1) Paints sign, positions leaf over fresh paint, and removes excess leaf after sign has dried, using cotton swab and knife blade. (2) Paints inside of window with watersize (glue), applies leaf, and paints sign in reverse on back of leaf, using paintbrush or airbrush. May cut out letters and apply background coating to construct and prepare signs, using tinning shears. May project layout image on paper and trace outline of design, using projector and electric needle. May specialize in maintenance of signs along railroad right-of-way and be designated Painter, Sign, Maintenance (r.r. trans.).
GOE: 01.06.03 STRENGTH: L GED: R4 M3 L3 SVP: 7 DLU: 77

970.381-030 RETOUCHER, PHOTOENGRAVING (print. & pub.)
Touches up photoengraving film reproductions of sketches or photographs to eliminate processing defects and distortions in design, or to create special effects on reproductions, utilizing knowledge of lithographic techniques: Compares film negatives or positives with original to locate portions of image, such as dots and lines that were lost during processing, spots on negatives or positives, and excessively dark or light tone values on film. Paints in lines and dots that were lost during processing, using brush, pen, or sponge and opaque. Scratches out spots and undesirable portions of image, using knife and pin. Paints in additional lines or dots to increase intensity of image on film or scratches out lines or dots to reduce intensity, following colors on original to restore specified tone values. May sketch designs on transparent paper preparatory to transferring to film. May retouch, correct, and create special effects on reproductions of photoengraved materials, using computer graphics system, and be designated Computer-Assisted Retoucher, Photoengraving (print. & pub.).
GOE: 01.06.01 STRENGTH: S GED: R3 M3 L3 SVP: 7 DLU: 86

970.381-034 SPOTTER, PHOTOGRAPHIC (photofinishing)
Covers or spots out imperfections on photographic prints, using gloved finger, brush, or pencil: Positions print under viewing light or on illuminated table and examines print to detect defects, such as surface blemishes, dust spots, and uneven margins. Selects premixed paint or mixes paint, using color charts, when repairing color prints. Applies paint to defective area of color print, using gloved finger or artists' brush. Shades light areas on black-and-white prints, using pencil. Rubs surface of photograph with cloth to remove debris and reduce gloss. Trims edges of print to enhance appearance, using scissors or paper cutter. Places prints in customer bag and records number per bag or mounts print in specified frame. May retouch film negatives and be designated Negative Spotter (photofinishing).
GOE: 01.06.03 STRENGTH: S GED: R3 M2 L1 SVP: 5 DLU: 77

970.381-038 STENCIL CUTTER (railroad equip.)
Designs, lays out, and cuts letters for stenciling railroad cars, according to specifications, using precision measuring and drawing instruments and handtools: Draws letter designs on stencil paper, using rule, triangle, T-square and pen or pencil. Brushes shellac and linseed oil on both sides of stencil paper to stiffen and preserve stencil. Cuts out letters, using knife or stencil-cutting machine. Constructs wood stencil frame, using miter box, saw, and hammer. Tacks stencil onto frame, using hammer or staple gun. May apply protective coating to exterior surfaces of locomotives, fixtures, and buildings, using brush, spray gun, or paint rollers. May stencil letters on cars, using brush or spray gun and be designated Car Letterer (railroad equip.).
GOE: 01.06.03 STRENGTH: L GED: R4 M3 L3 SVP: 7 DLU: 77

970.381-042 TYPE COPYIST (machinery mfg.)
Draws and cuts out type characters of plastic, such as letters, numbers, and logos for use in manufacturing phototypesetting type disks, using drawing and cutting instruments: Searches reference sources to determine availability of characters in type style specified on orders. Reproduces reference copies of new characters required to obtain working copies, using automatic film developer. Places tracing paper over working copies, and traces and draws new characters, using pencil and triangle. Measures width, thickness, and spacing of characters, using optical and other measuring instruments, and pencils in or erases markings of characters as necessary to arrive at specified size and spacing requirements. Places tracing paper with finalized characters in light box, positions plastic sheets over light box, and cuts plastic following character outlines on tracing paper to obtain plastic characters, using cutting tools and metal guides. Records identity of characters on card for filing with reference source and routes characters for further processing.
GOE: 01.06.03 STRENGTH: S GED: R4 M3 L3 SVP: 7 DLU: 86

970.581-010 MUSIC GRAPHER (print. & pub.) alternate titles: music autographer
Transcribes music symbols and lyrics from manuscript to sheet music master copy, using pen and ink, ink pad, rules, dies, and straightedge: Draws evenly spaced horizontal lines (staff lines) on master copy, using rule, straightedge, and pen. Reads manuscript to determine word and symbol dies needed. Presses dies in ink pad and transcribes words and symbols to master copy to prepare copy for reproduction.
GOE: 01.06.03 STRENGTH: S GED: R3 M2 L3 SVP: 6 DLU: 77

970.661-010 ENGROSSER (profess. & kin.) alternate titles: calligrapher; script artist
Letters formal documents, such as diplomas, testimonials, charters, citations, and appointments, using pen and ink. May design and cut script and display type faces for reproduction purposes. When designing and rendering borders, scrollwork, and initial letters for book or page, may be designated Illuminator (profess. & kin.).
GOE: 01.06.03 STRENGTH: S GED: R3 M2 L2 SVP: 8 DLU: 77

970.661-014 LETTERER (profess. & kin.) alternate titles: commercial artist, lettering
Paints or draws precise lettering to be reproduced in advertisements, books, and other printed materials, using lettering pen or brush and determining lettering design from layout sketches and instructions. May design lettering when style of letters is not specified.
GOE: 01.06.03 STRENGTH: S GED: R3 M2 L2 SVP: 6 DLU: 77

970.664-010 PAINTER HELPER, SIGN (any industry)
Assists PAINTER, SIGN (any industry) to lay out and paint letters and designs to make signs, using handtools: Cleans display boards or other display surfaces to remove foreign matter and rough places, using scraper or scouring brush. Beats dust bag against stencil on display area to create pounce pattern. Traces over pounce pattern to prepare outline for PAINTER, SIGN (any industry) to follow, using pencil. Applies coat of base paint to display surface and paints background of display, using brushes and hand rollers. May mix paint according to established formulas. Performs other duties as described under HELPER (any industry) Master Title.
GOE: 01.06.03 STRENGTH: L GED: R3 M2 L3 SVP: 5 DLU: 77

970.681-010 BEN-DAY ARTIST (print. & pub.) alternate titles: tint layer
Applies benday tints (shadings in form of dots of different intensities) to drawings or to zinc or aluminum plates with inked screen or pattern: Positions mask (protective covering) over parts of drawing or plate not to be shaded, or brushes protective coating over those parts as determined by inspection of copy. Applies ink to screen or pattern, places screen or pattern over drawing or plate, and applies pressure to transfer ink from screen, using roller or burnisher. Washes ink and protective coating from parts of drawing not to be shaded.
GOE: 01.06.03 STRENGTH: L GED: R3 M1 L2 SVP: 6 DLU: 77

970.681-014 COLORER (print. & pub.)
Colors by hand or sprays designs on cards, calendars, maps, and related articles, using colored inks and pens or airbrush, following instructions or working drawings: Applies color to article by stencil or freehand method, depending on article to be colored. May mix and blend paints. May paint monograms on stationery and sprinkle metallic powder over paint and be designated Bronzer (print. & pub.). May be designated according to article colored as Map Colorer (print. & pub.).
GOE: 01.06.03 STRENGTH: S GED: R3 M1 L2 SVP: 4 DLU: 77

970.681-018 INKER AND OPAQUER (motion picture)
Traces drawings prepared by CARTOONIST, MOTION PICTURES (motion picture; radio-tv broad.) and paints tracing to render drawing opaque, using tracing pen and brush: Positions celluloid sheet over original drawing. Traces original in ink on celluloid. Reverses celluloid and brushes thin coat of opaquing paint on reverse side to render drawing opaque.
GOE: 01.06.03 STRENGTH: S GED: R3 M1 L1 SVP: 7 DLU: 77

970.681-022 MANUGRAPHER (fabrication, nec)
Traces and paints advertising material on poster paper, using projector, brushes, and drawing instruments: Projects outline of advertisement on paper, using opaque projector, and traces magnified drawing of advertisement, using pencil. Applies paint to drawing according to color chart, using artists' brushes. Prints lettering on advertisement, using T-square, straightedge, and artists' brushes.
GOE: 01.06.03 STRENGTH: S GED: R3 M2 L2 SVP: 4 DLU: 77

970.681-026 PAINTER, ANIMATED CARTOONS (motion picture; radio-tv broad.)

Applies premixed color paints on back of inked celluloids to depict animated cartoon characters, using brush: Scans celluloid on which characters have been drawn to determine number codes of paints required. Brushes paint within outline of character, according to number code specified.
GOE: 01.06.03 STRENGTH: S GED: R3 M1 L1 SVP: 4 DLU: 77

970.681-030 PAINTER, PLATE (print. & pub.) alternate titles: plate colorer

Paints colors on zinc plates, using brushes and watercolors, following colors in original design, to guide PANTOGRAPHER (print. & pub.) in transferring design to cloth-printing rollers.
GOE: 01.06.03 STRENGTH: S GED: R3 M1 L2 SVP: 6 DLU: 77

971   PHOTOENGRAVING OCCUPATIONS

This group includes occupations concerned with reproducing line or continuous tone copy on metallic printing plates for use in letterpress printing, using photoetching process; mounting and photographing copy; developing latent images on plates; and etching plates to leave raised printing surface. Group also includes occupations concerned with the fabrication and assembly of silk screen stencils, using photoetching process.

971.131-010 SUPERVISOR, PHOTOENGRAVING (print. & pub.)

Supervises and coordinates activities of workers engaged in production of photoengraved printing plates by processes, such as photographing, developing, printing, and etching: Trains workers in techniques of photoengraving processes. Examines finished printing plates to ensure conformance with company standards or customer specifications, using magnifying glass. Requisitions parts, supplies, and materials and submits cost data to management for budget planning. Performs other duties as described under SUPERVISOR (any industry) Master Title.
GOE: 01.06.01 STRENGTH: L GED: R4 M3 L3 SVP: 8 DLU: 77

971.131-014 SUPERVISOR, SCREEN MAKING (textile)

Supervises and coordinates activities of workers engaged in preparing (by photographic process) and repairing screens used in printing textile materials: Confers with other supervisors to coordinate interdepartmental work flow, to determine type new screens to be produced, and estimate costs for repairing used screens. Trains new employees in techniques of photographic screen reproduction and repair or assigns employee to experienced worker for training. Interviews and hires personnel for department. Performs other duties as described under SUPERVISOR (any industry) Master Title.
GOE: 05.10.05 STRENGTH: M GED: R4 M3 L3 SVP: 8 DLU: 77

971.261-010 ETCHER, HAND (print. & pub.)

Etches images (designs) on surface of printing rollers coated with photo or acid resist on which images have been transferred photographically or engraved pantographically, utilizing knowledge of colors, fabrics, and etching and printing techniques: Studies design sheet to determine etching requirements based on colors in design, type and weight of fabric, and printing sequence. Lifts roller onto brackets of rinsing vat with aid of ETCHER HELPER, HAND (print. & pub.). Tapes ends of roller with masking tape to limit etching to specified width. Cleans rollers preparatory to etching, using sponge, cleaning chemicals, and water. Transfers roller from rinsing vat to acid vat with aid of ETCHER HELPER, HAND (print. & pub.), using electric hoist. Turns valve to agitate acid solution with compressed air and starts machine to rotate roller in solution. Periodically removes roller from acid bath, measures etch with depth gauge, and moves fingers over surface of roller and scans etching through magnifying lens to detect processing defects, such as pinholes and collapsing ground lines. Processes roller through series of acid baths to increase depth of etch and broaden ground lines without collapsing top (unengraved portion) of design. Verifies depth of etch, using depth gauge. Scratches charcoal into etched cavities to make ground lines stand out and examines engraving to determine whether roller will print with desired effect. Transfers etched roller to cleaning vats, starts machine to spin roller in cleaning solution, and lowers brush to surface of spinning roller to remove acid-resistant coating. Dilutes acid with water to obtain etching chemicals of specified concentration.
GOE: 01.06.01 STRENGTH: M GED: R4 M2 L3 SVP: 6 DLU: 77

971.381-010 ETCHER APPRENTICE, PHOTOENGRAVING (print. & pub.) alternate titles: etcher apprentice

Performs duties as described under APPRENTICE (any industry) Master Title.
GOE: 01.06.01 STRENGTH: L GED: R4 M2 L4 SVP: 8 DLU: 77

971.381-014 ETCHER, PHOTOENGRAVING (print. & pub.)

Etches metal photographic plates to produce photoengraved printing plates, using etching machines, handtools, and chemicals: Mixes caustic or acid solutions according to type metal plate being etched. Brushes protective (resist) solution on back and edges of metal plate to protect plate during etching process. Brushes protective (resist) powder over photographic emulsion on plate to protect printing design. Bakes plate to adhere powder to design, using gas heating plate. Mounts plate in etching machine and starts machine that sprays acid or caustic solution against plate to etch (eat away) areas not protected by resist solution or powder. Removes and measures plate to determine depth of etching,

using depth gauge, and remounts plate in machine when etching has not attained specified depth. Washes and scrubs etched plates to remove resist solutions and photographic emulsion, using brush and caustic solution. Dries plates, using chamois cloth. Matches colors with original artwork of multicolor photographic plates to produce balanced color valves, applying knowledge of photographic printing process. May weigh plates before and after etching to determine amounts of etching solutions to be added to machine, using scales. May be designated according to type of plate etched as Copper Etcher (print. & pub.); Zinc Etcher (print. & pub.).
GOE: 01.06.01 STRENGTH: L GED: R4 M2 L4 SVP: 8 DLU: 77

971.381-022 PHOTOENGRAVER (print. & pub.) alternate titles: engraving operator; photolith operator

Photographs copy, develops negatives, and prepares photosenitized metal plates, such as copper, zinc, aluminum, and magnesium for use in printing, using photography and developing equipment and engravers' handtools: Positions copy on copy board of darkroom camera and exposes film to copy. Fastens scoured metal plate to *whirling machine* table or suspension hooks, pours photosensitizing solution on plate, and starts machine which rotates plate to distribute and dry solution evenly over plate surface. Exposes negative and plate to bright light in vacuum type printing frame to transfer image onto plate. Rolls ink onto exposed plate and washes unexposed and unfixed emulsion from plate, using running water and cotton pad to expose bare metal. Places developed plate in acid bath or etching machine to erode unprotected metal to specified depth. Mounts etched plates on wood blocks, using hammer and nails or on metal base, using thermosetting adhesive to raise printing surface type to specified height. Removes excess metal from nonprinting areas of cut, using routing machine [ROUTER (print. & pub.)]. Cuts mortises in mounted plates, using power drill and jigsaw, for insertion of type or other cuts. Modifies and repairs finished plates, using engravers' handtools, etching brush, and acid. May be designated according to type of plate made as Plate Maker, Zinc (print. & pub.).
GOE: 01.06.01 STRENGTH: L GED: R4 M3 L3 SVP: 8 DLU: 77

971.381-026 PHOTOENGRAVER APPRENTICE (print. & pub.)

Performs duties as described under APPRENTICE (any industry) Master Title.
GOE: 01.06.01 STRENGTH: L GED: R4 M3 L3 SVP: 8 DLU: 77

971.381-030 PHOTOENGRAVING FINISHER (print. & pub.) alternate titles: plate finisher, photoengraving

Blocks out, re-etches, or intensifies designs to refine or repair copper, zinc, aluminum, and magnesium photoengraved printing plates according to copy and specifications, using artist's brushes and hand engraving and burnishing tools: Applies chalk to engraved surface and examines cut under magnifying glass to detect damaged halftone dots and evaluate quality of etching against copy. Outlines images, cuts border, blocks out backgrounds, and raises halftone dots, using engraving tools. Burnishes high halftone dots to correct defects in printing quality and contrast of cut, using burnishing tools. Repairs breaks in type, using handtools. May reetch or reengrave photographic plates to correct color tone valves or to intensify designs, using etching machine or engraver's handtools. May make proofs of completed monochrome and multicolor plates [PROOF-PRESS OPERATOR (print. & pub.)].
GOE: 01.06.01 STRENGTH: L GED: R4 M2 L2 SVP: 8 DLU: 77

971.381-034 PHOTOENGRAVING PRINTER (print. & pub.) alternate titles: proof-plate maker; stripper and printer

Exposes film or glass negatives or positives to artificial light to transfer image onto photosensitive metal plates used for printing, applying knowledge of photographic and layout techniques, using photographic equipment, handtools, and cutting machines: Washes plate to remove foreign matter, using brush, abrasive, and running water. Pours photosensitive solution onto face of plate and distributes solution evenly, using *whirling machine*. Positions sensitized plate in contact with photographic negative under vacuum frame and directs lights through negative for specified time to print image on sensitized coating of plate. Rolls ink onto face of plate or immerses plate in developing solution and washes with water to remove coating which has not been affected by light. Dusts ink-developed plates with protective powder and heats plates over gas flame to produce surface resistant to etching acid. Surprints line negatives over halftone print to introduce type or other solid matter and combines several subjects stripped to separate flats by successive printing onto plate in register. Cuts metal plates to size, using squaring shear, circle saw, or bandsaw. May mix chemicals. May strip negatives [STRIPPER (print. & pub.)].
GOE: 01.06.01 STRENGTH: L GED: R4 M2 L2 SVP: 8 DLU: 77

971.381-038 PHOTOENGRAVING PROOFER (print. & pub.) alternate titles: prover

Proves printing quality and register of photoengraved printing plates, using hand or power driven flatbed or cylinder press, and prepares data sheet on color matching or ink modification to improve printing quality and register according to copy or customer specifications: Clamps plates to press, applies ink to rollers, and positions guides, grippers, and fingers to guide paper through press. Wraps packing sheets and tympan around cylinder to form cushion. Cuts and pastes overlays under tympan sheet to increase impression of low areas. Depresses pedal to open grippers, inserts blank sheet, and turns crank or starts motor to print set of proofs for progressive proof book for both black and white and color plates. Prepares data on color matching and ink modification to guide

pressman. Examines proofs to determine printing quality of dots and lines, using magnifier, and marks corrections, such as reetching and additional finishing. May be designated according to work proofed as Proofer, Black And White (print. & pub.); Proofer, Color (print. & pub.).
GOE: 05.05.13 STRENGTH: L GED: R4 M2 L2 SVP: 8 DLU: 77

971.381-040 PHOTOENGRAVING-PROOFER APPRENTICE (print. & pub.) alternate titles: proofer apprentice
Performs duties as described under APPRENTICE (any industry) Master Title.
GOE: 05.05.13 STRENGTH: L GED: R4 M2 L2 SVP: 8 DLU: 77

971.381-046 SCREEN MAKER, TEXTILE (textile)
Prepares stencils used in screen printing of textile materials: Assembles prefabricated parts to construct silk screen frame, using handtools and wing nuts. Clamps frame and silk screen material in stretching machine and activates machine that stretches screen material over frame. Glues screen to frame and cuts excess material from around frame, using glue applicator and scissors. Coats screen with photosensitive emulsion, using brush. Positions negative on glass bed of photoprint machine and centers screen over negative. Activates photoprint machine that exposes screen and negative to high intensity light to develop pattern on screen. Washes unexposed emulsion from screen, using water and hose. Applies resist coating to screen to protect pattern, using brush, and removes resist coating from open areas of pattern, using suction machine.
GOE: 05.10.05 STRENGTH: M GED: R4 M2 L2 SVP: 7 DLU: 77

971.381-050 STRIPPER (print. & pub.) alternate titles: negative assembler; negative turner
Strips photographic negative from film base and mounts negative on glass plate or platemaking *flat* to be used in preparing photoengraving plates, using art layout, blueprint, and handtools: Examines negative to detect defective areas, using lighted viewing table. Spots or blocks out defective areas, using opaque and brush. Pours rubber solution and collodion over film base to toughen negative. Dries base, using blotter, and cuts negative to size, using knife and straightedge. Immerses glass or film base in acid bath to loosen negative. Strips negative from base. Mounts and aligns negative on glass plate or platemaking flat, according to art layout, blueprint, and color register. Rubs negative to remove excess water and to ensure adhesion to plate, using blotter. May control equipment to produce photographic negatives preparatory to stripping. May be designated according to type of negative stripped as Stripper, Black And White (print. & pub.); Stripper, Color (print. & pub.).
GOE: 01.06.01 STRENGTH: S GED: R4 M2 L3 SVP: 8 DLU: 77

971.381-054 STRIPPER APPRENTICE (print. & pub.) alternate titles: negative-turner apprentice; stripper-and-opaquer apprentice
Performs duties as described under APPRENTICE (any industry) Master Title.
GOE: 01.06.01 STRENGTH: S GED: R4 M2 L3 SVP: 8 DLU: 77

971.382-014 PHOTOGRAPHER, PHOTOENGRAVING (electron. comp.; print. & pub.) alternate titles: contact-frame operator; engraving photographer
Sets up and operates camera to photograph drawings, sketches, or other material to produce negatives for transfer to printing plates, rollers, or printed circuit boards: Mounts copy on holder, aligning centerline on copy with centerline on holder. Studies copy and order sheet to determine photographic techniques required to transfer desired effect onto film, according to plate or roller dimensions, type of design, colors in design, and engraving requirements. Computes camera settings required to reproduce sketch to specified scale according to dimensions of printing plates or rollers. Focuses camera, compensating for difference in size and distortions in copy. Measures opening in back of camera to verify settings, using steel tape. Positions film on vacuum board, closes board against back of camera, and locks board in position. Arranges arc lamps for even distribution of light and exposes film for specified length of time. Removes exposed film from camera and develops film in series of developing, rinsing, and fixing baths, or using automatic film processing equipment. Compares developed film with design to determine whether desired effect has been reproduced. Hangs film on line to dry. When producing negatives for halftone printing, inserts screen in front of film to reduce copy to dots for reproduction. When producing multicolor prints, fits color filters over lens. May process sensitized metal plates for subsequent etching [PHOTOENGRAVING PRINTER (print. & pub.)].
GOE: 01.06.01 STRENGTH: L GED: R4 M3 L3 SVP: 8 DLU: 77

971.382-018 REPEAT-PHOTOCOMPOSING-MACHINE OPERATOR (print. & pub.) alternate titles: composer
Operates photocomposing machine to repeat designs on film for transfer to sensitized copper rollers used in printing such products as wallpaper and oilcloth: Sketches design layout on worksheet according to sequence in which design is to be repeated around roller. Computes machine setting required to repeat design on film as laid out on worksheet, using standard formulas and tables. Mounts positive print on negative frame, aligning centerline on print with centerline on frame, and tapes print in position. Masks area around print with black paper. Centers film on backboard of machine and tapes film in position. Lifts backboard against negative frame and locks in position. Moves negative frame in position for exposing film to first repeat of design, following computations on worksheet. Starts compressor that creates vacuum between negative frame and backboard, drawing backboard against negative frame. Exposes

film to light through positive print for specified time, transferring image from print to film. Repeats process until design has been repeated along vertical and horizontal plane of film a specified number of times. Removes exposed film from machine and processes film through series of chemical baths to develop, fix, and rinse film. Examines developed film for exposure errors and misalignment of repeated designs. Agitates film in chemical solution to etch out overexposed film. Hangs developed film on line to dry.
GOE: 01.06.01 STRENGTH: L GED: R4 M3 L3 SVP: 7 DLU: 77

971.684-010 BLOCKER II (print. & pub.) alternate titles: film masker; film painter; negative checker
Examines photographic negatives for defects and paints over defects preparatory to transferring images to sensitized zinc plates or copper rollers, using measuring instruments, brushes, and handtools: Spreads negatives over illuminated table and marks register points on negatives, using straightedge, triangle, and scriber. Examines negatives to detect pinholes and to locate line along which design will be fitted around sensitized rollers or mounted on zinc plates. Masks (blocks out) pinholes and extra images on film, using brushes and opaque. Scratches out undesirable spots and lines, using knife or pin. Compares masked films with original design to verify conformance to specifications. May lay out and print customer's legend on films. May correct spelling, punctuation, and grammatical errors on negative proofs, using standard proofreading symbols.
GOE: 06.03.02 STRENGTH: S GED: R3 M2 L2 SVP: 4 DLU: 77

971.684-014 STAGER (print. & pub.) alternate titles: roller painter
Paints out specified portions of etched design on printing rollers to prevent further etching or paints around images on printing rollers to cover pinholes and scratches, using brushes and acid-resistant paint.
GOE: 05.12.14 STRENGTH: S GED: R3 M2 L1 SVP: 4 DLU: 77

971.685-010 ROLLER-PRINT TENDER (print. & pub.) alternate titles: roller printer
Tends equipment to transfer design images from master film to copper printing rollers: Marks register points on ends of rollers, using straightedge and scriber. Inserts mandrel through roller and lifts roller onto brackets of sensitizing machine, using hoist. Starts machine that rotates roller. Turns valve to spray roller with water and cleans coated roller, using cloth, cleaning solution, and pumice. Dries rollers, using paper towel. Fills spray gun with sensitizing solution and turns valve to spray solution onto rotating roller. Transfers sensitized roller to copy machine, using electric hoist. Positions master film over roller and aligns register points on film with register points on roller. Covers master film with sheet of transparent film and engages ends of transparent film in machine drive. Tapes master film to transparent film, using masking tape. Lifts ultraviolet light frame into position over roller and starts machine that rotates sensitized roller and film, exposing sensitized roller to images on film. Transfers exposed roller to developing bath, using electric hoist. Turns roller in developing solution for specified time to dissolve sensitized coating from areas of roller that were exposed to light through film. Transfers developed roller to dye bath and turns roller in bath to dye unexposed area of roller. Transfers dyed roller to wash vat and rinses excess dye from roller. Dries roller, using cloth.
GOE: 05.10.05 STRENGTH: V GED: R3 M2 L1 SVP: 3 DLU: 77

971.687-010 ETCHER HELPER, HAND (print. & pub.)
Assists ETCHER, HAND (print. & pub.) in etching designs on copper printing rollers: Trucks rollers from storage area to etching room. Inserts mandrel through roller and screws collar onto mandrel to hold roller in position. Assists ETCHER, HAND (print. & pub.) in lifting rollers onto machine brackets and in transferring rollers from one vat to another. Turns crank on mandrel to rotate rollers in rinsing and etching vats. Cleans solvent and acid-resistant coating from etched rollers by rubbing with sawdust or using absorbent cloth. Removes mandrel from etched rollers and trucks rollers to mending bench. Drains vats of spent etching solutions and performs other duties as described under HELPER (any industry) Master Title.
GOE: 05.12.03 STRENGTH: H GED: R2 M1 L1 SVP: 2 DLU: 77

972 LITHOGRAPHERS AND RELATED OCCUPATIONS

This group includes occupations concerned with reproducing line or continuous tone copy on metallic printing plates for use in lithographic printing using lithographic process; photographing, scanning and assembling copy to produce film; and exposing and developing latent images on plate.

972.137-010 SUPERVISOR, PREPRESS (print. & pub.) alternate titles: supervisor, prep
Supervises and coordinates activities of workers engaged in photography, image assembly, platemaking, and other prepress activities in preparation for offset lithographic printing: Examines work to ensure conformity to job specifications and company standards. Maintains inventory of supplies and materials, such as film, layout sheets, and plates. Oversees maintenance and repair of machines and equipment. Performs other duties as described under SUPERVISOR (any industry) Master Title. May perform minor maintenance and repair of machines and equipment. May be designated according to department supervised as Camera Supervisor (print. & pub.); Scanner Supervisor (print. & pub.); Supervisor, Offset-Plate Preparation (print. & pub.); Supervisor, Stripping (print. & pub.); Systems Manager (print. & pub.).

GOE: 01.06.01 STRENGTH: L GED: R4 M4 L4 SVP: 8 DLU: 89

972.281-010 DOT ETCHER (print. & pub.) alternate titles: color corrector; lithographer retoucher; process artist; tone artist

Increases or reduces size of photographic dots by chemical or photomechanical methods to make color corrections on halftone negatives or positives to be used in preparation of lithographic printing plates: Examines film on light table to determine specified color and color balance, using magnifying glass or densitometer. Compares proof print of color separation negative or positive with customer's original sample or copy and standard color chart to determine accuracy of reproduction. Identifies and marks color discrepancies on print and film. Prepares dyes or other chemical solutions according to standard formulas and applies solution to inaccurately colored areas of film to correct color by chemical method. Blocks out or modifies color shades of film, using template, brushes, and opaque. Prepares photographic masks to protect areas of film not needing correction, using contact frame and automatic film processor or by manually cutting masking material, to correct color by photomechanical method. Determines extent of correction and exposure length needed based on experience or predetermined exposure and color charts. Places masks over separation negatives or positives and exposes film for specified time, using contact frame and automatic film processor to reduce size of photographic dots to increase or reduce color. Applies opaque to defective areas of film to block out blemishes and pinholes.

GOE: 01.06.01 STRENGTH: L GED: R4 M3 L2 SVP: 8 DLU: 89

972.281-018 DOT ETCHER APPRENTICE (print. & pub.) alternate titles: lithographic retoucher apprentice; tone-artist apprentice

Performs duties as described under APPRENTICE (any industry) Master Title.

GOE: 01.06.01 STRENGTH: L GED: R4 M3 L2 SVP: 8 DLU: 77

972.281-022 STRIPPER, LITHOGRAPHIC I (print. & pub.) alternate titles: color stripper; commercial stripper; image assembler; process stripper

Plans composition of *film flat* according to customer's requirements, applying knowledge of film assembly; pieces together and positions negative or positive film on layout sheets; and makes composite film, using precision measuring instruments, artist's work aids and photographic equipment, to assemble multi- or single-color film flat used in production of lithographic printing plates: Examines materials received with order, such as pasteup, artwork, film, prints, or customer's instructions, to determine size and dimensions, number of colors on job, and camera work needed, such as number of base negatives, halftones, color separations (film for each primary color), and *screen tints*. Determines proportions needed to reduce or enlarge photographs and graphics to fit in designated areas of film flat and prevent color overlap, using calculator or proportion scale. Receives base negatives, halftones, and color separations from PHOTOGRAPHER, LITHOGRAPHIC (print. & pub.) 972.382-014 and SCANNER OPERATOR (print. & pub.) 972.282-010 to be used in composition of film flat. Touches up negatives to conceal pinholes and other imperfections, using artist's brush and opaque material, or examines positive film, using magnifier, and repairs broken lines and incomplete and missing half-tone dots, using needle and crayon pencil. Tapes layout sheet or grid to illuminated table and positions masking sheet and transparent plastic sheet over layout grid to prepare for positioning of film. Positions film negatives or positives on masking sheet or transparent plastic sheet according to predetermined reference marks on layout sheet and inserts illustrations, halftones, or four-color process negatives in windows of base negatives or complementary flats (flats that will be exposed onto same plate), using tape, triangles, straightedges, dividers, and magnifiers. Selects and inserts screen tints in film flat, using knowledge of dot percentages required to obtain specific colors. Cuts out masks, using razor blade, artist's knife, or mask cutting tool, and arranges negatives in order, to prepare for contact printing, plate exposure, or proof making. Aligns multiple negatives and masks over unexposed film in vacuum frame and activates light source to make negatives or positives for final film of each color. Determines or approves plans and page sequences to lay out job for specific printing press. Pieces together and aligns negatives or positives on masking sheet or transparent plastic sheet, applying knowledge acquired from experience in film assembly to assure register and fit with all units of color, to assemble film flat. Inverts assembled film flat on table and cuts windows behind image areas of negatives or positives, using razor blade or artist's knife, to allow exposure to plate or film. Routes completed negative or positive flat to proofing area for preparation of positive or negative proof. Examines proof returned by customer and makes corrections or remakes film to meet customer's specifications. Routes completed negative or positive flat to LITHOGRAPHIC PLATEMAKER (print. & pub.) 972.381-010 for preparation of positive or negative lithographic printing plate. May draw ruled lines and borders around negatives or positives, using scribing tools. May make proof from film flat to determine accuracy of flat.

GOE: 01.06.01 STRENGTH: L GED: R4 M3 L3 SVP: 8 DLU: 89

972.282-010 SCANNER OPERATOR (print. & pub.) alternate titles: electronic scanner operator; laser-beam-color-scanner operator

Analyzes original copy (material to be reproduced) and operates electronic scanner to produce color-separated positive or negative films for use in production of lithographic printing plates: Analyzes original copy to evaluate color density, gradation highlights, middle tones, and shadows, using densitometer and knowledge of light and color. Types on scanner keyboard or touches mouse to symbols on scanner video display unit to input software, or turns knobs or punches buttons to set scanner to specific color density, size, screen ruling, and exposure adjustments. Loads film into film holder, places holder in exposing chamber and starts automatic vacuum system mechanism that loads and secures film on scanner drum. Activates scanner to produce positive or negative films for each primary color and black in original copy. Unloads exposed film from scanner and places film in automatic processor to develop image on film. Inspects developed film for specified results and quality, using magnifying glass and scope, and forwards acceptable negatives or positives to STRIPPER, LITHOGRAPHIC (print. & pub.) I 972.281-022, PROOFER, PREPRESS (print. & pub.) 972.381-034, or customer. Performs tests to determine exposure adjustments on scanner and adjusts scanner controls until specified results are obtained. May position color transparency, negative, or reflection copy on scanning drum and mount drum and head on scanner.

GOE: 05.10.05 STRENGTH: L GED: R4 M3 L3 SVP: 7 DLU: 89

972.282-018 ELECTRONIC MASKING SYSTEM OPERATOR (print. & pub.) alternate titles: electronic plotting system operator

Operates computerized masking system to produce stripping masks used in production of offset lithographic printing plates: Positions artist's layout (comprehensive) on digitizing table of electronic masking system to prepare for data entry in system memory. Studies layout sheet to determine shapes of windows drawn on layout sheet. Selects options on menu of electronic masking system, such as shape, dimensions of designs to be drawn, register marks, and retrieval of stored designs. Touches symbol of option selected on menu with mouse (hand held input device) and presses button on mouse to activate option. Touches reference points of designs on layout sheet, using mouse, and presses button of mouse to enter coordinates of design in system memory. Views monitors for feedback and error prompts, for visual representations of work in progress, and for numerical information such as width of line and last point plotted. Presses button to transfer data from system memory to disk. Loads drafting unit with masking material to prepare for plotting and scoring of programmed figures or loads film into plotting drum to prepare for photographic mask exposure. Presses button to activate vacuum to hold masking material in place and to activate drafting unit that scores masking material with programmed figures or activates plotting drum to make photographic mask exposure. Removes scored masking material from drafting table, places material on light table and peels scored figures from masking material, using needle and tape, or removes film from plotting drum and puts film in automatic film processor, to create masks to be used by STRIPPER, LITHOGRAPHIC (print. & pub.) I 972.281-022. May operate electronic plotting system to draw artwork positions on pasteup.

GOE: 01.06.01 STRENGTH: L GED: R4 M3 L3 SVP: 8 DLU: 89

972.284-010 FILM FLAT INSPECTOR (print. & pub.)

Inspects *film flats* for quality, content, and positioning of elements at printing establishment: Places film flats and companion materials, such as artwork, pasteups, layouts, film, and corrected proofs, on light table and examines materials, using magnifying glass to view details in materials. Examines film flat label for identifying information, such as date and job number. Compares film flat to companion materials, using knowledge of film assembly, and measures film flat with ruler to verify conformance to specifications, such as positioning of pages in rotation for folding, trim marks, colors on pages, window sizes, and size, colors, and positioning of elements, such as halftones, screen tints, and type. Examines film flats for defects, such as holes or scratches on film, overlapping or unaligned elements, and incorrect dot percentages in halftones. Returns film flat to STRIPPER, LITHOGRAPHIC (print. & pub.) I 972.281-022 for corrections, or repairs defects, such as pinholes or incomplete and missing halftone dots, with opaque material or needle and crayon pencil.

GOE: 06.03.02 STRENGTH: L GED: R4 M3 L3 SVP: 7 DLU: 89

972.381-010 LITHOGRAPHIC PLATEMAKER (print. & pub.) alternate titles: platemaker

Exposes sensitized metal plate to positive or negative film, using vacuum frame, to produce offset lithographic printing plates: Punches holes in light-sensitive plate with register punch and inserts register pins in holes to prepare plate for contact with positive or negative film. Places plate on bed of vacuum frame and inserts positives or negatives on register pins to align positives or negatives with each other and with plate. Places masking paper on areas of plate not covered by positives or negatives to prevent exposure of those areas. Lowers top of vacuum frame onto plate and film assembly and activates vacuum to maintain contact between negative or positive film and plate. Sets timer to activate ultraviolet light that exposes plate to positives or negatives. Removes plate and film assembly from vacuum frame and places exposed plate in automatic processor to develop image and dry plate. Performs tests to determine time required for exposure by exposing plates and comparing exposure to gray scale (scale used to measure tone ranges). May replenish chemical solutions in automatic plate processor to maintain processor in working order. May expose plates, using step-and-repeat machines. May make proofs.

GOE: 01.06.01 STRENGTH: L GED: R4 M3 L3 SVP: 6 DLU: 89

972.381-014 LITHOGRAPHIC-PLATE-MAKER APPRENTICE (print. & pub.) alternate titles: lithographic-press-plate-maker apprentice, photomechanical

Performs duties as described under APPRENTICE (any industry) Master Title.

GOE: 01.06.01 STRENGTH: L GED: R4 M3 L3 SVP: 6 DLU: 77

972.381-018 SKETCH MAKER II (print. & pub.)

Sketches, photographs, and etches cloth designs on zinc plates in form that can be transferred to printing rollers by mechanical pantograph process, using precision measuring and drawing instruments, camera, and etching chemicals: Studies design and production sheet to determine number of times design will be repeated around roller, size of sketch, and number of plates required to complete sketch. Lays out reference lines on design according to location of one complete repeat of pattern and number of plates required to sketch pattern, using straightedge and pencil. Draws reference lines on zinc plates, using dividers, straightedge, and pencil. Places design under weighted door of camera and moves camera up graduated scale to enlarge pattern to specifications. Positions zinc plate on table beneath camera and aligns reference lines on plate with reference lines of reflected design. Traces around reflected outline of design, using diamond stylus, leaving specified spacing between colors to compensate for color, type of cloth, and etching process. Corrects flaws left in design by designer or artist, and reproduces design so that it will be practical for printing. Immerses sketched plate in acid solution to etch (deepen) lines of design. Washes etched plates, using water and brush. Records number of times design will be repeated around roller, number and size of plates in design, and spacings left between colors on production sheet.
GOE: 01.06.01 STRENGTH: S GED: R4 M2 L2 SVP: 7 DLU: 77

972.381-022 STRIPPER, LITHOGRAPHIC II (print. & pub.) alternate titles: book stripper; stripper, black and white; stripper-opaquer

Positions negative or positive film on layout sheets to assemble single or multiple color *film flats* used in production of lithographic printing plates, according to customer specifications, using precision measuring instruments and artist's work aids: Touches up negatives to conceal pinholes and other imperfections, using artist's brush and opaque material or examines positive film, using magnifier, and repairs broken lines and incomplete and missing halftone dots, using needle and crayon pencil. Tapes layout sheet or grid to illuminated table and positions masking sheet and transparent plastic sheet over layout sheet to prepare for positioning of film. Positions film negatives or positives on masking sheet or transparent plastic sheet according to predetermined reference marks on layout sheet and inserts halftones, *screen tints* or four-color process negatives in windows of base negatives or complementary flats (flats to be exposed onto same plate), using tape, triangles, straightedges, dividers, and magnifiers. Inverts assembled film flat on table and cuts windows behind image areas of negatives or positives, using razor blade or artist's knife to allow exposure to plate or film. Routes completed negative or positive flat to platemaking department for preparation of positive or negative lithographic printing plate or proof. May select screen tints to be inserted in film flat, using knowledge of dot percentages required to obtain specific colors. May draw ruled lines and borders around negatives or positives, using scribing tools.
GOE: 01.06.01 STRENGTH: L GED: R4 M3 L3 SVP: 7 DLU: 89

972.381-026 TRANSFERRER (print. & pub.) alternate titles: press-plate maker

Transfers images, by hand, from photographic negatives to zinc plates for printing by lithographic process: Covers surface of grained plates with coating of photosensitive chemicals, using brush, and allows plate to dry. Mounts negative and plate in camera and activates camera that exposes sensitized plate to strong artificial light through photographic negative for specified period of time, thus reproducing (transferring) image from negative to plate.
GOE: 01.06.01 STRENGTH: L GED: R3 M1 L1 SVP: 6 DLU: 77

972.381-030 PASTE-UP ARTIST (print. & pub.) alternate titles: keyliner; mechanical artist

Assembles typeset copy and artwork into pasteup for printing reproduction: Measures and marks board according to GRAPHIC DESIGNER (profess. & kin.) 141.061-018 or artist's layout to indicate position of artwork, typeset copy, page edges, folds, and colors, using ruler and drafting instruments. Measures artwork and layout space of artwork on pasteup and compares measurements, using ruler and proportion wheel to determine proportions needed to make reduced or enlarged photographic prints for pasteup. Cuts and trims typeset copy and artwork to specified size, applies adhesive, and aligns artwork and typeset copy on board, following position marks, and removes excess adhesive from board, using scissors, artist's knife, and drafting instruments. Tapes transparent plastic overlay to board, positions and applies copy to plastic, and applies masking film to artwork layout space on overlay to create clear space on negative where artwork can be added later by STRIPPER, LITHOGRAPHIC (print. & pub.) I 972.281-022. Indicates crop marks and enlargement or reduction measurements on photographs with grease pencil to prepare photographs for STRIPPER, LITHOGRAPHIC (print. & pub.) I and covers photographs with tissue paper to protect photographs. Tapes tracing paper to board to protect artwork and copy and writes specifications on tracing paper to provide information to PHOTOGRAPHER, LITHOGRAPHIC (print. & pub.) 972.382-014; STRIPPER, LITHOGRAPHIC (print. & pub.) I; and OFFSET-PRESS OPERATOR (print. & pub.) I 651.382-042. May make negatives or prints of artwork, using photographic equipment, to prepare artwork for pasteup. May operate phototypesetter to prepare typeset copy for pasteup. May operate electronic plotter to draw artwork positions on pasteup.
GOE: 01.06.01 STRENGTH: L GED: R4 M4 L3 SVP: 7 DLU: 89

972.381-034 PROOFER, PREPRESS (print. & pub.)

Makes single or multicolored prepress proofs of text and graphics, performing any combination of following duties: Places base material and color coated sheet or light sensitive film into laminating machine that transfers pigment from sheet or laminates light sensitive film to base. Exposes base to corresponding color-separated negative or positive film, using vacuum frame, and places color coated base in automatic processor that develops and reveals color image on base, or places light sensitive base into corresponding color bin of automatic toner machine that deposits powdered ink pigment onto image. Registers succeeding color negatives or positives over base, using magnifier or register device system, and repeats process to produce multicolor proof. Exposes film to proofing paper to make single-color proof. Exposes film to colored base material to produce overlay of each color, and assembles and aligns individual overlays on top of one another to form multicolor overlay proof. Compares test exposures to quality control color guides to determine data for exposure settings. Measures density levels of colors or color guides on proofs, using densitometer, and compares readings to set standards. Mixes powdered ink pigments, using ink matching book and measuring and mixing tools, to create nonstandard colors, and applies ink pigments to base by hand. Immerses exposed materials in chemical baths to hand-develop proofing materials. Method used to make proof is determined by brand of equipment and quality of proof required.
GOE: 05.10.05 STRENGTH: L GED: R3 M2 L3 SVP: 5 DLU: 89

972.381-038 PASTE-UP ARTIST APPRENTICE (print. & pub.)

Performs duties as described under APPRENTICE (any industry) Master Title.
GOE: 01.06.01 STRENGTH: L GED: R4 M4 L3 SVP: 7 DLU: 77

972.382-010 PHOTOGRAPHER APPRENTICE, LITHOGRAPHIC (print. & pub.) alternate titles: copy-camera-operator apprentice; lithographer apprentice; photolithographer apprentice

Performs duties as described under APPRENTICE (any industry) Master Title.
GOE: 01.06.01 STRENGTH: L GED: R4 M2 L3 SVP: 7 DLU: 77

972.382-014 PHOTOGRAPHER, LITHOGRAPHIC (print. & pub.) alternate titles: lithographic-camera operator; photolithographer; photolithographic process worker; process-camera operator

Sets up and operates horizontal or vertical process camera to photograph illustrations and printed material and produce film used in preparation of lithographic printing plates: Mounts material to be photographed on copyboard of camera and adjusts camera settings to enlarge or reduce size of copy to be reproduced. Selects and places screen over high contrast film in camera to reproduce image with dot pattern for halftone printing. Places color filters between lens and film to produce four-color separations. Performs exposure tests to determine line, halftone and color reproduction exposure lengths for various photographic factors, such as type of camera, screens, films, and light intensity. Measures degrees of darkness (density) of continuous tone images to be photographed, using densitometer, and enters readings into exposure control system of process camera to set exposure time for halftone images. Adjusts lens and copyboard for reduction or enlargement of copy and focus, adjusts lights, and exposes high contrast film for predetermined period of time. Places film in automatic film processor that develops, fixes, washes, and dries film. May immerse film in series of chemical baths to develop image on film and hang film on rack to dry for manual method of processing film. May measure original layouts and determine proportions needed to make reduced or enlarged photographic prints for pasteup.
GOE: 01.06.01 STRENGTH: L GED: R4 M2 L3 SVP: 7 DLU: 89

972.382-018 PHOTO MASK MAKER, ELECTRON-BEAM (electron. comp.) alternate titles: electron-beam operator

Operates computer-controlled electron-beam exposure equipment to transfer circuit pattern onto photoresist-coated photo mask plates for subsequent use in fabrication of semiconductor devices: Loads disk or tape of pattern information into equipment, and positions unexposed photo mask plate in vacuum chamber of equipment. Types commands to enter exposure specifications and production instructions and activate equipment that directs electron beam at specified locations on coated photo mask plate to expose photoresist. Develops and etches exposed photo mask plate, using automatic developing and etching equipment. Inspects pattern on photo mask plate for conformance to specifications, using microscope and specialized inspection devices.
GOE: 05.10.05 STRENGTH: L GED: R3 M2 L3 SVP: 6 DLU: 86

972.382-022 PHOTO MASK TECHNICIAN, ELECTRON-BEAM (electron. comp.)

Generates computer tape or disk of processing instructions for use in electron-beam fabrication of photo masks used in integrated circuit (IC) manufacture, using computer graphics system and software and applying knowledge of photo mask layout: Reviews work order and specification manuals to determine data required to lay out array (arrangement of integrated circuit layer patterns) for reproduction onto photo mask. Enters commands into computer, using keyboard, to retrieve from data file and display on display screen existing array format information. Calculates additional array information required, such as array center and coordinates, number of rows and columns in array, and location of test patterns in array, following specification manual and work order instructions. Locates file (computer tape) relating to specified IC layer and loads tape into computer tape drive. Enters specified commands into computer, using keyboard to retrieve IC layer pattern from file and display pattern on array format on computer display screen. Positions IC layer patterns and test

patterns within array format on display screen, using knowledge of photo mask layout and computer graphics. Enters electron-beam exposure instructions into computer and keys in commands to transfer array data and exposure instructions onto computer disk or tape for use by PHOTO MASK MAKER, ELECTRON-BEAM (electron. comp.) 972.382-018. May enter commands into computer, using keyboard, to transfer IC layer patterns onto hard copy (plots), using plotter peripheral equipment. May inspect plots of IC layer patterns for layout errors.
GOE: 05.10.05 STRENGTH: L GED: R3 M3 L3 SVP: 6 DLU: 86

972.384-014 PLATEMAKER, SEMICONDUCTOR PACKAGES (electron. comp.)
Prints and develops printing plates used in printing symbols and numbers on semiconductor packages: Types identifying symbols and numbers on paper or rubs transfer sheet to transfer symbols and numbers onto paper. Places paper containing identification information on camera grid. Places specified lens on camera holder and presses buttons and turns handles to adjust camera focus. Mounts film in guide slot of camera and pushes button to expose film to identify information. Removes exposed film from camera and places film in developer that automatically develops and dries negative. Inserts negative (containing image of identification information) and sheet of polymer into exposure machine. Activates machine to expose negative polymer sheet to print negative image on polymer and form printing plate. Removes polymer plate and places plate in envelope. Maintains production records and machines. May place semiconductor packages in oven to set or dry printing. May immerse printed packages in chemical solution to test durability of printing.
GOE: 05.10.05 STRENGTH: L GED: R3 M2 L3 SVP: 4 DLU: 86

972.681-010 MUSIC ENGRAVER (print. & pub.)
Engraves words and music on zinc plates used to print sheet music, following original manuscripts: Rules staff lines on plate, allowing for even margins. Stamps letters, words, and musical symbols in specified position on plate, using metal dies and hammer. Taps and scrapes engraved plates to smooth surface and prepare plates for use in printing presses, using ball peen hammers and hand scrapers.
GOE: 01.06.01 STRENGTH: S GED: R3 M1 L1 SVP: 6 DLU: 77

972.682-010 PLATE GRAINER (print. & pub.) alternate titles: plate preparer; zinc-plate grainer
Operates plate graining machine to roughen (grain) faces of flexible sheets of zinc or aluminum metal for use in offset-photolithographic printing: Operates power shear to cut sheets of aluminum and zinc to size, and clamps them to bed of graining machine tub (tray). Operates hydraulic lifting and tilting mechanism attached to machine to load and unload machine with specified amount of steel or wooden balls, water, and abrasive. Washes sediment from plates with water hose at end of graining cycle and places on conveyor for further washing under water jets and drying under heating unit. Examines each plate with magnifier at inspection table for uniformity, size, and structure of grain. Stacks plates in shipping crate. Rolls out and hammers used plates to remove gripper marks, dents, and bent corners. Lubricates machine and replaces worn bearings. May grain plates by wet or dry sandblasting. May feed plates through graining machine having reel-type nylon brush which roughens surface with abrasive and water. May grain plates with glass marbles.
GOE: 06.02.02 STRENGTH: L GED: R3 M2 L3 SVP: 7 DLU: 77

972.682-014 PLATE-GRAINER APPRENTICE (print. & pub.) alternate titles: stone-and-plate-preparer apprentice
Performs duties as described under APPRENTICE (any industry) Master Title.
GOE: 06.02.02 STRENGTH: L GED: R3 M2 L3 SVP: 7 DLU: 77

972.687-010 PLATE INSPECTOR (print. & pub.)
Inspects offset lithographic printing plates for quality and content at printing establishment: Visually examines plates for defects, such as spaces, spots, broken type, and crooked or overlapping halftones, and views film and *film flat* used to produce plates to determine cause of defect. Compares halftones and *screen tints* on plates to film flat, using magnifier, to detect overdevelopment or underdevelopment of plates. Measures plates with ruler and compares measurements and appearance of plates to prepress proofs to verify accuracy of positioning and presence of artwork and type for each color. Applies correcting solutions to plates or notifies supervisor of defects and suspected causes. Delivers plates meeting establishment criteria and companion materials, such as artwork, proofs, pasteups, film, and film flats, to press for printing.
GOE: 06.03.02 STRENGTH: L GED: R3 M2 L2 SVP: 5 DLU: 89

973   HAND COMPOSITORS, TYPESETTERS, AND RELATED OCCUPATIONS

This group includes occupations concerned with setting and distributing type by hand; making up and tearing down forms, including handset and machine-set type, mounted plates, and spacing material; locking forms; and pulling proofs. Occupations concerned with typesetting by word processing methods are found in Group 203.

973.137-010 SUPERVISOR, COMPOSING-ROOM (print. & pub.)
Supervises and coordinates activities of workers engaged in setting type by hand and machine for printing books, magazines, newspapers, catalogs, and pamphlets. Inspects typesetting operations to verify conformance with work order specifications. Performs duties as described under SUPERVISOR (any industry) Master Title.
GOE: 05.05.13 STRENGTH: L GED: R4 M2 L3 SVP: 7 DLU: 77

973.381-010 COMPOSITOR (print. & pub.) alternate titles: typesetter; typographer
Sets type by hand and machine, and assembles type and cuts in galley, for printing articles, headings, and other printed matter, determining type size, style, and compositional pattern from work order: Measures copy with line gauge to determine length of line. Sets composing stick to line length indicated on line gauge. Selects type from type case and sets it in compositional sequence, reading from copy. Inserts spacers between words or units to balance and justify lines. Transfers type from stick to galley when setup is complete. Inserts leads, slugs, or lines of quads between lines to adjust length of setup. Prepares proof copy of setup, using proof press. Examines proof for errors, corrects setup, and forwards it to imposing stone or bank. Cleans type after use and distributes it to specified boxes in type case. May set type to print copy that is unaccompanied by specifications, using knowledge of composition and printing processes. May be designated Job Compositor (print. & pub.) when setting type in commercial printing establishments or Ad Compositor (print. & pub.) when assembling type and cuts for display advertisements.
GOE: 05.05.13 STRENGTH: L GED: R4 M2 L3 SVP: 8 DLU: 77

973.381-014 COMPOSITOR APPRENTICE (print. & pub.) alternate titles: typesetter apprentice
Performs duties as described under APPRENTICE (any industry) Master Title.
GOE: 05.05.13 STRENGTH: L GED: R4 M2 L3 SVP: 8 DLU: 77

973.381-018 JOB PRINTER (print. & pub.) alternate titles: country printer; printer
Sets type according to copy and operates cylinder or automatic platen press to print complete job order: Selects type from type case and inserts type in printer's stick to reproduce material in copy. Inserts spacers between words and leads between lines. Slides type from stick into galley. Removes assembled type from galley and places type on composing stone. Places chase over type, inserts quoins, and locks chase to hold type. Lays form (type in locked chase) on bed of proof press, inks type, fastens sheet of paper to press roller, and pulls roller over form to make proof copy. Reads proof for errors and clarity of impression. Corrects errors by resetting type and improves impression by tapping face of type with hammer. Positions form (type in locked chase) on bed of press and tightens clamps, using wrench. Fills ink fountain and moves lever to adjust flow of ink. Sets feed guides according to size and thickness of paper. Runs proofsheet through press and examines sheet for clarity of impression. Pushes button to start press, examines printed sheets, and adjusts press when printing is defective. Cleans ink rollers at end of run.
GOE: 05.05.13 STRENGTH: M GED: R4 M2 L3 SVP: 8 DLU: 77

973.381-022 JOB-PRINTER APPRENTICE (print. & pub.) alternate titles: country-printer apprentice; printer's devil
Performs duties as described under APPRENTICE (any industry) Master Title.
GOE: 05.05.13 STRENGTH: M GED: R4 M2 L3 SVP: 8 DLU: 77

973.381-026 MAKE-UP ARRANGER (print. & pub.) alternate titles: stone hand
Arranges, groups, and locks galley setups of type, cuts, and headings in chases, according to dummy makeup sheet, for direct printing, reproduction proofs, or fabrication of sterotype and electrotype plates: Positions chase on imposing stone and transfers type and cuts from galley to chase, arranging type forms and units as specified on makeup sheet. Inserts lead or wooden strips between forms and units to maintain spacing during printing. Places quoins between type matter and chase frame and turns quoin key or setscrews in chase frame to lock type in place. May refile type in storage cabinets or dump type in remelt box subsequent to printing. May cut wood or lead strips to size to fabricate spacing inserts, using power saw.
GOE: 05.10.05 STRENGTH: L GED: R4 M2 L3 SVP: 8 DLU: 77

973.381-030 PROOFSHEET CORRECTOR (print. & pub.)
Replaces slugs in set type to correct errors indicated on proofsheet preparatory to printing of final copy: Arranges galleys of linotype slugs (takes) in sequence on correction table. Compares corrected type slugs against proof to detect errors. Compares guide symbols on proof with galley symbol, and reads portion of proof and galley text to locate positions for insertion of corrected slugs. Removes incorrect portion and manually inserts corrections. Cuts slugs to size to achieve specified fit, using electric saw. Keeps tabular material in specified sequence when correcting type line errors or adding new lines. Stores proofs in designated drawers and in sequence for specified period and disposes of obsolete proofs. Removes unwanted portions of lines from previously published editions, inserts new or corrected lines, and rearranges balance of slugs for next edition.
GOE: 05.05.13 STRENGTH: L GED: R4 M2 L3 SVP: 8 DLU: 77

973.681-010 GALLEY STRIPPER (print. & pub.)
Prepares page layouts, arranges, and mounts galleys of type, illustrations, sketches, and folios to be used in preparing printed material, using drafting and cutting instruments: Measures and marks paper according to artist's layout, cus-

tomer specifications, and instructions of supervisor to determine position of type and other material, using rules and drafting instruments. Cuts out and removes errors in galley, using cutting instruments, and strips in corrections or alterations, using tape. Cuts out illustrations, type matter, and other material, using scissors or knife, and arranges and fits material or positions material for emphasis on paper according to layout marks.
GOE: 05.10.05 STRENGTH: S GED: R3 M2 L2 SVP: 5 DLU: 77

974   ELECTROTYPERS, STEREOTYPERS, AND RELATED OCCUPATIONS

This group includes occupations concerned with reproducing printing surface of units of type, line or halftone plates, or full pages, using an electrochemical process that plates a mold of type surface with copper, chrome, or other metal to form a shell, backed with type metal; or by making a matrix of type and casting a curved or flat plate in stereotype metal; routing or planing cast plate to specified thickness; and mounting plates for printing.

974.131-010   SUPERVISOR, ELECTROTYPING AND STEREOTYPING (print. & pub.)
Supervises and coordinates activities of workers engaged in preparation of duplicate electrotype and stereotype printing plates: Examines items, such as plastic molds, proof prints, stereotype casting molds, and finished printing plates to ensure conformance to company standards or customer specifications. Requisitions parts, supplies, and materials. Performs other duties as described under SUPERVISOR (any industry) Master Title.
GOE: 05.05.13 STRENGTH: M GED: R4 M3 L3 SVP: 8 DLU: 77

974.381-010   ELECTROTYPER (print. & pub.)
Fabricates and finishes duplicate electrotype printing plates, according to specifications, using handtools, electroplating equipment, and metal casting, trimming, and forming machines: Forms plastic mold of composed type and cuts, using sheet-molding fiber and hydraulic press. Sprays mold with silver solution and immerses mold in plating tank. Separates mold from plated shell and fills back of shell with molten lead to form plate, using pouring ladle or casting machine. Removes excess metal from edges and back of plate, using power shear and milling machines. Examines plate to detect imperfect formation of halftone dots, lines, and type, using magnifier, and corrects defects, using engraver's handtools, punches, and hammer. Mounts finished plates on wood or metal blocks for flatbed presses or curves plate for cylinder presses, using hammer, nails, bonding press, or plate-curving machine. Removes excess metal from nonprinting areas of plate surface, using radial or cylindrical routing machine. May operate proof press to obtain proof of plate reproduction and registration. May revise plates to customer's specifications. May be known according to task performed as Electrotype Caster (print. & pub.); Electrotype Molder (print. & pub.).
GOE: 05.05.13 STRENGTH: M GED: R4 M3 L3 SVP: 8 DLU: 77

974.381-014   ELECTROTYPER APPRENTICE (print. & pub.)
Performs duties as described under APPRENTICE (any industry) Master Title.
GOE: 05.05.13 STRENGTH: M GED: R4 M3 L3 SVP: 8 DLU: 77

974.382-010   STEREOTYPER APPRENTICE (print. & pub.)
Performs duties as described under APPRENTICE (any industry) Master Title.
GOE: 05.05.13 STRENGTH: M GED: R4 M2 L2 SVP: 8 DLU: 77

974.382-014   STEREOTYPER (print. & pub.)
Operates machines to press face of composed type and plates into wood-fiber mat to form stereotype casting mold, pour molten metal into mold, and finish castings by cutting, shaving, and trimming to form plates for printing: Drills matching holes in series of mounted color plates to be duplicated and inserts pilot pins in base to register all plates to key plate for mat molding. Lays sheet of mat paper on form or plates, covers assembly with molding blanket and protective sheet, and pushes assembly to self-feeding rollers of mat-rolling machine or into cavity of hydraulic press. Adjusts time, temperature, and pressure controls to form and dry mold. Cuts and pastes pieces of paper felt or cardboard in large nonprinting areas of mat to prevent collapse during casting of plate. Aligns and notches mats of series with key color mat (mold), using matching machine with monocolor magnifier attachment. Aligns notches with pins of trimming machine and pushes lever to trim three edges of mat simultaneously. Lays mat on casting box platen and arranges steel bars on three sides of mat to confine molten type metal. Pours metal into casting box by hand or by operating automatic stereotype plate-casting machine. Trims plates to specified size [PLATE FINISHER (print. & pub.)]. Coats curved plates with nickel [PLATER (electroplating)]. May register series of color plates and mats by transparent acetate overlay process. May be designated according to task performed as Stereotype Caster (print. & pub.); Stereotype Molder (print. & pub.).
GOE: 05.05.13 STRENGTH: M GED: R4 M2 L2 SVP: 8 DLU: 77

974.682-010   BLOCKER, METAL BASE (print. & pub.)
Operates machines to cast blocks of type metal, mill blocks to specified size, and bond blocks to printing plates: Fills melting pot of stereotype casting machine with bars of metal alloy and sets thermostatic control. Tightens clamps on casting box cover and raises casting box to vertical position. Depresses lever on melting pot to open pouring gate or ladles molten metal into honeycomb

mold in casting box. Removes cast metal block from casting box after it has cooled and cuts to size on trim saw. Operates block leveling machine to mill block surface to specified height. Cuts sheet of thermoplastic bond film to size. Inserts film between plate back and block top and places on sliding table of heat press. Makes proof of cut on transparent plastic sheet to verify color register, using proof press. Marks plates for filing.
GOE: 05.10.05 STRENGTH: L GED: R4 M2 L2 SVP: 7 DLU: 77

976   DARKROOM OCCUPATIONS, N.E.C.

This group includes occupations, not elsewhere classified, concerned with photographing flat copy; enlarging or reducing copy by projection printing; contact printing; developing and fixing negatives, positives, and prints; developing and printing still or motion-picture black-and-white or color film; toning, dodging, or otherwise controlling resulting prints; and mixing photographic chemicals.

976.131-010   LABORATORY CHIEF (photofinishing) alternate titles: laboratory manager; photographic-laboratory supervisor
Supervises and coordinates activities of workers engaged in developing photographic prints from negatives, copying and enlarging prints, and in production of lantern slides, and airbrushing and retouching prints: Inspects finished film and prints for sharpness, color balance, and brilliance. Directs workers in care and setting up of field laboratory equipment. Requisitions and distributes materials and supplies. Assists workers in performance of tasks, such as airbrushing and retouching photographic prints. May set up and adjust laboratory equipment. May assist in classification of pictures as confidential or restricted before their release from laboratory. Performs other duties as described under SUPERVISOR (any industry) Master Title. May supervise and coordinate crew engaged in developing, printing, enlarging, and finishing prints in portable truck-drawn photographic laboratory and be designated Trailer Chief (photofinishing).
GOE: 05.10.05 STRENGTH: L GED: R4 M2 L3 SVP: 8 DLU: 77

976.131-014   SUPERVISOR, FILM PROCESSING (motion picture; photofinishing; radio-tv broad.) alternate titles: film technician; laboratory contact supervisor
Supervises and coordinates activities of workers engaged in developing exposed black-and-white and color motion picture film. Examines samples of developed film for defects, such as scratches, cracks, and contours. Directs workers to make machine adjustments to correct defects. Monitors gauges of developing solution tanks to ensure adherence to specifications. Sets up or corrects set-up of photographic processing machines. Collects and submits film strips and processing solutions to quality control department for analysis. Mends film breaks, replaces film reels, and performs minor repair work on machines, using handtools. Notifies maintenance supervisor when major repair is required. Performs other duties as described under SUPERVISOR (any industry) Master Title.
GOE: 06.01.01 STRENGTH: L GED: R4 M3 L3 SVP: 7 DLU: 77

976.131-018   SUPERVISOR, MICROFILM DUPLICATING UNIT (business ser.)
Supervises and coordinates activities of workers engaged in microfilm reproduction activities, including laboratory processing, computer output microfilming, optical character recognition and microfiche duplicating: Advises customer agencies of services available, equipment needs, and microfilming costs. Operates and repairs microfilming equipment as required to provide continuing service. Provides advice and counsel to units of local government and private agencies with respect to technical and procedural aspects of microfilming. Performs other duties as described under SUPERVISOR (any industry) Master Title.
GOE: 05.10.05 STRENGTH: L GED: R4 M3 L4 SVP: 7 DLU: 77

976.131-022   SUPERVISOR, QUALITY CONTROL (photofinishing)
Supervises and coordinates activities of workers engaged in inspecting, testing, and processing photographic materials and conducts tests to establish and maintain quality standards: Instructs workers in use of equipment and procedures and tours department to evaluate quality of work. Performs tests on film strips to determine photographic density, using densitometer, and records readings on chart to plot changes from established norms. Computes setup time factors for printing equipment to determine optional settings for color and density, using mathematical formulas, and sets up or notifies other workers to set up equipment accordingly. Authorizes adjustments when workers report significant change in temperature readings of equipment. Inspects equipment to detect mechanical malfunctioning and confers with maintenance personnel to authorize and schedule repairs. Advises management on adaptability of new processes or purchase of new equipment. Studies production records, company operational reports, customer comments, and manufacturers' recommendations for use and operation of photographic equipment to establish quality control standards. Prepares reports, such as budget of operational expenses, stock inventories, and personnel evaluation and submits reports to management. Confers with administrative and technical personnel to coordinate interdepartmental workflow. Performs other duties as described under SUPERVISOR (any industry) Master Title.
GOE: 05.10.05 STRENGTH: L GED: R4 M3 L3 SVP: 7 DLU: 77

976.131-026   SUPERVISOR, TYPE PHOTOGRAPHY (machinery mfg.)
Supervises and coordinates activities of workers engaged in photographing, developing, printing, examining, measuring, and sorting type characters used in

production of phototypesetting type disks: Schedules daily production activities, utilizing computerized production control system, and assigns work to staff based on priorities, knowledge of worker capability, and capacity of machines and equipment. Observes workflow to ensure schedules are maintained. Examines production operations at each station to ensure adherence to specifications and quality standards, using comparator-profile projector and rules. Confers with staff to resolve production problems and provide technical assistance. Interviews job applicants and trains new staff. Performs other duties as described under SUPERVISOR (any industry) Master Title.
GOE: 05.10.05 STRENGTH: L GED: R4 M3 L4 SVP: 8 DLU: 86

976.132-010 SUPERVISOR, FILM PROCESSING (photofinishing)
Supervises and coordinates activities of workers engaged in photofinishing operations, such as preparing photographic negatives and paper, and developing, sorting, and checking prints: Trains new workers and demonstrates new techniques to improve skills of experienced workers. Flips switches and turns controls on master panelboard to start photographic processing equipment, admit solutions to processing tanks, and to adjust solution temperature and flow rate. Monitors operation of machinery and equipment to detect defective parts. Repairs defects, such as loose nuts and bolts, and notifies maintenance department when major repairs are required. May perform duties of subordinates to maintain production or to replace absent worker. Performs other duties as described under SUPERVISOR (any industry) Master Title.
GOE: 05.10.05 STRENGTH: L GED: R4 M3 L3 SVP: 6 DLU: 77

976.134-010 SUPERVISOR, CUTTING AND SPLICING (motion picture; photofinishing)
Supervises and coordinates activities of workers engaged in numbering, cutting, assembling, splicing, and inspecting negative slide or motion picture film: Trains new workers in techniques, such as cutting out censored or defective scenes from film strip, assembling and splicing film strips together, and printing footage numbers on film rolls. Inserts film strip in splicing machine to test sealing unit and adjusts temperature controls of machine to obtain permanent seal without burning film. Inserts film strips in stapling machine to ascertain that film is secured in prescribed manner. Examines assembled film over bench lamp to detect cutting and splicing errors and to verify edited arrangement of picture sequence according to work order and editorial instructions. Performs other duties as described under SUPERVISOR (any industry) Master Title.
GOE: 05.12.01 STRENGTH: L GED: R4 M2 L3 SVP: 6 DLU: 77

976.137-014 SUPERVISOR, FINISHING DEPARTMENT (photofinishing) alternate titles: checking department supervisor; finishing department supervisor
Supervises and coordinates activities of workers engaged in cutting, checking, spotting, mounting, pricing, and packaging film negatives and prints to prepare orders for shipment: Plans and conducts training programs for new workers and to improve skills of experienced workers. Inspects work in progress to verify consistency of workers' decisions with company standards. Inspects equipment, makes minor adjustments, and confers with maintenance personnel to schedule major repairs. Reviews price listings of merchandise and indicates price changes on listings according to instructions from management. Requisitions supplies according to worker requirements and records of supplies on hand. Performs other duties as described under SUPERVISOR (any industry) Master Title. May perform duties of subordinates to prevent production lag.
GOE: 05.09.01 STRENGTH: L GED: R4 M2 L3 SVP: 6 DLU: 77

976.267-010 QUALITY-CONTROL TECHNICIAN (photofinishing)
Examines photographic prints, processed film, cameras and other photographic equipment for defects or faulty operation to determine course of action required to satisfy customer complaints: Reviews unresolved requests for adjustment of complaints and reads customer comments to determine basis of complaint and plan of action needed to resolve complaint. Spreads negatives and prints on illuminated worktable and uses magnifying glass to detect defects, such as incorrect coloring, shading, or cutting. Determines cause of defect and type correction required based on knowledge of photo processing and finishing techniques. Prepares memorandum to processing department and confers with SUPERVISOR, QUALITY CONTROL (photofinishing) to suggest remedies to prevent subsequent errors in processing. Contacts customer to explain causes for defects and confers with sales-service personnel to resolve technical questions and to demonstrate correct usage of photographic equipment. Prepares reports indicating complaints handled and dispositions made.
GOE: 05.10.05 STRENGTH: L GED: R4 M2 L3 SVP: 6 DLU: 77

976.360-010 PRINT CONTROLLER (photofinishing)
Sets up and adjusts photographic print developing equipment according to density, color, and size of prints: Positions film in densitometer, reads dials, and records findings on plot sheet to locate defects in density and color balance. Confers with SUPERVISOR, QUALITY CONTROL (photofinishing) to determine adjustments required to bring print machine into balance. Runs test film strip through print machine to evaluate machine exposure. Removes cover from control panel of print machine to gain access to control shafts and adjustment knobs, using wrench. Plugs electric timer into printer to determine time elapsed during printing operation. Starts equipment, observes timer, and adjusts shafts and knobs to attain specified process settings, using handtools. Locks control shafts of printer into position subsequent to final adjustment to prevent shifting in color or density balance during printing. Keeps record of adjustments made for departmental use.

GOE: 06.01.02 STRENGTH: L GED: R4 M3 L2 SVP: 6 DLU: 77

976.361-010 REPRODUCTION TECHNICIAN (any industry) alternate titles: copy-camera operator; photolith operator; vacuum-frame operator
Duplicates printed material on sensitized paper, cloth, or film according to customer specifications, using photographic equipment and handtools: Reads work order and confers with supervisor to determine processes, techniques, equipment, and materials required. Places original on sensitized material in vacuum frame. Mounts camera on tripod or stand and loads prescribed type and size film in camera. Sets camera controls to regulate exposure time according to line density of original and type of sensitized material. Activates camera to expose sensitized material, imprinting original on material. Develops exposed material [DEVELOPER (photofinishing) 976.681-010]. Examines developed reprint for defects, such as broken lines, spots, and blurs, and touches up defects, using chemicals, inks, brushes, and pens. May enlarge reprints [PROJECTION PRINTER (photofinishing) 976.381-018]. May reprint original in sections and piece sections together.
GOE: 05.10.05 STRENGTH: L GED: R4 M2 L2 SVP: 6 DLU: 77

976.362-010 FILM INSPECTOR (photofinishing) alternate titles: quality-control projectionist; reel-film inspector
Operates motion picture projector to inspect home movie film and visually examines slides for defects to determine need for reprocessing and repair: Randomly selects specified number of home movie reels and inserts reels in magazine of projector. Threads film through projector onto take-up reel. Starts projector and adjusts lens to focus image on screen. Examines projected image to detect defective exposure or color density and presence of scratches or foreign matter. Records findings on quality control sheet and notifies processing department personnel regarding need for machine adjustments or customer regarding defective camera lens. Measures width of film to determine accuracy of slitting, using precision measuring instrument, and notifies slitting department personnel when width is not within specified tolerances. Examines specified number of randomly selected photographic slides to detect scratches or defects in color density, accuracy, and exposure. Records type defect and reprocessing required on quality control form and routes form and defective slides to processing department. Conveys acceptable reels and slides to packaging department. Collects daily reports from production personnel, totals production figures, and calculates production averages to determine whether quotas have been met.
GOE: 05.10.05 STRENGTH: L GED: R4 M2 L2 SVP: 5 DLU: 77

976.380-010 COMPUTER-CONTROLLED-COLOR-PHOTOGRAPH-PRINTER OPERATOR (photofinishing)
Sets up and operates computerized photofinishing equipment to produce color photographic prints from negatives: Develops test film strip and prints test photographic prints from negative at specified intervals, using film processing and printing equipment, to ensure photofinishing equipment functions according to processing standards. Tests film strip and prints for conformance to color density values, using densitometer. Plots and records reading on charts and compares results with standards to ascertain color balance deviation and need for program changes, following processing control manual. Keys program changes into computer and posts changes in processing log to maintain record of changes. Measures and mixes specified chemicals and transfers solutions to reservoirs of photofinishing equipment. Reads customer photofinishing order to ascertain film type, number of prints desired, and delivery date and to determine machine settings and lens requirement for printing photos. Replaces lens and negative carrier in printer according to film type to be processed. Adjusts controls to regulate frame and paper size. Scans computer display unit to ensure specified program mode is operational and inputs code changes. Keys in billing information according to film type and number of exposures to be printed. Positions negatives in frame of carrier and depresses pedal to actuate printing action. Examines prints for variations from standards and keys in computer changes to maintain computer programming of color values in printing operation. Removes customer sales slip from billing unit and attaches slip to envelope containing customer film and prints.
GOE: 05.10.05 STRENGTH: S GED: R3 M3 L3 SVP: 3 DLU: 86

976.381-010 FILM LABORATORY TECHNICIAN I (motion picture)
Evaluates motion picture film to determine characteristics, such as sensitivity to light, density, and exposure time required for printing, using sensitometer, densitometer, and timer lights: Threads film strip through sensitometer, exposes film to light, and reads gauges to determine film's sensitivity to light. Threads film strip through densitometer and exposes film to light to determine density of film. Computes amount of light intensity needed to compensate for density of film, using standardized formulas. Exposes film strip to progressively timed lights to compare effects of various exposure times. Examines developed film strip to determine optimal exposure time and light intensity required for printing. Records test data and routes to FILM DEVELOPER (motion picture; photofinishing) and FILM PRINTER (motion picture). May be designated according to specialty as Densitometrist (motion picture); Sensitometrist (motion picture); Timer (motion picture).
GOE: 02.04.01 STRENGTH: L GED: R4 M4 L4 SVP: 7 DLU: 77

976.381-014 MICROFICHE DUPLICATOR (business ser.)
Prepares microfiche duplicates of microfilm, using contact printer and developing machine: Cuts roll of exposed microfilm to specified lengths, using paper cutter. Aligns film strips in lighted vacuum box and tapes strips together to as-

semble master print. Inserts master print and sensitized paper into vacuum frame of printer, sets timer, and activates printer to transfer image from master print to paper, producing microfiche print. Feeds print into machine that develops and fixes image by heat-ammonia process [BLUEPRINTING-MACHINE OPERATOR (any industry) 979.682-014]. Positions print on lighted table and examines print to detect imperfections, using magnifier. Affixes identification label to microfiche print.
GOE: 05.10.05 STRENGTH: L GED: R4 M2 L2 SVP: 6 DLU: 77

976.381-018 PROJECTION PRINTER (photofinishing) alternate titles: photograph enlarger; projection-camera operator
Produces enlarged or reduced photographic prints from original negative or positive, using projection printer: Sorts orders according to type, size, and processing requirements. Examines negative for contrast to determine grade of sensitized paper required for print. Places sensitized paper on easel and adjusts sliding arms of easel to outline specified area on paper, or threads paper through guides onto takeup spool and secures with tape. Places negative in holder and slides holder beneath light. Raises or lowers carriage of printer to focus image within outlined area on paper. Selects lens assembly according to size and type of negative to be printed and positions lens in holder. Adjusts lens opening, sets exposure timer, and starts machine. Varies contrast by shading darker image areas with hand or sheet of paper (dodging). Develops exposed paper [DEVELOPER (photofinishing)]. Examines developed prints to detect color deficiencies, scratches, and dust specks, and retouches print to remove defects, using paints, pencils, brush, and cloth. Computes customer charges and maintains production record.
GOE: 05.10.05 STRENGTH: L GED: R3 M2 L2 SVP: 7 DLU: 77

976.381-022 TEMPLATE REPRODUCTION TECHNICIAN (aircraft mfg.) alternate titles: tooling reproduction technician
Reproduces images of engineering drawings, tracings, stencils, layouts, templates, and other work aids onto base materials to produce working patterns used in manufacturing aircraft parts, using photographic and x-ray reproduction cameras, contact printers, and related equipment: Reads work order to determine nature of material to be copied, enlargement or reduction required, and equipment to be used. Sets up, operates, and adjusts photographic and reduction equipment to produce pattern negatives and to reproduce image from negative onto emulsion-treated or sensitized base material. Mixes developing and processing solutions, and immerses exposed materials in developing, processing, and rinsing solutions to produce image, manually or using material handling devices. Visually inspects image for quality. Cuts base material to specified dimensions, using power shear. May operate equipment to wash and dry processed materials. May operate photographic equipment to reproduce pattern on transparent plastic film. May laminate sensitized material onto base material.
GOE: 05.10.05 STRENGTH: L GED: R4 M2 L3 SVP: 7 DLU: 88

976.382-010 CAMERA OPERATOR, TITLE (motion picture)
Photographs title cards bearing foreign-language titles and dialogue on standard motion picture film for use with films for export: Sets title card on photographing rack. Switches on mercury light. Mounts rolls of film in camera and adjusts and focuses lens. Photographs title cards, removes film from camera, and forwards it for developing.
GOE: 05.10.05 STRENGTH: L GED: R4 M3 L3 SVP: 7 DLU: 77

976.382-014 COLOR-PRINTER OPERATOR (photofinishing)
Controls equipment to produce color prints from negatives: Reads customer instructions to determine processing requirement. Loads roll or magazine of printing paper into color printing equipment. Examines color negative to determine equipment control settings for production of prints meeting acceptable color-fidelity standards. Sets controls in accordance with examination, loads negative into machine, and starts machine to produce specified number of prints. Removes printed photographic paper from machine and places paper in film bag for further processing or in developing machine. Inspects finished prints for defects, such as dust and smudges, and removes defects, using brush, cloth, and cleaning fluid. Inserts processed negatives and prints into envelope for return to customer.
GOE: 05.10.05 STRENGTH: L GED: R3 M2 L2 SVP: 3 DLU: 87

976.382-018 FILM DEVELOPER (motion picture; photofinishing) alternate titles: developer operator
Operates machine to develop still or motion-picture film: Pulls reel of motion-picture film or rack of film strips through trapdoor into darkroom. Examines film to determine type processing required, utilizing knowledge of film developing techniques. Feels edges of film to detect tears and repairs film, using hand stapler. Mounts film in guide slot of developing machine according to length of time required for processing and pulls lever to lower film into processing position. Flips switch to start machine that transports film through series of solutions and into drying cabinet to develop and dry film. Observes film passing through machine to determine density of image and adjusts machine controls to shorten or lengthen path of film through solutions according to observation. May be designated according to type film developed as Negative Developer (motion picture; photofinishing); Positive Developer (motion picture; photofinishing).
GOE: 05.10.05 STRENGTH: L GED: R3 M1 L1 SVP: 6 DLU: 77

976.382-022 PHOTOSTAT OPERATOR (any industry) alternate titles: photocopy operator
Sets up and operates photostat machine to duplicate printed material, such as manuscripts: Places roll of sensitized paper in machine. Measures length and width of material to be copied, using rule. Computes percentage of enlargement or reproduction necessary, using chart or percentage scale. Mounts material on easel beneath lens, turns on light, and moves controls to focus lens on material. Estimates exposure time, according to size of lens aperture, grade of sensitized paper, and intensity of light. Places filter over lens to make color separation when copying color work. Sets automatic timer and starts exposure. Rolls exposed section of sensitized paper into developer tank inside machine and presses lever to cut section from roll. Turns crank to transfer print to pan of hypo (fixing fluid) attached to machine. Examines print for sharpness of line. Rinses developed print in water and places print in heated drying cabinet, between blotters, or on heated cylinders of roll-dryer. Trims excess margin from dried print, using cutting blade.
GOE: 05.10.05 STRENGTH: L GED: R3 M2 L2 SVP: 5 DLU: 77

976.382-030 PHOTOGRAPHIC ALIGNER, SEMICONDUCTOR WAFERS (electron. comp.) alternate titles: aligner
Operates photographic equipment to align and expose mask circuit pattern with photoresist-coated semiconductor wafer to produce image of circuit pattern on wafer surface: Inserts mask into aligning equipment. Places wafer in wafer holders, such as chuck or conveyor, using tweezers or vacuum wand, to load aligning equipment. Presses buttons to position wafers underneath microscope and aligning head. Observes wafer through microscope and turns knobs to align mask with index points on wafer. Presses button to activate wafer exposing cycle. Maintains production records.
GOE: 06.02.18 STRENGTH: L GED: R3 M2 L2 SVP: 4 DLU: 86

976.382-034 STEP-AND-REPEAT REDUCTION CAMERA OPERATOR (electron. comp.)
Operates step-and-repeat camera and film developer to reduce electronic drawings to specified size and to repeat pattern on photographic (photo mask) plates used in fabrication of semiconductor devices: Positions and aligns electronic drawing and photographic plates in holding fixtures of camera. Turns adjustment knobs to attain specified focus. Sets control panel dials according to specifications, or loads preprogrammed tape into computerized control panel, and activates camera. Feeds film into automatic machine that develops, fixes, washes, and dries film, or moves film from tank to tank in developing unit, using tongs or tweezers and utilizing knowledge of film development techniques to develop film. Records process information in production log. May inspect electronic drawing or exposed plate.
GOE: 05.10.05 STRENGTH: L GED: R3 M2 L2 SVP: 5 DLU: 86

976.382-038 PHOTO MASK PATTERN GENERATOR (electron. comp.) alternate titles: pattern generator operator
Operates pattern-generating machine to transfer integrated circuit pattern onto surface of *reticle* for use by PHOTO MASK PROCESSOR (electron. comp.) 976.384-014 in production of photo mask plates used in fabrication of semiconductor devices: Reads specifications to determine production data and enters data into pattern-generating machine, using keyboard. Loads digitizer tape into machine reader to control exposure process. Positions unexposed photoresist coated reticle on projection stage of machine and adjusts focus. Types commands to activate machine that exposes photoresist on reticle to circuit pattern. Tends developing and etching equipment to develop and etch pattern on reticle. Inspects reticle for defects, using microscope.
GOE: 05.10.05 STRENGTH: L GED: R3 M3 L3 SVP: 5 DLU: 86

976.384-010 PHOTO TECHNICIAN (electron. comp.)
Prints and develops film of circuit designs for use in fabricating printed circuit boards (PCB's), using photographic equipment and knowledge of photographic processing: Reads work order to determine photographic techniques required. Aligns artwork developed from circuitry blueprint and other specifications with duplicating film on darkroom light table, following prescribed procedures. Tapes materials to table or closes table lid and depresses control to activate vacuum device that holds work in alignment during processing. Adjusts camera settings for reduction or enlargement of image, according to work order specifications, and sets or activates timer that controls exposure time of film. Feeds exposed film into machine that develops, fixes, washes, and dries film [PRINT DEVELOPER, AUTOMATIC (photofinishing) 976.685-026]. Examines film to verify that reproduced image meets quality standards. May touch up artwork or developed film, using tape, knife, brush, or pen. May submerse exposed film in series of baths to develop and fix image, and dry film, using squeegee and electric dryer. May print and develop circuit image on diazo film, using automatic equipment, and be designated Diazo Technician (electron. comp.).
GOE: 05.10.05 STRENGTH: L GED: R3 M2 L3 SVP: 4 DLU: 86

976.384-014 PHOTO MASK PROCESSOR (electron. comp.)
Prints and develops working photo mask plates from master plate for subsequent use in fabrication of semiconductor devices: Reads work order to determine process specifications. Loads unexposed plates and master plate in holding fixture of printing machine. Adjusts controls and activates machine that exposes blank plates to image on master plate. Develops exposed plates, using developing equipment, chemicals, and dryer. Cleans developing equipment periodically and refills chemicals in developing sinks. Cleans master plate at specified intervals, using cleaning and rinsing solutions and ultrasonic equipment.
GOE: 05.10.05 STRENGTH: L GED: R3 M2 L2 SVP: 5 DLU: 88

976.385-010 MICROFILM PROCESSOR (business ser.)
Tends machine that automatically processes microfilm and examines processed film to ensure that quality of microfiche meets established standards:

Loads film into magazine of camera under darkroom conditions, attaches magazine to camera, and splices end of film to leader in machine to facilitate threading film, using splicing tape. Flips switches and turns valves to activate machine components and functions, such as blower, squeegee, water flow into processor, and rate of processing chemical replenishment. Monitors machine warning lights to detect processing malfunctions, such as break in film or leader, and takes action to correct malfunction, using knowledge of machine operation. Records film processing information, such as film type, developing speed, and rate of chemical replenishment to maintain film log. Examines processed film to ensure numerical order and clarity of microfiche, using film winder, light table, and magnifier. Marks defective microfiche section of film and lists identifying number of sections on identification sheet to indicate refilming required. Measures optical density of random film section to ensure standard processing, using densitometer. Places film on cutter, aligns markings on cutter and film, and moves cutting instrument across film to separate individual microfiche sections of film. Discards defective microfiche and places acceptable microfiche in envelope for further processing. Mixes processing chemicals to maintain supply, following specified formula, using mixing machine. Processes sample film and measures density of film to enable MICROFILM-CAMERA OPERATOR (business ser.) 976.682-022 to determine exposure settings for new batches of film.
GOE: 05.10.05 STRENGTH: L GED: R3 M2 L2 SVP: 2 DLU: 86

976.487-010 PHOTOGRAPH FINISHER (photofinishing) alternate titles: print finisher
Performs any combination of following tasks to dry, trim, and mount photographic prints: Places washed print on conveyor leading to heated rotating cylinder that dries and flattens print. Trims print edges, using paper cutter or scissors. Inserts print in specified frame or mounts print on material, such as paper, cardboard, or fabric, using cement or hand-operated press. Inserts print and corresponding negative in customer envelope. Computes price of order, according to size and number of prints, and marks price on customer envelope. May cut film lengthwise to separate individual print rolls, using slitting machine.
GOE: 05.10.05 STRENGTH: L GED: R2 M1 L1 SVP: 2 DLU: 77

976.564-010 DETAILER, SCHOOL PHOTOGRAPHS (photofinishing)
Performs variety of tasks to prepare and disseminate school photographs: Reads photographers' work orders and records information, such as number of prints and type finish specified as guide for processing film. Assigns control number to each order. Records customer charges on worksheet and submits to accounting department for billing. Sorts and bags film according to processing required. Cuts prints to prepare composite for group photographs, using chopping block, die, and mallet. Assembles composite and mails to picture service for processing of negative. Routes composite negative to printing section and records cost of composite service. Feeds specified photographs in gluing machine that automatically applies adhesive backing to photographs. Confers with photographers to discuss school programs available, costs, and shipping dates. Confers with customers to resolve complaints regarding missing or defective photographs. Cuts out, arranges, and pastes letters, numbers, and pictures to design advertising circulars. Maintains records indicating orders received, unit prices charged, and department earnings.
GOE: 07.05.03 STRENGTH: L GED: R3 M2 L2 SVP: 4 DLU: 77

976.567-010 FILM-REPLACEMENT ORDERER (motion picture)
Orders replacement footage for defective motion-picture negative film: Ascertains reel number of film, footage of film to be replaced, and intensity of light required for printing replacement. Transcribes this information on replacement ticket and delivers ticket to FILM PRINTER (motion picture).
GOE: 07.07.03 STRENGTH: L GED: R3 M2 L3 SVP: 3 DLU: 77

976.665-010 TAKE-DOWN SORTER (photofinishing)
Sorts and examines processed photographic film, repairs defective film, and tends drying cabinet that dries film: Flips switch to activate exhaust fan of drier, reads temperature gauge, and adjusts heat controls to maintain specified temperature in drier. Notifies supervisor or darkroom personnel concerning need for machine adjustments or solution changes if excessive amounts of film damage occurs. Monitors drying operation to detect dirty, twisted, or torn film in drier and removes defective film from drier. Washes film in negative cleaner to clean, soften, and straighten film and mends torn film, using tape, sealing solution, and scissors. Feels surface of film in drier to determine dryness and removes film from drier when completely dry. Examines film for clearness of image to determine printability and matches numbered label attached to film with number on customer envelope to avoid missorts. Sorts film into bins or attaches film to hooks according to size and type processing required. May compute customer charges, using pricelist.
GOE: 05.10.05 STRENGTH: L GED: R3 M1 L1 SVP: 3 DLU: 77

976.667-010 PHOTOGRAPHER HELPER (any industry)
Assists PHOTOGRAPHER, STILL (profess. & kin.) in taking and developing photographs: Arranges lights and screens, sets up camera at proper angle, and moves objects to secure desired background for photographs as directed. Assists in darkroom duties, such as mixing chemical solutions and developing films. May label photographs. Performs other duties as described under HELPER (any industry) Master Title.
GOE: 01.02.03 STRENGTH: M GED: R3 M2 L2 SVP: 4 DLU: 77

976.681-010 DEVELOPER (photofinishing) alternate titles: darkroom worker; doper; hand developer
Develops exposed photographic film or sensitized paper in series of chemical and water baths to produce negative or positive prints: Mixes developing and fixing solutions, following formula. Immerses exposed film or photographic paper in developer solution to bring out latent image. Immerses negative or paper in stop-bath to arrest developer action, in hyposolution to fix image, and in water to remove chemicals. Dries prints or negatives, using sponge or squeegee, or places them in mechanical air drier. May produce color photographs, negatives, and slides, using color reproduction processes, and be designated Color-Laboratory Technician (photofinishing). May perform duties as described under GROUP LEADER (any industry).
GOE: 05.10.05 STRENGTH: L GED: R3 M2 L2 SVP: 4 DLU: 77

976.682-010 FILM PRINTER (motion picture) alternate titles: daily release and dupe printer; positive printer operator
Sets up and operates motion picture film printing machine to produce positive images and soundtrack from negative film: Reads work orders to determine type film to be printed and type printing aperture required. Installs specified printing aperture in machine. Mounts rolls of positive and negative film on machine spindles and threads film through guide rollers, tension bars, picture and sound apertures and onto winding reel to synchronize negative and positive films for printing. Starts machine to pass films through printing apertures and produce positive images and soundtrack. Examines film passing through machine and turns lever of rheostat to adjust intensity of printing light according to control card specifications, or installs punched tape in machine that controls light and color densities during printing operation. Packages films in labled containers subsequent to printing. May operate printer equipped with negative viewer and evaluate scene frames to select frames with specified photographic characteristics preparatory to printing.
GOE: 05.10.05 STRENGTH: L GED: R3 M1 L1 SVP: 5 DLU: 77

976.682-014 PRINTER OPERATOR, BLACK-AND-WHITE (photofinishing) alternate titles: photograph printer
Operates printer to produce black-and-white photographic prints from negatives: Mounts roll of sensitized paper on spindle of printer and threads paper through guides, rollers, and onto take-up spindle. Prepares batch identification sheet, positions sheet in printer, and activates printer to transfer information from sheet to sensitized paper. Prints identification number on customer envelope, using stamping machine. Removes negative strip or single negative from envelope and cleans negatives to remove dust particles, using air blower or gloved finger. Inserts negative in printer and examines image to determine whether picture setting is in or out-of-doors. Activates printer and adjusts control knobs to produce photographic prints of required shading and density. Places printed roll in envelope and seals envelope to prevent exposure to light.
GOE: 05.10.05 STRENGTH: S GED: R3 M1 L1 SVP: 5 DLU: 77

976.682-018 RECTIFICATION PRINTER (any industry)
Operates rectification printer to remove aerial photograph distortions caused by variations in axis and tilt of airplane in relation to earth's surface: Positions roll of negative film in holder so that first negative is over lens in printer. Places print paper on easel of printer. Turns screws to regulate vertical and horizontal axis of printer and distance of printer from easel, following chart of axis, tilt, and scale settings received with film. Adjusts shutter speed and lens opening, according to kind of negative film and print paper used. Exposes negative and paper to light to print photograph.
GOE: 05.10.05 STRENGTH: L GED: R3 M2 L1 SVP: 4 DLU: 77

976.682-022 MICROFILM-CAMERA OPERATOR (business ser.)
Operates microfilm unit camera to film documents: Selects and inserts format disk, turns knobs and flips switches to set controls of unit operation, such as exposure time, margin space, and camera action, according to format instructions. Selects specified camera lens according to document reduction ratios desired on film and slides lens into position on unit. Loads film into camera and splices film to device that facilitates movement of film through unit, using splicing tape. Positions documents on unit feed belt, depresses pedal to activate camera, and observes control panel to monitor unit operation. Replaces film or realigns documents according to signal lights on control panel. Observes colors on printed documents to determine exposure settings based on predetermined standards, and adjusts unit controls to obtain desired effects. Removes film from unit and wraps film in light-resistant bag for further processing. Completes film identification sheet that indicates indexing numbers of microfilm and attaches sheet to bag for reference by MICROFILM PROCESSOR (business ser.) 976.385-010. May work in darkroom and develop exposed film through chemical processing.
GOE: 05.10.05 STRENGTH: L GED: R3 M1 L2 SVP: 3 DLU: 86

976.684-010 DENSITY CONTROL PUNCHER (motion picture)
Punches symbols in perforated tape or notches in negative film which control color and light density changes during printing of motion picture film, using electric tape puncher, film footage counter, and hand notcher: Punches density control symbols in tape according to timing specifications, using tape puncher. Feeds tape through viewing machine and observes light, color, and film footage recordings to verify accuracy of punched symbols. Mounts roll of filter tape or reel of negative film on bench spindle and threads material through footage counter onto takeup spindle. Turns crank to wind material through footage counter and observes footage recording or negative image to determine where density changes are required. Stops counter at point where density change is indicated and cuts filter tape, using cutting machine or notches film, using hand notcher. Routes tape and film to printing department. Maintains production records. May be designated according to method used as Matte Cutter (motion picture); Negative Notcher (motion picture).

GOE: 05.10.05 STRENGTH: L GED: R3 M1 L1 SVP: 4 DLU: 77

976.684-014 FILM LABORATORY TECHNICIAN (motion picture; photofinishing)

Performs any combination of following tasks to process motion picture film: Mixes specified chemicals according to formula to prepare solutions for use in processing film. Cuts and arranges film and splices film together according to written instructions or edited test print, using splicer. Compares film with edited print to detect irregularities in detail and color. Projects film on screen to detect defects in printing and developing, such as blurs, scratches, and perforations, using motion picture projector. Approves film for release, rejects defective film, or routes film to specified department for further processing. May be designated according to specialty as Film Inspector (motion picture); Film Splicer (motion picture).

GOE: 05.10.05 STRENGTH: L GED: R3 M2 L2 SVP: 3 DLU: 77

976.684-018 MOUNTER, HAND (photofinishing)

Cuts and mounts photographic film transparencies, using film cutter and heat-sealing press: Positions film roll on spindle of cutting machine and threads end of film into rack or along track in front of lighted screen, and under cutter knives. Inspects film for defects, such as blank or black film and double exposures. Aligns exposure separation line with cutter knives and depresses pedal to cut film along line. Positions cut film in center of mount and folds edges of mount over film. Inserts mount in heating press that automatically numbers, seals, and ejects mount into tray. Packs mounts in boxes for shipment.

GOE: 06.04.34 STRENGTH: S GED: R2 M1 L1 SVP: 2 DLU: 77

976.684-022 PRINT WASHER (photofinishing)

Washes and dries photographic prints, using print-washing pan, blotter, and wringer: Places developed prints in print-washing pan and activates mechanism that rotates pan to wash prints. Immerses prints in chemical solution subsequent to washing cycle to increase flexibility of prints. Dries prints, using blotter, or positions prints on metal plates, and dries prints, using wringer. Inserts prints in rack on open-faced frames to complete drying process. May examine prints for stains and other defects and return defective prints to developing room. May remove excess water from washed prints to prevent watermarks, using sponge or squeegee.

GOE: 05.10.05 STRENGTH: L GED: R2 M1 L1 SVP: 3 DLU: 77

976.684-026 SPLICER (photofinishing)

Joins strips of undeveloped film and winds film onto reels for subsequent processing, using splicing device and bench winder: Places one roll of film on spindle and another at end of splicer. Positions ends of each roll in splicing device. Depresses pedal to trim ends and form joint, or perforates film, using hand punch. Depresses pedal to drive staples into ends of film, pushes switch to lower heat-sealing head over film ends, or applies adhesive tape over joint to splice film ends. Removes film from splicing device and winds film on reel, using bench winder. Places film in container. May cut 16 mm. film into 8 mm. strips before splicing and be designated Slitter, Processed Film (photofinishing). May perform duties as described under GROUP LEADER (any industry) Master Title.

GOE: 06.04.34 STRENGTH: L GED: R2 M1 L1 SVP: 2 DLU: 77

976.684-030 CONTACT PRINTER, PRINTED CIRCUIT BOARDS (electron. comp.) alternate titles: exposure machine operator; imager; photo printer; photoresist printer

Prints circuit image on photoresist film-laminated panels for use in fabricating printed circuit boards (PCB's), using contact printer: Aligns (registers) one or more circuit negative films with film-laminated circuit board panel in drawer of contact printer vacuum frame. Activates printer controls to create vacuum and secure negative film against circuit board panel. Activates printer to expose negative and panel film to ultraviolet light and transfer circuit image onto panel film. Lifts drawer cover and removes PCB panel and negative. May measure light intensity of contact printer, using exposure meter, tapes, or radiometer, and adjust exposure time according to specifications. May secure negative and panel in vacuum frame, using jig or tape. May examine printed panels for defects in printed circuit. May feed circuit board panels into machine that develops exposed circuit pattern on panels. May tend equipment that laminates photoresist film to circuit board panels. May print circuit pattern on dry photoresist film for use in manufacturing double-sided and flexible PCB's and be designated Contact Printer, Dry Film (electron. comp.).

GOE: 05.10.05 STRENGTH: L GED: R2 M2 L2 SVP: 3 DLU: 86

976.684-034 CONTACT PRINTER, PHOTORESIST (inst. & app.; optical goods) alternate titles: reticle printer

Prints reticles or patterns on optical lenses, metal films, and other materials used in optical instruments, using printing equipment: Cleans material surfaces to facilitate adherence of photoresist solution, using solvents and pumice. Pours, brushes, or sprays photoresist solution onto material or dips material into photoresist tank to apply coating. Places material in drier to set photoresist. Positions material in vacuum printer, using handtools, such as tweezers and vacuum probe. Positions and aligns reticle pattern or mask over top of material, using binocular microscope, and activates vacuum to hold assembly in alignment. Sets printer time controls for specified exposure period and activates printer that exposes photoresist to light to print pattern onto material. Develops photoresist image on material, using developing solution, and places printed material into drier. May etch printed material, using etching equipment, or fill surfaces to specified thickness, using vacuum deposition equipment, to create reticle or pattern on material. May prepare photo masks for reticle-making process, using photographic equipment. May strip photoresist from material after etching or filling.

GOE: 05.05.11 STRENGTH: L GED: R3 M3 L3 SVP: 6 DLU: 86

976.684-038 CONTACT WORKER, LITHOGRAPHY (print. & pub.)

Combines multiple photographic film images onto single film to assist in film assembly (stripping) process for lithographic printing: Aligns negative or positive film image over unexposed film (duplicating or contact) and places film assembly into or on top of vacuum frame. Lowers top of frame or places vinyl sheeting over film and activates vacuum to maintain contact between original and unexposed film. Sets time controls and activates high intensity light source that exposes film to specified amount of time and light. Removes negative or positive and places exposed film in automatic processor that develops image on film.

GOE: 05.10.05 STRENGTH: L GED: R3 M2 L2 SVP: 6 DLU: 89

976.685-010 CUTTER (photofinishing) alternate titles: film cutter; print cutter

Tends automatic or semiautomatic machines that cut processed film or prints into single or multiple units: Examines film or print roll to determine size, number of cuts required, and type machine to use. Turns setscrews to adjust machine guides to roll width and sets density meter on automatic machine to coincide with sensitized marks on roll that control release of cutting blade. Threads roll through machine guides and starts machine that automatically cuts roll into individual or multiple units or depresses pedal of semiautomatic machine to cut roll. Cuts rolls of nonstandard width, using scissors or hand operated paper cutter. Inserts units in customer envelope. Keeps production records.

GOE: 06.04.09 STRENGTH: L GED: R2 M1 L1 SVP: 2 DLU: 77

976.685-014 DEVELOPER, AUTOMATIC (photofinishing) alternate titles: continuous process machine operator; film machine operator

Tends machine that develops sheets, strips, or continuous roll of film preparatory to printing: Pulls film through trapdoor into darkroom. Strips paper backing from film and attaches identifying label. Feels edges of film to detect tears and repairs film, using stapler. Reads work order or feels film for size or notches to determine type of process and developing time required. Positions racks of film on machine chain links according to developing time required or threads leader of continuous roll through machine preparatory to processing. Activates machine that automatically transports film through series of chemical baths to develop, fix, harden, bleach, and wash film. Listens for sounds that indicate machine malfunctioning and notifies supervisor or maintenance personnel when repairs are needed. May run test strip through machine for inspection by supervisor and add chemicals to or adjust machine as directed. May tend equipment that develops, fixes image, and dries x-ray plates and be designated X-Ray-Developing-Machine Operator (medical ser.).

GOE: 06.04.19 STRENGTH: L GED: R2 M1 L1 SVP: 2 DLU: 89

976.685-018 FILM LABORATORY TECHNICIAN II (motion picture)

Performs one or combination of following tasks to process motion picture film: Tends machine that automatically develops exposed film. Tends machine that dries film. Rewinds film by hand or tends machine that automatically inspects, cleans, counts footage, and rewinds reels of film. Numbers film by hand or tends machine that numbers film for identification purposes. Tends machine that brushes wax on splices to strengthen film at junctures and applies wax to sprocket holes of film to facilitate passage through projector. Removes damaged film sections or repairs defective sections, using handtools. May be designated according to specialty as Developing-Machine Tender (motion picture); Drying-Machine Tender (motion picture); Film Numberer (motion picture); Rewinder (motion picture); Waxer Tender (motion picture).

GOE: 05.12.14 STRENGTH: L GED: R3 M2 L2 SVP: 5 DLU: 77

976.685-022 MOUNTER, AUTOMATIC (photofinishing)

Tends automatic-mounting press that cuts film into individual transparencies, and inserts and seals transparencies in mounting frames: Loads mounting frames into machine and depresses lever to lock frames into feed position. Compares identifying labels to ensure numbers on film reel and customer envelope match. Records customer charges on envelope according to standard price listing. Mounts film reel on machine spindle and trims rough edges of film, using scissors. Threads film through machine guides and activates machine that automatically cuts film and mounts transparencies. Observes movement of film through machine to detect jamming and adjusts machine guides, using screwdriver. Notifies supervisor of major machine malfunction.

GOE: 06.04.20 STRENGTH: L GED: R2 M1 L1 SVP: 2 DLU: 77

976.685-026 PRINT DEVELOPER, AUTOMATIC (photofinishing)

Tends one or more machines that automatically develop, fix, wash, and dry photographic prints: Threads leaders (paper strips) around rollers, through processing tanks and dryer, around polished drum, and onto takeup reel. Turns valves to fill tanks with premixed solutions, such as developer, dyes, stop-baths, fixers, bleaches, and washes. Moves thermostatic control to keep steam-heated drum at specified temperature. Splices sensitized paper to leaders, using tape. Starts machine and throws switches to synchronize drive speeds of processing and drying units. Compares processed prints with color standard and reports variations to control department. Adds specified amounts of chemicals to renew solutions. Maintains production records.

GOE: 06.04.19 STRENGTH: L GED: R2 M1 L1 SVP: 4 DLU: 77

976.685-030 UTILITY WORKER, FILM PROCESSING (photofinishing)
Performs variety of tasks to assist or substitute for other workers in photofinishing laboratory: Sorts prints according to size and order number to facilitate handling. Tends automatic cutting machine that cuts roll into individual prints [CUTTER (photofinishing)]. Tends automatic film developing machine that develops and fixes image on film [DEVELOPER, AUTOMATIC (photofinishing)]. Removes prints from print developer rinse tray and tends drum-type drier that dries prints. Prepares daily production sheet, noting quantity and kind of work performed.
GOE: 06.04.19 STRENGTH: L GED: R3 M1 L2 SVP: 3 DLU: 77

976.685-034 DEVELOPER, PRINTED CIRCUIT BOARD PANELS (electron. comp.)
Tends equipment that develops photoresist image on panels of printed circuit boards (PCB's): Mixes specified amount of chemical solution and pours chemicals into equipment developing tank. Turns valves to admit specified amount of water into equipment reservoirs. Starts equipment and monitors conveyor systems, temperature gauges, and pumps. Adjusts controls to maintain specified temperature levels and speed of conveyor. Removes plastic protective film from upper and lower surfaces of photoresist laminated PCB panels. Places panels on conveyor that feeds panels into equipment that automatically develops photoresist circuit image on exposed photoresist film, dissolves unexposed photoresist film, and rinses and dries panels. Removes panels from conveyor and visually examines panels to detect development processing defects. Notifies supervisor of defective panels and equipment malfunctions.
GOE: 06.04.19 STRENGTH: M GED: R2 M2 L2 SVP: 2 DLU: 89

976.685-038 PHOTOGRAPHIC PROCESSOR, SEMICONDUCTOR WAFERS (electron. comp.) alternate titles: resist coater-developer
Tends photographic processing machines that coat semiconductor wafers with solutions, such as photoresist and developing chemicals: Places wafers in containers, such as boats, magazines, cassettes or chuck, using vacuum wand or tweezers. Loads wafer containers in photographic processing machine, such as photoresist coater or developer. Pushes buttons and turns knobs to start automatic coating cycle. Removes container of coated wafers from machine. Cleans and maintains machines. Maintains production records. May immerse wafers in baths of developing chemicals. May place coated wafers in oven to set and dry wafers. May enter production information into computer, using computer terminal keyboard. May immerse wafers in chemical baths to etch excess photoresist or to clean wafers. May visually inspect wafers to identify defects, such as misalignment, excess photoresist, and scratches.
GOE: 06.04.19 STRENGTH: L GED: R3 M1 L2 SVP: 2 DLU: 86

976.687-010 EDITOR, SCHOOL PHOTOGRAPH (photofinishing)
Compares negatives of several poses of an individual and selects best copy to be used in printing group or individual school photographs: Mounts reel of negative film in holding device or positions negatives on illuminated worktable to examine film images and determine degree of printability. Selects best copy of negatives viewed, considering factors, such as lighting, density, pose, and whether subjects eyes are open. Cuts out selected negative, using scissors and inserts negative into transparent holder to prevent damage. Attaches approved negative to card indicating work order number and processing instructions and routes negative to printing department. Discards unselected negatives.
GOE: 01.06.01 STRENGTH: L GED: R3 M1 L2 SVP: 5 DLU: 77

976.687-014 PHOTO CHECKER AND ASSEMBLER (photofinishing) alternate titles: checker; inspector
Inspects, assembles, and packs mounted or unmounted negatives, color film transparencies, and photographic prints: Examines items for natural color shading, density, sharpness of image, or identifying numbers, using lighted viewing screen. Marks defective prints, using grease pencil and standardized symbols to indicate nature of defect and corrective action required in reprinting. Removes defects, such as dust and smudges from prints, using brush, cloth, and cleaning fluid. Packages and labels satisfactory prints and negatives. Maintains daily production records. May cut negatives and prints from roll, using cutting machine. May be designated according to type of print inspected as Color-Print Inspector (photofinishing); Full-Roll Inspector (photofinishing); Mounting Inspector (photofinishing); Reversal-Print Inspector (photofinishing); May inspect prints for tears, dirt, scum, or other surface defects preparatory to mounting and be designated Take-Down Inspector (photofinishing).
GOE: 06.03.02 STRENGTH: L GED: R3 M1 L1 SVP: 4 DLU: 77

976.687-018 PHOTOFINISHING   LABORATORY   WORKER (photofinishing) alternate titles: film numberer; film sorter; pricer-bagger; proof sorter; racker; reprint sorter; sorter-packer
Performs any combination of following tasks to prepare and disseminate negatives, positives, and prints in photofinishing laboratory: Reads instructions written on orders, and examines contents of orders to ascertain size, type, and number of pieces. Sorts orders according to size and type processing required. Pastes identifying label on customer order envelopes and transfer bags to ensure matching of orders subsequent to processing. Removes finished work from transfer bags subsequent to processing and computes customer charges according to pricelist. Inserts order in bag or envelope, and staples bag together or seals envelope. Pastes address label on bag or envelope. Conveys orders between departments. Distributes supplies to other photofinishing workers. Maintains records of orders sorted and packaged.

GOE: 06.03.02 STRENGTH: L GED: R2 M2 L2 SVP: 3 DLU: 87

976.687-022 PRINT INSPECTOR (photofinishing)
Inspects photographic prints for defects, using film winder: Mounts roll of prints on spindle of film winder and tapes free end of film to crankshaft. Turns crank and inspects prints for defects as film winds onto crankshaft. Compares colors with standard image to ensure that prints meet specifications. Marks defective prints with code number, using chemical pencil, to indicate nature and degree of correction required.
GOE: 06.03.02 STRENGTH: L GED: R3 M1 L2 SVP: 5 DLU: 87

977   BOOKBINDERS AND RELATED OCCUPATIONS

This group includes occupations concerned with gathering pages, forms, folios, and tip-ins, and assembling them into pamphlets or books; trimming, gluing, and affixing endsheets, coverboards, or cover material; and applying decorations and lettering to fabricate books by hand, using handtools, presses, and other bench equipment. Occupations concerned with bookbinding machines are found in Group 653.

977.381-010 BOOKBINDER (print. & pub.) alternate titles: bookmaker
Cuts, assembles, glues, and sews components to bind books, according to specification, using automatic and manually operated machines, handtools, and equipment: Folds printed sheets to form signatures (pages) and assembles signatures in numerical order to form book body. Attaches endpapers to top and bottom of book body. Sews signatures and endpapers together along spine of book body, using sewing machine, or glues endpapers and signatures together along spine, using brush or glue machine. Compresses sewed or glued signatures to reduce book to required thickness, using handpress or smashing machine. Trims edges of book to size, using cutting or book trimming machine or hand cutter. Inserts book body in device that forms back edge of book into convex shape and produces grooves to facilitate attachment of cover. Applies glue to back of book, using brush or glue machine, and attaches cloth backing and headband. Applies color to edges of signatures, using brush, pad, or atomizer. Cuts binder board to specified dimension, using board shears, hand cutter, or cutting machine. Cuts cover material, such as leather or cloth, to specified dimensions and fits and glues material to binder board manually or by machine. Glues outside endpapers to cover. Places bound book in press that exerts pressure on cover until glue dries. May imprint and emboss lettering, designs, or numbers on cover, using gold, silver, or colored foil and stamping machine. May pack, weigh, and stack books on pallet for shipment. May specialize in repairing and rebinding damaged or worn books for resale or reuse.
GOE: 05.05.15 STRENGTH: M GED: R3 M2 L2 SVP: 7 DLU: 89

977.381-014 BOOKBINDER APPRENTICE (print. & pub.)
Performs duties as described under APPRENTICE (any industry) Master Title.
GOE: 05.05.15 STRENGTH: M GED: R3 M2 L2 SVP: 7 DLU: 77

977.684-010 BOOK REPAIRER (any industry) alternate titles: book mender
Repairs damaged or worn books for resale or reuse, using handtools: Erases disfigurations from pages. Cuts damaged pages, linings, or covers from book body, using knife. Trims pages, using knife or paper cutter. Positions and pastes repaired or new pages, linings, or covers to book body. Clamps book in press for specified time to bond edges. May operate sewing machine to sew pages into book body. May imprint or emboss lettering on cover, using stamping machine.
GOE: 05.12.19 STRENGTH: L GED: R2 M1 L1 SVP: 3 DLU: 77

977.684-014 INLAYER (print. & pub.)
Inserts or inlays pieces of leather, cloth, or paper in artistic formal patterns in surfaces of covered bookcases to form inlaid (mosaic) bindings: Cuts out out sections in bookcase cover, using pattern and knife or scissors. Positions and glues mosaic pieces in cut-out sections. Usually works from patterns.
GOE: 01.06.03 STRENGTH: S GED: R3 M1 L1 SVP: 4 DLU: 77

977.684-018 PRESSER (print. & pub.) alternate titles: caser-in; joint creaser; book paster
Folds prefabricated bookcases (separately made bindings) over book bodies and compresses assembled book in press to secure cases to bodies: Folds upper half of case over top sheet of book body; stretches case tight over back of book and holds book in place on lower half of case. Presses case down on book body; centers book in case with fingers. Stacks enfolded books in press and places pressboards at intervals in stack. Turns handwheel or depresses pedal to lower press head and clamp stack. Retains books in press until glue or paste has dried. Reverses handwheel or pushes lever to raise press head, removes books, and stacks books for finishing. May coat book bodies with paste, using brush, or position books over blade of machine and press button to lower book body between saturated rollers to coat body with paste prior to positioning case over book body and be designated Caser (print. & pub.) 977.684-018. May position enfolded books singly on press and press button to lower heated ram to crease and recrease joints on backbone of book. May wipe glue from endpapers, using cloth.
GOE: 06.02.26 STRENGTH: L GED: R2 M1 L1 SVP: 4 DLU: 89

977.684-022 STITCHER, HAND (print. & pub.)
Sews gathered and collated signatures by hand to form book preparatory to binding: Stretches holding cords over workbench frame. Positions signatures in

frame according to numbered sequence and attaches signatures to holding cords, using needle and thread. Wraps cloth tape around frame to compress signatures and sews signatures together to form book. Routes book to binding department.
GOE: 06.04.26 STRENGTH: L GED: R2 M1 L1 SVP: 4 DLU: 77

977.684-026 BENCH WORKER, BINDING (print. & pub.)
Examines, marks, measures, and prepares damaged, worn, and softbound publications for rebinding, following specifications: Reads job order for special instructions. Stacks publications on table and counts books or journals to ensure order is complete as listed on shipping or job slip. Removes cover and endpapers from book body or journal, using hands or scissors. Fans pages of publication and inspects publication for duplicate pages, incorrect numbering, and incorrect placement of pages. Removes advertisements, address cards, or coupons from publication as specified. Cuts and removes thread from spine of books, using scissors. Pulls staples, sensors, or spiral bindings from journals or other publications, using handtool. Measures and records book or journal dimensions on bindery slip. Locates, folds, and trims excess border from maps or other foldouts, using scissors. Inserts specifed colored paper markers between pages to identify book body with foldouts or narrow edges for BOOK TRIMMER (print. & pub.) 640.685-010. May pull endpapers' and reinforcing spine strip for attachment to book body. May remove dirt from cover, using cloth and cleaning solvent. May prepare and route slip and book case to printing or laminating area. May repair cover, using tape or glue. May operate machine to emboss name and address on nonmetallic plates [EMBOSSING-MACHINE OPERATOR (clerical) I 208.582-014].
GOE: 06.04.37 STRENGTH: L GED: R2 M1 L1 SVP: 3 DLU: 89

977.687-010 COLLATOR, HAND (print. & pub.)
Arranges and stacks printed or unprinted sheets on worktable according to size, weight, color or number sequence: Picks up one sheet at time from each stack to assemble complete set. Taps batch of sets on worktable or feeds sets into jogging machine to straighten and align sheets. Applies glue to top edges of sets, using brush or roller. Separates individual sets from glued stacks, using knife.
GOE: 06.04.26 STRENGTH: L GED: R2 M1 L1 SVP: 3 DLU: 77

979 OCCUPATIONS IN GRAPHIC ART WORK, N.E.C.

This group includes occupations, not elsewhere classified, concerned with graphic arts, such as engraving, roller making, silk screen printing, and other graphic arts and related activities.

979.130-010 SUPERVISOR, BLUEPRINTING-AND-PHOTOCOPY (any industry)
Supervises and coordinates activities of BLUEPRINTING-MACHINE OPERATOR (any industry), PHOTOSTAT OPERATOR (any industry), FILE CLERK (clerical) and other workers engaged in producing and filing blueprints, vandyke and ozalid prints, and photostats in an industrial plant or commercial photocopy laboratory: Sets up blueprint and photostat machines. Trains workers in operation of machines. Inspects finished prints for sharpness, density of line, and size. Consults with customers concerning work details, such as sizes of prints and prices. Performs other duties as described under SUPERVISOR (any industry) Master Title. May supervise workers engaged in making photostats only and be designated Supervisor, Photostat (any industry).
GOE: 05.10.05 STRENGTH: L GED: R4 M2 L2 SVP: 8 DLU: 77

979.130-014 SUPERVISOR, PRINTING-SHOP (print. & pub.) alternate titles: lead printer
Supervises and coordinates activities of workers engaged in photographing and assembling images, making plates, setting type, operating printing presses and related machines and equipment, and assembling and stitching pamphlets, leaflets, and books: Inspects film assembly, platemaking, printing, and binding operations to verify conformance to job order specifications. May repair printing presses, type-setting machines, and assembling and stitching equipment. May supervise workers in printing department of establishment and be designated Supervisor, Printing Department (print. & pub.). Performs other duties as described under SUPERVISOR (any industry) Master Title.
GOE: 05.05.13 STRENGTH: L GED: R4 M3 L4 SVP: 8 DLU: 89

979.131-010 SUPERVISOR, PUBLICATIONS PRODUCTION (print. & pub.) alternate titles: supervisor, layout
Supervises and coordinates activities of workers engaged in preparation and layout of printed material: Studies editorial matter to determine most effective form of presentation and number and type of illustrations required, in accordance with specifications of customer or editorial personnel and accepted standards of composition, limitations of equipment, and available funds. Prepares mockup of pages for use by other workers in setting type and making up pages. Marks copy to incorporate printing instructions and editorial changes, utilizing standard printing symbols. Routes artwork to reproduction department or outside contractor for retouching, photographing, and platemaking. Routes editorial material to composing room for typesetting. Reviews finished material for format, accuracy, and general appearance. Submits proofs for final review and routes corrected copy to pressroom for printing. Performs other duties as described under SUPERVISOR (any industry) Master Title. May plan technical drawings to supplement copy.
GOE: 01.02.03 STRENGTH: L GED: R4 M2 L4 SVP: 8 DLU: 77

979.131-014 SUPERVISOR, ROLLER SHOP (textile)
Supervises and coordinates activities of workers engaged in inspecting and repairing cloth printing rollers: Confers with technical and supervisory personnel in print department and analyzes customer orders and pattern sketches to determine specifications for printing rollers to be ordered and to plan department work schedule. Orders new and replacement printing rollers. Inspects new printing rollers for defects and rejects damaged rollers. Issues repair list and instructions for storing and transporting rollers to ROLLER INSPECTOR (textile). Confers with and assists ROLLER REPAIRER (textile) to repair defective rollers. Confers with engravers to resolve engraving problems. Performs other duties as described under SUPERVISOR (any industry) Master Title.
GOE: 06.02.01 STRENGTH: H GED: R4 M3 L3 SVP: 7 DLU: 77

979.131-018 SUPERVISOR, SILK-SCREEN CUTTING AND PRINTING (any industry)
Supervises and coordinates activities of workers engaged in fabricating and assembling silk screens and in handprinting, utilizing silk-screen method: Trains workers in performance of tasks, such as screen cutting by hand, photographic screen making, and screen printing. Examines screens for imperfections and compares screens with customer artwork to verify conformance to specifications. Compares paint colors with artwork, color swatches, or samples to verify correct color choice and to ascertain paint compatibility with stock to be printed. Examines sample print to verify specified register of colors and shifts register marks on silk-screen frame or brushes block-out lacquer on defective areas of screen to correct color register. Requisitions materials and supplies. Confers with other unit supervisors to coordinate interdepartmental workflow. May fabricate and assemble silk screens and sandblast stencils. May supervise workers engaged in sandblasting decorative designs on material. Performs other duties as described under SUPERVISOR (any industry) Master Title.
GOE: 06.02.01 STRENGTH: L GED: R4 M3 L3 SVP: 8 DLU: 77

979.132-010 SHIFT SUPERVISOR, FILM PROCESSING (print. & pub.)
Supervises and coordinates activities of workers engaged in production of computer tapes containing pattern design data or film positives or negatives of pattern designs for use in photoengraving processes: Analyzes work order and confers with supervisory personnel to determine most feasible method required to produce negative or positive film or computer tape of customer pattern design. Develops work procedures for producing customer design in accordance with computer limitations and customer specifications. Computes *mathematical model* for pattern designs adaptable to mathematical solution. Inspects film positives and negatives to verify conformance to specifications. May operate scanner, computer, display console, and color design console. Performs other duties as described under SUPERVISOR (any industry) Master Title.
GOE: 05.10.05 STRENGTH: L GED: R4 M3 L3 SVP: 8 DLU: 86

979.137-010 SUPERVISOR, FINISHING ROOM (print. & pub.)
Supervises and coordinates activities of workers engaged in finishing and assembling maps, charts, and globes. Performs duties as described under SUPERVISOR (any industry) Master Title.
GOE: 06.02.01 STRENGTH: L GED: R4 M2 L2 SVP: 7 DLU: 77

979.137-014 SUPERVISOR, INSPECTING (paper goods)
Supervises and coordinates activities of workers engaged in inspecting and packaging screen-printed wallpaper: Examines substandard wallpaper to determine repair procedures and corrective action required to prevent recurrence of defect. Rejects unsalvageable wallpaper. Compiles record of rejected wallpaper and reports probable causes to management for remedial action. Trains workers in inspecting and packaging procedures. Requisitions supplies and materials. Performs other duties as described under SUPERVISOR (any industry) Master Title.
GOE: 06.02.01 STRENGTH: L GED: R4 M2 L2 SVP: 7 DLU: 77

979.137-018 SUPERVISOR, PRODUCTION (paper goods)
Supervises and coordinates activities of workers engaged in handprinting and flocking wallcovering, utilizing silk-screen method: Monitors production activities and discusses methods and techniques with workers to improve performance. Performs other duties as described under SUPERVISOR (any industry) Master Title.
GOE: 06.02.01 STRENGTH: L GED: R4 M2 L2 SVP: 6 DLU: 77

979.137-022 SUPERVISOR, SAMPLE PREPARATION (textile)
Develops dye formulas according to customer specifications and supervises and coordinates activities of workers engaged in screen printing cloth samples by hand: Analyzes customer artwork and color card to determine number and type colors specified. Compares specified colors with standard color swatches to match colors and records mixing formulas from selected swatches. Monitors color weighing and mixing activities to ensure adherance with formula specifications. Observes cloth printing activities to ensure product conformance with standards. Examines printed samples for color penetration, off-center print, and to verify customer color specifications. Revises dye formulas to match shades desired by customer. Records data, such as customer name, pattern number, colors, and quantity desired and forwards data to production department. Performs other duties as described under SUPERVISOR (any industry) Master Title.
GOE: 06.02.01 STRENGTH: L GED: R4 M3 L3 SVP: 7 DLU: 77

979.137-026 SUPERVISOR, TYPE-DISK QUALITY CONTROL (machinery mfg.)
Supervises and coordinates activities of workers engaged in printing, developing, and examining type character proofsheets used to verify accuracy of

phototypesetting type disks: Schedules production activities, such as printing, developing, and proofing of copy used to verify accuracy of type characters on disks, applying knowledge of processing techniques and production requirements. Periodically examines proofs or type characters on disks, using magnifier, to ensure conformity to product specifications and quality standards. Interviews and hires job applicants, initiates training, and assigns new workers to work with experienced workers to continue on-the-job training. Performs other duties as described under SUPERVISOR (any industry) Master Title.
GOE: 06.01.01 STRENGTH: L GED: R4 M3 L4 SVP: 7 DLU: 86

979.281-010 DIE MAKER (print. & pub.) alternate titles: die cutter; die engraver

Engraves designs onto steel dies used to produce textile printing rollers, using engravers' handtools and machines: Measures dimensions of pattern to be engraved in die, using ruler. Operates engine lathe to turn steel roller down to size according to dimensions of pattern and copper printing roller. Sketches design on steel roller (die) utilizing one of following alternate methods: (1) Lays out reference points on design according to location of one complete pattern repeat, using ruler, dividers, and pencil. Covers design with transparent film and transfers reference points to film, using scriber and magnifying lens. Sketches design colors onto separate sheets of film, using brushes and ink. Examines design to detect errors in scribing and color quality and corrects or alters design, employing knowledge of colors, fabrics to be printed, and engraving and printing techniques. Immerses steel roller in electroplating solution to coat roller with copper. Wraps film around roller, allowing ink in design to react with copper coating to transfer design from film to roller. (2) Computes machine settings required to reproduce straight-line designs on roller, using mathematical tables and formulas. Plots machine settings on graph paper. Mounts steel roller in index-dividing machine and adjusts tracing carriage of machine according to computations on graph paper. Lowers tracing-carriage scriber to surface of roller and moves levers of machine to sketch vertical and horizontal lines on roller. Mounts sketched rollers in fixture on worktable and engraves outline of design following sketch lines, using gravers' tools. Cuts or stipples in ground lines as specified, using gravers' and stippling tools. Prints proof print of engraved design on wax paper to verify accuracy of etchings on roller. Removes scratches from and polishes roller die, using polishing lathe. Punches indentations into edges of die to facilitate transfer of design from die to *mill*, using hammer and punch. Controls furnace to harden and temper dies.
GOE: 01.06.01 STRENGTH: L GED: R4 M3 L3 SVP: 7 DLU: 77

979.281-014 ENGRAVER, BLOCK (print. & pub.) alternate titles: artist, woodblock; block cutter; engraver, wood; wood-cut engraver; wood-type finisher

Carves designs and lettering in wooden blocks or rollers used to print articles, such as cloth, greeting cards, and posters following sketch or photograph, using gravers handtools and machines: Traces or draws design on wooden block or roller, using pencil, ruler, dividers, or pantograph. Cuts design in block or roller, using wood-carving and engraving tools and power router. Rounds and bevels top edges, smooths sides and base, and cuts sharp angles, ridges, and joints to produce detail in printing and to finish type, using file and knife. Carves separate block for each color of multicolor pattern. May design pattern for use in cloth printing. May carve lettering and designs freehand. May cut and bend metal strips to conform to contours of design, using files, pliers, and pincers, and force strips into grooves of block to produce raised printing surface. May operate copy camera to produce negative from photograph or drawing of design [REPRODUCTION TECHNICIAN (any industry) 976.361-010].
GOE: 01.06.01 STRENGTH: L GED: R4 M2 L3 SVP: 7 DLU: 77

979.281-018 ENGRAVER, PICTURE (print. & pub.)

Engraves metal dies to represent portraits, landscapes, figures, and ornamental engravings used to make plates to print bonds, stamps, currency, diplomas, and other paper documents, following models and oral instructions: Traces model of drawing on gelatin sheet, using magnifying glasses and graver. Makes wax impression of tracing, transfers tracing to polished metal die, and stains design with weak acid solution. Engraves or etches lines, dots, and dashes in specified depths, widths, spacings, and directions to portray features, such as drapery, foliage, or flesh by either one or combination of following methods: (1) Draws design through transparent, acid-resistant background on metal plate, using tempered steel point, and washes design with acid that etches lines and other markings in metal surface to produce representations of images, such as wood, stone, foliage, and sky. (2) Cuts or carves lines of design in surface of metal die, using graver. Repeats cuts to obtain required depth for portrayal of images, such as flesh, hair, drapery, and clothing. Makes proof of engraved design, examines proof print, and reworks engraving as required. May engrave lettering on plates and be designated Engraver, Letter (print. & pub.).
GOE: 01.06.01 STRENGTH: L GED: R4 M3 L3 SVP: 8 DLU: 77

979.282-010 ELECTRONIC PREPRESS SYSTEM OPERATOR (print. & pub.) alternate titles: console operator; electronic imaging system operator; system operator

Operates prepress system to electronically assemble images into pages and to retouch and make color corrections to page elements to be used in production of lithographic printing plates or gravure cylinders: Enters digitized data, such as artist's layout, color separations, text, page dimensions, and layout instructions, into electronic prepress system computer memory, using components of system such as scanner, camera, keyboard, or mouse, or loads floppy disks or tapes containing information into system. Studies layout or other instructions

to determine work to be done and sequence of operations. Views monitors for visual representation of work in progress and for instructions and feedback throughout process. Activates options, such as masking or text processing; enters data, such as background color, shapes, and coordinates of images; and retrieves data from system memory to assemble elements on pages. Retrieves images from system memory; activates options, such as masking, pixel (picture element) editing, airbrushing, or image retouching; and enters data, such as coordinates of images and color specifications, into system to retouch and make color corrections. Saves completed work on floppy disks or magnetic tape. May create special effects, such as vignettes, mosaics, and image combining. May be designated according to area of specialization and be known as Electronic Color Correction Operator (print. & pub.); Electronic Page Makeup System Operator (print. & pub.); Pagination System Operator (print. & pub.).
GOE: 01.06.01 STRENGTH: S GED: R4 M3 L3 SVP: 7 DLU: 89

979.360-010 SCREEN-PRINTING-EQUIPMENT SETTER (paper goods)

Sets up and adjusts silk-screen printing equipment used to hand print multicolored designs on wallpaper: Adjusts feed rollers and spindle reel to specified tension, using wrench. Compares ink prepared for printing run with master color swatch to confirm accuracy of match. Examines printing screen for sharpness of stencil design and feels screen to verify specified tension on frame. Measures distance between printing guide marker on table and center of screen and adjusts distance as required to ensure specified color print registration. Starts drying oven and sets thermostat to temperature specified for printing run. Observes test run or manipulates equipment to produce test print. Examines print for defects and adjusts equipment to correct defective printing as required. Monitors production activities to ensure standard quality of printing. Trains workers in use of printing equipment.
GOE: 06.01.02 STRENGTH: L GED: R4 M2 L3 SVP: 7 DLU: 77

979.361-010 DOCUMENT RESTORER (profess. & kin.)

Restores and preserves documents for libraries, archives, and private and public historical societies: Cleans document, using cleaning compounds to remove dirt and stains, and removes foreign matter, such as rusted clips, pins, rotted bands, and adhesives. Tests document to determine if ink is fast, and to what extent map colors will fade. Immerses document in deacidification baths to remove acidity from paper and ink. Places document on rack to dry. Reinspects document for presence of foreign matter. Dampens document, places it between absorbent boards, and places boards in screw press to evenly distribute moisture content in document, and flatten all wrinkles and creases. Seals document in cellulose acetate film and places document in laminating machine to be laminated. Removes document and hones, presses, and trims it to specified size. Places document in cover, folder, or binder.
GOE: 05.05.13 STRENGTH: M GED: R4 M3 L3 SVP: 6 DLU: 77

979.362-010 INSTANT PRINT OPERATOR (print. & pub.) alternate titles: offset-duplicating machine operator, instant print; press operator, instant print shop; quick print operator

Operates offset-duplicating machine, photocopier, and related machines and equipment to produce copies of original materials for customers in instant print shop: Accepts printing orders from customers and computes and quotes prices to customers. Reads job orders to determine quantity of materials to be printed, and stock and ink specifications. Adjusts settings and operates camera plate maker to produce plastic or paper plates for use in offset duplicating. Operates offset duplicating machine to reproduce single or multicolor copies of text, drawings, graphs, or similar materials [OFFSET-DUPLICATING-MACHINE OPERATOR (print. & pub.) 651.682-014]. Operates copier to produce photocopies of single color or small run jobs [PHOTOCOPYING-MACHINE OPERATOR (clerical) 207.685-014]. Examines proof copy to assure accurate reproduction of color, centering of print, and conformance of copy to layout specifications. Operates auxiliary machines such as collator, pad and tablet making machine, stapler, and paper punching, folding, cutting, and perforating machines to assemble materials. May operate computerized typesetting machine to set type for printing. May assemble typeset copy and artwork into pasteup for printing reproduction. May receive payment from customers and box or wrap printed materials.
GOE: 05.10.05 STRENGTH: M GED: R3 M2 L3 SVP: 6 DLU: 88

979.380-010 PANTOGRAPH SETTER (print. & pub.)

Sets up pantograph machines to transfer designs in reduced form from 'zinc plates to varnished cloth-printing rollers: Inserts mandrel through roller and lifts roller onto headstocks on machine carriage, using electric hoist. Aligns centerline on zinc plate with centerline on machine table and tacks plate to table. Moves pantograph tracing arm through series of reference points on zinc plate and moves dimension levers backward or forward to adjust pantograph for specified reduction in scale of design. Tightens levers in position, using handtools. Positions diamond point on machine crossbar, moves tracing arm through reference points on zinc plate, and depresses pedal to mark corresponding marks on varnished roller. Aligns succeeding diamond point with marks on roller. Repeats procedure until diamond point has been spaced on crossbar for each side-repeat of pattern. Tightens diamond points in position, using pliers. Turns thumbscrew on diamond frame (holder) to raise diamond points equal distance from varnished roller. Weighs diamond points on miniature scales and adds or removes washers to compensate for differences in weight. Moves tracing arm through series of reference points on zinc plate, depresses pedal to mark corresponding crosses on roller, and examines marks on roller to verify alignment of diamond points. Determines ground setting accord-

ing to weight of fabric, type of design, and colors in design. Records ground setting, length of roller, width of engraving, and circumference of roller on production sheet.
GOE: 05.05.13 STRENGTH: M GED: R4 M2 L2 SVP: 6 DLU: 77

979.381-010 ENGRAVER I (print. & pub.) alternate titles: pantograph operator

Engraves lettering or designs in copper or steel printing plates, using pantograph engraving machine: Rubs blank plate with emery or charcoal and oil to polish surface. Clamps blank plate in position under diamond cutting point and master plate under tracing point of pantograph. Starts electric motor that revolves cutting point and lowers engraving control bar, simultaneously moving bar sideways until tracing point enters desired figure on master plate. Moves bar so that tracing point follows figure on master plate, reproducing figure on blank plate. Loosens thumbscrews and changes position of pantograph bar to reproduce figures larger or smaller than those on master plate. May be designated according to type of plate used as Engraver, Copperplate (print. & pub.); Engraver, Steel Plate (print. & pub.).
GOE: 05.10.05 STRENGTH: L GED: R3 M1 L2 SVP: 5 DLU: 77

979.381-014 LINE-UP EXAMINER (print. & pub.)

Examines proof sheets to detect errors in position and alignment of type, page elements, margins, trim, and fold areas: Positions proof sheet on glass top of lighted, line-up table. Moves geared straightedges into position over proof copy to verify alignment of printed material, page, position, and folio continuity. Compares colors on proof sheet with standard color key to verify specified color register. Records degree and direction plates or type must be shifted to correct alignment, or marks corrective information on proof sheet. Draws trim, stitch, and fold lines for bindery processes and plate trim lines for stereotype and electrotype plate fabrication, using straightedge and printer's line gauge.
GOE: 05.10.05 STRENGTH: L GED: R3 M2 L2 SVP: 8 DLU: 77

979.381-026 ROLLER REPAIRER (textile) alternate titles: engraved-roller inspector; roller inspector and mender

Examines engraved cloth-printing rollers for processing defects and repairs defects, using handtools: Lifts roller into brackets on table or turning device with aid of another worker and portable hoist. Examines rollers for defects, such as pinholes and scratches. Compares customer's design and printed proof to detect missed engravings, extra engravings, and uneven joining of design on circumference of roller, and examines roller to verify defects. Dusts engraved design with chalk and examines roller to determine whether engraving is too full or too dense to print desired effects on cloth. Plugs pinholes, extra engravings, and over-engraved areas with copper wire plugs, and forces plugs in place, using ball peen hammer and punch. Smooths rough spots, using file and removes scratches from roller surface, using burnishing tool. Traces outline of missed engraving on wax paper and transfers outline to roller, using scriber. Engraves additional lines or designs on roller surface freehand or following outline to fill in gaps in design or missing engravings, using gravers and magnifying lens. Rejects unrepairable rollers. Cleans and polishes rollers, using water, polishing paste, and cloth. May inspect rollers only and be designated Roller Inspector (textile).
GOE: 01.06.01 STRENGTH: H GED: R4 M2 L2 SVP: 7 DLU: 77

979.381-030 SIDEROGRAPHER (print. & pub.)

Reproduces original engravings on metal plates used to print banknotes, bonds, and other securities, using gravers' handtools and machines: Cuts around designs on roller die to remove undesirable parts of assembled die, using graver, and assembles die from several rollers on which parts of design have been engraved. Lays out construction lines on steel plate, using trammel point, dividers, steel scribers, and gauge, to align subjects to be transferred. Scrapes and burnishes plate surface to remove imperfections, aligns plate on transfer press bed, and positions engraved steel roll on plate, using magnifying glass to verify accuracy. Depresses lever that embeds engraved design on roll into steel plate. Examines transferred design and repeats process until exact reproduction is made. May reproduce design in soft steel rolls.
GOE: 01.06.01 STRENGTH: M GED: R4 M3 L2 SVP: 6 DLU: 77

979.381-034 SKETCH MAKER I (print. & pub.)

Traces designs on wood-printing blocks or rollers preparatory to engraving by ENGRAVER, BLOCK (print. & pub.), using stylus, ink, and burnishing tool: Places drawing of design over wax paper and traces design, using stylus. Pours ink over wax paper to fill depressions made by stylus and wipes away excess ink. Wraps inked paper around wood-printing roller or positions paper on printing block. Rubs back of paper, using burnishing tool (spoonlike instrument) to transfer inked design to roller or block. May print proof impression of design from etched printing rollers onto wax paper to verify accuracy of etchings and be designated Impression Printer (print. & pub.).
GOE: 01.06.01 STRENGTH: L GED: R3 M1 L1 SVP: 4 DLU: 77

979.381-038 STENCIL MAKER (carpet & rug)

Lays out and cuts stencils used to print multicolor designs on rugs, using opaque projector, knife, pencil, and brushes: Draws pencil copy of symmetrical design on tracing paper according to specified dimensions. Projects and enlarges scale drawing of nonsymmetrical design on tracing paper, using opaque projector, and reproduces enlargement, using pencil. Lays out shape of each stencil on drawing and traces shape onto stencil paper. Cuts stencil from paper, using knife. Brushes shellac onto stencils and attaches stencils to frames, using

handtools. May attach wires to brace frames. Prepares proof copy and inspects for accuracy of design reproduction. May mix paints to obtain specified colors for printing.
GOE: 01.06.02 STRENGTH: M GED: R3 M2 L2 SVP: 6 DLU: 77

979.382-010 CLAMPER (print. & pub.)

Operates clamp (rotary press) to transfer designs from engraved dies to *mills* used in transferring designs to copper printing rollers: Positions die in fixtures on bed of clamp. Mounts mill over die and turns handwheel to lower head of clamp against journals of mill, forcing mill against die. Rotates die specified number of times equal to number of times design is to repeat around circumference of mill. Examines impression of design on mill and determines from gap left between ends of impression amount reduction required in circumference of mill. Starts machine that turns die against mill to produce indentations on mill. Spreads acid-resistant wax over surface of mill and gradually increases pressure on head of clamp as die turns against mill, working wax away from area of mill corresponding to unengraved area of die. Removes mill from clamp and spins mill in acid bath to etch waxfree area of mill, leaving waxed area of mill in relief. Offsets head of clamp and works die against mill to round off end of design and make surface of mill oval to facilitate transfer of design from mill to surface of copper printing roller. Examines raised design on mill through magnifying lens to verify sharpness of lines. Inserts mill in heat-treating pot, fills pot with carbon-activated bonemeal, and places pot in electric furnace. Turns thermostat to set temperature of furnace according to type of steel. Removes mill from furnace at end of heating cycle, using tongs, and dips mill into brine solution to harden and temper steel. Cleans mill with wire brush. May operate engine lathe to reduce diameter of mill or to turn raised indentations off ends of mill [ENGINE-LATHE SET-UP OPERATOR (machine shop)].
GOE: 05.05.13 STRENGTH: M GED: R3 M2 L2 SVP: 6 DLU: 77

979.382-014 ENGRAVER, MACHINE (print. & pub.)

Sets up and operates engraving machine to transfer designs from *mills* to copper printing rollers used in color-printing cloth: Lifts printing roller into position on machine with aid of another worker. Places *truing I* roller in fixture on head of machine and lowers machine head until truing roller rests on surface of printing roller. Starts machine to rotate truing roller against printing roller and turns setscrews until truing roller rotates without horizontal motion to align head of machine with printing roller. Divides *register wheel* on machine into divisions, according to number of times design is to be repeated around printing roller, and marks divisions on wheel, using chalk. Inserts stud in specified slot on register wheel, replaces truing roller with mill, and moves *pitch finger* against stop on head of machine to set mill in register for engraving. Lowers mill to surface of printing roller, releases catch on weight lever to apply pressure on mill, and rotates mill one revolution to transfer one repeat of pattern to roller. Repeats procedure until design has been repeated around circumference of printing roller. Examines impression of design on roller to detect repeats of pattern that are out of register. Replaces mill with burnishing roller and works burnishing roller against printing roller to erase defective impressions. Increases pressure on mill if design is in register and starts machine that works mill against printing roller to increase depth of impression. Measures depth of engraving, using depth gauge. Measures width of embossed design on mill, using divider, and converts measurement into number of teeth on sideshift gear, using conversion tables. Releases pressure on mill and turns gear specified number of teeth to move mill into position for engraving design adjacent to first impression and repeats procedure as above until design has been engraved across length of roller. Engages dog in teeth of gear and pitches design in register. Repeats procedure until design has been engraved across length of roller. Mounts engraved roller on mandrel of polishing lathe and operates lathe to remove burrs and smooth roller [PRINTING-ROLLER POLISHER (machine shop)].
GOE: 05.10.05 STRENGTH: V GED: R4 M2 L2 SVP: 8 DLU: 77

979.382-018 PRINTER (print. & pub.) alternate titles: graphic arts technician; printer, small print shop

Reproduces and assembles graphic arts materials, performing any combination of following duties in small printing shop or printing department of establishment: Sets up and operates various types of cameras to produce plastic or paper plates, or negatives for later use in preparation of aluminum plates for reproduction in offset lithographic process. Touches up negatives, using opaque material, positions negatives on masking sheet, and cuts exposure windows in masking sheet to assemble *film flats* for reproduction. Places masked negative on aluminum plate, and exposes plate to negative under high intensity (ultraviolet) lamp to transfer image to plate, using vacuum frame. Places exposed plate in automatic processor or immerses plate in chemical solutions to develop image on plate. Operates offset-duplicating machine or small printing press to reproduce single or multicolor copies of line, drawings, graphs, or similar materials. Inspects printed material to verify specified color and clarity of print. Sets up and operates bindery equipment to cut, assemble, staple, or bind materials. Maintains machinery and equipment in operating condition.
GOE: 01.06.01 STRENGTH: M GED: R4 M2 L3 SVP: 5 DLU: 88

979.382-022 PANTOGRAPHER (print. & pub.)

Operates pantograph machine to transfer design in reduced form from zinc plate to varnished printing rollers: Moves stylus on tracing carriage through series of reference points on zinc plate, depresses pedal to lower diamond points to surface of roller, and observes alignment of diamond points with marks on

roller to verify machine setup. Sets ground point into slot on ground wheel according to instructions on design sheet. Moves lever to lock tracing carriage in position for inscribing ground lines on surface of varnished roller. Rotates ground wheel to advance tracing carriage specified distance, depresses pedal to lower diamond points to roller surface, and moves stylus back and forth within outline on zinc plate to inscribe oblique ground lines on roller. Releases tracing carriage and guides stylus around outline on zinc plate to transfer outline to roller. Engages register point in appropriate slot on *register wheel* and adjusts dimension levers, using handtools to set up machine for inscribing subsequent repeats of pattern around circumference of roller. Transfers portions of design represented by different colors onto separate rollers. Paints over pinholes, scratches, and reference points left on roller by PANTOGRAPH SETTER (print. & pub.), using brush and acid resistant paint. Marks register point on end of roller, using hammer and punch.
GOE: 05.10.05 STRENGTH: L GED: R3 M1 L1 SVP: 4 DLU: 77

979.382-026 COMPUTER TYPESETTER-KEYLINER (print. & pub.) alternate titles: desktop publisher

Lays out pages, selects size and style of type, and enters text and graphics into computer to produce printed materials, such as advertisements, brochures, newsletters, and forms, applying knowledge of graphic arts techniques and typesetting, and using computer: Reviews layout and customer order. Enters text into computer, using input device, such as mouse, keyboard, scanner, or modem. Scans artwork, using optical scanner which changes image into computer-readable form. Enters commands to position text and illustrations on page grid of computer monitor. Creates spaces between letters, columns, and lines, applying knowledge of typesetting, and enters commands, using input device. Arranges page according to aesthetic standards, layout specifications of GRAPHIC DESIGNER (profess. & kin.) 141.061-018, and applying knowledge of layout (keylining) and computer software. Prints paper or film copies of completed material. May alter illustration to enlarge, reduce, or clarify image. May operate stat camera to produce photostat. May operate automatic film developer to process photographs. May assemble art work into pasteup and perform keylining manually [PASTE-UP ARTIST (print. & pub.) 972.381-030].
GOE: 01.06.01 STRENGTH: S GED: R4 M3 L4 SVP: 6 DLU: 90

979.384-010 SCREEN MAKER, PHOTOGRAPHIC PROCESS (any industry)

Fabricates stencils for screen printing, applying knowledge of photochemical processing, using photographic equipment: Coats screen with photosensitive emulsion, using brush. Places and secures artwork and screen in frame of vacuum printer. Adjusts printer controls and activates printer to transfer image onto screen and form stencil. Washes unexposed emulsion from screen, using water and hose. Hangs screen in rack or places screen in oven to dry. May fabricate stencil by adhering film with specified image to screen, using vacuum frame. May insert screen in frame, using handtools and tension meters [PRINTING SCREEN ASSEMBLER (electron. comp.) 979.684-042]. May measure and mix ingredients used in photochemical process, according to standard formulas. May scrub screen for reuse, using solvents, brush, and hose. May pour ink or other printing material onto screen and move squeegee across screen to test screen or to screen print objects [SCREEN PRINTER (any industry) 979.684-034].
GOE: 05.10.05 STRENGTH: M GED: R3 M2 L2 SVP: 4 DLU: 88

979.581-010 ENGRAVER, RUBBER (print. & pub.)

Engraves rubber plates used in printing designs and lettering on fabric or other materials, using knife, mechanical drawing tools and handtools: Cuts strip of engraving gum (two- or three-ply rubber, cemented to cloth backing) from roll, using knife. Positions design over strip and traces outline or draws letters, using pencil and mechanical drawing tools, leaving impression in surface of strip. Cuts around impression with knife to one-ply depth and pulls cut rubber from strip, leaving raised design or lettering. Prepares additional rubber plates for jobs requiring colors by omitting different portions of design or lettering from each plate. Punches hole on either side of plate and inserts and clinches grommet around hole, using setting tool and hammer, for use in fastening plate to press.
GOE: 01.06.01 STRENGTH: S GED: R3 M1 L1 SVP: 6 DLU: 77

979.667-010 INSPECTOR, SCREEN PRINTING (print. & pub.)

Inspects stencils, silk screens, materials, and printed products at various stages of production to ensure conformance to specifications, applying knowledge of screen printing techniques: Reviews job order and examines customer artwork and material to be printed, such as vinyl, wood, glass, or paper products, to evaluate suitability of material for silk-screen printing. Inspects stencils for conformance to customers specifications and company standards and returns unsatisfactory stencils to cutter for modifications. Examines sample of screen printing prepared from stencil to verify print is complete and color is applied in conformity with customer's requirements. Feels surface of screen print for smoothness. Discusses corrections to silk-screen process with screen printer. Inspects final product to verify quality. Records inspection results on job order or quality control form.
GOE: 06.03.02 STRENGTH: L GED: R3 M2 L2 SVP: 3 DLU: 86

979.681-010 LETTERER (machinery mfg.) alternate titles: raiser; sketcher

Copies outline of type from lead type proof to furnish pattern for processing steel type: Places lead type under projectoscope that magnifies it. Traces outline of letter. Draws letter in detail, using drawing board, pencil, and paper.
GOE: 01.06.03 STRENGTH: S GED: R3 M1 L1 SVP: 6 DLU: 77

979.681-014 PRINTER (glass products)

Prints specified design on paper for use in etching glassware, using printing plate and artist's handtools: Warms printing plate and ink on electric heater preparatory to printing. Spreads ink on plate, using spatula and positions plate on paper. Rubs paper against plate to transfer design from plate to paper. Examines print for clarity and lays prints on worktable to dry. Cuts plate to produce new designs following outline on plate, using scriber. Applies acid to etch design into plate.
GOE: 01.06.01 STRENGTH: L GED: R3 M1 L2 SVP: 5 DLU: 77

979.681-018 ROLLER ENGRAVER, HAND (print. & pub.)

Engraves designs into copper textile printing rollers, using graver, punches, hammer, and sketches: Presses sketch on roller to produce impression of design. Cuts grooves of specified depth and uniformity into roller following lines of design impression. Refers to sketch to ensure that lines of only one printing color are engraved into each roller. May inspect design for defective engraving and reengrave roller to meet specifications. May engrave designs, using engraving machine [ENGRAVER, MACHINE (print. & pub.)].
GOE: 01.06.01 STRENGTH: S GED: R3 M2 L2 SVP: 7 DLU: 77

979.681-022 SILK-SCREEN CUTTER (any industry) alternate titles: film cutter; silk-screen maker; stencil cutter

Cuts stencils by hand for use in silk-screen printing: Superimposes transparent gelatinous film or shellacked onionskin paper on design or lettering to be reproduced, and cuts outline of design, using knife. Irons stencil on silk or fine copper mesh screen to transfer film or shellac onto screen. Cuts additional stencils for each color to be printed in design. May draw design directly on screen and fill in surfaces around design with glue, lacquer, or paper. May print designs [SCREEN PRINTER (any industry)]. May cut stencils for use in making computer circuit plug boards and be designated Silk-Screen-Layout Drafter (any industry).
GOE: 01.06.01 STRENGTH: L GED: R3 M1 L2 SVP: 5 DLU: 77

979.682-010 BLOCKER I (print. & pub.) alternate titles: mounter

Operates machines to mount finished stereotype and eletrotype printing plates on wood, synthetic, or metal blocks, and to trim, square, and smooth edges of mounted plates: Places plates face up on flat metal surface and taps plates with hammer and wooden block to straighten irregularities due to warping or bending. Cuts blocks to size on power saw. Lays plates on adhesive-coated block or inserts sheet of thermosetting bonding film between plate and block and places assembly on sliding table of heat press. Places bearers (steel bars) around assembled cut and covers assembly with heat resistant blanket to prevent mechanical damage to plate. Adjusts controls to regulate pressure and temperature of press. Pushes sliding table with plate into press cavity (oven) and depresses lever to apply pressure for specified time. Nails plate to block, using hammer or nailing machine. Operates machines, such as trim saw, rotary trimming machine, block planer, and block leveling machine to trim, square, and smooth edges of mounted plates and reduce blocks and mounted plates to type-high thickness. Adjusts microgauges, guides, and cutting blades of machines to produce specified cuts and verifies dimensions of blocks and mounted plates, using try square, snap gauge, and dial indicator type gauge. Patches plates with solder and sweats electrotypes to metal base, using electric soldering equipment. Cuts notches and mortises in mounted plates, using drill press and jig saw, to make openings for inserting type on other plates. May mount plates with double-coated pressure-sensitive tape and tap with woodblock and hammer to form bond. May operate routing machine to cut excess metal from nonprinting areas of electrotype, stereotype, and photoengraved printing plates [ROUTER (print. & pub.)].
GOE: 06.02.09 STRENGTH: L GED: R3 M2 L2 SVP: 7 DLU: 77

979.682-014 BLUEPRINTING-MACHINE OPERATOR (any industry) alternate titles: ammonia-print operator; blue-line operator; blueprint maker; diazo machine operator; whiteprinting-machine operator

Operates machine to make copies (blueprints) of printed material, such as documents or drawings: Examines negative of original for translucency. Selects sensitized paper according to color of line specified, and positions original over paper. Moves controls to regulate light intensity and exposure time, according to translucency of original and type of sensitized paper. Slides original and sensitized paper into printer to expose and develop print. Examines finished print for specified color, intensity, and sharpness of line. Pushes button to supply machine with ammonia, or manually pours ammonia into printer. May cover original negative with translucent sensitized paper and color filter to prepare autopositive (negative) of original. May be known according to trade name of printer operated.
GOE: 05.10.05 STRENGTH: L GED: R3 M2 L2 SVP: 5 DLU: 81

979.682-022 ROLLER VARNISHER (print. & pub.)

Operates machine to coat unengraved copper rollers or to top engraved copper rollers with acid-resistant varnish preparatory to inscribing design: Mounts roller on mandrel of machine, using electric hoist, and starts machine to rotate roller. Cleans roller, using rag or brush, detergents, and water. Dries roller, using paper towel or leather squeegee. Varnishes roller, using either of following methods: (1) Holds rubber varnishing roller against rotating copper roller and pours varnish between rollers. Guides varnishing roller back and forth over length of copper roller to distribute varnish evenly over surface of roller.

Inserts steam pipe through varnished roller and circulates steam through roller to smooth out pinholes and harden varnish. (2) Holds rubber topping roller against rotating steel (dummy) roller and pours varnish between rollers. Moves topping roller back and forth over dummy roller to work varnish into topping roller. Transfers topping roller to engraved roller as varnish becomes tacky and guides topping roller back and forth over engraved roller to top roller with varnish, leaving engravings exposed. Tops varnish coating with acid-resistant ink. Examines engravings on topped roller to detect ink smears or cavities filled with ink. Cleans and retops defective roller. Trucks varnished or topped rollers to storage area.
GOE: 06.02.21 STRENGTH: M GED: R3 M1 L1 SVP: 6 DLU: 77

979.682-026   ROUTER (print. & pub.) alternate titles: printing-plate router

Operates routing machine with free moving head to cut excess metal from nonprinting areas of electrotype, stereotype, and photoengraved printing plates: Clamps plate face onto routing machine table. Selects cutter bit and installs bit in chuck of routing spindle. Depresses pedal to start machine and moves hand guides to control direction of rotating cutter bit along outlines of design or letters set off by chemically darkened etching. Depresses pedal to raise cutter bit to avoid cutting printing areas of plate. Bevels edges of plates to form nailing surface for mounting plates to wood or synthetic blocks, using router or beveling machine. Mounts curved plates on saddle device in order to cut metal from nonprinting areas. May mount finished printing plates on wood, synthetic, or metal blocks to raise them to printing height, by hand or using automatic plate-mounting equipment [BLOCKER (print. & pub.) I].
GOE: 06.02.02 STRENGTH: L GED: R3 M1 L1 SVP: 5 DLU: 77

979.684-010   CARBON PRINTER (print. & pub.)

Transfers image onto polished surface of copper cylinder to be used in rotogravure process, using photographic equipment: Places sensitized carbon tissue in frame over setup form of matter to be reproduced, and exposes assembly to arc light. Removes tissue after exposure, trims to size, and affixes it to surface of cylinder. May mix chemicals to prepare sensitizing solution and immerse tissue in solution to produce sensitized coating on tissue.
GOE: 05.10.05 STRENGTH: R3 M1 L1 SVP: 5 DLU: 77

979.684-014   ENGRAVER II (print. & pub.)

Cuts letters and designs in linoleum and mounts cut articles on blocks for use in printing posters, using drawing and cutting instruments: Traces pattern of design and letters in reverse on linoleum, using ruler, pencil, and drawing instruments. Cuts around drawn pattern leaving raised design or letters, using cutting tools. Glues pattern to wooden block.
GOE: 01.06.01 STRENGTH: S GED: R3 M1 L1 SVP: 6 DLU: 77

979.684-018   LEGEND MAKER (fabrication, nec)

Arranges and mounts precut letters, numbers, symbols, and logos on paper backing to produce word groupings for signs and displays: Reads work order to determine wording of sign or display. Cuts transparent backing paper to specified size and positions and secures paper to graph grid on drafting table. Removes precut letters, numbers, symbols, or logos from strips or sheets, using knife, and positions them on pressure sensitive paper according to copy, following graph grid. Tapes letters to paper, using transparent tape. Removes completed graphic from table and cuts graphic to size according to customer specifications, using knife.
GOE: 06.04.26 STRENGTH: S GED: R2 M1 L2 SVP: 3 DLU: 77

979.684-022   MAP-AND-CHART MOUNTER (print. & pub.) alternate titles: bookmaker, map; finisher, map and chart

Performs any combination of following tasks to mount maps and charts according to oral or written specifications: Glues muslin or board backing to paper maps and charts, by hand or using mounting machine. Tends machine that automatically applies reinforcing tape to edges of unmounted charts and maps. Attaches spring roller and draw rod to roll-type maps and charts. Cuts maps into sections of specified size, using knife or razor. Spaces sections on muslin according to specifications and glues sections to muslin to assemble fold-mounted maps. Attaches brackets to corners of wooden strips to assemble map-mounting frame. Secures map or chart to frame, using glazier's points, screws, or tape. Inserts fold-mounted maps into binders, punches eyelet holes in binder, using hand press, and inserts and crimps eyelets to secure maps in binder, using hammer.
GOE: 06.02.26 STRENGTH: L GED: R3 M2 L2 SVP: 5 DLU: 77

979.684-026   PRINT-SHOP HELPER (print. & pub.)

Assists workers engaged in setting type, operating printing presses, and making plates, performing any combination of following duties: Moves material and supplies to and from various work areas. Assists in making ready and adjusting presses for production runs. Keeps presses supplied with paper stock. Cleans presses, printing plates, and type sections after use. Covers dampening rolls with wool or felt. Counts, stacks, and wraps finished printed material. Cleans electrotype shells prior to casting, and removes excess metal from edges or backs of cast printing plates, using metal trimming and shaving machines. Trims stereotype matrices to size and dries them between steam or flame-heated plates. Immerses cast plates in copper and chrome plating solutions. Nails wooden blocks to backs of prepared plates to bring plates to printing level. May set type by hand following copy. May be designated according to work involved as Electrotyper Helper (print. & pub.); Photoengraving Helper (print. & pub.); Stereotyper Helper (print. & pub.). Performs other duties as described under HELPER (any industry) Master Title.

GOE: 05.12.18 STRENGTH: M GED: R2 M1 L1 SVP: 3 DLU: 77

979.684-030   SCREEN PRINTER (textile) alternate titles: silk-screen printer

Prints designs on textiles, such as cloth, towels, bath cloths, sheets, and pillowcases, using screen and squeegee: Sets register guides along edge of printing table at intervals specified for pattern repeat. Pours color paste onto screen and positions screen against guides over cloth. Draws squeegee across screen to press color paste through open portion of screen and print design. Repeats process with different screen for each color in design. Washes screens with water or solvent to remove color paste.
GOE: 06.02.27 STRENGTH: L GED: R3 M2 L2 SVP: 3 DLU: 77

979.684-034   SCREEN PRINTER (any industry) alternate titles: decorator; letterer; screener; silk-screen operator; silk-screen painter

Prints lettering and designs on objects, such as posters, targets, instrument dials, furniture, glass, and toys, using screen printing device: Positions object against guides on setup board or holding fixture of screening device and lowers screen. Pours paint into screen frame or dips squeegee in paint and draws squeegee across screen to transfer design to object. Cleans screen with solvent at end of run and when using different colors. May mix paints according to standard formulas. May affix decals to parts and assemblies, using roller. May examine printed object for defects. May fabricate silk-screen stencil, using photographic equipment. May be designated according to object printed as Target-Face Maker (toy-sport equip.). May tend semiautomatic machine that advances wallpaper under printing screen and be designated Wallpaper Printer (paper goods) II. May screen print electrode material onto substrate used in electronic components, such as ceramic capacitors and film resistors, and be known as Silk-Screen Printer (electron. comp.). May screen print solder mask or nomenclature on printed circuit boards and be designated Screen Printer, Printed Circuit Boards (electron. comp.).
GOE: 06.04.34 STRENGTH: L GED: R2 M1 L1 SVP: 3 DLU: 86

979.684-038   SILK-SCREEN REPAIRER (any industry)

Repairs silk screens used in printing articles, such as glass, textile products, furniture, and toys, using handtools: Examines screens over lighted inspection table to detect holes in gelatin emulsion. Brushes blocking solution over holes. Measures alignment of design on article printed, using calipers, and adjusts registration guides and tightens screen in frame to correct misalignment.
GOE: 05.10.05 STRENGTH: L GED: R3 M2 L1 SVP: 3 DLU: 77

979.684-042   PRINTING SCREEN ASSEMBLER (electron. comp.) alternate titles: screen stretcher

Stretches and fastens screening material to metal frames to make printing screens, using either of following methods: (1) Positions frame in holding fixture of stretcher. Places specified length of screening material, such as silk, polyester, or metal mesh, over frame and secures edges of material in clamps of stretcher. Turns ratchet wheels on stretcher to stretch and straighten screening material. Examines and feels screening material to determine tension. Places tension measuring instrument on screening material to measure tension according to specifications. Glues screening material to frame and removes frame from stretcher. Trims excess material from frame, using knife. (2) Clamps specified length of screening material to screen frame. Tightens screws of frame to stretch and straighten screening material according to sequence diagram, using handtool. Examines screen for defects, such as runs or torn areas.
GOE: 06.04.34 STRENGTH: L GED: R2 M1 L1 SVP: 2 DLU: 86

979.685-010   SILK-SCREEN PRINTER, MACHINE (any industry) alternate titles: screen printer

Tends silk screen machine that prints designs, patterns, lettering, or other images on assorted materials and products, such as glassware, ceramics, metal, plastic, or electronic components: Bolts framed silk screen onto machine, and installs and adjusts workpiece holding fixture, stops, and guides, using handtools, ruler, and workpiece pattern. Attaches squeegee to pneumatic drive mechanism, using wrench, and connects air line to mechanism. Regulates air pressure and manipulates squeegee to adjust pressure and angle of sweep. Applies printing compound to screen, using spatula or brush. Places workpiece in or on holding fixture, presses button to lower screen, and depresses pedal or pushes button to activate squeegee. Observes silk screen and workpiece to detect printing defects caused by ripped screen and applies glue to rip to repair screen. Cleans silk screen, using brush and solvent. May thin printing compound, using specified thinner. May tend firing oven to dry printed workpiece. May sharpen squeegee on sanding machine. May transfer image of original artwork to screen, using vacuum printer. May be designated according to type of machine tended as Decorating-Machine Tender (glass mfg.); Squeegee-Machine Tender (glass mfg.); or Stenciling-Machine Tender (glass mfg.); glass products). May tend machine that screen-prints circuit pattern and nomenclature on printed circuit board (PCB) panels used in fabricating PCB's and be designated Screen-Printing-Machine Tender, Printed Circuit Boards (electron. comp.)
GOE: 06.04.09 STRENGTH: L GED: R2 M1 L2 SVP: 3 DLU: 89

979.687-010   EXAMINER (print. & pub.)

Inspects engraved letterheads, envelopes, cards, and stationery to detect defects in engraving and flaws in paper. Informs supervisor of defective engraving rollers and paper.
GOE: 06.03.02 STRENGTH: S GED: R2 M1 L2 SVP: 4 DLU: 77